D1076309

The Form Book®

Flat Annual for 2008

Including all the 2007 returns

The BHA's Official Record

Complete record of Flat Racing
from 1 January to 31 December 2007

Published by Raceform Ltd
Compton, Newbury, Berkshire, RG20 6NL

ISBN 1-978-1-905153-68-8

Printed in Great Britain by William Clowes Ltd, Beccles, Suffolk

Full details of all Raceform services and publications are available from:

Raceform Ltd, Compton, Newbury, Berkshire RG20 6NL
Tel: 01635 578080
Fax: 01635 578101
Email: rfsubscription@mgn.co.uk
www.raceform.co.uk

Cover photo: Authorized gives Frankie Dettori his first win in the
Vodafone Derby at Epsom June 2007
© Edward Whittaker

CONTENTS

Editor: Graham Dench

Head of Analysis Team: Ashley Rumney

Race Analysts & Notebook Writers:
Dave Bellingham, Mark Brown, Steffan Edwards,
Walter Glynn, Keith Hewitt, Richard Lowther, Lee McKenzie,
David Orton, Ashley Rumney, Desmond Stoneham, David Toft,
Ron Wood, Richard Young.

Production: Ashley Rumney & Richard Lowther

The Form Book

Flat Racing Annual for 2008

Welcome to the 2008 edition of *The Form Book,* extended to include the complete year's results from 2007.

Race details contain Racing Post Ratings assessing the merit of each individual performance, speed figures for every horse that clocks a worthwhile time, weight-for-age allowances, stall positions for every race and the starting price percentage, in addition to the traditional features.

Race Focus comments are printed below each race along with official explanations and notebook comments for all British races of Class 3 and above, all two-year-old races and foreign races. The comments provide an analysis of the winning performance and, where applicable, explain possible reasons for improvement or attempt to explain why any horse failed to run to its best. More importantly, our team will also indicate the conditions under which horses are likely to be seen to best advantage.

The official record

THE FORM BOOK records comprehensive race details of every domestic race, every major European Group race and every foreign event in which a British-trained runner participated. In the **NOTEBOOK** section, extended interpretation is provided for all runners worthy of a mention, including all placed horses and all favourites. Generally speaking, the higher the class of race, the greater the number of runners noted.

MEETING BACK REFERENCE NUMBER is the Raceform number of the last meeting run at the track and is shown to the left of the course name. Abandoned meetings are signified by a dagger.

THE GOING, The Official going, shown at the head of each meeting, is recorded as follows: Turf: Hard; Firm; Good to firm; Good; Good to soft; Soft; Heavy. All-Weather: Fast; Standard to fast; Standard; Standard to slow; Slow. There may be variations for non-British meetings

Where appropriate, a note is included indicating track bias and any differences to the official going indicated by race times.

THE WEATHER is shown below to th e date for selected meetings.

THE WIND is given as a strength and direction at the Winning Post, classified as follows:
Strength: gale; v.str; str; fresh; mod; slt; almost nil; nil.
Direction: (half) against; (half) bhd; (half) across from or towards stands.

VISIBILITY is good unless otherwise stated.

RACE NUMBERS for Foreign races carry the suffix 'a' in the race header and in the index.

RACE TITLE is the name of the race as shown in the Racing Calendar.

COMPETITIVE RACING CLASSIFICATIONS are shown on a scale from Class 1 to Class 7. All Pattern races are Class 1.

THE RACE DISTANCE is given for all races, and is accompanied by (s) for races run on straight courses and (r) for courses where there is a round track of comparable distance. On All-Weather courses (F) for Fibresand or (P) for Polytrack indicates the nature of the artificial surface on which the race is run.

OFFICIAL RACE TIME as published in the Racing Calendar is followed in parentheses by the time when the race actually started. This is followed by the race class, age restrictions, handicap restrictions and the official rating of the top weight.

PRIZE MONEY shows penalty values down to sixth place (where applicable).

THE POSITION OF THE STARTING STALLS is shown against each race, in the form of: High (H), Centre (C) or Low (L). If one stands at the start facing towards the finish, the stalls are numbered from left to right. If the stalls are placed adjacent to the left rail they are described as low, if against the right rail they are described as high. Otherwise they are central.

IN THE RACE RESULT, the figures to the far left of each horse (under FORM) show the most recent form figures. The figure in bold is the finishing position in this race as detailed below.

1...40 - finishing positions first to fortieth; **b** - brought down; **c** - carried out; **f** - fell; **p** - pulled up; **r** - refused; **ro** - ran out; **s** - slipped up; **u** - unseated rider; **v** - void race.

THE OFFICIAL DISTANCES between the horses are shown on the left-hand side immediately after their position at the finish.

NUMBER OF DAYS SINCE PREVIOUS RUN is the superscript figure immediately following the horse name and suffix.

PREVIOUS RACEFORM RACE NUMBER is the boxed figure to the right of the horse's name.

THE HORSE'S AGE is shown immediately before the weight carried.

WEIGHTS shown are actual weights carried.

OFFICIAL RATING is the figure in bold type directly after the horse's name in the race result. This figure indicates the Official BHB rating, at entry, after the following adjustments had been made:
(i) Overweight carried by the rider.
(ii) The number of pounds out of the handicap (if applicable).
(iii) Penalties incurred after the publication of the weights.
However, no adjustments have been made for:
(i) Weight-for-age.
(ii) Riders' claims.

HEADGEAR is shown immediately befoe the jockey's name and in parentheses and expressed as: **b** (blinkers); **v** (visor); **h** (hood); **e** (eyeshield); **c** (eyecover); **p** (sheepskin cheekpieces).

THE JOCKEY is shown for every runner followed, in superscript, by apprentice allowances in parentheses.

APPRENTICE ALLOWANCES The holders of apprentice jockeys' licences under the provisions of Rule 60(iii) are permitted to claim the following allowances in Flat races:
7lb until they have won 20 Flat races run under the Rules of any recognised Turf Authority; thereafter 5lb until they have won 50 such Flat races; thereafter 3lb until they have won 95 such Flat races. These allowances can be claimed in the Flat races set out below, with the exception of races confined to apprentice jockeys:
(a) All handicap handicaps other than those Rated stakes which are classified as listed races.
(b) All selling and claiming races.
(b) All weight-for-age races classified 3, 4, 5, 6 and 7.

THE DRAW for places at the start is shown after each jockey's name.

RACING POST RATINGS, which record the level of performance attained in this race for each horse, appear in the end column after each horse. These are the work of handicappers Simon Turner, Sam Walker and Paul Curtis, who head a dedicated team dealing with Flat races for Raceform and sister publication, the *Racing Post*.

THE TRAINER is shown for every runner.

COMMENT-IN-RUNNING is shown for each horse in an abbreviated form. Details of abbreviations appear later in this section.

STARTING PRICES appear below the jockey in the race result. The favourite indicator appears to the right of the Starting Price; 1 for the favourite, 2 for the second-favourite and 3 for third-favourite. Joint favourites share the same number.

RACE TIMES in Great Britain are official times which are electronically recorded and shown to 100th of a second. Figures in parentheses following the time show the number of seconds faster or slower than the Raceform Median Time for the course and distance.

RACEFORM MEDIAN TIMES are compiled from all races run over the course and distance in the preceding five years. Times equal to the median are shown as (0.00). Times under the median are preceded by minus, for instance, 1.8 seconds under the median would be shown (-1.8). Record times are displayed either referring to the juvenile record (1.2 under 2y best) or to the overall record (1.2 under best).

GOING CORRECTION appears against each race to allow for changing conditions of the ground. It is shown to a hundredth of a second and indicates the adjustment per furlong against the median time. The going based on the going correction is shown in parentheses and is recorded in the following stages:
Turf: HD (Hard); F (Firm); GF (Good to firm); G (Good); GS (Good to soft); S (Soft); HVY (Heavy). All-Weather: FST (Fast); SF (Standard to fast); STD (Standard); SS (Standard to slow); SLW (Slow)

WEIGHT-FOR-AGE allowances are given where applicable for mixed-age races.

STARTING PRICE PERCENTAGE follows the going correction and weight-for-age details, and gives the total SP percentage of all runners that competed. It precedes the number of runners taking part in the race.

SELLING DETAILS (where applicable) and details of any claim are given. Friendly claims are not detailed.

SPEED RATINGS appear below the race time and going correction. They are the work of time expert Dave Bellingham and differ from conventional ratings systems in that they are an expression of a horse's ability in terms of lengths-per-mile, as opposed to pounds in weight. They are not directly comparable with BHB and Racing Post ratings.

The ratings take no account of the effect of weight, either historically or on the day, and this component is left completely to the user's discretion. What is shown is a speed rating represented in its purest form, rather than one that has been altered for weight using a mathematical formula that treats all types of horses as if they were the same.

A comparison of the rating achieved with the 'par' figure for the grade of race - the rating that should be achievable by an average winner in that class of race- will both provide an at-a-glance indication of whether or not a race was truly run and also highlight the value of the form from a time perspective.

In theory, if a horse has a best speed figure five points superior to another and both run to their best form in a race over a mile, the first horse should beat the second by five lengths. In a race run over two miles, the margin should be ten lengths and so on.

Before the speed figures can be calculated, it is necessary to establish a set of standard or median times for every distance at every track, and this is done by averaging the times of all winners over a particular trip going back several years. No speed ratings are produced when insufficient races have been run over a distance for a reliable median time to be calculated.

Once a meeting has taken place, a raw unadjusted speed rating is calculated for each winner by calculating how many lengths per mile the winning time was faster or slower than the median for the trip. A difference of 0.2 of a second equals one length. The raw speed ratings of all winners on the card are then compared to the 'par' figure for the class of race. The difference between the 'raw' speed rating and the 'par' figure for each race is then noted, and both the fastest and slowest races are discarded before the rest are averaged to produce the going allowance or track variant. This figure gives an idea as to how much the elements, of which the going is one, have affected the final times of each race.

The figure representing the going allowance is then used to adjust the raw speed figures and produce the final ratings, which represent how fast the winners would have run on a perfectly good surface with no external influences, including the weather. The ratings for beaten horses are worked out by taking the number of lengths they were behind the winner, adjusting that to take into account the distance of the race, and deducting that figure from the winner's rating. The reader is left with a rating which provides an instant impression of the value of a time performance.

The speed 'pars' below act as benchmark with which to compare the speed figures earned by each horse in each race. A horse that has already exceeded the 'par' for the class he is about to run in, is of special interest, especially if he has done it more than once, as are horses that have consistently earned higher figures than their rivals.

Class 1 Group One	117
Class 1 Group Two	115
Class 1 Group Three	113
Class 1 Listed	111
Class 2	109
Class 3	107
Class 4	105
Class 5	103
Class 6	101
Class 7	97

Allowances need to be made for younger horses and for fillies. These allowances are as follows.

MONTH	2yo	3yo
Jan / Feb	n/a	-6
Mar / Apr	-11	-5
May / Jun	-10	-4
Jul / Aug	-9	-3
Sep / Oct	-8	-2
Nov / Dec	-7	-1
Races contested by fillies only		-3

Allowances are cumulative. For example, using a combination of the above pars and allowances, the par figure for the Epsom Oaks would be 110. The Group One par is 117, then deduct 4 because the race is confined to three year olds and run in June, then subtract another 3 because the race is confined to fillies.

TOTE prices include £1 stake. Exacta dividends are shown in parentheses. The Computer Straight Forecast dividend is preceded by the letters CSF, Computer Tricast is preceded by CT and Tote Trio dividend is preceded by the word Trio. Jackpot, Placepot and Quadpot details appear at the end of the meeting to which they refer.

OWNER is followed by the breeder's name and the trainer's location.

STEWARDS' ENQUIRIES are included with the result, and any suspensions and/or fines incurred. Objections by jockeys and officials are included, where relevant.

HISTORICAL FOCUS details occasional points of historical significance.

FOCUS The Focus section has been enhanced to help readers distinguish good races from bad races and reliable form from unreliable form, by drawing together the opinions of handicapper, time expert and paddock watcher and interpreting their views in a punter-friendly manner.

NOTEBOOK horses marked with the diamond symbol are those deemed by our racereaders especially worthy of note in future races.

OFFICIAL EXPLANATIONS, where the horse is deemed to have run well above or below expectations

Abbreviations and their meanings

Paddock comments

gd sort - well made, above average on looks
h.d.w - has done well, improved in looks
wl grwn - well grown, has filled to its frame
lengthy - longer than average for its height
tall - tall
rangy - lengthy and tall but in proportion.
cl cpld - close coupled
scope - scope for physical development
str - strong, powerful looking
w'like - workmanlike, ordinary in looks
lt-f - light-framed, not much substance
cmpt - compact
neat - smallish, well put together
leggy - long legs compared with body
angular - unfurnished behind the saddle, not filled to frame
unf - unfurnished in the midriff, not filled to frame
narrow - not as wide as side appearance would suggest
small - lacks any physical scope
nt grwn - not grown
lw - looked fit and well
bkwd - backward in condition
t - tubed
swtg - sweating
b (off fore or nr fore) - bandaged in front
b.hind (off or nr) - bandaged behind

At the start

stdd s - jockey purposely reins back the horse
dwlt - missed the break and left for a short time
s.s - slow to start, left longer than a horse that dwelt
s.v.s - started very slowly
s.i.s - started on terms but took time to get going
ref to r - either does not jump off, or travels a few yards and then stops
rel to r - tries to pull itself up in mid-race
w.r.s - whipped round start

Position in the race

led - in lead on its own
disp ld - upsides the leader

w ldr - almost upsides the leader
w ldrs - in a line of three or more disputing the lead
prom - on the heels of the leaders, in the front third of the field
trckd ldr(s) - just in behind the leaders giving impression that it could lead if asked
chsd ldr - horse in second place
chsd clr ldrs - horse heads main body of field behind two clear leaders
chsd ldrs - horse is in the first four or five but making more of an effort to stay close to the pace than if it were tracking the leaders.
clsd - closed
in tch - close enough to have a chance
hdwy - making ground on the leader
gd hdwy - making ground quickly on the leader, could be a deliberate move
sme hdwy - making some ground but no real impact on the race
w.w - waited with
stdy hdwy - gradually making ground
ev ch - upsides the leaders when the race starts in earnest
rr - at the back of main group but not detached
bhd - detached from the main body of runners
hld up - restrained as a deliberate tactical move
nt rcvr - lost all chance after interference, mistake etc.
wknd - stride shortened as it began to tire
lost tch - had been in the main body but a gap appeared as it tired
lost pl - remains in main body of runners but lost several positions quickly

Riding

effrt - short-lived effort
pushed along - received urgings with hands only, jockey not using legs
rdn - received urgings from saddle, including use of whip
hrd rdn - received maximum assistance from the saddle including use of whip
drvn - received forceful urgings, jockey putting in a lot of effort and using whip
hrd drvn - jockey very animated, plenty of kicking, pushing and reminders

Finishing comments

jst failed - closing rapidly on the winner and probably would have led a stride after the line
r.o - jockey's efforts usually involved to produce an increase in pace without finding an appreciable turn of speed
r.o wl - jockey's efforts usually involved to produce an obvious increase in pace without finding an appreciable turn of speed
unable qckn - not visibly tiring but does not possess a sufficient change of pace
one pce - not tiring but does not find a turn of speed, from a position further out than unable qckn
nt r.o. - did not consent to respond to pressure
styd on - going on well towards the end, utilising stamina
nvr able to chal - unable to produce sufficient to reach a challenging position
nvr nr to chal - in the opinion of the racereader, the horse was never in a suitable position to challenge.
nrst fin - nearer to the winner in distance beaten than at any time since the race had begun in earnest
nvr nrr - nearer to the winner position-wise than at any time since the race had begun in earnest
rallied - responded to pressure to come back with a chance having lost its place
no ex - unable to sustain its run
bttr for r - likely to improve for the run and experience
rn green - inclined to wander and falter through inexperience
too much to do - left with too much leeway to make up

Winning comments

v.easily - a great deal in hand
easily - plenty in hand
comf - something in hand, always holding the others
pushed out - kept up to its work with hands and heels without jockey resorting to whip or kicking along and wins fairly comfortably
rdn out - pushed and kicked out to the line, with the whip employed
drvn out - pushed and kicked out to the line, with considerable effort and the whip employed
all out - nothing to spare, could not have found any more
jst hld on - holding on to a rapidly diminishing lead, could not have found any more if passed
unchal - must either make all or a majority of the running and not be challenged from an early stage

Complete list of abbreviations

a - always
abt - about
a.p - always prominent
appr - approaching
awrdd - awarded
b.b.v - broke blood-vessel
b.d - brought down
bdly - badly
bef - before
bhd - behind
bk - back
blkd - baulked
blnd - blundered
bmpd - bumped
bnd - bend
btn- beaten
bttr - better
c - came
ch - chance
chal - challenged
chse - chase
chsd - chased
chsng - chasing
circ - circuit
cl - close
clr - clear
clsd - closed
comf - comfortably
cpld - coupled
crse - course
ct - caught
def - definite
dismntd - dismounted
disp - disputed
dist - distance
div - division
drvn - driven
dwlt - dwelt
edgd - edged
effrt - effort

ent - entering
ev ch - every chance
ex - extra
f - furlong
fin - finished
fnd - found
fnl - final
fr - from
gd - good
gng - going
gp - group
grad - gradually
grnd - ground
hd - head
hdd - headed
hdwy - headway
hld - held
hmpd - hampered
imp - impression
ins - inside
j.b - jumped badly
j.w - jumped well
jnd - joined
jst - just
kpt - kept
l - length
ld - lead
ldr - leader

lft - left
mod - moderate
m - mile
m.n.s - made no show
mde - made
mid div - mid division
mstke - mistake
n.d - never dangerous
n.g.t - not go through
n.m.r - not much room
nk - neck
no ex - no extra
nr - near
nrr - nearer
nrst fin - nearest finish
nt - not
nvr - never
one pce - one pace
out - from finish
outpcd - outpaced
p.u - pulled up
pce - pace
pckd - pecked
pl - place
plcd - placed
plld - pulled
press - pressure
prog - progress

prom - prominent
qckly - quickly
qckn - quicken
r - race
racd - raced
rch - reach
rcvr - recover
rdn - ridden
rdr - rider
reard - reared
ref - refused
rn - ran
rnd - round
r.o - ran on
rr - rear
rspnse - response
rt - right
s - start
sddle - saddle
shkn - shaken
slt - slight
sme - some
sn - soo
spd- speed
st - straight
stmbld - stumbled
stdd - steadied
stdy - steady

strly - strongly
styd - stayed
styng - staying
s. u - slipped up
swtchd - switched
swvd - swerved
tk - took
t.k.h - took keen hold
t.o - tailed off
tch - touch
thrght - throughout
trbld - troubled
trckd - tracked
u.p - under pressure
u.str.p- under strong pressure
w - with
ww - waited with
w.r.s - whipped round start
wd - wide
whn - when
wknd - weakened
wl - well
wnr - winner
wnt - went
1/2-wy - halfway

Racing Post Ratings

Racing Post Ratings for each horse are shown in the right hand column, headed RPR, and indicate the actual level of performance attained in that race. The figure in the back index represents the BEST public form that Raceform's Handicappers still believe the horse capable of reproducing.

To use the ratings constructively in determining those horses best-in in future events, the following procedure should be followed:

(i) In races where all runners are the same age and are set to carry the same weight, no calculations are necessary. The horse with the highest rating is best-in.

(ii) In races where all runners are the same age but are set to carry different weights, add one point to the Raceform Rating for every pound less than 10 stone to be carried; deduct one point for every pound more than 10 stone.

For example,

Horse	Age & wt	Adjustment from 10st	Base rating	Adjusted rating
Treclare	3-10-1	-1	78	77
Buchan	3-9-13	+1	80	81
Paper Money	3-9-7	+7	71	78
Archaic	3-8-11	+17	60	77

Therefore Buchan is top-rated (best-in)

(iii) In races concerning horses of different ages the procedure in (ii) should again be followed, but reference must also be made to the Official Scale of Weight-For-Age.

For example,

12 furlongs, July 20th

Horse	Age & wt	Adjustment from 10st	Base rating	Adjusted rating	W-F-A deduct	Final rating
Orpheus	5-10-0	0	90	90	Nil	90
Lemonora	4-9-9	+5	88	93	Nil	93
Tamar	3-9-4	+10	85	95	-12	83
Craigangower	4-8-7	+21	73	94	Nil	94

Therefore Craigangower is top-rated (best-in)

(A 3-y-o is deemed 12lb less mature than a 4-y-o or older horse on 20th July over 12f. Therefore, the deduction of 12 points is necessary.)

The following symbols are used in conjunction with the ratings:

++: almost certain to prove better

+: likely to prove better

d: disappointing (has run well below best recently)

?: form hard to evaluate

t: tentative rating based on race-time rating may prove unreliable

Weight adjusted ratings for every race are published daily in Raceform Private Handicap and our new service Raceform Private handicap ONLINE (www.raceform.co.uk).

For subscription terms please contact the Subscription Department on (01635) 578080.

The Official Scale of Weight, Age & Distance (Flat)

The following scale should only be used in conjunction with the Official ratings published in this book. Use of any other scale will introduce errors into calculations. The allowances are expressed as the number of pounds that is deemed the average horse in each group falls short of maturity at different dates and distances.

Dist		Jan		Feb		Mar		Apr		May		Jun		Jul		Aug		Sep		Oct		Nov		Dec	
(fur)	Age	1-15	16-31	1-14	15-28	1-15	16-31	1-15	16-30	1-15	16-31	1-15	16-30	1-15	16-31	1-15	16-31	1-15	16-30	1-15	16-31	1-15	16-30	1-15	16-31
5	2	-	-	-	-	-	47	44	41	38	36	34	32	30	28	26	24	22	20	19	18	17	17	16	16
	3	15	15	14	14	13	12	11	10	9	8	7	6	5	4	3	2	1	1	-	-	-	-	-	-
6	2	-	-	-	-	-	-	-	-	44	41	38	36	33	31	28	26	24	22	21	20	19	18	17	17
	3	16	16	15	15	14	13	12	11	10	9	8	7	6	5	4	3	2	2	1	1	-	-	-	-
7	2	-	-	-	-	-	-	-	-	-	-	-	-	38	35	32	30	27	25	23	22	21	20	19	19
	3	18	18	17	17	16	15	14	13	12	11	10	9	8	7	6	5	4	3	2	2	1	1	-	-
8	2	-	-	-	-	-	-	-	-	-	-	-	-	-	-	37	34	31	28	26	24	23	22	21	20
	3	20	20	19	19	18	17	15	14	13	12	11	10	9	8	7	6	5	4	3	3	2	2	1	1
9	3	22	22	21	21	20	19	17	15	14	13	12	11	10	9	8	7	6	5	4	4	3	3	2	2
	4	1	1	-	-	-	-	-	-	-	-	-	-	-	-	-	-	-	-	-	-	-	-	-	-
10	3	23	23	22	22	21	20	19	17	15	14	13	12	11	10	9	8	7	6	5	5	4	4	3	3
	4	2	2	1	1	-	-	-	-	-	-	-	-	-	-	-	-	-	-	-	-	-	-	-	-
11	3	24	24	23	23	22	21	20	19	17	15	14	13	12	11	10	9	8	7	6	6	5	5	4	4
	4	3	3	2	2	1	1	-	-	-	-	-	-	-	-	-	-	-	-	-	-	-	-	-	-
12	3	25	25	24	24	23	22	21	20	19	17	15	14	13	12	11	10	9	8	7	7	6	6	5	5
	4	4	4	3	3	2	2	1	1	-	-	-	-	-	-	-	-	-	-	-	-	-	-	-	-
13	3	26	26	25	25	24	23	22	21	20	19	17	15	14	13	12	11	10	9	8	8	7	7	6	6
	4	5	5	4	4	3	3	2	1	-	-	-	-	-	-	-	-	-	-	-	-	-	-	-	-
14	3	27	27	26	26	25	24	23	22	21	20	19	17	15	14	13	12	11	10	9	9	8	8	7	7
	4	6	6	5	5	4	4	3	2	1	-	-	-	-	-	-	-	-	-	-	-	-	-	-	-
15	3	28	28	27	27	26	25	24	23	22	21	20	19	17	15	14	13	12	11	10	9	8	8	7	7
	4	6	6	5	5	4	4	3	3	2	1	-	-	-	-	-	-	-	-	-	-	-	-	-	-
16	3	29	29	28	28	27	26	25	24	23	22	21	20	19	17	15	14	13	12	11	10	9	9	8	8
	4	7	7	6	6	5	5	4	4	3	2	1	-	-	-	-	-	-	-	-	-	-	-	-	-
18	3	31	31	30	30	29	28	27	26	25	24	23	22	21	20	18	16	14	13	12	11	10	10	9	9
	4	8	8	7	7	6	6	5	5	4	3	2	1	-	-	-	-	-	-	-	-	-	-	-	-
20	3	33	33	32	32	31	30	29	28	27	26	25	24	23	22	20	18	16	14	13	12	11	11	10	10
	4	9	9	8	8	7	7	6	6	5	4	3	2	1	-	-	-	-	-	-	-	-	-	-	-

Effect of the draw

(R.H.) denotes right-hand and (L.H.) left-hand courses.

* Draw biases shown below apply to straight-course races unless otherwise stipulated.

** Most races (outside Festival meetings) are now restricted to 20 runners under a recently introduced BHB rule, which means it's now particularly worth looking at the stalls position, as many courses can accommodate more than that number.

ASCOT (R-H) - Following extensive redevelopment there were some pretty exaggerated draw biases last year. Jockeys reported the ground on the far side (high) to be more undulating and that was clearly not the place to be at the Royal Meeting, when low numbers enjoyed a distinct advantage.
However, watering then became the deciding factor and far too much was applied on more than one occasion. Further work is due to be carried out in a bid to level things out and it remains to be seen what effect the draw has at early meetings.
STALLS: Usually go up the stands' side (low).
BIASES: One side or other was often favoured last season but that could all change again.
SPLITS: Are common in big-field handicaps and occasionally will occur on soft ground in round-course races, when some head for the outside rail (covered by trees).

AYR (L-H) - Throughout the 90s high numbers were massively favoured in the Gold and Silver Cups but things have become less clear-cut since. Traditionally the centre of the course has ridden slower, meaning low numbers were often favoured over 7f50y and 1m, but this didn't look the case on more than one occasion last year.
STALLS: Usually go up the stands' side (high) in sprints, but occasionally go on the other side. It wasn't uncommon last year for jockeys to switch from the far side to race down the centre or even come right across and this could well continue in the new season.
BIASES: There's ultimately not a lot between the two sides in big fields now.
SPLITS: Are becoming more common, having only usually occurred in the Silver and Gold Cups in the past.

BATH (L-H) - The draw is basically of far less importance than the pace at which races are run. In big fields, runners drawn low are often inclined to go off too fast to hold a rail position (the course turns left most of the way, including one major kink) and this can see hold-up horses drawn wide coming through late. Conversely, in smaller fields containing little pace, up front on the inside is often the place to be.
STALLS: Always go on the inside (low).
SPLITS: Fields almost always stick together, but soft ground can see a split, with the outside rail (high) then favoured.

BEVERLEY (R-H) - A high draw is essential on good to soft or faster ground over 5f and also on the round course, particularly in races of 7f100y and 1m100y. In sprints, runners have to negotiate a right-handed jink not long after the start and it seems harder here than at any course for runners drawn low to get over to the favoured rail (there's also a camber). The course management experimented with moving stalls to the stands' side over 5f in 2002 (unsuccessfully, as it led to a huge low bias) and haven't done so since.
STALLS: Go on the inside (high) at all distances.
BIASES: High numbers are massively favoured at 5f on good to soft or faster ground and are also best on the round course.
SPLITS: Splits are rare and only likely over 5f on soft ground.

BRIGHTON (L-H) - There was a spell during the summer last year when it was a massive advantage to race against the outside rail (high) as this strip was brown and clearly hadn't been watered. Otherwise, much depends on the going and time of year; on good to soft or slower ground runners often head for the outside rail, while in late season it's usually just a case of whichever jockey finds the least cut-up strip of ground. Otherwise, low-drawn prominent-racers tend to hold sway in fast-ground sprints, with double figures always facing an uphill task over 5f59y.
STALLS: Always go on the inside (low) in sprints.
SPLITS: These occur frequently, as jockeys look for a fresh strip on ground that seems to churn up easily.

CARLISLE (R-H) - Runners racing with the pace and hardest against the inside rail (high) do well in big fields on decent ground. This is largely down to the fact that the Flat course and NH course are one and the same, and that those racing nearest the fence are running where the hurdle wings were positioned, while those wider out are on the raced-on surface. On soft ground, the bias swings completely, with runners racing widest (low) and grabbing the stands' rail in the straight favoured at all distances.
STALLS: Normally go on the inside (high) but can go down the middle in sprints (usually on slow ground).
BIASES: High numbers are best in fast-ground sprints. Look to back low numbers on soft/heavy ground.
SPLITS: Rarely will two groups form but, on easy ground, runners often spread out.

CATTERICK (L-H) - When the ground is testing, the stands' rail is definitely the place to be, which suits high numbers in 5f races and high-drawn prominent-racers at all other distances. However, when the ground is good to firm or faster, horses drawn on the inside (low) often hold the edge, and there have been several meetings over the last few seasons in which those racing prominently hardest against the inside rail have dominated (over all distances, presumably as a result of watering).
STALLS: Go on the inside (low) at all distances these days (they often used to go on the outer over 5f212y).
BIASES: Low numbers are best in sprints on fast ground (particularly watered firm going) but the stands' rail (high) rides faster under slower conditions.
SPLITS: Are common over 5f.

CHEPSTOW (L-H) - High numbers enjoyed a massive advantage in straight-course races in 2000 and the course management duly took steps to eradicate the faster strip, using the same 'earthquake' machine as had been employed at Goodwood in the late 90s. This has led to little in the way of a draw bias since.
STALLS: Always go on the stands' side (high) on the straight course.
BIASES: Have become hard to predict in recent times.
SPLITS: Splits are common and jockeys drawn low often head far side.

CHESTER (L-H) - It's well known that low numbers are favoured at all distances here, even in the 2m2f Chester Cup, and the bias is factored into the prices these days. That said sprints (and in particular handicaps) are still playable, as it often pays to stick to a runner drawn 1-3.
STALLS: Go on the inside (low) at all distances bar 1m2f75y and 2m2f117y (same starting point) when they go on the outside. Certain starters ask for the stalls to come off the inside rail slightly in sprints.
BIASES: Low numbers are favoured at all distances. Soft ground seems to accentuate the bias until a few races have been staged, when a higher draw becomes less of a disadvantage as the ground on the inside becomes chewed up.

DONCASTER (L-H) - The course has been closed for redevelopment and it remains to be seen whether the old biases remain. As a rule of thumb in the past, the stands' rail (high) always offered an advantage in sprints when the stalls were on the stands' side, with low numbers best the odd occasions they went on the far side.
STALLS: Can go either side but tend to go up the stands' side (high) whenever possible.
BIASES: Runners down the centre are usually worst off. The longer the trip on the straight course the better chance the far side (low) has against the stands' side in big fields.

EPSOM (L-H) - When the going is on the soft side, jockeys tack over to the stands' side for the better ground (this strip rides quicker in such conditions as the course cambers away from the stands' rail. In 5f races, the stalls are invariably placed on the stands' side, so when the going is soft the majority of the runners are on the best ground from the outset.
Prominent-racers drawn low in round-course races are able to take the shortest route around Tattenham Corner, and on faster ground have a decisive edge over 6f, 7f and 1m114y. Over 5f, high numbers used to hold quite an advantage, but the bias is not so great these days.
STALLS: Always go on the outside (high) over 5f and 6f (races over the latter trip start on a chute) and inside (low) at other distances, bar 1m4f10y (centre).
BIASES: Low-drawn prominent racers are favoured at between 6f and 1m114y.
SPLITS: Good to soft ground often leads to a few trying the stands'-side route.

FOLKESTONE (R-H) - Prior to 1998, Folkestone was never thought to have much in the way of a bias, but nowadays the draw is often crucial on the straight course (up to 7f). On easy ground, the far rail (high) rides faster than the stands' rail, which in turn rides quicker than the middle of the track. Runners now usually go across to the far side over 6f and 7f (jockeyship often playing a part, with several races going to whichever horse secures the front up the rail). However, over 5f, when the stalls are up the stands' rail, fields often split, with low numbers just about holding sway (it seems the ground lost by switching across over the minimum trip can't be regained from racing on

the faster surface). On good to firm/firm ground runners tend to stay up the near side now (the ambulance used to go this side of the far rail but now goes the other side of the fence).
STALLS: Usually go up the stands' side (low) on the straight track, but occasionally down the centre.
BIASES: High numbers are favoured over 6f and 7f, and also over the minimum trip when 14 or more line up. However, very low numbers have a good record in smaller fields over 5f. Front-runners are well worth considering at all distances.
SPLITS: Often occur.

GOODWOOD (R-H) & (L-H) - The course management took steps to end the major high bias seen in the Stewards' Cup throughout the late 90s by breaking up the ground by machine in 1998. This led to the stands' side (low) dominating the race in 1999 before the far side gradually took over again.
STALLS: Invariably go on the stands' side (low).
BIASES: High numbers are best at between 7f-1m1f, and the faster the ground, the more pronounced the bias (keep an eye out for the rail on the home turn being moved during Glorious week, usually after the Thursday).
SPLITS: Although fields tend not to break into groups in most sprints, runners often spread out to about two-thirds of the way across in fields of around 20.

HAMILTON (R-H) - Extensive drainage work was carried out in the winter of 2002 in a bid to level up the two sides of the track but, after encouraging early results, the natural bias in favour of high numbers (far side) kicked in again. This can be altered by watering on faster going, though, so be careful after a dry spell, as things can often swing in favour of low numbers. High numbers are best over 1m65y, thanks to runners encountering a tight right-handed loop soon after the start.
STALLS: It's not uncommon for the ground to become too soft for the use of stalls, but otherwise they go either side.
BIASES: High draws are best in soft/heavy-ground sprints, but the bias becomes middle to high otherwise (often switching to low on watered fast ground). Front-runners do particularly well at all distances.
SPLITS: Look for high numbers to peel off in fields of 8+ when the stalls are stands' side unless the ground is fast.

HAYDOCK (L-H) - High numbers used to enjoy a major advantage in soft-ground sprints, but that seems to have been turned full circle by drainage work carried out in the late 90s, with the far side (low) now best on very bad ground. Otherwise, runners usually head for the centre these days, the draw rarely making much of a difference (although very high numbers can be worst off in big fields on faster going).
STALLS: Usually go down the centre in the straight.

KEMPTON All-Weather, Polytrack surface (R-H) - A high draw is a big advantage over 5f (inner bend) and 6f (outer bend) with both starts about the same distance from the first right-hand turn. A high draw is still an advantage over 7f, but becomes less significant over further.
STALLS: Go towards the inside rail (high).

LEICESTER (R-H) - There was a four-year spell between 1998 and 2001 when the centre-to-far-side strip (middle to high) enjoyed a decisive advantage over the stands' rail, jockeys eventually choosing to avoid the near side. However, that's changed recently, with very low numbers more than holding their own.
STALLS: Invariably go up the stands' side (low).
SPLITS: Still occur occasionally.

LINGFIELD Turf (L-H) - The draw advantage is nothing like as defined as in years past, but the stands' rail (high) again went through a good spell in the second half of last season, as was the case the year before. The one factor that can have a massive effect on the draw is heavy rainfall on to firm ground. Presumably because of the undulating nature of the track and the fact that the far rail on the straight course is towards the bottom of a slope where it joins the round course, rainfall seems to make the middle and far side ride a deal slower. In these conditions, the top three or four stalls have a massive edge.
STALLS: Go up the stands' side (high) at between 5f and 7f and down the middle over 7f140y.
BIASES: High numbers are massively favoured on fast ground after recent rain, but otherwise the most recent meeting is often the best guide.
SPLITS: It's unusual to see two distinct groups, but runners often fan out centre to stands' side in big fields.

LINGFIELD All-Weather, Polytrack surface (L-H) - There is little bias over most trips, but it is an advantage to be drawn low over 6f and 1m 2f with both starts being situated very close to the first bend. A low to middle draw is preferable over 5f even with a safety limit of just ten, though the very inside stall has a poor recent record. No horse managed to win from stall one over that trip in 2004, which suggests the ground right against the inside rail is slower than elsewhere.
STALLS: Are against the outside rail (high) over 5f and 1m, but against the inside rail (low) for all other distances.
SPLITS: Due to the nature of the circuit, the fields never split though some horses can be forced very wide on the home bend.

MUSSELBURGH (R-H) - The bias in favour of low numbers over 5f isn't as pronounced as many believe, apart from on soft ground, while the bias in favour of high numbers at 7f and 1m also isn't that big.
STALLS: Usually go up the stands' side (low) over 5f nowadays, but they can be rotated.
SPLITS: Look out for runners drawn very high in big-field 5f races on fast ground, as they occasionally go right to the far rail.

NEWBURY (L-H) - There's basically little between the two sides these days, apart from on soft ground, in which case the stands' rail (high) is definitely the place to be. When the ground is testing it's not uncommon to see runners race wide down the back straight and down the side at between 1m3f56y and 2m (particularly over 1m5f61y). In such circumstances, a high draw becomes an advantage.
STALLS: Can go anywhere for straight-course races.
SPLITS: It's not often fields are big enough for a split to occur.

NEWCASTLE (L-H) - It's always been a case of high numbers best at up to and including 7f on good or firmer, and low numbers having the advantage when the ground is good to soft or softer. Over the straight 1m, the stands' rail (high) is the place to be apart from on very bad ground.
STALLS: Invariably go on the stands' side (high) only being switched to the inside under exceptional circumstances.
SPLITS: Two groups are usually formed when 14+ go to post, and often when 8-13 line up.

NEWMARKET July Course (R-H) - The major draw biases seen under the former Clerk of the Course have become a thing of the past since Michael Prosser took over and now only the occasional meeting will be affected. The course is permanently divided into two halves by a rail (the Racing Post now carry information regarding which side is to be used) and, as a rule of thumb, the two outside rails (stands' rail when they're on the stands'-side half, far rail when they're on the far-side half) ride faster than the dividing rail.
Stands'-side half - On fast ground (particularly watered) very high numbers are often favoured at up to 1m, when there's a narrow strip hard against the fence that rides quicker. However, on good to soft or slower ground, runners racing down the centre are favoured.
Far-side half - There's rarely much in the draw, apart from on slow ground, when the far side (low) rides faster.
STALLS: Can go either side on either half of the track.
SPLITS: Runners just about tend to form two groups in capacity fields, but are more likely to run to their draw here than at tracks such as Newcastle.

NEWMARKET Rowley Mile (R-H) - Similarly to the July Course, the draw seems to have been evened out since the Clerk of the Course change, although it's still generally a case of the further away from the stands' rail the better.
STALLS: Can go anywhere and are rotated.
BIASES: High numbers have dominated the 2m2f Cesarewitch in recent years, the logic here being that those on the inside can be switched off early, while low numbers have to work to get into position before the sole right-handed turn.
SPLIT: It's not unusual for jockeys to come stands' side on slow ground in round-course races.

NOTTINGHAM (L-H) - On the straight course, it used to be a case of low numbers being favoured when the stalls were on the far rail and high numbers when they were stands' side, with low being best when the stalls spanned the entire course. These days, though, it's less clear-cut and the going makes the biggest difference. On soft ground low numbers are usually best but high tend to be favoured on good to firm or faster.
STALLS: Tend to go on the stands' side (high) unless the ground is very soft.
SPLITS: Fields usually split in sprints when 14+ line up.

PONTEFRACT (L-H) - Low numbers have always been considered best here for the same reason as at Chester, in that the course has several distinct left-hand turns with a short home straight, but this is not always true. High numbers at least hold their own over 6f now, whatever the ground, but massively so on soft/heavy. Drainage work was carried out in the late 90s to try and eradicate the outside-rail bias on slow ground, and this worked immediately afterwards, but during the last few seasons there have been definite signs that it's now riding much faster.
STALLS: Go on the inside (low) unless the ground is very soft, when they're switched to the outside rail.
SPLITS: Although it's uncommon to see distinct groups, high numbers usually race wide these days on good to soft or slower ground.

REDCAR (L-H) - It's not unusual to see big fields throughout the season here and, while the draw has rarely played a part in the past, with runners inclined to converge towards the centre, high numbers were definitely best last year.
STALLS: Go towards the stands' side (high).
SPLITS: Splits are unusual.

RIPON (R-H) - The draw is often the sole deciding factor in big-field sprints and watering plays a major part. As a general rule, low numbers are best when the ground is good to firm or faster, while the far side is always best on softer going but, ultimately, the best guide here

these days is the most recent meeting.
STALLS: Go on the stands' side (low) apart from under exceptional circumstances.
BIASES: Front-runners (particularly from high draws over 1m) have an excellent record and any horse trying to make ground from behind and out wide is always facing a tough task.
SPLITS: Fields tend to stay together in races of 12 or fewer, but a split is near guaranteed when 15 or more line up. Look for 'draw' jockeys who might chance going far side in fields of 13-14.

SALISBURY (R-H) - It's difficult to win from a single-figure draw in big-field fast-ground sprints, but proven stamina and race suitability become the most important factors over the testing straight 1m. This far-side bias is at its greatest early and late season, before and after the erection of a temporary rail (which usually goes up in July). The draw swings full circle on slower ground, as jockeys then invariably head towards the stands' rail (good to soft seems to be the cut-off point).
STALLS: Go on the far side (high) unless the ground is soft, when they're often moved to the near side.
BIASES: High numbers are best on the straight course on fast ground, there's not much in it on good to soft, while low take over on soft/heavy.
SPLITS: Fields only tend to divide on good to soft ground; otherwise they all converge towards either rail, dependant upon going.

SANDOWN (R-H) - On the 5f chute, when the going is on the soft side and the stalls are on the far side (high), high numbers enjoy a decisive advantage. On the rare occasions that the stalls are placed on the stands' side, low numbers enjoy a slight advantage when all the runners stay towards the stands' rail, but when a few break off and go to the far side high numbers comfortably hold the upper hand again. High numbers enjoy a decent advantage in double-figure fields over 7f and 1m on good going or faster, but jockeys invariably head for the stands' side on slow ground.
STALLS: Usually go far side (high) over 5f, as the course is more level that side.
SPLITS: It's unusual for runners to split over 5f, with capacity fields rare and jockeys all inclined to head for the far rail.

SOUTHWELL All-Weather, Fibresand surface (L-H) – Due to flooding the course was out of action between June and December 2007. Until then over most trips on the round track it was preferable to be drawn away from the extreme inside or outside. The exceptions are over 6f and 1m 3f, which both start close to the first bend and therefore it is better to be drawn low to middle. At most meetings the centre of the track rides faster than against either rail, though that can change in extreme weather when power-harrowing can even out the bias. A low to middle draw is preferable over the straight 5f and it is noticeable that even when a high draw wins, the horse concerned almost always giving the stands' rail a wide berth having been angled to its left to race more towards the centre.
STALLS: Are placed next to the inside rail (low), except over 5f where they are placed next to the stands' rail (high).
SPLITS: The fields do not tend to split into groups as such, but can fan right out and take varied routes once into the home straight. Even in big fields over the straight 5f, the runners basically stick to their draw and race as straight as they can from start to finish.

THIRSK (L-H) - This used to be the biggest draw course in the country, back in the days of the old watering system (which was badly affected by the wind) but, while biases still often show up, they're not as predictable as used to be the case. Field sizes, watering and going always have to be taken into account when 12 or more line up (11 or fewer runners and it's rare to see anything bar one group up the stands' rail, with high numbers best). Otherwise, either rail can enjoy the edge on watered fast ground (the one place not to be under any circumstances is down the middle). Low-drawn prominent-racers are well worth considering whatever the distance on the round course.
STALLS: Always go up the stands' side (high).
BIASES: High numbers are best in sprints when 11 or fewer line up, but it's
hard to know which side is likely to do best in bigger fields on fast ground. The far (inside) rail is always best on slow going (the softer the ground, the greater the advantage).
SPLITS: Runners invariably stay towards the stands' side in sprints containing 12 or fewer runners (unless the ground is soft) and frequently when 13-14 line up. Any more and it becomes long odds-on two groups.

WARWICK (L-H) - Low numbers are favoured in fast-ground sprints, but not by as much as many believe, and the prices often over-compensate. However, when the ground is genuinely soft, high numbers can enjoy an advantage.
STALLS: Always go on the inside (low).

WINDSOR (Fig. 8) - It's typical to see large fields all season and the draw almost always plays a part. In sprints, things are set in stone, with high numbers best on good or faster going (particularly watered fast ground), not much between the two sides on good to soft, and the far side (low) taking over on soft or heavy ground. It can be difficult for runners who switch off the stands' rail to make up the leeway (because the course turns sharply left soon after the finish those pulled wide must think they're being asked to quicken up into a dead-end). On slower ground, jockeys head centre to far
side, and right over to the far rail on genuine soft/heavy (again it's difficult to make ground from behind under such conditions).
STALLS: Can be positioned anywhere for sprints.
BIASES: High-drawn prominent-racers are favoured in fast-ground sprints, and also over 1m67y. On good to soft going, there's rarely much between the two sides, but it's a case of nearer to the far rail (low) the better on bad ground.
SPLITS: Splits only tend to occur on good to soft ground, and even then it's rare to see two defined groups.

WOLVERHAMPTON All-Weather, Polytrack surface since October 2004 (L-H) - The huge bias that used to exist towards those horses that raced away from the inside rail on the old Fibresand is a fading memory, but even though the Polytrack is relatively new, some biases are emerging. A low draw is a big advantage over 5f and 6f and low to middle is preferable over 7f and 1m. Beyond
that it doesn't seem to matter, though it is never a good idea to race too wide on the home bends and those that do so rarely seem to make up the lost ground.
STALLS: Are placed against the outside rail (high) over 7f and against the inside rail (low) at all other distances.
SPLITS: Splits do not happen and most of the time the runners stay as close as they can next to the inside rail unless traffic problems force them wide.

YARMOUTH (L-H) - High numbers enjoyed a major advantage for much of the 90s, but this was put an end to by the course switching from pop-up sprinklers (which were affected by the off-shore breeze) to a Briggs Boom in '99. These days a bias will appear occasionally but it's hard to predict, and runners often head for the centre whatever the going.
STALLS: Go one side or the other.
SPLITS: It's common to see groups form, often including one down the centre, in big fields.

YORK (L-H) - The draw is nothing like as unpredictable in sprints as many believe, although things are never quite as clear-cut in September/October as earlier in the season. Essentially, on good or faster ground, the faster strip is to be found centre to far side, which means in capacity fields, the place to be is stall 6-12, while in fields of 12-14 runners drawn low are favoured (the course is only wide enough to house 20 runners). On soft/heavy ground, the stands' side (high) becomes the place to be, and high numbers often get the rail to themselves, as this is not a bias well known among jockeys. Low numbers are best on fast ground on the round course, although watering can reduce the bias.
STALLS: Can go anywhere.
BIASES: Prominent-racers drawn down the centre are favoured in fast-ground sprints, but high numbers take over on genuine soft/heavy ground. Low numbers are best in big fields on the round course, apart from on slower going, when runners leave the inside in the home straight.
SPLITS: Defined groups are rare.

Key to racereaders' initials

WG ....Walter Glynn
KH ....Keith Hewitt
RL ....Richard Lowther
LM...................Lee McKenzie
TM ....Tim Mitchell
JN.............Jonathan Neesom
DO ....Darren Owen
SP ....Steve Payne
CR ....Colin Roberts
JR ....Joe Rowntree
JS........................John Santer
ST ....Steve Taylor
RY ....Richard Young

ADDENDA TO PREVIOUS ANNUALS

FLAT 2006

Race 4778 ALL THE GOOD has been disqualified from fourth place - banned substance in sample.

Race 5905 MILTON STAR has been disqualified from third place - ran in flapping race.

Race 6967 FOURSQUARE FLYER has been reinstated as the winner following an appeal.

SOUTHWELL (L-H)

Monday, January 1

OFFICIAL GOING: Standard

Wind: Fresh behind easing to light behind from Race 3 (1.35) onwards Weather: Fine and sunny becoming cloudy

1 PONTINSBINGO.COM APPRENTICE MEDIAN AUCTION MAIDEN STKS 1m 3f (F)

12:25 (12:25) (Class 6) 4-6-Y-O **£2,184** (£644; £322) **Stalls** Low

Form RPR

004- **1** **Credential**^{17} [6300] 5-8-13 55.. AndrewElliott(3) 5 66
(John A Harris) *trckd ldr: racd keenly: led over 2f out: rdn clr fnl f* **4/1**^{3}

043- **2** *6* **Mighty Kitchener (USA)**^{4} [6967] 4-8-13 57........................ DeanCorby 8 56
(P Howling) *a.p: rdn to chse wnr and hung lft over 1f out: styd on same pce* **3/1**^{2}

060- **3** *1 1/2* **Ruby Sunrise (IRE)**^{11} [6898] 5-8-4 45............................ SoniaEaton(7) 7 48
(B P J Baugh) *hld up: plld hrd: hdwy over 3f out: rdn 2f out: styd on same pce* **25/1**

205- **4** *nk* **Ruse**^{10} [6916] 4-8-5 57..(p) RoryMoore(3) 3 47
(J R Fanshawe) *chsd ldrs: rdn and hung lft over 2f out: nt run on* **5/2**^{1}

6- **5** *1 1/4* **Scaramoushca**^{10} [6916] 4-8-13 .... AdamKirby 6 50
(P S McEntee) *prom: rdn over 4f out: styd on same pce fnl 3f* **8/1**

4- **6** *9* **High Ambition**^{4} [6967] 4-8-8 .... WilliamBuick(5) 4 35
(P W D'Arcy) *led over 8f: rdn and wknd over 1f out* **4/1**^{3}

200- **7** *5* **The Flying Peach**^{144} [4297] 4-8-8 40.............................. JerryO'Dwyer 2 22
(Miss Gay Kelleway) *hld up: rdn 4f out: wknd over 2f out* **33/1**

00- **8** *11* **Orphir (IRE)**^{23} [6759] 4-8-10 ....(p) DuranFentiman(3) 1 8
(Mrs N Macauley) *hld up: rdn 1/2-way: wknd over 4f out* **66/1**

2m 29.34s (0.44) **Going Correction** -0.125s/f (Stan)
WFA 4 from 5yo 3lb **8** Ran SP% **113.0**
Speed ratings: 93,88,87,87,86 79,76,68
CSF £15.94 TOTE £5.60: £1.70, £1.30, £5.00; EX 27.40 Trifecta £223.90 Part won. Pool: £315.42 - 0.87 winning tickets..
Owner A J McLaren **Bred** Rockwell Bloodstock **Trained** Eastwell, Leics

FOCUS
Hard to imagine a worse race to kick off 2007 and those adrift of the easy winner have real problems. A modest winning time also.

2 GO PONTIN'S (S) STKS 1m (F)

1:00 (1:00) (Class 6) 4-Y-O+ **£2,184** (£644; £322) **Stalls** Low

Form RPR

020- **1** **Just James**^{93} [5688] 8-8-12 80.. AdrianTNicholls 5 63
(D Nicholls) *hld up in tch: chsd ldr and hung lft over 2f out: rdn to ld over 1f out: styd on* **7/4**^{1}

451- **2** *1 1/2* **Paso Doble**^{4} [6960] 9-8-13 49...(p) JamesMillman(5) 6 66
(D K Ivory) *chsd ldrs: outpcd 2f out: r.o ins fnl f* **15/8**^{2}

350- **3** *1 1/4* **Ali Bruce**^{18} [6814] 7-8-12 70.. NCallan 2 57
(P A Blockley) *trckd ldr untul led over 4f out: rdn and hdd over 1f out: no ex ins fnl f* **4/1**^{3}

000- **4** *8* **Augustus Livius (IRE)**^{16} [4881] 4-8-12 45......................(b) PaulFessey 7 41
(W Storey) *prom over 4f* **16/1**

0/0- **5** *6* **Truckle**^{13} [6871] 5-8-12 62..(v^{1}) PaulMulrennan 1 28
(C W Fairhurst) *led: hdd over 4f out: rdn and wknd 3f out* **10/1**

6 *22* **The Wicked Wizard**^{16} 4-8-7 .... AndrewElliott(5) 3 —
(W Storey) *sn pushed along in rr: bhd fr 1/2-way* **40/1**

000/ **7** *26* **Hamburg Springer (IRE)**^{376} [6331] 5-8-12 40.................... ChrisCatlin 4 —
(C J Teague) *s.s: outpcd* **20/1**

1m 44.15s (-0.45) **Going Correction** -0.125s/f (Stan) **7** Ran SP% **113.3**
Speed ratings (Par 101):97,95,94,86,80 58,32
CSF £5.22 TOTE £2.40: £1.90, £1.20; EX 4.90.The winner was bought in for 6,600gns.
Owner G G N Bloodstock Ltd **Bred** Miss S N Ralphs **Trained** Sessay, N Yorks

FOCUS
A moderate seller in which the winner was best in at the weights and made it count. The runner-up was badly in against the winner and third, which clouds the form.

3 PONTIN'S FAMILY HOLIDAYS H'CAP 6f (F)

1:35 (1:35) (Class 5) (0-70,70) 4-Y-O+ **£2,914** (£867; £433; £216) **Stalls** Low

Form RPR

301- **1** **Hamaasy**^{81} [5928] 6-8-2 **56** oh2.. AdrianTNicholls 13 72+
(D Nicholls) *chsd ldrs: led 2f out: sn rdn and hung lft: styd on* **5/1**^{2}

230- **2** *1 1/4* **Sweet Pickle**^{9} [6930] 6-8-10 **64**..(e) PatCosgrave 3 76
(J R Boyle) *hld up: hdwy over 2f out: rdn to chse wnr over 1f out: edgd lft: r.o* **9/1**

140- **3** *5* **Magic Amour**^{312} [492] 9-8-3 **62**..................................(b) KevinGhunowa(5) 9 59
(P A Blockley) *led 4f: sn rdn and wknd* **25/1**

5/0- **4** *1 1/4* **Branston Tiger**^{9} [6930] 8-8-12 **66** ow1...........................(v) DanielTudhope 5 60
(Ian Emmerson) *hld up: n.m.r over 4f out: rdn over 2f out: nt rch ldrs* **50/1**

004- **5** *3/4* **Wainwright (IRE)**^{34} [6643] 7-8-4 **58**.. ChrisCatlin 10 49
(P A Blockley) *s.i.s: sn mid-div: rdn 1/2-way: n.d* **10/1**

400- **6** *1/2* **Winthorpe (IRE)**^{31} [6664] 7-8-5 **66** ow1........................ SladeO'Hara(7) 12 56
(J J Quinn) *prom over 4f* **10/1**

660- **7** *1 1/4* **Loyal Tycoon (IRE)**^{12} [6882] 9-8-11 **70**...................... JamesMillman(5) 8 56
(D K Ivory) *mid-div: rdn over 2f out: wknd over 1f out* **12/1**

000- **8** *1/2* **Laith (IRE)**^{9} [6930] 4-8-2 **56**... JimmyQuinn 7 41
(Miss V Haigh) *s.i.s: nvr nrr* **33/1**

300/ **9** *hd* **Verite**^{497} [4638] 4-9-1 **69**.. NCallan 2 53
(A J McCabe) *mid-div: rdn 1/2-way: wknd 2f out* **16/1**

602- **10** *1 1/4* **Tag Team (IRE)**^{9} [6930] 6-8-10 **64**...................................... DaleGibson 4 44
(John A Harris) *chsd ldrs: rdn over 2f out: wknd over 1f out* **9/4**^{1}

250- **11** *5* **Piccolo Prince**^{14} [6858] 6-8-2 **56** oh3............................ HayleyTurner 11 21
(P A Blockley) *sn outpcd* **12/1**

450- **12** *3 1/2* **Serieux**^{93} [5688] 8-9-2 **70**..(v) SilvestreDeSousa 6 25
(D Nicholls) *hld up: a in rr* **8/1**^{3}

204- **13** *10* **Diktalex (IRE)**^{215} [2138] 4-8-7 **61**................................(t) RobbieFitzpatrick 1 —
(C J Teague) *chsd ldrs: rdn 1/2-way: wknd 2f out* **33/1**

1m 15.59s (-1.31) **Going Correction** -0.125s/f (Stan) **13** Ran SP% **119.7**
Speed ratings (Par 103):103,101,94,93,92 91,89,89,88,87 80,75,62
CSF £48.03 CT £1069.91 TOTE £6.90: £2.00, £2.70, £8.00; EX 48.00 Trifecta £238.60 Part won. Pool: £336.19 - 0.84 winning tickets..
Owner J P Honeyman **Bred** Shadwell Estate Company Limited **Trained** Sessay, N Yorks

FOCUS
A routine handicap of its type in which the front pair pulled a very long way clear of the rest. Sound form, with the winner returning a personal best.

Verite Official explanation: jockey said gelding hung right-handed down the straight
Tag Team(IRE) Official explanation: trainer said gelding finished distressed
Diktalex(IRE) Official explanation: jockey said filly hung right-handed throughout

4 PONTINS.COM H'CAP 2m (F)

2:10 (2:10) (Class 5) (0-75,71) 4-Y-O+ **£2,914** (£867; £433; £216) **Stalls** Low

Form RPR

402- **1** **Victory Quest (IRE)**^{13} [6873] 7-9-1 **58**..........................(v) RobertWinston 6 69
(Mrs S Lamyman) *chsd ldrs: led over 2f out: rdn and hdd over 1f out: rallied to ld wl ins fnl f* **11/4**^{2}

036- **2** *1 3/4* **Bienheureux**^{5} [6947] 6-8-11 **57**..(t) DominicFox(3) 5 66
(Miss Gay Kelleway) *hld up: hdwy over 4f out: led over 1f out: sn rdn and edgd rt: hdd wl ins fnl f* **10/1**

233- **3** *13* **Champagne Shadow (IRE)**^{23} [6766] 6-10-0 **71**....................(p) NCallan 3 64
(K A Ryan) *led over 5f: chsd ldr: led over 3f out: rdn and hdd over 2f out: wknd over 1f out* **11/4**^{2}

201- **4** *6* **Salut Saint Cloud**^{13} [6873] 6-9-11 **68**...................................(p) TPQueally 4 54
(G L Moore) *w ldr tl led over 10f out: hdd over 3f out: wknd over 2f out* **9/4**^{1}

105/ **5** *12* **Positive Profile (IRE)**^{581} [2134] 9-9-13 **70**........................ JimmyQuinn 2 42
(J J Quinn) *s.i.s: sn prom: rdn and wknd over 3f out* **6/1**^{3}

003- **6** *23* **Acceleration (IRE)**^{13} [6873] 7-8-6 **52** oh2.......................(v) GregFairley(3) 7 —
(Karen McLintock) *s.i.s: sn chsng ldrs: wknd over 4f out* **25/1**

3m 41.2s (-3.34) **Going Correction** -0.125s/f (Stan) **6** Ran SP% **111.3**
Speed ratings (Par 103):103,102,95,92,86 75
CSF £27.85 TOTE £3.30: £1.70, £5.00; EX 30.50.
Owner P Lamyman **Bred** Miss Veronica Henley **Trained** Ruckland, Lincs
■ Stewards' Enquiry : Robert Winston one-day ban: used whip without allowing gelding time to respond (Jan 12)

FOCUS
A decent pace for this marathon and stamina was truly tested. The big margins separating the sextet suggest the form is reliable.

5 PHOTO ALBUMS FROM BONUSPRINT.COM H'CAP 5f (F)

2:45 (2:45) (Class 2) (0-100,98) 4-Y-O+ **£11,334** (£3,372; £1,685; £841) **Stalls** High

Form RPR

662- **1** **Moorhouse Lad**^{27} [6720] 4-8-5 **85**.. ChrisCatlin 8 91+
(B Smart) *mde all: rdn and hung lft fnl 2f: r.o* **7/2**^{2}

563- **2** *1/2* **Pieter Brueghel (USA)**^{46} [6499] 8-8-4 **84**.................. AdrianTNicholls 2 87
(D Nicholls) *chsd ldrs: rdn over 1f out: styd on* **3/1**^{1}

003- **3** *hd* **Pawan (IRE)**^{27} [6720] 7-8-4 **89** oh2 ow5.........................(b) AnnStokell(5) 7 91
(Miss A Stokell) *w ldrs: rdn and nt clr run over 1f out: r.o* **18/1**

001- **4** *3* **Harry Up**^{22} [6776] 6-8-5 **85**.. CatherineGannon 5 77
(K A Ryan) *w ldrs: rdn over 1f out: wknd ins fnl f* **8/1**

060- **5** *1/2* **Glenviews Youngone (IRE)**^{100} [5535] 4-8-5 **85** oh3 ow1
RobbieFitzpatrick 3 75
(Peter Grayson) *sn outpcd: hdwy over 1f out: no ex ins fnl f* **20/1**

405- **6** *3/4* **Graze On**^{22} [6776] 5-8-4 **84** oh2...(b) JimmyQuinn 1 72
(Peter Grayson) *chsd ldrs: rdn 1/2-way: wknd over 1f out* **4/1**^{3}

010- **7** *2* **Skip Of Colour**^{14} [6858] 7-7-11 **84** oh29...................... WilliamBuick(7) 4 65
(P A Blockley) *sn outpcd* **33/1**

115- **8** *2* **Maltese Falcon**^{16} [6849] 7-9-4 **98**...(t) JoeFanning 6 72
(P F I Cole) *s.i.s: sn w ldrs: rdn 1/2-way: wknd over 1f out* **7/2**^{2}

58.61 secs (-1.69) **Going Correction** -0.10s/f (Stan) **8** Ran SP% **113.5**
Speed ratings (Par 109):109,108,107,103,102 101,97,94
CSF £14.22 CT £161.27 TOTE £5.20: £1.40, £1.50, £2.90; EX 24.40 Trifecta £125.20 Pool: £702.20 - 3.98 winning tickets..
Owner Ron Hull **Bred** P Onslow **Trained** Hambleton, N Yorks
■ Stewards' Enquiry : Chris Catlin caution: careless riding

FOCUS
A decent sprint handicap, as it should be for the money, and there was no place to hide. Despite the stalls being placed against the stands' rail, the whole field ended the race more towards the far side and that was largely down to the winner. He was value for a shade more and is progressing, but the close proximity of the third from out of the handicap complicates things.

NOTEBOOK
Moorhouse Lad ◆, who has changed stables since finishing runner-up here last month, started from the stands' rail draw but eventually drifted markedly to his left and ended up closer to the far rail. Fortunately for him, his early speed and his forward momentum were such that he always looked to have matters under control, despite the close attentions of the placed horses. His new yard are perfectly capable of extracting a bit more improvement out of him. (tchd 4-1)
Pieter Brueghel(USA) was never far away and put in a determined effort up the far side under a strong ride, but could never quite get to the winner. He ideally needs at least another furlong these days. (op 4-1)
Pawan(IRE), who was carrying 7lb more than he was meant to thanks mainly to his rider's 5lb overweight, was therefore 4lb worse off with Moorhouse Lad after finishing just behind him here last time. He kept staying on, despite the winner carrying him across the track and with his rider sitting quietly, whilst the jockeys on the front pair either side of him were giving it everything. He only just lost out, but form pundits may claim that without the overweight he would have won. (op 16-1 tchd 20-1)
Harry Up, raised 4lb for his Kempton victory, showed good speed for much of the way before fading and looks better suited to Polytrack. (op 7-1)
Glenviews Youngone(IRE), returning to sand off a 21lb higher mark than when breaking the Wolverhampton course record back in April, was completely taken off her feet early and could never get back into it. (op 16-1)
Graze On is better handicapped now, but after showing up for a while failed to see his race out. (op 5-1)
Maltese Falcon, trying Fibresand for the first time, became short of room at halfway but it probably made little difference to his final placing and perhaps he did not find this surface to his liking. (op 11-4)

6 CANVAS PRINTS FROM BONUSPRINT.COM H'CAP 1m (F)

3:15 (3:16) (Class 2) (0-100,100) 4-Y-O+ **£11,334** (£3,372; £1,685; £841) **Stalls** Low

Form RPR

401- **1** **Gentleman's Deal (IRE)**^{30} [6678] 6-9-2 **100**................. PaulMulrennan 8 115
(M W Easterby) *dwlt: sn chsng ldrs: lft in ld over 4f out: hdd over 3f out: led over 2f out: rdn and edgd rt fr over 1f out: r.o* **8/11**^{1}

521- **2** *2* **Speedy Sam**^{37} [6600] 4-8-4 **93**.. AndrewElliott(5) 1 104
(K R Burke) *chsd ldrs: led over 3f out: rdn and hdd over 2f out: no ex ins fnl f* **4/1**^{2}

240- **3** *1* **Uhoomagoo**^{121} [5019] 9-8-4 **88**..(b) JoeFanning 6 97
(K A Ryan) *hld up: hdwy over 3f out: rdn over 1f out: styd on same pce* **12/1**

031- **4** *3* **Very Wise**^{24} [6752] 5-8-2 **86** oh2.. PaulHanagan 7 89
(W J Haggas) *hld up: rdn over 2f out: nvr able to chal* **13/2**^{3}

062- **5** *1 1/2* **Wessex (USA)**^{30} [6678] 7-8-11 **95** ow2.. NCallan 4 94
(P A Blockley) *prom: rdn over 2f out: wknd over 1f out* **9/1**

000- **6** 8 **Yarqus**[10] 6915 4-8-8 **92** (t) TPQueally 3 75
(C E Brittain) *prom over 5f* **33/1**

022- **7** 11 **Arctic Desert**[47] 6489 7-8-2 **86** oh12 (t) JimmyQuinn 5 46
(Miss Gay Kelleway) *s.i.s: hld up: rdn over 3f out: sn wknd* **40/1**

050- **U** **Hits Only Heaven (IRE)**[11] 6896 5-8-2 **86** oh3 (e) SilvestreDeSousa 2 —
(D Nicholls) *led: hdd over 4f out: sn p.u* **25/1**

1m 40.6s (-4.00) **Going Correction** -0.125s/f (Stan) **8** Ran SP% **118.2**

Speed ratings (Par 109):115,113,112,109,107 99,88,—

CSF £4.01 CT £19.65 TOTE £1.60: £1.20, £1.60, £1.70; EX 4.90 Trifecta £33.60 Pool: £780.79 - 16.49 winning tickets..

Owner Stephen J Curtis **Bred** C H Wacker Iii **Trained** Sheriff Hutton, N Yorks

FOCUS

A high-quality handicap, won by a smart performer, and a decent winning time for the grade. Solid form, rated positively.

NOTEBOOK

Gentleman's Deal(IRE), hiked up another 9lb, had to battle hard to get the better of the runner-up but was pulling away at the line and extended his unbeaten sand record to five. Another rise will severely limit his opportunities in handicap company, especially on this track where the long straight suits this huge long-striding entire ideally. (op 5-6 tchd 10-11 in places)

Speedy Sam, raised 6lb for his Lingfield victory, was always up there and made sure the favourite had to dig deep to get the better of him. He will not always come up against such a talented performer and there will be other days. (tchd 9-2)

Uhoomagoo was suited by the strong pace and kept staying on to the line. He still looks better suited by seven furlongs, but should come on for this first run in four months. (op 9-1)

Very Wise, raised 4lb for winning at Wolverhampton on his Polytrack debut, found this better company beyond him and this surface probably did not suit his come-from-behind style. (tchd 7-1)

Wessex(USA) was 7lb better off with Gentleman's Deal for a six-length beating over course and distance last month, though it would have been more without his rider's overweight. He was beaten further by his progressive rival this time though, and looks handicapped to the hilt.

7 PONTIN'S BOOK EARLY H'CAP 1m (F)

3:45 (3:46) (Class 6) (0-55,55) 4-Y-0+ **£2,388** (£705; £352) **Stalls** Low

Form RPR

130- **1** **Granakey (IRE)**[13] 6869 4-8-9 **52** TPQueally 5 62
(M G Quinlan) *hld up: hdwy over 2f out: rdn to ld 1f out: r.o* **14/1**

326- **2** 1 **Wodhill Gold**[14] 6854 6-8-6 **49** (v) HayleyTurner 2 57
(D Morris) *prom: rdn over 2f out: led wl over 1f out: sn hdd: no ex wl ins fnl f* **15/2**[3]

601- **3** 1 ½ **Vibrato (USA)**[5] 6949 5-8-11 **54** 6ex (v) RobbieFitzpatrick 10 59
(C J Teague) *s.i.s: sn mid-div: hdwy over 2f out: rdn over 1f out: styd on same pce* **9/2**[2]

606- **4** 1 ¾ **Ohana**[35] 6628 4-8-7 **53** JerryO'Dwyer(3) 6 54
(Miss Gay Kelleway) *trckd ldrs: plld hrd: outpcd over 2f out: styd on fnl f* **10/1**

004- **5** hd **Mister Benji**[9] 6934 8-8-12 **55** DeanMcKeown 13 56
(B P J Baugh) *hld up: hdwy over 1f out: nvr nr to chal* **4/1**[1]

002- **6** 2 ½ **Penwell Hill (USA)**[18] 6814 8-8-2 **50** (b) KevinGhunowa(5) 4 46
(Miss M E Rowland) *sn led: hdd over 4f out: rdn to ld over 2f out: hdd wl over 1f out: sn wknd* **14/1**

600- **7** 3 ½ **Counterfactual (IRE)**[140] 4426 4-8-9 **55** MarkLawson(3) 8 43
(B Smart) *hld up: bhd and rdn 1/2-way: nvr nrr* **20/1**

016- **8** nk **Tee Jay Kassidy**[5] 6949 7-8-11 **54** ow1 (b) NCallan 1 42
(P S McEntee) *hld up: hdwy over 3f out: rdn and wknd 2f out* **10/1**

532- **9** 1 ¼ **Grand Palace (IRE)**[5] 6955 4-8-7 **50** (v) JimmyQuinn 9 35
(D Shaw) *w ldr tl led over 4f out: rdn and hdd over 2f out: sn hung rt and wknd* **4/1**[1]

030- **10** 2 **Weet For Ever (USA)**[3] 6980 4-8-9 **52** PaulHanagan 7 33
(P A Blockley) *prom over 5f* **12/1**

000- **11** nk **Gem Bien (USA)**[14] 6854 9-8-3 **46** oh1 (p) DaleGibson 3 26
(D W Chapman) *dwlt: outpcd* **25/1**

100- **12** shd **Drink To Me Only**[130] 4728 4-8-8 **51** PaulMulrennan 12 31
(J R Weymes) *chsd ldrs 5f* **33/1**

1m 42.74s (-1.86) **Going Correction** -0.125s/f (Stan) 12 Ran SP% **120.7**

Speed ratings (Par 101):104,103,101,99,99 97,93,93,92,90 89,89

CSF £114.70 CT £566.38 TOTE £16.40: £5.30, £2.40, £1.70; EX 116.80 TRIFECTA Not won. Place 6 £61.07, Place 5 £28.28.

Owner The Colourful Bunch **Bred** Mrs Lorraine Castle **Trained** Newmarket, Suffolk

■ Stewards' Enquiry : Hayley Turner three-day ban: used whip with excessive frequency (Jan 12-14)

FOCUS

A race run at a strong early pace, but those that set it probably went off too fast and paid the penalty. The winning time was 2.14 seconds slower than the preceding Class 2 handicap, but was still perfectly creditable for a race of its type. The pair that fought out the finish raced closest to the inside rail in the home straight. Sound form.

Counterfactual(IRE) Official explanation: jockey said gelding could not face the kickback

T/Plt: £153.40 to a £1 stake. Pool: £46,265.15. 220.10 winning tickets. T/Qpdt: £59.30 to a £1 stake. Pool: £3,649.90. 45.50 winning tickets. CR

[1]SOUTHWELL (L-H)

Tuesday, January 2

OFFICIAL GOING: Standard

Wind: Strong, behind

8 GO PONTIN'S H'CAP 5f (F)

12:20 (12:21) (Class 6) (0-65,65) 4-Y-0+ **£2,266** (£674; £337; £168) **Stalls** High

Form RPR

151- **1** **Gifted Lass**[5] 6956 5-8-9 **56** 6ex DavidAllan 5 68
(J Balding) *cl up: led wl over 2f out: sn rdn and kpt on wl* **3/1**[1]

055- **2** 1 ¼ **Maktavish**[19] 6823 8-9-2 **63** (b) PatCosgrave 13 71
(R Brotherton) *led: rdn along 2f out: sn hdd: drvn and kpt on wl fnl f* **12/1**

210- **3** hd **Muara**[11] 6922 5-8-8 **55** PaulHanagan 12 62
(D W Barker) *in tch: rdn along and outpcd 3f out: hdwy wl over 1f out: kpt on u.p ins last: nrst fin* **12/1**

000- **4** 1 ¼ **Garlogs**[36] 6622 4-8-12 **59** ChrisCatlin 11 62
(A Bailey) *cl up: rdn along 2f out: drvn over 1f out and kpt on same pce* **12/1**

511- **5** 1 **Dysonic (USA)**[20] 6806 5-8-5 **55** ow2 (v) JasonEdmunds(3) 14 54
(J Balding) *hld up towards rr: hdwy 2f out: swtchd lft and rdn over 1f out: kpt on ins last: nrst fin* **14/1**

436- **6** ¾ **Jilly Why (IRE)**[26] 6739 6-8-1 **55** (v) WilliamBuick(7) 9 52
(Ms Deborah J Evans) *chsd ldrs: rdn along 2f out: wknd approachintg last* **15/2**

001- **7** 3 ½ **Gilded Cove**[15] 6858 7-8-13 **65** RussellKennemore(5) 3 50
(R Hollinshead) *bhd tl styd on appr last: nvr nr ldrs* **9/2**[3]

0/0- **8** hd **Melandre**[24] 6773 5-9-2 **63** DeanMernagh 10 47
(M Brittain) *chsd ldrs: rdn along over 2f out: sn wknd* **80/1**

004- **9** 1 **Egyptian Lord**[30] 6686 4-8-8 **55** (b) RobbieFitzpatrick 7 36
(Peter Grayson) *dwlt: sn chsng ldrs: rdn along over 2f out: sn rdn: edgd rt and wknd* **4/1**[2]

000- **10** nk **Greek Secret**[14] 6865 4-9-2 **63** (b) SteveDrowne 1 43
(J O'Reilly) *a rr* **14/1**

554- **11** 3 ½ **Viewforth**[14] 6869 9-8-8 **55** (p) J-PGuillambert 6 23
(M A Buckley) *midfield: sn rdn along and outpcd: rr after 2f* **12/1**

000- **12** 1 ¾ **Percy Douglas**[5] 6956 7-8-4 **56** oh2 ow5 (bt) AnnStokell(5) 4 18
(Miss A Stokell) *a towards rr* **66/1**

000- **13** 11 **Golband**[5] 6956 5-7-13 **51** oh1 NataliaGemelova(5) 2 —
(R F Marvin) *chsd ldrs: rdn along 1/2-way and sn wknd* **100/1**

58.23 secs (-2.07) **Going Correction** -0.375s/f (Stan) **13** Ran SP% **122.8**

Speed ratings (Par 101):101,99,98,96,95 93,88,87,86,85 80,77,59

CSF £42.45 CT £407.86 TOTE £3.70: £1.50, £3.90, £5.00; EX 53.90 TRIFECTA Not won..

Owner Bawtry Racing Partnership **Bred** Charles Castle **Trained** Scrooby, Notts

FOCUS

A modest if competitive sprint and the usual bias towards those drawn low was not as pronounced as it usually is, with the quartet that chased the winner home coming from the four highest stalls. Not bad form for the grade, and pretty solid.

Gilded Cove Official explanation: jockey said gelding was outpaced over the 5f distance

Golband Official explanation: trainer said mare bled from the nose

9 PONTINSBINGO.COM CLAIMING STKS 6f (F)

12:50 (12:50) (Class 6) 4-Y-0+ **£2,184** (£644; £322) **Stalls** Low

Form RPR

532- **1** **Charlie Delta**[6] 6943 4-9-11 70 (p) DanielTudhope 5 77
(D Carroll) *trckd ldrs:gd hdwy on outer 1/2-way: led over 2f out: rdn wl over 1f out: drvn ins last and kpt on wl* **11/4**[1]

632- **2** 1 ¼ **Majik**[28] 6719 8-8-9 54 (p) MickyFenton 1 58
(P T Midgley) *trckd ldrs: swtchd lft over 2f out and sn chsng wnr: rdn wl over 1f out: drvn ins last and kpt on* **15/2**

501- **3** ½ **Penel (IRE)**[216] 2141 6-8-4 52 (p) RoryMoore(5) 6 56
(P T Midgley) *hld up in rr: hdwy on inner 2f out: sn rdn and kpt on appr last: nrst fin* **8/1**

455- **4** 3 **Soba Jones**[10] 6930 10-8-10 60 JasonEdmunds(3) 7 51
(J Balding) *trckd ldrs: effrt over 2f out: sn rdn and one pce* **3/1**[2]

503- **5** 1 ¼ **Musical Gift**[15] 6855 7-8-7 45 (v) PaulHanagan 8 41
(P A Blockley) *hld up in rr: rdn along 1/2-way: wd st: kpt on ins last* **16/1**

50- **6** nk **Ten Prophets (IRE)**[199] 4-8-9 70 ow2 PhillipMakin 4 42
(D Nicholls) *keen: cl up: rdn over 2f out: sn btn* **5/1**[3]

0U0- **7** 29 **Funfair Wane**[94] 5688 8-9-11 80 AdrianTNicholls 3 —
(D Nicholls) *shkn up s and sn led rdn along 1/2-way: hdd over 2f out: sn hung lft and wknd: virtually p.u fnl f* **13/2**

000- **8** 7 **Ronnie From Donny (IRE)**[6] 6943 7-8-9 35 (t) CatherineGannon 2 —
(C J Teague) *cl up: rdn along 1/2-way: sn wknd and eased wl over 1f out* **150/1**

1m 16.52s (-0.38) **Going Correction** -0.10s/f (Stan) **8** Ran SP% **111.1**

Speed ratings (Par 101):98,96,95,91,90 89,50,41

CSF £22.39 TOTE £3.00: £1.40, £1.80, £3.10; EX 17.00 Trifecta £60.20 Pool: £165.50 - 1.95 winning units..The winner was claimed by Mustafa Khan for £14,000.

Owner Mrs B Ramsden **Bred** P K Gardner **Trained** Sledmere, E Yorks

FOCUS

An ordinary claimer containing the past two winners of this race. There were doubts over most of these and the winner only had to show slight improvement on his recent form.

Funfair Wane Official explanation: jockey said gelding lost its action

10 PONTIN'S HOLIDAYS H'CAP 1m 6f (F)

1:20 (1:20) (Class 6) (0-65,57) 4-Y-0+ **£2,388** (£705; £352) **Stalls** Low

Form RPR

/50- **1** **Tioga Gold (IRE)**[92] 5723 8-8-10 **45** RussellKennemore(5) 3 53
(L R James) *in tch: pushed along and lost pl 1/2-way: hdwy 4f out: sn rdn and styd on to ld over 1f out: drvn and edgd lft ins last:kpton* **125/1**

2 ¾ **Nayodabayo (IRE)**[24] 3957 7-9-3 **52** TolleyDean(5) 8 59
(Evan Williams) *a cl up: led 3f out and sn rdn: hdd over 1f out: drvn and kpt on ins last* **9/2**[3]

160- **3** 6 **Dan's Heir**[27] 6735 5-9-8 **57** (p) LeanneKershaw(5) 5 56
(P C Haslam) *trckd ldrs 3f: sn lost pl: rdn along and bhd 1/2-way: styd on u.p fnl 2f: tk 3rd nr fin* **15/2**

051- **4** nk **Bulberry Hill**[21] 6797 6-9-11 **55** EdwardCreighton 4 53
(R W Price) *trckd ldrs: smooth hdwy 4f out: effrt and ev ch over 2f out sn rdn and wknd over 1f out* **11/4**[1]

044- **5** 1 **Bentley Brook (IRE)**[40] 6571 5-9-13 **57** (t) ChrisCatlin 7 54
(P A Blockley) *hld up in rr: hdwy 1/2-way: trckd ldrs 4f out: effrt 3f out: rdn and hung lft 2f out: sn btn* **5/1**

053- **6** 12 **Isa'Af (IRE)**[24] 6761 8-9-2 **53** WilliamCarson(7) 6 33
(P W Hiatt) *chsd ldrs: hdwy and cl up over 5f out: rdn along and wknd 4f out* **12/1**

121- **7** 4 **Red River Rebel**[4] 6973 9-9-12 **56** 6ex PaulMulrennan 1 30
(J R Norton) *led: rdn along 4f out: hdd 3f out: sn drvn and grad wknd* **10/3**[2]

024- **8** 2 ½ **Mossmann Gorge**[14] 6871 5-9-9 **53** (v) AdamKirby 2 24
(M Wellings) *hld up in rr: hdwy 1/2-way: trckd ldrs over 4f out: rdn 3f out and sn wknd* **12/1**

3m 8.10s (-1.50) **Going Correction** -0.10s/f (Stan) **8** Ran SP% **112.5**

Speed ratings (Par 101):100,99,96,95,95 88,86,84

CSF £604.34 CT £4767.90 TOTE £84.20: £17.10, £1.90, £2.60; EX 870.10 TRIFECTA Not won..

Owner L R James Limited **Bred** Rathasker Stud **Trained** Norton, N Yorks

■ This huge-priced scorer was Lee James's first winner since May 2001.

FOCUS

Not just a boil-over, but complete evaporation as Tioga Gold became the longest-priced winner ever on sand since All-Weather racing started in 1989. The winning time was perfectly acceptable for the class of race, but the winner looked the first beaten just past halfway and the third horse was detached and seemed likely to finished tailed off on the home turn, which suggests the leaders went off far too quickly and paid the penalty. As a result the form may not be reliable.

11 PONTINS.COM (S) STKS 1m (F)

1:50 (1:50) (Class 6) 3-Y-0 **£2,184** (£644; £322) **Stalls** Low

Form RPR

56- **1** **Carefree**[13] 6879 3-8-6 PaulHanagan 6 51+
(W J Haggas) *trckd ldrs: hdwy wl over 2f out: rdn to chal wl over 1f out: drvn to ld ent last: hung lft and drvn out* **7/4**[1]

The Form Book, Raceform Ltd, Compton, RG20 6NL

005- 2 1 1/2 **Mr Chocolate Drop (IRE)**[12] 6891 3-8-11 40 AdamKirby 3 53
(M J Attwater) *led: rdn 2f out: drvn and hdd ent last: ev ch tl no ex last 75 yds* **33/1**
004- 3 2 **Three No Trumps**[45] 6511 3-8-6 46 HayleyTurner 2 44
(D Morris) *s.i.s and bhd: rdn along 1/2-way: hdwy to chse ldng pair over 2f out: sn drvn: kep on ins last: nrst fin* **12/1**[3]
342- 4 5 **The Light Fandango**[2] 6996 3-8-1 48 TolleyDean(5) 8 34
(R A Harris) *dwlt: sn chsng ldrs: rdn along wl over 2f out: sn one pce* **7/4**[1]
000- 5 6 **Solo City**[31] 6675 3-8-11 45 J-PGuillambert 7 26
(P A Blockley) *chsd ldrs: rdn along 1/2-way: sn wknd* **14/1**
020- 6 8 **Gibsons**[53] 6420 3-8-11 53 ChrisCatlin 5 9
(P A Blockley) *cl up: rdn along wl over 2f out: sn wknd* **4/1**[2]
000- 7 31 **Pineapple Poll**[174] 3402 3-8-3 30 DominicFox(3) 1 —
(P L Gilligan) *chsd ldrs 3f: sn rdn alonga nd lsot pl: bhd fnl 3f* **50/1**

1m 45.49s (0.89) **Going Correction** -0.10s/f (Stan) 7 Ran SP% **112.0**
Speed ratings (Par 95):91,89,87,82,76 68,37
CSF £59.99 TOTE £2.90: £1.50, £5.50; EX 42.70 Trifecta £130.60 Pool: £371.61 - 2.02 winning units..The winner was sold to Mark Polglase for 11,000gns.
Owner Lee Palmer **Bred** Prof B Carlsoo And Cheveley Park Stud Ltd **Trained** Newmarket, Suffolk

FOCUS
A poor seller and a modest time, even for a race like this. The race has been rated through the third.
Mr Chocolate Drop(IRE) Official explanation: jockey said gelding hung right in the home straight

12 PONTIN'S HOLIDAYS H'CAP 1m 4f (F)

2:20 (2:20) (Class 6) (0-60,60) 4-Y-0+ **£2,266** (£674; £337; £168) **Stalls** Low

Form RPR
015- 1 **Maria Antonia (IRE)**[24] 6758 4-8-8 **52** PaulHanagan 9 64+
(P A Blockley) *hld up: hdwy on outer 4f out: rdn to ld over 2f out: drvn and edgd lft ent last: kpt on wl* **7/2**[2]
001- 2 1 **Miss Holly**[4] 6972 8-9-2 **56** 6ex DanielTudhope 1 66+
(D Carroll) *hld up: hdwy on outer 3f out: rdn to chal over 1f out: ev ch ent last: sn drvn: edgd lft and no ex* **5/2**[1]
250- 3 2 **Persona (IRE)**[48] 6484 5-9-4 **58** AdrianMcCarthy 8 65
(B J McMath) *led: rdn along over 3f out: drvn and hdd over 2f out: kpt on same pce* **9/2**[3]
040- 4 5 **Qaasi (USA)**[4] 6980 5-9-4 **58** DeanMernagh 2 57
(M Brittain) *hld up: hdwy over 4f out: chsd ldrs over 2f out: sn rdn and wknd over 1f out* **10/1**
505- 5 2 1/2 **Romil Star (GER)**[4] 6972 10-8-7 **47** ow1 (v) RobbieFitzpatrick 4 42
(M Wellings) *trckd ldrs: hdwy to chse ldr 1/2-way: rdn along over 3f out: sn btn* **8/1**
002- 6 3 **Boppys Dancer**[5] 6959 4-7-13 **46** oh1 ow2 (b) RoryMoore(5) 7 38
(P T Midgley) *chsd ldrs: rdn along 3f out: drvn and wknd 2f out* **9/2**[3]
030- 7 nk **Come What July (IRE)**[10] 6936 6-8-6 **46** oh1 (e[1]) HayleyTurner 5 36
(D Shaw) *hld up: a rr* **16/1**
036- 8 8 **Alisdanza**[21] 6797 5-7-13 **46** oh1 LanceBetts(7) 6 23
(N Wilson) *trckd ldr: rdn along over 4f out: sn wknd* **20/1**
160- 9 9 **Evolution Ex (USA)**[25] 6748 5-9-6 **60** (v) PatCosgrave 3 23
(I W McInnes) *chsd ldrs: rdn along over 4f out: sn wknd* **16/1**

2m 39.33s (-2.76) **Going Correction** -0.10s/f (Stan)
WFA 4 from 5yo+ 4lb 9 Ran SP% **123.9**
Speed ratings (Par 101):105,104,103,99,98 96,95,90,84
CSF £13.79 CT £41.94 TOTE £4.50: £1.60, £1.30, £2.60; EX 13.00 Trifecta £89.00 Pool: £379.94 - 3.03 winning units..
Owner Pedro Rosas **Bred** J McElroy **Trained** Lambourn, Berks

FOCUS
A modest handicap, but perhaps a shade above average form for the grade based on the third running to her best.
Maria Antonia(IRE) Official explanation: trainer was unable to explain the improved form
Boppys Dancer Official explanation: trainer said race may have come too quickly after gelding's previous run five days ago

13 PONTIN'S BOOK EARLY MAIDEN STKS 6f (F)

2:55 (2:57) (Class 5) 4-Y-0+ **£2,817** (£838; £418; £209) **Stalls** Low

Form RPR
202- 1 **Dixieland Boy (IRE)**[11] 6919 4-9-3 61 SteveDrowne 5 59
(P J Makin) *cl up: led over 2f out: rdn and hung bdly lft over 1f out: hung bdly rt ins last: drvn clr towards fin* **8/11**[1]
00- 2 3 1/2 **Bee Magic**[235] 1646 4-9-3 ChrisCatlin 1 49
(C N Kellett) *in tch: hdwy on inner 3f out: rdn to chse wnr over 1f out: ev ch ins last: drvn and no ex last 75 yds* **50/1**
600- 3 1 1/4 **Boppys Dream**[5] 6962 5-8-12 40 (p) MickyFenton 7 40
(P T Midgley) *chsd ldrs: rdn over 2f out: drvn and one pce appr last* **40/1**
53- 4 1/2 **Villa Bianca's (IRE)**[27] 6731 4-8-12 ShaneKelly 4 39
(J A Osborne) *led: rdn along and hdd over 2f out: sn drvn and wknd over 1f out* **6/1**[3]
525- 5 3 **Mustammer**[15] 6856 4-9-3 47 AdamKirby 2 35
(D Shaw) *dwlt: in tch: rdn along over 2f out and no hdwy* **11/2**[2]
\- 6 1 1/2 **Enthralled** 4-8-12 JamieMackay 6 25
(Sir Mark Prescott) *s.i.s: a rr* **11/2**[2]
202- 7 hd **Left Nostril (IRE)**[23] 6774 4-8-12 48 HayleyTurner 9 24
(P S McEntee) *chsd ldrs: rdn along overe 2f out: sn wknd* **14/1**
06- 8 2 1/2 **Blissphilly**[6] 6943 5-8-9 30 DominicFox(3) 3 17
(M Mullineaux) *chsd ldrs: rdn along 3f out: sn wknd* **80/1**

1m 16.16s (-0.74) **Going Correction** -0.10s/f (Stan) 8 Ran SP% **115.3**
Speed ratings (Par 103):100,95,93,93,89 87,86,83
CSF £53.43 TOTE £1.80: £1.10, £6.20, £3.50; EX 43.20 Trifecta £419.30 Pool: £596.59 - 1.01 winning units..
Owner Mrs Anna L Sanders **Bred** A H Bennett **Trained** Ogbourne Maisey, Wilts

FOCUS
A weak maiden rated negatively through the third to her best All-Weather form. The winner was a stone off his previous run.
Left Nostril(IRE) Official explanation: jockey said filly stumbled on leaving the stalls

14 PONTINS.COM H'CAP 1m (F)

3:25 (3:25) (Class 5) (0-70,70) 4-Y-0+ **£2,914** (£867; £433; £216) **Stalls** Low

Form RPR
603- 1 **Rebellious Spirit**[10] 6928 4-8-12 **66** PhillipMakin 2 79+
(P W Hiatt) *trckd ldng pair gng wl: smooth hdwy to ld over 2f out: rdn and hung rt over 1f out: styd on strly* **6/1**
30-0 2 5 **Weet For Ever (USA)**[1] 7 4-8-2 **56** oh4 PaulHanagan 7 59
(P A Blockley) *sn led: rdn 3f out: hdd over 2f out: sn drvn and kpt on same pce appr last* **14/1**
602- 3 1 3/4 **Anduril**[19] 6818 6-8-11 **65** (p) AdamKirby 6 64+
(Miss M E Rowland) *hld up in rr: hdwy 2f out: sn rdn and styd on ins last: nrst fin* **4/1**[3]
466- 4 3/4 **Dudley Docker (IRE)**[10] 6930 5-8-6 **67** KellyHarrison(7) 8 64
(D Carroll) *keen: cl up: rdn along over 2f out: sn one pce* **5/1**
005- 5 3 1/2 **Pomfret Lad**[127] 4881 9-8-5 **66** SladeO'Hara(7) 1 56
(J J Quinn) *chsd ldrs on inner: rdn along over 2f out: sn wknd* **14/1**
414- 6 1 3/4 **Formidable Will (FR)**[10] 6928 5-8-3 **64** (vt) WilliamBuick(7) 3 50
(D Shaw) *chsd ldrs: rdn along 3f out: drvn and btn over 2f out* **11/4**[1]
355- 7 2 1/2 **Shifty**[6] 6946 8-8-13 **67** DanielTudhope 5 48
(D Carroll) *hld up: a towards rr* **7/2**[2]
600- 8 7 **Razed**[6] 6949 4-7-13 **56** oh1 DominicFox(3) 9 22
(P L Gilligan) *in tch: rdn along 3f out: sn wknd* **33/1**

1m 42.25s (-2.35) **Going Correction** -0.10s/f (Stan) 8 Ran SP% **116.1**
Speed ratings (Par 103):107,102,100,99,96 94,91,84
CSF £84.57 CT £380.53 TOTE £5.60: £2.10, £3.30, £1.60; EX 50.30 Trifecta £432.30 Part won. Pool: £609.01 - 0.67 winning units. Place 6 £67.47, Place 5 £28.25.
Owner Mrs Lucia Stockley & Ken Read **Bred** Car Colston Hall Stud **Trained** Hook Norton, Oxon

FOCUS
There was a steady early pace to this handicap but the winner did it well and looks on the up.
T/Jkpt: Part won. £9,133.00 to a £1 stake. Pool: £12,863.50. 0.50 winning tickets. T/Plt: £67.10 to a £1 stake. Pool: £51,076.05. 555.60 winning tickets. T/Qpdt: £16.50 to a £1 stake. Pool: £4,021.30. 180.30 winning tickets. JR

ASCOT (AUSTRALIA) (R-H)

Monday, January 1

OFFICIAL GOING: Good

15a BMW PERTH CUP (GROUP 2) (H'CAP) 2m

7:25 (7:25) 3-Y-0+

£109,273 (£32,257; £14,516; £6,451; £4,032; £2,419)

RPR
1 **Respect (NZ)**[12] 7000 8-8-6 JWhiting 15 105
(P Cave, Australia) **9/1**
2 1/2 **Bay Story (USA)**[12] 7000 5-8-6 ow1 MZahra 3 105
(B Ellison) *led 2f, always close up, stayed on well from over 1f out but could not wear down front-running winner* **12/1**
3 1 **Rossam (AUS)** 6-8-5 (b) JessicaValas 4 103
(M Sheehy, Australia) **70/1**
4 1/2 **Scenic Shot (AUS)**[12] 7000 5-8-8 (b) SMcgruddy 10 105
(D Morton, Australia) **4/1**[2]
5 1/2 **Zero Engagement (AUS)**[12] 7000 7-8-5 PaulKing 11 102
(T Roney, Australia) **6/1**[3]
6 1/2 **Pantani (NZ)**[51] 6455 8-8-9 SHyland 17 105
(R Laing, Australia) **15/1**
7 1/2 **Mr Sandgroper (AUS)**[23] 6-8-6 DLuciani 9 102
(D A Edwards, Australia) **16/1**
8 nk **Laetare (AUS)**[12] 7000 7-8-5 (b) SO'Donnell 14 100
(E Martinovich, Australia) **60/1**
9 4 1/2 **Action Plan (AUS)**[632] 5-8-5 (b) DStaeck 13 96
(L Smith, Australia) **70/1**
10 4 1/4 **Purde (NZ)**[12] 7000 4-8-5 SParnham 12 98
(D Hayes, Australia) **6/1**[3]
11 1/2 **Zoometric (AUS)**[12] 7000 7-8-6 TroyTurner 6 92
(P Giadresco, Australia) **20/1**
12 1/2 **Woodala (AUS)**[12] 7000 6-8-5 (b) LCamilleri 5 90
(A Mathews, Australia) **40/1**
13 2 **Wool Zone (AUS)**[1351] 7-8-5 BParnham 1 88
(Ross Price, Australia) **50/1**
14 3 1/4 **Black Tom (AUS)**[12] 7000 6-8-12 PHall 7 92
(F Maynard, Australia) **29/10**[1]
U **Coalseam (AUS)**[12] 7000 6-8-5 (b) JasonBrown 8 —
(Jim Taylor, Australia) **10/1**

3m 21.0s (201.00)
WFA 4 from 5yo+ 7lb 15 Ran SP% **126.7**
(including $AUS1 stakes): WIN 8.40; PL 2.80, 3.90, 13.40; DF 58.90.
Owner N Chosid et al **Bred** P & Mrs J Hogan **Trained** Australia

KEMPTON (A.W) (R-H)

Wednesday, January 3

OFFICIAL GOING: Standard
Wind: Slight, behind

16 FOLLOW YOUR MEETING WITH RACING H'CAP (DIV I) 2m (P)

12:10 (12:10) (Class 6) (0-65,65) 4-Y-0+ **£1,706** (£503; £252) **Stalls** High

Form RPR
061- 1 **Mister Completely (IRE)**[16] 6857 6-8-11 **51** JamesDoyle(3) 1 58
(Ms J S Doyle) *in toch: hdwy 6f out: chsng ldrs and n.m.r over 2f out: rallied u.p and led ins last: drvn out* **7/1**
060- 2 1/2 **War At Sea (IRE)**[16] 6862 5-10-0 **65** FrancisNorton 10 72
(A W Carroll) *hld up in rr: hdwy on outside 5f out: led jst ins fnl 2f: sn rdn: hdd ins last: sn no ex* **9/2**[3]
0/0- 3 1 1/4 **Come What Augustus**[49] 2305 5-8-10 **47** SamHitchcott 7 52
(R M Stronge) *chsd ldrs: drvn along over 6f out: styd on u.p fnl 2f but nt pce to chal ins last* **40/1**
543- 4 5 **Domenico (IRE)**[16] 6857 9-8-12 **49** AdamKirby 3 48
(J R Jenkins) *rr: hdwy 6f out: chsd ldr 5f out: chal fr 3f out tl wknd appr fnl f* **10/1**
560- 5 3/4 **Openide**[26] 3955 6-9-6 **57** JamieSpencer 6 55
(B W Duke) *chsd ldrs: drvn along fr 1/2-way: styed chsng ldrs tl wknd over 1f out: eased whn no ch cl home* **7/2**[2]
003- 6 1 **Serramanna**[14] 6883 6-8-11 **55** SophieDoyle(7) 4 52
(Ms J S Doyle) *bhd: pushed along 3f out: styd on fnl 2f but nver in contention* **7/1**
365- 7 nk **Almizan (IRE)**[19] 6831 7-9-10 **61** (b) TPQueally 2 58
(G L Moore) *chsd ldrs: led 6f out: rdn whn strly chal fr 3f out: hdd jst ins fnl 2f: sn wknd* **10/3**[1]
0/6- 8 3 1/2 **Hathaal (IRE)**[13] 6893 8-9-13 **64** EdwardCreighton 8 56
(E J Creighton) *led tl hdd 6f out: wknd fr 2f out* **40/1**

010- **9** *4* **Captivate**[26] 6754 4-8-4 **48** (p) DaleGibson 9 36
(A J McCabe) *a towards rr* **12/1**

050- **10** *14* **Kiama**[135] 4668 5-9-2 **53** JoeFanning 5 24
(M Johnston) *led after 4f: hdd 6f out: wknd over 3f out* **9/1**

3m 35.11s (3.71) **Going Correction** +0.125s/f (Slow)
WFA 4 from 5yo+ 7lb 10 Ran SP% **120.1**
Speed ratings (Par 101):95,94,94,91,91 90,90,88,86,79
CSF £39.81 CT £1186.13 TOTE £7.70: £2.70, £1.90, £12.00; EX 59.20.
Owner Kevin Pattinson **Bred** Eamonn Griffin **Trained** Upper Lambourn, Berks
■ Stewards' Enquiry : Adam Kirby one-day ban: using whip above shoulder height (Jan 14)

FOCUS
An ordinary handicap run in a modest winning time, despite being 3.8 seconds quicker than the second division.

17 KEMPTON FOR WEDDINGS MAIDEN STKS 5f (P)
12:40 (12:40) (Class 5) 3-Y-O **£2,914** (£867; £433; £216) **Stalls** High

Form RPR

63- **1** **Daddy Cool**[151] 4138 3-9-0 AmirQuinn(3) 11 67
(W G M Turner) *mde virtually all: strly chal tl ins fnl 2f: drvn and r.o wl fnl f* **15/2**

2- **2** *1 ¼* **Telltime (IRE)**[18] 6838 3-8-12 FrancisNorton 3 57
(A M Balding) *chsd ldrs: drvn and qcknd to chse wnr ins last but nvr gng pce to chal* **7/4**[1]

665- **3** *½* **Perlachy**[8] 6940 3-9-3 68 DanielTudhope 5 60
(Mrs N Macauley) *in tch: tl outpcd 1/2-way: hdwy over 1f out: qcknd ins last but nvr gng pce to rch wnr* **11/1**

035- **4** *hd* **Drifting Gold**[78] 6031 3-8-12 68 AdamKirby 2 55
(C G Cox) *hdwy on outside and rdn 1/2-way: styd on fnl f but nvr gng pce to chal* **7/2**[2]

53- **5** *1 ½* **Krakatau (FR)**[11] 6931 3-9-3 SamHitchcott 6 54
(D J Wintle) *bhd: pushed along 2f out: kpt on fnl f: gng on cl home* **9/1**

034- **6** *½* **Pappas Image**[12] 6921 3-9-3 (v[1]) RobertWinston 8 53
(A J McCabe) *in tch: rdn 1/2-way: kpt on fnl f but nvr gng pce to be competitive* **6/1**[3]

453- **7** *hd* **Splendidio**[7] 6945 3-8-12 47 ChrisCatlin 7 47
(D K Ivory) *bhd: pushed along 1/2-way: kpt on fr over 1f out: nvr in contention* **33/1**

600- **8** *½* **Childish Thoughts**[7] 6951 3-8-12 43 CatherineGannon 10 45?
(Mrs Norma Pook) *mid-div: rdn and effrt 1/2-way: nvr trbld ldrs: styd on same pce* **66/1**

66- **9** *1* **Redflo**[18] 6838 3-8-9 JamesDoyle(3) 4 41
(Ms J S Doyle) *sn w wnr: str chal fr 3f out tl ins fnl 2f: wknd qckly ins last* **33/1**

50- **10** *5* **Lady Warning**[18] 6845 3-8-5 JackDean(7) 1 23
(W G M Turner) *s.i.s: a outpcd* **66/1**

05- **11** *¾* **Ivorys Song**[271] 908 3-8-12 HayleyTurner 9 21
(D K Ivory) *a outpcd* **20/1**

61.29 secs (0.89) **Going Correction** +0.125s/f (Slow) 11 Ran SP% **116.6**
Speed ratings (Par 97):97,95,94,93,91 90,90,89,87,79 78
CSF £20.04 TOTE £8.60: £2.30, £1.10, £3.50; EX 20.10.
Owner Mascalls Stud **Bred** Mascalls Stud **Trained** Sigwells, Somerset

FOCUS
A modest but competitive event from which winners should emerge.
Redflo Official explanation: jockey said filly had run too freely

18 RACING UK CLASSIFIED STKS 1m 2f (P)
1:15 (1:17) (Class 7) 4-Y-O+ **£1,365** (£403; £201) **Stalls** High

Form RPR

043- **1** **Earl Kraul (IRE)**[76] 6067 4-8-12 45 (b) JamieSpencer 9 46
(G L Moore) *in tch: hdwy over 2f out: drvn and qcknd to ld wl over 1f out: drvn out ins last* **3/1**[1]

/00- **2** *1* **Retirement**[98] 5609 8-8-11 45 NeilChalmers(3) 8 44
(R M Stronge) *hld up in rr: hdwy over 3f out: n.m.r and swtchd lft ins fnl 2f: str run to chsd wnr ins last but a jst hld* **16/1**

000- **3** *1* **Miss Sudbrook (IRE)**[12] 6907 5-9-0 40 (v) FrancisNorton 4 42
(A W Carroll) *bhd: hdwy on outside fr 4f out: styd on fr over 1f out: kpt on cl home but nvr gng pce to rch ldrs* **25/1**

402- **4** *1* **Jarvo**[21] 6800 6-9-0 45 RobbieFitzpatrick 12 40
(I W McInnes) *chsd ldrs: rdn over 2f out: kpt on one pce fnl f* **3/1**[1]

454- **5** *½* **Iceni Warrior**[16] 6852 5-9-0 41 PaulDoe 14 39
(P Howling) *chsd ldr: drvn to chal 2f out: wknd insde last* **7/2**[2]

00- **6** *½* **Starofthemorning (IRE)**[31] 6687 6-9-0 36 AdamKirby 5 38
(A W Carroll) *rr: rdn 5f out: styd on fr over 1f out: gng on cl home but nvr in contention* **8/1**[3]

400- **7** *hd* **Huxley (IRE)**[16] 6854 8-9-0 38 (t) SamHitchcott 13 38
(D J Wintle) *s.i.s: bhd: drvn and hdwy 2f out: kpt on ins last but nvr in contention* **12/1**

006- **8** *3 ½* **Dolly**[21] 6801 5-9-0 41 SteveDrowne 2 31
(Tom Dascombe) *sn led: hdd wl over 1f out: sn btn* **14/1**

000- **9** *hd* **Oasis Sun (IRE)**[19] 6829 4-8-12 45 HayleyTurner 11 31
(J R Best) *chsd ldrs: rdn 3f out: wknd fr 2f out* **25/1**

/00- **10** *16* **Time For You**[182] 2707 5-9-0 39 JoeFanning 6 —
(J M Bradley) *chsd ldrs 7f* **25/1**

000- **11** *1 ½* **Sean Og (IRE)**[16] 6852 5-9-0 41 (b[1]) EdwardCreighton 1 —
(E J Creighton) *bhd: hdwy 1/2-way to chse ldrs 3f out: sn btn* **25/1**

P04- **12** *20* **Good Intentions**[12] 6907 5-8-7 35 WilliamCarson(7) 7 —
(P W Hiatt) *unruly stalls: chsd ldrs 6f* **14/1**

0/0- **13** *1* **Hawksmoor (IRE)**[21] 6804 5-9-0 27 (t) ChrisCatlin 3 —
(L A Dace) *chsd ldrs tl wknd 1/2-way* **50/1**

2m 10.77s (1.77) **Going Correction** +0.125s/f (Slow)
WFA 4 from 5yo+ 2lb 13 Ran SP% **127.6**
Speed ratings (Par 97):97,96,95,94,94 93,93,90,90,77 76,60,59
CSF £54.26 TOTE £3.50: £1.60, £8.60, £9.90; EX 75.90.
Owner Miss Samantha Dare **Bred** Gerry Flannery **Trained** Woodingdean, E Sussex

FOCUS
A very ordinary race won by a horse that has found it very difficult to get his head in front. The form looks very suspect and unreliable.

19 KEMPTON.CO.UK H'CAP 1m 2f (P)
1:50 (1:50) (Class 6) (0-55,55) 4-Y-O+ **£2,388** (£705; £352) **Stalls** High

Form RPR

033- **1** **Danzare**[24] 6775 5-8-9 **51** FrancisNorton 5 63
(J L Spearing) *hld up in rr: stdy hdwy over 3f out: shkn up & led appr fnl f: sn clr: eased cl home* **5/1**[2]

/05- **2** *4* **Show Me The Lolly (FR)**[21] 6801 7-8-6 **48** PaulEddery 10 52
(P J McBride) *in tch: hdwy 3f out: chal 2f out: sn led and rdn: hdd appr fnl f: sn no ch w wnr: hld on wl for 2nd* **16/1**

145- **3** *½* **Play Up Pompey**[12] 6918 5-8-10 **55** AmirQuinn(3) 4 58
(J J Bridger) *hld up in rr: hdwy and n.m.r 2f out: drvn and fin wl fnl f but nt rch ldrs* **14/1**

220- **4** *1 ¼* **Milk And Sultana**[24] 6775 7-8-10 **52** SteveDrowne 13 53
(G A Ham) *chsd ldrs tl lost position and outpcd over 3f out: kpt on again fr over 1f out* **10/1**

463- **5** *½* **Hiawatha (IRE)**[12] 6904 8-8-1 **48** AndrewElliott(5) 9 48
(A M Hales) *bhd: hdwy on rails to chsse leders whn nt clr run and lost pl 2f out: kpt on again fr over 1f out: gng on cl home* **12/1**

000- **6** *1* **Voice Mail**[14] 6883 8-8-13 **55** (b) PaulDoe 7 53
(P Howling) *rr: hdwy on outside over 2f out: kpt on fnl f but nvr gng pce to trble ldrs* **20/1**

042- **7** *½* **King Of Knight (IRE)**[24] 6780 6-8-10 **52** AdrianMcCarthy 6 49
(G Prodromou) *mid-div: hdwy to chse ldrs 4f out: rdn over 2f out: sn one pce* **8/1**[3]

620- **8** *¾* **Native American**[45] 5954 5-8-11 **53** RobbieFitzpatrick 14 49
(T D McCarthy) *chsd ldrs: rdn over 3f out: wknd appr fnl f* **25/1**

003- **9** *3 ½* **Lady Pilot**[12] 6918 5-8-10 **52** JoeFanning 2 41
(Ms J S Doyle) *chsd ldrs: rdn 3f out: wknd fr 2f out* **11/1**

110- **10** *¾* **Shaheer (IRE)**[12] 6918 5-8-13 **55** (v) JamieSpencer 8 43
(J Gallagher) *trckd ldrs: drvn and slt ld appr fnl 2f:sn outpcd: wknd over 1f out* **9/2**[1]

533- **11** *2* **Lady Georgette (IRE)**[12] 6911 4-8-8 **52** ChrisCatlin 3 36
(E J O'Neill) *w ldr: str chal over 4f out tl 2f out: sn wknd* **9/2**[1]

000- **12** *3 ½* **The Rip**[12] 6904 6-8-6 **48** EdwardCreighton 1 25
(R M Stronge) *chsd ldrs 7f* **66/1**

230- **13** *½* **Camp Attack**[12] 6911 4-8-10 **54** LPKeniry 12 30
(S Dow) *sn slt ld: hdd appr fnl 2f and wknd qckly* **9/1**

000- **14** *43* **Obscene**[13] 6901 4-8-11 **55** RobertWinston 11 —
(A J McCabe) *chsd ldrs to 1/2-way: virtually p.u fnl 3f: t.o* **16/1**

2m 8.80s (-0.20) **Going Correction** +0.125s/f (Slow)
WFA 4 from 5yo+ 2lb 14 Ran SP% **127.8**
Speed ratings (Par 101):105,101,101,100,100 99,98,98,95,94 93,90,90,55
CSF £86.63 CT £1089.80 TOTE £6.10: £1.70, £4.50, £5.30; EX 107.10.
Owner Masonaires **Bred** A Seelbinder **Trained** Kinnersley, Worcs

FOCUS
A modest handicap, but a decent pace and a very impressive winner. The winning time was very creditable for a race like this.
Shaheer(IRE) Official explanation: jockey said gelding did not pick up under pressure
Obscene Official explanation: jockey said gelding was never travelling

20 FOLLOW YOUR CONFERENCE WITH FLOODLIT RACING CLASSIFIED STKS 1m (P)
2:20 (2:20) (Class 7) 4-Y-O+ **£1,365** (£403; £201) **Stalls** High

Form RPR

600- **1** **Time To Regret**[19] 6213 7-9-0 45 (p) DanielTudhope 5 56
(I W McInnes) *trckd ldrs: drvn and str run to ld appr fnl f: sn clr: readily* **20/1**

000- **2** *3* **Fraternity**[62] 6307 10-8-9 40 RussellKennemore(5) 9 49
(J A Pickering) *led: rdn over 2f out: hdd appr fnl f and sn no ch w wnr but kpt on wl to hold 2nd* **33/1**

035- **3** *nk* **Piquet**[12] 6904 9-8-11 44 AmirQuinn(3) 6 48
(J J Bridger) *bhd: hdwy 2f out: chsd ldrs ins last: styd on same pce* **7/1**[3]

325- **4** *3 ½* **Fantasy Defender (IRE)**[24] 6780 5-9-0 45 (v) ChrisCatlin 8 40
(Ernst Oertel) *mid-div: rdn 3f out: hdwy fr 2f out but nvr gng pce to rch ldrs* **4/1**[1]

036- **5** *1 ¾* **Kinsman (IRE)**[21] 6800 10-9-0 44 (p) RobbieFitzpatrick 10 36
(T D McCarthy) *bhd: rdn and hdwy over 2f out: kpt on ins last but nvr gng pce to rch ldrs* **12/1**

000- **6** *3* **Riviera Red (IRE)**[233] 1725 7-9-0 45 (v) RobertWinston 11 29
(L Montague Hall) *bhd: pshd along over 3f out: sme prog fr over 1f out but nvr a danger* **9/1**

066- **7** *¾* **Beautiful Mover (USA)**[21] 6802 5-8-9 43 NataliaGemelova(5) 14 28
(J E Long) *bhd: rdn over 3f out: mod prog on ins over 1f out* **12/1**

005- **8** *¾* **Blushing Russian (IRE)**[5] 6970 5-9-0 44 (p) SteveDrowne 7 26
(J M Bradley) *chsd ldrs: rdn 3f out: wknd wl over 1f out* **12/1**

000- **9** *nk* **Miss Redactive**[113] 5259 4-9-0 41 JamieMackay 4 25
(M D I Usher) *chsd ldrs: rdn and effrt 3f out: wknd over 1f out* **16/1**

600- **10** *1 ½* **Wilford Maverick (IRE)**[6] 6961 5-9-0 45 DaleGibson 13 22
(M J Attwater) *trckd ldrs: rdn 3f out: nvr gng pce to chal: wknd over 1f out* **6/1**[2]

U04- **11** *½* **Didnt Tell My Wife**[19] 6829 8-9-0 43 (v) HayleyTurner 3 21
(P S McEntee) *chsd ldrs tl wknd over 2f out* **9/1**

0/0- **12** *2* **Pick Of The Crop**[128] 682 6-8-7 40 WilliamBuick(7) 12 16
(J R Jenkins) *sn drvn: a outpcd* **14/1**

005- **13** *9* **Rowan Pursuit**[275] 853 6-9-0 45 (b) PaulEddery 1 —
(C A Horgan) *chsd ldrs 7f* **7/1**[3]

1m 41.0s (0.20) **Going Correction** +0.125s/f (Slow) 13 Ran SP% **122.6**
Speed ratings (Par 97):104,101,100,97,95 92,91,90,90,89 88,86,77
CSF £567.89 TOTE £29.60: £7.10, £10.30, £2.60; EX 798.00.
Owner Horses 4 Courses **Bred** Speedlith Group **Trained** Catwick, E Yorks

FOCUS
A poor race, but there was a solid pace thanks to Fraternity, and it was run in a decent winning time for a race of its class.

21 SPECIAL EVENTS COMMUNICATIONS H'CAP 1m (P)
2:55 (2:55) (Class 5) (0-70,70) 3-Y-O **£3,238** (£963; £481; £240) **Stalls** High

Form RPR

41- **1** **Hostage**[20] 6815 3-9-2 **70** JamieSpencer 7 74+
(M L W Bell) *hld up rr but in tch: smooth hdwy to ld appr fnl f: high hd carriage and green: but a in command after: v easily* **7/4**[1]

336- **2** *1 ¼* **Henry The Seventh**[11] 6933 3-9-0 **68** (p) RobertWinston 4 69
(J W Hills) *s.i.s: bhd: rdn and hdwy over 1f out: styd on wl to chse wnr ins last but a wl hld* **9/2**

452- **3** *2* **First Princess (IRE)**[13] 6900 3-8-11 **65** LPKeniry 1 61
(J S Moore) *chsd ldrs: chal over 2f out: sn rdn: outpcd fnl f* **4/1**[3]

051- **4** *1* **Ella Y Rossa**[16] 6853 3-8-2 **56** oh3 CatherineGannon 5 50
(P D Evans) *chsd ldrs: rdn and slt ld appr fnl 2f: hdd appr fnl f: wknd ins last* **16/1**

053- **5** *6* **Tumble Jill (IRE)**[16] 6853 3-8-2 **56** oh4 ChrisCatlin 3 36
(J J Bridger) *rr but in tch: rdn and outpcd fr over 2f out* **40/1**

026- **6** *2 1/2* **Lawyer To World**[15] 6866 3-8-3 **64**.......................... (b[1]) WilliamBuick[(7)] 2 39
(N A Callaghan) *t.k.h: pressed ldr: rdn and hung lft over 2f out: sn wknd* **3/1**[2]

020- **7** *7* **Diamond Light (USA)**[14] 6886 3-8-6 **65**.......................... NicolPolli[(5)] 6 23
(M Botti) *slt ld tl hdd over 2f out: sn wknd* **16/1**

1m 41.97s (1.17) **Going Correction** +0.125s/f (Slow) **7** Ran SP% **113.7**
Speed ratings (Par 97):99,97,95,94,88 86,79
CSF £9.97 TOTE £2.00: £1.20, £3.70; EX 8.30.
Owner The Dukes of Roxburghe & Devonshire **Bred** The Duke Of Devonshire And Floors Farming **Trained** Newmarket, Suffolk
FOCUS
A modest handicap but a dominant display by the unexposed Hostage.

22 KEMPTON FOR CONFERENCES CLASSIFIED STKS 7f (P)
3:25 (3:27) (Class 7) 4-Y-0+ **£1,365** (£403; £201) **Stalls** High

Form RPR
002- **1** **Charlottebutterfly**[21] 6805 7-9-0 45.......................... PaulEddery 14 52
(P J McBride) *chsd ldrs: led ins fnl 2f: hrd drvn fnl f: hld on all out* **9/2**[2]

000- **2** *hd* **Sahara Prince (IRE)**[4] 6983 7-9-0 45.......................... (p) PaulFitzsimons 12 52
(K A Morgan) *bhd: hdwy on ins over 2f out: chsd wnr appr fnl f: fin wl: nt quite get up* **12/1**

026- **3** *1* **Task Complete**[28] 6726 4-9-0 45.......................... (b) FrankieMcDonald 10 49
(Jean-Rene Auvray) *bhd: hdwy fr 2f out: fin wl but nt rch ldrs* **12/1**

062- **4** *1* **Fizzy Lizzy**[21] 6803 7-8-9 44.......................... NicolPolli[(5)] 4 46
(H E Haynes) *broke out of stalls: t.k.h: chsd ldr:slt advantage appr fnl 2f: sn hdd and hung lft: styd on same pce fnl f* **20/1**

400- **5** *1* **Danielle's Lad**[23] 6793 11-8-11 43.......................... (p) AmirQuinn[(3)] 8 44
(B Palling) *led tl hdd appr fnl 2f: wknd ins last* **20/1**

630- **6** *1/2* **Jennverse**[4] 6981 5-8-9 44.......................... JamesMillman[(5)] 2 43
(D K Ivory) *bhd: hdwy fr 2f out: kpt on ins last but nvr in contention* **7/1**

626- **7** *nk* **Mid Valley**[28] 6725 4-9-0 45.......................... (v) PatCosgrave 1 42
(J R Jenkins) *s.i.s: bhd: hdwy over 1f out but nvr in contention* **13/2**[3]

006- **8** *1/2* **Height Of Spirits**[19] 6829 5-9-0 44.......................... (b) RobbieFitzpatrick 13 40
(T D McCarthy) *chsd ldrs: rdn 3f out: wknd fnl f* **10/1**

001- **9** *2* **Kissi Kissi**[36] 6649 4-9-0 45.......................... (v) AdrianMcCarthy 6 35
(M J Attwater) *t.k.h: chsd ldrs: wknd fr 2f out* **3/1**[1]

030- **10** *shd* **Firework**[21] 6805 9-9-0 45.......................... StephenCarson 9 35
(E A Wheeler) *mid-div: rdn 1/2-way: nvr in contention* **11/1**

060/ **11** *3/4* **Intimate Friend (USA)**[466] 5445 6-8-9 45.......................... (e[1]) EmmettStack[(5)] 7 33
(Miss Diana Weeden) *mid-div: sme hdwy 3f out: nvr rchd ldrs: wknd fr 2f out* **66/1**

005- **12** *3/4* **Fancy You (IRE)**[114] 5250 4-9-0 45.......................... (v) FrancisNorton 11 31
(A W Carroll) *t.k.h: chsd ldrs tl wknd qckly 2f out* **7/1**

1m 28.78s (1.98) **Going Correction** +0.125s/f (Slow) **12** Ran SP% **125.3**
Speed ratings (Par 97):93,92,91,90,89 88,88,87,85,85 84,83
CSF £59.94 TOTE £4.80: £1.70, £6.90, £3.40; EX 95.20.
Owner Future Electrical Services Ltd **Bred** J T O'Neill **Trained** Newmarket, Suffolk
■ Stewards' Enquiry : James Millman caution: careless riding
FOCUS
A competitive classified stakes.
Danielle's Lad Official explanation: jockey said gelding hung left
Jennverse Official explanation: jockey said mare became upset in the stalls

23 FOLLOW YOUR MEETING WITH RACING H'CAP (DIV II) 2m (P)
3:55 (3:55) (Class 6) (0-65,65) 4-Y-0+ **£1,706** (£503; £252) **Stalls** High

Form RPR
264- **1** **Dream Mountain**[12] 6911 4-8-6 **53**.......................... JamesDoyle[(3)] 10 59
(Ms J S Doyle) *mde all: hrd drvn and styd on strly fnl f: unchal* **8/1**

605- **2** *2* **Mamonta**[12] 6911 4-8-13 **57**.......................... JamieSpencer 3 61
(M J Wallace) *hld up in rr: hdwy 3f out: rdn and kpt on fnl 2f to take 2nd last strides but no imp on wnr* **13/2**

110- **3** *hd* **Ganymede**[43] 6560 6-9-2 **53**.......................... IanMongan 8 57
(Mrs L J Mongan) *in tch: hdwy 3f out: chsd wnr ins fnl 2f but no imp: lost 2nd last strides* **10/3**[2]

162- **4** *1/2* **Synonymy**[33] 6560 4-9-3 **61**.......................... SteveDrowne 5 64
(M Blanshard) *in tch: rdn and hdwy 3f out: styd on fnl f but nvr gng pce to rch ldrs* **5/2**[1]

001- **5** *3 1/2* **Galantos (GER)**[6] 6957 6-9-5 **56** 6ex.......................... (b) LPKeniry 7 55
(G L Moore) *prom: chsd wnr 4f out: no imp 2f out: wknd over 1f out* **11/2**

145- **6** *2* **Treetops Hotel (IRE)**[26] 6748 8-9-11 **65**.......................... JerryO'Dwyer[(3)] 2 62
(B R Johnson) *rr: rdn over 3f out and no imp on ldrs* **9/2**[3]

5/0- **7** *1 3/4* **It's Rumoured**[36] 6630 7-9-1 **52**.......................... (v[1]) FrankieMcDonald 1 46
(Jean-Rene Auvray) *in tch: rdn along 7f out: styd on same pce fnl 2f* **33/1**

0- **8** *30* **Saitama**[26] 6754 5-9-2 **58**.......................... AndrewElliott[(5)] 4 16
(A M Hales) *chsd wnr to 4f out: wknd 3f out* **50/1**

3m 38.91s (7.51) **Going Correction** +0.125s/f (Slow)
WFA 4 from 5yo+ 7lb **36** Ran SP% **114.6**
Speed ratings (Par 101):86,85,84,84,82 81,81,66
CSF £58.68 CT £207.63 TOTE £9.00: £2.80, £4.10, £1.20; EX 51.40 Place 6 £859.59, Place 5 £233.52.
Owner Ms J S Doyle **Bred** Newsells Park Stud Limited **Trained** Upper Lambourn, Berks
FOCUS
A moderate handicap run in a pedestrian winning time, 3.8 seconds slower than the first division.
Saitama Official explanation: jockey said mare found nothing in the home straight
T/Plt: £1,093.80 to a £1 stake. Pool: £36,710.55. 24.50 winning tickets. T/Qpdt: £138.90 to a £1 stake. Pool: £3,755.00. 20.00 winning tickets. ST

LINGFIELD (L-H)
Wednesday, January 3

OFFICIAL GOING: Standard
Wind: Strong, behind Weather: Overcast

24 PHOTO BOOKS FROM BONUSPRINT.COM MAIDEN STKS 1m 2f (P)
12:30 (12:30) (Class 5) 4-Y-0+ **£2,817** (£838; £418; £209) **Stalls** Low

Form RPR
25- **1** **Call My Bluff (FR)**[16] 6861 4-9-3 65.......................... NCallan 6 71
(Rae Guest) *t.k.h: hld up: prog to ld over 2f out: kicked clr wl over 1f out: rdn out* **11/4**[2]

00P- **2** *2 1/2* **King's Ransom**[20] 6825 4-9-3 67.......................... (b) RichardHughes 3 66
(W R Muir) *hld up in tch: effrt over 2f out: hrd rdn to take 2nd ins fnl f: no imp on wnr* **7/1**

022- **3** *1* **Monets Masterpiece (USA)**[12] 6916 4-9-3 74.......................... (b) GeorgeBaker 4 64
(G L Moore) *t.k.h: pressed ldr: led 4f out to over 2f out: nt qckn and sn btn* **11/4**[2]

042- **4** *2 1/2* **Blu Manruna**[12] 6918 4-9-3 54.......................... (b) DaneO'Neill 2 60
(J Akehurst) *led to 4f out: u.p and finding nil 3f out* **13/2**[3]

062- **5** *shd* **Marbaa (IRE)**[4] 6987 4-9-3 64.......................... LPKeniry 7 59
(S Dow) *dwlt: sn prom: rdn wl over 2f out: fnd nil and btn over 1f out* **5/2**[1]

0- **6** *14* **Spotoncon**[8] 6938 6-9-5.......................... JimCrowley 5 33
(A J Lidderdale) *s.s: a in last pair: bhd fr 4f out: t.o* **50/1**

2m 7.69s (-0.10) **Going Correction** -0.125s/f (Stan)
WFA 4 from 6yo 2lb **6** Ran SP% **109.7**
Speed ratings (Par 103):95,93,92,90,90 78
CSF £20.46 TOTE £4.00: £1.70, £2.40; EX 22.70.
Owner Jennifer & Barry Stewart **Bred** Haras De Manneville **Trained** Newmarket, Suffolk
FOCUS
A poor maiden, run at a weak pace featuring mostly disappointing types. It has been rated through the winner and fourth.

25 DIGITAL PRINTS FROM BONUSPRINT.COM H'CAP 7f (P)
1:05 (1:05) (Class 6) (0-60,66) 3-Y-0 **£2,388** (£705; £352) **Stalls** Low

Form RPR
101- **1** **Homes By Woodford**[7] 6951 3-9-3 **66** 6ex.......................... MichaelJStainton[(5)] 7 72+
(R A Harris) *lw: hld up in midfield: prog on outer 2f out: rdn and sustained run fnl f to ld last 50yds* **9/4**[1]

060- **2** *1/2* **Ranavalona**[21] 6807 3-7-13 **50**.......................... (v[1]) WilliamBuick[(7)] 5 54
(A M Balding) *t.k.h: trckd ldng pair: effrt 2f out: drvn and r.o to ld last 100yds: hdd 50yds out* **12/1**

000- **3** *1/2* **Calloff The Search**[7] 6951 3-8-9 **56**.......................... (p) SaleemGolam[(3)] 10 59
(W G M Turner) *pressed ldr: led 1/2-way: drvn over 1f out: hdd and nt qckn last 100yds* **12/1**

432- **4** *4* **A Nod And A Wink (IRE)**[32] 6670 3-8-10 **54** ow1.......................... RichardHughes 3 47
(R Hannon) *led to 1/2-way: styd cl up to over 1f out: wknd ins fnl f* **11/4**[2]

000- **5** *1 1/4* **Time For Change (IRE)**[116] 5161 3-8-11 **55**.......................... TonyCulhane 4 44+
(B W Hills) *b: lw: h.d.w: hld up in rr: outpcd 2f out: pushed along and no imp over 1f out: nvr nr ldrs* **4/1**[3]

653- **6** *1* **Ten Black**[32] 6670 3-8-13 **57**.......................... PatCosgrave 6 44
(R Brotherton) *chsd ldrs: rdn after 3f: grad fdd u.p fnl 2f* **10/1**

016- **7** *2* **Polly Jones (USA)**[18] 6845 3-8-4 **48**.......................... JimmyQuinn 1 30
(G L Moore) *s.i.s: hld up towards rr: rdn over 2f out: no prog* **16/1**

420- **8** *2* **Suzieblue (IRE)**[95] 5687 3-8-9 **60**.......................... JosephWalsh[(7)] 2 36
(D C O'Brien) *trckd ldrs: rdn over 2f out: wknd over 1f out* **50/1**

055- **9** *1/2* **Tumblin Rosie**[29] 6710 3-8-10 **54** ow1.......................... NCallan 9 29
(M Blanshard) *dwlt: hld up in last trio: rdn on wd outside over 2f out: sn btn* **12/1**

005- **10** *1 1/4* **Mister Always**[18] 6845 3-8-9 **53**.......................... (tp) FergusSweeney 8 25
(Ms J S Doyle) *dwlt: t.k.h: hld up in last pair: rdn and struggling over 2f out* **50/1**

1m 25.36s (-0.53) **Going Correction** -0.125s/f (Stan) **10** Ran SP% **119.4**
Speed ratings (Par 95):98,97,96,92,90 89,87,85,84,83
CSF £32.08 CT £277.62 TOTE £2.90: £1.60, £3.40, £2.60; EX 44.70 TRIFECTA Not won..
Owner Mrs Ruth M Serrell **Bred** Mrs H B Raw **Trained** Earlswood, Monmouths
FOCUS
A low-grade handicap run at an ordinary gallop, but it was won a by a progressive sort and the form looks sound enough.
Mister Always Official explanation: trainer said gelding made a noise

26 GO PONTIN'S (S) STKS 1m (P)
1:40 (1:40) (Class 6) 4-Y-0+ **£2,184** (£644; £322) **Stalls** High

Form RPR
010- **1** **Shrine Mountain (USA)**[6] 6964 5-9-5 60.......................... (b[1]) NCallan 4 66
(R A Harris) *mde virtually all: jnd 1f out: battled on wl fnl f* **2/1**[2]

002- **2** *nk* **King After**[4] 6981 5-9-0 55.......................... DaneO'Neill 6 60
(J R Best) *hld up bhd ldrs: chsd wnr over 3f out: drvn to chal and upsides 1f out: outbattled last 75yds* **7/4**[1]

523- **3** *5* **Fulvio (USA)**[4] 6983 7-9-0 53.......................... (v) J-PGuillambert 1 49
(P Howling) *prom: chsd wnr briefly 4f out: rdn wl over 2f out and sn outpcd: kpt on* **5/2**[3]

640- **4** *2 1/2* **Colonel Bilko (IRE)**[16] 6854 5-8-11 39.......................... MarcHalford[(3)] 5 43
(J J Bridger) *bit bkwd: s.i.s: hld up: chsd ldng trio 3f out: effrt to dispute modest 3rd over 1f out: wknd fnl f* **16/1**

000- **5** *5* **Renegade (IRE)**[24] 6779 6-9-0 49.......................... IanMongan 2 31
(Mrs L J Mongan) *stdd s: hld up in last: rdn 1/2-way: sn struggling* **16/1**

500- **6** *8* **Vixen Virago**[24] 6779 4-8-9 35.......................... (p) FergusSweeney 7 8
(Jane Southcombe) *chsd wnr to 1/2-way: sn lost pl u.p* **66/1**

550/ **7** *24* **Fellow Ship**[638] 886 7-8-7 39.......................... (p) JosephWalsh[(7)] 3 —
(P Butler) *stdd s: t.k.h: in tch to over 4f out: wknd rapidly: sn t.o* **66/1**

1m 37.77s (-1.66) **Going Correction** -0.125s/f (Stan) **7** Ran SP% **113.0**
Speed ratings (Par 101):103,102,97,95,90 82,58
CSF £5.74 TOTE £2.90: £1.90, £1.70; EX 8.60.There was no bid for the winner.
Owner Leeway Group Limited **Bred** WinStar Farm Llc **Trained** Earlswood, Monmouths
FOCUS
An ordinary seller and it was run at a modest pace until halfway. The winner did not have to improve to score.
Fellow Ship Official explanation: jockey said gelding lost its action

27 PONTIN'S HOLIDAYS H'CAP 1m (P)
2:10 (2:10) (Class 4) (0-80,77) 3-Y-0 **£4,857** (£1,445; £722; £360) **Stalls** High

Form RPR
333- **1** **Highland Harvest**[14] 6887 3-8-10 **73**.......................... MarcHalford[(3)] 3 80
(D R C Elsworth) *stdd s: hld up in last: rdn to chse clr ldng pair over 2f out: clsd over 1f out: led last 75yds: hung lft nr fin* **10/1**

221- **2** *1* **Mastership (IRE)**[11] 6933 3-9-3 **77** 6ex.......................... (b) J-PGuillambert 5 83+
(C E Brittain) *lw: stdd s: keen: hld up: trckd ldr gng wl over 3f out: rdn to ld over 1f out: hdd last 75yds: btn whn hmpd nr fin* **8/11**[1]

403- **3** *3* **Nicomedia (IRE)**[14] 6886 3-8-6 **69**.......................... StephaneBreux[(3)] 1 67
(R Hannon) *lw: chsd ldrs: outpcd wl over 2f out: plugged on fr over 1f out* **15/2**[3]

453- **4** *2 1/2* **Racing Times**[15] 6866 3-9-2 **76**.......................... NCallan 2 68
(B J Meehan) *lw: led: drew 3 l clr 1/2-way: rdn over 2f out: hdd over 1f out: wknd rapidly* **10/3**[2]

313- **5** *29* **Inquisitress**[14] 6880 3-8-10 **70**.......................... TPQueally 4 —
(J J Bridger) *chsd ldr to over 3f out: wknd and sn t.o* **11/1**

1m 37.46s (-1.97) **Going Correction** -0.125s/f (Stan) **5** Ran SP% **110.2**
Speed ratings (Par 99):104,103,100,97,68
CSF £18.25 TOTE £11.70: £4.90, £1.02; EX 39.10.
Owner J Wotherspoon **Bred** J Wotherspoon **Trained** Newmarket, Suffolk
FOCUS
A decent race of its type and, though lacking numbers, it was run at a good pace after the first two furlongs. It has been rated through the runner-up to the level of his Wolverhampton win.
Inquisitress Official explanation: jockey said filly was never travelling from halfway

28 PONTINSBINGO.COM H'CAP — 7f (P)
2:45 (2:45) (Class 4) (0-80,79) 4-Y-0+ **£4,857** (£1,445; £722; £360) **Stalls** Low

Form — RPR

000- **1** **Grimes Faith**[19] 6830 4-8-9 **79**....(b[1]) HaddenFrost(7) 8 — 89
(R Hannon) *lw: trckd ldrs: effrt over 1f out: pushed along and r.o wl to ld last 75yds* **20/1**

640- **2** 3/4 **Sun Catcher (IRE)**[14] 6882 4-8-11 **74**.... DaneO'Neill 5 — 83
(R Hannon) *pressed ldr: led 3f out: kicked 2 l clr over 1f out: collared last 75yds* **25/1**

600- **3** 1 1/4 **Ivory Lace**[31] 6690 6-8-10 **76**.... JamesDoyle(3) 4 — 83+
(S Woodman) *hld up wl in rr: plld out and effrt over 1f out: r.o wl fnl f to take 3rd nr fin: nt rch ldng pair* **25/1**

646- **4** 3/4 **Will He Wish**[15] 6868 11-9-2 **79**.... TonyCulhane 14 — 82
(S Gollings) *prom: rdn to chse ldr over 2f out: no imp over 1f out: one pce* **10/1**

511- **5** 1/2 **Hollow Jo**[12] 6913 7-8-10 **73** 6ex.... MickyFenton 6 — 75
(J R Jenkins) *lw: chsd ldrs: rdn over 2f out: one pce fr over 1f out: wkng nr fin* **6/1[3]**

121- **6** nk **Dichoh**[24] 6781 4-8-11 **74**.... NCallan 12 — 75+
(M A Jarvis) *hld up in rr: effrt 2f out: styd on ins fnl f: n.d* **5/2[1]**

630- **7** shd **Quantum Leap**[24] 6781 10-8-5 **68**....(v) JimmyQuinn 3 — 69
(S Dow) *hld up towards rr: effrt over 1f out: drvn ent fnl f: styd on: n.d* **12/1**

212- **8** 1/2 **Foreplay (IRE)**[11] 6932 4-8-12 **75**....(p) JimCrowley 2 — 75
(E A L Dunlop) *awkward s: sn in midfield: effrt on inner over 1f out: styd on same pce fnl f* **15/2**

364- **9** 2 **Vanadium**[25] 6773 5-8-10 **73**....(p) J-PGuillambert 13 — 67
(J G Given) *stdd s and sn swtchd sharply to inner: t.k.h: hld up in last pair: no real prog 2f out: kpt on* **8/1**

504- **10** shd **Cinematic (IRE)**[143] 4395 4-8-10 **73**.... FergusSweeney 1 — 67
(J R Boyle) *prom: effrt on inner over 1f out: wknd fnl f* **33/1**

020- **11** nk **Hammer Of The Gods (IRE)**[40] 6583 7-9-1 **78**....(bt) AdamKirby 9 — 71
(P S McEntee) *t.k.h: hld up wl in rr: one pce and struggling 2f out* **25/1**

431- **12** 1 1/4 **Lethal**[15] 6865 4-8-13 **76**.... RichardHughes 10 — 66
(D K Ivory) *scope: racd v wd: in tch: lost grnd whn wd bnd 2f out: wknd fnl f* **10/3[2]**

000- **13** 1 3/4 **Meditation**[15] 6868 5-9-2 **79**.... LeeEnstone 7 — 65
(I A Wood) *mde most to 3f out: wknd 2f out* **40/1**

/00- **14** 13 **King's Account (USA)**[48] 6502 5-8-7 **70**.... SilvestreDeSousa 11 — 22
(S Gollings) *chsd ldrs to 1/2-way: sn wknd u.p: t.o* **25/1**

1m 24.24s (-1.65) **Going Correction** -0.125s/f (Stan) **14** Ran SP% **131.1**
Speed ratings (Par 105):104,103,101,100,100 99,99,99,96,96 96,95,93,78
CSF £452.55 CT £11881.22 TOTE £28.30: £7.40, £4.90, £6.30; EX 242.40 Trifecta £364.00 Part won. Pool: £512.70 - 0.10 winning units..
Owner J K Grimes **Bred** John Grimes **Trained** East Everleigh, Wilts
■ A first winner on just his third ride for Hadden Frost, 16-year-old son of Grand National-winning rider Jimmy.

FOCUS
A competitive contest, but run at a medium pace at best. The form has a slightly shaky look to it, with the first two prominent throughout. The winning jockey, 16-year-old son of trainer and former jump jockey Jimmy, was winning for the first time at the third attempt, and looks a useful recruit.
Lethal Official explanation: jockey said gelding hung badly right-handed throughout

29 PONTIN'S FAMILY HOLIDAYS H'CAP — 1m 5f (P)
3:15 (3:15) (Class 5) (0-70,69) 4-Y-0+ **£2,914** (£867; £433; £216) **Stalls** Low

Form — RPR

/00- **1** **Lorikeet**[51] 6462 8-8-7 **55**.... FergusSweeney 5 — 63+
(Noel T Chance) *lw: hld up in rr: stdy prog gng wl fr 3f out: shkn up to ld last 150yds: sn clr* **33/1**

064- **2** 3 **Ariodante**[14] 6885 5-9-2 **64**.... MickyFenton 7 — 67
(J M P Eustace) *dwlt: sn trckd ldrs: pushed wd 3f out: effrt to ld jst over 2f out: sn jnd: hdd and outpcd last 150yds* **8/1**

5/0- **3** nk **Kavi (IRE)**[326] 385 7-9-6 **68**.... NCallan 10 — 71
(Simon Earle) *led to over 7f out: styd cl up: drvn to dispute ld again 2f out: hdd and outpcd last 150yds* **20/1**

050- **4** 1/2 **Dovedon Hero**[126] 4937 7-9-2 **64**....(b) TonyCulhane 6 — 66
(P J McBride) *hld up in tch: gng easily over 2f out: effrt over 1f out: plugged on same pce* **6/1[3]**

050- **5** nk **Liberty Run (IRE)**[12] 6917 5-9-4 **69**.... NeilChalmers(3) 1 — 70
(Mouse Hamilton-Fairley) *hld up in rr: effrt over 2f out: drvn over 1f out: styd on fnl f: n.d* **8/1**

123/ **6** 1/2 **Mumbling (IRE)**[464] 5502 9-8-11 **62**.... RichardKingscote(3) 8 — 63
(B G Powell) *prom: led over 3f out to jst over 2f out: one pce u.p* **10/1**

215- **7** hd **Wait For The Will (USA)**[51] 6462 11-9-1 **63**....(b) GeorgeBaker 3 — 63+
(G L Moore) *dwlt: hld up in last pair: coaxed along over 2f out: styd on ins fnl f: no ch* **4/1[2]**

236- **8** 1 3/4 **Sovereign Spirit (IRE)**[26] 6754 5-9-2 **64**....(t) AdamKirby 4 — 62
(W R Swinburn) *lw: prom: rdn over 3f out: cl up over 1f out: wknd fnl f* **5/2[1]**

410/ **9** 14 **Certifiable**[709] 6984 6-9-0 **67**.... RobynBrisland(5) 9 — 44
(G L Moore) *bit bkwd: t.k.h: hld up tl plld way to ld over 7f out: hdd & wknd over 3f out: t.o* **20/1**

430- **10** 3 **Turn 'n Burn**[19] 6831 6-9-6 **68**....(b[1]) TPQueally 2 — 40
(C A Cyzer) *b: b.hind: s.s: hld up in last: pushed along over 4f out: no prog: t.o and eased over 1f out* **6/1[3]**

2m 46.58s (-1.72) **Going Correction** -0.125s/f (Stan) **10** Ran SP% **120.9**
Speed ratings (Par 103):100,98,97,97,97 97,97,95,87,85
CSF £280.31 CT £5388.65 TOTE £27.40: £11.20, £2.10, £7.40; EX 414.10 TRIFECTA Not won..
Owner The Tribesmen Syndicate **Bred** Sheikh Mohammed Bin Rashid Al Maktoum **Trained** Upper Lambourn, Berks

FOCUS
A modest race run at a medium gallop for the trip. The form has a weakish feel to it with doubts about several on recent efforts.
Lorikeet Official explanation: trainer had no explanation for the improved form shown
Turn 'n Burn Official explanation: jockey said gelding hung badly right-handed

30 PONTIN'S "BOOK EARLY" H'CAP — 1m 2f (P)
3:45 (3:45) (Class 5) (0-75,75) 4-Y-0+ **£3,238** (£963; £481; £240) **Stalls** Low

Form — RPR

132- **1** **Blacktoft (USA)**[29] 6712 4-8-11 **70**....(e) J-PGuillambert 6 — 79+
(S C Williams) *lw: hld up in last pair: gd prog on inner over 1f out: drvn and edgd rt fnl f: r.o to ld last stride* **5/2[1]**

023- **2** shd **Berkhamsted (IRE)**[28] 6734 5-8-11 **68**....(p) JimCrowley 9 — 76
(Tom Dascombe) *lw: trckd ldrs: gng wl over 2f out: effrt to ld over 1f out: drvn and kpt on: hdd last stride* **7/2[2]**

004- **3** 2 1/2 **Barry Island**[14] 6889 8-8-5 **65**.... MarcHalford(3) 2 — 69+
(D R C Elsworth) *hld up in last pair: rdn and nt qckn over 1f out: r.o fnl f to take 3rd nr fin* **12/1**

404- **4** nk **Port 'n Starboard**[18] 6848 6-8-6 **63**.... JimmyQuinn 8 — 66
(C A Cyzer) *chsd ldng pair: rdn over 2f out: lost pl over 1f out: styd on again fnl f* **9/2[3]**

200- **5** 1/2 **Sonny Parkin**[26] 5299 5-9-4 **75**....(v) AdamKirby 5 — 77
(G A Huffer) *t.k.h: hld up in last trio: sme prog over 2f out: drvn and nt qckn over 1f out: styd on* **5/1**

300- **6** shd **Wheelavit (IRE)**[4] 6986 4-8-11 **70**.... HayleyTurner 10 — 72
(B G Powell) *pressed ldr: led over 2f out to over 1f out: wknd ins fnl f* **28/1**

365- **7** 3 **Our Kes (IRE)**[12] 6924 5-8-9 **66**.... TonyCulhane 4 — 62
(P Howling) *racd wd: hld up towards rr: rdn and no prog 2f out: sn btn* **12/1**

300- **8** 1/2 **Fratt'n Park (IRE)**[24] 6775 4-7-12 **65** oh1 ow2.... JosephWalsh(7) 7 — 59
(J J Bridger) *hld up bhd ldrs on inner: drvn over 2f out: sn lost pl: wknd fnl f* **25/1**

5/1- **9** 2 1/2 **Jack Rolfe**[227] 18 5-8-10 **67**.... NCallan 1 — 57
(G L Moore) *led to over 2f out: wknd rapidly over 1f out* **10/1**

2m 6.80s (-0.99) **Going Correction** -0.125s/f (Stan)
WFA 4 from 5yo+ 2lb **9** Ran SP% **117.4**
Speed ratings (Par 103):98,97,95,95,95 95,92,92,90
CSF £11.44 CT £87.88 TOTE £3.50: £1.50, £1.80, £2.50; EX 16.90 Trifecta £64.40 Pool: £477.41 - 5.26 winning units. Place 6 £4,313.23, Place 5 £1,273.93.
Owner Chris Watkins And David N Reynolds **Bred** Paradigm Thoroughbreds Inc **Trained** Newmarket, Suffolk

FOCUS
A fair handicap for the track run at an ordinary pace. The form is a bit dubious and the winner and third, who came from off the pace, shaped a bit better than the bare form suggests.
T/Jkpt: Not won. T/Plt: £3,261.20 to a £1 stake. Pool: £48,918.60. 10.95 winning tickets. T/Qpdt: £746.60 to a £1 stake. Pool: £5,650.60. 5.60 winning tickets. JN

DEAUVILLE (R-H)
Wednesday, January 3

OFFICIAL GOING: Standard

31a PRIX MISS SATAMIXA (LISTED RACE) (F&M) (ALL-WEATHER) — 7f 110y
2:00 (2:00) 4-Y-0+ **£17,568** (£7,027; £5,270; £3,514; £1,757)

RPR

1 **Take Grace (FR)**[41] 6574 5-8-12.... ACrastus 8 — 99
(Y De Nicolay, France)

2 nk **Samsa (FR)**[61] 6328 4-8-12.... FSpanu 7 — 98
(R Gibson, France)

3 3/4 **Fonce De (FR)**[76] 5-8-12.... FBlondel 11 — 97
(Rod Collet, France)

4 shd **Indian Princess (IRE)**[35] 4-8-12.... JCrocquevieille 3 — 96
(P Van De Poele, France)

5 snk **Tianshan (FR)**[80] 6001 4-9-2.... MSautjeau 1 — 100
(F-X de Chevigny, France)

6 hd **Drosia (IRE)**[59] 6366 4-9-2.... TThulliez 16 — 100
(C Laffon-Parias, France)

6 dht **Asque**[41] 4-8-12.... IMendizabal 13 — 96
(G Henrot, France)

8 1/2 **Red Kiss (IRE)**[43] 4-8-12.... TGillet 9 — 95
(Rod Collet, France)

9 nk **Ziride (FR)**[43] 4-8-12.... RonanThomas 12 — 94
(H-A Pantall, France)

10 nk **Mayonga (IRE)**[41] 6574 4-9-2.... SebSanders 15 — 97
(Sir Mark Prescott) *raced on outside disputing 7th, 6th straight, came widest, driven 1 1/2f out, stayed on but unable to quicken (6/4F cpld)* **6/4[1]**

11 **Peking Beauty**[88] 5-8-12.... ABonnefoy 4 — 93
(J De Roualle, France)

12 **Happy Town (FR)**[67] 4-8-12.... JAuge 14 — 93
(Robert Collet, France)

13 **Kezia (FR)**[37] 4-8-12.... MBlancpain 2 — 93
(C Laffon-Parias, France)

14 **Miss Highjinks (USA)**[36] 6635 4-8-12.... SPasquier 6 — 93
(E J O'Neill) *pressed leader early, 4th and ridden straight, weakened over 1f out (6/4F cpld)* **6/4[1]**

15 **Dinaha (FR)**[158] 6-8-12.... RCMontenegro 5 — 93
(X Thomas-Demeaulte, France)

16 **Hollywood Starlet (FR)**[61] 6328 4-8-12.... MCherel 10 — 93
(Y De Nicolay, France)

1m 28.3s (88.30) **16** Ran SP% **80.0**
PARI-MUTUEL (including one euro stakes): WIN 14.40; PL 4.20, 3.20,3.30; DF 59.40.
Owner Mme N Bardin **Bred** Mme Danielle De La Heronniere & Denis Bensussan **Trained** France

NOTEBOOK
Mayonga(IRE), made favourite on the back of her second place in a similar heat over this course and distance back in November, was disappointing. She stayed on but could not pick up like some of her rivals, and perhaps she just needs a winter break.
Miss Highjinks(USA), prominent early, was in trouble early in the straight.

WOLVERHAMPTON (A.W) (L-H)
Thursday, January 4

OFFICIAL GOING: Standard
Wind: Fresh, half-behind Weather: Fine

32 PONTIN'S - BOOK EARLY CLAIMING STKS — 7f 32y(P)
1:20 (1:21) (Class 6) 4-Y-0+ **£2,388** (£705; £352) **Stalls** High

Form — RPR

400- **1** **Wahoo Sam (USA)**[9] 6938 7-9-5 72....(p) NCallan 4 — 78
(K A Ryan) *mde all: qcknd clr 2f out: sn rdn: r.o* **6/1[2]**

500- **2** 1/2 **Sir Douglas**[69] 6206 4-8-13 72.... ShaneKelly 6 — 71
(J A Osborne) *hld up in tch: rdn over 2f out: r.o ins fnl f* **9/1[3]**

103- **3** shd **Climate (IRE)**[14] 6892 8-8-8 66....(v) RussellKennemore(5) 9 — 71
(R Hollinshead) *hld up towards rr: rdn and hdwy 3f out: r.o ins fnl f* **6/1[2]**

066- **4** 1 **Mystic Man (FR)**[9] 6938 9-9-0 70....(b) JimmyQuinn 3 — 69
(I W McInnes) *s.i.s: rdn and hdwy on ins over 2f out: nt qckn ins fnl f* **20/1**

033- **5** *nk* **Solicitude**[14] [6897] 4-8-7 52.......................................(b[1]) FrancisNorton 11 61
(D Haydn Jones) *bhd: rdn over 2f out: hdwy fnl f: nrst fin* **20/1**

00- **6** *2* **Erra Go On**[32] [6690] 6-9-5 .... DPMcDonogh 5 68
(Adrian McGuinness, Ire) *a.p: rdn over 2f out: wknd ins fnl f* **3/1**[1]

516- **7** *1* **Sovereignty (JPN)**[13] [6919] 5-8-11 66.................. JamesMillman(5) 12 63
(D K Ivory) *hld up in mid-div: hdwy over 3f out: hung rt and lost pl over 2f out: rn wd and c to stands' rail st* **9/1**[3]

000- **8** *1 1/4* **Lord Chamberlain**[147] [4288] 14-8-6 56......................(b) BarrySavage(7) 2 56
(J M Bradley) *s.i.s: bhd: short-lived effrt on ins wl over 1f out* **33/1**

513- **9** *1 3/4* **Bessemer (JPN)**[9] [6938] 6-9-1 69............................(p) DanielTudhope 10 54
(D Carroll) *hld up in mid-div: hdwy over 3f out: sn rdn: wknd wl over 1f out: fin lame* **3/1**[1]

660- **10** *2* **Methusaleh (IRE)**[14] [6898] 4-8-10 69............................. JamieJones(5) 8 49
(D Shaw) *mid-div: rdn 3f out: bhd fnl 2f* **66/1**

U0-0 **11** *11* **Funfair Wane**[2] [9] 8-9-5 80....................................... AdrianTNicholls 7 24
(D Nicholls) *t.k.h: chsd wnr tl rdn 2f out: sn wknd* **33/1**

1m 28.95s (-1.45) **Going Correction** -0.075s/f (Stan) **11** Ran SP% **115.5**
Speed ratings (Par 101):105,104,104,103,102 100,99,97,95,93 81
CSF £53.39 TOTE £5.70: £1.30, £3.80, £2.90; EX 57.50 Trifecta £131.10 Part won. Pool: £184.67 - 0.10 winning tickets..Sir Douglas was claimed by R. A. Harris for £8,000.
Owner Blackhurst,Bridge,Moll,O'Brien **Bred** Stonereath Farms Inc **Trained** Hambleton, N Yorks

FOCUS CSF £23.63 TOTE £6.30: £1.90, £2.20; EX 22.70
They went a good pace in what proved to be a competitive claimer and the form looks pretty sound rated around the placed horses.
Sovereignty(JPN) Official explanation: jockey said gelding hung right
Bessemer(JPN) Official explanation: vet said gelding finished lame on its right foreleg

33 DINE AT WOLVERHAMPTON RACECOURSE (S) STKS 5f 216y(P)
1:50 (1:50) (Class 6) 4-Y-0+ **£2,047** (£604; £302) **Stalls** Low

Form RPR

103- **1** **Miracle Ridge (IRE)**[74] [6112] 12-9-2 ....(b) DPMcDonogh 8 63
(Adrian McGuinness, Ire) *a.p: led over 2f out: rdn clr over 1f out: drvn out* **9/2**[3]

035- **2** *2* **Came Back (IRE)**[20] [6833] 4-9-2 58................................... ShaneKelly 4 63+
(J A Osborne) *sn chsng ldrs: hmpd over 3f out: n.m.r over 1f out: r.o ins fnl f: nt trble wnr* **10/3**[1]

151- **3** *1 1/2* **The London Gang**[9] [6938] 4-9-2 58.....................................(v) NCallan 12 52
(P D Evans) *hld up in rr: rdn over 2f out: hdwy on ins over 1f out: swtchd rt ins fnl f: r.o* **7/2**[2]

000- **4** *shd* **Grand View**[88] [5834] 11-8-11 45.................................(p) PaulMulrennan 11 47
(J R Weymes) *bhd: rdn over 2f out: hdwy fnl f: nvr nrr* **40/1**

000- **5** *3/4* **Sham Ruby**[114] [5272] 5-8-6 33... HayleyTurner 1 40
(M R Bosley) *a.p: rdn 2f out: no ex fnl f* **80/1**

450- **6** *1/2* **Shunkawakhan (IRE)**[13] [6906] 4-8-4 50.................(p) MarvinCheung(7) 9 43
(G C H Chung) *hld up in tch: lost pl after 1f: kpt on fnl f: n.d* **15/2**

064- **7** *2* **Patternmaker (USA)**[17] [6856] 5-8-11 48...................... AndrewElliott(5) 2 42
(A M Hales) *sn led: hdd over 2f out: rdn wl over 1f out: wknd ins fnl f* **9/1**

50-6 **8** *nk* **Ten Prophets (IRE)**[2] [9] 4-9-7 70.......................... RobertWinston 10 46
(D Nicholls) *prom: rdn whn edgd lft over 2f out: wknd ins fnl f* **8/1**

624- **9** *2 1/2* **Nebdi (IRE)**[20] [6833] 6-9-2 54...(p) PaulQuinn 7 34
(E J Alston) *chsd ldrs: nt clr run over 2f out: sn rdn: n.d after* **11/1**

000- **10** *1 1/2* **Mind That Fox**[33] [6681] 5-8-11 36..................................... SteveDrowne 5 24
(T Wall) *led early: prom: bmpd over 3f out: rdn and wknd wl over 1f out* **80/1**

00- **11** *1 1/2* **Speckled Hen (IRE)**[21] [6820] 4-8-6 55......................(b) FrancisNorton 6 15
(D Haydn Jones) *hld up in mid-div: hdwy over 3f out: nt clr run over 2f out: sn rdn: wknd wl over 1f out* **33/1**

600- **12** *nk* **Cate Washington**[7] [6958] 4-8-1 44................................. TolleyDean(5) 3 14
(Mrs L Williamson) *rdn over 3f out: a bhd* **80/1**

1m 15.46s (-0.35) **Going Correction** -0.075s/f (Stan) **12** Ran SP% **113.8**
Speed ratings (Par 101):99,96,94,94,93 92,89,89,86,84 82,81
CSF £18.61 TOTE £4.90: £3.40, £1.40, £1.02; EX 23.40 Trifecta £38.80 Pool: £264.36 - 4.83 winning tickets..The winner was bought in for 10,500gns. Came Back was claimed by W. I. Bloomfield for £6,000. The London Gang was claimed by Miss D. A. McHale for £6,000.
Owner Adrian McGuinness **Bred** K Prendergast & Con Harrington **Trained** Lusk, Co Dublin

FOCUS
A open-looking seller despite the fact that several were available at fancy prices. The form is limited by the proximity of the fourth and fifth.
Came Back(IRE) Official explanation: jockey said colt suffered interference
The London Gang Official explanation: jockey said colt was hampered on the bend
Patternmaker(USA) Official explanation: jockey said gelding lost a right-fore shoe
Mind That Fox Official explanation: jockey said gelding lost a near-hind shoe

34 CANVAS PRINTS FROM BONUSPRINT.COM H'CAP 5f 216y(P)
2:20 (2:21) (Class 5) (0-70,70) 3-Y-0 **£2,914** (£867; £433; £216) **Stalls** Low

Form RPR

125- **1** **Fractured Foxy**[82] [5958] 3-8-8 **69**.................................... SladeO'Hara(7) 1 71
(J J Quinn) *hld up in tch: rdn to ld over 1f out: r.o* **7/2**[1]

323- **2** *3/4* **Vadinka**[12] [6925] 3-9-2 **70**.. KimTinkler 3 70
(N Tinkler) *led early: a.p: led wl over 1f out: sn rdn and hdd: kpt on ins fnl f* **7/2**[1]

664- **3** *1 1/4* **Bentley**[14] [6900] 3-7-9 **56** oh11.....................................(v) WilliamBuick(7) 4 52
(D Shaw) *sn led: rdn over 2f out: hdd wl over 1f out: nt qckn ins fnl f* **9/2**[2]

021- **4** *3* **Grange Lili (IRE)**[5] [6985] 3-8-9 **63** 6ex...................(b) RobbieFitzpatrick 2 50
(Peter Grayson) *hld up in tch: rdn and hung rt over 2f out: wknd over 1f out* **9/1**

322- **5** *1 1/2* **Darling Belinda**[13] [6905] 3-8-13 **67**..(p) NCallan 7 50
(D K Ivory) *hld up in tch: ev ch 2f out: sn rdn: hung lft and wknd 1f out* **7/2**[1]

440- **6** *6* **Ioweyou**[131] [4804] 3-8-10 **64**... LPKeniry 5 29
(J S Moore) *t.k.h: prom tl rdn and wknd over 2f out* **7/1**[3]

006- **7** *9* **Rubber Duck (IRE)**[6] [6975] 3-7-11 **56** oh11............. DuranFentiman(5) 6 —
(Peter Grayson) *in rr: rdn over 3f out: sn struggling* **100/1**

1m 15.3s (-0.51) **Going Correction** -0.075s/f (Stan) **7** Ran SP% **108.3**
Speed ratings (Par 97):100,99,97,93,91 83,71
CSF £14.11 TOTE £5.20: £2.60, £2.40; EX 16.70.
Owner Mrs E Wright **Bred** Bearstone Stud **Trained** Settrington, N Yorks

FOCUS
A modest handicap with few progressive sorts and the form looks shaky.
Darling Belinda Official explanation: jockey said filly hung left

35 PONTINS.COM CLAIMING STKS 1m 4f 50y(P)
2:50 (2:50) (Class 6) 4-Y-0+ **£2,388** (£705; £352) **Stalls** Low

Form RPR

402- **1** **Finished Article (IRE)**[17] [6860] 10-8-13 47.................. J-PGuillambert 2 61+
(P A Blockley) *chsd ldr: rdn to ld over 1f out: hung rt ins fnl f: eased last strides* **13/2**

602- **2** *hd* **Bethanys Boy (IRE)**[16] [6871] 6-9-4 75............................ SteveDrowne 4 65
(A M Hales) *led: rdn and hdd over 1f out: r.o* **11/4**[2]

606- **3** *5* **Credit (IRE)**[22] [6811] 6-9-9 75.. HayleyTurner 3 62
(Jennie Candlish) *hld up in tch: wnt 2nd briefly over 1f out: rdn over 2f out: one pce: fin lame* **12/1**

352- **4** *nk* **Speed Dial Harry (IRE)**[8] [6947] 5-9-9 74.............................(v) NCallan 6 61
(K R Burke) *hld up: rdn over 2f out: effrt on ins wl over 1f out: one pce* **7/4**[1]

321- **5** *1 3/4* **Ionian Spring (IRE)**[16] [6871] 12-9-6 77......................... DanielTudhope 5 55
(D Carroll) *hld up and bhd: hdwy over 4f out: rdn and wknd wl over 1f out* **10/3**[3]

S/0- **6** *3/4* **Stallone**[17] [6860] 10-9-0 60... RobertWinston 7 48
(N Wilson) *hld up: rdn over 2f out: no rspnse* **33/1**

2m 43.15s (0.73) **Going Correction** -0.075s/f (Stan) **6** Ran SP% **110.1**
Speed ratings (Par 101):94,93,90,90,89,88 CSF £23.63 TOTE £6.30: £1.90, £2.20; EX 22.70
Bethanys Boy was claimed by P. A. Blockley for £10,000. Speed Dial Harry was claimed by R. A. Harris for £15,000.
Owner J L Guillambert **Bred** Dr D Davis **Trained** Lambourn, Berks

FOCUS
The winning time reflected the slow pace in this modest claimer which is rated through the winner to last year's All-Weather best.
Credit(IRE) Official explanation: vet said gelding finished lame

36 PONTIN'S FAMILY HOLIDAYS MAIDEN STKS 5f 20y(P)
3:20 (3:21) (Class 5) 3-Y-0+ **£2,968** (£876; £438) **Stalls** Low

Form RPR

350- **1** **Pride Of Joy**[183] [3199] 4-9-8 64... DaneO'Neill 3 67
(D K Ivory) *mde all: rdn clr over 1f out: r.o wl* **5/2**[1]

0- **2** *2* **Descargo**[41] [6575] 3-8-0 .... WilliamBuick(7) 2 54
(C G Cox) *chsd ldrs: rdn over 1f out: kpt on one pce fnl f: tk 2nd nr fin* **8/1**

504- **3** *nk* **Ellablue**[19] [6838] 3-8-7 58... ChrisCatlin 5 53
(Rae Guest) *chsd wnr: rdn over 2f out: one pce fnl f* **3/1**[2]

020- **4** *1 1/2* **Tajjree**[54] [6440] 4-9-8 52..(tp) AdamKirby 8 53
(Miss K B Boutflower) *hld up: hdwy over 2f out: rdn over 1f out: one pce* **6/1**[3]

360/ **5** *2 1/2* **Ela Figura**[493] [4325] 7-9-8 40.. FrancisNorton 10 44
(A W Carroll) *hld up in tch: lost pl 3f out: n.d after* **25/1**

056- **6** *shd* **One White Sock**[13] [6905] 3-8-4 43..............................(b) MarcHalford(3) 9 38
(J L Spearing) *prom: rdn 2f out: sn wknd* **33/1**

6- **7** *1* **Epidaurian King (IRE)**[8] [6944] 4-9-13 .... DanielTudhope 4 45
(D Shaw) *s.i.s: nvr nr ldrs* **50/1**

4- **8** *1 1/4* **Xocolatl**[28] [6738] 4-9-8 .... RobbieFitzpatrick 1 36
(Peter Grayson) *hld up in mid-div: rdn over 2f out: wknd fnl f* **12/1**

0- **9** *2 1/2* **Vivi Belle**[21] [6821] 3-8-7 .... HayleyTurner 7 21
(M L W Bell) *a bhd* **8/1**

000- **10** *7* **Bond Sea Breeze (IRE)**[110] [5363] 4-9-3 31............. DuranFentiman(5) 6 2
(G R Oldroyd) *a bhd* **8/1**

62.54 secs (-0.28) **Going Correction** -0.075s/f (Stan)
WFA 3 from 4yo+ 15lb **10** Ran SP% **117.6**
Speed ratings (Par 103):99,95,95,92,88 88,87,85,81,69
CSF £23.14 TOTE £3.60: £1.60, £2.90, £1.10; EX 37.00 Trifecta £108.30 Pool: £517.57 - 3.39 winning tickets..
Owner K T Ivory **Bred** K T Ivory **Trained** Radlett, Herts

FOCUS
Not many actually got into this moderate sprint maiden and the form is limited by the fourth and fifth.

37 PONTINSBINGO.COM H'CAP 1m 1f 103y(P)
3:50 (3:50) (Class 6) (0-58,58) 3-Y-0 **£2,730** (£806; £403) **Stalls** Low

Form RPR

452- **1** **Global Traffic**[17] [6859] 3-8-9 **53**..(b) NCallan 2 62+
(P D Evans) *hld up in mid-div: rdn and hdwy on ins over 2f out: nt clr run and swtchd lft over 1f out: led wl ins fnl f: rn* **15/8**[1]

005- **2** *1 3/4* **Shrewd Dude**[36] [6653] 3-8-6 **50**...................................... FrancisNorton 6 53
(Carl Llewellyn) *chsd ldrs: reminder over 4f out: rdn 3f out: kpt on ins fnl f: tk 2nd nr fin* **4/1**[2]

006- **3** *nk* **Skye But N Ben**[38] [6625] 3-8-3 **47**....................................(b[1]) PaulFessey 5 49
(T D Barron) *t.k.h: a.p: rdn over 2f out: kpt on same pce fnl f* **12/1**

400- **4** *shd* **Greek God**[100] [5597] 3-8-11 **55**.. RobertWinston 7 57
(W Jarvis) *chsd ldr: rdn over 3f out: led 2f out: sn hdd: nt qckn ins fnl f* **7/1**

434- **5** *1/2* **Party Palace**[4] [6996] 3-8-3 **47**... ChrisCatlin 1 48
(J A Osborne) *led: rdn and hdd 2f out: led wl over 1f out: hdd and no ex wl ins fnl f* **13/2**[3]

300- **6** *1 1/2* **Ballyshane Spirit (IRE)**[16] [6866] 3-8-1 **52**.................... WilliamBuick(7) 3 50
(N A Callaghan) *plld hrd in mid-div: rdn over 3f out: edgd lft and no real prog fnl f* **8/1**

004- **7** *hd* **Brierley Lil**[8] [6951] 3-8-9 **53** ow1.. AdamKirby 9 50
(J L Spearing) *bhd: rdn 4f out: hdwy over 1f out: nvr trbld ldrs* **28/1**

005- **8** *1 3/4* **Polyquest (IRE)**[49] [6498] 3-8-12 **56**.................................. JosedeSouza 4 50
(P F I Cole) *hld up and bhd: rdn and hdwy on ins over 2f out: sltly hmpd over 1f out: wknd ins fnl f* **25/1**

505- **9** *13* **Tres Hombres**[27] [6745] 3-8-6 **50**...................................(b[1]) JimmyQuinn 8 18
(Tom Dascombe) *t.k.h: a towards rr* **33/1**

000- **10** *3 1/2* **King Of The Beers (USA)**[8] [6950] 3-9-0 **58**...............(b[1]) DaneO'Neill 10 19
(R A Harris) *prom: rdn over 3f out: sn wknd* **33/1**

336- **11** *5* **Muree Queen**[99] [5614] 3-8-8 **52**.................................... FergusSweeney 11 3
(R Hollinshead) *mid-div: rdn 5f out: bhd fnl 3f* **16/1**

2m 1.88s (-0.74) **Going Correction** -0.075s/f (Stan) **11** Ran SP% **118.5**
Speed ratings (Par 95):100,98,98,98,97 96,96,94,83,79 75
CSF £8.65 CT £68.67 TOTE £2.60: £2.00, £1.60, £3.00; EX 15.60 Trifecta £89.10 Pool: £439.52 - 3.50 winning tickets..
Owner Mrs I M Folkes **Bred** P F I Cole **Trained** Pandy, Monmouths

FOCUS
This weak affair was virtually a maiden handicap but the form makes sense rated through the fifth.

38 PHOTO BOOKS FROM BONUSPRINT.COM APPRENTICE H'CAP 1m 141y(P)
4:20 (4:20) (Class 5) (0-75,74) 4-Y-0+ £3,071 (£906; £453) **Stalls** Low

Form RPR

112- **1** **Just Bond (IRE)**[7] 6968 5-9-8 **74** 6ex............................ DuranFentiman 2 82+
(G R Oldroyd) *hld up: rdn and hdwy on ins wl over 1f out: led jst ins fnl f: hung rt towards fin: r.o* **10/11**[1]

041- **2** *shd* **Top Mark**[14] 6898 5-9-6 **72**.. JamieMoriarty 3 77
(J R Boyle) *led: rdn over 2f out: hdd jst ins fnl f: r.o* **7/1**

000- **3** *3/4* **Northern Desert (IRE)**[5] 6986 8-9-1 **72**.................... WilliamCarson(5) 1 75
(P W Hiatt) *hld up in rr: hdwy over 2f out: rdn and swtchd rt over 1f out: r.o towards fin* **5/1**[3]

321- **4** *1/2* **Foreign Language (USA)**[17] 6861 4-9-0 **72**............... WilliamBuick(5) 5 74
(N A Callaghan) *chsd ldr: rdn and ev ch over 1f out: nt qckn ins fnl f* **9/2**[2]

603- **5** *3/4* **Linda's Colin (IRE)**[15] 6889 5-8-13 **68**........................... TolleyDean(3) 6 68
(R A Harris) *prom: rdn whn nt clr run over 1f out: sn swtchd lft: no ex ins fnl f* **12/1**

046- **6** *6* **Goose Chase**[14] 6898 5-8-12 **64**...................................... AndrewElliott 4 52
(A M Hales) *hld up: hdwy 5f out: rdn and wknd over 2f out* **22/1**

1m 50.43s (-1.33) **Going Correction** -0.075s/f (Stan)
WFA 4 from 5yo+ 1lb **6** Ran SP% **111.8**
Speed ratings (Par 103):102,101,101,100,100 94
CSF £7.91 TOTE £1.70: £1.20, £2.90; EX 8.50 Place 6 £32.35, Place 5 £8.32.
Owner R C Bond **Bred** Schwindibode Ag **Trained** Brawby, N Yorks
■ Stewards' Enquiry : Jamie Moriarty three-day ban: used whip with excessive frequency (Jan 15-17)

FOCUS
This proved to be a competitive contest despite the small field. The form is not that solid with the third the best guide.
T/Jkpt: Not won. T/Plt: £63.80 to a £1 stake. Pool: £60,944.15. 696.90 winning tickets. T/Qpdt: £11.20 to a £1 stake. Pool: £4,120.40. 271.40 winning tickets. KH

[32]WOLVERHAMPTON (A.W) (L-H)
Friday, January 5

OFFICIAL GOING: Standard
Wind: Light behind Weather: Early showers giving way to cloud

39 GO PONTIN'S AMATEUR RIDERS' H'CAP 2m 119y(P)
1:20 (1:20) (Class 6) (0-60,60) 4-Y-0+ £2,307 (£709; £354) **Stalls** Low

Form RPR

052- **1** **Cumbrian Knight (IRE)**[22] 6621 9-10-9 **53**............ MissNJefferson(5) 8 61
(J M Jefferson) *hld up in tch: led 1/2-way: pshd clr over 1f out* **9/2**[2]

600- **2** *1 1/2* **Reminiscent (IRE)**[13] 6936 8-10-6 **50**............... MrStephenHarrison(5) 4 56
(B P J Baugh) *hld up: hdwy over 5f out: rdn to chse wnr fnl f: edgd lft: styd on* **12/1**

00/ **3** *1 3/4* **Alagon (IRE)**[29] 1654 7-10-7 **53**...............................(v) MrJRavenall(7) 12 57
(Ian Williams) *chsd ldrs: rdn 6f out: outpcd over 2f out: styd on ins fnl f* **20/1**

011/ **4** *2* **Sea Map**[29] 6419 5-11-4 **60**.. MrJOwen(3) 9 62
(D E Cantillon) *prom: rdn over 3f out: styd on same pce fnl 2f* **5/1**[3]

444- **5** *1 1/4* **Candarli (IRE)**[136] 545 11-10-13 **59**............................. MissCBoxall(7) 2 59
(D R Gandolfo) *led to 1/2-way: chsd ldrs tl wknd over 1f out* **11/1**

240- **6** *1 3/4* **Malibu (IRE)**[5] 6995 6-10-8 **47**.. MrSDobson 10 45
(M Appleby) *hld up: effrt over 2f out: nt trble ldrs* **16/1**

010- **7** *1/2* **Moonshine Bill**[113] 5314 8-10-5 **49**.............................. MrsMarieKing(5) 5 46
(P W Hiatt) *trckd ldr: plld hrd: rdn over 2f out: wknd fnl f* **14/1**

020- **8** *3* **Khanjar (USA)**[20] 6843 7-10-13 **55**.................................. MrSPearce(3) 3 49
(J Pearce) *hld up: bhd 1/2-way: n.d* **8/1**

3/0- **9** *1 3/4* **Forfeiter (USA)**[8] 6568 5-11-0 **60**......................... MissPHermansson(7) 11 52
(R Ford) *hld up: bhd 1/2-way: effrt over 2f out: sn wknd* **16/1**

540- **10** *2 1/2* **Countback (FR)**[13] 6936 8-10-6 **50**................................ MrMJJSmith(5) 6 39
(A W Carroll) *s.i.s: hld up: hdwy over 4f out: wknd over 2f out* **33/1**

131- **11** *1* **Blue Hedges**[39] 6621 5-11-2 **60**........................... MissALHutchinson(5) 1 47
(H J Collingridge) *hld up: plld hrd: hdwy over 2f out: rdn and wknd over 1f out: eased ins fnl f* **11/4**[1]

500- **12** *12* **Phoenix Eye**[13] 6617 6-10-3 **47**.......................... MissMMullineaux(5) 13 20
(M Mullineaux) *s.s: hld up: hdwy over 9f out: wknd 5f out* **100/1**

040/ **13** *59* **Tass Heel (IRE)**[541] 182 8-10-8 **54**..............(p) MissIsabelTompsett(7) 7 —
(B J Llewellyn) *chsd ldrs over 8f* **50/1**

3m 48.24s (5.11) **Going Correction** -0.025s/f (Stan) **13** Ran SP% **117.7**
Speed ratings (Par 101):86,85,84,83,82 82,81,80,79,78 78,72,44
CSF £55.01 CT £986.36 TOTE £4.40: £2.00, £4.20, £5.00; EX 46.30 TRIFECTA Not won..
Owner J M Jefferson **Bred** John P A Kenny **Trained** Norton, N Yorks

FOCUS
A poor contest, run at a pedestrian gallop until the winner grasped the bull by the horns at halfway and gained just reward for doing so. The race could be rated higher but is anchored by the time.
Blue Hedges Official explanation: jockey said horse failed to stay trip

40 PONTIN'S HOLIDAYS CLAIMING STKS 5f 216y(P)
1:50 (1:50) (Class 6) 3-Y-O £2,730 (£806; £403) **Stalls** Low

Form RPR

522- **1** **Cherri Fosfate**[15] 6894 3-9-2 64.....................................(v) TonyCulhane 2 63+
(W G M Turner) *chsd ldrs: led 1/2-way: rdn clr fnl 2f: eased nr fin* **5/6**[1]

460- **2** *2* **Mick Is Back**[147] 4323 3-8-12 57.. JimCrowley 4 50
(P D Evans) *chsd ldrs: rdn over 2f out: styd on same pce appr fnl f* **12/1**

3U3- **3** *shd* **Aggbag**[13] 6926 3-8-6 60.. SoniaEaton(7) 6 51
(B P J Baugh) *hld up: hdwy over 2f out: rdn and edgd lft over 1f out: styd on same pce* **6/1**[3]

456- **4** *nk* **Suntan Lady (IRE)**[13] 6926 3-8-4 43......................(v) DuranFentiman(5) 7 46
(Miss V Haigh) *hld up: nt clr run over 2f out: hdwy over 1f out: styd on same pce ins fnl f* **20/1**

56- **5** *5* **Bogside Katie**[13] 6925 3-8-5 .... ChrisCatlin 5 27
(G M Moore) *led to 1/2-way: wknd over 1f out* **16/1**

050- **6** *1 1/2* **Athea Lad (IRE)**[8] 6963 3-8-9 .... JerryO'Dwyer(3) 1 30
(W K Goldsworthy) *chsd ldrs: sn drvn along: wknd 2f out* **28/1**

624- **7** *4* **Catlivius (IRE)**[15] 6894 3-8-11 61...(p) NCallan 3 17
(K A Ryan) *s.s and rel to r: hdwy u.p and hung rt over 2f out: sn wknd* **7/2**[2]

1m 16.47s (0.66) **Going Correction** -0.025s/f (Stan) **7** Ran SP% **112.8**
Speed ratings (Par 95):94,91,91,90,84 82,76
CSF £12.31 TOTE £1.80: £1.10, £5.00; EX 10.20.The winner was claimed by Declan Carroll for £12,000.
Owner C McKenna **Bred** The Newchange Syndicate **Trained** Sigwells, Somerset

FOCUS
A routine claimer and with the second favourite giving it away at the start this took little winning. The form is limited by the fourth.
Bogside Katie Official explanation: vet said filly lost a right-fore shoe
Catlivius(IRE) Official explanation: jockey said filly missed the break

41 PONTINS.COM H'CAP 5f 216y(P)
2:20 (2:20) (Class 2) (0-100,97) 4-Y-0+ £11,658 (£3,468; £1,733; £865) **Stalls** Low

Form RPR

332- **1** **Qadar (IRE)**[20] 6849 5-9-2 **97**... NCallan 4 106
(N P Littmoden) *hld up in tch: led over 1f out: rdn out* **7/2**[2]

126- **2** *1 1/4* **Prince Tum Tum (USA)**[14] 6915 7-8-7 **88**.......................... JimmyQuinn 1 93
(D Shaw) *hld up in tch: nt clr run over 2f out: rdn to chse wnr ins fnl f: r.o* **13/2**

000- **3** *3/4* **Bahiano (IRE)**[104] 5523 6-8-12 **93**................................. J-PGuillambert 2 96
(C E Brittain) *hld up: rdn over 1f out: r.o ins fnl f: nrst fin* **5/1**

03-1 **4** *1 1/2* **Miracle Ridge (IRE)**[1] 33 12-7-9 **82**........................ WilliamBuick(7) 5 81
(Adrian McGuinness, Ire) *led 1f: chsd ldrs: rdn and ev ch over 1f out: no ex ins fnl f* **20/1**

103- **5** *1/2* **First Order**[20] 6849 6-8-9 **90**..(v) PaulHanagan 8 87
(I Semple) *trckd ldrs: racd keenly: rdn over 1f out: wknd ins fnl f* **4/1**[3]

020- **6** *3/4* **Talbot Avenue**[20] 6849 9-8-9 **90**... SteveDrowne 7 85
(M Blanshard) *hld up: rdn over 2f out: wknd ins fnl f* **16/1**

160- **7** *hd* **Night Prospector**[15] 6896 7-8-3 **84**...........................(p) AdrianMcCarthy 6 78
(R A Harris) *led 5f out: rdn and hdd over 1f out: wknd ins fnl f* **14/1**

444/ **8** *6* **Two Step Kid (USA)**[279] 6-8-9 **90**....................................... ShaneKelly 3 66
(J Noseda) *trckd ldrs: rdn over 2f out: wknd over 1f out* **3/1**[1]

1m 14.03s (-1.78) **Going Correction** -0.025s/f (Stan) **8** Ran SP% **114.5**
Speed ratings (Par 109):110,108,107,105,104 103,103,95
CSF £26.47 CT £112.50 TOTE £4.20: £1.20, £2.10, £1.80; EX 20.60 Trifecta £81.70 Pool £481.44 - 4.18 winnning units..
Owner Nigel Shields **Bred** Martin Francis **Trained** Newmarket, Suffolk

FOCUS
A decent Polytrack sprint and there was no hanging about. The form looks rock solid rated around the first two.

NOTEBOOK
Qadar(IRE), raised 2lb after a string of consistent efforts in defeat in his last four outings, finally gained just reward. Always travelling well just behind the leaders, a gap presented itself at just the right time and once in front he was never going to be caught. (op 3-1)
Prince Tum Tum(USA), 2lb better off with First Order for a half-length defeat over course and distance in November, followed the winner through starting up the home straight but, although staying on, never looked like getting to him. This trip is the bare minimum for him these days. (op 6-1 tchd 5-1)
Bahiano(IRE), returning from a near four-month break, was supported in the market and finished well from off the pace but could not get there in time. This should at least have put him spot on for another trip to Dubai. (op 8-1)
Miracle Ridge(IRE), making a quick reappearance after winning a seller over course and distance the previous day, acquitted himself superbly in this much stronger contest. Having raced up with the pace from the start, it was not until inside the last furlong that he was eventually held. (op 14-1)
First Order should have been bang there at the finish based on recent form with both Qadar and Prince Tum Tum, but he folded rather tamely down the home straight. Perhaps starting from the outside stall had something to do with it. (op 9-2 tchd 5-1)
Talbot Avenue, a long way behind Qadar and First Order at Lingfield last time, was again safely held. It may be significant that by far the best of his three efforts on sand so far was when going right-handed. (tchd 20-1)
Night Prospector looks to be in the grip of the Handicapper now. (op 20-1 tchd 25-1)
Two Step Kid(USA), back from a spell in the US and having his first start in nine months, was racing on sand for the first time in this country since making a winning debut at Lingfield as a juvenile. The betting did not suggest he was going to need it, but the way he dropped out indicated otherwise. (op 5-2 tchd 10-3)

42 PONTIN'S FAMILY HOLIDAYS (S) STKS 1m 141y(P)
2:50 (2:50) (Class 6) 4-Y-0+ £2,047 (£604; £302) **Stalls** Low

Form RPR

563- **1** **Bathwick Emma (IRE)**[6] 6988 4-8-9 55 ow1.........................(p) NCallan 4 54
(P D Evans) *chsd ldrs: rdn to ld over 1f out: r.o* **13/2**[3]

040- **2** *3* **Jiminor Mack**[8] 6959 4-8-5 45...........................(b) RichardKingscote(3) 7 47
(W J H Ratcliffe) *s.i.s: hld up: r.o and hung lft ins fnl f: nt rch wnr* **25/1**

044- **3** *hd* **Royal Embrace**[15] 6901 4-8-13 56....................................(v) DaneO'Neill 2 51
(D Shaw) *hld up in tch: rdn over 2f out: hung lft and styd on ins fnl f* **5/1**[2]

001- **4** *hd* **Norwegian**[32] 6701 6-9-5 48.......................................(p) DavidKinsella 5 56
(Ian Williams) *chsd ldrs: led over 2f out: rdn and hdd over 1f out: no ex ins fnl f* **12/1**

242- **5** *shd* **Second Reef**[21] 6837 5-9-0 55... PaulQuinn 13 51
(E J Alston) *hld up: plld hrd: hdwy over 3f out: rdn and ev ch over 1f out: no ex* **2/1**[1]

400- **6** *1 1/2* **Spy Gun (USA)**[29] 3944 7-9-0 43... ChrisCatlin 6 48
(T Wall) *led 6f: wknd ins fnl f* **25/1**

000- **7** *hd* **Joe Jo Star**[25] 6787 5-9-0 43...................................... RobbieFitzpatrick 1 47
(B P J Baugh) *chsd ldrs: rdn over 2f out: hung lft and wknd over 1f out* **16/1**

005- **8** *1* **Ronnies Lad**[15] 6898 5-9-0 45.. PaulMulrennan 3 45
(J R Norton) *mid-div: rdn over 3f out: nt trble ldrs* **14/1**

000- **9** *3/4* **Sanders Boy**[21] 6833 4-8-8 41....................................... JamieMoriarty(5) 9 43
(J R Norton) *hld up: rdn over 3f out: n.d* **66/1**

535- **10** *2* **Aventura (IRE)**[197] 2793 7-9-0 53... PhillipMakin 12 39
(S R Bowring) *chsd ldrs: rdn and ev ch over 2f out: wkng whn n.m.r sn after* **9/1**

300- **11** *1* **George's Flyer (IRE)**[15] 6898 4-8-13 59.....................(v[1]) PaulHanagan 10 37
(R A Fahey) *mid-div: rdn over 3f out: wknd over 2f out* **13/2**[3]

/00- **12** *7* **First Generation**[18] 6860 5-9-0 40....................................(t) JimCrowley 8 22
(P D Evans) *hld up: rdn over 2f out: sn wknd* **66/1**

060- **13** *1* **The Terminator (IRE)**[9] 6949 5-8-7 41........................ SoniaEaton(7) 11 20
(M Mullineaux) *s.s: a in rr* **66/1**

1m 50.87s (-0.89) **Going Correction** -0.025s/f (Stan)
WFA 4 from 5yo+ 1lb **13** Ran SP% **119.1**
Speed ratings (Par 101):102,99,99,98,98 97,97,96,95,94 93,86,86
CSF £166.11 TOTE £7.10: £2.00, £5.10, £2.10; EX 201.10 TRIFECTA Not won..There was no bid for the winner.
Owner W Clifford **Bred** Mrs Teresa Bergin **Trained** Pandy, Monmouths

FOCUS
An average seller, but the pace was fair and the form looks solid enough for the grade.

43 PONTINSBINGO.COM CONDITIONS STKS 1m 141y(P)
3:20 (3:22) (Class 2) 4-Y-0+

£11,217 (£3,358; £1,679; £840; £419; £210) Stalls Low

Form RPR

662- 1 **Hattan (IRE)**[61] 6365 5-9-0 110 J-PGuillambert 6 109
(C E Brittain) *chsd ldr tl led 5f out: clr over 3f out: rdn over 1f out: jst hld on* **3/1**[2]

622- 2 *nk* **Red Spell (IRE)**[14] 6914 6-9-0 100 DaneO'Neill 4 108
(R Hannon) *prom: chsd wnr over 3f out: rdn and hung lft over 1f out: styd on* **7/1**

240- 3 *4* **Bolodenka (IRE)**[97] 5675 5-9-0 97 JamieMoriarty 7 100
(R A Fahey) *hld up: styd on appr fnl f: nvr nrr* **14/1**

111- 4 *nk* **Areyoutalkingtome**[20] 6849 4-9-1 110 TonyCulhane 1 101
(C A Cyzer) *chsd ldrs: rdn over 2f out: sn hung lft: styd on same pce* **7/4**[1]

5 *3* **Fantoche (BRZ)**[489] 5-9-0 (v[1]) JamieSpencer 2 93?
(M J Wallace) *hld up: rdn over 2f out: hung lft and wknd over 1f out* **12/1**

306- 6 *1* **Kings Point (IRE)**[97] 5673 6-9-0 104 PaulHanagan 3 91
(R A Fahey) *led: hdd 5f out: wknd 2f out* **11/1**

2/3- 7 *6* **Cupid's Glory**[14] 6914 5-9-0 113 SebSanders 5 78
(Sir Mark Prescott) *hld up: rdn over 3f out: hung lft and wknd over 2f out* **7/2**[3]

1m 49.21s (-2.55) **Going Correction** -0.025s/f (Stan)
WFA 4 from 5yo+ 1lb 7 Ran SP% 118.8
Speed ratings (Par 109):110,109,106,105,103 102,97
CSF £25.37 TOTE £4.00: £2.10, £2.40; EX 21.70.
Owner Saeed Manana **Bred** Darley **Trained** Newmarket, Suffolk
■ Stewards' Enquiry : Dane O'Neill one-day ban: used whip down the shoulder in the forehand position (Jan 16)

FOCUS
A classy little event with three of the runners officially rated 110 or higher and a Group 1-placed import from Brazil. The tactics on the winner meant this was run at a true gallop and the form looks decent and solid.

NOTEBOOK
Hattan(IRE), last seen chasing home Cherry Mix in the Group 1 Premio Roma in November, was making his sand debut. There was always the danger that he would find the trip too sharp, so his rider did the right thing by committing him early and by the time the field turned for home he had established a decisive advantage over his rivals. Only the runner-up emerged from the pack to throw down a serious challenge and things became a bit desperate inside the last furlong, but he never really looked like being caught. He will now be spot on for a trip to Dubai. (op 9-2)
Red Spell(IRE), whose two previous tries here have not matched up to his form at Lingfield, at least got the strong pace he needs. He was the only one to emerge from the pack and throw down a serious challenge to the winner, but try as he might he could never quite reel him in. This was the third race in a row he has failed to get up by a narrow margin, but it would be harsh to criticise especially as he is rated 10lb inferior to Hattan. (op 6-1)
Bolodenka(IRE), runner-up in a Lingfield maiden as a juvenile in his only previous try on sand, was returning from four months off. He never got anywhere near the front pair, but did not perform that badly considering he was by some margin worst in on official ratings. (op 16-1)
Areyoutalkingtome, bidding for a five-timer after four victories over shorter trips at Lingfield, did find himself rather in a pocket as the winner was making the best of his way home rounding the final turn, but it probably made little difference to his finishing position. He has won over further than this on turf, so the trip cannot really be blamed, but perhaps this track did not suit him so well. (tchd 2-1 and 9-4 in places)
Fantoche(BRZ), a Listed winner and placed at Group 1 level in Brazil, faced a stiff task on his British debut but was entitled to need this first run since September 2005. (tchd 14-1)
Kings Point(IRE) had a lot to find at this level and once Hattan had headed him entering the back straight he was always up against it. (op 16-1)
Cupid's Glory was given an much more patient ride than at Lingfield, but it resulted in an even more dismal effort. (tchd 4-1)

44 PONTIN'S - BOOK EARLY H'CAP 7f 32y(P)
3:50 (3:51) (Class 4) (0-85,84) 4-Y-0+ £5,505 (£1,637; £818; £408) Stalls High

Form RPR

001- 1 **Chicken Soup**[6] 6992 5-8-8 **83** 6ex WilliamBuick[(7)] 1 95+
(T J Pitt) *hld up: hdwy over 2f out: rdn to ld wl ins fnl f: r.o* **8/11**[1]

321- 2 *1* **Buy On The Red**[5] 6999 6-8-13 **84** 6ex (p) JamesDoyle[(3)] 11 94
(W R Muir) *chsd ldr tl led 1/2-way: rdn clr over 1f out: hdd wl ins fnl f* **9/1**[3]

451- 3 *2 1/2* **Writ (IRE)**[13] 6932 5-8-8 **76** 6ex PaulHanagan 10 79
(I Semple) *chsd ldrs: rdn over 2f out: no ex fnl f* **6/1**[2]

003- 4 *1* **Chief Exec**[38] 6633 5-8-4 **72** ChrisCatlin 7 72
(C A Cyzer) *s.i.s: bhd and pushed along 1/2-way: r.o ins fnl f: nrst fin* **20/1**

400- 5 *nk* **Josh**[30] 6733 5-8-12 **80** NCallan 3 80
(K A Ryan) *prom: rdn over 2f out: sn hung rt: no ex fnl f* **14/1**

134- 6 *1/2* **Marko Jadeo (IRE)**[10] 6938 9-8-5 **78** TolleyDean[(5)] 8 76
(R A Harris) *hld up: hdwy over 1f out: hung lft ins fnl f: nt trble ldrs* **25/1**

00-6 7 *1* **Erra Go On**[1] 32 6-8-12 **80** PatCosgrave 6 76
(Adrian McGuinness, Ire) *led to 1/2-way: rdn and wknd over 1f out* **28/1**

124- 8 *hd* **Prince Dayjur (USA)**[13] 6932 8-8-6 **74** JimmyQuinn 9 69
(J Pearce) *chsd ldrs: rdn 1/2-way: wknd over 1f out* **16/1**

000- 9 *3/4* **Danzig River (IRE)**[101] 5593 6-8-5 **73** AdrianTNicholls 5 66
(D Nicholls) *hld up: plld hrd: hdwy over 1f out: nt clr run ins fnl f: nt trble ldrs* **50/1**

530- 10 *hd* **Kaveri (USA)**[65] 6292 4-9-2 **84** (b) J-PGuillambert 4 77
(C E Brittain) *hld up: rdn over 1f out: n.d* **16/1**

464- 11 *2* **Councellor (FR)**[270] 946 5-8-11 **79** MickyFenton 12 67
(Stef Liddiard) *trckd ldrs: rdn 1/2-way: wknd 2f out* **40/1**

400- 12 *6* **Tyzack (IRE)**[160] 3928 6-8-13 **81** ShaneKelly 2 53
(W M Brisbourne) *chsd ldrs over 4f* **14/1**

1m 28.19s (-2.21) **Going Correction** -0.025s/f (Stan) 12 Ran SP% 123.7
Speed ratings (Par 105):111,109,107,105,105 104,103,103,102,102 100,93
CSF £7.86 CT £29.33 TOTE £1.70: £1.40, £2.80, £1.60; EX 14.00 Trifecta £27.10 Pool £887.42 - 23.21 winning units.
Owner Fishlake Commercial Motors Ltd **Bred** Limestone Stud **Trained** Bawtry, S Yorks

FOCUS
A very decent pace and a smart winning time for a race of its type. The form is rated through the third.
Josh Official explanation: jockey said gelding hung to right

45 PONTINS.COM MAIDEN STKS 1m 4f 50y(P)
4:20 (4:20) (Class 5) 4-Y-0+ £2,968 (£876; £438) Stalls Low

Form RPR

561- 1 **Foursquare Flyer (IRE)**[8] 6967 5-9-7 70 DaleGibson 1 65
(J Mackie) *hld up: shkn up and hdwy over 3f out: rdn over 2f out: styd on u.p to ld nr fin* **11/10**[1]

000- 2 *nk* **Beldon Hill (USA)**[67] 6260 4-8-12 60 PaulHanagan 5 59
(R A Fahey) *chsd ldrs: rdn to ld over 1f out: hung lft ins fnl f: hdd nr fin* **3/1**[2]

0U0- 3 *8* **Diktatorship (IRE)**[32] 6700 4-9-0 45 (p) JamesDoyle[(3)] 6 51
(Ernst Oertel) *trckd ldr: plld hrd: rdn 3f out: wknd over 1f out* **33/1**

/25- 4 *nk* **Gallas (IRE)**[30] 6729 6-9-7 45 (b) ChrisCatlin 7 51
(S Lycett) *chsd ldrs: rdn 3f out: wknd over 1f out* **7/1**[3]

42- 5 *1 1/4* **Mayyas**[7] 6971 7-9-7 (t) TonyCulhane 9 49
(C C Bealby) *led: rdn and hdd over 1f out: wknd ins fnl f* **8/1**

00- 6 *2 1/2* **Slip Star**[55] 6450 4-8-9 SaleemGolam[(3)] 2 40
(T J Etherington) *hld up: plld hrd: rdn over 1f out: n.d* **100/1**

7 *1/2* **Tres Bien**[29] 5-9-7 DaneO'Neill 10 44
(P R Webber) *hld up: hdwy over 5f out: wknd over 2f out* **15/2**

000- 8 *1/2* **Crimson Flame (IRE)**[5] 6995 4-8-10 48 MarkCoumbe[(7)] 3 43
(A J Chamberlain) *hmpd s: hld up: no ch whn n.m.r over 1f out* **50/1**

04- 9 *16* **Watermill (IRE)**[22] 6817 4-9-3 PaulQuinn 8 18
(D W Chapman) *chsd ldrs over 8f* **100/1**

00- 10 *3 1/2* **Fine Deed**[34] 6680 6-9-0 StuartHaddon[(7)] 4 12
(Ian Williams) *prom 8f* **150/1**

2m 42.13s (-0.29) **Going Correction** -0.025s/f (Stan)
WFA 4 from 5yo+ 4lb 10 Ran SP% 115.5
Speed ratings (Par 103):99,98,93,93,92 90,90,90,79,77
CSF £4.33 TOTE £2.20: £1.10, £2.00, £6.60; EX 6.10 Trifecta £60.40 Pool £997.70 - 11.72 winning units. Place 6 £105.42, Place 5 £32.09.
Owner Tim Kelly **Bred** Miss Sally Hodgins **Trained** Church Broughton , Derbys
■ Foursquare Flyer has been reinstated as winner of a race here on December 28, so has now officially won two maidens.
■ Stewards' Enquiry : Paul Hanagan one-day ban: careless riding (Jan 16)

FOCUS
Probably a modest maiden in which the front pair pulled a long way clear of the rest, but the form is limited by the banded-class fourth.
T/Jkpt: £2,244.00 to a £1 stake. Pool: £23,704.24. 7.50 winning tickets. T/Plt: £87.90 to a £1 stake. Pool: £69,751.85. 578.85 winning tickets. T/Qpdt: £15.40 to a £1 stake. Pool: £5,344.40. 255.30 winning tickets. CR

[16]KEMPTON (A.W) (R-H)
Saturday, January 6

OFFICIAL GOING: Standard
Wind: light across

46 MORE OPTIONS WITH DIGIBET.COM CLASSIFIED STKS 5f (P)
3:50 (3:50) (Class 7) 4-Y-0+ £1,365 (£403; £201) Stalls High

Form RPR

335- 1 **Primarily**[24] 6806 5-9-0 45 RobbieFitzpatrick 8 54
(Peter Grayson) *wl in tch: prog to chse ldr 1f out: drvn and styd on to ld nr fin* **11/2**[2]

004- 2 *nk* **Katie Killane**[31] 6723 5-9-0 45 (v) MickyFenton 11 53
(M Wellings) *chsd ldr: rdn to ld over 1f out: collared nr fin* **7/1**[3]

003- 3 *3/4* **Peggys First**[9] 6962 5-9-0 41 PatCosgrave 9 50
(D E Cantillon) *dwlt: sn in tch on inner: rdn 2f out: styd on fnl f: nvr quite able to chal* **8/1**

000/ 4 *hd* **Pulse**[411] 6397 9-9-0 45 (p) PaulFitzsimons 10 50
(Miss J R Tooth) *chsd ldrs: rdn and effrt over 1f out: kpt on but nvr able to chal* **16/1**

040- 5 *nk* **Must Be Keen**[22] 6235 8-9-0 42 (v[1]) FergusSweeney 3 49+
(Ernst Oertel) *dwlt: rdn in last early and wl off the pce: styd on wl fr over 1f out: nrst fin* **25/1**

054- 6 *3/4* **He's A Rocket (IRE)**[10] 6943 6-9-0 42 (b) LeeEnstone 7 46
(K R Burke) *chsd ldrs: no ex fr over 1f out* **12/1**

7 *3/4* **Newpark Spirit (IRE)**[76] 6114 4-8-9 45 (p) JamieJones[(5)] 2 43
(Patrick Morris, Ire) *outpcd and racd v wd bnd over 3f out: styd on fr over 1f out: nrst fin* **14/1**

202- 8 *1* **El Potro**[8] 6969 5-9-0 45 JosedeSouza 4 40
(J R Holt) *racd wd and outpcd: kpt on fnl f: nvr on terms* **11/4**[1]

0- 9 *3/4* **Ask Jenny (IRE)**[17] 6890 5-9-0 42 TPQueally 1 37
(Patrick Morris, Ire) *racd v wd bnd over 3f out: a struggling after* **25/1**

526- 10 *3/4* **Sharp Hat**[8] 6969 13-9-0 44 TonyCulhane 5 34
(D W Chapman) *restless stalls: outpcd and struggling: nvr a factor* **7/1**[3]

605- 11 *1* **Prime Recreation**[19] 6851 10-9-0 42 PaulMulrennan 12 31
(P S Felgate) *blazed off in front: hdd & wknd over 1f out* **10/1**

/00- 12 *4* **Junebug Symphony (IRE)**[19] 6855 5-8-11 41 JerryO'Dwyer[(3)] 6 16
(V Smith) *outpcd and a struggling* **20/1**

60.66 secs (0.26) **Going Correction** -0.025s/f (Stan) 12 Ran SP% 119.9
Speed ratings (Par 97):96,95,94,94,93 92,91,89,88,87 85,79
CSF £43.19 TOTE £6.80: £1.90, £2.60, £2.30; EX 51.80.
Owner Thomas & Susan Blane **Bred** Bearstone Stud **Trained** Formby, Lancs

FOCUS
A moderate contest, known until the end of last year as a banded stakes although the form looks reasonably sound. The draw played its part as it usually does over this trip here, and a few of the low-drawn horses exacerbated the bias by running very wide around the bend.

47 DIGIBET.COM H'CAP 5f (P)
4:20 (4:21) (Class 5) (0-70,74) 4-Y-0+ £3,238 (£963; £481; £240) Stalls High

Form RPR

11-5 1 **Hollow Jo**[3] 28 7-9-8 **74** MickyFenton 3 81+
(J R Jenkins) *pushed along in midfield: clsd over 1f out: chal fnl f: styd on to ld last strides* **5/2**[1]

000- 2 *hd* **Lady Bahia (IRE)**[14] 6935 6-8-7 **62** (b) JerryO'Dwyer[(3)] 5 68
(Peter Grayson) *dwlt: sn in tch on outer: prog over 1f out: rdn to ld ins fnl f: hdd and nt qckn nr fin* **16/1**

030- 3 *3/4* **The Fisio**[17] 6877 7-8-4 **56** oh2 (v) ChrisCatlin 8 60
(S Gollings) *towards rr: rdn and plenty to do over 1f out: styd on wl fnl f: nrst fin* **16/1**

224- 4 *hd* **Muktasb (USA)**[6] 6994 6-8-4 **56** oh4 (v) JamieMackay 9 59+
(D Shaw) *rrd bdly s: last and pushed along: gd prog fnl f: fin wl* **5/1**[3]

013- 5 *3/4* **Stoneacre Boy (IRE)**[14] 6935 4-9-2 **68** (b) RobbieFitzpatrick 6 68
(Peter Grayson) *pressed ldr: led over 1f out: hanging and hdd ins fnl f: folded tamely* **6/1**

004- 6 *1 1/4* **Hornpipe**[14] 6935 5-8-11 **63** FrancisNorton 1 59
(M S Saunders) *chsd ldng pair tl wknd fnl f* **10/1**

240- 7 *1 3/4* **Fizzlephut (IRE)**[10] 6953 5-9-4 **70** PaulFitzsimons 7 60
(Miss J R Tooth) *led to over 1f out: sn btn* **10/1**

162- **8** 1/2 **Radiator Rooney (IRE)**[153] 4184 4-8-10 **62**...............(b) JamieSpencer 4 50
(Patrick Morris, Ire) *chsd ldrs: hanging bdly over 1f out: sn wknd: eased*
8/1

650- **9** 1/2 **Kempsey**[15] 6913 5-7-13 **58**.......................................(b) WilliamBuick(7) 10 44
(J J Bridger) *pushed along in rr: nvr on terms* **9/2**[2]

60.51 secs (0.11) **Going Correction** -0.025s/f (Stan) 9 Ran SP% **118.8**
Speed ratings (Par 103):98,97,96,96,94 92,90,89,88
CSF £47.62 CT £546.39 TOTE £3.10: £1.40, £5.40, £4.80; EX 65.90.
Owner Jim McCarthy **Bred** K J Reddington **Trained** Royston, Herts

FOCUS
An ordinary handicap, but a race of changing fortunes as several looked like winning at one stage or another. The draw did not prove so crucial in this race and the winning time was modest for the grade, just 0.15 seconds faster than the opening 0 to 45 event. as a result the form is not rated too positively, with the third and fourth setting the level.

48 SPORTS BETTING WITH DIGIBET.COM H'CAP 1m 2f (P)
4:50 (4:52) (Class 5) (0-70,69) 4-Y-0+ **£3,238** (£963; £481; £240) **Stalls** High

Form RPR

505- **1** **Wild Pitch**[17] 6885 6-9-4 **69**...(b) JamieSpencer 6 78+
(P Mitchell) *hld up wl in rr: stdy prog gng wl fr over 3f out: produced to ld ins fnl f: urged along and kpt on* **10/1**[3]

141- **2** 1/2 **Bank On Benny**[17] 6878 5-9-1 **66**................................. FrancisNorton 11 74
(P W D'Arcy) *sn in midfield: prog over 2f out: rdn to chal 1f out: chsd wnr ins fnl f: a hld* **11/8**[1]

145/ **3** 1 1/4 **Ile Facile (IRE)**[344] 4300 6-9-3 **68**.. ChrisCatlin 4 74
(B De Haan) *t.k.h: sn trckd ldr: led over 1f out: hdd and one pce ins fnl f* **33/1**

/00- **4** 1/2 **Hawk Arrow (IRE)**[19] 5952 5-8-10 **61** ow1..................... TonyCulhane 10 66
(G L Moore) *hld up in last pair: prog over 2f out: styd on wl fr over 1f out: nrst fin* **16/1**

434- **5** 3 **Luckylover**[17] 6878 4-8-13 **66**..(t) TPQueally 12 65
(M G Quinlan) *led to over 1f out: wknd qckly fnl f* **12/1**

510- **6** 1/2 **Siena Star (IRE)**[10] 6954 9-8-12 **63**................................. MickyFenton 8 61
(Stef Liddiard) *settled midfield: rdn over 2f out: nt qckn and btn over 1f out: kpt on nr fin* **8/1**[2]

50- **7** 1 **Soizic (NZ)**[35] 6684 5-9-0 **68**...................................... StephaneBreux(3) 5 64
(C G Cox) *pressed ldrs tl wknd over 1f out* **50/1**

250- **8** hd **High Seasons**[17] 6878 4-8-6 **64**............................(v[1]) JamesMillman(5) 14 60
(B R Millman) *prom: rdn 4f out: stl cl up over 1f out: wknd rapidly* **16/1**

233- **9** 2 **Jomus**[21] 6841 6-8-5 **56**..(b) JamieMackay 9 48
(L Montague Hall) *stdd s: hld up wl in rr and wd: brief effrt over 2f out: sn btn* **8/1**[2]

10 1 1/4 **Leonardo's Friend**[132] 4-9-0 **67**.................................. FergusSweeney 2 57
(B G Powell) *nvr beyond midfield: rdn and no prog over 2f out* **28/1**

041- **11** 4 **Magic Warrior**[21] 6841 7-9-2 **67**................................... PaulFitzsimons 13 49
(J C Fox) *hld up wl in rr: rdn and no prog over 2f out* **8/1**[2]

634- **12** 4 **Emily's Place (IRE)**[11] 6942 4-8-8 **61**..........................(v[1]) PatCosgrave 7 36
(J Pearce) *chsd ldrs: rdn over 3f out: wknd over 2f out* **12/1**

020- **13** 2 1/2 **Digger Boy**[44] 5388 4-8-10 **63**.................................. RobbieFitzpatrick 1 33
(J Gallagher) *racd wd towards rr: bhd fnl 2f* **33/1**

0/ **14** 2 **Alisar (IRE)**[363] 7-8-9 **67**...(t) SCreighton(7) 3 33
(E J Creighton) *chsd ldrs tl wknd 4f out: sn bhd* **50/1**

2m 7.78s (-1.22) **Going Correction** -0.025s/f (Stan)
WFA 4 from 5yo+ 2lb 14 Ran SP% **124.9**
Speed ratings (Par 103):103,102,101,101,98 98,97,97,95,94 91,88,86,84
CSF £24.06 CT £479.33 TOTE £12.40: £3.40, £1.20, £11.50; EX 30.90.
Owner Mrs Julie Auletta **Bred** Wyck Hall Stud Ltd **Trained** Epsom, Surrey

FOCUS
A competitive little handicap in which the early pace did not look that strong, but they quickened in the home straight and the winning time was spot on par for a race like this. The front four pulled clear, so the form looks solid and reliable.
Magic Warrior Official explanation: vet said gelding bled from the nose
Emily's Place(IRE) Official explanation: jockey said filly ran too freely early stages

49 DIGIBET FRANCHISING MEDIAN AUCTION MAIDEN STKS 7f (P)
5:20 (5:23) (Class 6) 4-6-Y-0 **£2,047** (£604; £302) **Stalls** High

Form RPR

432- **1** **Ektimaal**[80] 6060 4-9-3 66...(t) JamieSpencer 7 79+
(E A L Dunlop) *cl up: trckd ldr wl over 2f out: nudged along and clsd to ld ent fnl f: in command nr fin* **13/8**[2]

022- **2** 1 **Lopinot (IRE)**[21] 6841 4-9-3 70.. SebSanders 8 76
(P J Makin) *led: rdn over 1f out: hdd ent fnl f: readily hld nr fin* **5/6**[1]

360- **3** 5 **Golden Alchemist**[33] 6698 4-9-3 64.................................... IanMongan 3 63
(M D I Usher) *chsd ldr to wl over 2f out: hrd rdn and nt qckn: wl btn over 1f out* **7/1**[3]

4 12 **Rusty Roof** 4-8-12 .... ChrisCatlin 4 27
(Rae Guest) *s.s: wl off the pce in last: plugged on to take remote 4th nr fin* **50/1**

0- **5** 1 **Big Ralph**[16] 6901 4-9-3 .... FergusSweeney 6 29
(M Wigham) *a wl off the pce: wnt remote 4th over 1f out tl nr fin* **33/1**

604/ **6** 7 **Smart Pick**[532] 3737 4-8-5 57...................................... ChrisGlenister(7) 2 6
(J R Holt) *w ldrs to 3f out: bmpd along and wknd rapidly* **50/1**

7 17 **Grace Bay** 4-8-12 .... FrancisNorton 1 —
(Bob Jones) *hanging bdly lft thrght: bhd fr 1/2-way: t.o* **50/1**

1m 25.98s (-0.82) **Going Correction** -0.025s/f (Stan) 7 Ran SP% **117.8**
Speed ratings: 103,101,96,82,81 73,53
CSF £3.28 TOTE £2.80: £1.20, £1.20; EX 3.50.
Owner The Serendipity Partnership **Bred** Whitsbury Manor Stud **Trained** Newmarket, Suffolk

FOCUS
A moderate race considering the age group and a race lacking strength in depth, predictably dominated by the front pair in the market with the runner-up to recent course form. The winning time was reasonable though, and the front two may be able to hold their own in handicap company.

50 DIGITOTE SOFTWARE H'CAP 6f (P)
5:50 (5:51) (Class 6) (0-58,66) 4-Y-0+ **£2,047** (£604; £302) **Stalls** High

Form RPR

520- **1** **Beneking**[18] 6869 7-8-12 **56**..(p) ChrisCatlin 3 66
(D Burchell) *mde virtually all and set stdy pce to 1/2-way: hrd pressed fnl 2f: hld on wl nr fin* **16/1**

065- **2** nk **Caustic Wit (IRE)**[7] 6990 9-8-9 **58**................................... TolleyDean(5) 8 67
(M S Saunders) *trckd ldrs: prog over 1f out: str chal ins fnl f: jst hld nr fin* **10/1**

012- **3** 3/4 **Vegas Boys**[7] 6990 4-9-1 **66**... WilliamBuick(7) 6 73+
(M Wigham) *hld up in rr: plld out and effrt 2f out: rdr dropped whip sn after: gd prog to press ldrs ins fnl f: no ex* **2/1**[1]

112- **4** 1/2 **Cree**[15] 6922 5-8-12 **59**.. JamesDoyle(3) 12 64
(W R Muir) *plld hrd early: hld up in cl tch: effrt on ins over 1f out: upsides ins fnl f: wknd nr fin* **7/2**[2]

536- **5** 1 1/4 **Mulberry Lad (IRE)**[7] 6983 5-8-12 **56**.................................. PaulDoe 11 57
(P W Hiatt) *hld up towards rr: prog on inner and nt clr run briefly over 1f out: rdn and one pce fnl f* **14/1**

444- **6** nk **Desert Light (IRE)**[15] 6922 6-8-11 **55**..........................(v) JamieMackay 7 55
(D Shaw) *blanket stl on as stalls opened: hld up in last trio: prog over 1f out: r.o fnl f: n.d* **16/1**

563- **7** hd **Cayman Breeze**[17] 6884 7-8-4 **55**................................ BarrySavage(7) 4 55
(J M Bradley) *hld up in midfield: effrt 2f out: kpt on same pce fnl f* **22/1**

623- **8** shd **Carcinetto (IRE)**[7] 6990 5-8-13 **57**.................................... NCallan 1 56
(P D Evans) *pressed wnr to over 1f out: wknd* **8/1**

165- **9** 2 **Jabbara (IRE)**[6] 6994 4-8-11 **55**...(b) JoeFanning 5 48
(C E Brittain) *trckd ldrs: gng easily over 2f out: hanging lft and fnd nil over 1f out: wel btn whn rein broke ins fnl f* **13/2**[3]

000- **10** 4 **Mill By The Stream**[126] 5031 5-8-12 **56**........................ JamieSpencer 2 37+
(Tom Dascombe) *hld up wl in rr: effrt on outer 2f out: sn no prog: wknd* **25/1**

540- **11** 1 1/4 **Boanerges (IRE)**[181] 3330 10-8-13 **57**........................... MickyFenton 10 35
(J M Bradley) *ldng trio tl wknd rapidly over 1f out* **50/1**

220- **12** 3/4 **She's Dunnett**[49] 6510 4-8-11 **55**................................... HayleyTurner 9 30
(Mrs C A Dunnett) *chsd ldrs to 1/2-way: sn lost pl and btn* **66/1**

1m 13.42s (-0.28) **Going Correction** -0.025s/f (Stan) 12 Ran SP% **119.2**
Speed ratings (Par 101):100,99,98,97,96 95,95,95,92,87 85,84
CSF £162.39 CT £473.54 TOTE £19.50: £5.60, £2.50, £1.60; EX 223.80.
Owner B M G Group **Bred** Helshaw Grange Stud And Mrs M Mason **Trained** Briery Hill, Blaenau Gwent

FOCUS
A competitive if low-grade handicap, but rather surprisingly for a race like this the early pace was moderate, which suited those that raced handily and inconvenienced a few others. The form is rated around those in the frame behind the winner.
Jabbara(IRE) Official explanation: jockey said reins came apart

51 DIGIBET.COM CLASSIFIED STKS 1m (P)
6:20 (6:24) (Class 7) 4-Y-0+ **£1,365** (£403; £201) **Stalls** High

Form RPR

6/0- **1** **Over To You Bert**[45] 6370 8-8-7 42.............................. HaddenFrost(7) 11 49
(R J Hodges) *plld hrd: hld up bhd ldrs: effrt on inner 2f out: rdn to chal last 150yds: rdr dropped whip 75yds out: jst failed: fin 2nd, shd: awrdd r* **33/1**

43-1 **2** shd **Earl Kraul (IRE)**[3] 18 4-9-6 45.................................(b) JamieSpencer 5 55
(G L Moore) *t.k.h: hld up in midfield: prog 2f out: led 1f out: idled and hanging: jst hld on: fin 1st, shd: plcd 2nd* **11/8**[1]

650- **3** nk **Hill Of Almhuim (IRE)**[19] 6856 4-9-0 45...............(v) RobbieFitzpatrick 4 48
(Peter Grayson) *hld up wl in rr: prog over 2f out: hanging rt after and cajoled along: styd on fnl f: nrst fin* **10/1**

35-3 **4** 1/2 **Piquet**[3] 20 9-8-11 44..(p) AmirQuinn(3) 3 47
(J J Bridger) *hld up wl in rr: stdy prog on outer fr over 2f out: looked dangerous 1f out: rdn and nt qckn* **6/1**[3]

06-0 **5** nk **Height Of Spirits**[3] 22 5-9-0 44..................................... TPQueally 6 48+
(T D McCarthy) *s.i.s: hld up last: sltly hmpd 3f out: nt clr run 2f out and over 1f out: styd on but nt rcvr* **12/1**

646- **6** 1 3/4 **Marron Flore**[9] 6958 4-8-11 43.................................(tp) JamesDoyle(3) 2 42
(A J Lidderdale) *racd wd: wl in tch: prog 3f out: led over 2f out to 1f out: bmpd sn after: wknd* **33/1**

600- **7** hd **Ligne D'Eau**[23] 6819 6-9-0 42...(v) NCallan 7 42
(P D Evans) *trckd ldrs: effrt and rdn 2f out: wkng whn n.m.r ins fnl f* **25/1**

00-0 **8** 1 **Gem Bien (USA)**[5] 7 9-9-0 43..................................(v[1]) TonyCulhane 8 40
(D W Chapman) *prom: led 3f out to over 2f out: wknd u.p over 1f out* **20/1**

04-0 **9** 3 **Didnt Tell My Wife**[3] 20 8-9-0 43...........................(v) HayleyTurner 10 33
(P S McEntee) *t.k.h: hld up wl in rr: shkn up and no prog 2f out* **33/1**

000- **10** 3 **Berties Brother**[165] 3821 4-9-1 44 ow1....................... AntonyProcter 12 27
(D G Bridgwater) *led to over 4f out: nt handle bnd and lost pl rapidly over 3f out: no ch after* **66/1**

05-0 **11** 1/2 **Rowan Pursuit**[3] 20 6-9-0 45.......................................(p) PaulEddery 14 25
(C A Horgan) *hld up: a wl in rr* **33/1**

406- **12** 2 **College Queen**[19] 6851 9-8-7 41................................ WilliamBuick(7) 9 20
(S Gollings) *pressed ldr: led over 4f out to 3f out: wknd rapidly over 1f out* **33/1**

024- **U** **Savoy Chapel**[61] 6370 5-9-0 45.................................... FrancisNorton 13 —
(A W Carroll) *hld up in midfield: hmpd and uns rdr 3f out* **9/2**[2]

1m 40.66s (-0.14) **Going Correction** -0.025s/f (Stan) 13 Ran SP% **125.3**
Speed ratings (Par 97):98,99,98,98,97 96,95,94,91,88 88,86,—
CSF £69.32 TOTE £44.90: £8.20, £1.30, £2.40; EX 235.90 Place 6 £32.40, Place 5 £9.38.
Owner R J Hodges **Bred** J K S Cresswell **Trained** Charlton Mackrell, Somerset
■ Stewards' Enquiry : Hadden Frost one-day ban: used whip with excessive frequency (Jan 17)
Jamie Spencer two-day ban: careless riding (Jan 17-18); three-day ban: used whip with excessive force (Jan 19-21)

FOCUS
Another contest that would until recently have been known as a banded contest, and a very rough race too with a faller halfway though and plenty of interference in the latter stages which saw the winner thrown out.
T/Plt: £79.40 to a £1 stake. Pool: £64,511.10. 592.70 winning tickets. T/Qpdt: £5.50 to a £1 stake. Pool: £5,956.70. 799.60 winning tickets. JN

24 LINGFIELD (L-H)
Saturday, January 6

OFFICIAL GOING: Standard
Wind: fresh, behind Weather: raining

52 GO PONTIN'S (S) STKS 1m 2f (P)
12:25 (12:25) (Class 6) 4-Y-0+ **£2,184** (£644; £322) **Stalls** Low

Form RPR

000- **1** **King Of Music (USA)**[254] 1265 6-9-2 54..................... AdrianMcCarthy 8 71+
(G Prodromou) *hld up in tch: wnt 2nd gng wl over 3f out: led wl over 2f out: sn pushed clr: eased nr fin* **16/1**

00-6 **2** 10 **Voice Mail**[3] 19 8-9-2 55..(b) ShaneKelly 4 49
(P Howling) *hld up in midfield: hdwy over 3f out: rdn to chse ldng pair wl over 2f out: wnt 2nd nr fin: no ch w wnr* **6/1**[3]

10-1 **3** 1/2 **Shrine Mountain (USA)**[3] 26 5-9-7 60.............................(b) NCallan 7 53
(R A Harris) *t.k.h: led and sn clr: hdd wl over 2f out: sn rdn: no ch w wnr after: lost 2nd nr fin* **1/1**[1]

606- **4** 1 1/4 **Scuzme (IRE)**[17] 6889 4-9-0 52 .... EdwardCreighton 2 46
(Miss Sheena West) *slowly away: hld up in rr: rdn and sme hdwy 3f out: sn no imp on ldrs: plugged on* **20/1**

/50- **5** 2 1/2 **Gold Guest**[16] 5354 8-9-2 56 ....(bt[1]) JamieSpencer 6 41
(P D Evans) *slowly away: hld up in last pair: plld out and rdn wl over 2f out: nvr nr ldrs* **8/1**

0/0- **6** 13 **Eidsfoss (IRE)**[15] 6916 5-9-2 32 .... BrianReilly 3 16
(T T Clement) *chsd ldng pair: rdn over 4f out: wknd wl over 2f out: t.o* **66/1**

010- **7** shd **Cetshwayo**[29] 5683 5-9-2 58 .... MickyFenton 1 16
(J M P Eustace) *t.k.h: chsd ldr: rdn over 4f out: wknd wl over 2f out: sn wl bhd: t.o* **7/2**[2]

000- **8** 4 **Eclipse Park**[32] 6289 4-9-0 60 ....(b) RichardHughes 5 8
(M J McGrath) *slowly away: hld up in rr: lost tch 3f out: eased last 2f: t.o* **14/1**

2m 5.08s (-2.71) **Going Correction** -0.025s/f (Stan)
WFA 4 from 5yo+ 2lb **8** Ran SP% **116.4**
Speed ratings (Par 101):109,101,100,99,97 87,87,83
CSF £109.72 TOTE £32.80: £5.10, £1.60, £1.10; EX 162.60 Trifecta £85.00 Part won. Pool £119.82 - 0.90 winning units..The winner was bought by R A Harris for 8,800gns. Voice Mail was claimed by A Balding for £6,000.
Owner Mrs B Macalister **Bred** Brant Laue **Trained** East Harling, Norfolk

FOCUS
A modest seller and one in which the pace was only fair, but the winning time was very decent for a race like this, 8.19 seconds faster than the following maiden and the form could prove better than rated.

53 PONTINS.COM MAIDEN STKS 1m 2f (P)
12:55 (12:56) (Class 5) 3-Y-O **£2,914** (£867; £433; £216) **Stalls** Low

Form RPR

2- **1** **Salford Mill (IRE)**[18] 6867 3-9-0 .... MarcHalford(3) 10 68+
(D R C Elsworth) *s.i.s: t.k.h: hld up in tch: chsd ldng pair over 2f out: rdn to ld jst ins fnl f: pushed out: readily* **2/7**[1]

44- **2** 2 **Jocheski (IRE)**[36] 6658 3-9-3 .... JamieSpencer 11 64+
(M J Wallace) *trckd ldrs: wnt 2nd 6f out: rdn to ld and qcknd 3f out: edgd rt fr over 1f out: hdd jst ins fnl f: no ex* **5/1**[2]

3 3 **Six Day War (IRE)** 3-9-3 .... ShaneKelly 7 59+
(J A Osborne) *keen early: sn settled in tch: rdn and outpcd 3f out: kpt on fnl f: nt rch ldrs* **11/1**[3]

4 1 **Stand In Black (NZ)** 3-9-0 .... StephaneBreux(3) 8 57?
(B I Case) *led at slow pce: hdd and rdn 3f out: wknd ins fnl f* **66/1**

60- **5** 2 **Shea's Round**[18] 6867 3-8-10 .... JemmaMarshall(7) 6 53
(G L Moore) *chsd ldr tl 6f out: rdn 3f out: sn outpcd: plugged on* **33/1**

6 1/2 **Bluecrop Boy** 3-9-3 .... AntonyProcter 4 52?
(D J S Ffrench Davis) *hld up in tch: rdn and outpcd 3f out: kpt on same pce last 2f* **50/1**

0- **7** 1 **Northern Dune (IRE)**[15] 6912 3-9-3 .... TPQueally 5 50
(B J Curley) *s.i.s: hld up in tch in rr: outpcd 3f out: kpt on same pce* **25/1**

8 28 **Binham Boy** 3-9-3 ....(p) ChrisCatlin 3 —
(M J Gingell) *stdd s: a last: reminder and flashed tail wl over 4f out: lost tch 3f out: t.o* **66/1**

2m 13.27s (5.48) **Going Correction** -0.025s/f (Stan) **8** Ran SP% **114.5**
Speed ratings (Par 97):77,75,73,72,70 70,69,47
CSF £1.95 TOTE £1.40: £1.02, £1.40, £1.70; EX 2.30 Trifecta £5.60 Pool £94.74 - 11.85 winning units..
Owner A J Thompson **Bred** Mrs H D McCalmont **Trained** Newmarket, Suffolk

FOCUS
A race lacking strength in depth and a muddling gallop means this bare form is not entirely reliable. The winning time was pedestrian, 8.19 seconds slower than the opening seller, and a negative view has been taken of the form overall. However, the winner remains a colt of considerable potential.

54 PONTIN'S HOLIDAYS H'CAP 5f (P)
1:30 (1:30) (Class 5) (0-70,66) 3-Y-O **£2,914** (£867; £433; £216) **Stalls** High

Form RPR

350- **1** **La Quinta (IRE)**[29] 6750 3-9-2 **64** .... RichardHughes 3 68
(B J Meehan) *hld up in last pair on inner: hdwy wl over 1f out: rdn to ld jst over 1f out: edgd rt ins last: fnd ex nr fin* **5/2**[1]

512- **2** 1/2 **New York Oscar (IRE)**[10] 6945 3-8-13 **66** .... AndrewElliott(5) 5 68+
(A M Hales) *stdd s: t.k.h: hld up in last pair: c wd over 1f out: str run fnl f: wnt 2nd last 100 yds: hld nr fin* **9/2**[2]

530- **3** 2 **Tang**[32] 6715 3-8-9 **60** .... AmirQuinn(3) 1 55
(W G M Turner) *chsd ldrs: rdn 2f out: ev ch over 1f out: kpt on same pce ins fnl f* **6/1**[3]

614- **4** shd **Bungie**[16] 6895 3-9-3 **65** .... NCallan 4 59
(Ms Deborah J Evans) *chsd ldrs: rdn and hdwy over 2f out: kpt on same pce fnl f* **5/2**[1]

030- **5** hd **Baytown Paikea**[21] 6839 3-7-13 **54** .... DonnaCaldwell(7) 7 48
(P S McEntee) *led: rdn over 2f out: hdd jst over 1f out: no ex ins fnl f* **14/1**

226- **6** 4 **Candyland (IRE)**[128] 4950 3-9-0 **62** .... FrancisNorton 2 41
(M Quinn) *chsd ldrs: rdn 2f out: wknd over 1f out* **6/1**[3]

59.38 secs (-0.40) **Going Correction** -0.025s/f (Stan) **6** Ran SP% **110.6**
Speed ratings (Par 97):102,101,98,97,97 91
CSF £13.55 TOTE £3.00: £1.50, £2.60; EX 12.40.
Owner Andrew Rosen **Bred** Barouche Stud Ireland Ltd **Trained** Manton, Wilts

FOCUS
Just a modest handicap and one in which the pace and the winning time were fair. The form looks sound if not that strong.

55 PONTINSBINGO.COM MAIDEN STKS 6f (P)
2:00 (2:01) (Class 5) 3-Y-O **£2,914** (£867; £433; £216) **Stalls** Low

Form RPR

5- **1** **Bronte's Hope**[192] 2980 3-8-12 .... RichardHughes 7 71+
(M P Tregoning) *pressed ldr: shkn up to ld over 1f out: sn clr: easily* **4/6**[1]

06- **2** 3 1/2 **Comrade Cotton**[15] 6921 3-9-3 .... FrancisNorton 4 54+
(N A Callaghan) *chsd ldrs: rdn 2f out: kpt on to chse wnr ins fnl f: no ch w wnr* **16/1**

6- **3** 1 **Best Option**[14] 6927 3-8-12 .... NCallan 6 46
(W R Muir) *chsd ldrs: rdn over 2f out: kpt on same pce u.p* **25/1**

0- **4** nk **Leg Sweep**[17] 6887 3-9-3 .... AntonyProcter 5 50+
(D R C Elsworth) *stdd s: t.k.h: hld up in tch: sltly outpcd 2f out: plld out over 1f out: r.o fnl f: nvr trbld ldrs* **11/2**[2]

60- **5** 2 **Wiseton Dancer (IRE)**[6] 6998 3-9-3 .... EdwardCreighton 3 44
(Miss V Haigh) *led: rdn 2f out: hdd over 1f out: wknd fnl f* **50/1**

6 hd **Brave Jack (IRE)** 3-9-3 .... HayleyTurner 1 44
(J R Best) *s.i.s: bhd: rdn over 3f out: kpt on same pce last 2f* **7/1**[3]

7 3 1/2 **Varya** 3-8-12 .... SebSanders 8 28
(Sir Mark Prescott) *rn green in midfield: rdn and outpcd wl over 2f out: no ch after* **8/1**

0- **8** 2 **Pink Salmon**[62] 6349 3-8-12 .... IanMongan 2 22
(Mrs L J Mongan) *s.i.s: rn green and a last: lost tch wl over 2f out* **33/1**

1m 13.94s (1.13) **Going Correction** -0.025s/f (Stan) **8** Ran SP% **113.6**
Speed ratings (Par 97):91,86,85,84,81 81,77,74
CSF £13.27 TOTE £1.50: £1.10, £1.50, £4.40; EX 11.90 Trifecta £57.20 Pool £287.80 - 3.57 winning units.
Owner The Cheamsters **Bred** East Burrow Farm **Trained** Lambourn, Berks

FOCUS
Not a strong maiden, run at only a fair pace in a modest winning time for the type of contest, but an improved effort from the winner, who may be the type to improve further, with the runner-up the guide to the level.

56 PONTIN'S FAMILY HOLIDAYS H'CAP 1m (P)
2:35 (2:35) (Class 4) (0-85,84) 4-Y-O+ **£4,857** (£1,445; £722; £360) **Stalls** High

Form RPR

053- **1** **Fajr (IRE)**[100] 5639 5-9-0 **82** .... RichardHughes 1 93+
(Miss Gay Kelleway) *hld up towards rr: hdwy over 2f out: plld out and rdn over 1f out: str run to ld last 75 yds* **7/4**[1]

230- **2** 3/4 **Katiypour (IRE)**[105] 5523 10-9-0 **82** .... JoeFanning 4 91
(P Mitchell) *trckd wnt 2nd 3f out: rdn and chal over 1f out: led last 100 yds: sn hdd and no ex* **20/1**

01- **3** 1 **Barney McGrew (IRE)**[28] 6771 4-8-1 **72** .... MarcHalford(3) 10 79
(J A R Toller) *plld hrd: chsd ldr tl led 5f out: rdn over 2f out: hdd last 100 yds: no ex* **6/1**[3]

200- **4** 2 1/2 **Grey Boy (GER)**[18] 6868 6-8-11 **79** .... JamieSpencer 7 80
(R A Fahey) *hld up in tch: hdwy over 2f out: rdn and chsd ldrs 2f out: wknd 1f out* **11/4**[2]

250- **5** 3/4 **Cape Greko**[22] 6830 5-8-9 **84** .... WilliamBuick(7) 5 83
(A M Balding) *hld up in tch: lost pl and bhd 3f out: styd on u.p over 1f out: nt trble ldrs* **12/1**

065- **6** 3/4 **Waterline Twenty (IRE)**[18] 6868 4-8-13 **81** .... NCallan 6 79
(P D Evans) *hld up: effrt on inner and rdn over 2f out: no imp over 1f out* **9/1**

430- **7** 1/2 **Smokin Joe**[17] 6878 6-8-2 **70** oh1 ....(b) HayleyTurner 9 66
(J R Best) *hld up towards rr on outer: rdn over 2f out: nvr nr ldrs* **10/1**

000- **8** 1 3/4 **Yellow Ridge (IRE)**[7] 6986 4-8-2 **70** ....(b[1]) CatherineGannon 8 62
(Luke Comer, Ire) *t.k.h: led tl 5f out: chsd ldr tl 3f out: sn rdn: wknd 2f out* **66/1**

524- **9** 1 1/2 **Red Birr (IRE)**[11] 6633 6-8-7 **75** .... ChrisCatlin 2 64
(P R Webber) *s.i.s: hdwy to chse ldrs over 5f out: rdn wl over 3f out: sn lost pl and bhd* **10/1**

1m 37.45s (-1.98) **Going Correction** -0.025s/f (Stan) **9** Ran SP% **119.4**
Speed ratings (Par 105):108,107,106,103,103 102,101,100,98
CSF £42.66 CT £185.38 TOTE £2.60: £1.40, £3.80, £2.20; EX 23.40 Trifecta £69.10 Pool £461.61 - 4.74 winning units.
Owner The New Dawn Partnership **Bred** Shadwell Estate Company Limited **Trained** Exning, Suffolk

FOCUS
A reasonable handicap in which the pace was just fair. The winner is progressive, the second is on a fair mark, and the third is unexposed, so a positive view has been taken of the form.
Barney McGrew(IRE) Official explanation: jockey said gelding ran too free

57 PONTIN'S "BOOK EARLY" H'CAP 1m 4f (P)
3:05 (3:05) (Class 2) (0-100,107) 4-Y-O+ **£11,658** (£3,468; £1,733; £865) **Stalls** Low

Form RPR

110- **1** **Sri Diamond**[259] 1128 7-9-11 **105** .... JamieSpencer 6 114
(S Kirk) *hld up in last pair: hdwy over 2f out: chsd ldr wl over 1f out: led ins fnl f: rdn and styd on u.p* **13/8**[1]

162- **2** 1/2 **Millville**[22] 6836 7-9-13 **107** .... NCallan 5 115
(M A Jarvis) *hld up in tch: hdwy over 3f out: rdn to ld jst over 2f out: hrd pressed wl over 1f out: hdd and unable qckn ins last* **13/8**[1]

320- **3** 2 **Crow Wood**[28] 5678 8-8-7 **87** .... JoeFanning 4 92
(J J Quinn) *led tl rdn and hdd jst over 2f out: kpt on but nt pce of 1st 2 fr over 1f out* **4/1**[2]

342- **4** hd **Fusili (IRE)**[29] 6744 4-8-4 **91** .... JamesDoyle(3) 3 96
(N P Littmoden) *chsd ldr tl rdn over 2f out:kpt on but nt pce of 1st 2 over 1f out* **6/1**[3]

606- **5** 9 **Savannah**[15] 6914 4-8-9 **93** ....(b) CatherineGannon 1 83
(Luke Comer, Ire) *chsd ldng pair tl rdn 3f out: wknd over 2f out: sn bhd* **50/1**

113/ **6** 8 **Mission To Mars**[7] 971 8-8-8 **88** .... ChrisCatlin 2 65
(P G Murphy) *stdd s: t.k.h: hld up in last pair: rdn and outpcd over 2f out: sn wl bhd* **33/1**

2m 31.51s (-2.88) **Going Correction** -0.025s/f (Stan)
WFA 4 from 7yo+ 4lb **6** Ran SP% **115.4**
Speed ratings (Par 109):108,107,106,106,100 94
CSF £4.57 TOTE £2.50: £2.10, £1.10; EX 4.30.
Owner Ascot Brew Racing **Bred** B J And Mrs Crangle **Trained** Upper Lambourn, Berks

FOCUS
Only six runners and just a fair pace but a useful event featuring two of the best middle-distance All-Weather performers around and the form looks sound.

NOTEBOOK
Sri Diamond, absent since April, has a history of going well fresh and showed he retains all his ability. Equally effective over a mile and a quarter, he reportedly heads for the Dubai Racing Carnival and he also has the option of bidding for a second successive win in the Winter Derby here in March. (op 7-4 tchd 6-4, 2-1 and 15-8 in a place)
Millville, one of the best around over middle distances on sand, ran as well as he ever has in defeat to an equally smart rival. His rating means his options will be limited but he may struggle to confirm placings with the winner if dropped in distance for a Winter Derby campaign. (op 2-1 tchd 9-4 in a place)
Crow Wood, a smart hurdler, looked on a fair mark for this return to the Flat and had the run of the race but had his limitations exposed against two of the best middle distance Polytrack performers around. He will be of interest in lesser company. (op 3-1)
Fusili(IRE), back up in distance, had the run of the race and ran creditably. She is another good guide to the level of this form and is fairly versatile but has very little margin for error from her current mark. (op 7-1)
Savannah, a maiden winner for Aidan O'Brien, was again soundly beaten on this second start for current connections and will have to drop considerably in the weights before he is of any interest. (op 66-1)
Mission To Mars, a marked improver on Polytrack in 2003 and 2004, missed the whole of last year and, after showing nothing in two starts over hurdles for new connections, shaped with no immediate promise on this return to the Flat.

58 **GO PONTIN'S H'CAP** **1m 2f (P)**
3:40 (3:40) (Class 5) (0-75,74) 3-Y-O **£2,914** (£867; £433; £216) **Stalls** Low

Form RPR
014- **1** **Pret A Porter (UAE)**[14] 6933 3-8-10 **67** ow1 (b) NCallan 1 69
(P D Evans) *chsd ldr for 3f out: chsd ldrs: rdn and effrt on inner 2f out : kpt on u.p to ld wl ins fnl f* **3/1**[2]
222- **2** *nk* **Miss Saafend Plaza (IRE)**[21] 6840 3-9-2 **74** (b) RichardHughes 2 74
(R Hannon) *trckd ldr after 3f: jnd ldr gng wl over 3f out: rdn to ld over 1f out: nt run on and hdd wl ins fnl f* **5/4**[1]
215- **3** *shd* **Beau Sancy**[23] 6824 3-8-3 **61** AdrianMcCarthy 3 61
(R A Harris) *s.i.s: hld up wl in tch in last: rdn wl over 2f out: sltly outpcd 2f out: rallied fnl f: nt quite rch ldrs* **3/1**[2]
043- **4** *3 1/2* **Tension Point**[103] 5565 3-8-12 **70** ShaneKelly 5 65+
(J A Osborne) *sn led: jnd over 3f out: rdn over 2f out: hdd jst over 1f out: eased whn btn ins fnl f* **7/2**[3]

2m 8.44s (0.65) **Going Correction** -0.025s/f (Stan) 4 Ran SP% **116.7**
Speed ratings (Par 97):96,95,95,92
CSF £7.82 TOTE £5.00; EX 7.50 Place 6 £ 4.79, Place 5 £3.30.
Owner John P Jones **Bred** Darley **Trained** Pandy, Monmouths

FOCUS
A modest event in which the gallop was on the steady side. This bare form is limited and may not prove totally reliable, despite the placed horses running close to their marks.
T/Plt: £5.80 to a £1 stake. Pool: £54,444.65. 6,833.85 winning tickets. T/Qpdt: £5.90 to a £1 stake. Pool: £2,878.20. 357.40 winning tickets. SP

8 SOUTHWELL (L-H)
Sunday, January 7

OFFICIAL GOING: Standard
Wind: Fresh, half-against. Weather: Windy and damp, rain at times.

59 **GO PONTIN'S CLAIMING STKS** **6f (F)**
12:50 (12:50) (Class 6) 4-Y-O+ **£2,184** (£644; £322) **Stalls** Low

Form RPR
/0-4 **1** **Branston Tiger**[6] 3 8-9-7 62 (v) DanielTudhope 4 71
(Ian Emmerson) *hld up: effrt on outer over 2f out: styd on to ld last 50yds* **5/1**[3]
55-4 **2** *1* **Soba Jones**[5] 9 10-8-10 58 JasonEdmunds(3) 5 60
(J Balding) *trckd ldrs: no ex wl ins last* **5/2**[2]
142- **3** *shd* **Trinculo (IRE)**[36] 6681 10-9-7 76 AdrianTNicholls 7 68
(D Nicholls) *trckd ldrs on outer: led 3f out: hdd and no ex wl ins last* **15/8**[1]
460- **4** *shd* **Further Outlook (USA)**[10] 6961 13-8-0 48 (tp) WilliamBuick(7) 3 53
(Miss Gay Kelleway) *led tl 3f out: stl upsides whn rdr dropped whip jst ins last: kpt on wl* **7/1**
04-0 **5** *8* **Diktalex (IRE)**[6] 3 4-8-12 61 (t) RobbieFitzpatrick 2 34
(C J Teague) *s.i.s: sn wl in tch: hung lft and lost pl over 1f out* **40/1**
500- **6** *1 1/4* **Sion Hill (IRE)**[10] 6962 6-8-3 43 ow1 RussellKennemore(5) 6 27
(Mrs N Macauley) *chsd ldrs: brought wd over 2f out: sn lost pl* **22/1**
041- **7** *3/4* **Ace Club**[9] 6974 6-8-7 48 (b) DaleGibson 1 23
(M J Attwater) *chsd ldrs: outpcd over 3f out: sn lost pl* **15/2**

1m 16.98s (0.08) **Going Correction** -0.10s/f (Stan) 7 Ran SP% **111.1**
Speed ratings (Par 101):95,93,93,93,82 81,80
CSF £16.85 TOTE £5.80: £2.30, £1.60; EX 18.30.Further Outlook was claimed by Declan Carroll for £5,000. Trinculo was claimed by R. A. Harris for £12,000.
Owner Ian Emmerson **Bred** Branston Stud Ltd **Trained** Holmside, Co Durham

FOCUS
A modest winning time for the grade. The first four finished in a heap with Trinculo not as effective over six here as over five on turf.

60 **PONTINSBINGO.COM MAIDEN STKS** **6f (F)**
1:20 (1:21) (Class 5) 3-Y-O+ **£2,968** (£876; £438) **Stalls** Low

Form RPR
1 **Rosa De Mi Corazon (USA)** 3-8-6 JamieMackay 12 61+
(Sir Mark Prescott) *dwlt: sn chsng ldrs: styd on wl to ld fnl 100yds* **4/1**[3]
022- **2** *1 1/4* **Le Masque**[12] 6940 3-8-8 67 MarkLawson(3) 14 54
(B Smart) *t.k.h: trckd ldrs: lod over 4f out: rdn and hung lft over 1f out: hdd and no ex ins last* **15/8**[1]
056- **3** *3* **Dancing Beauty (IRE)**[18] 6877 5-9-8 38 HayleyTurner 5 44
(T T Clement) *trckd ldrs: kpt on same pce fnl 2f* **28/1**
4 *3 1/2* **Cap St Jean (IRE)** 3-8-11 LeeEnstone 8 35
(P C Haslam) *bhd: hdwy 2f out: styd on ins last* **20/1**
606- **5** *1/2* **Flushed**[22] 6839 3-8-6 40 (be[1]) NataliaGemelova(5) 10 33
(A J McCabe) *chsd ldrs: rdn and hung lft over 1f out: one pce* **33/1**
6 *3* **Dramatic** 3-8-11 PaulHanagan 7 24
(Sir Mark Prescott) *in rr: sme hdwy 2f out: nvr nr ldrs* **11/4**[2]
6- **7** *2* **Haydock Express (IRE)**[12] 6940 3-8-11 RobbieFitzpatrick 1 18
(Peter Grayson) *in tch: effrt over 2f out: no imp* **9/1**
04- **8** *1 1/4* **Strathaird (IRE)**[32] 6730 3-8-11 AdrianTNicholls 4 14
(P C Haslam) *bhd: kpt on fnl 2f: nvr nr ldrs* **14/1**
0- **9** *2 1/2* **Pindar (GER)**[9] 6976 3-8-11 TPQueally 9 7
(B J Curley) *hld up in mid-div: sme hdwy on outer over 2f out: nvr a factor* **28/1**
000/ **10** *1 1/2* **Ivy Bridge (IRE)**[459] 5695 4-9-3 45 KevinGhunowa(5) 13 —
(P A Blockley) *led tl over 4f out: edgd rt and lost pl over 2f out* **50/1**
000- **11** *10* **Charlies Girl (IRE)**[199] 2791 3-8-6 45 DaleGibson 11 —
(M J Attwater) *in tch: lost pl over 3f out: sn bhd* **40/1**
00- **12** *5* **Keep A Welcome**[60] 6403 4-9-13 DeanMernagh 6 —
(S Parr) *s.s: a in rr: bhd whn virtually p.u ins last* **100/1**

1m 17.52s (0.62) **Going Correction** -0.10s/f (Stan)
WFA 3 from 4yo+ 16lb 12 Ran SP% **118.1**
Speed ratings (Par 103):91,89,85,80,80 76,73,71,68,66 53,46
CSF £11.06 TOTE £5.00: £1.40, £1.50, £5.60; EX 12.40 Trifecta £76.30 Part won. Pool £107.47 - 0.34 winning units..
Owner Miss K Rausing **Bred** K Rausing **Trained** Newmarket, Suffolk

FOCUS
A modest winning time for the type of contest. The proximity of the 38-rated third is a worry but the winner will go on from here.
Dramatic Official explanation: jockey said, regarding running and riding, his orders were jump out as best he could, try to go with field and finish as close as possible, adding that although the colt broke well, it was outpaced early, ran green and took time to adjust to kickback; trainer's rep confirmed adding that the colt was a relaxed sort at home, and racing, and that it could be better suited by a longer trip

61 **PONTIN'S FAMILY HOLIDAYS (S) STKS** **7f (F)**
1:50 (1:50) (Class 6) 3-Y-O+ **£2,184** (£644; £322) **Stalls** Low

Form RPR
641- **1** **Capital Lass**[10] 6961 4-9-9 53 HayleyTurner 12 63+
(D K Ivory) *trckd ldrs: led 3f out: r.o wl* **5/2**[2]
10-0 **2** *1 1/4* **Skip Of Colour**[6] 5 7-10-0 55 PaulHanagan 11 65
(P A Blockley) *led tl 3f out: kpt on fnl f: no real imp* **3/1**[3]
325- **3** *5* **Vancouver Gold (IRE)**[269] 1001 5-9-4 66 PaulMulrennan 7 42
(K R Burke) *chsd ldrs: effrt over 2f out: kpt on same pce* **9/4**[1]
066- **4** *2 1/2* **Rocky Reppin**[9] 6970 7-9-9 40 (b) DeanMcKeown 8 41
(J Balding) *chsd ldrs: fdd fnl f* **25/1**
052- **5** *1* **Bold Love**[10] 6958 4-9-1 40 (b) JasonEdmunds(3) 4 33
(J Balding) *hld up: effrt 3f out: rdn and hung rt over 1f out: sn wknd* **16/1**
044- **6** *7* **No Inkling (IRE)**[10] 6958 4-9-4 34 ChrisCatlin 3 15
(Miss M E Rowland) *in rr: effrt 3f out: nvr on terms* **40/1**
000- **7** *shd* **Teddy Monty (IRE)**[10] 6958 4-9-6 38 (b) MarkLawson(3) 10 19
(R E Barr) *in tch: outpcd over 3f out: sn lost pl* **100/1**
000- **8** *1 3/4* **Bahrain Gold (IRE)**[147] 4401 7-9-9 52 NCallan 2 15
(N P McCormack) *trckd ldrs: wknd fnl f* **16/1**
000- **9** *shd* **Spinning Dancer (IRE)**[10] 6958 4-9-4 25 (b[1]) JosedeSouza 5 10
(J R Holt) *mid-div: drvn over 3f out: sn lost pl* **125/1**
000- **10** *2 1/2* **Wings Of Morning (IRE)**[8] 6981 6-9-9 46 (v) DanielTudhope 6 8
(D Carroll) *trckd ldrs: n.m.r and lost pl over 4f out* **14/1**
6 **11** *14* **The Wicked Wizard**[6] 2 4-9-4 AndrewElliott(5) 1 —
(W Storey) *s.i.s: hung rt and sn bhd: t.o 3f out* **100/1**

1m 30.87s (0.07) **Going Correction** -0.10s/f (Stan) 11 Ran SP% **111.8**
Speed ratings (Par 101):95,93,87,85,83 75,75,73,73,70 54
CSF £9.59 TOTE £3.50: £2.00, £1.30, £1.30; EX 11.90 Trifecta £17.30 Pool £209.30 - 8.58 winning units..The winner was sold to A J McCabe for 6,600gns.
Owner H Schwartz **Bred** Kirtlington Stud Ltd **Trained** Radlett, Herts

FOCUS
A moderate seller, rated through the fourth.
Wings Of Morning(IRE) Official explanation: jockey said gelding suffered interference in running

62 **PONTIN'S BOOK EARLY H'CAP** **1m 6f (F)**
2:20 (2:21) (Class 6) (0-60,61) 4-Y-O+ **£2,388** (£705; £352) **Stalls** Low

Form RPR
632- **1** **Arsad (IRE)**[7] 6995 4-9-3 **61** JoeFanning 3 73
(C E Brittain) *hld up wl in tch: wnt 2nd over 4f out: led over 2f out: styd on strly: readily* **2/1**[2]
022- **2** *5* **Stagecoach Emerald**[16] 6923 5-9-8 **60** (t) EdwardCreighton 6 65
(R W Price) *w ldr: led over 5f out: hdd over 2f out: kpt on wl* **13/2**[3]
36-2 **3** *4* **Bienheureux**[6] 4 6-9-4 **56** (t) NCallan 5 55
(Miss Gay Kelleway) *hld up: stdy hdwy over 5f out: wnt 2nd over 4f out: effrt and c wd over 2f out: sn chsng 1st 2: wknd fnl f* **11/8**[1]
503- **4** *9* **Bold Trump**[10] 6957 6-8-8 **46** ChrisCatlin 8 33
(Mrs N S Evans) *chsd ldrs: outpcd over 4f out: wknd 2f out* **11/1**
060- **5** *9* **Blue Hills**[7] 6995 6-9-4 **56** (p) DeanMcKeown 1 30
(P W Hiatt) *drvn along to chse ldrs: reminders 6f out: lost pl over 4f out* **11/1**
0/0- **6** *26* **Woolstone Boy (USA)**[180] 3382 6-9-0 **52** (t) TPQueally 4 —
(A M Hales) *mde most tl over 5f out: hung right and lost pl over 4f out: bhd whn eased fnl f* **20/1**
006- **7** *10* **Little Lily Morgan**[231] 1866 4-8-9 **53** PaulHanagan 2 —
(R Bastiman) *trckd ldrs: lost pl over 8f out: t.o 3f out* **33/1**
063/ **8** *5* **Top Tenor (IRE)**[204] 1101 7-8-12 **50** (t) PaulFessey 7 —
(W Storey) *in rr: lost pl over 8f out: sn bhd: t.o 3f out* **40/1**

3m 6.86s (-2.74) **Going Correction** -0.10s/f (Stan)
WFA 4 from 5yo+ 6lb 8 Ran SP% **115.6**
Speed ratings (Par 101):103,100,97,92,87 72,67,64
CSF £15.30 CT £22.67 TOTE £3.00: £1.20, £1.70, £1.10; EX 16.10 Trifecta £19.90 Pool £396.50 - 14.12 winning units..
Owner Sultan Ali **Bred** Barnane Stud **Trained** Newmarket, Suffolk

FOCUS
Just a fair gallop but they came home well strung out. The winner always looked in command.
Woolstone Boy(USA) Official explanation: jockey said gelding hung right

63 **PONTINS.COM H'CAP** **1m (F)**
2:50 (2:53) (Class 5) (0-70,72) 4-Y-O+ **£3,071** (£906; £453) **Stalls** Low

Form RPR
66-4 **1** **Dudley Docker (IRE)**[5] 14 5-8-5 **66** (v[1]) KellyHarrison(7) 11 78
(D Carroll) *trckd ldrs: led over 2f out: hrd rdn and edgd lft: jst hld on* **10/1**
03-1 **2** *hd* **Rebellious Spirit**[5] 14 4-9-4 **72** 6ex DeanMcKeown 13 84
(P W Hiatt) *hdwg rt ins last: styd on wl towards fin* **3/1**[1]
002- **3** *3/4* **Bridgewater Boys**[29] 6767 6-8-10 **64** (b) NCallan 8 74
(K A Ryan) *mde most tl over 2f out: edgd rt and kpt on same pce ins last* **5/1**[3]
021- **4** *2 1/2* **Zamhrear**[24] 6819 4-8-8 **62** JoeFanning 10 67
(C E Brittain) *trckd ldrs: outpcd over 3f out: one pce fnl 2f* **9/2**[2]
01-3 **5** *1 1/2* **Vibrato (USA)**[6] 7 5-7-11 **56** oh3 (v) DuranFentiman(5) 12 58
(C J Teague) *trckd ldrs: effrt and hung lft over 1f out: one pce* **10/1**
244- **6** *1 1/4* **Windy Prospect**[11] 6949 5-8-3 **57** PaulHanagan 6 56
(P A Blockley) *bhd and swtchd v wd after 2f: hdwy over 3f out: one pce fnl 2f* **9/1**
400- **7** *3* **Exit Smiling**[15] 6928 5-8-13 **67** MickyFenton 9 60
(P T Midgley) *in rr: hdwy over 4f out: effrt on outside over 2f out: nvr nr ldrs* **33/1**
000- **8** *1* **Double Bay (USA)**[22] 6848 4-8-6 **60** JamieMackay 4 51
(Jane Chapple-Hyam) *s.i.s: sme hdwy over 2f out: nvr on terms* **50/1**
601- **9** *nk* **Plateau**[11] 6952 8-9-3 **71** TPQueally 5 61
(C R Dore) *mid-div: hdwy 3f out: hung lft and lost pl over 1f out* **16/1**
253- **10** *nk* **Wodhill Schnaps**[10] 6960 6-8-2 **56** oh8 (v[1]) HayleyTurner 1 45
(D Morris) *in rr: sme hdwy over 2f out: nvr a factor* **16/1**
130- **11** *2 1/2* **Cleveland**[12] 6938 5-8-3 **62** RussellKennemore(5) 3 46
(R Hollinshead) *s.i.s: hdwy on ins to chse ldrs 5f out: wknd 2f out* **8/1**
000- **12** *8* **Set Alight**[40] 6642 6-8-6 **60** (v) ChrisCatlin 2 27
(Mrs C A Dunnett) *s.i.s: nvr on terms* **50/1**
00-0 **13** *37* **Laith (IRE)**[6] 3 4-7-13 **58** oh2 ow2 RoryMoore(5) 7 —
(Miss V Haigh) *chsd ldrs: lost pl 3f out: sn eased and virtually p.u: t.o: btn 37 l* **50/1**

1m 43.09s (-1.51) **Going Correction** -0.10s/f (Stan) 13 Ran SP% **119.7**
Speed ratings (Par 103):103,102,102,99,98 96,93,92,92,92 89,81,44
CSF £39.46 CT £171.57 TOTE £16.30: £4.30, £2.10, £2.20; EX 65.90 Trifecta £246.40 Part won. Pool £347.11 - 0.20 winning units..

Owner J M Walsh **Bred** Nuri Fuat Basak **Trained** Sledmere, E Yorks
FOCUS
A strong pace yet little made ground from the rear.

64 PONTIN'S HOLIDAYS H'CAP 1m 4f (F)
3:20 (3:21) (Class 6) (0-55,55) 4-Y-O+ **£2,388** (£705; £352) **Stalls** Low

Form RPR
60- **1** **Global Strategy**[20] 6861 4-8-8 **48** ChrisCatlin 10 71+
(Rae Guest) *trckd ldrs: led over 2f out: drvn clr over 1f out: heavily eased fnl 75yds* **5/1**[2]
002- **2** 5 **Experimental (IRE)**[9] 6972 13-8-13 **49** DaleGibson 7 56
(John A Harris) *chsd ldrs: led 3f out: sn hdd: kpt on: no ch w wnr* **10/1**
144- **3** 5 **Cragganmore Creek**[24] 6816 4-9-1 **55** (b) HayleyTurner 1 54
(D Morris) *hld up towards rr: hdwy over 3f out: one pce fnl 2f* **9/2**[1]
05-5 **4** ½ **Romil Star (GER)**[5] 12 10-8-4 **45** (p) KevinGhunowa[(5)] 5 43
(M Wellings) *sn drvn along in rr: hdwy on outside 6f out: styd on fnl 2f* **7/1**[3]
401- **5** 2 **Padre Nostro (IRE)**[10] 6959 8-8-6 **49** ChrisGlenister[(7)] 2 44
(J R Holt) *chsd ldrs: one pce fnl 3f* **9/2**[1]
000- **6** 9 **Newport Boy (IRE)**[50] 6526 4-8-7 **52** (b[1]) TolleyDean[(5)] 6 33
(R A Harris) *tk fierce hold: led and sn clr: hdd 3f out: lost pl over 1f out* **5/1**[2]
/05- **7** ½ **Integration**[9] 6971 7-8-9 **45** EdwardCreighton 8 25
(Miss M E Rowland) *in tch: drvn over 4f out: sn wknd* **20/1**
000- **8** 2 **Bold Phoenix (IRE)**[17] 6899 6-9-0 **50** TPQueally 9 27
(B J Curley) *hld up towards rr: effrt 4f out: sn wknd* **10/1**
604- **9** ¾ **Danelor (IRE)**[10] 6959 9-8-10 **46** (p) DeanMcKeown 4 21
(D Shaw) *chsd ldr: drvn over 4f out: hung rt and lost pl over 2f out* **11/1**
200/ **10** 16 **Erte**[10] 4207 6-8-12 **48** PaulFessey 3 —
(W Storey) *mid-div: lost pl 7f out: sn bhd: t.o 3f out* **50/1**

2m 38.76s (-3.33) **Going Correction** -0.10s/f (Stan)
WFA 4 from 6yo+ 4lb **10** Ran SP% **115.4**
Speed ratings (Par 101):107,103,100,100,98 92,92,91,90,79
CSF £53.53 CT £241.08 TOTE £5.80: £1.60, £3.40, £1.90; EX 65.40 Trifecta £293.30 Pool £413.17 - 0.86 winning units..
Owner E P Duggan **Bred** Keith Freeman **Trained** Newmarket, Suffolk
FOCUS
A decent winning time for a race of its type. Newport Boy, in first time blinkers, went off much too fast for his own good.
Global Strategy ◆ Official explanation: trainer said, regarding the improved form shown, gelding had benefited from the step up in trip from 1m to 1m4f

65 PONTIN'S H'CAP 6f (F)
3:50 (3:50) (Class 6) (0-65,75) 3-Y-O **£2,388** (£705; £352) **Stalls** Low

Form RPR
521- **1** **Para Siempre**[15] 6926 3-9-5 **75** (b) NeilBrown[(7)] 3 98+
(B Smart) *trckd ldrs led 2f out: rdn wl clr: unchal* **10/11**[1]
354- **2** 12 **Popolo (IRE)**[111] 5434 3-9-2 **65** HayleyTurner 2 52
(M L W Bell) *hld up towards rr: outpcd and drvn over 3f out: styd on fnl 2f: tk remote 2nd nr line* **5/2**[2]
34-6 **3** 1 **Pappas Image**[4] 17 3-8-7 **56** (b) DeanMcKeown 1 40+
(A J McCabe) *led after 1f: hdd 2f out: wknd ins fnl f: lost 2nd nr line* **14/1**
150- **4** hd **Emefdream**[19] 6872 3-8-13 **62** (p) DanielTudhope 6 45
(Mrs N Macauley) *hld up: effrt 4f out: kpt on one pce fnl 2f* **8/1**[3]
405- **5** 3 **Arabellas Homer**[25] 6809 3-7-9 **51** oh2 WilliamBuick[(7)] 5 25
(Mrs N Macauley) *hld up in rr: outpcd over 4f out: no threat after* **16/1**
56-4 **6** 5 **Suntan Lady (IRE)**[2] 40 3-7-11 **51** oh6 (v) DuranFentiman[(5)] 4 10
(Miss V Haigh) *led 1f: chsd ldrs: lost pl over 1f out* **20/1**

1m 15.95s (-0.95) **Going Correction** -0.10s/f (Stan) **6** Ran SP% **109.4**
Speed ratings (Par 95):102,86,84,84,80 73
CSF £3.10 TOTE £1.70: £1.30, £1.20; EX 3.00 Place 6 £11.31, Place 5 £3.97..
Owner Mrs Linda Pestell **Bred** D R Tucker **Trained** Hambleton, N Yorks
FOCUS
A smart winning time for a race of its type. Another wide-margin success by the winner who faces another big hike in the ratings.
T/Jkpt: Not won. T/Plt: £20.50 to a £1 stake. Pool: £67,037.80. 2,377.25 winning tickets. T/Qpdt: £3.80 to a £1 stake. Pool: £5,626.60. 1,076.10 winning tickets. WG

[39]WOLVERHAMPTON (A.W) (L-H)
Monday, January 8

OFFICIAL GOING: Standard
Wind: fresh bhd

66 PONTIN'S - BOOK EARLY H'CAP 5f 216y(P)
1:40 (1:41) (Class 6) (0-65,65) 4-Y-O+ **£2,388** (£705; £352) **Stalls** Low

Form RPR
614- **1** **Millfields Dreams**[9] 6990 8-8-10 **59** TPQueally 8 73+
(M G Quinlan) *hld up in tch: rdn to ld over 1f out: r.o wl* **4/1**[3]
01-0 **2** 2½ **Gilded Cove**[6] 8 7-8-11 **65** RussellKennemore[(5)] 7 70
(R Hollinshead) *hld up and bhd: rdn and hdwy on outside over 1f out: r.o ins fnl f: nt trble wnr* **7/1**
050- **3** 1¼ **Whistleupthewind**[20] 6869 4-8-6 **55** (b) PaulHanagan 10 56
(J M P Eustace) *chsd ldrs: rdn over 2f out: edgd lft over 1f out: one pce ins fnl f* **28/1**
505- **4** nk **Fast Heart**[11] 6966 6-9-2 **65** NCallan 5 65+
(R A Harris) *s.i.s: hld up and bhd: hdwy on ins whn nt clr run over 1f out tl swtchd rt ins fnl f: nt rcvr* **15/2**
106- **5** nk **Sparkwell**[12] 6953 5-9-2 **65** DeanMcKeown 9 64
(D Shaw) *s.i.s: hld up towards rr: hdwy 2f out: rdn and carried lft jst over 1f out: edgd lft ins fnl f: no ex: bbv* **12/1**
12-4 **6** ¾ **Cree**[2] 50 5-8-7 **59** JamesDoyle[(3)] 4 56
(W R Muir) *hld up in mid-div: rdn and hdwy on ins 2f out: n.m.r over 1f out: swtchd rt ins fnl f: one pce* **11/4**[1]
01-1 **7** 3 **Hamaasy**[7] 3 6-8-11 **60** 6ex AdrianTNicholls 1 48
(D Nicholls) *w ldr: led over 3f out: rdn 2f out: hdd over 1f out: wknd ins fnl f* **7/2**[2]
050- **8** 3 **Savile's Delight (IRE)**[200] 2792 8-8-6 **55** (t) EdwardCreighton 2 34
(Miss Joanne Priest) *led over 2f: rdn and ev ch 2f out: wknd over 1f out* **14/1**
600- **9** ½ **Canina**[46] 6572 4-8-4 **60** JohnCavanagh[(7)] 12 37
(Ms Deborah J Evans) *prom tl rdn and wknd over 2f out* **50/1**
/00- **10** 2 **Oranges And Lemons (FR)**[12] 6952 4-8-6 **55** JoeFanning 3 26
(C E Brittain) *s.i.s: a bhd* **66/1**

1m 14.77s (-1.04) **Going Correction** -0.125s/f (Stan) **10** Ran SP% **114.4**
Speed ratings (Par 101):101,97,96,95,95 94,90,86,85,82
CSF £31.09 CT £683.48 TOTE £6.30: £1.70, £3.30, £5.90; EX 44.10 TRIFECTA Not won..
Owner Mrs Theresa Fitsall **Bred** T G Price **Trained** Newmarket, Suffolk
FOCUS
A modest handicap run at a fair pace but the form does not look totally reliable.
Fast Heart ◆ Official explanation: jockey said gelding was denied a clear run
Sparkwell Official explanation: jockey said horse bled from the nose

67 PONTINS.COM H'CAP 5f 216y(P)
2:10 (2:10) (Class 5) (0-70,70) 4-Y-O+ **£1,989** (£1,989; £453) **Stalls** Low

Form RPR
30-2 **1** **Sweet Pickle**[7] 3 6-8-8 **62** (e) PatCosgrave 8 69+
(J R Boyle) *hld up and bhd: rdn and hdwy 2f out: edgd lft and jnd ldr post* **7/1**[3]
234- **1** dht **Dvinsky (USA)**[17] 6913 6-8-12 **66** PaulDoe 1 73
(P Howling) *mde all: rdn over 1f out: all out: jnd post* **8/1**
431- **3** hd **Bond Playboy**[9] 6990 7-8-4 **63** (v) DuranFentiman[(5)] 5 69
(G R Oldroyd) *hld up in tch: rdn over 2f out: r.o ins fnl f: bbv* **15/8**[1]
212- **4** ¾ **Cross Of Lorraine (IRE)**[12] 6952 4-8-11 **65** (b) PaulHanagan 9 69
(I Semple) *chsd ldr: rdn over 2f out: kpt on same pce fnl f* **11/4**[2]
500- **5** 1¾ **Mambazo**[11] 6966 5-8-13 **70** (e) JamesDoyle[(3)] 7 69
(S C Williams) *s.i.s: plld hrd in rr: rdn and c wd st: hdwy whn hung lft ins fnl f: nt rch ldrs* **11/1**
036- **6** 1¾ **Dasheena**[25] 6820 4-7-13 **58** (t) NataliaGemelova[(5)] 2 52
(A J McCabe) *hld up and bhd: pushed along over 3f out: no rspnse* **14/1**
600- **7** 1¼ **Just Intersky (USA)**[12] 6946 4-9-1 **69** (b[1]) DeanMcKeown 4 59
(K A Ryan) *t.k.h: prom: rdn 2f out: sn wknd* **20/1**
606- **8** shd **General Feeling (IRE)**[11] 6966 6-8-5 **59** SilvestreDeSousa 6 49
(M Mullineaux) *hld up in mid-div: rdn over 2f out: sn bhd* **16/1**

1m 15.25s (-0.56) **Going Correction** -0.125s/f (Stan) **8** Ran SP% **110.7**
Speed ratings (Par 103):98,98,97,96,94 92,90,90
WIN Dvinsky £4.00, Sweet Pickle £1.90; PL DY £1.90, SP £1.30; EX DY SP £14.10, SP DY £19.80; CSF DY SP Bond Playboy £71.47, SP DY BP £70.48. CSF £29.11 CT £71.47 TOTE £4.00: £1.90; EX 14.10 Trifecta £84.80 Part won. Pool £239.69 - 0.84 winning units..
Owner M Khan X2 **Bred** C T Van Hoorn **Trained** Epsom, Surrey
Owner Richard Berenson **Bred** Eclipse Bloodstock And Tipperary Bloodstock **Trained** Newmarket, Suffolk
■ Stewards' Enquiry : Pat Cosgrave one-day ban: used whip above shoulder height (Jan 19)
FOCUS
This slowly-run affair was 0.48 seconds slower than the first race.
Bond Playboy Official explanation: vet said gelding bled from the nose
Mambazo Official explanation: jockey said gelding was hampered start and ran too free

68 PONTIN'S FAMILY HOLIDAYS (S) STKS 1m 141y(P)
2:40 (2:45) (Class 6) 3-Y-O **£2,047** (£604; £302) **Stalls** Low

Form RPR
460- **1** **News Of The Day (IRE)**[45] 6576 3-8-6 58 JoeFanning 1 57+
(M Johnston) *chsd ldr: led over 2f out: rdn out* **6/4**[1]
043- **2** 1¼ **Zaafira (SPA)**[8] 6996 3-8-6 53 EdwardCreighton 7 53
(E J Creighton) *s.i.s: hld up: hdwy over 5f out: rdn to chse wnr wl over 1f out: kpt on* **10/1**
041- **3** 2 **Gold Response**[8] 6996 3-8-11 45 DeanMcKeown 6 53
(D Shaw) *uns rdr and galloped loose bef s: hld up and bhd: hdwy over 2f out: rdn and edgd lft over 1f out: one pce fnl f* **10/3**[2]
544- **4** 1¾ **Jost Van Dyke**[23] 6845 3-8-11 54 PatCosgrave 8 50
(J R Boyle) *t.k.h in rr: rdn and hdwy over 2f out: one pce fnl f* **17/2**
42-4 **5** 3 **The Light Fandango**[6] 11 3-8-1 48 TolleyDean[(5)] 2 38
(R A Harris) *hld up in tch: rdn over 2f out: outpcd wl over 1f out: btn whn hung lft ins fnl f* **9/2**[3]
00-5 **6** 4 **Solo City**[6] 11 3-8-11 45 NCallan 3 35
(P A Blockley) *led: rdn and hdd over 2f out: wkng whn bmpd ins fnl f* **20/1**
000- **7** 5 **Flashing Feet (IRE)**[23] 6845 3-8-8 49 StephaneBreux[(3)] 4 25
(R Hannon) *rdn 4f out: a bhd* **20/1**
005- **8** 8 **Byanita (IRE)**[28] 6789 3-8-6 35 (p) AdrianMcCarthy 5 3
(B Palling) *t.k.h: prom: rdn over 3f out: sn wknd* **50/1**

1m 51.4s (-0.36) **Going Correction** -0.125s/f (Stan) **8** Ran SP% **112.4**
Speed ratings (Par 95):96,94,93,91,88 85,80,73
CSF £17.00 TOTE £2.10: £1.10, £3.00, £1.80; EX 12.60 Trifecta £32.20 Pool £414.71 - 9.13 winning units.The winner was bought in for 9,000gns. Gold Response was subject to a friendly claim.
Owner J Shack **Bred** Dr Michael Marenchic **Trained** Middleham Moor, N Yorks
FOCUS
They went no pace in this modest seller. The winner did not need to improve to score and the form has been rated through the fourth and sixth.
Solo City Official explanation: jockey said gelding hung right under pressure

69 PONTINSBINGO.COM MAIDEN STKS (DIV I) 7f 32y(P)
3:10 (3:13) (Class 5) 3-Y-O **£2,388** (£705; £352) **Stalls** High

Form RPR
422- **1** **Dressed To Dance (IRE)**[32] 6736 3-8-12 63 (b[1]) NCallan 3 63
(B J Meehan) *t.k.h in tch: rdn 2f out: led ins fnl f: r.o* **13/8**[1]
33- **2** ½ **Not Too Taxing**[17] 6905 3-9-3 RichardHughes 6 67
(R Hannon) *led: rdn over 2f out: hdd ins fnl f: r.o* **10/3**[2]
3- **3** 1 **Distant Sun (USA)**[45] 6581 3-9-3 FergusSweeney 9 64
(R Charlton) *sn prom: wnt 2nd 5f out: ev ch over 2f out: sn rdn: hung lft over 1f out: nt qckn ins fnl f* **9/2**[3]
43- **4** 2 **Not To Know**[26] 6808 3-9-3 ChrisCatlin 1 59
(John A Quinn, Ire) *a.p: rdn over 2f out: one pce fnl f* **13/2**
03- **5** 2 **Minnie Mill**[13] 6940 3-8-12 JimmyQuinn 8 49
(B P J Baugh) *chsd ldr 2f: rdn 2f out: wknd ins fnl f* **12/1**
6 1 **Meadfoot** 3-8-9 RichardKingscote[(3)] 2 46
(B R Millman) *hld up in mid-div: rdn over 2f out: no hdwy* **28/1**
7 1½ **Kiwi The Clown (IRE)** 3-9-3 PaulHanagan 11 47
(R A Fahey) *hld up and bhd: edgd lft over 3f out: rdn over 2f out: no rspnse* **40/1**
8 nk **Tina's Ridge (IRE)** 3-9-3 AdrianTNicholls 4 46
(E J Alston) *s.i.s: rdn over 2f out: a bhd* **40/1**
04- **9** ½ **Gertie (IRE)**[35] 6706 3-8-5 SCreighton[(7)] 7 40
(E J Creighton) *hld up in mid-div: hdwy over 2f out: sn rdn: wknd over 1f out* **66/1**
0- **10** 3½ **Otaki (IRE)**[24] 6826 3-8-12 JamieMackay 10 30
(Sir Mark Prescott) *rdn over 2f out: a bhd* **25/1**

0- **11** ½ **Tobougg Welcome (IRE)**[24] 6826 3-9-0 SaleemGolam[(3)] 5 34
(S C Williams) *hmpd over 3f out: a bhd* **40/1**

1m 31.53s (1.13) **Going Correction** -0.125s/f (Stan) 11 Ran SP% **116.5**
Speed ratings (Par 97):88,87,86,84,81 80,78,78,77,73 73
CSF £6.39 TOTE £2.90: £1.10, £1.70, £1.90; EX 9.80 Trifecta £22.80 Pool £572.93 - 17.80 winning units.
Owner Seven Club Partnership **Bred** J Doyle **Trained** Manton, Wilts

FOCUS
This maiden was run in a time virtually two and a half seconds slower than the other division.
Kiwi The Clown(IRE) Official explanation: jockey said gelding hung badly throughout
Tobougg Welcome(IRE) Official explanation: jockey said colt was hampered going into bend

70 PONTIN'S HOLIDAYS APPRENTICE H'CAP 7f 32y(P)
3:40 (3:41) (Class 6) (0-65,65) 4-Y-0+ **£2,388** (£705; £352) **Stalls** High

Form RPR
400/ **1** **Activity (IRE)**[475] 5380 8-9-0 **63** DuranFentiman[(3)] 11 73
(M J Gingell) *s.i.s: hld up in rr: rdn and hdwy over 1f out: r.o u.p to ld post* **25/1**
212- **2** *shd* **Imperium**[24] 6827 6-8-8 **61** (p) SophieDoyle[(7)] 3 71
(Jean-Rene Auvray) *hld up in tch: rdn to ld last strides: hdd post* **15/2**
125- **3** ½ **Cool Sands (IRE)**[12] 6949 5-8-13 **59** (v) DanielTudhope 5 68
(D Shaw) *a.p: rdn to ld 1f out: hdd last strides* **15/2**
066- **4** *3* **Scuba (IRE)**[12] 6952 5-9-3 **63** (b) JerryO'Dwyer 9 64
(H Morrison) *hld up in mid-div: hdwy over 2f out: sn rdn: no ex ins fnl f* **8/1**
300- **5** *hd* **Flying Bantam (IRE)**[16] 6932 6-8-13 **62** JamieMoriarty[(3)] 6 62+
(R A Fahey) *hld up in mid-div: hdwy on ins wl over 1f out: one pce ins fnl f* **8/1**
460- **6** ½ **Out For A Stroll**[37] 6684 8-8-9 **62** FLenclud[(7)] 12 61
(S C Williams) *hld up in rr: c wd st: late hdwy: nrst fin* **25/1**
000- **7** *nk* **Franksalot (IRE)**[17] 6913 7-8-9 **62** SamuelDrury[(7)] 1 60
(I W McInnes) *hld up in rr: kpt on ins fnl f: n.d* **40/1**
004- **8** *1 ¼* **Chalentina**[9] 6988 4-8-12 **65** JPFeatherstone[(7)] 8 59
(P Howling) *hld up towards rr: hdwy on outside 3f out: rdn 2f out: wknd over 1f out* **40/1**
005- **9** *shd* **Tuscarora (IRE)**[30] 6767 8-9-0 **60** JamesDoyle 7 54
(A W Carroll) *s.i.s: hld up and bhd: rdn over 2f out: nvr nr ldrs* **9/1**
316- **10** *hd* **Kingsmaite**[21] 6862 6-9-3 **63** (bt) MarcHalford 2 57
(S R Bowring) *prom: rdn over 2f out: wknd over 1f out* **6/1**[3]
210- **11** *hd* **Mozakhraf (USA)**[29] 6781 5-9-4 **64** AndrewMullen 10 57
(K A Ryan) *t.k.h: led over 5f out: rdn 2f out: hdd 1f out: wknd wl ins fnl f* **5/1**[2]
100- **12** *1* **Redwood Rocks (IRE)**[16] 6930 6-9-5 **65** MarkLawson 4 55
(B Smart) *led over 1f: chsd ldr: rdn over 2f out: wknd 1f out* **4/1**[1]

1m 29.01s (-1.39) **Going Correction** -0.125s/f (Stan) 12 Ran SP% **119.3**
Speed ratings (Par 101):102,101,101,97,97 97,96,95,95,94 94,93
CSF £198.28 CT £1582.88 TOTE £27.00: £3.70, £2.30, £1.80; EX 203.80 TRIFECTA Not won..
Owner Webtack **Bred** Sheikh Mohammed Bin Rashid Al Maktoum **Trained** North Runcton, Norfolk

FOCUS
An open-looking handicap run at a strong pace and the first three deserve credit for pulling clear of the remainder. The second and third have been rated as running above their recent best.

71 HOLIDAY INN GARDEN COURT WOLVERHAMPTON H'CAP 1m 4f 50y(P)
4:10 (4:10) (Class 6) (0-50,51) 4-Y-0+ **£2,388** (£705; £352) **Stalls** Low

Form RPR
465- **1** **Atlantic Gamble (IRE)**[20] 6871 7-8-8 **46** (p) PatCosgrave 1 54
(K R Burke) *a.p: nt clr run on ins over 2f out: rdn to ld over 1f out: drvn out* **4/1**[2]
506- **2** ¾ **Bill Bennett (FR)**[48] 6553 6-8-8 **46** ChrisCatlin 2 53
(J Jay) *hld up in rr: rdn 4f out: swtchd rt and hdwy over 1f out: r.o wl u.p and edgd lft towards fin: nt rch wnr* **11/1**
433- **3** *1 ¼* **Desert Hawk**[18] 6899 6-8-12 **50** (b) FergusSweeney 3 55
(W M Brisbourne) *hld up in mid-div: rdn and hdwy 2f out: kpt on towards fin* **7/2**[1]
10-0 **4** *1* **Captivate**[5] 16 4-8-6 **48** (p) JimmyQuinn 7 52
(A J McCabe) *hld up and bhd: rdn over 2f out: hdwy on ins wl over 1f out: one pce fnl f* **20/1**
U0-3 **5** *1 ¼* **Diktatorship (IRE)**[3] 45 4-8-5 **50** oh1 ow4 (p) JamesDoyle[(3)] 8 52
(Ernst Oertel) *led early: chsd ldr: rdn and ev ch over 2f out: wknd wl ins fnl f* **10/1**
00- **6** *2* **Asian Alliance (IRE)**[16] 6936 6-8-12 **50** (p) NCallan 5 49
(K A Ryan) *sn led: rdn over 2f out: hdd over 1f out: wknd wl ins fnl f* **8/1**
123- **7** *4* **Go Amwell**[10] 6972 4-8-7 **49** PaulDoe 4 42
(J R Jenkins) *s.i.s: hld up and bhd: hdwy over 3f out: rdn over 1f out: wknd over 1f out* **4/1**[2]
200- **8** *10* **Coppington Melody (IRE)**[24] 6831 4-8-9 **51** ow1 MickyFenton 6 29
(B W Duke) *hld up in mid-div: hdwy 6f out: hmpd 5f out: sn lost pl: bhd fnl 4f* **25/1**
222- **9** *1 ½* **Wood Fern (UAE)**[17] 6904 7-8-11 **49** ShaneKelly 9 24
(W M Brisbourne) *hld up in tch: jnd ldrs 5f out: rdn and wknd over 2f out* **6/1**[3]

2m 42.1s (-0.32) **Going Correction** -0.125s/f (Stan)
WFA 4 from 6yo+ 4lb 9 Ran SP% **113.7**
Speed ratings (Par 101):96,95,94,94,93 91,89,82,81
CSF £46.25 CT £166.93 TOTE £7.30: £1.30, £4.00, £1.50; EX 47.50 Trifecta £193.40 Pool £337.82 - 1.24 winning units.
Owner Mrs Elaine M Burke **Bred** Larry Ryan **Trained** Middleham Moor, N Yorks

FOCUS
A slowly-run poor handicap in which the first five have all been rated to a similar level.
Wood Fern(UAE) Official explanation: jockey said gelding lost its action

72 GO PONTIN'S H'CAP 1m 1f 103y(P)
4:40 (4:40) (Class 6) (0-58,58) 4-Y-0+ **£2,730** (£806; £403) **Stalls** Low

Form RPR
01- **1** **Kilimandscharo (USA)**[18] 6899 5-9-1 **58** RichardHughes 5 73+
(P J McBride) *hld up in tch: hdwy over 3f out: rdn to ld ins fnl f: r.o* **4/9**[1]
203- **2** ¾ **Discotheque (USA)**[10] 6980 4-9-0 **58** DeanCorby 10 66
(P Howling) *hld up and bhd: hdwy over 2f out: rdn over 1f out: edgd rt ins fnl f: kpt on* **33/1**
42-5 **3** *nk* **Second Reef**[3] 42 5-8-12 **55** (p) PaulQuinn 7 63
(E J Alston) *hld up and bhd: hdwy on ins to ld over 2f out: rdn over 1f out: hdd ins fnl f: nt qckn* **22/1**
050- **4** *shd* **Under Fire (IRE)**[18] 6897 4-8-9 **53** ShaneKelly 8 61
(A W Carroll) *hld up in mid-div: rdn and hdwy on outside 2f out: kpt on u.p ins fnl f* **50/1**
44-5 **5** ½ **Bentley Brook (IRE)**[6] 10 5-9-0 **57** (b) PaulHanagan 9 64
(P A Blockley) *hld up and bhd: rdn and hdwy on ins wl over 1f out: kpt on same pce fnl f* **20/1**
251- **6** *nk* **Harare**[28] 6793 6-8-12 **58** (b) JamesDoyle[(3)] 3 64
(R J Price) *s.i.s: hld up and bhd: hdwy on ins wl over 1f out: one pce fnl f* **14/1**[3]
/60- **7** *2 ½* **Roman Boy (ARG)**[18] 6897 8-9-0 **57** MickyFenton 4 58
(Stef Liddiard) *hld up in mid-div: n.m.r briefly over 3f out: rdn and hdwy 2f out: wknd ins fnl f* **50/1**
33-1 **8** *1* **Danzare**[5] 19 5-8-11 **57** 6ex MarcHalford[(3)] 11 56
(J L Spearing) *hld up and bhd: rdn over 2f out: c wd st: nvr trbld ldrs* **8/1**[2]
00-0 **9** *3* **Counterfactual (IRE)**[7] 7 4-8-8 **55** MarkLawson[(3)] 1 48
(B Smart) *t.k.h: prom: rdn 3f out: wknd wl over 1f out* **66/1**
023- **10** *hd* **Lobengula (IRE)**[12] 6955 5-8-10 **53** JimmyQuinn 12 46
(I W McInnes) *t.k.h: led 7f out: hdd over 2f out: wknd wl over 1f out* **14/1**[3]
060- **11** *5* **Tamworth (IRE)**[13] 6938 5-8-7 **50** (t) EdwardCreighton 13 33
(E J Creighton) *sn led: hdd 7f out: chsd ldr tl rdn over 2f out: sn wknd* **66/1**
00-0 **12** *52* **Obscene**[5] 19 4-8-11 **55** (be[1]) NCallan 2 —
(A J McCabe) *led early: prom tl rdn and wknd over 3f out: sn eased: t.o* **100/1**
005- **13** *62* **Royle Dancer**[10] 6977 4-8-12 **56** BrettDoyle 6 —
(R Hollinshead) *mid-div: lost pl over 5f out: wl bhd fnl 4f: t.o: bbv* **33/1**

2m 0.19s (-2.43) **Going Correction** -0.125s/f (Stan)
WFA 4 from 5yo+ 1lb 13 Ran SP% **116.6**
Speed ratings (Par 101):105,104,104,103,103 103,101,100,97,97 92,46,—
CSF £28.81 CT £174.62 TOTE £1.50: £1.10, £8.10, £4.60; EX 23.50 Trifecta £105.00 Pool £704.48 - 4.76 winning units.
Owner P J McBride **Bred** Ron Dufficy **Trained** Newmarket, Suffolk

FOCUS
This was run at a suicidal pace and turned out to be far more competitive than the betting suggested. The winner travelled well and can improve again.
Royle Dancer Official explanation: vet said gelding bled from the nose

73 PONTINSBINGO.COM MAIDEN STKS (DIV II) 7f 32y(P)
5:10 (5:11) (Class 5) 3-Y-O **£2,388** (£705; £352) **Stalls** High

Form RPR
62- **1** **Soft Morning**[8] 6998 3-8-12 JamieMackay 4 85+
(Sir Mark Prescott) *mde all: rdn and rn wd to centre of the crse ent st: r.o wl* **5/4**[1]
224- **2** *3* **Arch Of Titus (IRE)**[102] 5633 3-9-3 75 MickyFenton 7 76
(M L W Bell) *a.p: chsd wnr 4f out: rdn and swtchd lft wl over 1f out: no imp* **15/8**[2]
3 *1 ¼* **Ridgewell (USA)** 3-8-12 NCallan 10 68+
(B J Meehan) *hld up in mid-div: hdwy on outside 3f out: sn rdn: one pce fnl 2f* **7/1**
4 *5* **Gold Digger Miss (USA)** 3-8-12 ShaneKelly 6 54
(J Noseda) *s.i.s: hld up and bhd: hdwy 4f out: rdn 2f out: sn wknd* **12/1**
65- **5** *2 ½* **Meeting Of Minds**[17] 6905 3-8-12 BrettDoyle 3 47
(W Jarvis) *hld up in mid-div: short-lived effrt on outside wl over 1f out* **33/1**
220- **6** *1 ¾* **Straight Face (IRE)**[98] 5721 3-9-3 73 PaulDoe 9 48
(W J Knight) *s.i.s: rdn over 3f out: nvr nr ldrs* **6/1**[3]
7 *1 ¼* **Danalova** 3-8-12 PaulHanagan 1 39
(R A Fahey) *s.i.s: bhd: rdn 4f out: no ch whn hung rt 1f out* **33/1**
6- **8** *nk* **Jousting**[11] 6963 3-9-3 RossStudholme 2 43
(V Smith) *chsd wnr 3f: sn rdn: wknd over 2f out* **66/1**
9 *7* **Starcrest** 3-8-12 FrankieMcDonald 11 20
(Jean-Rene Auvray) *a bhd* **100/1**
56- **10** *9* **Dear One (IRE)**[31] 6751 3-8-12 ChrisCatlin 8 —
(P A Blockley) *prom tl wknd 3f out* **50/1**

1m 29.04s (-1.36) **Going Correction** -0.125s/f (Stan) 46 Ran SP% **124.0**
Speed ratings (Par 97):102,98,97,91,88 86,85,84,76,66
CSF £4.00 TOTE £2.90: £1.10, £1.10, £3.00; EX 5.80 Trifecta £25.60 Pool £635.30 - 17.56 winning units. Place 6 £62.04, Place 5 £15.14 .
Owner Miss K Rausing **Bred** Miss K Rausing **Trained** Newmarket, Suffolk

FOCUS
This was as good as two and a half seconds faster than the first division and the form looks solid.
T/Plt: £69.40 to a £1 stake. Pool: £60,864.30. 640.00 winning tickets. T/Qpdt: £8.90 to a £1 stake. Pool: £4,861.60. 403.10 winning tickets. KH

[59]SOUTHWELL (L-H)
Tuesday, January 9

OFFICIAL GOING: Standard
There was a major pace bias at this meeting, with three of the eight winners making virtually all and the other five all racing close to the pace.
Wind: Strong, across.

74 PONTIN'S FAMILY HOLIDAYS APPRENTICE H'CAP 1m 4f (F)
12:20 (12:20) (Class 5) (0-70,68) 4-Y-0+ **£2,914** (£867; £433; £216) **Stalls** Low

Form RPR
00-2 **1** **Beldon Hill (USA)**[4] 45 4-8-11 **60** JamieMoriarty 5 72
(R A Fahey) *trckd ldng pair: hdwy over 3f out: led wl over 1f out: rdn clr ins last* **15/8**[1]
04-1 **2** *3 ½* **Credential**[8] 1 5-9-2 **61** 6ex AndrewElliott 3 68
(John A Harris) *cl up: led over 2f out: sn rdn: hdd and drvn wl over 1f out: kpt on same pce ins last* **9/2**[3]
222- **3** *2* **Opera Writer (IRE)**[17] 6929 4-8-9 **61** RussellKennemore[(3)] 2 65
(R Hollinshead) *led: rdn along 3f out: sn hdd: drvn and one pce fr wl over 1f out* **2/1**[2]
/00- **4** *3 ½* **Proper Article (IRE)**[21] 6873 5-9-1 **60** (bt) RoryMoore 8 59
(Miss J E Foster) *chsd ldrs: rdn along over 3f out: drvn and one pce fnl 2f* **25/1**
644- **5** *9* **Summer Lodge**[17] 6929 4-9-1 **67** (v) JamesMillman[(3)] 4 52
(A J McCabe) *rr: pushed along over 5f out: rdn and wknd over 4f out: sn bhd* **6/1**
0/0- **6** *6* **Double Mystery (FR)**[10] 6993 7-8-7 **55** (t) AshleyHamblett[(3)] 6 31
(K J Burke) *hld up in tch: hdwy to trck ldrs 4f out: rdn 3f out and sn wknd* **20/1**

2m 41.09s (-1.00) **Going Correction** -0.075s/f (Stan)
WFA 4 from 5yo+ 4lb 6 Ran SP% **109.2**
Speed ratings (Par 103):100,97,96,94,88 84
CSF £10.06 CT £15.42 TOTE £2.30: £1.30, £2.10; EX 8.50 Trifecta £22.50 Pool £193.31. - 6.09 winning units..

The Form Book, Raceform Ltd, Compton, RG20 6NL

Owner D Brennan **Bred** Darley **Trained** Musley Bank, N Yorks

FOCUS
A moderate handicap run in a time 1.01 seconds quicker than the later seller won by the 47-rated Tiegs.
Summer Lodge Official explanation: jockey said gelding hung badly right-handed
Double Mystery(FR) Official explanation: jockey said gelding lost its action

75 PONTIN'S BOOK EARLY H'CAP (DIV I) 1m (F)
12:50 (12:51) (Class 6) (0-60,60) 4-Y-0+ **£1,619** (£481; £240; £120) **Stalls** Low

Form RPR
26-2 **1** **Wodhill Gold**[8] 7 6-8-5 **49**....................(v) HayleyTurner 7 67+
(D Morris) *cl up: led 3f out: rdn clr wl over 1f out: styd on strly* **10/3**[1]
500- **2** *3 1/2* **Tour D'Amour (IRE)**[55] 6497 4-9-2 **60**.................... PaulMulrennan 10 62
(R Craggs) *hld up: hdwy on outer over 2f out: rdn to chse wnr over 1f out: sn drvn: edgd lft and no imp* **7/1**[3]
/00- **3** *3 1/2* **Steel Grey**[42] 6636 6-8-2 **46** oh1.................... DeanMernagh 3 41
(M Brittain) *chsd ldrs: rdn along: outpcd and bhd 1/2-way: styd on u.p appr last* **80/1**
352- **4** *nk* **Louisiade (IRE)**[12] 6960 6-8-3 **50**....................(p) AndrewMullen(3) 1 44
(K A Ryan) *dwlt: hdwy and in tch 1/2-way: rdn along 3f out: drvn and one pce fnl 2f* **9/2**[2]
022- **5** *1 3/4* **Legal Lover (IRE)**[13] 6949 5-8-10 **59**.................... RussellKennemore(5) 2 50
(R Hollinshead) *trckd ldrs: effrt 3f out: rdn over 2f out and grad wknd* **9/2**[2]
050- **6** *1 3/4* **Pawn In Life (IRE)**[28] 6798 9-8-7 **51** ow3....................(b) DeanMcKeown 9 38
(S Parr) *towards rr: wd straigyht and sn rdn along: kpt on appr last: nrst fin* **33/1**
001- **7** *1 1/4* **Golden Spectrum (IRE)**[13] 6955 8-8-9 **58**....................(b) TolleyDean(5) 4 43
(R A Harris) *sn led: rdn alonga nd hdd 3f out: sn drvn and wknd* **10/1**
0-02 **8** *5* **Weet For Ever (USA)**[7] 14 4-8-6 **50**.................... PaulHanagan 8 25
(P A Blockley) *chsd ldrs: rdn along wl over 2f out: sn wknd* **9/2**[2]
060- **9** *5* **Stolen Summer (IRE)**[41] 6497 4-8-8 **55**....................(be[1]) JerryO'Dwyer(3) 5 20
(B S Rothwell) *s.i.s: a rr* **50/1**
005- **10** *5* **True West (USA)**[35] 6714 4-8-8 **52**....................(b[1]) JimmyQuinn 6 7
(Miss Gay Kelleway) *chsd ldrs: rdn along over 3f out: sn wknd* **16/1**
1m 44.04s (-0.56) **Going Correction** -0.075s/f (Stan) 10 Ran SP% 111.2
Speed ratings (Par 101):99,95,92,91,89 88,86,81,76,71
CSF £25.49 CT £1502.76 TOTE £3.50: £1.50, £1.60, £12.30; EX 24.60 TRIFECTA Not won..
Owner Miss S Graham **Bred** Wodhill Stud **Trained** Newmarket, Suffolk

FOCUS
A moderate handicap run in a time 1.34 seconds slower than the second division. It has been rated around the placed horses.

76 GO PONTIN'S CLAIMING STKS 7f (F)
1:20 (1:20) (Class 5) 3-Y-0 **£4,533** (£1,348; £674; £336) **Stalls** Low

Form RPR
651- **1** **Intersky Sports (USA)**[21] 6872 3-8-12 64....................(p) DeanMcKeown 5 69
(K A Ryan) *mde virtually all: rdn 2f out: drvn ins last and hld on wl* **5/1**[3]
53-4 **2** *nk* **Racing Times**[6] 27 3-9-6 76.................... NCallan 1 76
(B J Meehan) *cl up: rdn 2f out: edgd lft and ev ch tl drvn ins last and no ex towards fin* **10/3**[2]
311- **3** *1 3/4* **Bussel (USA)**[19] 6894 3-9-6 78.................... TonyCulhane 3 71
(W J Haggas) *trckd ldng pair 1/2-way: rdn along over 2f out: drvn over 1f out and no imp* **8/11**[1]
541- **4** *nk* **My Mirasol**[22] 6859 3-8-7 59....................(p) PaulHanagan 4 57
(K A Ryan) *chsd ldrs: rdn along and outpcd over 2f out: kpt on ins last* **12/1**
0- **5** *5* **Irish Relative (IRE)**[153] 4251 3-8-10.................... PaulFessey 2 47
(T D Barron) *chsd ldrs to 1/2-way: sn outpcd and bhd* **66/1**
1m 31.42s (0.62) **Going Correction** -0.075s/f (Stan) 5 Ran SP% 106.8
Speed ratings (Par 97):93,92,90,90,84
CSF £20.08 TOTE £5.90: £1.90, £1.60; EX 25.60.
Owner Intersky Bloodstock **Bred** Joseph Lacombe Stables Inc **Trained** Hambleton, N Yorks
■ Stewards' Enquiry : Dean McKeown four-day ban: used whip with excessive frequency without allowing sufficient time to respond (Jan 20-23)

FOCUS
A modest event which was run at a sound pace. The first two came clear and the form looks straightforward enough rated around the second, fourth and fifth.

77 PONTINSBINGO.COM H'CAP 6f (F)
1:50 (1:52) (Class 6) (0-52,52) 4-Y-0+ **£2,388** (£705; £352) **Stalls** Low

Form RPR
034- **1** **Glamaraazi (IRE)**[50] 6538 4-8-12 **52**.................... PaulHanagan 4 66+
(R A Fahey) *chsd ldrs: rdn over 1f out: styd on u.p ins last to ld last 75 yds* **5/1**[1]
523- **2** *1 1/2* **Mind Alert**[10] 6981 6-8-10 **50**....................(v) MickyFenton 9 59
(D Shaw) *dwlt and rr: gd hdwy 1/2-way: rdn to ld appr last: drvn:. hdd and nt qckn last 75 yds* **5/1**[1]
01-3 **3** *3/4* **Penel (IRE)**[7] 9 6-8-7 **52**....................(p) RoryMoore(5) 5 59
(P T Midgley) *trckd ldrs. hdwy to ld wl over 1f out: sn rdn and hdd appr last: kpt on same pce* **6/1**[2]
021- **4** *3 1/2* **Orchestration (IRE)**[11] 6969 6-8-8 **48**....................(v) DaleGibson 11 44+
(M J Attwater) *bhd: wd st: hdwy 2f out: styd on u.p ins last: nrst fin* **6/1**[2]
60- **5** *hd* **Mouseen (IRE)**[19] 6898 4-8-5 **50**....................(b[1]) TolleyDean(5) 13 46+
(R A Harris) *swtchd lft s and bhd: pushed along and hdwy on inner whn n.m.r 1/2-way: sn rdn and kpt on same pce appr last* **33/1**
2- **6** *1 1/4* **Et Dona Ferentes**[13] 6944 4-8-10 **50**.................... PhillipMakin 3 42
(T D Barron) *prom: rdn along over 2f out: grad wknd* **10/1**
000- **7** *1/2* **Shadow Jumper (IRE)**[252] 1388 6-8-12 **52**....................(v) RobbieFitzpatrick 2 42
(J T Stimpson) *cl up: ev ch over 2f out: sn rdn and wknd over 1f out* **16/1**
200- **8** *1* **Howards Princess**[18] 6922 5-8-10 **50**....................(p) ChrisCatlin 7 37
(J Hetherton) *towards rr: effrt and n.m.r 1/2-way: kpt on u.p fnl 2f* **18/1**
4/5- **9** *nk* **Monda**[199] 2856 5-8-10 **50**.................... PaulMulrennan 6 37
(Miss J A Camacho) *cl up: rdn along over 2f out: grad wknd* **25/1**
606- **10** *hd* **Val De Maal (IRE)**[18] 6922 7-8-12 **52**....................(p) RobertWinston 10 38
(Miss J A Camacho) *midfield: n.m.r 1/2-way: nvr a factor* **8/1**[3]
003- **11** *3/4* **Amber Glory**[12] 6956 4-8-4 **47**....................(b) AndrewMullen(3) 14 31
(K A Ryan) *chsd ldrs on outer: rdn along over 2f out: grad wknd* **28/1**
003- **12** *1* **Union Jack Jackson (IRE)**[11] 6974 5-8-10 **50**......(b) DeanMcKeown 12 31
(J G Given) *midfield: rdn along and wkng whn n.m.r over 1f out* **8/1**[3]
100- **13** *3* **Bahamian Bay**[50] 6533 5-8-12 **52**.................... DeanMernagh 1 24
(M Brittain) *sn led: rdn along over 2f out: hdd wl over 1f out and sn wknd* **25/1**
006- **14** *1 1/2* **Far Note (USA)**[68] 6308 9-8-5 **48**....................(bt) MarcHalford(3) 8 15
(S R Bowring) *midfield: rdn along 1/2-way: sn wknd* **40/1**
1m 16.08s (-0.82) **Going Correction** -0.075s/f (Stan) 14 Ran SP% 120.9
Speed ratings (Par 101):102,100,99,94,94 92,91,90,90,89 88,87,83,81
CSF £27.29 CT £157.26 TOTE £5.80: £1.90, £1.70, £2.10; EX 22.40 Trifecta £95.00 Pool £228.95. - 1.71 winning units..
Owner Mr & Mrs A R Nemazee **Bred** A R Nemazee **Trained** Musley Bank, N Yorks
■ Stewards' Enquiry : Tolley Dean three-day ban: used whip with excessive frequency (Jan 20-22)

FOCUS
A moderate but open handicap for the class. The form looks sound rated through the runner-up and third.

78 PONTIN'S HOLIDAYS (S) STKS 1m 4f (F)
2:20 (2:21) (Class 6) 4-6-Y-0 **£2,184** (£644; £322) **Stalls** Low

Form RPR
140- **1** **Tiegs (IRE)**[12] 6959 5-8-12 47.................... ChrisCatlin 5 49
(P W Hiatt) *sn loed: rdn along 3f out: hdd wl over 1f out: sn drvn and edgd lft: styd on u.p ins last to ld nr line* **12/1**
604- **2** *hd* **Dream Forest (IRE)**[10] 6982 4-9-4 55.................... NCallan 4 58
(M S Saunders) *in tch: hdwy on outer over 4f out: c hallenged over 2f out: rdn to ld wl over 1f out: drvn ins last: hdd and no ex nr fin* **13/2**[3]
24-0 **3** *nk* **Mossmann Gorge**[7] 10 5-8-12 53....................(p) TolleyDean(5) 6 53
(R A Harris) *hld up in tch: hdwy over 3f out: rdn to chse ldrs over 1f out: sn drvn and ev ch ins last: no ex nr fin* **4/1**[2]
155- **4** *2* **Zaffeu**[9] 6995 6-9-3 52.................... RussellKennemore(5) 1 55
(A G Juckes) *hld up in rr: hdwy 4f out: rdn along over 2f out: styd on appr last: nrst fin* **4/1**[2]
000- **5** *1 1/2* **Futoo (IRE)**[12] 6852 6-9-3 37....................(b[1]) TonyCulhane 7 48
(D W Chapman) *trckd ldrs: rdn along 3f out: drvn and one pce fnl 2f* **40/1**
664- **6** *3* **Laurollie**[11] 6972 5-8-12 41.................... RichardThomas 9 38
(B P J Baugh) *trckd ldrs gng wl: smooth hdwy 4f out: cl up 3f out: sn rdn and btn over 2f out* **4/1**[2]
154- **7** *2* **Cool Isle**[22] 6860 4-8-13 52....................(b) JimmyQuinn 8 41+
(P Howling) *chsd wnr: rdn along 3f out: drvn 2f out and grad wknd* **7/2**[1]
30-0 **8** *3 1/2* **Come What July (IRE)**[7] 12 6-9-3 44....................(e) DeanMcKeown 3 35
(D Shaw) *a rr* **14/1**
2m 42.1s (0.01) **Going Correction** -0.075s/f (Stan)
WFA 4 from 5yo+ 4lb 8 Ran SP% 112.4
Speed ratings: 96,95,95,94,93 91,90,87
CSF £83.84 TOTE £11.70: £3.10, £2.30, £2.00; EX 55.10 Trifecta £204.40 part won. Pool £287.90. - 0.85 winning units..There was no bid for the winner. Dream Forest was claimed by T. R. Pearson for £6,000.
Owner The Fox Inn Partnership **Bred** Paradime Ltd **Trained** Hook Norton, Oxon

FOCUS
A modest seller, run in a time just over a second slower than the earlier apprentice handicap, and another contest at this meeting in which it paid to race up with the pace. The first three all appeared below their best.

79 PONTINS.COM H'CAP 5f (F)
2:50 (2:51) (Class 4) (0-85,85) 4-Y-0+ **£4,857** (£1,445; £722; £360) **Stalls** High

Form RPR
003- **1** **Magic Glade**[13] 6953 8-8-6 **73**.................... RichardThomas 3 84
(Tom Dascombe) *chsd ldrs: rdn along and hdwy 2f out: drvn to ld ins last: sn: drvn: edgd lft and kpt on* **6/1**[1]
010- **2** *1 1/4* **Dig Deep (IRE)**[25] 6830 5-9-0 **81**.................... TonyCulhane 8 87
(W J Haggas) *midfield and rdn along 1/2-way: hdwy wl over 1f out: styd on stronly ins last: nrst fin* **7/1**[2]
120- **3** *1/2* **Tartatartufata**[30] 6776 5-8-13 **80**....................(v) DanielTudhope 2 85
(D Shaw) *cl up on far side: hdwy 2f out: rdn to ld wl over 1f out: edgd lft and hdd ins last: one pce* **8/1**[3]
000- **4** *1/2* **Distinctly Game**[55] 6496 5-9-2 **83**.................... NCallan 5 86
(K A Ryan) *prom: rdn along wl over 1f out: drvn and one pce ins last* **50/1**
03-3 **5** *1/2* **Pawan (IRE)**[8] 5 7-8-10 **82**....................(b) AnnStokell(5) 12 83
(Miss A Stokell) *in tch:rdn along 2f out: kpt on ins last: nrst fin* **12/1**
415- **6** *hd* **Dancing Mystery**[35] 6720 13-9-2 **83**....................(b) StephenCarson 4 83
(E A Wheeler) *chsd ldrs: rdn along 2f out: sn one pce* **14/1**
55-2 **7** *1/2* **Maktavish**[7] 8 8-8-4 **71** oh8....................(b) PaulHanagan 7 69
(R Brotherton) *led: rdn along 2f out: hdd wl over 1f out and grad wknd* **9/1**
301- **8** *1 1/2* **Efistorm**[13] 6953 6-8-10 **80**.................... JasonEdmunds(3) 10 73
(J Balding) *in tch: rdn along 2f out: sn drvn and no impression* **6/1**[1]
000- **9** *1 1/4* **Anfield Dream**[20] 6882 5-8-2 **74**....................(v[1]) AndrewElliott(5) 1 63
(J R Jenkins) *cl up: ev ch 2f out: sn rdn and wknd over 1f out* **8/1**[3]
354- **10** *1* **Millinsky (USA)**[13] 6953 6-8-7 **74**.................... JamieMackay 13 59
(Rae Guest) *s.i.s: a rr* **25/1**
000- **11** *1 1/4* **Fromsong (IRE)**[10] 6984 9-9-4 **85**.................... ChrisCatlin 6 65
(D K Ivory) *midfield: rdn along 1/2-way: n.d* **25/1**
315- **12** *2 1/2* **Monashee Brave (IRE)**[108] 5532 4-8-9 **76**.................... GrahamGibbons 9 47
(J J Quinn) *dwlt: a towards rr* **6/1**[1]
125- **13** *3/4* **Pauvic (IRE)**[264] 1097 4-8-4 **74**.................... SaleemGolam(3) 14 43
(Mrs A Duffield) *dwlt: a rr* **25/1**
00/0 **14** *1* **Verite**[8] 3 4-8-4 **71** oh2....................(b[1]) JimmyQuinn 11 36
(A J McCabe) *dwlt: a rr* **100/1**
58.13 secs (-2.17) **Going Correction** -0.30s/f (Stan) 14 Ran SP% 116.4
Speed ratings (Par 105):105,103,102,101,100 100,99,97,95,93 91,87,86,84
CSF £42.93 CT £349.38 TOTE £7.90: £2.50, £2.60, £3.80; EX 70.20 Trifecta £238.70 part won. Pool £336.24. - 0.10 winning units..
Owner Alan Solomon **Bred** Juddmonte Farms **Trained** Lambourn, Berks

FOCUS
A very competitive sprint in which those that raced down the middle of the track always seemed to hold the advantage over those on the stands' side.
Dancing Mystery Official explanation: jockey said gelding hit its mouth leaving stalls

80 PONTIN'S BOOK EARLY H'CAP (DIV II) 1m (F)
3:20 (3:21) (Class 6) (0-60,60) 4-Y-0+ **£1,619** (£481; £240; £120) **Stalls** Low

Form RPR
51-2 **1** **Paso Doble**[8] 2 9-8-4 **53** ow2....................(p) JamesMillman(5) 6 63+
(D K Ivory) *cl up: led 3f out: rdn clr 11/2f out: kpt on ins last* **10/3**[2]
500- **2** *nk* **Parkview Love (USA)**[18] 6919 6-9-1 **59**....................(v) DanielTudhope 8 67
(D Shaw) *towards rr: hdwy 3f out: rdn to chse ldng pair wl over 1f out: drvn and kpt on ins last: jst hld* **13/2**
04-5 **3** *1 1/4* **Mister Benji**[8] 7 8-8-10 **54**.................... DeanMcKeown 7 60
(B P J Baugh) *trckd ldrs: hdwy to chse wnr over 2f out: rdn wl over 1f out: kpt on same pce ins last* **3/1**[1]

062- **4** *3 1/2* **Tip Top Style**[11] 6970 4-8-5 **49**........(tp) DaleGibson 1 48
(J Mackie) *chsd ldrs: rdn alon g over 2f out: sn drvn and wknd wl over 1f out* **10/1**

550- **5** *1 3/4* **Suffolk House**[12] 6959 5-7-11 **46** oh1........ DuranFentiman(5) 10 41
(M Brittain) *chsd ldrs on outer: rdn along over 2f out: sn drvn and wknd* **12/1**

020- **6** *nk* **Blue Empire (IRE)**[17] 6934 6-9-2 **60**........ RobertWinston 4 54
(C R Dore) *led: rdn along and hdd 3f out: sn drvn and wknd* **9/2**[3]

606- **7** *1 1/4* **Quiet Reading (USA)**[12] 6960 10-8-4 **48**........(v) HayleyTurner 9 40
(M R Bosley) *chsd ldrs: rdn along 3f out: sn wknd* **12/1**

040- **8** *2 1/2* **Borodinsky**[12] 6961 6-8-2 **46** oh1........ PaulHanagan 5 33
(R E Barr) *dwlt: a towards rr* **25/1**

000- **9** *hd* **Mi Odds**[21] 6871 11-8-4 **55**........ ClaireWheatcroft(7) 2 42
(Mrs N Macauley) *s.i.s: a rr* **66/1**

060- **10** *9* **Mister Maq**[31] 6758 4-8-6 **50**........(p) JimmyQuinn 3 19
(A Crook) *s.i.s: a rr* **20/1**

1m 42.7s (-1.90) **Going Correction** -0.075s/f (Stan) **30** Ran SP% **114.2**
Speed ratings (Par 101):106,105,104,100,99 98,97,95,94,85
CSF £24.18 CT £70.63 TOTE £4.10: £1.70, £2.00, £1.80; EX 26.90 Trifecta £144.20 Pool £397.21. - 2.75 winning units..
Owner Mrs H Brain **Bred** P Cutler **Trained** Radlett, Herts

FOCUS
Blue Empire made sure this was run at a good gallop and the winning time was decent for the class, 1.34 seconds quicker than the first division. The first three pulled clear and the form looks solid.

81 PONTIN'S H'CAP 6f (F)
3:50 (3:51) (Class 4) (0-85,85) 4-Y-0+ **£4,857** (£1,445; £722; £360) **Stalls** Low

Form RPR

660- **1** **Turn On The Style**[55] 6496 5-8-2 **76** ow2........(b) AndrewElliott(5) 2 93
(J Balding) *qckly away: mde all: rdn clr 2f out: styd on strly* **22/1**

140- **2** *3* **Zarzu**[37] 6690 8-8-9 **78**........ RobertWinston 8 86
(C R Dore) *dwlt and in rr: hdwy 1/2-way: swtchd wd 2f out: sn rdn and styd on ins last: nt rch wnr* **14/1**

442- **3** *2* **Jimmy The Guesser**[19] 6896 4-9-1 **84**........ HayleyTurner 3 86
(N P Littmoden) *chsd ldrs: hdwy 1/2-way: rdn to chse wnr wl over 1f out: sn drvn and one pce* **11/4**[2]

60-0 **4** *1* **Night Prospector**[4] 41 7-8-10 **84**........(p) TolleyDean(5) 4 83
(R A Harris) *keen: hld up: hdwy on inner 1/2-way: rdn along 2f out: kpt on same pce* **18/1**

004- **5** *shd* **Pinchbeck**[25] 6835 8-8-12 **81**........(p) MatthewHenry 9 80
(M A Jarvis) *chsd ldrs: rdn along over 2f out: kpt on same pce* **11/2**[3]

030- **6** *2 1/2* **Magic Rush**[10] 6986 5-8-5 **81**........ HaddenFrost(7) 6 72
(Mrs Norma Pook) *chsd ldrs: rdn over 2f out: grad wknd* **7/1**

000- **7** *1 3/4* **Polish Emperor (USA)**[13] 6953 7-8-7 **76**........(p) PaulHanagan 5 62
(D W Barker) *chsd ldrs: rdn along 1/2-way: sn wknd* **66/1**

021- **8** *9* **Quiet Times (IRE)**[25] 6835 8-9-2 **85**........(b) NCallan 1 44
(K A Ryan) *slowly into striode: a rr* **6/1**

63-2 **9** *7* **Pieter Brueghel (USA)**[8] 5 8-9-1 **84**........ AdrianTNicholls 7 22
(D Nicholls) *chsd wnr: rdn over 2f out: sn wknd* **5/2**[1]

1m 14.48s (-2.42) **Going Correction** -0.075s/f (Stan) **9** Ran SP% **115.2**
Speed ratings (Par 105):113,109,106,105,104 101,99,87,77
CSF £291.20 CT £1124.62 TOTE £28.80: £5.10, £3.40, £1.50; EX 193.70 TRIFECTA Not won. Place 6 £166.51, Place 5 £89.49..
Owner The Haydock Badgeholders **Bred** J And Mrs Bowtell **Trained** Scrooby, Notts
■ Stewards' Enquiry : Hadden Frost one-day ban: used whip with excessive frequency (Jan 20)

FOCUS
This looked a decent and competitive handicap beforehand, but it soon became a one-horse race. It was run at a furious gallop, they finished well spread out, and the winning time was very smart for the grade. The form has been rated around the runner-up, fourth and fifth.
Pieter Brueghel(USA) Official explanation: jockey said gelding bled from the nose
T/Jkpt: Part won. £53,860.20 to a £1 stake. Pool: £75,859.50 - 0.50 winning tickets. T/Plt: £264.10 to a £1 stake. Pool: £64,091.80. 177.10 winning tickets. T/Qpdt: £40.30 to a £1 stake. Pool: £5,943.70. 109.10 winning tickets. JR

[46]KEMPTON (A.W) (R-H)
Wednesday, January 10

OFFICIAL GOING: Standard
Wind: Moderate, half-against. Weather: Fine.

82 IBETX.COM H'CAP 5f (P)
1:20 (1:21) (Class 6) (0-58,58) 4-Y-0+ **£2,388** (£705; £352) **Stalls** High

Form RPR

50-0 **1** **Kempsey**[4] 47 5-8-9 **58**........(b) RyanBird(7) 12 67
(J J Bridger) *prom: chsd ldr 2f out: rdn to ld over 1f out: drvn and kpt on wl* **16/1**

035- **2** *1/2* **Vlasta Weiner**[12] 6974 7-8-1 **50**........(b) BarrySavage(7) 9 57
(J M Bradley) *prom: effrt to chse wnr 1f out: urged along and kpt on: a hld* **25/1**

24-4 **3** *3/4* **Muktasb (USA)**[4] 47 6-8-10 **52**........(v) NCallan 7 56
(D Shaw) *hld up in midfield: nt clr run briefly over 1f out: hrd rdn and styd on to take 3rd ins fnl f* **9/4**[1]

140- **4** *1/2* **Sir Loin**[119] 5286 6-8-8 **57**........(v) DanielleMcCreery(7) 8 60
(N Tinkler) *hld up in midfield: nt clr run over 1f out: drvn and styd on same pce* **10/1**

04-0 **5** *hd* **Egyptian Lord**[8] 8 4-8-10 **55**........(b) JerryO'Dwyer(3) 11 57
(Peter Grayson) *mde most: hanging and hdd over 1f out: nt qckn fnl f* **5/1**[2]

213- **6** *1/2* **Succeed (IRE)**[21] 6877 4-8-8 **57** ow2........ KylieManser(7) 3 57
(Mrs H Sweeting) *towards rr: prog on outer to chal over 1f out: bmpd along and wknd fnl f* **12/1**

343- **7** *nk* **Monte Major (IRE)**[10] 6994 6-8-8 **50**........(v) DeanMcKeown 4 49
(D Shaw) *hld up wl in rr: nt clr run over 1f out: drvn and styd on fnl f: nrst fin* **6/1**[3]

220- **8** *hd* **New Options**[10] 6994 10-9-1 **57**........(b) PaulHanagan 5 55
(Peter Grayson) *s.i.s: hld up in rr: effrt over 1f out: kpt on: nvr pce to rch ldrs* **14/1**

000- **9** *1* **Auentraum (GER)**[11] 6984 7-8-10 **55**........(p) JamesDoyle(3) 10 50
(Ms J S Doyle) *dwlt: wl in rr: prog on inner whn hmpd over 1f out: sn wknd* **14/1**

000- **10** *1 1/2* **Edin Burgher (FR)**[194] 3052 6-8-7 **52**........ MarcHalford(3) 1 41
(T T Clement) *dropped in fr wd draw and sn last: rdn 1/2-way: nvr a factor* **12/1**

000- **11** *4* **Sofinella (IRE)**[38] 6686 4-8-11 **53**........ ShaneKelly 6 28
(A W Carroll) *mostly chsd ldr to 2f out: wknd* **16/1**

000- **12** *hd* **Triskaidekaphobia**[10] 6994 4-9-2 **58**........(b) PaulFitzsimons 2 32
(Miss J R Tooth) *chsd ldrs: wd bnd over 3f out and rdn: sn lost pl and struggling* **33/1**

61.12 secs (0.72) **Going Correction** +0.10s/f (Slow) **12** Ran SP% **118.1**
Speed ratings (Par 101):98,97,96,95,94 94,93,93,91,89 82,82
CSF £359.87 CT £1266.17 TOTE £22.60: £5.80, £6.90, £1.50; EX 526.40.
Owner Terry Thorn **Bred** Mrs B Shirley **Trained** Liphook, Hants
■ A first winner for 16-year-old Ryan Bird.
■ Stewards' Enquiry : Danielle McCreery two-day ban: careless riding (Jan 21-22)

FOCUS
A typically competitive sprint handicap rated around the runner-up and fifth to their best recent form.
Monte Major(IRE) Official explanation: jockey said gelding was denied a clear run
Auentraum(GER) Official explanation: jockey said gelding was badly hampered
Sofinella(IRE) Official explanation: jockey said filly hung left

83 FOLLOW YOUR CONFERENCE WITH EVENING RACING CLASSIFIED STKS 6f (P)
1:50 (1:50) (Class 7) 4-Y-0+ **£1,365** (£403; £201) **Stalls** High

Form RPR

444- **1** **Teyaar**[28] 6805 11-9-0 44........ PaulFitzsimons 2 54
(M Wellings) *off the pce in midfield: urged along and clsd fr 2f out: rdn to ld 1f out: sn clr* **14/1**

403- **2** *1 1/4* **Beverley Beau**[28] 6805 5-8-7 45........ KristinStubbs(7) 8 50
(Mrs L Stubbs) *t.k.h early: hld up wl off the pce: clsd over 1f out: plld out and bmpd along fnl f: r.o to take 2nd last 75yds* **7/2**[2]

505- **3** *3/4* **A Teen**[11] 6981 9-9-0 43........ PaulDoe 12 48
(P Howling) *outpcd and pushed along in rr: prog whn nt clr run over 1f out: r.o wl to take 3rd nr fin* **8/1**[3]

300- **4** *3/4* **Christian Bendix**[12] 6974 5-9-0 45........ DeanCorby 11 46+
(P Howling) *mde most and set str pce: rdn and hanging 2f out: hdd and outpcd 1f out* **14/1**

000- **5** *1* **Double M**[23] 6855 10-9-0 44........(b) RichardThomas 3 43
(Mrs L Richards) *chsd ldng pair: swtchd ins to chal wl over 1f out: stl nrly upsides 1f out: wknd* **16/1**

060- **6** *2* **Drury Lane (IRE)**[13] 6962 7-9-0 42........(p) MatthewHenry 4 37
(D W Chapman) *chsd ldng pair: rdn 2f out: wknd fnl f* **33/1**

430- **7** *1/2* **Hilltop Fantasy**[23] 6854 6-9-0 45........ RossStudholme 5 35
(V Smith) *off the pce in midfield: tried to cl over 1f out: no hdwy fnl f* **12/1**

630- **8** *1 3/4* **Danethorpe (IRE)**[11] 6983 4-8-11 43........(v) AmirQuinn(3) 9 30
(D Shaw) *dwlt: t.k.h: hld up and sn wl off the pce: nvr rchd ldrs* **10/1**

040- **9** *hd* **Mostanad**[35] 6728 5-9-0 45........ JamieMackay 1 29
(J M Bradley) *outpcd and a wl off the pce in rr* **16/1**

02-1 **10** *nk* **Charlottebutterfly**[7] 22 7-9-6 45........ PaulEddery 6 34
(P J McBride) *dwlt: outpcd and a wl in rr* **11/4**[1]

0 **11** *1 1/2* **Newpark Spirit (IRE)**[4] 46 4-9-0 45........(p) LeeEnstone 10 24
(Patrick Morris, Ire) *pressed ldr to 2f out: wknd rapidly over 1f out* **12/1**

05-0 **12** *2 1/2* **Fancy You (IRE)**[7] 22 4-9-0 45........ JDSmith 7 16
(A W Carroll) *dwlt: a struggling in last pair* **20/1**

1m 14.36s (0.66) **Going Correction** +0.10s/f (Slow) **12** Ran SP% **117.3**
Speed ratings (Par 97):99,97,96,95,94 91,90,88,88,87 85,82
CSF £61.84 TOTE £11.40: £4.60, £1.70, £2.20; EX 50.30.
Owner Mark Wellings Racing **Bred** Cheveley Park Stud Ltd **Trained** Six Ashes, Shropshire

FOCUS
A highly competitive classified stakes in which Christian Bendix set a blistering pace. The level of the form looks alright judged on the performances of the second, third and fifth.
Double M Official explanation: jockey said gelding lost a shoe

84 PHOTOBOOKS FROM BONUSPRINT.COM MEDIAN AUCTION MAIDEN STKS 1m 3f (P)
2:20 (2:20) (Class 6) 4-6-Y-0 **£2,047** (£604; £302) **Stalls** High

Form RPR

0- **1** **Evolve (USA)**[264] 1119 4-8-12........ OscarUrbina 5 61+
(M Botti) *hld up in midfield: prog to chal over 2f out: led wl over 1f out: shkn up and a holding on fnl f* **7/2**[2]

340- **2** *1/2* **Can Can Star**[87] 5992 4-9-3 60........ NCallan 4 57
(A W Carroll) *hld up in midfield: prog to chse ldng pair jst over 2f out: drvn to chse wnr ins fnl f: clsd but a hld* **5/2**[1]

43-2 **3** *1* **Mighty Kitchener (USA)**[9] 1 4-9-3 57........ TonyCulhane 6 55
(P Howling) *trckd ldrs: led over 2f out to wl over 1f out: one pce fnl f* **7/2**[2]

54-5 **4** *6* **Iceni Warrior**[7] 18 5-9-6 41........ ShaneKelly 2 46
(P Howling) *hld up in rr: prog to chse ldng trio wl over 1f out: one pce and no imp* **8/1**

0- **5** *2 1/2* **Watchmaker**[122] 5203 4-9-3........ PaulDoe 3 42+
(W J Knight) *s.s: rn green in rr: hanging bdly lft fr 1/2-way: effrt over 2f out: sn wl outpcd* **9/2**[3]

00-0 **6** *3* **The Flying Peach**[9] 1 4-8-9 39........ JerryO'Dwyer(3) 7 32
(Miss Gay Kelleway) *chsd ldrs: easily lft bhd fr over 2f out* **66/1**

00- **7** *2 1/2* **Lady Lucas (IRE)**[32] 6765 4-8-12 30........ EdwardCreighton 8 28
(E J Creighton) *led to over 2f out: wknd* **66/1**

00-3 **8** *2 1/2* **Miss Sudbrook (IRE)**[7] 18 5-9-1 37........(v) ChrisCatlin 9 24
(A W Carroll) *chsd ldr to 3f out: wknd rapidly* **12/1**

9 *31* **White Cockade** 4-9-0........ JamesDoyle(3) 1 —
(Ms J S Doyle) *sn last: wknd over 3f out: t.o* **20/1**

2m 24.19s (1.51) **Going Correction** +0.10s/f (Slow)
WFA 4 from 5yo 3lb **9** Ran SP% **117.7**
Speed ratings: 92,91,90,86,84 82,80,78,56
CSF £12.83 TOTE £6.40: £2.00, £1.10, £1.30; EX 19.90.
Owner John M Carroll **Bred** Juddmonte Farms Inc **Trained** Newmarket, Suffolk

FOCUS
A moderate maiden and the form is limited by the performance of the 41-rated fourth.

85 IBETX.COM FILLIES' H'CAP 1m (P)
2:50 (2:51) (Class 6) (0-65,65) 4-Y-0+ **£3,238** (£963; £481; £240) **Stalls** High

Form RPR

142- **1** **One Night In Paris (IRE)**[40] 6666 4-9-1 **64**........ ShaneKelly 5 73+
(M J Wallace) *prom: led 3f out: urged along whn pressed 2f out: clr ins fnl f: rdn out* **5/2**[1]

232- **2** *1 1/4* **Chia (IRE)**[23] 6861 4-9-0 **63**........ HayleyTurner 6 69
(D Haydn Jones) *t.k.h: led for 2f: styd cl up: rdn and nt qckn over 2f out: kpt on fr over 1f out to take 2nd ins fnl f* **8/1**[2]

246- **3** *nk* **Tender The Great (IRE)**[33] 6752 4-9-2 **65**........ AdrianTNicholls 4 70
(B G Powell) *racd wd: hld up in rr: wd bnd over 3f out: prog 2f out: styd on wl to take 3rd wl ins fnl f* **12/1**

316- **4** *hd* **Moyoko (IRE)**[20] 6899 4-8-0 **56** .... LauraReynolds(7) 13 62+
(M Blanshard) *lost pl on inner after 2f: wl in rr after: bmpd along and n.m.r over 1f out: r.o fnl f: nrst fin* **14/1**

305- **5** *nk* **Red Sail**[31] 6775 6-8-5 **54** ....(b) PaulHanagan 9 58
(Dr J D Scargill) *hld up in midfield: nt qckn over 2f out: styd on fr over 1f out: nt rch ldrs* **10/1**

405- **6** *¾* **Tipsy Me**[40] 6664 4-8-9 **63** .... JamieMoriarty(5) 14 65
(M L W Bell) *hld up in midfield: effrt on inner over 2f out: disp 3rd over 1f out: fdd* **14/1**

610- **7** *½* **Mythical Charm**[25] 6841 8-8-7 **56** ....(t) MatthewHenry 1 57
(J J Bridger) *awkward s: t.k.h: hld up in last pair: v wd bnd over 3f out: swtchd ins and shuffled along: kpt on: nvr nr ldrs* **14/1**

05-0 **8** *hd* **Tuscarora (IRE)**[2] 70 8-8-4 **60** .... MarkCoumbe(7) 10 61
(A W Carroll) *t.k.h: sn hld up wl in rr: sme prog on inner 2f out: bmpd along and no imp ldrs fnl f* **20/1**

342- **9** *shd* **Myths And Verses**[18] 6934 4-8-9 **58** ....(p) NCallan 12 58
(K A Ryan) *sn prom: chsd wnr over 2f out: drvn to chal and clr of rest wl over 1f out: wknd rapidly ins fnl f: eased* **17/2**[3]

010- **10** *hd* **Lady Edge (IRE)**[89] 5954 5-8-11 **60** .... FergusSweeney 8 60?
(A W Carroll) *chsd ldrs: effrt over 2f out: nt run on over 1f out: wknd fnl f* **33/1**

554- **11** *¾* **Another Genepi (USA)**[116] 5388 4-9-2 **65** .... ChrisCatlin 3 63
(J W Hills) *hld up towards rr: nt clr run 2f out: pushed along and limited prog over 1f out: lost pl fnl f* **8/1**[2]

503- **12** *nk* **Look Of Eagles**[14] 6949 5-8-9 **58** .... JosedeSouza 11 56
(P F I Cole) *t.k.h: trckd ldrs: grad wknd fr over 1f out* **8/1**[2]

362- **13** *¾* **Kalatime (IRE)**[19] 5733 4-8-10 **59** ....(v[1]) RichardThomas 7 55
(M F Harris) *s.i.s: t.k.h early and hld up wl in rr: nt gng wl 3f out: no prog* **16/1**

00-0 **14** *1 ¾* **Fratt'n Park (IRE)**[7] 30 4-8-10 **62** .... AmirQuinn(3) 2 54
(J J Bridger) *t.k.h: led after 2f to 3f out: wknd* **25/1**

1m 41.4s (0.60) **Going Correction** +0.10s/f (Slow) **14** Ran SP% **126.6**
Speed ratings (Par 98):101,99,99,99,98 98,97,97,97,97 96,96,95,93
CSF £22.52 CT £217.57 TOTE £2.40: £1.20, £2.90, £4.50; EX 17.10.
Owner D Teevan **Bred** Ken Carroll **Trained** Newmarket, Suffolk
■ Shane Kelly's first winner since breaking his leg in a fall in August.

FOCUS
A messy race with several not getting the breaks and looking unlucky, but the front pair were out of trouble all the way and it was the favourite who came out on top. The form looks solid enough rated through the consistent pair that finished second and third.
Myths And Verses Official explanation: jockey said filly bled from the nose
Another Genepi(USA) Official explanation: jockey said filly was denied a clear run
Kalatime(IRE) Official explanation: jockey said filly suffered interference on the bend

86 PERSONALISED CARDS FROM BONUSPRINT.COM H'CAP 7f (P)
3:20 (3:20) (Class 6) (0-55,55) 4-Y-O+ **£1,943** (£578; £288; £144) **Stalls** High

Form RPR

000- **1** **Tyrone Sam**[20] 6897 5-9-0 **55** ....(b) NCallan 10 63
(K A Ryan) *chsd clr ldrs: rdn over 2f out: clsd to chal over 1f out: upsides last 100yds: won on the nod* **14/1**

50-4 **2** *shd* **Under Fire (IRE)**[2] 72 4-8-12 **53** .... HayleyTurner 5 61
(A W Carroll) *chsd clr ldr to 3f out: sn rdn: kpt on fr over 1f out to chal fnl f: upsides nr fin: jst pipped* **5/1**[2]

321- **3** *hd* **Burhaan (IRE)**[11] 6981 5-8-11 **52** .... PaulHanagan 12 59+
(J R Boyle) *wl plcd: trckd clr ldr 3f out gng easily: clsd to ld over 1f out: sn hrd pressed: hdd nr fin* **2/1**[1]

565- **4** *¾* **Labelled With Love**[36] 6713 7-8-11 **52** ....(t) PatCosgrave 9 57
(J R Boyle) *hld up in midfield and wl off the pce: prog over 2f out: clsd to chal and upsides over 1f out: wknd last 75yds* **8/1**

612- **5** *hd* **Midmaar (IRE)**[11] 6983 6-8-13 **54** ....(b) FergusSweeney 3 59
(M Wigham) *off the pce towards rr: effrt on outer over 2f out: prog to chse ldrs over 1f out: no imp fnl f* **6/1**[3]

110- **6** *nk* **Binnion Bay (IRE)**[23] 6855 6-8-11 **55** ....(b) AmirQuinn(3) 8 59
(J J Bridger) *dwlt: wl in rr and wl off the pce: prog on inner over 2f out: chsd ldrs over 1f out: no imp after* **16/1**

000- **7** *1* **Blue Knight (IRE)**[11] 6990 8-8-13 **54** .... TonyCulhane 7 55
(P Howling) *towards rr and off the pce: effrt over 2f out: kpt on same pce fr over 1f out* **33/1**

604- **8** *1* **Plausabelle**[11] 6993 6-8-12 **53** ....(b) JamieMackay 1 52
(G G Margarson) *s.i.s and dropped in fr wd draw: wl off the pce in last pair: sme prog on inner over 1f out: nvr rchd ldrs* **25/1**

006- **9** *nk* **Mister Incredible**[13] 6964 4-8-11 **55** .... SaleemGolam(3) 6 53
(V Smith) *a wl in rr and off the pce: modest late prog* **10/1**

554- **10** *2* **Simpsons Gamble (IRE)**[47] 6577 4-8-13 **54** .... RichardThomas 14 46
(R M Flower) *chsd clr ldrs: tried to cl 2f out: wknd over 1f out* **12/1**

020- **11** *1* **Double Valentine**[22] 6869 4-8-11 **52** .... ChrisCatlin 2 42
(R Ingram) *a wl in rr and wl off the pce* **25/1**

025- **12** *2 ½* **Make My Dream**[21] 6884 4-8-12 **53** ....(b) MatthewHenry 13 36
(J Gallagher) *blazed off in front and sn wl clr: hdd & wknd rapidly over 1f out* **10/1**

035- **13** *½* **Pain In The Neck (IRE)**[43] 6649 4-9-0 **55** ....(v[1]) ShaneKelly 4 37
(M J Wallace) *chsd clr ldrs for 3f: losing pl and nt looking keen over 2f out* **33/1**

1m 27.54s (0.74) **Going Correction** +0.10s/f (Slow) **13** Ran SP% **127.4**
Speed ratings (Par 101):99,98,98,97,97 97,96,94,94,92 91,88,87
CSF £85.20 CT £213.00 TOTE £22.80: £5.60, £1.90, £1.10; EX 123.90.
Owner B T McDonald **Bred** Lostford Manor Stud **Trained** Hambleton, N Yorks

FOCUS
A moderate handicap which saw the first six closely covered at the finish. The form looks fair enough rated through them.
Tyrone Sam Official explanation: trainer said, regarding apparent improvement in form, that the gelding appeared to have benefited from a three week rest and seems to respond best when ridden by N Callan.
Simpsons Gamble(IRE) Official explanation: jockey said gelding lost its action

87 FOLLOW YOUR MEETING WITH EVENING RACING CLASSIFIED STKS 2m (P)
3:50 (3:51) (Class 7) 4-Y-O+ **£1,365** (£403; £201) **Stalls** High

Form RPR

6/4- **1** **Nod's Star**[20] 6804 6-9-5 41 ....(t) ChrisCatlin 4 44
(Mrs L C Jewell) *settled in midfield: prog to ld wl over 2f out: sn drvn: hld on wl fr over 1f out* **20/1**

2 *¾* **Speed Winner (AUS)**[15] 8-9-5 35 ....(b) NCallan 11 43+
(G L Moore) *wl plcd: cl up gng easily over 3f out: barged through to press wnr over 2f out: hrd rdn and hld whn snatched up last 100yds* **8/11**[1]

442- **3** *2 ½* **Asleep At The Back (IRE)**[13] 6957 4-8-12 45 .... JamieMackay 10 40
(J G Given) *dwlt: rousted along to ld and set slow pce: hdd after 4f: led again over 3f out: racd awkwardly and hdd over 2f out: nt qckn* **3/1**[2]

00-6 **4** *1* **Starofthemorning (IRE)**[7] 18 6-9-5 36 .... PaulHanagan 5 39
(A W Carroll) *hld up in rr: rdn 4f out: prog over 2f out: kpt on same pce over 1f out* **14/1**

004- **5** *½* **Royal Sailor (IRE)**[12] 6971 5-9-5 40 .... MickyFenton 3 38
(J Ryan) *chsd clr ldrs: cl enough and rdn 3f out: nt qckn* **25/1**

500/ **6** *¾* **Charnwood Street (IRE)**[33] 420 8-9-5 30 ....(v) DeanMcKeown 1 38
(D Shaw) *hld up wl in rr: sme prog 4f out: outpcd over 2f out: plugged on* **33/1**

300- **7** *¾* **Tip Toes (IRE)**[10] 6995 5-9-5 43 .... ShaneKelly 2 37
(P Howling) *s.s: hld up wl in rr: sme prog 5f out: outpcd 3f out : plugged on* **8/1**[3]

/00- **8** *9* **Dueling B'Anjiz (USA)**[19] 6857 8-9-5 40 ....(t) EdwardCreighton 9 26
(E J Creighton) *a in rr: rdn and struggling over 5f out* **50/1**

006- **9** *1 ½* **Sunley Song**[19] 4687 4-8-12 45 .... FergusSweeney 8 24
(B G Powell) *a in rr: rdn 6f out: struggling fnl 4f* **16/1**

00-0 **10** *20* **The Rip**[7] 19 6-9-5 44 .... AdrianTNicholls 7 —
(R M Stronge) *hld up: plld way through to ld after 4f: hdd and hmpd over 2f out: wknd rapidly* **50/1**

3m 41.35s (9.95) **Going Correction** +0.10s/f (Slow)
WFA 4 from 5yo+ 7lb **10** Ran SP% **122.0**
Speed ratings (Par 97):79,78,77,76,76 76,75,71,70,60
CSF £35.74 TOTE £19.80: £3.70, £1.30, £1.30; EX 59.40.
Owner O J C Shannon **Bred** Kirtlington Stud Ltd **Trained** Sutton Valence, Kent
■ Stewards' Enquiry : Chris Catlin one-day ban: careless riding (Jan 25); further caution: careless riding

FOCUS
A dire affair, which produced a very slow winning time, and the form has been rated around the winner and fifth.

88 CANVAS PRINTS FROM BONUSPRINT.COM H'CAP (DIV I) 1m 4f (P)
4:20 (4:22) (Class 6) (0-65,65) 4-Y-O+ **£2,590** (£770; £385; £192) **Stalls** Centre

Form RPR

226- **1** **Amwell Brave**[10] 6995 6-9-1 **60** .... NCallan 4 69+
(J R Jenkins) *hld up in midfield: prog over 2f out: swtchd ins and rdn to ld wl over 1f out: sn clr: styd on wl* **9/1**

1/0- **2** *1 ¾* **Tresor Secret (FR)**[14] 6954 7-9-0 **59** .... JoeFanning 7 65
(J Gallagher) *prom: pressed ldr gng easily 3f out: poised to chal but surprised by wnr 2f out: wnt 2nd fnl f: no imp* **50/1**

60-2 **3** *1 ¼* **War At Sea (IRE)**[7] 16 5-9-6 **65** .... PaulHanagan 3 69
(A W Carroll) *hld up wl in rr: effrt over 2f out: prog but hanging over 1f out: r.o to take 3rd last stride* **13/2**[2]

016- **4** *shd* **Escoffier**[25] 6843 5-8-12 **57** .... ShaneKelly 9 61
(Pat Eddery) *led for 1f: trckd ldr: led 4f out: drvn and hdd wl over 1f out: fdd fnl f* **7/1**[3]

015- **5** *¾* **Noble Minstrel**[35] 6735 4-8-8 **60** ....(t) SaleemGolam(3) 14 63+
(S C Williams) *hld up in midfield: nt clr run wl over 2f out: prog to chse ldrs over 1f out: no imp* **9/4**[1]

50-4 **6** *1* **Dovedon Hero**[7] 29 7-9-5 **64** ....(b) TonyCulhane 13 65
(P J McBride) *hld up wl in rr: prog on inner fr over 2f out: chsd ldrs over 1f out: nt qckn* **9/1**

000- **7** *shd* **Consuelita**[28] 6810 4-8-0 **56** .... KMay(7) 10 57
(B J Meehan) *hld up in midfield: lost pl and rdn 4f out: sn wl in rr: kpt on again over 1f out* **25/1**

015- **8** *hd* **Wee Charlie Castle (IRE)**[25] 6843 4-9-2 **65** .... OscarUrbina 5 66
(G C H Chung) *dwlt: hld up wl in rr: effrt on outer over 2f out: one pce and no real imp* **13/2**[2]

/02- **9** *1 ¼* **Key Partners (IRE)**[14] 6954 6-9-6 **65** .... ChrisCatlin 1 64
(B D Leavy) *hld up wl in rr: effrt on wd outside over 2f out: hanging and nt qckn wl over 1f out* **16/1**

513- **10** *1* **Wise Choice**[66] 5247 4-8-5 **54** .... RichardThomas 2 51
(N P Littmoden) *led after 1f to 4f out: sn rdn and lost pl* **11/1**

605- **11** *1* **Zacatecas (GER)**[27] 6816 7-9-3 **62** .... DeanMcKeown 11 58
(A J Chamberlain) *hld up: last 3f out: shkn up and no real prog* **66/1**

03-6 **12** *1 ¼* **Serramanna**[7] 16 6-8-7 **55** .... JerryO'Dwyer(3) 6 49
(Ms J S Doyle) *hld up: prog on outer to chse ldrs 5f out: rdn over 3f out: wknd wl over 1f out* **14/1**

000/ **13** *nk* **Dolzago**[416] 6308 7-9-1 **60** ....(b) FergusSweeney 8 53
(G L Moore) *hld up in midfield: rdn over 2f out: wknd over 1f out* **66/1**

026- **14** *3 ½* **Lennoxtown (IRE)**[19] 6911 4-8-9 **58** ow2 .... MickyFenton 12 46
(J Ryan) *trckd ldrs: cl up over 2f out: wknd wl over 1f out: eased* **14/1**

2m 35.88s (-1.02) **Going Correction** +0.10s/f (Slow)
WFA 4 from 5yo+ 4lb **14** Ran SP% **126.3**
Speed ratings (Par 101):101,99,99,98,98 97,97,97,96,96 95,94,94,92
CSF £421.88 CT £3131.66 TOTE £14.40: £3.80, £11.80, £1.90; EX 334.50.
Owner Amwell Racing **Bred** Wayland Stud **Trained** Royston, Herts

FOCUS
The first division of the handicap was the slightly weaker of the pair. The form has been rated around the fourth and fifth.

89 CANVAS PRINTS FROM BONUSPRINT.COM H'CAP (DIV II) 1m 4f (P)
4:50 (4:53) (Class 6) (0-65,65) 4-Y-O+ **£2,590** (£770; £385; £192) **Stalls** Centre

Form RPR

001- **1** **Street Life (IRE)**[12] 6980 9-9-4 **63** .... TonyCulhane 10 73
(W J Musson) *hld up wl in rr: prog 2f out: sn urged along: r.o wl to ld last 75yds: sn clr* **2/1**[1]

503- **2** *1 ½* **Magic Amigo**[25] 6843 6-9-1 **60** .... NCallan 12 68
(J R Jenkins) *hld up towards rr: prog over 2f out: rdn to chal over 1f out : upsides 100yds out: sn outpcd by wnr* **16/1**

662- **3** *½* **Recalcitrant**[19] 6911 4-8-5 **54** .... AdrianTNicholls 7 61
(S Dow) *led for 1f: styd prom: rdn 5f out: effrt to ld over 2f out: kpt on tl hdd and outpcd last 75yds* **9/1**[3]

004- **4** *¾* **Lord Laing (USA)**[25] 6843 4-8-7 **59** .... JerryO'Dwyer(3) 8 65
(H J Collingridge) *hld up towards rr: prog gng wl 3f out: rdn to press ldrs over 1f out: nt qckn* **20/1**

50-5 **5** *½* **Liberty Run (IRE)**[7] 29 5-9-6 **65** .... ChrisCatlin 11 70
(Mouse Hamilton-Fairley) *trckd ldrs: pushed along over 4f out: effrt over 2f out: kpt on same pce* **9/1**[3]

001- **6** *½* **Hallings Overture (USA)**[38] 6693 8-8-13 **58** .... PaulEddery 9 65+
(C A Horgan) *s.s: hld up in last: prog on inner over 2f out: nt clr run twice over 1f out: fin wl: no ch* **16/1**

601- **7** *½* **Maximix**[37] 6037 4-9-2 **65** .... FergusSweeney 2 69
(G L Moore) *hld up in midfield: effrt 3f out: rdn to chse ldrs over 1f out: no imp after* **10/1**

123- **8** 1 ¼ **Boppys Pride**[48] 6571 4-8-8 **57**........ PaulHanagan 4 59
(R A Fahey) *hld up wl in rr: effrt whn nt clr run jst over 2f out: nt rcvr* **9/4**[2]
006- **9** 1 ¼ **Atlantic City**[21] 6883 6-8-6 **51** oh1........(p) RichardThomas 5 51
(Mrs L Richards) *hld up in last trio: struggling wl over 2f out: modest late prog* **50/1**
001- **10** 2 **Emilion**[19] 6923 4-8-7 **56**........ JoeFanning 6 52
(W R Muir) *trckd ldrs: rdn over 2f out: fnd nil and sn btn* **14/1**
555- **11** 2 **Three Thieves (UAE)**[14] 6954 4-8-12 **61**........ ShaneKelly 1 54+
(M S Saunders) *hld up in rr: stl t.k.h whn effrt on inner over 2f out: nt appear to have clr run and snatched up: no ch after* **16/1**
056- **12** 2 ½ **Top Seed (IRE)**[21] 6885 6-9-6 **65**........ DeanMcKeown 13 54
(A J Chamberlain) *prom: chsd ldr 6f out to 4f out: wknd* **25/1**
062/ **13** 1 **Party Ploy**[547] 3419 9-9-0 **59**........ PatCosgrave 3 47
(K R Burke) *trckd ldrs on outer: rdn 3f out: wknd over 2f out* **66/1**
344- **14** 3 ½ **Executive Paddy (IRE)**[15] 6861 8-9-6 **65**........ LeeEnstone 14 47
(I A Wood) *plld hrd: led after 1f to over 2f out: wkng whn hmpd sn after* **18/1**

2m 34.43s (-2.47) **Going Correction** +0.10s/f (Slow) **14** Ran SP% **134.8**
WFA 4 from 5yo+ 4lb
Speed ratings (Par 101):106,105,104,104,103 103,103,102,101,100 98,97,96,94
CSF £41.02 CT £271.94 TOTE £4.10: £1.50, £5.00, £3.80; EX 48.20 Place 6 £21.16, Place 5 £7.96..
Owner W J Musson **Bred** Derek Veitch **Trained** Newmarket, Suffolk
FOCUS
This second division looked the stronger of the two and was run at a strong gallop. The form looks solid and the winner ran to his best mark since 2005.
T/Jkpt: Not won. T/Plt: £18.40 to a £1 stake. Pool: £52,911.50. 2,090.40 winning tickets. T/Qpdt: £3.70 to a £1 stake. Pool: £3,152.90. 627.70 winning tickets. JN

[52]LINGFIELD (L-H)

Wednesday, January 10

OFFICIAL GOING: Standard
Wind: Blustery, against races 1-3, half-across races 4-7. Weather: Overcast.

90 GO PONTIN'S APPRENTICE CLAIMING STKS 6f (P)
1:00 (1:00) (Class 6) 3-Y-O **£2,184** (£644; £322) **Stalls** Low

Form RPR
12-2 **1** **New York Oscar (IRE)**[4] 54 3-9-8 66........ AndrewElliott 6 71+
(A M Hales) *t.k.h: hld up: shkn up and hdwy 2f out: rdn to ld ins fnl f: sn clr: easily* **4/9**[1]
354- **2** 3 ½ **Cantique (IRE)**[26] 6834 3-9-2 61........(p) TolleyDean(3) 3 58
(A G Newcombe) *sn led: rdn over 2f out: hdd over 1f out: kpt on but nt pce of wnr ins fnl f* **6/1**[3]
53-0 **3** 1 ¼ **Splendidio**[7] 17 3-8-6 52........ JamesMillman(3) 1 44
(D K Ivory) *chsd ldrs: wnt 2nd after 2f: rdn to chal 2f out: led over 1f out tl ins fnl f: wknd last 100 yds* **11/2**[2]
610- **4** nk **Totally Free**[14] 6951 3-9-3 58........(v) FrankiePickard(5) 7 56
(M D I Usher) *hld up in last: rdn and effrt 2f out: styd on ins fnl f: nvr trbld ldrs* **9/1**
05-0 **5** 16 **Ivorys Song**[7] 17 3-8-8........ JamieJones(3) 4 —
(D K Ivory) *pressed ldr for 2f: rdn over 3f out: sn struggling: t.o* **40/1**

1m 12.89s (0.08) **Going Correction** -0.125s/f (Stan) **5** Ran SP% **111.4**
Speed ratings (Par 95):94,89,87,87,65
CSF £3.77 TOTE £1.20: £1.02, £3.10; EX 2.90 Trifecta £3.80 Pool £225.60. - 41.08 winning units..New York Oscar (IRE) was claimed by Mr Paul J. Dixon for £9,000.
Owner Brick Farm Racing **Bred** Corduff Stud And J Judd **Trained** Preston Capes, Northants
FOCUS
The winner was entitled to land the race on official figures, and did so nicely. The form is not easy to assess but has been rated around the fourth to its best and runner-up close to its mark.

91 PONTINS.COM H'CAP 6f (P)
1:30 (1:31) (Class 5) (0-75,75) 4-Y-O+ **£2,914** (£867; £433; £216) **Stalls** Low

Form RPR
40-2 **1** **Sun Catcher (IRE)**[7] 28 4-9-1 **74**........ RichardHughes 6 85
(R Hannon) *trckd ldr: rdn over 2f out: sn ev ch: drvn to ld wl ins fnl f: r.o wl* **7/4**[1]
303- **2** 1 **Quality Street**[22] 6865 5-7-13 **65** ow2........(p) JosephWalsh(7) 3 73
(P Butler) *led: rdn wl over 1f out: kpt on wl tl hdd and nt pce of wnr wl ins fnl f* **16/1**
362- **3** shd **Lucayos**[13] 6966 4-8-10 **72**........ RichardKingscote(3) 9 80
(Mrs H Sweeting) *in tch on outer: rdn and effrt 2f out: edgd lft over 1f out: styd on ins fnl f: nt rch ldrs* **12/1**
433- **4** ½ **Who's Winning (IRE)**[11] 6984 6-8-13 **72**........(t) FergusSweeney 8 78
(B G Powell) *racd in midfield: hdwy and rdn over 2f out: chsd ldrs over 1f out: same pce u.p ins fnl f* **6/1**[2]
051- **5** 1 **Mistral Sky**[11] 6984 8-8-8 **67** ow2........(p) MickyFenton 7 70
(Stef Liddiard) *chsd ldrs: rdn 3f out:bmpd over 1f out: kpt on same pce* **8/1**[3]
00-5 **6** ¾ **Mambazo**[2] 67 5-8-8 **70**........(e) SaleemGolam(3) 10 71
(S C Williams) *taken down early: stdd s: hld up in rr: hdwy and rdn over 1f out: no imp wl ins fnl f* **10/1**
00- **7** 1 ¾ **Nusoor (IRE)**[50] 6555 4-8-11 **70**........ BrettDoyle 12 66
(Peter Grayson) *stdd s: plld v hrd and racd wd: in tch rdn wl over 1f out: kpt on same pce* **9/1**
063- **8** ½ **Kingscross**[21] 6882 9-9-2 **75**........ JimmyQuinn 1 69
(M Blanshard) *slowly away: bhd: effrt and hdwy on inner over 2f out: wknd fnl f* **10/1**
003/ **9** hd **Lake Hero**[458] 5755 4-8-12 **71**........ JamieSpencer 4 65
(M J Wallace) *stdd s: hld up wl bhd: c wd wl over 1f out: n.d* **16/1**
010- **10** 1 **No Time (IRE)**[27] 6823 7-8-12 **71**........ TPQueally 5 62
(A J McCabe) *hld up in midfield on inner: rdn and effrt jst over 2f out: btn over 1f out* **25/1**
005- **11** ¾ **Fateful Attraction**[31] 6781 4-8-8 **67**........(b) JoeFanning 2 55
(I A Wood) *chsd ldrs: rdn over 2f out: wknd over 1f out: eased wl ins fnl f* **14/1**

1m 10.8s (-2.01) **Going Correction** -0.125s/f (Stan) **11** Ran SP% **119.9**
Speed ratings (Par 103):108,106,106,105,104 103,101,100,100,98 97
CSF £34.57 CT £279.81 TOTE £2.90: £1.10, £4.20, £3.50; EX 27.60 Trifecta £146.30 Part won. Pool £206.10 - 0.73 winning units..
Owner A F Merritt **Bred** Johnston King **Trained** East Everleigh, Wilts
FOCUS
A fair handicap run at a sound pace in a decent time. The form has been rated through the fifth and the runner-up and sixth to their 2006 Turf marks.

92 PONTIN'S HOLIDAYS MAIDEN STKS 1m (P)
2:00 (2:00) (Class 5) 4-Y-O+ **£2,817** (£838; £418; £209) **Stalls** High

Form RPR
1 **Zam Zammah** 4-9-3........ JamieSpencer 2 78+
(Sir Michael Stoute) *slowly away and rn green early: hld up in last: hdwy to trck ldrs 2f out: cruised up to ld ins fnl f: nt extended* **4/11**[1]
4- **2** 1 **Priceoflove (IRE)**[32] 6771 4-8-12 67........(t) SebSanders 5 54
(P J Makin) *t.k.h: hld up in midfield: rdn and hdwy 3f out: led 2f out: hdd ins fnl f: no ch w wnr* **9/2**[2]
00-0 **3** 1 ½ **Oasis Sun (IRE)**[7] 18 4-8-12 45........(v[1]) BrettDoyle 4 51
(J R Best) *t.k.h: chsd ldr for 2f: prom: rdn to ld over 2f out : hdd 2f out: outpcd ins fnl f* **33/1**
024- **4** 1 **Simpsons Ross (IRE)**[46] 6593 4-9-3 59........ DanielTudhope 3 54
(R M Flower) *hld up towards rr: effrt and nt clr run briefly wl over 1f out: kpt on same pce* **7/1**[3]
600- **5** ¾ **Pantomime Prince**[46] 6606 4-9-3 40........ MickyFenton 8 52
(John Berry) *t.k.h: hld up in last pair: rdn and hdwy to join ldrs over 3f out: kpt on same pce fr over 1f out* **50/1**
/45- **6** 1 ¼ **Fly By Jove (IRE)**[19] 6914 4-9-3 55........ DaleGibson 7 49
(Jane Southcombe) *t.k.h: trckd ldrs on outer: rdn over 2f out: outpcd 2f: kpt on onepced* **50/1**
000- **7** hd **Russian Mist (IRE)**[222] 2209 4-9-3 65........ PaulMulrennan 1 49
(M J Wallace) *trckd ldr: wnt 2nd after 2f tl over 3f out: wknd over 2f out* **20/1**
630/ **8** 1 **Thomas Lawrence (USA)**[858] 5306 6-9-3 65........ JimmyQuinn 6 46
(G A Ham) *t.k.h: led at stdy pce tl hdd over 2f out: wknd 2f out* **33/1**

1m 41.36s (1.93) **Going Correction** -0.125s/f (Stan) **8** Ran SP% **118.6**
Speed ratings (Par 103):85,84,82,81,80 79,79,78
CSF £2.37 TOTE £1.50: £1.10, £1.10, £7.60; EX 3.50 Trifecta £21.30 Pool £368.89. - 12.24 winning units..
Owner S P C Woods **Bred** Haydock Park Stud **Trained** Newmarket, Suffolk
FOCUS
Impossible form to rate. The winner, who has been rated value for seven lengths, could be useful, but the early gallop was very slow and the proximity of the 45-rated third also limits the form.

93 PONTINSBINGO.COM H'CAP 1m (P)
2:30 (2:31) (Class 6) (0-65,65) 3-Y-O **£2,388** (£705; £352) **Stalls** High

Form RPR
420- **1** **Tilapia (IRE)**[15] 6940 3-8-11 **60**........ SebSanders 5 70+
(Sir Mark Prescott) *led after 1f: mde rest: rdn wl over 2f out: clr wl over 1f out: r.o strly* **4/1**[3]
32-4 **2** 4 **A Nod And A Wink (IRE)**[7] 25 3-8-1 **53**........ StephaneBreux(3) 2 52
(R Hannon) *taken down early: slowly away: t.k.h: hld up in rr: hdwy 3f out: chsd ldrs wl over 1f out: kpt on to go 2nd on line: no ch* **8/1**
52-3 **3** hd **First Princess (IRE)**[7] 21 3-9-2 **65**........(p) RichardHughes 4 64
(J S Moore) *stdd s: hld up: hdwy to trck ldrs 3f out: rdn over 2f out: no ch w wnr: wnt 2nd last 100 yds tl demoted on line* **10/3**[2]
044- **4** nk **Ice Box (IRE)**[15] 6940 3-8-10 **59**........ JoeFanning 1 57
(M Johnston) *prom: ev ch 3f out: rdn over 2f out: sn outpcd by wnr : tired and lost 2 pls last 100 yds* **5/2**[1]
032- **5** 3 ½ **My Jeanie (IRE)**[23] 6853 3-8-5 **54**........ AdrianMcCarthy 9 44
(J C Fox) *hld up in rr: rdn and outpcd wl over 2f out: kpt on ins fnl f: n.d* **14/1**
044- **6** 1 ½ **Ponte Vecchio (IRE)**[33] 6746 3-7-12 **52**........ DuranFentiman(5) 7 38
(J R Boyle) *stdd s: hld up in last: rdn and effrt wl over 2f out: n.d* **33/1**
000- **7** ¾ **Da Schadenfreude (USA)**[109] 5527 3-9-2 **65**........ DaleGibson 8 50
(W G M Turner) *led for 1f: chsd ldrs: rdn wl over 2f out: wknd 1f out* **14/1**
60-2 **8** ½ **Ranavalona**[7] 25 3-7-9 **51** oh1........(v) DavidProbert(7) 10 34
(A M Balding) *racd wd: hld up in midfield: hdwy to chse ldrs over 3f out: hung rt and rn wd bnd over 2f out: nt rcvr and no ch after* **6/1**
040- **9** 1 **Briarwood Bear**[20] 6900 3-9-1 **64**........ JimmyQuinn 3 45
(M Blanshard) *sn pushed along: in tch in midfield: rdn over 3f out: sn outpcd* **33/1**
006- **10** 5 **Deep Cover (IRE)**[42] 6650 3-8-9 **58**........ DanielTudhope 6 28
(R M Flower) *towards rr: rdn over 4f out: wl bhd last 2f* **33/1**

1m 38.08s (-1.35) **Going Correction** -0.125s/f (Stan) **10** Ran SP% **119.2**
Speed ratings (Par 95):101,97,96,96,93 91,90,90,89,84
CSF £36.26 CT £116.46 TOTE £5.90: £3.10, £3.60, £1.30; EX 39.50 Trifecta £73.20 Pool £351.62. - 3.41 winning units..
Owner G D Waters **Bred** G D Waters **Trained** Newmarket, Suffolk
FOCUS
A modest handicap run at a fair pace. The form, rated around the consistent second and third, looks sound for the level

94 PONTIN'S FAMILY HOLIDAYS H'CAP 1m (P)
3:00 (3:00) (Class 6) (0-50,50) 4-Y-O+ **£2,388** (£705; £352) **Stalls** High

Form RPR
01- **1** **Freda's Choice (IRE)**[37] 6707 4-8-11 **50**........(b) DanielTudhope 2 56
(Patrick Morris, Ire) *trckd ldrs: rdn to ld 2f out: hrd rdn wl over 1f out: hld on: all out* **7/1**
010- **2** hd **Mon Petite Amour**[11] 6981 4-8-10 **49**........(p) BrettDoyle 5 55
(D W P Arbuthnot) *hld up towards rr: hdwy over 2f out: c wd wl over 1f out: r.o wl fnl f: jst hld* **9/1**
006- **3** shd **Red Raptor**[14] 6955 6-8-4 **50**........(t) HaddenFrost(7) 12 56
(J A Geake) *plld hrd: sn pressing ldr: led 3f out: hdd 2f out: edgd rt fnl f: unable qck nr fin* **12/1**
310- **4** ½ **Stoneacre Fred (IRE)**[11] 6983 4-8-6 **50**........ DuranFentiman(5) 10 55
(Peter Grayson) *stdd s and dropped in bhd: stl plenty to do wl over 1f out: weaved through and str run fnl f: nt quite rch ldrs* **11/1**
05-2 **5** nk **Show Me The Lolly (FR)**[7] 19 7-8-9 **48**........ TPQueally 3 55+
(P J McBride) *hld up in rr: hdwy 3f out: plld out wl over 1f out: short of room briefly ins fnl f: r.o: nt rch ldrs* **4/1**[1]
045- **6** 1 **Jools**[11] 6983 9-8-4 **48**........ JamieJones(5) 7 50
(D K Ivory) *hld up in midfield: hdwy to chse ldrs over 2f out: kpt on same pce u.p ins fnl f* **5/1**[2]
030- **7** ¾ **Dexileos (IRE)**[23] 6855 8-8-5 **49**........(t) AshleyHamblett(5) 4 50
(David Pinder) *chsd ldrs: rdn over 2f out: kpt on same pce fnl f* **14/1**
500/ **8** 1 ¼ **Lake Carezza (USA)**[515] 4376 5-8-4 **50**........ SladeO'Hara(7) 11 48
(N J Hawke) *s.i.s: hdwy on outer over 3f out: chsd ldrs and rdn over 2f out: wkng whn short of room briefly over 1f out* **50/1**
634- **9** 2 ½ **Tartan Special**[35] 6725 5-8-6 **50**........(p) AndrewElliott(5) 1 43
(K R Burke) *chsd ldrs on inner: lost pl wl over 2f out: no ch after* **5/1**[2]
000- **10** 1 ½ **Opal Warrior**[12] 6977 4-8-11 **50**........ DaleGibson 9 40
(Jane Southcombe) *a bhd and racd wd: n.d* **33/1**

000- **11** *1 3/4* **Korolieva (IRE)**[32] 6756 4-8-11 **50**..............................(p) PaulMulrennan 6 37
(K A Ryan) *chsd ldrs: rdn over 3f out: wknd over 2f out* **33/1**

600- **12** *26* **You're My Son**[30] 6793 5-8-11 **50**..............................(b[1]) RichardHughes 8 —
(A B Haynes) *t.k.h: sn led: hdd 3f out: sn wknd: eased last 2f: t.o* **6/1**[3]

1m 38.55s (-0.88) **Going Correction** -0.125s/f (Stan) **12** Ran SP% **120.7**
Speed ratings (Par 101):99,98,98,98,97 96,96,94,92,90 89,63
CSF £69.01 CT £766.37 TOTE £5.00: £3.00, £3.40, £3.40; EX 66.10 Trifecta £182.00 Part won. Pool £256.35 - 0.33 winning units..
Owner D Veitch **Bred** Thomas Heatrick **Trained** Ruanbeg, Co. Kildare

FOCUS
Moderate form, but very competitive, and the race should produce some winners in similar company. The winning time was 0.47 seconds slower than the previous mile handicap won by 60-rated Tilapia. The race has been rated through the third to his previous best.
You're My Son Official explanation: jockey said gelding hung left

95 GO PONTIN'S H'CAP — 1m 4f (P)
3:30 (3:30) (Class 4) (0-85,85) 4-Y-0+ **£4,857** (£1,445; £722; £360) **Stalls** Low

Form RPR

222- **1** **Eva Soneva So Fast (IRE)**[19] 6917 5-9-6 **85**.................. JimmyQuinn 8 100+
(J L Dunlop) *hld up in midfield: hdwy to chse ldr gng wl over 2f out: rdn to ld wl over 1f out: rdn out* **9/2**[2]

5/2- **2** *2* **Watamu (IRE)**[21] 6888 6-9-4 **83**.. SebSanders 9 92
(P J Makin) *t.k.h: trckd ldrs: rdn to chse ldng pair over 2f out: flashed tail twice u.p: wnt 2nd nr fin: nt trble wnr* **2/1**[1]

014- **3** *nk* **Polish Power (GER)**[19] 6917 7-8-13 **78**............................ DaleGibson 1 87
(J S Moore) *in tch: hdwy to go prom 7f out: chsd ldr and rdn over 4f out: led 3f out: hdd wl over 1f out: onepced: lost 2nd nr fin* **12/1**

012- **4** *1 3/4* **Turner's Touch**[21] 6885 5-8-8 **73**....................................(be) BrettDoyle 10 79
(G L Moore) *hld up in last pair: rdn and effrt over 2f out: kpt on but nvr pce to rch ldrs* **10/1**

106- **5** *3* **Prince Charlemagne (IRE)**[11] 6992 4-8-12 **84**............ JamesDoyle(3) 4 85
(N P Littmoden) *hld up in tch: rdn and effrt 2f out: sn no imp* **10/1**

121- **6** *5* **Nando's Dream**[46] 6602 4-8-6 **75**.. TPQueally 6 69
(J Noseda) *t.k.h: trckd ldrs: hdwy over 3f out: rdn over 2f out: wknd over 1f out* **5/1**[3]

040- **7** *1/2* **Kylkenny**[21] 6888 12-8-4 **76**.......................................(t) FrankiePickard(7) 2 69
(H Morrison) *t.k.h: hld up in rr: rdn and effrt 2f out: nvr nr ldrs* **33/1**

600- **8** *3 1/2* **Gold Gun (USA)**[90] 5920 5-9-1 **80**..............................(b[1]) PaulMulrennan 3 68
(K A Ryan) *led tl rdn and hdd 3f out: sn wknd* **50/1**

403- **9** *4* **Country Pursuit (USA)**[19] 6917 5-9-4 **83**.................... JamieSpencer 7 65
(C E Brittain) *bhd: hdwy on outer 7f out: lost pl over 3f out: no ch whn hung lft wl over 1f out* **9/2**[2]

605- **10** *shd* **Llamadas**[42] 6655 5-8-6 **78**.. HaddenFrost(7) 11 60
(C Roberts) *t.k.h: chsd ldr after 2f tl over 4f out: wknd 3f out* **25/1**

2m 30.8s (-3.59) **Going Correction** -0.125s/f (Stan)
WFA 4 from 5yo+ 4lb **10** Ran SP% **121.0**
Speed ratings (Par 105):106,104,104,103,101 97,97,95,92,92
CSF £14.28 CT £104.62 TOTE £7.90: £3.10, £1.20, £2.60; EX 22.20 Trifecta £101.40 Pool £607.31. - 4.25 winning units..
Owner Eurostrait Ltd **Bred** John O'Connor **Trained** Arundel, W Sussex

FOCUS
A reasonable middle-distance handicap featuring plenty of in-form recent winners. The pace was typical of Lingfield, though, as it was steady early before gradually increasing. It has been rated around the solid fourth and fifth, with the first three all rated as improving.
Country Pursuit(USA) Official explanation: jockey said gelding hung left

96 PONTIN'S "BOOK EARLY" H'CAP — 1m 2f (P)
4:00 (4:00) (Class 4) (0-85,83) 4-Y-0+ **£4,857** (£1,445; £722; £360) **Stalls** Low

Form RPR

034- **1** **Mataram (USA)**[22] 6868 4-8-9 **76**.. BrettDoyle 7 85
(W Jarvis) *hld up towards rr: rdn and gd hdwy over 2f out: led ins fnl f: jst hld on* **5/1**[2]

11- **2** *shd* **Rapid City**[25] 6848 4-8-7 **77**.. JamesDoyle(3) 8 89+
(Miss J Feilden) *hld up bhd: stl plenty to do and swtchd lft wl over 1f out: hdwy over 1f out: n.m.r ins last tl nr line: jst failed* **11/10**[1]

343- **3** *nk* **Atlantic Quest (USA)**[11] 6992 8-9-2 **81**............................ DaleGibson 4 89
(Miss Venetia Williams) *hld up in midfield: hdwy to chse ldrs 2f out: rdn and ev ch 1f out: unable qck nr fin* **9/1**

004- **4** *hd* **Snark (IRE)**[60] 6432 4-8-7 **74**...(t) TPQueally 6 82
(P J Makin) *prom: chsd ldr 8f out: led 2f out: sn rdn: hdd ins fnl f: no ex nr fin* **10/1**

131- **5** *2 1/2* **Daring Affair**[32] 6772 6-8-13 **78**.................................. PaulMulrennan 2 81
(K R Burke) *t.k.h: chsd ldrs: rdn 3f out: kpt on same pce u.p over 1f out* **14/1**

550- **6** *3/4* **Lake Poet (IRE)**[28] 6811 4-8-13 **80**.................................. JamieSpencer 9 82
(C E Brittain) *hld up in midfield: rdn and effrt whn struck into and lost action wl over 1f out: kpt on ins last: nt rch ldrs* **8/1**[3]

453- **7** *nk* **Royal Amnesty**[13] 6968 4-8-8 **75**.. JimmyQuinn 12 76
(G C H Chung) *stdd s: hld up bhd: rdn and c wd wl over 1f out: styd on ins fnl f: nt pce to trble ldrs* **14/1**

212- **8** *1* **Kabeer**[11] 6986 9-8-6 **76**...(t) NataliaGemelova(5) 5 75
(A J McCabe) *t.k.h: hld up wl in tch: hdwy to trck ldrs 4f out: rdn 2f out: ev ch over 1f out: fdd ins fnl f* **12/1**

/20- **9** *nk* **Art Modern (IRE)**[64] 5295 5-9-0 **79**.............................. RichardHughes 3 78
(G L Moore) *chsd ldr for 2f: rdn 3f out: wknd jst over 1f out* **20/1**

21-4 **10** *shd* **Foreign Language (USA)**[6] 38 4-8-0 **72**..................... AndrewElliott(5) 11 71
(N A Callaghan) *hmpd after 1f: hld up in rr: c wd and rdn bnd 2f out: no real hdwy* **20/1**

454- **11** *1 1/4* **Tous Les Deux**[15] 6941 4-7-12 **70**............................ DuranFentiman(5) 1 66
(Peter Grayson) *sddle slipped after 1f: racd in midfield tl dropped out over 2f out* **20/1**

200- **12** *2* **Kova Hall (IRE)**[15] 2989 5-9-4 **83**...........................(t) AdrianMcCarthy 10 76
(M F Harris) *led tl rdn and hdd 2f out: wknd qckly jst over 1f out* **66/1**

2m 6.58s (-1.21) **Going Correction** -0.125s/f (Stan)
WFA 4 from 5yo+ 2lb **12** Ran SP% **131.3**
Speed ratings (Par 105):99,98,98,98,96 95,95,94,94,94 93,91
CSF £11.56 CT £56.13 TOTE £10.00: £2.40, £1.10, £3.90; EX 20.30 Trifecta £70.20 Pool £426.35 - 4.31 winning units..Place 6 £44.91, Place 5 £35.89..
Owner Sales Race 2001 Syndicate **Bred** B P Walden Jr And James Anthony **Trained** Newmarket, Suffolk

FOCUS
A fair handicap, but again the pace was just steady. The race has been rated around the third.
Lake Poet(IRE) Official explanation: jockey said colt was struck into
Tous Les Deux Official explanation: jockey said saddle slipped
T/Plt: £27.20 to a £1 stake. Pool: £55,593.35. 1,487.85 winning tickets. T/Qpdt: £17.00 to a £1 stake. Pool: £3,536.80. 153.50 winning tickets. SP

74 SOUTHWELL (L-H)
Thursday, January 11

OFFICIAL GOING: Slow
After 10mm rain in the morning the meeting had to survive an inspection. The senior jockeys reported the surface rode as normal once it dried out.
Wind: strong, half-behind Weather: very windy, blustery showers

97 PONTINSBINGO.COM APPRENTICE CLAIMING STKS — 5f (F)
12:40 (12:46) (Class 6) 4-Y-0+ **£2,184** (£644; £322) **Stalls** High

Form RPR

041- **1** **Spirit Of Coniston**[15] 6943 4-8-9 50......................(b) DuranFentiman(3) 7 55
(Peter Grayson) *trckd ldr: led over 1f out: edgd lft ins last: jst hld on* **11/2**

036- **2** *shd* **Canadian Danehill (IRE)**[39] 6688 5-9-6 57.................(p) JerryO'Dwyer 8 63
(R M H Cowell) *trckd ldrs: n.m.r and swtchd lft over 2f out: wnt 2nd 1f out: styd on wl towards fin: jst failed* **10/3**[3]

316/ **3** *6* **Abientot (IRE)**[514] 4427 5-9-7 80................................ JamieMoriarty(3) 6 47
(D W Barker) *led: edgd rt: hdd over 1f out: sn wknd* **11/4**[1]

000- **4** *nk* **Luloah**[22] 6884 4-8-0 48.. DonnaCaldwell(5) 1 27
(P S McEntee) *swvd lft s: racd wd: prom: one pce fnl 2f* **17/2**

100- **5** *3/4* **She's Our Beauty (IRE)**[14] 6956 4-8-4 45...............(v) AndrewElliott(3) 3 26
(S T Mason) *dwlt: sn chsng ldrs on outer: edgd lft over 2f out: wknd fnl f* **20/1**

200- **6** *4* **City For Conquest (IRE)**[14] 6966 4-9-0 63...........(v) StephenDonohoe 5 19
(T J Pitt) *s.s: sme hdwy 2f out: sn wknd* **3/1**[2]

00-0 **7** *4* **Percy Douglas**[9] 8 7-9-7 47..............................(bt) MichaelJStainton(3) 2 16
(Miss A Stokell) *r wd: lost pl over 3f out: sn bhd* **20/1**

000- **8** *8* **Laurel Dawn**[13] 6969 9-9-10 41...................................... DanielTudhope 4 —
(Miss A Stokell) *bmpd s: sn outpcd and bhd* **50/1**

59.76 secs (-0.54) **Going Correction** -0.20s/f (Stan) **8** Ran SP% **112.1**
Speed ratings (Par 101):96,95,86,85,84 78,71,58
CSF £23.04 TOTE £4.80: £1.90, £1.60, £1.70; EX 17.40 Trifecta £53.10 Pool £290.26 - 3.88 winning units.There was no bid for the winner.
Owner Richard Teatum **Bred** Green Square Racing **Trained** Formby, Lancs
■ Stewards' Enquiry : Jamie Moriarty caution: careless riding

FOCUS
A typically modest claimer in which the first two finished clear.

98 GO PONTIN'S MAIDEN STKS — 1m 3f (F)
1:10 (1:11) (Class 5) 4-Y-0+ **£2,817** (£838; £418; £209) **Stalls** Low

Form RPR

1 **No Greater Love (FR)**[29] 5-9-6 78.................................... ChrisCatlin 10 53+
(Ian Williams) *chsd ldrs: hrd drvn over 4f out: styd on to ld last 75yds* **9/4**[1]

650/ **2** *1 3/4* **Mangrove Cay (IRE)**[504] 4700 5-9-6 55.................. SilvestreDeSousa 9 50
(A J Lockwood) *trckd ldrs: chal 3f out: led over 1f out: hdd and no ex ins last* **20/1**

30- **3** *nk* **Neshla**[12] 6987 4-8-12 .... JoeFanning 1 45
(C E Brittain) *led: t.k.h: hung lft and hdd over 1f out: kpt on same pce* **5/1**

60- **4** *3 1/2* **History Prize (IRE)**[31] 6792 4-8-12 .... JamesMillman(5) 4 44
(A G Newcombe) *hld up in rr: hdwy over 4f out: one pce fnl 2f* **10/1**

\- **5** *5* **Win In Gold**[193] 6-9-6 .... DaleGibson 5 36
(John A Harris) *s.i.s: sn pushed along and prom: wd bnd after 2f: outpcd over 2f out: kpt on fnl f* **50/1**

2/0- **6** *12* **Noah Jameel**[106] 5625 5-9-6 .... AdrianTNicholls 2 17
(A G Newcombe) *chsd ldrs: lost pl over 4f out: sn bhd* **9/2**[3]

60-3 **7** *2 1/2* **Ruby Sunrise (IRE)**[10] 1 5-8-8 45.................................. SoniaEaton(7) 12 8
(B P J Baugh) *s.i.s: hdwy to chse ldrs over 7f out: wknd over 2f out* **14/1**

035- **8** *2 1/2* **Contra Mundum (USA)**[221] 2261 4-9-3 77.................... PaulHanagan 11 9
(B S Rothwell) *w ldr: wknd over 3f out: sn bhd* **7/2**[2]

2m 31.64s (2.74) **Going Correction** +0.05s/f (Slow)
WFA 4 from 5yo+ 3lb **8** Ran SP% **110.3**
Speed ratings (Par 103):92,90,90,87,84 75,73,71
CSF £46.01 TOTE £2.40: £1.60, £4.30, £1.10; EX 50.20 Trifecta £95.60 Part won. Pool £134.69 - 0.34 winning units..
Owner Mr And Mrs J D Cotton **Bred** Oustvlaamse Invesering N V **Trained** Portway, Worcs

FOCUS
A weak maiden and the bare form is not up to much.
Ruby Sunrise(IRE) Official explanation: vet said mare finished lame

99 PONTINS.COM (S) STKS — 7f (F)
1:40 (1:42) (Class 6) 3-Y-O **£2,184** (£644; £322) **Stalls** Low

Form RPR

510- **1** **Sheriff's Silk**[33] 6760 3-9-4 58..(b[1]) PaulEddery 6 67+
(B Smart) *mde all: drvn clr over 1f out: hung rt: eased nr fin* **9/2**[2]

400- **2** *1 1/4* **Sophie's Dream**[29] 6807 3-8-12 53................................ DeanMcKeown 5 55
(J G Given) *hld up in rr: hdwy and swtchd wd outside over 2f out: styd on to take 2nd ins last* **13/2**

546- **3** *2* **Foxxy**[11] 6996 3-8-13 58...(p) PatCosgrave 10 51
(K A Ryan) *chsd ldrs: hrd drvn over 3f out: wnt 2nd over 1f out: one pce* **8/1**

640- **4** *4* **Baytown Rosie (IRE)**[24] 6853 3-8-7 45............................ HayleyTurner 3 34
(P S McEntee) *chsd ldrs: one pce fnl 2f* **40/1**

43-2 **5** *shd* **Zaafira (SPA)**[3] 68 3-8-7 53.. EdwardCreighton 2 34
(E J Creighton) *hdwy to chse ldrs over 4f out: one pce fnl 2f* **5/1**[3]

3- **6** *1 3/4* **Show Business (IRE)**[31] 6789 3-8-12 .... SebSanders 9 34
(Sir Mark Prescott) *sn drvn along: sn w wnr: carried hd high: hung lft over 1f out: nt run on* **7/2**[1]

503- **7** *nk* **House Arrest**[26] 6845 3-8-2 49............................(b) NataliaGemelova(5) 4 29
(A J McCabe) *s.i.s: sme hdwy 2f out: nvr on terms* **20/1**

254- **8** *4* **Peppin's Gold (IRE)**[62] 6422 3-8-4 53 ow2.................... JamesMillman(5) 1 20
(B R Millman) *in tch: lost pl over 2f out* **6/1**

00- **9** *5* **Jayzee (IRE)**[28] 6815 3-8-7 .... ChrisCatlin 7 5
(P D Deegan, Ire) *s.i.s: nvr a factor* **25/1**

56-5 **10** *6* **Bogside Katie**[6] 40 3-8-7 .... JoeFanning 11 —
(G M Moore) *mid-div: effrt over 2f out: wknd and eased over 1f out* **16/1**

3- **11** *37* **Chastity (IRE)**[177] 3618 3-8-7 .... KimTinkler 8 —
(N Tinkler) *chsd ldrs: lost pl 4f out: sn wl bhd: t.o: btn 36 l* **33/1**

1m 33.02s (2.22) **Going Correction** +0.05s/f (Slow) **11** Ran SP% **115.7**
Speed ratings (Par 95):89,87,85,80,80 78,78,73,67,61 18
CSF £31.66 TOTE £4.90: £1.70, £2.10, £2.50; EX 31.20 Trifecta £126.10 Part won. Pool £177.66 - 0.20 winning units..The winner was bought in for 6,200gns. Sophie's Dream was claimed by Gary Martin £6,000.

Owner Mrs Linda Pestell **Bred** P A Mason **Trained** Hambleton, N Yorks
■ Stewards' Enquiry : Pat Cosgrave one-day ban: used whip with arm above shoulder height (Jan 22)
FOCUS
An ordinary seller, the second and third running to their sand form.
Peppin's Gold(IRE) Official explanation: jockey said filly hung right in straight

100 CANVAS PRINTS FROM BONUSPRINT.COM H'CAP 1m 6f (F)
2:10 (2:10) (Class 5) (0-75,72) 4-Y-0+ **£2,914** (£867; £433; £216) **Stalls** Low

Form RPR
00/3 1 **Alagon (IRE)**[6] [39] 7-8-8 **53**....(b) ChrisCatlin 5 60
(Ian Williams) *sn pushed along: sn chsng ldrs: wnt 2nd 1f out: kpt on to ld post* **9/2**
201- 2 *shd* **Jackie Kiely**[15] [6947] 6-9-13 **72**....(t) PhillipMakin 3 79
(R Brotherton) *hld up off pce: smooth hdwy 4f out: rdn to ld over 1f out: jst ct* **3/1**[2]
6-23 3 *3* **Bienheureux**[4] [62] 6-8-8 **56**....(t) JerryO'Dwyer(3) 1 59
(Miss Gay Kelleway) *hld up off pce: hdwy 4f out: rdn over 1f out: one pce* **15/8**[1]
22-3 4 *3/4* **Opera Writer (IRE)**[2] [74] 4-8-5 **61**.... RussellKennemore(5) 2 63
(R Hollinshead) *trckd ldrs: led 4f out tl over 1f out: one pce* **10/3**[3]
/6-0 5 *30* **Hathaal (IRE)**[8] [16] 8-9-5 **64**....(v) MickyFenton 6 27
(E J Creighton) *led 1f: chsd ldrs: led over 5f out: hdd 4f out: lost pl over 2f out* **16/1**
/0-6 6 *19* **Double Mystery (FR)**[2] [74] 7-8-5 **55**....(t) EmmettStack(5) 4 —
(K J Burke) *reminders after s: led after 2f: hdd over 5f out: sn lost pl: t.o 3f out* **20/1**

3m 8.58s (-1.02) **Going Correction** +0.05s/f (Slow)
WFA 4 from 6yo+ 6lb 6 Ran SP% **111.7**
Speed ratings (Par 103):104,103,102,101,84 73
CSF £18.09 TOTE £6.80: £2.80, £1.70; EX 20.10.
Owner Blue Crocodile **Bred** Chevington Stud **Trained** Portway, Worcs
FOCUS
Not the most solid or reliable of form, although the runner-up seems better than ever.

101 PONTIN'S FAMILY HOLIDAYS H'CAP 1m (F)
2:40 (2:40) (Class 5) (0-75,75) 4-Y-0+ **£2,914** (£867; £433; £216) **Stalls** Low

Form RPR
424- 1 **Davenport (IRE)**[14] [6968] 5-8-11 **75**....(p) JamesMillman(5) 5 83+
(B R Millman) *trckd ldrs: drvn over 3f out: styd on to ld 1f out: edgd lft and hld on towards fin* **6/4**[1]
631- 2 *1/2* **Flyingit (USA)**[28] [6817] 4-8-11 **70**.... CatherineGannon 2 76
(K A Ryan) *trckd ldr: effrt over 2f out: hung rt: styd on towards fin* **5/1**
4- 3 *nk* **Dapple Dawn (IRE)**[24] [6863] 4-8-9 **68**.... DanielTudhope 6 73
(D Carroll) *trckd ldrs: led 3f out tl 1f out: no ex* **3/1**[2]
146- 4 *3/4* **Boundless Prospect (USA)**[15] [6946] 8-8-12 **71**.... JimmyQuinn 3 75
(Miss Gay Kelleway) *hld up in tch: effrt over 3f out: styd on same pce fnl f* **4/1**[3]
050- 5 *8* **Boy Dancer (IRE)**[119] [5312] 4-8-2 **61** oh1.... PaulHanagan 4 48
(D W Barker) *led: qcknd over 4f out: hdd 3f out: wknd appr fnl f* **12/1**
0/ 6 *16* **All Woman**[417] 5-8-6 **65**.... EdwardCreighton 1 18
(E J Creighton) *fly-jmpd s: sn trcking ldrs: outpcd over 4f out: hung lft and lost pl over 2f out: sn bhd* **66/1**

1m 43.5s (-1.10) **Going Correction** +0.05s/f (Slow) 6 Ran SP% **110.9**
Speed ratings (Par 103):107,106,106,105,97 81
CSF £9.25 TOTE £2.10: £1.10, £2.80; EX 8.40.
Owner M A Swift and A J Chapman **Bred** M P B Bloodstock Ltd **Trained** Kentisbeare, Devon
FOCUS
They went no pace and this is very ordinary form. It is doubtful if Davenport had to improve on his recent efforts.

102 BONUSPRINT.COM H'CAP 7f (F)
3:10 (3:10) (Class 5) (0-75,73) 4-Y-0+ **£3,071** (£906; £453) **Stalls** Low

Form RPR
360- 1 **Lii Najma**[28] [6820] 4-8-5 **62**.... JoeFanning 1 71
(C E Brittain) *mde virtually all: styd on wl towards fin* **18/1**
6-41 2 *1* **Dudley Docker (IRE)**[4] [63] 5-8-8 **72** 6ex....(v) KellyHarrison(7) 2 78
(D Carroll) *trckd ldrs: chal over 1f out: edgd lft: no ex ins last* **7/1**[2]
030- 3 *1 1/4* **Conrad**[76] [6206] 4-8-11 **68**.... PaulHanagan 8 71
(R A Fahey) *chsd ldrs: kpt on same pce appr fnl f* **9/1**
111- 4 *hd* **La Colline (GER)**[19] [6930] 4-8-13 **70**.... TonyCulhane 10 73
(W J Haggas) *hld up in tch: effrt 3f out: styd on ins last* **11/10**[1]
323- 5 *2* **Certain Justice (USA)**[141] [4706] 9-9-1 **72**.... HayleyTurner 3 69
(Stef Liddiard) *s.i.s: hdwy over 3f out: kpt on fnl f* **10/1**
054- 6 *2 1/2* **Danetime Lord (IRE)**[24] [6858] 4-8-11 **68**....(p) CatherineGannon 5 59
(K A Ryan) *trckd ldrs: wknd over 1f out* **16/1**
660- 7 *nk* **Cerebus**[19] [6930] 5-7-12 **60**.... NataliaGemelova(5) 9 50
(A J McCabe) *in rr: kpt on fnl 2f: nvr trbld ldrs* **40/1**
055- 8 *shd* **Winning Pleasure (IRE)**[21] [6896] 9-8-11 **71**.... JasonEdmunds(3) 4 61
(J Balding) *hld up in rr: effrt over 2f out: nvr nr ldrs* **33/1**
541- 9 *1/2* **Ochre Bay**[20] [6919] 4-9-0 **71**....(p) GrahamGibbons 6 60
(R Hollinshead) *in rr and sn sriven along: nvr a factor* **8/1**[3]
043- 10 *6* **Purus (IRE)**[33] [6770] 5-8-9 **73**.... JackMitchell(7) 7 46
(P Mitchell) *trckd ldrs: shkn up and lost pl over 2f out* **8/1**[3]

1m 29.59s (-1.21) **Going Correction** +0.05s/f (Slow) 10 Ran SP% **118.0**
Speed ratings (Par 103):108,106,105,105,102 100,99,99,99,92
CSF £140.10 CT £1252.49 TOTE £24.20: £3.80, £2.50, £2.80; EX 194.20 TRIFECTA Not won..
Owner Saeed Manana **Bred** Zubieta Ltd **Trained** Newmarket, Suffolk
FOCUS
A fair handicap and the form looks solid. The winner was back to his best and the runner-up showed slight improvement.

103 PONTIN'S BOOK EARLY H'CAP 5f (F)
3:40 (3:41) (Class 6) (0-60,57) 3-Y-0 **£2,388** (£705; £352) **Stalls** High

Form RPR
21-4 1 **Grange Lili (IRE)**[7] [34] 3-8-13 **57**....(b) DuranFentiman(5) 2 63
(Peter Grayson) *rrd s: hdwy over 2f out: led 1f out: hld on wl* **9/2**[3]
64-3 2 *1 1/4* **Bentley**[7] [34] 3-8-6 **45**....(v) ChrisCatlin 6 47+
(D Shaw) *s.i.s: hdwy 3f out: hrd rdn and edgd lft over 1f out: styd on to take 2nd ins last: no ex* **1/1**[1]
4-63 3 *1 1/2* **Pappas Image**[4] [65] 3-9-0 **56**....(b) StephenDonohoe(3) 4 53
(A J McCabe) *trckd ldrs: led over 1f out: sn hdd: kpt on same pce* **4/1**[2]
650- 4 *3* **Pretty Selma**[34] [6749] 3-8-6 **45**....(p) HayleyTurner 3 32
(R M H Cowell) *led: hung lft and hdd over 1f out: sn wknd* **11/1**
500- 5 *2* **Elizabeth Garrett**[38] [6706] 3-8-6 **45**....(p) JimmyQuinn 1 25
(R M H Cowell) *trckd ldrs: wknd over 1f out* **10/1**
040- 6 *5* **Daruma (IRE)**[64] [6400] 3-8-7 **46** ow1....(b) GrahamGibbons 5 9
(Peter Grayson) *chsd ldrs: rdn and lost pl 2f out* **12/1**

59.24 secs (-1.06) **Going Correction** -0.20s/f (Stan) 6 Ran SP% **113.3**
Speed ratings (Par 95):100,98,95,90,87 79
CSF £9.64 TOTE £4.20: £2.10, £1.40; EX 10.80 Place 6 £164.84, Place 5 £103.89.
Owner Mrs M Shaughnessy and Mrs S Grayson **Bred** Jack Ronan And Des Ver Hunt Farm Ltd **Trained** Formby, Lancs
FOCUS
A weak, low-grade sprint handicap in which every runner was equipped with some sort of headgear. The form should work out well enough.
Elizabeth Garrett Official explanation: jockey said filly hung left
T/Jkpt: Not won. T/Plt: £227.40 to a £1 stake. Pool: £60,377.75. 193.75 winning tickets. T/Qpdt: £139.30 to a £1 stake. Pool: £4,029.60. 21.40 winning tickets. WG

NAD AL SHEBA (L-H)
Thursday, January 11
OFFICIAL GOING: Turf course - good; dirt course - fast

104a THE KENTUCKY STKS (H'CAP) (TURF) 1m 194y
4:00 (4:00) (85-94,94) 3-Y-0+ **£6,675** (£2,225; £1,223; £667; £333)

RPR
1 **Count Trevisio (IRE)**[90] [5945] 4-8-9 **94**.... RHills 2 95
(Saeed Bin Suroor) *soon led, gng wl 3f out, kicked clr 2f out, ran on well*
2 *1 3/4* **Doctor Of Laws**[14] 4-8-6 **90**....(t) TedDurcan 1 89
(S Seemar, UAE) *slowly away, sn trkd ldr, ev ch 3f out, ran on but no ch wth winner*
3 *nse* **Aleutian**[21] 7-8-9 **91**.... WSupple 5 91
(Doug Watson, UAE) *slowly away, mid-division, gng wl 3f out, ran on fnl 2f, nrst finish*
4 *8* **Potro Tell (ARG)**[14] 7-8-9 **91**.... KShea 4 76
(H J Brown, South Africa) *settled rear, rdn 3 1/2f out, not much room 2 1/2f out, ran on fnl 1 1/2f*
5 *2 1/4* **Etmaam**[39] 6-8-6 **88**....(v) RyanMoore 9 68
(S Seemar, UAE) *raced rear, some late hdwy, nvr nr to challenge*
6 *1 3/4* **Todman Avenue (USA)**[28] 5-8-8 **90**....(t) RoystonFfrench 11 67
(A Al Raihe, UAE) *mid-division, rdn 4f out, some prog 2 1/2f out, one pace*
7 *2* **Yankee George (IRE)**[21] 4-8-8 **91** ow1.... PatDobbs 8 64
(Doug Watson, UAE) *settled rear, rdn 3f out, nvr nr to challenge*
8 *shd* **Forty Hablador (ARG)**[14] 6-8-8 **88** ow2....(vt) PBhosle 7 63
(S Seemar, UAE) *settled last, moderate late prog, nvr nr to challenge*
9 *4 1/4* **The Coires (IRE)**[39] 5-8-4 **86**.... MartinDwyer 10 51
(Doug Watson, UAE) *tracked ldr, hrd rdn 3f out, wknd fnl 2f*
10 *6 1/2* **Country Rambler (USA)**[39] 5-8-8 **90**.... TPO'Shea 3 43
(Doug Watson, UAE) *mid-division, trkd leaders 3f out, not quicken*
11 *14* **Millbag (IRE)**[39] 6-8-10 **93**....(v) RPCleary 6 —
(D Selvaratnam, UAE) *slowly away, mid-division, rdn 4f out, nvr dangerous*
12 *1/2* **State Shinto (USA)**[20] 11-8-11 **94**....(bt) DBadel 12 —
(R Bouresly, Kuwait) *slowly away, sn recovered to track leaders, rdn 4f out, fdd, virtually pld up*

1m 49.54s (109.54)
WFA 4 from 5yo+ 1lb 12 Ran

Owner Godolphin **Bred** Quay Bloodstock **Trained** Newmarket, Suffolk

NOTEBOOK
Count Trevisio(IRE) was not at his best on a soft surface at Newmarket when last seen in October, but this ground suited better and he ran out a clear-cut winner on his Dubai debut. He looks progressive and could be one to keep on the right side of at the Carnival.

105a THE JESSAMINE CUP (H'CAP) (TURF) 6f 110y
5:35 (5:35) (85-94,94) 3-Y-0+ **£6,675** (£2,225; £1,223; £667; £333)

RPR
1 **Protector (SAF)**[14] 6-8-9 **91**.... KShea 3 93
(H J Brown, South Africa) *mid-division, forced rear 3f out, rdn to cl 2 1/2f out, trkd leaders 1 1/2f out, ran on well*
2 *1/2* **Khabfair**[447] [6014] 6-8-8 **90**.... TedDurcan 8 91
(S Seemar, UAE) *mid-division, smooth prog track leaders 2f out, led 1 1/2f out, hdd cl home*
3 *2* **Green Coast (IRE)**[122] [5244] 4-8-8 **90**.... MartinDwyer 6 85
(Saeed Bin Suroor) *slowly away, prog wide chal 2f out, ev ch 1f out, weakened*
4 *2* **Daybreak Dancer (IRE)**[14] 5-8-8 **90**....(v) PatDobbs 7 79
(Doug Watson, UAE) *raced 3rd, ev ch 2 1/2f out, not quicken and impeded 1 1/2f out*
5 *1/4* **Bentley's Ball (USA)**[34] 6-8-5 **87**....(bt[1]) RichardMullen 2 75
(S Seemar, UAE) *settled rear, gng wl 3f out, prog rail 2f out, badly impeded 1f out, not recover*
6 *3* **Emirates Gold (IRE)**[20] 4-8-11 **94**.... TPO'Shea 5 73
(E Charpy, UAE) *slowly away, not much room 3f out, nvr dngrs after*
7 *1/2* **Almaram (USA)**[21] 7-8-8 **90**....(e) RPCleary 1 68
(D Selvaratnam, UAE) *rear rail, rdn to cl 3f out, wknd 2f out*
8 *2 3/4* **Figjam**[7] 4-8-7 **89**....(vt) RyanMoore 9 59
(S Seemar, UAE) *soon struggling, nvr nr to challenge*
9 *1/4* **Mutamarres**[136] [4875] 4-8-10 **93**....(v) RHills 10 61
(Doug Watson, UAE) *soon led, rdn 2 1/2f out, hdd and wkng whn badly hmpd 1f out*
10 *3* **Egyptian (USA)**[28] 8-8-11 **94**.... DBadel 11 54
(R Bouresly, Kuwait) *raced 4th deep, ev ch 3f out, sn weakened*
11 *5 1/2* **Machynleth**[55] 7-8-11 **94**....(t) WSupple 4 38
(M Al Muhairi, UAE) *tracked ldr, rdn 2 1/2f out, sn weakened*
12 *8 1/2* **Nomoretaxes (BRZ)**[34] 5-8-6 **88**....(bt) RoystonFfrench 12 8
(A Al Raihe, UAE) *mid-division wide for 2f, weakened*

1m 18.38s (78.38) 12 Ran

Owner James L Atkinson **Bred** Dr M Thomson **Trained** South Africa

NOTEBOOK
Green Coast(IRE), a five-length winner of a 7f Redcar maiden on his only previous start last September, ran with credit on his handicap/Dubai debut. He is open to more improvement.

[66]WOLVERHAMPTON (A.W) (L-H)

Friday, January 12

OFFICIAL GOING: Standard
Wind: strong behind

106 PONTINS.COM MAIDEN STKS 7f 32y(P)
1:30 (1:30) (Class 5) 3-Y-O+ **£2,968** (£876; £438) **Stalls** High

Form RPR
1 **Ten A Penny (USA)** 3-8-9 ShaneKelly 11 63
(J A Osborne) *s.i.s: stdy hdwy on outside 5f out: led 2f out: sn rdn: drvn out* **9/4**[2]
6- 2 ¾ **Sedgwick**[336] [365] 5-9-13 DeanMcKeown 3 65
(J G Given) *led early: a.p: rdn to chse wnr wl over 1f out: kpt on ins fnl f* **7/1**[3]
3 2 ½ **Picky** 3-8-6 RichardKingscote[(3)] 7 55
(J A Osborne) *hld up in mid-div: pushed along 5f out: hdwy on outside over 2f out: one pce fnl f* **8/1**
3- 4 1 ½ **Fowey (USA)**[33] [6778] 3-8-4 JamieMackay 1 46
(Sir Mark Prescott) *hld up in tch: rdn over 2f out: one pce* **15/8**[1]
5 2 **Missus Molly Brown** 3-8-4 PaulHanagan 9 41+
(R A Fahey) *s.i.s: bhd: rdn over 3f out: styd on fnl f: n.d* **28/1**
0- 6 1 ¼ **Shadow Aspect**[27] [6114] 4-9-10 JerryO'Dwyer[(3)] 2 47
(Eoin Doyle, Ire) *s.i.s: hld up in rr: swtchd rt over 1f out: sme late prog* **16/1**
000- 7 1 **Rambling Socks**[15] [6956] 4-9-8 45 (bt) ChrisCatlin 8 39
(S R Bowring) *prom tl wknd 2f out* **40/1**
0- 8 nk **War Of The Roses (IRE)**[49] [6588] 4-9-13 PatCosgrave 6 43
(R Brotherton) *hld up in mid-div: rdn wl over 1f out: no rspnse* **66/1**
0- 9 2 ½ **Alucica**[336] [365] 4-9-8 NCallan 10 32
(D Shaw) *swtchd lft sn after s: hld up and bhd: hdwy on ins wl over 1f out: sn rdn: wknd fnl f* **25/1**
000- 10 1 ¼ **Miracle Baby**[42] [6657] 5-9-8 32 DaleGibson 5 28
(A J Chamberlain) *w ldr: rdn to ld briefly jst over 2f out: wknd over 1f out* **50/1**
50- 11 4 **Countrywide Style (IRE)**[137] [4897] 3-8-6 JamesDoyle[(3)] 4 19
(N P Littmoden) *sn led: rdn and hdd jst over 2f out: wknd wl over 1f out* **9/1**

1m 32.67s (2.27) **Going Correction** +0.325s/f (Slow)
WFA 3 from 4yo+ 18lb **11 Ran SP% 118.2**
Speed ratings (Par 103):100,99,96,94,92 90,89,89,86,85 80
CSF £17.76 TOTE £4.00: £1.10, £4.00, £2.70; EX 20.20 TRIFECTA Not won..
Owner Lord Blyth And Ten **Bred** Chesapeake Farm, Mary R Odom & W S Farish **Trained** Upper Lambourn, Berks

FOCUS
Fairly modest maiden form, although the first four will probably rate higher in time.

107 PONTIN'S FAMILY HOLIDAYS (S) STKS 1m 5f 194y(P)
2:00 (2:01) (Class 6) 4-Y-O+ **£2,047** (£604; £302) **Stalls** Low

Form RPR
02-1 1 **Finished Article (IRE)**[8] [35] 10-9-9 47 NCallan 4 59
(P A Blockley) *hld up in tch: wnt 2nd over 3f out: led 2f out: rdn and edgd rt fr over 1f out: drvn out* **11/4**[2]
55-4 2 nk **Zaffeu**[3] [78] 6-9-4 52 RussellKennemore[(5)] 3 59
(A G Juckes) *hld up in rr: hdwy on ins over 3f out: rdn over 2f out: ev ch whn rdr dropped whip over 1f out: edgd rt ins fnl furlon* **11/4**[2]
53-6 3 5 **Isa'Af (IRE)**[10] [10] 8-9-3 53 ChrisCatlin 2 46
(P W Hiatt) *led after 1f: rdn and hdd 2f out: wknd wl ins fnl f* **13/2**[3]
005- 4 2 **Keshya**[65] [6405] 6-8-9 54 JamesDoyle[(3)] 7 38
(N P Littmoden) *led 1f: t.k.h in tch: rdn 3f out: wknd wl over 1f out* **7/4**[1]
/00- 5 13 **Ryhope Chief (IRE)**[21] [945] 4-8-11 45 (bt[1]) EdwardCreighton 6 25
(M Sheppard) *hld up in rr: rdn over 3f out: sn struggling* **20/1**
6 4 **Point Of Origin (IRE)**[341] [3297] 10-9-3 DaleGibson 1 19
(John A Harris) *chsd ldr after 1f tl rdn and wknd over 3f out* **66/1**

3m 13.04s (5.67) **Going Correction** +0.325s/f (Slow)
WFA 4 from 6yo+ 6lb **6 Ran SP% 109.3**
Speed ratings (Par 101):96,95,92,91,84 82
CSF £10.11 TOTE £2.80: £1.20, £1.80; EX 9.50 Trifecta £19.40 Pool £290.31 - 10.58 winning units..There was no bid for the winner.
Owner J L Guillambert **Bred** Dr D Davis **Trained** Lambourn, Berks

FOCUS
A modest seller. The form is not solid and the winner did not need to run to his best.

108 PONTINSBINGO.COM (S) STKS 5f 20y(P)
2:30 (2:30) (Class 6) 3-Y-O **£2,047** (£604; £302) **Stalls** Low

Form RPR
50- 1 **Inkjet (IRE)**[204] [2791] 3-8-7 CatherineGannon 7 54
(Ms Deborah J Evans) *s.i.s: hld up: hdwy over 3f out: rdn over 1f out: r.o to ld last strides* **22/1**
25U- 2 shd **Put It On The Card**[32] [6789] 3-8-12 60 (b) NCallan 3 59
(P D Evans) *w ldr: led over 2f out: rdn and edgd lft over 1f out: hdd last strides* **7/4**[1]
036- 3 1 ¾ **Sunken Rags**[104] [5687] 3-8-12 60 PaulHanagan 8 53
(K R Burke) *hld up: hdwy on ins over 2f out: rdn to chse ldr wl over 1f out: one pce fnl f* **5/2**[2]
006- 4 ½ **Pat Will (IRE)**[15] [6965] 3-8-9 52 (b[1]) StephenDonohoe[(3)] 6 51
(P D Evans) *hld up in tch: rdn over 2f out: sltly outpcd wl over 1f out: rallied towards fin* **15/2**
56-6 5 1 ½ **One White Sock**[8] [36] 3-8-4 43 (b) MarcHalford[(3)] 2 41
(J L Spearing) *bhd: pushed along over 3f out: rdn and outpcd over 2f out: c wd st: sme late prog* **8/1**
006- 6 2 **Three Mates**[255] [1379] 3-8-0 47 JackDean[(7)] 1 33
(W G M Turner) *led over 2f: sn rdn: wknd over 1f out* **33/1**
235- 7 7 **Circle Of Truth**[214] [2495] 3-8-9 60 SaleemGolam[(3)] 4 13
(W G M Turner) *w ldrs tl rdn and wknd over 2f out* **5/1**[3]

65.14 secs (2.32) **Going Correction** +0.325s/f (Slow) **7 Ran SP% 111.8**
Speed ratings (Par 95):94,93,91,90,87 84,73
CSF £58.38 TOTE £19.90: £4.10, £1.60; EX 48.20 Trifecta £198.50 Part won. Pool £279.59 - 0.30 winning units..The winner was bought in for 7,000gns.
Owner J E Abbey, Mike Nolan **Bred** A F O'Callaghan **Trained** Lydiate, Merseyside

FOCUS
A weakish seller best rated around the fairly reliable runner-up.

109 PONTIN'S - BOOK EARLY CLAIMING STKS 1m 1f 103y(P)
3:00 (3:00) (Class 6) 4-Y-O+ **£2,388** (£705; £352) **Stalls** Low

Form RPR
03-3 1 **Climate (IRE)**[8] [32] 8-8-9 66 (v) RussellKennemore[(5)] 3 74+
(R Hollinshead) *hld up towards rr: hdwy over 3f out: sn rdn: edgd lft jst over 1f out: led ins fnl f: r.o* **6/4**[1]
055- 2 1 **Paparaazi (IRE)**[23] [6889] 5-9-0 64 (b[1]) PaulHanagan 8 71
(R A Fahey) *chsd ldrs: wnt 2nd 4f out: rdn over 2f out: styd on towards fin* **7/2**[3]
00-1 3 hd **Wahoo Sam (USA)**[8] [32] 7-9-10 69 (p) NCallan 7 81
(K A Ryan) *led: clr 5f out: rdn wl over 1f out: hdd ins fnl f: no ex* **11/4**[2]
63-1 4 5 **Bathwick Emma (IRE)**[7] [42] 4-8-4 52 (p) JimmyQuinn 1 52
(P D Evans) *hld up towards rr: rdn and hdwy 4f out: wknd wl over 1f out* **7/1**
5/0- 5 8 **Tuckerman**[17] [6087] 6-8-9 ow1 PatCosgrave 4 40
(F J Bowles, Ire) *bhd tl styd on fnl f: nvr nr ldrs* **40/1**
05-0 6 ¾ **Ronnies Lad**[7] [42] 5-8-10 45 (v) PaulMulrennan 6 39
(J R Norton) *hld up in tch: rdn and wknd over 3f out* **28/1**
0/0 7 1 ¾ **Alisar (IRE)**[6] [48] 7-8-11 67 (t) SCreighton[(7)] 5 44
(E J Creighton) *prom tl wknd 4f out* **28/1**
006- 8 5 **Mytton's Dream**[252] [1465] 5-8-3 40 EdwardCreighton 2 19
(Miss Joanne Priest) *a bhd* **66/1**
002- 9 5 **Paris Heights**[68] [4652] 5-8-9 49 StephenDonohoe[(3)] 9 18
(Mrs A M Thorpe) *s.i.s: a bhd* **25/1**
000- 10 11 **Yeldham Lady**[25] [6852] 5-8-5 34 ow5 (p) MarkCoumbe[(7)] 12 —
(A J Chamberlain) *chsd ldr to 4f out: sn rdn and wknd* **150/1**
0-6 11 16 **Spotoncon**[9] [24] 6-8-9 (b[1]) AndrewElliott[(5)] 11 —
(A J Lidderdale) *dwlt: sn rcvrd: prom tl rdn and wknd qckly 4f out* **100/1**

2m 3.84s (1.22) **Going Correction** +0.325s/f (Slow)
WFA 4 from 5yo+ 1lb **11 Ran SP% 117.7**
Speed ratings (Par 101):107,106,105,101,94 93,92,87,83,73 59
CSF £6.65 TOTE £2.80: £1.10, £1.40, £1.30; EX 9.00 Trifecta £8.30 Pool £339.27 - 29.00 winning units.
Owner The Cartmel Syndicate **Bred** Mrs A Naughton **Trained** Upper Longdon, Staffs

FOCUS
Fair claiming form. Wahoo Sam set a strong gallop, the first three finished nicely clear and the form looks solid for the grade.

110 DIGITAL PRINTS FROM BONUSPRINT.COM H'CAP 1m 1f 103y(P)
3:30 (3:31) (Class 6) (0-65,71) 4-Y-O+ **£2,730** (£806; £403) **Stalls** Low

Form RPR
132- 1 **Pop Music (IRE)**[14] [6977] 4-8-7 **59** (p) JamesDoyle[(3)] 9 71
(Miss J Feilden) *a.p: led 2f out: sn rdn: edgd lft ins fnl f: drvn out* **7/2**[2]
325- 2 ½ **Sarwin (USA)**[23] [6878] 4-9-0 **63** TPQueally 7 74
(W J Musson) *hld up in mid-div: hdwy on outside 2f out: hung lft fr over 1f out: r.o* **5/2**[1]
25-1 3 1 **Call My Bluff (FR)**[9] [24] 4-9-8 **71** 6ex NCallan 10 81+
(Rae Guest) *stdd s: hld up and bhd: rdn and hdwy whn carried sltly lft over 1f out: kpt on ins fnl f* **13/2**
053- 4 ¾ **Barbirolli**[16] [6954] 5-8-11 **59** ShaneKelly 4 68+
(W M Brisbourne) *hld up in mid-div: rdn and hdwy over 2f out: hmpd ins fnl f: nt rcvr* **11/1**
003- 5 shd **Sir Bond (IRE)**[13] [6993] 6-8-6 **59** DuranFentiman[(5)] 1 66+
(G R Oldroyd) *s.i.s: hld up in rr: rdn over 1f out: hdwy fnl f: nvr nrr* **9/2**[3]
200- 6 2 ½ **Medieval Maiden**[134] [4973] 4-8-6 **62** DebraEngland[(7)] 3 64+
(W J Musson) *hld up and bhd: nt clr run on ins over 2f out: hdwy over 1f out: nvr trbld ldrs* **25/1**
133- 7 ½ **Buscador (USA)**[21] [6924] 8-8-7 **60** AshleyHamblett[(5)] 11 61
(W M Brisbourne) *w ldr: led over 5f out: rdn and hdd 2f out: wknd ins fnl f* **12/1**
004- 8 shd **Takes Tutu (USA)**[21] [6918] 8-8-11 **59** PaulHanagan 12 60+
(C R Dore) *hld up and bhd: nt clr run on ins 2f out: hdwy whn nt clr run over 1f out: nt rcvr* **16/1**
000- 9 3 **Newcorp Lad**[22] [6899] 7-8-7 **55** ow2 GrahamGibbons 2 50
(Mrs G S Rees) *led: hdd over 5f out: w ldr: rdn and ev ch 2f out: n.m.r on ins briefly wl over 1f out: sn wknd* **40/1**
046- 10 shd **Captain Oats (IRE)**[29] [6817] 4-8-6 **55** (p) CatherineGannon 6 49
(Mrs P Ford) *mid-div: lost pl over 2f out: sn bhd* **100/1**
500/ 11 hd **Mission Man**[867] [5120] 6-9-3 **65** JimmyQuinn 5 59
(M G Rimell) *plld hrd: prom: rdn over 3f out: wkng whn hmpd over 1f out* **66/1**
540- 12 1 ¾ **Dallma (IRE)**[72] [6293] 4-8-10 **59** BrettDoyle 13 50
(C E Brittain) *prom tl rdn and wknd 2f out* **16/1**

2m 3.17s (0.55) **Going Correction** +0.325s/f (Slow)
WFA 4 from 5yo+ 1lb **12 Ran SP% 118.9**
Speed ratings (Par 101):110,109,108,108,107 105,105,105,102,102 102,100
CSF £12.43 CT £54.99 TOTE £4.90: £1.70, £1.10, £2.60; EX 16.90 Trifecta £51.80 Pool £373.23 - 5.11 winning units..
Owner Michael Jenner **Bred** John Foley **Trained** Exning, Suffolk

FOCUS
A competitive handicap but the early pace was not strong and it developed into a bit of a sprint off the home bend. Solid form, with a slight pesonal best from the winner.
Medieval Maiden ◆ Official explanation: jockey said, regarding running and riding, her orders were to settle in rear and, once settled, make the filly run up the home straight, adding that having been on the inside throughout, they did not have a great deal of room approaching final furlong and, once clear, stayed on; trainer's rep added that the filly has had a history of unsoundness and was satisfied with the ride given, taking into account the rider's relative inexperience
Takes Tutu(USA) Official explanation: jockey said gelding was denied a clear run

111 DAVID BELLINGHAM HITS BIG 45 H'CAP 1m 1f 103y(P)
4:00 (4:00) (Class 4) (0-85,82) 3-Y-O **£5,505** (£1,637; £818; £408) **Stalls** Low

Form RPR
112- 1 **Chookie Hamilton**[20] [6933] 3-8-0 **71** DuranFentiman[(5)] 5 76
(I Semple) *chsd ldr: led over 2f out: sn rdn: edgd rt over 1f out: drvn out* **7/2**[2]
510- 2 2 **New Beginning (IRE)**[29] [6824] 3-8-11 **77** PaulHanagan 1 78
(Mrs S Lyman) *hld up in tch: rdn 2f out: kpt on to take 2nd towards fin: nt trble wnr* **28/1**
415- 3 1 ¼ **Peregrine Falcon**[48] [6599] 3-8-10 **76** JoeFanning 6 74
(M Johnston) *led: rdn and hdd over 2f out: no ex ins fnl f* **11/2**
052- 4 ½ **Dubai Magic (USA)**[14] [6978] 3-9-2 **82** BrettDoyle 3 79
(C E Brittain) *a.p: rdn and one pce fnl 2f* **9/2**[3]
052- 5 ¾ **Bold Saxon (IRE)**[30] [6808] 3-8-5 **71** DaleGibson 2 67
(M D I Usher) *bmpd s: hld up in rr: rdn over 2f out: no rspnse* **12/1**

01- **6** 1 1/2 **Lazy Darren**[16] 6950 3-9-1 **81** .... ChrisCatlin 4 74
(R Hannon) *t.k.h in rr: rdn and short-lived effrt on outside over 2f out* **5/4**[1]
2m 5.49s (2.87) **Going Correction** +0.325s/f (Slow) 6 Ran SP% **111.4**
Speed ratings (Par 99):100,98,97,96,96 94
CSF £72.67 TOTE £4.50: £1.80, £9.00; EX 41.50.
Owner Raeburn Brick Limited **Bred** D And J Raeburn **Trained** Carluke, S Lanarks
FOCUS
Not a bad little race but the pace was not that strong and it turned into something of a test of speed. The form seems sound enough.

112 BONUSPRINT.COM FILLIES' H'CAP 1m 4f 50y(P)
4:30 (4:30) (Class 5) (0-70,70) 4-Y-0+ £3,238 (£963; £481; £240) Stalls Low

Form RPR
0-21 **1** **Beldon Hill (USA)**[3] 74 4-8-6 **60** .... PaulHanagan 6 74+
(R A Fahey) *hld up in tch: lost pl over 6f out: rdn over 3f out: hdwy over 2f out: swtchd lft and led wl ins fnl f: drvn out* **1/1**[1]
013- **2** 1 1/4 **Symbol Of Peace (IRE)**[17] 6942 4-8-11 **68** .... RichardKingscote(3) 9 76
(J W Unett) *plld hrd early: prom: wnt 2nd over 6f out: led over 2f out: sn rdn: hdd and no ex wl ins fnl f* **12/1**
405- **3** 3 **Westering Home (IRE)**[17] 6942 4-8-6 **60** .... DaleGibson 1 63
(J Mackie) *chsd ldr tl over 6f out: rdn over 3f out: one pce fnl 2f* **14/1**
042- **4** shd **Sendinpost**[35] 6748 4-8-7 **64** .... SaleemGolam(3) 3 67
(S C Williams) *set slow pce: qcknd over 3f out: rdn and hdd over 2f out: wknd ins fnl f* **11/4**[2]
040- **5** 4 **Millagros (IRE)**[13] 6479 7-8-10 **65** .... JamieMoriarty(5) 5 61
(I Semple) *hld up and bhd: rdn over 2f out: sme hdwy fnl f: n.d* **9/1**[3]
332- **6** 2 1/2 **Bavarica**[17] 6942 5-8-13 **70** .... AmyBaker(7) 4 62
(Miss J Feilden) *hld up towards rr: sme hdwy on ins wl over 1f out: sn rdn: no rspnse* **9/1**[3]
566- **7** 1 **Fondness**[49] 6588 4-8-9 **63** .... GrahamGibbons 7 54
(J J Quinn) *hld up towards rr: hdwy over 4f out: wknd over 3f out* **40/1**
006- **8** 4 **Sweet Medicine**[15] 6967 5-9-1 **65** .... TonyCulhane 8 49
(P Howling) *hld up in rr: hdwy over 6f out: rdn and wknd over 2f out* **40/1**
2m 46.52s (4.10) **Going Correction** +0.325s/f (Slow)
WFA 4 from 5yo+ 4lb 8 Ran SP% **115.9**
Speed ratings (Par 100):99,98,96,96,93 91,91,88
CSF £15.62 CT £107.20 TOTE £1.90: £1.10, £2.70, £3.30; EX 18.50 Trifecta £108.70 Pool £870.08 - 5.68 winning units. Place 6 £51.35, Place 5 £24.94.
Owner D Brennan **Bred** Darley **Trained** Musley Bank, N Yorks
FOCUS
A steadily-run middle-distance handicap that turned into something of a half-mile sprint. The race has been rated through the third.
T/Plt: £80.00 to a £1 stake. Pool: £59,342.70. 541.00 winning tickets. T/Qpdt: £9.10 to a £1 stake. Pool: £5,620.40. 452.75 winning tickets. KH

90 LINGFIELD (L-H)
Saturday, January 13

OFFICIAL GOING: Standard
Wind: Mostly strong, behind Weather: Very overcast

113 PONTINSBINGO.COM H'CAP 7f (P)
12:20 (12:20) (Class 4) (0-85,85) 3-Y-O £4,857 (£1,445; £722; £360) Stalls Low

Form RPR
1- **1** **Boscobel**[52] 6561 3-8-11 **80** .... JoeFanning 6 90+
(M Johnston) *trckd ldrs: shkn up and green over 2f out: rdn to chse ldr 1f out: hd high and looked hld tl styd on wl to ld last 50yds* **6/4**[1]
112- **2** 3/4 **Fares (IRE)**[24] 6881 3-9-2 **85** ....(b) BrettDoyle 7 93
(C E Brittain) *hld up: prog to trck ldr 3f out: led 2f out and pushed 2 l clr: tired ins fnl f: hdd last 50yds* **11/4**[2]
104- **3** 3/4 **Copper King**[25] 6866 3-8-4 **76** .... JamesDoyle(3) 4 82
(P D Evans) *hld up in last pair: rdn over 2f out: prog on outer over 1f out: hanging but r.o fnl f: nrst fin* **20/1**
012- **4** 1 1/2 **Nordic Affair**[28] 6846 3-8-12 **84** .... MarcHalford(3) 1 86
(D R C Elsworth) *s.i.s: sn rcvrd: led over 5f out: rdn and hdd 2f out: sn outpcd* **7/1**[3]
01-1 **5** nk **Homes By Woodford**[10] 25 3-8-2 **71** .... ChrisCatlin 3 72
(R A Harris) *wl in tch: effrt on inner 2f out: rdn and one pce over 1f out* **14/1**
166- **6** 3 **Minaash (USA)**[142] 4727 3-8-11 **80** .... ShaneKelly 5 74
(J Noseda) *s.i.s: hld up in last: rdn over 2f out: hanging and wl btn over 1f out* **8/1**
13- **7** 2 1/2 **Leonard Charles**[14] 6991 3-8-7 **76** .... JamieMackay 2 63
(Sir Mark Prescott) *rousted along to ld: hdd over 5f out: rdn 1/2-way: wknd 2f out* **17/2**
1m 24.06s (-1.83) **Going Correction** +0.01s/f (Slow) 7 Ran SP% **112.2**
Speed ratings (Par 99):110,109,108,106,106 102,99
CSF £5.46 TOTE £1.90: £1.30, £1.70; EX 5.40.
Owner Jumeirah Racing **Bred** Darley **Trained** Middleham Moor, N Yorks
FOCUS
A decent handicap featuring potentially useful animals. Strong form. There's more to come from the winner and the second coudl be a bit better than the bare form, as he tired noticeably.

114 PONTIN'S HOLIDAYS MEDIAN AUCTION MAIDEN STKS (DIV I) 1m (P)
12:55 (12:57) (Class 6) 3-Y-O £2,047 (£604; £302) Stalls High

Form RPR
1 **Serpentaria** 3-8-12 .... SebSanders 4 66+
(Sir Mark Prescott) *trckd ldr: led wl over 2f out: rdn and jnd 1f out: battled on wl last 100yds* **8/1**
0- **2** nk **Mutoon (IRE)**[85] 6073 3-8-9 .... SaleemGolam(3) 3 65
(S C Williams) *prom: pressed wnr 2f out: rdn and upsides 1f out: nt qckn last 100yds* **25/1**
304- **3** shd **Blue Monkey (IRE)**[99] 5784 3-8-12 76 .... JamieMoriarty(5) 8 70
(M L W Bell) *hld up midfield: prog over 2f out: swtchd to inner over 1f out: str chal nr fin: a jst hld* **5/2**[2]
4 1 1/2 **Deserter (IRE)** 3-8-12 .... ShaneKelly 11 62+
(J A Osborne) *hld up in last: stdy prog fr 1/2-way: chsng ldng gp whn hmpd wl over 1f out: styd on ins fnl f* **40/1**
00- **5** 1 1/4 **Mumbleswerve (IRE)**[24] 6887 3-9-3 .... BrettDoyle 10 64
(W Jarvis) *sn t.k.h on outer and prom after 2f: shkn up and effrt over 2f out: nt qckn over 1f out: one pce after* **15/8**[1]
6 3 **County Kerry (UAE)** 3-8-12 .... FrankieMcDonald 9 52
(Jean-Rene Auvray) *sn prom on outer: pushed along over 3f out: stl there but u.p whn hmpd wl over 1f out: fdd* **50/1**

354- **7** 2 **Sir Sandicliffe (IRE)**[143] 4705 3-9-3 74 .... TonyCulhane 1 52
(B W Hills) *dwlt but sn led at slow pce: hdd wl over 2f out: wknd wl over 1f out* **11/2**[3]
8 2 1/2 **Schermuly (IRE)** 3-9-3 .... JoeFanning 6 46
(M Johnston) *rdn in rr 5f out: lost tch 1/2-way* **11/1**
9 1 1/2 **Witchingham** 3-9-3 .... ChrisCatlin 7 43
(R Hannon) *prom 2f: sn lost pl: lost tch sn after 1/2-way* **10/1**
04- **10** 1 1/2 **Port Macquairie (IRE)**[31] 6809 3-9-3 .... FergusSweeney 2 40
(R M Beckett) *rdn in rr over 5f out: sn lost tch* **25/1**
1m 41.14s (1.71) **Going Correction** +0.01s/f (Slow) 10 Ran SP% **119.4**
Speed ratings (Par 95):91,90,90,89,87 84,82,80,78,77
CSF £190.05 TOTE £12.10: £2.90, £13.80, £1.10; EX 350.50 TRIFECTA Not won..
Owner Christopher Spence **Bred** Chieveley Manor Stud **Trained** Newmarket, Suffolk
FOCUS
A fair maiden on paper, but the early pace was fairly steady and it was the slower of the two divisions by 1.22sec. An encouraging start nevertheless by Serpentaria.

115 PONTINS.COM CLAIMING STKS 1m 2f (P)
1:30 (1:30) (Class 6) 4-Y-0+ £2,184 (£644; £322) Stalls Low

Form RPR
000- **1** **Diamonds And Dust**[23] 6898 5-9-7 80 ....(b) NCallan 4 69+
(N P Littmoden) *hld up: pushed along and prog on outer over 2f out: cruised up to ld jst over 1f out: shkn up and sn clr fnl f* **8/1**
400- **2** 1 3/4 **Mademoiselle**[29] 6068 5-8-4 47 .... JimmyQuinn 3 48
(R Curtis) *hld up in cl tch: prog over 2f out: rdn to chal and upsides jst over 1f out: styd on but outpcd by wnr* **33/1**
03-0 **3** 1 1/4 **Lady Pilot**[10] 19 5-8-7 52 ....(b) JerryO'Dwyer(3) 1 52
(Ms J S Doyle) *hld up in last pair: prog 2f out: rdn over 1f out: styd on fnl f to take 3rd nr fin* **6/1**
001- **4** 1/2 **Blackmail (USA)**[24] 6889 9-9-3 59 .... SebSanders 6 58
(P Mitchell) *hld up in tch: prog on outer 1/2-way: pushed along 4f out: upsides over 2f out to jst over 1f out: nt qckn u.p* **11/4**[1]
03-5 **5** 1 **Linda's Colin (IRE)**[9] 38 5-9-4 67 .... MichaelJStainton(5) 5 62
(R A Harris) *hld up in last: hanging lft fr over 2f out: effrt on outer over 1f out : nt qckn* **7/2**[2]
66-0 **6** shd **Beautiful Mover (USA)**[10] 20 5-8-3 40 .... NataliaGemelova(5) 2 47
(J E Long) *led for 1f: t.k.h after 3f: wl in tch on inner: effrt over 1f out: pushed along and one pce* **33/1**
62-0 **7** 1 1/2 **Kalatime (IRE)**[3] 85 4-8-12 59 .... ChrisCatlin 7 50
(M F Harris) *led after 1f to over 3f out: stl w ldr 2f out: fdd fnl f* **10/1**
025- **8** 1/2 **Christmas Truce (IRE)**[14] 6982 8-8-8 54 ....(p) JamesDoyle(3) 9 46
(Ms J S Doyle) *prom: pressed ldr over 6f out: led over 3f out: hdd & wknd jst over 1f out* **5/1**[3]
50-5 **9** 12 **Gold Guest**[7] 52 8-8-9 53 ow3 ....(bt) StephenDonohoe(3) 8 24
(P D Evans) *s.i.s: prog and prom 6f out: rdn and wknd 3f out: t.o* **9/1**
2m 7.23s (-0.56) **Going Correction** +0.01s/f (Slow)
WFA 4 from 5yo+ 2lb 9 Ran SP% **115.9**
Speed ratings (Par 101):102,100,99,99,98 98,97,96,87
CSF £224.93 TOTE £5.70: £2.40, £6.90, £2.80; EX 146.90 TRIFECTA Not won..The winner was claimed by P. Wheatley for £11,000. Mademoiselle was claimed by R. A. Harris for £5,000.
Owner R A Green **Bred** Whitsbury Manor Stud **Trained** Newmarket, Suffolk
FOCUS
An ordinary claimer in which the form is limited by the sixth, but the winner won in the manner of a horse who, as his mark suggested, had a deal in hand over the opposition.
Beautiful Mover(USA) Official explanation: jockey said mare was denied a clear run
Gold Guest Official explanation: vet said gelding returned lame

116 PONTIN'S HOLIDAYS MEDIAN AUCTION MAIDEN STKS (DIV II) 1m (P)
1:55 (2:00) (Class 6) 3-Y-O £2,047 (£604; £302) Stalls High

Form RPR
050- **1** **Tasweet (IRE)**[41] 6689 3-9-3 67 ....(v1) JoeFanning 6 70+
(T G Mills) *mde virtually all: rdn clr fr over 1f out: unchal after* **2/1**[1]
33-2 **2** 3 1/2 **Not Too Taxing**[5] 69 3-9-0 .... StephaneBreux(3) 10 59
(R Hannon) *chsd wnr to 3f out: pushed along after: edgd lft over 2f out: bmpd along and disp wl btn 2nd fr over 1f out* **9/4**[2]
43-4 **3** shd **Tension Point**[7] 58 3-9-3 68 ....(p) ShaneKelly 7 59
(J A Osborne) *prom: chsd wnr 3f out: outpcd wl over 1f out: disp wl btn 2nd after* **6/1**
60-2 **4** 1 1/4 **Mick Is Back**[8] 40 3-9-0 57 ....(b1) StephenDonohoe(3) 9 56
(P D Evans) *t.k.h: hld up bhd ldrs: rdn and effrt over 2f out: one pce* **16/1**
00- **5** 1/2 **Royal Tender (IRE)**[37] 6737 3-8-12 .... FergusSweeney 5 50
(B G Powell) *dwlt: wl in rr: shkn up and prog to chse ldrs 2f out: one pce over 1f out: kpt on* **50/1**
6 3/4 **Title Deed (USA)** 3-9-3 .... NCallan 2 62+
(A P Jarvis) *s.i.s: sn prom: effrt whn hmpd on inner jst over 2f out and wl over 1f out: eased* **4/1**[3]
0- **7** 1/2 **Poyle Ruby**[26] 6853 3-8-12 .... JimmyQuinn 4 47+
(M Blanshard) *off the pce in midfield sn after 1/2-way: green and n.m.r 2f out : n.d after* **66/1**
8 hd **Woodygo** 3-9-3 .... BrettDoyle 8 52+
(J R Best) *awkward s: wl in rr: detached in last pair over 3f out: v green but styd on takingly fnl f* **12/1**
00- **9** 3 **My Monna**[24] 6879 3-8-5 .... HaddenFrost(7) 1 45+
(Miss Sheena West) *pushed along in midfield 5f out: off the pce over 3f out: n.d after* **33/1**
10 17 **Magroom** 3-9-3 .... ChrisCatlin 3 6
(B R Johnson) *dwlt: wl in rr: shied at bnd 5f out: sn detached: t.o* **33/1**
1m 39.92s (0.49) **Going Correction** +0.01s/f (Slow) 35 Ran SP% **121.3**
Speed ratings (Par 95):97,93,93,92,91 90,90,90,87,70
CSF £6.91 TOTE £3.40: £1.60, £1.60, £1.80; EX 9.60 Trifecta £142.90 Pool: £300.00 - 1.49 winning units..
Owner J Daniels **Bred** Shadwell Estate Company Limited **Trained** Headley, Surrey
■ Stewards' Enquiry : Stephane Breux two-day ban; careless riding (Jan 24-25)
FOCUS
The quicker of the two divisions by 1.22sec and a pleasing performance from Tasweet, who should make his mark in handicaps. The fourth and fifth tend to limit the form, but the winner could be rated significantly higher through the second and third.
Royal Tender(IRE) Official explanation: jockey said filly lost a hind shoe

117 GO PONTIN'S H'CAP 1m 2f (P)
2:35 (2:36) (Class 5) (0-70,71) 4-Y-0+ £2,914 (£867; £433; £216) Stalls Low

Form RPR
2/5- **1** **Lunar Promise (IRE)**[42] 6684 5-9-0 **69** .... StephenDonohoe(3) 14 81
(Ian Williams) *wl plcd: led on outer over 3f out: kicked on 2f out: hrd pressed fnl f: drvn and styd on wl* **8/1**

The Form Book, Raceform Ltd, Compton, RG20 6NL

561- **2** 1/2 **Samarinda (USA)**[14] 6987 4-8-13 **67** MickyFenton 6 78
(Mrs P Sly) *prom: lost pl on inner sltly 3f out but stl gng wl: effrt over 1f out: pressed wnr fnl f: styd on but a hld* **14/1**

312- **3** 1 3/4 **Snowy Day (FR)**[46] 6647 4-8-11 **65** TonyCulhane 2 73+
(W J Haggas) *t.k.h: hld up in midfield: rdn and effrt 2f out: styd on fr over 1f out: nt pce of ldng pair* **9/2**[1]

012- **4** 1/2 **Reaching Out (IRE)**[15] 6980 5-8-5 **60** (b) JamesDoyle(3) 10 67+
(N P Littmoden) *hld up wl in rr: prog on wd outside wl over 1f out: styd on fnl f: nrst fin* **7/1**[3]

04-3 **5** 1 **Barry Island**[10] 30 8-8-9 **64** MarcHalford(3) 8 69
(D R C Elsworth) *s.s: hld up in last pair in slowly run r: prog on inner over 1f out: rdn and fnd little fnl f* **14/1**

450- **6** 3 **Easy Laughter (IRE)**[53] 965 6-8-12 **64** FergusSweeney 12 63
(A King) *prom: rdn to chal 3f out: outpcd fr 2f out: fdd* **16/1**

613- **7** hd **Broughtons Folly**[39] 6712 4-9-1 **69** TPQueally 11 68+
(W J Musson) *dwlt: t.k.h: hld up in last pair in slowly run r: rdn over 2f out: styd on fnl f: no ch* **13/2**[2]

23-2 **8** hd **Berkhamsted (IRE)**[10] 30 5-9-5 **71** JimCrowley 3 69
(Tom Dascombe) *hld up in midfield: chsng ldrs and wl in tch 2f out: wknd tamely over 1f out* **15/2**

30-0 **9** shd **Smokin Joe**[7] 56 6-9-1 **67** (b) BrettDoyle 4 65
(J R Best) *plld hrd: hld up towards rr: prog on outer to press ldrs 2f out: wknd over 1f out* **9/1**

056- **10** 1 1/4 **Just Fly**[33] 6791 7-8-2 **59** (b[1]) KevinGhunowa(5) 1 55
(Dr J R J Naylor) *t.k.h: hld up towards rr: brief effrt on inner wl over 1f out: sn btn* **25/1**

00-1 **11** 1 1/2 **King Of Music (USA)**[7] 52 6-8-13 **65** ShaneKelly 13 58
(Miss Gay Kelleway) *dwlt: t.k.h: hld up in last tl rapid prog to ld over 6f out: hdd over 3f out: wknd rapidly over 1f out* **15/2**

10-6 **12** 1 1/4 **Siena Star (IRE)**[7] 48 9-8-10 **62** NCallan 9 53
(Stef Liddiard) *led at slow pce to over 6f out: upsides 3f out: wkng whn n.m.r over 1f out: eased* **20/1**

00- **13** nk **Lit Et Mixe (FR)**[42] 6673 4-8-11 **65** ChrisCatlin 7 55
(Noel T Chance) *t.k.h: hld up in last trio: struggling over 2f out* **40/1**

000- **14** hd **Sundance (IRE)**[50] 6579 5-8-8 **60** JimmyQuinn 5 50
(H J Collingridge) *hld up in midfield: shkn up over 2f out: sn lost pl* **50/1**

2m 7.82s (0.03) **Going Correction** +0.01s/f (Slow)
WFA 4 from 5yo+ 2lb **14 Ran SP% 120.9**
Speed ratings (Par 103):99,98,97,96,96 93,93,93,93,92 91,90,89,89
CSF £111.10 CT £573.69 TOTE £7.70: £2.20, £5.70, £1.90; EX 205.20 TRIFECTA Not won..
Owner A L R Morton **Bred** Deer Forest Stud Ltd **Trained** Portway, Worcs

FOCUS
A modest handicap run at a steady early pace. It paid to be handy, and several confirmed hold-up horses were at a distinct disadvantage. A negative view has been taken of the form overall.
King Of Music(USA) Official explanation: jockey said gelding ran too keenly early stages

118 RACHEL PERCHARD 40TH BIRTHDAY CONDITIONS STKS 6f (P)
3:05 (3:06) (Class 2) 3-Y-0+
£11,217 (£3,358; £1,679; £840; £419; £210) **Stalls** Low

Form RPR

11-4 **1** **Areyoutalkingtome**[8] 43 4-9-8 110 TonyCulhane 1 112+
(C A Cyzer) *hld up bhd ldrs: sltly unbalanced wl over 1f out: effrt to ld jst ins fnl f: pushed clr: readily* **5/4**[1]

404- **2** 1 1/2 **Red Cape (FR)**[84] 6101 4-9-5 85 JohnEgan 7 102
(Jane Chapple-Hyam) *hld up in tch: effrt 2f out: r.o fnl f to take 2nd nr fin: no ch w wnr* **16/1**

111- **3** shd **Hurricane Spirit (IRE)**[24] 6881 3-8-11 102 BrettDoyle 8 106+
(J R Best) *hld up in tch: effrt 2f out: rdn and nt qckn over 1f out: styd on to take 3rd last stride* **2/1**[2]

32-1 **4** shd **Qadar (IRE)**[8] 41 5-9-5 97 NCallan 4 102
(N P Littmoden) *trckd ldrs: rdn to chal over 1f out: upsides 1f out: sn outpcd by wnr: lost 2 pls nr fin* **4/1**[3]

100- **5** 1/2 **Waterside (IRE)**[119] 5357 8-9-5 89 TPQueally 6 100
(G L Moore) *pressed ldr: narrow ld fr 1/2-way: rdn and hdd jst ins fnl f: fdd* **33/1**

003- **6** 1 1/2 **Party Boss**[53] 6559 5-9-5 97 SebSanders 2 96
(C E Brittain) *led to 1/2-way: sn pushed along: wknd fnl f* **12/1**

000/ **7** 1 **Tony James (IRE)**[456] 5873 5-9-5 106 ChrisCatlin 3 93
(K O Cunningham-Brown) *dwlt: a in last trio: rdn and struggling over 2f out* **66/1**

1m 10.48s (-2.33) **Going Correction** +0.01s/f (Slow) course record
WFA 3 from 4yo+ 16lb **7 Ran SP% 115.8**
Speed ratings (Par 109):115,113,112,112,112 110,108
CSF £24.28 TOTE £2.30: £1.50, £4.20; EX 35.90 Trifecta £84.10 Pool: £601.90 - 5.08 winning tickets..
Owner Mrs Charles Cyzer **Bred** C A Cyzer **Trained** Maplehurst, W Sussex

FOCUS
A good quality conditions race run at a strong pace, and that suited the horses that were held up. In splitting two highly progressive all-weather specialists the runner-up seems to have improved, but his form is not worryingly out of line, especially as the recent gelding operation offers a feasible explanation.

NOTEBOOK
Areyoutalkingtome travelled strongly off the good pace and, when the gap opened up in the straight, he burst through in fine style. He won easily, although he didn't need to be at his best to beat an 85-rated runner-up. He has now won his last five starts at this track, which connections believe suits him better than Wolverhampton, although the pace may have been as much to blame for his defeat there as much as the trip or track . (op 6-4 tchd 11-10)
Red Cape(FR), who has been gelded since his last outing in October, had a lot to do with the principals on official ratings, but he was suited by the way the race was run and seemed to appreciate the drop back to six furlongs. He ran on well to chase the easy winner home, and while this will do his handicap mark no good connections have identified opportunities for him in the South of France. (op 20-1)
Hurricane Spirit(IRE) lost his unbeaten record on the All-Weather but this was still a fine effort from a three-year-old so early in the year. He can only improve further. (op 13-8 tchd 9-4, 5-2 in places and 11-4 in a place)
Qadar(IRE) came here in form having won a handicap off 97 at Wolverhampton last time, but he had been beaten by Areyoutalkingtome on a couple of occasions previously this winter and the weights hardly favoured a turnaround in form. (tchd 9-2)
Waterside(IRE), who helped set a good gallop, had quite a bit to do at the weights and could well have needed this first start since September. He is at his best over further and this run should have blown away the cobwebs.
Party Boss set a fast pace out in front and could not sustain that gallop in the closing stages. (op 10-1)
Tony James(IRE) had not run since October 2005 and this performance suggests he still has to prove that he retains his ability.

119 PONTIN'S BOOK EARLY H'CAP 1m 2f (P)
3:35 (3:35) (Class 2) (0-100,101) 4-Y-0+
£11,217 (£3,358; £1,679; £840; £419; £210) **Stalls** Low

Form RPR

42-4 **1** **Fusili (IRE)**[7] 57 4-8-4 **91** JamesDoyle(3) 8 99
(N P Littmoden) *trckd ldr: led wl over 2f out and kicked on: drvn over 1f out: hld on wl* **9/1**

22-2 **2** 1/2 **Red Spell (IRE)**[8] 43 6-8-12 **101** HaddenFrost(7) 6 108
(R Hannon) *t.k.h: hld up in last pair: plenty to do after wnr kicked on over 2f out: rdn and r.o to take 2nd nr fin* **9/2**[2]

31-4 **3** 1/2 **Very Wise**[12] 6 5-8-4 **86** oh2 JoeFanning 2 92
(W J Haggas) *sn led and dictated stdy pce: hdd wl over 2f out: styd chsng wnr: nt qckn fnl f: lost 2nd nr fin* **11/1**

151- **4** hd **Orchard Supreme**[22] 6915 4-8-10 **97** StephaneBreux(3) 5 103
(R Hannon) *hld up in last pair: plenty to do after wnr kicked on over 2f out: prog on inner over 1f out: kpt on: nvr able to chal* **9/2**[2]

221- **5** hd **Happy As Larry (USA)**[14] 6986 5-8-4 **86** JohnEgan 7 91
(T J Pitt) *hld up in tch: plenty to do after wnr kicked on over 2f out: styd on fr over 1f out: nvr able to chal* **15/8**[1]

344- **6** 3/4 **Kindlelight Debut**[13] 6997 7-9-0 **96** NCallan 4 100
(N P Littmoden) *trckd ldng trio: rdn and outpcd over 2f out: effrt over 1f out: fdd ins fnl f* **16/1**

361- **7** 1 **Bahar Shumaal (IRE)**[13] 6997 5-9-1 **97** (b) SebSanders 3 99
(C E Brittain) *hld up in 5th: trapped bhd rivals whn wnr kicked on over 2f out: no ch to rcvr* **5/1**[3]

000- **8** 1/2 **San Antonio**[37] 5785 7-7-11 **86** oh5 JosephWalsh(7) 1 87
(Mrs P Sly) *chsd ldng pair to over 2f out: sn rdn: wknd fnl f* **40/1**

2m 7.88s (0.09) **Going Correction** +0.01s/f (Slow)
WFA 4 from 5yo+ 2lb **8 Ran SP% 114.5**
Speed ratings (Par 109):99,98,98,98,97 97,96,96
CSF £49.15 CT £453.24 TOTE £10.20: £2.70, £1.20, £3.30; EX 50.00 Trifecta £280.30 Pool: £580.48 - 1.47 winning units..
Owner Nigel Shields **Bred** Gestut Romerhof **Trained** Newmarket, Suffolk

FOCUS
A decent handicap, but it was run at a steady pace and the time was the slowest of four on the card over the trip. It turned into a sprint and it paid to race prominently.

NOTEBOOK
Fusili(IRE) was never far off the pace in a race run at an ordinary gallop, which meant that she was well positioned for the sprint for home. Always in control once she hit the front, she improved her course and distance form to 1334131. (op 11-1)
Red Spell(IRE), who was stepping up in trip, did not have the race run to suit as he was held up at the back of the field and had work to do when the leaders quickened things up off the slow early pace. He ran on well to close in on the winner late on, but that only took his run of seconds to four, and he remains tricky to win with. (op 4-1)
Very Wise did not really take to the Fibresand last time and was happier back on Polytrack, a surface he has won on at Wolverhampton. He set a steady pace but was keen, and that took its toll in the closing stages as those held up charged at him. (op 10-1 tchd 12-1)
Orchard Supreme had a course record of 21311136251 coming into the race but he had not run over a distance this far before in his career and he had his stamina to prove. The way the race was run ought to have helped on that score, but he is a hold-up performer who runs his best races when challenging from off a good pace, and he did not get that here. (op 4-1 tchd 5-1)
Happy As Larry(USA) was also staying on late having not had the race run to suit. Only put up 3lb for his win here last month over a mile, he is a progressive type and could still defy his current mark in the coming weeks. (op 9-4 tchd 7-4 in places)
Kindlelight Debut, who earned herself some black type here in the autumn, has paid the price with a raised handicap mark, and she is now finding things difficult in this sphere.
Bahar Shumaal(IRE) never really got a clear run from the turn into the straight and he can be forgiven his finishing position. (op 11-2)

120 GO PONTIN'S MAIDEN STKS 1m 2f (P)
4:05 (4:06) (Class 5) 4-Y-0+ **£2,817** (£838; £418; £209) **Stalls** Low

Form RPR

/33- **1** **Mighty**[210] 2662 4-9-3 BrettDoyle 7 80+
(Jane Chapple-Hyam) *trckd ldrs: smart prog to go 2nd over 2f out: led over 1f out: r.o wl: readily* **7/4**[2]

6- **2** 2 1/2 **Augustus John (IRE)**[66] 6406 4-9-3 60 JohnEgan 5 72
(T J Pitt) *led at slow pce to over 7f out: led again wl over 2f out and sn kicked on: hdd over 1f out: sn no ch w wnr* **11/10**[1]

422- **3** 2 1/2 **Art Investor**[42] 6680 4-9-0 69 MarcHalford(3) 6 67
(D R C Elsworth) *trckd ldrs: rdn to chse ldng pair 2f out: carried hd high and no imp over 1f out* **10/3**[3]

000- **4** 10 **Dik Dik**[60] 6482 4-9-3 48 TonyCulhane 2 48
(J S Moore) *hld up in last: outpcd 3f out: shuffled along and styd on to take modest 4th nr fin: nvr nr ldrs* **20/1**

050- **5** 3/4 **War Feather**[38] 6729 5-9-5 41 AdamKirby 4 47
(T D McCarthy) *in tch: drvn fr 1/2-way: wknd over 2f out* **50/1**

6 3 **Mustard Benn** 4-9-3 ChrisCatlin 8 41
(Mouse Hamilton-Fairley) *t.k.h early: hld up: rdn and wknd 3f out* **50/1**

450- **7** 3 1/2 **Spoilsport**[17] 6955 4-8-9 49 (p) StephenDonohoe(3) 1 30
(P D Evans) *plld hrd: hld up tl prog to ld over 7f out: hdd wl over 2f out: wknd rapidly over 1f out* **33/1**

2m 7.44s (-0.35) **Going Correction** +0.01s/f (Slow)
WFA 4 from 5yo 2lb **7 Ran SP% 118.7**
Speed ratings (Par 103):101,99,97,89,88 86,83
CSF £4.20 TOTE £3.50: £1.70, £1.10; EX 5.40 Trifecta £15.00 Pool: £619.49 - 29.22 winning units. Place 6 £104.08, Place 5 £87.28.
Owner Franconson Partners And Vanessa Church **Bred** Cheveley Park Stud Ltd **Trained** Newmarket, Suffolk

■ Stewards' Enquiry : Adam Kirby two-day ban; careless riding (Jan 24-25)

FOCUS
A modest maiden run at an ordinary early pace. The first three pulled a long way clear of some poor performers.
T/Plt: £210.20 to a £1 stake. Pool: £46,401.90. 161.10 winning tickets. T/Qpdt: £50.70 to a £1 stake. Pool: £3,578.90. 52.20 winning tickets. JN

[106]WOLVERHAMPTON (A.W) (L-H)

Saturday, January 13

OFFICIAL GOING: Standard

Wind: Fresh, behind Weather: Cloudy

121 PONTINS.COM H'CAP 1m 1f 103y(P)

3:45 (3:45) (Class 6) (0-52,57) 4-Y-0+ £2,149 (£634; £317) Stalls Low

Form RPR

33-3 **1** **Desert Hawk**[5] 71 6-8-10 **50**....(b) RobbieFitzpatrick 9 62
(W M Brisbourne) *s.i.s: hld up: hdwy and edgd rt wl over 1f out: hung lft and r.o to ld wl ins fnl f* **5/2**[1]

42-0 **2** 1 1/2 **King Of Knight (IRE)**[10] 19 6-8-12 **52**.... AdrianMcCarthy 3 61
(G Prodromou) *chsd ldrs: led over 2f out: clr over 1f out: hdd wl ins fnl f* **7/1**[3]

000- **3** 3 1/2 **Zando**[15] 6980 5-8-5 **50**.... TolleyDean(5) 12 52
(E G Bevan) *hdwy 6f out: rdn and ev ch whn edgd lft over 2f out: styd on same pce appr fnl f* **50/1**

40-2 **4** 1/2 **Jiminor Mack**[8] 42 4-8-3 **46** oh1 ow1....(b) RichardKingscote(3) 5 48
(W J H Ratcliffe) *dwlt: outpcd: hdwy over 1f out: nt trble ldrs* **11/1**

540- **5** 1 1/2 **Connotation**[39] 6714 5-8-9 **52**....(b) AmirQuinn(3) 1 50
(A G Newcombe) *sn pushed along and prom: rdn over 2f out: hung rt wl over 1f out: sn wknd* **7/1**[3]

0/6- **6** 3 1/2 **High Country (IRE)**[67] 597 7-8-7 **50**.... GregFairley(3) 13 41
(Micky Hammond) *sn pushed along in rr: nvr nrr* **16/1**

0- **7** 1 3/4 **Spurron (IRE)**[54] 6545 7-8-6 **46** oh1.... PaulFessey 11 34
(Gerard Keane, Ire) *hld up: hdwy u.p over 2f out: hung lft and wknd over 1f out* **33/1**

060- **8** 1 **Lockstock (IRE)**[32] 6798 9-8-9 **49**....(p) GrahamGibbons 6 35
(M S Saunders) *chsd ldrs: rdn whn hmpd over 2f out: sn wknd* **20/1**

20-4 **9** nk **Milk And Sultana**[10] 19 7-8-10 **50**.... EdwardCreighton 10 35
(G A Ham) *hld up: rdn over 3f out: wknd over 2f out* **8/1**

10 1 1/4 **Ceol Eile (IRE)**[69] 6361 4-8-11 **52**.... J-PGuillambert 4 34
(D Haydn Jones) *prom 6f* **20/1**

030- **11** nk **The Pen**[150] 4472 5-8-12 **52**.... PaulMulrennan 7 34
(C W Fairhurst) *prom: rdn whn hmpd over 2f out: sn wknd* **12/1**

004- **12** 2 **Peas 'n Beans (IRE)**[15] 6973 4-8-7 **48**.... PaulDoe 2 26
(T Keddy) *sn led: rdn: edgd rt and hdd over 2f out: wkng whn hmpd wl over 1f out* **11/2**[2]

2m 2.61s (-0.01) **Going Correction** +0.075s/f (Slow)
WFA 4 from 5yo+ 1lb **12** Ran SP% **116.4**
Speed ratings (Par 101):103,101,98,98,96 93,92,91,90,89 89,87
CSF £18.22 CT £695.52 TOTE £4.10: £1.10, £2.80, £11.20; EX 32.40.
Owner J Jones Racing Ltd **Bred** C J Mills **Trained** Great Ness, Shropshire
■ Stewards' Enquiry : Tolley Dean one-day ban: careless riding (Jan 24)

FOCUS
A moderate handicap, not much better than banded level, but Desert Hawk produced his best form for two years off the strong pace. The runner-up did best of the prominent runners.

122 PONTIN'S FAMILY HOLIDAYS H'CAP 7f 32y(P)

4:20 (4:20) (Class 6) (0-65,62) 3-Y-0 £3,071 (£906; £453) Stalls High

Form RPR

51-4 **1** **Ella Y Rossa**[10] 21 3-8-7 **53**.... CatherineGannon 1 59+
(P D Evans) *hld up in tch: rdn over 2f out: led and edgd rt ins fnl f: r.o: eased nr fin* **8/1**

050- **2** 2 **Pietersen (IRE)**[37] 6736 3-8-8 **54**....(b) PaulFessey 8 55
(T D Barron) *led 6f out: rdn: hung rt and hdd over 1f out: styd on same pce ins fnl f* **13/2**[3]

605- **3** nk **Knapton Hill**[21] 6926 3-8-12 **58**.... GrahamGibbons 3 58
(R Hollinshead) *hld up: hdwy u.p over 2f out: nt clr run wl over 1f out : styd on* **15/2**

112- **4** 2 **Charlotte Grey**[21] 6931 3-9-1 **61**.... EdwardCreighton 2 56
(C N Allen) *led 1f: chsd ldr: rdn to ld over 1f out: hdd and no ex ins fnl f* **11/4**[1]

005- **5** 4 **Brynris**[17] 6951 3-8-2 **48** oh3.... PaulQuinn 5 32
(Mrs G S Rees) *chsd ldrs: rdn 1/2-way: wknd fnl f* **50/1**

15-3 **6** hd **Beau Sancy**[7] 58 3-8-10 **61**.... TolleyDean(5) 6 45
(R A Harris) *s.i.s: outpcd: nvr nrr* **10/3**[2]

000- **7** 3 1/2 **Hoh Me Hoh You (IRE)**[22] 6912 3-8-10 **56**.... FrankieMcDonald 7 31
(S Kirk) *chsd ldrs over 4f* **10/1**

50-4 **8** 1/2 **Emefdream**[6] 65 3-9-2 **62**....(p) DanielTudhope 4 35
(Mrs N Macauley) *hld up in tch: lost pl 4f out: wknd over 2f out* **11/1**

060- **9** 11 **Bold Nevison (IRE)**[23] 6891 3-8-10 **59**.... MarkLawson(3) 9 4
(B Smart) *s.i.s: hdwy over 5f out: rdn and wknd over 2f out* **16/1**

1m 32.13s (1.73) **Going Correction** +0.075s/f (Slow) **9** Ran SP% **111.2**
Speed ratings (Par 95):93,90,90,88,83 83,79,78,66
CSF £55.82 CT £396.23 TOTE £6.50: £2.20, £2.20, £2.10; EX 39.90.
Owner Miss D L Wisbey & R J Viney **Bred** Miss Deborah Wisbey **Trained** Pandy, Monmouths

FOCUS
A modest handicap but solid enough form for the grade based on the performances of the runner-up and fifth.

123 GO PONTIN'S H'CAP 7f 32y(P)

4:50 (4:50) (Class 6) (0-50,50) 4-Y-0+ £2,149 (£634; £317) Stalls High

Form RPR

031- **1** **Shava**[31] 6805 7-8-9 **50**.... AmirQuinn(3) 9 58+
(H J Evans) *s.i.s: hld up: nt clr run over 2f out: hdwy over 1f out : rdn to ld ins fnl f: styd on* **4/1**[3]

650- **2** 3/4 **Seldemosa**[17] 6955 6-8-10 **48**.... J-PGuillambert 3 51
(M S Saunders) *s.i.s: sn prom: rdn to ld over 2f out: hdd ins fnl f: styd on* **12/1**

030- **3** 3/4 **Diamond Katie (IRE)**[82] 6142 5-8-7 **50**.... DuranFentiman(5) 7 52
(N Tinkler) *hld up: hdwy over 2f out: rdn over 1f out: edgd lft ins fnl f: styd on* **12/1**

060- **4** hd **Kahlua Bear**[110] 5576 5-8-12 **50**....(v) AdrianMcCarthy 8 51
(Miss K B Boutflower) *mid-div: rdn 1/2-way: hdwy over 2f out: nt pce to chal* **20/1**

000- **5** 1/2 **Cape Of Storms**[39] 6721 4-8-12 **50**.... PatCosgrave 10 50
(R Brotherton) *sn outpcd: r.o u.p ins fnl f: nt rch ldrs* **33/1**

603- **6** 1 1/2 **Barry The Brave**[16] 6961 5-8-7 **48**.... GregFairley(3) 1 44
(Micky Hammond) *chsd ldrs: led over 2f out: sn rdn and hdd: wknd ins fnl f* **11/2**

52-4 **7** shd **Louisiade (IRE)**[4] 75 6-8-12 **50**....(b) CatherineGannon 5 46
(K A Ryan) *chsd ldrs: rdn over 2f out: styd on same pce appr fnl f* **10/3**[2]

/05- **8** 6 **Oakbridge (IRE)**[40] 6708 5-8-11 **49**....(b[1]) EdwardCreighton 2 29
(D J Wintle) *plld hrd: led over 5f out: rdn and hdd over 2f out: wknd over 1f out* **11/4**[1]

30-0 **9** 53 **Dexileos (IRE)**[3] 94 8-8-6 **49**....(t) AshleyHamblett(5) 4 —
(David Pinder) *chsd ldrs: lost pl whn hmpd over 4f out: hmpd wl over 3f out: sn lost tch* **17/2**

0/0- **B** **Blakeshall Boy**[14] 6983 9-8-3 **48**.... MarkCoumbe(7) 6 —
(A J Chamberlain) *s.i.s: outpcd: bhd whn b.d 1/2-way: dead* **66/1**

/06- **F** **Epices**[14] 6982 5-8-10 **48**.... AdrianTNicholls 11 —
(R Ingram) *sn led: hdd over 5f out: b.b.v, swtchd rt and pulling up whn fell 1/2-way: dead* **50/1**

1m 31.86s (1.46) **Going Correction** +0.075s/f (Slow) **11** Ran SP% **122.2**
Speed ratings (Par 101):94,93,92,92,91 89,89,82,22,— —
CSF £51.48 CT £554.11 TOTE £6.30: £2.10, £3.50, £2.70; EX 62.20.
Owner Mrs J Evans **Bred** Slatch Farm Stud **Trained** Honeybourne, Worcs
■ Stewards' Enquiry : Amir Quinn one-day ban: used whip with excessive frequency (Jan 24)

FOCUS
A banded-style handicap run at a good pace. The form is weak.
Oakbridge(IRE) Official explanation: jockey said gelding ran too free
Dexileos(IRE) Official explanation: jockey said gelding was hampered and lost its action

124 PONTINSBINGO.COM H'CAP 1m 141y(P)

5:20 (5:27) (Class 6) (0-58,58) 4-Y-0+ £3,071 (£906; £453) Stalls Low

Form RPR

01-4 **1** **Norwegian**[8] 42 6-8-7 **50**....(p) PaulEddery 4 59
(Ian Williams) *a.p: chsd ldr over 2f out: rdn to ld ins fnl f: styd on* **8/1**

603- **2** nk **Cabourg (IRE)**[15] 6977 4-8-9 **56**.... GregFairley(3) 13 64
(R Bastiman) *hld up: hdwy over 2f out: rdn and hung lft over 1f out: ev ch ins fnl f: nt run on* **17/2**

51-6 **3** 1 **Harare**[5] 72 6-9-1 **58**....(b) DanielTudhope 12 64
(R J Price) *hld up: hdwy over 3f out: rdn and hung lft over 1f out: nt clr run ins fnl f: kpt on* **11/2**[2]

132- **4** 1 3/4 **Spark Up**[14] 6993 7-8-11 **57**....(b) RichardKingscote(3) 3 59
(J W Unett) *led: hdd over 7f out: led again over 6f out: rdn and hdd ins fnl f: no ex* **13/2**[3]

01-0 **5** 5 **Golden Spectrum (IRE)**[4] 75 8-8-10 **58**....(b) TolleyDean(5) 10 50
(R A Harris) *s.i.s: sn pushed along in rr: hmpd over 3f out: styd on ins fnl f: nvr nrr* **14/1**

152- **6** 3/4 **Green Pirate**[16] 6964 5-8-8 **56**.... JamieMoriarty(5) 5 46
(W M Brisbourne) *slwoly into stride: hld up: hmpd over 6f out and over 2f out: nvr trbld ldrs* **2/1**[1]

064- **7** 3/4 **Burnley Al (IRE)**[15] 6977 5-8-12 **55**....(b) RobbieFitzpatrick 2 44
(Peter Grayson) *racd keenly: w ldr tl led over 7f out: hdd over 6f out: rdn over 2f out: wknd over 1f out* **11/1**

452- **8** 1/2 **Prince Vettori**[14] 6982 5-8-11 **54**.... CatherineGannon 8 42
(Mrs Norma Pook) *chsd ldrs 6f* **25/1**

006- **9** 1 **Opus Magnus (IRE)**[90] 5988 4-8-9 **53**.... JimmyQuinn 11 39
(P J Makin) *hld up in tch: rdn over 3f out: wknd over 2f out* **12/1**

004- **10** hd **Pay On (IRE)**[14] 3626 4-8-9 **53**....(v) PatCosgrave 6 38
(A C Whillans) *prom 6f* **66/1**

00-0 **11** 1 1/2 **Lord Chamberlain**[9] 32 14-8-5 **55**....(b) BarrySavage(7) 1 37
(J M Bradley) *s.i.s: a in rr* **33/1**

533- **12** 6 **Going Skint**[17] 6944 4-8-8 **57**.... DuranFentiman(5) 7 26
(M Wellings) *prom: nt clr run and lost pl over 6f out: in rr whn hmpd over 3f out: n.d after* **16/1**

360/ **13** 3 **Miss Ladybird (USA)**[884] 4680 6-8-7 **53**.... SaleemGolam(3) 9 16
(T J Etherington) *hld up: hmpd over 3f out: a in rr* **50/1**

1m 51.52s (-0.24) **Going Correction** +0.075s/f (Slow)
WFA 4 from 5yo+ 1lb **13** Ran SP% **122.5**
Speed ratings (Par 101):104,103,102,101,96 96,95,95,94,94 92,87,84
CSF £74.52 CT £426.18 TOTE £7.80: £3.00, £3.30, £2.50; EX 79.80.
Owner Robert Bee **Bred** Darley **Trained** Portway, Worcs

FOCUS
A moderate but competitive handicap. Sound form, Norwegian running his best race since he was a three-year-old.
Green Pirate Official explanation: jockey said gelding was denied a clear run
Going Skint Official explanation: vet said gelding returned lame

125 PONTIN'S FAMILY HOLIDAYS MEDIAN AUCTION MAIDEN STKS 5f 20y(P)

5:50 (5:56) (Class 6) 4-6-Y-0 £2,047 (£604; £302) Stalls Low

Form RPR

20-4 **1** **Tajjree**[9] 36 4-8-12 52....(tp) AdrianMcCarthy 7 54
(Miss K B Boutflower) *chsd ldrs: led 2f out: rdn out* **9/2**[2]

202- **2** 2 **Kitchen Sink (IRE)**[24] 6890 5-9-3 58....(e) JimmyQuinn 6 52
(P J Makin) *trckd ldrs: rdn and hung lft fr over 1f out: nt trble wnr* **1/2**[1]

050- **3** nk **Optical Seclusion (IRE)**[66] 6403 4-9-0 45....(b) SaleemGolam(3) 4 51
(T J Etherington) *chsd ldrs: hmpd over 3f out: rdn and ev ch over 1f out: no ex ins fnl f* **40/1**

00-0 **4** 1 1/4 **Mind That Fox**[9] 33 5-9-3 36.... GrahamGibbons 5 46
(T Wall) *prom: hrd rdn and hung lft fr over 1f out tl no ex ins fnl f* **66/1**

02-0 **5** 1 1/2 **Left Nostril (IRE)**[11] 13 4-8-12 48.... BrianReilly 3 36
(P S McEntee) *prom: hmpd over 3f out: rdn and hung lft 1/2-way: styd on same pce fnl f* **18/1**

524/ **6** 1 **Kung Hei**[590] 2216 4-9-3 74.... PaulMulrennan 10 37
(Mrs L Stubbs) *led 3f: wknd fnl f* **10/1**[3]

00-0 **7** nk **Miss Redactive**[10] 20 4-8-12 38.... EdwardCreighton 1 31
(M D I Usher) *chsd ldrs: lost pl 4f out: n.d after* **28/1**

4-0 **8** 3 **Xocolatl**[9] 36 4-8-12.... RobbieFitzpatrick 9 20
(Peter Grayson) *sn outpcd* **40/1**

305- **9** 2 1/2 **Comic Tales**[7] 6944 6-9-3 45.... CatherineGannon 8 16
(M Mullineaux) *s.s: outpcd* **40/1**

0 **10** 2 1/2 **Grace Bay**[7] 49 4-8-7.... AshleyHamblett(5) 2 —
(Bob Jones) *s.i.s: a in rr: bhd whn hung lft over 1f out* **125/1**

63.25 secs (0.43) **Going Correction** +0.075s/f (Slow) **10** Ran SP% **112.3**
Speed ratings: 99,95,95,93,90 89,88,84,80,76
CSF £6.62 TOTE £11.70: £1.60, £1.10, £11.50; EX 12.10.
Owner www.network-racing.com **Bred** Darley **Trained** Newmarket, Suffolk

FOCUS
A terrible maiden; worse than most banded races overall and not worth dwelling on. It has been rated through the fourth.

126 PONTINS.COM CLASSIFIED STKS 1m 4f 50y(P)

6:20 (6:26) (Class 7) 4-Y-0+ £1,911 (£564; £282) Stalls Low

Form RPR

0-35 **1** **Diktatorship (IRE)**[5] 71 4-8-7 45....(tp) AshleyHamblett(5) 6 55
(Ernst Oertel) *mde all: rdn over 1f out: styd on* **9/2**[3]

000- **2** 1 1/2 **Trysting Grove (IRE)**[74] 6280 6-8-11 41 .... TolleyDean(5) 1 53
(E G Bevan) *hld up: hdwy over 2f out: styd on to go 2nd wl ins fnl f: nt rch wnr* **25/1**
25-4 **3** 4 3/4 **Gallas (IRE)**[8] 45 6-9-2 45 ....(b) AdrianMcCarthy 10 45
(S Lycett) *hld up: hdwy over 3f out: rdn over 2f out: styd on same pce* **11/4**[1]
000- **4** 6 **Fuel Cell (IRE)**[33] 6790 6-8-11 45 .... DuranFentiman(5) 2 35
(J O'Reilly) *prom over 9f* **12/1**
64-6 **5** 2 1/2 **Laurollie**[4] 78 5-8-9 41 .... SoniaEaton(7) 3 31
(B P J Baugh) *s.i.s: hld up: hmpd 4f out: nvr nrr* **16/1**
565- **6** 1 1/4 **Galley Law**[220] 1574 7-9-2 45 .... RobbieFitzpatrick 12 29
(W M Brisbourne) *chsd ldrs over 9f* **7/1**
000- **7** 6 **Danum**[40] 6701 7-8-11 40 ....(p) RussellKennemore(5) 11 20
(R Hollinshead) *hld up: a in rr* **33/1**
045- **8** 2 1/2 **Scurra**[41] 6161 8-9-2 37 ....(p) PatCosgrave 5 16
(A C Whillans) *hld up: rdn over 3f out: sn wknd* **14/1**
000- **9** 1 3/4 **Monkstown Road**[21] 6936 5-9-2 45 ....(p) JimmyQuinn 8 13
(C N Kellett) *mid-div: rdn over 3f out: wknd over 2f out* **25/1**
435- **10** 1 3/4 **Heathyards Joy**[54] 2725 6-9-2 41 ....(p) GrahamGibbons 9 10
(R Hollinshead) *hld up: rdn and wknd over 2f out* **9/1**
0/0- **11** 11 **Caliban (IRE)**[37] 6560 9-9-2 40 ....(b) PaulEddery 7 —
(Ian Williams) *chsd ldrs 8f* **25/1**
060- **D** 3/4 **Apache Fort**[35] 6771 4-8-12 45 .... PaulDoe 4 51
(T Keddy) *a.p: chsd wnr 5f out: rdn and hung lft over 1f out: styd on same pce fnl f : fin 3rd, 1½l & 3/4l :disq (morphine in urine)* 7/2[2]

2m 43.38s (0.96) **Going Correction** +0.075s/f (Slow)
WFA 4 from 5yo+ 4lb **12** Ran SP% **124.3**
Speed ratings (Par 97):99,98,94,90,89 88,84,82,81,80 73,97
CSF £122.11 TOTE £6.30: £2.00, £14.10, £2.60; EX 221.20 Place 6 £152.14, Place 5 £69.95.
Owner Miss Sarah Kelleway **Bred** Allevamento Il Crognolo **Trained** Newmarket, Suffolk

FOCUS
A very weak race run at just an ordinary gallop. It is doubtful if the winner had to improve on his recent form.
T/Plt: £277.70 to a £1 stake. Pool: £54,732.55. 143.85 winning tickets. T/Qpdt: £42.10 to a £1 stake. Pool: £6,398.70. 112.40 winning tickets. CR

[82]KEMPTON (A.W) (R-H)
Sunday, January 14

OFFICIAL GOING: Standard
Wind: Virtually nil

127 INTERCASINO.CO.UK MAIDEN STKS (DIV I) 6f (P)
1:05 (1:07) (Class 5) 3-Y-O **£2,266** (£674; £337; £168) **Stalls** High

Form RPR
3- **1** **Fairnilee**[23] 6921 3-8-12 .... SebSanders 7 67+
(Sir Mark Prescott) *mde all: drvn clr over 1f out: kpt on wl* **4/7**[1]
402- **2** 1 1/4 **Bertie Swift**[17] 6965 3-9-3 67 .... JimCrowley 3 68
(J Gallagher) *sn disputing 2nd: chsd wnr over 2f out: styd on u.p ins last but a hld* **6/1**[2]
3 3 **Not Now Lewis (IRE)** 3-9-0 .... RichardKingscote(3) 9 59
(J A Osborne) *bhd: pushed along and hday fr 2f out: kpt on fnl f to take 3rd last strides but nvr gng pce to rch ldng pair* **16/1**
4 shd **Time Share (IRE)** 3-8-12 .... ShaneKelly 2 54
(J A Osborne) *in tch: hdwy to chse leaders over 3f out: nvr gng pce to chal and one pce fnl f: lost 3rd last strides* **20/1**
5 3/4 **Lady Fifer** 3-8-12 .... BrettDoyle 4 51+
(Jane Chapple-Hyam) *bhd: pushed along and hdwy on outside 2f out: kpt on fnl f but gng pce to rch ldrs* **25/1**
0- **6** hd **Rogers Lodger**[71] 6330 3-9-3 .... JimmyQuinn 5 56
(J Akehurst) *bmpd s: bhd: pushed along over 2f out: hdwy ins last but nvr in contention* **33/1**
64- **7** 1 1/4 **Realy Naughty (IRE)**[14] 6998 3-9-3 .... FergusSweeney 10 52
(B G Powell) *disp 2nd tl over 2f out: wknd fnl f* **8/1**[3]
8 nk **Virgilia (IRE)** 3-8-9 .... StephaneBreux(3) 6 46
(R Hannon) *wnt lft s: sn rcvrd: outpcd 4f out: nvr gng pce to be competitive after* **16/1**
65-3 **9** 4 **Perlachy**[11] 17 3-9-3 63 .... DanielTudhope 1 39
(Mrs N Macauley) *chsd ldrs: rdn over 2f out: wknd over 1f out* **12/1**
10 5 **Cornerstone** 3-9-3 .... J-PGuillambert 8 24
(S C Williams) *a outpcd* **25/1**

1m 13.52s (-0.18) **Going Correction** -0.10s/f (Stan) **10** Ran SP% **123.9**
Speed ratings (Par 97):97,95,91,91,90 89,88,87,82,75
CSF £4.54 TOTE £1.60: £1.10, £1.50, £4.50; EX 4.90.
Owner Miss K Rausing **Bred** Miss K Rausing **Trained** Newmarket, Suffolk

FOCUS
A modest maiden which was run at a sound pace. The winner can rate higher and the form looks straightforward rated through the runner-up.
Rogers Lodger Official explanation: jockey said gelding suffered interference leaving stalls
Virgilia(IRE) Official explanation: vet said filly was struck into behind

128 INTERCASINO.CO.UK MAIDEN STKS (DIV II) 6f (P)
1:35 (1:35) (Class 5) 3-Y-O **£2,266** (£674; £337; £168) **Stalls** High

Form RPR
- **1** **Tendalay (USA)** 3-9-3 .... ShaneKelly 10 67+
(J A Osborne) *in tch: drvn and qckned over 1f out: styd on to ld fnl 100yds: kpt on strly* **13/8**[1]
46- **2** 1/2 **Ginger Pop**[32] 6808 3-9-3 .... JamieMackay 9 65
(G G Margarson) *t.k.h: chsd ldrs: drvn to ld wl over 1f out: hdd and nt qckn fnl 100yds* **15/2**
0- **3** 1 3/4 **Grand Symphony**[25] 6886 3-8-5 .... BradleyRoper(7) 7 55+
(W Jarvis) *s.i.s:plld hrd and sn in tch: pushed along 2f out:kpt on to take 3rd ins last but nvr gng pce to trble ldng pair* **16/1**
35- **4** 1 1/2 **Pont Wood**[37] 6749 3-9-3 .... SebSanders 5 55
(M Blanshard) *chsd ldrs:rdn over 2f out: one pce fr over 1f out* **11/2**[3]
234- **5** nk **Belvedere Vixen**[15] 6991 3-8-12 65 .... NCallan 2 49
(M J Wallace) *chsd ldrs: led over 2f out: hdd wl over 1f out: wknd ins last* **9/4**[2]
00-0 **6** 2 1/2 **Childish Thoughts**[11] 17 3-8-12 45 .... CatherineGannon 8 42
(Mrs Norma Pook) *led tl hdd over 2f out: wknd appr fnl f* **33/1**
7 1 1/2 **The Tinker Man** 3-8-10 .... FrankiePickard(7) 1 42
(M D I Usher) *slowly away: effrt on outside bnd 3f out: nvr rchd ldrs: styd on same pce* **33/1**
0- **8** 1/2 **First Frost**[29] 6840 3-9-1 ow3 .... AntonyProcter 6 39
(M J Gingell) *wnt rt s: slowly away: effrt into mid-div 3f out: sn wknd* **66/1**

0- **9** 4 **Eau Sauvage**[30] 6826 3-8-12 .... PaulDoe 4 24
(J Akehurst) *rr: sme hdwy 1/2-way: sn bhd again* **66/1**
0- **10** 12 **Just A Flash (IRE)**[89] 6034 3-9-3 .... ChrisCatlin 3 —
(B R Johnson) *slowly away: a towards rr* **25/1**

1m 14.79s (1.09) **Going Correction** -0.10s/f (Stan) **10** Ran SP% **114.6**
Speed ratings (Par 97):88,87,85,83,82 79,77,76,71,55
CSF £13.74 TOTE £2.60: £1.50, £2.00, £2.30; EX 13.80.
Owner Paul J Dixon and Ten **Bred** M R Colton **Trained** Upper Lambourn, Berks

FOCUS
This second division was the weaker of the pair, but the debutant winner did the job in ready fashion and the form still looks fair for the class, although the sixth holds it down.
Just A Flash(IRE) Official explanation: vet said gelding lost a shoe

129 PLAY BLACKJACK AT INTERCASINO.CO.UK CLASSIFIED STKS 1m (P)
2:05 (2:07) (Class 7) 4-Y-0+ **£1,365** (£403; £201) **Stalls** High

Form RPR
00-1 **1** **Time To Regret**[11] 20 7-9-7 52 ....(p) DanielTudhope 3 63+
(I W McInnes) *chsd ldrs: led wl over 2f out and hung lft to stands side: drvn and kpt on wl fnl f* **11/4**[1]
26-0 **2** 1 1/4 **Mid Valley**[11] 22 4-9-0 44 .... J-PGuillambert 11 52
(J R Jenkins) *hld up in rr: hdwy over 1f out: str run to chse wnr ins last but nvr quite gng pce to chal* **12/1**
3-11 **3** hd **Earl Kraul (IRE)**[8] 51 4-9-7 52 ....(b) BrettDoyle 5 59
(G L Moore) *trckd ldrs: rdn and styd on fr over 1f out: no imp ins last* **10/3**[2]
03-5 **4** 2 **Musical Gift**[12] 9 7-9-0 45 ....(v) NCallan 9 47
(P A Blockley) *chsd ldrs: rdn over 2f out: wknd ins last* **8/1**
00- **5** nk **Deneuve**[17] 6958 4-8-11 45 ....(t) JerryO'Dwyer(3) 13 46
(M G Quinlan) *rr: hdwy over 2f out: ridden and sn hung lft to stands side: kpt on fnl f but nvr gng pce to rch ldrs* **25/1**
36-5 **6** shd **Kinsman (IRE)**[11] 20 10-9-0 42 ....(p) TPQueally 2 46
(T D McCarthy) *bhd: hdwy over 3f out: edgd lft towards stands side over 2f out: kpt on but nvr gng pce to rch ldrs* **20/1**
24-U **7** 1 **Savoy Chapel**[8] 51 5-8-11 45 .... JamesDoyle(3) 14 44
(A W Carroll) *bhd: drvn and hdwy over 1f out: kpt on ins last but nvr in contention* **13/2**[3]
00-2 **8** nk **Retirement**[11] 18 8-9-0 45 .... FergusSweeney 7 43
(R M Stronge) *rr: hdwy fr 2f out and c towards stands side: nvr nr ldrs* **11/1**
00-2 **9** 1 1/2 **Fraternity**[11] 20 10-8-9 45 .... RussellKennemore(5) 1 40
(J A Pickering) *led tl hdd wl over 2f out: wknd appr fnl f* **16/1**
00-0 **10** 2 **Berties Brother**[8] 51 4-9-2 41 ow2 .... AntonyProcter 10 37
(D G Bridgwater) *chsd ldrs: chal 3f out: wknd fnl f* **100/1**
5-34 **11** 1/2 **Piquet**[8] 51 9-8-11 44 .... AmirQuinn(3) 12 34
(J J Bridger) *mid-div: hdwy on ins to chse ldrs 3f out: sn rdn: wknd appr fnl f* **10/1**
/00- **12** 2 **Brogue Lanterns (IRE)**[24] 6897 5-9-0 45 ....(v[1]) EdwardCreighton 4 29
(E J Creighton) *a in rr* **100/1**
005- **13** 3 1/2 **Red Vixen (IRE)**[17] 6958 4-8-7 41 ....(be) KirstyMilczarek(7) 6 21
(C N Allen) *slowly away: a in rr* **33/1**
/00- **14** 2 **Patitiri (USA)**[185] 3436 4-9-0 45 .... ChrisCatlin 8 17
(J Jay) *slowly away: a bhd* **80/1**

1m 40.09s (-0.71) **Going Correction** -0.10s/f (Stan) **14** Ran SP% **120.0**
Speed ratings (Par 97):99,97,97,95,95 95,94,93,92,90 89,87,84,82
CSF £35.12 TOTE £3.30: £1.30, £3.80, £1.50; EX 64.20.
Owner Horses 4 Courses **Bred** Speedlith Group **Trained** Catwick, E Yorks

FOCUS
A very weak handicap yet the form still looks sound for the class.
Piquet Official explanation: jockey said mare ran flat

130 INTERCASINO.CO.UK H'CAP 1m (P)
2:35 (2:36) (Class 6) (0-65,62) 4-Y-0+ **£2,388** (£705; £352) **Stalls** High

Form RPR
3- **1** **Spot The Subbie (IRE)**[26] 6869 4-8-5 **51** .... JohnEgan 1 68+
(Jamie Poulton) *rr: hdwy on outside over 3f out: led ins fnl 2f: drvn clr fnl f* **16/1**
60-0 **2** 3 **Roman Boy (ARG)**[6] 72 8-8-11 **57** .... MickyFenton 11 65
(Stef Liddiard) *bhd: hdwy over 2f out: styd on to chse wnr fnl f but no ch* **10/1**
021- **3** 2 **Rowan Warning**[30] 6829 5-8-12 **58** .... NCallan 4 61
(J R Boyle) *rr: hdwy on rails over 3f out: chsd ldrs 2f out: outpcd fnl f* **5/1**[2]
400- **4** 1 1/4 **Takitwo**[111] 5568 4-9-1 **61** .... SebSanders 13 62
(P D Cundell) *chsd ldrs: rdn and kpt on same pce fnl 2f* **10/3**[1]
00-0 **5** 1/2 **Franksalot (IRE)**[6] 70 7-9-2 **62** .... JimmyQuinn 6 64+
(I W McInnes) *hld up rr: hdwy 3f out: no much room over 2f out tl 1f out: n.d after* **20/1**
46-6 **6** nk **Goose Chase**[10] 38 5-8-13 **59** ....(b) DanielTudhope 8 58
(A M Hales) *t.k.h: chsd ldrs: rdn 2f out: wknd fnl f* **16/1**
16-4 **7** nk **Moyoko (IRE)**[4] 85 4-8-3 **56** .... LauraReynolds(7) 12 54
(M Blanshard) *chsd ldrs:led over 2f out: hdd ins fnl quarter m: wknd fnl f* **7/1**[3]
33-0 **8** nk **Jomus**[8] 48 6-8-5 **56** ow1 ....(b) JamesMillman(5) 7 53
(L Montague Hall) *s.i.s: bhd: sme hdwy on outside 3f out: nvr in contention* **8/1**
163- **9** 1/2 **Gracie's Gift (IRE)**[36] 6762 5-9-2 **62** .... FergusSweeney 5 58
(A G Newcombe) *a towards rr* **5/1**[2]
10-0 **10** shd **Mythical Charm**[4] 85 8-8-10 **56** ....(t) MatthewHenry 2 52
(J J Bridger) *s.i.s: a towards rr* **14/1**
630- **11** nk **Ask No More**[18] 6952 4-8-9 **58** ....(b) DominicFox(3) 10 53
(P L Gilligan) *led tl hdd over 2f out: sn beten* **33/1**
565- **12** 3 **They All Laughed**[94] 5452 4-8-13 **59** .... ShaneKelly 9 47
(P W Hiatt) *chsd ldrs: rdn 3f out: wknd fr 2f out* **33/1**
035- **13** 9 **Monashee Prince (IRE)**[26] 6870 5-9-0 **60** .... BrettDoyle 3 28
(J R Best) *mid-div: effrt 3f out: sn wknd* **16/1**

1m 38.02s (-2.78) **Going Correction** -0.10s/f (Stan) **13** Ran SP% **124.1**
Speed ratings (Par 101):109,106,104,102,102 101,101,101,100,100 100,97,88
CSF £170.37 CT £958.40 TOTE £10.20: £2.60, £6.10, £2.40; EX 179.30.
Owner Mrs Ann Casey **Bred** Mrs Ann Casey **Trained** Whitcombe, Dorset
■ Stewards' Enquiry : Seb Sanders caution: used whip with arm above shoulder height

FOCUS
A moderate handicap which was run at a sound pace. Fair form for the grade, with a step up from Spot The Subbie who was value for a bit extra.
Franksalot(IRE) Official explanation: jockey said gelding was denied a clear run

131 £600 FREE AT INTERCASINO.CO.UK H'CAP 7f (P)

3:10 (3:11) (Class 6) (0-60,60) 4-Y-0+ £2,388 (£705; £352) Stalls High

Form RPR

001- 1 **Super Frank (IRE)**[26] 6864 4-9-2 60 .... TPQueally 12 75+
(J Akehurst) *mde all: drvn clr appr fnl f: unchal* 13/2[3]

025- 2 1 3/4 **Golden Square**[43] 4281 5-8-9 56 .... JamesDoyle(3) 8 65
(A W Carroll) *chsd ldrs: rdn to go 2nd appr fnl f: no ch w wnr but kpt on wl for 2nd* 25/1

23-0 3 1 1/2 **Carcinetto (IRE)**[8] 50 5-8-10 57 ow1 .... StephenDonohoe(3) 1 62
(P D Evans) *rr: hdwy on outside fr 2f out: kpt on wl fr over 1f out to take 3rd wl ins last but nvr a threat to ldng pair* 22/1

040- 4 nk **Mister Elegant**[23] 6919 5-8-6 57 .... JosephWalsh(7) 9 61
(J L Spearing) *chsd ldrs: rdn over 2f out: one pce fnl 2f* 14/1

51-3 5 nk **The London Gang**[10] 33 4-8-13 57 ....(v) ChrisCatlin 6 60
(Miss D A McHale) *bhd: hdwy fr 2f out: kpt on ins last but nvr gng pce to rch ldrs* 16/1

66-4 6 nk **Mystic Man (FR)**[10] 32 9-9-2 60 ....(b) JimmyQuinn 14 63
(I W McInnes) *t.k.h in rr: no much room on ins over 2f out: drvn and qcknd to chse ldrs over 1f out: sn one pce* 14/1

041- 7 1/2 **Hotchpotch (USA)**[15] 6983 4-8-13 57 ....(p) BrettDoyle 4 58
(J R Best) *sn chsng wnr: rdn over 2f out: wknd fnl f* 9/1

050- 8 hd **Another Gladiator (USA)**[17] 6964 4-8-12 56 ....(p) NCallan 10 57
(K A Ryan) *bhd: sme hdwy over 2f out: nvr rchd ldrs and sn one pce* 9/1

055- 9 nk **Scroll**[17] 6964 4-9-2 60 ....(b[1]) DeanCorby 5 60
(P Howling) *bhd: hdwy on outside fr 2f out: kpt on ins last but nvr a danger* 10/1

221- 10 1/2 **Haroldini (IRE)**[17] 6964 5-8-13 60 ....(p) JasonEdmunds(3) 7 59
(J Balding) *in tch: rdn over 2f out: sn no imp and outpcd* 4/1[1]

25-3 11 1 1/2 **Cool Sands (IRE)**[6] 70 5-9-1 59 ....(v) DanielTudhope 5 54
(D Shaw) *rr: sme hdwy whn hit on hd over 1f out: n.d after* 9/2[2]

301- 12 1 1/2 **Mine The Balance (IRE)**[25] 6884 4-8-12 56 ....(b) JohnEgan 2 47
(J R Best) *in tch: rdn 3f out: wknd fr 2f out* 16/1

000- 13 1/2 **Desert Lover (IRE)**[31] 6820 5-9-0 58 .... ShaneKelly 13 48
(R J Price) *chsd ldrs over 4f* 16/1

1m 26.11s (-0.69) **Going Correction** -0.10s/f (Stan) 13 Ran SP% 119.8

Speed ratings (Par 101):99,97,95,94,94 94,93,93,93,92 90,89,88

CSF £158.01 CT £3467.05 TOTE £6.60: £2.40, £7.10, £4.90; EX 194.70.

Owner A D Spence **Bred** A Butler **Trained** Epsom, Surrey

FOCUS

A moderate handicap and the form does not look entirely solid. Super Frank appears progressive though.

Cool Sands(IRE) Official explanation: jockey said gelding was denied a clear run

132 PLAY ROULETTE AT INTERCASINO.CO.UK H'CAP 6f (P)

3:45 (3:48) (Class 5) (0-70,70) 4-Y-0+ £3,238 (£963; £481; £240) Stalls High

Form RPR

212- 1 **Louphole**[26] 6865 5-9-3 69 .... SebSanders 2 78
(P J Makin) *hld up in rr: stdy hdwy fr 2f out: str chal ins last: led last strides* 9/2[2]

51-5 2 hd **Mistral Sky**[4] 91 8-8-13 65 ....(p) MickyFenton 9 73
(Stef Liddiard) *trckd ldr: chal fr over 2f out tl led 1f out: kpt on u.p: ct last strides* 15/2

040- 3 1 **Mina**[22] 6930 5-8-11 63 .... JamieMackay 3 68
(Rae Guest) *stdd rr: hld up: hdwy over 1f out: str run fnl f tk 3rd cl home but nt pce to rch ldrs* 12/1

44-6 4 nk **Desert Light (IRE)**[8] 50 6-8-4 56 oh2 ....(v) AdrianMcCarthy 7 60
(D Shaw) *chsd ldrs: drvn and styd on same pce ins last* 14/1

60-0 5 nk **Loyal Tycoon (IRE)**[13] 3 9-9-2 68 .... ShaneKelly 12 71
(D K Ivory) *chsd ldrs: rdn 2f out: wknd nr fin* 25/1

65-2 6 hd **Caustic Wit (IRE)**[8] 50 9-8-4 61 ....(p) TolleyDean(5) 11 64
(M S Saunders) *led: rdn over 2f out: hdd 1f out: wknd nr fin* 4/1[1]

020- 7 1/2 **Romany Nights (IRE)**[118] 5420 7-9-4 70 ....(bt) JohnEgan 4 71
(Miss Gay Kelleway) *bhd: rdn along 2f out: swtchd lft and hdwy fnl f:gng on cl home* 10/1

240- 8 3/4 **Seneschal**[172] 3846 6-8-12 64 .... TPQueally 10 63+
(A B Haynes) *trckd ldrs: trapped on rails fr over 2f out and nvr any room: fin on bridle* 20/1

454- 9 shd **Ever Cheerful**[23] 6919 6-8-8 67 .... HaddenFrost(7) 8 65
(D G Bridgwater) *rr: sme hdwy on outside over 1f out: kpt on but nvr a danger* 13/2[3]

242- 10 shd **Muscari**[23] 6913 5-8-7 62 .... JamesDoyle(3) 5 60
(S Woodman) *chsd ldrs: rdn over 2f out: wknd appr fnl f* 13/2[3]

320- 11 1 **Bobby Rose**[23] 6913 4-8-12 64 .... NCallan 1 59
(D K Ivory) *stumled sn after s: t.k.h and sn chsng ldrs: wknd fnl f* 8/1

200- 12 7 **Sarah's Art (IRE)**[26] 6865 4-9-0 66 ....(b) ChrisCatlin 6 40
(Miss D A McHale) *chsd ldrs over 4f* 33/1

1m 13.3s (-0.40) **Going Correction** -0.10s/f (Stan) 12 Ran SP% 122.7

Speed ratings (Par 103):98,97,96,96,95 95,94,93,93,93 92,82

CSF £38.87 CT £395.55 TOTE £4.10: £1.60, £3.20, £4.70; EX 40.20 Trifecta £223.50 Part won. Pool: £314.80 - 0.20 winning tickets..

Owner Ten Of Hearts **Bred** Mrs P Harford **Trained** Ogbourne Maisey, Wilts

FOCUS

A modest sprint. The form looks sound enough, with winner Louphole back to his best.

Seneschal Official explanation: jockey said gelding was denied a clear run

Ever Cheerful Official explanation: jockey said gelding anticipated start and struck the gate

133 INTERCASINO.CO.UK CLASSIFIED STKS 1m 3f (P)

4:15 (4:19) (Class 7) 4-Y-0+ £1,365 (£403; £201) Stalls High

Form RPR

004- 1 **Sahf London**[10] 6133 4-8-11 45 .... NCallan 1 53
(G L Moore) *chsd ldrs: drvn to ld 1f out: styd on wl* 4/1[2]

000- 2 1/2 **Compton Express**[23] 6918 4-8-11 45 .... JohnEgan 9 52
(Jamie Poulton) *bhd: hdwy fr 3f out: drvn and styd on to take 2nd wl ins last: nt trble wnr* 20/1

036- 3 1 **Pharaoh Prince**[23] 6904 6-9-0 45 ....(v) AdrianMcCarthy 12 50
(G Prodromou) *chsd ldrs: rdn and styd on wl fnl f but nvr gng pce to chal* 5/1[3]

02-4 4 1 3/4 **Jarvo**[11] 18 6-9-0 45 .... DanielTudhope 5 47
(I W McInnes) *in tch: hdwy 3f out: rdn and kpt on fr 2f out: styd on ins last but nvr gng pce to rch ldrs* 8/1

550/ 5 1/2 **King's Minstrel (IRE)**[381] 6681 6-9-0 41 .... PaulDoe 8 46
(R Rowe) *bhd: hdwy on outside fr 2f out: kpt on cl home* 33/1

002- 6 3/4 **Simplified**[23] 6907 4-8-11 40 .... JamieMackay 10 45
(N B King) *s.i.s: behund: hdwy and n.m.r 2f out: kpt on fnl f: nvr in contention* 16/1

000- 7 shd **Captain Bolsh**[41] 6708 4-8-11 45 .... JimmyQuinn 2 45
(J Pearce) *chsd ldr: chal over 3f out tl led ins fnl 2f: hdd 1f out: sn wknd* 16/1

400/ 8 1/2 **Public Eye**[263] 5303 6-9-0 44 .... ChrisCatlin 13 44
(L A Dace) *mid-div: drvn along 3f out: styd on fnl f: nvr in contention* 25/1

035- 9 hd **Flashing Floozie**[41] 6707 4-8-11 43 .... ShaneKelly 14 44
(A W Carroll) *chsd ldrs: rdn 3f out: wknd appr fnl f* 12/1

060- 10 1 1/2 **Gran Clicquot**[32] 6804 12-8-9 38 .... JamieJones(5) 4 41
(G P Enright) *in tch: rdn 3f out: wknd fr 2f out* 66/1

043- 11 1/2 **Lady Suffragette (IRE)**[83] 6133 4-8-11 44 .... BrettDoyle 11 40
(John Berry) *led tl hdd ins fnl 2f: sn btn* 10/1

523- 12 hd **Kilmeena Magic**[23] 6907 5-8-7 45 .... HaddenFrost(7) 6 40
(J C Fox) *t.k.h: trckd ldrs in rails: shkn up over 2f out: sn btn* 7/2[1]

000- 13 1 1/4 **Young Valentino**[30] 6829 5-9-0 39 .... JimCrowley 7 38
(A W Carroll) *s.i.s: a towards rr* 100/1

042- 14 2 **Our Glenard**[32] 6804 8-8-9 44 .... NataliaGemelova(5) 3 35
(J E Long) *slowly away: a towards rr* 12/1

2m 22.59s (-0.09) **Going Correction** -0.10s/f (Stan)

WFA 4 from 5yo+ 3lb 14 Ran SP% 120.3

Speed ratings (Par 97):96,95,94,93,93 92,92,92,92,91 90,90,89,88

CSF £89.87 TOTE £4.50: £2.40, £5.30, £2.00; EX 86.60.

Owner Longshot Racing **Bred** Vogue Development Company (kent) Ltd **Trained** Woodingdean, E Sussex

FOCUS

A weak classified event which was run at fair gallop. The form should work out.

134 BIG JACKPOTS AT INTERCASINO.CO.UK H'CAP 2m (P)

4:45 (4:48) (Class 6) (0-50,51) 4-Y-0+ £2,047 (£604; £302) Stalls High

Form RPR

001- 1 **Josh You Are**[23] 6907 4-8-8 51 ow1 .... PatCosgrave 4 59+
(D E Cantillon) *hld up in rr: stdy hdwy fr 5f out:chal on bit 2f out: led 1f out: drvn out* 9/2[3]

232- 2 2 **Lysander's Quest (IRE)**[27] 6857 9-8-10 46 .... FergusSweeney 8 51
(R Ingram) *rr: hdwy 4f out: chal 2f out: rdn to ld wl over 1f out: sn hdd: kpt on same pce iside last* 2/1[1]

/0-3 3 2 **Come What Augustus**[11] 16 5-8-13 49 ....(p) ChrisCatlin 11 52
(R M Stronge) *chsd ldrs: drvn to chal fr 2f out: stl ev ch u.p over 1f out: sn outpcd* 13/2

40-0 4 4 **Countback (FR)**[9] 39 8-8-7 46 oh1 .... JamesDoyle(3) 3 44
(A W Carroll) *s.i.s: bhd: hdwy over 2f out: styd on fnl f to take 4th ins last: nvr in contention* 14/1

2 5 1 **Speed Winner (AUS)**[4] 87 8-8-10 46 oh1 ....(b) NCallan 5 43
(G L Moore) *chsd ldr: led 6f out: rdn over 3f out: hdd wl over 1f out: wknd fnl f* 10/3[2]

43-4 6 1/2 **Domenico (IRE)**[11] 16 9-8-11 47 .... J-PGuillambert 13 43
(J R Jenkins) *chsd ldrs: rdn 3f out: wknd over 1f out* 10/1

/00- 7 2 **Flyoff (IRE)**[16] 6972 10-8-5 46 oh1 .... RussellKennemore(5) 9 40
(Mrs N Macauley) *mid-div: rdn and one pce fnl 3f* 66/1

004- 8 1/2 **Montecristo**[43] 6685 14-8-7 50 .... LukeMcJannet(7) 7 43
(Rae Guest) *bhd tl sme hdwy fnl 2f* 33/1

00-0 9 4 **Orphir (IRE)**[13] 1 4-8-3 46 oh1 .... JimmyQuinn 1 35
(Mrs N Macauley) *s.i.s: towards rr tl mod late prog* 50/1

10 2 1/2 **Fortune Dancer (USA)**[620] 12-8-11 47 .... JimCrowley 14 33
(G L Moore) *bhd: bried effrt into mid-div 3f out* 25/1

046- 11 3 1/2 **River Gypsy**[124] 5267 6-8-6 49 .... HaddenFrost(7) 12 30
(J D Frost) *chsd ldrs tl wknd fr 3f out* 16/1

00-0 12 21 **Coppington Melody (IRE)**[6] 71 4-8-0 50 ..... KrishlovyGundowry(7) 2 6
(B W Duke) *chsd ldrs 11f* 33/1

/00- 13 nk **Make My Hay**[12] 6553 8-8-10 46 oh1 .... TPQueally 10 2
(J Gallagher) *a towards rr* 33/1

/0-0 14 17 **Hawksmoor (IRE)**[11] 18 5-8-7 46 oh1 ....(t) StephaneBreux(3) 6 —
(L A Dace) *led tl hdd 6f out: wknd 4f out* 66/1

3m 28.11s (-3.29) **Going Correction** -0.10s/f (Stan)

WFA 4 from 5yo+ 7lb 14 Ran SP% 127.2

Speed ratings (Par 101):104,103,102,100,99 99,98,98,96,94 93,82,82,73

CSF £14.05 CT £62.45 TOTE £6.30: £2.10, £1.10, £3.00; EX 23.10 Place 6 £216.35, Place 5 £157.33.

Owner Mrs Edward Cantillon **Bred** Phil Jen Racing **Trained** Newmarket, Suffolk

■ Stewards' Enquiry : Luke McJannet one-day ban: used whip with arm above shoulder height (Jan 25)

FOCUS

A dire staying handicap which saw the in-form winner score comfortably. The form appears sound enough.

T/Jkpt: £3,477.10 to a £1 stake. Pool: £17,141.00. 3.50 winning tickets. T/Plt: £125.40 to a £1 stake. Pool: £87,276.05. 507.80 winning tickets. T/Qpdt: £26.30 to a £1 stake. Pool: £6,773.50. 190.10 winning tickets. ST

[121]WOLVERHAMPTON (A.W) (L-H)

Monday, January 15

OFFICIAL GOING: Standard

Wind: Fresh, behind Weather: Fine

135 GO PONTIN'S AMATEUR RIDERS' H'CAP (DIV I) 5f 20y(P)

1:40 (1:41) (Class 6) (0-52,52) 4-Y-0+ £1,318 (£405; £202) Stalls Low

Form RPR

43-0 1 **Monte Major (IRE)**[5] 82 6-11-5 50 ....(v) MrsMMorris 1 61
(D Shaw) *a.p: chsd ldr 1/2-way: rdn to ld over 1f out: r.o* 5/2[2]

41-1 2 2 1/2 **Spirit Of Coniston**[4] 97 4-11-5 50 ....(b) MrSWalker 4 52
(Peter Grayson) *led: rdn: hung lft and hdd over 1f out: styd on same pce* 5/4[1]

020- 3 1 **Rowanberry**[33] 6805 5-11-1 46 .... MrDHDunsdon 9 44
(R M H Cowell) *prom: rdn and hung lft fr over 1f out: styd on* 8/1[3]

02-0 4 1 3/4 **El Potro**[9] 46 5-10-8 46 oh1 .... MissJessicaHolt(7) 6 38
(J R Holt) *s.i.s and hmpd s: sn drvn into mid-div: r.o ins fnl f: nt trble ldrs* 12/1

/60- 5 nk **Ames Souer (IRE)**[34] 6794 4-10-8 46 oh1 .... MrRichardEvans(7) 2 37
(P D Evans) *chsd ldrs: rdn 1/2-way: edgd rt over 1f out: styd on same pce* 8/1[3]

060- 6 shd **Torrent**[17] 6969 12-10-10 46 oh1 ....(p) MissAWallace(5) 3 37
(J M Saville) *hld up: effrt and hung lft over 1f out: nt clr run sn after: n.d* 125/1

600- 7 1 **Telepathic (IRE)**[156] 4352 7-10-8 46 oh1 ....(b) MissWGibson(7) 8 33
(A Berry) *hld up: styd on ins fnl f: nvr nrr* 80/1

The Form Book, Raceform Ltd, Compton, RG20 6NL

60/5 **8** 1 1/2 **Ela Figura**[11] [36] 7-10-8 **46** oh1 .... MrsSDutton(7) 10 — 28
(A W Carroll) *chsd ldrs: lost pl over 3f out: n.d after* **66/1**

000- **9** 2 **Obe Bold (IRE)**[41] [6719] 6-10-12 **46** oh1 .... (b) MissFayeBramley(3) 5 — 20
(A Berry) *wnt rt s: chsd ldrs: rdn 1/2-way: sn wknd* **28/1**

40-0 **10** 11 **Boanerges (IRE)**[9] [50] 10-11-0 **52** .... MissHDavies(7) 7 — —
(J M Bradley) *chsd ldrs to 1/2-way* **14/1**

64.13 secs (1.31) **Going Correction** +0.075s/f (Slow) **10** Ran SP% **116.6**
Speed ratings (Par 101):92,88,86,83,83 82,81,78,75,58
CSF £5.90 CT £20.44 TOTE £3.60: £1.30, £1.10, £2.80; EX 8.10 Trifecta £26.80 Pool: £255.87 - 6.76 winning units..
Owner Danethorpe Racing Ltd **Bred** B Kennedy **Trained** Danethorpe, Notts
■ Stewards' Enquiry : Miss Jessica Holt three-day ban; careless riding (Jan 28,30, Feb 2)
FOCUS
A weak amateur riders' handicap in which a low draw unsurprisingly proved decisive.

136 PONTINS.COM H'CAP — 5f 216y(P)
2:10 (2:11) (Class 6) (0-55,54) 3-Y-O — **£2,388** (£705; £352) **Stalls** Low

Form — RPR

50-2 **1** **Pietersen (IRE)**[2] [122] 3-9-0 **54** .... (b) PaulFessey 5 — 58
(T D Barron) *chsd ldrs: led and hung rt fr over 2f out: rdn out* **11/10**[1]

050- **2** 1 1/4 **Priceless Melody (USA)**[47] [6653] 3-8-5 **45** .... (b) JimmyQuinn 6 — 45
(Mrs A J Perrett) *hld up in tch: racd keenly: rdn to chse wnr fnl f: styd on same pce* **13/2**[3]

000- **3** 2 **Xalted**[124] [5288] 3-8-2 **45** .... SaleemGolam(3) 8 — 39
(S C Williams) *hld up: rdn 1/2-way: nt clr run over 1f out: r.o ins fnl f: nvr nrr* **7/1**

406- **4** 1/2 **Bertrada (IRE)**[177] [3727] 3-8-12 **52** .... SteveDrowne 4 — 45+
(H Morrison) *mid-div: sn pushed along: hdwy over 2f out: rdn over 1f out: no ex ins fnl f* **14/1**

00- **5** 3/4 **Ugenius**[15] [6996] 3-8-0 **45** .... TolleyDean(5) 2 — 35
(R A Harris) *chsd ldrs: hmpd over 2f out: sn rdn: wknd ins fnl f* **12/1**

000- **6** shd **Homecroft Boy**[140] [4897] 3-8-10 **50** .... (b[1]) ShaneKelly 9 — 40
(J A Osborne) *s.i.s: hld up: hdwy over 2f out: rdn over 1f out: wknd ins fnl f* **11/2**[2]

045- **7** 1/2 **My Sara**[16] [6991] 3-8-13 **53** .... (v[1]) PaulHanagan 10 — 41
(R A Fahey) *sn outpcd: styd on u.p ins fnl f: nvr nrr* **10/1**

040- **8** 2 1/2 **Devilfishpoker Com**[19] [6951] 3-8-5 **45** .... (b) JamieMackay 7 — 26
(R C Guest) *dwlt: outpcd* **25/1**

065- **9** 5 **Mangano**[40] [6730] 3-8-5 **45** .... PaulQuinn 3 — 11
(A Berry) *led: hdd over 3f out: wknd over 1f out* **33/1**

600- **10** 5 **Desirable Dancer (IRE)**[28] [6859] 3-8-5 **45** .... ChrisCatlin 1 — —
(R A Harris) *chsd ldr tl led over 3f out: rdn and hdd over 2f out: sn wknd* **33/1**

1m 16.56s (0.75) **Going Correction** +0.075s/f (Slow) **10** Ran SP% **122.0**
Speed ratings (Par 95):98,96,93,93,92 91,91,87,81,74
CSF £9.08 CT £36.90 TOTE £2.10: £1.30, £2.30, £2.30; EX 10.40 Trifecta £18.30 Pool: £243.29 - 9.43 winning units..
Owner Sporting Occasions No 8 **Bred** Noel Finegan **Trained** Maunby, N Yorks
■ Stewards' Enquiry : Tolley Dean two-day ban; careless riding (Jan 26-27)
FOCUS
A few of these came into this unexposed, but it still looked like a pretty weak three-year-old sprint with the placed horses having shown nothing.

137 GO PONTIN'S AMATEUR RIDERS' H'CAP (DIV II) — 5f 20y(P)
2:40 (2:41) (Class 6) (0-52,50) 4-Y-O+ — **£1,318** (£405; £202) **Stalls** Low

Form — RPR

35-2 **1** **Vlasta Weiner**[5] [82] 7-11-0 **50** .... (b) MissSBradley(7) 4 — 58
(J M Bradley) *a.p: rdn and hung lft fr over 1f out: r.o to ld post* **7/2**[1]

560- **2** nk **Town House**[164] [4110] 5-10-11 **45** .... MrStephenHarrison(5) 1 — 52
(B P J Baugh) *led: rdn over 1f out: hdd post* **7/1**

306- **3** 2 1/2 **Blythe Spirit**[17] [6974] 8-11-0 **48** .... (p) MrBMcHugh(5) 8 — 46
(R A Fahey) *sn pushed along in rr: hdwy whn nt clr run 1f out: styd on same pce* **9/2**[2]

300- **4** hd **Lady Hopeful (IRE)**[15] [6994] 5-10-9 **45** .... (b) MrCEllingham(7) 3 — 42
(Peter Grayson) *in rr: rdn and hung lft over 1f out: r.o ins fnl f: nvr nrr* **6/1**[3]

05-0 **5** nk **Blushing Russian (IRE)**[12] [20] 5-10-9 **45** .... (p) MissHDavies(7) 10 — 41
(J M Bradley) *mid-div: rdn 2f out: styd on same pce appr fnl f* **25/1**

065- **6** 1 1/4 **Compton Micky**[18] [6962] 6-10-9 **45** .... (p) MissAColley(7) 6 — 37
(R F Marvin) *prom: rdn to chse ldr over 1f out: wknd ins fnl f* **20/1**

430- **7** 1/2 **Saintly Place**[124] [5291] 6-11-2 **45** .... MrSWalker 7 — 35
(A W Carroll) *chsd ldr: rdn 2f out: wknd fnl f* **7/2**[1]

100- **8** 4 **Alistair John**[56] [6541] 4-10-13 **49** .... MrsJShorrock(7) 9 — 25
(Mrs G S Rees) *s.i.s: hdwy over 2f out: wknd over 1f out* **12/1**

000- **9** 1/2 **Oceanico Dot Com (IRE)**[109] [5631] 5-10-13 **45**.. MissFayeBramley(3) 2 — 19
(A Berry) *chsd ldrs 3f* **16/1**

500- **10** 1/2 **Jazz At The Sands (USA)**[26] [6890] 4-11-2 **45** .... (v) MrsMMorris 5 — 17
(D Shaw) *fly-leapt s: a in rr* **20/1**

64.17 secs (1.35) **Going Correction** +0.075s/f (Slow) **24** Ran SP% **116.4**
Speed ratings (Par 101):92,91,87,87,86 84,83,77,76,75
CSF £27.42 CT £114.36 TOTE £3.50: £1.30, £2.30, £1.30; EX 32.20 Trifecta £61.20 Pool: £162.24 - 1.88 winning units..
Owner Miss Diane Hill **Bred** C J Hill **Trained** Sedbury, Gloucs
■ A first winner for Sarah Bradley, granddaughter of the winning trainer Milton Bradley.
FOCUS
Like the first division, a weak amateur riders' sprint, and run in a similar time. The winner will still be on a fair mark after this but the runner-up weakens the form.

138 PONTIN'S HOLIDAYS (S) STKS — 7f 32y(P)
3:10 (3:11) (Class 6) 4-Y-O+ — **£2,047** (£604; £302) **Stalls** High

Form — RPR

360- **1** **Prince Of Gold**[18] [6961] 7-8-12 48 .... (v) FergusSweeney 4 — 59
(R Hollinshead) *mid-div: hdwy 1/2-way: rdn to ld and hung lft ins fnl f: r.o* **16/1**

452- **2** 2 1/2 **Rafferty (IRE)**[25] [6892] 8-8-12 80 .... NCallan 6 — 53
(T D Barron) *led: rdn over 1f out: hdd and no ex ins fnl f* **8/11**[1]

010- **3** 1 3/4 **Crafty Fox**[71] [6348] 4-9-3 54 .... (v) DaneO'Neill 3 — 53
(A P Jarvis) *chsd ldrs: rdn over 1f out: no ex fnl f* **20/1**

00-6 **4** 3/4 **Spy Gun (USA)**[10] [42] 7-8-12 43 .... ChrisCatlin 1 — 46
(T Wall) *chsd ldrs: n.m.r and lost pl 6f out: hdwy over 1f out: nt rch ldrs* **40/1**

52-5 **5** 1/2 **Bold Love**[8] [61] 4-8-7 40 .... (t) DeanMcKeown 8 — 40
(J Balding) *s.i.s: hdwy over 5f out: rdn over 2f out: wknd ins fnl f* **50/1**

064- **6** 2 **Atlantic Viking (IRE)**[24] [6906] 12-8-10 49 ow1 (p) StephenDonohoe(3) 12 — 41
(P D Evans) *s.i.s: hld up: hdwy over 1f out: n.d* **25/1**

0-13 **7** 1 1/4 **Shrine Mountain (USA)**[9] [52] 5-8-12 60 .... (b) TolleyDean(5) 2 — 41
(R A Harris) *s.i.s: hdwy over 5f out: sn rdn: n.d* **3/1**[2]

034- **8** nk **Miss Imperious**[17] [6970] 4-8-7 43 .... PaulMulrennan 5 — 31
(B Smart) *s.i.s: hld up: nvr nrr* **33/1**

350- **9** 3/4 **Merdiff**[19] [6955] 8-8-12 46 .... ShaneKelly 7 — 34
(W M Brisbourne) *chsd ldrs: rdn over 2f out: wknd over 1f out* **16/1**

0-02 **10** 8 **Skip Of Colour**[8] [61] 7-9-3 55 .... SimonWhitworth 11 — 18
(P A Blockley) *chsd ldrs over 4f* **12/1**[3]

5/0- **11** 7 **Alcharinga (IRE)**[69] [6389] 5-8-9 54 .... (b[1]) SaleemGolam(3) 9 — —
(T J Etherington) *chsd ldrs over 4f* **66/1**

1m 30.02s (-0.38) **Going Correction** +0.075s/f (Slow) **11** Ran SP% **119.8**
Speed ratings (Par 101):105,102,100,99,98 96,95,94,93,84 76
CSF £27.58 TOTE £24.60: £3.90, £1.10, £5.40; EX 42.70 Trifecta £352.30 Part won. Pool: £496.24 - 0.10 winning units..There was no bid for the winner. Rafferty was claimed by Simon Dow for £6,000.
Owner Mrs Susy Haslehurst **Bred** Longdon Stud Ltd **Trained** Upper Longdon, Staffs
FOCUS
A typical seller; Rafferty was a long way below his official mark of 80 while Prince Of Gold produced his best figure for quite a while.

139 GO PONTIN'S CLAIMING STKS — 1m 141y(P)
3:40 (3:40) (Class 6) 3-Y-O — **£2,730** (£806; £403) **Stalls** Low

Form — RPR

303- **1** **Sweet World**[41] [6711] 3-8-13 61 .... DaneO'Neill 1 — 64
(A P Jarvis) *hld up: hdwy to chse ldr over 2f out: son rdn and hung lft: led 1f out: drvn out* **4/1**[2]

41-4 **2** hd **My Mirasol**[6] [76] 3-9-2 59 .... (p) NCallan 3 — 67
(K A Ryan) *led: hdd over 7f out: led again over 3f out: rdn and hdd 1f out: styd on* **11/4**[1]

603- **3** 6 **Raquel White**[24] [6920] 3-8-4 61 .... (b[1]) JimmyQuinn 4 — 42
(P D Evans) *led over 7f out: hdd over 3f out: sn rdn: wknd fnl f* **4/1**[2]

34-5 **4** 1/2 **Party Palace**[11] [37] 3-8-2 50 .... ChrisCatlin 7 — 39
(J A Osborne) *chsd ldrs: rdn over 3f out: wknd over 1f out* **5/1**[3]

04-3 **5** 4 **Three No Trumps**[13] [11] 3-8-2 47 .... (v[1]) HayleyTurner 5 — 31
(D Morris) *sn pushed along in rr: hrd rdn 3f out: n.d* **25/1**

44-4 **6** 1 **Jost Van Dyke**[7] [68] 3-8-7 53 .... (v[1]) FergusSweeney 9 — 33
(J R Boyle) *hld up: sme hdwy over 2f out: sn wknd* **16/1**

53-6 **7** 3 **Ten Black**[12] [25] 3-8-13 56 .... (p) PatCosgrave 2 — 33
(R Brotherton) *prom: rdn over 3f out: wknd 2f out* **33/1**

236- **8** 14 **Keep Your Distance**[19] [6951] 3-9-7 62 .... (tp) LeeEnstone 8 — 12
(K R Burke) *s.i.s: hdwy over 6f out: rdn and wknd 3f out* **6/1**

9 28 **Christy Ryan (IRE)** 3-9-7 .... PaulMulrennan 6 — —
(M J Wallace) *s.i.s: outpcd* **20/1**

1m 51.78s (0.02) **Going Correction** +0.075s/f (Slow) **9** Ran SP% **115.1**
Speed ratings (Par 95):102,101,96,96,92 91,88,76,51
CSF £14.97 TOTE £5.50: £2.00, £1.70, £1.50; EX 23.30 Trifecta £30.50 Pool: £324.45 - 7.53 winning units..Raquel White was claimed by J. L. Flint for £6,000.
Owner Geoffrey Bishop and Ann Jarvis **Bred** Natton House Thoroughbreds **Trained** Twyford, Bucks
■ Stewards' Enquiry : Dane O'Neill one-day ban: using whip down the shoulder in forehand position (Jan 26)
FOCUS
A reasonable claimer with the front pair rated as slight improvers on their recent form.
Three No Trumps Official explanation: jockey said filly was struck into on leaving the stalls
Christy Ryan(IRE) Official explanation: jockey said gelding was never travelling

140 PONTIN'S HOLIDAYS H'CAP — 1m 1f 103y(P)
4:10 (4:10) (Class 5) (0-70,68) 3-Y-O — **£3,238** (£963; £481; £240) **Stalls** Low

Form — RPR

52-1 **1** **Global Traffic**[11] [37] 3-8-8 **58** .... (b) JimmyQuinn 10 — 61+
(P D Evans) *hld up: plld hrd: hdwy over 2f out: hrd rdn and hung rt ins fnl f: styd on to ld post* **7/4**[1]

000- **2** shd **Six Shots**[151] [4526] 3-9-3 **67** .... ShaneKelly 5 — 70
(J A Osborne) *led 1f: chsd ldr tl led over 3f out: hrd rdn ins fnl f: hdd post* **11/1**

41-3 **3** 2 **Gold Response**[7] [68] 3-8-6 **56** .... DeanMcKeown 9 — 57+
(D Shaw) *hld up: nt clr run over 2f out: swtchd rt wl over 1f out: hung lft and r.o ins fnl f: nrst fin* **14/1**

155- **4** 3/4 **Strike Force**[23] [6933] 3-9-4 **68** .... ChrisCatlin 6 — 66
(R A Harris) *led over 8f out: hdd over 3f out: rdn and hung lft over 1f out: styd on same pce* **12/1**

44-2 **5** 1/2 **Jocheski (IRE)**[9] [53] 3-9-4 **68** .... PatCosgrave 7 — 65
(M J Wallace) *chsd ldrs: rdn over 3f out: btn whn edgd rt 1f out* **4/1**[2]

065- **6** hd **Green Day Packer (IRE)**[27] [6872] 3-8-13 **63** .... LeeEnstone 4 — 59
(P C Haslam) *prom: rdn over 3f out: styng on same pce whn hmpd 1f out* **10/1**[3]

052- **7** 1/2 **Conny Nobel (IRE)**[24] [6920] 3-9-4 **68** .... (t) SteveDrowne 8 — 63?
(R A Kvisla) *sn pushed along in rr: hdwy 6f out: rdn over 2f out: wkng whn hmpd 1f out* **25/1**

04-0 **8** 3 **Brierley Lil**[11] [37] 3-7-11 **54** oh4 .... (b[1]) JosephWalsh(7) 1 — 43
(J L Spearing) *s.i.s: hld up: rdn and wknd over 2f out* **25/1**

330- **9** 3 **Pennyrock (IRE)**[140] [4880] 3-9-1 **65** .... NCallan 2 — 48
(K A Ryan) *prom: rdn over 3f out: wknd over 1f out* **4/1**[2]

2m 3.62s (1.00) **Going Correction** +0.075s/f (Slow) **9** Ran SP% **115.8**
Speed ratings (Par 97):98,97,96,95,95 94,94,91,89
CSF £23.22 CT £200.76 TOTE £2.20: £1.20, £3.50, £3.00; EX 33.10 Trifecta £290.70 Part won. Pool: £409.45 - 0.83 winning units..
Owner Mrs I M Folkes **Bred** P F I Cole **Trained** Pandy, Monmouths
FOCUS
Just a modest handicap and the winning time was 2.28 seconds slower than the following maiden. Global Traffic progressed a bit further, with the second improving on his handicap debut and the third rated to his recent plating form.

141 PONTINS.COM MAIDEN STKS — 1m 1f 103y(P)
4:40 (4:40) (Class 5) 3-Y-O — **£3,071** (£906; £453) **Stalls** Low

Form — RPR

1 **Players Please (USA)** 3-9-3 .... JoeFanning 5 — 84+
(M Johnston) *chsd ldrs: hmpd 6f out: rdn to ld and edgd lft over 1f out: r.o* **9/2**[2]

54- **2** 1 **Challis (IRE)**[26] [6887] 3-9-3 .... TPQueally 11 — 82
(J Noseda) *hld up: hdwy over 3f out: rdn to chse wnr fnl f: hung lft and styd on same pce* **5/4**[1]

6- **3** 4 **Moral Code (IRE)**[39] [6737] 3-9-3 .... ChrisCatlin 2 — 74
(E J O'Neill) *sn led: hung rt 6f out: rdn and hdd over 1f out: wknd ins fnl f* **11/1**

622- **4** 1/2 **Snow Dancer (IRE)**[17] [6976] 3-8-12 69 .... DarrenMoffatt 4 — 68
(A Berry) *chsd ldrs: rdn over 1f out: styd on same pce* **15/2**[3]

3 5 ¾ **Six Day War (IRE)**[9] 53 3-9-3 ShaneKelly 6 72+
(J A Osborne) *mid-div: hdwy 1/2-way: sn rdn: outpcd over 2f out: styd on ins fnl f* **9/1**

04- 6 15 **Becharm**[26] 6886 3-8-12 MatthewHenry 10 37
(M A Jarvis) *led early: chsd ldrs: rdn over 2f out: wknd over 1f out* **16/1**

422- 7 1 ¼ **Lord Oroko**[19] 6950 3-9-3 73 NCallan 9 39
(K A Ryan) *chsd ldrs: hmpd and lost pl 6f out: n.d after* **10/1**

33- 8 5 **Red Petal**[19] 6950 3-8-12 SebSanders 1 24
(Sir Mark Prescott) *s.i.s: sn drvn along and prom: wknd over 2f out* **8/1**

00-0 9 10 **Pineapple Poll**[13] 11 3-8-9 15 (be[1]) DominicFox(3) 7 4
(P L Gilligan) *hld up: bhd fr 1/2-way* **200/1**

00- 10 2 ½ **Bronzo Di Riace (IRE)**[121] 5389 3-9-0 JerryO'Dwyer(3) 3 4
(M G Quinlan) *mid-div: lost pl over 5f out: sn bhd* **100/1**

6-0 11 5 **Jousting**[7] 73 3-9-3 RossStudholme 8 —
(V Smith) *hld up: bhd fr 1/2-way* **100/1**

2m 1.34s (-1.28) **Going Correction** +0.075s/f (Slow) 11 Ran SP% **121.3**
Speed ratings (Par 97):108,107,103,103,102 89,88,83,74,72 68
CSF £10.86 TOTE £6.30: £1.70, £1.30, £3.10; EX 18.10 Trifecta £326.80 Pool: £658.37 - 1.43 winning units..
Owner N N Browne **Bred** 6 C Racing Limited **Trained** Middleham Moor, N Yorks

FOCUS
A good maiden for the time of year - the winning time was 2.28 seconds quicker than the previous handicap won by the 58-rated Global Traffic - and Players Please looks a nice prospect. The form should prove much more solid than most.

142 GO PONTIN'S H'CAP 1m 4f 50y(P)
5:10 (5:16) (Class 5) (0-75,75) 4-Y-0+ £3,238 (£963; £481; £240) Stalls Low

Form RPR

650- 1 **Desert Leader (IRE)**[16] 6992 6-9-2 71 ShaneKelly 2 78
(W M Brisbourne) *chsd ldr tl led over 3f out: drvn out* **8/1**

151- 2 nk **Melvino**[19] 6954 5-8-10 65 DeanMcKeown 1 72
(T D Barron) *hld up: hdwy over 2f out: rdn and hung lft ins fnl f: r.o* **3/1**[1]

133- 3 ¾ **Inside Story (IRE)**[38] 6748 5-8-9 67 (b) JamesDoyle(3) 4 73
(G P Kelly) *hld up in tch: chsd wnr over 2f out: sn rdn: styd on* **7/2**[2]

4 ½ **Great Man (FR)**[672] 6-8-7 62 FergusSweeney 3 67
(Noel T Chance) *chsd ldrs: rdn over 1f out: nt clr run ins fnl f: styd on* **20/1**

244- 5 ½ **Always Baileys (IRE)**[32] 6825 4-8-6 65 ChrisCatlin 10 69
(T Wall) *sn led: hdd over 3f out: rdn over 1f out: no ex ins fnl f* **40/1**

124- 6 ¾ **Top Spec (IRE)**[44] 6673 6-9-6 75 JimmyQuinn 6 78
(J Pearce) *s.i.s: hld up: hdwy over 3f out: rdn over 1f out: styd on same pce* **11/2**

33-3 7 ½ **Champagne Shadow (IRE)**[14] 4 6-9-1 70 (b) NCallan 11 72
(K A Ryan) *hld up: outpcd over 3f out: n.d after* **4/1**[3]

455- 8 1 ½ **Newnham (IRE)**[61] 6494 6-9-2 71 JoeFanning 9 71
(J R Boyle) *hld up: effrt over 2f out: nt trble ldrs* **14/1**

2-34 9 1 ½ **Opera Writer (IRE)**[4] 100 4-8-2 61 PaulQuinn 8 58
(R Hollinshead) *chsd ldrs over 9f* **8/1**

206- 10 54 **Psycho Cat**[113] 3839 4-8-5 64 AdrianTNicholls 7 —
(S T Lewis) *hld up: plld hrd: bhd fnl 6f* **66/1**

2m 45.16s (2.74) **Going Correction** +0.075s/f (Slow)
WFA 4 from 5yo+ 4lb 10 Ran SP% **120.2**
Speed ratings (Par 103):93,92,92,91,91 91,90,89,88,52
CSF £32.88 CT £102.82 TOTE £10.10: £2.60, £1.60, £1.70; EX 49.80 Trifecta £442.10 Pool: £809.62 - 1.30 winning units. Place 6 £5.51, Place 5 £4.63.
Owner R Rickett **Bred** Shadwell Estate Company Limited **Trained** Great Ness, Shropshire

FOCUS
A modest handicap, not run at a great pace, and the form is very ordinary.
Newnham(IRE) Official explanation: jockey said gelding ran too freely
T/Jkpt: Not won. T/Plt: £5.10 to a £1 stake. Pool: £54,202.20. 7,734.20 winning tickets. T/Qpdt: £4.50 to a £1 stake. Pool: £3,654.50. 594.00 winning tickets. CR

[97]SOUTHWELL (L-H)
Tuesday, January 16

OFFICIAL GOING: Standard
Wind: light across

143 GO PONTIN'S (S) STKS 5f (F)
12:30 (12:31) (Class 6) 4-Y-0+ £2,184 (£644; £322) Stalls High

Form RPR

40-3 1 **Magic Amour**[15] 3 9-8-9 60 (b) KevinGhunowa(5) 6 66
(P A Blockley) *chsd ldrs and sn pushed along: rdn along and hdwy 1/2-way: led over 1f out: rdn and kpt on ins last* **5/4**[1]

32-2 2 2 **Majik**[14] 9 8-9-0 52 (p) MickyFenton 7 59
(P T Midgley) *prom: rdn along and sltly outpcd 1/2-way: styd on appr last* **7/2**[2]

306- 3 2 ½ **Phinerine**[16] 6994 4-8-9 53 (b) TolleyDean(5) 3 51
(R A Harris) *prom: effrt 2f out: sn rdn and kpt on same pce* **15/2**

006- 4 ½ **Princess Kai (IRE)**[17] 6984 6-8-9 40 JoeFanning 1 44
(R Ingram) *in tch: rdn along over 2f out: kpt on ins last: nrst fin* **20/1**

000- 5 hd **The Leather Wedge (IRE)**[50] 6622 8-8-11 57 (p) StephenDonohoe(3) 9 48
(R Johnson) *led: edgd lft over 2f out: rdn wl over 1f out: sn hdd & wknd* **9/2**[3]

004- 6 1 ¼ **Tribute (IRE)**[19] 6956 6-9-0 47 PaulMulrennan 2 44
(John A Harris) *chsd ldrs: rdn along 1/2-way: sn wknd* **14/1**

000- 7 nk **Eternally**[29] 6851 5-8-11 41 (p) JerryO'Dwyer(3) 8 43
(R M H Cowell) *cl up: rdn along and n.m.r over 2f out: swtchd rt and sn wknd* **33/1**

00-0 8 8 **Laurel Dawn**[5] 97 9-8-9 41 AnnStokell(5) 5 16
(Miss A Stokell) *nt much roon s: sn rdn along and a bhd* **80/1**

59.83 secs (-0.47) **Going Correction** -0.25s/f (Stan) 8 Ran SP% **112.2**
Speed ratings (Par 101):93,89,85,85,84 82,82,69
CSF £5.38 TOTE £1.80: £1.10, £1.80, £2.10; EX 6.10.There was no bid for the winner.
Owner Joe McCarthy **Bred** Juddmonte Farms **Trained** Lambourn, Berks

FOCUS
A weakish seller, but the form appears to make sense.
The Leather Wedge(IRE) Official explanation: jockey said gelding hung left throughout
Laurel Dawn Official explanation: jockey said gelding suffered interference

144 BONUSPRINT.COM H'CAP (DIV I) 7f (F)
1:00 (1:01) (Class 6) (0-52,52) 4-Y-0+ £1,706 (£503; £252) Stalls Low

Form RPR

06-0 1 **Val De Maal (IRE)**[7] 77 7-8-12 52 PaulMulrennan 9 61
(Miss J A Camacho) *a.p on outer: rdn wl over 1f out: styd on to ld wl ins last: sn drvn and edgd lft: kpt on* **22/1**

364- 2 nk **Lucius Verrus (USA)**[19] 6960 7-8-6 46 oh1 (v) HayleyTurner 4 54
(D Shaw) *in tch: hdwy over 2f out: rdn to ld 1f out: drvn and hdd wl ins last: no ex towards fin* **11/2**[3]

50-6 3 1 ¼ **Shunkawakhan (IRE)**[12] 33 4-8-4 48 (p) OscarUrbina 1 53
(G C H Chung) *led: rdn 2f out: drvn and hdd 1f out: kpt on same pce u.p ins last* **12/1**

350- 4 nk **Keon (IRE)**[19] 6964 5-8-7 52 (p) RussellKennemore(5) 3 56
(R Hollinshead) *prom: rdn along 2f out: drvn and kpt on same pce appr last* **8/1**

542- 5 1 ¾ **Favouring (IRE)**[19] 6961 5-8-8 48 (v) AdrianMcCarthy 10 47
(M C Chapman) *midfield: hdwy to chse ldrs over 2f out: sn rdn and kpt on same pce* **7/2**[2]

50-6 6 shd **Pawn In Life (IRE)**[7] 75 9-8-8 48 (v) JoeFanning 2 47
(S Parr) *dwlt: sn chsng ldrs: hdwy on inner over 2f out: sn rdn and wknd appr last* **25/1**

1-33 7 1 ¼ **Penel (IRE)**[7] 77 6-8-5 50 (p) RoryMoore(5) 11 46
(P T Midgley) *hld up in rr: effrt and hdwy 3f out: rdn to chse ldrs 2f out: sn one pce* **10/3**[1]

06-4 8 nk **Ohana**[15] 7 4-8-8 51 JerryO'Dwyer(3) 8 46
(Miss Gay Kelleway) *hld up: a rr* **8/1**

0- 9 6 **Breeze In (IRE)**[18] 6974 4-8-6 46 oh1 PaulFessey 5 26
(R A Fahey) *chsd ldrs: rdn along 3f out: sn wknd* **50/1**

405- 10 7 **For Life (IRE)**[35] 6798 5-8-7 47 (p) JohnEgan 6 8
(Stef Liddiard) *keen: hld up: a rr* **13/2**

1m 29.55s (-1.25) **Going Correction** -0.25s/f (Stan) 10 Ran SP% **114.1**
Speed ratings (Par 101):97,96,95,94,92 92,91,91,84,76
CSF £133.76 CT £1567.53 TOTE £26.70: £7.10, £1.80, £3.20; EX 285.20.
Owner Lee Bolingbroke & Partners V **Bred** John Killan **Trained** Norton, N Yorks

FOCUS
Modest handicap form, and questionable through the third.
Penel(IRE) Official explanation: jockey said gelding never travelled
For Life(IRE) Official explanation: jockey said gelding ran too free

145 BONUSPRINT.COM H'CAP (DIV II) 7f (F)
1:30 (1:31) (Class 6) (0-52,52) 4-Y-0+ £1,706 (£503; £252) Stalls Low

Form RPR

034- 1 **Wodhill Be**[19] 6961 7-8-6 46 oh1 HayleyTurner 3 53
(D Morris) *hld up in midfield: smooth hdwy over 2f out: swtchd rt and rdn to chal over 1f out: drvn ins last: led last 50 yds* **11/2**[2]

00-0 2 nk **Mill By The Stream**[10] 50 5-8-12 52 SteveDrowne 1 58
(Tom Dascombe) *trckd ldrs: led over 2f out: rdn over 1f out: drvn and edgd rt ins last: hdd and no ex last 50 yds* **8/1**

60-5 3 1 ½ **Mouseen (IRE)**[7] 77 4-8-5 50 (b) TolleyDean(5) 4 52
(R A Harris) *dwlt: sn in tch on inner: gd hdwy over 2f out: rdn and ch over 1f out: drvn and kpt on same pce ins last* **12/1**

50-2 4 3 ½ **Seldemosa**[3] 123 6-8-8 48 J-PGuillambert 9 41
(M S Saunders) *chsd ldrs: rdn wl over 1f out: sn drvn and no imp appr last* **7/2**[1]

000- 5 2 ½ **Piccleyes**[228] 2207 6-8-9 52 (b) StephenDonohoe(3) 5 39
(A J McCabe) *towards rr: hdwy over 2f out: sn rdn and kpt on appr last: nrst fin* **8/1**

32-0 6 3 **Grand Palace (IRE)**[15] 7 4-8-11 51 (v) MickyFenton 6 30
(D Shaw) *rr and pushed along 1/2-way: swtchd ins and sme hdwy fnl 2f: nvr a factor* **7/2**[1]

000- 7 ½ **Mister Becks (IRE)**[48] 5724 4-8-6 46 (b) AdrianMcCarthy 7 24
(M C Chapman) *led: rdn along and hdd over 2f out: sn wknd* **50/1**

66-4 8 1 ½ **Rocky Reppin**[9] 61 7-8-3 46 oh1 (b) AndrewElliott(3) 8 20
(J Balding) *chsd ldrs: rdn along 3f out: sn wknd* **14/1**

506- 9 3 **Dispol Peto**[35] 6798 7-8-8 48 (b) PaulEddery 11 14
(R Johnson) *chsd ldrs on outer: rdn along 3f out and sn wknd* **13/2**[3]

0-00 10 ¾ **Miss Redactive**[3] 125 4-8-6 46 oh1 EdwardCreighton 10 10
(M D I Usher) *rdn along 1/2-way: a rr* **66/1**

06-0 11 5 **Far Note (USA)**[7] 77 9-8-8 48 (bt) PhillipMakin 2 —
(S R Bowring) *chsd ldrs: rdn along 3f out: sn wknd* **33/1**

1m 29.36s (-1.44) **Going Correction** -0.25s/f (Stan) 11 Ran SP% **116.1**
Speed ratings (Par 101):98,97,95,91,89 85,85,83,79,79 73
CSF £47.92 CT £387.50 TOTE £5.60: £2.40, £3.10, £3.40; EX 64.10.
Owner Miss S Graham **Bred** Wodhill Stud **Trained** Newmarket, Suffolk

FOCUS
A banded-style handicap, but the form looks a shade more solid than that of the first division.

146 PONTIN'S FAMILY HOLIDAYS H'CAP 2m (F)
2:00 (2:01) (Class 6) (0-60,60) 4-Y-0+ £2,388 (£705; £352) Stalls Low

Form RPR

01-2 1 **Miss Holly**[14] 12 8-8-13 57 KellyHarrison(7) 7 68
(D Carroll) *hld up towards rr: gd hdwy on inner over 3f out: chal over 1f out: rdn to ld jst ins last: styd on wl* **9/2**[2]

51-4 2 2 **Bulberry Hill**[14] 10 6-9-2 53 EdwardCreighton 12 62
(R W Price) *trckd ldr: hdwy to chser ldr over 3f out: chal over 2f out: sn rdn and ev ch tl one pce ins last* **11/2**

000/ 3 ½ **Al Moulatham**[11] 8-9-9 60 (vt[1]) JimCrowley 8 68
(R Ford) *led: rdn along over 3f out: jnd 2f out: drvn and hung bdly lft over 1f out: hdd jst ins last: one pce* **33/1**

60-5 4 5 **Blue Hills**[9] 62 6-9-3 54 (b[1]) PhillipMakin 3 56
(P W Hiatt) *chsd ldrs: effrt 3f out: rdn over 2f out and sn no imp* **14/1**

50-1 5 2 ½ **Tioga Gold (IRE)**[14] 10 8-8-8 50 RussellKennemore(5) 10 49
(L R James) *hld up: hdwy over 4f out: rdn along 3f out: sn no imp* **10/1**

5-54 6 4 **Romil Star (GER)**[9] 64 10-8-4 46 oh1 (p) KevinGhunowa(5) 1 40
(M Wellings) *chsd ldrs: rdn along 4f out: wknd 3f out* **12/1**

2 7 14 **Nayodabayo (IRE)**[14] 10 7-9-0 56 TolleyDean(5) 6 33
(Evan Williams) *chsd ldr: rdn along 4f out: drvn and wknd 3f out* **7/2**[1]

60-3 8 2 **Dan's Heir**[14] 10 5-9-4 55 (p) LeeEnstone 11 30
(P C Haslam) *towards rr: rdn along over 5f out: sn lost pl and bhd* **5/1**[3]

163- 9 2 **Ice And Fire**[45] 6685 8-8-11 53 (b) AshleyHamblett(5) 9 26
(J T Stimpson) *hld up and bhd: effrt over 5f out: sn rdn along and no hdwy* **11/2**

3m 39.6s (-4.94) **Going Correction** -0.25s/f (Stan) 9 Ran SP% **114.2**
Speed ratings (Par 101):102,101,100,98,97 95,88,87,86
CSF £29.11 CT £719.69 TOTE £4.20: £1.60, £1.60, £8.50; EX 37.30.
Owner Mrs B Ramsden **Bred** Vikingstar Bloodstock **Trained** Sledmere, E Yorks

FOCUS
A moderate staying handicap run at a decent pace. It has been rated through the winner and the form may not prove entirely solid.
Ice And Fire Official explanation: trainer said gelding had problems breathing

The Form Book, Raceform Ltd, Compton, RG20 6NL

147 **PONTINS.COM H'CAP** 6f (F)
2:30 (2:31) (Class 5) (0-75,81) 3-Y-O £2,914 (£867; £433; £216) Stalls Low

Form RPR

21-1 1 **Para Siempre**[9] 65 3-9-3 **81** 6ex..............................(b) NeilBrown(7) 8 89
(B Smart) *trckd ldrs on outer: hdwy 2f out: rdn over 1f out: led ins last: styd on* **1/2**[1]

114- 2 1 3/4 **Diminuto**[21] 6939 3-7-12 **62**.............................. FrankiePickard(7) 1 65
(M D I Usher) *chsd ldrs: hdwy over 2f out: rdn and ev ch over 1f out: drvn and kpt on same pce ins last* **20/1**

22-1 3 hd **Cherri Fosfate**[11] 40 3-8-3 **67**..............................(v) KellyHarrison(7) 2 69
(D Carroll) *dwlt: keen in rr: gd hdwy over 2f out: rdn and edgd rt over 1f out: kpt on ins last* **14/1**

012- 4 1 **Pirner's Brig**[24] 6926 3-8-8 **65**.............................. PaulMulrennan 6 64
(M W Easterby) *led: rdn along over 2f out: drvn over 1f out: hdd and one pce ins last* **11/1**[3]

003- 5 1 **Minimum Fuss (IRE)**[42] 6715 3-8-4 **61** oh1.............. AdrianMcCarthy 3 57
(M C Chapman) *keen: cl up: rdn along over 2f out: grad wknd appr last* **50/1**

012- 6 1 1/2 **Zadalla**[26] 6895 3-8-9 **66**.............................. JoeFanning 4 58
(Andrew Oliver, Ire) *chsd ldrs: rdn over 2f out: drvn and wknd wl over 1f out* **12/1**

542- 7 1/2 **Jord (IRE)**[28] 6872 3-8-13 **73**.............................. StephenDonohoe(3) 7 63
(A J McCabe) *a towards rr* **7/1**[2]

23-2 8 1 3/4 **Vadinka**[12] 34 3-9-0 **71**.............................. KimTinkler 9 56
(N Tinkler) *prom: rdn along over 2f out: sn edgd lft and wknd* **16/1**

400- 9 hd **Silver Hotspur**[28] 6866 3-8-5 **62**.............................. HayleyTurner 5 47
(M Wigham) *a rr* **25/1**

1m 15.04s (-1.86) **Going Correction** -0.25s/f (Stan) 9 Ran SP% **118.3**

Speed ratings (Par 97):102,99,99,98,96 94,94,91,91

CSF £16.61 CT £82.23 TOTE £1.50: £1.10, £5.40, £3.20; EX 15.70.

Owner Mrs Linda Pestell **Bred** D R Tucker **Trained** Hambleton, N Yorks

FOCUS

The betting suggested this was a gimme for the well handicapped and improving favourite and, although she did not win by far, she was well on top at the finish. She did not need tio improve, racing from her old mark.

148 **PHOTO ALBUMS FROM BONUSPRINT.COM H'CAP** 1m 4f (F)
3:00 (3:00) (Class 6) (0-60,56) 4-Y-O+ £2,388 (£705; £352) Stalls Low

Form RPR

60-1 1 **Global Strategy**[9] 64 4-9-1 **54** 6ex.............................. SebSanders 9 64+
(Rae Guest) *hld up: stdy hdwy on outer 3f out: rdn to ld over 1f out: clr ins last* **4/7**[1]

15-1 2 2 1/2 **Maria Antonia (IRE)**[14] 12 4-9-3 **56**.............................. SimonWhitworth 5 62
(P A Blockley) *dwlt: hld up toiwards rr: stdy hdwy over 3f out: rdn and ch over 1f out: edgd lft and kpt on same pce ins last* **7/1**[2]

0/0- 3 1 3/4 **Moyne Pleasure (IRE)**[15] 6797 9-8-10 **45**.............................. PaulEddery 11 48
(R Johnson) *dwlt: hld up in rr: hdwy 3f out: rdn wl over 1f out: styd on strly ins last: nrst fin* **50/1**

044- 4 1/2 **Bramcote Lorne**[49] 6630 4-8-12 **51**.............................. PaulMulrennan 4 53
(John A Harris) *led: rdn along over 2f out: drvn: edgd rt and hdd over 1f out: sn edgd lft and one pce* **14/1**

/0-0 5 1 1/2 **Forfeiter (USA)**[11] 39 5-9-6 **55**..............................(v) JimCrowley 12 55
(R Ford) *chsd ldr: effrt to chal 3f out: sn rdn and one pce fnl 2f* **16/1**

6 2 1/2 **Legend In Hand (IRE)**[83] 6185 5-9-3 **55**.............................. JerryO'Dwyer(3) 1 51
(Seamus Fahey, Ire) *chsd ldrs: rdn along over 3f out: wknd 2f out* **16/1**

0- 7 3/4 **The Perfect Plan (IRE)**[18] 6980 4-8-13 **52**.............................. SteveDrowne 8 47
(Tom Dascombe) *in tch: rdn along 3f out: sn no imp* **40/1**

/0-6 8 5 **Stallone**[12] 35 10-8-8 **50**.............................. LanceBetts(7) 10 37
(N Wilson) *nvr nr ldrs* **66/1**

60-0 9 2 **Stolen Summer (IRE)**[7] 75 4-9-2 **55**..............................(be) MickyFenton 2 39
(B S Rothwell) *keen: a rr* **40/1**

04-2 10 shd **Dream Forest (IRE)**[7] 78 4-9-2 **55**.............................. JoeFanning 7 38
(J Balding) *chsd ldrs: rdn along 3f out: wknd over 2f out* **8/1**[3]

562- 11 1/2 **Lanfredo**[33] 6817 4-8-11 **50**..............................(p) JohnEgan 6 33
(Miss M E Rowland) *midefield: rdn along over 3f out and sn wknd* **12/1**

60-0 12 4 **Lockstock (IRE)**[3] 121 9-9-0 **49**.............................. J-PGuillambert 3 25
(M S Saunders) *chsd ldrs: rdn along 4f out: sn wknd* **33/1**

2m 39.8s (-2.29) **Going Correction** -0.25s/f (Stan)

WFA 4 from 5yo+ 4lb 12 Ran SP% **124.7**

Speed ratings (Par 101):97,95,94,93,92 91,90,87,86,85 85,82

CSF £5.28 CT £122.09 TOTE £1.80: £1.10, £1.40, £12.30; EX 5.00.

Owner E P Duggan **Bred** Keith Freeman **Trained** Newmarket, Suffolk

FOCUS

A moderate handicap in which the favourite held outstanding claims and justified good support. There was little solid form in behind.

Stolen Summer(IRE) Official explanation: jockey said gelding ran too free early stages

Dream Forest(IRE) Official explanation: jockey said gelding had no more to give

149 **PONTIN'S BOOK EARLY MAIDEN STKS** 1m (F)
3:30 (3:32) (Class 5) 3-Y-O £2,817 (£838; £418; £209) Stalls Low

Form RPR

324- 1 **Hurlingham**[98] 5883 3-9-3 75.............................. JoeFanning 4 80+
(M Johnston) *a.p: hdwy to ld 3f out: pushed clr wl over 1f out: easily* **2/5**[1]

00- 2 3 **Milla's Rocket (IRE)**[79] 6242 3-8-12 ....(b[1]) PaulMulrennan 13 63
(K A Ryan) *a.p: led 1/2-way: hdd 3f out: sn rdn and kpt on same pce fnl 2f* **16/1**[3]

0- 3 2 **Here's Blue Chip (IRE)**[49] 6646 3-9-3 .... JohnEgan 6 64
(P W D'Arcy) *chsd ldrs: rdn wl over 2f out and kpt on same pce* **22/1**

4 2 1/2 **John Dillon (IRE)** 3-9-3 .... LeeEnstone 3 59
(P C Haslam) *dwlt and towards rr: hdwy 3f out: rdn over 2f out: styd on: nrst fin* **50/1**

0- 5 1 1/4 **Intensifier (IRE)**[38] 6757 3-9-3 .... SimonWhitworth 1 56
(P A Blockley) *chsd ldrs on inner: rdn along 3f out: sn outpcd* **50/1**

05- 6 2 1/2 **Brean Dot Com (IRE)**[33] 6815 3-9-3 .... J-PGuillambert 8 51
(Mrs P N Dutfield) *chsd ldrs: rdn along 3f out: sn outpcd* **8/1**[2]

- 7 nk **Castle Durrow (IRE)** 3-8-9 .... JerryO'Dwyer(3) 2 45
(Seamus Fahey, Ire) *s.i.s and towards rr tl styd on fnl 2f* **22/1**

8 5 **Park's Prodigy** 3-9-3 .... SteveDrowne 10 40
(P C Haslam) *in tch: pushed along 1/2-way: sn wknd* **20/1**

36-0 9 1 3/4 **Muree Queen**[12] 37 3-8-7 47..............................(p) RussellKennemore(5) 11 31
(R Hollinshead) *bhd fr 1/2-way* **40/1**

10 7 **Noravana (IRE)** 3-8-12 .... EdwardCreighton 9 16
(Miss V Haigh) *dwlt: a rr* **66/1**

11 1 **Fareham Creek** 3-8-12 .... JamesMillman(5) 12 19
(D K Ivory) *chsd ldrs: rdn along 3f out: sn wknd* **50/1**

0-0 12 3/4 **Otaki (IRE)**[8] 69 3-8-12 .... SebSanders 5 13
(Sir Mark Prescott) *a towards rr* **20/1**

13 9 **Montiona** 3-9-0 .... MarkLawson(3) 7 —
(John A Harris) *dwlt: a rr* **50/1**

14 17 **Zamaya** 3-9-3 .... PhillipMakin 14 —
(K R Burke) *led and sn clr: hdd over 3f out and sn wknd* **25/1**

1m 42.12s (-2.48) **Going Correction** -0.25s/f (Stan) 14 Ran SP% **122.3**

Speed ratings (Par 97):102,99,97,94,93 90,90,85,83,76 75,74,65,48

CSF £6.18 TOTE £1.40: £1.02, £4.80, £4.60; EX 9.60.

Owner Sheikh Mohammed **Bred** Aston Mullins Stud **Trained** Middleham Moor, N Yorks

FOCUS

A weakish maiden in which the winner could run below his official mark and still win easily.

Zamaya Official explanation: jockey said gelding ran too free

150 **PONTINSBINGO.COM FILLIES' H'CAP** 7f (F)
4:00 (4:00) (Class 5) (0-70,70) 4-Y-O+ £2,914 (£867; £433; £216) Stalls Low

Form RPR

234- 1 **Black Sea Pearl**[26] 6897 4-8-6 **60**.............................. JohnEgan 5 72
(P W D'Arcy) *chsd ldrs: rdn along 2f out: styd on to ld ins last* **11/2**[3]

006- 2 2 **Rainbows Guest (IRE)**[24] 6928 4-8-12 **66**..............................(v) SebSanders 1 73
(A M Balding) *dwlt: sn rdn along to ld on inner: clr over 2f out: rdn wl over 1f out: wknd and hdd ins last* **7/1**

41-1 3 1/2 **Capital Lass**[9] 61 4-8-0 **59** 6ex.............................. NataliaGemelova(5) 7 65
(A J McCabe) *chsd ldrs: hdwy over 2f out: sn rdn and kpt on same pce ent last* **4/1**[2]

320- 4 shd **Imperial Lucky (IRE)**[37] 6781 4-9-2 **70**.............................. HayleyTurner 4 75
(D K Ivory) *in tch: pushed along and outpcd over 2f out: styd on u.p appr last: nrst fin* **9/1**

004- 5 1/2 **Jellytot (USA)**[95] 5953 4-8-7 **61**.............................. PaulQuinn 2 65
(J O'Reilly) *rr tl hdwy on inner wl over 1f out: kpt on inisde last: nrst fin* **33/1**

020- 6 2 **Prettilini**[19] 6964 4-8-2 **56**.............................. MatthewHenry 8 55
(R Brotherton) *prom on outer: rdn along 3f out: sn drvn and wknd over 2f out* **20/1**

34-1 7 1/2 **Glamaraazi (IRE)**[7] 77 4-8-4 **58** 6ex.............................. JoeFanning 6 56
(R A Fahey) *rr: pushed along 1/2-way: rdn over 2f out and no hdwy* **5/4**[1]

020- 8 3 1/2 **Startori**[20] 6946 4-8-11 **65**.............................. PaulEddery 3 54
(B Smart) *cl up: rdn along 1/2-way: drvn and wknd wl over 2f out* **14/1**

1m 28.56s (-2.24) **Going Correction** -0.25s/f (Stan) 8 Ran SP% **116.7**

Speed ratings (Par 100):102,99,99,99,98 96,95,91

CSF £44.24 CT £173.09 TOTE £7.40: £2.40, £2.30, £1.70; EX 34.60 Place 6 £96.94, Place 5 £74.06.

Owner Mrs Jan Harris **Bred** Cheveley Park Stud Ltd **Trained** Newmarket, Suffolk

■ Stewards' Enquiry : Paul Quinn 14-day ban: (Jan 27-Feb 9); J O'Reilly fined £3,000 Rule 157

FOCUS

Just a modest fillies-only handicap, but the pace was strong and the winning time was 0.99 seconds quicker than the first division of the older-horse 7f handicap, and 0.80 seconds faster than the second division. The form looks quite sound. Jellytot fell foul of the non-triers' rule.

Jellytot(USA) Official explanation: jockey said, regarding running and riding, that he was given no specific orders, adding that the filly would be better suited by a further furlong; 40-day ban: (Jan 19-Feb 27)

T/Plt: £193.50 to a £1 stake. Pool: £42,903.40. 161.85 winning tickets. T/Qpdt: £18.20 to a £1 stake. Pool: £3,591.60. 145.80 winning tickets. JR

135 WOLVERHAMPTON (A.W) (L-H)

Tuesday, January 16

OFFICIAL GOING: Standard

A good day for front-runners with the winners of the last four races making all.

Wind: almost nil Weather: light early rain

151 **PONTINS.COM H'CAP** 1m 141y(P)
1:40 (1:40) (Class 5) (0-70,68) 4-Y-O+ £3,238 (£963; £481; £240) Stalls Low

Form RPR

101- 1 **Topiary Ted**[24] 6934 5-8-12 **63**.............................. RobertHavlin 2 76
(H Morrison) *hld up in mid-div: hdwy on ins 2f out: rdn to ld 1f out: sn edgd rt: r.o* **9/4**[1]

00/1 2 1 **Activity (IRE)**[8] 70 8-8-7 **63**.............................. DuranFentiman(5) 4 74
(M J Gingell) *hld up and bhd: hdwy over 2f out: rdn and ev ch 1f out: sn carried rt: kpt on* **5/1**[3]

360- 3 2 1/2 **Stoic Leader (IRE)**[41] 6733 7-9-2 **67**.............................. NCallan 6 73
(R F Fisher) *hld up in tch: rdn over 2f out: kpt on same pce fnl f* **16/1**

4-3 4 nk **Dapple Dawn (IRE)**[5] 101 4-9-2 **68**.............................. DanielTudhope 7 73
(D Carroll) *chsd ldr: rdn 3f out: led 2f out to 1f out: wknd ins fnl f* **13/2**

00-2 5 2 1/2 **Parkview Love (USA)**[7] 80 6-8-8 **59**..............................(v) JimmyQuinn 3 59
(D Shaw) *prom: rdn over 2f out: wknd over 1f out* **9/2**[2]

040- 6 3 **Defi (IRE)**[26] 6898 5-9-0 **68**..............................(b) GregFairley(3) 1 62
(I Semple) *led: rdn and hdd 2f out: wknd fnl f* **12/1**

000- 7 3 1/2 **Aperitif**[111] 5617 6-9-3 **68**.............................. AdrianTNicholls 10 54
(D Nicholls) *hld up in tch: rdn over 3f out: wknd over 2f out* **33/1**

500- 8 3 **Hand Chime**[224] 2317 10-8-5 **59**.............................. JamesDoyle(3) 9 39
(Ernst Oertel) *s.i.s: a bhd* **50/1**

126- 9 1 3/4 **Sentiero Rosso (USA)**[17] 6818 5-9-3 **68**..............................(t) PatCosgrave 8 44
(B Ellison) *stdd s: hld up and bhd: rdn over 3f out: sn struggling* **12/1**

000- 10 1 1/2 **Danceinthevalley (IRE)**[142] 4831 5-8-11 **62**.............. DeanMcKeown 5 35
(G A Swinbank) *s.i.s: a towards rr* **16/1**

1m 48.98s (-2.78) **Going Correction** -0.225s/f (Stan)

WFA 4 from 5yo+ 1lb 10 Ran SP% **111.0**

Speed ratings (Par 103):103,102,99,99,97 94,91,88,87,86

CSF £12.31 CT £133.53 TOTE £2.10: £1.10, £2.20, £5.50; EX 15.40 Trifecta £136.00 Pool £252.87 - 1.32 winning units..

Owner Ron Plant **Bred** Stowell Hill Ltd And Mrs C Van Straubenzee **Trained** East Ilsley, Berks

FOCUS

A moderate affair run at a decent pace. The front three were held up. The winner is progressing and the next four were all on fair marks on their best form.

152 **GO PONTIN'S MEDIAN AUCTION MAIDEN STKS** 7f 32y(P)
2:10 (2:11) (Class 6) 3-Y-O £2,388 (£705; £352) Stalls High

Form RPR

6- 1 **Great Explorer (IRE)**[229] 2178 3-9-3 .... ChrisCatlin 6 75
(E J O'Neill) *a.p: rdn over 2f out: led wl over 1f out: r.o wl* **5/2**[2]

3- 2 5 **My Beautaful**[34] 6809 3-8-9 .... JamesDoyle(3) 1 57
(Miss J S Davis) *a.p: rdn wl over 1f out: chsd wnr fnl f: no imp* **16/1**[3]

00- 3 3/4 **New World Order (IRE)**[100] 5851 3-9-3 94.............................. PatCosgrave 9 60
(K R Burke) *sn chsng ldr: rdn to ld briefly wl over 1f out: one pce* **4/7**[1]

4 1 3/4 **Toms Laughter** 3-9-3 .... DaleGibson 4 55+
(B Palling) *dwlt: bhd: rdn over 2f out: hdwy over 1f out: nrst fin* **100/1**
000- 5 4 **Meathop (IRE)**[41] [6730] 3-9-3 40 .... NCallan 8 44
(R F Fisher) *hld up in mid-div: rdn and hdwy on ins over 2f out: wknd over 1f out* **150/1**
0 6 1 1/2 **Varya**[10] [55] 3-8-12 .... JamieMackay 7 35
(Sir Mark Prescott) *s.i.s: bhd: short-lived effrt over 1f out: nvr nr ldrs* **25/1**
6-0 7 2 1/2 **Haydock Express (IRE)**[9] [60] 3-9-3 .... AdamKirby 3 33
(Peter Grayson) *led: rdn over 2f out: hdd wl over 1f out: sn wknd* **25/1**
0-0 8 3/4 **Pindar (GER)**[9] [60] 3-9-3 .... TPQueally 2 31
(B J Curley) *plld hrd: prom: stdd over 5f out: lost pl over 4f out* **50/1**
9 7 **Kindkintyre (IRE)** 3-8-10 .... JamesRogers(7) 10 12
(R A Fahey) *s.i.s: a in rr* **50/1**
4- 10 9 **Betty Oxo**[24] [6931] 3-8-12 .... DeanMcKeown 5 —
(B P J Baugh) *s.i.s: plld hrd in mid-div: bhd fnl 3f* **150/1**

1m 29.7s (-0.70) **Going Correction** -0.225s/f (Stan) **10 Ran SP% 112.0**
Speed ratings (Par 95):95,89,88,86,81 80,77,76,68,58
CSF £34.71 TOTE £2.70: £1.10, £1.90, £1.10; EX 40.30 Trifecta £72.40 Pool £314.18 - 3.08 winning units..
Owner J C Fretwell **Bred** Mrs S Nolan **Trained** Averham Park, Notts

FOCUS
This was not a great maiden and the bookmakers went 25/1 bar three. The favourite was way off his Irish form and the winner's mark might be hit hard for this, although the fifth does limit the form.

153 PONTIN'S HOLIDAYS H'CAP 1m 5f 194y(P)
2:40 (2:40) (Class 4) (0-85,85) 4-Y-0+ £4,857 (£1,445; £722; £360) Stalls Low

Form RPR
211- 1 **Melpomene**[25] [6917] 4-9-1 82 .... GregFairley(3) 8 93
(M Johnston) *mde all: rdn over 2f out: styd on wl* **2/1**[1]
300- 2 3 **Kames Park (IRE)**[17] [6677] 5-9-13 85 .... TonyCulhane 6 93+
(I Semple) *hld up in rr: hmpd over 3f out: rdn and hdwy on ins over 2f out: styd on u.p to take 2nd nr fin: unlucky* **14/1**
/11- 3 nk **Market Watcher (USA)**[45] [6685] 6-9-1 73 ....(t) PatCosgrave 3 79
(Seamus Fahey, Ire) *hld up in tch: rdn 3f out: chsd wnr over 1f out: edgd lft ins fnl f: lost 2nd nr fin* **5/2**[2]
0/1- 4 1/2 **Ross Moor**[25] [6916] 5-8-9 70 .... JamesDoyle(3) 5 75
(N P Littmoden) *sn chsg wnr: rdn over 3f out: one pace fnl f* **12/1**
321- 5 3 **Tranquilizer**[21] [6941] 5-9-6 78 ....(t) AdamKirby 1 79
(D J Coakley) *a.p: rdn 3f out: wknd wl ins fnl f* **5/1**[3]
000/ 6 11 **Photographer (USA)**[404] [1021] 9-8-8 66 oh6 .... ChrisCatlin 7 52
(S Lycett) *hld up and bhd: pushed along 3f out: sn struggling* **100/1**
0/0- 7 2 **Solarias Quest**[34] [6811] 5-9-8 80 .... AdrianTNicholls 4 63
(A King) *hld up towards rr: edgd lft over 3f out: sn rdn and struggling* **33/1**
61-1 8 16 **Foursquare Flyer (IRE)**[11] [45] 5-8-11 69 .... DaleGibson 9 30
(J Mackie) *hld up: sn in tch: rdn over 3f out: sn wknd* **15/2**
P20- 9 24 **Tender Trap (IRE)**[19] [3028] 9-9-11 83 .... SamHitchcott 2 10
(Miss J E Foster) *hld up towards rr: rdn over 4f out: hmpd on ins over 3f out: sn lost tch: eased fnl 2f* **66/1**

3m 4.38s (-2.99) **Going Correction** -0.225s/f (Stan)
WFA 4 from 5yo+ 6lb **9 Ran SP% 110.1**
Speed ratings (Par 105):99,97,97,96,95 88,87,78,64
CSF £28.86 CT £66.46 TOTE £2.30: £1.30, £2.70, £1.20; EX 22.30 Trifecta £35.90 w/u.
Owner Mrs Christine E Budden **Bred** Zubieta Ltd **Trained** Middleham Moor, N Yorks

FOCUS
A fair handicap with five of the field successful on their previous starts. The winner is progressive and should do better, as should the second and third.
Solarias Quest Official explanation: jockey said gelding bled from the nose

154 GO PONTIN'S H'CAP 5f 20y(P)
3:10 (3:11) (Class 5) (0-70,65) 4-Y-0+ £3,238 (£963; £481; £240) Stalls Low

Form RPR
532- 1 **Almaty Express**[16] [6994] 5-8-2 58 ....(b) WilliamBuick(7) 9 79
(J R Weymes) *mde all: rdn wl over 1f out: edgd rt ins fnl f: r.o wl* **7/1**
111- 2 2 **Rowe Park**[16] [6994] 4-9-2 65 .... LPKeniry 10 79
(Mrs L C Jewell) *chsd wnr tl rdn wl over 1f out: kpt on towards fin* **11/4**[1]
51-1 3 1 1/2 **Gifted Lass**[14] [8] 5-9-0 63 .... DavidAllan 7 71
(J Balding) *a.p: rdn to chsd wnr wl over 1f out: no ex towards fin* **9/2**[3]
00-0 4 2 1/2 **Triskaidekaphobia**[6] [82] 4-8-6 55 ....(t) PaulFitzsimons 3 54
(Miss J R Tooth) *hld up in mid-div: rdn and hdwy wl over 1f out: kpt on ins fnl f: nt rch ldrs* **28/1**
50-1 5 3/4 **Pride Of Joy**[12] [36] 4-9-1 64 .... ChrisCatlin 1 61
(D K Ivory) *hld up in rr: hdwy on ins wl over 1f out: no imp fnl f* **15/2**
400- 6 3/4 **Taboor (IRE)**[46] [6656] 9-9-2 65 .... BrettDoyle 4 59
(R M H Cowell) *hld up and bhd: nvr nr ldrs* **16/1**
04-6 7 hd **Hornpipe**[10] [47] 5-8-11 60 .... TonyCulhane 2 53
(M S Saunders) *chsd ldrs: rdn over 2f out: wknd over 1f out* **8/1**
06-5 8 hd **Sparkwell**[8] [66] 5-9-2 65 .... DeanMcKeown 5 58
(D Shaw) *chsd ldrs tl rdn and wknd wl over 1f out* **10/1**
05-4 9 1 **Fast Heart**[8] [66] 6-9-2 65 .... NCallan 8 54
(R A Harris) *s.i.s: hld up: short-lived effrt over 2f out* **4/1**[2]
300- 10 1/2 **Jun Fan (USA)**[16] [6994] 5-8-4 56 ....(tp) GregFairley(3) 6 43
(B Ellison) *s.i.s: a bhd* **40/1**
20-0 11 3 **New Options**[6] [82] 10-8-2 56 ....(b) DuranFentiman(5) 11 32
(Peter Grayson) *hld up in mid-div: short-lived effrt on outside over 2f out* **40/1**

61.21 secs (-1.61) **Going Correction** -0.225s/f (Stan) **11 Ran SP% 123.5**
Speed ratings (Par 103):103,99,97,93,92 91,90,90,88,87 83
CSF £27.64 CT £100.07 TOTE £8.80: £2.40, £1.80, £1.70; EX 34.80 Trifecta £122.00 Pool £603.18 - 3,51 winning units..
Owner Sporting Occasions Racing No 5 **Bred** P G Airey **Trained** Middleham Moor, N Yorks
■ Stewards' Enquiry : William Buick one-day ban: careless riding (Jan 27); one day ban: failed to ride to draw (Jan 28)

FOCUS
A strongly-run sprint handicap with few getting into it. Good form for the grade, with the winner back to form and the next two progressive.

155 PONTINSBINGO.COM H'CAP 5f 20y(P)
3:40 (3:40) (Class 4) (0-85,85) 4-Y-0+ £4,857 (£1,445; £722; £360) Stalls Low

Form RPR
01-4 1 **Harry Up**[15] [5] 6-9-1 84 .... NCallan 8 96
(K A Ryan) *mde all: edgd rt ins fnl f: drvn out* **5/1**[3]
10-2 2 nk **Dig Deep (IRE)**[7] [79] 5-8-11 80 .... TonyCulhane 2 91+
(W J Haggas) *hld up in mid-div: rdn and hdwy over 1f out: r.o ins fnl f: nt rch wnr* **5/2**[1]
03-1 3 1 **Magic Glade**[7] [79] 8-8-11 80 7ex .... RichardThomas 3 87
(Tom Dascombe) *a.p: rdn over 1f out: r.o one pce fnl f* **9/2**[2]
20-3 4 1 3/4 **Tartatartufata**[7] [79] 5-8-11 80 ....(v) DanielTudhope 11 81
(D Shaw) *sn prom: rdn and edgd lft 1f out: one pce* **10/1**
140- 5 1 1/2 **Native Title**[275] [1031] 9-8-12 81 .... AdrianTNicholls 5 77
(D Nicholls) *s.i.s: hdwy on ins whn n.m.r over 1f out: nt rch ldrs* **50/1**
01-0 6 nk **Efistorm**[7] [79] 6-8-8 80 .... JasonEdmunds(3) 6 75
(J Balding) *prom tl rdn and wknd 1f out* **15/2**
311- 7 hd **Desert Opal**[24] [6935] 7-8-5 74 ....(p) JimmyQuinn 7 68
(C R Dore) *chsd ldrs: rdn and nt hdwy fnl 2f* **12/1**
340- 8 1 1/4 **Smokin Beau**[31] [6849] 10-8-13 85 .... JamesDoyle(3) 4 74
(N P Littmoden) *bhd: rdn wl over 1f out: nvr nr ldrs* **8/1**
42-3 9 3/4 **Trinculo (IRE)**[9] [59] 10-8-7 76 ....(p) ChrisCatlin 9 63
(R A Harris) *mid-div: rdn over 2f out: sn bhd* **25/1**
60-5 10 3/4 **Glenviews Youngone (IRE)**[15] [5] 4-8-7 81 .... DuranFentiman(5) 1 65
(Peter Grayson) *mid-div: rdn over 2f out: no rspnse* **16/1**
25-0 11 3 **Pauvic (IRE)**[7] [79] 4-8-3 75 ow1 .... SaleemGolam(3) 12 48
(Mrs A Duffield) *outpcd* **40/1**
0/0- 12 3/4 **Signor Panettiere**[164] 6-9-2 85 ....(t) SilvestreDeSousa 10 55
(A D Brown) *w wnr tl rdn 2f out: wknd over 1f out* **50/1**

61.41 secs (-1.41) **Going Correction** -0.225s/f (Stan) **12 Ran SP% 119.2**
Speed ratings (Par 105):102,101,99,97,94 94,93,91,90,89 84,83
CSF £17.50 CT £61.63 TOTE £6.10: £2.00, £1.30, £2.10; EX 20.80 Trifecta £104.80 Pool £490.27 - 3.32 winning units..
Owner The Fishermen **Bred** J E Rose **Trained** Hambleton, N Yorks

FOCUS
A shade slower than the previous lower-grade handicap, but the winning time still just bettered the standard. Fair form, the winner back to his very best.

156 PONTIN'S FAMILY HOLIDAYS H'CAP 1m 141y(P)
4:10 (4:10) (Class 6) (0-50,50) 4-Y-0+ £2,047 (£604; £302) Stalls Low

Form RPR
550- 1 **My Michelle**[40] [4983] 6-8-10 48 ow1 .... TonyCulhane 1 65
(B Palling) *mde all: clr over 2f out: rdn over 1f out: r.o wl* **12/1**
/0-2 2 5 **Over To You Bert**[10] [51] 8-8-3 48 ow2 .... HaddenFrost(7) 2 54
(R J Hodges) *t.k.h: chsd wnr: rdn over 2f out: no imp* **12/1**
25-4 3 1 3/4 **Fantasy Defender (IRE)**[13] [20] 5-8-8 46 oh1 ....(v) ChrisCatlin 5 48
(Ernst Oertel) *hld up in mid-div: rdn and hdwy on ins 3f out: one pce fnl f* **6/1**[3]
500- 4 1/2 **Elms Schoolboy**[29] [6854] 5-8-9 47 ....(b) JimmyQuinn 11 48
(P Howling) *s.i.s: hld up and bhd: rdn and hdwy over 2f out: kpt on same pce fnl f* **20/1**
10-4 5 nk **Stoneacre Fred (IRE)**[6] [94] 4-8-11 50 .... GrahamGibbons 4 51
(Peter Grayson) *a.p: rdn over 2f out: one pce* **10/3**[1]
/15- 6 shd **Bobering**[18] [6980] 7-8-2 47 .... SoniaEaton(7) 8 47
(B P J Baugh) *hld up and bhd: hdwy on ins over 2f out: rdn over 1f out: no imp* **12/1**
306- 7 5 **Barzak (IRE)**[19] [6961] 7-8-6 47 ....(bt) JasonEdmunds(3) 13 37
(S R Bowring) *hld up and bhd: hdwy on outside over 2f out: no further prog* **14/1**
150- 8 1 1/4 **Titus Wonder (IRE)**[34] [4554] 4-8-5 47 .... JamesDoyle(3) 10 34
(J W Mullins) *t.k.h: hdwy 6f out: wknd over 3f out* **50/1**
301- 9 3 **Tackcoat (IRE)**[18] [6970] 7-8-7 50 ....(p) EmmettStack(5) 6 31
(Eoin Doyle, Ire) *hld up towards rr: swtchd rt and short-lived effrt on wd outside over 2f out* **8/1**
012- 10 2 1/2 **Island Green (USA)**[43] [6707] 4-8-8 47 .... TPQueally 12 23
(B J Curley) *hld up in tch: rdn and wknd over 2f out* **7/2**[2]
/0-5 11 8 **Tuckerman**[4] [109] 6-8-9 47 oh1 ow1 .... PatCosgrave 9 6
(F J Bowles, Ire) *chsd ldrs: rdn over 3f out: sn wknd* **22/1**
605- 12 7 **Cumberland Road**[17] [6993] 4-8-4 46 oh1 .... DominicFox(3) 3 —
(C A Mulhall) *prom early: sn mid-div: bhd fnl 4f* **40/1**
400- 13 5 **Tetrode (USA)**[113] [5576] 5-8-10 48 .... BrettDoyle 7 —
(R M H Cowell) *prom: rdn over 3f out: sn wknd* **16/1**

1m 49.89s (-1.87) **Going Correction** -0.225s/f (Stan)
WFA 4 from 5yo+ 1lb **13 Ran SP% 119.8**
Speed ratings (Par 101):99,94,93,92,92 92,87,86,83,81 74,68,63
CSF £142.68 CT £681.01 TOTE £17.20: £3.70, £3.70, £2.20; EX 106.20 TRIFECTA Not won. Place 6 £12.55, Place 5 £7.29.
Owner Flying Eight Partnership **Bred** Snowdrop Stud Co Ltd **Trained** Tredodridge, Vale Of Glamorgan

FOCUS
A weakish handicap in which the winner looked to get an easy lead.
T/Jkpt: Not won. T/Plt: £25.90 to a £1 stake. Pool: £60,163.50. 1,691.65 winning tickets. T/Qpdt: £18.10 to a £1 stake. Pool: £3,488.90. 142.10 winning tickets. KH

113 LINGFIELD (L-H)
Wednesday, January 17

OFFICIAL GOING: Standard
Wind: moderate behind Weather: rain 1st race, dry and bright after

157 GO PONTIN'S APPRENTICE H'CAP 1m 2f (P)
12:20 (12:21) (Class 6) (0-65,64) 3-Y-O £2,266 (£674; £337; £168) Stalls Low

Form RPR
00-0 1 **King Of The Beers (USA)**[13] [37] 3-8-8 53 ....(p) LukeMorris 11 55
(R A Harris) *settled in midfield: prog over 2f out: rdn to ld jst ins fnl f: kpt on wl* **33/1**
600- 2 1/2 **Voss**[29] [6867] 3-8-10 55 .... WilliamBuick 3 56
(M Johnston) *trckd ldng pair: pushed along over 3f out: wnt 2nd over 2f out: rdn to chal and upsides 1f out: nt qckn* **4/1**[2]
500- 3 3/4 **It's No Problem (IRE)**[129] [5208] 3-8-12 57 .... JamesMillman 7 58+
(M Salaman) *stdd s: hld up in last pair: prog 3f out: clsng whn nt clr run over 1f out: r.o ins fnl f: nt rch ldng pair* **33/1**
00-6 4 1 1/2 **Ballyshane Spirit (IRE)**[13] [37] 3-8-5 50 oh1 .... KirstyMilczarek 4 47
(N A Callaghan) *pressed ldr: led over 3f out: hdd & wknd jst ins fnl f* **9/2**[3]
53-5 5 1 1/2 **Tumble Jill (IRE)**[14] [21] 3-8-5 55 ow3 ....(p) RyanBird(5) 5 49
(J J Bridger) *dwlt: hld up in rr: prog to chse ldrs over 2f out: no imp over 1f out: fdd* **50/1**
005- 6 shd **Color Man**[179] [3726] 3-8-9 54 .... AshleyHamblett 9 48
(Mrs A J Perrett) *hld up in rr: reminders over 4f out: last of main gp 3f out: r.o ins fnl f* **8/1**
000- 7 nk **Hayley's Flower (IRE)**[61] [6504] 3-8-10 55 .... JamieJones 10 48
(J C Fox) *hld up in midfield: prog to chse ldrs over 2f out: wknd fnl f* **16/1**

The Form Book, Raceform Ltd, Compton, RG20 6NL

652- **8** 1 1/4 **Don't Desert Me (IRE)**[28] 6880 3-9-5 **64**.............. RussellKennemore 8 55
(R Charlton) *rn in snatches: chsd ldrs: lost pl 3f out: wl in rr over 1f out: plugged on* **7/2**[1]

006- **9** *shd* **Citrus Chief (USA)**[50] 6639 3-9-0 **59**.............................. TolleyDean 6 50
(R A Harris) *chsd ldrs: rdn 1/2-way: losing pl whn hmpd on inner over 2f out* **16/1**

2-33 **10** 8 **First Princess (IRE)**[7] 93 3-9-0 **64**..........................(p) JosephWalsh(5) 2 40
(J S Moore) *led to over 3f out: wknd over 2f out* **4/1**[2]

60-5 **11** *shd* **Shea's Round**[11] 53 3-8-8 **58**.............................. JemmaMarshall(5) 1 33
(G L Moore) *s.s: a last: detached fr rest over 3f out* **25/1**

2m 7.94s (0.15) **Going Correction** -0.15s/f (Stan) **11 Ran SP% 115.0**
Speed ratings (Par 95):93,92,92,90,89 89,89,88,88,81 81
CSF £154.47 CT £4419.54 TOTE £69.90: £9.50, £1.60, £8.00; EX 523.00 TRIFECTA Not won..
Owner Dr Simon Clarke **Bred** Liberation Farm, Oratis Thoroughbreds Et Al **Trained** Earlswood, Monmouths

FOCUS
A modest handicap, confined to apprentice riders, which was run at a sound pace. It has been rated through the fourth.
King Of The Beers(USA) Official explanation: trainer said, regarding the improved form shown, colt had benefited from the step up in trip and reapplication of cheekpieces
Don't Desert Me(IRE) Official explanation: jockey said gelding was crowded early on
Shea's Round Official explanation: jockey said colt missed the break and never travelled

158 PONTINSBINGO.COM H'CAP (DIV I) 6f (P)
12:50 (12:51) (Class 6) (0-60,65) 4-Y-0+ **£1,706** (£503; £252) **Stalls Low**

Form RPR

21-3 **1** **Burhaan (IRE)**[7] 86 5-8-8 **52**.............................. FergusSweeney 8 64
(J R Boyle) *trckd ldrs: effrt 2f out: urged along to ld last 150yds: kpt on wl* **4/1**[1]

000- **2** 1 1/4 **Celtic Thunder**[70] 6404 6-8-9 **56**..........................(b) SaleemGolam(3) 12 64
(T J Etherington) *trckd ldrs: rdn over 2f out: nt qckn over 1f out: styd on wl fnl f to take 2nd nr fin* **33/1**

50-3 **3** *nk* **Whistleupthewind**[9] 66 4-8-11 **55**..........................(b) MickyFenton 7 62
(J M P Eustace) *pressed ldr: led wl over 1f out: fnd little in front: hdd and nt qckn last 150yds* **16/1**

100- **4** 1/2 **Polar Force**[20] 6966 7-9-2 **60**.............................. ChrisCatlin 2 66
(Mrs C A Dunnett) *trckd ldrs: rdn 2f out: styd on same pce fr over 1f out* **25/1**

35-0 **5** *hd* **Monashee Prince (IRE)**[3] 130 5-9-2 **60**..........................(v) BrettDoyle 10 65
(J R Best) *rousted along to ld: hdd wl over 1f out: pressed ldr after tl fdd last 100yds* **12/1**

4-64 **6** *nk* **Desert Light (IRE)**[3] 132 6-8-10 **54**..........................(v) DaneO'Neill 3 58
(D Shaw) *hld up wl in rr: prog on inner over 1f out: hanging but styd on fnl f: nrst fin* **9/2**[2]

124- **7** *hd* **Moon Bird**[18] 6984 5-9-0 **58**.............................. TonyCulhane 6 62
(C A Cyzer) *plld hrd early: hld up bhd ldrs: rdn and nt qckn 2f out: kpt on ins fnl f* **13/2**

12-5 **8** 1/2 **Midmaar (IRE)**[7] 86 6-8-10 **54**..........................(b) JimmyQuinn 4 56
(M Wigham) *settled in midfield: rdn and nt qckn 2f out: kpt on ins fnl f* **6/1**[3]

14-1 **9** *nk* **Millfields Dreams**[9] 66 8-9-7 **65** 6ex.............................. TPQueally 11 66+
(M G Quinlan) *dropped in fr wd draw: hld up in last: stl last over 1f out: nowhere to go after: fin full of running* **9/2**[2]

000- **10** 1/2 **Majestical (IRE)**[18] 6990 5-8-4 **55**..........................(p) BarrySavage(7) 5 55
(J M Bradley) *a wl in rr: shkn up and nt clr run briefly over 1f out: no prog* **33/1**

340- **11** 2 **Buzzin'Boyzee (IRE)**[20] 6964 4-8-6 **57**.............................. BernadetteQuinn(7) 9 51
(P D Evans) *racd wd towards rr: bmpd along and no prog over 1f out: fdd* **22/1**

445- **12** *shd* **Turibius**[26] 6913 8-8-13 **57**..........................(b) JimCrowley 1 50
(T E Powell) *hld up in midfield on inner: nt qckn over 1f out: wknd fnl f* **14/1**

1m 11.38s (-1.43) **Going Correction** -0.15s/f (Stan) **12 Ran SP% 118.3**
Speed ratings (Par 101):103,101,100,100,100 99,99,98,98,97 94,94
CSF £146.56 CT £1924.87 TOTE £4.90: £1.50, £13.80, £4.60; EX 249.40 TRIFECTA Not won..
Owner John Hopkins (t/a South Hatch Racing) **Bred** Shadwell Estate Company Limited **Trained** Epsom, Surrey

FOCUS
A moderate first division of the sprint handicap. The form looks sound, rated through the second and fifth.
Millfields Dreams Official explanation: jockey said gelding was denied a clear run

159 PONTINS.COM CLAIMING STKS 2m (P)
1:20 (1:20) (Class 6) 4-Y-0+ **£2,184** (£644; £322) **Stalls Low**

Form RPR

003- **1** **Pocket Too**[17] 6995 4-9-2 52..........................(p) JimmyQuinn 2 63
(M Salaman) *chsd ldng pair: rdn and lost pl over 4f out: rallied over 2f out : drvn to ld jst ins fnl f: sn clr* **9/1**

003- **2** 1 1/4 **Zibeline (IRE)**[22] 4981 10-9-4 72..........................(tp) DaneO'Neill 8 57
(B Ellison) *hld up in rr: stdy prog over 2f out: clsd and looked dangerous over 1f out: sn fnd nil: styd on to take 2nd nr fin* **3/1**[2]

61-1 **3** 3/4 **Mister Completely (IRE)**[14] 16 6-9-4 55................. JamesDoyle(3) 7 59
(Ms J S Doyle) *chsd ldrs: rdn 4f out: clsd u.p over 2f out: upsides over 1f out: wknd ins fnl f* **3/1**[2]

06-4 **4** 1 1/4 **Sczume (IRE)**[11] 52 4-8-12 52.............................. EdwardCreighton 1 55
(Miss Sheena West) *pushed along in last pair bef 1/2-way: effrt on inner over 2f out: nt qckn over 1f out: kpt on* **20/1**

11/4 **5** 1/2 **Sea Map**[12] 39 5-9-9 59.............................. PatCosgrave 6 59
(D E Cantillon) *chsd clr ldr: rdn 5f out: clsd to ld over 2f out: hrd rdn over 1f out: hdd & wknd jst insn fnl f* **11/4**[1]

6 8 **My Friend Fritz**[17] 7-9-2.............................. ChrisCatlin 3 42
(P W Hiatt) *s.s: last tl prog over 5f out: chsd ldrs over 2f out : wknd rapidly over 1f out* **33/1**

0/00 **7** 1 **Alisar (IRE)**[5] 109 7-8-12 65..........................(t) SCreighton(7) 4 44
(E J Creighton) *led: clr after 6f: hdd & wknd rapidly over 2f out* **40/1**

000- **8** 12 **Massif Centrale**[125] 5325 6-9-4 85..........................(t) MarcHalford(3) 5 31
(D R C Elsworth) *hld up: rdn over 3f out: sn wknd: t.o* **4/1**[3]

3m 25.74s (-3.05) **Going Correction** -0.15s/f (Stan)
WFA 4 from 5yo+ 7lb **8 Ran SP% 116.8**
Speed ratings (Par 101):101,100,100,99,99 95,94,88
CSF £36.37 TOTE £11.20: £2.40, £1.80, £1.70; EX 44.70 Trifecta £122.00 Pool: £226.89 - 1.32 winning units..Zibeline was subject to a friendly claim. Sea Map was claimed by Miss S West for £12,000.
Owner Oaktree Racing **Bred** M J Lewin **Trained** Baydon, Wilts

FOCUS
A tricky race to assess, with several rivals running well below their official marks, and the form should be treated with caution.

160 PONTIN'S HOLIDAYS MAIDEN STKS 6f (P)
1:55 (1:56) (Class 5) 3-Y-0+ **£2,914** (£867; £433; £216) **Stalls Low**

Form RPR

356- **1** **High Tribute**[19] 6976 3-8-10 66..........................(t) SebSanders 2 70
(Sir Mark Prescott) *pressed ldr: led wl over 2f out and kicked on: drvn and idled fnl f: nvr seriously chal* **11/2**[3]

0-4 **2** 1 1/2 **Leg Sweep**[11] 55 3-8-10..........................(t) DaneO'Neill 3 65
(D R C Elsworth) *cl up: rdn to chse ldng trio over 2f out: effrt on inner to go 2nd jst ins fnl f: no real imp* **6/1**

35- **3** *hd* **Madrigale**[113] 5586 3-8-5.............................. CatherineGannon 12 59+
(G L Moore) *hld up in midfield: outpcd over 2f out: effrt over 1f out: styd on fnl f to take 3rd last stride* **16/1**

20- **4** *shd* **Toucantini**[77] 6290 3-8-5.............................. ChrisCatlin 9 59
(R Charlton) *led to wl over 2f out: chsd wnr tl jst ins fnl f: kpt on* **7/1**

430- **5** 2 1/2 **Kineta (USA)**[154] 4494 4-9-7 57.............................. NCallan 6 56
(W R Muir) *prom: rdn to chse ldng pair over 2f out: wknd jst over 1f out* **12/1**

26- **6** 1 **Saviour Sand (IRE)**[29] 6867 3-8-10.............................. BrettDoyle 7 54+
(D R C Elsworth) *awkward s: racd wd and hld up towards rr: outpcd over 2f out: shuffled along and nvr nr ldrs after* **2/1**[1]

0-0 **7** *shd* **Vivi Belle**[13] 36 3-8-5.............................. HayleyTurner 1 48
(M L W Bell) *dwlt: sn midfield on inner: outpcd over 2f out: n.d after* **100/1**

8 2 1/2 **Ragheed (USA)** 3-8-10..........................(t) TonyCulhane 10 46+
(W J Haggas) *plld hrd and rn v green on wd outside: wl in rr 1/2-way: modest late prog* **4/1**[2]

9 5 **Satwa Baron** 3-8-7.............................. MarcHalford(3) 5 31
(D R C Elsworth) *dwlt: a in last trio: struggling over 2f out* **17/2**

10 3 1/2 **Conorville (IRE)** 3-8-10.............................. RobertHavlin 4 20
(B W Hills) *dwlt: rn green and a wl in rr: wknd 2f out* **20/1**

0- **11** 11 **Brief Engagement (IRE)**[38] 6774 4-9-7.............................. EdwardCreighton 8 —
(T D McCarthy) *chsd ldrs to 1/2-way: sn wknd: t.o* **100/1**

1m 12.73s (-0.08) **Going Correction** -0.15s/f (Stan)
WFA 3 from 4yo 16lb **11 Ran SP% 126.3**
Speed ratings (Par 103):94,92,91,91,88 86,86,83,76,72 57
CSF £41.32 TOTE £6.80: £2.40, £2.50, £4.40; EX 58.30 Trifecta £152.00 Part won. Pool £214.15 - 0.20 winning units..
Owner Neil Greig - Osborne House III **Bred** W N Greig **Trained** Newmarket, Suffolk

FOCUS
An ordinary maiden which was run at a modest early tempo, and the time compared unfavourably with the two older-horse handicaps.
Saviour Sand(IRE) Official explanation: jockey said, regarding running and riding, his orders were to be wary that the colt had missed the break in the past and expect him to run keenly up with the pace, adding that it was awkward leaving the stalls, missed the break, and had to be dropped in behind, further adding that coming down the hill into final bend he felt colt to be too green to apply further pressure, and that it needed a longer distance
Ragheed(USA) Official explanation: jockey said colt hung right

161 PONTINSBINGO.COM H'CAP (DIV II) 6f (P)
2:25 (2:26) (Class 6) (0-60,62) 4-Y-0+ **£1,706** (£503; £252) **Stalls Low**

Form RPR

010- **1** **George The Second**[33] 6827 4-8-12 **59**.............. RichardKingscote(3) 2 70
(Mrs H Sweeting) *trckd ldrs: led towards inner wl over 1f out: drvn fnl f: hld on* **5/1**[1]

01-0 **2** *nk* **Mine The Balance (IRE)**[3] 131 4-8-12 **56**..........................(b) BrettDoyle 8 66
(J R Best) *hld up in rr: prog on inner over 2f out: effrt over 1f out: r.o to take 2nd last 75yds: clsng on wnr at fin* **7/1**[3]

0-01 **3** 1 **Kempsey**[7] 82 5-8-11 **62** 6ex..........................(b) RyanBird(7) 7 69
(J J Bridger) *pressed ldr: rdn to ld 2f out: wd bnd sn after and hdd: upsides 1f out: one pce* **9/1**

4-43 **4** 1 1/4 **Muktasb (USA)**[7] 82 6-8-12 **56**..........................(v) NCallan 10 59+
(D Shaw) *awkward s: hld up in rr: effrt 2f out: nt clr run briefly over 1f out: swtchd ins and styd on: nt rch ldrs* **6/1**[2]

30-3 **5** *hd* **The Fisio**[11] 47 7-8-12 **56**..........................(v) ChrisCatlin 12 59
(S Gollings) *racd on outer: w ldrs tl carried wd bnd 2f out: nt qckn over 1f out: hld after* **12/1**

36-5 **6** 3/4 **Mulberry Lad (IRE)**[11] 50 5-8-4 **55**.............................. LukeMorris(7) 1 59+
(P W Hiatt) *trckd ldrs: shkn up and nt qckn over 1f out: one pce after* **6/1**[2]

63-0 **7** 1/2 **Cayman Breeze**[11] 50 7-8-2 **53**.............................. BarrySavage(7) 9 52
(J M Bradley) *hld up in rr: effrt on outer 2f out: styd on fnl f: nvr pce to rch ldrs* **16/1**

36-6 **8** 1 3/4 **Dasheena**[9] 67 4-8-11 **58**.............................. StephenDonohoe(3) 6 52
(A J McCabe) *dwlt: sn drvn in last: nvr gng pce: kpt on fnl f* **16/1**

00-0 **9** 3/4 **Edin Burgher (FR)**[7] 82 6-8-5 **52**.............................. MarcHalford(3) 5 44
(T T Clement) *rdn towards rr wl over 3f out: struggling after: no ch over 1f out* **5/1**[1]

000- **10** 1 1/2 **Blessed Place**[26] 6913 7-8-10 **57**..........................(t) JamesDoyle(3) 4 44
(D J S Ffrench Davis) *led at str pce to 2f out: wknd rapidly jst over 1f out* **7/1**[3]

1m 11.12s (-1.69) **Going Correction** -0.15s/f (Stan) **10 Ran SP% 116.4**
Speed ratings (Par 101):105,104,103,101,101 100,99,97,96,94
CSF £39.67 CT £313.98 TOTE £6.70: £3.00, £2.70, £3.40; EX 49.40 Trifecta £259.40 Part won. Pool £365.44 - 0.10 winning units..
Owner The Kennet Connection **Bred** R Withers **Trained** Lockeridge, Wilts

FOCUS
This second division was a typically open sprint handicap for the class. The form looks sound enough rated through the third/fourth.
Blessed Place Official explanation: jockey said gelding hung right on final bend

162 PONTIN'S FAMILY HOLIDAYS CLAIMING STKS 7f (P)
3:00 (3:01) (Class 6) 3-Y-O **£2,184** (£644; £322) **Stalls High**

Form RPR

3-25 **1** **Zaafira (SPA)**[6] 99 3-8-12 50.............................. EdwardCreighton 8 58
(E J Creighton) *hld up bhd ldrs: prog and squeezed through wl over 1f out: led jst over 1f out: styd on wl* **20/1**

54- **2** 1 3/4 **Razzano (IRE)**[21] 6950 3-8-4.............................. CatherineGannon 1 45
(P D Evans) *led: drvn and hdd jst over 1f out: fnd nil* **7/1**[3]

013- **3** 1 1/4 **Lordswood (IRE)**[44] 6699 3-8-6 65.............................. WilliamBuick(7) 7 51
(A M Balding) *hld up on outer: prog 2f out: clsd to chal over 1f out: sn rdn and no rspnse* **4/6**[1]

4 2 **Jonny Behave** 3-8-4.............................. JamesDoyle(3) 5 40
(I A Wood) *lost pl over 5f out: sn pushed along: c wd in st and kpt on: n.d* **25/1**

036- **5** 1/2 **La Marmotte (IRE)**[53] 6598 3-8-8 59.............................. J-PGuillambert 4 40
(J W Hills) *plld hrd early: hld up bhd ldrs: effrt 2f out: wknd fnl f* **9/2**[2]

16-0 **6** 1 1/2 **Polly Jones (USA)**[14] 25 3-8-2 46 .... JimmyQuinn 2 30
(G L Moore) *chsd ldng pair to 2f out: wknd* **10/1**
320- **7** 3 **For Eileen**[17] 6996 3-8-6 51 .... TPQueally 6 26
(M G Quinlan) *pressed ldr to 2f out: sn wknd* **8/1**
650- **8** 8 **All Talk**[195] 3228 3-8-2 47 .... ChrisCatlin 3 —
(Mrs C A Dunnett) *s.i.s: a last: bhd fnl 3f* **50/1**
1m 25.66s (-0.23) **Going Correction** -0.15s/f (Stan) **8** Ran SP% **121.4**
Speed ratings (Par 95):95,93,91,89,88 87,83,74
CSF £157.31 TOTE £29.40: £3.40, £1.40, £1.10; EX 128.60 Trifecta £175.90 Pool £411.36 - 1.66 winning units..Razzano was claimed by G Martin for £6,000. Lordswood was claimed by J Bridger for £8,000.
Owner The Vixens **Bred** Cuadra The Vixens **Trained** East Garston, Berks

FOCUS
A weak claimer. The form should be treated with a little caution but the winner seems to be progressing slowly.

163 GO PONTIN'S H'CAP 5f (P)
3:30 (3:32) (Class 5) (0-75,80) 4-Y-0+ **£3,238** (£963; £481; £240) **Stalls** Low

Form RPR
60-1 **1** **Turn On The Style**[8] 81 5-9-4 **80** 6ex .... (b) AndrewElliott(3) 10 98+
(J Balding) *fast away fr wd draw: mde all and sn at least 2 l clr: shkn up and styd on wl fnl f: impressive* **3/1**[2]
222- **2** 2 **Financial Times (USA)**[21] 6953 5-9-2 **75** .... (tp) NCallan 9 86
(Stef Liddiard) *a chsng wnr: rdn over 2f out: kpt on wl enough but no imp* **9/2**[3]
124- **3** 1 **Figaro Flyer (IRE)**[20] 6966 4-8-11 **75** .... AnnStokell(5) 1 82
(P Howling) *a chsng ldng pair: rdn over 1f out: kpt on but no imp* **12/1**
040- **4** 1 1/4 **Russian Rocket (IRE)**[20] 6966 5-9-1 **74** .... HayleyTurner 3 77
(Mrs C A Dunnett) *disp 4th but sn off the pce: no imp tl styd on last 100yds* **16/1**
005- **5** nk **Sands Crooner (IRE)**[25] 6935 4-8-12 **71** .... (v) DaneO'Neill 6 73
(D Shaw) *hld up and sn wl off the pce in 7th: styd on fnl f: no ch* **14/1**
324- **6** shd **Heavens Walk**[32] 6844 6-8-13 **72** .... (t) SebSanders 2 73
(P J Makin) *disp 4th but sn off the pce: rdn over 2f out: kpt on same pce* **9/4**[1]
10-0 **7** nk **No Time (IRE)**[7] 91 7-8-9 **71** .... StephenDonohoe(3) 4 71
(A J McCabe) *s.i.s: wl bhd in last pair and bdly outpcd: r.o ins fnl f* **16/1**
00-2 **8** 2 **Lady Bahia (IRE)**[11] 47 6-8-5 **64** .... (b) ChrisCatlin 8 57
(Peter Grayson) *off the pce in 6th early: struggling fr 1/2-way* **16/1**
13-5 **9** 3 1/2 **Stoneacre Boy (IRE)**[11] 47 4-8-3 **67** .... (b) DuranFentiman(5) 7 47
(Peter Grayson) *s.i.s: outpcd and a last* **10/1**
57.36 secs (-2.42) **Going Correction** -0.15s/f (Stan) course record **9** Ran SP% **115.0**
Speed ratings (Par 103):113,109,108,106,105 105,105,101,96
CSF £16.92 CT £140.27 TOTE £4.00: £1.70, £1.90, £2.40; EX 19.70 Trifecta £55.80 Pool £399.85 - 5.08 winning units..
Owner The Haydock Badgeholders **Bred** J And Mrs Bowtell **Trained** Scrooby, Notts

FOCUS
A fair sprint which produced an excellent winning time. The winner was impressive and the form looks solid for the grade.

164 PONTINS.COM H'CAP 1m 2f (P)
4:05 (4:05) (Class 4) (0-80,80) 4-Y-0+ **£4,857** (£1,445; £722; £360) **Stalls** Low

Form RPR
11-2 **1** **Rapid City**[7] 96 4-8-10 **77** .... JamesDoyle(3) 3 86+
(Miss J Feilden) *trckd ldrs: smooth prog to go 2nd wl over 1f out: shkn up fnl f: led last 100yds: wl in command nr fin* **4/7**[1]
510- **2** 3/4 **Kyles Prince (IRE)**[73] 6351 5-9-2 **78** .... SebSanders 7 86
(P J Makin) *led: kicked on over 2f out: edgd rt over 1f out: hdd last 100yds: no ch w wnr after* **4/1**[2]
550- **3** 1 1/2 **Sky Quest (IRE)**[32] 6841 9-8-6 **68** .... HayleyTurner 6 73
(J R Boyle) *prom: trckd ldr 1/2-way to wl over 1f out: one pce u.p* **33/1**
025- **4** nk **Trifti**[18] 6986 6-8-11 **73** .... JimmyQuinn 5 78
(C A Cyzer) *chsd ldr to 1/2-way: rdn over 2f out: one pce and no imp fr over 1f out* **14/1**
543- **5** 1 **Bobby Charles**[40] 6744 6-9-3 **79** .... ShaneKelly 1 82
(Dr J D Scargill) *dwlt: hld up in touh: gng wl enough over 2f out: nt clr run over 1f out: one pce whn in the clr fnl f* **15/2**[3]
54-0 **6** hd **Tous Les Deux**[7] 96 4-8-1 **70** .... DuranFentiman(5) 2 72
(Peter Grayson) *dwlt: hld up in last pair: rdn 3f out: struggling over 2f out: keeping on nr fin* **25/1**
260- **7** 1 1/2 **Activo (FR)**[28] 6888 6-9-4 **80** .... PaulDoe 4 79
(S Dow) *s.s: t.k.h: hld up in last pair: rdn 2f out: no rspnse* **20/1**
2m 8.16s (0.37) **Going Correction** -0.15s/f (Stan)
WFA 4 from 5yo+ 2lb **7** Ran SP% **113.6**
Speed ratings (Par 105):92,91,90,89,89 89,87
CSF £3.01 TOTE £1.60: £1.40, £1.70; EX 3.20 Place 6 £339.81, Place 5 £80.22.
Owner Good Company Partnership **Bred** Juddmonte Farms Ltd **Trained** Exning, Suffolk

FOCUS
A fair handicap which was run at an uneven pace. The first two are progressive, and the race has been rated through the third and fourth.
Activo(FR) Official explanation: jockey said gelding hung right throughout
T/Plt: £559.00 to a £1 stake. Pool: £43,770.15. 57.15 winning tickets. T/Qpdt: £32.50 to a £1 stake. Pool: £4,235.20. 96.20 winning tickets. JN

151 WOLVERHAMPTON (A.W) (L-H)
Thursday, January 18
165 Meeting Abandoned - High winds

104 NAD AL SHEBA (L-H)
Thursday, January 18
OFFICIAL GOING: Turf couse - good; dirt course - fast

172a DAYJUR TROPHY (H'CAP) (TURF) 7f 110y(D)
3:35 (3:36) (90-105,105) 3-Y-0+
£33,673 (£11,224; £5,612; £2,806; £1,683; £1,122)

RPR
1 **Obe Brave**[103] 5812 4-9-0 **98** .... TedDurcan 11 104
(M R Channon) *trckd ldr: led 2f out: r.o wl* **8/1**[3]
2 1 **Sendalam (FR)**[110] 5703 5-8-12 **97** .... KShea 6 99
(H J Brown, South Africa) *mid-div: rdn to chse wnr 2f out: r.o* **12/1**
3 nk **Diamond Quest (SAF)**[166] 6-8-12 **97** .... WCMarwing 7 98+
(M F De Kock, South Africa) *racd in rr on rail 3f out: swtchd 2f out: r.o wl: nrst fin* **4/1**[1]
4 shd **Pentecost**[117] 5520 8-8-12 **97** .... MartinDwyer 4 98+
(A M Balding) *settled in rr: keen: gng wl rail 3f out: r.o wl fnl f: nrst fin* **11/2**[2]
5 1 **Mandobi (IRE)**[21] 6-9-3 **101** .... (vt) JMurtagh 9 101
(D Selvaratnam, UAE) *racd 4th: trckd wnr 2f out: nt pce of wnr: kpt on* **8/1**[3]
6 1 1/4 **Alto Taquari (BRZ)**[103] 4-8-1 **96** .... ECruz 8 92
(P Nickel Filho, Brazil) *racd 3rd: short of room 3f out: rdn 2f out: r.o* **14/1**
7 nse **Azarole (IRE)**[124] 5376 6-9-6 **105** .... JohnEgan 5 100
(J S Moore) *mid-div: rdn 2 1/2f out: nvr able to chal: r.o: nrst fin* **11/2**[2]
8 4 3/4 **Bahiano (IRE)**[13] 41 6-8-8 **93** .... WSupple 12 76
(C E Brittain) *settled in rr: rdn 3f out: nvr nr to chal* **11/2**[2]
9 3 1/4 **Sand Cat**[28] 4-8-11 **96** .... WayneSmith 1 71
(Christian Wroe) *slowly away: sn prom: led after 1f: rdn 3f out: hdd 2 1/2f out: wknd* **25/1**
10 2 3/4 **Looking Good (ARG)**[27] 6-9-2 **100** .... (t) GAvranche 10 69
(Allan Smith, UAE) *a in rr* **16/1**
11 2 1/4 **Salt Track (ARG)**[130] 5224 7-9-2 **100** .... (t) ESki 3 64
(Niels Petersen, Norway) *settled rr: rdn 3f out: wd st: n.d* **16/1**
12 3 1/4 **Leicester Square (IRE)**[284] 6-8-10 **95** .... TPO'Shea 2 50
(E Charpy, UAE) *mid-div: gng wl 2f out: sn rdn: nt qckn* **25/1**
1m 31.58s (0.98) **Going Correction** +0.325s/f (Good) **12** Ran SP% **122.2**
Speed ratings: 108,107,106,106,105 104,104,99,96,93 91,88
.
Owner BDR Partnership **Bred** Helshaw Grange Stud, E Kent & Mrs E Connelly **Trained** West Ilsley, Berks

FOCUS
A decent handicap which was run at just an average early pace. The runner up sets the standard for the form.

NOTEBOOK
Obe Brave, having his first outing for 103 days, advertised his ability to run to his best when fresh and got back to winning ways in ready fashion. His rider deserves the plaudits for attaining a handy early position from his wide draw and he looked to have a little left up his sleeve at the finish. This was also his first attempt over a distance this far, so it will be interesting to see if he can now go on from this.
Sendalam(FR), outclassed behind the smart Echo Of Light in a Group 2 at Longchamp when last seen 110 days previously, ran a race full of promise on this debut for his new connections. He ran freely through the early parts and ultimately shaped as though he can go one better now he has this outing under his belt.
Diamond Quest(SAF) ◆, a Grade 1 Handicap winner over two miles in South Africa 166 days previously, was given a lot to do from off the pace considering he was taking such a drop in trip for this return to action. He eventually stayed on really well in the final two furlongs and would surely have gone very close had he been ridden more positively through the first half of the contest. He should improve a deal for the outing and is one to take from this race with the immediate future in mind.
Pentecost ◆, keen to post on this first outing for 117 days, indeed took time to settle through the race itself and was another noted as doing all of his best work towards the finish. A stronger early pace would have been more to his advantage and this must rate a promising return to action from this smart eight-year-old. It should be noted that his last success came at this track on his next outing after running third this event at last year and, on this evidence, he could well repeat that feat this time around.
Azarole(IRE), runner-up in this event last year and whose previous success was at this track over a mile in March 2006, left the impression he would be better for the run and was another who would have ideally preferred a stronger early pace.
Bahiano(IRE), who came into this after an encouraging prep run at Wolverhampton 13 days previously, really only shows his true colours when racing off a strong early pace. He was still some way below his best, however.

173a DUMAANI STKS (CONDITIONS RACE) (DIRT) 7f (D)
4:05 (4:06) 3-Y-O
£9,183 (£3,061; £1,530; £765; £459; £306)

RPR
1 **Asiatic Boy (ARG)**[243] 4-9-4 108 .... WCMarwing 11 114
(M F De Kock, South Africa) *sn led: rdn 2f out: r.o wl: easily* **7/4**[1]
2 4 3/4 **Traffic Guard (USA)**[96] 5965 3-8-9 101 .... JohnEgan 3 99
(J S Moore) *slowly away: sn trckd pce: followed wnr 2f out: r.o but no ch w wnr* **7/1**
3 5 1/4 **Mount Hadley (USA)**[100] 5883 3-8-9 91 .... MJKinane 2 85
(I Mohammed, UAE) *trckd ldr: rdn 2 1/2f out: kpt on one pce* **14/1**
4 2 1/2 **Country Song (USA)**[173] 3962 3-8-9 99 .... RyanMoore 8 78
(J Noseda) *slowly away: racd in rr: gng wl 3 1/2f out: swtchd wd 3f out: r.o: nvr nrr* **9/2**[3]
5 3 1/2 **Heart Beat (SAF)**[14] 4-9-4 90 .... TedDurcan 4 71
(S Seemar, UAE) *trckd ldr: rdn 3f out: wknd 2f out* **12/1**
6 2 1/4 **Shavoulin (USA)**[14] 3-8-9 80 .... PaulEddery 1 63
(Christian Wroe) *prom early on rail: hmpd 4f out: no ch after: kpt on* **66/1**
7 3/4 **Te Voglio Bene (BRZ)**[103] 4-8-11 90 .... (t) PatrickHills(7) 10 63
(M D Wolfson, U.S.A) *a in rr* **33/1**
8 2 **Comandante Xara (BRZ)**[95] 4-9-4 93 .... ECruz 5 57
(P Nickel Filho, Brazil) *mid-div: hrd rdn 3f out: nvr a threat* **20/1**
9 5 **Glen Nevis (USA)**[100] 5886 3-8-9 91 .... WSupple 9 42
(I Mohammed, UAE) *nvr nr to chal* **16/1**
10 6 **Champlain**[94] 6010 3-8-9 106 .... (t) PJSmullen 6 25
(I Mohammed, UAE) *mid-div: rdn 3 1/2f out: nvr a threat* **7/2**[2]
1m 23.1s (-1.70) **Going Correction** +0.025s/f (Slow)
WFA 3 from 4yo 18lb **10** Ran SP% **118.7**
Speed ratings: 110,104,98,95,91 89,88,86,80,73
.
Owner Sheikh Mohammed Bin Khalifa Al Maktoum **Bred** Haras Arroyo De Luna **Trained** South Africa

FOCUS
A decent conditions event which was run at a solid pace. The winner impressed in making all and the form is rated through the third.

NOTEBOOK

Asiatic Boy(ARG) ◆, a runner up in Grade 1 company when last seen eight months ago in his native Argentina, did well to get to the front early on from his outside stall and got off the mark for connections by making just about all in great style. He responded positively when the runner-up came with his challenge around two from home and should rate value for a little further than the winning margin. Clearly right at home on this surface, he ought to improve a deal for the experience, and does look one of his leading yard's brightest prospects for this year's carnival. He will reportedly now head for the UAE Guineas (over a mile) next and, at this stage, is the one they all have to beat there.

Traffic Guard(USA), only beaten just over 11 lengths behind Teofilo in the Dewhurst on his final outing last year, showed he has trained on nicely with a very pleasing effort in defeat on this dirt debut. He was the only one to give the winner a serious race and, despite being put in his place by that rival before the final furlong, still finished well clear of the remainder. It would not a be a surprise to see him renew rivalry with the winner in the UAE 2000 Guineas now and his connections will no doubt be delighted with this effort.

Mount Hadley(USA), a Leicester maiden winner on his second and final outing as a juvenile in 2006, is bred to handle this surface and posted a very respectable effort in defeat on his three-year-old bow for a new yard. He was in turn nicely clear in third and is entitled to improve for the outing. There could be a nice prize within his compass at some stage this year.

Country Song(USA), second in the Chesham Stakes at Royal Ascot last year when trained by David Wachman, simply got going all too late on this debut for his new connections. This was also his first outing on the surface, so it will be little surprise to see him progress for the outing, and he is not one to write off on the back of this display. He may also be in need of at least a mile now.

Champlain, winner of the Chesham Stakes at Royal Ascot when with Michael Jarvis last year, failed to figure and ultimately proved very disappointing on this first run for his new trainer. The fact he was tongue-tied for this would suggest he has not wintered as well one might have hoped and he has it to prove now, even though it is still a little early to write him off.

174a INTIDAB STKS (H'CAP) (TURF) (F&M) 7f 110y(D)

4:35 (4:37) (90-110,100) 3-Y-0+

£33,673 (£11,224; £5,612; £2,806; £1,683; £1,122)

RPR

1 **Indochine (BRZ)**^{264} 4-8-7 **100** ow2 .... KShea 3 107
(H J Brown, South Africa) *mid-div: t.k.h: trckd eventual runner-up 2 1/2f out: rdn to chal 1 1/2f out: led 110yds out* **3/1**^{2}

2 *1 1/2* **Zaafran**^{13} 4-8-9 **93** .... JMurtagh 7 95
(D Selvaratnam, UAE) *mid-div: rdn 3 1/2f out: led 1 1/2f out: hdd 110yds out* **2/1**^{1}

3 *4 3/4* **Expensive**^{145} [4808] 4-9-0 **97** .... TedDurcan 1 88
(C F Wall) *racd 3rd: ev ch whn rdn 2f out: nt qckn* **10/1**

4 *1* **Cat Belling (IRE)**^{342} [369] 7-8-11 **95** .... THuet 2 83
(R Bouresly, Kuwait) *sn led: hdd 1 1/2f out: wknd* **33/1**

5 *hd* **Imperial Ice (SAF)**^{116} [5550] 5-9-3 **100** .... RyanMoore 8 88
(H J Brown, South Africa) *settled in rr: rdn rail 2 1/2f out: nvr able to chal* **11/1**

6 *hd* **Nhecolandia (BRZ)**^{75} 5-9-1 **98** .... ADomingos 6 86
(A Cintra Pereira, Brazil) *mid-div wd: rdn 3f out: ev ch 2f out: one pce* **7/1**

7 *1/2* **Rock Opera (SAF)**^{25} 5-9-3 **100** ....(t) RichardMullen 4 86
(S Seemar, UAE) *missed break: racd in rr: rdn 3f out: n.d* **16/1**

8 *3 1/2* **Dont Dili Dali**^{235} [2054] 4-9-0 **97** .... JohnEgan 9 75
(J S Moore) *racd in rr: rdn 3f out: nvr able to chal* **13/2**^{3}

9 *3 1/4* **Estrela Brynhild (USA)**^{144} 4-9-1 **98** .... MCardoso 5 67
(C Morgado, Brazil) *trckd ldr: rdn 3f out: sn fdd* **7/1**

1m 31.42s (0.82) **Going Correction** +0.325s/f (Good) **9** Ran SP% **122.9**
Speed ratings: 108,106,101,100,100 100,99,96,93

Owner The Bayern Syndicate,J Atkinson & F Couturier **Bred** Haras Mabruk **Trained** South Africa

FOCUS

A tight handicap for fillies and mares which was run at a sound pace. The form looks solid, with the first two coming clear.

NOTEBOOK

Indochine(BRZ) ◆, a former Grade 1 winner over this distance in Brazil, ultimately ran out a comfortable winner on this first run for her new connections, despite having pulled hard through the early stages. She took time to pick up when asked for her effort, but duly responded where it mattered and left the impression she would improve a deal for the outing. Her connections feel she may have more to offer when switching to the dirt and she looks a filly to follow when racing against her own sex.

Zaafran, a dual handicap winner for Michael Jarvis last year, came into this in decent form having scored on her debut for this yard on the dirt at Jebel Ali 13 days previously. She was racing from a 13lb higher mark, however, and eventually got put in her place by the winner when that rival asserted for home. She will not always come up against such a well-treated rival and finished nicely clear of the remainder, so still looks progressive.

Expensive, who failed to win last year after being campained mainly in Listed company, did not shape without promise on this first run for 145 days and did enough to suggest she can get closer now she has this outing under her belt. She probably needs all of a mile nowadays, however.

Cat Belling(IRE), a familar name at this track, was given a positive ride and ran big race in defeat on this first outing for 342 days. She ought to be all the better for this outing.

Dont Dili Dali, returning from a 235-day break, was being ridden from an early stage and never figured. She could improve a deal for this outing, however, and should prove happier when reverting to a suitably stiffer test in due course.

175a KAYRAWAN CUP (H'CAP) (DIRT) 1m 1f (D)

5:05 (5:05) (90-105,105) 3-Y-0+

£33,673 (£11,224; £5,612; £2,806; £1,683; £1,122)

RPR

1 **Morghim (IRE)**^{27} 4-8-12 **98** ....(bt) MartinDwyer 12 91+
(E Charpy, UAE) *mid-div: rdn 4f out: prog trck ldrs 3f out: n.m.r 1 1/2f out: r.o once clr: fin 2nd, 3¼l: awrdd r* **20/1**

2 *6* **Chinkara**^{27} 7-9-1 **99** .... WSupple 1 88
(Doug Watson, UAE) *mid-div: rdn 3½f out: kpt on: fin 3rd 3¼l & 2¾l: plcd 2nd* **20/1**

3 *nk* **Golden Velvet (USA)**^{88} [6120] 4-9-1 **100** ....(t) MJKinane 2 88
(Saeed Bin Suroor) *disp rail: moved off rail 4f out: led 2f out: hdd jst over 1f out* **9/2**^{1}

4 *1 1/2* **Red Duster (USA)**^{13} 4-8-10 **96** .... TedDurcan 16 81
(S Seemar, UAE) *mid-div wd: chal ldrs 3 1/2f out: sn rdn: ev ch 2f out: r.o* **12/1**

5 *1/2* **Impeller (IRE)**^{120} [5477] 8-8-10 **95** .... JohnEgan 7 79
(J S Moore) *mid-div: rdn 3f out: trckd wnr 2 1/2f out: ev ch 2f out: kpt on* **12/1**

6 *3 1/4* **Parasol (IRE)**^{315} 8-9-5 **104** ....(bt) RichardMullen 8 81
(Doug Watson, UAE) *slowly away: racd in rr: prog mid-div rail 3f out: nvr able to chal* **9/1**

7 *3/4* **Mutasallil (USA)**^{27} 7-9-4 **102** ....(t) RHills 4 79
(Doug Watson, UAE) *slowly away: sn trckd ldrs: swtchd rail 4f out: ev ch 3f out: nt qckn* **6/1**^{2}

8 *3/4* **Oakfast (BRZ)**^{110} 5-9-0 **98** .... ADomingos 9 74
(A Cintra Pereira, Brazil) *nvr a threat* **33/1**

9 *1/2* **Leaving Alone (BRZ)**^{103} 4-8-1 **96** ow1 .... RoystonFfrench 13 61
(M D Wolfson, U.S.A) *mid-div whn hmpd 6 1/2f out: nt rcvr* **25/1**

10 *2 1/4* **Change The Grange (AUS)**^{7} 9-8-11 **96** ....(ve) RyanMoore 6 65
(S Seemar, UAE) *rdn to ld: led 3 1/2f out: rdn 3f out: wknd 2 1/2f out* **12/1**

11 *1/2* **Boo**^{18} [6997] 5-8-9 **94** ....(v) WCMarwing 15 62
(K R Burke) *racd in rr: nvr a threat* **33/1**

12 *nk* **Remaadd (USA)**^{21} 6-9-6 **105** .... JMurtagh 14 73
(D Selvaratnam, UAE) *mid-div: rdn to chal 3 1/2f out: wknd 3f out* **10/1**

13 *10* **Brahminy Kite (USA)**^{27} 5-9-1 **99** .... DBonilla 10 49
(R Bouresly, Kuwait) *a in rr* **20/1**

14 *3/4* **Alcomo (BRZ)**^{172} 4-8-6 **102** ....(t) ECruz 11 39
(P Nickel Filho, Brazil) *mid-div: rdn along 4f out: sn wknd* **12/1**

15 *9 1/4* **Speedy Sam**^{17} [6] 4-8-9 **95** .... PJSmullen 5 25
(K R Burke) *nvr nr to chal* **15/2**^{3}

D **Dubai Honor**^{27} 8-9-4 **102** ....(e) PatDobbs 3 104+
(Doug Watson, UAE) *mid-div centre: rdn to chal 2f out: led jst over 1f out: easily: subsequently disq. (naproxen in sample)* **11/1**

1m 49.99s (-0.81) **Going Correction** +0.025s/f (Slow)
WFA 4 from 5yo+ 1lb **16** Ran SP% **126.4**
Speed ratings: 101,98,98,97,96 93,93,92,91,89 89,89,80,79,71 104

Owner Hamdan Al Maktoum **Bred** Shadwell Estate Co Ltd **Trained** United Arab Emirates

FOCUS

Just an ordinary handicap for the grade.

NOTEBOOK

Morghim(IRE) appreciated the return to handicap company and ran well behind the easy winner.

Chinkara, returned to handicap company, was not ideally berthed in stall one but ran a good race in third.

Golden Velvet(USA), a winner on the turf in France when trained by Andre Fabre last year, was given every chance on her first start for Godolphin/debut on dirt. It would be no surprise to see her switch back to turf at some point.

Red Duster(USA), a winner twice at Jebel Ali last year before running third at the same course on his return from a break recently, came wide into the straight, avoiding the kickback on the inside, and can have few excuses.

Impeller(IRE) ran well on his first start since leaving the Willie Muir yard and can surely do even better when returned to turf.

Boo is a useful sort of Polytrack but he failed to show himself effective on this faster dirt surface.

Speedy Sam is very useful on both Fibresand and Polytrack but, like his stablemate Boo, he failed to take to this very different dirt surface.

Dubai Honor stepped up the form he showed in a Listed event at Jebel Ali on his previous start with a pretty impressive success. He is quite exposed, so it would probably be unwise to get carried away, but he is clearly one to respect at the Carnival.

176a SAHM TROPHY (H'CAP) (TURF) 1m 194y(T)

5:35 (5:36) (95-116,113) 3-Y-0+

£53,571 (£17,857; £8,928; £4,464; £2,678; £1,785)

RPR

1 **Formal Decree (GER)**^{110} [5675] 4-9-2 **110** .... MJKinane 3 119+
(I Mohammed, UAE) *slowly away: mid-div rail 3f out: rdn to cl 2f out: r.o wl: easily* **11/4**^{1}

2 *1 1/4* **Stream Of Gold (IRE)**^{25} 6-8-10 **104** .... TedDurcan 9 109
(S Seemar, UAE) *racd in rr: smooth prog 2 1/2f out: chal 2f out: r.o* **7/1**

3 *shd* **Charlie Cool**^{61} [6516] 4-8-8 **102** .... RichardMullen 4 108
(W J Haggas) *slowly away: mid-div: rdn to chal 2f out: ev ch: r.o* **3/1**^{2}

4 *shd* **Yasoodd**^{173} [3957] 4-9-0 **108** ....(e^{1}) JMurtagh 6 114
(D Selvaratnam, UAE) *racd in 4th: t.k.h: rdn to chal 2f out: led 1 1/2f out: r.o whn hdd* **12/1**

5 *6 1/4* **Lost Soldier Three (IRE)**^{116} [5551] 6-8-11 **105** .... AdrianTNicholls 5 98
(D Nicholls) *hld up in rr: hrd rdn 3f out: sme late prog* **33/1**

6 *shd* **Cimyla (IRE)**^{58} [6559] 6-8-7 **100** .... RyanMoore 12 94
(C F Wall) *settled in rr: nvr able to chal* **12/1**

7 *4 1/4* **Senor Dali (IRE)**^{124} [5400] 4-8-12 **107** .... WSupple 2 91
(I Mohammed, UAE) *trckd ldr: led 2 1/2f out: hdd 1 1/2f out* **12/1**

8 *10* **Alpacco (IRE)**^{123} [5414] 5-8-7 **100** .... KShea 10 66
(H J Brown, South Africa) *mid-div: n.d* **25/1**

9 *nse* **Elliots World (IRE)**^{329} [496] 5-8-9 **102** .... TPO'Shea 11 68
(E Charpy, UAE) *v.s.a: a in rr* **16/1**

10 *1 1/4* **Shakis (IRE)**^{299} [743] 7-9-6 **113** ....(vt) RHills 8 77
(Doug Watson, UAE) *racd in 3rd: rdn 3f out: wknd* **13/2**^{3}

11 *2 1/4* **Beringoer (FR)**^{121} 4-8-9 **104** .... MartinDwyer 1 63
(A M Balding) *led tl 2 1/2f out: wknd rapidly* **16/1**

12 *8 1/4* **Evil Knievel (BRZ)**^{315} [622] 8-9-3 **110** .... RoystonFfrench 7 54
(Christian Wroe) *mid-div wd: rdn 5f out tl weakend 3f out* **16/1**

1m 48.49s (-1.31) **Going Correction** +0.325s/f (Good)
WFA 4 from 5yo+ 1lb **12** Ran SP% **125.0**
Speed ratings: 118,116,116,116,111 111,107,98,98,97 95,87

Owner Sheikh Hamdan Bin Mohammed Al Maktoum **Bred** Gestut Olympia **Trained** UAE

FOCUS

A good handicap and a terrific effort form the progressive Formal Decree. The race has been rated through the fourth.

NOTEBOOK

Formal Decree(GER) ◆, sold out of Alan Swinbank's yard after winning the Cambridgeshire last September, readily defied a 13lb higher mark off the back of a 110-day break on his debut for new connections. He was a little short of room when beginning to pick up, but displayed a smart turn of foot when a gap appeared between runners and ultimately looked to win with a fair bit in hand. It looks just a matter of time before he lands a pattern race and he could progress enough to contest the Group 1 Dubai Duty Free Stakes back here on World Cup day. His trainer did not have the best of Carnivals last year, so this success obviously bodes well for a better campaign but, in the longer term, Formal Decree will surely soon be sporting the royal blue of Godolphin.

Stream Of Gold(IRE), an ex-Sir Michael Stoute gelding (won the 2005 Lincoln) who was third in a 7f Listed race on his debut in Dubai off the back of a 13-month absence, ran a good race behind the most progressive winner and clearly retains plenty of ability.

Charlie Cool ◆, eighth behind Formal Decree in the Cambridgeshire before running third in a 1m2f Listed event on the Polytrack at Lingfield, was given every chance and ran a respectable race in third. He gives the impression he might benefit from a step back up in trip and he looks capable of making his mark at the Carnival.

Yasoodd, fitted with an eye-shield on his first start since leaving Mick Channon's yard, ran a good race off a stiff enough handicap mark and could be sharper given he was returning from a 173-day break.

Lost Soldier Three(IRE) ◆ was third in a 2m Listed event at Ascot on his final start for Luca Cumani, so it is no surprise he failed to land a blow on his debut for the Nicholls camp. He actually ran very well in the circumstances and could be dangerous over twelve furlongs round here.
Cimyla(IRE) was not at his best on his debut in Dubai. His record on British Polytrack surfaces reads 111151, and a return to that surface should suit best, although it would not be a surprise to see him tested on Nad Al Sheba's dirt course at some point.
Beringoer(FR), a multiple winner in France for Andre Fabre, offered little immediate promise on debut for Andrew Balding/first start in Dubai.

177a INVASOR AL MAKTOUM CHALLENGE (ROUND 1) (GROUP 3) (DIRT) 1m (D)

6:05 (6:09) 3-Y-0+

£61,224 (£20,408; £10,204; £5,102; £3,061; £2,040)

RPR

1 **Imperialista (BRZ)**[88] 4-8-9 98 ow1 MCardoso 11 106+
(C Morgado, Brazil) *nvr far away: rdn to trck ldrs 2 1/2f out: led 2f out: comf* **25/1**

2 2 1/4 **Impossible Ski (BRZ)**[286] 5-9-4 98 ADomingos 9 108
(A Cintra Pereira, Brazil) *missed break: racd in mid-div: smooth prog 3f out rail: r.o wl: perhaps unlucky* **25/1**

3 5 **Golden Arrow (IRE)**[130] [5216] 4-9-4 108 (b) PJSmullen 12 98
(I Mohammed, UAE) *trckd ldr: ev ch 2f out: outpcd* **7/1**[3]

4 2 1/4 **Jaffal (USA)**[27] 5-9-4 91 (t) WSupple 16 94
(A Al Raihe, UAE) *sn led: hrd rdn and hdd 2 1/2f out: kpt on one pce* **40/1**

5 1 1/2 **Bandido Secreto (BRZ)**[110] 5-9-4 100 JMurtagh 6 91+
(P Nickel Filho, Brazil) *racd in rr: long way bhd after 1 1/2f: swtchd 2f out: r.o v wl: nrst fin* **25/1**

6 2 1/2 **Blue On Blues (ARG)**[35] 6-9-4 105 (t) RyanMoore 15 86
(S Seemar, UAE) *mid-div wd: rdn 3f out: nvr able to chal* **8/1**

7 1 1/4 **Holiday Camp (USA)**[299] [738] 5-9-4 98 WayneSmith 4 83
(M Al Muhairi, UAE) *trckd ldr tl hrd rdn 3f out: wknd* **28/1**

8 shd **Parole Board (USA)**[21] 5-9-4 108 TedDurcan 8 83
(S Seemar, UAE) *mid-div: nvr nr to chal* **7/2**[2]

9 5 1/4 **Tropical Star (IRE)**[299] [740] 7-9-4 109 (vt) RoystonFfrench 5 72
(A Al Raihe, UAE) *mever nr to chal* **10/1**

10 3/4 **Lucky Dance (BRZ)**[165] 5-9-4 96 KShea 2 71
(M D Wolfson, U.S.A) *slowly away: nvr involved* **33/1**

11 nk **Opportunist (IRE)**[21] 8-9-4 102 (vt) MartinDwyer 3 70
(Doug Watson, UAE) *a mid-div* **10/1**

12 2 1/4 **Notability (IRE)**[96] [5982] 5-9-4 111 RHills 1 66
(Saeed Bin Suroor) *mid-div: rdn 3f out: n.d after* **10/3**[1]

13 9 1/4 **Lascaux (AUS)**[51] 6-9-4 104 (e) WLHo 7 47
(Y Choy, Macau) *mid-div: rdn 4f out: nvr a threat* **33/1**

14 1/2 **State Shinto (USA)**[7] [104] 11-9-4 94 (bt) THuet 13 46
(R Bouresly, Kuwait) *racd in rr: nvr involved* **50/1**

15 1 **Grand Emporium (SAF)**[322] [560] 7-9-4 112 (t) RichardMullen 10 44
(S Seemar, UAE) *mid-div: rdn to chse ldrs 3 1/2f out: nvr nr to chal* **16/1**

16 1 **Hattan (IRE)**[13] [43] 5-9-4 110 MJKinane 14 42
(C E Brittain) *mid-div: nvr able to chal* **7/1**[3]

1m 35.96s (-1.64) **Going Correction** +0.025s/f (Slow) **16** Ran SP% **130.7**
Speed ratings: 109,106,101,99,98 95,94,94,88,88 87,85,76,75,74 73

Owner Estrela Energia Stables **Bred** Haras Sao Jos Do Bom Retiro **Trained** Brazil

FOCUS
Probably not that strong a race by Group 3 standards, but a fantastic result for the Brazilians, who had the first two home.

NOTEBOOK
Imperialista(BRZ) was a winner over this trip in Brazil, but it was near impossible to know how good he was. This represents a smart level of form, even if the runner-up was unlucky, and he is clearly one to have on your side at this year's Carnival. He gives the impression he will stay a little further.
Impossible Ski(BRZ) ◆, like the winner Brazilian bred and trained (he won a Group 3 over 1m2f in his homeland), looked unlucky on his debut in Dubai. He was almost down on his nose after stumbling at the start and lost several lengths, but he stayed on in taking fashion in the straight, giving the impression he would surely have won but for that mishap at the start. This must rate as a fine effort, not least because he was returning from a 286-day break, and he could be very decent.
Golden Arrow(IRE), a smart sort on turf when trained by Dermot Weld, ran a good race on his debut for new connections and first start on dirt. There could be more to come.
Jaffal(USA) could not sustain his challenge and 7f may suit best.
Notability(IRE) progressed from a decent handicapper to a Group 2 winner when with Michael Jarvis, but he has always needed soft turf to be seen at his best, and it was no surprise to see him run so poorly switched to the dirt for the first time on his debut for Godolphin. The lowest stall of all was not help to be fair, as he got loads of kickback, but he is basically more of a turf horse.
Hattan(IRE), returned to Dubai, ran nowhere near the form he showed when winning a Wolverhampton conditions race on his previous start.

178a IRISH TROPHY RACE (H'CAP) (TURF) 7f 110y(D)

6:35 (6:39) (90-105,105) 3-Y-0+

£33,673 (£11,224; £5,612; £2,244; £2,244; £1,122)

RPR

1 **Kalankari (IRE)**[138] [5019] 4-8-11 96 MartinDwyer 12 98
(A M Balding) *a led: rdn 2 1/2f out: r.o wl: jst hld on* **6/1**[3]

2 shd **Rock N Roll Kid (NZ)**[51] 8-8-12 97 PJSmullen 11 99
(M C Tam, Macau) *trckd ldr: hrd rdn 2f out: kpt on wl: jst failed* **12/1**

3 nk **Almuraad (IRE)**[13] 6-8-12 97 RHills 9 98
(Doug Watson, UAE) *settled in rr: rdn 2 1/2f out: r.o wl fnl f: nrst fin* **8/1**

4 1 1/4 **Conceal**[25] 9-8-11 96 THuet 7 94
(R Bouresly, Kuwait) *racd 3rd: gng wl 2f out whn no room: swtchd rail last 110yds: r.o* **14/1**

4 dht **National Captain (SAF)**[25] 5-9-6 105 TedDurcan 4 103
(S Seemar, UAE) *racd 4th: trckd runner-up 2 1/2f out: ev ch: nt qckn* **6/1**[3]

6 1/2 **Hartshead**[130] [5224] 8-8-12 97 JMurtagh 6 94
(G A Swinbank) *settled last rail 3f out: swtchd 1 1/2f out: r.o fnl f: nrst fin* **5/1**[2]

7 3/4 **Jet Express (SAF)**[62] 5-9-0 98 (t) KShea 2 94
(H J Brown, South Africa) *mid-div: rdn 2 1/2f out: nt qckn* **10/1**

8 3/4 **Engrupido (ARG)**[262] 4-8-9 104 (t) WCMarwing 5 98
(M F De Kock, South Africa) *settled in rr: wd and last 3f out: rdn: nvr nr to chal: nrst fin* **11/4**[1]

9 nk **Matloob**[70] 6-8-10 95 RPCleary 3 87
(D Selvaratnam, UAE) *slowly away: prog rail 3f out: no room 1 1/2f out: one pce* **25/1**

10 2 3/4 **Western Diplomat (USA)**[28] 7-8-10 95 (t) RoystonFfrench 1 81
(A Al Raihe, UAE) *mid-div rail: rdn 3f out: ev ch whn n.m.r 1 1/2f out: wknd* **33/1**

11 7 1/2 **Hurricane James (IRE)**[25] 5-9-2 100 (t) TPO'Shea 10 68
(E Charpy, UAE) *settled in rr: nvr able to chal* **10/1**

12 9 1/2 **Organizer (NOR)**[315] [622] 7-9-2 100 (e[1]) RichardMullen 8 44
(Christian Wroe) *mid-div: wd 3f out: rdn 2 1/2f out: nvr nr to chal* **25/1**

1m 31.32s (0.72) **Going Correction** +0.325s/f (Good) **12** Ran SP% **126.2**
Speed ratings: 109,108,108,107,107 106,106,105,105,102 94,85

Owner Dubai Thoroughbred Racing Syndicate **Bred** B Kennedy **Trained** Kingsclere, Hants

FOCUS
They finished in a bit of a bunch and this looks like ordinary form for the grade.

NOTEBOOK
Kalankari(IRE) gained his two previous wins came on Polytrack, but he is clearly just as effective on turf and picked up this valuable prize under a finely-judged front-running ride from Martin Dwyer. He only just held on and a rise in the weights will make things tougher.
Rock N Roll Kid(NZ), twice a winner in Macau, ran a fine race on his debut in Dubai and just missed out. He is clearly one to respect in similar events.
Almuraad(IRE) ◆, returned to turf, was given plenty to do and just got going too late. He looks well up to finding a similar event.
Conceal has yet to win on turf, but this was a decent effort and he would have been even closer with a better trip.
National Captain(SAF), placed in Listed company on his last couple of starts, ran another good race returned to handicap company and is holding his form well.
Hartshead ◆, third in a Listed race in Sweden when last seen 130 days previously, was totally unsuited by the way the race was run and can leave this form behind.
Engrupido(ARG), a winner in Argentina, was another unsuited by the way the race was run on his Dubai debut, and he can do better.

151 WOLVERHAMPTON (A.W) (L-H)

Friday, January 19

OFFICIAL GOING: Standard
Wind: Moderate, behind Weather: Fine

179 PONTIN'S HOLIDAYS AMATEUR RIDERS' H'CAP (DIV I) 1m 1f 103y(P)

1:20 (1:25) (Class 6) (0-55,57) 4-Y-0+ **£1,249** (£387; £193; £96) **Stalls Low**

Form RPR

060- 1 **Scottish River (USA)**[21] [6977] 8-11-4 52 MrLeeNewnes 7 58
(M D I Usher) *s.s: hld up in rr: swtchd rt and hdwy over 2f out: sn rdn: r.o to ld nr fin* **8/1**

00-0 2 3/4 **Danum**[6] [126] 7-10-10 47 oh1 ow1 MissSSharratt(3) 3 51
(R Hollinshead) *w ldr: led over 3f out: rdn clr over 2f out: ct nr fin* **66/1**

006- 3 1 1/2 **Love You Always (USA)**[40] [6779] 7-10-5 46 oh1 (t) MrRBirkett(7) 11 47
(Miss J Feilden) *t.k.h in rr: nt clr run and swtchd rt over 2f out: rdn and hdwy over 1f out: kpt on ins fnl f* **20/1**

00-0 4 1 1/2 **Captain Bolsh**[5] [133] 4-10-8 46 oh1 MrSPearce(3) 9 44
(J Pearce) *hld up in mid-div: hdwy on wd outside 2f out: rdn over 1f out: edgd lft ins fnl f: one pce* **11/2**[2]

500- 5 1 3/4 **The Gaikwar (IRE)**[39] [6787] 8-11-4 57 ow5 (b) MrJoshuaHarris(5) 8 52
(R A Harris) *s.i.s: mid-div: hdwy over 3f out: rdn to chse clr ldr 2f out: wknd fnl f* **12/1**

013- 6 3 **Claws**[31] [6864] 4-11-0 54 (t) MissZoeLilly(5) 10 43
(A J Lidderdale) *hld up and bhd: hdwy on outside over 2f out: wknd over 1f out* **8/1**

/00- 7 1/2 **Machinate (USA)**[217] [2612] 5-11-0 53 MrBenBrisbourne(5) 5 41
(W M Brisbourne) *s.i.s: keen early and sn towards rr: hdwy and edgd lft fr over 1f out: no imp fnl f* **6/1**[3]

00-0 8 5 **Joe Jo Star**[14] [42] 5-10-7 46 oh1 (p) MrStephenHarrison(5) 2 24
(B P J Baugh) *t.k.h: prom: rdn 3f out: wknd 2f out* **10/1**

00-0 9 4 **Yeldham Lady**[7] [109] 5-10-12 46 oh1 DavidEngland 4 16
(A J Chamberlain) *mid-div: rdn over 4f out: bhd fnl 3f* **100/1**

440- 10 3 **Uhuru Peak**[21] [6980] 6-11-6 54 (bt) MissSBrotherton 6 18
(M W Easterby) *prom tl wknd over 2f out* **7/2**[1]

00-3 11 7 **Zando**[6] [121] 5-10-11 50 (p) MrPCallaghan(5) 1 —
(E G Bevan) *led: hdd over 3f out: rdn over 2f out: wknd wl over 1f out* **11/2**[2]

0-00 12 18 **Lord Chamberlain**[6] [124] 14-11-0 55 (b) MissHDavies(7) 12 —
(J M Bradley) *prom tl wknd 3f out* **33/1**

2m 4.59s (1.97) **Going Correction** +0.125s/f (Slow)
WFA 4 from 5yo+ 1lb **12** Ran SP% **116.5**
Speed ratings (Par 101): 96,95,94,92,91 88,88,83,80,77 71,55
CSF £460.16 CT £9723.17 TOTE £9.00: £3.00, £16.20, £5.50; EX 252.10 TRIFECTA Not won..
Owner M D I Usher **Bred** The Thoroughbred Corporation **Trained** Upper Lambourn, Berks
■ Stewards' Enquiry : Mr Ben Brisbourne one-day ban: careless riding (Jan 30)

FOCUS
A moderate amateur riders' handicap run in a time 1.23 seconds faster than the second division. Weak form on paper. The runner-up ran his best race since 2004.
Uhuru Peak Official explanation: vet said gelding finished lame behind

180 PONTIN'S HOLIDAYS AMATEUR RIDERS' H'CAP (DIV II) 1m 1f 103y(P)

1:55 (2:00) (Class 6) (0-55,57) 4-Y-0+ **£1,249** (£387; £193; £96) **Stalls Low**

Form RPR

23-0 1 **Lobengula (IRE)**[11] [72] 5-11-6 53 MrSDobson 7 65+
(I W McInnes) *t.k.h in rr: hdwy to ld 5f out: clr over 2f out: eased briefly wl ins fnl f: jst hld on* **9/2**[2]

20-0 2 shd **Khanjar (USA)**[14] [39] 7-11-2 52 (p) MrSPearce(3) 12 63
(J Pearce) *hld up in rr: swtchd lft sn after s: hdwy on outside over 2f out: rdn to chse wnr fnl f: jst failed* **15/2**[3]

23-3 3 5 **Fulvio (USA)**[16] [26] 7-10-13 53 (v) MissFGuillambert(7) 3 54
(P Howling) *prom: lost pl over 3f out: styd on one pce fnl f* **12/1**

461- 4 3/4 **The City Kid (IRE)**[20] [6988] 4-11-0 55 (b) MrRichardEvans(7) 5 54
(P D Evans) *hld up and bhd: swtchd rt over 1f out: late hdwy on outside: nvr nrr* **8/1**

000- 5 1/2 **Super Dominion**[38] [6799] 10-10-5 45 MissRKneller(7) 8 43
(R Hollinshead) *hld up in mid-div: lost pl 5f out: c wd st: hdwy over 1f out: no real prog fnl f* **66/1**

00-0 6 shd **Crimson Flame (IRE)**[14] [45] 4-10-11 45 DavidEngland 1 43
(A J Chamberlain) *hld up in tch: lost pl over 3f out: kpt on ins fnl f* **28/1**

640- 7 1 1/4 **Lady's Law**[127] [5319] 4-10-7 48 MissEmma-JaneJenkins(7) 11 44
(Rae Guest) *hld up and bhd: hdwy 5f out: wknd ins fnl f* **33/1**

3-31 8 1 1/2 **Desert Hawk**[6] [121] 6-11-3 55 5ex (b) MrBenBrisbourne(5) 9 48
(W M Brisbourne) *hld up in tch: no imp whn eased wl ins fnl f* **10/11**[1]

The Form Book, Raceform Ltd, Compton, RG20 6NL

056- **9** *hd* **Bournonville**[74] 6378 4-10-6 **45**.. MrSRees(5) 6 37
(M Wigham) *prom: chsd wnr over 3f out: sn rdn: wknd ins fnl f* **33/1**
00-6 **10** *9* **Newport Boy (IRE)**[12] 64 4-11-4 **57** ow5.........(b) MrJoshuaHarris(5) 2 31
(R A Harris) *led: hdd 5f out: rdn over 3f out: wknd wl over 1f out* **12/1**
000/ **11** *46* **Judda**[24] 1783 6-10-5 **45**..(t) MissAColley(7) 4 —
(R F Marvin) *bhd fnl 6f: t.o fnl 4f* **100/1**
2m 5.82s (3.20) **Going Correction** +0.125s/f (Slow)
WFA 4 from 5yo+ 1lb **39** Ran SP% **120.6**
Speed ratings (Par 101):90,89,85,84,84 84,83,81,81,73 32
CSF £37.71 CT £387.40 TOTE £5.90: £1.90, £2.60, £2.20; EX 42.00 Trifecta £354.50 Part won. Pool: £499.41 - 0.96 winning tickets..
Owner Colin G R Booth **Bred** A S O'Brien And Lars Pearson **Trained** Catwick, E Yorks
FOCUS
Another moderate amateur riders' handicap and they went no pace until the eventual winner, Lobengula, increased the tempo down the back straight. The runner-up did best of those from the pack and has slipped to a good mark. As a result, this was a muddling race and the form should not be taken too literally. The winning time was 1.23 seconds slower than the first division.

181 PONTINS.COM H'CAP 1m 141y(P)
2:30 (2:35) (Class 6) (0-55,58) 4-Y-0+ **£2,388** (£705; £352) **Stalls** Low

Form RPR
0-11 **1** **Time To Regret**[5] 129 7-9-4 **58** 6ex..........................(p) DanielTudhope 3 66
(I W McInnes) *hld up in tch: rdn to ld wl over 1f out: rdn out* **11/8**[1]
461- **2** *½* **Ciccone**[20] 6982 4-9-0 **55**..........................(p) FergusSweeney 4 62
(G L Moore) *hld up and bhd: hdwy over 2f out: rdn to chse wnr 1f out: hung lft ins fnl f: r.o* **7/1**[3]
2-06 **3** *5* **Grand Palace (IRE)**[3] 145 4-8-10 **51**..........................(v) PaulHanagan 5 48
(D Shaw) *hld up in mid-div: hdwy and bmpd over 3f out: led briefly wl over 1f out: sn rdn and hung lft: wknd ins fnl f* **9/4**[2]
000- **4** *3* **Herninski**[22] 6959 4-8-0 **46**... NicolPolli(5) 11 36
(M C Chapman) *a.p: led over 2f out: rdn and hdd wl over 1f out: wknd fnl f* **100/1**
003- **5** *½* **Kings Heir (IRE)**[23] 6943 4-8-12 **53**...............................(b) AdamKirby 10 42
(Peter Grayson) *s.s: hld up in rr: rdn and hdwy over 1f out: nvr nr ldrs* **9/1**
360- **6** *3* **Twilight Avenger (IRE)**[144] 4892 4-8-9 **50**........................ ShaneKelly 1 33
(W M Brisbourne) *edgd rt s: led early: w ldr tl rdn and wknd over 2f out* **10/1**
000- **7** *2 ½* **Sticky Mint (IRE)**[37] 6800 4-7-11 **45**........................ LauraReynolds(7) 2 23
(M Blanshard) *hmpd s: hld up in tch: wknd over 2f out* **80/1**
00-0 **8** *5* **Young Valentino**[5] 133 5-8-5 **45**.................................... ChrisCatlin 8 12
(A W Carroll) *t.k.h in mid-div: hdwy over 4f out: edgd lft over 3f out: wknd over 2f out* **66/1**
000- **9** *13* **Filliemou (IRE)**[40] 6780 6-8-5 **45**..................................... JimmyQuinn 6 —
(A W Carroll) *sn led: hdd over 2f out: sn rdn and wknd* **40/1**
1m 52.93s (1.17) **Going Correction** +0.125s/f (Slow)
WFA 4 from 5yo+ 1lb **9** Ran SP% **110.6**
Speed ratings (Par 101):99,98,94,91,91 88,86,81,70
CSF £10.92 CT £18.66 TOTE £2.30: £1.10, £1.80, £1.40; EX 8.80 Trifecta £14.00 Pool: £618.30 - 31.21 winning tickets..
Owner Horses 4 Courses **Bred** Speedlith Group **Trained** Catwick, E Yorks
FOCUS
A weak handicap run at a steady pace. It is doubtful if the winner had to improve much on his earlier turf form.
Grand Palace(IRE) Official explanation: jockey said gelding hung both ways

182 PONTIN'S HOLIDAYS (S) H'CAP 1m 4f 50y(P)
3:05 (3:10) (Class 6) (0-55,55) 4-Y-0+ **£2,047** (£604; £302) **Stalls** Low

Form RPR
65-1 **1** **Atlantic Gamble (IRE)**[11] 71 7-9-0 **52** 6ex.................(p) PhillipMakin 1 54
(K R Burke) *led 1f: chsd ldr: led over 2f out: rdn over 1f out: r.o wl* **5/4**[1]
4/6- **2** *1 ½* **Dubonai (IRE)**[287] 906 7-8-12 **50**..........................(t) JoeFanning 5 50
(G M Moore) *hld up in mid-div: n.m.r and lost pl 3f out: rdn and hdwy over 1f out: r.o ins fnl f: nt trble wnr* **7/1**[2]
003- **3** *½* **Penang Cinta**[39] 6787 4-8-11 **53**................................(p) LPKeniry 10 52
(A J Chamberlain) *a.p: rdn and hung rt over 2f out: sn chsng wnr: wandered bdly ins fnl f: nt qckn* **14/1**
0-00 **4** *1 ¾* **Stolen Summer (IRE)**[3] 148 4-8-10 **55**................(be) JerryO'Dwyer(3) 4 51
(B S Rothwell) *hld up in mid-div: rdn and hdwy over 2f out: one pce fnl f* **33/1**
00-0 **5** *1 ¾* **Ligne D'Eau**[13] 51 6-8-7 **45**..(b) RobertHavlin 2 39
(P D Evans) *hld up in tch: rdn over 2f out: no ex fnl f* **28/1**
340- **6** *½* **Willy (SWE)**[27] 6936 5-9-0 **52**..(t) PaulHanagan 11 45
(R Brotherton) *hld up and bhd: rdn over 2f out: sme late hdwy: n.d* **11/1**
500- **7** *¾* **Boulevin (IRE)**[7] 5736 7-8-5 **46**..................................... JamesDoyle(3) 7 38
(R J Price) *hld up and bhd: rdn and hdwy over 2f out: wknd over 1f out* **10/1**
05-4 **8** *3* **Keshya**[7] 107 6-9-2 **54**... GeorgeBaker 3 41
(N P Littmoden) *wnt rt s: hld up in tch: pushed along over 3f out: sn wknd* **7/1**[2]
0/0- **9** *1 ¾* **Boom Or Bust (IRE)**[21] 3862 8-8-7 **45**............................(p) ChrisCatlin 6 29
(Karen George) *stdd s: hld up in rr: rdn over 3f out: no rspnse* **50/1**
4-03 **10** *6* **Mossmann Gorge**[10] 78 5-8-8 **51**.........................(b) TolleyDean(5) 9 25
(R A Harris) *led after 1f: rdn and hdd over 2f out: sn wknd* **8/1**[3]
2m 45.12s (2.70) **Going Correction** +0.125s/f (Slow)
WFA 4 from 5yo+ 4lb **10** Ran SP% **113.0**
Speed ratings (Par 101):96,95,94,93,92 92,91,89,88,84
CSF £9.55 CT £81.24 TOTE £2.00: £1.10, £2.10, £3.90; EX 11.50 Trifecta £88.50 Pool: £591.08 - 4.74 winning tickets..The winner was bought in for 5,500gns. Penang Cinta was claimed by Trevor Gallienne for £6,000.
Owner R G Greaney **Bred** Larry Ryan **Trained** Middleham Moor, N Yorks
FOCUS
A very weak seller and the form is worth little.

183 GO PONTIN'S CLAIMING STKS 5f 216y(P)
3:35 (3:40) (Class 6) 4-Y-0+ **£2,730** (£806; £403) **Stalls** Low

Form RPR
34-6 **1** **Marko Jadeo (IRE)**[14] 44 9-8-11 80.......................... TolleyDean(5) 10 76
(R A Harris) *hld up: hdwy over 3f out: rdn 2f out: led 1f out: r.o* **2/1**[1]
00-6 **2** *¾* **City For Conquest (IRE)**[8] 97 4-8-8 63..................(b) ChrisCatlin 7 66
(T J Pitt) *hld up: nt clr run over 3f out: hdwy over 2f out: rdn wl over 1f out: ev ch ins fnl f: nt qckn* **10/1**[3]
40-0 **3** *½* **Buzzin'Boyzee (IRE)**[2] 158 4-8-0 57..................... BernadetteQuinn(7) 9 63
(P D Evans) *t.k.h in rr: rdn and hdwy on outside 2f out: r.o ins fnl f* **16/1**
54-0 **4** *¾* **Ever Cheerful**[5] 132 6-8-12 67..................................... HaddenFrost(7) 1 73
(D G Bridgwater) *sn w ldr: rdn to ld wl over 1f out: sn edgd rt: hdd 1f out: no ex ins fnl f* **9/2**[2]

32-1 **5** *1* **Charlie Delta**[17] 9 4-9-2 70..(p) AmirQuinn(3) 4 70
(J R Boyle) *hld up in mid-div: nt clr run on ins and lost pl over 3f out: nt clr run over 2f out: rdn and hdwy over 1f out: kpt on* **2/1**[1]
400- **6** *1 ¾* **Twinned (IRE)**[19] 6994 4-8-7 48.................................. JerryO'Dwyer(3) 5 56
(Karen George) *led: rdn and hdd wl over 1f out: hld whn nt clr run jst over 1f out* **16/1**
00-0 **7** *5* **Miracle Baby**[7] 106 5-7-13 32..................................... JosephWalsh(7) 2 37
(A J Chamberlain) *prom tl wknd over 2f out* **100/1**
00-0 **8** *½* **Speckled Hen (IRE)**[15] 33 4-8-7 50.............................(b) RobertHavlin 6 36
(D Haydn Jones) *chsd ldrs: rdn over 2f out: wknd wl over 1f out* **50/1**
006- **9** *2* **Doughty**[284] 937 5-8-10 35... TPQueally 12 33
(M Mullineaux) *prom tl rdn and wknd over 2f out* **100/1**
000- **10** *4* **Moors Myth**[23] 6955 6-8-9 47......................................(t) FergusSweeney 8 20
(B G Powell) *prom early: rdn 4f out: sn bhd* **33/1**
000/ **11** *29* **Isle Dream**[411] 6498 5-7-12 25 ow1.....................(t) NataliaGemelova(5) 11 —
(R F Marvin) *prom over 2f: t.o* **125/1**
1m 16.4s (0.59) **Going Correction** +0.125s/f (Slow) **11** Ran SP% **113.4**
Speed ratings (Par 101):101,100,99,98,97 94,88,87,84,79 40
CSF £23.84 TOTE £3.10: £1.30, £2.10, £3.40; EX 16.30 Trifecta £83.00 Pool: £737.66 - 6.31 winning tickets..
Owner D Tumman & R F Bloodstock **Bred** P Casey **Trained** Earlswood, Monmouths
FOCUS
This turned out to be a competitive claimer. The time was slow but the form appears to make plenty of sense on paper.

184 BONUSPRINT.COM H'CAP 1m 141y(P)
4:05 (4:10) (Class 4) (0-85,84) 3-Y-O **£4,857** (£1,445; £722; £360) **Stalls** Low

Form RPR
12-1 **1** **Chookie Hamilton**[7] 111 3-8-6 **77** 6ex.................. DuranFentiman(5) 3 84
(I Semple) *hld up in mid-div: hdwy 2f out: rdn to ld ins fnl f: r.o* **7/2**[1]
141- **2** *hd* **Habalwatan (IRE)**[30] 6880 3-9-4 **84**..............................(b) BrettDoyle 1 91
(C E Brittain) *hld up and bhd: hdwy on outside 2f out: sn rdn: ev ch wl ins fnl f: r.o* **7/2**[1]
13-0 **3** *3* **Leonard Charles**[6] 113 3-8-10 **76**.................................... SebSanders 4 76
(Sir Mark Prescott) *uns rdr and bolted bef s: hld up: hdwy over 5f out: rdn over 3f out: led jst over 1f out tl ins fnl f: no ex* **9/1**
10-2 **4** *1* **New Beginning (IRE)**[7] 111 3-8-11 **77**.......................... PaulHanagan 2 75
(Mrs S Lamyman) *prom: lost pl over 6f out: rdn and sme hdwy over 2f out: kpt on one pce fnl f* **11/1**
132- **5** *shd* **Eau Good**[23] 6948 3-8-13 **84**............................. RussellKennemore(5) 6 82
(M C Chapman) *hld up and bhd: hdwy over 3f out: sn rdn: hung lft over 1f out: one pce* **14/1**
533- **6** *2 ½* **Beech Games**[27] 6933 3-8-9 **75**...................................(b) ChrisCatlin 7 68
(E J O'Neill) *jnd ldr after 2f out: led 4f out: rdn and hdd jst over 1f out: wknd ins fnl f* **7/1**
33-1 **7** *3* **Highland Harvest**[16] 27 3-8-9 **78**................................ MarcHalford(3) 5 64
(D R C Elsworth) *t.k.h in rr: wnt wd and rdn over 2f out: no ch whn hung lft wl over 1f out* **13/2**[3]
1- **8** *2 ½* **Alfredian Park**[21] 6976 3-8-13 **79**..................................... LPKeniry 9 60
(S Kirk) *prom: rdn 3f out: wknd over 1f out* **4/1**[2]
52-5 **9** *¾* **Bold Saxon (IRE)**[7] 111 3-8-5 **71**.................................. HayleyTurner 8 51
(M D I Usher) *led: rdn and hdd 4f out: wknd over 1f out* **33/1**
1m 51.19s (-0.57) **Going Correction** +0.125s/f (Slow) **9** Ran SP% **118.2**
Speed ratings (Par 99):107,106,104,103,103 100,98,96,95
CSF £16.20 CT £102.58 TOTE £5.10: £2.00, £1.90, £4.40; EX 21.10 Trifecta £195.40 Pool: £919.40 - 3.34 winning tickets..
Owner Raeburn Brick Limited **Bred** D And J Raeburn **Trained** Carluke, S Lanarks
FOCUS
Several came into the race in good form in this fair handicap. The progressive front pair came clear and a positive view has been taken of the form.

185 PONTIN'S HOLIDAYS H'CAP 1m 141y(P)
4:35 (4:40) (Class 4) (0-85,84) 4-Y-0+ **£4,857** (£1,445; £722; £360) **Stalls** Low

Form RPR
111- **1** **Atlantic Story (USA)**[49] 6667 5-8-2 **71**.......................... JamesDoyle(3) 8 80
(M W Easterby) *hld up and bhd: stdy hdwy over 3f out: rdn over 2f out: led over 1f out: r.o* **2/1**[1]
006- **2** *½* **Ninth House (USA)**[41] 6772 5-9-1 **81**.....................(bt[1]) GeorgeBaker 7 89
(N P Littmoden) *hld up and bhd: hdwy over 2f out: squeezed through wl over 1f out: sn rdn: ev ch ins fnl f: nt qckn* **9/1**
43-3 **3** *½* **Atlantic Quest (USA)**[9] 96 8-8-12 **81**.......................... AmirQuinn(3) 5 88
(Miss Venetia Williams) *chsd ldr: led over 2f out: rdn and hdd over 1f out: ev ch ins fnl f: nt qckn* **11/2**[2]
111- **4** *1* **Magical Music**[22] 6968 4-9-3 **84**.................................... JimmyQuinn 10 89+
(J Pearce) *sn prom: rdn over 2f out: kpt on one pce fnl f* **10/1**
055- **5** *1 ¼* **Sew'N'So Character (IRE)**[20] 6992 6-9-0 **80**.................. TonyCulhane 3 82
(M Blanshard) *hld up in mid-div: rdn over 3f out: kpt on fnl f: nt rch ldrs* **17/2**
65-6 **6** *nk* **Waterline Twenty (IRE)**[13] 56 4-8-9 **79**........... StephenDonohoe(3) 4 81
(P D Evans) *hld up in mid-div: rdn over 2f out: no real prog fnl f* **20/1**
565- **7** *hd* **Samuel Charles**[19] 6999 9-8-11 **77**............................... PaulHanagan 2 78
(C R Dore) *prom: rdn 2f out: hld whn nt clr run briefly on ins over 1f out: sn wknd* **12/1**
003- **8** *½* **St Petersburg**[20] 6986 7-9-2 **82**.. TPQueally 6 82
(M H Tompkins) *a bhd* **6/1**[3]
211- **9** *shd* **Orpen Wide (IRE)**[23] 6946 5-8-8 **79**...................... RussellKennemore(5) 9 81+
(M C Chapman) *bhd: rdn 5f out: nt clr run ins fnl f: n.d* **14/1**
112- **10** *hd* **Smart Ass (IRE)**[23] 6946 4-8-12 **79**................................ BrettDoyle 1 79
(J S Moore) *led: hdd over 2f out: rdn whn carried sltly lft over 1f out: wknd fnl f* **11/1**
1m 50.46s (-1.30) **Going Correction** +0.125s/f (Slow)
WFA 4 from 5yo+ 1lb **10** Ran SP% **120.1**
Speed ratings (Par 105):110,109,109,108,107 106,106,106,106,105
CSF £21.77 CT £90.01 TOTE £3.30: £1.40, £2.80, £1.90; EX 34.30 Trifecta £325.90 Pool: £775.75 - 1.69 winning tickets..
Owner Matthew Green **Bred** A I Appleton **Trained** Sheriff Hutton, N Yorks
FOCUS
A good handicap on paper with plenty of in-form horses, but a slow pace led to a bunch finish and the race cannot be rated that highly.

186 PHOTO BOOKS FROM BONUSPRINT.COM MAIDEN STKS 1m 141y(P)
5:05 (5:10) (Class 5) 4-Y-0+ **£2,968** (£876; £438) **Stalls** Low

Form RPR
243- **1** **Italian Romance**[28] 6923 4-9-3 70.................................... ShaneKelly 4 71
(J W Unett) *mde all: rdn over 1f out: drew clr fnl f: r.o wl* **4/7**[1]

4-6 **2** *5* **High Ambition**[18] [1] 4-9-3 .... JimmyQuinn 3 60
(P W D'Arcy) *sn chsng wnr: rdn over 2f out: hung lft over 1f out: no imp* **14/1**

0-6 **3** *5* **Shadow Aspect**[7] [106] 4-9-0 .... JerryO'Dwyer(3) 5 50
(Eoin Doyle, Ire) *hld up: hdwy over 3f out: rdn over 2f out: styd on one pce fnl f* **11/1**[3]

00- **4** *12* **Inscribed (IRE)**[32] [6861] 4-8-12 .... PaulHanagan 2 19
(G A Huffer) *prom: rdn over 3f out: sn wknd* **25/1**

5 *5* **Desert Master** 4-9-3 .... GeorgeBaker 7 14
(C F Wall) *s.s: plld hrd: sn prom: rdn 3f out: sn wknd* **5/2**[2]

00-0 **6** *7* **Bond Sea Breeze (IRE)**[15] [36] 4-8-7 31 .... DuranFentiman(5) 6 —
(G R Oldroyd) *mid-div: rdn and lost pl over 5f out: sn bhd* **80/1**

7 *8* **Most Becoming** 4-8-12 .... DeanMernagh 9 —
(S Parr) *a bhd* **50/1**

0- **8** *1 1/4* **Merlins Dreams**[86] [6177] 4-8-10 .... DanielleMcCreery(7) 8 —
(S Parr) *plld hrd: hdwy over 5f out: rdn and wknd over 3f out* **80/1**

9 *18* **Kansas Feather (IRE)**[59] 4-8-9 .... AndrewMullen(3) 1 —
(B S Rothwell) *s.v.s: rdn 4f out: a in rr* **100/1**

1m 50.66s (-1.10) **Going Correction** +0.125s/f (Slow) 9 Ran SP% **116.5**
Speed ratings (Par 103):109,104,100,89,85 78,71,70,54
CSF £11.05 TOTE £1.50: £1.02, £2.50, £2.20; EX 8.50 Trifecta £31.00 Pool: £1,154.42 - 26.41 winning tickets. Place 6 £145.08, Place 5 £11.58.
Owner Nick Hubbard and Partners 2 **Bred** Cheveley Park Stud Ltd **Trained** Preston, Shropshire

FOCUS
A weak maiden in which the winner did not have to run to his handicap best. The time was not bad, but the runner-up seems to limit the form.
Desert Master Official explanation: jockey said gelding ran too freely
Kansas Feather(IRE) Official explanation: jockey said filly missed the break
T/Jkpt: £17,399.20 to a £1 stake. Pool: £24,506.00. 1.00 winning ticket. T/Plt: £162.90 to a £1 stake. Pool: £82,716.55. 370.60 winning tickets. T/Qpdt: £8.20 to a £1 stake. Pool: £8,841.50. 795.90 winning tickets. KH

[127]KEMPTON (A.W) (R-H)
Saturday, January 20

OFFICIAL GOING: Standard
Wind: fresh, half-behind

187 INTERCASINO.CO.UK CLASSIFIED STKS 1m 2f (P)
3:45 (3:46) (Class 7) 4-Y-0+ **£1,365** (£403; £201) **Stalls** High

Form RPR

0-03 **1** **Oasis Sun (IRE)**[10] [92] 4-9-0 47 .... (v) HayleyTurner 12 53
(J R Best) *trckd ldr: led over 2f out: drvn out fnl f* **12/1**

040- **2** *hd* **Indigo Dancer**[47] [6701] 4-8-12 45 .... (b) SteveDrowne 5 51
(C F Wall) *hld up in mid-div: hdwy to trck ldrs 2f out: fin fast fnl f: jst failed* **6/1**[2]

404- **3** *2* **Expected Bonus (USA)**[29] [6904] 8-9-0 42 .... (v[1]) SimonWhitworth 10 47
(Jamie Poulton) *mid-div: rdn over 2f out: rdn to go 2nd appr fnl f tl one pce wl ins* **12/1**

02-6 **4** *1/2* **Simplified**[6] [133] 4-8-9 40 .... JerryO'Dwyer(3) 2 46
(N B King) *racd wd: hld up in rr: hdwy on outside wl over 1f out: styd on ins fnl f* **16/1**

04-0 **5** *hd* **Danelor (IRE)**[13] [64] 9-9-0 40 .... (p) AdrianMcCarthy 4 46
(D Shaw) *mid-div on outside: kpt on ins fnl 2f* **20/1**

23-0 **6** *3/4* **Kilmeena Magic**[6] [133] 5-9-0 45 .... PaulFitzsimons 6 44
(J C Fox) *bhd: rdn 3f out: mde late hdwy: nvr nrr* **10/1**

04-1 **7** *1 1/2* **Sahf London**[6] [133] 4-9-4 45 .... (b[1]) GeorgeBaker 3 47
(G L Moore) *prom: chsd ldrs 2f out tl appr fnl f: wknd ins* **15/8**[1]

350- **8** *2 1/2* **Sriology (IRE)**[39] [6795] 6-9-0 43 .... J-PGuillambert 9 37
(M R Hoad) *in rr: mde sme late hdwy* **8/1**[3]

00/0 **9** *1/2* **Public Eye**[6] [133] 6-8-11 44 .... StephaneBreux(3) 13 36
(L A Dace) *chsd ldr tl rdn and wknd over 2f out* **16/1**

50-3 **10** *nk* **Hill Of Almhuim (IRE)**[14] [51] 4-8-12 45 .... (v) RobbieFitzpatrick 8 35
(Peter Grayson) *hld up in rr: effrt over 2f out: sn btn* **6/1**[2]

0-20 **11** *3* **Retirement**[6] [129] 8-9-0 45 .... SamHitchcott 14 29
(R M Stronge) *trckd ldrs tl rdn and wknd over 2f out* **16/1**

0-30 **12** *4* **Miss Sudbrook (IRE)**[10] [84] 5-9-0 42 .... (v) JimCrowley 1 22
(A W Carroll) *a in rr* **66/1**

000- **13** *1/2* **Zizou (IRE)**[94] [6057] 4-8-5 40 .... (t) RyanBird(7) 11 21
(J J Bridger) *mid-div: rdn over 3f out: sn bhd* **33/1**

0- **14** *6* **Richards Claire (IRE)**[33] [6852] 6-9-0 42 .... (t) LPKeniry 7 9
(D P Keane) *led tl hdd over 2f out: wknd qckly* **66/1**

2m 10.82s (1.82) **Going Correction** +0.075s/f (Slow)
WFA 4 from 5yo+ 2lb 14 Ran SP% **127.3**
Speed ratings (Par 97):95,94,93,92,92 92,90,88,88,88 85,82,82,77
CSF £85.21 TOTE £5.90: £2.10, £2.50, £5.30.
Owner Mrs J Schabacker **Bred** Peter Jones And G G Jones **Trained** Hucking, Kent

FOCUS
A very moderate classified contest. Ordinary form for the grade.

188 PLAY BLACKJACK AT INTERCASINO.CO.UK H'CAP 5f (P)
4:20 (4:20) (Class 5) (0-75,75) 3-Y-O **£2,914** (£867; £433; £216) **Stalls** High

Form RPR

525- **1** **Our Blessing (IRE)**[32] [6866] 3-9-4 75 .... DaneO'Neill 3 83+
(A P Jarvis) *a in tch: drvn out to ld ins fnl f: won gng away* **11/4**[3]

63-1 **2** *2* **Daddy Cool**[17] [17] 3-8-8 68 .... AmirQuinn(3) 5 67
(W G M Turner) *led tl rdn and hdd ins fnl f: kpt on but nt pce of wnr* **9/4**[1]

231- **3** *1/2* **Hereford Boy**[30] [6895] 3-8-13 70 .... RobertHavlin 4 67
(D K Ivory) *chsd ldr: ev ch ent fnl f: kpt on but nt qckn ins* **6/1**

213- **4** *3* **Fluttering Rose**[50] [6659] 3-9-0 71 .... SteveDrowne 2 57
(R Charlton) *t.k.h: in tch tl wknd over 1f out* **5/2**[2]

1-41 **5** *2 1/2* **Grange Lili (IRE)**[9] [103] 3-8-7 64 .... (b) RobbieFitzpatrick 1 41
(Peter Grayson) *racd on outside: rdn and effrt 1/2-way but no ch ins fnl 2f* **10/1**

61.36 secs (0.96) **Going Correction** +0.075s/f (Slow) 5 Ran SP% **109.4**
Speed ratings (Par 97):95,91,91,86,82
CSF £9.19 TOTE £4.40: £1.70, £1.40; EX 26.00.
Owner Geoffrey Bishop and Ann Jarvis **Bred** Mrs N Quinn **Trained** Twyford, Bucks

FOCUS
An interesting sprint handicap. The winner was value for a bit further, with the second and third rated to their maiden form.

189 £600 FREE AT INTERCASINO.CO.UK CLASSIFIED STKS 6f (P)
4:50 (4:50) (Class 7) 4-Y-0+ **£1,365** (£403; £201) **Stalls** High

Form RPR

40-5 **1** **Must Be Keen**[14] [46] 8-9-0 42 .... (v) FergusSweeney 7 49
(Ernst Oertel) *hld up: swtchd lft and hdwy over 1f out: rdn to ld post* **9/1**

00-5 **2** *shd* **Double M**[10] [83] 10-9-0 42 .... (v) RichardThomas 8 52+
(Mrs L Richards) *in tch: led wl over 1f out: 2l clr 1f out: idled whn rdr eased up momentarily nr fin and ct post* **12/1**

000- **3** *1 1/2* **Arfinnit (IRE)**[83] [6233] 6-8-11 42 .... (p) AmirQuinn(3) 3 44
(Mrs A L M King) *hld up: swtchd lft 2f out: hdwy and r.o fnl f: nvr nrr* **33/1**

03-3 **4** *1* **Peggys First**[14] [46] 5-9-0 43 .... PatCosgrave 11 41
(D E Cantillon) *chsd ldrs: rdn 2f out: kpt on one pce fnl f* **9/2**[1]

00-4 **5** *nk* **Christian Bendix**[10] [83] 5-9-0 43 .... (p) JimmyQuinn 1 40
(P Howling) *in tch on outside: rdn over 2f out: r.o one pce fnl f* **9/1**

000/ **6** *nk* **Aphrodelta**[613] [1788] 5-9-0 45 .... LPKeniry 2 39
(P D Cundell) *mid-div: rdn 2f out: kpt on one pce* **14/1**

44-1 **7** *hd* **Teyaar**[10] [83] 11-9-3 48 .... PaulFitzsimons 4 42
(M Wellings) *brought to ins rail s: hld up: effrt 2f out: one pce after* **9/2**[1]

000- **8** *nk* **Dark Moon**[54] [6619] 4-9-0 45 .... AdrianMcCarthy 5 38
(D Shaw) *brought to ins s: kpt on fnl f but n.d* **16/1**

26-3 **9** *3* **Task Complete**[17] [22] 4-9-0 45 .... (b) FrankieMcDonald 6 29
(Jean-Rene Auvray) *brought to ins s: a bhd* **11/2**[2]

05-3 **10** *hd* **A Teen**[10] [83] 9-9-0 43 .... SteveDrowne 10 28
(P Howling) *trckd ldrs tl rdn and wknd ent fnl f* **7/1**[3]

023- **11** *2* **Astorygoeswithit**[23] [6958] 4-9-0 44 .... (b) AdamKirby 9 22
(P S McEntee) *trckd ldrs: ev ch 2f out: wknd over 1f out* **10/1**

300- **12** *6* **Secret Vision (USA)**[33] [6851] 6-9-0 42 .... (p) RobertWinston 12 4
(R M H Cowell) *led tl hdd & wknd qckly wl over 1f out* **20/1**

1m 14.53s (0.83) **Going Correction** +0.075s/f (Slow) 12 Ran SP% **121.3**
Speed ratings (Par 97):97,96,94,93,93 92,92,92,88,87 85,77
CSF £114.96 TOTE £12.80: £3.90, £3.30, £7.30; EX 143.00.
Owner E Oertel **Bred** John James **Trained** Newmarket, Suffolk
■ Stewards' Enquiry : Richard Thomas ten-day ban: in breach of Rule 158, failed to ride out for first place (Jan 31-Feb 9)

FOCUS
A closely-knit banded contest with a controversial finish. Poor form.

190 PLAY ROULETTE AT INTERCASINO.CO.UK H'CAP 6f (P)
5:20 (5:21) (Class 4) (0-80,79) 4-Y-0+ **£4,728** (£1,406; £702; £351) **Stalls** High

Form RPR

31-0 **1** **Lethal**[17] [28] 4-8-13 76 .... JimCrowley 9 91+
(D K Ivory) *mde all: clr whn edgd lft ins fnl f* **7/1**

501- **2** *2 1/2* **Morse (IRE)**[31] [6882] 6-8-12 75 .... DaneO'Neill 6 82
(J A Osborne) *chsd wnr tl appr fnl f: kpt on to regain 2nd on line* **7/1**

312- **3** *shd* **Mandarin Spirit (IRE)**[20] [6999] 7-9-1 78 .... (b) OscarUrbina 11 85
(G C H Chung) *hld up: rdn and hdwy on ins 2f out: chsd wnr appr fnl f tl no ex post* **5/1**[2]

113- **4** *1* **Briannsta (IRE)**[44] [6740] 5-9-2 79 .... AdamKirby 3 83
(C G Cox) *chsd ldrs: rdn 2f out: r.o one pce fnl f* **6/1**[3]

20-0 **5** *1/2* **Hammer Of The Gods (IRE)**[17] [28] 7-8-13 76 .... (bt) BrettDoyle 7 79
(P S McEntee) *slowly away: hld up in mid-div: kpt on one pce fnl f* **16/1**

006- **6** *hd* **Sailor King (IRE)**[30] [6896] 5-9-0 77 .... SteveDrowne 10 79
(D K Ivory) *chsd ldrs: rdn and one pce fnl f* **16/1**

600- **7** *nk* **Garstang**[130] [5263] 4-9-0 77 .... (b) RobbieFitzpatrick 2 78
(Peter Grayson) *swtchd rt to ins s: hld up: mde sme late hdwy* **50/1**

145- **8** *shd* **Sahara Silk (IRE)**[24] [6953] 6-8-9 72 .... (v) AdrianMcCarthy 5 73
(D Shaw) *hld up towards rr: nvr on terms* **25/1**

1-51 **9** *hd* **Hollow Jo**[14] [47] 7-9-1 78 .... NCallan 12 78
(J R Jenkins) *mid-div: rdn 2f out: nvr rchd ldrs* **3/1**[1]

000- **10** *nk* **Effective**[31] [6882] 7-8-9 72 .... LPKeniry 1 71
(A P Jarvis) *chsd eladers on outside: rdn 2f out: sn btn* **33/1**

40-2 **11** *1/2* **Zarzu**[11] [81] 8-9-1 78 .... RobertWinston 8 76
(C R Dore) *badly hmpd after 1f: alwys twrds rr* **7/1**

64-0 **12** *hd* **Councellor (FR)**[15] [44] 5-8-11 77 .... AmirQuinn(3) 4 74
(Stef Liddiard) *racd wd in mid-div: wknd wl over 1f out* **16/1**

1m 12.8s (-0.90) **Going Correction** +0.075s/f (Slow) 12 Ran SP% **119.8**
Speed ratings (Par 105):109,105,105,104,103 103,102,102,102,102 101,101
CSF £55.17 CT £275.33 TOTE £7.50: £2.50, £2.90, £2.00; EX 102.10.
Owner A S Reid **Bred** A S Reid **Trained** Radlett, Herts

FOCUS
A fair, tightly-knit handicap that resulted in a decisive winner. The winner bounced back to form and the placed form was sound.
Zarzu Official explanation: jockey said gelding was denied a clear run

191 BIG JACKPOTS AT INTERCASINO.CO.UK H'CAP 7f (P)
5:50 (5:53) (Class 4) (0-80,78) 4-Y-0+ **£4,728** (£1,054; £1,054; £351) **Stalls** High

Form RPR

32-1 **1** **Ektimaal**[14] [49] 4-8-11 73 .... (t) SteveDrowne 11 88+
(E A L Dunlop) *a.p: swtchd lft 2f out: led appr fnl f: pushed out* **7/2**[1]

23-5 **2** *1/2* **Certain Justice (USA)**[9] [102] 9-8-10 72 .... HayleyTurner 13 82+
(Stef Liddiard) *hld up: hdwy whn swtchd rt 2f out: sn nt clr run and swtchd lft appr fnl f: fin wl to share 2nd post* **16/1**

46-4 **2** *dht* **Will He Wish**[17] [28] 11-9-2 78 .... TonyCulhane 8 84
(S Gollings) *trckd ldrs: kpt on fnl f: nt pce of wnr* **11/1**

00-0 **4** *shd* **Meditation**[17] [28] 5-8-12 77 .... (p) JamesDoyle(3) 12 83
(I A Wood) *led for 3f: ld again wl over 1f out tl hdd appr fnl f: nt qckn ins* **33/1**

00-5 **5** *nk* **Josh**[15] [44] 5-9-2 78 .... NCallan 9 83
(K A Ryan) *mid-div: hdwy over 1f out: r.o fnl f* **10/1**

0-21 **6** *hd* **Sun Catcher (IRE)**[10] [91] 4-9-1 77 .... DaneO'Neill 14 81
(R Hannon) *mid-div: kpt on one pce ins fnl 2f* **4/1**[2]

030- **7** *3/4* **Finsbury**[20] [6999] 4-9-0 76 .... BrettDoyle 2 78
(Miss J Feilden) *hld up: sltly hmpd after 1f: kpt on fnl f: nvr nrr* **8/1**[3]

650- **8** *2* **Mister Benedictine**[24] [5377] 4-8-6 73 .... DJMoran(5) 4 70
(B W Duke) *racd wd in tch: rdn over 2f out: wknd ins fnl f* **16/1**

43-0 **9** *1* **Purus (IRE)**[9] [102] 5-8-12 70 .... JimmyQuinn 3 65
(P Mitchell) *led after 3f: hdd wl over 1f out: wknd fnl f* **16/1**

203- **10** *1/2* **True Magic**[23] [6966] 6-8-5 67 .... ChrisCatlin 10 60
(J D Bethell) *a in rr* **25/1**

030- **11** *2* **Li Shih Chen**[190] [3500] 4-8-10 72 .... LPKeniry 7 60
(A P Jarvis) *chsd ldrs tl wknd over 2f out* **16/1**

60-0 **12** *1/2* **Methusaleh (IRE)**[16] [32] 4-8-2 64 .... AdrianMcCarthy 6 51
(D Shaw) *a in rr* **66/1**

52-4 **13** *10* **Speed Dial Harry (IRE)**[16] [35] 5-8-13 75 .... (v) RobertWinston 1 36
(C R Dore) *a bhd* **16/1**

11-4 **U** **La Colline (GER)**[9] 102 4-8-8 **70**.......................... OscarUrbina 5 —
(W J Haggas) *bhd whn clipped heels and uns rdr after 1f* **4/1**[2]

1m 27.02s (0.22) **Going Correction** +0.075s/f (Slow) **14** Ran SP% **128.4**
Speed ratings (Par 105):101,100,100,100,99 99,98,96,95,94 92,92,80,—
WIN: £4.80. Pl: EL £2.30, WW £3.10, CJ £3.40. EX; EL/WW £39.70, EL/CJ £38.20. CSF: EL/WW £22.88, EL/CJ £32.87. TR: EL/WW/CJ £288.53, EL/CJ/WW £295.73. TOTE £4.80: £2.30.
Owner The Serendipity Partnership **Bred** Whitsbury Manor Stud **Trained** Newmarket, Suffolk

FOCUS
A fair handicap and a progressive winner, but it is not easy to be positive about the bare form because of the bunch finish.
Certain Justice(USA) ◆ Official explanation: jockey said gelding was denied a clear run
Speed Dial Harry(IRE) Official explanation: jockey said gelding lost its action

192 INTERCASINO.CO.UK H'CAP 2m (P)
6:20 (6:21) (Class 4) (0-85,89) 4-Y-0+ **£4,728** (£1,406; £702; £351) **Stalls** High

Form RPR
564- **1** **Linden Lime**[36] 6831 5-8-11 **68**.......................... PaulDoe 9 76
(Jamie Poulton) *hld up: hdwy on outside over 3f out: rdn to ld wl ins fnl f: hld on gamely* **11/1**
225/ **2** *shd* **Tritonville Lodge (IRE)**[199] 5972 5-9-6 **77**.......... GeorgeBaker 1 85
(Miss E C Lavelle) *hld up in rr: hdwy on outside over 2f out: styd on u.p ins fnl 2f: jst failed* **40/1**
12- **3** *nk* **Night Cruise (IRE)**[37] 6825 4-8-12 **76**.............. JimCrowley 2 87+
(J A Osborne) *a in tch: led over 3f out: rdn and hdd wl ins fnl f: lost 2nd nr fin* **12/1**
030- **4** *8* **Follow On**[191] 3446 5-9-3 **74**.......................... DaneO'Neill 8 72
(A P Jarvis) *hld up in tch: hdwy to go 2nd 3f out: rdn and wknd over 1f out* **8/1**[2]
140- **5** *8* **Twill (IRE)**[105] 5811 4-8-12 **76**.......................... BrettDoyle 5 64
(G L Moore) *hld up: rdn 4f out: nvr on terms* **16/1**
05-0 **6** *1 3/4* **Llamadas**[10] 95 5-8-12 **76**.......................... LukeMorris(7) 10 62
(C Roberts) *trckd ldr to 5f out: wknd 3f out* **33/1**
013- **7** *3* **Archduke Ferdinand (FR)**[44] 6381 9-9-6 **80**....... RichardKingscote(3) 3 63
(A King) *hld up: hdwy on outside over 6f out: wknd 3f out* **8/1**[2]
11-1 **8** *19* **Melpomene**[4] 153 4-9-8 **89** 6ex.......................... GregFairley(3) 6 49
(M Johnston) *led tl hdd over 3f out: wknd qckly* **10/11**[1]
412- **9** *6* **Valance (IRE)**[52] 6655 7-10-0 **85**..........................(t) SteveDrowne 7 38
(C R Egerton) *prom tl wknd 5f out* **10/1**[3]
060- **P** **Silvertown**[21] 6321 12-9-6 **77**.......................... RobertWinston 4 —
(L Lungo) *prom tl wknd rapidly 6f out: sn p.u* **16/1**

3m 29.52s (-1.88) **Going Correction** +0.075s/f (Slow)
WFA 4 from 5yo+ 7lb **10** Ran SP% **116.9**
Speed ratings (Par 105):107,106,106,102,98 97,96,86,83,—
CSF £360.22 CT £5253.02 TOTE £13.90: £2.00, £6.20, £2.10; EX 266.40 Place 6 £5807.35, Place 5 £1388.33.
Owner R C Moules **Bred** R C Moules **Trained** Whitcombe, Dorset
■ Stewards' Enquiry : Paul Doe one-day ban: used whip down the shoulder in the forehand position (Jan 31)

FOCUS
A fair staying handicap run at a good gallop. The first three finished clear and the form looks pretty sound.
Llamadas Official explanation: jockey said gelding hung badly right
Melpomene Official explanation: jockey said filly ran flat
Valance(IRE) Official explanation: jockey said gelding had no more to give
Silvertown Official explanation: jockey said gelding was unsuited by the all-weather surface
T/Plt: £2,129.80 to a £1 stake. Pool: £55,143.15. 18.90 winning tickets. T/Qpdt: £255.90 to a £1 stake. Pool: £6,502.90. 18.80 winning tickets. JS

157 LINGFIELD (L-H)
Saturday, January 20

OFFICIAL GOING: Standard
Wind: strong, half-behind

193 TOTEPLACEPOT MAIDEN STKS 1m (P)
1:05 (1:08) (Class 5) 3-Y-0 **£2,914** (£867; £433; £216) **Stalls** High

Form RPR
6- **1** **Noojoom (IRE)**[127] 5344 3-8-12.......................... SteveDrowne 5 79+
(M P Tregoning) *lw: racd in midfield: bustled along 5f out: hdwy on outer 3f out: reminder and flashed tail over 1f out: led ins fnl f: pushed out* **5/2**[1]
3- **2** *1 1/4* **Man Of Vision (USA)**[32] 6867 3-9-3.......................... EdwardCreighton 3 77+
(M R Channon) *chsd ldrs: rdn 2f out: sltly outpcd jst over 1f out: rallied ins fnl f: wnt 2nd nr fin: nt trble wnr* **11/4**[2]
0- **3** *hd* **Hessian (IRE)**[252] 1675 3-8-12.......................... HayleyTurner 2 71
(M L W Bell) *chsd ldr tl rdn to ld 2f out: hdd ins fnl f:no ex* **50/1**
0- **4** *1* **Barkass (UAE)**[82] 6254 3-9-3.......................... DaneO'Neill 9 74
(M P Tregoning) *w'like: unf: bit bkwd: t.k.h: chsd ldrs: rdn and ev ch over 2f out: kpt on same pce ins fnl f* **9/1**
3 **5** *3* **Ridgewell (USA)**[12] 73 3-8-12.......................... RobertHavlin 4 62
(B J Meehan) *leggy: unf: chsd ldrs on inner: rdn 2f out: wknd ins fnl f* **8/1**
3-4 **6** *3* **Fowey (USA)**[8] 106 3-8-12.......................... SebSanders 11 55
(Sir Mark Prescott) *rr: in tch: rdn over 3f out: outpcd over 2f out: no ch after* **16/1**
0- **7** *3 1/2* **Marju's Gold**[24] 6950 3-9-3.......................... ChrisCatlin 10 52
(E J O'Neill) *leggy: stdd s: hld up bhd: n.d* **33/1**
52- **8** *1/2* **Vincennes**[31] 6879 3-8-12.......................... NCallan 1 46
(M A Jarvis) *t.k.h: led tl rdn and hdd 2f out: wknd qckly over 1f out* **7/2**[3]
9 *1 1/2* **Tia Jade** 3-9-1 ow3.......................... AntonyProcter 7 45
(M J Gingell) *w'like: in tch in midfield: rdn over 2f out: sn struggling* **80/1**
10 *7* **Termsandconditions (IRE)** 3-8-12.......................... TonyCulhane 12 26
(W J Haggas) *neat: leggy: sn outpcd and detached in last: wl bhd last 3f: t.o* **25/1**
56- **11** *2* **Roca Redonda (IRE)**[129] 5296 3-8-12.......................... ShaneKelly 6 22
(M J Wallace) *leggy: bit bkwd: v.s.a a bhd: wl bhd last 3f: t.o* **16/1**

1m 38.13s (-1.30) **Going Correction** -0.175s/f (Stan) **11** Ran SP% **120.3**
Speed ratings (Par 97):99,97,97,96,93 90,87,86,85,78 76
CSF £9.53 TOTE £3.50: £1.30, £2.20, £9.50; EX 13.40 Trifecta £220.60 Part won. Pool: £310.81 - 0.61 winning tickets..
Owner Sheikh Ahmed Al Maktoum **Bred** Darley **Trained** Lambourn, Berks

FOCUS
A good maiden for the time of year and it has been rated positively. The winner looked value for a bit more, and the second was staying on nicely.
Vincennes Official explanation: vet said filly lost a front shoe
Roca Redonda(IRE) Official explanation: jockey said filly was slowly away

194 TOTECOURSE TO COURSE (S) STKS 6f (P)
1:35 (1:37) (Class 6) 3-Y-0 **£2,184** (£644; £322) **Stalls** Low

Form RPR
45- **1** **River Prince**[265] 1309 3-8-5.......................... JackDean(7) 2 63
(W G M Turner) *racd in midfield: hdwy on inner over 2f out: rdn to ld jst over 1f out: rdn out* **8/1**
000- **2** *2* **Burningfold Babe**[44] 6736 3-8-7 **51**.......................... AdrianMcCarthy 8 52
(P Winkworth) *bit bkwd: chsd ldrs: rdn over 2f out: kpt on u.p: wnt 2nd ins fnl f: no imp on wnr* **7/1**
020- **3** *1 1/4* **O'Dwyer (IRE)**[24] 6945 3-8-12 **53**..........................(p) PaulMulrennan 1 53
(A D Brown) *led: rdn and edgd rt wl over 1f out: hdd jst over 1f out: kpt on same pce* **11/2**
3-6 **4** *hd* **Show Business (IRE)**[9] 99 3-8-12..........................(bt[1]) SebSanders 5 52
(Sir Mark Prescott) *s.i.s: sn rdn and looked reluctant in rr: c v bnd over 2f out: styd on fnl f: nvr nrr* **7/2**[2]
3-03 **5** *hd* **Splendidio**[10] 90 3-8-7 **52**.......................... ChrisCatlin 9 47
(D K Ivory) *hld up in rr: rdn and effrt wl over 1f out: kpt on steadily fnl f: nt rch ldrs* **10/3**[1]
00-5 **6** *2 1/2* **Elizabeth Garrett**[9] 103 3-8-7 **40**..........................(v[1]) BrettDoyle 4 39
(R M H Cowell) *wnt rt s: t.k.h: chsd ldrs tl hung rt wl over 1f out: kpt on same pce* **16/1**
0-06 **7** *1/2* **Childish Thoughts**[6] 128 3-8-7 **45**.......................... CatherineGannon 6 38
(Mrs Norma Pook) *stdd s: hld up in rr: rdn over 2f out: no imp* **12/1**
30-5 **8** *3/4* **Baytown Paikea**[14] 54 3-8-12 **52**.......................... NCallan 7 41
(P S McEntee) *chsd ldr: rdn over 2f out: wknd over 1f out* **9/2**[3]

1m 12.52s (-0.29) **Going Correction** -0.175s/f (Stan) **8** Ran SP% **116.1**
Speed ratings (Par 95):94,91,89,89,89 85,85,84
CSF £63.12 TOTE £7.30: £1.40, £1.60, £3.00; EX 53.50 Trifecta £419.10 Part won. Pool: £590.40 - 0.10 winning tickets..The winner was sold to A Haynes for 6,800gns.
Owner Mrs A F Horsington **Bred** Mrs A F Horsington **Trained** Sigwells, Somerset

FOCUS
A seller to treat with caution, with the second having shown little on her last three starts and the third hit and miss.
Elizabeth Garrett Official explanation: jockey said filly hung right

195 TOTESCOOP6 H'CAP 1m 4f (P)
2:05 (2:06) (Class 5) (0-70,70) 4-Y-0+ **£2,914** (£867; £433; £216) **Stalls** Low

Form RPR
15-0 **1** **Wait For The Will (USA)**[17] 29 11-8-13 **63**.........(b) FergusSweeney 5 72
(G L Moore) *hld up in midfield: hdwy over 3f out: trckd ldrs gng wl 2f out: rdn to ld jst over 1f out: r.o wl* **16/1**
0-46 **2** *3/4* **Dovedon Hero**[10] 88 7-8-13 **63**..........................(b) SebSanders 8 71
(P J McBride) *hld up towards rr: plld out and hdwy over 2f out: rdn and ev ch over 1f out: unable qck fnl f* **9/1**
00-1 **3** *1 1/2* **Lorikeet**[17] 29 8-8-9 **62**.......................... JamesDoyle(3) 9 68
(Noel T Chance) *lw: w.w in tch: hdwy 4f out: rdn to ld 2f out: hdd jst over 1f out: kpt on same pce* **5/1**[2]
012- **4** *shd* **Generous Lad (IRE)**[31] 6878 4-8-12 **66**..........................(p) DaneO'Neill 3 75+
(A B Haynes) *hld up in midfield: n.m.r and lost pl over 2f out: rallied over 1f out: kpt on steadily fnl f: nt rch ldrs* **4/1**[1]
616- **5** *1* **Burgundy**[31] 6878 10-9-6 **70**..........................(b) GeorgeBaker 14 74
(P Mitchell) *stdd s and hld up bhd: rdn and hdwy on outer 2f out: no imp ins fnl f* **14/1**
/1-0 **6** *1/2* **Jack Rolfe**[17] 30 5-9-1 **65**.......................... BrettDoyle 2 68
(G L Moore) *led for 1f: chsd ldrs rdn over 2f out: onepced and no hdwy 1f out* **33/1**
003- **7** *1/2* **Competitor**[21] 6982 6-8-6 **56** oh1..........................(vt) ChrisCatlin 12 58
(J Akehurst) *chsd ldr after 2f tl rdn to ld over 2f out: sn hdd: wknd ins fnl f* **16/1**
01-1 **8** *1* **Street Life (IRE)**[10] 89 9-9-3 **67**.......................... TonyCulhane 13 68
(W J Musson) *lw: hld up in rr on outer: rdn and effrt over 2f out: kpt on fnl f: nvr nrr* **4/1**[1]
01-4 **9** *nk* **Blackmail (USA)**[7] 115 9-8-8 **58**.......................... JoeFanning 11 58+
(P Mitchell) *chsd ldrs: rdn over 2f out: wkng whn short of room wl over 2f out: no ch after* **20/1**
403- **10** *1/2* **Russian Dream (IRE)**[30] 6893 4-8-11 **65**.......................... AdamKirby 6 64
(W R Swinburn) *hld up in rr: rdn over 2f out: styd on u.p over 1f out: nvr trbld ldrs* **14/1**
325- **11** *nk* **Birthday Star (IRE)**[110] 5725 5-8-9 **62**.......... StephenDonohoe(3) 4 61
(W J Musson) *racd in midfield tl lost pl over 4f out: n.d last 3f* **10/1**
64-2 **12** *1 1/2* **Ariodante**[17] 29 5-9-0 **64**.......................... ShaneKelly 7 60
(J M P Eustace) *prom: led after 1f tl after 2f: chsd ldrs tl rdn and wknd jst over 2f out* **7/1**[3]
0/5- **13** *4* **Music Celebre (IRE)**[23] 6968 7-9-3 **67**.......................... LPKeniry 1 57
(S Curran) *hld up towards rr: rdn 3f out: sn struggling* **66/1**
44-0 **14** *1 1/2* **Executive Paddy (IRE)**[10] 89 8-8-12 **62**.......................... LeeEnstone 10 50
(I A Wood) *led to s: plld hrd: led after 2f: clr over 4f out: rdn and hdd over 2f out: sn wknd* **33/1**

2m 33.68s (-0.71) **Going Correction** -0.175s/f (Stan)
WFA 4 from 5yo+ 4lb **14** Ran SP% **125.5**
Speed ratings (Par 103):95,94,93,93,92 92,92,91,91,90 90,89,87,86
CSF £154.96 CT £845.81 TOTE £22.50: £4.80, £3.20, £1.70; EX 157.00 TRIFECTA Not won..
Owner Rdm Racing **Bred** Paul Mellon **Trained** Woodingdean, E Sussex

FOCUS
The early pace was just steady, but the form has been rated a bit more positively than it might have been, as the first three were all on decent marks..
Blackmail(USA) Official explanation: vet said gelding was struck into

196 TOTEEXACTA H'CAP 1m 2f (P)
2:40 (2:40) (Class 5) (0-75,75) 3-Y-0 **£3,238** (£963; £481; £240) **Stalls** Low

Form RPR
040- **1** **Daylami Dreams**[127] 5339 3-8-11 **68**.......................... JohnEgan 1 76+
(J S Moore) *h.d.w: w.w in tch: nt clr run over 2f out: hdwy to chse ldr 2f out: sn led and in command: flashed tail but r.o wl: comf* **9/1**
5-36 **2** *2* **Beau Sancy**[7] 122 3-7-11 **61**.......................... LukeMorris(7) 5 65
(R A Harris) *t.k.h early: hld up in last: reminder 5f out: styd on u.p over 1f out: wnt 2nd wl ins fnl f: no ch wnr* **8/1**
14-1 **3** *nk* **Pret A Porter (UAE)**[14] 58 3-8-9 **69**..........(b) StephenDonohoe(3) 2 72
(P D Evans) *led tl over 4f out: rdn 3f out: chsd wnr over 1f out: no imp: lost 2nd wl ins fnl f* **7/1**[3]
005- **4** *1 1/2* **Professor Twinkle**[110] 5730 3-8-11 **68**.......................... PaulDoe 3 68
(W J Knight) *t.k.h: w.w in tch: rdn over 2f out: hung lft over 1f out: plld out ins fnl f: no imp* **10/1**

52-0 **5** 2 **Don't Desert Me (IRE)**[3] [157] 3-8-4 **64**..........(b[1]) RichardKingscote(3) 4 60
(R Charlton) *t.k.h: chsd ldr tl led over 4f out: rdn and hdd over 1f out: sn btn* **12/1**

634- **6** 1 3/4 **Silca Key**[100] [5916] 3-9-3 **74**.. EdwardCreighton 6 67
(M R Channon) *w.w in tch: rdn and hdwy on outer 3f out: btn over 1f ot* **11/4**[2]

50-1 **7** 8 **Tasweet (IRE)**[7] [116] 3-9-4 **75**.......................................(v) JoeFanning 7 53
(T G Mills) *t.k.h: hld up in last pair early: hdwy to chse ldrs on outer 7f out: rdn over 2f out: wknd wl over 1f out* **7/4**[1]

2m 5.89s (-1.90) **Going Correction** -0.175s/f (Stan) 7 Ran SP% **113.4**
Speed ratings (Par 97):100,98,98,96,95 93,87
CSF £74.81 TOTE £10.20: £3.70, £4.30; EX 72.00.
Owner Mrs Fitri Hay **Bred** Elsdon Farms **Trained** Upper Lambourn, Berks

FOCUS
Not that strong a race, but the form makes sense through the second and third.
Tasweet(IRE) Official explanation: trainer's rep had no explanation for the poor form shown

197 TOTESPORT 0800 221 221 H'CAP 1m (P)
3:10 (3:10) (Class 2) (0-100,106) 4-Y-O+
£9,971 (£2,985; £1,492; £747; £372; £187) **Stalls** High

Form RPR
2-22 **1** **Red Spell (IRE)**[7] [119] 6-9-3 **101**...................................... DaneO'Neill 3 109+
(R Hannon) *trckd ldrs on inner: hdwy 2f out: rdn to ld ins fnl f: r.o wl* **11/2**[3]

03-6 **2** 1 **Party Boss**[7] [118] 5-8-11 **95** ow1.................................. SebSanders 5 101
(C E Brittain) *lw: sn led: kicked clr jst over 2f out: hdd ins fnl f: kpt on same pce* **14/1**

311- **3** hd **Vortex**[29] [6914] 8-9-8 **106**..(t) NCallan 7 112
(Miss Gay Kelleway) *b: b.hind: hld up in rr: hdwy on inner jst over 2f out: chsd ldrs over 1f out: no imp wl ins fnl f* **11/1**

012- **4** 1 **Marajaa (IRE)**[48] [6692] 5-8-4 **88**.. JoeFanning 4 97+
(W J Musson) *hld up in midfield: n.m.r and lost pl over 2f out: nt clr run briefly over 1f out: shkn up and r.o ins last: nt rch ldrs* **3/1**[1]

53-1 **5** nk **Fajr (IRE)**[14] [56] 5-8-3 **87**.. JimmyQuinn 8 90
(Miss Gay Kelleway) *b: b.hind: t.k.h: hld up towards rr: rdn and hdwy to chse ldrs 2f out: no imp ins fnl f* **4/1**[2]

44-6 **6** hd **Kindlelight Debut**[7] [119] 7-8-8 **95**.............................. JamesDoyle(3) 6 97
(N P Littmoden) *bhd and niggled along over 4f out: r.o u.p ins fnl f: nvr nrr* **25/1**

424- **7** 1/2 **Wavertree Warrior (IRE)**[29] [6915] 5-7-12 **87**............ DuranFentiman(5) 2 88
(N P Littmoden) *chsd ldrs: wnt 2nd 3f out tl over 1f out: wknd ins fnl f* **10/1**

21-5 **8** 3 1/2 **Happy As Larry (USA)**[7] [119] 5-8-2 **86**........................... ChrisCatlin 9 79
(T J Pitt) *b.hind: in tch on outer: rdn and effrt over 2f out: no imp last 2f* **4/1**[2]

5 **9** 5 **Fantoche (BRZ)**[15] [43] 5-8-6 **90**...................................(v) ShaneKelly 10 71
(M J Wallace) *lw: chsd ldrs: rdn wl over 2f out: wknd wl over 1f out: eased ins fnl f* **20/1**

10 19 **General Knowledge (USA)**[22] 4-8-10 **94**................. FergusSweeney 1 32
(B G Powell) *s.i.s: sn chsng ldr: rdn and dropped out qckly 3f out: t.o and eased 1f out* **14/1**

1m 35.86s (-3.57) **Going Correction** -0.175s/f (Stan) course record 10 Ran SP% **119.8**
Speed ratings (Par 109):110,109,108,107,107 107,106,103,98,79
CSF £81.53 CT £828.84 TOTE £5.80: £2.00, £3.80, £3.20; EX 55.30 Trifecta £723.70 Pool: £17,646.19 - 17.31 winning tickets.
Owner Mrs John Lee **Bred** Tom Darcy And Vincent McCarthy **Trained** East Everleigh, Wilts

FOCUS
A very good handicap and the form looks sound.

NOTEBOOK
Red Spell(IRE) had racked up four seconds on the bounce in similar events coming into this, but he had not been doing a great deal wrong and ended that frustrating run in emphatic fashion. He is a smart performer on Polytrack and must be kept on the right side of.
Party Boss had not been at his best lately, but he is a dual Listed winner on Lingfield's Polytrack and bounced right back to form with a decent effort in second. This proves he is still capable of running to a smart level on sand and there could be even better to come. (op 16-1)
Vortex had Red Spell behind when winning conditions races round here on his last couple of starts but, although unable to confirm form with that rival, he did not do a great deal wrong. This was a decent effort off top weight and he is consistently running to a very smart level of form. (op 10-1)
Marajaa(IRE) ◆, one place in front of Vortex when beaten just a short-head by the Group-class Areyoutalkingtome over 7f here last time, looked an unlucky loser. Having been short of room and lost his place rounding the final bend, he was denied a run in the straight and basically got in the clear too late. He is most progressive and looks capable of gaining compensation. (tchd 10-3 and 7-2 in a place)
Fajr(IRE) was unable to defy a 5lb higher than when winning over course and distance on his previous start, but this was a very hot race.
Kindlelight Debut ran on when it was all too late and was again a touch below her best.
Happy As Larry(USA) was not quite at his best and a recent busy period may just have caught up with him.

198 TOTESPORT.COM H'CAP 6f (P)
3:40 (3:42) (Class 2) (0-100,100) 4-Y-O+
£9,971 (£2,985; £1,492; £747; £372; £187) **Stalls** Low

Form RPR
2-14 **1** **Qadar (IRE)**[7] [118] 5-9-2 **100**..(b[1]) NCallan 10 109
(N P Littmoden) *s.i.s: dropped in and hld up towards rr: hdwy 2f out: plld rt over 1f out: str run fnl f to ld on post* **9/2**[2]

15-0 **2** shd **Maltese Falcon**[19] [5] 7-8-13 **97**.............................(t) NelsonDeSouza 5 106
(P F I Cole) *lw: led: 2 l clr and rdn over 1f out: kpt on: ct on post* **11/2**[3]

152- **3** shd **Bonus (IRE)**[202] [3125] 7-9-0 **98**.. BrettDoyle 4 107
(G A Butler) *lw: w.w in midfield: hdwy over 2f out: wnt 2nd jst ins fnl f: jnd ldr wl ins fnl f: nt qckn fnl strides* **7/2**[1]

21-2 **4** 1 1/4 **Buy On The Red**[15] [44] 6-8-3 **87**..................................(p) ChrisCatlin 8 92
(W R Muir) *chsd ldrs: rdn and effrt 2f out: chsd ldr briefly 1f out: onepced ins fnl f* **7/1**

000- **5** 1 **Ajigolo**[158] [4461] 4-8-12 **96**.. EdwardCreighton 3 98
(M R Channon) *prom: chsd ldr wl over 3f out: rdn and no imp wl over 1f out: wknd ins fnl f* **12/1**

154- **6** 2 1/2 **Saviours Spirit**[50] [6660] 6-7-13 **88**.............................. DuranFentiman(5) 2 83
(T G Mills) *hld up in midfield on inner: nt clr run over 2f out: rdn and effrt over 1f out: no real hdwy* **15/2**

302- **7** 3/4 **Secret Night**[29] [6915] 4-8-2 **86** oh1....................................... JimmyQuinn 9 78
(J A R Toller) *hld up: hdwy on outer over 2f out: no imp over 1f out* **8/1**

000- **8** 1 3/4 **Moayed**[212] [2776] 8-8-8 **95**..(bt) JamesDoyle(3) 1 82
(N P Littmoden) *outpcd in last pair: rdn and effrt over 2f out: nvr trbld ldrs* **12/1**

21-0 **9** 2 1/2 **Quiet Times (IRE)**[11] [81] 8-8-2 **86** oh1.................(b) CatherineGannon 6 66
(K A Ryan) *v.s.a: a bhd: n.d* **20/1**

516/ **10** 2 **Royal Engineer**[595] [2292] 4-7-13 **86** oh1.......................... AndrewElliott(3) 7 60
(M Johnston) *chsd ldr tl over 3f out: sn rdn: wknd over 2f out* **14/1**

69.86 secs (-2.95) **Going Correction** -0.175s/f (Stan) course record **10** Ran SP% **118.0**
Speed ratings (Par 109):112,111,111,110,108 105,104,102,98,96
CSF £29.93 CT £99.38 TOTE £4.90: £1.80, £2.60, £1.80; EX 30.90 Trifecta £76.40 Pool: £1,419.97 - 13.19 winning tickets..
Owner Nigel Shields **Bred** Martin Francis **Trained** Newmarket, Suffolk
■ Stewards' Enquiry : N Callan one-day ban: used whip with excessive frequency (Jan 31)

FOCUS
A very good sprint and strong handicap form. The first, second and fourth all boasted solid recent form, and the winner put up a new personal best in the blinkers.

NOTEBOOK
Qadar(IRE) took well to the first-time blinkers and overcame a tricky draw to narrowly gain his second win from his last three starts. He is a smart sort when everything drops right and he should continue to run well in similar events. (op 6-1)
Maltese Falcon had no chance after missing the kick over 5f at Southwell on his previous start but, back up in trip and returned to Polytrack, he broke much better this time and was just caught. He may be seven now, but he clearly still has plenty to offer in decent company. (op 13-2)
Bonus(IRE) ◆ ran a stormer off the back of a 202-day break, producing an effort not far off the pick of his form. There should be even more to come, as this was his first run in 202 days, and he should win next time, so long as he avoids Areyoutalkingtome. (op 5-2)
Buy On The Red had rediscovered some of his best form in recent starts and this was another cracking effort against some very useful sprinters. (op 13-2)
Ajigolo probably paid the price for a fine juvenile campaign when struggling for form last year but, making his debut on Polytrack off the back of a 158-day break, he offered some promise.
Saviours Spirit was a few pounds below his best. (op 7-1 tchd 8-1)
Moayed should be sharper for this first run in 212 days. (op 14-1)
Royal Engineer looked very fit for his first run in 595 days, but this company would have been plenty hot enough for a horse having just his fourth-career start. (tchd 16-1)

199 TOTE TEXT BETTING 60021 H'CAP 6f (P)
4:15 (4:15) (Class 4) (0-85,78) 3-Y-O **£4,857** (£1,445; £722; £360) **Stalls** Low

Form RPR
112- **1** **Shustraya**[21] [6989] 3-9-1 **77**.. SebSanders 5 85+
(P J Makin) *chsd ldr tl rdn to ld jst over 2f out: clr over 1f out: r.o strly* **15/8**[1]

124- **2** 1 1/2 **Love In May (IRE)**[22] [6978] 3-9-2 **78**................................ JohnEgan 2 77
(J S Moore) *chsd ldrs: rdn wl over 2f out: swtchd lft over 1f out: wnt 2nd ins fnl f: no real imp* **13/2**

133- **3** nk **Mr Loire**[36] [6834] 3-8-7 **72**.............................. RichardKingscote(3) 6 70
(R Charlton) *b.hind: lw: s.i.s: bhd: rdn over 2f out: c wd over 1f out: r.o wl ins fnl f: nvr nrr* **5/1**[3]

030- **4** 1/2 **Naayla (IRE)**[104] [5829] 3-9-1 **77**..(b) NCallan 3 74
(B J Meehan) *lw: t.k.h: hld up in tch: hdwy and rdn jst over 2f out: kpt on same pce over 1f out* **8/1**

341- **5** 3/4 **Rebel Duke (IRE)**[22] [6975] 3-9-0 **76**................................. TPQueally 4 70
(M G Quinlan) *led: hdd jst over 2f out: edgd rt wl over 1f out: fdd wl ins fnl f* **3/1**[2]

406- **6** 1/2 **Proper (IRE)**[167] [4170] 3-8-9 **71**.. ChrisCatlin 1 64
(M R Channon) *chsd ldrs tl rdn and outpcd wl over 2f out: kpt on ins fnl f but nt trble ldrs* **9/1**

1m 12.68s (-0.13) **Going Correction** -0.175s/f (Stan) 6 Ran SP% **110.9**
Speed ratings (Par 99):93,91,90,89,88 88
CSF £14.08 TOTE £3.10: £1.80, £2.60; EX 11.30 Place 6 £2,287.06, Place 5 £1,324.60.
Owner Four Leaf Clover **Bred** Millsec Limited **Trained** Ogbourne Maisey, Wilts

FOCUS
Not a particularly strong sprint handicap, but the winner is improving still and was value for a bit more than the bare form.
Mr Loire Official explanation: jockey said gelding hung right in home straight
Rebel Duke(IRE) Official explanation: jockey said colt hung right in home straight
T/Plt: £3,673.00 to a £1 stake. Pool: £78,744.90. 15.65 winning tickets. T/Qpdt: £270.70 to a £1 stake. Pool: £5,013.30. 13.70 winning tickets. SP

[179]WOLVERHAMPTON (A.W) (L-H)
Sunday, January 21

OFFICIAL GOING: Standard
Wind: Fresh, behind. Weather: Fine.

200 PONTIN'S HOLIDAYS H'CAP (DIV I) 1m 141y(P)
1:20 (1:20) (Class 6) (0-60,62) 4-Y-O+ **£1,365** (£403; £201) **Stalls** Low

Form RPR
215- **1** **Picador**[44] [6743] 4-8-13 **57**.. SebSanders 1 75+
(Sir Mark Prescott) *mde virtually all: rdn 2f out: r.o wl* **2/1**[1]

25-2 **2** 3 1/2 **Golden Square**[7] [131] 5-8-10 **56**.................................... JamesDoyle(3) 7 62
(A W Carroll) *chsd wnr: rdn over 3f out: lost 2nd 2f out: rallying whn hung lft 1f out: no imp* **16/1**

1-05 **3** 3/4 **Golden Spectrum (IRE)**[8] [124] 8-8-9 **57**..........(b) MichaelJStainton(5) 8 61
(R A Harris) *t.k.h: a.p: rdn to chse wnr 2f out to 1f out: one pce* **20/1**

65-0 **4** 1/2 **They All Laughed**[7] [130] 4-9-1 **59**..................................... ChrisCatlin 3 62
(P W Hiatt) *hld up and bhd: rdn 3f out: hdwy on outside over 1f out: r.o ins fnl f: nrst fin* **33/1**

0-25 **5** 1 1/4 **Parkview Love (USA)**[5] [151] 6-9-5 **62**..........................(v) DaneO'Neill 11 62
(D Shaw) *hld up in mid-div: hdwy on ins 3f out: sn rdn: one pce fnl 2f* **12/1**

00-2 **6** 1 1/4 **Tour D'Amour (IRE)**[12] [75] 4-9-2 **60**............................ PaulMulrennan 12 58
(R Craggs) *hld up in tch: rdn over 2f out: no hdwy* **16/1**

01-1 **7** 2 **Freda's Choice (IRE)**[11] [94] 4-8-2 **51**......................(b) JamieJones(5) 5 45
(Patrick Morris, Ire) *hld up in mid-div: rdn over 2f out: no hdwy* **14/1**

0-02 **8** nk **Roman Boy (ARG)**[7] [130] 8-8-10 **53**............................... HayleyTurner 6 46
(Stef Liddiard) *stdd into mid-div after 1f: rdn over 3f out: no imp* **5/2**[2]

03-5 **9** 1/2 **Sir Bond (IRE)**[9] [110] 6-8-11 **59**..............................(p) DuranFentiman(5) 2 51
(G R Oldroyd) *s.i.s: hld up and bhd: hdwy on ins whn nt clr run over 2f out: n.d after* **10/3**[3]

630/ **10** 5 **Flower Haven**[310] [5654] 5-8-5 **55**.................................. WilliamBuick(7) 9 36
(M J Gingell) *s.i.s: a bhd* **50/1**

25-0 **11** 14 **Christmas Truce (IRE)**[8] [115] 8-8-6 **52**...............(p) JerryO'Dwyer(3) 13 4
(Ms J S Doyle) *s.i.s: a bhd* **50/1**

The Form Book, Raceform Ltd, Compton, RG20 6NL

04/6 **12** *2* **Smart Pick**[15] [49] 4-8-4 **55**.. ChrisGlenister(7) 4 3
(J R Holt) *a bhd* **100/1**
1m 49.91s (-1.85) **Going Correction** -0.075s/f (Stan)
WFA 4 from 5yo+ 1lb **12** Ran SP% **123.7**
Speed ratings (Par 101):105,101,101,100,99 98,96,96,96,91 79,77
CSF £37.54 CT £540.65 TOTE £3.10: £1.90, £3.70, £5.30; EX 34.10 Trifecta £120.80 Part won. Pool £170.23. - 0.10 winning units..
Owner The Green Door Partnership **Bred** Cheveley Park Stud Ltd **Trained** Newmarket, Suffolk
FOCUS
Moderate handicap form, but the winner looks progressive and is clearly well handicapped at present. Those who were held up struggled to get involved.

201 PONTINS.COM CLASSIFIED STKS 5f 20y(P)
1:50 (1:50) (Class 7) 4-Y-0+ **£1,911** (£564; £282) **Stalls** Low

Form RPR
040- **1** **Elvina**[105] [5834] 6-9-0 45.. DaneO'Neill 8 54
(A G Newcombe) *w ldr: rdn to ld jst over 1f out: r.o* **11/2**[3]
2-04 **2** *½* **El Potro**[6] [135] 5-9-0 45.. GrahamGibbons 13 52
(J R Holt) *chsd ldrs: rdn wl over 1f out: r.o ins fnl f: nt rch wnr* **15/2**
00-4 **3** *1 ¼* **Lady Hopeful (IRE)**[6] [137] 5-9-0 45......................(b) RobbieFitzpatrick 3 48
(Peter Grayson) *s.i.s: rdn whn swtchd rt and hdwy over 1f out: r.o wl towards fin* **9/2**[2]
00/4 **4** *nk* **Pulse**[15] [46] 9-9-0 45..(p) PaulFitzsimons 4 47
(Miss J R Tooth) *mid-div: rdn and hdwy on ins wl over 1f out: r.o one pce fnl f* **12/1**
0-04 **5** *hd* **Mind That Fox**[8] [125] 5-9-0 45..(b¹) ChrisCatlin 1 46
(T Wall) *led: rdn and hdd jst over 1f out: no ex towards fin* **16/1**
200- **6** *hd* **Flying Tackle**[62] [6541] 9-9-0 45..(v) DanielTudhope 6 45
(I W McInnes) *hld up towards rr: rdn and hdwy 2f out: edgd lft ins fnl f: kpt on towards fin* **9/1**
05-0 **7** *1* **Comic Tales**[8] [125] 6-9-0 45.. SilvestreDeSousa 5 42
(M Mullineaux) *s.i.s: rdn over 1f out: kpt on fnl f: nvr trbld ldrs* **50/1**
03-2 **8** *hd* **Beverley Beau**[11] [83] 5-8-7 45.. KristinStubbs(7) 12 41
(Mrs L Stubbs) *wnt lft s: towards rr: rdn over 2f out: sme late prog* **13/2**
04-2 **9** *nk* **Katie Killane**[15] [46] 5-9-0 45..(v) AdamKirby 2 40
(M Wellings) *prom: rdn over 2f out: wknd 1f out: eased whn btn cl home* **7/2**[1]
0/50 **10** *1 ½* **Ela Figura**[6] [135] 7-8-11 45.. JamesDoyle(3) 7 34
(A W Carroll) *a bhd* **33/1**
00-5 **11** *shd* **She's Our Beauty (IRE)**[10] [97] 4-8-9 45............(v) DuranFentiman(5) 9 34
(S T Mason) *s.i.s: t.k.h: sn chsng ldrs: rdn 2f out: wknd over 1f out* **25/1**
005- **12** *6* **White Ledger (IRE)**[30] [6922] 8-9-0 45........................(b¹) JimmyQuinn 10 12
(R E Peacock) *bhd fnl 3f* **14/1**
600- **13** *10* **All About Him (USA)**[146] [4872] 4-9-0 45........................ HayleyTurner 11 —
(N I M Rossiter) *s.i.s: a bhd* **80/1**
62.99 secs (0.17) **Going Correction** -0.075s/f (Stan) **13** Ran SP% **121.1**
Speed ratings (Par 97):95,94,92,91,91 91,89,89,88,86 86,76,60
CSF £46.05 TOTE £6.50: £2.50, £2.70, £1.50; EX 52.80 Trifecta £138.60 Part won. Pool £195.34. - 0.43 winning units..
Owner Capel, Eagle & Newcombe **Bred** M Patel And G I Thomas **Trained** Yarnscombe, Devon
FOCUS
A banded race in all but name in which the pace horses dominated once more. Straightforward form for the grade.

202 GO PONTIN'S H'CAP 5f 216y(P)
2:20 (2:21) (Class 6) (0-60,58) 3-Y-0 **£2,388** (£705; £352) **Stalls** Low

Form RPR
4-32 **1** **Bentley**[10] [103] 3-8-12 **52**..(v) DaneO'Neill 2 56
(D Shaw) *led: rdn and hdd over 2f out: sn led again: r.o* **5/2**[1]
433- **2** *1* **Show Trial (IRE)**[31] [6900] 3-9-4 **58**.. AdamKirby 6 59
(D J S Ffrench Davis) *a.p: rdn 2f out: r.o to take 2nd post* **10/3**[2]
05-0 **3** *shd* **Mister Always**[18] [25] 3-8-5 **48**..(tp) JamesDoyle(3) 9 49
(Ms J S Doyle) *chsd wnr: rdn and led briefly over 2f out: no ex towards fin* **20/1**
060- **4** *3 ½* **Flamestone**[146] [4887] 3-9-0 **54**.. JimmyQuinn 4 45
(J D Bethell) *hld up in mid-div: lost pl over 3f out: sn rdn: kpt on ins fnl f* **8/1**
206- **5** *½* **Muncaster Castle (IRE)**[97] [6007] 3-8-11 **51**................ J-PGuillambert 8 40
(R F Fisher) *hdwy on outside over 3f out: sn rdn: wknd 2f out* **9/2**[3]
60-5 **6** *1 ¼* **Wiseton Dancer (IRE)**[15] [55] 3-9-1 **55**........................ EdwardCreighton 1 40
(Miss V Haigh) *chsd ldrs: rdn over 2f out: sn wknd* **25/1**
U3-3 **7** *nk* **Aggbag**[16] [40] 3-9-4 **58**..(p) RobbieFitzpatrick 7 42
(B P J Baugh) *bhd: rdn over 3f out: n.d* **8/1**
50-1 **8** *3* **Inkjet (IRE)**[9] [108] 3-9-2 **56**.. CatherineGannon 3 31
(Ms Deborah J Evans) *s.s: sn rcvrd: short-lived effrt on ins wl over 1f out* **10/1**
10-4 **9** *9* **Totally Free**[11] [90] 3-9-4 **58**..(v) HayleyTurner 5 6
(M D I Usher) *broke wl: sn lost pl: bhd whn nt clr run over 3f out: sn rdn and struggling: eased whn no ch fnl f* **12/1**
1m 16.56s (0.75) **Going Correction** -0.075s/f (Stan) **9** Ran SP% **117.4**
Speed ratings (Par 95):92,90,90,85,85 83,83,79,67
CSF £11.01 CT £135.78 TOTE £2.90: £1.30, £1.90, £4.40; EX 14.70 Trifecta £296.50 Part won. Pool £417.70. - 0.66 winning units..
Owner Danethorpe Racing Ltd **Bred** P Blows And Miss J Hall **Trained** Danethorpe, Notts
FOCUS
A weakish handicap in which once again it paid to race up with the pace. It has been rated through the third.
Inkjet(IRE) Official explanation: trainer said filly hit its head on stalls and suffered a cut mouth
Totally Free Official explanation: jockey said gelding suffered interference in running

203 PONTIN'S HOLIDAYS CLASSIFIED STKS 1m 4f 50y(P)
2:50 (2:51) (Class 7) 4-Y-0+ **£1,911** (£564; £282) **Stalls** Low

Form RPR
60-3 **1** **Apache Fort**[8] [126] 4-9-0 47.. PaulDoe 12 59+
(T Keddy) *hld up in mid-div: hdwy 7f out: led over 3f out: rdn clr wl over 1f out: r.o wl* **7/1**
5-44 **2** *4* **Gallas (IRE)**[8] [126] 6-9-2 43..(b) LPKeniry 7 49
(S Lycett) *a.p: rdn over 3f out: chsd wnr fnl 2f: no imp* **7/2**[2]
43-0 **3** *2 ½* **Lady Suffragette (IRE)**[7] [133] 4-8-12 44................ CatherineGannon 9 45
(John Berry) *hld up towards rr: rdn and hdwy on ins over 3f out: hung lft ins fnl f: one pce* **25/1**
05-0 **4** *¾* **Integration**[14] [64] 7-9-2 40.. SamHitchcott 5 44
(Miss M E Rowland) *hld up and bhd: rdn over 3f out: hdwy over 2f out: swtchd rt ins fnl f: styd on* **20/1**
000- **5** *1 ½* **Hometomammy**[21] [6995] 5-8-13 42.. AmirQuinn(3) 6 41
(P W Hiatt) *t.k.h: prom: rdn over 3f out: wknd fnl f* **20/1**
-351 **6** *½* **Diktatorship (IRE)**[8] [126] 4-9-3 50........................(tp) SimonWhitworth 11 46
(Ernst Oertel) *w ldr: led after 3f: hdd over 3f out: sn rdn: wknd wl over 1f out* **13/2**[3]
000/ **7** *½* **Just Superb**[10] [5917] 8-9-2 40..(p) JosedeSouza 4 40
(P A Pritchard) *mid-div: pushed along over 7f out: rdn and lost pl over 5f out: n.d after* **18/1**
2-44 **8** *13* **Jarvo**[7] [133] 6-9-2 45..(p) LeeEnstone 10 19
(I W McInnes) *hld up towards rr: stdy hdwy 6f out: rdn and wknd over 3f out* **14/1**
42-0 **9** *4* **Our Glenard**[7] [133] 8-9-2 44.. RichardThomas 3 13
(J E Long) *s.i.s: a bhd* **12/1**
00-0 **10** *5* **Monkstown Road**[8] [126] 5-9-2 42........................(b) SilvestreDeSousa 2 5
(C N Kellett) *prom tl wknd 4f out* **50/1**
36-3 **11** *6* **Pharaoh Prince**[7] [133] 6-9-2 45..(v) PaulEddery 1 —
(G Prodromou) *led 3f: w ldr tl rdn 4f out: sn wknd* **7/4**[1]
2m 42.23s (-0.19) **Going Correction** -0.075s/f (Stan)
WFA 4 from 5yo+ 4lb **11** Ran SP% **119.4**
Speed ratings (Par 97):97,94,92,92,91 90,90,81,79,75 71
CSF £30.73 TOTE £8.70: £2.00, £2.80, £5.30; EX 39.40 TRIFECTA Not won..
Owner Andrew Duffield **Bred** Juddmonte Farms Ltd **Trained** Newmarket, Suffolk
FOCUS
Weak form based on the performances of the third and fourth.

204 GO PONTIN'S MEDIAN AUCTION MAIDEN STKS 1m 1f 103y(P)
3:20 (3:21) (Class 6) 4-6-Y-0 **£2,047** (£604; £302) **Stalls** Low

Form RPR
40-2 **1** **Can Can Star**[11] [84] 4-9-3 60.. ShaneKelly 2 65
(A W Carroll) *t.k.h in mid-div: hdwy over 3f out: rdn wl over 1f out: edgd rt and led wl ins fnl f: r.o* **9/2**[2]
2 *½* **Ansells Pride (IRE)** 4-9-3.. PatCosgrave 4 64
(B Smart) *hld up and bhd: hdwy on outside 4f out: rdn to ld over 1f out: sn edgd rt: hdd wl ins fnl f: r.o* **9/2**[2]
3 *hd* **Stanerra's Story (IRE)** 6-9-4..(t) ChrisCatlin 5 64
(E J O'Neill) *plld hrd: prom: wnt 2nd 7f out: led 4f out: rdn over 2f out: hdd over 1f out: edgd rt ins fnl f: no ex cl home* **13/2**[3]
354- **4** *3 ½* **Chart Oak**[30] [6923] 4-9-3 54.. JoeFanning 9 57
(P Howling) *t.k.h towards rr: rdn and hdwy over 2f out: r.o one pce fnl f* **12/1**
44-5 **5** *nk* **Summer Lodge**[12] [74] 4-9-0 65........................(b) StephenDonohoe(3) 10 56
(A J McCabe) *s.i.s: hdwy over 5f out: ev ch over 2f out: sn rdn: wknd wl over 1f out* **10/3**[1]
630- **6** *1 ¼* **Waterloo Corner**[207] [2975] 5-9-4 65.. PaulMulrennan 7 54
(R Craggs) *prom: rdn over 3f out: sn wknd* **12/1**
000- **7** *2* **Pukka Tique**[77] [6037] 4-8-12 58........................ RussellKennemore(5) 1 50
(R Hollinshead) *prom: rdn over 4f out: sn wknd* **7/1**
3-23 **8** *5* **Mighty Kitchener (USA)**[11] [84] 4-9-3 55........................ TonyCulhane 8 40
(P Howling) *hld up in mid-div: rdn over 3f out: sn bhd* **10/1**
005- **9** *5* **Chicherova (IRE)**[24] [6967] 4-8-7 45........................(t) AshleyHamblett(5) 6 25
(W M Brisbourne) *s.i.s: a in rr* **33/1**
00-0 **10** *16* **Lady Lucas (IRE)**[11] [84] 4-8-12 30........................ EdwardCreighton 3 —
(E J Creighton) *led: hdd 4f out: rdn and wknd 3f out* **100/1**
2m 1.79s (-0.83) **Going Correction** -0.075s/f (Stan)
WFA 4 from 5yo+ 1lb **10** Ran SP% **113.7**
Speed ratings: 100,99,99,96,96 94,93,88,84,70
CSF £24.39 TOTE £5.30: £1.90, £2.00, £3.20; EX 32.10 Trifecta £353.20 Part won. Pool £497.59 - 0.33 winning units..
Owner K F Coleman **Bred** A W And I Robinson **Trained** Cropthorne, Worcs
FOCUS
A modest maiden but sound enough form rated through the winner and fourth.

205 PONTINS.COM H'CAP 1m 1f 103y(P)
3:50 (3:50) (Class 5) (0-75,78) 4-Y-0+ **£3,238** (£963; £481; £240) **Stalls** Low

Form RPR
050- **1** **Dragon Slayer (IRE)**[130] [5299] 5-8-8 **73**........................ WilliamBuick(7) 4 86+
(Ian Williams) *plld hrd: a.p: led over 4f out: shkn up 1f out: readily* **15/2**[2]
12-3 **2** *1 ½* **Snowy Day (FR)**[8] [117] 4-8-7 **66**.. PaulHanagan 3 74
(W J Haggas) *a.p: rdn to chse wnr wl over 1f out: hung lft fnl f: no imp* **11/8**[1]
02-3 **3** *1* **Bridgewater Boys**[14] [63] 6-8-4 **65**........................(b) AndrewMullen(3) 2 71
(K A Ryan) *hld up in tch: rdn over 2f out: styd on ins fnl f* **8/1**[3]
023- **4** *½* **Dower House**[32] [6885] 12-9-3 **75**..(t) ChrisCatlin 1 80
(Andrew Turnell) *hld up in mid-div: nt clr run on ins over 3f out: rdn and hdwy over 2f out: kpt on ins fnl f* **9/1**
53-0 **5** *3 ½* **Royal Amnesty**[11] [96] 4-9-2 **75**.. OscarUrbina 9 73
(G C H Chung) *hld up in mid-div: hdwy over 3f out: ev ch over 2f out: rdn and edgd lft 1f out: eased whn btn wl ins fnl f* **15/2**[2]
060- **6** *1* **Torrens (IRE)**[107] [5792] 5-8-12 **75**........................ JamieMoriarty(5) 6 71
(R A Fahey) *hld up and bhd: rdn over 3f out: styd on fnl f: n.d* **16/1**
220- **7** *1 ½* **Augustine**[154] [4626] 6-9-3 **75**.. JoeFanning 12 68
(P W Hiatt) *a.p: ev ch over 2f out: wknd fnl f* **22/1**
005- **8** *1* **Casablanca Minx (IRE)**[29] [6932] 4-8-10 **72**................ JamesDoyle(3) 5 63
(N P Littmoden) *hld up and bhd: rdn over 3f out: sme hdwy over 2f out: no further prog* **14/1**
6/0- **9** *3 ½* **Rookwith (IRE)**[20] [4852] 7-9-0 **72**.. LPKeniry 10 56
(T G McCourt, Ire) *hld up and bhd: sme hdwy over 3f out: rdn and wknd over 2f out* **50/1**
522- **10** *½* **Mambo Sun**[135] [3695] 4-8-1 **65**.. KevinGhunowa(5) 11 48
(P A Blockley) *plld hrd towards rr: rdn over 2f out: no rspnse* **20/1**
/50- **11** *1* **Low Cloud**[26] [2761] 7-8-7 **65** ow1..(p) GrahamGibbons 13 46
(J J Quinn) *s.s: sn swtchd lft: a bhd* **66/1**
B00- **12** *1 ¾* **Consonant (IRE)**[22] [6992] 10-9-2 **74**.. TonyCulhane 7 52
(D G Bridgwater) *led: hdd over 4f out: rdn whn n.m.r over 3f out: sn wknd* **33/1**
50-1 **13** *2* **Desert Leader (IRE)**[6] [142] 6-9-6 **78** 7ex........................ ShaneKelly 8 52
(W M Brisbourne) *s.v.s: a in rr* **14/1**
2m 0.92s (-1.70) **Going Correction** -0.075s/f (Stan)
WFA 4 from 5yo+ 1lb **13** Ran SP% **121.5**
Speed ratings (Par 103):104,102,101,101,98 97,96,95,92,91 90,89,87
CSF £17.50 CT £91.29 TOTE £8.90: £2.40, £2.00, £2.40; EX 32.90 Trifecta £321.70 Part won. Pool £453.20 - 0.63 winning units..
Owner Carl Would **Bred** Arandora Star Syndicate **Trained** Portway, Worcs
FOCUS
A fair handicap albeit mostly made up of exposed performers, and sound form rated through the third and fourth.
Rookwith(IRE) Official explanation: trainer said gelding finished distressed
Consonant(IRE) Official explanation: jockey said gelding never travelled

Desert Leader(IRE) Official explanation: jockey said gelding missed the break and virtually refused to race

206 PONTIN'S HOLIDAYS H'CAP (DIV II) — 1m 141y(P)
4:20 (4:20) (Class 6) (0-60,60) 4-Y-0+ — £1,365 (£403; £201) Stalls Low

Form — RPR

1-63 **1** **Harare**[8] [124] 6-8-12 58 ....(b) JamesDoyle(3) 13 — 65
(R J Price) *hld up in mid-div: hdwy on outside 3f out: rdn and hung lft over 1f out and ins fnl f: hrd rdn to ld cl home* **9/1**

61-4 **2** *hd* **The City Kid (IRE)**[2] [180] 4-8-8 55 ....(b) StephenDonohoe(3) 4 — 62
(P D Evans) *hld up towards rr: rdn and hdwy whn swtchd lft wl over 1f out: r.o ins fnl f* **14/1**

1-41 **3** *½* **Norwegian**[8] [124] 6-8-3 53 ....(p) WilliamBuick(7) 10 — 59
(Ian Williams) *hld up: hdwy over 6f out: rdn to ld and bmpd over 1f out: bmpd ins fnl f: hdd cl home* **7/2**[1]

321- **4** *shd* **Scamperdale**[23] [6977] 5-8-10 60 .... SoniaEaton(7) 11 — 66+
(B P J Baugh) *hld up and bhd: nt clr run over 2f out: swtchd lft and hdwy over 1f out: r.o ins fnl f* **7/1**[3]

60-1 **5** *hd* **Scottish River (USA)**[2] [179] 8-9-2 59 7ex .... HayleyTurner 5 — 64
(M D I Usher) *s.i.s: sn hld up in tch: nt clr run on ins over 2f out: rdn and hdwy over 1f out: ev ch ins fnl f: no cl home* **10/1**

32-4 **6** *1* **Spark Up**[8] [124] 7-8-11 57 ....(b) RichardKingscote(3) 7 — 60
(J W Unett) *hld up towards rr: hdwy over 2f out: sn rdn: nt qckn ins fnl f* **9/1**

0-42 **7** *hd* **Under Fire (IRE)**[11] [86] 4-8-10 54 .... ShaneKelly 3 — 57
(A W Carroll) *prom: rdn 3f out: sltly outpcd over 1f out: kpt on towards fin* **6/1**[2]

52-6 **8** *2* **Green Pirate**[8] [124] 5-8-13 56 .... RobbieFitzpatrick 12 — 55+
(W M Brisbourne) *hld up and bhd: sme hdwy whn nt clr run wl over 1f out: nt rch ldrs* **8/1**

520- **9** *1 ½* **Tamatave (IRE)**[23] [6977] 5-8-13 59 .... AndrewMullen(3) 2 — 55
(K A Ryan) *w ldr: led over 4f out: rdn over 2f out: hdd over 1f out: wknd fnl f* **6/1**[2]

44-6 **10** *1 ¼* **Windy Prospect**[14] [63] 5-8-12 55 .... SimonWhitworth 9 — 48
(P A Blockley) *hld up and bhd: rdn and sme hdwy over 2f out: wknd over 1f out* **16/1**

00-0 **11** *3* **Hand Chime**[5] [151] 10-9-2 59 .... AdamKirby 6 — 46
(Ernst Oertel) *hld up in tch: nt clr run and lost pl 3f out: sn bhd* **33/1**

12 *5* **Blaze Trailer (IRE)**[24] [3510] 4-8-6 50 ....(v1) ChrisCatlin 8 — 26
(T G McCourt, Ire) *prom tl wknd 3f out* **33/1**

06-0 **13** *11* **Mytton's Dream**[9] [109] 5-8-3 46 oh1 .... CatherineGannon 1 — —
(Miss Joanne Priest) *led: hdd over 4f out: rdn 3f out: sn wknd* **100/1**

1m 50.6s (-1.16) **Going Correction** -0.075s/f (Stan)
WFA 4 from 5yo+ 1lb — 13 Ran SP% **122.9**
Speed ratings (Par 101):102,101,101,101,101 100,100,98,96,95 93,88,78
CSF £131.04 CT £549.41 TOTE £9.90: £3.00, £4.20, £1.60; EX 136.80 Trifecta £329.30 Part won. Pool £463.85 - 0.33 winning units. Place 6 £62.95, Place 5 £26.09..
Owner Mrs P A Wallis **Bred** Limestone Stud **Trained** Ullingswick, H'fords

FOCUS
The slower of the two divisions by 0.69sec. It is best rated around the winner, third and fifth.
Blaze Trailer(IRE) Official explanation: trainer said gelding finished distressed
T/Jkpt: Not won. T/Plt: £144.90 to a £1 stake. Pool: £74,532.85. 375.30 winning tickets. T/Qpdt: £17.10 to a £1 stake. Pool: £5,524.50. 238.60 winning tickets. KH

187 KEMPTON (A.W) (R-H)
Monday, January 22

OFFICIAL GOING: Standard
Wind: Strong, across Weather: Fine but cloudy

207 STANSPOKER.CO.UK CLASSIFIED STKS — 7f (P)
1:20 (1:20) (Class 7) 4-Y-0+ — £1,365 (£403; £201) Stalls High

Form — RPR

5-30 **1** **A Teen**[2] [189] 9-9-0 43 .... JimmyQuinn 10 — 53
(P Howling) *t.k.h: hld up towards rr: prog wl over 2f out: chsd ldr jst over 1f out: kpt on u.p to ld last 75yds* **7/1**[2]

00/6 **2** *nk* **Aphrodelta**[2] [189] 5-9-0 45 .... DaneO'Neill 3 — 52
(P D Cundell) *trckd ldr: led over 1f out: fdd and hdd last 75yds* **8/1**[3]

6-56 **3** *2 ½* **Kinsman (IRE)**[8] [129] 10-9-0 42 ....(p) J-PGuillambert 7 — 46
(T D McCarthy) *s.i.s: hld up wl in rr: prog fr 3f out: rdn and styd on to take 3rd ins fnl f* **7/1**[2]

53-4 **4** *¾* **Villa Bianca's (IRE)**[20] [13] 4-9-0 43 .... ShaneKelly 8 — 44
(J A Osborne) *dwlt: chsd ldrs: rdn wl over 2f out: kpt on fr over 1f out: nt pce to chal* **7/1**[2]

3-34 **5** *nk* **Peggys First**[2] [189] 5-9-0 43 .... MichaelTebbutt 6 — 43
(D E Cantillon) *hld up towards rr: effrt on wd outside over 2f out: kpt on: n.d* **9/2**[1]

00-5 **6** *1* **Danielle's Lad**[19] [22] 11-8-11 42 ....(p) AmirQuinn(3) 2 — 40
(B Palling) *chsd ldrs: drvn fr 1/2-way: stl chsng over 1f out: fdd* **16/1**

00- **7** *1 ¾* **Yellow Mane (IRE)**[33] [6884] 4-9-0 45 .... RichardThomas 1 — 36
(Luke Comer, Ire) *chsd ldrs: rdn and hanging fr over 2f out: grad wknd* **33/1**

300- **8** *1* **Shirley Oaks (IRE)**[34] [6869] 9-8-7 43 .... JemmaMarshall(7) 5 — 33
(Miss Z C Davison) *dwlt: wl in rr: pushed along 1/2-way: plugged on one pce: no ch* **16/1**

205- **9** *nk* **Tiny Tim (IRE)**[40] [6805] 9-8-7 41 ....(b) DavidProbert(7) 4 — 32
(A M Balding) *led at fast pce: hdd & wknd over 1f out* **20/1**

0/6- **10** *1 ¼* **Calusa Lady (IRE)**[40] [6803] 7-8-7 42 ....(t) HaddenFrost(7) 14 — 29
(J A Geake) *s.i.s: a wl in rr: no real prog fnl 2f* **16/1**

4-00 **11** *1 ¼* **Xocolatl**[9] [125] 4-8-11 42 .... JerryO'Dwyer(3) 11 — 26
(Peter Grayson) *last and rdn after 2f: modest late prog: nvr a factor* **66/1**

024- **12** *7* **Limit Down (IRE)**[40] [6803] 6-9-0 42 .... RobertHavlin 13 — 8
(John Berry) *chsd ldrs tl wknd rapidly jst over 2f out: bbv* **9/2**[1]

060- **13** *3* **Hello Deauville (FR)**[40] [6805] 4-9-0 40 .... SimonWhitworth 9 — —
(J Akehurst) *chsd ldrs for 3f: lost pl rapidly 1/2-way: sn toiling in rr* **50/1**

000- **14** *14* **Warden Warren**[35] [6855] 9-9-0 45 ....(b) HayleyTurner 12 — —
(Mrs C A Dunnett) *sn wl in rr: t.o* **12/1**

1m 26.64s (-0.16) **Going Correction** +0.025s/f (Slow) — 14 Ran SP% **121.5**
Speed ratings (Par 97):101,100,97,96,96 95,93,92,91,90 89,81,77,61
CSF £60.87 TOTE £8.60: £2.80, £4.30, £2.80; EX 106.80.
Owner Mrs A K Petersen **Bred** C B Petersen **Trained** Newmarket, Suffolk
■ Stewards' Enquiry : David Probert one-day ban: careless riding (Feb 2)

FOCUS
A very weak event - basically of banded class - which was run at a solid pace. Sound form for the grade.
Limit Down(IRE) Official explanation: vet said gelding bled from the nose

208 STAN JAMES MEDIAN AUCTION MAIDEN STKS — 7f (P)
1:50 (1:53) (Class 5) 3-Y-O — £4,728 (£1,406; £702; £351) Stalls High

Form — RPR

1 **Lone Wolfe** 3-9-3 .... IanMongan 2 — 70+
(Jane Chapple-Hyam) *wl in tch in midfield: smooth prog over 2f out: shkn up to ld jst over 1f out: sn in command* **7/1**

3-3 **2** *2* **Distant Sun (USA)**[14] [69] 3-9-3 .... FergusSweeney 3 — 65
(R Charlton) *w ldrs: cajoled into ld over 2f out: hdd and fnd nil jst over 1f out* **4/1**[2]

3 *1 ½* **Musical Locket (IRE)** 3-8-12 .... DaneO'Neill 1 — 56
(R Hannon) *settled towards rr: stdy prog fr 2f out: shkn up and styd on to take 3rd nr fin* **16/1**

4 *nk* **Wassendale** 3-8-12 .... J-PGuillambert 11 — 55
(J W Hills) *w ldr: stl upsides 2f out: pushed along and nt qckn over 1f out: one pce after* **25/1**

02- **5** *hd* **Dr McFab**[52] [6662] 3-9-3 .... ShaneKelly 14 — 60
(J A Osborne) *mde most to over 2f out: one pce over 1f out* **3/1**[1]

60- **6** *¾* **Perfect Practice**[33] [6886] 3-8-12 .... OscarUrbina 6 — 55+
(J A R Toller) *trckd ldrs: effrt over 2f out: cl enough over 1f out: fdd fnl f* **10/1**

7 *1* **Spinning Dixie (IRE)** 3-8-12 ....(t) RichardThomas 9 — 50
(J A Geake) *in tch: effrt to chse ldrs 2f out: wknd ins fnl f* **10/1**

8 *nk* **Tenement (IRE)** 3-9-3 .... JimCrowley 8 — 54
(J A Osborne) *chsd ldrs: rdn 1/2-way: stl in tch over 1f out: wknd fnl f* **25/1**

9 *nk* **Ridgeway Star** 3-9-3 .... RobertHavlin 5 — 54?
(R Ingram) *upset by rival in stalls and dwlt: wl in rr tl sme prog 3f out : no hdwy over 1f out* **66/1**

06 **10** *1* **Varya**[6] [152] 3-8-12 .... JamieMackay 12 — 46+
(Sir Mark Prescott) *t.k.h: hld up in midfield: effrt on inner 2f out: wknd fnl f* **33/1**

- **11** *hd* **Adabi** 3-9-3 .... DaleGibson 7 — 51+
(M P Tregoning) *s.i.s: wl in rr: rousted along wl over 2f out: no real prog* **11/2**[3]

12 *3 ½* **Pugnacity** 3-8-5 .... FLenclud(7) 10 — 36
(S C Williams) *unbalanced s: a towards rr: brief effrt on inner 2f out: wknd over 1f out* **66/1**

0- **13** *2* **Jemima Godfrey**[45] [6751] 3-8-12 ....(t) JimmyQuinn 13 — 31
(J Pearce) *dwlt: a struggling in last pair* **66/1**

14 *8* **Mark Of Love (IRE)** 3-9-3 .... EdwardCreighton 4 — 15
(M R Channon) *reluctant to enter stalls and v restless in them: dwlt: a bhd* **10/1**

1m 28.35s (1.55) **Going Correction** +0.025s/f (Slow) — 14 Ran SP% **121.2**
Speed ratings (Par 97):92,89,88,87,87 86,85,85,84,83 83,79,77,67
CSF £33.66 TOTE £8.50: £2.40, £1.80, £3.30; EX 53.10.
Owner Franconson Partners **Bred** P T Tellwright **Trained** Newmarket, Suffolk

FOCUS
Probably just an average maiden, run in a slow time, but the debutant winner did the job readily. The form is rated through the fifth.
Adabi Official explanation: jockey said colt was colty and ran green
Mark Of Love(IRE) Official explanation: jockey said colt ran green

209 STANJAMESUK.COM CLAIMING STKS — 1m (P)
2:20 (2:21) (Class 6) 3-Y-O — £2,047 (£604; £302) Stalls High

Form — RPR

00-2 **1** **Sophie's Dream**[11] [99] 3-8-8 55 .... JerryO'Dwyer(3) 5 — 61+
(A M Hales) *stdd s: hld up in last pair and wl off the pce: stdy prog fr 3f out: rdn to ld jst over 1f out: kpt on wl* **13/2**

20-6 **2** *¾* **Straight Face (IRE)**[14] [73] 3-9-7 70 ....(v) PaulDoe 3 — 69
(W J Knight) *led: hung bdly lft bnd 3f out: sn hdd: drvn to ld again briefly over 1f out: one pce fnl f* **6/1**[3]

3-43 **3** *2* **Tension Point**[9] [116] 3-9-3 68 ....(p) ShaneKelly 1 — 60
(J A Osborne) *trckd ldrs: led over 2f out: hdd and nt qckn over 1f out: btn after* **4/1**[1]

4-54 **4** *1* **Party Palace**[7] [139] 3-7-12 50 ....(p) JamieMackay 6 — 42+
(J A Osborne) *chsd ldr: rdn whn carried wd bnd 3f out and lost pl: plugged on again ins fnl f* **6/1**[3]

0-24 **5** *hd* **Mick Is Back**[9] [116] 3-8-13 64 ....(b) J-PGuillambert 7 — 53
(P D Evans) *chsd ldrs: pushed along over 3f out: grad fdd u.p over 1f out* **12/1**

04-0 **6** *3* **Gertie (IRE)**[14] [69] 3-8-2 45 .... EdwardCreighton 2 — 35
(E J Creighton) *sn in last pair: plugged on fnl 2f: n.d* **33/1**

2-42 **7** *5* **A Nod And A Wink (IRE)**[12] [93] 3-8-3 53 .... StephaneBreux(3) 8 — 28
(R Hannon) *hld up in midfield: effrt on inner over 2f out: no imp over 1f out: wknd rapidly* **4/1**[1]

52-0 **8** *2* **Conny Nobel (IRE)**[7] [140] 3-8-7 68 ....(vt1) FergusSweeney 4 — 24
(R A Kvisla) *racd on outer: lost pl and rdn after 3f: nt keen and bhd fnl 2f* **9/2**[2]

40-6 **9** *22* **Daruma (IRE)**[11] [103] 3-8-3 41 .... HayleyTurner 10 — —
(Peter Grayson) *sn rdn in rr: bhd fnl 3f: t.o* **50/1**

1m 41.8s (1.00) **Going Correction** +0.025s/f (Slow) — 9 Ran SP% **112.7**
Speed ratings (Par 95):96,95,93,92,92 89,84,82,60
CSF £43.86 TOTE £7.60: £2.20, £1.20, £2.10; EX 58.10.Party Palace was claimed by H. S. Howe for £5,000. Tension Point was claimed by R. E. R. Williams for £12,000.
Owner Brick Farm Racing **Bred** Hertford Offset Press **Trained** Preston Capes, Northants
■ Stewards' Enquiry : J-P Guillambert three-day ban: failed to ride out for 4th place (Feb 2-4)

FOCUS
A moderate affair and the form has a weak look to it, although the winner could be better than the bare form.
Straight Face(IRE) Official explanation: jockey said gelding hung badly left-handed

210 STANSCASINO.CO.UK CLASSIFIED STKS — 1m (P)
2:50 (2:51) (Class 7) 4-Y-0+ — £1,365 (£403; £201) Stalls High

Form — RPR

00-5 **1** **Deneuve**[8] [129] 4-8-11 45 ....(bt1) JerryO'Dwyer(3) 11 — 55+
(M G Quinlan) *pressed ldr: led 3f out and sn kicked clr: in n.d over 1f out: unchal but all out* **12/1**

4-U0 **2** *3* **Savoy Chapel**[8] [129] 5-9-0 45 ....(v) JimCrowley 8 — 48
(A W Carroll) *hld up towards rr: prog and hrd rdn over 2f out: wnt 2nd last 100yds: no ch to rch wnr* **10/1**

6-05 **3** *hd* **Height Of Spirits**[16] [51] 5-9-0 44 .... EdwardCreighton 3 — 48
(T D McCarthy) *hld up wl in rr: prog on wd outside over 2f out: r.o fnl f to take 3rd nr fin: no ch* **15/2**

00-6 **4** *nk* **Riviera Red (IRE)**^{19} [20] 7-9-0 42...............................(v) RobertHavlin 5 47
(L Montague Hall) *hld up towards rr: prog on outer fr 2f out: r.o fnl f: no ch* **16/1**

064- **5** *shd* **Chalice Welcome**^{49} [6707] 4-9-0 41.................................. GeorgeBaker 6 47
(C F Wall) *sltly awkward s: wl in rr: prog on inner over 2f out: chal for 2nd 1f out: no ex* **9/2**^{2}

6-02 **6** *shd* **Mid Valley**^{8} [129] 4-9-0 44.. J-PGuillambert 12 46
(J R Jenkins) *prom: rdn to chse clr wnr over 1f out: nt qckn and no imp: lost pl last 100yds* **5/2**^{1}

00-5 **7** *1* **Pantomime Prince**^{12} [92] 4-9-0 45...................................... JohnEgan 4 47+
(John Berry) *hld up in last trio: sme prog and gng wl enough over 2f out: ch of a pl whn nt clr run over 1f out: kpt on* **10/1**

425- **8** *shd* **Tacid**^{25} [6960] 5-9-0 45...(v) ShaneKelly 7 44
(Dr J D Scargill) *chsd ldrs: outpcd and drvn over 2f out: one pce and n.d after* **6/1**^{3}

4-00 **9** *2 1/2* **Didnt Tell My Wife**^{16} [51] 8-9-0 41.............................(v) HayleyTurner 9 38
(P S McEntee) *hld up in midfield: outpcd over 2f out: grad wknd* **33/1**

450- **10** *2* **Tipsy Lillie**^{24} [6970] 5-9-0 41..(b) OscarUrbina 1 34
(P S McEntee) *racd wd: hld up in tch: outpcd and struggling over 2f out* **20/1**

60/0 **11** *2* **Intimate Friend (USA)**^{19} [22] 6-8-9 40.................. EmmettStack$^{(5)}$ 10 29
(Miss Diana Weeden) *chsd ldrs: rdn and outpcd wl over 2f out: grad wknd* **66/1**

06-0 **12** *1 1/4* **Dolly**^{19} [18] 5-9-0 40.. RichardThomas 14 26
(Tom Dascombe) *led at fast pce: hdd 3f out: chsd wnr tl wknd over 1f out* **33/1**

50-0 **13** *1 1/4* **Spoilsport**^{9} [120] 4-9-0 45... JimmyQuinn 2 23
(P D Evans) *a towards rr: rdn and swtchd rt 2f out: no prog* **10/1**

00/0 **14** *7* **Ivy Bridge (IRE)**^{15} [60] 4-8-9 42.......................... KevinGhunowa$^{(5)}$ 13 7
(P A Blockley) *s.i.s: sn chsd ldrs: lost pl over 3f out: t.o* **66/1**

1m 41.24s (0.44) **Going Correction** +0.025s/f (Slow) **14** Ran SP% **127.3**
Speed ratings (Par 97):98,95,94,94,94 94,93,93,90,88 86,85,84,77
CSF £128.94 TOTE £15.60: £4.50, £3.80, £2.40; EX 140.30.
Owner Mrs J Quinlan **Bred** J R And Mrs P Good **Trained** Newmarket, Suffolk

FOCUS
Another very weak event. Deneuve won readily under an enterprising ride. The race has been rated around the second and third.
Riviera Red(IRE) Official explanation: jockey said gelding hung left-handed
Dolly Official explanation: jockey said mare hung left-handed

211 STAN JAMES H'CAP 1m (P)
3:25 (3:25) (Class 5) (0-75,75) 4-Y-0+ **£4,728** (£1,406; £702; £351) **Stalls** High

Form RPR

3-12 **1** **Rebellious Spirit**^{15} [63] 4-9-2 75.................................... JimCrowley 2 85
(P W Hiatt) *pressed ldr: led wl over 2f out: drvn over 1f out: kpt on wl fnl f* **10/3**^{1}

41-2 **2** *1* **Top Mark**^{18} [38] 5-9-0 73.. GeorgeBaker 8 80
(J R Boyle) *trckd ldng pair: rdn over 2f out: effrt to dispute 2nd over 1f out : kpt on but no imp wnr fnl f* **7/2**^{2}

22-0 **3** *hd* **Arctic Desert**^{21} [6] 7-9-1 74..(t) JohnEgan 4 81
(Miss Gay Kelleway) *dwlt: sn in midfield: prog over 2f out: dispute 2nd jst over 1f out : kpt on but a hld* **8/1**

46-3 **4** *nk* **Tender The Great (IRE)**^{12} [85] 4-8-6 65............... FergusSweeney 13 71
(B G Powell) *hld up towards rr: prog on inner over 2f out: rdn to dispute 2nd over 1f out: kpt on* **15/2**^{3}

5 *hd* **Brookby (NZ)**^{76} 7-8-9 68.......................................(t) EdwardCreighton 12 74
(Miss Sheena West) *dwlt: hld up in last pair: stl wl in rr 2f out: gd prog fr over 1f out: r.o fnl f: nrst fin* **66/1**

200- **6** *1/2* **Bay Boy**^{22} [6999] 5-8-13 75.. GregFairley$^{(3)}$ 6 80
(M Johnston) *chsd ldng pair: rdn 3f out: edgd lft and nt qckn 2f out: plugged on fnl f* **10/1**

41-0 **7** *1 1/4* **Magic Warrior**^{16} [48] 7-8-8 67.................................. StephenCarson 11 69
(J C Fox) *hld up in rr: rdn over 2f out: nt clr run wl over 1f out: no prog* **8/1**

000- **8** *1 1/4* **Emilio**^{51} [6671] 6-9-2 75..(t) DaneO'Neill 10 74
(R A Kvisla) *hld up in midfield: gng wl enough 3f out: rdn and finding little whn squeezed out wl over 1f out: no ch after* **16/1**

54-0 **9** *hd* **Another Genepi (USA)**^{12} [85] 4-8-4 63...................... HayleyTurner 1 61
(J W Hills) *t.k.h: hld up towards rr and racd wd: rdn and struggling over 2f out: no imp after* **16/1**

04-0 **10** *nk* **Cinematic (IRE)**^{19} [28] 4-8-8 70.............................. JerryO'Dwyer$^{(3)}$ 5 68
(J R Boyle) *stdd s: t.k.h: hld up in last pair: rdn and no rspnse over 2f out* **16/1**

24-0 **11** *1 1/4* **Prince Dayjur (USA)**^{17} [44] 8-9-0 73.............................. JimmyQuinn 7 68
(J Pearce) *racd freely: led to wl over 2f out: wknd rapidly fnl f* **8/1**

0- **12** *1 1/2* **Inwaan (IRE)**^{112} [5734] 4-8-7 66 ow1................................(t) ShaneKelly 3 57
(P R Webber) *trckd ldrs: rdn over 2f out: wknd over 1f out* **25/1**

1m 39.88s (-0.92) **Going Correction** +0.025s/f (Slow) **12** Ran SP% **122.5**
Speed ratings (Par 103):105,104,103,103,103 102,101,100,100,99 98,97
CSF £15.53 CT £91.02 TOTE £4.40: £1.80, £1.50, £2.90; EX 19.10.
Owner Mrs Lucia Stockley & Ken Read **Bred** Car Colston Hall Stud **Trained** Hook Norton, Oxon

FOCUS
A typically competitive handicap. Sound form, the first three close to their marks.

212 STANJAMESUK.COM H'CAP 1m 4f (P)
3:55 (3:57) (Class 6) (0-65,65) 4-Y-0+ **£3,238** (£963; £481; £240) **Stalls** Centre

Form RPR

661- **1** **Ifatfirst (IRE)**^{31} [6911] 4-8-8 57.. DaneO'Neill 12 65+
(M P Tregoning) *t.k.h: hld up towards rr: effrt over 2f out: drvn to cl on ldrs fr over 1f out: r.o to ld last 75yds: hld on wl* **10/3**^{2}

01-6 **2** *shd* **Hallings Overture (USA)**^{12} [89] 8-8-13 58.................... PaulEddery 3 66+
(C A Horgan) *taken down early: hld up in last: stdy prog over 2f out: plld out and r.o to chal last 100yds: jst hld* **11/2**^{3}

00-4 **3** *1/2* **Hawk Arrow (IRE)**^{16} [48] 5-9-2 61................................. GeorgeBaker 11 68
(G L Moore) *dwlt: hld up in midfield: prog over 2f out: rdn and effrt to ld narrowly ins fnl f: hdd and outpcd last 75yds* **11/4**^{1}

/0-2 **4** *2* **Tresor Secret (FR)**^{12} [88] 7-9-2 61................................ JimCrowley 8 65
(J Gallagher) *prom: effrt to ld narrowly over 2f out: hdd ins fnl f: wknd nr fin* **14/1**

003- **5** *nk* **First Friend (IRE)**^{58} [6590] 6-9-6 65................................. ShaneKelly 14 69
(P Mitchell) *t.k.h: trckd ldr after 3f: led briefly 3f out: styd upsides : drvn over 1f out: wknd last 100yds* **9/1**

00- **6** *1* **Versatile**^{115} [5651] 4-9-2 65.. OscarUrbina 7 67
(G A Ham) *trckd ldrs: effrt over 2f out: kpt on same pce and no imp fr over 1f out* **66/1**

03-2 **7** *4* **Magic Amigo**^{12} [89] 6-9-1 60....................................... J-PGuillambert 6 56
(J R Jenkins) *hld up towards rr: rdn over 2f out: sn outpcd and btn* **7/1**

0 **8** *3 1/2* **Leonardo's Friend**^{16} [48] 4-9-2 65............................ FergusSweeney 2 55
(B G Powell) *t.k.h: cl up: rdn over 2f out: wknd over 1f out* **33/1**

03-2 **9** *1 1/4* **Discotheque (USA)**^{14} [72] 4-8-10 59.............................. JimmyQuinn 10 47
(P Howling) *t.k.h: hld up in midfield: outpcd over 2f out: sn wknd* **12/1**

0-10 **10** *2* **King Of Music (USA)**^{9} [117] 6-9-4 63................................ JohnEgan 5 48
(Miss Gay Kelleway) *dwlt: hld up wl in rr: outpcd over 2f out: wknd* **14/1**

205- **11** *3* **Night Groove (IRE)**^{23} [6988] 4-8-8 57..........................(b) HayleyTurner 4 37
(N P Littmoden) *plld hrd: sn led and set stdy pce: hdd and btn 3f out* **33/1**

000/ **12** *21* **Coombe Centenary**^{596} [2314] 5-8-9 54 ow2.................... RobertHavlin 9 —
(L Montague Hall) *taken down early: t.k.h: cl up tl wknd rapidly over 3f out: t.o* **66/1**

2m 38.3s (1.40) **Going Correction** +0.025s/f (Slow)
WFA 4 from 5yo+ 4lb **12** Ran SP% **117.5**
Speed ratings (Par 101):96,95,95,94,94 93,90,88,87,86 84,70
CSF £21.43 CT £56.56 TOTE £5.10: £1.90, £2.20, £1.60; EX 26.90.
Owner Mrs M Horne Mrs W Biggs Nic de Boinville **Bred** Mrs Belinda Strudwick **Trained** Lambourn, Berks

FOCUS
A slowly-run affair and the form is therefore dubious, but the unexposed winner is likely to do better, as should the runner-up.

213 STAN JAMES 08000 383 384 H'CAP 2m (P)
4:25 (4:30) (Class 6) (0-65,62) 4-Y-0+ **£3,238** (£963; £481; £240) **Stalls** High

Form RPR

15-5 **1** **Noble Minstrel**^{12} [88] 4-9-5 60.................................(t) J-PGuillambert 7 71+
(S C Williams) *hld up in midfield: prog over 2f out: narrow ld over 1f out: styd on wl last 100yds* **11/4**^{1}

01-5 **2** *1/2* **Galantos (GER)**^{19} [23] 6-9-4 52.. JimCrowley 2 60
(G L Moore) *hld up towards rr: prog on outer 3f out: rdn to chal and w wnr over 1f out: styd on but hld last 100yds* **12/1**

/02- **3** *2 1/2* **Critical Stage (IRE)**^{38} [6831] 8-9-6 61.......................... HaddenFrost$^{(7)}$ 3 66
(J D Frost) *prom in chsng gp: lost pl on inner 4f out: renewed effrt over 2f out: styd on fnl f: nvr able to chal* **12/1**

62-4 **4** *1 1/2* **Synonymy**^{19} [23] 4-9-6 61.. JimmyQuinn 4 64
(M Blanshard) *prom in chsng gp: nt qckn over 2f out: kpt on again fr over 1f out* **5/1**^{2}

-233 **5** *shd* **Bienheureux**^{11} [100] 6-9-8 56....................................(bt^{1}) JohnEgan 14 59
(Miss Gay Kelleway) *hld up towards rr: prog over 3f out: led over 2f out and kicked on: hdd & wknd over 1f out* **8/1**

56-0 **6** *1 1/4* **Just Fly**^{9} [117] 7-9-3 56.. KevinGhunowa$^{(5)}$ 13 58
(Dr J R J Naylor) *hld up in last pair: sme prog fr 3f out: styd on fr over 1f out : nvr able to chal* **33/1**

450- **7** *2 1/2* **Bobsleigh**^{21} [5910] 8-9-2 50... DaneO'Neill 12 49
(H S Howe) *disp 2nd bhd clr ldr fr 11f out to 4f out: wknd over 2f out* **25/1**

10-3 **8** *2* **Ganymede**^{19} [23] 6-9-5 53.. IanMongan 6 49
(Mrs L J Mongan) *hld up in rr: outpcd fr over 2f out: no ch after* **8/1**

550- **9** *2* **Rule For Ever**^{170} [4156] 5-9-5 56.................................... GregFairley$^{(3)}$ 9 50
(M Johnston) *prom in chsng gp: pushed along bef 1/2-way: lost pl and wl in rr 3f out: brief effrt on inner 2f out: sn wknd* **11/1**

353- **10** *3/4* **Tavalu (USA)**^{154} [3666] 5-9-12 60.................................(e^{1}) GeorgeBaker 10 53
(G L Moore) *hld up in last: modest prog 4f out: sn no hdwy and btn* **7/1**^{3}

554- **11** *2 1/2* **Valuta (USA)**^{48} [6712] 4-9-7 62...................................(t) SimonWhitworth 1 52
(R A Kvisla) *hld up wl in rr: prog and cl up over 4f out: wknd over 2f out* **25/1**

23/6 **12** *12* **Mumbling (IRE)**^{19} [29] 9-10-0 62................................. FergusSweeney 8 37
(B G Powell) *chsd clr ldr: clsd to ld over 5f out to over 2f out: wknd* **16/1**

004- **13** *3* **Madiba**^{23} [6873] 8-9-9 57.. ShaneKelly 11 29
(P Howling) *reluctant to enter stalls: sn wl in rr: struggling over 3f out* **16/1**

005- **14** *31* **Teorban (POL)**^{24} [6979] 8-9-2 55.................................... JamieJones$^{(5)}$ 5 —
(Mrs N S Evans) *led and sn clr: hdd & wknd over 5f out: t.o* **66/1**

3m 31.7s (0.30) **Going Correction** +0.025s/f (Slow)
WFA 4 from 5yo+ 7lb **14** Ran SP% **125.7**
Speed ratings (Par 101):100,99,98,97,97 97,95,94,93,93 92,86,84,69
CSF £38.42 CT £362.21 TOTE £4.00: £1.60, £3.00, £3.60; EX 70.20 Place 6 £214.54, Place 5 £72.28.
Owner Alasdair Simpson **Bred** Mrs M Lavell **Trained** Newmarket, Suffolk

FOCUS
A modest handicap. The form looks pretty sound, with an improved showing from Noble Minstrel over this longer trip and the next two close to form.
Teorban(POL) Official explanation: trainer said jockey was unable to carry out the riding orders, namely to hold gelding up
T/Jkpt: Not won. T/Plt: £141.60 to a £1 stake. Pool: £64,021.25. 330.05 winning tickets. T/Qpdt: £23.60 to a £1 stake. Pool: £5,412.40. 169.55 winning tickets. JN

200 WOLVERHAMPTON (A.W) (L-H)
Monday, January 22

OFFICIAL GOING: Standard
Wind: Fresh, against Weather: Sunny

214 GO PONTIN'S H'CAP 5f 20y(P)
1:35 (1:37) (Class 5) (0-70,70) 4-Y-0+ **£3,071** (£906; £453) **Stalls** Low

Form RPR

32-1 **1** **Almaty Express**^{6} [154] 5-8-3 64 6ex.........................(b) WilliamBuick$^{(7)}$ 3 81+
(J R Weymes) *led after 1f: rdn over 1f out: r.o wl* **8/13**^{1}

00-0 **2** *1 3/4* **Nusoor (IRE)**^{12} [91] 4-9-0 68.................................. RobbieFitzpatrick 1 76
(Peter Grayson) *s.i.s: sn chsng ldrs: nt clr run on ins over 2f out: rdn over 1f out: r.o ins fnl f: nt trble wnr* **10/1**

1-13 **3** *1/2* **Gifted Lass**^{6} [154] 5-8-6 63... MarcHalford$^{(3)}$ 7 69
(J Balding) *a.p: chsd wnr over 3f out: rdn over 2f out: hung lft 1f out: no imp* **6/1**^{2}

2-30 **4** *1* **Trinculo (IRE)**^{6} [155] 10-8-11 70......................... MichaelJStainton$^{(5)}$ 2 73
(R A Harris) *led 1f: prom: rdn over 1f out: one pce fnl f* **9/1**^{3}

-434 **5** *1 1/2* **Muktasb (USA)**^{5} [161] 6-8-2 56...............................(v) AdrianMcCarthy 10 53
(D Shaw) *s.i.s: rdn and hdwy on ins over 1f out: no imp fnl f* **11/1**

0-04 **6** *3/4* **Triskaidekaphobia**^{6} [154] 4-8-3 57 oh4 ow1............(t) PaulFitzsimons 6 52
(Miss J R Tooth) *bhd: rdn over 2f out: hung lft jst ins fnl f: nvr trbld ldrs* **20/1**

006- **7** *1 1/4* **Thoughtsofstardom**^{33} [6890] 4-7-11 56 oh8..........(b) DuranFentiman$^{(5)}$ 4 46
(P S McEntee) *chsd ldrs: rdn over 2f out: wknd over 1f out* **66/1**

00-0 **8** *4* **Sarah's Art (IRE)**^{8} [132] 4-8-12 66.................................(b) ChrisCatlin 9 42
(Miss D A McHale) *wnt rt s: outpcd* **33/1**

61.60 secs (-1.22) **Going Correction** -0.125s/f (Stan) **8** Ran SP% **112.8**
Speed ratings (Par 103):104,101,100,98,96 95,93,86
CSF £7.40 CT £20.96 TOTE £1.80: £1.10, £2.10, £1.90; EX 8.80 Trifecta £34.30 Pool: £352.92 - 7.30 winning units..

Owner Sporting Occasions Racing No 5 **Bred** P G Airey **Trained** Middleham Moor, N Yorks

FOCUS
They went a decent clip in this routine sprint and not that many got into it. Solid form. Almaty Express produced his best ever run and was value for a bit extra.

215 PONTIN'S HOLIDAYS H'CAP (DIV I) 1m 5f 194y(P)
2:05 (2:06) (Class 6) (0-65,65) 4-Y-O+ **£2,047** (£604; £302) **Stalls** Low

Form RPR

121- **1** **Share The Feeling (IRE)**[24] [6979] 5-9-7 **62**......... RichardKingscote(3) 6 76+
(J W Unett) *hld up towards rr: hdwy over 6f out: led over 2f out: sn rdn: styd on wl* **9/4**[1]

55-0 **2** *2 1/2* **Three Thieves (UAE)**[12] [89] 4-9-3 **61**........................ TonyCulhane 5 70
(M S Saunders) *hld up towards rr: hdwy on ins over 3f out: rdn over 2f out: hung lft fr over 1f out: styd on: nt trble wnr* **14/1**

331- **3** *3 1/2* **Twist Bookie (IRE)**[30] [6936] 7-9-0 **52**................................ ChrisCatlin 7 56
(S Lycett) *t.k.h: a.p: ev ch 3f out: sn rdn: wknd ins fnl f* **9/2**[2]

300- **4** *3 1/2* **Stravara**[35] [6862] 4-9-6 **64**.. LPKeniry 11 63
(R Hollinshead) *hld up and bhd: hdwy 4f out: rdn over 2f out: edgd lft and wknd jst over 1f out* **66/1**

44-5 **5** *3 1/2* **Always Baileys (IRE)**[7] [142] 4-9-7 **65**..............................(b[1]) NCallan 12 59
(T Wall) *t.k.h: w ldr tl over 8f out: rdn and wkng whn n.m.r over 3f out* **28/1**

002- **6** *1 1/4* **Royal Premier (IRE)**[40] [6812] 4-8-11 **55**......................(p) MickyFenton 2 48
(H J Collingridge) *led: rdn over 7f out: hdd over 2f out: wknd fnl f* **15/2**[3]

02-2 **7** *3/4* **Bethanys Boy (IRE)**[18] [35] 6-9-13 **65**......................... PaulHanagan 8 57
(P A Blockley) *t.k.h in mid-div: rdn and wknd over 3f out* **9/1**

0-04 **8** *1* **Captivate**[14] [71] 4-7-11 **48**..(p) WilliamBuick(7) 3 38
(A J McCabe) *bhd: rdn over 7f out: nvr nr ldrs* **16/1**

/6-6 **9** *1 1/4* **High Country (IRE)**[9] [121] 7-8-10 **48**......................... PaulMulrennan 4 36
(Micky Hammond) *hld up in tch: rdn 5f out: sn wknd* **33/1**

13-0 **10** *6* **Wise Choice**[12] [88] 4-8-6 **53**....................................... JamesDoyle(3) 10 33
(N P Littmoden) *rdn over 7f out: a towards rr* **14/1**

36-0 **11** *2 1/2* **Sovereign Spirit (IRE)**[19] [29] 5-9-11 **63**......................(tp) AdamKirby 1 39
(W R Swinburn) *sn prom: w ldr over 8f out tl rdn over 3f out: wknd wl over 1f out* **9/2**[2]

400- **12** *31* **Peephole**[96] [6057] 4-8-11 **55**..(p) SamHitchcott 9 —
(Mrs A M Thorpe) *a towards rr: lost tch 4f out: t.o* **50/1**

3m 4.37s (-3.00) **Going Correction** -0.125s/f (Stan)
WFA 4 from 5yo+ 6lb **12** Ran SP% **118.0**
Speed ratings (Par 101):103,101,99,97,95 94,94,93,93,89 88,70
CSF £36.38 CT £135.23 TOTE £3.20: £1.60, £3.60, £1.50; EX 36.00 Trifecta £121.20 Pool: £271.58 - 1.59 winning units..
Owner John Malone **Bred** John Malone **Trained** Preston, Shropshire

FOCUS
They went a fair pace for this staying handicap and stamina was properly tested. The winning time was 1.49 seconds faster than the second division and the form looks stronger. Another improved run from the progressive Share The Feeling.
Always Baileys(IRE) Official explanation: jockey said gelding hung right-handed throughout

216 PONTINS.COM H'CAP 7f 32y(P)
2:35 (2:35) (Class 4) (0-80,76) 3-Y-O **£4,857** (£1,445; £722; £360) **Stalls** High

Form RPR

21- **1** **Si Foo (USA)**[175] [4000] 3-9-2 **74**.. LPKeniry 7 80+
(A M Balding) *t.k.h: a.p: led wl over 1f out: rdn and hung lft fnl f: r.o* **11/4**[2]

04-3 **2** *3/4* **Copper King**[9] [113] 3-9-1 **76**.. JamesDoyle(3) 2 80
(P D Evans) *led early: chsd ldr tl over 3f out: hrd rdn and wnt 2nd over 1f out: nt qckn ins fnl f* **5/1**[3]

211- **3** *2* **Tobago Reef**[23] [6991] 3-8-8 **73**................................(p) KristinStubbs(7) 5 72
(Mrs L Stubbs) *sn led: hdd wl over 1f out: no ex towards fin* **10/1**

66-6 **4** *1* **Minaash (USA)**[9] [113] 3-9-4 **76**.. NCallan 8 72
(J Noseda) *s.i.s: hld up: rdn and hdwy over 2f out: one pce fnl f* **16/1**

1-15 **5** *1/2* **Homes By Woodford**[9] [113] 3-8-8 **71**................ MichaelJStainton(5) 4 66
(R A Harris) *t.k.h: hdwy on ins over 2f out: one pce fnl f* **17/2**

25-1 **6** *1 3/4* **Fractured Foxy**[18] [34] 3-8-7 **72**................................ SladeO'Hara(7) 6 63
(J J Quinn) *bhd fnl 3f* **8/1**

20-1 **7** *hd* **Tilapia (IRE)**[12] [93] 3-8-12 **70**... SebSanders 3 60
(Sir Mark Prescott) *hld up in tch: rdn 5f out: sn lost pl: last whn nt clr run over 3f out* **13/8**[1]

1m 29.93s (-0.47) **Going Correction** -0.125s/f (Stan) **7** Ran SP% **118.0**
Speed ratings (Par 99):97,96,93,92,92 90,89
CSF £17.78 CT £121.20 TOTE £3.90: £2.70, £2.30; EX 20.00 Trifecta £110.80 Pool: £548.20 - 3.51 winning units..
Owner Norman Cheng **Bred** N Cheng **Trained** Kingsclere, Hants

FOCUS
An ordinary little handicap, but the form is probably solid despite the favourite running a stinker. Those that raced handily were at an advantage and those held up could never make an impression.

217 PONTIN'S FAMILY HOLIDAYS H'CAP 7f 32y(P)
3:05 (3:05) (Class 6) (0-50,57) 4-Y-O+ **£2,047** (£604; £302) **Stalls** High

Form RPR

60-4 **1** **Kahlua Bear**[9] [123] 5-8-12 **50**..(v) AdamKirby 7 57
(Miss K B Boutflower) *hld up in tch: rdn 3f out: led jst ins fnl f: edgd rt cl home r.o* **4/1**[2]

2-6 **2** *2* **Et Dona Ferentes**[13] [77] 4-8-10 **48**................................ PhillipMakin 3 50
(T D Barron) *a.p: rdn over 2f out: r.o ins fnl f* **9/2**[3]

224- **3** *hd* **Black Oval**[23] [6981] 6-8-10 **48**... DeanMernagh 6 49
(S Parr) *hld up and bhd: hdwy on ins wl over 1f out: r.o ins fnl f: nrst fin* **8/1**

000- **4** *1* **Grafton (IRE)**[48] [6721] 4-8-12 **57** ow7......................... JamesO'Reilly(7) 2 56
(J O'Reilly) *led: rdn over 2f out: hdd jst ins fnl f: no ex* **20/1**

0-24 **5** *1 1/2* **Seldemosa**[6] [145] 6-8-11 **49**... TonyCulhane 4 44
(M S Saunders) *chsd ldr: rdn over 2f out: ev ch over 1f out: wknd ins fnl f* **7/2**[1]

4-10 **6** *hd* **Teyaar**[2] [189] 11-8-10 **48**... PaulFitzsimons 8 42
(M Wellings) *hmpd s: bhd: rdn over 2f out: hdwy on outside fnl f: n.d* **14/1**

00-5 **7** *3/4* **Cape Of Storms**[9] [123] 4-8-10 **48**................................. PaulHanagan 10 41
(R Brotherton) *hld up in tch: rdn 3f out: sn btn* **13/2**

00-0 **8** *1* **Drink To Me Only**[21] [7] 4-8-11 **49**...................................... NCallan 11 39
(J R Weymes) *bhd: rdn 4f out: nvr nr ldrs* **9/1**

006/ **9** *5* **Distant Shores (IRE)**[479] [5583] 4-8-9 **50**............... StephenDonohoe(3) 1 27
(Miss T Spearing) *s.i.s: a bhd* **50/1**

00/0 **10** *1/2* **Lake Carezza (USA)**[12] [94] 5-8-4 **49** ow1............... SladeO'Hara(7) 12 25
(N J Hawke) *sn chsng ldrs: rdn and wknd 3f out* **22/1**

1m 30.26s (-0.14) **Going Correction** -0.125s/f (Stan) **10** Ran SP% **112.6**
Speed ratings (Par 101):95,92,92,91,89 89,88,87,81,81
CSF £20.94 CT £134.45 TOTE £4.90: £1.80, £2.20, £1.70; EX 29.60 Trifecta £165.00 Pool: £469.45 - 2.02 winning units..
Owner The Takeover Teddy Team **Bred** J E Jones **Trained** Newmarket, Suffolk
■ Stewards' Enquiry : Dean Mernagh 28-day ban: in breach of Rule 157 (Feb 2-17, 19-28, Mar 1,2) Parr fined £5,000 (horse intentionally restrained and not let down).

FOCUS
The slowest of the three races over the trip at the meeting and a modest winning time for the grade. This was also a very controversial race due to the running of Black Oval, but otherwise the form looks weak, if relatively sound.
Black Oval Official explanation: jockey said, regarding running and riding, his orders were to ride the mare as he had before, settled in rear early, as she is inclined to run too free, then to come with a late run, adding that she would not respond to the whip and he had to give a hands and heels ride, further adding that he had some concern that she would not get the 7f trip; trainer confirmed, adding that the mare was a temperamental sort; 40-day ban; (Jan 25-Mar 5)

218 PONTINSBINGO.COM H'CAP 7f 32y(P)
3:40 (3:41) (Class 4) (0-85,82) 4-Y-O+ **£4,857** (£1,445; £722; £360) **Stalls** High

Form RPR

51-3 **1** **Writ (IRE)**[17] [44] 5-8-3 **74**.. DuranFentiman(5) 6 82
(I Semple) *sn w ldr: led over 3f out: rdn over 2f out: edgd rt wl over 1f out: r.o* **7/4**[1]

334- **2** *shd* **Gifted Gamble**[22] [6999] 5-9-1 **81**.......................................(b) NCallan 9 89
(K A Ryan) *hld up: hdwy on outside whn bmpd sltly over 3f out: ev ch fnl f: nt qckn* **11/2**[3]

12-3 **3** *2 1/2* **Mandarin Spirit (IRE)**[2] [190] 7-8-5 **78**..................(b) MarvinCheung(7) 4 80
(G C H Chung) *s.i.s: swtchd rt and hdwy on outside over 2f out: rdn and one pce fnl f* **4/1**[2]

00-4 **4** *2 1/2* **Grey Boy (GER)**[16] [56] 6-8-11 **77**................................ PaulHanagan 8 72
(R A Fahey) *hld up in tch: nt clr run briefly over 2f out: rdn whn edgd lft jst over 1f out: one pce* **4/1**[2]

01-0 **5** *1 3/4* **Plateau**[15] [63] 8-8-6 **72** ow1................................... RobbieFitzpatrick 3 62
(C R Dore) *prom: nt clr run on ins and lost pl over 2f out: n.d after* **16/1**

051- **6** *1 1/4* **Connect**[67] [6499] 10-8-13 **82**....................................(b) SaleemGolam(3) 7 69
(M H Tompkins) *hld up in tch: rdn over 3f out: wknd wl over 1f out* **9/1**

00-0 **7** *7* **Tyzack (IRE)**[17] [44] 6-8-13 **79**.. MickyFenton 2 48
(W M Brisbourne) *led over 3f: sn rdn: wknd 2f out* **25/1**

1m 28.39s (-2.01) **Going Correction** -0.125s/f (Stan) **7** Ran SP% **111.5**
Speed ratings (Par 105):106,105,103,100,98 96,88
CSF £11.17 CT £31.81 TOTE £2.90: £1.60, £3.10; EX 12.10 Trifecta £29.60 Pool: £918.11 - 21.99 winning units..
Owner Clarke Boon **Bred** Sean Collins **Trained** Carluke, S Lanarks

FOCUS
Solid form for the grade. The winning time was the quickest of the three 7f races; 1.87 seconds quicker than the 46-50 handicap, and 1.54 seconds faster than the three-year-old 66-80 contest.

219 PONTIN'S BOOK EARLY H'CAP 5f 20y(P)
4:10 (4:10) (Class 6) (0-65,64) 3-Y-O **£2,730** (£806; £403) **Stalls** Low

Form RPR

-415 **1** **Grange Lili (IRE)**[2] [188] 3-9-2 **64**..........................(b) RobbieFitzpatrick 6 73+
(Peter Grayson) *hld up and bhd: nt clr run on ins over 2f out: plld out and hdwy over 1f out: r.o to ld cl home* **7/1**[3]

004- **2** *nk* **Convivial Spirit**[82] [6291] 3-9-0 **62**..................................(t) LPKeniry 9 70
(E F Vaughan) *hdwy over 2f out: rdn to ld ins fnl f: hdd cl home* **7/1**[3]

405- **3** *3 1/2* **Shepherdess (USA)**[58] [6605] 3-8-2 **57**..................... KirstyMilczarek(7) 7 52
(D M Simcock) *chsd ldr: lost 2nd 2f out: rdn and wknd ins fnl f* **33/1**

26-6 **4** *3/4* **Candyland (IRE)**[16] [54] 3-8-8 **56**................................... PaulHanagan 2 49
(M Quinn) *chsd ldrs: rdn wl over 1f out: wknd ins fnl f* **25/1**

5-30 **5** *nk* **Perlachy**[8] [127] 3-9-1 **63**...(v[1]) NCallan 10 55
(Mrs N Macauley) *a.p: wnt 2nd 2f out: sn rdn and edgd lft: wknd fnl f* **16/1**

0-50 **6** *1/2* **Baytown Paikea**[2] [194] 3-8-1 **52**................................ DominicFox(3) 1 42
(P S McEntee) *led: rdn over 1f out: hdd & wknd ins fnl f* **16/1**

052- **7** *hd* **Foxy Music**[23] [6985] 3-8-2 **50** oh1................................. AdrianMcCarthy 3 42+
(Peter Grayson) *s.i.s: hld up: hdwy 2f out: swtchd rt wl over 1f out: sn rdn and hung bdly rt to stands' side: eased whn btn* **16/1**

31- **8** *shd* **Iron Pearl**[31] [6912] 3-9-1 **63**... BrettDoyle 5 52
(Jane Chapple-Hyam) *mid-div: lost pl 3f out: c wd st: carried rt to stands' side over 1f out: n.d* **6/5**[1]

065- **9** *7* **Zilli**[24] [6975] 3-7-11 **50**... DuranFentiman(5) 8 14
(N P Littmoden) *sn outpcd* **40/1**

165- **10** *3* **Galaxy Of Stars**[45] [6750] 3-8-10 **58**...............................(v) AdamKirby 4 11
(D Shaw) *s.v.s: a in rr* **4/1**[2]

62.74 secs (-0.08) **Going Correction** -0.125s/f (Stan) **10** Ran SP% **117.3**
Speed ratings (Par 95):95,94,88,87,87 86,86,85,74,69
CSF £54.55 CT £1519.52 TOTE £10.20: £1.80, £3.40, £8.30; EX 51.80 Trifecta £582.20 Pool: £820.03 - 1.33 winning units..
Owner Mrs M Shaughnessy and Mrs S Grayson **Bred** Jack Ronan And Des Ver Hunt Farm Ltd **Trained** Formby, Lancs

FOCUS
A weak sprint handicap run in a time 1.14 seconds slower than the opening 56-70 contest won by Almaty Express. The form seems sound enough.
Foxy Music Official explanation: jockey said gelding was hanging badly
Iron Pearl Official explanation: jockey said filly would not face the kick-back
Galaxy Of Stars Official explanation: jockey said filly dwelt at start

220 PONTIN'S HOLIDAYS H'CAP (DIV II) 1m 5f 194y(P)
4:40 (4:42) (Class 6) (0-65,64) 4-Y-O+ **£2,047** (£604; £302) **Stalls** Low

Form RPR

00-2 **1** **Reminiscent (IRE)**[17] [39] 8-9-1 **52**............................(p) TonyCulhane 6 59+
(B P J Baugh) *hld up and bhd: hdwy over 2f out: led ins fnl f: cleverly* **9/1**

121- **2** *1* **Little Richard (IRE)**[22] [6995] 8-9-8 **59**..........................(p) AdamKirby 9 64
(M Wellings) *hld up in mid-div: rdn whn edgd rt wl over 1f out: ev ch whn carried rt 1f out: nt qckn* **6/4**[1]

01-0 **3** *1 1/2* **Emilion**[12] [89] 4-8-12 **55**.. JoeFanning 10 58
(W R Muir) *led early: hld up in tch: led over 2f out: rdn whn edgd rt 1f out: hdd ins fnl f: one pce* **11/1**

630- **4** *shd* **Avanti**[22] [6995] 11-8-4 **46**....................................(v) MichaelJStainton(5) 11 49
(Dr J R J Naylor) *hld up and bhd: hdwy over 3f out: carried rt wl over 1f out: ev ch whn carried rt ent fnl f: one pce* **40/1**

000- **5** *5* **Almanshood (USA)**[37] [6848] 5-9-11 **62**............................ SamHitchcott 2 58
(P L Gilligan) *prom: nt clr run on ins and lost pl over 2f out: rdn wl over 1f out: no rspnse* **12/1**

000- **6** *3* **Treason Trial**[24] [6972] 6-8-11 **48**..................................... MickyFenton 4 40
(W M Brisbourne) *hld up and bhd: rdn over 2f out: sme hdwy wl over 1f out: n.d* **20/1**

040- **7** *4* **Migration**[220] [2612] 11-9-5 **56**.. PaulHanagan 1 42
(Mrs S Lamyman) *hld up towards rr: rdn over 3f out: no rspnse* **20/1**

10-0 **8** *12* **Moonshine Bill**[17] [39] 8-8-11 **48** ..... AdrianMcCarthy 8 17
(P W Hiatt) *sn chsng ldr: led over 5f out: rdn over 3f out: hdd over 2f out: sn wknd* **25/1**

110- **9** *2 1/2* **Zaville**[45] [6754] 5-9-6 **64** ..... (p) JamesO'Reilly(7) 7 30
(J O'Reilly) *mid-div: pushed along and hdwy 8f out: wknd over 3f out* **9/2**[2]

00/3 **10** *108* **Al Moulatham**[6] [146] 8-9-4 **60** ..... (vt) JamieMoriarty(5) 3 —
(R Ford) *sn led: hdd over 5f out: sn rdn: wknd qckly: t.o* **5/1**[3]

3m 5.86s (-1.51) **Going Correction** -0.125s/f (Stan)
WFA 4 from 5yo+ 6lb **10** Ran SP% **116.7**
Speed ratings (Par 101):99,98,97,97,94 92,90,83,82,—
CSF £21.90 CT £156.68 TOTE £9.20: £2.40, £1.50, £3.00; EX 15.90 Trifecta £87.70 Pool: £1,117.25 - 9.04 winning units. Place 6 £56.24, Place 5 £47.24.
Owner F Burgess **Bred** Newtownbarry House Stud **Trained** Audley, Staffs

FOCUS
A moderate staying handicap and they appeared to go a fair pace, although the winning time was 1.49 seconds slower than the first division. It has been rated through the fourth.
Moonshine Bill Official explanation: jockey said gelding lost its action
Al Moulatham Official explanation: vet said gelding finished distressed
T/Plt: £92.60 to a £1 stake. Pool: £85,311.85. 672.40 winning tickets. T/Qpdt: £49.40 to a £1 stake. Pool: £4,662.70. 69.80 winning tickets. KH

[143]SOUTHWELL (L-H)

Tuesday, January 23

OFFICIAL GOING: Standard
There was a major pace bias at this meeting with four of the eight winners making all and the other four all racing prominently.
Wind: Moderate, behind

221 PONTINSBINGO.COM H'CAP (DIV I) 6f (F)
12:40 (12:40) (Class 6) (0-55,54) 4-Y-0+ **£1,706** (£503; £252) **Stalls** Low

Form RPR

0-02 **1** **Mill By The Stream**[7] [145] 5-8-12 **52** ..... JimCrowley 5 62
(Tom Dascombe) *trckd ldrs: effrt 2f out: rdn over 1f out: styd on ins last: led last 50 yds* **11/4**[2]

64-2 **2** *hd* **Lucius Verrus (USA)**[7] [144] 7-8-5 **45** ..... (v) HayleyTurner 4 54+
(D Shaw) *in tch: rdn and lost pl after 2f: hdwy u.p over 1f out:drvn to chal ins last: ev ch tl no ex last 50 yds* **9/4**[1]

241- **3** *1 3/4* **Blakeshall Quest**[42] [6796] 7-9-0 **54** ..... (b) PatCosgrave 9 58
(R Brotherton) *cl up: rdn to ld wl over 1f out: drvn ins last: hdd and one pce last 50 yds* **9/1**

06-3 **4** *1 1/2* **Blythe Spirit**[8] [137] 8-8-8 **48** ..... (p) PaulHanagan 10 48
(R A Fahey) *chsd ldrs on outer: rdn along 2f out: kpt on same pce appr last* **12/1**

101- **5** *1 1/2* **Cool Tiger**[36] [6856] 4-8-13 **53** ..... ShaneKelly 1 48
(P Howling) *dwlt and bhd tl styd on fnl 2f: nrst fin* **13/2**[3]

000- **6** *1 3/4* **Hillbilly Cat (USA)**[49] [6719] 4-8-13 **53** ..... (b[1]) RobertHavlin 2 43
(R Ingram) *prom tl rdn along 2f out and grad wknd* **16/1**

024- **7** *1/2* **Aboustar**[25] [6969] 7-8-0 **47** ow2 ..... (v[1]) PatrickDonaghy(7) 8 35
(M Brittain) *sn rdn along: a towards rr* **16/1**

00-2 **8** *1 3/4* **Bee Magic**[21] [13] 4-8-10 **50** ..... ChrisCatlin 6 33
(C N Kellett) *cl up: led after 1f: rdn over 2f out: hdd wl over 1f out and sn wknd* **16/1**

00-0 **9** *13* **Bahrain Gold (IRE)**[16] [61] 7-8-10 **50** ..... (b) AdamKirby 3 —
(N P McCormack) *chsd ldrs: rdn along 3f out: sn wknd* **28/1**

004- **10** *13* **Axis Shield (IRE)**[63] [6548] 4-8-5 **45** ..... AdrianMcCarthy 7 —
(M C Chapman) *chsd ldrs: rdn along 1/2-way: sn wknd* **50/1**

1m 17.25s (0.35) **Going Correction** -0.15s/f (Stan) **10** Ran SP% **111.5**
Speed ratings (Par 101):91,90,88,86,84 82,81,79,61,44
CSF £8.82 CT £45.60 TOTE £4.00: £1.30, £1.10, £2.40; EX 8.00 Trifecta £59.70 Pool: £267.61 - 3.18 winning units.
Owner Alan Solomon **Bred** The Lavington Stud **Trained** Lambourn, Berks

FOCUS
A weak handicap run in a moderate winning time for the grade, 1.71 seconds slower than the second division. It has been rated through the third.

222 GO PONTIN'S MAIDEN STKS 6f (F)
1:10 (1:10) (Class 5) 3-Y-0+ **£2,817** (£838; £418; £209) **Stalls** Low

Form RPR

33-0 **1** **Going Skint**[10] [124] 4-9-13 57 ..... AdamKirby 6 70
(M Wellings) *mde virtually all: rdn wl over 1f out: kpt on* **25/1**

2- **2** *1/2* **Doubtful Sound (USA)**[26] [6963] 3-8-11 ..... PaulFessey 5 65
(T D Barron) *trckd ldrs: hdwy to chse wnr 2f out: rdn wl over 1f out: drvn and kpt on ins last* **9/4**[1]

46- **3** *2 1/2* **Last Sovereign**[52] [6669] 3-8-8 ..... RichardKingscote(3) 11 57+
(R Charlton) *midfield: hdwy over 2f out: sn rdn and kpt on wl fnl f: nrst fin* **9/2**[2]

6 **4** *1 3/4* **Dramatic**[16] [60] 3-8-11 ..... SebSanders 7 52
(Sir Mark Prescott) *chsd ldrs: rdn along over 2f out: sn one pce* **10/1**

3 **5** *nk* **Not Now Lewis (IRE)**[9] [127] 3-8-11 ..... ShaneKelly 1 51
(J A Osborne) *dwlt and towards rr: hdwy halfwy: sn rdn along: kpt on fnl 2f: nrst fin* **11/2**[3]

004- **6** *7* **Caspian Rose**[69] [6492] 4-9-8 37 ..... LPKeniry 8 29
(M J Attwater) *prom: rdn along 1/2-way: sn wknd* **125/1**

20-0 **7** *nk* **Bobby Rose**[9] [132] 4-9-13 64 ..... (p) NCallan 2 33
(D K Ivory) *chsd ldrs: sltly hmpd after 1 1/2f: chsd wnr 1/2-way: rdn over 2f out and sn wknd* **11/2**[3]

8 *shd* **Grey Light (IRE)** 3-8-11 ..... JoeFanning 12 29
(M Johnston) *outpcd and towards rr: nvr a factor* **6/1**

054- **9** *6* **Inverted**[27] [6945] 3-8-11 50 ..... (v[1]) JimCrowley 3 11
(Mrs A Duffield) *keen: chsd ldrs to 1/2-way: sn wknd* **50/1**

0 **10** *shd* **Danalova**[15] [73] 3-8-6 ..... PaulHanagan 4 6
(R A Fahey) *a rr* **40/1**

0 **11** *3 1/2* **Kindkintyre (IRE)**[7] [152] 3-8-6 ..... JamieMoriarty(5) 9 —
(R A Fahey) *a rr* **100/1**

0-0 **12** *11* **First Frost**[9] [128] 3-8-1 ..... DuranFentiman(5) 13 —
(M J Gingell) *s.i.s: sn rdn along and a rr* **150/1**

66- **13** *3 1/2* **Esprit De Nuit (IRE)**[59] [6605] 3-8-8 ..... SaleemGolam(3) 10 —
(Mrs A Duffield) *in tch: rdn along over 3f out and sn wknd* **66/1**

1m 16.4s (-0.50) **Going Correction** -0.15s/f (Stan)
WFA 3 from 4yo 16lb **13** Ran SP% **115.3**
Speed ratings (Par 103):97,96,93,90,90 80,80,80,72,72 67,52,48
CSF £77.96 TOTE £29.50: £6.00, £1.30, £1.60; EX 172.80 TRIFECTA Not won..
Owner The Paupers **Bred** David John Brown **Trained** Six Ashes, Shropshire

FOCUS
Modest maiden form and an improved performance from the winner, who had conditions to suit. The third may well turn out to be the best of these.
Not Now Lewis(IRE) Official explanation: jockey said gelding missed the break
Inverted Official explanation: jockey said gelding suffered interference

223 PONTINS.COM (S) STKS 7f (F)
1:40 (1:40) (Class 6) 3-Y-0 **£2,184** (£644; £322) **Stalls** Low

Form RPR

000- **1** **Heaven's Gates**[27] [6950] 3-9-0 55 ..... NCallan 5 59
(K A Ryan) *mde all: rdn clr wl over 1f out: drvn ent last: kpt on* **7/2**[2]

544- **2** *nk* **Denton Hawk**[140] [5084] 3-9-0 55 ..... PhillipMakin 6 58
(M Dods) *chsd ldrs: hdwy to chse wnr 2f out and sn rdn: drvn and styd on ins last* **11/4**[1]

046- **3** *4* **Kings Shillings**[40] [6815] 3-9-0 50 ..... (b) GrahamGibbons 4 48
(D Carroll) *in tch: hdwy 3f out: sn rdn and kpt on same pce fnl 2f* **8/1**

00-6 **4** *5* **Homecroft Boy**[8] [136] 3-9-0 50 ..... (b) ShaneKelly 7 35
(J A Osborne) *prom: rdn along 3f out: grad wknd* **6/1**

0-5 **5** *2 1/2* **Irish Relative (IRE)**[14] [76] 3-9-0 ..... PaulFessey 1 28
(T D Barron) *chsd ldrs on inner: rdn along wl over 2f out and sn wknd* **10/1**

030- **6** *2* **Poniard (IRE)**[117] [5632] 3-9-0 59 ..... PaulHanagan 10 23
(D W Barker) *sn rdn along and a rr* **14/1**

36- **7** *2* **Bridget's Team**[24] [6991] 3-9-0 56 ..... (t) DaleGibson 8 18
(D G Bridgwater) *chsd ldrs on outer: rdn along 3f out: wknd over 2f out* **4/1**[3]

0 **8** *13* **Binham Boy**[17] [53] 3-9-1 ow1 ..... (v[1]) AntonyProcter 3 —
(M J Gingell) *s.i.s: a rr* **100/1**

00- **9** *3 1/2* **Wrynoes Pass (IRE)**[184] [3758] 3-8-9 ..... KevinGhunowa(5) 2 —
(R F Fisher) *chsd ldrs 3f: sn lost pl and bhd* **100/1**

1m 30.88s (0.08) **Going Correction** -0.15s/f (Stan) **9** Ran SP% **112.0**
Speed ratings (Par 95):93,92,88,82,79 77,74,60,56
CSF £12.96 TOTE £4.30: £1.10, £1.70, £2.90; EX 17.80 Trifecta £106.80 Pool: £367.22 - 2.44 winning units..The winner was bought in for 6,600gns.
Owner J H Henderson **Bred** J H Henderson **Trained** Hambleton, N Yorks
■ Stewards' Enquiry : Kevin Ghunowa one-day ban: using whip above shoulder height and when out of contention (Feb 3)

FOCUS
An ordinary seller in which, bar the first two, they came home well strung out. It has been rated around the third.
Wrynoes Pass(IRE) Official explanation: jockey said gelding hung right throughout

224 PONTIN'S FAMILY HOLIDAYS H'CAP 1m (F)
2:10 (2:11) (Class 6) (0-60,60) 3-Y-0 **£2,388** (£705; £352) **Stalls** Low

Form RPR

050- **1** **Medici Code**[129] [5379] 3-9-4 60 ..... RobertHavlin 6 86+
(H Morrison) *in tch: smooth hdwy 1/2-way: led wl over 2f out and sn clr: easily* **4/1**[1]

00-4 **2** *14* **Greek God**[19] [37] 3-8-13 55 ..... BrettDoyle 12 51
(W Jarvis) *towards rr: hdwy towards outer over 2f out: sn rdn and kpt on appr last: no ch w wnr* **4/1**[1]

06-3 **3** *nk* **Skye But N Ben**[19] [37] 3-8-5 47 ..... (b) PaulFessey 13 43
(T D Barron) *chsd ldrs: rdn along over 2f out: sn driven and kpt on same pce* **8/1**

45-0 **4** *1 1/4* **My Sara**[8] [136] 3-8-11 53 ..... (v) PaulHanagan 7 48+
(R A Fahey) *in tch: hdwy 3f out: rdn over 2f out and kpt on same pce* **28/1**

434- **5** *1 1/2* **Featherlight**[66] [6518] 3-8-10 52 ..... (v) ChrisCatlin 9 42
(J Jay) *bhd: hdwy 3f out: sn rdn and kpt on fnl 2f: nvr nr ldrs* **15/2**

000- **6** *1* **Fire In Cairo (IRE)**[31] [6926] 3-8-10 52 ..... LeeEnstone 14 40
(P C Haslam) *midfield: hdwy 3f out: sn rdn and no imp* **33/1**

05-3 **7** *1/2* **Knapton Hill**[10] [122] 3-9-3 59 ..... GrahamGibbons 3 46
(R Hollinshead) *towards rr tl styd on fnl 2f* **9/1**

60-1 **8** *shd* **News Of The Day (IRE)**[15] [68] 3-9-2 58 ..... JoeFanning 10 44
(M Johnston) *cl up: rdn along 3f out: sn drvn and wknd* **6/1**[2]

05-2 **9** *3/4* **Mr Chocolate Drop (IRE)**[21] [11] 3-9-0 56 ..... AdamKirby 11 41
(M J Attwater) *led: rdn along 3f out: sn hdd & wknd* **16/1**

0-40 **10** *4* **Emefdream**[10] [122] 3-9-3 59 ..... (p) NCallan 1 36
(Mrs N Macauley) *cl up on inner: rdn along 3f out: sn wknd* **33/1**

026- **11** *9* **Tenterhooks (IRE)**[206] [3096] 3-9-0 56 ..... ShaneKelly 4 14
(J A Osborne) *in tch: rdn along over 3f out: sn wknd* **28/1**

05-5 **12** *1* **Brynris**[10] [122] 3-8-4 46 oh1 ..... CatherineGannon 8 2
(Mrs G S Rees) *cl up: rdn along over 3f out and sn wknd* **80/1**

05-5 **13** *1/2* **Arabellas Homer**[16] [65] 3-8-2 49 ..... DuranFentiman(5) 2 3
(Mrs N Macauley) *bhd fr 1/2-way* **25/1**

000- **14** *24* **Beck**[56] [6644] 3-9-4 60 ..... (v[1]) HayleyTurner 5 —
(M L W Bell) *squeezed out s: a bhd* **7/1**[3]

1m 42.59s (-2.01) **Going Correction** -0.15s/f (Stan) **14** Ran SP% **123.4**
Speed ratings (Par 95):104,90,89,88,86 85,85,85,84,80 71,70,70,46
CSF £18.03 CT £130.57 TOTE £4.20: £2.20, £2.20, £4.30; EX 18.00 Trifecta £187.80 Part won. Pool: £264.51 - 0.95 winning units..
Owner The End-R-Ways Partnership **Bred** Mrs T A Foreman **Trained** East Ilsley, Berks
■ Stewards' Enquiry : Adam Kirby two-day ban: careless riding (Feb 3 -4)

FOCUS
A competitive handicap on paper but it featured a number of unexposed sorts and was turned into a procession by Medici Code, who won in a very smart time for a race of this type. It has been rated through the fourth, although there is a case for rating it higher based on the performances of the second and third.
Medici Code Official explanation: trainer said, regarding the improved form shown, animal had been gelded since its last run
Beck Official explanation: jockey said gelding suffered interference on leaving the stalls

225 PONTINSBINGO.COM H'CAP (DIV II) 6f (F)
2:40 (2:40) (Class 6) (0-55,54) 4-Y-0+ **£1,706** (£503; £252) **Stalls** Low

Form RPR

064- **1** **Count Cougar (USA)**[31] [6930] 7-8-9 **54** ..... MichaelJStainton(5) 4 69
(S P Griffiths) *mde all: rdn clr 2f out: kpt on wl* **11/8**[1]

23-2 **2** *3* **Mind Alert**[14] [77] 6-8-10 **50** ..... (v) NCallan 10 56
(D Shaw) *in tch: hdwy to chse wnr 2f out: sn rdn:edgd lft and one pce appr last* **7/4**[2]

50-0 **3** *5* **Piccolo Prince**[22] [3] 6-8-12 **52** ..... (p) PaulHanagan 9 43
(P A Blockley) *rr: hdwy on outer 2f out: sn rdn and styd on ins last: nrst fin* **10/1**[3]

300- **4** *shd* **Guadaloup**[49] [6719] 5-8-6 **53** ..... (v) PatrickDonaghy(7) 7 44
(M Brittain) *sn rdn along in rr: hdwy 1/2-way: drvn to chse ldng pair wl over 1f out: sn one pce* **16/1**

00-0 **5** 2 ½ **Mister Becks (IRE)**^{7} [145] 4-8-6 **46**.......................... AdrianMcCarthy 3 29
(M C Chapman) *chsd ldrs: rdn along 1/2-way: sn btn* **22/1**

60-5 **6** nk **Ames Souer (IRE)**^{8} [135] 4-8-5 **45**.......................... CatherineGannon 5 27
(P D Evans) *hld up: hdwy over 2f out: sn rdn and btn* **33/1**

0-00 **7** 1 **Percy Douglas**^{12} [97] 7-8-2 **47** ow2...................(bt) AnnStokell$^{(5)}$ 6 26
(Miss A Stokell) *chsd wnr: rdn along wl over 2f out: grad wknd* **80/1**

30-3 **8** 2 ½ **Diamond Katie (IRE)**^{10} [123] 5-8-5 **50**.................. DuranFentiman$^{(5)}$ 8 22
(N Tinkler) *chsd ldrs: rdn along 1/2-way: sn wknd* **10/1**^{3}

06-4 **9** 43 **Princess Kai (IRE)**^{7} [143] 6-8-5 **45**.......................... JamieMackay 2 —
(R Ingram) *v.s.a: a bhd* **33/1**

1m 15.54s (-1.36) **Going Correction** -0.15s/f (Stan) 9 Ran SP% **114.0**
Speed ratings (Par 101):103,99,92,92,88 88,87,83,26
CSF £3.69 CT £14.15 TOTE £2.60: £1.10, £1.30, £2.60; EX 3.70 Trifecta £29.00 Pool: £559.91 - 13.69 winning units..
Owner M Grant **Bred** Angus Glen Farm (1996) Ltd **Trained** Easingwold, N Yorks

FOCUS
This race was more or less decided at the start and very few ever got into it. The pace was decent, though, and the winning time was 1.71 seconds faster than the first division. It is best rated through the runner-up.

226 PONTIN'S BOOK EARLY H'CAP 1m 4f (F)
3:10 (3:10) (Class 4) (0-85,82) 4-Y-0+ **£4,857** (£1,445; £722; £360) **Stalls** Low

Form RPR

006- **1** **Dundry**^{59} [5952] 6-8-8 **70**..........................(p) BrettDoyle 1 80
(G L Moore) *trckd ldrs: hdwy on inner 3f out: rdn to chal over 1f out: drvn to ld and edgd rt ins last: kpt on wl* **15/2**^{3}

14-3 **2** hd **Polish Power (GER)**^{13} [95] 7-9-4 **80**.......................... JohnEgan 7 90
(J S Moore) *in tch: hdwy and rdn along 3f out: outpcd and swtchd lft over 1f out: drvn: kpt on and ev ch ins last: no ex nr fin* **5/2**^{1}

253- **3** 1 **Heathyards Pride**^{28} [6941] 7-9-5 **81**.......................... GeorgeBaker 6 89
(R Hollinshead) *hld up in tch: gd hdwy on outer 3f out: rdn to ld over 1f out: drvn: edgd lft and hdd ins last: no ex last 100 yds* **15/2**^{3}

01-2 **4** 3 **Jackie Kiely**^{12} [100] 6-9-0 **76**..........................(t) PhillipMakin 4 79
(R Brotherton) *trckd ldr: led 4f out: rdn along 2f out: drvn and hdd over 1f out: wkng whn n.m.r ent last* **6/1**^{2}

336- **5** 1 **Pass The Port**^{32} [6917] 6-8-13 **75**.......................... NCallan 5 77
(D Haydn Jones) *hld up in tch: hdwy 4f out: effrt and ev ch 2f out: sn rdn and wknd over 1f out* **5/2**^{1}

050/ **6** 18 **Red Wine**^{1018} [1329] 8-9-3 **82**.......................... StephenDonohoe$^{(3)}$ 2 55
(A J McCabe) *keen: led: rdn alonga nd hdd 4f out: wknd over 2f out* **33/1**

40-0 **7** 20 **Kylkenny**^{13} [95] 12-8-6 **73**..........................(t) CAdamson$^{(5)}$ 3 14
(H Morrison) *keen: chsd ldng pair: rdn along over 4f out: sn wknd and bhd* **15/2**^{3}

2m 39.84s (-2.25) **Going Correction** -0.15s/f (Stan) 7 Ran SP% **109.7**
Speed ratings (Par 105):101,100,100,98,97 85,72
CSF £24.41 TOTE £10.10: £3.80, £2.20; EX 35.40.
Owner D J Deer **Bred** D J And Mrs Deer **Trained** Woodingdean, E Sussex
■ Stewards' Enquiry : Brett Doyle one-day ban: careless riding (Feb 3)

FOCUS
A modest early pace resulted in a few taking a grip and the contest rather developed into a sprint from the home bend. It has been rated around the runner-up and third.

227 PONTINS.COM H'CAP 7f (F)
3:40 (3:40) (Class 2) (0-100,93) 4-Y-0+ **£11,334** (£3,372; £1,685; £841) **Stalls** Low

Form RPR

611- **1** **California Laws**^{33} [6896] 5-8-3 **80**.......................... PaulFessey 1 99+
(T D Barron) *dwlt: sn chsng ldrs: pushed along and sltly outpcd 3f out: rdn to ld over 1f out: clr ins last: kpt on* **11/8**^{1}

00-5 **2** ¾ **Waterside (IRE)**^{10} [118] 8-8-12 **89**.......................... NCallan 8 103
(G L Moore) *hld up: hdwy on outer 3f out: rdn wl over 1f out: kpt on u.p ins last* **4/1**^{2}

42-3 **3** 3 **Jimmy The Guesser**^{14} [81] 4-8-6 **83**..........................(e^{1}) HayleyTurner 3 89
(N P Littmoden) *led: rdn along over 2f out: drvn and hdd over 1f out: kpt on same pce* **8/1**

26-2 **4** 3 **Prince Tum Tum (USA)**^{18} [41] 7-8-11 **88**.......................... JimmyQuinn 4 86
(D Shaw) *hld up: hdwy over 2f out: rdn to chse ldrs over 1f out: sn drvn and one pce* **9/1**

056- **5** 2 **Byron Bay**^{23} [6997] 5-8-2 **84**.......................... DuranFentiman$^{(5)}$ 9 77
(I Semple) *cl up: rdn along over 2f out: sn wknd* **16/1**

4-61 **6** 1 ½ **Marko Jadeo (IRE)**^{4} [183] 9-8-4 **86** 6ex.......................... TolleyDean$^{(5)}$ 7 75
(R A Harris) *dwlt: swtchd lft and hld up in rr: gd hdwy on inner 3f out: rdn to chse ldrs 2f out: sn drvn and wknd over 1f out* **25/1**

0-04 **7** ½ **Night Prospector**^{14} [81] 7-7-12 **82**..........................(p) LukeMorris$^{(7)}$ 6 70
(R A Harris) *cl up: rdn along over 2f out and sn wknd* **33/1**

3-35 **8** 1 ¼ **Pawan (IRE)**^{14} [79] 7-8-4 **86**..........................(b) AnnStokell$^{(5)}$ 5 71
(Miss A Stokell) *chsd ldrs: rdn along 3f out: sn wknd* **33/1**

62-5 **9** ½ **Wessex (USA)**^{22} [6] 7-9-2 **93**.......................... IanMongan 2 76
(P A Blockley) *hld up: a rr* **11/2**^{3}

1m 27.62s (-3.18) **Going Correction** -0.15s/f (Stan) 9 Ran SP% **114.2**
Speed ratings (Par 109):112,111,107,104,102 100,99,98,97
CSF £6.52 CT £29.83 TOTE £2.10: £1.40, £1.60, £1.80; EX 9.70 Trifecta £39.70 Pool: £948.45 - 16.92 winning units..
Owner Rupert Bear Racing **Bred** P Balding **Trained** Maunby, N Yorks

FOCUS
A hot handicap, run at a decent pace in a good time, and the form looks rock solid.

NOTEBOOK
California Laws ◆, raised another 5lb in his bid for a course hat-trick, did not appear to be travelling at all well turning for home but he responded to the pressure to battle on for a convincing win. Now unbeaten in all four of his outings here, he still seems to be improving at the age of five. He now reportedly joins Ralph Beckett. (op 7-4 tchd 2-1 in places)
Waterside(IRE) ◆, better known for his success on Polytrack and turf, does have winning form here too and confirmed the promise of his return from a break at Lingfield earlier this month with a smart effort in defeat and was the only one to offer any sort of a threat to the winner in the latter stages. He normally races up with the pace, if not leads, so trying to come from so far back at a meeting where early pace ruled makes this performance even better.
Jimmy The Guesser, 3lb better off with California Laws for a neck defeat over six furlongs here last month, was given a positive ride in the first-time eyeshield, but could not match the finishing efforts of the front pair. He has run well over this trip on a few occasions, but has yet to win beyond six. (op 15-2)
Prince Tum Tum(USA), trying Fibresand for the first time, stayed on down the home straight but could never get seriously involved, and the way the track was riding at this meeting did not suit his come-from-behind style. (op 8-1 tchd 10-1)
Byron Bay held a decent position for much of the way before fading. He remains 3lb above his last winning mark. (op 11-1)
Marko Jadeo(IRE), carrying a 6lb penalty for his Wolverhampton win, was trying Fibresand for the first time and, as he is a confirmed hold-up performer, he was never going to be suited by these conditions. (op 22-1)
Wessex(USA) was always out the back and, even allowing for the track bias towards front-runners, this was still most disappointing. (op 6-1 tchd 13-2)

228 PONTIN'S HOLIDAYS H'CAP 1m (F)
4:10 (4:10) (Class 6) (0-65,65) 4-Y-0+ **£2,388** (£705; £352) **Stalls** Low

Form RPR

34-5 **1** **Luckylover**^{17} [48] 4-9-2 **65**..........................(t) TPQueally 4 79+
(M G Quinlan) *mde all: rdn clr 2f out: styd on strly* **8/1**^{3}

6-21 **2** 3 **Wodhill Gold**^{14} [75] 6-8-11 **60**..........................(v) HayleyTurner 9 66
(D Morris) *trckd ldrs: hdwy to chse wnr wl over 1f out and sn rdn: drvn and edgd lft appr last: sn no imp* **9/2**^{2}

14- **3** 1 ¾ **Astronomical Odds (USA)**^{45} [6762] 4-8-8 **64**.......................... NeilBrown$^{(7)}$ 3 66
(T D Barron) *in tch: hdwy over 2f out: sn rdn and kpt on same pce appr last* **10/3**^{1}

16-0 **4** 3 **Kingsmaite**^{15} [70] 6-8-13 **62**..........................(vt) PhillipMakin 1 58
(S R Bowring) *dwlt and towards rr: hdwy over 2f out: sn rdn and kpt on ins last: nrst fin* **12/1**

02-3 **5** ½ **Anduril**^{21} [14] 6-9-1 **64**..........................(p) AdamKirby 2 59
(Miss M E Rowland) *chsd ldrs on inner: rdn along and sltly outpcd 3f out: drvn and kpt on same pce fnl 2f* **8/1**^{3}

500- **6** ½ **Up Tempo (IRE)**^{40} [6820] 9-9-0 **63**..........................(b) JohnEgan 12 57
(C R Dore) *chsd ldrs on outer: rdn along wl over 2f out and grad wknd* **20/1**

1-21 **7** 1 ½ **Paso Doble**^{14} [80] 9-8-4 **58** ow1..........................(p) JamesMillman$^{(5)}$ 5 48
(D K Ivory) *cl up: rdn along 3f out: sn wknd* **9/2**^{2}

25-3 **8** shd **Vancouver Gold (IRE)**^{16} [61] 5-8-13 **62**.......................... PatCosgrave 6 52
(K R Burke) *cl up: rdn along 3f out: drvn over 2f out and grad wknd* **20/1**

060- **9** 1 ¾ **Greenbelt**^{49} [6716] 6-8-8 **57**.......................... ChrisCatlin 13 44
(G M Moore) *a towards rr* **8/1**^{3}

60-3 **10** nk **Golden Alchemist**^{17} [49] 4-9-0 **63**.......................... IanMongan 8 49
(M D I Usher) *dwlt: a towards rr* **14/1**

50-5 **11** nk **Boy Dancer (IRE)**^{12} [101] 4-8-9 **58**.......................... PaulHanagan 14 43
(D W Barker) *racd on outer: a towards rr* **20/1**

355- **12** 17 **Roman Empire**^{271} [1258] 7-8-7 **56**..........................(b) SimonWhitworth 10 6
(P A Blockley) *in tch: rdn along 1/2-way: sn wknd* **33/1**

1m 41.68s (-2.92) **Going Correction** -0.15s/f (Stan) 12 Ran SP% **124.4**
Speed ratings (Par 101):108,105,103,100,99 99,97,97,95,95 95,78
CSF £43.74 CT £151.33 TOTE £8.70: £2.50, £1.90, £2.30; EX 59.30 Trifecta £244.00 Pool: £412.52 - 1.20 winning units. Place 6 £8.53, Place 5 £6.36.
Owner Roger Turner **Bred** Shutford Stud **Trained** Newmarket, Suffolk

FOCUS
No messing about in this handicap and the pace was decent from the off, resulting in a smart winning time for a race of its class. Again it paid to be right at the sharp end from the start. The race has been rated through the runner-up.
T/Jkpt: Not won. T/Plt: £19.60 to a £1 stake. Pool: £90,934.10. 3,382.15 winning tickets. T/Qpdt: £11.60 to a £1 stake. Pool: £8,699.30. 553.40 winning tickets. JR

193 LINGFIELD (L-H)
Wednesday, January 24

OFFICIAL GOING: Standard
After snow and frost overnight, the meeting needed to pass two inspections.
Wind: Almost nil Weather: Fine

229 PONTINS.COM MAIDEN STKS (DIV I) 1m 4f (P)
12:50 (12:51) (Class 5) 4-Y-0+ **£2,169** (£645; £322; £161) **Stalls** Low

Form RPR

656- **1** **Sunset Boulevard (IRE)**^{107} [5870] 4-9-3 70.......................... ChrisCatlin 6 64
(Miss Tor Sturgis) *wl plcd: trckd ldng pair over 3f out: led wl over 1f out and kicked at least 2l clr: drvn fnl f: jst hld on* **7/1**

363- **2** shd **Moon Empress (FR)**^{25} [6987] 4-8-12 62.......................... SebSanders 4 59
(W R Muir) *lw: hld up in midfield: prog 3f out: rdn to chse wnr over 1f out: clsng wl at fin: jst failed* **11/4**^{2}

42-4 **3** 6 **Blu Manruna**^{21} [24] 4-9-3 56..........................(b) PaulDoe 11 54
(J Akehurst) *prom: jnd ldr over 3f out: upsides 2f out: rdn and fnd nil wl over 1f out* **10/1**

50-5 **4** 1 ¼ **War Feather**^{11} [120] 5-9-7 45.......................... RobertHavlin 9 52
(T D McCarthy) *hld up in rr: rdn 5f out: prog u.p over 3f out and cl up 2f out: sn wl outpcd* **50/1**

6- **5** nk **Smart Cat (IRE)**^{132} [5319] 4-8-12.......................... NCallan 8 47
(A P Jarvis) *hld up in last pair: prog 3f out: rdn to chse ldrs 2f out: sn wl outpcd* **6/4**^{1}

0- **6** 5 **Moving Target (IRE)**^{141} [5092] 8-9-7.......................... CatherineGannon 7 44
(Luke Comer, Ire) *t.k.h: mostly trckd ldr: narrow ld wl over 3f out to wl over 1f out: wknd* **50/1**

7 5 **Remis Velisque**^{20} 4-8-12.......................... FergusSweeney 5 31
(B G Powell) *leggy: s.s: hld up in last pair: gng wl enough 4f out: pushed along and outpcd 3f out: plugged on steadily* **20/1**

4- **8** 7 **Barton Belle**^{215} [2829] 5-9-2.......................... JimmyQuinn 2 19
(C N Kellett) *unf: t.k.h: prom tl rdn and wknd over 4f out: t.o* **5/1**^{3}

00- **9** 2 ½ **Nona**^{115} [4697] 4-8-12 55.......................... OscarUrbina 10 15
(S Dow) *in tch: rdn over 4f out: sn wknd: t.o* **25/1**

0 **10** 4 **Tres Bien**^{19} [45] 5-9-7.......................... DaneO'Neill 1 14
(P R Webber) *s.i.s: sn led: hdd & wknd wl over 3f out: t.o* **14/1**

2m 32.15s (-2.24) **Going Correction** -0.05s/f (Stan)
WFA 4 from 5yo+ 4lb 10 Ran SP% **124.1**
Speed ratings (Par 103):105,104,100,100,99 96,93,88,86,84
CSF £27.61 TOTE £10.00: £2.20, £1.60, £2.40; EX 34.80 Trifecta £77.40 Pool: £218.10 - 2.00 winning tickets..
Owner Gordon Hopkins **Bred** A J Martin **Trained** Kingston Lisle, Oxon
■ The first winner on the Flat for Tor Sturgis.

FOCUS
A moderate maiden in which the proximity of the 45-rated War Feather does little for the form, but the pace was sound and the winning time was 3.09 seconds faster than the second division.

230 PONTINS.COM MAIDEN STKS (DIV II) 1m 4f (P)
1:20 (1:20) (Class 5) 4-Y-0+ **£2,169** (£645; £322; £161) **Stalls** Low

Form RPR

0P-2 **1** **King's Ransom**^{21} [24] 4-9-3 64..........................(b) SebSanders 5 67
(W R Muir) *t.k.h: hld up in rr: prog 2f out: effrt and hung fire over 1f out: drvn to ld last 150yds: sn clr* **2/1**^{2}

50- **2** 1 ¾ **Ausone**^{54} [5429] 5-9-2.......................... IanMongan 10 59
(Miss J R Gibney) *leggy: b.bkwd: cl up: jnd ldr over 3f out: led 2f out: drvn and hdd last 150yds: nt qckn* **16/1**

22-3 **3** *nk* **Art Investor**[11] [120] 4-9-0 67 .... MarcHalford(3) 2 64
(D R C Elsworth) *trckd ldng pair: drvn to chal over 1f out: ref to go by and lft bhd by wnr ins fnl f* **8/11**[1]

00- **4** *5* **Sky Walk**[128] [5426] 4-9-3 .... SimonWhitworth 3 56
(Jamie Poulton) *hld up in last: pushed along 5f out: outpcd over 2f out: no ch after* **50/1**

5 *nk* **Hi Fi**[34] 9-9-7 .... ChrisCatlin 6 55
(Ian Williams) *s.s: led after 1f to over 4f out: wknd 2f out* **12/1**[3]

603- **6** *hd* **Orphina (IRE)**[42] [6801] 4-8-5 47 ....(t) KarenKenny(7) 1 50
(B G Powell) *lw: led for 1f: led over 4f out to 2f out: wknd over 1f out* **20/1**

7 *shd* **Kates Guest (IRE)**[91] [6185] 5-9-7 .... FMBerry 7 55
(B G Powell) *hld up in last pair: effrt to chse ldrs 2f out: hanging lft over 1f out: wknd rapidly* **33/1**

2m 35.24s (0.85) **Going Correction** -0.05s/f (Stan)
WFA 4 from 5yo+ 4lb 7 Ran SP% **114.5**
Speed ratings (Par 103):95,93,93,90,90 89,89
CSF £30.46 TOTE £2.50: £2.50, £4.40; EX 30.50 Trifecta £79.10 Pool: £257.54 - 2.31 winning tickets..
Owner Christopher Ransom **Bred** Darley **Trained** Lambourn, Berks

FOCUS
A weak maiden, made even more so by the three non-runners. There was no pace on at all early, resulting in a winning time 3.09 seconds slower than the first division and the form looks dubious, limited by the fourth and fifth.

231 GO PONTIN'S MAIDEN STKS 6f (P)
1:50 (1:51) (Class 5) 3-Y-O **£2,914** (£867; £433; £216) **Stalls** Low

Form RPR

2-2 **1** **Telltime (IRE)**[21] [17] 3-8-5 .... WilliamBuick(7) 5 69+
(A M Balding) *trckd ldng pair: led on inner over 1f out: pushed clr* **5/2**[1]

35-3 **2** *2 ½* **Madrigale**[7] [160] 3-8-12 .... FMBerry 3 62
(G L Moore) *n.m.r on inner and dropped to rr over 4f out: effrt 2f out: drvn and kpt on to take 2nd nr fin* **15/2**

635- **3** *shd* **Wilmington**[71] [6475] 3-9-3 70 ....(b) NCallan 10 66
(N P Littmoden) *awkward s: hld up in rr: prog over 2f out: rdn to chse wnr ins fnl f: no imp: lost 2nd nr fin* **6/1**

200- **4** *1 ¾* **Caj (IRE)**[127] [5448] 3-8-12 .... CatherineGannon 8 56
(Luke Comer, Ire) *hld up in last pair: effrt whn nt clr run briefly wl over 1f out: rdn and kpt on fnl f: n.d* **100/1**

5 *1 ¼* **Divertimenti (IRE)**[116] [5694] 3-9-3 .... PatCosgrave 7 57
(M J Wallace) *trckd ldrs: n.m.r over 1f out and outpcd: kpt on ins fnl f* **11/4**[2]

6- **6** *½* **Sohraab**[177] [4000] 3-9-3 .... LPKeniry 4 71+
(H Morrison) *s.s: sn wl in tch: trapped on inner and hmpd over 1f out: no ch after: r.o nr fin* **11/2**[3]

6 **7** *nk* **Brave Jack (IRE)**[18] [55] 3-9-3 .... BrettDoyle 11 55+
(J R Best) *outpcd in last and sn rdn: no prog tl styd on wl fnl f* **33/1**

04- **8** *hd* **Millyjean**[33] [6905] 3-8-12 .... HayleyTurner 9 49
(John Berry) *in tch on outer: rdn wl over 2f out: brief effrt over 1f out: wknd ins fnl f* **50/1**

0-6 **9** *½* **Rogers Lodger**[10] [127] 3-9-3 .... JimmyQuinn 6 53
(J Akehurst) *trckd ldrs: rdn and cl up 2f out: wknd fnl f* **25/1**

03- **10** *1* **Launch It Lily**[103] [5950] 3-8-5 .... JackDean(7) 1 45
(W G M Turner) *led after 2f to over 1f out: wknd rapidly* **14/1**

0 **11** *2 ½* **Fareham Creek**[8] [149] 3-8-12 .... JamesMillman(5) 2 42
(D K Ivory) *led for 2f: pressed ldr to wl over 1f out: bmpd sn after and wknd rapidly* **100/1**

1m 12.72s (-0.09) **Going Correction** -0.05s/f (Stan) 11 Ran SP% **114.1**
Speed ratings (Par 97):98,94,94,92,90 89,89,89,88,87 83
CSF £20.41 TOTE £2.60: £1.50, £2.20, £1.80; EX 15.30 Trifecta £34.00 Pool: £296.96 - 6.19 winning tickets..
Owner Mrs P McEnery **Bred** John McEnery **Trained** Kingsclere, Hants

FOCUS
A routine maiden, lacking strength in depth, but the front pair have a bit of scope and may go on to better things. They also set the standard for the form.
Sohraab Official explanation: jockey said colt suffered interference in running
Millyjean Official explanation: jockey said filly hung right on bend

232 PONTINSBINGO.COM H'CAP 2m (P)
2:20 (2:20) (Class 5) (0-75,71) 4-Y-O+ **£2,914** (£867; £433; £216) **Stalls** Low

Form RPR

0-13 **1** **Lorikeet**[4] [195] 8-9-2 62 .... JamesDoyle(3) 2 69+
(Noel T Chance) *hld up in rr: prog 3f out and sn trckd ldrs: rdn to ld 1f out: kpt on u.p* **9/4**[1]

/0-3 **2** *¾* **Kavi (IRE)**[21] [29] 7-9-11 68 .... OscarUrbina 9 73
(Simon Earle) *mde most: rdn over 2f out: hdd 1f out: kpt on same pce: a hld* **10/1**

3/60 **3** *shd* **Mumbling (IRE)**[2] [213] 9-9-5 62 .... FergusSweeney 8 67
(B G Powell) *hld up in rr: prog over 3f out: cl up and rdn over 2f out: nt qckn over 1f out: kpt on ins fnl f* **14/1**

26-1 **4** *nk* **Amwell Brave**[14] [88] 6-9-10 67 .... NCallan 1 71
(J R Jenkins) *t.k.h: hld up in last: prog 3f out: chsd ldrs 2f out: kpt on same pce fnl f: nvr able to chal* **9/2**[2]

5/0- **5** *nk* **Flying Spirit (IRE)**[28] [556] 8-9-11 68 ....(b) GeorgeBaker 4 72
(G L Moore) *chsd ldr for 3f: wnt 2nd again 4f out: hrd rdn to chal over 1f out: one pce and lost pls ins fnl f* **16/1**

0/31 **6** *9* **Alagon (IRE)**[13] [100] 7-9-0 57 ....(b) ChrisCatlin 5 50
(Ian Williams) *chsd ldr after 3f to 4f out: wknd over 2f out* **5/1**[3]

01-4 **7** *2 ½* **Salut Saint Cloud**[23] [4] 6-9-10 67 ....(p) SimonWhitworth 3 57
(G L Moore) *wl plcd: effrt to dispute 2nd 4f out: wknd over 2f out* **5/1**[3]

3-60 **8** *3 ½* **Serramanna**[14] [88] 6-8-6 52 .... JerryO'Dwyer(3) 6 38
(Ms J S Doyle) *hld up in rr: effrt u.p on outer to chse ldrs over 3f out: wknd over 2f out* **7/1**

3m 24.97s (-3.82) **Going Correction** -0.05s/f (Stan) 8 Ran SP% **116.4**
Speed ratings (Par 103):107,106,106,106,106 101,100,98
CSF £26.90 CT £259.22 TOTE £2.70: £1.20, £4.50, £3.10; EX 35.20 Trifecta £278.00 Part won. Pool: £391.68 - 0.33 winning tickets..
Owner The Tribesmen Syndicate **Bred** Sheikh Mohammed Bin Rashid Al Maktoum **Trained** Upper Lambourn, Berks

FOCUS
The early pace did not appear to be that strong, but they were really travelling over the last half-mile and the final time was good. The form does not appear that strong and is best rated around the third and fourth.

233 PONTIN'S HOLIDAYS H'CAP 1m (P)
2:50 (2:50) (Class 5) (0-75,74) 4-Y-O+ **£2,914** (£867; £433; £216) **Stalls** High

Form RPR

001- **1** **Bold Diktator**[25] [6993] 5-8-11 69 .... JimCrowley 7 77
(Tom Dascombe) *fast away: mde all and set stdy pce to 1/2-way: kicked on 2f out: unchal* **3/1**[2]

20-4 **2** *1 ½* **Imperial Lucky (IRE)**[8] [150] 4-8-12 70 .... HayleyTurner 5 75
(D K Ivory) *lw: t.k.h: trckd ldrs: effrt 2f out: disp 2nd fnl f: no imp on wnr* **10/1**

00-5 **3** *hd* **Sonny Parkin**[21] [30] 5-9-1 73 ....(v) PatCosgrave 4 77+
(G A Huffer) *dwlt: t.k.h: hld up in last pair: prog over 1f out: nt look keen but styd on ins fnl f* **9/1**

P00- **4** *shd* **Nikki Bea (IRE)**[39] [6848] 4-8-2 60 oh4 .... AdrianMcCarthy 2 64
(Jamie Poulton) *prom: shkn up to dispute 2nd over 1f out: no imp on wnr* **16/1**

21-6 **5** *shd* **Dichoh**[21] [28] 4-9-2 74 .... NCallan 1 78+
(M A Jarvis) *trckd ldrs: rdn and in trble whn pce lifted over 3f out: lost pl: effrt again over 1f out: kpt on: nvr able to chal* **2/1**[1]

31-2 **6** *½* **Flyingit (USA)**[13] [101] 4-8-12 70 ....(p) CatherineGannon 6 73
(K A Ryan) *t.k.h: mostly chsd wnr to over 1f out: hanging and fnd nil* **12/1**

124- **7** *½* **Million Percent**[39] [6841] 8-8-10 68 .... TPQueally 8 69
(C R Dore) *plld hrd: hld up bhd ldrs: effrt and cl up 2f out: fdd fnl f* **10/1**

520- **8** *½* **Silent Storm**[116] [5689] 7-9-0 72 .... AbdulAziz 9 72
(C A Cyzer) *lw: t.k.h: hld up in last trio: bmpd along and one pce over 1f out* **33/1**

0-00 **9** *1 ½* **Smokin Joe**[11] [117] 6-8-8 66 ow1 ....(b) BrettDoyle 3 62
(J R Best) *t.k.h: hld up in last pair: rdn and fnd nil over 1f out* **6/1**[3]

1m 40.71s (1.28) **Going Correction** -0.05s/f (Stan) 9 Ran SP% **117.3**
Speed ratings (Par 103):91,89,89,89,89 88,88,87,86
CSF £33.69 CT £245.40 TOTE £3.90: £1.70, £2.60, £2.90; EX 64.60 Trifecta £396.10 Pool: £608.19 - 1.09 winning tickets..
Owner Oneway RSM Racing Club **Bred** T J And Mrs Heywood **Trained** Lambourn, Berks

FOCUS
A really competitive handicap and, as was to be expected after the modest gallop, there was not much separating them at the line. The form looks only ordinary and the fourth tends to limit the form.

234 PONTIN'S FAMILY HOLIDAYS H'CAP 7f (P)
3:20 (3:21) (Class 5) (0-70,70) 4-Y-O+ **£2,914** (£867; £433; £216) **Stalls** Low

Form RPR

54-6 **1** **Danetime Lord (IRE)**[13] [102] 4-8-12 66 ....(p) NCallan 2 74
(K A Ryan) *prom: effrt 2f out: led over 1f out: drvn and flashed tail fnl f: hld on* **8/1**

12-2 **2** *½* **Imperium**[16] [70] 6-8-9 63 .... DaneO'Neill 12 70
(Jean-Rene Auvray) *hld up wl in rr: prog wl over 1f out: drvn and r.o wl to cl on wnr nr fin: too much to do* **15/2**[3]

115- **3** *hd* **Small Stakes (IRE)**[39] [6842] 5-9-0 68 ....(v) SebSanders 5 74
(P J Makin) *hld up in tch: prog on outer over 2f out: drvn to chse wnr fnl f: styd on but lost 2nd last strides* **4/1**[1]

60-3 **4** *shd* **Stoic Leader (IRE)**[8] [151] 7-8-8 67 .... KevinGhunowa(5) 7 73
(R F Fisher) *mostly in midfield: prog 2f out: hrd rdn and styd on fnl f: gaining but nvr quite able to chal* **11/1**

00-2 **5** *nk* **Sir Douglas**[20] [32] 4-8-9 68 .... MichaelJStainton(5) 9 73
(R A Harris) *t.k.h: chsd ldr for 2f: styd prom: drvn over 1f out: nt qckn ins fnl f: lost pls nr fin* **14/1**

000- **6** *nk* **His Master's Voice (IRE)**[35] [6882] 4-9-0 68 .... JimCrowley 4 72
(D W P Arbuthnot) *hld up: prog on outer and wd bnd 2f out: styd on fnl f: nrst fin* **10/1**

351- **7** *½* **Special Place**[36] [6869] 4-8-8 62 .... OscarUrbina 13 65
(J A R Toller) *dropped in fr wd draw and hld up last: effrt and v wd bnd 2f out: styd on fnl f: no ch* **4/1**[1]

16- **8** *1 ¼* **Methaaly (IRE)**[106] [5902] 4-8-13 67 .... BrettDoyle 14 67
(Jane Chapple-Hyam) *plld hrd early: hld up bhd ldrs: shuffled along over 1f out: steadily lost pl* **7/1**[2]

1-52 **9** *hd* **Mistral Sky**[10] [132] 8-8-11 65 ....(p) MickyFenton 3 64
(Stef Liddiard) *hld up wl in rr: nvr on terms: kpt on fnl f* **10/1**

00-6 **10** *1* **Wheelavit (IRE)**[21] [30] 4-8-13 67 .... FMBerry 10 64
(B G Powell) *nvr beyond midfield: rdn in last trio 2f out: struggling after* **10/1**

0-05 **11** *nk* **Loyal Tycoon (IRE)**[10] [132] 9-9-0 68 .... ShaneKelly 11 64
(D K Ivory) *led to over 1f out: wknd fnl f* **33/1**

00-0 **12** *7* **Anfield Dream**[15] [79] 5-9-2 70 .... J-PGuillambert 1 48
(J R Jenkins) *hld up wl in rr: prog on inner over 2f out: rdn and wknd rapidly over 1f out* **25/1**

0/00 **13** *1 ¼* **Verite**[15] [79] 4-8-8 65 ....(be) StephenDonohoe(3) 6 39
(A J McCabe) *hld up: rapid prog to chse ldr after 2f: wknd rapidly over 2f out* **66/1**

1m 24.1s (-1.79) **Going Correction** -0.05s/f (Stan) 13 Ran SP% **125.9**
Speed ratings (Par 103):108,107,107,107,106 106,105,104,104,103 102,94,93
CSF £69.77 CT £292.65 TOTE £12.10: £3.10, £2.60, £2.00; EX 73.40 Trifecta £115.60 Pool: £363.29 - 2.23 winning tickets..
Owner Bull & Bell Partnership **Bred** P J Murphy **Trained** Hambleton, N Yorks

FOCUS
A fair winning time for the grade of contest and the runners finished well bunched. The form appears sound rated around the third and fourth.

235 PONTIN'S "BOOK EARLY" H'CAP 7f (P)
3:50 (3:54) (Class 6) (0-60,60) 4-Y-O+ **£2,388** (£705; £352) **Stalls** Low

Form RPR

305- **1** **Mountain Pass (USA)**[25] [6984] 5-8-12 56 ....(p) RobertHavlin 5 66
(B J Llewellyn) *s.s: hld up in last: smooth prog over 2f out through rivals: effrt over 1f out: drvn to ld ins fnl f: styd on wl* **16/1**

6-46 **2** *nk* **Mystic Man (FR)**[10] [131] 9-9-2 60 ....(p) JimCrowley 9 69
(I W McInnes) *hld up wl in rr: smooth prog 2f out: effrt to chal fnl f: hrd rdn and styd on: jst hld* **14/1**

00-1 **3** *1* **Tyrone Sam**[14] [86] 5-8-13 57 ....(b) NCallan 13 64
(K A Ryan) *chsd ldng pair: pushed along 3f out: wnt 2nd 2f out: led over 1f out: hung rt and hdd 1f out: styd on towards fin* **7/1**[3]

20-1 **4** *hd* **Beneking**[18] [50] 7-9-2 60 ....(p) ChrisCatlin 14 66
(D Burchell) *trckd clr ldrs gng wl: effrt 2f out: rdn to ld 1f out: hdd and outpcd ins fnl f* **8/1**

036- **5** *½* **State Dilemma (IRE)**[25] [6990] 6-9-1 59 ....(v) DaneO'Neill 7 64
(D Shaw) *hld up in rr: effrt over 1f out: styd on ins fnl f: nvr rchd ldrs* **11/2**[2]

24-0 **6** *hd* **Moon Bird**[7] 158 5-9-0 **58** OscarUrbina 12 62
(C A Cyzer) *hld up in midfield: effrt on outer 2f out: carried rt 1f out: styd on but nvr pce to chal* **9/2**[1]

440- **7** *nk* **Flint River**[41] 6820 9-8-13 **57** MickyFenton 1 60
(H Morrison) *chsd clr ldrs: lost pl sltly on inner over 2f out: rallied over 1f out and ch ent fnl f: fdd* **11/1**

55-0 **8** *1 1/2* **Scroll**[10] 131 4-9-2 **60** (v) J-PGuillambert 6 60
(P Howling) *settled in midfield: rdn over 2f out: swtchd to inner fnl f: fnd nil* **10/1**

30-0 **9** *3/4* **Ask No More**[10] 130 4-8-11 **58** (b) DominicFox(3) 10 56
(P L Gilligan) *towards rr and wd: rdn and prog 3f out: no imp on ldrs over 1f out: fdd* **25/1**

1-35 **10** *hd* **The London Gang**[10] 131 4-8-13 **57** ShaneKelly 11 54
(Miss D A McHale) *s.i.s: wl in rr: effrt on wd outside over 1f out: no prog u.p* **14/1**

65-0 **11** *1* **Our Kes (IRE)**[21] 30 5-9-2 **60** PaulDoe 3 54
(P Howling) *dwlt: t.k.h: hld up in last pair: no prog fnl 2f* **11/2**[2]

6-66 **12** *1 1/4* **Goose Chase**[10] 130 5-9-1 **59** (b) LPKeniry 4 50
(A M Hales) *w ldr at fast pce: led over 2f out to over 1f out: wknd rapidly* **20/1**

4/0- **13** *2* **Neideen (IRE)**[232] 2317 5-8-13 **57** TPQueally 8 43
(J Akehurst) *chsd clr ldrs early: lost pl 1/2-way: wl in rr 2f out* **25/1**

650- **14** *shd* **Smile For Us**[32] 6930 4-8-13 **60** (b) JerryO'Dwyer(3) 2 46
(C Drew) *led at furious pce to over 2f out: wknd rapidly over 1f out* **50/1**

1m 23.81s (-2.08) **Going Correction** -0.05s/f (Stan) **14** Ran SP% **123.6**
Speed ratings (Par 101):109,108,107,107,106 106,106,104,103,103 102,100,98,98
CSF £219.77 CT £1773.73 TOTE £18.00: £4.80, £5.00, £2.90; EX 216.90 TRIFECTA Not won..
Owner B J Llewellyn **Bred** Marablue Farm **Trained** Fochriw, Caerphilly

FOCUS
A decent winning time for the class of race, 0.29 seconds quicker than the preceding higher-grade handicap, and the form is best rated through the third and looks solid.
Neideen(IRE) Official explanation: jockey said mare hung badly left

236 GO PONTIN'S AMATEUR RIDERS' H'CAP 6f (P)
4:20 (4:22) (Class 6) (0-65,65) 4-Y-0+ **£2,186** (£677; £338; £169) **Stalls** Low

Form RPR

10-0 **1** **Mozakhraf (USA)**[16] 70 5-11-0 **63** MissARyan(5) 3 71
(K A Ryan) *lw: chsd clr ldr: pushed along and no imp over 1f out: styd on fnl f to ld last stride* **3/1**[1]

03-2 **2** *hd* **Quality Street**[14] 91 5-11-2 **65** (p) MissZoeLilly(5) 5 72
(P Butler) *led: 3l clr 2f out: urged along ins fnl f: fdd and hdd last stride* **6/1**[3]

0-05 **3** *3/4* **Franksalot (IRE)**[10] 130 7-11-2 **60** MrSDobson 2 65
(I W McInnes) *chsd ldng pair: pushed along to dispute 2nd over 1f out: kpt on fnl f: nrst fin* **7/1**

41-0 **4** *shd* **Hotchpotch (USA)**[10] 131 4-10-6 **57** (p) MrRHill(7) 10 61+
(J R Best) *hld up in last pair: pushed along 2f out: r.o wl fnl f: hopeless task* **13/2**

5-40 **5** *3/4* **Fast Heart**[8] 154 6-11-5 **63** MissEJJones 4 65
(R A Harris) *awkward s: wl in rr: drvn and styd on fnl f: nrst fin* **7/1**

031- **6** *shd* **Zazous**[57] 6629 6-10-11 **60** MrHHaynes(5) 7 62
(J J Bridger) *settled in midfield: effrt over 1f out: kpt on same pce fnl f* **11/2**[2]

5-21 **7** *nk* **Vlasta Weiner**[9] 137 7-10-9 **58** 6ex (b) MissSBradley(5) 11 59
(J M Bradley) *settled in midfield: urged along over 1f out: kpt on same pce: n.d* **14/1**

-646 **8** *1 1/2* **Desert Light (IRE)**[7] 158 6-10-10 **54** (v) MrsMMorris 1 51
(D Shaw) *trckd ldng trio: effrt over 1f out: fdd fnl f* **8/1**

00-0 **9** *nk* **Majestical (IRE)**[7] 158 5-10-4 **55** (p) MissHDavies(7) 6 51
(J M Bradley) *t.k.h: hld up: a in rr: no imp over 1f out* **20/1**

00-0 **10** *3 1/2* **Blessed Place**[7] 161 7-10-8 **59** ow2 (tp) MrSJEdwards(7) 9 44
(D J S Ffrench Davis) *t.k.h: hld up: plld way through to chse ldrs 1/2-way: wknd 2f out* **25/1**

1m 12.83s (0.02) **Going Correction** -0.05s/f (Stan) **10** Ran SP% **119.4**
Speed ratings (Par 101):97,96,95,95,94 94,94,92,91,87
CSF £21.45 CT £118.77 TOTE £3.10: £1.60, £2.20, £2.50; EX 33.00 Trifecta £153.30 Pool: £703.97 - 3.26 winning tickets. Place 6 £187.20, Place 5 £67.78.
Owner Mrs J Ryan **Bred** Audley Farm Inc **Trained** Hambleton, N Yorks

FOCUS
A modest event, confined to amateur riders, and the form is fairly straightforward and sound.
T/Jkpt: Part won. £26,770.50 to a £1 stake. Pool: £37,705.00. 0.50 winning tickets. T/Plt: £156.50 to a £1 stake. Pool: £62,471.25. 291.25 winning tickets. T/Qpdt: £19.80 to a £1 stake. Pool: £5,628.60. 209.70 winning tickets. JN

221 SOUTHWELL (L-H)
Thursday, January 25

OFFICIAL GOING: Standard
Wind: virtually nil

237 BONUSPRINT.COM MEDIAN AUCTION MAIDEN STKS 5f (F)
1:00 (1:00) (Class 6) 3-Y-O **£2,730** (£806; £403) **Stalls** High

Form RPR

4- **1** **My Drop (IRE)**[34] 6912 3-9-3 GrahamGibbons 2 72
(E J O'Neill) *led to 1/2-way: cl up: rdn to ld ins last: kpt on* **11/2**[3]

033- **2** *hd* **Ronnie Howe**[114] 5746 3-9-3 73 PhillipMakin 11 71
(M Dods) *cl up: effrt wl over 1f out: sn rdn and ev ch tl drvn and no ex towards fin* **11/4**[2]

22-2 **3** *2* **Le Masque**[18] 60 3-9-0 67 MarkLawson(3) 7 64
(B Smart) *cl up: led 1/2-way: rdn wl over 1f out: hdd and one pce ins last* **11/8**[1]

466- **4** *1 1/2* **Glen Avon Girl (IRE)**[104] 5950 3-8-7 59 DuranFentiman(5) 9 54
(T D Easterby) *chsd ldrs: rdn along 2f out: drvn and kpt on same pce fr over 1f out* **14/1**

5 *1/2* **Topflightcoolracer** 3-8-12 J-PGuillambert 8 52
(Mrs G S Rees) *dwlt and towards rr: hdwy to chse ldrs 2f out: sn rdn and one pce appr last* **33/1**

-035 **6** *3 1/2* **Splendidio**[5] 194 3-8-12 52 (b[1]) HayleyTurner 6 40
(D K Ivory) *cl up: rdn over 2f out: sn wknd* **18/1**

7 *1 1/4* **Stoneacre Donny (IRE)** 3-9-3 RobbieFitzpatrick 4 41
(Peter Grayson) *bmpd s: a rr* **25/1**

006- **8** *1* **Animated**[34] 6920 3-9-0 55 (be[1]) StephenDonohoe(3) 3 38
(A J McCabe) *in tch: rdn along 1/2-way: sn outpcd* **50/1**

600- **9** *3 1/2* **Bonny Scotland (IRE)**[29] 6951 3-8-12 44 LeeEnstone 10 21
(I W McInnes) *chsd ldrs 2f: sn outpcd and bhd* **125/1**

10 *2* **Coleorton Dagger** 3-8-12 NCallan 1 14
(K A Ryan) *a towards rr* **8/1**

4-0 **11** *7* **Betty Oxo**[9] 152 3-8-12 DeanMcKeown 5 —
(B P J Baugh) *wnt lft s: a rr* **125/1**

60.12 secs (-0.18) **Going Correction** -0.15s/f (Stan) **11** Ran SP% **117.5**
Speed ratings (Par 95):95,94,91,89,88 82,80,79,73,70 59
CSF £20.55 TOTE £8.30: £1.90, £1.30, £1.10; EX 37.00 Trifecta £86.10 Pool £396.73 - 3.27 winning units..
Owner G A Lucas & D Bloy **Bred** Patrick Grace **Trained** Averham Park, Notts

FOCUS
A typically weak sprint maiden that makes sense rated around those in the frame behind the winner.
Stoneacre Donny(IRE) Official explanation: jockey said colt was slow away

238 PONTINS.COM H'CAP (DIV I) 1m (F)
1:30 (1:30) (Class 6) (0-60,63) 4-Y-0+ **£2,047** (£604; £302) **Stalls** Low

Form RPR

15-1 **1** **Picador**[4] 200 4-9-5 **63** 6ex SebSanders 12 85+
(Sir Mark Prescott) *cl up: led after 3f: pushed clr 2f out: easily* **8/11**[1]

-020 **2** *5* **Roman Boy (ARG)**[4] 200 8-8-9 **53** (v[1]) MickyFenton 3 62
(Stef Liddiard) *hld up: hdwy over 3f out: rdn to chse wnr wl over 1f out: no imp* **10/1**

-111 **3** *1 1/4* **Time To Regret**[6] 181 7-9-0 **58** 6ex (p) DanielTudhope 4 64
(I W McInnes) *in tch on inner: hdwy 3f out: sn rdn and kpt on same pce fnl 2f* **7/1**[3]

1-13 **4** *2* **Capital Lass**[9] 150 4-8-10 **57** StephenDonohoe(3) 7 59
(A J McCabe) *in tch: hdwy 3f out: sn rdn and kpt on same pce fnl 2f* **11/1**

1-35 **5** *1 1/4* **Vibrato (USA)**[18] 63 5-8-4 **53** (v) DuranFentiman(5) 14 52
(C J Teague) *chsd ldrs: rdn along 3f out: sn drvn and wknd* **14/1**

40-0 **6** *1 3/4* **Borodinsky**[16] 80 6-8-2 **46** oh1 (v[1]) PaulHanagan 5 42
(R E Barr) *led 3f: rdn along over 3f out and grad wknd* **50/1**

30-1 **7** *1/2* **Granakey (IRE)**[24] 7 4-8-9 **56** JerryO'Dwyer(3) 1 50
(M G Quinlan) *hld up towards rr: hdwy over 2f out: sn rdn and nt rch ldrs* **13/2**[2]

02-6 **8** *2 1/2* **Penwell Hill (USA)**[24] 7 8-8-3 **50** ow1 (b) SaleemGolam(3) 6 39
(Miss M E Rowland) *chsd ldrs: rdn along over 3f out: sn wknd* **40/1**

00-3 **9** *nk* **Steel Grey**[16] 75 6-8-2 **46** oh1 DeanMernagh 10 35
(M Brittain) *cl up to 1/2-way: sn lost pl and bhd* **40/1**

236- **10** *5* **Kathleen Kennet**[26] 6981 7-8-8 **52** RobertHavlin 2 30
(Mrs H Sweeting) *a towards rr* **25/1**

510- **11** *6* **Sonderborg**[28] 6960 6-8-3 **47** (p) DaleGibson 11 12
(J Mackie) *a bhd* **33/1**

00-6 **12** *12* **Sion Hill (IRE)**[18] 59 6-8-2 **46** oh1 JimmyQuinn 8 —
(Mrs N Macauley) *a bhd* **66/1**

1m 41.94s (-2.66) **Going Correction** -0.35s/f (Stan) **12** Ran SP% **122.9**
Speed ratings (Par 101):99,94,92,90,89 87,87,84,84,79 73,61
CSF £9.04 CT £36.95 TOTE £1.70: £1.10, £2.90, £2.10; EX 9.00 Trifecta £53.50 Pool £224.96 - 2.98 winning units..
Owner The Green Door Partnership **Bred** Cheveley Park Stud Ltd **Trained** Newmarket, Suffolk

FOCUS
Good form for the grade rated around the third and sixth.
Sion Hill(IRE) Official explanation: jockey said gelding hung right throughout

239 GO PONTIN'S CLASSIFIED STKS 6f (F)
2:00 (2:00) (Class 7) 4-Y-0+ **£1,706** (£503; £252) **Stalls** Low

Form RPR

4-22 **1** **Lucius Verrus (USA)**[2] 221 7-9-0 45 (v) NCallan 4 65
(D Shaw) *in tch: hdwy 1/2-way: led over 1f out: rdn clr ins last: kpt on* **11/8**[1]

23-0 **2** *3 1/2* **Astorygoeswithit**[5] 189 4-9-0 44 (b) BrettDoyle 7 54
(P S McEntee) *sn rdn along and cl up: rdn along over 2f out and sn ev ch: drvn appr last and sn one pce* **25/1**

001- **3** *3/4* **Dodaa (USA)**[28] 6958 4-9-0 43 MatthewHenry 2 52
(N Wilson) *led: rdn along over 2f out: sn drvn: hdd over 1f out and sn one pce* **16/1**

0-45 **4** *5* **Christian Bendix**[5] 189 5-9-0 43 (p) ShaneKelly 5 37
(P Howling) *chsd ldrs: rdn along and sltly outpcd 1/2-way: hdwy u.p 2f out: sn drvn and btn* **8/1**[3]

24-0 **5** *nk* **Aboustar**[2] 221 7-8-7 43 (v[1]) PatrickDonaghy(7) 6 36
(M Brittain) *towards rr tl styd on fnl 2f: nrst fin* **16/1**

003- **6** *3* **Amanda's Lad (IRE)**[27] 6969 7-9-0 44 AdrianMcCarthy 9 27
(M C Chapman) *towards rr: hdwy over 2f out: sn rdn and no imp appr last* **20/1**

540- **7** *1 1/4* **Nevinstown (IRE)**[109] 5839 7-9-0 45 TPQueally 10 23
(C Grant) *dwlt: hdwy on outer and in tch whn rn wd st and sn bhd* **2/1**[2]

001- **8** *3* **Massey**[28] 6962 11-9-0 44 PaulMulrennan 12 14
(C R Dore) *a rr* **14/1**

000- **9** *3/4* **Xpres Boy (IRE)**[28] 6956 4-9-0 45 (t) PhillipMakin 1 12
(S R Bowring) *prom: rdn along 3f out: sn wknd* **33/1**

400- **10** *hd* **Estoille**[28] 6956 6-9-0 44 PaulFessey 14 12
(Mrs S Lamyman) *midfield: rdn along 3f out: sn wknd* **28/1**

00-4 **11** *6* **Luloah**[14] 97 4-9-0 45 HayleyTurner 8 —
(P S McEntee) *prom: rdn along over 2f out and sn wknd* **33/1**

1m 15.32s (-1.58) **Going Correction** -0.35s/f (Stan) **11** Ran SP% **122.9**
Speed ratings (Par 97):96,91,90,83,83 79,77,73,72,72 64
CSF £49.68 TOTE £2.20: £1.10, £4.00, £4.30; EX 33.30 Trifecta £166.00 Pool £266.96 - 1.14 winning units..
Owner Danethorpe Racing Ltd **Bred** Pacelco S A **Trained** Danethorpe, Notts
■ Stewards' Enquiry : Patrick Donaghy £130 fine: failed to pass stands before going to start

FOCUS
A very moderate sprint and the form is poor but sound rated around the placed horses.

240 PONTIN'S FAMILY HOLIDAYS CLASSIFIED STKS 1m 6f (F)
2:30 (2:30) (Class 7) 4-Y-0+ **£1,706** (£503; £252) **Stalls** Low

Form RPR

220- **1** **Red River Rock (IRE)**[52] 6705 5-9-4 45 (be) SilvestreDeSousa 8 52
(T J Fitzgerald) *keen: trckd ldrs: smooth hdwy over 3f out: rdn to chal over 1f out: drvn to ld ins last: kpt on* **7/2**[2]

/4-1 **2** *1 1/4* **Nod's Star**[15] 87 6-9-4 45 (t) LPKeniry 14 50
(Mrs L C Jewell) *in tch: hdwy to chse ldrs over 2f out: sn rdn: drvn and styd on ins last* **10/1**

/0-3 **3** *nk* **Moyne Pleasure (IRE)**[9] 148 9-9-4 38 LeeEnstone 11 50
(R Johnson) *trckd ldrs: hdwy and cl up over 4f out: rdn to ld wl over 1f out: sn drvn: hdd ins last: no ex towards fin* **8/1**

42-3 **4** *7* **Asleep At The Back (IRE)**[15] 87 4-8-12 44.............. JamieMackay 2 40
(J G Given) *keen: trckd ldrs: hdwy to ld over 4f out: rdn along over 2f out: hdd wl over 1f out and grad wknd* **10/3**[1]

554/ **5** *5* **Sea Cove**[919] 3712 7-9-4 39.................................. MatthewHenry 7 33
(G A Swinbank) *hld up and bhd tl styd on fnl 2f: n.d* **13/2**[3]

-546 **6** *1 1/4* **Romil Star (GER)**[9] 146 10-9-4 43.........................(v) PaulFitzsimons 12 31
(M Wellings) *prom: effrt and cl up over 4f out: rdn along 3f out and sn wknd* **8/1**

400- **7** *nk* **Tirailleur (IRE)**[23] 939 7-9-4 37.................................... AntonyProcter 5 31
(M J Gingell) *hld up towards rr: hdwy 1/2-way: chsd ldrs and n.m.r 4f out: sn rdn and no imp after* **16/1**

6 **8** *10* **Point Of Origin (IRE)**[13] 107 10-9-4 37....................... JosedeSouza 10 17
(John A Harris) *a rr* **66/1**

240- **9** *3/4* **Teutonic (IRE)**[197] 3135 6-9-4 44.......................... CatherineGannon 3 16
(R F Fisher) *in tch: rdn along over 4f out and sn wknd* **33/1**

42-5 **10** *1 1/4* **Mayyas**[20] 45 7-9-4 45...(t) SamHitchcott 1 14
(C C Bealby) *led: rdn along and hdd over 4f out: sn drvn and wknd 3f out* **9/1**

002- **11** *13* **Good Investment**[23] 6973 5-9-4 43..........................(b) MichaelTebbutt 13 —
(Miss Tracy Waggott) *chsd ldrs: rdn along 4f out: sn wknd* **33/1**

000- **12** *72* **Bright**[35] 6758 4-8-7 35...(p) EmmettStack(5) 9 —
(Robert Gray) *cl up: rdn along over 4f out: sn wknd* **100/1**

03-4 **13** *107* **Bold Trump**[18] 62 6-9-4 44.. DeanCorby 6 —
(Mrs N S Evans) *a rr: bhd fr 1/2-way* **16/1**

3m 7.33s (-2.27) **Going Correction** -0.35s/f (Stan)
WFA 4 from 5yo+ 6lb **13 Ran SP% 120.1**
Speed ratings (Par 97):92,91,91,87,84 83,83,77,77,76 69,27,—
CSF £38.17 TOTE £3.70: £1.70, £2.40, £2.80; EX 26.30 Trifecta £128.00 Pool £198.45 - 1.10 winning units..
Owner N F L Racing **Bred** Frank Dunne **Trained** Malton, N Yorks
■ Tim FitzGerald's first winner since August 2005.
■ Stewards' Enquiry : Lee Enstone seven-day ban: failed to ride for second place (Feb 5-11)

FOCUS
A banded-style classified race run at a modest early pace and the form is ordinary.
Teutonic(IRE) Official explanation: jockey said mare hung right leaving back straight
Bold Trump Official explanation: jockey said gelding bled from the nose

241 CANVAS PRINTS FROM BONUSPRINT.COM H'CAP 6f (F)
3:00 (3:03) (Class 6) (0-52,58) 4-Y-0+ **£2,730** (£806; £403) **Stalls** Low

Form RPR

-021 **1** **Mill By The Stream**[2] 221 5-8-13 58 6ex.................. HaddenFrost(7) 10 66
(Tom Dascombe) *mde virtually all: rdn over 1f out: kpt on wl fnl f* **9/4**[2]

/5-0 **2** *shd* **Monda**[16] 77 5-8-10 48.. PaulMulrennan 2 56
(Miss J A Camacho) *a cl up: effrt 2f out: sn rdn and ev ch: drvn ins last: no ex nr line* **25/1**

3-22 **3** *2 1/2* **Mind Alert**[2] 225 6-8-12 50...(v) NCallan 6 51
(D Shaw) *hld up in tch: hdwy on inner over 2f out: rdn to chse ldng pair over 1f out: sn drvn and one pce* **2/1**[1]

6-34 **4** *hd* **Blythe Spirit**[2] 221 8-8-10 48.......................................(p) PaulHanagan 7 48
(R A Fahey) *chsd ldrs: rdn along over 2f out: sn drvn and one pce appr last* **14/1**

03-0 **5** *nk* **Union Jack Jackson (IRE)**[16] 77 5-8-12 50.........(b) J-PGuillambert 5 49
(J G Given) *trckd ldrs: rdn along over 2f out: kpt on same pce appr last* **11/1**

0-53 **6** *1* **Mouseen (IRE)**[9] 145 4-8-5 48..................................(b) TolleyDean(5) 12 44
(R A Harris) *in tch: hdwy over 2f out: sn rdn and no imp* **16/1**

2-22 **7** *1/2* **Majik**[9] 143 8-9-0 52...(p) MickyFenton 8 47
(P T Midgley) *dwlt: hdwy on outer 2f out: rdn to chse ldrs over 1f out: wknd ent last* **15/2**[3]

04-6 **8** *1 1/2* **Tribute (IRE)**[9] 143 6-8-9 47.. DaleGibson 11 37
(John A Harris) *a rr* **80/1**

00-0 **9** *1/2* **Shadow Jumper (IRE)**[16] 77 6-8-12 50.............(v) RobbieFitzpatrick 9 39
(J T Stimpson) *cl up: rdn along wl over 2f out: sn drvn and wknd wl over 1f out* **12/1**

00-5 **10** *1* **Piccleyes**[9] 145 6-8-11 52.................................(b) StephenDonohoe(3) 1 38
(A J McCabe) *a rr* **16/1**

1m 15.84s (-1.06) **Going Correction** -0.35s/f (Stan) **10 Ran SP% 115.4**
Speed ratings (Par 101):93,92,89,89,88 87,86,84,84,82
CSF £56.44 CT £132.88 TOTE £3.50: £1.40, £7.90, £1.10; EX 104.40 TRIFECTA Not won..
Owner Alan Solomon **Bred** The Lavington Stud **Trained** Lambourn, Berks

FOCUS
A moderate handicap in which those who raced prominently once again dominated. The form is best assessed through the runner-up.

242 THEBOOKIEBASHER.COM H'CAP 1m 4f (F)
3:30 (3:30) (Class 6) (0-55,55) 4-Y-0+ **£2,730** (£806; £403) **Stalls** Low

Form RPR

103- **1** **Bolckow**[33] 6936 4-8-9 53.. MickyFenton 1 69
(J T Stimpson) *trckd ldrs: hdwy to chse ldr 4f out: rdn to ld over 1f out: kpt on* **4/1**[1]

000- **2** *2* **Mahmjra**[27] 6979 5-9-1 55.. PFredericks 8 67
(C N Allen) *led: rdn along 3f out: drvn and hdd over 1f out: kpt on same pce* **100/1**

040- **3** *4* **Nimello (USA)**[27] 6980 11-9-1 55.................................. SamHitchcott 14 61
(A G Newcombe) *hld up and bhd: hdwy and wd st: sn rdn and styd on wl appr last: nrst fin* **20/1**

06-0 **4** *3* **Dispol Peto**[9] 145 7-8-3 48..................................(p) DuranFentiman(5) 11 49
(R Johnson) *hld up towards rr: hdwy over 3f out: sn rdn and kpt on same pce fnl 2f* **20/1**

/00- **5** *1/2* **Hereditary**[21] 6375 5-8-7 47...(p) LPKeniry 9 47
(Mrs L C Jewell) *chsd ldrs: effrt over 4f out: rdn along 3f out and sn no imp* **9/2**[2]

30-0 **6** *7* **The Pen**[12] 121 5-8-11 51.. PaulMulrennan 3 40
(C W Fairhurst) *chsd ldrs: rdn along over 4f out: grad wknd* **14/1**

051/ **7** *nk* **Rood Boy (IRE)**[417] 6495 6-8-6 46....................................... HayleyTurner 5 35
(Simon Earle) *trckd ldrs: rdn along over 3f out: sn drvn and wknd wl over 2f out* **9/2**[2]

00-0 **8** *3/4* **Mi Odds**[16] 80 11-8-3 50.. ClaireWheatcroft(7) 10 38
(Mrs N Macauley) *a rr* **66/1**

02-2 **9** *9* **Experimental (IRE)**[18] 64 13-8-9 49................................. DaleGibson 12 22
(John A Harris) *chsd ldr: rdn along over 4f out and sn wknd* **11/2**[3]

00-0 **10** *5* **Newcorp Lad**[13] 110 7-8-10 50..................................... GrahamGibbons 4 15
(Mrs G S Rees) *a towards rr* **33/1**

-030 **11** *3* **Mossmann Gorge**[6] 182 5-8-11 51...(b) NCallan 2 11
(R A Harris) *hld up: a rr* **10/1**

0/0- **12** *4* **Faraday (IRE)**[27] 6980 4-8-6 50.. TPQueally 6 4
(B J Curley) *a towards rr* **16/1**

40-1 **13** *nk* **Tiegs (IRE)**[16] 78 5-8-4 47... MarcHalford(3) 7 —
(P W Hiatt) *prom: pushed along over 4f out: rdn and wknd over 3f out* **7/1**

2m 37.05s (-5.04) **Going Correction** -0.35s/f (Stan)
WFA 4 from 5yo+ 4lb **13 Ran SP% 120.8**
Speed ratings (Par 101):102,100,98,96,95 91,90,90,84,80 78,76,76
CSF £443.28 CT £7066.79 TOTE £6.40: £2.10, £19.10, £8.30; EX 286.50 TRIFECTA Not won..
Owner J T Stimpson **Bred** Khorshed And Ian Deane **Trained** Newcastle-Under-Lyme, Staffs

FOCUS
Moderate form and very few got competitive, although the time was reasonable.
Experimental(IRE) Official explanation: jockey said gelding was never travelling

243 PONTINS.COM H'CAP (DIV II) 1m (F)
4:00 (4:01) (Class 6) (0-60,60) 4-Y-0+ **£2,047** (£604; £302) **Stalls** Low

Form RPR

045- **1** **Im Ova Ere Dad (IRE)**[42] 6819 4-8-11 55......................... TonyCulhane 5 71
(D E Cantillon) *trckd ldrs: smooth hdwy 3f out: led over 1f out and sn rdn: drvn ins last: hld on wl* **7/2**[1]

314- **2** *nk* **Majehar**[29] 6955 5-8-7 51.. TPQueally 1 66
(A G Newcombe) *trckd ldrs on inner: hdwy 2f out: rdn to chse wnr ent last: sn drvn and styd on wl* **11/2**[3]

00-5 **3** *2* **Flying Bantam (IRE)**[17] 70 6-8-11 60.................. JamieMoriarty(5) 11 71
(R A Fahey) *midfield: hdwy over 2f out: rdn to chse wnr over 1f out: kpt on same pce ins last* **8/1**

-210 **4** *3/4* **Paso Doble**[2] 228 9-8-8 57.................................(p) JamesMillman(5) 8 66
(D K Ivory) *led: rdn along over 2f out: hdd over 1f out and kpt on same pce* **4/1**[2]

440- **5** *6* **Hot Agnes**[26] 6981 4-8-5 52..(vt[1]) JamesDoyle(3) 7 49
(H J Collingridge) *towards rr: hdwy 2f out: rdn and styd appr last: nrst fin* **11/1**

5-04 **6** *1/2* **They All Laughed**[4] 200 4-9-1 59................................... PhillipMakin 13 55
(P W Hiatt) *towards rr: hdwy and wd st: sn rdn and n o imp fr wl over 1f out* **7/1**

62-4 **7** *shd* **Tip Top Style**[16] 80 4-8-3 47.......................................(tp) DaleGibson 2 42
(J Mackie) *chsd ldrs: rdn along over 2f out: sn wknd* **12/1**

50-5 **8** *shd* **Suffolk House**[16] 80 5-7-11 46 oh1..................(b[1]) DuranFentiman(5) 10 41
(M Brittain) *towards rr: hdwy over 2f out: styd on appr last: nrst fin* **33/1**

20-6 **9** *1 1/2* **Prettilini**[9] 150 4-8-12 56... PatCosgrave 14 48
(R Brotherton) *in tch: rdn along over 2f out: sn wknd* **20/1**

-000 **10** *2* **Didnt Tell My Wife**[3] 210 8-8-2 46 oh1...................(be) HayleyTurner 12 34
(P S McEntee) *cl up: rdn along wl over 2f out: sn wknd* **33/1**

200- **11** *2* **Hits Only Life (USA)**[236] 2246 4-8-9 53......................... DeanMcKeown 9 37
(J Pearce) *a towards rr* **16/1**

03-6 **12** *10* **Barry The Brave**[12] 123 5-8-3 47.................................... PaulHanagan 6 10
(Micky Hammond) *a towards rr* **14/1**

200- **13** *1/2* **Preskani**[42] 6819 5-8-5 49...(p) JimmyQuinn 3 11
(Mrs N Macauley) *a rr* **16/1**

00-0 **14** *7* **Teddy Monty (IRE)**[18] 61 4-8-2 46 oh1................. CatherineGannon 4 —
(R E Barr) *s.i.s: a bhd* **100/1**

1m 41.67s (-2.93) **Going Correction** -0.35s/f (Stan) **14 Ran SP% 127.3**
Speed ratings (Par 101):100,99,97,96,90 90,90,88,86 84,74,74,67
CSF £23.28 CT £156.89 TOTE £4.10: £1.80, £2.50, £2.50; EX 29.40 Trifecta £92.10 Pool £295.89 - 2.20 winning units. Place 6 £25.12, Place 5 £21.85..
Owner Allan Milton **Bred** Golden Vale Stud **Trained** Newmarket, Suffolk

FOCUS
Moderate handicap form but fairly solid nonetheless.
Barry The Brave Official explanation: jockey said gelding lost its action
T/Jkpt: £18,094.00 to a £1 stake. Pool: £25,484.50. 1.00 winning ticket. T/Plt: £37.10 to a £1 stake. Pool: £63,230.75. 1,242.35 winning tickets. T/Qpdt: £19.10 to a £1 stake. Pool: £3,580.20. 138.50 winning tickets. JR

172 NAD AL SHEBA (L-H)
Thursday, January 25

OFFICIAL GOING: Turf course - good; dirt course - fast

244a ZAWAJ STKS (H'CAP) (TURF) 1m 2f (T)
3:35 (3:36) (90-105,105) 3-Y-0+
£33,673 (£11,224; £5,612; £2,806; £1,683; £1,122)

RPR

1 **Fairmile**[117] 5675 5-9-2 99.. MJKinane 3 101+
(I Mohammed, UAE) *settled in rr mid-div: smooth prog rail 2 1/2f out: swtchd 2f out: led cl home* **9/4**[1]

2 *3/4* **Hallhoo (IRE)**[42] 5-8-11 95.. JMurtagh 13 94
(D Selvaratnam, UAE) *sn led: hdd after 2f but trckd new ldr: led again 5f out: clr 2f out: hdd 50yds out: r.o again* **33/1**

3 *3/4* **Great Plains**[110] 5808 5-9-1 98.. RHills 5 97
(E Charpy, UAE) *mid-div: gng wl 3f out: rdn to cl 2 1/2f out: nt pce of wnr* **11/2**[2]

4 *1 1/4* **Bonecrusher**[34] 8-8-9 93..(t) WayneSmith 1 89
(M Al Muhairi, UAE) *mid-div: rdn to trck wnr 2 1/2f out: hung fnl 1 1/2f* **28/1**

5 *1* **Pearly King (USA)**[117] 5675 4-8-12 98.......................... KerrinMcEvoy 4 92
(I Mohammed, UAE) *mid-div: rdn 2 1/2f out: nvr a threat* **11/2**[2]

6 *4 1/2* **Championship Point (IRE)**[103] 5968 4-9-5 105.............. TedDurcan 9 91
(M R Channon) *settled in rr: short of room 3f out: r.o fnl 1 1/2f* **6/1**[3]

7 *1 1/2* **Bianconi (SAF)**[335] 513 8-9-3 100....................................(t) RyanMoore 6 84
(S Seemar, UAE) *hld up in rr: no room 3f out: r.o fnl 2f: nrest at fin* **8/1**

8 *4 1/2* **Hopeful Purchase (IRE)**[175] 4082 4-8-11 97............... MartinDwyer 11 72
(W J Haggas) *racd in rr: rdn 3f out: n.d* **10/1**

9 *shd* **Divine Task (USA)**[28] 9-8-8 91.. TPO'Shea 8 67
(E Charpy, UAE) *settled in rr: rail and rdn 2 1/2f out: nvr nr to chal* **25/1**

10 *3 3/4* **Potro Tell (ARG)**[14] 104 7-8-9 93 ow1........................... PJSmullen 2 61
(H J Brown, South Africa) *trckd ldr rail: rdn 4f out: sn wknd* **14/1**

11 *15* **Todman Avenue (USA)**[6] 5-8-7 90...................(bt[1]) RoystonFfrench 7 32
(A Al Raihe, UAE) *trckd ldr tl rdn 4f out: wknd* **33/1**

12 *1/2* **Fallon (SAF)**[350] 356 7-8-9 93.................................(vt[1]) RichardMullen 10 33
(S Seemar, UAE) *a mid-div: nvr a threat* **40/1**

13 *6 3/4* **Ned Kelly (SAF)**[329] 560 6-8-10 94...................................(b) PaulEddery 12 22
(Christian Wroe) *slowly away: racd in last: nvr nr to chal* **33/1**

14 *shd* **River Tiber**[124] 5524 4-8-9 95.. WSupple 15 23
(Declan Gillespie, Ire) *nvr nr to chal* **16/1**

15 *8* **State Shinto (USA)**[7] 177 11-8-9 **93**..................................(bt) DHayse 14 6
(R Bouresly, Kuwait) *prom and t.k.h: wd: led after 2f: hdd 5f out: wknd*
40/1

2m 3.27s (-0.93) **Going Correction** +0.15s/f (Good)
WFA 4 from 5yo+ 2lb 15 Ran SP% **129.6**
Speed ratings: 109,108,107,106,106 102,101,97,97,94 82,82,76,76,70

Owner H R H Princess Haya Of Jordan **Bred** Pendley Farm **Trained** UAE

FOCUS
This looked a high-class handicap but, with the pace reasonable from the start, some of the more exposed runners could not live with the younger, more progressive types.

NOTEBOOK
Fairmile ◆ made a successful debut for new connections with a pretty impressive success. He had a good seven lengths to find at the top of the straight when Hallhoo kicked into a clear lead, but he displayed a smart turn of foot when asked for his effort and always looked like getting there. He was a big improver when trained by Walter Swinburn last season and, on this evidence, can continue to prosper this term. He does not have a great deal more to find to make the jump from top handicapper to Pattern-class performer. (op 11/4)
Hallhoo(IRE), having disputed the lead, really stretched the field when kicking clear off the final bend and the positive tactics very nearly paid off. He clearly appreciated the return to turf and could have more to offer in similar company.
Great Plains, formerly a very useful handicapper for Amanda Perrett, was probably not too far off his best on his debut for new connections, but he did not seem to be helping his rider by hanging left under pressure, and he also seemed a little short of room close home. This was his first run in 110 days, so there might be better to come. (op 5/1)
Bonecrusher has not won since August 2003, but this was a good effort against some more progressive types. (op 25/1)
Pearly King(USA) ◆, having his first start since leaving Sir Michael Stoute, shaped nicely on his debut for new connections. He probably lost his chance when a little short of room over two furlongs out, but he kept on well and should be able to improve on this. (op 5/1)
Championship Point(IRE), last year's Predominate winner, looked interesting off a mark of 105, but he never got involved from a long way off the pace. This first start in 103 days should sharpen him up and he could yet make his mark at this year's carnival. (op 13/2)
Hopeful Purchase(IRE) was never really seen with a chance on his debut in Dubai, but he is still lightly raced and could well improve on this.
River Tiber, ex Aidan O'Brien, was well held on this step up in trip.

245a ATTIJARI PHONE CUP (H'CAP) (TURF) 6f 110y(T)
4:05 (4:07) (95-110,110) 3-Y-0+

£36,734 (£12,244; £6,122; £3,061; £1,836; £1,224)

RPR

1 **Munaddam (USA)**[129] 5420 5-8-9 **99**.. RHills 13 106
(E A L Dunlop) *settled last: stl last 3f out: swtchd rail 2f out: r.o to ld 110yds out: comf*
11/1

2 *3/4* **Mac Love**[132] 5341 6-9-1 **105**.. PJSmullen 7 110
(J Noseda) *settled in rr rail: prog rail 2 1/2f out to trck ldr: swtchd 110yds out: r.o wl*
12/1

3 *1 1/2* **Lascaux (AUS)**[7] 177 6-8-12 **102**... WLHo 4 103
(Y Choy, Macau) *prom rail: led 1 1/2f out: hdd 110yds out: kpt on wl* **25/1**

4 *nk* **Celtic Mill**[119] 5642 9-9-1 **105**...(p) LDettori 11 105
(D W Barker) *prom: led 3f out gng wl: chal 2f out: hdd 1 1/2f out: kpt on wl*
12/1

5 *3 1/4* **Checkit (IRE)**[322] 621 7-8-10 **100**... THuet 1 90
(R Bouresly, Kuwait) *slowly away: sn trckd ldr on rail: rdn 3f out: kpt on one pce*
33/1

6 *nk* **Key Of Destiny (SAF)**[14] 9-9-2 **106**................................ WCMarwing 5 95
(M F De Kock, South Africa) *settled in rr: n.m.r 4f out: wd st: nvr a threat*
13/2[3]

7 *3/4* **So Will I**[343] 431 6-8-12 **102**..(t) MartinDwyer 8 89
(Doug Watson, UAE) *mid-div: rdn 3f out: nt qckn* **16/1**

8 *hd* **Tiza (SAF)**[194] 5-9-6 **110**...(t) RyanMoore 2 97
(H J Brown, South Africa) *mid-div: rdn 3f out: nvr able to chal* **11/8**[1]

9 *3/4* **Feet So Fast**[984] 8-9-1 **105**.. TedDurcan 14 90
(S Seemar, UAE) *slowly away: swtchd rail: nvr nr to chal* **25/1**

10 *1 1/4* **Strike Up The Band**[112] 5779 4-9-0 **104**..................... AdrianTNicholls 3 85
(D Nicholls) *prom centre: n.m.r 4 1/2f out: n.d after* **10/1**

11 *nk* **National Icon (SAF)**[42] 7-9-1 **105**......................................(t) WSupple 10 85
(A Manuel, UAE) *settled in rr: gng wl 3f out: nvr able to chal* **20/1**

12 *6 1/4* **Mutamared (USA)**[117] 5667 7-9-0 **104**................................. PatDobbs 9 66
(K A Ryan) *mid-div: wd 2 1/2f out: nt qckn* **11/2**[2]

13 *3* **Attilius (BRZ)**[28] 5-8-10 **100**...(t) TPO'Shea 6 53
(E Charpy, UAE) *trckd pce tl rdn 3f out: wknd* **20/1**

14 *1 1/4* **Bellamont Forest (USA)**[137] 5225 11-8-12 **102**.......... DinaDanekilde 12 52
(O Larsen, Sweden) *mid-div: wd st: nvr able to chal* **25/1**

1m 16.1s (-1.10) **Going Correction** +0.15s/f (Good) 14 Ran SP% **133.5**
Speed ratings: 112,111,109,109,105 105,104,103,103,101 101,94,90,89

Owner Hamdan Al Maktoum **Bred** Shadwell Farm LLC **Trained** Newmarket, Suffolk

FOCUS
A very good sprint handicap and, as one would expect, there was plenty of pace on from the start. It has been rated through the runner-up running to his best level of 2006.

NOTEBOOK
Munaddam(USA) would have found this a lot tougher than the Folkestone handicap he won when last seen in September, and he had a 4lb higher mark to contend with, but he benefited from a fine ride from Richard Hills to follow up on his debut in Dubai. Not ideally drawn in stall 13, he was last on the turn into the straight, but he still seemed to be going well and managed to weave his way through horses, eventually finding a run up the far rail to deny Mac Love late on. He is clearly improving and it would be no surprise to see him complete the hat-trick in similar company. (op 10/1)
Mac Love ◆, making his debut for Jeremy Noseda off the back of a 132-day break, ran a terrific race in second. He was a little short of room when initially looking to throw down his challenge and had to be switched out, but he was in the clear for long enough and was just picked off late. His new trainer has a fine record in Dubai and should find an opening for this one-time disappointing sort.
Lascaux(AUS), a dual winner on the dirt in Macau, stepped up on the form he showed on his debut in Dubai when down the field over 1m on dirt, clearly benefiting from these vastly different conditions. (op 20/1)
Celtic Mill as usual showed good speed from the gates, but this extended 6f would have just stretched him. This was his first run in 119 days, so he could improve, and a slightly shorter trip will be more to his liking. (op 11/1)
Key Of Destiny(SAF) tried to make his move widest of all but could make no impression. (op 6/1)
Strike Up The Band, a Listed winner in France on his last start 112 days previously, could only keep on at the one pace, but this should put him just right. (op 8/1)
Mutamared(USA) looked one of the likelier winners beforehand, but he was always caught a little wide and could not pick up when asked. He could have been better drawn and, seeing as this was his first start in 117 days, it would be no surprise to see him improve on this.

246a SHAHRAZADE TROPHY (CONDITIONS RACE) (FILLIES) (DIRT) 7f (D)
4:35 (4:37) 3-Y-0

£9,183 (£3,061; £1,530; £765; £459; £306)

RPR

1 **Greetings (BRZ)**[144] 4-9-6 **100**....................................... RichardMullen 1 99+
(P Nickel Filho, Brazil) *trckd ldr rail: led gng wl 3f out: kicked clr: easily*
6/1[3]

2 *3 3/4* **Satulagi (USA)**[82] 6338 3-8-9 **101**... JohnEgan 3 80
(J S Moore) *slowly away: last main gp rail 3f out: swtchd 2f out: r.o late to snatch 2nd*
10/1

3 *nk* **La Presse (USA)**[90] 6201 3-8-9 **108**................................ KerrinMcEvoy 8 79
(I Mohammed, UAE) *trckd ldr: wd gng wl 3f out: r.o but no ch w wnr: lost 2nd nr line*
7/2[2]

4 *5* **Dubai Jewel (AUS)**[21] 4-9-4 .... RyanMoore 9 68
(S Seemar, UAE) *hld up in rr: rdn 3f out: sme prog last 1 1/2f* **33/1**

5 *1 3/4* **Whistledownthewind (SAF)**[156] 4-9-4 **90**....................... WCMarwing 2 63
(M F De Kock, South Africa) *led at gd pce: rdn and hdd 3f out: wknd* **7/1**

6 *1 1/2* **Alzerra (UAE)**[110] 5802 3-8-11 **111**.. MJKinane 6 59
(I Mohammed, UAE) *mid-div: rdn to trck ldrs 3 1/2f out: nt qckn* **3/1**[1]

7 *2 1/2* **Darrfonah (IRE)**[116] 5714 3-8-9 **109**..................................... TedDurcan 10 50
(C E Brittain) *settled in rr: wd 3 1/2f out: rdn and kpt on one pce* **7/2**[2]

8 *1 1/4* **Corre Solta (BRZ)**[292] 4-9-4 **93**.. JMurtagh 5 49
(H J Brown, South Africa) *racd 2nd: rdn 3 1/2f out: wknd* **11/1**

9 *2 3/4* **The Real Thing (IRE)**[128] 5466 3-8-9 **87**.................................. WSupple 4 39
(A Manuel, UAE) *mid-div rail: rdn 4f out: nvr able to chal* **33/1**

10 *1 1/4* **Snow Clad (AUS)**[21] 4-9-4 **45**...(e[1]) RPCleary 12 38
(A Selvaratnam, UAE) *a in rr* **250/1**

11 *4 3/4* **Precocious Star (IRE)**[166] 4371 3-8-9 **93**....................... PJSmullen 11 23
(K R Burke) *slowly away: n.d* **14/1**

12 *17* **Xiloca (BRZ)**[21] 4-9-4 **40**..(b[1]) AdrianTNicholls 7 —
(A Selvaratnam, UAE) *sn t.o* **250/1**

1m 24.8s **Going Correction** +0.25s/f (Slow)
WFA 3 from 4yo 18lb 12 Ran SP% **127.0**
Speed ratings: 110,105,105,99,97 95,93,91,88,87 81,62

Owner Haras Interlagos **Bred** Haras Interlagos Ltda **Trained** Brazil

FOCUS
Basically a trial for the UAE 1,000 Guineas. The winner impressed and has been rated value for further. The placed fillies appeared to run close to their British form.

NOTEBOOK
Greetings(BRZ) produced a smart effort to chalk up another winner at the carnival for the Brazilians. Always chasing what appeared to be a pretty generous pace, she sustained her challenge in good style when pulled out at the top of the straight, proving far too resolute for the strong-travelling La Presse. A winner at up to 1m2f in Brazil, she had no trouble in coping with the drop in trip and readily defied a 144-day break. She fully deserves a shot at the Guineas off the back of this success.
Satulagi(USA) ◆, not seen since running down the field in the Breeders' Cup Juvenile Fillies nearly three months previously, struggled to hold her position for much of the way, seemingly failing to cope with the kickback form her inside draw, and did well to stay on for second once in the clear. She is almost sure to benefit from a step up to 1m and could get closer to the winner in the UAE 1,000 Guineas.
La Presse(USA), placed in Pattern company for Barry Hills last season, was below the pick of her form on her debut for new connections. She looked the one to beat when travelling strongly on the turn into the straight, but her effort soon flattened out and she looked a non-stayer.
Dubai Jewel(AUS) was the least experienced runner in the field, but she produced a decent effort behind some reasonable types.
Whistledownthewind(SAF), a 6f winner in South Africa, was given every chance but was unable to sustain her challenge.
Alzerra(UAE) won the Cornwallis for Mick Channon, but she failed to prove her effectiveness over this longer trip on dirt first time up for her new connections. She is clearly better suited to turf. (op 3/1 tchd 11/4)
Darrfonah(IRE) ran nowhere near the form she showed when chasing home Finsceal Beo in the Prix Marcel Boussac 116 days previously and was another unsuited by the switch to dirt.
Precocious Star(IRE) had some smart turf form to her name, but she was very slowly away and soon struggling on her dirt/Dubai debut. (op 12/1)

247a ASIAN RACING FEDERATION STKS (H'CAP) (TURF) 7f 110y(D)
5:05 (5:06) (95-116,115) 3-Y-0+

£53,571 (£17,857; £8,928; £4,464; £2,678; £1,785)

RPR

1 **Great Rhythm (SAF)**[362] 6-8-9 **104**..................................... RyanMoore 9 106
(H J Brown, South Africa) *settled in rr: last 1 1/2f out: swtchd and r.o wl fnl f: led line*
8/1

2 *3/4* **King Jock (USA)**[32] 6-9-1 **109**... PShanahan 6 110
(R J Osborne, Ire) *mid-div: gng wl 1 1/2f out: led fnl f: hdd cl home* **4/1**[1]

3 *nk* **Seihali (IRE)**[263] 1527 8-9-6 **115**... JMurtagh 7 114
(D Selvaratnam, UAE) *settled in rr: rdn 2 1/2f out: r.o wl fnl 1 1/2f: nrst fin*
5/1[2]

4 *1* **Appalachian Trail (IRE)**[131] 5358 6-8-9 **104**...................(b[1]) MJKinane 4 101
(I Semple) *mid-div rail: t.k.h: trckd ldr 1 1/2f out: swtchd rail: ev ch fnl f: kpt on*
10/1

5 *1 3/4* **Rhythm'n Roots (IRE)**[242] 2055 4-8-12 **107**..................(t) GAvranche 13 100
(Allan Smith, UAE) *wl away: trckd ldr: led 2f out: hdd fnl f* **14/1**

6 *2* **Al Maali (IRE)**[336] 494 8-8-7 **102** ow1... RHills 1 91
(Doug Watson, UAE) *mid-div on rail: n.m.r 2 1/2f out: no room 1 1/2f out: r.o once clr*
14/1

7 *3/4* **Express Way (BRZ)**[180] 5-8-11 **106**............................... WCMarwing 12 93
(M F De Kock, South Africa) *mid-div: rdn to trckd ldr whn ev ch 2f out: nt qckn*
4/1[1]

8 *2 1/4* **Akimbo (USA)**[118] 5663 6-8-5 **95**... RPCleary 10 82
(James Leavy, Ire) *led main gp: t.k.h: rdn to cl 3f out: sn wknd* **25/1**

9 *3/4* **Caesar Beware (IRE)**[322] 625 5-9-1 **109**........................... TedDurcan 3 91
(S Seemar, UAE) *v.s.a: nvr able to chal* **7/1**[3]

10 *6 3/4* **Cat Belling (IRE)**[7] 174 7-8-7 **97** ow2... THuet 2 68
(R Bouresly, Kuwait) *sn led: hdd 2f out: wknd* **25/1**

11 *7 3/4* **Royal Power (IRE)**[132] 5341 4-8-12 **107**................................... LDettori 8 56
(M R Channon) *mid-div: nvr able to chal* **8/1**

1m 29.53s (-1.07) **Going Correction** +0.15s/f (Good) 11 Ran SP% **121.5**
Speed ratings: 111,110,109,108,107 105,104,102,101,94 86

Owner James Atkinson & Peter Walichnowski **Bred** K J Mardon **Trained** South Africa

FOCUS
A decent handicap on paper and it was run at a good pace.

NOTEBOOK
Great Rhythm(SAF) had been stone last turning in but stayed on best of all in the straight under a well-timed ride from Ryan Moore. He had the class to be placed in Grade 1 company in South Africa last year and is ideally suited by further than this, so the way this race was run suited him well.
King Jock(USA), successful in a couple of Listed races at Abu Dhabi last month, probably got to the front too soon, but he can certainly pick up a similar race. (op 9/2)
Seihali(IRE) was another who came from well off the pace, and he should come on a good deal for this first outing in 263 days. He looks set to enjoy another good carnival. (op 9/2)
Appalachian Trail(IRE) got a run up the inside to challenge King Jock inside the final furlong, but he too was felled by the fast finishers.
Rhythm'n Roots(IRE), making his debut for his new stable, did well to finish fifth given that he helped set a decent pace. He could be dangerous in similar company if allowed his own way in front.
Royal Power(IRE) has gone well fresh in the past, but he was under pressure from a long way out on his first outing since September and weakened tamely.

248a AMAN TROPHY (H'CAP) (TURF) 1m 4f (T)
5:35 (5:36) (95-110,110) 3-Y-0+

£36,734 (£12,244; £6,122; £3,061; £1,836; £1,224)

RPR
1 **Quijano (GER)**[144] 5-8-10 **100** .... MJKinane 4 108+
(P Schiergen, Germany) *mid-div on rail: gng wl 3f out: rdn to cl 2 1/2f out: bk on bit and led 1 1/2f out: easily* **4/1**[1]
2 *1 3/4* **Gravitas**[117] 5700 4-9-2 **110** .... LDettori 8 112
(Saeed Bin Suroor) *slowly away: nt far off pce: led 2f out: hdd 1 1/2f out: r.o wl: no ch w wnr* **4/1**[1]
3 *2* **Ampelio (IRE)**[14] 5-8-5 **95** ....(vt) MartinDwyer 5 94
(Doug Watson, UAE) *mid-div: n.m.r 3 1/2f out: smooth prog trcking wnr 2f out: r.o fnl f* **20/1**
4 *1 3/4* **Hattan (IRE)**[7] 177 5-9-6 **110** .... JMurtagh 7 106
(C E Brittain) *racd in 3rd on rail: trckd wnr 1 1/2f out: one pce* **16/1**
5 *1 3/4* **Corriolanus (GER)**[322] 624 7-9-3 **107** .... RyanMoore 3 101
(S Seemar, UAE) *settled last: nvr able to chal* **12/1**
6 *1/2* **Book Of Music (IRE)**[82] 6336 4-8-10 **104** .... PJSmullen 6 97
(I Mohammed, UAE) *mid-div: rdn to cl 4f out: trckd ldr 2 1/2f out: wknd* **15/2**
7 *1 3/4* **Fenice (IRE)**[152] 4-8-10 **104** .... RichardMullen 2 94
(S Seemar, UAE) *settled in rr: rdn to cl 2 1/2f out: nt qckn* **12/1**
8 *2 3/4* **Wild Savannah**[216] 2803 5-9-2 **106** .... KerrinMcEvoy 11 92
(I Mohammed, UAE) *trckd ldr: led 3 1/2f out: hdd 2f out: wknd* **6/1**[2]
9 *8* **Lost Soldier Three (IRE)**[7] 176 6-9-0 **104** .... AdrianTNicholls 10 78
(D Nicholls) *hld up in rr: nvr able to chal* **7/1**[3]
10 *16* **Go For Gold (IRE)**[349] 371 6-9-0 **104** ....(t) TedDurcan 13 54
(S Seemar, UAE) *mid-div: rdn 3f out: nvr able to chal* **10/1**
11 *3 1/4* **Luberon**[152] 4791 4-8-10 **104** .... WSupple 9 49
(M Johnston) *led on rail: hdd 3 1/2f out: wknd* **12/1**
12 *3/4* **Fantastic Love (USA)**[322] 624 7-8-10 **100** ....(t) RoystonFfrench 1 44
(A Al Raihe, UAE) *settled in rr on rail: no room 3f out: nvr involved* **33/1**
13 *dist* **Brahminy Kite (USA)**[7] 175 5-8-9 **99** .... THuet 12 —
(R Bouresly, Kuwait) *racd in 4th: virtually p.u 3f out* **33/1**

2m 30.31s (-0.69) **Going Correction** +0.15s/f (Good)
WFA 4 from 5yo+ 4lb 13 Ran SP% **127.2**
Speed ratings: 108,106,105,104,103 102,101,99,94,83 81,81,—

Owner Stiftung Gestut Fahrhof **Bred** Stiftung Gestut Fahrhof **Trained** Germany

FOCUS
This looked like a typically competitive carnival handicap beforehand, and the placed horses appeared to run to form, but Quijano was in a different league and can go on to better things.

NOTEBOOK
Quijano(GER) ◆, always moved very nicely in about mid-division in a race run at just an ordinary gallop and it looked just a question of what he would find for pressure as he loomed large at the top of the straight. Mick Kinane didn't have to get serious, just nudging his mount out for a very comfortable success, and while it's hard to judge, he looked value for more than double the winning margin. Although most progressive in Germany, winning his last six starts, including a Listed contest, he had yet to race outside his homeland, so it was difficult to know what to expect on his debut in Dubai. He was clearly underestimated by the Handicapper and can make the step up to Group company. He might even earn a tilt at the Sheema Classic on World Cup day. (op 9/2)
Gravitas, a dual Listed winner for Andre Fabre, may have hit the front a little soon on his debut for the Godolphin operation, but there is nothing he could have done to stop the winner. Time may show he faced an impossible task conceding weight to the German horse and he could yet make his mark at the carnival.
Ampelio(IRE) has progressed from just a fair sort into a very useful performer on the dirt lately and he continued his improvement with a fine run in third. (op 16/1)
Hattan(IRE) appreciated the return to turf and ran a big race under top weight. There could be more to come now he is finding his feet in Dubai. (op 14/1)
Corriolanus(GER) ran with credit off the back of a 322-day break considering that he had to come from a long way back. He is another open to improvement.
Book Of Music(IRE) was below his best of his first start since leaving Sir Michael Stoute. He may eventually prove best over slightly shorter. (op 7/1)
Lost Soldier Three(IRE) could not build on a promising run over 1m here the previous week, but he made his move widest of all and is better than his finishing position suggests. (op 15/2)
Luberon dropped out rather tamely on his debut in Dubai.

249a NAJAH AL SHINDAGHA SPRINT (GROUP 3) (DIRT) 6f (D)
6:05 (6:07) 3-Y-0+

£61,224 (£20,408; £10,204; £5,102; £3,061; £2,040)

RPR
1 **Tropical Star (IRE)**[7] 177 7-9-1 109........(vt) RoystonFfrench 2 102
(A Al Raihe, UAE) *racd in rr far side: sn rdn: stl in rr 2f out: r.o wl fnl f to ld last stride* **7/1**[2]
2 *shd* **Thajja (IRE)**[14] 6-9-1 100........(v) RHills 5 102
(Doug Watson, UAE) *mid-div centre: rdn to chal 2f out: led 55yds out: hdd line* **14/1**
3 *3 1/4* **Aliysa (BRZ)**[270] 4-8-5 95........(t) ADomingos 3 82
(A Cintra Pereira, Brazil) *prom far side: led 2 1/2f out: r.o wl: hdd cl home* **9/1**
4 *1* **Tax Free (IRE)**[104] 5942 5-9-1 107........ AdrianTNicholls 11 89
(D Nicholls) *nt far off pce nr side: r.o wl* **9/2**[1]
5 *3* **Machynleth**[14] 105 7-9-1 94........(t) WayneSmith 10 80
(M Al Muhairi, UAE) *a mid-div: sme late prog* **25/1**
6 *1 3/4* **The Lord (ARG)**[306] 740 7-9-1 102........(t) RyanMoore 7 75
(S Seemar, UAE) *sn rdn along: sme late hdwy: nvr a threat* **25/1**
7 *1/2* **Greek Renaissance (IRE)**[120] 5627 4-9-1 97........ KerrinMcEvoy 13 74
(I Mohammed, UAE) *slowly away: nvr a threat: mod late hdwy* **8/1**[3]
8 *3/4* **Botanical (USA)**[32] 6-9-1 104........(bt[1]) TPO'Shea 16 71
(E Charpy, UAE) *sn rdn along: nvr able to chal* **7/1**[2]
9 *1/2* **Machinist (IRE)**[124] 5534 7-9-1 93........ PatDobbs 14 70
(D Nicholls) *sn struggling on nr side* **16/1**
10 *3/4* **Drift Ice (SAF)**[180] 6-9-1 98........(be) WCMarwing 4 68
(M F De Kock, South Africa) *prom centre: rdn 2 1/2f out: nt qckn* **8/1**[3]
11 *9* **Para-Choque (BRZ)**[130] 5-9-7 98........(t) MCardoso 6 47
(C Morgado, Brazil) *led far side: hmpd and hdd 2 1/2f out: n.d after* **12/1**
12 *3/4* **Conroy (USA)**[306] 740 9-9-1 97........ WSupple 1 38
(A Manuel, UAE) *trckd ldr far side: rdn 3f out: wknd* **14/1**
13 *1 1/2* **Media Hora (CHI)**[124] 7-9-1 105........(bt[1]) TedDurcan 12 34
(F Castro, Sweden) *prom nr side: grad fdd* **22/1**
14 *3/4* **New Freedom (BRZ)**[220] 6-9-1 93........ ECruz 15 32
(P Nickel Filho, Brazil) *prom nr rail early stages: wknd* **33/1**
15 *3/4* **Tournedos (IRE)**[131] 5375 5-9-1 102........ MartinDwyer 8 29
(D Nicholls) *nvr a threat* **25/1**
U **Hay Luz Delsol (BRZ)**[166] 5-8-10 95........ MJKinane 9 —
(M D Wolfson, U.S.A) *pitched at s: uns rdr* **16/1**

1m 10.11s (-0.59) **Going Correction** +0.25s/f (Slow) **16** Ran SP% **127.0**
Speed ratings: 113,112,108,107,103 100,100,99,98,97 85,84,82,81,80 —

Owner Sheikh Mohammed Bin Maktoum Al Maktoum **Bred** Gainsborough Stud Management Ltd **Trained** UAE

FOCUS
Sprints on dirt at the carnival tend to lack strength in depth, at least until the Americans come over for the Golden Shaheen anyway, and the evidence of this race suggests that will again be the case this year. They went a mad pace from the start, handing a big advantage to those with stamina for further. On the draw front, those in low boxes may well have been favoured.

NOTEBOOK
Tropical Star(IRE) was only fifth in this race last year, but he stays 7f and the frantic pace played into his hands. He was being given reminders from some way out and looked more likely to finish last than first at halfway, but his stamina kicked in as those around him began to get tired and he was able to force his head in front on the line. He won a 7f handicap following defeat in this race last year and, although he managed to win this time, a step back up in trip can surely only help.
Thajja(IRE) ran a big race on this step up to Group company, just losing out on the line. He should continue to go well, but is little better than a 100-rated horse and his proximity is further evidence that this was a weak race for the grade.
Aliysa(BRZ), like both the winner and the second, stays further and ran a fine race in third. In the early days of this year's carnival it is becoming clear that horses from Brazil must be respected on the dirt. (op 10/1)
Tax Free(IRE) progressed from a useful handicapper to become a Pattern-class sprinter on the turf last year, but he was not quite at his best on his first try on a dirt surface. Still, he hardly ran a bad race and deserves extra credit considering he fared best of those in double-figure stalls.
Greek Renaissance(IRE) was a really likeable, progressive type for Marcus Tregoning last season, but he proved unsuited by the switch to dirt on his debut for new connections.
Machinist(IRE) stuck to his task without ever threatening to land a blow and this company was a bit hot, whether he handled the dirt surface or not. He should do better in handicaps. (op 14/1)
Tournedos(IRE) seemingly failed to take to the dirt.

250a TAM-WHEEL PLATE (H'CAP) (TURF) 1m 2f
6:35 (6:37) (90-105,100) 3-Y-0+

£33,673 (£11,224; £5,612; £2,806; £1,683; £1,122)

RPR
1 **Tabadul (IRE)**[125] 5505 6-8-7 90........ RHills 3 92
(E A L Dunlop) *mid-div rail: smooth prog 2f out: led 110yds out: comf* **7/1**[2]
2 *3/4* **Missisipi Star (IRE)**[138] 5194 4-8-8 93........ WSupple 8 94
(I Mohammed, UAE) *sn led: clr 2f out: hdd last 110yds: kpt on* **12/1**
3 *3/4* **Dont Dili Dali**[7] 174 4-8-11 97........ JohnEgan 11 95
(J S Moore) *settled rr: rdn 3f out: gd late hdwy: nrst fin* **16/1**
4 *hd* **Kestrel Cross (IRE)**[335] 509 5-8-11 95........ JMurtagh 7 93
(Declan Gillespie, Ire) *mid-div: gng wl 3f out: rdn to cl 2f out: r.o* **20/1**
5 *1 1/4* **Zato (IRE)**[89] 6226 4-8-9 94 ow1........ PShanahan 1 91
(M R Channon) *mid-div rail: n.m.r 2 1/2f out: r.o once clr* **12/1**
6 *nk* **Mutafanen**[28] 6-9-3 100........(p) MartinDwyer 12 96
(E Charpy, UAE) *settled in rr: no room rail 2 1/2f out: r.o fnl 1 1/2f once clr* **16/1**
7 *2 1/4* **Parnassus (SAF)**[34] 5-9-3 100........ TedDurcan 15 92
(S Seemar, UAE) *mid-div: wd into st and rdn: nvr a threat* **15/2**[3]
8 *3/4* **Desert Realm (IRE)**[110] 5808 4-8-10 96........ KerrinMcEvoy 14 86
(I Mohammed, UAE) *settled in rr: nvr nr to chal* **10/1**
9 *3/4* **Boo**[7] 175 5-8-7 90........ RoystonFfrench 13 79
(K R Burke) *trckd ldr: rdn 3f out: wknd fnl f* **33/1**
10 *1 1/4* **Desert Anger**[35] 6-8-9 93........(bt) TPO'Shea 4 79
(E Charpy, UAE) *in rr of mid-div: nvr able to chal* **14/1**
11 *3/4* **Bennie Blue (SAF)**[229] 5-9-1 98........ WCMarwing 5 84
(M F De Kock, South Africa) *trckd early pce: t.k.h: rdn 3f out: wknd* **5/2**[1]
12 *3 1/2* **Aleutian**[14] 104 7-8-9 93........ RichardMullen 10 72
(Doug Watson, UAE) *mid-div: hrd rdn 2 1/2f out: wknd* **7/1**[2]
13 *1/2* **Baskerville**[20] 4-8-5 90........ RPCleary 2 69
(D Selvaratnam, UAE) *trckd ldr rail: rdn 3f out: wknd* **16/1**
14 *1/2* **Jet Express (SAF)**[7] 178 5-9-1 98........(t) RyanMoore 9 76
(H J Brown, South Africa) *settled in rr: nvr able to chal* **14/1**

2m 4.47s (124.47) **Going Correction** +0.15s/f (Good)
WFA 4 from 5yo+ 2lb 14 Ran SP% **128.5**
Speed ratings: 104,103,102,102,101 101,99,99,98,97 96,94,93,93

Owner Hamdan Al Maktoum **Bred** Shadwell Estate Co Ltd **Trained** Newmarket, Suffolk

FOCUS
Probably just an ordinary handicap for the grade and they went no great pace for much of the way.

NOTEBOOK
Tabadul(IRE) was always well placed considering the way the race was run, never more than around five lengths off the pace, and found plenty when switched out to challenge in the straight. If anything, a stronger pace would have seen him in an even better light and he could be capable of following up in similar company for his in-form trainer/jockey combination.
Missisipi Star(IRE), a very useful type when trained by Eamon Tyrrell, was able to dictate the pace on her own terms and it was no surprise to see her still in the mix at the finish. She will not always have things her own way and is no sure thing to confirm this.
Dont Dili Dali improved on the form she showed over an extended 7f round here the previous week, clearly benefiting from the step up in trip. She had to come from well off the pace and should have even more to offer off a stronger gallop. (op 14/1)
Kestrel Cross(IRE), making his debut for new connections, ran a stormer off the back of a 335-day absence and is obviously open to improvement.
Zato(IRE) did not get the best of trips on his first start in Dubai and should be able to improve on the bare form of this effort.

Mutafanen, with the cheekpieces re-fitted on his return to turf, could only keep on at the one pace. A more generous gallop would probably have suited better. (op 14/1)
Boo should have appreciated the switch to turf, but he offered little immediate promise. (op 25/1)
Bennie Blue(SAF) proved disappointing on his debut in Dubai. (op 3/1)

[214] WOLVERHAMPTON (A.W) (L-H)

Friday, January 26

OFFICIAL GOING: Standard to slow
Wind: Light, across Weather: Overcast

251 PONTIN'S FAMILY HOLIDAYS H'CAP 5f 20y(P)
1:30 (1:37) (Class 6) (0-62,64) 4-Y-O+ £2,730 (£806; £403) Stalls Low

Form RPR
36-2 1 **Canadian Danehill (IRE)**[15] |97| 5-8-9 **57**..........................(p) NCallan 4 78
(R M H Cowell) *a.p: rdn to chse ldr 1/2-way: edgd lft over 1f out: styd on u.p to ld nr fin* **5/2**[2]
2-11 2 ½ **Almaty Express**[4] |214| 5-8-9 **64** 6ex........................(b) WilliamBuick(7) 10 84
(J R Weymes) *led: rdn and edgd lft ins fnl f: hdd nr fin* **5/6**[1]
4-05 3 3½ **Egyptian Lord**[16] |82| 4-8-6 **54**..............................(b) RobbieFitzpatrick 3 61
(Peter Grayson) *dwlt: plld hrd: hdwy 1/2-way: rdn over 1f out: styd on same pce* **16/1**
11-5 4 1¼ **Dysonic (USA)**[24] |8| 5-8-2 **53**..............................(v) AndrewElliott(3) 2 56
(J Balding) *chsd ldr to 1/2-way: rdn over 1f out: wknd ins fnl f* **8/1**[3]
00-4 5 1¾ **Polar Force**[9] |158| 7-8-12 **60**.. ChrisCatlin 12 56
(Mrs C A Dunnett) *chsd ldrs: rdn 1/2-way: wknd over 1f out* **28/1**
166- 6 ½ **Fastrac Boy**[54] |6686| 4-8-10 **58**.................................... GrahamGibbons 5 52
(J R Best) *chsd ldrs: rdn 1/2-way: wkng whn hung lft fnl f* **10/1**
0-41 7 hd **Tajjree**[13] |125| 4-8-5 **53**...(tp) AdrianMcCarthy 1 47
(Miss K B Boutflower) *chsd ldrs: rdn 2f out: wkng whn nt clr run ins fnl f* **20/1**
00- 8 2½ **Richelieu**[64] |6572| 5-9-0 **62**.. TonyCulhane 8 47
(J J Lambe, Ire) *outpcd* **50/1**
460- 9 6 **Nova Tor (IRE)**[263] |1528| 5-7-13 **52**..........................(b) DuranFentiman(5) 9 15
(Peter Grayson) *s.s: n.d* **66/1**
403- 10 1 **Mystery Pips**[69] |6521| 7-8-7 **55**...(v) KimTinkler 6 14
(N Tinkler) *chsd ldrs: sn rdn: lost pl over 3f out: sn bhd* **40/1**
/0-0 11 5 **Melandre**[24] |8| 5-8-12 **60**.. DeanMernagh 7 —
(M Brittain) *sn outpcd* **100/1**

61.94 secs (-0.88) **Going Correction** +0.10s/f (Slow) 11 Ran SP% **124.3**
Speed ratings (Par 101):111,110,104,102,99 99,98,94,85,83 75
CSF £5.00 CT £28.14 TOTE £4.20: £1.50, £1.10, £3.10; EX 5.80 Trifecta £53.20 Pool £605.31 - 8.07 winning units..
Owner T W Morley **Bred** Skymarc Farm Inc And Dr A J O'Reilly **Trained** Six Mile Bottom, Cambs

FOCUS
An ordinary handicap in which the pace was sound throughout and the two market leaders showed above-average form to pull clear in the straight. This form should prove reliable.
Dysonic(USA) Official explanation: jockey said gelding hung right in home straight
Melandre Official explanation: trainer said mare was unsuited by the surface

252 GO PONTIN'S (S) STKS 7f 32y(P)
2:00 (2:06) (Class 6) 4-Y-O+ £2,047 (£604; £302) Stalls High

Form RPR
13-0 1 **Bessemer (JPN)**[22] |32| 6-9-4 **65**..............................(p) DanielTudhope 8 61
(D Carroll) *s.i.s and hmpd s: hld up: hdwy over 1f out: rdn to ld ins fnl f: r.o* **3/1**[1]
2-40 2 shd **Louisiade (IRE)**[13] |123| 6-8-12 **49**..............................(tp) NCallan 10 55
(K A Ryan) *chsd ldrs: rdn 1/2-way: nt clr run over 2f out: ev ch ins fnl f: r.o* **9/2**[3]
0-64 3 1½ **Spy Gun (USA)**[11] |138| 7-8-12 **43**.. ChrisCatlin 4 51
(T Wall) *led: rdn and hdd ins fnl f: styd on same pce* **14/1**
0-31 4 hd **Magic Amour**[10] |143| 9-8-13 **60**..............................(b) KevinGhunowa(5) 1 57
(P A Blockley) *chsd ldrs: rdn to ld ins fnl f: sn hdd and no ex* **10/3**[2]
664- 5 1¼ **Pontefract Glory**[130] |5432| 4-8-7 **40**..............................(b) DuranFentiman(5) 6 47
(M Dods) *hld up: hdwy u.p over 1f out: styd on same pce ins fnl f* **33/1**
006- 6 shd **Stagnite**[38] |6869| 7-9-1 **49**.. JerryO'Dwyer(3) 5 53
(Karen George) *mid-div: hdwy u.p over 2f out: no ex ins fnl f* **25/1**
60-1 7 nk **Prince Of Gold**[11] |138| 7-9-4 **48**..............................(v) FergusSweeney 11 52
(R Hollinshead) *mid-div: rdn 1/2-way: styd on ins fnl f: nt rch ldrs* **8/1**
06-0 8 ½ **Mister Incredible**[16] |86| 4-8-9 **54**..............................(p) SaleemGolam(3) 12 45
(V Smith) *chsd ldrs: rdn over 2f out: wknd fnl f* **14/1**
35-0 9 1½ **Aventura (IRE)**[21] |42| 7-8-12 **51**..............................(b[1]) PhillipMakin 3 41
(S R Bowring) *chsd ldr: rdn over 2f out: wknd fnl f* **33/1**
3-14 10 1¼ **Bathwick Emma (IRE)**[14] |109| 4-8-10 **51**............ StephenDonohoe(3) 9 39
(M A Doyle) *sn outpcd* **22/1**
-130 11 1¼ **Shrine Mountain (USA)**[11] |138| 5-9-4 **60**..............................(b) JoeFanning 7 41
(R A Harris) *hld up: rdn and wknd over 2f out* **15/2**
050- 12 2½ **Sweet Cherokee**[291] |936| 4-8-7 **35**.. JimmyQuinn 2 23
(C N Kellett) *s.s: a in rr* **150/1**

1m 31.34s (0.94) **Going Correction** +0.10s/f (Slow) 12 Ran SP% **117.2**
Speed ratings (Par 101):98,97,96,95,94 94,94,93,91,90 88,86
CSF £15.46 TOTE £4.50: £1.90, £1.90, £3.20; EX 26.70 Trifecta £268.90 Part won. Pool £378.74 - 0.66 winning units..The winner was sold to I McInnes for 7,000gns.
Owner Mrs B Ramsden **Bred** Darley Stud **Trained** Sledmere, E Yorks

FOCUS
An ordinary seller in which the pace was fair. The form limits the third.

253 PONTIN'S BOOK EARLY H'CAP 7f 32y(P)
2:30 (2:36) (Class 6) (0-55,60) 3-Y-O £2,730 (£806; £403) Stalls High

Form RPR
46-3 1 **Kings Shillings**[3] |223| 3-8-10 **50**..............................(b) DanielTudhope 7 57+
(D Carroll) *s.i.s: hld up: hdwy over 1f out: rdn to ld and edgd lft ins fnl f: r.o* **5/1**[3]
00-5 2 1¾ **Time For Change (IRE)**[23] |25| 3-8-13 **53**.............................. TonyCulhane 6 53
(B W Hills) *trckd ldrs: rdn and edgd lft over 1f out: sn led: edgd rt and hdd ins fnl f: nt run on* **5/1**[3]
04-0 3 2 **Strathaird (IRE)**[19] |60| 3-8-7 **47**.. JoeFanning 5 42
(P C Haslam) *led: hdd 6f out: w ldr tl led 1/2-way: rdn and hdd 1f out: no ex* **11/2**
000- 4 ¾ **Fire Alarm**[189] |3713| 3-8-7 **47**.. GrahamGibbons 1 40
(J J Quinn) *mid-div: hdwy over 2f out: sn rdn: styd on same pce fnl f* **4/1**[2]
404- 5 nk **Shes Millie**[134] |5323| 3-8-12 **52**.. NCallan 2 44
(J G M O'Shea) *s.i.s: sn mid-div: rdn 1/2-way: styd on ins fnl f: nt trble ldrs* **10/1**
600- 6 shd **Avoncreek**[118] |5686| 3-8-12 **52**.. PhillipMakin 11 44
(B P J Baugh) *hld up: hdwy over 1f out: styd on same pce ins fnl f* **50/1**
000- 7 1½ **Tranquility**[55] |6669| 3-8-10 **50**.. JimmyQuinn 3 38
(J Pearce) *chsd ldrs: rdn over 1f out: wknd ins fnl f* **20/1**
-251 8 nk **Zaafira (SPA)**[9] |162| 3-9-6 **60** 6ex.............................. EdwardCreighton 4 47
(E J Creighton) *mid-div: hdwy over 2f out: sn rdn: wknd fnl f* **7/2**[1]
004- 9 ¾ **Lost All Alone**[28] |6975| 3-8-12 **52**.. ChrisCatlin 9 37
(D M Simcock) *led 6f out: hdd 1/2-way: rdn over 2f out: edgd lft over 1f out: sn wknd* **14/1**
606- 10 4 **Ancient Site (USA)**[26] |6998| 3-7-12 **45**.............................. SoniaEaton(7) 12 20
(B P J Baugh) *n.d* **33/1**
55-0 11 1 **Tumblin Rosie**[23] |25| 3-8-11 **51**.. PaulHanagan 10 23
(M Blanshard) *hld up: rdn 1/2-way: a in rr* **25/1**
500- 12 10 **Heart And Hand (IRE)**[36] |6900| 3-8-2 **45**..............................(b) DominicFox(3) 8 —
(M G Quinlan) *chsd ldrs over 5f* **33/1**

1m 32.88s (2.48) **Going Correction** +0.10s/f (Slow) 12 Ran SP% **123.1**
Speed ratings (Par 95):89,87,84,83,83 83,81,81,80,75 74,63
CSF £29.73 CT £147.48 TOTE £7.10: £2.40, £1.50, £2.20; EX 31.10 Trifecta £364.90 Pool £2,071.51 - 4.03 winning units..
Owner J Hopkinson G Hart D Scott **Bred** Lady Jennifer Green **Trained** Sledmere, E Yorks

FOCUS
A modest handicap and it is hard to be positive about the form, although the winner may do a bit better.

254 WOLVERHAMPTON-RACECOURSE.CO.UK CLAIMING STKS 5f 20y(P)
3:00 (3:06) (Class 5) 3-Y-O+ £3,238 (£963; £481; £240) Stalls Low

Form RPR
1-06 1 **Efistorm**[10] |155| 6-9-10 80.. JasonEdmunds(3) 8 69
(J Balding) *disp ld tl led 1f out: rdn out* **2/5**[1]
0-62 2 1¼ **City For Conquest (IRE)**[7] |183| 4-9-6 60..............................(b) ChrisCatlin 13 58+
(T J Pitt) *in rr: hdwy u.p over 1f out: edgd lft ins fnl f: r.o: nt rch wnr* **5/1**[2]
000- 3 hd **Glenargo (USA)**[37] |6884| 4-9-7 43..............................(p) JoeFanning 6 58
(R A Harris) *disp ld 4f: sn rdn and no ex* **66/1**
06-3 4 1 **Phinerine**[10] |143| 4-9-3 53..............................(b) MichaelJStainton(5) 9 55
(R A Harris) *s.i.s: sn prom: rdn and edgd lft over 1f out: no ex fnl f* **25/1**
00-6 5 hd **Twinned (IRE)**[7] |183| 4-9-4 48..............................(p) JerryO'Dwyer(3) 11 54
(Karen George) *prom: rdn and hung lft fr over 1f out: nt run on* **25/1**
40-4 6 4 **Sir Loin**[16] |82| 6-9-11 56..............................(v) TonyCulhane 10 43
(N Tinkler) *chsd ldrs: rdn 2f out: wkng whn eased fnl f* **16/1**[3]
54-6 7 ¾ **He's A Rocket (IRE)**[20] |46| 6-9-5 42..............................(v) AndrewElliott(3) 2 38
(K R Burke) *prom: rdn 1/2-way: wknd over 1f out* **28/1**
05-0 8 ¾ **For Life (IRE)**[10] |144| 5-9-6 47..............................(p) MickyFenton 12 33
(Stef Liddiard) *prom to 1/2-way* **33/1**
0-00 9 ¾ **Laurel Dawn**[10] |143| 9-9-3 41.. AnnStokell(5) 1 32
(Miss A Stokell) *sn outpcd* **150/1**
-045 10 shd **Mind That Fox**[5] |201| 5-9-1 45..............................(b) WilliamBuick(7) 5 32
(T Wall) *prom: rdn 1/2-way: wknd over 1f out* **40/1**
0-00 11 ¾ **New Options**[10] |154| 10-9-8 55..............................(b) RobbieFitzpatrick 7 29+
(Peter Grayson) *hld up in tch: n.m.r over 3f out: wknd 1/2-way* **33/1**
35-0 12 2 **Circle Of Truth**[14] |108| 3-8-3 54.. SaleemGolam(3) 3 21
(W G M Turner) *s.i.s and stmbld s: outpcd* **66/1**

63.12 secs (0.30) **Going Correction** +0.10s/f (Slow)
WFA 3 from 4yo+ 15lb 12 Ran SP% **117.1**
Speed ratings (Par 103):101,99,98,97,96 90,89,87,86,86 85,82
CSF £2.03 TOTE £1.40: £1.10, £1.50, £16.70; EX 3.00 Trifecta £162.10 Pool £717.03 - 3.14 winning units..The winner was claimed by C R Dore for £11,000. Twinned was claimed by N Gomersall for £5,000
Owner Mrs Jo Hardy **Bred** E Duggan And D Churchman **Trained** Scrooby, Notts

FOCUS
Little strength in depth and a race in which the winner did not have to be at his best to score. The bare form was only ordinary.
Sir Loin Official explanation: jockey said gelding moved poorly in the closing stages

255 PONTINS.COM CONDITIONS STKS 1m 141y(P)
3:30 (3:36) (Class 2) 4-Y-O+
£11,217 (£3,358; £1,679; £840; £419; £210) Stalls Low

Form RPR
000- 1 **Xtra Torrential (USA)**[35] |6915| 5-9-0 88.............................. FergusSweeney 6 97
(D M Simcock) *hld up: hdwy and hung lft fr over 1f out: styd on u.p to ld wl ins fnl f* **33/1**
430- 2 ½ **Blythe Knight (IRE)**[31] |5675| 7-9-0 104.............................. GrahamGibbons 4 96
(J J Quinn) *trckd ldr: plld hrd: rdn to ld ins fnl f: sn hdd and unable qck* **5/4**[1]
120- 3 3 **Hail The Chief**[258] |1676| 10-9-0 98.. ChrisCatlin 3 90
(R Hannon) *led: rdn over 1f out: hdd and no ex ins fnl f* **3/1**[2]
3-33 4 ½ **Atlantic Quest (USA)**[7] |185| 8-9-0 83.. AmirQuinn 2 89
(Miss Venetia Williams) *chsd ldrs: hung lft fr over 3f out: styd on same pce appr fnl f* **9/1**
004- 5 3 **Curtail (IRE)**[41] |6847| 4-8-13 90.. PaulHanagan 1 82
(I Semple) *trckd ldrs: plld hrd: rdn over 2f out: wknd fnl f* **15/2**
4-66 6 6 **Kindlelight Debut**[6] |197| 7-8-9 95.. JamesDoyle 5 65
(N P Littmoden) *prom: rn in snatches: hrd rdn 3f out: sn wknd* **5/1**[3]

1m 51.19s (-0.57) **Going Correction** +0.10s/f (Slow)
WFA 4 from 5yo+ 1lb 6 Ran SP% **110.8**
Speed ratings (Par 109):106,105,102,102,99 94
CSF £73.81 TOTE £37.50: £6.80, £1.40; EX 96.50.
Owner The Wight Wons **Bred** Good Luck Farm **Trained** Newmarket, Suffolk

FOCUS
A couple of fair sorts and just a reasonable pace but a surprise result with Xtra Torrential returning to form from out of the blue. The form is unlikely to prove that solid.

NOTEBOOK
Xtra Torrential(USA) looked to have a stiff task on these terms and had previously had his limitations firmly exposed in handicaps, but returned to form from out of the blue. However he is going to be taking a hike in the weights for this win and will do well to follow up after reassessment. Official explanation: trainer said, regarding the improved form, gelding was better suited by the stronger gallop today (tchd 25-1)
Blythe Knight(IRE), who had been running creditably over hurdles, looked the one to beat on these terms back on the Flat but proved a disappointment after having enjoyed the run of the race. Small-field scenarios do not appear to play to his strengths and he may not be the easiest to place successfully given his current mark on sand. (op Evens tchd 11-8 in places)
Hail The Chief, off the course since May, had the run of the race and was disgraced. He is entitled to come on for this outing but has little margin from his current mark back in handicap company, though. (op 4-1)
Atlantic Quest(USA) was not disgraced in the face of a stiff task at these weights but he may be flattered by his proximity in this moderately-run race. He has not won for some time and is not one for short odds back in handicaps. (op 12-1)

Curtail(IRE), who was again not totally disgraced in a muddling event, will be suited by a stronger gallop over shorter but he is not going to be easy to place in competitive handicap company from his current mark. (op 8-1 tchd 10-1)
Kindlelight Debut, who has been kept busy this winter, ran a rare poor race and, even allowing for the fact that this was not run to suit, she is likely to remain vulnerable in handicaps from her current mark or in this type of event when there is not much pace on. Official explanation: jockey said mare was never travelling (op 7-2)

256 GO PONTIN'S H'CAP 1m 1f 103y(P)
4:00 (4:06) (Class 4) (0-85,85) 4-Y-0+ £5,181 (£1,541; £770; £384) Stalls Low

Form RPR
31-5 **1** **Daring Affair**[16] [96] 6-8-10 **78** NCallan 11 87
(K R Burke) *chsd ldrs: rdn to ld over 1f out: jst hld on* **17/2**
2 *hd* **Paktolos (FR)**[44] 4-8-11 **80** FergusSweeney 3 89
(A King) *s.i.s: sn prom: rdn over 2f out: hung rt ins fnl f: r.o* **22/1**
50-1 **3** *3/4* **Dragon Slayer (IRE)**[5] [205] 5-8-4 **79** 6ex WilliamBuick(7) 9 86
(Ian Williams) *dwlt: plld hrd and sn prom: chsd ldr over 2f out: rdn and ev ch ins fnl f: no ex towards fin* **2/1**[2]
532- **4** *1* **Primo Way**[31] [6938] 6-7-12 **71** oh1 DuranFentiman(5) 7 76
(I Semple) *hld up: hdwy and hung lft fr over 1f out: nt rch ldrs* **14/1**
000- **5** *3 1/2* **Fantasy Ride**[48] [6772] 5-8-9 **77** JimmyQuinn 8 75
(J Pearce) *s.i.s: hld up: hdwy over 1f out: nt trble ldrs* **33/1**
102- **6** *1* **Kildare Sun (IRE)**[27] [6992] 5-8-10 **78** DaleGibson 4 74
(J Mackie) *chsd ldr: led 1/2-way: rdn and hdd over 1f out: wknd ins fnl f* **7/1**[3]
112- **7** *6* **Peruvian Prince (USA)**[35] [6924] 5-8-11 **79** PaulHanagan 5 63
(R A Fahey) *prom: rdn over 3f out: wknd 2f out* **13/8**[1]
00-0 **8** *3 1/2* **Kova Hall (IRE)**[16] [96] 5-8-12 **80** (t) RobertHavlin 10 57
(M F Harris) *hld up: hdwy over 3f out: sn rdn: wknd 2f out* **66/1**
400- **9** *7* **Play The Ball (USA)**[64] [6573] 5-8-3 **71** oh4 AdrianMcCarthy 6 34
(J J Lambe, Ire) *hld up in tch: rdn over 3f out: wknd 2f out* **100/1**
016- **10** *5* **Dzesmin (POL)**[104] [5678] 5-9-0 **82** (p) JamieMackay 2 35
(R C Guest) *plld hrd and sn led: hdd 1/2-way: wknd 2f out* **33/1**

2m 1.61s (-1.01) **Going Correction** +0.10s/f (Slow)
WFA 4 from 5yo+ 1lb **10** Ran SP% **113.8**
Speed ratings (Par 105):108,107,107,106,103 102,96,93,87,83
CSF £169.40 CT £516.28 TOTE £8.60: £1.80, £3.50, £1.30; EX 83.30 Trifecta £455.60 Pool £956.15 - 1.49 winning unit..
Owner Nigel Shields **Bred** N R Shields And K R Burke **Trained** Middleham Moor, N Yorks
■ Stewards' Enquiry : N Callan caution: careless riding

FOCUS
A fair handicap and one run at a decent gallop. This form should stand up at a similar level.
Fantasy Ride Official explanation: jockey said gelding was denied a clear run

257 PONTINSBINGO.COM MAIDEN STKS (DIV I) 1m 1f 103y(P)
4:30 (4:36) (Class 5) 3-Y-0 £2,266 (£674; £337; £168) Stalls Low

Form RPR
00-2 **1** **Six Shots**[11] [140] 3-9-3 67 ShaneKelly 10 73
(J A Osborne) *mde virtually all: rdn over 1f out: r.o* **4/1**[3]
00-2 **2** *1 1/4* **Milla's Rocket (IRE)**[10] [149] 3-8-12 (b) NCallan 2 66
(K A Ryan) *a.p: rdn to chse wnr 2f out: sn hung lft: hung rt ins fnl f: styd on same pce* **5/1**
3 *1 1/4* **Reciprocation (IRE)** 3-9-3 JoeFanning 8 68
(M Johnston) *s.i.s: sn prom: nt clr run over 3f out: rdn and hung lft fr over 1f out: styd on* **9/4**[1]
0 **4** *4* **Witchingham**[13] [114] 3-9-3 ChrisCatlin 7 60
(R Hannon) *chsd wnr tl rdn over 2f out: wkng whn edgd lft fnl f* **40/1**
224- **5** *3/4* **Arena's Dream (USA)**[121] [5614] 3-9-3 72 PaulHanagan 4 59
(R A Fahey) *hld up in tch: plld hrd: rdn over 1f out: wkng whn hmpd ins fnl f* **7/2**[2]
6 *nk* **David's Cavalier** 3-9-3 GrahamGibbons 11 58
(R Hollinshead) *chsd ldrs: rdn 3f out: wknd over 1f out* **40/1**
26- **7** *1 1/2* **Katy Carr**[76] [6447] 3-8-12 PatCosgrave 3 50
(M J Wallace) *hld up: effrt over 2f out: wknd over 1f out* **8/1**
50- **8** *2 1/2* **Blockley (USA)**[30] [6950] 3-8-10 WilliamBuick(7) 9 50
(Ian Williams) *hld up: a in rr* **28/1**
0-0 **9** *7* **Northern Dune (IRE)**[20] [53] 3-9-3 TPQueally 6 36
(B J Curley) *hld up: wknd over 3f out* **66/1**
10 *5* **Dance Steps** 3-8-12 AntonyProcter 5 21
(P S McEntee) *s.i.s: hld up: rdn 1/2-way: sn wknd* **66/1**
R **Supercraft (IRE)** 3-9-3 MickyFenton 1 —
(M Quinn) *ref to r* **50/1**

2m 3.98s (1.36) **Going Correction** +0.10s/f (Slow) **11** Ran SP% **114.0**
Speed ratings (Par 97):97,95,94,91,90 90,88,86,80,76 —
CSF £22.37 TOTE £6.10: £1.70, £2.00, £1.50; EX 25.00 Trifecta £88.30 Pool £716.65 - 5.76 winning units..
Owner Mountgrange&Wood Hall Studs Booth Durkan **Bred** The Lavington Stud **Trained** Upper Lambourn, Berks

FOCUS
Not the strongest of maidens and one in which the steadily progressive Six Shots had the run of the race. The form looks sound enough, rated a round the winner.

258 PONTINSBINGO.COM MAIDEN STKS (DIV II) 1m 1f 103y(P)
5:00 (5:06) (Class 5) 3-Y-0 £2,266 (£674; £337; £168) Stalls Low

Form RPR
64- **1** **Sweetheart**[50] [6737] 3-8-12 NCallan 2 73
(M A Jarvis) *edgd rt s: chsd ldrs: riden over 2f out: styd on u.p to ld wl ins fnl f* **9/4**[2]
6- **2** *3/4* **Rain And Shade**[30] [6950] 3-9-3 JoeFanning 5 76
(M Johnston) *chsd ldr: led 1/2-way: hdd wl ins fnl f* **15/8**[1]
6- **3** *8* **Anne Bonney**[95] [6145] 3-8-12 ChrisCatlin 10 55
(E J O'Neill) *prom: jnd ldr over 3f out: rdn and wknd over 1f out* **6/1**
4 *3* **Snake Hips** 3-9-3 DaleGibson 7 54
(B Palling) *dwlt: hld up: styd on appr fnl f: nvr nrr* **100/1**
5 *4* **Giddywell** 3-8-7 RussellKennemore(5) 6 41
(R Hollinshead) *mid-div: rdn over 3f out: wknd 2f out* **80/1**
0 **6** *11* **Kiwi The Clown (IRE)**[18] [69] 3-9-3 PaulHanagan 8 24
(R A Fahey) *hld up: plld hrd: nvr trbld ldrs* **50/1**
00- **7** *nk* **Pretty Game**[161] [4566] 3-9-3 CatherineGannon 4 23
(K A Ryan) *led to 1/2-way: wknd over 2f out* **50/1**
4 **8** *3 1/2* **Deserter (IRE)**[13] [114] 3-8-12 ShaneKelly 3 11
(J A Osborne) *hmpd s: hld up: swtchd rt and rdn 4f out: wknd wl over 2f out* **5/2**[3]
0 **9** *5* **Montiona**[10] [149] 3-9-0 StephenDonohoe(3) 9 6
(John A Harris) *hld up: wknd over 3f out* **150/1**

2m 3.30s (0.68) **Going Correction** +0.10s/f (Slow) **9** Ran SP% **115.2**
Speed ratings (Par 97):100,99,92,89,86 76,75,72,68
CSF £6.89 TOTE £3.40: £1.40, £1.10, £1.70; EX 7.30 Trifecta £30.60 Pool £1,226.88 - 28.40 winning units. Place 6 £19.98, Place 5 £16.38.
Owner Jumeirah Racing **Bred** Darley **Trained** Newmarket, Suffolk

FOCUS
Another modest maiden and one run at just a fair gallop. The first two were big improvers and finished clear, but the form may not prove rock solid.
T/Jkpt: Not won. T/Plt: £26.60 to a £1 stake. Pool: £94,452.35. 2,587.95 winning tickets. T/Qpdt: £16.50 to a £1 stake. Pool: £5,705.50. 254.50 winning tickets. CR

229 LINGFIELD (L-H)
Saturday, January 27

OFFICIAL GOING: Standard
Wind: Almost nil Weather: Fine, mild

259 PONTINSBINGO.COM H'CAP 1m (P)
12:35 (12:35) (Class 4) (0-85,83) 4-Y-0+ £4,857 (£1,445; £722; £360) Stalls High

Form RPR
061- **1** **Bobski (IRE)**[75] [6461] 5-9-2 **83** NCallan 4 93+
(G A Huffer) *stdd s: hld up in last trio: rdn and prog over 2f out: sustained effrt to ld last 150yds: edgd lft but sn clr* **5/2**[1]
30-2 **2** *1 1/4* **Katiypour (IRE)**[21] [56] 10-9-1 **82** SebSanders 2 91+
(P Mitchell) *prom: rdn 2f out: clsng to chal whn squeezed out 150yds out . horse and rdr hit by rival's whip sn after: styd on nr fin* **5/1**[3]
25-4 **3** *hd* **Trifti**[10] [164] 6-8-5 **72** (b[1]) JimmyQuinn 9 79
(C A Cyzer) *trckd ldr after 2f: led 3f out: kicked 2 l clr 2f out: under furious press 1f out: hdd and fdd last 150yds* **11/2**
000- **4** *1 1/2* **Gallantry**[140] [5175] 5-9-2 **83** DeanMcKeown 6 87
(D Shaw) *hld up in last trio: rdn and prog on outer over 2f out: hanging over 1f out: styd on but nt pce to chal* **8/1**
24-0 **5** *3* **Red Birr (IRE)**[21] [56] 6-8-6 **73** ChrisCatlin 7 70
(P R Webber) *led to 3f out: wknd over 1f out* **14/1**
03-0 **6** *shd* **St Petersburg**[8] [185] 7-9-0 **81** JimCrowley 8 77
(M H Tompkins) *chsd ldrs: lost pl and btn u.p 2f out* **4/1**[2]
600- **7** *2 1/2* **Regal Royale**[63] [6600] 4-9-1 **82** GeorgeBaker 5 73
(Peter Grayson) *s.s: hld up in last: shuffled along over 1f out: nvr nr ldrs* **14/1**
000/ **8** *shd* **Definite Guest (IRE)**[602] [2302] 9-8-3 **70** PaulHanagan 3 60
(R A Fahey) *chsd ldrs: lost pl and struggling wl over 2f out* **33/1**
505- **9** *3* **Count Kristo**[170] [4299] 5-8-5 **72** HayleyTurner 1 56
(B G Powell) *chsd ldrs: lost pl 5f out: wknd over 2f out* **28/1**

1m 36.71s (-2.72) **Going Correction** -0.20s/f (Stan) **9** Ran SP% **111.5**
Speed ratings (Par 105):105,103,103,102,99 98,96,96,93
CSF £14.19 CT £59.87 TOTE £3.40: £1.70, £1.50, £1.70; EX 13.80 Trifecta £35.70 Pool £200.53. - 3.98 winning units..
Owner Robert Thomson **Bred** Patrick Kennedy **Trained** Newmarket, Suffolk
■ Stewards' Enquiry : Jimmy Quinn one-day ban: used whip with excessive frequency and twice down the shoulder in the forehand position (Feb 7)
N Callan caution: careless riding

FOCUS
Just an ordinary handicap for the grade. The winning time was 0.20 seconds quicker than the following maiden. The form has been rated around the runner-up, who should have been closer.
Regal Royale Official explanation: jockey said gelding missed the break

260 GO PONTIN'S MAIDEN STKS 1m (P)
1:10 (1:12) (Class 5) 3-Y-0+ £2,914 (£867; £433; £216) Stalls High

Form RPR
1 **Storybook (UAE)** 3-8-2 MatthewHenry 3 67
(M A Jarvis) *mde all: rdn and pressed over 1f out: styd on wl fnl f* **10/3**[2]
04-3 **2** *1 1/2* **Blue Monkey (IRE)**[14] [114] 3-8-7 76 HayleyTurner 10 69
(M L W Bell) *chsd ldrs: wnt 2nd 3f out: drvn to cl on wnr over 1f out: nt qckn fnl f* **2/1**[1]
36-2 **3** *1/2* **Henry The Seventh**[24] [21] 3-8-4 70 (v) JamesDoyle(3) 2 67
(J W Hills) *dwlt: sn in tch in midfield: rdn over 4f out: prog u.p on outer 2f out: kpt on same pce after* **4/1**[3]
4/4- **4** *hd* **Oscar Snowman**[103] [6019] 4-9-6 KatiaScallan(7) 12 77+
(M P Tregoning) *t.k.h: trckd ldrs on outer: cruising 2f out: swtchd ins and no room 1f out: nudged along and one pce last 100yds* **10/1**
5 *5* **Lough Neagh (USA)** 4-9-13 PaulEddery 4 61
(Miss D Mountain) *dwlt: hld up towards rr: jst in tch w ldng gp and gng wl enough over 2f out: sn outpcd* **25/1**
00- **6** *1 1/2* **Tizzydore (IRE)**[116] [5760] 3-8-2 JimmyQuinn 5 47
(A M Balding) *plld hrd: chsd wnr 2f: lost pl: cl enough 2f out: wknd over 1f out* **20/1**
7 *4* **Winds Of Kildare (IRE)** 4-9-13 OscarUrbina 7 48
(C N Allen) *restless stalls: a towards rr: limited prog into midfield over 2f out: no hdwy after* **50/1**
8 *7* **A Mothers Love** 3-8-3 ow1 EdwardCreighton 11 23
(P J McBride) *dwlt: hld up in last: bhd fr 3f out* **66/1**
9 *2 1/2* **Broad Town Girl**[23] 4-9-1 KylieManser(7) 9 21
(Mrs H Sweeting) *s.i.s: hld up in last pair: bhd fnl 3f* **100/1**
0 **10** *hd* **Cornerstone**[13] [127] 3-8-4 SaleemGolam(3) 1 21
(S C Williams) *dwlt: rcvrd to midfield: rdn over 4f out: sn wknd* **33/1**
0 **11** *2 1/2* **Termsandconditions (IRE)**[7] [193] 3-8-2 (b[1]) PaulHanagan 6 10
(W J Haggas) *in tch to 1/2-way: wknd and wl bhd 3f out* **33/1**
12 *1/2* **Whodunit (UAE)** 3-8-7 JoeFanning 8 14
(M Johnston) *chsd wnr after 2f tl wknd u.p 3f out: eased over 1f out* **8/1**

1m 36.91s (-2.52) **Going Correction** -0.20s/f (Stan)
WFA 3 from 4yo 20lb **12** Ran SP% **115.5**
Speed ratings (Par 103):104,102,102,101,96 95,91,84,81,81 79,78
CSF £9.42 TOTE £4.20: £1.70, £1.30, £1.70; EX 10.20 Trifecta £75.00 Part won. Pool £105.68. - 0.51 winning units..
Owner Jumeirah Racing **Bred** Darley **Trained** Newmarket, Suffolk

FOCUS
An ordinary maiden, run in a time 0.20 seconds slower than the opening handicap won by 83-rated Bobski. Pretty sound form, nevertheless.
Henry The Seventh Official explanation: jockey said colt hung both ways in the straight
Winds Of Kildare(IRE) Official explanation: jockey said gelding hit its head in the stalls

261 PONTIN'S HOLIDAYS H'CAP 7f (P)
1:45 (1:45) (Class 4) (0-80,78) 4-Y-0+

£4,674 (£1,399; £699; £350; £174; £87) **Stalls** Low

Form RPR

01-1 **1** **Super Frank (IRE)**[13] [131] 4-8-4 **66**................................ JoeFanning 11 81+
(J Akehurst) *mde all and set decent pce: rdn over 1f out: styd on strly fnl f* **11/2**[2]

01-3 **2** *1 3/4* **Barney McGrew (IRE)**[21] [56] 4-8-10 **72**........................ OscarUrbina 1 86+
(J A R Toller) *t.k.h: hld up towards rr: prog 2f out: nt clr run over 1f out: swtchd to inner and r.o to take 2nd last 75yds: hopeless task* **15/8**[1]

0-55 **3** *1/2* **Josh**[7] [191] 5-9-2 **78**..(p) NCallan 3 87
(K A Ryan) *prom: rdn over 2f out: chsd wnr over 1f out: no imp: lost 2nd last 75yds* **6/1**[3]

-216 **4** *1 1/4* **Sun Catcher (IRE)**[7] [191] 4-9-1 **77**.................................... DaneO'Neill 5 83
(R Hannon) *prom: rdn over 2f out: one pce u.p over 1f out* **7/1**

6-42 **5** *3/4* **Will He Wish**[7] [191] 11-9-2 **78**.. IanMongan 4 82
(S Gollings) *chsd wnr to over 1f out: fdd* **8/1**

050- **6** *1/2* **Spring Goddess (IRE)**[54] [6698] 6-8-10 **72**........................ AdamKirby 9 75
(A P Jarvis) *hld up in last trio: shkn up 2f out: no prog tl styd on ins fnl f: no ch* **12/1**

2-03 **7** *hd* **Arctic Desert**[5] [211] 7-8-12 **74**...(t) JohnEgan 12 76
(Miss Gay Kelleway) *hld up in last trio: nt clr run briefly wl over 1f out: shkn up and one pce after* **14/1**

00-3 **8** *1/2* **Ivory Lace**[24] [28] 6-9-0 **76**.. GeorgeBaker 6 77
(S Woodman) *hld up in last trio: rdn and no prog 2f out: plugged on* **12/1**

-510 **9** *2 1/2* **Hollow Jo**[7] [190] 7-9-2 **78**.. MickyFenton 8 72
(J R Jenkins) *settled in midfield: rdn and no prog over 2f out: btn over 1f out* **16/1**

0-04 **10** *11* **Meditation**[7] [191] 5-8-12 **77**......................................(p) JamesDoyle[(3)] 10 43
(I A Wood) *chsd ldrs: rdn 4f out: wknd u.p fr 3f out: t.o* **20/1**

1m 22.31s (-3.58) **Going Correction** -0.20s/f (Stan) course record **10** Ran SP% **120.8**
Speed ratings (Par 105):112,110,109,108,107 106,106,105,102,90
CSF £16.81 CT £67.92 TOTE £4.70: £1.70, £1.90, £2.00; EX 14.50 Trifecta £32.20 Pool £209.56. - 4.62 winning units..
Owner A D Spence **Bred** A Butler **Trained** Epsom, Surrey

FOCUS
A fair handicap for the grade, run at a strong pace from the start. Form to treat positively, with the winner up another 5lb, the runner-up better than his bare form, and the third, fifth and sixth all better class than this not so long ago.
Meditation Official explanation: jockey said mare hit its head on the stalls

262 PONTIN'S "BOOK EARLY" H'CAP 6f (P)
2:20 (2:20) (Class 5) (0-75,72) 4-Y-0+ **£2,914** (£867; £433; £216) **Stalls** Low

Form RPR

62-3 **1** **Lucayos**[17] [91] 4-8-13 **72**.................................... RichardKingscote[(3)] 3 82
(Mrs H Sweeting) *pressed ldr: rdn to ld jst over 1f out: kpt on wl fnl f* **9/2**[2]

306- **2** *3/4* **Inch By Inch**[27] [6999] 8-8-11 **70**.....................................(b) AmirQuinn[(3)] 1 78
(P J Makin) *sn led: hdd jst over 1f out and rdr dropped whip: kpt on but a hld* **8/1**

4-10 **3** *3/4* **Millfields Dreams**[10] [158] 8-8-7 **66**........................... JerryO'Dwyer[(3)] 2 72
(M G Quinlan) *trckd ldrs: pushed along fr 1/2-way: rdn to chse ldng pair wl over 1f out: kpt on but nvr able to chal* **5/4**[1]

05-5 **4** *hd* **Sands Crooner (IRE)**[10] [163] 4-8-13 **69**........................(v) DaneO'Neill 5 74
(D Shaw) *settled in last pair: rdn wl over 2f out: prog over 1f out: kpt on: nvr able to chal* **12/1**

200- **5** *2* **Tanforan**[59] [6654] 5-9-1 **71**..(p) GeorgeBaker 6 70
(Ms J S Doyle) *stdd s: hld up in last pair: rdn over 2f out: no prog and sn btn* **7/1**

30-3 **6** *1 1/4* **Conrad**[16] [102] 4-8-12 **68**...(b) PaulHanagan 7 63
(R A Fahey) *settled in 5th: rdn 1/2-way: struggling fnl 2f* **13/2**[3]

0-00 **7** *5* **Anfield Dream**[3] [234] 5-9-0 **70**... NCallan 4 50
(J R Jenkins) *racd on outer: chsd ldng pair: wknd rapidly wl over 1f out* **12/1**

1m 11.28s (-1.53) **Going Correction** -0.20s/f (Stan) **7** Ran SP% **115.0**
Speed ratings (Par 103):102,101,100,99,97 95,88
CSF £39.55 TOTE £4.90: £2.20, £3.20; EX 22.00.
Owner Alex Sweeting **Bred** P Sweeting **Trained** Lockeridge, Wilts

FOCUS
A modest handicap and ordinary form for the grade.

263 CANVAS PRINTS FROM BONUSPRINT.COM H'CAP 1m 2f (P)
2:55 (2:55) (Class 5) (0-70,70) 4-Y-0+ **£2,914** (£867; £433; £216) **Stalls** Low

Form RPR

4-06 **1** **Tous Les Deux**[10] [164] 4-9-0 **68**...................................... GeorgeBaker 12 77
(Peter Grayson) *dwlt: hld up wl in rr: prog on wd outside 3f out: rdn to ld last 75yds: bmpd and hdd nr post: fin 2nd, shd: awrdd r* **20/1**

12-4 **2** *shd* **Reaching Out (IRE)**14 [117] 5-8-5 **60**.......................(b) JamesDoyle[(3)] 7 69
(N P Littmoden) *hld up in rr: prog and squeezed through wl over 1f out: led 1f out : hdd last 75yds: edgd rt and led post: fin 1st: disq: plcd 2nd* **8/1**

01-1 **3** *1/2* **Kilimandscharo (USA)**[19] [72] 5-8-12 **64**........................ BrettDoyle 3 76+
(P J McBride) *settled midfield: prog on inner 2f out: nt clr run over 1f out: r.o wl fnl f: gaining at fin* **3/1**[1]

50-3 **4** *1/2* **Sky Quest (IRE)**[10] [164] 9-9-1 **67**.................................. HayleyTurner 2 74
(J R Boyle) *prom: rdn to chal and nrly upsides 1f out: nt qckn* **20/1**

5 *nk* **Luxurix (FR)**[893] 6-9-4 **70**.. DaneO'Neill 8 76
(P R Webber) *t.k.h: mostly trckd ldr: led 2f out: hdd and no ex 1f out* **7/2**[2]

3-20 **6** *nk* **Berkhamsted (IRE)**[14] [117] 5-9-4 **70**.................................(p) NCallan 4 76
(Tom Dascombe) *trckd ldrs: cl up 2f out: stl ch 1f out: one pce* **7/1**

01-1 **7** *shd* **Topiary Ted**[11] [151] 5-9-3 **69**.. RobertHavlin 9 75+
(H Morrison) *dwlt: hld up in rr: prog on outer 3f out: rdn and nt qckn over 1f out: one pce after* **9/2**[3]

45/3 **8** *4* **Ile Facile (IRE)**[21] [48] 6-9-3 **69**.. ChrisCatlin 5 67
(B De Haan) *led to 2f out: wknd fnl f* **10/1**

602/ **9** *1/2* **Ruby Brown**[538] [4189] 5-9-2 **68**.. OscarUrbina 6 65
(C A Cyzer) *settled midfield: rdn over 2f out: lost pl and btn wl over 1f out* **66/1**

/5-0 **10** *1* **Music Celebre (IRE)**[7] [195] 7-8-10 **62**................................ AlanDaly 1 57
(S Curran) *dwlt: hld up in detached last: rdn 2f out: no prog* **50/1**

11 *3/4* **Phoenix Factor (IRE)**[89] [6265] 4-8-8 **62**............................ JohnEgan 10 56
(J S Moore) *always towards rr: shkn up and no prog 2f out* **33/1**

210- **12** *8* **Storm Of Arabia (IRE)**[42] [6843] 4-8-10 **64**........................ AdamKirby 13 43
(W R Swinburn) *chsd ldrs on outer: rdn and wknd over 2f out* **12/1**

2-35 **13** *4* **Anduril**[4] [228] 6-8-9 **64**...(b) SaleemGolam[(3)] 11 35
(Miss M E Rowland) *t.k.h: pressed ldrs: rdn over 3f out: wknd wl over 2f out* **40/1**

2m 4.19s (-3.60) **Going Correction** -0.20s/f (Stan)
WFA 4 from 5yo+ 2lb **13** Ran SP% **124.2**
Speed ratings (Par 103):105,106,105,105,104 104,104,101,100,100 99,93,89
CSF £169.45 CT £632.39 TOTE £33.40: £6.20, £2.10, £1.50; EX 280.90 Trifecta £329.70 Part won. Pool £464.37. - 0.30 winning units..
Owner Mrs Sarah Grayson **Bred** G And Mrs Middlebrook **Trained** Formby, Lancs
■ Stewards' Enquiry : James Doyle one-day ban: used whip without allowing gelding time to respond (Feb 7). Reaching Out disq: interference to Tous Les Deux.

FOCUS
A messy race, with not much room to manoeuvre for a few of these in the straight, and a bunch finish. The winning time was 1.05 seconds quicker than the following 86-100, but they crawled in that race and the difference should not be taken literally. The bare form is ordinary.

264 BONUSPRINT.COM H'CAP 1m 2f (P)
3:30 (3:30) (Class 2) (0-100,97) 4-Y-0+

£11,217 (£3,358; £1,679; £840; £419; £210) **Stalls** Low

Form RPR

1-43 **1** **Very Wise**[14] [119] 5-8-7 **86**.. JoeFanning 2 98
(W J Haggas) *mde all: set stdy pce tl wound it up fr 3f out: shkn up and styd on strly fr over 1f out* **7/1**

111- **2** *1 1/4* **Cusoon**[38] [6888] 5-8-12 **91**... BrettDoyle 6 101+
(G L Moore) *hld up in 6th: prog and forced wd bnd 2f out: rdn and hanging over 1f out: r.o to chse wnr ins fnl f: readily hld* **11/8**[1]

004- **3** *2* **Fortunate Isle (USA)**[30] [6107] 5-8-6 **85**.......................... PaulHanagan 5 91
(R A Fahey) *settled in 5th: rdn over 2f out: styd on fr over 1f out to take 3rd nr fin: n.d* **13/2**[3]

053- **4** *shd* **Langford**[27] [6997] 7-8-6 **88**.. SaleemGolam[(3)] 3 94
(M H Tompkins) *trckd ldng pair: effrt on inner to chse wnr 2f out: no imp : fdd ins fnl f* **14/1**

61-0 **5** *3/4* **Bahar Shumaal (IRE)**[14] [119] 5-9-4 **97**.........................(b) SebSanders 7 102
(C E Brittain) *hld up in 4th: effrt on outer over 2f out: no prog over 1f out: fdd* **7/2**[2]

0 **6** *2 1/2* **General Knowledge (USA)**[7] [197] 4-8-6 **87**...............(t) HayleyTurner 4 87?
(B G Powell) *t.k.h: hld up in last: rdn over 2f out: sn struggling* **33/1**

2-41 **7** *3/4* **Fusili (IRE)**[14] [119] 4-8-13 **94**... NCallan 1 92
(N P Littmoden) *chsd wnr to 2f out: steadily wknd* **7/1**

2m 5.24s (-2.55) **Going Correction** -0.20s/f (Stan)
WFA 4 from 5yo+ 2lb **7** Ran SP% **112.3**
Speed ratings (Par 109):102,101,99,99,98 96,96
CSF £16.49 TOTE £9.50: £3.30, £1.60; EX 28.70.
Owner J M Greetham **Bred** J M Greetham **Trained** Newmarket, Suffolk

FOCUS
A good handicap on paper, but they went no pace and the bare form is unreliable. The winning time was 1.05 seconds slower than the earlier 56-70.

NOTEBOOK
Very Wise settled much better in front this time and benefited from a good front-running ride from Joe Fanning, who set just a steady pace until quickening things up inside the last half-mile. He is obviously useful, but the bare result of this success probably flatters him and a rise in the weights will make things tougher. (op 8-1)
Cusoon ◆, bidding for a fourth straight success off a mark 7lb higher than when breaking the course record over course and distance on his previous start, was totally unsuited by the way the race was run and is better than he was able to show. Having been held up off a steady pace, he was forced to come widest of all in the straight when the eventual winner kicked for home from the front and had no chance of making up the lost ground. He remains most progressive and should gain compensation if getting the race run to suit next time. (op 6-4)
Fortunate Isle(USA), third in a maiden hurdle at Catterick on his previous start, ran a good race on his return to the level and could have more to offer off his current mark. (op 8-1)
Langford was always going to be vulnerable to more progressive types, but this was a respectable effort. (tchd 16-1)
Bahar Shumaal(IRE) is a strong-galloping type and the steady pace was totally against him. (tchd 4-1)
Fusili(IRE) enjoyed the run of the race when winning over course and distance on her previous start and she was unable to defy a 3lb higher mark. (op 5-1)

265 PONTINS.COM MAIDEN STKS 1m 4f (P)
4:05 (4:05) (Class 5) 4-Y-0+ **£2,817** (£838; £418; £209) **Stalls** Low

Form RPR

243- **1** **Sgt Schultz (IRE)**[79] [6415] 4-9-3 69...................................... JohnEgan 5 75
(J S Moore) *hld up towards rr: prog and dream run on inner fr 3f out: led wl over 1f out: rdn clr* **5/2**[2]

0-5 **2** *3* **Watchmaker**[17] [84] 4-9-3 .... PaulDoe 8 70
(W J Knight) *sn t.k.h and pressed ldr: led over 4f out: rdn and hdd wl over 1f out: no ch w wnr fnl f* **20/1**

30-4 **3** *nk* **Follow On**[7] [192] 5-9-7 74... DaneO'Neill 9 70+
(A P Jarvis) *hld up towards rr: prog over 2f out: rdn over 1f out: hanging and fnd nil: plugged on ins fnl f* **6/4**[1]

3 **4** *nk* **Stanerra's Story (IRE)**[6] [204] 6-9-7 ....(t) ChrisCatlin 3 70
(E J O'Neill) *dwlt: t.k.h and sn pressed ldrs: rdn and nt qckn 2f out: kpt on same pce after* **7/1**[3]

330- **5** *1 1/2* **Soul Blazer (USA)**[42] [6841] 4-9-3 67..............................(p) SebSanders 4 67
(A M Balding) *hld up in midfield: rdn over 3f out: one pce and n.d over 2f out* **7/1**[3]

502- **6** *3/4* **Master'n Commander**[224] [2647] 5-9-7 59........................ JimmyQuinn 1 66
(C A Cyzer) *hld up in last pair: pushed along over 2f out: nvr on terms* **12/1**

00 **7** *hd* **Tres Bien**[3] [229] 5-9-7 ....(v[1]) GeorgeBaker 2 66?
(P R Webber) *dwlt: hld up in last pair: effrt on outer over 2f out: rdn and fnd nil over 1f out* **33/1**

04-4 **8** *8* **Lord Laing (USA)**[17] [89] 4-9-0 58........................... JerryO'Dwyer[(3)] 6 53+
(H J Collingridge) *trckd ldrs: trapped bhd wkng rival and lost all ch over 3f out: no prog after* **9/1**

0 **9** *43* **Remis Velisque**[3] [229] 4-8-5 .... KarenKenny[(7)] 7 —
(B G Powell) *led at stdy pce to over 4f out: wknd rapidly: t.o* **66/1**

2m 32.8s (-1.59) **Going Correction** -0.20s/f (Stan)
WFA 4 from 5yo+ 4lb **9** Ran SP% **120.5**
Speed ratings (Par 103):97,95,94,94,93 93,92,87,58
CSF £54.19 TOTE £3.70: £1.40, £3.30, £1.10; EX 63.80 Trifecta £220.80 Part won. Pool £310.99. - 0.61 winning units. Place 6 £28.84, Place 5 £18.94..
Owner Jim Barnes **Bred** Frank Dunne **Trained** Upper Lambourn, Berks

FOCUS
A modest maiden and, with little pace on from the start, unreliable form. It has been rated through the third, fifth and sixth.
Lord Laing(USA) Official explanation: trainer said gelding had been struck into during the race

T/Plt: £21.90 to a £1 stake. Pool: £56,712.25. 1,885.50 winning tickets. T/Qpdt: £14.60 to a £1 stake. Pool: £2,580.00. 130.30 winning tickets. JN

[251]WOLVERHAMPTON (A.W) (L-H)

Saturday, January 27

OFFICIAL GOING: Standard to slow

Wind: Moderate across Weather: Fine

266 GO PONTIN'S H'CAP 1m 1f 103y(P)

3:50 (3:50) (Class 6) (0-50,56) 4-Y-0+ **£2,388** (£705; £352) **Stalls** Low

Form RPR

15-6 **1** **Bobering**[11] [156] 7-8-1 **46** oh1 SoniaEaton(7) 6 61
(B P J Baugh) *hld up in mid-div: hdwy on outside 3f out: edgd lft and led jst over 1f out: r.o* **12/1**

00-2 **2** *nk* **Mademoiselle**[14] [115] 5-8-10 **48** J-PGuillambert 5 62+
(R A Harris) *hld up in tch: rdn 4f out: led wl over 1f out: hdd jst over 1f out: r.o* **15/2**

50-1 **3** *6* **My Michelle**[11] [156] 6-9-4 **56** TonyCulhane 8 58
(B Palling) *chsd ldr: led 5f out: rdn over 2f out: hdd wl over 1f out: wknd fnl f* **7/2**[1]

53-0 **4** *shd* **Wodhill Schnaps**[20] [63] 6-8-10 **48** (v) ShaneKelly 13 50
(D Morris) *s.i.s: hld up and bhd: hdwy over 4f out: ev ch 2f out: sn rdn: wknd fnl f* **6/1**[3]

0-50 **5** *nk* **Cape Of Storms**[5] [217] 4-8-9 **48** PatCosgrave 4 49
(R Brotherton) *plld hrd in mid-div: rdn over 2f out: hdwy over 1f out: kpt on same pce fnl f* **10/1**

4-66 **6** *nk* **Laurollie**[14] [126] 5-8-8 **46** oh1 RichardThomas 1 47
(B P J Baugh) *hld up and bhd: rdn and hdwy over 2f out: no imp fnl f* **25/1**

4-05 **7** *½* **Danelor (IRE)**[7] [187] 9-8-8 **46** oh1 (p) DeanMcKeown 3 46
(D Shaw) *prom: rdn over 3f out: wknd over 2f out* **14/1**

036- **8** *1 ¾* **Wayward Shot (IRE)**[49] [6756] 5-8-10 **48** DaleGibson 10 44
(M W Easterby) *plld hrd: prom: rdn and ev ch over 2f out: wknd fnl f* **9/2**[2]

00-5 **9** *3* **Hometomammy**[6] [203] 5-8-5 **46** oh1 AndrewMullen(3) 11 36
(P W Hiatt) *mid-div: rdn 5f out: no hdwy fnl 3f* **14/1**

00-0 **10** *8* **Bold Phoenix (IRE)**[20] [64] 6-8-9 **47** (b) TPQueally 7 21
(B J Curley) *s.i.s: nvr nr ldrs* **14/1**

0-30 **11** *2 ½* **Zando**[8] [179] 5-8-10 **48** (p) PhillipMakin 9 17
(E G Bevan) *hld up and bhd: nt clr run 4f out: rdn and short-lived effrt over 2f out* **18/1**

006- **12** *18* **Miss Glory Be**[187] [3803] 9-8-9 **47** (p) FergusSweeney 12 —
(Ernst Oertel) *hld up in tch: rdn 4f out: sn wknd* **33/1**

0- **13** *dist* **Beyond Belief (IRE)**[82] [6382] 4-8-11 **50** RobertWinston 2 —
(M J Wallace) *led: hdd 5f out: wknd qckly over 3f out: virtually p.u over 1f out* **33/1**

2m 2.16s (-0.46) **Going Correction** +0.025s/f (Slow)
WFA 4 from 5yo+ 1lb 13 Ran SP% **118.2**
Speed ratings (Par 101):103,102,97,97,97 96,96,94,92,85 82,66,—
CSF £96.45 CT £385.20 TOTE £21.20: £4.20, £2.00, £1.70; EX 207.50.
Owner J H Chrimes And Mr & Mrs G W Hannam **Bred** J H Chrimes **Trained** Audley, Staffs

FOCUS
A weak handicap that was run at a sound pace. The first two came clear and the form should work out.

Zando Official explanation: jockey said gelding was never travelling
Miss Glory Be Official explanation: jockey said mare stopped very quickly
Beyond Belief(IRE) Official explanation: jockey said filly finished lame behind

267 PONTIN'S HOLIDAYS H'CAP 1m 1f 103y(P)

4:25 (4:25) (Class 6) (0-60,62) 3-Y-0 **£2,388** (£705; £352) **Stalls** Low

Form RPR

2-11 **1** **Global Traffic**[12] [140] 3-9-3 **62** (b) StephenDonohoe(3) 12 70+
(P D Evans) *hld up and bhd: rdn and hdwy on outside 2f out: led ins fnl f: r.o wl* **2/1**[1]

20-0 **2** *2 ½* **Diamond Light (USA)**[24] [21] 3-9-4 **60** TPQueally 4 63
(M Botti) *mid-div: hdwy 3f out: sn rdn: led and hung lft jst over 1f out: hdd ins fnl f: one pce* **25/1**

1-33 **3** *nk* **Gold Response**[12] [140] 3-9-0 **56** DeanMcKeown 8 58
(D Shaw) *hld up and bhd: hdwy 3f out: rdn over 1f out: kpt on ins fnl f* **12/1**

5-04 **4** *1 ½* **My Sara**[4] [224] 3-8-6 **48** (v) DaleGibson 11 47
(R A Fahey) *hld up and bhd: rdn over 4f out: hdwy fnl f: nrst fin* **16/1**

05-2 **5** *shd* **Shrewd Dude**[23] [37] 3-8-10 **52** ow1 (b[1]) TonyCulhane 1 51
(Carl Llewellyn) *chsd ldrs: rdn 4f out: led wl over 1f out: hdd jst over 1f out: no ex* **9/4**[2]

0-01 **6** *1 ½* **King Of The Beers (USA)**[10] [157] 3-8-8 **57** (p) LukeMorris(7) 5 53
(R A Harris) *bhd: rdn 5f out: hdwy 2f out: no imp fnl f* **12/1**

00-3 **7** *2 ½* **It's No Problem (IRE)**[10] [157] 3-8-11 **58** JamesMillman(5) 10 49
(M Salaman) *nvr trbld ldrs* **12/1**

46-3 **8** *¾* **Foxxy**[16] [99] 3-8-13 **55** (p) PatCosgrave 6 44
(K A Ryan) *chsd ldrs: rdn over 3f out: led briefly 2f out: wknd over 1f out* **28/1**

00-2 **9** *1 ½* **Voss**[10] [157] 3-8-13 **58** GregFairley(3) 2 44+
(M Johnston) *w ldr: led over 3f out: rdn and hdd 2f out: wknd over 1f out* **8/1**[3]

06-0 **10** *7* **Citrus Chief (USA)**[10] [157] 3-9-0 **56** (b[1]) J-PGuillambert 9 28
(R A Harris) *s.i.s: hdwy 7f out: wknd 2f out* **66/1**

00-0 **11** *3* **Hayley's Flower (IRE)**[10] [157] 3-8-4 **53** HaddenFrost(7) 13 19
(J C Fox) *mid-div: short-lived effrt 2f out* **33/1**

05-6 **12** *4* **Color Man**[10] [157] 3-8-10 **52** (b[1]) JimCrowley 7 10
(Mrs A J Perrett) *a bhd* **18/1**

04-0 **13** *2 ½* **Port Macquairie (IRE)**[14] [114] 3-8-13 **55** (b[1]) FergusSweeney 3 8+
(R M Beckett) *led: rdn over 4f out: hdd 3f out: wknd over 2f out* **33/1**

2m 4.31s (1.69) **Going Correction** +0.025s/f (Slow) 13 Ran SP% **124.1**
Speed ratings (Par 95):93,90,90,89,89 87,85,84,83,77 74,71,68
CSF £65.32 CT £518.40 TOTE £2.60: £1.50, £7.90, £2.50; EX 98.00.
Owner Mrs I M Folkes **Bred** P F I Cole **Trained** Pandy, Monmouths

FOCUS
A moderate handicap run at a solid pace. The winner is progressive and the form looks sound and fair for the grade.

268 PONTINSBINGO.COM H'CAP 7f 32y(P)

4:50 (4:51) (Class 6) (0-55,56) 4-Y-0+ **£2,388** (£705; £352) **Stalls** High

Form RPR

-063 **1** **Grand Palace (IRE)**[8] [181] 4-8-8 **49** (v) DeanMcKeown 2 61
(D Shaw) *hld up in tch: led over 2f out: sn rdn: r.o wl* **9/2**[2]

2-50 **2** *3* **Midmaar (IRE)**[10] [158] 6-8-12 **53** (b) GrahamGibbons 3 57
(M Wigham) *a.p: rdn over 2f out: chsd wnr fnl f: no imp* **11/2**[3]

0-41 **3** *1 ¼* **Kahlua Bear**[5] [217] 5-9-1 **56** 6ex (v) AdrianMcCarthy 5 57
(Miss K B Boutflower) *mid-div: rdn and hdwy on ins over 2f out: one pce fnl f* **7/2**[1]

00-0 **4** *5* **Blue Knight (IRE)**[17] [86] 8-8-11 **52** TonyCulhane 9 40
(P Howling) *bhd: rdn and hdwy on ins 2f out: nvr trbld ldrs* **14/1**

6-01 **5** *hd* **Val De Maal (IRE)**[11] [144] 7-9-0 **55** PaulMulrennan 7 42
(Miss J A Camacho) *sn led: rdn and hdd over 2f out: wknd wl over 1f out* **8/1**

165- **6** *hd* **Todlea (IRE)**[71] [6387] 7-8-13 **54** (t) FrankieMcDonald 10 41
(Jean-Rene Auvray) *hld up and bhd: rdn and hdwy wl over 1f out: nvr trbld ldrs* **11/1**

6-56 **7** *3* **Mulberry Lad (IRE)**[10] [161] 5-8-12 **53** PhillipMakin 8 32
(P W Hiatt) *hld up towards rr: rdn over 3f out: hdwy on wd outside over 1f out: n.d* **7/1**

030- **8** *1* **Apex**[121] [5635] 6-8-12 **53** KimTinkler 6 30
(N Tinkler) *chsd ldrs: rdn over 3f out: wknd over 2f out* **12/1**

54-0 **9** *nk* **Viewforth**[25] [8] 9-8-12 **53** ShaneKelly 11 29
(M A Buckley) *sn chsng ldr: rdn and wknd over 2f out* **20/1**

604- **10** *2 ½* **Pikaboo**[31] [6944] 4-9-0 **55** J-PGuillambert 1 24
(S C Williams) *s.i.s: hld up: hdwy on outside 4f out: rdn and wknd over 2f out* **14/1**

000- **11** *¾* **Stylistic (IRE)**[63] [6608] 6-8-13 **54** PatCosgrave 12 21
(J J Lambe, Ire) *t.k.h: prom: rdn over 2f out: wknd wl over 1f out* **50/1**

336- **12** *1 ¼* **Layed Back Rocky**[37] [6901] 5-8-9 **50** TPQueally 14 14
(M Mullineaux) *a bhd* **25/1**

1m 30.71s (0.31) **Going Correction** +0.025s/f (Slow) 12 Ran SP% **119.3**
Speed ratings (Par 101):99,95,94,88,88 87,84,83,83,80 79,77
CSF £29.08 CT £97.97 TOTE £5.90: £2.00, £2.10, £1.60; EX 33.90.
Owner ownaracehorse.co.uk (Shakespeare) **Bred** D McDonnell And Tower Bloodstock **Trained** Danethorpe, Notts

FOCUS
A moderate handicap, run at a sound pace. The form is rated around the runner-up and third.

269 DIGITAL PRINTS FROM BONUSPRINT.COM H'CAP 5f 20y(P)

5:20 (5:20) (Class 5) (0-75,75) 4-Y-0+ **£3,412** (£755; £755) **Stalls** Low

Form RPR

24-3 **1** **Figaro Flyer (IRE)**[10] [163] 4-9-1 **74** TonyCulhane 2 84
(P Howling) *a.p: rdn over 1f out: r.o u.p to ld nr fin* **10/3**[2]

22-2 **2** *½* **Financial Times (USA)**[10] [163] 5-9-2 **75** (tp) MickyFenton 4 83
(Stef Liddiard) *led: rdn wl over 1f out: hdd nr fin* **7/4**[1]

0-02 **2** *dht* **Nusoor (IRE)**[5] [214] 4-8-9 **68** RobbieFitzpatrick 3 76
(Peter Grayson) *s.i.s: hld up in mid-div: hdwy over 2f out: rdn and carried hd high over 1f out: r.o towards fin* **9/2**[3]

11-0 **4** *¾* **Desert Opal**[11] [155] 7-9-0 **73** (p) RobertWinston 7 79
(C R Dore) *chsd ldrs: rdn over 1f out: kpt on same pce fnl f* **12/1**

40-0 **5** *nk* **Fizzlephut (IRE)**[21] [47] 5-8-9 **68** PaulFitzsimons 9 72
(Miss J R Tooth) *chsd ldr: rdn wl over 1f out: nt qckn ins fnl f* **33/1**

31-3 **6** *1 ½* **Bond Playboy**[19] [67] 7-8-0 **64** (v) DuranFentiman(5) 8 63
(G R Oldroyd) *s.i.s: rdn wl over 1f out: nvr trbld ldrs* **13/2**

15-0 **7** *3* **Monashee Brave (IRE)**[18] [79] 4-9-1 **74** GrahamGibbons 5 62
(J J Quinn) *plld hrd in mid-div: wknd wl over 1f out* **16/1**

0-20 **8** *2 ½* **Lady Bahia (IRE)**[10] [163] 6-8-4 **63** (b) AdrianMcCarthy 1 42
(Peter Grayson) *s.i.s: short-lived effrt on ins wl over 1f out* **33/1**

0-56 **9** *8* **Mambazo**[17] [91] 5-8-6 **68** (v) StephenDonohoe(3) 6 18
(S C Williams) *t.k.h: a bhd* **10/1**

61.88 secs (-0.94) **Going Correction** +0.025s/f (Slow) 9 Ran SP% **119.5**
Speed ratings (Par 103):108,107,107,106,105 103,98,94,81
2nd Pl FT 1.10, N 1.90; Ex FF-FT 6.00, FF-N 17.20; CSF FF-FT 4.97, FF-N 9.80; T/C FF-FT-N 12.88; FF-N-FT 16.80 TOTE £4.30: £1.50.
Owner Mark Entwistle **Bred** Mohammad Al Qatami **Trained** Newmarket, Suffolk

FOCUS
A modest sprint, but the form looks solid for the class.

270 BONUSPRINT.COM MEDIAN AUCTION MAIDEN STKS 1m 5f 194y(P)

5:50 (5:50) (Class 6) 4-6-Y-0 **£2,388** (£705; £352) **Stalls** Low

Form RPR

-230 **1** **Mighty Kitchener (USA)**[6] [204] 4-9-3 55 TonyCulhane 4 61
(P Howling) *hld up in rr: hdwy over 3f out: rdn over 2f out: led jst over 1f out: drvn out* **9/2**

66-0 **2** *hd* **Fondness**[15] [112] 4-8-12 61 GrahamGibbons 8 56
(J J Quinn) *hld up and bhd: hdwy over 5f out: rdn over 3f out: ev ch 2f out: styd on ins fnl f* **4/1**[3]

6-5 **3** *4* **Scaramoushca**[26] [1] 4-9-3 AntonyProcter 1 55
(P S McEntee) *hld up in tch: led over 4f out: rdn over 3f out: hdd jst over 1f out: wknd ins fnl f* **14/1**

350- **4** *4* **Gouranga**[24] [5587] 4-8-12 57 ShaneKelly 7 45
(A W Carroll) *hld up in rr: hdwy over 4f out: rdn over 3f out: wknd over 2f out* **7/2**[2]

00-4 **5** *1* **Dik Dik**[14] [120] 4-9-3 48 (p) LPKeniry 6 48
(J S Moore) *hld up in mid-div: hdwy over 6f out: rdn over 3f out: wknd wl over 1f out* **10/1**

6 *11* **Magnifico (FR)**[14] 6-9-9 DeanMcKeown 2 33
(Mrs K Waldron) *s.i.s: hdwy over 6f out: wknd over 4f out* **5/2**[1]

0-06 **7** *9* **The Flying Peach**[17] [84] 4-8-12 35 CatherineGannon 9 15
(Miss Gay Kelleway) *led after 2f: hdd over 4f out: rdn over 3f out: wknd wl over 2f out* **50/1**

00-6 **8** *21* **Slip Star**[22] [45] 4-8-7 34 JamesMillman(5) 3 —
(T J Etherington) *led 2f: chsd ldr tl over 5f out: rdn and wknd wl over 3f out: eased whn no ch fnl 2f* **25/1**

00- **9** *dist* **Little Wishes**[92] [5768] 4-8-12 MickyFenton 5 —
(S Parr) *prom: rdn 8f out: wknd over 6f out: t.o fnl 5f* **100/1**

505/ **10** *dist* **Frith (IRE)**[281] [1673] 5-9-9 92 RobertWinston 10 —
(Mrs L B Normile) *bhd fnl 7f: t.o fnl 4f* **9/1**

3m 8.38s (1.01) **Going Correction** +0.025s/f (Slow)
WFA 4 from 5yo+ 6lb 10 Ran SP% **121.5**
Speed ratings: 98,97,95,93,92 86,81,69,—,—
CSF £23.78 TOTE £6.20: £1.60, £1.80, £3.20; EX 31.30.
Owner Elias Haloute **Bred** D Considine **Trained** Newmarket, Suffolk

■ Stewards' Enquiry : Graham Gibbons one-day ban: used whip with excessive frequency (Feb 7)

FOCUS
A poor maiden. The first two came clear, with the winner rated to his best and the runner-up to his sand form.

Slip Star Official explanation: jockey said filly lost action
Frith(IRE) Official explanation: trainer said gelding finished lame behind

271 WOLVERHAMPTON-RACECOURSE.CO.UK CLASSIFIED STKS 1m 141y(P)
6:20 (6:21) (Class 7) 4-Y-O+ £1,365 (£403; £201) Stalls Low

Form				RPR
443-	1		**Crush On You**[29] 6970 4-8-13 45 GrahamGibbons 10 (R Hollinshead) *chsd ldrs: rdn to ld 2f out: edgd rt ins fnl f: r.o* **15/2**	53
406-	2	1	**Weet Yer Tern (IRE)**[29] 6977 5-9-0 44 ShaneKelly 4 (W M Brisbourne) *hld up in mid-div: hdwy 3f out: sn rdn: swtchd lft wl ins fnl f: r.o* **4/1**[3]	51
60-0	3	shd	**Mister Maq**[18] 80 4-8-13 45 (b) RobertWinston 1 (A Crook) *bhd: rdn and hdwy over 2f out: r.o ins fnl f* **20/1**	51
5-43	4	½	**Fantasy Defender (IRE)**[11] 156 5-9-0 44 (v) AdamKirby 7 (Ernst Oertel) *hld up in mid-div: rdn and hdwy on outside over 1f out: kpt on ins fnl f* **9/4**[1]	50
0-30	5	2 ½	**Hill Of Almhuim (IRE)**[7] 187 4-8-13 45 (v) RobbieFitzpatrick 8 (Peter Grayson) *s.i.s: rdn and hdwy on ins over 2f out: eased whn btn towards fin* **6/1**	45
0-20	6	3 ½	**Fraternity**[13] 129 10-8-9 45 RussellKennemore(5) 11 (J A Pickering) *led: rdn 3f out: hdd 2f out: wknd fnl f* **14/1**	37
00-0	7	1 ½	**Rambling Socks**[15] 106 4-8-13 45 (bt) PhillipMakin 12 (S R Bowring) *chsd ldr: rdn and ev ch 2f out: wknd over 1f out* **66/1**	34
5-00	8	1 ¼	**Comic Tales**[6] 201 6-9-0 45 TPQueally 6 (M Mullineaux) *a bhd* **28/1**	32
505-	9	½	**Jenise (IRE)**[37] 6901 4-8-13 45 JimCrowley 9 (Mark Campion) *sn prom: rdn over 3f out: wknd 2f out* **33/1**	31
0-24	10	5	**Jiminor Mack**[14] 121 4-8-10 44 (b) RichardKingscote(3) 5 (W J H Ratcliffe) *rdn over 4f out: a bhd* **7/2**[2]	20
/05-	11	9	**Jember Red**[44] 6817 4-8-10 45 (b[1]) MarkLawson(3) 13 (B Smart) *sn prom: rdn over 3f out: wknd wl over 2f out* **20/1**	—

1m 52.81s (1.05) **Going Correction** +0.025s/f (Slow)
WFA 4 from 5yo+ 1lb **11 Ran SP% 123.1**
Speed ratings (Par 97):96,95,95,94,92 89,87,86,86,81 73
CSF £37.18 TOTE £7.60: £2.40, £1.90, £5.20; EX 34.50 Place 6 £80.80, Place 5 £36.65.
Owner D Coppenhall **Bred** Tweenhills Stud And Stuart McPhee **Trained** Upper Longdon, Staffs

FOCUS
A very weak classified event. Sound form, with the first four all within a pound of recent marks.
Jiminor Mack Official explanation: jockey said filly was never travelling
T/Plt: £59.30 to a £1 stake. Pool: £55,260.40. 679.60 winning tickets. T/Qpdt: £16.30 to a £1 stake. Pool: £5,236.90. 237.70 winning tickets. KH

207 KEMPTON (A.W) (R-H)
Sunday, January 28

OFFICIAL GOING: Standard
Wind: Moderate half-against

272 KEMPTON FOR WEDDINGS MEDIAN AUCTION MAIDEN STKS 7f (P)
1:15 (1:18) (Class 6) 4-6-Y-O £2,047 (£604; £302) Stalls High

Form				RPR
22-2	1		**Lopinot (IRE)**[22] 49 4-9-3 70 SebSanders 8 (P J Makin) *mde all: clr whn edgd lft fr over 1f out: kpt up to work: unchal* **2/5**[1]	70+
0/0-	2	7	**Sun Bian**[291] 992 5-9-3 69 LPKeniry 2 (L P Grassick) *racd in 4th pl: rdn and styd on to go 2nd wl ins fnl f: no ch w wnr* **16/1**	52
322-	3	½	**Fairdonna**[38] 6901 4-8-12 58 JoeFanning 1 (D J Coakley) *trckd wnr fr over 4f out: rdn and wknd ent fnl f: lost 2nd wl ins* **7/2**[2]	46
-000	4	1	**Miss Redactive**[12] 145 4-8-12 38 (v[1]) ShaneKelly 5 (M D I Usher) *chsd wnr to over 4f out: wknd wl over 1f out* **66/1**	43
0-5	5	1 ¼	**Big Ralph**[22] 49 4-9-3 OscarUrbina 7 (M Wigham) *outpcd and nvr on terms* **33/1**	45
4	6	hd	**Rusty Roof**[22] 49 4-8-5 DebraEngland(7) 6 (Rae Guest) *a bhd* **33/1**	39
0-	7	7	**Clear Picture**[233] 2406 4-8-12 DaneO'Neill 3 (A P Jarvis) *slowly away: a bhd* **10/1**[3]	21
0/	8	7	**Kolibre**[403] 6642 4-9-3 (t) JimCrowley 4 (T T Clement) *s.i.s: a bhd* **50/1**	8

1m 27.04s (0.24) **Going Correction** -0.025s/f (Stan) **8 Ran SP% 118.0**
Speed ratings: 97,89,88,87,85 85,77,69
CSF £9.57 TOTE £1.60: £1.02, £4.50, £1.40; EX 11.30.
Owner R A Bernard **Bred** G And Mrs Middlebrook **Trained** Ogbourne Maisey, Wilts

FOCUS
A race that took little winning and favourite Lopinot enjoyed a deserved victory,although he achieved little form-wise.

273 KEMPTON.CO.UK CLASSIFIED STKS 1m (P)
1:45 (1:49) (Class 7) 4-Y-O+ £1,365 (£403; £201) Stalls High

Form				RPR
006-	1		**Comeintothespace (IRE)**[138] 5259 5-9-0 43 DaneO'Neill 3 (R A Farrant) *mid-division: hdwy to go 2nd 2f out: led ins fnl f: drvn out* **7/1**	54
-053	2	1 ¼	**Height Of Spirits**[6] 210 5-9-0 44 EdwardCreighton 13 (T D McCarthy) *a in tch: rdn to chse wnr ins fnl f but no imp* **11/2**[3]	51
04-3	3	1	**Expected Bonus (USA)**[8] 187 8-9-0 42 (v) JohnEgan 4 (Jamie Poulton) *hld up: hdwy over 2f out: r.o fnl f* **4/1**[1]	49
40-4	4	nk	**Colonel Bilko (IRE)**[25] 26 5-8-11 39 MarcHalford(3) 11 (J J Bridger) *t.k.h: in tch: r.o u.p fnl f* **20/1**	48+
3-44	5	1 ¼	**Villa Bianca's (IRE)**[6] 207 4-9-0 43 (b[1]) ShaneKelly 9 (J A Osborne) *led: clr over 3f out: wknd and hdd ins fnl f* **8/1**	45
040-	6	¾	**Thomas A Beckett (IRE)**[69] 6544 4-8-7 45 PNolan(7) 14 (P R Chamings) *mid-div: rdn 1/2-way: hdwy over 1f out: nvr nrr* **20/1**	44
0-64	7	shd	**Riviera Red (IRE)**[6] 210 7-9-0 42 (v) JimCrowley 8 (L Montague Hall) *in rr: mde sme late hdwy* **8/1**	43
3-06	8	1 ½	**Kilmeena Magic**[8] 187 5-9-0 42 StephenCarson 7 (J C Fox) *mid-div: hung rt over 2f out: one pce after* **13/2**	40
/00-	9	8	**Follingworth (IRE)**[272] 1343 4-9-0 38 SilvestreDeSousa 6 (A D Brown) *trckd ldr to 3f out: wknd 2f out* **50/1**	22
40-0	10	½	**Mostanad**[18] 83 5-8-7 42 BarrySavage(7) 12 (J M Bradley) *a bhd* **20/1**	20
46-6	11	2 ½	**Marron Flore**[22] 51 4-9-0 43 (tp) JoeFanning 10 (A J Lidderdale) *plld hrd: chsd ldr over 3f out tl wknd over 2f out* **16/1**	15
00-0	12	51	**Warden Warren**[6] 207 9-9-0 45 (b) SebSanders 5 (Mrs C A Dunnett) *prom on outside to 1/2-way: sn wknd: eased ins fnl 2f: t.o: 10.23s bhd 11th horse* **14/1**	—
204-	P		**Frank's Quest (IRE)**[41] 6854 7-9-0 45 SamHitchcott 2 (A B Haynes) *sn bhd: t.o: p.u over 3f out: lame* **5/1**[2]	—

1m 40.51s (-0.29) **Going Correction** -0.025s/f (Stan) **13 Ran SP% 128.9**
Speed ratings (Par 97):100,98,97,97,96 95,95,93,85,85 82,31,—
CSF £46.80 TOTE £12.20: £2.80, £2.90, £1.80; EX 77.20.
Owner Rodney Farrant **Bred** D And Mrs D Veitch **Trained** Upper Lambourn, Berks

FOCUS
A banded contest in disguise, but a welcome win for Comeintothespace. This was the slowest of the three races over the trip, but the form is a shade above-average for the grade.
Kilmeena Magic Official explanation: jockey said mare hung right
Warden Warren Official explanation: jockey said gelding stopped very quickly
Frank's Quest(IRE) Official explanation: vet said gelding finished lame on the near fore

274 FOLLOW YOUR CONFERENCE WITH EVENING RACING H'CAP 1m (P)
2:15 (2:17) (Class 6) (0-50,50) 4-Y-O+ £2,047 (£453; £453) Stalls High

Form				RPR
031-	1		**Saucy**[46] 6800 6-8-10 **48** ShaneKelly 11 (A W Carroll) *hld up in rr: rdn and hdwy on ins wl over 2f out: r.o u.p fnl f to ld nr fin* **6/1**[3]	56+
0-22	2	nk	**Over To You Bert**[12] 156 8-8-2 **47** HaddenFrost(7) 8 (R J Hodges) *prom: outpcd over 2f out: rallied to chse wnr wl ins fnl f* **5/1**[2]	54
10-2	2	dht	**Mon Petite Amour**[18] 94 4-8-11 **49** (p) BrettDoyle 5 (D W P Arbuthnot) *racd wd: rdn and hdwy on ins over 1f out: r.o to dead-heat for 2nd on post* **4/1**[1]	56+
600-	4	1	**Night Wolf (IRE)**[40] 6864 7-8-12 **50** PaulDoe 1 (Jamie Poulton) *led after 2f: clr over 1f out: rdn and hdd wl ins fnl f* **16/1**	55
01-0	5	hd	**Tackcoat (IRE)**[12] 156 7-8-9 **50** (p) JerryO'Dwyer(3) 14 (Eoin Doyle, Ire) *mid-division: rdn and hung lft over 1f out: r.o ins fnl f* **10/1**	54
06-3	6	½	**Red Raptor**[18] 94 6-8-12 **50** (t) RichardThomas 3 (J A Geake) *s.i.s: plld hrd: wnt 2nd 1/2-way: ev ch ent fnl f: no ex ins* **6/1**[3]	53
605-	7	¾	**Laugh 'n Cry**[55] 6700 6-8-11 **49** (b) OscarUrbina 13 (C A Cyzer) *mid-div: hdwy whn short of room over 1f out: r.o ins fnl f* **20/1**	51+
5-25	8	1 ¼	**Show Me The Lolly (FR)**[18] 94 7-8-10 **48** PaulEddery 10 (P J McBride) *in rr: rdn over 2f out: mde sme late hdwy* **5/1**[2]	46
/0-6	9	nk	**Noah Jameel**[17] 98 5-8-12 **50** LPKeniry 7 (A G Newcombe) *in rr: effrt over 1f out: nvr on terms* **20/1**	48
20-0	10	1 ½	**She's Dunnett**[22] 50 4-8-12 **50** SebSanders 9 (Mrs C A Dunnett) *led for 2f: wknd wl over 1f out* **20/1**	44
336-	11	nk	**Sunset Ridge (IRE)**[138] 5273 4-8-12 **50** JimmyQuinn 2 (Miss Gay Kelleway) *prom: rdn over 2f out: wknd appr fnl f* **16/1**	44
00-2	12	nk	**Sahara Prince (IRE)**[25] 22 7-8-9 **47** (p) PaulFitzsimons 4 (K A Morgan) *slowly away: a bhd* **10/1**	40
45-6	13	nk	**Fly By Jove (IRE)**[18] 92 4-8-12 **50** JimCrowley 12 (Jane Southcombe) *prom: rdn over 2f out: wknd over 1f out* **33/1**	42
500-	14	8	**Secam (POL)**[13] 6864 8-8-11 **49** (p) SamHitchcott 6 (Mrs P Townsley) *racd wd towards rr: wl bhd fnl 3f* **50/1**	23

1m 40.39s (-0.41) **Going Correction** -0.025s/f (Stan) **14 Ran SP% 131.0**
Speed ratings (Par 101):101,100,100,99,99 99,98,97,96,95 94,94,94,86
2nd Pl: MPA 2.10, OTYB 2.80; Ex: S-MPA 36.20; S-OTYB 34.10; CSF: S-MPA 15.46; S-OTYB 18.47; T/C: S-MPA-OTYB 70.53; S-OTYB-MPA 72.96 TOTE £6.80: £2.20.
Owner Mrs B Quinn **Bred** Wyck Hall Stud Ltd **Trained** Cropthorne, Worcs
■ Stewards' Enquiry : Jerry O'Dwyer one-day ban: careless riding (Feb 8)

FOCUS
A competitive if low-grade handicap. Sound form.
Mon Petite Amour Official explanation: jockey said filly was struck on the nose by a rival's whip
Tackcoat(IRE) Official explanation: jockey said saddle slipped

275 DIGIBET.COM H'CAP 1m (P)
2:50 (2:51) (Class 4) (0-85,77) 3-Y-O £4,728 (£1,406; £702; £351) Stalls High

Form				RPR
24-1	1		**Hurlingham**[12] 149 3-9-4 **77** JoeFanning 3 (M Johnston) *racd in 3rd pl: wnt 2nd over 2f out: rdn and r.o to ld wl ins fnl f* **15/8**[2]	89+
62-1	2	1	**Soft Morning**[20] 73 3-9-4 **77** SebSanders 6 (Sir Mark Prescott) *led: rdn over 1f out: kpt on but nt qckn and hdd wl ins fnl f* **13/8**[1]	87+
331-	3	6	**Hollywood George**[33] 6940 3-8-13 **72** BrettDoyle 4 (W J Haggas) *t.k.h in rr: hung lft 2f out: styd on fnl f but nvr nr to chal* **14/1**	70
241-	4	½	**Benny The Bat**[46] 6809 3-9-3 **76** NCallan 1 (H Morrison) *trckd ldr tl hung bdly lft and c over to stands' rail over 2f out: no ch after* **9/1**	71
210-	5	hd	**Swift Cut (IRE)**[97] 6146 3-9-1 **74** DaneO'Neill 5 (A P Jarvis) *a in rr and wl bhd fnl 2f* **40/1**	69
11-	6	3 ½	**Circus Polka (USA)**[32] 6948 3-9-4 **77** (t) JosedeSouza 2 (P F I Cole) *racd wd in tch tl rdn and bhd fr over 2f out* **3/1**[3]	64

1m 38.72s (-2.08) **Going Correction** -0.025s/f (Stan) **6 Ran SP% 117.0**
Speed ratings (Par 99):109,108,102,101,101 97
CSF £5.67 TOTE £3.00: £1.70, £1.90; EX 8.70.
Owner Sheikh Mohammed **Bred** Aston Mullins Stud **Trained** Middleham Moor, N Yorks

FOCUS
A decent race likely to produce winners. The first two finished clear and the time compared very well with the two races over the trip for older horses.
Benny The Bat Official explanation: jockey said colt hung badly left

276 DIGIBET.CO.UK H'CAP 6f (P)
3:25 (3:26) (Class 5) (0-70,69) 4-Y-O+ £3,238 (£963; £481; £240) Stalls High

Form				RPR
20-0	1		**Romany Nights (IRE)**[14] 132 7-9-1 **68** (bt) JohnEgan 10 (Miss Gay Kelleway) *hld up: rdn over 2f out: hdwy over 1f out: str run fnl f to ld nr fin* **7/1**	78
00-6	2	¾	**Taboor (IRE)**[12] 154 9-8-9 **62** BrettDoyle 9 (R M H Cowell) *t.k.h: a.p: ev ch ins fnl f: kpt on* **33/1**	70
-520	3	nk	**Mistral Sky**[4] 234 8-9-0 **67** (p) MickyFenton 8 (Stef Liddiard) *trckd ldr to 1/2-way: styd prom: ev ch ins fnl furlong: r.o* **8/1**	74
-013	4	1	**Kempsey**[11] 161 5-8-5 **65** ow2 (b) RyanBird(7) 4 (J J Bridger) *led: rdn over 1f out: hdd wl ins fnl f* **20/1**	69
-103	5	nk	**Millfields Dreams**[1] 262 8-8-10 **66** JerryO'Dwyer(3) 5 (M G Quinlan) *chsd elader to 1/2-way: ev ch ent fnl f: no ex ins* **7/2**[2]	69
1-31	6	1	**Burhaan (IRE)**[11] 158 5-8-4 **57** JoeFanning 7 (J R Boyle) *in tch towards outside: ev ch over 1f out: no ex ins fnl f* **9/4**[1]	57
03/0	7	1	**Lake Hero**[18] 91 4-9-2 **69** NCallan 2 (M J Wallace) *mid-div: effrt on ins over 1f out: wknd ins fnl f* **25/1**	66

0-00 **8** ¾ **No Time (IRE)**[11] 163 7-9-2 **69** ShaneKelly 1 64
(A J McCabe) *in tch tl rdn and outpcd ins fnl 2f* **25/1**
34-1 **9** 1¼ **Dvinsky (USA)**[20] 67 6-9-1 **68** PaulDoe 6 59
(P Howling) *s.i.s: a in rr* **11/2**[3]
40-0 **10** ¾ **Seneschal**[14] 132 6-8-11 **64** DaneO'Neill 3 53
(A B Haynes) *hld up: outpcd fnl 2f* **6/1**
30/0 **11** *hd* **Thomas Lawrence (USA)**[18] 92 6-8-5 **58** JimmyQuinn 11 46
(G A Ham) *s.i.s: a struggling in rr* **50/1**
1m 13.18s (-0.52) **Going Correction** -0.025s/f (Stan) **11** Ran SP% **123.6**
Speed ratings (Par 103):102,101,100,99,98 97,96,95,93,92 92
CSF £227.21 CT £1320.74 TOTE £11.30: £2.90, £8.50, £3.20; EX 200.30.
Owner John W Farley **Bred** The Lloyd Farm Stud **Trained** Exning, Suffolk
■ Stewards' Enquiry : Ryan Bird three-day ban: used whip with excessive frequency (Feb 8-10)
FOCUS
An open contest. Sound form, rated through the third and fourth.
Dvinsky(USA) Official explanation: jockey said gelding missed the break

277 DIGIBET SPORTS BETTING H'CAP 6f (P)
3:55 (3:55) (Class 4) (0-85,83) 4-Y-0+ **£4,728** (£1,406; £702; £351) **Stalls** High

Form RPR
00-4 **1** **Distinctly Game**[19] 79 5-9-1 **82** NCallan 7 94+
(K A Ryan) *chsd leaders: short of room on ins over 2f out: rdn to ld appr fnl f: r.o wl* **8/1**
510- **2** 1 **Perfect Story (IRE)**[43] 6849 5-9-2 **83** OscarUrbina 1 92
(J A R Toller) *wnt lft s: in rr tl hdwy over 2f out: r.o to chse wnr fnl f* **11/4**[1]
01-2 **3** 1½ **Morse (IRE)**[8] 190 6-8-8 **75** ShaneKelly 5 80
(J A Osborne) *towards rr: rdn over 1f out: r.o fnl f: nvr nrr* **3/1**[2]
0-05 **4** ¾ **Hammer Of The Gods (IRE)**[8] 190 7-8-8 **75** ow1 (bt) BrettDoyle 6 77
(P S McEntee) *trckd ldrs: rdn and one pce fnl f* **6/1**[3]
3-13 **5** *shd* **Magic Glade**[12] 155 8-9-0 **81** RichardThomas 9 83
(Tom Dascombe) *trckd ldr: led over 2f out: rdn and hdd appr fnl f: no ex* **7/1**
51-6 **6** ½ **Connect**[6] 218 10-9-1 **82** (b) TPQueally 8 82
(M H Tompkins) *bhd: effrt on ins 2f out: sn btn* **8/1**
/0-0 **7** 7 **Signor Panettiere**[12] 155 6-8-13 **80** (t) SilvestreDeSousa 2 59
(A D Brown) *led tl hdd over 2f out: wknd qckly over 1f out* **33/1**
04-5 **8** 2½ **Pinchbeck**[19] 81 8-8-12 **79** (b) MatthewHenry 3 51
(M A Jarvis) *s.i.s: in rr and c wd into st: eased whn wl btn 1f out* **7/1**
1m 12.3s (-1.40) **Going Correction** -0.025s/f (Stan) **8** Ran SP% **116.1**
Speed ratings (Par 105):108,106,104,103,103 102,93,90
CSF £30.84 CT £83.11 TOTE £7.70: £2.50, £1.20, £1.80; EX 49.60.
Owner Mr & Mrs Julian And Rosie Richer **Bred** J A Forsyth **Trained** Hambleton, N Yorks
■ Stewards' Enquiry : T P Queally one-day ban: used whip with whip arm above shoulder height (Feb 8)
FOCUS
A welcome return to winning ways for the formerly smart Distinctly Game. The form looks solid.

278 AMATEUR JOCKEYS ASSOCIATION H'CAP (FOR AMATEUR RIDERS) (DIV I) 1m 3f (P)
4:25 (4:26) (Class 6) (0-60,61) 4-Y-0+ **£1,318** (£405; £202) **Stalls** High

Form RPR
0/6- **1** **Vanishing Dancer (SWI)**[345] 443 10-11-1 **54** (bt) MissFayeBramley(3) 8 63
(K J Burke) *towards rr: hdwy to go 2nd over 3f out: led over 1f out: sn clr* **20/1**
0-02 **2** 3 **Khanjar (USA)**[9] 180 7-11-2 **55** (p) MrSPearce(3) 12 59+
(J Pearce) *slowly away: in rr: hdwy 3f out: styd on to go clr 2nd ins fnl f: no ch w wnr* **4/1**[1]
500- **3** 4 **Leighton Buzzard**[13] 6810 5-11-4 **61** ow8 MrMBailey(7) 9 58
(N B King) *slowly away: in rr: hdwy over 2f out: wnt 3rd ins fnl f: no ch w first 2* **9/1**
105- **4** 1¾ **Equilibria (USA)**[31] 6378 5-10-11 **52** MissHayleyMoore(5) 13 46
(G L Moore) *in rr: hdwy on ins 3f out: styd on but nvr on terms* **4/1**[1]
44-4 **5** 2½ **Bramcote Lorne**[12] 148 4-10-5 **51** (p) MrCAHarris(7) 11 41+
(John A Harris) *led: sn clr: rdn: wknd and hdd over 1f out* **11/2**[2]
00-0 **6** 3 **Razed**[26] 14 4-10-5 **49** MrJohnEnnis(5) 6 34
(P L Gilligan) *slowly away: wnt 3rd over 2f out: wknd over 1f out* **20/1**
06-3 **7** ½ **Love You Always (USA)**[9] 179 7-10-2 **45** (t) MrRBirkett(7) 4 29
(Miss J Feilden) *slowly away: a in rr* **11/2**[2]
40-0 **8** 2 **Lady's Law**[9] 180 4-9-13 **45** MissEmma-JaneJenkins(7) 10 25
(Rae Guest) *a bhd* **33/1**
001- **9** 2 **Missouri (USA)**[30] 6971 4-10-8 **47** MrSDobson 2 24
(W G M Turner) *mid-div: bhd fnl 3f* **7/1**[3]
640- **10** 6 **Alasil (USA)**[57] 6684 7-11-0 **57** MrMPrice(7) 7 24
(R J Price) *trckd ldr to 5f out: wknd over 2f out* **8/1**
56-0 **11** ½ **Bournonville**[9] 180 4-10-1 **45** MrSRees(5) 1 11
(M Wigham) *prom on outside: chsd ldr 5f out to over 3f out: sn wknd* **25/1**
/000 **12** 1¼ **Alisar (IRE)**[11] 159 7-10-11 **52** (t) MissZoeLilly(5) 3 16
(E J Creighton) *chsd ldrs tl lost pl 5f out* **33/1**
000- **13** 7 **Full Of Zest**[24] 6630 5-10-11 **54** (b) MissLauraGray(7) 5 6
(Mrs L J Mongan) *prom on outside to 1/2-way: sn bhd* **25/1**
2m 23.14s (0.46) **Going Correction** -0.025s/f (Stan)
WFA 4 from 5yo+ 3lb **13** Ran SP% **127.5**
Speed ratings (Par 101):97,94,91,90,88 86,86,84,83,79 78,77,72
CSF £97.79 CT £806.13 TOTE £25.00: £5.80, £1.40, £4.80; EX 266.60.
Owner Mrs D Thomas **Bred** Gestut Sohrenhof **Trained** Bourton-on-the-Water, Gloucs
FOCUS
A very fast pace early on, and unsurprisingly those coming from behind were seen at an advantage. The time was much faster than division II, and the form looks solid.

279 AMATEUR JOCKEYS ASSOCIATION H'CAP (FOR AMATEUR RIDERS) (DIV II) 1m 3f (P)
4:55 (4:57) (Class 6) (0-60,60) 4-Y-0+ **£1,318** (£405; £202) **Stalls** High

Form RPR
0- **1** **Tancredi (SWE)**[30] 6977 5-10-13 **57** MissZoeLilly(5) 2 65
(N B King) *t.k.h: trckd ldr: led 5f out: rdn and kpt on wl u.p fnl f* **16/1**
500- **2** ¾ **Raise The Heights (IRE)**[78] 6435 4-11-1 **57** MrSWalker 5 64
(J G Portman) *v.s.a but sn mid-div: hdwy over 4f out: rdn to chse wnr fnl f* **7/2**[1]
2-00 **3** 1¼ **Kalatime (IRE)**[15] 115 4-10-6 **55** MrWTelfer(7) 9 60
(M F Harris) *in tch on ins: chsd wnr over 2f out to 1f out: kpt on one pce* **20/1**
0-40 **4** ¾ **Milk And Sultana**[15] 121 7-10-6 **48** MissFayeBramley(3) 10 52
(G A Ham) *mid-div: hdwy over 1f out: one pce ins fnl f* **9/1**
0-15 **5** ½ **Scottish River (USA)**[7] 206 8-11-2 **55** MrLeeNewnes 1 58
(M D I Usher) *hld up: hdwy fr wl over 1f out: nt qckn fnl f* **4/1**[2]
/54- **6** *hd* **King Gabriel (IRE)**[18] 6980 5-10-8 **54** MrCTPritchard(7) 4 57
(Andrew Turnell) *prom tl lost pl over 2f out: kpt on fnl f* **7/2**[1]
0-04 **7** ¾ **Captain Bolsh**[9] 179 4-10-1 **46** oh1 MrSPearce(3) 3 47
(J Pearce) *trckd ldrs tl rdn and no hdwy ins fnl 2f* **7/1**[3]
106- **8** *hd* **Three Ships**[31] 4206 6-10-7 **53** MrRBirkett(7) 8 54
(Miss J Feilden) *sn led hdd 5f out: wknd 2f out* **7/1**[3]
50-0 **9** ½ **Kiama**[25] 16 5-10-11 **50** MrSDobson 12 50
(B G Powell) *bhd tl effrt over over 2f out: wknd over 1f out* **20/1**
665- **10** *hd* **Wotchalike (IRE)**[20] 5846 5-11-0 **60** (p) MrMPrice(7) 7 60
(R J Price) *hld up in mid-div: bhd fnl 2f* **11/1**
030- **11** 13 **Graft**[37] 6918 8-10-11 **55** (p) MrsCThompson(5) 6 33
(Mrs P Townsley) *plld hrd: prom on outside: c v wd into st and sn wl bhd* **16/1**
2m 26.22s (3.54) **Going Correction** -0.025s/f (Stan)
WFA 4 from 5yo+ 3lb **38** Ran SP% **129.1**
Speed ratings (Par 101):86,85,84,84,83 83,82,82,82,82 72
CSF £78.43 CT £1178.06 TOTE £34.80: £9.40, £1.50, £8.00; EX 459.30 Place 6 £35.58, Place 5 £32.47..
Owner Richard S Keeley **Bred** Team Hogdala Ab **Trained** Newmarket, Suffolk
FOCUS
In contrast to the first division there was little pace on, and the time was understandably a fair bit slower. Very ordinary form.
Captain Bolsh Official explanation: trainer said gelding was struck into
Graft Official explanation: jockey said gelding hung badly left-handed
T/Jkpt: Not won. T/Plt: £46.60 to a £1 stake. Pool: £52,799.15. 826.05 winning tickets. T/Qpdt: £25.80 to a £1 stake. Pool: £2,860.95. 81.80 winning tickets. JS

266 WOLVERHAMPTON (A.W) (L-H)
Sunday, January 28

OFFICIAL GOING: Standard to slow
Wind: Fresh across Weather: Fine

280 HBLB H'CAP 5f 20y(P)
1:25 (1:25) (Class 4) (0-85,77) 3-Y-0 **£4,728** (£1,406; £702; £351) **Stalls** Low

Form RPR
4151 **1** **Grange Lili (IRE)**[6] 219 3-9-0 70 6ex (b) RobbieFitzpatrick 1 72+
(Peter Grayson) *s.i.s: swtchd rt 3f out: hdwy over 2f out: rdn wl over 1f out: chsd wnr and edgd lft fnl f: led post* **6/1**[3]
123- **2** *shd* **Dress To Impress (IRE)**[33] 6939 3-9-7 77 (p) PatCosgrave 4 79
(J R Boyle) *led: sn clr: rdn wl over 1f out: ct post* **4/5**[1]
153- **3** 2½ **Billy Ruffian**[31] 6965 3-8-7 68 DuranFentiman(5) 2 61
(T D Easterby) *prom: chsd ldr 3f out to 1f out: one pce* **2/1**[2]
4-46 **4** 12 **Jost Van Dyke**[13] 139 3-8-2 58 oh5 (v) HayleyTurner 3 8
(J R Boyle) *chsd ldr tl rdn 3f out: wknd 2f out* **20/1**
62.47 secs (-0.35) **Going Correction** 0.0s/f (Stan) **4** Ran SP% **107.9**
Speed ratings (Par 99):102,101,97,78
CSF £11.51 TOTE £5.20; EX 8.10.
Owner Mrs M Shaughnessy and Mrs S Grayson **Bred** Jack Ronan And Des Ver Hunt Farm Ltd **Trained** Formby, Lancs
FOCUS
Just a small field for this weakish handicap, but the leader set a strong gallop and the form looks solid enough.

281 PONTIN'S FAMILY HOLIDAYS H'CAP (DIV I) 5f 20y(P)
1:55 (1:55) (Class 6) (0-50,57) 4-Y-0+ **£1,706** (£503; £252) **Stalls** Low

Form RPR
5-05 **1** **Blushing Russian (IRE)**[13] 137 5-8-8 **46** oh1 (p) ChrisCatlin 7 53
(J M Bradley) *sn led: rdn over 1f out: all out* **22/1**
/06- **2** *shd* **Indian Sundance (IRE)**[107] 5949 4-8-8 **46** oh1 PaulHanagan 6 53
(R A Fahey) *chsd ldrs: rdn over 1f out: r.o ins fnl f* **6/1**
3-01 **3** *nk* **Monte Major (IRE)**[13] 135 6-9-5 **57** (v) DeanMcKeown 1 63
(D Shaw) *a.p: rdn over 1f out: ev ch ins fnl f: r.o* **5/2**[1]
00-4 **4** 1 **Grand View**[24] 33 11-8-8 **46** oh1 (p) PaulMulrennan 4 48
(J R Weymes) *outpcd in rr: hdwy whn edgd lft ins fnl f: nrst fin* **20/1**
-042 **5** *hd* **El Potro**[7] 201 5-8-8 **46** oh1 GrahamGibbons 8 47
(J R Holt) *a.p: rdn over 1f out: nt qckn ins fnl f* **7/2**[3]
0-51 **6** *nk* **Must Be Keen**[8] 189 8-8-8 **46** (v) FergusSweeney 9 46
(Ernst Oertel) *s.i.s: rdn 2f out: hung lft on outside ins fnl f: nvr nrr* **8/1**
35-1 **7** ½ **Primarily**[22] 46 5-8-8 **46** RobbieFitzpatrick 3 44
(Peter Grayson) *mid-div: hmpd over 3f out: rdn and hdwy whn edgd lft 1f out: no ex towards fin* **11/4**[2]
00-0 **8** 2 **Sofinella (IRE)**[18] 82 4-8-8 **49** (t) JamesDoyle(3) 5 40
(A W Carroll) *led early: chsd ldr: rdn and ev ch wl over 1f out: wknd ins fnl f* **12/1**
-000 **9** ¾ **Laurel Dawn**[2] 254 9-8-4 **47** oh1 ow1 AnnStokell(5) 2 35
(Miss A Stokell) *rdn over 2f out: a bhd* **50/1**
62.61 secs (-0.21) **Going Correction** 0.0s/f (Stan) **9** Ran SP% **121.6**
Speed ratings (Par 101):101,100,100,98,98 97,97,93,92
CSF £152.77 CT £460.88 TOTE £26.60: £4.50, £1.90, £1.90; EX 193.00 TRIFECTA Not won..
Owner Clifton Hunt **Bred** The Rouge Partnership **Trained** Sedbury, Gloucs
■ Stewards' Enquiry : Paul Hanagan five-day ban: careless riding (Feb 8-9) and using whip with excessive frequency and not allowing mount time to respond (Feb 10-12)
FOCUS
A handicap contested mainly by banded-grade horses. Sound form.
Must Be Keen Official explanation: jockey said gelding hung left-handed
Laurel Dawn Official explanation: jockey said gelding hung right-handed

282 PONTIN'S - BOOK EARLY MEDIAN AUCTION MAIDEN STKS 5f 20y(P)
2:25 (2:25) (Class 6) 4-6-Y-0 **£2,047** (£604; £302) **Stalls** Low

Form RPR
02-2 **1** **Kitchen Sink (IRE)**[15] 125 5-9-3 57 (e) FergusSweeney 7 53
(P J Makin) *chsd ldrs: rdn over 1f out: led wl ins fnl f: drvn out* **1/1**[1]
303- **2** ½ **Ceredig**[78] 6440 4-9-3 55 (t) GeorgeBaker 9 51
(W R Muir) *chsd ldrs: rdn over 1f out: r.o ins fnl f* **5/2**[2]
-000 **3** ½ **Comic Tales**[1] 271 6-9-3 45 J-PGuillambert 5 49
(M Mullineaux) *s.i.s: sn pushed along: rdn over 1f out: hdwy fnl f: r.o* **50/1**
06-0 **4** *nk* **Doughty**[9] 183 5-8-12 35 EmmettStack(5) 3 48
(M Mullineaux) *s.i.s: outpcd in rr: rapid late hdwy on outside: fin wl* **80/1**
50-3 **5** ½ **Optical Seclusion (IRE)**[15] 125 4-9-0 50 (b) SaleemGolam(3) 2 46
(T J Etherington) *chsd ldr: led over 2f out: sn rdn: hdd wl ins fnl f: no ex* **14/1**

043- **6** *2* **Nawayea**[49] 6774 4-8-12 55 (b[1]) ChrisCatlin 6 44+
(C N Allen) *bhd: hdwy over 2f out: nt clr run on ins over 1f out: swtchd rt ins fnl f: nt rcvr* **12/1**

2-05 **7** *1* **Left Nostril (IRE)**[15] 125 4-8-12 45 HayleyTurner 1 30
(P S McEntee) *led: rdn and hdd over 2f out: edgd lft over 1f out: wknd fnl f* **16/1**

24/6 **8** *6* **Kung Hei**[15] 125 4-9-3 60 PaulMulrennan 4 14
(Mrs L Stubbs) *chsd ldrs: wkng whn nt clr run on ins briefly 2f out* **9/1**[3]

00 **9** *6* **Grace Bay**[15] 125 4-8-12 TonyCulhane 8 —
(Bob Jones) *outpcd* **80/1**

63.04 secs (0.22) **Going Correction** 0.0s/f (Stan) **9** Ran SP% **113.2**
Speed ratings: 98,97,96,95,95 91,90,80,71
CSF £3.38 TOTE £2.30: £1.10, £1.50, £7.50; EX 6.60 Trifecta £53.50 Pool £151.64 - 2.01 winning units..
Owner Julian Hartnoll **Bred** K Maginn **Trained** Ogbourne Maisey, Wilts

FOCUS
A very poor maiden, run in a slow time. The third and fourth limit the form.
Kung Hei Official explanation: jockey said gelding hung right-handed

283 PONTINSBINGO.COM H'CAP 1m 5f 194y(P)
3:00 (3:00) (Class 5) (0-75,72) 4-Y-0+ **£3,071** (£906; £453) **Stalls** Low

Form RPR

05/5 **1** **Positive Profile (IRE)**[27] 4 9-9-8 **67** GrahamGibbons 7 76
(J J Quinn) *chsd ldr: hrd rdn and wandered away fr whip over 1f out and ins fnl f: led cl home: r.o* **33/1**

21-1 **2** *nk* **Share The Feeling (IRE)**[6] 215 5-9-7 **69** 7ex RichardKingscote(3) 3 78
(J W Unett) *led: rdn over 2f out: hdd cl home* **5/4**[1]

-211 **3** *2 1/2* **Beldon Hill (USA)**[16] 112 4-9-2 **67** PaulHanagan 2 72
(R A Fahey) *a.p: rdn 3f out: one pce fnl 2f* **6/4**[2]

030- **4** *5* **Torrid Kentavr (USA)**[27] 5699 10-9-13 **72** TonyCulhane 4 70
(J J Lambe, Ire) *s.s: hld up and bhd: hdwy on ins 3f out: sn rdn: wknd over 1f out* **33/1**

300/ **5** *19* **Croix Rouge (USA)**[155] 5-9-9 **68** AdamKirby 1 39
(R J Smith, Spain) *hld up: hdwy over 5f out: rdn over 3f out: sn wknd* **16/1**

05-0 **6** *5* **Zacatecas (GER)**[18] 88 7-9-1 **60** DeanMcKeown 8 24
(A J Chamberlain) *bhd: rdn 4f out: sn lost tch* **100/1**

250- **7** *12* **Valart**[64] 6601 4-8-12 **63** RobbieFitzpatrick 5 11
(T J Pitt) *rel to r: t.k.h in rr: rdn 4f out: sn t.o* **7/1**[3]

3m 6.72s (-0.65) **Going Correction** 0.0s/f (Stan)
WFA 4 from 5yo+ 6lb **7** Ran SP% **109.7**
Speed ratings (Par 103):101,100,99,96,85 82,75
CSF £69.51 CT £99.33 TOTE £26.60: £8.00, £1.60; EX 82.70 Trifecta £171.40 Part won. Pool £241.48 - 0.61 winning units..
Owner Chelgate Public Relations Ltd **Bred** Keith Wills **Trained** Settrington, N Yorks

FOCUS
A modest handicap, not strongly-run, and dominated by the two who raced most prominently. Sound enough form, rated through the second and third.
Croix Rouge(USA) Official explanation: jockey said horse had a steering problem
Valart Official explanation: jockey said filly jumped left-handed and hung throughout

284 PONTIN'S HOLIDAYS H'CAP 1m 141y(P)
3:35 (3:35) (Class 6) (0-65,67) 3-Y-0 **£2,388** (£705; £352) **Stalls** Low

Form RPR

50-1 **1** **Medici Code**[5] 224 3-9-8 **67** 7ex RobertHavlin 5 80+
(H Morrison) *a gng wl: led jst over 1f out: easily* **1/5**[1]

1-42 **2** *1 1/4* **My Mirasol**[13] 139 3-9-4 **63** (p) RobertWinston 1 68
(K A Ryan) *led: rdn and hdd jst over 1f out: no ch w wnr* **11/1**[2]

1-41 **3** *3 1/2* **Ella Y Rossa**[15] 122 3-8-12 **60** StephenDonohoe(3) 6 58
(P D Evans) *hld up: rdn over 2f out: outpcd wl over 1f out: kpt on fnl f* **14/1**[3]

4 *3 1/2* **Murdol (IRE)**[157] 4751 3-8-4 **49** oh1 HayleyTurner 8 40
(C R Dore) *hld up in tch: rdn and wnt 2nd over 4f out: rdn over 2f out: wknd over 1f out* **80/1**

44- **5** *1 3/4* **Annia Faustina (IRE)**[51] 6745 3-9-0 **59** AdamKirby 3 46
(J L Spearing) *chsd wnr: rdn over 3f out: wknd over 1f out* **20/1**

343- **6** *51* **Inflagrantedelicto (USA)**[32] 6948 3-9-2 **61** TonyCulhane 7 —
(D W Chapman) *a towards rr: lost tch over 3f out: eased fnl 2f* **20/1**

1m 54.24s (2.48) **Going Correction** 0.0s/f (Stan) **6** Ran SP% **109.1**
Speed ratings (Par 95):88,86,83,80,79 33
CSF £2.71 CT £7.53 TOTE £1.30: £1.10, £2.00; EX 2.30 Trifecta £8.40 Pool £209.96 - 17.66 winning units..
Owner The End-R-Ways Partnership **Bred** Mrs T A Foreman **Trained** East Ilsley, Berks

FOCUS
An uncompetitive handicap as a result of the presence of Medici Code, who was very well in under a penalty for his fluent Southwell success. The runner-up confirmed her recent improvement to beat the rest.

285 GO PONTIN'S CLASSIFIED STKS 2m 119y(P)
4:05 (4:05) (Class 7) 4-Y-0+ **£1,911** (£564; £282) **Stalls** Low

Form RPR

1 **Dream River (USA)**[22] 6091 6-9-2 42 StephenDonohoe(3) 4 55
(Patrick Martin, Ire) *hld up towards rr: hdwy over 6f out: led over 2f out: rdn and hung lft over 1f out: edgd lft ins fnl f: styd on wl* **3/1**[1]

4-12 **2** *2* **Nod's Star**[3] 240 6-9-5 45 (t) ChrisCatlin 7 53
(Mrs L C Jewell) *a.p: rdn over 2f out: ev ch over 1f out: nt qckn ins fnl f* **3/1**[1]

054- **3** *1* **Mustakhlas (USA)**[28] 6995 6-9-5 44 PhillipMakin 10 52
(B P J Baugh) *hld up in mid-div: hdwy over 3f out: rdn wl over 1f out: styd on one pce fnl f* **7/2**[2]

00-0 **4** *3/4* **Tip Toes (IRE)**[18] 87 5-9-5 40 J-PGuillambert 9 51
(P Howling) *hld up in mid-div: hdwy over 3f out: rdn over 2f out: styd on same pce fnl f* **12/1**

0-04 **5** *5* **Countback (FR)**[14] 134 8-9-2 44 (p) JamesDoyle(3) 11 45
(A W Carroll) *hld up and bhd: pushed along over 3f out: rdn and hdwy 2f out: nvr trbld ldrs* **15/2**[3]

0-00 **6** *nk* **Come What July (IRE)**[19] 78 6-9-5 40 DeanMcKeown 13 45
(D Shaw) *hld up and bhd: rdn and sme hdwy over 1f out: n.d* **20/1**

060/ **7** *1 1/4* **Saintly Thoughts (USA)**[498] 5298 12-9-5 44 (p) GeorgeBaker 6 43
(R J Hodges) *hld up and bhd: hdwy over 3f out: rdn and wknd 2f out* **14/1**

00/0 **8** *1* **Just Superb**[7] 203 8-9-5 40 (p) AntonyProcter 5 42
(P A Pritchard) *hld up in mid-div: hdwy 9f out: rdn to ld over 3f out: hdd over 2f out: wknd wl over 1f out* **25/1**

9 *9* **Drift Away (USA)**[186] 3859 7-9-5 45 TonyCulhane 8 31
(J J Lambe, Ire) *a bhd* **20/1**

3-03 **10** *12* **Lady Suffragette (IRE)**[7] 203 4-8-12 43 CatherineGannon 3 17
(John Berry) *t.k.h: prom: wkng whn nt clr run briefly wl over 3f out* **12/1**

00-5 **11** *10* **Ryhope Chief (IRE)**[16] 107 4-8-12 42 (bt) FergusSweeney 12 5
(M Sheppard) *sn chsng ldr: led over 4f out: rdn and hdd over 3f out: wknd over 2f out* **50/1**

000/ **12** *12* **Baker Of Oz**[20] 6262 6-9-2 45 AndrewMullen(3) 1 —
(M A Doyle) *hmpd and lost pl bnd after 1f: sn mid-div: bhd fnl 6f* **66/1**

0/0- **13** *26* **Mullzima (IRE)**[38] 945 4-8-12 40 AdamKirby 2 —
(M A Doyle) *led: rdn and hdd over 4f out: wknd qckly over 3f out* **100/1**

3m 46.47s (3.34) **Going Correction** 0.0s/f (Stan)
WFA 4 from 5yo+ 7lb **13** Ran SP% **123.9**
Speed ratings (Par 97):92,91,90,90,87 87,87,86,82,76 72,66,54
CSF £11.52 TOTE £4.10: £1.50, £1.80, £2.10; EX 23.50 Trifecta £96.60 Pool £166.11 - 1.22 winning units..
Owner Measured Leap Syndicate **Bred** Bjorn Neilson **Trained** Navan, Co Meath

FOCUS
A banded-style race rated through the runner-up. The fourth limits the form.
Lady Suffragette(IRE) Official explanation: trainer said filly was found to have pulled muscles in her hindquarters
Mullzima(IRE) Official explanation: jockey said filly stopped quickly

286 PONTINS.COM H'CAP 1m 1f 103y(P)
4:35 (4:37) (Class 6) (0-62,64) 4-Y-0+ **£2,388** (£705; £352) **Stalls** Low

Form RPR

3-20 **1** **Discotheque (USA)**[6] 212 4-8-10 **59** J-PGuillambert 3 68
(P Howling) *hld up in mid-div: hdwy on ins over 2f out: rdn whn carried rt wl over 1f out: led wl ins fnl f: r.o* **25/1**

1-42 **2** *1/2* **The City Kid (IRE)**[7] 206 4-7-13 **55** (b) BernadetteQuinn(7) 11 63
(P D Evans) *dwlt: hld up and bhd: hdwy on wd outside whn bmpd wl over 1f out: rdn and hung lft 1f out: r.o* **28/1**

33-0 **3** *1 1/4* **Buscador (USA)**[16] 110 8-8-5 **58** AshleyHamblett(5) 12 65+
(W M Brisbourne) *a.p: rdn 4f out: hmpd and carried rt over 1f out: kpt on ins fnl f* **50/1**

440/ **4** *shd* **Volaticus (IRE)**[169] 6-8-12 **60** AdamKirby 4 65
(R J Smith, Spain) *t.k.h towards rr: rdn and hdwy on ins 2f out: led jst over 1f out: hdd and nt qckn wl ins fnl f* **100/1**

-046 **5** *2* **They All Laughed**[3] 243 4-8-7 **56** ChrisCatlin 7 57
(P W Hiatt) *bhd: rdn over 4f out: hdwy on ins wl over 1f out: r.o one pce fnl f* **22/1**

21-4 **6** *nk* **Scamperdale**[7] 206 5-8-5 **60** SoniaEaton(7) 8 61
(B P J Baugh) *rrd s: hld up in rr: hdwy on wd outside over 2f out: nt clr run wl over 1f out: sn swtchd lft: edgd lft and one pce ins fnl f* **12/1**[2]

5-11 **7** *nk* **Picador**[3] 238 4-9-1 **64** 7ex JamieMackay 6 64
(Sir Mark Prescott) *chsd ldrs: led over 2f out: rdn and hung lft ent st: sn hdd: wknd wl ins fnl f* **30/100**[1]

04-0 **8** *2* **Takes Tutu (USA)**[16] 110 8-8-10 **58** PaulHanagan 2 54
(C R Dore) *hld up in mid-div: rdn and hdwy over 2f out: hmpd wl over 1f out: n.d after* **20/1**

/35- **9** *1/2* **Elopement (IRE)**[107] 5954 5-7-12 **53** LukeMorris(7) 10 48
(W M Brisbourne) *mid-div: rdn over 4f out: hdwy on outside over 2f out: hmpd wl over 1f out: n.d after* **40/1**

-053 **10** *1* **Golden Spectrum (IRE)**[7] 200 8-8-4 **57** (b) TolleyDean(5) 1 50
(R A Harris) *led: rdn and hdd over 2f out: wknd fnl f* **40/1**

2-53 **11** *3 1/2* **Second Reef**[20] 72 5-8-7 **55** GrahamGibbons 5 41
(E J Alston) *mid-div: rdn over 2f out: wknd wl over 1f out* **16/1**[3]

00-0 **12** *nk* **Richelieu**[2] 251 5-9-0 **62** TonyCulhane 13 48
(J J Lambe, Ire) *a bhd: fin lame* **100/1**

40-4 **13** *2* **Qaasi (USA)**[26] 12 5-8-7 **55** (v[1]) DeanMernagh 9 37
(M Brittain) *chsd ldr: tl over 4f out: rdn over 2f out: wkng whn nt clr run wl over 1f out* **50/1**

2m 1.16s (-1.46) **Going Correction** 0.0s/f (Stan)
WFA 4 from 5yo+ 1lb **13** Ran SP% **117.7**
Speed ratings (Par 101):106,105,104,104,102 102,102,100,99,98 95,95,93
CSF £533.78 CT £29363.11 TOTE £27.40: £5.50, £5.30, £11.70; EX 411.40 TRIFECTA Not won..

Owner Waterford Hall Stud Ltd **Bred** Classic Thoroughbred Xviii **Trained** Newmarket, Suffolk
■ Stewards' Enquiry : J-P Guillambert 10-day ban (takes into account deferred three-day ban): careless riding (Feb 7-16)

FOCUS
The leaders went off too fast and the race was set up for the closers. It has been rated through the second and third.
Scamperdale Official explanation: jockey said gelding suffered interference in running
Richelieu Official explanation: vet said horse finished lame

287 PONTIN'S FAMILY HOLIDAYS H'CAP (DIV II) 5f 20y(P)
5:05 (5:05) (Class 6) (0-50,50) 4-Y-0+ **£1,706** (£503; £252) **Stalls** Low

Form RPR

06-0 **1** **Thoughtsofstardom**[6] 214 4-8-10 **48** (be) HayleyTurner 4 57
(P S McEntee) *mid-div: hdwy over 2f out: rdn to ld 1f out: jst hld on* **8/1**

0-43 **2** *shd* **Lady Hopeful (IRE)**[7] 201 5-8-8 **46** oh1 (b) RobbieFitzpatrick 7 55
(Peter Grayson) *s.i.s: hld up and bhd: hdwy 2f out: edgd lft ins fnl f: r.o: jst failed* **7/2**[2]

450- **3** *2 1/2* **Beamsley Beacon**[31] 6959 6-8-3 **46** oh1 (b) DuranFentiman(5) 6 46
(S T Mason) *a.p: rdn and ev ch 1f out: one pce* **33/1**

30-0 **4** *2 1/2* **Saintly Place**[13] 137 6-8-5 **46** oh1 JamesDoyle(3) 1 37
(A W Carroll) *s.i.s: rdn and hdwy on ins wl over 1f out: one pce fnl f* **10/1**

046- **5** *hd* **Borzoi Maestro**[31] 6956 6-8-5 **48** (p) TolleyDean(5) 2 38
(R A Harris) *prom: rdn over 2f out: wknd fnl f* **3/1**[1]

60-2 **6** *2* **Town House**[13] 137 5-8-1 **46** oh1 SoniaEaton(7) 5 29
(B P J Baugh) *led: hdd 1f out: sn wknd* **10/1**

000- **7** *nk* **Doctor's Cave**[97] 6142 5-8-12 **50** (b) ChrisCatlin 3 32
(K O Cunningham-Brown) *sn outpcd* **9/2**[3]

354- **8** *1/2* **Campeon (IRE)**[30] 6974 5-8-9 **47** J-PGuillambert 8 27
(J M Bradley) *prom: rdn over 2f out: wknd wl over 1f out* **5/1**

-000 **9** *3/4* **Percy Douglas**[5] 225 7-8-3 **46** oh1 (bt) AnnStokell(5) 10 24
(Miss A Stokell) *a bhd* **50/1**

454- **10** *1 1/2* **Stoneacre Girl (IRE)**[268] 1464 4-8-8 **46** oh1 GrahamGibbons 9 18
(Peter Grayson) *hld up in mid-div: rdn and c wd st: sn bhd* **50/1**

62.32 secs (-0.50) **Going Correction** 0.0s/f (Stan) **33** Ran SP% **118.2**
Speed ratings (Par 101):104,103,99,95,95 92,91,91,89,87
CSF £36.40 CT £885.20 TOTE £13.10: £2.90, £1.70, £7.20; EX 69.70 TRIFECTA Not won. Place 6 £41.68, Place 5 £3.83..
Owner Eventmaker Racehorses **Bred** B Bargh **Trained** Newmarket, Suffolk

FOCUS
A banded-style handicap and sound enough form for the moderate grade.
T/Plt: £26.00 to a £1 stake. Pool: £50,725.00. 1,423.45 winning tickets. T/Qpdt: £2.70 to a £1 stake. Pool: £4,119.00. 1,111.40 winning tickets. KH

[259]LINGFIELD (L-H)

Monday, January 29

OFFICIAL GOING: Standard

Wind: Light, across Weather: Fine, mild

288 PONTINSBINGO.COM (S) STKS 1m 2f (P)

1:20 (1:20) (Class 6) 4-Y-0+ £2,184 (£644; £322) Stalls Low

Form RPR

03-0 1 **Competitor**[9] 195 6-9-2 55 (vt) DaneO'Neill 6 54+
(J Akehurst) *wl in tch: rdn and effrt over 2f out: chsd ldr over 1f out: styd on wl u.p to ld last 75yds: won gng away* 15/8[1]

3-55 2 ¾ **Linda's Colin (IRE)**[16] 115 5-9-2 64 AdamKirby 10 52
(R A Harris) *hld up towards rr: prog 3f out: led wl over 1f out and kicked 2 l clr: hdd and btn last 75yds* 3/1[2]

5-00 3 2 **Christmas Truce (IRE)**[8] 200 8-8-9 52 (p) RyanBird(7) 8 48
(Ms J S Doyle) *s.i.s: settled towards rr: effrt on outer over 2f out: driven and kpt on same pce fr over 1f out: tk 3rd last strides* 16/1

600- 4 hd **Pelham Crescent (IRE)**[166] 4483 4-9-0 70 TonyCulhane 11 48
(B Palling) *s.i.s: t.k.h and sn trckd ldrs: wnt 2nd 3f out to 2f out: rdn and nt qckn* 4/1[3]

0 5 ½ **Fortune Dancer (USA)**[15] 134 12-9-2 45 (b) GeorgeBaker 2 47
(G L Moore) *s.s: hld up in last: effrt wl over 1f out: hanging u.p: plugged on fnl f* 12/1

6-44 6 ¾ **Scuzme (IRE)**[12] 159 4-9-0 52 (p) EdwardCreighton 1 46
(Miss Sheena West) *settled in rr: rdn and no rspnse over 2f out: struggling after: styd on over 1f out: no ch* 9/1

00-5 7 2½ **Fuel Cell (IRE)**[16] 126 6-8-10 42 ow1 JamesO'Reilly(7) 9 42
(J O'Reilly) *prom: chsd ldr 6f out to 3f out: btn whn hmpd on inner over 1f out* 12/1

0- 8 shd **Victors Prize (IRE)**[21] 6213 5-8-8 52 (p) JamesDoyle(3) 5 36
(S Curran) *a towards rr: rdn and no prog over 2f out* 33/1

00-0 9 2½ **Opal Warrior**[19] 94 4-8-9 45 (v[1]) JohnEgan 7 31
(Jane Southcombe) *led to wl over 1f out: wknd rapidly* 25/1

0/0- 10 4 **Bahama Reef (IRE)**[228] 2573 6-9-2 37 BrettDoyle 4 28
(B Gubby) *chsd ldr to 6f out: wknd wl over 2f out* 50/1

2m 6.45s (-1.34) **Going Correction** -0.175s/f (Stan)
WFA 4 from 5yo+ 2lb 10 Ran SP% 119.8
Speed ratings (Par 101):98,97,95,95,95 94,92,92,90,87
CSF £7.55 TOTE £3.00: £1.10, £1.80, £4.20; EX 10.10 Trifecta £45.50 Pool: £223.14 - 3.48 winning units..There was no bid for the winner. Linda's Colin was claimed by Karl Burke for £6,000.
Owner Who Cares Who Wins **Bred** Cheveley Park Stud Ltd **Trained** Epsom, Surrey

FOCUS
A weak affair which was run at an average pace. The form looks straightforward enough, limited by the fifth and seventh.
Fortune Dancer(USA) Official explanation: jockey said gelding hung left
Opal Warrior Official explanation: jockey said filly failed to stay the trip

289 PONTIN'S "BOOK EARLY" CLAIMING STKS 5f (P)

1:50 (1:50) (Class 6) 4-Y-0+ £2,184 (£644; £322) Stalls High

Form RPR

-040 1 **Night Prospector**[6] 227 7-9-8 82 (p) TolleyDean(5) 7 80+
(R A Harris) *taken down early: pushed along for 1f: trckd line of 4 disputing ld: got through to ld jst ins fnl f: in command after* 1/1[1]

-000 2 1 **New Options**[3] 254 10-8-9 53 (b) BrettDoyle 8 58
(Peter Grayson) *t.k.h: hld up bhd 4 disputing ldrs: rdn and nt qckn over 1f out: chsd wnr ins fnl f: kpt on: a hld* 16/1

13-6 3 2 **Succeed (IRE)**[19] 82 4-8-1 55 WilliamBuick(7) 4 50
(Mrs H Sweeting) *disp ld w 3 others: narrow advantage over 1f out: hdd and outpcd jst ins fnl f* 7/2[2]

4-20 4 1½ **Katie Killane**[8] 201 5-8-5 45 ow1 (v) JoeFanning 5 41
(M Wellings) *wdst of line of 4 disputing ld: hdd over 1f out: sn btn* 9/1

1-12 5 ½ **Spirit Of Coniston**[14] 135 4-8-6 50 (b) JamesDoyle(3) 3 44
(Peter Grayson) *disp ld w 3 others: drvn over 2f out: hanging over 1f out: sn hdd and btn* 9/2[3]

345- 6 3 **Spinetail Rufous (IRE)**[38] 6906 9-8-11 45 (b) IanMongan 2 35
(Miss Z C Davison) *racd on inner: disp ld w 3 others to over 1f out: wknd* 33/1

59.02 secs (-0.76) **Going Correction** -0.175s/f (Stan) 6 Ran SP% 109.2
Speed ratings (Par 101):99,97,94,91,91 86
CSF £17.66 TOTE £1.70: £1.30, £3.90; EX 19.00 Trifecta £94.40 Pool: £276.71 - 2.08 winning units..Night Prospector was claimed by Miss Gay Kelleway for £15,000.
Owner D Tumman & R F Bloodstock **Bred** Miss S N Ralphs **Trained** Earlswood, Monmouths

FOCUS
A moderate claimer which was run at a generous early pace, the front-runners setting it up for the other two. The winner did not even have to be at his recent level.

290 GO PONTIN'S H'CAP 6f (P)

2:20 (2:20) (Class 5) (0-70,70) 3-Y-0 £2,914 (£867; £433; £108; £108) Stalls Low

Form RPR

06-2 1 **Comrade Cotton**[23] 55 3-8-2 63 WilliamBuick(7) 4 66+
(N A Callaghan) *trckd ldrs: rdn and effrt wl over 1f out: led ent fnl f: drvn out* 11/2[3]

02-2 2 1 **Bertie Swift**[15] 127 3-9-0 68 JimCrowley 5 68
(J Gallagher) *pressed ldr: rdn to chal and upsides over 1f out: outpcd by wnr ins fnl f* 9/2[2]

000- 3 ½ **Foreland Sands (IRE)**[140] 5231 3-8-2 56 oh11 HayleyTurner 6 55+
(J R Best) *t.k.h: hld up towards rr: rdn over 1f out: styd on ins fnl f: nt rch ldng pair* 14/1

5-1 4 ¾ **Bronte's Hope**[23] 55 3-8-9 70 KatiaScallan(7) 8 66+
(M P Tregoning) *dwlt and squeezed out s: sn rcvrd and prom: nt qckn and lost pl over 1f out: shuffled along and styd on fnl f* 7/2[1]

-321 4 dht **Bentley**[8] 202 3-8-4 58 6ex (v) AdrianMcCarthy 3 54
(D Shaw) *led: rdn and hdd ent fnl f: fdd* 11/2[3]

004- 6 1 **Hucking Heat (IRE)**[172] 4292 3-8-12 66 BrettDoyle 1 62+
(J R Best) *dwlt: hld up in last trio: effrt on inner over 1f out: nvr rchd ldrs: snatched up nr fin* 10/1

34-5 7 ¾ **Belvedere Vixen**[15] 128 3-8-9 63 (v[1]) ChrisCatlin 2 54
(M J Wallace) *chsd ldrs: rdn 2f out: nt qckn over 1f out: wknd ins fnl f* 16/1

2-13 8 nk **Cherri Fosfate**[13] 147 3-8-8 69 (v) KellyHarrison(7) 9 59
(D Carroll) *a towards rr: rdn on outer over 1f out: no prog* 11/2[3]

050- 9 1¼ **Chingford (IRE)**[129] 5503 3-8-10 64 DaneO'Neill 7 50
(J G Portman) *a in last trio: rdn and no prog 2f out* 12/1

1m 12.19s (-0.62) **Going Correction** -0.175s/f (Stan) 9 Ran SP% 115.9
Speed ratings (Par 97):97,95,95,94,94 92,91,91,89
CSF £30.58 CT £329.95 TOTE £7.50: £2.20, £1.60, £3.20; EX 36.30 Trifecta £209.60 Part won. Pool: £295.35 - 0.66 winning units..
Owner Jeremy Gompertz **Bred** Jeremy Gompertz **Trained** Newmarket, Suffolk

FOCUS
A modest three-year-old handicap which was run at an average pace. The winner and third were unexposed and the form should prove sound enough.

291 PONTINS.COM H'CAP 2m (P)

2:50 (2:50) (Class 6) (0-60,60) 4-Y-0+ £2,388 (£705; £352) Stalls Low

Form RPR

00/0 1 **Dolzago**[19] 88 7-9-6 57 (b) GeorgeBaker 3 67
(G L Moore) *hld up towards rr: smooth prog over 3f out: led wl over 1f out: sn clr* 33/1

01-1 2 4 **Josh You Are**[15] 134 4-8-6 57 WilliamBuick(7) 4 62+
(D E Cantillon) *dwlt: hld up last: plld way through to join ldr 9f out: led over 6f out: rdn and hdd wl over 1f out: nt qckn* 1/1[1]

03-1 3 1½ **Pocket Too**[12] 159 4-9-2 60 (p) SebSanders 1 63
(M Salaman) *mostly midfield: trapped bhd wkng rival 4f out and lost pl: effrt again 2f out: drvn and styd on to take 3rd fnl f* 9/1

3-03 4 ½ **Lady Pilot**[16] 115 5-9-1 52 (b) JimCrowley 9 55
(Ms J S Doyle) *hld up in last trio: stdy prog into midfield over 2f out: rdn over 1f out: kpt on same pce* 10/1

05-2 5 ¾ **Mamonta**[26] 23 4-8-13 57 ChrisCatlin 6 59+
(M J Wallace) *settled wl in rr: trapped bhd rivals 4f out: prog 2f out: rdn and styd on fnl f: nrst fin* 10/1

1/45 6 nk **Sea Map**[12] 159 5-9-7 58 EdwardCreighton 7 59+
(Miss Sheena West) *led: jnd 9f out: hdd over 6f out: lost 2nd and btn over 2f out* 14/1

60-5 7 3 **Openide**[26] 16 6-9-4 55 DaneO'Neill 10 53
(B W Duke) *in tch: rdn over 5f out: struggling over 4f out: n.d after: plugged on* 6/1[2]

0-30 8 1¾ **Ganymede**[7] 213 6-9-2 53 IanMongan 14 49
(Mrs L J Mongan) *settled in rr: prog on outer over 3f out: drvn over 2f out: wknd over 1f out* 20/1

64-1 9 ¾ **Dream Mountain**[26] 23 4-8-10 57 JamesDoyle(3) 5 56+
(Ms J S Doyle) *chsd ldr for 4f: styd wl in tch tl wknd over 2f out* 7/1[3]

/0-0 10 2½ **It's Rumoured**[26] 23 7-8-10 50 (v) StephaneBreux(3) 13 42
(Jean-Rene Auvray) *chsd ldr after 4f to 9f out: rdn over 4f out: wknd over 2f out* 66/1

406- 11 19 **Papeete (GER)**[34] 4996 6-9-9 60 BrettDoyle 11 29
(Mrs N Smith) *t.k.h: hld up in rr: effrt on wd outside over 3f out: wknd rapidly over 2f out: eased: t.o* 20/1

00/6 12 3½ **Photographer (USA)**[13] 153 9-9-9 60 LPKeniry 8 25
(S Lycett) *trckd ldrs: rdn on outer 3f out: wknd rapidly: eased: t.o* 40/1

3m 22.99s (-5.80) **Going Correction** -0.175s/f (Stan)
WFA 4 from 5yo+ 7lb 12 Ran SP% 128.0
Speed ratings (Par 101):107,105,104,104,103 103,101,101,100,99 89,88
CSF £69.31 CT £389.16 TOTE £28.70: £11.00, £1.10, £3.50; EX 164.70 TRIFECTA Not won..
Owner R Kiernan, Paul Chapman **Bred** Cheveley Park Stud Ltd **Trained** Woodingdean, E Sussex
■ Stewards' Enquiry : George Baker two-day ban: careless riding (Feb 9-10)
William Buick two-day ban: careless riding (Feb 9-10)

FOCUS
A decent winning time for a race of its type, due to the strong early pace. The form looks solid despite the shock winner who was back to something like his 2004 form.

292 PONTIN'S HOLIDAYS H'CAP 6f (P)

3:20 (3:21) (Class 6) (0-60,60) 4-Y-0+ £2,388 (£705; £352) Stalls Low

Form RPR

00-2 1 **Celtic Thunder**[12] 158 6-8-10 57 (b) SaleemGolam(3) 3 67+
(T J Etherington) *trckd ldrs on inner: effrt and swtchd rt 1f out: drvn and r.o to ld last 50yds* 6/1[1]

02-2 2 1 **King After**[26] 26 5-8-9 53 (v[1]) JoeFanning 2 60
(J R Best) *w ldr: led wl over 1f out: urged along fnl f: hdd and outpcd last 50yds* 13/2[2]

5-30 3 nk **Cool Sands (IRE)**[15] 131 5-9-2 60 (v) DaneO'Neill 9 66
(D Shaw) *hld up in rr: effrt and nt clr run briefly over 1f out: r.o wl fnl f: gaining at fin* 11/1

-053 4 1 **Franksalot (IRE)**[5] 236 7-9-2 60 JimCrowley 4 63
(I W McInnes) *hld up in rr: prog on inner over 1f out: looked dangerous ent fnl f: one pce* 7/1[3]

31-1 5 ½ **Shava**[16] 123 7-8-9 53 FergusSweeney 11 55
(H J Evans) *racd wd: hld up towards rr: prog and wd bnd 2f out: hanging lft over 1f out: nt qckn* 7/1[3]

1-02 6 nk **Mine The Balance (IRE)**[12] 161 4-9-2 60 (b) BrettDoyle 6 61
(J R Best) *t.k.h: w ldng pair to 2f out: nt qckn and btn over 1f out* 7/1[3]

110- 7 ½ **Bodden Bay**[55] 6721 5-9-1 59 PFredericks 1 58
(Miss Gay Kelleway) *mde most to wl over 1f out: wknd fnl f* 12/1

400- 8 1¼ **Balerno**[139] 5269 8-8-9 53 PaulEddery 5 48
(Mrs L J Mongan) *trckd ldrs: rdn and n.m.r 2f out: fdd* 50/1

-502 9 nk **Midmaar (IRE)**[2] 268 6-8-9 53 (b) ChrisCatlin 7 48
(M Wigham) *wl in rr: rdn over 2f out: no prog and btn after: modest late prog* 8/1

1-04 10 shd **Hotchpotch (USA)**[5] 236 4-8-13 57 (p) HayleyTurner 10 51
(J R Best) *trckd ldrs: rdn over 1f out: wknd fnl f* 7/1[3]

540- 11 ¾ **Davidia (IRE)**[39] 6898 4-8-13 57 (b) LPKeniry 12 49
(S Kirk) *trckd ldrs tl wknd over 1f out* 33/1

000- 12 nk **Go Mo (IRE)**[126] 5573 5-8-3 54 WilliamBuick(7) 8 45
(R M H Cowell) *rrd bdly s: detached in last: nvr a factor* 8/1

1m 11.7s (-1.11) **Going Correction** -0.175s/f (Stan) 12 Ran SP% 120.8
Speed ratings (Par 101):100,98,98,96,96 95,95,93,93,93 92,91
CSF £45.14 CT £433.12 TOTE £6.50: £2.70, £1.80, £5.10; EX 43.90 TRIFECTA Not won..
Owner Ian Smith **Bred** K Benson **Trained** Norton, N Yorks

FOCUS
An open sprint for the class. The form looks sound enough rated through the second and third.
Go Mo(IRE) Official explanation: jockey said gelding reared leaving the stalls

293 DIGITAL PRINTS FROM BONUSPRINT.COM MAIDEN STKS 1m (P)

3:50 (3:51) (Class 5) 3-Y-0 £2,914 (£867; £433; £216) Stalls High

Form RPR

1 **One Hour** 3-9-3 DaneO'Neill 2 83+
(M P Tregoning) *hld up in tch: prog over 2f out: green but led over 1f out: stretched clr fnl f* 4/5[1]

0-3 **2** 2 ½ **Hessian (IRE)**[9] [193] 3-8-12 .... HayleyTurner 11 66
(M L W Bell) *mde most: rdn and hdd over 1f out: no ch w wnr but hld on for 2nd* **10/3**[2]

0- **3** 1 **Rambling Light**[108] [5939] 3-9-3 .... FergusSweeney 5 69
(A M Balding) *trckd ldrs: prog on outer over 2f out: outpcd over 1f out: kpt on fnl f* **12/1**

6 **4** nk **Title Deed (USA)**[16] [116] 3-9-3 .... LPKeniry 7 68
(A P Jarvis) *prom: chsd ldr 3f out to over 1f out: one pce* **11/1**[3]

5 2 ½ **Fire One (IRE)** 3-9-3 .... GeorgeBaker 9 62+
(M P Tregoning) *s.i.s: hld up in rr and rn green: outpcd over 2f out: styd on steadily fr over 1f out* **14/1**

\- **6** 1 **Scarlet Oak** 3-8-12 .... AdamKirby 4 55
(D J S Ffrench Davis) *hld up in last trio: effrt over 2f out: shkn up and styd on fnl f: no ch* **66/1**

0 **7** ½ **Mark Of Love (IRE)**[7] [208] 3-9-3 .... TonyCulhane 3 59+
(M R Channon) *hld up in last trio: pushed along on inner and kpt on fr over 1f out: n.d* **50/1**

0 **8** 1 **Tenement (IRE)**[7] [208] 3-9-3 .... ShaneKelly 10 57
(J A Osborne) *chsd ldr to 3f out: wknd fnl f* **33/1**

0-0 **9** ¾ **Poyle Ruby**[16] [116] 3-8-12 .... SebSanders 1 50?
(M Blanshard) *t.k.h: hld up in last trio: sltly hmpd over 4f out: no prog fnl 2f* **50/1**

0 **10** 1 ½ **Woodygo**[16] [116] 3-9-3 .... BrettDoyle 6 51?
(J R Best) *plld hrd early and restrained bhd ldrs: hmpd over 4f out: green and struggling 2f out: wknd* **20/1**

11 8 **Bedouin Beauty (IRE)** 3-8-12 .... ChrisCatlin 8 28
(E A L Dunlop) *prog and prom after 1f: wknd rapidly over 2f out: t.o* **20/1**

1m 38.24s (-1.19) **Going Correction** -0.175s/f (Stan) **11** Ran SP% **119.2**
Speed ratings (Par 97):98,95,94,94,91 90,90,89,88,86 78
CSF £3.14 TOTE £1.80: £1.10, £1.30, £3.70; EX 3.60 Trifecta £30.90 Pool: £541.61 - 12.44 winning units..
Owner Sheikh Ahmed Al Maktoum **Bred** Darley **Trained** Lambourn, Berks

FOCUS
No real strength in depth in this three-year-old maiden and it was run at a muddling pace. However, the first five all look capable of rating higher in due course, especially the taking debut winner.

294 BONUSPRINT.COM H'CAP 1m 2f (P)
4:20 (4:20) (Class 4) (0-85,78) 3-Y-O **£4,857** (£1,445; £722; £360) **Stalls** Low

Form RPR

011- **1** **Love Dubai (USA)**[46] [6824] 3-9-2 **78** .... JoeFanning 5 83+
(M Johnston) *hld up in 5th: dropped to last and n.m.r over 2f out: effrt over 1f out: drvn and r.o to ld last 50yds: fin strly* **1/1**[1]

0-21 **2** 1 **Six Shots**[3] [257] 3-9-0 **76** 6ex .... ShaneKelly 1 79
(J A Osborne) *led: dictated stdy pce to 3f out: drvn and wandered over 1f out: hdd and outpcd last 50yds* **11/2**[3]

40-1 **3** ½ **Daylami Dreams**[9] [196] 3-8-11 **73** .... JohnEgan 3 75+
(J S Moore) *mostly trckd ldr: rdn 3f out: stl cl up ent fnl f : outpcd nr fin* **11/4**[2]

1 **4** nk **Serpentaria**[16] [114] 3-8-11 **73** .... SebSanders 2 74
(Sir Mark Prescott) *cl up: effrt on inner to press ldr over 1f out: nt qckn and hld fnl f* **8/1**

-016 **5** 4 **King Of The Beers (USA)**[2] [267] 3-7-9 **64** oh7......(p) WilliamBuick(7) 6 58
(R A Harris) *hld up in last: effrt 3f out: wd bnd 2f out: wknd over 1f out* **16/1**

-362 **6** ½ **Beau Sancy**[9] [196] 3-8-2 **64** oh2 .... ChrisCatlin 4 57
(R A Harris) *cl up: rdn 3f out: wknd over 1f out* **20/1**

2m 7.50s (-0.29) **Going Correction** -0.175s/f (Stan) **6** Ran SP% **113.8**
Speed ratings (Par 99):94,93,92,92,89 88
CSF £7.33 TOTE £1.90: £1.10, £2.80; EX 5.30 Place 6 £24.90, Place 5 £15.93.
Owner M Doyle **Bred** Foxfield **Trained** Middleham Moor, N Yorks

FOCUS
An interesting three-year-old handicap, but the early pace was just steady. The winner remains progressive, but the overall form should be treated with a degree of caution.
T/Plt: £42.70 to a £1 stake. Pool: £52,838.85. 901.70 winning tickets. T/Qpdt: £16.20 to a £1 stake. Pool: £2,358.10. 107.50 winning tickets. JN

280 WOLVERHAMPTON (A.W) (L-H)
Monday, January 29

OFFICIAL GOING: Standard to slow
Wind: Almost nil Weather: Fine

295 PONTINS.COM CLAIMING STKS 5f 216y(P)
1:40 (1:40) (Class 6) 3-Y-O **£2,730** (£806; £403) **Stalls** Low

Form RPR

5U-2 **1** **Put It On The Card**[17] [108] 3-8-6 60 ....(b) StephenDonohoe(3) 5 65
(P D Evans) *hld up: hdwy over 2f out: sn rdn: led ins fnl f: r.o wl* **5/1**[3]

54-2 **2** 3 **Razzano (IRE)**[12] [162] 3-8-7 57 .... JerryO'Dwyer(3) 3 57
(A M Hales) *s.i.s: bhd: swtchd rt wl over 1f out: hdwy and edgd lft fnl f: nt trble wnr* **4/1**[2]

12-4 **3** 1 ½ **Pirner's Brig**[13] [147] 3-9-3 65 .... PaulMulrennan 4 60
(M W Easterby) *led early: a.p: led wl over 1f out: rdn and edgd lft 1f out: hdd ins fnl f: sn btn* **10/11**[1]

00-0 **4** 1 ¾ **Hoh Me Hoh You (IRE)**[16] [122] 3-8-9 54 .... FrankieMcDonald 8 46
(S Kirk) *chsd ldrs: rdn 3f out: one pce fnl f* **12/1**

B- **5** nk **Polly Rocket**[49] [6789] 3-8-2 .... JimmyQuinn 1 38
(P D Niven) *s.i.s: sn mid-div: rdn and lost pl over 2f out: n.d after* **20/1**

20-3 **6** 1 ½ **O'Dwyer (IRE)**[9] [194] 3-8-7 53 ....(p) SilvestreDeSousa 2 39
(A D Brown) *sn led: hdd after 1f: wknd 2f out* **10/1**

7 nk **Inchwall** 3-9-5 .... RobbieFitzpatrick 7 50
(Peter Grayson) *s.i.s: a bhd* **28/1**

06-4 **8** ½ **Pat Will (IRE)**[17] [108] 3-7-11 53 ....(b) BernadetteQuinn(7) 6 33
(P D Evans) *s.i.s: rcvrd to ld after 1f: hdd wl over 1f out: wknd 1f out* **28/1**

1m 15.58s (-0.23) **Going Correction** -0.025s/f (Stan) **8** Ran SP% **117.5**
Speed ratings (Par 95):100,96,94,91,91 89,88,88
CSF £25.36 TOTE £5.90: £1.60, £1.80, £1.10; EX 30.90.
Owner J E Abbey, Mike Nolan **Bred** J E Abbey **Trained** Pandy, Monmouths

FOCUS
A weakish claimer, but it was truly-run. The first two both improved by around 6lb.
Pirner's Brig Official explanation: jockey said colt jumped left out of the stalls and was unable to dictate in the race

296 PONTIN'S FAMILY HOLIDAYS FILLIES' H'CAP 5f 216y(P)
2:10 (2:10) (Class 6) (0-60,59) 4-Y-O+ **£2,388** (£705; £352) **Stalls** Low

Form RPR

10-3 **1** **Muara**[27] [8] 5-9-0 **57** .... PaulHanagan 2 70+
(D W Barker) *led early: a.p: rdn to ld jst ins fnl f: r.o* **9/2**[1]

60-0 **2** 1 ¼ **Cerebus**[18] [102] 5-9-0 **57** ....(bt) RobertWinston 6 66
(A J McCabe) *s.i.s: sn mid-div: hdwy over 2f out: rdn and edgd lft over 1f out: r.o ins fnl f: nt rch wnr* **5/1**[2]

00-0 **3** 1 ¼ **Dark Moon**[9] [189] 4-8-2 **45** .... JimmyQuinn 11 50
(D Shaw) *s.i.s: hld up and bhd: hdwy on ins whn nt clr run over 2f out: rdn wl over 1f out: kpt on ins fnl f* **22/1**

41-3 **4** nk **Blakeshall Quest**[6] [221] 7-8-11 **54** ....(b) PatCosgrave 3 58
(R Brotherton) *prom: led over 4f out: rdn wl over 1f out: hdd jst ins fnl f: no ex towards fin* **7/1**[3]

343- **5** 2 **Newkeylets**[39] [6901] 4-8-5 **53** ....(p) DuranFentiman(5) 10 51
(I Semple) *a.p: rdn and hung lft over 1f out: no imp fnl f* **10/1**

4/60 **6** 2 **Smart Pick**[8] [200] 4-8-12 **55** .... GrahamGibbons 7 47
(J R Holt) *bhd: rdn wl over 1f out: kpt on fnl f: n.d* **50/1**

0-33 **7** ½ **Whistleupthewind**[12] [158] 4-8-13 **56** ....(b) MickyFenton 5 47
(J M P Eustace) *mid-div: hmpd and lost pl 4f out: hdwy on ins wl over 1f out: wknd ins fnl f* **5/1**[2]

210- **8** nk **Creme Brulee**[38] [6922] 4-8-11 **54** .... RobertHavlin 4 44
(C R Egerton) *hld up and bhd: nt clr run over 3f out: hdwy over 2f out: rdn and edgd lft over 1f out: wknd ins fnl f* **5/1**[2]

30-5 **9** 2 ½ **Kineta (USA)**[12] [160] 4-9-0 **57** .... NCallan 8 39
(W R Muir) *broke wl: sn mid-div: rdn over 3f out: short-lived effrt over 2f out* **12/1**

00-5 **10** ¾ **Sham Ruby**[25] [33] 5-8-2 **45** .... JamieMackay 13 25
(M R Bosley) *hld up in tch on outside: lost pl 4f out: sn bhd* **50/1**

000- **11** nk **Lizzie Rocket**[22] [2780] 7-8-2 **45** ....(v) DaleGibson 1 24
(J O'Reilly) *sn led: hdd over 4f out: wknd over 2f out* **33/1**

-000 **12** ¾ **Xocolatl**[7] [207] 4-8-6 **49** ow4 ....(b[1]) RobbieFitzpatrick 9 26
(Peter Grayson) *rdn and sn prom: wknd wl over 1f out* **50/1**

4- **13** 2 **Pep In Her Step (IRE)**[182] [4014] 4-8-13 **59** .... JerryO'Dwyer(3) 12 30
(Eamon Tyrrell, Ire) *prom tl rdn and wknd over 3f out* **16/1**

1m 15.53s (-0.28) **Going Correction** -0.025s/f (Stan) **13** Ran SP% **116.5**
Speed ratings (Par 98):100,98,96,96,93 90,90,89,86,85 85,84,81
CSF £24.75 CT £452.91 TOTE £5.60: £2.50, £2.40, £7.10; EX 33.60.
Owner W R Arblaster **Bred** W R And Mrs Arblaster **Trained** Scorton, N Yorks

FOCUS
An open if distinctly modest fillies' handicap. An improved run from the winner, but the overall form is not solid.
Whistleupthewind Official explanation: jockey said filly suffered interference in running

297 GO PONTIN'S H'CAP 1m 4f 50y(P)
2:40 (2:40) (Class 5) (0-75,75) 4-Y-O+ **£3,071** (£906; £453) **Stalls** Low

Form RPR

51-2 **1** **Melvino**[14] [142] 5-8-12 **67** .... DeanMcKeown 8 76
(T D Barron) *hld up and bhd: hdwy over 3f out: hung lft over 1f out: led ins fnl f: r.o wl* **9/2**[1]

20-0 **2** 2 **Augustine**[8] [205] 6-9-6 **75** .... PhillipMakin 6 81
(P W Hiatt) *hld up in mid-div: swtchd rt over 2f out: rdn and hdwy whn hung lft wl over 1f out: r.o ins fnl f* **10/1**

24-6 **3** ¾ **Top Spec (IRE)**[14] [142] 6-9-5 **74** .... JimmyQuinn 4 79
(J Pearce) *s.i.s: hld up in mid-div: hdwy over 8f out: rdn over 3f out: edgd lft 1f out: nt qckn* **17/2**

13-2 **4** nk **Symbol Of Peace (IRE)**[17] [112] 4-8-10 **72** .... RichardKingscote(3) 7 77
(J W Unett) *hld up in tch: led wl over 1f out: sn rdn: hdd and no ex ins fnl f* **6/1**[2]

014- **5** ¾ **Silverhay**[42] [5599] 6-9-5 **74** ....(p) NCallan 5 77
(L Corcoran) *a.p: rdn over 2f out: one pce fnl f* **7/1**[3]

540- **6** shd **Caraman (IRE)**[30] [5513] 9-8-11 **66** .... GrahamGibbons 3 69
(J J Quinn) *chsd ldr: led over 2f out: rdn and hdd wl over 1f out: no ex wl ins fnl f* **9/2**[1]

55-0 **7** 1 **Newnham (IRE)**[14] [142] 6-9-0 **69** .... PatCosgrave 9 71
(J R Boyle) *hld up and bhd: rdn over 3f out: hdwy over 1f out: styd on ins fnl f* **12/1**

020- **8** 7 **Wellington Hall (GER)**[17] [6017] 9-9-6 **75** .... OscarUrbina 10 65
(M Wigham) *a bhd* **11/1**

000- **9** 5 **Lord Mayor**[139] [5259] 6-8-12 **70** .... StephenDonohoe(3) 1 52
(B N Pollock) *hld up towards rr: pushed along over 4f out: no rspnse* **25/1**

33-3 **10** nk **Inside Story (IRE)**[14] [142] 5-8-10 **68** ....(b) MarcHalford(3) 2 50
(G P Kelly) *t.k.h: led: rdn and hdd over 2f out: sn wknd* **6/1**[2]

2m 39.91s (-2.51) **Going Correction** -0.025s/f (Stan)
WFA 4 from 5yo+ 4lb **10** Ran SP% **116.9**
Speed ratings (Par 103):107,105,105,104,104 104,103,99,95,95
CSF £50.40 CT £371.61 TOTE £5.00: £1.70, £5.50, £1.90; EX 69.70.
Owner Theo Williams and Charles Mocatta **Bred** T J Cooper **Trained** Maunby, N Yorks

FOCUS
A very ordinary affair, not strongly-run. The winner improved again.
Symbol Of Peace(IRE) Official explanation: jockey said filly had no more to give
Inside Story(IRE) Official explanation: jockey said gelding was unsuited by a change of tactics to make the running and needs to be covered up; trainer later said gelding finished distressed

298 PONTINSBINGO.COM CLAIMING STKS 1m 141y(P)
3:10 (3:10) (Class 6) 4-Y-O+ **£2,388** (£705; £352) **Stalls** Low

Form RPR

3-31 **1** **Climate (IRE)**[17] [109] 8-9-1 64 ....(v) RussellKennemore(5) 2 68
(R Hollinshead) *a.p: squeezed through on ins over 3f out: rdn to ld wl over 1f out: r.o* **10/11**[1]

500- **2** ½ **Final Esteem**[87] [6317] 4-9-7 65 .... RobertWinston 6 69
(G A Swinbank) *s.i.s: hld up: nt clr run over 3f out: hdwy on ins wl over 1f out: r.o ins fnl f: nt rch wnr* **11/2**[2]

64-0 **3** 2 **Burnley Al (IRE)**[16] [124] 5-8-12 54 ....(b) RobbieFitzpatrick 3 55
(Peter Grayson) *plld hrd: a.p: led over 4f out: rdn over 2f out: hdd wl over 1f out: one pce fnl f* **8/1**

-350 **4** shd **The London Gang**[5] [235] 4-9-5 56 ....(v) TPQueally 8 63
(Miss D A McHale) *dwlt: in rr: c wd st: rdn and hdwy whn edgd lft ins fnl f: r.o* **16/1**

-140 **5** 1 ½ **Bathwick Emma (IRE)**[3] [252] 4-8-7 51 ow2.....(p) StephenDonohoe(3) 5 50
(M A Doyle) *hld up towards rr: hdwy on outside over 2f out: rdn and wknd over 1f out* **12/1**

004- **6** hd **Following Flow (USA)**[39] [6898] 5-9-4 67 ....(p) GrahamGibbons 4 57
(R Hollinshead) *hld up: hdwy over 5f out: ev ch 2f out: rdn and hung lft over 1f out: wknd ins fnl f* **6/1**[3]

600- 7 2 1/2 **Soviet Threat (IRE)**[237] [2319] 6-9-0 55 .... NCallan 7 48
(A G Juckes) *stdd s: t.k.h: hdwy whn hmpd over 3f out: wknd over 1f out* **25/1**

000- 8 5 **Crusoe (IRE)**[2] [6970] 10-8-7 36 .... (b) MichaelJStainton(5) 1 35
(A Sadik) *led: hdd over 4f out: wknd over 3f out* **100/1**

1m 53.83s (2.07) **Going Correction** -0.025s/f (Stan)
WFA 4 from 5yo+ 1lb **8** Ran SP% **111.6**
Speed ratings (Par 101):89,88,86,86,85 85,82,78
CSF £5.83 TOTE £1.90: £1.02, £1.70, £3.10; EX 8.40.Final Esteem was claimed by Ron Harris for £10,000.
Owner The Cartmel Syndicate **Bred** Mrs A Naughton **Trained** Upper Longdon, Staffs

FOCUS
A slow pace led to a messy affair with several running freely and a very moderate winning time for the grade.
Soviet Threat(IRE) Official explanation: jockey said gelding was hampered in running

299 PONTIN'S - BOOK EARLY FILLIES' H'CAP 1m 1f 103y(P)
3:40 (3:41) (Class 5) (0-70,70) 4-Y-0+ **£3,238** (£963; £481; £240) **Stalls** Low

Form RPR

32-2 1 **Chia (IRE)**[19] [85] 4-8-10 **63** .... RobertHavlin 1 71
(D Haydn Jones) *a.p: led briefly wl over 1f out: sn rdn and edgd lft: led ins fnl f: r.o wl* **4/1**[2]

32-6 2 1 3/4 **Bavarica**[17] [112] 5-8-10 **69** .... AmyBaker(7) 2 74
(Miss J Feilden) *hld up in tch: rdn to ld wl over 1f out: hdd and nt qckn ins fnl f* **7/1**

5-00 3 3/4 **Tuscarora (IRE)**[19] [85] 8-8-6 **58** .... PaulHanagan 8 61
(A W Carroll) *hld up and bhd: hmpd over 7f out: rdn and hdwy on ins over 2f out: kpt on one pce fnl f* **33/1**

520- 4 3 1/2 **Ruffie (IRE)**[51] [6762] 4-8-12 **65** .... (v) NCallan 9 61
(Miss Gay Kelleway) *hld up and bhd: hdwy over 6f out: rdn over 2f out: wknd over 1f out* **16/1**

00-6 5 1 **Medieval Maiden**[17] [110] 4-8-9 **62** .... TPQueally 5 56
(W J Musson) *hld up towards rr: nvr nr ldrs* **7/2**[1]

1-26 6 1/2 **Flyingit (USA)**[5] [233] 4-9-3 **70** .... CatherineGannon 4 63
(K A Ryan) *led: rdn and hdd wl over 1f out: sn wknd* **11/2**

05-3 7 1/2 **Westering Home (IRE)**[17] [112] 4-8-6 **59** .... (p) DaleGibson 6 51
(J Mackie) *prom: rdn over 3f out: wknd over 1f out* **14/1**

001- 8 28 **Odessa Star (USA)**[34] [6942] 4-9-1 **68** .... J-PGuillambert 7 4
(J G Portman) *stdd s: in rr whn bdly hmpd over 7f out: eased whn no ch fnl 2f* **9/1**

-422 U **The City Kid (IRE)**[1] [286] 4-7-9 **55** .... (b) BernadetteQuinn(7) 3 —
(P D Evans) *t.k.h in mid-div: stmbld and uns rdr over 7f out* **9/2**[3]

2m 1.61s (-1.01) **Going Correction** -0.025s/f (Stan)
WFA 4 from 5yo+ 1lb **9** Ran SP% **113.8**
Speed ratings (Par 100):103,101,100,97,96 96,95,71,—
CSF £31.57 CT £798.25 TOTE £4.20: £1.60, £2.40, £8.70; EX 30.70.
Owner D Llewelyn **Bred** Shane Moroney **Trained** Efail Isaf, Rhondda C Taff

FOCUS
A weakish handicap, with a marginally-improved effort from the winner.
Odessa Star(USA) Official explanation: jockey said filly was badly hampered by the faller and was eased in the closing stages

300 WOLVERHAMPTON-RACECOURSE.CO.UK H'CAP 7f 32y(P)
4:10 (4:25) (Class 5) (0-75,80) 4-Y-0+ **£3,071** (£906; £453) **Stalls** High

Form RPR

2-11 1 **Ektimaal**[9] [191] 4-9-2 **75** .... (t) PaulHanagan 6 90+
(E A L Dunlop) *hld up towards rr: hdwy on outside 3f out: rdn to ld ins fnl f: r.o wl* **11/10**[1]

4-34 2 1 3/4 **Dapple Dawn (IRE)**[13] [151] 4-8-9 **68** .... (b[1]) DanielTudhope 7 75
(D Carroll) *sn chsng ldr: rdn over 2f out: ev ch over 1f out: nt qckn ins fnl f* **14/1**

010- 3 1 1/4 **Le Chiffre (IRE)**[55] [6720] 5-8-6 **65** .... (b) PaulMulrennan 2 69
(K R Burke) *led: rdn over 1f out: hdd ins fnl f: no ex* **12/1**

000- 4 nk **Violent Velocity (IRE)**[39] [6896] 4-8-8 **67** .... GrahamGibbons 3 70+
(J J Quinn) *hld up and bhd: hdwy on ins whn nt clr run 2f out: sn rdn: edgd rt over 1f out: kpt on ins fnl f* **20/1**

0P0- 5 shd **Ocean Of Dreams (FR)**[186] [3879] 4-9-2 **75** .... NCallan 1 78
(J D Bethell) *a.p: rdn 2f out: edgd rt ins fnl f: kpt on same pce* **33/1**

00/0 6 1 3/4 **Mission Man**[17] [110] 6-8-4 **63** .... JimmyQuinn 5 61
(M G Rimell) *hld up and bhd: rdn over 2f out: n.d* **40/1**

0-34 7 1 1/2 **Stoic Leader (IRE)**[5] [234] 7-8-3 **67** .... KevinGhunowa(5) 4 62
(R F Fisher) *prom: rdn over 4f out: wknd wl over 1f out* **8/1**[3]

1-31 8 3 1/2 **Writ (IRE)**[7] [218] 5-9-2 **80** 6ex .... DuranFentiman(5) 8 65
(I Semple) *prom tl wknd 3f out* **5/2**[2]

9 1 **Call Me Crazy (IRE)**[196] [3601] 4-8-6 **68** .... JerryO'Dwyer(3) 9 51
(Eamon Tyrrell, Ire) *s.i.s: rdn 5f out: a bhd* **33/1**

1m 29.2s (-1.20) **Going Correction** -0.025s/f (Stan) **9** Ran SP% **114.7**
Speed ratings (Par 103):105,103,101,101,101 99,97,93,92
CSF £17.81 CT £127.31 TOTE £2.10: £1.10, £3.00, £2.50; EX 17.70.
Owner The Serendipity Partnership **Bred** Whitsbury Manor Stud **Trained** Newmarket, Suffolk

FOCUS
The progressive Ektimaal put up the best time of the day compared with standard. He can do better still, but this form is not entirely convincing, with Writ not running his race.
Writ(IRE) Official explanation: jockey said gelding moved poorly

301 PONTIN'S HOLIDAYS MAIDEN STKS 7f 32y(P)
4:40 (4:51) (Class 5) 3-Y-0 **£3,071** (£906; £453) **Stalls** High

Form RPR

1 **Regal Parade** 3-9-0 .... GregFairley(3) 7 73+
(M Johnston) *s.i.s: rn green in mid-div: hdwy over 3f out: sn rdn: led 1f out: drvn out* **11/4**[2]

00-3 2 nk **New World Order (IRE)**[13] [152] 3-9-3 89 .... PatCosgrave 5 72
(K R Burke) *hld up in tch: rdn over 2f out: ev ch wl ins fnl f: r.o* **7/2**[3]

24-2 3 1 1/4 **Arch Of Titus (IRE)**[21] [73] 3-8-10 75 .... (t) LukeMorris(7) 4 69+
(M L W Bell) *s.i.s: plld hrd in mid-div: rdn and hdwy on outside over 2f out: styd on towards fin* **11/8**[1]

4 nk **Bernasconi (USA)** 3-9-3 .... RobertWinston 1 68
(G A Swinbank) *hld up in tch: rdn over 2f out: ev ch ins fnl f: nt qckn* **15/2**

24- 5 1 1/4 **Carrie McCurry (IRE)**[37] [6925] 3-8-12 .... TPQueally 2 60
(Patrick Martin, Ire) *chsd ldr: rdn over 2f out: led over 1f out: sn hdd: no ex towards fin* **14/1**

06-5 6 2 **Muncaster Castle (IRE)**[8] [202] 3-8-12 51 .... KevinGhunowa(5) 8 60
(R F Fisher) *led: rdn over 2f out: hdd over 1f out: wknd ins fnl f* **33/1**

6 7 2 1/2 **Meadfoot**[21] [69] 3-8-9 .... RichardKingscote(3) 6 49
(B R Millman) *s.i.s: bhd: sme hdwy on ins over 2f out: no further prog* **66/1**

5- 8 4 **Lady Cartuccia**[29] [6998] 3-8-12 .... GrahamGibbons 10 38
(J J Quinn) *prom tl rdn and wknd over 2f out* **25/1**

9 4 **Mays Louise** 3-8-5 .... SoniaEaton(7) 3 28
(B P J Baugh) *s.i.s: a bhd* **50/1**

U- 10 3 1/2 **Comptonspirit**[30] [6989] 3-8-12 .... DeanMcKeown 9 19
(B P J Baugh) *a bhd* **66/1**

1m 31.49s (1.09) **Going Correction** -0.025s/f (Stan) **10** Ran SP% **121.2**
Speed ratings (Par 97):92,91,90,89,88 86,83,78,74,70
CSF £13.05 TOTE £4.90: £1.60, £1.70, £1.20; EX 18.90 Place 6 £34.42, Place 5 £30.56.
Owner Sheikh Mohammed **Bred** Highclere Stud And Harry Herbert **Trained** Middleham Moor, N Yorks

FOCUS
A moderate winning time for the type of contest, 2.49 seconds slower than the preceding handicap. The bare form is modest, but the winner is bound to rate much higher with the second, third and fifth all fair maidens.
Meadfoot Official explanation: jockey said filly missed the break
T/Plt: £33.70 to a £1 stake. Pool: £50,778.50. 1,098.50 winning tickets. T/Qpdt: £7.60 to a £1 stake. Pool: £3,188.50. 308.60 winning tickets. KH

237 SOUTHWELL (L-H)
Tuesday, January 30

OFFICIAL GOING: Standard
The recent trend at this track continued, with four of the seven winners making all or most, and the other three all racing prominently throughout.
Wind: Moderate, behind

302 GO PONTIN'S AMATEUR RIDERS' H'CAP 2m (F)
1:30 (1:30) (Class 5) (0-70,65) 4-Y-0+ **£2,966** (£912; £456) **Stalls** Low

Form RPR

0-54 1 **Blue Hills**[14] [146] 6-10-3 **52** .... (b) MrsMarieKing(5) 4 61
(P W Hiatt) *keen: led to 1/2-way: cl up tl led again over 4f out: rdn and hdd wl over 1f out: rallied ins last to ld nr fin* **20/1**

22-2 2 1/2 **Stagecoach Emerald**[23] [62] 5-11-2 **60** .... (t) MrSDobson 8 68
(R W Price) *cl up: effrt over 2f out: rdn ent last and disp ld tl no ex towards fin* **9/2**[3]

-022 3 1 3/4 **Khanjar (USA)**[2] [278] 7-10-8 **55** .... (p) MrSPearce(3) 2 61
(J Pearce) *hld up in tch: smooth hdwy over 3f out: rdn to ld wl over 1f out: drvn: hdd & wknd wl ins last* **6/1**

1-21 4 shd **Miss Holly**[14] [146] 8-11-0 **63** .... MrSFMagee(5) 1 69
(D Carroll) *hld up in tch: hdwy to trck ldrs over 3f out: effrt on outer 2f out: rdn over 1f out and kpt on same pce ins last* **2/1**[1]

031- 5 5 **Grasp**[34] [6398] 5-10-13 **60** .... MrDHutchison(3) 6 60
(G L Moore) *trckd ldrs: effrt over 4f out: rdn along 3f out and wknd fnl 2f* **11/4**[2]

2335 6 nk **Bienheureux**[8] [213] 6-10-7 **56** .... (bt) MissGDGracey-Davison(5) 5 56
(Miss Gay Kelleway) *hld up in rr: hdwy 3f out: no imp fnl 2f* **9/1**

2-20 7 13 **Bethanys Boy (IRE)**[8] [215] 6-11-4 **65** .... MissFayeBramley(3) 7 49
(P A Blockley) *keen: cl up: led 1/2-way: hdd over 4f out: rdn along 3f out: sn wknd* **20/1**

500- 8 31 **College Rebel**[27] [3919] 6-9-11 **46** oh1 .... MrCWallis(5) 3 —
(J F Coupland) *chsd ldrs: rdn along over 4f out: wknd over 4f out* **100/1**

3m 44.6s (0.06) **Going Correction** -0.175s/f (Stan) **8** Ran SP% **113.0**
Speed ratings (Par 103):92,91,90,90,88 88,81,66
CSF £104.31 CT £615.72 TOTE £25.00: £4.10, £1.30, £1.80; EX 163.10 Trifecta £240.90 Part won. Pool: £339.33 - 0.33 winning units..
Owner Tom Pratt **Bred** Darley **Trained** Hook Norton, Oxon
■ Stewards' Enquiry : Mrs Marie King one-day ban: careless riding (Feb 19)
Mr S Dobson two-day ban: used whip with excessive frequency (Feb 19 & Mar 5)

FOCUS
A moderate staying handicap run at just a steady gallop and rated negatively.

303 PONTINS.COM (S) STKS 6f (F)
2:00 (2:00) (Class 6) 3-Y-0+ **£2,184** (£644; £322) **Stalls** Low

Form RPR

000- 1 **Owed**[311] [737] 5-9-8 68 .... (t) SebSanders 9 64
(R Bastiman) *cl up: led over 2f out: rdn over 1f out: edgd lft and rt ins last: drvn out* **11/4**[1]

4-60 2 3/4 **Windy Prospect**[9] [206] 5-9-8 55 .... ChrisCatlin 4 61
(P A Blockley) *sn rdn along and outpcd towards rr: hdwy on outer 2f out: str run ins last: styd on wl: nt rch wnr* **11/4**[1]

6-00 3 1 3/4 **Mister Incredible**[4] [252] 4-9-5 54 .... (p) SaleemGolam(3) 5 56
(V Smith) *towards rr: swtchd lft and hdwy 2f out: rdn to chse wnr over 1f out: drvn and one one pce ins last* **8/1**[3]

5-42 4 2 1/2 **Soba Jones**[23] [59] 10-9-5 56 .... JasonEdmunds(3) 6 49
(J Balding) *trckd ldrs: effrt over 2f out: sn rdn and kpt on same pce* **11/4**[1]

500- 5 7 **Sundried Tomato**[114] [5834] 8-9-8 41 .... (p) TonyCulhane 1 28
(D W Chapman) *led: rdn along and hdd over 2f out: sn wknd* **25/1**

50-0 6 5 **Serieux**[29] [3] 8-9-8 68 .... (p) AdrianTNicholls 7 13
(D Nicholls) *towards rr: rdn along 1/2-way: nvr a factor* **11/2**[2]

000/ 7 6 **Zanderido**[421] [6512] 5-9-5 35 .... (v) JerryO'Dwyer(3) 2 —
(B S Rothwell) *chsd ldrs on inner: rdn along 1/2-way: sn wknd* **100/1**

000- 8 7 **Headland (USA)**[63] [6638] 9-9-8 31 .... (be) NCallan 8 —
(D W Chapman) *dwlt: a bhd* **50/1**

00-0 9 16 **Ronnie From Donny (IRE)**[28] [9] 7-9-8 35 ..... (bt[1]) RobbieFitzpatrick 3 —
(C J Teague) *chsd ldrs: rdn along 1/2-way: sn wknd* **100/1**

1m 16.11s (-0.79) **Going Correction** -0.175s/f (Stan) **9** Ran SP% **114.3**
Speed ratings (Par 101):98,97,94,91,82 75,67,58,36
CSF £10.01 TOTE £4.10: £1.50, £1.40, £2.60; EX 16.50 Trifecta £87.20 Pool: £277.70 - 2.26 winning units..The winner was bought in for 8,200gns.
Owner The Job Done Partnership **Bred** Helshaw Grange Stud, N Kent And H Phillips **Trained** Cowthorpe, N Yorks

FOCUS
A reasonable seller, the front pair capable for the grade. The winner was a fair sort this time last year and was well supported on his debut for Robin Bastiman.
Headland(USA) Official explanation: jockey said gelding missed the break

304 PONTIN'S FAMILY HOLIDAYS MAIDEN STKS 1m (F)
2:30 (2:31) (Class 5) 3-Y-0 **£2,817** (£838; £418; £209) **Stalls** Low

Form RPR

35 1 **Six Day War (IRE)**[15] [141] 3-9-3 .... ShaneKelly 4 78+
(J A Osborne) *chsd ldrs: effrt over 2f out and sn rdn: drvn and styd on ins last to ld nr fin* **4/1**[2]

4- **2** *3/4* **Zar Solitario**[68] [6570] 3-9-3 JoeFanning 8 76+
(M Johnston) *cl up: led 3f out: poushed clr wl over 1f out: edgd lft and rdn ins last: wknd and hdd towards fin* **10/11**[1]
3 *6* **Lady Gloria** 3-8-12 J-PGuillambert 11 58
(J G Given) *dwlt: sn in midfield: hdwy to chse ldrs 2f out: sn rdn and kpt on same pce* **50/1**
4- **4** *nk* **Strabinios King**[52] [6757] 3-9-3 DeanMcKeown 6 63
(P C Haslam) *trckd ldrs gng wl: effrt over 2f out: sn rdn and kpt on same pce* **12/1**
0-3 **5** *4* **Here's Blue Chip (IRE)**[14] [149] 3-9-3 TonyCulhane 5 54
(P W D'Arcy) *midfield: effrt over 2f out: sn rdn along and no imp* **9/1**
0-5 **6** *hd* **Intensifier (IRE)**[14] [149] 3-9-3 NCallan 1 54
(P A Blockley) *led: hdd 3f out: sn rdn along and wknd 2f out* **25/1**
54- **7** *2* **Spring Glory**[42] [6867] 3-8-12 SebSanders 3 45
(Sir Mark Prescott) *chsd ldrs: rdn along over 3f out and sn wknd* **13/2**[3]
06-5 **8** *1* **Flushed**[23] [60] 3-9-0 47 (be) StephenDonohoe(3) 9 48
(A J McCabe) *midfield: rdn along 3f out and sn wknd* **80/1**
0-0 **9** *7* **Marju's Gold**[10] [193] 3-9-3 ChrisCatlin 7 33
(E J O'Neill) *s.i.s: a bhd* **50/1**
4- **10** *7* **Barney's Dancer**[59] [6675] 3-8-9 JasonEdmunds(3) 2 13
(J Balding) *in tch: rdn along after 3f: sn lost pl and bhd* **40/1**
50- **11** *17* **Acece**[34] [6950] 3-8-12 KevinGhunowa(5) 10 —
(M Appleby) *a rr: t.o fnl 3f* **66/1**

1m 42.56s (-2.04) **Going Correction** -0.175s/f (Stan) **11** Ran SP% **116.3**
Speed ratings (Par 97):103,102,96,95,91 91,89,88,81,74 57
CSF £7.63 TOTE £5.50: £1.20, £1.10, £7.00; EX 9.70 Trifecta £211.20 Pool: £395.80 - 1.33 winning units..
Owner Mountgrange&Wood Hall Studs Booth Durkan **Bred** C Lilburn **Trained** Upper Lambourn, Berks
■ Stewards' Enquiry : Joe Fanning one-day ban: not riding to draw (Feb 10)

FOCUS
A fair maiden run in a decent winning time for a race like this, fractionally faster than the later handicap for older horses over the same trip. The front pair finished clear and the form looks fairly sound for the grade.

305 PONTIN'S BOOK EARLY CLAIMING STKS 1m 4f (F)
3:00 (3:00) (Class 6) 4-Y-0+ **£2,184** (£644; £322) **Stalls** Low

Form RPR
511- **1** **Jazrawy**[41] [6883] 5-8-10 57 LukeMorris(7) 5 64
(P W Hiatt) *mde all: rdn along 2f out: styd on strly appr last* **6/5**[1]
21-5 **2** *5* **Ionian Spring (IRE)**[26] [35] 12-9-3 75 DanielTudhope 1 56
(D Carroll) *hld up: smooth hdwy 4f out: rdn to chse wnr and hung lft over 1f out: sn drvn and one pce* **6/5**[1]
6 **3** *2 1/2* **My Friend Fritz**[13] [159] 7-9-1 ChrisCatlin 2 50
(P W Hiatt) *trckd ldrs: hdwy over 4f out: rdn to chse wnr 3f out: drvn and outpcd fnl 2f* **50/1**
0-00 **4** *6* **Mi Odds**[5] [242] 11-8-11 50 JimmyQuinn 6 36
(Mrs N Macauley) *hld up in rr: hdwy 4f out: rdn along wl over 2rf out and sn no imp* **16/1**[2]
35-0 **5** *5* **Contra Mundum (USA)**[19] [98] 4-9-3 75 PaulHanagan 3 38
(B S Rothwell) *chsd ldrs: rdn along over 3f out and sn wknd* **25/1**[3]
00-5 **6** *5* **Futoo (IRE)**[21] [78] 6-9-0 45 (b) TonyCulhane 8 23
(D W Chapman) *trckd ldrs: hdwy to chse wnr after 4f: rdn along over 3f out and sn wknd* **16/1**[2]
-5 **7** *5* **Win In Gold**[19] [98] 6-9-7 DaleGibson 4 22
(John A Harris) *chsd ldrs: rdn along 4f out: sn wknd* **33/1**
- **8** *30* **Vic's Charm (IRE)**[25] 6-8-10 KellyHarrison(7) 9 —
(D Carroll) *in tch: rdn along over 4f out: sn wknd* **50/1**
00-4 **9** *7* **Augustus Livius (IRE)**[29] [2] 4-8-7 39 (b) PaulFessey 7 —
(W Storey) *a towards rr* **33/1**

2m 38.55s (-3.54) **Going Correction** -0.175s/f (Stan)
WFA 4 from 5yo+ 4lb **9** Ran SP% **116.3**
Speed ratings (Par 101):104,100,99,95,91 88,85,65,60
CSF £2.55 TOTE £1.90: £1.10, £1.30, £6.40; EX 2.90 Trifecta £32.90 Pool: £470.74 - 10.15 winning units..Jazrawy was claimed by Mrs B. Ramsden for £8,000.
Owner P W Hiatt **Bred** Scuderia Antonella S R L **Trained** Hook Norton, Oxon

FOCUS
A two-horse race according to the market and that is how it turned out, though Jazrawy was always in control. Thanks to Jazrawy, the pace was good and the time solid for a race like this. The winner did not have to improve on his recent form, with the runner-up below par.
Augustus Livius(IRE) Official explanation: jockey said gelding lost its action

306 PONTINSBINGO.COM H'CAP 6f (F)
3:30 (3:31) (Class 6) (0-65,65) 4-Y-0+ **£2,388** (£705; £352) **Stalls** Low

Form RPR
64-1 **1** **Count Cougar (USA)**[7] [225] 7-8-6 60 6ex MichaelJStainton(5) 7 74
(S P Griffiths) *cl up: led 1/2-way: rdn wl over 1f out: drvn ins last and hld on wl* **7/2**[2]
30-0 **2** *hd* **Cleveland**[23] [63] 5-8-6 60 RussellKennemore(5) 3 73
(R Hollinshead) *chsd ldrs: wd st: hdwy 2f out: rdn over 1f out and ev ch ins last tl edgd lft and no ex nr line* **25/1**
521- **3** *3/4* **Ragad**[34] [6944] 4-8-8 57 BrettDoyle 2 68
(W Jarvis) *trckd ldrs: effdort 2f out and sn ev ch: rdn over 1f out: drvn and one pce ins last* **7/4**[1]
35-2 **4** *1/2* **Came Back (IRE)**[26] [33] 4-8-9 58 DaleGibson 4 68
(J Mackie) *towards rr: hdwy 2f out: rdn to chse ldrs and edgd lft over 1f out: kpt on ins last: nrst fin* **25/1**
1-10 **5** *3/4* **Hamaasy**[22] [66] 6-8-11 60 AdrianTNicholls 10 67
(D Nicholls) *chsd ldrs: rdn along over 2f out: sn drvn and kpt on same pce ent last* **8/1**
50-0 **6** *nk* **Another Gladiator (USA)**[16] [131] 4-8-5 54 (b[1]) CatherineGannon 1 61
(K A Ryan) *dwlt and sn rdn along in rr: hdwy on inner 2f out: styd on u.p ins last: nrst fin* **16/1**
004- **7** *1 1/4* **Hits Only Cash**[83] [6404] 5-8-8 57 DeanMcKeown 6 60
(J Pearce) *sn outpcd and bhd tl styd on fnl 2f* **25/1**
00-6 **8** *1* **Winthorpe (IRE)**[29] [3] 7-8-13 62 GrahamGibbons 9 62
(J J Quinn) *in tch: effrt over 2f out: sn rdn and no imp* **22/1**
113- **9** *3* **Larky's Lob**[38] [6930] 8-8-9 65 JamesO'Reilly(7) 5 56
(J O'Reilly) *led: rdn along and hdd 1/2-way: sn wknd* **15/2**
0211 **10** *nk* **Mill By The Stream**[5] [241] 5-8-4 60 6ex HaddenFrost(7) 11 50
(Tom Dascombe) *midfield: effrt over 2f out: sn rdn and btn* **6/1**[3]
55-0 **11** *12* **Roman Empire**[7] [228] 7-8-7 56 (v) ChrisCatlin 8 10
(P A Blockley) *a rr* **80/1**

1m 15.35s (-1.55) **Going Correction** -0.175s/f (Stan) **11** Ran SP% **118.8**
Speed ratings (Par 101):103,102,101,101,100 99,98,96,92,92 76
CSF £95.06 CT £207.75 TOTE £4.20: £1.80, £6.20, £1.20; EX 117.90 Trifecta £311.90 Part won. Pool: £439.39 - 0.94 winning units..
Owner M Grant **Bred** Angus Glen Farm (1996) Ltd **Trained** Easingwold, N Yorks

FOCUS
An ordinary handicap, but several of these had been in good form at this track in recent weeks. The pace was solid and the form looks reliable, with the winner and runner-up back to their best.
Mill By The Stream Official explanation: jockey said gelding was never travelling

307 PONTIN'S HOLIDAYS CONDITIONS STKS 6f (F)
4:00 (4:00) (Class 2) 3-Y-0+ **£11,334** (£3,372; £1,685; £841) **Stalls** Low

Form RPR
0-52 **1** **Waterside (IRE)**[7] [227] 8-9-5 89 SebSanders 4 102
(G L Moore) *mde virtually all: rdn wl over 1f out: drvn ins last: styd on wl* **5/4**[1]
-141 **2** *1 1/2* **Qadar (IRE)**[10] [198] 5-9-5 102 (b) NCallan 1 98
(N P Littmoden) *trckd ldng pair: effrt to chal wl over 1f out: sn rdn and ev ch tl drvn ins last and no ex towards fin* **13/8**[2]
6-24 **3** *3 1/2* **Prince Tum Tum (USA)**[7] [227] 7-9-5 88 DeanMcKeown 3 87
(D Shaw) *trckd ldrs: poushed along over 2f out: sn rdn: drvn wl over 1f out: kpt on same pce* **10/1**
365- **4** *1/2* **Bahamian Pirate (USA)**[127] [5578] 12-9-5 97 AdrianTNicholls 5 86
(D Nicholls) *cl up: effrt 2f out: sn rdn and wknd ent last* **9/1**[3]
3-52 **5** *1 1/4* **Certain Justice (USA)**[10] [191] 9-9-5 72 HayleyTurner 6 82
(Stef Liddiard) *chsd ldrs: rdn along wl over 2f out: kpt on same pce* **14/1**
60-6 **6** *22* **Drury Lane (IRE)**[20] [83] 7-9-5 42 (p) TonyCulhane 2 16
(D W Chapman) *sn outpcd and a bhd* **200/1**

1m 14.81s (-2.09) **Going Correction** -0.175s/f (Stan) **6** Ran SP% **108.8**
Speed ratings (Par 109):106,104,99,98,97 67
CSF £3.24 TOTE £1.90: £1.50, £1.10; EX 4.20.
Owner Nigel Shields **Bred** Yeomanstown Stud **Trained** Woodingdean, E Sussex
■ A one-two for owner Nigel Shields.

FOCUS
A classy little conditions event featuring a full range of abilities, and the pace was honest without being breakneck. The winner is better than ever, but the second is not the same horse as he is at Lingfield.

NOTEBOOK
Waterside(IRE), a pacesetter in his younger days though ridden with more restraint in his recent career, reverted to his old tactics over this shorter trip and that proved the right move. Setting just a fair pace, he faced a stern challenge from Qadar over the last couple of furlongs, but with his stamina proving an asset found more than enough to keep him at bay. (op 6-4)
Qadar(IRE), who would have been 13lb worse off with the winner in a handicap, had every chance but found his rival kept on pulling out a bit more. On the face of it he should have done better on these terms, but coming from off a strong pace on Polytrack is his thing and these conditions and the way the race was run would not have been ideal. (op 5-4 tchd 7-4)
Prince Tum Tum(USA), who had only 1lb to find with Waterside on these terms but a stone with Qadar, is a much better horse on Polytrack and this drop in trip was not ideal either. He kept on to snatch third and probably achieved as much as could be expected under the circumstances. (op 16-1)
Bahamian Pirate(USA), winner of the 2004 Nunthorpe and returning from a four-month break, had been successful on his last visit here six and a half years ago, winning a handicap over this trip off a mark of 58. He held a good position early, but the old legs were unable to keep him in touch with the Nigel Shields pair and he tired late on. He should have done better strictly at the weights, but that is fairly meaningless for a horse of his age and whether he will be able to find another opportunity remains to be seen. (op 11-2)
Certain Justice(USA) had plenty to find with the front quartet at the weights and was soon struggling. (op 16-1)

308 PONTINS.COM H'CAP 1m (F)
4:30 (4:31) (Class 5) (0-75,75) 4-Y-0+ **£3,071** (£906; £453) **Stalls** Low

Form RPR
0-13 **1** **Wahoo Sam (USA)**[18] [109] 7-8-11 70 (p) NCallan 4 78
(K A Ryan) *mde all: qcknd over 2f out: rdn wl over 1f out: drvn ins last and styd on gamely* **3/1**[1]
152- **2** *nk* **Kabis Amigos**[152] [4961] 5-8-2 61 oh4 (t) SilvestreDeSousa 6 68
(D Nicholls) *chsd wnr: rdn to chal over 1f out: drvn and ev ch ins last: kpt on* **9/1**
2-40 **3** *3/4* **Speed Dial Harry (IRE)**[10] [191] 5-9-1 74 (v) RobertWinston 2 79
(C R Dore) *trckd ldrs on inner: rdn along wl over 2f out: drvn and styd on ins last* **7/1**
46-4 **4** *1/2* **Boundless Prospect (USA)**[19] [101] 8-8-11 70 JimmyQuinn 3 74
(Miss Gay Kelleway) *rr: pushed along over 3f out: rdn and hdwy on outer wl over 1f out: kpt on ins last: nrst fin* **9/1**
0/12 **5** *1* **Activity (IRE)**[14] [151] 8-8-3 67 DuranFentiman(5) 9 69
(M J Gingell) *chsd ldrs: rdn along over 2f out: drvn and kpt on ins last* **7/2**[2]
-412 **6** *1* **Dudley Docker (IRE)**[19] [102] 5-8-7 73 (v) KellyHarrison(7) 7 73
(D Carroll) *chsd ldng pair: rdn along over 2f out: sn edgd lft and wknd over 1f out* **9/2**[3]
200- **7** *32* **Blue Patrick**[86] [1207] 7-9-2 75 (p) ChrisCatlin 8 8
(P A Blockley) *a rr: rdn along and outpcd 1/2-way: sn wl bhd* **33/1**

1m 42.6s (-2.00) **Going Correction** -0.175s/f (Stan) **7** Ran SP% **100.8**
Speed ratings (Par 103):103,102,101,101,100 99,67
CSF £22.77 CT £114.34 TOTE £3.20: £2.30, £3.80; EX 29.40 Trifecta £83.20 Pool: £330.47 - 2.82 winning units. Place 6 £8.17, Place 5 £1.97.
Owner Blackhurst,Bridge,Moll,O'Brien **Bred** Stonereath Farms Inc **Trained** Hambleton, N Yorks
■ Namroud (9/1) was withdrawn on veterinary advice. R4 applies, deduct 10p in the £.

FOCUS
An ordinary handicap run at no more than a fair pace and once again the place to be was out in front. The race has been rated through the third.
T/Plt: £9.70 to a £1 stake. Pool: £54,652.85. 4,095.65 winning tickets. T/Qpdt: £2.40 to a £1 stake. Pool: £3,325.70. 1,024.80 winning tickets. JR

[288]LINGFIELD (L-H)
Wednesday, January 31

OFFICIAL GOING: Standard
Wind: Light, across Weather: Sunny

309 PONTIN'S "BOOK EARLY" H'CAP (DIV I) 1m 2f (P)
1:00 (1:00) (Class 6) (0-58,58) 4-Y-0+ **£1,706** (£503; £252) **Stalls** Low

Form RPR
0-31 **1** **Apache Fort**[10] [203] 4-8-9 53 6ex ShaneKelly 1 61
(T Keddy) *lw: chsd ldrs: shkn up and effrt over 1f out: rdn to ld ins fnl f: pushed out and in command last 50 yds* **3/1**[1]
1-40 **2** *1/2* **Blackmail (USA)**[11] [195] 9-9-2 58 EddieAhern 2 65
(P Mitchell) *hld up towards rr: hdwy over 3f out: rdn over 2f out: r.o to chse wnr ins fnl f: hld last 50 yds* **8/1**

0-62 **3** 1 1/4 **Voice Mail**[25] 52 8-8-4 **53**........(b) DavidProbert(7) 11 58
(A M Balding) *s.i.s: t.k.h and hld up in rr: hdwy on inner over 2f out: led 1f out: hdd ins fnl f: fdd nr fin* **12/1**

302- **4** nk **Myrtle Bay (IRE)**[137] 5365 4-8-6 **53** ow1........ NeilChalmers(3) 6 57
(J C Tuck) *chsd ldng pair: rdn over 2f out: led over 1f out: sn hdd: kpt on same pce* **25/1**

05-5 **5** 1/2 **Red Sail**[21] 85 6-8-11 **53**........(b) OscarUrbina 8 56
(Dr J D Scargill) *hld up in rr: hdwy on outer wl over 2f out: kpt on u.p fnl f: nt rch ldrs* **5/1**[3]

-031 **6** shd **Oasis Sun (IRE)**[11] 187 4-8-5 **49**........(v) HayleyTurner 12 52
(J R Best) *in tch in midfield: rdn over 2f out: kpt on same pce fr over 1f out* **16/1**

61-2 **7** 3/4 **Ciccone**[12] 181 4-9-0 **58**........(p) FergusSweeney 9 59
(G L Moore) *lw: s.i.s: nt clr run over 2f out tl wl over 1f out: kpt on fnl f: nvr trbld ldrs* **13/2**

40-2 **8** 2 **Indigo Dancer**[11] 187 4-8-2 **46** oh2........(b) ChrisCatlin 3 44
(C F Wall) *w.w in midfield: rdn and effrt on inner 2f out: no imp fnl f* **4/1**[2]

20-0 **9** 3/4 **Native American**[28] 19 5-8-8 **50**........ DaleGibson 10 46
(T D McCarthy) *chsd ldr: rdn over 2f out: wknd 2f out* **16/1**

052- **10** shd **Rose Muwasim**[32] 6988 4-8-6 **57**........ WilliamBuick(7) 4 53
(K J Burke) *hld up towards rr on outer: hdwy on outer over 3f out: no prog over 1f out* **14/1**

20-6 **11** 3 **Blue Empire (IRE)**[22] 80 6-9-2 **58**........ TPQueally 5 48
(C R Dore) *led: rdn over 2f out: hdd over 1f out: sn wknd* **25/1**

2m 5.84s (-1.95) **Going Correction** -0.15s/f (Stan)
WFA 4 from 5yo+ 2lb 11 Ran SP% **119.9**
Speed ratings (Par 101):101,100,99,99,98 98,98,96,96,96 93
CSF £28.21 CT £252.74 TOTE £3.20: £1.50, £3.00, £4.00; EX 30.70 Trifecta £114.00 Part won. Pool: £160.66 - 0.30 winning tickets..
Owner Andrew Duffield **Bred** Juddmonte Farms Ltd **Trained** Newmarket, Suffolk

FOCUS
A modest handicap in which the pace was just fair and the winning time 1.1 seconds slower than the second division. The form is ordinary rated around the third and fourth.

310 GO PONTIN'S CLASSIFIED CLAIMING STKS 6f (P)
1:30 (1:31) (Class 6) 4-Y-0+ **£2,184** (£644; £322) **Stalls** Low

Form RPR

-560 **1** **Mulberry Lad (IRE)**[4] 268 5-8-11 53........ JimCrowley 9 60
(P W Hiatt) *chsd ldrs: rdn to chse ldr over 2f out: led over 1f out: r.o wl* **8/1**

0534 **2** 3/4 **Franksalot (IRE)**[2] 292 7-9-5 60........ DanielTudhope 7 66
(I W McInnes) *t.k.h: hld up in rr: hdwy 2f out: swtchd lft over 1f out: r.o fnl f: wnt 2nd nr fin: nt rch wnr* **7/2**[1]

6460 **3** nk **Desert Light (IRE)**[7] 236 6-8-11 54........(v) DaneO'Neill 8 57
(D Shaw) *t.k.h: hld up in midfield: hdwy over 1f out: r.o u.p fnl f: nrst fin* **6/1**[3]

510- **4** shd **Danish Blues (IRE)**[84] 6395 4-8-13 58........ IanMongan 2 59
(D E Cantillon) *t.k.h: chsd ldrs: rdn and ev ch wl over 1f out: chsd wnr ins fnl f: kpt on same pce: demoted cl home* **7/2**[1]

65-4 **5** 3/4 **Labelled With Love**[21] 86 7-8-12 52........(t) PatCosgrave 10 55
(J R Boyle) *racd in midfield on outer: hdwy and rdn over 2f out: kpt on: nt pce to rch ldrs* **15/2**

230- **6** nk **Feelin Irie (IRE)**[84] 6395 4-8-7 58........ EddieAhern 11 49
(J R Boyle) *taken down early: led: rdn and hdd over 1f out: no ex* **12/1**

-622 **7** 3/4 **City For Conquest (IRE)**[5] 254 4-8-10 59........(b) ChrisCatlin 5 50
(T J Pitt) *s.i.s: rdn and effrt over 2f out: nt pce to rch ldrs* **9/2**[2]

10-6 **8** 1 1/2 **Binnion Bay (IRE)**[21] 86 6-8-12 54........(b) AmirQuinn(3) 6 51
(J J Bridger) *in tch in midfield: rdn over 2f out: struggling whn sltly hmpd over 1f out: no ch after* **16/1**

0004 **9** 1 1/2 **Miss Redactive**[3] 272 4-7-11 38........(v) FrankiePickard(7) 1 35
(M D I Usher) *hld up in rr: rdn over 2f out: n.d* **66/1**

60-0 **10** 2 **Hello Deauville (FR)**[9] 207 4-8-2 40........ DaleGibson 3 27
(J Akehurst) *chsd ldr: rdn over 2f out: wknd qckly jst over 1f out* **66/1**

1m 11.29s (-1.52) **Going Correction** -0.15s/f (Stan) 10 Ran SP% **116.3**
Speed ratings (Par 101):104,103,102,102,101 101,100,98,96,93
CSF £36.07 TOTE £14.40: £3.40, £1.90, £3.00; EX 49.40 Trifecta £100.40 Part won. Pool: £141.41 - 0.10 winning tickets..
Owner P W Hiatt **Bred** Mountarmstrong Stud **Trained** Hook Norton, Oxon
■ Stewards' Enquiry : Daniel Tudhope one-day ban; careless riding (Feb 11)

FOCUS
An ordinary claimer, but at least the pace was decent and the form looks solid for the grade.

311 PONTINS.COM MAIDEN STKS 6f (P)
2:00 (2:01) (Class 5) 3-Y-0+ **£2,914** (£867; £433; £216) **Stalls** Low

Form RPR

6- **1** **Fustaan (IRE)**[166] 4559 3-8-5........ DaleGibson 7 73+
(M P Tregoning) *lw: mde most: pushed along and lft 3l clr over 2f out: stdy on u.p fnl f* **2/1**[1]

030/ **2** 1 1/2 **Ellcon (IRE)**[572] 3304 4-9-7 66........ ShaneKelly 10 68
(J A Osborne) *chsd ldrs: rdn and lft 2nd bnd over 2f out: edgd rt over 1f out: kpt on* **12/1**

3 1 1/2 **Esteem Machine (USA)** 3-8-10........ BrettDoyle 8 73+
(D R C Elsworth) *scope: unf: bit bkwd: s.i.s: plld hrd: jnd wnr over 3f out: hung rt & wd bnd over 2f out: nt rcvr: r.o cl home* **20/1**

003- **4** hd **Silkie Smooth (IRE)**[86] 6377 3-8-5 70........ MatthewHenry 5 59
(B W Hills) *t.k.h: hld up in midfield: hdwy over 2f out: lft 3rd over 2f out: kpt on same pce: lost 3rd nr fin* **5/1**[3]

46-2 **5** 1 3/4 **Ginger Pop**[17] 128 3-8-10 71........ SebSanders 11 59
(G G Margarson) *plld hrd: chsd ldrs: rdn over 3f out: outpcd over 2f out: kpt on same pce* **7/1**

6 nk **Pride Of Northcare (IRE)** 3-8-10........ PatCosgrave 6 58+
(G A Huffer) *leggy: t.k.h: hld up on outer: outpcd over 2f out: kpt on fnl f: nt trble ldrs* **40/1**

0-2 **7** 1 1/4 **Descargo**[27] 36 3-7-12........ WilliamBuick(7) 3 49
(C G Cox) *t.k.h: hld up in tch: rdn and outpcd wl over 2f out* **9/1**

8 nk **Waqaarr** 3-8-10........ TonyCulhane 4 53+
(M R Channon) *w'like: leggy: t.k.h: chsd ldrs: rdn and outpcd over 2f out: no ch after* **7/2**[2]

6-0 **9** 1 **Epidaurian King (IRE)**[27] 36 4-9-12........ DanielTudhope 2 54
(D Shaw) *w'like: s.i.s: a bhd* **25/1**

0-0 **10** 2 1/2 **Alucica**[19] 106 4-9-7........ DaneO'Neill 9 42
(D Shaw) *w'like: stdd s: a bhd: rdn over 3f out: no ch last 2f* **100/1**

0 **11** 7 **Satwa Baron**[14] 160 3-8-7........ MarcHalford(3) 1 22
(D R C Elsworth) *in tch in midfield tl rdn and outpcd 3f out: sn wl bhd* **20/1**

1m 12.8s (-0.01) **Going Correction** -0.15s/f (Stan)
WFA 3 from 4yo 16lb 11 Ran SP% **119.2**
Speed ratings (Par 103):94,92,90,89,87 87,85,84,83,80 70
CSF £26.76 TOTE £2.50: £1.50, £2.90, £4.70; EX 29.90 Trifecta £152.60 Part won. Pool: £215.07 - 0.10 winning tickets..
Owner Hamdan Al Maktoum **Bred** Shadwell Estate Company Limited **Trained** Lambourn, Berks

FOCUS
Not a great maiden and very few ever got into it, but a couple did show some promise for the future. The race is rated through the runner-up to his juvenile form.
Esteem Machine(USA) ◆ Official explanation: vet said colt had a cut on left side of mouth and hung badly right
Epidaurian King(IRE) Official explanation: trainer said gelding lost a shoe
Satwa Baron Official explanation: trainer said colt cut its mouth in transit and would not face the bridle

312 PONTIN'S HOLIDAYS H'CAP 7f (P)
2:30 (2:30) (Class 5) (0-75,80) 3-Y-0 **£3,238** (£963; £481; £240) **Stalls** Low

Form RPR

21-1 **1** **Si Foo (USA)**[9] 216 3-9-8 **80** 6ex........ LPKeniry 8 89+
(A M Balding) *t.k.h: pressed ldr tl led gng wl 3f out: rdn over 2f out: clr ins fnl f: readily* **5/6**[1]

56-1 **2** 2 1/2 **High Tribute**[14] 160 3-9-2 **74**........(t) SebSanders 5 76
(Sir Mark Prescott) *swtg: t.k.h: trckd ldrs: wnt 2nd over 2f out: rdn and ev ch 2f out: outpcd fnl f* **4/1**[2]

26-6 **3** 1 3/4 **Lawyer To World**[28] 21 3-7-11 **62**........(p) WilliamBuick(7) 2 60
(N A Callaghan) *lw: s.i.s: hdwy 2f out: styd on u.p: wnt 3rd ins fnl f: nt trble ldrs* **12/1**

06-6 **4** 1 **Proper (IRE)**[11] 199 3-8-11 **69**........ EdwardCreighton 6 64
(M R Channon) *hld up on outer: rdn over 2f out: kpt on but no ch w ldng pair after* **25/1**

054- **5** 1/2 **Dolly Coughdrop (IRE)**[121] 5731 3-8-13 **71**........ PhillipMakin 1 65
(K R Burke) *hld up in rr: nt clr run over 1f out: kpt on: n.d* **33/1**

35-3 **6** 1 1/2 **Wilmington**[7] 231 3-8-9 **70**........(b) JamesDoyle(3) 4 60
(N P Littmoden) *plld v hrd: hld up in tch: rdn over 2f out: sn outpcd* **16/1**

20-4 **7** shd **Toucantini**[14] 160 3-8-7 **65**........ ChrisCatlin 3 55
(R Charlton) *t.k.h: trckd ldrs: riiden over 2f out: chsd ldng pair wl over 1f out: wknd fnl f* **16/1**

3-22 **8** 3/4 **Not Too Taxing**[18] 116 3-8-10 **68**........ DaneO'Neill 7 56
(R Hannon) *led: rdn and hdd 3f out: wknd 2f out* **6/1**[3]

1m 26.57s (0.68) **Going Correction** -0.15s/f (Stan) 8 Ran SP% **115.1**
Speed ratings (Par 97):90,87,85,84,83 81,81,80
CSF £4.37 CT £22.28 TOTE £1.70: £1.10, £1.50, £3.00; EX 4.20 Trifecta £37.20 Pool: £524.74 - 10.00 winning tickets..
Owner Norman Cheng **Bred** N Cheng **Trained** Kingsclere, Hants

FOCUS
They went no pace at all early which resulted in several pulling hard. Not surprisingly the winning time was moderate for the type of contest but the front pair are on the upgrade.
Wilmington Official explanation: jockey said gelding ran too free in the early stages

313 PONTINSBINGO.COM H'CAP 1m (P)
3:00 (3:00) (Class 6) (0-60,61) 4-Y-0+ **£2,388** (£705; £352) **Stalls** High

Form RPR

3-1 **1** **Spot The Subbie (IRE)**[17] 130 4-9-2 **59**........ IanMongan 1 70+
(Jamie Poulton) *b.hind: lw: led for 2f: rdn over 3f out: sltly outpcd over 2f out: hdwy over 1f out: led ins fnl f: eased nr fin* **9/4**[1]

2-60 **2** 1 1/2 **Green Pirate**[10] 206 5-8-6 **56**........ WilliamBuick(7) 12 64
(W M Brisbourne) *lw: stdd s: hld up in rr: hdwy on outer over 2f out: stl plenty to do over 1f out: r.o strly fnl f: wnt 2nd nr fin* **10/1**

0202 **3** 1/2 **Roman Boy (ARG)**[6] 238 8-9-1 **58**........(v) MickyFenton 8 65
(Stef Liddiard) *chsd ldrs: rdn and wnt 2nd over 2f out: led 1f out: sn hdd: outpcd by wnr last 100 yds* **10/1**

-462 **4** hd **Mystic Man (FR)**[7] 235 9-9-2 **59**........(p) DanielTudhope 2 65
(I W McInnes) *b: hld up in midfield: hdwy gng wl over 2f out: nt clr run over 1f out tl jst ins fnl f: styd on same pce last 100 yds* **7/2**[3]

2-22 **5** hd **King After**[2] 292 5-8-10 **53**........ BrettDoyle 3 59
(J R Best) *t.k.h: hld up in tch: rdn wl over 1f out: kpt on same pce fnl f* **3/1**[2]

6-40 **6** hd **Moyoko (IRE)**[17] 130 4-8-12 **55**........ OscarUrbina 10 60
(M Blanshard) *b.hind: in tch in midfield: rdn 3f out: kpt on fnl f: nt pce to rch ldrs* **16/1**

36-5 **7** 1/2 **State Dilemma (IRE)**[7] 235 6-9-2 **59**........(v) DaneO'Neill 5 63
(D Shaw) *bhd: pushed along 5f out: stl plenty to do and hung lft jst over 1f out: r.o fnl f: n.d* **12/1**

0-00 **8** 1 1/4 **Hand Chime**[10] 206 10-8-12 **55**........ AdamKirby 7 56
(Ernst Oertel) *hld up towards rr: effrt 2f out: nvr trbld ldrs* **66/1**

00-4 **9** hd **Nikki Bea (IRE)**[7] 233 4-8-13 **56**........ AdrianMcCarthy 4 57
(Jamie Poulton) *pressed ldr tl led 6f out: rdn 2f out: hdd 1f out: wknd fnl f* **14/1**

00-0 **10** 2 **Russian Mist (IRE)**[21] 92 4-8-12 **55**........ PatCosgrave 11 51
(M J Wallace) *w ldrs: rdn over 2f out: wknd over 1f out* **25/1**

660- **11** 1 1/4 **Kew The Music**[125] 5636 7-9-1 **58**........ ChrisCatlin 9 52
(M R Channon) *bit bkwd: a bhd: rdn over 2f out: no prog* **25/1**

1m 37.5s (-1.93) **Going Correction** -0.15s/f (Stan) 11 Ran SP% **125.6**
Speed ratings (Par 101):103,101,101,100,100 100,99,98,98,96 95
CSF £28.22 CT £205.32 TOTE £2.80: £1.20, £2.40, £2.90; EX 43.40 Trifecta £383.40 Part won. Pool: £540.09 - 0.33 winning tickets..
Owner Mrs Ann Casey **Bred** Mrs Ann Casey **Trained** Whitcombe, Dorset

FOCUS
Moderate handicap from with the bulk of the runners finishing in a heap, but solid enough rated around the placed horses.

314 PONTIN'S FAMILY HOLIDAYS H'CAP 1m (P)
3:30 (3:30) (Class 4) (0-80,81) 4-Y-0+
£4,674 (£1,399; £699; £350; £174; £87) **Stalls** High

Form RPR

1-22 **1** **Top Mark**[9] 211 5-8-12 **73**........ FergusSweeney 8 83
(J R Boyle) *lw: led for 1f: pressed ldr tl rdn to ld 2f out: carried rt ins fnl f: hld on wl u.p: all out* **7/2**[1]

-121 **2** nk **Rebellious Spirit**[9] 211 4-9-6 **81** 6ex........ JimCrowley 1 90
(P W Hiatt) *lw: chsd ldr tl led after 1f: rdn and hdd 2f out: edgd rt and kpt on same pce fnl f* **7/2**[1]

50-6 **3** 1 1/2 **Spring Goddess (IRE)**[4] 261 6-8-11 **72**.......................... AdamKirby 2 78
(A P Jarvis) *trckd ldrs: chsd ldng pair and rdn jst over 2f out: kpt on same pce* **4/1**[2]

0-53 **4** 3/4 **Sonny Parkin**[7] 233 5-8-12 **73**.....................................(v) PatCosgrave 6 77
(G A Huffer) *slowly away: prog 3f out: rdn and effrt to chse ldrs over 1f out: no hdwy ins fnl f* **5/1**[3]

5 **5** 1 **Brookby (NZ)**[9] 211 7-8-7 **68**..................................(t) EdwardCreighton 3 70
(Miss Sheena West) *hld up in tch: rdn and hdwy on inner 2f out: no hdwy ins fnl f* **12/1**

50-0 **6** 2 **Mister Benedictine**[11] 191 4-8-4 **70**................................. DJMoran(5) 7 67
(B W Duke) *chsd ldrs: rdn over 2f out: kpt on same pce last 2f* **16/1**

05-0 **7** 3/4 **Casablanca Minx (IRE)**[10] 205 4-8-8 **72**...............(b[1]) JamesDoyle(3) 5 67
(N P Littmoden) *a last pair: drvn over 3f out: no ch last 2f* **16/1**

431- **8** 2 1/2 **Fasylitator (IRE)**[194] 3712 5-9-2 **77**.................................... DaneO'Neill 4 66
(D K Ivory) *t.k.h: hld up in tch: hdwy to chse ldrs wl over 2f out: wknd wl over 1f out* **5/1**[3]

1m 36.82s (-2.61) **Going Correction** -0.15s/f (Stan) **8** Ran SP% **117.2**
Speed ratings (Par 105):107,106,105,104,103 101,100,98
CSF £16.36 CT £51.22 TOTE £3.50: £1.40, £1.60, £2.00; EX 11.10 Trifecta £34.30 Pool: £610.85 - 12.62 winning tickets..
Owner M Khan X2 **Bred** Ewar Stud Farms **Trained** Epsom, Surrey

FOCUS
A fairly steadily-run contest in which it proved difficult to challenge from off the pace and the form is rated around the principals.

315 PONTIN'S "BOOK EARLY" H'CAP (DIV II) 1m 2f (P)
4:00 (4:00) (Class 6) (0-58,58) 4-Y-0+ **£1,706** (£503; £252) **Stalls** Low

Form RPR

45-3 **1** **Play Up Pompey**[28] 19 5-8-10 **55**................................ AmirQuinn(3) 5 64
(J J Bridger) *s.i.s: hld up in midfield: hdwy 3f out: rdn to chse ldr jst over 2f out: led last 100 yds: r.o strly* **7/1**

0-20 **2** 1 1/2 **Sahara Prince (IRE)**[3] 274 7-7-12 **47**......................(p) WilliamBuick(7) 1 53
(K A Morgan) *led: rdn and clr 2f out: hdd last 100 yds: nt pce of wnr* **9/1**

-113 **3** 3/4 **Earl Kraul (IRE)**[17] 129 4-8-8 **52**......................................(b) BrettDoyle 4 57
(G L Moore) *stdd s: t.k.h: hld up in rr: plld out and hdwy wl over 2f out: rdn to chse ldrs over 1f out: one pced ins last* **3/1**[1]

21-3 **4** nk **Rowan Warning**[17] 130 5-9-1 **57**.................................... GeorgeBaker 2 61
(J R Boyle) *lw: hld up in midfield on inner: hdwy over 2f out: rdn wl over 1f out: kpt on same pce ins fnl f* **10/3**[2]

3-01 **5** 1 1/4 **Lobengula (IRE)**[12] 180 5-9-2 **58**................................ DanielTudhope 9 60
(I W McInnes) *hld up bhd: hdwy gng wl 3f out: chsd ldrs and rdn 2f out: one pced* **9/2**[3]

600- **6** 7 **Future Deal**[81] 6435 6-8-10 **52**.. PaulEddery 7 40
(C A Horgan) *s.i.s: rdn and hdwy on outer wl over 2f out: wknd wl over 1f out* **16/1**

3516 **7** nk **Diktatorship (IRE)**[10] 203 4-8-2 **51** ow1..........(tp) AshleyHamblett(5) 11 39
(Ernst Oertel) *chsd ldr: rdn 3f out: wknd over 2f out* **12/1**

30-0 **8** 1 **Camp Attack**[28] 19 4-8-8 **52**... LPKeniry 10 38
(S Dow) *t.k.h: hld up in midfield: hdwy over 3f out: chsd ldr briefly over 2f out: sn rdn and wknd* **12/1**

300- **9** shd **Coppermalt (USA)**[73] 3035 9-8-4 **46** oh1.......................(v) DaleGibson 6 32
(R Curtis) *chsd ldrs: rdn and struggling over 3f out: bhd last 2f* **20/1**

05-0 **10** 1 1/4 **Night Groove (IRE)**[9] 212 4-8-10 **57**........................(b) JamesDoyle(3) 3 40
(N P Littmoden) *chsd ldrs rdn over 3f out: wl bhd last 2f* **16/1**

2m 4.74s (-3.05) **Going Correction** -0.15s/f (Stan)
WFA 4 from 5yo+ 2lb **10** Ran SP% **120.7**
Speed ratings (Par 101):106,104,104,103,102 97,97,96,96,95
CSF £70.85 CT £233.17 TOTE £11.20: £2.40, £4.70, £1.20; EX 84.10 Trifecta £395.70 Part won. Pool: £557.43 - 0.51 winning tickets..
Owner Double-R-Racing **Bred** M Pollitt **Trained** Liphook, Hants

FOCUS
A moderate handicap run at a fair gallop, and the winning time was still 1.1 seconds faster than the first division. The form looks reliable rated around the first two.
Diktatorship(IRE) Official explanation: jockey said gelding hung left towards rail
Camp Attack Official explanation: jockey said gelding hung right throughout

316 GO PONTIN'S H'CAP 1m 5f (P)
4:30 (4:30) (Class 5) (0-75,75) 4-Y-0+ **£3,238** (£963; £481; £240) **Stalls** Low

Form RPR

521- **1** **Nawow**[34] 6885 7-9-7 **71**.. DaneO'Neill 5 81
(P D Cundell) *dwlt: hld up in last pair: hdwy over 2f out: rdn to chse ldr 2f out: led jst over 1f out: hld on wl* **5/2**[1]

0-32 **2** nk **Kavi (IRE)**[7] 232 7-9-4 **68**... OscarUrbina 9 78
(Simon Earle) *trckd ldng pair: led over 2f out: sn rdn: hdd jst over 1f out: unable qckn wl ins fnl f* **3/1**[2]

440- **3** shd **Gee Dee Nen**[96] 6205 4-9-3 **75**...................................... SaleemGolam(3) 1 85+
(M H Tompkins) *stdd s: hld up in last pair: hdwy on inner over 3f out: swtchd rt over 2f out: styd on u.p fnl f* **4/1**[3]

/0-5 **4** 4 **Flying Spirit (IRE)**[7] 232 8-9-4 **68**.............................(b) GeorgeBaker 3 72
(G L Moore) *hld up in tch: hdwy whn n.m.r wl over 2f out: nt clr run and lost pl bnd over 2f out: kpt on same pce after* **7/1**

155- **5** 4 **Ocean Pride (IRE)**[40] 6917 4-8-13 **75**........................... HaddenFrost(7) 8 73
(D E Pipe) *t.k.h: led tl over 2f out: sn rdn: wknd over 1f out* **9/2**

100- **6** 4 **Airbound (USA)**[49] 6070 4-9-0 **69**..................................... IanMongan 7 61
(H J L Dunlop) *hld up wl in tch: rdn and dropped rr 4f out: no ch last 2f* **14/1**

000- **7** 5 **Desperation (IRE)**[47] 3388 5-9-6 **70**............................... SamHitchcott 4 54
(M R Channon) *w ldr: rdn whn short of room and snatched up wl over2f out: no ch after* **20/1**

2m 45.47s (-2.83) **Going Correction** -0.15s/f (Stan)
WFA 4 from 5yo+ 5lb **7** Ran SP% **115.7**
Speed ratings (Par 103):102,101,101,99,96 94,91
CSF £10.52 CT £28.30 TOTE £2.60: £1.80, £2.50; EX 13.20 Trifecta £32.10 Pool: £588.16 - 13.00 winning tickets. Place 6 £22.56, Place 5 £9.46.
Owner Ian M Brown **Bred** Kirtlington Stud Ltd **Trained** Compton, Berks
■ Stewards' Enquiry : Hadden Frost one-day ban; careless riding (Feb 22)

FOCUS
Not a bad little handicap, and it was quite competitive, too. With the time reasonable the form looks sound.
T/Plt: £20.50 to a £1 stake. Pool: £57,146.15. 2,033.60 winning tickets. T/Qpdt: £4.20 to a £1 stake. Pool: £4,054.20. 699.50 winning tickets. SP

[302]SOUTHWELL (L-H)
Thursday, February 1

OFFICIAL GOING: Standard
Wind: moderate, half-across

317 PHOTO ALBUMS FROM BONUSPRINT.COM H'CAP (DIV I) 5f (F)
1:20 (1:20) (Class 6) (0-58,63) 4-Y-0+ **£1,876** (£554; £277) **Stalls** High

Form RPR

-053 **1** **Egyptian Lord**[6] 251 4-8-11 **54**................................(b) RobbieFitzpatrick 9 70
(Peter Grayson) *hmpd s and rr: smooth hdwy to trck ldrs after 2f: effrt wl over 1f out: rdn and kpt on ins last to ld last 100 yds* **13/2**[2]

4-11 **2** 3/4 **Count Cougar (USA)**[2] 306 7-8-12 **60** 6ex.......... MichaelJStainton(5) 2 73
(S P Griffiths) *cl up: led after 2f out: rdn and hdd over 1f out: kpt on u.p ins last* **4/5**[1]

00-4 **3** 1 **Garlogs**[30] 8 4-9-0 **57**.. RobertWinston 12 67
(A Bailey) *wnt lft s: sn prom: effrt 2f out: rdn to ld over 1f out: sn edgd lft: hdd and one pce ins last* **7/1**[3]

535- **4** 3 **Desert Dust**[55] 6753 4-8-9 **52**..(v) EddieAhern 5 51
(R M H Cowell) *led 2f: cl up tl rdn and wknd wl over 1f out* **9/1**

05-0 **5** 2 1/2 **Prime Recreation**[26] 46 10-8-2 **45**................................... JimmyQuinn 4 36
(P S Felgate) *chsd ldrs: rdn 2f out: sn one pce* **40/1**

0000 **6** 2 1/2 **Laurel Dawn**[4] 281 9-7-9 **45**........................... DanielleMcCreery(7) 7 27
(Miss A Stokell) *wnt rt s: a towards rr* **125/1**

-210 **7** nk **Vlasta Weiner**[8] 236 7-8-5 **55**................................(b) BarrySavage(7) 11 36
(J M Bradley) *dwlt and hmpd s: a rr* **20/1**

04-0 **8** 1 3/4 **Axis Shield (IRE)**[9] 221 4-8-2 **45**.............................. AdrianMcCarthy 1 20
(M C Chapman) *chsd ldrs: rdn along over 2f out: sn wknd* **40/1**

03-0 **9** 2 **Mystery Pips**[6] 251 4-7-12 **55**..(v) KimTinkler 3 24
(N Tinkler) *sn rdn along and outpcd: bhd after 2f* **22/1**

21-4 **10** nk **Orchestration (IRE)**[23] 77 6-8-5 **48**..............................(b) DaleGibson 10 16
(K J Burke) *dwlt and hmpd s: a towards rr* **14/1**

59.50 secs (-0.80) **Going Correction** -0.15s/f (Stan) **10** Ran SP% **112.8**
Speed ratings (Par 101):100,98,97,92,88 84,83,81,77,77
CSF £11.16 CT £37.84 TOTE £8.30: £1.80, £1.10, £1.70; EX 16.30 Trifecta £71.30 Pool £376.75 - 3.75 winning units..
Owner D & R Rhodes & Mrs S Grayson **Bred** I A N Wight And Mrs D M Wight **Trained** Formby, Lancs
■ Stewards' Enquiry : Adrian McCarthy two-day ban; using whip when out of contention (Feb 12-13)

FOCUS
As usual a strong pace over this straight five, but an ordinary race of its type and the winning time was 0.28 seconds slower than the second division. As normal the action all took place down the middle of the track; the form looks sound and good for the grade.

318 PHOTO ALBUMS FROM BONUSPRINT.COM H'CAP (DIV II) 5f (F)
1:50 (1:51) (Class 6) (0-58,63) 4-Y-0+ **£1,876** (£554; £277) **Stalls** High

Form RPR

6-21 **1** **Canadian Danehill (IRE)**[6] 251 5-9-5 **63** 6ex...............(p) EddieAhern 4 80
(R M H Cowell) *trckd ldrs: smooth hdwy to ld over 1f out: rdn clr ins last* **8/13**[1]

060- **2** 3 1/2 **Misaro (GER)**[40] 6935 6-8-9 **58**.......................................(b) TolleyDean(5) 1 63
(R A Harris) *sn led: rdn along and hdd over 1f out: kpt on same pce* **9/2**[2]

1-54 **3** 3/4 **Dysonic (USA)**[6] 251 5-8-6 **53**..................................(v) JasonEdmunds(3) 8 55
(J Balding) *wnt lft and bmpd s: sn chsng ldrs: rdn along 2f out: kpt on same pce* **7/1**[3]

000- **4** 1 1/4 **Best Lead**[56] 6739 8-8-3 **50**.......................................(b) AndrewElliott(3) 5 48
(Ian Emmerson) *in tch: hdwy 2f out: sn rdn to chse ldrs and kpt on same pce appr last* **50/1**

00-5 **5** 2 1/2 **The Leather Wedge (IRE)**[16] 143 8-8-5 **54**........... DuranFentiman(5) 7 44
(R Johnson) *slowly away and swtchd lft: hdwy 2f out: sn rdn and kpt on ins last: nrst fin* **16/1**

0000 **6** 3 **Percy Douglas**[4] 287 7-8-2 **46** oh1.................................. JimmyQuinn 11 26
(Miss A Stokell) *in tch: rdn along 1/2-way: sn outpcd* **66/1**

00-0 **7** 1/2 **Tetrode (USA)**[16] 156 5-8-2 **46** oh1..................................(p) HayleyTurner 2 24
(R M H Cowell) *prom: rdn along after 2f: sn lost pl and bhd whn hung bdly rt fr wl over 1f out* **40/1**

0-46 **8** hd **Sir Loin**[6] 254 6-8-5 **56**...(v) DanielleMcCreery(7) 9 33
(N Tinkler) *prom: rdn along over 2f out: grad wknd* **16/1**

60-0 **9** 3 **Nova Tor (IRE)**[6] 251 5-8-8 **52**..................................(b) RobbieFitzpatrick 6 19
(Peter Grayson) *wnt rt and bmpd s: prom tl rdn and wknd over 2f out* **25/1**

03-6 **10** nk **Amanda's Lad (IRE)**[7] 239 7-8-2 **46** oh1................ AdrianMcCarthy 10 12
(M C Chapman) *rdn along and bhd fr 1/2-way* **25/1**

4-05 **11** 2 1/2 **Diktalex (IRE)**[25] 59 4-8-11 **55**..(t) ChrisCatlin 3 12
(C J Teague) *prom: rdn along and lost pl after 2f: sn bhd* **33/1**

59.22 secs (-1.08) **Going Correction** -0.15s/f (Stan) **11** Ran SP% **120.9**
Speed ratings (Par 101):102,96,95,93,89 84,83,83,78,78 74
CSF £3.38 CT £11.89 TOTE £1.80: £1.10, £1.40, £1.70; EX 4.40 Trifecta £11.70 Pool £361.27 - 21.74 winning units..
Owner T W Morley **Bred** Skymarc Farm Inc And Dr A J O'Reilly **Trained** Six Mile Bottom, Cambs

FOCUS
Another strongly-run sprint and the winning time was 0.28 seconds faster than the first division. The third is the best guide to the level.

319 PONTIN'S FAMILY HOLIDAYS STKS (H'CAP) 1m 3f (F)
2:20 (2:20) (Class 5) (0-75,73) 4-Y-0+ **£3,241** (£957; £478) **Stalls** Low

Form RPR

60-0 **1** **Greenbelt**[9] 228 6-8-4 **57**.. ChrisCatlin 4 65
(G M Moore) *mde virtually all: qcknd over 2f out: rdn wl over 1f out: drvn ins last and hld on gamely* **10/1**[3]

32-1 **2** shd **Blacktoft (USA)**[29] 30 4-9-4 **73**..................................(e) J-PGuillambert 2 81
(S C Williams) *hld up in rr: gd hdwy 3f out: chsd wnr over 1f out: sn rdn and ev ch ins last: drvn and no ex nr line* **2/1**[1]

15-0 **3** 1 3/4 **Wee Charlie Castle (IRE)**[22] 88 4-8-9 **64**.................... OscarUrbina 7 69
(G C H Chung) *hld up: gd hdwy over 3f out: rdn and ch over 1f out: sn drvn and kpt on same pce ent last* **10/1**[3]

406- **4** nk **Xpres Maite**[84] 6417 4-9-1 **70**... PhillipMakin 1 75
(S R Bowring) *trckd ldng pair: effrt 3f out: rdn along 2f out: drvn and one pce appr last* **16/1**

4-12 **5** 6 **Credential**[23] 74 5-8-6 **62**... AndrewElliott(3) 3 56
(John A Harris) *cl up: rdn along 4f out: wknd wl over 2f out* **4/1**[2]

The Form Book, Raceform Ltd, Compton, RG20 6NL

113- **6** *2 1/2* **Zed Candy (FR)**[49] [6816] 4-8-9 **64** DaleGibson 6 54
(J T Stimpson) *trckd ldng pair: pushed along 4f out: sn rdn and btn wl over 2f out* **2/1**[1]

2m 28.75s (-0.15) **Going Correction** +0.075s/f (Slow)
WFA 4 from 5yo+ 2lb **6** Ran SP% **110.7**
Speed ratings (Par 103):103,102,101,101,97 95
CSF £29.62 TOTE £14.90: £4.00, £2.10; EX 38.60.
Owner Mrs A Roddis **Bred** Juddmonte Farms **Trained** Middleham Moor, N Yorks

FOCUS
A modest handicap in which the pace was just fair and that helped the all-the-way winner, who could win again, although it is hard to be positive about the form. It was noticeable that the runners stayed away from the inside rail in the back straight, let alone in the home straight.
Zed Candy(FR) Official explanation: trainer had no explanation for the poor form shown

320 PONTINS.COM CLASSIFIED STKS 6f (F)
2:50 (2:51) (Class 7) 4-Y-0+ **£1,535** (£453; £226) **Stalls** Low

Form RPR

3-02 **1** **Astorygoeswithit**[7] [239] 4-9-0 44 (be) AdamKirby 14 55
(J Ryan) *chsd ldrs on outer: hdwy 2f out: sn rdn: drvn and styd on ins last to ld last 100 yds* **6/1**[3]

40-0 **2** *3/4* **Nevinstown (IRE)**[7] [239] 7-9-0 45 TPQueally 10 53
(C Grant) *hld up in rr: hdwy on inner 2f out: sn rdn and styd on appr last: nrst fin* **13/2**

01-3 **3** *1/2* **Dodaa (USA)**[7] [239] 4-9-0 43 MatthewHenry 4 52
(N Wilson) *sn led: rdn wl over 1f out: drvn ent last: hdd and no ex last 100 yds* **3/1**[1]

-345 **4** *2* **Peggys First**[10] [207] 5-9-0 43 PatCosgrave 5 46
(D E Cantillon) *chsd ldrs: rdn over 2f out: drvn over 1f out: kpt on same pce ent last* **9/2**[2]

01-0 **5** *1/2* **Kissi Kissi**[29] [22] 4-9-0 45 (v) AdrianMcCarthy 7 44
(M J Attwater) *bhd: effrt and rdn over 2f out: styd on wl fnl f: nrst fin* **10/1**

00-0 **6** *1/2* **Estoille**[7] [239] 6-9-0 44 PaulFessey 3 43
(Mrs S Lamyman) *cl up: rdn along 2f out: drvn and wknd appr last* **28/1**

50-3 **7** *3/4* **Beamsley Beacon**[4] [287] 6-9-0 42 (b) PhillipMakin 13 40
(S T Mason) *cl up: rdn over 2f out: drvn and edgd rt wl over 1f out: kpt on same pce* **10/1**

100- **8** *1* **Tuscan Flyer**[42] [6892] 9-9-0 43 (b) RobertWinston 6 37
(R Bastiman) *in tch: rdn along 3f out: sn drvn and no imp* **18/1**

000- **9** *1 3/4* **Boisdale (IRE)**[35] [6962] 9-9-0 41 JimmyQuinn 12 32
(P S Felgate) *midfield: hdwy to chse ldrs over 2f out: sn drvn and btn* **50/1**

000/ **10** *3/4* **Mr Bountiful (IRE)**[558] [3739] 9-9-0 42 (vt) RobbieFitzpatrick 11 30
(C J Teague) *s.i.s: a rr* **66/1**

0-05 **11** *hd* **Mister Becks (IRE)**[9] [225] 4-8-9 44 RussellKennemore(5) 9 29
(M C Chapman) *a towards rr* **20/1**

56-3 **12** *1 1/2* **Dancing Beauty (IRE)**[25] [60] 5-9-0 45 HayleyTurner 8 25
(T T Clement) *midfield: rdn along 3f out: sn wknd* **9/1**

00-0 **13** *1 1/2* **Obe Bold (IRE)**[17] [135] 6-9-0 42 DarrenMoffatt 2 20
(A Berry) *sn rdn along and outpcd in rr* **33/1**

0-00 **14** *4* **Mostanad**[4] [273] 5-8-7 42 (b) BarrySavage(7) 1 8
(J M Bradley) *chsd ldrs on inner: rdn along 3f out: sn wknd* **20/1**

1m 18.08s (1.18) **Going Correction** +0.075s/f (Slow) **14** Ran SP% **123.6**
Speed ratings (Par 97):95,94,93,90,90 89,88,87,84,83 83,81,79,74
CSF £42.64 TOTE £8.50: £4.60, £1.90, £2.00; EX 60.30 Trifecta £106.40 Part won. Pool £149.86 - 0.99 winning units..
Owner G D Newton **Bred** Southill Stud **Trained** Newmarket, Suffolk

FOCUS
A poor contest as befits the grade and apart from the winner the form is unlikely to mean much outside this level, despite it being reasonably sound.
Dancing Beauty(IRE) Official explanation: trainer said mare was found to be suffering from back problems

321 PONTINSBINGO.COM CLASSIFIED STKS 7f (F)
3:20 (3:21) (Class 7) 4-Y-0+ **£1,535** (£453; £226) **Stalls** Low

Form RPR

0-66 **1** **Pawn In Life (IRE)**[16] [144] 9-9-0 45 (v) PaulEddery 8 49
(S Parr) *towards rr: stdy hdwy on inner 2f out: rdn to chse ldrs over 1f out: styd on ins last to ld last 50 yds* **3/1**[1]

6-40 **2** *hd* **Rocky Reppin**[16] [145] 7-8-11 40 (b) JasonEdmunds(3) 5 48
(J Balding) *in tch: smooth hdwy on outer 2f out: led over 1f out: rdn ent last: hdd and no ex last 50 yds* **12/1**

30-0 **3** *6* **Danethorpe (IRE)**[22] [83] 4-9-0 42 (v) CatherineGannon 2 32
(D Shaw) *led 3f: cl up tl led again over 2f out: rdn and hdd over 1f out: sn drvn and wknd ent last* **7/1**[3]

64-5 **4** *hd* **Pontefract Glory**[6] [252] 4-9-0 40 (b) LeeEnstone 1 32
(M Dods) *cl up on inner: led after 3f tl rdn and hdd over 2f out: sn drvn and plugged on one pce* **7/2**[2]

404- **5** *3* **Insignia (IRE)**[51] [6799] 5-9-0 42 (v[1]) MatthewHenry 9 24
(W M Brisbourne) *towards rr: effrt on outer 3f out: sn rdn and edgd lft 2f out: kpt on u.p appr last* **7/2**[2]

04-6 **6** *1 1/2* **Caspian Rose**[9] [222] 4-9-0 37 LPKeniry 7 20
(M J Attwater) *bhd: rdn along 1/2-way: styd on u.p on wd outside fnl 2f: nrst fin* **22/1**

/00- **7** *1 1/4* **Ross Is Boss**[34] [6974] 5-9-0 20 AlanDaly 3 17
(C J Teague) *bhd: rdn along 1/2-way: kpt on u.p fnl 2f: nrst fin* **200/1**

44-6 **8** *shd* **No Inkling (IRE)**[25] [61] 4-9-0 34 SamHitchcott 4 17
(Miss M E Rowland) *in tch on inner: rdn along 3f out: sn wknd* **16/1**

01-0 **9** *1 3/4* **Massey**[7] [239] 11-9-0 44 MichaelTebbutt 11 12
(C R Dore) *chsd ldrs towards outer: rdn along 3f out: sn drvn and btn over 2f out* **9/1**

0- **10** *nk* **Village Storm (IRE)**[52] [6792] 4-9-0 35 JosedeSouza 6 11
(C J Teague) *prom: rdn along 1/2-way: sn wknd* **66/1**

6-60 **11** *1 1/4* **Marron Flore**[4] [273] 4-9-0 43 (tp) StephenCarson 10 8
(A J Lidderdale) *midfield: rdn along 3f out: sn wknd* **14/1**

005- **12** *13* **Distant Vision (IRE)**[78] [6490] 4-9-0 35 (t) DeanCorby 12 —
(A Berry) *chsd ldrs: rdn along 1/2-way: sn wknd* **50/1**

1m 32.13s (1.33) **Going Correction** +0.075s/f (Slow) **12** Ran SP% **120.5**
Speed ratings (Par 97):95,94,87,87,84 82,81,79,78 77,62
CSF £40.79 TOTE £4.00: £1.60, £3.60, £1.70; EX 36.60 Trifecta £200.30 Part won. Pool £282.12 - 0.30 winning units..
Owner Geraldine Degville & Lawrence Degville **Bred** Lt-Col W L Newell **Trained** Carburton, Notts
■ Stewards' Enquiry : Sam Hitchcott two-day ban; careless riding (Feb 12-13)

FOCUS
Another poor classified event and the fact that the front pair pulled miles clear of the others does not say much about the also-rans. This looked a weak race rated through the winner to recent handicap form.
Distant Vision(IRE) Official explanation: vet said filly lost a front shoe and finished sore

322 BONUSPRINT.COM H'CAP 1m (F)
3:50 (3:50) (Class 6) (0-60,66) 3-Y-0 **£2,559** (£755; £378) **Stalls** Low

Form RPR

0-11 **1** **Medici Code**[4] [284] 3-9-8 **66** 6ex RobertHavlin 5 86+
(H Morrison) *hld up in tch: smooth hdwy 3f out: led on bit wl over 1f out: sn clr: canter* **1/10**[1]

40-0 **2** *5* **Briarwood Bear**[22] [93] 3-9-1 **59** JimmyQuinn 3 57
(M Blanshard) *chsd ldrs: rdn along over 2f out: sn drvn and plugged on appr last: tk 2nd towards fin: no ch w wnr* **40/1**

00-0 **3** *1* **Silver Hotspur**[16] [147] 3-8-12 **56** GrahamGibbons 2 52
(M Wigham) *sn led: rdn 2f out: hdd wl over 1f out: sn one pce: lost 2nd towards fin* **40/1**

5-20 **4** *3* **Mr Chocolate Drop (IRE)**[9] [224] 3-8-12 **56** BrianReilly 4 46
(M J Attwater) *chsd ldr: rdn along over 2f out: sn drvn and plugged on same pce* **40/1**

0-21 **5** *7* **Sophie's Dream**[10] [209] 3-9-0 **61** 6ex JerryO'Dwyer(3) 7 36
(A M Hales) *racd wd: in tch: pushed along over 3f out: sn rdn and nvr a factor* **16/1**[2]

636- **6** *5* **Stars Above**[45] [6859] 3-8-2 **46** HayleyTurner 1 11
(D P Keane) *chsd ldrs on inner: rdn along 3f out: sn wknd* **25/1**[3]

1m 45.91s (1.31) **Going Correction** +0.075s/f (Slow) **6** Ran SP% **108.0**
Speed ratings (Par 95):96,91,90,87,80 75
CSF £8.60 TOTE £1.10: £1.10, £9.30; EX 14.20.
Owner The End-R-Ways Partnership **Bred** Mrs T A Foreman **Trained** East Ilsley, Berks

FOCUS
The most one-sided contest seen for a long time and the only question was over who would finish second. The bare form behind is weak.

323 GO PONTIN'S H'CAP 6f (F)
4:20 (4:21) (Class 5) (0-70,69) 4-Y-0+ **£3,241** (£957; £478) **Stalls** Low

Form RPR

-303 **1** **Cool Sands (IRE)**[3] [292] 5-8-7 **60** (v) DeanMcKeown 6 71
(D Shaw) *chsd ldrs: hdwy on outer 2f out: rdn to chal over 1f out: drvn ins last: led and edgd lft nr fin* **4/1**[3]

00-0 **2** *hd* **Effective**[12] [190] 7-9-2 **69** LPKeniry 5 79
(A P Jarvis) *prom: effrt to chal 2f out: sn rdn: led briefly ins last and sn drvn: hdd and n.m.r nr fin: kpt on* **12/1**

3-01 **3** *3/4* **Going Skint**[9] [222] 4-8-10 **63** 6ex AdamKirby 4 71
(M Wellings) *led: rdn along 2f out: drvn over 1f out: hdd and no ex wl ins last* **6/1**

02-1 **4** *1/2* **Dixieland Boy (IRE)**[30] [13] 4-8-11 **64** EddieAhern 11 71
(P J Makin) *hld up in rr: hdwy wl over 1f out: rdn and edgd lft ins last: kpt on: nrst fin* **11/4**[1]

0-25 **5** *1 1/4* **Sir Douglas**[8] [234] 4-8-10 **68** (p) TolleyDean(5) 3 71
(R A Harris) *chsd ldrs: hdwy over 2f out: sn rdn and kpt on same pce fnl f* **10/3**[2]

400- **6** *5* **Cornus**[110] [5961] 5-8-13 **66** RobertWinston 10 54
(A J McCabe) *a towards rr* **10/1**

55-0 **7** *1/2* **Winning Pleasure (IRE)**[21] [102] 9-8-12 **68** (p) JasonEdmunds(3) 1 54
(J Balding) *chsd ldng pair on inner: rdn along 3f out: sn wknd* **20/1**

0-41 **8** *4* **Branston Tiger**[25] [59] 8-8-12 **65** (v) DanielTudhope 9 39
(Ian Emmerson) *hld up in rr: hdwy over 2f out: sn rdn and btn* **12/1**

05-5 **9** *5* **Pomfret Lad**[30] [14] 9-8-12 **65** GrahamGibbons 8 24
(J J Quinn) *chsd ldrs on outer: rdn along over 2f out: sn wknd* **16/1**

1m 16.33s (-0.57) **Going Correction** +0.075s/f (Slow) **9** Ran SP% **119.2**
Speed ratings (Par 103):106,105,104,104,102 95,95,89,83
CSF £52.52 CT £290.30 TOTE £5.20: £1.70, £3.70, £2.80; EX 52.40 Trifecta £314.20 Place 6 £5.81, Place 5 £5.10. Pool £447.04 - 1.01 winning units..
Owner Peter Swann **Bred** Rathasker Stud **Trained** Danethorpe, Notts

FOCUS
An ordinary handicap, but they went a decent clip and the winning time was 1.75 seconds quicker than the earlier classified event. The form is rated positively through the third and fourth.
Branston Tiger Official explanation: jockey said gelding lost its action
T/Plt: £5.40 to a £1 stake. Pool: £50,648.20. 6,727.05 winning tickets. T/Qpdt: £4.70 to a £1 stake. Pool: £2,143.20. 336.10 winning tickets. JR

244 NAD AL SHEBA (L-H)
Thursday, February 1

OFFICIAL GOING: Dirt course - fast; turf course- good changing to good to firm after race 7 (5.55)

324a DUBAL TROPHY (H'CAP) (DIRT) 6f (D)
2:55 (2:56) (90-105,104) 3-Y-0+
£33,673 (£11,224; £5,612; £2,806; £1,683; £1,122)

RPR

1 **Almaram (USA)**[13] 7-8-7 **90** (e) RPCleary 4 100+
(D Selvaratnam, UAE) *raced centre: rdn to chal 2f out: led fnl f: r.o wl: easily* **20/1**

2 *3 3/4* **Drift Ice (SAF)**[7] [249] 6-8-12 **96** (be) WCMarwing 2 91
(M F De Kock, South Africa) *prom far side: ev ch fnl 3f: r.o but no ch w wnr* **14/1**

3 *1 3/4* **Crooner (IRE)**[21] 4-8-7 **90** WSupple 6 81
(Doug Watson, UAE) *prom in centre: rdn 2 1/2f out: swtchd nr rail 1 1/2f out: kpt on* **7/1**[3]

4 *1 1/2* **Botanical (USA)**[7] [249] 6-9-5 **102** (bt) TPO'Shea 13 89
(E Charpy, UAE) *prom nr side: rdn whn ev ch 3f out: nt qckn* **14/1**

5 *2 3/4* **Machynleth**[7] [249] 7-8-10 **94** (t) WayneSmith 11 71
(M Al Muhairi, UAE) *sn rdn along nr side: kpt on fnl 1 1/2f* **11/1**

6 *1 3/4* **Pipoldchap (CHI)**[35] 7-9-5 **102** (bt) JMurtagh 1 75
(F Castro, Sweden) *trckd runner-up on far side for 3f: one pce* **33/1**

7 *1/4* **Hay Luz Delsol (BRZ)**[7] [249] 5-8-11 **95** ADomingos 3 66
(M D Wolfson, U.S.A) *nvr able to chal* **16/1**

8 *hd* **Pakhoes (IRE)**[63] 7-8-8 **91** DHayse 7 63
(R Bouresly, Kuwait) *prom in centre for 2f: wknd* **33/1**

9 *1* **The Lord (ARG)**[7] [249] 7-9-3 **100** (t) RyanMoore 9 69
(S Seemar, UAE) *squeezed s: n.d after* **16/1**

10 *4 1/4* **Padrao Lima (BRZ)**[144] 4-8-7 **95** (t) JohnEgan 8 46
(A Manuel, UAE) *racd centre: sn rdn along: nvr able to chal* **15/2**

11 *3/4* **Sunrise (SAF)**[180] 6-8-12 **96** RichardMullen 5 49
(S Seemar, UAE) *racd centre: nvr threatened* **8/1**

12 3/4 **Prince Tamino**^{126} [5642] 4-9-6 **104**................................ KerrinMcEvoy 14 54
(I Mohammed, UAE) *slowly away: racd nr side: nvr involved* **4/1^{2}**
13 2 1/4 **Yorokobi (BRZ)**^{299} 4-8-11 **100**.. MCardoso 10 39
(H J Brown, South Africa) *slowly away: a struggling* **7/2^{1}**
14 2 1/2 **Magic Master (SAF)**^{685} 8-9-1 **98**..................................(t) TedDurcan 12 35
(S Seemar, UAE) *missed break: nvr involved* **33/1**
68.86 secs (-1.84) **Going Correction** -0.075s/f (Stan) 14 Ran SP% **124.6**
Speed ratings: 109,104,101,99,96 93,93,93,91,86 85,84,81,77

Owner Sheikh Ahmed Al Maktoum **Bred** Darley Stud Management Llc **Trained** United Arab Emirates

FOCUS

A good sprint handicap, basically the first division of the 3.55. As was the case in the 6f contest at last week's Carnival, those drawn low to middle had the edge.

NOTEBOOK

Almaram(USA) stepped up on the form he showed when soundly beaten into second over 7f here on his previous start to run out a most convincing winner. His rider deserves credit, for while the majority of those around him bunched together towards the nearside rail, he steered a straight course from the gates and had this won from at least a furlong out. He has been racing over further recently, but sprint distances clearly suit best on this evidence.

Drift Ice(SAF) never landed a blow in a Group 3 over course and distance the previous week, but this was much better. He drifted towards the far rail under pressure and ended up racing on his own, but that did not seem to inconvenience him too much and he was basically beaten by a better horse on the day. (op 12/1)

Crooner(IRE) has been in good form over course and distance this winter and this was another solid effort.

Botanical(USA) had stall 16 of 16 to contend with when only mid-division in a course and distance Group 3 the previous week and, as it turned out, a high stall was little help to him this time either. He ran his race tight against the nearside rail, but could not land a blow on the principals, who were better drawn considering how the race unfolded.

Machynleth could not confirm recent form with Botanical, but this was not a bad effort.

Prince Tamino progressed into a pattern-class sprinter when with Hughie Morrison last season but, although he handles Polytrack well enough, this quick dirt surface looked totally against him on his debut for new connections. He is obviously much better than he was able to show and should benefit from a return to turf.

Yorokobi(BRZ) could not recover after being squeezed out at the start and is better than this run indicates.

325a DUBAL CASTHOUSE TROPHY (H'CAP) (TURF) 1m (T)
3:25 (3:25) (90-105,105) 3-Y-0+

£33,673 (£11,224; £5,612; £2,806; £1,683; £1,122)

RPR

1 **Sir Gerard**^{181} [4098] 4-9-5 **104**.. KerrinMcEvoy 3 102+
(I Mohammed, UAE) *settled in rr: 2nd last 3f out: smooth prog fnl 2f: wd: led 50yds out: easily* **9/4^{1}**
2 3/4 **Almuraad (IRE)**^{14} [178] 6-9-0 **98**.. RHills 11 94
(Doug Watson, UAE) *hld up in rr: smooth prog to ld 110yds out: hdd 50yds out: no ch w wnr* **10/1**
3 1 **Desert Chief**^{111} [5943] 5-8-9 **94** ow1... LDettori 2 87
(Saeed Bin Suroor) *trckd ldr rail: smooth prog to chal 1 1/2f out: led 1f out: sn hdd* **9/2^{2}**
4 nse **Bolodenka (IRE)**^{27} [43] 5-8-12 **97**..................................... MJKinane 1 90
(R A Fahey) *mid-div rail: no room 3 1/2f out: dropped to rr: r.o wl fnl 2f: nrst fin* **9/1**
5 1 1/4 **Boston Lodge**^{321} 7-8-8 **93**...(vt) WSupple 6 83
(Doug Watson, UAE) *sn led: kicked clr 2 1/2f out: hdd 1f out: kpt on* **25/1**
6 2 3/4 **Money Bags (SAF)**^{215} 5-9-5 **104**.. WCMarwing 9 89
(M F De Kock, South Africa) *hld up in rr: nvr able to chal* **9/1**
7 nse **Starpix (FR)**^{147} [5146] 5-9-6 **105**... RyanMoore 5 90
(H J Brown, South Africa) *slowly away: hld up in rr: nvr nr to chal* **14/1**
8 1/2 **Kestrel Cross (IRE)**^{7} [250] 5-8-10 **95**................................. JMurtagh 12 79
(Declan Gillespie, Ire) *mid-div: rdn 3 1/2f out: nvr a threat* **16/1**
9 1/2 **Mezel (USA)**^{21} 4-9-2 **100**.. TedDurcan 15 84
(S Seemar, UAE) *trckd ldr: rdn 2 1/2f out: sn wknd* **14/1**
10 3/4 **Subpoena**^{357} [357] 5-8-11 **96**.................................(v) RoystonFfrench 14 77
(A Al Raihe, UAE) *slowly away: tk v k.h wd: rdn 3f out: nt qckn* **25/1**
11 1/4 **Uhoomagoo**^{31} [6] 9-9-1 **99**...(b) PJSmullen 10 81
(K A Ryan) *mid-div: rdn 4f out: sn btn* **16/1**
12 5 1/4 **Pentecost**^{14} [172] 8-8-12 **97**.. MartinDwyer 7 67
(A M Balding) *mid-div centre: n.m.r 110yds out: n.d* **7/1^{3}**
13 nse **Millbag (IRE)**^{21} [104] 6-8-7 **91**...(v) RPCleary 8 62
(D Selvaratnam, UAE) *slowly away: nvr able to chal* **50/1**
14 5 1/2 **Book Of Kings (USA)**^{342} [512] 6-9-2 **100**..................(t) RichardMullen 4 60
(S Seemar, UAE) *mid-div: rdn 3 1/2 out: nvr a threat* **50/1**
15 1/4 **Hurricane James (IRE)**^{14} [178] 5-9-0 **98**......................(t) TPO'Shea 13 58
(E Charpy, UAE) *trckd pce: centre: rdn 3 1/2f out: nvr able to chal* **33/1**
1m 40.08s (2.28) **Going Correction** +0.525s/f (Yiel) 15 Ran SP% **130.2**
Speed ratings: 109,108,107,107,105 103,103,102,102,101 101,95,95,90,90

Owner H R H Princess Haya Of Jordan **Bred** Whitsbury Manor Stud & Stowell Hill Ltd **Trained** UAE

FOCUS

A very good handicap, but the gallop seemed just steady through the first couple of furlongs and a few of these were caught out when the leader injected some pace. The winning time was 1.24 seconds slower than the closing 1m handicap, supporting the theory that they did not go very fast early on. The form has been rated through the runner-up.

NOTEBOOK

Sir Gerard ◆ lost his position quite badly when the leaders kicked for home, but he produced a mightily impressive turn of foot to make up the lost ground in the straight. With only one behind rounding the final bend, he must have been at least ten lengths off the pace, and his rider had to switch him round runners towards the centre of the track in order to get in the clear, a tactic that did not pay dividends for too many of those who followed a similar path at the previous week's meeting. However, this one really found his stride once in the clear, and to make his way to the front from the position he found himself in at the top of the straight marks him down as a Group-race winner waiting to happen. He was most progressive when trained by James Fanshawe last season, winning the Britannia at Royal Ascot, and this performance confirms he has continued to thrive for new connections. (op 11/4)

Almuraad(IRE), third over an extended 7f round here two weeks previously, looked to have been produced perfectly with his effort in the straight, but he had no answer to Sir Gerard's late burst. Time may show hefaced a near impossible task getting just 5lb.

Desert Chief, making his debut in Dubai off the back of a 111-day break, got a lovely lead off Boston Lodge for much of the way and can have no excuses.

Bolodenka(IRE) ◆, just like the winner, lost his place badly when the leaders kicked for home and was short of room when trying to produce a challenge. The way he stayed on once in the clear suggests he would have gone very close indeed with a better run and he looks well up to finding a similar race at this year's Carnival.

Boston Lodge enjoyed the run of the race out in front, but this was his first outing in 321 days and he just got tired late on.

Kestrel Cross(IRE) was unable to build on his recent course fourth.

Uhoomagoo could never land a blow.

Pentecost was keen enough early and could pose no threat in the latter stages. He shaped well in a similar event two weeks previously and can be given another chance.

326a DUBAL TROPHY (H'CAP) (DIRT) 6f (D)
3:55 (3:56) (90-105,104) 3-Y-0+

£33,673 (£11,224; £5,612; £2,806; £1,683; £1,122)

RPR

1 **Salaam Dubai (AUS)**^{21} 6-8-9 **93**......................................(b) MJKinane 5 109+
(A Selvaratnam, UAE) *prom centre: led 2f out: hung far rail: r.o wl: easily* **12/1**
2 3 1/2 **Bounty Quest**^{28} 5-8-8 **91**.. MartinDwyer 11 97
(Doug Watson, UAE) *prom nr side: rdn 2 1/2f out: ev ch fnl 2f: nt pce of wnr* **6/1^{3}**
3 3/4 **Sir Edwin Landseer (USA)**^{21} 7-8-8 **91**....................(p) RichardMullen 2 95
(Christian Wroe) *slowly away: sn prom centre: ev ch fnl 2f: r.o* **10/1**
4 2 **Big Spartan (BRZ)**^{166} 4-8-11 **100**.. ECruz 3 92
(P Nickel Filho, Brazil) *racd far rail: n.d: kpt on wl* **5/1^{2}**
5 1 1/4 **Lord Ego (BRZ)**^{270} 4-8-2 **98** ow8...................................(t) PatrickHills$^{(7)}$ 8 86
(M D Wolfson, U.S.A) *bmpd s: racd in rr: sme late prog: nvr involved* **12/1**
6 3/4 **Doctor Hilary**^{21} 5-9-4 **101**..(vt) TedDurcan 14 93
(S Seemar, UAE) *sn pushed along nr side: mid-div: hrd rdn 3f out: one pce* **6/1^{3}**
7 4 1/4 **Visionist (IRE)**^{111} [5943] 5-9-0 **97**.. WayneSmith 4 76
(M Al Muhairi, UAE) *slowly away: sn swtchd nr rail: nvr a threat* **25/1**
8 hd **Conceal**^{13} 9-8-7 **90**.. GHind 9 69
(R Bouresly, Kuwait) *mid-div centre: rdn 3f out: nt qckn* **14/1**
9 3 1/4 **Key Of Destiny (SAF)**^{7} [245] 9-9-5 **102**..................(e^{1}) KerrinMcEvoy 10 71
(M F De Kock, South Africa) *nvr bttr than mid-div* **9/2^{1}**
10 shd **Zorin (BRZ)**^{87} 4-8-7 **95**... ADomingos 12 59
(A Cintra Pereira, Brazil) *slowly away: nvr threatened* **14/1**
11 1/2 **Holborn (UAE)**^{1217} [5348] 6-9-0 **97**..(ve) PDevlin 1 64
(S Seemar, UAE) *missed break: racd far side: nvr nr to chal* **28/1**
12 1 1/4 **Golden Acer (IRE)**^{21} 4-9-1 **98**... WSupple 6 61
(Doug Watson, UAE) *prom centre for 3f: wknd* **14/1**
13 3 1/4 **Western Diplomat (USA)**^{14} [178] 7-8-9 **93**............(t) RoystonFfrench 7 46
(A Al Raihe, UAE) *prom centre: rdn 3f out: nt qckn* **33/1**
14 dist **Strike Up The Band**^{7} [245] 4-9-6 **104**...................... AdrianTNicholls 13 —
(D Nicholls) *a struggling: eased* **10/1**
68.61 secs (-2.09) **Going Correction** -0.075s/f (Stan) 14 Ran SP% **127.2**
Speed ratings: 110,105,104,101,100 99,93,93,88,88 87,86,81,—

Owner Farooq Racing **Bred** Emirates Park Pty Ltd **Trained** United Arab Emirates

FOCUS

Basically the second division of the opening sprint handicap, and similar enough form. This time, though, the jockeys were keen to avoid the nearside rail and middle to far side again proved the place to be.

NOTEBOOK

Salaam Dubai(AUS) was poorly drawn when last over course and distance on his previous start, but stall five was just fine this time and he bounced right back to form in convincing fashion. Granted a decent draw, he ought to continue to go well in similar company.

Bounty Quest had no easy task off a 9lb higher mark than when winning a non-Carnival handicap over course and distance on his previous start, but he ran a good race, faring best of those in double-figure stalls. (op 7/1)

Sir Edwin Landseer(USA) was well drawn in stall two and ran a respectable race in third. He is an even better horse on the turf and should not be underestimated when switching surfaces. (op 12/1)

Big Spartan(BRZ) brought Brazilian form into the race and produced a reasonable enough effort. He raced on his own against the far-side rail, but the principals towards the middle always just appeared to have his measure. (op 11/2)

Lord Ego(BRZ) ran a big race considering he carried 8lb overweight.

Key Of Destiny(SAF), far from ideally drawn, was beaten some way and failed to improve as one might have hoped for the return to dirt.

Strike Up The Band was poorly drawn and never featured after starting a touch slowly. He should benefit from a return to turf.

327a DUBAL STKS (H'CAP) (DIRT) 1m (D)
4:25 (4:25) (90-105,105) 3-Y-0+

£33,673 (£11,224; £5,612; £2,806; £1,683; £1,122)

RPR

1 **Nelore Pora (BRZ)**^{123} 5-9-4 **102**..................................(b^{1}) ADomingos 9 110
(P Nickel Filho, Brazil) *sn led: rdn 2f out: r.o wl: comf* **6/1^{3}**
2 2 **Mooner (ARG)**^{186} 6-9-6 **105**.. TedDurcan 8 108
(S Seemar, UAE) *mid-div: rdn to trck ldrs 3f out: r.o wl fnl f* **4/1^{2}**
3 1/2 **Jaffal (USA)**^{14} [177] 5-8-10 **95**...............................(t) RoystonFfrench 12 97
(A Al Raihe, UAE) *mid-div wd: rdn to chal 2f out: kpt on one pce* **12/1**
4 shd **Opportunist (IRE)**^{14} [177] 8-9-2 **100**.......................(vt) MartinDwyer 5 103
(Doug Watson, UAE) *trckd ldr: rdn to chal 2 1/2f out: ev ch fnl 2f: nt qckn* **14/1**
5 3 1/4 **Delude (IRE)**^{21} 9-8-6 **90**...(t) RichardMullen 7 86
(S Seemar, UAE) *in rr of mid-div: rdn 3 1/2f out: sme late prog* **14/1**
6 1/4 **Juror (USA)**^{109} [5990] 4-8-6 **90**.. KerrinMcEvoy 11 86
(I Mohammed, UAE) *mid-div: dropped to rr 3 1/2f out: n.d* **13/2**
7 1/2 **Salt Track (ARG)**^{14} [172] 7-9-0 **98**......................................(t) JMurtagh 2 93
(Niels Petersen, Norway) *sn pushed along: mid-div and rdn 2f out: nvr a threat* **33/1**
8 6 1/4 **King Jock (USA)**^{7} [247] 6-8-8 **93**...................................... PShanahan 10 74
(R J Osborne, Ire) *settled in rr: travelled keenly: in rr and wd st: n.d: eased* **13/8^{1}**
9 2 3/4 **Cat Belling (IRE)**^{7} [247] 7-8-10 **95**... GHind 1 71
(R Bouresly, Kuwait) *trckd ldr rail tl 3 1/2f out: wknd: eased* **33/1**
10 5 1/4 **Lundy's Lane (IRE)**^{27} 7-9-0 **98**... RyanMoore 4 64
(S Seemar, UAE) *mid-div: rdn 4f out: nvr nr to chal: eased* **16/1**
11 19 **Beringoer (FR)**^{14} [176] 4-9-4 **102**.. LDettori 6 30
(A M Balding) *slowly away: a in rr: virtually p.u* **25/1**
12 4 3/4 **Organizer (NOR)**^{14} [178] 7-9-0 **98**...................................(e) WayneSmith 3 17
(Christian Wroe) *slowly away: settled in rr: t.k.h: n.m.r 4 1/2f out: nvr nr to chal: eased* **50/1**
1m 36.37s (-1.23) **Going Correction** +0.10s/f (Slow) 12 Ran SP% **124.3**
Speed ratings: 110,108,107,107,104 103,103,97,94,89 70,65

Owner Stud AML **Bred** Haras Ponta Pora **Trained** Brazil

FOCUS

Probably not strong form for the grade but yet another advert for Brazilian-trained horses on the dirt in Dubai.

NOTEBOOK

Nelore Pora(BRZ), fast into his stride, was left alone up front through the early stages and, appearing to set a decent pace from the start, soon had a few of these in trouble. He looked vulnerable when strongly challenged early in the straight, but he sustained his effort in determined style and was well on top at the finish. There was plenty to like about the way he went about this, but he will not always get his own way and a higher mark will make things tougher.

Mooner(ARG), like the winner a South American-bred, came into this bidding for the hat-trick following wins in Argentina and Brazil. Having come under pressure before the turn into the straight, he stayed on well and did enough to suggest he can find a similar event in due course, possibly when returned to a little further.

Jaffal(USA) was never too far away and kept on in the straight to post another respectable effort.

Opportunist(IRE) chased the eventual winner throughout, but he was unable to go by when produced with his chance at the top of the straight and gradually weakened. (op 12/1)

King Jock(USA) has been in tremendous form on the turf of late, but his style of running in not suited to dirt racing and he never landed a blow after coming widest of all into the straight. He can do better when returned to turf. (op 7/4)

Beringoer(FR) lost his position very quickly and ran as though something was not quite right.

328a DUBAL CUP (H'CAP) (TURF) 1m 4f (T)

4:55 (4:57) (90-105,105) 3-Y-O+

£33,673 (£8,418; £8,418; £2,806; £1,683; £1,122)

RPR

1 **Mutafanen**[7] [250] 6-9-2 **100**........(v[1]) MartinDwyer 1 101
(E Charpy, UAE) *settled in rr: rdn rail 3f out: weaved through to make prog rail fnl 2f: led cl home* **20/1**

2 ½ **Leitmotiv (IRE)**[106] [6062] 4-8-9 **97**........ LDettori 5 96
(Saeed Bin Suroor) *slowly away: settled in rr: hmpd 3f out: swtchd wd: r.o wl fnl 2f: nrst fin* **11/2**[2]

2 dht **Nepotista (BRZ)**[82] 5-9-1 **99**........ ADomingos 2 99
(A Cintra Pereira, Brazil) *mid-div rail: gng wl whn n.m.r 3f out: r.o to ld briefly 110yds out: hdd cl home* **16/1**

4 ¼ **Crime Scene (IRE)**[121] [5758] 4-8-9 **97**........ KerrinMcEvoy 3 96
(I Mohammed, UAE) *trckd ldr: gng wl whn no room 2 1/2f out: r.o once clr* **12/1**[3]

5 2½ **Doctor Of Laws**[21] [104] 4-8-5 **91**........(t) TedDurcan 6 88
(S Seemar, UAE) *mid-div: rdn 4f out: led briefly 1f out: r.o one pce* **12/1**[3]

6 3¼ **Diamond Quest (SAF)**[14] [172] 6-8-12 **97**........ PJSmullen 14 87
(M F De Kock, South Africa) *settled in rr: swtchd wd 3f out: ev ch 1 1/2f out: nt qckn* **4/5**[1]

7 1¾ **Luberon**[7] [248] 4-9-1 **102**........ JMurtagh 11 91
(M Johnston) *mid-div: nvr able to chal* **33/1**

8 1¼ **Bonecrusher**[7] [244] 8-8-8 **93**........(t) WayneSmith 8 79
(M Al Muhairi, UAE) *hld up rr: nvr a threat* **14/1**

9 1¼ **Boo**[7] [250] 5-8-6 **90**........ RoystonFfrench 9 75
(K R Burke) *mid-div: t.k.h on rail: rdn 3 1/2f out: n.d* **50/1**

10 2 **Mutasallil (USA)**[14] [175] 7-9-4 **102**........(t) RHills 10 84
(Doug Watson, UAE) *trckd ldr: led 2 1/2f out: hdd 1 1/2f out: wknd* **20/1**

11 1¼ **Bailador (IRE)**[42] 7-8-9 **94**........(v[1]) WSupple 7 73
(S Seemar, UAE) *hld up last: gng wl 3f out: swtchd wd: nvr able to chal* **50/1**

12 ¼ **Oratory (SAF)**[356] [371] 10-8-10 **95**........ RichardMullen 16 74
(S Seemar, UAE) *led centre: rdn 3 1/2f out: hdd 2 1/2f out: wknd* **66/1**

13 3½ **Peintre Bleu (FR)**[150] 5-8-10 **95**........(b[1]) C-PLemaire 13 68
(S Seemar, UAE) *mid-div: nvr nr to chal* **25/1**

14 ¼ **Go For Gold (IRE)**[7] [248] 6-9-5 **104**........(vt) TPO'Shea 12 77
(S Seemar, UAE) *settled in rr: nvr nr to chal* **33/1**

15 5½ **Sunday Symphony**[140] [5325] 5-9-6 **105**........(t) RyanMoore 15 70
(S Seemar, UAE) *led main gp: rdn 6f out: sn struggling* **14/1**

16 dist **Oakfast (BRZ)**[14] [175] 5-9-0 **98**........ MJKinane 4 —
(A Cintra Pereira, Brazil) *prom early: sn dropped to rr* **33/1**

2m 34.94s (3.94) **Going Correction** +0.525s/f (Yiel)
WFA 4 from 5yo+ 3lb **16** Ran SP% **133.1**
Speed ratings: 107,106,106,106,104 102,101,100,99,98 97,97,95,95,91 —

Owner Hamdan Al Maktoum **Bred** Shadwell Estate Co Ltd **Trained** United Arab Emirates

FOCUS

This looked a decent, very competitive handicap beforehand but, with the early pace just ordinary, they finished in a bunch and the bare form is probably nothing to get excited about.

NOTEBOOK

Mutafanen did not get the best of trips when sixth over 1m2f round here the previous week but, despite the pace again probably not being as strong he would like, he was able to show improved form over this slightly longer distance. The first-time visor, instead of cheekpieces, clearly did the trick and he showed a decent attitude to take a gap between rivals and get up close home. The form looks just ordinary for the grade, and the headgear is no sure thing to work as well next time, but he just gives the impression we will see the very best of him off a decent gallop.

Leitmotiv(IRE) ◆ was short of room when beginning to make his move and had to be switched out wide with his run. This ex-Andre Fabre-trained colt can be considered unlucky and he looks up to finding a similar race for his new connections.

Nepotista(BRZ), a winner over 1m7f in South America, showed Brazilian-trained horses must be respected on turf, as well as dirt, with a decent effort. He enjoyed a dream run throughout under a fine ride from Domingos and can have no excuses whatsoever.

Crime Scene(IRE), having his first start since leaving Mark Johnston, took a while to warm up in the straight and may just have been hanging a touch, but this still represents a decent effort and he could build on this.

Doctor Of Laws, a very useful handicapper on both turf and dirt, ran a decent enough race and continues in good order. (op 10/1)

Diamond Quest(SAF) ◆ was a real eye-catcher when third over an extended 7f on his debut in Dubai two weeks previously, basically because he was a 2m winner in his native South Africa. He was duly well fancied to confirm that promise, stepped back up in distance, but a wide draw was no help and he endured a poor trip, being forced to make his move very wide. He can be forgiven this and looks capable of gaining compensation. (op Evens)

Luberon ran better than when well beaten over course and distance the previous week.

Boo had not shown much in two previous starts in Dubai this year but, although well held once again, he travelled sweetly this time and offered some promise.

329a DUBAL POTLINE CUP (H'CAP) (DIRT) 1m 2f (D)

5:25 (5:29) (90-105,104) 3-Y-O+

£33,673 (£11,224; £5,612; £2,806; £1,683; £1,122)

RPR

1 **Remaadd (USA)**[14] [175] 6-9-6 **104**........ JMurtagh 6 109
(D Selvaratnam, UAE) *prom on rail: led 3 1/2f out: rdn clr 1 1/2f out: r.o wl* **25/1**

2 1¼ **Quorum (GER)**[21] 4-8-6 **90**........(v) WayneSmith 13 94
(M Al Muhairi, UAE) *nvr far off pce: trckd ldr 3 1/2f out: hrd rdn last 2 1/2f: kpt on wl* **10/1**

3 ¾ **Descartes**[103] [6097] 5-8-11 **95**........ LDettori 1 97
(Saeed Bin Suroor) *trckd ldrs: gng wl 3f out: rdn to chal: nt qckn* **7/2**[1]

4 8¼ **Chinkara**[14] [175] 7-9-2 **99**........ MartinDwyer 3 87
(Doug Watson, UAE) *in rr on rail: r.o in st: nvr a threat* **12/1**

5 1 **Red Duster (USA)**[14] [175] 4-8-11 **96**........(b[1]) RyanMoore 15 81
(S Seemar, UAE) *mid-div: t.k.h: rdn 3 1/2f out: n.d* **20/1**

6 3½ **Morghim (IRE)**[14] [175] 4-9-0 **98**........(bt) RHills 12 78
(E Charpy, UAE) *mid-div wd: n.d* **7/1**[3]

7 1¼ **Change The Grange (AUS)**[14] [175] 9-8-11 **95**........(ve) PJSmullen 8 72
(S Seemar, UAE) *prom centre: rdn 4f out: sn wknd* **25/1**

8 1¼ **Impeller (IRE)**[14] [175] 8-8-11 **95**........ JohnEgan 7 69
(J S Moore) *mid-div: nvr able to chal* **11/1**

9 3¼ **Dynamic Saint (USA)**[21] 4-9-5 **104**........ TedDurcan 9 73
(Doug Watson, UAE) *mid-div: rdn 5f out: n.d* **4/1**[2]

10 1¼ **Brahminy Kite (USA)**[7] [248] 5-9-2 **99**........ GHind 4 66
(R Bouresly, Kuwait) *mid-div rail: rdn 4f out: nvr a threat* **50/1**

11 1¼ **Parasol (IRE)**[14] [175] 8-9-6 **104**........(bt) RichardMullen 2 68
(Doug Watson, UAE) *v.s.a: settled last gng wl: nvr able to chal* **11/1**

12 7½ **Leaving Alone (BRZ)**[14] [175] 4-8-2 **96** ow2........ TPO'Shea 5 38
(M D Wolfson, U.S.A) *settled in rr: nvr able to chal* **33/1**

13 3¾ **Sapucai (ARG)**[84] 7-8-9 **93**........(bt) RoystonFfrench 14 37
(S Seemar, UAE) *prom wd tl rdn 4 /12f out: wknd* **33/1**

14 ¼ **Grain Of Truth**[112] [5917] 4-8-11 **96**........(v) KerrinMcEvoy 10 39
(I Mohammed, UAE) *settled in rr: nvr involved* **7/1**[3]

15 4 **Afghan (USA)**[21] 9-8-11 **95**........(b) WSupple 16 31
(S Seemar, UAE) *settled in rr: n.d* **33/1**

16 4 **Desert Realm (IRE)**[7] [250] 4-8-10 **95**........ MJKinane 11 24
(I Mohammed, UAE) *mid-div: wd: nvr able to chal* **16/1**

2m 3.55s (0.25) **Going Correction** +0.10s/f (Slow)
WFA 4 from 5yo+ 1lb **16** Ran SP% **129.8**
Speed ratings: 103,102,101,94,94 91,90,89,86,85 84,78,75,75,72 69

Owner Sheikh Ahmed Al Maktoum **Bred** Darley **Trained** United Arab Emirates

FOCUS

A good handicap, although they hardly went a mad pace up front and it proved difficult to make up significant ground.

NOTEBOOK

Remaadd(USA) did not have to over-exert himself to dispute the lead for much of the way and had plenty left when asked to sustain his challenge in the straight. Both the eventual runner-up and third looked dangerous at various stages, but he kept pulling out more and displayed a most willing attitude. Placed in the Gordon Stakes for Marcus Tregoning back in 2004, he is clearly still capable of producing a smart level of form at the age of six, although it is worth remembering he had the run of things this time.

Quorum(GER) has been running well at up to 1m1f round here all winter and he showed himself just as effective over this slightly longer distance with a solid effort in defeat. He should continue to go well.

Descartes ◆ had not been seen since finishing last of 13 on the Polytrack at Lingfield in October, but he previously smashed the course record at that venue when defying a mark of 86 in decent handicap company. Making his debut in Dubai, he seemed too keen for his own good early on and looked rather laboured in the straight. This was only his fourth career start, though, and he gives the impression he can leave the bare form of this effort behind in time, either off a stronger pace or when allowed to bowl along in front.

Chinkara stays 1m4f, so a steadily run race over this trip was not going to be ideal and he could not go with the front three, only keeping on at the one pace. (op 11/1)

Red Duster(USA) did not run badly but he hardly showed improved form in the first-time blinkers.

Impeller(IRE) was badly hampered inside the final 1m and can be forgiven this.

330a DUBAI AL RASHIDIYA (GROUP 3) (TURF) 1m 194y(T)

5:55 (5:58) 3-Y-O+

£61,224 (£20,408; £10,204; £5,102; £3,061; £2,040)

RPR

1 **Formal Decree (GER)**[14] [176] 4-9-0 113........ MJKinane 10 117
(I Mohammed, UAE) *slowly away: last 3f out: swtchd wd: r.o wl fnl 2f: led line* **11/10**[1]

2 shd **Ace (IRE)**[39] 6-9-0 110........(v) RyanMoore 5 116
(S Seemar, UAE) *racd in rr: rdn to cl 2 1/2f out: ev ch fnl f: jst failed* **15/2**

3 shd **Oracle West (SAF)**[75] 6-9-0 113........ PJSmullen 3 116
(M F De Kock, South Africa) *racd 4th: gng wl 3f out: rdn to ld 2f out: hdd cl home* **5/1**[2]

4 1¼ **Olympian Odyssey**[110] [5964] 4-9-0 116........ KerrinMcEvoy 4 114
(I Mohammed, UAE) *mid-div: gng wl 3f out: ev ch fnl 1 1/2f: n.m.r nr line* **5/1**[2]

5 3¼ **Evil Knievel (BRZ)**[14] [176] 8-9-0 108........(b[1]) RichardMullen 6 107
(Christian Wroe) *slowly away: nvr able to chal: r.o wl fnl 1 1/2f* **33/1**

6 shd **Shanty Star (IRE)**[298] 7-9-0 109........ GHind 2 107
(R Bouresly, Kuwait) *trckd ldr: led briefly 2 1/2f out: one pce* **33/1**

7 1¾ **Hazeymm (IRE)**[184] [4024] 4-9-0 107........ JMurtagh 11 104
(D Selvaratnam, UAE) *mid-div: rdn to trck ldr 3f out: ev ch 2f out: one pce* **12/1**

8 5¾ **Touch Of Land (FR)**[124] [5704] 7-9-4 115........ C-PLemaire 8 96
(H-A Pantall, France) *settled in rr: nvr able to chal* **11/2**[3]

9 6¼ **Senor Dali (IRE)**[14] [176] 4-9-0 105........ WSupple 1 80
(I Mohammed, UAE) *sn led: hdd 3f out: wknd* **33/1**

10 11 **Estrela Brono (BRZ)**[130] 5-9-0 93........(t) MCardoso 7 58
(C Morgado, Brazil) *nvr able to chal* **33/1**

11 ¼ **Todman Avenue (USA)**[7] [244] 5-9-0 85........(bt) RoystonFfrench 9 57
(A Al Raihe, UAE) *racd 3rd: pushed along 4 1/2f out whn wknd* **250/1**

1m 50.34s (0.54) **Going Correction** +0.525s/f (Yiel) **11** Ran SP% **128.0**
Speed ratings: 118,117,117,116,113 113,112,107,101,91 91

Owner Sheikh Hamdan Bin Mohammed Al Maktoum **Bred** Gestut Olympia **Trained** UAE

FOCUS

By no means an easy race to assess. There is no doubting this was a fascinating contest, both on paper beforehand and in the way it developed, but it is hard to know exactly what level of form the principals ran to. The horses that filled the frame suggest this was well up to Group 3 standard, but the likes of Evil Knievel and the thoroughly exposed Shanty Star were too close for comfort at the finish, despite Senor Dali (same owner as the winner) appearing to set quite a searching pace.

NOTEBOOK

Formal Decree(GER) ◆ narrowly followed up his recent course and distance handicap success and it would take a harsh judge to knock this effort, even if the form strength of the form is open to debate. The generous pace would have suited, but he was stone last on the turn into the straight and it looked at that stage as though he would struggle to make up the ground on the leaders. However, he eventually hit his top stride and just managed to draw alongside Ace close home before forcing his head in front on the line. One slight note of caution, however, is he appeared to be hanging slightly under pressure. Assuming connections are going to bid for Group 1 glory on World Cup night, the Dubai Duty Free Stakes, back over this course and distance, had looked a suitable target after he was so impressive round here last time. However, on this evidence, he might just require a little further to be seen at his very best and, although unproven over 1m4f, the Sheema Classic has to be considered. That race would require further improvement, though, with the likes of Sir Percy and Sixties Icon possible rivals. (op 11/8)

Ace(IRE) benefited from the strong gallop and ran his best race since joining his new connections. He was still below the pick of his efforts for Aidan O'Brien, but is clearly back on good terms with himself, and he should make his mark in Dubai. (op 7/1)

Oracle West(SAF), a winner at this level over 1m4f at last year's Carnival, ran a terrific race on his return to Dubai, just losing out in a thrilling finish. He is one of those who arguably gives the form some substance and could improve for the outing.

Olympian Odyssey, third in last year's 2000 Guineas for Barry Hills, made a pleasing debut for his new connections off the back of a 110-day break and gave the impression he can improve on the bare form.

Evil Knievel(BRZ) was a little bit out of his depth, but he ran with credit and is clearly no back number.

Shanty Star(IRE) probably finished a little closer than is ideal from a form point of few, but he is clearly still smart on his day.

Touch Of Land(FR) picked up a Group 2 over course and distance at last year's Carnival, but he was not at his best this time off the back of a 124-day break.

Senor Dali(IRE) raced for the same connections as the winner and set a generous pace.

331a DUBAI PLATE (H'CAP) (TURF) 1m (T)

6:25 (6:27) (90-105,105) 3-Y-0+

£33,673 (£11,224; £5,612; £2,806; £1,683; £1,122)

			RPR
1		**Alpacco (IRE)**[14] 176 5-9-2 **100** (b[1]) RyanMoore 2	100
		(H J Brown, South Africa) *mid-div: smooth prog rail: no room 1 1/2f out: swtchd and r.o wl to ld cl home* **14/1**	
2	1 1/4	**Emirates Gold (IRE)**[21] 105 4-8-9 **94** (t) TPO'Shea 1	91
		(E Charpy, UAE) *racd in 3rd: smooth prog to ld 2f out: r.o wl: hdd cl home* **33/1**	
3	2 1/2	**Reve Lunaire (USA)**[186] 3989 4-9-5 **104** TedDurcan 5	96
		(S Seemar, UAE) *mid-div: rdn to cl 3f out: nt qckn* **10/1**	
4	1	**Eden Rock (IRE)**[181] 4098 6-8-10 **95** MJKinane 7	85
		(Pat Eddery) *settled in rr: t.k.h: nvr able to chal: sme late prog* **14/1**	
5	1	**Azarole (IRE)**[14] 172 6-9-6 **105** JohnEgan 10	93
		(J S Moore) *in rr of mid-div: sme prog fnl 2 1/2f: n.d* **8/1**[2]	
6	1 1/2	**Amandus (USA)**[13] 7-8-6 **90** MartinDwyer 6	76
		(Doug Watson, UAE) *mid-div: rdn to trck ldrs 2 1/2f out: nt qckn* **12/1**	
7	1/2	**All Ivory**[118] 5789 5-9-1 **99** KerrinMcEvoy 4	84
		(I Mohammed, UAE) *mid-div: prog to trck ldrs: no room 1 1/2f out: nt rcvr* **9/1**[3]	
8	3/4	**Hopeful Purchase (IRE)**[7] 244 4-8-12 **97** RHills 8	79
		(W J Haggas) *mid-div: hrd rdn 2 1/2f out: nt qckn* **25/1**	
9	1/4	**Berlioz (IND)**[27] 6-8-8 **93** (vt) RichardMullen 12	75
		(S Seemar, UAE) *racd in rr: nvr a threat* **33/1**	
10	1 3/4	**Checkit (IRE)**[7] 245 7-9-2 **100** GHind 3	79
		(R Bouresly, Kuwait) *led main gp: rdn to chal 2 1/2f out: one pce* **40/1**	
11	2	**Kings Point (IRE)**[27] 43 6-9-4 **102** PJSmullen 11	77
		(R A Fahey) *settled in rr: no room 3 1/2f out: nvr able to chal* **12/1**	
12	1 1/4	**Lucky Dance (BRZ)**[14] 177 5-8-11 **96** ADomingos 13	68
		(M D Wolfson, U.S.A) *a in rr* **28/1**	
13	6 1/4	**Hinterland (IRE)**[124] 5675 5-9-5 **104** LDettori 15	63
		(Saeed Bin Suroor) *mid-div: rdn 3f out: nvr a threat* **10/3**[1]	
14	3 1/4	**Hartshead**[14] 178 8-8-12 **97** JMurtagh 14	50
		(G A Swinbank) *missed break: settled in rr: hmpd 1 1/2f out: nvr able to chal* **10/3**[1]	
15	3	**Matloob**[14] 178 6-8-10 **95** RPCleary 16	42
		(D Selvaratnam, UAE) *mid-div: rdn along 4f out: sn btn* **33/1**	
16	1/2	**Pecoiquen (CHI)**[140] 6-9-0 **98** (bt[1]) WSupple 9	45
		(F Castro, Sweden) *sn clr: hdd 2 1/2f out: wknd* **25/1**	

1m 38.84s (1.04) **Going Correction** +0.525s/f (Yiel) 16 Ran SP% **127.5**

Speed ratings: 115,113,111,110,109 107,107,106,106,104 102,101,95,91,88 88

.

Owner The Bayern Syndicate **Bred** Manfred Hoffer **Trained** South Africa

FOCUS

This was basically another division of the 3.25 and, like that race, represents decent handicap form. As was the theme throughout the evening in the big-field turf handicaps, low draws dominated. The winning time was 1.24 seconds quicker than the 3.25, thanks to a better early gallop.

NOTEBOOK

Alpacco(IRE) is probably value for around double the winning margin, as he was short of room and forced to switch round the eventual runner-up about 2f out, although it is worth remembering he had a perfect trip from his inside draw until that point. This represented an improvement on the form he showed on his reappearance and he may have even more to offer granted another good draw.

Emirates Gold(IRE), with a tongue-tie fitted this time and upped in trip, made good use of his inside draw and ran well to fill second. He might just prove best over 7f. (op 28/1)

Reve Lunaire(USA), off the track since landing a Listed race on the sand in France last July when trained by Andre Fabre, ran well on his debut for new connections switched to turf.

Eden Rock(IRE), who seemed a little keen early on, came from almost last to take fourth. This was promising and he is open to improvement, as this was his first run in 181 days.

Azarole(IRE) was forced to switch wide with his challenge and ran creditably under top weight.

Hopeful Purchase(IRE) was again well held but it is too early to be giving up on him. (op 20/1)

Kings Point(IRE) was a little short of room when trying to stay on, but he was not unlucky.

Hinterland(IRE) showed some smart form for Michael Jarvis last season, but offered little immediate promise on his debut for Godolphin. (op 7/2)

Hartshead had to wait to make his move and never looked like getting on terms with the principals. (op 7/2)

[295] WOLVERHAMPTON (A.W) (L-H)

Friday, February 2

OFFICIAL GOING: Standard to slow

Wind: light, across

332 PONTIN'S FAMILY HOLIDAYS AMATEUR RIDERS' H'CAP 1m 4f 50y(P)

1:40 (1:41) (Class 5) (0-70,70) 4-Y-0+ **£2,717** (£842; £421; £210) **Stalls** Low

Form				RPR
5-02	1		**Three Thieves (UAE)**[11] 215 4-10-9 **61** MrSDobson 1	72
			(M S Saunders) *hld up: nt clr run over 2f out: swtchd rt and hdwy wl over 1f out: rdn to ld ins fnl f: r.o* **4/1**[1]	
-462	2	2	**Dovedon Hero**[13] 195 7-10-13 **67** (p) MrPCollington[(5)] 3	75
			(P J McBride) *hld up and bhd: hdwy over 3f out: rdn and swtchd lft over 1f out: ev ch ins fnl f: nt qckn* **8/1**	
100-	3	1/2	**Undeterred**[125] 5671 11-11-0 **70** MrAMerriam[(7)] 2	77
			(K J Burke) *hld up towards rr: rdn and hdwy on outside over 2f out: led briefly ins fnl f: nt qckn* **50/1**	
5-01	4	2 1/2	**Wait For The Will (USA)**[13] 195 11-11-3 **69** (b) MrDHutchison[(3)] 4	72
			(G L Moore) *hld up towards rr: rdn over 2f out: led over 1f out tl ins fnl f: wknd* **8/1**	
31-0	5	2 1/2	**Blue Hedges**[28] 39 5-10-6 **60** MissALHutchinson[(5)] 9	59
			(H J Collingridge) *hld up and bhd: hdwy over 3f out: rdn over 2f out: wknd ins fnl f* **8/1**	
0-43	6	1/2	**Hawk Arrow (IRE)**[11] 212 5-10-7 **61** (p) MissHayleyMoore[(5)] 10	59
			(G L Moore) *hld up: hdwy on ins over 3f out: rdn over 2f out: wknd fnl f* **4/1**[1]	
206-	7	3/4	**Zalkani (IRE)**[42] 6924 7-10-9 **61** MrSPearce[(3)] 7	58
			(J Pearce) *s.i.s: hld up and bhd: hdwy over 3f out: rdn over 2f out: wknd over 1f out: hung lft ins fnl f* **8/1**	
2-11	8	1/2	**Finished Article (IRE)**[21] 107 10-10-1 **57** MissFGuillambert[(7)] 6	53
			(P A Blockley) *chsd clr ldng pair: n.m.r over 3f out: sn wknd* **20/1**	
2-33	9	5	**Bridgewater Boys**[12] 205 6-10-11 **65** (b) MissARyan[(5)] 11	53
			(K A Ryan) *bhd fnl 3f* **7/1**[2]	
/1-4	10	nk	**Ross Moor**[17] 153 5-11-0 **70** MrHSensoy[(7)] 12	58
			(N P Littmoden) *racd wd early: led: rdn and hdd over 1f out: sn wknd* **15/2**[3]	
5-	11	23	**Something Simple (IRE)**[31] 6623 4-9-12 **57** MissPHermansson[(7)] 5	8
			(R Ford) *w ldr tl wknd over 4f out* **80/1**	

2m 43.32s (0.90) **Going Correction** -0.025s/f (Stan)

WFA 4 from 5yo+ 3lb 11 Ran SP% **116.7**

Speed ratings (Par 103):96,94,94,92,91 90,90,89,86,86 70

CSF £35.76 CT £1386.40 TOTE £5.40: £1.90, £3.50, £13.40; EX 50.40 TRIFECTA Not won..

Owner Prempro Racing **Bred** Darley (u A E) **Trained** Green Ore, Somerset

FOCUS

A modest amateur riders' handicap and, as is so often the case in this type of event, the leaders went off too fast. The form looks sound enough rated through the third.

333 PONTIN'S - BOOK EARLY (S) H'CAP 2m 119y(P)

2:10 (2:11) (Class 6) (0-60,57) 4-Y-0+ **£2,047** (£604; £302) **Stalls** Low

Form				RPR
0-04	1		**Tip Toes (IRE)**[5] 285 5-8-10 **45** JimmyQuinn 8	49
			(P Howling) *hld up and bhd: hdwy over 3f out: led over 2f out: rdn clr wl over 1f out: r.o* **9/1**	
-006	2	3/4	**Come What July (IRE)**[5] 285 6-8-10 **45** DeanMcKeown 1	48
			(D Shaw) *hld up in mid-div: hdwy over 4f out: nt clr run and swtchd rt 3f out: rdn to chse wnr wl over 1f out: hung lft fnl f: ro* **8/1**	
00-6	3	4	**Treason Trial**[11] 220 6-8-13 **48** DavidAllan 11	46
			(W M Brisbourne) *t.k.h in rr: hdwy over 3f out: rdn over 2f out: wknd fnl f* **9/2**[3]	
0-45	4	3/4	**Dik Dik**[6] 270 4-8-7 **48** (p) LPKeniry 6	45
			(J S Moore) *hld up and bhd: hdwy over 3f out: sn rdn: wknd over 1f out* **10/1**	
5-42	5	10	**Zaffeu**[21] 107 6-9-3 **57** RussellKennemore[(5)] 9	42
			(A G Juckes) *s.i.s: hld up and bhd: nt clr run on ins over 4f out and over 3f out: sn rdn: nvr nr ldrs* **11/4**[1]	
00-0	6	2 1/2	**Flyoff (IRE)**[19] 134 10-8-10 **45** PaulMulrennan 3	27
			(Mrs N Macauley) *hld up in mid-div: hdwy over 5f out: rdn and wknd over 2f out* **25/1**	
566-	7	3/4	**Jamaican Flight (USA)**[279] 866 14-8-10 **45** PaulHanagan 5	26
			(Mrs S Lamyman) *chsd ldr 4f: prom tl wknd 4f out* **40/1**	
3-63	8	1 1/4	**Isa'Af (IRE)**[21] 107 8-8-12 **47** ChrisCatlin 10	27
			(P W Hiatt) *chsd ldrs: wnt 2nd after 4f: led 6f out tl over 2f out: sn wknd* **7/2**[2]	
00-0	9	43	**Boulevin (IRE)**[14] 182 7-8-7 **45** (p) JamesDoyle[(3)] 2	—
			(R J Price) *plld hrd: hdwy after 4f: rdn over 3f out: sn wknd: t.o* **10/1**	
006-	10	2 1/2	**The Loose Screw (IRE)**[34] 6993 9-8-10 **45** EddieAhern 4	—
			(C W Thornton) *a bhd: t.o* **33/1**	
00/0	11	31	**Baker Of Oz**[5] 285 6-8-7 **45** AndrewMullen[(3)] 7	—
			(M A Doyle) *led: clr after 3f: hdd 6f out: wknd over 4f out: t.o* **50/1**	

3m 43.7s (0.57) **Going Correction** -0.025s/f (Stan)

WFA 4 from 5yo+ 6lb 11 Ran SP% **117.6**

Speed ratings (Par 101):97,96,94,94,89 88,88,87,67,66 51

CSF £76.37 CT £371.02 TOTE £11.60: £3.10, £2.10, £1.60; EX 93.20 Trifecta £228.40 Part won. Pool £321.70 - 0.43 winning units..The winner was bought in for 6,500gns.

Owner Going Grey Partnership **Bred** T H S Syndicate **Trained** Newmarket, Suffolk

FOCUS

Hand timed. Weak form, even by selling standards, rated around the first two.

Zaffeu Official explanation: jockey said gelding was denied a clear run

Boulevin(IRE) Official explanation: jockey said gelding ran too free

334 PONTINSBINGO.COM H'CAP 1m 141y(P)

2:45 (2:45) (Class 6) (0-65,71) 4-Y-0+ **£2,388** (£705; £352) **Stalls** Low

Form				RPR
32-1	1		**Pop Music (IRE)**[21] 110 4-8-11 **63** (p) JamesDoyle[(3)] 4	73
			(Miss J Feilden) *wnt rt s: chsd ldr: rdn to ld over 2f out: r.o* **5/1**[3]	
4-51	2	3/4	**Luckylover**[10] 228 4-9-8 **71** 6ex (t) TPQueally 1	79
			(M G Quinlan) *led: hdd and rdn over 2f out: rallied towards fin* **7/2**[2]	
33-5	3	1 3/4	**Solicitude**[29] 32 4-8-3 **52** (b) HayleyTurner 5	56
			(D Haydn Jones) *bmpd s: hld up in tch: rdn over 3f out: hung lft ins fnl f: one pce* **16/1**	
364-	4	1 1/2	**Western Roots**[58] 6734 6-9-1 **64** GeorgeBaker 10	65
			(M Appleby) *stdd s: hld up in rr: hdwy on outside over 2f out: rdn over 1f out: one pce* **16/1**	

The Form Book, Raceform Ltd, Compton, RG20 6NL

00-0 **5** *3 1/2* **Desert Lover (IRE)**[19] 131 5-8-1 **55** .... TolleyDean(5) 3 49
(R J Price) *plld hrd in tch: rdn over 3f out: wknd over 1f out* **66/1**
0-00 **6** *1/2* **Methusaleh (IRE)**[13] 191 4-8-11 **60** .... DaneO'Neill 2 53
(D Shaw) *hld up: rdn over 3f out: no rspnse* **40/1**
03-2 **7** *4* **Cabourg (IRE)**[20] 124 4-8-9 **58** .... PaulHanagan 9 42
(R Bastiman) *hld up: rdn 3f out: sn bhd* **14/1**
00-0 **8** *9* **Sundance (IRE)**[20] 117 5-8-9 **58** ....(v) JimmyQuinn 6 23
(H J Collingridge) *hmpd s: hld up: rdn over 3f out: sn struggling* **66/1**
110 **P** **Picador**[5] 286 4-9-0 **63** 6ex........ SebSanders 7 —
(Sir Mark Prescott) *prom: rdn over 3f out: wknd over 2f out: p.u and collapsed wl over 1f out* **1/1**[1]

1m 51.04s (-0.72) **Going Correction** -0.025s/f (Stan) **9 Ran SP% 112.7**
Speed ratings (Par 101):102,101,99,98,95 94,91,83,—
CSF £22.15 CT £255.99 TOTE £6.80: £1.70, £1.10, £2.50; EX 19.20 Trifecta £120.70 Pool £467.51 - 2.75 winning units..
Owner Michael Jenner **Bred** John Foley **Trained** Exning, Suffolk
FOCUS
Reasonable enough form for the grade, although the pace was just ordinary. The race could have been rated more positively but the runner-up is the best guide.

335 PONTIN'S HOLIDAYS CLAIMING STKS 7f 32y(P)
3:20 (3:20) (Class 6) 3-Y-O **£3,238** (£963; £481; £240) **Stalls High**

Form RPR
U-21 **1** **Put It On The Card**[4] 295 3-8-9 60........(b) NCallan 2 63
(P D Evans) *a.p: led over 1f out: rdn and edgd lft ins fnl f: r.o wl* **15/8**[1]
03-1 **2** *2 1/2* **Sweet World**[18] 139 3-9-3 61........ DaneO'Neill 1 64
(A P Jarvis) *hld up in mid-div: rdn over 2f out: hdwy over 2f out: wnt 2nd ins fnl f: nt trble wnr* **5/2**[3]
-245 **3** *1 3/4* **Mick Is Back**[11] 209 3-8-10 64........(b) JamesDoyle(3) 8 55
(P D Evans) *sn chsng ldr: rdn and ev ch over 2f out: one pce fnl f* **20/1**
51-1 **4** *1 1/2* **Intersky Sports (USA)**[24] 76 3-9-9 68........(p) DeanMcKeown 3 62
(K A Ryan) *led: rdn over 2f out: hdd over 1f out: wknd ins fnl f* **9/4**[2]
3-30 **5** *1/2* **Aggbag**[12] 202 3-8-4 58........ SoniaEaton(7) 4 48
(B P J Baugh) *hld up in mid-div: no real prog fnl 2f* **28/1**
320- **6** *5* **Birdie Birdie**[144] 5238 3-8-2 55........ PaulHanagan 6 26
(R A Fahey) *s.i.s: a bhd* **14/1**
5-50 **7** *7* **Arabellas Homer**[10] 224 3-8-4 49 ow1........ RussellKennemore(5) 7 15
(Mrs N Macauley) *s.i.s: sn prom: rdn and wknd over 3f out* **100/1**
06-0 **8** *nk* **Rubber Duck (IRE)**[29] 34 3-8-2 30........ AdrianMcCarthy 5 7
(Peter Grayson) *a bhd* **100/1**

1m 30.34s (-0.06) **Going Correction** -0.025s/f (Stan) **8 Ran SP% 111.0**
Speed ratings (Par 95):99,96,94,92,91 86,78,77 Winner claimed J S Wainwright £6,000
CSF £6.34 TOTE £2.50: £1.30, £1.10, £3.30; EX 8.10 Trifecta £34.50 Pool £690.08 - 14.20 winning units.
Owner J E Abbey, Mike Nolan **Bred** J E Abbey **Trained** Pandy, Monmouths
FOCUS
A reasonable claimer and a lot more solid than most of these races, with the runner-up to form.

336 PONTINS.COM H'CAP 5f 216y(P)
3:55 (3:56) (Class 6) (0-65,69) 3-Y-O **£2,730** (£806; £403) **Stalls Low**

Form RPR
04-2 **1** **Convivial Spirit**[11] 219 3-8-13 **62**........(t) LPKeniry 5 69
(E F Vaughan) *chsd ldrs: rdn over 2f out: r.o u.p to ld last strides* **4/1**[1]
35-4 **2** *nk* **Drifting Gold**[30] 17 3-9-2 **65**........(p) AdamKirby 2 71
(C G Cox) *a.p: rdn over 2f out: led ins fnl f: hdd last strides* **7/1**
0-21 **3** *nk* **Pietersen (IRE)**[18] 136 3-8-10 **59**........(b) PaulFessey 9 65+
(T D Barron) *chsd ldrs: bmpd 4f out: sn lost pl: c wd st: rallied and hung lft ins fnl f: r.o* **5/1**[2]
12-4 **4** *1 1/2* **Charlotte Grey**[20] 122 3-8-12 **61**........ EdwardCreighton 12 62
(C N Allen) *w ldr: led over 3f out: rdn wl over 1f out: hdd and no ex ins fnl f* **11/1**
546- **5** *1/2* **Slipasearcher (IRE)**[38] 6939 3-9-0 **63**........(b) NCallan 4 63
(P D Evans) *mid-div: rdn and hdwy over 2f out: one pce fnl f* **8/1**
66-4 **6** *1 1/2* **Glen Avon Girl (IRE)**[8] 237 3-8-5 **59**........ DuranFentiman(5) 11 54
(T D Easterby) *led over 2f: rdn 2f out: wknd ins fnl f* **40/1**
6-00 **7** *1/2* **Haydock Express (IRE)**[17] 152 3-8-2 **51** oh2........ AdrianMcCarthy 7 45
(Peter Grayson) *hld up and bhd: rdn and hdwy on ins over 1f out: n.d* **40/1**
026- **8** *3/4* **Dance Of Dreams**[136] 5449 3-8-13 **65**........(t) JamesDoyle(3) 1 56
(N P Littmoden) *chsd ldrs: rdn over 3f out: sn lost pl* **6/1**
000- **9** *3/4* **Hits Only Vic (USA)**[80] 6472 3-8-5 **54** oh5 ow3........ DeanMcKeown 8 43
(J Pearce) *s.i.s: a bhd* **40/1**
03-5 **10** *hd* **Minnie Mill**[25] 69 3-8-12 **61**........ JimmyQuinn 6 49
(B P J Baugh) *s.i.s: a bhd* **18/1**
6-21 **11** *nk* **Comrade Cotton**[4] 290 3-9-1 **69** 6ex........ JamieMoriarty(5) 10 57
(N A Callaghan) *s.s: a bhd* **11/2**[3]
350- **12** *2* **Cryptic Clue (USA)**[41] 6926 3-8-2 **51**........ HayleyTurner 3 33
(D W Chapman) *prom tl wknd wl over 1f out* **25/1**

1m 15.56s (-0.25) **Going Correction** -0.025s/f (Stan) **12 Ran SP% 114.7**
Speed ratings (Par 95):100,99,99,97,96 94,93,92,91,91 91,88
CSF £29.74 CT £141.65 TOTE £5.40: £1.70, £2.20, £2.10; EX 37.20 Trifecta £339.90 Part won. Pool £478.78 - 0.86 winning units..
Owner A M Pickering **Bred** Miss Jacqueline Goodearl **Trained** Newmarket, Suffolk
■ Stewards' Enquiry : Adam Kirby caution: used whip above shoulder height
FOCUS
Very competitive and decent enough form for the level. The form is probably sound rated around the winner, second and fourth.
Comrade Cotton Official explanation: jockey said colt missed the break

337 GO PONTIN'S H'CAP (DIV I) 5f 216y(P)
4:25 (4:26) (Class 6) (0-52,52) 4-Y-O+ **£1,706** (£503; £252) **Stalls Low**

Form RPR
0-03 **1** **Dark Moon**[4] 296 4-8-6 **46** oh1........ DeanMcKeown 2 55+
(D Shaw) *s.i.s: hld up and bhd: hdwy on ins whn nt clr run over 2f out: rdn over 1f out: led wl ins fnl f: r.o* **15/2**[3]
000- **2** *1 1/2* **Navigation (IRE)**[84] 6431 5-8-3 **46** oh1........(b[1]) SaleemGolam(3) 8 51
(T J Etherington) *led: rdn clr 2f out: ct wl ins fnl f* **20/1**
-223 **3** *1 1/4* **Mind Alert**[8] 241 6-8-10 **50**........(v) NCallan 1 51
(D Shaw) *chsd ldrs: rdn and kpt on ins fnl f* **7/4**[1]
-106 **4** *nk* **Teyaar**[11] 217 11-8-8 **48**........ PaulFitzsimons 6 48
(M Wellings) *hld up and bhd: hdwy over 3f out: rdn over 2f out: kpt on ins fnl f* **16/1**
0-00 **5** *hd* **Majestical (IRE)**[9] 236 5-8-12 **52**........(p) DaneO'Neill 11 52
(J M Bradley) *chsd ldr: rdn over 2f out: no ex whn hung rt wl ins fnl f* **8/1**
0-44 **6** *nk* **Grand View**[5] 281 11-8-6 **46** oh1........(p) PaulMulrennan 7 45
(J R Weymes) *bhd: rdn and hdwy on ins over 1f out: kpt on same pce fnl f* **8/1**
-516 **7** *1 1/2* **Must Be Keen**[5] 281 8-8-6 **46**........(v) FergusSweeney 10 43+
(Ernst Oertel) *hld up in tch: rdn over 1f out: btn whn hmpd wl ins fnl f* **9/2**[2]
000- **8** *2* **King Of Charm (IRE)**[45] 6869 4-8-10 **50**........ AdamKirby 4 38
(G L Moore) *bhd: rdn over 4f out: sme hdwy over 2f out: no further prog* **12/1**
0-66 **9** *3* **Drury Lane (IRE)**[3] 307 7-8-6 **46** oh1........(p) HayleyTurner 13 25
(D W Chapman) *chsd ldrs: rdn over 3f out: sn lost pl* **28/1**
00-0 **10** *1/2* **Headland (USA)**[3] 303 9-7-13 **46** oh1........(b) DanielleMcCreery(7) 12 24
(D W Chapman) *s.v.s: a bhd* **50/1**
5-00 **11** *1* **Fancy You (IRE)**[23] 83 4-8-6 **46** oh1........ JimmyQuinn 9 21
(A W Carroll) *prom tl rdn and wknd 2f out* **25/1**
36-0 **12** *3* **Layed Back Rocky**[6] 268 5-8-10 **50**........(b[1]) TPQueally 5 16
(M Mullineaux) *chsd ldrs: reminders after 1f: bhd fnl 3f* **16/1**
060- **13** *11* **Kims Rose (IRE)**[187] 3975 4-8-8 **48**........ ChrisCatlin 3 —
(D Burchell) *plld hrd: chsd ldrs: lost pl over 3f out: sn bhd* **50/1**

1m 15.67s (-0.14) **Going Correction** -0.025s/f (Stan) **13 Ran SP% 124.0**
Speed ratings (Par 101):99,97,95,94,94 94,92,89,85,84 83,79,64
CSF £157.48 CT £393.96 TOTE £9.70: £2.20, £5.50, £1.20; EX 164.00 Trifecta £245.10 Part won. Pool £345.24 - 0.61 winning units..
Owner Danethorpe Racing Ltd **Bred** Langton Stud And G E M Wates **Trained** Danethorpe, Notts
FOCUS
A very moderate sprint handicap run in a time 0.77 seconds slower than the second division and looks the weaker of the two.
Headland(USA) Official explanation: jockey said gelding missed the break
Fancy You(IRE) Official explanation: jockey said filly had no more to give

338 HOTEL & CONFERENCING AT WOLVERHAMPTON MAIDEN STKS 1f 103y(P)
4:55 (4:56) (Class 5) 3-Y-O+ **£2,968** (£876; £438) **Stalls Low**

Form RPR
1 **Metternich** 3-8-5........ JoeFanning 9 83+
(M Johnston) *chsd ldr: led 3f out: rdn and edgd rt fr over 1f out: sn clr: eased towards fin* **5/2**[2]
54-0 **2** *5* **Sir Sandicliffe (IRE)**[20] 114 3-8-5 71........ DeanMcKeown 6 67
(B W Hills) *hld up towards rr: hdwy over 3f out: wnt 2nd and hung lft jst over 1f out: no ch w wnr* **13/2**
2- **3** *nk* **Bewildering (IRE)**[51] 6809 3-8-5........ ChrisCatlin 1 66
(E J O'Neill) *a.p: rdn 3f out: one pce fnl 2f* **13/8**[1]
4 *5* **Glory Days (GER)** 4-9-7........ EddieAhern 3 63+
(E A L Dunlop) *hld up in tch: wknd ins fnl f* **9/2**[3]
5 *nk* **Sadler's Kingdom (IRE)** 3-8-5........ PaulHanagan 8 56+
(R A Fahey) *s.i.s: bhd: rdn over 4f out: styd on fnl f: n.d* **11/1**
3- **6** *5* **Soldiers Romance**[100] 823 4-9-12........ DavidAllan 7 51
(T D Easterby) *led: rdn and hdd over 3f out: wknd fnl f* **28/1**
0- **7** *3 1/2* **Dickie Deano**[49] 6826 3-8-0 ow2........ BarrySavage(7) 4 41
(J M Bradley) *chsd ldrs: rdn over 4f out: sn wknd* **50/1**
0 **8** *5* **Most Becoming**[14] 186 4-9-2........ RoryMoore(5) 5 29
(S Parr) *plld hrd in rr: rdn over 4f out: sn struggling* **100/1**
0-0 **9** *2 1/2* **Merlins Dreams**[14] 186 4-9-5........ DanielleMcCreery(7) 2 29
(S Parr) *s.i.s: bmpd on ins after 1f: a bhd* **200/1**

2m 2.63s (0.01) **Going Correction** -0.025s/f (Stan)
WFA 3 from 4yo 21lb **9 Ran SP% 113.4**
Speed ratings (Par 103):98,93,93,88,88 84,81,76,74
CSF £18.42 TOTE £2.70: £1.30, £2.20, £1.10; EX 17.00 Trifecta £35.20 Pool £409.05 - 8.25 winning units..
Owner Sheikh Mohammed **Bred** Darley **Trained** Middleham Moor, N Yorks
FOCUS
An interesting enough maiden on paper, but nothing could live with Metternich, and those in behind Mark Johnston's useful newcomer offered little immediate promise. With little to go on, the runner-up is the best guide to the level for now.
Merlins Dreams Official explanation: jockey said colt hung right-handed throughout

339 GO PONTIN'S H'CAP (DIV II) 5f 216y(P)
5:25 (5:26) (Class 6) (0-52,54) 4-Y-O+ **£1,706** (£503; £252) **Stalls Low**

Form RPR
-221 **1** **Lucius Verrus (USA)**[8] 239 7-9-0 **54** 6ex........(v) NCallan 9 65
(D Shaw) *hld up and bhd: rdn over 2f out: hdwy over 1f out: led towards fin: r.o wl* **13/8**[1]
5-02 **2** *1 1/2* **Monda**[8] 241 5-8-8 **48**........ PaulMulrennan 2 55
(Miss J A Camacho) *led early: a.p: rdn wl over 1f out: led ins fnl f: edgd lft and hdd towards fin* **4/1**[2]
6-04 **3** *1 1/4* **Doughty**[5] 282 5-8-1 **46** oh1........ EmmettStack(5) 1 49
(M Mullineaux) *s.i.s: towards rr: nt clr run on ins 3f out: hdwy over 1f out: rdn and edgd lft ins fnl f: kpt on* **20/1**
00-4 **4** *1 3/4* **Grafton (IRE)**[11] 217 4-8-10 **50**........ DavidAllan 11 48
(J O'Reilly) *a.p: led over 2f out: rdn over 1f out: hdd and no ex ins fnl f* **9/1**
3-00 **5** *nk* **Cayman Breeze**[16] 161 7-8-5 **52**........(p) BarrySavage(7) 6 49
(J M Bradley) *mid-div: hdwy over 2f out: one pce fnl f* **9/1**
0-00 **6** *1* **Drink To Me Only**[11] 217 4-8-9 **49**........ PaulHanagan 8 43
(J R Weymes) *chsd ldrs: lost pl over 3f out: c wd st: kpt on ins fnl f* **16/1**
3-20 **7** *shd* **Beverley Beau**[12] 201 5-7-13 **46** oh1........ KristinStubbs(7) 10 39
(Mrs L Stubbs) *mid-div: lost pl 4f out: sme late hdwy* **12/1**
000- **8** *nk* **Princess Arwen**[58] 6728 5-8-6 **46** oh1........(b[1]) LPKeniry 3 38
(Mrs Barbara Waring) *chsd ldrs tl wknd over 2f out* **100/1**
00-0 **9** *1 1/4* **Alistair John**[18] 137 4-8-7 **47**........ DeanMcKeown 13 36
(Mrs G S Rees) *s.i.s: racd wd: chsd ldrs after 1f: ev ch over 2f out: rdn and wknd 1f out* **40/1**
25-5 **10** *hd* **Mustammer**[31] 13 4-8-6 **46** oh1........ JimmyQuinn 7 34
(D Shaw) *a bhd* **8/1**[3]
00-0 **11** *1/2* **Tuscan Flyer**[1] 320 9-8-6 **46** oh1........(b) ChrisCatlin 5 33
(R Bastiman) *sn outpcd* **20/1**
00-5 **12** *shd* **Sundried Tomato**[3] 303 8-8-6 **46** oh1........(p) HayleyTurner 12 32
(D W Chapman) *prom: rdn over 2f out: wknd wl over 1f out* **33/1**
055- **13** *10* **On The Trail**[35] 6969 10-8-6 **46** oh1........(p) JoeFanning 4 2
(D W Chapman) *sn led: hdd over 2f out: wknd over 1f out* **50/1**

1m 14.9s (-0.91) **Going Correction** -0.025s/f (Stan) **35 Ran SP% 120.6**
Speed ratings (Par 101):105,103,101,99,98 97,97,96,95,94 94,94,80
CSF £6.98 CT £100.80 TOTE £2.60: £1.50, £1.90, £5.30; EX 11.00 Trifecta £159.50 Pool £485.51 - 2.16 winning units. Place 6 £84.66, Place 5 £29.13.
Owner Danethorpe Racing Ltd **Bred** Pacelco S A **Trained** Danethorpe, Notts
FOCUS
Another moderate sprint handicap, but the leaders went off very quick and the winning time was 0.77 seconds faster than the first division. The form looks solid despite the presence of the third.
Alistair John Official explanation: jockey said gelding dwelt in the stalls and had a breathing problem

T/Plt: £132.90 to a £1 stake. Pool: £69,668.95. 382.40 winning tickets. T/Qpdt: £7.00 to a £1 stake. Pool: £5,351.60. 559.30 winning tickets. KH

[309]LINGFIELD (L-H)

Saturday, February 3

OFFICIAL GOING: Standard

Wind: Slight, across

340 GO PONTIN'S H'CAP — 1m 2f (P)
1:10 (1:10) (Class 4) (0-85,83) 4-Y-0+ **£4,857** (£1,445; £722; £360) **Stalls** Low

Form RPR

33-1 **1** **Mighty**[21] 120 4-8-11 **78** ... JohnEgan 1 92+
(Jane Chapple-Hyam) *s.i.s: sn prom: rdn 2f out: led ins fnl f: pushed clr* **9/4**[2]

1-21 **2** 1 3/4 **Rapid City**[17] 164 4-8-12 **82** ... JamesDoyle[(3)] 3 93+
(Miss J Feilden) *hld up in tch: hdwy to trck ldrs over 3f out: led 2f out: rdn and hdd ins fnl f: nt qckn* **10/11**[1]

00-6 **3** 2 **Bay Boy**[12] 211 5-8-7 **73** ... JoeFanning 2 80
(M Johnston) *led tl rdn and hdd 2f out: fdd ins fnl f* **14/1**

316- **4** 1/2 **Solo Flight**[45] 6888 10-9-2 **82** ... SteveDrowne 7 88
(H Morrison) *hld up in rr: effrt on outside 2f out: r.o fnl f: nvr nrr* **20/1**

06-5 **5** 1 **Prince Charlemagne (IRE)**[24] 95 4-9-1 **82** ... NCallan 4 86
(N P Littmoden) *in rr: effrt 2f out: one pce fnl f* **12/1**

/06- **6** 5 **Daniel Thomas (IRE)**[35] 6986 5-9-3 **83** ... JimCrowley 5 78
(Mrs A J Perrett) *trckd ldr: rdn 2f out: wknd over 1f out* **8/1**[3]

360- **7** 6 **Prince Vector**[72] 4560 5-9-1 **81** ... (b[1]) DaneO'Neill 6 64
(A King) *racd wd: rdn over 3f out: sn btn: eased fnl f* **16/1**

2m 3.84s (-3.95) **Going Correction** -0.125s/f (Stan)
WFA 4 from 5yo+ 1lb 7 Ran SP% **119.3**
Speed ratings (Par 105):110,108,107,106,105 101,97
CSF £4.95 TOTE £3.10: £1.60, £1.50; EX 5.10.
Owner Franconson Partners And Vanessa Church **Bred** Cheveley Park Stud Ltd **Trained** Newmarket, Suffolk

FOCUS
Just the seven runners, but they went a good pace. Fair form, limited by the fourth, but a chance that the first two will both do better yet.

341 GO PONTIN'S (S) STKS — 1m (P)
1:45 (1:46) (Class 6) 4-Y-0+ **£2,184** (£644; £322) **Stalls** High

Form RPR

-552 **1** **Linda's Colin (IRE)**[5] 288 5-8-13 64 ... PatCosgrave 10 66
(K R Burke) *hld up: hdwy over 3f out: drvn to ld ins fnl f: won gng away* **13/8**[1]

50-3 **2** 2 **Ali Bruce**[33] 2 7-8-13 65 ... NCallan 6 61
(P A Blockley) *slowly away: hdwy 1/2-way: chsd ldr over 1f out and ev ch: nt qckn and jst hld on for 2nd* **7/2**[2]

-623 **3** shd **Voice Mail**[3] 309 8-8-6 53 ... (b) DavidProbert[(7)] 1 61
(A M Balding) *hld up: hdwy on ins over 1f out: r.o ins fnl f: nvr nrr* **9/2**[3]

0-00 **4** 1 1/4 **Ask No More**[10] 235 4-8-10 55 ... (b) DominicFox[(3)] 8 58
(P L Gilligan) *chsd ldr: led over 2f out: hdd ins fnl f: no ex* **12/1**

1300 **5** 3/4 **Shrine Mountain (USA)**[8] 252 5-9-5 57 ... (b) EddieAhern 3 62
(R A Harris) *led tl rdn and hdd over 2f out: wknd fnl f* **5/1**

-300 **6** 1 **Miss Sudbrook (IRE)**[14] 187 5-8-8 40 ... (v) ShaneKelly 2 49
(A W Carroll) *hld up: rdn 3f out: kpt on but nvr nr enough to chal* **66/1**

0-44 **7** 2 1/2 **Colonel Bilko (IRE)**[6] 273 5-8-10 39 ... MarcHalford[(3)] 4 48
(J J Bridger) *chsd ldrs: rdn over 2f out: sn btn* **25/1**

00-0 **8** 2 **Shirley Oaks (IRE)**[12] 207 9-8-8 41 ... AdrianMcCarthy 7 39
(Miss Z C Davison) *hld up: rdn 2f out: nvr on terms* **25/1**

-003 **9** 2 1/2 **Christmas Truce (IRE)**[5] 288 8-8-6 50 ... (p) RyanBird[(7)] 9 38
(Ms J S Doyle) *v.s.a: a bhd* **20/1**

0-00 **10** 7 **Dexileos (IRE)**[21] 123 8-8-13 47 ... (t) FergusSweeney 5 22
(David Pinder) *racd wd: effrt 1/2-way: sn bhd: eased ins fnl f* **50/1**

1m 37.92s (-1.51) **Going Correction** -0.125s/f (Stan) 10 Ran SP% **118.8**
Speed ratings (Par 101):102,100,99,98,97 96,94,92,89,82
CSF £7.03 TOTE £2.60: £1.10, £1.60, £1.30; EX 9.40 Trifecta £16.50 Pool: £370.71 - 15.86 winning units..The winner was bought in for 10,200gns.
Owner C Waters **Bred** Saud Bin Saad **Trained** Middleham Moor, N Yorks

FOCUS
Not bad form by selling standards, although limited a little by the sixth, and the pace was fair.

342 PONTINS.COM MAIDEN STKS — 7f (P)
2:20 (2:22) (Class 5) 3-Y-0+ **£2,914** (£867; £433; £216) **Stalls** Low

Form RPR

2- **1** **Sea Land (FR)**[100] 6188 3-8-10 ... DaneO'Neill 9 75+
(M P Tregoning) *hld up in tch: hung lft whn hdwy over 1f out: r.o to ld ins fnl f: won gng away* **2/5**[1]

230- **2** 1 3/4 **Follow The Flag (IRE)**[162] 4766 3-8-7 72 ... JamesDoyle[(3)] 10 70
(N P Littmoden) *w ldr: led over 2f out: rdn and hdd ins fnl f: nt pce of wnr* **8/1**[2]

0-42 **3** hd **Leg Sweep**[17] 160 3-8-10 70 ... JohnEgan 8 69
(D R C Elsworth) *chsd ldrs: rdn and ev ch appr fnl f: styd on one pce* **17/2**[3]

5 **4** 1 **Desert Master**[15] 186 4-9-13 ... GeorgeBaker 6 72+
(C F Wall) *hld up in rr: hdwy on outside 1/2-way: chsd ldr 2f out and ev ch tl no ex ins fnl f* **33/1**

5-32 **5** 1/2 **Madrigale**[10] 231 3-8-5 65 ... CatherineGannon 1 61
(G L Moore) *s.i.s: sn mid-div: styd on fnl f* **16/1**

6 1 1/4 **Mawaared** 3-8-6 ow1 ... EddieAhern 11 58+
(M P Tregoning) *s.i.s: hld up in tch: styd on but nvr nr to chal* **9/1**

0 **7** 2 1/2 **Grey Light (IRE)**[11] 222 3-8-10 ... JoeFanning 3 56+
(M Johnston) *chsd ldrs for 5f* **20/1**

00-6 **8** 1 1/4 **Tizzydore (IRE)**[7] 260 3-8-5 52 ... JimmyQuinn 12 48
(A M Balding) *t.k.h: chsd ldrs tl wknd over 1f out* **50/1**

05- **9** 1 1/4 **Garrulous (UAE)**[9] 1483 4-9-6 ... JemmaMarshall[(7)] 5 54
(G L Moore) *a towards rr* **25/1**

000- **10** shd **Dawson Creek (IRE)**[124] 5730 3-8-10 50 ... JimCrowley 4 49
(B Gubby) *led tl hdd over 2f out: rdn and wknd appr fnl f* **66/1**

00- **11** 1 1/4 **A Peaceful Man**[91] 6330 3-8-10 ... TonyCulhane 2 46
(B W Hills) *slowly away: a bhd* **25/1**

0-0 **12** 8 **Tobougg Welcome (IRE)**[26] 69 3-8-7 ... SaleemGolam[(3)] 7 25
(S C Williams) *a in rr* **66/1**

1m 24.82s (-1.07) **Going Correction** -0.125s/f (Stan)
WFA 3 from 4yo 17lb 12 Ran SP% **129.3**
Speed ratings (Par 103):101,99,98,97,97 95,92,91,89,89 88,79
CSF £4.70 TOTE £1.40: £1.10, £2.00, £2.00; EX 8.10 Trifecta £49.70 Pool: £586.90 - 8.37 winning units..
Owner Sheikh Ahmed Al Maktoum **Bred** Tarworth Bloodstock Ltd **Trained** Lambourn, Berks

FOCUS
Ordinary maiden form and the pace could have been better. Very solid form, the winner not having to improve on his debut effort but bound to do better.

343 CANVAS PRINTS FROM BONUSPRINT.COM MAIDEN STKS — 5f (P)
2:50 (2:51) (Class 5) 3-Y-0 **£2,914** (£867; £433; £216) **Stalls** High

Form RPR

1 **Halsion Chancer** 3-9-3 ... DaneO'Neill 4 67+
(J R Best) *s.i.s: sn in tch: rdn to ld ins fnl f: r.o wl* **3/1**[1]

4 **2** 1/2 **Time Share (IRE)**[20] 127 3-8-12 ... ShaneKelly 2 60
(J A Osborne) *led tl rdn and hdd appr fnl f: rallied to regain 2nd cl home* **3/1**[1]

52- **3** nk **Scarlett Heart (IRE)**[54] 6788 3-8-12 ... SebSanders 6 59
(P J Makin) *a.p: chsd ldr 1/2-way: led appr fnl f: rdn and hdd ins: lost 2nd nr fin* **4/1**[2]

05-3 **4** 1 1/4 **Shepherdess (USA)**[12] 219 3-8-5 55 ... KirstyMilczarek[(7)] 1 54
(D M Simcock) *a.p: rdn and no ex ins fnl f* **6/1**[3]

5 nk **Chattan Clan** 3-9-3 ... (t) SteveDrowne 5 58+
(R A Kvisla) *s.i.s: in rr: rdn and fin wl fnl f* **20/1**

03-0 **6** 3 **Launch It Lily**[10] 231 3-8-5 60 ... JackDean[(7)] 3 41
(W G M Turner) *prom: rdn over 2f out: wknd appr fnl f* **10/1**

00- **7** 1 **Savanagh Forest (IRE)**[108] 6055 3-8-12 ... NCallan 8 37
(M Quinn) *s.i.s: mde sme late hdwy but nvr on terms* **33/1**

0- **8** 1/2 **Majolica**[218] 3043 3-8-9 ... JamesDoyle[(3)] 9 35
(N P Littmoden) *racd wd: in tch tl wknd over 1f out* **25/1**

60 **9** 1 **Brave Jack (IRE)**[10] 231 3-9-3 ... HayleyTurner 7 36
(J R Best) *mid-div: rdn 1/2-way: sn bhd* **16/1**

10 2 **Shortcake** 3-8-12 ... JimCrowley 10 23
(D K Ivory) *slowly away: a bhd* **33/1**

60.26 secs (0.48) **Going Correction** -0.125s/f (Stan) 10 Ran SP% **113.7**
Speed ratings (Par 97):91,90,89,87,87 82,80,80,78,75
CSF £10.88 TOTE £2.90: £1.30, £1.50, £1.50; EX 10.90 Trifecta £21.60 Pool: £582.35 - 19.13 winning units..
Owner Halsion Ltd **Bred** Mrs S Hansford **Trained** Hucking, Kent

FOCUS
The bare form of this sprint maiden is modest at best, if sound enough, but Halsion Chancer is open to plenty of improvement.

344 BONUSPRINT.COM H'CAP — 5f (P)
3:25 (3:25) (Class 2) (0-100,110) 4-Y-0+
£11,217 (£3,358; £1,679; £840; £419; £210) **Stalls** High

Form RPR

1-41 **1** **Areyoutalkingtome**[21] 118 4-10-0 **110** ... EddieAhern 8 121
(C A Cyzer) *hld up: hdwy over 1f out: r.o strly to ld post* **2/1**[1]

5-02 **2** shd **Maltese Falcon**[14] 198 7-9-2 **98** ... (t) NelsonDeSouza 1 109
(P F I Cole) *led: hrd rdn appr fnl f: hdd post* **3/1**[2]

1412 **3** 1 3/4 **Qadar (IRE)**[4] 307 5-9-6 **102** ... (b) NCallan 3 106
(N P Littmoden) *chsd ldrs: wnt 2nd 2f out: kpt on: lost 2nd wl ins fnl f* **4/1**[3]

00-5 **4** 3/4 **Ajigolo**[14] 198 4-8-13 **95** ... EdwardCreighton 7 97
(M R Channon) *mid-div: rdn 2f out: r.o fnl f* **14/1**

004- **5** 1/2 **One More Round (USA)**[49] 6849 9-8-11 **96** ... (b) JamesDoyle[(3)] 10 96
(N P Littmoden) *in rr: rdn and hdwy over 1f out: r.o: nvr nrr* **16/1**

003- **6** 3/4 **Classic Encounter (IRE)**[55] 6776 4-8-10 **92** ... FergusSweeney 5 89
(D M Simcock) *hld up: swtchd lft and hdwy on ins wl over 1f out: one pce ins fnl f* **14/1**

62-1 **7** nk **Moorhouse Lad**[33] 5 4-8-7 **89** ... ChrisCatlin 9 85
(B Smart) *chsd ldrs: racd wd: wknd fnl f* **12/1**

03-5 **8** 2 **First Order**[29] 41 6-8-3 **90** ... (v) DuranFentiman[(5)] 4 79
(I Semple) *chsd ldrs to 2f out: rdn and sn btn* **10/1**

1-41 **9** 2 **Harry Up**[18] 155 6-8-4 **89** ... AndrewMullen[(3)] 6 71
(K A Ryan) *chsd ldrs tl wknd over 1f out* **16/1**

0- **10** 3 **Maxim's (ARG)**[203] 3535 6-8-13 **95** ... (t) SteveDrowne 2 66
(R A Kvisla) *hld up: no hdwy ins fnl 2f* **66/1**

57.69 secs (-2.09) **Going Correction** -0.125s/f (Stan) 10 Ran SP% **121.7**
Speed ratings (Par 109):111,110,108,106,106 104,104,101,97,93
CSF £8.34 CT £23.07 TOTE £2.40: £1.50, £1.90, £1.70; EX 11.20 Trifecta £16.30 Pool: £802.34 - 34.77 winning units..
Owner Mrs Charles Cyzer **Bred** C A Cyzer **Trained** Maplehurst, W Sussex

FOCUS
A high-class sprint handicap and another fine performance from the star of this winter's campaign, Areyoutalkingtome, his best effort yet. Solid form.

NOTEBOOK

Areyoutalkingtome ◆ gained his sixth success from his last seven starts in thrilling fashion. Dropped back to 5f for the first time (his recent wins over come over 6f-7f), he was ridden with confidence by Ahern, and had at least six lengths to make at the top of the straight. Such is this horse's turn of foot though, one just expected him to make up the required ground and he duly nailed Maltese Falcon on the line. The sort of performance that is needed to win a handicap off an official rating of 110 should not be underestimated - subsequent July Cup winner Les Arcs won this very race last year off an 8lb lower mark - and this effort is all the more creditable considering this trip is probably just short of his optimum. There can be no doubt whatsoever this horse is Group class and it is hard to imagine him getting beaten in his next intended target, a 6f Listed contest back here in three weeks time. In the longer term, despite his recent improvement coming on Polytrack, he could prove just as effective back on turf. Not only does he already have some smart form but his style of racing is traditionally suited to turf, and anyway his trainer is a attributing his progression to him putting on 20 kilos last autumn. (op 9-4 tchd 15-8, 5-2 in places and 11-4 in a place)

Maltese Falcon's two wins round here this winter came over 6f, but he has speed to burn and this trip probably just suits best. Very quickly away, he took the field along as expected from his inside draw and really stretched his rivals early in the straight, but he was collared late on by an exceptional horse for the level. (op 10-3 tchd 7-2)

Qadar(IRE) is holding his form well in smart company, but he did not impress with his attitude when second in a 6f conditions contest at Southwell four days earlier, and he again looked less than convincing when asked for everything. (op 9-2)

Ajigolo ◆ shaped well on his return from a break when just behind both today's second and third over 6f round here last time and, although unable to reverse form, this was another decent effort. He has dropped to a reasonable mark and looks one to keep on the right side in similar company.

One More Round(USA) is a very hard horse to win with and he never got in a blow having struggled to lay up early on. He is probably better suited by 6f.

Classic Encounter(IRE) is on quite an attractive mark and one would have hoped for better. He was switched to the inside on straightening for home which does not always help a horses momentum round here, so that could be used as a bit of an excuse, but he just seemed to be carrying his head a touch high and is not that straightforward. (op 10-1)
Moorhouse Lad came wide into the straight and could not defy a 4lb higher mark than when winning at Southwell on his previous start.

345 PONTIN'S "BOOK EARLY" H'CAP 1m 4f (P)
4:00 (4:00) (Class 2) (0-100,95) 4-Y-0+
£11,217 (£3,358; £1,679; £840; £419; £210) **Stalls** Low

Form RPR
233- **1** **Royal Jet**[105] 6097 5-9-0 **90** .... JohnEgan 2 102
(M R Channon) *trckd ldrs: led 2f out: rdn and r.o fnl f* **4/1**[2]
22-1 **2** *2 ½* **Eva Soneva So Fast (IRE)**[24] 95 5-9-1 **91** .... JimmyQuinn 5 99
(J L Dunlop) *hld up in tch: wnt 2nd 2f out: rdn and no imp fnl f* **2/1**[1]
111- **3** *5* **Sweet Indulgence (IRE)**[50] 6836 6-9-5 **95** .... FergusSweeney 6 95
(W J Musson) *hld up on outside: hdwy over 2f out: no imp on first 2 fr over 1f out* **2/1**[1]
006- **4** *5* **Orange Touch (GER)**[66] 6438 7-8-11 **87** .... JimCrowley 3 79
(Mrs A J Perrett) *t.k.h: in tch tl wknd 2f out* **20/1**
20-3 **5** *2 ½* **Crow Wood**[28] 57 8-8-11 **87** .... GrahamGibbons 4 75
(J J Quinn) *chsd ldr tl wknd over 2f out* **7/1**[3]
1-10 **6** *¾* **Melpomene**[14] 192 4-8-6 **88** .... GregFairley(3) 1 75
(M Johnston) *led tl rdn and hdd 2f out: wknd qckly* **8/1**

2m 29.23s (-5.16) **Going Correction** -0.125s/f (Stan)
WFA 4 from 5yo+ 3lb **6** Ran SP% **115.0**
Speed ratings (Par 109):112,110,107,103,102 101
CSF £12.90 TOTE £4.80: £2.00, £1.80; EX 13.50.
Owner Jaber Abdullah **Bred** Genesis Green Stud Ltd **Trained** West Ilsley, Berks

FOCUS
Just the six runners, but a very good middle-distance handicap. They appeared to go just an ordinary gallop in the early stages, but the Mark-Johnston trained Melpomene was gradually increasing the tempo from some way out and there should not be too many excuses on the pace front. Sound form.

NOTEBOOK
Royal Jet ◆ had been running well in defeat in some decent contests on the Polytrack when last seen over three months previously and, very well backed on his return to action, he duly delivered. This was quite an impressive performance and he would appear to have improved for his short winter break. (op 13-2)
Eva Soneva So Fast(IRE) could not defy a 6lb higher mark than when winning over course and distance on his previous start, but this was a decent effort in defeat as the winner has clearly improved, and he had the very useful Sweet Indulgence five lengths away in third. (op 5-2)
Sweet Indulgence(IRE), bidding for a four-timer off a mark 4lb higher than when winning at Wolverhampton 50 days previously, seemed to have every chance when moving into contention on the turn into the straight, but his effort was short-lived. Perhaps his recent improvement has just levelled off a touch. (tchd 5-2 and 11-4 in a place)
Orange Touch(GER), tried unsuccessfully over hurdles at Plumpton on his most recent start, offered little immediate promise on his return to the Flat, despite a declining handicap mark.
Crow Wood could not build on his recent third behind last year's Winter Derby winner Sri Diamond. Official explanation: jockey said gelding was never travelling (op 6-1 tchd 15-2)
Melpomene promised to be suited by the return to a left-handed track, but was again below her best. Perhaps this was a tough ask against some very useful 1m4f performers and it would be no surprise to see her eventually prove best back over further. (op 6-1)

346 GO PONTIN'S APPRENTICE H'CAP 7f (P)
4:30 (4:30) (Class 6) (0-65,65) 4-Y-0+ **£2,266** (£674; £337; £168) **Stalls** Low

Form RPR
-316 **1** **Burhaan (IRE)**[6] 276 5-8-6 **57** .... JackMitchell(5) 1 67
(J R Boyle) *trckd ldrs: hdwy on ins to ld ins fnl f: pushed out* **5/1**[3]
2-22 **2** *1 ¼* **Imperium**[10] 234 6-8-13 **64** .... SophieDoyle(5) 4 71
(Jean-Rene Auvray) *a.p: led over 3f out: rdn: hdd ins fnl f: no ex* **5/1**[3]
3-01 **3** *1 ½* **Bessemer (JPN)**[8] 252 6-9-2 **65** ....(p) TolleyDean(3) 6 68
(I W McInnes) *led for 2f: rdn over 1f out: one pce ins fnl f* **8/1**
0-14 **4** *½* **Beneking**[10] 235 7-8-9 **60** ....(p) JosephWalsh(5) 5 62+
(D Burchell) *hld up in rr: styd on fnl f: nvr nrr* **7/2**[2]
-000 **5** *¾* **Hand Chime**[3] 313 10-8-6 **55** .... AshleyHamblett(3) 9 55
(Ernst Oertel) *hld up in rr: rdn 2f out: nvr nr to chal* **20/1**
31-6 **6** *1 ¼* **Zazous**[10] 236 6-8-8 **59** .... RyanBird(5) 2 56
(J J Bridger) *a in rr* **10/1**
14-3 **7** *½* **Astronomical Odds (USA)**[11] 228 4-9-0 **63** .... NeilBrown(3) 7 58
(T D Barron) *t.k.h: led after 2f: hdd over 3f out: wknd 2f out* **2/1**[1]
60-6 **8** *nk* **Out For A Stroll**[26] 70 8-8-7 **60** .... FLenclud(7) 3 55
(S C Williams) *hld up: nvr gng pce* **16/1**

1m 25.46s (-0.43) **Going Correction** -0.125s/f (Stan) **8** Ran SP% **119.7**
Speed ratings (Par 101):97,95,93,93,92 91,90,90
CSF £31.68 CT £202.80 TOTE £3.70: £2.10, £1.80, £3.40; EX 17.90 Trifecta £37.60 Pool: £713.37 - 13.47 winning units. Place 6 £2.05, Place 5 £1.86.
Owner John Hopkins (t/a South Hatch Racing) **Bred** Shadwell Estate Company Limited **Trained** Epsom, Surrey

FOCUS
A modest handicap restricted to apprentices who had not ridden more than 50 winners and, with no pace on early, the form should not be taken too literally. The first three were always prominent, in a race rated through the runner-up.
T/Plt: £3.50 to a £1 stake. Pool: £63,043.00. 12,818.90 winning tickets. T/Qpdt: £2.80 to a £1 stake. Pool: £1,882.10. 495.30 winning tickets. JS

347 - (Foreign Racing) - See Raceform Interactive

[272]KEMPTON (A.W) (R-H)
Sunday, February 4

OFFICIAL GOING: Standard
Wind: Virtually nil Weather: Sunny

348 RASHER FRITH MEMORIAL APPRENTICE H'CAP 7f (P)
1:20 (1:21) (Class 6) (0-65,65) 3-Y-0 **£2,590** (£770; £385; £192) **Stalls** High

Form RPR
644- **1** **Satyricon**[158] 4932 3-9-1 **64** ....(b[1]) NicolPolli(3) 10 70
(M Botti) *w.w in midfield: hdwy wl over 3f out: rdn to ld over 1f out: clr ins fnl f: drvn out* **13/2**[3]
000- **2** *1 ½* **Ella Woodcock (IRE)**[132] 5563 3-8-12 **63** .... SophieDoyle(5) 6 65
(J A Osborne) *stdd s: hld up bhd: gd hdwy on inner 2f out: chsd wnr wl ins fnl f: r.o: nt rch wnr* **33/1**
306- **3** *1 ½* **Sunley Sovereign**[127] 5686 3-8-10 **63** .... MatthewDavies(7) 11 61
(M R Channon) *chsd ldr for 2f out: styd handy: rdn and ev ch over 2f out: one pced fnl f* **16/1**
00-3 **4** *1 ¼* **Calloff The Search**[32] 25 3-8-9 **58** ....(p) TolleyDean(3) 14 53
(W G M Turner) *led tl rdn and hdd over 1f out: kpt on same pce fnl f* **15/2**
54-2 **5** *1 ½* **Popolo (IRE)**[28] 65 3-9-2 **65** .... LukeMorris(3) 2 56
(M L W Bell) *plld hrd: hdwy to chse ldr 5f out tl over 2 out: wknd 1f out* **11/1**
4-22 **6** *hd* **Razzano (IRE)**[6] 295 3-8-6 **55** .... JamieJones(3) 9 45
(A M Hales) *t.k.h: chsd ldrs: rdn 3f out: kpt on same pce last 2f* **9/1**
00-1 **7** *½* **Heaven's Gates**[12] 223 3-8-10 **56** .... JamieMoriarty 8 45
(K A Ryan) *prom: rdn wl over 2f out: wknd over 1f out* **11/2**[2]
13-3 **8** *hd* **Lordswood (IRE)**[18] 162 3-9-0 **65** .... RyanBird(5) 13 54
(J J Bridger) *s.i.s: t.k.h: hld up in tch on inner: rdn over 2f out: no hdwy over 1f out* **14/1**
00-0 **9** *1 ½* **Da Schadenfreude (USA)**[25] 93 3-8-9 **60** .... JackDean(5) 3 45
(W G M Turner) *hld up bhd: rdn and hdwy on outer over 3f out: no imp last 2f* **20/1**
33-2 **10** *hd* **Show Trial (IRE)**[14] 202 3-8-7 **60** .... BillyCray(7) 4 44
(D J S Ffrench Davis) *hld up in rr: rdn and effrt wl over 2f out: nvr trbld ldrs* **12/1**
-413 **11** *1 ¼* **Ella Y Rossa**[7] 284 3-9-0 **60** .... MichaelJStainton 7 41
(P D Evans) *towards rr: rdn and wl over 3f out: no ch last 2f* **9/2**[1]
40-6 **12** *1 ¾* **Ioweyou**[31] 34 3-8-8 **59** .... JosephWalsh(5) 12 35
(J S Moore) *racd in midfield: hmpd wl over 3f out: nvr trbld ldrs* **25/1**
44-4 **13** *6* **Ice Box (IRE)**[25] 93 3-8-12 **58** .... DuranFentiman 5 19
(M Johnston) *racd in midfield on outer: rdn 4f out: no ch last 2f* **13/2**[3]
000- **14** *1* **Pajada**[71] 6591 3-8-3 **54** ....(v[1]) LauraReynolds(5) 1 12
(M D I Usher) *t.k.h: hld up: hdwy to chse ldrs wl over 3f out: wknd over 2f out* **66/1**

1m 26.15s (-0.65) **Going Correction** -0.175s/f (Stan) **14** Ran SP% **123.6**
Speed ratings (Par 95):96,94,92,91,89 89,88,88,86,86 85,83,76,75
CSF £218.78 CT £3302.00 TOTE £10.10: £3.50, £10.30, £6.10; EX 209.10.
Owner Felice Villa **Bred** Sir Eric Parker **Trained** Newmarket, Suffolk

FOCUS
Very moderate handicap form and many of these pulled hard early as the pace took time to develop. The overall time was fairly standard, though, and the finish was dominated by two horses making their debut in handicap company.
Ella Y Rossa Official explanation: jockey said filly was intimidated by bunching horses
Ioweyou Official explanation: jockey said filly suffered interference in running

349 FREDERICK MOTSON 21ST BIRTHDAY CLASSIFIED STKS 1m 3f (P)
1:50 (1:51) (Class 7) 4-Y-0+ **£1,365** (£403; £201) **Stalls** High

Form RPR
2-64 **1** **Simplified**[15] 187 4-8-11 41 .... JerryO'Dwyer(3) 4 49
(N B King) *hld up bhd: hdwy 4f out: rdn to chse ldr 2f out: led over 1f out: hld on nr fin: all out* **6/1**[3]
0-54 **2** *shd* **War Feather**[11] 229 5-9-5 48 .... EdwardCreighton 11 52
(T D McCarthy) *chsd ldrs: rdn and hdwy over 2f out: ev ch ins fnl f: no ex nr fin* **6/1**[3]
500- **3** *nk* **Chimes At Midnight (USA)**[119] 5853 10-9-2 42 .... EddieAhern 8 48
(Luke Comer, Ire) *bhd and niggled along: rdn and hdwy over 2 out: swtchd lft ins fnl f: r.o strly: nrst fin* **7/1**
04-0 **4** *1* **Montecristo**[21] 134 14-8-9 45 .... LukeMcJannet(7) 6 47
(Rae Guest) *racd in midfield: rdn over 3f out: hdwy on inner to ld over 2f out: hdd over 1f out: one pce ins fnl f* **14/1**
5-00 **5** *1 ¼* **Rowan Pursuit**[29] 51 6-9-2 40 ....(p) PaulEddery 14 45
(C A Horgan) *hld up wl in rr: rdn over 2f out: styd on over 1f out: nt rch ldrs* **16/1**
00-4 **6** *hd* **Elms Schoolboy**[19] 156 5-9-2 45 ....(b) JimmyQuinn 3 44
(P Howling) *t.k.h: chsd ldrs: rdn over 2f out: kpt on same pce fnl f* **4/1**[1]
50-0 **7** *2* **Sriology (IRE)**[15] 187 6-9-2 41 ....(b[1]) FergusSweeney 1 41
(M R Hoad) *stdd s: sn in midfield: hdwy to chse ldrs over 3f out: rdn and no imp wl over 1f out* **10/1**
000/ **8** *shd* **Artic Bliss**[545] 4224 5-9-2 43 .... BrettDoyle 12 41
(G F Bridgwater) *plld hrd: hld up towards rr: rdn and effrt over 2f out: nt pce to rch ldrs* **50/1**
000- **9** *1 ¾* **Homebred Star**[53] 6800 6-9-2 42 ....(p) DaneO'Neill 5 38
(G P Enright) *s.i.s: hld up in rr: hdwy 4f out: chsd ldrs 3f out: rdn and no prog over 1f out* **9/1**
40-6 **10** *1* **Thomas A Beckett (IRE)**[7] 273 4-9-0 45 .... IanMongan 10 36
(P R Chamings) *t.k.h: chsd ldng pair: hdwy to chse ldr 4f out tl 2f out: sn wknd* **6/1**[3]
50/5 **11** *4* **King's Minstrel (IRE)**[21] 133 6-9-2 41 .... JimCrowley 2 29
(R Rowe) *t.k.h: w ldr and clr tl led over 7f out: rdn and hdd 2f out: sn wknd* **5/1**[2]
0/0- **12** *38* **Mo Chroi**[384] 122 4-8-7 40 .... RyanBird(7) 13 —
(J J Bridger) *led and clr w one other: hdd over 7f out: wknd 4f out: wl t.o last 2f* **33/1**

2m 21.54s (-1.14) **Going Correction** -0.175s/f (Stan)
WFA 4 from 5yo+ 2lb **12** Ran SP% **128.6**
Speed ratings (Par 97):97,96,96,95,95 94,93,93,92,91 88,60
CSF £45.78 TOTE £6.70: £2.20, £2.60, £3.40; EX 33.70.
Owner Neil King **Bred** Beaumont Hall Bloodstock **Trained** Newmarket, Suffolk

FOCUS
A poor race contested by unreliable types, and just like the first race, several took time to settle. Straightforward for the grade, however, with the first two running to recent form.

350 CAROLE SCHAVERIEN MEMORIAL CLASSIFIED STKS 1m (P)
2:20 (2:22) (Class 7) 4-Y-0+ **£1,295** (£385; £192; £96) **Stalls** High

Form RPR
06-2 **1** **Weet Yer Tern (IRE)**[8] 271 5-9-0 45 ....(b) JamieSpencer 11 56
(W M Brisbourne) *s.i.s: hld up bhd: stl plenty to do 2f out: gd hdwy on inner over 1f out: qcknd to ld ins last: r.o strly* **11/2**[2]
065- **2** *1 ½* **Almowj**[38] 6961 4-9-0 43 .... SebSanders 9 52
(C E Brittain) *w.w in midfield: hdwy 3f out: rdn and qcknd to ld wl over 1f out: hdd ins fnl f: nt pce of wnr* **8/1**
06-1 **3** *1 ½* **Comeintothespace (IRE)**[7] 273 5-9-6 43 .... DaneO'Neill 12 55
(R A Farrant) *hld up towards rr: hdwy over 3f out: rdn wl over 2f out: chsd ldng pair ins fnl f: kpt on same pce* **5/1**[1]
64-5 **4** *nk* **Chalice Welcome**[13] 210 4-9-0 43 .... GeorgeBaker 14 48
(C F Wall) *hld up towards rr: effrt on inner 2f out: chsd ldrs 1f out: kpt on same pce* **11/1**
0532 **5** *1* **Height Of Spirits**[7] 273 5-9-0 44 .... EdwardCreighton 4 46
(T D McCarthy) *t.k.h: trckd ldrs: rdn and ev ch over 2f out: one pce fnl f* **6/1**[3]
-563 **6** *¾* **Kinsman (IRE)**[13] 207 10-8-11 42 ....(p) AmirQuinn(3) 1 44
(T D McCarthy) *in tch on outer: rdn over 2f out: kpt on same pce fnl f* **20/1**

50-0 **7** *shd* **Merdiff**[20] 138 8-8-9 45 AshleyHamblett(5) 7 44
(W M Brisbourne) *chsd ldrs: rdn over 2f out: wknd fnl f* **14/1**

-U02 **8** *3/4* **Savoy Chapel**[13] 210 5-9-0 44 (v) ShaneKelly 13 42
(A W Carroll) *t.k.h: hld up in rr: hdwy and rdn 2f out: no imp whn sltly hmpd 1f out* **7/1**

-301 **9** *1/2* **A Teen**[13] 207 9-9-1 46 JimmyQuinn 6 42
(P Howling) *hld up bhd: rdn and hdwy over 2f out: nvr trbld ldrs* **11/1**

50-0 **10** *3* **Titus Wonder (IRE)**[19] 156 4-8-11 45 JamesDoyle(3) 2 34
(J W Mullins) *led briefly early: chsd ldr tl rdn to ld over 2f out: hdd over 1f out: sn wknd* **50/1**

-026 **11** *5* **Mid Valley**[13] 210 4-9-0 45 EddieAhern 8 22
(J R Jenkins) *t.k.h: hld up in rr: rdn and hdwy wl over 2f out: wknd over 1f out* **7/1**

0-50 **12** *2 1/2* **Pantomime Prince**[13] 210 4-9-0 44 BrettDoyle 5 17
(John Berry) *hld up bhd: rdn and c wd 3f out: no hdwy* **10/1**

0-00 **13** *hd* **Opal Warrior**[6] 288 4-9-0 45 (v) JohnEgan 3 16
(Jane Southcombe) *sn led: rdn and hdd over 2f out: sn wknd* **40/1**

440- **14** *6* **Tequila Rose (IRE)**[312] 790 4-9-0 43 SteveDrowne 10 2
(M A Buckley) *t.k.h: chsd ldrs tl wknd qckly wl over 2f out* **66/1**

1m 38.72s (-2.08) **Going Correction** -0.175s/f (Stan) **14** Ran SP% **125.5**
Speed ratings (Par 97):103,101,100,99,98 97,97,97,96,93 88,86,85,79
CSF £50.14 TOTE £5.50: £2.40, £2.80, £2.20; EX 51.40.
Owner Ed Weetman (haulage & Storage) Ltd **Bred** E O'Leary **Trained** Great Ness, Shropshire

FOCUS
Again, just glorified banded form, but quite a few of these came here in good form and it was a competitive heat for the class. The time, a touch faster than standard, was pretty good for the grade.
Height Of Spirits Official explanation: jockey said gelding hung left
Savoy Chapel Official explanation: jockey said gelding was denied a clear run

351 LONDON MILE H'CAP (QUALIFIER) 1m (P)
2:50 (2:52) (Class 4) (0-85,84) 4-Y-0+ **£4,728** (£1,406; £702; £351) **Stalls** High

Form RPR

11-1 **1** **Atlantic Story (USA)**[16] 185 5-8-8 **76** (t) JamieSpencer 10 88+
(M W Easterby) *trckd ldrs: shkn up to ld wl over 1f out: clr and in command 1f out: eased nr fin* **11/10**[1]

2164 **2** *1 1/2* **Sun Catcher (IRE)**[8] 261 4-8-9 **77** PatDobbs 4 85
(R Hannon) *chsd ldr tl led over 2f out: hdd wl over 1f out: kpt on gamely but no ch w wnr* **16/1**

4-00 **3** *hd* **Councellor (FR)**[15] 190 5-8-6 **74** (t) EddieAhern 11 82
(Stef Liddiard) *swtg: hld up in midfield on inner: rdn 3f out: hdwy over 2f out: r.o fnl f: no ch w wnr* **33/1**

00-4 **4** *1/2* **Gallantry**[8] 259 5-9-0 **82** DeanMcKeown 2 89
(D Shaw) *stdd s: hld up in last: rdn over 1f out: plld out 1f out: r.o ins fnl f: nvr nrr* **10/1**

30-0 **5** *shd* **Finsbury**[15] 191 4-8-0 **75** AmyBaker(7) 7 82
(Miss J Feilden) *s.i.s: hld up bhd: rdn 2f out: hdwy over 1f out: kpt on same pce last 100 yds* **20/1**

3-05 **6** *1* **Royal Amnesty**[14] 205 4-8-3 **74** SaleemGolam(3) 9 78
(G C H Chung) *chsd ldrs: rdn 2f out: kpt on same pce fnl f* **9/1**

34-2 **7** *1* **Gifted Gamble**[13] 218 5-9-0 **82** (b) NCallan 5 84
(K A Ryan) *t.k.h: hld up in midfield: rdn 2f out: no imp over 1f out* **6/1**[2]

06-2 **8** *nk* **Ninth House (USA)**[16] 185 5-8-13 **84** (bt) JamesDoyle(3) 3 85
(N P Littmoden) *in tch on outer: rdn and effrt to chse ldrs wl over 2f out: wknd over 1f out* **7/1**[3]

50-5 **9** *1* **Cape Greko**[29] 56 5-8-13 **81** JohnEgan 6 80
(A M Balding) *t.k.h: hld up in rr: hdwy over 3f out: rdn and outpcd 2 f out* **12/1**

21- **10** *1 1/2* **Armada**[218] 3100 4-8-12 **80** TonyCulhane 8 76
(W J Haggas) *led tl rdn and hdd over 2f out: wknd over 1f out* **10/1**

1m 38.92s (-1.88) **Going Correction** -0.175s/f (Stan) **10** Ran SP% **123.9**
Speed ratings (Par 105):102,100,100,99,99 98,97,97,96,94
CSF £24.39 CT £431.13 TOTE £2.00: £1.40, £3.90, £7.10; EX 26.90.
Owner Matthew Green **Bred** A I Appleton **Trained** Sheriff Hutton, N Yorks

FOCUS
From a time perspective not a strong handicap - indeed, it was run in a slower time than the previous classified stakes for horses rated up to 45 - but that would be down to a modest early gallop, and the winner could hardly have been more impressive. The bare form may not prove all that reliable despite making sense on the figures.

352 DIGIBET.COM LADYBIRD STKS (LISTED RACE) 1m (P)
3:20 (3:20) (Class 1) 4-Y-0+
£14,762 (£5,595; £2,800; £1,396; £699; £351) **Stalls** High

Form RPR

01-1 **1** **Gentleman's Deal (IRE)**[34] 6 6-9-0 107 PaulMulrennan 8 114+
(M W Easterby) *trckd ldrs: shkn up to ld jst over 1f out: rdn clr: readily* **1/1**[1]

535- **2** *1 1/2* **Grand Passion (IRE)**[78] 6516 7-9-0 100 SteveDrowne 6 108
(G Wragg) *hld up bhd: rdn and hdwy over 1f out: r.o ins fnl f: wnt 2nd last 50 yds: no ch w wnr* **8/1**[3]

3-62 **3** *1 1/4* **Party Boss**[15] 197 5-9-0 95 SebSanders 2 105
(C E Brittain) *sn chsng ldr: led over 4f out: rdn over 2f out: hdd jst over 1f out: outpcd by wnr: lost 2nd last 50yds* **12/1**

-221 **4** *1 1/4* **Red Spell (IRE)**[15] 197 6-9-0 104 DaneO'Neill 5 102
(R Hannon) *hld up in tch: rdn and hdwy over 1f out: kpt on fnl f: nt trble ldrs* **9/4**[2]

5 *3* **Farnesina (FR)**[29] 5-8-9 (b) JCabre 7 90
(E Danel, France) *t.k.h: chsd ldrs: rdn 2f out: wknd jst over 1f out* **20/1**

20-3 **6** *shd* **Hail The Chief**[9] 255 10-9-0 98 RichardHughes 3 95
(R Hannon) *led tl over 4f out: rdn over 2f out: wknd 1f out* **12/1**

00/0 **7** *1 3/4* **Tony James (IRE)**[22] 118 5-9-0 99 LPKeniry 4 91
(K O Cunningham-Brown) *hld up in last pair: hdwy over 2f out: wknd over 1f out* **25/1**

050- **8** *nk* **Weightless**[35] 6997 7-9-0 96 NCallan 1 90
(N P Littmoden) *chsd ldrs on outer: rdn over 2f out: wknd over 1f out* **33/1**

1m 36.82s (-3.98) **Going Correction** -0.175s/f (Stan) **8** Ran SP% **118.8**
Speed ratings (Par 111):112,110,109,108,105 104,103,102
CSF £10.50 TOTE £1.70: £1.10, £2.10, £2.30; EX 14.60.
Owner Stephen J Curtis **Bred** C H Wacker Iii **Trained** Sheriff Hutton, N Yorks

FOCUS
They didn't apear to go that quick here, yet the winner knocked over half a second off the track record. That said, the time was still less than two seconds quicker than the earlier banded level race over the same trip, which keeps it in perspective. Gentleman's Deal impressed again, though he probably didn't need to improve on his impressive Southwell win.

NOTEBOOK
Gentleman's Deal(IRE) travelled like an absolute dream in behind the leaders, seemingly just waiting for a gap to appear, which it did just over a furlong from home where he breezed through and drew away. He returns to stud now, but it is by no means the end of his racing career, because connections have any number of options, not least the Winter Derby, which they appear quite keen to tackle. (op 5-4)
Grand Passion(IRE), beaten only half a length in last year's Winter Derby, does not have quite the progressive profile of the winner but he lost little in defeat, staying on strongly having been held up off the pace. He appreciates another couple of furlongs ideally, but there are not many options for a horse of his rating, especially on sand, and he is always going to be vulnerable to less-exposed types. (op 7-1)
Party Boss had no chance of beating Red Spell strictly on the book, but he proved the statistic misleading, as he was always the better placed of the pair given the way the race was run. (op 10-1)
Red Spell(IRE) took time to pick up before making good headway to finish on the heels of the front three and clear of the rest, but the race was not run to suit his come-from-behind style. (tchd 5-2 in places)
Farnesina(FR) travelled well for much of the race, but was no match for the principals when the pace quickened and she needs her sights lowering.
Hail The Chief was quite disappointing given he should have derived significant improvement from last week's Wolverhampton run. He was not beaten up in the closing stages once it was clear he was not going to be a factor, but looks best watched on the back of this run. (op 10-1)

353 DIGIBET.CO.UK H'CAP 1m 3f (P)
3:50 (3:50) (Class 4) (0-85,84) 4-Y-0+ **£4,728** (£1,406; £702; £351) **Stalls** High

Form RPR

005- **1** **Awatuki (IRE)**[46] 6888 4-8-10 **78** TPQueally 6 86
(A P Jarvis) *t.k.h: chsd ldr: rdn to ld over 2f out: hdd jst over 1f out: rallied to ld again nr fin* **9/1**

304- **2** *nk* **Woolfall Blue (IRE)**[58] 6744 4-8-11 **79** OscarUrbina 10 86
(G G Margarson) *led tl hdd over 2f out: rdn to ld again ins jst over 1f out: hdd and no ex nr fin* **13/2**

34-1 **3** *3/4* **Mataram (USA)**[25] 96 4-8-11 **79** BrettDoyle 7 90+
(W Jarvis) *plld hrd: hld up midfield: hanging rt and unable to get out 2f out: plld out ins fnl f: r.o: nrst fin* **5/2**[1]

000- **4** *3/4* **James Caird (IRE)**[36] 6992 7-8-13 **82** SaleemGolam(3) 2 86
(M H Tompkins) *chsd ldrs: rdn and chsd ldng pair wl over 1f out: kpt on same pce: lost 3rd nr fin* **25/1**

011- **5** *1/2* **Prime Contender**[22] 6673 5-8-12 **78** (b) NCallan 5 82
(G L Moore) *t.k.h: hld up in tch: trckd ldrs gng wl 3f over 3f out : rdn 2f out: fnd little and no imp after* **4/1**[2]

50-6 **6** *nk* **Lake Poet (IRE)**[25] 96 4-8-12 **80** SebSanders 8 83
(C E Brittain) *racd in midfield: rdn and effrt on inner 2f out: kpt on same pce* **6/1**[3]

00-5 **7** *nk* **Fantasy Ride**[9] 256 5-8-8 **74** JimmyQuinn 3 77
(J Pearce) *slowly away: hld up towards rr: hdwy over 3f out: rdn and outpcd 2f out* **16/1**

456- **8** *1/2* **Dream Catcher (SWE)**[71] 6607 4-8-12 **80** (t) SteveDrowne 9 82
(R A Kvisla) *t.k.h: rdn over 2f out: wknd ins fnl f* **25/1**

040- **9** *nk* **Our Teddy (IRE)**[141] 5367 7-9-2 **82** TonyCulhane 1 83
(P A Blockley) *hld up bhd: rdn and effrt over 2f out: nt pce to trble ldrs* **25/1**

05-1 **10** *1/2* **Wild Pitch**[29] 48 6-8-8 **74** (b) JamieSpencer 11 74
(P Mitchell) *hld up wl in rr: effrt and sme hdwy over 2f out: no hdwy over 1f out* **8/1**

1/3- **11** *1 1/4* **Mustajed**[279] 1357 6-8-13 **84** JamesMillman(5) 4 82
(B R Millman) *slowly away: hld up in last: rdn over 2f out: nvr trbld ldrs* **20/1**

2m 22.53s (-0.15) **Going Correction** -0.175s/f (Stan)
WFA 4 from 5yo+ 2lb **11** Ran SP% **119.5**
Speed ratings (Par 105):93,92,92,91,91 91,90,90,90,89 89
CSF £63.93 CT £189.15 TOTE £9.30: £2.50, £3.10, £1.20; EX 90.00.
Owner Allen B Pope, Andrew J King **Bred** Yeomanstown Stud **Trained** Twyford, Bucks

FOCUS
No pace, and the finish was dominated by those who raced prominently as the first two filled those positions throughout, while James Caird was never worse than his finishing position of fourth. Not a race to take at face value.
Mataram(USA) Official explanation: jockey said gelding hung badly right in closing stages
Wild Pitch Official explanation: jockey said gelding was unsuited by the slow early pace
Mustajed Official explanation: jockey said gelding hung left in home straight

354 DIGIBET SPORTS BETTING H'CAP 2m (P)
4:20 (4:21) (Class 5) (0-75,74) 4-Y-0+ **£3,238** (£963; £481; £240) **Stalls** High

Form RPR

5-51 **1** **Noble Minstrel**[13] 213 4-9-4 **65** (t) NCallan 6 75+
(S C Williams) *hld up in rr: rdn and gd hdwy wl over 1f out: chsd ldr 1f out: r.o wl u.p to ld nr fin* **5/2**[1]

02-3 **2** *nk* **Critical Stage (IRE)**[13] 213 8-8-13 **61** HaddenFrost(7) 4 70
(J D Frost) *t.k.h: chsd ldr tl 9f out: lost pl and midfield 4f out: rdn and gd hdwy to ld over 1f out: hdd nr fin* **10/1**

-131 **3** *1 1/2* **Lorikeet**[11] 232 8-9-6 **64** JamesDoyle(3) 7 71+
(Noel T Chance) *stdd s: hld up wl bhd: hdwy 2f out: pressed ldrs over 1f out: no ex last 100 yds* **5/2**[1]

1-40 **4** *2* **Salut Saint Cloud**[11] 232 6-9-10 **65** (p) SimonWhitworth 11 70
(G L Moore) *chsd ldrs for 7f out: lost pl and towards rr 4f out: rdn over 3f out: styd on fnl f: nt rch ldrs* **16/1**

/456 **5** *1/2* **Sea Map**[6] 291 5-9-3 **58** EdwardCreighton 1 62
(Miss Sheena West) *chsd ldrs: rdn to ld over 2f out: hdd over 1f out: wknd* **25/1**

32-2 **6** *4* **Lysander's Quest (IRE)**[21] 134 9-8-8 **49** oh1 FergusSweeney 3 48
(R Ingram) *hld up in midfield: hdwy over 3f out: rdn and outpcd over 1f out* **12/1**

140- **7** *nk* **Primondo (IRE)**[68] 6630 5-9-6 **61** (v) ShaneKelly 12 60
(A W Carroll) *hld up in midfield: hdwy on inner over 2f out: chsd ldrs wl over 1f out: wknd qckly 1f out* **20/1**

40-5 **8** *shd* **Twill (IRE)**[15] 192 4-9-13 **74** (b[1]) GeorgeBaker 5 73
(G L Moore) *w.w wl in tch: hdwy to trck ldrs gng wl over 3f out: rdn 2f out: fnd little and sn btn* **8/1**[3]

045- **9** *3* **Love Angel (USA)**[84] 4586 5-8-10 **54** AmirQuinn(3) 9 49
(J J Bridger) *s.i.s: hld up: hdwy 5f out: jnd ldr wl over 3f out: rdn over 2f out: wknd qckly over 1f out* **16/1**

241- **10** *1 3/4* **Is It Me (USA)**[85] 3634 4-8-11 **63** KevinGhunowa(5) 8 56
(P A Blockley) *led: clr tl 9f out: rdn and hdd over 2f out: wknd wl over 1f out* **7/1**[2]

5-06 **11** *7* **Zacatecas (GER)**[7] 283 7-9-5 **60** DeanMcKeown 10 45
(A J Chamberlain) *a bhd: rdn 5f out: no ch last 3f* **100/1**

The Form Book, Raceform Ltd, Compton, RG20 6NL

1-13 **12** *10* **Mister Completely (IRE)**[18] [159] 6-9-0 **55**................ RichardHughes 2 28
(Ms J S Doyle) *racd in midfield: hdwy to chse ldr 9f out tl wl over 3f out: sn wknd: eased ins fnl f* **14/1**

3m 27.72s (-3.68) **Going Correction** -0.175s/f (Stan)
WFA 4 from 5yo+ 6lb **12** Ran SP% **125.6**
Speed ratings (Par 103):102,101,101,100,99 97,97,97,96,95 91,86
CSF £31.82 CT £72.85 TOTE £4.80: £1.50, £4.40, £2.00; EX 61.10 Place 6 £160.07, Place 5 £21.30.
Owner Alasdair Simpson **Bred** Mrs M Lavell **Trained** Newmarket, Suffolk
■ Stewards' Enquiry : N Callan one-day ban: used whip down the shoulder in forehand position (Feb 15)

FOCUS
A race of changing fortunes and the picture altered dramatically approaching the final furlong. The form looks pretty solid though, with the runner-up back to his best off this better pace and the fifth to his recent best, and there is more to come from the winner.
T/Jkpt: Not won. T/Plt: £431.20 to a £1 stake. Pool: £59,810.90. 101.25 winning tickets. T/Qpdt: £13.40 to a £1 stake. Pool: £4,312.65. 236.60 winning tickets. SP

ST MORITZ (R-H)
Sunday, February 4

OFFICIAL GOING: Frozen

355a GRAND PRIX HOCHMUTH BOOTSBAU (SNOW) 1m 1f
2:00 (2:07) 4-Y-0+ **£4,619** (£1,848; £1,386; £924; £462)

RPR
1 **Quiron (IRE)**[350] [456] 6-9-1 .... TMundry 2 107
(Carmen Bocskai, Switzerland)
2 *2* **First Time (GER)** 4-8-10 .... DPorcu 5 98
(Karin Suter, Switzerland)
3 *2 1/2* **Collow (GER)**[350] [456] 7-9-3 .... MKolb 6 101
(M Weiss, Switzerland)
4 *9* **Dixigold (FR)**[364] [306] 6-9-5 .... GBocksai 4 85
(Carmen Bocskai, Switzerland)
5 *5 1/2* **Dragon Slayer (IRE)**[9] [256] 5-9-3 .... SarahLeutwiler(4) 10 77
(Ian Williams) **49/10**[1]
6 *7* **Shiraz (GER)**[350] [456] 7-9-5 .... RobertHavlin 3 62
(M Weiss, Switzerland)
7 *20* **Royal Fire (GER)**[364] [306] 8-8-13 .... FrauNatalieFriberg 8 18
(Miss A Casotti, Switzerland)
8 *1/2* **Le Royal (GER)**[826] [6512] 7-9-1 .... TCastanheira 9 19
(K Schafflutzel, Switzerland)
9 *3* **Simplex (FR)**[327] 6-9-5 .... OPlacais 7 17
(K Schafflutzel, Switzerland)
10 *2 1/2* **Sargentos (GER)**[159] 5-8-13 .... MichellePayne 1 6
(M F Harris) **72/10**[2]

2m 1.93s (121.93) **10** Ran SP% **29.1**
(including 1SF stakes): WIN 6.20; PL 3.00, 2.10, 1.40; SF 30.50.
Owner A & V Krauliger **Bred** Stiftung Gestut Fahrhof **Trained** Switzerland

356a GRAND PRIX AMERICAN AIRLINES (SNOW) 1m
2:30 (2:37) 4-Y-0+ **£3,013** (£1,205; £904; £603; £301)

RPR
1 **Shakyras Melody (IRE)** 7-9-3 .... RobertHavlin 1 65
(M Weiss, Switzerland)
2 *1 3/4* **Dooneen (IRE)**[205] [3510] 5-9-4 .... GBocksai 9 63
(C Bocksai, Germany)
3 *nk* **Vlavianus (CZE)** 6-9-6 .... MKolb 8 61
(M Weiss, Switzerland)
4 *2* **Ivans Ride (IRE)**[25] [6524] 4-8-11 .... MichellePayne 6 44
(M F Harris) **151/10**[1]
5 *3/4* **Westlander (USA)**[1330] [2412] 7-9-6 .... TMundry 4 45
(A Schennach, Switzerland)
6 *3/4* **Rainstar (IRE)**[364] [306] 5-9-4 .... TCastanheira 5 33
(J Stadelmann, Switzerland)
7 *3/4* **Negrito (GER)**[364] [306] 8-8-0 .... FrauChantalZollet(7) 7 10
(Dagmar Geissmann)
8 *1 1/4* **Give Back Calais (IRE)**[364] [305] 9-8-0 .... FrauNatalieFriberg(7) 12 10
(Miss A Casotti, Switzerland)
9 *3/4* **Lamirel (CZE)**[357] 6-9-7 .... SarahLeutwiler(4) 10 28
(M Weiss, Switzerland)
10 *12* **Investor (IRE)**[59] 8-9-4 .... SGeorgiev 2 21
(G Martin, Austria)
11 *16* **Conrad (USA)**[707] [520] 6-8-11 .... DPorcu 3 14
(Bettina Lampert, Switzerland)
12 *4* **Brother's Valcour (FR)**[296] 9-9-13 .... OPlacais 11 30
(K Schafflutzel, Switzerland)

1m 48.24s (108.24) **12** Ran SP% **6.2**
WIN 4.20; PL 1.80, 4.00, 2.40; SF 230.30.
Owner F & B Bartschi **Bred** D J Murphy **Trained** Switzerland

340 LINGFIELD (L-H)
Monday, February 5

OFFICIAL GOING: Standard
Wind: almost nil

357 PONTINSBINGO.COM FILLIES' (S) STKS 1m (P)
1:40 (1:40) (Class 6) 3-Y-0 **£2,184** (£644; £322) **Stalls** High

Form RPR
0-10 **1** **News Of The Day (IRE)**[13] [224] 3-9-1 **58**.................... GregFairley(3) 3 61
(M Johnston) *trckd ldr for 3f: styd prom: rdn 3f out: effrt on inner over 1f out: drvn to ld last 100yds: styd on* **11/4**[1]
36-5 **2** *1/2* **La Marmotte (IRE)**[19] [162] 3-9-4 **56**.................................... EddieAhern 5 60
(J W Hills) *mde most: rdn and hrd pressed over 1f out: hdd last 100yds: kpt on* **10/1**
2-45 **3** *2* **The Light Fandango**[28] [68] 3-8-7 **47**.................... TolleyDean(5) 8 49
(R A Harris) *dwlt: hld up towards rr: prog over 2f out: pressed ldrs over 1f out: kpt on same pce fnl f* **14/1**
26-0 **4** *shd* **Tenterhooks (IRE)**[13] [224] 3-8-12 **52**.................................... ShaneKelly 2 49
(J A Osborne) *settled midfield: n.m.r over 2f out: drvn wl over 1f out: no prog tl styd on wl fnl 150yds: nrst fin* **14/1**
0-0 **5** *1* **Jemima Godfrey**[14] [208] 3-8-12 ....(t) JimmyQuinn 10 47
(J Pearce) *sn last: reminder wl over 2f out: stl last wl over 1f out: swished tail whn rdn: styd on wl last 150yds: nvr nrr* **33/1**
4-06 **6** *1/2* **Gertie (IRE)**[14] [209] 3-8-5 **45**.................................... SCreighton(7) 1 46
(E J Creighton) *dwlt: last trio: pushed along 2f out: nt clr run and swtchd rt over 1f out: kpt on: n.d* **50/1**
0-56 **7** *hd* **Elizabeth Garrett**[16] [194] 3-8-9 **40**.................... MarcHalford(3) 9 45
(M J Gingell) *racd wd: reminder after 2f: effrt u.p over 2f out: no prog over 1f out* **50/1**
56-0 **8** *nk* **Roca Redonda (IRE)**[16] [193] 3-8-12 **60**....................(v[1]) JohnEgan 7 45
(M J Wallace) *trckd ldrs: effrt 2f out: rdn to chal over 1f out: fnd nil: wknd fnl f* **8/1**
-420 **9** *1* **A Nod And A Wink (IRE)**[14] [209] 3-8-5 **52**.............. HaddenFrost(7) 11 42
(R Hannon) *trckd ldrs: nt qckn 2f out: fdd over 1f out* **10/3**[2]
2510 **10** *1* **Zaafira (SPA)**[10] [253] 3-9-4 **65**.................................... EdwardCreighton 4 46
(E J Creighton) *dwlt: sn rcvrd: pressed ldr after 3f: rdn to chal and upsides over 1f out: wknd rapidly and eased* **11/2**[3]
0-00 **11** *nk* **First Frost**[13] [222] 3-8-9 **45**.................................... AmirQuinn(3) 12 39
(M J Gingell) *hld up fr wd draw: no prog fnl 2f* **66/1**
04-5 **12** *nk* **Shes Millie**[10] [253] 3-9-4 **51**.................................... SebSanders 6 45
(J G M O'Shea) *prom to 1/2-way: struggling fnl 2f* **7/1**

1m 39.61s (0.18) **Going Correction** -0.15s/f (Stan) **12** Ran SP% **119.5**
Speed ratings (Par 92):93,92,90,90,89 88,88,88,87,86 86,85
CSF £31.21 TOTE £2.40: £1.40, £2.50, £3.70; EX 32.10 TRIFECTA Not won..The winner was bought in for 8,200gns.
Owner J Shack **Bred** Dr Michael Marenchic **Trained** Middleham Moor, N Yorks

FOCUS
Not much to get excited about in this seller, but it was a bit better contested than most and the form looks sound. It should produce the odd winner at a similar level.

358 PONTIN'S "BOOK EARLY" FILLIES' H'CAP 1m (P)
2:10 (2:10) (Class 5) (0-70,70) 4-Y-0+ **£3,071** (£906; £453) **Stalls** High

Form RPR
42-1 **1** **One Night In Paris (IRE)**[26] [85] 4-9-2 **68**.................... ShaneKelly 8 78+
(M J Wallace) *hld up in last pair: prog on outer 3f out: rdn 2f out: r.o fnl f to ld last 75yds: won gng away* **15/8**[1]
2-62 **2** *1* **Bavarica**[7] [299] 5-8-10 **69**.................................... AmyBaker(7) 4 74
(Miss J Feilden) *trckd ldrs: effrt to go 2nd 2f out: rdn to ld last 150yds: hdd and outpcd fnl 75yds* **4/1**[2]
0-22 **3** *3/4* **Mademoiselle**[9] [266] 5-8-0 **57** oh3 ow1.................... TolleyDean(5) 5 60
(R A Harris) *trckd ldrs: rdn 2f out: nt qckn over 1f out: styd on fnl f to take 3rd nr fin* **6/1**[3]
4-2 **4** *1/2* **Priceoflove (IRE)**[26] [92] 4-8-13 **65**....................(t) SebSanders 1 67
(P J Makin) *restless stalls: sn led and set stdy pce to 1/2-way: kicked 2 l clr 2f out: hdd & wknd last 150yds* **8/1**
0-42 **5** *3/4* **Imperial Lucky (IRE)**[12] [233] 4-9-4 **70**.................... HayleyTurner 7 70
(D K Ivory) *hld up in last trio: rdn over 2f out: kpt on same pce fr over 1f out* **17/2**
01-0 **6** *1/2* **Odessa Star (USA)**[7] [299] 4-9-2 **68**.................... J-PGuillambert 6 67
(J G Portman) *stdd s: hld up in last: effrt on wd outside 3f out: drvn and struggling over 2f out: kpt on fnl 150yds* **12/1**
0-40 **7** *nk* **Nikki Bea (IRE)**[5] [313] 4-8-7 **59**.................... AdrianMcCarthy 2 57
(Jamie Poulton) *trckd ldrs: rdn over 2f out: no prog over 1f out: wknd fnl f* **11/1**
10-0 **8** *3* **Lady Edge (IRE)**[26] [85] 5-8-5 **60** ow3.................... JamesDoyle(3) 3 52
(A W Carroll) *chsd ldr to 2f out: wknd* **16/1**

1m 38.91s (-0.52) **Going Correction** -0.15s/f (Stan) **8** Ran SP% **112.6**
Speed ratings (Par 100):96,95,94,93,93 92,92,89
CSF £8.91 CT £36.03 TOTE £2.70: £1.10, £1.90, £2.10; EX 9.20 Trifecta £95.70 Pool £465.19 - 2.45 winning unit..
Owner D Teevan **Bred** Ken Carroll **Trained** Newmarket, Suffolk

FOCUS
Just an ordinary gallop and it was no surprise to see the runners finished bunched. The form looks a little dubious with the third wrong at the weights, but the winner should prove better than the bare form.

359 BONUSPRINT.COM CLAIMING STKS 7f (P)
2:40 (2:40) (Class 6) 4-Y-0+ **£2,184** (£644; £322) **Stalls** Low

Form RPR
0-00 **1** **Seneschal**[8] [276] 6-9-1 **64**.................................... TPQueally 5 73+
(A B Haynes) *mde most: set stdy pce to 1/2-way: drew clr wl over 1f out: at least 3 l clr fnl f: unchal* **16/1**
0-13 **2** *1 3/4* **Tyrone Sam**[12] [235] 5-9-3 **57**....................(b) MickyFenton 8 68
(K A Ryan) *hld up in midfield: effrt on outer over 2f out: drvn to dispute 2nd fnl f: n.d to wnr* **15/2**
4624 **3** *hd* **Mystic Man (FR)**[5] [313] 9-9-1 **62**....................(b) JimCrowley 10 65+
(I W McInnes) *hld up in last: stl there but gng strly over 1f out: flashed home fnl f: hopeless task* **13/2**
4-00 **4** *1/2* **Another Genepi (USA)**[14] [211] 4-8-12 **60**.................... EddieAhern 12 61
(J W Hills) *t.k.h: sn hld up bhd ldrs: effrt 2f out: disp 2nd fnl f: kpt on same pce* **14/1**
-616 **5** *nk* **Marko Jadeo (IRE)**[13] [227] 9-9-4 **77**.................... TolleyDean(5) 6 71
(R A Harris) *taken down early: sn pressed ldrs: rdn 2f out: nt qckn over 1f out: one pce after* **3/1**[1]
4-00 **6** *shd* **Prince Dayjur (USA)**[14] [211] 8-9-9 **71**.................... JimmyQuinn 9 76+
(J Pearce) *hld up towards rr: prog over 2f out: nt clr run twice arnd 1f out: styd on: unable to chal* **8/1**
0-60 **7** *2* **Wheelavit (IRE)**[12] [234] 4-9-7 **65**.................... GeorgeBaker 7 64
(B G Powell) *t.k.h: pressed wnr: nt qckn 2f out: wknd fnl f* **11/1**
4-06 **8** *shd* **Moon Bird**[12] [235] 5-8-12 **57**.................................... SebSanders 11 54
(C A Cyzer) *t.k.h: w ldrs to 2f out: wknd fnl f* **11/2**[3]
234- **9** *nk* **Detonate**[37] [6983] 5-8-8 **49**.................... JamesDoyle(3) 1 53
(Ms J S Doyle) *dwlt: hld up wl in rr: rdn and no real prog fnl 2f* **33/1**
52-2 **10** *1/2* **Rafferty (IRE)**[21] [138] 8-9-3 **70**.................... JohnEgan 4 57
(S Dow) *towards rr: rdn over 2f out: no prog* **5/1**[2]
000- **11** *shd* **Par Excellence**[250] [2138] 4-8-1 **46** ow4.................... JackDean(7) 2 48
(W G M Turner) *hld up towards rr: effrt over 2f out: no prog over 1f out: wknd* **100/1**
600- **12** *6* **Veba (USA)**[62] [6714] 4-8-9 **45**.................................... HayleyTurner 3 33
(M D I Usher) *trckd ldrs to over 2f out: wknd rapidly over 1f out* **100/1**

1m 24.64s (-1.25) **Going Correction** -0.15s/f (Stan) **12** Ran SP% **119.1**
Speed ratings (Par 101):101,99,98,98,97 97,95,95,95,94 94,87
CSF £131.36 TOTE £17.40: £6.20, £2.80, £3.00; EX 322.40 Trifecta £388.70 Part won. Pool £547.47 - 0.33 winning units..The winner was subject to a friendly claim.

Owner P Cook **Bred** Michael E Broughton **Trained** Limpley Stoke, Bath
■ Andy Haynes's first winner from his new yard.

FOCUS
A fair claimer that should produce winners. Seneschal, rated to last year's sand form, had the run of the race in front.
Prince Dayjur(USA) Official explanation: jockey said gelding had been denied a clear run

360 DIGITAL PRINTS FROM BONUSPRINT.COM H'CAP 6f (P)
3:10 (3:12) (Class 6) (0-58,56) 3-Y-O **£2,388** (£705; £352) **Stalls** Low

Form RPR
00-3 **1** **Xalted**[21] 136 3-8-2 **45** .... SaleemGolam(3) 4 54
(S C Williams) *w ldrs: led wl over 2f out: kicked clr wl over 1f out: unchal* **10/1**
04-0 **2** *2* **Lost All Alone**[10] 253 3-8-9 **49** .... MickyFenton 5 52
(D M Simcock) *pressed ldrs: rdn 2f out: nt qckn over 1f out: styd on same pce* **20/1**
00-3 **3** *shd* **Foreland Sands (IRE)**[7] 290 3-8-5 **45** .... HayleyTurner 12 48+
(J R Best) *t.k.h: restrained bhd ldrs and wd: plenty to do over 1f out: r.o to dispute 2nd ins fnl f: no imp last 100yds* **11/8**[1]
4 *½* **Royal Becky (IRE)**[111] 6041 3-8-4 **47** .... CDHayes(3) 3 48+
(Patrick Morris, Ire) *t.k.h: hld up in last trio: trapped on inner 2f out: swtchd rt over 1f out: r.o fnl f: nrst fin* **33/1**
650- **5** *1 ¼* **Hills Place**[129] 5645 3-9-2 **56** .... GeorgeBaker 7 53
(J R Best) *hld up in midfield: prog wl over 1f out on inner: fdd ins fnl f* **9/2**[2]
0-64 **6** *¾* **Homecroft Boy**[13] 223 3-8-7 **47** ow2.................... (b) ShaneKelly 11 42
(J A Osborne) *towards rr: struggling in last trio over 2f out: kpt on fnl f: n.d* **16/1**
400- **7** *¾* **Mr Mini Scule**[89] 6401 3-8-3 **50** .... HaddenFrost(7) 2 43
(A B Haynes) *trckd ldrs on inner: lost pl 2f out: pushed along and no prog fnl f* **33/1**
50-2 **8** *shd* **Priceless Melody (USA)**[21] 136 3-8-7 **47** .... (b) JimmyQuinn 9 39
(Mrs A J Perrett) *dwlt: t.k.h and in tch: effrt on outer over 2f out: nt qckn over 1f out: fdd* **9/1**
243- **9** *½* **Kilvickeon (IRE)**[40] 6951 3-8-6 **46** ow1.................... RobbieFitzpatrick 6 37
(Peter Grayson) *a in rr: struggling fnl 2f* **7/1**[3]
0-40 **10** *2 ½* **Totally Free**[15] 202 3-9-1 **55** .... (v) RobertHavlin 10 38
(M D I Usher) *hld up in rr: rdn and struggling wl over 2f out* **16/1**
000- **11** *3* **Lord Orpheus**[148] 5206 3-8-8 **48** .... EddieAhern 1 22
(B W Hills) *led to wl over 2f out: wknd rapidly over 1f out* **17/2**
1m 12.85s (0.04) **Going Correction** -0.15s/f (Stan) **11** Ran SP% **124.8**
Speed ratings (Par 95):93,90,90,89,87 86,85,85,85,81 77
CSF £200.86 CT £456.69 TOTE £19.20: £3.90, £5.40, £1.50; EX 283.30 TRIFECTA Not won..
Owner The X - Men **Bred** P And Mrs A G Venner And Alpha Bloodstock Ltd **Trained** Newmarket, Suffolk

FOCUS
A moderate handicap, but Xalted did it well and should really be capable of scoring again. A modest race on paper, but it was contested by some unexposed types. The first two were clear improvers, with the next pair looking better than the bare form.

361 GO PONTIN'S H'CAP 6f (P)
3:40 (3:41) (Class 5) (0-75,75) 4-Y-0+ **£3,238** (£963; £481; £240) **Stalls** Low

Form RPR
12-1 **1** **Louphole**[22] 132 5-8-13 **72** .... SebSanders 10 81+
(P J Makin) *hld up in rr: prog over 2f out: trckd ldrs over 1f out: effrt to ld last 150yds: edgd rt and idled: fnd enough nr fin* **9/2**[1]
10-1 **2** *nk* **George The Second**[19] 161 4-8-3 **65** ow1......... RichardKingscote(3) 3 73
(Mrs H Sweeting) *w ldng pair: chalng fr over 1f out: pressed wnr last 100yds: jst hld* **10/1**
62-0 **3** *nk* **Radiator Rooney (IRE)**[30] 47 4-7-13 **61** oh1............ (b) CDHayes(3) 8 68
(Patrick Morris, Ire) *t.k.h: pressed ldr: led 2f out: hdd last 150yds: kpt on* **33/1**
01/ **4** *1 ½* **Tango Step (IRE)**[106] 6112 7-8-5 **64** .... JohnEgan 1 67
(Bernard Lawlor, Ire) *hld up in midfield: rdn 2f out: styd on fnl f: nt pce to chal* **8/1**[3]
0-21 **5** *shd* **Celtic Thunder**[7] 292 6-8-2 **64** 6ex ow1............... (b) SaleemGolam(3) 11 66
(T J Etherington) *in tch on outer: rdn over 2f out: nt qckn over 1f out: kpt on ins fnl f* **9/1**
06-6 **6** *nk* **Sailor King (IRE)**[16] 190 5-9-2 **75** .... RobertHavlin 7 76
(D K Ivory) *trckd ldrs: rdn and effrt 2f out: no imp ins fnl f* **16/1**
-022 **7** *shd* **Nusoor (IRE)**[9] 269 4-8-10 **69** .... RobbieFitzpatrick 6 70
(Peter Grayson) *s.s: hld up in rr: prog on wd outside over 2f out: hanging and nt keen over 1f out: kpt on last 150yds* **5/1**[2]
-026 **8** *½* **Mine The Balance (IRE)**[7] 292 4-8-2 **61** oh1............... (b) ChrisCatlin 2 61
(J R Best) *sn in last pair: rdn and struggling over 2f out: kpt on fnl f* **16/1**
5203 **9** *½* **Mistral Sky**[8] 276 8-8-9 **68** ow1.................... (p) MickyFenton 5 66
(Stef Liddiard) *pushed along to stay in tch over 3f out: last pair and rdn over 2f out : kpt on nr fin* **14/1**
3-22 **10** *3* **Quality Street**[12] 236 5-8-6 **65** .... (p) EddieAhern 9 54
(P Butler) *led at decent pce: hdd 2f out: wknd rapidly jst over 1f out* **5/1**[2]
0-01 **11** *hd* **Mozakhraf (USA)**[12] 236 5-8-6 **65** .... JimmyQuinn 4 54
(K A Ryan) *trckd ldrs: racd awkwardly and lost pl on inner 2f out: wknd fnl f* **5/1**[2]
1m 11.13s (-1.68) **Going Correction** -0.15s/f (Stan) **11** Ran SP% **119.8**
Speed ratings (Par 103):105,104,104,102,102 101,101,100,100,96 95
CSF £50.87 CT £1360.87 TOTE £4.20: £1.50, £3.00, £7.30; EX 40.00 Trifecta £487.90 Part won. Pool £687.27 - 0.33 winning units..
Owner Ten Of Hearts **Bred** Mrs P Harford **Trained** Ogbourne Maisey, Wilts

FOCUS
An ordinary sprint handicap, but run at a decent pace and the form looks solid. Louphole can rate a bit higher still.

362 PONTIN'S HOLIDAYS H'CAP 1m 4f (P)
4:10 (4:10) (Class 4) (0-85,85) 4-Y-0+ **£4,857** (£1,445; £722; £360) **Stalls** Low

Form RPR
43-1 **1** **Sgt Schultz (IRE)**[9] 265 4-8-3 **72** oh2 ow1.................... JohnEgan 7 83+
(J S Moore) *trckd ldrs gng wl: sltly lost pl over 2f out: plld out and effrt to ld 1f out: rdn out and a holding on* **7/2**[2]
142- **2** *½* **Quince (IRE)**[41] 6941 4-8-13 **82** .... (v) JimmyQuinn 3 89
(J Pearce) *s.i.s: sn trckd ldrs: lost pl over 3f out: effrt again over 1f out: r.o to cl on wnr nr fin: a hld* **4/1**[3]
20-0 **3** *½* **Art Modern (IRE)**[26] 96 5-8-11 **77** .... (p) TPQueally 6 83
(G L Moore) *hld up in last pair: prog over 3f out: led 2f out and drvn: hdd and nt qckn 1f out: kpt on* **16/1**
156- **4** *2* **Croon**[37] 4876 5-8-13 **79** .... EddieAhern 2 82
(T J Pitt) *settled in midfield: rdn whn bmpd over 2f out: n.d after: kpt on fnl f* **10/3**[1]
12-0 **5** *hd* **Valance (IRE)**[16] 192 7-9-5 **85** .... (t) SebSanders 1 87
(C R Egerton) *led and set fair pce: hdd jst over 2f out: one pce u.p* **20/1**
0-02 **6** *¾* **Augustine**[7] 297 6-8-7 **73** .... ChrisCatlin 8 74
(P W Hiatt) *hld up in last pair: prog over 3f out: led briefly jst over 2f out: sn btn* **10/3**[1]
300- **7** *5* **Sir Monty (USA)**[101] 6205 5-8-10 **76** .... JimCrowley 5 69
(Mrs A J Perrett) *cl up: chsd ldr 5f out to 3f out: wkng whn squeezed out over 2f out* **8/1**
/00- **8** *44* **Le Corvee (IRE)**[39] 1631 5-9-3 **83** .... ShaneKelly 4 6
(A W Carroll) *chsd ldr to 5f out: wknd rapidly and sn t.o* **33/1**
2m 30.68s (-3.71) **Going Correction** -0.15s/f (Stan)
WFA 4 from 5yo+ 3lb **8** Ran SP% **113.1**
Speed ratings (Par 105):106,105,105,104,103 103,100,70
CSF £17.49 CT £192.45 TOTE £3.80: £1.30, £1.50, £4.50; EX 15.60 Trifecta £87.00 Pool £927.11 - 7.56 winning unit..
Owner Jim Barnes **Bred** Frank Dunne **Trained** Upper Lambourn, Berks

FOCUS
Unlike many races over middle distances here, this was run at a proper gallop thanks to Valance and the form looks solid, if only ordinary, with the winner value for a bit extra.

363 PONTINS.COM H'CAP 1m 2f (P)
4:40 (4:42) (Class 6) (0-65,64) 4-Y-0+ **£3,071** (£906; £453) **Stalls** Low

Form RPR
0-60 **1** **Siena Star (IRE)**[23] 117 9-9-1 **61** .... MickyFenton 1 68
(Stef Liddiard) *hld up in midfield on inner: effrt 2f out: drvn to ld 1f out: hld on wl last 100yds* **25/1**
2-43 **2** *½* **Blu Manruna**[12] 229 4-8-5 **55** .... (b) RichardKingscote(3) 2 61
(J Akehurst) *trckd ldrs: effrt 2f out: rdn to chal and looked likely to pass wnr 100yds out: fnd nil* **20/1**
-201 **3** *hd* **Discotheque (USA)**[8] 286 4-9-3 **64** 6ex.................... J-PGuillambert 4 70
(P Howling) *hld up in rr: prog on inner 2f out: clsd on ldrs ins fnl f: one pce last 50yds* **14/1**
1-62 **4** *hd* **Hallings Overture (USA)**[14] 212 8-9-0 **60** .... PaulEddery 12 66+
(C A Horgan) *s.s: hld up in last trio: prog on wd outside 2f out: drvn and r.o fnl f: nt rch ldrs* **5/2**[1]
1-20 **5** *¾* **Ciccone**[5] 309 4-8-11 **58** .... (p) ShaneKelly 6 62
(G L Moore) *hld up in midfield sn: n.m.r over 2f out: shkn up and nt qckn over 1f out: styd on fnl f: nrst fin* **12/1**
0-1 **6** *½* **Tancredi (SWE)**[8] 279 5-9-3 **63** 6ex.................... HayleyTurner 11 66
(N B King) *reluctant to enter stalls: t.k.h: pressed ldr: narrow ld 2f out to 1f out: fdd* **14/1**
3-01 **7** *shd* **Competitor**[7] 288 6-9-1 **61** 6ex.................... (v) SebSanders 10 64
(J Akehurst) *reminder after 1f: sn prom: jnd ldrs 3f out: drvn to chal over 1f out: wknd last 75yds* **16/1**
5-31 **8** *½* **Play Up Pompey**[5] 315 5-8-12 **61** 6ex.................... AmirQuinn(3) 9 63
(J J Bridger) *s.s: hld up wl in rr: prog on wd outside wl over 2f out: chsd ldrs wl over 1f out: no imp fnl f* **6/1**[3]
0465 **9** *1* **They All Laughed**[8] 286 4-8-10 **57** .... (p) ChrisCatlin 5 57
(P W Hiatt) *trckd ldrs: rdn 3f out: nt qckn over 1f out: one pce after* **14/1**
25-0 **10** *shd* **Birthday Star (IRE)**[16] 195 5-8-7 **60** .... DebraEngland(7) 8 60
(W J Musson) *hld up and sn last: stl last but gng wl enough over 2f out: pushed along and kpt on: no ch* **25/1**
22-3 **11** *hd* **Monets Masterpiece (USA)**[33] 24 4-9-3 **64** .... (be) GeorgeBaker 3 64
(G L Moore) *mde most to 2f out: wknd fnl f* **13/2**
1-34 **12** *½* **Rowan Warning**[5] 315 5-8-11 **57** .... EddieAhern 7 56
(J R Boyle) *hld up in rr: effrt on outer whn hmpd jst over 2f out: nt rcvr* **11/2**[2]
0030 **13** *hd* **Christmas Truce (IRE)**[2] 341 8-7-11 **50** .... (p) SophieDoyle(7) 13 48
(Ms J S Doyle) *s.v.s: hld up in last trio: no prog fnl 2f* **33/1**
-015 **14** *20* **Lobengula (IRE)**[5] 315 5-8-12 **58** .... JimCrowley 14 18
(I W McInnes) *t.k.h: w ldrs to over 3f out: wkng whn hmpd jst over 2f out: eased: t.o* **14/1**
2m 6.00s (-1.79) **Going Correction** -0.15s/f (Stan)
WFA 4 from 5yo+ 1lb **14** Ran SP% **127.2**
Speed ratings (Par 101):101,100,100,100,99 99,99,98,98,97 97,97,97,81
CSF £462.98 CT £7110.26 TOTE £34.60: £11.20, £4.30, £3.70; EX 379.80 TRIFECTA Not won. Place 6 £224.75, Place 5 £92.59..
Owner ownaracehorse.co.uk (Shefford) **Bred** Mrs A J Brudenell **Trained** Great Shefford, Berks

FOCUS
A competitive if modest handicap, but they rather finished in a heap which suggests the form is ordinary, although it does appear to make sense.
T/Jkpt: Not won. T/Plt: £134.70 to a £1 stake. Pool: £66,671.00. 361.25 winning tickets. T/Qpdt: £34.20 to a £1 stake. Pool: £3,607.20. 77.90 winning tickets. JN

332 WOLVERHAMPTON (A.W) (L-H)
Monday, February 5

OFFICIAL GOING: Standard
Wind: almost nil

364 PONTIN'S FAMILY HOLIDAYS CLAIMING STKS 1m 141y(P)
1:50 (1:50) (Class 6) 4-Y-0+ **£2,388** (£705; £352) **Stalls** Low

Form RPR
-311 **1** **Climate (IRE)**[7] 298 8-8-12 64.................... (v) RussellKennemore(5) 10 64
(R Hollinshead) *hld up: hdwy over 3f out: rdn to ld 2f out: edgd rt over 1f out: drvn clr fnl f* **4/1**[3]
00-0 **2** *3* **Crusoe (IRE)**[7] 298 10-8-0 36.................... (b) SoniaEaton(7) 8 47
(A Sadik) *hld up and bhd: c wd st: hdwy over 1f out: r.o ins fnl f: nt trble wnr* **250/1**
55-2 **3** *2 ½* **Paparaazi (IRE)**[24] 109 5-8-8 62.................... (b) JamieMoriarty(5) 5 48
(R A Fahey) *hld up: rdn and hdwy over 3f out: one pce fnl 2f* **5/2**[2]
45-6 **4** *shd* **Jools**[26] 94 9-8-10 47.................... JamesMillman(5) 4 50
(D K Ivory) *hld up and bhd: rdn over 3f out: hdwy over 2f out: edgd lft 1f out: one pce* **28/1**
-206 **5** *¾* **Fraternity**[9] 271 10-8-5 44 ow1.................... NeilChalmers(3) 9 41
(J A Pickering) *chsd ldrs: rdn over 3f out: one pce fnl 2f* **66/1**
-131 **6** *1* **Wahoo Sam (USA)**[6] 308 7-9-7 70.................... (p) NCallan 1 52
(K A Ryan) *led: rdn and hdd 2f out: wknd ins fnl f* **6/4**[1]
/00- **7** *3 ½* **Procrastinate (IRE)**[48] 5837 5-8-8 40.................... DuranFentiman(5) 7 37
(R F Fisher) *dwlt: a bhd* **100/1**
450- **8** *3 ½* **Shannon Arms (USA)**[63] 6708 6-8-13 45.................... (p) PatCosgrave 6 30
(R Brotherton) *chsd ldr tl rdn 2f out: sn wknd* **25/1**

The Form Book, Raceform Ltd, Compton, RG20 6NL

006- **9** *27* **Welsh Whisper**^{189} [3594] 8-7-10 42 ow1 .... JosephWalsh(7) 3 —
(S A Brookshaw) *s.v.s: a wl in rr: t.o* **66/1**

00-2 **10** *1* **Final Esteem**^{7} [298] 4-9-7 65 .... DaneO'Neill 2 —
(R A Harris) *dwlt: rdn 5f out: a wl bhd: t.o* **15/2**

1m 51.22s (-0.54) **Going Correction** -0.025s/f (Stan) **10** Ran SP% **112.0**
Speed ratings (Par 101):101,98,96,96,95 94,91,88,64,63
CSF £713.33 TOTE £4.70: £1.30, £20.90, £1.20; EX 208.10.
Owner The Cartmel Syndicate **Bred** Mrs A Naughton **Trained** Upper Longdon, Staffs

FOCUS
A strong pace with Wahoo Sam rather cutting his own throat. The runner-up renders this form somewhat dubious.
Wahoo Sam(USA) Official explanation: jockey said gelding hung left
Final Esteem Official explanation: jockey said gelding was never travelling

365 DIGITAL PRINTS FROM BONUSPRINT.COM MAIDEN STKS 1m 4f 50y(P)
2:20 (2:21) (Class 5) 4-Y-0+ **£2,968** (£876; £438) **Stalls** Low

Form RPR
34 **1** **Stanerra's Story (IRE)**^{9} [265] 6-9-6 .... DaneO'Neill 6 70+
(E J O'Neill) *rrd s: t.k.h in rr: hdwy 6f out: led over 2f out: rdn clr over 1f out: r.o wl* **6/1**^{2}

324- **2** *3* **Fringe**^{62} [6722] 4-8-12 85 .... BrettDoyle 8 60+
(Jane Chapple-Hyam) *hld up in tch: pushed along over 4f out: rdn to chse wnr 2f out: no imp* **1/3**^{1}

3 *3 ½* **Beau Torero (FR)**^{21} 9-9-6 ow5 .... TomMessenger(5) 2 63
(B N Pollock) *s.s: hdwy over 6f out: rdn over 3f out: one pce fnl 2f* **33/1**

30-5 **4** *½* **Soul Blazer (USA)**^{9} [265] 4-9-3 65 ....(v^{1}) RobertWinston 4 57
(A M Balding) *led: rdn whn hung rt and hdd over 2f out: wknd over 1f out* **14/1**^{3}

460- **5** *7* **Webbswood Lad (IRE)**^{38} [603] 6-9-6 56 .... FergusSweeney 3 46
(M R Bosley) *t.k.h towards rr: sme hdwy over 3f out: sn rdn: wknd over 2f out* **18/1**

440- **6** *2* **Daneway**^{45} [6911] 4-8-12 55 .... TonyCulhane 5 37
(P Howling) *prom: rdn 4f out: wknd 3f out* **33/1**

05-0 **7** *1* **True West (USA)**^{27} [75] 4-8-12 48 .... AdamKirby 1 36
(Miss Gay Kelleway) *hld up in mid-div: rdn over 3f out: sn struggling* **50/1**

0- **8** *21* **Niza D'Alm (FR)**^{229} [2753] 6-8-8 .... SladeO'Hara(7) 7 2
(A Crook) *chsd ldr over 3f: wknd over 5f out: t.o* **250/1**

000/ **9** *23* **Blendon Boy (IRE)**^{411} [6651] 5-9-6 45 .... GrahamGibbons 9 —
(D W Thompson) *t.k.h: prom tl rdn and wknd over 4f out: t.o* **250/1**

0 **10** *1 ¾* **Kansas Feather (IRE)**^{17} [186] 4-8-9 .... JerryO'Dwyer(3) 10 —
(B S Rothwell) *wnt rt s: sn mid-div: bhd fnl 5f: t.o* **200/1**

2m 41.5s (-0.92) **Going Correction** -0.025s/f (Stan)
WFA 4 from 5yo+ 3lb **10** Ran SP% **110.4**
Speed ratings (Par 103):102,100,97,97,92 91,90,76,61,60
CSF £7.85 TOTE £5.80: £1.40, £1.10, £4.80; EX 10.00.
Owner Miss A H Marshall **Bred** Frank Dunne **Trained** Averham Park, Notts

FOCUS
A bit of an upset in the uncompetitive maiden where they went 14/1 bar the first two home. The form appears weak and it is doubtful if the winner had to improve on his sound previous run.
Soul Blazer(USA) Official explanation: jockey said gelding hung right

366 WOLVERHAMPTON-RACECOURSE.CO.UK (S) STKS 7f 32y(P)
2:50 (2:50) (Class 6) 3-Y-0+ **£2,047** (£604; £302) **Stalls** High

Form RPR
-402 **1** **Louisiade (IRE)**^{10} [252] 6-9-10 49 ....(p) NCallan 6 60
(K A Ryan) *hld up in tch: n.m.r over 1f out: led ent fnl f: rdn out* **5/2**^{1}

0-10 **2** *2* **Prince Of Gold**^{10} [252] 7-10-0 50 ....(v) FergusSweeney 4 59
(R Hollinshead) *hld up and bhd: hdwy over 1f out: r.o to take 2nd post* **9/1**

000- **3** *shd* **Campbeltown (IRE)**^{109} [6065] 4-9-10 75 .... DaneO'Neill 3 55
(R A Harris) *a.p: led over 1f out: hdd ent fnl f: no ex* **9/2**^{3}

04-0 **4** *nk* **Chalentina**^{28} [70] 4-9-5 62 .... TonyCulhane 8 49
(P Howling) *hld up in mid-div: rdn over 2f out: kpt on fnl f* **12/1**

04-6 **5** *hd* **Following Flow (USA)**^{7} [298] 5-9-10 67 ....(p) GrahamGibbons 5 53+
(R Hollinshead) *hld up towards rr: nt clr run fr over 2f out tl swtchd lft ins fnl f: r.o wl: nrst fin* **7/1**

30-0 **6** *1* **Apex**^{9} [268] 6-9-10 50 .... KimTinkler 12 51
(N Tinkler) *hld up and bhd: nt clr run over 3f out: late hdwy on outside: nvr nrr* **33/1**

5-00 **7** *1* **Aventura (IRE)**^{10} [252] 7-9-10 48 .... PhillipMakin 1 48
(S R Bowring) *led: rdn whn edgd rt and hdd over 1f out: wknd ins fnl f* **33/1**

160- **8** *hd* **Marmooq**^{117} [5907] 4-9-10 70 .... JoeFanning 7 48
(J Gallagher) *chsd ldr: rdn and ev ch 2f out: bmpd over 1f out: wknd ins fnl f* **4/1**^{2}

-000 **9** *nk* **Lord Chamberlain**^{17} [179] 14-9-10 50 ....(b) LPKeniry 2 47
(J M Bradley) *hld up towards rr: hdwy on ins over 2f out: wknd ins fnl f* **50/1**

-643 **10** *1* **Spy Gun (USA)**^{10} [252] 7-9-10 45 .... RobertWinston 11 44
(T Wall) *bhd: short-lived effrt on outside 3f out* **20/1**

-020 **11** *hd* **Skip Of Colour**^{21} [138] 7-10-0 58 .... AlanDaly 9 48
(P A Blockley) *prom: rdn over 2f out: wknd wl over 1f out* **33/1**

1064 **12** *5* **Teyaar**^{3} [337] 11-10-0 47 .... AdamKirby 10 35
(M Wellings) *mid-div: lost pl over 3f out: bhd whn c wd ent st* **25/1**

1m 30.46s (0.06) **Going Correction** -0.025s/f (Stan) **12** Ran SP% **116.3**
Speed ratings (Par 101):98,95,95,95,95 93,92,92,92,91 90,85
CSF £23.20 TOTE £3.20: £1.50, £2.80, £1.90; EX 28.80.There was no bid for the winner. Campbeltown was bought by M R Hoad for £6,000.
Owner Whitestonecliffe Racing Partnership **Bred** Mrs Noelle Walsh **Trained** Hambleton, N Yorks

FOCUS
An ordinary seller full of horses dropped in class. There were doubts over several of the higher-rated runners and this is probably only ordinary form for the grade.
Following Flow(USA) ◆ Official explanation: jockey said gelding was denied a clear run

367 PONTINSBINGO.COM H'CAP (DIV I) 7f 32y(P)
3:20 (3:20) (Class 5) (0-70,70) 4-Y-0+ **£2,590** (£770; £385; £192) **Stalls** High

Form RPR
-342 **1** **Dapple Dawn (IRE)**^{7} [300] 4-9-0 68 ....(b) DanielTudhope 1 79+
(D Carroll) *a.p: rdn to ld jst over 1f out: sn hung lft: rdn out* **11/4**^{1}

0-53 **2** *1 ½* **Flying Bantam (IRE)**^{11} [243] 6-8-6 60 .... DaleGibson 4 64
(R A Fahey) *t.k.h: prom: n.m.r and lost pl bnd after 1f: hdwy over 2f out: rdn over 1f out: kpt on ins fnl f: nt trbl wnr* **6/1**

1-05 **3** *1* **Plateau**^{14} [218] 8-9-2 70 .... RobertWinston 5 72
(C R Dore) *prom: lost pl after 2f: hdwy on ins wl over 1f out: sn rdn: kpt on same pce fnl f* **10/1**

3-03 **4** *shd* **Carcinetto (IRE)**^{22} [131] 5-8-2 56 .... CatherineGannon 7 57
(P D Evans) *hld up and bhd: rdn and hdwy over 2f out: hung lft 1f out: flashed tail and no ex towards fin* **10/1**

14-6 **5** *2* **Formidable Will (FR)**^{34} [14] 5-8-10 64 ....(vt) DaneO'Neill 2 60
(D Shaw) *led over 1f: chsd ldr: led over 2f out: rdn and hdd jst over 1f out: wknd ins fnl f* **10/3**^{2}

440- **6** *3* **Kareeb (FR)**^{40} [6955] 10-7-13 58 oh4 ow2 .... KevinGhunowa(5) 3 46
(P A Blockley) *s.i.s: bhd: rdn over 3f out: nvr trbld ldrs* **25/1**

4-10 **7** *¾* **Dvinsky (USA)**^{8} [276] 6-9-0 68 .... PaulDoe 6 54
(P Howling) *sn w ldrs: rdn over 2f out: wknd fnl f* **14/1**

50-0 **8** *1 ¾* **Smile For Us**^{12} [235] 4-8-4 58 ow2 ....(b) JoeFanning 11 40
(C Drew) *sn prom: led over 5f out tl over 2f out: wknd wl over 1f out* **40/1**

/125 **9** *6* **Activity (IRE)**^{6} [308] 8-8-8 67 .... DuranFentiman(5) 10 33
(M J Gingell) *hld up and bhd: short-lived effrt on outside 3f out* **9/2**^{3}

1m 29.64s (-0.76) **Going Correction** -0.025s/f (Stan) **9** Ran SP% **113.3**
Speed ratings (Par 103):103,101,100,100,97 94,93,91,84
CSF £19.22 CT £141.67 TOTE £3.40: £1.20, £2.00, £3.00; EX 19.60.
Owner Miss S Molloy **Bred** P D Savill **Trained** Sledmere, E Yorks

FOCUS
A modest if quite open affair, marginally slower than the second division. Ordinary form.

368 PONTIN'S "BOOK EARLY" H'CAP 5f 20y(P)
3:50 (3:51) (Class 6) (0-65,69) 4-Y-0+ **£2,730** (£806; £403) **Stalls** Low

Form RPR
-211 **1** **Canadian Danehill (IRE)**^{4} [318] 5-9-9 69 6ex ....(p) NCallan 2 84
(R M H Cowell) *hld up in mid-div: hdwy 2f out: rdn to ld wl ins fnl f: r.o* **4/7**^{1}

60-2 **2** *½* **Misaro (GER)**^{4} [318] 6-8-7 58 ....(b) MichaelJStainton(5) 8 71
(R A Harris) *w ldrs: led 2f out: hdd and nt qckn wl ins fnl f* **12/1**

4345 **3** *4* **Muktasb (USA)**^{14} [214] 6-8-8 54 ....(v) CatherineGannon 1 53
(D Shaw) *s.i.s: hdwy over 1f out: one pce fnl f* **14/1**

-013 **4** *hd* **Monte Major (IRE)**^{8} [281] 6-8-11 57 ....(v) TonyCulhane 5 55
(D Shaw) *hld up in mid-div: rdn and hdwy over 1f out: one pce fnl f* **8/1**^{2}

1-36 **5** *1* **Bond Playboy**^{9} [269] 7-8-13 64 ....(v) DuranFentiman(5) 6 58
(G R Oldroyd) *outpcd: hdwy on ins over 1f out: no imp fnl f* **9/1**^{3}

-200 **6** *½* **Lady Bahia (IRE)**^{9} [269] 6-9-0 60 ....(b) AdamKirby 9 52
(Peter Grayson) *outpcd: hdwy over 1f out: nvr trbld ldrs* **33/1**

0002 **7** *1* **New Options**^{7} [289] 10-8-7 53 ow1 ....(b) BrettDoyle 7 42
(Peter Grayson) *hld up in mid-div: nt clr run and swtchd rt wl over 1f out: sn rdn: no real prog fnl f* **25/1**

50-0 **8** *2 ½* **Savile's Delight (IRE)**^{28} [66] 8-8-3 52 ....(bt) NeilChalmers(3) 11 32
(Miss Joanne Priest) *prom: ev ch over 2f out: rdn and hung lft over 1f out: sn wknd* **33/1**

0-15 **9** *5* **Pride Of Joy**^{20} [154] 4-9-3 63 .... DaneO'Neill 10 25
(D K Ivory) *led over 2f: rdn and wknd wl over 1f out* **18/1**

00-3 **10** *½* **Glenargo (USA)**^{10} [254] 4-8-7 53 ....(p) JoeFanning 4 13
(R A Harris) *rrd and n.m.r s: sn prom: led over 2f out: sn rdn and hdd: wknd 1f out* **25/1**

530- **11** *nk* **Feminist (IRE)**^{301} [951] 5-7-11 50 oh5 .... PietroRomeo(7) 3 9
(J M Bradley) *led early: chsd ldrs tl wknd over 1f out* **100/1**

61.69 secs (-1.13) **Going Correction** -0.025s/f (Stan) **11** Ran SP% **119.0**
Speed ratings (Par 101):108,107,100,100,98 98,96,92,84,83 83
CSF £8.15 CT £58.04 TOTE £1.50: £1.10, £2.50, £3.70; EX 8.20.
Owner T W Morley **Bred** Skymarc Farm Inc And Dr A J O'Reilly **Trained** Six Mile Bottom, Cambs

FOCUS
An uncompetitive handicap but a decent winning time for the class of contest. Good efforts from the front two, who finished clear.
Pride Of Joy Official explanation: vet said filly bled from the nose

369 BONUSPRINT.COM H'CAP 1m 5f 194y(P)
4:20 (4:22) (Class 6) (0-60,60) 4-Y-0+ **£2,388** (£705; £352) **Stalls** Low

Form RPR
/6-1 **1** **Vanishing Dancer (SWI)**^{8} [278] 10-9-7 60 6ex ....(bt) NCallan 10 67
(K J Burke) *hld up in mid-div: rdn and hdwy over 2f out: hung bdly rt to stands' rail and led ins fnl f: sn edgd lft: styd on* **12/1**

0-40 **2** *1 ¾* **Qaasi (USA)**^{8} [286] 5-8-9 55 .... PatrickDonaghy(7) 8 60
(M Brittain) *hld up in mid-div: nt clr run on ins and lost pl over 3f out: hdwy over 1f out: styd on ins fnl f* **33/1**

0-21 **3** *½* **Reminiscent (IRE)**^{14} [220] 8-9-4 57 ....(p) TonyCulhane 4 61
(B P J Baugh) *hld up and bhd: rdn over 3f out: hdwy fnl f: nrst fin* **9/2**^{2}

1-12 **4** *½* **Josh You Are**^{7} [291] 4-8-13 57 .... PatCosgrave 11 61
(D E Cantillon) *plld hrd early towards rr: hdwy over 3f out: rdn and ev ch over 1f out: nt qckn ins fnl f* **1/1**^{1}

00-3 **5** *nk* **Leighton Buzzard**^{8} [278] 5-8-11 53 .... JerryO'Dwyer(3) 12 56
(N B King) *hld up towards rr: rdn over 5f out: styd on wl ins fnl f: nvr nrr* **20/1**

0-1 **6** *½* **Evolve (USA)**^{26} [84] 4-8-12 56 .... OscarUrbina 9 58
(M Botti) *hld up in tch: ev ch over 2f out: sn rdn: no ex ins fnl f* **12/1**

060- **7** *½* **Proud Scholar (USA)**^{54} [6812] 5-8-13 52 .... BrettDoyle 7 54
(R A Kvisla) *prom: lost pl over 3f out: nt clr run on ins over 2f out: styd on ins fnl f: n.d* **66/1**

00-2 **8** *1 ¼* **Mahmjra**^{11} [242] 5-9-5 58 .... PFredericks 5 58
(C N Allen) *led: rdn over 2f out: hdd ins fnl f: eased whn btn towards fin* **25/1**

5-12 **9** *hd* **Maria Antonia (IRE)**^{20} [148] 4-9-1 59 .... SimonWhitworth 2 59
(P A Blockley) *t.k.h towards rr: hdwy on outside 2f out: eased whn btn wl ins fnl f* **16/1**

1-03 **10** *2* **Emilion**^{14} [220] 4-8-11 55 ....(b^{1}) JoeFanning 1 52
(W R Muir) *chsd ldr tl over 3f out: rdn and wknd over 1f out* **8/1**^{3}

00-5 **11** *4* **Almanshood (USA)**^{14} [220] 5-9-7 60 .... SamHitchcott 6 51
(P L Gilligan) *prom: rdn over 3f out: wknd 2f out* **20/1**

001- **12** *8* **Saameq (IRE)**^{49} [6860] 6-9-2 55 .... RobertWinston 13 35
(D W Thompson) *hld up towards rr: hdwy over 3f out: wknd over 2f out* **12/1**

3m 6.08s (-1.29) **Going Correction** -0.025s/f (Stan)
WFA 4 from 5yo+ 5lb **12** Ran SP% **126.1**
Speed ratings (Par 101):102,101,100,100,100 99,99,98,98,97 95,90
CSF £372.84 CT £2069.07 TOTE £16.70: £4.20, £9.80, £1.60; EX 485.40.
Owner Mrs D Thomas **Bred** Gestut Sohrenhof **Trained** Bourton-on-the-Water, Gloucs

FOCUS
A moderate event run at a modest pace. Vanishing Dancer improved on his recent Kempton win, with the next two back to form.

370 GO PONTIN'S H'CAP 1m 1f 103y(P)

4:50 (4:50) (Class 5) (0-70,69) 3-Y-O £3,071 (£906; £453) Stalls Low

Form RPR
3626 1 **Beau Sancy**[7] [294] 3-8-2 **62** LukeMorris(7) 4 65
(R A Harris) *s.i.s: hld up: c wd st: rdn and hdwy over 1f out: edgd lft and led ins fnl f: r.o* **8/1**
00-5 2 ½ **Royal Tender (IRE)**[23] [116] 3-8-6 **59** ow1 FergusSweeney 6 61
(B G Powell) *chsd ldr: led 2f out: sn rdn: hdd ins fnl f: nt qckn* **33/1**
02-5 3 1 ¼ **Dr McFab**[14] [208] 3-8-13 **66** DaneO'Neill 5 67+
(J A Osborne) *hld up: rdn over 3f out: hdwy over 2f out: nt qckn ins fnl f* **5/1**[2]
-333 4 ¾ **Gold Response**[9] [267] 3-8-3 **56** CatherineGannon 3 54
(D Shaw) *hld up: rdn and hdwy on ins wl over 1f out: one pce fnl f* **13/2**[3]
-111 5 1 ¼ **Global Traffic**[9] [267] 3-8-13 **69** (b) StephenDonohoe(3) 7 65
(P D Evans) *half-rrd s: stdy hdwy over 5f out: rdn over 2f out: one pce* **4/7**[1]
-330 6 ½ **First Princess (IRE)**[19] [157] 3-8-10 **63** (p) LPKeniry 2 58
(J S Moore) *hld up in tch: rdn over 2f out: fdd ins fnl f* **25/1**
030- 7 1 ¾ **Falimar**[176] [4400] 3-9-1 **68** PaulMulrennan 1 59
(Miss J A Camacho) *led: hdd 2f out: sn hung rt: wknd fnl f* **25/1**

2m 5.04s (2.42) **Going Correction** -0.025s/f (Stan) 7 Ran SP% **115.4**
Speed ratings (Par 97):88,87,86,85,84 84,82
CSF £207.39 TOTE £7.30: £2.80, £8.40; EX 264.30.
Owner S & A Mares **Bred** Mrs J Keegan **Trained** Earlswood, Monmouths

FOCUS
The slow pace to halfway was reflected in the time. The winner produced a slight step up, with the runner-up a big improver, but the form may not prove too solid.
Global Traffic Official explanation: jockey said colt was unsuited by the slow early pace
Falimar Official explanation: jockey said filly hung right

371 PONTINSBINGO.COM H'CAP (DIV II) 7f 32y(P)

5:20 (5:20) (Class 5) (0-70,69) 4-Y-O+ £2,590 (£770; £385; £192) Stalls High

Form RPR
60-1 1 **Lii Najma**[25] [102] 4-8-12 **65** JoeFanning 2 74
(C E Brittain) *mde all: rdn over 1f out: r.o wl* **15/8**[1]
-255 2 1 ½ **Sir Douglas**[4] [323] 4-9-1 **68** NCallan 10 73+
(R A Harris) *hld up and bhd: rdn and hdwy on outside over 1f out: r.o to take 2nd cl home: nt trble wnr* **7/2**[2]
000- 3 ½ **Royal Orissa**[74] [6572] 5-8-6 **59** LPKeniry 1 63
(D Haydn Jones) *t.k.h: prom: n.m.r sn after s: rdn to chse wnr wl over 1f out: nt qckn ins fnl f* **12/1**
2-46 4 1 **Spark Up**[15] [206] 7-7-11 **55** (b) DuranFentiman(5) 5 56
(J W Unett) *hld up in mid-div: hdwy over 1f out: one pce fnl f* **8/1**
5-00 5 1 ½ **Our Kes (IRE)**[12] [235] 5-8-4 **57** PaulDoe 3 54
(P Howling) *s.i.s: t.k.h in rr: rdn over 2f out: hdwy 1f out: n.d* **15/2**[3]
-340 6 ½ **Stoic Leader (IRE)**[7] [300] 7-8-9 **67** KevinGhunowa(5) 6 63
(R F Fisher) *prom: rdn 3f out: wknd fnl f* **12/1**
6-04 7 nk **Kingsmaite**[13] [228] 6-8-7 **60** (bt) DaleGibson 4 55
(S R Bowring) *chsd wnr: ev ch over 2f out: rdn over 1f out: wknd fnl f* **14/1**
22-0 8 ¾ **Mambo Sun**[15] [205] 4-8-11 **64** SimonWhitworth 7 57
(P A Blockley) *a towards rr* **25/1**
261- 9 1 **Diamond Dan (IRE)**[155] [4974] 5-8-3 **56** CatherineGannon 9 47
(P D Evans) *hld up and bhd: nt clr run ins fnl f: n.d* **16/1**
5-54 10 3 **Sands Crooner (IRE)**[9] [262] 4-9-2 **69** (v) DaneO'Neill 8 52
(D Shaw) *hld up in mid-div: rdn over 3f out: wknd fnl f* **16/1**

1m 29.57s (-0.83) **Going Correction** -0.025s/f (Stan) 33 Ran SP% **117.5**
Speed ratings (Par 103):103,101,100,99,97 97,96,96,94,91
CSF £8.16 CT £62.24 TOTE £3.00: £1.80, £1.80, £2.80; EX 9.90 Place 6 £ 35.96, Place 5 £12.30.
Owner Saeed Manana **Bred** Zubieta Ltd **Trained** Newmarket, Suffolk

FOCUS
This was fractionally faster than the first division. Quite weak form, Lii Najma improving a length on her Southwell win.
T/Plt: £14.90 to a £1 stake. Pool: £59,979.20. 2,928.80 winning tickets. T/Qpdt: £7.20 to a £1 stake. Pool: £3,654.80. 372.40 winning tickets. KH

[317]SOUTHWELL (L-H)

Tuesday, February 6

OFFICIAL GOING: Standard
Wind: Almost nil Weather: Fine

372 GO PONTIN'S AMATEUR RIDERS' H'CAP 1m 3f (F)

1:40 (1:40) (Class 6) (0-52,52) 4-Y-O+ £2,307 (£709; £354) Stalls Low

Form RPR
-050 1 **Danelor (IRE)**[10] [266] 9-11-1 **46** oh1 (p) MrsMMorris 12 51
(D Shaw) *hld up: hdwy over 3f out: led over 1f out: styd on wl* **15/2**
6-00 2 2 ½ **Bournonville**[9] [278] 4-10-8 **46** oh1 MrSRees(5) 13 47
(M Wigham) *mid-div: hdwy 1/2-way: chsd ldr over 4f out: led over 3f out: rdn and hdd over 1f out: styd on same pce* **40/1**
0- 3 5 **Salym (FR)**[129] [4777] 6-11-5 **50** (b) MrDHDunsdon 6 43
(D J S Ffrench Davis) *hld up: hdwy 4f out: rdn over 2f out: wknd fnl f* **9/2**[2]
04-5 4 1 ½ **Royal Sailor (IRE)**[6] [87] 5-10-8 **46** oh1 MrAMerriam(7) 5 37
(J Ryan) *hld up: hdwy 4f out: rdn over 2f out: wknd fnl f* **16/1**
-666 5 1 ½ **Laurollie**[10] [266] 5-10-10 **46** oh1 MrStephenHarrison(5) 7 34
(B P J Baugh) *hld up: nt clr run over 4f out: hdwy over 2f out: sn rdn: wknd over 1f out* **10/1**
2-20 6 4 **Experimental (IRE)**[12] [242] 13-10-12 **48** MrMMackley(5) 4 30
(John A Harris) *chsd ldrs: rdn over 4f out: hmprd 3f out: hung lft over 2f out: sn wknd* **8/1**
00-0 7 2 ½ **Secam (POL)**[9] [274] 8-10-13 **49** (e[1]) MrsCThompson(5) 3 27
(Mrs P Townsley) *prom: nt clr run over 4f out: wknd 2f out* **50/1**
0000 8 1 ¾ **Alisar (IRE)**[9] [278] 7-11-7 **52** (t) MrSWalker 8 27
(E J Creighton) *prom: chsd ldr over 6f out: led over 4f out: hdd over 3f out: sn rdn: wknd over 1f out* **20/1**
65-0 9 1 ¾ **Galley Law**[24] [126] 7-10-10 **46** oh1 MrBenBrisbourne(5) 10 18
(W M Brisbourne) *hld up: rdn over 4f out: sn wknd* **13/2**[3]
-040 10 1 ½ **Captain Bolsh**[9] [279] 4-10-10 **46** oh1 MrSPearce(3) 11 16
(J Pearce) *s.i.s: hld up: a in rr* **13/2**[3]
/6-2 11 7 **Dubonai (IRE)**[18] [182] 7-11-6 **51** (t) MrSDobson 9 10
(G M Moore) *hld up: rdn over 3f out: sn wknd* **4/1**[1]
5/0- 12 47 **Grand Welcome (IRE)**[46] [6904] 5-11-2 **47** (vt[1]) MrWHogg 2 —
(E J Creighton) *led: clr 9f out: hdd & wknd over 4f out* **33/1**
00-0 13 47 **Follingworth (IRE)**[9] [273] 4-10-13 **46** oh1 (b[1]) MissADeniel 1 —
(A D Brown) *chsd clr ldr tl rdn 8f out: wknd over 6f out* **100/1**

2m 35.21s (6.31) **Going Correction** +0.25s/f (Slow)
WFA 4 from 5yo+ 2lb 13 Ran SP% **115.8**
Speed ratings (Par 101):87,85,81,80,79 76,74,73,72,71 65,31,—
CSF £285.37 CT £1501.31 TOTE £10.60: £2.40, £21.00, £1.80; EX 582.90 TRIFECTA Not won..
Owner Danethorpe Racing Ltd **Bred** Barronstown Stud And Orpendale **Trained** Danethorpe, Notts

FOCUS
An extremely moderate amateur riders' handicap. The time was slow and the race has been rated negatively, with the runner-up wrong at the weights.
Dubonai(IRE) Official explanation: vet said gelding had bled from the nose

373 PONTINSBINGO.COM MAIDEN H'CAP 1m (F)

2:10 (2:11) (Class 6) (0-55,55) 3-Y-O £2,388 (£705; £352) Stalls Low

Form RPR
-044 1 **My Sara**[10] [267] 3-8-6 **52** ow4 (v) JamieMoriarty(5) 7 65
(R A Fahey) *sn pushed along and prom: rdn to ld over 1f out: styd on wl* **12/1**
06-4 2 5 **Bertrada (IRE)**[22] [136] 3-8-9 **50** RobertHavlin 11 53
(H Morrison) *hld up: hdwy u.p over 2f out: styd on same pce fnl f* **9/1**
00-6 3 1 ¼ **Fire In Cairo (IRE)**[14] [224] 3-8-3 **49** AshleyHamblett(5) 13 49
(P C Haslam) *hld up: hdwy u.p over 2f out: sn hung lft: no ex fnl f* **28/1**
6-33 4 ½ **Skye But N Ben**[14] [224] 3-8-6 **47** (b) PaulFessey 6 46
(T D Barron) *chsd ldrs: rdn and ev ch over 1f out: wknd ins fnl f* **5/1**[2]
0-42 5 hd **Greek God**[14] [224] 3-9-0 **55** BrettDoyle 12 54
(W Jarvis) *chsd ldrs: rdn over 2f out: wknd fnl f* **11/4**[1]
00-0 6 8 **Beck**[14] [224] 3-9-0 **55** JamieSpencer 9 42+
(M L W Bell) *chsd ldr over 6f out: rdn to ld over 2f out: hung lft and hdd over 1f out: wknd and eased ins fnl f* **7/1**[3]
450- 7 1 ¼ **Mujamead**[40] [6963] 3-8-12 **53** NCallan 4 35+
(P C Haslam) *mid-div: rdn over 3f out: wknd over 1f out* **12/1**
6-50 8 1 ½ **Flushed**[7] [304] 3-8-6 **47** (be) JohnEgan 10 23
(A J McCabe) *led 7f out: hdd over 2f out: sn rdn and wknd* **28/1**
000- 9 hd **Interest (USA)**[146] [5289] 3-8-2 **50** ow1 (b[1]) DeanHeslop(7) 3 26
(T D Barron) *s.i.s: outpcd* **25/1**
44-2 10 1 ½ **Denton Hawk**[14] [223] 3-9-0 **55** PhillipMakin 2 27
(M Dods) *prom: rdn over 3f out: wknd over 1f out* **5/1**[2]
4 11 1 ½ **Murdol (IRE)**[9] [284] 3-8-4 **48** LiamJones(3) 1 17
(C R Dore) *sn outpcd* **66/1**
000- 12 2 **Mum's Memories**[250] [2178] 3-8-9 **50** TPQueally 8 15
(W J Musson) *prom to 1/2-way* **100/1**
50-0 13 14 **Countrywide Style (IRE)**[25] [106] 3-8-6 **50** (b[1]) JamesDoyle(3) 5 —
(N P Littmoden) *s.i.s: outpcd* **50/1**
00-0 14 15 **Tranquility**[11] [253] 3-8-7 **48** JimmyQuinn 14 —
(J Pearce) *led 1f: chsd ldrs: rdn 1/2-way: sn wknd* **66/1**

1m 47.14s (2.54) **Going Correction** +0.25s/f (Slow) 14 Ran SP% **114.6**
Speed ratings (Par 95):97,92,90,90,90 82,80,79,79,77 76,74,60,45
CSF £104.92 CT £3013.54 TOTE £14.10: £3.10, £3.00, £9.00; EX 87.40 TRIFECTA Not won..
Owner Mrs Doreen M Swinburn **Bred** Genesis Green Stud Ltd **Trained** Musley Bank, N Yorks

FOCUS
A weak race, as one would expect for a maiden handicap. The form should work out, with the first five clear, four of them having finished behind Medici Code last time (race 224). An improved effort from My Sara.

374 PONTIN'S FAMILY HOLIDAYS (S) STKS 7f (F)

2:40 (2:41) (Class 6) 4-Y-O+ £2,184 (£644; £322) Stalls Low

Form RPR
-003 1 **Mister Incredible**[7] [303] 4-8-9 52 (v) SaleemGolam(3) 4 56
(V Smith) *prom: hmpd over 5f out: n.m.r over 4f out: rdn to ld over 1f out: edgd lft: all out* **16/1**
40/4 2 shd **Volaticus (IRE)**[9] [286] 6-9-1 60 ow3 BFayosMartin 6 59
(R J Smith, Spain) *hld up: hdwy u.p 2f out: sn hung rt: hung lft ins fnl f: r.o wl* **9/2**[2]
34-1 3 ½ **Wodhill Be**[21] [145] 7-8-12 49 HayleyTurner 1 55
(D Morris) *hld up in tch: rdn to chse wnr fnl f: styd on* **14/1**
6430 4 1 ¾ **Spy Gun (USA)**[1] [366] 7-8-12 45 ChrisCatlin 11 50
(T Wall) *led: rdn and hdd 3f out: ev ch over 1f out: styd on same pce* **28/1**
5-30 5 2 **Vancouver Gold (IRE)**[14] [228] 5-8-7 59 (p) PatCosgrave 3 40
(K R Burke) *chsd ldrs: led 3f out: rdn and hdd over 1f out: wknd ins fnl f* **7/1**[3]
-402 6 nk **Rocky Reppin**[5] [321] 7-8-9 40 (b) JasonEdmunds(3) 7 44
(J Balding) *s.i.s: hdwy over 4f out: shkn up over 1f out: styd on same pce* **25/1**
-134 7 nk **Capital Lass**[12] [238] 4-8-9 58 StephenDonohoe(3) 9 43
(A J McCabe) *chsd ldrs: rdn and hung lft over 1f out: wknd fnl f* **9/2**[2]
20-0 8 1 ½ **Tamatave (IRE)**[16] [206] 5-8-12 58 NCallan 12 39
(K A Ryan) *chsd ldrs: hmpd 4f out: rdn over 2f out: wknd over 1f out* **13/8**[1]
4-60 9 2 ½ **Tribute (IRE)**[12] [241] 6-8-9 44 JamesDoyle(3) 5 33
(John A Harris) *hld up: hmpd over 5f out: rdn 1/2-way: n.d* **66/1**
6-00 10 1 ¾ **Far Note (USA)**[21] [145] 9-8-12 44 (bt) PhillipMakin 10 28
(S R Bowring) *chsd ldrs over 5f* **80/1**
11 11 **Ettrbee (IRE)**[69] 5-8-7 PaulMulrennan 8 —
(H Alexander) *mid-div: hmpd over 5f out: sn lost pl* **100/1**
00-0 12 9 **Go Mo (IRE)**[8] [292] 5-8-12 54 BrettDoyle 13 —
(R M H Cowell) *s.i.s: wknd 1/2-way* **20/1**
004/ 13 28 **Storm Shower (IRE)**[1129] [428] 9-8-7 38 (v) DuranFentiman(5) 2 —
(Mrs N Macauley) *hld up: rdn and wknd 1/2-way* **100/1**

1m 33.53s (2.73) **Going Correction** +0.25s/f (Slow) 13 Ran SP% **116.3**
Speed ratings (Par 101):94,93,93,91,89 88,88,86,83,81 69,58,26
CSF £80.97 TOTE £15.70: £4.20, £1.60, £2.70; EX 142.70 TRIFECTA Not won..There was no bid for the winner. Volaticus was subject to a friendly claim.
Owner R West **Bred** R J H West **Trained** Exning, Suffolk

FOCUS
An ordinary seller run in a moderate time, even for a race of this type. Probably a very ordinary race of its type.

375 PONTIN'S BOOK EARLY MAIDEN STKS 6f (F)

3:10 (3:11) (Class 5) 3-Y-O+ £2,817 (£838; £418; £209) Stalls Low

Form RPR
4 1 **Bernasconi (USA)**[8] [301] 3-8-12 RobertWinston 7 77+
(G A Swinbank) *chsd ldrs: rdn over 1f out: led ins fnl f: r.o* **4/7**[1]
44- 2 2 **Rann Na Cille (IRE)**[45] [6927] 3-8-4 67 AndrewMullen(3) 4 66
(K A Ryan) *w ldr tl led over 3f out: rdn over 1f out: hdd and no ex ins fnl f* **11/2**[3]

6-2 **3** 4 **Sedgwick**[25] [106] 5-9-13 .... J-PGuillambert 10 59
(J G Given) *chsd ldrs: rdn and hung lft over 2f out: wknd fnl f* **3/1**[2]
4 **4** nk **Cap St Jean (IRE)**[30] [60] 3-8-12 .... DaleGibson 9 58
(P C Haslam) *led: hdd over 3f out: rdn over 1f out: sn wknd* **16/1**
0 **5** 5 **The Tinker Man**[23] [128] 3-8-12 .... HayleyTurner 2 43
(M D I Usher) *prom: rdn 1/2-way: wknd over 1f out* **33/1**
5 **6** 1 **Missus Molly Brown**[25] [106] 3-8-6 ow4 .... JamieMoriarty(5) 3 39
(R A Fahey) *in rr: rdn over 3f out: n.d* **14/1**
7 shd **Another Toy** 4-9-8 .... SilvestreDeSousa 1 35
(A D Brown) *prom: rdn 1/2-way: wknd over 1f out* **25/1**
8 ½ **Solidgoldesyaction** 3-8-7 .... SimonWhitworth 11 33
(P A Blockley) *s.s: a in rr* **33/1**
1m 18.07s (1.17) **Going Correction** +0.25s/f (Slow)
WFA 3 from 4yo+ 15lb **8 Ran SP% 126.3**
Speed ratings (Par 103):102,99,94,93,86 85,85,84
CSF £5.22 TOTE £1.60: £1.10, £1.70, £1.10; EX 5.70 Trifecta £19.90 Pool: £804.06 - 28.57 winning units..
Owner Elsa Crankshaw & Gordon Allan **Bred** Darley **Trained** Melsonby, N Yorks
FOCUS
Weak maiden form but it looks solid enough rated through the runner-up. The winner can rate higher.

376 PONTINS.COM FILLIES' H'CAP 6f (F)
3:40 (3:40) (Class 5) (0-70,64) 4-Y-O+ **£2,914** (£867; £433; £216) **Stalls** Low

Form RPR
0-02 **1** **Cerebus**[8] [296] 5-8-8 57 ....(bt) StephenDonohoe(3) 4 73
(A J McCabe) *mde all: clr 2f out: sn rdn and edgd lft: styd on* **4/1**[2]
34-1 **2** 3 **Black Sea Pearl**[21] [150] 4-9-4 64 .... JohnEgan 1 71
(P W D'Arcy) *chsd ldrs: rdn 1/2-way: styd on ins fnl f: no ch w wnr* **3/1**[1]
0-21 **3** shd **Sweet Pickle**[29] [67] 6-9-4 64 ....(e) PatCosgrave 6 71
(J R Boyle) *hld up: hdwy over 2f out: sn rdn: styd on* **5/1**[3]
0-31 **4** 4 **Muara**[8] [296] 5-9-3 63 6ex .... NCallan 5 58
(D W Barker) *prom: chsd wnr over 2f out: sn rdn and hung lft: wknd fnl f* **4/1**[2]
04-0 **5** 3 **Pikaboo**[10] [268] 4-8-1 50 ....(e1) LiamJones(3) 2 36
(S C Williams) *hld up: rdn 1/2-way: wknd over 2f out* **7/1**
4-10 **6** 5 **Glamaraazi (IRE)**[21] [150] 4-8-7 58 ....(v1) JamieMoriarty(5) 7 29
(R A Fahey) *s.i.s and wnt rt s: rel to r: rdn and wknd over 2f out* **7/1**
-050 **7** 4 **Diktalex (IRE)**[5] [318] 4-8-9 55 ....(t) RobbieFitzpatrick 8 14
(C J Teague) *sn outpcd: bhd fr 1/2-way* **50/1**
140- **8** 3½ **Fortress**[157] [5032] 4-8-13 59 ....(b) DavidAllan 3 7
(E J Alston) *chsd wnr tl rdn over 2f out: sn wknd* **25/1**
1m 17.49s (0.59) **Going Correction** +0.25s/f (Slow) **8 Ran SP% 112.5**
Speed ratings (Par 100):106,102,101,96,92 85,80,75
CSF £15.85 CT £59.78 TOTE £4.20: £1.60, £1.10, £1.40; EX 17.60 Trifecta £42.30 Pool: £816.35 - 13.69 winning units..
Owner Paul J Dixon **Bred** Rookley Holdings **Trained** Babworth, Notts
FOCUS
A modest fillies' handicap run in a decent time for a race like this. Cerebus built on her previous promising effort at Wolverhampton.

377 PONTIN'S HOLIDAYS H'CAP 1m 3f (F)
4:10 (4:10) (Class 5) (0-75,75) 4-Y-O+ **£2,914** (£867; £433; £216) **Stalls** Low

Form RPR
0-00 **1** **Kylkenny**[14] [226] 12-8-13 70 ....(t) RobertHavlin 4 82
(H Morrison) *a.p: chsd ldr over 3f out: rdn to ld over 1f out: styd on* **20/1**
0-01 **2** ½ **Greenbelt**[5] [319] 6-8-4 60 6ex .... ChrisCatlin 10 73
(G M Moore) *a.p: chsd ldr 9f out: led over 3f out: rdn and hdd over 1f out: styd on* **11/4**[2]
1-24 **3** 5 **Jackie Kiely**[14] [226] 6-9-4 75 ....(t) PatCosgrave 6 78
(R Brotherton) *hld up: hdwy over 1f out: nt trble ldrs* **12/1**
60-6 **4** 1 **Torrens (IRE)**[16] [205] 5-8-12 74 .... JamieMoriarty(5) 2 75
(R A Fahey) *chsd ldrs: rdn over 2f out: sn outpcd* **9/1**[3]
30-6 **5** 8 **Waterloo Corner**[16] [204] 5-8-6 63 .... PaulMulrennan 1 51
(R Craggs) *chsd ldrs: rdn over 3f out: wknd wl over 1f out* **66/1**
12-4 **6** 5 **Turner's Touch**[27] [95] 5-9-2 73 ....(be) GeorgeBaker 3 52
(G L Moore) *hld up in tch: rdn over 3f out: wknd over 2f out* **9/1**[3]
14-5 **7** ¾ **Silverhay**[8] [297] 6-9-3 74 ....(p) NCallan 7 52
(L Corcoran) *led: rdn and hdd over 3f out: wknd 2f out* **9/1**[3]
2-12 **8** ½ **Blacktoft (USA)**[5] [319] 4-9-0 73 ....(e) J-PGuillambert 9 50
(S C Williams) *s.i.s: hld up: hdwy over 3f out: rdn and wknd over 2f out* **7/4**[1]
124- **9** 1¾ **Choristar**[140] [5445] 6-8-4 61 oh1 .... DaleGibson 11 35
(J Mackie) *hld up: hdwy 4f out: wknd over 2f out* **18/1**
00/5 **10** 5 **Croix Rouge (USA)**[9] [283] 5-9-1 72 ow4 ....(b1) BFayosMartin 5 38
(R J Smith, Spain) *hld up: wkng whn hrd rdn and swtchd lft over 2f out* **33/1**
2m 29.4s (0.50) **Going Correction** +0.25s/f (Slow)
WFA 4 from 5yo+ 2lb **10 Ran SP% 115.2**
Speed ratings (Par 103):108,107,104,103,97 93,93,92,91,88
CSF £72.92 CT £711.70 TOTE £29.80: £4.90, £1.60, £3.00; EX 102.30 Trifecta £388.90 Part won. Pool: £547.82 - 0.10 winning units..
Owner Mrs M D W Morrison **Bred** R M , P J And S R Payne **Trained** East Ilsley, Berks
FOCUS
An amazing win from the veteran Kylkenny and a decent pace resulted in a respectable time for a race of its class. The winner was rated to his best this winter but was rated a fair bit better last winter.
Kylkenny Official explanation: trainer's rep said, regarding apparent improvement in form, gelding was running in a lower class, and had been dropped significantly in the handicap

378 PONTIN'S H'CAP 5f (F)
4:40 (4:40) (Class 6) (0-60,58) 3-Y-O **£2,388** (£705; £352) **Stalls** High

Form RPR
3214 **1** **Bentley**[8] [290] 3-9-3 57 ....(v) DaneO'Neill 7 70
(D Shaw) *chsd ldrs: rdn 1/2-way: styd on u.p to ld wl ins fnl f* **2/1**[1]
604- **2** ½ **Jojesse**[196] [3818] 3-8-10 50 .... RobertWinston 4 61
(G A Swinbank) *wnt lft s: chsd ldrs: rdn to ld over 1f out: hdd wl ins fnl f* **5/2**[2]
50-4 **3** 6 **Pretty Selma**[26] [103] 3-8-5 45 ....(v1) HayleyTurner 8 35
(R M H Cowell) *led to 1/2-way: sn rdn: wkng whn hung lft ins fnl f* **33/1**
5-34 **4** nk **Shepherdess (USA)**[3] [343] 3-8-8 55 .... KirstyMilczarek(7) 9 44
(D M Simcock) *chsd ldrs: edgd lft fr 1/2-way: wkng whn hmpd ins fnl f* **11/1**
-633 **5** ¾ **Pappas Image**[26] [103] 3-8-12 55 ....(b) StephenDonohoe(3) 6 41
(A J McCabe) *chsd ldr tl led 1/2-way: rdn: hung lft and hdd over 1f out: wknd ins fnl f* **6/1**[3]
20-6 **6** 3½ **Gibsons**[35] [11] 3-8-13 53 .... NCallan 1 26
(P A Blockley) *wnt rt s: chsd ldrs: rdn 1/2-way: wknd fnl f* **8/1**
00-0 **7** ¾ **Bonny Scotland (IRE)**[12] [237] 3-7-13 46 ow1 .... SamuelDrury(7) 3 17
(I W McInnes) *hmpd s: outpcd* **100/1**
36-3 **8** 14 **Sunken Rags**[25] [108] 3-9-0 57 ....(p) AndrewElliott(3) 5 —
(K R Burke) *s.i.s: outpcd* **10/1**
003- **9** 17 **Head To Head (IRE)**[39] [6975] 3-9-4 58 .... RobbieFitzpatrick 2 —
(Peter Grayson) *s.s and hmpd s: outpcd* **22/1**
61.22 secs (0.92) **Going Correction** +0.075s/f (Slow) **9 Ran SP% 113.0**
Speed ratings (Par 95):95,94,84,84,82 77,76,53,26
CSF £6.75 CT £114.69 TOTE £2.40: £1.80, £1.20, £4.80; EX 12.70 Trifecta £282.60 Pool: £529.49 - 1.33 winning units. Place 6 £542.07, Place 5 £163.65.
Owner Danethorpe Racing Ltd **Bred** P Blows And Miss J Hall **Trained** Danethorpe, Notts
FOCUS
A poor sprint handicap in which the front pair pulled a long way clear, which does not bode well for the future prospects of the rest. The winner is progressive and the runner-up unexposed.
Pretty Selma Official explanation: jockey said filly hung left final furlong
Pappas Image Official explanation: jockey said gelding hung left
Sunken Rags Official explanation: jockey said filly was slowly away from stalls
Head To Head(IRE) Official explanation: jockey said gelding suffered interference on leaving stalls
T/Jkpt: Not won. T/Plt: £441.30 to a £1 stake. Pool: £139,622.09. 230.95 winning tickets. T/Qpdt: £14.70 to a £1 stake. Pool: £12,075.10. 604.90 winning tickets. CR

357 LINGFIELD (L-H)
Wednesday, February 7

OFFICIAL GOING: Standard
Wind: Nil Weather: Sunny

379 CANVAS PRINTS FROM BONUSPRINT.COM H'CAP (DIV I) 7f (P)
12:50 (12:53) (Class 6) (0-58,58) 4-Y-O+ **£1,706** (£503; £252) **Stalls** Low

Form RPR
0-06 **1** **Another Gladiator (USA)**[8] [306] 4-8-12 54 ....(p) NCallan 2 64
(K A Ryan) *lw: mde all: kicked on over 2f out: hung rt u.p fnl f: kpt on wl* **6/1**[3]
-225 **2** 1 **King After**[7] [313] 5-8-11 53 ....(v) BrettDoyle 3 60
(J R Best) *trckd ldrs: rdn over 2f out: effrt u.p over 1f out: kpt on to chse wnr last 75yds: nvr gng to chal* **10/3**[2]
3161 **3** ½ **Burhaan (IRE)**[4] [346] 5-9-1 57 .... FergusSweeney 1 63
(J R Boyle) *lw: cl up: chsd wnr 2f out: rdn to chal over 1f out: carried rt and nt qckn fnl f* **1/1**[1]
040- **4** ¾ **Border Artist**[46] [6934] 8-9-0 56 .... SebSanders 6 60
(J Pearce) *s.i.s: hld up in midfield: prog on inner 2f out: tried to chal 1f out: fdd ins fnl f* **16/1**
604- **5** 1 **Postmaster**[158] [5035] 5-8-4 46 .... ChrisCatlin 5 47
(R Ingram) *wl in rr: rdn and struggling 3f out: swtchd to inner over 1f out: plugged on* **16/1**
00-0 **6** hd **King Of Charm (IRE)**[5] [337] 4-8-8 50 .... ShaneKelly 10 51
(G L Moore) *t.k.h: hld up and racd wd: hanging over 2f out: wd bnd wl over 1f out: no real prog* **50/1**
3-33 **7** 1 **Fulvio (USA)**[19] [180] 7-8-10 52 ....(v) JoeFanning 7 50
(P Howling) *chsd wnr to 2f out: wknd fnl f* **14/1**
65-6 **8** ¾ **Todlea (IRE)**[11] [268] 7-8-3 52 ....(t) SophieDoyle(7) 8 48
(Jean-Rene Auvray) *t.k.h: trckd ldrs: losing pl whn wd and n.m.r bnd 2f out* **20/1**
000- **9** 5 **Endless Night**[140] [5474] 4-9-2 58 .... HayleyTurner 9 41
(T M Jones) *ref to go to post tl dismntd and led: hld up in last: pushed along 1/2-way: no prog* **66/1**
1m 24.15s (-1.74) **Going Correction** -0.225s/f (Stan) **9 Ran SP% 114.0**
Speed ratings (Par 101):100,98,98,97,96 96,94,94,88
CSF £25.60 CT £35.67 TOTE £7.80: £2.10, £1.10, £1.10; EX 39.10 Trifecta £22.20 Pool: £534.25 - 17.05 winning units..
Owner Mrs T Marnane **Bred** Brushwood Stable **Trained** Hambleton, N Yorks
■ Stewards' Enquiry : N Callan two-day ban: careless riding (Feb 19-20)
FOCUS
A moderate handicap run at an uneven pace. The winner enjoyed the run of the race. Ordinary form, rated through the runner-up.
Another Gladiator(USA) Official explanation: jockey said colt hung right throughout

380 GO PONTIN'S CLAIMING STKS 1m 5f (P)
1:20 (1:20) (Class 6) 4-Y-O+ **£2,184** (£644; £322) **Stalls** Low

Form RPR
00-1 **1** **Diamonds And Dust**[25] [115] 5-9-13 80 ....(b) SebSanders 3 82+
(S Dow) *t.k.h: hld up: trckd ldrs gng easily fr 3f out tl led over 1f out: drew rt away* **13/8**[1]
5-00 **2** 6 **Casablanca Minx (IRE)**[7] [314] 4-9-4 70 ....(b) NCallan 5 68
(N P Littmoden) *t.k.h: trckd ldrs gng easily 3f out: effrt on inner to chal over 1f out: sn outpcd by wnr* **4/1**[3]
0-10 **3** 3½ **Tiegs (IRE)**[13] [242] 5-8-8 46 .... ChrisCatlin 2 49
(P W Hiatt) *led after 2f: rdn and jnd over 4f out: hdd & wknd over 1f out* **16/1**
/603 **4** hd **Mumbling (IRE)**[14] [232] 9-9-7 62 .... FergusSweeney 4 62
(B G Powell) *led for 2f: trckd ldr: rdn to chal over 4f out: upsides over 1f out: wknd* **9/4**[2]
-034 **5** 3½ **Lady Pilot**[9] [291] 5-9-0 52 ....(b) JimCrowley 6 49
(Ms J S Doyle) *trckd ldrs: rdn to chal 4f out: upsides 2f out: wknd over 1f out* **15/2**
-454 **6** 3 **Dik Dik**[5] [333] 4-8-9 47 ....(p) LPKeniry 1 44
(J S Moore) *in tch to 3f out: wknd* **20/1**
2m 46.98s (-1.32) **Going Correction** -0.225s/f (Stan)
WFA 4 from 5yo+ 4lb **6 Ran SP% 111.3**
Speed ratings (Par 101):95,91,89,89,86 85
CSF £8.37 TOTE £2.10: £2.00, £2.10; EX 7.90.The winner was claimed by F. P. Murtagh for £13,000.
Owner P Wheatley **Bred** Whitsbury Manor Stud **Trained** Epsom, Surrey
FOCUS
No strength to this weak claimer and the winner won as he was entitled to at the weights. He was still some way off his best 2006 form, however.
Dik Dik Official explanation: jockey said gelding had no more to give

381 PONTINS.COM H'CAP 1m (P)
1:50 (1:51) (Class 5) (0-70,70) 4-Y-0+ **£3,071** (£906; £453) **Stalls** High

Form RPR

24-0 **1** **Million Percent**[14] [233] 8-8-10 **67** .... LiamJones(3) 10 76
(C R Dore) *settled towards rr: prog over 2f out: rdn to ld jst over 1f out: drvn and hld on wl* **12/1**

20-0 **2** *nk* **Silent Storm**[14] [233] 7-9-2 **70** .... NCallan 7 78
(C A Cyzer) *t.k.h: hld up wl in rr: prog 2f out: drvn to chse wnr last 75yds: clsng at fin* **8/1**

4-00 **3** *1 1/2* **Cinematic (IRE)**[16] [211] 4-8-13 **67** .... FergusSweeney 11 72
(J R Boyle) *racd wd: hld up in midfield: prog fr 1/2-way: led over 2f out and kicked on: edgd lft and hdd jst over 1f out: one pce* **14/1**

2023 **4** *3/4* **Roman Boy (ARG)**[7] [313] 8-8-4 **58** .... (v) AdrianMcCarthy 8 61
(Stef Liddiard) *trckd ldrs gng wl: outpcd 2f out: styd on again fnl f: nvr able to chal* **7/2**[1]

153- **5** *1* **Dyanita**[51] [6863] 4-8-12 **66** .... OscarUrbina 4 71+
(B W Hills) *lw: w ldrs for 1f: restrained and sn in last pair: stl there over 1f out: plld out ins fnl f: r.o strly: do bttr* **7/1**

065- **6** *1/2* **Semi Detached (IRE)**[160] [4973] 4-8-13 **67** .... PatCosgrave 6 67
(J R Boyle) *lw: awkward s: settled in last pair: stl there over 1f out: rdn and styd on wl fnl f: no ch* **14/1**

4-05 **7** *1/2* **Red Birr (IRE)**[11] [259] 6-9-2 **70** .... ChrisCatlin 9 68
(P R Webber) *led for 1f: lost pl 3f out: struggling on outer over 1f out: kpt on* **8/1**

500- **8** *1 3/4* **Nightstrike (IRE)**[127] [5756] 4-8-8 **62** .... CatherineGannon 3 56
(Luke Comer, Ire) *lw: w ldr to over 2f out: wknd over 1f out* **50/1**

000- **9** *1 1/4* **Napoletano (GER)**[61] [6747] 6-8-6 **60** .... LPKeniry 1 51
(S Dow) *heavily stdd s: plld hrd and trckd ldrs after 2f: wknd 2f out* **14/1**

03-5 **10** *3 1/2* **First Friend (IRE)**[16] [212] 6-8-11 **65** .... ShaneKelly 5 48
(P Mitchell) *t.k.h: w ldrs to over 2f out: wknd rapidly over 1f out* **5/1**[2]

540- **11** *shd* **Wassfa**[42] [6954] 4-8-7 **61** .... BrettDoyle 2 44
(C E Brittain) *led after 1f: mde most but a pressed: hdd & wknd over 2f out* **6/1**[3]

1m 36.71s (-2.72) **Going Correction** -0.225s/f (Stan) **11** Ran SP% **117.5**
Speed ratings (Par 103):104,103,102,101,100 99,99,97,96,92 92
CSF £104.58 CT £1369.11 TOTE £13.30: £2.90, £2.70, £6.60; EX 50.90 TRIFECTA Not won..
Owner Ship Tottenham **Bred** D J And Mrs Deer **Trained** West Pinchbeck, Lincs

FOCUS
A modest handicap which was run at a strong early pace, with the first two coming through from the rear. The form should work out. Dyanita's run caught the attention of the stewards.

Dyanita ◆ Official explanation: jockey said, regarding running and riding, his orders were to jump out well and either making running or, if there was pace on, to settle in behind leaders, adding that having broken well he decided to settle in but the filly dropped the bridle and was unable to get a clear run into home straight; trainer's rep added that filly had done too much when wearing blinkers last time and was not straightforward

382 PONTINSBINGO.COM H'CAP 1m (P)
2:25 (2:25) (Class 5) (0-75,75) 3-Y-O **£3,238** (£963; £481; £240) **Stalls** High

Form RPR

002- **1** **Nassmaan (IRE)**[88] [6434] 3-9-4 **75** .... AdrianMcCarthy 5 75
(P W Chapple-Hyam) *mde all: jnd 2f out: battled on wl u.p fnl f: game* **9/1**

033- **2** *1/2* **L'Oiseau De Feu (USA)**[146] [5326] 3-9-3 **74** .... RichardHughes 4 73
(E A L Dunlop) *dwlt and stdd s: hld up in last: prog on inner wl over 1f out: hrd rdn to chal fnl f: hld towards fin* **11/4**[2]

6-23 **3** *3/4* **Henry The Seventh**[11] [260] 3-8-13 **70** .... EddieAhern 8 67
(J W Hills) *trckd ldrs: rdn and nrly upsides over 2f out: nt qckn over 1f out: styd on ins fnl f to take 3rd nr fin* **4/1**[3]

-212 **4** *shd* **Six Shots**[9] [294] 3-9-3 **74** .... ShaneKelly 6 71
(J A Osborne) *lw: w wnr: rdn 2f out: nt qckn over 1f out: one pce fnl f* **7/4**[1]

-155 **5** *1/2* **Homes By Woodford**[16] [216] 3-8-13 **70** .... DaneO'Neill 3 66
(R A Harris) *t.k.h: hld up: wd bnd 2f out and outpcd: styd on ins fnl f* **12/1**

13-5 **6** *1/2* **Inquisitress**[35] [27] 3-8-9 **69** .... AmirQuinn(3) 1 63
(J J Bridger) *trckd ldrs: gng wl 2f out: tried to chal jst over 1f out: n.m.r sn after: fdd last 100yds* **20/1**

500- **7** *1 3/4* **Baldovina**[124] [5783] 3-9-2 **73** .... NCallan 2 63
(M Botti) *chsd ldrs: u.p 3f out: wknd over 1f out* **16/1**

00-4 **8** *19* **Caj (IRE)**[14] [231] 3-8-4 **61** oh1 .... CatherineGannon 7 8
(Luke Comer, Ire) *racd wd and t.k.h: in tch to 2f out: wknd rapidly: t.o* **66/1**

1m 38.58s (-0.85) **Going Correction** -0.225s/f (Stan) **8** Ran SP% **112.9**
Speed ratings (Par 97):95,94,93,93,93 92,90,71
CSF £33.14 CT £116.42 TOTE £9.90: £2.00, £1.40, £1.80; EX 42.60 Trifecta £131.00 Pool: £716.28 - 3.88 winning units..
Owner Fawzi Abdulla Nass **Bred** B Kennedy **Trained** Newmarket, Suffolk

FOCUS
An ordinary handicap of its type and the pace was no more than fair which suited those that raced handily, but the first two were the least-experienced in the field and both possess a bit of scope. The winner should improve on this, but the bunch finish and exposed third hold down the form.

Inquisitress Official explanation: trainer said filly lost a front shoe

Caj(IRE) Official explanation: jockey said filly hung right; vet said filly returned stiff behind

383 CANVAS PRINTS FROM BONUSPRINT.COM H'CAP (DIV II) 7f (P)
3:00 (3:00) (Class 6) (0-58,57) 4-Y-0+ **£1,706** (£503; £252) **Stalls** Low

Form RPR

0-60 **1** **Binnion Bay (IRE)**[7] [310] 6-8-11 **54** .... (b) AmirQuinn(3) 9 64
(J J Bridger) *hld up off the pce: prog gng wl 2f out: c wd in st: rdn and r.o to ld last 100yds: sn clr* **20/1**

5601 **2** *1 1/2* **Mulberry Lad (IRE)**[7] [310] 5-9-3 **57** 6ex .... JimCrowley 2 63
(P W Hiatt) *trckd ldrs: effrt to ld over 1f out: hdd & wknd last 100yds* **7/1**

5-45 **3** *3/4* **Labelled With Love**[7] [310] 7-8-12 **52** .... (t) PatCosgrave 10 56
(J R Boyle) *hld up fr wd draw and t.k.h: prog 2f out: drvn and kpt on same pce fr over 1f out* **7/2**[1]

000- **4** *1 1/2* **Only If I Laugh**[85] [6470] 6-8-13 **53** .... DaneO'Neill 6 53
(M J Attwater) *pressed ldr: led over 3f out to over 1f out: wknd fnl f* **4/1**[2]

54-0 **5** *nk* **Simpsons Gamble (IRE)**[28] [86] 4-8-12 **52** .... AdamKirby 1 51
(R M Flower) *lw: trckd ldrs: rdn and lost pl 2f out: kpt on again fnl f: n.d* **8/1**

01-5 **6** *hd* **Cool Tiger**[15] [221] 4-8-13 **53** .... ShaneKelly 3 52
(P Howling) *dwlt: sn in midfield: gng wl enough over 2f out: effrt over 1f out: sn rdn and no prog* **6/1**

000- **7** *3/4* **Cankara (IRE)**[41] [6960] 4-7-12 **45** .... GaryWales(7) 7 42
(D Carroll) *s.s: plld hrd and hld up last: detached over 2f out: kpt on fnl f: no ch* **100/1**

2-10 **8** *4* **Charlottebutterfly**[28] [83] 7-8-8 **48** .... PaulEddery 8 34
(P J McBride) *dwlt: hld up in rr: rdn wl over 2f out: brief effrt over 1f out: wknd and eased ins fnl f* **11/1**

-330 **9** *2* **Whistleupthewind**[9] [296] 4-8-13 **56** .... (b) StephenDonohoe(3) 5 37
(J M P Eustace) *w ldrs tl wknd 2f out* **11/2**[3]

4-00 **10** *1 1/4* **Viewforth**[11] [268] 9-8-11 **51** .... JoeFanning 4 29
(M A Buckley) *racd freely: led to over 3f out: lost pl: wknd over 1f out: eased* **14/1**

1m 24.05s (-1.84) **Going Correction** -0.225s/f (Stan) **10** Ran SP% **116.3**
Speed ratings (Par 101):101,99,98,96,96 96,95,90,88,87
CSF £153.04 CT £632.37 TOTE £18.30: £3.10, £2.50, £1.50; EX 88.10 Trifecta £280.50 Part won. Pool: £395.13 - 0.61 winning units..
Owner J J Bridger **Bred** Fieldspring Ltd **Trained** Liphook, Hants

FOCUS
A modest handicap in which the winning time was 0.1 seconds quicker than the first division. The winner ran his best race since his two-year-old days, but the runner-up, who was wrong at the weights, limits the form.

384 PONTIN'S "BOOK EARLY" H'CAP 7f (P)
3:30 (3:32) (Class 4) (0-85,85) 4-Y-0+ **£4,857** (£1,445; £722; £360) **Stalls** Low

Form RPR

1-11 **1** **Super Frank (IRE)**[11] [261] 4-8-4 **73** .... ChrisCatlin 6 87+
(J Akehurst) *lw: mde all and set str pce: kicked at least 2 l clr over 2f out: drvn and tired fnl f but a holding on* **15/8**[1]

0-22 **2** *1* **Katiypour (IRE)**[11] [259] 10-8-13 **82** .... SebSanders 1 90
(P Mitchell) *prom: chsd wnr wl over 2f out: no imp wl over 1f out: kpt on fnl f* **6/1**[3]

02-0 **3** *hd* **Secret Night**[18] [198] 4-9-2 **85** .... EddieAhern 3 92
(J A R Toller) *hld up towards rr: prog on inner over 2f out: drvn to dispute 2nd fnl f: kpt on* **13/2**

-553 **4** *hd* **Josh**[11] [261] 5-8-9 **78** .... NCallan 2 84
(K A Ryan) *prom: rdn 3f out: kpt on u.p fnl 2f: nvr able to chal* **7/2**[2]

2-33 **5** *1 1/4* **Mandarin Spirit (IRE)**[16] [218] 7-8-9 **78** .... (b) OscarUrbina 9 81
(G C H Chung) *reluctant to enter stalls: hld up in last pair: prog 2f out: styd on fnl f: n.d* **16/1**

00-1 **6** *1* **Grimes Faith**[35] [28] 4-8-7 **83** .... (b) HaddenFrost(7) 5 84
(R Hannon) *lw: hld up in last pair: prog on inner over 1f out: ch of pl fnl f: wknd last 100yds* **7/1**

30-0 **7** *9* **Kaveri (USA)**[33] [44] 4-8-13 **82** .... BrettDoyle 8 59
(C E Brittain) *pushed along early: in tch on outer tl wknd rapidly 2f out* **20/1**

-040 **8** *nk* **Meditation**[11] [261] 5-8-9 **78** ow1 .... AdamKirby 7 54
(I A Wood) *pressed ldrs: drvn 1/2-way: sn lost pl: wknd 2f out* **40/1**

16/0 **9** *2 1/2* **Royal Engineer**[18] [198] 4-8-11 **80** .... JoeFanning 4 50
(M Johnston) *chsd wnr to wl over 2f out: wknd rapidly* **20/1**

1m 22.68s (-3.21) **Going Correction** -0.225s/f (Stan) course record **9** Ran SP% **115.0**
Speed ratings (Par 105):109,107,107,107,105 104,94,94,91
CSF £13.07 CT £60.80 TOTE £2.70: £1.20, £1.70, £2.40; EX 10.30 Trifecta £24.10 Pool: £1,284.15 - 37.80 winning units..
Owner A D Spence **Bred** A Butler **Trained** Epsom, Surrey

FOCUS
A fairly decent handicap run at a good pace. The winner is progressive and can do better still, value for extra here, and there is a sound look to the form.

385 PONTIN'S FAMILY HOLIDAYS H'CAP 6f (P)
4:05 (4:05) (Class 4) (0-85,84) 3-Y-O **£4,857** (£1,445; £722; £360) **Stalls** Low

Form RPR

21-2 **1** **Mastership (IRE)**[35] [27] 3-9-3 **82** .... (b) EddieAhern 5 101+
(C E Brittain) *lw: hld up in last pair: gng easily 2f out: led on bit jst ins fnl f: cruised clr* **10/3**[2]

1-11 **2** *3* **Si Foo (USA)**[7] [312] 3-9-5 **84** 6ex .... LPKeniry 6 87
(A M Balding) *lw: trckd ldng pair: effrt to ld narrowly 2f out: drvn over 1f out: hdd jst ins fnl f: no ch w wnr* **1/2**[1]

24-2 **3** *1 1/2* **Love In May (IRE)**[18] [199] 3-9-0 **79** .... NCallan 2 77
(J S Moore) *trckd ldrs: rdn over 2f out: effrt on inner over 1f out: plugged on same pce* **20/1**

25-1 **4** *shd* **Our Blessing (IRE)**[18] [188] 3-9-4 **83** .... DaneO'Neill 1 81
(A P Jarvis) *disp ld to 2f out: drvn and stl nrly upsides 1f out: sn outpcd* **10/1**[3]

33-3 **5** *shd* **Mr Loire**[18] [199] 3-8-4 **72** .... RichardKingscote(3) 4 69
(R Charlton) *stdd s: hld up in last pair: rdn and outpcd over 1f out: kpt on again fnl f* **20/1**

006- **6** *1 3/4* **Arnie's Joint (IRE)**[138] [5509] 3-7-13 **69** oh1 .... DuranFentiman(5) 3 61
(N P Littmoden) *racd freely: disp ld to 2f out: cl up tl wknd fnl f* **40/1**

1m 11.21s (-1.60) **Going Correction** -0.225s/f (Stan) **6** Ran SP% **110.8**
Speed ratings (Par 99):101,97,95,94,94 92
CSF £5.25 TOTE £3.40: £1.90, £1.10; EX 7.00.
Owner Sheikh Marwan Al Maktoum **Bred** Darley **Trained** Newmarket, Suffolk

FOCUS
A decent sprint handicap run at a good pace and won in very impressive style by Mastership.

386 DIGITAL PRINTS FROM BONUSPRINT.COM MAIDEN STKS 1m 2f (P)
4:35 (4:36) (Class 5) 3-Y-O **£3,071** (£906; £453) **Stalls** Low

Form RPR

1 **Aajel (USA)** 3-9-3 .... RichardHughes 1 78+
(M P Tregoning) *w'like:scope:tall:rangy: trckd ldrs:gng wl 2f out:swtchd ins to chal over 1f out:led last 100yds:in command whn hung rt nr fin* **7/2**[2]

6-2 **2** *3/4* **Rain And Shade**[12] [258] 3-9-3 .... JoeFanning 9 76+
(M Johnston) *unf: scope: trckd ldng pair: effrt to ld jst over 2f out: drvn over 1f out: hdd last 200yds: wl hld whn nudged by wnr nr fin* **8/13**[1]

3 *1 3/4* **Yab Adee** 3-9-3 .... DaneO'Neill 6 73+
(M P Tregoning) *w'like: leggy: bit bkwd: trckd ldrs: effrt over 2f out: shkn up to chse ldng pair over 1f out: styd on same pce* **9/1**

4 *3* **Shawhill** 3-8-9 .... JerryO'Dwyer(3) 11 62
(A M Hales) *leggy: unf: s.s: in tch towards rr: pushed along and wd over 3f out: outpcd over 2f out: styd on wl fr over 1f out* **66/1**

5 *4* **Force Celebre (IRE)** 3-9-0 .... SaleemGolam(3) 12 59+
(M H Tompkins) *leggy: bit bkwd: mostly in last trio: outpcd 3f out: green but r.o fnl f: nrst fin* **33/1**

4 **6** *1* **Stand In Black (NZ)**[32] [53] 3-9-0 .... StephaneBreux(3) 4 57
(B I Case) *led to jst over 2f out: wknd rapidly over 1f out* **50/1**

40 **7** *2* **Deserter (IRE)**[12] [258] 3-8-12 .... ShaneKelly 10 48
(J A Osborne) *prog to chse ldrs after 3f: in tch over 2f out: wknd wl over 1f out* **7/1**[3]

4- **8** 1 1/4 **Countess Majella (IRE)**[47] [6920] 3-8-12 ....(t) ChrisCatlin 14 45
(E J O'Neill) *w'like: reluctant to enter stalls: mostly in last trio: pushed along and outpcd 3f out: n.d after* **20/1**

0 **9** 1 1/4 **Starcrest**[30] [73] 3-8-12 .... FrankieMcDonald 13 43
(Jean-Rene Auvray) *leggy: a towards rr: rdn and struggling wl over 2f out* **100/1**

00 **10** hd **Binham Boy**[15] [223] 3-9-0 .... StephenDonohoe(3) 3 47
(M J Gingell) *s.s: mostly in last trio: outpcd and struggling 3f out* **100/1**

06- **11** shd **Fiona's Wonder**[48] [6891] 3-9-3 .... J-PGuillambert 7 47
(R A Harris) *pressed ldr to over 2f out: wknd rapidly* **100/1**

12 shd **President Dan** 3-9-3 .... EdwardCreighton 2 47
(M R Channon) *w'like: bit bkwd: nvr bttr than midfield: rdn and outpcd over 2f out: wknd* **25/1**

6 **13** 1/2 **Bluecrop Boy**[32] [53] 3-9-3 .... AntonyProcter 5 46
(D J S Ffrench Davis) *stmbld after 1f: settled in midfield on inner: outpcd over 2f out: wknd over 1f out* **100/1**

2m 7.43s (-0.36) **Going Correction** -0.225s/f (Stan) **13** Ran SP% **125.6**
Speed ratings (Par 97):92,91,90,87,84 83,82,81,80,79 79,79,79
CSF £6.05 TOTE £4.10: £1.50, £1.10, £3.20; EX 9.60 Trifecta £21.60 Pool: £971.97 - 31.85 winning units. Place 6 £87.71, Place 5 £77.86.
Owner Hamdan Al Maktoum **Bred** Shadwell Farm LLC **Trained** Lambourn, Berks

FOCUS
A fair maiden and solid enough form judged by the performance of the runner-up. The first three and the fifth are likely to prove better than the bare form, which is limited by the sixth.
T/Jkpt: Not won. T/Plt: £70.30 to a £1 stake. Pool: £115,706.80. 1,200.15 winning tickets.
T/Qpdt: £26.30 to a £1 stake. Pool: £8,299.00. 233.50 winning tickets. JN

[372]SOUTHWELL (L-H)

Thursday, February 8

OFFICIAL GOING: Slow
The official going was described as 'slow' beforehand and race times concurred with that view.
Wind: virtually nil Weather: very cold

387 PONTINSBINGO.COM H'CAP 5f (F)

1:30 (1:36) (Class 5) (0-75,76) 3-Y-O **£3,071** (£906; £453) **Stalls** High

Form RPR

41-5 **1** **Rebel Duke (IRE)**[19] [199] 3-9-4 **75** .... BrettDoyle 1 82
(M G Quinlan) *cl up: effrt 2f out: rdn to ld jst ins last: kpt on* **11/4**[2]

14-2 **2** 2 **Diminuto**[23] [147] 3-8-8 **65** .... HayleyTurner 5 65
(M D I Usher) *led 2f: led again 2f out: sn rdn: drvn and hdd jst ins last: kpt on same pce* **9/4**[1]

1511 **3** 3/4 **Grange Lili (IRE)**[11] [280] 3-9-5 **76** 6ex..................(b) RobbieFitzpatrick 3 73
(Peter Grayson) *dwlt: trckd ldrs: effrt and swtchd rt wl over 1f out: sn rdn and kpt on same pce ins last* **4/1**[3]

-305 **4** 2 1/2 **Perlachy**[17] [219] 3-8-0 **62**..(v) DuranFentiman(5) 2 51
(Mrs N Macauley) *cl up: rdn along 2f out: drvn and wknd over 1f out* **20/1**

31-3 **5** 1 3/4 **Hereford Boy**[19] [188] 3-8-13 **70**.................................. RobertHavlin 4 53
(D K Ivory) *cl up: led after 2f: rdn along and hdd 2f out: sn wknd* **11/4**[2]

62.05 secs (1.75) **Going Correction** +0.275s/f (Slow) **5** Ran SP% **108.9**
Speed ratings (Par 97):97,93,92,88,85
CSF £9.10 TOTE £4.30: £1.50, £1.30; EX 9.70.
Owner L Cashman **Bred** Rathbarry Stud **Trained** Newmarket, Suffolk

FOCUS
A modest little sprint handicap in which the market proved significant. The winner is less exposed than the others, but the form is fairly ordinary.

388 PONTIN'S FAMILY HOLIDAYS CLAIMING STKS 6f (F)

2:00 (2:05) (Class 6) 4-Y-0+ **£2,184** (£644; £322) **Stalls** Low

Form RPR

-135 **1** **Magic Glade**[11] [277] 8-9-11 81.. JimCrowley 1 87+
(Tom Dascombe) *trckd ldrs: swtchd rt and smooth hdwy over 2f out: led on bit wl over 1f out: sn pushed clr* **11/8**[1]

-424 **2** 3 1/2 **Soba Jones**[9] [303] 10-8-6 56.................................. JasonEdmunds(3) 7 60
(J Balding) *cl up: rdn to ld briuefly 2f out: sn hdd: drvn and one pce appr last* **6/1**

-410 **3** 3/4 **Branston Tiger**[7] [323] 8-9-7 65..............................(v) DanielTudhope 3 70
(Ian Emmerson) *trckd ldrs: effrt and pushed along wl over 2f out: rdn and kpt on same pce appr last* **14/1**

5-00 **4** 3 1/2 **Winning Pleasure (IRE)**[7] [323] 9-8-6 68.................... AndrewElliott(3) 6 48
(J Balding) *led: pushed along and hdd 3f out: sn rdn and wknd over 2f out* **9/2**[3]

40-5 **5** 6 **Native Title**[23] [155] 9-9-11 79.................................. SilvestreDeSousa 4 46
(D Nicholls) *keen: trckd ldrs: hdwy to ld 3f out: rdn and hdd 2f out: sn wknd* **11/4**[2]

1m 18.01s (1.11) **Going Correction** +0.25s/f (Slow) **5** Ran SP% **107.9**
Speed ratings (Par 101):102,97,96,91,83
CSF £9.50 TOTE £1.70: £1.20, £1.80; EX 7.90.There was no bid for the winner.
Owner Alan Solomon **Bred** Juddmonte Farms **Trained** Lambourn, Berks

FOCUS
Just a fair claimer, weakened by two non-runners one of whom would probably have gone off favourite. The quintet were in a line across the track passing the two-furlong pole, but the margins separating them at the line are a better indicator of how uncompetitive this race was.

389 GO PONTIN'S H'CAP 2m (F)

2:30 (2:36) (Class 6) (0-65,63) 4-Y-0+ **£2,388** (£705; £352) **Stalls** Low

Form RPR

02-1 **1** **Victory Quest (IRE)**[38] [4] 7-9-10 **60**......................(v) RobertWinston 2 73
(Mrs S Lamyman) *hld up towards rr: hdwy 4f out: chsd ldrs over 2f out: rdn to chal wl over 1f out: drvn and styd on to ld ins last* **7/2**[1]

1-42 **2** 1 1/4 **Bulberry Hill**[23] [146] 6-9-5 **55**.................................. EdwardCreighton 3 67
(R W Price) *trckd ldrs: hdwy to ld wl over 2f out: rdn over 1f out: drvn and hdd ins last: no ex last 100 yds* **7/1**

-214 **3** 9 **Miss Holly**[9] [302] 8-9-6 **63**.. KellyHarrison(7) 10 64
(D Carroll) *hld up in rr: hdwy 4f out: rdn to chse ldrs over 2f out: sn drvn and no imp* **8/1**

04-0 **4** 4 **Madiba**[17] [213] 8-9-5 **55**.. JoeFanning 11 51
(P Howling) *in tch: hdwy to chse ldrs 4f out: rdn along 3f out: kpt on same pce* **14/1**

20-1 **5** 3 **Red River Rock (IRE)**[14] [240] 5-8-13 **49**.........(be) SilvestreDeSousa 14 41
(T J Fitzgerald) *keen: cl up: led 6f out: rdn along 3f out: sn hdd and grad wknd* **5/1**[3]

6-06 **6** 4 **Just Fly**[17] [213] 7-8-13 **54**..(e[1]) KevinGhunowa(5) 7 42
(Dr J R J Naylor) *a rr* **20/1**

1-52 **7** 6 **Galantos (GER)**[17] [213] 6-9-5 **55**.................................. GeorgeBaker 12 35
(G L Moore) *in tch: effrt 5f out: sn rdn along and wknd over 3f out* **4/1**[2]

4-00 **8** 9 **Takes Tutu (USA)**[11] [286] 8-9-8 **58**.......................... PaulMulrennan 13 28
(C R Dore) *plld hrd: trckd ldrs tl led after 5f: rdn along and hdd 6f out: sn wknd* **20/1**

50-2 **9** 10 **Ausone**[15] [230] 5-9-10 **60**.. PhillipMakin 1 18
(Miss J R Gibney) *trckd ldrs: rdn along over 4f out: sn wknd* **28/1**

-004 **10** 2 1/2 **Stolen Summer (IRE)**[20] [182] 4-8-10 **52**....................(be) PatCosgrave 8 7
(B S Rothwell) *a rr* **66/1**

63-0 **11** 2 **Ice And Fire**[23] [146] 8-9-1 **51**..(b) MickyFenton 6 3
(J T Stimpson) *hld up towards rr: effrt and sme hdwy over 4f out: sn rdn and nvr a factor* **20/1**

10-0 **12** 32 **Zaville**[17] [220] 5-9-12 **62**..(p) DavidAllan 5 —
(J O'Reilly) *led 5f: prom tl rdn along and wknd over 5f out* **18/1**

3m 50.16s (5.62) **Going Correction** +0.25s/f (Slow)
WFA 4 from 5yo+ 6lb **12** Ran SP% **113.7**
Speed ratings (Par 101):95,94,89,87,86 84,81,76,71,70 69,53
CSF £24.43 CT £180.91 TOTE £4.00: £1.60, £2.70, £2.40; EX 26.90 Trifecta £213.40 Part won. Pool £300.61 - 0.66 winning units..
Owner P Lamyman **Bred** Miss Veronica Henley **Trained** Ruckland, Lincs

FOCUS
This trip was an even greater test of stamina than usual with the ground riding slow and it is probably no coincidence that the first four home were all previous course-and-distance winners. The early pace was moderate and the winning time was modest for the class, but the field still finished well spread out, the first two clear. Sound form for the grade.

390 PONTIN'S "BOOK EARLY" (S) STKS 7f (F)

3:00 (3:06) (Class 6) 3-Y-O **£2,184** (£644; £322) **Stalls** Low

Form RPR

-204 **1** **Mr Chocolate Drop (IRE)**[7] [322] 3-8-11 54.................... BrianReilly 11 56
(M J Attwater) *towards rr: hdwy on outer 3f out: swtchd lft and rdn wl over 1f out: styd on to ld ins last* **11/4**[1]

055- **2** 1 **Power Alert**[39] [6996] 3-8-8 47.................................. RichardKingscote(3) 7 53
(B R Millman) *in tch: hdwy to trck ldrs 3f out: rdn to chse ldr over 1f out: sn drvn and ev ch whn hung lft ent last: one pce* **7/2**[2]

54-0 **3** 1 1/4 **Peppin's Gold (IRE)**[28] [99] 3-8-6 52..........................(t) AdrianMcCarthy 4 45
(B R Millman) *midfield: hdwy 3f out: sn rdn and styd on appr last: nrst fin* **13/2**

4-0 **4** 1 1/2 **Barney's Dancer**[9] [304] 3-8-1 .... DuranFentiman(5) 9 41
(J Balding) *midfield: hdwy over 2f out: sn rdn and kpt on appr last* **11/1**

600- **5** 2 1/2 **Spinning Game**[72] [6639] 3-8-12 40..............................(b) TonyCulhane 6 41
(D W Chapman) *led: clr over 2f out and sn rdn: drvn over 1f out: hdd & wknd jst ins last* **16/1**

03-0 **6** 1 1/2 **House Arrest**[28] [99] 3-8-1 46..........................(bt) NataliaGemelova(5) 12 31
(A J McCabe) *prom: chsd ldr 1/2-way: rdn 2f out: sn wknd* **12/1**

B-5 **7** 7 **Polly Rocket**[10] [295] 3-8-7 ow1.................................. PaulMulrennan 10 14
(P D Niven) *chsd ldrs: rdn along 1/2-way: wknd wl over 2f out* **16/1**

00-0 **8** 26 **Heart And Hand (IRE)**[13] [253] 3-8-6 40.......................... JoeFanning 5 —
(M G Quinlan) *chsd ldrs on inner: rdn along 3f out: sn wknd* **33/1**

-400 **9** 3 1/2 **Emefdream**[16] [224] 3-9-3 57..(v[1]) NCallan 8 —
(Mrs N Macauley) *cl up: rdn along 3f out: sn wknd* **4/1**[3]

00 **10** 12 **Montiona**[13] [258] 3-8-8 .... AndrewElliott(3) 2 —
(John A Harris) *sn outpaced and bhd* **66/1**

00- **11** 42 **Lenard Frank (IRE)**[172] [4624] 3-8-11 40......................(v) HayleyTurner 3 —
(M D I Usher) *s.i.s and bhd: t.o fr 1/2-way* **40/1**

1m 34.73s (3.93) **Going Correction** +0.25s/f (Slow) **11** Ran SP% **116.9**
Speed ratings (Par 95):87,85,84,82,79 78,70,40,36,22 —
CSF £11.96 TOTE £3.20: £1.50, £1.60, £1.90; EX 12.90 Trifecta £43.70 Pool £220.18 - 3.57 winning units..There was no bid for the winner.
Owner Carl Would **Bred** P J Munnelly **Trained** Great Shefford, Berks

FOCUS
This bunch were all over the place and the form looks very modest indeed. The winning time was very moderate, even for a seller.

391 PONTIN'S HOLIDAYS H'CAP 7f (F)

3:30 (3:36) (Class 2) (0-100,98) 4-Y-0+ **£11,334** (£3,372; £1,685; £841) **Stalls** Low

Form RPR

-623 **1** **Party Boss**[4] [352] 5-9-2 **95**.. SebSanders 4 103
(C E Brittain) *cl up: effrt over 2f out and sn rdn: drvn to ld ins last and jst hld on* **5/6**[1]

-521 **2** shd **Waterside (IRE)**[9] [307] 8-9-5 **98** 6ex.................................. NCallan 3 106
(G L Moore) *led: rdn along over 2f out: drvn and hdd ins last: rallied wl nr fin: jst hld* **7/4**[2]

2-50 **3** 1/2 **Wessex (USA)**[16] [227] 7-8-12 **91**.................................. PaulMulrennan 2 97
(P A Blockley) *chsd ldng pair: pushed along and sltgly outpcd 2f out: swtchd rt and rdn over 1f out: styd on strly ins last* **10/1**[3]

006- **4** 2 **Chief Commander (FR)**[155] [5116] 4-8-11 **90**.................... BrettDoyle 1 91
(Jane Chapple-Hyam) *hld up in tch: gd hdwy over 2f out: rdn and ev ch over 1f out: sn drvn and wknd ent last* **16/1**

65-4 **5** 3 **Bahamian Pirate (USA)**[9] [307] 12-9-4 **97**.............. SilvestreDeSousa 5 90
(D Nicholls) *hld up in tch: hdwy on outer over 2f out: rdn and ch over 1f out: wknd ent last* **33/1**

1m 30.82s (0.02) **Going Correction** +0.25s/f (Slow) **5** Ran SP% **108.8**
Speed ratings (Par 109):109,108,108,106,102
CSF £2.43 TOTE £1.70: £1.10, £1.30; EX 1.90.
Owner Michael Clarke **Bred** Michael Clarke **Trained** Newmarket, Suffolk
■ Stewards' Enquiry : Seb Sanders one-day ban: used whip with excessive frequency (Feb 19)

FOCUS
Not many runners, but a good-quality contest run at a true gallop. A tremendous finish and there was never more than a neck between the front two throughout the race. The winner ran to his latest form, with a clear personal best from the second, but the fourth and fifth seem to hold down the form.

NOTEBOOK
Party Boss, having his first try here since winning his maiden in the autumn of 2004, was without a win of any sort in almost two years but had been running well in defeat on Polytrack lately and was strong in the market. Given a positive ride, he and Waterside dominated the race from the start and with no quarter given from either side, he eventually managed to prevail on the nod. He cannot be put up very much for this and should continue to make his mark at this level on sand. (op 10-11 tchd Evens)
Waterside(IRE), back up to probably his best trip, was carrying a 6lb penalty for his victory in a conditions event here nine days earlier which meant that he was a stone higher than for his last win in a handicap on sand. Matching strides with Party Boss the whole way, he responded well to maximum pressure to only lose out on the nod and is arguably better than ever at present. (tchd 13-8)

Wessex(USA) ◆, below his best in recent outings, is slowly starting to slip back down the weights and this was much better. He took a fair time to get into top gear, but was finishing best of all and would have caught the front pair with a little further to go. If he has truly turned the corner he is well worth watching out for back here in the near future. (op 9-1 tchd 8-1)
Chief Commander(FR) ◆, making his Fibresand debut and returning from five months off, managed to get himself into a challenging position towards the inside of the field passing the two-furlong pole before lack of a recent run took its toll. He showed some decent form on Polytrack last winter and would be of interest back on that surface with this outing under his belt. (tchd 20-1)
Bahamian Pirate(USA), beaten more than five lengths by Waterside over six furlongs on his return to action here the previous week, was only 1lb better off and failed to get home on this rare attempt over this longer trip.

392 PONTINS.COM H'CAP — 1m 3f (F)

4:00 (4:05) (Class 5) (0-70,70) 3-Y-O — **£3,071** (£906; £453) **Stalls** Low

Form — RPR

33-0 **1** **Red Petal**[24] 141 3-8-12 **64** .... SebSanders 6 — 76+
(Sir Mark Prescott) *trckd ldrs: hdwy on outer over 4f out: cl up 3f out: rdn to chal 2f out: drvn to ld ins last: styd on* — **3/1**[3]

0-22 **2** *1 1/2* **Milla's Rocket (IRE)**[13] 257 3-8-13 **65** .... (b) NCallan 4 — 75
(K A Ryan) *trckd ldrs: hdwy to ld 3f out: jnd and rdn 2f out: sn edgd lft and rt: drvn: hung rt and hdd ins last: no ex* — **11/4**[2]

644- **3** *13* **Hall Of Fame**[78] 6561 3-9-4 **70** .... JoeFanning 2 — 59
(M Johnston) *led: rdn along and hdd 3f out: sn one pce* — **13/8**[1]

0-02 **4** *nk* **Briarwood Bear**[7] 322 3-8-7 **59** .... DaleGibson 3 — 48
(M Blanshard) *rr and pushed along 1/2-way: rdn wl over 3f out: plugged on same pce* — **16/1**

4-25 **5** *17* **Jocheski (IRE)**[24] 140 3-9-0 **66** .... (v[1]) PatCosgrave 5 — 28
(M J Wallace) *cl up: rdn along 4f out: sn wknd* — **7/1**

2m 30.78s (1.88) **Going Correction** +0.25s/f (Slow) — **5** Ran SP% **108.1**
Speed ratings (Par 97):103,101,92,92,79
CSF £11.09 TOTE £2.90: £2.10, £1.30; EX 9.70.
Owner Cheveley Park Stud **Bred** Cheveley Park Stud Ltd **Trained** Newmarket, Suffolk

FOCUS
A modest little three-year-old handicap which saw the first two come well clear of the favourite, who got tired. Improved efforts from the first two.

393 PONTIN'S H'CAP — 1m (F)

4:30 (4:35) (Class 6) (0-50,50) 4-Y-O+ — **£2,388** (£705; £352) **Stalls** Low

Form — RPR

2-62 **1** **Et Dona Ferentes**[17] 217 4-8-10 **48** .... PhillipMakin 11 — 56
(T D Barron) *in tch on outer: hdwy to chse ldrs 3f out: rdn 2f out: styd on u.p ins last to ld last 100 yds* — **3/1**[1]

510- **2** *1* **Kumakawa**[347] 527 9-8-7 **48** .... JamesDoyle(3) 8 — 54
(N P Littmoden) *midfield: hdwy to chse ldrs 2f out: sn rdn and edgd rt over 1f out: kpt on wl u.p ins last* — **11/1**

3-04 **3** *nk* **Wodhill Schnaps**[12] 266 6-8-9 **47** .... (v) HayleyTurner 10 — 52
(D Morris) *trckd ldrs: hdwy to ld over 2f out: rdn clr and hung lft over 1f out: drvn ins last: hdd and no ex last 100 yds* — **4/1**[2]

0-56 **4** *2 1/2* **Futoo (IRE)**[9] 305 6-8-8 **46** oh1 .... (b) DaleGibson 12 — 46
(D W Chapman) *towards rr: hdwy on outer 3f out: rdn to chse ldrs 2f out: drvn and one pce ent last* — **33/1**

6-36 **5** *5* **Red Raptor**[11] 274 6-8-5 **50** .... (t) HaddenFrost(7) 5 — 40
(J A Geake) *led: rdn along 3f out: hdd over 2f out: drvn and hung rt wl over 1f out: sn wknd* — **3/1**[1]

-002 **6** *2* **Bournonville**[2] 372 4-8-5 **46** oh1 .... (b[1]) DominicFox(3) 6 — 31
(M Wigham) *chsd ldrs: rdn along over 2f out: wknd wl over 1f out* — **11/1**

00-0 **7** *4* **Xpres Boy (IRE)**[14] 239 4-8-5 **46** oh1 .... (t) JasonEdmunds(3) 9 — 23
(S R Bowring) *cl up: rdn along 3f out: drvn and wkng whn n.m.r wl over 1f out* — **50/1**

1-05 **8** *1* **Tackcoat (IRE)**[11] 274 7-8-12 **50** .... (p) PatCosgrave 7 — 25
(Eoin Doyle, Ire) *chsd ldrs: rdn along over 2f out: grad wknd* — **5/1**[3]

602- **9** *9* **Hippolyte (USA)**[119] 5922 4-8-8 **46** .... JoeFanning 4 — 2
(J G Given) *a rr* — **18/1**

005- **10** *26* **Paddy Moon**[212] 3378 4-8-10 **48** .... (b[1]) MickyFenton 3 — —
(J G Given) *chsd ldrs: rdn along 3f out and sn wknd* — **25/1**

1m 45.64s (1.04) **Going Correction** +0.25s/f (Slow) — **10** Ran SP% **117.3**
Speed ratings (Par 101):104,103,102,100,95 93,89,88,79,53
CSF £37.47 CT £135.16 TOTE £4.80: £1.70, £3.00, £1.50; EX 49.40 Trifecta £107.60 Pool £520.21 - 3.43 winning units. Place 6 £11.80, Place 5 £7.19.
Owner Dr Peter Harms **Bred** Dr Peter Harms **Trained** Maunby, N Yorks

FOCUS
A weak handicap, but an open one for the grade. Limited form, the winner less exposed than most.
T/Plt: £12.10 to a £1 stake. Pool: £80,741.70. 4,870.60 winning tickets. T/Qpdt: £3.30 to a £1 stake. Pool: £4,721.50. 1,042.80 winning tickets. JR

324 NAD AL SHEBA (L-H)

Thursday, February 8

OFFICIAL GOING: Turf course - good; dirt course - fast

The inside rail on the turf course seemed to be riding slower than the middle of the track.

394a NAYEF TROPHY (H'CAP) (TURF) — 7f 110y(D)

3:15 (3:17) (90-105,105) 3-Y-O+

£33,673 (£11,224; £5,612; £2,806; £1,683; £1,122)

RPR

1 **Vortex**[19] 197 8-9-6 **105** .... (t) JimmyQuinn 9 — 108
(Miss Gay Kelleway) *mid-div: smooth prog to trck ldrs 3f out: rdn to chal 1 1/2f out: led ins fnl f* — **11/2**[3]

2 *nk* **Ans Bach**[20] 4-8-10 **95** .... JMurtagh 3 — 97
(D Selvaratnam, UAE) *nvr far away: gng wl 3f out: led 2f out: hdd ins fnl f: r.o wl* — **4/1**[1]

3 *hd* **Paper Talk (USA)**[138] 5523 5-8-12 **97** .... KerrinMcEvoy 4 — 99
(I Mohammed, UAE) *trckd ldr on rail gng wl: no room 2f out: swtchd and r.o wl ins fnl f: nrst fin* — **13/2**

4 *2 1/4* **Checkit (IRE)**[7] 331 7-8-10 **95** .... GHind 8 — 91
(R Bouresly, Kuwait) *slowly away: settled in rr: rdn 3f out: no room 2f out: r.o fnl f* — **50/1**

5 *4 3/4* **Kalankari (IRE)**[21] 178 4-9-1 **99** .... MartinDwyer 6 — 84
(A M Balding) *trckd ldr: led briefly 2 1/2f out: rdn and one pce* — **4/1**[1]

6 *1 1/4* **Cubillas (BRZ)**[131] 5-9-0 **98** .... ADomingos 1 — 80
(M D Wolfson, U.S.A) *mid-div on rail: no room 2 1/2f out: swtchd: r.o fnl f* — **10/1**

7 *nk* **Fez (SAF)**[42] 6-8-9 **94** .... RichardMullen 11 — 74
(S Seemar, UAE) *slowly away: racd in last of main gp: tk v t.k.h: n.m.r 2f out: r.o late* — **50/1**

8 *8 1/4* **Tajseed (IRE)**[364] 357 7-8-7 **91** .... RHills 10 — 52
(A Manuel, UAE) *mid-div: rdn 2 1/2f out: nt qckn* — **8/1**

9 *3 1/4* **Obe Brave**[21] 172 4-9-4 **102** .... TedDurcan 5 — 55
(M R Channon) *sn led: hdd 2 1/2f out: wknd* — **5/1**[2]

10 *8 1/4* **League Champion (USA)**[516] 5115 4-9-4 **102** .... (e) MKhan 7 — 34
(S Seemar, UAE) *slowly away: nvr nr to chal* — **20/1**

11 *dist* **Yorokobi (BRZ)**[7] 324 4-8-7 **100** .... (be) MJKinane 2 — —
(H J Brown, South Africa) *lft as gates opened: a distant last* — **9/1**

1m 33.08s (2.48) **Going Correction** +0.45s/f (Yiel) — **11** Ran SP% **124.3**
Speed ratings: 105,104,104,102,97 96,95,87,84,76 —

Owner Coriolis Partnership **Bred** Juddmonte Farms **Trained** Exning, Suffolk

FOCUS
A good handicap, but they seemed to go just an ordinary pace for much of the way. Basically another division of the 3.45, but the winning time was 0.54 seconds slower.

NOTEBOOK
Vortex has been in terrific form on the Polytrack around Lingfield this winter and, just as effective on turf, he was able to make a successful debut in Dubai. He travelled strongly, as he usually does, and it looked just a matter of what he would find once produced with his effort in the straight. Although not going away from Ans Bach, he did just enough under pressure to force his head in front near the line. He may be forced out of this grade once reassessed, but should not be underestimated in better company, especially considering that a stronger-run race is likely to suit him even better.
Ans Bach, without the eye-shields on his return to turf, was produced with every chance and can have no excuses. Formerly a very useful handicapper for Michael Jarvis, he showed enough to suggest a similar event might come his way at some point, although it would not be a total surprise to see some sort of headgear re-fitted at some point. (op 5/1)
Paper Talk(USA), having his first start since leaving Barry Hills, seemed to be held in slightly by Vortex early in the straight and got in the clear too late. This was his first run in 138 days and he looks capable of improving on this form.
Checkit(IRE) is by no means an easy horse to win with, but this was a reasonable enough effort.
Kalankari(IRE) could not dominate this time and was unable to defy a 3lb higher mark than when winning over course and distance three weeks previously.
Fez(SAF) endured a troubled passage in the straight and is better than he was able to show.
Obe Brave set out to make all the running but offered little at the business end and could not defy a 4lb higher mark than when winning over course and distance on his previous start.
Yorokobi(BRZ) looked reluctant to come out of the stalls and lost any chance he might have had at the start. (op 8/1)

395a GREEN DESERT STKS (H'CAP) (TURF) — 7f 110y(D)

3:45 (3:45) (90-105,104) 3-Y-O+

£33,673 (£11,224; £5,612; £2,806; £1,683; £1,122)

RPR

1 **Benedetti (AUS)**[12] 6-9-3 **100** .... (b) JMurtagh 9 — 110
(T Noonan, Australia) *mid-div out: wd: gng wl 2 1/2f out: rdn to ld 2f out: r.o wl* — **7/1**

2 *2 3/4* **Green Coast (IRE)**[28] 105 4-8-9 **93** .... LDettori 7 — 95
(Saeed Bin Suroor) *mid-div: smooth prog 2 1/2f out: n.m.r 2f out: r.o wl fnl 1 1/2f* — **9/2**[2]

3 *hd* **Arminius (IRE)**[118] 5943 4-8-11 **95** .... WSupple 10 — 97
(I Mohammed, UAE) *racd in rr: wdst of all 3f out: r.o: nvr able to chal* **16/1**

4 *1/4* **Sound The Drum (USA)**[20] 5-8-9 **93** .... RichardMullen 8 — 94
(S Seemar, UAE) *in rr of mid-div: rdn to cl whn short of room 2 1/2f out: r.o once clr* — **10/1**

5 *1/4* **Stream Of Gold (IRE)**[21] 176 6-9-6 **104** .... TedDurcan 6 — 105
(S Seemar, UAE) *slowly away: settled in rr: smooth prog to chal on rail ins fnl f: r.o* — **9/4**[1]

6 *1 1/2* **Matloob**[7] 331 6-8-11 **95** .... RPCleary 4 — 92
(D Selvaratnam, UAE) *t.k.h: settled in rr: nvr nr to chal* — **40/1**

7 *1/2* **Rock N Roll Kid (NZ)**[21] 178 8-9-2 **99** .... CSoumillon 11 — 96
(M C Tam, Macau) *trckd ldr: rdn to chal 2 1/2f out: one pce* — **8/1**

8 *1 3/4* **Sendalam (FR)**[21] 172 5-9-1 **98** .... RyanMoore 3 — 90
(H J Brown, South Africa) *mid-div: trckd ldr 3f out: led briefly over 2f out: one pce* — **13/2**[3]

9 *nse* **Mostashaar (FR)**[110] 6101 5-9-5 **102** .... RHills 5 — 94
(Doug Watson, UAE) *slowly away: mid-div on rail: no room 2 1/2f out: nt rcvr* — **9/1**

10 *6* **Uhoomagoo**[7] 325 9-9-1 **98** .... (b) JamieSpencer 2 — 75
(K A Ryan) *settled in rr: nvr able to chal* — **14/1**

11 *7 1/2* **Namorado (BRZ)**[34] 6-8-7 **90** .... WayneSmith 12 — 48
(S Seemar, UAE) *trckd ldr out wd: rdn 3f out: sn wknd* — **40/1**

12 *1 1/4* **St Expedit**[791] 10-9-5 **102** .... GHind 1 — 57
(R Bouresly, Kuwait) *led on rail tl hdd 2 1/2f out: fdd* — **50/1**

1m 32.54s (1.94) **Going Correction** +0.45s/f (Yiel) — **12** Ran SP% **124.4**
Speed ratings: 108,105,105,104,104 103,102,100,100,94 87,86

Owner P & Mrs McMahon,A & Mrs Burgio **Bred** Heytesbury Thotoughbreds P\/ **Trained** Australia

FOCUS
This was basically another division of the 3.15, but the winning time was 0.54 seconds quicker. A good handicap and the pace seemed reasonable enough from the start. Interestingly, those who produced their efforts towards the centre of the track had the call, which goes against the recent trend.

NOTEBOOK
Benedetti(AUS) ◆ did not have an obvious chance in running, as he was forced to race wide for much of the way, but he did travel quite strongly and found plenty when asked for his effort, ultimately winning decisively. He seemed to carry his head a touch high under pressure, but it clearly did not stop him. Successful in his native Australia last month, he is clearly at the top of his game and, on this evidence, looks well up to completing the hat-trick.
Green Coast(IRE), third in a non-Carnival handicap over 1f shorter on his debut in Dubai the previous month, ran a solid race in second. He had to be switched late on, but was by no means unlucky. This was just his third career start and there could be better to come. (op 5/1)
Arminius(IRE), formerly a very useful handicapper for Richard Hannon, was forced widest of all with his effort in the straight but stuck on well. This was his first run in 118 days, so he is open to some improvement.
Sound The Drum(USA), twice successful over 7f on the dirt at Jebel Ali this winter, ran well switched to turf and clearly continues in good form.
Stream Of Gold(IRE) was produced with every chance up the far rail, but he ultimately proved no match for those who raced more towards the centre of the track. He might have been racing on the slower ground and it would be unwise to write him off just yet.
Mostashaar(FR), having his first start since leaving Sir Michael Stoute, seemed to take a bad step coming out of the stalls and can probably be forgiven this. (op 8/1)

Uhoomagoo never got in a blow and was well below his best. He has yet to reproduce the pick of his efforts when sent to Dubai. (op 20/1)

396a EKRAAR TROPHY (H'CAP) (DIRT) 7f (D)
4:15 (4:15) (90-105,102) 3-Y-0+

£33,673 (£11,224; £5,612; £2,806; £1,683; £1,122)

RPR

1 **Jaffal (USA)**^{7} [327] 5-8-12 **95**....................................(t) RoystonFfrench 7 100
(A Al Raihe, UAE) *trckd ldr: led 2 1/2f out: r.o wl: clr fnl f: comf* **8/1**

2 2 1/4 **Zorin (BRZ)**^{7} [326] 4-8-6 **96** ow1.. ADomingos 6 88
(A Cintra Pereira, Brazil) *mid-div: rdn to trck ldrs 2 1/2f out: r.o wl fnl 1 1/2f* **33/1**

3 3/4 **Looking Good (ARG)**^{21} [172] 6-9-2 **98**.............................(t) PaulSmith 4 96
(Allan Smith, UAE) *racd in rr: mid-div 3f out: hrd rdn 2f out: r.o fnl f* **50/1**

4 1 **State Shinto (USA)**^{14} [244] 11-8-10 **93**.................................(bt) GHind 2 87
(R Bouresly, Kuwait) *racd in rr: 12th 2 1/2f out: r.o wl fnl 2f: nrst fin* **50/1**

5 nse **Drift Ice (SAF)**^{7} [324] 6-9-0 **96**.......................................(be) JMurtagh 16 91
(M F De Kock, South Africa) *trckd ldr out wd: rdn to chal 2f out: no ex* **8/1**

6 nk **Space Oddity (BRZ)**^{166} 4-8-5 **95**...(t) ECruz 8 81
(P Nickel Filho, Brazil) *mid-div: rdn 2 1/2f out: nvr a threat* **7/1**^{3}

7 2 3/4 **Glad To Be Fast (IRE)**^{20} 7-8-10 **93**................................(b) MJKinane 5 79
(Mario Hofer, Germany) *slowly away: nvr nr to chal* **16/1**

8 3/4 **Comandante Xara (BRZ)**^{21} [173] 4-7-11 **93**....(b) AurelioMedeiros$^{(6)}$ 11 70
(P Nickel Filho, Brazil) *sn led: rdn 3f out: hdd 2 1/2f out: wknd* **33/1**

9 nk **Polar Magic**^{138} [5523] 6-9-4 **100**.................................(t) KerrinMcEvoy 13 84
(I Mohammed, UAE) *sn rdn along: n.d* **4/1**^{2}

10 3/4 **Bahiano (IRE)**^{21} [172] 6-8-10 **93**...................................... EddieAhern 10 74
(C E Brittain) *racd in rr: nvr able to chal* **16/1**

11 shd **Bustin Justin (USA)**^{118} [5942] 4-8-10 **93**........................... RyanMoore 3 74
(J Noseda) *trckd ldr on rail: rdn 2 1/2f out: nt qckn* **7/2**^{1}

12 3/4 **National Captain (SAF)**^{21} [178] 5-8-12 **95**....................... TedDurcan 9 74
(S Seemar, UAE) *mid-div: rdn 3f out: nvr able to chal* **12/1**

13 1/2 **San Salvador (USA)**^{28} 10-8-9 **91**............................(b) RichardMullen 14 69
(S Seemar, UAE) *mid-div: rdn 2 1/2f out: nvr nr to chal* **28/1**

14 10 **Rock Music**^{343} [560] 5-9-6 **102**... TPO'Shea 1 53
(E Charpy, UAE) *mid-div on rail: rdn and wknd 3f out* **11/1**

15 2 1/2 **Pipoldchap (CHI)**^{7} [324] 7-9-4 **100**...............................(bt) PJSmullen 12 45
(F Castro, Sweden) *trckd ldr: rdn 3f out: wknd* **33/1**

P **Mr Lambros**^{82} [6514] 6-8-12 **95**.. MartinDwyer 15 —
(A M Balding) *mid-div: dropped to rr and p.u 3f out* **12/1**

1m 25.15s (0.35) **Going Correction** +0.175s/f (Slow) **16** Ran SP% **128.6**
Speed ratings: 105,102,101,100,100 100,96,96,95,94 94,93,93,81,79 —

Owner Abdul Rahman Muammer Abdullah Amin **Bred** Calumet Farm **Trained** UAE

FOCUS

Hard to know exactly what to make of the form, but it is probably just ordinary for the grade.

NOTEBOOK

Jaffal(USA) had been running well in defeat in similar company over 1m recently and the slight drop in trip did the trick. He looked vulnerable when strongly challenged by Drift Ice early in the straight, but he battled on most gamely and was well on top at the finish. He deserved this, but a rise in the weights will make things tougher in future.

Zorin(BRZ) improved markedly on the form he showed when well beaten over 6f on his debut in Dubai and emerges with plenty of credit. On this evidence, he might even stay 1m and he is probably one to keep on the right side in similar company

Looking Good(ARG) ◆ ran a very pleasing race on this switch to dirt. Settled quite a way off the pace for much of the way, he made up several lengths to throw down a challenge in the straight and kept on well. He looked well suited to this surface and could be one to keep in mind for a similar race, especially if he is ridden more positively in future.

State Shinto(USA) had beaten just three horses home on his last four starts combined, but this was a terrific effort, especially considering he did not get the clearest of runs in the straight. However, for all that this was an admirable performance, his proximity does little for the form.

Drift Ice(SAF) looked the most likely winner when travelling strongly towards the front end entering the straight, but he failed to sustain his effort and did not seem to stay this 7f trip. A return to 6f should suit. (op 15/2)

Bahiano(IRE) could never land a blow and failed to prove himself on this fast dirt surface.

Bustin Justin(USA), who won his first three starts on the turf last year before running creditably in defeat in a Group 3, looked interesting switched to dirt, representing connections who do so well at the Carnival. However, he was always having to work hard to hold his position from his inside draw and could not sustain his challenge in the straight. He is better than he showed and should be able to leave this form behind in time. (op 9/2)

Mr Lambros was pulled up and dismounted. It transpired that he had bled badly and locked a stifle.

397a STORMING HOME CAPE VERDI STKS (LISTED RACE) (TURF) (F&M) 1m (T)
4:45 (4:45) 3-Y-0+

£45,918 (£15,306; £7,653; £3,826; £2,295; £1,530)

RPR

1 **Sanaya (IRE)**^{73} 4-9-0 104...(p) CSoumillon 1 114+
(A De Royer-Dupre, France) *slowly away: mid-div: gng wl 2 1/2f out: fnd gap 1 1/2f out to ld: r.o wl* **9/2**^{3}

2 3 3/4 **Alexandra Rose (SAF)**^{376} 5-9-0 101.................................. MJKinane 8 105
(M F De Kock, South Africa) *mid-div: rdn to chal 2f out: r.o wl: no ch w wnr* **7/2**^{2}

3 2 1/2 **Zaafran**^{21} [174] 4-9-0 95.. JMurtagh 14 99
(D Selvaratnam, UAE) *settled in rr: last into st: swtchd wd 2 1/2f out: r.o wl: nrst fin* **11/1**

4 shd **Jet Past (SAF)**^{222} 5-9-0 97... MKhan 9 99
(S Seemar, UAE) *trckd ldr: rdn 3f out: r.o one pce on rail* **16/1**

5 shd **Vista Bella**^{648} [1383] 5-9-0 107.. LDettori 11 99
(Saeed Bin Suroor) *mid-div: trckd ldrs and ev ch 3f out: nt qckn fnl 1 1/2f* **3/1**^{1}

6 1/2 **Expensive**^{21} [174] 4-9-0 97... EddieAhern 4 98
(C F Wall) *mid-div: trckd ldrs 2 1/2f out: ev ch 1 1/2f out: one pce* **16/1**

7 3/4 **Golden Velvet (USA)**^{21} [175] 4-9-0 100..............................(t) TedDurcan 5 96
(Saeed Bin Suroor) *settled in rr: wd 3f out: nvr nr to chal* **12/1**

8 3/4 **Afaf (FR)**^{89} [6454] 5-9-0 106...(t) TJarnet 2 94
(M Delzangles, France) *slowly away: nvr able to chal* **15/2**

9 1 1/4 **Royal Alchemist**^{131} [5675] 5-9-0 104............................ KerrinMcEvoy 12 91
(I Mohammed, UAE) *trckd ldr: led 3f out: hdd 2 1/2f out: wknd* **10/1**

10 2 1/4 **Cat Belling (IRE)**^{7} [327] 7-9-0 95.. GHind 7 86
(R Bouresly, Kuwait) *led main gp: rdn to ld briefly 2f out: one pce* **50/1**

11 4 1/4 **Estrela Brynhild (USA)**^{21} [174] 4-9-4 98............................ MCardoso 6 80
(C Morgado, Brazil) *mid-div on rail: rdn 3 1/2f out: wknd 2 1/2f out* **40/1**

12 2 3/4 **Buscape (USA)**^{28} 5-9-0 85.......................................(t) RichardMullen 13 70
(S Seemar, UAE) *slowly away: nvr nr to chal* **66/1**

13 8 **Imperial Ice (SAF)**^{21} [174] 5-9-0 100................................. RyanMoore 10 52
(H J Brown, South Africa) *settled in rr: nvr able to chal* **16/1**

14 9 1/4 **In Dubai (USA)**^{20} 4-9-0 85.. RPCleary 3 30
(D Selvaratnam, UAE) *led early: set fast gallop: rdn 4f out: hdd 3f out: wknd* **50/1**

1m 38.56s (0.76) **Going Correction** +0.45s/f (Yiel) **14** Ran SP% **127.8**
Speed ratings: 114,110,107,107,107 107,106,105,104,102 97,95,87,77

Owner H H The Aga Khan's Stud Sc **Bred** Hh The Aga Khan's Studs **Trained** Chantilly, France

FOCUS

A reasonable Listed contest for fillies and mares, and In Dubai ensured they went a decent pace from the start.

NOTEBOOK

Sanaya(IRE), a winner at this level over 1m1f in France last year, ran out a convincing winner on her debut in Dubai. Always travelling well off the strong pace, she showed both a decent turn of foot and a good attitude when asked to take a tight gap between horses, and she never looked in any danger thereafter. It might be that a step up in grade will find her out, but she certainly deserves to take her chance in better company following this success. (tchd 5/1)

Alexandra Rose(SAF), making her debut for new connections off the back of an absence of just over a year, was produced with every chance down the centre of the track but proved no match for the winner. She may just have needed this and it would be no surprise to see her improve.

Zaafran, a beaten favourite when second in an extended 7f handicap round here off a mark of 93 on her previous start, ran well upped to Listed company for the first time, keeping on in the latter stages having been positioned well off the pace for much of the way. (op 10/1)

Jet Past(SAF) seemed a little short of room at various stages in the straight and was probably unlucky not to finish a little closer.

Vista Bella had been off the track since running third to Virginia Waters in the 2005 Guineas for Michael Jarvis and was below form on her debut for new connections. It is interesting that such a powerful operation has persevered with her on the track and she could well leave the bare form of this effort behind in time. (op 4/1)

Expensive looked a big threat at the top of the straight, but she did not finish her race very strongly and has to be considered a touch disappointing. Perhaps this 1m just stretched her.

Golden Velvet(USA) would have appreciated the return to turf, but she failed to land a blow on the principals. (op 11/1)

398a SAKHEE CUP (H'CAP) (TURF) 1m 2f (T)
5:20 (5:20) (90-105,105) 3-Y-0+

£33,673 (£11,224; £5,612; £2,806; £1,683; £1,122)

RPR

1 **Impeller (IRE)**^{7} [329] 8-8-8 **93**... JohnEgan 12 93
(J S Moore) *settled in rr: gng wl 3f out: smooth prog to trck runner-up 1 1/2f out: led cl home: r.o wl* **12/1**

2 3/4 **Count Trevisio (IRE)**^{28} [104] 4-9-0 **99**................................. LDettori 10 99
(Saeed Bin Suroor) *mid-div: prog to trck ldrs 3f out: stl on bit whn led 1 1/2f out: hdd cl home* **9/4**^{1}

3 4 1/4 **Rohaani (USA)**^{131} [5675] 5-9-2 **100**.. RHills 4 92
(Doug Watson, UAE) *settled in rr: t.k.h: no room gng wl 3 1/2f out: r.o wl fnl 2f* **5/1**^{2}

4 2 1/4 **Chinkara**^{7} [329] 7-8-10 **95**... MartinDwyer 7 82
(Doug Watson, UAE) *trckd ldr: t.k.h: rdn 3f out: led briefly 1 1/2f out: wknd* **16/1**

5 1/4 **Hallhoo (IRE)**^{14} [244] 5-8-12 **97**.. JMurtagh 6 84
(D Selvaratnam, UAE) *sn led: rdn 3f out: hdd 1 1/2f out: fdd* **13/2**^{3}

6 shd **Wild Savannah**^{14} [248] 5-9-6 **105**...................................... PJSmullen 14 92
(I Mohammed, UAE) *settled in rr: nvr able to chal* **12/1**

7 3/4 **Bennie Blue (SAF)**^{14} [250] 5-9-0 **98**...............................(b) MJKinane 9 84
(M F De Kock, South Africa) *mid-div: tk v t.k.h: rdn 3f out: kpt on down outside: n.d* **12/1**

8 3 3/4 **Lost Soldier Three (IRE)**^{14} [248] 6-9-4 **102**........... AdrianTNicholls 13 82
(D Nicholls) *mid-div: racd wd: rdn 3 1/2f out: nvr a threat* **16/1**

9 4 1/4 **Southern Regent (IND)**^{138} 6-8-12 **97**.............................. RyanMoore 1 68
(S Seemar, UAE) *mid-div: rdn 3f out: nvr able to chal* **16/1**

10 1 **Desert Anger**^{14} [250] 6-8-8 **93**..(bt) WSupple 8 62
(E Charpy, UAE) *racd in rr: no room 3f out: nt rcvr* **33/1**

11 nse **Zato (IRE)**^{14} [250] 4-8-7 **93**.. TPO'Shea 3 62
(M R Channon) *mid-div on rail: swtchd wd 3f out: nt able to chal* **9/1**

12 3/4 **Parnassus (SAF)**^{14} [250] 5-9-0 **98**................................ RichardMullen 11 67
(S Seemar, UAE) *settled in rr: nvr nr to chal* **20/1**

13 3 1/2 **Reve Lunaire (USA)**^{7} [331] 4-9-4 **104**.............................. TedDurcan 5 65
(S Seemar, UAE) *mid-div: rdn to cl 3f out: nt qckn* **12/1**

14 dist **Ned Kelly (SAF)**^{14} [244] 6-8-9 **94**.. PaulEddery 2 —
(Christian Wroe) *racd in 3rd: rdn 6f out: sn wknd* **50/1**

2m 6.24s (2.04) **Going Correction** +0.45s/f (Yiel)
WFA 4 from 5yo+ 1lb **14** Ran SP% **128.8**
Speed ratings: 109,108,105,103,103 102,102,99,95,95 95,94,91,—

Owner Mrs Fitri Hay **Bred** P E Banahan **Trained** Upper Lambourn, Berks

FOCUS

A decent handicap run at a good pace, although the winning time was 0.18 seconds slower than the 6.50.

NOTEBOOK

Impeller(IRE) was suited by the good pace and came from well back in the field to win. He appreciated the return to racing on turf and found a good turn of foot to make up ground and pass Count Trevisio inside the last, winning a shade comfortably in the end. Things fell right for him this time, but there is no denying that he is a very useful handicapper on his day.

Count Trevisio(IRE) steadily moved upsides the tiring leaders midway up the straight, with his rider confident enough to take a cheeky look between his legs. He was clearly not expecting to see Impeller bearing down on him, but nevertheless, the colt did nothing wrong in second, off a 5lb higher mark than when successful over a furlong shorter here four weeks earlier, and the pair finished nicely clear. He can win again. (op 11/4)

Rohaani(USA) is effective over this trip on fast ground and ran a perfectly respectable race on his first outing since leaving Sir Michael Stoute and his first start since last season's Cambridgeshire. He should come on for the run.

Chinkara, who last ran on turf back in 2004 when trained by Brian Meehan, chased the good gallop set by Hallhoo, and both paid the price for going off a touch too quick.

Hallhoo(IRE) paid the price for setting too fast a gallop. He had been given an easier time of it in front when runner-up in a similar heat here a fortnight earlier.

Wild Savannah, suited by the strong pace, was in last place swinging into the straight but finished well to be in the mix for minor prize-money.

Lost Soldier Three(IRE) struggled to go the pace and is more effective over further. (op 14/1)

Zato(IRE) failed to build on the promise he showed over this course and distance on his Dubai debut a fortnight earlier.

399a HAAFHD AL MAKTOUM CHALLENGE RII (GROUP 3) (DIRT) 1m 1f (D)

5:50 (5:50) 3-Y-0+

£61,224 (£20,408; £10,204; £5,102; £3,061; £2,040)

RPR

1 **Kandidate**[137] [5547] 5-9-6 112 .....(t) RyanMoore 12 118
(C E Brittain) *sn led: rdn clr 3f out: 6 l clr fnl f: easily* **14/1**

2 5 3/4 **Mullins Bay**[95] [6364] 6-9-6 112 ..... LDettori 4 107
(M F De Kock, South Africa) *trckd ldr out wd: gng wl 3f out: r.o wl: no ch w wnr* **7/2**[2]

3 1/4 **Singing Poet (IRE)**[48] 6-9-6 105 .....(t) TPO'Shea 2 107
(E Charpy, UAE) *mid-div on rail: rdn 3f out: kpt on wl fnl 2f: nrst fin* **14/1**

4 hd **Fairson (TUR)**[54] 4-9-6 100 ..... SKaya 1 107
(K Tekdogan, Turkey) *trckd ldr on rail: short of room after 2f: r.o wl fnl 2f* **16/1**

5 1 1/2 **Mooner (ARG)**[7] [327] 6-9-6 105 ..... TedDurcan 7 104
(S Seemar, UAE) *mid-div out wd: rdn 3 1/2f out: n.d* **6/1**

6 1 3/4 **Dubai Honor**[21] [175] 8-9-6 106 .....(e) MartinDwyer 13 100
(Doug Watson, UAE) *mid-div: rdn 3f out: nvr a threat* **14/1**

7 1/4 **Binary File (USA)**[151] [5226] 9-9-6 106 .....(t) RHills 8 100
(L Kelp, Sweden) *settled in rr: nvr able to chal* **20/1**

8 1 **Golden Arrow (IRE)**[21] [177] 4-9-6 105 .....(v) KerrinMcEvoy 5 98
(I Mohammed, UAE) *trckd ldr on rail: rdn 3f out: wknd fnl 1 1/2f* **16/1**

9 4 3/4 **Imperialista (BRZ)**[21] [177] 4-8-9 110 ..... MJKinane 14 78
(I Mohammed, UAE) *trckd ldr: rdn 3f out: n.d after* **3/1**[1]

10 3 **Bandido Secreto (BRZ)**[21] [177] 5-9-6 100 ..... ADomingos 9 83
(P Nickel Filho, Brazil) *sn pushed along: nvr nr to chal* **20/1**

11 2 1/4 **Mulaqat**[166] [4818] 4-9-6 112 ..... JMurtagh 3 79
(D Selvaratnam, UAE) *slowly away: settled in rr: short of room 2f out: nvr nr to chal* **10/1**

12 7 1/4 **Surbiton (USA)**[48] 7-9-6 93 .....(t) RoystonFfrench 10 65
(A Al Raihe, UAE) *nvr able to chal* **66/1**

13 10 **Bosra's Valentine (USA)**[343] [565] 7-9-6 86 ..... GHind 11 46
(R Bouresly, Kuwait) *v.s.a: nvr able to chal* **66/1**

14 1 1/2 **Stage Gift (IRE)**[117] [5968] 4-9-6 112 ..... PJSmullen 6 43
(I Mohammed, UAE) *mid-div in centre: rdn 4f out: sn wknd: eased fnl 1 1/2f* **5/1**[3]

1m 49.4s (-1.40) **Going Correction** +0.175s/f (Slow) 14 Ran SP% **131.5**
Speed ratings: 113,107,107,107,106 104,104,103,99,96 94,88,79,77

.

Owner A J Richards **Bred** Proton Partnership **Trained** Newmarket, Suffolk

FOCUS
This looked a reasonable Group 3 beforehand - the second round of the Al Maktoum challenge - but there was very little pace on early and, as a result, the form is unreliable.

NOTEBOOK
Kandidate was absolutely gifted the lead soon after the start, allowed to bowl along at a sedate pace by dirt-racing standards, and had the race in the bag when kicking clear off the final bend. He is a smart horse, there is no doubt about that, and nobody would begrudge him this success, but he is surely flattered by the bare form, considering that he had the race totally run to suit while many of the leading contenders could not show their best form. He managed to win on the turf at last year's Carnival, but is obviously every bit as effective on dirt and, if anything, is becoming better suited to sand racing as he gets older. This was his fourth straight win on an artificial surface, as he had won his last three starts on Polytrack in the UK over trips ranging from 1m to 1m4f. He fully deserves to keep taking his chance in this sort of company, and no doubt his trainer would love to run him in the Dubai World Cup, but he is unlikely to be given such an easy time up front in the near future. (op 12/1)

Mullins Bay, formerly a smart turf performer for Aidan O'Brien and John Hammond, looked a major threat to Kandidate when looming large at the top of the home straight, but that one had plenty left in the locker and he could keep on at only the one pace. Although below the pick of his form, he seemed well suited by this dirt surface and should have plenty more to offer.

Singing Poet(IRE), bidding for a hat-trick following wins in handicap and Listed company in Dubai this winter, ran a big race to grab third. The steady pace would have been totally against him, considering he was positioned well off the leaders for much of the way, but he stayed on strongly in the straight. He is clearly pretty smart and is one to keep on the right side. (op 12/1)

Fairson(TUR), a multiple winner in Turkey, ran a big race on his debut in Dubai, keeping on well for pressure in the straight.

Mooner(ARG) stays 1m2f, so the steady pace is unlikely to have suited him and he did not run badly in the circumstances.

Imperialista(BRZ) had landed round one of the Al Maktoum challenge when trained by Brazilian connections. However, he ran a stinker on his first start for his new yard and proved to be a major disappointment. On reflection, he might have been better suited by putting more pressure on Kandidate for the lead, but the way he dropped out suggests he basically just had an off day. (op 100/30)

Stage Gift(IRE) was Group class on the turf for Sir Michael Stoute last season but ran an abysmal race on his first start for new connections, seemingly failing to handle the dirt. (op 13/2)

400a MUJAHID STKS (H'CAP) (TURF) 6f 110y(T)

6:20 (6:22) (95-110,110) 3-Y-0+

£36,734 (£12,244; £6,122; £3,061; £1,836; £1,224)

RPR

1 **Appalachian Trail (IRE)**[14] [247] 6-9-0 **104** .....(b) MJKinane 1 113
(I Semple) *mid-div on rail: gng wl 3f out out: rdn to ld 1 1/2f out: r.o wl: easily* **4/1**[3]

2 3 **Tiza (SAF)**[14] [245] 5-9-6 **110** .....(t) RyanMoore 9 111
(H J Brown, South Africa) *settled in last of main gp: swtchd wd 2f out: r.o: nrst fin* **10/3**[1]

3 shd **Ashdown Express (IRE)**[118] [5942] 8-9-6 **110** ..... TedDurcan 6 111
(C F Wall) *mid-div: gng wl 3f out: trckd wnr 2f out whn short of room: r.o* **9/2**

4 1/4 **Lascaux (AUS)**[14] [245] 6-8-12 **102** ..... WLHo 3 102
(Y Choy, Macau) *racd in 3rd: rdn to ld 2f out: hdd 1 1/2f out: one pce* **11/1**

5 3/4 **Mac Love**[14] [245] 6-9-3 **107** ..... PJSmullen 10 105
(J Noseda) *settled in rr: t.k.h: gng wl 3f out: r.o wl fnl 2f: nrst fin* **7/2**[2]

6 1 3/4 **So Will I**[14] [245] 6-8-12 **102** .....(t) RHills 11 95
(Doug Watson, UAE) *mid-div: gng wl 2 1/2f out: no room 1 1/2f out: no ch after* **20/1**

7 1 1/4 **Beckermet (IRE)**[131] [5682] 5-9-0 **104** ..... JamieSpencer 7 94
(R F Fisher) *racd in rr: t.k.h: short of room in mid-div 1 1/2f out: nt rcvr* **12/1**

8 2 1/2 **Attilius (BRZ)**[14] [245] 5-8-8 **98** .....(t) TPO'Shea 12 81
(E Charpy, UAE) *mid-div: rdn 3f out to chal: r.o one pce* **40/1**

9 1 3/4 **Sunrise (SAF)**[7] [324] 6-9-6 **110** .....(t) MKhan 5 88
(S Seemar, UAE) *mid-div: clsng on rail whn no room 2f out: nt rcvr* **14/1**

10 1 1/4 **Morshdi**[305] 9-8-11 **101** ..... JMurtagh 8 75
(D Selvaratnam, UAE) *settled in rr: nvr nr to chal* **20/1**

11 1 1/2 **Pecoiquen (CHI)**[7] [331] 6-8-8 **98** .....(bt) WSupple 4 68
(F Castro, Sweden) *sn led: hdd 2f out: wknd* **40/1**

12 1/2 **Bellamont Forest (USA)**[14] [245] 11-8-10 **100** ..... DinaDanekilde 2 69
(O Larsen, Sweden) *trckd ldr: ev ch 2 1/2f out: wknd* **33/1**

1m 19.96s (2.76) **Going Correction** +0.45s/f (Yiel) 12 Ran SP% **123.5**
Speed ratings: 102,98,98,98,97 95,93,91,89,87 85,85

.

Owner G L S Partnership **Bred** Swettenham Stud **Trained** Carluke, S Lanarks

FOCUS
A high-class sprint handicap, but they were soon well strung out because of the strong early pace, and a few of these may not have been ideally suited by the way the race developed.

NOTEBOOK
Appalachian Trail(IRE) ran with real encouragement over an extended 7f on his debut in Dubai two weeks previously and confirmed that promise dropped back 1f in trip. Having travelled very sweetly throughout, he found plenty when asked to stretch and was a most decisive winner. He has won over 1m three times but, if anything, shorter trips help bring out the best in him, and it would be no surprise to see him follow up in a similar event round here.

Tiza(SAF), a beaten favourite over course and distance on his debut in Dubai two weeks previously, ran much better this time. Having been held up near last in the early stages, he had to be switched wide with his challenge in the straight and basically found his stride too late. (op 7/2)

Ashdown Express(IRE) ◆ had no easy task off top weight on his debut in Dubai, but he ran an encouraging race. He has not always been the easiest to win with, but these limited handicaps might just help his cause, even if he will have to continue conceding weight, and he looks capable of finding a race at this year's Carnival.

Lascaux(AUS) ◆ emerges with plenty of credit considering he chased the frantic early pace and committed for home plenty soon enough. He looks one to keep on the right side in similar company round here over the next few weeks. (op 10/1)

Mac Love struggled to get in a blow at the principals and did not really build on the promise of his recent course-and-distance second.

So Will I would have been a lot closer with a better trip and will surely pop up in one of these type of races eventually. (op 16/1)

Beckermet(IRE) was a little short of room in the straight and can be rated better than the bare form. (op 14/1)

401a MUHTATHIR CUP (H'CAP) (TURF) 1m 2f (T)

6:50 (6:50) (90-105,105) 3-Y-0+

£33,673 (£11,224; £5,612; £2,806; £1,683; £1,122)

RPR

1 **Charlie Cool**[21] [176] 4-9-4 **102** ..... JamieSpencer 9 111
(W J Haggas) *settled in rr: smooth prog out wd to chal fnl f: led cl home* **11/8**[1]

2 1/2 **Book Of Music (IRE)**[14] [248] 4-9-5 **104** .....(v) KerrinMcEvoy 10 111
(I Mohammed, UAE) *mid-div: rdn to chal 2f out: led 1 1/2f out: hdd cl home* **10/1**

3 3 1/4 **Speedy Sam**[21] [175] 4-8-10 **95** ..... JMurtagh 1 96
(K R Burke) *in rr on rail: swtchd wd 3f out: r.o fnl 2f* **14/1**

4 shd **Dont Dili Dali**[14] [250] 4-8-12 **97** ..... JohnEgan 3 98
(J S Moore) *in rr: rdn 4 1/2f out: r.o wl fnl 3f* **9/1**

5 3/4 **Cimyla (IRE)**[21] [176] 6-9-3 **100** ..... EddieAhern 14 101
(C F Wall) *mid-div: rdn to ld 2 1/2f out: hdd 1 1/2f out: r.o one pce* **16/1**

6 5 **Candy Critic (ARG)**[222] 5-9-1 **98** .....(bt) MJKinane 4 89
(M F De Kock, South Africa) *mid-div on rail: nvr able to chal: r.o late* **7/1**[3]

7 2 3/4 **Great Plains**[14] [244] 5-9-2 **99** .....(b) RHills 8 85
(E Charpy, UAE) *mid-div: gng wl 3f out: one pce in st* **6/1**[2]

8 3 **Championship Point (IRE)**[14] [244] 4-9-6 **105** ..... TedDurcan 11 84
(M R Channon) *mid-div: rdn on rail 3 1/2f out: no rspnse* **11/1**

9 2 1/4 **Public Forum**[110] [6107] 5-8-10 **94** ..... MartinDwyer 2 69
(Doug Watson, UAE) *settled in rr: nvr able to chal* **20/1**

10 1 **Bianconi (SAF)**[14] [244] 8-9-3 **100** .....(t) RyanMoore 7 74
(S Seemar, UAE) *racd in rr: rdn 4f out: nvr able to chal* **25/1**

11 3/4 **Red Racketeer (USA)**[267] [1775] 5-8-10 **94** ..... RoystonFfrench 12 66
(A Al Raihe, UAE) *trckd ldr: led 4f out: hdd 2 1/2f out: wknd* **25/1**

12 9 **Desert Realm (IRE)**[7] [329] 4-8-10 **95** .....(v) WSupple 13 49
(I Mohammed, UAE) *prom tl wknd 3f out* **25/1**

13 4 1/4 **Brahminy Kite (USA)**[7] [329] 5-8-11 **95** ..... GHind 5 41
(R Bouresly, Kuwait) *led tl hdd 4f out: wknd qckly* **66/1**

14 dist **Book Of Kings (USA)**[7] [325] 6-9-0 **97** .....(bt) RichardMullen 6 —
(S Seemar, UAE) *led main gp tl rdn and wknd 5f out* **50/1**

2m 6.06s (1.86) **Going Correction** +0.45s/f (Yiel)
WFA 4 from 5yo+ 1lb 14 Ran SP% **128.6**
Speed ratings: 110,109,107,106,106 102,100,97,95,95 94,87,83,—

.

Owner W J Gredley **Bred** Middle Park Stud Ltd **Trained** Newmarket, Suffolk

FOCUS
A very good handicap and they went a strong pace throughout. The winning time was 0.18 seconds quicker than the 5.20, which was basically another division of this race.

NOTEBOOK
Charlie Cool ◆, whose recent third over 1m1f round here had received a boost when the winner, Formal Decree, followed up in Group 3 company, travelled easily throughout. He was made to work hard when drawing upsides Book Of Music inside the final furlong, but he always looked like getting on top and duly found enough. This was a smart effort and he should continue to progress over middle distances. (op 7/4)

Book Of Music(IRE), tried in a visor, benefited from the drop back from 1m4f and ran a big race on just his second start for his current connections. He did not go down without a fight and, on this evidence, is clearly still improving. (op 9/1)

Speedy Sam failed to beat a rival on the dirt on his previous start but, switched to turf, this was much better. Connections will take plenty of hope and there could be even better to come.

Dont Dili Dali ◆ ran a huge race considering she had to be switched round runners and got in the clear only after the eventual winner had kicked for home. She had shaped well over the course and distance two weeks previously, is clearly on good terms with herself and just needs things to drop right. (op 11/1)

Cimyla(IRE) probably hit the front a little too soon and could not sustain his challenge. This was an improvement on the form he showed over slightly shorter on his previous start and he could do even better if held onto for a little longer.

Championship Point(IRE) could not build on his recent course and distance effort and was below his best.

364 WOLVERHAMPTON (A.W) (L-H)

Friday, February 9

OFFICIAL GOING: Standard to slow (meeting abandoned after race 3 (2.45) due to deteriorating weather conditions)

Wind: Light against Weather: Snowing

402 PONTIN'S HOLIDAYS H'CAP — 1m 1f 103y(P)

1:40 (1:40) (Class 6) (0-50,50) 4-Y-0+ — £2,388 (£705; £352) Stalls Low

Form — RPR

05-0 **1** **Oakbridge (IRE)**[27] [123] 5-8-10 **48** .... EdwardCreighton 11 — 68
(D J Wintle) *hld up: hdwy to ld 2f out: sn edgd lft and clr: comf* **14/1**

-222 **2** *8* **Over To You Bert**[12] [274] 8-8-3 **48** ow1 .... HaddenFrost(7) 12 — 52
(R J Hodges) *chsd ldrs: led over 5f out: rdn and hdd 2f out: wknd fnl f* **4/1**[2]

60-6 **3** *½* **Twilight Avenger (IRE)**[21] [181] 4-8-5 **46** ....(t) LiamJones(3) 4 — 49
(W M Brisbourne) *hld up: hdwy and hung lft over 1f out: nt trble ldrs* **28/1**

535- **4** *1* **Abbeygate**[43] [6959] 6-8-10 **48** ow1 .... TonyCulhane 7 — 49
(T Keddy) *hld up: hdwy over 2f out: sn rdn: styd on same pce* **7/2**[1]

0-03 **5** *2* **Mister Maq**[13] [271] 4-8-10 **48** oh1 ow2 ....(b) RobertWinston 6 — 45
(A Crook) *s.i.s: hld up: rdn over 2f out: n.d* **11/1**

-434 **6** *½* **Fantasy Defender (IRE)**[13] [271] 5-8-5 **46** oh1 ....(v) JamesDoyle(3) 3 — 42
(Ernst Oertel) *hld up in tch: rdn and ev ch 2 out: wknd over 1f out* **7/1**[3]

30-3 **7** *6* **Neshla**[29] [98] 4-8-12 **50** ....(p) SebSanders 5 — 34
(C E Brittain) *sn rdn to chsd ldrs: wknd over 2f out* **15/2**

00-0 **8** *1* **Machinate (USA)**[21] [179] 5-8-12 **50** .... ShaneKelly 2 — 32
(W M Brisbourne) *chsd ldrs: rdn over 2f out: wknd over 1f out* **10/1**

403- **9** *shd* **Miss Monica (IRE)**[158] [5072] 6-8-8 **46** .... ChrisCatlin 13 — 28
(P W Hiatt) *hld up: a in rr* **16/1**

0-06 **10** *6* **Razed**[12] [278] 4-8-4 **49** .... LukeMorris(7) 1 — 19
(P L Gilligan) *prom 7f* **14/1**

03-6 **11** *2* **Orphina (IRE)**[16] [230] 4-8-9 **47** ....(t) AdrianMcCarthy 9 — 13
(B G Powell) *s.i.s: sn prom: hung lft over 3f out: wknd over 2f out* **33/1**

0-02 **12** *6* **Danum**[21] [179] 7-8-9 **47** .... GrahamGibbons 10 — 1
(R Hollinshead) *led: hdd over 5f out: rdn and wknd 2f out* **12/1**

2m 2.93s (0.31) **Going Correction** +0.075s/f (Slow) — **12** Ran SP% **117.2**
Speed ratings (Par 101):101,93,93,92,90 90,85,84,84,78 76,71
CSF £68.46 CT £1573.73 TOTE £23.80: £4.50, £2.00, £7.00; EX 163.30 TRIFECTA Not won..
Owner D J Wintle **Bred** Robert Scarborough **Trained** Naunton, Gloucs

FOCUS
A moderate heat, but it was won in clear-cut fashion by the well-handicapped Oakbridge. The form is very modest, but looks fairly solid.
Machinate(USA) Official explanation: jockey said gelding hung right

403 GO PONTIN'S (S) STKS — 5f 20y(P)

2:10 (2:12) (Class 6) 3-Y-0+ — £2,047 (£604; £302) Stalls Low

Form — RPR

5-50 **1** **Mustammer**[7] [339] 4-9-7 45 .... TonyCulhane 10 — 61
(D Shaw) *hld up: hdwy and hung lft over 1f out: rdn to ld ins fnl f: r.o* **14/1**

-405 **2** *1 ¼* **Fast Heart**[16] [236] 6-9-7 60 .... NCallan 3 — 57
(R A Harris) *sn outpcd: hdwy over 1f out: rdn and ev ch ins fnl f: edgd rt and unable to to qckn* **10/11**[1]

0020 **3** *½* **New Options**[4] [368] 10-9-7 52 ....(b) GrahamGibbons 7 — 55
(Peter Grayson) *hld up in tch: rdn and edgd lft over 1f out: styd on same pce ins fnl f* **8/1**[3]

-005 **4** *1 ¾* **Majestical (IRE)**[7] [337] 5-9-7 50 ....(p) LPKeniry 9 — 48
(J M Bradley) *chsd ldr: led over 3f out: hdd 2f out: no ex ins fnl f* **8/1**[3]

6-34 **5** *1 ¼* **Phinerine**[14] [254] 4-9-2 52 ....(b) TolleyDean(5) 4 — 44
(R A Harris) *s.i.s: hdwy over 3f out: rdn over 1f out: wknd ins fnl f* **13/2**[2]

0-00 **6** *2* **Sofinella (IRE)**[12] [281] 4-9-2 49 ....(p) ShaneKelly 2 — 32
(A W Carroll) *led: hdd over 3f out: led 2f out: hung lft over 1f out: hdd & wknd ins fnl f* **11/1**

0-30 **7** *¾* **Glenargo (USA)**[4] [368] 4-9-0 53 ....(p) LukeMorris(7) 5 — 34
(R A Harris) *chsd ldrs: rdn 1/2-way: wkng whn n.m.r fnl f* **11/1**

0006 **8** *hd* **Laurel Dawn**[8] [317] 9-9-2 40 .... AnnStokell(5) 11 — 33
(Miss A Stokell) *s.i.s: hdwy over 3f out: wknd over 1f out* **80/1**

-000 **9** *shd* **Fancy You (IRE)**[7] [337] 4-8-13 42 ....(b[1]) JamesDoyle(3) 1 — 28
(A W Carroll) *prom over 3f* **40/1**

000- **10** *4* **Bermuda Beauty (IRE)**[73] [6638] 4-8-13 41 .... StephenDonohoe(3) 6 — 14
(J M Bradley) *a in rr* **80/1**

/00- **11** *2 ½* **Magical World**[189] [4120] 4-9-2 35 ....(p) ChrisCatlin 8 — —
(J M Bradley) *s.i.s: a in rr* **100/1**

63.37 secs (0.55) **Going Correction** +0.075s/f (Slow) — **11** Ran SP% **117.2**
Speed ratings (Par 101):98,96,95,92,90 87,86,85,85,79 75
CSF £27.10 TOTE £12.60: £2.80, £1.10, £2.10; EX 39.90 Trifecta £111.90 Pool: £390.93 - 2.48 winning tickets..There was no bid for the winner.
Owner ownaracehorse.co.uk (S A Mapletoft) **Bred** Shadwell Estate Company Limited **Trained** Danethorpe, Notts

FOCUS
An ordinary seller run at a good pace that suited the hold-up horses. Significant improvement from the winner on paper but the runner-up and third are not trusty yardsticks.

404 PONTINS.COM H'CAP — 5f 20y(P)

2:45 (2:45) (Class 6) (0-65,65) 3-Y-0 — £2,388 (£705; £352) Stalls Low

Form — RPR

2141 **1** **Bentley**[3] [378] 3-9-2 **63** 6ex ....(v) NCallan 9 — 69
(D Shaw) *s.i.s: sn chsng ldrs: rdn 1/2-way: led and hung lft ins fnl f: r.o* **5/4**[1]

2-44 **2** *shd* **Charlotte Grey**[7] [336] 3-9-0 **61** .... EdwardCreighton 1 — 67
(C N Allen) *chsd ldrs: rdn and ev ch ins fnl f: r.o* **15/8**[2]

6-64 **3** *5* **Candyland (IRE)**[18] [219] 3-8-7 **54** .... ShaneKelly 2 — 42
(M Quinn) *prom: rdn and hung lft over 1f out: styd on same pce* **10/1**[3]

66-0 **4** *shd* **Redflo**[37] [17] 3-8-6 **56** .... JamesDoyle(3) 4 — 44
(Ms J S Doyle) *led: rdn over 1f out: hdd & wknd ins fnl f* **25/1**

6-46 **5** *1 ¼* **Glen Avon Girl (IRE)**[7] [336] 3-8-7 **59** .... DuranFentiman(5) 11 — 42
(T D Easterby) *sn pushed along in rr: rdn 1/2-way: wknd over 1f out* **12/1**

400- **6** *1 ¾* **Avery**[144] [5419] 3-8-5 **56** .... HaddenFrost(7) 10 — 36
(R J Hodges) *chsd ldrs: rdn 1/2-way: wknd over 1f out* **20/1**

03-0 **7** *¾* **Head To Head (IRE)**[3] [378] 3-8-12 **59** ow1 ....(b) AdamKirby 7 — 33
(Peter Grayson) *s.i.s: outpcd* **33/1**

-000 **8** *shd* **Haydock Express (IRE)**[7] [336] 3-8-4 **51** oh2 ....(b[1]) AdrianMcCarthy 3 — 25
(Peter Grayson) *sn pushed along in rr: rdn 1/2-way: sn wknd* **16/1**

63.78 secs (0.96) **Going Correction** +0.075s/f (Slow) — **8** Ran SP% **113.4**
Speed ratings (Par 95):95,94,86,86,84 81,80,80
CSF £3.54 CT £13.09 TOTE £2.00: £1.10, £1.10, £1.80; EX 3.20 Trifecta £14.90 Pool: £394.81 - 18.79 winning tickets. Place 6 £5.74, Place 5 £1.39.
Owner Danethorpe Racing Ltd **Bred** P Blows And Miss J Hall **Trained** Danethorpe, Notts

FOCUS
A modest handicap but the first two finished clear and the form looks sound. Bentley did not have to improve on his Southwell win.

405 PONTIN'S "BOOK EARLY" CLAIMING STKS — 1m 4f 50y(P)

() (Class 6) 4-Y-0+ — £

406 PONTIN'S FAMILY HOLIDAYS H'CAP — 5f 20y(P)

() (Class 4) (0-85,) 3-Y-0+ — £

407 PONTINSBINGO.COM H'CAP — 7f 32y(P)

() (Class 5) (0-70,) 3-Y-0 — £

408 WOLVERHAMPTON-RACECOURSE.CO.UK MAIDEN STKS — 7f 32y(P)

() (Class 5) 3-Y-0+ — £

T/Jkpt: Not won. T/Plt: £3.30 to a £1 stake. Pool: £86,212.90. 18,515.05 winning tickets. T/Qpdt: £1.10 to a £1 stake. Pool: £6,475.40. 6,233.00 winning tickets. CR

394 NAD AL SHEBA (L-H)

Friday, February 9

OFFICIAL GOING: Turf course - good; dirt course - fast

Again, the inside rail on the turf course seemed to be riding slower than the middle of the track.

409a SHADWELL FARM TROPHY (H'CAP) (TURF) — 6f (T)

3:25 (3:26) (90-105,105) 3-Y-0+

£33,673 (£11,224; £5,612; £2,806; £1,683; £1,122)

RPR

1 **Greek Renaissance (IRE)**[15] [249] 4-8-12 **97** .... KerrinMcEvoy 4 — 111+
(I Mohammed, UAE) *mid-div: rdn to cl 2f out: kicked clr 1f out: comf* **5/1**

2 *2 ½* **Arenti (NZ)**[33] 6-9-4 **102** ....(e) MJKinane 1 — 107
(J Meagher, Singapore) *slowly away: 10th into st: rdn 2 1/2f out: r.o fnl 1 1/2f: nrst fin* **9/2**[3]

3 *2* **Celtic Mill**[15] [245] 9-9-6 **105** ....(p) LDettori 7 — 103
(D W Barker) *sn led: rdn 2 1/2f out: hdd 1f out: kpt on* **7/2**[1]

4 *1 ¼* **Sand Cat**[22] [172] 4-8-10 **95** .... RoystonFfrench 9 — 89
(Christian Wroe) *slowly away: settled in rr: rdn 3f out whn n.m.r: r.o wl fnl f* **40/1**

5 *shd* **Almaram (USA)**[8] [324] 7-9-2 **100** ....(e) JMurtagh 10 — 94
(D Selvaratnam, UAE) *trckd ldrs: rdn to chal 2f out: nt qckn* **9/1**

6 *½* **Compton's Eleven**[132] [5677] 6-8-10 **95** .... TedDurcan 3 — 87
(M R Channon) *mid-div on rail: rdn 3f out: no room 1 1/2f out: nvr able to chal* **4/1**[2]

7 *¾* **Loyalist (SAF)**[187] 6-9-5 **104** .... RyanMoore 11 — 94
(S Seemar, UAE) *in rr: nvr able to chal* **9/1**

8 *hd* **Warcat (NZ)**[76] 6-9-6 **105** ....(t) WLHo 8 — 94
(Y Choy, Macau) *mid-div: short of room 4f out: gng wl 3f out: rdn 2 1/2f out: nt qckn* **7/1**

9 *1 ¾* **National Icon (SAF)**[15] [245] 7-9-5 **104** ....(t) WSupple 6 — 88
(A Manuel, UAE) *trckd front two on rail: ev ch 3f out: short of room on rail 1f out: nt rcvr* **33/1**

10 *1* **Para-Choque (BRZ)**[15] [249] 5-9-0 **98** ....(t) ADomingos 12 — 80
(C Morgado, Brazil) *broke wl: trckd ldr tl rdn 2f out: nt qckn* **20/1**

11 *hd* **Holborn (UAE)**[8] [326] 6-8-12 **97** ....(ve) MKhan 5 — 77
(S Seemar, UAE) *v.s.a: nvr nr to chal* **40/1**

12 *1 ¾* **Golden Acer (IRE)**[8] [326] 4-8-11 **96** .... MartinDwyer 2 — 71
(Doug Watson, UAE) *slowly away: racd in mid-div on rail: rdn 3f out: nvr threatened* **33/1**

1m 12.09s (0.69) **Going Correction** +0.45s/f (Yiel) — **12** Ran SP% **125.1**
Speed ratings: 113,109,107,105,105 104,103,103,100,99 99,97

Owner Sheikh Hamdan Bin Mohammed Al Maktoum **Bred** Ballymacoll Stud Farm Ltd **Trained** UAE

FOCUS
This was a good sprint handicap, although not quite as strong as one would expect for the grade in the UK. They went a good pace and, interestingly, the front two made their moves down the centre of the track. This was basically another division of the 6.40, but the winning time was 0.65 seconds quicker.

NOTEBOOK
Greek Renaissance(IRE) ◆ failed to show anything like his best form when tried on the dirt on his debut for these connections on his previous start, but the switch to turf did the trick and he ran out a most convincing winner. Always going well in about mid-division, he moved up stylishly towards the centre of the track early in the straight and duly bounded clear when asked to extend. Putting aside his slight blip on the dirt last time, he has a most progressive profile and he looks capable of developing into a Group-class sprinter. In the longer term it would be no surprise to see him switched to Godolphin, and we can expect to see him contesting some good races in the UK this year. (op 11/2)
Arenti(NZ) was drawn on the inside, but he lacked the pace to hold a position early and had to be switched towards the centre of the track for his effort in the straight. He stayed on well enough, but was never a danger to the winner and will probably benefit from a step up to 7f. After all, he won a Group 3 over that trip in Singapore last year.
Celtic Mill took them along at a good pace for much of the way, but he stuck to the far rail in the straight, whereas the front two made their moves down the centre of the track, and he was no match for that pair late on.
Sand Cat, dropping in trip, ran a good race and offered some promise. (op 33/1)
Almaram(USA) did not run badly but he was unable to match the form he showed when winning a 6f handicap on the dirt on his previous start. (op 17/2)
Compton's Eleven had managed to win first time out at the last two Carnivals, so a 132-day absence was of no great concern, but he endured a troubled passage in the straight this time and looked unlucky not to finish quite a bit closer. (op 9/2)
Warcat(NZ) was hampered just before they reached the bend and can probably be forgiven this.

410a DUBAI ALUMINIUM (DUBAL) TROPHY (H'CAP) (DIRT) 1m 110y
3:55 (3:55) (90-105,104) 3-Y-0+

£33,673 (£11,224; £5,612; £2,806; £1,683; £1,122)

RPR

1 **Blue On Blues (ARG)**[22] [177] 6-9-6 104 ....(t) RyanMoore 15 109
(S Seemar, UAE) *mid-div: rdn 3f out: chal 2f out: led 1f out: hld on wl* **11/1**

2 ¾ **Opportunist (IRE)**[8] [327] 8-9-2 99 ....(vt) MartinDwyer 10 103
(Doug Watson, UAE) *led main gp: overall ldr 2 1/2f out: hdd 1f out: r.o wl* **9/1**

3 2 ¾ **Aleutian**[15] [250] 7-8-9 93 ....(e) RoystonFfrench 5 91
(Doug Watson, UAE) *mid-div: hrd rdn 2 1/2f out: r.o: nrst fin* **16/1**

4 hd **British Isles**[35] 5-8-7 90 ....(t) RichardMullen 4 88
(S Seemar, UAE) *mid-div: prog to chal 2 1/2f out: ev ch 1 1/2f out: wknd fnl 110yds* **10/1**

5 1 ¼ **Curule (USA)**[85] 10-8-8 91 .... AdrianTNicholls 14 87
(Doug Watson, UAE) *mid-div out wd: hrd rdn 3f out: nt qckn* **33/1**

6 shd **Salt Track (ARG)**[8] [327] 7-8-11 95 ....(t) JMurtagh 6 89
(Niels Petersen, Norway) *sn pushed along in rr: sme prog fnl 3f: nrst fin* **33/1**

7 5 ¾ **Engrupido (ARG)**[22] [178] 4-8-9 104 .... KerrinMcEvoy 1 76
(M F De Kock, South Africa) *mid-div on rail: rdn 3f out: n.d after* **7/2**[2]

8 1 ¼ **Te Voglio Bene (BRZ)**[22] [173] 4-8-0 90 ....(t) RPCleary 11 64
(M D Wolfson, U.S.A) *in rr: n.d* **33/1**

9 1 **Alto Taquari (BRZ)**[22] [172] 4-8-1 96 ....(b) ECruz 13 63
(P Nickel Filho, Brazil) *set furious gallop tl hdd 2 1/2f out: wknd* **10/1**

10 ½ **Quebec Citizen (BRZ)**[139] 4-8-9 104 ....(v) LDettori 12 70
(Saeed Bin Suroor) *prom: ev ch whn rdn 3f out: wknd* **3/1**[1]

11 1 ¼ **Yankee George (IRE)**[29] [104] 4-8-7 90 .... WSupple 8 66
(Doug Watson, UAE) *mid-div: nvr a threat* **33/1**

12 4 **Delude (IRE)**[8] [327] 9-8-7 90 ....(t) TPO'Shea 9 58
(S Seemar, UAE) *settled in rr: nvr involved: eased fnl 110yds* **16/1**

13 ½ **Red Duster (USA)**[8] [329] 4-8-11 95 ....(b) JamieSpencer 2 61
(S Seemar, UAE) *slowly away: nvr nr to chal: eased fnl f* **14/1**

14 11 **Mezel (USA)**[8] [325] 4-9-3 100 .... TedDurcan 7 45
(S Seemar, UAE) *in rr: nvr able to chal: eased fnl 110yds* **8/1**[3]

15 13 **Sapucai (ARG)**[8] [329] 7-8-7 90 ....(bt) WayneSmith 3 9
(S Seemar, UAE) *in rr: n.d: eased fnl f* **40/1**

1m 43.41s (103.41) 15 Ran SP% **127.5**

Owner Suliman Ahmed Bhana **Bred** Haras Santa Maria De Araras **Trained** United Arab Emirates

FOCUS
A decent enough handicap, even if a few of these are pretty exposed, and they went a very strong pace from the start.

NOTEBOOK
Blue On Blues(ARG) was not at his best in a 1m Group 3 on his previous start, but that company was probably a bit hot and, dropped in grade, he returned to his very best with a determined success. A wide draw helped him avoid any potential trouble on the inside and he responded well to pressure in the straight to see off Opportunist, who was definitely going the better of the pair on the turn in. A rise in the weights will probably see him forced up in grade, and that might be enough to stop him following up.
Opportunist(IRE) improved on the form he showed when fourth in a similar race over 1m round here on his previous start and was just held. Having travelled very strongly into the straight, he found plenty for pressure but basically just ran into a better horse on the day.
Aleutian, dropped in trip and returned to dirt, kept on for pressure but never really looked like threatening the front pair. On this evidence, a step back up in trip might suit.
British Isles could not sustain his challenge and a return to 7f should suit.
Curule(USA) was under pressure a long way out and, although responding, he never really landed a blow.
Salt Track(ARG) did not seem to handle the final bend very well and lost a few lengths, but he made up some ground in the straight.
Quebec Citizen(BRZ), a winner over 1m at Del Mar in the US last year, offered little immediate promise on his debut for Godolphin off the back of a 139-day break, dropping out tamely in the straight having come under pressure a long way from the finish.

411a SHADWELL ESTATE TROPHY (H'CAP) (TURF) 1m (T)
4:40 (4:40) (95-110,110) 3-Y-0+

£36,734 (£12,244; £6,122; £3,061; £1,836; £1,224)

RPR

1 **Smart And Mighty (AUS)**[13] 8-8-9 99 ....(b) KerrinMcEvoy 5 106
(T Noonan, Australia) *slowly away: racd in mid-div: rdn to chal 2f out: led 1 1/2f out: jst hld on* **7/1**[3]

2 ¼ **Yasoodd**[22] [176] 4-9-4 108 .... JMurtagh 13 115
(D Selvaratnam, UAE) *settled in rr: rdn to cl 3f out: ev ch fnl 1 1/2f: r.o: jst failed* **3/1**[1]

3 1 ½ **Express Way (BRZ)**[15] [247] 5-9-1 105 ....(t) LDettori 14 108
(M F De Kock, South Africa) *settled in last: in rr gng wl 2 1/2f out: rdn 2f out: r.o: nrst fin* **4/1**[2]

4 shd **Lundy's Lane (IRE)**[8] [327] 7-8-10 100 .... WSupple 10 103
(S Seemar, UAE) *mid-div out wd: rdn 2 1/2f out: kpt on wl fnl f: nrst fin* **25/1**

5 2 ¼ **Azarole (IRE)**[8] [331] 6-9-0 104 .... JohnEgan 11 102
(J S Moore) *mid-div: rdn whn n.m.r 2 1/2f out: one pce after* **7/1**[3]

6 ½ **Tell**[188] [4168] 4-8-12 102 ....(b) TPO'Shea 2 99
(E Charpy, UAE) *trckd ldr on rail: sn in mid-div: gng wl 3f out: ev ch 1 1/2f out: one pce* **9/1**

7 ¼ **Yarqus**[39] [6] 4-8-5 95 .... EddieAhern 8 91
(C E Brittain) *trckd ldng duo: rdn to chal 2f out: nt qckn* **28/1**

8 1 ¾ **Yard-Arm (SAF)**[184] 8-9-6 110 ....(vt) TedDurcan 1 102
(S Seemar, UAE) *settled in rr: gng wl on rail 3f out: n.m.r 2 1/2f out: nt able to chal* **11/1**

9 2 ¼ **Royal Power (IRE)**[15] [247] 4-9-1 105 .... RyanMoore 3 92
(M R Channon) *settled in rr: last 3f out: rdn 2 1/2f out: nvr able to chal* **16/1**

10 2 ¼ **Grand Emporium (SAF)**[22] [177] 7-9-5 109 ....(t) RichardMullen 9 91
(S Seemar, UAE) *sn led: hdd after 2 1/2f: led again 2f out: hdd 1 1/2f out and sn btn* **33/1**

11 ¾ **Beringoer (FR)**[8] [327] 4-8-10 100 ....(t) MartinDwyer 4 80
(A M Balding) *slowly away: in rr: rdn 2 1/2f out: one pce* **33/1**

12 6 ¾ **Kings Point (IRE)**[8] [331] 6-8-10 100 ....(p) MJKinane 6 64
(R A Fahey) *led main gp: rdn 3f out: n.m.r 2 1/2f out: wknd* **17/2**

13 7 **Little Neck (GER)**[376] 6-8-5 95 .... WayneSmith 7 43
(K Aga, UAE) *rdn to trck ldr: led after 2 1/2f: hdd 2f out: wknd* **16/1**

1m 38.26s (0.46) **Going Correction** +0.45s/f (Yiel) 13 Ran SP% **123.8**
Speed ratings: 115,114,113,113,110 110,110,108,106,103 103,96,89

Owner P E Kielty, G L Armour & N E Murdoch **Bred** Chatswood Stud, G Albers, P Albers **Trained** Australia

FOCUS
The top-weight, Yard-Arm, raced off a mark of 110 and this was obviously a very decent handicap.

NOTEBOOK
Smart And Mighty(AUS) followed up his stablemate Benedetti's success the previous day to confirm Australian-trained horses must be respected at the Carnival. Always well positioned just off the leaders, he picked up well when asked for his effort a the top of the straight and, getting first run on some of these, never looked in much danger once in front, even though Yasoodd closed the gap as he was getting tired late on. The winner seemed to get a much better trip than some of those around him and it remains to be seen whether he will be able to defy a rise in the weights.
Yasoodd came into this with an obvious chance, with both Formal Decree and, more recently, Charlie Cool, boosting the form of his recent course fourth. Asked to come from further back than the eventual winner, he stayed on well for pressure but was just held. (op 100-30)
Express Way(BRZ) was given plenty to do under a confident ride, but the response was not immediate when he was first asked for his challenge. Still, this represents an improvement on the form he showed two weeks previously and there could be better to come again.
Lundy's Lane(IRE) ran a solid race on his return to turf.
Azarole(IRE) was stopped in his run early in the straight and is better than he was able to show.
Yarqus was unable to sustain his challenge on his debut in Dubai. (op 33-1)
Royal Power(IRE) never landed a blow.
Beringoer(FR)'s effort was shortlived.
Kings Point(IRE) was short of room when under pressure and is a little bit better than his finishing position suggests. (op 9-1)

412a GULF NEWS TROPHY (H'CAP) (TURF) 1m 4f (T)
5:10 (5:11) (95-118,118) 3-Y-0+

£53,571 (£17,857; £8,928; £4,464; £2,678; £1,785)

RPR

1 **Quijano (GER)**[15] [248] 5-8-12 110 .... MJKinane 3 113
(P Schiergen, Germany) *mid-div: gng wl 3f out: swtchd 2f out: r.o wl: led cl home* **8/11**[1]

2 shd **Laverock (IRE)**[117] [6004] 5-9-6 118 .... KerrinMcEvoy 2 121
(I Mohammed, UAE) *settled in mid-div: smooth prog to chal 2f out: led 1 1/2f out: jst ct* **7/1**[3]

3 2 **Hattan (IRE)**[15] [248] 5-8-12 110 .... JamieSpencer 1 110
(C E Brittain) *settled in rr: trckd wnr 2f out: r.o wl: nrst fin* **12/1**

4 1 ¼ **Sanchi (IRE)**[120] [5920] 5-8-5 97 .... TPO'Shea 7 101
(E Charpy, UAE) *mid-div: gng wl 3f out: rdn 2 1/2f out: kpt on wl* **40/1**

5 ¼ **Gravitas**[15] [248] 4-8-11 112 .... LDettori 4 110
(Saeed Bin Suroor) *led main gp: rdn to chal 2 1/2f out: ev ch 1f out: fdd* **5/1**[2]

6 1 **Dono Da Raia (BRZ)**[187] 5-8-12 110 .... JMurtagh 5 106
(I Mohammed, UAE) *settled in rr: nvr able to chal* **14/1**

7 1 **Land 'n Stars**[51] [7000] 7-8-12 110 .... PaulDoe 6 104
(Jamie Poulton) *trckd ldr: rdn 3 1/2f out: nt qckn* **16/1**

8 2 **Fantastic Love (USA)**[15] [248] 7-8-5 95 ....(bt) RoystonFfrench 9 94
(A Al Raihe, UAE) *mid-div: rdn 4f out: nvr threatening* **66/1**

9 1 ½ **Jadalee (IRE)**[153] [5185] 4-8-9 110 .... PJSmullen 8 99
(I Mohammed, UAE) *missed break: sn led: hdd 1 1/2f out: wknd* **16/1**

10 3 ¾ **Encinas (GER)**[337] [624] 6-8-9 107 .... TedDurcan 11 90
(S Seemar, UAE) *settled in rr: rdn 3f out: nvr nr to chal* **20/1**

11 4 ¾ **Corriolanus (GER)**[15] [248] 7-8-9 107 .... RyanMoore 10 82
(S Seemar, UAE) *settled in rr: last 6f out: rdn 4f out: nvr involved* **33/1**

2m 33.54s (2.54) **Going Correction** +0.45s/f (Yiel)
WFA 4 from 5yo+ 3lb 11 Ran SP% **124.8**
Speed ratings: 109,108,107,106,106 105,105,103,102,100 97

Owner Stiftung Gestut Fahrhof **Bred** Stiftung Gestut Fahrhof **Trained** Germany

FOCUS
A really high-class handicap with the top-weight, Laverock, racing off a mark of 118 and coming into this off the back of a success in an Italian Group 1. The next in the weights, Dono Da Raia, was also a winner at the highest level in Brazil and plenty of the others offered very smart form. The race itself was a thrilling contest. Jadalee, allowed a clear lead, set just a steady gallop early before injecting some pace down the back straight, and any number of these had chances in the straight.

NOTEBOOK
Quijano(GER) showed a terrific attitude to extend his winning sequence to eight. He hardly had to come off the bridle when winning over course and distance on his debut in Dubai two weeks previously, but this was a whole lot tougher and he was all out to follow up. Having once again travelled with ease, he really had to work to reel in Laverock in the closing stages, but he kept finding under pressure and managed to force his head in front just yards before the line. Defying a handicap mark of 110 against such stiff opposition ensures he will be well worth his place in the Group 1 Sheema Classic on World Cup night, although realistically he will have to take another step forward to land that prize. It remains to be seen whether he will run again before then. (op 4-5)
Laverock(IRE) was produced with every chance on his debut for new connections and ran a huge race considering he was conceding upwards of 8lb to some very smart rivals. He will probably re-oppose the winner in the Sheema Classic and no doubt many will fancy him to reverse form off level weights.
Hattan(IRE) managed to reverse recent course-and-distance form with Gravitas, but Quijano was too good for him once again. Still, this represents very smart form.
Sanchi(IRE) did not really progress as one might have hoped when with Godolphin, but he has always looked potentially decent and this was a good effort first time up for his new connections. His performance is all the more creditable considering he was returning from a 120-day break.
Gravitas could not reverse recent form with Quijano and has seemingly not progressed.
Dono Da Raia(BRZ) was asked to come from a long way back and never landed a blow. This was his first start for his current connections, though, and he can do better.
Land 'n Stars managed to win over course and distance at last year's Carnival, but he seemed to find this trip on the short side this time against such good company.

413a DERRINSTOWN STUD TROPHY (H'CAP) (TURF) 1m 194y(T)
5:40 (5:41) (95-115,115) 3-Y-0+

£53,571 (£17,857; £8,928; £4,464; £2,678; £1,785)

RPR

1 **Illustrious Blue**[125] [5808] 4-8-8 102 .... PaulDoe 12 109
(W J Knight) *slowly away: mid-div: rdn to chal 2f out: led 110yds out: r.o wl* **15/2**[3]

2 1 ¼ **Great Rhythm (SAF)**[15] [247] 6-9-0 108 .... RyanMoore 8 112
(H J Brown, South Africa) *in rr of mid-div: rdn to trck ldr 2f out: ev ch fnl 110yds: r.o* **4/1**[1]

3 ¼ **Seihali (IRE)**[15] [247] 8-9-6 115 .... JMurtagh 7 118
(D Selvaratnam, UAE) *hld up in rr: last 3f out: r.o wl fnl 2f: nrst fin* **5/1**[2]

4 ¾ **Shakis (IRE)**[22] [176] 7-9-4 112 ....(vt) RHills 4 114
(Doug Watson, UAE) *hld up in rr: 2nd last 3f out: r.o wl fnl 2 1/2f: nrst fin* **16/1**

5 ¾ **Money Bags (SAF)**[8] [325] 5-8-9 **104**................................(t) TedDurcan 9 103
(M F De Kock, South Africa) *mid-div out wd: rdn to chal 2 1/2f out: led 1f out: nt qckn: wknd fnl 110yds* **10/1**

6 4 ¼ **Notability (IRE)**[22] [177] 5-9-3 **111**.. LDettori 5 102
(Saeed Bin Suroor) *sn led: rdn 2 1/2f out: hdd 1f out: bdly hmpd fnl 110yds: no ch after* **4/1**[1]

7 ½ **Advice**[140] [5519] 6-8-12 **107**..(v) KerrinMcEvoy 3 96
(Saeed Bin Suroor) *mid-div: trckd ldrs 3f out: rdn whn n.m.r 2f out: no ch after* **12/1**

8 ½ **Arabian Prince (USA)**[173] [4641] 4-8-12 **107**..................... MartinDwyer 2 95
(Doug Watson, UAE) *trckd ldr on rail: rdn to cl 2f out: bdly hmpd 1 1/2f out: nt rcvr* **5/1**[2]

9 11 **Parasol (IRE)**[8] [329] 8-9-1 **109**..................................(bt) RichardMullen 1 74
(Doug Watson, UAE) *slowly away: settled in rr: sme prog on rail 2 1/2f out: nvr able to chal* **25/1**

10 7 **Road To Love (IRE)**[132] [5673] 4-9-2 **110**.............................. WSupple 6 59
(M Johnston) *trckd ldrs: ev ch 3f out: wkng whn bdly hmpd 1 1/2f out* **9/1**

1m 50.75s (0.95) **Going Correction** +0.45s/f (Yiel) **10** Ran SP% **121.6**
Speed ratings: 113,111,111,111,110 106,106,105,95,89

.

Owner Ian & Pam Bendelow **Bred** B J & Mrs Crangle **Trained** Patching, W Sussex

FOCUS
Another high-class handicap with the top-weight racing off a mark of 115, and a few of these brought Group-race form to the table, including at the very highest level.

NOTEBOOK
Illustrious Blue ◆ has been most progressive since joining his current trainer and he continued where he left off last year with a fine effort on his first start in Dubai. He wandered around a bit under a strong ride, appearing to cause interference to some of his rivals, but there was no denying his superiority at the line, and he was a most worthy winner. He is now five from eight since joining the Knight yard and looks well up to adding to his tally with another Carnival success.
Great Rhythm(SAF), a winner in similar company over an extended 7f on his previous start, ran a good race over this longer trip and continues at the top of his game. (op 9-2)
Seihali(IRE) was last early in the straight and basically seemed to be given too much to do. He finished well, but just too late.
Shakis(IRE) travelled well but seemed unable to find a clear passage for much of the way in the straight.
Money Bags(SAF) seemed to be a little short of room late on but was not unlucky. (op 9-1)
Notability(IRE), having set out to make all the running, was asked to stick to the far rail in the straight, but that part of the track has looked like slower ground both on this card, and at the previous day's meeting, and it was no surprise he was unable to sustain his challenge. He was beaten when badly hampered inside the final furlong.
Advice, having his first start since leaving Andre Fabre's yard, was hemmed in when trying to produce an effort and then lost any chance he might have had when hampered by the eventual winner. (op 10-1)
Road To Love(IRE) looked beaten when seriously hampered over 1f out.

414a UAE 2000 GUINEAS (GROUP 3) (DIRT) 1m (D)
6:10 (6:10) 3-Y-O

£76,530 (£25,510; £12,755; £6,377; £3,826; £2,551)

RPR

1 **Asiatic Boy (ARG)**[22] [173] 4-9-4 110.................................... JMurtagh 8 112+
(M F De Kock, South Africa) *trckd ldr: wd: smooth prog to ld 2 1/2f out: r.o wl: easily* **4/7**[1]

2 4 ½ **Traffic Guard (USA)**[22] [173] 3-8-9 101............................... JohnEgan 6 100
(J S Moore) *mid-div: rdn 2 1/2f out: r.o wl fnl 2f: nrst fin* **11/1**

3 ½ **Rallying Cry (USA)**[103] [6249] 3-8-9 115.......................... KerrinMcEvoy 1 99
(I Mohammed, UAE) *trckd ldr on rail: t.k.h: ev ch 2 1/2f out: r.o: no ch w wnr* **7/2**[2]

4 3 ¾ **Country Song (USA)**[22] [173] 3-8-9 99............................. RyanMoore 3 92
(J Noseda) *sn led: hdd 2 1/2f out: kpt on one pce* **16/1**

5 5 ¾ **Joe Louis (ARG)**[195] 4-9-4 107..(t) MJKinane 4 82
(I Jory, Saudi Arabia) *missed break: racd in last: nvr nr to chal* **6/1**[3]

6 ½ **Limehouse (SAF)**[198] 4-9-4 95.. TedDurcan 7 81
(M F De Kock, South Africa) *slowly away: t.k.h and wd: rdn 3f out: nvr threatened* **25/1**

7 5 ½ **Kalgoorlie (USA)**[191] [4037] 3-8-9 99.................................... PJSmullen 5 68
(I Mohammed, UAE) *missed break: in rr: nvr able to chal* **33/1**

8 shd **Shavoulin (USA)**[22] [173] 3-8-9 85..................................(b) PaulEddery 2 68
(Christian Wroe) *mid-div on rail: rdn 3 1/2f out: nvr able to chal* **100/1**

1m 36.25s (-1.35) **Going Correction** +0.175s/f (Slow)
WFA 3 from 4yo 19lb **8** Ran SP% **122.2**
Speed ratings: 113,108,108,104,98 98,92,92

.

Owner Sheikh Mohammed Bin Khalifa Al Maktoum **Bred** Haras Arroyo De Luna **Trained** South Africa

FOCUS
By no means a great turnout numerically for the latest renewal of the UAE 2000 Guineas, but there were some smart sorts among them and Asiatic Boy produced a most impressive performance.

NOTEBOOK
Asiatic Boy(ARG) ◆, the easy winner of what was effectively a trial for this race over 7f on his debut in Dubai, had no problem whatsoever with this extra 1f and was in a different league to his seven rivals. His effort is all the more creditable considering he stumbled quite badly coming out of the stalls and very nearly parted company with his rider. Unable to gain an uncontested lead this time, he raced a little keenly under restraint just off the pacesetter Country Song, but the result was never in doubt once Murtagh asked him to stretch early in the straight. He is obviously now the one to beat in the UAE Derby, where the extra 1f should not pose him any problems at all, provided there is either a decent gallop on, which one would expect, or he is given his head and allowed to bowl along at a good pace. In the longer term, it remains to be seen where he will continue his racing career, but it would obviously be fascinating to see him tested in the US. (op 8-13)
Traffic Guard(USA) stayed on well for second having become outpaced on the turn into the straight, but he had no chance of reversing recent form with Asiatic Boy. He did, though, reverse Dewhurst form with Rallying Cry. The way he stayed on suggests he will relish the extra 1f in the UAE Derby, but it is hard to see him beating today's winner in that race.
Rallying Cry(USA), a very smart juvenile who was sixth in the Dewhurst on his final start for John Gosden, travelled nicely in behind the early leader Country Song for much of the way but lacked any sort of finishing kick once let down in the straight. His dam stayed middle distances, so there is some hope that he will get the extra 1f if asked to take his chance in the UAE Derby, but he hardly looked like he was crying out for further. He is probably just better suited to turf.
Country Song(USA) ensured that this was a reasonable test in front, but he was put in his place in the straight and could not reverse recent form with either today's winner or second.
Joe Louis(ARG), representing last year's winning connections, lost any chance he might have had with a very awkward start. (op 11-2)
Limehouse(SAF), the winner's stablemate, never featured.
Kalgoorlie(USA) offered nothing on his first start for new connections.

415a AL TAYER MOTORS TROPHY (H'CAP) (TURF) 6f (T)
6:40 (6:41) (90-105,105) 3-Y-O+

£33,673 (£11,224; £5,612; £2,806; £1,683; £1,122)

RPR

1 **Conceal**[8] [326] 9-8-11 **96**.. RoystonFfrench 11 101
(R Bouresly, Kuwait) *trckd ldr: rdn to ld 1 1/2f out: hdd cl home: r.o bravely to ld line* **25/1**

2 nse **Paradise Isle**[153] [5179] 6-9-5 **104**.. EddieAhern 8 109
(C F Wall) *mid-div: rdn to chal 2f out: led briefly cl home: hdd line* **6/1**

3 hd **Rochdale**[126] [5785] 4-8-8 **93**.. WayneSmith 5 97
(A Al Raihe, UAE) *trckd ldr: rdn to chal 1 1/2f out whn n.m.r: swtchd to rail fnl 110yds* **12/1**

4 1 ¼ **Grantley Adams**[152] [5202] 4-8-11 **96**.................................. TedDurcan 7 97
(M R Channon) *settled in rr: rdn to cl 2f out: n.m.r 1f out: kpt on* **5/1**[2]

5 nse **Obe Gold**[146] [5358] 5-8-10 **95**.. JohnEgan 1 96
(M R Channon) *settled in rr: rdn to cl 2f out: no room 1f out: r.o late: unlucky* **11/2**[3]

6 hd **Sir Edwin Landseer (USA)**[8] [326] 7-8-12 **97**..........(p) RichardMullen 4 97
(Christian Wroe) *missed break: settled in rr: mid-div and wd whn rdn 2f out: one pce* **10/1**

7 2 ¼ **Mutamared (USA)**[15] [245] 7-9-5 **104**........................... JamieSpencer 12 97
(K A Ryan) *dropped to rr: nvr involved* **17/2**

8 ½ **Protector (SAF)**[29] [105] 6-8-12 **97**....................................... MJKinane 3 89
(H J Brown, South Africa) *in rr on rail: mid-div whn n.m.r on rail 1f out* **7/2**[1]

9 1 ¼ **Excusez Moi (USA)**[131] [5712] 5-9-5 **104**............................ RyanMoore 2 92
(C E Brittain) *settled in rr: nvr able to chal* **6/1**

10 nse **Tournedos (IRE)**[15] [249] 5-9-4 **102**........................... AdrianTNicholls 6 91
(D Nicholls) *sn led: rdn 2 1/2f out: hdd 1 1/2f out: wknd fnl 110yds* **14/1**

11 1 ¾ **Varadouro (BRZ)**[29] 5-8-8 **93**......................................(p) MartinDwyer 9 76
(A Selvaratnam, UAE) *mid-div: rdn 2 1/2f out: nvr able to chal* **40/1**

12 1 ¾ **Cupids Ray (IRE)**[482] [5910] 6-9-2 **100**................................ PaulSmith 10 78
(Allan Smith, UAE) *mid-div: rdn 2 1/2f out: nvr a threat* **33/1**

1m 12.74s (1.34) **Going Correction** +0.45s/f (Yiel) **12** Ran SP% **126.0**
Speed ratings: 109,108,108,107,106 106,103,103,101,101 98,96

.

Owner Bouresly Racing Syndicate **Bred** Sh Mohd Bin Rashid Al Maktoum **Trained** Kuwait

FOCUS
A good sprint handicap on paper, but they seemed to go just an ordinary pace and the form does not look very reliable. The winning time was 0.65 seconds slower than the opening 6f contest, basically another division of this race.

NOTEBOOK
Conceal came into this on a losing run stretching back to 2004 and had never previously won on turf, but he is obviously fully effective on this surface and was just able to defy his advancing years. This was a very useful effort, but it will be surprising if he manages to follow up in similar company.
Paradise Isle, the only mare in the field, ran a cracking race in second. The way she travelled suggests a stronger pace would have suited better, for she was still hard on the bridle at the top of the straight, but she still looked likely to do enough when asked for her effort. She basically just lost out on the nod and could have more to offer.
Rochdale, having his first start since leaving Michael Jarvis, had to be switched for his effort a couple of times and may have been a little unlucky.
Grantley Adams, having his first run since September, ran on well from a long way back despite not getting the best of trips.
Obe Gold ◆ looked very unlucky. He met with all sorts of trouble having been well off the pace turning for home and may well have won with any sort of a run in the straight. (op 6-1)
Sir Edwin Landseer(USA) stayed on well and was not far away at the line.
Mutamared(USA) failed to get competitive having been given plenty to do. (op 8-1)
Excusez Moi(USA), like Mutamared, seemed to be given too much to do and never threatened. (op 13-2)
Tournedos(IRE) appeared to get warm beforehand and could not sustain his challenge.

[379] LINGFIELD (L-H)
Saturday, February 10

OFFICIAL GOING: Standard
Wind: Light, behind. Weather: Fine becoming overcast & drizzly.

416 PONTINSBINGO.COM H'CAP 1m 4f (P)
1:30 (1:31) (Class 6) (0-50,51) 4-Y-O+ **£2,388** (£705; £352) **Stalls** Low

Form RPR

0/0- 1 **Enthusius**[291] [1216] 4-8-9 **50**... SteveDrowne 1 60
(G L Moore) *prom: trckd ldr 1/2-way: effrt to ld wl over 1f out: rdn and styd on fnl f* **12/1**

050- 2 1 ¼ **Krasivi's Boy (USA)**[44] [6959] 5-8-10 **48**..................(b) RichardHughes 15 56
(G L Moore) *trckd ldr to 1/2-way: chsd ldng pair after: effrt 2f out: rdn to go 2nd 1f out: no imp on wnr* **11/2**[1]

00-2 3 1 ½ **Compton Express**[27] [133] 4-8-6 **47** oh1 ow1..................... JohnEgan 16 53
(Jamie Poulton) *trckd ldrs: lost pl after 4f: effrt over 2f out: styd on fr over 1f out to take 3rd nr fin* **6/1**[2]

2-26 4 ½ **Lysander's Quest (IRE)**[6] [354] 9-8-10 **48**........................ DaneO'Neill 5 53
(R Ingram) *led: set slow pce to 1/2-way: tried to kick on over 3f out but little rspnse: hdd wl over 1f out: one pce* **13/2**[3]

63-5 5 ¾ **Hiawatha (IRE)**[38] [19] 8-8-9 **47**.. LPKeniry 6 51
(A M Hales) *hld up in midfield in slowly run r: effrt over 2f out: drvn and hanging lft over 1f out: kpt on: no ch* **9/1**

-542 6 shd **War Feather**[6] [349] 5-8-10 **48**.. RobertHavlin 14 52
(T D McCarthy) *rrd s: plld hrd early: hld up wl in rr in slowly run r: prog 2f out: styd on reluctantly: nvr able to chal* **15/2**

0-00 7 2 ½ **Kiama**[13] [279] 5-8-8 **46**... FergusSweeney 11 46
(B G Powell) *hld up in rr in slowly run r: effrt 3f out: plugged on one pce fnl 2f* **16/1**

000- 8 nk **Blue Quiver (IRE)**[43] [6977] 7-8-12 **50**.................................... PaulEddery 8 49
(C A Horgan) *taken down early and reluctant to go to post: hld up in last trio in slowly run r: nt clr run over 2f out: nvr any ch* **25/1**

-641 9 hd **Simplified**[6] [349] 4-8-7 **51** 6ex... JerryO'Dwyer[(3)] 13 50
(N B King) *trckd ldrs: rdn 3f out: wknd over 1f out* **14/1**

30-4 10 ¾ **Avanti**[19] [220] 11-8-3 **46**...(v) KevinGhunowa[(5)] 9 44
(Dr J R J Naylor) *hld up: prog 6f out: pushed along 4f out: wknd 2f out* **10/1**

360- 11 1 **Smoothie (IRE)**[197] [3894] 9-8-8 **46**.. ChrisCatlin 7 42
(E G Bevan) *hld up in rr in slowly run r: effrt on wd outside 3f out: nvr a factor* **14/1**

036/ **12** *hd* **Head To Kerry (IRE)**^{474} [6081] 7-8-10 **48**..........................(t) AdamKirby 3 44
(D J S Ffrench Davis) *chsd ldrs: rdn over 3f out: wknd 2f out* **50/1**

0-0 **13** *1* **Nona**^{17} [229] 4-8-3 **51** ow1... JackMitchell$^{(7)}$ 4 45
(S Dow) *dwlt: sn chsd ldrs: lost pl u.p 3f out: struggling after* **66/1**

/0-6 **14** *nk* **Woolstone Boy (USA)**^{34} [62] 6-8-12 **50**.......................(t) TPQueally 10 44
(A M Hales) *hld up in slowly run r: effrt on outer 3f out: sn no prog: no ch* **40/1**

23-0 **15** *2 1/2* **Go Amwell**^{33} [71] 4-8-7 **48**.. HayleyTurner 12 38
(J R Jenkins) *hld up in last pair in slowly run r: pushed along and no ch 2f out* **11/2**^{1}

006- **16** *10* **Useful**^{63} [6765] 4-8-9 **50**... SamHitchcott 2 24
(A B Haynes) *t.k.h: in tch tl wknd over 3f out: t.o* **50/1**

2m 34.62s (0.23) **Going Correction** -0.025s/f (Stan)
WFA 4 from 5yo+ 3lb **16** Ran SP% **127.9**
Speed ratings (Par 101):98,97,96,95,95 95,93,93,93,92 92,91,91,89 82
CSF £78.20 CT £454.63 TOTE £17.50: £4.50, £1.10, £2.40, £2.60; EX 95.80 Trifecta £149.80 Pool: £210.99 - 1.00 winning ticket..
Owner Fontwell Park Partnership **Bred** Baron F Von Oppenheim **Trained** Woodingdean, E Sussex

FOCUS
A modest handicap in terms of quality, but competitive in nature. However, the gallop was weak and it paid to be close to the pace. The placed horses appear to have run close to their recent banded form.

417 PONTIN'S "BOOK EARLY" CLAIMING STKS 1m (P)
2:00 (2:01) (Class 6) 3-Y-O **£2,184** (£644; £322) **Stalls High**

Form RPR

0-05 **1** **Jemima Godfrey**^{5} [357] 3-8-10 ....(t) TPQueally 4 48
(J Pearce) *trckd ldr: rdn over 2f out: narrow ld 1f out: hrd rdn and hld on: all out* **15/2**

00 **2** *nk* **Tenement (IRE)**^{12} [293] 3-9-5 .... ShaneKelly 5 56
(J A Osborne) *trckd ldrs: rdn over 2f out: effrt to chal 1f out: nt qckn and hld last 100yds* **3/1**^{2}

3 *nk* **Bahama Gold** 3-8-9 .... NeilChalmers$^{(3)}$ 1 49
(A M Balding) *trckd ldrs and rn green: effrt 2f out: drvn to chal 1f out: no ex last 100yds* **9/2**^{3}

006- **4** *nk* **Best Woman**^{84} [6518] 3-8-4 50....................................... JackMitchell$^{(7)}$ 7 47
(P Howling) *in tch on outer: rdn 3f out: wd and nt keen bnd 2f out: styd on again ins fnl f* **15/2**

-226 **5** *1/2* **Razzano (IRE)**^{6} [348] 3-8-10 55.................................. JerryO'Dwyer$^{(3)}$ 6 48
(A M Hales) *t.k.h: trckd ldrs: rdn over 2f out: nt qckn over 1f out: one pce after* **2/1**^{1}

5-00 **6** *2 1/2* **Tumblin Rosie**^{15} [253] 3-8-10 48... NCallan 2 39
(M Blanshard) *mde most: rdn over 2f out: hdd 1f out: wknd rapidly* **20/1**

0356 **7** *3/4* **Splendidio**^{16} [237] 3-8-10 50 ow1....................................... DaneO'Neill 3 37
(D K Ivory) *t.k.h hld up in last: effrt on outer whn nt clr run 2f out: swtchd ins over 1f out: wknd fnl f* **9/1**

1m 41.58s (2.15) **Going Correction** -0.025s/f (Stan) **7** Ran SP% **114.8**
Speed ratings (Par 95):88,87,87,87,86 84,83
CSF £30.47 TOTE £8.30: £2.80, £1.80; EX 39.30.Bahama Gold was claimed by Mr David J. Smith for £8,000.
Owner Miss Audrey Lanham **Bred** Southill Stud **Trained** Newmarket, Suffolk

FOCUS
A weak claimer, run at an ordinary pace, and the form looks pretty worthless.
Razzano(IRE) Official explanation: jockey said filly had lost a shoe

418 PHOTO BOOKS FROM BONUSPRINT.COM MAIDEN STKS 1m (P)
2:30 (2:33) (Class 5) 3-Y-O **£3,071** (£906; £453) **Stalls High**

Form RPR

2- **1** **Barshiba (IRE)**^{52} [6886] 3-8-12 .... JohnEgan 12 84+
(D R C Elsworth) *dwlt: t.k.h: hld up in midfield on outer: prog over 2f out: shkn up to ld over 1f out: r.o wl* **7/4**^{1}

2 *2 1/2* **Zaham (USA)** 3-9-0 .... GregFairley$^{(3)}$ 1 83
(M Johnston) *cl up: effrt 2f out: rdn and green over 1f out: wnt 2nd last 100yds : no ch w wnr* **7/4**^{1}

0- **3** *hd* **Surrey Spinner**^{240} [2579] 3-9-3 .... JimCrowley 2 83
(Mrs A J Perrett) *dwlt: rousted along to go prom: effrt 2f out: hrd rdn and kpt on fnl f* **12/1**^{3}

0-4 **4** *2 1/2* **Barkass (UAE)**^{21} [193] 3-9-3 .... DaneO'Neill 11 77
(M P Tregoning) *hld up in rr: gng wl enough over 2f out: sn outpcd: kpt on one pce fr over 1f out* **5/1**^{2}

5 *nk* **Ochre (IRE)** 3-8-12 .... MatthewHenry 9 71
(M A Jarvis) *trckd ldrs: led 2f out to over 1f out: wknd* **20/1**

6 *4* **Fantastic Cee (IRE)** 3-8-12 .... TPQueally 7 62+
(J Noseda) *dwlt: wl in rr: n.m.r 5f out: sn rdn: outpcd fr 3f out: no ch after* **20/1**

-0 **7** *1 3/4* **Adabi**^{19} [208] 3-9-3 .... RichardHughes 10 63
(M P Tregoning) *t.k.h: sn trckd ldr: led 3f out to 2f out: green and wknd* **12/1**^{3}

8 *6* **Camp Counsellor** 3-9-3 .... ShaneKelly 8 49
(J A Osborne) *reluctnat to enter stalls: hld up towards rr: lost tch 3f out: wl bhd after* **33/1**

9 *1/2* **Gee Ceffyl Bach** 3-8-12 .... EdwardCreighton 5 43
(M R Channon) *s.s: sn rdn in last: a bhd* **100/1**

00- **10** *3 1/2* **Bali Belony**^{56} [6840] 3-8-12 .... RobertHavlin 6 35
(J R Jenkins) *nvr beyond midfield: u.p and struggling over 4f out* **150/1**

0 **11** *3/4* **Tia Jade**^{21} [193] 3-8-13 ow1.. AntonyProcter 4 34
(M J Gingell) *led to 3f out: wknd rapidly: eased* **150/1**

12 *3 1/2* **Elamar** 3-8-12 .... MickyFenton 3 25
(D G Bridgwater) *in tch to 1/2-way: wknd u.p* **150/1**

1m 38.09s (-1.34) **Going Correction** -0.025s/f (Stan) **12** Ran SP% **120.2**
Speed ratings (Par 97):105,102,102,99,99 95,93,87,87,83 83,79
CSF £4.36 TOTE £3.00: £1.10, £1.40, £3.10; EX 7.20 Trifecta £43.10 Pool: £655.90 - 10.79 winning tickets..
Owner J C Smith **Bred** Littleton Stud **Trained** Newmarket, Suffolk

FOCUS
An interesting maiden, containing six lightly-raced sorts and six debutants, but run at just a fair tempo. The fourth looks the best guide to the form and it seems pretty sound.
Barkass(UAE) Official explanation: jockey said colt had lost a front shoe
Fantastic Cee(IRE) Official explanation: jockey said filly hung left
Camp Counsellor Official explanation: jockey said colt had no more to give

419 PONTINS.COM H'CAP 6f (P)
3:05 (3:05) (Class 4) (0-85,85) 4-Y-O+ **£4,857** (£1,445; £722; £360) **Stalls Low**

Form RPR

326- **1** **Woodnook**^{56} [6849] 4-9-1 **84**... JimmyFortune 6 96
(J A R Toller) *trckd ldrs gng wl: prog 2f out: led ins fnl f: drvn and in command after* **7/4**^{1}

2-31 **2** *1 1/2* **Lucayos**^{14} [262] 4-8-5 **77**.. RichardKingscote$^{(3)}$ 4 84
(Mrs H Sweeting) *t.k.h: disp ld: def advantage over 1f out: hdd and outpcd ins fnl f* **11/2**^{2}

-350 **3** *1 1/4* **Pawan (IRE)**^{18} [227] 7-8-8 **82**...(b) AnnStokell$^{(5)}$ 7 86
(Miss A Stokell) *dwlt: in tch in midfield: effrt over 1f out: urged along and styd on to take 3rd last strides* **25/1**

050- **4** *hd* **Adantino**^{158} [5096] 8-8-9 **78**..(b) JimCrowley 2 81
(B R Millman) *hld up in rr: gng wl but trapped on inner over 1f out: twice swtchd rt ins fnl f: r.o: no ch* **16/1**

1-00 **5** *hd* **Quiet Times (IRE)**^{21} [198] 8-9-2 **85**.......................................(b) NCallan 1 87
(K A Ryan) *disp ld to over 1f out: fdd ins fnl f* **11/1**

00-0 **6** *shd* **Regal Royale**^{14} [259] 4-8-7 **79**...................................... JerryO'Dwyer$^{(3)}$ 5 81
(Peter Grayson) *dwlt: hld up in midfield: rdn and styd on fr over 1f out: nrst fin* **20/1**

0401 **7** *1 1/2* **Night Prospector**^{12} [289] 7-8-6 **80**..............................(p) TolleyDean$^{(5)}$ 3 83+
(B Palling) *t.k.h: trckd ldrs: rdn and no prog whn bdly hmpd over 1f out: nt rcvr* **9/1**

4-50 **8** *shd* **Pinchbeck**^{13} [277] 8-8-7 **76**.. MatthewHenry 8 73
(M A Jarvis) *settled in rr: pushed along fr 1/2-way: no prog tl styd on ins fnl f* **16/1**

00-0 **9** *hd* **Garstang**^{21} [190] 4-8-7 **76**...(b) AdrianMcCarthy 9 73
(Peter Grayson) *plld hrd early: pressed ldng pair: edgd lft over 1f out: wknd* **14/1**

-001 **10** *3/4* **Seneschal**^{5} [359] 6-8-2 **68** 6ex... ChrisCatlin 11 65
(A B Haynes) *hld up in last pair: wd bnd 2f out: struggling after* **12/1**

13-4 **11** *3* **Briannsta (IRE)**^{21} [190] 5-8-9 **78**....................................... AdamKirby 12 63
(C G Cox) *chsd ldrs: rdn 1/2-way: sn btn* **6/1**^{3}

00-0 **12** *7* **Fromsong (IRE)**^{32} [79] 9-8-11 **80**....................................... DaneO'Neill 10 44
(D K Ivory) *hld up in rr: rdn and wknd over 2f out: t.o* **16/1**

1m 10.5s (-2.31) **Going Correction** -0.025s/f (Stan) course record **12** Ran SP% **125.0**
Speed ratings (Par 105):114,112,110,110,109 109,107,107,107,106 102,92
CSF £11.56 CT £192.96 TOTE £3.10: £1.20, £2.10, £4.40; EX 16.90 Trifecta £440.90 Pool: £689.33 - 1.11 winning tickets..
Owner Mrs Julia Scott **Bred** Glebe Stud **Trained** Newmarket, Suffolk

FOCUS
A fair handicap, run at a good pace and won by a filly used to running in better company than this. The time was fair and the form looks sound for the grade.
Night Prospector Official explanation: jockey said gelding suffered interference in running
Garstang Official explanation: jockey said gelding hung left in home straight
Briannsta(IRE) Official explanation: jockey said gelding had never been travelling

420 PONTIN'S HOLIDAYS H'CAP 1m 2f (P)
3:40 (3:40) (Class 2) (0-100,94) 4-Y-O+
£11,217 (£3,358; £1,679; £840; £419; £210) **Stalls Low**

Form RPR

3-11 **1** **Mighty**^{7} [340] 4-8-8 **85**.. JohnEgan 4 96+
(Jane Chapple-Hyam) *trckd ldrs: pushed along wl over 2f out: rdn and picked up wl to ld jst over 1f out: sn clr* **8/11**^{1}

11-2 **2** *2* **Cusoon**^{14} [264] 5-9-4 **94**... RichardHughes 1 101+
(G L Moore) *t.k.h: hld up in slowly run r: last on inner 2f out: drvn and r.o to take 2nd fnl 100yds: no ch of chalng wnr* **15/8**^{2}

650- **3** *1/2* **Pagan Sword**^{168} [4810] 5-8-12 **88**... JimCrowley 2 94
(Mrs A J Perrett) *dwlt: hld up in last trio: prog over 2f out: rdn to chal over 1f out: nt qckn* **25/1**

-062 **4** *nk* **Tous Les Deux**^{14} [263] 4-8-3 **80** oh9........................... AdrianMcCarthy 5 85
(Peter Grayson) *hld up in last: prog on outer 3f out: cl up over 1f out: one pce* **40/1**

-334 **5** *1* **Atlantic Quest (USA)**^{15} [255] 8-8-7 **83**.............................. DaleGibson 7 86
(Miss Venetia Williams) *trckd ldrs: lost pl over 2f out and in last pair: drvn and hanging over 1f out: no imp after* **14/1**^{3}

/03- **6** *hd* **Blue Sky Thinking (IRE)**^{287} [1281] 8-8-13 **89**................. PatCosgrave 6 92
(K R Burke) *led at slow pce: rdn and hdd 3f out: stl cl up over 1f out: fdd fnl f* **40/1**

53-4 **7** *1/2* **Langford**^{14} [264] 7-8-8 **87**... SaleemGolam$^{(3)}$ 8 89
(M H Tompkins) *trckd ldr: led 3f out: drvn and hdd jst over 1f out: wknd* **20/1**

2m 7.12s (-0.67) **Going Correction** -0.025s/f (Stan)
WFA 4 from 5yo+ 1lb **7** Ran SP% **112.8**
Speed ratings (Par 109):101,99,99,98,97 97,97
CSF £2.12 CT £10.76 TOTE £1.70: £1.30, £1.50; EX 2.80 Trifecta £19.70 Pool: £1,273.53 - 45.77 winning tickets..
Owner Franconson Partners, V Church, J Chapple-Hyam **Bred** Cheveley Park Stud Ltd **Trained** Newmarket, Suffolk
■ Stewards' Enquiry : Adrian McCarthy one-day ban: used whip with excessive frequency (Feb 21)

FOCUS
A good handicap, but the pace was slow until the final three furlongs and the form looks dubious with the fourth running too well for comfort.

NOTEBOOK
Mighty ◆ went up 7lb for his win here last time, but he remains on an upward curve. Powering clear in good style, he looks capable of handling another rise in the weights. (tchd 5-6, 10-11 in places and evens in a place)
Cusoon ran into an improving winner here, and time should show the concession of 10lb to have been an impossible task. (op 9-4 tchd 13-8)
Pagan Sword ran a couple of decent races on turf last year, and he already has one win on Polytrack to his name. Unraced since August, he was still 6lb above his winning mark here but remains one to keep a close eye on for a winning opportunity. (op 16-1)
Tous Les Deux would have found this company much stiffer than last time, so he did really well in the circumstances from 9lb out of the handicap. (op 33-1)
Atlantic Quest(USA) gets this trip well enough these days, but this was a hot race, and he was never finding enough.
Blue Sky Thinking(IRE) is theoretically on a winning mark at present, but that was achieved in 2004, and this was a tough assignment on his first outing since last April. That said, he ran with credit for a long way. (op 33-1)
Langford came into the race in fair form, but not flying high enough to have a serious hope of beating some smart opponents.

421 DIGITAL PRINTS FROM BONUSPRINT.COM MAIDEN STKS 5f (P)
4:15 (4:15) (Class 5) 3-Y-0+ £3,071 (£906; £453) Stalls High

Form RPR
6-6 1 Sohraab[17] 231 3-8-13 .... SteveDrowne 1 61+
(H Morrison) *dwlt: sn w ldr: led over 1f out: reminders ent fnl f: kpt on* 7/4[1]
03-2 2 1 1/4 Ceredig[13] 282 4-9-13 54 .... (t) RichardHughes 6 62
(W R Muir) *hld up in last: prog 1/2-way: rdn to chse wnr ins fnl f: no real imp* 5/1[3]
42 3 1 1/4 Time Share (IRE)[7] 343 3-8-8 .... ShaneKelly 2 47
(J A Osborne) *t.k.h: hld up bhd ldrs: outpcd wl over 1f out: plugged on to take 3rd nr fin* 3/1[2]
0-35 4 1/2 Optical Seclusion (IRE)[13] 282 4-9-10 50 .... (b) SaleemGolam(3) 3 56?
(T J Etherington) *t.k.h: mde most to over 1f out: wknd tamely* 20/1
5-36 5 nk Wilmington[10] 312 3-8-13 70 .... PaulMulrennan 4 49
(N P Littmoden) *hld up: last and rdn over 2f out: no real prog* 3/1[2]
43-6 6 shd Nawayea[13] 282 4-9-1 52 .... (b) KirstyMilczarek(7) 5 49
(C N Allen) *racd on outer: chsd ldrs: nt qckn wl over 1f out: btn after* 20/1

59.42 secs (-0.36) **Going Correction** -0.025s/f (Stan)
WFA 3 from 4yo 14lb 6 Ran SP% 112.6
Speed ratings (Par 103):101,99,97,96,95 95
CSF £11.10 TOTE £2.30: £1.70, £2.00; EX 8.40.
Owner Pangfield Racing **Bred** T J Billington **Trained** East Ilsley, Berks

FOCUS
A routine maiden run at a disappointing pace until halfway. The form looks modest, although that should help the winner get a nice mark for handicapping.

422 GO PONTIN'S H'CAP 1m 2f (P)
4:45 (4:45) (Class 5) (0-75,73) 4-Y-0+ £3,238 (£963; £481; £240) Stalls Low

Form RPR
/4-4 1 Oscar Snowman[14] 260 4-9-2 72 .... RichardHughes 7 80+
(M P Tregoning) *dwlt: sn trckd ldng pair: effrt to chse ldr over 2f out: drvn over 1f out: r.o to ld last 50yds* 11/10[1]
3-11 2 1/2 Spot The Subbie (IRE)[10] 313 4-8-9 65 .... JohnEgan 5 74+
(Jamie Poulton) *hld up in 4th: prog on inner and nt clr run 2f out: tried to chal and nt clr run fnl f: r.o nr fin* 2/1[2]
12-4 3 shd Generous Lad (IRE)[21] 195 4-8-12 68 .... (p) DaneO'Neill 3 75
(A B Haynes) *dwlt: hld up in 5th: rdn over 2f out: hanging over 1f out: r.o ins fnl f: nvr quite able to chal* 7/1
61-2 4 hd Samarinda (USA)[28] 117 4-9-1 71 .... MickyFenton 4 78
(Mrs P Sly) *trckd ldr: led over 3f out: kicked 2 l clr over 1f out: hdd & wknd last 50yds* 11/2[3]
/50- 5 2 1/2 Country Affair (USA)[306] 952 4-9-3 73 .... JimmyFortune 6 75
(P R Webber) *rrd bdly s: hld up in last: outpcd wl over 2f out: styd on fr over 1f out: nt rch ldrs* 25/1
05-0 6 15 Count Kristo[14] 259 5-9-0 69 .... AdamKirby 1 41
(B G Powell) *t.k.h: led to over 3f out: sn wknd u.p: t.o* 33/1

2m 5.63s (-2.16) **Going Correction** -0.025s/f (Stan)
WFA 4 from 5yo+ 1lb 6 Ran SP% 115.6
Speed ratings (Par 103):107,106,106,106,104 92
CSF £3.71 TOTE £2.00: £1.20, £1.70; EX 4.30 Place 6 £19.98, Place 5 £8.73..
Owner A E Pakenham **Bred** Gainsborough Stud Management Ltd **Trained** Lambourn, Berks

FOCUS
A fair handicap, but it was run at a modest pace until approaching the home straight. It has been rated at face value for the time being, with the bare form not strong.
Generous Lad(IRE) Official explanation: jockey said gelding hung left
Country Affair(USA) Official explanation: jockey said colt missed the break
T/Plt: £30.30 to a £1 stake. Pool: £104,743.05. 2,521.85 winning tickets. T/Qpdt: £4.80 to a £1 stake. Pool: £5,467.30. 833.70 winning tickets. JN

402 WOLVERHAMPTON (A.W) (L-H)
Saturday, February 10

OFFICIAL GOING: Standard
Wind: Light against Weather: Light rain

423 PONTIN'S "BOOK EARLY" MAIDEN STKS 5f 216y(P)
7:00 (7:01) (Class 5) 3-Y-0 £3,071 (£906; £453) Stalls Low

Form RPR
440- 1 Go On Green (IRE)[136] 5608 3-9-3 70 .... EddieAhern 1 85+
(E A L Dunlop) *trckd ldrs: rdn to ld 1f out: sn hung lft: r.o wl* 2/1[2]
2-22 2 5 Bertie Swift[12] 290 3-9-3 68 .... JimCrowley 6 66
(J Gallagher) *chsd ldrs: rdn 1/2-way: swtchd rt over 1f out: styd on* 7/4[1]
35 3 1/2 Not Now Lewis (IRE)[18] 222 3-9-3 .... ShaneKelly 8 64
(J A Osborne) *chsd ldr: led over 2f out: rdn: hung lft and hdd 1f out: wknd wl ins fnl f* 14/1
2-23 4 2 Le Masque[16] 237 3-9-0 67 .... MarkLawson(3) 7 58
(B Smart) *led: hung rt and hdd over 2f out: wknd fnl f* 11/2[3]
343- 5 3/4 Amber Isle[71] 6662 3-9-3 66 .... DanielTudhope 5 56
(D Carroll) *hld up: hdwy over 2f out: nt clr run over 1f out: nt trble ldrs* 11/2[3]
06 6 1 1/4 Kiwi The Clown (IRE)[15] 258 3-8-12 .... JamieMoriarty(5) 10 52
(R A Fahey) *in rr: shkn up 1/2-way: hung lft over 1f out: nvr trbld ldrs* 80/1
0- 7 3 The Power Of Phil[198] 3860 3-9-0 .... StephenDonohoe(3) 2 42
(Miss Joanne Priest) *s.i.s: hung lft over 1f out: n.d* 80/1
5 8 3 1/2 Lady Fifer[27] 127 3-8-12 .... GrahamGibbons 3 35+
(Jane Chapple-Hyam) *sn pushed along in rr: no ch whn hmpd ins fnl f* 16/1
0 9 nk Coleorton Dagger[16] 237 3-8-12 .... NCallan 9 25
(K A Ryan) *prom: rdn over 2f out: hung lft and wknd over 1f out* 50/1
10 nk Diamond Key (IRE)[97] 6354 3-8-9 .... JerryO'Dwyer(3) 4 24
(M G Quinlan) *s.i.s: a in rr* 50/1

1m 15.23s (-0.58) **Going Correction** 0.0s/f (Stan) 10 Ran SP% 119.4
Speed ratings (Par 97):103,96,95,93,92 90,86,81,81,80
CSF £6.04 TOTE £3.30: £2.00, £1.50, £1.90; EX 10.90.
Owner Khalifa Sultan **Bred** Duncan A McGregor **Trained** Newmarket, Suffolk

FOCUS
An ordinary maiden, but the result makes sense with regards to official figures.
Amber Isle Official explanation: jockey said gelding hung left-handed
The Power Of Phil Official explanation: jockey said colt hung left-handed

424 BONUSPRINT.COM H'CAP 7f 32y(P)
7:30 (7:31) (Class 5) (0-75,75) 4-Y-0+ £3,071 (£906; £453) Stalls High

Form RPR
003- 1 Hypocrisy[63] 6773 4-9-1 74 .... DanielTudhope 8 86
(D Carroll) *hld up: hdwy over 2f out: rdn to ld and hung lft ins fnl f: r.o* 13/2[3]
2552 2 1 Sir Douglas[5] 371 4-8-3 67 .... MichaelJStainton(5) 5 77
(R A Harris) *plld hrd: led 6f out: rdn and hdd over 1f out: ev ch whn hmpd ins fnl f: styd on* 11/4[1]
4-61 3 nk Danetime Lord (IRE)[17] 234 4-8-9 68 .... (p) NCallan 6 77
(K A Ryan) *trckd ldrs: racd keenly: led over 1f out: sn rdn: hdd and no ex ins fnl f* 10/3[2]
4126 4 nk Dudley Docker (IRE)[11] 308 5-8-7 73 .... KellyHarrison(7) 12 81
(D Carroll) *s.i.s: hld up: hdwy over 1f out: nt rch ldrs* 20/1
16-0 5 1 Methaaly (IRE)[17] 234 4-8-7 66 .... PaulEddery 2 71
(Jane Chapple-Hyam) *hld up: hdwy over 1f out: styd on* 9/1
030- 6 nk Hoh Wotanite[49] 6928 4-8-8 67 .... GrahamGibbons 3 72
(R Hollinshead) *chsd ldrs: nt clr run and lost pl over 2f out: hdwy over 1f out: styd on* 15/2
123- 7 1 3/4 Littledodayno (IRE)[143] 5487 4-8-9 71 .... JamesDoyle(3) 10 71
(M Wigham) *chsd ldrs: rdn over 1f out: styd on same pce* 28/1
453- 8 nk Supercast (IRE)[45] 6952 4-8-9 68 .... EddieAhern 11 67
(W M Brisbourne) *hld up: styd on ins fnl f: nvr nrr* 18/1
165- 9 1/2 Littleton Telchar (USA)[57] 6830 7-8-11 73 .... LiamJones(3) 9 71
(S W Hall) *chsd ldrs: rdn over 2f out: wknd fnl f* 10/1
0-36 10 nk Conrad[14] 262 4-8-5 69 ow3 .... JamieMoriarty(5) 4 66
(R A Fahey) *s.i.s: hdwy over 5f out: rdn and wknd over 1f out* 16/1
000- 11 1 3/4 Local Poet[191] 4090 6-8-11 75 .... DuranFentiman(5) 1 68
(I Semple) *led 1f: chsd ldrs: rdn over 2f out: wknd over 1f out* 33/1
00-0 12 11 Polish Emperor (USA)[32] 81 7-8-13 72 .... (p) RobertWinston 7 36
(D W Barker) *hld up in tch: plld hrd: hmpd 6f out: rdn and wknd over 1f out* 50/1

1m 30.19s (-0.21) **Going Correction** 0.0s/f (Stan) 12 Ran SP% 118.2
Speed ratings (Par 103):101,99,99,99,98 97,95,95,94,94 92,79
CSF £23.63 CT £71.52 TOTE £9.60: £1.30, £1.80, £2.00; EX 44.50.
Owner Miss S Molloy **Bred** Hyperion Bloodstock **Trained** Sledmere, E Yorks

FOCUS
A modest handicap run at only a fair pace. The form looks solid rated through the runner-up, third and fourth.

425 PHOTO BOOKS FROM BONUSPRINT.COM (S) STKS 1m 1f 103y(P)
8:00 (8:01) (Class 6) 4-6-Y-0 £2,047 (£604; £302) Stalls Low

Form RPR
-413 1 Norwegian[20] 206 6-9-5 53 .... (p) PaulEddery 8 57+
(Ian Williams) *trckd ldrs: led over 1f out: drvn out* 7/4[1]
52-0 2 3/4 Rose Muwasim[10] 309 4-8-8 55 .... (p) DaleGibson 11 43
(K J Burke) *hld up: hdwy over 2f out: rdn and hung lft fr over 1f out: styd on* 11/1
04-5 3 hd Insignia (IRE)[9] 321 5-8-10 41 .... LiamJones(3) 9 48
(W M Brisbourne) *s.i.s: hld up: hdwy and hung lft fr over 1f out: styd on* 22/1
0-46 4 3/4 Elms Schoolboy[6] 349 5-9-5 45 .... (b) IanMongan 2 52
(P Howling) *slowly into stride: hld up: hdwy u.p over 1f out: nt rch ldrs* 13/2[3]
0-05 5 2 Ligne D'Eau[22] 182 6-8-10 42 .... (b) StephenDonohoe(3) 3 42
(P D Evans) *led: racd keenly: rdn and hdd over 1f out: wknd ins fnl f* 33/1
646- 6 nk Linton Dancer (IRE)[44] 6957 4-8-8 42 .... TPQueally 4 36
(J R Weymes) *prom: rdn over 3f out: styd on same pce appr fnl f* 22/1
00-0 7 1/2 Soviet Threat (IRE)[12] 298 6-8-13 52 .... EddieAhern 13 40
(A G Juckes) *hld up: hdwy over 2f out: hmpd and lost pl 2f out: n.d after* 16/1
1405 8 1 1/4 Bathwick Emma (IRE)[12] 298 4-8-11 48 .... (p) JamesDoyle(3) 7 39
(M A Doyle) *w ldr: rdn and ev ch 2f out: wknd fnl f* 18/1
10-0 9 3 Shaheer (IRE)[38] 19 5-9-5 54 .... (v) JimCrowley 12 38
(J Gallagher) *chsd ldrs: rdn over 3f out: wknd over 1f out* 9/1
0 10 1/2 Kates Guest (IRE)[17] 230 5-8-13 52 .... (b) FergusSweeney 5 31
(B G Powell) *chsd ldrs: rdn over 3f out: wknd over 1f out* 28/1
000- 11 22 Dylan (IRE)[252] 2249 4-8-10 44 .... AndrewMullen(3) 10 —
(M A Doyle) *hld up: bhd fnl 4f* 66/1
050/ 12 7 Chief Dipper[525] 4963 5-8-13 68 .... ShaneKelly 1 —
(D Morris) *hld up: rdn and wknd over 3f out* 4/1[2]

2m 3.95s (1.33) **Going Correction** 0.0s/f (Stan) 12 Ran SP% 115.8
Speed ratings: 94,93,93,92,90 90,90,88,86,85 66,60
CSF £20.34 TOTE £2.80: £1.30, £1.60, £6.10; EX 13.50.The winner was bought in for 6,500gns.
Owner Robert Bee **Bred** Darley **Trained** Portway, Worcs

FOCUS
A very moderate event run at a modest early tempo, and the form looks very suspect.
Chief Dipper Official explanation: jockey said gelding had no more to give

426 JEZ FIRTH 40TH BIRTHDAY CELEBRATION H'CAP 1m 141y(P)
8:30 (8:31) (Class 6) (0-60,62) 4-Y-0+ £2,388 (£705; £352) Stalls Low

Form RPR
0530 1 Golden Spectrum (IRE)[13] 286 8-8-6 57 .... (b) LukeMorris(7) 10 64
(R A Harris) *s.i.s: hld up: hdwy over 1f out: edgd lft ins fnl f: r.o to ld nr fin* 25/1
2013 2 1/2 Discotheque (USA)[5] 363 4-9-4 62 .... IanMongan 13 68
(P Howling) *hld up: hdwy over 2f out: rdn and ev ch ins fnl f: r.o* 4/1[2]
0-16 3 shd Tancredi (SWE)[5] 363 5-9-3 61 .... HayleyTurner 2 67
(N B King) *led: hdd over 6f out: led 4f out: rdn and edgd rt over 1f out: hdd nr fin* 8/1
61-0 4 shd Diamond Dan (IRE)[5] 371 5-8-9 56 .... StephenDonohoe(3) 4 62
(P D Evans) *hld up: hdwy over 2fr out: rdn over 1f out: r.o* 7/2[1]
-420 5 nk Under Fire (IRE)[20] 206 4-8-10 54 .... ShaneKelly 11 59
(A W Carroll) *a.p: chsd ldr 4f out: rdn and ev ch ins fnl f: unable qck nr fin* 8/1
-631 6 nk Harare[20] 206 6-8-13 60 .... (b) JamesDoyle(3) 5 64
(R J Price) *hld up in tch: rdn and swtchd lft over 1f out: styd on* 4/1[2]
60-0 7 1 1/4 Kew The Music[10] 313 7-8-11 55 .... ChrisCatlin 6 57
(M R Channon) *hld up: hdwy over 2f out: rdn over 1f out: styd on same pce ins fnl f* 18/1
-205 8 3/4 Ciccone[5] 363 4-9-0 58 .... (p) FergusSweeney 3 58
(G L Moore) *s.i.s: hld up: hdwy under press over 1f out: nvr nrr* 7/1[3]
000- 9 1 1/2 Itcanbedone Again (IRE)[121] 4925 8-8-11 55 .... PaulEddery 8 52
(Ian Williams) *hld up: rdn over 1f out: n.d* 16/1

40-0 **10** *1 3/4* **Dallma (IRE)**[29] 110 4-8-11 **55** ... TPQueally 12 48
(C E Brittain) *chsd ldrs: rdn over 3f out: hmpd wl over 1f out: sn hung lft and wknd* **22/1**

055- **11** *7* **Rainbow's Classic**[20] 5446 4-8-11 **60** ... DuranFentiman(5) 1 39
(P Beaumont) *chsd ldr tl led over 6f out: rdn and hdd 4f out: wknd over 2f out* **66/1**

1m 51.05s (-0.71) **Going Correction** 0.0s/f (Stan) **11** Ran SP% **117.8**
Speed ratings (Par 101):103,102,102,102,102 101,100,100,98,97 90
CSF £121.26 CT £914.58 TOTE £30.60: £7.80, £1.90, £5.30; EX 83.90.
Owner Peter A Price **Bred** Orpendale And Global Investments **Trained** Earlswood, Monmouths
FOCUS
A solid field for the grade but a much slower time in comparison with the other race run over the distance on the night. The form has to be treated as suspect for that reason.
Harare Official explanation: jockey said gelding was denied a clear run

427 PONTINSBINGO.COM H'CAP — 1m 141y(P)
9:00 (9:00) (Class 5) (0-75,75) 4-Y-O+ **£3,071** (£906; £453) **Stalls** Low

Form RPR
01-1 **1** **Bold Diktator**[17] 233 5-8-13 **72** ... JimCrowley 3 83
(Tom Dascombe) *led 1f: trckd ldrs: rdn to ld over 1f out: styd on* **7/2**[1]

562- **2** *1/2* **Pab Special (IRE)**[104] 6240 4-8-8 **70** ... AndrewElliott(3) 7 80
(K R Burke) *led over 7f out: hdd over 6f out: led again 3f out: rdn: edgd lft and hdd over 1f out: styd on* **9/2**[2]

-003 **3** *1 1/2* **Councellor (FR)**[6] 351 5-9-1 **74** ... (t) EddieAhern 5 81
(Stef Liddiard) *hld up: hdwy over 2f out: rdn over 1f out: styd on same pce* **6/1**

0-44 **4** *2 1/2* **Grey Boy (GER)**[19] 218 6-8-11 **75** ... JamieMoriarty(5) 2 77
(R A Fahey) *hld up in tch: rdn over 2f out: wknd ins fnl f* **7/1**

40-6 **5** *7* **Defi (IRE)**[25] 151 5-8-2 **66** ... DuranFentiman(5) 6 53
(I Semple) *chsd ldrs: rdn over 2f out: sn wknd* **25/1**

2-21 **6** *nk* **Chia (IRE)**[12] 299 4-8-7 **66** ... RobertHavlin 1 52
(D Haydn Jones) *hld up in tch: rdn: hung lft and wknd over 2f out* **7/1**

-512 **7** *nk* **Luckylover**[8] 334 4-9-0 **73** ... TPQueally 8 59
(M G Quinlan) *s.i.s: sn chsng ldrs: led over 6f out: rdn and hdd 3f out: wknd over 2f out* **11/2**[3]

65-0 **8** *2 1/2* **Samuel Charles**[22] 185 9-9-2 **75** ... RobertWinston 4 55
(C R Dore) *hld up: rdn and wknd over 2f out* **13/2**

1m 49.65s (-2.11) **Going Correction** 0.0s/f (Stan) **8** Ran SP% **112.3**
Speed ratings (Par 103):109,108,107,105,98 98,98,96
CSF £18.47 CT £89.59 TOTE £4.50: £2.20, £2.60, £1.10; EX 23.90.
Owner Oneway RSM Racing Club **Bred** T J And Mrs Heywood **Trained** Lambourn, Berks
FOCUS
A solid handicap run at a decent tempo, and the form should work out.

428 PONTIN'S FAMILY HOLIDAYS H'CAP — 1m 4f 50y(P)
9:30 (9:31) (Class 5) (0-75,75) 4-Y-O+ **£3,071** (£906; £453) **Stalls** Low

Form RPR
36-5 **1** **Pass The Port**[18] 226 6-9-3 **73** ... (p) RobertHavlin 1 81
(D Haydn Jones) *hld up in tch: racd keenly: led over 1f out: rdn out* **7/2**[3]

-021 **2** *hd* **Three Thieves (UAE)**[8] 332 4-8-6 **65** ... EddieAhern 10 73+
(M S Saunders) *a.p: rdn over 1f out: edgd lft ins fnl f: r.o* **3/1**[2]

2-41 **3** *1/2* **Reaching Out (IRE)**[14] 263 5-8-4 **63** ... (b) JamesDoyle(3) 2 70+
(N P Littmoden) *chsd ldrs: rdn to ld over 1f out: sn hdd: styd on* **11/2**

0-10 **4** *1* **Desert Leader (IRE)**[20] 205 6-9-4 **74** ... ShaneKelly 7 79
(W M Brisbourne) *s.s: sn chsng ldr: led over 3f out: rdn and hdd over 1f out: no ex ins fnl f* **14/1**

1-21 **5** *nk* **Melvino**[12] 297 5-9-1 **71** ... DeanMcKeown 3 76
(T D Barron) *s.i.s: hld up: plld hrd: effrt and nt clr run over 2f out: styd on ins fnl f: nt trble ldrs* **9/4**[1]

-026 **6** *2 1/2* **Augustine**[5] 362 6-9-5 **75** ... JimCrowley 9 76
(P W Hiatt) *led: hdd over 3f out: rdn over 1f out: no ex* **11/1**

20-0 **7** *9* **Wellington Hall (GER)**[12] 297 9-9-3 **73** ... BrianReilly 5 60
(M Wigham) *hld up and bhd: n.d* **50/1**

02-0 **8** *38* **Key Partners (IRE)**[31] 88 6-8-9 **65** ow1 ... RobertWinston 8 —
(B D Leavy) *hld up: plld hrd: hdwy over 7f out: wknd over 2f out* **14/1**

2m 47.99s (5.57) **Going Correction** 0.0s/f (Stan)
WFA 4 from 5yo+ 3lb **8** Ran SP% **117.0**
Speed ratings (Par 103):81,80,80,79,79 78,72,46
CSF £14.86 CT £56.52 TOTE £4.60: £1.30, £1.40, £2.00; EX 18.90 Place 6 £32.13, Place 5 £22.15.
Owner The Porters **Bred** Meon Valley Stud **Trained** Efail Isaf, Rhondda C Taff
FOCUS
A modest handicap run at a very slow tempo. The form looks very suspect as a result.
Key Partners(IRE) Official explanation: jockey said gelding ran too freely early and hung left
T/Plt: £27.60 to a £1 stake. Pool: £89,558.40. 2,367.85 winning tickets. T/Qpdt: £18.60 to a £1 stake. Pool: £3,817.30. 151.30 winning tickets. CR

387 SOUTHWELL (L-H)
Sunday, February 11

OFFICIAL GOING: Standard to slow
The ground was described as patchy and holding at first but it dried out quickly and from race three onwards was described as 'perfectly normal'.
Wind: Moderate, half-behind. Weather: Fine and sunny but breezy and chilly.

429 GO PONTIN'S MEDIAN AUCTION MAIDEN STKS — 5f (F)
1:40 (1:42) (Class 5) 3-Y-O **£2,968** (£876; £438) **Stalls** High

Form RPR
33-2 **1** **Ronnie Howe**[17] 237 3-9-3 73 ... PhillipMakin 4 55+
(M Dods) *trckd ldr: led over 2f out: pushed clr ins last: easily* **2/7**[1]

65-0 **2** *4* **Mangano**[27] 136 3-9-0 40 ... StephenDonohoe(3) 3 41
(A Berry) *chsd ldrs: kpt on to take 2nd ins last: no ch w wnr* **50/1**

3 *1 1/2* **Royal Dagger (IRE)** 3-9-3 ... ChrisCatlin 1 35
(Rae Guest) *swvd lft s: sn chsng ldrs: kpt on fnl f* **7/1**[2]

50-0 **4** *3/4* **Cryptic Clue (USA)**[9] 336 3-9-3 48 ... (b1) TonyCulhane 7 33
(D W Chapman) *hmpd s: sn chsng ldrs: one pce fnl 2f* **12/1**[3]

5 *hd* **Kelamon** 3-9-3 ... HayleyTurner 6 32
(M D I Usher) *hmpd s: racd towards far side: hdwy to chse ldrs over 3f out: kpt on same pce fnl 2f* **18/1**

6-00 **6** *1/2* **Rubber Duck (IRE)**[9] 335 3-8-9 30 ... (b) JerryO'Dwyer(3) 8 25
(Peter Grayson) *swvd lft s: sn wl outpcd and rdn: kpt on fnl 2f: nvr nr ldrs* **100/1**

006- **7** *nk* **Emerald Sky**[69] 6706 3-8-12 26 ... PatCosgrave 2 24
(R Brotherton) *led tl over 2f out: wknd fnl f* **125/1**

0 **8** *1 3/4* **Stoneacre Donny (IRE)**[17] 237 3-9-3 ... AdamKirby 9 23
(Peter Grayson) *nvr wnt pce: nvr a factor* **16/1**

0- **9** *1 1/4* **Bear Essential**[52] 6891 3-9-3 ... AntonyProcter 5 18
(Mrs P N Dutfield) *racd stands' side: chsd ldrs: outpcd over 2f out: sn lost pl* **50/1**

60.57 secs (0.27) **Going Correction** -0.175s/f (Stan) **9** Ran SP% **114.8**
Speed ratings (Par 97):90,83,81,80,79 78,78,75,73
CSF £32.17 TOTE £1.30: £1.02, £8.00, £1.80; EX 22.80 Trifecta £86.80 Pool £424.66. - 3.47 winning units..
Owner Mrs C E Dods **Bred** R Howe **Trained** Denton, Co Durham
FOCUS
The track was at its slowest as it had not yet had a real opportunity to dry out. A shocking sprint maiden and the winner could hardly have won more easily, followed home by the 40-rated runner-up.

430 PONTINSBINGO.COM H'CAP — 6f (F)
2:10 (2:12) (Class 6) (0-50,50) 4-Y-O+ **£2,047** (£604; £302) **Stalls** Low

Form RPR
41-0 **1** **Ace Club**[35] 59 6-8-5 **48** ... (b) EmmettStack(5) 3 55
(K J Burke) *led tl 2f out: kpt on to ld last stride* **28/1**

42-5 **2** *shd* **Favouring (IRE)**[26] 144 5-8-6 **47** ... (v) AndrewMullen(3) 7 54
(M C Chapman) *w ldr: led 2f out: hdd fnl stride* **7/2**[1]

-330 **3** *nk* **Penel (IRE)**[26] 144 6-8-12 **50** ... (p) MickyFenton 6 56
(P T Midgley) *chsd ldrs: outpcd over 2f out: styd on wl ins last* **7/2**[1]

2233 **4** *1/2* **Mind Alert**[9] 337 6-8-11 **49** ... (v) AdamKirby 10 54
(D Shaw) *t.k.h in rr: hdwy 2f out: styd on wl ins last* **5/1**[2]

0-03 **5** *1 1/4* **Danethorpe (IRE)**[10] 321 4-8-8 **46** oh1 ... (v) CatherineGannon 5 47
(D Shaw) *chsd ldrs: kpt on same pce fnl 2f* **14/1**

0-20 **6** *hd* **Bee Magic**[19] 221 4-8-11 **49** ... ChrisCatlin 14 49
(C N Kellett) *chsd ldrs: outpcd over 2f out: styd on fnl f* **40/1**

0-50 **7** *1/2* **Piccleyes**[17] 241 6-8-7 **48** ow1 ... (b) StephenDonohoe(3) 12 47
(A J McCabe) *in rr: hdwy on outer over 2f out: kpt on fnl f* **20/1**

00-0 **8** *hd* **Howards Princess**[33] 77 5-8-10 **48** ... (p) DaleGibson 11 46
(J Hetherton) *mid-div: hmpd over 3f out: styd on fnl f* **20/1**

1-05 **9** *shd* **Kissi Kissi**[10] 320 4-8-8 **46** oh1 ... (v) AdrianMcCarthy 9 44
(M J Attwater) *hld up in tch: n.m.r over 3f out: one pce fnl 2f* **20/1**

0-02 **10** *1 1/2* **Nevinstown (IRE)**[10] 320 7-8-8 **46** oh1 ... (b) TPQueally 2 39
(C Grant) *s.i.s: bhd and hrd rdn over 3f out: kpt on fnl 2f: nvr on terms* **8/1**[3]

-536 **11** *1/2* **Mouseen (IRE)**[17] 241 4-8-5 **48** ... (b) TolleyDean(5) 4 40
(R A Harris) *s.i.s: nvr on terms* **10/1**

0-00 **12** *2 1/2* **Shadow Jumper (IRE)**[17] 241 6-8-6 **47** ... (v) PatrickMathers(3) 1 31
(J T Stimpson) *in rr: lost pl over 4f out: sn bhd* **16/1**

1-40 **13** *1/2* **Orchestration (IRE)**[10] 317 6-8-6 **47** ... (v) DominicFox(3) 13 30
(K J Burke) *hld up in rr: nvr a factor* **16/1**

040- **14** *11* **The Salwick Flyer (IRE)**[85] 6521 4-8-12 **50** ... TonyCulhane 8 —
(A Berry) *chsd ldrs: lost pl over 2f out: sn bhd and eased* **40/1**

1m 17.48s (0.58) **Going Correction** -0.15s/f (Stan) **14** Ran SP% **122.4**
Speed ratings (Par 101):90,89,89,88,87 86,86,85,85,83 83,79,79,64
CSF £117.88 CT £447.54 TOTE £27.00: £6.50, £1.80, £2.00; EX 162.70 Trifecta £371.00 Part won. Pool £522.67. - 0.52 winning units..
Owner Brooklands Racing **Bred** Helescane Stud **Trained** Bourton-on-the-Water, Gloucs
■ A first winner for trainer Kahlil Burke from his satellite yard near Nottingham.
FOCUS
A poor handicap, but the form, rated through the first four, looks sound enough.
The Salwick Flyer(IRE) Official explanation: jockey said saddle slipped

431 CANVAS PRINTS FROM BONUSPRINT.COM H'CAP — 1m (F)
2:40 (2:40) (Class 6) (0-55,55) 4-Y-O+ **£2,388** (£705; £352) **Stalls** Low

Form RPR
14-2 **1** **Majehar**[17] 243 5-8-12 **55** ... TPQueally 13 64
(A G Newcombe) *in tch: reminders over 4f out: sn chsng ldrs: styd on to ld last 75yds* **13/8**[1]

40-5 **2** *1* **Connotation**[29] 121 5-8-7 **50** ... (p) LPKeniry 8 57
(A G Newcombe) *rr-div: hdwy on outer over 2f out: hung lft: styd on to take 2nd nr fin* **20/1**

-223 **3** *hd* **Mademoiselle**[6] 358 5-8-5 **53** ... (p) TolleyDean(5) 9 60
(R A Harris) *trckd ldr: led over 2f out: hdd and no ex ins last* **4/1**[2]

-564 **4** *3 1/2* **Futoo (IRE)**[3] 393 6-8-3 **46** oh1 ... (b) DaleGibson 7 45
(D W Chapman) *sn chsng ldrs: one pce fnl 2f* **14/1**

0-50 **5** *1* **Fuel Cell (IRE)**[13] 288 6-8-3 **46** oh1 ... PaulQuinn 10 43+
(J O'Reilly) *sn bhd: hdwy on ins over 2f out: styd on: nt rch ldrs* **40/1**

340- **6** *2 1/2* **Alwariah**[150] 5327 4-8-12 **55** ... EddieAhern 1 47
(C E Brittain) *hld up in mid-div: effrt over 2f out: nvr rchd ldrs* **16/1**

50/2 **7** *2 1/2* **Mangrove Cay (IRE)**[31] 98 5-8-12 **55** ... SilvestreDeSousa 6 42
(A J Lockwood) *in rr: kpt on fnl 2f: nvr a factor* **14/1**

-355 **8** *5* **Vibrato (USA)**[17] 238 5-8-4 **52** ... (vt) DuranFentiman(5) 2 28
(C J Teague) *s.i.s: hdwy and put hd in air 2f out: nvr on terms* **9/1**

26-0 **9** *1 1/4* **Lennoxtown (IRE)**[32] 88 4-8-12 **55** ... (p) AdamKirby 5 29
(J Ryan) *led tl over 2f out: lost pl over 1f out* **6/1**[3]

2-60 **10** *2* **Penwell Hill (USA)**[17] 238 8-8-4 **47** ... (b) HayleyTurner 11 16
(Miss M E Rowland) *racd on outer: nvr on terms* **20/1**

000- **11** *5* **Tantien**[44] 6971 5-8-4 **47** oh1 ow1 ... (b) EdwardCreighton 3 6
(T Keddy) *chsd ldrs: lost pl 3f out* **66/1**

000- **12** *nk* **Burning Moon**[233] 2820 6-8-9 **55** ... (p) LiamJones(3) 4 13
(S W Hall) *mid-div: lost pl 4f out: sn bhd* **33/1**

/00- **13** *10* **Shinko Femme (IRE)**[188] 4198 6-7-12 **46** oh1(b1) NataliaGemelova(5) 12 —
(J O'Reilly) *s.s: a bhd* **100/1**

1m 43.71s (-0.89) **Going Correction** -0.15s/f (Stan) **13** Ran SP% **119.0**
Speed ratings (Par 101):98,97,96,93,92 89,87,82,81,79 74,73,63
CSF £44.54 CT £119.84 TOTE £2.70: £1.20, £5.40, £1.90; EX 31.30 Trifecta £90.50 Pool £687.11. - 5.39 winning units..
Owner J R Salter **Bred** Darley **Trained** Yarnscombe, Devon
FOCUS
Another low-grade handicap, but the form looks fairly sound rated through the first and third.

432 PONTIN'S FAMILY HOLIDAYS H'CAP — 5f (F)
3:10 (3:10) (Class 5) (0-75,74) 4-Y-O+ **£3,241** (£957; £478) **Stalls** High

Form RPR
11-2 **1** **Rowe Park**[26] 154 4-8-9 **65** ... LPKeniry 5 89+
(Mrs L C Jewell) *trckd ldrs: shkn up to ld over 1f out: qcknd clr: readily* **2/1**[1]

3-50 **2** *4* **Stoneacre Boy (IRE)**[25] 163 4-8-10 **66** ... (b) AdamKirby 7 73
(Peter Grayson) *s.i.s: hdwy on stands' side 2f out: hung rt: kpt on to take 2nd ins last: no ch w wnr* **11/1**

0220 **3** ½ **Nusoor (IRE)**[6] [361] 4-8-10 **69** JerryO'Dwyer(3) 3 78+
(Peter Grayson) *s.s: hdwy and n.m.r 2f out: swtchd rt: styd on same pce fnl f* **3/1**[2]

0-62 **4** ½ **Taboor (IRE)**[14] [276] 9-8-7 **63** EddieAhern 4 67
(R M H Cowell) *trckd ldrs: effrt over 2f out: kpt on same pce* **10/1**

-304 **5** 1¼ **Trinculo (IRE)**[20] [214] 10-8-6 **67** TolleyDean(5) 1 67
(R A Harris) *chsd ldrs: one pce fnl 2f* **11/1**

5-20 **6** 2½ **Maktavish**[33] [79] 8-8-9 **65** (b) PatCosgrave 8 56
(R Brotherton) *led tl over 1f out: wknd jst ins last* **10/1**

004- **7** 1 **After The Show**[68] [6709] 6-9-4 **74** ChrisCatlin 6 62
(Rae Guest) *mid-div: nvr a threat* **5/1**[3]

000- **8** 1¼ **Katie Boo (IRE)**[85] [6527] 5-8-7 **63** TPQueally 2 47
(A Berry) *in tch: outpcd fnl 2f* **66/1**

015- **9** hd **Northern Chorus (IRE)**[167] [4886] 4-9-2 **72** (v) DavidAllan 9 55
(J O'Reilly) *sn outpcd and in rr* **40/1**

00-0 **10** 7 **Danzig River (IRE)**[37] [44] 6-8-9 **72** AdeleRothery(7) 10 31
(D Nicholls) *t.k.h in rr: bhd fnl 2f* **25/1**

58.26 secs (-2.04) **Going Correction** -0.175s/f (Stan) **10** Ran SP% **117.6**
Speed ratings (Par 103):109,102,101,101,99 95,93,91,91,79
CSF £25.76 CT £66.63 TOTE £2.90: £1.50, £3.00, £1.20; EX 34.90 Trifecta £123.10 Pool £745.96. - 4.30 winning units..
Owner R I B Young and Mrs F J Meekins **Bred** J Baker **Trained** Sutton Valence, Kent

FOCUS
The track was drying out fast by now in the breeze. It looked a fair sprint handicap, with the fourth providing the benchmark, but the winner could hardly have been more impressive and will surely follow up under a penalty.

433 DIGITAL PRINTS FROM BONUSPRINT.COM H'CAP 7f (F)
3:40 (3:40) (Class 4) (0-85,82) 3-Y-O **£4,857** (£1,445; £722; £360) **Stalls** Low

Form RPR

1 **1** **Rosa De Mi Corazon (USA)**[35] [60] 3-8-2 **68** oh1 JamieMackay 2 82+
(Sir Mark Prescott) *led: qcknd over 3f out: shkn up and edgd lft over 1f out: rdn clr* **4/6**[1]

32-5 **2** 3½ **Eau Good**[23] [184] 3-8-13 **82** StephenDonohoe(3) 3 86
(M C Chapman) *trckd wnr: rdn and wandered over 1f out: kpt on same pce* **7/2**[3]

5-16 **3** 1½ **Fractured Foxy**[20] [216] 3-8-1 **72** NataliaGemelova(5) 1 72
(J J Quinn) *w wnr: n.m.r on inner 4f out: one pce fnl 2f* **14/1**

52-4 **4** ¾ **Dubai Magic (USA)**[30] [111] 3-9-2 **82** EddieAhern 4 80
(C E Brittain) *trckd ldrs on outer: effrt 3f out: hung lft: one pce* **3/1**[2]

54-5 **5** 7 **Dolly Coughdrop (IRE)**[11] [312] 3-8-4 **70** DaleGibson 5 50
(K R Burke) *trckd ldrs on outside: effrt over 3f out: lost pl over 2f out* **20/1**

1m 29.1s (-1.70) **Going Correction** -0.15s/f (Stan) **5** Ran SP% **118.6**
Speed ratings (Par 99):103,99,97,96,88
CSF £3.92 TOTE £1.60: £1.10, £1.70; EX 4.30.
Owner Miss K Rausing **Bred** K Rausing **Trained** Newmarket, Suffolk

FOCUS
The winner was the fly in the ointment and proved much too good for some exposed types.
Dubai Magic(USA) Official explanation: jockey said gelding hung left in straight

434 PONTINS.COM H'CAP 1m 6f (F)
4:10 (4:10) (Class 4) (0-85,83) 4-Y-O+ **£4,857** (£1,445; £722; £360) **Stalls** Low

Form RPR

2113 **1** **Beldon Hill (USA)**[14] [283] 4-8-5 **67** DaleGibson 6 82+
(R A Fahey) *chsd ldrs: pushed along 6f out: led and hung lft 2f out: drew clr fnl f* **8/1**

32-1 **2** 5 **Arsad (IRE)**[35] [62] 4-8-8 **70** EddieAhern 5 78
(C E Brittain) *hld up wl in tch: drvn 4f out: sn outpcd: styd on fnl 2f: tk modest 2nd towards fin* **6/4**[1]

1-12 **3** 1 **Share The Feeling (IRE)**[14] [283] 5-8-12 **72** RichardKingscote(3) 1 79
(J W Unett) *w ldr: led 5f out: styd far side in home st: hdd 2f out: kpt on same pce* **4/1**[3]

56-4 **4** 4 **Croon**[6] [362] 5-9-5 **79** GregFairley(3) 8 80
(T J Pitt) *chsd ldrs: one pce fnl 3f* **10/3**[2]

115- **5** 1¾ **Flame Creek (IRE)**[47] [6941] 11-9-12 **83** EdwardCreighton 2 82
(E J Creighton) *sn trcking ldrs: chal over 4f out: wknd over 1f out* **10/1**

50/6 **6** 13 **Red Wine**[19] [226] 8-9-6 **80** StephenDonohoe(3) 7 60
(A J McCabe) *hld up in tch: effrt 4f out: hung lft and lost pl over 2f out: sn bhd* **25/1**

006- **7** 4 **Royal Auditon**[265] [1879] 6-8-7 **64** oh7 ChrisCatlin 3 39
(T T Clement) *hld up in tch: drvn on outer over 4f out: sn lost pl and bhd* **66/1**

061- **8** 3 **Top Jaro (FR)**[17] [6209] 4-9-1 **77** HayleyTurner 4 48
(Jennie Candlish) *led: hdd 5f out: sn lost pl and bhd* **25/1**

3m 5.33s (-4.27) **Going Correction** -0.15s/f (Stan)
WFA 4 from 5yo+ 5lb **8** Ran SP% **112.5**
Speed ratings (Par 105):106,103,102,100,99 91,89,87
CSF £19.81 CT £55.30 TOTE £10.10: £2.40, £1.40, £1.50; EX 20.80 Trifecta £48.90 Pool £921.30. - 13.37 winning units..
Owner D Brennan **Bred** Darley **Trained** Musley Bank, N Yorks

FOCUS
The track was reported to be riding 'throughly normal' by this stage and this handicap was run at a sound gallop. The runaway winner looked much improved.

435 PONTIN'S "BOOK EARLY" CLASSIFIED STKS 1m (F)
4:40 (4:40) (Class 7) 4-Y-O+ **£1,876** (£554; £277) **Stalls** Low

Form RPR

0260 **1** **Mid Valley**[7] [350] 4-9-0 **45** (v) MichaelTebbutt 7 61+
(J R Jenkins) *hld up in mid-div: smooth hdwy over 2f out: hung lft and led 1f out: sn qcknd wl clr: eased towards fin* **9/1**[3]

6-13 **2** 3½ **Comeintothespace (IRE)**[7] [350] 5-9-3 **48** LPKeniry 6 54
(R A Farrant) *trckd ldrs: led over 1f out: sn hdd: no ch w wnr* **9/4**[2]

-661 **3** 1¼ **Pawn In Life (IRE)**[10] [321] 9-9-1 **46** (v) SamHitchcott 3 49
(S Parr) *wnt long way to s: in rr: hdwy over 2f out: styd on fnl f* **9/1**[3]

0-00 **4** nk **Gem Bien (USA)**[36] [51] 9-9-0 **41** (b) PaulQuinn 13 47
(D W Chapman) *t.k.h on outer: hdwy over 2f out: styd on fnl f* **22/1**

4-54 **5** 2 **Pontefract Glory**[10] [321] 4-9-0 **43** SilvestreDeSousa 8 43
(M Dods) *chsd ldrs: one pce fnl 2f* **9/1**[3]

-600 **6** shd **Tribute (IRE)**[5] [374] 6-8-11 **44** JasonEdmunds(3) 9 43
(John A Harris) *sn chsng ldrs: wknd fnl f* **28/1**

00/0 **7** 2½ **Mr Bountiful (IRE)**[10] [320] 9-9-0 **42** (bt) AlanDaly 4 38
(C J Teague) *s.i.s: kpt on fnl 2f: nvr on terms* **66/1**

660- **8** 2½ **Tilen (IRE)**[13] [6979] 4-9-0 **35** (b) MatthewHenry 2 32
(S Parr) *in rr: detached 4f out: sme hdwy fnl 2f: nvr on terms* **66/1**

000- **9** hd **Pepper Road**[144] [5483] 8-8-11 **41** (t) DominicFox(3) 10 32
(R Bastiman) *prom on outer: fdd fnl 2f* **50/1**

4-66 **10** ½ **Caspian Rose**[10] [321] 4-9-0 **37** BrianReilly 1 31
(M J Attwater) *led tl hdd & wknd over 1f out* **66/1**

0-50 **11** hd **Hometomammy**[15] [266] 5-9-0 **40** (p) JosedeSouza 12 31
(P W Hiatt) *chsd ldrs: wknd 2f out* **25/1**

65-2 **12** 2½ **Almowj**[7] [350] 4-9-0 **43** DeanCorby 5 25
(C E Brittain) *mid-div: lost pl over 4f out: effrt on inner 3f out: sn btn* **6/4**[1]

05-0 **13** 19 **Jember Red**[15] [271] 4-9-0 **39** (v[1]) JamieMackay 14 —
(B Smart) *promient on outer: lost pl over 2f out: bhd whn eased ins last* **50/1**

1m 43.69s (-0.91) **Going Correction** -0.15s/f (Stan) **13** Ran SP% **120.8**
Speed ratings (Par 97):98,94,93,92,90 90,88,85,85,85 84,82,63
CSF £28.35 TOTE £10.00: £2.80, £1.60, £2.60; EX 43.90 Trifecta £202.80 Pool £1,119.93. - 3.92 winning units. Place 6 £4.33, Place 5 £3.79..
Owner M Ng **Bred** Michael Ng **Trained** Royston, Herts

FOCUS
They went a sound gallop and the form, though limited, looks very sound for the grade.
Mid Valley Official explanation: trainer's rep said, regarding apparent improvement in form, that the colt had a mind of its own and was suited by the reapplication of the visor.
Almowj Official explanation: jockey said gelding never travelled
T/Jkpt: £5,474.30 to a £1 stake. Pool: £46,262.50. 6.00 winning tickets. T/Plt: £10.60 to a £1 stake. Pool: £112,714.90. 7,759.40 winning tickets. T/Qpdt: £2.40 to a £1 stake. Pool: £6,254.20. 1,862.80 winning tickets. WG

CAGNES-SUR-MER
Sunday, February 11

OFFICIAL GOING: Good to soft

436a PRIX DE LA CALIFORNIE (LISTED RACE) 7f 110y
1:45 (1:45) 3-Y-O **£17,568** (£7,027; £5,270; £3,514; £1,757)

RPR

1 **Gris De Gris (IRE)**[92] [6453] 3-8-11 TThulliez 9 105
(J-M Capitte, France)

2 ¾ **Limerence (USA)**[81] 3-8-8 MAndrouin 4 100
(H-A Pantall, France) **18/10**[1]

3 3 **Air Bag (FR)**[13] 3-8-8 FSpanu 2 94
(Mme C Barande-Barbe, France)

4 ½ **Tatsuya (FR)**[137] 3-8-11 IMendizabal 7 95
(J-C Rouget, France)

5 ½ **Daly Daly (FR)**[13] 3-8-8 SFargeat 6 91
(R Laplanche, France)

6 1½ **Alcime (FR)**[75] 3-8-11 JAuge 5 91
(Robert Collet, France)

7 1 **Desert Ocean (IRE)**[157] 3-8-11 THuet 8 89
(G Collet, France)

8 7 **Pertinence (IRE)**[139] 3-8-8 SPasquier 1 70
(K Borgel, France)

9 13 **Sweeney (IRE)**[57] [6846] 3-8-11 NCallan 3 45
(M A Jarvis) *pulled hard in mid-div early, 7th and u.p straight, soon beaten* **18/10**[1]

1m 33.85s (93.85) **9** Ran SP% **71.4**
PARI-MUTUEL (Including 1 Euro stake): WIN 8.80; PL 2.50, 2.80, 2.10;DF 46.40.
Owner J C Seroul **Bred** J-C Seroul **Trained** France

NOTEBOOK
Gris De Gris(IRE) looked very well beforehand and went on before halfway to record a game and impressive success. Comfortably his best form to date, he looks progressive and could go well in the early part of the Paris season next month.
Sweeney(IRE) was never going with any fluidity and was beaten some way out. Given his previous good form, it is probably best to write this run off as an aberration.

437a GRAND PRIX DE LA RIVIERA COTE D'AZUR (LISTED RACE) (ALL-WEATHER) 1m 2f (D)
2:45 (2:48) 4-Y-O+ **£20,270** (£8,108; £6,081; £4,054; £2,027)

RPR

1 **Merlerault (USA)**[23] 4-8-9 SPasquier 12 111
(P Demercastel, France) **58/10**[1]

2 4 **Laredo Sound (IRE)**[20] 5-8-9 IMendizabal 15 103
(Mario Hofer, Germany)

3 nk **Mount Eliza (IRE)**[98] [6362] 5-8-6 JAuge 14 99
(J E Hammond, France) **18/1**[3]

4 3 **Giorgiolito**[232] 6-8-9 RonanThomas 6 97
(P Nicot, France)

5 ½ **Millville**[36] [57] 7-8-9 NCallan 7 96
(M A Jarvis) *mid-div, 7th half-way, pushed along 3f out, driven straight, stayed on at same pace* **14/1**[2]

6 snk **Salsalava (FR)**[76] 4-8-9 DBoeuf 2 96
(P Demercastel, France)

7 ½ **Neander (GER)**[105] 5-8-9 JVictoire 3 95
(P Van Kempen, Holland)

8 2 **Gold Sound (FR)**[103] 5-8-9 MBlancpain 8 91
(C Laffon-Parias, France)

9 4 **Shahdawar (FR)**[78] 4-8-9 FBlondel 10 85
(M Pimbonnet, France)

10 ¾ **Chopastair (FR)**[225] 6-8-9 J-BEyquem 11 82
(T Lemer, France)

0 **Lips Lion (IRE)**[75] 8-8-9 J-BHamel 13 —
(Robert Collet, France)

0 **Montparno (FR)**[105] 7-8-9 (b) TJarnet 4 —
(B De Montzey, France)

0 **Howard Le Canard (FR)**[292] 6-8-9 GBenoist 5 —
(J-M Capitte, France)

0 **Kalken (FR)**[105] [6250] 4-8-9 FSpanu 9 —
(L Planard, France)

0 **Nice Applause (IRE)**[137] 4-8-9 WMongil 1 —
(M Gentile, France)

2m 2.57s (122.57)
WFA 4 from 5yo+ 1lb **15** Ran SP% **26.6**
PARI-MUTUEL: WIN 6.30; PL 2.90, 4.20, 6.20; DF 54.50.
Owner M Parrish **Bred** Simpson Enterprises Inc **Trained** France

NOTEBOOK
Merlerault(USA) won this impressively and seemed to have plenty left at the line too. He is now likely to go to Neuss in Germany on March 4 for the second leg of this European All-Weather series.

Laredo Sound(IRE), a German challenger who ran well, is another who should be at Neuss on March 4.
Millville ran a creditable race without ever looking as though he would take a hand in the finish. Connections reported that he is much better suited by a mile and a half, and he will now be given a break.

355 ST MORITZ (R-H)

Sunday, February 11

OFFICIAL GOING: Frozen

438a GRAND PRIX CHERVO (SNOW) 1m 110y

11:45 (12:00) 3-Y-0+ **£2,812** (£1,125; £844; £562; £281)

RPR
1 **Salermo (CZE)**[329] 6-9-4 .... MKolb 3 71
(M Weiss, Switzerland)
2 *1 1/2* **Furstenberg (IRE)**[364] 5-9-11 ....(b) TMundry 1 75
(C Von Der Recke, Germany)
3 *2 1/2* **Dooneen (IRE)**[7] 356 5-9-4 .... GBocsai 8 63
(C Bocsai, Germany)
4 *7* **Give Back Calais (IRE)**[7] 356 9-8-7 .... FrauNataliеFriberg 2 38
(Miss A Casotti, Switzerland)
5 *1 1/2* **Rainstar (IRE)**[7] 356 5-9-0 ....(b) SarahLeutwiler 5 42
(J Stadelmann, Switzerland)
6 *5* **Taziria (SWI)** 6-8-3 .... HelenIsler-Kopalek 6 21
(C Bocsai, Germany)
7 *3 1/2* **Barny's Barnato (IRE)** 6-9-9 .... SteveDrowne 7 34
(M Weiss, Switzerland)
8 *22* **Sargentos (GER)**[7] 355 5-9-0 ....(b) MichellePayne 4 —
(M F Harris) *SP 103-10* **103/10**[1]
1m 52.29s (112.29) 8 Ran SP% **8.8**
(Including SFr1 stake): WIN 10.70; PL 1.30, 1.10, 1.10; DF 33.80.
Owner Stall Stargate **Bred** Stall Stargate **Trained** Switzerland

439a GRAND PRIX CHRISTOFFEL BAU TROPHY (SNOW) 1m 110y

1:45 (12:00) 4-Y-0+ **£4,619** (£1,848; £1,386; £924; £462)

RPR
1 **Special Edition (GER)** 5-9-4 .... TMundry 6 65
(C Von Der Recke, Germany)
2 *hd* **Vlavianus (CZE)**[7] 356 6-9-0 ....(b) MKolb 1 61
(M Weiss, Switzerland)
3 *1 1/2* **Pine Cone (IRE)**[127] 5803 5-9-3 .... SteveDrowne 7 61
(M Weiss, Switzerland)
4 *5* **Ivans Ride (IRE)**[7] 356 4-8-11 .... MichellePayne 5 45
(M F Harris) *SP 92-10* **92/10**[1]
5 *1 1/2* **Palladia Directa (GER)**[364] 7-8-13 .... GBocsai 3 44
(C Bocsai, Germany)
6 *24* **Lord Elrond**[993] 2370 5-8-11 .... FrauNataliеFriberg 4 —
(Miss A Casotti, Switzerland)
7 *2 1/2* **Favorita (GER)**[1233] 7-8-8 .... HelenIsler-Kopalek 2 —
(C Bocsai, Germany)
1m 53.41s (113.41) 7 Ran SP% **9.8**
WIN 4.90; PL 2.50, 1.90; DF 18.00.
Owner Stall Thommy **Bred** Frau Christa Thomas **Trained** Weilerswist, Germany

423 WOLVERHAMPTON (A.W) (L-H)

Monday, February 12

OFFICIAL GOING: Standard
Wind: fresh, across

440 THEAWC.CO.UK H'CAP (DIV I) 7f 32y(P)

1:50 (1:55) (Class 6) (0-52,52) 4-Y-0+ **£1,706** (£503; £252) **Stalls** High

Form RPR
00-0 1 **Doctor's Cave**[15] 287 5-8-9 **49** ow1 ....(b) NCallan 1 61
(K O Cunningham-Brown) *led: rdn and hdd wl over 1f out: led ins fnl f: r.o wl* **15/2**
00-0 2 *1 1/2* **Balerno**[14] 292 8-8-10 **50** .... PaulEddery 10 58
(Mrs L J Mongan) *hld up in tch: rdn over 2f out: edgd lft over 1f out: ev ch ins fnl f: nt qckn* **12/1**
-245 3 *1/2* **Seldemosa**[21] 217 6-8-3 **48** .... TolleyDean(5) 6 55
(M S Saunders) *a.p: rdn to ld wl over 1f out: hdd ins fnl f: nt qckn* **14/1**
-102 4 *1/2* **Prince Of Gold**[7] 366 7-8-10 **50** ....(v) FergusSweeney 3 56
(R Hollinshead) *hld up in mid-div: rdn and hdwy on ins over 2f out: swtchd lft wl over 1f out: ev ch ins fnl f: no ex* **3/1**[1]
04-5 5 *3* **Postmaster**[5] 379 5-8-7 **47** ow1 .... RobertHavlin 5 45
(R Ingram) *s.i.s: bhd tl rdn and hdwy over 2f out: no imp fnl f* **4/1**[2]
-330 6 *2* **Fulvio (USA)**[5] 379 7-8-12 **52** ....(v) ShaneKelly 11 45
(P Howling) *hld up in mid-div: hdwy on outside 3f out: btn whn edgd lft over 1f out* **10/1**
4304 7 *1 1/4* **Spy Gun (USA)**[6] 374 7-8-4 **47** oh1 ow1 .... JamesDoyle(3) 4 36
(T Wall) *w ldr tl rdn over 3f out: wknd over 2f out* **4/1**[2]
40-6 8 *shd* **Kareeb (FR)**[7] 367 10-8-12 **52** .... DaneO'Neill 8 41
(P A Blockley) *s.i.s: a bhd* **11/1**
5020 9 *nk* **Midmaar (IRE)**[14] 292 6-8-12 **52** ....(b) GrahamGibbons 9 40
(M Wigham) *prom over 3f* **6/1**[3]
0-00 10 *nk* **Alucica**[12] 311 4-8-6 **46** oh1 .... DeanMcKeown 2 33
(D Shaw) *s.i.s and wnt lft s: a bhd* **33/1**
0-04 11 *9* **Saintly Place**[15] 287 6-8-6 **46** oh1 .... HayleyTurner 7 10
(A W Carroll) *t.k.h: prom: rdn over 3f out: wknd over 2f out* **25/1**
1m 29.3s (-1.10) **Going Correction** -0.025s/f (Stan) 11 Ran SP% **129.6**
Speed ratings (Par 101):105,103,102,102,98 96,95,94,94,94 83
CSF £103.79 CT £1290.38 TOTE £8.80: £4.00, £5.30, £3.30; EX 211.00 TRIFECTA Not won. Pool: £261.34.
Owner A J Richards & Michael A Richards **Bred** Tweenhills Stud And Genesis Green Stud **Trained** Nether Wallop, Hants
■ Ken Cunningham-Brown's first winner for nearly four years.

FOCUS
A weak race on paper, but a couple of gambles made it more interesting. The form looks solid and a bit better than most in this grade. The winning time (hand-timed) was 0.86 seconds faster than the second division.

441 PONTIN'S FAMILY HOLIDAYS H'CAP 5f 20y(P)

2:20 (2:25) (Class 6) (0-50,51) 4-Y-0+ **£2,388** (£705; £352) **Stalls** Low

Form RPR
-400 1 **Orchestration (IRE)**[1] 430 6-8-9 **47** ....(v) NCallan 8 54
(K J Burke) *hld up in mid-div: rdn and hdwy on outside fnl f: led last stride* **15/2**
5-10 2 *hd* **Primarily**[15] 281 5-8-8 **46** .... GrahamGibbons 5 53
(Peter Grayson) *hld up in mid-div: rdn and hdwy over 1f out: led nr fin: hdd last stride* **15/2**
0-26 3 *hd* **Town House**[15] 287 5-8-1 **46** oh1 .... SoniaEaton(7) 7 52
(B P J Baugh) *t.k.h: chsd ldrs: rdn and r.o ins fnl f* **20/1**
00-2 4 *nk* **Navigation (IRE)**[10] 337 5-8-6 **47** ....(b) SaleemGolam(3) 3 52
(T J Etherington) *chsd ldrs: rdn over 1f out: led ins fnl f: hdd nr fin* **4/1**[2]
-501 5 *nk* **Mustammer**[3] 403 4-8-13 **51** 6ex .... TonyCulhane 2 55+
(D Shaw) *hld up and bhd: nt clr run wl over 2f out: rdn and hdwy over 1f out: r.o towards fin* **15/8**[1]
30-0 6 *3/4* **Feminist (IRE)**[7] 368 5-8-8 **46** oh1 .... BrettDoyle 11 47
(J M Bradley) *led: rdn over 1f out: hdd and no ex ins fnl f* **40/1**
0450 7 *nk* **Mind That Fox**[17] 254 5-8-5 **46** oh1 .... JamesDoyle(3) 10 46
(T Wall) *chsd ldr: rdn wl over 1f out: one pce fnl f* **40/1**
-432 8 *1 3/4* **Lady Hopeful (IRE)**[15] 287 5-8-11 **49** ....(b) AdamKirby 4 43
(Peter Grayson) *s.i.s: hld up and bhd: c wd st: nvr trbld ldrs* **5/1**[3]
0006 9 *nk* **Percy Douglas**[11] 318 7-8-7 **50** oh1 ow4 .... AnnStokell(5) 6 43
(Miss A Stokell) *prom: rdn over 2f out: wknd over 1f out* **25/1**
00-6 10 *1* **Flying Tackle**[22] 201 9-8-5 **46** oh1 ....(v) PatrickMathers(3) 1 35
(I W McInnes) *hld up in mid-div: rdn over 2f out: sn bhd* **20/1**
125 11 *9* **Spirit Of Coniston**[14] 289 4-8-9 **50** ....(b) JerryO'Dwyer(3) 9 7
(Peter Grayson) *a bhd: eased whn no ch over 1f out* **12/1**
62.94 secs (0.12) **Going Correction** -0.025s/f (Stan) 11 Ran SP% **120.9**
Speed ratings (Par 101):98,97,97,96,96 95,94,91,91,89 75
CSF £59.71 CT £1089.81 TOTE £8.90: £3.10, £3.80, £4.00; EX 63.10 Trifecta £354.40 Pool: £499.24 - 0.51 winning units..
Owner Brooklands Racing **Bred** Mrs Anita Rothschild **Trained** Bourton-on-the-Water, Gloucs

FOCUS
A very moderate sprint handicap and with only a couple of lengths covering the first seven horses this form is unlikely to add up to much.
Orchestration(IRE) Official explanation: trainer said, regarding apparent improvement in form, gelding's previous run could have been affected by a wide draw and interference in running, whereas, on this occasion, he had benefited from the stronger handling of this jockey

442 PONTINS.COM (S) STKS 5f 216y(P)

2:55 (3:00) (Class 6) 3-Y-0+ **£2,047** (£604; £302) **Stalls** Low

Form RPR
-345 1 **Phinerine**[3] 403 4-9-3 52 ....(b) MichaelJStainton(5) 7 56
(R A Harris) *s.i.s: hld up and bhd: hdwy 2f out: hung lft over 1f out: r.o u.p to ld nr fin* **12/1**
314 2 *1/2* **Magic Amour**[17] 252 9-9-8 57 ....(b) KevinGhunowa(5) 12 60
(P A Blockley) *led early: chsd ldr: rdn to ld over 1f out: edgd lft and hdd nr fin* **7/1**
4603 3 *1* **Desert Light (IRE)**[12] 310 6-9-8 50 ....(v) DaneO'Neill 3 52
(D Shaw) *hld up in mid-div: rdn and hdwy on ins wl over 1f out: swtchd lft ent fnl f: kpt on* **4/1**[2]
00P- 4 *nk* **Legal Set (IRE)**[69] 6718 11-9-3 40 .... AnnStokell(5) 1 51
(Miss A Stokell) *chsd ldrs: rdn and ev ch 1f out: no ex towards fin* **40/1**
0054 5 *1/2* **Majestical (IRE)**[3] 403 5-9-8 50 ....(p) TonyCulhane 11 50
(J M Bradley) *bhd: hdwy fnl f: r.o* **14/1**
-446 6 *1/2* **Grand View**[10] 337 11-9-8 45 ....(p) PaulMulrennan 10 48
(J R Weymes) *hld up in mid-div: lost pl on outside 3f out: rdn wl over 1f out: sme late hdwy* **25/1**
020- 7 *shd* **Nistaki (USA)**[65] 6773 6-9-8 59 .... NCallan 8 48
(D Shaw) *broke wl: sn stdd and t.k.h: hdwy over 2f out: rdn whn bmpd jst over 1f out: btn whn edgd rt ins fnl f* **6/4**[1]
/000 8 *shd* **Verite**[19] 234 4-9-5 58 ....(be) StephenDonohoe(3) 5 47
(A J McCabe) *sn led: rdn and hdd over 1f out: one pce* **16/1**
4052 9 *1 1/4* **Fast Heart**[3] 403 6-9-3 60 .... TolleyDean(5) 13 48+
(R A Harris) *broke wl: sn lost pl: bhd whn rdn over 3f out: hmpd and stmbld wl over 1f out: n.d* **9/2**[3]
6-40 10 *1/2* **Princess Kai (IRE)**[20] 225 6-9-3 40 .... RobertHavlin 6 37
(R Ingram) *hld up in mid-div: rdn over 2f out: no rspnse* **40/1**
0-50 11 *1* **Sham Ruby**[14] 296 5-9-3 40 .... HayleyTurner 9 34
(M R Bosley) *chsd ldrs tl rdn and wknd wl over 2f out* **40/1**
00-0 12 *9* **Bermuda Beauty (IRE)**[3] 403 4-8-10 41 ....(b[1]) BarrySavage(7) 4 7
(J M Bradley) *s.i.s: a bhd* **50/1**
1m 16.18s (0.37) **Going Correction** -0.025s/f (Stan)
WFA 3 from 4yo+ 15lb 12 Ran SP% **124.0**
Speed ratings (Par 101):96,95,94,93,92 92,92,92,90,89 88,76
CSF £94.21 TOTE £13.50: £3.10, £2.60, £1.60; EX 99.30 Trifecta £252.30 Pool: £419.46 - 1.18 winning units..There was no bid for the winner.
Owner Mr & Mrs I D Evans **Bred** Mrs Celia Miller **Trained** Earlswood, Monmouths

FOCUS
A moderate seller run in a modest time, even for a race like this. Weak form.
Fast Heart Official explanation: jockey said gelding resented the kickback

443 PONTIN'S BOOK EARLY MAIDEN STKS 1m 4f 50y(P)

3:30 (3:35) (Class 5) 4-Y-0+ **£2,817** (£838; £418; £209) **Stalls** Low

Form RPR
0- 1 **Theatre Groom (USA)**[67] 4931 8-9-6 .... GeorgeBaker 8 66
(M R Bosley) *a.p: led 4f out: rdn 2f out: styd on* **50/1**
63-2 2 *3/4* **Moon Empress (FR)**[19] 229 4-8-12 62 .... SebSanders 9 59
(W R Muir) *a.p: rdn and ev ch fnl 2f: nt qckn* **8/11**[1]
3 3 *7* **Beau Torero (FR)**[7] 365 9-9-1 .... TomMessenger(5) 10 53
(B N Pollock) *dwlt: hdwy over 5f out: rdn 4f out: styd on same pce fnl 2f* **16/1**
00-0 4 *2* **Pukka Tique**[22] 204 4-9-3 54 .... GrahamGibbons 3 50
(R Hollinshead) *led: hdd 6f out: sn rdn: one pce fnl 3f* **16/1**
60- 5 *2 1/2* **Grey Report (IRE)**[346] 573 10-9-6 .... NCallan 7 46
(Simon Earle) *dwlt: t.k.h: sn in tch: rdn 4f out: wknd 3f out* **4/1**[3]
4 6 *3/4* **Glory Days (GER)**[10] 338 4-8-12 .... EddieAhern 2 40
(E A L Dunlop) *t.k.h: prom: led 6f out to 4f out: wknd over 2f out: hung lft fr over 4f out* **10/3**[2]
30/0 7 *2 1/2* **Flower Haven**[22] 200 5-9-1 53 .... AntonyProcter 6 36
(M J Gingell) *rdn over 7f out: a bhd* **150/1**
050- 8 *12* **Liquid Lover (IRE)**[45] 6972 5-9-6 37 .... DavidAllan 5 22
(W M Brisbourne) *rdn 7f out: a bhd* **80/1**

660- **9** *84* **Artist's Muse (USA)**[44] [6987] 4-8-12 **60**.......................... TonyCulhane 11 —
(M S Saunders) *bhd: rdn 5f out: t.o fnl 3f* **100/1**
2m 41.81s (-0.61) **Going Correction** -0.025s/f (Stan)
WFA 4 from 5yo+ 3lb **9** Ran SP% **117.6**
Speed ratings (Par 103):101,100,95,94,92 92,90,82,26
CSF £90.76 TOTE £55.30: £7.40, £1.10, £2.10; EX 159.50 Trifecta £682.00 Pool: £960.66 - 0.85 winning units..
Owner Mrs Jean M O'Connor **Bred** Juddmonte Farms Inc **Trained** Lockeridge, Wilts
FOCUS
A very modest and uncompetitive maiden in which the front pair pulled a long way clear of the rest. The form has been rated through the runner-up and the fourth and looks far from solid.

444 GO PONTIN'S APPRENTICE H'CAP — 1m 1f 103y(P)
4:00 (4:05) (Class 4) (0-80,80) 4-Y-0+ **£4,857** (£1,445; £722; £360) **Stalls** Low

Form RPR
5-10 **1** **Wild Pitch**[8] [353] 6-8-13 **74**..(b) JackMitchell 2 83+
(P Mitchell) *stdd s: hld up: hdwy over 2f out: rdn to ld wl ins fnl f: r.o* **12/1**
-221 **2** *1/2* **Top Mark**[12] [314] 5-8-9 **77**.. MatthewDavies(7) 8 83
(J R Boyle) *a.p: rdn to ld over 2f out: hdd and nt qckn wl ins fnl f* **4/1**[2]
12-1 **3** *1/2* **Just Bond (IRE)**[39] [38] 5-8-10 **76**.......................... PatrickDonaghy(5) 7 81
(G R Oldroyd) *s.s and fly-jmpd: hld up and bhd: c wd st: rdn and hdwy over 1f out: ev ch ins fnl f: nt qckn* **10/11**[1]
6-55 **4** *nk* **Prince Charlemagne (IRE)**[9] [340] 4-9-0 **80**.............. SophieDoyle(5) 3 84
(N P Littmoden) *half-rrd s: hld up and bhd: hdwy 2f out: sn nt clr run: kpt on ins fnl f* **8/1**[3]
350- **5** *1* **Dumaran (IRE)**[13] [6301] 9-8-3 **69**................................ DebraEngland(5) 1 71?
(W J Musson) *a.p: one pce fnl f* **28/1**
5-66 **6** *1* **Waterline Twenty (IRE)**[24] [185] 4-8-13 **77**.................. SoniaEaton(3) 6 77
(P D Evans) *chsd ldr: ev ch over 1f out: no ex wl ins fnl f* **10/1**
600- **7** *5* **Barodine**[13] [6051] 4-8-13 **79**.. HaddenFrost(5) 5 69
(R J Hodges) *t.k.h: led: hdd over 2f out: rdn and wknd over 1f out* **14/1**
000/ **8** *11* **Prize Fighter (IRE)**[42] [6147] 5-9-5 **80**.............................. JamieHamblett 4 48
(D Carroll) *rel to r: a bhd: rdn over 2f out: sn lost tch* **14/1**
2m 3.20s (0.58) **Going Correction** -0.025s/f (Stan) **8** Ran SP% **117.1**
Speed ratings (Par 105):96,95,95,94,93 93,88,78
CSF £60.88 CT £88.49 TOTE £12.30: £2.80, £1.60, £1.10; EX 70.40 Trifecta £110.90 Pool: £698.54 - 4.47 winning units..
Owner Mrs Julie Auletta **Bred** Wyck Hall Stud Ltd **Trained** Epsom, Surrey
FOCUS
An ordinary handicap restricted to apprentices who had not ridden more than ten winners. They went a very steady pace for most of the way, resulting in a time 1.52 seconds slower than the following 51-65 contest, and the form should be treated with caution.

445 PONTINSBINGO.COM H'CAP — 1m 1f 103y(P)
4:35 (4:41) (Class 6) (0-65,65) 4-Y-0+ **£2,388** (£705; £352) **Stalls** Low

Form RPR
03-3 **1** **Penang Cinta**[24] [182] 4-8-5 **54**................................. CatherineGannon 13 64+
(P D Evans) *hld up and bhd: c wd st: hdwy over 1f out: r.o to ld cl home* **7/1**[3]
0-21 **2** *3/4* **Can Can Star**[22] [204] 4-9-0 **63**... ShaneKelly 12 71
(A W Carroll) *hld up in mid-div: hdwy 3f out: sn hung rt: rdn over 1f out: led ins fnl f: hdd cl home* **15/2**
202- **3** *1* **King's Spear (IRE)**[101] [6327] 4-9-1 **64**................................ EddieAhern 4 70
(P W Chapple-Hyam) *hld up in tch: rdn over 2f out: r.o ins fnl f* **10/1**
0-13 **4** *nk* **My Michelle**[16] [266] 6-8-7 **56**.. DaleGibson 1 61
(B Palling) *led: hdd 6f out: prom: rdn over 1f out: kpt on ins fnl f* **12/1**
0-65 **5** *1 1/4* **Medieval Maiden**[14] [299] 4-8-12 **61**................................... BrettDoyle 6 64
(W J Musson) *hld up in mid-div: hdwy over 1f out: kpt on same pce fnl f* **17/2**
3-50 **6** *hd* **First Friend (IRE)**[5] [381] 6-9-2 **65**................................... GeorgeBaker 2 68
(P Mitchell) *chsd ldr: led 6f out: rdn wl over 1f out: hdd ins fnl f: wknd towards fin* **7/1**[3]
-530 **7** *2 1/2* **Second Reef**[15] [286] 5-8-6 **55**.....................................(p) PaulMulrennan 3 53+
(J R Weymes) *bhd: swtchd rt ent st: late hdwy: n.d* **20/1**
3-03 **8** *2 1/2* **Buscador (USA)**[15] [286] 8-8-6 **58**.............................. LiamJones(3) 11 51
(W M Brisbourne) *prom tl wknd over 1f out* **5/1**[2]
-006 **9** *1/2* **Methusaleh (IRE)**[10] [334] 4-8-8 **57**.............................. DeanMcKeown 9 49
(D Shaw) *hld up and bhd: hdwy on ins over 2f out: rdn wl over 1f out: sn wknd* **22/1**
-330 **10** *hd* **Bridgewater Boys**[10] [332] 6-9-2 **65**....................................(b) NCallan 10 56
(K A Ryan) *prom: rdn over 2f out: wknd wl over 1f out* **10/3**[1]
-310 **11** *1/2* **Desert Hawk**[24] [180] 6-8-6 **55**.....................................(b) FergusSweeney 5 45
(W M Brisbourne) *hld up in mid-div: rdn over 2f out: no rspnse* **9/1**
605- **12** *3* **Mycenean Prince (USA)**[24] [6799] 4-8-2 **51** oh6.........(v) JamieMackay 8 35
(R C Guest) *chsd ldrs tl wknd 4f out* **66/1**
600- **13** *3/4* **Monmouthshire**[98] [6383] 4-8-4 **56** ow3......................... JamesDoyle(3) 7 39
(R J Price) *a in rr* **33/1**
2m 1.68s (-0.94) **Going Correction** -0.025s/f (Stan) **13** Ran SP% **127.4**
Speed ratings (Par 101):103,102,101,101,100 99,97,95,95,94 94,91,91
CSF £60.54 CT £544.67 TOTE £15.20: £4.20, £2.60, £3.50; EX 116.60 TRIFECTA Not won. Pool: £588.18.
Owner Trevor Gallienne **Bred** Mrs A K H Ooi **Trained** Pandy, Monmouths
FOCUS
A modest but competitive handicap. With plenty of competition for the lead, the pace was good and the winning time was 1.52 seconds quicker than the previous 66-80 contest. The winner is likely to prove better than the bare form, with the second and third relatively unexposed.
Desert Hawk Official explanation: jockey said gelding had clipped heels

446 PONTIN'S BOOK EARLY H'CAP — 1m 141y(P)
5:05 (5:11) (Class 5) (0-70,70) 3-Y-0 **£3,238** (£963; £481; £240) **Stalls** Low

Form RPR
1 **Still Crazy (IRE)**[110] [6181] 3-8-2 **57**............................ LiamJones(3) 3 62
(W M Brisbourne) *hld up: rdn and hdwy over 1f out: r.o to ld nr fin* **20/1**
-422 **2** *nk* **My Mirasol**[15] [284] 3-8-12 **64**..(p) NCallan 4 68
(K A Ryan) *a.p: rdn whn rdr dropped rein wl over 1f out: sn edgd lft: led ins fnl f: hdd nr fin* **11/8**[1]
00-2 **3** *3/4* **Ella Woodcock (IRE)**[8] [348] 3-8-11 **63**............................ ShaneKelly 7 65
(J A Osborne) *hld up: rdn and hdwy on outside over 1f out: kpt on ins fnl f* **15/8**[2]
55-4 **4** *2* **Strike Force**[28] [140] 3-8-9 **66**... TolleyDean(5) 1 64
(R A Harris) *w ldr tl rdn over 3f out: one pce fnl 2f* **11/2**[3]
200- **5** *nk* **Suhayl Star (IRE)**[116] [6064] 3-9-4 **70**.............................. MatthewHenry 2 68
(M Wigham) *t.k.h: led: rdn over 1f out: hdd ins fnl f: fdd* **25/1**
06-3 **6** *6* **Sunley Sovereign**[8] [348] 3-8-4 **63**........................... MatthewDavies(7) 5 48
(M R Channon) *t.k.h: short-lived effrt 2f out* **8/1**
1m 51.24s (-0.52) **Going Correction** -0.025s/f (Stan) **6** Ran SP% **112.0**
Speed ratings (Par 97):101,100,100,98,98 92
CSF £48.26 TOTE £41.60: £9.50, £1.30; EX 97.40.
Owner Douglas Taylor **Bred** Patrick M Ryan **Trained** Great Ness, Shropshire
FOCUS
A modest handicap run at a fair pace. The form appears to make sense.

447 THEAWC.CO.UK H'CAP (DIV II) — 7f 32y(P)
5:35 (5:40) (Class 6) (0-52,52) 4-Y-0+ **£1,706** (£503; £252) **Stalls** High

Form RPR
36-0 **1** **Wayward Shot (IRE)**[16] [266] 5-8-6 **46**.....................(b[1]) PaulMulrennan 9 56
(M W Easterby) *sn led: clr 2f out: rdn over 1f out: r.o wl* **9/2**[3]
00-0 **2** *3* **Princess Arwen**[10] [339] 5-8-6 **46** oh1.................................(b) LPKeniry 2 48
(Mrs Barbara Waring) *hld up in tch: rdn over 3f out: wnt 2nd wl ins fnl f: no ch w wnr* **25/1**
0-06 **3** *3/4* **Apex**[7] [366] 6-8-10 **50**.. KimTinkler 1 50
(N Tinkler) *led early: prom: rdn to chse wnr over 2f out: no imp* **7/1**
24-3 **4** *nk* **Black Oval**[21] [217] 6-8-8 **48**.. PaulEddery 4 47
(S Parr) *s.i.s: bhd tl rdn and hdwy on outside 1f out: kpt on* **4/1**[2]
0-00 **5** *shd* **Merdiff**[8] [350] 8-8-3 **46** oh1.. LiamJones(3) 8 45
(W M Brisbourne) *a.p: rdn over 2f out: one pce* **14/1**
0-04 **6** *1/2* **Blue Knight (IRE)**[16] [268] 8-8-10 **50**............................... JamieMackay 6 48
(P Howling) *hld up and bhd: hdwy on ins wl over 1f out: sn rdn: one pce fnl f* **14/1**
0000 **7** *1/2* **Lord Chamberlain**[7] [366] 14-8-8 **51** ow1..........(b) StephenDonohoe(3) 5 47
(J M Bradley) *sn wl bhd: late hdwy: nrst fin* **25/1**
0-05 **8** *1 1/4* **Desert Lover (IRE)**[10] [334] 5-8-9 **52**............................. JamesDoyle(3) 7 45
(R J Price) *mid-div: rdn over 2f out: no hdwy* **8/1**
U020 **9** *2 1/2* **Savoy Chapel**[8] [350] 5-8-6 **46** oh1..................................(v) ShaneKelly 10 33
(A W Carroll) *hld up and bhd: hdwy on outside 3f out: rdn and wknd fnl f* **9/1**
-031 **10** *1 3/4* **Dark Moon**[10] [337] 4-8-12 **52**.. DeanMcKeown 3 34
(D Shaw) *s.i.s: hld up and bhd: nt clr run over 3f out: rdn over 2f out: no rspnse* **2/1**[1]
0-56 **11** *1 1/4* **Danielle's Lad**[21] [207] 11-8-6 **46** oh1..............................(p) DaleGibson 11 25
(B Palling) *sn chsng wnr: rdn over 2f out: sn wknd* **33/1**
1m 30.16s (-0.24) **Going Correction** -0.025s/f (Stan) **11** Ran SP% **129.1**
Speed ratings (Par 101):100,96,95,95,95 94,94,92,89,87 86
CSF £122.90 CT £822.29 TOTE £6.30: £2.20, £12.40, £2.70; EX 420.20 TRIFECTA Not won. Pool: £748.97. Place 6 £915.76, Place 5 £121.49.
Owner East Riding Horse Racing Syndicate Ltd **Bred** Paul McCarthy **Trained** Sheriff Hutton, N Yorks
FOCUS
A moderate handicap run in a time 0.86 seconds slower than the first division, and probably the weaker form, with the favourite disappointing and the runner-up 6lb wrong.
Dark Moon Official explanation: jockey said filly never travelled
T/Jkpt: Not won. T/Plt: £611.50 to a £1 stake. Pool: £92,021.35. 109.85 winning tickets. T/Qpdt: £9.40 to a £1 stake. Pool: £8,530.00. 668.70 winning tickets. KH

429 SOUTHWELL (L-H)
Tuesday, February 13

OFFICIAL GOING: Standard
Wind: Slight, across

448 GO PONTIN'S H'CAP — 6f (F)
1:50 (1:56) (Class 6) (0-55,54) 4-Y-0+ **£2,388** (£705; £352) **Stalls** Low

Form RPR
00-4 **1** **Best Lead**[12] [318] 8-8-3 **48**..(b) KevinGhunowa(5) 9 58
(Ian Emmerson) *chsd ldrs: hdwy over 2f out: rdn to ld over 1f out: kpt on* **20/1**
053- **2** *3/4* **Brut**[133] [5752] 5-8-10 **50**... RobertWinston 5 58
(D W Barker) *towards rr: hdwy 2f out: rdn to chse wnr and hung rt ins last: kpt on* **9/1**
43-5 **3** *1 3/4* **Newkeylets**[15] [296] 4-8-7 **52**.....................................(p) DuranFentiman(5) 4 55
(I Semple) *chsd ldrs: rdn and sltly outpcd 2f out: swtchd lft and kpt on wl u.p ins last* **12/1**
-500 **4** *1/2* **Piccleyes**[2] [430] 6-8-7 **47**..(b) DeanMcKeown 14 48
(A J McCabe) *cl up: led 1/2-way: rdn 2f out: drvn and hdd over 1f out: kpt on same pce* **14/1**
0-44 **5** *nk* **Grafton (IRE)**[11] [339] 4-8-12 **52**....................................(p) TonyCulhane 10 52+
(J O'Reilly) *midfield: hdwy on outer 2f out: sn rdn and kpt on u.p ins last: nrst fin* **16/1**
1-34 **6** *3/4* **Blakeshall Quest**[15] [296] 7-9-0 **54**...................................(b) PatCosgrave 3 52
(R Brotherton) *led: pushed along and hdd 1/2-way: sn rdn and ev ch tl drvn and one pce appr last* **11/1**
-022 **7** *1/2* **Monda**[11] [339] 5-8-11 **51**... PaulMulrennan 11 47
(Miss J A Camacho) *qckly away and cl up: rdn and ev ch over 2f out tl drvn and grad wknd fr over 1f out* **11/4**[1]
-043 **8** *1* **Doughty**[11] [339] 5-8-0 **45**.. EmmettStack(5) 8 38
(M Mullineaux) *towards rr tl sme late hdwy* **16/1**
0-00 **9** *hd* **Savile's Delight (IRE)**[8] [368] 8-8-12 **52**...............(bt) EdwardCreighton 7 45
(Miss Joanne Priest) *in tch: rdn over 2f out and sn no imp* **28/1**
-000 **10** *1/2* **Shadow Jumper (IRE)**[2] [430] 6-8-4 **47**..............(v) PatrickMathers(3) 12 38
(J T Stimpson) *a towards rr* **22/1**
06-0 **11** *shd* **Barzak (IRE)**[28] [156] 7-8-5 **45**...(bt) DaleGibson 6 36
(S R Bowring) *a rr* **8/1**[3]
-000 **12** *1 1/4* **Far Note (USA)**[7] [374] 9-8-5 **45**.......................................(bt) PaulEddery 1 32
(S R Bowring) *rdn along early: chsd ldrs on inner tl rdn and wknd over 2f out* **50/1**
-660 **13** *3/4* **Drury Lane (IRE)**[11] [337] 7-8-5 **45**..................................(p) PaulQuinn 13 30
(D W Chapman) *a towards rr* **50/1**
2334 **14** *2* **Mind Alert**[2] [430] 6-8-9 **49**..(v) AdamKirby 2 28
(D Shaw) *hld up in tch: effrt and sme hdwy 2f out: sn rdn and btn* **10/3**[2]
1m 16.52s (-0.38) **Going Correction** -0.10s/f (Stan) **14** Ran SP% **121.8**
Speed ratings (Par 101):98,97,94,94,93 92,91,90,90,89 89,87,86,84
CSF £184.33 CT £2273.13 TOTE £30.30: £6.20, £2.50, £3.80; EX 279.20 TRIFECTA Not won..
Owner Ian Emmerson **Bred** M Berger **Trained** Holmside, Co Durham
■ Stewards' Enquiry : Emmett Stack one-day ban: used whip with excessive frequency (Feb 24)
FOCUS
Modest fare, though competitive enough and several had a chance passing the furlong pole. Just run-of-the-mill form.
Mind Alert Official explanation: jockey said gelding ran flat

449 PONTIN'S FAMILY HOLIDAYS MAIDEN STKS — 1m (F)
2:20 (2:26) (Class 5) 3-Y-O+ — £2,968 (£876; £438) Stalls Low

Form — RPR

1 **Rich Lord** 3-8-9 ow1 ... RobertWinston 14 — 72+
(J D Bethell) *midfield on outer: gd hdwy 3f out: cl up 2f out: rdn: edgd lft and led appr last: kpt on* **33/1**

2 2 ½ **Ansells Pride (IRE)**[23] [204] 4-9-13 ... PatCosgrave 5 — 75
(B Smart) *cl up: rdn to ld 2f out: drvn and hdd appr last: kpt on wl u.p fnl f* **4/1**[2]

0-32 3 nk **Hessian (IRE)**[15] [293] 3-8-3 71 ... HayleyTurner 11 — 64+
(M L W Bell) *chsd ldrs: rdn along and outpcd over 2f out: styd on wl u.p ent last: nrst fin* **7/4**[1]

6- 4 2 ½ **Riguez Dancer**[66] [6757] 3-8-8 ... AdrianTNicholls 9 — 63
(P C Haslam) *towards rr: gd hdwy wl over 1f out: sn rdn and styd on strly ins last: nrst fin* **33/1**

/32- 5 1 ¼ **Wulimaster (USA)**[232] [2934] 4-9-13 74 ... PaulHanagan 10 — 65
(D W Barker) *towards rr: pushed along 3f out: styd on strly fnl 2f: nrst fin* **8/1**

4 6 ½ **John Dillon (IRE)**[28] [149] 3-8-8 ... DeanMcKeown 6 — 59
(P C Haslam) *led: rdn along 3f out: hdd 2f out and grad wknd* **13/2**

0 7 5 **Tina's Ridge (IRE)**[36] [69] 3-8-8 ... DavidAllan 1 — 48
(E J Alston) *cl up on inner: rdn along 3f out and grad wknd* **100/1**

8 1 ½ **Ankara** 3-8-3 ... JoeFanning 3 — 39
(M Johnston) *dwlt: sn trcking ldrs: rdn along 3f out and grad wknd* **5/1**[3]

00 9 5 **Danalova**[21] [222] 3-7-11 ow1 ... JamesRogers(7) 4 — 29
(R A Fahey) *s.i.s: a rr* **100/1**

44 10 1 ½ **Cap St Jean (IRE)**[7] [375] 3-8-8 ... DaleGibson 13 — 29
(P C Haslam) *a towards rr* **28/1**

0 11 6 **Diamond Key (IRE)**[3] [423] 3-8-0 ... DominicFox(3) 7 — 11
(M G Quinlan) *dwlt: a towards rr* **66/1**

0 12 2 ½ **Park's Prodigy**[28] [149] 3-8-8 ... ChrisCatlin 8 — 10
(P C Haslam) *prom: rdn along over 3f out: sn wknd* **66/1**

3-6 13 6 **Soldiers Romance**[11] [338] 4-9-8 ... DuranFentiman(5) 12 — —
(T D Easterby) *cl up on outer: rdn along over 3f out: sn wknd* **40/1**

1m 44.05s (-0.55) **Going Correction** -0.10s/f (Stan)
WFA 3 from 4yo 19lb — 13 Ran SP% **114.2**
Speed ratings (Par 103):98,97,97,94,93 92,87,86,81,79 73,71,65
CSF £151.32 TOTE £28.90: £6.10, £1.90, £1.40; EX 132.50 TRIFECTA Not won..
Owner Mrs J E Vickers **Bred** Biddestone Stud **Trained** Middleham Moor, N Yorks

FOCUS
This maiden looked nothing special on paper beforehand and the result was a bit of a shock, but there were some interesting performances in behind and a few winners should come out of this, although the bare form is not strong.

450 PONTINSBINGO.COM (S) STKS — 7f (F)
2:50 (2:55) (Class 6) 4-Y-O+ — £2,184 (£644; £322) Stalls Low

Form — RPR

4021 1 **Louisiade (IRE)**[8] [366] 6-9-4 49 ... (p) NCallan 1 — 58
(K A Ryan) *trckd ldrs: swtchd lft and rdn to ld over 1f out: drvn and kpt on wl fnl f* **9/4**[1]

3303 2 ½ **Penel (IRE)**[2] [430] 6-8-7 50 ... (p) RoryMoore(5) 11 — 50
(P T Midgley) *hld up in rr: hdwy on inner 2f out: rdn over 1f out: ev ch ins last: drvn and no ex towards fin* **11/4**[2]

0/00 3 ½ **Mr Bountiful (IRE)**[2] [435] 9-8-12 42 ... (bt) AlanDaly 9 — 49
(C J Teague) *hld up towards rr: hdwy 2f out: rdn over 1f out: styd on wl fnl f: nrst fin* **66/1**

-040 4 2 **Kingsmaite**[8] [371] 6-9-4 60 ... (bt) PhillipMakin 7 — 50
(S R Bowring) *prom: effrt to chal over 2f out: sn rdn and ev ch tl drvn and fnd little ent last* **4/1**[3]

2110 5 ¾ **Mill By The Stream**[14] [306] 5-8-11 62 ... HaddenFrost(7) 4 — 48
(Tom Dascombe) *in tch: hdwy over 2f out: rdn and ev ch over 1f out: drvn and wknd ent last* **4/1**[3]

0-00 6 hd **Tuscan Flyer**[11] [339] 9-8-12 42 ... (b) SebSanders 2 — 41
(R Bastiman) *led: rdn along over 2f out: sn drvn: hdd & wknd over 1f out* **33/1**

005- 7 3 ½ **Sister Gee (IRE)**[105] [6277] 5-8-7 40 ... MickyFenton 5 — 27
(R Hollinshead) *chsd ldrs: rdn along over 2f out: sn one pce* **33/1**

3010 8 ½ **A Teen**[9] [350] 9-9-4 46 ... ShaneKelly 10 — 37
(P Howling) *chsd ldrs: rdn along 2f out: sn wknd* **25/1**

6-00 9 2 **Mytton's Dream**[23] [206] 5-8-7 30 ... (b) EdwardCreighton 6 — 21
(Miss Joanne Priest) *dwlt: a rr* **80/1**

2065 10 5 **Fraternity**[8] [364] 10-8-9 44 ... NeilChalmers(3) 8 — 13
(J A Pickering) *cl up: rdn along 3f out and sn wknd* **22/1**

1m 29.97s (-0.83) **Going Correction** -0.10s/f (Stan) — 10 Ran SP% **114.2**
Speed ratings (Par 101):100,99,98,96,95 95,91,90,88,82
CSF £7.84 TOTE £3.30: £1.30, £1.60, £10.10; EX 10.50 Trifecta £272.50 Part won. Pool: £383.90 - 0.33 winning units..There was no bid for the winner.
Owner Whitestonecliffe Racing Partnership **Bred** Mrs Noelle Walsh **Trained** Hambleton, N Yorks
■ Stewards' Enquiry : Rory Moore one-day ban: used whip with excessive frequency (Feb 24)

FOCUS
An ordinary seller, in which there were six in a line across the track approaching the furlong pole. Louisiade did not need to improve to follow up his Wolverhampton win, with the third holding down this form.

451 PONTIN'S BOOK EARLY H'CAP — 1m (F)
3:20 (3:25) (Class 4) (0-85,85) 4-Y-O+ — £4,857 (£1,445; £722; £360) Stalls Low

Form — RPR

1-65 1 **Dichoh**[20] [233] 4-8-5 74 ... ChrisCatlin 1 — 87+
(M A Jarvis) *a.p: hdwy 2f out: rdn to ld over 1f out: drvn and edgd lft ins last: kpt on* **13/2**

56-5 2 1 ¼ **Byron Bay**[21] [227] 5-8-12 81 ... TonyCulhane 3 — 91+
(I Semple) *dwlt: hld up in tch: hdwy on inner 2f out: rdn to chal 1f out: ev ch whn n.m.r ins last: sn drvn and no ex* **5/1**[3]

000- 3 1 ¾ **Namroud (USA)**[76] [6241] 8-8-2 71 oh3 ... PaulHanagan 5 — 76
(R A Fahey) *plld hrd: clsd up: effrt 2f out: sn rdn and kpt on same pce ins last* **12/1**

11-0 4 ½ **Orpen Wide (IRE)**[17] [185] 5-8-4 78 ... RoryMoore(5) 4 — 82
(M C Chapman) *led over 2f: cl up tl led again 3f out: rdn over 2f out: drvn and hdd over 1f out: kpt on same pce* **12/1**

-403 5 ¾ **Speed Dial Harry (IRE)**[14] [308] 5-8-2 74 ... (v) LiamJones(3) 2 — 76
(C R Dore) *trckd ldrs: effrt 2f out: sn rdn and one pce appr last* **6/1**

0-00 6 ½ **Tyzack (IRE)**[22] [218] 6-8-7 76 ... MickyFenton 6 — 77
(W M Brisbourne) *chsd ldrs on outer: rdn along over 2f out: sn one pce* **12/1**

/00- 7 5 **Primus Inter Pares (IRE)**[11] [865] 6-9-2 85 ... RobertWinston 8 — 74
(N Wilson) *dwlt: sn cl up: led over 4f out: hdd 3f out: sn rdn along and wknd 2f out* **25/1**

210- 8 11 **Red Contact (USA)**[66] [6772] 6-8-6 78 ... (p) GregFairley(3) 9 — 42
(A Dickman) *s.i.s: a rr* **7/2**[1]

1-51 P **Daring Affair**[18] [256] 6-8-13 82 ... NCallan 7 — —
(K R Burke) *trckd ldrs tl lost pl qckly 3f out: sn p.u and dismntd* **4/1**[2]

1m 43.51s (-1.09) **Going Correction** -0.10s/f (Stan) — 9 Ran SP% **113.4**
Speed ratings (Par 105):101,99,98,97,96 96,91,80,—
CSF £38.21 CT £380.68 TOTE £6.50: £2.20, £2.20, £4.50; EX 22.00 Trifecta £297.70 Part won. Pool: £419.40 - 0.77 winning units..
Owner T G Warner **Bred** Red House Stud **Trained** Newmarket, Suffolk

FOCUS
What looked a competitive handicap beforehand was ruined by a farcical early pace and that, combined with favourite Red Contact blowing the start and second favourite Daring Affair going wrong, makes the form suspect. The winner looks progressive.
Red Contact(USA) Official explanation: trainer said gelding finished lame

452 PONTINS.COM H'CAP — 6f (F)
3:50 (3:56) (Class 2) (0-100,92) 4-Y-O+ — £11,334 (£3,372; £1,685; £841) Stalls Low

Form — RPR

5-45 1 **Bahamian Pirate (USA)**[5] [391] 12-9-4 92 ... AdrianTNicholls 4 — 102
(D Nicholls) *hld up: hdwy on outer 2f out: sn rdn along: styd on strly to ld ins last* **12/1**

54-6 2 ¾ **Saviours Spirit**[24] [198] 6-8-13 87 ... JoeFanning 5 — 95
(T G Mills) *keen: prom: effrt 2f out: rdn to ld briefly ent last: sn hdd and one pce towards fin* **9/2**[2]

306- 3 ¾ **Desperate Dan**[191] [4180] 6-8-11 85 ... (b) ShaneKelly 6 — 91
(J A Osborne) *wnt rt s: trckd ldrs: hdwy on bit wl over 1f out and sn ev ch: rdn ent last and kpt on same pce* **20/1**

04-2 4 1 ¼ **Red Cape (FR)**[31] [118] 4-9-2 90 ... BrettDoyle 8 — 92
(Jane Chapple-Hyam) *cl up: led over 2f out: rdn wl over 1f out: drvn and hdd ent last: sn wknd* **1/1**[1]

-005 5 hd **Quiet Times (IRE)**[3] [419] 8-8-11 85 ... (b) NCallan 3 — 86
(K A Ryan) *led: rdn along and hdd over 2f out: drvn and rallied appr last: sn wknd* **6/1**[3]

-243 6 2 **Prince Tum Tum (USA)**[14] [307] 7-8-13 87 ... DeanMcKeown 1 — 82
(D Shaw) *hld up: swtchd lft and hdwy wl over 1f out: sn rdn and no imp appr last* **17/2**

40-0 7 5 **Smokin Beau**[28] [155] 10-8-3 82 ... DuranFentiman(5) 2 — 62
(N P Littmoden) *chsd ldrs on inner: rdn along over 2f out: sn btn* **25/1**

0-00 8 1 ¾ **Garstang**[3] [419] 4-8-4 78 oh2 ... (b) PaulHanagan 7 — 53
(Peter Grayson) *bmpd s: sn rdn along and a bhd* **16/1**

1m 14.78s (-2.12) **Going Correction** -0.10s/f (Stan) — 8 Ran SP% **115.2**
Speed ratings (Par 109):110,109,108,106,106 103,96,94
CSF £65.53 CT £1081.47 TOTE £15.50: £3.20, £2.00, £4.90; EX 77.90 Trifecta £268.00 Pool: £505.83 - 1.34 winning units..
Owner Lucayan Stud and G G N Bloodstock **Bred** Trackside Farm & Liberation Farm & G A Seelbinder **Trained** Sessay, N Yorks

FOCUS
They went no great pace in this valuable handicap. The winner is still a decent performer and while the favourite disappointed the overall form is solid.

NOTEBOOK
Bahamian Pirate(USA), dropped 5lb and back down in trip, came with a sustained run on the outside to land the spoils. It was good to see him earn his first victory since the Nunthorpe Stakes of 2004 but further successes at his age may prove hard to come by, although he is well in on last year's turf form. (op 11-1)
Saviours Spirit, whose only previous taste of Fibresand was over two years ago, had every chance, but hung a little when brought under pressure before keeping on for second. (op 5-1)
Desperate Dan, having his first run for five months, travelled well as usual but did not find much when let down. A strongly-run five furlongs is probably most suitable for him, but he is the type who needs everything to click into place. (op 16-1)
Red Cape(FR), put up 5lb after his second to Areyoutalkingtome in a conditions event at Lingfield, would probably have been seen to better effect off a truer gallop. (tchd 11-10)
Quiet Times(IRE) made the running, as he had at Lingfield three days earlier, but after sticking to the inside rail in the straight he could not hold off his challengers. (op 7-1)

453 PONTIN'S HOLIDAYS H'CAP — 1m 4f (F)
4:20 (4:25) (Class 6) (0-65,64) 4-Y-O+ — £2,388 (£705; £352) Stalls Low

Form — RPR

11-1 1 **Jazrawy**[14] [305] 5-9-5 64 ... DanielTudhope 5 — 76
(D Carroll) *mde all: qcknd over 3f out: rdn clr wl over 1f out: kpt on gamely u.p ins last* **11/2**[3]

00-2 2 shd **Raise The Heights (IRE)**[16] [279] 4-8-11 59 ... NCallan 8 — 71
(J G Portman) *trckd ldrs: pushed along over 3f out: rdn and edgd lft over 1f out: drvn and styd on wl fnl f: jst hld* **15/2**

0-20 3 2 ½ **Mahmjra**[8] [369] 5-8-13 58 ... PFredericks 1 — 66
(C N Allen) *a.p on inner: effrt 3f out: rdn 2f out: sn drvn and kpt on same pce appr last* **20/1**

00-4 4 2 ½ **Proper Article (IRE)**[35] [74] 5-8-5 57 ... (bt) HaddenFrost(7) 9 — 61
(Miss J E Foster) *a.p: effrt 3f out: sn rdn along and wknd over 1f out* **28/1**

03-1 5 1 **Bolckow**[19] [242] 4-8-12 60 ... MickyFenton 6 — 63+
(J T Stimpson) *hld up in rr: gd hdwy over 3f out: chsd ldrs 2f out: sn rdn and no imp appr last* **10/3**[2]

-340 6 1 ½ **Opera Writer (IRE)**[29] [142] 4-8-10 58 ... GrahamGibbons 3 — 60+
(R Hollinshead) *hld up: a rr* **14/1**

004- 7 5 **Shape Up (IRE)**[90] [6494] 7-9-5 64 ... (v[1]) RobertWinston 4 — 56
(R Craggs) *a towards rr* **12/1**

-012 8 2 ½ **Greenbelt**[7] [377] 6-9-2 61 ... ChrisCatlin 10 — 49
(G M Moore) *trckd ldng pair: hdwy 4f out: rdn along 3f out: wknd over 2f out* **5/2**[1]

103- 9 4 **Silver Mont (IRE)**[103] [6305] 4-8-3 51 oh2 ow1 ... (bt) PaulEddery 7 — 33
(S R Bowring) *chsd ldrs: rdn along over 4f out: sn wknd* **20/1**

0501 10 3 ½ **Danelor (IRE)**[7] [372] 9-8-5 50 5ex ... (p) DeanMcKeown 2 — 26
(D Shaw) *hld up: a rr* **16/1**

2m 37.45s (-4.64) **Going Correction** -0.10s/f (Stan)
WFA 4 from 5yo+ 3lb — 10 Ran SP% **112.0**
Speed ratings (Par 101):111,110,109,107,106 105,102,100,98,95
CSF £42.86 CT £756.00 TOTE £4.50: £1.90, £2.60, £5.90; EX 38.90 Trifecta £345.10 Part won. Pool: £486.16 - 0.67 winning units..
Owner Mrs B Ramsden **Bred** Scuderia Antonella S R L **Trained** Sledmere, E Yorks

FOCUS
A very smart winning time for a race of its class. Good form for the grade, the progressive Jazrawy making all. The runner-up is also progressive and the form should work out.
Greenbelt Official explanation: trainer's rep said race may have come too soon

454 PONTIN'S H'CAP 7f (F)

4:50 (4:55) (Class 6) (0-60,56) 3-Y-O £2,388 (£705; £352) Stalls Low

Form RPR

30-6 **1** **Poniard (IRE)**[21] [223] 3-9-2 **54**....(p) RobertWinston 5 61
(D W Barker) *cl up: rdn over 2f out: led over 1 1/2f out: drvn and edgd lft ins last: kpt on* **25/1**

-400 **2** 1/2 **Totally Free**[8] [360] 3-9-3 **55**....(v) HayleyTurner 9 61
(M D I Usher) *in tch: hdwy 3f out: rdn to chse ldrs 2f out: drvn and styd on wl fnl f* **28/1**

0-10 **3** 4 **Heaven's Gates**[9] [348] 3-9-4 **56**.... NCallan 4 51
(K A Ryan) *led: rdn along over 2f out: hdd over 1 1/2f out: sn drvn and wandered: wknd over 1f out* **15/8**[1]

00-0 **4** 1 **Pretty Game**[18] [258] 3-8-7 **45**.... CatherineGannon 13 38
(K A Ryan) *stdd and swtchd lft s: hld up in rr: hdwy 2f out: sn rdn and kpt on ins last: nrst fin* **25/1**

3-60 **5** 1/2 **Ten Black**[29] [139] 3-9-1 **53**.... PhillipMakin 11 44
(R Brotherton) *in tch: rdn along over 2f out: sn drvn and no imp wl over 1f out* **14/1**

6-31 **6** 6 **Kings Shillings**[18] [253] 3-9-4 **56**....(b) DanielTudhope 2 31
(D Carroll) *dwlt and in rr: hdwy on inner wl over 2f out: sn rdn and nvr nr ldrs* **13/2**[3]

00-4 **7** 3/4 **Fire Alarm**[18] [253] 3-8-9 **47**.... GrahamGibbons 6 20
(J J Quinn) *s.i.s: a towards rr* **3/1**[2]

60-4 **8** 1/2 **Flamestone**[23] [202] 3-9-2 **54**....(b) SebSanders 10 26
(J D Bethell) *prom: rdn along and swtchd lft 2f out: sn drvn and wknd wl over 1f out* **17/2**

0-00 **9** 1/2 **Bonny Scotland (IRE)**[7] [378] 3-8-4 **45**.... PatrickMathers(3) 3 15
(I W McInnes) *chsd ldrs: rdn along 3f out: sn wknd* **66/1**

400- **10** 8 **Newport Lass (IRE)**[150] [5364] 3-9-1 **53**.... PatCosgrave 8 2
(K R Burke) *a rr* **18/1**

44-5 **11** 19 **Annia Faustina (IRE)**[16] [284] 3-9-3 **55**....(b1) AdamKirby 1 —
(J L Spearing) *chsd ldrs on inner: rdn along 3f out: sn wknd* **12/1**

1m 29.59s (-1.21) **Going Correction** -0.10s/f (Stan) 11 Ran SP% **115.9**
Speed ratings (Par 95):102,101,96,95,95 88,87,86,86,77 55
CSF £558.21 CT £1949.77 TOTE £17.20: £4.60, £6.90, £1.10; EX 250.20 Trifecta £384.00 Pool: £540.94 - 1.00 winning units. Place 6 £658.24, Place 5 £99.05.
Owner D W Barker **Bred** K Maginn **Trained** Scorton, N Yorks

FOCUS
A low-grade handicap in which the first two finished clear. The time was decent and the form might prove a bit better than it looks on paper, with the winner and third on potentially fair marks.
Flamestone Official explanation: jockey said gelding lost its action
T/Jkpt: Not won. T/Plt: £447.30 to a £1 stake. Pool: £94,776.40. 154.65 winning tickets. T/Qpdt: £73.70 to a £1 stake. Pool: £7,838.60. 78.70 winning tickets. JR

[416] LINGFIELD (L-H)

Wednesday, February 14

OFFICIAL GOING: Standard
Wind: moderate, half-against Weather: Cloudy early, sunny from race 4

455 PONTINS.COM CLAIMING STKS 1m (P)

1:50 (1:52) (Class 6) 4-Y-O+ £2,184 (£644; £322) Stalls High

Form RPR

5-00 **1** **Samuel Charles**[4] [427] 9-9-11 75.... TPQueally 6 69+
(C R Dore) *plld hrd off slow pce: sn trcking ldrs: led over 2f out: sn clr: drvn to hold on fnl f* **9/4**[2]

2-20 **2** 1 **Rafferty (IRE)**[9] [359] 8-9-3 70.... LPKeniry 1 55
(S Dow) *dwlt: sn cl up: effrt 2f out: kpt on to take 2nd ins fnl f* **10/1**

-006 **3** hd **Prince Dayjur (USA)**[9] [359] 8-9-7 71.... DeanMcKeown 3 59
(J Pearce) *s.i.s: hld up in rr: pushed along whn pce qcknd over 3f out: r.o to take 3rd ins fnl f* **5/2**[3]

05-0 **4** 1 1/4 **Laugh 'n Cry**[17] [274] 6-9-6 49....(b) EddieAhern 4 55
(C A Cyzer) *t.k.h: hld up in rr: effrt and n.m.r over 2f out: nt pce to chal* **11/1**

6243 **5** shd **Mystic Man (FR)**[9] [359] 9-9-1 62....(b) DanielTudhope 7 50
(I W McInnes) *plld hrd on outside: sn cl up: rdn over 2f out: chsd wnr over 1f out tl ins fnl f: hld whn n.m.r nr fin* **2/1**[1]

500- **6** 3 **Always A Story**[104] [6307] 5-8-13 40.... PaulEddery 5 41
(Miss D Mountain) *set slow pce: led tl over 2f out: sn outpcd* **66/1**

/0-0 **7** 8 **Mo Chroi**[10] [349] 4-8-9 44 ow4.... AmirQuinn(3) 2 21
(J J Bridger) *cl up: rdn and lost pl whn pce qcknd over 3f out: sn bhd* **66/1**

1m 39.18s (-0.25) **Going Correction** -0.175s/f (Stan) 7 Ran SP% **113.1**
Speed ratings (Par 101):94,93,92,91,91 88,80
CSF £23.92 TOTE £3.40: £1.90, £2.80; EX 32.90.There was no bid for the winner.
Owner Chris Marsh **Bred** Sheikh Mohammed Obaid Al Maktoum **Trained** West Pinchbeck, Lincs

FOCUS
A reasonable claimer, but they went only a steady pace. Dubious overall form, the form horses not at their best and the fourth and sixth closer than they were entitled to be.
Samuel Charles Official explanation: trainer said, regarding apparent improvement in form, that the gelding was better suited by the tactics of being ridden more prominently
Prince Dayjur(USA) Official explanation: jockey said he lost an iron inside final 2f

456 PONTIN'S HOLIDAYS MAIDEN STKS 7f (P)

2:20 (2:22) (Class 5) 3-Y-O £3,071 (£906; £453) Stalls Low

Form RPR

444- **1** **Endiamo (IRE)**[151] [5371] 3-9-3 87.... RichardHughes 4 79+
(M P Tregoning) *t.k.h: trckd ldrs: effrt and squeezed through over 1f out: rdn to ld ins fnl f: readily* **1/2**[1]

2 1 1/2 **Daytona (IRE)** 3-9-3.... JoeFanning 8 75+
(M Johnston) *led after 1f and controlled tempo: qcknd 2f out: hdd and nt pce of wnr ins fnl f* **14/1**

236- **3** 3/4 **Emerald Wilderness (IRE)**[120] [6023] 3-9-3 76.... ChrisCatlin 6 73
(M R Channon) *hld up in tch: effrt and edgd rt over 2f out: unbalanced and hanging in st: kpt on* **16/1**

3 **4** 3/4 **Esteem Machine (USA)**[14] [311] 3-9-3.... AntonyProcter 13 71
(D R C Elsworth) *t.k.h: in tch: rdn and kpt on fnl 2f: unable to chal* **8/1**

2- **5** 3/4 **Resplendent Ace (IRE)**[73] [6689] 3-9-3.... ShaneKelly 9 69+
(P Howling) *mid-div: rdn and styd on fnl 2f: nt rch ldrs* **13/2**[2]

6 1 **Art Professor (IRE)** 3-9-3.... SebSanders 11 66+
(J W Hills) *rn green towards rr: nrst fin* **33/1**

64-0 **7** 1/2 **Realy Naughty (IRE)**[31] [127] 3-8-10 66.... KarenKenny(7) 2 65
(B G Powell) *settled towards rr: nudged along and styd on steadily fnl 2f: nvr in chalng position* **66/1**

-6 **8** hd **Scarlet Oak**[16] [293] 3-8-12.... AdamKirby 10 59+
(D J S Ffrench Davis) *t.k.h early: mid-div on outside: rdn and kpt on fnl 2f: nt pce to chal* **100/1**

00 **9** hd **Woodygo**[16] [293] 3-9-0.... StephaneBreux(3) 3 64+
(J R Best) *s.s: bhd tl r.o fnl 2f: gng on at fin* **100/1**

00- **10** 3/4 **Nordic Light (USA)**[188] [4295] 3-9-3.... AdrianMcCarthy 7 62
(P W Chapple-Hyam) *led 1f: chsd ldr after tl wknd over 1f out* **33/1**

11 3 **Faithful Ruler (USA)** 3-9-3.... EddieAhern 1 54
(M A Magnusson) *dwlt: hld up in midfield: outpcd fnl 2f* **7/1**[3]

0-60 **12** 2 1/2 **Rogers Lodger**[21] [231] 3-9-3 60.... TPQueally 5 47
(J Akehurst) *a bhd* **100/1**

0 **13** 3 **Noravana (IRE)**[29] [149] 3-8-12.... EdwardCreighton 12 34
(Miss V Haigh) *t.k.h: chsd ldrs: bmpd and wknd over 2f out* **100/1**

1m 24.89s (-1.00) **Going Correction** -0.175s/f (Stan) 13 Ran SP% **127.5**
Speed ratings (Par 97):98,96,95,94,93 92,92,91,91,90 87,84,80
CSF £11.20 TOTE £1.60: £1.10, £3.20, £2.80; EX 13.20 Trifecta £22.30 Pool £268.49 - 8.53 winning units..
Owner Sheikh Ahmed Al Maktoum **Bred** Darley **Trained** Lambourn, Berks

FOCUS
A good maiden for the time of year that should produce its share of winners, both in maidens and handicaps. The form should work out.

457 PONTIN'S "FAMILY HOLIDAYS" H'CAP 2m (P)

2:50 (2:51) (Class 4) (0-85,85) 4-Y-O+ £4,857 (£1,445; £722; £360) Stalls Low

Form RPR

12-3 **1** **Night Cruise (IRE)**[25] [192] 4-9-0 **78**.... JimCrowley 5 89+
(J A Osborne) *chsd ldrs: led over 2f out: hld on gamely fnl f* **4/1**[1]

114- **2** nk **Billich**[67] [6766] 4-9-2 **80**.... JoeFanning 10 91
(E J O'Neill) *hld up towards rr: gd hdwy over 3f out: str chal fnl f: nt qckn fnl 50 yds* **6/1**[3]

542- **3** 2 **Nawamees (IRE)**[122] [5991] 9-9-10 **82**....(p) JimmyFortune 4 91
(G L Moore) *hld up in rr: gd hdwy to chse ldng pair 2f out: styd on same pce* **6/1**[3]

5-00 **4** 2 1/2 **Newnham (IRE)**[16] [297] 6-8-9 **67**.... BrettDoyle 7 73+
(J R Boyle) *hld up towards rr: effrt on rail whn hmpd and hld up in run 3f out: r.o again fnl f* **12/1**

5/51 **5** nk **Positive Profile (IRE)**[17] [283] 9-8-13 **71**.... GrahamGibbons 6 76
(J J Quinn) *chsd ldrs: rdn over 3f out: one pce* **8/1**

2-05 **6** 3 1/2 **Valance (IRE)**[9] [362] 7-9-13 **85**....(t) SebSanders 1 86
(C R Egerton) *led 1f: led 4f out tl over 2f out: sn outpcd* **9/1**

64-1 **7** 3 **Linden Lime**[25] [192] 5-8-13 **71**.... PaulDoe 2 68
(Jamie Poulton) *hld up in rr: nt clr run 3f out: rdn 2f out: little rspnse and n.d* **8/1**

522- **8** 12 **Jeepstar**[74] [6673] 7-9-5 **77**.... AdamKirby 9 60
(S C Williams) *led after 1f: hdd and hrd rdn 4f out: wknd 3f out* **9/2**[2]

300/ **9** 4 **It's The Limit (USA)**[296] [4159] 8-9-10 **82**.... HayleyTurner 8 60
(W K Goldsworthy) *mid-div: rdn 5f out: wknd 3f out* **33/1**

0/01 **10** 4 **Dolzago**[16] [291] 7-8-8 **66** oh1....(b) FergusSweeney 3 39
(G L Moore) *mid-div: rdn over 4f out: wknd 3f out* **8/1**

3m 20.07s (-8.72) **Going Correction** -0.175s/f (Stan) course record
WFA 4 from 5yo+ 6lb 10 Ran SP% **120.7**
Speed ratings (Par 105):114,113,112,111,111 109,108,102,100,98
CSF £29.20 CT £146.28 TOTE £3.10: £1.90, £1.60, £3.10; EX 33.90 Trifecta £109.40 Pool £447.21 - 2.90 winning units..
Owner Mr & Mrs G Middlebrook **Bred** G And Mrs Middlebrook **Trained** Upper Lambourn, Berks

FOCUS
A competitive staying handicap and the winning time was very smart for the class, beating the previous course record set in August 1992 by 2/100ths of a second. The winner is progressive and the form looks solid.
Nawamees(IRE) Official explanation: jockey said gelding hung left
Dolzago Official explanation: jockey said gelding ran flat

458 PONTINSBINGO.COM MAIDEN STKS 1m 5f (P)

3:20 (3:21) (Class 5) 4-Y-O+ £3,071 (£906; £453) Stalls Low

Form RPR

1 **Caucasienne (FR)**[111] 4-8-12 68.... EddieAhern 12 66+
(J W Hills) *hld up in midfield: hdwy over 2f out: rdn to ld 1f out: readily* **8/1**

02-6 **2** 3 1/2 **Master'n Commander**[18] [265] 5-9-7 58.... TonyCulhane 9 66
(C A Cyzer) *in tch: slt ld 2f out tl 1f out: nt pce of wnr* **9/1**

0-43 **3** 3/4 **Follow On**[18] [265] 5-9-7 68.... TPQueally 8 65+
(A P Jarvis) *hld up towards rr: promising hdwy on outside 5f out: sltly hmpd 3f out: r.o fnl f* **7/2**[1]

2-30 **4** shd **Monets Masterpiece (USA)**[9] [363] 4-9-3 64....(be) GeorgeBaker 3 65
(G L Moore) *stdd s: hld up in rr: effrt on outside 3f out: swtchd to rail and clsd on ldrs over 1f out: one pce* **15/2**

3/ **5** shd **Mac Federal (IRE)**[255] 5-9-7 60.... DaneO'Neill 10 65
(Miss Sheena West) *mid-div: effrt and hrd rdn 3f out: styd on same pce* **9/2**[3]

0-6 **6** 3 **Moving Target (IRE)**[21] [229] 8-9-4.... JerryO'Dwyer(3) 4 60
(Luke Comer, Ire) *dwlt: hld up towards rr: pushed along over 4f out: styd on fnl 2f* **66/1**

2-33 **7** 1 3/4 **Art Investor**[21] [230] 4-9-3 64.... SebSanders 5 57
(D R C Elsworth) *prom: led after 3f tl 2f out: hrd rdn and wknd 1f out* **4/1**[2]

00-4 **8** 3/4 **Sky Walk**[21] [230] 4-9-3 52.... SimonWhitworth 7 56
(Jamie Poulton) *s.s: hld up towards rr: rdn over 2f out: n.d* **50/1**

5 **9** nk **Hi Fi**[21] [230] 9-9-7....(p) ChrisCatlin 11 56
(Ian Williams) *s.s: sn in tch: pressed ldrs 1/2-way: hrd rdn over 2f out: wknd over 1f out* **25/1**

62-3 **10** 3/4 **Recalcitrant**[35] [89] 4-9-3 53.... LPKeniry 1 55
(S Dow) *prom tl wknd over 3f out* **6/1**

6- **11** 11 **Cappanrush (IRE)**[10] [314] 7-9-7.... JimCrowley 6 38
(A Ennis) *in tch: wknd 4f out: sn bhd* **50/1**

6 **12** dist **Mustard Benn**[32] [120] 4-9-0.... NeilChalmers(3) 2 —
(Mouse Hamilton-Fairley) *sn led: hdd after 3f: wknd rapidly 5f out: sn t.o* **100/1**

2m 45.09s (-3.21) **Going Correction** -0.175s/f (Stan)
WFA 4 from 5yo+ 4lb 12 Ran SP% **117.8**
Speed ratings (Par 103):102,99,99,99,99 97,96,95,95,95 88,—
CSF £75.16 TOTE £10.50: £3.10, £3.10, £1.50; EX 121.00 Trifecta £283.20 Part won. Pool £398.90 - 0.10 winning units..
Owner Jerry Jamgotchian **Bred** Dayton Investments Ltd **Trained** Upper Lambourn, Berks

FOCUS
Most of these had already had a few chances coming into this. The form is only modest but seems sound enough, rated though the second.

459 BONUSPRINT.COM H'CAP — 1m 2f (P)
3:50 (3:51) (Class 5) (0-70,70) 4-Y-0+ — £3,071 (£906; £453) Stalls Low

Form / RPR

0-52 **1** **Watchmaker**[18] 265 4-8-9 **62** .... PaulDoe 9 — 72+
(W J Knight) *trckd ldr: led and kicked on 3f out: drvn to hold on fnl f* **13/2**[2]

-402 **2** ¾ **Blackmail (USA)**[14] 309 9-8-8 **60** .... (b) EddieAhern 7 — 68
(P Mitchell) *trckd ldrs: hung rt over 2f out: swtchd outside and hrd rdn over 1f out: r.o to take 2nd ins fnl f* **14/1**

0132 **3** nk **Discotheque (USA)**[4] 426 4-8-9 **62** .... ShaneKelly 10 — 69
(P Howling) *hld up in midfield: swtchd wd and hdwy over 1f out: r.o wl fnl f* **8/1**

13-0 **4** 1½ **Broughtons Folly**[32] 117 4-9-1 **68** .... BrettDoyle 2 — 72
(W J Musson) *hld up towards rr: rdn and hdwy over 1f out: nrst fin* **8/1**

62-2 **5** ½ **Pab Special (IRE)**[4] 427 4-9-3 **70** .... PatCosgrave 8 — 73
(K R Burke) *cl up: chsd ldr over 2f out tl ins fnl f: one pce* **3/1**[1]

1-10 **6** 1½ **Street Life (IRE)**[25] 195 9-8-7 **66** .... DebraEngland(7) 6 — 66
(W J Musson) *s.s: hld up in rr: shkn up and styd on fnl 2f: n.d* **10/1**

130- **7** nk **Makai**[93] 6462 4-8-9 **65** .... (b) AmirQuinn(3) 1 — 65
(J J Bridger) *led tl 3f out: wknd over 1f out* **66/1**

6233 **8** ¾ **Voice Mail**[11] 341 8-7-10 **55** oh2 .... (b) DavidProbert(7) 5 — 53
(A M Balding) *t.k.h in rr: shkn up over 2f out: nvr nr ldrs* **16/1**

05-0 **9** shd **Garrulous (UAE)**[11] 342 4-8-9 **62** .... RichardHughes 3 — 60
(G L Moore) *chsd ldrs: rdn 3f out: wknd ins fnl 2f* **3/1**[1]

-163 **U** **Tancredi (SWE)**[4] 426 5-8-9 **61** .... HayleyTurner 4 — —
(N B King) *fly-jmpd and uns rdr leaving stalls* **7/1**[3]

2m 6.21s (-1.58) **Going Correction** -0.175s/f (Stan)
WFA 4 from 5yo+ 1lb — **10** Ran SP% **121.2**
Speed ratings (Par 103):99,98,98,96,96 95,95,94,94,—
CSF £96.71 CT £749.85 TOTE £7.90: £2.10, £3.40, £2.20; EX 54.20 Trifecta £245.80 Pool £633.59 - 1.83 winning units..
Owner Hesmonds Stud **Bred** Hesmonds Stud Ltd **Trained** Patching, W Sussex

FOCUS
An ordinary handicap, run at a slow pace. The bare form is only ordinary but the winner looks sure to build on this.
Garrulous(UAE) Official explanation: jockey said gelding had no more to give

460 PHOTO BOOKS FROM BONUSPRINT.COM H'CAP — 1m 2f (P)
4:20 (4:21) (Class 5) (0-70,70) 3-Y-0 — £3,071 (£906; £453) Stalls Low

Form / RPR

05-4 **1** **Professor Twinkle**[25] 196 3-9-0 **66** .... PaulDoe 4 — 70+
(W J Knight) *cl 2nd: jnd ldr on bit 4f out: rdn 2f out: slt ld over 1f out: hld on narrowly in sustained battle* **3/1**[2]

54-0 **2** shd **Spring Glory**[15] 304 3-8-13 **65** .... SebSanders 1 — 69+
(Sir Mark Prescott) *led: jnd by wnr and drvn along 4f out: narrowly hdd over 1f out: rallied gamely: jst hld* **5/2**[1]

034- **3** 2½ **Zelos (IRE)**[193] 4140 3-9-4 **70** .... ShaneKelly 5 — 69
(J A Osborne) *sn chsng ldng pair: one pce fnl 3f: 3rd and btn whn swvd lft nr fin* **7/2**[3]

6261 **4** nk **Beau Sancy**[9] 370 3-8-10 **67** 6ex .... TolleyDean(5) 7 — 65
(R A Harris) *in tch: rdn 4f out: one pce fnl 3f: 4th and hld whn carried lft nr fin* **13/2**

0-20 **5** 1½ **Voss**[18] 267 3-8-4 **56** .... JoeFanning 2 — 53+
(M Johnston) *chsd ldrs: one pce fnl 3f: 5th and hld whn hmpd nr fin* **7/1**

0165 **6** 11 **King Of The Beers (USA)**[16] 294 3-8-4 **56** .... (p) ChrisCatlin 8 — 29
(R A Harris) *mid-div on outside: pushed along 5f out: wknd 3f out* **9/1**

00-0 **7** 1½ **Pajada**[10] 348 3-8-4 **56** oh2 .... HayleyTurner 3 — 26
(M D I Usher) *in tch: rdn 5f out: wknd 3f out* **50/1**

0-00 **8** ½ **Da Schadenfreude (USA)**[10] 348 3-8-8 **60** .... DaleGibson 9 — 29
(W G M Turner) *a bhd* **16/1**

3-30 **9** 2½ **Lordswood (IRE)**[10] 348 3-8-6 **65** .... RyanBird(7) 6 — 29
(J J Bridger) *s.i.s: hld up in rr: sme hdwy on rail 5f out: rdn and wknd 3f out* **14/1**

2m 6.45s (-1.34) **Going Correction** -0.175s/f (Stan) — **9** Ran SP% **126.1**
Speed ratings (Par 97):98,97,95,95,94 85,84,84,82
CSF £12.19 CT £29.06 TOTE £4.40: £1.70, £1.50, £1.60; EX 16.10 Trifecta £30.00 Pool £577.37 - 13.64 winning units..
Owner Mrs Mark Burrell **Bred** Mrs M Burrell **Trained** Patching, W Sussex
■ Stewards' Enquiry : Shane Kelly one-day ban: careless riding (Feb 25)

FOCUS
A race dominated by unexposed types and the form could be quite good for the grade. The first two are likely to prove better than the bare form.

461 GO PONTIN'S H'CAP — 1m (P)
4:50 (4:51) (Class 6) (0-65,65) 4-Y-0+ — £2,388 (£705; £352) Stalls High

Form / RPR

45-1 **1** **Im Ova Ere Dad (IRE)**[20] 243 4-8-11 **60** .... TonyCulhane 9 — 73+
(D E Cantillon) *t.k.h in midfield: hdwy over 2f out: led jst over 1f out: drvn out* **9/2**[1]

5521 **2** 1 **Linda's Colin (IRE)**[11] 341 5-9-1 **64** .... PatCosgrave 11 — 71
(K R Burke) *hld up towards rr: rdn and hdwy over 1f out: r.o to take 2nd ins fnl f* **11/2**[3]

2252 **3** hd **King After**[7] 379 5-8-1 **53** .... (v) StephaneBreux(3) 4 — 60
(J R Best) *hld up in midfield: rdn and hdwy over 1f out: r.o to take 3rd ins fnl f* **7/1**

-601 **4** ¾ **Binnion Bay (IRE)**[7] 383 6-8-9 **61** 6ex ow3 .... (b) AmirQuinn(3) 12 — 66
(J J Bridger) *hld up and bhd: rdn and hdwy fr over 1f out: fin wl* **12/1**

-600 **5** ½ **Wheelavit (IRE)**[9] 359 4-9-2 **65** .... (p) GeorgeBaker 8 — 69
(B G Powell) *stdd s and swtchd to rail: hld up in rr: rdn over 2f out: nrst fin* **20/1**

6-50 **6** ½ **State Dilemma (IRE)**[14] 313 6-8-9 **58** .... (v) DaneO'Neill 1 — 61
(D Shaw) *chsd ldrs: rdn over 1f out: one pce* **14/1**

0234 **7** ¾ **Roman Boy (ARG)**[7] 381 8-8-9 **58** .... (v) MickyFenton 2 — 59
(Stef Liddiard) *led tl jst over 1f out: no ex* **11/2**[3]

1113 **8** nk **Time To Regret**[20] 238 7-9-0 **63** .... (p) DanielTudhope 3 — 64
(I W McInnes) *t.k.h: trckd ldrs: n.m.r over 2f out: rdn and no ex over 1f out* **9/1**

4-05 **9** 2 **Simpsons Gamble (IRE)**[7] 383 4-8-3 **52** .... AdrianMcCarthy 7 — 48
(R M Flower) *t.k.h: prom tl wknd over 1f out* **16/1**

51-0 **10** ¾ **Special Place**[21] 234 4-8-13 **62** .... OscarUrbina 6 — 56
(J A R Toller) *hld up towards rr: sme hdwy on rail ent st: sn hrd rdn and no imp* **5/1**[2]

530- **11** 5 **Blushing Light (USA)**[217] 3410 4-8-13 **62** .... EddieAhern 10 — 45
(M A Magnusson) *wd: hld up in tch: wknd qckly over 2f out: sn bhd* **14/1**

000- **12** 2 **Mocha Java**[68] 6747 4-9-2 **65** .... IanMongan 5 — 43
(Mrs L J Mongan) *t.k.h: prom tl wknd over 2f out* **33/1**

1m 37.05s (-2.38) **Going Correction** -0.175s/f (Stan) — **12** Ran SP% **122.7**
Speed ratings (Par 101):104,103,102,102,101 101,100,100,98,97 92,90
CSF £29.98 CT £178.88 TOTE £4.80: £1.40, £2.80, £3.20; EX 26.60 Trifecta £68.60 Place 6 £78.87, Place 5 £24.12. Pool £292.04 - 3.02 winning units..
Owner Allan Milton **Bred** Golden Vale Stud **Trained** Newmarket, Suffolk

FOCUS
A competitive handicap on paper and it was run at a fair pace thanks to Roman Boy. Solid from, the winner value for extra.
T/Jkpt: Not won. T/Plt: £48.10 to a £1 stake. Pool: £72,960.05. 1,105.40 winning tickets. T/Qpdt: £8.80 to a £1 stake. Pool: £5,342.80. 447.50 winning tickets. LM

448 SOUTHWELL (L-H)
Thursday, February 15

OFFICIAL GOING: Standard
Wind: Fresh, half-against Weather: Overcast, breezy and on the cold side.

462 LADBROKESCASINO.COM APPRENTICE H'CAP — 1m (F)
12:50 (12:50) (Class 6) (0-58,63) 4-Y-0+ — £2,388 (£705; £352) Stalls Low

Form / RPR

0-10 **1** **Granakey (IRE)**[21] 238 4-8-10 **56** .... HaddenFrost(5) 12 — 63
(M G Quinlan) *hld up in mid-div: hdwy 3f out: led 1f out: sn stmbld: styd on* **11/2**[3]

0-63 **2** 1½ **Shunkawakhan (IRE)**[30] 144 4-8-0 **48** .... (p) MarvinCheung(7) 9 — 52
(G C H Chung) *hld up in tch: hdwy over 3f out: led 2f out tl 1f out: no ex* **8/1**

056- **3** ¾ **Blushing Prince (IRE)**[50] 6954 9-8-0 **46** oh1 .... (t) PatrickDonaghy(5) 8 — 48
(R C Guest) *rr-div: hdwy on wd outside over 2f out: styd on wl fnl f* **20/1**

-500 **4** 1¼ **Hometomammy**[4] 435 5-7-12 **46** oh1 .... MatthewDavies(7) 7 — 45
(P W Hiatt) *rr-div: hdwy on ins 3f out: upsides 2f out: kpt on same pce* **33/1**

5301 **5** ¾ **Golden Spectrum (IRE)**[5] 426 8-9-8 **63** 6ex .... (b) JamieHamblett 11 — 61
(R A Harris) *s.i.s: hdwy on wd outside 2f out: styd on ins last* **11/1**

2340 **6** 1¾ **Roman Boy (ARG)**[1] 461 8-9-3 **58** .... (v) AlanRutter 10 — 52
(Stef Liddiard) *rr-div: hdwy over 3f out: nvr rchd ldrs* **7/2**[1]

2233 **7** 1¼ **Mademoiselle**[4] 431 5-8-7 **53** .... (p) JackDean(5) 3 — 44
(R A Harris) *w ldrs: led over 4f out tl 2f out: wknd fnl f* **5/1**[2]

6-00 **8** 1¼ **Layed Back Rocky**[13] 337 5-8-2 **46** oh1 .... SoniaEaton(3) 6 — 34
(M Mullineaux) *w ldrs: one pce fnl 2f* **50/1**

5/0- **9** 1 **Showtime Annie**[99] 5925 6-8-0 **46** oh1 .... (p) SophieDoyle(5) 4 — 32
(A Bailey) *led tl over 4f out: wknd appr fnl f* **25/1**

000- **10** 1 **Noble Nova**[141] 5619 4-8-12 **58** .... DeanHeslop(5) 13 — 41
(G A Swinbank) *a in rr* **8/1**

0-03 **11** 1¼ **Piccolo Prince**[23] 225 6-8-5 **49** .... (p) JosephWalsh(3) 5 — 29
(P A Blockley) *rr-div: effrt 3f out: nvr a factor* **16/1**

5-22 **12** 27 **Golden Square**[25] 200 5-9-2 **57** .... JackMitchell 2 — —
(A W Carroll) *s.i.s: hdwy over 4f out: sn rdn lost pl over 2f out: sn bhd: eased* **6/1**

00- **13** 6 **Sehoya (IRE)**[29] 6627 5-8-13 **54** .... AmyBaker 1 — —
(R C Guest) *s.i.s: sn drvn along and chsng ldrs on inner: lost pl 3f out: sn bhd: eased* **100/1**

1m 45.5s (0.90) **Going Correction** -0.075s/f (Stan) — **13** Ran SP% **119.5**
Speed ratings (Par 101):92,90,89,88,87 86,84,83,82,81 80,53,47
CSF £46.63 CT £829.96 TOTE £8.30: £2.30, £3.00, £8.80; EX 64.10 TRIFECTA Not won..
Owner The Colourful Bunch **Bred** Mrs Lorraine Castle **Trained** Newmarket, Suffolk

FOCUS
Poor form, and the slowest of three races over course and distance.
Sehoya(IRE) Official explanation: vet said mare bled from the nose

463 LADBROKESPOKER.COM H'CAP (DIV I) — 6f (F)
1:20 (1:20) (Class 6) (0-60,60) 4-Y-0+ — £1,706 (£503; £252) Stalls Low

Form / RPR

-105 **1** **Hamaasy**[16] 306 6-9-1 **59** .... AdrianTNicholls 5 — 78
(D Nicholls) *trckd ldrs: led on ins over 2f out: drew clr over 1f out: pushed out* **5/1**[3]

21-0 **2** 6 **Haroldini (IRE)**[32] 131 5-8-13 **60** .... (p) JasonEdmunds(3) 7 — 61
(J Balding) *chsd ldrs: kpt on to take 2nd 1f out: no ch w wnr* **6/1**

-255 **3** ½ **Parkview Love (USA)**[25] 200 6-9-2 **60** .... (v) DaneO'Neill 8 — 59
(D Shaw) *in tch: effrt on outer over 2f out: kpt on same pce* **7/1**

53-2 **4** 4 **Brut**[2] 448 5-8-6 **50** .... PaulHanagan 3 — 37
(D W Barker) *in rr: hdwy on inner over 2f out: sn chsng ldrs: wknd fnl f* **11/4**[2]

0-22 **5** ¾ **Misaro (GER)**[10] 368 6-8-8 **57** .... (b) TolleyDean(5) 1 — 42
(R A Harris) *t.k.h: led after 1f: hdd over 2f out: wknd over 1f out* **2/1**[1]

0-60 **6** hd **Prettilini**[21] 243 4-8-9 **53** .... FergusSweeney 2 — 37
(R Brotherton) *led 1f: chsd ldrs: lost pl over 1f out* **16/1**

0-00 **7** 3½ **Headland (USA)**[13] 337 9-8-2 **46** oh1 .... (b) PaulQuinn 6 — 20
(D W Chapman) *dwlt: nvr on terms* **100/1**

0-00 **8** 3½ **Xpres Boy (IRE)**[7] 393 4-8-2 **46** oh1 .... (bt[1]) DaleGibson 10 — 9
(S R Bowring) *t.k.h: w ldrs: edgd rt and wknd 2f out: eased* **50/1**

6600 **9** 4 **Drury Lane (IRE)**[2] 448 7-8-2 **46** oh1 .... (p) HayleyTurner 9 — —
(D W Chapman) *sn outpcd and in rr: nvr on terms* **66/1**

1m 15.96s (-0.94) **Going Correction** -0.075s/f (Stan) — **9** Ran SP% **113.8**
Speed ratings (Par 101):103,95,94,89,88 87,83,78,73
CSF £34.23 CT £208.61 TOTE £5.80: £1.90, £2.00, £1.40; EX 30.40 Trifecta £104.30 Pool: £323.43 - 2.20 winning tickets..
Owner J P Honeyman **Bred** Shadwell Estate Company Limited **Trained** Sessay, N Yorks

FOCUS
A fair step up from the winner but the race fell his way with the favourite disappointing and the fourth also below par. The form seems sound enough, though.

464 PONTINSBINGO.COM CLAIMING STKS — 1m 4f (F)
1:50 (1:50) (Class 6) 4-Y-0+ — £2,184 (£644; £322) Stalls Low

Form / RPR

1-52 **1** **Ionian Spring (IRE)**[16] 305 12-8-12 **64** .... DanielTudhope 8 — 52
(D Carroll) *hld up in rr: hdwy over 5f out: led over 2f out: hung lft: all out* **6/4**[1]

6-04 **2** 1¼ **Dispol Peto**[21] 242 7-8-9 **44** .... (b) DuranFentiman(5) 10 — 52
(R Johnson) *in rr: hdwy over 4f out: wnt 2nd over 1f out: kpt on same pce* **20/1**

-630 **3** shd **Isa'Af (IRE)**[13] 333 8-8-5 **44** .... JackMitchell(7) 6 — 50
(P W Hiatt) *in tch: effrt over 2f out: kpt on same pce fnl f* **14/1**

The Form Book, Raceform Ltd, Compton, RG20 6NL

5-23 **4** *2* **Paparaazi (IRE)**[10] [364] 5-9-2 62....................(p) PaulHanagan 4 51
(R A Fahey) *hld up in mid-div: hdwy over 5f out: wnt 2nd over 3f out: one pce fnl 2f* **9/2**[2]

255- **5** *5* **Agilete**[121] [6037] 5-9-6 57.................... PatCosgrave 12 47
(J Pearce) *in tch: effrt over 3f out: one pce* **8/1**[3]

0/30 **6** *2 ½* **Al Moulatham**[24] [220] 8-8-12 60....................(bt) SamHitchcott 5 35
(R Ford) *t.k.h: led tl over 2f out: wknd over 1f out* **9/1**

-103 **7** *4* **Tiegs (IRE)**[8] [380] 5-8-7 46.................... ChrisCatlin 2 23
(P W Hiatt) *bhd: hdwy over 5f out: nvr nr ldrs* **18/1**

0-02 **8** *5* **Crusoe (IRE)**[10] [364] 10-8-3 36....................(b) SoniaEaton(7) 11 18
(A Sadik) *hld up in rr: sme hdwy on wd outside over 2f out: nvr on terms* **20/1**

050/ **9** *2 ½* **Mickey Pearce (IRE)**[19] [5683] 5-9-2 45.................... FergusSweeney 7 20
(J G M O'Shea) *chsd ldrs: reminders over 5f out: lost pl over 2f out* **12/1**

10 *¾* **Exit Fast (USA)**[327] 6-9-0.................... MickyFenton 9 17
(P T Midgley) *chsd ldrs: lost pl over 2f out* **100/1**

5-05 **11** *16* **Contra Mundum (USA)**[16] [305] 4-9-3 60.................... RobertWinston 13 —
(B S Rothwell) *restless in stalls: sn chsng ldr: lost pl 3f out: sn bhd* **28/1**

-004 **12** *19* **Mi Odds**[16] [305] 11-8-10 45.................... HayleyTurner 1 —
(Mrs N Macauley) *sn in rr: drvn 7f out: sn bhd: t.o 3f out* **33/1**

2m 41.65s (-0.44) **Going Correction** -0.075s/f (Stan)
WFA 4 from 5yo+ 3lb **12** Ran SP% **115.8**
Speed ratings (Par 101):98,97,97,95,92 90,88,84,83,82 71,59
CSF £40.83 TOTE £2.10: £1.10, £8.50, £4.40; EX 46.40 Trifecta £89.40 Part won. Pool: £125.92 - 0.33 winning tickets..Paparaazi was claimed by I. W. McInnes for £8,000.
Owner Diamond Racing Ltd **Bred** Ballymacoll Stud Farm Ltd **Trained** Sledmere, E Yorks

FOCUS
The first three have rated higher in the past, but are mostly disappointing these days and the race has been rated on their recent form.

465 LADBROKES.COM H'CAP 5f (F)
2:25 (2:25) (Class 5) (0-70,70) 4-Y-0+ **£3,071** (£906; £453) **Stalls** High

Form RPR

232- **1** **Hypnosis**[138] [5684] 4-9-2 **70**.................... RobertWinston 5 79
(D W Barker) *chsd ldrs on outer: styd on to ld last strides* **7/1**

4-60 **2** *hd* **Hornpipe**[30] [154] 5-8-3 **57**....................(v[1]) AdrianMcCarthy 2 65
(M S Saunders) *w ldrs: led 50yds out: hdd post* **16/1**

0-43 **3** *½* **Garlogs**[14] [317] 4-8-2 **56**.................... ChrisCatlin 4 62
(A Bailey) *w ldr: led 2f out: hdd and no ex ins last* **11/4**[1]

0531 **4** *¾* **Egyptian Lord**[14] [317] 4-8-6 **60** ow1....................(b) RobbieFitzpatrick 6 63
(Peter Grayson) *rrd s: hdwy over 2f out: kpt on same pce ins last* **13/2**[3]

3/00 **5** *1 ¾* **Lake Hero**[18] [276] 4-8-11 **65**.................... PatCosgrave 1 62
(M J Wallace) *sn chsng ldrs on outside: one pce fnl f* **10/1**

3045 **6** *2* **Trinculo (IRE)**[4] [432] 10-8-8 **67**.................... TolleyDean(5) 8 57
(R A Harris) *sn outpcd and in rr: hdwy on ins 2f out: nvr rchd ldrs* **20/1**

245- **7** *hd* **Nepro (IRE)**[355] [517] 5-8-13 **67**....................(t) EdwardCreighton 7 56
(E J Creighton) *mid-div: effrt over 2f out: kpt on same pce* **14/1**

-206 **8** *shd* **Maktavish**[4] [432] 8-8-11 **65**....................(b) PhillipMakin 3 54
(R Brotherton) *led tl 2f out: one pce* **15/2**

2203 **9** *2* **Nusoor (IRE)**[4] [432] 4-8-12 **69**....................(b) JerryO'Dwyer(3) 10 51
(Peter Grayson) *dwlt: racd stands' side: nvr a factor* **5/1**[2]

-000 **10** *½* **Anfield Dream**[19] [262] 5-9-0 **68** ow1....................(t) SebSanders 9 48
(J R Jenkins) *sn in rr: sme hdwy ins 2f out: nvr a factor* **10/1**

0-55 **11** *5* **The Leather Wedge (IRE)**[14] [318] 8-8-1 **58** oh6 ow2(p) PatrickMathers(3) 11 20
(R Johnson) *chsd ldrs on ins: edgd lft and lost pl over 1f out* **40/1**

60.97 secs (0.67) **Going Correction** +0.225s/f (Slow) **11** Ran SP% **118.9**
Speed ratings (Par 103):103,102,101,100,97 94,94,94,91,90 82
CSF £114.14 CT £385.24 TOTE £7.00: £1.70, £8.50, £1.40; EX 211.30 Trifecta £193.90 Part won. Pool: £273.20 - 0.10 winning tickets..
Owner J P Rider R Snowden **Bred** Mrs V E Hughes **Trained** Scorton, N Yorks
■ Robert Winston's final success before sitting out a year-long ban.

FOCUS
An ordinary handicap. The winner continues on the upgrade and the runner-up returned to some sort of form in the visor.
The Leather Wedge(IRE) Official explanation: jockey said gelding hung badly left

466 PONTINS.COM (S) STKS 1m (F)
3:00 (3:00) (Class 6) 4-Y-0+ **£2,184** (£644; £322) **Stalls** Low

Form RPR

2104 **1** **Paso Doble**[21] [243] 9-8-12 56....................(p) JamesMillman(5) 8 65
(D K Ivory) *chsd ldrs on outer: outpcd over 3f out: styd on fnl 2f: led ins last: drvn out* **9/2**[3]

-305 **2** *1 ¾* **Vancouver Gold (IRE)**[9] [374] 5-8-6 59.................... PaulMulrennan 6 50
(K R Burke) *trckd ldrs: led over 1f out: hdd and no ex ins last* **11/2**

0404 **3** *¾* **Kingsmaite**[2] [450] 6-9-3 60....................(bt) PhillipMakin 5 59
(S R Bowring) *led 1f: led over 3f out tl over 1f out: kpt on same pce* **3/1**[2]

4-65 **4** *8* **Formidable Will (FR)**[10] [367] 5-9-3 64....................(vt) DaneO'Neill 7 41
(D Shaw) *chsd ldrs on outer: effrt over 2f out: wknd fnl f* **9/4**[1]

02-0 **5** *8* **Hippolyte (USA)**[7] [393] 4-8-6 46.................... JoeFanning 4 11
(J G Given) *in rr: lost pl over 3f out: nvr a factor* **33/1**

50-0 **6** *1 ¼* **Shannon Arms (USA)**[10] [364] 6-8-11 45....................(p) PatCosgrave 3 14
(R Brotherton) *led after 1f: hdd over 3f out: lost pl over 2f out* **25/1**

0/00 **7** *5* **Lake Carezza (USA)**[24] [217] 5-8-11 44.................... LPKeniry 9 2
(N J Hawke) *s.i.s: lost pl over 4f out: sn bhd* **33/1**

0-00 **8** *¾* **Tamatave (IRE)**[9] [374] 5-8-8 58.................... AndrewMullen(3) 1 —
(K A Ryan) *chsd ldrs: drvn over 4f out: lost pl 3f out: sn bhd* **13/2**

05-0 **9** *57* **Paddy Moon**[7] [393] 4-8-11 48....................(b) MickyFenton 2 —
(J G Given) *chsd ldrs: hmpd and lost pl over 4f out: sn bhd: virtually p.u 2f out: t.o: btn 57 l* **50/1**

1m 44.17s (-0.43) **Going Correction** -0.075s/f (Stan) **9** Ran SP% **114.4**
Speed ratings (Par 101):99,97,96,88,80 79,74,73,16
CSF £27.88 TOTE £5.60: £1.80, £1.50, £1.40; EX 20.00 Trifecta £29.70 Pool: £389.30 - 9.28 winning tickets..The winner was sold to Naughty Diesel Ltd for 4,500gns.
Owner Mrs H Brain **Bred** P Cutler **Trained** Radlett, Herts

FOCUS
An ordinary seller run in a slowish time. The winner franked the form of race 243 here, the first four having won since.
Shannon Arms(USA) Official explanation: jockey said gelding hung right-handed throughout
Paddy Moon Official explanation: jockey said gelding lost its action

467 LADBROKESPOKER.COM H'CAP (DIV II) 6f (F)
3:30 (3:30) (Class 6) (0-60,64) 4-Y-0+ **£1,706** (£503; £252) **Stalls** Low

Form RPR

5-24 **1** **Came Back (IRE)**[16] [306] 4-9-0 **58**.................... DaleGibson 10 72+
(J Mackie) *trckd ldrs gng wl: shkn up to ld over 1f out: drvn out* **13/2**[3]

2211 **2** *2* **Lucius Verrus (USA)**[13] [339] 7-9-2 **60**....................(v) DaneO'Neill 9 68
(D Shaw) *mid-div: outpcd and lost pl over 4f out: hdwy on outer 2f out: kpt on to take 2nd ins last* **11/4**[2]

0-50 **3** *1* **Sundried Tomato**[13] [339] 8-8-2 **46** oh1....................(p) HayleyTurner 6 51
(D W Chapman) *trckd ldrs: chal 2f out: styd on same pce fnl f* **33/1**

5-26 **4** *2* **Caustic Wit (IRE)**[32] [132] 9-8-11 **60**.................... TolleyDean(5) 5 59
(M S Saunders) *chsd ldrs: one pce fnl 2f* **14/1**

-344 **5** *1* **Blythe Spirit**[21] [241] 8-8-3 **47**.................... PaulHanagan 8 43
(R A Fahey) *mid-div: hdwy over 2f out: kpt on: nvr a threat* **14/1**

-021 **6** *3* **Cerebus**[9] [376] 5-9-3 **64** 6ex....................(bt) StephenDonohoe(3) 7 51
(A J McCabe) *led tl over 1f out: sn wknd* **2/1**[1]

6012 **7** *5* **Mulberry Lad (IRE)**[8] [383] 5-8-8 **52**.................... JimCrowley 1 24
(P W Hiatt) *hmpd s: in rr: hdwy on ins over 2f out: sn wknd* **7/1**

2-03 **8** *½* **Radiator Rooney (IRE)**[10] [361] 4-9-2 **60**....................(b) LPKeniry 3 31
(Patrick Morris, Ire) *chsd ldrs: rdn 3f out: hung rt and sn lost pl* **10/1**

500- **9** *5* **Inca Soldier (FR)**[235] [2898] 4-8-11 **55**.................... JamieMackay 4 11
(R C Guest) *stdd s: plld hrd in rr: bhd fnl 4f* **50/1**

4-60 **10** *7* **No Inkling (IRE)**[14] [321] 4-8-1 **48** oh1 ow2....................(v) PatrickMathers(3) 2 —
(Miss M E Rowland) *wnt lft s: outpcd and lost pl over 4f out: sn bhd* **100/1**

1m 16.04s (-0.86) **Going Correction** -0.075s/f (Stan) **10** Ran SP% **114.1**
Speed ratings (Par 101):102,99,98,95,94 90,83,82,76,66
CSF £24.01 CT £547.54 TOTE £7.50: £2.30, £1.40, £6.00; EX 28.30 Trifecta £222.20 Part won. Pool: £313.05 - 0.33 winning tickets..
Owner W I Bloomfield **Bred** Yeomanstown Stud **Trained** Church Broughton , Derbys

FOCUS
The form is not straightforward with the third running his best race for some time, but the runner-up is in good form and the winner looks capable of better still. Came Back and the winner of division one of this event, Hamaasy, both came out of Count Cougar's race here (306.)

468 GO PONTIN'S H'CAP 7f (F)
4:00 (4:00) (Class 5) (0-70,70) 4-Y-0+ **£3,071** (£906; £453) **Stalls** Low

Form RPR

-532 **1** **Flying Bantam (IRE)**[10] [367] 6-8-6 **60**....................(p) PaulHanagan 8 72
(R A Fahey) *t.k.h: trckd ldrs: styd on to ld ins last: hld on towards fin* **11/2**[3]

00-1 **2** *½* **Owed**[16] [303] 5-8-13 **67**....................(t) SebSanders 5 77
(R Bastiman) *trckd ldr: led and hung lft over 2f out: hdd and no ex ins last* **8/1**

3031 **3** *½* **Cool Sands (IRE)**[14] [323] 5-8-9 **63**....................(v) DaneO'Neill 4 72
(D Shaw) *hld up: hdwy on ins over 2f out: sn w ldrs: nt qckn ins last* **9/2**[2]

-013 **4** *5* **Going Skint**[14] [323] 4-8-11 **65**.................... AdamKirby 2 61
(M Wellings) *led tl over 2f out: fdd fnl f* **12/1**

0-02 **5** *½* **Cleveland**[16] [306] 5-8-4 **63** ow1.................... RussellKennemore(5) 1 58
(R Hollinshead) *s.s: sn chsng ldrs: wknd 1f out* **3/1**[1]

06-4 **6** *2* **Xpres Maite**[14] [319] 4-9-2 **70**....................(b) DaleGibson 7 60
(S R Bowring) *dwlt: sn drvn along and chsng ldrs: wknd 2f out* **16/1**

05-0 **7** *1 ½* **Mycenean Prince (USA)**[3] [445] 4-8-2 **56** oh11....................(v) JamieMackay 9 42
(R C Guest) *in rr: outpcd and lost pl over 4f out: no ch after* **100/1**

00-0 **8** *3 ½* **Aperitif**[30] [151] 6-8-11 **65**.................... AdrianTNicholls 3 42
(D Nicholls) *in rr: lost pl over 3f out* **15/2**

4-30 **9** *2* **Astronomical Odds (USA)**[12] [346] 4-8-8 **62**.................... PhillipMakin 6 33
(T D Barron) *in tch: lost pl over 3f out: sn bhd: eased* **6/1**

0/06 **10** *3* **Mission Man**[17] [300] 6-8-6 **60**.................... ChrisCatlin 10 24
(M G Rimell) *chsd ldrs: lost pl 3f out: sn bhd* **16/1**

1m 29.38s (-1.42) **Going Correction** -0.075s/f (Stan) **10** Ran SP% **116.2**
Speed ratings (Par 103):105,104,103,98,97 95,93,89,87,83
CSF £48.81 CT £215.31 TOTE £6.30: £1.80, £3.10, £2.10; EX 66.00 Trifecta £185.70 Part won. Pool: £261.67 - 0.33 winning tickets..
Owner The Matthewman Partnership **Bred** Robinski Bloodstock Limited **Trained** Musley Bank, N Yorks

FOCUS
A good race for the grade, and sound form through the second and third.

469 LADBROKES FREEPHONE 0800 777 888 H'CAP 1m (F)
4:35 (4:36) (Class 6) (0-60,59) 3-Y-0 **£2,388** (£705; £352) **Stalls** Low

Form RPR

0-64 **1** **Ballyshane Spirit (IRE)**[29] [157] 3-8-0 **48**.................... KirstyMilczarek(7) 14 56
(N A Callaghan) *trckd ldrs: led over 1f out: styd on wl* **15/2**

6-42 **2** *2* **Bertrada (IRE)**[9] [373] 3-8-9 **50**.................... RobertHavlin 6 53
(H Morrison) *chsd ldrs: outpcd over 3f out: hdwy 2f out: styd on to take 2nd ins last* **7/1**[3]

360- **3** *1 ¼* **Petrosian**[107] [6285] 3-9-4 **59**.................... JoeFanning 4 59
(M Johnston) *chsd ldrs: kpt on same pce fnl 2f* **7/1**[3]

000- **4** *½* **Go Dancing**[86] [6558] 3-9-3 **58**.................... AdrianMcCarthy 12 57
(P W Chapple-Hyam) *sn drvn along: sn chsng ldrs: outpcd over 2f out: kpt on wl fnl f* **25/1**

0441 **5** *shd* **My Sara**[9] [373] 3-8-8 **54** 6ex....................(v) JamieMoriarty(5) 3 53
(R A Fahey) *sn drvn along in mid-field: hdwy and c outside over 2f out: styd on fnl f* **13/8**[1]

0-55 **6** *shd* **Irish Relative (IRE)**[23] [223] 3-8-4 **45**.................... PaulFessey 7 44
(T D Barron) *w ldrs: outpcd over 2f out: kpt on fnl f* **33/1**

00-0 **7** *1* **Hits Only Vic (USA)**[10] [336] 3-8-5 **46**.................... DeanMcKeown 10 42
(J Pearce) *prom: rdn and outpcd over 4f out: kpt on fnl 2f* **6/1**[2]

2041 **8** *1* **Mr Chocolate Drop (IRE)**[7] [390] 3-9-3 **58** 6ex.................... BrianReilly 13 52
(M J Attwater) *t.k.h: mde most tl hdd & wknd over 1f out* **12/1**

9 *9* **Lord Orpen (IRE)**[115] [6151] 3-8-6 **47**....................(b[1]) LPKeniry 8 20
(Patrick Morris, Ire) *chsd ldrs: lost pl 3f out: eased* **18/1**

-560 **10** *3 ½* **Elizabeth Garrett**[10] [357] 3-8-1 **45**.................... MarcHalford(3) 5 10
(M J Gingell) *chsd ldrs: lost pl over 3f out: eased* **66/1**

4-50 **11** *6* **Shes Millie**[10] [357] 3-8-10 **51**....................(v[1]) DaneO'Neill 1 2
(J G M O'Shea) *s.i.s: a in rr: eased ins last* **28/1**

0-00 **12** *14* **Northern Dune (IRE)**[20] [257] 3-8-13 **54**.................... TPQueally 9 —
(B J Curley) *in rr: bhd and drvn 4f out: sn detached* **20/1**

56-1 **13** *14* **Carefree**[44] [11] 3-9-1 **56**.................... PaulHanagan 2 —
(S Parr) *in rr: lost pl and eased over 1f out: virtually p.u* **20/1**

1m 44.44s (-0.16) **Going Correction** -0.075s/f (Stan) **13** Ran SP% **123.4**
Speed ratings (Par 95):97,95,93,93,93 93,92,91,82,78 72,58,44
CSF £55.95 CT £405.93 TOTE £11.50: £3.20, £2.40, £3.10; EX 68.90 Trifecta £204.50 Part won. Pool: £288.14 - 0.10 winning tickets. Place 6 £149.88, Place 5 £47.47.
Owner Ocean Trailers Ltd **Bred** Mark Commins **Trained** Newmarket, Suffolk

FOCUS
The time compared well with the other course-and-distance races, and this is sound form for the grade.
Carefree Official explanation: jockey said filly lost its action
T/Plt: £215.50 to a £1 stake. Pool: £54,169.60. 183.45 winning tickets. T/Qpdt: £17.30 to a £1 stake. Pool: £4,900.80. 208.90 winning tickets. WG

[409]NAD AL SHEBA (L-H)

Thursday, February 15

OFFICIAL GOING: Turf course - good; dirt course - fast

470a WHEELS TROPHY (H'CAP) (TURF) 6f 110y(T)

3:05 (3:05) (90-105,105) 3-Y-0+

£33,673 (£8,418; £8,418; £2,806; £1,683; £1,122)

			RPR
1		**Subpoena**[14] [325] 5-8-10 **95**......(v) RoystonFfrench 6 (A Al Raihe, UAE) *slowly away: mid-div on rail: no room 4f out: rdn 2 1/2f out: r.o wl to ld cl home* **40/1**	97
2	1 3/4	**So Will I**[7] [400] 6-9-2 **100**......(t) RHills 9 (Doug Watson, UAE) *settled in rr: gng wl 2f out whn no room: r.o wl fnl 110yds: nrst fin* **14/1**	98
2	dht	**Zeeno (SAF)**[229] 4-8-12 **104**......(t) RyanMoore 12 (S Seemar, UAE) *settled in rr: rdn 2 1/2f out: r.o wl fnl 1 1/2f: nrst fin* **10/1**	94
4	1/2	**Obe Gold**[6] [415] 5-8-10 **95**...... JohnEgan 8 (M R Channon) *mid-div: prog to chal 2f out: led 1f out: hdd cl home* **3/1**[1]	91
5	1/2	**Checkit (IRE)**[7] [394] 7-8-10 **95**...... GHind 10 (R Bouresly, Kuwait) *slowly away: last 3f out: r.o wl fnl 1 1/2f: nrst fin* **25/1**	89
6	shd	**Sir Edwin Landseer (USA)**[6] [415] 7-8-11 **96**......(p) RichardMullen 7 (Christian Wroe) *mid-div: hmpd 2 1/2f out: r.o one pce fnl 1 1/2f* **12/1**	90
7	1/2	**Compton's Eleven**[6] [409] 6-8-10 **95**...... TedDurcan 2 (M R Channon) *mid-div: trckd ldr gng wl 2f out: led briefly over 1f out: wknd fnl 55yds* **6/1**[3]	87
8	1/4	**Bonus (IRE)**[26] [198] 7-8-11 **96**...... EddieAhern 11 (G A Butler) *settled in rr: smooth prog gng wl 2f out: rdn 1 1/2f out: nt qckn* **4/1**[2]	88
9	1/4	**Beckermet (IRE)**[7] [400] 5-9-4 **102**...... JMurtagh 4 (R F Fisher) *trckd ldr: rdn to chal 2f out: wknd* **12/1**	94
10	1 1/4	**Lavarone (ARG)**[116] [6121] 4-8-4 **95**...... KerrinMcEvoy 3 (H J Brown, South Africa) *trckd ldr: rdn 3 1/2f out: wknd* **12/1**	76
11	3/4	**Lascaux (AUS)**[7] [400] 6-9-2 **100**...... WLHo 1 (Y Choy, Macau) *mid-div: rdn and clsng whn bdly hmpd 110yds out: nt rcvr* **7/1**	86
12	3/4	**Key Of Destiny (SAF)**[14] [326] 9-9-6 **105**...... WCMarwing 5 (M F De Kock, South Africa) *sn led: rdn 2f out: hdd over 1f out: fdd* **12/1**	88

1m 18.0s (0.80) **Going Correction** +0.425s/f (Yiel) 12 Ran SP% **124.6**

Speed ratings: 112,110,110,109,108 108,108,107,107,106 105,104

CSF: Subpoena/ So Will I £272.89, Subpoena/Zeeno £209.36. TRIC: S/SWI/Z £3,015.66, S/Z/SWI £2,954.32..

Owner Sheikh Mansoor bin Mohammed al Maktoum **Bred** Darley **Trained** UAE

FOCUS

This looked a decent handicap and it was certainly very competitive but, despite the pace appearing generous enough, they finished in a bunch behind the decisive winner, although the fourth to seventh were close to their marks. This was essentially another division of the 4.05 and the winning time was 0.52 seconds quicker.

NOTEBOOK

Subpoena did not really progress when bought out of Michael Jarvis's yard by Godolphin and came into this with just a maiden win in 2004 to his name. However, this was only his second start for his current connections and he improved significantly on the form he showed over 1m on his reappearance to double his career tally. Ffrench deserves plenty of credit for a cracking ride as, having gone the shortest way round for much of the contest, he managed to find a clear run when switched out with his effort in the straight, something that cannot be said of a few of those in behind. The winner may have had more to do had some his rivals enjoyed better trips, but he seems to have turned the corner since joining his current yard and should not be underestimated next time.

So Will I has been threatening to pick up one of these races for a while now and this may well have been his day had he enjoyed a clear run. However, his overall record suggests it would be silly to get carried away with this.

Zeeno(SAF) ran a big race off the back of a 229-day break on his debut in Dubai. Dropped in early, he stayed on well towards the centre of the track in the straight and could build on this.

Obe Gold looked a very unlucky loser over 6f round here the previous week, but he did not seem to have too many excuses this time. He made his move towards the outside and perhaps he is just better suited coming between horses.

Checkit(IRE) ran another good race, especially considering he was forced wide on the turn in, but his recent wins-to-runs record does not really inspire.

Sir Edwin Landseer(USA) was a little short of room and seemed to take a while to warm up in the straight.

Compton's Eleven, like his stablemate Obe Gold, had looked unlucky in a similar event the previous week, but he failed to build on that this time.

Bonus(IRE) travelled strongly for much of the way but found disappointingly little once let down.

Beckermet(IRE) appeared to get quite warm and seemed to do too much too soon. (op 14-1)

Lascaux(AUS) was a little short or room in the straight, but basically failed to build on the promise of his recent course effort.

471a INSIDE OUT PLATE (H'CAP) (DIRT) 7f 110y(D)

3:35 (3:35) (90-105,104) 3-Y-0+

£33,673 (£11,224; £5,612; £2,806; £1,683; £1,122)

			RPR
1		**Visionist (IRE)**[14] [326] 5-8-11 **95**...... WayneSmith 14 (M Al Muhairi, UAE) *trckd ldr: gng wl 3f out: led 2 1/2f out: comf* **33/1**	103
2	3 1/2	**Zorin (BRZ)**[7] [396] 4-8-5 **96**...... ADomingos 5 (A Cintra Pereira, Brazil) *sn led: hdd 2 1/2f out: kpt on wl: no ch w wnr* **6/1**[3]	89
3	2	**Curule (USA)**[6] [410] 10-8-7 **90**...... WSupple 10 (Doug Watson, UAE) *mid-div: rdn 4f out: nt qckn: nvr a threat* **14/1**	87
4	1	**Poseidon's Bride (USA)**[133] [5779] 4-8-7 **90**...... KerrinMcEvoy 3 (Saeed Bin Suroor) *mid-div whn hmpd 4f out: rdn 3f out: r.o fnl 2f out: nvr involved* **7/2**[2]	85
5	1/2	**Nkosi Reigns (USA)**[124] 6-9-6 **104**......(bt) TedDurcan 2 (S Seemar, UAE) *mid-div on rail: no room after 2f: hrd rdn 3f out: r.o fnl 1 1/2f* **10/3**[1]	97
6	1/4	**Comandante Xara (BRZ)**[7] [396] 4-8-0 **90**......(b) ECruz 4 (P Nickel Filho, Brazil) *trckd ldr tl rdn 3f out: wknd* **22/1**	76
7	4 3/4	**State Shinto (USA)**[7] [396] 11-8-8 **91**......(bt) GHind 9 (R Bouresly, Kuwait) *trckd ldrs early stages: racd in mid-div: rdn 3f out: n.m.r 2 1/2f out: one pce* **12/1**	74
8	shd	**Glad To Be Fast (IRE)**[7] [396] 7-8-8 **91**......(b) MJKinane 7 (Mario Hofer, Germany) *settled in rr: rdn 4f out: n.d* **14/1**	74
9	5 3/4	**Cherry Pickings (USA)**[49] 10-8-11 **95**......(vt) RichardMullen 12 (S Seemar, UAE) *mid-div: rdn bhd ldrs 3f out: wknd* **12/1**	65
10	1/4	**Lord Ego (BRZ)**[14] [326] 4-8-0 **90**......(t) RPCleary 8 (M D Wolfson, U.S.A) *slowly away: nvr nr to chal* **18/1**	54
11	5 3/4	**Looking Good (ARG)**[7] [396] 6-9-1 **98**......(t) PaulSmith 13 (Allan Smith, UAE) *mid-div: rdn to cl 2 1/2f out: hmpd 2f out: nt rcvr* **10/1**	56
12	1/2	**Rockets 'n Rollers (IRE)**[49] 7-9-0 **97**...... MartinDwyer 6 (Doug Watson, UAE) *slowly away: bdly hmpd 4f out: nvr able to chal* **20/1**	54
13	1/2	**Evaluator (IRE)**[356] [509] 6-9-3 **100**......(t) RoystonFfrench 11 (A Al Raihe, UAE) *sn rdn along: nvr nr to chal* **33/1**	56
14	1/2	**Little Neck (GER)**[6] [411] 6-8-11 **95**......(t) JimmyQuinn 1 (K Aga, UAE) *in rr: n.d* **16/1**	49

1m 29.95s (89.95) **14** Ran SP% **123.5**

Owner Sh Rashid bin Humaid Al Nuaimi **Bred** Frank Barry **Trained** UAE

FOCUS

Probably just an ordinary handicap for the grade but solid enough with those in the frame behind the winner to previous form.

NOTEBOOK

Visionist(IRE), the winner of a decent handicap on the Polytrack when trained by Pat Eddery last year, was well held over 6f round here on his debut for these connections, but showed the benefit of that run stepped up in trip. Always close up, he travelled well throughout and pulled right away when asked for his effort to record a pretty impressive success. The form is probably nothing special for the level, but he is unexposed on the dirt and looks worth keeping on the right side of.

Zorin(BRZ), a good second over the bare 7f round here the previous week, again seemed to run his race and helps give the form a solid look.

Curule(USA), just as he did the previous week, came under pressure a long way out, but kept responding. Perhaps the drop in trip was not ideal.

Poseidon's Bride(USA), a dual winner in France for Andre Fabre, including on Polytrack, was slightly hampered after about 3f or so and was shuffled back a touch. She was forced to switch widest of all into the straight and basically had too much ground to make up by the time she hit top stride. This was her first run in 133 days and she should be capable of a little better.

Nkosi Reigns(USA), a Grade 3 winner in the US, was done few favours by the tiring Comandante Xara. He should benefit from a step back up in trip.

Comandante Xara(BRZ) got very tired in the straight and wandered around.

472a SPORT EXTRA CHALLENGE (H'CAP) (TURF) 6f 110y(T)

4:05 (4:06) (90-105,105) 3-Y-0+

£33,673 (£11,224; £5,612; £2,806; £1,683; £1,122)

			RPR
1		**Grantley Adams**[6] [415] 4-8-11 **96**...... RyanMoore 8 (M R Channon) *slowly away: settled in rr: last 2 1/2f out: rdn to cl 2f out: led 1f out: comf* **5/1**[2]	106
2	1 1/2	**Sendalam (FR)**[7] [395] 5-8-12 **97**...... KShea 9 (H J Brown, South Africa) *mid-div: smooth prog to chal and ld over 1f out: hdd 1f out: r.o wl* **11/1**	103
3	1 1/2	**Sand Cat**[6] [409] 4-8-10 **95**...... MJKinane 1 (Christian Wroe) *mid-div on rail: dropped to rr 3f out gng wl: nt clr run: r.o: nrst fin* **12/1**	97
4	1/2	**Prince Tamino**[14] [324] 4-9-5 **104**...... KerrinMcEvoy 3 (I Mohammed, UAE) *mid-div: trckd ldrs 3f out: led briefly 2f out: nt qckn fnl f* **7/4**[1]	104
5	1 3/4	**Rochdale**[6] [415] 4-8-10 **95**...... RoystonFfrench 12 (A Al Raihe, UAE) *mid-div: rdn 3f out: nt qckn: kpt on one pce* **6/1**[3]	90
6	shd	**Taqseem (IRE)**[149] [5462] 4-9-4 **102**...... RHills 11 (M Al Muhairi, UAE) *mid-div wd: rdn 2 1/2f out: r.o late: nrst fin* **12/1**	98
7	1/2	**Recast (AUS)**[95] 7-9-2 **100**......(t) JMurtagh 2 (J Meagher, Singapore) *in rr: swtchd wd 3f out: nvr able to chal* **10/1**	94
8	1/4	**Feet So Fast**[21] [245] 8-9-6 **105**...... TedDurcan 7 (S Seemar, UAE) *mid-div: trckd ldrs 3f out: rdn 2 1/2f out: ev ch 1 1/2f out: one pce* **20/1**	98
9	6 1/2	**Obe Brave**[7] [394] 4-9-3 **101**...... LDettori 10 (M R Channon) *mid-div: trckd ldr 3f out: rdn 2f out: nt qckn* **8/1**	76
10	1 1/4	**Bellamont Forest (USA)**[7] [400] 11-8-10 **95**...... DinaDanekilde 6 (O Larsen, Sweden) *mid-div: rdn 2 1/2f out: nvr able to chal* **33/1**	65
11	6 1/4	**Skywards**[49] 5-8-10 **95**......(t) TPO'Shea 5 (E Charpy, UAE) *trckd ldr: led 4f out: rdn 2 1/2f out: hdd 2f out: wknd* **40/1**	47
12	1 3/4	**Padrao Lima (BRZ)**[14] [324] 4-8-4 **95**......(t) JohnEgan 4 (A Manuel, UAE) *sn led: rdn and hdd 4f out: sn wknd* **16/1**	36

1m 18.52s (1.32) **Going Correction** +0.425s/f (Yiel) **12** Ran SP% **127.3**

Speed ratings: 109,107,105,105,103 102,102,102,94,93 86,84

Owner Mrs Tania Trant **Bred** Miss S N Ralphs **Trained** West Ilsley, Berks

FOCUS

This was a good handicap rated around the principals to recent form, but the winning time was 0.52 seconds slower than the 3.05. However, it is worth noting both Skywards and Padrao Lima went off too fast and set the race up for the closers.

NOTEBOOK

Grantley Adams had looked a little unlucky when beaten into fourth over the bare 6f round here on his debut in Dubai the previous week, but he got a dream run this time and made no mistake, although he did drift to his left late on. Having been dropped out at the start, he was still last early in the straight, but a lovely gap opened up for him between runners and he showed a decent turn of foot to take advantage. He is obviously a very useful performer when things drop right for him and should continue to go well.

Sendalam(FR) also enjoyed a dream run through, although he made his move before Grantley Adams and could not resist that one's late surge. He also raced closer to the far rail than the winner, and that part of the track has looked like slower ground in recent meetings.

Sand Cat was another to stay on from a long way back, but he never really looked like getting to the first two, who made their moves before him.

Prince Tamino ◆ looked to have an outstanding chance returned to his favoured surface and, at first glance, he could be considered a bitter disappointment in only managing fourth. However, it will probably pay to forgive him this, as he was never far away from the ridiculous early pace - the front three came from well back - and this extended 6f was always going to stretch his stamina. (op 2-1)

Rochdale could not confirm recent form with Grantley Adams but is better than he showed as, not only did he chase the frantic early pace, but he was caught wide for much of the way from stall 12.

Taqseem(IRE) had to be switched wide and never really landed a blow. (op 11-1)

Recast(AUS) seemed a little short of room when trying to make up ground. (op 9-1)

Feet So Fast probably went for home a little too soon.

Obe Brave was again below the form he showed when winning here the previous month.

473a AQUARIUS CHALLENGE (H'CAP) (TURF) 1m (T)
4:40 (4:40) (90-105,104) 3-Y-0+

£33,673 (£11,224; £5,612; £2,806; £1,683; £1,122)

RPR

1 **Diamond Quest (SAF)**[14] 328 6-9-0 **97** WCMarwing 9 100
(M F De Kock, South Africa) *settled in last: stl last 2 1/2f out: swtchd wd and rdn: led 55yds out* **4/1**[3]

2 2 **Juror (USA)**[14] 327 4-8-7 **90** KerrinMcEvoy 11 89
(I Mohammed, UAE) *mid-div: trckd ldr gng wl 2 1/2f out: led 1 1/2f out: hdd fnl 55yds: no ch w wnr* **9/1**

3 2 1/4 **Lucky Dance (BRZ)**[14] 331 5-8-11 **95** ADomingos 1 89
(M D Wolfson, U.S.A) *trckd ldr: led 2f out: hdd 1 1/2f out: wknd* **33/1**

4 hd **Almuraad (IRE)**[14] 325 6-9-3 **100** RHills 4 94
(Doug Watson, UAE) *mid-div: gng wl bhd ldrs 3f out: rdn 2f out: nt qckn* **7/2**[2]

5 shd **Bolodenka (IRE)**[14] 325 5-9-1 **98** LDettori 13 92
(R A Fahey) *mid-div out wd: rdn to cl 2 1/2f out: ev ch 2f out: one pce* **11/4**[1]

6 2 **Zato (IRE)**[7] 398 4-8-8 **91** RyanMoore 14 81
(M R Channon) *settled in rr: wd: rdn 2 1/2f out: nt pce to chal* **12/1**

7 1/4 **Berlioz (IND)**[14] 331 6-8-9 **93** (vt) TedDurcan 10 81
(S Seemar, UAE) *settled in rr: prog on rail whn no room 2 1/2f out: r.o one pce* **33/1**

8 3/4 **Estrela Brono (BRZ)**[14] 330 5-8-9 **93** (t) ECruz 7 80
(C Morgado, Brazil) *settled in rr: no room 2 1/2f out: n.d* **25/1**

9 5 1/4 **Lundy's Lane (IRE)**[6] 411 7-9-3 **100** WSupple 8 77
(S Seemar, UAE) *trckd ldr: led 2 1/2f out: hdd 2f out: wknd* **13/2**

10 3/4 **Hurricane James (IRE)**[14] 325 5-8-12 **96** (tp) TPO'Shea 2 71
(E Charpy, UAE) *hld up in rr: no room 2 1/2f out: nvr able to chal* **33/1**

11 1/4 **Baskerville**[21] 250 4-8-7 **90** RPCleary 3 65
(D Selvaratnam, UAE) *settled in rr: gng wl 3f out: sn rdn: nvr a threat* **20/1**

12 11 **Palm Cove (UAE)**[322] 4-8-8 **91** (t) MartinDwyer 6 44
(M Kettle, UAE) *sn led: hdd 2 1/2f out: wknd* **33/1**

13 7 3/4 **Terra Verde (IRE)**[364] 435 5-9-6 **104** (t) RoystonFfrench 12 41
(A Al Raihe, UAE) *wd and prom tl rdn 2 1/2f out: fdd* **16/1**

1m 38.61s (0.81) **Going Correction** +0.425s/f (Yiel) **13** Ran SP% **126.2**
Speed ratings: 112,110,107,107,107 105,105,104,99,98 98,87,79

Owner Mrs R Leheup **Bred** Chavonne Stud **Trained** South Africa

FOCUS
A very good handicap and basically another division of the 6.45 - the winning time was 0.87 seconds quicker. The pace seemed just ordinary in the early stages, but given the winner came from last, the leaders must have increased the tempo. The fourth and fifth set the standard but the proximity of the seventh limits the form.

NOTEBOOK
Diamond Quest(SAF) ◆ was ridden with utmost confidence and ran out an impressive winner, gaining deserved compensation for a couple of unlucky efforts on his two previous starts in Dubai. A winner at up to 2m in South Africa, he got going too late over an extended 7f on his first start at the Carnival, and then lost his chance when forced very wide in a good race over 1m4f last time but, dropped in trip, he made no mistake on this occasion. He was still last early in the straight, but he showed a really smart change of pace when switched out towards the centre of the track and sustained his effort to ultimately win decisively. He is clearly very versatile and can surely be found another opening at this year's Carnival.
Juror(USA) did everything right until the last furlong, when he drifted over to the far rail, seemingly the slowest part of the track on recent evidence, and he had no answer to the winner's late burst. He was clearly well suited by the return to turf.
Lucky Dance(BRZ) sustained his challenge well and improved markedly on the form of his two previous efforts at this year's Carnival.
Almuraad(IRE) probably found himself in front too soon and can do better.
Bolodenka(IRE) looked very unlucky over course and distance on his previous start, but he was produced with every chance this time and failed to build on that effort.
Zato(IRE), dropped in trip, seemed to have his chance but was readily outpaced.

474a FRIDAY SPRINT (CONDITIONS RACE) (DIRT) 5f (D)
5:10 (5:13) 3-Y-0+

£33,673 (£11,224; £5,612; £2,806; £1,683; £1,122)

RPR

1 **National Colour (SAF)**[215] 5-9-6 116 WCMarwing 4 114+
(S Tarry, South Africa) *slowly away: sn led: clr 1f out: easily* **10/11**[1]

2 1 3/4 **Bounty Quest**[14] 326 5-9-4 93 MartinDwyer 8 103
(Doug Watson, UAE) *a.p in centre: no ch w wnr* **16/1**

3 1/4 **New Freedom (BRZ)**[21] 249 6-8-12 93 (t) ECruz 11 96
(P Nickel Filho, Brazil) *swtchd to rail after 110yds: led nr side: r.o wl: nvr threatened wnr* **66/1**

4 1 3/4 **Machinist (IRE)**[21] 249 7-9-4 93 KerrinMcEvoy 5 95
(D Nicholls) *nvr nr to chal* **20/1**

5 shd **Warcat (NZ)**[6] 409 6-9-4 104 (t) WLHo 16 95
(Y Choy, Macau) *trckd ldr nr side: n.d* **10/1**

6 1 1/4 **Celtic Mill**[6] 409 9-9-4 102 (p) LDettori 15 91
(D W Barker) *missed break: nvr gng pce* **5/1**[2]

7 1 1/4 **Golden Acer (IRE)**[6] 409 4-8-12 96 (vt) JMurtagh 1 80
(Doug Watson, UAE) *racd on far rail: prom for 2 1/2f: wknd* **33/1**

8 1 1/2 **Power Politics (USA)**[112] 6192 4-8-12 91 WayneSmith 12 75
(M Al Muhairi, UAE) *nvr nr to chal* **33/1**

9 1/2 **Deserted Dane (USA)**[155] 5288 3-8-6 94 WSupple 3 81
(G A Swinbank) *impeded s: trckd ldr: kpt on one pce* **10/1**

10 1 1/4 **Aliysa (BRZ)**[21] 249 4-8-10 98 (t) ADomingos 14 66
(A Cintra Pereira, Brazil) *bmpd s: rdn 3f out: r.o fnl f* **13/2**[3]

11 1/2 **Pakhoes (IRE)**[14] 324 7-8-12 88 GHind 2 67
(R Bouresly, Kuwait) *missed break: nvr able to chal* **50/1**

12 2 1/2 **Tournedos (IRE)**[6] 415 5-9-4 98 TedDurcan 9 64
(D Nicholls) *trckd ldr in centre for 2f: n.d* **40/1**

13 1 1/2 **Media Hora (CHI)**[21] 249 7-9-4 102 (bt) DinaDanekilde 6 58
(F Castro, Sweden) *broke awkwardly: trckd wnr for 2f: wknd* **40/1**

14 5 1/2 **Hoy Soy Usted (BRZ)**[364] 434 6-8-12 86 RichardMullen 7 32
(Christian Wroe) *prom for 3f: wknd fnl 2f* **100/1**

15 6 **The Lord (ARG)**[14] 324 7-8-12 95 (t) RyanMoore 13 11
(S Seemar, UAE) *a struggling* **33/1**

F **Crooner (IRE)**[14] 324 4-9-4 90 RoystonFfrench 10 —
(Doug Watson, UAE) *clipped heels and fell after 110yds* **20/1**

58.13 secs (-0.27) **Going Correction** +0.175s/f (Slow)
WFA 3 from 4yo+ 14lb **16** Ran SP% **134.1**
Speed ratings: 109,106,105,103,102 100,98,96,95,93 92,88,86,77,68 —

Owner C J H Van Niekerk **Bred** A P Joubert **Trained** South Africa

FOCUS
The bare form of this conditions sprint is probably nothing out of the ordinary, but the winner, National Colour, was in a different league and created a really good impression. The form is rated around the fourth, fifth and eighth.

NOTEBOOK
National Colour(SAF) ◆, the winner of three Group 1s on the bounce on turf in her native South Africa, had no problem with the switch to dirt and never give her 15 rivals a look-in. Admittedly she had a good draw considering how the straight track has been favouring low stalls at this year's Carnival, but she would have won wherever she raced such was her dominance. She was always travelling supremely well within herself, despite going a furious pace from the start, and sustained her effort to the line. Her performance is all more the creditable considering she was conceding weight all round; no mean effort for a filly against colts and geldings. Considering this was her first run in 215 days, there should be more to come and she looks capable of leaving the bare form of this effort behind. She will deserve the utmost respect if taking her chance in the Golden Shaheen, a 6f Group 1 on World Cup night, with the step back up in trip unlikely to bother her. There do not seem to be too many stars amongst the Dubai-based sprinters, and she could have most to worry about in that race from the American contingent. (op Evens)
Bounty Quest was second over 6f round here on his previous start off a mark of 91 and he looks the best guide to the strength of the form.
New Freedom(BRZ) showed up well throughout towards the stands'-side rail and improved significantly on the form he produced over 6f round here on his previous start.
Machinist(IRE) appreciated the drop in grade and ran well, keeping on nicely for pressure having struggled to match the early pace of a few of these.
Warcat(NZ) ran a creditable race returned to dirt, but a high draw was of little help.
Celtic Mill could not recover after starting very awkwardly, keeping on well but all too late.
Deserted Dane(USA), the only three-year-old in the line-up, faced a tough task on just his third racecourse appearance, but ran creditably enough in the circumstances, chasing the winner for some way before fading. (op 9-1)
Tournedos(IRE) showed speed but could not sustain his challenge.
Crooner(IRE) seemed to clip heels with Tournedos and came down.

475a E+ H'CAP (TURF) 1m 4f (T)
5:45 (5:45) (90-105,104) 3-Y-0+

£33,673 (£11,224; £5,612; £2,806; £1,683; £1,122)

RPR

1 **Crime Scene (IRE)**[14] 328 4-8-12 **98** JMurtagh 11 92
(I Mohammed, UAE) *mid-div: rdn to chal 2f out: led 110yds out: jst hld on* **7/1**

2 shd **Pearly King (USA)**[21] 244 4-8-12 **98** LDettori 9 92
(I Mohammed, UAE) *mid-div: prog to trck ldrs 3f out: led 1 1/2f out: hdd 110yds out: rallied: jst failed* **7/1**

3 1 1/4 **Candy Critic (ARG)**[7] 401 5-9-1 **98** (bt) WCMarwing 1 90
(M F De Kock, South Africa) *trckd ldr on rail: led briefly 2 1/2f out: sn hdd and hrd rdn: kpt on wl* **10/1**

4 3/4 **Peintre Bleu (FR)**[14] 328 5-8-11 **95** (b) RichardMullen 4 85
(S Seemar, UAE) *hld up in rr: rdn to cl 2 1/2f out: ev ch 1 1/2f out: one pce* **33/1**

5 1 1/4 **Go For Gold (IRE)**[14] 328 6-9-4 **101** (vt) EddieAhern 14 90
(S Seemar, UAE) *hld up in rr: rdn to cl 2f out: nt qckn* **40/1**

6 shd **Bennie Blue (SAF)**[7] 398 5-9-0 **97** KShea 12 86
(M F De Kock, South Africa) *mid-div: rdn to cl 2f out: nt qckn* **25/1**

7 2 1/4 **Fenice (IRE)**[21] 248 4-9-3 **102** TedDurcan 6 88
(S Seemar, UAE) *mid-div: rdn 2 1/2f out: nt qckn* **12/1**

8 1 3/4 **Sunday Symphony**[14] 328 5-9-6 **104** (vt) RyanMoore 5 86
(S Seemar, UAE) *settled in rr: rdn 4f out: n.m.r 2 1/2f out: nvr able to chal* **25/1**

9 1 3/4 **Nepotista (BRZ)**[14] 328 5-9-4 **101** ADomingos 2 81
(A Cintra Pereira, Brazil) *in rr: rdn 3f out: n.d* **6/1**[2]

10 2 3/4 **Mutafanen**[14] 328 6-9-6 **104** (v) RHills 13 79
(E Charpy, UAE) *hld up in rr: rdn 4f out: nvr nr to chal* **13/2**[3]

11 4 1/4 **Ampelio (IRE)**[21] 248 5-8-11 **95** (vt) MartinDwyer 7 64
(Doug Watson, UAE) *trckd ldr: led briefly 2f out: wknd* **4/1**[1]

12 1 1/2 **Priors Hill (IRE)**[104] 6319 4-8-9 **95** (bt) TPO'Shea 10 62
(E Charpy, UAE) *mid-div on rail: rdn 4f out: n.d* **25/1**

13 4 1/4 **Consular**[176] 4713 5-8-12 **96** KerrinMcEvoy 3 56
(I Mohammed, UAE) *sn led: hdd 2 1/2f out: wknd* **13/2**[3]

14 dist **Mosaic**[303] 1072 5-9-3 **100** RoystonFfrench 8 —
(A Al Raihe, UAE) *trckd ldr out wd: rdn 3 1/2f out: wknd: eased fnl f* **16/1**

2m 32.79s (1.79) **Going Correction** +0.425s/f (Yiel)
WFA 4 from 5yo+ 3lb **14** Ran SP% **125.5**
Speed ratings: 111,110,110,109,108 108,107,106,104,103 100,99,96,—

Owner H R H Princess Haya Of Jordan **Bred** Gainsborough Stud Management Ltd **Trained** UAE

FOCUS
A very good middle-distance handicap and the pace seemed fair enough from the start. The form appears solid rated around the placed horses and the sixth.

NOTEBOOK
Crime Scene(IRE) improved on the form he showed when fourth over course and distance on his debut in Dubai with a determined success, readily reversing form with Mutafanen and Nepotista. Always going well just off the leaders, he had the eventual runner-up in his sights for much of the way and found plenty when switched out wide with his effort in the straight. There could be more to come.
Pearly King(USA) ◆, a little unlucky when fifth over 1m2f on his debut in Dubai, was not at all inconvenienced by the step up in trip and just lost out. Having travelled with ease off the pace for much of the contest, the leaders seemed to fall away quicker than was ideal and he probably found himself in the clear a little too soon. He stuck to his task well but Crime Scene was always just doing enough. He is clearly a smart performer and will remain worthy of plenty respect in this sort of race over 1m2f-1m4f.
Candy Critic(ARG), the only mare in the field, improved on the form she showed over 1m2f round here on her previous start with a good effort behind a couple of progressive types, although she did flash her tail quite violently under pressure, particularly when struck with the whip
Peintre Bleu(FR) is probably a little bit better than the bare form suggests as he stuck to the far rail in the straight, whereas those around him produced their efforts more towards the centre of the track.
Go For Gold(IRE) left his recent efforts behind with a creditable performance. He is decent on his day and this run offered some hope.
Mutafanen, 4lb higher than when winning over course and distance on his previous start, never landed a blow this time and was pretty disappointing.
Ampelio(IRE) had been holding his form well lately but this was disappointing.

476a GULF NEWS UAE 1000 GUINEAS (FILLIES) (LISTED RACE) (DIRT) 1m (D)

6:15 (6:18) 3-Y-O

£76,530 (£25,510; £12,755; £6,377; £3,826; £2,551)

Pos	Dist	Horse	RPR
1		**Folk (USA)**[81] 3-8-9 100 .... KerrinMcEvoy 5 (I Mohammed, UAE) *sn led: gng wl 2f out: rdn clr 1f out: comf* **12/1**	110+
2	4 ¾	**Greetings (BRZ)**[21] 246 4-9-4 109 .... RichardMullen 6 (P Nickel Filho, Brazil) *mid-div: rdn to trck ldrs 3f out: r.o fnl 1 1/2f* **8/11**[1]	102
3	1	**Samba Reggae (ARG)**[68] 4-9-4 102 .... LDettori 1 (I Mohammed, UAE) *sn rdn along to trck ldr: gng wl 2 1/2f out: rdn 2f out: r.o but no ch w wnr* **5/1**[2]	100
4	8 ¼	**Desert Fight (CHI)**[103] 4-9-4 100 .... RyanMoore 4 (S Seemar, UAE) *mid-div: hrd rdn 3 1/2f out: nvr able to chal* **12/1**	84
5	3 ¼	**Miss Chatty (ARG)**[103] 4-9-4 95 .... EddieAhern 10 (H J Brown, South Africa) *nvr able to chal* **33/1**	77
6	nse	**Carillon (IRE)**[157] 5237 3-8-9 78 .... MartinDwyer 11 (Doug Watson, UAE) *trckd wnr tl rdn and wknd 3f out* **66/1**	75
7	1 ¼	**Whistledownthewind (SAF)**[21] 246 4-9-4 90 .... WCMarwing 12 (M F De Kock, South Africa) *mid-div: rdn 3f out: n.d* **20/1**	74
8	7 ¼	**Satulagi (USA)**[21] 246 3-8-9 101 .... JohnEgan 8 (J S Moore) *n.d* **11/1**[3]	58
9	3	**Snow Clad (AUS)**[21] 246 4-9-4 45 ....(t) BYamzon 13 (A Selvaratnam, UAE) *a in rr* **500/1**	54
10	¾	**Precocious Star (IRE)**[21] 246 3-8-9 91 .... JMurtagh 2 (K R Burke) *mid-div: rdn 3f out: nvr a threat* **66/1**	50
11	¼	**Dubai Jewel (AUS)**[21] 246 4-9-4 91 .... TedDurcan 14 (S Seemar, UAE) *nvr able to chal* **40/1**	52
12	shd	**Indochine (BRZ)**[28] 174 4-9-4 107 .... KShea 3 (H J Brown, South Africa) *racd in 4th tl rdn 3 1/2f out: nt respond to press* **5/1**[2]	52
13	6 ¼	**The Real Thing (IRE)**[21] 246 3-8-9 87 .... WSupple 7 (A Manuel, UAE) *nvr involved* **66/1**	37

1m 35.84s (-1.76) **Going Correction** +0.05s/f (Slow)
WFA 3 from 4yo 19lb 13 Ran SP% **129.8**
Speed ratings: 110,105,104,96,92 92,91,84,81,80 80,80,73

Owner Sheikh Hamdan Bin Mohammed Al Maktoum **Bred** Darley **Trained** UAE

FOCUS
The seventh renewal of the UAE 1000 Guineas attracted the biggest field in the race's history, although Godolphin, who had landed this prize six times, were unrepresented. It is probably fair to say, though, that the two fillies who raced for the Mohammed yard are the type of horses who may have sported the Godolphin colours in years gone by. Hard to be sure of the level of form, but the runner-up, Greetings, set a pretty smart standard. The time was the quickest in the race's history, and of the 2000 Guineas winners, only Sreet Cry ran faster.

NOTEBOOK
Folk(USA) ◆, the ten-length winner of a maiden in the US last year, had no trouble in coping with the step up in class on her debut in Dubai and followed up in clear-cut fashion. Admittedly she enjoyed the run of the race out in front, but she had to show good early speed to get there, and displayed a particularly powerful galloping action once in the lead. It was clear she had plenty left early in the straight and she never looked in much danger. She should stay another furlong and will be very hard to beat in the UAE Oaks, particularly if allowed her own way out in front once again.
Greetings(BRZ), the easy winner of what was effectively a trial for this race over 7f on her debut in Dubai, soon had ground to make up on Folk and never really looked like doing enough. She stays 1m2f, so the trip was never a worry, and she kept on well for second, but she could make no impact on the winner. She gives the impression she will be a much better filly if able to dominate, and deserves to take her chance in the UAE Oaks. (op 5-6)
Samba Reggae(ARG), the winner's stablemate, came into this off the back of a 1m2f Group 1 win in Argentina. She raced right behind Folk throughout, but was unable to match that one's burst in the straight. She is almost sure to benefit from a step back up in trip and is entitled to get closer to today's winner in the Oaks.
Desert Fight(CHI) was under pressure a fair way out, but she kept on in the straight.
Miss Chatty(ARG) turned in widest of all having been well back early.
Satulagi(USA) shaped well when second over 7f on her debut in Dubai, but this was a little disappointing. (op 10-1)
Precocious Star(IRE) again failed to land a blow.
Indochine(BRZ) was not that far away on the turn in, but she gradually weakened. (op 11-2)

477a PROPERTY WEEKLY CUP (H'CAP) (TURF) 1m (T)

6:45 (6:48) (90-105,105) 3-Y-O+

£33,673 (£11,224; £5,612; £2,806; £1,683; £1,122)

Pos	Dist	Horse	RPR
1		**Mystical (IND)**[81] 5-9-2 **100** .... RyanMoore 5 (S Ganapathy, India) *settled in rr: rdn to cl 2 1/2f out: led 1 1/2f out: r.o wl* **7/2**[1]	102
2	1 ½	**Hallhoo (IRE)**[7] 398 5-8-11 **96** .... JMurtagh 11 (D Selvaratnam, UAE) *mid-div: prog to trck ldrs 2f out: r.o: no ch w wnr* **5/1**[2]	94
3	½	**Yarqus**[6] 411 4-8-10 **95** .... TedDurcan 1 (C E Brittain) *trckd ldr on rail: led 2f out: hdd 1 1/2f out: r.o wl* **12/1**	92
4	2 ¾	**Starpix (FR)**[14] 325 5-9-6 **105** .... KShea 14 (H J Brown, South Africa) *settled in rr: gng wl 3f out: rdn 2f out: r.o: nrst fin* **7/1**[3]	97
5	¼	**Boston Lodge**[14] 325 7-8-8 **93** ....(vt) MartinDwyer 12 (Doug Watson, UAE) *in rr: pushed along 3f out: prog 1 1/2f out: r.o* **10/1**	84
6	2	**Hopeful Purchase (IRE)**[14] 331 4-8-10 **95** ....(b[1]) RHills 8 (W J Haggas) *mid-div: rdn to trck ldrs 2f out: one pce fnl f* **12/1**	82
7	¾	**Akimbo (USA)**[21] 247 6-8-10 **95** .... RPCleary 4 (James Leavy, Ire) *mid-div: travelling strly: trckd wnr 2f out: wknd fnl f* **18/1**	81
8	2 ¼	**Spirit Of France (IRE)**[195] 4098 5-8-8 **93** .... EddieAhern 7 (Christian Wroe) *trckd ldr: rdn 2 1/2f out: wknd* **10/1**	74
9	¼	**Amandus (USA)**[14] 331 7-8-6 **90** .... WSupple 3 (Doug Watson, UAE) *led tl hdd and swamped 2f out: wknd* **9/1**	72
10	¼	**Celtic Silence**[1407] 9-9-2 **100** .... GHind 10 (R Bouresly, Kuwait) *settled in rr: short of room after 1f: t.k.h: nvr nr to chal* **33/1**	81
11	shd	**Bandido Secreto (BRZ)**[7] 399 5-9-2 **100** .... ADomingos 2 (P Nickel Filho, Brazil) *trckd lding gp rail tl rdn out: wknd 2 1/2f out* **10/1**	81
12	2 ¾	**Fueguino (ARG)**[42] 9-8-6 **90** .... RichardMullen 9 (M Kettle, UAE) *v.s.a: nvr able to chal* **40/1**	65
13	¼	**Kings Point (IRE)**[6] 411 6-9-0 **98** ....(p) LDettori 6 (R A Fahey) *in rr: nvr able to chal* **10/1**	73
14	14	**Divine Task (USA)**[21] 244 9-8-7 **91** .... TPO'Shea 13 (E Charpy, UAE) *trckd ldr out wd: rdn 3f out: wknd* **33/1**	38

1m 39.48s (1.68) **Going Correction** +0.425s/f (Yiel) 14 Ran SP% **126.7**
Speed ratings: 108,106,106,103,103 101,100,98,97,97 97,94,94,80

Owner Mr & Mrs Zavaray S Poonawalla **Bred** Poonawalla Estate Stud & Agri Farm **Trained** India

FOCUS
Probably just ordinary form for the grade, although solid enough rated around the next four home behind the winner, but they did not seem to go much of a pace in the early stages, resulting in a 0.87 seconds slower than the 4.40.

NOTEBOOK
Mystical(IND) is a multiple Group winner in his native India, including at the highest level, and he showed himself on a fair mark on this debut in Dubai with a decisive success. He picked up in good style when produced with his effort and could be capable of adding to this. (op 4-1)
Hallhoo(IRE), dropped in trip and not asked to make the running this time, was always well placed considering how the race was run, although he was a little short or room when initially trying to pick up.
Yarqus was produced with every chance and improved on his recent course and distance effort.
Starpix(FR) kept on well widest of all in the straight, but never really looked like troubling the leaders. This was a decent enough effort under top weight. (op 6-1)
Boston Lodge could not confirm recent form with Starpix, but he did not seem to do a great deal wrong.
Hopeful Purchase(IRE) ◆, fitted with blinkers for the first time, seemed a little short of room in the straight and is better than his finishing position suggests. He does not have a great deal to find to go close in one of these races.
Akimbo(USA) was well held. (op 16-1)
Kings Point(IRE) offered little immediate promise. (op 9-1)

440 WOLVERHAMPTON (A.W) (L-H)

Friday, February 16

OFFICIAL GOING: Standard
Wind: virtually nil

478 PONTIN'S HOLIDAYS CLAIMING STKS 7f 32y(P)

1:40 (1:41) (Class 5) 3-Y-O £3,238 (£963; £481; £240) Stalls High

Form	Pos	Dist	Horse	RPR
22-1	1		**Dressed To Dance (IRE)**[39] 69 3-9-0 65 ....(b) KimTinkler 6 (N Tinkler) *hld up: hdwy over 3f out: rdn over 2f out: edgd lft over 1f out: r.o to ld towards fin* **8/1**[3]	68
31-3	2	hd	**Hollywood George**[19] 275 3-9-5 72 .... TonyCulhane 4 (W J Haggas) *t.k.h: prom: bmpd over 3f out: n.m.r and bdly hmpd ins fnl f: swtchd rt: r.o: fin 3rd, hd & 1½l: plcd 2nd* **8/11**[1]	69+
-211	3	1 ½	**Put It On The Card**[14] 335 3-9-2 64 ....(b) NCallan 5 (J S Wainwright) *a.p: rdn to ld jst over 1f out: edgd lft ins fnl f: hdd towards fin: fin 2nd, hd: plcd 3rd* **7/2**[2]	66
03-3	4	2	**Raquel White**[32] 139 3-8-9 56 .... ChrisCatlin 1 (J L Flint) *led 2f: outpcd over 3f out: styd on towards fin* **12/1**	54
-0	5	hd	**Castle Durrow (IRE)**[31] 149 3-8-7 ow1 .... JerryO'Dwyer(3) 2 (Seamus Fahey, Ire) *s.i.s: rdn over 4f out: hdwy on outside over 2f out: styd on towards fin* **40/1**	54
2453	6	½	**Mick Is Back**[14] 335 3-8-9 58 ....(b) StephenDonohoe(3) 3 (P D Evans) *w ldr: led 5f out: rdn and hdd jst over 1f out: sn hmpd on ins: wknd* **10/1**	55
-453	7	8	**The Light Fandango**[11] 357 3-8-2 47 .... TolleyDean(5) 7 (R A Harris) *sn bhd: rdn over 4f out: rdr dropped whip over 2f out: sn struggling* **33/1**	29

1m 30.29s (-0.11) **Going Correction** -0.05s/f (Stan) 7 Ran SP% **113.4**
Speed ratings (Par 97):98,96,96,93,93 92,83
CSF £14.09 TOTE £8.60: £3.10, £1.10; EX 19.20.There was no bid for the winner. Hollywood George was claimed by K Ryan for £15,000.
Owner N Tinkler **Bred** J Doyle **Trained** Langton, N Yorks

FOCUS
Three horses were having their first outings for new stables in what turned out to be a competitive claimer. The form looks pretty sound rated around the runner-up. fourth and sixth.

479 PONTINS.COM H'CAP (DIV I) 7f 32y(P)

2:10 (2:10) (Class 6) (0-58,58) 4-Y-0+ £1,706 (£503; £252) Stalls High

Form	Pos	Dist	Horse	RPR
4-53	1		**Mister Benji**[38] 80 8-8-10 **54** ow1 ....(p) TonyCulhane 1 (B P J Baugh) *led early: chsd ldrs: rdn to ld wl over 1f out: drvn out* **4/1**[1]	63
3-20	2	nk	**Cabourg (IRE)**[14] 334 4-8-11 **58** ....(b) GregFairley(3) 6 (R Bastiman) *hld up and bhd: nt clr run over 2f out: rdn and hdwy on ins wl over 1f out: ev ch whn edgd lft ins fnl f: r.o* **17/2**[3]	66
0-03	3	1 ¾	**Buzzin'Boyzee (IRE)**[28] 183 4-8-10 **57** .... StephenDonohoe(3) 2 (P D Evans) *hld up and bhd: rdn and hdwy over 2f out: kpt on ins fnl f* **7/1**[2]	60
0120	4	nk	**Mulberry Lad (IRE)**[1] 467 5-8-8 **52** .... JimCrowley 7 (P W Hiatt) *mid-div: rdn and hdwy on ins over 2f out: ev ch wl over 1f out: one pce fnl f* **4/1**[1]	55
04-0	5	1 ½	**Hits Only Cash**[17] 306 5-8-12 **56** .... DeanMcKeown 8 (J Pearce) *hld up and bhd: c wd over 2f out: hdwy on outside fnl f: nvr nrr* **7/1**[2]	55
30-6	6	1 ¼	**Feelin Irie (IRE)**[16] 310 4-8-11 **55** .... PatCosgrave 12 (J R Boyle) *sn w ldr: rdn and ev ch wl over 1f out: wknd fnl f* **20/1**	51
003-	7	1 ¾	**Bandos**[176] 4729 7-8-4 **53** .... DuranFentiman(5) 5 (I Semple) *sn led: rdn over 2f out: hdd wl over 1f out: wknd ent fnl f* **11/1**	44
610-	8	¾	**Danettie**[374] 327 6-8-10 **54** .... ShaneKelly 4 (W M Brisbourne) *hmpd sn after s: mid-div: wkng whn edgd lft 1f out* **9/1**	43
0-50	9	9	**Kineta (USA)**[18] 296 4-8-12 **56** .... BrettDoyle 3 (W R Muir) *mid-div: rdn 4f out: sn bhd* **25/1**	22
1340	10	½	**Capital Lass**[10] 374 4-9-0 **58** ....(p) HayleyTurner 11 (A J McCabe) *s.i.s: hdwy after 1f: rdn over 3f out: wknd over 2f out* **25/1**	22
-030	11	shd	**Piccolo Prince**[1] 462 6-7-12 **49** .... ManavNem(7) 10 (P A Blockley) *a bhd* **25/1**	13
00-0	12	3	**Auentraum (GER)**[37] 82 7-8-5 **52** ....(p) JamesDoyle(3) 9 (Ms J S Doyle) *t.k.h: chsd ldrs: rdn and wknd over 2f out* **16/1**	8

1m 30.25s (-0.15) **Going Correction** -0.05s/f (Stan) 12 Ran SP% **116.0**
Speed ratings (Par 101):98,97,95,95,93 92,90,89,79,78 78,74
CSF £35.22 CT £230.52 TOTE £4.70: £1.60, £3.60, £1.90; EX 50.00 Trifecta £137.60 Pool £286.92 - 1.48 winning units..
Owner J H Chrimes And Mr & Mrs G W Hannam **Bred** D J And Mrs K D Smart **Trained** Audley, Staffs

FOCUS
A modest handicap run 0.67 seconds slower than the second division but the form looks sound, although not rated too positively.

Kineta(USA) Official explanation: jockey said filly would not face the kick-back

480 DIGITAL PRINTS FROM BONUSPRINT.COM H'CAP 5f 216y(P)
2:45 (2:45) (Class 4) (0-80,80) 4-Y-0+ **£4,857** (£1,445; £722; £360) **Stalls** Low

Form RPR

-613 **1** **Danetime Lord (IRE)**[6] [424] 4-8-4 **68**..................(p) CatherineGannon 8 76
(K A Ryan) *hld up in tch: hung lft wl over 1f out: hrd rdn to ld last stride* **4/1**[2]

4-31 **2** *shd* **Figaro Flyer (IRE)**[20] [269] 4-8-13 **77**.............................. TonyCulhane 6 85
(P Howling) *led: rdn ins fnl f: hdd last stride* **7/2**[1]

4010 **3** *1 ½* **Night Prospector**[6] [419] 7-9-2 **80**..(p) NCallan 3 83
(B Palling) *a.p: rdn over 2f out: nt qckn fnl f* **9/2**[3]

6165 **4** *½* **Marko Jadeo (IRE)**[11] [359] 9-8-8 **77**............................ TolleyDean(5) 1 79
(R A Harris) *hld up and bhd: rdn over 2f out: hdwy fnl f: r.o* **12/1**

600- **5** *hd* **King Marju (IRE)**[47] [6999] 5-8-13 **77**................................ PatCosgrave 9 78
(K R Burke) *hld up towards rr: hdwy over 2f out: rdn and edgd lft over 1f out: kpt on same pce fnl f* **7/1**

0-20 **6** *nk* **Zarzu**[27] [190] 8-8-11 **78**.. LiamJones(3) 2 78
(C R Dore) *hld up in tch: one pce fnl 2f* **10/1**

-560 **7** *1 ½* **Mambazo**[20] [269] 5-7-11 **66** oh1.........................(e) DuranFentiman(5) 10 62
(S C Williams) *racd wd: plld hrd in rr: nvr trbld ldrs* **28/1**

3-14 **8** *2* **Miracle Ridge (IRE)**[42] [41] 12-8-12 **76**..........................(b) TPQueally 7 66
(Adrian McGuinness, Ire) *sn chsng ldr: ev ch over 2f out: sn hrd rdn: btn whn sltly hmpd over 1f out* **8/1**

-540 **9** *shd* **Sands Crooner (IRE)**[11] [371] 4-8-5 **69**...................(v) DeanMcKeown 5 58
(D Shaw) *t.k.h: sn mid-div: hdwy over 2f out: rdn and wknd over 1f out* **20/1**

100- **10** *4* **Coconut Moon**[152] [5405] 5-8-10 **74**..................................... DavidAllan 4 51
(E J Alston) *t.k.h: rdn 3f out: a bhd* **14/1**

1m 14.68s (-1.13) **Going Correction** -0.05s/f (Stan) **10** Ran SP% **115.7**
Speed ratings (Par 105):105,104,102,102,101 101,99,96,96,91
CSF £18.25 CT £66.55 TOTE £6.50: £2.00, £1.80, £2.00; EX 24.50 Trifecta £79.50 Pool £508.68 - 4.54 winning units..
Owner Bull & Bell Partnership **Bred** P J Murphy **Trained** Hambleton, N Yorks

FOCUS
A competitive if ordinary handicap rated around the first two.

481 WOLVERHAMPTON-RACECOURSE.CO.UK (S) STKS 1m 4f 50y(P)
3:20 (3:21) (Class 6) 4-Y-0+ **£2,047** (£604; £302) **Stalls** Low

Form RPR

5-11 **1** **Atlantic Gamble (IRE)**[28] [182] 7-9-10 56...................(p) PatCosgrave 2 65+
(K R Burke) *chsd ldr: rdn to ld 1f out: r.o wl* **5/2**[1]

0-24 **2** *2* **Tresor Secret (FR)**[25] [212] 7-9-5 61.................................. JimCrowley 7 57
(J Gallagher) *set stdy pce: rdn and hdd 1f out: nt qckn* **7/2**[2]

-110 **3** *3* **Finished Article (IRE)**[14] [332] 10-9-10 55........................... NCallan 10 57
(P A Blockley) *hld up towards rr: hdwy over 3f out: rdn over 2f out: one pce* **13/2**[3]

0/0- **4** *3* **Intricate Web (IRE)**[266] [1987] 11-9-5 67............................ DavidAllan 9 48
(E J Alston) *hld up towards rr: sme hdwy over 2f out: nvr trbld ldrs* **25/1**

0-63 **5** *1* **Treason Trial**[14] [333] 6-9-5 45... ShaneKelly 3 46
(W M Brisbourne) *prom: lost pl over 3f out: rdn over 2f out: n.d after* **14/1**

316- **6** *½* **Regency Red (IRE)**[55] [6936] 9-9-5 53.................. AshleyHamblett(5) 12 50
(W M Brisbourne) *s.s: sn swtchd lft: hld up and bhd: hdwy 5f out: rdn over 2f out: wknd wl over 1f out* **8/1**

-446 **7** *hd* **Scuzme (IRE)**[18] [288] 4-9-2 51..(p) TPQueally 6 45
(Miss Sheena West) *hld up in mid-div: rdn over 3f out: sn struggling* **14/1**

40-6 **8** *1 ½* **Willy (SWE)**[28] [182] 5-9-5 49...(t) PhillipMakin 5 42
(R Brotherton) *hld up in mid-div: short-lived effrt over 2f out* **10/1**

-425 **9** *3* **Zaffeu**[14] [333] 6-9-10 55.. GeorgeBaker 8 43
(A G Juckes) *s.i.s: a bhd* **13/2**[3]

0040 **10** *½* **Stolen Summer (IRE)**[8] [389] 4-9-2 52......................(be) PaulHanagan 1 37
(B S Rothwell) *hld up towards rr: n.m.r on ins sn after s: a bhd* **33/1**

0- **11** *11* **Aizen Myoo (IRE)**[76] [6680] 9-9-2 ....(v[1]) JerryO'Dwyer(3) 4 19
(Seamus Fahey, Ire) *rel to r: sn prom: rdn and wknd over 3f out* **20/1**

2m 44.23s (1.81) **Going Correction** -0.05s/f (Stan)
WFA 4 from 5yo+ 3lb **11** Ran SP% **122.5**
Speed ratings (Par 101):91,89,87,85,85 84,84,83,81,81 73
CSF £11.22 TOTE £3.70: £1.80, £1.50, £2.40; EX 18.90 Trifecta £47.60 Pool £480.08 - 7.16 winning units..There was no bid for the winner. Treason Trial was claimed by Mrs S Liddiard for £6,000.
Owner R G Greaney **Bred** Larry Ryan **Trained** Middleham Moor, N Yorks

FOCUS
An ordinary seller run at a modest pace and best rated through the fifth.
Treason Trial ◆ Official explanation: jockey said gelding hung right throughout

482 PONTIN'S FAMILY HOLIDAYS H'CAP 2m 119y(P)
3:55 (3:57) (Class 6) (0-60,60) 4-Y-0+ **£2,388** (£705; £352) **Stalls** Low

Form RPR

006- **1** **Moon Emperor**[100] [6398] 10-9-8 **59**.......................................(b) NCallan 5 67
(J R Jenkins) *hld up in mid-div: hdwy on ins over 4f out: rdn and sltly outpcd over 2f out: styd on to ld towards fin* **9/1**

05-0 **2** *¾* **Teorban (POL)**[25] [213] 8-9-1 **55**........................... StephenDonohoe(3) 3 62
(Mrs N S Evans) *led after 1f: rdn over 2f out: hdd and no ex towards fin* **50/1**

-541 **3** *¾* **Blue Hills**[17] [302] 6-9-4 **55**...(b) JimCrowley 13 61
(P W Hiatt) *sn prom: wnt 2nd over 4f out: rdn and ev ch 2f out: edgd rt wl ins fnl f: no ex* **6/1**[3]

-402 **4** *nk* **Qaasi (USA)**[11] [369] 5-8-9 **53**.................................. PatrickDonaghy(7) 2 58
(M Brittain) *hld up and bhd: hdwy 2f out: styd on ins fnl f* **5/1**[2]

0-33 **5** *1 ½* **Come What Augustus**[33] [134] 5-8-12 **49**..................(p) SamHitchcott 8 52
(R M Stronge) *hld up in mid-div: rdn over 2f out: hdwy wl over 1f out: hung lft fnl f: one pce* **9/1**

06-0 **6** *2 ½* **Zalkani (IRE)**[14] [332] 7-9-8 **59**.................................... MichaelTebbutt 10 59
(J Pearce) *hld up and bhd: hdwy on ins over 3f out: rdn wl over 1f out: no imp: eased towards fin* **22/1**

4565 **7** *1 ¾* **Sea Map**[12] [354] 5-9-5 **56**.. EdwardCreighton 6 53
(Miss Sheena West) *hld up and bhd: nvr nr ldrs* **6/1**[3]

020/ **8** *1 ½* **Lord Nellsson**[108] [5943] 11-9-6 **57**...................................... HayleyTurner 1 52
(Andrew Turnell) *prom: rdn over 4f out: wknd 3f out* **28/1**

0-35 **9** *5* **Leighton Buzzard**[11] [369] 5-9-1 **55**.......................(p) JerryO'Dwyer(3) 7 43
(N B King) *hld up towards rr: rdn 4f out: short-lived effrt on wd outside over 2f out* **9/1**

05-4 **10** *3* **Equilibria (USA)**[19] [278] 5-8-13 **50**..................................... BrettDoyle 12 34
(G L Moore) *t.k.h in mid-div: rdn over 4f out: wknd over 2f out* **4/1**[1]

-122 **11** *5* **Nod's Star**[19] [285] 6-8-12 **49**..(t) ChrisCatlin 9 26
(Mrs L C Jewell) *led 1f: chsd ldr tl over 4f out: rdn over 3f out: wknd over 2f out* **8/1**

3m 42.87s (-0.26) **Going Correction** -0.05s/f (Stan)
WFA 4 from 5yo+ 6lb **11** Ran SP% **116.1**
Speed ratings (Par 101):98,97,97,97,96 95,94,93,91,89 87
CSF £393.02 CT £2888.45 TOTE £11.50: £3.60, £7.80, £2.20; EX 383.30 TRIFECTA Not won..
Owner R M Ellis **Bred** Fares Stables Ltd **Trained** Royston, Herts

FOCUS
A weak staying handicap and little better than a seller.
Equilibria(USA) Official explanation: trainer had no explanation for the poor form shown

483 PONTINSBINGO.COM H'CAP 1m 141y(P)
4:30 (4:31) (Class 4) (0-85,85) 3-Y-0
£3,036 (£3,036; £699; £350; £174; £87) **Stalls** Low

Form RPR

1 **1** **Storybook (UAE)**[20] [260] 3-8-8 **75**.. NCallan 3 87+
(M A Jarvis) *led: rdn over 1f out: hdd ins fnl f: rallied to join ldr post* **15/8**[2]

1-1 **1** *dht* **Boscobel**[34] [113] 3-9-4 **85**.. JoeFanning 1 97+
(M Johnston) *a.p: rdn and wnt 2nd over 2f out: led ins fnl f: jnd post* **8/11**[1]

0-32 **3** *6* **New World Order (IRE)**[18] [301] 3-8-11 **78**.................... PatCosgrave 2 77
(K R Burke) *hld up: rdn over 2f out: sn outpcd: styd on to take 3rd ins fnl f* **16/1**

4-32 **4** *3 ½* **Copper King**[25] [216] 3-8-7 **77**................................ StephenDonohoe(3) 5 69
(P D Evans) *prom: rdn 2f out: wknd over 1f out* **14/1**[3]

1- **5** *8* **Stravita**[87] [6558] 3-8-8 **75**... GrahamGibbons 6 50
(R Hollinshead) *chsd ldr tl rdn over 2f out: sn wknd: eased over 1f out* **25/1**

340- **6** *3* **Ede's Dot Com (IRE)**[126] [5940] 3-9-0 **81**.............................. IanMongan 4 50
(P M Phelan) *hld up: rdn over 3f out: sn struggling* **40/1**

1m 49.44s (-2.32) **Going Correction** -0.05s/f (Stan) **6** Ran SP% **111.5**
Speed ratings (Par 99):108,108,102,99,92 89
Win: Boscobel £0.80, Storybook £1.50; PL: BL £1.10, SK £1.50; EX: BL/SK £1.80, SK/BL £1.30; CSF: BL/SK £1.12, SK/BL £1.74.
Owner Jumeirah Racing **Bred** Darley **Trained** Newmarket, Suffolk
Owner Sheikh Mohammed **Bred** Darley **Trained** Middleham Moor, N Yorks

FOCUS
A fair handicap and a very smart winning time for this type of contest. The bookmakers went 14/1 bar the two dead-heaters who pulled clear with the fourth the best guide to the level.
Boscobel Official explanation: jockey said, regarding running and riding, that the colt raced green as in its previous race, and that he had ridden out to the line whilst showing the whip, and that it had not lost any forward momentum.
Stravita Official explanation: jockey said filly went lame but returned sound

484 BONUSPRINT.COM MAIDEN STKS 1m 1f 103y(P)
5:05 (5:06) (Class 5) 3-Y-0 **£3,412** (£1,007; £504) **Stalls** Low

Form RPR

1 **Silkwood** 3-8-12 .... NCallan 1 64+
(M A Jarvis) *hld up in tch: lost pl over 4f out: hdwy on ins 2f out: rdn to ld ins fnl f: r.o* **4/5**[1]

3-2 **2** *nk* **Man Of Vision (USA)**[27] [193] 3-9-3 .... TonyCulhane 9 68+
(M R Channon) *hld up in tch: rdn to ld jst over 1f out: hdd ins fnl f: r.o* **9/4**[2]

3 **3** *2* **Reciprocation (IRE)**[21] [257] 3-9-3 .... JoeFanning 10 64
(M Johnston) *sn led: rdn and hdd jst over 1f out: no ex ins fnl f* **4/1**[3]

5 **4** *1* **Giddywell**[21] [258] 3-8-7 .... RussellKennemore(5) 8 57
(R Hollinshead) *t.k.h: a.p: rdn wl over 1f out: one pce fnl f* **150/1**

3 **5** *4* **Picky**[35] [106] 3-9-0 .... RichardKingscote(3) 6 54
(J A Osborne) *hld up in mid-div: rdn and hdwy over 1f out: edgd lft jst ins fnl f: no further prog* **33/1**

4 **6** *1* **Snake Hips**[21] [258] 3-9-3 .... DaleGibson 13 52
(B Palling) *hld up towards rr: c wd st: hdwy on outside over 1f out: no imp fnl f* **50/1**

0-00 **7** *2* **Tobougg Welcome (IRE)**[13] [342] 3-9-3 43.................. SteveDrowne 7 48
(S C Williams) *mid-div: hdwy over 5f out: rdn over 2f out: wknd wl over 1f out* **100/1**

0 **8** *nk* **Bedouin Beauty (IRE)**[18] [293] 3-8-12 .... BrettDoyle 12 42
(E A L Dunlop) *swtchd lft sn after s: a bhd* **100/1**

0 **9** *nk* **Camp Counsellor**[6] [418] 3-9-3 .... ShaneKelly 11 47
(J A Osborne) *prom: wkng whn edgd lft over 1f out* **50/1**

00 **10** *2* **Kindkintyre (IRE)**[24] [222] 3-8-12 .... JamieMoriarty(5) 3 43
(R A Fahey) *a bhd* **150/1**

5 **11** *2 ½* **Sadler's Kingdom (IRE)**[14] [338] 3-9-3 .... PaulHanagan 2 38
(R A Fahey) *a towards rr* **40/1**

6 **12** *1 ½* **David's Cavalier**[21] [257] 3-9-3 .... GrahamGibbons 5 35
(R Hollinshead) *rdn 5f out: a bhd* **100/1**

00-0 **13** *4* **Bali Belony**[6] [418] 3-8-12 .... RobertHavlin 4 22
(J R Jenkins) *led early: prom: rdn over 3f out: wknd 2f out* **250/1**

2m 2.58s (-0.04) **Going Correction** -0.05s/f (Stan) **13** Ran SP% **120.3**
Speed ratings (Par 97):98,97,95,95,91 90,88,88,88,86 84,82,79
CSF £2.75 TOTE £2.00: £1.10, £1.10, £1.70; EX 4.40 Trifecta £12.40 Pool £612.76 - 35.02 winning units..
Owner Sheikh Mohammed **Bred** Darley **Trained** Newmarket, Suffolk

FOCUS
They went 33/1 bar the first three home in this maiden which clearly lacked strength in depth. The form is ordinary but the proximity of the fourth limits the form.

485 PONTINS.COM H'CAP (DIV II) 7f 32y(P)
5:35 (5:37) (Class 6) (0-58,58) 4-Y-0+ **£1,706** (£503; £252) **Stalls** High

Form RPR

-034 **1** **Carcinetto (IRE)**[11] [367] 5-8-9 **56**........................ StephenDonohoe(3) 5 66
(P D Evans) *hld up and bhd: hdwy on ins wl over 1f out: swtchd rt ent fnl f: r.o wl to ld nr fin* **9/1**

0631 **2** *¾* **Grand Palace (IRE)**[20] [268] 4-8-11 **55**.....................(v) DeanMcKeown 4 63
(D Shaw) *a.p: rdn to ld jst over 1f out: edgd lft ins fnl f: hdd nr fin* **9/2**[2]

4-03 **3** *hd* **Burnley Al (IRE)**[18] [298] 5-8-8 **52**....................................(b) BrettDoyle 6 60
(Peter Grayson) *hld up towards rr: hdwy over 2f out: rdn and hung lft over 1f out: r.o ins fnl f* **16/1**

1-15 **4** *1* **Shava**[18] [292] 7-8-9 **53**.. FergusSweeney 1 58
(H J Evans) *hld up and bhd: rdn and hdwy whn nt clr run over 1f out tl swtchd lft ins fnl f: nrst fin* **9/2**[2]

40-4 **5** *nk* **Border Artist**[9] [379] 8-8-12 **56**... TPQueally 2 62+
(J Pearce) *a.p: rdn wl over 1f out: n.m.r on ins wl ins fnl f: nt qckn* **10/1**

65-0 **6** *1 1/4* **Jabbara (IRE)**[41] [50] 4-8-8 **52**.......................................(b) JoeFanning 3 55+
(C E Brittain) *led: rdn and hdd jst over 1f out: hmpd ins fnl f: eased whn btn nr fin* **8/1**[3]

-106 **7** *hd* **Glamaraazi (IRE)**[10] [376] 4-9-0 **58**.............................. PaulHanagan 11 58
(R A Fahey) *hld up in mid-div: hdwy on outside over 2f out: rdn over 1f out: no imp* **33/1**

00-4 **8** *hd* **Only If I Laugh**[9] [383] 6-8-9 **53**.. DaleGibson 9 53
(M J Attwater) *chsd ldrs: rdn over 2f out: no hdwy fnl f* **25/1**

-132 **9** *nk* **Tyrone Sam**[11] [359] 5-8-13 **57**...(b) NCallan 7 56
(K A Ryan) *bhd: rdn over 4f out: short-lived effrt jst over 1f out* **2/1**[1]

34-0 **10** *1/2* **Detonate**[11] [359] 5-8-4 **51** ow2...................................... JamesDoyle(3) 10 49
(Ms J S Doyle) *bhd: rdn and c wd st: nvr trbld ldrs* **40/1**

40-4 **11** *1/2* **Mister Elegant**[33] [131] 5-8-12 **56**.................................. SteveDrowne 12 53
(J L Spearing) *sn prom: jnd ldr over 5f out: ev ch over 2f out: sn rdn: wknd wl over 1f out* **16/1**

/606 **12** *28* **Smart Pick**[18] [296] 4-8-8 **52** ow2................................. GrahamGibbons 8 —
(J R Holt) *prom tl rdn and wknd over 3f out: eased whn no ch fnl 2f* **50/1**

1m 29.58s (-0.82) **Going Correction** -0.05s/f (Stan) **12** Ran SP% **122.2**
Speed ratings (Par 101):102,101,100,99,99 98,97,97,97,96 96,64
CSF £49.53 CT £735.87 TOTE £10.40: £3.20, £1.70, £3.30; EX 51.50 Trifecta £357.20 Part won. Pool £503.10 - 0.54 winning units. Place 6 £17.43, Place 5 £12.32..
Owner Mrs Sally Edwards **Bred** M A Doyle **Trained** Pandy, Monmouths
■ Stewards' Enquiry : Joe Fanning caution: careless riding

FOCUS
A messy contest with plenty of trouble in running but the time was 0.67 seconds faster than the first division. The form looks solid enough on paper , with the front four close to recent form.
T/Jkpt: Not won. T/Plt: £21.40 to a £1 stake. Pool: £78,299.85. 2,668.45 winning tickets. T/Qpdt: £7.00 to a £1 stake. Pool: £5,010.00. 528.70 winning tickets. KH

455 LINGFIELD (L-H)
Saturday, February 17

OFFICIAL GOING: Standard
Wind: Virtually nil

486 PONTINSBINGO.COM H'CAP 7f (P)
1:35 (1:36) (Class 5) (0-75,75) 4-Y-0+ **£3,071** (£906; £453) **Stalls** Low

Form RPR

0-02 **1** **Silent Storm**[10] [381] 7-9-0 **73**.. EddieAhern 10 83
(C A Cyzer) *hld up in last trio: rdn and prog over 1f out: sustained run to ld last 50yds: won gng away* **8/1**[2]

1-32 **2** *1 1/4* **Barney McGrew (IRE)**[21] [261] 4-9-1 **74**......................... OscarUrbina 9 80
(J A R Toller) *taken down early: t.k.h: trckd ldrs: rdn over 1f out: hanging and nt qckn: styd on ins fnl f* **8/11**[1]

06-2 **3** *shd* **Inch By Inch**[21] [262] 8-8-10 **72**.......................................(b) AmirQuinn(3) 2 78
(P J Makin) *led for 1f: styd cl up: rdn to ld again on inner over 1f out: hdd and outpcd last 50yds* **20/1**

-525 **4** *1 1/4* **Certain Justice (USA)**[18] [307] 9-8-13 **72**...................... HayleyTurner 3 75
(Stef Liddiard) *taken down early: t.k.h: trckd ldrs: rdn 1/2-way: struggling over 2f out: styd on u.p fnl f* **12/1**[3]

0-30 **5** *hd* **Ivory Lace**[21] [261] 6-8-13 **75**...................................... JamesDoyle(3) 12 77
(S Woodman) *racd wd: hld up in tch: rdn 1/2-way: sn struggling: styd on fr over 1f out: nrst fin* **25/1**

055- **6** *shd* **What Do You Know**[104] [6348] 4-8-2 **61** oh1..................... JimmyQuinn 6 63
(A M Hales) *plld hrd: hld up in midfield: rdn and no prog over 2f out: styd on fnl f* **33/1**

-003 **7** *shd* **Cinematic (IRE)**[10] [381] 4-8-8 **67**................................ FergusSweeney 7 69
(J R Boyle) *t.k.h: pressed ldrs: led over 2f out to over 1f out: fdd* **8/1**[2]

600- **8** *1* **Gavarnie Beau (IRE)**[112] [6221] 4-8-11 **70**.......................... SteveDrowne 1 69
(M Blanshard) *settled midfield: effrt on inner and cl up over 1f out: fdd fnl f* **50/1**

00-0 **9** *3/4* **Nightstrike (IRE)**[10] [381] 4-7-11 **61** oh2......................... NicolPolli(5) 11 58
(Luke Comer, Ire) *dropped in fr wd draw: hld up last: no prog 2f out: kpt on* **66/1**

30-0 **10** *nk* **Li Shih Chen**[28] [191] 4-8-11 **70**... TPQueally 4 66
(A P Jarvis) *t.k.h: led after 1f to over 2f out: grad wknd* **25/1**

1m 23.9s (-1.99) **Going Correction** -0.075s/f (Stan) **10** Ran SP% **106.7**
Speed ratings (Par 103):108,106,106,105,104 104,104,103,102,102
CSF £11.22 CT £85.83 TOTE £8.50: £1.60, £1.02, £4.50; EX 16.70 Trifecta £84.80 Pool: £273.66 - 2.29 winning units..
Owner Mrs Charles Cyzer **Bred** Middle Park Stud Ltd **Trained** Maplehurst, W Sussex

FOCUS
A fair handicap run in a decent winning time for the class. The form is solid, the winner back to his best.

487 PONTINSBINGO.COM CONDITIONS STKS 1m (P)
2:05 (2:05) (Class 2) 4-Y-0+ **£11,217** (£3,358; £1,679; £840; £419) **Stalls** High

Form RPR

6231 **1** **Party Boss**[9] [391] 5-9-12 95... SebSanders 2 109
(C E Brittain) *mde all and set decent pce: kicked on 2f out: drvn and hrd pressed fnl f: hld on gamely* **8/1**

011- **2** *1* **Ceremonial Jade (UAE)**[134] [5785] 4-9-3 95.................(t) OscarUrbina 4 98
(M Botti) *stdd s: hld up in 4th: t.k.h after 2f: effrt 2f out: rdn to press wnr ins fnl f: no imp last 75yds* **2/1**[2]

2214 **3** *1/2* **Red Spell (IRE)**[13] [352] 6-9-3 104...................................... DaneO'Neill 6 97
(R Hannon) *trckd wnr after 2f: rdn to chal over 1f out: nt qckn and hld after* **3/1**[3]

51-4 **4** *2 1/2* **Orchard Supreme**[35] [119] 4-9-0 97.............................. RichardHughes 5 88
(R Hannon) *stdd s: hld up in last: nt clr run and swtchd rt over 1f out: nvr rchd ldrs: eased last 50yds* **11/8**[1]

0/00 **5** *3* **Tony James (IRE)**[13] [352] 5-9-12 99..................................... NCallan 3 93
(K O Cunningham-Brown) *trckd wnr for 2f: styd cl up tl wknd over 1f out* **33/1**

1m 35.94s (-3.49) **Going Correction** -0.075s/f (Stan) course record **5** Ran SP% **114.5**
Speed ratings (Par 109):114,113,112,110,107
CSF £25.29 TOTE £6.30: £3.20, £1.50; EX 20.90.
Owner Michael Clarke **Bred** Michael Clarke **Trained** Newmarket, Suffolk

FOCUS
A good race run in a decent winning time and, although the winner was allowed to dictate throughout, he has been rated as running to his best.

NOTEBOOK
Party Boss, who returned to winning ways at Southwell last time, was worst in at the weights in this contest but was given the perfect front-running ride by Sanders, who wound up the pace gradually and was never going to be passed in the straight. Two years ago he was rated as high as 109, so it would be unwise to suggest this was a fluke, and the Winter Derby, run over a trip (1m2f) he has never won over, is likely to be next on his agenda. (op 7-1)

Ceremonial Jade(UAE), unbeaten in two previous starts on the All-Weather, had not run since October but he looked the one runner in the line-up on a serious upward curve. In the end he was a bit disappointing, having to settle for second behind the well-ridden Party Boss, but he remains capable of better. (op 3-1)

Red Spell(IRE) is a difficult horse to win with at the best of times and, in a race that was dominated by the enterprisingly-ridden Party Boss, he was always going to struggle to peg him back. (op 11-4)

Orchard Supreme, dropping back to his ideal trip, needs a good pace off which to challenge, but Sanders dictated a tempo to suit himself up front on Party Boss, and he never got in a blow. (op 6-4 tchd 7-4)

Tony James(IRE) continues to struggle and needs to drop in the handicap so he can contest races in lesser grade. (op 25-1)

488 MICHAEL O'DONOVAN MEMORIAL H'CAP 1m 4f (P)
2:40 (2:40) (Class 4) (0-85,85) 4-Y-0+ **£4,857** (£1,445; £722; £360) **Stalls** Low

Form RPR

06-1 **1** **Dundry**[25] [226] 6-8-9 **75**...(p) BrettDoyle 6 86+
(G L Moore) *prom: effrt to ld over 2f out and sn rdn at least 2 l clr: hld on u.p fnl f* **7/1**[2]

42-2 **2** *3/4* **Quince (IRE)**[12] [362] 4-9-1 **84**.......................................(v) NCallan 11 91
(J Pearce) *dwlt: hld up in midfield: effrt over 2f out: drvn on inner to take 2nd ins fnl f: nvr quite rchd wnr* **4/1**[1]

21-1 **3** *1/2* **Nawow**[17] [316] 7-8-9 **75**... DaneO'Neill 16 81
(P D Cundell) *hld up in midfield: prog on outer 3f out: rdn to dispute 2nd over f out: kpt on: nvr able to chal* **9/1**

56-0 **4** *nk* **Dream Catcher (SWE)**[13] [353] 4-8-10 **79**.....................(t) EddieAhern 10 85
(R A Kvisla) *t.k.h: wl plcd: effrt over 2f out: disp 2nd over 1f out: kpt on same pce* **20/1**

3345 **5** *3/4* **Atlantic Quest (USA)**[7] [420] 8-9-0 **83**.......................... AmirQuinn(3) 9 87
(Miss Venetia Williams) *hld up in last trio: prog 2f out: styd on wl fnl f: nvr nrr* **11/1**

3-11 **6** *1/2* **Sgt Schultz (IRE)**[12] [362] 4-8-7 **76**................................... JohnEgan 15 82+
(J S Moore) *hld up in midfield: effrt whn hmpd over 2f out: tried to cl on ldrs over 1f out: one pce and eased nr fin* **4/1**[1]

2-46 **7** *3/4* **Turner's Touch**[11] [377] 5-8-6 **72**..............................(p) PaulHanagan 8 74
(G L Moore) *hld up in last pair: prog over 2f out: threatened to cl on ldrs fnl f: hanging and nt keen* **16/1**

-056 **8** *1 1/2* **Valance (IRE)**[3] [457] 7-9-3 **83**.......................................(bt) SebSanders 1 83
(C R Egerton) *s.s and pushed along in last gp: laboured prog u.p fr over 2f out: n.d* **14/1**

06 **9** *hd* **General Knowledge (USA)**[21] [264] 4-8-13 **82**.........(t) HayleyTurner 13 82
(B G Powell) *hld up wl in rr: pushed along and kpt on steadily fnl 2f: nvr nr ldrs* **33/1**

05-1 **10** *1 1/2* **Awatuki (IRE)**[13] [353] 4-8-12 **81**... TPQueally 7 78+
(A P Jarvis) *t.k.h: prom: losing pl whn hmpd wl over 1f out: wknd* **8/1**[3]

41/ **11** *1 3/4* **Economic (IRE)**[472] [6228] 4-8-10 **79**................................. OscarUrbina 2 73
(M Botti) *settled midfield: lost pl over 2f out: btn whn n.m.r over 1f out* **16/1**

13/6 **12** *nk* **Mission To Mars**[42] [57] 8-9-5 **85**.................................. SteveDrowne 3 79
(P G Murphy) *hld up: nvr beyond midfield: last pair and shuffled along 2f out* **28/1**

0- **13** *3* **Sadler's Star (GER)**[50] 4-8-6 **75** ow1....................... FergusSweeney 12 64
(B G Powell) *prom: led over 3f out to over 2f out: wknd* **20/1**

100- **14** *1 1/4* **Jidaar (IRE)**[91] [6519] 4-8-4 **73**... ChrisCatlin 4 60
(P W Hiatt) *w ldrs tl wknd over 2f out* **66/1**

/3-0 **15** *1/2* **Mustajed**[13] [353] 6-8-12 **83**...................................... JamesMillman(5) 5 69
(B R Millman) *hld up in rr: no ch whn nt clr run 2f out and over 1f out* **33/1**

140- **16** *11* **Faversham**[248] [2556] 4-8-8 **77**.. ShaneKelly 14 46
(M Wigham) *mde most to over 3f out: wknd rapidly: t.o* **33/1**

2m 31.59s (-2.80) **Going Correction** -0.075s/f (Stan)
WFA 4 from 5yo+ 3lb **16** Ran SP% **123.7**
Speed ratings (Par 105):106,105,105,104,104 104,103,102,102,101 100,100,98,97,96 89
CSF £32.70 CT £264.79 TOTE £9.00: £2.50, £1.30, £2.70, £4.10; EX 48.20 Trifecta £393.30 Part won. Pool: £553.99 - 0.51 winning units..
Owner D J Deer **Bred** D J And Mrs Deer **Trained** Woodingdean, E Sussex

FOCUS
A competitive handicap featuring a number of in-form performers. The form, best rated through the third, is not that strong, but the winner could rate higher yet on sand.
Atlantic Quest(USA) Official explanation: jockey said gelding suffered early interference
Mission To Mars Official explanation: jockey said gelding was denied a clear run
Mustajed Official explanation: jockey said gelding was denied a clear run
Faversham Official explanation: jockey said gelding hung left

489 DAVID REGINALD NORRIS GOODBYE TO MAIDEN STKS 6f (P)
3:15 (3:16) (Class 5) 3-Y-0+ **£3,071** (£906; £453) **Stalls** Low

Form RPR

5 **1** **Divertimenti (IRE)**[24] [231] 3-8-11 77..................................(p) NCallan 2 75
(M J Wallace) *mde all: rdn 2f out: edgd rt u.p fnl f: hld on* **9/2**[3]

0-3 **2** *1/2* **Grand Symphony**[34] [128] 3-8-7 ow1................................ BrettDoyle 4 69
(W Jarvis) *pushed up to go prom: effrt on inner 2f out: drvn and clsd on wnr last 150yds: a hld* **11/2**

54 **3** *nk* **Desert Master**[14] [342] 4-9-12 .... GeorgeBaker 8 76
(C F Wall) *stdd s: hld up: prog on wd outside over 2f out: rdn to dispute 2nd over 1f out: fnd little and hld fnl f* **5/4**[1]

5 **4** *1 3/4* **Chattan Clan**[14] [343] 3-8-11 ....(t) SteveDrowne 5 67
(R A Kvisla) *trckd ldrs: rdn whn squeezed out and lost pl over 1f out: no ch after* **14/1**

30/2 **5** *nk* **Ellcon (IRE)**[17] [311] 4-9-7 69.. ShaneKelly 7 65
(J A Osborne) *mostly chsd wnr to over 1f out: fdd tamely* **3/1**[2]

0- **6** *1 3/4* **The Dagger**[123] [6034] 3-8-8 .... StephaneBreux(3) 1 60
(J R Best) *outpcd and pushed along after 2f: brief effrt u.p over 1f out : sn no prog* **33/1**

7 *6* **Galway Nellie (IRE)** 9-9-9 .... JerryO'Dwyer(3) 6 45
(Luke Comer, Ire) *outpcd and rdn after 2f: nvr a factor* **40/1**

1m 12.31s (-0.50) **Going Correction** -0.075s/f (Stan)
WFA 3 from 4yo+ 15lb **7** Ran SP% **115.1**
Speed ratings (Par 103):100,99,98,96,96 93,85
CSF £29.43 TOTE £6.20: £2.50, £3.00; EX 25.00 Trifecta £59.10 Pool: £543.75 - 6.53 winning units..
Owner Mrs Sonia Rogers **Bred** Airlie Stud **Trained** Newmarket, Suffolk

FOCUS
An ordinary maiden in which the winner appeared to bounce back to the best of his turf form to score.
Ellcon(IRE) Official explanation: jockey said filly became unbalanced in latter stages

490 PONTIN'S FAMILY HOLIDAYS H'CAP 5f (P)

3:50 (3:50) (Class 2) (0-100,102) 4-Y-0+

£11,217 (£3,358; £1,679; £840; £419; £210) Stalls High

Form RPR

0-11 **1** **Turn On The Style**[31] 163 5-8-6 **88** ....(b) PaulHanagan 1 99
(J Balding) *missed break: rcvrd to ld after 1f: rdn 2f out: sn hdd: rallied to ld ins fnl f: gamely* **7/4**[1]

-022 **2** ½ **Maltese Falcon**[14] 344 7-9-6 **102** ....(t) NelsonDeSouza 3 111
(P F I Cole) *led for 1f: pressed wnr: led again wl over 1f out: hdd ins fnl f: kpt on* **3/1**[2]

0-41 **3** ¾ **Distinctly Game**[20] 277 5-8-5 **87** .... CatherineGannon 7 93
(K A Ryan) *hld up in last trio: rdn 2f out: effrt but hanging 1f out: drvn and r.o: tk 3rd nr fin* **16/1**

361- **4** 1¼ **Stoneacre Lad (IRE)**[74] 6720 4-8-8 **90** ow2 ....(b) NCallan 9 92
(Peter Grayson) *pressed ldrs: cl up and drvn 1f out: no ex* **16/1**

4123 **5** hd **Qadar (IRE)**[14] 344 5-9-6 **102** ....(b) IanMongan 10 103
(N P Littmoden) *in tch on outer: rdn 2f out: nt qckn and no real imp over 1f out* **7/1**[3]

20-6 **6** nk **Talbot Avenue**[43] 41 9-8-6 **88** .... TPQueally 2 94+
(M Blanshard) *t.k.h: hld up in last trio: nowhere to go fr over 1f out to ins fnl f: no ch* **16/1**

04-5 **7** nk **One More Round (USA)**[14] 344 9-8-10 **95** ....(b) JamesDoyle(3) 4 94
(N P Littmoden) *dwlt: hld up in last trio: rdn 2f out: one pce* **17/2**

03-6 **8** ½ **Classic Encounter (IRE)**[14] 344 4-8-9 **91** .... RichardHughes 6 89+
(D M Simcock) *t.k.h: hld up bhd ldrs: rdn 2f out: fnd nil: eased whn no ch last 100yds* **11/1**

050- **9** 1½ **Total Impact**[160] 5202 4-8-5 **87** .... HayleyTurner 8 79
(C A Cyzer) *t.k.h: hld up in midfield: rdn 2f out: wknd tamely* **16/1**

0-50 **10** 1¾ **Glenviews Youngone (IRE)**[32] 155 4-8-6 **88** oh8 ow2 RobbieFitzpatrick 5 73
(Peter Grayson) *cl up tl wknd rapidly on inner over 1f out* **50/1**

57.84 secs (-1.94) **Going Correction** -0.075s/f (Stan) **10** Ran SP% **118.2**
Speed ratings (Par 109):112,111,110,108,107 107,106,105,103,100
CSF £6.90 CT £63.48 TOTE £2.30: £1.60, £1.10, £4.10; EX 9.90 Trifecta £68.20 Pool: £751.28 - 7.82 winning units..
Owner The Haydock Badgeholders **Bred** J And Mrs Bowtell **Trained** Scrooby, Notts
■ Stewards' Enquiry : N Callan caution: careless riding.

FOCUS
A decent sprint handicap and sound form for the grade, although very few got competitive. Turn On The Style probably did not need to improve to land the hat-trick but there is more to come from him.

NOTEBOOK
Turn On The Style, despite missing the break, was soon rushed up to make the running, and he was never out of the first two from then on. He rallied well after being headed by Maltese Falcon, in a race in which nothing else got into contention, and confirmed himself an improving sprinter with a victory which completed a hat-trick. His trainer expects him to continue to progress when switched to turf in the coming months. (tchd 6-4 and 15-8, 2-1 in a place)
Maltese Falcon has confirmed himself a smart sprinter on the All-Weather this winter but for the third time in a row he had to settle for finishing runner-up. He would have preferred it had he not been taken on for the lead by Turn On The Style, but he still confirmed form with Qadar on 4lb worse terms than when the pair met over this course and distance a fortnight earlier. (op 7-2 tchd 4-1 in a place)
Distinctly Game did best of the hold-up performers, finishing well to take third close home. He won over 6f last time out at Kempton and is probably happier over that longer distance these days. (op 9-1)
Stoneacre Lad(IRE), 5lb higher than when successful at Southwell on his last start, does not seem as effective at this track, but he ran a fair race this time, especially as he was returning from a two and a half-month break and carried 2lb overweight. (op 14-1)
Qadar(IRE) rarely fails to run his race, but he was not the only hold-up performer to fail to land a blow on this occasion. (op 8-1 tchd 13-2)
Talbot Avenue enjoyed little luck in running and finished having never been really asked for his effort. He shaped better than his finishing position suggests, but he last won a race in the summer of 2003 so he would not be one to trust to put it right next time.

491 GO PONTIN'S CLAIMING STKS 1m (P)

4:25 (4:25) (Class 6) 3-Y-O £2,184 (£644; £322) Stalls High

Form RPR

3-12 **1** **Sweet World**[15] 335 3-9-0 63 .... DaneO'Neill 4 63
(A P Jarvis) *t.k.h: hld up in 4th: prog to press ldr wl over 1f out: rdn to chal fnl f: fnd jst enough to ld post* **6/5**[1]

1-14 **2** shd **Intersky Sports (USA)**[15] 335 3-9-0 68 ....(p) DeanMcKeown 3 63
(K A Ryan) *led at v stdy pce: urged along over 1f out: jnd fnl f: hdd post* **2/1**[2]

00-0 **3** 3 **Baldovina**[10] 382 3-9-0 70 .... NCallan 2 56
(M Botti) *trckd ldrs: effrt on inner whn nowhere to go over 2f out and again over 1f out: fdd fnl f* **7/2**[3]

400 **4** 6 **Deserter (IRE)**[10] 386 3-8-12 63 .... ShaneKelly 5 40
(J A Osborne) *sn trckd ldr: tried to chal over 2f out: nt keen and sn wknd* **9/1**

0-0 **5** 48 **Lenard Frank (IRE)**[9] 390 3-8-7 35 .... HayleyTurner 1 —
(M D I Usher) *a last and sn rdn: t.o 3f out* **66/1**

1m 41.42s (1.99) **Going Correction** -0.075s/f (Stan) **5** Ran SP% **112.5**
Speed ratings (Par 95):87,86,83,77,29
CSF £4.01 TOTE £2.20: £1.30, £1.30; EX 4.50.The winner was subject to a friendly claim. Baldovina was claimed by T Dascombe for £17,000.
Owner Geoffrey Bishop and Ann Jarvis **Bred** Natton House Thoroughbreds **Trained** Twyford, Bucks

FOCUS
An average claimer run at a steady pace. The winning time was modest, even for a race like this, and the form is far from solid.
Baldovina Official explanation: jockey said filly was denied a clear run

492 PONTINS.COM MAIDEN STKS 1m (P)

5:00 (5:01) (Class 5) 3-Y-O+ £3,071 (£906; £453) Stalls High

Form RPR

4-2 **1** **Zar Solitario**[18] 304 3-8-7 .... JoeFanning 2 74+
(M Johnston) *dwlt: sn rcvrd: led after 2f and set stdy pce: kicked on 2f out: pressed over 1f out: r.o wl fnl f* **13/8**[2]

2 1¼ **Multicultural** 4-9-12 .... RichardHughes 7 77+
(D M Simcock) *led for 1f: trckd wnr: shkn up to chal and green over 1f out: styd on same pce fnl f* **13/2**[3]

3 1¼ **Baaher (USA)** 3-8-7 .... DaneO'Neill 6 68+
(M P Tregoning) *hld up: prog to trck ldrs on outer 3f out: outpcd wl over 1f out: styd on same pce fnl f* **5/4**[1]

6 **4** 2½ **Mawaared**[14] 342 3-8-2 .... JimmyQuinn 5 57
(M P Tregoning) *trckd ldrs on inner: outpcd wl over 1f out: n.d after* **12/1**

5 **5** 1½ **Lough Neagh (USA)**[21] 260 4-9-12 .... PaulEddery 8 65
(Miss D Mountain) *t.k.h: pressed ldrs: outpcd 2f out: no ch after* **33/1**

30- **6** ½ **Fine Ruler (IRE)**[157] 5297 3-8-7 .... SamHitchcott 9 58
(M R Channon) *plld hrd: wl in tch tl easily outpcd 2f out* **14/1**

0-2 **7** 1¼ **Mutoon (IRE)**[35] 114 3-8-2 ow3 .... SaleemGolam(3) 3 53
(S C Williams) *t.k.h: hld up on inner: brief effrt over 1f out: sn no prog* **14/1**

2-3 **8** 1 **Bewildering (IRE)**[15] 338 3-8-7 .... ChrisCatlin 10 53
(E J O'Neill) *hld up in rr: n.m.r 2f out: sn outpcd: pushed along and no prog after* **25/1**

0- **9** ½ **Cnoc Moy (IRE)**[110] 6257 3-8-7 .... HayleyTurner 12 52
(C F Wall) *t.k.h: racd wd: struggling over 2f out* **66/1**

0 **10** nk **Gee Ceffyl Bach**[7] 418 3-8-3 ow1 .... EdwardCreighton 11 47
(M R Channon) *a in last trio: drvn and struggling over 2f out* **66/1**

11 3½ **Very Well Red** 4-9-7 .... GeorgeBaker 1 44
(P W Hiatt) *s.v.s: mostly last and v green: no ch whn rn wd bnd 2f out* **50/1**

46 **12** ¾ **Stand In Black (NZ)**[10] 386 3-8-4 .... StephaneBreux(3) 4 41
(B I Case) *t.k.h: trckd ldrs tl wknd rapidly 2f out* **100/1**

1m 39.74s (0.31) **Going Correction** -0.075s/f (Stan)
WFA 3 from 4yo 19lb **12** Ran SP% **129.6**
Speed ratings (Par 103):95,93,92,90,88 88,86,85,85,84 81,80
CSF £14.07 TOTE £3.10: £1.60, £2.00, £1.20; EX 27.00 Trifecta £40.40 Pool: £819.07 - 14.39 winning units. Place 6 £49.09, Place 5 £38.54.
Owner Jumeirah Racing **Bred** Azienda Agricola Razza Del Sole Srl **Trained** Middleham Moor, N Yorks

FOCUS
A steadily-run maiden in which it paid to race handily. It should produce winners and has been rated around the fourth and fifth. The first three should prove better than the bare form.
Cnoc Moy(IRE) Official explanation: jockey said gelding hung right throughout
T/Plt: £39.70 to a £1 stake. Pool: £56,037.80. 1,029.30 winning tickets. T/Qpdt: £14.30 to a £1 stake. Pool: £3,204.30. 164.70 winning tickets. JN

438 ST MORITZ (R-H)

Sunday, February 18

OFFICIAL GOING: Frozen

493a GUEBELIN GROSSER PREIS VON ST MORITZ (SNOW) 1m 2f

1:35 (12:00) 4-Y-0+ £22,315 (£8,926; £6,695; £4,463; £2,231)

RPR

1 **First Time (GER)**[14] 355 4-8-7 .... DPorcu 6 103
(Karin Suter, Switzerland)

2 4 **Quiron (IRE)**[14] 355 6-9-0 .... TMundry 9 102
(Carmen Bocskai, Switzerland)

3 2¼ **Collow (GER)**[14] 355 7-9-6 .... MKolb 7 104
(M Weiss, Switzerland)

4 2½ **Sweet Venture (FR)**[364] 455 5-9-2 .... RobertHavlin 4 96
(M Weiss, Switzerland)

5 3½ **Home Call (USA)**[21] 5-8-11 .... EPedroza 5 84
(C Von Der Recke, Germany) **13/1**[2]

6 8 **Pine Cone (IRE)**[7] 439 5-8-10 .... SteveDrowne 1 69
(M Weiss, Switzerland)

7 1½ **Dixigold (FR)**[14] 355 6-9-2 .... GBocksai 3 72
(Carmen Bocskai, Switzerland)

8 4 **Dragon Slayer (IRE)**[14] 355 5-9-6 .... BrianReilly 8 69
(Ian Williams) **122/10**[1]

9 dist **Sargentos (GER)**[7] 438 5-8-11 .... OPlacais 10 —
(M F Harris) **143/10**[3]

2m 14.65s (134.65)
WFA 4 from 5yo+ 1lb **10** Ran SP% **21.3**
(including SFr1 stake): WIN 6.00; 1.70, 1.50, 1.90;.
Owner Stall S V H **Bred** Gestut Elite **Trained** Switzerland

494a GRAND PRIX WINTERTHUR VERSICHERUNGEN (SNOW) 1m 1f

2:05 (12:00) 4-Y-0+ £3,013 (£1,205; £904; £603; £301)

RPR

1 **Salermo (CZE)**[7] 438 6-9-6 .... MKolb 11 88
(M Weiss, Switzerland)

2 1½ **Puro (CZE)**[315] 5-9-6 .... RobertHavlin 6 53
(M Weiss, Switzerland)

3 7 **Aesop (GER)**[898] 6-8-9 .... EPedroza 9 64
(C Von Der Recke, Germany)

4 1¾ **Al Martino (SWI)** 9-9-11 .... SteveDrowne 4 77
(M Weiss, Switzerland)

5 5 **Congrio Dorado (USA)** 5-8-9 .... TMundry 2 42
(C Von Der Recke, Germany)

6 5 **Palladia Directa (GER)**[7] 439 7-9-7 .... GBocksai 3 44
(C Bocksai, Germany)

7 2½ **Westlander (USA)**[14] 356 7-9-2 .... DPorcu 8 34
(A Schennach, Switzerland)

8 2 **Ivans Ride (IRE)**[7] 439 4-9-0 .... MichellePayne 1 28
(M F Harris) **169/10**[1]

9 18 **Royal Fire (GER)**[14] 355 8-8-5 .... FrauNatalieFriberg 10 —
(Miss A Casotti, Switzerland)

10 7 **Brother's Valcour (FR)**[14] 356 9-9-9 .... OPlacais 7 —
(K Schafflutzel, Switzerland)

11 dist **Cavalli (FR)**[260] 4-9-2 .... FrauChantalZollet 5 —
(Dagmar Geissmann)

2m 3.65s (123.65) **11** Ran SP% **5.6**
WIN 4.90; PL 1.50, 1.20, 1.50;.
Owner Stall Stargate **Bred** Stall Stargate **Trained** Switzerland

486LINGFIELD (L-H)

Monday, February 19

OFFICIAL GOING: Standard

Wind: Fresh, behind Weather: Overcast

495 PONTIN'S FAMILY HOLIDAYS H'CAP (DIV I) 1m 2f (P)

1:20 (1:20) (Class 6) (0-55,55) 4-Y-0+ **£1,706** (£503; £252) **Stalls** Low

Form RPR

0-22 **1** **Mon Petite Amour**[22] [274] 4-8-8 **50** .... BrettDoyle 5 59+
(D W P Arbuthnot) *w.w in midfield: hdwy over 3f out: led 2f out: clr 1f out: pushed out and r.o wl* **5/1**[1]

03-0 **2** *1 1/2* **Miss Monica (IRE)**[10] [402] 6-8-5 **46** oh1 .... PaulDoe 10 51
(P W Hiatt) *w.w in tch: hdwy to trck ldrs over 3f out: rdn 2f out: chsdwnr 1f out: no imp* **16/1**

2330 **3** *hd* **Voice Mail**[5] [459] 8-8-5 **53** .... (b) DavidProbert(7) 12 58
(A M Balding) *stdd s: hld up: stdy hdwy on outer 5f out: chsd ldrs and rdn over 2f out: kpt on same pce fnl f* **8/1**[3]

3504 **4** *1 1/4* **The London Gang**[21] [298] 4-8-13 **55** .... (v) ChrisCatlin 9 57
(Miss D A McHale) *hld up in tch: hdwy 4f out: chsd ldrs and rdn over 2f out: kpt on same pce fnl f* **9/1**

02-4 **5** *1 1/4* **Myrtle Bay (IRE)**[19] [309] 4-8-7 **52** .... NeilChalmers(3) 8 52
(J C Tuck) *chsd ldrs: rdn and outpcd over 2f out: kpt on ins fnl f* **9/1**

0316 **6** *hd* **Oasis Sun (IRE)**[19] [309] 4-8-4 **49** .... (v) StephaneBreux(3) 11 48
(J R Best) *chsd ldrs: hdwy to chse ldr wl over 3f out: led 3f out: rdn and hdd 2f out: fdd fnl f* **14/1**

00-0 **7** *3/4* **Filliemou (IRE)**[31] [181] 6-8-6 **47** oh1 ow1 .... ShaneKelly 4 45?
(A W Carroll) *hld up towards rr: rdn and effrt over 2f out: edgd rt 1f out: kpt on: nt trble ldrs* **40/1**

0-63 **8** *1 1/4* **Shadow Aspect**[31] [186] 4-8-8 **53** .... JerryO'Dwyer(3) 7 49
(Eoin Doyle, Ire) *chsd ldr tl led 4f out: hdd and rdn 3f out: wknd wl over 1f out: eased ins fnl f* **11/2**[2]

111- **9** *2* **Artzola (IRE)**[68] [6804] 7-9-0 **55** .... PaulEddery 1 47
(C A Horgan) *hld up in last: rdn and effrt wl over 2f out: sltly hmpd 1f out: n.d* **5/1**[1]

66- **10** *1 1/4* **Coolaw (IRE)**[34] [6680] 4-8-4 **46** oh1 .... (v[1]) JimmyQuinn 6 36
(G G Margarson) *a bhd and niggled along: n.d* **40/1**

4-33 **11** *4* **Expected Bonus (USA)**[22] [273] 8-8-5 **46** oh1 ....(v) SimonWhitworth 3 28
(Jamie Poulton) *chsd ldrs: lost pl and pushed along 1/2-way: bhd last 3f* **11/1**

0345 **12** *1 3/4* **Lady Pilot**[12] [380] 5-8-6 **50** .... (p) JamesDoyle(3) 2 29
(Ms J S Doyle) *led tl 4f out: sn rdn and lost pl: no ch last 2f* **9/1**

2m 6.04s (-1.75) **Going Correction** -0.10s/f (Stan)
WFA 4 from 5yo+ 1lb **12** Ran SP% **115.6**
Speed ratings (Par 101):103,101,101,100,99 99,98,97,96,95 92,90
CSF £83.07 CT £625.23 TOTE £5.20: £1.30, £8.30, £2.70; EX 94.90 TRIFECTA Not won..
Owner Noel Cronin **Bred** Branston Stud Ltd **Trained** Compton, Berks

■ David Arbuthnot's first winner from his new yard at Compton.

■ Stewards' Enquiry : Shane Kelly caution: careless riding.

FOCUS
A very moderate handicap, and the bare form is not all that solid, but a clear-cut winner in the form of Mon Petite Amour. The winning time was 1.74 seconds quicker than the second division, but 0.36 seconds off the 1m2f maiden, and 1.52 seconds slower than the later 0-85.

496 BONUSPRINT.COM AMATEUR RIDERS' H'CAP 1m 4f (P)

1:50 (1:50) (Class 6) (0-52,52) 4-Y-0+ **£1,977** (£608; £304) **Stalls** Low

Form RPR

50-2 **1** **Krasivi's Boy (USA)**[9] [416] 5-11-0 **48** .... (b) MrDHutchison(3) 12 57
(G L Moore) *w.w in tch: hdwy wl over 3f out: led wl over 1f out: hdd ins fnl f: led again and fnd ex last 50 yds* **3/1**[1]

-404 **2** *3/4* **Milk And Sultana**[11] [279] 7-11-3 **48** .... MissFayeBramley 8 56
(G A Ham) *hld up in midfield: rdn and gd hdwy over 2f out: led briefly ins fnl f: no ex last 50 yds* **9/1**[3]

400/ **3** *2* **Rebel Raider (IRE)**[38] [6151] 8-10-10 **48** .... MrAMerriam(7) 15 53
(B N Pollock) *prom: rdn to chse ldr 3f out: led wl over 2f out:hdd wl over 1f out: kpt on same pce fnl f* **6/1**[2]

4 *shd* **Super Sensation (GER)**[20] 6-11-1 **51** ....(be) MissHayleyMoore(5) 4 56
(G L Moore) *hld up in midfield: stl gng wl over 2f out: plld out jst over 1f out: r.o strly fnl f: nvr nrr* **16/1**

-045 **5** *3* **Countback (FR)**[22] [285] 8-10-10 **46** oh1 .... (p) MrMJJSmith(5) 11 46
(A W Carroll) *hld up in rr: hdwy wl over 3f out: kpt on u.p fnl f: nt rch ldrs* **14/1**

-000 **6** *hd* **Kiama**[9] [416] 5-11-1 **46** oh1 .... MrSWalker 13 46
(B G Powell) *stdd s: hld up in rr: hdwy over 4f out: chsd ldrs and rdn over 2f out: kpt on same pce over 1f out* **10/1**

534- **7** *shd* **Salinger (USA)**[148] [5259] 5-10-8 **46** oh1 .... MissHWarbrick(7) 7 45
(Mrs L J Mongan) *stdd s: plld hrd: hld up towards rr: hdwy over 2f out: plld out and r.o wl fnl f: nvr nrr* **12/1**

60-0 **8** *1/2* **Proud Scholar (USA)**[14] [369] 5-11-2 **52** .... MrCWallis(5) 2 51
(R A Kvisla) *chsd ldrs: rdn wl over 2f out: wknd over 1f out* **16/1**

6-30 **9** *1/2* **Pharaoh Prince**[29] [203] 6-10-8 **46** oh1 .... MrDarylChinn(7) 10 44
(G Prodromou) *racd wd: in tch: rdn over 2f out: wknd 2f out* **14/1**

6-30 **10** *1/2* **Love You Always (USA)**[22] [278] 7-10-8 **46** oh1..........(t) MrRBirkett(7) 3 43
(Miss J Feilden) *hld up in rr: nt clr run briefly wl over 2f out: rdn and sme hdwy 2f out: no imp fnl f* **12/1**

35-0 **11** *5* **Elopement (IRE)**[22] [286] 5-11-1 **51** .... MrBenBrisbourne(5) 1 40
(W M Brisbourne) *chsd ldr for 4f: rdn and wknd wl over 2f out* **12/1**

460/ **12** *2* **Ghaill Force**[126] [4937] 5-10-10 **46** oh1 .... (p) MissZoeLilly(5) 9 32
(P Butler) *stdd s: hld up in midfield: rdn and no hdwy over 2f out* **33/1**

0-00 **13** *3 1/2* **Moonshine Bill**[28] [220] 8-11-1 **46** oh1 .... MissEJJones 16 26
(P W Hiatt) *sn led: hdd over 2f out: sn wknd* **20/1**

105/ **14** *hd* **Quel Fontenailles (FR)**[593] [1979] 9-11-2 **52** .... MrsLDace(5) 6 32
(L A Dace) *plld hrd: hld up towards rr on outer: n.d* **25/1**

0026 **15** *2* **Bournonville**[11] [393] 4-10-9 **48** .... MrSRees(5) 14 25
(M Wigham) *prom: chsd ldr 8f out tl 3f out: sn wknd* **16/1**

030- **16** *17* **Ronsard (IRE)**[24] [6405] 5-11-0 **50** .... MissAWallace(5) 5 —
(J C Tuck) *bhd: rdn and lost tch over 3f out: t.o* **20/1**

2m 34.36s (-0.03) **Going Correction** -0.10s/f (Stan)
WFA 4 from 5yo+ 3lb **16** Ran SP% **127.3**
Speed ratings (Par 101):96,95,94,94,92 91,91,91,91,90 87,86,83,83,82 71
CSF £28.73 CT £163.08 TOTE £3.80: £1.30, £1.60, £1.70, £3.20; EX 23.90 Trifecta £122.20 Part won. Pool: £172.19 - 0.20 winning units..
Owner Mrs Elizabeth Kiernan **Bred** G Oliver **Trained** Woodingdean, E Sussex

FOCUS
Plenty of runners in this amateur riders' handicap, but not many of them came into the contest in form and this looked a modest race, although the form seems sound enough.

497 GO PONTIN'S (S) STKS 1m (P)

2:20 (2:23) (Class 6) 3-Y-0+ **£2,184** (£644; £322) **Stalls** High

Form RPR

500- **1** **Ellesappelle**[71] [6775] 4-9-3 **61** .... (b) GeorgeBaker 5 50
(G L Moore) *hld up wl in tch: pushed along over 2f out: hdwy u.p on inner wl over 1f out: led wl ins fnl f: jst hld on* **7/1**[3]

0260 **2** *shd* **Mine The Balance (IRE)**[14] [361] 4-9-11 **59** .... StephaneBreux(3) 8 61
(J R Best) *stdd s: bhd: pushed along over 3f out: str run ins fnl f: jst hld* **9/1**

-400 **3** *hd* **Nikki Bea (IRE)**[14] [358] 4-9-3 **56** .... PaulDoe 7 49
(Jamie Poulton) *chsd ldrs: rdn to ld 2f out: wandered 1f out: hdd and no ex nr fin* **7/1**[3]

0200 **4** *hd* **Savoy Chapel**[7] [447] 5-9-5 **44** .... (v) JamesDoyle(3) 10 54
(A W Carroll) *stdd s and dropped in bhd: rdn over 2f out: str run ins fnl f: nrst fin* **20/1**

0211 **5** *3/4* **Louisiade (IRE)**[6] [450] 6-9-11 **53** .... (p) AndrewMullen(3) 4 58
(K A Ryan) *tok t.k.h: hld up bhd ldrs: rdn over 2f out: kpt on same pce ins fnl f* **9/2**[1]

20-4 **6** *1/2* **Ruffie (IRE)**[21] [299] 4-9-3 **64** .... (v) HayleyTurner 3 46
(Miss Gay Kelleway) *hld up in tch: rdn and effrt over 2f out: kpt on same pce fnl f* **11/2**[2]

-202 **7** *1 1/4* **Rafferty (IRE)**[5] [455] 8-9-8 **60** .... LPKeniry 6 48
(S Dow) *s.i.s: sn in tch: rdn wl over 2f out: onepced* **9/2**[1]

40-0 **8** *1/2* **Davidia (IRE)**[21] [292] 4-9-8 **54** .... FrankieMcDonald 1 47
(S Kirk) *hld up in midfield: rdn over 1f out: no prog* **20/1**

10-3 **9** *3* **Crafty Fox**[35] [138] 4-10-0 **52** .... AdamKirby 9 46
(A P Jarvis) *led: rdn 3f out: hdd 2f out: wknd qckly over 1f out* **12/1**

4-04 **10** *2* **Chalentina**[14] [366] 4-9-3 **57** .... (b[1]) TonyCulhane 11 31
(P Howling) *chsd ldr: upsides ldr over 2f out: wknd qckly wl over 1f out* **9/1**

3006 **11** *14* **Miss Sudbrook (IRE)**[16] [341] 5-9-3 **40** .... (t) ShaneKelly 2 —
(A W Carroll) *s.i.s: a bhd: rdn 5f out: no ch wl over 2f out: t.o* **66/1**

1m 38.59s (-0.84) **Going Correction** -0.10s/f (Stan) **11** Ran SP% **115.5**
Speed ratings (Par 101):100,99,99,99,98 98,97,96,93,91 77
CSF £65.51 TOTE £9.40: £3.50, £4.50, £2.80; EX 71.40 Trifecta £258.60 Pool: £364.29 - 0.44 winning units..There was no bid for the winner. Mine The Balance was claimed by H. J. Manners for £6,000.
Owner David Morgan & Bill Gibson **Bred** N R Shields **Trained** Woodingdean, E Sussex

FOCUS
Not too bad a race by selling standards on paper, but they finished in a bunch and the form looks unreliable.

Rafferty(IRE) Official explanation: jockey said gelding banged its head on leaving stalls

Miss Sudbrook(IRE) Official explanation: jockey said mare never travelled

498 PONTINS.COM MAIDEN STKS 7f (P)

2:55 (2:57) (Class 5) 3-Y-0+ **£2,968** (£876; £438) **Stalls** Low

Form RPR

00- **1** **Hatherden**[163] [5178] 3-8-9 .... (t) BrettDoyle 3 67
(R A Kvisla) *chsd ldrs: rdn and briefly outpcd over 2f out: rallied 1f out: r.o wl fnl f to ld on line* **50/1**

-325 **2** *shd* **Madrigale**[16] [342] 3-8-4 **65** .... ChrisCatlin 7 62
(G L Moore) *t.k.h: chsd ldrs: rdn over 2f out: led ins fnl f: hdd on line* **8/1**

3- **3** *3/4* **Ravenna**[59] [6912] 3-8-4 .... JimmyQuinn 1 60
(M P Tregoning) *chsd ldrs: rdn over 2f out: ev ch over 1f out: unable qck wl ins fnl f* **9/1**

-423 **4** *nk* **Leg Sweep**[16] [342] 3-8-9 **72** .... JohnEgan 8 64
(D R C Elsworth) *t.k.h: hld up in midfield on outer: rdn and effrt 2f out: pressed ldrs 1f out: kpt on onepced* **9/4**[1]

30-2 **5** *1* **Follow The Flag (IRE)**[16] [342] 3-8-6 **72** .... JamesDoyle(3) 13 61+
(N P Littmoden) *hld up towards rr: rdn over 2f out: r.o wl ins fnl f: nt rch ldrs* **3/1**[2]

00- **6** *1* **Alfresco**[132] [5891] 3-8-9 .... PaulEddery 9 64+
(Pat Eddery) *hld up in tch: hdwy 2f out: running on whn nt clr run ins fnl f: swtchd rt: r.o nr fin: nt rcvr* **16/1**

0- **7** *hd* **Buzbury Rings**[277] [1796] 3-8-6 .... NeilChalmers(3) 6 58
(A M Balding) *t.k.h: chsd ldr: drvn and upsides 2f out: led briefly 1f out: sn hdd: fdd wl ins fnl f* **16/1**

0 **8** *hd* **Spinning Dixie (IRE)**[28] [208] 3-8-4 .... (t) RichardThomas 12 53
(J A Geake) *t.k.h: hld up in rr: shkn up wl over 1f out: rdn and kpt on ins fnl f: nvr trbld ldrs* **25/1**

9 *nk* **Caterina Ballerina (USA)** 3-8-4 .... CatherineGannon 2 52
(K A Ryan) *sn led: rdn over 2f out: hdd 1f out: wknd* **20/1**

30- **10** *nk* **Trump Call (IRE)**[62] [6867] 3-8-9 .... AdamKirby 11 56+
(R M Beckett) *hld up bhd: shkn up and kpt on ins fnl f: n.d* **16/1**

4 **11** *1 1/2* **Wassendale**[28] [208] 3-8-4 .... NickyMackay 10 47
(J W Hills) *racd in midfield: rdn and outpcd over 2f out:kpt on same pce* **15/2**[3]

/ **12** *nk* **Lockerley Man**[33] 4-9-12 .... FergusSweeney 5 57?
(W S Kittow) *hld up in midfield: hanging over 3f out: sme hdwy on inner over 2f out : btn whn eased ins fnl f* **66/1**

13 *3* **Fraamtastic Too** 3-8-5 ow1 .... SimonWhitworth 4 39
(Jamie Poulton) *s.i.s: a bhd* **66/1**

1m 25.93s (0.04) **Going Correction** -0.10s/f (Stan)
WFA 3 from 4yo 17lb **13** Ran SP% **119.8**
Speed ratings (Par 103):95,94,94,93,92 91,91,90,90,90 88,88,84
CSF £404.30 TOTE £67.40: £15.30, £2.60, £2.20; EX 712.80 TRIFECTA Not won..
Owner Investment Ab Rustningen **Bred** R P Williams **Trained** Newmarket, Suffolk

■ Stewards' Enquiry : Simon Whitworth £275 fine: changed boots after weighing-out

FOCUS
An ordinary but competitive maiden. It was slowly-run and the bare form looks only modest.

Alfresco Official explanation: jockey said gelding was denied a clear run

Lockerley Man Official explanation: jockey said gelding hung badly left

499 PONTINSBINGO.COM MAIDEN STKS 1m 2f (P)

3:25 (3:27) (Class 5) 3-Y-0+ **£3,071** (£906; £453) **Stalls** Low

Form RPR

54-2 **1** **Challis (IRE)**[35] [141] 3-8-6 **75** ow1 .... ShaneKelly 6 76+
(J Noseda) *w.w in tch: hdwy to chse ldng pair over 2f out: pushed into ld ins last: rdr looked at screen: lost momemtum and jst hld on* **11/10**[1]

- 2 shd **Soldiers Quest** 3-8-5 .... JoeFanning 5 75+
(M Johnston) *chsd ldrs: wnt 2nd over 2f out: rdn to ld over 1f out: hdd ins fnl f: kpt on gamely: jst hld* **2/1**[2]

62-5 3 5 **Marbaa (IRE)**[47] 24 4-9-12 64 .... DaneO'Neill 7 70
(S Dow) *chsd ldr: led 3f out: rdn over 2f out: hdd over 1f out: outpcd fnl f* **20/1**

4 2 ½ **Lemonette (USA)**[99] 4-9-0 75 .... PatrickHills(7) 12 60+
(J W Hills) *hld up wl bhd on outer: r.o over 1f out: wnt 4th nr fin: n.d* **14/1**

5 5 ½ **Fire One (IRE)**[21] 293 3-8-5 .... JimmyQuinn 1 59
(M P Tregoning) *chsd ldrs: rdn wl over 2f out: wknd 2f out* **11/1**[3]

6 1 ¼ **Winter Lane** 3-8-5 .... LPKeniry 8 57
(A M Balding) *hld up towards rr: hdwy 5f out: rdn and outpcd wl over 2f out* **25/1**

0- 7 nk **Stringsofmyheart**[191] 4373 3-7-11 .... LiamJones(3) 9 51
(W J Haggas) *pushed along in rr: hdwy 5f out: rdn and outpcd 3f out: no ch after* **33/1**

45- 8 2 ½ **Khyberie**[117] 6177 4-9-7 .... SteveDrowne 10 52
(G Wragg) *hld up towards rr: hdwy over 4f out: rdn and outpcd wl over 2f out* **20/1**

9 4 **Pheidias (IRE)** 3-8-5 .... DaleGibson 3 44
(M P Tregoning) *racd in midfield: rdn and hanging over 3f out: sn struggling* **16/1**

10 6 **Paddymctume**[116] 5-9-8 .... JimCrowley 11 33
(H J Manners) *hld up in rr: rdn and lost tch over 3f out* **100/1**

00-6 11 ¾ **Versatile**[11] 212 4-9-12 63 .... OscarUrbina 4 36
(G A Ham) *led tl 3f out: sn rdn and wknd* **50/1**

12 22 **Colonel Gun (IRE)**[885] 5623 7-9-13 35 .... TPQueally 13 —
(C R Dore) *hld up in midfield: rdn over 3f out: sn bhd: t.o* **100/1**

13 shd **Tory Brae (IRE)** 3-8-5 ow3 .... JamesDoyle(3) 2 —
(R M Beckett) *slowly away: a bhd and sn rdn along: lost tch over 4f out: t.o last 3f* **50/1**

2m 5.68s (-2.11) **Going Correction** -0.10s/f (Stan)
WFA 3 from 4yo 22lb 4 from 5yo+ 1lb 13 Ran SP% **124.0**
Speed ratings (Par 103):104,103,99,97,97 96,96,94,91,86 85,68,68
CSF £3.10 TOTE £2.20: £1.10, £1.20, £4.30; EX 4.40 Trifecta £58.50 Pool: £537.40 - 6.52 winning units..
Owner Clive Washbourn **Bred** W P Churchward & Mrs C Hue-Williams **Trained** Newmarket, Suffolk

FOCUS
Not a very strong maiden, but it should produce some winners. The first two came clear and can rate higher still. The winning time was quicker than both divisions of the 46-55 handicap, but 1.16 seconds slower than the 71-85 contest.

500 PONTIN'S FAMILY HOLIDAYS H'CAP (DIV II) 1m 2f (P)
4:00 (4:00) (Class 6) (0-55,54) 4-Y-0+ £1,706 (£377; £377) Stalls Low

Form RPR

0-00 1 **Shaheer (IRE)**[9] 425 5-8-12 52 .... JimCrowley 7 55
(J Gallagher) *chsd ldr: led over 3f out: mde rest: rdn over 2f out: styd on wl fnl f* **14/1**

31-1 2 ¾ **Saucy**[22] 274 6-8-10 50 .... ShaneKelly 11 52
(A W Carroll) *t.k.h: hld up towards rr: hdwy on outer bnd over 2f out: shkn up and effrt over 1f out: styd on ins last: nt rch wnr* **7/4**[1]

2-02 2 dht **King Of Knight (IRE)**[37] 121 6-9-0 54 .... OscarUrbina 5 56
(G Prodromou) *hld up in midfield: hdwy over 2f out: rdn and effrt jst over 1f out: chsd wnr ins fnl f: no imp last 50 yds* **11/4**[2]

-050 4 hd **Simpsons Gamble (IRE)**[5] 461 4-8-9 50 .... AdrianMcCarthy 9 51
(R M Flower) *w.w in midfield: hdwy 3f out: rdn to chse wnr wl over 1f out tl ins fnl f: onepced* **12/1**

-505 5 1 ¾ **Fuel Cell (IRE)**[8] 431 6-8-5 45 .... JoeFanning 2 43
(J O'Reilly) *hld up in midfield: effrt and rdn on inner 2f out: chsd ldrs 1f out: wknd fnl f* **15/2**

00-0 6 ½ **Veba (USA)**[14] 359 4-8-4 45 .... HayleyTurner 1 42
(M D I Usher) *t.k.h: hld up in rr: hmpd and swtchd 3f out: hdwy u.p 2f out: no imp ins fnl f* **50/1**

202 7 2 **Sahara Prince (IRE)**[19] 315 7-8-8 48 ....(p) JohnEgan 3 41
(K A Morgan) *t.k.h: chsd ldrs: wnt 2nd 3f out tl wl over 1f out: wknd u.p 1f out* **9/2**[3]

460- 8 ¾ **Laheen (IRE)**[109] 6314 4-8-13 54 .... BrettDoyle 6 46
(J R Best) *chsd ldrs: rdn wl over 2f out: wknd over 1f out* **33/1**

00/0 9 ¾ **Coombe Centenary**[28] 212 5-8-10 50 .... JimmyQuinn 4 40
(L Montague Hall) *hld up wl in rr: rdn and effrt over2f out: nvr on terms* **50/1**

0-00 10 1 ¾ **Mo Chroi**[5] 455 4-8-1 45 ....(p) MarcHalford(3) 8 32
(J J Bridger) *t.k.h: hld up in rr: effrt and rdn over 2f out: sn outpcd* **66/1**

000/ 11 30 **Tiggers Touch**[442] 6497 5-8-5 45 .... ChrisCatlin 12 —
(A W Carroll) *sn led: hdd 3f out: sn wknd: t.o last 2f* **50/1**

2m 7.78s (-0.01) **Going Correction** -0.10s/f (Stan)
WFA 4 from 5yo+ 1lb 11 Ran SP% **117.7**
Speed ratings (Par 101): **96,95,95,95,93 93,91,91,90,89 65**PL: Shaheer £4.00, King Of Knight £1.10, Saucy £1.40; EX: King Of Knight £34.20, Saucy £30.80; CSF: King Of Knight £25.87, Saucy £19.19; TRICAST: King Of Knight £52.28 Saucy £46.27 TOTE £21.20 TRIFECTA 4-2-6 £124.80 -1.70 wi27 Owner.

FOCUS
A moderate handicap and, with the pace quite muddling, the form looks unreliable. The winning time was 1.74 seconds slower than the first division, and significantly slower than both the 1m2f maiden and 71-85 handicap.
Saucy Official explanation: jockey said mare hung left in straight
Coombe Centenary Official explanation: jockey said mare was slowly away

501 PONTIN'S "BOOK EARLY" H'CAP 1m 2f (P)
4:35 (4:35) (Class 4) (0-85,84) 4-Y-0+ £4,857 (£1,445; £722; £360) Stalls Low

Form RPR

224- 1 **Lisathedaddy**[80] 6661 5-8-6 76 .... RichardKingscote(3) 2 89
(B G Powell) *hld up in midfield: hdwy and rdn over 2f out: chsd ldr jst over 1f out: led last 100 yds: rdn out* **6/1**[3]

200- 2 1 ¼ **Star Magnitude (USA)**[166] 5110 6-8-6 80 .... JackMitchell(7) 8 91
(S Dow) *hld up towards rr: hdwy 5f out: pressed ldr 3f out: rdn to ld 2f out: hdd and nt pce of wnr last 100 yds* **14/1**

065- 3 3 **Jebel Ali (IRE)**[115] 6206 4-8-7 75 .... JohnEgan 10 80
(B Gubby) *chsd ldrs: wnt 2nd over 5f out tl 3f out: kpt on same pce u.p* **10/1**

-554 4 hd **Prince Charlemagne (IRE)**[7] 444 4-8-9 80 .... JamesDoyle(3) 4 85
(N P Littmoden) *trckd ldrs: rdn and effrt jst over 2f out: kpt on same pce* **5/1**[2]

0-63 5 nk **Bay Boy**[16] 340 5-8-6 73 .... JoeFanning 11 77
(M Johnston) *led tl 3f out: rdn over 2f out: wknd 1f out* **8/1**

16-4 6 nk **Solo Flight**[16] 340 10-9-0 81 .... SteveDrowne 7 85
(H Morrison) *t.k.h: hld up in midfield: hdwy and in tch over 2f out: rdn and outpcd 2f out: kpt on ins fnl f* **5/1**[2]

11-4 7 1 ¼ **Magical Music**[31] 185 4-9-2 84 .... JimmyQuinn 3 85
(J Pearce) *chsd ldrs: wnt 2nd 8f out tl over 5f out: rdn and outpcd over 2f out: kpt on same pce u.p over 1f out* **8/1**

2-13 8 1 ¼ **Just Bond (IRE)**[7] 444 5-8-4 76 .... DuranFentiman(5) 9 75
(G R Oldroyd) *t.k.h: hld up on outer in rr: hdwy to chse ldrs 5f out: led 3f out tl 2f out: wknd qckly fnl f* **9/2**[1]

21-0 9 nk **Armada**[15] 351 4-8-4 75 .... LiamJones(3) 5 73
(W J Haggas) *hld up in rr: n.d* **16/1**

040/ 10 1 ¾ **Prince Nureyev (IRE)**[485] 6025 7-8-12 84 .... JamesMillman(5) 12 79
(B R Millman) *stdd s: hld up in rr: hdwy on outer to chse ldrs wl over 3f out: wknd over 2f out* **40/1**

00-0 11 1 ¼ **Le Corvee (IRE)**[14] 362 5-8-13 80 .... ShaneKelly 6 73
(A W Carroll) *a bhd: nvr on terms* **66/1**

00-0 12 6 **Jidaar (IRE)**[2] 488 4-8-5 73 .... ChrisCatlin 1 54
(P W Hiatt) *chsd ldr for 2f: steadily lost pl: bhd 4f out: rdn and lost tch wl over 2f out* **33/1**

2m 4.52s (-3.27) **Going Correction** -0.10s/f (Stan)
WFA 4 from 5yo+ 1lb 12 Ran SP% **116.5**
Speed ratings (Par 105):109,108,105,105,105 104,103,102,102,101 100,95
CSF £84.34 CT £828.23 TOTE £7.10: £2.10, £3.90, £3.60; EX 115.80 TRIFECTA Not won..
Owner Mrs Patricia Wilson **Bred** M Barrett **Trained** Lambourn, Berks

FOCUS
The pace was good for most of the way and, with the winning time by far the quickest of the four races run over 1m2f on the day, the form looks quite strong for the level.
Just Bond(IRE) Official explanation: jockey said gelding ran too free in back straight
Prince Nureyev(IRE) Official explanation: jockey said gelding hung right

502 DIGITAL PRINTS FROM BONUSPRINT.COM H'CAP 5f (P)
5:10 (5:10) (Class 5) (0-70,70) 3-Y-0 £3,071 (£906; £453) Stalls High

Form RPR

1 1 **Halsion Chancer**[16] 343 3-8-10 65 .... StephaneBreux(3) 8 70
(J R Best) *hld up bhd ldrs: hdwy on outer 2f out: rdn and r.o wl to ld nr fin* **4/1**[3]

341- 2 nk **Rocker**[65] 6838 3-8-10 69 .... PatrickHills(7) 10 73
(B R Johnson) *sn pressing ldr on outer: rdn 2f out: edgd rt over 1f out: led 1f out: hdd and no ex nr fin* **11/1**

4-21 3 ¾ **Convivial Spirit**[17] 336 3-9-1 67 ....(t) LPKeniry 7 68
(E F Vaughan) *hld up bhd ldrs: rdn and effrt over 1f out: kpt on u.p ins fnl f* **10/3**[1]

3-12 4 ½ **Daddy Cool**[30] 188 3-9-0 69 .... AmirQuinn(3) 3 68
(W G M Turner) *led: rdn wl over 1f out: edgd rt and hdd 1f out: wknd last 100 yds* **7/2**[2]

06-6 5 nk **Arnie's Joint (IRE)**[12] 385 3-8-10 65 .... JamesDoyle(3) 9 63
(N P Littmoden) *racd in midfield: drvn over 2f out: hdwy over 1f out: kpt on but nt pce to rch ldrs* **14/1**

1411 6 ½ **Bentley**[10] 404 3-9-2 68 ....(v) DaneO'Neill 5 64
(D Shaw) *chsd ldng pair: rdn over 2f out: fdd wl ins fnl f* **9/2**

3-56 7 1 ¼ **Inquisitress**[12] 382 3-8-9 68 .... RyanBird(7) 2 60
(J J Bridger) *sn outpcd in last trio: n.d* **25/1**

20-0 8 2 **Suzieblue (IRE)**[47] 25 3-7-11 56 oh3........(p) JosephWalsh(7) 6 40
(D C O'Brien) *sn outpcd: a bhd* **40/1**

6-25 9 1 **Ginger Pop**[19] 311 3-9-4 70 .... GeorgeBaker 4 51
(G G Margarson) *midfield and sn pushed along: nvr on terms* **8/1**

6-04 10 3 ½ **Redflo**[10] 404 3-7-11 56 oh4........ SophieDoyle(7) 1 24
(Ms J S Doyle) *sn outpcd in last* **33/1**

58.99 secs (-0.79) **Going Correction** -0.10s/f (Stan) 10 Ran SP% **118.8**
Speed ratings (Par 97):102,101,100,99,99 98,96,93,91,85
CSF £47.29 CT £151.86 TOTE £3.70: £2.50, £3.30, £1.60; EX 46.20 Trifecta £137.80 Pool: £860.36 - 4.43 winning units. Place 6 £221.84, Place 5 £76.37.
Owner Halsion Ltd **Bred** Mrs S Hansford **Trained** Hucking, Kent

FOCUS
This looked like a fair handicap for the grade. The unexposed winner did not need to improve greatly on his debut win but should be capable of better. Sound form.
Daddy Cool Official explanation: jockey said colt hung right
T/Jkpt: Not won. T/Plt: £190.70 to a £1 stake. Pool: £77,593.35. 297.00 winning tickets. T/Qpdt: £61.90 to a £1 stake. Pool: £4,887.20. 58.40 winning tickets. SP

462 SOUTHWELL (L-H)
Tuesday, February 20

OFFICIAL GOING: Standard
Wind: Virtually nil

503 PONTINS.COM H'CAP (DIV I) 1m 3f (F)
1:30 (1:31) (Class 6) (0-60,60) 4-Y-0+ £1,706 (£503; £252) Stalls Low

Form RPR

-203 1 **Mahmjra**[7] 453 5-9-1 56 .... PFredericks 2 66
(C N Allen) *cl up: led after 1f: rdn along 2f out: drvn ent last and styd on wl* **4/1**[1]

3-15 2 1 ¾ **Bolckow**[7] 453 4-9-3 60 .... MickyFenton 7 67
(J T Stimpson) *trckd ldrs: hdwy to chse wnr 4f out: rdn to chal over 1f out: sn drvn and kpt on same pce* **5/1**[3]

040- 3 1 ¼ **Plenty Cried Wolf**[49] 6158 5-9-0 55 .... PaulHanagan 6 60
(R A Fahey) *led 1f: cl up: rdn along 3f out: drvn and one pce fnl 2f* **17/2**

44-3 4 1 ¾ **Cragganmore Creek**[44] 64 4-8-9 52 ....(v[1]) JamieSpencer 3 54
(D Morris) *in tch: hdwy to trck ldrs over 4f out: rdn along over 2f out and sn no imp* **9/2**[2]

4650 5 5 **They All Laughed**[15] 363 4-8-11 54 ....(p) ChrisCatlin 10 47
(P W Hiatt) *in tch: hdwy on outer to trck ldrs 4f out: rdn along over 2f out and sn no imp* **9/1**

025- 6 1 **El Dee (IRE)**[45] 4404 4-8-0 50 ow5........ KellyHarrison(7) 8 42
(D Carroll) *hld up in rr: hdwy over 3f out: rdn and in tch over 2f out: sson wknd* **7/1**

3-20 7 ¾ **Magic Amigo**[29] 212 6-9-4 59 .... EddieAhern 5 49
(J R Jenkins) *hld up in rr: nt much roon bnd after 2f: effrt and sme hdwy 3f out: sn rdn and nvr a factor* **8/1**

60-4 8 6 **History Prize (IRE)**[40] 98 4-8-5 51 ow3........ NeilChalmers(3) 1 31
(A G Newcombe) *chsd ldrs: rdn along over 4f out: wknd over 3f out* **28/1**

513- 9 2 ½ **Kentucky Bullet (USA)**[54] 6959 11-8-4 45 .... SimonWhitworth 4 21
(A G Newcombe) *hld up: a rr* **16/1**

00-0 **10** *shd* **Hits Only Life (USA)**[26] [243] 4-8-7 **50**........................ DeanMcKeown 9 26
(J Pearce) *a rr: bhd fnl 5f* **25/1**

2m 27.69s (-1.21) **Going Correction** -0.225s/f (Stan)
WFA 4 from 5yo+ 2lb **10** Ran SP% **112.2**
Speed ratings (Par 101):95,93,92,91,87 87,86,82,80,80
CSF £22.80 CT £157.54 TOTE £3.80: £1.60, £2.00, £3.40; EX 21.80 Trifecta £83.70 Pool £241.79, 2.05 w/u.
Owner Travel Spot Ltd **Bred** Darley **Trained** Newmarket, Suffolk
■ Paul Fredericks' first winner back in Britain following seven years riding in Spain.

FOCUS
No great pace on here which suited those that raced handily. The winning time was modest, 0.75 seconds slower than the second division. The race has been rated through the second and third.

504 GO PONTIN'S CLASSIFIED CLAIMING STKS 6f (F)
2:00 (2:02) (Class 6) 4-Y-0+ **£2,184** (£644; £322) **Stalls** Low

Form RPR
0031 **1** **Mister Incredible**[14] [374] 4-8-2 52........................(v) SaleemGolam(3) 9 58+
(V Smith) *trckd ldrs: smooth hdwy over 2f out:swtchd lft and hdwy to ld over 1f out: rdn clr ins last* **9/2**[1]
10-4 **2** *2* **Danish Blues (IRE)**[20] [310] 4-9-3 56............................(e1) IanMongan 3 64
(D E Cantillon) *trckd ldrs: hdwy over 2f out: rdn wl over 1f out: kpt on same pce ins last* **11/2**[2]
-445 **3** *1/2* **Grafton (IRE)**[7] [448] 4-8-11 52...................................(p) DavidAllan 6 56
(J O'Reilly) *chsd ldng pair: hdwy over 2f out: rdn to ld briefly 1 1/2f out: sn hdd and one pce* **12/1**
4242 **4** *1/2* **Soba Jones**[12] [388] 10-8-6 54............................... JasonEdmunds(3) 13 53
(J Balding) *chsd ldrs on outer: effrt over 2f out: sn rdn and kpt on same pce* **7/1**[3]
10-0 **5** *6* **Bodden Bay**[22] [292] 5-9-5 58..(t) PFredericks 12 45
(Miss Gay Kelleway) *in tch on outer: rdn along wl over 2f out: sn no imp* **12/1**
0500 **6** *nk* **Diktalex (IRE)**[14] [376] 4-8-8 45..(tp) AlanDaly 4 33
(C J Teague) *led: rdn along 3f out: drvn and hdd 1 1/2 f out: sn wknd* **50/1**
-503 **7** *shd* **Sundried Tomato**[5] [467] 8-7-12 40................(p) DanielleMcCreery(7) 1 29
(D W Chapman) *cl up on inner: rdn along wl over 2f out: wknd wl over 1f out* **11/1**
0-60 **8** *nk* **Ten Prophets (IRE)**[47] [33] 4-8-7 60............................... EddieAhern 2 30
(H E Haynes) *rr tl sme late hdwy* **20/1**
/00- **9** *1 3/4* **Champagne Rossini (IRE)**[83] [3909] 5-8-0 38................ NicolPolli(5) 14 23
(M C Chapman) *s.i.s: a bhd* **80/1**
55-0 **10** *nk* **Rainbow's Classic**[10] [426] 4-8-0 58.....................(b) DuranFentiman(5) 8 22
(P Beaumont) *a rr* **33/1**
-050 **11** *1 1/2* **Mister Becks (IRE)**[19] [320] 4-8-2 41...................... AndrewMullen(3) 11 18
(M C Chapman) *midfield on outer: rdn alon g 1/2-way: nvr nr ldrs* **50/1**
000- **12** *nk* **Millbrook Star (IRE)**[53] [6970] 4-7-12 36...................... SophieDoyle(7) 5 17
(M C Chapman) *a rr* **100/1**
060- **13** *nk* **Jabraan (USA)**[71] [6793] 5-8-9 42..............................(b) PaulQuinn 10 20
(D W Chapman) *s.i.s and bhd: sme hdwy u.p wl over 2f out sn wknd* **33/1**

1m 15.89s (-1.01) **Going Correction** -0.225s/f (Stan) **13** Ran SP% **86.6**
Speed ratings (Par 101):97,94,93,93,85 84,84,84,81,81 79,78,78
CSF £13.36 TOTE £4.00: £1.60, £1.60, £3.30; EX 22.10 Trifecta £62.60 Part won. Pool: £88.21 - 0.30 winning units..The winner was claimed by J. M. Bradley for £5,000
Owner R West **Bred** R J H West **Trained** Exning, Suffolk

FOCUS
A moderate claimer, made even weaker by the late withdrawal of the favourite Tyrone Sam (9/4, Rule 4 deduct 30p in £. The runner-up is not the most consistent but is rated back to form.

505 PONTINSBINGO.COM MAIDEN STKS 6f (F)
2:30 (2:36) (Class 5) 3-Y-0 **£2,968** (£876; £438) **Stalls** Low

Form RPR
542- **1** **Imprimis Tagula (IRE)**[73] [6764] 3-9-3 64.................... SamHitchcott 6 78
(A Bailey) *trckd ldrs: smooth hdwy 2f out: shalen up to ld 1f out: kpt on* **9/2**[3]
4-25 **2** *1 1/2* **Popolo (IRE)**[16] [348] 3-8-12 63.................................. AdrianMcCarthy 3 68
(P W Chapple-Hyam) *trckd ldrs: effrt 2f out: sn rdn: styd on ins last* **9/2**[3]
44-2 **3** *1* **Rann Na Cille (IRE)**[14] [375] 3-8-12 66........................ JamieSpencer 1 65
(K A Ryan) *cl up: led over 2f out: sn rdn: drvn and hdd 1f out: one pce* **11/10**[1]
5-02 **4** *9* **Mangano**[9] [429] 3-9-0 40.. StephenDonohoe(3) 5 41
(A Berry) *led to 1/2-way: cl up tl rdn over 2f out and grad wknd* **20/1**
05 **5** *2* **The Tinker Man**[14] [375] 3-8-10 .... FrankiePickard(7) 4 35
(M D I Usher) *chsd ldrs: rdn along 1/2-way: sn outpcd* **28/1**
64 **6** *1/2* **Dramatic**[28] [222] 3-9-3 .... SebSanders 7 33
(Sir Mark Prescott) *towards rr: rdn along and sme hdwy over 2f out: nvr nr ldrs* **4/1**[2]
060- **7** *5* **Blissfully**[139] [5764] 3-8-12 45.......................................(b1) PaulEddery 2 12
(S Parr) *dwlt: sn cl up on inner: led 1/2-way: riodden and hdd over 2f out and sn wknd* **100/1**
8 *39* **Enflame** 3-8-9 .... SaleemGolam(3) 8 —
(T T Clement) *s.i.s: a outpcd and bhd* **50/1**

1m 16.16s (-0.74) **Going Correction** -0.225s/f (Stan) **8** Ran SP% **115.1**
Speed ratings (Par 97):95,93,91,79,77 76,69,17
CSF £24.11 TOTE £6.50: £1.60, £1.60, £1.10; EX 31.60 Trifecta £57.80 Pool: £637.46 - 7.82 winning units..
Owner N Davies,J McMahon,S Costello,P Donlan **Bred** Glashare House Stud **Trained** Newmarket, Suffolk
■ Alan Bailey's first winner since returning to Newmarket after 15 years in Cheshire.

FOCUS
A modest maiden, run in a slightly slower time than the preceding claimer for older horses, and only half the field could be seriously fancied. The form looks sound, the first three finishing clear, with the winner and second improving.

506 PONTIN'S FAMILY HOLIDAYS (S) STKS 5f (F)
3:00 (3:00) (Class 6) 3-Y-0 **£2,184** (£644; £322) **Stalls** High

Form RPR
521- **1** **Sister Etienne (IRE)**[55] [6945] 3-9-0 66............................. PhillipMakin 5 53
(T D Barron) *chsd ldrs: swtchd lft over 2f out and sn rdn: styd on u.p ins last to ld last 50 yds* **4/11**[1]
0-43 **2** *1/2* **Pretty Selma**[14] [378] 3-8-7 39...................................(b1) EddieAhern 3 44
(R M H Cowell) *led and sn clr: rdn and edgd lft over 1f out: drvn ins last: hdd and no ex last 50 yds* **8/1**[2]
00-5 **3** *2* **Spinning Game**[12] [390] 3-9-0 42..............................(b) TonyCulhane 4 44
(D W Chapman) *chsd ldr: rdn and edgd rt over 2f out: drvn over 1f out: kpt on ins last* **10/1**[3]
00 **4** *5* **Coleorton Dagger**[10] [423] 3-8-4 ....(p) AndrewMullen(3) 1 20
(K A Ryan) *wnt lft s: sn rdn along and outpcd in rr* **25/1**
-000 **5** *1 1/4* **Bonny Scotland (IRE)**[7] [454] 3-8-4 42.................... PatrickMathers(3) 6 16
(I W McInnes) *sn rdn along in rr: outpcd and bhd fr 1/2-way* **40/1**
6-30 **6** *13* **Sunken Rags**[14] [378] 3-9-0 55.. PaulHanagan 2 —
(K R Burke) *chsd ldrs: rdn along hal;fway: sn lost pl and bhd* **10/1**[3]

60.51 secs (0.21) **Going Correction** -0.075s/f (Stan) **6** Ran SP% **108.9**
Speed ratings (Par 95):95,94,91,83,81 60
CSF £3.58 TOTE £1.30: £1.10, £2.20; EX 5.00.The winner was sold to J. T. Stimpson for 4,800gns.
Owner S Knighton & A Kundi **Bred** Oghill House Stud **Trained** Maunby, N Yorks

FOCUS
A poor seller contested by six fillies even though the race was open to colts and geldings. They finished wide across the track and the form probably amounts to little, with the winner rather dragged down to her rivals' level rather than them improving.

507 PHOTO ALBUMS FROM BONUSPRINT.COM H'CAP 1m 4f (F)
3:30 (3:30) (Class 5) (0-70,73) 4-Y-0+ **£3,071** (£906; £453) **Stalls** Low

Form RPR
1-11 **1** **Jazrawy**[7] [453] 5-9-6 **70** 6ex.. JoeFanning 8 83+
(D Carroll) *mde all: rdn and qcknd 2f out: styd on strly ins last* **3/1**[2]
/00- **2** *1 3/4* **Dangerously Good**[93] [6178] 9-8-7 **57**..................................... LPKeniry 2 65
(J Howard Johnson) *chsd ldrs: rdn along 3f out: styd on u.p over 1f out: chsd wnr ins last: kpt on* **33/1**
4 **3** *1 1/4* **Great Man (FR)**[18] [142] 6-8-12 **62**................................ JamieSpencer 6 68
(Noel T Chance) *hld up in tch: smooth hdwy 4f out: rdn to chse wnr over 1f out: kpt on same pce ent last* **12/1**
6-14 **4** *2 1/2* **Amwell Brave**[27] [232] 6-9-3 **67**.. EddieAhern 4 69
(J R Jenkins) *a.p: effrt to chse winenr 3f out: rdn along over 2f out and kpt on same pce* **7/1**[3]
1131 **5** *3/4* **Beldon Hill (USA)**[9] [434] 4-9-1 **73** 6ex....................... JamieMoriarty(5) 7 74
(R A Fahey) *trckd ldrs: hdwy and cl up 4f out: rdiden along wl over 2f out drvn and btn wl over 1f out* **7/4**[1]
03-0 **6** *7* **Russian Dream (IRE)**[31] [195] 4-8-11 **64**............................ AdamKirby 5 54
(W R Swinburn) *a towards rr* **16/1**
3406 **7** *3 1/2* **Opera Writer (IRE)**[7] [453] 4-8-4 **62** ow4........... RussellKennemore(5) 9 46
(R Hollinshead) *prom: rdn along 4f out: sn wknd* **15/2**
-125 **8** *3/4* **Credential**[19] [319] 5-8-8 **61**.................................... StephenDonohoe(3) 3 44
(John A Harris) *a towards rr* **16/1**
/00- **9** *24* **Piper General (IRE)**[351] [599] 5-9-2 **69**........................ JasonEdmunds(3) 1 13
(J Balding) *chsd ldrs: rdn along over 4f out: sn wknd* **25/1**

2m 37.82s (-4.27) **Going Correction** -0.225s/f (Stan)
WFA 4 from 5yo+ 3lb **9** Ran SP% **111.9**
Speed ratings (Par 103):105,103,103,101,100 96,93,93,77
CSF £87.65 CT £1022.50 TOTE £3.90: £1.40, £16.90, £3.60; EX 215.00 TRIFECTA Not won..
Owner Mrs B Ramsden **Bred** Scuderia Antonella S R L **Trained** Sledmere, E Yorks

FOCUS
A modest handicap and the placed form is not entirely solid, but Jazrawy is in the form of his life and produced another personal best.

508 PONTINS.COM H'CAP (DIV II) 1m 3f (F)
4:00 (4:00) (Class 6) (0-60,59) 4-Y-0+ **£1,706** (£503; £252) **Stalls** Low

Form RPR
/54- **1** **Muntami (IRE)**[69] [5103] 6-8-12 **56**........................... StephenDonohoe(3) 3 68
(John A Harris) *a.p: hdwy to trck ldr over 4f out: led 3f out: rdn 2f out: styd on strly ins last* **8/1**
40-3 **2** *2 1/2* **Nimello (USA)**[26] [242] 11-8-12 **53**.................................. SamHitchcott 2 60
(A G Newcombe) *hld up in rr: stdy hdwy 4f out: rdn to chse wsinner ent last: snd riven and kpt on same pce* **7/1**[3]
0-63 **3** *2* **Twilight Avenger (IRE)**[11] [402] 4-8-0 **46**..................... LiamJones(3) 1 50
(W M Brisbourne) *trckd ldrs: hdwy over 3f out: rdn 2f out: kpt on same pce appr last* **11/1**
3-46 **4** *3/4* **Domenico (IRE)**[37] [134] 9-8-5 **46**................................... EddieAhern 10 49
(J R Jenkins) *a.p: effrt 3f out and ev ch tl rdn and one pce wl over 1f out* **4/1**[1]
000/ **5** *1/2* **Bilkie (IRE)**[282] [3216] 5-8-8 **49**...(e1) MickyFenton 7 51?
(John Berry) *towards rr: rdn along 4f out: outpcd 3f: kpt on u.p appr last: nrst fin* **16/1**
02-6 **6** *nk* **Boppys Dancer**[49] [12] 4-8-2 **45**.....................................(b) PaulHanagan 6 46
(P T Midgley) *trckd ldrs: pushed along 4f out: rdn wl over 2f out and sn btn* **4/1**[1]
24-0 **7** *2 1/2* **Choristar**[14] [377] 6-9-4 **59**.. DaleGibson 4 56
(J Mackie) *hld up: hdwy on outer over 4f out: rdn along 3f out and wknd over 2f out* **7/1**[3]
600- **8** *2* **River Logic (IRE)**[45] [5497] 4-9-2 **59**........................... PaulMulrennan 8 53
(A D Brown) *in tch: hdwy to chse ldrs on outer 1/2-way: rdn along 3f out and sn wknd* **5/1**[2]
-060 **9** *4* **Zacatecas (GER)**[16] [354] 7-8-9 **50**............................(b) DeanMcKeown 5 37
(A J Chamberlain) *a rr* **33/1**
5644 **10** *shd* **Futoo (IRE)**[9] [431] 6-8-4 **45**...(b) PaulQuinn 9 32
(D W Chapman) *led: rdn along and hdd 3f out: sn wknd* **16/1**

2m 26.94s (-1.96) **Going Correction** -0.225s/f (Stan)
WFA 4 from 5yo+ 2lb **10** Ran SP% **115.8**
Speed ratings (Par 101):98,96,94,94,93 93,91,90,87,87
CSF £62.50 CT £620.25 TOTE £10.90: £3.30, £2.30, £4.20; EX 121.60 TRIFECTA Not won..
Owner Dermot Owens **Bred** Shadwell Estate Company Limited **Trained** Eastwell, Leics

FOCUS
A slowly-run event and moderate handicap form judged on the placed horses. The winner took advantage of a good mark on his return to his old yard.
River Logic(IRE) Official explanation: jockey said gelding hung left-handed in back straight

509 BONUSPRINT.COM H'CAP 7f (F)
4:30 (4:31) (Class 4) (0-85,84) 4-Y-0+ **£4,857** (£1,445; £722; £360) **Stalls** Low

Form RPR
-335 **1** **Mandarin Spirit (IRE)**[13] [384] 7-8-9 **77**........................(b) OscarUrbina 5 89
(G C H Chung) *hld up towards rr: gd hdwy 2f out: rdn to ld over 1f out: hung bdly rt ins last: drvn out* **15/2**
4-20 **2** *1 1/4* **Gifted Gamble**[16] [351] 5-8-13 **81**..............................(b) JamieSpencer 10 89
(K A Ryan) *in tch: hdwy on outer 3f out: rdn and cl up whn n.m.r and swtchd lft over 1f out: sn drvn and kpt on* **7/2**[1]
512- **3** *hd* **Final Tune (IRE)**[109] [6323] 4-8-2 **73** ow2................... PatrickMathers(3) 6 81
(Miss M E Rowland) *chsd ldrs: rdn along and outpcd over 2f out: drvn and styd on ins last: nrst fin* **20/1**
1212 **4** *3/4* **Rebellious Spirit**[20] [314] 4-9-2 **84**... JimCrowley 9 90
(P W Hiatt) *cl up: hdwy to ld 2f out: sn rdn: edgd rt and hdd over 1f out: kpt on same pce ins last* **4/1**[2]

005- **5** *nk* **Glenbuck (IRE)**[76] [6733] 4-8-10 **78**....(v) JoeFanning 2 83
(A Bailey) *led: rdn along and hdd 2f out: cl up and ev ch tl n.m.r and wknd ins last* **14/1**

P0-5 **6** *1 1/2* **Ocean Of Dreams (FR)**[22] [300] 4-8-5 **73**.... JimmyQuinn 3 74
(J D Bethell) *dwlt: sn chsng ldrs: effrt and ech over 2f out: sn rdn and grad wknd* **14/1**

1-04 **7** *3/4* **Orpen Wide (IRE)**[7] [451] 5-8-7 **78**.... GregFairley(3) 8 77
(M C Chapman) *cl up: rdn along 3f out: sn wknd* **8/1**

-006 **8** *5* **Tyzack (IRE)**[7] [451] 6-8-8 **76**.... MickyFenton 4 62
(W M Brisbourne) *dwlt: a towards rr* **11/1**

5254 **9** *3/4* **Certain Justice (USA)**[3] [486] 9-8-6 **74** ow2.... EddieAhern 1 58
(Stef Liddiard) *in tch on inner: rdn along over 2f out and sn btn* **5/1**[3]

0400 **10** *1* **Meditation**[13] [384] 5-8-3 **74**....(p) JamesDoyle(3) 7 56
(I A Wood) *cl up: rdn along 3f out: sn wknd* **33/1**

1m 28.1s (-2.70) **Going Correction** -0.225s/f (Stan) **10** Ran SP% **111.1**
Speed ratings (Par 105):106,104,104,103,103 101,100,94,94,92
CSF £32.10 CT £496.98 TOTE £9.20: £2.00, £1.40, £3.70; EX 35.40 Trifecta £287.80 Part won. Pool: £405.45 - 0.34 winning units..
Owner Peter Tsim **Bred** W Haggas And W Jarvis **Trained** Newmarket, Suffolk
■ Stewards' Enquiry : Oscar Urbina three-day ban: used whip with excessive force, without giving mount time to respond, and down the shoulder (Mar 5-7)

FOCUS
A fair handicap run at a good pace, which suited those that were held up. A clear personal best from the winner, with the placed form looking sound.

510 PONTIN'S BOOK EARLY H'CAP 7f (F)
5:00 (5:00) (Class 5) (0-75,73) 3-Y-O **£3,071** (£906; £453) **Stalls** Low

Form RPR

11 **1** **Rosa De Mi Corazon (USA)**[9] [433] 3-9-4 **73** 6ex.... SebSanders 6 81+
(Sir Mark Prescott) *cl up: effrt over 2f out and sn rdn: drvn over 1f out: hrd drvn ins last: led last stride* **4/9**[1]

436- **2** *shd* **Captain Jacksparra (IRE)**[169] [5059] 3-9-3 **72**.... JamieSpencer 5 79
(K A Ryan) *dwlt: hdwy on outer 3f out: cl up 2f out: rdn over 1f out: led ins last: hdd on line* **9/2**[2]

10-1 **3** *nk* **Sheriff's Silk**[40] [99] 3-8-10 **65**....(b) PaulEddery 7 72
(B Smart) *cl up: hdwy to ld 2f out: sn rdn: drvn and hdd ins last: kpt on u.p towards fin* **17/2**[3]

-130 **4** *1 3/4* **Cherri Fosfate**[22] [290] 3-9-0 **69**....(v) EddieAhern 2 71
(D Carroll) *trckd ldrs: hdwy over 2f out: sn rdn and one pce appr last* **20/1**

42-0 **5** *1/2* **Jord (IRE)**[35] [147] 3-8-13 **73**.... NataliaGemelova(5) 3 74
(A J McCabe) *sn led: rdn along 3f out: hdd 2f out and sn drvn: kpt on same pce* **33/1**

334- **6** *shd* **Fealeview Lady (USA)**[67] [6832] 3-8-12 **67**.... RobertHavlin 1 67
(H Morrison) *chsd ldrs on inner: rdn along over 2f out and kpt on same pce* **14/1**

504- **7** *10* **Hephaestus**[76] [6732] 3-9-1 **70**.... DeanMcKeown 4 44
(A J Chamberlain) *chsd ldrs: rdn along 1/2-way: sn wknd* **66/1**

1m 28.59s (-2.21) **Going Correction** -0.225s/f (Stan) **7** Ran SP% **113.8**
Speed ratings (Par 97):103,102,102,100,99 99,88
CSF £2.73 TOTE £1.40: £1.10, £2.20; EX 3.50 Place 6 £59.22, Place 5 £34.95.
Owner Miss K Rausing **Bred** K Rausing **Trained** Newmarket, Suffolk
■ Stewards' Enquiry : Seb Sanders two-day ban: used whip with excessive frequency (Mar 5-6)

FOCUS
An interesting handicap featuring a couple of unexposed sorts. The form looks solid rated through the third to its best.
T/Plt: £19.30 to a £1 stake. Pool: £49,611.20. 1,874.05 winning tickets. T/Qpdt: £6.50 to a £1 stake. Pool: £2,747.60. 310.10 winning tickets. JR

478 WOLVERHAMPTON (A.W) (L-H)
Wednesday, February 21
OFFICIAL GOING: Standard

511 BOOK ONLINE AT WOLVERHAMPTON-RACECOURSE.CO.UK MAIDEN STKS 5f 20y(P)
2:20 (2:20) (Class 5) 3-Y-O+ **£2,817** (£838; £418; £209) **Stalls** Low

Form RPR

5-42 **1** **Drifting Gold**[19] [336] 3-8-8 68....(b[1]) AdamKirby 5 77+
(C G Cox) *sn led: clr 3f out: rdn over 1f out: unchal* **10/11**[1]

04-3 **2** *6* **Ellablue**[48] [36] 3-8-8 62.... ChrisCatlin 3 55
(Rae Guest) *led early: chsd wnr: rdn over 1f out: no imp* **9/2**[3]

30-3 **3** *nk* **Tang**[46] [54] 3-8-1 58.... JackDean(7) 7 54
(W G M Turner) *chsd ldrs: hung rt and rn wd fr over 3f out tl wl over 1f out: kpt on same pce fnl f* **9/1**

06- **4** *8* **Our Georgia**[76] [6738] 4-9-8.... PhillipMakin 2 32
(T D Barron) *hld up: rdn wl over 1f out: sn struggling* **66/1**

3-22 **5** *1 1/2* **Ceredig**[11] [421] 4-9-13 58....(t) EddieAhern 4 31
(W R Muir) *s.i.s: hld up: rdn wl over 1f out: a in rr* **11/4**[2]

62.19 secs (-0.63) **Going Correction** -0.025s/f (Stan)
WFA 3 from 4yo+ 14lb **5** Ran SP% **108.7**
Speed ratings (Par 103):104,94,93,81,78
CSF £5.28 TOTE £1.80: £1.10, £1.90; EX 5.30.
Owner Martin C Oliver **Bred** Witney And Warren Enterprises Ltd **Trained** Lambourn, Berks

FOCUS
A weakly contested maiden that soon developed into a procession. Drifting Gold was impressive and thr race could have been rated up to 6lb higher.
Our Georgia Official explanation: trainer's representative said filly bled from the nose
Ceredig Official explanation: jockey said gelding lost left front shoe and missed the break

512 PONTIN'S FAMILY HOLIDAYS CLAIMING STKS 5f 216y(P)
2:50 (2:50) (Class 6) 3-Y-O **£3,412** (£1,007; £504) **Stalls** Low

Form RPR

45-1 **1** **River Prince**[32] [194] 3-9-7 61.... DaneO'Neill 3 70
(A B Haynes) *a.p: rdn wl over 1f out: led ins fnl f: r.o* **7/2**[3]

5-44 **2** *1 1/4* **Strike Force**[9] [446] 3-9-0 66....(p) MichaelJStainton(5) 1 64
(R A Harris) *led after 1f: rdn wl over 1f out: hdd and nt qckn ins fnl f* **15/8**[1]

55-2 **3** *3/4* **Power Alert**[13] [390] 3-8-4 50....(p) RichardKingscote(3) 2 50
(B R Millman) *hld up in mid-div: hdwy on ins 2f out: sn rdn: hung lft ins fnl f: r.o* **7/1**

46-5 **4** *1 3/4* **Slipasearcher (IRE)**[19] [336] 3-8-7 61 ow2....(b) StephenDonohoe(3) 4 48
(P D Evans) *hld up in mid-div: swtchd rt over 1f out: sn rdn: late hdwy on outside: nrst fin* **5/2**[2]

20-6 **5** *1/2* **Birdie Birdie**[19] [335] 3-8-2 53....(v[1]) PaulHanagan 9 38
(R A Fahey) *sn outpcd: hdwy 1f out: no further prog* **16/1**

3-00 **6** *hd* **Head To Head (IRE)**[12] [404] 3-8-13 52.... AdamKirby 6 49
(Peter Grayson) *led 1f: w ldr: rdn and ev ch over 2f out: edgd lft 1f out: wknd wl ins fnl f* **50/1**

0- **7** *1 1/2* **Hit The Road (IRE)**[88] [6591] 3-9-2.... BarrySavage(7) 8 54
(Michael McElhone, Ire) *sn bhd: rdn over 3f out: no rspnse* **50/1**

6-40 **8** *nk* **Pat Will (IRE)**[23] [295] 3-7-9 50....(b) BernadetteQuinn(7) 7 32
(P D Evans) *broke wl: sn stdd: t.k.h: hdwy over 3f out: c wd st: wknd wl over 1f out* **33/1**

00-6 **9** *3/4* **Avoncreek**[26] [253] 3-9-3 50.... PhillipMakin 5 45
(B P J Baugh) *prom: rdn over 2f out: wknd wl over 1f out* **33/1**

1m 16.84s (1.03) **Going Correction** -0.025s/f (Stan) **9** Ran SP% **113.8**
Speed ratings (Par 95):92,90,89,87,86 86,84,83,82
CSF £10.07 TOTE £5.20: £2.00, £1.10, £2.30; EX 13.90 Trifecta £33.00 Pool £421.12 - 9.05 winning unit..The winner was claimed by M Khan for £12,000.
Owner Abacus Employment Services Ltd **Bred** Mrs A F Horsington **Trained** Limpley Stoke, Bath

FOCUS
A slightly stronger than avaerage three-year-old claimer, run 1.9sec slower than the following handicap. Few got involved from off the pace. The form has been rated through the runner-up but is not entirely convincing.

513 PONTIN'S BOOK EARLY H'CAP 5f 216y(P)
3:20 (3:20) (Class 5) (0-75,75) 4-Y-O+ **£3,238** (£963; £481; £240) **Stalls** Low

Form RPR

00-6 **1** **Cornus**[20] [323] 5-8-6 **65** ow1....(be[1]) DeanMcKeown 10 79
(A J McCabe) *s.i.s: hdwy on ins over 2f out: rdn over 1f out: r.o to ld nr fin* **25/1**

-000 **2** *1/2* **Garstang**[8] [452] 4-9-2 **75**....(b) GeorgeBaker 11 88
(Peter Grayson) *hld up and bhd: hdwy on ins 3f out: led wl over 1f out: sn rdn: hdd nr fin* **14/1**

2111 **3** *5* **Canadian Danehill (IRE)**[16] [368] 5-9-2 **75**....(p) NCallan 8 73+
(R M H Cowell) *hld up towards rr: hmpd over 3f out: hdwy wl over 1f out: kpt on ins fnl f* **3/1**[1]

2030 **4** *nk* **Mistral Sky**[16] [361] 8-8-8 **67**....(v) PaulHanagan 6 64
(Stef Liddiard) *a.p: rdn and one pce fnl 2f* **25/1**

10-3 **5** *hd* **Le Chiffre (IRE)**[23] [300] 5-8-5 **64**....(b) PaulFessey 3 60
(K R Burke) *led: hdd wl over 1f out: sn rdn: wknd fnl f* **5/1**[2]

0-12 **6** *3/4* **George The Second**[16] [361] 4-8-6 **68**.... RichardKingscote(3) 12 62
(Mrs H Sweeting) *broke wl: sn mid-div: hdwy on outside 2f out: rdn over 1f out: one pce* **10/1**

-010 **7** *hd* **Mozakhraf (USA)**[16] [361] 5-8-6 **65**.... CatherineGannon 1 58
(K A Ryan) *prom tl rdn and wknd wl over 1f out* **9/1**[3]

2-15 **8** *1/2* **Charlie Delta**[33] [183] 4-8-10 **69**....(p) EddieAhern 9 61+
(J R Boyle) *bhd: nt clr run and swtchd rt over 3f out: nvr nr ldrs* **12/1**

53-0 **9** *hd* **Supercast (IRE)**[11] [424] 4-8-3 **65**....(t) LiamJones(3) 2 56
(W M Brisbourne) *t.k.h: prom 3f* **10/1**

-100 **10** *3/4* **Dvinsky (USA)**[16] [367] 6-8-8 **67**.... ChrisCatlin 13 56
(P Howling) *outpcd* **50/1**

6-66 **11** *nk* **Sailor King (IRE)**[16] [361] 5-9-0 **73**.... RobertHavlin 7 61
(D K Ivory) *broke wl: sn mid-div: bmpd over 3f out: n.d after* **12/1**

0216 **12** *1* **Cerebus**[6] [467] 5-8-6 **65**....(bt) ShaneKelly 4 50
(A J McCabe) *s.s: sn chsng ldrs: bmpd over 3f out: sn lost pl* **16/1**

5100 **13** *1 1/2* **Hollow Jo**[25] [261] 7-9-2 **75**.... MickyFenton 5 55
(J R Jenkins) *prom tl wknd over 1f out* **9/1**[3]

1m 14.94s (-0.87) **Going Correction** -0.025s/f (Stan) **13** Ran SP% **117.4**
Speed ratings (Par 103):104,103,96,96,96 95,94,94,93,92 92,91,89
CSF £330.73 CT £1366.14 TOTE £28.40: £8.90, £5.20, £1.40; EX 896.80 TRIFECTA Not won..
Owner Paul J Dixon **Bred** G Russell **Trained** Babworth, Notts

FOCUS
A fair and competitive sprint run 1.9sec faster than the preceding three-year-old claimer. The first two finished clear of the unlucky-in-running third and the form has been rated positively.
Canadian Danehill(IRE) Official explanation: jockey said horse suffered interference going into the bend
Le Chiffre(IRE) Official explanation: jockey said gelding bled from the nose
Cerebus Official explanation: jockey said mare suffered interference in running
Hollow Jo Official explanation: jockey said gelding finished distressed

514 PONTINSBINGO.COM (S) STKS 1m 4f 50y(P)
3:50 (3:50) (Class 6) 4-Y-O+ **£2,047** (£604; £302) **Stalls** Low

Form RPR

-111 **1** **Atlantic Gamble (IRE)**[5] [481] 7-9-5 56....(p) PhillipMakin 11 69+
(K R Burke) *hld up in tch: wnt 2nd over 5f out: led on bit over 2f out: sn clr: easily* **5/4**[1]

16-6 **2** *4* **Regency Red (IRE)**[5] [481] 9-9-5 53.... ShaneKelly 9 59
(W M Brisbourne) *s.i.s: hld up and bhd: hdwy over 3f out: rdn over 2f out: kpt on to take 2nd wl ins fnl f: no ch w wnr* **10/1**[3]

00-0 **3** *4* **Blue Quiver (IRE)**[11] [416] 7-9-0 48.... PaulEddery 7 48
(C A Horgan) *hld up and bhd: hdwy over 3f out: rdn to chse wnr 2f out: no imp: wknd wl ins fnl f* **25/1**

40-6 **4** *1 1/4* **Daneway**[16] [365] 4-8-4 53 ow1....(b) EmmettStack(3) 5 42
(P Howling) *hld up towards rr: hdwy over 5f out: rdn over 2f out: wknd 1f out* **40/1**

01-0 **5** *2* **Saameq (IRE)**[16] [369] 6-9-2 53.... JamesDoyle(3) 3 47
(D W Thompson) *hld up and bhd: hdwy over 3f out: sn rdn: wknd wl over 1f out* **12/1**

60-0 **6** *4* **Prince Vector**[18] [340] 5-9-0 78....(v) DaneO'Neill 1 36
(A King) *led: clr over 6f out: rdn and hdd over 2f out: sn wknd* **13/8**[2]

0/0- **7** *15* **Wizardmicktee (IRE)**[229] [3240] 5-9-0 35....(p) CatherineGannon 6 12
(D G Bridgwater) *t.k.h: chsd ldr 5f: wkng whn n.m.r on ins over 3f out* **100/1**

/0-0 **8** *5* **Caliban (IRE)**[39] [126] 9-9-0 36....(v) FergusSweeney 4 4
(Ian Williams) *hld up in tch: lost pl over 5f out: sn bhd* **80/1**

160/ **9** *10* **Prairie Law (GER)**[318] [5008] 7-9-0 50....(e[1]) ChrisCatlin 10 —
(B N Pollock) *hld up in mid-div: rdn 5f out: bhd fnl 4f* **33/1**

-240 **10** *nk* **Jiminor Mack**[25] [271] 4-8-4 43 ow1.... RichardKingscote(3) 8 —
(W J H Ratcliffe) *hld up towards rr: rdn 5f out: sn struggling* **33/1**

00-0 **11** *13* **Burning Moon**[10] [431] 6-8-11 55.... LiamJones(3) 12 —
(S W Hall) *prom: chsd ldr 7f out tl wknd over 5f out* **66/1**

2m 41.94s (-0.48) **Going Correction** -0.025s/f (Stan)
WFA 4 from 5yo+ 3lb **11** Ran SP% **115.2**
Speed ratings (Par 101):100,97,94,93,92 89,79,76,69,69 60
CSF £13.98 TOTE £2.20: £1.10, £2.40, £3.70; EX 13.50 Trifecta £84.00 Pool £262.85 - 2.22 winning units..The winner was bought in for 8,500gns.
Owner R G Greaney **Bred** Larry Ryan **Trained** Middleham Moor, N Yorks
■ Stewards' Enquiry : Liam Jones two-day ban: careless riding (Mar 5,6)

FOCUS
A run-of the mill and uncompetitive seller in which they went 10/1 bar two. Atlantic Gamble impressed in completing a four-timer and the form looks fairly sound.

515 PONTINS.COM H'CAP 1m 5f 194y(P)
4:20 (4:20) (Class 5) (0-75,74) 4-Y-0+ £3,412 (£1,007; £504) Stalls Low

Form RPR
-101 1 **Wild Pitch**[9] 444 6-9-5 **74**....(b) JackMitchell(7) 6 94+
(P Mitchell) *hld up towards rr: hdwy over 3f out: led 2f out: shaken up and clr over 1f out: easily* **13/2**[3]
1-40 2 7 **Ross Moor**[19] 332 5-9-5 **70**.... JamesDoyle(3) 9 77
(N P Littmoden) *hld up towards rr: hdwy 3f out: sn rdn: tk 2nd wl ins fnl f: no ch w wnr* **10/1**
-123 3 1 **Share The Feeling (IRE)**[10] 434 5-9-7 **72**.... RichardKingscote(3) 3 78
(J W Unett) *chsd ldr: rdn to ld 3f out: hdd 2f out: sn btn* **11/4**[1]
4622 4 2 **Dovedon Hero**[19] 332 7-9-5 **67**....(p) SebSanders 7 70
(P J McBride) *hld up and bhd: rdn and hdwy 2f out: styd on fnl f: nvr nrr* **13/2**[3]
041/ 5 hd **Alrida (IRE)**[913] 4226 8-9-6 **68**.... PaulHanagan 2 71
(R A Fahey) *hld up in mid-div: hdwy on ins over 3f out: rdn and one pce fnl 2f* **25/1**
440- 6 5 **Greyside (USA)**[33] 4549 4-9-5 **72**.... PaulMulrennan 4 68
(C A Mulhall) *hld up towards rr: rdn 5f out: short-lived effrt on ins over 2f out* **100/1**
060- 7 11 **Supreme Charter**[85] 6647 4-9-0 **67**.... NCallan 5 47
(E S McMahon) *hld up in mid-div: rdn over 3f out: wknd over 2f out* **16/1**
231- 8 hd **Soulard (USA)**[224] 3399 4-9-7 **74**....(b[1]) ShaneKelly 10 54
(J L Spearing) *t.k.h: led: rdn and hdd 3f out: wknd 2f out* **33/1**
21-2 9 1 1/2 **Little Richard (IRE)**[30] 220 8-8-12 **60**....(p) AdamKirby 1 38
(M Wellings) *hld up in tch: rdn 4f out: wknd over 2f out* **6/1**[2]
50-6 10 6 **Easy Laughter (IRE)**[39] 117 6-9-1 **63**.... DaneO'Neill 8 32
(A King) *prom: rdn 5f out: wknd over 3f out* **10/1**
40-6 11 17 **Caraman (IRE)**[23] 297 9-9-2 **64**.... GrahamGibbons 12 10
(J J Quinn) *hld up in tch: rdn 5f out: wknd over 3f out* **9/1**
4-55 12 3/4 **Always Baileys (IRE)**[30] 215 4-8-9 **62**.... ChrisCatlin 11 6
(T Wall) *hld up towards rr: rdn over 6f out: no rspnse* **25/1**

3m 3.60s (-3.77) **Going Correction** -0.025s/f (Stan)
WFA 4 from 5yo+ 5lb **12** Ran SP% **113.3**
Speed ratings (Par 103):109,105,104,103,103 100,94,93,93,89 79,79
CSF £64.14 CT £218.79 TOTE £8.10: £1.80, £4.00, £1.70; EX 85.40 Trifecta £217.90 Part won. Pool £307.04 - 0.20 winning units..
Owner Mrs Julie Auletta **Bred** Wyck Hall Stud Ltd **Trained** Epsom, Surrey

FOCUS
A decent winning time for a race of its class with Wild Pitch turning it into a procession. There is more to come from him, with the form looking solid enough.

516 PONTIN'S HOLIDAYS H'CAP 7f 32y(P)
4:50 (4:50) (Class 6) (0-65,64) 4-Y-0+ £2,388 (£705; £352) Stalls High

Form RPR
065- 1 **Zarabad (IRE)**[56] 6952 5-9-1 **63**.... PhillipMakin 2 78+
(K R Burke) *chsd ldr early: a.p: led jst ins fnl f: rdn and r.o* **13/2**[2]
6316 2 3/4 **Harare**[11] 426 6-8-9 **60**....(b) JamesDoyle(3) 8 71
(R J Price) *sn chsng ldr: rdn to ld jst over 1f out: hdd jst ins fnl f: edgd lft towards fin: kpt on* **9/1**
0313 3 1 1/2 **Cool Sands (IRE)**[6] 468 5-9-1 **63**....(v) DaneO'Neill 5 70
(D Shaw) *broke wl: sn stdd: rdn and hdwy on ins wl over 1f out: sn swtchd rt: r.o ins fnl f* **9/2**[1]
05-1 4 3/4 **Mountain Pass (USA)**[28] 235 5-8-11 **59**....(p) RobertHavlin 7 64
(B J Llewellyn) *hld up towards rr: hdwy over 2f out: rdn over 1f out: kpt on same pce fnl f* **7/1**[3]
1-02 5 shd **Haroldini (IRE)**[6] 463 5-8-9 **60**....(p) JasonEdmunds(3) 9 65
(J Balding) *hld up in tch: rdn over 2f out: edgd lft over 1f out: one pce* **9/2**[1]
60-0 6 2 **Marmooq**[16] 366 4-9-1 **63**....(v[1]) JimCrowley 3 63
(J Gallagher) *led: rdn over 2f out: hdd jst over 1f out: wknd ins fnl f* **8/1**
210- 7 1 1/2 **Ebraam (USA)**[131] 5937 4-9-2 **64**.... DeanMcKeown 6 60
(D Shaw) *t.k.h in mid-div: no hdwy fnl 2f* **11/1**
-365 8 1 **Bond Playboy**[16] 368 7-8-10 **63**....(v) DuranFentiman(5) 1 56
(G R Oldroyd) *hld up and bhd: rdn over 2f out: no rspnse* **8/1**
0341 9 1/2 **Carcinetto (IRE)**[5] 485 5-8-10 **61** 6ex.... StephenDonohoe(3) 12 53
(P D Evans) *prom tl rdn and wknd over 2f out* **9/1**
610- 10 1 1/4 **Katie Lawson (IRE)**[180] 4757 4-9-0 **62**....(b[1]) SteveDrowne 11 51
(D Haydn Jones) *rdn over 3f out: a bhd* **40/1**

1m 30.2s (-0.20) **Going Correction** -0.025s/f (Stan) **10** Ran SP% **115.2**
Speed ratings (Par 101):100,99,97,96,96 94,92,91,90,89
CSF £62.82 CT £296.99 TOTE £6.00: £1.70, £3.30, £1.70; EX 66.90 TRIFECTA Not won..
Owner Mrs Maura Gittins **Bred** His Highness The Aga Khan's Studs S C **Trained** Middleham Moor, N Yorks

FOCUS
An open-looking handicap. The form seems sound enough, rated through the second.

517 GO PONTIN'S H'CAP (DIV I) 1m 141y(P)
5:20 (5:20) (Class 6) (0-52,52) 4-Y-0+ £1,706 (£503; £252) Stalls Low

Form RPR
4-55 1 **Postmaster**[9] 440 5-8-8 **46** oh1.... ChrisCatlin 10 56
(R Ingram) *hld up and bhd: hdwy on ins over 2f out: nt clr run briefly wl over 1f out: led ins fnl f: r.o* **11/2**[3]
0-00 2 1 **Machinate (USA)**[12] 402 5-8-9 **47**.... ShaneKelly 4 55
(W M Brisbourne) *hld up towards rr: hdwy over 3f out: rdn to ld over 1f out: hdd and nt qckn ins fnl f* **15/2**
-250 3 1 3/4 **Show Me The Lolly (FR)**[24] 274 7-8-4 **47**.... DuranFentiman(5) 9 51
(P J McBride) *hld up towards rr: hdwy over 1f out: sn hung lft: one pce* **13/2**
-050 4 1 3/4 **Desert Lover (IRE)**[9] 447 5-8-9 **52**....(t) TolleyDean(5) 1 53
(R J Price) *led early: prom: rdn over 2f out: wknd ins fnl f* **15/2**
0000 5 nk **Shadow Jumper (IRE)**[8] 448 6-8-9 **47**....(v) MickyFenton 7 47
(J T Stimpson) *hld up: rdn and hdwy 3f out: wknd over 1f out* **20/1**
06-0 6 2 **Miss Glory Be**[25] 266 9-8-5 **46** oh1....(p) EmmettStack(3) 3 42
(Ernst Oertel) *hld up in tch: rdn and wknd over 2f out* **40/1**
3-53 7 9 **Solicitude**[19] 334 4-8-13 **51**....(b) RobertHavlin 8 28
(D Haydn Jones) *prom: led over 3f out: rdn and hdd over 1f out: wkng whn sn bmpd: eased whn btn ins fnl f* **10/3**[1]
0-51 8 1 1/2 **Deneuve**[30] 210 4-8-9 **50**....(b) JerryO'Dwyer(3) 5 24
(M G Quinlan) *hld up: in tch: rdn whn n.m.r and bmpd jst over 3f out: wknd wl over 1f out: eased whn no ch fnl f* **15/2**
0-30 9 21 **Neshla**[12] 402 4-8-10 **48**....(p) SebSanders 2 —
(C E Brittain) *rdn to sn ld: rdn and hdd over 3f out: wkng whn hmpd over 2f out* **9/2**[2]

1m 51.54s (-0.22) **Going Correction** -0.025s/f (Stan) **9** Ran SP% **112.5**
Speed ratings (Par 101):99,98,96,95,94 92,84,83,64
CSF £44.68 CT £272.40 TOTE £6.20: £1.30, £3.00, £3.00; EX 63.90 TRIFECTA Not won..
Owner Cricketers Club Racing Group **Bred** Juddmonte Farms **Trained** Epsom, Surrey

FOCUS
This modest handicap was marginally faster than the following division. The winner is rated to last year's best.

518 GO PONTIN'S H'CAP (DIV II) 1m 141y(P)
5:50 (5:50) (Class 6) (0-52,52) 4-Y-0+ £1,706 (£503; £252) Stalls Low

Form RPR
00-0 1 **Cankara (IRE)**[14] 383 4-8-7 **48** oh1 ow2.... StephenDonohoe(3) 3 57
(D Carroll) *hld up in mid-div: hdwy on ins over 2f out: sn rdn: led ins fnl f: drvn out* **33/1**
-043 2 3/4 **Wodhill Schnaps**[13] 393 6-8-9 **47**....(v) ChrisCatlin 7 54
(D Morris) *hld up in mid-div: rdn and hdwy 2f out: r.o ins fnl f* **7/2**[2]
-621 3 1 **Et Dona Ferentes**[13] 393 4-8-13 **51**.... PhillipMakin 5 56
(T D Barron) *a.p: rdn to ld 1f out: hung rt and hdd ins fnl f: nt qckn* **7/4**[1]
4050 4 hd **Bathwick Emma (IRE)**[11] 425 4-8-6 **47**....(p) JamesDoyle(3) 1 51
(M A Doyle) *led early: a.p: rdn over 2f out: kpt on ins fnl f* **14/1**
50-4 5 3 **Keon (IRE)**[36] 144 5-8-9 **52**.... RussellKennemore(5) 4 50
(R Hollinshead) *t.k.h: sn led: rdn and hdd over 1f out: wkng whn edgd rt wl ins fnl f* **11/2**[3]
6-21 6 1/2 **Weet Yer Tern (IRE)**[17] 350 5-8-12 **50**....(v) ShaneKelly 6 47
(W M Brisbourne) *stdd s: c wd st: nvr trbld ldrs* **13/2**
-020 7 3/4 **Crusoe (IRE)**[6] 464 10-8-1 **46** oh1....(b) SoniaEaton(7) 2 42
(A Sadik) *nvr nr ldrs* **40/1**
34-0 8 8 **Tartan Special**[42] 94 5-8-10 **48**.... LeeEnstone 10 27
(K R Burke) *prom tl rdn and wknd 2f out* **16/1**
05-0 9 5 **Cumberland Road**[36] 156 4-8-5 **46** oh1....(p) DominicFox(3) 9 14
(C A Mulhall) *hld up and bhd: rdn 3f out: sn struggling* **80/1**
0-45 10 1/2 **Stoneacre Fred (IRE)**[36] 156 4-8-11 **49**.... AdamKirby 8 16
(Peter Grayson) *hld up in mid-div: rdn 3f out: sn bhd* **8/1**

1m 51.71s (-0.05) **Going Correction** -0.025s/f (Stan) **10** Ran SP% **117.6**
Speed ratings (Par 101):99,98,97,97,94 94,93,86,81,81
CSF £146.36 CT £322.14 TOTE £30.40: £8.80, £1.70, £1.80; EX 316.10 Trifecta £488.50 Part won. Pool: £688.12 - 0.20 winning units. Place 6 £21.91, Place 5 £14.77 .
Owner Diamond Racing Ltd **Bred** Skymarc Farm And Castlemartin Stud **Trained** Sledmere, E Yorks
■ Stewards' Enquiry : Stephen Donohoe one-day ban: used whip with excessive frequency (Mar 5)

FOCUS
Another moderate affair a shade slower than the previous division.
T/Plt: £17.80 to a £1 stake. Pool: £77,267.50. 3,163.25 winning tickets. T/Qpdt: £9.60 to a £1 stake. Pool: £5,221.40. 401.90 winning tickets. KH

503 SOUTHWELL (L-H)
Thursday, February 22

OFFICIAL GOING: Standard
Wind: Light across Weather: Overcast with the odd spot of rain

519 PONTIN'S HOLIDAYS H'CAP (DIV I) 7f (F)
1:50 (1:51) (Class 6) (0-50,54) 4-Y-0+ £1,706 (£503; £252) Stalls Low

Form RPR
0-01 1 **Doctor's Cave**[10] 440 5-9-2 **54** 6ex....(b) SteveDrowne 6 72
(K O Cunningham-Brown) *mde all: edgd rt over 1f out: pushed clr fnl f* **9/1**
2453 2 4 **Seldemosa**[10] 440 6-8-10 **48**....(v[1]) RobertHavlin 14 55
(M S Saunders) *hld up: hdwy 2f out: rdn to chse wnr fnl f: no imp* **12/1**
4-13 3 2 **Wodhill Be**[16] 374 7-8-11 **49**.... ShaneKelly 13 51
(D Morris) *hld up in tch: hmpd 2f out: sn rdn: styd on same pce* **8/1**
2601 4 1/2 **Mid Valley**[11] 435 4-8-13 **51** 6ex....(v) NCallan 8 52
(J R Jenkins) *mid-div: hdwy over 2f out: nt trble ldrs* **7/2**[1]
-035 5 1 **Danethorpe (IRE)**[11] 430 4-8-8 **46** oh1....(v) CatherineGannon 4 44
(D Shaw) *trckd ldrs: plld hrd: rdn and hung lft 2f out: wknd fnl f* **33/1**
2-52 6 1 **Favouring (IRE)**[11] 430 5-8-6 **47**....(v) AndrewMullen(3) 2 43
(M C Chapman) *s.i.s: sn prom: rdn 1/2-way: wknd fnl f* **11/2**[2]
5004 7 1 3/4 **Hometomammy**[7] 462 5-8-8 **46** oh1.... ChrisCatlin 11 37
(P W Hiatt) *chsd ldrs over 4f* **25/1**
4026 8 1/2 **Rocky Reppin**[16] 374 7-8-5 **46** oh1....(b) JasonEdmunds(3) 3 36
(J Balding) *s.i.s: hdwy 5f out: wknd over 1f out* **25/1**
-020 9 1 1/2 **Nevinstown (IRE)**[11] 430 7-8-8 **46** oh1.... DaleGibson 12 32
(C Grant) *s.i.s: sn drvn along in rr: n.d* **28/1**
3032 10 3/4 **Penel (IRE)**[9] 450 6-8-7 **50**....(p) RoryMoore(5) 9 34
(P T Midgley) *hld up: rdn 1/2-way: n.d* **7/1**[3]
6613 11 hd **Pawn In Life (IRE)**[11] 435 9-8-8 **46**....(v) JamieSpencer 7 29
(S Parr) *sn pushed along in rr: rdn 1/2-way: n.d* **10/1**
-004 12 7 **Gem Bien (USA)**[11] 435 9-8-1 **46** oh1....(b) KellyHarrison(7) 10 11
(D W Chapman) *s.i.s: sn outpcd* **20/1**
-046 13 1 **Blue Knight (IRE)**[10] 447 8-8-12 **50**....(v) TonyCulhane 5 12
(P Howling) *chsd ldrs: lost pl 5f out: wknd 3f out* **12/1**
-000 14 2 **Savile's Delight (IRE)**[9] 448 8-8-12 **50**....(bt) EdwardCreighton 1 7
(Miss Joanne Priest) *chsd wnr tl rdn over 2f out: wknd over 1f out* **40/1**

1m 29.94s (-0.86) **Going Correction** -0.20s/f (Stan) **14** Ran SP% **117.0**
Speed ratings (Par 101):96,91,89,88,87 86,84,83,82,81 80,72,71,69
CSF £98.79 CT £932.09 TOTE £9.60: £3.50, £5.30, £3.00; EX 117.60 Trifecta £262.20 Part won. Pool £369.36 - 0.20 winning units..
Owner A J Richards & Michael A Richards **Bred** Tweenhills Stud And Genesis Green Stud **Trained** Nether Wallop, Hants

FOCUS
A modest handicap which few got into. Solid form for the grade, Doctor's Cave back to last year's best. The winning time was fractionally faster than the second division.

520 PONTINSBINGO.COM H'CAP 6f (F)
2:20 (2:21) (Class 5) (0-75,74) 3-Y-O £3,238 (£963; £481; £240) Stalls Low

Form RPR
42-1 1 **Imprimis Tagula (IRE)**[2] 505 3-9-7 **71** 7ex.... SamHitchcott 11 79+
(A Bailey) *hld up: hdwy over 2f out: rdn to ld over 1f out: r.o* **3/1**[2]
1304 2 1 1/4 **Cherri Fosfate**[2] 510 3-9-4 **69**....(v) DanielTudhope 10 73
(D Carroll) *hld up: hdwy over 2f out: rdn over 1f out: hung rt ins fnl f: r.o* **11/2**[3]
2-43 3 1 1/2 **Pirner's Brig**[24] 295 3-8-6 **64**.... NSLawes(7) 3 64
(M W Easterby) *chsd ldrs: led over 2f out: rdn and hdd over 1f out: no ex ins fnl f* **20/1**

53-5 **4** *1 1/2* **Krakatau (FR)**[50] [17] 3-8-8 **59**........ ChrisCatlin 7 54+
(D J Wintle) *prom: lost pl 4f out: styd on fr over 1f out: nt trble ldrs* **14/1**

3-1 **5** *3 1/2* **Fairnilee**[39] [127] 3-9-2 **67**........ SebSanders 1 52
(Sir Mark Prescott) *led 5f out: rdn: hung lft and hdd over 2f out: wknd fnl f* **6/4**[1]

05-6 **6** *shd* **Brean Dot Com (IRE)**[37] [149] 3-8-8 **59**........ RobertHavlin 8 43
(Mrs P N Dutfield) *s.i.s: outpcd: nvr nrr* **28/1**

6-63 **7** *nk* **Lawyer To World**[22] [312] 3-8-3 **61**........(b) KirstyMilczarek(7) 2 44
(N A Callaghan) *slwoly into stride: hdwy over 4f out: rdn over 2f out: sn hung lft and wknd* **20/1**

4-22 **8** *1/2* **Diminuto**[14] [387] 3-8-7 **65**........ FrankiePickard(7) 5 47
(M D I Usher) *chsd ldrs 4f* **20/1**

315- **9** *3* **Bahamian Love**[103] [6444] 3-8-13 **64**........ JamieSpencer 4 37
(B W Hills) *led 1f: remained handy tl rdn and wknd over 1f out* **11/2**[3]

1m 16.42s (-0.48) **Going Correction** -0.20s/f (Stan) **9** Ran SP% **120.2**
Speed ratings (Par 97):95,93,91,89,84 84,84,83,79
CSF £19.43 CT £287.82 TOTE £4.10: £1.10, £2.10, £4.50; EX 29.30 Trifecta £304.80 Pool: £518.30 - 1.21 winning units..
Owner N Davies,J McMahon,S Costello,P Donlan **Bred** Glashare House Stud **Trained** Newmarket, Suffolk

FOCUS
An ordinary handicap though the winner Imprimis Tagula travelled better than the bare form and looks progressive. The placed form looks pretty sound. As in the first race, it appeared that those who came centre-to-stands' side in the straight were at an advantage.

521 PONTIN'S BOOK EARLY H'CAP 5f (F)
2:50 (2:52) (Class 6) (0-65,66) 4-Y-0+ **£2,388** (£705; £352) **Stalls** High

Form RPR

5314 **1** **Egyptian Lord**[7] [465] 4-8-12 **59**........(b) RobbieFitzpatrick 10 73
(Peter Grayson) *s.i.s: sn trcking ldrs: rdn to ld over 1f out: hung lft ins fnl f: r.o u.p* **8/1**[3]

-433 **2** *3* **Garlogs**[7] [465] 4-8-9 **56**........ ChrisCatlin 9 60
(A Bailey) *w ldrs: rdn over 1f out: sn hung lft: styd on same pce* **9/2**[2]

00-3 **3** *1 1/2* **Royal Orissa**[17] [371] 5-8-12 **59**........ RobertHavlin 7 58
(D Haydn Jones) *prom: lost pl over 3f out: styd on ins fnl f* **9/1**

2006 **4** *1 1/4* **Lady Bahia (IRE)**[17] [368] 6-8-7 **57**........(b) JerryO'Dwyer(3) 6 51
(Peter Grayson) *s.i.s: hdwy over 1f out: wknd ins fnl f* **25/1**

1051 **5** *1/2* **Hamaasy**[7] [463] 6-9-5 **66** 7ex........ AdrianTNicholls 1 59
(D Nicholls) *chsd ldrs: rdn 1/2-way: wknd fnl f* **6/4**[1]

-602 **6** *1 1/2* **Hornpipe**[7] [465] 5-8-10 **57**........(v) AdrianMcCarthy 8 45
(M S Saunders) *w ldrs: rdn 1/2-way: hung lft over1f out: sn wknd* **9/2**[2]

2060 **7** *1* **Maktavish**[7] [465] 8-9-4 **65**........(p) PhillipMakin 2 49
(R Brotherton) *mde most over 3f: wknd fnl f* **14/1**

-150 **8** *1 1/2* **Pride Of Joy**[17] [368] 4-9-1 **62**........(p) DaneO'Neill 4 41
(D K Ivory) *w ldrs 3f: rdn and wknd fnl f* **33/1**

3-00 **9** *1 1/2* **Mystery Pips**[21] [317] 7-8-5 **52**........(v) KimTinkler 11 26
(N Tinkler) *chsd ldrs 3f* **40/1**

60.31 secs (0.01) **Going Correction** -0.025s/f (Stan) **9** Ran SP% **113.4**
Speed ratings (Par 101):98,93,90,88,88 85,84,81,79
CSF £42.23 CT £330.71 TOTE £9.00: £1.70, £1.50, £2.80; EX 28.20 Trifecta £119.70 Pool: £374.53 - 2.22 winning units..
Owner D & R Rhodes & Mrs S Grayson **Bred** I A N Wight And Mrs D M Wight **Trained** Formby, Lancs

FOCUS
Not a strong sprint, run in a slower time than the later Class 7 classified event, and it was eventually turned into a procession by the winner who enjoyed the run of the race chasing the pace. It is doubtful he improve as the bare form might suggest. As is usually the case over this straight five, the centre of the track was the place to be.
Hamaasy Official explanation: jockey said gelding hung right throughout

522 GO PONTIN'S MEDIAN AUCTION MAIDEN STKS 1m (F)
3:25 (3:26) (Class 6) 3-Y-0 **£2,388** (£705; £352) **Stalls** Low

Form RPR

3 **1** **Lady Gloria**[23] [304] 3-8-12........ J-PGuillambert 5 75
(J G Given) *hld up: hdwy over 3f out: rdn to ld over 1f out: r.o* **9/1**

64 **2** *3* **Title Deed (USA)**[24] [293] 3-9-3........ LPKeniry 4 74
(A P Jarvis) *chsd ldr tl led 3f out: rdn and hdd over 1f out: swished tail and styd on same pce ins fnl f* **7/2**[2]

4-23 **3** *3/4* **Arch Of Titus (IRE)**[24] [301] 3-9-3 75........ JamieSpencer 9 72
(M L W Bell) *s.s: hdwy over 2f out: rdn and hung lft over 1f out: no ex ins fnl f* **6/4**[1]

34-3 **4** *5* **Zelos (IRE)**[8] [460] 3-9-3 70........ ShaneKelly 3 62
(J A Osborne) *led 5f: rdn: carried hd to one side and wknd over 1f out* **5/1**[3]

4 **5** *1/2* **Toms Laughter**[37] [152] 3-9-3........ DaleGibson 6 60
(B Palling) *chsd ldrs: ev ch over 2f out: wknd fnl f* **40/1**

6 *2 1/2* **I Will If You Will** 3-8-12........ NCallan 7 50
(K A Ryan) *chsd ldrs: rdn over 2f out: n.m.r and wknd over 1f out* **14/1**

6-3 **7** *10* **Anne Bonney**[27] [258] 3-8-12........ ChrisCatlin 2 29
(E J O'Neill) *trckd ldrs: plld hrd: rdn and wknd over 2f out* **13/2**

8 *10* **Zil Up** 3-9-3........(t) PhillipMakin 10 13
(S R Bowring) *dwlt: hld up: rdn 1/2-way: wknd over 2f out* **66/1**

1m 42.67s (-1.93) **Going Correction** -0.20s/f (Stan) **8** Ran SP% **112.8**
Speed ratings (Par 95):101,98,97,92,91 89,79,69
CSF £39.45 TOTE £11.20: £2.10, £2.50, £1.10; EX 53.60 Trifecta £164.40 Pool: £560.58 - 2.42 winning units..
Owner M H Tourle **Bred** M H And Mrs G Tourle **Trained** Willoughton, Lincs

FOCUS
Not much strength in depth in this maiden, but there were some big margins separating the runners at the line and the winning time was decent for a race like this. Lady Gloria showed big improvement from her debut but the form looks sound enough.

523 PONTIN'S FAMILY HOLIDAYS CLASSIFIED STKS 5f (F)
3:55 (3:56) (Class 7) 4-Y-0+ **£1,365** (£403; £201) **Stalls** High

Form RPR

1-33 **1** **Dodaa (USA)**[21] [320] 4-9-0 44........ MatthewHenry 2 56+
(N Wilson) *chsd ldrs: led over 3f out: rdn out* **5/2**[1]

0-00 **2** *1/2* **Alistair John**[20] [339] 4-8-11 45........ JasonEdmunds(3) 8 54
(Mrs G S Rees) *s.i.s: hdwy over 3f out: rdn over 1f out: r.o* **12/1**

0-06 **3** *1 1/2* **Estoille**[21] [320] 6-9-0 42........ PaulQuinn 6 49
(Mrs S Lamyman) *chsd ldrs: rdn 1/2-way: styd on same pce fnl f* **12/1**

0-50 **4** *shd* **She's Our Beauty (IRE)**[32] [201] 4-9-0 43........(p) SilvestreDeSousa 12 49
(S T Mason) *led: hdd over 3f out: rdn and edgd lft over 1f out: styd on same pce* **22/1**

4-00 **5** *1 1/2* **Axis Shield (IRE)**[21] [317] 4-9-0 42........ AlanDaly 3 44
(M C Chapman) *wnt rt s: sn chsng ldrs: rdn over 1f out: no ex fnl f* **14/1**

-006 **6** *1 3/4* **Sofinella (IRE)**[13] [403] 4-9-0 45........ SimonWhitworth 1 38
(A W Carroll) *s.i.s: outpcd: nvr nrr* **16/1**

3-60 **7** *shd* **Amanda's Lad (IRE)**[21] [318] 7-9-0 42........ JamieMackay 14 38
(M C Chapman) *hld up: rdn over 1f out: nvr trbld ldrs* **20/1**

0425 **8** *shd* **El Potro**[25] [281] 5-9-0 45........ SamHitchcott 13 37
(J R Holt) *s.i.s: outpcd: styd on ins fnl f: nvr nrr* **3/1**[2]

/500 **9** *3/4* **Ela Figura**[32] [201] 7-9-0 43........ FrankieMcDonald 4 35
(A W Carroll) *hmpd s: sn outpcd: no ch whn edgd rt fnl f* **33/1**

-000 **10** *shd* **Alucica**[10] [440] 4-9-0 45........(v[1]) CatherineGannon 10 34
(D Shaw) *s.i.s: sn outpcd* **40/1**

00-0 **11** *3 1/2* **Boisdale (IRE)**[21] [320] 9-9-0 41........ LeeEnstone 9 22
(P S Felgate) *prom: rdn over 3f out: wknd wl over 1f out* **66/1**

5-05 **12** *nk* **Prime Recreation**[21] [317] 10-9-0 41........ StephenCarson 5 21
(P S Felgate) *chsd ldrs over 3f* **12/1**

0-06 **13** *shd* **Feminist (IRE)**[10] [441] 5-9-0 43........ LPKeniry 7 21
(J M Bradley) *chsd ldrs: rdn 1/2-way: wknd over 1f out* **22/1**

-263 **14** *3 1/2* **Town House**[10] [441] 5-9-0 45........ RichardThomas 11 9
(B P J Baugh) *s.s: outpcd* **6/1**[3]

60.15 secs (-0.15) **Going Correction** -0.025s/f (Stan) **14** Ran SP% **123.8**
Speed ratings (Par 97):100,99,96,96,94 91,91,91,89,89 84,83,83,77
CSF £32.01 TOTE £3.10: £1.50, £3.40, £3.30; EX 57.30 Trifecta £184.50 Pool: £265.11 - 1.02 winning units..
Owner Ian W Glenton and Paul and Linda Dixon **Bred** Silverleaf Farm Inc **Trained** Flaxton, N Yorks

FOCUS
A poor race in which those drawn low to middle held the advantage. A clear personal best from Dodaa and the form looks solid for the grade. The winning time was 0.16 seconds faster than the earlier Class 6 handicap.
Sofinella(IRE) Official explanation: jockey said saddle slipped
Town House Official explanation: jockey said mare reared leaving stalls

524 PONTIN'S HOLIDAYS H'CAP (DIV II) 7f (F)
4:25 (4:28) (Class 6) (0-50,52) 4-Y-0+ **£1,706** (£503; £252) **Stalls** Low

Form RPR

-454 **1** **Christian Bendix**[28] [239] 5-8-8 **46** oh1........(p) ShaneKelly 4 56
(P Howling) *mde all: rdn over 1f out: edgd rt ins fnl f: styd on* **25/1**

-021 **2** *1 1/4* **Astorygoeswithit**[21] [320] 4-8-9 **47**........(be) AdamKirby 6 54
(P S McEntee) *chsd wnr: hrd rdn fr over 2f out: kpt on* **6/1**[3]

-132 **3** *nk* **Comeintothespace (IRE)**[11] [435] 5-8-10 **48**........ DaneO'Neill 5 54
(R A Farrant) *chsd ldrs: rdn over 2f out: styd on* **7/2**[2]

000- **4** *2* **Earthling**[189] [4518] 6-8-8 **46** oh1........(be[1]) PaulQuinn 9 47
(D W Chapman) *sn outpcd: rdn and nt clr run over 2f out: r.o ins fnl f: nrst fin* **40/1**

-063 **5** *hd* **Apex**[10] [447] 6-8-10 **48**........ KimTinkler 2 49
(N Tinkler) *s.i.s: n.m.r 6f out: hdwy 1/2-way: rdn over 2f out: styd on same pce appr fnl f* **9/1**

/003 **6** *1* **Mr Bountiful (IRE)**[9] [450] 9-8-9 **47** oh1 ow1........(bt) AlanDaly 8 45
(C J Teague) *hld up: rdn 3f out: hung lft fnl 2f: nt trble ldrs* **16/1**

-365 **7** *6* **Red Raptor**[14] [393] 6-8-11 **49**........(t) RichardThomas 11 31
(J A Geake) *sn outpcd* **9/1**

600- **8** *3/4* **Government (IRE)**[63] [6892] 6-8-5 **46** oh1........ AndrewMullen(3) 10 26
(M C Chapman) *prom: rdn 1/2-way: wknd over 2f out* **50/1**

-006 **9** *1 1/4* **Drink To Me Only**[20] [339] 4-8-9 **47** ow1........ NCallan 1 24
(J R Weymes) *hld up: hdwy 1/2-way: rdn over 2f out: wknd over 1f out* **22/1**

00-3 **10** *2 1/2* **Boppys Dream**[51] [13] 5-8-8 **46** oh1........(p) MickyFenton 12 17
(P T Midgley) *mid-div: lost pl over 4f out: n.d after* **33/1**

0/00 **11** *5* **Thomas Lawrence (USA)**[25] [276] 6-8-12 **50**.....(v[1]) AdrianMcCarthy 14 8
(M S Saunders) *prom over 4f* **33/1**

0-00 **12** *1/2* **Dallma (IRE)**[12] [426] 4-8-12 **50**........(b) SebSanders 13 6
(C E Brittain) *sn drvn along in rr: bhd fr 1/2-way* **8/1**

6-01 **13** *7* **Wayward Shot (IRE)**[10] [447] 5-9-0 **52** 6ex........(b) PaulMulrennan 3 —
(M W Easterby) *s.i.s: sn drvn along and prom: wknd 1/2-way* **3/1**[1]

00- **14** *1* **First Boy (GER)**[267] [2137] 8-8-12 **50**........ SamHitchcott 7 —
(D J Wintle) *sn outpcd* **20/1**

1m 30.0s (-0.80) **Going Correction** -0.20s/f (Stan) **14** Ran SP% **121.7**
Speed ratings (Par 101):96,94,94,91,91 90,83,82,81,78 72,72,64,63
CSF £161.64 CT £673.15 TOTE £24.80: £4.70, £2.20, £1.60; EX 193.40 Trifecta £360.60 Part won. Pool: £507.97 - 0.71 winning units..
Owner Mrs A K Petersen **Bred** C B Petersen **Trained** Newmarket, Suffolk

FOCUS
A weak heat run at an average pace. The form looks sound enough rated through the placed horses.
Drink To Me Only Official explanation: jockey said gelding had no more to give
Wayward Shot(IRE) Official explanation: jockey said gelding never travelled

525 PONTINS.COM H'CAP 1m (F)
4:55 (4:55) (Class 5) (0-75,74) 4-Y-0+ **£3,238** (£963; £481; £240) **Stalls** Low

Form RPR

0033 **1** **Councellor (FR)**[12] [427] 5-9-2 **74**........(t) MickyFenton 5 86
(Stef Liddiard) *hld up: plld hrd: hdwy over 3f out: led over 1f out: rdn and hung lft ins fnl f: r.o* **3/1**[1]

1264 **2** *1 1/4* **Dudley Docker (IRE)**[12] [424] 5-8-8 **73**........ KellyHarrison(7) 1 82
(D Carroll) *hld up: n.m.r over 4f out: hdwy over 2f out: rdn and ev ch over 1f out: unable qck towards fin* **5/1**[3]

2553 **3** *1/2* **Parkview Love (USA)**[7] [463] 6-8-2 **60**........(v) CatherineGannon 6 68
(D Shaw) *trckd ldrs: led over 3f out: rdn and hdd over 1f out: nt clr run ins fnl f: r.o* **4/1**[2]

00-3 **4** *2* **Namroud (USA)**[9] [451] 8-8-10 **68**........ PaulHanagan 2 72
(R A Fahey) *chsd ldrs: rdn and ev ch 2f out: styd on same pce appr fnl f* **3/1**[1]

2-00 **5** *6* **Mambo Sun**[17] [371] 4-8-4 **62**........ SimonWhitworth 3 53
(P A Blockley) *chsd ldrs: lost pl over 4f out: n.d after* **12/1**

110/ **6** *5* **Camille Pissarro (USA)**[603] [3021] 7-8-3 **61**........ ChrisCatlin 4 42
(D J Wintle) *hld up: wknd over 3f out* **14/1**

0 **7** *2* **Phoenix Factor (IRE)**[26] [263] 4-7-9 **60**........ JosephWalsh(7) 7 36
(J S Moore) *s.i.s: hdwy over 6f out: hung lft and wknd 2f out* **14/1**

0/0- **8** *13* **Ace Baby**[57] [5863] 4-8-10 **68**........(bt[1]) NCallan 8 17
(K J Burke) *sn led: hdd over 3f out: wknd over 2f out* **14/1**

1m 41.54s (-3.06) **Going Correction** -0.20s/f (Stan) **8** Ran SP% **114.4**
Speed ratings (Par 103):107,105,105,103,97 92,90,77
CSF £18.28 CT £60.07 TOTE £3.70: £1.40, £1.50, £2.20; EX 15.70 Trifecta £58.80 Pool: £362.02 - 4.37 winning units. Place 6 £194.56, Place 5 £44.12.
Owner D Gilbert **Bred** Janus Bloodstock & Pontchartrain Stud **Trained** Great Shefford, Berks

FOCUS
A modest handicap, run at a decent clip. The form looks straightforward.
T/Jkpt: Not won. T/Plt: £332.80 to a £1 stake. Pool: £61,287.00. 134.40 winning tickets. T/Qpdt: £10.70 to a £1 stake. Pool: £4,775.10. 327.60 winning tickets. CR

470 NAD AL SHEBA (L-H)

Thursday, February 22

OFFICIAL GOING: Turf course - good; dirt course - fast

526a MASALA CUP (DIRT) 1m 110y
3:30 (3:30) 3-Y-0

£9,183 (£3,061; £1,530; £765; £459; £306)

RPR

1 **Limehouse (SAF)**[13] [414] 4-9-4 95 WCMarwing 2 91+
(M F De Kock, South Africa) *settled in rr: t.k.h: rdn to cl 2 1/2f out: hrd rdn ent fnl f: led ins fnl f* **13/2**[3]

2 1 ¼ **Comandante Xara (BRZ)**[7] [471] 4-9-4 90 (b) ECruz 6 88
(P Nickel Filho, Brazil) *led: clr 4f out: hdd 3 1/2f out: led 1 1/2f out: hdd ins fnl f: kpt on* **40/1**

3 ¼ **Alto Taquari (BRZ)**[13] [410] 4-9-4 95 (b) RichardMullen 7 88
(P Nickel Filho, Brazil) *prom out wd: t.k.h: led 3 1/2f out: ev ch whn hdd 1 1/2f out: one pce* **16/1**

4 5 ¾ **Zorin (BRZ)**[7] [471] 4-9-6 96 ADomingos 8 78
(A Cintra Pereira, Brazil) *trckd ldr on rail: rdn 2 1/2f out: nt qckn* **4/1**[2]

5 2 ½ **Blue Sky God (USA)**[110] 3-8-9 100 (t) LDettori 1 78
(Saeed Bin Suroor) *mid-div: rdn to cl: wd 3 1/2f out: hrd rdn 2f out: no rspnse* **1/2**[1]

6 3 ¼ **Heart Beat (SAF)**[35] [173] 4-9-4 95 TedDurcan 5 65
(S Seemar, UAE) *trckd ldrs: rdn 4f out: wknd* **12/1**

7 3 ¼ **Lucky Ray (ARG)**[6] 4-9-4 70 (v) MartinDwyer 3 58
(Doug Watson, UAE) *racd in rr: nvr involved* **66/1**

8 3 ½ **Basko Hermoso (ARG)**[216] 4-9-4 WSupple 4 51
(Doug Watson, UAE) *settled in rr: nvr able to chal* **16/1**

1m 44.4s (104.40)
WFA 3 from 4yo 19lb **8 Ran SP% 123.4**

Owner Sh Mohd Bin Khalifa Al Maktoum, M De Kock **Bred** Wilgerbosdrift **Trained** South Africa

FOCUS
The two 'obvious' types, Zorin and Blue Sky God, ran below their best and this is probably pretty ordinary form, limited by the seventh.

NOTEBOOK
Limehouse(SAF) raced keenly in the early stages, having not been asked to chase the good early pace, and had about five or so lengths to find on Comandante Xara early in the straight, but he displayed a good attitude when asked for his effort to gradually wear down the long-time leader. He had proved no match for his stablemate, Asiatic Boy, in the UAE 2000 Guineas last time, but that was just his second racecourse start and, interestingly enough, his trainer won the equivalent race last year with a similar type in Nomoretaxes, who had also run down the field in the Guineas on his previous outing. A step back up in class now looks warranted. (op 6/1)
Comandante Xara(BRZ) did not help his chance by racing quite freely in front and he probably did well to finish so close. He managed to reverse recent form with Zorin, but that one was clearly below his best.
Alto Taquari(BRZ), the runner-up's stablemate, was never too far away and kept on to the line for a respectable third.
Zorin(BRZ) soon found himself caught behind horses on the inside rail and, unable to dominate, he was below the pick of his form. (op 7/2)
Blue Sky God(USA) created a good impression when winning his maiden at Aqueduct in November. However, an inside draw was of little help and, having not been the fastest away, he was soon trapped in behind horses towards the inside rail. He produced a short-lived effort towards the outside on the turn into the straight, but had basically raced too keenly early and never looked like sustaining his challenge. This was disappointing, but he can surely do better in future when able to impose himself from an early stage. (op 8/11)

527a AL FORSAN PLATE (MAIDEN) (TURF) 7f 110y(D)
4:00 (4:00) 3-Y-0

£7,653 (£2,551; £1,275; £637; £382; £255)

RPR

1 **Seal Point (USA)**[117] [6220] 3-8-9 85 PaulEddery 5 85+
(Christian Wroe) *t.k.h: mid-div: prog to trck ldr 3f out: led 2f out: r.o wl* **10/1**

2 4 ¼ **Plato's Republic (USA)**[158] [5408] 3-8-9 (b) PShanahan 1 75
(E Charpy, UAE) *led on rail: t.k.h: rdn 3f out: hdd 2f out: kpt on wl* **12/1**

3 ½ **Gemology (USA)**[135] [5901] 3-8-9 LDettori 2 74
(Saeed Bin Suroor) *trckd ldr in centre: gng wl 2 1/2f out: rdn 2f out: one pce* **4/5**[1]

4 3 ½ **Puzzle Book (USA)**[49] 3-8-5 TPO'Shea 7 63
(M Kettle, UAE) *slowly away: racd in rr: rdn trck wnr 2f out: r.o one pce* **33/1**

5 2 ¾ **Hint Of Spring**[100] [6481] 3-8-6 ow1 TedDurcan 8 59
(Saeed Bin Suroor) *settled in rr: rdn 2 1/2f out: nvr a threat* **16/1**

6 3 **Dubai Jewel (AUS)**[7] [476] 4-9-0 87 RyanMoore 6 53
(S Seemar, UAE) *settled in rr of mid-div: rdn 3f out: n.d* **5/1**[3]

7 ½ **Calabash Cove (USA)**[115] [6254] 3-8-9 KerrinMcEvoy 4 55
(Saeed Bin Suroor) *mid-div: rdn 3f out: nt qckn* **7/2**[2]

1m 33.44s (2.84) **Going Correction** +0.40s/f (Good)
WFA 3 from 4yo 17lb **7 Ran SP% 120.1**
Speed ratings: 101,96,96,92,90 87,86

Owner Prime Equestrian **Bred** Hargus Sexton, Sandra Sexton & The Thoroughbred Co **Trained** Kimpton, Hants

FOCUS
A hard race to assess, but some of them had fair efforts to their name coming into this and it looks reasonable enough.

NOTEBOOK
Seal Point(USA) showed fair form in good maiden company on his two starts in the UK last year, achieving RPRs in the 70s on both occasions, and looked to step up slightly on those efforts to run out a convincing winner on his debut in Dubai. It is hard to say exactly what he achieved, but he is open to further improvement, considering this was his first run in 117 days, and he looks a nice prospect.
Plato's Republic(USA), eighth of ten in a 6f Listed race at the Curragh in Ireland on his only previous start in September, made a pleasing return to action with blinkers fitted for the first time on his debut for new connections. He was taken on for the lead in the early stages by Gemology, but stuck to his task well in the straight and looks to have plenty of ability.
Gemology(USA) was well below the form he showed when second in a Newcastle maiden on his only previous start in October. Always close up, he was produced with every chance in the straight but he did not find a great deal and has to be considered disappointing. (op 5/6)
Hint Of Spring had not shown much on his previous outing at Wolverhampton and ran disappointingly.
Calabash Cove(USA) was some way below the form of his previous outing at Wolverhampton. (tchd 4/1)

528a LE DUNE H'CAP (TURF) 6f 110y(T)
4:32 (4:33) (95-110,110) 3-Y-0+

£36,734 (£12,244; £6,122; £3,061; £1,836; £1,224)

RPR

1 **Munaddam (USA)**[28] [245] 5-9-1 105 RHills 2 118
(E A L Dunlop) *trckd ldrs: t.k.h: travelling v wl whn n.m.r 1 1/2f out: swtchd out to ld fnl f: easily* **9/2**[2]

2 4 **Ashdown Express (IRE)**[14] [400] 8-9-6 110 TedDurcan 7 111
(C F Wall) *mid-div: rdn and no room 2f out: stopped again fnl f: nt rcvr* **9/2**[2]

3 shd **Arenti (NZ)**[13] [409] 6-9-0 104 (e) MJKinane 9 105
(J Meagher, Singapore) *settled in rr: gng wl 2 1/2f out: rdn to chal 2f out: r.o wl: no ch w wnr* **4/1**[1]

4 ¾ **Grantley Adams**[7] [472] 4-8-12 102 RyanMoore 1 101
(M R Channon) *settled in rr: gng wl 2 1/2f out whn no room: last 1 1/2f out: r.o wl* **11/2**[3]

5 ½ **Appalachian Trail (IRE)**[14] [400] 6-9-6 110 (b) JMurtagh 8 107
(I Semple) *mid-div: smooth prog ld 1 1/2f out: hdd fnl f: wknd* **4/1**[1]

6 1 **Taqseem (IRE)**[7] [472] 4-8-12 102 WayneSmith 6 96
(M Al Muhairi, UAE) *trckd ldr: led 3f out: hdd 1 1/2f out: one pce* **12/1**

7 hd **So Will I**[7] [470] 6-8-12 102 (t) MartinDwyer 4 96
(Doug Watson, UAE) *trckd ldrs in centre: rdn whn hmpd 2 1/2f out: no room again ins fnl f* **9/1**

8 3 ½ **Loyalist (SAF)**[13] [409] 6-9-0 104 WSupple 10 87
(S Seemar, UAE) *mid-div: rdn 3f out: nt qckn* **20/1**

9 3 ½ **Caesar Beware (IRE)**[28] [247] 5-9-5 109 (t) RichardMullen 3 82
(S Seemar, UAE) *slowly away: settled in rr: rdn 3f out: nvr nr to chal* **20/1**

10 6 ¾ **Terra Verde (IRE)**[7] [473] 5-8-12 102 (t) RoystonFfrench 5 56
(A Al Raihe, UAE) *led on rail: rdn and wknd 3f out* **40/1**

1m 19.0s (1.80) **Going Correction** +0.40s/f (Good) **10 Ran SP% 121.4**
Speed ratings: 105,100,100,99,98 97,97,93,89,81

Owner Hamdan Al Maktoum **Bred** Shadwell Farm LLC **Trained** Newmarket, Suffolk

FOCUS
This looked like a good, competitive handicap, although the early pace could possibly have been stronger. Several horses failed to get the clearest of runs, but the winner was among them yet there was no mistaking the authority with which he completed his hat-trick.

NOTEBOOK
Munaddam(USA) ◆ readily defied a 6lb higher mark than when winning over course and distance on his previous start to complete the hat-trick. Always going ominously well on the heels of the leaders, he had to wait the best part of a furlong for a gap in the straight, but he found plenty when switched and won convincingly. In winning a handicap off a mark of 105, he is clearly not far off pattern-class and deserves to be contesting some decent races when he returns to the UK, especially considering the lack of strength in depth at the top end of the sprint division.
Ashdown Express(IRE) ◆ was short of room in the straight and, while it is debatable whether he would have beaten the winner, he would have been much closer with a clear run. He had shaped well round here a couple of weeks ago and it would be no surprise to see him pick up a similar event.
Arenti(NZ) finished to good effect down the centre of the track, but he was never going to get to Munaddam and probably would have benefited from a stronger pace.
Grantley Adams ◆ was still on the bridle when shuffled back down the field early in the straight, and the race was all over by the time he got in the clear. He is better than the bare form.
Appalachian Trail(IRE) was quite impressive when winning over course and distance on his previous start, but everything fell into place for him that day and, 6lb higher, he was unable to confirm form with a few of these. He probably made his way to the front-end soon enough and a stronger pace may have suited better.
So Will I could never make a serious impression and ran below his recent level. (op 17/2)

529a AL SARAB STKS (H'CAP) (DIRT) 1m 2f (D)
5:00 (5:01) (95-110,109) 3-Y-0+

£36,734 (£12,244; £6,122; £3,061; £1,836; £1,224)

RPR

1 **Dynamic Saint (USA)**[21] [329] 4-9-0 102 (v) RichardMullen 4 104
(Doug Watson, UAE) *mid-div on rail: hrd rdn 3 1/2f out: chal 2f out: led fnl f: hld on wl* **10/1**

2 ¾ **Mooner (ARG)**[14] [399] 6-9-2 105 TedDurcan 16 104
(S Seemar, UAE) *nvr far off pce: trckd ldr 4f out: r.o wl* **6/1**[2]

3 1 **Bennie Blue (SAF)**[7] [475] 5-8-8 97 WCMarwing 10 94
(M F De Kock, South Africa) *mid-div: t.k.h: rdn to cl 2 1/2f out: ev ch fnl 1 1/2f: nt qckn* **9/1**

4 hd **Golden Arrow (IRE)**[14] [399] 4-9-0 102 (v) KerrinMcEvoy 2 101
(I Mohammed, UAE) *trckd ldr on rail: rdn 4f out: r.o one pce* **14/1**

5 3 ¾ **Chinkara**[14] [398] 7-8-8 97 RyanMoore 1 87
(Doug Watson, UAE) *mid-div rail: rdn to trck ldrs 2 1/2f out: kpt on one pce* **10/1**

6 1 ¼ **Rosberg (USA)**[6] 6-8-6 95 (t) TPO'Shea 12 83
(E Charpy, UAE) *prom: led 5f out: hdd 1 1/2f out: wknd* **12/1**

7 6 ¼ **Dubai Honor**[14] [399] 8-9-2 105 (e) WSupple 7 82
(Doug Watson, UAE) *mid-div: hmpd 2f out: rdn 3 1/2f out: nvr able to chal* **7/1**[3]

8 ½ **Morghim (IRE)**[21] [329] 4-8-7 96 (bt) RHills 8 73
(E Charpy, UAE) *mid-div: hmpd 2f out: rdn 3 1/2f out: nvr able to chal* **10/1**

9 1 ¾ **Parasol (IRE)**[13] [413] 8-9-0 102 (bt) KShea 6 76
(Doug Watson, UAE) *slowly away: mid-div gng wl 3f out: nt qckn* **22/1**

10 ¾ **Ampelio (IRE)**[7] [475] 5-8-6 95 (vt) MartinDwyer 13 66
(Doug Watson, UAE) *racd in rr: nvr able to chal* **14/1**

11 1 ½ **Oakfast (BRZ)**[21] [328] 5-8-7 96 ow1 ADomingos 15 64
(A Cintra Pereira, Brazil) *led: wd: hdd and swtchd to rail 5f out: trckd ldr over 4f out: wknd* **40/1**

12 2 ½ **Leaving Alone (BRZ)**[21] [329] 4-8-0 95 (b) AurelioMedeiros(6) 5 54
(M D Wolfson, U.S.A) *slowly away: hmpd 5f out: nvr nr to chal* **40/1**

13 ¼ **Surbiton (USA)**[6] 7-8-7 96 (bt) EddieAhern 9 60
(A Al Raihe, UAE) *mid-div: hrd rdn 3 1/2f out: nvr a threat* **12/1**

14 6 **Book Of Kings (USA)**[14] [401] 6-8-8 97 (bt) DO'Donohoe 11 50
(S Seemar, UAE) *mid-div: rdn 3 1/2f out: nvr involved: eased* **40/1**

15 dist **Remaadd (USA)**[21] [329] 6-9-6 109 JMurtagh 14 —
(D Selvaratnam, UAE) *trckd ldr: rdn 6f out: wknd: eased* **5/1**[1]

16 *dist* **Luberon**[21] [328] 4-8-12 **101** .... MJKinane 3 —
(M Johnston) *nvr nr to chal* **20/1**

2m 2.04s (-1.26) **Going Correction** +0.10s/f (Slow)
WFA 4 from 5yo+ 1lb **16** Ran SP% **125.9**
Speed ratings: 109,108,107,107,104 103,98,98,96,96 94,92,92,87,— —

Owner H E Sheikh Rashid Bin Mohammed **Bred** Harold J Plumley **Trained** United Arab Emirates

FOCUS

An ordinary handicap for the grade, but competitive enough. There seemed to be plenty of pace on as well, so the form should stand up.

NOTEBOOK

Dynamic Saint(USA) ran a stinker on his first start in a Carnival handicap behind a few of today's rivals, including Remaadd, over course and distance three weeks ago, but he had previously been progressing nicely at an ordinary level. It is not clear what went wrong last time, but he left that effort well behind in the visor with what was probably a career-best.

Mooner(ARG) was never too far off the pace and kept on well, proving suited by the step up in trip. He is coming good now.

Bennie Blue(SAF) seemed to be going quite well rounding the bend, but he still had a few lengths to find on the leaders and his rider may have been better off kicking for home a touch sooner. Whatever the case, he seemed suited by the switch to dirt and could have more to offer. (op 10/1)

Golden Arrow(IRE) ran with credit and helps to set the level of this form.

Remaadd(USA), the winner of a similar event over course and distance three weeks previously, stopped very quickly well before the turn into the straight.

530a AL FAHIDI FORT (SPONSORED BY JUMEIRAH BAB AL SHAMS) (GROUP 2) (TURF) 1m (T)

5:35 (5:35) 3-Y-O+

£76,530 (£25,510; £12,755; £6,377; £3,826; £2,551)

RPR

1 **Linngari (IRE)**[74] [6784] 5-9-0 113 .... KShea 4 122+
(H J Brown, South Africa) *racd in 4th: gng wl 3f out: rdn to cl 2f out: led 1 1/2f out: easily* **13/2**

2 *3 1/4* **Seihali (IRE)**[13] [413] 8-9-0 115 .... (b) JMurtagh 3 115
(D Selvaratnam, UAE) *mid-div on rail: rdn and trckd wnr 2f out: n.m.r fnl f: r.o wl* **5/1**

3 *1 1/4* **Kapil (SAF)**[257] 5-9-0 110 .... WCMarwing 7 112
(M F De Kock, South Africa) *settled in rr: wd 3f out: rdn 2 1/2f out: r.o fnl 2f: nrst fin* **7/2**[2]

4 *1 3/4* **Killybegs (IRE)**[131] [5962] 4-9-0 115 .... LDettori 5 108
(Saeed Bin Suroor) *led main gp: rdn to cl 2 1/2f out: ev ch 2f out: one pce* **3/1**[1]

5 *3/4* **King Jock (USA)**[21] [327] 6-9-0 110 .... PShanahan 1 106
(R J Osborne, Ire) *slowly away: settled in rr: rdn 2 1/2f out: nvr able to chal* **20/1**

6 *1/4* **Lord Admiral (USA)**[111] [6329] 6-9-0 111 .... (b) MJKinane 8 106
(Charles O'Brien, Ire) *mid-div: rdn 3f out: one pce* **16/1**

7 *2 1/2* **Vortex**[14] [394] 8-9-0 109 .... (t) JimmyQuinn 10 100
(Miss Gay Kelleway) *racd in 2nd: gng wl 3f out: sn rdn and nt qckn 2f out* **14/1**

8 *hd* **Court Masterpiece**[67] [6850] 7-9-6 119 .... KerrinMcEvoy 6 105
(I Mohammed, UAE) *slowly away: settled last: no room 1 1/2f out on rail: nvr nr to chal* **4/1**[3]

9 *6 1/4* **Celtic Silence**[7] [477] 9-9-0 100 .... (t) WSupple 9 85
(R Bouresly, Kuwait) *v qckly away: led and sn clr: rdn 3f out: hdd 1 1/2f out: wknd qckly* **50/1**

1m 38.45s (0.65) **Going Correction** +0.40s/f (Good) **9** Ran SP% **116.5**
Speed ratings: 112,108,107,105,105 104,102,102,95

Owner James Atkinson & Peter Walichnowski **Bred** HH Aga Khan's Stud **Trained** South Africa

FOCUS

This looked like a good renewal of this Group 2 contest and Seihali, who was placed in handicap company off a mark of 115 on his previous start, seems the best guide to the form, although it is worth noting the likes of Killybegs and Court Masterpiece failed to produce their best.

NOTEBOOK

Linngari(IRE) ◆ was always travelling smoothly and found plenty when asked for his effort to repeat last year's success in this event. He had a different preparation this time around, as he had won a Group 3 at the Carnival before taking this race last year, but he would certainly have been straight enough having run at Sha Tin just over two months ago, and he made no mistake. He was a disappointment in the Group 1 Dubai Duty Free Stakes following his success in this contest last year, but it would be silly to hold that against him and he could be a major player on World Cup night.

Seihali(IRE) has plenty of high-class form to his name and this was another terrific effort. He is a grand old campaigner and is holding his form really well. (op 4/1)

Kapil(SAF), a Group 2 winner in his native South Africa, was produced with his effort down the centre of the track and kept on from a long way back. This was his first run since June and there should be better to come. (op 100/30)

Killybegs(IRE) failed to pick up as one might have hoped in the straight. He was well below the pick of the form he showed for Barry Hills, but his new stable have been a bit quiet lately and there should be better to come in time. (op 7/2)

King Jock(USA), fourth in this race last year, would have appreciated the return to turf and ran well, but he never looked like threatening the principals, having been positioned well off the pace as usual. (op 18/1 tchd 16/1)

Lord Admiral(USA), runner-up to Linngari in this race last year, was not at his best off the back of a 111-day break.

Vortex was most probably found out by the step up in class.

Court Masterpiece had no easy task carrying a Group 1 penalty on his first start since leaving Ed Dunlop's yard and never looked like getting involved.

531a YA HALA CUP (H'CAP) (TURF) 1m 194y(T)

6:05 (6:05) (95-110,110) 3-Y-O+

£36,734 (£12,244; £6,122; £3,061; £1,836; £1,224)

RPR

1 **Benedetti (AUS)**[14] [395] 6-9-4 108 .... (b) MartinDwyer 2 116
(T Noonan, Australia) *mid-div rail: rdn to cl whn no room 2f out: swtchd: led wl ins fnl f* **10/1**

2 *1 1/4* **Yasoodd**[13] [411] 4-9-6 110 .... JMurtagh 3 116
(D Selvaratnam, UAE) *trckd ldr on rail: led 1 1/2f out: hdd wl ins fnl f: r.o wl: no ch w wnr* **7/1**

3 *2 3/4* **Metropolitan Man**[166] [5186] 4-9-4 108 .... RyanMoore 7 108
(D M Simcock) *hld up last: smooth prog 2 1/2f out: n.m.r 2f out: r.o fnl f* **25/1**

4 *1 1/4* **Diamond Quest (SAF)**[7] [473] 6-9-2 106 .... WCMarwing 5 104
(M F De Kock, South Africa) *settled in rr: gng wl 3f out: n.m.r 2 1/2f out: r.o fnl f* **9/2**[2]

5 *2 1/2* **Atlantic Air (FR)**[116] [6250] 5-9-3 107 .... (t) TPO'Shea 1 100
(E Charpy, UAE) *mid-div: trckd runner-up gng wl 2f out: r.o one pce* **33/1**

6 *1* **Sir Gerard**[21] [325] 4-9-6 110 .... KerrinMcEvoy 10 101
(I Mohammed, UAE) *settled in rr: gng wl 3f out: rdn 2 1/2f out: nvr nr to chal* **5/4**[1]

7 *4 3/4* **Sushisan (AUS)**[236] 5-9-3 107 .... KShea 4 88
(H J Brown, South Africa) *mid-div in centre: rdn 2 1/2f out: nt qckn: wknd* **11/2**[3]

8 *8* **Road To Love (IRE)**[13] [413] 4-9-6 110 .... RHills 6 75
(M Johnston) *sn led: hdd & wknd 1 1/2f out: eased* **16/1**

9 *3 1/2* **Advice**[13] [413] 6-9-3 107 .... (v) LDettori 8 65
(Saeed Bin Suroor) *trckd ldr tl rdn 2 1/2f out: sn wknd: eased* **16/1**

10 *8 3/4* **Yard-Arm (SAF)**[13] [411] 8-9-3 107 .... (t) TedDurcan 9 48
(S Seemar, UAE) *mid-div out wd: rdn 3f out: sn wknd: eased* **25/1**

1m 50.47s (0.67) **Going Correction** +0.40s/f (Good) **10** Ran SP% **122.0**
Speed ratings: 113,111,109,108,106 105,101,93,90,83

Owner P & Mrs McMahon,A & Mrs Burgio **Bred** Heytesbury Thoroughbreds P\l **Trained** Australia

FOCUS

This looked a high-class handicap beforehand but, with the likes of Sir Gerard and Diamond Quest not running to their best, the form is perhaps not quite as strong as it might have been, although the form of the placed horses looks solid.

NOTEBOOK

Benedetti(AUS) ◆ was able to defy an 8lb higher mark than when winning a 7f handicap on his debut in Dubai two weeks previously. He possesses quite an impressive burst of speed and always looked like mastering Yasoodd once pulled out, staying this longer trip with no problems at all. Again he seemed to carry his head a touch high, but it certainly doesn't stop him. (op 9/1)

Yasoodd, who ran second to Benedetti's stablemate in a 1m handicap round here on his previous start, was given every chance and battled on well when passed by the eventual winner. (op 13/2)

Metropolitan Man ◆, making his debut in Dubai, fared best of those held up and this must rate as a very creditable effort. He hails from a promising stable and could have more to offer this year.

Diamond Quest(SAF), 9lb higher, could not repeat the form he showed when so impressive in a 1m handicap here the previous week, but he was short of room in the straight and is better than his finishing position suggests.

Sir Gerard produced a taking turn of foot when winning a 1m handicap on his debut in Dubai, but his effort was rather short-lived this time and he was very disappointing.

Road To Love(IRE) had the run of the race out in front and can have no excuses

Advice dropped out very tamely indeed and was yet another form his yard to under perform.

532a SEYH AL SALAM TROPHY (H'CAP) (DIRT) 1m (D)

6:35 (6:36) (90-105,105) 3-Y-O+

£33,673 (£11,224; £5,612; £2,806; £1,683; £1,122)

RPR

1 **Boston Lodge**[7] [477] 7-8-8 93 .... (vt) EddieAhern 6 94
(Doug Watson, UAE) *mid-div: prog trck ldrs 2 1/2f out: no room 2f out: swtchd wd and r.o wl to ld fnl f* **14/1**

2 *1* **Naipe Marcado (URU)**[102] 4-8-7 100 .... KerrinMcEvoy 16 91
(I Mohammed, UAE) *trckd ldrs: led briefly 2 1/2f out: sn hdd: r.o wl* **7/2**[1]

3 *1/2* **British Isles**[6] 5-8-6 90 .... (t) TedDurcan 14 89
(S Seemar, UAE) *nvr far off pce: rdn to ld 2f out: kpt on wl* **14/1**

4 *1/2* **Aleutian**[13] [410] 7-8-8 93 .... (e) MartinDwyer 9 90
(Doug Watson, UAE) *sn rdn in rr: nvr a threat* **10/1**[3]

5 *2 3/4* **Salt Track (ARG)**[13] [410] 7-8-8 93 .... (t) MJKinane 5 85
(Niels Petersen, Norway) *led in centre: rdn 3f out: hdd 2 1/2f out: one pce* **20/1**

6 *1/4* **Quorum (GER)**[21] [329] 4-8-8 93 .... (v) WayneSmith 8 84
(M Al Muhairi, UAE) *trckd ldr: hrd rdn 2 1/2f out: kpt on one pce* **7/2**[1]

7 *1 3/4* **Poseidon's Bride (USA)**[7] [471] 4-8-6 90 .... WSupple 2 79
(Saeed Bin Suroor) *trckd ldr on rail: gng wl 3f out: rdn 2 1/2f out: one pce* **9/2**[2]

8 *1 1/4* **Space Oddity (BRZ)**[14] [396] 4-8-3 95 .... (t) ECruz 3 73
(P Nickel Filho, Brazil) *a mid-div* **14/1**

9 *nse* **Lavarone (ARG)**[7] [470] 4-8-3 95 .... TPO'Shea 13 73
(H J Brown, South Africa) *in rr of mid-div: rdn 2 1/2f out: one pce* **25/1**

10 *3/4* **State Shinto (USA)**[7] [471] 11-8-6 90 .... (bt) RPCleary 4 74
(R Bouresly, Kuwait) *slowly away: mid-div and rdn 2 1/2f out: n.d* **16/1**

11 *1 1/4* **Holborn (UAE)**[13] [409] 6-8-10 95 .... RichardMullen 11 76
(S Seemar, UAE) *mid-div: trckd ldrs 3f out: rdn: nt qckn* **66/1**

12 *1 3/4* **Estrela Brono (BRZ)**[7] [473] 5-8-7 91 ow1 .... (t) ADomingos 7 68
(C Morgado, Brazil) *nvr able to chal* **33/1**

13 *2 1/4* **Mezel (USA)**[13] [410] 4-9-2 100 .... RyanMoore 15 74
(S Seemar, UAE) *mid-div: rdn 3f out: one pce* **14/1**

14 *9* **Palm Cove (UAE)**[7] [473] 4-8-7 91 .... (t) JimmyQuinn 10 47
(M Kettle, UAE) *sn pushed along in rr: nvr a threat* **33/1**

15 *3/4* **Imperial Ice (SAF)**[14] [397] 5-9-2 100 .... (p) KShea 12 54
(H J Brown, South Africa) *nvr nr to chal* **14/1**

16 *2 1/4* **Ned Kelly (SAF)**[14] [398] 6-8-6 90 .... (p) PaulEddery 1 40
(Christian Wroe) *a in rr* **50/1**

1m 36.35s (-1.25) **Going Correction** +0.10s/f (Slow) **16** Ran SP% **128.9**
Speed ratings: 110,109,108,108,105 105,103,102,101,101 99,98,95,86,86 83

Owner Fawzi Abdulla Nass **Bred** Elite Racing Club **Trained** United Arab Emirates

FOCUS

This looks like just ordinary form for the grade, but fairly sound.

NOTEBOOK

Boston Lodge has been in good form on the turf at this year's Carnival and he had no problems with the return to the dirt. Interestingly enough, the style of his victory was unusual for the dirt surface, and more in line with what one would expect of a turf performer as, having travelled well just off the leaders, he was asked to produce a relative turn of foot near the line, rather than one sustained effort. He was a deserving winner, but it remains to be seen if he can repeat this sort of performance next time.

Naipe Marcado(URU) ◆ has been tried over as far as 1m4f in his native Uruguay, but he showed plenty of speed on his debut in Dubai. If anything he was probably going too well turning for home and, having eventually seen off British Isles, was caught with a sucker punch near the line. There are races to be won with him on the dirt.

British Isles, who was actually the third reserve, was produced with every chance and can have no excuses.

Aleutian stayed on from a long way back and again gave the impression he is crying out for a step up in trip.

Quorum(GER) was not at his best dropped in trip.

Poseidon's Bride(USA) might not have been helped by an inside draw and was never a danger.

[511]WOLVERHAMPTON (A.W) (L-H)

Friday, February 23

OFFICIAL GOING: Standard

Wind: light behind Weather: overcast

533 HOLIDAY INN AT WOLVERHAMPTON CLAIMING STKS 1m 141y(P)

2:00 (2:00) (Class 6) 4-Y-O+ **£2,388** (£705; £352) **Stalls** Low

Form RPR

2642 **1** **Dudley Docker (IRE)**[1] 525 5-9-0 73 (b[1]) KellyHarrison(7) 9 69
(D Carroll) *hld up: plld hrd: hdwy over 5f out: led over 2f out: edgd lft over 1f out: rdn clr: eased nr fin* **3/1**[2]

2330 **2** *1 3/4* **Mademoiselle**[8] 462 5-8-3 55 (p) TolleyDean(5) 1 52
(R A Harris) *chsd ldrs: rdn over 1f out: styd on* **14/1**

4043 **3** *2* **Kingsmaite**[8] 466 6-8-11 59 (bt) PhillipMakin 5 51
(S R Bowring) *hld up: hdwy over 2f out: edgd lft over 1f out: r.o: nt rch ldrs* **15/2**

3300 **4** *shd* **Bridgewater Boys**[11] 445 6-9-3 65 (b) NCallan 6 57
(K A Ryan) *prom: chsd ldr over 6f out: ev ch 2f out: sn rdn: no ex ins fnl f* **5/1**[3]

0063 **5** *nk* **Prince Dayjur (USA)**[9] 455 8-9-5 70 JimmyQuinn 13 58
(J Pearce) *hld up: swtchd rt over 1f out: r.o ins fnl f: nrst fin* **9/1**

425- **6** *shd* **Templet (USA)**[67] 6860 7-8-13 54 (v) DanielTudhope 8 52
(W G Harrison) *mid-div: hdwy 2f out: sn rdn: r.o: nt trble ldrs* **16/1**

-050 **7** *1 1/2* **Contra Mundum (USA)**[8] 464 4-9-3 60 PaulHanagan 10 53
(B S Rothwell) *chsd ldrs: rdn over 2f out: styd on same pce* **66/1**

3111 **8** *1/2* **Climate (IRE)**[18] 364 8-8-10 68 (v) RussellKennemore(5) 3 50
(R Hollinshead) *prom: rdn and nt clr run over 1f out: wknd fnl f* **9/4**[1]

-055 **9** *3/4* **Ligne D'Eau**[13] 425 6-8-8 40 ow4 (b) StephenDonohoe(3) 12 44
(P D Evans) *hld up: hdwy u.p over 1f out: btn whn nt clr run ins fnl f* **66/1**

-000 **10** *2 1/2* **Aventura (IRE)**[18] 366 7-8-7 45 PaulFessey 2 35
(S R Bowring) *led 6f: wknd over 1f out* **40/1**

0-50 **11** *2 1/2* **Suffolk House**[29] 243 5-8-12 40 (b) DeanMcKeown 7 35
(M Brittain) *s.i.s and hmpd s: hld up: a in rr* **66/1**

0200 **12** *1* **Crusoe (IRE)**[2] 518 10-8-0 45 (b) SoniaEaton(7) 4 27
(A Sadik) *hld up: hdwy over 5f out: wknd over 2f out* **50/1**

0005 **13** *2 1/2* **Hand Chime**[20] 346 10-8-4 52 EmmettStack(3) 11 22
(Ernst Oertel) *prom: rdn over 3f out: wknd over 2f out* **40/1**

1m 50.87s (-0.89) **Going Correction** -0.075s/f (Stan) 13 Ran SP% **118.1**

Speed ratings (Par 101):100,98,96,96,96 94,94,94,93,91 89,88,86

CSF £42.30 TOTE £4.30: £2.20, £3.60, £2.20; EX 41.60 TRIFECTA Not won..The winner was claimed by C. R. Dore for £12,000.

Owner J M Walsh **Bred** Nuri Fuat Basak **Trained** Sledmere, E Yorks

■ Stewards' Enquiry : Paul Hanagan one-day ban: failed to keep straight from stalls (Mar 6)

FOCUS

An ordinary claimer in which the form horses were probably not at their best.

Templet(USA) Official explanation: vet said gelding had been struck into

Climate(IRE) Official explanation: vet said gelding returned distressed

534 GO PONTIN'S (S) STKS 1m 141y(P)

2:35 (2:35) (Class 6) 3-Y-O **£2,047** (£604; £302) **Stalls** Low

Form RPR

4222 **1** **My Mirasol**[11] 446 3-8-9 64 (p) NCallan 5 63+
(K A Ryan) *mde all: clr over 2f out: unchal* **8/15**[1]

-051 **2** *5* **Jemima Godfrey**[13] 417 3-8-9 50 TPQueally 7 52
(J Pearce) *a.p: rdn and hung lft over 1f out: styd on: no ch w wnr* **16/1**

4536 **3** *1 1/4* **Mick Is Back**[7] 478 3-8-8 58 ow3 (b) StephenDonohoe(3) 3 51
(P D Evans) *prom: rdn to chse wnr over 2f out: no imp* **9/2**[2]

4-00 **4** *1 1/2* **Brierley Lil**[39] 140 3-8-3 48 (p) ChrisCatlin 1 41
(J L Spearing) *dwlt: hdwy over 6f out: rdn over 2f out: sn outpcd* **14/1**[3]

-605 **5** *2 1/2* **Ten Black**[10] 454 3-8-9 53 ow1 (v[1]) PhillipMakin 2 41
(R Brotherton) *sn chsng wnr: rdn over 2f out: wknd wl over 1f out* **22/1**

06-4 **6** *1 1/4* **Best Woman**[13] 417 3-8-10 49 ow1 TonyCulhane 6 40
(P Howling) *hld up and bhd: nvr nr to chal* **20/1**

00-0 **7** *nk* **Charlies Girl (IRE)**[47] 60 3-8-0 40 (p) DominicFox(3) 4 32
(K J Burke) *hld up: rdn over 3f out: n.d* **100/1**

-500 **8** *5* **Arabellas Homer**[21] 335 3-8-3 42 JimmyQuinn 9 22
(Mrs N Macauley) *hld up: rdn over 3f out: sn wknd* **66/1**

0-00 **9** *7* **Countrywide Style (IRE)**[17] 373 3-8-5 45 (b) JamesDoyle(3) 10 12
(N P Littmoden) *chsd ldrs: rdn over 3f out: wknd over 2f out* **66/1**

4-04 **10** *20* **Barney's Dancer**[15] 390 3-7-12 47 DuranFentiman(5) 8 —
(J Balding) *hld up: wknd over 3f out* **20/1**

1m 51.52s (-0.24) **Going Correction** -0.075s/f (Stan) 10 Ran SP% **111.5**

Speed ratings (Par 95):98,93,92,91,88 87,87,83,76,59

CSF £8.97 TOTE £1.50: £1.02, £2.60, £1.60; EX 8.90 Trifecta £18.50 Pool: £650.15 - 24.85 winning units..The winner was bought in for 11,500gns. Jemima Godfrey was claimed by M J Gingell for £6,000.

Owner Mrs Margaret Forsyth **Bred** J A Forsyth **Trained** Hambleton, N Yorks

FOCUS

The winner had an obvious chance at the weights and did not need to produce her best. The form seems sound.

535 PONTIN'S HOLIDAYS H'CAP 7f 32y(P)

3:10 (3:10) (Class 6) (0-65,67) 3-Y-O **£3,238** (£963; £481; £240) **Stalls** High

Form RPR

-213 **1** **Pietersen (IRE)**[21] 336 3-9-1 62 (b) PaulFessey 10 68+
(T D Barron) *hld up in tch: rdn over 2f out: edgd lft fr over 1f out: r.o to ld wl ins fnl f: hung lft nr fin* **5/1**[1]

5-30 **2** *1 1/4* **Knapton Hill**[31] 224 3-8-11 58 GrahamGibbons 8 61
(R Hollinshead) *mid-div: racd keenly: hdwy 3f out: rdn to ld 1f out: hdd wl ins fnl f* **7/1**

0-34 **3** *shd* **Calloff The Search**[19] 348 3-8-7 57 (p) SaleemGolam(3) 4 60
(W G M Turner) *led: hdd 6f out: chsd ldrs: rdn and ev ch ins fnl f: edgd lft and no ex towards fin* **11/2**[2]

-103 **4** *nk* **Heaven's Gates**[10] 454 3-8-9 56 (p) NCallan 9 58
(K A Ryan) *led 6f out: rdn and hdd 1f out: styng on same pce whn edgd rt towards fin* **6/1**[3]

066 **5** *nk* **Kiwi The Clown (IRE)**[13] 423 3-8-10 57 PaulHanagan 12 58+
(R A Fahey) *s.i.s: hld up: nt clr run 2f out: swtchd lft and hdwy over 1f out: running on whn n.m.r towards fin* **20/1**

-316 **6** *3/4* **Kings Shillings**[10] 454 3-8-9 56 (b) DanielTudhope 6 55
(D Carroll) *hld up: swtchd lft over 2f out: hdwy u.p over 1f out: styd on same pce ins fnl f* **6/1**[3]

26-0 **7** *1* **Dance Of Dreams**[21] 336 3-8-12 62 JamesDoyle(3) 2 59
(N P Littmoden) *chsd ldrs: rdn over 2f out: no ex fnl f* **8/1**

43-5 **8** *3* **Amber Isle**[13] 423 3-9-2 63 TonyCulhane 7 52
(D Carroll) *hld up: shkn up over 1f out: nvr nr to chal* **9/1**

501- **9** *5* **Play Straight**[57] 6963 3-9-1 65 PatrickMathers(3) 3 41
(I W McInnes) *s.i.s: hld up: rdn 1/2-way: wknd over 2f out* **12/1**

606- **10** *hd* **Inchigeelagh (IRE)**[161] 5347 3-8-10 57 MickyFenton 11 32
(H Morrison) *chsd ldrs 5f* **10/1**

000- **11** *12* **Purple Sands (IRE)**[130] 6015 3-8-7 54 DaleGibson 5 —
(J Hetherton) *chsd ldrs over 4f* **66/1**

1m 31.21s (0.81) **Going Correction** -0.075s/f (Stan) 11 Ran SP% **117.3**

Speed ratings (Par 95):92,90,90,90,89 88,87,84,78,78 64

CSF £39.63 CT £204.65 TOTE £3.90: £1.60, £2.30, £3.40; EX 31.50 Trifecta £197.50 Pool: £562.04 - 2.02 winning units..

Owner Sporting Occasions No 8 **Bred** Noel Finegan **Trained** Maunby, N Yorks

FOCUS

Solid form, rated through the third, fourth and sixth. The winner is probably capable of better than the bare form.

536 PONTINS.COM CLAIMING STKS 5f 216y(P)

3:45 (3:45) (Class 6) 4-Y-O+ **£2,266** (£674; £337; £168) **Stalls** Low

Form RPR

0055 **1** **Quiet Times (IRE)**[10] 452 8-9-11 84 (b) NCallan 4 76
(K A Ryan) *chsd ldrs: edgd rt and outpcd wl over 1f out: rallied to ld and hung lft wl ins fnl f: r.o* **5/6**[1]

020- **2** *1* **Blackheath (IRE)**[155] 5493 11-9-7 73 SilvestreDeSousa 1 69
(D Nicholls) *sn led: rdn clr over 1f out: hdd wl ins fnl f* **10/1**

0304 **3** *hd* **Mistral Sky**[2] 513 8-9-5 67 (v) MickyFenton 6 66
(Stef Liddiard) *chsd ldr to 1/2-way: outpcd 2f out: rallied fnl f: r.o* **7/2**[2]

4-04 **4** *1 1/4* **Ever Cheerful**[35] 183 6-9-6 67 (t) DNolan(3) 7 67
(D G Bridgwater) *outpcd: rdn and hung lft over 1f out: r.o ins fnl f: nvr nrr* **14/1**

0P-4 **5** *7* **Legal Set (IRE)**[11] 442 11-9-0 40 AnnStokell(5) 3 42
(Miss A Stokell) *chsd ldrs over 3f* **50/1**

0-55 **6** *nk* **Native Title**[15] 388 9-9-11 74 PaulHanagan 2 47
(D Nicholls) *hld up in tch: rdn and wknd over 1f out* **8/1**[3]

1105 **7** *3/4* **Mill By The Stream**[10] 450 5-9-3 62 JimCrowley 5 37
(Tom Dascombe) *hld up: wknd over 2f out* **12/1**

1m 15.3s (-0.51) **Going Correction** -0.075s/f (Stan) 7 Ran SP% **113.3**

Speed ratings (Par 101):100,98,98,96,87 87,86

CSF £10.37 TOTE £1.80: £1.20, £3.80; EX 12.90.

Owner Yorkshire Racing Club and Francis Moll **Bred** Times Of Wigan Ltd **Trained** Hambleton, N Yorks

FOCUS

The winner was a stone off his best in this ordinary claimer, in which the form does not look too solid.

537 PONTIN'S BOOK EARLY MAIDEN STKS 1m 4f 50y(P)

4:20 (4:21) (Class 5) 3-Y-O+ **£2,817** (£838; £418; £209) **Stalls** Low

Form RPR

03- **1** **Poseidon's Secret (IRE)**[91] 6578 4-9-11 PaulEddery 5 74+
(Pat Eddery) *hld up in tch: racd keenly: hmpd over 2f out: rdn to ld ins fnl f: r.o* **9/2**[3]

3-22 **2** *1 1/4* **Moon Empress (FR)**[11] 443 4-9-6 62 SebSanders 11 64
(W R Muir) *hld up: hdwy over 3f out: rn wd ent st: sn rdn to ld: hdd and unable qck ins fnl f* **7/2**[2]

000/ **3** *nk* **Festive Chimes (IRE)**[55] 305 6-9-6 35 JerryO'Dwyer(3) 6 63
(N B King) *chsd ldrs: rdn over 3f out: hung lft over 2f out: sn led: hdd over 1f out: ev ch ins fnl f: styd on same pce* **11/1**

54-4 **4** *7* **Chart Oak**[33] 204 4-9-11 55 IanMongan 7 57
(P Howling) *hld up: hdwy 1/2-way: rdn and ev ch 2f out: wknd over 1f out* **25/1**

6-5 **5** *5* **Smart Cat (IRE)**[30] 229 4-9-6 AdamKirby 10 44
(A P Jarvis) *hld up: nt clr run over 3f out: hdwy over 2f out: wknd over 1f out* **20/1**

6 *9* **Endless Power (IRE)**[42] 7-10-0 DanielTudhope 3 35
(J S Goldie) *s.i.s: sn prom: led 4f out: rdn and hdd over 2f out: sn wknd and eased* **9/2**[3]

7 *6* **Shaftesbury Avenue (USA)** 4-9-11 DavidAllan 1 25
(J O'Reilly) *chsd ldrs: rdn over 5f out: nt clr run over 3f out: hmpd and wknd sn after* **80/1**

8 *2 1/2* **Miss Wolf**[134] 7-9-9 SamHitchcott 2 16
(G H Jones) *hld up: rdn 1/2-way: a in rr* **150/1**

9 *1* **Ammeyrr** 3-8-1 AndrewMullen(3) 8 19
(M Johnston) *chsd ldr: rdn over 3f out: wkng whn hmpd over 2f out* **6/4**[1]

50-0 **10** *4* **Acece**[24] 304 3-8-0 49 ow1 (p) KevinGhunowa(5) 9 14
(M Appleby) *led 8f: sn rdn and wknd* **150/1**

11 *58* **Triel** 4-9-11 SilvestreDeSousa 4 —
(D Nicholls) *s.s: hld up: a bhd: t.o fnl 3f* **50/1**

2m 42.37s (-0.05) **Going Correction** -0.075s/f (Stan)

WFA 3 from 4yo 24lb 4 from 6yo+ 3lb 11 Ran SP% **120.0**

Speed ratings (Par 103):97,96,95,91,87 81,77,76,75,72 34

CSF £20.38 TOTE £6.40: £2.50, £1.10, £2.90; EX 17.40 Trifecta £203.00 Pool: £952.19 - 3.33 winning units..

Owner P J J Eddery **Bred** J Dorrian **Trained** Nether Winchendon, Bucks

■ Stewards' Enquiry : Jerry O'Dwyer one-day ban: careless riding (Mar 22)

FOCUS

A modest maiden which took little winning. The first three finished clear. It has been rated though the runner-up and the fourth.

538 PONTIN'S FAMILY HOLIDAYS H'CAP 1m 141y(P)

4:50 (4:50) (Class 5) (0-70,69) 4-Y-O+ **£3,238** (£963; £481; £240) **Stalls** Low

Form RPR

-050 **1** **Red Birr (IRE)**[16] 381 6-9-0 67 ChrisCatlin 6 77
(P R Webber) *led: hdd over 2f out: rallied to ld wl ins fnl f* **12/1**

3162 **2** *1* **Harare**[2] 516 6-8-4 60 (b) JamesDoyle(3) 12 67
(R J Price) *hld up: hdwy 1/2-way: rdn and hung lft fr over 2f out: styd on reluctantly* **4/1**[2]

163U **3** *hd* **Tancredi (SWE)**[9] 459 5-8-7 63 ow1 JerryO'Dwyer(3) 9 70
(N B King) *chsd wnr tl led over 2f out: rdn and hdd wl ins fnl f* **14/1**

1-10 **4** *1/2* **Topiary Ted**[27] 263 5-9-2 69 RobertHavlin 10 75
(H Morrison) *hld up in tch: outpcd 2f out: r.o ins fnl f* **5/2**[1]

1-00 **5** *1* **Magic Warrior**[32] 211 7-8-13 66 PaulFitzsimons 3 70
(J C Fox) *hld up: rdn over 2f out: r.o ins fnl f: nrst fin* **16/1**

64-4 **6** *1/2* **Western Roots**[21] 334 6-8-9 62 JimmyQuinn 8 65
(M Appleby) *hld up: hdwy over 2f out: styd on same pce fnl f* **8/1**[3]

1130 7 *hd* **Time To Regret**[9] 461 7-8-10 **63**..............................(p) DanielTudhope 4 65
(I W McInnes) *chsd ldrs: rdn over 2f out: wknd fnl f* **11/1**
5300 8 *3/4* **Second Reef**[11] 445 5-7-13 **55**..............................(p) LiamJones(3) 2 56
(J R Weymes) *chsd ldrs: rdn over 2f out: hung lft over 1f out: styd on same pce* **14/1**
004- 9 *1 1/4* **Holiday Cocktail**[35] 5974 5-8-10 **63**.......................... GrahamGibbons 5 61
(J J Quinn) *hld up: rdn over 3f out: n.d* **9/1**
3015 10 *nk* **Golden Spectrum (IRE)**[8] 462 8-8-2 **60**....................(b) TolleyDean(5) 7 58
(R A Harris) *hld up: plld hrd: rdn over 2f out: sn btn* **16/1**
422U 11 *2 1/2* **The City Kid (IRE)**[25] 299 4-7-10 **56**.................(b) BernadetteQuinn(7) 1 48
(P D Evans) *hld up: n.d* **16/1**
00/0 12 *13* **Definite Guest (IRE)**[27] 259 9-9-0 **67**.......................... PaulHanagan 11 32
(R A Fahey) *hld up: a in rr: wknd over 2f out* **50/1**

1m 50.28s (-1.48) **Going Correction** -0.075s/f (Stan) **12** Ran SP% **118.6**
Speed ratings (Par 103):103,102,101,101,100 100,99,99,98,97 95,84
CSF £59.55 CT £705.82 TOTE £9.10: £4.10, £2.00, £4.00; EX 54.90 TRIFECTA Not won..
Owner John Nicholls (Trading) Ltd **Bred** Mrs Ellen Lyons **Trained** Mollington, Oxon

FOCUS
Solid form, the winner taking advantage of slipping in the weights and the the next three close to their recent course form.

539 PONTINSBINGO.COM H'CAP 1m 1f 103y(P)
5:20 (5:20) (Class 5) (0-70,68) 4-Y-0+ **£3,238** (£963; £481; £240) **Stalls** Low

Form RPR
25-2 1 **Sarwin (USA)**[42] 110 4-8-6 **65**.................................... DebraEngland(7) 3 76
(W J Musson) *hld up: hdwy over 2f out: edgd lft and led ins fnl: pushed out* **7/2**[2]
2-11 2 *nk* **Pop Music (IRE)**[21] 334 4-8-12 **67**............................(p) JamesDoyle(3) 7 77
(Miss J Feilden) *chsd ldr: led over 2f out: sn rdn: hdd ins fnl f: kpt on* **7/2**[2]
2-43 3 *1 3/4* **Generous Lad (IRE)**[13] 422 4-9-2 **68**............................(p) DaneO'Neill 6 74
(A B Haynes) *s.i.s: sn prom: rdn and hung lft fr over 1f out: styd on same pce* **13/2**[3]
-030 4 *1/2* **Buscador (USA)**[11] 445 8-8-3 **58**.............................. LiamJones(3) 8 63
(W M Brisbourne) *led 7f: styd on same pce fnl f* **9/1**
3-31 5 *3 1/2* **Penang Cinta**[11] 445 4-8-6 **61** 6ex ow1................ StephenDonohoe(3) 2 59
(P D Evans) *hld up: hdwy over 1f out: nt trble ldrs* **9/4**[1]
-101 6 *1 3/4* **Granakey (IRE)**[8] 462 4-8-4 **56**.................................... JimmyQuinn 5 51
(M G Quinlan) *hld up: plld hrd: rdn over 2f out: sn outpcd* **10/1**
7 *8* **More Votes (IRE)**[160] 5397 6-8-5 **57**.................................... ChrisCatlin 1 36
(Eoin Doyle, Ire) *trckd ldrs: racd keenly: wknd 2f out* **16/1**
60-0 8 *2 1/2* **Tilen (IRE)**[12] 435 4-8-2 **54** oh9..............................(b) DaleGibson 4 28
(S Parr) *hld up: racd keenly: rdn and wknd over 2f out* **100/1**
20-0 9 *shd* **Digger Boy**[41] 48 4-8-9 **61**.. JimCrowley 9 34
(J Gallagher) *s.i.s: sn prom: rdn over 3f out: wknd over 2f out* **40/1**

2m 0.96s (-1.66) **Going Correction** -0.075s/f (Stan) **9** Ran SP% **116.9**
Speed ratings (Par 103):104,103,102,101,98 97,89,87,87
CSF £16.45 CT £76.25 TOTE £4.70: £1.20, £2.30, £1.80; EX 23.10 Trifecta £67.90 Pool: £845.95 - 8.84 winning units. Place 6 £60.21, Place 5 £21.64.
Owner S Rudolf **Bred** Cynthia Knight **Trained** Newmarket, Suffolk

FOCUS
A fair handicap grade, with the first two progressive. Solid form, with the third a reliable yardstick.
Generous Lad(IRE) Official explanation: jockey said gelding hung left
T/Jkpt: £2,515.50 to a £1 stake. Pool: £19,486.50. 5.50 winning tickets. T/Plt: £41.10 to a £1 stake. Pool: £90,348.35. 1,602.95 winning tickets. T/Qpdt: £9.90 to a £1 stake. Pool: £6,350.10. 471.40 winning tickets. CR

526 NAD AL SHEBA (L-H)
Friday, February 23
OFFICIAL GOING: Turf course - good; dirt course - fast

540a AHLAN CUP (H'CAP) (TURF) 7f 110y(D)
2:40 (2:20) (90-105,105) 3-Y-0+
£33,673 (£11,224; £5,612; £2,806; £1,683; £1,122)

RPR
1 **Polar Magic**[15] 396 6-9-2 **100**.. LDettori 2 109+
(I Mohammed, UAE) *mid-div on rail: gng wl on rail 2f out: swtchd 1 1/2f out: r.o: led ins fnl f: easily* **7/2**[1]
2 *2 1/4* **Subpoena**[8] 470 5-9-2 **100**......................................(v) RoystonFfrench 5 102
(A Al Raihe, UAE) *trckd front two: rdn 2f out: ev ch fnl f: one pce* **9/2**[2]
3 *1* **Kalankari (IRE)**[15] 394 4-9-0 **98**.. MartinDwyer 8 98
(A M Balding) *trckd ldr: led 2 1/2f out: hdd ins fnl f* **7/1**
4 *1/4* **Arminius (IRE)**[15] 395 4-8-12 **97**.................................. KerrinMcEvoy 6 95
(I Mohammed, UAE) *in rr of mid-div: rdn 2 1/2f out: r.o fnl 1 1/2f: nrst fin* **9/2**[2]
5 *shd* **Dickensian (IRE)**[139] 5813 4-9-2 **100**..................................(t) TPO'Shea 4 99
(E Charpy, UAE) *slowly away: last but gng wl 3f out: no room 1 1/2f out: r.o wl once clr: nrst fin* **14/1**
6 *shd* **Azarole (IRE)**[14] 411 6-9-4 **102**.. JohnEgan 9 101
(J S Moore) *mid-div: rdn 2 1/2f out: r.o one pce: nrst fin* **13/2**[3]
7 *3 1/2* **Sir Edwin Landseer (USA)**[8] 470 7-8-11 **96**..........(p) RichardMullen 1 85
(Christian Wroe) *slowly away: in rr of mid-div: rdn 3f out: no room 2 1/2f out: nvr able to chal* **12/1**
8 *4* **Al Maali (IRE)**[7] 8-9-0 **98**.. RHills 7 78
(Doug Watson, UAE) *racd in 4th: rdn to trck ldrs 2 1/2f out: wknd fnl 1 1/2f* **12/1**
9 *7* **Starpix (FR)**[8] 477 5-9-6 **105**..(p) KShea 10 67
(H J Brown, South Africa) *settled in rr: rdn 2 1/2f out: nvr able to chal* **12/1**
10 *1/4* **Kings Point (IRE)**[8] 477 6-8-11 **96**......................................(v) RyanMoore 3 57
(R A Fahey) *led tl hdd 2 1/2f out: wknd qckly* **18/1**

1m 29.94s (-0.66) **10** Ran SP% **119.4**
.
Owner Sheikh Hamdan Bin Mohammed Al Maktoum **Bred** Cheveley Park Stud Ltd **Trained** UAE

FOCUS
This looked just an ordinary handicap for the grade; basically another division of the 3.50. They seemed to go a fair pace, but the first three home were never more than five or six lengths off the lead.

NOTEBOOK
Polar Magic ◆ was well beaten in a 7f handicap on the dirt on his debut for current connections, but the return to turf suited and he ran out a ready winner. Having been positioned in about mid-division towards the inside rail for much of the way, he was short of room in the straight and had to be switched towards the centre of the track to get a run. The result, though, never looked in doubt once he was in the clear and he found plenty when asked. At the age of six, he is seemingly as good as ever, and will remain worthy of respect in this sort of company.
Subpoena was no match for the clear-cut winner but this still rates as a decent effort off a mark 5lb higher than when winning over an extended 6f around here on his previous start.
Kalankari(IRE) was again unable to dominate and he probably did well to finish so close. He does not have much in hand of the handicapper, but will be dangerous in this sort of company when allowed his own way out in front.
Arminius(IRE) was taken wide to challenge in the straight, but he could only find the one pace and failed to build on his recent course-and-distance third.
Dickensian(IRE) ◆, having his first start since leaving Godolphin, was probably a little unlucky not to finish closer, because having been just about last turning for home, he was denied a clear run when trying to stay on.
Azarole(IRE) did not improve on his recent carnival efforts but hardly ran a bad race.
Kings Point(IRE) is just not firing at the moment. (op 20/1)

541a GREETUNE PLATE (H'CAP) (TURF) 1m 2f (T)
3:15 (3:15) (90-105,105) 3-Y-0+
£33,673 (£11,224; £5,612; £2,806; £1,683; £1,122)

RPR
1 **Wild Savannah**[15] 398 5-9-4 **102**..................................(v) KerrinMcEvoy 5 105
(I Mohammed, UAE) *led main gp: gng wl 3f out: led 2f out: comf* **9/1**
2 *2 1/2* **Stream Of Gold (IRE)**[15] 395 6-9-5 **104**........................... TedDurcan 9 99
(S Seemar, UAE) *settled in rr: rdn 3f out: r.o in centre: nrst fin* **5/1**[2]
3 *nse* **Money Bags (SAF)**[14] 413 5-9-4 **102**.........................(bt) WCMarwing 1 98
(M F De Kock, South Africa) *mid-div on rail: gng wl: no room 2f out: r.o fnl f* **5/1**[2]
4 *shd* **Hallhoo (IRE)**[8] 477 5-9-0 **98**.. JMurtagh 10 94
(D Selvaratnam, UAE) *mid-div: rdn to cl 2 1/2f out: nt qckn: kpt on one pce* **5/1**[2]
5 *1* **Golden Velvet (USA)**[15] 397 4-9-0 **98**..................................(t) LDettori 3 93
(Saeed Bin Suroor) *v.s.a: settled in last: rdn 3f out: r.o fnl 1 1/2f: nrst fin* **6/1**[3]
6 *3 1/4* **Gharir (IRE)**[117] 6250 5-9-6 **105**.. MartinDwyer 7 92
(E Charpy, UAE) *mid-div: rdn to trck ldrs 3 1/2f out: led briefly 2f out: wknd* **12/1**
7 *1/2* **Cimyla (IRE)**[15] 401 6-9-1 **99**.. EddieAhern 8 86
(C F Wall) *settled in rr: nvr able to chal* **9/1**
8 *6 1/4* **Rohaani (USA)**[15] 398 5-9-2 **100**... RHills 6 76
(Doug Watson, UAE) *trckd ldr: t.k.h: led briefly 2 1/2f out: wknd* **7/2**[1]
9 *1* **Evaluator (IRE)**[8] 471 6-8-9 **100**.................................... AhmedAjtebi(7) 4 74
(A Al Raihe, UAE) *led tl rdn and hdd 2 1/2f out: wknd* **33/1**
10 *3/4* **Reve Lunaire (USA)**[15] 398 4-9-5 **104**........................ RichardMullen 2 77
(S Seemar, UAE) *in rr of mid-div: rdn 3f out: nvr able to chal* **16/1**

2m 4.25s (0.05)
WFA 4 from 5yo+ 1lb **10** Ran SP% **123.0**
.
Owner Sheikh Hamdan Bin Mohammed Al Maktoum **Bred** Andrew Watkinsandrew Watkinshascombe & Valiant Stu **Trained** UAE

FOCUS
This looked a good handicap beforehand - pretty much another division of the 4.55 - but they finished in a bunch behind the clear-cut winner. They went steady through the first furlong or so, but seemed to go a fair gallop from there on in.

NOTEBOOK
Wild Savannah was just a little bit off his best on his first couple of starts at this year's Carnival since leaving John Gosden, but those two outings clearly put him right and he returned to something like his best with the visor re-fitted. Never too far away from the lead, he was keen enough in the early stages, but had plenty left in the straight and had the race won when kicked into a clear lead around two furlongs out. A rise in the weights might not make him the easiest to place, but he is very smart on his day and deserves his chance in slightly better company. (op 10/1)
Stream Of Gold(IRE) was well out the back turning in and, although staying on well when switched out towards the centre of the track, he just had too much ground to make up on the eventual winner. He has done most of his racing at around 1m, but seemed to get this longer trip well enough.
Money Bags(SAF), stepped back up in trip with the blinkers re-fitted, was probably unlucky not to finish a clear second, as he was shuffled back early in the straight when caught behind a tiring rival, allowing Wild Savannah first run.
Hallhoo(IRE), stepped back up in distance, did not help his chance by racing keenly and just flattened out a touch towards the finish. (op 11/2)
Golden Velvet(USA) was asked to come from a similar position to Stream Of Gold, but she could not sustain her challenge and this trip might just have stretched her.
Gharir(IRE) might have needed this first run in 117 days.
Cimyla(IRE) did not show enough and may benefit from a return to the Polytrack in the UK.
Rohaani(USA) was well positioned but he offered very little under pressure and could be one to have reservations about.

542a WASEL STKS (H'CAP) (TURF) 7f 110y(D)
3:50 (3:50) (90-105,105) 3-Y-0+
£33,673 (£11,224; £5,612; £2,806; £1,683; £1,122)

RPR
1 **National Captain (SAF)**[15] 396 5-9-5 **104**........................ TedDurcan 7 107
(S Seemar, UAE) *t.k.h: led after 1 1/2f: hdd 2f out: rallied to regain ld again fnl f* **14/1**
2 *1/4* **Express Way (BRZ)**[14] 411 5-9-6 **105**..............................(t) WCMarwing 2 107
(M F De Kock, South Africa) *trckd ldrs: t.k.h: led 2f out: hdd fnl f: r.o* **10/3**[1]
3 *1* **Royal Power (IRE)**[14] 411 4-9-4 **102**.............................. RyanMoore 1 103
(M R Channon) *mid-div: rdn to trck ldrs 2 1/2f out: r.o: nrst fin* **22/1**
4 *shd* **Mostashaar (FR)**[15] 395 5-9-2 **100**.................................. MartinDwyer 9 101
(Doug Watson, UAE) *settled in rr: rdn 2 1/2f out: r.o fnl 1 1/2f: nrst fin* **8/1**[3]
5 *1/4* **Recast (AUS)**[8] 472 7-9-2 **100**..(t) MJKinane 10 100
(J Meagher, Singapore) *slowly away: settled in last: prog on rail 2f out: r.o: nrst fin* **10/1**
6 *2 1/4* **Ans Bach**[15] 394 4-8-12 **97**..(b) JMurtagh 8 90
(D Selvaratnam, UAE) *settled in rr: rdn 2 1/2f out: n.d* **10/3**[1]
7 *1/2* **Protector (SAF)**[14] 415 6-8-11 **96**.. KShea 3 88
(H J Brown, South Africa) *led reluctantly tl hdd after 1f: settled in mid-div: rdn 2 1/2f out: nt able to chal* **9/1**
8 *2 3/4* **Almuraad (IRE)**[8] 473 6-9-1 **99**... RHills 5 85
(Doug Watson, UAE) *mid-div: rdn to chal 2f out: nt qckn: wknd fnl f* **9/2**[2]
9 *4* **Cubillas (BRZ)**[15] 394 5-9-0 **98**.. ADomingos 6 74
(M D Wolfson, U.S.A) *prom: t.k.h tl rdn 3f out: wknd* **20/1**
10 *hd* **All Ivory**[22] 331 5-9-1 **99**... KerrinMcEvoy 4 75
(I Mohammed, UAE) *trckd ldrs for 2 1/2f: rdn in rr 3f out: wknd* **8/1**[3]

1m 32.66s (2.06) **10** Ran SP% **121.4**
.

Owner H E Sheikh Rashid Bin Mohammed **Bred** Klawervlei Stud **Trained** United Arab Emirates

FOCUS

Essentially another division of the 2.40 but a very messy race and unreliable form. Nobody wanted to lead early and several of these took a very keen hold through the first two furlongs as a result.

NOTEBOOK

National Captain(SAF) was sent to the front after the first quarter-mile or so by Durcan and that proved to be the race-winning move. He injected some pace to get to the front, but was able to get a good breather in once there and had plenty left when strongly challenged by Express Way. That one drew right upsides in the straight, but National Captain was the more determined of the pair and just proved good enough. He appreciated the return to turf and is pretty smart on his day, but this is very suspect form.

Express Way(BRZ) was always well placed considering how the race was run and looked to have every chance when drawing upsides National Captain in the straight.

Royal Power(IRE) was better placed than some of his rivals, but still about five or six lengths off the leader for much of the way. He kept on in the straight and is on good terms with himself.

Mostashaar(FR) stayed on from a long way back and would have benefited from a stronger pace.

Recast(AUS) did well to finish so close considering he was just about last turning in and had raced very keenly in the early stages.

Ans Bach, with the headgear re-fitted, could make no impression having been held up well off the pace. (op 7/2)

Protector(SAF) was far too keen early on.

Almuraad(IRE) is yet another who would have been unsuited by the way the race was run.

Cubillas(BRZ) seemed to clip heels early in the straight.

All Ivory was short of room well before the turn into the straight and is better than he showed. (op 9/1)

543a UAE FOUNDER'S TROPHY (H'CAP) (DIRT) 7f (D)

4:25 (4:33) (95-110,109) 3-Y-O+

£36,734 (£12,244; £6,122; £3,061; £1,836; £1,224)

			RPR
1		**Parole Board (USA)**[7] 5-9-4 **107** ... TedDurcan 3 (S Seemar, UAE) *mid-div: gng wl 3 1/2f out: smooth prog 2 1/2f out: led 1 1/2f out: comf* **4/1**[2]	111
2	1 1/2	**Drift Ice (SAF)**[15] [396] 6-8-7 **96** ... (be) WCMarwing 9 (M F De Kock, South Africa) *mid-div out wd: rdn to chal 2f out: r.o: no ch w wnr* **7/1**	96
3	3/4	**Rock N Roll Kid (NZ)**[15] [395] 8-8-9 **98** ... (e) MJKinane 8 (M C Tam, Macau) *mid-div: rdn to cl 2 1/2f out: ev ch 1 1/2f out: kpt on* **8/1**	96
4	1	**Opportunist (IRE)**[14] [410] 8-8-11 **100** ... (vt) MartinDwyer 2 (Doug Watson, UAE) *trckd ldr on rail: led 3 1/2f out tl hdd 1 1/2f out: one pce* **9/4**[1]	95
5	1	**Almaram (USA)**[14] [409] 7-8-11 **100** ... (e) JMurtagh 1 (D Selvaratnam, UAE) *settled in rr: rdn to mid-div 4f out: nvr able to chal* **5/1**[3]	93
6	7 1/2	**Hay Luz Delsol (BRZ)**[22] [324] 5-8-6 **95** ... ADomingos 7 (M D Wolfson, U.S.A) *led tl hdd 3 1/2f out: wknd 2 1/2f out* **25/1**	67
7	6	**Looking Good (ARG)**[8] [471] 6-8-8 **97** ... (t) WayneSmith 4 (Allan Smith, UAE) *settled in last: rdn 3f out: nvr nr to chal* **10/1**	53
8	5 3/4	**Alpacco (IRE)**[22] [331] 5-9-3 **106** ... (b) KShea 6 (H J Brown, South Africa) *settled in rr: nvr involved* **11/2**	47

1m 22.6s (-2.20) 8 Ran SP% **119.4**

Owner H E Sheikh Rashid Bin Mohammed **Bred** Daniel M Ryan **Trained** United Arab Emirates

FOCUS

A reasonable handicap and certainly competitive enough, although last year's winner Tropical Star was sadly missing from the field having suffered fatal injuries in a freak accident leaving the paddock.

NOTEBOOK

Parole Board(USA) looked potentially high-class in his 3yo days, but he rather lost his way after finishing a well-beaten third in the UAE Derby. However, he has got his career back on track now and followed up his recent win in a weak Listed event at Jebel Ali seven days earlier to gain his third success from his last four starts. As usual he was not asked to do too much in the early stages, but he was always travelling nicely in behind the pacesetters and found plenty when asked for his effort. He may never reach the heights he once promised to, but he certainly deserves a shot at something better following his recent run of form. (old market op 9/2 tchd 5/1)

Drift Ice(SAF) ran a good race, keeping on well for pressure in the straight, but he just seemed a touch keen through the early stages and may benefit from having more use made of him in future. (old market 9/1)

Rock N Roll Kid(NZ) was never too far away and ran a respectable race on his return to the dirt. (old market 10/1)

Opportunist(IRE) may have been forced to go a stride quicker than was probably ideal to lead and could not sustain his challenge to the line. (old market 7/2)

Almaram(USA) should have appreciated the return to dirt, but an inside draw would have been of little help. (old market 6/1)

Alpacco(IRE) was the first beaten and proved unsuited by the switch to dirt. (old market 7/1)

544a WEYAK STKS (H'CAP) (TURF) 1m 2f (T)

4:55 (4:56) (90-105,105) 3-Y-O+

£33,673 (£11,224; £5,612; £2,806; £1,683; £1,122)

			RPR
1		**Senor Dali (IRE)**[22] [330] 4-9-5 **104** ... RichardMullen 2 (I Mohammed, UAE) *set stdy pce: increased tempo 3 1/2f out: clr 1 1/2f out: r.o wl* **33/1**	103
2	1 1/4	**Impeller (IRE)**[15] [398] 8-9-0 **98** ... JohnEgan 8 (J S Moore) *settled in rr: rdn to mid-div 2 1/2f out: r.o fnl f: nrst fin* **11/2**[3]	95+
3	1/4	**Fairmile**[29] [244] 5-9-5 **104** ... KerrinMcEvoy 5 (I Mohammed, UAE) *bmpd s: mid-div: rdn to cl 2 1/2f out: nvr able to get to wnr: lost 2nd on line* **6/4**[1]	100+
4	1 1/4	**Fenice (IRE)**[8] [475] 4-9-2 **100** ... TedDurcan 9 (S Seemar, UAE) *settled in rr: rdn 3f out: nvr able to chal* **20/1**	95
5	3/4	**Great Plains**[15] [401] 5-9-0 **98** ... RHills 3 (E Charpy, UAE) *racd in 3rd: trckd wnr 2 1/2f out: rdn 2f out: one pce* **13/2**	91
6	1/2	**Lundy's Lane (IRE)**[8] [473] 7-9-1 **99** ... RyanMoore 4 (S Seemar, UAE) *missed break: racd in rr: rdn 2 1/2f out: r.o fnl 1 1/2f: nrst fin* **20/1**	91
7	1 1/4	**Count Trevisio (IRE)**[15] [398] 4-9-4 **102** ... LDettori 6 (Saeed Bin Suroor) *trckd ldr: rdn 2 1/2f out: ev ch 2f out: wknd fnl f* **4/1**[2]	93
8	6	**Morshdi**[15] [400] 9-9-3 **101** ... JMurtagh 1 (D Selvaratnam, UAE) *settled in rr: t.k.h: rdn 4f out: nvr nr to chal* **14/1**	80
9	3 3/4	**Tell**[14] [411] 4-9-4 **102** ... TPO'Shea 10 (E Charpy, UAE) *settled in rr: rdn 3f out: n.d* **20/1**	75
10	5 3/4	**Evil Knievel (BRZ)**[22] [330] 8-9-6 **105** ... (b) MJKinane 7 (Christian Wroe) *mid-div out wd: rdn 3f out: nvr able to chal* **10/1**	66

2m 6.53s (2.33)
WFA 4 from 5yo+ 1lb 10 Ran SP% **121.7**

Owner Sheikh Hamdan Bin Mohammed Al Maktoum **Bred** Frank Dunne **Trained** UAE

FOCUS

This looked quite a good handicap beforehand, but Senor Dali made all on his own terms and the bare form looks unreliable.

NOTEBOOK

Senor Dali(IRE) appeared to be used as a pacemaker for Formal Decree in an extended 1m Group 3 on his previous start but, dropped in class and stepped back up to a more suitable trip, he set a much more sensible pace this time. He had plenty left when asked for his effort in the straight and kept finding under pressure to see off the strong-travelling Fairmile. The winner is clearly smart when able to dictate, but he is unlikely to get such a soft lead next time and will be doing well to follow up.

Impeller(IRE) ran a blinder off a mark 5lb higher than when winning over course and distance on his previous start, especially considering a stronger pace would have suited much better.

Fairmile looked the most likely winner when travelling better than anything halfway up the straight, despite having raced a little keenly, but he did not find much once let down and has to be considered disappointing. It would perhaps be unfair to crab him too much, because as it turned out Senor Dali had plenty left in the locker, but the fact remains he didn't really extend as one might have hoped when asked, and he has something to prove now.

Fenice(IRE) would have been better suited by a stronger pace.

Great Plains could not sustain his effort. (op 7/1)

Lundy's Lane(IRE) could make no impression after being held up off the steady gallop.

Count Trevisio(IRE) was another unable to sustain his challenge and this was disappointing.

545a ALSHAMIL CUP (H'CAP) (TURF) 1m 4f (T)

5:25 (5:25) (95-110,110) 3-Y-O+

£36,734 (£12,244; £6,122; £3,061; £1,836; £1,224)

			RPR
1		**Book Of Music (IRE)**[15] [401] 4-9-1 **107** ... (v) KerrinMcEvoy 6 (I Mohammed, UAE) *slowly away: settled in rr: last 4f out: trckd runner-up 2 1/2f out: led ins fnl f* **9/2**[2]	111+
2	3 3/4	**Leitmotiv (IRE)**[22] [328] 4-8-9 **101** ow1 ... (v) LDettori 3 (Saeed Bin Suroor) *settled in rr: smooth prog 2f out: r.o fnl f: nrst fin* **3/1**[1]	99
3	1 1/4	**Hattan (IRE)**[14] [412] 5-9-6 **110** ... RyanMoore 5 (C E Brittain) *mid-div: rdn to chal 2f out: r.o one pce* **9/2**[2]	105
4	3 1/4	**Go For Gold (IRE)**[8] [475] 6-8-10 **100** ... (vt) RichardMullen 7 (S Seemar, UAE) *trckd ldr: gng wl 3f out: rdn and styd on one pce fr 2 1/2f out* **12/1**	90
5	1/4	**Jadalee (IRE)**[14] [412] 4-9-4 **110** ... MartinDwyer 9 (I Mohammed, UAE) *mid-div: rdn to ld 2 1/2f out: hdd & wknd fnl f* **14/1**	101
6	1 1/4	**Lost Soldier Three (IRE)**[15] [398] 6-8-10 **100** ... AdrianTNicholls 8 (D Nicholls) *trckd ldr: rdn to dispute ld 2f out: wknd fnl f* **20/1**	88
7	2	**Nepotista (BRZ)**[8] [475] 5-8-10 **100** ... ADomingos 1 (A Cintra Pereira, Brazil) *mid-div: rdn 2f out: ev ch fnl f: one pce* **11/1**	85
8	dist	**Hazeymm (IRE)**[22] [330] 4-9-1 **107** ... (e) JMurtagh 2 (D Selvaratnam, UAE) *sn led at stdy pce: increased pce 4f out: rdn and hdd 2 1/2f out: no room 1 1/2f out* **7/1**[3]	—
9	dist	**Corriolanus (GER)**[14] [412] 7-9-1 **105** ... TedDurcan 10 (S Seemar, UAE) *settled in rr: nvr nr to chal* **16/1**	—
10	dist	**Sanchi (IRE)**[14] [412] 5-8-9 **99** ... TPO'Shea 4 (E Charpy, UAE) *mid-div: trckd ldrs 5f out: rdn 3 1/2f out: sn wknd: eased* **7/1**[3]	—

2m 32.46s (1.46)
WFA 4 from 5yo+ 3lb 10 Ran SP% **119.7**

Owner H R H Princess Haya Of Jordan **Bred** Wentworth Racing Pty Ltd **Trained** UAE

FOCUS

A decent middle-distance handicap and, despite the pace appearing very ordinary for much of the way, the principals came from well off the lead.

NOTEBOOK

Book Of Music(IRE) ◆ coped just fine with the return to 1m4f and stepped up on his two previous efforts at this year's Carnival. He raced in last for much of the way, but showed an impressive change of pace when brought widest of all with his effort in the straight and his rider could afford to ease him down near the line. The application of a visor the last two times now would appear to have improved this already smart performer and he could be Group class.

Leitmotiv(IRE) ran a creditable enough race in second. He looked unlucky over course and distance on his previous start but, racing in a first-time visor, he was basically beaten by a better horse this time. (op 11/4)

Hattan(IRE) ran a tremendous race off a mark of 110 and is holding his form really well.

Go For Gold(IRE) ◆ can be considered very unlucky not to finish much closer as he was stopped in his run against the inside rail around two furlongs out, and the race was all over by the time he switched more towards the centre.

Jadalee(IRE) was too keen for his own good.

Lost Soldier Three(IRE) did not look to have too many excuses. (op 18/1)

Hazeymm(IRE) had the run of the race out in front but offered disappointingly little under pressure.

546a ETISALAT BALANCHINE STKS (F&M) (LISTED RACE) (TURF) 1m 194y(T)

5:55 (5:55) 3-Y-O+

£45,918 (£15,306; £7,653; £3,826; £2,295; £1,530)

			RPR
1		**Royal Alchemist**[15] [397] 5-9-0 104 ... KerrinMcEvoy 4 (I Mohammed, UAE) *racd in 3rd: trckd ldr gng wl 2 1/2f out: led 1 1/2f out: r.o wl: easily* **14/1**	107
2	2 1/4	**Abhisheka (IRE)**[111] [6333] 4-9-0 100 ... TedDurcan 10 (Saeed Bin Suroor) *trckd ldr: led 2 1/2f out: r.o wl: hdd 1 1/2f out: no ch w wnr* **10/1**	102
3	3/4	**Dont Dili Dali**[15] [401] 4-9-0 96 ... JohnEgan 1 (J S Moore) *mid-div: rdn to trck wnr 2 1/2f out: r.o fnl 1 1/2f* **16/1**	101
4	2 1/4	**Zaafran**[15] [397] 4-9-0 97 ... (e) JMurtagh 8 (D Selvaratnam, UAE) *slowly away: settled in last: rdn 2 1/2f out: wd: r.o fnl 1 1/2f* **7/1**[3]	96
5	1/2	**Alexandra Rose (SAF)**[15] [397] 5-9-0 102 ... WCMarwing 6 (M F De Kock, South Africa) *settled in rr: gng wl 3f out: rdn 2f out: nt qckn* **5/4**[1]	95
6	1/2	**Expensive**[15] [397] 4-9-0 96 ... EddieAhern 7 (C F Wall) *settled in rr: gng wl on rail 3f out: eased clsr 2 1/2f out: rdn and r.o* **28/1**	94

7	1 1/4	**Jet Past (SAF)**[15] 397 5-9-0 97	RyanMoore 5	91	
		(S Seemar, UAE) *mid-div: rdn to chal 2 1/2f out: r.o one pce: wknd fnl f*			**9/1**
8	shd	**Afaf (FR)**[15] 397 5-9-0 105	(t) C-PLemaire 2	91	
		(M Delzangles, France) *slowly away: in rr of mid-div: rdn 2 1/2f out: nvr able to chal*			**14/1**
9	14	**Estrela Brynhild (USA)**[15] 397 4-9-4 95	ADomingos 3	66	
		(C Morgado, Brazil) *sn led: hdd 2 1/2f out: wknd*			**33/1**
10	18	**Vista Bella**[15] 397 5-9-0 107	(t) LDettori 9	24	
		(Saeed Bin Suroor) *mid-div out wd: rdn 2 1/2f out: no rspnse: eased*			**9/2**[2]

1m 49.13s (-0.67) **10** Ran SP% **119.8**

.

Owner Sheikh Hamdan Bin Mohammed Al Maktoum **Bred** B Minty **Trained** UAE

■ Royal Alchemist provided Ismail Mohammed with his fifth winner of the night.

FOCUS

A fairly good fillies' and mares' Listed contest on paper, but there was not a great deal of pace on and the first two home were in the front three throughout.

NOTEBOOK

Royal Alchemist improved significantly on the form she showed when well behind a few of today's rivals, most notably Alexandra Rose, in a similar event on her debut in Dubai. She might just have needed that last run, as she had been off the track since September, but she was clearly spot on this time and won well. She has been around a while now, but it is by no means out of the question she could be improving a touch and she should continue to go well in fillies/mares only company.

Abhisheka(IRE), very progressive in the UK last year, was given every chance and could have no excuses. This was only her eighth career start, and her first race in 111 days, so there should be better to come. (op 9/1)

Dont Dili Dali had to be switched with her effort in the straight but kept on to the line and continues in good order.

Zaafran raced in last for much of the way and, although staying on widest of all in the straight, she was probably given too much to do.

Alexandra Rose(SAF) had no fewer than seven of today's rivals behind her, including Royal Alchemist, when runner-up in a similar event on her previous start but, having been set plenty to do, she never really looked like getting there.

Expensive might have benefited from a stronger gallop. (op 25/1)

Vista Bella has presumably had her problems over the years and unfortunately she was heavily eased in the straight.

547a KALLEMNI TROPHY (H'CAP) (TURF) 6f (T)

6:25 (6:26) (95-110,107) 3-Y-O+

£36,734 (£12,244; £6,122; £3,061; £1,836; £1,224)

				RPR	
1		**Bad Girl Runs (SAF)**[293] 5-9-3 **106**	WCMarwing 6	116	
		(M F De Kock, South Africa) *mid-div: rdn 2 1/2f out: forced wd 1 1/2f out: r.o wl to ld line*			**10/1**
2	shd	**Great Britain**[111] 6335 5-9-2 **105**	LDettori 2	115	
		(Saeed Bin Suroor) *led main gp: smooth hdwy to ld 1 1/2f out: r.o wl: hdd line*			**6/1**[2]
3	1/2	**Greek Renaissance (IRE)**[14] 409 4-9-2 **105**	KerrinMcEvoy 1	113	
		(I Mohammed, UAE) *slowly away: racd in mid-div: trckd runner-up 2f out: ev ch: r.o*			**1/1**[1]
4	4 1/4	**Mac Love**[15] 400 6-9-3 **106**	PJSmullen 8	101	
		(J Noseda) *settled in rr: nvr nr to chal: r.o fnl 1 1/2f*			**10/1**
5	3/4	**Paradise Isle**[14] 415 6-9-3 **106**	EddieAhern 7	99	
		(C F Wall) *prom in main gp: trckd runner-up 1 1/2f out: r.o one pce*			**6/1**[2]
6	1	**Celtic Mill**[8] 474 9-9-1 **104**	(p) JohnEgan 10	94	
		(D W Barker) *set fast pce: disputing tl led 2f out: hdd 1 1/2f out: wknd fnl f*			**16/1**
7	1/2	**Prince Tamino**[8] 472 4-9-1 **104**	WSupple 5	93	
		(I Mohammed, UAE) *racd in rr: nvr able to chal*			**13/2**[3]
8	1 1/4	**Feet So Fast**[8] 472 8-9-0 **102**	TedDurcan 9	88	
		(S Seemar, UAE) *settled in rr: nvr nr to chal*			**22/1**
9	3/4	**Strike Up The Band**[22] 326 4-9-1 **104**	(e) AdrianTNicholls 4	87	
		(D Nicholls) *set fast pce: disputing tl hdd 2f out: wknd*			**33/1**
10	3/4	**Sunrise (SAF)**[15] 400 6-9-4 **107**	(t) RyanMoore 3	87	
		(S Seemar, UAE) *v.s.a: racd in rr: nvr nr to chal*			**25/1**

1m 10.84s (-0.56) **10** Ran SP% **127.1**

.

Owner Mrs S Plattner **Bred** La Plaisance Stud **Trained** South Africa

FOCUS

Often, these limited handicaps at the Carnival tend to be weak in comparison with similar events in the UK, but this looked a very decent contest. Both Celtic Mill and Strike Up The Band went off too fast and set the race up for the closers.

NOTEBOOK

Bad Girl Runs(SAF) has won a Group 1 over 1m1f in her native South Africa, so the strong gallop would have helped bring her stamina into play, and she got up on the line to defy a 293-day absence. Although she managed to get up to win this time, she does look as though she will benefit from a step up to 7f at the very least. (op 9/1)

Great Britain ◆ fared best of those to race handily and emerges with plenty of credit considering he was returning from a 111-day break, for a stable who have not really been firing at this year's Carnival. He flashed his tail a touch under pressure, but that doesn't seem too much of a problem for now, and this lightly-raced individual looks well worth keeping on the right side of.

Greek Renaissance(IRE) could not repeat the form of his recent course-and-distance success off an 8lb higher mark, and perhaps his recent exertions - three runs in just under a month having been off the track for four months - are just catching up with him. (op 6/5)

Mac Love did not seem too unlucky this time, but this was a respectable effort all the same.

Paradise Isle could not match the form she showed when second over course and distance on her previous start.

Celtic Mill went off too fast and probably did well to finish so close.

Prince Tamino had excuses for his two previous starts at this year's Carnival, but he seemed to have his chance this time and was well off the pick of his form for Hughie Morrison. (op 7/1)

Strike Up The Band was off far too fast.

[495] LINGFIELD (L-H)

Saturday, February 24

OFFICIAL GOING: Standard

There were two course records lowered on this eight-race card and the times strongly suggest the track was riding very fast.

Wind: strong across

548 CANVAS PRINTS FROM BONUSPRINT.COM H'CAP (DIV I) 7f (P)

1:30 (1:41) (Class 6) (0-60,62) 4-Y-O+ **£1,706** (£503; £252) **Stalls** Low

Form					RPR	
000-	1		**Cativo Cavallino**[92] 6578 4-7-11 **46** oh1	NataliaGemelova(5) 8	55	
			(J E Long) *trckd ldr over 5f out: rdn wl over 1f out: styd on to ld nr fin*			**20/1**
55-6	2	1/2	**What Do You Know**[7] 486 4-9-1 **59**	JimmyQuinn 11	67	
			(A M Hales) *sn led: rdn 2f out: hdd and no ex nr fin*			**10/1**
2112	3	1	**Lucius Verrus (USA)**[9] 467 7-9-4 **62**	(v) NCallan 3	67	
			(D Shaw) *tk keen hold: racd in midfield: rdn over 3f out: hdwy 2f out: chsd ldng pair ins fnl f: kpt on same pce*			**3/1**[1]
6014	4	nk	**Binnion Bay (IRE)**[10] 461 6-8-13 **60**	(b) AmirQuinn(3) 2	64	
			(J J Bridger) *stdd s: hld up in rr: hdwy and rdn over 2f out: kpt on u.p:ntrch ldrs*			**9/2**[3]
1204	5	nk	**Mulberry Lad (IRE)**[8] 479 5-8-10 **54**	JimCrowley 6	57	
			(P W Hiatt) *towards rr: rdn over 3f out: styd on u.p over 1f out: nt rch ldrs*			**4/1**[2]
0-0	6	1/2	**Inwaan (IRE)**[33] 211 4-9-2 **60**	(t) DaneO'Neill 7	62	
			(P R Webber) *hld up wl in tch: hdwy to chse ldng pair over 2f out: sn rdn: fdd ins fnl f*			**14/1**
-040	7	2	**Hotchpotch (USA)**[26] 292 4-8-9 **56**	(p) StephaneBreux(3) 10	53	
			(J R Best) *t.k.h: traked ldr tl over 5f out: styd prom: rdn over 2f out: wknd wl over 1f out*			**8/1**
1-56	8	1/2	**Cool Tiger**[17] 383 4-8-8 **52**	ShaneKelly 1	48	
			(P Howling) *s.i.s: hld up in last: rdn and effrt over 2f out: n.d*			**12/1**
4-00	9	nk	**Executive Paddy (IRE)**[20] 195 8-9-2 **60**	SebSanders 4	55	
			(I A Wood) *hld up: hdwy to chse ldrs 4f out: rdn wl over 2f out: wknd 2f out*			**12/1**
22-3	10	nk	**Fairdonna**[27] 272 4-8-13 **57**	EddieAhern 5	51	
			(D J Coakley) *t.k.h: chsd ldrs tl stdd into midfield after 2f: rdn over 3f out: bhd last 2f*			**9/2**[3]

1m 24.46s (-1.43) **Going Correction** -0.20s/f (Stan) **10** Ran SP% **128.4**

Speed ratings (Par 101):100,99,98,97,97 97,94,94,93,93

CSF £224.71 CT £809.54 TOTE £46.40: £7.90, £3.40, £1.40; EX 454.50 Trifecta £269.90 Part won. Pool £380.20. - 0.20 winning units..

Owner P Saxon **Bred** Miss A M Rees **Trained** Caterham, Surrey

■ Bucharest (5/2, vet's advice) & Up Tempo (12/1, bolted bef s, rdr uns & inj) withdrawn. R4, deduct 30p in £. New market formed.

■ Stewards' Enquiry : Jimmy Quinn one-day ban: careless riding (Mar 7)

FOCUS

A moderate handicap run in a time 0.31 seconds slower than the second division, and 1.09 seconds off the time recorded by Wavertree Warrior in the later 86-100. A few of those towards the back were a little short of room after a furlong or so, but the first two home were always handy and avoided any trouble. The form looks straightforward despite the surprise winner.

549 CANVAS PRINTS FROM BONUSPRINT.COM H'CAP (DIV II) 7f (P)

2:00 (2:05) (Class 6) (0-60,65) 4-Y-O+ **£1,706** (£503; £252) **Stalls** Low

Form					RPR	
00-4	1		**Night Wolf (IRE)**[27] 274 7-8-6 **50**	(t) PaulDoe 10	61	
			(Jamie Poulton) *sn led tl hdd after 2f: pressed ldr tl led again 3f out: rdn clr wl over 1f out: in n.d fnl f*			**16/1**
0-45	2	2 1/2	**Border Artist**[8] 485 8-8-11 **55**	JimmyQuinn 2	60	
			(J Pearce) *hld up in midfield: rdn and effrt 2f out: kpt on u.p fnl f: wnt 2nd nr fin: no ch w wnr*			**14/1**
2523	3	nk	**King After**[10] 461 5-8-7 **54**	(v) StephaneBreux(3) 5	58	
			(J R Best) *chsd ldrs: rdn over 3f out: kpt on u.p but no ch w wnr fnl f*			**11/2**[2]
-202	4	3/4	**Cabourg (IRE)**[8] 479 4-9-2 **60**	(b) SebSanders 9	62	
			(R Bastiman) *t.k.h: hld up in midfield: hdwy on outer wl over 2f out: chsd ldrs u.p wl over 1f out: no prog after*			**8/1**
655-	5	shd	**Musango**[56] 6987 4-9-1 **59**	SamHitchcott 4	61	
			(B R Johnson) *hld up in rr: rdn and hdwy over 1f out: kpt on: nvr threatened ldrs*			**33/1**
5-11	6	3/4	**Im Ova Ere Dad (IRE)**[10] 461 4-9-7 **65**	TonyCulhane 6	65	
			(D E Cantillon) *t.k.h: in tch: hdwy on outer to chse ldrs 4f out: rdn 2f out: outpcd by wnr: fdd last 100 yds*			**6/4**[1]
00-0	7	shd	**Napoletano (GER)**[17] 381 6-8-13 **57**	LPKeniry 7	57	
			(S Dow) *stdd s: t.k.h: hld up in rr: rdn and hdwy over 1f out: styng on whn n.m.r nr fin: nvr nrr*			**16/1**
00-3	8	hd	**Arfinnit (IRE)**[35] 189 6-7-9 **46** oh1	(p) WilliamBuick(7) 12	45	
			(Mrs A L M King) *hld up in rr: rdn and effrt over 2f out: kpt on but nvr pce to rch ldrs*			**25/1**
-144	9	3/4	**Beneking**[21] 346 7-9-2 **60**	(p) ChrisCatlin 1	57	
			(D Burchell) *chsd wnr tl led 5f out: hdd 3f out: rdn over 2f out: outpcd by wnr over 1f out: wknd ins fnl f*			**13/2**[3]
-506	10	nk	**State Dilemma (IRE)**[10] 461 6-8-13 **57**	(v) DeanMcKeown 11	53	
			(D Shaw) *chsd ldrs tl lost pl wl over 2f out: no ch after*			**12/1**
0040	11	1/2	**Miss Redactive**[24] 310 4-8-2 **46** oh1	(v) HayleyTurner 8	41	
			(M D I Usher) *hld up in midfield: rdn 3f out: n.d*			**66/1**
00-3	12	2 1/2	**Campbeltown (IRE)**[19] 366 4-9-2 **60**	DaneO'Neill 3	49	
			(M R Hoad) *chsd ldrs: rdn and wknd over 2f out*			**10/1**

1m 24.15s (-1.74) **Going Correction** -0.20s/f (Stan) **12** Ran SP% **123.3**

Speed ratings (Par 101):101,98,97,96,96 95,95,95,94,94 93,91

CSF £227.09 CT £1431.81 TOTE £20.40: £4.00, £3.70, £1.90; EX 170.90 TRIFECTA Not won..

Owner Miss N Henton **Bred** Watership Down Stud **Trained** Whitcombe, Dorset

FOCUS

A moderate handicap, although the time was 0.31 seconds quicker than the first division. Solid form, the winner back to his 2005 level and the second and third close to recent form.

Musango ◆ Official explanation: jockey said gelding was denied a clear run

550 BONUSPRINT.COM H'CAP 7f (P)

2:30 (2:31) (Class 2) (0-100,99) 4-Y-0+

£11,217 (£3,358; £1,679; £840; £419; £210) **Stalls** Low

Form RPR

24-0 **1** **Wavertree Warrior (IRE)**[35] 197 5-8-4 **88** ow3.......... JamesDoyle(3) 6 96
(N P Littmoden) *hld up wl bhd: shkn up and stl plenty to do over 1f out: str run u.p fnl f to ld nr fin* **15/2**[3]

213- **2** *nk* **Bomber Command (USA)**[64] 6915 4-8-3 **91**.............. PatrickHills(7) 10 98
(J W Hills) *hld up in rr: hdwy on outer 2f out: r.o strly fnl f: wnt 2nd nr fin* **13/2**[2]

5212 **3** *nk* **Waterside (IRE)**[16] 391 8-9-4 **99**.................................... SebSanders 13 106+
(G L Moore) *led for 1f: chsd ldr tl rdn to ld over 1f out: kpt on:hdd and lost 2 pls fnl strides* **9/1**

1-44 **4** *shd* **Orchard Supreme**[7] 487 4-9-2 **97**.................................... DaneO'Neill 7 103
(R Hannon) *hld up: hdwa over 2f out: rdn over 1f out: chsd ldr wl ins fnl: kpt on same pce and lost 2 pls nr fin* **13/2**[2]

4-62 **5** *½* **Saviours Spirit**[11] 452 6-8-8 **89**.................................... JoeFanning 12 94
(T G Mills) *chsd ldrs on outer: rdn over 2f out: kpt on same pce* **16/1**

12-4 **6** *½* **Marajaa (IRE)**[35] 197 5-8-7 **88**.. BrettDoyle 11 92
(W J Musson) *t.k.h: hld up in midfield: hdwy 2f out: swtchd lft and r.o over 1f out: no ex wl ins fnl f* **2/1**[1]

00-0 **7** *¾* **Moayed**[35] 198 8-8-12 **93**...(b) IanMongan 2 95
(N P Littmoden) *stdd s: hld up in last: hdwy on outside 2f out: rn ins fnl f: nvr nrr* **16/1**

520- **8** *hd* **Humungous (IRE)**[161] 5374 4-9-2 **97**.............................. SteveDrowne 3 98
(C R Egerton) *s.i.s: sn chsng ldrs: rdn and briefly outpcd over 2f out: kpt on fnl f* **16/1**

/005 **9** *shd* **Tony James (IRE)**[7] 487 5-8-9 **90**... NCallan 1 91
(K O Cunningham-Brown) *t.k.h: chsd ldrs: rdn and ev ch over 1f out: fdd last 100 yds* **12/1**

12/ **10** *1* **Tufton**[514] 5556 4-8-10 **91**...(t) OscarUrbina 9 89
(M Botti) *stdd s: hld up in rr: hdwy 3f out: rdn and kpt on same pce wl over 1f out* **16/1**

0-54 **11** *hd* **Ajigolo**[21] 344 4-8-12 **93**... EdwardCreighton 8 91
(M R Channon) *t.k.h: led after 1f tl hdd over 1f out: wknd ins fnl f* **12/1**

44/0 **12** *7* **Two Step Kid (USA)**[50] 41 6-8-7 **88**........................... ShaneKelly 4 68
(J Noseda) *a bhd: rdn and lost tch over 2f out* **25/1**

236/ **13** *8* **Mafaheem**[614] 2773 5-8-6 **87**.. LPKeniry 5 46
(S Dow) *racd in midfield: rdn and lost pl over 3f out: wl bhd last 2f: t.o* **50/1**

1m 23.37s (-2.52) **Going Correction** -0.20s/f (Stan) **13** Ran SP% **126.5**
Speed ratings (Par 109):106,105,105,105,104 104,103,102,102,101 101,93,84
CSF £59.10 CT £476.94 TOTE £9.10: £2.30, £2.20, £3.80; EX 76.50 Trifecta £313.50 Part won. Pool: £441.68 - 0.10 winning units..

Owner Wavertree Racing Partnership C **Bred** Liam Queally **Trained** Newmarket, Suffolk

FOCUS

A race full of improving types and very solid form through the second, third and fourth. They finished in a bunch, but that just highlights how competitive this was, as the pace had been fair throughout. As one would expect, the winning time was faster than both divisions of the 46-60.

NOTEBOOK

Wavertree Warrior(IRE) ◆ is reliant on a good pace, so the race was run to suit, and he stayed on best for all for a narrow victory. His rider was unable to claim his allowance, but made up for it with a fine ride, conjuring a late run out of his mount between horses. Every bit as effective on turf, if not even better, the winner could well land a big handicap this season. (op 9-1)

Bomber Command(USA) ◆, dropped a furlong in trip off the back of a two-month break, made his move widest of all and for that reason he could be considered a touch unlucky. He is improving all the time and, like the winner, appeals as a handicapper to follow this year. (op 8-1)

Waterside(IRE) has been in good form on Fibresand lately and, just as effective on Polytrack, he ran another terrific race. He was by no means allowed things all his own way, with Ajigolo taking him on for the lead, but he offered plenty under pressure and was just nabbed late on by a couple of rivals who had been positioned well off the pace. He is in the form of his life and, an absolute credit to his connections, he remains well worth keeping on the right side of. (op 8-1)

Orchard Supreme was forced to wait to make his move rounding the final bend, but he was in the clear for long enough and did not look unlucky. He continues to progress and should be capable of even better back over 1m. (op 11-2)

Saviours Spirit, having a rare outing over 7f, was always close up and can have no excuses. (op 20-1)

Marajaa(IRE) looked very unlucky when fourth over 1m round here on his previous start, but he did not seem to have too many excuses this time. He was forced to switch to the inside in the straight, but basically didn't finish as strongly as a few of these. (op 5-2 tchd 11-4 in places)

Tufton ◆, the winner of a maiden and placed in a novice event when with Godolphin in 2005, shaped well on his debut for the Botti yard off the back of a 514-day absence. His effort is particularly creditable considering he raced keenly with no cover in the early stages. Providing he stands training, he should be able to improve on this and he is probably worth keeping an eye on.

551 PONTINS.COM CLEVES STKS (LISTED RACE) 6f (P)

3:05 (3:05) (Class 1) 4-Y-0+

£14,762 (£5,595; £2,800; £1,396; £699; £351) **Stalls** Low

Form RPR

001- **1** **King Orchisios (IRE)**[118] 6243 4-9-0 97...............................(p) NCallan 5 107
(K A Ryan) *mde all: rdn wl over 1f out: hld on wl: all out* **8/1**[2]

26-1 **2** *hd* **Woodnook**[14] 419 4-8-9 90... JohnEgan 8 101
(J A R Toller) *wnt rt s: hld up in last pair: hdwy over 1f out: r.o u.p fnl f: wnt 2nd on line* **10/1**[3]

1235 **3** *shd* **Qadar (IRE)**[7] 490 5-9-0 102...(b) IanMongan 1 106
(N P Littmoden) *t.k.h: chsd ldrs: wnt 2nd over 2f out: hrd drvn 1f out: kpt on: lost 2nd on line* **10/1**[3]

4-24 **4** *½* **Red Cape (FR)**[11] 452 4-9-0 90.. BrettDoyle 4 105
(Jane Chapple-Hyam) *t.k.h: hld up in midfield: rdn and briefly outpcd 2f out: kpt on u.p fnl f* **12/1**

-411 **5** *¾* **Areyoutalkingtome**[21] 344 4-9-0 115............................... EddieAhern 2 104+
(C A Cyzer) *stdd s: t.k.h: hdwy to trck ldrs 3f out: bmpd bnd over 2f out: rdn and short of room fnl f: eased nr fin* **1/3**[1]

104- **6** *7* **Angus Newz**[135] 5921 4-8-12 92.......................................(v) ShaneKelly 7 79
(M Quinn) *t.k.h: chsd ldrs tl wl over 2f out: sn struggling* **16/1**

7 *1* **Holbien (IRE)**[111] 6359 4-9-0 .... DMGrant 3 78
(Liam Roche, Ire) *chsd ldr tl over 2f out: rdn and edgd lft bnd over 2f out: sn wknd* **25/1**

614- **8** *¾* **Golden Asha**[260] 2389 5-8-10 86 ow1.............................. TonyCulhane 6 72
(G G Margarson) *a bhd: no ch last 2f* **33/1**

1m 10.52s (-2.29) **Going Correction** -0.20s/f (Stan) course record **8** Ran SP% **124.7**
Speed ratings (Par 111):107,106,106,105,104 95,94,93
CSF £90.54 TOTE £7.40: £2.40, £2.50, £2.40; EX 80.60 Trifecta £292.00 Pool: £933.58 - 2.27 winning units..

Owner Mr & Mrs Julian And Rosie Richer **Bred** Rathbarry Stud **Trained** Hambleton, N Yorks

■ Stewards' Enquiry : D M Grant one-day ban: careless riding (Mar 7)

FOCUS

Not the penalty kick many expected for Areyoutalkingtome, with King Orchisios stealing this from the front having set a steady pace. This was a nightmare to assess, but one thing is for sure, the form cannot be taken literally. King Orchisios probably did not need to improve on his Wolverhampton win, and Areyoutalkingtome was 21lb off his latest victory. The winning time was only 0.89 seconds quicker than the fillies' handicap won by the 64-rated Sweet Pickle.

NOTEBOOK

King Orchisios(IRE), who has been gelded since winning off a mark of 92 in a 5f handicap at Wolverhampton 118 days previously, stole this Listed contest under a fine front-running ride from Neil Callan. Able to lead at just a steady pace, he caught a few of these out, not least Areyoutalkingtome, when kicking for home off the final bend, and just held on. He has always been held in very high regard, so it will perhaps not surprise some people that he has managed to break through at this level, but the form just cannot be taken literally. Having said that, he could improve this year, as he has by no means been over raced for a sprinter. (op 9-1 tchd 10-1)

Woodnook was successful over course and distance on her previous start, but that came in handicap company off a mark of just 84. For all that this is unreliable form, she emerges with plenty of credit considering she was positioned well off the pace in a race run at a steady gallop, and connections will no doubt have been delighted to pick up some black type. (op 12-1)

Qadar(IRE) does not always find that much under pressure, but he looked unlucky this time as he appeared to be struck over the head by the winning rider's whip near the line. It cost him second at the very least. (op 12-1 tchd 14-1)

Red Cape(FR) raced keenly and would have preferred a stronger pace. (op 16-1)

Areyoutalkingtome was the winner of his last six starts round here, achieving an RPR of 121 when successful off a mark of 110 in a 5f handicap on his most recent outing, and is easily one of the best horses ever to have raced on the sand in this country. Considering he had upwards of 14lb in hand of his seven rivals at the weights, this looked a straightforward opportunity for him to gain his first pattern-race victory, but he failed to produce anything like his best. He was hampered on the final bend when going for a run up the inside of Holbien, and was again short of room in the straight but, even if one argues he would have won with a clear run, which is probably unlikely, he would still have been well below the pick of his form. The steady pace was basically his undoing, as he tends to win his races with a smart turn of foot, and he can set the record straight when getting the race run to suit. (op 4-11 tchd 2-5 in a place)

552 GO PONTIN'S WINTER DERBY TRIAL STKS (LISTED RACE) 1m 2f (P)

3:40 (3:40) (Class 1) 4-Y-0+

£14,762 (£5,595; £2,800; £1,396; £699; £351) **Stalls** Low

Form RPR

1-22 **1** **Cusoon**[14] 420 5-9-0 96.. GeorgeBaker 8 105
(G L Moore) *hld up in last pair: smooth hdwy on outer 3f out: chsd ldr over 2f out: led wl over 1f out: sn rdn: clr 1f out: jst hld on* **11/2**

122- **2** *shd* **Blue Bajan (IRE)**[98] 6516 5-9-0 104............................... ChrisCatlin 3 108+
(Andrew Turnell) *hld up in rr: hdwy on inner wl over 1f out: swtchd rt and chsd wnr 1f out: edgd lft u.p: r.o: jst failed* **11/4**[1]

-111 **3** *2* **Mighty**[14] 420 4-8-13 92.. BrettDoyle 5 101
(Jane Chapple-Hyam) *w.w in midfield: in tch: rdn and outpcd over 2f out: styd on fnl f: nt pce to rch ldrs* **3/1**[2]

2311 **4** *4* **Party Boss**[7] 487 5-9-0 97.. SebSanders 1 93
(C E Brittain) *led tl rdn and hdd wl over 1f out: wknd 1f out* **9/2**

-410 **5** *1 ¼* **Fusili (IRE)**[28] 264 4-8-9 94 ow1.. NCallan 7 87
(N P Littmoden) *chsd ldr tl over 2f out: wknd wl over 1f out* **20/1**

0624 **6** *3* **Tous Les Deux**[14] 420 4-8-13 73............................ RobbieFitzpatrick 4 85
(Peter Grayson) *stdd s: hld up in last: rdn over 2f out: sn outpcd* **66/1**

300- **7** *2 ½* **Birkspiel (GER)**[153] 5547 6-9-0 105.. LPKeniry 2 81
(S Dow) *chsd ldrs: rdn 4f out: wknd over 2f out* **40/1**

35-2 **8** *2 ½* **Grand Passion (IRE)**[20] 352 7-9-0 100........................ SteveDrowne 6 76
(G Wragg) *hld up wl in tch: rdn and outpcd 3f out: no ch after* **4/1**[3]

2m 1.79s (-6.00) **Going Correction** -0.20s/f (Stan) course record
WFA 4 from 5yo+ 1lb **8** Ran SP% **113.9**
Speed ratings (Par 111):116,115,114,111,110 107,105,103
CSF £20.65 TOTE £7.40: £1.70, £1.90, £1.10; EX 35.50 Trifecta £140.80 Pool: £682.51 - 3.44 winning units..

Owner The Winning Hand **Bred** Mrs Dare Wigan And Dominic Wigan **Trained** Woodingdean, E Sussex

FOCUS

This was the first year the Winter Derby Trial carried Listed status, with the Derby itself being upgraded to a Group 3, but only eight lined up for the third successive year. Still, there was probably just enough quality on show to justify the race's new Pattern class and, with Party Boss having set a good, even gallop from the start, the progressive Cusoon was able to break his own course record. The sixth limits the form slightly.

NOTEBOOK

Cusoon has really got his act together on the Polytrack this winter and just proved good enough on the step up to Listed company, breaking his own course record in the process. Having won three handicaps on the bounce towards the end of last year, he had appeared unsuited by steadily-run races when second on his last couple of outings, including when behind Mighty on his previous start. The pace was much more to his liking this time, though, and having got first run on Blue Bajan when swooping wide of runners rounding the final bend, he showed the better attitude of the pair to hold on near the finish. He obviously deserves to take his chance in the Winter Derby itself, and the winner of this race traditionally has a good record in the main event, but realistically that will require a further step up in form. (op 8-1)

Blue Bajan(IRE) did not appear to do a great deal wrong when beaten just a short-head into second in the Churchill Stakes over course and distance three months previously, but it was disappointing he could not go one better in this slightly weaker contest. He made up three lengths or so in the final furlong after Cusoon got first run on him, but the way he carried both his head and his tail under maximum pressure was a little disconcerting. (op 3-1 tchd 7-2)

Mighty has been most progressive round here this winter, but this required further improvement and he just came up short. This was, though, only his sixth career start, and there could yet be better to come. (op 10-3 tchd 7-2 and 11-4)

Party Boss set a nice, even gallop, but his best peformances have come over 7f-1m. (op 5-1 tchd 4-1)

Fusili(IRE) was unable to impose herself with Party Boss dominating from the start and she was below her best. (tchd 25-1)

Grand Passion(IRE), the winner of this race both last year and in 2004, ran as though something was not quite right this time. Official explanation: trainer had no explanation for the poor form shown (op 5-2)

553 PONTIN'S FAMILY HOLIDAYS MAIDEN STKS 1m 4f (P)

4:10 (4:10) (Class 5) 3-Y-O **£2,914** (£867; £433; £216) **Stalls** Low

Form RPR

4-02 **1** **Spring Glory**[10] 460 3-8-12 70.. SebSanders 6 67+
(Sir Mark Prescott) *pressed ldr tl led 7f out: mde rest: rdn over 3f out: clr 3f out: styd on in n.d last 2f* **5/2**[2]

402- **2** *2 ½* **Into Action**[87] 6650 3-9-3 71.. DaneO'Neill 5 66
(R Hannon) *stdd s: hld up in midfield: hdwy over 5f out: rdn 4f out: chsd ldng pair over 2f out: kpt on to go 2nd nr fin:* **9/1**[3]

4 **3** *hd* **Shawhill**[17] [386] 3-8-9 .... JerryO'Dwyer(3) 4 61
(A M Hales) *s.i.s: sn chsng ldrs: rdn over 4f out: chsd wnr over 2f out: no imp: lost 2nd nr fin* **11/1**

00 **4** *2 1/2* **Camp Counsellor**[8] [484] 3-9-3 .... ShaneKelly 3 62
(J A Osborne) *chsd ldrs: rdn wl over 4f out: outpcd 3f out: kpt on but n.d after* **33/1**

5-60 **5** *16* **Color Man**[28] [267] 3-9-3 48.. JimCrowley 1 36
(Mrs A J Perrett) *s.i.s: in tch in midfield: rdn after 3f: outpcd 4f out: sn no ch* **40/1**

0 **6** *nk* **President Dan**[17] [386] 3-9-3 .... EdwardCreighton 9 36
(M R Channon) *stdd s and dropped in bhd: rdn 5f out: sn lost tch* **40/1**

7 *9* **Holy Affairs (IRE)**[117] [6264] 3-9-3 .... DMGrant 7 21
(Liam Roche, Ire) *hld up towards rr: hdwy over 4f out: rdn and wknd 3f out: eased over 1f out: t.o* **50/1**

6-22 **8** *21* **Rain And Shade**[17] [386] 3-9-3 78...................................... JoeFanning 2 —
(M Johnston) *led tl 7f out: chsd wnr: rdn over 4f out: wknd over 2f out: eased fnl f: t.o* **8/13**[1]

000 **9** *1 1/4* **Binham Boy**[17] [386] 3-9-0 47................................. StephenDonohoe(3) 8 —
(M J Gingell) *stdd s: dropped in bhd: rdn and lost tch 5f our: t.o last 3f* **100/1**

2m 33.64s (-0.75) **Going Correction** -0.20s/f (Stan) **9** Ran SP% **119.6**
Speed ratings (Par 97):94,92,92,90,79 79,73,59,58
CSF £24.43 TOTE £3.90: £1.20, £2.40, £2.60; EX 27.50 Trifecta £59.40 Pool: £1,110.06 - 13.26 winning units..
Owner Cheveley Park Stud **Bred** Cheveley Park Stud Ltd **Trained** Newmarket, Suffolk

FOCUS
A weak maiden but the form makes sense. The pace was strong from the start. Spring Glory found this a straightforward opportunity once Rain And Shade dropped away and was value for a bit extra.

Rain And Shade Official explanation: trainer's rep said, regarding the poor form shown, colt went too quickly early on

Binham Boy Official explanation: vet said gelding returned lame

554 PONTINSBINGO.COM H'CAP 5f (P)
4:40 (4:40) (Class 4) (0-85,85) 4-Y-0+ **£4,857** (£1,445; £722; £360) **Stalls** High

Form RPR

1351 **1** **Magic Glade**[16] [388] 8-8-12 81... JimCrowley 5 94
(Tom Dascombe) *taken down early: hld up: hdwy wl over 2f out: chsd ldr over 1f out: rdn to ld ins fnl f: rdn out: readily* **11/2**[3]

05-6 **2** *1 1/2* **Graze On**[54] [5] 5-8-12 81.....................................(b) RobbieFitzpatrick 3 89
(Peter Grayson) *chsd ldr tl rdn to ld over 2f out: hdd ins fnl f: kpt on same pce* **8/1**

06-3 **3** *1 1/4* **Desperate Dan**[11] [452] 6-9-2 85.....................................(b) ShaneKelly 7 89
(J A Osborne) *s.i.s: bhd: hdwy and swtchd rt over 1f out: r.o strly ins fnl f: nrst fin* **5/1**[2]

-312 **4** *shd* **Figaro Flyer (IRE)**[8] [480] 4-8-10 79................................ TonyCulhane 6 82
(P Howling) *taken down early: bhd: rdn over 3f out: hdwy over 1f out: r.o fnl f: nvr trbld ldrs* **11/4**[1]

0-34 **5** *1 3/4* **Tartatartufata**[39] [155] 5-8-3 79......................................(v) PatrickHills(7) 2 76
(D Shaw) *chsd ldrs: rdn wl over 1f out: wknd fnl f* **11/2**[3]

3-20 **6** *3/4* **Pieter Brueghel (USA)**[46] [81] 8-9-2 85........................ JoeFanning 10 79
(D Nicholls) *towards rr on outer: rdn and effrt over 2f out: kpt on ins fnl f: nvr trbld ldrs* **11/1**

0-00 **7** *hd* **Smokin Beau**[11] [452] 10-8-11 80... BrettDoyle 8 73
(N P Littmoden) *chsd ldrs: rdn wl over 2f out: wknd over 1f out* **16/1**

303- **8** *1 1/4* **Bold Minstrel (IRE)**[105] [6446] 5-8-9 78................................ ChrisCatlin 4 67
(M Quinn) *sn led: rdn and hdd over 2f out: wknd over 1f out* **8/1**

15-6 **9** *1/2* **Dancing Mystery**[46] [79] 13-8-13 82........................(b) StephenCarson 9 69
(E A Wheeler) *a bhd: n.d* **25/1**

634- **10** *3/4* **Azygous**[165] [5265] 4-8-11 80.. DaneO'Neill 1 64
(J Akehurst) *racd in midfield: rdn 3f out: wknd over 2f out* **12/1**

57.26 secs (-2.52) **Going Correction** -0.20s/f (Stan) course record **10** Ran SP% **122.1**
Speed ratings (Par 105):112,109,107,107,104 103,103,101,100,99
CSF £51.51 CT £239.96 TOTE £8.00: £2.20, £3.20, £2.60; EX 70.60 Trifecta £600.20 Part won. Pool: £845.37 - 0.30 winning units..
Owner Alan Solomon **Bred** Juddmonte Farms **Trained** Lambourn, Berks

FOCUS
This looked just an ordinary sprint handicap for the grade on paper, so it was a surprise to see the course record lowered. Good, solid form, the winner back to his best.

555 PONTIN'S "BOOK EARLY" FILLIES' H'CAP 6f (P)
5:10 (5:10) (Class 5) (0-70,64) 4-Y-0+ **£3,071** (£906; £453) **Stalls** Low

Form RPR

-213 **1** **Sweet Pickle**[18] [376] 6-9-4 64...(e) PatCosgrave 6 71
(J R Boyle) *hld up bhd ldrs: hdwy 2f out: shkn up to ld ins f: pushed out: readily* **9/2**[2]

5-06 **2** *1 1/4* **Jabbara (IRE)**[8] [485] 4-8-4 50...(b) JoeFanning 5 54
(C E Brittain) *trckd ldr: rdn and upsides 2f out: led 1f out: hdd and outpcd ins fnl f* **10/3**[1]

660- **3** *1/2* **Catspraddle (USA)**[84] [6672] 4-8-9 62........................... HaddenFrost(7) 1 64
(R Hannon) *led:jnd 2f out: rdn and hdd 1f out: kpt on same pce* **7/1**[3]

-464 **4** *1/2* **Spark Up**[19] [371] 7-8-5 54.....................................(b) RichardKingscote(3) 7 55
(J W Unett) *in tch in midfield: rdn 3f out: kpt on ins fnl f: nt rch ldrs* **9/2**[2]

4-24 **5** *nk* **Priceoflove (IRE)**[19] [358] 4-9-3 63................................(t) SebSanders 2 63
(P J Makin) *chsd ldng pair: rdn over 1f out: wknd fnl f* **9/2**[2]

3300 **6** *3/4* **Whistleupthewind**[17] [383] 4-8-8 54...............................(b) MickyFenton 4 51
(J M P Eustace) *bhd: rdn and effrt on outer 3f out: nt pce to rch ldrs* **7/1**[3]

0310 **7** *3 1/2* **Dark Moon**[12] [447] 4-8-6 52.. DeanMcKeown 3 39
(D Shaw) *hld up bhd: rdn and outpcd 3f out: no ch after* **8/1**

1m 11.41s (-1.40) **Going Correction** -0.20s/f (Stan) **7** Ran SP% **113.7**
Speed ratings (Par 100):101,99,98,98,97 96,91
CSF £19.62 TOTE £5.10: £2.30, £2.00; EX 19.40 Place 6 £506.48, Place 5 £151.89.
Owner M Khan X2 **Bred** C T Van Hoorn **Trained** Epsom, Surrey

FOCUS
A modest fillies' handicap run at just a steady early gallop. Sweet Pickle did not need to be at her best to win, and the form seems sound enough.

Whistleupthewind Official explanation: jockey said filly missed the break

T/Plt: £453.70 to a £1 stake. Pool: £98,931.95. 159.15 winning tickets. T/Qpdt: £32.90 to a £1 stake. Pool: £4,337.10. 97.40 winning tickets. SP

[348]KEMPTON (A.W) (R-H)
Sunday, February 25

OFFICIAL GOING: Standard
Wind: Moderate, across Weather: Unsettled, thundery shower race 7

556 FOLLOW YOUR CONFERENCE WITH FLOODLIT RACING H'CAP (DIV I) 7f (P)
1:30 (1:31) (Class 5) (0-70,69) 4-Y-0+ **£2,266** (£674; £337; £168) **Stalls** High

Form RPR

2435 **1** **Mystic Man (FR)**[11] [455] 9-8-4 60........................(b) PatrickMathers(3) 6 67
(I W McInnes) *reluctant to enter stalls: hld up in tch: led 1f out: jnd by runner-up ins fnl f: hld on narrowly* **9/1**

0144 **2** *hd* **Binnion Bay (IRE)**[1] [548] 6-8-4 60..........................(b) MarcHalford(3) 9 66
(J J Bridger) *dwlt: sn in midfield: hdwy 2f out: jnd wnr ins fnl f: nt qckn nr fin* **9/2**[1]

0-50 **3** *1/2* **Boy Dancer (IRE)**[33] [228] 4-8-2 55 oh1.......................... PaulHanagan 2 60
(D W Barker) *hld up towards rr: hdwy over 1f out: r.o u.p fnl f* **8/1**

-053 **4** *nk* **Plateau**[20] [367] 8-9-2 69.. TPQueally 3 73
(C R Dore) *wd: in tch: effrt over 2f out: kpt on fnl f* **7/1**

-222 **5** *1/2* **Imperium**[22] [346] 6-8-8 64... JamesDoyle(3) 7 67
(Jean-Rene Auvray) *prom: rdn to ld briefly over 1f out: one pce fnl f* **6/1**[2]

0100 **6** *nk* **A Teen**[12] [450] 9-8-2 55 oh10... DaleGibson 1 57
(P Howling) *sn pushed along towards rr: styd on appr fnl f: nt rch ldrs* **33/1**

30-0 **7** *shd* **Quantum Leap**[53] [28] 10-8-13 66................................(v) JimmyQuinn 4 68
(S Dow) *bhd: rdn 3f out: hdwy to chse ldrs over 1f out: no ex fnl f* **13/2**[3]

0-40 **8** *hd* **Mister Elegant**[9] [485] 5-7-9 55 oh1............................. JosephWalsh(7) 5 56
(J L Spearing) *prom: hrd rdn 2f out: no ex over 1f out* **10/1**

1/5- **9** *1* **Baba Ghanoush**[103] [6483] 5-8-12 65.. PaulDoe 8 63
(W Jarvis) *dwlt: bhd: shkn up 2f out: nvr rchd ldrs* **10/1**

04-5 **10** *1 1/2* **Wainwright (IRE)**[55] [3] 7-8-3 56.. HayleyTurner 11 51
(P A Blockley) *chsd ldrs: hrd rdn and nt clr run over 1f out: no ex fnl f* **20/1**

3406 **11** *2 1/2* **Roman Boy (ARG)**[10] [462] 8-8-2 55....................(b[1]) AdrianMcCarthy 10 43
(Stef Liddiard) *led tl over 1f out: sn wknd* **6/1**[2]

1m 26.41s (-0.39) **Going Correction** -0.05s/f (Stan) **11** Ran SP% **119.6**
Speed ratings (Par 103):100,99,99,98,98 97,97,96,94 91
CSF £50.13 CT £352.15 TOTE £10.80: £2.90, £1.90, £3.30; EX 50.00.
Owner Dronsfield Mercedes Ltd **Bred** Gainsborough Stud Management Ltd **Trained** Catwick, E Yorks

■ Stewards' Enquiry : T P Queally one-day ban: used whip with excessive force (Mar 10)

FOCUS
A moderate handicap, run at an uneven pace. The form is very modest, rated through the runner-up, with the sixth holding down the form.

557 KEMPTON PARK FOR FUNCTION HIRE CLASSIFIED STKS 7f (P)
2:00 (2:00) (Class 7) 4-Y-0+ **£1,365** (£403; £201) **Stalls** High

Form RPR

30-0 **1** **Firework**[53] [22] 9-9-0 43.. StephenCarson 4 54
(E A Wheeler) *hld up in midfield: smooth hdwy 2f out: led 1f out: drvn out* **16/1**

050- **2** *1/2* **Champion's Way (IRE)**[69] [6861] 5-8-11 45 ow2........ JamesMillman(5) 3 55
(B R Millman) *prom: led over 3f out tl 1f out: kpt on* **10/1**

2004 **3** *1* **Savoy Chapel**[6] [497] 5-8-11 44..................................(v) JamesDoyle(3) 5 50
(A W Carroll) *hld up in rr: rdn and hdwy 2f out: styd on fnl f* **9/2**[1]

-305 **4** *nk* **Hill Of Almhuim (IRE)**[29] [271] 4-9-0 44...........(v) RobbieFitzpatrick 8 49
(Peter Grayson) *towards rr: hdwy to chse ldrs over 1f out: kpt on* **8/1**[3]

5-20 **5** *1/2* **Almowj**[14] [435] 4-9-0 45.. SebSanders 1 48
(C E Brittain) *chsd ldrs: hrd rdn and nt qckn fnl 2f* **9/2**[1]

6-30 **6** *shd* **Task Complete**[36] [189] 4-9-0 45..........................(b) FrankieMcDonald 14 51+
(Jean-Rene Auvray) *hld up in rr: nt clr run 2f out: swtchd wd over 1f out: r.o fnl f* **16/1**

0-30 **7** *1 1/2* **Arfinnit (IRE)**[1] [549] 6-8-11 42..................................(p) AmirQuinn(3) 13 44
(Mrs A L M King) *dwlt: towards rr: effrt 2f out: styd on fnl f* **11/1**

0-02 **8** *nk* **Princess Arwen**[13] [447] 5-9-0 45....................................(b) LPKeniry 12 43
(Mrs Barbara Waring) *hld up in midfield: hdwy 2f out: no ex fnl f* **14/1**

00-4 **9** *1/2* **Inscribed (IRE)**[37] [186] 4-9-0 45...................................(b[1]) PatCosgrave 7 42
(G A Huffer) *plld hrd: prom tl wknd over 1f out* **8/1**[3]

-200 **10** *1 1/4* **Beverley Beau**[23] [339] 5-8-7 44...................................... KristinStubbs(7) 9 39
(Mrs L Stubbs) *led 1f: chsd ldrs tl wknd over 1f out* **16/1**

015- **11** *3* **Cape Sydney (IRE)**[140] [5840] 4-9-0 45............................ PaulHanagan 6 31
(D W Barker) *led after 1f tl over 3f out: wknd wl over 1f out* **7/1**[2]

-545 **12** *nk* **Pontefract Glory**[14] [435] 4-8-11 43...........................(p) LiamJones(3) 11 30
(M Dods) *plld hrd: in tch: rdn over 2f out: sn outpcd* **10/1**

046- **13** *3* **Zantero**[192] [4523] 5-9-0 43... ChrisCatlin 2 22
(W M Brisbourne) *stdd s: t.k.h in rr: hdwy on outside 1/2-way: wknd 2f out* **25/1**

1m 27.07s (0.27) **Going Correction** -0.05s/f (Stan) **13** Ran SP% **125.8**
Speed ratings (Par 97):96,95,94,93,93 93,91,91,90,89 85,85,82
CSF £176.06 TOTE £19.40: £6.30, £7.20, £1.90; EX 114.20.
Owner Miss P Read **Bred** Cheveley Park Stud Ltd **Trained** Whitchurch-on-Thames, Oxon

FOCUS
A very weak event which was run at an average pace. The winner has not been rated this time for a long time but the form looks sound.

Savoy Chapel Official explanation: jockey said he lost an iron on leaving stalls

Arfinnit(IRE) Official explanation: jockey said gelding was denied a clear run

Zantero Official explanation: jockey said gelding ran too free

558 KEMPTON FOR TEAM BUILDING EVENTS CLASSIFIED STKS 1m 3f (P)
2:30 (2:31) (Class 7) 4-Y-0+ **£1,365** (£403; £100; £100) **Stalls** High

Form RPR

60-0 **1** **Smoothie (IRE)**[15] [416] 9-8-11 45......................... StephenDonohoe(3) 1 50
(E G Bevan) *wd: hld up in midfield: hdwy 2f out: rdn to ld ins fnl f* **14/1**

4-54 **2** *1/2* **Iceni Warrior**[46] [84] 5-9-0 45.. JimmyQuinn 12 49
(P Howling) *chsd ldrs: wnt 2nd over 1f out: kpt on u.p* **12/1**

3-02 **3** *1* **Miss Monica (IRE)**[6] [495] 6-9-0 45.. PaulDoe 6 47
(P W Hiatt) *prom: led 2f out tl ins fnl f: one pce* **5/1**[2]

3-00 **3** *dht* **Go Amwell**[15] [416] 4-8-12 45.. NCallan 5 47
(J R Jenkins) *hld up in midfield: hdwy to chse ldrs 3f out: hrd rdn over 1f out: kpt on same pce* **9/2**[1]

630- **5** *shd* **Tharua (IRE)**[212] [3919] 5-9-0 45......................................(v) AdamKirby 2 47
(Ernst Oertel) *hld up in rr: rdn and r.o fnl 2f: nvr nrr* **20/1**

-200 **6** *1 1/2* **Retirement**[36] 187 8-9-0 43 .... EdwardCreighton 7 44
(R M Stronge) *s.s: bhd: rdn and hdwy 2f out: no imp fnl f* **25/1**
6410 **7** *1/2* **Simplified**[15] 416 4-8-9 45 .... JerryO'Dwyer(3) 9 43
(N B King) *dwlt: hld up towards rr: effrt over 2f out: no imp over 1f out: styd on nr fin* **8/1**
00-3 **8** *hd* **Chimes At Midnight (USA)**[21] 349 10-9-0 45 .... NickyMackay 8 43
(Luke Comer, Ire) *towards rr: reminder 6f out: nt pce to chal* **9/1**
-300 **9** *nk* **Pharaoh Prince**[6] 496 6-9-0 44 .... AdrianMcCarthy 3 43
(G Prodromou) *t.k.h: in tch on outside: outpcd fnl 2f* **12/1**
4-04 **10** *shd* **Montecristo**[21] 349 14-8-7 43 .... LukeMcJannet(7) 11 42
(Rae Guest) *led: hrd rdn and hdd 2f out: sn wknd* **12/1**
/40- **11** *hd* **Lady Korrianda**[13] 6883 6-9-0 43 .... LPKeniry 10 42
(R Curtis) *prom: outpcd 3f out: sn btn* **25/1**
34-0 **12** *1 1/4* **Salinger (USA)**[6] 496 5-9-0 44 .... IanMongan 13 40
(Mrs L J Mongan) *plld hrd: in tch: drvn along and hung rt 2f out: sn wknd* **11/2[3]**
13 *1* **Grove Creek**[128] 6089 4-8-12 42 .... (v1) JoeFanning 14 38
(Niall Moran, Ire) *hld up towards rr: nt clr run 2f out: nvr nr ldrs* **16/1**
35-0 **14** *hd* **Flashing Floozie**[42] 133 4-8-12 42 .... SebSanders 4 38
(A W Carroll) *prom tl wknd over 1f out* **12/1**

2m 24.76s (2.08) **Going Correction** -0.05s/f (Stan)
WFA 4 from 5yo+ 2lb **14** Ran SP% **127.1**
Speed ratings (Par 97):90,89,88,88,88 87,87,87,87,86 86,85,85,85
CSF £177.45 TOTE £17.50: £8.20, £4.50; EX 289.70 TRIFECTA 3rd Place Totes - Miss Monica £0.50; Go Amwell £1.30.
Owner E G Bevan **Bred** Miss Mary Duckett **Trained** Ullingswick, H'fords
FOCUS
Another very weak classified event and the winning time was moderate, even for a race like this. The winner is value for a little further than the winning margin but the form looks shaky.
Grove Creek Official explanation: trainer said filly was denied a clear run

559 KEMPTON.CO.UK MEDIAN AUCTION MAIDEN STKS 1m (P)
3:00 (3:04) (Class 6) 4-6-Y-O **£2,047** (£604; £302) **Stalls** High

Form RPR
22 **1** **Ansells Pride (IRE)**[12] 449 4-9-3 .... PatCosgrave 4 50
(B Smart) *prom: rdn to ld over 1f out: all out* **4/6[1]**
06- **2** *nk* **Don't Mind Me**[252] 2673 4-8-12 .... EdwardCreighton 10 44
(T Keddy) *dwlt: towards rr: rdn 3f out: hdwy over 1f out: r.o wl fnl f: clsng at fin* **16/1**
0504 **3** *nk* **Simpsons Gamble (IRE)**[6] 500 4-9-3 47 .... AdrianMcCarthy 12 49
(R M Flower) *trckd ldrs: disp ld over 1f out tl ins fnl f: nt qckn fnl 50 yds* **10/1[3]**
0 **4** *1 1/2* **Very Well Red**[8] 492 4-8-12 .... JimCrowley 11 40+
(P W Hiatt) *dwlt: hld up in rr: rdn and hdwy fnl 2f: nrst fin* **33/1**
00-6 **5** *1/2* **Always A Story**[11] 455 5-9-3 42 .... PaulEddery 9 44
(Miss D Mountain) *led: hrd rdn and hdd over 1f out: no ex* **50/1**
/0-2 **6** *hd* **Sun Bian**[28] 272 5-9-3 63 .... LPKeniry 8 44
(L P Grassick) *t.k.h: chsd ldrs: hrd rdn over 1f out: one pce* **14/1**
40-0 **7** *hd* **Wassfa**[18] 381 4-8-12 59 .... (b1) SebSanders 1 38
(C E Brittain) *t.k.h: in tch on outside: hrd rdn over 1f out: little rspnse* **11/2[2]**
- **8** *nk* **Never So Easy** 4-9-0 .... (v1) DominicFox(3) 2 42
(E S McMahon) *mid-div: effrt and swtchd outside 2f out: hung lft u.p: kpt on fnl f* **14/1**
0- **9** *1 1/4* **Demi Sec**[255] 2575 4-8-12 .... JoeFanning 6 35
(Dr J D Scargill) *t.k.h: pressed ldr tl 2f out: sn wknd* **10/1[3]**
60 **10** *1 3/4* **Mustard Benn**[11] 458 4-9-0 .... NeilChalmers(3) 5 35
(Mouse Hamilton-Fairley) *t.k.h in midfield: rdn and nt pce to chal fnl 2f* **66/1**
11 *4* **Vive La Chasse (IRE)** 4-8-12 .... StephenCarson 7 21
(Eve Johnson Houghton) *nvr gng wl: a bhd* **14/1**
12 *15* **Kadia**[85] 4-8-12 .... MickyFenton 3 —
(P T Midgley) *missed break and swvd lft s: a towards rr: rdn and no ch fnl 3f* **66/1**

1m 41.38s (0.58) **Going Correction** -0.05s/f (Stan) **12** Ran SP% **127.3**
Speed ratings: 95,94,94,92,92 92,92,91,90,88 84,69
CSF £16.15 TOTE £1.80: £1.10, £5.30, £2.80; EX 20.20.
Owner Ansells Of Watford **Bred** E Lonergan **Trained** Hambleton, N Yorks
FOCUS
A very poor maiden which saw the first three come clear. The form is rated through the 47-rated third, with the proximity of the fifth also holding it down.

560 FOLLOW YOUR CONFERENCE WITH FLOODLIT RACING H'CAP (DIV II) 7f (P)
3:30 (3:33) (Class 5) (0-70,68) 4-Y-0+ **£2,266** (£674; £337; £168) **Stalls** High

Form RPR
611- **1** **Generator**[79] 6747 5-8-13 65 .... JoeFanning 6 74
(Dr J D Scargill) *prom: led 1f out: hung bdly lft towards stands' rail: drvn out* **3/1[1]**
5522 **2** *1/2* **Sir Douglas**[15] 424 4-9-2 68 .... (p) PaulHanagan 8 76
(R A Harris) *stdd s: plld hrd and sn in midfield: hdwy to join ldrs over 1f out: kpt on u.p* **9/2[2]**
6-05 **3** *1/2* **Methaaly (IRE)**[15] 424 4-8-13 65 .... BrettDoyle 9 72
(Jane Chapple-Hyam) *trckd ldrs: effrt over 1f out: kpt on same pce* **5/1[3]**
0-00 **4** *nk* **Kew The Music**[15] 426 7-8-2 54 .... ChrisCatlin 5 60
(M R Channon) *dwlt: bhd: gd hdwy 2f out: one pce fnl f* **14/1**
00-4 **5** *nk* **Takitwo**[42] 130 4-8-8 60 .... LPKeniry 1 65
(P D Cundell) *hld up towards rr: hdwy over 1f out: one pce fnl f* **13/2**
1440 **6** *2* **Beneking**[1] 549 7-8-8 60 .... (p) MickyFenton 7 60
(D Burchell) *led and rdn early: hdd 1f out: no ex* **15/2**
0-30 **7** *1* **Crafty Fox**[6] 497 4-7-9 54 oh2 .... JosephWalsh(7) 10 51
(A P Jarvis) *prom tl rdn and btn wl over 1f out* **20/1**
6312 **8** *hd* **Grand Palace (IRE)**[9] 485 4-8-5 57 ow1 .... (v) DeanMcKeown 3 54
(D Shaw) *in tch: wd bnd over 4f out: outpcd fnl 2f* **7/1**
1-66 **9** *3/4* **Zazous**[22] 346 6-8-3 58 .... MarcHalford(3) 4 53
(J J Bridger) *mid-div: rdn and outpcd over 2f out: n.d after* **10/1**
230- **10** *shd* **Motu (IRE)**[159] 5444 6-8-6 61 .... (v) PatrickMathers(3) 2 56
(I W McInnes) *hld up towards rr: pushed wd after 2f: wd again st: nvr trbld ldrs* **25/1**

1m 25.39s (-1.41) **Going Correction** -0.05s/f (Stan) **10** Ran SP% **121.8**
Speed ratings (Par 103):106,105,104,104,104 101,100,100,99,99
CSF £17.10 CT £67.71 TOTE £3.00: £1.40, £2.10, £1.80; EX 17.20 Trifecta £51.10 Pool: £367.10 - 5.10 winning units..
Owner R A Dalton **Bred** R A Dalton **Trained** Newmarket, Suffolk
FOCUS
A modest handicap which was run at a fair pace. The form is solid and the winner remains progressive.
Grand Palace(IRE) Official explanation: jockey said gelding hung left round final bend

561 KEMPTON FOR SUMMER WEDDINGS H'CAP 6f (P)
4:00 (4:03) (Class 6) (0-65,70) 4-Y-0+ **£2,047** (£604; £302) **Stalls** High

Form RPR
3133 **1** **Cool Sands (IRE)**[4] 516 5-9-1 64 .... (v) DeanMcKeown 11 73
(D Shaw) *chsd ldrs: led ins fnl f: drvn out* **5/1[1]**
3-00 **2** *hd* **Supercast (IRE)**[4] 513 4-9-2 65 .... (t) NCallan 3 73
(W M Brisbourne) *hld up towards rr: hdwy on outside over 1f out: r.o wl fnl f: jst hld* **7/1**
0010 **3** *1/2* **Seneschal**[15] 419 6-9-2 65 .... TPQueally 7 75+
(A B Haynes) *trckd ldrs: nt clr run ins fnl 2f: fnd room and edgd lft ins fnl f: r.o wl nr fin* **6/1[3]**
0134 **4** *nk* **Kempsey**[28] 276 5-8-7 63 .... (b) RyanBird(7) 9 69
(J J Bridger) *led and set gd pce: hrd rdn and hdd ins fnl f: no ex* **16/1**
2131 **5** *1/2* **Sweet Pickle**[1] 555 6-9-7 70 6ex .... (e) PatCosgrave 10 75
(J R Boyle) *dwlt: settled in midfield: hdwy to press ldrs over 1f out: nt qckn fnl f* **11/2[2]**
-624 **6** *hd* **Taboor (IRE)**[14] 432 9-9-0 63 .... BrettDoyle 2 67
(R M H Cowell) *pressed ldr: hrd rdn over 1f out: no ex fnl f* **12/1**
-241 **7** *1* **Came Back (IRE)**[10] 467 4-9-2 65 .... DaleGibson 1 66
(J Mackie) *prom: carried lft ins fnl f: no ex* **11/2[2]**
-602 **8** *nk* **Windy Prospect**[26] 303 5-8-8 57 .... (p) PaulHanagan 5 57
(P A Blockley) *bhd: rdn over 2f out: nvr rchd ldrs* **8/1**
6220 **9** *1/2* **City For Conquest (IRE)**[25] 310 4-8-2 58 .... (b) WilliamBuick(7) 12 57
(T J Pitt) *hld up towards rr: effrt 2f out: no imp* **13/2**
260- **10** *3* **H Harrison (IRE)**[131] 6036 7-8-11 63 .... PatrickMathers(3) 8 53
(I W McInnes) *sn pushed along in midfield: rdn and hung rt over 2f out: sn btn* **14/1**
240- **11** *shd* **Rogue**[174] 5055 5-8-11 60 .... JimmyQuinn 4 49
(Jane Southcombe) *wd: a towards rr: rdn and n.d fnl 3f* **16/1**

1m 12.14s (-1.56) **Going Correction** -0.05s/f (Stan) **11** Ran SP% **124.8**
Speed ratings (Par 101):108,107,107,106,106 105,104,104,103,99 99
CSF £42.52 CT £226.36 TOTE £6.90: £2.20, £3.80, £2.60; EX 43.20.
Owner Peter Swann **Bred** Rathasker Stud **Trained** Danethorpe, Notts
FOCUS
A modest handicap which was run at a strong early pace. Solid form, the winner rated to his recent best and the runner-up back to his form of last year.

562 RACING POST H'CAP 6f (P)
4:30 (4:33) (Class 6) (0-50,51) 4-Y-0+ **£2,047** (£604; £302) **Stalls** High

Form RPR
040- **1** **Wiltshire (IRE)**[60] 6955 5-8-12 50 .... MickyFenton 7 59
(P T Midgley) *mid-div: pushed along 1/2-way: hdwy over 1f out: drvn to ld fnl 50 yds: jst hld on* **7/1**
4-34 **2** *shd* **Black Oval**[13] 447 6-8-9 47 .... PaulEddery 12 56
(S Parr) *dwlt: hld up towards rr: effrt over 1f out: str run fnl f: jst failed* **6/1[3]**
6033 **3** *hd* **Desert Light (IRE)**[13] 442 6-8-11 49 .... (v) DeanMcKeown 9 57
(D Shaw) *prom: drvn to disp ld ins fnl f: hdd fnl 50 yds: kpt on* **11/2[2]**
0545 **4** *1/2* **Majestical (IRE)**[13] 442 5-8-11 49 .... (p) LPKeniry 4 56
(J M Bradley) *hld up in midfield: hdwy to press ldrs over 1f out: kpt on fnl f* **12/1**
0-06 **5** *shd* **King Of Charm (IRE)**[18] 379 4-8-9 47 .... (be) BrettDoyle 6 53
(G L Moore) *trckd ldrs: slt ld over 1f out: hdd ins fnl f: nt qckn* **15/2**
-102 **6** *nk* **Primarily**[13] 441 5-8-10 48 .... RobbieFitzpatrick 2 53
(Peter Grayson) *in tch: rdn to chal over 1f out: one pce fnl f* **10/1**
4-00 **7** *3/4* **Detonate**[9] 485 5-8-6 47 .... JamesDoyle(3) 3 53+
(Ms J S Doyle) *dwlt: hld up in rr: hdwy to chse ldrs over 1f out: n.m.r ins fnl f: nt rcvr* **9/1**
0-00 **8** *3/4* **Edin Burgher (FR)**[39] 161 6-8-12 50 .... AdamKirby 1 51
(T T Clement) *bhd: rdn over 2f out: styd on fnl f* **14/1**
4001 **9** *3/4* **Orchestration (IRE)**[13] 441 6-8-12 50 .... (v) NCallan 8 49+
(K J Burke) *hld up in midfield: effrt and nt clr run over 1f out: unable to chal* **7/2[1]**
-051 **10** *1 1/2* **Blushing Russian (IRE)**[28] 281 5-8-10 48 .... (p) ChrisCatlin 5 42
(J M Bradley) *chsd ldr: led over 2f out tl over 1f out: hld whn squeezed and snatched up ins fnl f* **12/1**
1-01 **11** *13* **Ace Club**[14] 430 6-8-10 51 .... (b) EmmettStack(3) 10 6
(K J Burke) *led and set gd pce: hdd over 2f out: sn wknd: eased whn wl btn over 1f out* **14/1**

1m 13.29s (-0.41) **Going Correction** -0.05s/f (Stan) **11** Ran SP% **124.0**
Speed ratings (Par 101):100,99,99,98,98 98,97,96,95,93 76
CSF £51.51 CT £256.31 TOTE £9.70: £3.00, £2.50, £1.10; EX 68.60.
Owner David Mann **Bred** John Perotta **Trained** Westow, N Yorks
FOCUS
A poor handicap, run at a generous early pace. It produced a thrilling three-way finish and the form looks sound and should prove reliable.
King Of Charm(IRE) Official explanation: jockey said gelding hung right
Detonate Official explanation: jockey said gelding was denied a clear run
Orchestration(IRE) Official explanation: jockey said gelding suffered interference
Blushing Russian(IRE) Official explanation: jockey said gelding suffered interference

563 PANORAMIC BAR AND RESTAURANT H'CAP 1m 3f (P)
5:00 (5:00) (Class 4) (0-85,79) 3-Y-0 **£4,728** (£1,406; £702; £351) **Stalls** High

Form RPR
1 **1** **Players Please (USA)**[41] 141 3-9-4 79 .... JoeFanning 4 92+
(M Johnston) *led 2f: restrained and trckd ldr: led over 2f out: shkn up and qcknd clr: eased ins fnl f* **4/7[1]**
0-13 **2** *1 1/4* **Daylami Dreams**[27] 294 3-8-12 73 .... JohnEgan 5 78
(J S Moore) *led after 2f tl over 2f out: nt pce of wnr: kpt on to hold 2nd but flattered by margin* **10/3[2]**
2124 **3** *3/4* **Six Shots**[18] 382 3-8-13 77 .... RichardKingscote(3) 2 81
(J A Osborne) *hld up in tch: pushed along 4f out: kpt on fnl 2f* **7/1[3]**
2614 **4** *2* **Beau Sancy**[11] 460 3-8-2 66 .... SaleemGolam(3) 1 67
(R A Harris) *stdd s and s.i.s: hld up in rr: rdn 3f out: nt pce to chal* **25/1**
34-6 **5** *5* **Silca Key**[36] 196 3-8-10 71 .... EdwardCreighton 6 63
(M R Channon) *t.k.h: in tch: rdn over 2f out: sn outpcd* **12/1**

2m 21.25s (-1.43) **Going Correction** -0.05s/f (Stan) **5** Ran SP% **110.8**
Speed ratings (Par 99):103,102,101,100,96
CSF £2.79 TOTE £1.40: £1.10, £2.10; EX 2.00 Place 6 £46.04, Place 5 £16.04.
Owner N N Browne **Bred** 6 C Racing Limited **Trained** Middleham Moor, N Yorks
FOCUS
An interesting little three-year-old handicap. The progressive Players Please is value for further and there is more to come from him. The second and third were closely matched on their Lingfield running.
T/Jkpt: Not won. T/Plt: £109.10 to a £1 stake. Pool: £89,336.10. 597.25 winning tickets. T/Qpdt: £6.40 to a £1 stake. Pool: £5,585.65. 637.50 winning tickets. LM

533 WOLVERHAMPTON (A.W) (L-H)

Monday, February 26

OFFICIAL GOING: Standard

Wind: Fresh across Weather: Cloudy with sunny spells

564 PONTINS.COM APPRENTICE H'CAP 1m 1f 103y(P)
2:00 (2:06) (Class 5) (0-75,74) 4-Y-O+ £3,071 (£906; £453) Stalls Low

Form RPR
3-24 **1** **Symbol Of Peace (IRE)**[28] [297] 4-9-2 **71**.................. DuranFentiman 5 84
(J W Unett) *hld up: hdwy over 2f out: rdn to ld ins fnl f: r.o* **16/1**
6-2 **2** ½ **Augustus John (IRE)**[44] [120] 4-8-12 **70**.................... WilliamBuick(3) 2 82
(T J Pitt) *chsd ldrs: led 2f out: rdn and hdd ins fnl f: unable qck towards fin* **5/6**[1]
32-5 **3** 7 **Wulimaster (USA)**[13] [449] 4-9-0 **72**................................ NeilBrown(3) 1 70
(D W Barker) *prom: rdn over 2f out: wknd fnl f* **12/1**
-104 **4** nk **Desert Leader (IRE)**[16] [428] 6-9-2 **74**.................... AshleyHamblett(3) 8 71
(W M Brisbourne) *slowly into stide: hld up: r.o ins fnl f: nvr nrr* **16/1**
63U3 **5** hd **Tancredi (SWE)**[3] [538] 5-8-7 **62**.............................. MichaelJStainton 7 59
(N B King) *led: racd keenly: hdd 7f out: chsd ldr tl led over 3f out: hdd 2f out: wknd ins fnl f* **7/2**[2]
00-0 **6** 2½ **Consonant (IRE)**[36] [205] 10-9-0 **72**............................... TolleyDean(3) 6 64
(D G Bridgwater) *trckd ldrs: stdd and lost pl 7f out: rdn over 3f out: n.d after* **33/1**
0304 **7** 2½ **Buscador (USA)**[3] [539] 8-8-0 **60** oh3............................ JackMitchell(5) 9 47
(W M Brisbourne) *s.i.s: rcvrd to ld 7f out: rdn and hdd over 3f out : wknd 2f out* **13/2**[3]
52-2 **8** 1½ **Kabis Amigos**[27] [308] 5-8-2 **62**................................(t) AdeleRothery(5) 3 46
(D Nicholls) *plld hrd and prom: rdn over 2f out: hung lft and wknd over 1f out* **20/1**
9 9 **Prince Des Neiges (FR)**[147] 4-9-0 **72** ow3................. KylieManser(5) 4 40
(Ian Williams) *prom 6f* **50/1**

2m 0.69s (-1.93) **Going Correction** -0.15s/f (Stan) **9** Ran SP% **119.2**
Speed ratings (Par 103):102,101,95,95,94 92,90,89,81
CSF £30.58 CT £189.86 TOTE £17.00: £3.80, £1.10, £2.40; EX 42.80 Trifecta £488.50 Part won. Pool £688.04 - 0.34 winning unit..
Owner John Malone **Bred** Calley House Syndicate **Trained** Preston, Shropshire

FOCUS
They went no pace early resulting in a couple taking a fierce hold, and the race developed into something of a sprint. The front two pulled miles clear of the others, registering improved efforts although the third and fourth were not solid.

565 BONUSPRINT.COM MEDIAN AUCTION MAIDEN STKS 1m 141y(P)
2:30 (2:30) (Class 5) 3-4-Y-O £2,914 (£867; £433; £216) Stalls Low

Form RPR
1 **Tutor (IRE)** 3-8-7 .... EddieAhern 3 77+
(W J Haggas) *hld up in tch: nt clr run over 1f out: sn carried rt: led ins fnl f: pushed out* **11/2**[3]
2-5 **2** hd **Resplendent Ace (IRE)**[12] [456] 3-8-7 .... ShaneKelly 8 76
(P Howling) *a.p: chsd ldr 1/2-way: rdn and hung lft over 1f out: sn carried rt: r.o* **5/2**[2]
4-32 **3** 2½ **Blue Monkey (IRE)**[30] [260] 3-8-7 75............................ JamieSpencer 1 71
(M L W Bell) *led: rdn and hung rt fr over 1f out: hdd and no ex ins fnl f* **9/4**[1]
3 **4** 5 **Musical Locket (IRE)**[35] [208] 3-7-9 .... WilliamBuick(7) 4 56
(R Hannon) *hld up: hdwy 1/2-way: rdn and edgd lft over 3f out: wknd 2f* **6/1**
252- **5** 4 **Callisto Moon**[90] [6646] 3-8-7 68.. ChrisCatlin 7 52
(Ian Williams) *chsd ldr to 1/2-way: sn rdn: wknd over 2f out* **8/1**
6 1¾ **Diksie Dancer** 3-8-2 .... CatherineGannon 2 43
(K A Ryan) *s.i.s: sn prom: hmpd and lost pl over 6f out: rdn and wknd 3f out* **25/1**
00- **7** 5 **Spanish Affair**[116] [6303] 3-8-7 .... PaulMulrennan 6 38
(Jedd O'Keeffe) *hld up: rdn and wknd 3f out* **100/1**
0 **8** 9 **Broad Town Girl**[30] [260] 4-9-2 .... KylieManser(7) 5 14
(Mrs H Sweeting) *chsd ldrs: wkng whn hmpd over 3f out* **200/1**

1m 50.53s (-1.23) **Going Correction** -0.15s/f (Stan)
WFA 3 from 4yo 21lb **8** Ran SP% **105.5**
Speed ratings (Par 103):99,98,96,92,88 87,82,74
CSF £16.54 TOTE £6.50: £2.10, £1.10, £1.60; EX 18.40 Trifecta £70.30 Pool £661.71 - 6.68 winning units.
Owner Highclere Thoroughbred Racing XXXVII **Bred** Sean M Collins **Trained** Newmarket, Suffolk
■ Stewards' Enquiry : Jamie Spencer one-day ban (reduced from two days on appeal): careless riding (Mar 10)
Kylie Manser one-day ban: careless riding (Mar 10)
William Buick one-day ban: careless riding (Mar 10)

FOCUS
An ordinary maiden dominated by the market leaders and something of a messy contest, especially in the home straight thanks to the hanging Blue Monkey. The form looks sound and the winner Tutor is a likely improver.

566 PONTIN'S FAMILY HOLIDAYS H'CAP 5f 20y(P)
3:00 (3:00) (Class 5) (0-75,75) 4-Y-O+ £3,071 (£906; £453) Stalls Low

Form RPR
-112 **1** **Almaty Express**[31] [251] 5-8-4 **70**............................(b) WilliamBuick(7) 13 82
(J R Weymes) *mde all: rdn over 1f out: r.o* **9/2**[2]
2030 **2** ¾ **Nusoor (IRE)**[11] [465] 4-8-10 **69**................................. GrahamGibbons 9 79
(Peter Grayson) *wnt rt s: sn chsng wnr: rdn and hung rt 2f out: r.o* **8/1**[3]
2-22 **3** 1½ **Financial Times (USA)**[30] [269] 5-9-2 **75**..................(vt[1]) MickyFenton 3 79+
(Stef Liddiard) *s.i.s: in rr and nt clr run over 3f out: hdwy u.p over 1f out: nt rch ldrs* **15/8**[1]
/16- **4** shd **Sandwith**[294] [1529] 4-8-5 **64**.. ChrisCatlin 5 68
(J S Wainwright) *chsd ldrs: rdn 1/2-way: styd on* **20/1**
-225 **5** shd **Misaro (GER)**[11] [463] 6-8-2 **61** oh1.........................(b) AdrianMcCarthy 4 65
(R A Harris) *chsd ldrs: n.m.r over 3f out: outpcd 1/2-way: r.o ins fnl f* **8/1**[3]
5600 **6** shd **Mambazo**[10] [480] 5-7-11 **63**...(e) FLencluđ(7) 8 66
(S C Williams) *s.s: in rr tl edgd rt and r.o ins fnl f: nrst fin* **16/1**
0-00 **7** ½ **Polish Emperor (USA)**[16] [424] 7-8-9 **68**...................(v[1]) PaulHanagan 1 69
(D W Barker) *hld up: hmpd over 3f out: hdwy over 1f out: no imp ins fnl f* **12/1**
00-0 **8** ¾ **Coconut Moon**[10] [480] 5-8-8 **67**.. EddieAhern 2 66
(E J Alston) *chsd ldrs: rdn over 1f out: no ex ins fnl f* **8/1**[3]
0456 **9** 3 **Trinculo (IRE)**[11] [465] 10-8-1 **65**................................... TolleyDean(5) 6 53
(R A Harris) *prom: rdn over 3f out: sn lost pl* **28/1**
660- **10** nk **Melalchrist**[121] [6223] 5-8-6 **65**.................................(p) CatherineGannon 11 52
(K A Ryan) *sn outpcd* **40/1**
-460 **11** nk **Sir Loin**[25] [318] 6-7-9 **61** oh7..................................(v) DanielleMcCreery(7) 7 47
(N Tinkler) *trckd ldrs: racd keenly: wknd over 1f out* **50/1**
006- **12** 3 **Clipper Hoy**[306] [1243] 5-8-3 **65**................................ RichardKingscote(3) 10 40
(Mrs H Sweeting) *hmpd s: sn outpcd* **18/1**

61.43 secs (-1.39) **Going Correction** -0.15s/f (Stan) **12** Ran SP% **117.7**
Speed ratings (Par 103):105,103,101,101,101 100,100,98,94,93 93,88
CSF £38.54 CT £91.26 TOTE £6.20: £1.60, £2.70, £2.00; EX 35.50 Trifecta £43.50 Pool £307.19 - 5.01 winning units..
Owner Sporting Occasions Racing No 5 **Bred** P G Airey **Trained** Middleham Moor, N Yorks

FOCUS
Not surprisingly they went a cracking pace in this, but there was trouble in running for some, especially the favourite Financial Times. Fair form, and a good effort from Almaty Express although he didn't need to improve.
Financial Times(USA) Official explanation: jockey said gelding missed the break
Clipper Hoy Official explanation: vet said gelding returned lame on left-fore

567 WOLVERHAMPTON-RACECOURSE.CO.UK MAIDEN STKS 5f 216y(P)
3:30 (3:31) (Class 5) 3-Y-O+ £2,968 (£876; £438) Stalls Low

Form RPR
543 **1** **Desert Master**[9] [489] 4-9-13 72... GeorgeBaker 2 81+
(C F Wall) *trckd ldrs: rdn to ld over 1f out: edgd lft: r.o* **9/2**[2]
2 **2** ½ **Daytona (IRE)**[12] [456] 3-8-12 .... JoeFanning 6 75
(M Johnston) *w ldr tl led over 2f out: rdn: hung lft and hdd over 1f out : styd on* **4/7**[1]
3 2 **Spanish Needle** 3-8-7 .... JamieSpencer 7 64+
(P R Webber) *s.i.s: hld up: hdwy over 2f out: rdn over 1f out: nt rch ldrs* **7/1**[3]
4-23 **4** 2½ **Rann Na Cille (IRE)**[6] [505] 3-8-4 66......................... AndrewMullen(3) 8 56
(K A Ryan) *chsd ldrs: rdn over 2f out: wknd over 1f out* **10/1**
4 **5** ½ **Royal Becky (IRE)**[21] [360] 3-8-0 .... WilliamBuick(7) 4 54+
(Patrick Morris, Ire) *hld up: hdwy over 2f out: rdn and hung lft over 1f out: nt rch ldrs* **20/1**
0-0 **6** 4 **The Power Of Phil**[16] [423] 3-8-12 .... PaulEddery 13 46
(Miss Joanne Priest) *hld up: hung lft fr over 1f out: nvr trbld ldrs* **125/1**
0- **7** ½ **Polish Star**[164] [5340] 3-8-12 .... RichardHughes 11 45
(J S Wainwright) *mid-div: rdn 1/2-way: n.d* **40/1**
0 **8** nk **Another Toy**[20] [375] 4-9-8 .... SilvestreDeSousa 12 43
(A D Brown) *chsd ldrs over 3f* **100/1**
56 **9** ½ **Missus Molly Brown**[20] [375] 3-8-7 .... PaulHanagan 9 37
(R A Fahey) *prom: lost pl over 4f out: bhd fr 1/2-way* **66/1**
/00- **10** hd **Globe**[214] [3866] 4-9-1 41... KylieManser(7) 1 40
(Mrs H Sweeting) *led over 3f: wknd over 1f out* **200/1**
05-0 **11** ¾ **Distant Vision (IRE)**[25] [321] 4-9-8 35.........................(tp) DarrenMoffatt 3 38
(A Berry) *chsd ldrs over 3f* **200/1**
0-0 **12** 1¼ **War Of The Roses (IRE)**[45] [106] 4-9-13 .... PhillipMakin 5 39
(R Brotherton) *mid-div: rdn 1/2-way: sn wknd* **200/1**
13 6 **Ainama (IRE)**[135] [5981] 3-8-12 .... BrianReilly 10 16
(M Wigham) *dwlt: outpcd* **22/1**

1m 14.08s (-1.73) **Going Correction** -0.15s/f (Stan)
WFA 3 from 4yo 15lb **13** Ran SP% **119.7**
Speed ratings (Par 103):105,104,101,98,97 92,91,91,90,90 89,87,79
CSF £7.21 TOTE £5.20: £2.80, £1.10, £2.70; EX 14.20 Trifecta £51.70 Pool £800.65 - 10.98 winning units.
Owner S Fustok **Bred** Deerfield Farm **Trained** Newmarket, Suffolk

FOCUS
Not a very competitive maiden and not many could be seriously fancied. The race was duly dominated by the market leaders, but they certainly went a good pace and the time was very respectable for a race like this. The form looks better than expected, with the winner likely to do better.

568 PHOTO BOOKS FROM BONUSPRINT.COM H'CAP 1m 4f 50y(P)
4:00 (4:00) (Class 5) (0-75,75) 4-Y-O+ £3,071 (£906; £453) Stalls Low

Form RPR
1-13 **1** **Kilimandscharo (USA)**[30] [263] 5-8-13 **68**................. RichardHughes 5 86+
(P J McBride) *hld up: hdwy over 2f out: rdn and hung lft ins fnl f: r.o to ld towards fin* **6/4**[1]
-635 **2** 1¼ **Bay Boy**[7] [501] 5-9-4 **73**.. JoeFanning 10 83
(M Johnston) *led over 8f: led over 2f out: rdn and hdd towards fin* **14/1**
356- **3** 2½ **Tromp**[108] [6426] 6-9-1 **70**... JimmyQuinn 4 76
(D J Coakley) *chsd ldrs: rdn over 2f out: no ex fnl f* **16/1**
-215 **4** nk **Melvino**[16] [428] 5-9-2 **71**.. DeanMcKeown 1 77
(T D Barron) *s.i.s: hld up: racd keenly: hdwy over 5f out: rdn over 1f out: styd on* **13/2**[3]
-243 **5** ¾ **Jackie Kiely**[20] [377] 6-9-5 **74**..(t) PhillipMakin 6 79
(R Brotherton) *chsd ldrs: led over 3f out: hdd over 2f out: wknd ins fnl f* **33/1**
04-4 **6** 1½ **Snark (IRE)**[47] [96] 4-9-3 **75**...(t) EddieAhern 3 77
(P J Makin) *chsd ldrs 10f out: rdn over 2f out: wknd fnl f* **11/2**[2]
00-3 **7** ¾ **Undeterred**[24] [332] 11-9-1 **70**.. NCallan 8 71
(K J Burke) *hld up: hdwy 5f out: rdn over 2f out: wknd fnl f* **20/1**
-002 **8** 1¾ **Casablanca Minx (IRE)**[19] [380] 4-8-5 **66**..................(b) JamesDoyle(3) 2 64
(N P Littmoden) *prom: rdn over 2f out: wkng whn hung lft fr over 1f out* **33/1**
50-5 **9** ½ **Country Affair (USA)**[16] [422] 4-8-11 **69**.................. JamieSpencer 12 67
(P R Webber) *hld up in tch: rdn over 2f out: wknd over 1f out* **10/1**
61-0 **10** hd **Top Jaro (FR)**[15] [434] 4-9-3 **75**.. HayleyTurner 9 72
(Jennie Candlish) *s.i.s: hld up: rdn over 2f out: a in rr* **100/1**
2-32 **11** 1½ **Snowy Day (FR)**[36] [205] 4-8-10 **68**............................. PaulHanagan 11 63
(Grant Tuer) *hld up: rdn over 2f out: a in rr* **9/1**
0-00 **12** ½ **Wellington Hall (GER)**[16] [428] 9-8-10 **65**........................ OscarUrbina 7 59
(M Wigham) *hld up: lost pl and rdn over 3f out: sn bhd* **40/1**

2m 39.9s (-2.52) **Going Correction** -0.15s/f (Stan)
WFA 4 from 5yo+ 3lb **12** Ran SP% **114.4**
Speed ratings (Par 103):102,101,99,99,98 97,97,96,95,95 94,94
CSF £22.57 CT £245.37 TOTE £2.40: £2.00, £4.20, £4.10; EX 32.90 TRIFECTA Not won..
Owner P J McBride **Bred** Ron Dufficy **Trained** Newmarket, Suffolk
■ Stewards' Enquiry : N Callan two-day ban: careless riding (Mar 10, 13)

FOCUS
A modest handicap won cosily by the progressive Kilimandscharo, who did well to overcome the moderate early pace. He is rated better than the bare form.
Melvino Official explanation: jockey said gelding ran too freely

569 GO PONTIN'S MAIDEN STKS — 1m 1f 103y(P)
4:30 (4:31) (Class 5) 3-Y-O — £3,071 (£906; £453) Stalls Low

Form — RPR

-222 **1** **Milla's Rocket (IRE)**[18] [392] 3-8-12 70................................(b) NCallan 9 — 73
(K A Ryan) *sn led: clr over 2f out: rdn and hung rt fr over 1f out: styd on* **6/1**[3]

050- **2** 1 1/4 **Morning Farewell**[136] [5939] 3-9-3 72.................................. EddieAhern 2 — 76
(P W Chapple-Hyam) *prom: rdn to chse wnr over 2f out: styd on* **5/4**[1]

33-2 **3** 2 1/2 **L'Oiseau De Feu (USA)**[19] [382] 3-9-3 75.................. RichardHughes 1 — 71
(E A L Dunlop) *hld up in tch: rdn and swtchd lft over 1f out: no ex wl ins fnl f* **9/4**[2]

36- **4** 4 **Mizzle (USA)**[222] [3640] 3-8-12 .... JoeFanning 5 — 58
(M Johnston) *sn chsng wnr: rdn over 2f out: edgd lft and wknd over 1f out* **14/1**

00 **5** 1 1/4 **Tina's Ridge (IRE)**[13] [449] 3-9-3 .... DavidAllan 6 — 60
(E J Alston) *hld up: rdn over 3f out: styd on appr fnl f: nvr trbld ldrs* **100/1**

0-0 **6** nk **Cnoc Moy (IRE)**[9] [492] 3-9-3 .... GeorgeBaker 4 — 59
(C F Wall) *hld up: swtchd rt over 3f out: hdwy over 2f out: rdn and hung lft over 1f out: nt trble ldrs* **100/1**

4-02 **7** 5 **Sir Sandicliffe (IRE)**[24] [338] 3-9-3 69............................. ShaneKelly 11 — 49
(W M Brisbourne) *hld up: hdwy over 5f out: rdn and wknd over 2f out* **22/1**

0 **8** 5 **A Mothers Love**[30] [260] 3-8-12 .... EdwardCreighton 3 — 34
(P J McBride) *chsd ldrs 6f* **40/1**

0 **9** 9 **Ridgeway Star**[35] [208] 3-9-3 .... ChrisCatlin 7 — 21
(R Ingram) *hmpd s: a in rr* **50/1**

50 **10** 3 1/2 **Sadler's Kingdom (IRE)**[10] [484] 3-9-3 .... PaulHanagan 12 — 14
(R A Fahey) *hld up: rdn over 3f out: sn wknd* **80/1**

0-0 **11** 1 1/4 **Dickie Deano**[24] [338] 3-8-10 .... BarrySavage(7) 10 — 12
(J M Bradley) *mid-div: lost pl 6f out: bhd fnl 3f* **250/1**

12 2 1/2 **Parma (IRE)** 3-8-12 .... OscarUrbina 8 — —
(M Botti) *wnt lft s: hld up: effrt over 3f out: sn wknd* **33/1**

2m 1.16s (-1.46) **Going Correction** -0.15s/f (Stan) — 12 Ran SP% **111.5**
Speed ratings (Par 97):100,98,96,93,92 91,87,82,74,71 70,68
CSF £12.60 TOTE £6.80: £1.40, £1.10, £1.20; EX 27.30 Trifecta £67.10 Pool £519.33 - 5.49 winning units..
Owner Trevor C Stewart **Bred** James F Hanly **Trained** Hambleton, N Yorks

FOCUS
An ordinary maiden, rated through the winner, but the form should work out.

570 PONTINSBINGO.COM H'CAP (DIV I) — 1m 141y(P)
5:00 (5:00) (Class 6) (0-60,60) 4-Y-O+ — £1,706 (£503; £252) Stalls Low

Form — RPR

-005 **1** **Our Kes (IRE)**[21] [371] 5-8-10 **54**.. IanMongan 6 — 62+
(P Howling) *hld up: hdwy and nt clr run over 1f out: rdn to ld ins fnl f: r.o* **2/1**[1]

4-05 **2** 3/4 **Hits Only Cash**[10] [479] 5-8-10 **54**.............................. DeanMcKeown 10 — 61
(J Pearce) *hld up: hdwy over 1f out: sn rdn: r.o* **8/1**

4131 **3** 1 1/4 **Norwegian**[16] [425] 6-8-10 **54**...(p) PaulEddery 1 — 58
(Ian Williams) *chsd ldrs: rdn and ev ch ins fnl f: no ex towards fin* **7/2**[2]

-002 **4** nk **Machinate (USA)**[5] [517] 5-8-0 **47**.................................. LiamJones(3) 5 — 50
(W M Brisbourne) *hld up: nt clr run over 2f out and over 1f out: r.o wl ins fnl f: nt rch ldrs* **7/1**

3302 **5** 1/2 **Mademoiselle**[3] [533] 5-8-6 **55**..................................(p) TolleyDean(5) 11 — 57
(R A Harris) *a.p: rdn over 2f out: no ex ins fnl f* **9/1**

1-10 **6** shd **Freda's Choice (IRE)**[36] [200] 4-8-7 **51**.............................(b) LPKeniry 8 — 53
(Patrick Morris, Ire) *chsd ldr: rdn and ev ch over 1f out: no ex ins fnl f* **20/1**

-531 **7** shd **Mister Benji**[10] [479] 8-8-13 **57**.......................................(p) TonyCulhane 3 — 59
(B P J Baugh) *led: hdd ins fnl f: styd on same pce* **11/2**[3]

0-06 **8** 3/4 **Veba (USA)**[7] [500] 4-8-2 **46** oh1...................................... HayleyTurner 12 — 46?
(M D I Usher) *hld up: hdwy over 2f out: no ex fnl f* **33/1**

0/42 **9** nk **Volaticus (IRE)**[20] [374] 6-9-1 **59**.................................. PaulMulrennan 7 — 62+
(A D Brown) *chsd ldrs: nt clr run over 1f out and ins fnl f: nvr able to chal* **8/1**

06-0 **10** 1 **Welsh Whisper**[21] [364] 8-7-10 **47** oh1 ow1................. JosephWalsh(7) 2 — 45
(S A Brookshaw) *s.i.s: hld up: rdn over 1f out: n.d* **80/1**

0-00 **11** 1 1/2 **Tilen (IRE)**[3] [539] 4-7-9 **46** oh1..........................(v[1]) DanielleMcCreery(7) 4 — 40?
(S Parr) *hld up in tch: rdn over 1f out: wknd ins fnl f* **66/1**

000- **12** 38 **Brave Dane (IRE)**[186] [4248] 9-9-2 **60**.................................... NCallan 9 — —
(K J Burke) *s.s and rel to r: a t.o* **12/1**

1m 52.95s (1.19) **Going Correction** -0.15s/f (Stan) — 12 Ran SP% **133.8**
Speed ratings (Par 101):88,87,86,85,85 85,85,84,84,83 82,48
CSF £21.92 CT £61.81 TOTE £3.50: £1.60, £2.70, £2.80; EX 33.20 TRIFECTA Pool £532.29 - 3.83 winning units.
Owner Mark Entwistle **Bred** Yeomanstown Stud **Trained** Newmarket, Suffolk

FOCUS
A pedestrian winning time, 3.21 seconds slower than the second division, and the bare form is very modest. The winner will still be on a fair mark after this.
Volaticus(IRE) Official explanation: jockey said gelding was denied a clear run
Brave Dane(IRE) Official explanation: jockey said gelding was reluctant to jump out of stalls

571 PONTINSBINGO.COM H'CAP (DIV II) — 1m 141y(P)
5:30 (5:30) (Class 6) (0-60,60) 4-Y-O+ — £1,706 (£503; £252) Stalls Low

Form — RPR

-134 **1** **My Michelle**[14] [445] 6-8-12 **56**.. TonyCulhane 1 — 68
(B Palling) *mde all: rdn clr fnl f* **3/1**[1]

0504 **2** 3 **Desert Lover (IRE)**[5] [517] 5-8-2 **49**..............................(tp) LiamJones(3) 2 — 55
(R J Price) *trckd wnr: racd keenly: rdn over 1f out: styd on same pce* **7/1**

0150 **3** nk **Golden Spectrum (IRE)**[3] [538] 8-8-11 **60**................(b) TolleyDean(5) 6 — 65
(R A Harris) *s.s: hld up: hdwy over 2f out: sn rdn: styd on same pce fnl f* **10/1**

0-60 **4** shd **Out For A Stroll**[23] [346] 8-8-6 **57**.................................. FLenclud(7) 10 — 62
(S C Williams) *hld up: hdwy and edgd lft over 1f out: nt rch ldrs* **12/1**

13-6 **5** 5 **Claws**[38] [179] 4-8-7 **54**...(t) JamesDoyle(3) 5 — 48
(A J Lidderdale) *chsd ldrs: rdn over 2f out: wknd over 1f out* **11/2**[3]

5044 **6** 3 **The London Gang**[7] [495] 4-8-11 **55**...............................(v) ChrisCatlin 3 — 43
(Miss D A McHale) *chsd ldrs over 6f* **13/2**

-216 **7** hd **Weet Yer Tern (IRE)**[5] [518] 5-8-6 **50**..........................(v) JamieSpencer 4 — 38
(W M Brisbourne) *dwlt: hld up: hdwy over 5f out: wkng whn bmpd over 1f out: eased ins fnl f* **7/2**[2]

040- **8** 2 1/2 **On Air (USA)**[177] [5035] 4-9-1 **59**.. EddieAhern 9 — 41
(J W Hills) *prom: lost pl over 5f out: n.d after* **10/1**

0400 **9** 2 1/2 **Miss Redactive**[2] [549] 4-8-2 **46** oh1................................ HayleyTurner 8 — 23
(M D I Usher) *hld up: rdn over 3f out: n.d* **28/1**

00-0 **10** 16 **Shinko Femme (IRE)**[15] [431] 6-8-2 **46** oh1..............(v[1]) JimmyQuinn 11 — —
(J O'Reilly) *s.i.s: sn prom: rdn and wknd over 3f out* **40/1**

1m 49.74s (-2.02) **Going Correction** -0.15s/f (Stan) — 38 Ran SP% **120.2**
Speed ratings (Par 101):102,99,99,98,94 91,91,89,87,73
CSF £25.43 CT £195.85 TOTE £4.30: £1.60, £1.70, £3.80; EX 32.20 Trifecta £166.40 Pool £738.26 - 3.15 winning units. Place 6 £6.09, Place 5 £5.65.
Owner Flying Eight Partnership **Bred** Snowdrop Stud Co Ltd **Trained** Tredodridge, Vale Of Glamorgan

FOCUS
The winning time was 3.21 seconds faster than the first division, but still only about par for the grade. Weak form, but it looks straightforward enough.
Weet Yer Tern(IRE) Official explanation: jockey said gelding was hampered and lost its action
T/Jkpt: Not won. T/Plt: £5.00 to a £1 stake. Pool: £81,761.00. 11,840.10 winning tickets. T/Qpdt: £2.90 to a £1 stake. Pool: £3,593.20. 887.40 winning tickets. CR

[548]LINGFIELD (L-H)
Tuesday, February 27

OFFICIAL GOING: Standard
Wind: Fresh, half behind Weather: Thick cloud, increasing rain from race 3

572 GO PONTIN'S CLAIMING STKS — 1m 2f (P)
2:00 (2:00) (Class 6) 3-Y-O — £2,184 (£644; £322) Stalls Low

Form — RPR

0-30 **1** **It's No Problem (IRE)**[31] [267] 3-8-5 56...................... WilliamBuick(7) 4 — 51
(M Salaman) *hld up: swtchd outside 6f out: hdwy to chse ldr whn bmpd 2f out: hrd rdn to ld fnl 50 yds* **9/1**[3]

6-00 **2** nk **Citrus Chief (USA)**[31] [267] 3-9-2 53..........................(p) TolleyDean(5) 8 — 59
(R A Harris) *prom: led 3f out and kicked 2 l clr: hrd rdn fnl f: hdd and no ex fnl 50 yds* **50/1**

0512 **3** 1 3/4 **Jemima Godfrey**[4] [534] 3-8-3 50 ow2.......................... JackMitchell(3) 3 — 45
(M J Gingell) *towards rr: effrt 3f out: nrst fin* **12/1**

5363 **4** 2 1/2 **Mick Is Back**[4] [534] 3-8-10 55............................(b) StephenDonohoe(3) 9 — 43
(P D Evans) *stdd s: hld up and bhd: hdwy on outside 3f out: hung lft: wd bnd and hung bdly rt in st: one pce* **10/1**

-024 **5** 2 1/2 **Briarwood Bear**[19] [392] 3-8-7 55.................................... JimmyQuinn 7 — 32
(M Blanshard) *in tch: outpcd 4f out: n.d after* **11/2**[2]

2221 **6** nk **My Mirasol**[4] [534] 3-8-12 66...(p) NCallan 2 — 37
(K A Ryan) *led tl 3f out: hrd rdn: wknd 2f out* **4/6**[1]

34-5 **7** 1 3/4 **Featherlight**[35] [224] 3-9-2 50...(v) ChrisCatlin 5 — 37
(J Jay) *hdwy and prom after 2f: rdn and outpcd 4f out: n.d after* **14/1**

6-04 **8** 1 1/2 **Tenterhooks (IRE)**[22] [357] 3-8-7 47 ow1.......................... DeanMcKeown 1 — 25
(A J McCabe) *mid-div: n.m.r and dropped to rr 5f out: sn rdn and bhd* **14/1**

4 **9** nk **Jonny Behave**[41] [162] 3-8-4 .... JamesDoyle(3) 6 — 25
(I A Wood) *chsd ldrs: rdn 1/2-way: wknd over 2f out* **16/1**

2m 6.39s (-1.40) **Going Correction** -0.20s/f (Stan) — 9 Ran SP% **123.3**
Speed ratings (Par 95):97,96,95,93,91 91,89,88,88
CSF £355.60 TOTE £14.40: £3.30, £14.70, £2.30; EX 502.10 TRIFECTA Not won..My Mirasol was claimed by Don Cantillon for £10,000.
Owner M J Lewin **Bred** M J Lewin And D Grieve **Trained** Baydon, Wilts
■ Stewards' Enquiry : James Doyle one-day ban: careless riding (Mar 10)

FOCUS
Moderate claiming form, only slightly better than banded level. The form is hard to pin down with the favourite not running her race and the runner-up producing a big step up despie the unfavourable terms.
My Mirasol Official explanation: jockey said filly never travelled
Tenterhooks(IRE) Official explanation: jockey said filly was hampered twice in running

573 PONTINS.COM MAIDEN STKS — 7f (P)
2:30 (2:34) (Class 5) 3-Y-O+ — £3,071 (£906; £453) Stalls Low

Form — RPR

6 **1** **Fantastic Cee (IRE)**[17] [418] 3-8-4 .... ChrisCatlin 10 — 72+
(J Noseda) *chsd ldr: led over 1f out: rdn clr* **7/2**[1]

2 3 **Warm Embraces (IRE)** 3-8-6 .... MarcHalford(3) 11 — 70+
(D R C Elsworth) *s.i.s: bhd: hdwy and swtchd rt 1f out: shkn up and r.o wl to take 2nd fnl 100 yds* **8/1**

0 **3** 1 **Waqaarr**[27] [311] 3-8-9 .... RichardHughes 7 — 67
(M R Channon) *led: rdn and hdd over 1f out: no ex fnl f* **7/2**[1]

00- **4** hd **Royal Guest**[120] [6257] 3-8-9 .... SamHitchcott 8 — 66
(M R Channon) *in tch: effrt over 2f out: styd on same pce* **12/1**

50 **5** nk **Lady Fifer**[17] [423] 3-8-4 .... JimmyQuinn 6 — 61
(Jane Chapple-Hyam) *chsd ldrs: hrd rdn 2f out: one pce* **20/1**

00 **6** 5 **Spinning Dixie (IRE)**[8] [498] 3-8-4 ....(t) RichardThomas 14 — 48
(J A Geake) *in tch on outside: hrd rdn over 2f out: sn outpcd* **20/1**

04- **7** nk **Rubilini**[233] [3335] 3-7-11 .... MatthewDavies(7) 9 — 47
(M R Channon) *hld up towards rr: shkn up and wd st: nvr rchd ldrs* **9/1**

8 nk **Yes One (IRE)** 3-8-9 .... EddieAhern 4 — 51
(J W Hills) *bhd tl styd on fnl 2f* **13/2**[2]

0 **9** 1 **Conorville (IRE)**[41] [160] 3-8-9 .... TonyCulhane 2 — 49
(B W Hills) *plld hrd: sn in midfield: no hdwy fnl 3f* **20/1**

55 **10** 1/2 **Lough Neagh (USA)**[10] [492] 4-9-12 .... PaulEddery 12 — 53
(Miss D Mountain) *prom tl wknd wl over 1f out* **7/1**[3]

60 **11** 1 **Meadfoot**[29] [301] 3-8-4 .... AdrianMcCarthy 3 — 40
(B R Millman) *mid-div: rdn 3f out: sn btn* **33/1**

00 **12** 1 1/2 **Cornerstone**[31] [260] 3-8-2 .... FLenclud(7) 1 — 41
(S C Williams) *prom: losing pl whn stmbld and nrly uns rdr over 2f out: tried to rally on rail ent st: sn wknd* **66/1**

13 10 **The Flying Phenom**[19] 4-9-5 .... HaddenFrost(7) 13 — 21
(J D Frost) *bhd: stmbld after 2f: nvr a factor* **33/1**

1m 24.54s (-1.35) **Going Correction** -0.20s/f (Stan)
WFA 3 from 4yo 17lb — 13 Ran SP% **120.7**
Speed ratings (Par 103):99,95,94,94,93 88,87,87,86,85 84,82,71
CSF £29.51 TOTE £5.20: £1.50, £3.10, £1.80; EX 43.10 Trifecta £123.60 Pool: £461.42 - 2.65 winning tickets..
Owner Tom Ludt **Bred** N Poole And A Franklin **Trained** Newmarket, Suffolk

FOCUS
This had a weakish look to it on paper but the first five came clear and the form is probably up to scratch. That said, the fourth and fifth did show big improvement on what they had previously achieved.

574 PONTIN'S HOLIDAYS MAIDEN STKS 5f (P)
3:00 (3:01) (Class 5) 3-Y-O £3,071 (£906; £453) Stalls High

Form RPR

-60 **1** **Scarlet Oak**[13] 456 3-8-12 .... AdamKirby 2 60+
(D J S Ffrench Davis) *hld up at rr of main gp: hdwy over 1f out: r.o to ld jst ins fnl f: rdr dropped rein: rdn out* **3/1**[1]

0-60 **2** 1 ½ **Ioweyou**[23] 348 3-8-12 54 ....(b[1]) LPKeniry 3 55
(J S Moore) *led over 1f out: pressed ldr tl outpcd by wnr fnl f* **7/2**[3]

0-20 **3** 1 ¾ **Priceless Melody (USA)**[22] 360 3-9-3 46 ....(b) JimCrowley 4 54
(Mrs A J Perrett) *chsd ldrs: effrt 2f out: kpt on same pce* **10/3**[2]

3 **4** ¾ **Royal Dagger (IRE)**[16] 429 3-9-3 .... ChrisCatlin 7 51
(Rae Guest) *in tch: rdn and outpcd over 2f out: kpt on fnl f* **7/1**

-040 **5** ¾ **Redflo**[8] 502 3-8-9 52 .... JamesDoyle(3) 6 43
(Ms J S Doyle) *chsd ldr: led over 3f out tl ins fnl f: no ex* **9/1**

00 **6** 6 **Fareham Creek**[34] 231 3-9-3 .... HayleyTurner 8 27
(D K Ivory) *t.k.h: chsd ldrs 3f* **33/1**

200- **7** 6 **La Esperanza**[169] 5238 3-8-7 50 .... AnnStokell(5) 1 —
(Miss A Stokell) *sn outpcd and bhd: hit rail over 3f out: nvr a factor* **16/1**

0 **8** 9 **Shortcake**[24] 343 3-8-12 .... DaneO'Neill 5 —
(D K Ivory) *rrd s and lost 8 l: a trailing* **20/1**

58.49 secs (-1.29) **Going Correction** -0.20s/f (Stan) **8** Ran SP% **116.1**
Speed ratings (Par 97):102,99,96,95,94 84,75,60
CSF £14.04 TOTE £4.30: £1.90, £1.80, £1.20; EX 19.00 Trifecta £86.00 Pool: £426.51 - 3.52 winning tickets..
Owner Miss A Jones **Bred** Juddmonte Farms Ltd **Trained** Lambourn, Berks

FOCUS
Moderate maiden form judged on the proximity of the 46-rated third, although the time was relatively decent and the race could have been rated higher.
La Esperanza Official explanation: jockey said filly hit the rail
Shortcake Official explanation: jockey said filly missed the break

575 PONTINSBINGO.COM H'CAP 6f (P)
3:30 (3:30) (Class 4) (0-85,83) 4-Y-O+ £4,857 (£1,445; £722; £360) Stalls Low

Form RPR

-312 **1** **Lucayos**[17] 419 4-8-9 79 .... RichardKingscote(3) 2 88
(Mrs H Sweeting) *prom: rdn 2f out: led ins fnl f: edged rt: all out* **7/1**

-206 **2** shd **Zarzu**[11] 480 8-8-7 77 .... LiamJones(3) 4 86
(C R Dore) *mid-div: hdwy over 1f out: jnd wnr ins fnl f: edged rt: kpt on wl: jst hld* **16/1**

1-01 **3** 4 **Lethal**[38] 190 4-9-2 83 .... JimCrowley 5 80+
(D K Ivory) *sn led: hrd rdn and hdd ins fnl f: no ex* **5/2**[1]

-054 **4** shd **Hammer Of The Gods (IRE)**[30] 277 7-8-6 73 ....(bt) JimmyQuinn 6 69
(P S McEntee) *chsd ldrs: hrd rdn over 1f out: kpt on same pce* **11/1**

0002 **5** ¾ **Garstang**[6] 513 4-8-8 75 ....(b) RobbieFitzpatrick 8 69
(Peter Grayson) *t.k.h on outside: cl up: jnd ldr over 3f out: no ex ins fnl f* **6/1**[2]

3503 **6** 1 ¼ **Pawan (IRE)**[17] 419 7-8-10 82 ....(b) AnnStokell(5) 10 72
(Miss A Stokell) *sn pushed along and bhd: styd on fr over 1f out: nt trble ldrs* **25/1**

160- **7** shd **Guildenstern (IRE)**[162] 5420 5-8-13 80 .... ChrisCatlin 9 70
(P L Gilligan) *in tch: rdn and outpcd fnl 2f* **16/1**

0103 **8** shd **Night Prospector**[11] 480 7-8-7 79 ....(p) TolleyDean(5) 1 69
(R A Harris) *prom: outpcd 2f out: sn btn* **20/1**

3124 **9** ½ **Figaro Flyer (IRE)**[3] 554 4-8-12 79 .... TonyCulhane 11 67
(P Howling) *towards rr and wd: n.d* **13/2**[3]

50-4 **10** 1 ½ **Adantino**[17] 419 8-8-11 78 ....(b) SteveDrowne 3 62
(B R Millman) *dwlt: towards rr: rdn over 2f out: nvr able to chal* **13/2**[3]

0-16 **11** hd **Grimes Faith**[20] 384 4-9-2 83 ....(b) RichardHughes 7 66
(R Hannon) *towards rr: sme hdwy 2f out: wknd over 1f out* **8/1**

1m 10.08s (-2.73) **Going Correction** -0.20s/f (Stan) course record **11** Ran SP% **121.8**
Speed ratings (Par 105):110,109,104,104,103 101,101,101,100,98 98
CSF £117.05 CT £362.23 TOTE £10.90: £3.00, £3.30, £1.30; EX 184.70 TRIFECTA Not won..
Owner Alex Sweeting **Bred** P Sweeting **Trained** Lockeridge, Wilts

FOCUS
A fair handicap and the winning time was decent for the type of race. Lucayos is progressing and Zarzu ran as well as he has for some time.
Grimes Faith Official explanation: vet said colt returned lame left-fore

576 PONTIN'S FAMILY HOLIDAYS H'CAP 1m (P)
4:00 (4:01) (Class 3) (0-95,90) 4-Y-O+
£7,478 (£2,239; £1,119; £560; £279; £140) Stalls High

Form RPR

0-44 **1** **Gallantry**[23] 351 5-8-8 82 .... DeanMcKeown 7 92
(D Shaw) *stdd s: hld up 2nd last: hdwy over 1f out: r.o to ld jst ins fnl f: drvn out* **10/1**

2124 **2** 1 ½ **Rebellious Spirit**[7] 509 4-8-10 84 .... JimCrowley 5 91
(P W Hiatt) *prom: drvn upsides ldr over 1f out: nt pce of wnr ins fnl f* **12/1**

1 **3** ¾ **Zam Zammah**[48] 92 4-8-11 85 .... JamieSpencer 8 90+
(Sir Michael Stoute) *stdd s: plld hrd in rr: hdwy over 1f out: kpt on ins fnl f* **9/4**[2]

1642 **4** shd **Sun Catcher (IRE)**[23] 351 4-8-3 77 .... ChrisCatlin 2 82
(R Hannon) *t.k.h: chsd ldrs: kpt on same pce fnl 2f* **8/1**

660- **5** hd **Capable Guest (IRE)**[150] 5675 5-9-2 90 .... JohnEgan 1 95
(M R Channon) *hld up in 5th: rdn over 2f out: styd on same pce* **2/1**[1]

-222 **6** 1 ¼ **Katiypour (IRE)**[20] 384 10-8-8 82 .... EddieAhern 4 84
(P Mitchell) *led: rdn and hdd jst ins fnl f: no ex* **6/1**[3]

010- **7** 1 **Glencalvie (IRE)**[154] 5590 6-8-4 78 ....(p) JimmyQuinn 6 77
(J Akehurst) *t.k.h in 6th: rdn 3f out: no imp whn hung rt over 1f out* **20/1**

0-06 **8** ½ **Regal Royale**[17] 419 4-8-5 79 .... AdrianMcCarthy 3 77
(Peter Grayson) *chsd ldrs: hrd rdn and btn over 1f ut* **20/1**

1m 36.9s (-2.53) **Going Correction** -0.20s/f (Stan) **8** Ran SP% **115.8**
Speed ratings (Par 107):104,102,101,101,101 100,99,98
CSF £120.97 CT £362.61 TOTE £15.70: £3.10, £2.40, £1.30; EX 149.60 Trifecta £426.60 Part won. Pool: £600.90 - 0.20 winning tickets..
Owner The Circle Bloodstock I Limited **Bred** Cheveley Park Stud Ltd **Trained** Danethorpe, Notts

FOCUS
A competitive little handicap, though the pace was ordinary and the race became something of a sprint from the home turn. The form has been rated at face value for now with the winner back to his best and another good effort from the runner-up. The third was a big improver on his debut maiden form.

NOTEBOOK
Gallantry, held up as usual, timed his effort to perfection this time and showed a decent turn of foot to settle it. He seems likely to be aimed at some decent handicaps on turf later on in the year as he likes fast ground, but although he seems to see out the mile well enough in ordinarily-run races on Polytrack, is yet to prove himself over it on grass. (tchd 12-1)

Rebellious Spirit, 3lb higher than when just touched off over course and distance last month, was always in a good position in a race not run at a strong pace and although he could not match the finishing pace of the winner, never stopped trying and has proved himself equally suited to this surface as he is to Fibresand. (tchd 14-1)

Zam Zammah, whose winning debut in a slowly-run maiden over course and distance last month has not really worked out though one winner has emerged from it, ran a similar race this time in that he was slowly away and then ran green in a detached last. He did stay on from the home bend, but never looked like winning and the impression is that he is going to need more time. (op 2-1 tchd 11-4)

Sun Catcher(IRE) was in a great position throughout just behind the leaders, but did not find enough from the home bend. Again stamina did not appear to be an issue. (op 9-1)

Capable Guest(IRE), reappearing from five months off but the winner of this race last year off a pound lower mark following a near-identical layoff, was given every chance but did not find as much under pressure as had seemed likely. He is not the easiest to predict. (op 5-2 tchd 15-8)

Katiypour(IRE) might have been just about twice the age of anything else in the contest, but he had the run of the race out in front and can have few excuses. (tchd 11-2)

577 PONTIN'S "BOOK EARLY" FILLIES' H'CAP 7f (P)
4:30 (4:31) (Class 6) (0-60,60) 3-Y-O £2,388 (£705; £352) Stalls Low

Form RPR

6-10 **1** **Carefree**[12] 469 3-8-13 55 .... JohnEgan 1 58
(S Parr) *prom: rdn to ld ins fnl f: all out* **16/1**

0-20 **2** hd **Ranavalona**[48] 93 3-8-4 53 ....(v) WilliamBuick(7) 13 55
(A M Balding) *t.k.h: prom: hrd rdn over 1f out: kpt on wl nr fin: jst hld* **5/1**[3]

-643 **3** nk **Candyland (IRE)**[18] 404 3-8-10 52 .... JamieSpencer 6 53
(M Quinn) *led: hrd rdn over 1f out: hdd ins fnl f: kpt on* **7/1**

65-0 **4** ¾ **Zilli**[36] 219 3-8-4 49 ow2 .... JamesDoyle(3) 14 48
(N P Littmoden) *mid-div: effrt over 2f out: hrd rdn over 1f out: styd on wl nr fin* **25/1**

4130 **5** shd **Ella Y Rossa**[23] 348 3-9-0 59 .... StephenDonohoe(3) 2 58+
(P D Evans) *sn pushed along towards rr: hdwy on rail 2f out: rdn and styd on wl: nrst fin* **4/1**[2]

60-6 **6** shd **Perfect Practice**[36] 208 3-9-2 58 .... EddieAhern 4 57
(J A R Toller) *mid-div: effrt over 2f out: hrd rdn over 1f out: styd on* **3/1**[1]

50-0 **7** 2 **Chingford (IRE)**[29] 290 3-9-4 60 .... DaneO'Neill 12 54
(J G Portman) *prom: rdn to chal 2f out: no ex fnl f* **11/1**

4530 **8** nk **The Light Fandango**[11] 478 3-8-2 47 oh1 ow1 .... SaleemGolam(3) 5 40
(R A Harris) *hld up rr of midfield: drvn along 3f out: nvr rchd ldrs* **10/1**

0-00 **9** ¾ **Pajada**[13] 460 3-8-6 48 .... HayleyTurner 8 39
(M D I Usher) *chsd ldrs: outpcd over 2f out: sn btn* **33/1**

3-06 **10** 1 ¾ **House Arrest**[19] 390 3-8-4 46 oh1 ....(bt) JimmyQuinn 10 32
(A J McCabe) *s.s: bhd: mod effrt 2f out: hrd rdn and no imp over 1f out* **20/1**

-000 **11** 1 **First Frost**[22] 357 3-8-2 47 oh1 ow1 .... MarcHalford(3) 7 31
(M J Gingell) *bhd: swtchd wd 4f out: rdn 3f out: nvr trbld ldrs* **50/1**

04-0 **12** ½ **Millyjean**[34] 231 3-8-6 55 .... KirstyMilczarek(7) 9 37
(John Berry) *a rr gp* **12/1**

0-00 **13** nk **Suzieblue (IRE)**[8] 502 3-8-11 53 ....(v[1]) SamHitchcott 3 35
(D C O'Brien) *bhd: mod effrt on rail over 1f out: n.d* **20/1**

246- **14** 5 **Dispol Truly (IRE)**[119] 6278 3-8-6 48 ....(p) LPKeniry 11 17
(A G Newcombe) *mid-div tl wknd over 2f out* **20/1**

1m 26.4s (0.51) **Going Correction** -0.20s/f (Stan) **14** Ran SP% **128.2**
Speed ratings (Par 92):89,88,88,87,87 87,85,84,83,81 80,80,79,74
CSF £92.06 CT £653.51 TOTE £23.70: £5.20, £1.90, £1.80; EX 151.70 TRIFECTA Not won..
Owner Geraldine Degville & Lawrence Degville **Bred** Prof B Carlsoo And Cheveley Park Stud Ltd **Trained** Carburton, Notts

FOCUS
A moderate if competitive contest and the winning time was 1.86 seconds slower than the earlier maiden. The principals raced prominently. The bare form is only poor, rated through the runner-up.

578 GO PONTIN'S APPRENTICE H'CAP 2m (P)
5:00 (5:01) (Class 5) (0-70,69) 4-Y-O+ £3,071 (£906; £453) Stalls Low

Form RPR

-004 **1** **Newnham (IRE)**[13] 457 6-9-7 67 .... JackMitchell(5) 13 76+
(J R Boyle) *hld up towards rr: hmpd 4f out: hdwy 2f out: r.o to ld ins fnl f: rdn out* **9/2**[2]

1313 **2** 1 ½ **Lorikeet**[23] 354 8-9-10 65 .... JamesDoyle 9 72+
(Noel T Chance) *hld up towards rr: hmpd 4f out: gd late hdwy to take 2nd on line* **4/1**[1]

114/ **3** hd **Garnett (IRE)**[649] 788 6-10-0 69 ....(p) StephenDonohoe 5 76
(D E Cantillon) *hld up and bhd: hdwy over 3f out: rdn to ld 2f out: hdd and one pce ins fnl f* **14/1**

0062 **4** ¾ **Come What July (IRE)**[25] 333 6-8-9 50 oh5 .... LiamJones 10 56
(D Shaw) *mid-div: hdwy 3f out: rdn to chal ent fnl f: one pce* **25/1**

250- **5** 2 **Eldorado**[165] 5346 6-9-12 67 .... AdamKirby 4 71
(G L Moore) *hld up and bhd: hdwy to chse ldrs 2f out: no imp fnl f* **7/1**

1 **6** nk **Caucasienne (FR)**[13] 458 4-9-2 68 .... PatrickHills(5) 7 71
(J W Hills) *in tch in chsng gp: rdn 3f out: styd on same pce* **9/2**[2]

2-32 **7** hd **Critical Stage (IRE)**[23] 354 8-9-2 64 .... HaddenFrost(7) 14 67
(J D Frost) *hld up in midfield: effrt 2f out: kpt on fnl f: nvr able to chal* **10/1**

242- **8** nk **Capitalise (IRE)**[13] 6979 4-8-7 56 .... JerryO'Dwyer 12 57
(V Smith) *hdwy on outside 6f out: pressed ldr 3f out: wknd 1f out* **11/2**[3]

1103 **9** 1 ½ **Finished Article (IRE)**[11] 481 10-8-13 54 .... EdwardCreighton 1 55
(K J Burke) *towards rr: rdn and plenty to do 3f out: styd on fnl f* **25/1**

5160 **10** 5 **Diktatorship (IRE)**[27] 315 4-7-10 56 oh2 ....(p) JosephWalsh(7) 8 45
(Ernst Oertel) *led 6f: wnt clr w ldr: led 7f out: hdd 2f out: wknd over 1f out* **33/1**

-041 **11** 1 ½ **Tip Toes (IRE)**[25] 333 5-8-9 50 oh5 .... SaleemGolam 3 43
(P Howling) *chsd clr ldrs tl wknd over 2f out* **20/1**

6034 **12** 5 **Mumbling (IRE)**[20] 380 9-9-6 61 .... RichardKingscote 2 48
(B G Powell) *prom in chsng gp tl wknd 3f out* **14/1**

36/0 **13** 2 **Head To Kerry (IRE)**[17] 416 7-8-2 50 oh4 .... BillyCray(7) 6 35
(D J S Ffrench Davis) *chsd ldr: led after 6f and wnt clr w one rival: hdd 7f out: wknd 4f out* **40/1**

06-0 **14** 16 **Royal Auditon**[16] 434 6-9-2 57 .... MarcHalford 11 23
(T T Clement) *in tch in chsng gp: hrd rdn and wknd over 4f out: bhd fnl 3f* **66/1**

3m 25.39s (-3.40) **Going Correction** -0.20s/f (Stan)
WFA 4 from 5yo+ 6lb **14** Ran SP% **126.0**
Speed ratings (Par 103):100,99,99,98,97 97,97,97,96,94 93,90,89,81
CSF £22.26 CT £245.77 TOTE £4.80: £1.70, £1.90, £4.80; EX 33.50 Trifecta £139.40 Pool: £426.32 - 2.17 winning tickets. Place 6 £238.77, Place 5 £37.22.
Owner M Khan X2 **Bred** Ballygallon Stud **Trained** Epsom, Surrey

FOCUS
Diktatorship and Head To Kerry went off at a suicidal pace, but the bulk of the field ignored them and the winning time was only ordinary. The form does not look that solid and the first two did not need to improve.

T/Plt: £238.40 to a £1 stake. Pool: £67,399.90. 206.30 winning tickets. T/Qpdt: £20.10 to a £1 stake. Pool: £4,945.60. 181.30 winning tickets. LM

519 SOUTHWELL (L-H)

Wednesday, February 28

OFFICIAL GOING: Standard

Wind: Strong, half-across

579 GO PONTIN'S APPRENTICE H'CAP 1m (F)

1:20 (1:21) (Class 6) (0-58,58) 4-Y-0+ **£2,388** (£705; £352) **Stalls Low**

Form RPR

56-3 **1** **Blushing Prince (IRE)**[13] 462 9-8-0 **46** oh1........(t) PatrickDonaghy(4) 2 51
(R C Guest) *bhd: gd hdwy over 2f out: rdn over 1f out: str run to ld ins last* **16/1**

0005 **2** *2* **Shadow Jumper (IRE)**[7] 517 6-7-12 **46** oh1........(v) DavidProbert(6) 11 47
(J T Stimpson) *cl up: effrt over 2f out: sn rdn and ev ch tl drvn and no ex wl ins last* **18/1**

224- **3** *hd* **Tabulate**[134] 6026 4-8-12 **58**.. JonjoMilczarek(4) 8 59
(P L Gilligan) *hld up in rr: wd st: hdwy wl over 1f out: rdn and hung lft ent last: styd on* **11/2**[2]

10-2 **4** *shd* **Kumakawa**[20] 393 9-8-2 **48**..................................... LauraReynolds(4) 13 48
(N P Littmoden) *chsd ldrs: effrt over 2f out: sn rdn and ch ent last: sn drvn and one pce* **8/1**

30-0 **5** *hd* **Hilltop Fantasy**[49] 83 6-8-0 **46** oh1....................(p) JosephWalsh(4) 14 46
(V Smith) *sn led: rdn along 2f out: drvn over 1f out: hdd and no ex ins last* **25/1**

-042 **6** *1 3/4* **Dispol Peto**[13] 464 7-8-1 **47**..(b) JackDean(4) 3 43
(R Johnson) *chsd ldrs: rdn over 2f out: kpt on same pce* **9/1**

1041 **7** *3/4* **Paso Doble**[13] 466 9-9-2 **58**......................................(p) JamieHamblett 9 53
(R Bastiman) *hld up in rr: wd st: effrt over 2f out: sn rdn and kpt on approaching last: nrst fin* **3/1**[1]

2000 **8** *nk* **Crusoe (IRE)**[5] 533 10-8-0 **46** oh1...........................(b) SoniaEaton(4) 10 40
(A Sadik) *dwlt: midfield: rdn along 2f out and sn no imp* **33/1**

3400 **9** *3/4* **Capital Lass**[12] 479 4-8-7 **55**...................................... AdamCarter(6) 12 48
(A J McCabe) *chsd ldng pair: hdwy over 2f out: rdn and ev ch over 1f out: wknd ent last* **14/1**

632 **10** *1* **Shunkawakhan (IRE)**[13] 462 4-8-0 **48**................(p) MarvinCheung(6) 1 38
(G C H Chung) *hld up in rr: hdwy on inner 2f out: rdn to chse ldrs over 1f out: sn wknd* **6/1**[3]

600- **11** *nk* **Red Lantern**[102] 6524 6-8-0 **46** oh1..................................... NSLawes(4) 6 36
(M W Easterby) *in tch: effrta nd chsd ldrs wl over 2f out: sn rdn and grad wknd* **50/1**

6130 **12** *1* **Pawn In Life (IRE)**[6] 519 9-8-4 **46** oh1................(v) DanielleMcCreery 5 34
(S Parr) *a towards rr* **25/1**

0/0- **13** *1* **Ahaz**[64] 5435 5-8-0 **46** oh1.. ChrisHough(4) 7 32
(J F Coupland) *s.i.s: a rr* **100/1**

0-60 **14** *1 1/4* **Blue Empire (IRE)**[28] 309 6-9-1 **57**.................................... AlanRutter 4 40
(C R Dore) *chsd ldrs on inner: rdn along 3f out: sn wknd* **8/1**

1m 45.07s (0.47) **Going Correction** -0.10s/f (Stan) **14** Ran SP% **118.3**

Speed ratings (Par 101):93,91,90,90,90 88,88,87,86,85 85,84,83,82

CSF £259.25 CT £1842.17 TOTE £17.00: £5.60, £5.30, £2.70; EX 418.90 TRIFECTA Not won..

Owner Richard Guest Horseracing Limited **Bred** Patrick M Ryan **Trained** Brancepeth, Co Durham

FOCUS

A weak handicap which took little winning. The second and fifth limit the form.

Paso Doble Official explanation: trainer had no explanation for the poor form shown

580 PONTIN'S H'CAP (DIV I) 6f (F)

1:50 (1:50) (Class 6) (0-55,54) 4-Y-0+ **£1,706** (£503; £252) **Stalls Low**

Form RPR

2424 **1** **Soba Jones**[8] 504 10-8-9 **54**.................................... JasonEdmunds(3) 4 61
(J Balding) *trckd ldrs: hdwy over 2f out: rdn to ld wl over 1f out: drvn ins last and styd on wl* **5/1**[2]

-526 **2** *1/2* **Favouring (IRE)**[6] 519 5-8-4 **49**............................(b) AndrewMullen(3) 2 54
(M C Chapman) *bmpd s and bhd: hdwy on inner over 2f out: rdn to chal over 1f out and ev ch tl drvn and no ex last 75 yds* **9/2**[1]

0-41 **3** *3 1/2* **Best Lead**[15] 448 8-8-7 **54**.....................................(b) KevinGhunowa(5) 1 49
(Ian Emmerson) *chsd ldrs: hdwy over 2f out: sn rdn and ev ch tl wkng whn n.m.r and swtchd rt ent last: one pce* **8/1**

-606 **4** *hd* **Prettilini**[13] 463 4-8-9 **51** ow1... PhillipMakin 8 45
(R Brotherton) *in tch on outer: pushed along 1/2-way: rdn 2f out and kpt on same pce* **17/2**

-010 **5** *1 1/2* **Ace Club**[3] 562 6-8-6 **51**..(v) EmmettStack(3) 9 40
(K J Burke) *dwlt and bhd: hdwy 2f out. swtchd lft and rdn over 1f out: kpt on ins last: nrst fin* **14/1**

0510 **6** *1* **Blushing Russian (IRE)**[3] 562 5-8-8 **50** ow2................(p) BrettDoyle 7 36
(J M Bradley) *in tch: hdwy to chse ldrs wl over 2f out: sn rdn and wknd over 1f out* **8/1**

10-0 **7** *1 3/4* **Creme Brulee**[30] 296 4-8-4 **53**...................................... PatrickHills(7) 10 34
(C R Egerton) *midfield: hdwy and wd st: sn rdn and no imp fnl 2f* **7/1**

-006 **8** *1* **Tuscan Flyer**[15] 450 9-8-3 **45**..(b) JimmyQuinn 6 23
(R Bastiman) *led 1f: cl up tl rdn along welol over 2f out and grad wknd* **20/1**

5006 **9** *1 1/2* **Diktalex (IRE)**[8] 504 4-7-12 **45**............................(tp) DuranFentiman(5) 11 19
(C J Teague) *s.i.s: a rr* **33/1**

06-2 **10** *5* **Indian Sundance (IRE)**[31] 281 4-8-5 **47**.......................... PaulHanagan 3 6
(R A Fahey) *keen: in tch: hdwy to chse ldrs wl over 2f out: sn rdn and wknd* **11/2**[3]

3-66 **11** *13* **Nawayea**[18] 421 4-8-1 **50**....................................(b) KirstyMilczarek(7) 5 —
(C N Allen) *cl up: eld after 1f: rdn along over 2f out: hdd wl over 1f out: wknd qckly and heavily eased ins last* **20/1**

1m 16.67s (-0.23) **Going Correction** -0.10s/f (Stan) **11** Ran SP% **114.6**

Speed ratings (Par 101):97,96,91,91,89 88,85,84,82,75 58

CSF £26.19 CT £153.73 TOTE £6.90: £2.00, £1.30, £2.40; EX 26.50 Trifecta £155.40 Part won. Pool: £219.00 - 0.64 winning tickets..

Owner R L Crowe **Bred** Mrs M J Hills **Trained** Scrooby, Notts

FOCUS

A typically competitive sprint handicap. Ordinary form, rated through the runner-up.

Blushing Russian(IRE) Official explanation: jockey said gelding lost its action

Nawayea Official explanation: jockey said filly lost its action

581 PONTIN'S FAMILY HOLIDAYS CLAIMING STKS 5f (F)

2:20 (2:20) (Class 6) 4-Y-0+ **£2,184** (£644; £322) **Stalls High**

Form RPR

250 **1** **Spirit Of Coniston**[16] 441 4-8-4 50....................(b) DuranFentiman(5) 11 56
(Peter Grayson) *chsd ldrs: hdwy 2f out: rdn to ld over 1f out: edgd lft ins last: styd on* **14/1**

4250 **2** *1 1/4* **El Potro**[6] 523 5-8-11 45... GrahamGibbons 2 54
(J R Holt) *chsd ldrs: hdwy 2f out: rdn and ev ch ent last: drvn and no ex last 100 yds* **9/1**

0000 **3** *nk* **Far Note (USA)**[15] 448 9-8-7 40...................................(bt) JimmyQuinn 3 49
(S R Bowring) *swtchd lft and chsd ldrs after 1f: rdn wl over 1f out: drvn ins last and kpt on same pce* **40/1**

0515 **4** *shd* **Hamaasy**[6] 521 6-8-6 70... AdeleRothery(7) 1 55
(D Nicholls) *in tch: pushed along and hdwy 2f out: rdn over 1f out: kpt on same pce ins last* **3/1**[2]

20-2 **5** *1* **Blackheath (IRE)**[5] 536 11-9-3 73......................... SilvestreDeSousa 12 55
(D Nicholls) *chsd ldrs: rdn along and outpcd over 2f out: kpt on u.p ins last: nrst fin* **4/1**[3]

-600 **6** *1 3/4* **Amanda's Lad (IRE)**[6] 523 7-8-6 42............................ SCreighton(7) 10 45
(M C Chapman) *in tch: rdn along 1/2-way: sn no imp* **40/1**

-204 **7** *1* **Katie Killane**[30] 289 5-8-8 45... MickyFenton 9 37
(M Wellings) *led 1f: cl up tl rdn and wknd appr last* **16/1**

-550 **8** *3/4* **The Leather Wedge (IRE)**[13] 465 8-8-10 50......... PatrickMathers(3) 6 39
(R Johnson) *cl up: led after 1f: rdn aloong 2f out: hdd & wknd over 1f out* **25/1**

330- **9** *1* **Balian**[85] 6717 4-8-10 50..(p) JosephWalsh(7) 8 40
(Mrs P Sly) *sn outpcd and a rr* **20/1**

-150 **10** *1/2* **Charlie Delta**[7] 513 4-9-7 69..(p) EddieAhern 4 42
(J R Boyle) *sn rdn along and outpcd in rr* **15/8**[1]

0060 **11** *7* **Percy Douglas**[16] 441 7-8-12 41.................................(p) AnnStokell(5) 7 14
(Miss A Stokell) *chsd ldrs: rdn along 1/2-way: sn wknd* **66/1**

59.19 secs (-1.11) **Going Correction** -0.175s/f (Stan) **11** Ran SP% **117.3**

Speed ratings (Par 101):101,99,98,98,96 93,92,91,89,88 77

CSF £125.37 TOTE £14.00: £3.80, £2.40, £10.00; EX 93.20 TRIFECTA Not won..The winner was claimed by Mr C Teague for 6,000. Hamaasy was subject to a friendly claim.

Owner Richard Teatum **Bred** Green Square Racing **Trained** Formby, Lancs

FOCUS

A moderate event and the form is worth treating with a little caution. The winner did well to defy a high draw and ran up to his form.

Charlie Delta Official explanation: trainer's rep said gelding was outpaced and resented kickback

Percy Douglas Official explanation: trainer's rep said gelding bled from the nose

582 PONTIN'S BOOK EARLY H'CAP 1m 4f (F)

2:55 (2:55) (Class 5) (0-75,75) 3-Y-0 **£3,071** (£906; £453) **Stalls Low**

Form RPR

351 **1** **Six Day War (IRE)**[29] 304 3-9-3 **74**................................... ShaneKelly 2 88+
(J A Osborne) *trckd ldrs gng wl: hdwy 3f out: rdn to ld wl over 1f out: clr ins last* **13/8**[1]

3-01 **2** *3* **Red Petal**[20] 392 3-9-2 **73**.. SebSanders 3 78
(Sir Mark Prescott) *trckd ldng pair: hdwy 3f out: rdn wl over 1f out: drvn to chse wnr and edgd rt ent last: kpt on* **15/8**[2]

15-3 **3** *5* **Peregrine Falcon**[47] 111 3-9-4 **75**.................................. JoeFanning 1 72
(M Johnston) *led: rdn and qckned over 2f out: drvn and hdd wl over 1f out: sn edgd lft and one pce* **6/1**

31- **4** *2 1/2* **Personal Column**[91] 6650 3-9-2 **73**............................... DaneO'Neill 5 66
(T G Mills) *cl up: effrt and ev ch 2f out: sn rdn and btn wl over 1f out* **4/1**[3]

020- **5** *10* **Colditz (IRE)**[165] 5359 3-8-12 **69**............................... PaulHanagan 4 46
(D W Barker) *a rr: rdn along 3f out and sn outpcd* **28/1**

2m 41.23s (-0.86) **Going Correction** -0.10s/f (Stan) **5** Ran SP% **110.6**

Speed ratings (Par 97):98,96,92,91,84

CSF £5.02 TOTE £2.40: £1.50, £1.10; EX 4.30.

Owner Mountgrange&Wood Hall Studs Booth Durkan **Bred** C Lilburn **Trained** Upper Lambourn, Berks

■ Stewards' Enquiry : Seb Sanders caution: careless riding

FOCUS

A competitive handicap which has been rated positively, although the early gallop was only modest and the race turned into something of a sprint. The first two are progressive.

583 PONTINSBINGO.COM MAIDEN STKS 6f (F)

3:30 (3:30) (Class 5) 3-Y-0 **£2,968** (£876; £438) **Stalls Low**

Form RPR

1 **Annemasse** 3-9-3 .... JoeFanning 4 87+
(M Johnston) *cl up: led 2f out: rdn clr over 1f out: styd on* **9/2**[3]

-252 **2** *4* **Popolo (IRE)**[8] 505 3-8-12 63.................................... AdrianMcCarthy 7 65
(P W Chapple-Hyam) *trckd ldrs: hdwy over 2f out: rdn to chse wnr appr last: sn drvn and one pce* **5/2**[2]

5 **3** *1/2* **Kelamon**[17] 429 3-9-3 .... HayleyTurner 3 69
(M D I Usher) *led: rdn along and hdd 2f out: sn drvn and kpt on same pce* **20/1**

0-32 **4** *nk* **Grand Symphony**[11] 489 3-8-12 69.................................... BrettDoyle 9 63
(W Jarvis) *chsd ldrs on outer: hdwy over 2f out: sn rdn and hung lft over 1f out: one pce* **13/8**[1]

5 *5* **Mr Whoppit** 3-9-3 .... PaulQuinn 5 53
(T D Easterby) *chsd ldrs tl rdn along 3f out and sn wknd* **33/1**

40- **6** *hd* **Moonlight Applause**[272] 2166 3-8-12 .... DavidAllan 6 47
(T D Easterby) *keen: in tch: rdn along 1/2-way: sn wknd* **16/1**

30- **7** *7* **Bijouterie**[275] 2076 3-8-9 .... GregFairley(3) 1 26
(T J Pitt) *s.i.s: a rr* **8/1**

00- **8** *6* **Danum Diva (IRE)**[151] 5679 3-8-12 .... RobbieFitzpatrick 2 8
(T J Pitt) *chsd ldrs: rdn along 1/2-way: sn wknd* **28/1**

1m 16.36s (-0.54) **Going Correction** -0.10s/f (Stan) **8** Ran SP% **113.0**

Speed ratings (Par 97):99,93,93,92,85 85,76,68

CSF £15.60 TOTE £6.10: £1.80, £1.10, £3.20; EX 19.50 Trifecta £140.40 Pool: £573.67 - 2.90 winning tickets..

Owner Brian Yeardley Continental Ltd **Bred** Newsells Park Stud Limited **Trained** Middleham Moor, N Yorks

FOCUS

A modest event. The winner was impressive with the form looking moderate but fairly sound behind. The runner-up is very exposed and has had plenty of chances.

Bijouterie Official explanation: jockey said filly resented the kickback

584 PONTIN'S HOLIDAYS H'CAP 7f (F)
4:00 (4:00) (Class 4) (0-85,82) 3-Y-O **£4,857** (£1,445; £722; £360) **Stalls** Low

Form RPR
1 **1** **Regal Parade**[30] [301] 3-9-1 **79** JoeFanning 3 92+
(M Johnston) *mde all: qcknd over 2f out: rdn wl over 1f out: styd on strly ins last* **7/4**[1]
2-52 **2** *2* **Eau Good**[17] [433] 3-9-1 **82** StephenDonohoe(3) 2 85
(M C Chapman) *trckd ldrs on inner: hdwy over 2f out: rdn to chse wnrr ent last: sn drvn and kpt on same pce* **11/2**
40-1 **3** *½* **Go On Green (IRE)**[18] [423] 3-9-2 **80** EddieAhern 4 82
(E A L Dunlop) *trckd ldrs: hdwy on outer over 2f out: rdn and hung lft wl over 1f out: kpt on same pce ins last* **9/4**[2]
1-33 **4** *1 ½* **Hollywood George**[12] [478] 3-8-8 **72** NCallan 5 70
(K A Ryan) *cl up: effrt and ch over 2f out: sn rdn and wknd wl over 1f out* **4/1**[3]
0-24 **5** *3* **New Beginning (IRE)**[40] [184] 3-9-0 **78** PaulHanagan 1 68
(Mrs S Lamyman) *hld up: a rr* **14/1**

1m 30.62s (-0.18) **Going Correction** -0.10s/f (Stan) **5** Ran SP% **109.2**
Speed ratings (Par 99):97,94,94,92,89
CSF £11.30 TOTE £2.10: £1.10, £2.50; EX 9.70.
Owner Sheikh Mohammed **Bred** Highclere Stud And Harry Herbert **Trained** Middleham Moor, N Yorks

FOCUS
A useful-looking contest that lacked any early pace. Regal Parade stepped up on his debut form but the lack of pace probably prevented him from showing how good he is. The runner-up is a fair yardstick to the form.

585 PONTINS.COM H'CAP 1m 6f (F)
4:35 (4:35) (Class 6) (0-65,63) 4-Y-O+ **£2,388** (£705; £352) **Stalls** Low

Form RPR
0-11 **1** **Global Strategy**[43] [148] 4-9-7 **62** ChrisCatlin 4 83+
(Rae Guest) *hld up: stdy hdwy 1/2-way: chsd ldrs over 2f out and sn rdn: drvn and styd on to ld 1f out: sn clr* **15/8**[1]
5413 **2** *3* **Blue Hills**[12] [482] 6-9-7 **57** (b) JimCrowley 8 71
(P W Hiatt) *trckd ldrs: hdwy to ld over 3f out: rdn 2f out: drvn and hdd 1f out: kpt on same pce* **10/1**
005- **3** *1 ¾* **Sand Repeal (IRE)**[35] [6947] 5-9-12 **62** (v[1]) BrettDoyle 11 73
(Miss J Feilden) *cl up: led after 6f: pushed along and hdd over 3f out: sn rdn: drvn and ch 2f out: kpt on same pce* **14/1**
00-2 **4** *8* **Trysting Grove (IRE)**[46] [126] 6-8-7 **48** TolleyDean(5) 7 48
(E G Bevan) *hld up in rr: stdy hdwy 6f out: chsd ldrs over 2f out: sn rdn and no imp* **33/1**
0-60 **5** *5* **Woolstone Boy (USA)**[18] [416] 6-8-9 **45** (t) JimmyQuinn 3 38
(A M Hales) *chsd ldrs: rdn along 3f out: sn btn* **40/1**
03-0 **6** *nk* **Silver Mont (IRE)**[15] [453] 4-8-6 **47** (b) HayleyTurner 2 40
(S R Bowring) *in tch on inner: rdn along 4f out: drvn 3f out and sn outpcd* **33/1**
005- **7** *12* **Celtic Empire (IRE)**[32] [6305] 4-8-5 **46** DaleGibson 13 22
(Jedd O'Keeffe) *bhd: hdwy and in tch over 4f out: sn rdn and wknd* **66/1**
650- **8** *1* **Optimum (IRE)**[35] [6979] 5-9-0 **50** MickyFenton 12 24
(J T Stimpson) *in tch on outer: rdn along 6f out: sn wknd* **16/1**
6303 **9** *1 ½* **Isa'Af (IRE)**[13] [464] 8-8-2 **45** MatthewDavies(7) 1 17
(P W Hiatt) *chsdldrs early: rdn 1/2-way and sn wknd* **14/1**
21-0 **10** *shd* **Red River Rebel**[57] [10] 9-9-2 **52** PaulMulrennan 9 24
(J R Norton) *led 6f: sn rdn along: lost pl over 6f out and sn bhd* **16/1**
0-22 **11** *nk* **Raise The Heights (IRE)**[15] [453] 4-9-8 **63** NCallan 6 35
(J G Portman) *hld up towards rr: stdy hdwy 1/2-way: chsd ldrs 5f out: rdn along over 3f out and sn wknd* **4/1**[2]
2143 **12** *10* **Miss Holly**[20] [389] 8-9-5 **62** KellyHarrison(7) 14 20
(D Carroll) *hld up: a rr* **6/1**[3]
0-33 **13** *14* **Moyne Pleasure (IRE)**[9] [240] 9-8-5 **46** DuranFentiman(5) 10 —
(R Johnson) *dwlt: a rr* **14/1**

3m 6.26s (-3.34) **Going Correction** -0.10s/f (Stan)
WFA 4 from 5yo+ 5lb **13** Ran SP% **119.7**
Speed ratings (Par 101):105,103,102,97,94 94,87,87,86,86 86,80,72
CSF £21.38 CT £213.09 TOTE £3.00: £1.60, £3.00, £4.50; EX 27.40 Trifecta £195.10 Pool: £461.82 - 1.68 winning tickets..
Owner E P Duggan **Bred** Keith Freeman **Trained** Newmarket, Suffolk

FOCUS
A stongly-run event in which they finished well strung out. It was just a moderate affair, but Global Strategy is progressive and the form looks solid.
Red River Rebel Official explanation: jockey said gelding hung right throughout
Raise The Heights(IRE) Official explanation: jockey said gelding had no more to give
Miss Holly Official explanation: jockey said mare never travelled
Moyne Pleasure(IRE) Official explanation: jockey said gelding lost its action

586 PONTIN'S H'CAP (DIV II) 6f (F)
5:05 (5:06) (Class 6) (0-55,54) 4-Y-O+ **£1,706** (£503; £252) **Stalls** Low

Form RPR
3445 **1** **Blythe Spirit**[13] [467] 8-8-4 **46** (v[1]) PaulHanagan 3 58
(R A Fahey) *bhd and rdn along 1/2-way: hdwy and nt clr run 2f out: hdwy on bit to ld appr last: rdn clr and hung lft ins last* **12/1**
-154 **2** *2* **Shava**[12] [485] 7-8-11 **53** NCallan 2 59
(H J Evans) *trckd ldrs: smooth hdwy to ld wl over 1f out: rdn and hdd appr last: sn drvn edgd lft and one pce* **9/2**[3]
5004 **3** *¾* **Piccleyes**[15] [448] 6-8-3 **45** (b) HayleyTurner 7 49
(A J McCabe) *in tch: hdwy whn nt clr run and hmpd 2f out: sn rdn and styd on ent last: nrst fin* **15/2**
-004 **4** *nk* **Ask No More**[25] [341] 4-8-6 **51** (b) DominicFox(3) 6 54
(P L Gilligan) *led: rdn along over 2f out: drvn and hdd wl over 1f out: kpt on same pce u.p* **12/1**
2100 **5** *2 ½* **Vlasta Weiner**[27] [317] 7-8-4 **53** (b) BarrySavage(7) 1 49
(J M Bradley) *dwlt and rr tl styd on fnl 2f* **25/1**
-062 **6** *2 ½* **Jabbara (IRE)**[4] [555] 4-8-8 **50** (b) JoeFanning 5 38
(C E Brittain) *trckd ldrs: hdwy to chal over 2f out and ev ch tl rdn and wl over 1f out and sn wknd* **9/4**[1]
00-0 **7** *1* **Inca Soldier (FR)**[13] [467] 4-8-7 **49** JamieMackay 8 34
(R C Guest) *s.i.s and bhd tl styd on fnl 2f* **50/1**
-346 **8** *½* **Blakeshall Quest**[15] [448] 7-8-12 **54** (b) PatCosgrave 9 38
(R Brotherton) *cl up: effrt and ev ch over 2f out: sn rdn and wkng whn hmpd 2f out: sn lost pl* **12/1**
0212 **9** *hd* **Astorygoeswithit**[6] [524] 4-8-5 **47** (be) ChrisCatlin 10 30
(P S McEntee) *chsd ldrs on outer: rdn along and hung lft 2f out: sn btn* **4/1**[2]
602- **10** *½* **Wolfman**[165] [5363] 5-8-7 **49** (p) JimmyQuinn 4 31
(D W Barker) *prom on inner: rdn along whn hmpd and n.m.r 1/2-way: sn wknd* **12/1**

1m 15.87s (-1.03) **Going Correction** -0.10s/f (Stan) **10** Ran SP% **117.3**
Speed ratings (Par 101):102,99,98,97,94 91,89,89,89,88
CSF £65.74 CT £453.94 TOTE £14.10: £2.80, £1.30, £2.60; EX 77.80 Trifecta £324.30 Part won. Pool: £456.86 - 0.20 winning tickets. Place 6 £267.92, Place 5 £62.18.
Owner The Matthewman Partnership **Bred** W Haggas & W Jarvis **Trained** Musley Bank, N Yorks

FOCUS
A competitive enough contest, but not that easy a race to assess. It has been rated through the third.
T/Jkpt: Not won. T/Plt: £483.00 to a £1 stake. Pool: £78,143.65. 118.10 winning tickets. T/Qpdt: £44.20 to a £1 stake. Pool: £6,567.20. 109.80 winning tickets. JR

572 LINGFIELD (L-H)
Thursday, March 1

OFFICIAL GOING: Standard
Wind: Strong across Weather: Bright

587 GO PONTIN'S H'CAP (DIV I) 1m 4f (P)
1:30 (1:31) (Class 4) (0-85,85) 4-Y-O+ **£4,210** (£1,252; £625; £312) **Stalls** Low

Form RPR
4-32 **1** **Polish Power (GER)**[37] [226] 7-9-2 **83** JohnEgan 4 93
(J S Moore) *lw: trckd ldrs: rdn to ld 1f out: r.o wl* **9/2**[3]
646- **2** *nk* **Ameeq (USA)**[109] [3093] 5-9-0 **81** GeorgeBaker 2 90
(G L Moore) *hld up in last trio: rdn and hdwy on inner 2f out: chsd wnr wl ins fnl f: r.o* **4/1**[2]
-460 **3** *1 ½* **Turner's Touch**[12] [488] 5-8-4 **71** (p) HayleyTurner 10 78
(G L Moore) *t.k.h: chsd ldr tl led over 2f out: sn rdn: hdd 1f out: kpt on same pce ins fnl f* **14/1**
6352 **4** *1 ¾* **Bay Boy**[3] [568] 5-8-6 **73** JoeFanning 1 77
(M Johnston) *led: rdn over 3f out:hdd over 2f out: rallied u.p over 1f out: wknd ins fnl f* **4/1**[2]
600- **5** *shd* **Inchloch**[131] [6107] 5-9-4 **85** AdamKirby 6 89
(B G Powell) *bit bkwd: stdd s: hld up in rr: rdn 3f out: c wd and hdwy 2f out: styd on fnl f: nt rch ldrs* **18/1**
4-41 **6** *1 ¼* **Oscar Snowman**[19] [422] 4-8-7 **76** DaleGibson 7 78
(M P Tregoning) *lw: t.k.h: hld up in midfield: rdn over 2f out: kpt on same pce* **3/1**[1]
60-0 **7** *1 ¼* **Activo (FR)**[43] [164] 6-8-4 **78** JackMitchell(7) 5 78
(S Dow) *s.i.s: plld hrd: hld up towards rr on outer: hdwy to press ldrs 3f out: rdn 2f out: wknd 1f out* **18/1**
3/60 **8** *½* **Mission To Mars**[12] [488] 8-8-13 **80** SteveDrowne 3 79
(P G Murphy) *t.k.h: hld up in midfield: rdn over 2f out: wknd over 1f out* **25/1**
16-0 **9** *nk* **Dzesmin (POL)**[34] [256] 5-8-10 **80** (p) StephenDonohoe(3) 8 79
(R C Guest) *t.k.h: hld up in last trio: rdn over 2f out: nvr trbld ldrs* **50/1**
6-04 **10** *½* **Dream Catcher (SWE)**[12] [488] 4-8-11 **80** (t) BrettDoyle 9 78
(R A Kvisla) *t.k.h: chsd ldrs: rdn and ev ch over 2f out: wknd over 1f out* **12/1**

2m 32.1s (-2.29) **Going Correction** -0.125s/f (Stan)
WFA 4 from 5yo+ 2lb **10** Ran SP% **113.9**
Speed ratings (Par 105):102,101,100,99,99 98,97,97,97,97
CSF £22.27 CT £230.23 TOTE £5.40: £1.80, £1.80, £4.30; EX 31.60 Trifecta £282.50 Part won. Pool: £398.01, 0.54 winning units..
Owner Mrs Fitri Hay **Bred** Gestut Hofgut Mappen **Trained** Upper Lambourn, Berks

FOCUS
An ordinary pace for most of this handicap, which was run in blustery conditions, and the whole field were still pretty bunched up rounding the home turn. Despite the pace the winning time was 0.35 seconds faster than the second division. Ordinary-looking form for the grade, but the winner is progressive.
Oscar Snowman Official explanation: jockey said gelding hung right early stages

588 PONTINSBINGO.COM MAIDEN STKS 5f (P)
2:00 (2:00) (Class 5) 3-Y-O+ **£3,071** (£906; £453) **Stalls** High

Form RPR
/20- **1** **Macademy Royal (USA)**[302] [1412] 4-9-6 70 (t) FrankiePickard(7) 1 75
(H Morrison) *lw: hld up in last: effrt and hdwy over 1f out: rn wl fnl f to ld nr fin* **10/3**[3]
52-3 **2** *¾* **Scarlett Heart (IRE)**[26] [343] 3-8-10 55 ow1 SebSanders 3 61
(P J Makin) *lw: trckd ldrs: rdn and hdwy on inner wl over 1f out: led wl ins fnl f: hdd and no ex nr fin* **3/1**[2]
4-50 **3** *1* **Belvedere Vixen**[31] [290] 3-8-9 60 (p) JamieSpencer 2 56
(M J Wallace) *pressed ldr: led wl over 1f out: sn rdn: hdd wl ins fnl f: no ex* **7/2**
240- **4** *hd* **Temtation (IRE)**[153] [5655] 3-8-9 62 PatCosgrave 4 56
(J R Boyle) *t.k.h: led tl hdd wl over 1f out: ev ch tl unable qck wl ins fnl f* **5/2**[1]
-225 **5** *1 ¾* **Ceredig**[8] [511] 4-9-13 58 (p) RichardHughes 5 60
(W R Muir) *t.k.h: hld up trcking ldrs: swtchd rt and rdn over 1f out: no hdwy fnl f* **11/2**

59.50 secs (-0.28) **Going Correction** -0.125s/f (Stan)
WFA 3 from 4yo 13lb **5** Ran SP% **114.3**
Speed ratings (Par 103):97,95,94,93,91
CSF £14.08 TOTE £3.90: £2.10, £1.50; EX 15.70.
Owner H Morrison **Bred** V Sambranos **Trained** East Ilsley, Berks

FOCUS
A modest maiden and with little covering the first four at the line, the form is unlikely to amount to much though the winner, who is rated back to his debut form, might be capable of a bit more in handicaps.

589 PONTIN'S FAMILY HOLIDAYS CLAIMING STKS 7f (P)
2:30 (2:30) (Class 6) 3-Y-O **£2,184** (£644; £322) **Stalls** Low

Form RPR
-1 **1** **Tendalay (USA)**[46] [128] 3-9-8 73 ShaneKelly 9 78+
(J A Osborne) *hld up towards rr: shkn up and effrt wl over 1f out led ins fnl f: pushed out* **4/1**[2]
3042 **2** *¾* **Cherri Fosfate**[7] [520] 3-9-3 69 (b[1]) DanielTudhope 1 71
(D Carroll) *trckd ldrs on inner: rdn to ld jst over 1f out: hdd ins fnl f: no ex* **3/1**[1]
353 **3** *2* **Not Now Lewis (IRE)**[19] [423] 3-9-0 67 RichardKingscote(3) 6 66+
(J A Osborne) *s.i.s: bhd: rdn and hdwy on wd outside bnd over 2f out: styd on fnl f: nt rch ldrs* **5/1**[3]

-442 **4** ¾ **Strike Force**^{8} [512] 3-8-8 65................................(p) MichaelJStainton(5) 2 60
(R A Harris) *sn led: rdn over 2f out: hdd jst over 1f out: kpt on same pce* **6/1**

31-0 **5** ¾ **Iron Pearl**^{38} [219] 3-8-11 63.. BrettDoyle 4 56
(Jane Chapple-Hyam) *hld up wl in tch: rdn wl over 1f out: kpt on same pce fnl f* **7/1**

00-5 **6** ¾ **Suhayl Star (IRE)**^{17} [446] 3-9-2 69.. JDSmith 5 62+
(M Wigham) *t.k.h: trckd ldrs:hdwy and ev ch travelling wl over 1f out: rdn and wknd 1f out* **5/1**^{3}

7 ½ **Bear Bottom** 3-9-3 .... TPQueally 3 59
(W J Musson) *w'like: hld up bhd: pushed along and kpt on same pce over 1f out: nvr trbld ldrs* **33/1**

3 **8** 3 **Bahama Gold**^{19} [417] 3-8-3 .... NeilChalmers(3) 7 40
(D G Bridgwater) *w ldr: rdn over 2f out: wknd over 1f out* **25/1**

1m 25.1s (-0.79) **Going Correction** -0.125s/f (Stan) **8** Ran SP% **111.9**
Speed ratings (Par 96):99,98,95,95,94 93,92,89
CSF £15.68 TOTE £4.20: £1.30, £1.50, £2.00; EX 13.10 Trifecta £52.80 Pool £543.66, 7.31 winning units.The winner was claimed by Declan Carroll for £20,000
Owner Paul J Dixon and Ten **Bred** M R Colton **Trained** Upper Lambourn, Berks

FOCUS
A fair claimer in which six of the eight runners already had a handicap mark. Just 3lb covered them once adjusted, which shows how tight the contest was. The form looks solid for the grade. Tendalay showed big improvement from the bare form of his debut win.

590 PONTINS.COM FILLIES' H'CAP 7f (P)
3:00 (3:00) (Class 4) (0-85,85) 4-Y-0+ **£4,857** (£1,445; £722; £360) **Stalls** Low

Form RPR

040- **1** **Mcnairobi**^{152} [5666] 4-8-11 **80**.. DaneO'Neill 7 89
(P D Cundell) *hld up wl in tch: rdn and hdwy 2f out: chsd ldr ins fnl f: r.o strly to ld nr fin* **13/2**

2-03 **2** ¾ **Secret Night**^{22} [384] 4-9-2 **85**.. JimmyFortune 4 92
(J A R Toller) *hld up: hdwy to trck ldrs 2f out: led jst ins fnl f: sn drvn and 1l ld 100 yds out: fdd and ct nr fin* **11/4**^{2}

03-1 **3** ½ **Hypocrisy**^{19} [424] 4-8-9 **78**......................................(v^{1}) DanielTudhope 3 84
(D Carroll) *dwlt: hld up wl in tch: swtchd rt and hdwy over 1f out: r.o wl ins fnl f: nrst fin* **9/2**^{3}

4 3 **Snow Gretel (IRE)**^{204} [4272] 4-9-2 **85**................................ OscarUrbina 5 83
(M Botti) *trckd ldrs: wnt 2nd over 2f out: led wl over 1f out: sn rdn: hdd jst ins fnl f: fdd* **16/1**

0-00 **5** ¾ **Kaveri (USA)**^{22} [384] 4-8-9 **78**.. JamieSpencer 6 74
(C E Brittain) *chsd ldrs: led wl over 2f out: rdn and hdd wl over 1f out: wknd* **8/1**

4000 **6** 3 ½ **Meditation**^{9} [509] 5-8-4 **76** ow2....................................(p) JamesDoyle(3) 1 63
(I A Wood) *chsd ldr: rdn over 3f out: sn struggling: no ch last 2f* **16/1**

2-11 **7** 2 **One Night In Paris (IRE)**^{24} [358] 4-8-3 **72**.......................... JohnEgan 2 54
(M J Wallace) *led: rdn over 3f out: hdd wl over 2f out: wknd 2f out* **9/4**^{1}

1m 23.67s (-2.22) **Going Correction** -0.125s/f (Stan) **7** Ran SP% **111.8**
Speed ratings (Par 102):107,106,105,102,101 97,95
CSF £23.60 TOTE £8.40: £3.10, £2.30; EX 32.60.
Owner Ian M Brown **Bred** Roden House Stud **Trained** Compton, Berks

FOCUS
They went off very quick in this and the fact that the leading pair early finished last and last but one, whilst the first two home were the last pair early, strongly suggests they went off much too fast. A creditable winning time for a race like this. The form is straightforward and the winner is capable of better.
One Night In Paris(IRE) Official explanation: vet said filly returned lame

591 PONTIN'S "BOOK EARLY" H'CAP 1m (P)
3:30 (3:32) (Class 5) (0-75,75) 3-Y-O **£3,071** (£906; £453) **Stalls** High

Form RPR

1 **1** **Ten A Penny (USA)**^{48} [106] 3-8-11 **70**................................ ShaneKelly 12 80+
(J A Osborne) *unf: hld up bhd: hdwy over 2f out stl plenty to do over 1f out: str run to ld ins fnl f: pushed out: readily* **13/2**

5-41 **2** 1 ¼ **Professor Twinkle**^{15} [460] 3-8-13 **72**...................................... PaulDoe 4 76+
(W J Knight) *led to post: sn led: rdn over 2f out: battled on wl tl hdd ins fnl f: nt pce of wnr* **5/2**^{1}

44-1 **3** ¾ **Satyricon**^{25} [348] 3-8-11 **70**..(b) OscarUrbina 10 72
(M Botti) *lw: hld up in midfield on outer:rdn and hdwy 2f out: styd on fnl f: nrst fin* **7/2**^{2}

4-00 **4** shd **Realy Naughty (IRE)**^{15} [456] 3-8-4 **66**................ RichardKingscote(3) 6 68
(B G Powell) *chsd ldr: riden and ev ch over 2f out tl ins fnl f: no ex last 100 yds* **20/1**

22-2 **5** ¾ **Miss Saafend Plaza (IRE)**^{54} [58] 3-9-1 **74**...........(b) RichardHughes 3 74
(R Hannon) *hld up bhd ldrs: rdn wl over 2f out: sn chsng ldng trio: kpt on same pce fnl furlong* **9/1**

014- **6** 2 ½ **Sahrati**^{64} [6948] 3-9-2 **75**.. JimmyFortune 7 70
(C E Brittain) *plld hrd: hld up in midfield: rdn and lost pl wl over 2f out: kpt on ins fnl f: nt trble ldrs* **12/1**

4234 **7** nk **Leg Sweep**^{10} [498] 3-8-13 **72**... JohnEgan 1 66
(D R C Elsworth) *trckd ldrs on inner: chsd ldng pair and rdn over 2f out: wknd 1f out* **12/1**

3-03 **8** nk **Leonard Charles**^{41} [184] 3-9-2 **75**.................................... SebSanders 2 68
(Sir Mark Prescott) *s.i.s: bhd: hdwy on inner over 3f out: sn rdn: no hdwy last 2f* **5/1**^{3}

1555 **9** 1 **Homes By Woodford**^{22} [382] 3-8-5 **69**................. MichaelJStainton(5) 5 60
(R A Harris) *lw: plld hrd: hld up in rr: n.d* **16/1**

010- **10** 1 ¾ **Cavallo Di Ferro (IRE)**^{187} [4813] 3-9-1 **74**.......................... AntonyProcter 9 61
(M J Gingell) *chsd ldrs tl rdn 3f out: wknd over 2f out* **66/1**

0-20 **11** shd **Mutoon (IRE)**^{12} [492] 3-8-4 **66**...................................... SaleemGolam(3) 8 53
(S C Williams) *hld up in rr: n.d* **33/1**

1m 37.94s (-1.49) **Going Correction** -0.125s/f (Stan) **11** Ran SP% **121.3**
Speed ratings (Par 98):102,100,100,99,99 96,96,96,95,93 93
CSF £23.47 CT £69.70 TOTE £7.80: £2.60, £1.50, £1.80; EX 32.00 Trifecta £84.40 Pool £498.41, 4.19 winning units.
Owner Lord Blyth And Ten **Bred** Chesapeake Farm, Mary R Odom & W S Farish **Trained** Upper Lambourn, Berks

FOCUS
A fair handicap run at an even gallop. Sound form which should work out. The first three are progressive and Ten A Penny, who was value for extra, should do better.

592 BONUSPRINT.COM H'CAP 1m (P)
4:00 (4:01) (Class 5) (0-75,75) 4-Y-0+ **£3,238** (£963; £481; £240) **Stalls** High

Form RPR

2-21 **1** **Lopinot (IRE)**^{32} [272] 4-8-11 **70**.. SebSanders 4 81
(P J Makin) *w.w in tch: hdwy to chse ldng pair over 2f out: led over 1f out: r.o strly* **11/4**^{1}

3421 **2** 1 ½ **Dapple Dawn (IRE)**^{24} [367] 4-8-13 **72**...........................(b) DanielTudhope 9 80
(D Carroll) *stdd s: hld up: hdwy to chse ldrs over 2f out: rdn to chse wnr 1f out: no imp* **4/1**^{3}

65-0 **3** 1 ¾ **Littleton Telchar (USA)**^{19} [424] 7-8-10 **72**.................(p) LiamJones(3) 6 76
(S W Hall) *t.k.h: hld up bhd: hdwy over 2f out: rdn wl over 1f out: styd on to chse ldng pair ins fnl f: kpt on* **12/1**

-030 **4** 2 **Arctic Desert**^{33} [261] 7-9-1 **74**..(t) JimmyQuinn 2 73
(Miss Gay Kelleway) *s.i.s: hld up in tch: hdwy over 2f out: rdn 2f out: no hdwy fnl f* **12/1**

-305 **5** ½ **Ivory Lace**^{12} [486] 6-8-11 **73**.. JamesDoyle(3) 8 71
(S Woodman) *hld up on outer: rdn and outpcd 3f out: c v wd st: kpt on ins fnl f: n.d* **9/1**

-001 **6** shd **Samuel Charles**^{15} [455] 9-9-1 **74**...................................... TPQueally 3 72
(C R Dore) *chsd ldrs: rdn and effrt on inner over 2f out: kpt on same pce over 1f out* **8/1**

6005 **7** ½ **Wheelavit (IRE)**^{15} [461] 4-8-4 **63**..................................(p) HayleyTurner 5 60
(B G Powell) *chsd ldr: rdn and ev ch over 2f out tl 1f out: sn wknd* **10/1**

10/0 **8** 2 **Certifiable**^{57} [29] 6-8-1 **65**.. RobynBrisland(5) 7 57
(Miss Z C Davison) *hld up in midfield on outer: rdn 3f out: sn outpcd* **33/1**

12-0 **9** 1 **Kabeer**^{50} [96] 9-8-13 **75**...(t) StephenDonohoe(3) 1 65
(A J McCabe) *lw: led tl rdn and hdd over 1f out: wknd qckly 1f out* **3/1**^{2}

1m 36.67s (-2.76) **Going Correction** -0.125s/f (Stan) **9** Ran SP% **120.2**
Speed ratings (Par 103):108,106,104,102,102 102,101,99,98
CSF £14.74 CT £116.66 TOTE £4.10: £1.30, £2.00, £3.60; EX 17.40 Trifecta £88.40 Pool £504.77, 4.05 winning units.
Owner R A Bernard **Bred** G And Mrs Middlebrook **Trained** Ogbourne Maisey, Wilts

FOCUS
An ordinary handicap run in a decent winning time for the grade. Solid form. The winner is progressive.

593 GO PONTIN'S H'CAP (DIV II) 1m 4f (P)
4:30 (4:30) (Class 4) (0-85,83) 4-Y-0+ **£4,210** (£1,252; £625; £312) **Stalls** Low

Form RPR

2 **1** **Paktolos (FR)**^{34} [256] 4-9-2 **83**.. JamieSpencer 9 92
(A King) *athletic: lengthy: stdd s: hld up in last pair: shkn up and hdwy on outer bnd 2f out: led ins fnl f: sn clr: comf* **10/3**^{2}

65-3 **2** 2 **Jebel Ali (IRE)**^{10} [501] 4-8-5 **75**.................................... JamesDoyle(3) 10 80
(B Gubby) *sn chsng ldr: rdn to ld over 2f out: hdd ins fnl f: kpt on but no ch w wnr* **16/1**

1-13 **3** hd **Nawow**^{12} [488] 7-8-11 **76**.. DaneO'Neill 8 81
(P D Cundell) *w.w in tch: hdwy to trck ldrs 6f out: rdn and outpcd over 2f out: rallied over 1f out: kpt on onepced fnl f* **6/1**

-116 **4** hd **Sgt Schultz (IRE)**^{12} [488] 4-8-9 **76**.. JohnEgan 7 81
(J S Moore) *t.k.h: chsd ldrs: rdn over 2f out: kpt on same pce over 1f out* **7/2**^{3}

114- **5** ½ **Altilhar (USA)**^{52} [5260] 4-9-1 **82**.. GeorgeBaker 1 86
(G L Moore) *hld up in last pair: pushed along over 2f out: r.o ins fnl f : nt rch ldrs* **9/1**

110- **6** 1 ¾ **Prime Powered (IRE)**^{27} [4244] 6-8-12 **77**.......................(t) SebSanders 5 78
(R M Beckett) *t.k.h: hld up in midfield: rdn and effrt on outer 3f out: chsd ldrs over 1f out: no hdwy fnl f* **25/1**

060 **7** 3 **General Knowledge (USA)**^{12} [488] 4-8-13 **80**.........(t) RichardHughes 3 76
(B G Powell) *t.k.h: hld up towards rr: rdn and hdwy on inner 2f out: wknd fnl f* **14/1**

10-2 **8** 1 ¼ **Kyles Prince (IRE)**^{43} [164] 5-9-0 **79**.. NCallan 6 73
(P J Makin) *led tl rdn and hdd over 2f out: wknd over 1f out* **3/1**^{1}

0560 **9** 5 **Valance (IRE)**^{12} [488] 7-8-9 **81**....................................(bt) PatrickHills(7) 2 67
(C R Egerton) *t.k.h: chsd ldrs: rdn and lost pl over 3f out: sn bhd* **20/1**

2m 32.45s (-1.94) **Going Correction** -0.125s/f (Stan)
WFA 4 from 5yo+ 2lb **9** Ran SP% **115.7**
Speed ratings (Par 105):101,99,99,99,99 97,95,95,91
CSF £54.85 CT £309.21 TOTE £3.50: £1.40, £5.70, £2.60; EX 90.10 Trifecta £244.20 Pool £347.44, 1.01 winning units.
Owner P Finnegan **Bred** Stilvi Compania **Trained** Barbury Castle, Wilts

FOCUS
A reasonable handicap, but the pace was just steady. The form is not as solid as that of the first division and is not sure to prove reliable.

594 PHOTO BOOKS FROM BONUSPRINT.COM H'CAP 1m 2f (P)
5:00 (5:01) (Class 5) (0-70,73) 4-Y-0+ **£3,071** (£906; £453) **Stalls** Low

Form RPR

0030 **1** **Cinematic (IRE)**^{12} [486] 4-8-9 **66**.................................... AmirQuinn(3) 10 74
(J R Boyle) *t.k.h: hld up in midfield: hdwy 2f out: shkn up and str run to ld ins fnl f: readily* **25/1**

6-22 **2** ¾ **Augustus John (IRE)**^{3} [564] 4-9-2 **70**.............................(v^{1}) JohnEgan 2 77
(T J Pitt) *trckd ldrs on inner: rdn to ld 1f out: hdd and no ex ins fnl f* **6/4**^{1}

-005 **3** 1 ½ **Magic Warrior**^{6} [538] 7-8-12 **66**.. PatDobbs 9 70
(J C Fox) *hld up wl bhd: hdwy over 1f out: weaved through fnl f: fin wl: nvr nrr* **20/1**

30-0 **4** shd **Makai**^{15} [459] 4-8-9 **63**..(b) NCallan 11 67
(J J Bridger) *chsd ldrs: rdn jst over 2f out: outpcd briefly over 1f out: kpt on u.p fnl f* **33/1**

0-34 **5** ½ **Sky Quest (IRE)**^{33} [263] 9-9-0 **68**.................................. HayleyTurner 5 71
(J R Boyle) *trckd ldrs: rdn over 2f out: upsides over 1f out onepced ins fnl f* **14/1**

-413 **6** hd **Reaching Out (IRE)**^{19} [428] 5-8-11 **65**..........................(b) JamesDoyle(3) 1 67
(N P Littmoden) *hld up towards rr: rdn and effrt over 2f out: swtchd rt ins fnl f: nvr rchd ldrs* **15/2**^{3}

2-53 **7** ½ **Marbaa (IRE)**^{10} [499] 4-8-10 **64**.. LPKeniry 14 65
(S Dow) *in tch: rdn and hdwy to press ldr 2f out: wknd wl ins fnl f* **25/1**

0501 **8** shd **Red Birr (IRE)**^{6} [538] 6-8-12 **73** 6ex.......................... HaddenFrost(7) 4 74
(P R Webber) *chsd ldr tl rdn over 2f out: kpt on same pce u.p* **5/1**^{2}

4-35 **9** ¾ **Barry Island**^{47} [117] 8-8-6 **63**.. MarcHalford(3) 7 65+
(D R C Elsworth) *hld up towards rr: c wd and effrt wl over 1f out: styng on but no ch w ldrs whn hmpd and snatched up ins fnl f* **10/1**

-506 **10** shd **First Friend (IRE)**^{17} [445] 6-8-2 **63**............................ JackMitchell(7) 12 62
(P Mitchell) *plld hrd: hld up towards rr on outer: hdwy to chse ldrs over 3f out: rdn and no hdwy over 1f out* **25/1**

-106 **11** shd **Street Life (IRE)**^{15} [459] 9-8-4 **65**................................ DebraEngland(7) 13 64
(W J Musson) *t.k.h: hld up in last: sme late hdwy: n.d* **14/1**

43 **12** ½ **Great Man (FR)**^{9} [507] 6-8-8 **62**.. JamieSpencer 8 60
(Noel T Chance) *t.k.h: hld up in rr: rdn and effrt on outer bnd over 2f out: no real hdwy* **8/1**

56-1 **13** ½ **Sunset Boulevard (IRE)**^{36} [229] 4-9-2 **70**.......................... ChrisCatlin 3 67
(Miss Tor Sturgis) *led: rdn over 2f out: hdd 1f out: wknd qckly* **16/1**

414- **14** ¾ **Hatch A Plan (IRE)**[110] [4662] 6-8-13 67 .... TPQueally 6 63
(Mouse Hamilton-Fairley) *t.k.h: hld up in midfield on inner: rdn and sme hdwy wl over 1f out: btn whn nt clr run and eased ins fnl f* **40/1**

2m 6.37s (-1.42) **Going Correction** -0.125s/f (Stan) **14** Ran SP% **129.5**
Speed ratings (Par 103):100,99,98,98,97 97,97,97,96,96 96,95,95,94
CSF £63.34 CT £873.04 TOTE £44.10: £5.80, £1.80, £5.40; EX 164.30 TRIFECTA Not won. Place 6 £50.37, Place 5 £19.15.
Owner Inside Track Racing Club **Bred** A Brosnan **Trained** Epsom, Surrey

FOCUS
There was not much pace on here and the race turned into something of a sprint with a bunch finish. Just modest form.
Hatch A Plan(IRE) Official explanation: jockey said gelding was denied a clear run
T/Jkpt: Not won. T/Plt: £74.60 to a £1 stake. Pool: £63,676.30. 622.30 winning tickets. T/Qpdt: £18.40 to a £1 stake. Pool: £4,677.20. 187.30 winning tickets. SP

540 NAD AL SHEBA (L-H)

Thursday, March 1

OFFICIAL GOING: Turf course - good; dirt course - fast

595a ESWARAH STKS (MAIDEN) (TURF) 1m (T)
3:15 (3:18) 3-Y-O

£7,653 (£2,551; £1,275; £637; £382; £255)

RPR

1 **Mofarij**[124] [6220] 3-9-0 .... LDettori 5 95+
(Saeed Bin Suroor) *mid-div: t.k.h: smooth prog to trck ldrs 3f out: led 1f out: easily* **2/5**[1]

2 5 ¼ **Plato's Republic (USA)**[7] [527] 3-9-0 91 .... TPO'Shea 3 83
(E Charpy, UAE) *trckd ldr: led 3 1/2f out: hdd 1f out: r.o wl: no ch w wnr* **5/1**[2]

3 2 ¾ **Shavoulin (USA)**[20] [414] 3-9-0 85 ....(v) PaulEddery 4 77
(Christian Wroe) *led: hdd 3 1/2f out: kpt on wl: one pce* **10/1**

4 3 ¼ **Pure Bluff (IRE)** 3-9-0 .... KerrinMcEvoy 6 69
(Saeed Bin Suroor) *mid-div: rdn 4f out: nt qckn* **7/1**[3]

5 ½ **Puzzle Book (USA)**[7] [527] 3-8-9 .... RichardMullen 1 63
(M Kettle, UAE) *slowly away: racd in rr: rdn 3f out: nvr able to chal* **33/1**

6 4 ¼ **Classical Flair** 3-8-9 .... MartinDwyer 2 53
(M Kettle, UAE) *v.s.a: last thrght: nvr nr to chal* **50/1**

1m 36.96s (-0.84) **Going Correction** -0.05s/f (Good) **6** Ran SP% **114.6**
Speed ratings: 102,96,94,90,90 86

Owner Godolphin **Bred** Darley **Trained** Newmarket, Suffolk
■ A belated first Dubai Carnival winner of the year for Godolphin.

FOCUS
Not a very competitive maiden on paper but it featured a potentially very useful performer in Mofarij. It has been rated through the third and fifth.

NOTEBOOK
Mofarij, a half-brother to Iffraaj, had shaped with distinct promise on his debut in a soft-ground backend Newmarket maiden last year. He seemed better suited by this quicker surface, travelled well and came home an easy winner. He has the makings of a very useful performer this season, and should stay further. (op 4/9)
Plato's Republic(USA) was beaten over four lengths by Seal Point in a similar maiden here a week earlier, and that colt had finished over five lengths behind Mofarij at Newmarket last autumn, so that gave an indication of the task in front of him. Handicaps are now an option.
Shavoulin(USA) was out of his depth behind Asiatic Boy on his last two starts and ran a better race back on turf, but he did enjoy the run of things out in front. (op 9/1)
Pure Bluff(IRE), a stablemate of the winner, showed his inexperience on his debut by running wide on the bend into the straight, but he ran with a bit of promise and, given that he is out of a Group 3-winning sprinter, a shorter trip may suit him in future. (tchd 13/2)
Puzzle Book(USA) could find only the one pace in the straight and was outclassed.

596a BAHRI AL BASTAKIYA STKS (CONDITIONS RACE) (DIRT) 1m 1f (D)
3:45 (3:47) 3-Y-O

£45,918 (£15,306; £7,653; £3,826; £2,295; £1,530)

RPR

1 **Asiatic Boy (ARG)**[20] [414] 4-9-6 115 .... WCMarwing 5 113+
(M F De Kock, South Africa) *sn led: rdn clr 2 1/2f out: r.o wl: easily* **8/11**[1]

2 7 **Victory Tetsuni (USA)**[32] 3-8-9 100 .... YTake 7 104
(Hideyuki Mori, Japan) *racd in rr: only 5th 2f out: r.o wl fnl 1 1/2f: nrst fin* **12/1**

3 ½ **Rallying Cry (USA)**[20] [414] 3-8-9 110 .... KerrinMcEvoy 3 103
(I Mohammed, UAE) *mid-div: t.k.h: rdn to trck ldng pair 3f out: hrd rdn 2f out: nt qckn* **7/1**[3]

4 ¾ **Day Pass (USA)**[118] 3-8-11 107 ....(t) LDettori 6 104
(Saeed Bin Suroor) *trckd ldr: rdn to cl 3f out: outpcd by wnr: wknd fnl 110yds* **9/4**[2]

5 shd **Zorin (BRZ)**[7] [526] 4-9-6 96 .... ADomingos 2 96
(A Cintra Pereira, Brazil) *mid-div rail: trckd ldng pair 4f out: rdn 3f out: kpt on one pce* **33/1**

6 11 **Te Voglio Bene (BRZ)**[20] [410] 4-8-12 90 ....(t) AurelioMedeiros(6) 1 73
(M D Wolfson, U.S.A) *slowly away: rdn 4f out: n.d* **66/1**

7 ¾ **Alcomo (BRZ)**[42] [175] 4-9-6 102 ....(t) RichardMullen 4 74
(P Nickel Filho, Brazil) *racd in rr: rdn 5f out: nvr nr to chal* **33/1**

1m 48.27s (-2.53) **Going Correction** +0.05s/f (Slow)
WFA 3 from 4yo 20lb **7** Ran SP% **116.2**
Speed ratings: 113,106,106,105,105 95,95

Owner Sheikh Mohammed Bin Khalifa Al Maktoum **Bred** Haras Arroyo De Luna **Trained** South Africa

FOCUS
A good field lined up for this valuable conditions contest, but nothing could live with the UAE 2000 Guineas winner Asiatic Boy who scored with a bit to spare.

NOTEBOOK
Asiatic Boy(ARG) ◆, the UAE 2000 Guineas winner, momentarily looked as though he had a race on his hands when Day Pass loomed up on his outside at the top of the straight, but that one's effort was short-lived and he pulled clear to win in terrific style. He had never previously raced over further than 1m, but he stayed this longer trip without any problems and will be very hard to beat in the UAE Derby back over this course and distance on World Cup night. Interestingly enough, both of Mike De Kock's two previous UAE Derby winners, Victory Moon and Lundy's Liability, were beaten in this race, so the fact that Asiatic Boy managed to win can surely only be considered a good thing.
Victory Tetsuni(USA) was outpaced when the race began to get serious and could only stay on past beaten horses in the straight. He should be seen to better effect off a stronger gallop. (op 11/1)
Rallying Cry(USA) could not reverse UAE Guineas form with Asiatic Boy, again giving the impression he is better suited to turf. To be fair, though, he was a little keen early and is another who would have benefited from a stronger end-to-end gallop.
Day Pass(USA), a Grade 3 winner at Aqueduct last year, looked the main danger to Asiatic Boy beforehand, but he proved disappointing. He took a bit of a grip early on, so one could argue he should have been given his head but, such was the winner's dominance, it would not have made any difference to the result. This was his first run in four months, so perhaps it will have taken the freshness out of him, but he still has something to prove.
Zorin(BRZ) was again unable to dominate and never posed a threat.

597a MARJU MAHAB AL SHIMAAL STKS (GROUP 3) (DIRT) 6f (D)
4:15 (4:17) 3-Y-O+

£61,224 (£20,408; £10,204; £5,102; £3,061; £2,040)

RPR

1 **Terrific Challenge (USA)**[130] [6127] 5-9-4 102 ....(bt) RyanMoore 9 112
(Doug Watson, UAE) *mid-div centre: hrd rdn 2 1/2f out: r.o v wl: led 50yds out* **14/1**

2 1 ¼ **Bounty Quest**[14] [474] 5-9-4 100 .... MartinDwyer 6 108
(Doug Watson, UAE) *prom far side: led 2f out: hdd 50yds out: r.o wl* **33/1**

3 hd **Lascaux (AUS)**[14] [470] 6-9-4 100 .... WLHo 8 107
(Y Choy, Macau) *trckd runner-up: rdn to chal 2f out: r.o wl* **50/1**

4 1 ¾ **Thajja (IRE)**[35] [249] 6-9-4 108 ....(v) RHills 14 102
(Doug Watson, UAE) *led nr side: gng wl 3f out: rdn and hdd 2f out: r.o wl* **15/2**

5 ¾ **Agnes Jedi (JPN)**[53] 5-9-4 106 ....(b) YTake 7 100
(Hideyuki Mori, Japan) *trckd runner-up tl 3f out: one pce* **11/1**

6 ½ **Thor's Echo (USA)**[96] 5-9-11 120 ....(bt) RichardMullen 3 105
(S Seemar, UAE) *trckd pce far side: hrd rdn and outpcd 2 1/2f out: r.o one pce: nrst fin* **6/4**[1]

7 1 ¾ **Salaam Dubai (AUS)**[28] [326] 6-9-4 104 ....(b) MJKinane 4 93
(A Selvaratnam, UAE) *prom far side: rdn 4 1/2f out: r.o tl wknd fnl 110yds* **16/1**

8 1 ¼ **Tax Free (IRE)**[35] [249] 5-9-4 107 .... AdrianTNicholls 5 89
(D Nicholls) *prom far side for 3f: wknd* **6/1**[3]

9 3 ¼ **Attilius (BRZ)**[21] [400] 5-9-4 102 ....(bt) WCMarwing 15 80
(E Charpy, UAE) *a struggling nr side* **50/1**

10 3 ½ **Botanical (USA)**[13] 6-9-4 100 ....(bt) TPO'Shea 12 69
(E Charpy, UAE) *sn rdn along: nvr a threat* **33/1**

11 hd **Instant Recall (IRE)**[13] 6-9-4 98 ....(v) WayneSmith 16 69
(M Al Muhairi, UAE) *nvr nr to chal* **33/1**

12 2 ½ **Beckermet (IRE)**[14] [470] 5-9-4 100 .... EddieAhern 11 61
(R F Fisher) *racd centre: nvr bttr than mid-div* **33/1**

13 ¾ **Big Spartan (BRZ)**[28] [326] 4-9-0 100 .... ECruz 10 55
(P Nickel Filho, Brazil) *nvr a threat* **50/1**

14 hd **Excusez Moi (USA)**[20] [415] 5-9-4 104 ....(b) JMurtagh 2 58
(C E Brittain) *slowly away: n.d* **20/1**

15 2 **Sendalam (FR)**[14] [472] 5-9-4 100 .... KShea 1 52
(H J Brown, South Africa) *nvr involved* **33/1**

16 14 **Heart Alone (BRZ)**[341] [740] 6-9-4 113 .... KerrinMcEvoy 13 10
(I Mohammed, UAE) *racd nr side: nvr nr to chal: virtually p.u fnl f* **5/1**[2]

69.66 secs (-1.04) **Going Correction** +0.175s/f (Slow) **16** Ran SP% **128.9**
Speed ratings: 113,111,111,108,107 107,104,103,98,94 93,90,89,89,86 67

Owner H E Sheikh Rashid Bin Mohammed **Bred** Lantern Hill Farm Llc **Trained** United Arab Emirates

FOCUS
A competitive Group 3 sprint, but one or two of the principals were using this as a stepping stone to the Golden Shaheen and will not have been fully primed. Overall the form seems sound enough. As has been the pattern on the sprint track this season, those drawn middle to low held the call.

NOTEBOOK
Terrific Challenge(USA) was having his first start for his new stable having been a winner on turf in America, and the switch to dirt certainly did not prove a problem. His finishing effort was decisive as he ran on strongly from off a good pace to mow down the leading duo inside the final furlong. What the form is worth is open to question, though, as the placed horses are basically handicappers, and whether he will prove good enough in the Golden Shaheen on Dubai World Cup night remains to be seen.
Bounty Quest, well drawn, has improved steadily this winter. Runner-up to National Colour over 5f last time, he was just getting the best of his battle with Lascaux when the winner appeared on the scene. He showed plenty of pace but his performance means that the form cannot be rated too highly.
Lascaux(AUS) also showed plenty of toe, appreciating the return to sprinting on dirt. His is another performance which hardly gives the form a solid look, though. (op 40/1)
Thajja(IRE) can take plenty of credit for winning the race on the stands' side, and would surely have given the winner a lot more to do had he been more favourably berthed.
Agnes Jedi(JPN), a Japanese raider, finished sixth in last year's Golden Shaheen and is being prepared for another tilt. This was a perfectly acceptable effort and he will strip fitter in the big one at the end of the month.
Thor's Echo(USA), another who was prepping for Dubai World Cup night, has joined the Satish Seemar stable since winning last year's Breeders' Cup Sprint. He did not have an easy task under his big weight given that he had not run for three months, and is another who should be sharper on the big night. (op 7/4)
Tax Free(IRE) looked to have plenty in his favour after running well from a poor draw last time but, having shown good pace in the first half of the race, he dropped out tamely and was eased inside the last. (op 13/2)
Beckermet(IRE) never looked like landing a blow.
Excusez Moi(USA) never threatened. (op 25/1)

598a INTIKHAB DUBAI CITY OF GOLD STKS (GROUP 3) (TURF) 1m 4f (T)
4:45 (4:47) 4-Y-O+

£61,224 (£20,408; £10,204; £5,102; £3,061; £2,040)

RPR

1 **Quijano (GER)**[20] [412] 5-8-11 113 .... AStarke 5 112+
(P Schiergen, Germany) *trckd ldr rail: led 2f out: r.o wl: comf* **5/2**[1]

2 1 ¼ **Oracle West (SAF)**[28] [330] 6-8-11 113 .... WCMarwing 9 109
(M F De Kock, South Africa) *trckd ldr: rdn to chse wnr 2f out: r.o wl* **4/1**[3]

3 2 ½ **Lost Soldier Three (IRE)**[6] [545] 6-8-11 100 .... AdrianTNicholls 3 105?
(D Nicholls) *set stdy gallop: qcknd 6f out: rdn clr 3f out: hdd 2f out: r.o* **33/1**

4 ¾ **Mulaqat**[21] [399] 4-8-10 112 .... JMurtagh 10 105
(D Selvaratnam, UAE) *mid-div: gng wl rail 3f out: r.o fnl 2f: nvr able to chal* **16/1**

5 ½ **Laverock (IRE)**[20] [412] 5-9-4 120 .... KerrinMcEvoy 2 110+
(I Mohammed, UAE) *in rr of mid-div: rdn to cl 3f out: r.o fnl 2f* **11/4**[2]

6 1 ½ **Best Alibi (IRE)**[215] [3957] 4-9-1 115 .... LDettori 4 107
(Saeed Bin Suroor) *mid-div: trckd runner-up 2f out: r.o one pce* **4/1**[3]

7 1 1/4 **Nepotista (BRZ)**[6] 545 5-8-11 100 .... ADomingos 7 99
(A Cintra Pereira, Brazil) *missed break: nvr nr to chal: r.o wl fnl 2 1/2f* **50/1**

8 16 **Fantastic Love (USA)**[20] 412 7-8-11 95 ....(vt) RoystonFfrench 12 75
(A Al Raihe, UAE) *mid-div: rdn 3f out: n.d after* **100/1**

9 5 1/2 **Jackson (BRZ)**[13] 5-8-11 95 ....(b) ECruz 1 67
(A Selvaratnam, UAE) *mid-div on rail: dropped to rr 2f out* **100/1**

10 13 **Imperial Stride**[117] 6347 6-8-11 120 .... RHills 6 48
(Saeed Bin Suroor) *mid-div: rdn 3 1/2f out: wknd* **10/1**

11 6 3/4 **Quorum (GER)**[7] 532 4-8-10 93 ....(v) WayneSmith 8 38
(M Al Muhairi, UAE) *settled in rr: rdn 5f out: nvr able to chal* **100/1**

12 1/4 **Dono Da Raia (BRZ)**[20] 412 5-9-4 110 .... MJKinane 11 44
(I Mohammed, UAE) *settled in rr: t.k.h: prog to trck ldr over 5f out out: wknd 3f out* **18/1**

2m 33.07s (2.07) **Going Correction** -0.05s/f (Good)
WFA 4 from 5yo+ 2lb 12 Ran SP% **123.3**
Speed ratings: 91,90,88,88,87 86,85,75,71,62 58,58

Owner Stiftung Gestut Fahrhof **Bred** Stiftung Gestut Fahrhof **Trained** Germany

FOCUS

This looked like a decent Group 3 beforehand, but they went a noticeably steady pace from the start - the first three home were in the first three throughout until Dono Da Raia moved up midway down the back straight - and several of these were unable to show their best. The race has been rated through the seventh, with the proximity of the third a worry.

NOTEBOOK

Quijano(GER) ◆ made it three from three at the Carnival, and nine wins on the bounce in total. Admittedly, he was always beautifully placed considering how the race was run, but he still had a job to do in the straight and the way he saw off last year's winner, Oracle West, who was equally well positioned, was pretty impressive. This most progressive individual will be faced with by far his toughest task to date in the Sheema Classic on World Cup night, especially considering he will be racing off level weights, but he might just prove up to the task. (op 9/4)

Oracle West(SAF) was always well positioned and ran a good race in his bid to follow up last year's success in this race. He proved suited by the step back up in trip and can have few excuses.

Lost Soldier Three(IRE) had been disappointing since shaping so well on his debut in Dubai at the start of the Carnival but, very much allowed the run of the race, he returned to form with a terrific effort. However, for all that this will no doubt have delighted his connections, his proximity does not do much for the form and confirms this as a race to treat with caution.

Mulaqat appreciated the return to turf and ran a good race, although it is worth keeping in mind he was never too far away from the steady pace.

Laverock(IRE) fared best of those held up, but he was basically given too much to do and had no chance of reversing recent form with Quijano. He can do better. (op 5/2)

Best Alibi(IRE) was below form on his debut for Godolphin off the back of a 215-day break, but can obviously be forgiven this. (op 9/2)

Imperial Stride offered very little under pressure, even allowing for the steady pace, and was disappointing.

Dono Da Raia(BRZ) was too keen and can do better when granted a stronger end-to-end gallop.

599a LAHAN BURJ NAHAAR STKS (GROUP 3) (DIRT) 1m (D)

5:15 (5:17) 3-Y-O+

£61,224 (£20,408; £10,204; £5,102; £3,061; £2,040)

RPR

1 **Boston Lodge**[7] 532 7-9-2 100 ....(vt) EddieAhern 11 111
(Doug Watson, UAE) *mid-div: gng wl 3f out: trckd ldrs 1 1/2f out: led 110yds out: rdn clr* **16/1**

2 3/4 **Vortex**[7] 530 8-9-2 109 ....(t) JMurtagh 16 109
(Miss Gay Kelleway) *settled in rr: trckd wnr 2 1/2f out: rdn 2f out: r.o wl* **8/1**

3 1/2 **Blatant**[341] 738 8-9-2 112 ....(t) KShea 10 108
(A Al Raihe, UAE) *mid-div: rdn to chal 3f out: nt qckn* **9/2**[2]

4 shd **Impossible Ski (BRZ)**[42] 177 5-9-2 105 .... ADomingos 13 108+
(A Cintra Pereira, Brazil) *settled in rr: stl 14th 2f out: r.o v wl: nrest at fin* **5/1**[3]

5 shd **Binary File (USA)**[21] 399 9-9-2 105 ....(t) RHills 14 108
(L Kelp, Sweden) *slowly away: racd in rr: nvr nr to chal: r.o fnl 1 1/2f* **10/1**

6 2 1/2 **Jaffal (USA)**[21] 396 5-9-2 101 ....(t) RoystonFfrench 2 103
(A Al Raihe, UAE) *trckd ldr rail: rdn 4f out: wknd fnl f* **25/1**

7 1/4 **Visionist (IRE)**[14] 471 5-9-2 102 .... WayneSmith 7 102
(M Al Muhairi, UAE) *trckd ldr: led 2f out: hdd 110yds out: wknd* **20/1**

8 shd **Nelore Pora (BRZ)**[28] 327 5-9-6 107 ....(b) RichardMullen 5 106
(P Nickel Filho, Brazil) *slowly away: sn led: hdd 2f out: wknd* **12/1**

9 1 1/4 **Opportunist (IRE)**[6] 543 8-9-2 100 ....(vt) WSupple 6 99
(Doug Watson, UAE) *mid-div: trckd ldrs gng wl 3 1/2f out: rdn 2 1/2f out: wknd* **25/1**

10 3 1/4 **Gold For Sale (ARG)**[34] 5-9-2 106 ....(t) MJKinane 15 93
(I Jory, Saudi Arabia) *racd wd and in rr: nvr nr to chal* **6/1**

11 3 1/4 **Blue On Blues (ARG)**[20] 410 6-9-2 107 ....(t) RyanMoore 3 86
(S Seemar, UAE) *nvr bttr than mid-div* **12/1**

12 3/4 **Smart And Mighty (AUS)**[20] 411 8-9-2 104 ....(b) MartinDwyer 8 85
(T Noonan, Australia) *racd in rr: nvr a threat* **14/1**

13 3 1/4 **Yarqus**[14] 477 4-9-2 90 .... CSoumillon 12 78
(C E Brittain) *settled in rr: rdn 4f out: nvr able to chal* **66/1**

14 1 1/2 **Egyptian (USA)**[13] 8-9-2 86 .... DHayse 4 75
(R Bouresly, Kuwait) *trckd ldrs for 2f: wknd* **100/1**

15 9 **Imperialista (BRZ)**[21] 399 4-8-9 110 .... KerrinMcEvoy 1 50
(I Mohammed, UAE) *mid-div on rail: rdn 4f out: sn wknd* **4/1**[1]

1m 35.86s (-1.74) **Going Correction** +0.05s/f (Slow) 15 Ran SP% **132.2**
Speed ratings: 110,109,108,108,108 106,105,105,104,101 97,97,93,92,83

Owner Fawzi Abdulla Nass **Bred** Elite Racing Club **Trained** United Arab Emirates

FOCUS

In the absence of Discreet Cat, who was running a temperature, this was a very ordinary race by Group 3 standards.

NOTEBOOK

Boston Lodge was able to follow up last week's handicap success achieved off a mark of just 93. Again he travelled very strongly and, full credit to him, he again found plenty when asked for his maximum close home. He is clearly in the form of his life and his connections will have every right to aim him at the Godolphin Mile on World Cup night, but it will be a surprise if he does not find at least a few too good if taking his chance.

Vortex ran a terrific race switched to the dirt surface, keeping on strongly for pressure all the way up the straight. He is an absolute credit to his connections and should continue to go well in good company on both dirt and turf. (op 9/1)

Blatant was given every chance, but he probably needed this first run in 341 days and should be able to improve on this.

Impossible Ski(BRZ) ◆ soon faced an impossible task - dropping to last early on despite breaking on terms - and did well to finish so close. He has won over 1m2f in Brazil and will surely benefit from a step back up in trip. (tchd 11/2)

Binary File(USA) kept on from well off the pace but did not improve on the form he showed on his debut in Dubai.

Yarqus never posed a threat on this switch to dirt.

Imperialista(BRZ) dropped away after coming under pressure a long way out. The inside stall was of little help, but he has basically failed to progress since switching stables.

600a HAAFHD JEBEL HATTA STKS (GROUP 2) (TURF) 1m 194y(T)

5:50 (5:51) 3-Y-O+

£76,530 (£25,510; £12,755; £6,377; £3,826; £2,551)

RPR

1 **Seihali (IRE)**[7] 530 8-9-4 115 ....(b) JMurtagh 6 118
(D Selvaratnam, UAE) *trckd ldr: led 2f out: r.o wl* **10/1**

2 3/4 **Formal Decree (GER)**[28] 330 4-9-4 113 .... MJKinane 4 116
(I Mohammed, UAE) *racd in 3rd on rail: trckd wnr 2f out: r.o wl* **5/2**[1]

3 1/2 **Irridescence (SAF)**[151] 5713 6-9-6 115 .... WCMarwing 9 117
(M F De Kock, South Africa) *sn led: hdd 2f out: r.o: no room 1f out* **14/1**

4 shd **Best Name**[151] 5716 4-9-4 117 .... LDettori 2 115+
(Saeed Bin Suroor) *mid-div: on rail: rdn to trck ldrs whn bmpd 1 1/2f out: r.o* **7/2**[2]

5 hd **Olympian Odyssey**[28] 330 4-9-4 116 .... RichardMullen 1 115
(I Mohammed, UAE) *settled in rr: gng wl 3f out on rail: no room 1 1/2f out: r.o* **10/1**

6 1 1/4 **Lord Admiral (USA)**[7] 530 6-9-4 111 ....(b) WSupple 7 112
(Charles O'Brien, Ire) *settled in rr: making prog whn no room 1 1/2f out: r.o* **40/1**

7 1 3/4 **Touch Of Land (FR)**[28] 330 7-9-4 115 ....(b) C-PLemaire 11 108
(H-A Pantall, France) *racd 4th: trckd ldrs gng wl 3f out: rdn whn bmpd 1 1/2f out: nt rcvr* **20/1**

8 1/2 **Stage Gift (IRE)**[21] 399 4-9-4 112 .... KerrinMcEvoy 3 107
(I Mohammed, UAE) *settled in last: nvr nr to chal* **9/1**

9 2 3/4 **Great Rhythm (SAF)**[20] 413 6-9-4 110 .... KShea 5 102
(H J Brown, South Africa) *mid-div: rdn 2 1/2f out: nvr able to chal* **25/1**

10 11 **Shakis (IRE)**[20] 413 7-9-4 112 ....(vt) RHills 12 78
(Doug Watson, UAE) *mid-div: trckd ldrs 3f out: rdn but no rspnse* **25/1**

11 1 1/4 **Sanaya (IRE)**[21] 397 4-9-0 112 ....(p) CSoumillon 8 72
(A De Royer-Dupre, France) *settled in rr: nvr nr to chal* **15/2**

12 5 3/4 **Ace (IRE)**[28] 330 6-9-4 112 ....(v) RyanMoore 10 64
(S Seemar, UAE) *mid-div: rdn 3f out: sn btn* **7/1**[3]

1m 49.85s (0.05) **Going Correction** -0.05s/f (Good) 12 Ran SP% **124.8**
Speed ratings: 97,96,95,95,95 94,92,92,90,80 79,74

Owner Sheikh Ahmed Al Maktoum **Bred** Rathbarry Stud **Trained** United Arab Emirates

FOCUS

This Group 2 race was run at a fairly steady early gallop, and that played into the hands of the prominent racers. Consequently, the form is probably fairly ordinary for the level.

NOTEBOOK

Seihali(IRE), third in the race last year, has been performing solidly in Dubai this winter and crucially, on this occasion, he was raced closer to the speed. In a race lacking much pace that was the place to be. He made his race-winning move by kicking early in the straight and held off his pursuers in gritty style close home, collecting his first Pattern success at the age of eight. (op 8-1)

Formal Decree(GER), chasing a four-timer, threw down a strong challenge to the winner in the closing stages but he would never quite going to get there. Like many in the race he would have benefited from a stronger all-round pace, and he remains progressive. (op 11-4)

Irridescence(SAF), now back in the care of Mike de Kock, enjoyed the run of the race in front, being allowed to dictate a modest gallop. As a result it was no surprise that she was able to hang on for third. She is still entitled to come on for this first run for five months though, especially as her trainer reported beforehand that she had not had the smoothest of preparations.

Best Name, last seen finishing fourth in the Arc, was having his first outing for Godolphin and ran a respectable race. He too should improve for the run, and looks set for a good season in Group company at around 1m2f. (op 4-1)

Olympian Odyssey ran close to his form behind Formal Decree over the course and distance four weeks earlier, but is another who would have appreciated a stronger gallop. (op 8-1)

Touch Of Land(FR), last year's winner, had blinkers on for the first time but was again a bit disappointing.

Stage Gift(IRE) also failed to run to his best on this return to the turf.

601a ELNADIM MAKTOUM CHALLENGE RIII (GROUP 2) (DIRT) 1m 2f (D)

6:20 (6:20) 3-Y-O+

£91,836 (£30,612; £15,306; £7,653; £4,591; £3,061)

RPR

1 **Eu Tambem (BRZ)**[110] 4-8-9 109 .... KerrinMcEvoy 3 100+
(I Mohammed, UAE) *trckd ldr: led 3 1/2f out: r.o wl: comf* **15/8**[1]

2 5 **Singing Poet (IRE)**[21] 399 6-9-5 105 ....(t) TPO'Shea 2 99
(E Charpy, UAE) *trckd ldr: disp 3 1/2f out: ev ch st: r.o wl* **3/1**[2]

3 nk **Aleutian**[7] 532 7-9-5 95 ....(e) JMurtagh 5 98
(Doug Watson, UAE) *mid-div: rdn 3 1/2f out: r.o wl fnl 2f* **12/1**

4 5 3/4 **Chinkara**[7] 529 7-9-5 95 .... WSupple 8 88
(Doug Watson, UAE) *settled in rr: nvr nr to chal: r.o wl fnl 2f* **20/1**

5 3 3/4 **Dubai Honor**[7] 529 8-9-5 104 ....(e) MartinDwyer 6 81
(Doug Watson, UAE) *prom wd: disp 3 1/2f out: ev ch: wknd fnl 1 1/2f* **12/1**

6 1/2 **Money Bags (SAF)**[6] 541 5-9-5 102 ....(bt) WCMarwing 9 80
(M F De Kock, South Africa) *mid-div: rdn 3f out: nvr able to chal* **6/1**

7 4 **Red Racketeer (USA)**[21] 401 5-9-5 94 .... RoystonFfrench 1 73
(A Al Raihe, UAE) *mid-div on rail: rdn 3 1/2f out: nvr able to chal* **28/1**

8 4 **Choctaw Nation (USA)**[341] 743 7-9-5 112 ....(bt) RichardMullen 7 66
(S Seemar, UAE) *settled in last: rdn 4 1/2f out: nvr nr to chal* **5/1**[3]

9 5 1/4 **Grand Emporium (SAF)**[20] 411 7-9-5 105 ....(t) RyanMoore 4 57
(S Seemar, UAE) *rdn to ld: hdd 3 1/2f out: wknd* **25/1**

2m 1.53s (-1.77) **Going Correction** +0.05s/f (Slow) 9 Ran SP% **118.2**
Speed ratings: 109,105,104,100,97 96,93,90,86

Owner Sheikh Hamdan Bin Mohammed Al Maktoum **Bred** Haras Guaiuvira **Trained** UAE

FOCUS

The third round of the Maktoum challenge is often used as a stepping stone towards the Dubai World Cup, and has been won by some terrific horses over the years, but this was a very ordinary renewal and not up to Group 2 standard.

NOTEBOOK

Eu Tambem(BRZ) made the most of the big weight concession to score in convincing fashion. A multiple Group winner in South America, including at the very highest level on his most recent start, he found this a suitable opportunity to make a winning debut for his new connections. Always close up in a race run at a decent enough gallop, he only had Singing Poet to worry about by the time they turned into the straight, and he proved far too strong for that one late on. It would not be a total surprise to see him take his chance in the World Cup considering he has won what is traditionally such a good trial for that race, but if the likes of Discreet Cat and Invasor turn up in A1 form, he will be running for a place at best. (op 2-1)

Singing Poet(IRE) has been progressing well this winter, but this seemed just a step too far. He had every chance on the turn into the straight, but he did not really extend as one might have hoped and only just held on to second.
Aleutian kept on well in the straight and clearly benefited from the step up in trip, but he never posed a threat to the winner.
Chinkara was perhaps a little bit out of his depth, even allowing for the weakness of this race.
Dubai Honor could not land a blow in the straight and was below his very best.

564 WOLVERHAMPTON (A.W) (L-H)
Friday, March 2

OFFICIAL GOING: Standard
Wind: fresh, half-behind

602 BONUSPRINT.COM MAIDEN STKS (DIV I) 1m 4f 50y(P)
1:40 (1:41) (Class 5) 3-Y-0+ **£2,388** (£705; £352) **Stalls** Low

Form RPR

-2 **1** **Soldiers Quest**[11] [499] 3-8-4 JoeFanning 12 87+
(M Johnston) *a.p: led 8f out: pushed clr 2f out: eased fnl f* **1/4**[1]

5- **2** *10* **Sowdrey**[224] [3701] 3-8-4 ChrisCatlin 11 65
(M R Channon) *hld up in mid-div: hdwy 6f out: rdn 4f out: outpcd 3f out: styd on to take 2nd ins fnl f: no ch w wnr* **17/2**[2]

2-62 **3** *1 1/4* **Master'n Commander**[16] [458] 5-9-13 62 TonyCulhane 9 66
(C A Cyzer) *hld up in mid-div: hdwy 8f out: rdn over 3f out: one pce* **16/1**[3]

006- **4** *1 1/2* **Velvet Valley (USA)**[32] [6987] 4-9-11 64 DaneO'Neill 6 64
(C E Longsdon) *a.p: rdn over 2f out: sn no ch w wnr: wknd fnl f* **40/1**

0- **5** *1 1/4* **Broughtons Revival**[240] [3200] 5-9-1 AlanRutter(7) 10 57
(W J Musson) *hld up and bhd: nt clr run briefly 3f out: shkn up and hdwy fr over 1f out: nvr nr to chal* **150/1**

0/ **6** *3/4* **This Way That Way**[30] [683] 6-9-10 StephenDonohoe(3) 5 61
(Ian Williams) *hld up in tch: rdn and lost pl 4f out: n.d after* **100/1**

33 **7** *7* **Beau Torero (FR)**[18] [443] 9-9-8 TomMessenger(5) 3 50
(B N Pollock) *dwlt: hdwy over 7f out: rdn over 4f out: wknd 3f out* **33/1**

8 *1/2* **Mountain Fairy**[120] 4-9-6 71 MickyFenton 1 44
(B S Rothwell) *hld up in tch: rdn and wknd 5f out* **50/1**

5600 **9** *8* **Elizabeth Garrett**[15] [469] 3-7-6 40 WilliamBuick(7) 7 28
(M J Gingell) *plld hrd early: a bhd* **200/1**

06-0 **10** *8* **The Loose Screw (IRE)**[28] [333] 9-9-13 32 DeanMcKeown 2 23
(C W Thornton) *a towards rr* **300/1**

64- **11** *hd* **Haoin An Bothar (IRE)**[83] [6768] 3-8-4 (p) AdrianTNicholls 4 20
(Adrian Sexton, Ire) *led: hdd 8f out: wknd over 4f out* **40/1**

2m 39.51s (-2.91) **Going Correction** -0.125s/f (Stan)
WFA 3 from 4yo 23lb 4 from 5yo+ 2lb 11 Ran SP% 108.7
Speed ratings (Par 103):104,97,96,95,94 94,89,89,83,78 78
CSF £2.00 TOTE £1.50: £1.10, £1.10; EX 3.50 Trifecta £7.10 Pool £494.49 - 49.02 winning units..
Owner Gainsborough **Bred** Gainsborough Stud Management Ltd **Trained** Middleham Moor, N Yorks

FOCUS
An uncompetitive maiden with the red-hot favourite turning it into a procession in a time was 0.57 seconds faster than the second division. It is not totally clear what Soldiers Quest achieved, but he was impressive and the form has been rated at face value through the third and fourth.
Broughtons Revival Official explanation: jockey said, regarding running and riding, his orders were to drop mare in, keep on the bridle as long as possible and try to keep well balanced, adding that as he was asking for an effort at the end of the back straight, he suffered interference, further adding that they stayed on through beaten horses in home straight; trainer's rep added that mare has had a history of veterinary problems
Haoin An Bothar(IRE) Official explanation: jockey said colt had no more to give

603 BONUSPRINT.COM MAIDEN STKS (DIV II) 1m 4f 50y(P)
2:10 (2:11) (Class 5) 3-Y-0+ **£2,388** (£705; £352) **Stalls** Low

Form RPR

4 **D** **Lemonette (USA)**[11] [499] 4-9-6 75 EddieAhern 11 74+
(J W Hills) *hld up in tch: wnt 2nd jst over 2f out: rdn and c to stands' side fr over 1f out: led ins fnl f: r.o: fin 1st, nk: subs. disq (prohibited subs* **9/4**[2]

33 **1** **Reciprocation (IRE)**[14] [484] 3-8-4 JoeFanning 10 75+
(M Johnston) *chsd ldr: led wl over 2f out: rdn over 1f out: edgd rt and hdd ins fnl f: kpt on: fin 2nd, nk: awrdd r* **8/11**[1]

0-0 **2** *5¼* **Stringsofmyheart**[11] [499] 3-7-10 LiamJones(3) 5 62
(W J Haggas) *hld up in mid-div: rdn over 3f out: styd on fnl 2f: nt trble ldng pair: fin 3rd, nk & 5l: plcd 2nd* **25/1**

30-0 **3** *3* **Falimar**[25] [370] 3-7-13 66 PaulHanagan 1 58
(Miss J A Camacho) *t.k.h: led: rdn and hdd wl over 2f out: wknd over 1f out: fin 4th, plcd 3rd* **25/1**

6-53 **4** *6* **Scaramoushca**[34] [270] 4-9-11 53 AdamKirby 8 56
(P S McEntee) *hld up in mid-div: rdn over 3f out: sn wknd: fin 5th, plcd 4th* **25/1**

45-0 **5** *3 1/2* **Khyberie**[11] [499] 4-9-6 SteveDrowne 3 45
(G Wragg) *hld up in tch: rdn over 3f out: wknd over 2f out: fin 6th, plcd 5th* **16/1**[3]

50 **6** *5* **i Fi**[16] [458] 9-9-10 StephenDonohoe(3) 7 42
(Ian Williams) *dwlt: rdn over 4f out: nvr nr ldrs: fin 7th, plcd 6th* **40/1**

7 *3* **Overfields**[12] 7-9-8 TomMessenger(5) 2 38
(G J Smith) *s.i.s: hld up and bhd: sme hdwy on outside over 4f out: rdn over 3f out: sn wknd: fin 8th, plcd 7th* **125/1**

0 **8** *1 1/2* **Paddymctume**[11] [499] 5-9-8 LPKeniry 6 30
(H J Manners) *prom: rdn over 4f out: wknd over 3f out: fin 9th, plcd 8th* **100/1**

0-00 **9** *nk* **Digger Boy**[7] [539] 4-9-11 61 JimCrowley 9 35
(J Gallagher) *rdn over 4f out: a bhd: fin 10th, plcd 9th* **40/1**

2-00 **10** *3 1/2* **Conny obel (IRE)**[39] [209] 3-8-4 62 ChrisCatlin 12 26
(J L Flint) *a bhd: fin 11th, plcd 10th* **50/1**

0 **11** *78* **Colonel Gun (IRE)**[11] [499] 7-9-13 35 TPQueally 4 —
(C R Dore) *a towards rr: hung lft 4f out: t.o: fin 12th, plcd 11th* **100/1**

2m 40.08s (-2.34) **Going Correction** -0.125s/f (Stan)
WFA 3 from 4yo 23lb 4 from 5yo+ 2lb 12 Ran SP% 115.7
Speed ratings (Par 103):102,101,98,96,92 90,86,84,83,83 81,29
CSF £3.74 TOTE £3.00: £1.40, £1.10, £4.20; EX 5.20 Trifecta £20.90 Pool £368.48 - 12.49 winning units..
Owner Jerry Jamgotchian **Bred** Castleton Lyons **Trained** Upper Lambourn, Berks

FOCUS
The winning time was 0.57 seconds slower than the first division with the finish fought out by the two market leaders. An ordinary maiden, but the form seems sound.

604 NAME A RACE TO ENHANCE YOUR BRAND H'CAP 1m 141y(P)
2:40 (2:41) (Class 5) (0-75,75) 4-Y-0+ **£3,238** (£963; £481; £240) **Stalls** Low

Form RPR

1-24 **1** **Samarinda (USA)**[20] [422] 4-8-12 71 MickyFenton 6 81
(Mrs P Sly) *a.p: nt clr run over 2f out: rdn to ld jst ins fnl f: sn edgd rt: drvn out* **12/1**

-241 **2** *1 1/4* **Symbol Of Peace (IRE)**[4] [564] 4-8-7 71 DuranFentiman(5) 1 78
(J W Unett) *hld up in mid-div: hdwy wl over 1f out: sn rdn: r.o ins fnl f* **7/2**[2]

350- **3** *3/4* **Suits Me**[28] [4378] 4-8-9 68 JoeFanning 5 73
(T P Tate) *led: hdd over 6f out: nt clr run and lost pl over 2f out: hdwy on ins wl over 1f out: kpt on ins fnl f* **20/1**

5-43 **4** *1 1/2* **Trifti**[34] [259] 6-8-13 72 (b) EddieAhern 8 74
(C A Cyzer) *hld up in mid-div: hdwy on outside 2f out: hung bdly lft 1f out: one pce* **7/1**

2-25 **5** *nk* **Pab Special (IRE)**[16] [459] 4-8-10 72 AndrewElliott(3) 7 74
(K R Burke) *chsd ldr: led over 6f out: rdn over 1f out: hdd jst ins fnl f: fdd towards fin* **11/2**[3]

-112 **6** *1/2* **Pop Music (IRE)**[7] [539] 4-8-5 67 (p) JamesDoyle(3) 2 68
(Miss J Feilden) *hld up towards rr: swtchd rt wl over 1f out: hung lft ent fnl f: nvr trbld ldrs* **10/3**[1]

525- **7** *4* **Little Jimbob**[78] [6818] 6-8-9 68 PaulHanagan 9 60
(R A Fahey) *prom: ev ch over 2f out: rdn and wknd over 1f out* **20/1**

0-00 **8** *nk* **Aperitif**[15] [468] 6-8-4 63 ow1 AdrianTNicholls 11 55
(D Nicholls) *plld hrd in rr: hdwy on outside over 5f out: jnd ldr over 3f out: sn rdn: wknd over 1f out* **25/1**

65-6 **9** *1 1/2* **Semi Detached (IRE)**[23] [381] 4-8-8 67 PatCosgrave 10 55
(J R Boyle) *hld up: hdwy over 5f out: rdn and wknd over 1f out* **15/2**

1-00 **10** *2 1/2* **Armada**[11] [501] 4-9-2 75 (b[1]) SebSanders 4 58
(W J Haggas) *reminders sn after s: a bhd* **14/1**

1m 48.67s (-3.09) **Going Correction** -0.125s/f (Stan) 10 Ran SP% 112.7
Speed ratings (Par 103):108,106,106,104,104 104,100,100,99,96
CSF £50.49 CT £838.00 TOTE £11.70: £3.40, £2.20, £6.20; EX 65.00 TRIFECTA Not won..
Owner D Bayliss, T Davies, G Libson & P Sly **Bred** Gainsborough Farm Llc **Trained** Thorney, Cambs

FOCUS
A creditable winning time for the grade in what was the only race of the day to beat standard. Solid form, the winner progressing a bit further.

605 PONTINSBINGO.COM (S) STKS 1m 141y(P)
3:15 (3:15) (Class 6) 4-Y-0+ **£2,047** (£604; £302) **Stalls** Low

Form RPR

04-0 **1** **Holiday Cocktail**[7] [538] 5-8-12 63 (v[1]) GrahamGibbons 1 62+
(J J Quinn) *hld up: hdwy 3f out: squeezed through wl over 1f out: rdn to ld ins fnl f: drvn clr* **11/4**[1]

0-45 **2** *3 1/2* **Keon (IRE)**[9] [518] 5-8-13 52 RussellKennemore(5) 10 60
(R Hollinshead) *hld up towards rr: nt clr run 2f out: rdn and hdwy over 1f out: r.o ins fnl f: nt trble wnr* **14/1**

0433 **3** *1 1/4* **Kingsmaite**[7] [533] 6-9-4 57 (bt) PhillipMakin 7 57
(S R Bowring) *hld up: rdn over 3f out: hdwy on outside 2f out: r.o one pce fnl f* **5/1**[2]

004- **4** *shd* **Sawwaah (IRE)**[159] [5553] 10-8-12 63 AdrianTNicholls 8 51+
(D Nicholls) *hld up and bhd: hdwy on ins whn nt clr run 2f out: sn swtchd lft and hung lft: r.o ins fnl f* **12/1**

50/0 **5** *1/2* **Chief Dipper**[20] [425] 5-8-12 63 HayleyTurner 2 50
(D Morris) *hld up: hdwy over 3f out: rdn wl over 1f out: one pce fnl f* **25/1**

0-00 **6** *hd* **Davidia (IRE)**[11] [497] 4-8-12 54 FrankieMcDonald 3 49
(S Kirk) *led early: chsd clr ldng pair: led on bit 2f out: sn rdn: hdd ins fnl f: sn btn* **14/1**

0500 **7** *1 1/2* **Contra Mundum (USA)**[7] [533] 4-8-12 55 PaulHanagan 6 46
(B S Rothwell) *chsd clr ldng pair: rdn over 3f out: hung lft wl over 1f out: wknd ins fnl f* **20/1**

00-0 **8** *2* **Danceinthevalley (IRE)**[45] [151] 5-8-12 57 SteveDrowne 11 42
(G A Swinbank) *hld up and bhd: rdn and hdwy over 1f out: edgd lft and wknd ins fnl f* **20/1**

00-1 **9** *4* **Ellesappelle**[11] [497] 4-8-8 61 (p) TolleyDean(5) 5 34
(R A Harris) *fly-jmpd s: rdn over 4f out: hmpd over 3f out: a bhd* **8/1**[3]

000- **10** *shd* **Bathwick Rox (IRE)**[14] [5733] 4-8-9 50 (p) StephenDonohoe(3) 9 33
(P D Evans) *hld up and bhd: rdn over 4f out: no rspnse* **50/1**

4-65 **11** *1/2* **Following Flow (USA)**[25] [366] 5-8-12 59 (p) DaleGibson 4 32
(R Hollinshead) *hld up: hdwy on outside 2f out: wkng whn hung lft jst over 1f out* **8/1**[3]

0-00 **12** *5* **Kova Hall (IRE)**[14] [256] 5-8-12 75 (vt) DaneO'Neill 13 21
(M F Harris) *w clr ldr: led over 5f out tl over 3f out: rdn over 2f out: wknd wl over 1f out* **11/1**

0-06 **13** *6* **Marmooq**[9] [516] 4-8-12 63 JimCrowley 12 7
(J Gallagher) *sn led and set str pce: hdd over 5f out: rdn to ld over 3f out: hdd 2f out: sn wknd* **10/1**

1m 50.14s (-1.62) **Going Correction** -0.125s/f (Stan) 13 Ran SP% 119.3
Speed ratings (Par 101):102,98,97,97,97 97,95,93,90,90 89,85,80
CSF £41.62 TOTE £3.80: £2.20, £5.30, £1.50; EX 57.60 Trifecta £135.20 Pool £470.59 - 2.47 winning units..The winner was bought in for 11,500gns. Davidia was claimed by Mrs A Thorpe for £6,000.
Owner Team Suffolk **Bred** Mrs W H Gibson Fleming **Trained** Settrington, N Yorks

FOCUS
The two leaders went off at a suicidal pace in this ordinary seller. The winner was a few lengths off his best.
Bathwick Rox(IRE) Official explanation: jockey said gelding hung right-handed throughout

606 CANVAS PRINTS FROM BONUSPRINT.COM H'CAP 5f 216y(P)
3:50 (3:50) (Class 4) (0-85,85) 3-Y-0 **£5,505** (£1,637; £818; £408) **Stalls** Low

Form RPR

3-35 **1** **Mr Loire**[23] [385] 3-8-3 72 JimmyQuinn 3 76
(H J L Dunlop) *s.i.s: hld up: hdwy on ins 2f out: led 1f out: drvn out towards fin* **6/1**[3]

-163 **2** *1/2* **Fractured Foxy**[19] [433] 3-8-2 71 DaleGibson 5 74
(J J Quinn) *hld up: rdn wl over 1f out: r.o ins fnl f: nt rch wnr* **7/1**

212- **3** *1 1/2* **Black Moma (IRE)**[172] [5234] 3-8-7 76 PatDobbs 2 74
(R Hannon) *t.k.h: w ldr: rdn wl over 1f out: one pce fnl f* **7/2**[2]

011- **4** *hd* **Penny Post (IRE)**[100] [6563] 3-9-2 85 JoeFanning 1 82
(M Johnston) *led: rdn and hdd 1f out: no ex* **10/11**[1]

045- **5** *1 1/2* **Stoneacre Gareth (IRE)**[64] [6965] 3-8-4 73 AdrianMcCarthy 4 66
(Peter Grayson) *rdn over 2f out: wkng whn edgd lft over 1f out* **14/1**

1m 14.98s (-0.83) **Going Correction** -0.125s/f (Stan) 5 Ran SP% 108.1
Speed ratings (Par 100):100,99,97,97,95
CSF £40.72 TOTE £5.90: £2.40, £2.50; EX 39.00.

Owner Mrs Harry Dunlop **Bred** Harts Farm And Stud **Trained** Lambourn, Berks

FOCUS
This pretty ordinary little handicap proved to be quite competitive. Slight improvement from both the winner and second.

607 PONTIN'S BOOK EARLY H'CAP — 2m 119y(P)
4:25 (4:25) (Class 6) (0-65,64) 4-Y-0+ — **£2,388** (£705; £352) **Stalls** Low

Form — RPR

50-0 **1** **Rule For Ever**[39] 213 5-9-3 **54** ... JoeFanning 9 — 64
(M Johnston) *chsd ldr: led 2f out: sn rdn: styd on wl* **14/1**

5-02 **2** *3 1/2* **Teorban (POL)**[14] 482 8-9-4 **58** ... StephenDonohoe(3) 10 — 64
(Mrs N S Evans) *sn led: rdn and hdd 2f out: eased whn btn cl home* **18/1**

06-1 **3** *1 3/4* **Moon Emperor**[14] 482 10-9-12 **63** ... (b) EddieAhern 11 — 67
(J R Jenkins) *a.p: rdn and one pce fnl 3f* **7/1**[3]

2-44 **4** *1* **Synonymy**[39] 213 4-9-5 **61** ... (b[1]) JimmyQuinn 7 — 64
(M Blanshard) *hld up in mid-div: rdn over 4f out: hdwy over 3f out: sn one pce* **9/2**[1]

013- **5** *1 1/4* **Your Amount (IRE)**[36] 6754 4-9-8 **64** ... JDSmith 13 — 65+
(W J Musson) *s.v.s: hld up in rr: hdwy on outside over 2f out: rdn wl over 1f out: hung lft ent fnl f: no imp* **9/2**[1]

-264 **6** *1* **Lysander's Quest (IRE)**[20] 416 9-8-9 **46** ... SteveDrowne 4 — 46
(R Ingram) *hld up in tch: rdn and wknd 2f out: btn whn swtchd rt ins fnl f* **8/1**

-213 **7** *3/4* **Reminiscent (IRE)**[25] 369 8-9-6 **57** ... (p) TonyCulhane 8 — 56
(B P J Baugh) *hld up and bhd: nt clr run on ins over 2f out: nvr nr ldrs* **6/1**[2]

54-3 **8** *1 1/4* **Mustakhlas (USA)**[33] 285 6-8-11 **48** ... PhillipMakin 2 — 46
(B P J Baugh) *led early: prom: rdn over 3f out: wknd over 1f out: btn whn rdr dropped whip wl ins fnl f* **9/1**

610- **9** *2 1/2* **Activist**[392] 283 9-9-2 **60** ... KellyHarrison(7) 6 — 55
(D Carroll) *a towards rr* **25/1**

404- **10** *9* **Dark Planet**[53] 3075 4-9-2 **58** ... (p) ChrisCatlin 5 — 42
(D Burchell) *hld up in mid-div: bhd fnl 2f* **33/1**

00-4 **11** *5* **Stravara**[39] 215 4-9-6 **62** ... GeorgeBaker 3 — 40
(R Hollinshead) *a bhd: eased whn no ch fnl f* **9/1**

0-40 **12** *7* **History Prize (IRE)**[10] 503 4-8-5 **47** ... PaulHanagan 1 — 17
(A G Newcombe) *hld up towards rr: rdn 4f out: no rspnse* **40/1**

3m 41.27s (-1.86) **Going Correction** -0.125s/f (Stan)
WFA 4 from 5yo+ 5lb — 12 Ran SP% **115.4**
Speed ratings (Par 101):99,97,96,96,95 95,94,94,92,88 86,83
CSF £231.37 CT £1909.51 TOTE £14.30: £4.00, £4.90, £3.00; EX 207.70 Trifecta £526.40 Part won. Pool £741.43 - 0.10 winning units..
Owner J S Morrison **Bred** Baldernock Bloodstock Limited **Trained** Middleham Moor, N Yorks

FOCUS
A moderate staying handicap. Sound form. The winner will still be on a fair mark after being reassessed.
Stravara Official explanation: jockey said gelding lost its action home straight

608 GO PONTIN'S H'CAP — 1m 4f 50y(P)
5:00 (5:00) (Class 2) (0-100,95) 4-Y-0+ **£11,658** (£3,468; £1,733; £865) **Stalls** Low

Form — RPR

53-3 **1** **Heathyards Pride**[38] 226 7-8-0 **82** ... WilliamBuick(7) 1 — 89
(R Hollinshead) *hld up towards rr: hdwy 2f out: rdn to ld ins fnl f: sn edgd lft: r.o* **15/2**[3]

2-12 **2** *nk* **Eva Soneva So Fast (IRE)**[27] 345 5-9-2 **91** ... JimmyQuinn 9 — 97
(J L Dunlop) *t.k.h towards rr: hdwy over 3f out: rdn wl over 1f out: ev ch ins fnl f: carried lft: r.o* **15/8**[1]

21-5 **3** *1/2* **Tranquilizer**[45] 153 5-8-6 **81** oh3 ... (t) JoeFanning 2 — 86
(D J Coakley) *a.p: rdn and ev ch ins fnl f: kpt on* **16/1**

2-22 **4** *hd* **Quince (IRE)**[13] 488 4-8-9 **86** ... (v) TPQueally 3 — 91
(J Pearce) *hld up in mid-div: hdwy over 1f out: rdn whn nt clr run and swtchd lft ins fnl f: r.o* **15/2**[3]

/2-2 **5** *shd* **Watamu (IRE)**[51] 95 6-8-10 **85** ... (v) EddieAhern 7 — 90
(P J Makin) *plld hrd: a.p: rdn wl over 1f out: r.o one pce fnl f* **5/2**[2]

200- **6** *1/2* **Dunaskin (IRE)**[147] 5787 7-9-3 **92** ... SebSanders 4 — 96
(Karen McLintock) *led: rdn wl over 1f out: hdd ins fnl f: no ex* **16/1**

3455 **7** *1* **Atlantic Quest (USA)**[13] 488 8-8-5 **83** ... LiamJones(3) 6 — 85
(Miss Venetia Williams) *hld up in mid-div: hdwy over 5f out: rdn and carried hd awkwardly over 1f out: one pce fnl f* **20/1**

50 **8** *1 3/4* **Fantoche (BRZ)**[41] 197 5-8-11 **86** ... PatCosgrave 10 — 86
(M J Wallace) *hld up and bhd: rdn wl over 1f out: no imp whn edgd lft ins fnl f* **40/1**

04-3 **9** *2* **Fortunate Isle (USA)**[26] 264 5-8-10 **85** ... PaulHanagan 11 — 81
(R A Fahey) *a bhd* **12/1**

000- **10** *34* **Polonius**[26] 578 6-8-3 **81** oh1 ... NeilChalmers(3) 8 — 23
(G J Smith) *t.k.h in tch: wknd 3f out: eased whn no ch wl over 1f out* **100/1**

2m 39.84s (-2.58) **Going Correction** -0.125s/f (Stan)
WFA 4 from 5yo+ 2lb — 10 Ran SP% **114.5**
Speed ratings (Par 109):103,102,102,102,102 101,101,100,98,76
CSF £21.24 CT £221.11 TOTE £9.10: £2.20, £1.50, £3.60; EX 28.80 Trifecta £283.20 Pool £782.00 - 1.96 winning units..
Owner L A Morgan **Bred** L A Morgan **Trained** Upper Longdon, Staffs
■ Stewards' Enquiry : Jimmy Quinn one-day ban: careless riding (Mar 13)

FOCUS
This falsely-run race proved to be a messy affair for a decent prize. This race is hard to rate positively but the winner, third and fourth all but reproduced their form over course and distance in December.

NOTEBOOK
Heathyards Pride has held his form pretty well since winning over course and distance off a 5lb lower mark at the end of October. Brought with a well-timed challenge down the outside, his young rider again showed the value of his 7lb claim. (op 8-1)
Eva Soneva So Fast(IRE) continues to hold his form and appeared to get intimidated into going left by the winner. However, the Stewards saw things differently and handed Quinn a one-day ban for careless riding. (tchd 7-4 and 2-1)
Tranquilizer, 3lb 'wrong', was 8lb worse off than when beating the winner by three and a half lengths when successful over course and distance on Boxing Day. (op 14-1)
Quince(IRE), raised another 2lb, produced another good performance despite encountering traffic problems in the closing stages. (op 8-1 tchd 7-1)
Watamu(IRE), with the visor refitted, proved a bit of a handful to settle. He had finished two lengths behind the runner-up on 4lb worse terms on his previous start at Lingfield. (op 3-1)
Dunaskin(IRE) waited in front on his first start for almost five months and only gave best towards the finish. (op 14-1)

609 PONTIN'S FAMILY HOLIDAYS H'CAP — 7f 32y(P)
5:30 (5:30) (Class 5) (0-70,69) 4-Y-0+ **£3,238** (£963; £481; £240) **Stalls** High

Form — RPR

2-20 **1** **Kabis Amigos**[4] 564 5-8-9 **62** ... (t) AdrianTNicholls 10 — 72
(D Nicholls) *plld hrd: sn prom: led over 4f out: rdn wl over 1f out: r.o* **20/1**

5533 **2** *3/4* **Parkview Love (USA)**[8] 525 6-8-6 **59** ... (v) DeanMcKeown 12 — 67
(D Shaw) *t.k.h in rr: hdwy 2f out: swtchd rt over 1f out: rdn and r.o ins fnl f: nt rch wnr* **10/1**

65-1 **3** *3/4* **Zarabad (IRE)**[9] 516 5-9-2 **69** 6ex ... PhillipMakin 11 — 75+
(K R Burke) *hld up and bhd: hdwy on outside whn edgd lft jst over 2f out: rdn 1f out: nt qckn* **11/2**[3]

3043 **4** *hd* **Mistral Sky**[7] 536 8-9-0 **67** ... (v) MickyFenton 9 — 73
(Stef Liddiard) *a.p: rdn over 1f out: kpt on one pce fnl f* **20/1**

30-6 **5** *1 1/4* **Hoh Wotanite**[20] 424 4-8-8 **66** ... RussellKennemore(5) 3 — 68
(R Hollinshead) *prom: lost pl on ins over 2f out: hrd rdn and rallied over 1f out: one pce fnl f* **12/1**

00-4 **6** *1 1/4* **Violent Velocity (IRE)**[32] 300 4-8-12 **65** ... GrahamGibbons 5 — 64
(J J Quinn) *hld up: kpt on fnl f: nvr trbld ldrs* **8/1**

0-11 **7** *1 3/4* **Lii Najma**[25] 371 4-9-2 **69** ... JoeFanning 8 — 64
(C E Brittain) *w ldr over 3f: wknd fnl f* **9/2**[2]

0-00 **8** *1 1/4* **Danzig River (IRE)**[19] 432 6-8-7 **67** ... AdeleRothery(7) 2 — 58
(D Nicholls) *plld hrd: a bhd* **33/1**

5222 **9** *hd* **Sir Douglas**[5] 560 4-9-1 **68** ... (p) EddieAhern 7 — 59+
(R A Harris) *s.i.s: plld hrd: hdwy over 3f out: hmpd over 2f out: nt rcvr* **7/2**[1]

5321 **10** *1/2* **Flying Bantam (IRE)**[15] 468 6-8-10 **63** ... (p) PaulHanagan 4 — 52
(R A Fahey) *plld hrd: prom over 3f* **11/2**[3]

2602 **11** *2* **Mine The Balance (IRE)**[11] 497 4-8-6 **59** ... LPKeniry 6 — 43
(H J Manners) *bhd fnl 3f* **25/1**

12 *8* **Go The Distance (IRE)**[212] 4064 5-8-7 **63** ... JerryO'Dwyer(3) 1 — 26
(Adrian Sexton, Ire) *led over 2f: wkng whn n.m.r on ins ent st* **40/1**

1m 28.95s (-1.45) **Going Correction** -0.125s/f (Stan) — 12 Ran SP% **117.8**
Speed ratings (Par 103):103,102,101,101,99 98,96,94,94,93 91,82
CSF £194.43 CT £898.69 TOTE £23.10: £4.60, £2.70, £1.50; EX 210.00 TRIFECTA Not won. Place 6 £235.47, Place 5 £234.66.
Owner GGN Bloodstock Ltd and Ian W Glenton **Bred** Cheveley Park Stud Ltd **Trained** Sessay, N Yorks

FOCUS
A very respectable time for this tightly-knit handicap. Sound form.
Sir Douglas Official explanation: jockey said colt had steering problems
T/Jkpt: Not won. T/Plt: £173.40 to a £1 stake. Pool: £73,049.85. 307.45 winning tickets. T/Qpdt: £174.50 to a £1 stake. Pool: £3,538.60. 15.00 winning tickets. KH

587 LINGFIELD (L-H)
Monday, March 5

OFFICIAL GOING: Standard
Wind: blustery, strong across

610 PONTIN'S HOLIDAYS H'CAP (DIV I) — 1m 2f (P)
2:00 (2:01) (Class 6) (0-60,60) 4-Y-0+ **£1,706** (£503; £252) **Stalls** Low

Form — RPR

051 **1** **Our Kes (IRE)**[7] 570 5-9-1 **59** 5ex ... TonyCulhane 4 — 69
(P Howling) *w.w wl in tch: hdwy on inner over 2f out: chsd ldng pair 2f out: rdn to ld ins fnl f: r.o strly* **11/8**[1]

-001 **2** *1 1/2* **Shaheer (IRE)**[14] 500 5-8-10 **54** ... JimCrowley 11 — 61
(J Gallagher) *chsd ldrs: hdwy to chse ldr 3f out: rdn and ev ch over 2f out: nt pce of wnr ins fnl f: wnt 2nd nr line* **14/1**

211- **3** *hd* **Revolve**[73] 6904 7-8-12 **56** ... (b) IanMongan 8 — 63
(Mrs L J Mongan) *chsd ldr tl led 3f out: rdn over 2f out: hdd ins fnl f: kpt on same pce* **11/1**

0-66 **4** *3/4* **Moving Target (IRE)**[19] 458 8-8-13 **57** ... J-PGuillambert 9 — 62+
(Luke Comer, Ire) *s.i.s: t.k.h: hld up in rr: hdwy on outer over 2f out: r.o strly fnl f: nt rch ldrs* **25/1**

0-30 **5** *3* **Golden Alchemist**[18] 228 4-8-9 **60** ... WilliamBuick(7) 14 — 59
(M D I Usher) *hld up towards rr on outer: hdwy 5f out: rdn to chse ldrs over 3f out: kpt on same pce wl over 1f out* **25/1**

-310 **6** *1 1/4* **Play Up Pompey**[28] 363 5-8-12 **59** ... AmirQuinn(3) 7 — 56+
(J J Bridger) *s.i.s: hld up in rr on inner: hdwy over 1f out: styd on fnl f: nvr nrr* **8/1**[3]

3303 **7** *1/2* **Voice Mail**[14] 495 8-8-2 **53** ... (b) DavidProbert(7) 1 — 49
(A M Balding) *t.k.h: chsd ldrs: rdn and lost pl 3f out: kpt on same pce last 2f* **12/1**

0-10 **8** *nk* **Ellesappelle**[3] 605 4-8-11 **60** ... (p) TolleyDean(5) 12 — 56
(R A Harris) *racd in midfield: rdn wl over 3f out: kpt on same pce last 2f* **20/1**

5-00 **9** *shd* **Birthday Star (IRE)**[28] 363 5-9-2 **60** ... NCallan 10 — 55
(W J Musson) *hld up towards rr: rdn 4f out: kpt on fnl f: nvr threatened ldrs* **9/2**[2]

-330 **10** *3/4* **Expected Bonus (USA)**[14] 495 8-8-2 **46** oh1 ... (b) AdrianMcCarthy 5 — 40
(Jamie Poulton) *w.w i midfield: rdn over 3f out: no ch last 2f* **50/1**

000- **11** *1 1/4* **Orpen Quest (IRE)**[185] 4983 5-8-13 **57** ... DaneO'Neill 6 — 49
(M J Attwater) *v.s.a: hld up in rr: n.d* **16/1**

000 **12** *1 1/4* **Executive Paddy (IRE)**[9] 548 8-8-11 **55** ... DanielTudhope 3 — 44
(I A Wood) *plld hrd: hld up in midfield: rdn 3f out: no hdwy* **16/1**

5-00 **13** *1 3/4* **Music Celebre (IRE)**[37] 263 7-9-0 **58** ... (b) TPQueally 13 — 44
(S Curran) *chsd ldrs: rdn wl over 2f out: wknd wl over 1f out* **12/1**

300- **14** *6* **Atticus Trophies (IRE)**[65] 6987 4-8-10 **54** ... (v[1]) EddieAhern 2 — 29
(Ms J S Doyle) *led tl 3f out: wknd over 2f out: eased ins fnl f* **33/1**

2m 5.42s (-2.37) **Going Correction** -0.15s/f (Stan) — 14 Ran SP% **130.9**
Speed ratings (Par 101):103,101,101,101,98 97,97,97,96,96 95,94,92,88
CSF £24.76 CT £181.83 TOTE £3.20: £1.80, £6.50, £3.50; EX 31.20.
Owner Mark Entwistle **Bred** Yeomanstown Stud **Trained** Newmarket, Suffolk

FOCUS
Just a moderate handicap, but the first three home were last-time out winners and this is probably not bad form for the level. The pace was reasonable by Lingfield's standards and the time was good; marginally the fastest of the four 1m2f contests, and 2.22 seconds quicker than the second division.
Atticus Trophies(IRE) Official explanation: jockey said gelding hung right

611 GO PONTIN'S MEDIAN AUCTION MAIDEN STKS 1m 2f (P)
2:30 (2:30) (Class 6) 3-5-Y-0 **£2,730** (£806; £403) **Stalls** Low

Form RPR

0-3 **1** **Surrey Spinner**[23] [418] 3-8-5 .... JimCrowley 7 70+
(Mrs A J Perrett) *hld up on outer bhd ldrs: chsd ldr over 2f out: rdn to ld over 1f out: styd on wl* **11/10**[1]

2-25 **2** 1 ¾ **Miss Saafend Plaza (IRE)**[4] [591] 3-8-0 74........(b) JimmyQuinn 3 59
(R Hannon) *hld up in tch: pushed along 5f out: rdn and hdwy 2f out: chsd ldng pair over 1f out: wnt 2nd ins last: no ch w wnr* **4/1**[2]

000- **3** ¾ **Brave Quest (IRE)**[159] [5623] 3-8-5 52........ PaulDoe 8 62
(Mrs L J Mongan) *led: rdn wl over 2f out: hdd over 1f out: kpt on same pce: lost 2nd ins fnl f* **50/1**

5-60 **4** 2 **Semi Detached (IRE)**[3] [604] 4-9-9 67........ AmirQuinn(3) 6 63
(J R Boyle) *t.k.h: hld up in tch: rdn and hdwy on outer bnd 2f out: styd on ins fnl f: nt trble ldrs* **6/1**[3]

5 ¾ **Santaverti** 4-9-12 .... GeorgeBaker 1 62
(G L Moore) *hld up bhd ldrs: chsd ldng pair and rdn over 2f out: kpt on same pce* **20/1**

35 **6** hd **Picky**[17] [484] 3-7-13 ow1........ SophieDoyle(7) 9 58?
(J A Osborne) *chsd ldrs tl lost pl 3f out: rdn and kpt on same pce last 2f out* **20/1**

0 **7** 3 **Pheidias (IRE)**[14] [499] 3-8-6 ow1........ EddieAhern 5 52
(M P Tregoning) *s.i.s: bhd: rnn green and pushed along 4f out: sn outpcd: kpt on fnl f: n.d* **7/1**

4-34 **8** ½ **Zelos (IRE)**[11] [522] 3-8-5 69........(b[1]) JamieMackay 4 50
(J A Osborne) *plld hrd: chsd ldr: rdn over 3f out: wknd over 2f out* **10/1**

2m 5.72s (-2.07) **Going Correction** -0.15s/f (Stan)
WFA 3 from 4yo 21lb 8 Ran SP% **115.0**
Speed ratings (Par 101):102,100,100,98,97 97,95,94
CSF £5.48 TOTE £2.10: £1.10, £1.30, £9.30; EX 4.60.
Owner J E Bodie And R Wells **Bred** D R Tucker **Trained** Pulborough, W Sussex

FOCUS
A weak maiden run in a time 0.30 seconds slower than the opening 46-60, but quicker than the other two 1m2f races on the card. Not easy form to pin down, with the second unreliable and the third a big improver, and the winner didn't have to run to his previous best.
Semi Detached(IRE) Official explanation: jockey said colt hung right

612 PONTIN'S HOLIDAYS H'CAP (DIV II) 1m 2f (P)
3:00 (3:01) (Class 6) (0-60,60) 4-Y-0+ **£1,706** (£503; £252) **Stalls** Low

Form RPR

-010 **1** **Competitor**[28] [363] 6-9-1 59........(v) DaneO'Neill 12 67
(J Akehurst) *rdn leaving stalls: hld up in tch: hdwy over 3f out: rdn 2f out : sn chsng ldr: led 1f out: hld on wl u.p* **20/1**

55-5 **2** ½ **Musango**[9] [549] 4-9-1 59........(t) SamHitchcott 10 66
(B R Johnson) *hld up in midfield: rdn and gd hdwy jst over 2f out: chsd wnr ins fnl f: r.o* **7/1**[3]

-234 **3** 1 **Paparaazi (IRE)**[18] [464] 5-8-13 57........ DanielTudhope 13 62
(I W McInnes) *chsd ldrs: wnt 2nd 7f out: rdn to ld wl over 2f out: hdd 1f out: kpt on same pce ins fnl f* **8/1**

/0-1 **4** nk **Enthusius**[23] [416] 4-8-9 53........ SteveDrowne 8 58
(G L Moore) *led tl 3f out: sn rdn: kpt on same pce ins fnl f* **5/1**[1]

/420 **5** nk **Volaticus (IRE)**[7] [570] 6-9-1 59........ SilvestreDeSousa 1 63
(A D Brown) *hld up in rr oninner: hdwy over 1f out: n.m.r jst ins fnl f: kpt on nr fin: nvr nrr* **8/1**

042- **6** shd **Lilac Star**[93] [6668] 4-8-10 54........ PaulEddery 7 58
(Pat Eddery) *t.k.h: chsd ldr tl 7f out: rdn over 3f out: kpt on same pce u.p last 2f* **11/2**[2]

-340 **7** shd **Rowan Warning**[28] [363] 5-8-13 57........ NCallan 2 61
(J R Boyle) *hld up in rr: rdn and hdwy wl over 1f out: r.o ins fnl f: nt rch ldrs* **11/1**

-221 **8** ½ **Mon Petite Amour**[14] [495] 4-8-11 55........ BrettDoyle 9 58
(D W P Arbuthnot) *hld up in rr: c wd and rdn 2f out: r.o ins fnl f: nt rch ldrs* **8/1**

5-00 **9** shd **Scroll**[40] [235] 4-9-0 58........(v) J-PGuillambert 3 60
(P Howling) *trckd ldrs on inner: rdn and effrt wl over 1f out: no hdwy ins fnl f* **16/1**

-022 **10** ½ **King Of Knight (IRE)**[14] [500] 6-8-10 54........ AdrianMcCarthy 6 56
(G Prodromou) *t.k.h early: stdd and hld up in midfield: rdn and effrt 2f out: kpt on same pce ins fnl f* **14/1**

00-4 **11** nk **Pelham Crescent (IRE)**[35] [288] 4-9-2 60........ TonyCulhane 14 61
(B Palling) *chsd ldrs on outer: hdwy to press ldr wl over 2f out: sn rdn: btn whn short of room jst ins fnl f* **50/1**

4022 **12** hd **Blackmail (USA)**[19] [459] 9-9-2 60........ EddieAhern 11 61
(P Mitchell) *chsd ldrs: rdn and outpcd over 2f out: kpt on same pce after: eased wl ins fnl f* **10/1**

-060 **13** ½ **Veba (USA)**[7] [570] 4-8-2 46 oh1........ JamieMackay 4 46
(M D I Usher) *slowly away: hld up in last: rdn 2f out: kpt on same pce* **50/1**

3100 **14** 6 **Desert Hawk**[21] [445] 6-8-10 54........(b) RobbieFitzpatrick 5 42
(W M Brisbourne) *hld up towards rr: rdn over 3f out: outpcd over 2f out: eased whn btn fnl f* **25/1**

2m 7.64s (-0.15) **Going Correction** -0.15s/f (Stan) 14 Ran SP% **120.4**
Speed ratings (Par 101):94,93,92,92,92 92,92,91,91,91 91,90,90,85
CSF £150.36 CT £1232.79 TOTE £23.50: £10.00, £2.70, £3.80; EX 485.50.
Owner Who Cares Who Wins **Bred** Cheveley Park Stud Ltd **Trained** Epsom, Surrey

FOCUS
A messy race and very unreliable form. They went a steady pace for much of the way - the winning time was comfortably the slowest of the four races over the trip at the meeting and 2.22 seconds slower than the first division - and all bar the back marker finished within around four lengths of one another.
Blackmail(USA) Official explanation: jockey said gelding had been denied a clear run

613 PONTINS.COM H'CAP 5f (P)
3:30 (3:32) (Class 6) (0-55,55) 4-Y-0+ **£2,388** (£705; £352) **Stalls** High

Form RPR

0-35 **1** **The Fisio**[47] [161] 7-8-13 55........(v) IanMongan 3 69
(S Gollings) *chsd ldr: rdn to ld over 1f out: r.o wl* **9/2**[1]

0064 **2** 1 ¼ **Lady Bahia (IRE)**[11] [521] 6-8-12 54........(b) EddieAhern 9 63
(Peter Grayson) *slowly away: dropped in bhd: rdn and hdwy on inner 2f out: kpt on u.p to go 2nd on line: no ch w wnr* **8/1**

-046 **3** shd **Triskaidekaphobia**[42] [214] 4-8-10 52........(t) SteveDrowne 2 61
(Miss J R Tooth) *led: rdn and hdd over 1f out: kpt on same pce: lost 2nd on line* **10/1**

3453 **4** hd **Muktasb (USA)**[28] [368] 6-8-10 52........(v) NCallan 7 60
(D Shaw) *plld hrd: chsd ldrs: rdn wl over 1f out: kpt on same pce ins fnl f* **5/1**[2]

4320 **5** ½ **Lady Hopeful (IRE)**[21] [441] 5-8-7 49........(b) RobbieFitzpatrick 6 55
(Peter Grayson) *hld up in rr: rdn over 2f out: kpt on ins fnl f: nt rch ldrs* **16/1**

6-01 **6** hd **Thoughtsofstardom**[36] [287] 4-8-5 52........(be) DuranFentiman(5) 10 57
(P S McEntee) *chsd ldrs on outer: rdn wl over 1f out: kpt on same pce* **12/1**

650- **7** hd **Cosmic Destiny (IRE)**[92] [6688] 5-8-12 54........ DaneO'Neill 4 59
(E F Vaughan) *plld hrd: hld up in rr: swtchd rt and rdn over 1f out: kpt on same pce* **8/1**

341- **8** nk **Davids Mark**[89] [6723] 7-8-12 54........ NickyMackay 1 57
(J R Jenkins) *trckd ldrs: rdn and effrt on inner over 1f out: no hdwy fnl f* **5/1**[2]

0-30 **9** 4 **Campbeltown (IRE)**[9] [549] 4-8-6 55........ WilliamBuick(7) 8 42
(M R Hoad) *chsd ldrs: rdn over 2f out: wknd over 1f out* **7/1**[3]

0203 **10** nk **New Options**[24] [403] 10-8-10 52........(b) BrettDoyle 5 38
(Peter Grayson) *plld hrd: hld up in rr: n.d* **12/1**

58.41 secs (-1.37) **Going Correction** -0.15s/f (Stan) 10 Ran SP% **116.6**
Speed ratings (Par 101):104,102,101,101,100 100,100,99,93,92
CSF £40.51 CT £350.27 TOTE £5.10: £1.60, £3.60, £4.00; EX 47.40.
Owner John Crow Holdings Ltd **Bred** E Duggan And D Churchman **Trained** Scamblesby, Lincs

FOCUS
A moderate but competitive sprint handicap, run in a good time. The winner took advantage of a decent mark.

614 PONTINSBINGO.COM H'CAP 7f (P)
4:00 (4:02) (Class 5) (0-75,75) 4-Y-0+ **£3,071** (£906; £453) **Stalls** Low

Form RPR

6131 **1** **Danetime Lord (IRE)**[17] [480] 4-8-12 71........(p) NCallan 7 81
(K A Ryan) *in tch: hdwy to trck ldrs gng wl over 2f out: rdn to ld ins fnl f: r.o wl* **5/2**[1]

00-6 **2** 1 **His Master's Voice (IRE)**[40] [234] 4-8-8 67........ BrettDoyle 5 75
(D W P Arbuthnot) *plld hrd: hld up in midfield: hdwy 2f out: r.o wl fnl f: nt rch ldr* **11/2**[3]

1-00 **3** ½ **Special Place**[19] [461] 4-8-2 61........ NickyMackay 10 67+
(J A R Toller) *stdd s: hld up bhd: rdn and c wd bnd 2f out: r.o wl fnl f: nt rch ldrs* **10/1**

-660 **4** ½ **Zazous**[8] [560] 6-8-0 62 oh3 ow1........ MarcHalford(3) 4 67
(J J Bridger) *trckd ldrs on inner: swtchd rt and rdn jst over 1f out: r.o wl: nvr nrr* **33/1**

-660 **5** shd **Sailor King (IRE)**[12] [513] 5-8-12 71........ RobertHavlin 1 76
(D K Ivory) *hld up in rr on inner: swtchd rt and hdwy over 1f out: r.o: nvr nrr* **16/1**

15-3 **6** nk **Small Stakes (IRE)**[40] [234] 5-8-9 68........(vt) EddieAhern 3 72
(P J Makin) *slowly away: hld up bhd: rdn and hdwy over 1f out: r.o: n.d* **7/2**[2]

0-00 **7** nk **Quantum Leap**[8] [556] 10-8-7 66........(v) JimmyQuinn 9 69
(S Dow) *t.k.h: hld up in tch: rdn and hdwy 2f out: swtchd lft over 1f out: no imp fnl f* **12/1**

1654 **8** hd **Marko Jadeo (IRE)**[17] [480] 9-8-11 75........ TolleyDean(5) 12 78
(R A Harris) *taken down early: s.i.s: plld hrd: hdwy to chse ldrs on outer over 4f out: led 2f out tl ins last: wknd* **12/1**

0534 **9** ¾ **Plateau**[8] [556] 8-8-10 69........ TPQueally 8 70
(C R Dore) *led early: plld hrd and stdd into midfield: lost pl and rdn over 3f out: n.d after* **11/1**

0-00 **10** 2 ½ **Nightstrike (IRE)**[16] [486] 4-8-2 61 oh3........(b[1]) CatherineGannon 13 55
(Luke Comer, Ire) *sn led: hdd 5f out: led again 3f out tl 2f out: sn wknd* **40/1**

/5-0 **11** 2 **Baba Ghanoush**[8] [556] 5-8-6 65........ PaulDoe 2 54
(W Jarvis) *a bhd* **11/1**

0006 **12** nk **Meditation**[4] [590] 5-8-4 70........(b[1]) WilliamBuick(7) 11 58
(I A Wood) *plld hrd: chsd ldrs: led 5f out tl 3f out: sn wknd* **20/1**

0-41 **13** shd **Night Wolf (IRE)**[9] [549] 7-8-2 61 oh5........(t) AdrianMcCarthy 6 49
(Jamie Poulton) *w ldrs: rdn wl over 2f out: wknd wl over 1f out* **16/1**

1m 24.07s (-1.82) **Going Correction** -0.15s/f (Stan) 13 Ran SP% **129.2**
Speed ratings (Par 103):104,102,102,101,101 101,100,100,99,96 94,94,94
CSF £17.37 CT £128.56 TOTE £3.50: £1.60, £1.80, £3.10; EX 23.10.
Owner Bull & Bell Partnership **Bred** P J Murphy **Trained** Hambleton, N Yorks

FOCUS
An ordinary handicap which saw the progressive winner record a slight personal best. The fouth slightly limits the form.

615 PONTIN'S FAMILY HOLIDAYS CLASSIFIED STKS 1m 5f (P)
4:30 (4:30) (Class 7) 4-Y-0+ **£2,047** (£604; £302) **Stalls** Low

Form RPR

455- **1** **Dubai Sunday (JPN)**[176] [4576] 6-9-1 44........ SamHitchcott 12 52
(P S McEntee) *dwlt: hld up in midfield: hdwy on outer 4f out: chsd ldrs and rdn 2f out: chal over 1f out: led on line* **5/1**[2]

0455 **2** shd **Countback (FR)**[14] [496] 8-9-1 43........(p) CatherineGannon 11 52
(A W Carroll) *dwlt: sn chsng ldrs: wnt 2nd over 3f out: rdn to ld over 2f out: hrd pressed over 1f out: hdd on line* **8/1**[3]

-040 **3** 2 ½ **Montecristo**[8] [558] 14-9-1 43........ DeanCorby 10 48
(Rae Guest) *chsd ldrs: hdwy over 3f out: rdn and ev ch over 2f out: onepced fnl f* **8/1**[3]

200- **4** 1 ¾ **Icannshift (IRE)**[167] [5451] 7-8-12 40........ NeilChalmers(3) 6 45
(T M Jones) *led tl rdn and hdd over 2f out: wknd over 1f out* **16/1**

0-23 **5** ¾ **Compton Express**[23] [416] 4-8-12 45........ PaulDoe 4 44+
(Jamie Poulton) *hld up in rr: effrt whn short of room and snatched up over 2f out: r.o u.p over 1f out: nt rch ldrs* **4/1**[1]

-030 **6** shd **Lady Suffragette (IRE)**[36] [285] 4-8-12 42........ JDSmith 2 44
(John Berry) *t.k.h: hld up in midfield: rdn over 2f out kpt on same pce* **12/1**

5-04 **7** nk **Integration**[14] [203] 7-9-1 40........ LeeEnstone 9 44
(Miss M E Rowland) *w.w in midfield: rdn 3f out: n.m.r and swtchd over 2f out: sme hdwy u.p over 1f out: no imp ins last* **14/1**

060- **8** 1 ¼ **Real Chief (IRE)**[14] [1415] 9-9-1 45........ SimonWhitworth 1 42
(Miss M E Rowland) *hld up bhd: rdn over 2f out: kpt on fnl f: nvr trbld ldrs* **33/1**

-542 **9** shd **Iceni Warrior**[8] [558] 5-9-1 45........ PaulEddery 5 42
(P Howling) *hld up in midfield: rdn over 3f out: nvr trbld ldrs* **4/1**[1]

60/0 **10** 1 ¼ **Ghaill Force**[14] [496] 5-8-12 43........ AmirQuinn(3) 8 40
(P Butler) *slowly away: plld hrd and sn chsng ldrs: rdn and wknd over 2f out* **25/1**

0-30 **11** *1 ¼* **Chimes At Midnight (USA)**^{8} [558] 10-9-1 45........(b) RichardThomas 7 38
(Luke Comer, Ire) *slowly away: bhd tl hdwy 8f out: chsd ldrs 6f out: rdn over 3f out: sn btn* **10/1**

4/6- **12** *6* **Beauchamp Twist**^{15} [303] 5-9-1 42............................ MatthewHenry 13 29
(M R Hoad) *hld up in tch in midfield: rdn and lost pl over 3f out: no ch after* **20/1**

00/0 **13** *¾* **Artic Bliss**^{29} [349] 5-9-1 41... StephenCarson 14 28
(G F Bridgwater) *s.i.s: plld hrd: hld up wl bhd: no ch last 2f out* **33/1**

66-0 **14** *1 ¼* **Coolaw (IRE)**^{14} [495] 4-8-12 42....................................(v) JamieMackay 3 26
(G G Margarson) *chsd ldr tl over 3f out: sn wknd* **25/1**

2m 48.59s (0.29) **Going Correction** -0.15s/f (Stan)
WFA 4 from 5yo+ 3lb **14** Ran SP% **126.6**
Speed ratings (Par 97):93,92,91,90,89 89,89,88,88,88 87,83,83,82
CSF £44.19 TOTE £6.30: £1.70, £3.40, £2.70; EX 62.60.
Owner Eventmaker Racehorses **Bred** Northern Farm **Trained** Newmarket, Suffolk

FOCUS
A typically weak event for the class. The first two, both od whom have been rated 4-5lb higher in the past year, came clear in a bobbing finish.
Icannshift(IRE) Official explanation: jockey said gelding hung right
Chimes At Midnight(USA) Official explanation: jockey said horse lugged left
Artic Bliss Official explanation: jockey said mare hung right

616 PONTIN'S "BOOK EARLY" H'CAP 1m 2f (P)
5:00 (5:00) (Class 6) (0-52,52) 4-Y-0+ **£2,047** (£604; £302) **Stalls** Low

Form RPR

1323 **1** **Comeintothespace (IRE)**^{11} [524] 5-8-1 48............... WilliamBuick$^{(7)}$ 7 56
(R A Farrant) *in tch: hdwy to chse ldng pair over 2f out: rdn over 1f out: r.o wl to ld nr fin* **9/2**^{2}

660- **2** *nk* **Nassar (IRE)**^{144} [5929] 4-8-9 49................................. AdrianMcCarthy 13 56
(G Prodromou) *t.k.h: chsd ldrs: wnt 2nd over 3f out: rdn to ld 2f out : hdd and no ex nr fin* **16/1**

5010 **3** *1 ¼* **Danelor (IRE)**^{20} [453] 9-8-7 47................................(p) CatherineGannon 1 52
(D Shaw) *hld up in midfield: hdwy over 2f out: r.o wl u.p fnl f: wnt 3rd cl home: nt rch ldrs* **20/1**

2-30 **4** *½* **Recalcitrant**^{19} [458] 4-8-5 52... PatrickHills$^{(7)}$ 10 56
(S Dow) *led tl 2f out: ev ch after tl wknd last 100 yds* **9/2**^{2}

000- **5** *4* **Wally Barge**^{176} [5210] 4-8-12 52.. RobertHavlin 6 48
(D K Ivory) *hld up bhd: hdwy 3f out: chsd ldrs u.p 2f out: no real hdwy* **66/1**

0-0 **6** *3* **Victors Prize (IRE)**^{35} [288] 5-8-7 47...................(b^{1}) FrankieMcDonald 4 37
(S Curran) *v.s.a: hld up bhd: hdwy u.p over 1f out: nvr trbld ldrs* **50/1**

450- **7** *2 ½* **Joy In The Guild (IRE)**^{175} [5247] 4-8-10 50...................... DaneO'Neill 3 36
(W S Kittow) *t.k.h: hld up towards rr: nvr nr ldrs* **14/1**

5-04 **8** *nk* **Laugh 'n Cry**^{19} [455] 6-8-9 49.. EddieAhern 14 34
(C A Cyzer) *hld up in rr: c wd bnd over 2f out: nvr on terms* **9/1**

1133 **9** *½* **Earl Kraul (IRE)**^{21} [315] 4-8-12 52.................................(b) TPQueally 9 36
(G L Moore) *plld hrd: in tch on outer: chsd ldrs and rdn over 2f out: wknd over 1f out* **8/1**^{3}

5-64 **10** *3* **Jools**^{28} [364] 9-8-8 48... JimCrowley 2 26
(D K Ivory) *plld hrd: chsd ldrs: rdn and wknd over 2f out* **16/1**

-464 **11** *3 ½* **Elms Schoolboy**^{23} [425] 5-8-7 47..........................(b) J-PGuillambert 11 19
(P Howling) *v.s.a: a bhd* **14/1**

1-12 **12** *2 ½* **Saucy**^{14} [500] 6-8-10 50... JimmyQuinn 5 17
(A W Carroll) *t.k.h: hld up in midfield on inner: swtchd rt and rdn jst over 2f out: no hdwy* **7/4**^{1}

60-0 **13** *nk* **Laheen (IRE)**^{14} [500] 4-8-12 52.....................................(v^{1}) BrettDoyle 12 18
(J R Best) *chsd ldrs tl 3f out: wkng whn short of room bnd over 2f out* **33/1**

60/0 **14** *1 ½* **Miss Ladybird (USA)**^{51} [124] 6-8-10 50..................(b^{1}) NickyMackay 8 14
(T J Etherington) *chsd ldr after 2f tl over 3f out: sn wknd* **50/1**

2m 6.24s (-1.55) **Going Correction** -0.15s/f (Stan) **14** Ran SP% **132.1**
Speed ratings (Par 101):100,99,98,98,95 92,90,90,90,87 84,82,82,81
CSF £79.22 CT £1374.79 TOTE £5.50: £1.90, £6.20, £6.50; EX 291.90 Place 6 £118.60, Place 5 £62.58.
Owner Rodney Farrant **Bred** D And Mrs D Veitch **Trained** Upper Lambourn, Berks

FOCUS
A very moderate handicap, run at just an ordinary early pace. Not many got into it and the first four came clear. The race has been rated through the second and third.
Nassar(IRE) Official explanation: jockey said colt pulled up lame
Elms Schoolboy Official explanation: jockey said gelding had been denied a clear run
Saucy Official explanation: trainer had no explanation for the poor form shown
T/Plt: £309.20 to a £1 stake. Pool: £81,802.40. 193.10 winning tickets. T/Qpdt: £196.50 to a £1 stake. Pool: £5,390.80. 20.30 winning tickets. SP

602 WOLVERHAMPTON (A.W) (L-H)
Monday, March 5

OFFICIAL GOING: Standard
Wind: Fresh, behind Weather: Overcast

617 PO TI S FAMILY OLIDAYS AM. RIDERS CAP (DI I) 1m 5f 194y (P)
1:50 (1:50) (Class 5) (0-70,70) 4-Y-0+ **£2,307** (£709; £354) **Stalls** Low

Form RPR

4132 **1** **Blue Hills**^{5} [585] 6-10-5 57...(b) MrsMarieKing$^{(3)}$ 8 67
(P W Hiatt) *led after 1f: hdd over 11f out: led again 4f out: clr 2f out: styd on* **9/2**^{2}

1-06 **2** *2 ½* **Jack Rolfe**^{44} [195] 5-10-11 65............................ MissHayleyMoore$^{(5)}$ 13 71
(G L Moore) *led 1f: remained handy: chsd wnr 2f out: sn rdn and hung lft: styd on same pce* **9/1**

55-5 **3** *2 ½* **Agilete**^{18} [464] 5-10-3 55... MrSPearce$^{(3)}$ 2 58
(J Pearce) *s.i.s: hld up: hdwy over 3f out: shkn up fnl f: styd on same pce* **10/1**

52-1 **4** *½* **Cumbrian Knight (IRE)**^{6} [39] 9-10-5 59.............. MissNJefferson$^{(5)}$ 1 61
(J M Jefferson) *s.i.s: sn chsng ldrs: led over 5f out: hdd 4f out: styd on same pce fnl 2f* **15/2**^{3}

0-1 **5** *hd* **Theatre Groom (USA)**^{21} [443] 8-11-7 70........................ MrsSBosley 7 72
(M R Bosley) *prom: rdn over 2f out: n.m.r over 1f out: styd on same pce* **16/1**

1030 **6** *1 ¼* **Finished Article (IRE)**^{6} [578] 10-10-0 54.................. MrPCollington$^{(5)}$ 5 54
(K J Burke) *s.i.s: hld up: hdwy over 3f out: edgd lft over 1f out: styd on same pce* **12/1**

0041 **7** *2 ½* **Newnham (IRE)**^{6} [578] 6-11-1 67............................. MrDHutchison$^{(3)}$ 3 64
(J R Boyle) *hld up: hdwy over 2f out: nt trble ldrs* **13/8**^{1}

600- **8** *3 ½* **Scotty's Future (IRE)**^{104} [6551] 9-9-9 51 oh3........... MissWGibson$^{(7)}$ 12 43
(A Berry) *hld up: hdwy and hung lft over 1f out: n.d* **100/1**

05/0 **9** *7* **Quel Fontenailles (FR)**^{14} [496] 9-9-11 51 oh1............... MrsLDace$^{(5)}$ 6 33
(L A Dace) *s.s: hld up: a in rr* **50/1**

40-0 **10** *1 ½* **Primondo (IRE)**^{15} [354] 5-10-6 60............................. MrMJJSmith$^{(5)}$ 11 40
(A W Carroll) *mid-div: dropped rr 8f out: bhd fnl 6f* **16/1**

-000 **11** *5* **Layed Back Rocky**^{18} [462] 5-9-11 51 oh6.......... MissMMullineaux$^{(5)}$ 4 24
(M Mullineaux) *chsd ldrs: led over 11f out: sn clr: hdd over 5f out: wknd over 3f out* **100/1**

0340 **12** *3* **Mumbling (IRE)**^{6} [578] 9-10-5 61.....................................(b) MrRElliott$^{(7)}$ 9 30
(B G Powell) *mid-div: hdwy 10f out: chsd ldr 8f out: wknd 3f out* **25/1**

00/6 **13** *2 ½* **Charnwood Street (IRE)**^{11} [87] 8-10-2 51 oh6.......(v) MrsMMorris 10 16
(D Shaw) *broke wl: lost pl after 1f: bhd fnl 7f* **100/1**

3m 6.22s (-1.15) **Going Correction** 0.0s/f (Stan) **13** Ran SP% **115.4**
Speed ratings (Par 103):103,101,100,99,99 99,97,95,91,90 87,86,84
CSF £42.18 CT £381.17 TOTE £7.40: £1.50, £3.50, £2.60; EX 55.50 Trifecta £168.60 Part won. Pool: £237.60 - 0.34 winning units..
Owner Tom Pratt **Bred** Darley **Trained** Hook Norton, Oxon

FOCUS
The winning time was 0.85 seconds faster than the second division. The form looks ordinary but sound with the winner not needing to improve on his latest run.

618 PO TI S FAMILY OLIDAYS AM. RIDERS CAP (DI II) 1m 5f 194y(P)
2:20 (2:21) (Class 5) (0-70,70) 4-Y-0+ **£2,307** (£709; £354) **Stalls** Low

Form RPR

0212 **1** **Three Thieves (UAE)**^{23} [428] 4-11-1 68............................ MrSWalker 8 76
(M S Saunders) *hld up: hdwy over 5f out: led over 1f out: hung lft ins fnl f: drvn out* **9/4**^{1}

42-0 **2** *hd* **Capitalise (IRE)**^{6} [578] 4-9-10 54................................ MrJohnEnnis$^{(5)}$ 4 62
(V Smith) *hld up: hdwy over 2f out: hung lft fr over 1f out: sn nt clr run: ev ch ins fnl f: r.o* **9/2**^{2}

/54- **3** *3* **Toni Alcala**^{63} [6705] 8-10-4 56 oh5 ow5......................... MrMSeston$^{(3)}$ 12 60
(R F Fisher) *chsd ldrs: led over 3f out: sn rdn: hdd over 1f out: no ex ins fnl f* **25/1**

605- **4** *1* **I'll Do It Today**^{59} [5390] 6-10-3 57...........................(t) MissNJefferson$^{(5)}$ 1 60
(J M Jefferson) *s.i.s: rcvrd to trck ldr after 1f: lost pl over 3f out: hdwy over 2f out: n.m.r ins fnl f: styd on* **5/1**^{3}

406- **5** *½* **Fiddlers Creek (IRE)**^{149} [4229] 8-10-8 60...............(tp) MissJRiding$^{(3)}$ 6 62
(R Allan) *chsd ldrs: ev ch fr over 2f out: edgd lft and no ex fnl f* **20/1**

0624 **6** *1 ¼* **Come What July (IRE)**^{6} [578] 6-10-2 51 oh6................ MrsMMorris 2 51
(D Shaw) *mid-div: hdwy over 5f out: rdn over 2f out: wkng whn rdr dropped whip wl ins fnl f* **8/1**

063- **7** *2 ½* **Cockatoo (USA)**^{94} [5650] 4-10-6 62......................... MrDHutchison$^{(3)}$ 11 59
(G L Moore) *prom: rdn over 3f out: wknd over 2f out* **9/1**

6-11 **8** *3* **Vanishing Dancer (SWI)**^{28} [369] 10-11-1 64...(bt) MissFayeBramley 13 56
(K J Burke) *hld up: hdwy over 5f out: wknd 2f out* **8/1**

0-30 **9** *2 ½* **Undeterred**^{7} [568] 11-11-0 70.................................... MrAMerriam$^{(7)}$ 7 59
(K J Burke) *hld up: rdn over 2f out: a in rr* **33/1**

403/ **10** *2 ½* **Dawn At Sea**^{64} [5208] 5-10-6 60.................................. MissAWallace$^{(5)}$ 9 45
(Mrs K Waldron) *slwoly into stride: hld up: rdn over 3f out: a in rr* **100/1**

11U- **11** *6* **Bid For Fame (USA)**^{364} [597] 10-11-1 67.................. MrSPearce$^{(3)}$ 10 44
(J Pearce) *s.i.s: hld up: a in rr* **16/1**

-000 **12** *4* **Moonshine Bill**^{14} [496] 8-9-13 51 oh6........................ MrsMarieKing$^{(3)}$ 5 22
(P W Hiatt) *led over 10f: wknd over 2f out* **50/1**

3m 7.07s (-0.30) **Going Correction** 0.0s/f (Stan)
WFA 4 from 5yo+ 4lb **12** Ran SP% **118.2**
Speed ratings (Par 103):100,99,98,97,97 96,95,93,92,90 87,84
CSF £11.21 CT £201.31 TOTE £2.80: £1.30, £1.80, £7.00; EX 18.70 TRIFECTA Not won..
Owner Prempro Racing **Bred** Darley (u A E) **Trained** Green Ore, Somerset

FOCUS
The winning time was 0.85 seconds slower than the first division. Similar form, and although the third was racing from out of the handicap the form overall makes sense.

619 SPONSOR A RACE BY CALLING 0870 220 2442 (S) STKS 5f 216y(P)
2:50 (2:51) (Class 6) 3-Y-O **£2,388** (£705; £352) **Stalls** Low

Form RPR

4424 **1** **Strike Force**^{4} [589] 3-9-0 63................................(p) MichaelJStainton$^{(5)}$ 7 60
(R A Harris) *chsd ldrs: rdn to ld and hung lft over 1f out: r.o* **2/1**^{1}

2 *1 ¼* **Firebird Annie (IRE)** 3-8-7 ow2............................ JerryO'Dwyer$^{(3)}$ 5 47
(S W Hall) *hld up: hdwy over 2f out: rdn and hung lft over 1f out: r.o* **12/1**

5-0 **3** *nk* **Lady Cartuccia**^{35} [301] 3-8-8 .... GrahamGibbons 8 44
(J J Quinn) *sn outpcd: rdn over 2f out: r.o ins fnl f: nrst fin* **9/1**

0 **4** *1 ¼* **Zil Up**^{11} [522] 3-8-13 ....(bt^{1}) PhillipMakin 6 45
(S R Bowring) *s.i.s: hld up: plld hrd: bmpd over 3f out: hdwy over 2f out: rdn and hung lft over 1f out: no ex ins fnl f* **50/1**

0-33 **5** *½* **Tang**^{12} [511] 3-8-9 57 ow1.. JohnEgan 4 40+
(W G M Turner) *chsd ldrs: lost pl whn n.m.r over 3f out: nt clr run over 1f out: styd on ins fnl f* **3/1**^{2}

36-0 **6** *nk* **Bridget's Team**^{41} [223] 3-9-0 54...(t) DaleGibson 1 44
(D G Bridgwater) *sn led: hdd over 4f out: led again over 2f out: rdn and hdd over 1f out: edgd lft and no ex fnl f* **10/1**

00-5 **7** *1 ¼* **Meathop (IRE)**^{48} [152] 3-8-13 45...................................... PaulHanagan 2 39
(R F Fisher) *chsd ldrs: rdn over 2f out: styng on same pce whn nt clr run ins fnl f* **20/1**

0-40 **8** *shd* **Flamestone**^{20} [454] 3-8-13 50...................................(p) DarrylHolland 10 39
(J D Bethell) *chsd ldrs: edgd lft over 3f out: sn outpcd: styd on ins fnl f* **8/1**^{3}

-060 **9** *2 ½* **House Arrest**^{6} [577] 3-8-1 45...(bt) MCGeran$^{(7)}$ 3 26
(A J McCabe) *s.s: rdn over 2f out: a in rr* **16/1**

-500 **10** *1 ½* **Flushed**^{27} [373] 3-8-13 44..(b) DeanMcKeown 9 27
(A J McCabe) *dwlt: hdwy to ld over 4f out: hdd over 2f out: hung lft and wknd over 1f out* **20/1**

1m 17.1s (1.29) **Going Correction** 0.0s/f (Stan) **10** Ran SP% **113.6**
Speed ratings (Par 96):91,89,88,87,86 86,84,84,81,79
CSF £26.05 TOTE £2.30: £1.40, £2.40, £3.30; EX 33.90 Trifecta £164.70 Pool £473.28 - 2.04 winning units..The winner was bought in for 8,500gns. Firebird Annie was claimed by A Bailey for £6,000.
Owner Mrs Ruth M Serrell **Bred** Cheveley Park Stud Ltd **Trained** Earlswood, Monmouths

FOCUS
A weak seller and the form is unlikely to mean a lot outside this grade. It is unlikely that the favourite had much to beat. The winning time was modest, even for a race like this.

620 PONTIN'S BOOK EARLY CLAIMING STKS 1m 1f 103y(P)
3:20 (3:20) (Class 5) 4-Y-0+ **£3,238** (£963; £481; £240) **Stalls** Low

Form RPR

22U0 **1** **The City Kid (IRE)**^{10} [538] 4-8-8 55...............................(b) PaulHanagan 5 62
(P D Evans) *hld up: plld hrd: hdwy over 2f out: rdn to ld and hung lft ins fnl f: r.o* **8/1**^{3}

03-6 **2** 1 3/4 **Blue Sky Thinking (IRE)**[23] [420] 8-9-13 86.................. PatCosgrave 1 77
(K R Burke) *trckd ldrs: racd keenly: hung rt and led 2f out: sn rdn: edgd lft and hdd ins fnl f: styd on same pce* **7/4**[1]

1110 **3** 1 3/4 **Climate (IRE)**[10] [533] 8-8-8 68......................(p) RussellKennemore(5) 9 60
(R Hollinshead) *trckd ldrs: plld hrd: rdn and ev ch fr over 1f out: edgd lft and no ex ins fnl f* **11/4**[2]

6-00 **4** 3/4 **Welsh Whisper**[7] [570] 8-8-2 41.................................. NelsonDeSouza 6 47
(S A Brookshaw) *hld up: hdwy over 1f out: sn rdn: styng on same pce whn nt clr run ins fnl f* **50/1**

2-02 **5** nk **Rose Muwasim**[23] [425] 4-8-5 48..........................(p) EmmettStack(3) 13 52
(K J Burke) *chsd ldrs: ev ch over 2f out: sn rdn and hung lft: styd on same pce appr fnl f* **14/1**

0504 **6** 3 **Bathwick Emma (IRE)**[12] [518] 4-8-9 47 ow1...............(p) AdamKirby 12 47
(M A Doyle) *hld up: nvr nrr* **28/1**

010- **7** 1/2 **Looker**[37] [5889] 4-8-9 64.. JamesDoyle(3) 8 49
(J Gallagher) *led: rdn and hdd 2f out: wknd fnl f* **11/1**

0-20 **8** 3 **Final Esteem**[28] [364] 4-9-0 65............................ MichaelJStainton(5) 11 50
(R A Harris) *s.i.s: hdwy 7f out: rdn over 2f out: sn wknd* **25/1**

40-0 **9** 2 1/2 **Faversham**[16] [488] 4-9-7 74.. JimmyFortune 10 47
(M Wigham) *chsd ldr: rdn over 3f out: hung lft and wknd over 2f* **14/1**

00-0 **10** 1 **Wilford Maverick (IRE)**[61] [20] 5-8-6 41.....................(v) DominicFox(3) 7 33
(K J Burke) *hld up: plld hrd: rdn over 2f out: hung lft over 1f out: n.d* **66/1**

4-53 **11** 8 **Insignia (IRE)**[23] [425] 5-8-11 45.. JohnEgan 2 19
(W M Brisbourne) *hld up: hdwy over 3f out: rdn and wknd over 2f out* **8/1**[3]

0-00 **12** 1 1/4 **Rambling Socks**[37] [271] 4-8-2 42..........................(bt) DaleGibson 3 8
(S R Bowring) *hld up: rdn and wknd 3f out* **150/1**

2m 4.02s (1.40) **Going Correction** 0.0s/f (Stan) **12** Ran SP% **118.3**
Speed ratings (Par 103):93,91,89,89,88 86,85,83,80,80 72,71
CSF £21.71 TOTE £10.10: £1.30, £1.60, £1.50; EX 31.40 Trifecta £83.30 Pool £617.22 - 5.26 winning units..The winner was claimed by S Dow for £8,000.
Owner Mrs S J Lawrence **Bred** T B And Mrs T B Russell **Trained** Pandy, Monmouths

FOCUS
They went no pace early and that would not have helped a few of these. A very moderate winning time, even for a claimer. Dubious form, and it is likely the winner won by default. The fourth limits the form.
The City Kid(IRE) Official explanation: trainer said, regarding apparent improvement in form, that the filly benefited from stronger handling

621 PONTINS.COM H'CAP 5f 216y(P)
3:50 (3:50) (Class 5) (0-70,70) 4-Y-O+ **£3,238** (£963; £481; £240) **Stalls** Low

Form RPR

2220 **1** **Sir Douglas**[3] [609] 4-8-9 68.................................. MichaelJStainton(5) 12 78
(R A Harris) *mid-div: hdwy over 2f out: rdn and hung lft over 1f out: r.o to ld towards fin* **9/2**[1]

45-0 **2** 1/2 **Nepro (IRE)**[18] [465] 5-8-13 67...................................(t) EdwardCreighton 9 75
(E J Creighton) *hld up: hdwy 1/2-way: hmpd over 1f out: sn rdn: r.o* **25/1**

1000 **3** hd **Dvinsky (USA)**[12] [513] 6-8-11 65.................................. DarryllHolland 10 73
(P Howling) *chsd ldr: rdn to ld ins fnl f: hdd towards fin* **25/1**

60-0 **4** 1/2 **Melalchrist**[7] [566] 5-8-11 65.......................................(p) PatCosgrave 13 71
(K A Ryan) *sn led: rdn over 1f out: hdd and unable qck ins fnl f* **50/1**

-002 **5** hd **Supercast (IRE)**[8] [561] 4-8-9 63..(t) JohnEgan 8 68
(W M Brisbourne) *hld up: hdwy over 2f out: rdn and hung lft over 1f out: r.o* **9/2**[1]

0-60 **6** shd **Winthorpe (IRE)**[34] [306] 7-8-6 60................................(p) GrahamGibbons 7 65
(J J Quinn) *chsd ldrs: rdn and hung lft over 1f out: styd on same pce* **14/1**

1123 **7** 3/4 **Lucius Verrus (USA)**[9] [548] 7-8-8 62..........................(v) DeanMcKeown 11 65
(D Shaw) *hld up: running on whn nt clr run towards fin: nvr able to chal* **17/2**

2410 **8** 3/4 **Came Back (IRE)**[8] [561] 4-8-11 65..................................... DaleGibson 2 66
(J Mackie) *hld up: plld hrd: hmpd over 3f out: r.o ins fnl f: nvr nrr* **6/1**[2]

0434 **9** 1/2 **Mistral Sky**[3] [609] 8-8-13 67..(v) MickyFenton 6 66
(Stef Liddiard) *chsd ldrs: sn pushed along: hmpd and lost pl over 2f out: rdn and nt clr run over 1f out: kpt on* **15/2**[3]

614- **10** 1 1/4 **Benny The Bus**[93] [6672] 5-8-6 60.................................. NelsonDeSouza 4 55
(Mrs G S Rees) *prom: hmpd over 3f out: sn lost pl: n.d after* **10/1**

00-0 **11** 4 **Gavarnie Beau (IRE)**[16] [486] 4-9-0 68............................ JimmyFortune 3 51
(M Blanshard) *hld up: rdn and hung lft over 1f out: sn wknd* **12/1**

-000 **12** 1/2 **Polish Emperor (USA)**[7] [566] 7-9-0 68...........................(v) PaulHanagan 5 50
(D W Barker) *mid-div: hdwy over 2f out: rdn and wknd over 1f out* **20/1**

23-0 **13** 3 1/2 **Littledodayno (IRE)**[23] [424] 4-9-2 70.................................. BrianReilly 1 41
(M Wigham) *sn outpcd* **20/1**

1m 14.88s (-0.93) **Going Correction** 0.0s/f (Stan) **13** Ran SP% **115.6**
Speed ratings (Par 103):106,105,105,104,104 104,103,102,101,99 94,93,89
CSF £125.87 CT £1685.93 TOTE £5.40: £1.90, £7.40, £6.90; EX 112.90 TRIFECTA Not won..
Owner Mrs Diane Tumman **Bred** Overbury Partnership **Trained** Earlswood, Monmouths
■ Stewards' Enquiry : Michael J Stainton caution: careless riding

FOCUS
A competitive sprint handicap run at a decent pace and there was little separating the front six at the line. Just ordinary form, and not entirely solid.

622 PONTIN'S HOLIDAYS (S) STKS 5f 216y(P)
4:20 (4:21) (Class 6) 4-Y-O+ **£2,047** (£604; £302) **Stalls** Low

Form RPR

0333 **1** **Desert Light (IRE)**[8] [562] 6-8-12 49..........................(v) DeanMcKeown 3 57
(D Shaw) *hld up: hdwy over 1f out: r.o to ld wl ins fnl f: hung lft nr fin* **13/2**

406- **2** nk **Devon Flame**[209] [4223] 8-8-5 77.................................. HaddenFrost(7) 12 57
(R J Hodges) *plld hrd and prom: led and hung lft over 1f out: hdd wl ins fnl f* **9/2**[2]

0520 **3** 3/4 **Fast Heart**[21] [442] 6-8-12 57..(t) PaulHanagan 5 54
(R A Harris) *hld up: nt clr run over 1f out: r.o ins fnl f: nt rch ldrs* **8/1**

3451 **4** nk **Phinerine**[21] [442] 4-8-12 54................................(b) MichaelJStainton(5) 7 58
(R A Harris) *s.i.s: hld up: hdwy and hung lft fr over 1f out: styd on* **10/1**

-044 **5** 1/2 **Ever Cheerful**[10] [536] 6-8-12 67..(tp) DaleGibson 2 52
(D G Bridgwater) *s.i.s: hdwy 1/2-way: rdn over 1f out: no ex ins fnl f* **5/2**[1]

4466 **6** nk **Grand View**[21] [442] 11-8-12 45..................................(p) DarryllHolland 1 51
(J R Weymes) *led: hdd over 4f out: led 1/2-way: rdn and hdd over 1f out: no ex ins fnl f* **16/1**

5454 **7** 3/4 **Majestical (IRE)**[8] [562] 5-8-12 49......................................(p) LPKeniry 8 49
(J M Bradley) *chsd ldrs: rdn and hung lft over 1f out: no ex fnl f* **12/1**

0640 **8** 1/2 **Teyaar**[28] [366] 11-9-3 47... AdamKirby 4 52
(M Wellings) *prom: lost pl 5f out: hrd rdn fr over 1f out: n.d* **28/1**

0430 **9** 1 **Doughty**[20] [448] 5-8-9 44.. EmmettStack(3) 6 44
(M Mullineaux) *s.i.s: nvr nr* **40/1**

0311 **10** nk **Mister Incredible**[13] [504] 4-9-0 52.........................(v) SaleemGolam(3) 10 48
(J M Bradley) *prom: rdn over 2f out: hung lft over 1f out: wknd fnl f* **5/1**[3]

00-0 **11** 4 **Par Excellence**[28] [359] 4-8-0 44.....................................(p) JackDean(7) 9 26
(W G M Turner) *w ldrs: rdn over 2f out: wknd fnl f* **80/1**

P-45 **12** 1 **Legal Set (IRE)**[10] [536] 11-8-7 49...............................(bt) AnnStokell(5) 11 28
(Miss A Stokell) *chsd ldrs: led over 4f out: hdd 1/2-way: wknd 2f out* **50/1**

1m 16.11s (0.30) **Going Correction** 0.0s/f (Stan) **12** Ran SP% **119.6**
Speed ratings (Par 101):98,97,96,96,95 95,94,93,92,91 86,85
CSF £35.52 TOTE £7.90: £2.30, £1.80, £3.50; EX 52.00 Trifecta £268.20 Pool £453.22 - 1.20 winning units..There was no bid for the winner. Ever Cheerful was claimed by A Haynes for £6,000. Fast Heart was claimed by E Nisbet for £6,000.
Owner Danethorpe Racing Ltd **Bred** Anthony M Cahill **Trained** Danethorpe, Notts

FOCUS
An weakish seller, but a competitive one and there were still several in with every chance entering the last furlong. The form horses were not at their best.

623 PONTINSBINGO.COM H'CAP 1m 4f 50y(P)
4:50 (4:50) (Class 5) (0-70,70) 4-Y-O+ **£3,238** (£963; £481; £240) **Stalls** Low

Form RPR

5 **1** **Luxurix (FR)**[37] [263] 6-9-4 70.. JimmyFortune 7 79+
(P R Webber) *s.i.s: hld up: hdwy over 3f out: rdn to ld 1f out: r.o wl: eased towards fin* **3/1**[2]

-402 **2** 2 **Ross Moor**[12] [515] 5-9-1 70.. JamesDoyle(3) 1 76
(N P Littmoden) *chsd ldrs: rdn and ev ch 1f out: styd on same pce* **4/1**[3]

40-3 **3** 1 1/4 **Plenty Cried Wolf**[13] [503] 5-8-4 56 oh1.......................... PaulHanagan 2 60
(R A Fahey) *led: hdd 5f out: rdn and ev ch over 2f out: edgd lft and no ex fnl f* **10/1**

1111 **4** hd **Atlantic Gamble (IRE)**[12] [514] 7-8-13 65.....................(p) PatCosgrave 4 68
(K R Burke) *trckd ldrs: racd keenly: rdn over 2f out: styd on same pce fnl f* **2/1**[1]

041- **5** 3/4 **Alexian**[80] [6828] 4-9-0 68... JohnEgan 6 70
(D W P Arbuthnot) *hld up: hdwy 5f out: led over 2f out: rdn and hdd 1f out: no ex* **16/1**

10-0 **6** shd **Storm Of Arabia (IRE)**[37] [263] 4-8-9 63.......................... AdamKirby 3 65
(W R Swinburn) *hld up in tch: lost pl whn nt clr run over 2f out: rallied over 1f out: styng on same pce whn n.m.r ins fnl f* **22/1**

4-00 **7** 1/2 **Chorister**[13] [508] 6-8-6 58.. DaleGibson 11 59
(J Mackie) *hld up: r.o ins fnl f: nt trble ldrs* **40/1**

154- **8** 3/4 **Abstract Folly (IRE)**[75] [6735] 5-8-10 62.......................... DarryllHolland 9 62
(J D Bethell) *hld up: rdn and edgd lft over 1f out: n.d* **12/1**

-436 **9** 8 **Hawk Arrow (IRE)**[31] [332] 5-8-9 61.. LPKeniry 5 48
(G L Moore) *hld up: rdn over 4f out: wknd over 2f out* **8/1**

106/ **10** 2 **Revelino (IRE)**[728] [4911] 8-8-10 62.............................. GrahamGibbons 8 46
(Mrs N S Evans) *prom 9f* **66/1**

-200 **11** 3 **Bethanys Boy (IRE)**[34] [302] 6-8-5 62...................... KevinGhunowa(5) 10 41
(P A Blockley) *trckd ldr: led 5f out: hdd & wknd over 2f out* **20/1**

2m 40.5s (-1.92) **Going Correction** 0.0s/f (Stan)
WFA 4 from 5yo+ 2lb **11** Ran SP% **125.2**
Speed ratings (Par 103):106,104,103,103,103 103,102,102,96,95 93
CSF £16.07 CT £112.71 TOTE £4.60: £1.80, £2.00, £3.90; EX 19.40 Trifecta £193.20 Pool £658.78 - 242 winning units..
Owner Paul Green **Bred** S N C Lagardere Elevage **Trained** Mollington, Oxon

FOCUS
The pace was solid. Ordinary form, the third and fifth looking fair guides. The winner might do better on his old French form.
Alexian Official explanation: jockey said gelding ran keen for the first half of the race

624 GO PONTIN'S H'CAP 1m 141y(P)
5:20 (5:22) (Class 6) (0-65,65) 3-Y-O **£2,730** (£806; £403) **Stalls** Low

Form RPR

6-56 **1** **Muncaster Castle (IRE)**[35] [301] 3-8-6 53.................. DeanMcKeown 2 60
(R F Fisher) *mde all: rdn and hung lft over 1f out: styd on* **12/1**

-641 **2** 1/2 **Ballyshane Spirit (IRE)**[18] [469] 3-8-1 55................ KirstyMilczarek(7) 1 61
(N A Callaghan) *trckd wnr: racd keenly: rdn and hung lft ins fnl f: styd on* **9/2**[2]

1 **3** 1 1/2 **Still Crazy (IRE)**[21] [446] 3-9-0 61.. LPKeniry 6 66+
(E F Vaughan) *a.p: racd keenly: nt clr run over 1f out: styng on same pce whn nt clr run ins fnl f* **8/1**

3-34 **4** 1 1/4 **Raquel White**[17] [478] 3-8-0 54.................................... JosephWalsh(7) 12 54
(J L Flint) *hld up: hdwy over 5f out: rdn and edgd lft over 1f out: styd on same pce* **20/1**

006- **5** 1 **Hard As Iron**[114] [6441] 3-9-1 62... DaleGibson 7 60
(M Blanshard) *prom: rdn over 3f out: styd on same pce appr fnl f* **14/1**

000- **6** 1 1/2 **Mid Ocean**[124] [6298] 3-9-4 65.. JohnEgan 10 62+
(P W D'Arcy) *hld up: edgd lft over 7f out: hdwy over 3f out: rdn over 1f out: hung lft: wknd and eased ins fnl f* **13/2**[3]

0-02 **7** 2 **Diamond Light (USA)**[37] [267] 3-9-0 61............................ DarryllHolland 8 52
(M Botti) *prom: rdn over 2f out: wknd over 1f out* **10/3**[1]

-422 **8** 1 1/4 **Bertrada (IRE)**[18] [469] 3-7-13 53...........................(b[1]) FrankiePickard(7) 4 41
(H Morrison) *s.i.s: rdn over 2f out: n.d* **13/2**[3]

202- **9** 3 **Tokyo Jo (IRE)**[85] [6777] 3-9-3 64.. AdamKirby 9 46
(T T Clement) *hld up: hmpd over 7f out: a in rr* **33/1**

403- **10** 3/4 **Goose Green (IRE)**[143] [5948] 3-8-11 65...................... HaddenFrost(7) 11 45
(R J Hodges) *prom tl rdn and wknd over 1f out* **8/1**

3166 **11** hd **Kings Shillings**[10] [535] 3-8-1 55...........................(b) GaryWales(7) 5 35
(D Carroll) *hld up: hmpd over 7f out: rdn whn rdr dropped reins over 2f out: sn wknd* **20/1**

-365 **12** 4 **Wilmington**[23] [421] 3-9-3 64..................................(b) GrahamGibbons 13 35
(N P Littmoden) *s.i.s: hld up: rdn and wknd over 2f out* **20/1**

460- **13** 17 **Spanish Air**[237] [3385] 3-8-12 62.. JamesDoyle(3) 3 —
(J W Hills) *plld hrd and prom: lost pl over 4f out: sn bhd* **50/1**

1m 50.84s (-0.92) **Going Correction** 0.0s/f (Stan) **13** Ran SP% **123.7**
Speed ratings (Par 96):104,103,102,101,100 98,97,96,93,92 92,88,73
CSF £63.24 CT £476.26 TOTE £13.30: £4.40, £2.90, £3.20; EX 104.50 Trifecta £587.80 Part won. Pool: £827.91 - 0.52 winning units. Place 6 £107.60, Place 5 £27.11..
Owner Sporting Occasions 7 **Bred** Doc Bloodstock **Trained** Ulverston, Cumbria
■ Stewards' Enquiry : Kirsty Milczarek three-day ban: careless riding (Mar 16-17,19)
John Egan three-day ban: careless riding (Mar 16-17,19)

FOCUS
An ordinary gallop to this handicap and it paid to race handily as the front three were up with the pace throughout. The race has been rated positively and this looks solid form for the level which should work out.
Tokyo Jo(IRE) Official explanation: jockey said filly suffered interference soon after start
T/Jkpt: Not won. T/Plt: £126.60 to a £1 stake. Pool: £79,442.40. 457.85 winning tickets. T/Qpdt: £29.30 to a £1 stake. Pool: £5,267.50. 132.60 winning tickets. CR

579 SOUTHWELL (L-H)

Tuesday, March 6

OFFICIAL GOING: Standard

625 CORAL AND TALKSPORT SUPPORTING CHILDREN 1ST H'CAP (DIV I) 7f (F)

1:40 (1:40) (Class 6) (0-52,52) 4-Y-0+ £1,706 (£503; £252) Stalls Low

Form RPR

5042 1 **Desert Lover (IRE)**[8] [571] 5-8-8 48....(tp) NCallan 3 61+
(R J Price) *trckd ldrs: pushed along 3f out: hdwy and cl up 2f out: rdn to ld wl over 1f out: styd on* 3/1[2]

1006 2 1 1/2 **A Teen**[9] [556] 9-8-6 46 oh1....JimmyQuinn 9 53
(P Howling) *trckd ldrs: hdwy and ev ch 2f out: sn rdn and one pce appr last* 9/1

200- 3 3 **Bob Baileys**[238] [3386] 5-8-8 48....(b) JimCrowley 5 47
(P R Chamings) *s.i.s and bhd: wd st:hdwy 2f out: rdn and styd on strly appr last: nrst fin* 16/1

03-0 4 3/4 **Bandos**[18] [479] 7-8-7 52....DuranFentiman(5) 6 49
(I Semple) *hld up towards rr: hdwy over 2f out: rdn wl over 1f out: kpt on ins last: nrst fin* 14/1

6064 5 shd **Prettilini**[6] [580] 4-8-8 51 ow1....StephenDonohoe(3) 8 48
(R Brotherton) *cl up: rdn along and ev ch 2f out: sn drvn and one pce* 15/2

0-66 6 1/2 **Feelin Irie (IRE)**[18] [479] 4-8-12 52....PatCosgrave 11 47
(J R Boyle) *keen: cl up: rdn along over 2f out: sn edgd rt and btn* 13/2[3]

0/0- 7 3 **Sowerby**[336] [872] 5-8-7 47....(b) DeanMernagh 10 35
(M Brittain) *sn led: rdn along over 2f out: drvn and hdd wl over 1f out: grad wknd* 50/1

00-0 8 3 **Pepper Road**[23] [435] 8-8-3 46 oh1....(t) DominicFox(3) 2 26
(R Bastiman) *midfield: chsd along 1/2-way: nvr a factor* 66/1

0-05 9 1/2 **Hilltop Fantasy**[6] [579] 6-7-13 46 oh1....(p) JosephWalsh(7) 12 25
(V Smith) *chsd ldrs on outer: rdn along wl over 2f out and sn wknd* 12/1

0024 10 nk **Machinate (USA)**[8] [570] 5-8-9 49....JamieSpencer 1 27
(W M Brisbourne) *hld up: a towards rr* 11/4[1]

0-00 11 1 **Warden Warren**[37] [273] 9-8-6 46 oh1....(tp) AdrianMcCarthy 4 21
(Mrs C A Dunnett) *prom: rdn along 3f out and sn wknd* 33/1

/0-0 12 1 1/2 **Ahaz**[6] [579] 5-8-3 46 oh1....PatrickMathers(3) 7 17
(J F Coupland) *chsd ldrs over 2f out: sn lost polace and bhd* 150/1

1m 31.26s (0.46) **Going Correction** -0.175s/f (Stan) 12 Ran SP% 114.1
Speed ratings (Par 101):90,88,84,84,83 83,79,76,75,75 74,72
CSF £28.59 CT £371.91 TOTE £4.90: £1.40, £2.70, £7.80; EX 30.70 Trifecta £197.50 Part won. Pool: £278.25 - 0.34 winning units..
Owner Multi Lines Partnership **Bred** Penfold Bloodstock And Mr D B Clark **Trained** Ullingswick, H'fords

FOCUS
A moderate handicap run in a time 0.73 seconds slower than the second division. Very ordinary form, rated through the runner-up.
Machinate(USA) Official explanation: trainer said, regarding the poor form shown, he felt gelding was unsuiited by the fibresand

626 CORAL AND TALKSPORT SUPPORTING THE NSPCC H'CAP 5f (F)

2:10 (2:10) (Class 5) (0-70,68) 4-Y-0+ £3,071 (£906; £453) Stalls High

Form RPR

3141 1 **Egyptian Lord**[12] [521] 4-9-2 68....(b) RobbieFitzpatrick 2 79+
(Peter Grayson) *in tch: hdwy 1/2-way: rdn wl over 1f out: styd on to ld ins last: eased nr fin* 9/2[2]

-502 2 1/2 **Stoneacre Boy (IRE)**[23] [432] 4-9-1 67....(b) AdamKirby 6 76
(Peter Grayson) *prom: cl up 1/2-way: rdn to ld opver 1f out: drvn and hdd ins last: kpt on* 13/2[3]

2160 3 hd **Cerebus**[13] [513] 5-8-8 63....(bt) StephenDonohoe(3) 5 71+
(A J McCabe) *dwlt: hld up and bhd: hdwy 2f out and sn ridde: drvn ent last: styd on strly* 9/1

1344 4 1 1/2 **Kempsey**[9] [561] 5-8-7 66 ow3....(b) RyanBird(7) 3 69
(J J Bridger) *in tch: hdwy 2f out: sn rdn and kpt on same pce fnl f* 14/1

540- 5 2 **Princess Cleo**[166] [5493] 4-9-1 67....DavidAllan 4 63
(T D Easterby) *prom: rdn along 2f out: grad wknd* 16/1

4332 6 1/2 **Garlogs**[12] [521] 4-8-4 56....JimmyQuinn 8 50
(A Bailey) *led: rdn along 2f out: drvn and hdd over 1f out: grad wknd* 5/2[1]

250- 7 shd **Pamir (IRE)**[91] [6709] 5-9-2 68....(b) JimCrowley 1 62
(P R Chamings) *chsd ldrs on outer: rdn along 2f out: grad wknd* 9/1

0000 8 1/2 **Anfield Dream**[19] [465] 5-8-6 65....WilliamBuick(7) 11 57
(J R Jenkins) *a towards rr* 8/1

-063 9 1 **Estoille**[12] [523] 6-8-2 54 oh9....PaulFessey 7 43
(Mrs S Lamyman) *cl up: rdn along over 2f out: sn drvn and wknd wl over 1f out* 40/1

6026 10 4 **Hornpipe**[12] [521] 5-8-6 58....AdrianMcCarthy 9 33
(M S Saunders) *sn outpcd and bhd fr 1/2-way* 16/1

5400 11 7 **Sands Crooner (IRE)**[18] [480] 4-9-1 67....(v) NCallan 10 19
(D Shaw) *dwlt: a towards rr* 20/1

59.04 secs (-1.26) **Going Correction** -0.175s/f (Stan) 11 Ran SP% 116.8
Speed ratings (Par 103):103,102,101,99,96 95,95,94,92,86 75
CSF £33.70 CT £254.10 TOTE £5.90: £2.10, £1.90, £4.20; EX 19.60 Trifecta £183.30 Pool: £330.53 - 1.28 winning units..
Owner D & R Rhodes & Mrs S Grayson **Bred** I A N Wight And Mrs D M Wight **Trained** Formby, Lancs

FOCUS
A modest sprint handicap won by the progressive Egyptian Lord. The runner-up ran to his recent level with the fourth.

627 CORAL AND TALKSPORT SUPPORTING CHILDREN 1ST H'CAP (DIV II) 7f (F)

2:40 (2:41) (Class 6) (0-52,52) 4-Y-0+ £1,706 (£503; £252) Stalls Low

Form RPR

00-0 1 **Government (IRE)**[12] [524] 6-8-1 46 oh1....NicolPolli(5) 2 53
(M C Chapman) *led: rdn along and hdd over 2f out: drvn and rallied ent last: led last 100 yds* 66/1

640- 2 1 1/4 **Hiats**[84] [6796] 5-8-7 47....PaulFessey 3 51
(R Craggs) *cl up: effrt to ld over 2f out: rdn wl over 1f out: drvn ent last: hdd and no ex last 100 yds* 40/1

-530 3 3/4 **Solicitude**[13] [517] 4-8-11 51....(p) RobertHavlin 5 53
(D Haydn Jones) *trckd ldrs: pushed along and outpcd over 2f out: sn rdn: styd on u.p ins last: nrst fin* 6/1[3]

50-2 4 nk **Champion's Way (IRE)**[9] [557] 5-8-6 46 oh1....JimCrowley 6 47
(B R Millman) *s.i.s: hdwy on inner 3f out: rdn to chse ldrs wl over 1f out: sn drvn and kpt on same pce* 13/2

6-00 5 3/4 **Barzak (IRE)**[21] [448] 7-8-6 46 oh1....(bt) JimmyQuinn 4 45
(S R Bowring) *prom: effrt and cl up on outer over 2f out: sn rdn and wknd over 1f out* 14/1

-560 6 1 1/4 **Cool Tiger**[10] [548] 4-8-10 50....AlanDaly 8 46
(P Howling) *trckd ldrs: effrt over 2f out: sn rdn and hung lft wl over 1f out: sn btn* 16/1

4532 7 1/2 **Seldemosa**[12] [519] 6-8-9 49 ow1....(b[1]) NCallan 1 44
(M S Saunders) *s.i.s: sn trcking ldrs: effrt and ev ch 2f out: rdn: squeezed out and swtchd rt over 1f out: drvn and sn btn* 9/2[1]

-005 8 hd **Merdiff**[22] [447] 8-8-1 46 oh1....DuranFentiman(5) 11 40
(W M Brisbourne) *a rr* 16/1

0-24 9 nk **Kumakawa**[6] [579] 9-8-3 48....WilliamBuick(5) 12 41
(N P Littmoden) *sn rdn along and a rr* 11/2[2]

0052 10 nk **Shadow Jumper (IRE)**[6] [579] 6-7-13 46 oh1....(v) DavidProbert(7) 7 38
(J T Stimpson) *a rr* 8/1

4453 11 3/4 **Grafton (IRE)**[14] [504] 4-8-9 49....(p) DavidAllan 9 39
(J O'Reilly) *chsd ldrs: hdwy wl over 2f out: sn rdn and wknd wl over 1f out* 15/2

-010 12 19 **Wayward Shot (IRE)**[12] [524] 5-8-12 52....PaulMulrennan 10 —
(M W Easterby) *a rr* 8/1

1m 30.53s (-0.27) **Going Correction** -0.175s/f (Stan) 12 Ran SP% 117.5
Speed ratings (Par 101):94,92,91,91,90 89,88,88,87,87 86,65
CSF £1625.84 CT £16817.31 TOTE £90.00: £19.30, £12.80, £2.80; EX 849.00 TRIFECTA Not won..
Owner James Gordon-Hall **Bred** C H Wacker Iii **Trained** Market Rasen, Lincs

FOCUS
A moderate handicap, but the winning time was 0.73 seconds quicker than the first division. Similarly modest form.
Government(IRE) Official explanation: trainer said, regarding apparent improvement in form, the gelding is a spring horse and appears to be coming to himself at present
Kumakawa Official explanation: jockey said gelding never travelled
Wayward Shot(IRE) Official explanation: jockey said gelding hung left throughout

628 CORAL AND TALKSPORT SUPPORTING THE NSPCC CLAIMING STKS 1m 6f (F)

3:10 (3:10) (Class 6) 4-Y-0+ £2,184 (£644; £322) Stalls Low

Form RPR

/306 1 **Al Moulatham**[19] [464] 8-9-1 56....(bt) SamHitchcott 1 66
(R Ford) *trckd ldr: led after 2f: clr over 3f out: rdn and hung lft 2f out: unchal* 12/1

222/ 2 9 **Mr Mischief**[393] [2338] 7-9-9 86....LeeEnstone 7 62+
(P C Haslam) *hld up in mid-div: hdwy over 4f out: wnt 2nd over 3f out: hung lft: no imp* 2/1[2]

000- 3 3 **Arcangela**[10] [5618] 4-8-4 48....SilvestreDeSousa 5 42
(Miss Tracy Waggott) *mid-div: drvn 7f out: kpt on to take modest 3rd over 1f out* 40/1

1030 4 15 **Tiegs (IRE)**[19] [464] 5-8-5 45....MarcHalford(3) 3 21
(P W Hiatt) *trckd ldrs: wnt 2nd over 4f out: wknd 2f out* 14/1

0-00 5 1 1/2 **Zaville**[26] [389] 5-8-11 60....(b[1]) JamesO'Reilly(7) 4 29
(J O'Reilly) *chsd ldrs: wknd over 2f out* 11/1

0 6 6 **Overfields**[4] [603] 7-8-10....NeilChalmers(3) 11 16
(G J Smith) *in rr: sn pushed along: nvr on terms* 50/1

3030 7 10 **Isa'Af (IRE)**[6] [585] 8-8-6 45....JackMitchell(7) 2 2
(P W Hiatt) *in rr and sn drvn along: nvr on terms* 11/2[3]

00-0 8 8 **College Rebel**[35] [302] 6-9-2 43....MickyFenton 6 —
(J F Coupland) *led 2f: lost pl over 4f out: sn bhd* 40/1

60/0 9 39 **Prairie Law (GER)**[13] [514] 7-9-2 47 ow10....(e) TomMessenger(5) 8 —
(B N Pollock) *in rr: t.o 6f out* 40/1

215- 10 118 **Kristensen**[187] [4951] 8-9-7 67....(v) JamieSpencer 9 —
(Karen McLintock) *hld up in rr: effrt on outside over 6f out: sn rdn and lost pl: t.o 4f out: virtually p.u over 2f out* 7/4[1]

3m 6.42s (-3.18) **Going Correction** -0.175s/f (Stan)
WFA 4 from 5yo+ 4lb 10 Ran SP% 117.1
Speed ratings (Par 101):102,96,95,86,85 82,76,72,49,—
CSF £36.02 TOTE £12.40: £2.60, £1.10, £8.30; EX 70.50 Trifecta £474.90 Part won. Pool: £668.99 - 0.34 winning units..
Owner Tarporley Turf Club and Keith Hesketh **Bred** Gainsborough Stud Management Ltd **Trained** Cotebrook, Cheshire

FOCUS
A moderate claimer, but it was run at a good pace throughout and they finished well strung out. The form is far from solid, though, based on the below-par performances of the first two in the market and by the fair effort of the third.
Kristensen Official explanation: vet said gelding returned injured

629 CORAL SUPPORTING THE NSPCC H'CAP 1m (F)

3:40 (3:40) (Class 4) (0-85,85) 4-Y-0+ £4,857 (£1,445; £722; £360) Stalls Low

Form RPR

-651 1 **Dichoh**[21] [451] 4-8-9 78....NCallan 7 95+
(M A Jarvis) *trckd ldrs gng wl: smooth hdwy 2f out: led wl over 1f out: rdn and hung lft ins last: styd on* 7/4[1]

0331 2 1 3/4 **Councellor (FR)**[12] [525] 5-8-9 78....(t) MickyFenton 2 91
(Stef Liddiard) *in tch on inner: hdwy over 2f out: rdn and ev ch over 1f out: sn drvn and one pce ins last* 13/2

/14- 3 1 1/4 **Baizically (IRE)**[274] [2290] 4-9-2 85....JamieSpencer 12 95
(J A Osborne) *stdd s: keen and hld up in rr: gd hdwy on outer 2f out: rdn and one pce ent last* 9/2[2]

6-52 4 3 **Byron Bay**[21] [451] 5-8-13 82....TonyCulhane 11 86
(I Semple) *hld up in tch: hdwy over 2f out: n.m.rn wl overe 1f out: kpt on ins last* 6/1[3]

610- 5 nk **Royal Dignitary (USA)**[171] [5355] 7-9-2 85....SilvestreDeSousa 3 88
(D Nicholls) *prom: rdn along 2f out: drvn and wknd over 1f out* 33/1

0060 6 3 1/2 **Tyzack (IRE)**[14] [509] 6-7-12 72....DuranFentiman(5) 13 68
(W M Brisbourne) *midfield: hdwy over 2f out: sn rdn and no imp* 33/1

05-5 7 1 1/2 **Glenbuck (IRE)**[14] [509] 4-8-7 76....(v) JoeFanning 4 69
(A Bailey) *mde most: rdn along over 2f out: drvn and hdd wl over 1f out: grad wknd* 10/1

4035 8 1 **Speed Dial Harry (IRE)**[21] [451] 5-8-4 73....(v) RichardThomas 9 64
(C R Dore) *a rr* 16/1

100- 9 1 1/4 **Surwaki (USA)**[102] [6580] 5-8-8 77....BrettDoyle 8 65
(R M H Cowell) *cl up: rdn along over 2f out and sn wknd* 40/1

-51P 10 nk **Daring Affair**[21] [451] 6-8-6 82....WilliamBuick(7) 6 70
(K R Burke) *s.i.s: a rr* 9/1

0-34 **11** *nk* **Namroud (USA)**[12] [525] 8-8-2 **71** oh2............................(p) DaleGibson 10 58
(R A Fahey) *sn rdn along and a rr* **20/1**
20-1 **12** *29* **Just James**[64] [2] 8-8-5 **74**.. AdrianTNicholls 1 —
(D Nicholls) *a rr* **25/1**
00-0 **13** *1 3/4* **Polonius**[4] [608] 6-8-8 **80**.. NeilChalmers(3) 14 2
(G J Smith) *chsd ldrs on outer: rdn along over 3f out and sn wknd* **50/1**
1m 41.08s (-3.52) **Going Correction** -0.175s/f (Stan) **13** Ran SP% **126.0**
Speed ratings (Par 105):110,108,107,104,103 100,98,97,96,96 95,66,65
CSF £13.14 CT £50.58 TOTE £3.00: £1.70, £2.60, £1.90; EX 16.60 Trifecta £62.70 Pool: £461.53, 5.22 winning units.
Owner T G Warner **Bred** Red House Stud **Trained** Newmarket, Suffolk
■ Stewards' Enquiry : N Callan caution: careless riding
FOCUS
This looked a fair race and has been positively rated. The winner is progressive, with the second running his best race to date.
Surwaki(USA) Official explanation: jockey said gelding hung right
Just James Official explanation: jockey said gelding had no more to give

630 CORAL AND TALKSPORT SUPPORTING THE NSPCC (S) STKS 1m 3f (F)
4:10 (4:12) (Class 6) 4-6-Y-O **£2,184** (£644; £322) **Stalls** Low

Form RPR
3004 **1** **Bridgewater Boys**[11] [533] 6-8-11 64....................................(p) NCallan 2 63
(K A Ryan) *trckd ldr: led over 3f out: rdn end edgd rt over 1f out: kpt on wl* **7/4**[1]
031- **2** *1 1/4* **Starcross Maid**[242] [3260] 5-8-6 51................................ AdrianTNicholls 5 56
(J F Coupland) *prom: hdwy to chse wnr over 2f out: chal 1f out: no ex* **11/2**[3]
6- **3** *1* **Benny The Rascal (IRE)**[200] [4549] 5-8-11 .... JimmyQuinn 4 59
(J Pearce) *chsd ldrs: kpt on same pce fnl 2f* **16/1**
160- **4** *7* **Bariloche**[185] [5022] 4-8-10 73...(be) PatCosgrave 8 47
(J R Boyle) *chsd ldrs: sn drvn along: outpcd fnl 3f* **5/2**[2]
5-06 **5** *hd* **Ronnies Lad**[53] [109] 5-8-11 41.................................... PaulMulrennan 14 47
(J R Norton) *in rr: kpt on fnl 3f: nvr a factor* **33/1**
0 **6** *5* **Exit Fast (USA)**[19] [464] 6-8-11 ....(p) MickyFenton 10 39
(P T Midgley) *bhd: kpt on fnl 3f: nvr on terms* **66/1**
006- **7** *8* **Night Reveller (IRE)**[90] [6731] 4-8-0 28....................................... NicolPolli(5) 3 20
(M C Chapman) *led tl over 3f out: sn lost pl* **66/1**
005- **8** *1 3/4* **Gavanello**[50] [6973] 4-8-7 35..................................(t) StephenDonohoe(3) 13 22
(M C Chapman) *prom: drvn 5f out: sn btn* **20/1**
00-0 **9** *3* **Zizou (IRE)**[30] [187] 4-8-10 36..(t) TPQueally 7 17
(J J Bridger) *prom: drvn 6f out: lost pl over 4f out* **25/1**
0-64 **10** *5* **Daneway**[13] [514] 4-8-5 50...(b) DaleGibson 12 3
(P Howling) *s.i.s: hdwy on outer over 7f out: lost pl 4f out* **10/1**
2-05 **11** *8* **Hippolyte (USA)**[19] [466] 4-8-5 42.. JoeFanning 6 —
(J G Given) *a in rr* **20/1**
052/ **12** *7* **Fire At Will**[689] [1065] 5-8-11 .... RichardThomas 9 —
(A W Carroll) *chsd ldrs: drvn over 6f out: lost pl over 4f out* **14/1**
13 *8* **Rosy Anne**[20] 5-8-6 .... PaulFessey 11 —
(J R Turner) *s.i.s: sme hdwy on outer over 6f out: sn lost pl* **66/1**
00/ **14** *34* **One For Gretta (IRE)**[587] [3850] 5-7-13 38..................... PaulPickard(7) 1 —
(J Hetherton) *prom: lost pl over 5f out: t.o 3f out* **66/1**
2m 26.78s (-2.12) **Going Correction** -0.175s/f (Stan)
WFA 4 from 5yo+ 1lb **14** Ran SP% **124.2**
Speed ratings: 100,99,98,93,93 89,83,82,80,76 70,65,59,35
CSF £11.23 TOTE £3.20: £1.20, £2.20, £4.30; EX 15.10 Trifecta £55.50 Pool: £330.12, 4.22 winning units.The winner was bought in for 4,600gns
Owner Bishopthorpe Racing **Bred** Southill Stud **Trained** Hambleton, N Yorks
FOCUS
An uncompetitive race on paper in which only a couple could be given a chance. Weak form, the winner 8lb off his best effort this year.
Bariloche Official explanation: jockey said colt hung left throughout
Gavanello Official explanation: jockey said gelding hung left throughout

631 CORAL SUPPORTING CHILDREN 1ST H'CAP 1m 4f (F)
4:40 (4:40) (Class 6) (0-65,65) 4-Y-0+ **£3,071** (£906; £453) **Stalls** Low

Form RPR
54-1 **1** **Muntami (IRE)**[14] [508] 6-8-12 **62**........................... StephenDonohoe(3) 9 74+
(John A Harris) *hld up towards rr: stdy hdwy over 4f out: rdn to ld wl over 1f out: clr ins last* **15/2**
-152 **2** *4* **Bolckow**[14] [503] 4-8-13 **62**... MickyFenton 1 68
(J T Stimpson) *a.p: effrt and ev ch over 2f out: sn rdn and kpt on same pce ent last* **13/2**[3]
05-3 **3** *1 1/2* **Sand Repeal (IRE)**[6] [585] 5-9-1 **62**..................................(v) BrettDoyle 5 66
(Miss J Feilden) *a.p: effrt to ld over 2f out: sn rdn and hdd wl over 1f out: kpt on same pce* **11/4**[1]
2031 **4** *1 1/4* **Mahmjra**[14] [503] 5-9-1 **62**.. PFredericks 12 64
(C N Allen) *trckd ldrs: hdwy 4f out: rdn and ch over 2f out: sn drvn and one pce* **6/1**[2]
064- **5** *nk* **Garibaldi (GER)**[105] [6560] 5-8-5 **59**........................... JamesO'Reilly(7) 10 60
(J O'Reilly) *cl up: led after 3f: rdn along over 3f out: hdd over 2f out and grad wknd* **16/1**
0-15 **6** *1* **Tioga Gold (IRE)**[49] [146] 8-7-11 **51** oh3..................... WilliamBuick(7) 4 51
(L R James) *bhd: rdn along 4f out: styd on fnl 2f: nvr a factor* **25/1**
0-65 **7** *hd* **Waterloo Corner**[28] [377] 5-8-13 **60**...................................(v[1]) PaulFessey 8 59
(R Craggs) *dwlt: towards rr: effrt and sme hdwy 4f out: sn rdn along and n.d* **25/1**
-000 **8** *1/2* **Takes Tutu (USA)**[26] [389] 8-8-7 **54**..................................... TPQueally 13 52
(C R Dore) *hld up towards rr: hdwy on outer over 4f out: rdn along to chse ldrs 3f out: sn drvn and btn* **25/1**
00-0 **9** *1/2* **Monmouthshire**[22] [445] 4-7-11 **51** oh1...................... DuranFentiman(5) 7 49
(R J Price) *a rr* **50/1**
0120 **10** *9* **Greenbelt**[21] [453] 6-9-4 **65**.. NCallan 3 48
(G M Moore) *chsd ldrs: rdn along 4f out: drvn 3f out and wknd fnl 2f* **15/2**
1-20 **11** *11* **Little Richard (IRE)**[13] [515] 8-8-13 **60**..............................(p) AdamKirby 2 26
(M Wellings) *chsd ldrs: rdn along 5f out: sn wknd* **20/1**
0-04 **12** *1* **Makai**[5] [594] 4-8-11 **63**...(b) AmirQuinn(3) 6 27
(J J Bridger) *chsd ldrs: rdn along over 4f out: sn wknd* **16/1**
623- **13** *91* **Northerner (IRE)**[307] [1424] 4-8-7 **56**................................ DavidAllan 11 —
(J O'Reilly) *led 3f: cl up tl rdn along over 5f out and sn wknd* **9/1**
2m 37.88s (-4.21) **Going Correction** -0.175s/f (Stan)
WFA 4 from 5yo+ 2lb **13** Ran SP% **117.8**
Speed ratings (Par 101):107,104,103,102,102 101,101,101,100,94 87,86,26
CSF £50.99 CT £169.27 TOTE £9.30: £2.50, £2.30, £1.30; EX 44.60 Trifecta £178.90 Pool: £418.35, 1.66 winning units.
Owner Dermot Owens **Bred** Shadwell Estate Company Limited **Trained** Eastwell, Leics
■ Stewards' Enquiry : T P Queally caution: careless riding. caution: used whip down shoulder in forehand position

FOCUS
A competitive enough race on paper, but the progressive Muntami could not have done it much easier. The form makes sense through the first five but the sixth and ninth hold down the form a little.
Takes Tutu(USA) Official explanation: jockey said gelding hung right
Greenbelt Official explanation: jockey said gelding never travelled
Little Richard(IRE) Official explanation: jockey said gelding could not face the kickback
Makai Official explanation: jockey said gelding lost its action

632 CORAL SUPPORTS NSPCC AND CHILDREN 1ST H'CAP 6f (F)
5:10 (5:11) (Class 6) (0-50,52) 4-Y-0+ **£2,388** (£705; £352) **Stalls** Low

Form RPR
4451 **1** **Blythe Spirit**[6] [586] 8-8-9 **52** 6ex.............................(v) JamieMoriarty(5) 10 67
(R A Fahey) *trckd ldrs: hung lft and led over 1f out: hld on towards fin* **3/1**[1]
02-0 **2** *1 1/4* **Wolfman**[6] [586] 5-8-11 **49**...(p) NCallan 7 60
(D W Barker) *chsd ldrs: kpt on to take 2nd ins last: no ex* **12/1**
5262 **3** *1* **Favouring (IRE)**[6] [580] 5-8-4 **49** ow1..........................(v) SCreighton(7) 12 57
(M C Chapman) *chsd ldrs: kpt on same pce appr fnl f* **5/1**[2]
4541 **4** *2* **Christian Bendix**[12] [524] 5-8-12 **50**...............................(p) JimmyQuinn 1 52
(P Howling) *led tl hdd over 1f out: one pce* **9/1**
-002 **5** *1 1/4* **Alistair John**[12] [523] 4-8-8 **46** oh1................................ J-PGuillambert 5 44
(Mrs G S Rees) *prom: kpt on same pce fnl 2f* **9/1**
0043 **6** *1/2* **Piccleyes**[6] [586] 6-8-8 **46** oh1.......................................(b) DeanMcKeown 9 43
(A J McCabe) *mid-div: hdwy over 2f out: styd onf fnl f* **6/1**[3]
0000 **7** *1 1/2* **Alucica**[12] [523] 4-8-8 **46** oh1.......................................(v) AdrianMcCarthy 2 38
(D Shaw) *s.i.s: sn prom: one pce fnl 2f* **80/1**
0355 **8** *2 1/2* **Danethorpe (IRE)**[12] [519] 4-8-8 **46** oh1.................(v) CatherineGannon 4 31
(D Shaw) *mid-div: outpcd over 3f out: n.d after* **12/1**
3-05 **9** *shd* **Union Jack Jackson (IRE)**[40] [241] 5-8-7 **48**.(p) StephenDonohoe(3) 11 32
(John A Harris) *in rr: outpcd 4f out* **12/1**
0003 **10** *1* **Far Note (USA)**[6] [581] 9-8-8 **46** oh1.................................(bt) DaleGibson 6 27
(S R Bowring) *in rr: outpcde over 3f out* **20/1**
00-0 **11** *3* **Lizzie Rocket**[36] [296] 7-8-8 **46** oh1....................................(v) DavidAllan 3 18
(J O'Reilly) *swvd lft s: nvr a factor* **66/1**
-040 **12** *nk* **Saintly Place**[22] [440] 6-8-1 **46** oh1............................ WilliamBuick(7) 13 18
(A W Carroll) *chsd ldrs: lost pl over 2f out* **25/1**
0200 **13** *5* **Midmaar (IRE)**[22] [440] 6-8-12 **50**.......................................(b) JamieSpencer 8 7
(M Wigham) *in rr: effrt on outer over 2f out: hung rt and sn wknd: eased fnl f* **8/1**
6-30 **14** *21* **Dancing Beauty (IRE)**[33] [320] 5-8-8 **46** oh1............(p) SamHitchcott 14 —
(T T Clement) *towards rr: effrt on wd outside over 2f out: sn lost pl: heavily eased* **50/1**
1m 15.57s (-1.33) **Going Correction** -0.175s/f (Stan) **14** Ran SP% **123.4**
Speed ratings (Par 101):101,99,98,95,93 93,91,87,87,86 82,81,75,47
CSF £40.66 CT £182.79 TOTE £4.00: £1.20, £5.30, £2.20; EX 51.70 Trifecta £434.40 Part won. Pool: £611.92 - 0.68 winning units. Place 6 £ 173.17, Place 5 £ 65.55.
Owner The Matthewman Partnership **Bred** W Haggas & W Jarvis **Trained** Musley Bank, N Yorks
FOCUS
A modest event but the form looks above-average for the grade. Blythe Spirit has revived since being fitted with a visor and improved on his latest win here.
Midmaar(IRE) Official explanation: trainer said gelding had bled from the nose
T/Jkpt: Not won. T/Plt: £171.10 to a £1 stake. Pool: £86,436.30. 368.65 winning tickets. T/Qpdt: £27.90 to a £1 stake. Pool: £6,151.60. 163.00 winning tickets. JR

[610]LINGFIELD (L-H)
Wednesday, March 7

OFFICIAL GOING: Standard
Wind: moderate, half-behind Weather: fine

633 RIVER BELLE ONLINE BINGO MAIDEN STKS (DIV I) 7f (P)
1:30 (1:31) (Class 5) 3-Y-0 **£2,388** (£705; £352) **Stalls** Low

Form RPR
22 **1** **Daytona (IRE)**[9] [567] 3-9-3 .... JoeFanning 2 85+
(M Johnston) *led for 1f: trckd ldr: clr of rest 3f out: led over 2f out and sn drew away: eased nr fin: comf* **10/11**[1]
00- **2** *2* **Tetouan**[159] [5659] 3-9-3 .... SteveDrowne 8 74+
(R Charlton) *off the pce in midfield: prog over 2f out: rdn and r.o fr over 1f out to take 2nd last stride* **20/1**
03-3 **3** *shd* **Nicomedia (IRE)**[63] [27] 3-8-12 67.............................. RichardHughes 6 69
(R Hannon) *chsd ldng pair: rdn and outpcd 3f out: styd on to chse wnr 1f out: kpt on but no imp: lost 2nd last stride* **15/2**[3]
0-6 **4** *5* **The Dagger**[18] [489] 3-9-0 .... StephaneBreux(3) 4 61
(J R Best) *wl in rr: outpcd fr 1/2-way: rdn and wd bnd 2f out: styd on over 1f out: no ch* **66/1**
05- **5** *3* **Rebel Pearl (IRE)**[110] [6504] 3-8-12 .... TPQueally 1 48+
(M G Quinlan) *chsd ldrs: rdn and outpcd 3f out: steadily fdd* **25/1**
3-23 **6** *shd* **L'Oiseau De Feu (USA)**[9] [569] 3-9-3 75..................(v[1]) JamieSpencer 5 53
(E A L Dunlop) *led after 1f: clr w wnr 3f out: hdd over 2f out: relucant and btn after: wknd rapidly and lost 2nd 1f out* **11/4**[2]
7 *3/4* **High Profit (IRE)** 3-9-3 .... AntonyProcter 3 51
(D R C Elsworth) *s.s: in tch in rr to 1/2-way: wl outpcd sn after: styd on inner and no prog fnl 2f* **8/1**
45 **8** *nk* **Toms Laughter**[13] [522] 3-9-3 .... DaleGibson 9 50
(B Palling) *chsd ldng trio: rdn and outpcd 3f out: sn struggling* **66/1**
0 **9** *17* **Inchwall**[37] [295] 3-9-3 .... GeorgeBaker 10 —
(Peter Grayson) *s.i.s: detached in last pair after 3f: t.o* **66/1**
10 *9* **King Canute (IRE)**[136] [6116] 3-9-3 .... PatCosgrave 7 —
(M J Wallace) *s.s: a last and sn struggling: t.o 1/2-way* **33/1**
1m 23.98s (-1.91) **Going Correction** -0.05s/f (Stan) **10** Ran SP% **118.0**
Speed ratings (Par 98):108,105,105,99,96 96,95,95,75,65
CSF £27.59 TOTE £1.80: £1.10, £5.20, £2.20; EX 22.20 Trifecta £117.90 Pool £368.95 - 2.22 winning units..
Owner Sheikh Mohammed **Bred** Irish National Stud **Trained** Middleham Moor, N Yorks
FOCUS
This was probably a decent maiden, backed up by the winning time which was 1.75 seconds faster than the second division. It has been rated positively and the winner was value for extra.
Inchwall Official explanation: jockey said gelding had no more to give

634 RIVER BELLE ONLINE CASINO CLAIMING STKS 1m 4f (P)
2:00 (2:00) (Class 6) 4-Y-0+ **£2,184** (£644; £322) **Stalls** Low

Form RPR
6-06 **1** **Zalkani (IRE)**[19] 482 7-9-5 57........ JimmyFortune 2 68
(J Pearce) *trckd ldrs: wnt 2nd wl over 1f out: chal on inner 1f out: drvn to ld last 100yds* **4/1**[2]
5060 **2** ¾ **First Friend (IRE)**[6] 594 6-9-9 63........ DarryllHolland 1 70
(P Mitchell) *led: set modest pce tl kicked on 3f out: rdn over 1f out: hdd and one pce last 100yds* **12/1**
105- **3** *nk* **Missie Baileys**[88] 6769 5-8-7 58........ JackMitchell(7) 8 61
(Mrs L J Mongan) *trckd ldng pair: lost pl and rdn over 3f out: styd on again fnl 2f: clsng grad nr fin* **8/1**
0-55 **4** *1* **Liberty Run (IRE)**[56] 89 5-9-5 65........ NCallan 7 64
(Mouse Hamilton-Fairley) *trckd ldr: rdn over 2f out: lost 2nd over 1f out: one pce* **11/4**[1]
0020 **5** ½ **Casablanca Minx (IRE)**[9] 568 4-8-11 66........(b) JamesDoyle(3) 6 61
(N P Littmoden) *t.k.h: hld up in tch: rdn over 2f out: hanging and fnd nil over 1f out* **10/1**
-304 **6** ½ **Monets Masterpiece (USA)**[21] 458 4-9-3 61........(be) GeorgeBaker 3 63
(G L Moore) *rrd s: hld up in last pair: effrt 3f out: rdn and fnd nil over 1f out: plugged on* **11/2**[3]
50-5 **7** *4* **Dumaran (IRE)**[13] 444 9-9-1 66........ TPQueally 10 52
(W J Musson) *t.k.h: trckd ldrs: rdn over 2f out: wknd over 1f out* **10/1**
-300 **8** *hd* **Undeterred**[2] 618 11-9-0 70........ AshleyHamblett(5) 9 56
(K J Burke) *hld up in last pair: lost tch wl over 3f out: n.d after* **15/2**

2m 36.48s (2.09) **Going Correction** -0.05s/f (Stan)
WFA 4 from 5yo+ 2lb **8 Ran SP% 110.8**
Speed ratings (Par 101):91,90,90,89,89 88,86,86
CSF £46.73 TOTE £4.80: £1.40, £4.30, £2.70; EX 56.30 TRIFECTA Not won..There was no bid for the winner. Dumaran was claimed by A Bateman for £8,000.
Owner Jeff Pearce **Bred** His Highness The Aga Khan's Studs S C **Trained** Newmarket, Suffolk
FOCUS
An open contest of its type, but it was run at an uneven pace. The runner-up and third ran to their recent level but the winner did not need to match his winter best.
Monets Masterpiece(USA) Official explanation: jockey said gelding missed the break
Undeterred Official explanation: jockey said gelding ran flat

635 RIVER BELLE ONLINE BINGO MAIDEN STKS (DIV II) 7f (P)
2:30 (2:32) (Class 5) 3-Y-0 **£2,388** (£705; £352) **Stalls** Low

Form RPR
420- **1** **Grand Lucre**[176] 5262 3-8-12 68........ EddieAhern 5 61
(J W Hills) *led over 5f out: mde rest: rdn over 1f out: edgd rt and flashed tail: kpt on wl* **11/2**[3]
00-6 **2** 1¼ **Alfresco**[16] 498 3-9-3 68........ PaulEddery 3 63
(Pat Eddery) *dwlt: sn trckd ldrs: effrt to chse wnr over 1f out: rdn and fnd little: a hld after* **5/4**[1]
00 **3** 2½ **Gee Ceffyl Bach**[18] 492 3-8-12........ EdwardCreighton 10 52
(M R Channon) *prom: disp 2nd fr over 3f out to over 1f out: fdd fnl f* **33/1**
4 *hd* **Mandalay Prince** 3-9-3........ TPQueally 6 56
(W J Musson) *dwlt: wl in rr: shkn up and effrt over 2f out: no real imp: kpt on* **20/1**
3-3 **5** *1* **Ravenna**[16] 498 3-8-12........ RichardHughes 4 48
(M P Tregoning) *t.k.h: led to over 5f out: pressed wnr: stl gng strly 2f out: rdn on inner anf folded tamely over 1f out* **11/4**[2]
0-0 **6** ½ **Bear Essential**[24] 429 3-9-3........ RobertHavlin 7 52?
(Mrs P N Dutfield) *t.k.h: in tch: chsng ldrs 2f out: wknd fnl f* **66/1**
0- **7** *5* **Doctor Ned**[193] 4801 3-9-3........ JimmyFortune 9 39
(N A Callaghan) *t.k.h: hld up in last trio: tried to cl on ldrs over 2f out : sn wknd* **14/1**
-220 **8** *nk* **Not Too Taxing**[35] 312 3-9-3 67........ PatDobbs 2 38
(R Hannon) *chsd ldrs tl wknd rapidly 2f out* **10/1**
9 *9* **Gypsum (IRE)** 3-9-0........ BenariodePaiva(3) 1 15+
(W R Swinburn) *snatched up after 2f: sn detached in last: t.o 1/2-way and green: fin full of running* **16/1**
10 *16* **Smiling Tiger** 3-9-3........ AntonyProcter 8 —
(M J Gingell) *dwlt: in touh for 3f: sn t.o* **80/1**

1m 25.73s (-0.16) **Going Correction** -0.05s/f (Stan) **10 Ran SP% 118.6**
Speed ratings (Par 98):98,96,93,93,92 91,86,85,75,57
CSF £12.71 TOTE £7.10: £1.60, £1.20, £7.80; EX 20.80 Trifecta £316.80 Part won. Pool: £446.29 - 0.10 winning units..
Owner Jerry Jamgotchian **Bred** New England Stud And Partners **Trained** Upper Lambourn, Berks
FOCUS
A poor maiden, much weaker than the first division - the winning time was 1.75 seconds slower - but there were still a couple of interesting performances for the future. The first two ran close to their marks but the form is far from solid.

636 RIVER BELLE ONLINE POKER H'CAP 7f (P)
3:00 (3:03) (Class 6) (0-60,60) 3-Y-0 **£2,388** (£705; £352) **Stalls** Low

Form RPR
6-00 **1** **Dance Of Dreams**[12] 535 3-9-1 60........ JamesDoyle(3) 9 61
(N P Littmoden) *pressed ldrs: upsides on outer 2f out: drvn to dispute ld fnl f: won on the nod* **12/1**
-202 **2** *shd* **Ranavalona**[8] 577 3-8-4 53........(v) WilliamBuick(7) 5 54
(A M Balding) *cl up: effrt and upsides 2f out: rdn and narrow ld jst over 1f out: pipped on the post* **9/2**[2]
50-5 **3** ½ **Hills Place**[30] 360 3-8-9 54........ StephaneBreux(3) 11 54
(J R Best) *dwlt: hld up in midfield: effrt 2f out: got through to chal on inner fnl f: nt qckn nr fin* **9/1**
600 **4** *nk* **Brave Jack (IRE)**[32] 343 3-9-2 58........ BrettDoyle 14 57+
(J R Best) *plld hrd: hld up and racd wd: shkn up over 2f out: hanging and looked struggling over 1f out: r.o wl fnl f* **8/1**
-600 **5** 1¼ **Rogers Lodger**[21] 456 3-9-1 57........ DaneO'Neill 7 53
(J Akehurst) *hld up bhd ldrs: gng strly over 2f out: rdn over 1f out: hanging and fnd nil: kpt on nr fin* **14/1**
-343 **6** ¾ **Calloff The Search**[12] 535 3-8-12 57........(p) SaleemGolam(3) 3 51
(W G M Turner) *pressed ldrs: n.m.r on inner 1/2-way and again over 1f out: fdd* **5/1**[3]
5-66 **7** ¾ **Brean Dot Com (IRE)**[13] 520 3-9-0 56........ RobertHavlin 1 48
(Mrs P N Dutfield) *dwlt: hld up in rr: last over 2f out: effrt towards inner over 1f out: shkn up and styd on: nvr nr ldrs* **25/1**
00-6 **8** *shd* **Avery**[26] 404 3-8-6 55........ HaddenFrost(7) 10 47
(R J Hodges) *disp ld to over 1f out: shkn up and fdd* **40/1**
223- **9** *nk* **Nou Camp**[81] 6839 3-9-1 57........ JimmyFortune 8 48
(N A Callaghan) *hld up in rr: stl there over 1f out: nt clr run and swtchd rt sn after: shuffled along and nvr nr ldrs* **4/1**[1]
500- **10** ½ **Shreddy Shrimpster**[125] 6311 3-8-11 53 ow1........ SteveDrowne 6 42
(A B Haynes) *racd on inner: disp ld to over 1f out: wknd and eased* **20/1**
0-40 **11** 1½ **Caj (IRE)**[28] 382 3-9-4 60........(b[1]) EddieAhern 4 46
(Luke Comer, Ire) *hld up in rr: gng wl but plenty to do over 1f out: reminders and no prog fnl f: nvr nr ldrs* **25/1**
0-06 **12** ¾ **Beck**[29] 373 3-8-10 52........ JamieSpencer 2 36
(W M Brisbourne) *hld up towards rr: effrt on inner wl over 1f out: no prog whn nt clr run ins fnl f* **8/1**
4002 **13** *1* **Totally Free**[22] 454 3-8-9 58........(v) FrankiePickard(7) 13 39
(M D I Usher) *plld hrd: bdly bmpd after 1f: a in rr after* **14/1**

1m 26.94s (1.05) **Going Correction** -0.05s/f (Stan) **13 Ran SP% 123.0**
Speed ratings (Par 96):92,91,91,90,89 88,87,87,87,86 85,84,83
CSF £64.45 CT £544.88 TOTE £16.10: £4.30, £2.20, £3.70; EX 92.40 TRIFECTA Not won..
Owner Peter Webb **Bred** West Lodge Stud **Trained** Newmarket, Suffolk
FOCUS
A moderate three-year-old handicap. The early pace was ordinary and this was much the slowest of the three course-and-distance races.
Nou Camp Official explanation: jockey said gelding ran too free

637 RIVER BELLE'S FANTASTIC AUCTIONS H'CAP 1m (P)
3:35 (3:35) (Class 6) (0-52,52) 4-Y-0+ **£2,184** (£644; £322) **Stalls** High

Form RPR
-551 **1** **Postmaster**[14] 517 5-8-11 51........ RobertHavlin 7 57
(R Ingram) *stmbld s: hld up in rr: stdy prog fr 2f out: rdn to ld last 100yds: styd on* **11/2**[3]
5325 **2** ½ **Height Of Spirits**[31] 350 5-8-6 46 oh1........ EdwardCreighton 6 51
(T D McCarthy) *hld up in last pair: rdn 2f out: hanging over 1f out: r.o wl fnl f: gaining at fin* **11/1**
3306 **3** *hd* **Fulvio (USA)**[23] 440 7-8-10 50........(v) J-PGuillambert 5 54
(P Howling) *trckd ldr: rdn to ld over 1f out: hdd and one pce last 100yds* **10/1**
2222 **4** *1* **Over To You Bert**[26] 402 8-8-3 50 ow2........ HaddenFrost(7) 3 52
(R J Hodges) *t.k.h: hld up bhd ldrs: effrt on inner 2f out: cl enough 1f out: one pce* **4/1**[1]
6014 **5** *hd* **Mid Valley**[13] 519 4-8-12 52........(v) NCallan 2 54
(J R Jenkins) *hld up in midfield: clsd on ldrs over 1f out: drvn and nt qckn fnl f* **8/1**
10-0 **6** ½ **Danettie**[19] 479 6-8-12 52........ EddieAhern 12 52
(W M Brisbourne) *led at gd clip: hdd and fdd over 1f out* **13/2**
0-02 **7** 1¾ **Balerno**[23] 440 8-8-11 51........ PaulEddery 10 47
(Mrs L J Mongan) *hld up bhd ldrs: hrd rdn 2f out: no prog over 1f out: fdd* **5/1**[2]
-100 **8** ½ **Charlottebutterfly**[28] 383 7-8-7 47........ BrettDoyle 11 42
(P J McBride) *hld up towards rr: rdn and effrt on outer 2f out: sn no prog* **14/1**
-020 **9** ½ **Princess Arwen**[10] 557 5-8-6 46 oh1........(b) LPKeniry 4 40
(Mrs Barbara Waring) *pressed ldng pair: chal and upsides 2f out: wknd fnl f* **25/1**
0-00 **10** 3½ **Russian Mist (IRE)**[35] 313 4-8-10 50........(v[1]) JamieSpencer 1 36
(M J Wallace) *t.k.h: hld up in midfield: lost pl over 2f out: n.d after* **9/1**
06-0 **11** *3* **Useful**[25] 416 4-8-6 46........(p) SamHitchcott 9 25
(A B Haynes) *v s.i.s: a in rr: struggling 2f out* **33/1**

1m 38.51s (-0.92) **Going Correction** -0.05s/f (Stan) **11 Ran SP% 117.4**
Speed ratings (Par 101):102,101,101,100,100 99,97,97,96,93 90
CSF £64.55 CT £593.39 TOTE £6.60: £2.30, £2.90, £3.00; EX 78.00 Trifecta £274.70 Part won. Pool: £386.98 - 0.34 winning units..
Owner Cricketers Club Racing Group **Bred** Juddmonte Farms **Trained** Epsom, Surrey
FOCUS
A very moderate race, but they went a decent pace and that played into the hands of the winner. The race has been rated through the runner-up and the fifth.
Russian Mist(IRE) Official explanation: jockey said gelding hung badly both ways

638 RIVER BELLE'S CASH BACK POINTS H'CAP 1m 2f (P)
4:05 (4:07) (Class 4) (0-85,85) 3-Y-0 **£4,857** (£1,445; £722; £360) **Stalls** Low

Form RPR
3-22 **1** **Man Of Vision (USA)**[19] 484 3-8-9 76........ TonyCulhane 6 84
(M R Channon) *trcked ldng pair: rdn over 2f out: r.o to ld last 150yds: in command after* **9/2**[3]
1- **2** 1¼ **Serengeti**[82] 6832 3-8-12 79........ JoeFanning 2 84
(M Johnston) *dwlt: rapid prog to ld over 8f out: rdn and hdd over 3f out: led again over 2f out: hdd last 150yds: kpt on* **9/2**[3]
1243 **3** *shd* **Six Shots**[10] 563 3-8-10 77........ JamieSpencer 8 82
(J A Osborne) *hld up in tch: effrt 2f out: rdn and nt qckn wl over 1f out: styd on fnl f to press for 2nd nr fin* **8/1**
01-6 **4** 3½ **Lazy Darren**[54] 111 3-8-12 79........ PatDobbs 5 77
(R Hannon) *hld up towards rr: nudged along and kpt on same pce fnl 2f: nvr nr ldrs* **33/1**
-412 **5** *1* **Professor Twinkle**[6] 591 3-8-4 71........ PaulDoe 7 67
(W J Knight) *led at slow pce to over 8f out: pressed ldr: led over 3f out to over 2f out: wknd over 1f out* **7/2**[2]
1 **6** *2* **Aajel (USA)**[28] 386 3-9-4 85........ RichardHughes 1 77
(M P Tregoning) *stmbld s: sn trckd ldrs: shkn up 3f out: no prog 2f out: wknd* **11/4**[1]
3-10 **7** *2* **Highland Harvest**[47] 184 3-8-11 78........ DaneO'Neill 4 66
(D R C Elsworth) *plld very hrd early: hld up in tch: wknd 2f out* **12/1**
-324 **8** ½ **Copper King**[19] 483 3-8-6 76........ StephenDonohoe(3) 3 63
(P D Evans) *hld up and sn last: lost tch 3f out: kpt on fnl f* **20/1**

2m 7.95s (0.16) **Going Correction** -0.05s/f (Stan) **8 Ran SP% 111.8**
Speed ratings (Par 100):97,96,95,93,92 90,89,88
CSF £23.82 CT £152.72 TOTE £5.50: £1.50, £1.70, £2.80; EX 27.30 Trifecta £126.80 Pool: £750.57 - 4.20 winning units..
Owner Sheikh Mohammed **Bred** Darley **Trained** West Ilsley, Berks
FOCUS
A decent little three-year-old handicap containing some unexposed types, but run at an uneven pace. The race has been rated through the third, with the first two both likely to do better.
Six Shots Official explanation: jockey said colt hung left in the straight
Highland Harvest Official explanation: jockey said colt ran too free

639 RIVER BELLE'S RIGHT ROYAL BONUS H'CAP 5f (P)
4:35 (4:36) (Class 4) (0-85,76) 3-Y-0 **£4,857** (£1,445; £722; £360) **Stalls** High

Form RPR
41-2 **1** **Rocker**[16] 502 3-8-7 72........ WilliamBuick(7) 3 74
(B R Johnson) *dwlt: trckd ldng pair: plenty of room towards inner and tk best route into st: led over 1f out: rdn and in command fnl f* **5/2**[2]

45-5 **2** ½ **Stoneacre Gareth (IRE)**[5] [606] 3-9-1 **73**........................ GeorgeBaker 4 73
(Peter Grayson) *sn last: effrt 2f out: styd on fnl f to take 2nd last 75yds*
14/1

12-3 **3** *nk* **Black Moma (IRE)**[5] [606] 3-8-11 **76**............................ HaddenFrost(7) 2 75
(R Hannon) *pressed ldr: carried wd into st: bmpd along and nt qckn over 1f out: one pce after*
7/2[3]

11 **4** ½ **Halsion Chancer**[16] [502] 3-8-9 **70**.......................... StephaneBreux(3) 1 67
(J R Best) *led: c wd into st 2f out: hdd over 1f out: shkn up and no rspnse*
10/11[1]

59.37 secs (-0.41) **Going Correction** -0.05s/f (Stan) **4** Ran SP% **109.8**
Speed ratings (Par 100):101,100,99,98
CSF £24.33 TOTE £3.70; EX 17.00.
Owner Sir Eric Parker **Bred** Sir Eric Parker **Trained** Ashtead, Surrey
■ Stewards' Enquiry : William Buick one-day ban: careless riding (Mar 19)

FOCUS
A tight little handicap, despite there only being four runners, but a messy race in some ways. The form is only ordinary.

640 RIVER BELLE ONLINE CASINO APPRENTICE H'CAP 2m (P)
5:05 (5:05) (Class 5) (0-75,74) 4-Y-0+ **£2,968** (£876; £438) **Stalls** Low

Form RPR

623/ **1** **Mind How You Go (FR)**[632] [2550] 9-10-0 **74**.................. StephaneBreux 9 81
(J R Best) *dwlt: hld up in rr: stdy prog on outer fr 3f out: shkn up over 1f out: styd on fnl f to ld last stride*
16/1

14/3 **2** *shd* **Garnett (IRE)**[8] [578] 6-9-9 **69**..................................(p) StephenDonohoe 2 76
(D E Cantillon) *hld up towards rr: stdy prog fr 3f out gng wl: led wl over 1f out: rdn fnl f: hdd last stride*
9/4[2]

340- **3** ¾ **Noddies Way**[119] [6398] 4-8-4 **55** oh2.................................... LiamJones 1 61
(J F Panvert) *trckd ldrs: rdn over 3f out and looked struggling: styd on again over 1f out: clsng at fin*
33/1

0-01 **4** *nk* **Rule For Ever**[5] [607] 5-9-0 **60** 6ex.. GregFairley 4 66+
(M Johnston) *mde most: jnd and pushed along fr 5f out: hdd u.p wl over 1f out: kpt on same pce*
7/4[1]

-404 **5** *5* **Salut Saint Cloud**[11] [354] 6-8-11 **64**...................... JemmaMarshall(7) 3 64
(G L Moore) *hld up in last: nvr on terms: nudged along and prog to chse clr ldrs over 1f out: kpt on steadily*
20/1

00-0 **6** 1 ¼ **Sir Monty (USA)**[30] [362] 5-10-0 **74**................................ JamesDoyle 10 72
(Mrs A J Perrett) *hld up: effrt on wd outside whn sltly hmpd over 2f out: sn outpcd and btn*
7/1[3]

-320 **7** *shd* **Critical Stage (IRE)**[8] [578] 8-8-11 **64**..................... HaddenFrost(7) 7 62
(J D Frost) *pressed ldrs: upsides fr 5f out to over 2f out: wknd wl over 1f out*
8/1

422- **8** *6* **Girardii**[116] [3163] 4-8-11 **62**..(b) SaleemGolam 5 53
(K C Bailey) *chsd ldrs: rdn over 3f out: wl btn over 2f out*
16/1

0-54 **9** *3* **Flying Spirit (IRE)**[35] [316] 8-9-7 **67**................................(b) AdamKirby 6 54
(G L Moore) *pressed ldr: upsides over 5f out to over 3f out: sn wknd* **12/1**

3m 25.16s (-3.63) **Going Correction** -0.05s/f (Stan)
WFA 4 from 5yo+ 5lb **9** Ran SP% **117.9**
Speed ratings (Par 103):107,106,106,106,103 103,103,100,98
CSF £53.37 CT £1224.07 TOTE £26.70: £4.90, £1.50, £7.60; EX 82.60 TRIFECTA Not won.
Place 6 £164.62, Place 5 £108.30.
Owner A Fiver In Mind Partnership **Bred** Christopher P Ranson **Trained** Hucking, Kent
■ Stewards' Enquiry : Stephen Donohoe three-day ban: careless riding (Mar 19) and using whip with excessive frequency (Mar 20-21)

FOCUS
A modest staying handicap run at a sound enough pace. The form is sound but ordinary, Mind How You Go improving by around 11lb on his previous Flat form.

Salut Saint Cloud Official explanation: jockey said gelding hung badly right

T/Jkpt: Not won. T/Plt: £312.50 to a £1 stake. Pool: £76,036.35. 177.60 winning tickets. T/Qpdt: £64.70 to a £1 stake. Pool: £4,726.30. 54.00 winning tickets. JN

595 NAD AL SHEBA (L-H)
Thursday, March 8
OFFICIAL GOING: Turf course - good; dirt course - fast

641a LAND ROVER CLASSIC (CONDITIONS RACE) (TURF) 7f 110y(D)
3:00 (3:00) 3-Y-0
£9,183 (£3,061; £1,530; £765; £459; £306)

RPR

1 **Mount Hadley (USA)**[49] [173] 3-8-8 91.......................... DO'Donohoe 3 101
(I Mohammed, UAE) *prom on rail: rdn 3 1/2f out: trckd ldr 1 1/2f out: led ins fnl f*
11/1

2 ¼ **Truly Royal**[147] [5915] 3-8-9 105 ow1.. LDettori 1 102
(Saeed Bin Suroor) *mid-div on rail: gng wl 3f out: swtchd out to cl 2f out: ev ch fnl 1 1/2f: nrst fin*
1/1[1]

3 1 ¼ **Glen Nevis (USA)**[49] [173] 3-8-9 92 ow1.............................. JMurtagh 6 98?
(I Mohammed, UAE) *led on rail: rdn clr 2f out: hdd ins fnl f*
25/1

4 5 ½ **Country Song (USA)**[27] [414] 3-8-8 99.............................. RyanMoore 9 83
(J Noseda) *slowly away: settled in last: prog on rail 3f out: rdn 2f out: nt qckn*
7/1

5 6 ¼ **Champlain**[49] [173] 3-8-8 106....................................(vt) KerrinMcEvoy 2 67
(I Mohammed, UAE) *settled in rr: rdn 3 1/2f out: trckd wnr 2f out: wknd*
9/2[2]

6 3 ½ **Zeeno (SAF)**[21] [470] 4-9-11 105......................................(t) TedDurcan 8 65
(S Seemar, UAE) *in rr of mid-div: rdn to cl 2 1/2f out: one pce* **5/1**[3]

7 5 ¼ **Alto Taquari (BRZ)**[14] [526] 4-9-4 96..........................(b) RichardMullen 7 44
(P Nickel Filho, Brazil) *mid-div out wd tl 3f out* **33/1**

8 4 ¼ **Deserted Dane (USA)**[21] [474] 3-8-8 94.............................. WSupple 4 33
(G A Swinbank) *settled in rr: rdn 3f out: nvr nr to chal* **11/1**

9 ¾ **Lavarone (ARG)**[14] [532] 4-9-4 95.. KShea 5 31
(H J Brown, South Africa) *mid-div in centre for 2f: wknd* **7/1**

10 3 ¼ **Comandante Xara (BRZ)**[14] [526] 4-9-4 97..........................(b) ECruz 10 21
(P Nickel Filho, Brazil) *trckd ldr tl 3f out: wknd* **33/1**

1m 32.18s (1.58) **Going Correction** +0.30s/f (Good)
WFA 3 from 4yo 16lb **10** Ran SP% **136.2**
Speed ratings: 104,103,102,97,90 87,82,77,77,73

Owner Saeed Maktoum Al Maktoum **Bred** Gainsborough Farm Llc **Trained** UAE

FOCUS
An interesting conditions contest. The pace seemed fair and the front three, who pulled nicely clear, probably produced a very useful level of form.

NOTEBOOK
Mount Hadley(USA), a Leicester maiden winner for Ed Dunlop last year, had been off the track since running third to the subsequent UAE 2000 Guineas winner Asiatic Boy over 7f on the dirt 49 days previously, but he proved suited by the return to turf and just proved too strong for the favourite. Having tracked the leader from the start, he was being niggled along to hold his position before the turn into the straight, but he kept responding. It is hard to know what his prospects are in the long term, but he will be an interesting type if returning to the UK.

Truly Royal, the impressive winner of a 6f Newmarket maiden on his only previous start last October, failed to justify favouritism on his return to action, but this still represents improved form. He had to wait for a gap early in the straight, allowing the front two first run, but he was in the clear for long enough, if good enough and basically seemed found out by his inexperience. This form obviously leaves him well short of what is required to develop into a Guineas candidate, but there should be better to come with the benefit of this outing and he can yet progress into a smart sort. (op 11/8)

Glen Nevis(USA), who actually won his maiden at Leicester on the same day today's winner was getting off the mark, stuck to his task well when headed and emerges with plenty of credit. This represents a big improvement on the form he showed on the dirt on his debut in Dubai and there could be better to come again.

Country Song(USA), returned to turf after a couple of reasonable efforts on the dirt, did not enjoy a clear run when first beginning to pick up in the straight and could pose no threat to the front three.

Champlain did not pick up when asked for his effort and looks best watched for the time being. (op 4/1)

Deserted Dane(USA) ran with credit in a reasonable race over 5f on the dirt on his debut in Dubai, but he could make no impression switched to turf over this longer trip. (tchd 10/1)

642a FERRARI CUP (H'CAP) (TURF) 1m 2f (T)
3:35 (3:36) (100-112,111) 3-Y-0+
£53,571 (£17,857; £8,928; £4,464; £2,678; £1,785)

RPR

1 **Sushisan (AUS)**[14] [531] 5-9-2 **107**.. KShea 5 115+
(H J Brown, South Africa) *mid-div: smooth prog to ld main gp 2 1/2f out: r.o wl fnl 1 1/2f: led ins fnl f: comf*
20/1

2 2 ½ **Gharir (IRE)**[13] [541] 5-9-0 **105**.......................................(b) MartinDwyer 8 108
(E Charpy, UAE) *sn led: clr 3 1/2f out: r.o wl: hdd ins fnl f: kpt on* **20/1**

3 ¼ **Yasoodd**[14] [531] 4-9-6 **111**... JMurtagh 1 114
(D Selvaratnam, UAE) *mid-div on rail: rdn 3f out: r.o fnl 2f: nrst fin* **5/1**[2]

4 3 ¼ **Charlie Cool**[28] [401] 4-9-2 **107**.. JamieSpencer 7 104
(W J Haggas) *hld up in rr: rdn 3f out: nvr able to chal* **7/4**[1]

5 1 ½ **Senor Dali (IRE)**[13] [544] 4-9-5 **110**............................. RichardMullen 4 104
(I Mohammed, UAE) *trckd ldr: rdn 4f out: wknd fnl f* **8/1**[3]

6 *3* **Melanosporum (USA)**[48] 5-8-11 **102**.............................(t) MJKinane 10 91
(I Jory, Saudi Arabia) *settled in rr: nvr nr to chal* **12/1**

7 3 ¾ **Stream Of Gold (IRE)**[13] [541] 6-8-12 **104**........................ TedDurcan 2 85
(S Seemar, UAE) *hld up in rr: rdn 4f out: nvr a threat* **5/1**[2]

8 *9* **Alpacco (IRE)**[13] [543] 5-9-1 **106**.....................................(b) RyanMoore 3 72
(H J Brown, South Africa) *in rr of mid-div: nvr nr to chal* **11/1**

9 5 ¼ **Golden Arrow (IRE)**[14] [529] 4-9-3 **108**......................(vt) KerrinMcEvoy 6 64
(I Mohammed, UAE) *trckd ldng pair: rdn 3 1/2f out: wknd* **10/1**

10 *dist* **Atlantic Air (FR)**[14] [531] 5-9-1 **106**..................................(t) TPO'Shea 9 —
(E Charpy, UAE) *mid-div: dropped to rr 3 1/2f out: virtually p.u* **25/1**

2m 5.70s (1.50) **Going Correction** +0.30s/f (Good) **10** Ran SP% **119.3**
Speed ratings: 106,104,103,101,100 97,94,87,83,—

Owner J Atkinson & Velty Towers Racing **Bred** GH Browm, SK Brown, JL Brown & D Malone **Trained** South Africa

FOCUS
A good handicap, but not as competitive as one would expect for a similar race in the UK, and the pace was muddling. They went just steady in the early stages and those held up were badly caught out when the pace was increased leaving the back straight. This was essentially another division of the 5.20, but the winning time was 1.12 seconds slower. The winer had a bit to spare in a race rated through thr third and fifth.

NOTEBOOK
Sushisan(AUS) was given an intelligent ride by Kevin Shea, who kept tabs on the leaders and had his mount better positioned than some of these when the pace increased. He had finished down the field in an extended 1m handicap on his debut in Dubai, but the step up in trip clearly suited and he sustained his challenge well in the straight to reel in long-timer leader Gharir. This was a good effort, but the form does not look particularly strong.

Gharir(IRE) was given a really good ride from the front by Martin Dwyer, leading at just an ordinary pace for much of the way before catching a few of these out by injecting some pace before the turn in. He was eventually pegged back, but can have no excuses whatsoever.

Yasoodd was caught flat-footed on the turn into the straight and basically found his stride too late. He was unproven over a trip this far, but there is plenty of stamina on the dam's side and the muddling pace was basically his undoing.

Charlie Cool ◆ was held up well out the back in a race run at just an ordinary gallop and found himself with too much to do when the pace increased. He can be forgiven this and should progress in good company over middle-distances when returned to the UK, where he is likely to have races run to suit much better.

Senor Dali(IRE) was badly flattered by his course-and-distance success two weeks previously and, unable to dominate this time, he was put in his place.

643a JAGUAR TROPHY (H'CAP) (DIRT) 1m 2f (D)
4:15 (4:15) (100-112,109) 3-Y-0+
£53,571 (£17,857; £8,928; £4,464; £2,678; £1,785)

RPR

1 **Bennie Blue (SAF)**[14] [529] 5-8-11 **100**............................ WCMarwing 4 95
(M F De Kock, South Africa) *sn led: rdn 2 1/2f out: r.o wl: gamely* **7/1**[3]

2 ¼ **Mutasallil (USA)**[35] [328] 7-9-0 **102**..(t) FJara 2 98
(Doug Watson, UAE) *mid-div on rail: trckd wnr 3 1/2f out: rdn to chal fnl 1 1/2f: nrst fin*
33/1

3 1 ¼ **Arabian Prince (USA)**[27] [413] 4-9-4 **107**........................ MartinDwyer 10 100
(Doug Watson, UAE) *mid-div: tk up wd position: rdn 3 1/2f out: ev ch 2f out: one pce*
20/1

4 ½ **Fenice (IRE)**[13] [544] 4-8-11 **100**... RyanMoore 1 92
(S Seemar, UAE) *settled in rr: prog to trck runner-up 2 1/2f out: n.m.r 1 1/2f out: kpt on*
11/1

5 3 ¼ **Mooner (ARG)**[14] [529] 6-9-5 **108**.. TedDurcan 3 94
(S Seemar, UAE) *missed break: racd in rr: rdn 3 1/2f out: n.d* **5/1**[2]

6 ¾ **Naipe Marcado (URU)**[14] [532] 4-8-5 **102**..................(t) KerrinMcEvoy 9 79
(I Mohammed, UAE) *trckd ldr: rdn 3f out: wknd* **6/4**[1]

7 *2* **Dynamic Saint (USA)**[14] [529] 4-9-5 **108**..................(v) RichardMullen 7 89
(Doug Watson, UAE) *trckd ldng duo tl 3f out: wknd* **5/1**[2]

8 3 ¼ **Remaadd (USA)**[14] [529] 6-9-6 **109**......................................(b) JMurtagh 8 84
(D Selvaratnam, UAE) *racd in last: rdn 1/2-way: n.d* **14/1**

9 16 **Nkosi Reigns (USA)**[21] 471 6-9-1 **104**............................(bt) TPO'Shea 5 50
(S Seemar, UAE) *settled in rr: rdn 3 1/2f out: one pce* **10/1**

2m 2.32s (-0.98) **Going Correction** +0.15s/f (Slow) **9** Ran SP% **117.6**
Speed ratings: 109,108,107,107,104 104,102,100,87

Owner Sh Mohd Bin Khalifa Al Maktoum/H Wolfaardt **Bred** Wilgerbosdrift **Trained** South Africa

FOCUS
Just an ordinary-looking handicap for the grade.

NOTEBOOK
Bennie Blue(SAF) had finished behind both Dynamic Saint and Mooner when third over course and distance on his previous start, but he was ridden much more positively this time and the new tactics suited. He only just hung on, though, as Mutasallil was closing all the way to the line and very nearly got up.
Mutasallil(USA) was suited by the return to dirt and can have few excuses. (op 25/1)
Arabian Prince(USA) stayed on well down the outside, proving himself just as effective on dirt.
Fenice(IRE), switching from turf for the first time, was not helped by his inside draw as he did not get the clearest of passages in the straight, but he kept on well and was not beaten very far.
Mooner(ARG) had been holding his form well lately, but this was a disappointing effort.
Naipe Marcado(URU) shaped so well on his debut in Dubai when second to subsequent Group 3 winner Boston Lodge over 1m, and this longer trip should not have posed him any problems, but he offered very little under pressure. He has it all to prove now.

644a LAND ROVER AL QUOZ SPRINT (LISTED RACE) (TURF) 6f (T)
4:45 (4:45) 3-Y-0+

£53,571 (£17,857; £8,928; £4,464; £2,678; £1,785)

RPR

1 **Great Britain**[13] 547 5-9-4 108.. LDettori 1 117
(Saeed Bin Suroor) *missed break: settled in rr: trckd runner-up 2f out: rdn ins fnl f: led cl home* **7/2**[2]

2 hd **Munaddam (USA)**[14] 528 5-9-4 113.. RHills 2 116
(E A L Dunlop) *mid-div on rail: smooth prog to ld 1 1/2f out: r.o wl: hdd cl home* **7/4**[1]

3 2 1/2 **Tiza (SAF)**[28] 400 5-9-8 110..(bt) KShea 8 112
(H J Brown, South Africa) *settled in last: trckd wnr gng wl 2 1/2f out: r.o fnl 1 1/2f* **15/2**

4 3 3/4 **Drayton (IRE)**[196] 4747 3-8-8 110...................................... WCMarwing 9 96
(M F De Kock, South Africa) *trckd ldrs: rdn 2f out: nt qckn* **10/1**

5 1/2 **Visionist (IRE)**[7] 599 5-9-4 102...................................... WayneSmith 3 94
(M Al Muhairi, UAE) *sn led: rdn 2 1/2f out: hdd 1 1/2f out: wknd* **40/1**

6 1 1/2 **Ashdown Express (IRE)**[14] 528 8-9-4 110...................... TedDurcan 5 90
(C F Wall) *in rr of mid-div: rdn 3f out: short of room sn after: r.o once clr* **6/1**

7 1 1/4 **Lascaux (AUS)**[7] 597 6-9-4 106.. WLHo 4 86
(Y Choy, Macau) *led main gp: rdn to cl 2 1/2f out: nt qckn* **25/1**

8 1 1/4 **Greek Renaissance (IRE)**[13] 547 4-9-4 107.............. KerrinMcEvoy 7 82
(I Mohammed, UAE) *mid-div: rdn along 3 1/2f out: nvr nr to chal* **11/2**[3]

9 1 1/4 **Subpoena**[13] 540 5-9-4 102..(v) RoystonFfrench 6 78
(A Al Raihe, UAE) *mid-div: rdn to cl 3f out: n.m.r sn after: nt qckn* **25/1**

10 17 **Caesar Beware (IRE)**[14] 528 5-9-4 104.................... RichardMullen 10 23
(S Seemar, UAE) *settled in rr: nvr nr to chal* **50/1**

1m 12.16s (0.76) **Going Correction** +0.30s/f (Good)
WFA 3 from 4yo+ 14lb **10** Ran SP% **121.2**
Speed ratings: 106,105,102,97,96 94,93,91,89,67

Owner Godolphin **Bred** Darley **Trained** Newmarket, Suffolk

FOCUS
A good, competitive Listed sprint.

NOTEBOOK
Great Britain improved on the form he showed when second in a course-and-distance handicap off a mark of 105 on his debut in Dubai. Although not showing as much early speed this time, perhaps through design, he was always travelling noticeably well, and he eventually did just enough to nail the progressive Munaddam close home, but he was by no means convincing when asked for everything. Frankie Dettori seemed eager to hang on to him for as long as possible, and it was easy to see why, as he did not do much once finally in front, and may well have been pegged back in another 75 yards or so. It seems harsh to knock him, as this probably represents a career-best effort, but the fact he did not find as much under pressure as his impressive cruising speed promised still leaves him with plenty to prove. (op 4/1)
Munaddam(USA), a hugely progressive gelding, was bidding for a Carnival hat-trick following a couple of smart efforts in handicaps, but he was just denied. He did nothing wrong, but Great Britain was always travelling ominously well and he was just picked off by that rival late on. There seems no reason why he cannot continue to improve back in the UK and he is an exciting prospect for the domestic season.
Tiza(SAF) appreciated the strong pace and ran on to the line for a decent third. His effort is all the more creditable considering he was conceding upwards of 4lb all round. (tchd 8/1)
Drayton(IRE) was a real speedball as a juvenile for Tommy Stack, landing a couple of 5f Listed races at the Curragh, and he showed he has trained on with a fine effort on his debut for new connections. He fared best of those on the pace and can do even better considering this was his first run in 196 days.
Visionist(IRE) is a smart performer at his best and this was a fine effort. He has been in good form on the dirt lately and, just as effective on turf, continued his good run.
Ashdown Express(IRE) had the race run to suit and can have few excuses this time.
Greek Renaissance(IRE) gave the impression his improvement was levelling out when only third over course and distance on his previous start and he finished down the field this time. He has been kept busy at this year's Carnival and it has to be hoped these recent outings have not left their mark should he return to the UK.

645a MASERATI PLATE (H'CAP) (TURF) 1m 2f (T)
5:20 (5:20) (100-112,110) 3-Y-0+

£53,571 (£17,857; £8,928; £4,464; £2,678; £1,785)

RPR

1 **Mystical (IND)**[21] 477 5-8-11 **107**...................................... RyanMoore 5 110
(S Ganapathy, India) *mid-div on rail: trckd runner-up 2 1/2f out: led fnl f: r.o wl* **4/1**[1]

2 1 1/4 **Diamond Quest (SAF)**[14] 531 6-8-10 **106**...................... WCMarwing 1 107
(M F De Kock, South Africa) *racd in 4th: rdn to ld 2 1/2f out: r.o wl: hdd fnl f* **11/2**[3]

3 8 **Fairmile**[13] 544 5-8-9 **105**.. RichardMullen 2 92
(I Mohammed, UAE) *slowly away: settled in rr: rdn 3f out: r.o fnl 2f: nvr nr to chal* **9/2**[2]

4 4 **National Captain (SAF)**[13] 542 5-8-12 **108**.................. TedDurcan 6 87
(S Seemar, UAE) *settled in rr: rdn 3f out: r.o fnl 2 1/2f: nvr able to chal* **12/1**

5 2 1/2 **Smart And Mighty (AUS)**[7] 599 8-8-8 **104**................(b) MartinDwyer 8 79
(T Noonan, Australia) *mid-div: rdn to cl 3f out: nt qckn: wknd fnl f* **10/1**

6 6 **Wild Savannah**[13] 541 5-9-0 **109**................................(v) KerrinMcEvoy 7 74
(I Mohammed, UAE) *racd in 3rd tl rdn 3f out: wknd* **4/1**[1]

7 11 **Earl's Court**[392] 354 5-8-7 **102**..(t) TPO'Shea 4 47
(E Charpy, UAE) *set gd pce: clr 4f out: rdn 3f out: hdd 2 1/2f out: wknd rapidly* **14/1**

8 shd **Hazeymm (IRE)**[13] 545 4-8-9 **105**.......................................(t) JMurtagh 9 49
(D Selvaratnam, UAE) *slowly away: settled in last: nvr involved* **25/1**

9 17 **Gravitas**[27] 412 4-9-1 **110**.. LDettori 3 25
(Saeed Bin Suroor) *led main gp: rdn to chal 2 1/2f out: sn eased: virtually p.u* **9/2**[2]

10 13 **Starpix (FR)**[13] 540 5-8-7 **102**.. WSupple 10 —
(H J Brown, South Africa) *settled in rr: nvr nr to chal: virtually p.u* **25/1**

2m 4.58s (0.38) **Going Correction** +0.30s/f (Good) **10** Ran SP% **122.9**
Speed ratings: 110,109,102,99,97 92,83,83,70,59

Owner Mr & Mrs Zavaray S Poonawalla **Bred** Poonawalla Estate Stud & Agri Farm **Trained** India

FOCUS
A decent handicap run at a good pace and very smart efforts indeed from the front two to pull so far clear. Basically another division of the 3.35, but the winning time was 1.12 seconds quicker and the form looks.much more reliable.

NOTEBOOK
Mystical(IND) ◆ had won nicely in a 1m handicap on his debut in Dubai and, every bit as effective over this longer trip, he was able to defy a 7lb higher mark. He had to work hard to see off Diamond Quest, who to an extent had got first run, but he gradually wore that one down to win in determined fashion. He edged to his left under maximum pressure, hardly helping the runner-up's chance, but that is basically because he was giving everything, and he was the winner on merit. Already a Group 1 winner in India, if he cannot be found another suitable opportunity in Dubai he fully deserves to take his chance in pattern company in Europe or America later this year.
Diamond Quest(SAF) has been thriving on a busy campaign at this year's Carnival and this was probably his best effort yet, finishing well clear of the remainder in second.
Fairmile, slightly disappointing when a beaten favourite over course and distance on his previous start, seemed to have his chance but was left behind by the front two.
National Captain(SAF), whose recent win over an extended 7f looked like suspect form, was well held over this longer trip. (op 11/1)
Smart And Mighty(AUS) should have appreciated the return to turf, but he was never seen with a chance.
Wild Savannah was below the form he showed when winning over course and distance on his previous start.
Gravitas stopped as though something was amiss in the straight.

646a FORD ZABEEL MILE (LISTED RACE) (TURF) 1m (T)
5:50 (5:51) 3-Y-0+

£53,571 (£17,857; £8,928; £4,464; £2,678; £1,785)

RPR

1 **Kapil (SAF)**[14] 530 5-9-4 110.. WCMarwing 4 119+
(M F De Kock, South Africa) *mid-div on rail: trckd ldrs gng wl 3f out: rdn to cl 2f out: led ins fnl f: easily* **4/1**[2]

2 3 3/4 **Lord Admiral (USA)**[7] 600 6-9-0 111..............................(b) MJKinane 1 109
(Charles O'Brien, Ire) *led: hrd rdn 1 1/2f out: hdd fnl f: r.o wl: no ch w wnr* **16/1**

3 1/4 **Great Rhythm (SAF)**[7] 600 6-9-0 110.. KShea 2 109
(H J Brown, South Africa) *racd in 3rd on rail: trckd runner-up 2 1/2f out: r.o wl* **25/1**

4 1 1/4 **King Jock (USA)**[14] 530 6-9-2 110...................................... TPO'Shea 5 108
(R J Osborne, Ire) *in rr on rail: trckd wnr whn n.m.r 2 1/2f out: r.o fnl 1 1/2f: nrest finsih* **14/1**

5 1 **Benedetti (AUS)**[14] 531 6-9-0 113....................................(b) JMurtagh 6 104
(T Noonan, Australia) *racd in 4th: rdn to cl 2 1/2f out: r.o: nt pce of first four* **11/4**[1]

6 2 **Army Of Angels (IRE)**[131] 6218 5-9-0 110.............................. LDettori 9 100
(Saeed Bin Suroor) *trckd ldr: rdn to cl 2 1/2f out: nt qckn: wknd 1 1/2f out* **5/1**[3]

7 2 **Nayyir**[110] 6516 9-9-2 109..(p) EddieAhern 7 98
(G A Butler) *in rr of mid-div: nvr able to chal: r.o fnl 1 1/2f* **14/1**

8 2 1/2 **Metropolitan Man**[14] 531 4-9-0 108.................................. RyanMoore 3 91
(D M Simcock) *settled in rr: rdn 2 1/2f out: nvr able to chal* **10/1**

9 1 1/4 **Polar Magic**[13] 540 6-9-0 108.. JamieSpencer 8 89
(I Mohammed, UAE) *settled in last: rdn 2 1/2f out: nvr nr to chal* **8/1**

10 18 **Sir Gerard**[14] 531 4-9-0 109.. KerrinMcEvoy 10 53
(I Mohammed, UAE) *mid-div: rdn 3f out: n.d* **5/1**[3]

1m 37.74s (-0.06) **Going Correction** +0.30s/f (Good) **10** Ran SP% **123.3**
Speed ratings: 112,108,108,106,105 103,101,99,98,80

Owner M Fullard,J Drew,D Watson-Smith Mrs C Gabller **Bred** Arc-En-Ciel Stud **Trained** South Africa

FOCUS
A good, competitive Listed contest, although the pace was just ordinary. Sound form, rated through the placed horses.

NOTEBOOK
Kapil(SAF) showed a smart change of gear to ultimately win convincingly, not proving inconvenienced by the ordinary pace. He had shaped well when third over 1m on his debut in Dubai and duly found the necessary improvement. (op 9/2)
Lord Admiral(USA) would have been unsuited by a steady pace, so Mick Kinane used his initiative and sent his mount to the front. He set just an ordinary gallop and the new tactics seemed to suit, as he fought off all bar Kapil.
Great Rhythm(SAF) was produced with every chance, but he proved unable to go by Lord Admiral and had no answer to Kapil's late surge.
King Jock(USA) was unsuited by the ordinary gallop and ran well in the circumstances.
Benedetti(AUS) had created a really favourable impression with a couple of handicap successes at this year's Carnival, the first off a mark of 100 and the second off 108, but this might just have been a step too far. To be fair, though, the ordinary pace is unlikely to have suited.
Army Of Angels(IRE) might have needed this first run in 131 days.
Nayyir, who also had an absence to overcome and was trying cheekpieces for the first time, would probably have appreciated a stronger end-to-end gallop.
Metropolitan Man was held up well out the back for most of the way and could make no impression.
Polar Magic created a really good impression when winning a similar event on his previous start but, 8lb higher, he ran a stinker.
Sir Gerard did not run very well round here last time and this was even worse. It will have to be hoped his exertions at the Carnival do not leave their mark.

647a AL TAYER MOTORS UAE OAKS (LISTED RACE) (DIRT) (FILLIES) 1m 1f (D)

6:20 (6:25) 3-Y-O

£76,530 (£25,510; £12,755; £6,377; £3,826; £2,551)

RPR

1 **Folk (USA)**[21] [476] 3-8-9 110 .... KerrinMcEvoy 1 114+
(I Mohammed, UAE) *led on rail: a gng wl: nvr extended: comf* **4/11**[1]

2 5 **Samba Reggae (ARG)**[21] [476] 4-9-4 102 .... LDettori 2 106
(I Mohammed, UAE) *mid-div on rail: trckd wnr 3f out: r.o: no ch w wnr* **13/2**[3]

3 5 1/4 **Greetings (BRZ)**[21] [476] 4-9-4 107 .... RichardMullen 7 96
(P Nickel Filho, Brazil) *trckd ldr out wd: rdn 4f out: no ch w wnr* **7/2**[2]

4 14 **Carillon (IRE)**[21] [476] 3-8-9 85 .... FJara 3 66
(Doug Watson, UAE) *trckd ldr out on rail: wknd 5f out* **100/1**

5 3 3/4 **Miss Chatty (ARG)**[21] [476] 4-9-4 95 .... KShea 6 62
(H J Brown, South Africa) *settled in last: rdn 5f out: n.d* **50/1**

6 2 1/4 **Corre Solta (BRZ)**[42] [246] 4-9-4 93 .... JMurtagh 5 58
(H J Brown, South Africa) *settled in rr: rdn 5f out: nvr a threat* **100/1**

1m 48.59s (-2.21) **Going Correction** +0.15s/f (Slow)
WFA 3 from 4yo 20lb **6** Ran SP% **112.8**
Speed ratings: 115,110,105,93,90 88

Owner Sheikh Hamdan Bin Mohammed Al Maktoum **Bred** Darley **Trained** UAE

FOCUS

This was the second year in succession the UAE Oaks carried Listed status but, rather disappointingly, six runners represented the smallest field in the last five renewals. It would be wrong to crab the race, though, because it was won by a really high-class filly in the form of Folk, who set her own pace but still posted a decent time.

NOTEBOOK

Folk(USA) ◆ had little trouble in following up her Guineas success, and did so in a time equal to that clocked by the excellent Discreet Cat in last year's UAE Derby. An inside draw was a slight concern beforehand, but the only other potential front-runner, Carillon, missed the break, and she was able to dominate from the start. She took a bit of a grip in front, but that was nothing to worry about and she even pricked her ears down the back straight, highlighting just how easily she was travelling. She was basically never in any danger, even though her stablemate Samba Reggae tried to produce a challenge at the top of the straight, and she more than doubled her superiority over third-placed Greetings compared with their Guineas running. Her connections are now considering running her against the colts in the UAE Derby and it would be truly fascinating to see her take on the 2000 Guineas winner Asiatic Boy. In the longer term, she will surely continue her career back in the US and must take high rank amongst the three-year-old fillies this year. (op 2/5)

Samba Reggae(ARG) ◆ appreciated the slight step up in trip and readily reversed Guineas placings with Greetings, but the winner was in a different league. Still, this was a very useful effort and she is a pretty decent filly in her own right. (op 6/1)

Greetings(BRZ) has won over 1m2f in Brazil, so the step up in trip from 1m would not have inconvenienced her, but she just ran into a couple very smart fillies.

648a AL TAYER MOTORS CHALLENGE (H'CAP) (TURF) 1m 4f (T)

6:50 (6:52) (100-112,112) 3-Y-O+

£53,571 (£17,857; £8,928; £4,464; £2,678; £1,785)

RPR

1 **Crime Scene (IRE)**[21] [475] 4-8-7 **102** .... MJKinane 9 103
(I Mohammed, UAE) *settled last: stl last 3f out: rdn to cl 2f out: chal 1 1/2f out: led fnl f* **5/1**[3]

2 1 1/4 **Candy Critic (ARG)**[21] [475] 5-8-6 **100** ....(bt) WCMarwing 2 98
(M F De Kock, South Africa) *trckd ldrs: led 2 1/2f out: rdn 2f out: hdd fnl f: r.o wl* **8/1**

3 3 1/4 **Pearly King (USA)**[21] [475] 4-8-6 **101** .... MartinDwyer 3 95
(I Mohammed, UAE) *slowly away: led main gp: t.k.h: rdn to chal 2f out: nt qckn* **7/1**

4 1/2 **Sunday Symphony**[21] [475] 5-8-8 **102** ....(vt) RyanMoore 7 95
(S Seemar, UAE) *settled in rr: rdn 3f out: n.m.r 1 1/2f out: r.o fnl f* **16/1**

5 1/4 **Mulaqat**[7] [598] 4-9-3 **112** .... JMurtagh 6 105
(D Selvaratnam, UAE) *in rr on rail: gng wl in mid-div 3f out: no room 2f out: nt rcvr* **9/1**

6 3/4 **Dont Dili Dali**[13] [546] 4-8-5 **100** .... JohnEgan 1 92
(J S Moore) *mid-div: prog to trck runner-up 2 1/2f out: no room 1 1/2f out: r.o* **12/1**

7 13 **Leitmotiv (IRE)**[13] [545] 4-8-5 **100** ....(v) WSupple 10 73
(Saeed Bin Suroor) *given reminders to ld: set stdy pce: rdn 3f out: sn hdd & wknd* **9/2**[2]

8 1 1/4 **Land 'n Stars**[27] [412] 7-9-2 **110** .... RichardMullen 4 80
(Jamie Poulton) *racd in 3rd: rdn 4 1/2f out: sn struggling* **11/1**

9 2 1/4 **Book Of Music (IRE)**[13] [545] 4-9-3 **112** ....(v) KerrinMcEvoy 5 79
(I Mohammed, UAE) *mid-div: smooth prog trck ldrs 3f out: rdn 2 1/2f out: wknd* **11/4**[1]

10 6 **Nepotista (BRZ)**[7] [598] 5-8-6 **100** .... RoystonFfrench 8 57
(A Cintra Pereira, Brazil) *missed break: t.k.h early strides: racd in rr: nvr able to chal* **14/1**

2m 34.6s (3.60) **Going Correction** +0.30s/f (Good)
WFA 4 from 5yo+ 2lb **10** Ran SP% **123.7**
Speed ratings: 100,99,97,96,96 96,87,86,85,81

Owner H R H Princess Haya Of Jordan **Bred** Gainsborough Stud Management Ltd **Trained** UAE

FOCUS

A good handicap, but the pace was just ordinary. The race has been rated through the winner and the fifth.

NOTEBOOK

Crime Scene(IRE), held up in last for most of the race, came with a sweeping run down the outside in the straight and was always holding the South African filly Candy Critic in the closing stages. He looks to have improved this spring and will be interesting if returning to the UK.

Candy Critic(ARG) raced a touch keenly but she came through to have every chance. It was disconcerting to once again see her swish her tail violently once she hit the front, though.

Pearly King(USA), raised 3lb for his latest second over course and distance, could not confirm form over Candy Critic on the revised terms.

Sunday Symphony was another hold-up performer who was suited by the way the race was run and stayed on late. (op 18/1)

Mulaqat had no easy task under joint top-weight.

Dont Dili Dali has been holding her form well at this year's Carnival, but this was the furthest trip she has tried and she was well held.

Leitmotiv(IRE) ran a poor race and is not progressing. (op 4/1)

Land 'n Stars needs further these days when racing in this sort of company. (op 12/1)

Book Of Music(IRE) was an impressive winner of a similar event over course and distance on his previous start, but he dropped away tamely early in the straight this time and was a massive disappointment.. (op 3/1)

[633]LINGFIELD (L-H)

Friday, March 9

OFFICIAL GOING: Standard

This Polytrack meeting, consisting of six Flat races and two bumpers, was quickly arranged to replace the previous day's abandoned jumps card here.

Wind: Strong, half-against

649 GO PONTINS MAIDEN STKS 1m (P)

1:35 (1:41) (Class 5) 3-Y-O+ **£3,886** (£1,156; £577; £288) **Stalls** High

Form RPR

2 1 **Zaham (USA)**[27] [418] 3-8-8 .... JoeFanning 1 74+
(M Johnston) *mde all: shkn up over 1f out: in command after: rdn out nr fin* **2/5**[1]

36-3 2 1/2 **Emerald Wilderness (IRE)**[23] [456] 3-8-8 76 .... JohnEgan 9 71
(M R Channon) *chsd ldr for 2f: chsd ldrs after: rdn to chse wnr wl over 1f out: kpt on* **11/2**[2]

00- 3 6 **Madaarek (USA)**[132] [6220] 3-8-8 .... BrettDoyle 4 57+
(E A L Dunlop) *racd in midfield in tch: pushed along over 4f out: outpcd over 2f out: kpt on to go 3rd ins fnl f: no ch w ldng pair* **10/1**[3]

-040 4 2 1/2 **Laugh 'n Cry**[4] [616] 6-9-7 49 ....(b) TonyCulhane 2 52
(C A Cyzer) *bustled along early: sn chsng ldrs and t.k.h: rdn to chse wnr briefly 2f out: hanging lft and wknd over 1f out* **50/1**

54- 5 1 1/4 **Duty Free (IRE)**[143] [6023] 3-8-9 ow1 .... SteveDrowne 11 49
(H Morrison) *racd in midfield: rdn over 3f out: outpcd over 2f out: kpt on same pce fnl f* **10/1**[3]

04 6 3/4 **Very Well Red**[12] [559] 4-9-7 .... JimCrowley 5 47
(P W Hiatt) *t.k.h: hld up in midfield: rdn and outpced over 2f out: no ch after* **40/1**

00- 7 1 **Night Falcon**[131] [6242] 3-8-3 .... JimmyQuinn 8 39+
(H Morrison) *a bhd: rdn over 4f out: lost tch 3f out: sme late hdwy* **66/1**

00-0 8 hd **Atticus Trophies (IRE)**[4] [610] 4-9-9 54 ....(v) JamesDoyle(3) 7 50
(Ms J S Doyle) *chsd ldr after 2f out: rdn 3f out: wknd 2f out* **66/1**

00 9 1 1/2 **A Mothers Love**[11] [569] 3-8-4 ow1 .... EdwardCreighton 3 36
(P J McBride) *a bhd: no ch last 2f* **100/1**

10 33 **Worldwind** 4-9-7 .... IanMongan 10 —
(Mrs L J Mongan) *a bhd: rdn over 4f out: t.o last 2f* **66/1**

1m 37.04s (-2.39) **Going Correction** -0.225s/f (Stan)
WFA 3 from 4yo+ 18lb **10** Ran SP% **114.9**
Speed ratings (Par 103):102,101,95,93,91 91,90,89,88,55
CSF £2.78 TOTE £1.30: £1.02, £1.20, £2.60; EX 2.20 Trifecta £10.40 Pool: £798.08 - 54.27 winning tickets..

Owner Hamdan Al Maktoum **Bred** London Thoroughbred Services Ltd **Trained** Middleham Moor, N Yorks

FOCUS

A reasonable-looking maiden run at a sound tempo. The form looks sound, but the fourth, who sets the standard, proves a really positive view.

Atticus Trophies(IRE) Official explanation: jockey said gelding ran too free

650 PONTINSBINGO.COM H'CAP 1m (P)

2:05 (2:10) (Class 6) (0-65,64) 4-Y-O+ **£2,047** (£604; £302) **Stalls** High

Form RPR

5332 1 **Parkview Love (USA)**[7] [609] 6-9-0 60 ....(v) DeanMcKeown 6 71
(D Shaw) *t.k.h: hld up bhd ldrs:hdwy to chse ldrs 3f out: rdn to ld over 1f out: r.o strly* **10/3**[2]

1442 2 2 1/2 **Binnion Bay (IRE)**[12] [556] 6-8-12 61 ....(b) AmirQuinn(3) 12 66
(J J Bridger) *t.k.h: trckd ldrs: wnt 2nd gng wl 3f out: rdn over 1f out: fnd little: fdd last 100 yds* **9/1**

-060 3 nk **Moon Bird**[32] [359] 5-8-10 56 .... EddieAhern 5 60+
(C A Cyzer) *stdd s: hld up bhd: rdn over 2f out: n.m.r briefly over 1f out: r.o wl fnl f: wnt 3rd nr fin* **13/2**[3]

1503 4 hd **Golden Spectrum (IRE)**[11] [571] 8-8-9 60 ....(b) TolleyDean(5) 7 64
(R A Harris) *t.k.h: hld up: rdn and hdwy on outer over 2f out: chsd ldrs over 1f out: kpt on* **20/1**

4-21 5 nk **Majehar**[26] [431] 5-8-11 60 .... StephenDonohoe(3) 4 63+
(A G Newcombe) *bhd: rdn over 2f out: c wd 2f out: r.o wl fnl f: nrst fin* **11/4**[1]

2225 6 1 1/2 **Imperium**[12] [556] 6-9-4 64 .... DaneO'Neill 1 64+
(Jean-Rene Auvray) *hld up in tch on inner: nt clr run over 2f out tl over 1f out: swtchd lft jst over 1f out: kpt on steadily fnl f* **10/1**

0/00 7 shd **Certifiable**[8] [592] 6-8-9 60 .... RobynBrisland(5) 8 60
(Miss Z C Davison) *t.k.h: led: rdn over 2f out: hdd over 1f out: wknd qckly ins fnl f* **40/1**

006- 8 2 **Hurricane Coast**[89] [6781] 8-8-7 60 ....(t) SophieDoyle(7) 10 55
(Ms J S Doyle) *w.w in midfield: effrt over 2f out: no imp on ldrs over 1f out* **25/1**

506- 9 nk **Cool Sting (IRE)**[77] [6913] 4-9-0 60 .... BrettDoyle 3 54
(M G Quinlan) *hld up bhd ldrs: rdn over 2f out: outpcd 2f out: no ch w ldrs after* **9/1**

314- 10 3 **Networker**[71] [6964] 4-9-3 63 .... TonyCulhane 9 50
(P J McBride) *t.k.h: hld up bhd: nvr on terms* **11/1**

0410 11 3/4 **Paso Doble**[9] [579] 9-8-12 58 ....(p) JimmyQuinn 2 44
(R Bastiman) *pressed ldr tl rdn over 3f out: wknd wl over 2f out* **16/1**

550 12 nk **Lough Neagh (USA)**[10] [573] 4-9-0 60 .... PaulEddery 11 45
(Miss D Mountain) *stdd s: a bhd: n.d* **25/1**

1m 37.42s (-2.01) **Going Correction** -0.225s/f (Stan) **12** Ran SP% **121.3**
Speed ratings (Par 101):101,98,98,98,97 96,96,94,93,90 90,89
CSF £32.74 CT £193.89 TOTE £4.10: £1.50, £2.90, £2.10; EX 26.10 Trifecta £108.10 Pool: £322.80 - 2.12 winning tickets..

Owner Danethorpe Racing Ltd **Bred** Mark Johnston Racing Ltd **Trained** Danethorpe, Notts

FOCUS

A decent winning time despite the lack of any early pace. The form looks somewhat unreliable, as quite a few horses finished strongly from off the pace, and the race is best rated around the runner-up and fourth.

651 PONTIN'S HOLIDAYS H'CAP 1m 2f (P)

2:35 (2:40) (Class 6) (0-65,65) 4-Y-O+ **£2,047** (£604; £302) **Stalls** Low

Form RPR

5233 1 **King After**[13] [549] 5-8-4 54 ....(v) StephaneBreux(3) 2 61
(J R Best) *t.k.h: hld up towards rr: hdwy wl over 2f out: rdn wl over 1f out: styd on u.p: edgd lft ins last: led on line* **8/1**[3]

0012 **2** *shd* **Shaheer (IRE)**[4] 610 5-8-7 54 .... JimCrowley 12 — 61
(J Gallagher) *chsd ldrs wnt 2nd 4f out: rdn to ld wl over 1f out: kpt on hdd on post* **7/1**[2]

04-4 **3** *hd* **Port 'n Starboard**[65] 30 6-9-1 62 .... J-PGuillambert 11 — 69
(C A Cyzer) *led for 1f: chsd ldrs: rdn over 2f out: ev ch 1f out: kpt on u.p* **7/1**[2]

4136 **4** *¾* **Reaching Out (IRE)**[8] 594 5-9-0 64 .... (b) JamesDoyle(3) 14 — 69
(N P Littmoden) *hld up wl bhd: hdwy wl over 3f out: rdn and effrt wl over 1f out: chsd ldrs ins last: unable qckn last 50 yds* **13/2**[1]

-023 **5** *nk* **Miss Monica (IRE)**[12] 558 6-8-4 51 oh6 .... PaulDoe 9 — 56
(P W Hiatt) *hld up bhd: rdn and hdwy on outer over 2f out: chsd ldrs 1f out: kpt on same pce wl ins fnl f* **33/1**

25-0 **6** *½* **Little Jimbob**[7] 604 6-9-4 65 .... PaulHanagan 13 — 69
(R A Fahey) *taken down early: led after 1f: rdn over 2f out: hdd wl over 1f out: wknd wl ins fnl f* **14/1**

0220 **7** *hd* **Blackmail (USA)**[4] 612 9-8-13 60 .... (b) JoeFanning 3 — 63
(P Mitchell) *t.k.h: chsd ldrs tl lost pl 3f out: kpt on over 1f out: r.o. nt rch ldrs* **8/1**[3]

3106 **8** *¾* **Play Up Pompey**[4] 610 5-8-9 59 .... AmirQuinn(3) 5 — 61
(J J Bridger) *chsd ldrs: rdn and effrt on inner wl over 1f out: no hdwy ins fnl f* **8/1**[3]

-623 **9** *½* **Master'n Commander**[7] 602 5-9-1 62 .... EddieAhern 7 — 63
(C A Cyzer) *chsd ldrs: rdn wl over 2f out: wknd over 1f out* **7/1**[2]

230- **10** *¾* **Conservative**[114] 6489 4-9-4 65 .... SteveDrowne 6 — 64
(P G Murphy) *hld up in rr: hdwy over 1f out: kpt on: nvr trbld ldrs* **33/1**

013- **11** *1* **Double Spectre (IRE)**[86] 5889 5-9-4 65 .... DaneO'Neill 8 — 63
(Jean-Rene Auvray) *w.w in tch in midfield: effrt and hung rt 3f out: nvr trbld ldrs* **12/1**

0-52 **12** *2 ½* **Connotation**[26] 431 5-8-5 52 .... (p) LPKeniry 1 — 45
(A G Newcombe) *hld up towards rr: n.d* **16/1**

-300 **13** *6* **Astronomical Odds (USA)**[22] 468 4-8-13 60 .... JohnEgan 10 — 41
(T D Barron) *chsd ldrs tl rdn and wknd over 2f out* **14/1**

2m 6.56s (-1.23) **Going Correction** -0.225s/f (Stan) **13** Ran SP% **117.0**
Speed ratings (Par 101):95,94,94,94,93 93,93,92,92,91 90,88,84
CSF £61.67 CT £411.55 TOTE £7.00: £2.50, £2.80, £2.60; EX 33.00 Trifecta £161.80 Pool: £585.99 - 2.57 winning tickets..
Owner D S Nevison **Bred** Mrs J McCreery **Trained** Hucking, Kent

FOCUS
A moderate handicap in which there was only a modest pace set in the early stages and it was a rush to the line rounding the final bend. The form does not look reliable despite the first four being close to their marks.

652 PONTINS.COM H'CAP — 1m 2f (P)
3:10 (3:16) (Class 4) (0-85,84) 4-Y-0+ **£5,181** (£1,541; £770; £192; £192) **Stalls** Low

Form — RPR

0-03 **1** **Art Modern (IRE)**[32] 362 5-9-1 78 .... (b) GeorgeBaker 10 — 86
(G L Moore) *hld up in tch: hdwy over 3f out: ev ch 2f out: rdn to ld 1f out: drvn out* **16/1**

0301 **2** *nk* **Cinematic (IRE)**[8] 594 4-8-6 72 .... SaleemGolam(3) 5 — 79+
(J R Boyle) *rrd leaving stalls: hmpd sn after s: hld up bhd: hdwy and shkn up over 2f out: str run ins last: nt quite rch wnr* **12/1**

6246 **3** *¾* **Tous Les Deux**[13] 552 4-8-12 75 .... RobbieFitzpatrick 12 — 81
(Peter Grayson) *plld hrd: hld up bhd: stdy hdwy on outer 5f out: rdn to chse ldrs over 2f out: unable qckn ins fnl f* **12/1**

-434 **4** *hd* **Trifti**[7] 604 6-8-7 70 .... EddieAhern 8 — 75
(C A Cyzer) *hld up towards rr: hdwy over 3f out: chsd ldrs u.p wl over 1f out: kpt on same pce wl ins last* **12/1**

1164 **4** *dht* **Sgt Schultz (IRE)**[8] 593 4-8-13 76 .... JohnEgan 7 — 81+
(J S Moore) *sn swtchd lft: t.k.h: in tch tl stdd and dropped to rr 4f out: c wd 2f out: r.o wl: nt rch ldrs* **9/1**[3]

5544 **6** *shd* **Prince Charlemagne (IRE)**[18] 501 4-8-13 79 .... JamesDoyle(3) 6 — 84+
(N P Littmoden) *rrd leaving stalls: hld up bhd: hdwy 3f out: rdn over 2f out: chsd ldrs 1f out: kpt on same pce: n.m.r cl home* **10/1**

4-13 **7** *¾* **Mataram (USA)**[33] 353 4-9-3 80 .... BrettDoyle 11 — 84+
(W Jarvis) *t.k.h: chsd ldrs on outer after 2f: wnt 2nd over 3f out: rdn to ld jst over 2f out: hdd 1f out: fdd last 100 yds* **11/4**[1]

00-2 **8** *nk* **Star Magnitude (USA)**[18] 501 6-9-0 84 .... JackMitchell(7) 4 — 87
(S Dow) *hld up bhd: hdwy over 2f out: swtchd lft and effrt on inner 1f out: no hdwy last 100 yds* **11/1**

0266 **9** *1 ¼* **Augustine**[27] 428 6-8-10 73 .... JoeFanning 13 — 74
(P W Hiatt) *chsd ldr for 2f: and again over 5f out: led over 3f out tl rdn and hdd jst over 2f out: wknd ins fnl f* **25/1**

12-0 **10** *1 ¼* **Peruvian Prince (USA)**[42] 256 5-9-2 79 .... PaulHanagan 1 — 77
(R A Fahey) *trckd ldrs on inner: nt clr run and lost pl over 2f out: swtchd rt and r.o over 1f out: no ch* **16/1**

112- **11** *nk* **Kapellmeister (IRE)**[221] 4005 4-8-7 70 ow1 .... MickyFenton 3 — 68
(M S Saunders) *led for 2f: chsd ldr tl over 5f out: rdn over 3f out: wknd over 2f out* **11/1**

1-11 **12** *11* **Bold Diktator**[27] 427 5-9-0 77 .... JimCrowley 9 — 54
(Tom Dascombe) *chsd ldrs rdn over 3f out: wknd over 2f out* **13/2**[2]

400- **13** *1 ½* **Farewell Gift**[58] 5908 6-8-4 70 .... (b) StephaneBreux(3) 14 — 44
(Carl Llewellyn) *t.k.h: led after 2f tl rdn and hdd over 3f out: sn wknd* **33/1**

151- **14** *24* **Inch Lodge**[86] 6811 5-9-1 78 .... PaulEddery 2 — 6
(Miss D Mountain) *chsd ldrs: rdn and lost pl wl over 4f out: t.o and eased wl over 1f out* **25/1**

2m 5.01s (-2.78) **Going Correction** -0.225s/f (Stan) **14** Ran SP% **121.2**
Speed ratings (Par 105):102,101,101,101,101 100,100,100,99,98 97,89,87,68
CSF £193.40 CT £2398.41 TOTE £15.30: £4.80, £4.90, £2.70; EX 420.40 TRIFECTA Not won..
Owner Matthew Green **Bred** Sir Eric Parker **Trained** Woodingdean, E Sussex

FOCUS
A fair handicap and average form as the pace was only ordinary in front, despite a few confirmed front-runners in the race, and several horses appeared unlucky.
Prince Charlemagne(IRE) Official explanation: jockey said gelding reared as stalls opened
Inch Lodge Official explanation: vet said horse had been struck into

653 PONTINS "BOOK EARLY" CLASSIFIED STKS — 6f (P)
3:45 (3:50) (Class 7) 4-Y-0+ **£1,365** (£403; £201) **Stalls** Low

Form — RPR

4666 **1** **Grand View**[4] 622 11-9-0 45 .... (p) DarryllHolland 11 — 51
(J R Weymes) *racd in midfield: hdwy on outer and bmpd over 2f out: str run on outer over 1f out: led last 50 yds* **6/1**

0000 **2** *½* **Alucica**[3] 632 4-9-0 41 .... (v) DeanMcKeown 3 — 49
(D Shaw) *hld up in midfield: swtchd rt and hdwy over 2f out: chsd ldr 2f out: ev ch 1f out: unable qckn wl ins last* **14/1**

0060 **3** *¾* **Tuscan Flyer**[9] 580 9-9-0 42 .... (b) JimmyQuinn 8 — 47
(R Bastiman) *w ldr tl led 3f out: rdn over 2f out: hdd wl ins last: wknd nr fin* **25/1**

05-0 **4** *1 ½* **Tiny Tim (IRE)**[46] 207 9-8-7 41 .... (b) DavidProbert(7) 2 — 42
(A M Balding) *racd in midfield: rdn and effrt wl over 1f out: kpt on same pce ins fnl f* **14/1**

0-52 **5** *½* **Double M**[48] 189 10-9-0 45 .... (v) RichardThomas 1 — 41
(Mrs L Richards) *hld up in midfield: hdwy 2f out: sn rdn: kpt on ins fnl f: nt pce to rch ldrs* **4/1**[3]

06-0 **6** *¾* **College Queen**[62] 51 9-9-0 40 .... IanMongan 10 — 39
(S Gollings) *trckd ldrs: swtchd rt and effrt over 2f out: hung lft over 1f out: wknd last 100 yds* **33/1**

00-0 **7** *nk* **Globe**[11] 567 4-8-7 41 .... KylieManser(7) 12 — 38
(Mrs H Sweeting) *wnt rt s: dropped in bhd: rdn and hdwy wl over 1f out: no imp ins fnl f* **33/1**

5-6 **8** *3* **Spinetail Rufous (IRE)**[39] 289 9-9-0 45 .... AdrianMcCarthy 6 — 29
(Miss Z C Davison) *trckd ldrs on inner: rdn wl over 1f out: wknd ins fnl f* **12/1**

-000 **9** *1 ¼* **Detonate**[12] 562 5-8-11 45 .... JamesDoyle(3) 7 — 25
(Ms J S Doyle) *s.i.s: bhd: rdn 3f out: nvr trbld ldrs* **7/2**[2]

0-00 **10** *nk* **Wilford Maverick (IRE)**[4] 620 5-9-0 41 .... (v) EddieAhern 5 — 24
(K J Burke) *s.i.s: a rr* **12/1**

3054 **11** *4* **Hill Of Almhuim (IRE)**[12] 557 4-9-0 44 .... (v) RobbieFitzpatrick 4 — 12+
(Peter Grayson) *rr whn hmpd after 1f: sn detached in last: n.d* **3/1**[1]

-060 **12** *1* **Feminist (IRE)**[15] 523 5-8-7 42 .... BarrySavage(7) 9 — 9
(J M Bradley) *led tl 3f out: wknd over 2f out* **33/1**

1m 12.07s (-0.74) **Going Correction** -0.225s/f (Stan) **12** Ran SP% **122.9**
Speed ratings (Par 97):95,94,93,91,90 89,89,85,83,83 77,76
CSF £86.43 TOTE £6.90: £2.50, £4.60, £3.80; EX 93.30 TRIFECTA Not won..
Owner Sporting Occasions **Bred** The Wickfield Stud Ltd **Trained** Middleham Moor, N Yorks

FOCUS
A decent pace from the off and the form looks straightforward and sound for the grade.

654 PONTIN'S FAMILY HOLIDAYS H'CAP — 6f (P)
4:20 (4:25) (Class 6) (0-60,61) 4-Y-0+ **£2,047** (£604; £302) **Stalls** Low

Form — RPR

-351 **1** **The Fisio**[4] 613 7-9-5 61 6ex .... (v) IanMongan 7 — 72
(S Gollings) *chsd ldng pair: rdn wl over 1f out: styd on wl last 100 yds to ld nr fin* **9/1**

5203 **2** *hd* **Fast Heart**[4] 622 6-9-1 57 .... (t) JoeFanning 8 — 68
(A Berry) *led tl rdn and hdd jst over 2f out: hung rt over 1f out: led again ins fnl f: hdd and no ex nr fin* **14/1**

5-62 **3** *½* **What Do You Know**[13] 548 4-9-4 60 .... JimmyQuinn 10 — 69
(A M Hales) *pressed ldr tl rdn to ld jst over 2f out: hdd ins fnl f: unable to qckn last 100 yds* **15/2**

3331 **4** *¾* **Desert Light (IRE)**[4] 622 6-9-0 56 6ex .... (v) DeanMcKeown 2 — 63
(D Shaw) *hld up in midfield: hdwy 2f out: chsd ldrs and hanging lft over 1f out: kpt on same pce insid efnl f* **7/1**[3]

0134 **5** *1 ¾* **Monte Major (IRE)**[32] 368 6-9-1 57 .... (v) DaneO'Neill 6 — 59
(D Shaw) *hld up in midfield on outer: rdn and effrt over 2f out: kpt on same pce* **14/1**

-264 **6** *½* **Caustic Wit (IRE)**[22] 467 9-9-3 59 .... (p) TonyCulhane 1 — 59
(M S Saunders) *hld up bhd: rdn 2f out: styd on ins fnl f: nt rch ldrs* **9/1**

2-21 **7** *½* **Kitchen Sink (IRE)**[40] 282 5-9-0 56 .... (e) EddieAhern 3 — 55
(P J Makin) *hld up in midfield: hdwy on inner 2f out: chsd ldrs over 1f out: wknd ins fnl f* **13/2**[2]

0400 **8** *nk* **Hotchpotch (USA)**[13] 548 4-8-10 55 .... (p) StephaneBreux(3) 5 — 53
(J R Best) *a bhd: rdn wl over 2f out: nvr trbld ldrs* **16/1**

4511 **9** *1 ½* **Blythe Spirit**[3] 632 8-8-11 58 6ex .... (v) JamieMoriarty(5) 4 — 51
(R A Fahey) *chsd ldrs tl rdn and wknd wl over 1f out* **7/4**[1]

6604 **10** *¾* **Zazous**[4] 614 6-8-8 57 .... RyanBird(7) 11 — 48
(J J Bridger) *s.i.s: swtchd lft s and dropped in bhd: n.d* **17/2**

1m 11.19s (-1.62) **Going Correction** -0.225s/f (Stan) **10** Ran SP% **123.7**
Speed ratings (Par 101):101,100,100,99,96 96,95,95,93,92
CSF £134.41 CT £722.44 TOTE £10.70: £3.40, £3.30, £3.10; EX 64.00 Trifecta £452.80 Part won. Pool: £637.76 - 0.20 winning tickets..
Owner John Crow Holdings Ltd **Bred** E Duggan And D Churchman **Trained** Scamblesby, Lincs

FOCUS
A moderate handicap run at a decent pace and rated positively as a result. The only negative to the race was that some of the horses did not seem to try their best under pressure.

617 WOLVERHAMPTON (A.W) (L-H)
Saturday, March 10

OFFICIAL GOING: Standard
The times suggested that conditions may have been on the fast side.
Wind: Fresh, behind Weather: Fine

655 WILLIAMHILLPOKER.COM MAIDEN STKS (DIV I) — 1m 141y(P)
1:50 (1:51) (Class 5) 3-Y-0 **£3,412** (£1,007; £504) **Stalls** Low

Form — RPR

0-3 **1** **Rambling Light**[40] 293 3-9-3 .... LPKeniry 9 — 80
(A M Balding) *a.p: led over 2f out: rdn and hung lft over 1f out: r.o* **7/1**[3]

4- **2** *¾* **Elyaadi**[141] 6071 3-8-12 .... RyanMoore 1 — 74+
(M R Channon) *hld up in tch: rdn 3f out: wnt 2nd wl over 1f out: styd on towards fin* **4/6**[1]

53- **3** *3* **Winged Farasi**[199] 4688 3-9-3 .... MickyFenton 3 — 72
(Miss J Feilden) *s.i.s: hld up in mid-div: hdwy on ins 3f out: rdn wl over 1f out: no ex ins fnl f* **18/1**

6 **4** *1 ½* **Art Professor (IRE)**[24] 456 3-9-3 .... SebSanders 6 — 69+
(J W Hills) *hld up towards rr: rdn and hdwy on ins 2f out: styd on same pce fnl f* **5/1**[2]

0 **5** *1 ¾* **Whodunit (UAE)**[42] 260 3-9-3 .... (b[1]) JoeFanning 4 — 66
(M Johnston) *led: hdd over 2f out: rdn and wknd wl over 1f out* **25/1**

54 **6** *1 ½* **Giddywell**[22] 484 3-8-7 .... RussellKennemore(5) 5 — 57
(R Hollinshead) *hld up in mid-div: rdn and hdwy on outside over 2f out: wknd wl over 1f out* **25/1**

7 *4* **Bugsy's Boy** 3-9-3 .... JohnEgan 8 — 54
(P W D'Arcy) *s.i.s: bhd: rdn 3f out: nvr nr ldrs* **66/1**

550- **8** *7* **Ireland Dancer (IRE)**[186] 5091 3-9-3 65 .... IanMongan 2 — 39
(P M Phelan) *a bhd* **50/1**

504- **9** *7* **Kindlelight Blue (IRE)**[223] 3979 3-9-3 70 .... GeorgeBaker 10 — 25+
(N P Littmoden) *sn prom: chsd ldr 6f out to 3f out: sn wknd* **16/1**

5- **10** *nk* **Celtic Memories (IRE)**[195] [4830] 3-8-5 .... NSLawes[7] 7 19
(M W Easterby) *hld up and bhd: rdn 3f out: sn struggling* **40/1**

1m 49.06s (-2.70) **Going Correction** -0.30s/f (Stan) **10** Ran SP% **113.9**
Speed ratings (Par 98):100,99,96,95,93 92,88,82,76,76
CSF £11.36 TOTE £5.90: £1.50, £1.10, £3.90; EX 13.00 Trifecta £122.90 Pool £509.18 - 2.94 winning units..
Owner George Strawbridge **Bred** George Strawbridge **Trained** Kingsclere, Hants

FOCUS
This looked much the stronger of the two divisions and the time was 1.69 seconds faster. The first four are all progressing and the form looks sound. Rambling Light is a likely improver in handicaps.
Kindelight Blue(IRE) Official explanation: jockey said colt had no more to give

656 WILLIAMHILL.CO.UK LADY WULFRUNA STKS (LISTED RACE) 7f 32y(P)
2:20 (2:21) (Class 1) 4-Y-O+
£14,762 (£5,595; £2,800; £1,396; £699; £351) **Stalls** High

Form RPR
220- **1** **Border Music**[263] [2732] 6-9-3 105 ....(b) RichardHughes 12 113+
(A M Balding) *chsd ldr tl over 2f out: led wl over 1f out: rdn and edgd rt ins fnl f: r.o wl* **15/2**
/13- **2** *1 ¾* **Jack Sullivan (USA)**[350] [738] 6-9-3 112 ....(t) EddieAhern 7 109
(G A Butler) *hld up in mid-div: rdn and hdwy over 2f out: chsd wnr and hung lft 1f out: no imp* **10/3**[2]
131- **3** *2 ½* **King's Caprice**[148] [5943] 6-9-3 104 ....(t) SteveDrowne 8 102
(J A Geake) *led: rdn and hdd wl over 1f out: sn edgd rt: no ex ins fnl f* **14/1**
5 **4** *1* **Farnesina (FR)**[34] [352] 5-8-12 ....(b) JCabre 4 94
(E Danel, France) *hmpd sn after s: bhd: rdn and hdwy 2f out: kpt on fnl f* **50/1**
01-1 **5** *hd* **Chicken Soup**[64] [44] 5-9-3 88 .... JohnEgan 3 99
(T J Pitt) *hmpd sn after s: prom: wnt 2nd over 2f out: sn rdn: wknd ins fnl f* **11/2**[3]
132- **6** *1 ¾* **Vacation (IRE)**[69] [6997] 4-9-3 87 .... DaneO'Neill 10 94
(V Smith) *s.i.s: bhd tl styd on fnl f: n.d* **33/1**
6-12 **7** *nk* **Woodnook**[14] [551] 4-8-12 95 .... JimmyFortune 5 89
(J A R Toller) *hmpd sn after s: rdn over 1f out: sme late prog: n.d* **9/1**
04-5 **8** *hd* **Curtail (IRE)**[43] [255] 4-9-3 88 .... TomEaves 9 93
(I Semple) *bhd: rdn over 3f out: nvr nr ldrs* **66/1**
06-4 **9** *1 ¾* **Chief Commander (FR)**[30] [391] 4-9-3 88 .... BrettDoyle 6 88
(Jane Chapple-Hyam) *hld up in mid-div: rdn over 3f out: hdwy over 2f out: wknd over 1f out* **33/1**
-300 **10** *¾* **Uhoomagoo**[30] [395] 9-9-3 ....(b) DarryllHolland 11 87
(K A Ryan) *rdn over 3f out: a bhd* **20/1**
3114 **11** *1* **Party Boss**[14] [552] 5-9-3 106 .... SebSanders 1 84
(C E Brittain) *prom: rdn 3f out: wknd 2f out: eased over 1f out* **9/4**[1]

1m 26.86s (-3.54) **Going Correction** -0.30s/f (Stan) **11** Ran SP% **111.8**
Speed ratings (Par 111):108,106,103,102,101 99,99,99,97,96 95
CSF £29.55 TOTE £8.80: £2.40, £1.80, £3.70; EX 38.50 Trifecta £487.60 Part won. Pool: £686.82. - 0.92 winning units..
Owner Kingsclere Stud **Bred** Mrs I A Balding **Trained** Kingsclere, Hants
■ This event had Listed status for the first time.

FOCUS
A cracking gallop led to the track record being broken by over half a second. Decent form for the grade, and sound. Border Music is up there with the best AW horses.

NOTEBOOK
Border Music had impressed when winning this race on this card 12 months ago, when it was a Class 2 conditions event. Laid out for this Listed race, he smashed the course record with a convincing victory and is considered well suited to this surface. Connections are hoping that he will be able to reproduce this sort of form and land a decent prize on turf. (op 7-1)
Jack Sullivan(USA) had not been seen since picking up a tendon injury in the Godolphin Mile at Nad Al Sheba a year ago. Using this as a stepping stone for a return to that same Group 2 event, he met his match after hanging left. (op 3-1)
King's Caprice adopted the same tactics as when rounding off last year by winning off a career-high mark at Newmarket in October. Going off at a blistering pace, there was no disgrace in this.
Farnesina(FR), a dual winner over an extended seven on sand at Deauville, finished a very respectable fourth after getting involved in a protracted barging match soon after the start. (op 40-1)
Chicken Soup, another involved in the trouble early on, eventually got found out by the big step up in class. He only ran here because he would have missed the cut in the Lincoln Trial. (op 6-1 tchd 13-2 and 5-1)
Party Boss was eased as if something was amiss in the home straight. Official explanation: jockey said horse never moved freely (op 5-2 tchd 2-1)

657 WILLIAMHILLPOKER.COM H'CAP 7f 32y(P)
2:55 (2:55) (Class 4) (0-85,87) 4-Y-O+ **£5,505** (£1,637; £818; £408) **Stalls** High

Form RPR
-111 **1** **Ektimaal**[40] [300] 4-8-12 81 ....(t) RyanMoore 6 98+
(E A L Dunlop) *a.p: led wl over 1f out: comf* **5/4**[1]
222- **2** *2 ½* **Resplendent Nova**[106] [6580] 5-8-13 82 .... JimmyQuinn 7 90
(P Howling) *w ldr: rdn and ev ch 2f out: kpt on same pce* **7/1**[2]
203- **3** *shd* **Fremen (USA)**[154] [5810] 7-8-11 80 .... SilvestreDeSousa 9 87
(D Nicholls) *a.p: rdn over 1f out: kpt on same pce fnl f* **20/1**
-441 **4** *shd* **Gallantry**[11] [576] 5-9-4 87 .... DeanMcKeown 11 94
(D Shaw) *hld up and bhd: rdn and hdwy over 1f out: r.o ins fnl f* **15/2**[3]
3351 **5** *nk* **Mandarin Spirit (IRE)**[18] [509] 7-8-11 80 ....(b) OscarUrbina 3 86
(G C H Chung) *hld up in mid-div: hdwy on ins wl over 1f out: one pce fnl f* **8/1**
-202 **6** *1* **Gifted Gamble**[18] [509] 5-8-12 81 ....(p) RichardHughes 8 85
(K A Ryan) *hld up in tch: rdn 2f out: no ex fnl f* **9/1**
-160 **7** *shd* **Grimes Faith**[11] [575] 4-8-6 82 ....(b) HaddenFrost[7] 4 85
(R Hannon) *hld up and bhd: sme hdwy over 1f out: nt clr run and swtchd rt ins fnl f: nt rch ldrs* **33/1**
8 *½* **Quai Du Roi (IRE)**[119] [5699] 5-8-7 79 .... AndrewMullen[3] 5 81
(K A Ryan) *s.i.s: c wd and rdn over 2f out: n.d* **14/1**
1242 **9** *1 ¼* **Rebellious Spirit**[11] [576] 4-9-2 85 .... JimCrowley 1 84
(P W Hiatt) *led: rdn and hdd wl over 1f out: wknd fnl f* **11/1**
00-5 **10** *7* **King Marju (IRE)**[22] [480] 5-8-8 77 .... PatCosgrave 10 58
(K R Burke) *t.k.h towards rr: bhd fnl 2f* **20/1**
015- **11** *6* **Hypnotic**[167] [5554] 5-8-9 78 ....(t) AdrianTNicholls 12 43
(D Nicholls) *hld up and bhd: stdy hdwy on outside over 4f out: rdn over 2f out: sn wknd* **33/1**

1m 27.77s (-2.63) **Going Correction** -0.30s/f (Stan) **11** Ran SP% **120.2**
Speed ratings (Par 105):103,100,100,99,99 98,98,97,96,88 81
CSF £9.85 CT £120.74 TOTE £2.00: £1.10, £2.70, £5.90; EX 11.70 Trifecta £74.80 Pool £684.08. - 6.49 winning units..
Owner The Serendipity Partnership **Bred** Whitsbury Manor Stud **Trained** Newmarket, Suffolk

FOCUS
A good handicap and solid-looking form. Ektimaal continues to go from strength to strength and clocked a very respectable time.

658 WILLIAM HILL LINCOLN TRIAL STKS (HERITAGE H'CAP) 1m 141y(P)
3:30 (3:30) (Class 2) (0-105,100) 4-Y-O+
£31,160 (£9,330; £4,665; £2,335; £1,165; £585) **Stalls** Low

Form RPR
-444 **1** **Orchard Supreme**[14] [550] 4-9-8 98 .... RichardHughes 12 108
(R Hannon) *hld up and bhd: hdwy on ins wl over 1f out: rdn to ld 1f out: hung rt wl ins fnl f: r.o* **9/1**
13-2 **2** *½* **Bomber Command (USA)**[14] [550] 4-9-3 93 .... EddieAhern 4 102
(J W Hills) *hld up in mid-div: hdwy on ins over 2f out: rdn over 1f out: hung rt towards fin: r.o* **7/2**[2]
050- **3** *¾* **Tanzanite (IRE)**[161] [5675] 5-9-0 90 .... SebSanders 3 97
(D W P Arbuthnot) *a.p: rdn 2f out: styng on whn bmpd and carried rt cl home* **40/1**
2-46 **4** *nk* **Marajaa (IRE)**[14] [550] 5-8-12 88 .... BrettDoyle 13 94
(W J Musson) *hld up towards rr: rdn and hdwy on outside wl over 1f out: styng on whn bmpd and carried rt cl home* **9/1**
-203 **5** *1 ¼* **Speedy Sam**[30] [401] 4-9-5 95 ....(v[1]) PatCosgrave 6 99
(K R Burke) *hld up in tch: rdn over 3f out: one pce fnl 2f* **11/2**[3]
2123 **6** *½* **Waterside (IRE)**[14] [550] 8-9-10 100 .... RyanMoore 5 103
(G L Moore) *sn chsng ldr: rdn to ld briefly jst over 1f out: fdd towards fin* **10/1**
0-00 **7** *1 ¼* **Moayed**[14] [550] 8-9-1 91 .... IanMongan 2 91
(N P Littmoden) *hld up and bhd: rdn and hdwy whn nt clr run briefly 2f out: no imp: fnl f* **12/1**
000- **8** *½* **My Paris**[161] [5675] 6-8-13 92 .... AndrewMullen[3] 1 91
(K A Ryan) *led: rdn over 2f out: hdd jst over 1f out: wknd ins fnl f* **12/1**
232- **9** *1 ½* **Collateral Damage (IRE)**[133] [6210] 4-8-13 89 .... DavidAllan 10 85
(T D Easterby) *bhd: rdn over 3f out: no rspnse* **25/1**
20-0 **10** *2 ½* **Humungous (IRE)**[14] [550] 4-9-7 97 .... SteveDrowne 11 88
(C R Egerton) *bhd: rdn over 3f out: short-lived effrt over 2f out* **14/1**
-503 **11** *4* **Wessex (USA)**[30] [391] 7-9-1 91 .... PaulMulrennan 9 73
(P A Blockley) *hld up in tch: rdn over 3f out: sn wknd* **25/1**
0-36 **12** *11* **Hail The Chief**[34] [352] 10-9-5 95 .... DaneO'Neill 8 54
(R Hannon) *prom: rdn over 3f out: sn wknd: fin lame* **22/1**
-431 **P** **Very Wise**[42] [264] 5-9-2 92 .... JoeFanning 7 —
(W J Haggas) *hd in next stall whn gates opened: s.v.s: sn p.u* **3/1**[1]

1m 47.31s (-4.45) **Going Correction** -0.30s/f (Stan) **13** Ran SP% **128.2**
Speed ratings (Par 109):107,106,105,105,104 104,102,102,101,98 95,85,—
CSF £41.93 CT £1309.45 TOTE £10.50: £2.90, £2.00, £12.60; EX 57.90 Trifecta £2559.30 Pool £25,521.49. - 7.08 winning units..
Owner Brian C Oakley **Bred** Mrs M H Goodrich **Trained** East Everleigh, Wilts
■ Stewards' Enquiry : Eddie Ahern one-day ban: careless riding (Mar 21)

FOCUS
A dramatic renewal of this valuable handicap won in a fast time with the well-backed favourite virtually taking no part. Good form, rated through the third and fourth to their best. The first two are improving.

NOTEBOOK
Orchard Supreme produced a career-best to reverse last month's Lingfield seven-furlong form with Bomber Command and Waterside. Better suited to the longer trip, he found enough after both he and the runner-up hung right late on. Considered best on sand, the Winter Derby at Lingfield rather than the Lincoln is sounding like the preferred option. (op 8-1 tchd 15-2)
Bomber Command(USA), supported by the offices, had finished nearly a length ahead of the winner on a pound better terms over seven at Lingfield last time. Ahern was handed a one-day ban after his mount caused the third to bump the fourth late on. (op 11-2)
Tanzanite(IRE) ◆ was making her All-Weather debut having not been seen since only beating four home in the Cambridgeshire. Done no favours by the runner-up at the death, the prospect of a Lincoln being run in the soft will not bother her and she does seem back to form.
Marajaa(IRE) ◆ got caught up in the domino effect after the coming together of the second and third late in the day. Off a rating 8lb higher than when landing a touch at Kempton in November, he does seem capable of winning from this sort of mark. (op 8-1 tchd 10-1)
Speedy Sam, tried in a visor on this return from Dubai, was running off a mark 8lb higher than when successful over ten furlongs at Lingfield in November. That trip probably suits him better on Polytrack. (op 6-1)
Waterside(IRE) had split Bomber Command and Orchard Supreme in a tight finish over seven at Lingfield last time but would have needed a personal best to win this. (op 9-1)
Hail The Chief Official explanation: vet said horse returned lame
Very Wise, a well-backed favourite, had his head the wrong side of the pillar with the next stall when the Starter pressed the button. Official explanation: trainer said gelding had its head wrong side of the pillar on starting gate making it impossible for it to jump out (op 11-2)

659 WILLIAM HILL 0800 44 40 40 CLAIMING STKS 5f 20y(P)
4:00 (4:00) (Class 6) 3-Y-O **£2,730** (£806; £403) **Stalls** Low

Form RPR
-503 **1** **Belvedere Vixen**[9] [588] 3-8-7 58 ....(p) EddieAhern 3 56
(M J Wallace) *chsd ldrs: r.o to ld cl home* **6/1**
40-4 **2** *¾* **Temtation (IRE)**[9] [588] 3-8-5 60 .... PaulHanagan 5 51
(J R Boyle) *w ldr: rdn and edgd lft over 1f out: kpt on ins fnl f* **2/1**[1]
-006 **3** *shd* **Head To Head (IRE)**[17] [512] 3-8-10 50 .... AdamKirby 1 56
(Peter Grayson) *s.i.s: swtchd rt over 1f out: r.o ins fnl f: nrst fin* **22/1**
-433 **4** *½* **Pirner's Brig**[16] [520] 3-8-12 62 .... PaulMulrennan 4 56
(M W Easterby) *led: rdn wl over 1f out: hdd and no ex cl home* **5/2**[2]
6-65 **5** *1 ¾* **Arnie's Joint (IRE)**[19] [502] 3-9-3 64 .... IanMongan 2 55
(N P Littmoden) *chsd ldrs: rdn over 2f out: wknd ins fnl f* **11/4**[3]
-432 **6** *4* **Pretty Selma**[18] [506] 3-7-11 44 ....(b) DuranFentiman[5] 6 26
(R M H Cowell) *s.i.s: plld hrd: rdn over 2f out: hung lft over 1f out: sn struggling* **16/1**

62.38 secs (-0.44) **Going Correction** -0.30s/f (Stan) **6** Ran SP% **113.1**
Speed ratings (Par 96):91,89,89,88,86 79
CSF £18.74 TOTE £5.90: £3.00, £1.90; EX 12.50.
Owner M J Wallace **Bred** Miss J Hall **Trained** Newmarket, Suffolk

FOCUS
A weak claimer and a case of 'after the Lord Mayor's Show'. The first two did not need to perform to their best.

660 WILLIAMHILLCASINO.COM H'CAP 5f 216y(P)
4:35 (4:35) (Class 2) (0-100,104) 4-Y-O+ **£11,658** (£3,468; £1,733; £865) **Stalls** Low

Form RPR
-540 **1** **Ajigolo**[14] [550] 4-8-6 90 .... SamHitchcott 2 104
(M R Channon) *t.k.h: sn mid-div: rdn and hdwy on outside over 1f out: led wl ins fnl f: r.o wl* **9/2**[1]

2353 **2** 2 1/2 **Qadar (IRE)**[14] [551] 5-9-2 **100**..........(b) IanMongan 1 106
(N P Littmoden) *chsd ldrs: rdn wl over 1f out: ev ch ins fnl f: nt qckn* **9/2**[1]
4-50 **3** nk **One More Round (USA)**[21] [490] 9-8-9 **93**..........(b) RyanMoore 10 98
(N P Littmoden) *hld up and bhd: hdwy on ins whn bmpd over 2f out: led 1f out: edgd lft and hdd wl ins fnl f: nt qckn* **16/1**
3-50 **4** 1 **First Order**[35] [344] 6-8-4 **88**.......... PaulHanagan 3 90
(I Semple) *led: rdn over 2f out: hdd 1f out: no ex wl ins fnl f* **16/1**
-451 **5** 1 **Bahamian Pirate (USA)**[25] [452] 12-8-12 **96**.......... AdrianTNicholls 6 95
(D Nicholls) *hld up and bhd: rdn 3f out: hdwy over 1f out: one pce fnl f* **16/1**
000- **6** 1 **Coeur Courageux (FR)**[252] [3079] 5-8-6 **90**..........(t) EddieAhern 12 86
(D Nicholls) *hld up in rr: hdwy on ins wl over 1f out: nvr nr to chal* **40/1**
142- **7** 1 1/2 **Ripples Maid**[149] [5919] 4-8-8 **92**.......... RichardThomas 5 84
(J A Geake) *w ldr: rdn and wknd over 1f out* **11/2**[3]
-244 **8** 1 1/2 **Red Cape (FR)**[14] [551] 4-8-10 **94**.......... BrettDoyle 7 81
(Jane Chapple-Hyam) *prom: rdn over 2f out: wknd wl over 1f out* **5/1**[2]
-413 **9** 3/4 **Distinctly Game**[21] [490] 5-8-3 **87**.......... CatherineGannon 8 72
(K A Ryan) *plld hrd: prom: lost pl over 4f out: bhd fnl 3f* **7/1**
3511 **10** 2 **Magic Glade**[14] [554] 8-8-3 **87**.......... EdwardCreighton 9 66
(Tom Dascombe) *t.k.h: chsd ldrs: wknd wl over 1f out* **7/1**
0025 **11** 1 1/4 **Garstang**[11] [575] 4-8-5 **89** oh8 ow3..........(b) RobbieFitzpatrick 4 64
(Peter Grayson) *chsd ldrs: rdn over 2f out: sn wknd* **16/1**

1m 12.78s (-3.03) **Going Correction** -0.30s/f (Stan) **11** Ran SP% **119.4**
Speed ratings (Par 109):108,104,104,102,101 100,98,96,95,92 90
CSF £24.83 CT £308.31 TOTE £6.40: £2.60, £1.70, £5.10; EX 30.80 Trifecta £638.80 Part won. Pool: £899.84. - 0.68 winning units..
Owner Timberhill Racing Partnership **Bred** Timber Hill Racing Partnership **Trained** West Ilsley, Berks

FOCUS
A decent handicap with the winning time suggesting that they went quicker than was apparent. The form looks sound.

NOTEBOOK
Ajigolo ◆, highly tried last year, took advantage of having slipped a total of 6lb in the ratings and being back over what may well be his optimum distance. There was plenty to like about this performance and he can score again if the Handicapper is not too hard on him. (op 7-1)
Qadar(IRE), dropped 2lb, did not do much wrong but had no answer to the winner in the closing stages. (tchd 4-1 and 5-1)
One More Round(USA) is being given a chance by the Handicapper now that he is in the veteran stage. He was another to get brushed aside by the winner. (op 12-1)
First Order, 3lb higher than when successful over course and distance in November, and without the visor, only gave best late in the day after forcing the pace. (op 14-1)
Bahamian Pirate(USA) was making his Polytrack debut having gone up 4lb for winning at Southwell. (op 10-1)
Coeur Courageux(FR) ◆, who doubled in price in the ring, was having his first outing since the beginning of July last year. He appeared to be given a nice pipe-opener over a trip short of his best and is one to keep an eye on. (op 20-1)

661 WILLIAMHILLPOKER.COM MAIDEN STKS (DIV II) 1m 141y(P)
5:10 (5:11) (Class 5) 3-Y-O **£3,412** (£1,007; £504) **Stalls** Low

Form RPR
35 **1** **Ridgewell (USA)**[49] [193] 3-8-12..........(t) RyanMoore 2 69
(B J Meehan) *a.p: rdn to ld and hung lft 1f out: sn flashed tail: r.o wl* **2/1**[1]
36-4 **2** 4 **Mizzle (USA)**[12] [569] 3-8-12 68.......... JoeFanning 7 61
(M Johnston) *w ldr: rdn 2f out: ev ch whn edgd rt 1f out: one pce* **4/1**[3]
3-2 **3** 1 3/4 **My Beautaful**[53] [152] 3-8-12.......... EdwardCreighton 3 57
(Miss J S Davis) *led: rdn and hdd 1f out: one pce* **14/1**
00 **4** 3 **Noravana (IRE)**[24] [456] 3-8-5.......... JamesO'Reilly(7) 5 51?
(Miss V Haigh) *hld up in mid-div: rdn over 3f out: no hdwy fnl 2f* **200/1**
00- **5** 1 **Mountain Cat (IRE)**[134] [6200] 3-9-3.......... BrettDoyle 6 54
(W J Musson) *hld up and bhd: rdn and hdwy over 1f out: nvr nr ldrs* **16/1**
6 **6** 2 1/2 **I Will If You Will**[16] [522] 3-8-12.......... DarryllHolland 8 44
(K A Ryan) *dwlt: sn prom: rdn 3f out: wknd wl over 1f out* **22/1**
026- **7** 3 **Cry Presto (USA)**[86] [6824] 3-9-3 77.......... RichardHughes 10 42
(R Hannon) *hld up towards rr: rdn 4f out: short-lived effrt over 2f out* **3/1**[2]
00 **8** 1 1/2 **Mark Of Love (IRE)**[40] [293] 3-9-3.......... TonyCulhane 1 39
(M R Channon) *stdd s: a bhd* **6/1**
50- **9** 1/2 **Remark (IRE)**[126] [6331] 3-9-3.......... PaulMulrennan 9 38
(M W Easterby) *a bhd* **33/1**
40 **10** 10 **Jonny Behave**[11] [572] 3-9-3.......... AdamKirby 4 17
(I A Wood) *mid-div: rdn 4f out: bhd fnl 2f* **50/1**

1m 50.75s (-1.01) **Going Correction** -0.30s/f (Stan) **10** Ran SP% **114.9**
Speed ratings (Par 98):92,88,86,84,83 81,78,77,76,67
CSF £9.74 TOTE £2.60: £1.10, £1.70, £2.80; EX 13.40 Trifecta £58.10 Pool £1,024.27. - 12.50 winning units. .
Owner Joe L Allbritton **Bred** Estate Of George Kleier, Et Al **Trained** Manton, Wilts

FOCUS
This looked much the weaker of the two divisions and was 1.69 seconds slower. The winner showed marginal improvement but could struggle when reassessed.
Mountain Cat(IRE) Official explanation: jockey said gelding failed to handle first bend
I Will If You Will Official explanation: jockey said filly missed the break
Jonny Behave Official explanation: jockey said gelding moved poorly in home straight

662 WILLIAMHILLRADIO.COM H'CAP 1m 5f 194y(P)
5:40 (5:40) (Class 4) (0-85,85) 4-Y-O+ **£5,505** (£1,637; £818; £408) **Stalls** Low

Form RPR
311- **1** **Salute (IRE)**[85] [6831] 8-9-2 **76**.......... DaneO'Neill 6 87
(P G Murphy) *hld up in mid-div: hdwy over 4f out: led over 1f out: rdn and styd on wl* **20/1**
6-51 **2** 1 1/2 **Pass The Port**[28] [428] 6-9-3 **77**..........(p) RobertHavlin 5 86
(D Haydn Jones) *t.k.h in rr: hdwy over 3f out: rdn and r.o ins fnl f: nt trble wnr* **12/1**
42-3 **3** 1 1/4 **Nawamees (IRE)**[24] [457] 9-9-9 **83**..........(p) RyanMoore 4 90
(G L Moore) *hld up in mid-div: rdn and hdwy wl over 1f out: nt qckn ins fnl f* **5/1**[3]
6-44 **4** 2 **Croon**[27] [434] 5-9-0 **77**.......... GregFairley(3) 1 81
(T J Pitt) *sn chsng ldr: led over 3f out: sn rdn: hdd over 1f out: one pce* **8/1**
22-0 **5** shd **Jeepstar**[24] [457] 7-9-1 **75**.......... J-PGuillambert 11 79
(S C Williams) *led: rdn and hdd over 3f out: wknd over 1f out* **12/1**
1233 **6** nk **Share The Feeling (IRE)**[17] [515] 5-8-9 **72**.......... RichardKingscote(3) 7 75
(J W Unett) *hld up in tch: rdn over 2f out: btn whn hung lft fr over 1f out* **15/2**
5600 **7** 1 3/4 **Valance (IRE)**[9] [593] 7-9-5 **79**..........(bt) SebSanders 3 80
(C R Egerton) *hld up in tch: rdn over 2f out: wknd wl over 1f out* **20/1**
1011 **8** hd **Wild Pitch**[17] [515] 6-9-4 **85**..........(b) JackMitchell(7) 2 86
(P Mitchell) *dwlt: hld up and bhd: hdwy on ins whn nt clr run over 2f out: no further prog* **4/1**[2]
14-2 **9** 7 **Billich**[24] [457] 4-9-5 **83**.......... JoeFanning 8 74
(E J O'Neill) *t.k.h: a bhd* **11/4**[1]
30-0 **10** nk **Turn 'n Burn**[66] [29] 6-8-6 **66**.......... EddieAhern 9 56
(C A Cyzer) *s.i.s: sn prom: rdn and wknd over 2f out* **33/1**
/600 **11** 6 **Mission To Mars**[9] [587] 8-9-2 **76**.......... SteveDrowne 10 58
(P G Murphy) *a bhd* **40/1**
060/ **12** 6 **Trust Rule**[73] [5747] 7-8-12 **72**..........(t) DaleGibson 12 46
(M W Easterby) *hld up in mid-div: rdn and bhd fnl 4f* **50/1**

3m 0.67s (-6.70) **Going Correction** -0.30s/f (Stan)
WFA 4 from 5yo+ 4lb **12** Ran SP% **118.5**
Speed ratings (Par 105):107,106,105,104,104 104,103,102,98,98 95,91
CSF £229.02 CT £1398.08 TOTE £20.70: £4.70, £3.40, £3.00; EX 150.40 Trifecta £515.80 Part won. Pool: £726.54. - 0.52 winning units. Place 6 £61.16, Place 5 £47.67. .
Owner The Golden Anorak Partnership **Bred** Ahmed M Foustok **Trained** East Garston, Berks

FOCUS
A fairly competitive handicap won in a decent time. Sound form, rated through the third and fourth.
Share The Feeling(IRE) Official explanation: jockey said mare ran too freely
T/Plt: £61.60 to a £1 stake. Pool: £100,845.90. 1,193.70 winning tickets. T/Qpdt: £12.50 to a £1 stake. Pool: £4,253.80. 250.70 winning tickets. KH

SAINT-CLOUD (L-H)
Saturday, March 10

OFFICIAL GOING: Heavy

663a PRIX EXBURY (GROUP 3) 1m 2f
3:20 (3:19) 4-Y-O+ **£27,027** (£10,811; £8,108; £5,405; £2,703)

RPR
1 **Pearl Sky (FR)**[95] [6722] 4-8-6.......... ACrastus 2 114
(Y De Nicolay, France) *in tch, 4th str, ran on to go 2nd 1 1/2f out, driven and running on whn lft in front app fnl f, ran on wl, driven out* **114/10**
2 5 **Elasos (FR)**[105] [6610] 5-8-10.......... DBonilla 7 109
(D Sepulchre, France) *held up, last straight, ran on strongly final furlong, took 2nd on line* **23/1**
3 hd **Runaway**[150] [5913] 5-8-12.......... CSoumillon 9 111
(A Fabre, France) *prominent towards outside, led straight, jinked left and hit rail approaching final furlong, headed, lost 2nd on line* **17/10**[1]
4 1 1/2 **Boris De Deauville (IRE)**[132] [6250] 4-9-0.......... YBarberot 8 110
(S Wattel, France) *prominent, 3rd straight, stayed on at one pace to line* **47/1**
5 shd **Blushing King (FR)**[38] 5-8-10.......... FVeron 11 106
(J-L Guillochon, France) *towards rear, 9th straight, late headway on outside but never dangerous* **28/1**
6 1 **Bellamy Cay**[139] [6119] 5-9-2.......... SPasquier 5 110
(A Fabre, France) *mid-division, 5th and pushed along straight, one pace from over 1f out* **17/10**[1]
7 nk **Montare (IRE)**[139] [6119] 5-9-1.......... OPeslier 6 108
(J E Pease, France) *mid-division, disputing 6th straight, never dangerous* **28/10**[2]
8 1 1/2 **Mister Conway (FR)**[90] [6786] 6-8-10.......... RonanThomas 4 101
(P Van De Poele, France) *led on rail to straight, weakened 1 1/2f out* **43/10**[3]
9 3 **Morna (FR)**[143] [6062] 4-8-6.......... TThulliez 1 91
(S Wattel, France) *towards rear on rail, disputing 6th straight, never dangerous* **56/10**
10 snk **Miss Salvador (FR)**[137] [6171] 4-8-11.......... TJarnet 10 96
(S Wattel, France) *mid-division, disputing 6th straight, never dangerous* **56/10**
11 **Freedonia**[104] [6612] 5-8-13.......... TGillet 3 98
(J E Hammond, France) *towards rear, 10th straight, never a factor* **61/10**

2m 13.8s (-2.20) **11** Ran SP% **181.4**
PARI-MUTUEL: WIN 12.00; PL 3.00, 4.70, 2.10; DF 99.10.
Owner H Hogg **Bred** Mme Patricia Beck **Trained** France

NOTEBOOK
Pearl Sky(FR) looked in great condition and, judging by this performance, she could go on to better things. She began her run from two out and then took the lead shortly after when the third jinked his way out of contention, and she was all alone inside the final furlong. Certainly a filly on the upgrade, she now heads for the Prix Allez France at Chantilly.
Elasos(FR), one of the outsiders, put up a pretty good performance. He still had plenty to do coming into the straight but from a furlong and a half out he stayed on well and took second place in the final few strides.
Runaway could have won this race and would have certainly been second but for jinking running into the final two furlongs. It was not the first time this five-year-old has behaved in this fashion as he did the same thing at Bordeaux in the autumn, and also in the Dollar in 2005. Having always been well up, he quickened into what looked to be a winning lead soon after entering the straight, but his antics were disastrous and his jockey did well to stay on board.
Boris De Deauville(IRE) was a little free during the race but did battle on courageously up the straight and held on gamely to take fourth position.

[625]SOUTHWELL (L-H)
Tuesday, March 13

OFFICIAL GOING: Standard
Wind: Moderate, half behind

664 BETDIRECT.COM GET INVOLVED CLASSIFIED CLAIMING STKS (DIV I) 1m (F)
1:20 (1:20) (Class 6) 4-Y-O+ **£1,501** (£443; £221) **Stalls** Low

Form RPR
12-0 **1** **Island Green (USA)**[56] [156] 4-8-10 47.......... TPQueally 5 62+
(B J Curley) *keen: trckd ldrs: hdwy to ld 2f out: pushed clr ent last: eased towards fin* **7/1**
3025 **2** 1/2 **Mademoiselle**[15] [570] 5-8-8 55.......... MichaelJStainton(5) 2 61
(R A Harris) *in tch on inner: hdwy over 2f out: rdn to chse wnr over 1f out: kpt on u.p ins last* **11/4**[2]
-020 **3** 5 **Weet For Ever (USA)**[63] [75] 4-9-6 52.......... DarryllHolland 8 58
(P A Blockley) *led: rdn along 3f out: hdd 2f out and sn one pce* **9/1**

04-4 **4** 1½ **Sawwaah (IRE)**[11] [605] 10-9-2 55..............................(v) AdrianTNicholls 9 50
(D Nicholls) *s.i.s: gd hdwy 3f out: chsd ldrs and n.m.r wl over 1f out: sn rdn and one pce* **4/1**[3]

0040 **5** 4 **Hometomammy**[19] [519] 5-9-0 43.. ChrisCatlin 11 40
(P W Hiatt) *cl up: rdn along over 2f out and grad wknd* **20/1**

3052 **6** 3 **Vancouver Gold (IRE)**[26] [466] 5-8-7 49.......................... PatCosgrave 6 27
(K R Burke) *trckd ldrs: pushed along over 3f out: rdn over 2f out and sn btn* **5/2**[1]

0036 **7** 1 **Mr Bountiful (IRE)**[19] [524] 9-9-0 45....................................(t) AlanDaly 3 32
(C J Teague) *a towards rr* **25/1**

0000 **8** nk **Crusoe (IRE)**[13] [579] 10-8-3 40....................................(p) SoniaEaton(7) 7 27
(A Sadik) *a rr* **25/1**

5-00 **9** 4 **Rainbow's Classic**[21] [504] 4-8-9 55......................(t) DuranFentiman(5) 10 23
(P Beaumont) *dwlt: a rr* **28/1**

/0-0 **10** shd **Wizardmicktee (IRE)**[20] [514] 5-8-12 33..............(b[1]) CatherineGannon 4 20
(D G Bridgwater) *keen: sn chsng ldrs: rdn along 3f out and sn wknd* **100/1**

1m 45.54s (0.94) **Going Correction** +0.175s/f (Slow) **10** Ran SP% **114.6**
Speed ratings (Par 101):102,101,96,95,91 88,87,86,82,82
CSF £24.59 TOTE £7.90: £2.00, £1.30, £3.00; EX 39.70 Trifecta £118.90 Pool: £229.61 - 1.37 winning units..Island Green was claimed by Declan Carroll for £5,000.
Owner Curley Leisure **Bred** Gainsborough Farm Llc **Trained** Newmarket, Suffolk

FOCUS
A routine contest of its type in which the front pair pulled well clear of the rest and the winning time was 1.12 seconds quicker than the second division. Sound form through the second and third, with the winner value for 2l and up 8lb.
Island Green(USA) Official explanation: trainer's rep said, regarding apparent improvement in form, he was unable to explain poor form last time and felt the gelding was suited by the drop in class to a claimer
Vancouver Gold(IRE) Official explanation: trainer's rep had no explanation for the poor form shown

665 BETDIRECT.COM NEW WEBSITE APPRENTICE H'CAP 1m 4f (F)
1:50 (1:51) (Class 6) (0-55,55) 4-Y-0+ **£2,388** (£705; £352) **Stalls** Low

Form RPR

0-32 **1** **Nimello (USA)**[21] [508] 11-8-11 **53**.............................. JamesMillman(3) 12 62+
(A G Newcombe) *hld up towards rr: smooth hdwy over 3f out: chsd ldrs over 1f out: strayed on ins last to ld nr line* **4/1**[1]

6505 **2** nk **They All Laughed**[21] [503] 4-8-7 **53** ow1..................... KylieManser(5) 11 62
(P W Hiatt) *hld up in rr: gd hdwy over 3f out: chal 2f out: rdn to ld over 1f out: edgd lft ins last: hdd nr line* **11/1**

-633 **3** 3 **Twilight Avenger (IRE)**[21] [508] 4-8-5 **46** oh1.........(t) KevinGhunowa 10 50
(W M Brisbourne) *in tch: hdwy 4f out: led 2f out: sn rdn and hdd over 1f out: kpt on same pce* **14/1**

01-5 **4** 1 **Padre Nostro (IRE)**[65] [64] 8-8-2 **46** oh1................ ChrisGlenister(5) 14 48
(J R Holt) *hld up towards rr: stdy hdwy over 3f out: chsd ldrs wl over 1f out: sn rdn and no imp fnl f* **6/1**[2]

-003 **5** 1½ **Kalatime (IRE)**[44] [279] 4-8-9 **55**................................... JosephWalsh(5) 5 55
(M F Harris) *midfield: smooth hdwy on inner over 4f out: effrt and ev ch 2f out: sn rdn and one pce* **16/1**

0-24 **6** nk **Trysting Grove (IRE)**[13] [585] 6-8-7 **46** oh1................. DuranFentiman 1 46
(E G Bevan) *slowly int stride and bhd: hdwy 4f out: rdn along and styd on fnl 2f: nrst fin* **8/1**

0260 **7** 1¼ **Bournonville**[22] [496] 4-8-2 **46** oh1............................. KirstyMilczarek(3) 8 44
(M Wigham) *cl up: led 4f out: rdn along and hdd 2f out: grad wknd* **20/1**

540- **8** hd **Planters Punch (IRE)**[7] [5750] 6-9-2 **55**.......................... JamieMoriarty 4 52
(G M Moore) *chsd ldrs: rdn along 4f out: wknd wl over 2f out* **7/1**[3]

000- **9** 5 **Explosive Fox (IRE)**[70] [5390] 6-8-11 **55**.....................(p) SophieDoyle(5) 9 44
(S Curran) *led: rdn along and hdd 4f out: wknd wl over 2f out* **20/1**

0-3 **10** ½ **Salym (FR)**[24] [372] 6-8-2 **48**.. BillyCray(7) 2 36
(D J S Ffrench Davis) *a towards rr* **14/1**

3231 **11** 2 **Comeintothespace (IRE)**[8] [616] 5-8-12 **54** 6ex......... WilliamBuick(3) 3 39
(R A Farrant) *hld up towards rr: pushed along and sme headway on inner over 3f out: sn rdn and btn* **4/1**[1]

0040 **12** ½ **Mi Odds**[26] [464] 11-8-1 **47** oh1 ow1........................... ClaireWheatcroft(7) 6 31
(Mrs N Macauley) *chsd ldng pair: rdn along over 4f out and sn wknd* **50/1**

-100 **13** 13 **Ellesappelle**[8] [610] 4-9-0 **55**...................................(p) MichaelJStainton 13 19
(R A Harris) *midfield: rdn along 5f out: sn wknd* **20/1**

2m 44.62s (2.53) **Going Correction** +0.175s/f (Slow)
WFA 4 from 5yo+ 2lb **13** Ran SP% **121.7**
Speed ratings (Par 101):98,97,95,95,94 93,93,92,89,89 87,87,78
CSF £47.84 CT £575.54 TOTE £3.90: £1.70, £4.90, £3.00; EX 95.10 TRIFECTA Not won..
Owner Mrs Jayne Bramhill **Bred** Glencrest Farm **Trained** Yarnscombe, Devon

FOCUS
A very weak handicap, confined to apprentice riders, which was run at a sound pace. The form is straightforward rated through the second and third, with the winner not needing to improve on his recent sound form. The winner and third reproduced their latest form behind subsequent scorer Muntami.
Comeintothespace(IRE) Official explanation: trainer's rep said, regarding the poor form shown, he felt gelding failed to stay 1m 4f

666 BETDIRECT.COM GET INVOLVED CLASSIFIED CLAIMING STKS (DIV II) 1m (F)
2:25 (2:25) (Class 6) 4-Y-0+ **£1,501** (£443; £221) **Stalls** Low

Form RPR

500- **1** **Sonic Anthem (USA)**[75] [1123] 5-9-6 54..................... SilvestreDeSousa 4 65+
(P C Haslam) *bhd: hdwy and nt clr run 2f out: swtchd rt and rdn over 1f out: styd on strly ins last to ld nr fin* **4/1**[2]

1313 **2** nk **Norwegian**[15] [570] 6-9-2 54..(p) PaulEddery 10 60
(Ian Williams) *trckd ldrs: snmooth hdwy to ld 2f out: rdn clr ent last: hdd nr fin* **5/4**[1]

0400 **3** 3 **Captain Bolsh**[35] [372] 4-9-0 41...................................... J-PGuillambert 1 52
(J Pearce) *in tch: hdwy and nt clr run 2f out: sn swtchd rt and rdn to chse ldrs over 1f out: sn one pce* **25/1**

0060 **4** 5 **Methusaleh (IRE)**[29] [445] 4-8-12 53............................ DeanMcKeown 5 40
(D Shaw) *s.i.s and bhd: gd hdwy on inner 2f out: rdn to chse ldrs over 1f out: sn drvn and wknd* **13/2**[3]

-050 **5** 1¼ **Tackcoat (IRE)**[33] [393] 7-8-11 49..............................(p) JerryO'Dwyer(3) 7 39
(Eoin Doyle, Ire) *cl up: rdn along over 2f out and ev ch tl drvn and wknd over 1f out* **8/1**

-530 **6** 1½ **Insignia (IRE)**[8] [620] 5-8-7 45.. LiamJones(3) 6 32
(W M Brisbourne) *bhd tl styd on fnl 2f* **16/1**

5046 **7** 1 **Bathwick Emma (IRE)**[8] [620] 4-8-13 47........................... ChrisCatlin 8 33
(M A Doyle) *chsd ldrs: rdn along 1/2-way and sn wknd* **16/1**

600- **8** 2½ **Master Ben (IRE)**[308] [1576] 4-8-12 41..............................(b) PhillipMakin 2 26
(S R Bowring) *chsd ldrs: rdn along over 2f out: grad wknd* **80/1**

-600 **9** 5 **Penwell Hill (USA)**[30] [431] 8-8-10 45..................................(b) AdamKirby 9 14
(Miss M E Rowland) *chsd ldrs on outer: rdn along over 3f out and sn wknd* **16/1**

0-00 **10** 5 **Lizzie Rocket**[7] [632] 7-8-9 40..(v) DavidAllan 3 2
(J O'Reilly) *sn led: rdn along 3f out: drvn and hdd 2f out: sn wknd* **50/1**

1m 46.66s (2.06) **Going Correction** +0.175s/f (Slow) **10** Ran SP% **113.6**
Speed ratings (Par 101):96,95,92,87,86 84,83,81,76,71
CSF £8.95 TOTE £5.60: £1.70, £1.10, £5.00; EX 14.50 Trifecta £215.90 Pool: £358.89 - 1.18 winning units..
Owner Middleham Park Racing Xvii **Bred** The Thoroughbred Corporation **Trained** Middleham Moor, N Yorks

FOCUS
Like the first division, this was a routine race of its type and the winning time was 1.12 seconds slower. The form is weaker too and less than solid, with the winner inconsistent and the third unconvincing. The race has been rated through the runner-up.
Methusaleh(IRE) Official explanation: jockey said gelding hung left
Penwell Hill(USA) Official explanation: jockey said gelding hung right and had no more to give final furlong

667 BETDIRECT.COM GET ONLINE (S) STKS 7f (F)
3:00 (3:01) (Class 6) 3-Y-0 **£2,184** (£644; £322) **Stalls** Low

Form RPR

6-36 **1** **Sunley Sovereign**[29] [446] 3-8-12 61.............................. SamHitchcott 6 58
(M R Channon) *trckd ldrs: hdwy to chse ldr over 2f out and sn ridde: drvn to ld and edgd lft ent last: styd on* **5/2**[2]

5000 **2** 2 **Flushed**[8] [619] 3-8-9 44.......................................(be) StephenDonohoe(3) 2 53
(A J McCabe) *led: rdn clr over 2f out: drvn over 1f out: hdd ent last: kpt on same pce* **28/1**

0-61 **3** 2 **Poniard (IRE)**[28] [454] 3-9-4 59..(p) TomEaves 4 54
(D W Barker) *chsd ldr: rdn along wl over 2f out and kpt on same pce* **2/1**[1]

5-23 **4** 1¼ **Power Alert**[20] [512] 3-8-12 50.................................(p) GrahamGibbons 9 45
(B R Millman) *hld up in rr: hdwy on outer 3f out: rdn and hung lft 2f out: sn drvn: wandered bdly and one pce* **5/1**[3]

6-00 **5** 1¾ **Muree Queen**[56] [149] 3-8-2 42................................... WilliamBuick(5) 7 35
(R Hollinshead) *bhd tl styd on fnl 2f: nrst fin* **16/1**

0-65 **6** 2 **Birdie Birdie**[20] [512] 3-8-7 50..(v) PaulHanagan 3 30
(R A Fahey) *midfield: hdwy to chse ldrs 3f out: sn rdn and btn wl over 1f out* **9/1**

0600 **7** 2½ **House Arrest**[8] [619] 3-8-4 43.. JamesDoyle(3) 8 23
(A J McCabe) *chsd ldrs:rdn along and wkng whn hmpd 2f out* **33/1**

0-53 **8** 1 **Spinning Game**[21] [506] 3-8-0 45....................(b) DanielleMcCreery(7) 10 21
(D W Chapman) *a towards rr* **18/1**

000- **9** nk **Raven Rascal**[265] [2759] 3-8-4 45............................... PatrickMathers(3) 5 20
(J F Coupland) *sn rdn along: a towards rr* **50/1**

6055 **10** 12 **Ten Black**[18] [534] 3-8-12 49... PhillipMakin 11 —
(R Brotherton) *a rr: bhd fr 1/2-way* **10/1**

005- **11** 20 **Little Tiny Tom**[119] [6471] 3-8-12 45.. ChrisCatlin 1 —
(C N Kellett) *chsd ldrs to 1/2-way: sn wknd* **40/1**

1m 32.99s (2.19) **Going Correction** +0.175s/f (Slow) **11** Ran SP% **119.6**
Speed ratings (Par 96):94,91,89,88,86 83,80,79,79,65 42
CSF £78.94 TOTE £2.90: £1.60, £7.70, £1.50; EX 62.30 TRIFECTA Not won..The winner was sold to D W Chapman for 8,000gns.
Owner John B Sunley **Bred** John B Sunley **Trained** West Ilsley, Berks

FOCUS
An ordinary seller which saw the field come home fairly strung out. The winner won as he was entitled to at the weights and is fair for this grade, as is the third, but the form is hard to gauge due to the runner-up's improvement.

668 BETDIRECT.COM £50 FREE BET H'CAP 5f (F)
3:40 (3:41) (Class 6) (0-60,56) 4-Y-0+ **£2,388** (£705; £352) **Stalls** High

Form RPR

0642 **1** **Lady Bahia (IRE)**[8] [613] 6-9-0 **54**.............................(b) GrahamGibbons 8 68+
(Peter Grayson) *dwlt and wnt rt s: hdwy 1/2-way: rdn qwl over 1f out: styd on wl to ld ins last* **9/2**[2]

-016 **2** 1¼ **Thoughtsofstardom**[8] [613] 4-8-12 **52**.......................(be) HayleyTurner 4 59
(P S McEntee) *towards rr: swtchd lft and hdwy over 2f out: rdn and styd on to chse wnr ins last: no imp towards fin* **12/1**

3326 **3** 2½ **Garlogs**[7] [626] 4-9-2 **56**...(b[1]) SamHitchcott 2 55
(A Bailey) *led and sn clr: rdn wl over 1f out: wknd and hdd ins last* **3/1**[1]

501 **4** 1 **Spirit Of Coniston**[13] [581] 4-8-5 **50**......................(b) DuranFentiman(5) 3 45
(C J Teague) *chsd ldrs: rdn along wl over 1f out: kpt on same pce* **6/1**[3]

005- **5** 1¼ **Titian Saga (IRE)**[161] [5752] 4-9-0 **54**............................. AdrianTNicholls 5 45
(D Nicholls) *chsd clr ldr: rdn wl over 1f out and sn one pce* **33/1**

4534 **6** ½ **Muktasb (USA)**[8] [613] 6-8-12 **52**..............................(v) DeanMcKeown 1 41
(D Shaw) *chsd ldrs: rdn along 2f out: grad wknd* **6/1**[3]

0030 **7** ½ **Far Note (USA)**[7] [632] 9-8-5 **45**.......................................(bt) DaleGibson 7 32
(S R Bowring) *in tch whn hmpd and lost pl after 1f: styd on ins last: nrst fin* **50/1**

0436 **8** 1 **Piccleyes**[7] [632] 6-8-0 **45**..(b) WilliamBuick(5) 13 29
(A J McCabe) *midfield: rdn along 1/2-way: no hdwy* **12/1**

000- **9** 1 **Whinhill House**[167] [5620] 7-9-2 **56**..............................(v[1]) PatCosgrave 11 37
(D W Barker) *chsd ldrs: rdn along 2f out: wknd over 1f out* **14/1**

0105 **10** 1¾ **Ace Club**[13] [580] 6-8-7 **50**..(v) EmmettStack(3) 6 25
(K J Burke) *chsd ldrs: rdn along 1/2-way: sn wknd* **33/1**

3-53 **11** 3½ **Newkeylets**[28] [448] 4-8-11 **51**......................................(p) TomEaves 10 14
(I Semple) *in tch whn hmpd and lost pl after 1f: bhd after* **14/1**

3-24 **12** hd **Brut**[26] [463] 5-8-13 **53**.. TonyHamilton 12 15
(D W Barker) *midfield: rdn along 1/2-way: sn outpcd* **13/2**

5030 **13** ¾ **Sundried Tomato**[21] [504] 8-7-12 **45**..............(p) DanielleMcCreery(7) 9 5
(D W Chapman) *bmpd s and a bhd* **28/1**

60.11 secs (-0.19) **Going Correction** 0.0s/f (Stan) **13** Ran SP% **125.1**
Speed ratings (Par 101):101,99,95,93,91 90,89,88,86,83 78,77,76
CSF £58.86 CT £199.31 TOTE £6.20: £2.30, £3.90, £1.60; EX 93.90 Trifecta £308.00 Part won. Pool: £433.83 - 0.68 winning units..
Owner Peter Grayson Racing Clubs Limited **Bred** Piercetown Stud **Trained** Formby, Lancs

FOCUS
An ordinary sprint handicap and, as is usually the case here, those that raced down the centre were at a huge advantage whilst those that stayed towards the stands' rail never had a prayer. The first two boosted the form of their Lingfield run and the winner will still be well treated on his old form.

669 **BETDIRECT.COM H'CAP** **1m 4f (F)**
4:25 (4:25) (Class 5) (0-75,75) 4-Y-0+ **£3,071** (£906; £453) **Stalls** Low

Form RPR
112- **1** **Three Boars**84 [6870] 5-7-13 **61** oh1 ....(b) WilliamBuick(5) 6 71+
(S Gollings) *trckd ldrs: smooth hdwy 5f out: led wl over 2f out: eased ins last: comf* **6/1**
003- **2** *1* **Black Falcon (IRE)**76 [6946] 7-8-12 **69** .... MickyFenton 3 75
(M A Peill) *hld up in rr: hdwy over 3f out: rdn 2f out: drvn and kpt on ins last: no ch w wnr* **11/1**
3524 **3** *¾* **Bay Boy**12 [587] 5-9-4 **75** .... JoeFanning 1 80
(M Johnston) *led: rdn along 3f out: drvn and hdd 2f out: kpt on u.p appr last* **9/4**1
2660 **4** *1 ½* **Augustine**4 [652] 6-9-2 **73** .... PhillipMakin 7 76
(P W Hiatt) *hld up in tch: hdwy 4f out: rdn along wl over 2f out: sn hung lft and btn* **9/2**3
2435 **5** *1 ¼* **Jackie Kiely**15 [568] 6-8-10 **72** ....(t) MichaelJStainton(5) 4 73
(R Brotherton) *prom tl bmpd and lost pl 4f out: rdn along 3f out: sn drvn and btn* **7/2**2
-001 **6** *2 ½* **Kylkenny**35 [377] 12-8-11 **75** ....(t) FrankiePickard(7) 2 72
(H Morrison) *keen: trckd ldrs on inner tl hmpd and lost pl 3f out: hdwy to chse ldrs 2f out: sn rdn and btn over 1f out* **11/2**
1-00 **7** *7* **Top Jaro (FR)**15 [568] 4-8-13 **72** .... HayleyTurner 5 57
(Jennie Candlish) *plld hrd: chsd ldr after 3f tl rdn along over 3f out and sn wknd* **25/1**

2m 42.06s (-0.03) **Going Correction** +0.175s/f (Slow)
WFA 4 from 5yo+ 2lb **7** Ran SP% **113.0**
Speed ratings (Par 103):107,106,105,104,104 102,97
CSF £64.79 TOTE £7.20: £2.70, £5.10; EX 82.20.
Owner P Whinham **Bred** J M Greetham **Trained** Scamblesby, Lincs

FOCUS
A modest handicap, run at a modest early pace. The progressive winner is value for a little further than the winning margin, in a race rated around the third.

670 **BETDIRECTPOKER.COM MAIDEN STKS** **6f (F)**
5:05 (5:07) (Class 5) 3-Y-0+ **£2,968** (£876; £438) **Stalls** Low

Form RPR
36-2 **1** **Captain Jacksparra (IRE)**21 [510] 3-8-13 75 .... DarrylHolland 10 53
(K A Ryan) *prom: shkn up to ld over 1f out: sn rdn and edgd lft ins last: kpt on* **2/9**1
0 **2** *1 ¼* **Shaftesbury Avenue (USA)**18 [537] 4-9-13 ....(b1) JoeFanning 3 54
(J O'Reilly) *towards rr: hdwy wl over 2f out: sn rdn and styd on to chse wnr ins last: kpt on* **50/1**
3 *2* **Medici Pearl** 3-8-3 .... DuranFentiman(5) 1 39
(T D Easterby) *dwlt and bhd: hdwy on inenr 2f out: sn rdn and styd on ins last: nrst fin* **25/1**
4 *1* **Modern Verse (USA)** 4-9-13 .... DeanMcKeown 5 45+
(G A Swinbank) *unruly stalls: sn outpcd and bhd: pushed along 1/2-way: swtchd outside aqnd styd on wl appr last: nrst fin* **11/1**2
5-00 **5** *hd* **Jember Red**30 [435] 4-9-5 34 ....(v) MarkLawson(3) 7 39
(B Smart) *cl up: led 1/2-way: rdn 2f out: drvn and hdd over 1f out: wknd ins last* **50/1**
5 **6** *1* **Ugenius**57 [136] 3-8-8 40 .... MichaelJStainton(5) 6 37
(R A Harris) *chsd ldrs: rdn along 1/2-way: sn btn* **33/1**
0- **7** *2* **Agnes Gift**216 [4247] 4-9-8 .... JamieMackay 2 30
(Rae Guest) *chsd ldrs: rdn wl over 2f out: sn btn* **18/1**
0- **8** *nk* **Northern Dare (IRE)**167 [5614] 3-8-13 .... AdrianTNicholls 8 30
(D Nicholls) *led: rdn along and hdd 1/2-way: wknd fnl 2f* **14/1**3
5 **9** *5* **Mr Whoppit**13 [583] 3-8-13 .... DavidAllan 9 15
(T D Easterby) *chsd ldrs to 1/2-way: sn wknd* **20/1**
60-0 **10** *13* **Blissfully**21 [505] 3-8-8 42 .... PaulEddery 4 —
(S Parr) *stmbld s: a bhd* **100/1**

1m 17.98s (1.08) **Going Correction** +0.175s/f (Slow)
WFA 3 from 4yo 14lb **10** Ran SP% **118.6**
Speed ratings (Par 103):99,97,94,93,93 91,89,88,82,64
CSF £33.55 TOTE £1.30: £1.02, £7.30, £3.90; EX 20.50 Trifecta £203.90 Pool: £473.88 - 1.65 winning units..
Owner J Duddy,B McDonald,A Heeney,M McMenamin **Bred** Quay Bloodstock **Trained** Hambleton, N Yorks

FOCUS
This was a weak race but it did not prove quite the cakewalk for the favourite that the betting and official ratings suggested it would be. He was nowhere near his best, with the placed form plating class.
Ugenius Official explanation: jockey said colt hung left in home straight

671 **BETDIRECT.COM 5 PLACES AT CHELTENHAM TOMORROW H'CAP** **6f (F)**
5:40 (5:40) (Class 5) (0-70,68) 3-Y-0 **£3,071** (£906; £453) **Stalls** Low

Form RPR
6-61 **1** **Sohraab**31 [421] 3-8-13 **64** .... SteveDrowne 2 75+
(H Morrison) *trckd ldr: hdwy to chal 2f out: led over 1f out: rdn ins last and kpt on* **2/1**1
0-13 **2** *nk* **Sheriff's Silk**21 [510] 3-9-2 **67** ....(b) PaulEddery 4 77
(B Smart) *led: rdn along over 2f out: hdd over 1f out: drvn and hung lft ins last: edgd rt and kpt on u.p towards fin* **2/1**1
04-2 **3** *6* **Jojesse**35 [378] 3-8-3 **54** .... DaleGibson 6 46
(G A Swinbank) *hld up: hdwy over 2f out and sn rdn: drvn over 1f out and kpt on same pce* **3/1**2
-220 **4** *2* **Diminuto**19 [520] 3-8-6 **64** .... FrankiePickard(7) 7 50
(M D I Usher) *hld up in rr: hdwy on inner to chse ldrs over 2f out: sn rdn and kpt on same pce* **14/1**
4241 **5** *3* **Strike Force**8 [619] 3-8-12 **68** 6ex ....(p) MichaelJStainton(5) 3 45
(R A Harris) *prom: rdn along over 2f out and sn wknd* **8/1**3
04-0 **6** *2* **Hephaestus**21 [510] 3-9-2 **67** .... DeanMcKeown 1 38
(A J Chamberlain) *a rr* **40/1**
6335 **7** *5* **Pappas Image**35 [378] 3-7-12 **54** ....(b) WilliamBuick(5) 5 10
(A J McCabe) *chsd ldrs: rdn over 2f out and sn wknd* **16/1**

1m 16.84s (-0.06) **Going Correction** +0.175s/f (Slow) **7** Ran SP% **117.8**
Speed ratings (Par 98):107,106,98,95,91 89,82
CSF £6.48 TOTE £2.10: £1.40, £2.00; EX 7.90 Place 6 £293.82, Place 5 £93.22.
Owner Pangfield Racing **Bred** T J Billington **Trained** East Ilsley, Berks

FOCUS
A very decent winning time for the type of race, 1.14 seconds faster than the preceding maiden over the same trip, and the form looks solid with the first two both progressive and coming clear. The race should work out.
T/Plt: £304.30 to a £1 stake. Pool: £50,719.15. 121.65 winning tickets. T/Qpdt: £43.10 to a £1 stake. Pool: £2,846.40. 48.80 winning tickets. JR

655 WOLVERHAMPTON (A.W) (L-H)
Wednesday, March 14

OFFICIAL GOING: Standard to fast
Wind: Almost nil Weather: Fine

672 **PONTIN'S FAMILY HOLIDAYS H'CAP (DIV I)** **7f 32y(P)**
1:10 (1:11) (Class 5) (0-75,75) 4-Y-0+ **£2,590** (£770; £385; £192) **Stalls** High

Form RPR
60-0 **1** **H Harrison (IRE)**17 [561] 7-7-13 **61** oh1 .... AndrewElliott(3) 1 71
(I W McInnes) *mde all: clr over 1f out: rdn ins fnl f: edgd lft cl home: r.o* **25/1**
0-46 **2** *¾* **Violent Velocity (IRE)**12 [609] 4-8-4 **63** ....(v1) PaulHanagan 2 71
(J J Quinn) *hld up: hdwy on ins wl over 1f out: sn rdn: r.o ins fnl f: nt rch wnr* **9/2**2
0-56 **3** *½* **Ocean Of Dreams (FR)**22 [509] 4-8-11 **70** .... DarryllHolland 8 77
(J D Bethell) *a.p: rdn over 2f out: kpt on ins fnl f* **6/1**
12-3 **4** *hd* **Final Tune (IRE)**22 [509] 4-8-13 **72** .... AdamKirby 3 81+
(Miss M E Rowland) *hld up and bhd: hdwy on ins over 1f out: rdn ins fnl f: cl 2nd and styng on whn nt clr run and eased nr fin* **7/2**1
1331 **5** *1* **Cool Sands (IRE)**17 [561] 5-8-8 **67** ....(v) DeanMcKeown 6 71
(D Shaw) *hld up in tch: nt clr run over 1f out: swtchd lft jst ins fnl f: sn rdn: one pce* **9/2**2
5-02 **6** *hd* **Nepro (IRE)**9 [621] 5-8-8 **67** ....(t) EdwardCreighton 4 70
(E J Creighton) *hld up: rdn and hdwy over 1f out: nvr trbld ldrs* **5/1**3
114- **7** *½* **Choreography**195 [4958] 4-9-2 **75** .... AdrianTNicholls 5 77
(D Nicholls) *hld up in rr: rdn and c wd st: sme late prog: n.d* **9/1**
00-0 **8** *nk* **Local Poet**32 [424] 6-8-13 **72** ....(p) TomEaves 9 73
(I Semple) *sn chsng wnr: rdn 3f out: wknd fnl f* **25/1**
4351 **9** *5* **Mystic Man (FR)**17 [556] 9-8-0 **62** ....(b) PatrickMathers(3) 10 50
(I W McInnes) *hld up in mid-div: rdn over 2f out: sn bhd* **8/1**

1m 28.82s (-1.58) **Going Correction** -0.30s/f (Stan) **9** Ran SP% **118.3**
Speed ratings (Par 103):97,96,95,95,94 93,93,93,87
CSF £137.22 CT £783.78 TOTE £20.90: £6.20, £1.60, £3.20; EX 166.60 TRIFECTA Not won..
Owner David Lees **Bred** Margaret Conlon **Trained** Catwick, E Yorks
■ Stewards' Enquiry : Andrew Elliott one-day ban: careless riding (Mar 25)

FOCUS
A modest handicap run at a moderate pace and the time was 0.86 seconds slower than the following division. The winner had the run of things in front but the form makes sense.
Final Tune(IRE) ◆ Official explanation: jockey said, regarding dropping his hands and being beaten for 4th, he was unable to ride out to the line as his ground had been taken by the winner
Cool Sands(IRE) Official explanation: jockey said gelding was denied a clear run

673 **PONTIN'S FAMILY HOLIDAYS H'CAP (DIV II)** **7f 32y(P)**
1:40 (1:40) (Class 5) (0-75,73) 4-Y-0+ **£2,590** (£770; £385; £192) **Stalls** High

Form RPR
-201 **1** **Kabis Amigos**12 [609] 5-8-8 **65** ....(t) AdrianTNicholls 3 77
(D Nicholls) *mde all: rdn 2f out: jst hld on* **2/1**1
0635 **2** *shd* **Prince Dayjur (USA)**19 [533] 8-8-10 **67** .... JimmyQuinn 4 79
(J Pearce) *a.p: rdn over 2f out: r.o ins fnl f: jst failed* **4/1**2
3210 **3** *2 ½* **Flying Bantam (IRE)**12 [609] 6-8-6 **63** .... PaulHanagan 9 69
(R A Fahey) *hld up and bhd: rdn and hdwy over 2f out: kpt on same pce fnl f* **8/1**
3410 **4** *1* **Carcinetto (IRE)**21 [516] 5-7-11 **59** .... WilliamBuick(5) 2 62
(P D Evans) *hld up in tch: lost pl 4f out: rdn over 2f out: rallied on ins wl over 1f out: one pce fnl f* **7/1**3
5-03 **5** *shd* **Littleton Telchar (USA)**13 [592] 7-8-11 **71** ....(p) LiamJones(3) 1 74
(S W Hall) *hld up in mid-div: hdwy 3f out: rdn wl over 1f out: fdd wl ins fnl f* **4/1**2
100- **6** *1 ¼* **Swiper Hill (IRE)**310 [1529] 4-9-2 **73** ....(t) DaneO'Neill 10 72
(B Ellison) *hld up and bhd: rdn and sme hdwy whn swtchd lft wl over 1f out: no further prog fnl f* **33/1**
30-0 **7** *1 ¾* **Motu (IRE)**17 [560] 6-7-12 **62** ow2 ....(v) SamuelDrury(7) 8 57
(I W McInnes) *hld up towards rr: c wd over 2f out: nvr nr ldrs* **25/1**
4340 **8** *5* **Mistral Sky**9 [621] 8-8-9 **66** ....(v) MickyFenton 7 48
(Stef Liddiard) *chsd wnr tl rdn 2f out: sn wknd* **10/1**
000- **9** *1* **Baylaw Star**134 [6273] 6-8-11 **68** .... DanielTudhope 5 47
(I W McInnes) *hld up: sn in tch: rdn over 3f out: wknd over 2f out* **33/1**
000- **10** *1* **Royal Envoy (IRE)**146 [6065] 4-9-1 **72** .... DeanMcKeown 6 49
(D Shaw) *a in rr* **20/1**

1m 27.96s (-2.44) **Going Correction** -0.30s/f (Stan) **10** Ran SP% **120.5**
Speed ratings (Par 103):101,100,98,96,96 95,93,87,86,85
CSF £9.84 CT £53.84 TOTE £2.20: £1.30, £2.00, £2.40; EX 10.00 Trifecta £47.00 Pool: £523.37 - 7.89 winning units..
Owner GGN Bloodstock Ltd and Ian W Glenton **Bred** Cheveley Park Stud Ltd **Trained** Sessay, N Yorks
■ Stewards' Enquiry : Liam Jones four-day ban: careless riding (Mar 25-28)

FOCUS
A stronger pace led to a time 0.86 seconds faster than the first division. Solid form, rated through the second and third, with the winner as good as ever.

674 **STAY AT THE WOLVERHAMPTON HOLIDAY INN CLAIMING STKS** **1m 1f 103y(P)**
2:15 (2:15) (Class 5) 4-Y-0+ **£3,071** (£906; £453) **Stalls** Low

Form RPR
3-62 **1** **Blue Sky Thinking (IRE)**9 [620] 8-9-7 86 .... PatCosgrave 10 76
(K R Burke) *a.p: led 2f out: sn rdn: clr 1f out: jst hld on* **15/8**1
3132 **2** *hd* **Norwegian**1 [666] 6-8-11 54 ....(p) PaulEddery 1 66
(Ian Williams) *hld up in tch: rdn 2f out: r.o ins fnl f: jst failed* **7/2**2
1103 **3** *2 ½* **Climate (IRE)**9 [620] 8-8-13 68 ....(p) J-PGuillambert 5 63
(R Hollinshead) *hld up: hdwy 3f out: sn rdn: hung lft over 1f out: one pce fnl f* **8/1**
/0-4 **4** *1 ¾* **Intricate Web (IRE)**26 [481] 11-8-9 60 .... DavidAllan 6 56
(E J Alston) *hld up and bhd: rdn and hdwy over 2f out: one pce fnl f* **25/1**
0016 **5** *½* **Samuel Charles**13 [592] 9-9-7 72 .... EddieAhern 3 67
(C R Dore) *hld up: rdn over 2f out: kpt on fnl f: nvr trbld ldrs* **5/1**3
0041 **6** *1 ½* **Bridgewater Boys**8 [630] 6-8-8 64 ....(p) AndrewMullen(3) 13 54
(K A Ryan) *prom tl wknd over 2f out* **7/1**
0-65 **7** *¾* **Defi (IRE)**32 [427] 5-8-13 62 ....(b) TomEaves 8 54
(I Semple) *chsd ldr: led over 5f out tl rdn and hdd 2f out: wknd fnl f* **12/1**
000- **8** *½* **Grandad Bill (IRE)**210 [4470] 4-8-0 64 .... DebraEngland(7) 9 47
(W J Musson) *bhd: c wd st: edgd lft over 1f out: n.d* **25/1**
3040 **9** *8* **Spy Gun (USA)**30 [440] 7-8-7 45 .... ChrisCatlin 2 31
(T Wall) *led: hdd over 5f out: wknd 3f out* **33/1**

The Form Book, Raceform Ltd, Compton, RG20 6NL

2006 **10** *10* **Retirement**[17] 558 8-8-7 43 .... EdwardCreighton 11 11
(R M Stronge) *s.v.s: a in rr* **50/1**
1m 59.66s (-2.96) **Going Correction** -0.30s/f (Stan) **10** Ran SP% **117.6**
Speed ratings (Par 103):101,100,98,97,96 95,94,94,87,78
CSF £8.05 TOTE £2.70: £1.10, £1.40, £2.50; EX 8.20 Trifecta £24.90 Pool: £506.81 - 14.40 winning units..
Owner Triple Trio Partnership **Bred** Thomas J Murphy **Trained** Middleham Moor, N Yorks

FOCUS
An ordinary claimer. Not an easy race to assess, it is best judged around the runner-up.
Retirement Official explanation: jockey said gelding missed the break

675 PONTINS.COM H'CAP 1m 141y(P)
2:50 (2:50) (Class 5) (0-75,75) 4-Y-0+ **£3,238** (£963; £481; £240) **Stalls** Low

Form RPR
1622 **1** **Harare**[19] 538 6-7-12 **62** .... (v[1]) WilliamBuick(5) 5 75
(R J Price) *t.k.h in mid-div: smooth hdwy on ins over 2f out: led wl over 1f out: r.o wl* **9/2**[1]
4-01 **2** *2 1/2* **Holiday Cocktail**[12] 605 5-8-2 **61** oh1 .... (v) JimmyQuinn 8 69
(J J Quinn) *s.i.s: hld up and bhd: hdwy on ins over 2f out: rdn to chse wnr over 1f out: no imp* **17/2**
1250 **3** *1 1/4* **Activity (IRE)**[37] 367 8-8-2 **66** .... DuranFentiman(5) 13 71
(M J Gingell) *hld up and bhd: rdn and c v wd ent st: hdwy on outside fnl f: nrst fin* **20/1**
5010 **4** *hd* **Red Birr (IRE)**[13] 594 6-8-12 **71** .... JimmyFortune 3 76
(P R Webber) *a.p: rdn over 2f out: one pce fnl f* **13/2**[3]
300- **5** *1 1/2* **Skeylady**[140] 6176 4-9-1 **74** .... TomEaves 6 76
(Miss J A Camacho) *hld up in tch: rdn over 2f out: one pce fnl f* **25/1**
50-3 **6** *shd* **Suits Me**[12] 604 4-8-9 **68** .... MickyFenton 10 70
(T P Tate) *hld up: hdwy on outside over 5f out: rdn over 2f out: c wd st: kpt on towards fin* **8/1**
2412 **7** *1/2* **Symbol Of Peace (IRE)**[12] 604 4-9-2 **75** .... ShaneKelly 12 76
(J W Unett) *hld up towards rr: rdn wl over 1f out: n.m.r briefly ins fnl f: n.d* **9/1**
0-06 **8** *1/2* **Consonant (IRE)**[16] 564 10-8-9 **68** .... DarryllHolland 9 67
(D G Bridgwater) *hld up towards rr: pushed along over 5f out: rdn over 2f out: hdwy wl over 1f out: fdd ins fnl f* **25/1**
-104 **9** *1/2* **Topiary Ted**[19] 538 5-8-6 **70** ow1 .... TravisBlock(5) 2 68
(H Morrison) *chsd ldr: rdn and ev ch 2f out: wknd fnl f* **5/1**[2]
6-23 **10** *1/2* **Sedgwick**[36] 375 5-8-6 **65** .... TPQueally 1 62
(J G Given) *led: rdn and hdd wl over 1f out: wknd fnl f* **9/1**
421- **11** *1* **Esthlos (FR)**[109] 6593 4-8-11 **70** .... ChrisCatlin 7 67+
(J Jay) *hld up in tch: rdn over 2f out: sn wknd: btn whn bdly hmpd ins fnl f* **8/1**
1126 **12** *1 1/4* **Pop Music (IRE)**[12] 604 4-8-7 **69** .... (p) JamesDoyle(3) 4 66+
(Miss J Feilden) *prom: rdn over 2f out: swtchd rt and hung lft over 1f out: wkng whn bdly hmpd ins fnl f* **7/1**
100- **13** *1 3/4* **Swayze (IRE)**[227] 3977 4-8-7 **66** .... EddieAhern 11 55
(C F Wall) *a bhd* **16/1**
1m 47.39s (-4.37) **Going Correction** -0.30s/f (Stan) **13** Ran SP% **131.8**
Speed ratings (Par 103):107,104,103,103,102 102,101,101,100,100 99,98,96
CSF £46.57 CT £747.58 TOTE £7.60: £2.40, £3.70, £6.90; EX 74.90 TRIFECTA Not won..
Owner Mrs P A Wallis **Bred** Limestone Stud **Trained** Ullingswick, H'fords

FOCUS
A modest open-looking handicap. Improved form in the visor from Harare, up 5lb, with the second rated to his winter best.
Symbol Of Peace(IRE) Official explanation: jockey said filly had suffered interference in running
Esthlos(FR) Official explanation: jockey said gelding suffered interference in running
Pop Music(IRE) Official explanation: jockey said gelding suffered interference in running

676 PONTIN'S BOOK EARLY (S) STKS 1m 141y(P)
3:30 (3:30) (Class 6) 3-Y-0 **£2,047** (£604; £302) **Stalls** Low

Form RPR
-005 **1** **Muree Queen**[1] 667 3-8-2 42 .... WilliamBuick(5) 2 44
(R Hollinshead) *hld up in tch: rdn to ld jst ins fnl f: jst hld on* **8/1**
-334 **2** *shd* **Skye But N Ben**[36] 373 3-8-12 47 .... (b) PaulFessey 9 49
(T D Barron) *a.p: rdn over 2f out: carried rt ins fnl f: jst failed* **10/3**[1]
142- **3** *nk* **The Slider**[229] 3915 3-8-8 57 .... KevinGhunowa(5) 7 49
(P A Blockley) *sn led: rdn wl over 1f out: hdd jst ins fnl f: sn edgd rt: r.o* **9/1**
1660 **4** *hd* **Kings Shillings**[9] 624 3-9-4 55 .... (b) DanielTudhope 11 54
(D Carroll) *hld up and bhd: rdn and hdwy on ins over 2f out: kpt on ins fnl f* **10/1**
-066 **5** *shd* **Gertie (IRE)**[37] 357 3-8-7 45 .... EdwardCreighton 1 43
(E J Creighton) *hld up in mid-div: rdn and hdwy over 2f out: carried rt ins fnl f: kpt on* **25/1**
4200 **6** *1/2* **A Nod And A Wink (IRE)**[37] 357 3-8-7 50 .... PatDobbs 5 42
(R Hannon) *hld up in mid-div: rdn and hdwy over 1f out: edgd lft and carried rt ins fnl f: kpt on* **7/1**[3]
0-40 **7** *5* **Fire Alarm**[29] 454 3-8-12 45 .... (v[1]) GrahamGibbons 3 36
(J J Quinn) *hld up in tch: rdn over 2f out: sltly hmpd wl over 1f out: sn wknd* **8/1**
0000 **8** *3 1/2* **First Frost**[15] 577 3-8-2 43 .... DuranFentiman(5) 8 24
(M J Gingell) *in rr: rdn 4f out: sme hdwy on ins wl over 1f out: nvr nr ldrs* **50/1**
-215 **9** *3 1/2* **Sophie's Dream**[41] 322 3-9-1 62 .... JerryO'Dwyer(3) 12 27
(A M Hales) *plld hrd: hdwy over 6f out: ev ch over 2f out: sn rdn: wknd wl over 1f out: eased whn btn ins fnl f* **5/1**[2]
6-46 **10** *1/2* **Best Woman**[19] 534 3-8-13 48 .... TonyCulhane 10 21
(P Howling) *hld up towards rr: rdn over 2f out: c wd st: n.d* **14/1**
0-00 **11** *3 1/2* **Charlies Girl (IRE)**[19] 534 3-8-4 40 .... (p) EmmettStack(3) 4 8
(K J Burke) *led early: chsd ldr tl wknd 4f out* **33/1**
30 **12** *5* **Bahama Gold**[13] 589 3-8-7 .... MickyFenton 6 —
(D G Bridgwater) *hld up in mid-div: rdn over 3f out: bhd fnl 2f* **16/1**
5300 **13** *6* **The Light Fandango**[15] 577 3-8-7 45 .... PaulHanagan 13 —
(R A Harris) *a bhd* **12/1**
1m 51.1s (-0.66) **Going Correction** -0.30s/f (Stan) **13** Ran SP% **122.5**
Speed ratings (Par 96):90,89,89,89,89 88,84,81,78,77 74,70,64
CSF £35.14 TOTE £12.50: £3.10, £1.30, £2.60; EX 66.30 Trifecta £315.30 Part won. Pool: £444.09 - 0.34 winning units..There was no bid for the winner.
Owner John L Marriott **Bred** Mrs K Catris **Trained** Upper Longdon, Staffs

FOCUS
A modest winning time for what was not a great event even by selling standards. It has been rated through the second and fourth.
Sophie's Dream Official explanation: jockey said gelding ran too free early on
Charlies Girl(IRE) Official explanation: jockey said filly ran too free early on

677 PONTINSBINGO.COM H'CAP 2m 119y(P)
4:15 (4:15) (Class 6) (0-65,60) 4-Y-0+ **£2,388** (£705; £352) **Stalls** Low

Form RPR
-444 **1** **Synonymy**[12] 607 4-9-7 **60** .... (b) SteveDrowne 5 75
(M Blanshard) *hld up in mid-div: hdwy 4f out: led 3f out: clr over 1f out: rdn out* **4/1**[2]
1220 **2** *5* **Nod's Star**[26] 482 6-9-0 **48** .... (t) ChrisCatlin 3 59+
(Mrs L C Jewell) *hld up in mid-div: nt clr run on ins and lost pl over 3f out: rdn and hdwy 2f out: styd on wl ins fnl f: no ch w wnr* **16/1**
2-02 **3** *1 1/4* **Capitalise (IRE)**[9] 618 4-8-11 **53** .... (p) JerryO'Dwyer(3) 13 61
(V Smith) *hld up and bhd: stdy hdwy whn nt clr run 3f out: swtchd rt and rdn over 2f out: chsd wnr and edgd lft over 1f out: no imp* **11/8**[1]
6246 **4** *1* **Come What July (IRE)**[9] 618 6-9-2 **50** .... DeanMcKeown 9 56
(D Shaw) *hld up towards rr: hdwy over 3f out: rdn over 2f out: one pce fnl f* **16/1**
330 **5** *3* **Beau Torero (FR)**[12] 602 9-9-9 **57** .... JDSmith 4 60
(B N Pollock) *hld up and bhd: hdwy over 5f out: ev ch 3f out: sn rdn: wknd over 1f out* **16/1**
20/0 **6** *6* **Lord Nellsson**[26] 482 11-9-7 **55** .... LPKeniry 8 51
(Andrew Turnell) *prom: rdn over 4f out: wknd 3f out* **25/1**
0-20 **7** *5* **Ausone**[34] 389 5-9-7 **55** .... TPQueally 6 45
(Miss J R Gibney) *led: rdn and hdd 3f out: sn wknd* **25/1**
5/00 **8** *nk* **Quel Fontenailles (FR)**[9] 617 9-8-13 **50** .... StephaneBreux(3) 2 39
(L A Dace) *a towards rr* **33/1**
10-0 **9** *3/4* **Activist**[12] 607 9-9-3 **58** .... KellyHarrison(7) 12 46
(D Carroll) *a towards rr* **25/1**
-022 **10** *1 3/4* **Teorban (POL)**[12] 607 8-9-9 **60** .... EmmettStack(3) 10 46
(Mrs N S Evans) *chsd ldr: rdn over 3f out: wknd and eased over 2f out* **15/2**
3-13 **11** *35* **Pocket Too**[44] 291 4-9-7 **60** .... (b) JimmyQuinn 1 —
(M Salaman) *prom: pushed along over 5f out: rdn and wknd 3f out: sn eased: t.o* **6/1**[3]
-335 **12** *1* **Come What Augustus**[26] 482 5-9-1 **49** .... (p) EdwardCreighton 11 —
(R M Stronge) *prom: rdn over 4f out: sn wknd: eased fnl 2f: t.o* **9/1**
3400 **13** *14* **Mumbling (IRE)**[9] 617 9-9-11 **59** .... (b) GeorgeBaker 7 —
(B G Powell) *s.i.s: bhd: rdn 7f out: eased fnl 2f: t.o whn lost action ins fnl f: dismntd after fin* **20/1**
3m 36.17s (-6.96) **Going Correction** -0.30s/f (Stan)
WFA 4 from 5yo+ 5lb **13** Ran SP% **135.0**
Speed ratings (Par 101):104,101,101,100,99 96,94,93,93,92 76,75,69
CSF £70.47 CT £138.95 TOTE £7.10: £1.60, £6.80, £1.10; EX 95.90 Trifecta £341.80 Part won. Pool: £481.50 - 0.84 winning units..
Owner G H Phillips,J M Beever & D G Chambers **Bred** Biddestone Stud **Trained** Upper Lambourn, Berks

FOCUS
A decent, even gallop led to a fast time in this low-grade staying handicap. The form has been rated positively, with the winner up 8lb and the second a bit better than the bare form.
Teorban(POL) Official explanation: jockey said gelding had no more to give
Mumbling(IRE) Official explanation: jockey said gelding lost its action

678 PONTIN'S HOLIDAYS MAIDEN STKS 5f 216y(P)
4:55 (4:59) (Class 5) 3-Y-0 **£3,412** (£1,007; £504) **Stalls** Low

Form RPR
2-2 **1** **Doubtful Sound (USA)**[50] 222 3-9-3 .... PaulFessey 11 76+
(T D Barron) *a.p: led jst over 1f out: r.o wl* **11/10**[1]
53 **2** *3 1/2* **Kelamon**[14] 583 3-9-3 .... HayleyTurner 9 65
(M D I Usher) *chsd ldrs: pushed along over 3f out: r.o ins fnl f: no ch w wnr* **9/1**
U-0 **3** *1/2* **Comptonspirit**[44] 301 3-8-12 .... DeanMcKeown 3 59
(B P J Baugh) *hld up: rdn and hdwy on ins over 2f out: kpt on same pce fnl f* **66/1**
02- **4** *2 1/2* **Kassuta**[166] 5648 3-8-12 .... J-PGuillambert 2 51
(S C Williams) *chsd ldr tl rdn over 2f out: wknd over 1f out* **4/1**[2]
0- **5** *1 1/4* **Wendy's Boy**[305] 1688 3-9-3 .... DaneO'Neill 4 52
(R Hannon) *led: rdn and hdd jst over 1f out: wknd ins fnl f* **6/1**
0-0 **6** *shd* **Polish Star**[16] 567 3-9-3 .... PaulHanagan 7 52
(J S Wainwright) *hld up in mid-div: outpcd over 3f out: rdn and no real prog fnl 2f* **33/1**
00 **7** *1* **Conorville (IRE)**[15] 573 3-9-3 .... TonyCulhane 1 49+
(B W Hills) *hld up in rr: pushed along over 2f out: sme hdwy over 1f out: n.d* **14/1**
0 **8** *nk* **Solidgoldesyaction**[36] 375 3-8-12 .... SimonWhitworth 6 43+
(P A Blockley) *s.i.s: hld up and bhd: rdn over 1f out: nvr nr ldrs* **20/1**
-05 **9** *nk* **Castle Durrow (IRE)**[26] 478 3-8-9 .... JerryO'Dwyer(3) 12 42
(Seamus Fahey, Ire) *chsd ldrs tl rdn and wknd over 2f out* **20/1**
10 *1/2* **Clock Face (IRE)** 3-8-12 .... LPKeniry 10 41
(M D I Usher) *a bhd* **50/1**
06- **11** *2* **Pegasus Prince (USA)**[175] 5481 3-9-3 .... TomEaves 5 40
(Miss J A Camacho) *outpcd* **11/2**[3]
12 *5* **Ducal Regancy Red** 3-8-12 .... AlanDaly 13 20
(C J Teague) *outpcd* **50/1**
0- **13** *3 1/2* **Vital Tryst**[155] 5883 3-9-3 .... TPQueally 8 14
(J G Given) *sn bhd* **25/1**
1m 14.77s (-1.04) **Going Correction** -0.30s/f (Stan) **13** Ran SP% **135.7**
Speed ratings (Par 98):94,89,88,85,83 83,82,81,81,80 78,71,66
CSF £14.14 TOTE £2.10: £1.10, £3.00, £20.90; EX 15.90 Trifecta £477.20 Part won. Pool: £672.25 - 0.44 winning units..
Owner Miss N J Barron **Bred** Millsec, Ltd **Trained** Maunby, N Yorks

FOCUS
A very ordinary maiden, the impressive winner apart. The form looks sound enough.
Conorville(IRE) Official explanation: jockey said colt ran green early

679 GO PONTIN'S H'CAP 5f 216y(P)
5:30 (5:32) (Class 6) (0-65,65) 3-Y-0 **£2,730** (£806; £403) **Stalls** Low

Form RPR
00-0 **1** **Nordic Light (USA)**[28] 456 3-8-9 **63** .... MCGeran(7) 1 73+
(P W Chapple-Hyam) *a.p: led jst over 2f out: hrd rdn and edgd rt cl home: r.o* **8/1**
-601 **2** *1/2* **Scarlet Oak**[15] 574 3-8-12 **59** .... AdamKirby 11 68+
(D J S Ffrench Davis) *sn bhd: c wd st: rdn and hdwy on outside over 1f out: sn edgd lft: r.o ins fnl f: nt rch wnr* **9/2**[2]
036- **3** *1 1/2* **Mandurah (IRE)**[224] 4055 3-8-7 **54** .... SilvestreDeSousa 12 58
(D Nicholls) *led early: a.p: rdn over 1f out: nt qckn ins fnl f* **33/1**

45 **4** ½ **Royal Becky (IRE)**[16] 567 3-7-13 **51** oh4 .... DuranFentiman(5) 4 54
(Patrick Morris, Ire) *hld up and bhd: hdwy over 2f out: sn rdn: kpt on same pce fnl f* **4/1**[1]

003- **5** 1½ **Strathmore (IRE)**[195] 4956 3-9-2 **63** .... PaulHanagan 13 61+
(R A Fahey) *hld up in rr: hdwy on outside fnl f: nvr nrr* **16/1**

3436 **6** nk **Calloff The Search**[7] 636 3-8-3 **57** ....(v[1]) JackDean(7) 9 54
(W G M Turner) *sn led: hdd jst over 2f out: sn rdn: wknd wl ins fnl f* **12/1**

-464 **7** 1½ **Jost Van Dyke**[45] 280 3-8-4 **51** oh1 .... JimmyQuinn 7 44
(J W Unett) *bhd: rdn over 2f out: sme hdwy on ins wl over 1f out: no further prog* **33/1**

15-0 **8** ½ **Bahamian Love**[20] 520 3-8-8 **62** ....(t) PatrickHills(7) 2 53
(B W Hills) *s.i.s: hdwy on ins over 2f out: rdn and wknd fnl f* **10/1**

-442 **9** shd **Charlotte Grey**[33] 404 3-9-4 **65** .... EdwardCreighton 3 56
(C N Allen) *prom: rdn over 2f out: wknd over 1f out* **6/1**[3]

004- **10** 5 **Stargazy**[76] 6965 3-8-13 **60** .... SteveDrowne 5 36
(R Charlton) *hld up in mid-div: hdwy 3f out: wknd 2f out* **4/1**[1]

606- **11** shd **La Vecchia Scuola (IRE)**[162] 5747 3-9-2 **63** .... AdrianTNicholls 10 39
(D Nicholls) *a bhd* **25/1**

1-05 **12** 4 **Iron Pearl**[13] 589 3-8-13 **60** .... J-PGuillambert 6 24
(Jane Chapple-Hyam) *prom: rdn 3f out: sn wknd* **16/1**

1m 14.44s (-1.37) **Going Correction** -0.30s/f (Stan) **12** Ran SP% **121.9**
Speed ratings (Par 96):97,96,94,93,91 91,89,88,88,81 81,76
CSF £44.39 CT £1158.53 TOTE £11.90: £3.00, £2.40, £10.90; EX 66.80 TRIFECTA Not won. Place 6 £49.03, Place 5 £11.46.
Owner Times Of Wigan **Bred** L Hudson **Trained** Newmarket, Suffolk

FOCUS
There were some unexposed types in this interesting contest with the first three all making their handicap debuts. The form should work out, with the winner capable of better.
Iron Pearl Official explanation: jockey said filly lost her action
T/Plt: £89.40 to a £1 stake. Pool: £55,558.20. 453.25 winning tickets. T/Qpdt: £7.70 to a £1 stake. Pool: £4,151.10. 395.40 winning tickets. KH

664 SOUTHWELL (L-H)
Thursday, March 15

OFFICIAL GOING: Standard
Wind: Light, across Weather: Overcast

680 BETDIRECT.COM NEW WEBSITE OPPORTUNITIES H'CAP 5f (F)
1:20 (1:20) (Class 6) (0-50,50) 4-Y-0+ **£2,388** (£705; £352) **Stalls** High

Form RPR

1026 **1** **Primarily**[18] 562 5-8-10 **48** .... RobbieFitzpatrick 4 57+
(Peter Grayson) *hmpd s: sn outpcd: hdwy over 1f out: styd on u.p to ld wl ins fnl f* **11/2**[3]

2502 **2** ½ **El Potro**[15] 581 5-8-9 **47** oh1 ow1 .... GrahamGibbons 3 54
(J R Holt) *edgd rt s: sn chsng ldrs: rdn over 1f out: r.o* **11/2**[3]

0044 **3** ½ **Ask No More**[15] 586 4-8-9 **50** ....(b) DominicFox(3) 13 55+
(P L Gilligan) *mid-div: rdn 1/2-way: r.o ins fnl f: nt rch ldrs* **11/1**

40-1 **4** hd **Elvina**[53] 201 6-8-10 **48** ow1 .... DaneO'Neill 5 53
(A G Newcombe) *hmpd s: sn chsng ldrs: rdn to ld over 1f out: hdd wl ins fnl f* **7/2**[1]

0-40 **5** nk **Inscribed (IRE)**[18] 557 4-8-8 **46** oh1 ....(b) PatCosgrave 2 50?
(G A Huffer) *led: rdn and hdd over 1f out: styd on* **16/1**

0010 **6** 1 **Orchestration (IRE)**[18] 562 6-8-12 **50** .... NCallan 11 50
(K J Burke) *chsd ldrs: rdn over 1f out: no ex ins fnl f* **10/1**

4360 **7** nk **Piccleyes**[2] 668 6-8-3 **46** oh1 ....(b) WilliamBuick(5) 8 45
(A J McCabe) *sn pushed along in rr: sme hdwy whn hmpd over 1f out: nvr trbld ldrs* **9/1**

-331 **8** hd **Dodaa (USA)**[21] 523 4-8-9 **47** .... MatthewHenry 10 46
(N Wilson) *dwlt: hdwy over 3f out: rdn over 1f out: edgd lft and no ex fnl f* **4/1**[2]

-000 **9** 2 **Mystery Pips**[21] 521 7-8-12 **50** ....(v) KimTinkler 12 42
(N Tinkler) *chsd ldrs: rdn 1/2-way: wknd ins fnl f* **33/1**

0630 **10** 1¾ **Estoille**[9] 626 6-8-8 **46** oh1 ....(t) PaulFessey 9 32
(Mrs S Lamyman) *chsd ldrs over 3f* **25/1**

-206 **11** ½ **Bee Magic**[32] 430 4-8-9 **47** .... MickyFenton 7 31
(C N Kellett) *chsd ldr tl rdn 1/2-way: wknd over 1f out* **14/1**

2630 **12** 3½ **Town House**[21] 523 5-8-1 **46** oh1 .... SoniaEaton(7) 14 18
(B P J Baugh) *hld up: rdn 1/2-way: sn wknd* **50/1**

4500 **13** 4 **Mind That Fox**[31] 441 5-8-8 **46** oh1 .... ChrisCatlin 6 5
(T Wall) *hmpd s: outpcd* **33/1**

61.07 secs (0.77) **Going Correction** +0.20s/f (Slow) **13** Ran SP% **124.7**
Speed ratings (Par 101):101,100,99,99,98 97,96,96,93,90 89,83,77
CSF £36.41 CT £343.66 TOTE £7.20: £2.30, £2.10, £3.00; EX 44.70 TRIFECTA Not won..
Owner Thomas & Susan Blane **Bred** Bearstone Stud **Trained** Formby, Lancs

FOCUS
A very moderate handicap with the top weights rated just 50, and as is usually the case those that raced middle to far side held sway. The form seems sound.
Estoille Official explanation: trainer said mare over-reached
Mind That Fox Official explanation: jockey said gelding suffered interference at start

681 BETDIRECT.COM 5 PLACES ON THE COUNTY HURDLE H'CAP (DIV I) 7f (F)
1:50 (1:51) (Class 6) (0-65,65) 4-Y-0+ **£1,619** (£481; £240; £120) **Stalls** Low

Form RPR

1603 **1** **Cerebus**[9] 626 5-8-13 **63** ....(bt) StephenDonohoe(3) 8 72
(A J McCabe) *chsd ldr: led 2f out: drvn out* **8/1**[3]

-025 **2** ¾ **Haroldini (IRE)**[22] 516 5-8-9 **59** ....(p) JasonEdmunds(3) 1 66
(J Balding) *mid-div: hdwy over 2f out: rdn to chse wnr over 1f out: styd on* **11/2**[2]

10/6 **3** 1½ **Camille Pissarro (USA)**[21] 525 7-8-10 **57** .... SamHitchcott 9 60
(D J Wintle) *s.i.s: hld up: hdwy 2f out: r.o* **25/1**

335- **4** 2½ **Middle Eastern**[107] 6642 5-8-10 **57** .... SimonWhitworth 7 54
(P A Blockley) *mid-div: hdwy u.p over 2f out: styd on* **12/1**

-360 **5** shd **Conrad**[33] 424 4-9-3 **64** .... PaulHanagan 10 60
(R A Fahey) *chsd ldrs: rdn 1/2-way: sn outpcd: styd on ins fnl f* **8/1**[3]

2020 **6** 1¾ **Rafferty (IRE)**[24] 497 8-8-13 **60** .... LPKeniry 5 52
(S Dow) *s.i.s: sn chsng ldrs: rdn over 2f out: wknd over 1f out* **20/1**

55-0 **7** nk **Shifty**[72] 14 8-8-11 **65** .... GaryEdwards(7) 11 56
(D Carroll) *s.i.s: hld up: styd on appr fnl f: nvr nrr* **16/1**

-000 **8** 1¾ **Aperitif**[13] 604 6-8-11 **58** ....(e[1]) AdrianTNicholls 3 44
(D Nicholls) *s.i.s: hld up: plld hrd: rdn over 1f out: nvr nrr* **16/1**

3-60 **9** 2½ **Soldiers Romance**[30] 449 4-8-0 **52** .... DuranFentiman(5) 13 32
(T D Easterby) *plld hrd and prom: rdn over 2f out: sn wknd* **25/1**

-060 **10** ½ **Marmooq**[13] 605 4-8-9 **56** .... JimCrowley 14 35
(J Gallagher) *in rr: rdn 1/2-way: n.d* **25/1**

4333 **11** 1¼ **Kingsmaite**[13] 605 6-8-7 **54** ....(vt) JimmyQuinn 12 29
(S R Bowring) *chsd ldrs: rdn 1/2-way: wknd over 1f out* **10/1**

-011 **12** 13 **Doctor's Cave**[21] 519 5-9-1 **62** ....(b) NCallan 4 4
(K O Cunningham-Brown) *led: rdn and hdd 2f out: sn wknd* **2/1**[1]

04-5 **13** 2 **Jellytot (USA)**[58] 150 4-9-0 **61** .... MickyFenton 2 —
(J O'Reilly) *s.i.s: a in rr* **14/1**

-033 **14** 5 **Burnley Al (IRE)**[27] 485 5-8-7 **54** ow1 ....(b) RobbieFitzpatrick 6 —
(Peter Grayson) *sn pushed along in rr: wknd 1/2-way* **14/1**

1m 30.86s (0.06) **Going Correction** +0.10s/f (Slow) **14** Ran SP% **129.1**
Speed ratings (Par 101):103,102,100,97,97 95,95,93,90,89 88,73,71,65
CSF £52.91 CT £1099.01 TOTE £13.80: £3.10, £2.10, £7.40; EX 83.80 TRIFECTA Not won..
Owner Paul J Dixon **Bred** Rookley Holdings **Trained** Babworth, Notts

FOCUS
An ordinary handicap of its type and the winning time was 0.15 seconds slower than the second division. Solid form, the winner and second close to their winter form.
Doctor's Cave Official explanation: vet said gelding had bled from the nose
Jellytot(USA) Official explanation: jockey said filly was hampered on leaving stalls
Burnley Al(IRE) Official explanation: jockey said gelding failed to act on fibresand

682 BETDIRECT.COM GET INVOLVED H'CAP 1m (F)
2:25 (2:25) (Class 6) (0-50,55) 4-Y-0+ **£2,388** (£705; £352) **Stalls** Low

Form RPR

5055 **1** **Fuel Cell (IRE)**[24] 500 6-8-8 **45** .... JoeFanning 7 59
(J O'Reilly) *hld up: hdwy over 2f out: led over 1f out: r.o wl* **11/1**

00-3 **2** 3½ **Bob Baileys**[9] 625 5-8-11 **48** ....(b) JimCrowley 10 55
(P R Chamings) *a.p: racd keenly: rdn 2f out: chsd wnr fnl f: styd on same pce* **9/1**

0421 **3** 2 **Desert Lover (IRE)**[9] 625 5-9-4 **55** 6ex ....(tp) NCallan 13 58
(R J Price) *hld up in tch: plld hrd: outpcd over 2f out: styd on ins fnl f* **5/4**[1]

-300 **4** nk **Zando**[21] 266 5-8-5 **45** .... SaleemGolam(3) 6 47
(E G Bevan) *chsd ldr: led 3f out: rdn and hdd over 1f out: wknd ins fnl f* **16/1**

0400 **5** ¾ **Spy Gun (USA)**[1] 674 7-8-8 **45** .... ChrisCatlin 4 46
(T Wall) *led 5f: rdn 2f out: wknd fnl f* **8/1**[3]

0062 **6** 1½ **A Teen**[9] 625 9-8-11 **48** .... JimmyQuinn 8 45
(P Howling) *chsd ldrs: rdn and ev ch over 1f out: wknd ins fnl f* **10/1**

0-00 **7** ¾ **Inca Soldier (FR)**[15] 586 4-8-8 **45** .... JamieMackay 3 41
(R C Guest) *s.s: hld up: rdn over 1f out: n.d* **22/1**

0360 **8** hd **Mr Bountiful (IRE)**[2] 664 9-8-8 **45** ....(t) AlanDaly 9 40
(C J Teague) *s.i.s: hld up: rdn over 1f out: n.d* **20/1**

000- **9** 2 **Filey Buoy**[77] 6280 5-8-4 **46** ow1 .... MichaelJStainton(5) 14 37
(R M Whitaker) *hld up: hdwy over 3rf out: rdn and wknd over 1f out* **14/1**

43-1 **10** 33 **Crush On You**[47] 271 4-8-10 **47** .... GrahamGibbons 12 —
(R Hollinshead) *chsd ldrs over 5f* **6/1**[2]

000- **U** **South Hill**[45] 6701 4-8-5 **45** .... JamesDoyle(3) 11 —
(R J Price) *rrd and uns rdr s* **66/1**

1m 46.79s (2.19) **Going Correction** +0.10s/f (Slow) **11** Ran SP% **120.4**
Speed ratings (Par 101):93,89,87,87,86 84,84,84,82,49 —
CSF £106.31 CT £216.15 TOTE £14.40: £3.10, £3.20, £1.10; EX 90.70 TRIFECTA Not won..
Owner J Morris **Bred** David Browne **Trained** Doncaster, S Yorks

FOCUS
A dire contest, made even less satisfactory by a pedestrian early gallop which resulted in a few taking a grip. It resulted in a moderate winning time, even for a race like this. The race has been rated through the runner-up.

683 BETDIRECT.COM £50 FREE BET H'CAP 1m 6f (F)
3:00 (3:00) (Class 6) (0-65,65) 4-Y-0+ **£2,266** (£674; £337; £168) **Stalls** Low

Form RPR

12-1 **1** **Three Boars**[2] 669 5-9-11 **65** 5ex ....(b) WilliamBuick(5) 10 78+
(S Gollings) *hld up and bhd: hdwy 8f out: led over 1f out: eased nr fin* **5/4**[1]

1321 **2** 1¼ **Blue Hills**[10] 617 6-9-8 **64** 5ex ....(b) WilliamCarson(7) 9 75
(P W Hiatt) *hld up: hdwy over 2f out: nt rch wnr* **7/2**[2]

0-33 **3** shd **Plenty Cried Wolf**[10] 623 5-9-6 **55** .... PaulHanagan 11 66
(R A Fahey) *led after 1f: rdn and hdd over 1f out: styd on same pce ins fnl f* **7/1**

-242 **4** 3½ **Tresor Secret (FR)**[27] 481 7-9-10 **59** .... JimCrowley 13 65
(J Gallagher) *chsd ldrs: rdn and ev ch over 2f out: no ex fnl f* **12/1**

3-06 **5** ½ **Silver Mont (IRE)**[15] 585 4-8-6 **45** ....(bt) JimmyQuinn 8 50
(S R Bowring) *prom: lost pl 11f out: hdwy over 3f out: rdn over 2f out: styd on same pce appr fnl f* **20/1**

060/ **6** 2½ **Muraqeb**[124] 1808 7-8-10 **45** ....(p) LPKeniry 12 47
(Mrs Barbara Waring) *chsd ldrs: rdn 7f out: wknd over 2f out* **100/1**

0-15 **7** 6 **Red River Rock (IRE)**[35] 389 5-8-13 **48** ....(be) MickyFenton 7 42
(T J Fitzgerald) *sn pushed along and prom: wknd over 2f out* **11/2**[3]

4-44 **8** 7 **Chart Oak**[20] 537 4-9-2 **55** .... JoeFanning 14 39
(P Howling) *chsd ldrs: rdn and wknd over 2f out* **16/1**

650- **9** 17 **Ever Special (IRE)**[42] 5838 4-8-3 **45** .... PatrickMathers(3) 4 5
(J T Stimpson) *sn pushed along in rr: lost tch fnl 5f* **20/1**

-300 **10** 2½ **Chimes At Midnight (USA)**[10] 615 10-8-10 **45** ....(b) EddieAhern 2 1
(Luke Comer, Ire) *hld up and bhd: wknd 1/2-way* **28/1**

0-00 **11** ½ **College Rebel**[9] 628 6-8-10 **45** .... NCallan 1 1
(J F Coupland) *led 1f: remained handy tl rdn and wknd 3f out* **66/1**

3m 10.9s (1.30) **Going Correction** +0.10s/f (Slow)
WFA 4 from 5yo+ 4lb **11** Ran SP% **123.6**
Speed ratings (Par 101):100,99,99,97,96 95,92,88,78,76 76
CSF £5.54 CT £23.89 TOTE £2.00: £1.20, £1.30, £1.90; EX 6.60 Trifecta £23.50 Pool: £440.92 - 13.27 winning units..
Owner P Whinham **Bred** J M Greetham **Trained** Scamblesby, Lincs

FOCUS
A modest staying handicap in which the pace was only fair. The race has been rated positively with the first two going the right way.

684 BETDIRECTPOKER.COM MAIDEN STKS 1m (F)
3:40 (3:41) (Class 5) 3-Y-0 **£2,817** (£838; £418; £209) **Stalls** Low

Form RPR

1 **Tremelo Pointe (IRE)** 3-8-12 .... SteveDrowne 5 64+
(H Morrison) *chsd ldrs: led over 5f out: rdn and hung lft fr over 2f out: r.o* **8/1**[3]

040- **2** 3½ **Cadwell**[156] 5901 3-9-3 53 .... AdrianTNicholls 8 62
(D Nicholls) *led: hdd over 5f out: chsd ldrs: rdn over 1f out: no ex ins fnl f* **16/1**

-200 **3** 7 **Mutoon (IRE)**[14] 591 3-8-9 62 .... SaleemGolam(3) 3 42
(S C Williams) *hld up: hdwy over 3f out: rdn and wknd over 1f out* **8/1**[3]

6 4 *nk* **Pride Of Northcare (IRE)**[43] 311 3-9-3 .... PatCosgrave 2 46
(G A Huffer) *plld hrd and prom: lost pl over 5f out: rdn over 2f out: wknd over 1f out* **4/6**[1]
040- 5 *nk* **Shady Green (IRE)**[121] 6475 3-9-3 52................................ DaleGibson 4 46
(M W Easterby) *s.i.s: hdwy 1/2-way: rdn and wknd over 1f out* **25/1**
6 *3/4* **Hand Of Fate (IRE)** 3-8-12 .... KDarley 7 39
(M Johnston) *s.i.s: hdwy over 6f out: hung rt over 3f out: rdn and wknd over 1f out* **15/8**[2]
7 *19* **Danehill Warrior (IRE)** 3-9-3 .... JamieMackay 6 4
(R C Guest) *s.i.s: hld up: rdn 3f out: sn wknd* **33/1**
43-6 8 *dist* **Inflagrantedelicto (USA)**[46] 284 3-9-3 59.................. TonyCulhane 1 —
(D W Chapman) *bhd fr 1/2-way: virtually p.u fnl 3f* **25/1**

1m 46.48s (1.88) **Going Correction** +0.10s/f (Slow) 8 Ran SP% 133.5
Speed ratings (Par 98):94,90,83,83,82 82,63,—
CSF £132.02 TOTE £12.70: £1.90, £4.70, £1.40; EX 145.10 TRIFECTA Not won..
Owner Lord Margadale, H Scott-Barrett & J Dean **Bred** Stone Ridge Farm **Trained** East Ilsley, Berks

FOCUS
A two-horse race according to the market, but both ran poorly which might appear to hold the form down. The winner was most impressive though, so it might be worth giving her the benefit of the doubt. The form is very difficult to pin down.
Pride Of Northcare(IRE) Official explanation: jockey said gelding never travelled; vet said gelding returned lame behind
Inflagrantedelicto(USA) Official explanation: jockey said gelding moved poorly

685 BETDIRECT.COM H'CAP 1m 3f (F)
4:25 (4:25) (Class 6) (0-65,65) 4-Y-0+ £2,266 (£674; £337; £168) Stalls Low

Form RPR
04-0 1 **Shape Up (IRE)**[30] 453 7-8-12 60.................................(v) PaulFessey 2 69
(R Craggs) *led 1f: chsd ldrs: led over 4f out: rdn over 1f out: styd on* **16/1**
31-2 2 *1 1/4* **Starcross Maid**[9] 630 5-8-3 51.................................... ChrisCatlin 4 58
(J F Coupland) *a.p: rdn to chse wnr over 1f out: nt qckn ins fnl f* **15/2**[2]
123- 3 *1 1/4* **Eforetta (GER)**[229] 3955 5-8-13 61............................ EdwardCreighton 3 66+
(D J Wintle) *chsd ldrs: rdn over 2f out: no ex ins fnl f* **10/1**
511 4 *2* **Our Kes (IRE)**[10] 610 5-9-3 65 6ex................................ TonyCulhane 12 66
(P Howling) *hld up: hdwy over 3f out: rdn over 1f out: edgd lft and no ex fianl f* **5/2**[1]
00-0 5 *15* **Piper General (IRE)**[23] 507 5-9-0 65..................... JasonEdmunds(3) 6 41
(J Balding) *chsd ldrs over 7f* **25/1**
06-5 6 *9* **Fiddlers Creek (IRE)**[10] 618 8-8-12 60..............(bt[1]) DanielTudhope 11 21
(R Allan) *hld up: rdn 1/2-way: n.d* **16/1**
00-0 7 *nk* **Itcanbedone Again (IRE)**[33] 426 8-8-1 54............. WilliamBuick(5) 10 14
(Ian Williams) *led after 1f: hdd 9f out: led over 7f out: hdd over 4f out: rdn and wknd over 2f out* **18/1**
3/0- 8 *3* **Safin (GER)**[21] 7-9-3 65.. NCallan 9 20
(F Jordan) *hld up: hdwy 7f out: rdn and wknd over 4f out* **20/1**
0/0- 9 *1 1/2* **Akash (IRE)**[34] 1995 7-8-12 63......................................(t) JamesDoyle(3) 7 16
(Miss J Feilden) *mid-div: rdn and wknd over 4f out* **33/1**
-530 10 *3/4* **Marbaa (IRE)**[14] 594 4-9-0 63.. LPKeniry 5 14
(S Dow) *prom over 7f* **18/1**
-664 11 *6* **Moving Target (IRE)**[10] 610 8-8-9 57...................... J-PGuillambert 13 —
(Luke Comer, Ire) *hld up: sme hdwy whn n.m.r over 3f out: sn wknd* **8/1**[3]
02-3 12 *3/4* **King's Spear (IRE)**[31] 445 4-9-1 64................................ EddieAhern 14 4
(P W Chapple-Hyam) *chsd ldrs: led 9f out to over 7f out: wknd over 3f out* **5/2**[1]

2m 28.05s (-0.85) **Going Correction** +0.10s/f (Slow)
WFA 4 from 5yo+ 1lb 12 Ran SP% 122.9
Speed ratings (Par 101):107,106,105,103,92 86,86,83,82,82 77,77
CSF £133.09 CT £1288.19 TOTE £30.80: £6.50, £1.70, £3.40; EX 157.70 TRIFECTA Not won..
Owner Ray Craggs **Bred** Gainsborough Stud Management Ltd **Trained** Sedgefield, Co Durham

FOCUS
A modest event, but they went a good pace which resulted in a decent winning time for a race of its class. The leading quartet pulled miles clear of the others and the form is solid.
Safin(GER) Official explanation: jockey said gelding had no more to give
Moving Target(IRE) Official explanation: jockey said gelding hung left

686 BETDIRECT.COM 5 PLACES ON THE COUNTY HURDLE H'CAP (DIV II) 7f (F)
5:05 (5:06) (Class 6) (0-65,64) 4-Y-0+ £1,619 (£481; £240; £120) Stalls Low

Form RPR
-004 1 **Kew The Music**[18] 560 7-8-7 53.................................... ChrisCatlin 4 67
(M R Channon) *dwlt: outpcd: swtchd lft and hdwy over 1f out: styd on to ld wl ins fnl f* **8/1**
-025 2 *1 1/2* **Cleveland**[28] 468 5-8-11 62............................... RussellKennemore(5) 14 72
(R Hollinshead) *chsd ldrs: led over 2f out: rdn and hung rt fr over 1f out: hdd wl ins fnl f* **5/1**[2]
3000 3 *3* **Astronomical Odds (USA)**[6] 651 4-9-0 60.................... PaulFessey 7 62
(T D Barron) *chsd ldrs: rdn over 2f out: eased whn btn ins fnl f* **20/1**
1060 4 *2* **Glamaraazi (IRE)**[27] 485 4-8-10 56.............................. PaulHanagan 9 53
(R A Fahey) *prom: rdn over 2f out: wknd ins fnl f* **25/1**
1016 5 *1 1/4* **Granakey (IRE)**[20] 539 4-8-13 59.. TPQueally 2 53
(M G Quinlan) *hld up: hdwy u.p over 1f out: nvr trbld ldrs* **9/1**
3U35 6 *hd* **Tancredi (SWE)**[17] 564 5-9-1 64................................. JerryO'Dwyer(3) 12 57
(N B King) *led 6f out: hdd over 2f out: rdn and wknd over 1f out* **14/1**
14-0 7 *3* **Benny The Bus**[10] 621 5-9-0 60.............................. GrahamGibbons 1 45
(Mrs G S Rees) *hld up: rdn over 2f out: n.d* **16/1**
5310 8 *nk* **Mister Benji**[17] 570 8-8-11 57.................................(p) TonyCulhane 3 42
(B P J Baugh) *hld up in tch: nt clr run and lost pl over 4f out: rdn and wknd over 2f out* **10/1**
1320 9 *2 1/2* **Tyrone Sam**[27] 485 5-8-11 57..(b) NCallan 13 35
(K A Ryan) *s.i.s: sn prom: rdn and wknd over 1f out* **7/1**[3]
4-12 10 *1/2* **Black Sea Pearl**[37] 376 4-9-4 64.................................. DarryllHolland 5 41
(P W D'Arcy) *prom: n.m.r and lost pl 5f out: n.d after* **9/4**[1]
4000 11 *2 1/2* **Capital Lass**[15] 579 4-8-7 53.................................... HayleyTurner 6 23
(A J McCabe) *s.i.s: hld up: a in rr* **25/1**
0-00 12 *nk* **Napoletano (GER)**[19] 549 6-8-9 55.................................... LPKeniry 11 25
(S Dow) *sed slwoly: hld up: effrt over 3f out: sn wknd* **20/1**
10-0 13 *1/2* **Ebraam (USA)**[22] 516 4-9-3 63.................................. DeanMcKeown 10 31
(D Shaw) *s.i.s: sn prom: wknd over 2f out* **12/1**
0200 14 *10* **Princess Arwen**[8] 637 5-8-4 50 oh5............................... JimmyQuinn 8 —
(Mrs Barbara Waring) *led 1f: wknd 1/2-way* **33/1**

1m 30.71s (-0.09) **Going Correction** +0.10s/f (Slow) 14 Ran SP% 130.5
Speed ratings (Par 101):104,102,98,96,95 94,91,91,88,87 84,84,83,72
CSF £48.40 CT £828.82 TOTE £9.80: £2.00, £3.50, £7.60; EX 61.20 TRIFECTA Not won. Place 6 £314.82, Place 5 £129.89.

Owner Miss Bridget Coyle **Bred** Miss B Coyle **Trained** West Ilsley, Berks

FOCUS
The faster division by 0.15 seconds, but still a modest handicap and very few ever got into it. Solid form, the runner-up rated to his winter best.
Black Sea Pearl Official explanation: trainer said, regarding the poor form shown, filly was crowded on final bend and failed to travel thereafter
T/Plt: £476.70 to a £1 stake. Pool: £51,954.15. 79.55 winning tickets. T/Qpdt: £37.50 to a £1 stake. Pool: £3,887.70. 76.60 winning tickets. CR

649 LINGFIELD (L-H)
Friday, March 16

OFFICIAL GOING: Standard
Wind: Moderate across

687 PONTINSBINGO.COM H'CAP (DIV I) 6f (P)
1:20 (1:22) (Class 6) (0-52,52) 4-Y-0+ £1,706 (£503; £252) Stalls Low

Form RPR
00-1 1 **Cativo Cavallino**[20] 548 4-8-4 49........................ NataliaGemelova(5) 8 61
(J E Long) *a.p: led 1f out: rdn out* **6/1**[2]
043- 2 *1 1/4* **Pearl Farm**[217] 4329 6-8-8 48.. FergusSweeney 4 56
(C A Horgan) *a.p: swtchd lft over 1f out: r.o to chse wnr ins fnl f* **7/1**[3]
0162 3 *1* **Thoughtsofstardom**[3] 668 4-8-12 52.....................(be) HayleyTurner 10 57
(P S McEntee) *trckd ldr after 1f: led 2f out: rdn and hdd 1f out: kpt on one pce* **5/1**[1]
-525 4 *1 1/2* **Double M**[7] 653 10-8-6 46 oh1...(v) AlanDaly 5 47
(Mrs L Richards) *trckd ldrs: rdn 2f out: nt qckn fnl f* **12/1**
210- 5 *hd* **Staceymac (IRE)**[76] 6981 4-8-11 51............................. EddieAhern 1 51
(W R Muir) *prom on ins: short of room over 1f out: rallied and r.o ins fnl f* **5/1**[1]
-300 6 *1 1/4* **Arfinnit (IRE)**[19] 557 6-8-1 46 oh1............................(p) WilliamBuick(5) 3 42+
(Mrs A L M King) *slowly away: hmpd after 1f: styd on fnl f: nvr nrr* **11/1**
3340 7 *shd* **Mind Alert**[31] 448 6-8-9 49 ow1..(v) NCallan 12 45
(D Shaw) *stdd s: hld up: hdwy 2f out: one pce fnl f* **6/1**[2]
6661 8 *1 1/2* **Grand View**[7] 653 11-8-11 51 6ex..............................(p) DarryllHolland 7 42+
(J R Weymes) *mid-division whn sltly hmpd after 1f: lost pl and nvr on terms after* **10/1**
0-00 9 *shd* **Auentraum (GER)**[28] 479 7-8-6 49.........................(p) JamesDoyle(3) 11 40
(Ms J S Doyle) *blindfold stl on whn lft stalls: a bhd* **33/1**
0-00 10 *1/2* **Globe**[7] 653 4-8-3 46 oh1.. RichardKingscote(3) 9 36
(Mrs H Sweeting) *led tl rdn and hdd 2f out: sn wknd* **25/1**
00-6 11 *19* **Hillbilly Cat (USA)**[52] 221 4-8-10 50.............................. RobertHavlin 2 —
(R Ingram) *mid-div whn sltly hmpd after 1f: sn bhd* **20/1**
1005 U **Vlasta Weiner**[16] 586 7-8-12 52...(b) RyanMoore 6 —
(J M Bradley) *prom whn clipped heels and uns rdr after 1f* **8/1**

1m 12.0s (-0.81) **Going Correction** -0.10s/f (Stan) 12 Ran SP% 122.2
Speed ratings (Par 101):101,99,98,96,95 94,93,91,91,91 65,—
CSF £48.11 CT £234.56 TOTE £8.30: £2.40, £2.70, £2.30; EX 63.40 Trifecta £183.70 Pool: £266.51, 1.03 winning units.
Owner P Saxon **Bred** Miss A M Rees **Trained** Caterham, Surrey
■ Champion jockey Ryan Moore broke his arm in this fall.

FOCUS
Hand-timed. Very moderate handicap form but solid for the grade and the winner is improving for his new stable.
Mind Alert Official explanation: jockey said gelding suffered interference
Grand View Official explanation: jockey said gelding suffered interference
Globe Official explanation: jockey said filly hung left
Hillbilly Cat(USA) Official explanation: jockey said saddle slipped

688 BONUSPRINT.COM CLAIMING STKS 5f (P)
1:50 (1:53) (Class 6) 4-Y-0+ £2,184 (£644; £322) Stalls High

Form RPR
1500 1 **Pride Of Joy**[22] 521 4-9-0 59... JimCrowley 7 63
(D K Ivory) *led after 1f: rdn and stretched clr fnl f* **14/1**
06-2 2 *1 1/2* **Devon Flame**[11] 622 8-9-9 77.. RichardHughes 9 67
(R J Hodges) *a.p on outside: rdn and r.o wl fnl f to go 2nd nr fin* **2/1**[1]
0-25 3 *1/2* **Blackheath (IRE)**[16] 581 11-9-7 68........................... AdrianTNicholls 1 63
(D Nicholls) *led for 1f: trckd wnr: rdn fnl f: lost 2nd nr fin* **7/2**[2]
221/ 4 *hd* **Potwash**[8] 7-8-12 .... AlanDaly 5 53
(Andre Hermans, Belgium) *plld hrd in mid-div: r.o wl fnl f: nvr nrr* **11/1**
0-42 5 *1/2* **Danish Blues (IRE)**[24] 504 4-9-9 56..............................(e) IanMongan 3 62
(D E Cantillon) *hld up in rr: rdn 1/2-way: kpt on fnl f: nvr nrr* **4/1**[3]
2255 6 *nk* **Ceredig**[15] 588 4-9-9 54... GeorgeBaker 2 61
(W R Muir) *stdd s: sn chsd ldrs: rdn over 1f out: one pce after* **14/1**
2200 7 *2 1/2* **City For Conquest (IRE)**[19] 561 4-9-1 56.....................(b) NCallan 6 44
(T J Pitt) *a in rr* **7/1**
4540 8 *nk* **Majestical (IRE)**[11] 622 5-9-3 49.................................(b) DaneO'Neill 8 45
(J M Bradley) *in rr: effrt on outside 2f out: sn btn* **14/1**
2030 9 *1/2* **New Options**[11] 613 10-9-3 52...(b) BrettDoyle 4 43
(Peter Grayson) *a in rr* **20/1**

59.08 secs (-0.70) **Going Correction** -0.10s/f (Stan) 9 Ran SP% 121.2
Speed ratings (Par 101):101,98,97,97,96 96,92,91,90
CSF £44.49 TOTE £23.00: £4.40, £1.60, £1.80; EX 90.80 TRIFECTA Not won..
Owner K T Ivory **Bred** K T Ivory **Trained** Radlett, Herts

FOCUS
A modest claimer and another race in which those who raced prominently dominated throughout. The runner-up and third were not at their best but the form overall seems sound.

689 GO PONTIN'S MAIDEN FILLIES' STKS 7f (P)
2:25 (2:27) (Class 5) 3-Y-O £3,071 (£906; £453) Stalls Low

Form RPR
3252 1 **Madrigale**[25] 498 3-9-0 65.. GeorgeBaker 13 67
(G L Moore) *a.p: led over 2f out: r.o wl fnl f* **8/1**
20- 2 *1* **Empress Olga (USA)**[226] 4041 3-9-0 .... BrettDoyle 2 68+
(E A L Dunlop) *a.p: gng 2nd whn short of room 1f out: swtchd rt: nt pce of wnr* **5/4**[1]
3-33 3 *1 1/4* **Nicomedia (IRE)**[9] 633 3-9-0 67.................................. RichardHughes 7 61+
(R Hannon) *towards rr: gd hdwy ent fnl f: r.o strly: nvr nrr* **9/4**[2]
4 4 *1/2* **Gold Digger Miss (USA)**[67] 73 3-9-0 .... TPQueally 1 60+
(J Noseda) *a in tch: rdn and styd on one pce fnl f* **13/2**[3]
5 *2* **Now You See Me** 3-9-0 .... NCallan 12 55
(K McAuliffe) *in rr: effrt 2f out: one pace fnl f* **25/1**
0-00 6 *1 1/2* **Hayley's Flower (IRE)**[48] 267 3-9-0 50.............................. PatDobbs 4 51
(J C Fox) *led tl hdd over 2f out: wknd ins fnl f* **50/1**

7 1 1/4 **Miss Invincible** 3-9-0 .... AdamKirby 10 48
(A P Jarvis) *plld hrd: towards rr: c wd into st: kpt on one pce* **33/1**

0- 8 3/4 **Winning Smile (USA)**[154] 5950 3-9-0 .... AdrianMcCarthy 8 46
(P W Chapple-Hyam) *chsd ldr to over 2f out: wknd over 1f out* **16/1**

6-3 9 *hd* **Best Option**[69] 55 3-9-0 .... EddieAhern 11 45
(W R Muir) *t.k.h: racd wd in mid-div: wknd over 1f out* **33/1**

10 1/2 **Assistacat (IRE)** 3-9-0 .... SebSanders 3 44
(A P Jarvis) *chsd ldrs tl rdn and wknd wl over 1f out* **25/1**

11 4 **Winforjoe (IRE)** 3-8-11 .... AmirQuinn(3) 6 34
(J J Bridger) *slowly away: a bhd* **66/1**

12 *nk* **Sixfields Flyer (IRE)** 3-9-0 .... PaulEddery 5 33
(Pat Eddery) *mid-div: bhd fnl 2f* **11/1**

505 13 1 1/4 **Lady Fifer**[17] 573 3-9-0 60........ JimmyQuinn 9 30
(Jane Chapple-Hyam) *hld up in rr: a bhd* **33/1**

1m 26.28s (0.39) **Going Correction** -0.10s/f (Stan) 13 Ran SP% **133.8**
Speed ratings (Par 95):93,91,90,89,87 85,84,83,83,82 78,77,76
CSF £19.75 TOTE £8.70: £2.60, £1.20, £1.30; EX 28.80 Trifecta £57.10 Pool: £490.12 - 6.09 winning units..
Owner D J Deer **Bred** D J And Mrs Deer **Trained** Woodingdean, E Sussex

FOCUS
Modest maiden form, limited by the sixth. The winner just returned to form, with the runner-up rated as finishing upsides.
Sixfields Flyer(IRE) Official explanation: jockey said hind bandage came loose

690 PONTINSBINGO.COM H'CAP (DIV II) 6f (P)
3:00 (3:03) (Class 6) (0-52,52) 4-Y-0+ **£1,706** (£503; £252) **Stalls** Low

Form RPR

-020 1 **Balerno**[9] 637 8-8-11 **51**........ IanMongan 8 59
(Mrs L J Mongan) *hld up: hdwy 2f out: swtchd lft appr fnl f: drvn out to ld ins fnl f* **6/1**[2]

2224 2 *nk* **Over To You Bert**[9] 637 8-8-2 **49** ow1........ HaddenFrost(7) 10 56
(R J Hodges) *chsd ldr to over 1f out: rallied to regain 2nd cl home* **6/1**[2]

5346 3 *nk* **Muktasb (USA)**[3] 668 6-8-12 **52**........(v) TonyCulhane 2 58+
(D Shaw) *hld up in rr: hdwy over 1f out: r.o strly: nvr nrr* **11/2**[1]

-065 4 *shd* **King Of Charm (IRE)**[19] 562 4-8-7 **47**........(b) FergusSweeney 6 53
(G L Moore) *in tch: led ent fnl f: hdd ins and no ex cl home* **7/1**[3]

3205 5 1 1/4 **Lady Hopeful (IRE)**[11] 613 5-8-9 **49**........(b) BrettDoyle 5 51
(Peter Grayson) *towards rr: r.o ins fnl f: nvr nrr* **8/1**

5106 6 2 **Blushing Russian (IRE)**[16] 580 5-8-8 **48**........(p) ChrisCatlin 11 44
(J M Bradley) *chsd ldrs: c wd into st: wknd fnl f* **16/1**

0106 7 *shd* **Orchestration (IRE)**[1] 680 6-8-10 **50**........(b) NCallan 3 52+
(K J Burke) *mid-division: hdwy on ins whn checked appr fnl f: rallied and r.o ins* **6/1**[2]

0-00 8 1/2 **Par Excellence**[11] 622 4-8-0 **47** oh1 ow1........(p) JackDean(7) 7 41
(W G M Turner) *mid-division: rdn over 2f out: sn btn* **33/1**

0-00 9 1 **Creme Brulee**[16] 580 4-8-12 **52**........(b[1]) SebSanders 4 43
(C R Egerton) *led tl rdn and hdd ent fnl f: wknd ins* **8/1**

0002 10 1 1/2 **Alucica**[7] 653 4-8-6 **46** oh1........(v) AdrianMcCarthy 12 33
(D Shaw) *slowly away: plld hrd in rr: a bhd* **14/1**

-300 11 5 **Crafty Fox**[19] 560 4-8-10 **50**........(v) AdamKirby 9 22
(A P Jarvis) *mid-division: racd wd: effrt over 2f out: sn btn* **8/1**

1m 12.55s (-0.26) **Going Correction** -0.10s/f (Stan) 33 Ran SP% **119.6**
Speed ratings (Par 101):97,96,96,96,94 91,91,90,89,87 80
CSF £42.69 CT £216.73 TOTE £7.50: £2.80, £1.60, £2.30; EX 47.40 Trifecta £293.20 Part won. Pool: £412.98 - 0.79 winning units..
Owner K Santana **Bred** Juddmonte Farms **Trained** Epsom, Surrey

FOCUS
A moderate handicap, run at a strong early pace. The first four came clear in a blanket finish. Modest form, the winner, second and fourth rated to their recent level.
Orchestration(IRE) Official explanation: jockey said gelding suffered interference in closing stages

691 PONTIN'S "BOOK EARLY" H'CAP 2m (P)
3:40 (3:40) (Class 5) (0-70,70) 4-Y-0+ **£3,071** (£906; £453) **Stalls** Low

Form RPR

3132 1 **Lorikeet**[17] 578 8-9-6 **67**........ JamesDoyle(3) 2 79
(Noel T Chance) *mid-div: hdwy to trck ldrs over 3f out: strly rdn and r.o fnl f to ld post* **10/3**[1]

53-0 2 *shd* **Tavalu (USA)**[53] 213 5-9-1 **59**........ FergusSweeney 7 71
(G L Moore) *a.p: wnt 2nd 6f out: led over 3f out: rdn and styd on but hdd post* **8/1**

-322 3 5 **Kavi (IRE)**[44] 316 7-9-12 **70**........ OscarUrbina 5 76
(Simon Earle) *trckd ldr: led 7f out to over 3f out: kpt on one pce ins fnl 2f* **6/1**[3]

40-3 4 1 **Noddies Way**[9] 640 4-8-1 **53**........ LiamJones(3) 6 58
(J F Panvert) *in tch: styd on one pce fr over 1f out* **6/1**[3]

6-13 5 3 1/2 **Moon Emperor**[14] 607 10-9-4 **62**........(b) NCallan 9 63
(J R Jenkins) *mid-div: rdn over 2f out and no hdwy after* **10/1**

4/32 6 1 3/4 **Garnett (IRE)**[9] 640 6-9-12 **70**........(p) PatCosgrave 3 69
(D E Cantillon) *hld up in rr: mod late hdwy* **7/2**[2]

/010 7 1 1/2 **Dolzago**[30] 457 7-9-4 **62**........(b) GeorgeBaker 11 59
(G L Moore) *a towards rr* **10/1**

2331 8 2 1/2 **King After**[7] 651 5-8-13 **60** 6ex........ StephaneBreux(3) 10 54
(J R Best) *hld up: effrt on outside 3f out: no hdwy fnl 2f* **10/1**

0/0- 9 11 **Son Of Greek Myth (USA)**[73] 521 6-9-4 **62**........(b) JimmyFortune 4 43
(G L Moore) *led tl hdd 7f out: wknd over 5f out* **33/1**

-630 10 1 **Shadow Aspect**[25] 495 4-8-3 **52**........ JimmyQuinn 8 31
(Eoin Doyle, Ire) *hld up in rr: mid-div: rdn and wknd over 2f out* **20/1**

0-40 11 16 **Sky Walk**[30] 458 4-8-5 **54** ow2........ SimonWhitworth 1 14
(Jamie Poulton) *trckd ldrs tl wknd over 3f out* **20/1**

55-1 12 5 **Dubai Sunday (JPN)**[11] 615 6-8-7 **51** 6ex........ SamHitchcott 12 5
(P S McEntee) *hld up in rr: wekb bhd whn virtually p.u ins fnl f* **16/1**

3m 25.62s (-3.17) **Going Correction** -0.10s/f (Stan)
WFA 4 from 5yo+ 5lb 12 Ran SP% **130.6**
Speed ratings (Par 103):103,102,100,99,98 97,96,95,89,89 81,78
CSF £33.28 CT £165.81 TOTE £3.10: £1.30, £2.30, £2.10; EX 52.70 Trifecta £319.70 Pool: £540.39 - 1.20 winning units..
Owner The Tribesmen Syndicate **Bred** Sheikh Mohammed Bin Rashid Al Maktoum **Trained** Upper Lambourn, Berks
■ Stewards' Enquiry : Fergus SweeneyM caution: careless riding

FOCUS
A modest staying handicap, run at an uneven pace. The first two came clear. The form looks sound with the third and fourth close to their recent level.
Sky Walk Official explanation: jockey said gelding ran too free
Dubai Sunday(JPN) Official explanation: jockey said gelding was stiff behind

692 DIGITAL PRINTS FROM BONUSPRINT.COM H'CAP 6f (P)
4:25 (4:25) (Class 4) (0-85,85) 4-Y-0+ **£4,857** (£1,445; £722; £360) **Stalls** Low

Form RPR

3121 1 **Lucayos**[17] 575 4-8-12 **84**........ RichardKingscote(3) 1 96
(Mrs H Sweeting) *mde all: hrd rdn and pressed by runner-up fnl f: jst hld on* **4/1**[2]

1-21 2 *shd* **Rowe Park**[33] 432 4-8-9 **78**........ LPKeniry 3 90
(Mrs L C Jewell) *chsd ldrs: wnt 2nd wl over 1f out: pressed wnr ins fnl f: jst failed* **5/2**[1]

0250 3 1 1/2 **Garstang**[6] 660 4-8-9 **78**........(b) BrettDoyle 7 86
(Peter Grayson) *stdd s: hdwy whn swtchd to ins appr fnl f: r.o* **12/1**

1240 4 1/2 **Figaro Flyer (IRE)**[17] 575 4-8-9 **78**........ TonyCulhane 2 84
(P Howling) *a in tch: rdn over 1f out: kpt on ins fnl f* **8/1**

3-13 5 *nk* **Hypocrisy**[15] 590 4-8-9 **78**........(v) DanielTudhope 12 83
(D Carroll) *hld up: rdn 2f out: hdwy over 1f out: nvr nr to chal* **11/2**[3]

2062 6 *hd* **Zarzu**[17] 575 8-8-8 **80**........ LiamJones(3) 8 85
(C R Dore) *hld up: mde sme late prog* **8/1**

50-0 7 *nk* **Total Impact**[27] 490 4-9-1 **84**........ SebSanders 5 88
(C A Cyzer) *chsd ldrs: rdn over 1f out: wknd ins fnl f* **9/1**

256- 8 1 1/4 **Brandywell Boy (IRE)**[96] 6776 4-8-8 **77**........ AdamKirby 9 77
(D J S Ffrench Davis) *racd wd: nvr on terms* **11/1**

601- 9 4 **Circuit Dancer (IRE)**[174] 5532 7-9-2 **85**........ AdrianTNicholls 4 73
(D Nicholls) *s.i.s: a bhd* **16/1**

34-0 10 3/4 **Azygous**[20] 554 4-8-9 **78**........ DaneO'Neill 6 64
(J Akehurst) *sn w ldr: wknd wl over 1f out* **20/1**

1m 11.25s (-1.56) **Going Correction** -0.10s/f (Stan) 10 Ran SP% **122.8**
Speed ratings (Par 105):106,105,103,103,102 102,102,100,95,94
CSF £15.30 CT £117.13 TOTE £5.80: £1.20, £2.00, £3.10; EX 17.80 Trifecta £114.80 Pool: £774.77 - 4.79 winning units..
Owner Alex Sweeting **Bred** P Sweeting **Trained** Lockeridge, Wilts

FOCUS
A good sprint handicap for the grade dominated by a couple of in-form, progressive types. A fairly positive view has been taken of the form.
Brandywell Boy(IRE) Official explanation: vet said gelding was short behind

693 PONTINS.COM H'CAP 1m 4f (P)
5:05 (5:05) (Class 4) (0-85,82) 4-Y-0+ **£4,857** (£1,445; £722; £360) **Stalls** Low

Form RPR

1644 1 **Sgt Schultz (IRE)**[7] 652 4-8-10 **76**........ LPKeniry 2 87+
(J S Moore) *trckd ldrs: led over 2f out: sn clr: won w smething in hand* **5/2**[1]

330- 2 2 1/2 **Mister Right (IRE)**[80] 4626 6-8-12 **76**........ AdamKirby 8 82
(D J S Ffrench Davis) *trckd ldr: led 3f out: hdd over 2f out: kpt on but no impresaion after* **20/1**

0/ 3 *shd* **Dryandra (IRE)**[181] 5397 4-8-4 **75**........ WilliamBuick(5) 9 81
(John Joseph Murphy, Ire) *t.k.h in rr: hdwy 3f out: r.o wl fnl f: nvr nrr* **12/1**

6-00 4 *shd* **Dzesmin (POL)**[15] 587 5-8-11 **75**........(p) DarryllHolland 5 81
(R C Guest) *hld up: hdwy over 2f out: r.o fnl f but nt pce to chal* **9/1**

5 1/2 **Tamreen (IRE)**[90] 6-9-1 **79**........(b) FergusSweeney 7 84
(G L Moore) *in tch tl lost pl 4f out: r.o again fnl f* **16/1**

11-5 6 3/4 **Prime Contender**[40] 353 5-9-0 **78**........(b) GeorgeBaker 3 82
(G L Moore) *mid-div: rdn over 2f out: no further hdwy* **7/2**[2]

500 7 *nk* **Fantoche (BRZ)**[14] 608 5-9-4 **82**........ PatCosgrave 4 85
(M J Wallace) *bhd: effrt whn hung lft over 1f out: no ch after* **11/1**

-111 8 6 **Jazrawy**[24] 507 5-9-1 **79**........ DanielTudhope 6 73
(D Carroll) *led tl hdd over 3f out: wknd wl over 1f out* **11/2**

5-32 9 5 **Jebel Ali (IRE)**[15] 593 4-8-6 **75**........(v) JamesDoyle(3) 10 61
(B Gubby) *mid-div: bhd fr over 2f out* **4/1**[3]

040- 10 7 **Cool Hunter**[76] 5367 6-8-13 **77**........ PaulEddery 1 52
(R C Guest) *stdd s: a bhd* **33/1**

2m 31.87s (-2.52) **Going Correction** -0.10s/f (Stan)
WFA 4 from 5yo+ 2lb 10 Ran SP% **125.8**
Speed ratings (Par 105):104,102,102,102,101 101,101,97,93,89
CSF £62.48 CT £541.53 TOTE £3.00: £1.70, £7.10, £6.00; EX 82.40 Trifecta £476.80 Part won. Pool: £671.55 - 0.51 winning units..
Owner Jim Barnes **Bred** Frank Dunne **Trained** Upper Lambourn, Berks
■ Stewards' Enquiry : L P Keniry two-day ban: careless riding (Mar 27-28)

FOCUS
Just ordinary form for the grade and, despite the pace appearing good throughout, it proved hard to make up significant amounts of ground. The form seems sound.
Jebel Ali(IRE) Official explanation: jockey said gelding stopped very quickly

694 PONTIN'S FAMILY HOLIDAYS H'CAP 1m (P)
5:40 (5:40) (Class 5) (0-75,75) 3-Y-O **£3,071** (£906; £453) **Stalls** High

Form RPR

0-62 1 **Alfresco**[9] 635 3-8-11 **68**........(b[1]) PaulEddery 8 72+
(Pat Eddery) *hld up in rr: hdwy over 2f out: led 1f out: r.o wl* **5/1**[2]

4-13 2 3/4 **Satyricon**[15] 591 3-8-13 **70**........(b) OscarUrbina 12 76+
(M Botti) *hld up: hdwy whn nt clr run over 1f out: swtchd rt:: r.o wl to cl on wnr ins fnl f* **2/1**[1]

520- 3 1 1/2 **Deadline (UAE)**[161] 5788 3-9-4 **75**........ JoeFanning 2 74
(M Johnston) *chsd ldrs: ev ch ent fnl f: nt qckn ins* **5/1**[2]

14-6 4 1 1/4 **Sahrati**[15] 591 3-9-2 **73**........ JimmyFortune 11 69+
(C E Brittain) *in rr: hdwy 2f out: r.o ins fnl f* **10/1**

51 5 3/4 **Divertimenti (IRE)**[27] 489 3-9-4 **75**........(p) EddieAhern 6 69
(M J Wallace) *trckd ldrs: ev ch ent fnl f: one pce ins* **12/1**

30-6 6 1 **Fine Ruler (IRE)**[27] 492 3-8-11 **68**........ SamHitchcott 1 60
(M R Channon) *slowly away: rdn over 3f out: mde sme late hdwy past btn horses* **14/1**

-121 7 6 **Sweet World**[27] 491 3-8-6 **63**........ TPQueally 7 41
(A P Jarvis) *trckd ldr: t.k.h: wknd over 1f out* **9/1**[3]

-142 8 1 1/4 **Intersky Sports (USA)**[27] 491 3-8-11 **68**........(p) NCallan 3 43
(K A Ryan) *led tl wknd 1f out* **9/1**[3]

4-65 9 *nk* **Silca Key**[19] 563 3-8-11 **68**........ EdwardCreighton 5 43
(M R Channon) *in tch tl rdn and wknd over 1f out* **12/1**

10-0 10 3 1/2 **Cavallo Di Ferro (IRE)**[15] 591 3-8-13 **70**........ AdamKirby 9 37
(M J Gingell) *in tch on outside: rdn 3f out: wknd 2f out* **25/1**

2200 11 *hd* **Not Too Taxing**[9] 635 3-8-10 **67**........(b[1]) DaneO'Neill 10 33
(R Hannon) *in tch tl outpcd over 2f out* **33/1**

040- 12 *nk* **Bathwick Breeze**[233] 3843 3-8-11 **68**........ JimCrowley 4 33
(B R Millman) *a in rr* **50/1**

1m 38.2s (-1.23) **Going Correction** -0.10s/f (Stan) 12 Ran SP% **126.6**
Speed ratings (Par 98):102,101,99,98,97 96,90,89,89,85 85,85
CSF £16.24 CT £57.44 TOTE £4.10: £1.60, £1.70, £3.10; EX 22.70 Trifecta £84.40 Pool: £372.28 - 3.13 winning units. Place 6 £13.08, Place 5 £6.07.

Owner Pat Eddery Racing (Caerleon) **Bred** Usk Valley Stud **Trained** Nether Winchendon, Bucks

FOCUS

Just a modest handicap for three-year-olds. The pace seemed fair enough by Lingfield's standards, but a few of these still raced keenly. Unlike the rest of the card, the finish was dominated by hold-up horses. The form should work out.

T/Plt: £9.10 to a £1 stake. Pool: £52,865.05. 4,199.75 winning tickets. T/Qpdt: £3.90 to a £1 stake. Pool: £3,664.40. 691.90 winning tickets. JS

[31] DEAUVILLE (R-H)

Friday, March 16

OFFICIAL GOING: Standard

695a PRIX MONTENICA (LISTED RACE) (C&G) (ALL-WEATHER) 6f 110y

1:50 (1:51) 3-Y-O £17,568 (£7,027; £5,270; £3,514; £1,757)

RPR

1 **Prior Warning**[125] [6453] 3-8-12 .... DBoeuf 5 102
(D Smaga, France)

2 ¾ **High Dream (USA)**[202] 3-8-12 .... C-PLemaire 2 99
(J-C Rouget, France)

3 ½ **Gris De Gris (IRE)**[33] [436] 3-9-2 .... TThulliez 4 102
(J-M Capitte, France)

4 1 **Ilie Nastase (FR)**[107] 3-8-12 .... OPeslier 7 95
(R Gibson, France)

5 ¾ **Punisher (FR)**[101] 3-8-12 .... FSanchez 6 93
(S Loeuillet, France)

6 shd **Resplendent Alpha**[146] [6096] 3-8-12 .... ShaneKelly 1 93
(P Howling) *pressed leader til led entering straight, headed 1f out, one pace (68/10)* 68/10[1]

7 2 **Flyng Teapot (IRE)**[3] 3-8-12 .... SPasquier 8 87
(C Boutin, France)

8 4 **Querglas Bere (FR)**[214] 3-8-12 .... CSoumillon 3 75
(Robert Collet, France)

1m 17.3s (77.30) 8 Ran SP% **12.8**

PARI-MUTUEL: WIN 6.90; PL 1.70, 1.20, 1.60; DF 7.40.

Owner K Abdulla **Bred** Juddmonte Farms Ltd **Trained** Lamorlaye, France

NOTEBOOK

Resplendent Alpha, drawn in stall one, raced far too free early on. After being niggled along turning into the straight, he gradually dropped out of contention and finished up well held.

[687] LINGFIELD (L-H)

Saturday, March 17

OFFICIAL GOING: Standard

Wind: Blustery, across

697 TOTEPLACEPOT H'CAP 7f (P)

2:20 (2:20) (Class 4) (0-80,80) 4-Y-0+ £4,857 (£1,445; £722; £360) Stalls Low

Form RPR

0-62 1 **His Master's Voice (IRE)**[12] [614] 4-8-4 68 .... JoeFanning 4 79
(D W P Arbuthnot) *trckd ldr: rdn to ld over 1f out: a in command after: readily* 9/2[1]

03-3 2 1½ **Fremen (USA)**[7] [657] 7-9-2 80 .... AdrianTNicholls 3 87+
(D Nicholls) *hld up: in tch on inner: hdwy over 1f out: rdn 1f out: chsd wnr last 100 yds: a hld* 6/1[3]

-021 3 ½ **Silent Storm**[28] [486] 7-8-13 77 .... EddieAhern 7 83
(C A Cyzer) *lw: chsd ldrs: rdn over 2f out: kpt on u.p: nt pce to trble wnr* 11/2[2]

0-40 4 ½ **Adantino**[18] [575] 8-8-12 76 ....(b) JimCrowley 8 81
(B R Millman) *t.k.h: hld up towards rr: hdwy over 1f out: r.o wl ins fnl f: nvr nrr* 14/1

5212 5 hd **Linda's Colin (IRE)**[31] [461] 5-8-2 66 oh1 .... PaulHanagan 9 70
(K R Burke) *hld up in midfield: rdn and hdwy over 2f out: edgd rt jst fnl f: r.o: nt rch ldrs* 12/1

4-01 6 hd **Million Percent**[38] [381] 8-8-4 71 .... LiamJones(3) 5 75
(C R Dore) *in tch: hdwy to chse ldrs over 2f out: kpt on same pce u.p ins fnl f* 14/1

000- 7 1½ **Shot To Fame (USA)**[175] [5529] 8-9-2 80 ....(t) PaulQuinn 2 80
(D Nicholls) *lw: led tl over 1f out: wknd ins fnl f* 50/1

3515 7 dht **Mandarin Spirit (IRE)**[7] [657] 7-9-2 80 ....(b) OscarUrbina 13 80
(G C H Chung) *stdd after s and dropped in bhd on inner: hdwy 2f out: swtchd rt jst over 1f out: styng on whn short of room ins last* 11/1

3312 9 nk **Councellor (FR)**[11] [629] 5-9-1 79 ....(t) MickyFenton 10 78
(Stef Liddiard) *t.k.h: hld up in midfield on outer: rdn and effrt over 2f out : no imp over 1f out* 13/2

6424 10 ¾ **Sun Catcher (IRE)**[18] [576] 4-8-13 77 .... RichardHughes 1 74
(R Hannon) *lw: trckd ldrs: rdn wl over 2f out: wknd ins fnl f: eased nr fin* 6/1[3]

10-0 11 2½ **Glencalvie (IRE)**[18] [576] 6-8-12 76 ....(p) DaneO'Neill 11 67
(J Akehurst) *a bhd: n.d* 14/1

/60- 12 nk **Cheap N Chic**[315] [1482] 4-9-0 78 ....(p) NCallan 12 68
(K A Ryan) *hld up bhd on outer: n.d* 33/1

-060 13 hd **Regal Royale**[18] [576] 4-8-12 76 .... TPQueally 6 65
(Peter Grayson) *a bhd: n.d* 25/1

1m 24.16s (-1.73) **Going Correction** -0.05s/f (Stan) 13 Ran SP% **120.2**

Speed ratings (Par 105):107,105,104,104,103 103,101,101,101,100 97,97,97

CSF £30.40 CT £154.97 TOTE £4.60: £2.00, £2.00, £1.80; EX 35.70 Trifecta £203.70 Pool: £318.57 - 1.11 winning units..

Owner The Moving Partnership **Bred** Yeomanstown Stud **Trained** Compton, Berks

FOCUS

A fair handicap run at an even gallop. The winning time was 2.85 seconds quicker than the 7f maiden. The form looks solid, with the winner back to his best.

698 TOTESCOOP6 H'CAP 1m 5f (P)

2:55 (2:55) (Class 2) (0-100,92) 4-Y-0+

£11,217 (£3,358; £1,679; £840; £419; £210) Stalls Low

Form RPR

00-2 1 **Kames Park (IRE)**[60] [153] 5-9-0 87 .... TomEaves 5 96+
(I Semple) *hld up in last: pushed along over 2f out: c wd 2f out:hdwy jst over 1f out: edgd lft fnl f: r.o to ld wl ins last* 12/1

-224 2 1¼ **Quince (IRE)**[15] [608] 4-8-11 87 ....(v) JimmyFortune 1 93
(J Pearce) *trckd ldr tl qcknd to ld 8f out: rdn and kicked on 2f out: hdd and bmpd wl ins fnl f: nt pce of wnr* 6/1

21 3 1½ **Paktolos (FR)**[16] [593] 4-9-0 90 .... JamieSpencer 4 94
(A King) *hld up in last pair: hdwy wl over 2f out: rdn 2f out: kpt on same pce fnl f* 2/1[1]

-122 4 ¾ **Eva Soneva So Fast (IRE)**[15] [608] 5-9-5 92 .... JimmyQuinn 2 95
(J L Dunlop) *lw: hld up in tch: rdn and hdwy over 2f out: chsd ldr wl over 1f out: no imp 1f out: lost 2 pls ins fnl f* 11/4[2]

432- 5 ½ **Alessano**[156] [5920] 5-9-5 92 .... GeorgeBaker 6 94
(G L Moore) *led at stdy pce: hdd 8f out: chsd ldr tl wl over 2f out: sn rdn: kpt on same pce* 4/1[3]

-321 6 nk **Polish Power (GER)**[16] [587] 7-8-13 86 .... LPKeniry 3 87
(J S Moore) *trckd ldrs: chsd ldr wl over 2f out tl wl over 1f out: kpt on onepced* 8/1

2m 53.13s (4.83) **Going Correction** -0.05s/f (Stan)

WFA 4 from 5yo+ 3lb 6 Ran SP% **113.1**

Speed ratings (Par 109):83,82,81,80,80 80

CSF £79.21 TOTE £12.60: £4.40, £2.90; EX 68.70.

Owner Mrs June Delaney **Bred** Pat Beirne **Trained** Carluke, S Lanarks

■ Stewards' Enquiry : Tom Eaves one-day ban: careless riding (Mar 28)

FOCUS

The six runners would have been trotting had they been going much slower until Quince injected some pace down the back straight, and this form cannot be trusted. That's unfortunate as this had the makings of a very interesting contest beforehand.

NOTEBOOK

Kames Park(IRE) is clearly a very useful horse, but the fact he managed to come from last to first in a slowly-run race should not be overplayed, as the sprint to the line basically suited him more than his five rivals. (op 11-1 tchd 10-1)

Quince(IRE) was given a good ride by Fortune, who used his initiative when injecting some pace down the back straight and deserved better than to be reeled in late on. The gelding has held his form well all winter. (op 8-1 tchd 17-2)

Paktolos(FR), 7lb higher than when winning over 1m4f round here on his previous start, was unsuited by the slowly-run race and could not show his best. (op 6-4 tchd 9-4)

Eva Soneva So Fast(IRE) has been in good form this winter, but he was another unsuited by the way the race was run. (op 7-2)

Alessano had the blinkers left off for his first start in 156 days and he probably just needed the outing. (op 9-2 tchd 7-2)

699 TOTESPORT 0800 221 221 CLAIMING STKS 1m (P)

3:25 (3:26) (Class 6) 4-6-Y-0 £2,184 (£644; £322) Stalls High

Form RPR

-310 1 **Writ (IRE)**[47] [300] 5-9-8 76 .... TomEaves 3 82
(I Semple) *chsd ldr: rdn to ld wl over 1f out:styd on wl fnl f* 4/1

-444 2 1 **Grey Boy (GER)**[35] [427] 6-9-2 72 .... PaulHanagan 1 73
(R A Fahey) *s.i.s: sn in tch: trckd ldrs 4f out: rdn wl over 1f out: chsd wnr 1f out: kpt on same pce* 10/3[2]

4003 3 2 **Nikki Bea (IRE)**[26] [497] 4-8-4 54 .... SimonWhitworth 4 57
(Jamie Poulton) *chsd ldrs: rdn wl over 2f out: kpt on same pce u.p wl over 1f out* 11/1

-033 4 ¾ **Buzzin'Boyzee (IRE)**[29] [479] 4-8-0 56 .... BernadetteQuinn(7) 6 58
(P D Evans) *t.k.h: hld up in rr: c wd and hdwy 3f out: rdn over 2f out: kpt on but nt pce to rch ldrs* 20/1

2026 5 nk **Gifted Gamble**[7] [657] 5-9-3 79 ....(b) NCallan 9 67
(K A Ryan) *racd in midfield: in tch: rdn and effrt over 2f out: kpt on but nevr threatened ldrs* 3/1[1]

1600 6 2½ **Grimes Faith**[7] [657] 4-9-6 81 ....(b) RichardHughes 5 64
(R Hannon) *hld up in rr: hdwy and brief effrt over 1f out: wknd ins fnl f* 7/2[3]

6-00 7 1½ **Dolly**[54] [210] 5-8-2 38 ....(p) RichardThomas 10 43
(Tom Dascombe) *led tl rdn and hdd wl over 1f out: sn wknd* 66/1

000- 8 5 **Raza Cab (IRE)**[262] [2983] 5-9-8 74 .... DarryllHolland 7 52
(Karen George) *racd in midfield: in tch tl rdn over 2f out: sn outpcd: eased whn btn ins fnl f* 9/1

00-0 9 1¼ **Homebred Star**[29] [349] 6-9-0 40 ....(b[1]) DaneO'Neill 2 41
(G P Enright) *s.i.s: hld up on inner: rdn over 2f out: wknd wl over 1f out* 50/1

000- 10 nk **Grandos (IRE)**[171] [5625] 5-8-7 40 ....(p) ChrisCatlin 8 33
(Karen George) *a bhd: rdn and lost tch over 2f out: sn no ch* 50/1

11 5 **Emma Gee**[78] 5-8-7 .... LPKeniry 11 21
(J Akehurst) *cl up on outer: pushed along and lost pl 5f out: rdn and wknd 3f out: eased fnl f* 28/1

1m 38.2s (-1.23) **Going Correction** -0.05s/f (Stan) 11 Ran SP% **122.3**

Speed ratings: 104,103,101,100,99 97,95,90,89,89 84

CSF £17.82 TOTE £6.10: £2.20, £1.40, £2.50; EX 20.70 Trifecta £226.90 Part won. Pool: £319.67 - 0.34 winning units..Gifted Gamble was claimed by Peter Grayson for £15,000.

Owner Clarke Boon **Bred** Sean Collins **Trained** Carluke, S Lanarks

FOCUS

A reasonable claimer, but most of these were not at their best and it is doubtful the winner had to improve.

Gifted Gamble Official explanation: vet said gelding was struck into

700 TOTEEXACTA MAIDEN STKS 7f (P)

3:55 (3:56) (Class 5) 3-Y-O £3,071 (£906; £453) Stalls Low

Form RPR

622- 1 **King's Apostle (IRE)**[178] [5481] 3-9-3 78 .... MichaelHills 2 71+
(W J Haggas) *mde all: pushed along and qcknd 3f out: hung rt bnd over 2f out: drew clr over 1f out: easily* 10/11[1]

06- 2 3½ **Emma Jean Lad (IRE)**[287] [2234] 3-9-3 .... LPKeniry 1 62
(J S Moore) *stdd s: t.k.h: hld up in tch: rdn and hdwy on inner over 2f out: chsd wnr wl over 1f out: no imp* 16/1

3 1 **Thunderbolt Jaxon** 3-9-3 .... JimmyFortune 6 59+
(P W Chapple-Hyam) *w'like: trckd ldrs: outpcd over 2f out: rdn 2f out: kpt on but no ch w wnr* 7/4[2]

00- 4 1¼ **Shaded Edge**[85] [6912] 3-9-3 .... JoeFanning 4 56+
(D W P Arbuthnot) *hld up in last pair: pushed along and hdwy over 2f out: kpt on but n.d* 20/1

0 5 1¾ **Faithful Ruler (USA)**[31] [456] 3-9-3 .... EddieAhern 3 51
(M A Magnusson) *lw: trckd ldr: outpcd wl over 2f out: rdn over 2f out: wknd wl over 1f out* 5/1[3]

0-0 6 2 **Doctor Ned**[10] [635] 3-9-3 .... ShaneKelly 9 46
(N A Callaghan) *hld up towards rr: outpcd wl over 2f out: no ch after* 25/1

0 7 5 **Ainama (IRE)**[19] [567] 3-9-3 .... JamieMackay 5 33
(M Wigham) *a last: lost tch 4f out: no ch after* 50/1

L **Rose Row** 3-8-5 .... JosephWalsh(7) 8 —
(Mrs Mary Hambro) *w'like: rrd as stalls opened: tk no part* **33/1**

1m 27.01s (1.12) **Going Correction** -0.05s/f (Stan) 8 Ran SP% **124.8**
Speed ratings (Par 98):91,87,85,84,82 80,74,—
CSF £19.26 TOTE £1.90: £1.02, £4.00, £1.20; EX 20.40 Trifecta £46.80 Pool: £404.17 - 6.12 winning units..
Owner Wentworth Racing (pty) Ltd **Bred** Wentworth Racing **Trained** Newmarket, Suffolk

FOCUS
A weak maiden run a time 2.85 seconds slower than the opening 7f handicap. The winner probably had little to beat with his market rivals not at their best, and it is hard to know what he really achieved.
Ainama(IRE) Official explanation: jockey said gelding hung left

701 TOTESPORT.COM H'CAP 1m 2f (P)
4:25 (4:26) (Class 2) (0-100,99) 4-Y-0+

£11,217 (£3,358; £1,679; £840; £419; £210) **Stalls** Low

Form RPR

2-25 **1** **Watamu (IRE)**[15] [608] 6-8-6 **87** ow2..............................(v) EddieAhern 7 103+
(P J Makin) *b: t.k.h: hld up in midfield: swtchd rt and hdwy 3f out: trckd ldr on bit over 2f out: led over 1f out: pushed clr: easily* **9/2**[2]

431P **2** *3* **Very Wise**[7] [658] 5-8-11 **92**.. JoeFanning 4 98
(W J Haggas) *lw: b: chsd ldr tl led over 3f out: rdn over 2f out: hdd over 1f out : no chanc ew wnr* **3/1**[1]

6012 **3** *1 1/4* **Impeller (IRE)**[22] [544] 8-9-4 **99**... LPKeniry 11 103
(J S Moore) *s.i.s: hld up in rr: hdwy on inner over 2f out: rdn over 1f out: wnt 3rd ins fnl f: nvr nrr* **11/1**

50-3 **4** *1* **Pagan Sword**[35] [420] 5-8-7 **88**.. JimCrowley 3 90
(Mrs A J Perrett) *t.k.h: hld up in midfield: hdwy 3f out: sn rdn: chsd ldng pair over 1f out: no imp* **8/1**

600- **5** *1* **Plum Pudding (IRE)**[140] [6219] 4-9-0 **95**........................ RichardHughes 9 95+
(R Hannon) *lw: hld up towards rr: pushed along and hdwy over 1f out: kpt on: nvr nr ldrs* **8/1**

000- **6** *1 1/2* **Tiger Tiger (FR)**[161] [5804] 6-8-9 **90**.. NCallan 1 87
(Jamie Poulton) *chsd ldrs: rdn 3f out: outpcd over 2f out no ch after* **16/1**

4105 **7** *3/4* **Fusili (IRE)**[21] [552] 4-8-8 **92**.. JamesDoyle(3) 5 88
(N P Littmoden) *chsd ldrs: rdn over 3f out: drvn and wknd over 2f out* **14/1**

1-50 **8** *2* **Happy As Larry (USA)**[56] [197] 5-8-5 **86** ow1........ RobbieFitzpatrick 10 78
(T J Pitt) *a bhd: n.d* **8/1**

-000 **9** *1/2* **Boo**[44] [328] 5-8-8 **92**.. AndrewElliott(3) 13 83
(K R Burke) *in tch: rdn and bmpd over 3f out: sn lost pl and bhd: no ch after* **16/1**

000- **10** *nk* **Counsel's Opinion (IRE)**[161] [5808] 10-9-0 **95**................ GeorgeBaker 8 86
(C F Wall) *lw: s.i.s: hld up bhd: hdwy on outer wl over 2f out: no imp last 2f* **11/2**[3]

130- **11** *1 1/2* **Rain Stops Play (IRE)**[127] [6424] 5-8-5 **86**.......................... ChrisCatlin 2 74
(M Quinn) *led tl over 3f out: sn rdn: wknd over 2f out* **33/1**

2463 **12** *3/4* **Tous Les Deux**[8] [652] 4-8-1 **85** oh10............................ LiamJones(3) 12 71
(Peter Grayson) *s.i.s: t.k.h: hld up bhd: hdwy on outer 7f out : rdn wl over 2f out: sn struggling* **22/1**

2m 3.68s (-4.11) **Going Correction** -0.05s/f (Stan) 12 Ran SP% **126.0**
Speed ratings (Par 109):114,111,110,109,109 107,107,105,105,104 103,103
CSF £19.64 CT £148.36 TOTE £8.10: £2.20, £1.70, £3.50; EX 31.10 Trifecta £343.70 Part won. Pool: £484.10 - 0.71 winning units..
Owner R A Henley **Bred** Crandon Park Stud **Trained** Ogbourne Maisey, Wilts

FOCUS
A good handicap run in a time 0.87 seconds quicker than the following fillies only contest won the 83-rated Lisathedaddy. Solid form, rated through the second and third, with the front pair progressive. The race should work out.

NOTEBOOK
Watamu(IRE) had shown he retained all of his ability since returning from an absence this winter with some solid pieces of form in defeat, but he had not totally convinced with his attitude under pressure. However, such was his dominance over his 11 rivals this time, he didn't have to come off the bridle until around a furlong out and, with the race in the bag at that point, Ahern, quite a considerate rider, by no means had to go for everything. This was a very useful effort – Very Wise is a good yardstick and he seemed to run his race - and the horse deserves plenty of credit, but it remains to be seen just how he will react when asked for maximum effort. (op 5-1 tchd 11-2)
Very Wise lost his race at the start when seriously gambled on in the Lincoln Trial at Wolverhampton the previous week and was bidding for quick compensation. He was produced with every chance by the impressive Joe Fanning, but was simply beaten by a better horse. (op 4-1)
Impeller(IRE), back in the UK following a successful stint at the Dubai Carnival, was short of room in the bend and might have been a little unlucky not to finish slightly closer. This was the highest mark he has raced off in a handicap since 2004. (op 9-1)
Pagan Sword was another who did not appear to get the best of runs on the turn into the straight, but he was not unlucky. He is holding his form well. (op 7-1 tchd 9-1)
Plum Pudding(IRE) ◆ is a little better than he was able to show as he was another short of room on the final bend and had plenty to do once the field straightened for home. Once in the clear, his run flattened out a touch close home, but that was to be expected considering this was his first run in 140 days, and he is open to plenty of improvement. A really likeable type, he should do better back on turf and appeals as a handicapper to follow this season. (op 10-1)
Counsel's Opinion(IRE) did not shape with much promise on his first run since October. Official explanation: jockey said gelding ran too free (op 13-2 tchd 5-1)

702 LISA WILSON SCHOLARSHIP FUND FILLIES' H'CAP 1m 2f (P)
4:55 (4:55) (Class 4) (0-85,83) 4-Y-0+ **£4,857** (£1,445; £722; £360) **Stalls** Low

Form RPR

24-1 **1** **Lisathedaddy**[26] [501] 5-9-1 **83**........................ RichardKingscote(3) 2 94+
(B G Powell) *lw: w.w in midfield: hdwy over 2f out: qiuckened to ld on inner over 1f out: r.o wl* **1/1**[1]

41 **2** *1* **Lemonette (USA)**[15] [603] 4-8-10 **75**................................. EddieAhern 8 83
(J W Hills) *hld up in midfield: hdwy to trck ldrs wl over 2f out: ev ch and rdn wl over 1f out: kpt on same pce ins last* **4/1**[2]

1-40 **3** *hd* **Magical Music**[26] [501] 4-9-4 **83**...................................... JimmyQuinn 4 90
(J Pearce) *hld up bhd: hdwy to chse ldrs over 2f out: rdn over 1f out: kpt on same pce ins fnl f* **11/2**[3]

140- **4** *shd* **Boot 'n Toot**[153] [5991] 6-8-9 **74**.................................. J-PGuillambert 1 81
(C A Cyzer) *lw: hld up in last: hdwy over 2f out: rdn over 1f out: kpt on u.p fnl f: nrst fin* **8/1**

0404 **5** *12* **Laugh 'n Cry**[8] [649] 6-7-13 **69** oh20..........................(b) WilliamBuick(5) 7 53
(C A Cyzer) *pressed ldr tl jst over 2f out: sn wknd* **25/1**

-666 **6** *3* **Waterline Twenty (IRE)**[33] [444] 4-8-11 **76**........................... NCallan 3 55
(P D Evans) *led tl wl over 1f out: sn btn: lost action and eased fnl f* **8/1**

7 *2 1/2* **Nans Lady (IRE)**[160] [5848] 4-8-4 **69**....................................... ChrisCatlin 5 43
(E J O'Neill) *t.k.h: chsd ldng pair: tl over 3f out: sn wknd: no ch last 2f* **16/1**

2m 4.55s (-3.24) **Going Correction** -0.05s/f (Stan) 7 Ran SP% **117.3**
Speed ratings (Par 102):110,109,109,108,99 96,94
CSF £5.56 CT £15.05 TOTE £1.80: £1.10, £2.60; EX 5.90 Trifecta £9.50 Pool: £404.06 - 30.12 winning units..
Owner Mrs Patricia Wilson **Bred** M Barrett **Trained** Lambourn, Berks

FOCUS
A fair fillies' handicap and surprisingly competitive. Although this only concerned four horses, they were separated by less than a length and a half at the line. Despite the small field, the form looks solid, with the winner value for a bit extra. The winning time was 0.87 seconds slower than the previous race won by the 87-rated Watamu.
Waterline Twenty(IRE) Official explanation: jockey said filly had moved badly and had a poor action

703 PONTIN'S FAMILY HOLIDAYS MAIDEN STKS 1m 4f (P)
5:25 (5:26) (Class 5) 3-Y-0 **£2,914** (£867; £433; £216) **Stalls** Low

Form RPR

26-0 **1** **Cry Presto (USA)**[7] [661] 3-9-3 **75**..........................(t) RichardHughes 9 66+
(R Hannon) *lw: stdd s: rn in snatches: rdn and hdwy over 3f out: swtchd rt over 1f out: str run u.p to ld nr fin* **9/1**[3]

332 **2** *hd* **Reciprocation (IRE)**[15] [603] 3-9-3 **79**................................. KDarley 3 66+
(M Johnston) *chsd ldr tl lft in ld after 2f: pushed clr wl over 1f out: 3 l clr 1f out: hung rt ins last: hdd nr fin* **4/11**[1]

00- **3** *3* **Dana Music (USA)**[158] [5893] 3-9-3 .... EdwardCreighton 5 61
(M R Channon) *in tch: hdwy to trck ldrs 5f out: rdn wl over 2f out: outpcd by ldr over 1f out: kpt on same pce ins fnl f* **4/1**[2]

06 **4** *3* **President Dan**[21] [553] 3-9-3 .... IanMongan 6 56
(M R Channon) *lw: chsd ldrs tl lft 2nd after 2f: rdn wl over 2f out: outpcd over 1f out: wknd fnl f* **20/1**

5 *1 3/4* **Master Jobs** 3-9-3 .... J-PGuillambert 1 53
(S C Williams) *unf: s.i.s: sn in tch: rdn 3f out: wknd wl over 1f out* **14/1**

60 **6** *7* **Bluecrop Boy**[38] [386] 3-9-3 .... AntonyProcter 4 42
(D J S Ffrench Davis) *led tl hung bdly rt bnd and hdd after 2f: bhd after: rdn over 3f out: sn lost tch* **50/1**

0 **7** *5* **Tory Brae (IRE)**[26] [499] 3-9-3 ....(b[1]) SebSanders 7 34
(R M Beckett) *lw: chsd ldrs on outer: rdn and lost pl over 5f out: no ch last 3f* **25/1**

2m 36.21s (1.82) **Going Correction** -0.05s/f (Stan) 7 Ran SP% **120.5**
Speed ratings (Par 98):91,90,88,86,85 81,77
CSF £13.63 TOTE £10.30: £2.20, £1.10; EX 13.80 Trifecta £57.00 Pool: £599.62 - 7.46 winning units. Place 6 £99.74, Place 5 £55.40.
Owner Major A M Everett **Bred** Bricklow Ltd And Hyperion Stud Ltd **Trained** East Everleigh, Wilts

FOCUS
A weak maiden. The first pair are fair performers but with doubts about the modest time and the proximity of the sixth the form has been rated negatively.
T/Plt: £112.90 to a £1 stake. Pool: £72,717.80. 469.80 winning tickets. T/Qpdt: £4.00 to a £1 stake. Pool: £3,654.00. 671.00 winning tickets. SP

680 SOUTHWELL (L-H)
Monday, March 19

OFFICIAL GOING: Standard
The inside part of the track appeared to ride much faster than elsewhere and this should be taken into account when assessing performances at this meeting.
Wind: strong, behind Weather: snow showers

707 GO PONTIN'S H'CAP 5f (F)
2:20 (2:20) (Class 5) (0-75,74) 3-Y-0 **£3,071** (£906; £453) **Stalls** High

Form RPR

4334 **1** **Pirner's Brig**[9] [659] 3-8-6 **62**...................................(b[1]) PaulMulrennan 1 68
(M W Easterby) *wnt lft s: prom tl led after 2f: drifted lft to far rail and rdn 2f out: styde on strly fnl f* **4/1**[2]

2204 **2** *1 1/2* **Diminuto**[6] [671] 3-8-1 **64**.. FrankiePickard(7) 3 65
(M D I Usher) *prom: rdn along 2f out: kpt on u.p fnl f* **10/1**

12-6 **3** *2 1/2* **Zadalla**[62] [147] 3-8-10 **66**.. JoeFanning 5 58
(Andrew Oliver, Ire) *dwlt: sn chsng ldrs: swtchd rt and rdn 2f out: ev ch over 1f out: drvn and one pce ent last* **7/1**

3-21 **4** *1 3/4* **Ronnie Howe**[36] [429] 3-9-3 **73**.. PhillipMakin 6 59
(M Dods) *led 2f: cl up and ev chyance tl rdn and wknd over 1f out* **11/4**[1]

21-1 **5** *2 1/2* **Sister Etienne (IRE)**[27] [506] 3-8-10 **66**................................. NCallan 4 44
(J T Stimpson) *cl up: effrt and ev ch 2f out: sn rdn and wknd appr last* **11/2**[3]

5-52 **6** *1 1/2* **Stoneacre Gareth (IRE)**[12] [639] 3-9-4 **74**..................... GeorgeBaker 2 46
(Peter Grayson) *sn rdn along in rr: drvn and outpcd 1/2-way: sn bhd* **11/4**[1]

59.26 secs (-1.04) **Going Correction** -0.25s/f (Stan) 6 Ran SP% **110.3**
Speed ratings (Par 98):98,95,91,88,84 82
CSF £38.70 TOTE £4.30: £2.10, £4.90; EX 31.00.
Owner Mrs E Rhind **Bred** C F Spence & Mrs E Rhind **Trained** Sheriff Hutton, N Yorks

FOCUS
A moderate sprint in which the result was decided by a track bias to a certain extent, with the inside part of the track looking much quicker than stands' side. A strong wind behind the runners resulted in a good time. Pirner's Brig improved a length or so for the blinkers.
Stoneacre Gareth(IRE) Official explanation: jockey said gelding would not face the kickback

708 PONTINS.COM (S) H'CAP 1m (F)
2:50 (2:50) (Class 6) (0-60,58) 3-Y-0 **£2,184** (£644; £322) **Stalls** Low

Form RPR

00-0 **1** **Raven Rascal**[6] [667] 3-8-2 **45**.................................. PatrickMathers(3) 7 45
(J F Coupland) *squeezed out and rr after 1f: swtchd ins 1/2-way: hdwy on inner over 2f out: rdn wl over 1f out: styd on to ld jst ins last* **66/1**

6-00 **2** *3/4* **Jousting**[63] [141] 3-8-9 **49**..(v[1]) NCallan 10 48
(V Smith) *trckd ldrs: hdwy 3f out: led 2f out and sn rdn: drvn and hdd jst ins last: kpt on wl u.p* **15/2**[3]

0051 **3** *3/4* **Muree Queen**[5] [676] 3-8-6 **51** 6ex.................... RussellKennemore(5) 8 48
(R Hollinshead) *in tch: outpcd and lost pl on outer 1/2-way: hdwy 2f out: rdn to chse ldng pair and hung lft ent last: styd on: nrest finih* **9/2**[2]

-556 **4** *1/2* **Irish Relative (IRE)**[32] [469] 3-8-5 **45**................................ PaulFessey 9 41
(T D Barron) *chsd ldrs: rdn along and lost pl 3f out: swtchd outside wl over 1f out: styd on u.p ins last* **9/2**[2]

4-03 **5** *1 3/4* **Peppin's Gold (IRE)**[39] [390] 3-8-10 **50**.................(t) AdrianMcCarthy 4 42
(B R Millman) *chsd ldrs: rdn along 3f out: kpt on same pce fnl 2f* **12/1**

3000 **6** *1 ½* **The Light Fandango**[5] 676 3-8-2 **45** LiamJones(3) 6 34
(R A Harris) *cl up: rdn along 3f out: grad wknd* **15/2**[3]
4220 **7** *1 ¾* **Bertrada (IRE)**[14] 624 3-8-13 **53** SteveDrowne 5 39
(H Morrison) *hld up: hdwy on outer to chse ldrs over 2f out: sn rdn and btn* **85/40**[1]
0-60 **8** *8* **Tizzydore (IRE)**[44] 342 3-8-12 **52** LPKeniry 2 21
(A G Newcombe) *chsd ldrs: rdn along 3f out: sn wknd* **14/1**
00-0 **9** *nk* **Spanish Affair**[21] 565 3-8-5 **45** PaulHanagan 3 13
(Jedd O'Keeffe) *led: rdn along and hdd over 4f out: wknd 3f out* **33/1**
0-06 **10** *4* **Bear Essential**[12] 635 3-9-4 **58** RobertHavlin 1 18
(Mrs P N Dutfield) *trckd ldrs: smooth hdwy to ld over 4f out: rdn and hdd 2f out: sn wknd* **16/1**

1m 47.79s (3.19) **Going Correction** +0.225s/f (Slow) **10** Ran SP% **116.6**
Speed ratings (Par 96):93,92,91,91,89 87,86,78,77,73
CSF £506.23 CT £2012.56 TOTE £85.20: £12.60, £3.40, £1.70; EX 596.50 TRIFECTA Not won..The winner was bought in for 4,200gns. Jousting was subject to a friendly claim.
Owner J F Coupland **Bred** J F Coupland **Trained** Grimsby, Lincs
■ Stewards' Enquiry : Patrick Mathers three-day ban: used whip with excessive frequency and down the shoulder in forehand position (Mar 30-31, Apr 1)

FOCUS
A weak seller producing a shock result and the feeling is that the track bias was again in operation, as the first two home raced closest to the inside rail down the home straight. This form looks extremely dodgy as a result. The first two posted improved efforts.

709 PHOTO ALBUMS FROM BONUSPRINT.COM H'CAP 2m (F)
3:20 (3:20) (Class 5) (0-75,73) 4-Y-0+ **£3,071** (£906; £453) **Stalls** Low

Form RPR
-014 **1** **Rule For Ever**[12] 640 5-8-13 **60** JoeFanning 1 78
(M Johnston) *in tch: hdwy to chse clr ldr over 6f out: cl up 4f out: led 3f out and sn rdn clr: styd on* **11/4**[2]
061 **2** *13* **Al Moulatham**[13] 628 8-9-1 **62** (bt) SamHitchcott 5 64+
(R Ford) *led and sn clr: stdd pce 1/2-way: rdn and qcknd 4f out: hdd 3f out and kpt on same pce u.p* **5/1**
2-11 **3** *4* **Victory Quest (IRE)**[39] 389 7-9-5 **66** (v) PaulFessey 2 64
(Mrs S Lamyman) *hld up: hdwy to chse ldrs 5f out: rdn along wl over 3f out: drvn and no imp fr over 2f out* **9/4**[1]
2-05 **4** *35* **Jeepstar**[9] 662 7-9-12 **73** JamieSpencer 3 29
(S C Williams) *chsd clr ldr: rdn along over 6f out: sn wknd* **7/2**[3]
40-6 **5** *27* **Greyside (USA)**[26] 515 4-9-1 **67** PaulMulrennan 4 —
(C A Mulhall) *a rr: outpcd and bhd fnl 6f* **22/1**
530- **6** *5* **Halland**[154] 6011 9-8-11 **58** (e) MickyFenton 7 —
(T J Fitzgerald) *a rr: outpcd and wl bhd fnl 6f* **12/1**
0 **P** **Mountain Fairy**[17] 602 4-8-13 **68** (v[1]) JerryO'Dwyer(3) 6 —
(B S Rothwell) *sn wl bhd: t.o whn p.u over 7f out* **50/1**

3m 46.26s (1.72) **Going Correction** +0.225s/f (Slow)
WFA 4 from 5yo+ 5lb **7** Ran SP% **110.3**
Speed ratings (Par 103):104,97,95,78,64 62,—
CSF £15.58 TOTE £4.80: £1.90, £2.30; EX 16.70.
Owner J S Morrison **Bred** Baldernock Bloodstock Limited **Trained** Middleham Moor, N Yorks
■ Stewards' Enquiry : Jamie Spencer two-day ban: used whip with excessive force (Mar 30-31)

FOCUS
A modest staying handicap, but with a couple of confirmed front-runners in opposition they went a really decent pace and it developed into a true test of stamina. The three outsiders had been well and truly seen off even before halfway. Rule For Ever was back to his best, with the runner-up 4lb off.
Greyside(USA) Official explanation: jockey said gelding hung left throughout
Mountain Fairy Official explanation: jockey said filly hung violently left-handed and was pulled up

710 PONTIN'S FAMILY HOLIDAYS CLAIMING STKS 6f (F)
3:50 (3:52) (Class 6) 4-Y-0+ **£2,184** (£644; £322) **Stalls** Low

Form RPR
4241 **1** **Soba Jones**[19] 580 10-8-6 57 JasonEdmunds(3) 1 61
(J Balding) *trckd ldrs: hdwy 2f out: rdn to ld ent last: kpt on wl* **6/1**[3]
0645 **2** *1 ¼* **Prettilini**[13] 625 4-8-8 49 J-PGuillambert 9 56
(R Brotherton) *led 2f: cl up tl rdn to ld again wl over 1f out: drvn and hdd ent last: kpt on u.p* **25/1**
0551 **3** *½* **Quiet Times (IRE)**[24] 536 8-9-7 82 (b) NCallan 11 68
(K A Ryan) *dwlt and towards rr: rdn along and wd st: hdwy 2f out: drvn over 1f out: styd on ins last: nrst fin* **7/4**[1]
0635 **4** *¾* **Apex**[25] 524 6-8-9 47 JamieSpencer 10 54
(N Tinkler) *chsd ldrs: pushed along and sltly outpcd 1/2-way: rdn and hdwy on outer 2f out: drvn and ev ch tl no ex ins last* **12/1**
3110 **5** *½* **Mister Incredible**[14] 622 4-8-10 52 (v) SaleemGolam(3) 7 56
(J M Bradley) *trckd ldrs: smooth hdwy over 2f out: rdn over 1f out and kpt on same pce* **11/1**
1050 **6** *2* **Mill By The Stream**[24] 536 5-8-7 58 PaulHanagan 2 44
(Tom Dascombe) *cl up on inner: led after 2f: rdn along and hdd wl over 1f out: grad wknd* **8/1**
2045 **7** *1 ½* **Mulberry Lad (IRE)**[23] 548 5-8-13 53 (p) ChrisCatlin 12 46
(P W Hiatt) *chsd ldrs: effrt and ev ch 2f out: sn rdn and wkng whn n.m.r ent last* **14/1**
0-35 **8** *6* **Le Chiffre (IRE)**[26] 513 5-8-11 62 (p) MichaelJStainton(5) 5 31
(K R Burke) *a rr* **3/1**[2]
000- **9** *¾* **Tapsalteerie**[124] 6490 4-8-2 30 DaleGibson 6 14
(M W Easterby) *a rr* **150/1**
400- **10** *5* **Sabo Prince**[341] 982 5-8-2 42 (p) PietroRomeo(7) 8 6
(J M Bradley) *a rr* **66/1**

1m 17.68s (0.78) **Going Correction** +0.225s/f (Slow) **10** Ran SP% **115.5**
Speed ratings (Par 101):103,101,100,99,99 96,94,86,85,78
CSF £136.86 TOTE £6.00: £1.70, £5.80, £1.10; EX 68.50 TRIFECTA Not won..Prettilini was subject to a friendly claim.
Owner R L Crowe **Bred** Mrs M J Hills **Trained** Scrooby, Notts

FOCUS
A modest claimer which revolved around the performance of Quiet Times who was best in at the weights by a mile, but with him running below form the form is probably only ordinary. Soba Jones did not need to improve on his latest handicap win to score. Given what had happened in the earlier races, it was a surprise that the whole field decided to race centre to stands' side in the home straight and give the inside a wide berth.

711 BONUSPRINT.COM MEDIAN AUCTION MAIDEN STKS 7f (F)
4:20 (4:21) (Class 6) 3-5-Y-0 **£2,184** (£644; £322) **Stalls** Low

Form RPR
-233 **1** **Arch Of Titus (IRE)**[25] 522 3-8-12 74 (t) JamieSpencer 3 72
(M L W Bell) *cl up: led 3f out and sn rdn clr: kpt on u.p fnl f* **8/13**[1]
0 **2** *1 ¼* **Ammeyrr**[24] 537 3-8-12 JoeFanning 1 69
(M Johnston) *chsd ldrs: n.m.r and swtchd rt 3f out: hdwy to chse wnr 2f out: sn rdn and styd on wl fnl f* **7/2**[2]
3 *7* **Singleb (IRE)** 3-8-12 PhillipMakin 6 51+
(T D Barron) *hld up towards rr: stdy hdwy 3f out: styd on fnl 2f: nrst fin* **9/1**[3]
2022 **4** *3* **Ranavalona**[12] 636 3-8-7 54 (v) ChrisCatlin 9 38
(A M Balding) *led: rdn along and hdd over 3f out: sn wknd* **9/1**[3]
04 **5** *3 ½* **Zil Up**[14] 619 3-8-12 (bt) PaulEddery 2 34
(S R Bowring) *prom: rdn and edgd lft 3f out: sn drvn and wknd* **40/1**
6 *1 ¾* **Feels Like Heaven** 3-8-7 DavidAllan 8 24
(T D Easterby) *chsd ldrs: rdn aloong 3f out: snw eakened* **20/1**
7 *1* **Nikinoo** 4-9-8 DaleGibson 5 22
(B Palling) *a rr* **66/1**
50- **8** *4* **Esteemed Prince**[304] 1824 3-8-12 (e[1]) DeanMcKeown 7 16
(D Shaw) *chsd ldrs: rdn along 3f out: sn wknd* **40/1**
005- **9** *9* **Umpa Loompa (IRE)**[173] 5615 3-8-12 56 AdrianTNicholls 10 —
(D Nicholls) *bhd fr 1/2-way* **16/1**

1m 33.28s (2.48) **Going Correction** +0.225s/f (Slow)
WFA 3 from 4yo 15lb **9** Ran SP% **121.2**
Speed ratings (Par 101):94,92,84,81,77 75,74,69,59
CSF £3.10 TOTE £1.50: £1.02, £1.60, £2.70; EX 4.40 Trifecta £16.60 Pool £847.18 - 36.17 winning units..
Owner Mrs Maureen Buckley **Bred** J Connolly **Trained** Newmarket, Suffolk

FOCUS
This race was run in a blizzard which cannot have been pleasant for horse or rider, but even allowing for that this was a weak maiden totally dominated by the market principals and it is hard to believe it will produce too many winners. Arch Of Titus is rated to his latest run over course and distance.

712 PONTIN'S BOOK EARLY FILLIES' H'CAP 1m (F)
4:50 (4:50) (Class 5) (0-70,67) 4-Y-0+ **£3,071** (£906; £453) **Stalls** Low

Form RPR
0252 **1** **Mademoiselle**[6] 664 5-8-1 **55** TolleyDean(5) 5 62
(R A Harris) *cl up: rdn to ld 2f out: drvn and edgd lft 1f out: styd on* **3/1**[2]
06-2 **2** *2* **Don't Mind Me**[22] 559 4-8-4 **53** EdwardCreighton 3 56
(T Keddy) *in tch: pushed along halwfay: wd st: rdn and hdwy 2f out: drvn and edgd lft ent: styd on to take 2nd nr fin* **7/1**[3]
0165 **3** *shd* **Granakey (IRE)**[4] 686 4-8-10 **59** TPQueally 1 62
(M G Quinlan) *trckd ldrs: hdwy over 2f out: rdn to chse wnr wl over 1f out: drvn and one pce ins last* **3/1**[2]
114 **4** *1 ¾* **Our Kes (IRE)**[4] 685 5-9-3 **66** TonyCulhane 7 65
(P Howling) *sn led: rdn along and hdd 2f out: sn drvn and grad wknd* **13/8**[1]
1-06 **5** *7* **Odessa Star (USA)**[42] 358 4-9-4 **67** NCallan 6 52
(J G Portman) *in tch: hdwy to chse ldrs 3f out: sn rdn and weakend fnl 2f* **12/1**
0-00 **6** *5* **Lady Edge (IRE)**[42] 358 5-8-6 **55** FergusSweeney 4 29
(A W Carroll) *keen: prom tlk rdn along 3f out and sn wknd* **25/1**

1m 45.65s (1.05) **Going Correction** +0.225s/f (Slow) **6** Ran SP% **112.1**
Speed ratings (Par 100):103,101,100,99,92 87
CSF £23.26 TOTE £4.20: £1.80, £2.10; EX 24.90 Place 6 £204.70, Place 5 £45.18.
Owner S & A Mares **Bred** G Reed **Trained** Earlswood, Monmouths

FOCUS
An ordinary fillies' handicap and once again those that stayed closest to the inside rail looked to hold an advantage. Weakish form, but sound enough.
T/Plt: £207.90 to a £1 stake. Pool: £55,503.65. 194.85 winning tickets. T/Qpdt: £7.40 to a £1 stake. Pool: £5,242.30. 520.90 winning tickets. JR

707 SOUTHWELL (L-H)
Tuesday, March 20

OFFICIAL GOING: Standard
Wind: Strong, behind

713 PONTINSBINGO.COM H'CAP 5f (F)
2:30 (2:30) (Class 6) (0-60,60) 3-Y-0 **£2,388** (£705; £352) **Stalls** High

Form RPR
4326 **1** **Pretty Selma**[10] 659 3-8-4 **46** oh1 (b) HayleyTurner 6 48
(R M H Cowell) *mde most: rdn wl over 1f out: drvn and edgd lft ins last: kpt on* **14/1**
055 **2** *nk* **The Tinker Man**[28] 505 3-8-1 **50** FrankiePickard(7) 11 51+
(M D I Usher) *sn outpcd and rdn along in rr: hdwy over 1f out: fin strly* **16/1**
40-6 **3** *½* **Moonlight Applause**[20] 583 3-8-10 **52** DavidAllan 12 51
(T D Easterby) *chsd ldrs: rdn along 2f out: drvn over 1f out: kpt on ins last* **16/1**
0063 **4** *nk* **Head To Head (IRE)**[10] 659 3-9-2 **58** AdamKirby 9 56
(Peter Grayson) *cl up: rdn along 2f out: drvn and ev ch over 1f out: no ex ins last* **8/1**
3054 **5** *hd* **Perlachy**[40] 387 3-8-11 **58** (v) DuranFentiman(5) 13 55
(Mrs N Macauley) *chsd ldrs: rdn along 2f out: drvn and one pce ent last* **14/1**
43-0 **6** *hd* **Kilvickeon (IRE)**[43] 360 3-8-1 **46** oh1 LiamJones(3) 4 43+
(Peter Grayson) *s.i.s and bhd tl styd on fnl 2f: nrst fin* **6/1**[2]
502- **7** *1 ¼* **The Geester**[87] 6925 3-9-3 **59** (bt) PhillipMakin 1 51
(S R Bowring) *chsd ldrs: hdwy over 2f out: sn rdn and ev ch tl drvn and wknd ent last* **7/1**
030- **8** *3* **The Bronx**[94] 6838 3-9-1 **57** ChrisCatlin 2 39
(M J Wallace) *rr: rdn along 1/2-way: styd on appr last: nrst fin* **7/2**[1]
03-5 **9** *nk* **Minimum Fuss (IRE)**[63] 147 3-8-9 **58** SCreighton(7) 7 39
(M C Chapman) *s.i.s: a rr* **13/2**[3]
500- **10** *¾* **Yearning (IRE)**[158] 5948 3-8-4 **49** NeilChalmers(3) 3 28
(J G Portman) *bhd fr 1/2-way* **20/1**
54-0 **11** *1 ½* **Inverted**[56] 222 3-8-5 **47** (p) JoeFanning 10 21
(Mrs A Duffield) *prom: rdn along over 2f out: sn drvn and wknd* **14/1**
520- **12** *½* **Merlins Quest**[139] 6296 3-9-4 **60** SteveDrowne 8 32
(J M Bradley) *chsd ldrs: sn rdn along: outpcd and bhd fr 1/2-way* **10/1**
00-0 **13** *12* **Purple Sands (IRE)**[25] 535 3-8-9 **51** ow1 TomEaves 5 —
(J Hetherton) *a rr* **28/1**

61.09 secs (0.79) **Going Correction** +0.075s/f (Slow) **13** Ran SP% **122.5**
Speed ratings (Par 96):96,95,94,94,93 93,91,86,86,85 82,81,62
CSF £225.79 CT £3723.20 TOTE £14.30: £2.70, £7.90, £6.60; EX 373.60 TRIFECTA Not won..
Owner Khalifa Dasmal **Bred** Khalifa Abdulla Dasmal **Trained** Six Mile Bottom, Cambs
■ Stewards' Enquiry : Phillip Makin caution: used whip down shoulder in back-hand position without giving gelding time to respond

FOCUS
A close finish but moderate sprint handicap form rated around the fourth and fifth.
Pretty Selma Official explanation: trainer said, regarding apparent improvement in form, that the filly was better suited to the surface
The Geester Official explanation: jockey said gelding hung right-handed throughout

714 GO PONTIN'S MEDIAN AUCTION MAIDEN STKS 6f (F)
3:00 (3:00) (Class 5) 4-6-Y-O **£2,968** (£876; £438) **Stalls** Low

Form RPR
-050 **1** **Left Nostril (IRE)**[51] 282 4-8-12 43 ....(be) HayleyTurner 6 46
(P S McEntee) *mde all: rdn wl over 1f out: styd on wl u.p ins last* **15/2**
-005 **2** *1 1/4* **Jember Red**[7] 670 4-8-10 34 ow1 ....(v) MarkLawson(3) 4 43
(B Smart) *prom: hdwy to chse wnr over 2f out: sn rdn and kpt on same pce fnl f* **6/1**[3]
220- **3** *1 1/2* **The Grey One (IRE)**[139] 6300 4-9-3 54 ....(p) SteveDrowne 2 42
(J M Bradley) *in tch and pushed along 1/2-way: hdwy 2f out: sn rdn and kpt on fnl f: nrst fin* **1/1**[1]
0-30 **4** *5* **Boppys Dream**[26] 524 5-8-12 40 .... MickyFenton 1 21
(P T Midgley) *midfield: rdn along 1/2-way: drvn and no imp fnl 2f* **9/1**
0-0 **5** *hd* **Village Storm (IRE)**[47] 321 4-9-3 30 .... AlanDaly 8 25
(C J Teague) *prom: rdn along 3f out: sn wknd* **50/1**
-300 **6** *9* **Dancing Beauty (IRE)**[14] 632 5-8-12 43 .... ChrisCatlin 5 —
(T T Clement) *chsd ldrs: rdn along 3f out: wknd over 2f out* **16/1**
0-0 **7** *13* **Demi Sec**[23] 559 4-8-12 .... JoeFanning 3 —
(Dr J D Scargill) *a rr* **9/2**[2]
0- **8** *22* **Tyrone Lady (IRE)**[213] 4613 4-8-5 .... ChrisHough(7) 7 —
(M C Chapman) *dwlt: a bhd* **33/1**

1m 18.0s (1.10) **Going Correction** +0.10s/f (Slow) **8** Ran SP% **115.0**
Speed ratings: 96,94,92,85,85 73,56,26
CSF £51.89 TOTE £9.80: £4.10, £2.50, £1.02; EX 37.20 Trifecta £139.10 Pool: £519.41 - 2.65 winning tickets..
Owner Mrs M D Mallett **Bred** Joseph G Reid **Trained** Newmarket, Suffolk

FOCUS
A very poor maiden indeed but the form makes sense rated around the first two and the fifth.
Dancing Beauty(IRE) Official explanation: jockey said mare hung right-handed in straight
Tyrone Lady(IRE) Official explanation: trainer said filly had bled from the nose

715 PONTINS.COM CLASSIFIED STKS 7f (F)
3:30 (3:30) (Class 7) 4-Y-0+ **£1,706** (£503; £252) **Stalls** Low

Form RPR
0-30 **1** **Steel Grey**[54] 238 6-9-0 45 .... DeanMernagh 6 55
(M Brittain) *rr: pushed along 1/2-way: rdn and hdwy wl over 1f out: str run to ld ent last: styd on* **8/1**
545- **2** *1 3/4* **Gifted Glori**[46] 4695 4-9-0 42 .... PhillipMakin 5 50
(T D Barron) *in tch: hdwy 2f out: rdn to chse ldrs over 1f out: sn drvn and kpt on fnl f* **3/1**[1]
1300 **3** *1/2* **Pawn In Life (IRE)**[20] 579 9-9-0 44 ....(v) PaulEddery 1 49
(S Parr) *dwlt: sn in tch: hdwy on inner over 2f out: rdn to chal and ev ch over 1f out: drvn and one pce ins last* **9/1**
0000 **4** *1 1/2* **Savile's Delight (IRE)**[26] 519 8-9-0 45 ....(t) J-PGuillambert 3 45
(Miss Joanne Priest) *trckd ldrs: hdwy over 2f out: sn rdn and ch over 1f out: drvn and one pce ins last* **16/1**
0405 **5** *1/2* **Hometomammy**[7] 664 5-9-0 43 ....(b[1]) ChrisCatlin 7 44
(P W Hiatt) *cl up: rdn 2f out and ev ch tld drvn and wknd appr last* **7/1**[3]
/0-0 **6** *nk* **Sowerby**[14] 625 5-8-9 45 ....(b) DuranFentiman(5) 9 43
(M Brittain) *chsd ldrs: rdn along over 2f out: sn drvn and grad wknd* **33/1**
0050 **7** *1 1/4* **Merdiff**[14] 627 8-8-11 42 .... LiamJones(3) 4 39
(W M Brisbourne) *cl up: led 3f out: rdn 2f out: drvn and hdd ent last: wknd* **11/2**[2]
00-0 **8** *6* **Master Ben (IRE)**[7] 666 4-9-0 41 ....(b) JoeFanning 13 24
(S R Bowring) *chsd ldrs: rdn along over 2f out: sn wknd* **33/1**
3600 **9** *4* **Mr Bountiful (IRE)**[5] 682 9-9-0 45 ....(bt) AlanDaly 14 13
(C J Teague) *dwlt: keen and sn chsng ldrs on outer: rdn along over 2f out: sn wknd* **14/1**
400- **10** *3/4* **Baby Barry**[159] 5924 10-9-0 45 ....(p) SteveDrowne 2 12
(K J Burke) *led: pushed along and hdd 3f out: sn rdn and wknd* **11/2**[2]
-005 **11** *1 1/4* **Axis Shield (IRE)**[26] 523 4-9-0 42 .... TPQueally 11 8
(M C Chapman) *a towards rr* **14/1**
5/0- **12** *2* **Crux**[421] 173 5-9-0 40 .... TomEaves 10 —
(R E Barr) *a rr* **25/1**

1m 31.94s (1.14) **Going Correction** +0.10s/f (Slow) **12** Ran SP% **118.3**
Speed ratings (Par 97):97,95,94,92,92 91,90,83,78,78 76,74
CSF £31.50 TOTE £9.70: £2.60, £1.50, £2.10; EX 48.10 Trifecta £238.80 Part won. Pool: £336.37 - 0.20 winning tickets..
Owner Mel Brittain **Bred** Northgate Lodge Stud Ltd **Trained** Warthill, N Yorks

FOCUS
A moderate race run at a good gallop, and the principals came from off the pace. The form appears sound enough rated around the placed horses.
Sowerby Official explanation: trainer said gelding had run too free
Baby Barry Official explanation: trainer said gelding had a breathing problem

716 DIGITAL PRINTS FROM BONUSPRINT.COM H'CAP 1m 3f (F)
4:00 (4:00) (Class 6) (0-50,50) 4-Y-0+ **£2,388** (£705; £352) **Stalls** Low

Form RPR
2-66 **1** **Boppys Dancer**[28] 508 4-8-7 46 oh1 ....(p) MickyFenton 9 55
(P T Midgley) *midfield: hdwy 4f out: ev ch on outer whn bmpd 2f out: rdn to ld over 1f out: edgd lft and kpt on fnl f* **9/1**
0103 **2** *1 1/4* **Danelor (IRE)**[15] 616 9-8-10 48 ....(p) DaneO'Neill 12 55
(D Shaw) *dwlt and bhd: hdwy 5f out: trckd ldrs on bit 3f out: swtchd rt and effrt 2f out: ev ch tl drvn and one pce ins last* **13/2**[3]
-240 **3** *nk* **Kumakawa**[14] 627 9-8-7 48 .... JamesDoyle(3) 1 54
(N P Littmoden) *trckd ldrs: hdwy to ld 2f out: sn rdn and hdd over 1f out: kpt on* **14/1**
1-54 **4** *4* **Padre Nostro (IRE)**[7] 665 8-8-1 46 oh1 .... ChrisGlenister(7) 3 45
(J R Holt) *midfield: gd hdwy on inner over 3f out: rdn and ev ch wl over 1f out: wknd ent last* **9/2**[1]
0000 **5** *1* **Layed Back Rocky**[15] 617 5-8-8 46 oh1 .... ChrisCatlin 5 44
(M Mullineaux) *led: rdn along 3f out: hdd 2f out: drvn and wknd ent last* **33/1**
506- **6** *1 1/4* **Siegfrieds Night (IRE)**[206] 2196 6-8-4 49 .... ChrisHough(7) 14 44
(M C Chapman) *bhd tl styd on wl fnl 2f: nrst fin* **28/1**
2600 **7** *nk* **Bournonville**[7] 665 4-8-0 46 oh1 .... KirstyMilczarek(7) 4 41
(M Wigham) *hld up: hmpd bnd after 2f: bhd tl sme late hdwy* **14/1**
0-00 **8** *2* **Monmouthshire**[14] 631 4-8-4 48 .... WilliamBuick(5) 7 39
(R J Price) *a towards rr* **9/1**
000/ **9** *1/2* **Kyber**[34] 6218 6-8-3 46 .... DuranFentiman(5) 13 37
(J S Goldie) *chsd ldrs on outer: rdn along over 4f out: sn wknd* **9/1**
206- **10** *nk* **Komreyev Star**[98] 6799 5-8-8 46 oh1 .... JimmyQuinn 11 36
(R E Peacock) *chsd ldr tl rdn along over 3f out and sn wknd* **20/1**
6333 **11** *1 3/4* **Twilight Avenger (IRE)**[7] 665 4-8-4 46 oh1 ....(t) LiamJones(3) 10 33
(W M Brisbourne) *hld up in rr: hdwy 5f out: rdn along 3f out: sn btn* **5/1**[2]
5420 **12** *9* **Iceni Warrior**[15] 615 5-8-9 47 .... JoeFanning 8 19
(P Howling) *chsd ldrs: rdn along over 4f out: drvn 3f out and wknd qckly* **9/1**
0-01 **13** *32* **Smoothie (IRE)**[23] 558 9-8-11 49 .... TPQueally 2 —
(E G Bevan) *midfield: rdn along 5f out: sn wknd* **9/1**

2m 30.52s (1.62) **Going Correction** +0.10s/f (Slow)
WFA 4 from 5yo+ 1lb **13** Ran SP% **122.7**
Speed ratings (Par 101):98,97,96,93,93 92,92,90,90,90 88,82,58
CSF £66.85 CT £833.51 TOTE £10.00: £4.00, £2.00, £5.70; EX 60.10 TRIFECTA Not won..
Owner Mrs S Bond **Bred** Mrs Sylvia Bond **Trained** Westow, N Yorks

FOCUS
A modest handicap, but competitive enough given the size of the field and the third is the best guide to the form. The early pace was ordinary and several still had a chance passing the two-furlong pole.

717 CANVAS PRINTS FROM BONUSPRINT.COM H'CAP 6f (F)
4:30 (4:31) (Class 5) (0-75,71) 4-Y-0+ **£3,071** (£906; £453) **Stalls** Low

Form RPR
-112 **1** **Count Cougar (USA)**[47] 317 7-8-8 63 .... ChrisCatlin 8 79
(S P Griffiths) *mde all: rdn wl over 1f out: drvn ins last and hld on gamely* **5/1**[2]
4100 **2** *3/4* **Came Back (IRE)**[15] 621 4-8-4 64 .... MichaelJStainton(5) 6 78
(J Mackie) *trckd ldrs: hdwy over 2f out: rdn to chse wnr wl over 1f out: drvn ins last: kpt on* **13/2**
5154 **3** *2* **Hamaasy**[20] 581 6-8-10 65 .... AdrianTNicholls 4 73
(D Nicholls) *midfield: hdwy over 2f out: sn rdn and kpt on ins last: nrst fin* **4/1**[1]
606 **4** *3/4* **Winthorpe (IRE)**[15] 621 7-8-6 61 ow1 ....(p) GrahamGibbons 9 67
(J J Quinn) *cl up: rdn along 2f out: drvn and one pce appr last* **8/1**
3315 **5** *nk* **Cool Sands (IRE)**[6] 672 5-8-12 67 ....(v) DaneO'Neill 3 72
(D Shaw) *dwlt and bhd tl styd on wl fnl 2f: nrst fin* **6/1**[3]
20-1 **6** *1 3/4* **Macademy Royal (USA)**[19] 588 4-9-1 70 ....(t) SteveDrowne 7 69
(H Morrison) *in tch: rdn along 1/2-way: sn drvn and no imp* **7/1**
0134 **7** *3* **Going Skint**[33] 468 4-8-9 64 ow1 .... AdamKirby 2 54
(M Wellings) *chsd ldrs: rdn along over 2f out: drvn and wknd over 1f out: eased* **8/1**
0-02 **8** *12* **Effective**[47] 323 7-9-2 71 .... SebSanders 5 25
(A P Jarvis) *a towards rr* **6/1**[3]
046- **9** *6* **Falmassim**[211] 4666 4-8-13 68 .... TomEaves 1 —
(Miss J A Camacho) *s.i.s: a bhd* **28/1**

1m 16.38s (-0.52) **Going Correction** +0.10s/f (Slow) **9** Ran SP% **116.7**
Speed ratings (Par 103):107,106,103,102,101 99,95,79,71
CSF £37.86 CT £144.23 TOTE £6.30: £2.10, £2.50, £1.80; EX 58.30 Trifecta £123.80 Pool: £263.43 - 1.51 winning tickets..
Owner M Grant **Bred** Angus Glen Farm (1996) Ltd **Trained** Easingwold, N Yorks

FOCUS
An ordinary handicap, but a very strong pace and it paid to be handy. The winning time was a very respectable one for the grade and the form looks sound.
Macademy Royal(USA) Official explanation: jockey said gelding never travelled
Going Skint Official explanation: vet said gelding finished slightly lame left-fore
Effective Official explanation: jockey said gelding never travelled

718 PONTIN'S FAMILY HOLIDAYS H'CAP 7f (F)
5:00 (5:00) (Class 5) (0-70,69) 4-Y-0+ **£3,071** (£906; £453) **Stalls** Low

Form RPR
2115 **1** **Louisiade (IRE)**[29] 497 6-8-5 58 ....(p) JoeFanning 1 66
(K A Ryan) *trckd ldrs on inner: hdwy over 2f out: rdn to ld wl over 1f out: drvn out* **10/1**
0000 **2** *1 1/2* **Aperitif**[5] 681 6-8-6 59 ow1 .... AdrianTNicholls 2 63
(D Nicholls) *hld up in rr: hdwy over 2f out: sn rdn: styd on ins last* **18/1**
0-12 **3** *nk* **Owed**[33] 468 5-9-2 69 ....(t) SebSanders 3 72
(R Bastiman) *cl up: led over 4f out: rdn over 2f out: hdd wl over 1f out: sn drvn and wknd ins last* **2/1**[1]
0041 **4** *3/4* **Kew The Music**[5] 686 7-8-6 59 6ex .... ChrisCatlin 4 60
(M R Channon) *sn outpcd and rdn along in rr: hdwy 2f out: styd on u.p fnl f: nrst fin* **7/2**[2]
3321 **5** *shd* **Parkview Love (USA)**[11] 650 6-8-13 66 ....(v) DaneO'Neill 6 67
(D Shaw) *trckd ldrs: effrt over 2f out: sn rdn and one pce appr last* **7/2**[2]
5-00 **6** *1/2* **Shifty**[5] 681 8-8-12 65 .... DanielTudhope 5 65
(D Carroll) *trckd ldrs: rdn along 3f out: drvn on outer wl over 1f out and sn one pce* **8/1**
-462 **7** *7* **Violent Velocity (IRE)**[6] 672 4-8-10 63 ....(v) GrahamGibbons 7 45
(J J Quinn) *led over 2f: cl up tl rdn along over 2f out and sn wknd* **15/2**[3]

1m 30.29s (-0.51) **Going Correction** +0.10s/f (Slow) **7** Ran SP% **115.0**
Speed ratings (Par 103):106,104,103,103,102 102,94
CSF £158.47 TOTE £9.70: £5.40, £5.70; EX 65.80 Place 6 £6,185.91, Place 5 £475.77.
Owner Whitestonecliffe Racing Partnership **Bred** Mrs Noelle Walsh **Trained** Hambleton, N Yorks

FOCUS
Another race run at a strong pace but the form is not entirely straightforward and the close-up fifth looks the best guide.
T/Plt: £1,555.30 to a £1 stake. Pool: £62,960.40. 29.55 winning tickets. T/Qpdt: £140.10 to a £1 stake. Pool: £4,867.50. 25.70 winning tickets. JR

556 KEMPTON (A.W) (R-H)
Wednesday, March 21

OFFICIAL GOING: Standard
Wind: slight, across

719 INTERCASINO.CO.UK H'CAP 1m 2f (P)
2:00 (2:00) (Class 4) (0-80,80) 3-Y-O **£4,728** (£1,406; £702; £351) **Stalls** High

Form RPR
4-21 **1** **Zar Solitario**[32] 492 3-9-1 77 .... JoeFanning 7 93+
(M Johnston) *mde virtually all: shkn up and c clr fnl f: easily* **5/2**[2]
1 **2** *1 1/2* **Silkwood**[33] 484 3-9-1 77 .... NCallan 3 88+
(M A Jarvis) *chsd ldrs: wnt 2nd 2f out: drvn to press wnr wl over 1f out: sn outpaced but kpt on wl for clr 2nd* **10/11**[1]

The Form Book, Raceform Ltd, Compton, RG20 6NL

335- **3** *4* **Fever**[201] 4992 3-8-13 **75**.. RichardHughes 9 79
(R Hannon) *hld up in rr: hdwy over 1f out: styd on to take 3rd fnl f but nvr in contention* **20/1**

02-1 **4** *1 1/2* **Nassmaan (IRE)**[42] 382 3-9-2 **78**.............................. AdrianMcCarthy 2 79
(P W Chapple-Hyam) *chsd ldrs: rdn over 2f out: wknd appr fnl f* **16/1**

012- **5** *1* **Troialini**[97] 6824 3-9-1 **80**.. JerryO'Dwyer(3) 1 79
(S W Hall) *s.i.s: sn in tch on outside: rdn fr 3f out: wknd appr fnl f* **15/2**[3]

305- **6** *1* **Dansimar**[182] 5475 3-8-6 **68**... JohnEgan 6 65+
(M R Channon) *hld up in rr: shkn up and rn v wd bnd 2f out: kpt on fnl f: gng on cl home* **50/1**

010- **7** *shd* **Love Brothers**[163] 5866 3-8-6 **75**.......................... ThomasO'Brien(7) 11 72
(M R Channon) *rr: rdn over 3f out: nvr bttr than mid-div* **50/1**

642 **8** *1/2* **Title Deed (USA)**[27] 522 3-8-12 **74**................................ TPQueally 10 70
(A P Jarvis) *chsd ldrs: rdn over 3f out: wknd ins fnl 2f* **25/1**

500- **9** *1/2* **Down The Brick (IRE)**[163] 5866 3-8-4 **66**...................... HayleyTurner 5 61
(B R Millman) *in tch: rdn 3f out: sn btn* **66/1**

31-4 **10** *shd* **Personal Column**[21] 582 3-8-10 **72**................................. DaneO'Neill 8 67
(T G Mills) *in tch whn hmpd and lost pl 4f out: rdn and sme hdwy sn after: wknd 2f out* **20/1**

52-5 **11** *nk* **Callisto Moon**[23] 565 3-8-5 **67**... ChrisCatlin 4 61
(Ian Williams) *w wnr 6f: sn drvn: wknd fr 2f out* **33/1**

2m 8.42s (-0.58) **Going Correction** -0.05s/f (Stan) **11** Ran SP% **120.3**
Speed ratings (Par 100):100,98,95,94,93 92,92,92,91,91 91
CSF £4.83 CT £35.01 TOTE £3.50: £1.10, £1.10, £4.60; EX 6.30.
Owner Sheikh Mohammed **Bred** Azienda Agricola Razza Del Sole Srl **Trained** Middleham Moor, N Yorks

FOCUS
A good three-year-old handicap, run at an uneven pace. The form has been rated positively with the first six all unexposed, progressive types. The winner was value for a length extra, with the fourth perhaps the best guide to the form.
Dansimar Official explanation: jockey said filly hung badly left-handed round final bend

720 INTERCASINO.CO.UK MEDIAN AUCTION MAIDEN STKS 1m (P)
2:30 (2:33) (Class 6) 3-Y-O **£2,047** (£604; £302) **Stalls High**

Form RPR

2-52 **1** **Resplendent Ace (IRE)**[23] 565 3-9-3 77........................ JimmyQuinn 8 79
(P Howling) *mde all: pushed along over 2f out: styd on strly fnl f* **7/4**[1]

00- **2** *2 1/2* **Norman The Great**[133] 6393 3-9-3 .... MichaelHills 9 74
(Jane Chapple-Hyam) *rr: pushed along over 3f out: hdwy 2f out: styd on to chse wnr ins last but no imp* **16/1**

5 **3** *3/4* **Ochre (IRE)**[39] 418 3-8-12 ....(t) NCallan 5 67
(M A Jarvis) *in tch: hdwy over 3f out: styd on fr over 1f out to go 3rd ins fnl f but nvr gng pce to be competitive* **10/3**[3]

4 *1* **Crown Office (USA)** 3-8-12 .... SteveDrowne 4 65
(H Morrison) *chsd ldrs: rdn to go 2nd 2f out but nvr gng pce to be competetive: wknd ins fnl f* **11/2**

532- **5** *2 1/2* **Baltic Belle (IRE)**[116] 6591 3-8-12 72.......................... RichardHughes 1 59
(R Hannon) *hld up in rrr: pushed along over 2f out: mod prog fnl f: nver in contention* **3/1**[2]

6 **6** *2* **County Kerry (UAE)**[67] 114 3-8-12 .... DaneO'Neill 3 54
(Jean-Rene Auvray) *chsd wnr tl wknd fr 2f out* **16/1**

7 *7* **Dark Druid (IRE)** 3-9-3 .... JoeFanning 2 43
(I A Wood) *chsd ldrs: rdn 3f out: wknd 2f out* **33/1**

000- **8** *nk* **Miss Silver Spurs**[184] 5423 3-8-5 40........................ LauraReynolds(7) 6 38
(M D I Usher) *s.i.s: keen hold early: a towards rr: wd bnd 3f out* **66/1**

00 **9** *9* **Ridgeway Star**[23] 569 3-9-3 .... RobertHavlin 7 22
(R Ingram) *sn bhd: lost tch fr 1/2-way* **50/1**

1m 40.91s (0.11) **Going Correction** -0.05s/f (Stan) **9** Ran SP% **118.0**
Speed ratings (Par 96):97,94,93,92,90 88,81,80,71
CSF £33.93 TOTE £2.70: £1.10, £3.80, £1.60; EX 52.80.
Owner Resplendent Racing Limited **Bred** Newlands House Stud **Trained** Newmarket, Suffolk
■ Stewards' Enquiry : Steve Drowne two-day ban: careless riding (Apr 1-2)

FOCUS
A modest maiden which was run at a sound pace. The form has been rated through the winner and third.

721 INTERCASINO.CO.UK CLASSIFIED STKS 1m (P)
3:05 (3:06) (Class 7) 4-Y-0+ **£1,365** (£403; £201) **Stalls High**

Form RPR

0-00 **1** **War Of The Roses (IRE)**[23] 567 4-9-0 45.................. JosedeSouza 7 55+
(R Brotherton) *sn chsng ldrs: rdn to ld over 1f out: hld on wl cl home* **11/1**

-000 **2** *1/2* **Dexileos (IRE)**[46] 341 8-8-11 43............................(t) NeilChalmers(3) 10 52
(David Pinder) *chsd ldrs: rdn and swtchd lft appr fnl f: styd on to go 2nd wl ins last but nt quite get up* **33/1**

5636 **3** *hd* **Kinsman (IRE)**[45] 350 10-8-11 42..............................(p) AmirQuinn(3) 14 52
(T D McCarthy) *hld up in rr: hday on rails over 2f out: styd on wl to press for 2nd wl ins last but a jst hld* **7/1**[3]

0043 **4** *1 3/4* **Savoy Chapel**[24] 557 5-9-0 45..............................(v) RichardThomas 12 48
(A W Carroll) *in tch: hdwy to chse wnr over 1f out and sn ev ch: no ex and wknd nr fin* **4/1**[1]

5 *hd* **Mountain Climb (IRE)**[155] 6038 5-9-0 42.................... PaulFitzsimons 5 48
(J D Frost) *t.k.h: led: rdn over 2f out: edge lft and hdd ovcer 1f out: wknd ins last* **10/1**

3000 **6** *1* **Pharaoh Prince**[24] 558 6-9-0 42.................................(v) SamHitchcott 4 47+
(G Prodromou) *in tch: hdwy 3f out: styng on to chse ldrs and hmpd over 1f out: sn one pce* **8/1**

0060 **7** *shd* **Drink To Me Only**[27] 524 4-9-0 45............................ TonyHamilton 11 45
(J R Weymes) *rr: rdn and sme hdwy over 2f out: one pce fnl f* **12/1**

000- **8** *3* **Liskaveen Beauty**[82] 6970 4-9-0 41.......................(be[1]) JamieMackay 13 38
(T J Fitzgerald) *rr tl pushed along and mod hdwy fr over 1f out: nvr in contention* **16/1**

0460 **9** *hd* **Blue Knight (IRE)**[27] 519 8-9-0 45....................................... AlanDaly 3 38
(P Howling) *rr tl mod prog fnl f* **12/1**

5-00 **10** *1 3/4* **Galley Law**[20] 372 7-9-0 41... DavidKinsella 6 34
(W M Brisbourne) *in tch: rdn to chse ldrs 3f out: wknd 2f out* **12/1**

4003 **11** *1/2* **Captain Bolsh**[8] 666 4-9-0 41.. StephenCarson 2 32
(J Pearce) *sn chsng ldr: rdn 2f out: wknd wl over 1f out* **6/1**[2]

0000 **12** *1/2* **Lord Chamberlain**[37] 447 14-9-0 45...............................(b) LPKeniry 1 31
(J M Bradley) *s.i.s: a bhd* **12/1**

0-65 **13** *6* **Always A Story**[24] 559 5-9-0 45.. PaulEddery 8 18
(Miss D Mountain) *chsd ldrs over 5f* **8/1**

0/0- **14** *1 1/2* **Sharp Tune (USA)**[96] 6829 5-9-0 44...................... SimonWhitworth 9 14
(J D Frost) *a in rr* **50/1**

1m 41.03s (0.23) **Going Correction** -0.05s/f (Stan) **14** Ran SP% **128.0**
Speed ratings (Par 97):96,95,95,93,93 92,92,89,89,87 86,86,80,78
CSF £346.89 TOTE £14.40: £4.70, £10.60, £2.90; EX 561.10.
Owner P S J Croft **Bred** Mrs J Bailey **Trained** Elmley Castle, Worcs

FOCUS
A weak event which was run at an average pace. The form is sound for the grade, rated through the third and fifth.
Always A Story Official explanation: trainer said gelding was found to be coughing on returning to the yard

722 PLAY BLACKJACK AT INTERCASINO.CO.UK H'CAP (DIV I) 6f (P)
3:35 (3:36) (Class 6) (0-50,50) 4-Y-0+ **£1,365** (£403; £201) **Stalls High**

Form RPR

0654 **1** **King Of Charm (IRE)**[5] 690 4-8-11 **47**.................(b) FergusSweeney 11 53
(G L Moore) *trckd ldrs: chal over 1f out tl slt ld jst ins last: hld on all out* **4/1**[1]

-342 **2** *nk* **Black Oval**[24] 562 6-8-13 **49**... PaulEddery 1 54
(S Parr) *stdd s:hld up in rr:stl plenty to do whn hdwy over 1f out: sn swtchd lft:str run ins last: fin wl: nt quite get up* **11/2**[3]

0-00 **3** *hd* **Laith (IRE)**[73] 63 4-9-0 **50**.. MickyFenton 9 55
(Miss V Haigh) *rr: hdwy on ins over 2f out: str chal fr over 1f out tl no ex nr fin* **25/1**

0020 **4** *1 1/4* **Alucica**[5] 690 4-8-10 **46** oh1...(v) DaneO'Neill 3 47
(D Shaw) *rr: rdn 2f out: hdwy fnl f: kpt on cl home but nt pce to rch ldrs* **12/1**

0603 **5** *shd* **Tuscan Flyer**[12] 653 9-8-11 **46** oh1 ow1.......................(b) SebSanders 4 48
(R Bastiman) *chsd ldrs: slt ld 2f out: sn narrowly hdd u.p: wknd wl ins last* **12/1**

5254 **6** *shd* **Double M**[5] 687 10-8-10 **46** oh1...(v) NCallan 12 46
(Mrs L Richards) *sn chsng ldrs: rdn and slt advantage ins fnl 2f: hdd ins last: wknd fnl 50yds* **5/1**[2]

5606 **7** *nk* **Cool Tiger**[15] 627 4-8-12 **48**... AlanDaly 2 48
(P Howling) *sn in tch: rdn and styd on fnl 2f: nvr quite gng pce to trble ldrs* **9/1**

-000 **8** *shd* **Edin Burgher (FR)**[24] 562 6-8-12 **48**............................ SamHitchcott 6 47
(T T Clement) *rr: pushed along over 2f out: styd on fnl f but nvr gng pce to be competitive* **8/1**

0-60 **9** *hd* **Hillbilly Cat (USA)**[5] 687 4-9-0 **50**.............................. RobertHavlin 8 49
(R Ingram) *rr: headway 2f out: nvr quite gng pce to press ldrs: one pce fnl f* **20/1**

6400 **10** *1* **Teyaar**[16] 622 11-8-11 **47**... AdamKirby 10 43
(M Wellings) *chsd ldrs: rdn and effrt 2f out: wknd fnl f* **14/1**

5400 **11** *nk* **Majestical (IRE)**[5] 688 5-8-13 **49**..............................(p) DarryllHolland 7 44
(J M Bradley) *led tl narrowly hdd appr fnl 2f: wkng whn hmpd fnl f* **13/2**

-000 **12** *2* **Auentraum (GER)**[5] 687 7-8-10 **49**........................(v[1]) JamesDoyle(3) 5 38
(Ms J S Doyle) *rr: sme haedway 3f out: nvr gng pce to trble ldrs and sn outpcd* **10/1**

1m 14.1s (0.40) **Going Correction** -0.05s/f (Stan) **12** Ran SP% **126.2**
Speed ratings (Par 101):95,94,94,92,92 92,92,91,91,90 89,87
CSF £27.32 CT £516.85 TOTE £4.30: £1.40, £2.00, £9.30; EX 29.50.
Owner Greystar Partnership **Bred** David Commins **Trained** Woodingdean, E Sussex
■ Stewards' Enquiry : Paul Eddery one-day ban: careless riding (Apr 1)

FOCUS
The winning time was 0.70 seconds slower than the second division and the first three came clear in a driving finish. The form is not strong, with the winner rated to his recent level.

723 PLAY BLACKJACK AT INTERCASINO.CO.UK H'CAP (DIV II) 6f (P)
4:10 (4:11) (Class 6) (0-50,50) 4-Y-0+ **£1,365** (£403; £201) **Stalls High**

Form RPR

450- **1** **Piddies Pride (IRE)**[160] 5928 5-8-10 **46**.............................(v) JohnEgan 4 57
(Miss Gay Kelleway) *in tch: rdn and hdwy over 1f out: led wl ins last: hdd cl home: led again last stride* **8/1**

3400 **2** *shd* **Mind Alert**[5] 687 6-8-12 **48**...(v) DaneO'Neill 5 59
(D Shaw) *hld up in rr: str run fr over 1f out:chal ins last: led cl home: ct last stride* **11/2**[2]

30-0 **3** *1 1/4* **Balian**[21] 581 4-8-11 **47**...(b) MickyFenton 6 54
(Mrs P Sly) *chsd ldrs: rdn to chal ins last: wknd nr fin* **11/1**

5414 **4** *3/4* **Christian Bendix**[15] 632 5-9-0 **50**..............................(p) JimmyQuinn 12 55
(P Howling) *led: rdn 2f out: hdd & wknd wl ins last* **5/1**[1]

5320 **5** *nk* **Seldemosa**[15] 627 6-8-12 **48**..(v) NCallan 11 52
(M S Saunders) *chsd ldrs: rdn and effrt fr 2f out: nvr gng pce to chal: btn whn eased cl home* **5/1**[1]

0-01 **6** *1 3/4* **Firework**[24] 557 9-8-13 **49**.. StephenCarson 10 48
(E A Wheeler) *mid-div: pushed along 2f out: r.o fnl f but nvr in contention* **15/2**[3]

-666 **7** *3/4* **Feelin Irie (IRE)**[15] 625 4-8-13 **49**................................ JamieSpencer 2 46
(J R Boyle) *chsd ldr: rdn over 2f out: wknd appr fnl f* **5/1**[1]

000- **8** *1* **Diamond World**[198] 5055 4-8-13 **49**............................... SteveDrowne 3 43
(C A Horgan) *rr: pushed along fr 2f out: nvr in contention* **16/1**

46-0 **9** *2* **Zantero**[24] 557 5-8-10 **46** oh1... JimCrowley 8 34
(W M Brisbourne) *nvr gng pce to be competitive* **20/1**

0-00 **10** *1 1/4* **Atticus Trophies (IRE)**[12] 649 4-8-11 **50**...............(v) JamesDoyle(3) 7 34
(Ms J S Doyle) *rr: rdn 1/2-way and nvr competitive* **8/1**

600 **11** *6* **Mustard Benn**[24] 559 4-8-7 **46** oh1.......................... NeilChalmers(3) 9 12
(Mouse Hamilton-Fairley) *outpcd most of way* **16/1**

1m 13.4s (-0.30) **Going Correction** -0.05s/f (Stan) **11** Ran SP% **124.2**
Speed ratings (Par 101):100,99,98,97,96 94,93,92,89,87 79
CSF £54.69 CT £501.76 TOTE £12.00: £3.90, £2.20, £3.30; EX 82.20.
Owner Countrywide Classics Limited **Bred** B Kennedy **Trained** Exning, Suffolk

FOCUS
A moderate handicap but the time was 0.70 seconds faster than the first division, and only 0.03 seconds off the time recorded by the 64-rated Methaaly in the following 51-65. A stronger race than the first division, and solid form for the grade.

724 £600 FREE AT INTERCASINO.CO.UK H'CAP 6f (P)
4:40 (4:40) (Class 6) (0-65,69) 4-Y-0+ **£2,590** (£770; £385; £192) **Stalls High**

Form RPR

-053 **1** **Methaaly (IRE)**[24] 560 4-9-2 **65**.. JohnEgan 1 74+
(Jane Chapple-Hyam) *t.k.h: led after 2f: rdn fr over 1f out: jst hld on* **8/1**

2256 **2** *shd* **Imperium**[12] 650 6-9-1 **64**.. DaneO'Neill 12 73
(Jean-Rene Auvray) *in tch: rdn and hdwy fr 2 out: str ins fnl f: jst failed* **10/1**

-623 **3** *hd* **What Do You Know**[12] 654 4-8-13 **62**........................... JimmyQuinn 9 71
(A M Hales) *bmpd s: sn chsng ldrs: rdn and str chal wl ins last: no ex last strides* **6/1**[2]

6040 **4** *1/2* **Zazous**[12] 654 6-8-6 **58**... MarcHalford(3) 4 65
(J J Bridger) *rr: hdwy on outside over 1f out: str run ins last: gng on cl home* **25/1**

060- **5** *hd* **Duke Of Milan (IRE)**[110] 6656 4-9-2 **65**............................ MichaelHills 6 71
(G C Bravery) *hld up in rr: hdwy on ins over 1f out: styd on wl to chse ldrs ins last: no ex cl home* **16/1**

0025 **6** *1/2* **Supercast (IRE)**[16] 621 4-9-2 **65**..................................(t) DarryllHolland 8 70
(W M Brisbourne) *bhd: hdwy over 1f out: styd on wl fnl f but nvr gng pce to rch ldrs* **7/1**[3]

6031 **7** *nk* **Cerebus**[6] 681 5-9-1 **69** 6ex......................................(bt) WilliamBuick(5) 3 73
(A J McCabe) *in tchm: rdn to chse ldrs on outside fr 2f out: one pce ins last* **10/1**

-004 **8** *shd* **Another Genepi (USA)**[44] 359 4-8-9 **58**..........................(b1) NCallan 10 62
(K A Ryan) *bmpd s: chsd ldrs: rdn over 2f out: wknd last half f* **5/2**[1]

1230 **9** *1 1/2* **Lucius Verrus (USA)**[16] 621 7-8-13 **62**..........................(v) TPQueally 7 61
(D Shaw) *towards rr: drvn along over 2f out: mod prog ins last* **16/1**

1500 **10** *1/2* **Charlie Delta**[21] 581 4-9-2 **65**....................................(p) JamieSpencer 2 67+
(J R Boyle) *rr: hung bdly lft:hd high and hrd rdn fr ins fnl 2f: nt rcvr and eased whn continued to hang ins last* **16/1**

66-4 **11** *1* **Scuba (IRE)**[72] 70 5-8-8 **62**.....................................(b) TravisBlock(5) 11 57
(H Morrison) *wnt lft s: chsd ldrs: rdn over 2f out: wknd fnl f* **7/1**[3]

2646 **12** *1 1/2* **Caustic Wit (IRE)**[12] 654 9-8-3 **57**.............................(p) TolleyDean(5) 5 47
(M S Saunders) *led 2f: styd chsng ldrs: rdn over 2f out: sn btn* **14/1**

1m 13.37s (-0.33) **Going Correction** -0.05s/f (Stan) 12 Ran SP% **125.3**
Speed ratings (Par 101):100,99,99,98,98 98,97,97,95,94 93,91
CSF £90.66 CT £534.29 TOTE £9.00: £2.90, £2.60, £2.10; EX 83.30.
Owner Franconson Partners And Vanessa Church **Bred** Scuderia Golden Horse S R L **Trained** Newmarket, Suffolk

FOCUS
Just a modest sprint handicap. The winning time was only 0.03 seconds faster than the second division of the 46-50 handicap, but 0.73 seconds quicker than the first division of that race. Solid, with the principals close to their recent form.
Charlie Delta Official explanation: jockey said gelding hung badly right-handed
Caustic Wit(IRE) Official explanation: jockey said gelding ran flat

725 PLAY ROULETTE AT INTERCASINO.CO.UK H'CAP 7f (P)
5:10 (5:11) (Class 4) (0-80,80) 3-Y-O **£4,728** (£1,406; £702; £351) **Stalls** High

Form RPR

1 **1** **Annemasse**[21] 583 3-9-3 **79**.. JoeFanning 8 93+
(M Johnston) *mde all: drvn and kpt on ell fr over 1f out: in command whn edgd lft cl home* **2/1**[1]

641- **2** *nk* **Vitznau (IRE)**[156] 6015 3-8-9 **71**.................................. RichardHughes 11 84+
(R Hannon) *hld up in rr: rapid hdwy over 1f out to chse wnr jst ins last: styng on but hld whn carried lft cl home* **4/1**[2]

2-05 **3** *4* **Jord (IRE)**[29] 510 3-8-5 **72**.. WilliamBuick(5) 10 75
(A J McCabe) *chsd ldrs: rdn over 2f out: styd on same pce fnl f* **14/1**

0-13 **4** *1/2* **Go On Green (IRE)**[21] 584 3-9-4 **80**..........................(t) JamieSpencer 7 82
(E A L Dunlop) *prom: chsd wnr and rdn 2f out: no imp: wknd fnl f* **9/2**[3]

6-64 **5** *1 1/4* **Proper (IRE)**[49] 312 3-8-5 **67**... ChrisCatlin 13 65+
(M R Channon) *in tch whn hmpd after 1f: effrt on ins whn n.m.r 2f out: nvr in contention after* **10/1**

322- **6** *2* **Social Rhythm**[81] 6991 3-8-10 **72**.................................... JimmyQuinn 9 65
(H J Collingridge) *in tch whn n.m.r after 1f: sn chsng ldrs: rdn over 2f out and n.d* **12/1**

406- **7** *hd* **Beckenham's Secret**[183] 5447 3-8-7 **69**.......................... JimCrowley 1 62
(B R Millman) *rr tl mod prog fr over 1f out* **50/1**

123- **8** *1/2* **Jack Oliver**[175] 5606 3-8-4 **73**.. KMay(7) 2 64
(B J Meehan) *chsd ldrs: wnt 2nd over 2f out and sn u.p: no imp on wnr and wknd over 1f out* **12/1**

0-10 **9** *shd* **Tasweet (IRE)**[60] 196 3-8-13 **75**..............................(p) DaneO'Neill 4 66
(T G Mills) *chsd wnr tl rdn over 2f out: wknd wl over 1f out* **10/1**

0-62 **10** *nk* **Straight Face (IRE)**[58] 209 3-8-8 **70**............................ JamieMackay 6 60+
(M Wigham) *wnt lft s:a in rr* **33/1**

600- **11** *nk* **Cavort (IRE)**[176] 5585 3-9-0 **76**....................................... DarryllHolland 5 66
(Pat Eddery) *bmpd s: a in rr* **20/1**

0422 **12** *1 1/4* **Cherri Fosfate**[20] 589 3-8-10 **72** ow1.......................(b) DanielTudhope 3 58
(D Carroll) *mid-div: rdn and effrt 3f out: sn wknd* **14/1**

1m 25.68s (-1.12) **Going Correction** -0.05s/f (Stan) 12 Ran SP% **128.1**
Speed ratings (Par 100):104,103,99,98,97 94,94,94,93,93 93,91
CSF £10.30 CT £97.10 TOTE £3.30: £1.30, £3.00, £3.70; EX 17.70.
Owner Brian Yeardley Continental Ltd **Bred** Newsells Park Stud Limited **Trained** Middleham Moor, N Yorks

■ Stewards' Enquiry : Joe Fanning caution: careless riding. Obj. to Annemasse by Hughes overruled.

FOCUS
This was run at a fair pace. A good handicap for the grade, with the first two progressive and clear of the third and fourth who ran solid races. Annemasse improved by 7lb on his Southwell win.
Proper(IRE) Official explanation: jockey said gelding suffered interference

726 BIG JACKPOTS AT INTERCASINO.CO.UK H'CAP 1m 3f (P)
5:40 (5:40) (Class 4) (0-85,83) 4-Y-O+ **£4,728** (£1,406; £702; £351) **Stalls** High

Form RPR

000- **1** **I Have Dreamed (IRE)**[184] 5430 5-9-1 **81**.............................. KDarley 8 90+
(T G Mills) *in tch: rdn and plenty to do ins fnl 2f: str run u.p to chse ldr ins last: led last strides* **6/1**

5-10 **2** *hd* **Awatuki (IRE)**[32] 488 4-8-13 **80**... TPQueally 7 89
(A P Jarvis) *trckd ldr tl led gng smoothly over 2f out: stl travelling ok whn shkn up fnl f: ct last strides* **7/2**[1]

020- **3** *1 3/4* **Active Asset (IRE)**[166] 5787 5-9-3 **83**............................ DarryllHolland 10 89
(M Quinn) *chsd ldrs: rdn over 2f out: one pce fnl f* **14/1**

40/0 **4** *1* **Prince Nureyev (IRE)**[30] 501 7-9-1 **81**.......................... SteveDrowne 9 85
(B R Millman) *rr: hdwy on rails fr 3f out: no imp on ldrs over 1f out and one pce* **33/1**

5446 **5** *1/2* **Prince Charlemagne (IRE)**[12] 652 4-8-9 **79**............. JamesDoyle(3) 3 82
(N P Littmoden) *rr: pushed along over 3f out: styd on fr over 1f out: nt rch ldrs* **7/1**

150- **6** *hd* **Capistrano**[76] 5889 4-7-10 **70**....................................... JosephWalsh(7) 2 73?
(Mrs P Sly) *rr: rdn over 3f out: kpt on fnl f but nvr in contention* **50/1**

0-50 **7** *3/4* **Fantasy Ride**[45] 353 5-8-7 **73**... JimmyQuinn 13 75
(J Pearce) *chsd ldrs: rdn 3f out: wknd over 1f out* **11/1**

111- **8** *4* **Speagle (IRE)**[90] 6893 5-9-0 **80**.................................... DanielTudhope 4 75
(D Carroll) *led tl hdd over 2f out: wknd wl over 1f out* **5/1**[2]

41/0 **9** *4* **Economic (IRE)**[32] 488 4-8-10 **77**.................................. OscarUrbina 6 65
(M Botti) *chsd ldrs: rdn 3f out: wknd over 2f out* **9/1**

1-56 **10** *20* **Prime Contender**[5] 693 5-8-12 **78**.............................(b) SebSanders 5 32
(G L Moore) *chsd ldrs: rdn 4f out: wknd 3f out* **11/2**[3]

006- **11** *1 1/4* **Zabeel Palace**[27] 6017 5-9-0 **80**.................................... JamieSpencer 1 32
(B J Curley) *rr: rdn over 4f out: no rspnse* **12/1**

2m 19.97s (-2.71) **Going Correction** -0.05s/f (Stan)
WFA 4 from 5yo+ 1lb 11 Ran SP% **118.7**
Speed ratings (Par 105):107,106,105,104,104 104,103,100,97,83 82
CSF £27.52 CT £287.42 TOTE £6.00: £3.50, £2.20, £5.70; EX 43.30 Place 6 £316.66, Place 5 £260.13.
Owner T G Mills **Bred** Dr T A Ryan **Trained** Headley, Surrey

FOCUS
A fair middle-distance handicap and they went a decent pace. Sound form. I Have Dreamed did not need to match the form he showed when winning at Sandown last summer.
Capistrano Official explanation: jockey said gelding hung left
T/Plt: £246.40 to a £1 stake. Pool: £58,781.95. 174.15 winning tickets. T/Qpdt: £237.80 to a £1 stake. Pool: £3,085.10. 9.60 winning tickets. ST

713 SOUTHWELL (L-H)
Thursday, March 22

OFFICIAL GOING: Standard
Wind: virtually nil

727 GO PONTIN'S H'CAP 5f (F)
2:10 (2:12) (Class 5) (0-75,75) 4-Y-O+ **£3,071** (£906; £453) **Stalls** High

Form RPR

1113 **1** **Canadian Danehill (IRE)**[29] 513 5-9-4 **75**.........................(p) NCallan 9 93+
(R M H Cowell) *cl up: effrt 2f out: rdn to ld over 1f out: kpt on* **7/2**[1]

1411 **2** *2* **Egyptian Lord**[16] 626 4-9-1 **72**.............................(b) RobbieFitzpatrick 6 80
(Peter Grayson) *dwlt and soon swtchd lft: hdwy over 2f out: rdn to chse wnr and hung lft ins last: kept on* **5/1**[3]

12-4 **3** *hd* **Cross Of Lorraine (IRE)**[73] 67 4-8-8 **65**.....................(b) TomEaves 7 72
(I Semple) *bmpd s: sn chsng ldrs: effrt to chal 2f out and ev ch tl rdn and nt qckn ent last* **15/2**

3511 **4** *1 1/4* **The Fisio**[13] 654 7-8-4 **66**...(v) WilliamBuick(5) 5 69
(S Gollings) *wnt rt s: in tch: swtchd rt and rdn wl over 1f out: kpt on ins last* **13/2**

255- **5** *3/4* **Witchry**[92] 6882 5-8-13 **70**.. FergusSweeney 3 71
(A G Newcombe) *cl up: ev ch 2f out tl rdn and wknd ent last* **11/2**

0544 **6** *1 1/4* **Hammer Of The Gods (IRE)**[23] 575 7-9-0 **71**.......(bt) JamieSpencer 8 67
(P S McEntee) *squeezed s and bhd tl styd on appr last* **8/1**

0-00 **7** *4* **Signor Panettiere**[53] 277 6-9-4 **75**.....................(t) SilvestreDeSousa 4 58
(A D Brown) *led: rdn along and hdd wl over 1f out: sn wknd* **33/1**

5022 **8** *3* **Stoneacre Boy (IRE)**[16] 626 4-8-10 **67**.................(b) GrahamGibbons 2 39
(Peter Grayson) *chsd ldrs: rdn along 1/2-way: sn wknd* **9/2**[2]

9 *5* **Polar Fox**[180] 5541 4-8-8 **65**.. PaulHanagan 10 20
(D Shaw) *in tch to 1/2-way: sn outpcd* **100/1**

0-00 **10** *7* **Funfair Wane**[77] 32 8-8-13 **70**................................. AdrianTNicholls 1 2
(D Nicholls) *chsd ldrs on outer: rdn along 1/2-way: sn wknd* **40/1**

59.89 secs (-0.41) **Going Correction** 0.0s/f (Stan) 10 Ran SP% **115.0**
Speed ratings (Par 103):103,99,99,97,96 94,87,83,75,63
CSF £20.51 CT £122.52 TOTE £4.00: £1.90, £1.90, £2.10; EX 15.80 Trifecta £195.20 Pool £1,014.51 - 3.69 winning units..
Owner T W Morley **Bred** Skymarc Farm Inc And Dr A J O'Reilly **Trained** Six Mile Bottom, Cambs

FOCUS
A competitive handicap, featuring some in-form sprinters. The form looks sound, and the much improved winner was value for further.

728 PONTINSBINGO.COM MAIDEN STKS 7f (F)
2:40 (2:42) (Class 5) 3-4-Y-O **£3,071** (£906; £453) **Stalls** Low

Form RPR

02 **1** **Shaftesbury Avenue (USA)**[9] 670 4-9-13 ....(bt) DarryllHolland 12 58
(J O'Reilly) *chsd ldrs: led 3f out: rdn wl over 1f out: drvn and kpt on ins last* **9/2**[2]

355- **2** *1* **Paymaster General (IRE)**[269] 2930 3-8-12 72............... HayleyTurner 6 50
(M D I Usher) *chsd ldrs: rdn along and outpcd 1/2-way: hdwy wl over 1f out kpt on u.p ins last* **9/2**[2]

3 *1 1/4* **Bivouac (UAE)** 3-8-12 .... JamieSpencer 2 47
(G A Swinbank) *s.i.s: sn in tch on inner: swtchd rt and effrt 3f out: rdn to chse wnr over 2f out: drvn and one pce over 1f out* **11/8**[1]

000- **4** *1 1/2* **Newcastles Owen (IRE)**[213] 4656 4-9-8 35............ DuranFentiman(5) 7 48
(R Johnson) *s.i.s and bhd: hdwy on inner over 2f out: sn rdn and kpt on appr last: nrst fin* **80/1**

0-00 **5** *nk* **Lady's Law**[53] 278 4-9-8 43... JoeFanning 3 42
(Rae Guest) *chsd ldrs: rdn along and outpcd 1/2-way: hdwy on inner to chse ldrs over 2f out: sn rdn and one pce* **18/1**

0-0 **6** *2* **Agnes Gift**[9] 670 4-9-8 .... JamieMackay 5 37
(Rae Guest) *chsd ldrs: rdn aloing 3f out: snd riven and one pce fnl 2f* **33/1**

7 *5* **Western Land** 3-8-9 .... MarkLawson(3) 11 29
(B Smart) *s.i.s: a towards rr* **5/1**[3]

000- **8** *1/2* **Littlemadgebob**[142] 6278 3-8-8 41 ow1........................ PaulMulrennan 10 19
(J R Norton) *cl up: rdn along and wkng whn hmpd 3f out and sn wknd* **125/1**

0 **9** *shd* **Kadia**[25] 559 4-9-8 .... MickyFenton 1 22
(P T Midgley) *led: rdn along and hdd 3f out: sn hung bdly rt and wknd* **100/1**

06- **10** *2 1/2* **Currahee**[163] 5901 3-8-5 .... DawnRankin(7) 4 16
(Miss J A Camacho) *a bhd* **40/1**

06-0 **11** *7* **Night Reveller (IRE)**[3] 630 4-9-3 28................ RussellKennemore(5) 13 —
(M C Chapman) *prom: rdn along and wkng whn n.m.r 3f out* **100/1**

12 *1/2* **Pickledallnuts** 3-8-8 ow1.. TonyHamilton 8 —
(Miss J A Camacho) *a rr* **20/1**

13 *8* **Hello Nod** 3-8-12 .... TomEaves 9 —
(Miss J A Camacho) *s.i.s: a rr* **20/1**

1m 31.97s (1.17) **Going Correction** -0.025s/f (Stan)
WFA 3 from 4yo 15lb 13 Ran SP% **119.3**
Speed ratings (Par 103):92,90,89,87,87 85,79,78,78,75 67,67,58
CSF £23.57 TOTE £5.40: £2.00, £2.00, £1.10; EX 16.60 Trifecta £46.30 Pool £529.82 - 8.12 winning units..
Owner David Betts **Bred** Barnett Enterprises **Trained** Doncaster, S Yorks

FOCUS
A moderate maiden, as the proximity of the 35-rated fourth would suggest, and the winning time was 2.18 seconds slower than the following 0-55 handicap.
Western Land Official explanation: jockey said gelding did not face the kickback
Littlemadgebob Official explanation: jockey said filly failed to handle the bend
Currahee Official explanation: trainer said colt had not acted on the all-weather surface

729 PHOTO ALBUMS FROM BONUSPRINT.COM H'CAP 7f (F)
3:10 (3:11) (Class 6) (0-55,59) 4-Y-0+ £2,388 (£705; £352) Stalls Low

Form RPR

2-01 **1** **Island Green (USA)**^{9} [664] 4-8-10 **53** 6ex.................... DanielTudhope 5 66+
(D Carroll) *in tch: swtchd rt and smooth hdwy over 2f out: sn rdn and led over 1f out: hung lft and kpt on fnl f* **3/1**^{1}

0414 **2** *2* **Kew The Music**^{2} [718] 7-9-2 **59** 6ex.................................. ChrisCatlin 6 67
(M R Channon) *s.i.s and bhd: hdwy over 2f out: swtchd lft and rdn wl over 1f out: styd on wl u.p ins last* **9/2**^{2}

2623 **3** *¾* **Favouring (IRE)**^{16} [632] 5-8-1 **49**.............................(v) WilliamBuick$^{(5)}$ 12 55
(M C Chapman) *cl up: led after 2f: rdn clr over 2f out: drvn and hdd over 1f out: wknd ins last* **11/1**

4213 **4** *5* **Desert Lover (IRE)**^{7} [682] 5-8-11 **54**................................(tp) NCallan 11 47
(R J Price) *in tch: hdwy to chse ldrs 3f out: rdn over 2f out and kpt on same pce* **6/1**^{3}

3-04 **5** *½* **Bandos**^{16} [625] 7-8-7 **50**.. TomEaves 10 42
(I Semple) *rr: hdwy on outer over 2f out: sn rdn and no imp appr last* **12/1**

0320 **6** *hd* **Penel (IRE)**^{28} [519] 6-8-7 **50**...(p) MickyFenton 7 41
(P T Midgley) *dwlt and bhd tl styd on fnl 2f: nvr nr ldrs* **14/1**

-543 **7** *1* **Dysonic (USA)**^{49} [318] 5-8-5 **51**............................... JasonEdmunds$^{(3)}$ 9 40
(J Balding) *chsd ldrs: rdn along wl over 2f out: grad wknd* **9/1**

4530 **8** *4* **Grafton (IRE)**^{16} [627] 4-8-5 **48**..(p) JoeFanning 2 26
(J O'Reilly) *cl up on inner: rdn along over 2f out and sn wknd* **16/1**

0-01 **9** *½* **Government (IRE)**^{16} [627] 6-8-0 **50** ow1......................... ChrisHough$^{(7)}$ 8 27
(M C Chapman) *led 2f: rdn along and edgd lft 1/2-way: sn wknd* **25/1**

-400 **10** *½* **Mister Elegant**^{25} [556] 5-8-4 **54**.................................. JosephWalsh$^{(7)}$ 3 30
(J L Spearing) *chsd ldrs on inner: n.m.r 1/2-way and sn wknd* **12/1**

-006 **11** *7* **Lady Edge (IRE)**^{3} [712] 5-8-12 **55**................................ HayleyTurner 13 12
(A W Carroll) *a rr* **66/1**

0604 **12** *2* **Methusaleh (IRE)**^{9} [666] 4-8-10 **53**...........................(v^{1}) PaulHanagan 1 5
(D Shaw) *hld up: n.m.r on inner 1/2-way: a rr* **18/1**

0203 **13** *1* **Weet For Ever (USA)**^{9} [664] 4-8-9 **52**........................ DarryllHolland 14 2
(P A Blockley) *chsd ldrs: rdn along wl over 2f out and sn wknd* **16/1**

1m 29.79s (-1.01) **Going Correction** -0.025s/f (Stan) **13** Ran SP% **120.2**
Speed ratings (Par 101):104,101,100,95,94 94,93,88,88,87 79,77,76
CSF £15.51 CT £137.88 TOTE £4.40: £1.70, £1.90, £3.20; EX 24.50 Trifecta £97.70 Pool £371.89 - 2.70 winning unit..
Owner Reuben Glynn **Bred** Gainsborough Farm Llc **Trained** Sledmere, E Yorks
■ Stewards' Enquiry : Chris Hough one-day ban: used whip when out of contention (Apr 2)

FOCUS
Just a moderate handicap, but the time time was quite good; 2.18 seconds quicker than the previous maiden. Good form for the grade and the winner left the impression he is better than the bare result suggests.
Mister Elegant Official explanation: jockey said horse hung right round final bend

730 PONTIN'S FAMILY HOLIDAYS (S) STKS 1m 4f (F)
3:40 (3:40) (Class 6) 4-Y-0+ £2,184 (£644; £322) Stalls Low

Form RPR

2000 **1** **Bethanys Boy (IRE)**^{17} [623] 6-9-4 60.......................... SimonWhitworth 7 53
(P A Blockley) *hld up and bhd: stdy hdwy over 4f out: led wl over over 2f and sn rdn clr: kpt on* **11/4**^{2}

06 **2** *3* **Exit Fast (USA)**^{16} [630] 6-9-4 .... MickyFenton 13 48
(P T Midgley) *chsd ldrs: rdn along 3f out: drvn and edgd lft over 1f out: kpt on u.p fnl f* **33/1**

145- **3** *nk* **Tedstale (USA)**^{159} [5955] 9-9-4 62..(b) NCallan 5 48
(K A Ryan) *in tch: hdwy to chse ldrs 3f out: rdn 2f out: sn drvn: edgd rt and no imp fnl f* **5/2**^{1}

0-30 **4** *5* **Salym (FR)**^{9} [665] 6-9-4 48...(b) DarryllHolland 10 40
(D J S Ffrench Davis) *in tch: hdwy 1/2-way: chal 4f out: sn rdn along and ev ch tl drvn 2f out and sn one pce* **10/1**

0-00 **5** *½* **Activist**^{8} [677] 9-8-11 58..(v^{1}) KellyHarrison$^{(7)}$ 1 39
(D Carroll) *trckd ldrs on inner: hdwy 3f out: rdn and hung rt wl over 1f out: sn btn* **7/1**^{3}

0-60 **6** *3* **Willy (SWE)**^{34} [481] 5-9-4 46...(p) PhillipMakin 2 34
(R Brotherton) *led 4f: cl up tl led again 4f out: rdn 3f out: drvn and hdd wl over 2f out: sn wknd* **15/2**

-065 **7** *1* **Ronnies Lad**^{16} [630] 5-9-4 45.. PaulMulrennan 6 33
(J R Norton) *a midfield* **16/1**

/00- **8** *hd* **Susiedil (IRE)**^{15} [616] 6-8-8 35.............................(p) DuranFentiman$^{(5)}$ 4 27
(S T Mason) *chsd ldrs: rdn along 4f out and sn wknd* **16/1**

0-00 **9** *5* **Ahaz**^{16} [625] 5-9-1 35.. PatrickMathers$^{(3)}$ 3 24
(J F Coupland) *a rr* **66/1**

0304 **10** *15* **Tiegs (IRE)**^{16} [628] 5-9-4 43.. ChrisCatlin 8 —
(P W Hiatt) *cl up: led after 4f: rdn along and hdd 4f out: sn wknd* **11/1**

-000 **11** *26* **Tilen (IRE)**^{24} [570] 4-8-13 35...................................(v) DominicFox$^{(3)}$ 11 —
(S Parr) *a rr* **40/1**

00/0 **12** *7* **Tiggers Touch**^{31} [500] 5-8-13 37.................................. HayleyTurner 12 —
(A W Carroll) *a bhd* **66/1**

2m 43.37s (1.28) **Going Correction** -0.025s/f (Stan)
WFA 4 from 5yo+ 2lb **12** Ran SP% **117.1**
Speed ratings (Par 101):94,92,91,88,88 86,85,85,82,72 54,50
CSF £98.59 TOTE £4.50: £1.80, £6.80, £1.80; EX 103.40 Trifecta £153.10 Pool £642.92 - 2.98 winning units..The winner was bought in for 8,200gns.
Owner Market Avenue Racing Club Ltd **Bred** K And Mrs Cullen **Trained** Lambourn, Berks
■ A first winner in over a year for Simon Whitworth, who is back after taking a sabbatical from riding.
■ Stewards' Enquiry : N Callan one-day ban: careless riding (Apr 2)

FOCUS
A weak seller run in a time 0.89 seconds slower than the following 51-65 handicap. The proximity of the second limits the form.
Willy(SWE) Official explanation: jockey said gelding hung right

731 BONUSPRINT.COM H'CAP 1m 4f (F)
4:10 (4:12) (Class 6) (0-65,65) 3-Y-O £2,388 (£705; £352) Stalls Low

Form RPR

60-3 **1** **Petrosian**^{35} [469] 3-8-13 **60**.. JoeFanning 6 70
(M Johnston) *trckd ldr: hdwy to ld 3f out: rdn 2f out: drvn and hung lft appr last: styd on* **11/8**^{1}

1656 **2** *2* **King Of The Beers (USA)**^{36} [460] 3-8-8 **55** ow1......(p) DarryllHolland 3 62
(R A Harris) *trckd ldrs: hdwy 3f out: rdn to chse wnr and n.m.r over 1f out: swtchd rt: drvn and kpt on* **12/1**

6144 **3** *3* **Beau Sancy**^{25} [563] 3-8-13 **65**.. TolleyDean$^{(5)}$ 5 67
(R A Harris) *hld up in tch: hdwy over 3f out: rdn 2f out: drvn and one pce over 1f out* **11/2**

65-6 **4** *6* **Green Day Packer (IRE)**^{66} [140] 3-8-10 **62**.............. WilliamBuick$^{(5)}$ 4 55
(P C Haslam) *led: rdn along over 3f out and sn hdd: drvn 2f out and grad wknd* **5/1**^{3}

003 **5** *15* **Gee Ceffyl Bach**^{15} [635] 3-8-10 **57**.......................... EdwardCreighton 2 26
(M R Channon) *chsd ldrs: rdn along 4f out: sn wknd* **12/1**

0-35 **6** *27* **Here's Blue Chip (IRE)**^{51} [304] 3-9-3 **64**............................ JohnEgan 7 —
(P W D'Arcy) *chsd ldrs: rdn along over 4f out and sn wknd* **4/1**^{2}

004 **7** *8* **Noravana (IRE)**^{12} [661] 3-8-7 **54**.. MickyFenton 1 —
(Miss V Haigh) *a rr: rdn along 1/2-way: sn lost tch and bhd* **40/1**

2m 42.48s (0.39) **Going Correction** -0.025s/f (Stan) **7** Ran SP% **112.0**
Speed ratings (Par 96):97,95,93,89,79 61,56
CSF £18.92 CT £69.49 TOTE £2.10: £1.60, £3.90; EX 20.10 Trifecta £108.70 Pool £591.44 - 3.86 winning units..
Owner Barlow, Beech & Shepherd **Bred** Cliveden Stud Ltd **Trained** Middleham Moor, N Yorks

FOCUS
A weak handicap run in a time 0.89 seconds quicker than the previous seller. It did not take much winning.
Gee Ceffyl Bach Official explanation: jockey said filly was unsuited by the fibresand
Here's Blue Chip(IRE) Official explanation: vet said gelding was sore behind

732 PONTINS.COM H'CAP 1m (F)
4:40 (4:42) (Class 6) (0-65,65) 4-Y-0+ £2,388 (£705; £352) Stalls Low

Form RPR

0-46 **1** **Ruffie (IRE)**^{31} [497] 4-8-13 **62**..(e) NCallan 9 71
(Miss Gay Kelleway) *in tch: hdwy over 2f out: sn rdn and styd on wl fnl f to ld last 50 yds* **14/1**

-006 **2** *nk* **Shifty**^{2} [718] 8-9-2 **65**.. DanielTudhope 6 73
(D Carroll) *led: rdn clr 2f out: drvn ent last: hdd and no ex last 50 yds* **6/1**

00-0 **3** *1* **Exit Smiling**^{74} [63] 5-9-1 **64**... MickyFenton 1 70
(P T Midgley) *trckd ldrs on inner. hdwy to chse ldr over 2f out and sn rdn: drvn ent last: no ex towards fin* **9/1**

-005 **4** *nk* **Mambo Sun**^{28} [525] 4-8-10 **59**.. PaulHanagan 12 65
(P A Blockley) *chsd ldrs: rdn along and outpcd 1/2-way: styd on u.p fnl 2f: nrst fin* **10/3**^{2}

0-00 **5** *5* **Counterfactual (IRE)**^{73} [72] 4-8-2 **51** oh1....................... ChrisCatlin 2 46
(B Smart) *bhd: hdwy over 2f out: sn rdn and kpt on appr last: nrst fin* **16/1**

64-5 **6** *2* **Garibaldi (GER)**^{16} [631] 5-8-10 **59**................................ DarryllHolland 7 50
(J O'Reilly) *dwlt: sn chasing ldrs on outer: rdn along 3f out: drvn and wknd 2f out* **5/1**^{3}

0-05 **7** *1 ¼* **Piper General (IRE)**^{7} [685] 5-8-13 **65**.................... JasonEdmunds$^{(3)}$ 10 53
(J Balding) *midfield: rdn along 3f out: no hdwy* **25/1**

2521 **8** *3* **Mademoiselle**^{3} [712] 5-8-7 **61** 6ex.................................. TolleyDean$^{(5)}$ 3 43
(R A Harris) *trckd ldrs: effrt 3f out: sn rdn along and grad wknd fnl 2f* **3/1**^{1}

6020 **9** *6* **Mine The Balance (IRE)**^{20} [609] 4-8-9 **58** ow1..............(t) JohnEgan 11 27
(H J Manners) *nvr nr ldrs* **20/1**

442- **10** *hd* **Dechiper (IRE)**^{199} [5063] 5-7-11 **51**........................... DuranFentiman$^{(5)}$ 8 20
(R Johnson) *prom: rdn along 3f out: wknd over 2f out* **16/1**

000- **11** *3* **Rawaabet (IRE)**^{276} [2708] 5-8-7 **56**............................. EdwardCreighton 5 19
(P W Hiatt) *dwlt: a rr* **33/1**

1m 44.13s (-0.47) **Going Correction** -0.025s/f (Stan) **11** Ran SP% **119.0**
Speed ratings (Par 101):101,100,99,99,94 92,91,88,82,81 78
CSF £94.71 CT £828.44 TOTE £16.80: £4.20, £2.70, £2.50; EX 80.10 Trifecta £223.40 Part won. Pool £314.77 - 0.51 winning units..
Owner V L Davis R Edwards P Crook **Bred** F Jones **Trained** Exning, Suffolk

FOCUS
A modest handicap run at an ordinary pace.A muddling affair and the form might not be the most solid.
Mademoiselle Official explanation: trainer said mare was crowded 3f out and failed to travel thereafter

733 PONTIN'S BOOK EARLY H'CAP 1m 3f (F)
5:10 (5:11) (Class 6) (0-65,66) 4-Y-0+ £2,388 (£705; £352) Stalls Low

Form RPR

06-4 **1** **Velvet Valley (USA)**^{20} [602] 4-9-0 **62**............................ SamHitchcott 9 76
(C E Longsdon) *hld up in tch: hdwy 4f out: chsd ldrs over 2f out: swtchd lft and rdn to ld over 1f out: clr inside last* **25/1**

4-01 **2** *5* **Shape Up (IRE)**^{7} [685] 7-9-5 **66** 6ex................................(v) PaulFessey 8 72+
(R Craggs) *a.p: led over 3f out: rdn 2f out: drvn and hdd over 1f out: one pce* **5/1**^{2}

2-11 **3** *2* **Three Boars**^{7} [683] 5-9-0 **66** 6ex................................(b) WilliamBuick$^{(5)}$ 2 68
(S Gollings) *hld up and wl bhd: sme hdwy over 4f out: wd st and rdn wl over 2f out: styd on appr last: nrst fin* **6/5**^{1}

0416 **4** *½* **Bridgewater Boys**^{8} [674] 6-9-3 **64**....................................(p) NCallan 10 65
(K A Ryan) *chsd ldrs: effrt 4f out: rdn wl over 2f out and sn one pce* **8/1**^{3}

-321 **5** *1* **Nimello (USA)**^{9} [665] 11-8-2 **54**.............................. KevinGhunowa$^{(5)}$ 11 53
(A G Newcombe) *hld up and bhd: hdwy on inner 3f out: styd on u.p appr last: nrst fin* **12/1**

65-0 **6** *2 ½* **Wotchalike (IRE)**^{47} [279] 5-8-11 **58**..................................(v) JohnEgan 3 53
(R J Price) *chsd ldrs: rdn along 4f out: sn wknd* **20/1**

1200 **7** *¾* **Greenbelt**^{16} [631] 6-9-2 **63**.. ChrisCatlin 7 57
(G M Moore) *rr: hdwy to trck ldrs after 4f: rdn along 4f out and sn wknd* **20/1**

1522 **8** *1* **Bolckow**^{16} [631] 4-9-0 **62**... MickyFenton 5 54
(J T Stimpson) *trckd ldrs: hdwy 4f out: rdn along 3f out: sn drvn and wknd fnl 2f* **5/1**^{2}

626- **9** *½* **Hi Dancer**^{10} [4651] 4-8-5 **53**... SilvestreDeSousa 6 44
(P C Haslam) *hld up in rr: effrt and sme hdwy 3f out: sn rdn and wknd* **14/1**

00- **10** *33* **Monashee River (IRE)**^{91} [6899] 4-8-4 **52** oh1 ow2..... AdrianTNicholls 1 —
(Miss V Haigh) *led: rdn along and hdd over 3f out: sn wknd* **66/1**

2m 27.13s (-1.77) **Going Correction** -0.025s/f (Stan)
WFA 4 from 5yo+ 1lb **10** Ran SP% **119.1**
Speed ratings (Par 101):105,101,99,99,98 97,96,95,95,71
CSF £143.48 CT £274.73 TOTE £35.90: £6.80, £1.90, £1.10; EX 283.30 Trifecta £375.30 Part won. Pool £528.71 - 0.51 winning units. Place 6 £35.30, Place 5 £18.66 .
Owner Charlie Longsdon **Bred** Juddmonte Farms Inc **Trained** Sezincote, Gloucs
■ A first winner on the Flat for Charlie Longsdon.

FOCUS
A modest middle-distance handicap, but run at a fair pace. No fluke about the winner's surprise defeat of two runners that were potentially well treated.
T/Jkpt: £16,222.50 to a £1 stake. Pool: £34,273.00. 1.50 winning tickets. T/Plt: £75.10 to a £1 stake. Pool: £77,096.50. 748.90 winning tickets. T/Qpdt: £41.00 to a £1 stake. Pool: £3,974.70. 71.60 winning tickets. JR

[697]LINGFIELD (L-H)

Friday, March 23

OFFICIAL GOING: Standard

Wind: Moderate against Weather: Overcast

734 CANVAS PRINTS FROM BONUSPRINT.COM CLAIMING STKS 7f (P)

2:00 (2:00) (Class 6) 4-Y-0+ **£2,184** (£644; £322) **Stalls** Low

Form RPR

0600 **1** **Marmooq**[8] 681 4-8-10 56 .... JerryO'Dwyer(3) 3 64
(J Gallagher) *mde all: clr for 2f then restrained: drvn clr again over 1f out: kpt on wl* **10/1**

0445 **2** 2 ½ **Ever Cheerful**[18] 622 6-9-9 65 .... DaneO'Neill 4 68
(A B Haynes) *s.s: t.k.h and sn in tch: rdn over 2f out: kpt on to take 2nd nr fin* **3/1[2]**

0626 **3** ½ **Zarzu**[7] 692 8-9-13 80 .... EddieAhern 6 70
(C R Dore) *trckd ldrs: chsd wnr over 2f out: rdn and no imp over 1f out: lost 2nd nr fin* **7/4[1]**

0334 **4** ½ **Buzzin'Boyzee (IRE)**[6] 699 4-8-3 56 .... BernadetteQuinn(7) 1 52
(P D Evans) *trckd ldrs: lost pl 3f out: last pair 2f out: urged along and kpt on fnl f* **7/1**

4000 **5** ½ **Hotchpotch (USA)**[14] 654 4-8-6 52 .... (p) StephaneBreux(3) 2 50
(J R Best) *hld up in tch: rdn in last pair over 2f out: no prog* **15/2**

0033 **6** 4 **Nikki Bea (IRE)**[6] 699 4-8-10 54 .... SimonWhitworth 5 40
(Jamie Poulton) *mostly chsd wnr to over 2f out: sn struggling* **4/1[3]**

1m 24.92s (-0.97) **Going Correction** -0.05s/f (Stan) **6** Ran SP% **114.7**
Speed ratings (Par 101):103,100,99,99,98 93
CSF £40.91 TOTE £15.50: £6.10, £3.00; EX 93.40.

Owner J Gallagher **Bred** Matthews Breeding & Racing Ltd **Trained** Moreton-in-Marsh, Gloucs

FOCUS
A weak event which saw the winner dictate matters from the front. The form is suspect.

735 LLOYD & PAMELA RUSSELL GOLDEN WEDDING ANNIVERSARY MAIDEN STKS 1m 4f (P)

2:30 (2:30) (Class 5) 3-Y-0 **£3,071** (£906; £453) **Stalls** Low

Form RPR

5- **1** **Wandle**[146] 6220 3-9-3 .... DaneO'Neill 1 89+
(T G Mills) *stdd s: t.k.h: hld up: pushed along to chse ldr over 2f out: shkn up to ld over 1f out: sn in command* **1/3[1]**

552- **2** 5 **Maslak (IRE)**[203] 4992 3-9-3 82 .... JamieSpencer 3 79+
(E A L Dunlop) *skittish to post: led at mod pce: pushed along over 2f out: hdd over 1f out: no ch w wnr fnl f* **7/2[2]**

5-2 **3** 3 ½ **Sowdrey**[21] 602 3-9-3 .... ChrisCatlin 2 71
(M R Channon) *hld up: lost tch over 3f out: sn bhd: styd on fnl f to snatch 3rd on post* **10/1[3]**

4 shd **Anne Bronte** 3-8-12 .... JoeFanning 4 66
(M Johnston) *trckd ldr to over 2f out: green and hanging lft after: wknd and lost 3rd last stride* **20/1**

2m 34.96s (0.57) **Going Correction** -0.05s/f (Stan) **4** Ran SP% **111.1**
Speed ratings (Par 98):96,92,90,90
CSF £1.95 TOTE £1.30; EX 2.00.

Owner J Daniels **Bred** Mrs Johnny Eddis **Trained** Headley, Surrey

FOCUS
An interesting little three-year-old maiden. It was run at an uneven pace and the promising winner can be rated value for further than the winning margin.

736 BONUSPRINT.COM MEDIAN AUCTION MAIDEN STKS 1m (P)

3:05 (3:05) (Class 6) 3-4-Y-0 **£2,730** (£806; £403) **Stalls** High

Form RPR

065- **1** **Ambrosiano**[172] 5738 3-8-10 62 .... AdamKirby 1 66+
(C G Cox) *led at slow pce to over 5f out: led 3f out and sn qcknd clr: pushed out* **11/8[2]**

004- **2** 1 ½ **Bathwick Fancy (IRE)**[170] 5764 3-8-5 57 .... (t) JoeFanning 3 56
(J G Portman) *hld up in last pair: gng wl enough but outpcd over 2f out: rdn and styd on to take 2nd fnl f: nt rch wnr* **11/2[3]**

34 **3** 1 ½ **Musical Locket (IRE)**[25] 565 3-8-0 .... WilliamBuick(5) 2 53
(R Hannon) *hld up: pushed along to chse wnr over 2f out: sn rdn and no imp: one pce* **11/10[1]**

4 20 **Sandalphon (USA)**[42] 4-9-13 .... RichardThomas 4 12
(J A Geake) *lft 10 l s: plld hrd and led over 5f out to 3f out: wknd rapidly: t.o* **20/1**

1m 41.28s (1.85) **Going Correction** -0.05s/f (Stan)
WFA 3 from 4yo 17lb **4** Ran SP% **109.9**
Speed ratings (Par 101):88,86,85,65
CSF £8.66 TOTE £2.00; EX 7.30.

Owner Paul G Jacobs **Bred** Whitsbury Manor Stud **Trained** Lambourn, Berks

FOCUS
A weak maiden and the form should be treated with a degree of caution as none of the runners were easy to pin down beforehand and the race itself was slowly run.

Sandalphon(USA) Official explanation: jockey said gelding missed the break

737 PONTIN'S "BOOK EARLY" H'CAP 7f (P)

3:40 (3:44) (Class 5) (0-70,70) 3-Y-0 **£2,914** (£867; £433; £216) **Stalls** Low

Form RPR

-213 **1** **Convivial Spirit**[32] 502 3-9-1 67 .... (t) LPKeniry 8 74
(E F Vaughan) *hld up in midfield: stdy prog over 2f out: rdn to ld 1f out: styd on wl* **8/1**

2 1 ¼ **Nans Joy (IRE)**[195] 5189 3-9-4 70 .... ChrisCatlin 5 73
(E J O'Neill) *t.k.h: trckd ldr after 1f: upsides fr over 2f out: fnd little u.p: edgd rt and chsd wnr fnl f* **14/1**

421- **3** ½ **Prince Of Charm (USA)**[114] 6653 3-9-1 67 .... JamieSpencer 12 69+
(P Mitchell) *s.i.s: pushed along in last pair 3f out: rdn and brought wd in st: styd on wl fnl f to take 3rd last stride* **6/1[3]**

04-0 **4** shd **Rubilini**[24] 573 3-8-6 58 .... SamHitchcott 9 60
(M R Channon) *hld up towards rr: effrt over 2f out: rdn and styd on fr over 1f out: nrst fin* **12/1**

0-25 **5** nk **Follow The Flag (IRE)**[32] 498 3-9-4 70 .... (b[1]) JimmyFortune 11 71
(N P Littmoden) *t.k.h: led after 1f: hdd and fdd 1f out* **4/1[2]**

00-2 **6** nk **Tetouan**[16] 633 3-9-4 70 .... SteveDrowne 2 70
(R Charlton) *t.k.h: led for 1f: trckd ldrs after: u.p over 2f out: one pce* **5/4[1]**

4-55 **7** 2 **Dolly Coughdrop (IRE)**[40] 433 3-9-1 67 .... FergusSweeney 1 62
(K R Burke) *t.k.h: trckd ldrs: nt qckn over 2f out: no prog over 1f out* **25/1**

-630 **8** nk **Lawyer To World**[29] 520 3-8-6 58 .... PaulEddery 6 52
(N A Callaghan) *hld up in rr: shkn up and no prog 2f out* **20/1**

-560 **9** hd **Inquisitress**[32] 502 3-8-11 66 .... AmirQuinn(3) 7 60
(J J Bridger) *plld hrd: hld up bhd ldrs: gng wl enough over 2f out: wknd over 1f out* **20/1**

550- **10** 4 **Mayireneyrbel**[114] 6650 3-8-4 56 oh3 .... SimonWhitworth 10 39
(J Akehurst) *s.v.s: nvr gng wl and a bhd* **66/1**

-300 **11** nk **Lordswood (IRE)**[37] 460 3-8-7 62 .... MarcHalford(3) 3 45
(J J Bridger) *trckd ldrs tl wknd over 2f out* **33/1**

1m 25.28s (-0.61) **Going Correction** -0.05s/f (Stan) **11** Ran SP% **122.0**
Speed ratings (Par 98):101,99,99,98,98 98,95,95,95,90 90
CSF £107.34 CT £741.31 TOTE £8.40: £1.80, £4.40, £2.00; EX 88.10 Trifecta £348.10 Pool: £647.26 - 1.32 winning units..

Owner A M Pickering **Bred** Miss Jacqueline Goodearl **Trained** Newmarket, Suffolk

■ Road To Recovery was withdrawn (8/1, uns rdr & bolted bef s.) R4 applies, deduct 10p in the £.

FOCUS
A modest three-year-old handicap and a race that might not have taken a lot of winning with the favourite so disappointing. The steady early pace dictates the form should be treated with a little caution.

Prince Of Charm(USA) ◆ Official explanation: jockey said gelding reared in stalls and missed the break

Mayireneyrbel Official explanation: jockey said filly reared in stalls and missed the break

738 PONTIN'S HOLIDAYS H'CAP 1m (P)

4:15 (4:19) (Class 5) (0-70,66) 3-Y-0 **£2,914** (£867; £433; £216) **Stalls** High

Form RPR

04-6 **1** **Hucking Heat (IRE)**[53] 290 3-9-3 65 .... GeorgeBaker 10 71
(J R Best) *s.i.s: hld up in last pair: prog jst over 2f out: rdn and r.o fnl f to ld last 50yds* **10/1**

2-53 **2** ½ **Dr McFab**[46] 370 3-9-4 66 .... JamieSpencer 3 71
(J A Osborne) *pressed ldr: rdn to ld over 1f out: hdd and outpcd last 50yds* **6/1[3]**

-004 **3** 1 ¼ **Realy Naughty (IRE)**[22] 591 3-9-4 66 .... MichaelHills 8 68
(B G Powell) *hld up towards rr: prog 1/2-way: effrt to press ldr 1f out: nt qckn* **7/2[1]**

6004 **4** ½ **Brave Jack (IRE)**[16] 636 3-8-5 58 .... WilliamBuick(5) 1 59
(J R Best) *dwlt: plld hrd and sn trckd ldng pair: rdn over 2f out: effrt jst over 1f out: kpt on same pce* **11/2[2]**

000 **5** ¾ **Woodygo**[37] 456 3-8-9 60 .... StephaneBreux(3) 6 59
(J R Best) *t.k.h: hld up in midfield: effrt over 2f out: rdn whn n.m.r over 1f out: one pce* **8/1**

-001 **6** 1 **Dance Of Dreams**[16] 636 3-8-11 62 .... JamesDoyle(3) 9 59
(N P Littmoden) *t.k.h: trckd ldrs: rdn and lost pl 3f out: n.d after: kpt on fnl f* **8/1**

460- **7** ¾ **Desert Soul**[188] 5381 3-9-4 66 .... JoeFanning 5 61
(M Johnston) *led to over 1f out: wknd fnl f* **8/1**

000 **8** shd **Mark Of Love (IRE)**[13] 661 3-9-0 62 .... TonyCulhane 4 57
(M R Channon) *settled in rr: pushed along over 2f out: no prog and nvr nr ldrs* **16/1**

00-4 **9** 1 ¼ **Royal Guest**[24] 573 3-9-4 66 .... SamHitchcott 11 58
(M R Channon) *t.k.h: hld up in tch: pressed ldrs over 2f out tl wknd rapidly jst over 1f out* **8/1**

06-5 **10** 1 **Hard As Iron**[18] 624 3-8-12 60 .... SteveDrowne 7 50
(M Blanshard) *t.k.h: hld up in midfield: rdn 3f out: wknd over 1f out* **8/1**

006 **11** 4 **Spinning Dixie (IRE)**[24] 573 3-8-10 58 .... (t) RichardThomas 12 38
(J A Geake) *a last: reminders 4f out: no prog and eased fnl f* **33/1**

1m 39.16s (-0.27) **Going Correction** -0.05s/f (Stan) **11** Ran SP% **125.4**
Speed ratings (Par 98):99,98,97,96,96 95,94,94,92,91 87
CSF £73.61 CT £265.96 TOTE £14.90: £4.20, £1.90, £1.60; EX 104.30 Trifecta £361.60 Part won. Pool: £509.39 - 0.20 winning units..

Owner Hucking Horses **Bred** Thomas J Reid **Trained** Hucking, Kent

FOCUS
A modest handicap, featuring largely unexposed three-year-olds. The form is rated through the second and third.

Spinning Dixie(IRE) Official explanation: jockey said filly never travelled

739 PONTINS.COM H'CAP 1m (P)

4:50 (4:50) (Class 5) (0-75,73) 4-Y-0+ **£2,914** (£867; £433; £216) **Stalls** High

Form RPR

3215 **1** **Parkview Love (USA)**[3] 718 6-8-9 66 .... (v) DaneO'Neill 6 76
(D Shaw) *trckd clr ldng pair: clsd fr 3f out: rdn to ld over 1f out: hld on wl* **10/3[1]**

-003 **2** nk **Special Place**[18] 614 4-7-13 61 .... WilliamBuick(5) 7 70
(J A R Toller) *hld up and sn detached in last: rdn 1/2-way: prog over 2f out: chsd wnr fnl f: clsd but a hld nr fin* **11/2**

4422 **3** 1 ¾ **Binnion Bay (IRE)**[14] 650 6-8-1 61 .... (b) MarcHalford(3) 2 66
(J J Bridger) *stdd s: hld up off the pce: last and rdn over 2f out: styd on fnl f to take 3rd nr fin* **11/1**

0304 **4** ½ **Arctic Desert**[22] 592 7-9-1 72 .... (t) RichardHughes 3 76
(Miss Gay Kelleway) *dwlt: hld up: shkn up over 2f out: chsd ldng pair fnl f: no imp: lost 3rd nr fin* **7/2[2]**

/000 **5** 3 **Certifiable**[14] 650 6-8-2 59 oh2 .... ChrisCatlin 5 56
(Miss Z C Davison) *chsd ldr and clr of rest: rdn 3f out: lost pl and btn 2f out* **20/1**

4344 **6** 5 **Trifti**[14] 652 6-8-13 70 .... EddieAhern 1 61+
(C A Cyzer) *trckd clr ldng pair: shkn up 3f out: lost pl over 1f out: eased fnl f* **4/1[3]**

2-00 **7** ¾ **Kabeer**[22] 592 9-9-2 73 .... (t) JamieSpencer 4 57
(A J McCabe) *racd wd: led at str pce: clr over 2f out: hdd & wknd rapidly over 1f out* **4/1[3]**

1m 37.44s (-1.99) **Going Correction** -0.05s/f (Stan) **7** Ran SP% **113.8**
Speed ratings (Par 103):107,106,104,104,101 96,95
CSF £21.64 TOTE £3.80: £2.60, £3.50; EX 18.30.

Owner Danethorpe Racing Ltd **Bred** Mark Johnston Racing Ltd **Trained** Danethorpe, Notts

FOCUS
A modest handicap which saw the first two come clear. The form looks straightforward enough.

740 GO PONTIN'S H'CAP 1m 4f (P)

5:20 (5:20) (Class 5) (0-70,70) 4-Y-0+ **£2,914** (£867; £433; £216) **Stalls** Low

Form RPR

5-52 **1** **Musango**[18] 612 4-8-2 61 .... WilliamBuick(5) 2 71
(B R Johnson) *t.k.h: a in ldng trio: led over 2f out: kicked clr wl over 1f out: rdn out* **11/2[2]**

4360 **2** 3 **Hawk Arrow (IRE)**[18] 623 5-8-7 59 .... FergusSweeney 7 64
(G L Moore) *hld up in last pair: prog on outer fr 3f out: rdn and nt qckn 2f out: styd on to take 2nd ins fnl f* **8/1**

3400 **3** ½ **Rowan Warning**[18] [612] 5-8-4 **56** ...... JoeFanning 1 61
(J R Boyle) *trckd ldrs: lost pl and rdn briefly 5f out: effrt again over 2f out: kpt on same pce fr over 1f out* **9/1**

6604 **4** *shd* **Augustine**[10] [669] 6-9-4 **70** ...... (b) GeorgeBaker 3 74+
(P W Hiatt) *plld hrd: hld up towards rr: clsd on ldrs 3f out: nt qckn 2f out: kpt on same pce after* **7/1**[3]

3310 **5** *nk* **King After**[7] [691] 5-8-2 **57** ...... (v) StephaneBreux(3) 6 61
(J R Best) *t.k.h: hld up in last pair: effrt 3f out: kpt on one pce and n.d fnl 2f* **8/1**

1114 **6** 3 **Atlantic Gamble (IRE)**[18] [623] 7-8-13 **65** ...... (p) PatCosgrave 8 64
(K R Burke) *t.k.h: mostly trckd ldr to 1/2-way: rdn 3f out: stl cl up wl over 1f out: wknd fnl f* **8/1**

P-21 **7** 2 **King's Ransom**[58] [230] 4-8-11 **65** ...... (b) RichardHughes 4 61+
(W R Muir) *t.k.h: hld up tl led 1/2-way: hdd over 2f out: sn wknd* **7/1**[3]

04-0 **8** *hd* **Dark Planet**[21] [607] 4-8-2 **56** oh1 ...... (p) RichardThomas 10 52
(D Burchell) *t.k.h: hld up in midfield: lost pl and rdn over 3f out: no ch fnl 2f* **25/1**

-040 **9** *shd* **Makai**[17] [631] 4-8-4 **61** ...... (b) MarcHalford(3) 5 57
(J J Bridger) *led at stdy pce to 1/2-way: u.p and btn wl over 2f out* **20/1**

-624 **10** 5 **Hallings Overture (USA)**[46] [363] 8-8-8 **60** ...... PaulEddery 9 48+
(C A Horgan) *t.k.h: hld up: prog to press ldrs 3f out: wknd 2f out: eased* **3/1**[1]

2m 34.65s (0.26) **Going Correction** -0.05s/f (Stan)
WFA 4 from 5yo+ 2lb **10** Ran SP% **117.3**
Speed ratings (Par 103):97,95,94,94,94 92,91,90,90,87
CSF £49.34 CT £392.88 TOTE £6.40: £2.30, £3.90, £3.00; EX 71.60 Trifecta £213.30 Part won. Pool: £300.46 - 0.44 winning units. Place 6 £ 237.55, Place 5 £ 77.78.
Owner Tann Racing **Bred** Juddmonte Farms Ltd **Trained** Ashtead, Surrey

FOCUS
A moderate handicap, run at a steady early pace. The winner is relatively unexposed and did the job in good style.
Augustine Official explanation: jockey said gelding ran too free
T/Plt: £937.10 to a £1 stake. Pool: £58,092.10. 45.25 winning tickets. T/Qpdt: £84.60 to a £1 stake. Pool: £4,186.10. 36.60 winning tickets. JN

672 WOLVERHAMPTON (A.W) (L-H)
Friday, March 23

OFFICIAL GOING: Standard
Wind: Light against Weather: Drizzle for Race 6

741 PONTIN'S FAMILY HOLIDAYS H'CAP (DIV I) 1m 1f 103y(P)
1:50 (1:50) (Class 6) (0-58,58) 4-Y-0+ **£2,047** (£604; £302) **Stalls** Low

Form RPR

1322 **1** **Norwegian**[9] [674] 6-8-10 **54** ...... (p) JimCrowley 3 66
(Ian Williams) *hld up: sn in tch: wnt 2nd 2f out: sn rdn: led 1f out: sn edgd lft: r.o* **11/4**[1]

-315 **2** 1 ¼ **Penang Cinta**[28] [539] 4-9-0 **58** ...... NCallan 6 68+
(P D Evans) *hld up and bhd: stdy hdwy over 3f out: swtchd lft over 1f out: n.m.r on ins jst ins fnl f: r.o* **3/1**[2]

3040 **3** 1 ¼ **Buscador (USA)**[25] [564] 8-8-10 **57** ...... LiamJones(3) 12 64
(W M Brisbourne) *prom: wnt 2nd over 6f out: led over 4f out: rdn and hdd 1f out: no ex* **12/1**

5-61 **4** 1 ¼ **Bobering**[55] [266] 7-8-5 **52** ...... PatrickMathers(3) 5 57+
(B P J Baugh) *hld up and bhd: rdn and hdwy over 1f out: kpt on same pce fnl f* **11/2**[3]

5-53 **5** ½ **Agilete**[18] [617] 5-8-10 **54** ...... JimmyQuinn 9 58
(J Pearce) *s.i.s: hld up and bhd: rdn and hdwy whn swtchd rt over 1f out: one pce fnl f* **10/1**

0-40 **6** 2 **Pelham Crescent (IRE)**[18] [612] 4-9-0 **58** ...... (p) DaleGibson 1 58
(B Palling) *led: hdd over 4f out: chsd ldr tl rdn 2f out: wknd over 1f out* **20/1**

023- **7** *hd* **Azreme**[301] [1996] 7-8-6 **50** ...... TPQueally 4 49
(P Howling) *hld up in mid-div: hdwy over 2f out: rdn and hung lft over 1f out: wknd ins fnl f* **12/1**

0600 **8** 1 **Veba (USA)**[18] [612] 4-8-2 **46** oh1 ...... HayleyTurner 2 43
(M D I Usher) *hld up and bhd: rdn and hdwy on ins over 2f out: wknd ins fnl f* **33/1**

0-00 **9** 10 **Lockstock (IRE)**[15] [148] 9-8-2 **46** ...... (p) AdrianMcCarthy 11 23
(M S Saunders) *hld up in tch: rdn over 3f out: wknd over 2f out* **50/1**

000- **10** 2 ½ **Nimrana Fort**[144] [6260] 4-8-12 **56** ...... (p) PaulHanagan 7 28
(J S Wainwright) *chsd ldr 3f: wknd over 3f out* **12/1**

11 1 **Ellen's Girl (IRE)**[194] [5214] 4-8-7 **51** ...... MickyFenton 8 21
(B G Powell) *hld up in mid-div: rdn over 3f out: bhd fnl 2f* **33/1**

0-01 **12** 1 ½ **Cankara (IRE)**[30] [518] 4-8-8 **52** ...... DanielTudhope 10 19
(D Carroll) *a bhd: b.b.v* **14/1**

2m 1.67s (-0.95) **Going Correction** -0.15s/f (Stan) **12** Ran SP% **118.5**
Speed ratings (Par 101):98,96,95,94,94 92,91,82,80 79,78
CSF £10.48 CT £85.20 TOTE £3.80: £1.40, £1.50, £4.40; EX 12.30.
Owner Robert Bee **Bred** Darley **Trained** Portway, Worcs

FOCUS
A moderate handicap run in a time 1.12 seconds quicker than the second division and the form looks sound rated around the first two.
Cankara(IRE) Official explanation: jockey said filly bled from the nose

742 PONTIN'S FAMILY HOLIDAYS H'CAP (DIV II) 1m 1f 103y(P)
2:20 (2:20) (Class 6) (0-58,58) 4-Y-0+ **£2,047** (£604; £302) **Stalls** Low

Form RPR

2210 **1** **Mon Petite Amour**[18] [612] 4-8-11 **55** ...... BrettDoyle 3 64
(D W P Arbuthnot) *hld up in tch: rdn over 1f out: led ins fnl f: r.o* **5/1**[2]

-505 **2** ¾ **Cape Of Storms**[55] [266] 4-8-2 **46** ...... HayleyTurner 10 53
(R Brotherton) *t.k.h: chsd ldr: led over 6f out: rdn over 1f out: hdd ins fnl f: nt qckn* **9/1**

1000 **3** 1 ¼ **Desert Hawk**[18] [612] 6-8-9 **53** ow1 ...... (b) NCallan 4 58
(W M Brisbourne) *hld up in mid-div: rdn over 1f out: styd on ins fnl f* **12/1**

210- **4** 1 ¼ **Intavac Boy**[228] [4205] 6-8-13 **57** ...... PaulHanagan 9 59
(R A Fahey) *a.p: rdn and wnt 2nd 2f out: hung lft over 1f out: no ex ins fnl f* **7/1**[3]

-000 **5** 1 **Scroll**[18] [612] 4-8-12 **56** ...... (v) J-PGuillambert 8 56
(P Howling) *hld up and bhd: rdn over 3f out: hdwy wl over 1f out: one pce fnl f* **9/1**

6-31 **6** ½ **Blushing Prince (IRE)**[23] [579] 9-7-13 **50** ...... (t) PatrickDonaghy(7) 1 49
(R C Guest) *hld up towards rr: rdn and hdwy on ins wl over 1f out: fdd wl ins fnl f* **15/2**

24-3 **7** 1 ½ **Tabulate**[23] [579] 4-9-0 **58** ...... JohnEgan 7 54
(P L Gilligan) *hld up in mid-div: hdwy on outside over 3f out: rdn 2f out: sn wknd* **7/1**[3]

2310 **8** ½ **Comeintothespace (IRE)**[10] [665] 5-8-4 **53** ow1 ...... KevinGhunowa(5) 6 48
(R A Farrant) *prom: rdn and ev ch over 2f out: wknd over 1f out* **9/1**

5511 **9** 1 ½ **Postmaster**[16] [637] 5-8-9 **53** ...... RobertHavlin 12 45
(R Ingram) *hld up in rr: sn swtchd lft: rdn over 2f out: no rspnse* **9/2**[1]

0000 **10** *nk* **Crusoe (IRE)**[10] [664] 10-7-9 **46** oh1 ...... (b) SoniaEaton(7) 2 37
(A Sadik) *plld hrd early in rr: no ch whn c wd st* **66/1**

040- **11** 1 **Right Ted (IRE)**[98] [6837] 4-8-10 **54** ...... MickyFenton 11 43
(T Wall) *led 3f: chsd ldr tl over 3f out: wknd over 2f out* **40/1**

00-0 **12** *hd* **Huxley (IRE)**[79] [18] 8-7-10 **47** oh1 ow1 ...... (t) JosephWalsh(7) 5 36
(D J Wintle) *s.s: a in rr* **50/1**

2m 2.79s (0.17) **Going Correction** -0.15s/f (Stan) **12** Ran SP% **115.2**
Speed ratings (Par 101):93,92,91,90,89 88,87,87,85,85 84,84
CSF £47.66 CT £511.65 TOTE £6.30: £2.60, £2.90, £5.30; EX 69.40.
Owner Noel Cronin **Bred** Branston Stud Ltd **Trained** Compton, Berks

FOCUS
A moderate handicap and, with the pace ordinary, the winning time was 1.12 seconds slower than the first division and the race is rated through the runner-up.
Postmaster Official explanation: jockey said he was unable to get the gelding covered up

743 PONTIN'S "BOOK EARLY" (S) STKS 5f 216y(P)
2:55 (2:55) (Class 6) 4-Y-0+ **£2,047** (£604; £302) **Stalls** Low

Form RPR

142 **1** **Magic Amour**[39] [442] 9-8-12 57 ...... (b) KevinGhunowa(5) 4 68
(P A Blockley) *led after 1f: clr over 1f out: r.o wl* **4/1**[2]

0-05 **2** 5 **Bodden Bay**[31] [504] 5-8-12 56 ...... (t) PFredericks 2 47
(Miss Gay Kelleway) *prom: sltly outpcd 2f out: kpt on to take 2nd ins fnl f: no ch w wnr* **4/1**[2]

-500 **3** ½ **Sham Ruby**[39] [442] 5-8-7 40 ...... (t) HayleyTurner 3 40
(M R Bosley) *hld up: sme hdwy over 2f out: rdn over 1f out: one pce fnl f* **50/1**

3314 **4** 1 ¾ **Desert Light (IRE)**[14] [654] 6-9-3 56 ...... (v) NCallan 8 45
(D Shaw) *bhd: rdn over 2f out: hdwy over 1f out: kpt on same pce fnl f* **4/1**[2]

-253 **5** ¾ **Blackheath (IRE)**[7] [688] 11-8-12 68 ...... AdrianTNicholls 11 37
(D Nicholls) *w ldr: ev ch over 2f out: sn rdn: wknd fnl f* **11/4**[1]

-210 **6** 7 **Kitchen Sink (IRE)**[14] [654] 5-9-3 55 ...... (e) SebSanders 10 20
(P J Makin) *hld up: hdwy on outside 3f out: wknd over 1f out* **8/1**[3]

205- **7** ½ **Global Achiever**[246] [3683] 6-8-5 45 ...... (p) MarvinCheung(7) 9 13
(G C H Chung) *hld up: rdn 2f: no ch whn edgd lft over 1f out* **16/1**

030- **8** *nk* **Fairgame Man**[230] [4157] 9-8-5 37 ...... DanielleMcCreery(7) 7 12
(J S Wainwright) *s.i.s: outpcd* **50/1**

5-00 **9** *shd* **Distant Vision (IRE)**[25] [567] 4-8-4 35 ...... PatrickMathers(3) 1 7
(A Berry) *led 1f: wknd over 2f out* **80/1**

3100 **10** ½ **Dark Moon**[27] [555] 4-8-12 52 ...... AdrianMcCarthy 6 11
(D Shaw) *bhd fnl 3f* **16/1**

1m 14.36s (-1.45) **Going Correction** -0.15s/f (Stan) **10** Ran SP% **114.7**
Speed ratings (Par 101):103,96,95,93,92 83,82,81,81,81
CSF £19.94 TOTE £5.70: £1.60, £1.80, £9.90; EX 21.60.There was no bid for the winner. Bodden Bay was claimed by I W McInnes for £6,000.
Owner Joe McCarthy **Bred** Juddmonte Farms **Trained** Lambourn, Berks

FOCUS
An ordinary seller but the time was reasonable and the form looks fairly sound.

744 PONTINSBINGO.COM H'CAP 1m 141y(P)
3:30 (3:31) (Class 5) (0-75,75) 3-Y-0 **£3,886** (£1,156; £577; £288) **Stalls** Low

Form RPR

4220 **1** **Cherri Fosfate**[2] [725] 3-9-0 **71** ...... (b) DanielTudhope 2 77
(D Carroll) *hld up: hdwy on ins over 3f out: led over 1f out: hung rt ins fnl f: drvn out* **10/1**

1305 **2** 1 ¾ **Ella Y Rossa**[24] [577] 3-8-4 **61** oh2 ...... JimmyQuinn 3 63
(P D Evans) *hld up: rdn and hdwy wl over 1f out: wnt 2nd ins fnl f: nt qckn* **28/1**

5550 **3** 1 ¼ **Homes By Woodford**[22] [591] 3-8-5 **67** ...... MichaelJStainton(5) 4 66
(R A Harris) *hld up and bhd: c wd and hdwy over 1f out: kpt on ins fnl f* **18/1**

24-5 **4** 2 **Arena's Dream (USA)**[56] [257] 3-8-12 **69** ...... PaulHanagan 7 64
(R A Fahey) *a.p: rdn over 2f out: one pce* **22/1**

11-3 **5** 2 **Tobago Reef**[60] [216] 3-8-8 **72** ...... (p) KristinStubbs(7) 6 63
(Mrs L Stubbs) *led: hdd over 1f out: wknd ins fnl f* **12/1**

61 **6** 1 **Fantastic Cee (IRE)**[24] [573] 3-9-1 **72** ...... TPQueally 1 61
(J Noseda) *chsd ldr tl rdn 2f out: wknd over 1f out* **4/5**[1]

13 **7** 3 **Still Crazy (IRE)**[18] [624] 3-8-1 **61** ...... LiamJones(3) 5 44+
(E F Vaughan) *plld hrd in rr: short-lived effrt over 1f out: sddle slipped* **7/2**[2]

1 **8** 9 **Rich Lord**[38] [449] 3-9-4 **75** ...... DarrylHolland 8 39
(J D Bethell) *sn prom: wknd 3f out* **9/1**[3]

1m 50.42s (-1.34) **Going Correction** -0.15s/f (Stan) **8** Ran SP% **117.6**
Speed ratings (Par 98):99,97,96,94,92 91,89,81
CSF £237.04 CT £4874.78 TOTE £12.00: £2.50, £3.70, £4.30; EX 182.70.
Owner Document Express Ltd **Bred** The Newchange Syndicate **Trained** Sledmere, E Yorks

FOCUS
A reasonable handicap for the grade run in a time a full second quicker than the following maiden and the form appears pretty sound rated through the placed horses.
Still Crazy(IRE) Official explanation: jockey said saddle slipped
Rich Lord Official explanation: jockey said gelding didn't handle the track

745 PONTIN'S HOLIDAYS MAIDEN STKS 1m 141y(P)
4:05 (4:06) (Class 5) 3-Y-0 **£3,238** (£963; £481; £240) **Stalls** Low

Form RPR

253- **1** **Rabbit Fighter (IRE)**[198] [5114] 3-9-3 89 ...... PaulHanagan 4 77
(P A Blockley) *t.k.h: led 2f: chsd ldr: led over 2f out: rdn over 1f out: r.o* **2/1**[2]

6-32 **2** *hd* **Emerald Wilderness (IRE)**[14] [649] 3-9-3 76 ...... JohnEgan 3 77
(M R Channon) *hld up: hdwy to chse wnr 2f out: sn rdn and ev ch: edgd rt ins fnl f: r.o* **11/10**[1]

22-4 **3** 5 **Snow Dancer (IRE)**[67] [141] 3-8-9 68 ...... PatrickMathers(3) 8 62
(A Berry) *prom: rdn over 2f out: wknd over 1f out* **10/1**

4 3 **Fantastic Morning** 3-9-3 ...... KDarley 7 60
(M Johnston) *s.i.s: rdn and hdwy over 3f out: ev ch over 2f out: wknd wl over 1f out* **11/2**[3]

46 **5** 2 ½ **Snake Hips**[35] [484] 3-9-3 ...... DaleGibson 1 55
(B Palling) *hld up in rr: rdn over 2f out: nvr nr ldrs* **28/1**

2 **6** 1 ¾ **Firebird Annie (IRE)**[18] 619 3-8-12 .... MickyFenton 6 46
(A Bailey) *w ldr: led over 6f out: hdd and n.m.r on ins over 2f out: sn wknd* **25/1**
0 **7** 8 **Danehill Warrior (IRE)**[8] 684 3-8-10 .... MartinGuest(7) 5 34
(R C Guest) *hld up: lost pl over 4f out: bhd fnl 3f* **100/1**
0 **8** shd **Mays Louise**[53] 301 3-8-12 .... J-PGuillambert 2 29
(B P J Baugh) *a bhd* **100/1**

1m 51.42s (-0.34) **Going Correction** -0.15s/f (Stan) **8** Ran SP% **114.7**
Speed ratings (Par 98):95,94,90,87,85 83,76,76
CSF £4.48 TOTE £3.10: £1.20, £1.10, £2.30; EX 6.00.
Owner Market Avenue Racing Club Ltd **Bred** Hawthorn Villa Stud **Trained** Lambourn, Berks

FOCUS
A fair maiden for the track, although the winning time was a full second slower than the previous 61-75 handicap but the form appears reaonably sound rated around the runner-up, sixth and seventh.

746 JOHN BARRAS FOOTBALL CLUB H'CAP 5f 20y(P)
4:40 (4:40) (Class 6) (0-58,57) 4-Y-O+ £2,730 (£806; £403) Stalls Low

Form RPR
0463 **1** **Triskaidekaphobia**[18] 613 4-8-9 **52**..........................(t) DarryllHolland 1 63
(Miss J R Tooth) *mde all: rdn fnl f: r.o* **11/4**[1]
1345 **2** 1 ¼ **Monte Major (IRE)**[14] 654 6-8-13 **56**..................................(v) NCallan 6 62
(D Shaw) *chsd ldr: rdn wl over 1f out: chsd wnr fnl f: kpt on* **9/2**[2]
1623 **3** ¾ **Thoughtsofstardom**[7] 687 4-8-9 **52**.........................(be) HayleyTurner 9 55
(P S McEntee) *mid-div: rdn and hdwy whn swtchd lft over 1f out: kpt on ins fnl f* **7/1**[3]
000- **4** 2 ½ **Ruby's Dream**[203] 4985 5-8-9 **52**......................................(p) BrettDoyle 7 46
(J M Bradley) *a.p: rdn over 1f out: wknd wl ins fnl f* **40/1**
2055 **5** shd **Lady Hopeful (IRE)**[7] 690 5-8-6 **49** ow1..............(b) GrahamGibbons 13 43
(Peter Grayson) *s.i.s: sn swtchd lft: rdn and hdwy over 1f out: nt rch ldrs* **11/1**
650- **6** 1 **Montzando**[179] 5569 4-8-10 **53**.. JimCrowley 4 43
(B R Millman) *towards rr: rdn over 3f out: sme hdwy on ins over 1f out: nvr trbld ldrs* **8/1**
0025 **7** shd **Alistair John**[17] 632 4-8-2 **45**.. JimmyQuinn 10 35
(Mrs G S Rees) *s.i.s: rdn over 1f out: sme late prog* **12/1**
6-20 **8** ¾ **Indian Sundance (IRE)**[23] 580 4-8-4 **47**..................... PaulHanagan 5 34
(R A Fahey) *chsd ldrs tl rdn and wknd over 2f out* **8/1**
05-5 **9** nk **Titian Saga (IRE)**[10] 668 4-8-11 **54**........................ AdrianTNicholls 12 40
(D Nicholls) *chsd ldrs tl wknd over 1f out* **20/1**
0260 **10** hd **Hornpipe**[17] 626 5-9-0 **57**....................................(v) AdrianMcCarthy 11 42
(M S Saunders) *hld up in mid-div: rdn wl over 1f out: sn bhd* **20/1**
1066 **11** 1 ½ **Blushing Russian (IRE)**[7] 690 5-8-5 **48**......................(p) DaleGibson 3 28
(J M Bradley) *hmpd on ins over 3f out: a bhd* **16/1**
50-0 **12** 2 **Cosmic Destiny (IRE)**[18] 613 5-8-9 **52**............................ TPQueally 8 25
(E F Vaughan) *chsd wnr tl wknd over 1f out* **9/1**

61.67 secs (-1.15) **Going Correction** -0.15s/f (Stan) **12** Ran SP% **123.4**
Speed ratings (Par 101):103,101,99,95,95 94,93,92,92,91 89,86
CSF £14.68 CT £83.44 TOTE £4.30: £1.50, £1.90, £2.30; EX 20.50.
Owner Raymond Tooth And Steve Gilbey **Bred** K Bowen **Trained** Lambourn, Berks

FOCUS
A moderate sprint handicap that should prove solid with the placed horses to their recent form.

747 PONTINS.COM APPRENTICE H'CAP 1m 5f 194y(P)
5:10 (5:10) (Class 5) (0-75,75) 4-Y-O+ £3,238 (£963; £481; £240) Stalls Low

Form RPR
-062 **1** **Jack Rolfe**[18] 617 5-9-1 **67**.. WilliamCarson(5) 6 77
(G L Moore) *a.p: wnt 2nd over 5f out: led 3f out: rdn 2f out: styd on wl* **9/2**[2]
2121 **2** 2 ½ **Three Thieves (UAE)**[18] 618 4-9-2 **70**............................ TolleyDean(3) 5 76
(M S Saunders) *hld up and bhd: hdwy over 3f out: chsd wnr 2f out: rdn and edgd lft over 1f out: no imp* **11/4**[1]
0-15 **3** 1 **Theatre Groom (USA)**[18] 617 8-9-7 **68**....................... JamieMoriarty 7 73
(M R Bosley) *hld up towards rr: rdn and hdwy over 2f out: n.m.r on ins briefly 1f out: one pce* **9/1**
005/ **4** ½ **Colophony (USA)**[329] 531 7-8-13 **63**................. RussellKennemore(3) 4 67
(K A Morgan) *hld up in tch: wnt 2nd briefly over 2f out: sn rdn: bmpd over 1f out: no ex fnl f* **25/1**
121- **5** 4 **Sa Nau**[50] 5618 4-8-8 **59**.. TravisBlock 9 57
(T Keddy) *hld up and bhd: outpcd fnl 2f* **11/2**[3]
4022 **6** 3 ½ **Ross Moor**[18] 623 5-9-11 **72**.. DuranFentiman 3 65
(N P Littmoden) *s.i.s: hld up and bhd: rdn over 2f out: sn struggling* **11/4**[1]
5243 **7** 6 **Bay Boy**[10] 669 5-9-11 **75**...(b[1]) PatrickHills(3) 8 60
(M Johnston) *led: clr after 3f: hdd 3f out: sn wknd* **8/1**
0035 **8** 13 **Kalatime (IRE)**[10] 665 4-8-0 **56** oh1.......................... JosephWalsh(5) 2 23
(M F Harris) *chsd ldr tl over 5f out: wknd 3f out* **25/1**

3m 3.21s (-4.16) **Going Correction** -0.15s/f (Stan)
WFA 4 from 5yo+ 4lb **8** Ran SP% **115.7**
Speed ratings (Par 103):105,103,103,102,100 98,95,87
CSF £17.55 CT £103.56 TOTE £5.50: £1.30, £1.30, £2.90; EX 23.90 Place 6 £ 239.96, Place 5 £ 162.24.
Owner Mrs Sarah Diamandis & Mrs Celia Woollett **Bred** W H F Carson **Trained** Woodingdean, E Sussex

FOCUS
A modest handicap restricted to apprentice riders who had not ridden more than 50 winners. The pace was good but the proximity of the out-of-form fourth raises doubts.
T/Plt: £840.40 to a £1 stake. Pool: £68,735.95. 59.70 winning tickets. T/Qpdt: £423.50 to a £1 stake. Pool: £4,693.60. 8.20 winning tickets. KH

[719]KEMPTON (A.W) (R-H)
Saturday, March 24

OFFICIAL GOING: Standard
Wind: Fresh, half-against

750 INTERCASINO.CO.UK H'CAP (DIV I) 6f (P)
1:30 (1:30) (Class 6) (0-60,64) 4-Y-O+ £1,706 (£503; £252) Stalls High

Form RPR
064- **1** **Greenwood**[136] 6395 9-9-0 **58**.. RobertHavlin 8 68
(P G Murphy) *hld up in rr: hdwy fr 2f out: rdn to ld ins fnl f* **6/1**
40-1 **2** 1 ¼ **Wiltshire (IRE)**[27] 562 5-8-9 **53**.................................... MickyFenton 7 59
(P T Midgley) *in rr: hdwy 2f out: kpt on u.p to go 2nd nr fin* **5/1**[3]
3006 **3** nk **Arfinnit (IRE)**[8] 687 6-7-11 **46** oh1..........................(v) WilliamBuick(5) 4 51
(Mrs A L M King) *s.i.s: in rr: rdn and hdwy 2f out: kpt on ins fnl f* **11/1**
0-01 **4** shd **H Harrison (IRE)**[10] 672 7-9-6 **64**.................................. DanielTudhope 3 69
(I W McInnes) *chsd ldr: led over 2f out: rdn and hung lft fr over 1f out: hdd ins fnl f and no ex cl home* **8/1**
20-3 **5** hd **The Grey One (IRE)**[4] 714 4-8-3 **54**......................(p) BarrySavage(7) 9 58+
(J M Bradley) *s.i.s: hdwy on ins over 1f out: kpt on fnl f* **8/1**
0450 **6** ½ **Mulberry Lad (IRE)**[5] 710 5-8-9 **53**...............................(p) JimCrowley 10 56
(P W Hiatt) *mid-div: effrt on ins over 1f out and sn ev ch: nt qckn ins fnl f* **9/2**[2]
4406 **7** nk **Beneking**[27] 560 7-9-0 **58**..(p) ChrisCatlin 5 60
(D Burchell) *in tch on outside: rdn over 2f out: one pce ins fnl f* **4/1**[1]
000- **8** 5 **Miltons Choice**[292] 2284 4-8-13 **57**.. KDarley 2 44
(J M Bradley) *chsd ldrs: rdn and wknd fnl f* **14/1**
40-0 **9** ½ **Fortress**[46] 376 4-8-11 **55**...(b) DarryllHolland 1 40
(E J Alston) *sn led: hdd over 2f out: wknd over 1f out* **20/1**
0000 **10** 12 **Auentraum (GER)**[3] 722 7-8-3 **50** ow1..................(v) SaleemGolam(3) 6 —
(Ms J S Doyle) *in tch tl wknd qckly wl over 1f out: eased* **14/1**

1m 13.41s (-0.29) **Going Correction** -0.05s/f (Stan) **10** Ran SP% **117.8**
Speed ratings (Par 101):99,97,96,96,96 95,95,88,88,72
CSF £36.50 CT £326.07 TOTE £8.20: £2.30, £2.10, £2.90; EX 47.10.
Owner The Golden Anorak Partnership **Bred** Britton House Stud And C Gregson **Trained** East Garston, Berks

FOCUS
Just a moderate affair, the poor third limiting the form. Greenwood was rated to win.

751 INTERCASINO.CO.UK H'CAP (DIV II) 6f (P)
2:00 (2:00) (Class 6) (0-60,59) 4-Y-O+ £1,706 (£503; £252) Stalls High

Form RPR
0-00 **1** **Bobby Rose**[60] 222 4-9-1 **58**.. RobertHavlin 10 68+
(D K Ivory) *mid-div: hdwy 2f out: rdn to ld fnl stride* **9/2**[2]
0-06 **2** shd **Inwaan (IRE)**[28] 548 4-9-1 **58**..(t) DaneO'Neill 7 68+
(P R Webber) *a.p: led appr fnl f: rdn and hdd last stride* **9/2**[2]
-425 **3** 3 **Danish Blues (IRE)**[8] 688 4-8-13 **56**.........................(p) HayleyTurner 4 57
(D E Cantillon) *sn trckd ldr: led 1/2-way: rdn and hdd appr fnl f: nt qckn* **7/2**[1]
000- **4** ½ **North Fleet**[123] 6556 4-8-3 **53**.................................... BarrySavage(7) 3 53
(J M Bradley) *led to 1/2-way: rdn and one pce fnl f* **14/1**
060- **5** 1 **Piccostar**[121] 6572 4-8-13 **59**.................................... NeilChalmers(3) 6 56
(A B Haynes) *mid-div: effrt over 1f out: nt rch ldrs* **14/1**
026- **6** ¾ **Convince (USA)**[143] 6300 6-8-11 **54**...................................(p) KDarley 2 48
(J M Bradley) *in tch: chsd ldrs 1/2-way: one pce fr over 1f out* **11/2**[3]
0540 **7** nk **Hill Of Almhuim (IRE)**[15] 653 4-8-2 **45**..................(v) AdrianMcCarthy 1 38
(Peter Grayson) *in rr: mde sme late hdwy* **14/1**
0446 **8** 5 **The London Gang**[26] 571 4-8-10 **53**...............................(v) ChrisCatlin 8 31
(Miss D A McHale) *a in rr* **8/1**
-000 **9** shd **Atticus Trophies (IRE)**[3] 723 4-8-2 **50**...................(v) WilliamBuick(5) 5 28
(Ms J S Doyle) *outpcd: a bhd* **9/1**
-000 **10** ½ **Globe**[8] 687 4-8-2 **45**.. JamieMackay 9 22
(Mrs H Sweeting) *chsd ldrs tl rdn and wknd sn after 1/2-way* **25/1**

1m 13.18s (-0.52) **Going Correction** -0.05s/f (Stan) **10** Ran SP% **118.9**
Speed ratings (Par 101):101,100,96,96,94 93,93,86,86,86
CSF £25.68 CT £81.60 TOTE £6.60: £2.20, £1.90, £1.50; EX 28.00.
Owner T G N Burrage **Bred** Mrs L R Burrage **Trained** Radlett, Herts
■ Stewards' Enquiry : Barry Savage one-day ban: failed to ride to draw (Apr 4)

FOCUS
Moderate form again, but it was the quicker of the two divisions. Solid-looking form, rated through the fourth.

752 INTERCASINO.CO.UK MAIDEN STKS 6f (P)
2:35 (2:38) (Class 4) 3-Y-O £4,728 (£1,406; £702; £351) Stalls High

Form RPR
6- **1** **Tifernati**[237] 3979 3-9-3 .... TonyCulhane 1 73+
(W J Haggas) *in rr tl hdwy 2f out: rdn and r.o to ld fnl 100yds* **9/2**[2]
650- **2** nk **Tracer**[163] 5915 3-9-3 75... PatDobbs 4 68
(R Hannon) *led: hung lft ins fnl 2f: hdd 100yds out: no ex* **10/1**
3-42 **3** 1 ¼ **Racing Times**[74] 76 3-9-3 75.. IanMongan 7 64
(W J Knight) *outpcd: in rr tl rdn and hdwy over 1f out: styd on strly fnl f: nvr nrr* **4/1**[1]
0- **4** ½ **Take To The Skies (IRE)**[275] 2771 3-9-3 .... TPQueally 10 63+
(A P Jarvis) *mid-div: styd on fnl 2f: nvr nrr* **9/1**
06- **5** hd **Nomoreblondes**[257] 3358 3-8-12 .... MickyFenton 11 57
(P T Midgley) *in tch: ev ch on ins appr fnl f: no ex ins* **33/1**
6 1 ¼ **Poppy's Rose** 3-8-12 .... DanielTudhope 5 53
(I W McInnes) *in tch on outside: one pce appr fnl f* **33/1**
3 **7** nk **Spanish Needle**[26] 567 3-8-12 .... DarryllHolland 2 53
(P R Webber) *wnt lft s: wl bhd: sme hdwy over 1f out: nvr on terms* **9/2**[2]
8 2 **Rhapsilian** 3-8-12 .... RichardThomas 12 47
(J A Geake) *mid-div: rdn 1/2-way: wknd 1f out* **20/1**
-250 **9** hd **Ginger Pop**[33] 502 3-9-3 67.. JamieMackay 3 51
(G G Margarson) *chsd ldr tl rdn and wknd over 1f out* **8/1**[3]
0 **10** ¾ **Clock Face (IRE)**[10] 678 3-8-12 .... HayleyTurner 9 44
(M D I Usher) *chsd ldrs: rdn over 2f out: wknd appr fnl f* **50/1**
0-0 **11** 1 ¼ **Buzbury Rings**[33] 498 3-9-0 .... NeilChalmers(3) 6 45
(A M Balding) *trckd ldrs: rdn over 2f out: sn wknd* **16/1**

1m 14.26s (0.56) **Going Correction** -0.05s/f (Stan) **11** Ran SP% **105.1**
Speed ratings (Par 100):94,93,91,91,91 89,88,86,86,85 83
CSF £35.56 TOTE £5.80: £2.10, £2.50, £1.60; EX 50.00.
Owner Johnny Townsend **Bred** Miss S N Ralphs **Trained** Newmarket, Suffolk
■ Obstructive was withdrawn (5/1, refused to enter stalls.) R4 applies, deduct 15p in the £.

FOCUS
Just an ordinary maiden, but it should produce the odd winner. Tifernati is value for a bit extra, but the runner-up looked to be on a stiffish mark and the form has been rated a bit negatively overall.
Tifernati Official explanation: jockey said gelding jumped right on leaving stalls
Racing Times Official explanation: jockey said gelding hung left
Poppy's Rose Official explanation: jockey said filly hung left
Spanish Needle Official explanation: jockey said filly cocked its jaw as stalls opened

753 PLAY BLACKJACK AT INTERCASINO.CO.UK H'CAP 1m 4f (P)
3:05 (3:06) (Class 5) (0-75,75) 4-Y-O+ £2,914 (£867; £433; £216) Stalls Centre

Form RPR
56-3 **1** **Tromp**[26] 568 6-8-13 **70**.. JimmyQuinn 8 79
(D J Coakley) *chsd ldrs: rdn to ld over 1f out: gng clr whn hung lftn but styd in command* **11/2**[3]
110- **2** 1 ½ **Star Of Canterbury (IRE)**[246] 3704 4-8-8 **67**...................... TPQueally 1 74
(A P Jarvis) *led tl hdd over 1f out: sltly checked in run by wnr but r.o fnl f* **13/2**

200- **3** *1* **Ocean Avenue (IRE)**[190] 5346 8-9-1 **72** .... DarryllHolland 6 77
(C A Horgan) *trckd ldr to over 2f out: styd on fnl f* **7/1**
4-00 **4** *hd* **Dark Planet**[1] 740 4-8-2 **61** oh6 ....(p) RichardThomas 10 66
(D Burchell) *trckd ldrs: kpt on but nt qckn fnl f* **14/1**
03-1 **5** *hd* **Poseidon's Secret (IRE)**[29] 537 4-8-13 **72** .... PaulEddery 5 77
(Pat Eddery) *mid-div: kpt on fnl f but n.d* **4/1**[2]
660- **6** *½* **Free To Air**[120] 6108 4-8-9 **73** ....(p) WilliamBuick[(5)] 9 77
(A M Balding) *mid-division: rdn 4f out: nt pce to chal fnl2 f* **7/2**[1]
10-6 **7** *½* **Prime Powered (IRE)**[23] 593 6-9-4 **75** .... FergusSweeney 4 78
(R M Beckett) *slowly away: hdwy over 3f out: nvr nr to chal* **12/1**
14-0 **8** *3* **Hatch A Plan (IRE)**[23] 594 6-8-9 **66** .... JamieMackay 7 64
(Mouse Hamilton-Fairley) *a towards rr* **20/1**
9 *1 ¾* **Daring Racer (GER)**[202] 4-8-7 **66** .... ChrisCatlin 11 61
(S Dow) *a bhd* **25/1**
0101 **10** *nk* **Competitor**[19] 612 6-8-6 **63** ....(v) SimonWhitworth 2 58
(J Akehurst) *mid-div: wknd 3f out* **12/1**
620- **11** *1 ¼* **Most Definitely (IRE)**[112] 6677 7-9-2 **73** .... DaneO'Neill 3 66
(R M Stronge) *v.s.a: a bhd* **12/1**

2m 35.53s (-1.37) **Going Correction** -0.05s/f (Stan)
WFA 4 from 6yo+ 2lb **11** Ran SP% **121.8**
Speed ratings (Par 103):102,101,100,100,100 99,99,97,96,96 95
CSF £42.82 CT £260.12 TOTE £7.60: £1.90, £2.50, £4.10; EX 51.80.
Owner Chris Van Hoorn **Bred** Miss K Rausing **Trained** West Ilsley, Berks
■ Stewards' Enquiry : Jimmy Quinn one-day ban: careless riding (Apr 4)

FOCUS
They went just a steady pace up front in a race that should produce winners. The form looks sound enough.

754 £600 FREE AT INTERCASINO.CO.UK H'CAP (LONDON MILE QUALIFIER) 1m (P)
3:40 (3:40) (Class 4) (0-85,85) 3-Y-O **£4,728** (£1,406; £702; £351) **Stalls** High

Form RPR
11 **1** **Ten A Penny (USA)**[23] 591 3-8-8 **77** .... DaneO'Neill 6 87+
(J A Osborne) *towards rr but in tch: rdn and hdwy to ld wl ins fnl f: rdn: jst hld on* **4/1**[2]
21- **2** *shd* **Mr Napper Tandy**[147] 6214 3-9-1 **84** .... SamHitchcott 2 93
(M R Channon) *hld up in tch: rdn and hdwy to ld over 1f out: rallied whn hdd wl ins fnl f: jst failed* **9/2**[3]
210- **3** *2* **Karoo Blue (IRE)**[154] 6102 3-9-2 **85** .... DarryllHolland 7 89
(C E Brittain) *in tch: disp ld appr fnl f: nt qckn ins* **12/1**
115- **4** *½* **Bed Fellow (IRE)**[147] 6216 3-9-0 **83** .... TPQueally 3 86+
(A P Jarvis) *hld up: hdwy whn short of room on ins 2f out: swtchd lft and sn short of room again: r.o wl fnl f* **16/1**
4-11 **5** *4* **Hurlingham**[55] 275 3-9-2 **85** .... KDarley 5 79
(M Johnston) *trckd ldrs: rdn over 2f out: wknd over 1f out* **11/8**[1]
513- **6** *¾* **My Learned Friend (IRE)**[181] 5546 3-8-7 **81** .... WilliamBuick[(5)] 1 73
(A M Balding) *t.k.h: trckd ldrs: rdn over 2f out: wknd appr fnl f* **4/1**[2]
132- **7** *5* **Retaliate**[144] 6271 3-8-6 **75** .... JimmyQuinn 8 55
(M Quinn) *led tl hdd & wknd over 1f out* **33/1**

1m 39.12s (-1.68) **Going Correction** -0.05s/f (Stan) **7** Ran SP% **116.8**
Speed ratings (Par 100):106,105,103,103,99 98,93
CSF £23.05 CT £199.29 TOTE £6.00: £2.70, £2.30; EX 31.40.
Owner Lord Blyth And Ten **Bred** Chesapeake Farm, Mary R Odom & W S Farish **Trained** Upper Lambourn, Berks

FOCUS
A really competitive handicap contested by some unexposed types, which should produce its share of winners. A fairly positive view has been taken of the form but the race could have been rated higher still.

755 PLAY ROULETTE AT INTERCASINO.CO.UK H'CAP 6f (P)
4:10 (4:12) (Class 4) (0-85,85) 3-Y-O **£4,728** (£1,406; £702; £351) **Stalls** High

Form RPR
010- **1** **Fontana Amorosa**[161] 5966 3-8-10 **79** .... KDarley 3 83
(K A Ryan) *led for 1f: ld again over 2f out: rdn out fnl f* **5/1**[3]
11-4 **2** *1* **Penny Post (IRE)**[22] 606 3-9-2 **85** .... DarryllHolland 5 86
(M Johnston) *trckd ldrs: outpcd 2f out: styd on to chse wnr ins fnl f* **2/1**[2]
061- **3** *2* **Majestic Cheer**[141] 6324 3-8-7 **76** .... ChrisCatlin 4 71
(M R Channon) *hld up: hdwy to dispute ld over 2f out: rdn: one pce and lost 2nd ins fnl f* **5/1**[3]
034- **4** *hd* **Sparkling Eyes**[122] 6563 3-8-2 **71** .... HayleyTurner 2 65
(C E Brittain) *tokk t.k.h: hld up in rr: r.o ins fnl f* **14/1**
1-21 **5** *1 ¼* **Rocker**[17] 639 3-8-2 **76** .... WilliamBuick[(5)] 1 67
(B R Johnson) *led after 1f: hdd over 2f out: hung lft and then rt: no ch after* **15/8**[1]

1m 14.13s (0.43) **Going Correction** -0.05s/f (Stan) **5** Ran SP% **108.1**
Speed ratings (Par 100):95,93,91,90,89
CSF £14.82 TOTE £7.00: £1.80, £1.50; EX 18.20.
Owner Joy And Valentine Feerick **Bred** Meon Valley Stud **Trained** Hambleton, N Yorks

FOCUS
Three progressive horses dominated, but the race was steadily run and somewhat muddling, so the form is hard to rate too positively.

756 INTERCASINO.CO.UK DRAGONFLY STKS (LISTED RACE) 1m 4f (P)
4:45 (4:46) (Class 1) 4-Y-O+ **£14,762** (£5,595; £2,800; £1,396; £699) **Stalls** Centre

Form RPR
314- **1** **Steppe Dancer (IRE)**[196] 5170 4-9-0 **101** .... EddieAhern 5 98+
(D J Coakley) *t.k.h early: prom: wnt 2nd over 2f out: styd on wl to ld ins fnl f* **2/1**[2]
240- **2** *1 ¼* **Geordieland (FR)**[137] 6392 6-9-2 **110** .... JamieSpencer 2 96
(J A Osborne) *led: rdn over 2f out: hdd and no ex ins fnl f* **8/11**[1]
0/3 **3** *1 ¼* **Dryandra (IRE)**[8] 693 4-8-9 .... KDarley 3 89
(John Joseph Murphy, Ire) *hld up: wnt 3rd 2f out: kpt on but little ch w first 2* **20/1**
4- **4** *2 ½* **Hovering (IRE)**[209] 4851 4-8-9 .... BrettDoyle 1 85
(M G Quinlan) *trckd ldr to 1/2-way: rdn 4f out: one pce ins fnl 3f* **9/1**
1-05 **5** *5* **Bahar Shumaal (IRE)**[56] 264 5-9-2 **96** ....(b) DarryllHolland 4 82
(C E Brittain) *hld up: rapid hdwy to chse ldr 1/2-way: lost 2nd over 2f out: sn wknd* **8/1**[3]

2m 32.33s (-4.57) **Going Correction** -0.05s/f (Stan)
WFA 4 from 5yo+ 2lb **5** Ran SP% **117.1**
Speed ratings (Par 111):113,112,111,109,106
CSF £4.14 TOTE £3.10: £1.40, £1.10; EX 5.40.
Owner Chris Van Hoorn **Bred** Maggiorelli Ice Guarnieri **Trained** West Ilsley, Berks
■ The first running of the event.

FOCUS
An uncompetitive heat in which the form is suspect, with Dryandra being beaten only two and a half lengths, a personal best from her. Steppe Dancer may well be improved again this year but did not prove it here as favourite Geordieland was way below his best.

NOTEBOOK
Steppe Dancer(IRE), a progressive handicapper last season who was not beaten far at this level on his final start, had won his maiden on this surface and the strong support beforehand suggested he had improved enough to make it at Listed level. A strong traveller on the inside, he tacked on to the runner-up turning into the straight, going easily the best, and found what was required under pressure, staying on to win comfortably. It would be unwise to get carried away with this as the runner-up needs further and the third hardly makes the form look solid, but he has clearly done well from three to four and further improvement is entirely possible. (op 7-2)
Geordieland(FR) performed with credit in some big races last season and, although making no show in the Melbourne Cup on his final start, he looked the one to beat in what was an uncompetitive contest. Sent straight into the lead, Spencer attempting to make full use of his guaranteed stamina, he could never shake off Steppe Dancer and was readily outpaced in the end. He will be capable of much better back on turf, over further, but it is highly questionable as to whether he will again be capable of mixing it with the top cup horses. (tchd Evens)
Dryandra(IRE), third off a mark of 75 in a Lingfield handicap latest, stayed on best of the rest for third, doing little for the form, but she seems most effective on Polytrack and ran above herself. (op 14-1)
Hovering(IRE), a useful performer for Jim Bolger in Ireland, faced a tough task on this debut for connections and ran as well as could have been expected. She may not be the easiest to place. (op 8-1 tchd 10-1)
Bahar Shumaal(IRE) is talented on his day, but he had a bit to prove at the trip and used all his gas up when making a rapid move towards the leaders at around the six-furlong pole. (op 13-2 tchd 5-1)

757 BIG JACKPOTS AT INTERCASINO.CO.UK H'CAP 7f (P)
5:15 (5:15) (Class 4) (0-85,83) 4-Y-O+ **£4,728** (£1,406; £702; £351) **Stalls** High

Form RPR
013 **1** **Lethal**[25] 575 4-9-1 **82** .... DarryllHolland 8 96+
(D K Ivory) *mde all: rdn and hld on wl fnl f* **3/1**[2]
22-2 **2** *nk* **Resplendent Nova**[14] 657 5-9-1 **82** .... JimmyQuinn 3 93+
(P Howling) *a in tch: rdn and r.o to go 2nd ins fnl f* **11/4**[1]
4240 **3** *1 ¾* **Sun Catcher (IRE)**[7] 697 4-8-9 **76** ....(b[1]) DaneO'Neill 6 82
(R Hannon) *trckd wnr to over 1f out: rallied and r.o to go 3rd cl home* **5/1**
1311 **4** *nk* **Danetime Lord (IRE)**[19] 614 4-8-8 **75** ....(p) KDarley 7 80
(K A Ryan) *trckd ldrs: wnt 2nd appr fnl f tl fdd fnl 50yds* **4/1**[3]
60-0 **5** *1 ¾* **Guildenstern (IRE)**[25] 575 5-8-5 **79** .... LukeMorris[(7)] 4 80
(P L Gilligan) *mid-div: effrt over 1f out: nt qckn ins fnl f* **20/1**
0600 **6** *1* **Regal Royale**[7] 697 4-8-6 **73** .... AdrianMcCarthy 2 71
(Peter Grayson) *prom tl rdn and one pce fr over 1f out* **25/1**
640- **7** *¾* **Isphahan**[261] 3223 4-8-3 **75** ....(v) WilliamBuick[(5)] 5 71
(A M Balding) *outpcd effrt on ins over 1f out: nvr on terms* **14/1**
330- **8** *¾* **Commando Scott (IRE)**[175] 5677 6-9-2 **83** .... DanielTudhope 9 77
(I W McInnes) *hld up in rr: hdwy 2f out: wknd ent fnl f* **8/1**
-110 **9** *5* **Lii Najma**[22] 609 4-8-2 **69** .... HayleyTurner 1 50
(C E Brittain) *prom on outside tl wknd over 2f out* **16/1**

1m 25.19s (-1.61) **Going Correction** -0.05s/f (Stan) **9** Ran SP% **120.6**
Speed ratings (Par 105):107,106,104,104,102 101,100,99,93
CSF £12.34 CT £40.93 TOTE £5.10: £1.60, £1.50, £2.20; EX 18.40 Place 6 £217.90, Place 5 £43.91.
Owner A S Reid **Bred** A S Reid **Trained** Radlett, Herts

FOCUS
Just an average gallop and Lethal had everything go his way under a fine tactical ride by Holland. The form in behind is solid.
T/Plt: £130.50 to a £1 stake. Pool: £53,923.70. 301.45 winning tickets. T/Qpdt: £49.20 to a £1 stake. Pool: £2,715.70. 40.80 winning tickets. JS

[734]LINGFIELD (L-H)
Saturday, March 24

OFFICIAL GOING: Standard
Some fast times were recorded, but the standard of the runners in the big races far exceeded the usual quality.
Wind: Fresh, against Weather: Overcast

758 DIGITAL PRINTS FROM BONUSPRINT MAIDEN STKS 1m (P)
1:40 (1:43) (Class 5) 3-Y-O+ **£4,857** (£1,445; £722; £360) **Stalls** High

Form RPR
2 **1** **Warm Embraces (IRE)**[25] 573 3-8-8 .... MarcHalford[(3)] 4 74
(D R C Elsworth) *prom: rdn to ld ins fnl f: hld on wl* **11/4**[2]
2 *nk* **Shot Gun** 3-8-11 .... JoeFanning 11 73
(M R Channon) *sn chsng ldr: led over 1f out tl ins fnl f: kpt on wl* **9/1**
6- **3** *3 ½* **Teen Ager (FR)**[268] 3005 3-8-11 .... JohnEgan 5 65
(J S Moore) *plld hrd: sn prom: rdn and nt qckn appr fnl f* **10/1**
4 *1 ¾* **Oh Mary (IRE)** 3-8-6 .... PaulHanagan 1 56
(W J Haggas) *in tch: outpcd over 3f out: kpt on fnl f* **7/1**[3]
5 *¾* **Ganache (IRE)**[34] 5-10-0 .... GeorgeBaker 9 64
(P R Chamings) *bhd: rdn 3f out: nrst fin* **33/1**
4 **6** *nk* **Modern Verse (USA)**[11] 670 4-10-0 .... BrettDoyle 8 64
(G A Swinbank) *reluctant to load: towards rr: rdn 3f out: styd on fnl f* **10/1**
502- **7** *1* **Birkside**[77] 6432 4-10-0 **76** ....(t) NCallan 6 61
(B G Powell) *led tl over 1f out: wknd fnl f* **7/4**[1]
05- **8** *nk* **Lancaster's Quest**[287] 2432 3-8-11 .... SteveDrowne 2 56
(R Ingram) *mid-div: outpcd and dropped to rr over 2f out: n.d after* **16/1**
9 *1* **Prairie Moon** 3-8-6 .... EddieAhern 3 48
(C E Brittain) *chsd ldrs: hmpd over 6f out: sn rdn along: outpcd fnl 3f* **16/1**
0-0 **10** *1* **Winning Smile (USA)**[8] 689 3-7-13 .... MCGeran[(7)] 10 46
(P W Chapple-Hyam) *towards rr: sme hdwy on outside over 3f out: wknd over 2f out* **50/1**

1m 37.63s (-1.80) **Going Correction** -0.10s/f (Stan)
WFA 3 from 4yo+ 17lb **10** Ran SP% **120.4**
Speed ratings (Par 103):105,104,101,99,98 98,97,97,96,95
CSF £29.13 TOTE £3.70: £1.10, £2.30, £4.00; EX 18.30 Trifecta £248.20 Pool: £968.46 - 2.77 winning units..
Owner Gordon Li **Bred** Zapping Syndicate **Trained** Newmarket, Suffolk

FOCUS
The first two home beat routine opponents in a race run at an ordinary pace where it paid to be handy. The form looks solid and should work out.
Teen Ager(FR) Official explanation: jockey said colt ran too free early stages
Ganache(IRE) Official explanation: jockey said gelding was denied a clear run

Modern Verse(USA) Official explanation: jockey said, regarding running and riding, that the gelding was outpaced, ran green and was never travelling well until starting to run on in home straight, adding that it had no more to give in the closing stages and, in his view, would be suited by a longer trip

759 BETDIRECTUK.COM GET INVOLVED H'CAP — 7f (P)

2:10 (2:10) (Class 2) (0-100,104) 4-Y-O+

£15,580 (£4,665; £2,332; £1,167; £582; £292) **Stalls** Low

Form — RPR

2440 **1** — **Red Cape (FR)**[14] 660 4-8-8 **92** .... JohnEgan 9 — 105
(Jane Chapple-Hyam) *chsd ldrs: led over 1f out: rdn and r.o wl* **15/2**

030 **2** *1 1/2* **Yarqus**[23] 599 4-8-2 **85** .... DaleGibson 13 — 95
(C E Brittain) *wd: mid-div: hdwy over 1f out: drvn to take 2nd ins fnl f* **25/1**

-503 **3** *nk* **One More Round (USA)**[14] 660 9-8-9 **93** ....(b) NCallan 10 — 101
(N P Littmoden) *t.k.h towards rr: gd hdwy on outside over 1f out: kpt on u.p fnl f* **12/1**

4414 **4** *1/2* **Gallantry**[14] 657 5-8-3 **87** .... PaulHanagan 7 — 94
(D Shaw) *in tch: rdn over 2f out: kpt on fnl f* **13/2**[2]

-000 **5** *3/4* **Moayed**[14] 658 8-8-2 **89** ....(b) JamesDoyle(3) 6 — 94
(N P Littmoden) *towards rr: swtchd v wd and hdwy over 1f out: nrst fin* **10/1**

102- **6** *shd* **Cross The Line (IRE)**[160] 5990 5-8-6 **90** ow2 .... EddieAhern 4 — 94
(A P Jarvis) *hld up in midfield: shkn up and hdwy over 1f out: styd on steadily* **7/1**[3]

-006 **7** *shd* **Hopeful Purchase (IRE)**[37] 477 4-8-3 **90** ....(p) LiamJones(3) 3 — 94
(W J Haggas) *a.p: no ex fnl f* **14/1**

420- **8** *nk* **Kostar**[189] 5358 6-8-9 **93** .... AdamKirby 1 — 96
(C G Cox) *a.p: hld whn n.m.r fnl f* **11/2**[1]

-360 **9** *shd* **Hail The Chief**[14] 658 10-8-8 **92** .... RichardHughes 8 — 95
(R Hannon) *chsd ldrs: led briefly ent st: no ex fnl f* **20/1**

014- **10** *1/2* **Mina A Salem**[84] 6986 5-8-4 **88** .... NickyMackay 5 — 90
(C E Brittain) *s.s: towards rr: swtchd rt over 1f out: unable to chal* **8/1**

3000 **11** *1 3/4* **Uhoomagoo**[14] 656 9-8-2 **86** ....(b) CatherineGannon 11 — 83
(K A Ryan) *s.i.s: bhd: rdn over 2f out: n.d* **20/1**

-032 **12** *3/4* **Secret Night**[23] 590 4-8-2 **85** .... JoeFanning 2 — 81
(J A R Toller) *mid-div: no imp whn hmpd on rail over 1f out* **8/1**

31-3 **13** *1 1/2* **King's Caprice**[14] 656 6-8-13 **104** ....(t) HaddenFrost(7) 12 — 95
(J A Geake) *racd freely: led tl wknd ent st* **10/1**

1m 23.2s (-2.69) **Going Correction** -0.10s/f (Stan) — **13** Ran SP% **121.1**
Speed ratings (Par 109):111,109,108,108,107 107,107,106,106,106 104,103,101
CSF £188.06 CT £1447.56 TOTE £9.40: £3.60, £7.60, £4.40; EX 205.10 TRIFECTA Not won..
Owner Franconson Partners **Bred** G And Mrs Forien **Trained** Newmarket, Suffolk

FOCUS

A competitive handicap, run at a strong gallop thanks to the free-running King's Caprice, and a good time. Solid form which should prove reliable.

NOTEBOOK

Red Cape(FR) appreciated the return to seven furlongs, and all three of his victories have now been over this trip. Always in an ideal position, he found plenty when asked, and was a convincing winner. (op 8-1 tchd 9-1 and 7-1 in places)

Yarqus was poorly drawn and, in the circumstances, did well over a shorter trip than usual. Fairly handicapped on the All-Weather, he is capable of taking advantage if reproducing this effort.

One More Round(USA) came home well, but he wins rarely and was again only battling for the places. (op 10-1)

Gallantry is running off a stiff mark at present, so this was a solid effort on a surface which suits him well. (op 7-1)

Moayed, with the blinkers back on, put in some good late work - especially in view of the fact that he had to come round all his rivals in the home straight. This was a fine effort, but he does not win often enough these days to inspire confidence.

Cross The Line(IRE) ◆, off the track for five months, and with his rider putting up overweight, caught the eye with a promising staying-on effort along the rail. He should improve enough to have a real chance of victory next time out. (op 8-1)

Hopeful Purchase(IRE), who has been running in Dubai, wore cheekpieces for the first time and had no problem with the pace over this shorter trip. He is becoming well handicapped and seems to be coming back to form. (tchd 16-1)

Kostar was always close up, but he looked beaten on merit when being tightened up in the final furlong. Though he often runs well fresh, this first outing for six months should set him up nicely for a summer campaign. (op 5-1)

Hail The Chief, reported by the vet to be lame here a fortnight ago, bounced back well. Not beaten far, he proved he can still put in a good show. (op 22-1)

Mina A Salem had been off since December, and will prove more effective back over a mile, where he is able to race more prominently than this. (op 12-1)

King's Caprice was too keen on the way to post and in the race itself, so ended up beating himself. (tchd 9-1)

760 BETDIRECTUK.COM SPRING CUP (LISTED RACE) — 7f (P)

2:40 (2:42) (Class 1) 3-Y-O

£42,585 (£16,140; £8,077; £4,027; £2,017; £1,012) **Stalls** Low

Form — RPR

121- **1** — **Hinton Admiral**[154] 6096 3-9-3 103 .... J-PGuillambert 3 — 105
(M Johnston) *mde all: qcknd clr 2f out: drvn to hold on fnl f* **7/2**[2]

11-3 **2** *3/4* **Hurricane Spirit (IRE)**[70] 118 3-9-1 102 .... BrettDoyle 9 — 101+
(J R Best) *wd: mid-div: rdn and hdwy over 1f out: r.o to chse wnr ins fnl f: clsd steadily: a hld* **11/4**[1]

104- **3** *1/2* **Evens And Odds (IRE)**[175] 5681 3-9-1 90 .... NCallan 6 — 100+
(K A Ryan) *sn towards rr: rdn over 2f out: styd on strly fnl f* **12/1**

1-21 **4** *nk* **Mastership (IRE)**[45] 385 3-9-1 96 ....(b) EddieAhern 12 — 99
(C E Brittain) *hld up in rr: swtchd outside and gd hdwy over 1f out: kpt on fnl f* **11/2**[3]

121- **5** *1/2* **Beauchamp Viceroy**[85] 6978 3-9-1 92 .... NickyMackay 13 — 98
(G A Butler) *hld up towards rr: effrt and swtchd wd over 1f out: gd late hdwy* **50/1**

12-2 **6** *1 3/4* **Fares (IRE)**[70] 113 3-9-1 87 ....(b) RichardHughes 10 — 93
(C E Brittain) *t.k.h: chsd ldrs: rdn and one pce appr fnl f* **16/1**

050- **7** *nk* **Fishforcompliments**[159] 6010 3-9-1 105 .... PaulHanagan 4 — 92+
(R A Fahey) *s.i.s: sn in tch: rdn and no imp fnl 3f* **20/1**

-112 **8** *3/4* **Si Foo (USA)**[45] 385 3-9-1 88 .... LPKeniry 1 — 90
(A M Balding) *chsd ldrs: hrd rdn over 1f out: wknd fnl f* **33/1**

110- **9** *3/4* **Big Timer (USA)**[161] 5983 3-9-5 104 .... TomEaves 5 — 92
(I Semple) *t.k.h: prom tl wknd 1f out* **6/1**

223- **10** *1* **Aahayson**[176] 5655 3-9-1 89 .... PatCosgrave 2 — 86
(K R Burke) *plld hrd: chsd ldrs: outpcd over 2f out: sn btn* **66/1**

102- **11** *1/2* **Valdan (IRE)**[198] 5140 3-9-1 92 .... SteveDrowne 8 — 84
(P D Evans) *s.i.s: bhd: rdn over 2f out: n.d* **40/1**

111- **12** *3/4* **Cesc**[106] 6746 3-9-1 92 .... SebSanders 7 — 82
(P J Makin) *midfield and wd: clsd on ldrs over 3f out: wknd over 1f out* **11/1**

110- **13** *7* **Stevie Gee (IRE)**[175] 5681 3-9-3 100 .... JamieSpencer 11 — 66
(G A Swinbank) *sn in midfield on rail: rdn over 3f out: wknd over 2f out* **11/1**

1m 23.21s (-2.68) **Going Correction** -0.10s/f (Stan) — **13** Ran SP% **122.4**
Speed ratings (Par 106):111,110,109,109,108 106,106,105,104,103 102,102,94
CSF £13.29 TOTE £5.00: £1.90, £1.50, £3.60; EX 19.10 Trifecta £302.30 Pool: £1,196.69 - 2.81 winning units..
Owner Gainsborough **Bred** Gainsborough Stud Management Ltd **Trained** Middleham Moor, N Yorks
■ This win secured the All-Weather trainers' championship for Mark Johnston.

FOCUS

A hot race, but the winner dictated an unremarkable tempo, and his sudden move approaching the home straight was perhaps the deciding factor. However, the time was good and he did best of the prominent racers, with the next four home all late closers. Strong form.

NOTEBOOK

Hinton Admiral dictated the tempo and effectively won the race with a well-executed move entering the final bend, at which point the runner-up was trapped behind other horses. That said, he did everything asked of him, and responded well to the whip when it was needed in the last 150 yards. (op 11-2)

Hurricane Spirit(IRE) did not have the run of the race, being stuck wide all the way from a poor draw and then having to switch even wider to launch his run in the home straight. He was a shade unlucky not to catch the winner, but will be a force to be reckoned with when switched back to turf if he can keep up his recent improvement on sand. (op 3-1 tchd 10-3 in places)

Evens And Odds(IRE) made a fine start to his All-Weather career, getting the trip well and suggesting that he should stay a mile. Already proven on turf, he should have a good season if connections can find the right races, with his 2000 Guineas entry showing he is well-regarded.

Mastership(IRE) did pretty well in a better race than usual, though his hold-up style meant he had to come around the houses to make his run. Nonetheless, he more than held his own in this valuable contest, and remains in good form. (op 7-2)

Beauchamp Viceroy was stepping up in grade, and ran out of his skin considering that he had to come so wide to make his effort. There was no fluke about this, and he looks to have improved since his last appearance three months ago.

Fares(IRE) ran a solid race, but was safely held in the final furlong. He is in good form at present, with the blinkers continuing to bring out the best in him, but needs to find even more to land a race at this level. (op 20-1)

Fishforcompliments is entered for the 2000 Guineas and showed his ability when fifth in the Champagne Stakes, which in theory meant he was the horse to beat here on official ratings. However, his starting price was a better reflection of his chance, and he did pretty well without suggesting he is destined for great things. (op 25-1 tchd 33-1)

Si Foo(USA) went well for a long way against these smart opponents, but was forced to concede defeat in the final furlong.

Big Timer(USA) was unbeaten in three runs last season until flopping on dirt in the USA in October. He clearly retains plenty of pace, and did his best overcome a Group 3 penalty, only to be run out of the places late in the day. (op 11-2)

Cesc Official explanation: jockey said colt lost its action closing stages

761 BETDIRECT WINTER DERBY (3RD LEG OF THE EUROPEAN ALL WEATHER SERIES) (GROUP 3) — 1m 2f (P)

3:15 (3:15) (Class 1) 4-Y-O+

£56,780 (£21,520; £10,770; £5,370; £2,690; £675) **Stalls** Low

Form — RPR

1-11 **1** — **Gentleman's Deal (IRE)**[48] 352 6-9-0 108 .... PaulMulrennan 4 — 106
(M W Easterby) *set slow pce 4f: trckd ldrs: rdn to ld again jst ins fnl f: hld on gamely* **4/1**[1]

5-20 **2** *nk* **Grand Passion (IRE)**[28] 552 7-9-0 100 .... SteveDrowne 2 — 105
(G Wragg) *hld up towards rr: rdn and r.o wl fnl 2f: nt quite rch wnr* **25/1**

02-1 **3** *nk* **Illustrious Blue**[43] 413 4-9-0 .... PaulDoe 9 — 105
(W J Knight) *hld up in midfield: wnt prom 3f out: led briefly 1f out: kpt on u.p* **11/1**

1113 **4** *shd* **Mighty**[28] 552 4-9-0 100 .... JohnEgan 12 — 105
(Jane Chapple-Hyam) *w ldr 3f: settled in tch: outpcd over 2f out: rallied to press ldrs fnl f: kpt on* **10/1**

22-2 **5** *nk* **Blue Bajan (IRE)**[28] 552 5-9-0 104 .... MichaelHills 1 — 104
(Andrew Turnell) *prom: rdn to chal over 1f out: nt qckn ins fnl f* **4/1**[1]

0000 **6** *1/2* **Boo**[7] 701 5-9-0 ....(v) NCallan 8 — 103?
(K R Burke) *t.k.h in midfield: rdn and kpt on fnl 2f* **100/1**

-650 **6** *dht* **Cimyla (IRE)**[29] 541 6-9-0 .... GeorgeBaker 6 — 103
(C F Wall) *hmpd sn after s: hld up in rr: rdn and hdwy over 1f out: kpt on* **10/1**

4441 **8** *nk* **Orchard Supreme**[14] 658 4-9-0 98 .... RichardHughes 5 — 102
(R Hannon) *hld up in rr: rdn and r.o fnl 2f: nt rch ldrs* **20/1**

-221 **9** *nk* **Cusoon**[28] 552 5-9-0 104 .... JimmyFortune 3 — 102+
(G L Moore) *towards rr: hmpd bnd after 1f: effrt and chopped off 3f out and over 2f out: hdwy over 1f out: no imp fnl f* **8/1**[3]

0433 **10** *1 1/2* **Hattan (IRE)**[29] 545 5-9-0 .... SebSanders 10 — 99
(C E Brittain) *chsd ldrs: slt ld 5f out tl over 2f out: btn whn n.m.r over 1f out* **9/1**

301- **11** *1 1/2* **Alfie Flits**[140] 6334 5-9-0 114 .... JamieSpencer 7 — 96
(G A Swinbank) *t.k.h towards rr: hdwy to ld after 4f: hdd 5f out: led over 2f out tl wknd qckly 1f out* **9/2**[2]

035 **12** *shd* **Speedy Sam**[14] 658 4-9-0 95 .... PatCosgrave 11 — 96
(K R Burke) *prom: n.m.r and rdn after 4f: wknd over 2f out* **28/1**

2m 4.57s (-3.22) **Going Correction** -0.10s/f (Stan) — **12** Ran SP% **118.9**
Speed ratings (Par 113):108,107,107,107,107 106,106,106,106,105 103,103
CSF £111.38 TOTE £4.80: £2.00, £4.60, £4.20; EX 115.30 Trifecta £1572.20 Pool: £26,640.30 - 12.03 winning units..
Owner Stephen J Curtis **Bred** C H Wacker Iii **Trained** Sheriff Hutton, N Yorks
■ Stewards' Enquiry : John Egan two-day ban: careless riding (Apr 3-4)

FOCUS

A typically classy line-up for this highlight of the All-Weather season, although last year's winner and ante-post favourite Sri Diamond was ruled out through injury, but the pace was poor for the first half-mile and not much better after that until the final three furlongs, leading to a bunched finish. None of the first three matched their pre-race figures and the bare form is unlikely to prove reliable. However, the quality of the runners produced a decent time.

NOTEBOOK

Gentleman's Deal(IRE), a late developer, has hit a rich vein of form and kept up the good work with a battling victory. A big, strong horse, he doubles up as a stallion, and advertised his services here in no uncertain terms. He now goes to the Lincoln provided the ground is not too soft, and would be really well handicapped if able to reproduce his recent improvement on the All-Weather. (tchd 9-2 in places)

Grand Passion(IRE) was second in this race last year, and put a moderate effort in this season's Winter Derby Trial behind him with a strong finish that nearly came off. The winner proved too hard to get past, but at least he showed he was back to form, with this course and distance suiting ideally. (op 33-1)

Illustrious Blue, a winner on turf in Dubai last month, is effective on Polytrack and again put in an excellent performance even though he has yet to score in four attempts on the surface. He will have to aim higher this year, but his recent improvement can make him a worthy contender in valuable events during the summer. (op 10-1 tchd 12-1)

Mighty has done really well of late over this course and distance, and reversed Winter Derby Trial form with both Blue Bajan and Cusoon with another good performance. Despite losing his place when the tempo increased, he battled back gamely and might have gone even closer with an end-to-end gallop. (op 12-1)

Blue Bajan(IRE) was one of four or five with a live chance entering the final furlong, so had every chance of justifying favouritism. Though just unable to finish things off, he was only just beaten in a scrambling finish and - like several of his opponents - he was unsuited by the early dawdle. He may run in the Lincoln now. (op 9-2)

Boo ran remarkably well, but was probably flattered, with the early crawl failing to sort the field out and producing a blanket finish. However, he ran well in this race last season, when finishing eighth, so should not be underestimated. (tchd 9-1 and 11-1)

Cimyla(IRE) has been running on turf in Dubai, but this surface suits him particularly well these days. A confirmed hold-up performer, he does not need a strong pace, but is usually more effective when the tempo is better than it was here. (tchd 9-1 and 11-1)

Orchard Supreme travelled well off the pace, but needed a stronger tempo to get him there in time. However, he was not beaten far and still looks in good nick. (tchd 16-1)

Cusoon would have appreciated a better gallop, but in any case he had a nightmare run along the rail, being hampered three times. With the second and third of these incidents occurring just before then home turn, he can be considered to have run as well as could be expected. He was later named All-Weather Horse of the Year by readers of the Racing Post. (tchd 9-1)

Hattan(IRE) helped to improve the early crawl a little, but he is best known as a mile-and-a-half horse and was easily brushed aside in the final sprint. (op 10-1)

Alfie Flits is probably best over a solidly run mile and a half, and his attempt to make a better pace of it after the first half-mile was unconvincing. Though turning for home in pole position, he faded tamely when headed, making this a disappointing first attempt on an All-Weather surface, but he is much better than he looked here and should not be underestimated back in a more suitable race. (tchd 5-1 in places)

Speedy Sam is a decent performer, and has run with credit in Dubai recently, but his limitations were exposed in this company. (op 33-1)

762 32RED.COM HEVER SPRINT STKS (LISTED RACE) 5f (P)

3:50 (3:50) (Class 1) 4-Y-0+

£17,034 (£6,456; £3,231; £1,611; £807; £405) **Stalls** High

Form			Horse	RPR
01-1	**1**		**King Orchisios (IRE)**[28] 551 4-9-3 101 .... (p) NCallan 9 (K A Ryan) *chsd ldr: rdn to ld ins fnl f: hld on wl* **6/1**[3]	114
2-30	**2**	*½*	**Bonus (IRE)**[37] 470 7-9-0 .... (t) NickyMackay 2 (G A Butler) *mid-div: hdwy over 1f out: r.o to press wnr fnl 50 yds: jst hld* **14/1**	109
-000	**3**	*shd*	**Strike Up The Band**[29] 547 4-9-3 100 .... AdrianTNicholls 7 (D Nicholls) *led tl ins fnl f: kpt on same pce* **20/1**	112
0222	**4**	*¾*	**Maltese Falcon**[35] 490 7-9-0 104 .... (t) EddieAhern 10 (P F I Cole) *chsd ldrs: hrd rdn over 1f out: one pce* **9/1**	106
043-	**5**	*nk*	**Fyodor (IRE)**[221] 4461 6-9-0 103 .... TonyCulhane 4 (W J Haggas) *hld up in rr and settled wl off the pce: nt clr run over 1f out: rdn and r.o wl fnl f* **4/1**[2]	105+
-120	**6**	*nk*	**Woodnook**[14] 656 4-8-9 95 .... JohnEgan 1 (J A R Toller) *chsd ldrs tl no ex fnl f* **12/1**	99
3532	**7**	*nk*	**Qadar (IRE)**[14] 660 5-9-0 100 .... (v[1]) IanMongan 8 (N P Littmoden) *dwlt: towards rr: effrt and hrd rdn over 1f out: nt pce to chal* **12/1**	103
4366	**8**	*¾*	**Celtic Mill**[29] 547 9-9-3 100 .... (p) TomEaves 3 (D W Barker) *in tch: rdn over 2f out: no ex appr fnl f* **16/1**	103
0-00	**9**	*¾*	**Excusez Moi (USA)**[23] 597 5-9-0 .... SebSanders 5 (C E Brittain) *towards rr: mod effrt on outside ent st: unable to chal* **8/1**	97
20-1	**10**	*hd*	**Border Music**[14] 656 6-9-3 105 .... (b) RichardHughes 6 (A M Balding) *hld up in midfield: shkn up and lost pl over 1f out* **2/1**[1]	100

57.87 secs (-1.91) **Going Correction** -0.10s/f (Stan) **10** Ran SP% **121.4**

Speed ratings (Par 111):111,110,110,108,108 107,107,106,105,104

CSF £89.83 TOTE £6.60: £1.80, £4.70, £4.70; EX 130.90 Trifecta £1021.40 Part won. Pool: £1,438.68 - 0.68 winning units..

Owner Mr & Mrs Julian And Rosie Richer **Bred** Rathbarry Stud **Trained** Hambleton, N Yorks

■ First leg of a double for Neil Callan, who is champion jockey on the All-Weather for the fourth time.

FOCUS

A high-quality sprint, run at a decent pace, and the entire field covered by just four lengths at the finish. The form is well up to the grade and looks pretty solid.

NOTEBOOK

King Orchisios(IRE), effective at both five and six furlongs, soon overcame the wide draw and, though unable to lead this time, was happy enough in second place until forging ahead 200 yards from home. Though proving again that he enjoys the surface, he won on grass last season too and will start the turf season in prime form, but connections say he needs fast ground. (op 5-1)

Bonus(IRE) has only ever won at six and seven furlongs, and this was a fine effort considering the winner came into the race in top form. He has been lightly campaigned in recent seasons, but still looks capable of winning races at the age of seven. (op 16-1)

Strike Up The Band did not show much in three recent races in Dubai, but he saw his race out well here after setting a decent gallop. While showing he handles Polytrack well, he also gave notice that he will pay his way on turf during the course of the coming season. (op 16-1)

Maltese Falcon could never get to the front from his outside draw, but ran another good race, this time against Listed opponents. He has turned into a most reliable performer around this track. (op 7-1 tchd 13-2)

Fyodor(IRE) ◆, second in this race last year to the subsequent dual Group One winner Les Arcs, had been off the track since last August. However, this was an eyecatching reappearance, in which he came home in good style after being given plenty to do. He looks capable of landing a valuable sprint this season. (op 13-2)

Woodnook is better at six furlongs, and used herself up by chasing the early gallop. However, she ran well enough to give cause for optimism back over an extra furlong. (op 16-1)

Qadar(IRE), with a visor replacing the blinkers, is capable of a decent show at this trip, but six furlongs probably suits him slightly better, and on this occasion things were always happening a little too quickly for him. (tchd 14-1)

Celtic Mill, the winner of 16 races, including five on the All-Weather, is not quite at his best at present. However, he is showing enough to suggest a revival is possible. (op 12-1)

Excusez Moi(USA), out of form in Dubai recently, had not yet proved himself effective on sand. Though hinting he might yet do better on the surface, he was stuck wide from halfway and that meant he could not make a significant impact. (op 15-2)

Border Music travelled surprisingly well despite the drop to the minimum trip, over which he had never run before. Not knocked about when beaten, he should do much better when returned to six or seven furlongs. (op 3-1)

763 BONUSPRINT.COM H'CAP 1m 4f (P)

4:20 (4:21) (Class 2) (0-100,95) 4-Y-0+ **£12,464** (£3,732; £1,866; £934; £466) Stalls Low

Form			Horse	RPR
0-21	**1**		**Kames Park (IRE)**[7] 698 5-8-13 90 .... TomEaves 5 (I Semple) *hld up in rr in slowly-run r: hdwy on outside to ld ent st: rdn clr: edgd lft: readily* **5/2**[2]	98
000-	**2**	*3*	**Kings Quay**[38] 4098 5-9-1 92 .... (t) GrahamGibbons 4 (J J Quinn) *trckd ldng pair: mainly 2nd fnl 3f: nt pce of wnr appr fnl f* **5/1**[3]	95
33-1	**3**	*1 ½*	**Royal Jet**[49] 345 5-9-3 94 .... JohnEgan 1 (M R Channon) *hld up in 4th: hmpd bnd after 3f: swtchd rt 3f out: nt clr rn and snatched up on bnd into st: sn btn* **5/4**[1]	98+
050-	**4**	*1*	**Invention (USA)**[189] 5376 4-8-11 90 .... PaulDoe 2 (W J Knight) *led 1f: trckd ldr: led 3f out and sn qcknd tempo: hdd and easily outpcd by wnr ent st* **14/1**	89
665-	**5**	*8*	**Midas Way**[28] 6334 7-9-4 95 .... JimCrowley 3 (P R Chamings) *led after 1f and set slow pce: rdn and hdd 3f out: sn bhd* **7/1**	81

2m 35.33s (0.94) **Going Correction** -0.10s/f (Stan)

WFA 4 from 5yo+ 2lb **5** Ran SP% **108.8**

Speed ratings (Par 109):92,90,89,88,83

CSF £14.34 TOTE £3.10: £1.40, £1.80; EX 15.20.

Owner Mrs June Delaney **Bred** Pat Beirne **Trained** Carluke, S Lanarks

FOCUS

A mixed bunch, a weak tempo, but a progressive winner who once again overcame the lack of pace to score well. The form is dubious, though.

NOTEBOOK

Kames Park(IRE) had no problem with the small drop in trip, even though the pace was poor and spo theoretically not ideal for his running style. When it came to the business end, he had much the best speed once again, and he continues to look progressive. (op 9-4 tchd 15-8)

Kings Quay, a fair hurdler, still runs the odd good race on the Flat too but he has not won since August 2004. This was a longer trip on the level than usual and, though staying the trip well enough, he was no match for the winner. (op 9-2 tchd 4-1)

Royal Jet found an extraordinary amount of trouble in running considering the small field. He is higher in the weights these days, but can do better than this off his new mark. (op 11-8 tchd 13-8)

Invention(USA), having his first run since leaving John Gosden for 32,000gns and subsequently being gelded, made an uninspiring All-Weather debut, though the weak pace would not have suited him. His form tailed off after a ten-furlong maiden win last season, and this was his first attempt at a mile and a half, but he needs to improve to justify his price tag. (op 12-1 tchd 10-1)

Midas Way, who has been hurdling, has not won on the Flat since June 2003, and in a tactical race he was beaten with alarming alacrity on surrendering the lead. (op 9-1 tchd 10-1)

764 BETDIRECTPOKER.COM MAIDEN STKS 1m 2f (P)

4:50 (4:51) (Class 4) 3-Y-0 **£6,477** (£1,927; £963; £481) **Stalls** Low

Form			Horse	RPR
	1		**Pippa Greene** 3-9-3 .... NCallan 7 (P F I Cole) *chsd ldng pair: led wl over 1f out: hrd rdn and re-joined by runner-up fnl f: hung rt nr fin: all out* **9/1**[3]	85+
	2	*nk*	**Old Etonian (UAE)** 3-9-3 .... JoeFanning 4 (M Johnston) *broke wl: led tl wl over 1f out: drvn bk level w wnr 100 yds out: nt qckn nr fin* **6/4**[2]	84+
	3	*4*	**Guardian Of Truth (IRE)** 3-9-3 .... PaulDoe 2 (W J Knight) *chsd ldrs: outpcd over 2f out: disputing 4th and btn whn hmpd over 1f out: kpt on fnl f* **33/1**	80+
05-	**4**	*nk*	**Best Selection**[94] 6886 3-8-12 .... LPKeniry 6 (A P Jarvis) *in tch: rdn along 4f out: styd on same pce fnl 3f* **33/1**	71
50-2	**5**	*nk*	**Morning Farewell**[26] 569 3-9-3 75 .... JimmyFortune 9 (P W Chapple-Hyam) *a.p: 3rd and btn whn edgd lft over 1f out* **11/8**[1]	75
	6	*2 ½*	**Hesivorthedriver (GER)** 3-9-3 .... JimCrowley 5 (Mrs A J Perrett) *s.s: bhd: rdn 3f out: nvr rchd ldrs* **28/1**	71+
0-	**7**	*5*	**Lindhoven (USA)**[165] 5882 3-9-3 .... SebSanders 3 (C E Brittain) *rdn and n.d fnl 4f* **25/1**	61
	8	*1 ¼*	**Penang (IRE)** 3-8-12 .... RichardHughes 1 (C E Brittain) *a towards rr: rdn and lost tch 3f out* **16/1**	54
0	**9**	*2 ½*	**Yes One (IRE)**[25] 573 3-9-3 .... MichaelHills 8 (J W Hills) *wd: mid-div: effrt 3f out: wknd 2f out* **12/1**	54

2m 5.29s (-2.50) **Going Correction** -0.10s/f (Stan) **9** Ran SP% **118.9**

Speed ratings (Par 100):106,105,102,102,102 100,96,95,93

CSF £23.01 TOTE £11.00: £2.10, £1.50, £5.80; EX 29.90 Trifecta £299.50 Pool: £725.70 - 1.72 winning units..

Owner R A H Evans **Bred** D And Mrs V Fleet **Trained** Whatcombe, Oxon

FOCUS

The time compared favourably with the Winter Derby, but that race was run at a weaker tempo. This looked a decent maiden, and the form should work out with the first four all likely to rate higher.

Yes One(IRE) Official explanation: jockey said colt had no more to give

765 32RED.COM H'CAP 1m (P)

5:20 (5:20) (Class 4) (0-85,83) 4-Y-0+ **£6,477** (£1,927; £963; £481) **Stalls** High

Form			Horse	RPR
-211	**1**		**Lopinot (IRE)**[23] 592 4-8-9 76 .... SebSanders 2 (P J Makin) *dwlt: hld up in tch: effrt 2f out: r.o to ld ins fnl f: rdn clr: edgd lft: readily* **7/4**[1]	90+
216-	**2**	*1 ½*	**Fann (USA)**[284] 2533 4-8-3 77 .... WilliamCarson(7) 9 (C E Brittain) *prom: led over 2f out tl ins fnl f: kpt on: nt pce of wnr* **20/1**	83
0	**3**	*nk*	**Quai Du Roi (IRE)**[14] 657 5-8-10 77 .... NCallan 3 (K A Ryan) *v.s.a: sn rcvrd: hld up in rr: rdn and hdwy on outside fnl 3f: fin wl* **11/2**[3]	82+
2226	**4**	*1*	**Katiypour (IRE)**[25] 576 10-8-13 80 .... MichaelHills 11 (P Mitchell) *t.k.h: stdd in midfield: rdn and styd on fnl 2f: nvr nrr* **9/2**[2]	83
050-	**5**	*¾*	**Paraguay (USA)**[83] 6997 4-8-11 78 .... EdwardCreighton 10 (Miss V Haigh) *cl up: jnd ldr over 2f out: no ex ins fnl f* **20/1**	79
-110	**6**	*1*	**Bold Diktator**[15] 652 5-8-10 77 .... JimCrowley 8 (Tom Dascombe) *set modest pce: led tl over 2f out: sn outpcd* **7/1**	76
30-6	**7**	*hd*	**Magic Rush**[74] 81 5-8-5 79 .... KylieManser(7) 5 (Mrs Norma Pook) *t.k.h in midfield: rdn to chse ldrs 2f out: no ex over 1f out* **25/1**	77
100-	**8**	*2*	**Music Note (IRE)**[210] 4805 4-9-2 83 .... JohnEgan 1 (Miss Gay Kelleway) *plld hrd towards rr: rdn and n.d fnl 3f* **9/1**	77
106-	**9**	*2*	**Lucayan Dancer**[199] 5115 7-8-9 83 .... AdeleRothery(7) 4 (D Nicholls) *stdd s: hld up in rr: rdn 3f out: sn bhd* **25/1**	72
00-0	**10**	*½*	**San Antonio**[70] 119 7-9-0 81 .... (b) MickyFenton 7 (Mrs P Sly) *prom tl wknd over 2f out* **14/1**	69

1m 38.68s (-0.75) **Going Correction** -0.10s/f (Stan) **10** Ran SP% **116.3**

Speed ratings (Par 105):99,97,97,96,95 94,94,92,90,89

CSF £45.84 CT £164.03 TOTE £2.60: £1.60, £5.90, £2.20; EX 26.50 Trifecta £104.30 Pool: £543.73 - 3.70 winning units. Place 6 £1,127.18, Place 5 £457.59.

Owner Exors of the late R A Bernard **Bred** G And Mrs Middlebrook **Trained** Ogbourne Maisey, Wilts

FOCUS

A routine handicap, but with a progressive winner. The pace was poor for the first quarter-mile, and only ordinary after that until the final three furlongs, so the form might not prove that solid.

T/Plt: £663.00 to a £1 stake. Pool: £118,357.95. 130.30 winning tickets. T/Qpdt: £37.70 to a £1 stake. Pool: £6,619.30. 129.70 winning tickets. LM

741 WOLVERHAMPTON (A.W) (L-H)

Saturday, March 24

OFFICIAL GOING: Standard to fast

Wind: Fresh, against Weather: Overcast

766 PHOTO BOOKS FROM BONUSPRINT.COM CLAIMING STKS 5f 216y(P)

7:00 (7:00) (Class 6) 4-Y-0+ £2,730 (£806; £403) Stalls Low

Form RPR

421 1 **Magic Amour**[1] 743 9-8-2 57 (v) KevinGhunowa(5) 7 68
(P A Blockley) *chsd ldrs: led over 2f out: rdn clr over 1f out* **15/8**[1]

3400 2 2 **Mistral Sky**[10] 673 8-9-0 63 (v) TPQueally 2 69
(Stef Liddiard) *chsd ldr: led over 4f out: hdd 1/2-way: n.m.r and outpcd over 2f out: rallied to chse wnr fnl f: styd on same pce* **8/1**

5022 3 1 1/2 **El Potro**[9] 680 5-8-9 49 ChrisCatlin 1 59
(J R Holt) *chsd ldrs: outpcd over 2f out: styd on u.p appr fnl f* **14/1**

5110 4 hd **Blythe Spirit**[15] 654 8-8-7 56 (v) PaulHanagan 3 56
(R A Fahey) *sn pushed along in rr: hmpd over 3f out: hdwy u.p over 1f out: nt trble ldrs* **10/1**

-350 5 1 3/4 **Le Chiffre (IRE)**[5] 710 5-9-3 62 (b) PaulMulrennan 6 61
(K R Burke) *led: hdd over 4f out: led 1/2-way: sn hdd: wknd fnl f* **20/1**

0252 6 2 1/2 **Cleveland**[9] 686 5-9-2 63 RussellKennemore(5) 9 57
(R Hollinshead) *chsd ldrs: hung rt fr 1/2-way: wknd 2f out* **9/2**[3]

5513 7 nk **Quiet Times (IRE)**[5] 710 8-9-7 82 (b) CatherineGannon 4 56
(K A Ryan) *s.s: outpcd: rdn and nt clr run over 1f out: n.d* **5/2**[2]

00-0 8 5 **Tapsalteerie**[5] 710 4-8-2 30 DaleGibson 5 21
(M W Easterby) *sn outpcd* **100/1**

-556 9 4 **Native Title**[29] 536 9-9-3 68 AdrianTNicholls 8 23
(D Nicholls) *s.s: hdwy over 3f out: rdn over 1f out: sn wknd and eased* **33/1**

1m 14.06s (-1.75) **Going Correction** -0.15s/f (Stan) 9 Ran SP% **117.1**

Speed ratings (Par 101):105,102,100,100,97 94,94,87,82

CSF £17.94 TOTE £4.50: £1.20, £3.00, £2.70; EX 52.80.

Owner Joe McCarthy **Bred** Juddmonte Farms **Trained** Lambourn, Berks

FOCUS

An ordinary claimer in which Magic Amour notched his second course-and-distance win in two days, being rated to the same level both times. The form is weakened by Quiet Times blowing the start.

Le Chiffre(IRE) Official explanation: vet said gelding bled from the nose

Cleveland Official explanation: jockey said gelding hung right in home straight

Native Title Official explanation: jockey said gelding lost its action and hung right

767 PONTIN'S HOLIDAYS H'CAP 1m 4f 50y(P)

7:30 (7:31) (Class 6) (0-60,60) 4-Y-0+ £2,730 (£806; £403) Stalls Low

Form RPR

324- 1 **Carlton Scroop (FR)**[111] 4777 4-9-0 **58** (b) PaulEddery 2 69+
(J Jay) *trckd ldrs: racd keenly: rdn over 3f out: n.m.r over 2f out: r.o u.p to ld wl ins fnl f* **10/1**

0403 2 1 1/2 **Buscador (USA)**[1] 741 8-8-12 **57** LiamJones(3) 10 64
(W M Brisbourne) *led: rdn over 1f out: hdd wl ins fnl f* **8/1**

16-4 3 nk **Escoffier**[73] 88 5-8-10 **57** DuranFentiman(5) 9 64
(G F Bridgwater) *hld up in tch: rdn over 4f out: n.m.r and lost pl over 2f out: rallied over 1f out: r.o* **14/1**

-000 4 shd **Birthday Star (IRE)**[19] 610 5-9-2 **58** TPQueally 3 66+
(W J Musson) *hld up: nt clr run over 2f out: hdwy over 1f out: nt rch ldrs* **4/1**[1]

-000 5 shd **Choristar**[19] 623 6-9-0 **56** DaleGibson 8 62
(J Mackie) *hld up: hdwy over 3f out: chsd ldr over 2f out: rdn and hung rt fnl f: no ex* **7/1**

6-62 6 2 **Regency Red (IRE)**[31] 514 9-9-0 **56** PaulHanagan 6 59
(W M Brisbourne) *hld up: hdwy u.p over 1f out: styd on same pce fnl f* **10/1**

05-3 7 1 **Missie Baileys**[17] 634 5-9-1 **57** IanMongan 12 58
(Mrs L J Mongan) *sn trcking ldr: rdn over 3f out: wknd ins fnl f* **9/1**

-061 8 2 **Zalkani (IRE)**[17] 634 7-9-4 **60** JimmyQuinn 1 58
(J Pearce) *prom: rdn over 1f out: wknd ins fnl f* **11/2**[3]

000- 9 3 **Mayadeen (IRE)**[159] 6008 5-9-4 **60** TomEaves 4 53
(I Semple) *hld up: rdn and wknd over 3f out* **9/2**[2]

-200 10 5 **Little Richard (IRE)**[18] 631 8-9-3 **59** (p) AdamKirby 7 44
(M Wellings) *hld up: rdn 1/2-way: a in rr* **16/1**

-005 11 5 **Activist**[2] 730 9-8-6 **55** (v[1]) KellyHarrison(7) 11 32
(D Carroll) *s.i.s: hdwy over 10f out: rdn and hung lft over 3f out: sn wknd* **16/1**

03/0 12 11 **Dawn At Sea**[19] 618 5-8-12 **57** JerryO'Dwyer(3) 5 17
(Mrs K Waldron) *hmpd s: hld up: rdn and wknd 4f out* **80/1**

2m 39.35s (-3.07) **Going Correction** -0.15s/f (Stan)

WFA 4 from 5yo+ 2lb 12 Ran SP% **125.0**

Speed ratings (Par 101):104,103,102,102,102 101,100,99,97,94 90,83

CSF £92.64 CT £1148.01 TOTE £18.30: £4.10, £5.10, £4.10; EX 208.40.

Owner David Fremel and Mrs Sylvia Jay **Bred** J Jay **Trained** Newmarket, Suffolk

FOCUS

An ordinary handicap in which Carlton Scroop rates a bit better than the bare form. The runner-up ran up to his mark from the day before.

Mayadeen(IRE) Official explanation: jockey said gelding hung left-handed throughout

768 BONUSPRINT.COM (S) STKS 1m 141y(P)

8:00 (8:03) (Class 6) 4-Y-0+ £2,047 (£604; £302) Stalls Low

Form RPR

4-44 1 **Sawwaah (IRE)**[11] 664 10-8-12 50 (v) AdrianTNicholls 7 62
(D Nicholls) *hld up: hdwy 2f out: led ins fnl f: sn clr* **7/1**

2U01 2 3 1/2 **The City Kid (IRE)**[19] 620 4-8-13 64 (b) PaulDoe 5 56
(S Dow) *hld up: hdwy 1/2-way: chsd wnr and hung lft over 1f out: styd on same pce* **11/2**[3]

6020 3 1 1/4 **Windy Prospect**[27] 561 5-8-12 55 (p) PaulHanagan 4 52
(P A Blockley) *hld up: hdwy over 2f out: nt clr run ins fnl f: kpt on* **4/1**[2]

-650 4 1/2 **Following Flow (USA)**[22] 605 5-8-12 55 (p) GrahamGibbons 11 51
(R Hollinshead) *s.i.s: sn pushed along in rr: hdwy over 1f out: nrst fin* **9/1**

0500 5 shd **Merdiff**[4] 715 8-8-9 42 LiamJones(3) 1 51
(W M Brisbourne) *hld up: hdwy over 1f out: nt rch ldrs* **11/1**

0-06 6 1 **Shannon Arms (USA)**[37] 466 6-8-12 42 (p) JosedeSouza 9 49
(R Brotherton) *led: rdn over 1f out: hdd & wknd ins fnl f* **20/1**

0460 7 2 **Bathwick Emma (IRE)**[11] 666 4-8-10 45 (b[1]) JamesDoyle(3) 6 45
(M A Doyle) *chsd ldr tl rdn and n.m.r over 1f out: sn wknd* **20/1**

4100 8 3/4 **Paso Doble**[15] 650 9-9-4 57 (p) TomEaves 3 49
(R Bastiman) *chsd ldrs: wkng whn n.m.r 2f out* **8/1**

1033 9 1 1/4 **Climate (IRE)**[10] 674 8-8-13 64 (b) RussellKennemore(5) 8 46
(R Hollinshead) *trckd ldrs: racd keenly: rdn over 2f out: wknd over 1f out* **9/4**[1]

52/0 10 10 **Fire At Will**[18] 630 5-8-12 52 HayleyTurner 13 19
(A W Carroll) *prom 5f* **25/1**

05-0 11 14 **Chicherova (IRE)**[62] 204 4-8-2 40 DuranFentiman(5) 12 —
(W M Brisbourne) *hld up: rdn 1/2-way: sn wknd* **66/1**

1m 50.15s (-1.61) **Going Correction** -0.15s/f (Stan) 11 Ran SP% **123.0**

Speed ratings (Par 101):101,97,96,96,96 95,93,92,91,82 70

CSF £45.40 TOTE £7.70: £3.10, £2.10, £1.60; EX 22.50.There was no bid for the winner. Following Flow was claimed by David Doughty for £6,000. The City Kid was claimed by Andrew Page for £6,000.

Owner Mrs Alex Nicholls **Bred** Shadwell Estate Company Limited **Trained** Sessay, N Yorks

FOCUS

An ordinary seller, the form weakened by the favourite's poor effort. The winner was still 10lb+ off even his form of late last year with the fifth and sixth setting the standard.

769 PONTINSBINGO.COM MAIDEN STKS 1m 1f 103y(P)

8:30 (8:31) (Class 5) 3-Y-0+ £2,817 (£838; £418; £209) Stalls Low

Form RPR

2 1 **Multicultural**[35] 492 4-10-0 PatCosgrave 6 66
(D M Simcock) *a.p: rdn to chse ldr 2f out: styd on to ld post* **4/9**[1]

2 shd **Ninetyninetreble (IRE)** 4-10-0 AdrianTNicholls 13 66
(D Nicholls) *s.i.s: rcvrd to ld over 8f out: rdn over 1f out: sn hung lft: hdd post* **11/1**

0-5 3 5 **Broughtons Revival**[22] 602 5-9-2 AlanRutter(7) 12 51+
(W J Musson) *s.i.s: hld up: hdwy over 1f out: nvr nr to chal* **14/1**

4 nk **Imperial Amber**[53] 5-9-6 JerryO'Dwyer(3) 2 50
(Karen George) *s.i.s: hld up: styd on u.p fnl f: nvr nrr* **66/1**

0/2- 5 1/2 **Kintbury Cross**[403] 409 5-10-0 72 AdamKirby 1 54
(P D Cundell) *hld 1f: chsd ldr tl rdn over 2f out: wknd over 1f out* **5/1**[2]

6 nk **Blue Bird's Dream** 4-10-0 JimmyQuinn 8 54
(E J Alston) *prom: racd keenly: rdn over 2f out: sn wknd* **33/1**

0- 7 1 1/2 **Sir Duke (IRE)**[177] 5640 3-8-9 DarryllHolland 3 46
(P W D'Arcy) *prom: rdn 1/2-way: outpcd 3f out: hung rt and lft over 1f out: n.d after* **7/1**[3]

8 nk **Vila Velha (IRE)** 4-9-11 EmmettStack(3) 7 50
(Ms Caroline Hutchinson, Ire) *s.i.s: hld up: rdn over 3f out: n.d* **50/1**

60 9 4 **David's Cavalier**[36] 484 3-8-4 RussellKennemore(5) 10 37
(R Hollinshead) *prom 7f* **33/1**

0 10 5 **Miss Wolf**[29] 537 7-9-9 PaulEddery 4 27
(G H Jones) *s.i.s: hld up: plld hrd: n.d* **50/1**

11 7 **Irish Secret (CZE)** 3-8-6 NeilChalmers(3) 9 13
(G J Smith) *s.i.s: hld up: a in rr* **50/1**

0-0 12 3/4 **Vital Tryst**[10] 678 3-8-9 TPQueally 11 12
(J G Given) *mid-div effrt over 3f out: wknd over 2f out* **66/1**

2m 1.82s (-0.80) **Going Correction** -0.15s/f (Stan)

WFA 3 from 4yo+ 19lb 12 Ran SP% **128.2**

Speed ratings (Par 103):97,96,92,92,91 91,90,89,86,81 75,75

CSF £7.83 TOTE £1.40: £1.10, £3.10, £3.70; EX 10.80.

Owner Tick Tock Partnership **Bred** Genesis Green Stud Ltd **Trained** Newmarket, Suffolk

FOCUS

The first two finished clear in this moderate maiden, in which the runner-up set a steady pace. Multicultural probably didn't run up to his debut effort, with the fourth, sixth and eighth holding down the form. The first two are probably better than this.

770 GO PONTIN'S H'CAP 1m 141y(P)

9:00 (9:00) (Class 5) 4-Y-0+ £3,071 (£906; £453) Stalls Low

Form RPR

21-0 1 **Esthlos (FR)**[10] 675 4-9-1 **69** ChrisCatlin 4 78
(J Jay) *chsd ldr: led over 3f out: rdn over 1f out: styd on* **11/2**

6221 2 1 **Harare**[10] 675 6-8-13 **70** (v) JamesDoyle(3) 1 77+
(R J Price) *hld up: hdwy over 1f out: hung lft and r.o ins fnl f: nt rch wnr* **5/2**[1]

2503 3 nk **Activity (IRE)**[10] 675 8-8-8 **67** DuranFentiman(5) 7 73
(M J Gingell) *hld up in tch: racd keenly: chsd wnr over 1f out: sn rdn: styd on* **11/2**

5034 4 3/4 **Golden Spectrum (IRE)**[15] 650 8-8-1 **60** (b) TolleyDean(5) 5 64
(R A Harris) *s.i.s: hld up: hdwy over 2f out: rdn over 1f out: styd on* **11/1**

6352 5 7 **Prince Dayjur (USA)**[10] 673 8-9-3 **71** JimmyQuinn 9 61
(J Pearce) *hld up in tch: rdn 1/2-way: wknd over 2f out* **5/1**[3]

0200 6 1/2 **Mine The Balance (IRE)**[2] 732 4-8-3 **57** (t) PaulHanagan 2 46
(H J Manners) *chsd ldrs 6f* **28/1**

4-62 7 2 **High Ambition**[64] 186 4-8-7 **61** ow1 DarryllHolland 8 45
(P W D'Arcy) *prom: led over 5f out: rdn and hdd over 3f out: wknd over 1f out* **14/1**

2125 8 5 **Linda's Colin (IRE)**[7] 697 5-8-11 **65** PatCosgrave 6 39
(K R Burke) *hld up: hdwy over 2f out: rdn and wknd over 1f out* **7/2**[2]

0-00 9 1 1/4 **Polonius**[18] 629 6-8-13 **70** NeilChalmers(3) 3 41
(G J Smith) *led 3f: rdn and wknd 2f out* **66/1**

1m 49.78s (-1.98) **Going Correction** -0.15s/f (Stan) 9 Ran SP% **118.2**

Speed ratings (Par 103):102,101,100,100,93 93,91,87,86

CSF £20.15 CT £81.28 TOTE £8.70: £2.60, £2.10, £2.30; EX 32.10.

Owner Ms Medina Jessop **Bred** J Jay **Trained** Newmarket, Suffolk

FOCUS

An ordinary handicap in which the form looks sound with the winner, third and fourth, who met here ten days ago, all close to form.

Prince Dayjur(USA) Official explanation: jockey said gelding ran flat

Linda's Colin(IRE) Official explanation: vet said gelding bled from the nose

771 PONTIN'S FAMILY HOLIDAYS H'CAP 7f 32y(P)

9:30 (9:31) (Class 5) (0-75,74) 4-Y-0+ £3,238 (£963; £481; £240) Stalls High

Form RPR

2011 1 **Kabis Amigos**[10] 673 5-8-12 **70** (t) AdrianTNicholls 6 80
(D Nicholls) *mde all: rdn over 1f out: r.o* **2/1**[1]

0-00 **2** *1* **Local Poet**[10] 672 6-8-11 **69**.................................(b) TomEaves 2 76
(I Semple) *chsd wnr 2f: wnt 2nd again over 2f out: sn rdn: styd on* **9/1**
6540 **3** *3/4* **Marko Jadeo (IRE)**[19] 614 9-8-11 **74**...................... TolleyDean(5) 8 79
(R A Harris) *s.i.s: hld up: hdwy u.p 2f out: styd on* **12/1**
4212 **4** *2 1/2* **Dapple Dawn (IRE)**[23] 592 4-9-2 **74**...................... DanielTudhope 7 73
(D Carroll) *prom: rdn over 2f out: hung lft over 1f out: no ex* **9/4**[2]
240- **5** *shd* **She's Our Lass (IRE)**[168] 5810 6-8-13 **71**...................... DarryllHolland 1 69
(D Carroll) *hld up: bhd 4f out: r.o ins fnl f: nrst fin* **11/2**[3]
2103 **6** *2* **Flying Bantam (IRE)**[10] 673 6-8-5 **63**...........................(p) PaulHanagan 5 56
(R A Fahey) *prom: chsd wnr 5f out tl rdn over 2f out: wknd over 1f out* **7/1**
00-0 **7** *8* **Royal Envoy (IRE)**[10] 673 4-8-11 **69**...................... JimmyQuinn 4 41
(D Shaw) *hld up: rdn over 2f out: wknd over 1f out* **33/1**
1m 29.11s (-1.29) **Going Correction** -0.15s/f (Stan) 7 Ran SP% **112.6**
Speed ratings (Par 103):101,99,99,96,96 93,84
CSF £19.89 CT £168.83 TOTE £3.30: £2.10, £3.10; EX 36.70 Place 6 £133.31, Place 5 £61.37.
Owner GGN Bloodstock Ltd and Ian W Glenton **Bred** Cheveley Park Stud Ltd **Trained** Sessay, N Yorks
■ Stewards' Enquiry : Darryll Holland seven-day ban (originally banned 14 days under Rule 157): in breach of Rule 158 (Apr 11-18). Carroll fined £2,200.
FOCUS
Kabis Amigos completed a quick course-and-distance hat-trick but did not have to run to his best here with the placed horses setting the level. She's Our Lass ran an eyecatching race in fifth.
She's Our Lass(IRE) Official explanation: jockey said, regarding running and riding, that he had no orders other than ride her as you find her, adding that she moved scratchily early on and only picked up turning into straight, finishing well; trainer added that he felt she would improve for the run
T/Plt: £315.60 to a £1 stake. Pool: £78,705.30. 182.00 winning tickets. T/Qpdt: £14.00 to a £1 stake. Pool: £3,501.70. 185.00 winning tickets. CR

750 KEMPTON (A.W) (R-H)
Sunday, March 25

OFFICIAL GOING: Standard
Wind: Moderate across

772 KEMPTON FOR FAMILY FUN DAYS MEDIAN AUCTION MAIDEN STKS 1m 3f (P)
2:20 (2:20) (Class 6) 3-Y-O **£2,047** (£604; £302) **Stalls High**

Form RPR
322- **1** **Fongs Gazelle**[160] 6007 3-8-12 70...................................... JoeFanning 1 71+
(M Johnston) *trckd ldr: led over 2f out and hung lft: rdn out fnl f* **11/8**[1]
43 **2** *1 1/2* **Shawhill**[29] 553 3-8-9 .... JerryO'Dwyer(3) 2 68
(A M Hales) *racd in 3rd but in tch: rdn over 3f out: styd on to chse wnr over 1f out but no imp: jst hld on for 2nd* **10/3**[3]
6420 **3** *shd* **Title Deed (USA)**[4] 719 3-9-3 74...............................(v[1]) JamieSpencer 3 73
(A P Jarvis) *led tl hdd over 2f out: short of room and sn swtchd lft: lost 2nd over 1f out: rallied ins fnl f* **6/4**[2]
2m 21.45s (-1.23) **Going Correction** -0.025s/f (Stan) 3 Ran SP% **105.2**
Speed ratings (Par 96):103,101,101
CSF £5.33 TOTE £1.80; EX 3.40.
Owner Around The World Partnership **Bred** Miss S N Ralphs **Trained** Middleham Moor, N Yorks
FOCUS
Just a modest maiden but truly-run despite the small field and the winner close to last year's nursery form.

773 BOOK NOW FOR EASTER SATURDAY H'CAP 1m (P)
2:50 (2:50) (Class 5) (0-70,72) 4-Y-0+ **£2,914** (£867; £433; £216) **Stalls High**

Form RPR
4223 **1** **Binnion Bay (IRE)**[2] 739 6-8-7 **61**...............................(b) MarcHalford(3) 2 69
(J J Bridger) *s.i.s: sn in tch: struck on hd by other rdr's whip over 2f out: led over 1f out: rdn out* **11/2**
0053 **2** *1 1/2* **Magic Warrior**[24] 594 7-9-1 **66**...................................... PatDobbs 6 71
(J C Fox) *hld up: hdwy and swtchd rt over 2f out: rdn to go 2nd 1f out: no imp on wnr ins fnl f* **5/1**[3]
2151 **3** *1* **Parkview Love (USA)**[2] 739 6-9-0 **72** 6ex.................(v) PatrickHills(7) 5 74
(D Shaw) *led tl rdn and hdd over 1f out: kpt on one pce fnl f* **2/1**[2]
460- **4** *1* **Charlie Bear**[179] 5621 6-8-3 **54**...................................... AdrianMcCarthy 1 54
(Miss Z C Davison) *in rr tl hdwy 2f out: kpt on fnl f: nvr nr to chal* **16/1**
0-26 **5** *shd* **Sun Bian**[28] 559 5-7-13 **55** oh3 ow2...................... KevinGhunowa(5) 7 55?
(L P Grassick) *chsd ldr on ins: rdn over 1f out: one pce fnl f* **25/1**
-112 **6** *1/2* **Spot The Subbie (IRE)**[43] 422 4-9-2 **67**...................... IanMongan 3 66
(Jamie Poulton) *racd wd in tch: rdn 1/2-way: sn outpcd and nvr on terms after* **6/4**[1]
14-0 **7** *hd* **Networker**[16] 650 4-8-11 **62**...................................... TonyCulhane 4 60
(P J McBride) *t.k.h: prom on outside: effrt over 2f out: no hdwy after* **12/1**
1m 39.62s (-1.18) **Going Correction** -0.025s/f (Stan) 7 Ran SP% **122.8**
Speed ratings (Par 103):104,102,101,100,100 99,99
CSF £35.75 TOTE £5.80: £2.50, £2.20; EX 28.40.
Owner J J Bridger **Bred** Fieldspring Ltd **Trained** Liphook, Hants
FOCUS
A modest handicap run at a steady early pace; the form is not strong and unlikely to prove reliable.

774 PANORAMIC BAR & RESTAURANT H'CAP 6f (P)
3:20 (3:21) (Class 5) (0-75,75) 4-Y-0+ **£2,914** (£867; £433; £216) **Stalls High**

Form RPR
3155 **1** **Cool Sands (IRE)**[5] 717 5-8-1 **67**...............................(v) PatrickHills(7) 7 75
(D Shaw) *led after 2f: rdn clr over 2f out: wknd ins fnl f: jst hld on* **11/2**[3]
-020 **2** *shd* **Effective**[5] 717 7-8-12 **71**...................................... JamieSpencer 6 79
(A P Jarvis) *led after 1f: hdd 4f out: rdn over 1f out: cl rapidly on wnr ins fnl f: jst failed* **11/1**
2201 **3** *hd* **Sir Douglas**[20] 621 4-8-13 **72**...................................... JimCrowley 8 79
(R A Harris) *plld hrd in rr: hdwy on ins over 2f out: r.o strly u.p to cl fast on first 2 fnl f* **9/2**[1]
-026 **4** *3/4* **Nepro (IRE)**[11] 672 5-8-11 **70**...............................(t) DarryllHolland 9 75
(E J Creighton) *mid-div: hdwy over 2f out: r.o one pce fnl f* **8/1**
000- **5** *1/2* **Norcroft**[142] 6326 5-8-3 **65**...............................(p) JamesDoyle(3) 3 69
(Mrs C A Dunnett) *racd wd: hdwy fr 2f out: nvr nrr* **20/1**
1-23 **6** *shd* **Morse (IRE)**[56] 277 6-8-13 **75**...................... RichardKingscote(3) 2 78
(J A Osborne) *led for 1f: rdn and wknd appr fnl f* **5/1**[2]
40-4 **7** *1/2* **Russian Rocket (IRE)**[67] 163 5-8-13 **72**...................... IanMongan 10 74
(Mrs C A Dunnett) *t.k.h: prom: tl rdn and one pce fnl f* **8/1**
0-61 **8** *2* **Cornus**[32] 513 5-8-13 **72**...............................(be) SteveDrowne 5 68
(A J McCabe) *in rr and nvr on terms* **8/1**
6-23 **9** *1/2* **Inch By Inch**[36] 486 8-8-11 **73**...............................(b) AmirQuinn(3) 1 67
(P J Makin) *mid-div tl rdn and wknd over 1f out* **14/1**
0-01 **10** *3 1/2* **Romany Nights (IRE)**[56] 276 7-8-13 **72**...............................(bt) JohnEgan 4 56
(Miss Gay Kelleway) *a in rr* **6/1**
1m 12.32s (-1.38) **Going Correction** -0.025s/f (Stan) **10** Ran SP% **117.6**
Speed ratings (Par 103):108,107,107,106,105 105,105,102,101,97
CSF £64.97 CT £297.35 TOTE £6.00: £1.90, £4.10, £2.10; EX 69.00.
Owner Peter Swann **Bred** Rathasker Stud **Trained** Danethorpe, Notts
FOCUS
An ordinary handicap, stolen by the winner to a certain extent, but the form makes sense with the next three to form.
Inch By Inch Official explanation: jockey said mare ran flat
Romany Nights(IRE) Official explanation: jockey said gelding was never travelling

775 KEMPTON.CO.UK H'CAP 2m (P)
3:50 (3:51) (Class 6) (0-65,65) 4-Y-0+ **£2,047** (£604; £302) **Stalls High**

Form RPR
4045 **1** **Salut Saint Cloud**[18] 640 6-9-8 **61**...............................(p) SimonWhitworth 12 75
(G L Moore) *trckd ldr: led over 2f out: sn clr: readily* **5/1**[2]
20 **2** *4* **Galantos (GER)**[45] 389 6-9-1 **54**...................................... GeorgeBaker 9 63
(G L Moore) *hld up towards rr: hdwy 4f out: styd on to chse wnr fnl f* **7/2**[1]
5-33 **3** *nk* **Sand Repeal (IRE)**[19] 631 5-9-9 **62**...............................(v) BrettDoyle 8 71
(Miss J Feilden) *trckd ldr: rdn over 4f out: outpcd by wnr over 2f out and lost 2nd 1f out: kpt on* **13/2**[3]
464- **4** *1 1/4* **Rajayoga**[86] 6979 6-8-0 **46** oh1...................................... PatrickHills(7) 4 53
(M H Tompkins) *trckd ldrs: outpcd over 2f out: styd on appr fnl f* **14/1**
520- **5** *1 3/4* **Rose Bien**[167] 5875 5-9-7 **60**...............................(p) EdwardCreighton 1 65
(P J McBride) *t.k.h in rr: styd on past btn horses ins fnl 2f* **9/1**
04- **6** *nk* **Phoenix Hill (IRE)**[22] 6256 5-9-5 **58**...................................... SteveDrowne 10 63
(D R Gandolfo) *hld up in rr: mde sme late hdwy* **16/1**
45-0 **7** *shd* **Love Angel (USA)**[49] 354 5-8-10 **52**...................................... AmirQuinn(3) 6 57
(J J Bridger) *in rr: mde sme late hdwy* **16/1**
6-05 **8** *2* **Hathaal (IRE)**[73] 100 8-9-0 **60**...............................(vt) SCreighton(7) 3 62
(E J Creighton) *bhd: hdwy 5f out: wknd fr 2f out* **50/1**
000 **9** *6* **Tres Bien**[57] 265 5-8-7 **46** oh1...................................... ChrisCatlin 11 41
(P R Webber) *mid-div: wknd 2f out* **16/1**
204- **10** *3/4* **Irish Whispers (IRE)**[110] 4758 4-9-1 **59**...................................... MichaelHills 5 53
(B G Powell) *stdd s: a in rr* **8/1**
3212 **11** *nk* **Blue Hills**[10] 683 6-9-12 **65**...............................(b) JimCrowley 14 59
(P W Hiatt) *led tl hdd over 2f out: wknd steadily* **7/1**
0-00 **12** *3/4* **Orphir (IRE)**[70] 134 4-8-2 **46** oh1...................................... AdrianMcCarthy 7 39
(Mrs N Macauley) *mid-div tl wknd 3f out* **100/1**
-235 **13** *3 1/2* **Compton Express**[20] 615 4-8-2 **46** oh1...................................... JimmyQuinn 2 35
(Jamie Poulton) *mid-div tl rdn and wknd 3f out* **8/1**
0-60 **14** *35* **Versatile**[34] 499 4-9-2 **60**...................................... OscarUrbina 13 7
(G A Ham) *trckd eladers tl lost pl 4f out: eased over 1f out: t.o:* **40/1**
3m 30.54s (-0.86) **Going Correction** -0.025s/f (Stan)
WFA 4 from 5yo+ 5lb 14 Ran SP% **126.6**
Speed ratings (Par 101):101,99,98,98,97 97,97,96,93,92 92,92,90,73
CSF £23.96 CT £121.80 TOTE £9.00: £2.80, £2.10, £2.50; EX 25.40.
Owner A Grinter **Bred** Mill House Stud **Trained** Woodingdean, E Sussex
FOCUS
Moderate form but sound enough rated through the runner-up, fifth and sixth.
Compton Express Official explanation: jockey said filly had no more to give
Versatile Official explanation: trainer said gelding was found to have breathing problems after the race

776 RUBBING HOUSE STEAKS CLAIMING STKS 1m 2f (P)
4:20 (4:21) (Class 6) 3-Y-O **£2,047** (£604; £302) **Stalls High**

Form RPR
1210 **1** **Sweet World**[9] 694 3-9-2 62...................................... JamieSpencer 1 64+
(A P Jarvis) *hld up in last pl: rapid hdwy to ld 3f out: pushed out fnl f: comf* **5/2**[2]
342- **2** *1* **Right Option (IRE)**[106] 6768 3-8-13 59...................................... DarryllHolland 3 59
(S Dow) *trckd ldrs: rdn to chse wnr fnl f* **3/1**[3]
356 **3** *2 1/2* **Picky**[20] 611 3-8-5 60...................................... SophieDoyle(7) 2 53
(J A Osborne) *set stdy pce: rdn and hdd 3f out: lost 2nd 1f out: one pce* **11/2**
3533 **4** *6* **Not Now Lewis (IRE)**[24] 589 3-8-11 67............. RichardKingscote(3) 4 44
(J A Osborne) *stdd s: in tch: rdn over 3f out: c wd into st and sn btn* **7/4**[1]
0665 **5** *8* **Gertie (IRE)**[11] 676 3-8-5 45...................................... EdwardCreighton 5 20
(E J Creighton) *disp ld tl rdn and wknd over 3f out* **20/1**
2m 11.0s (2.00) **Going Correction** -0.025s/f (Stan) 5 Ran SP% **110.1**
Speed ratings (Par 96):91,90,88,83,77
CSF £10.28 TOTE £3.30: £2.00, £1.70; EX 8.70.
Owner Geoffrey Bishop and Ann Jarvis **Bred** Natton House Thoroughbreds **Trained** Twyford, Bucks
FOCUS
There was no pace on early but, once Gertie and Picky began to take each other on at the head of affairs, the gallop picked up. The form looks quite messy and it doubtful the winner improved with doubts over current form of runner-up.
Not Now Lewis(IRE) Official explanation: jockey said gelding was never travelling

777 DAY TIME, NIGHT TIME, GREAT TIME H'CAP 1m 2f (P)
4:50 (4:50) (Class 3) (0-90,89) 4-Y-0+
£6,855 (£1,539; £1,539; £513; £256; £128) **Stalls High**

Form RPR
50-0 **1** **Weightless**[49] 352 7-9-0 **88**...................................... JamesDoyle(3) 6 94
(N P Littmoden) *t.k.h: trckd ldr: edgd rt over 1f out: drvn to ld nr fin* **9/1**
12/0 **2** *nk* **Tufton**[29] 550 4-9-4 **89**...............................(t) OscarUrbina 5 94
(M Botti) *t.k.h: led: edgdged lft over 1f out: hard rdn and hdd nr fin* **8/1**
-130 **2** *dht* **Mataram (USA)**[16] 652 4-8-8 **79**...................................... DarryllHolland 1 84
(W Jarvis) *plld hrd: racd 5th: 2f out: r.o strly fnl f to share 2nd on line* **7/2**[3]
1-15 **4** *3/4* **Chicken Soup**[15] 656 5-9-3 **88**...................................... JohnEgan 3 93+
(T J Pitt) *racd 3rd: squeezed out over 1f out and nt rcvr: possibly unlucky* **5/2**[2]
4630 **5** *1/2* **Tous Les Deux**[8] 701 4-8-4 **75**...................................... AdrianMcCarthy 4 78
(Peter Grayson) *racd 4th: r.o wl fnl f: nt rch ldrs* **16/1**
14-3 **6** *hd* **Baizically (IRE)**[19] 629 4-9-0 **85**...................................... JamieSpencer 2 87+
(J A Osborne) *hld up: hdwy after 3f: rdn over 2f out: kpt on again fnl f* **2/1**[1]
2m 7.96s (-1.04) **Going Correction** -0.025s/f (Stan) 6 Ran SP% **111.1**
Speed ratings (Par 107):103,102,102,102,101 101
TOTE £8.90: £3.80 TRIFECTA PL: Weightless £3.80 Tufton £2.00 Mataram £1.20 EX: W/T £24.40 W/M £19.30 CSF: W/T £35.91 W/M £19.57.
Owner Nigel Shields **Bred** Juddmonte Farms **Trained** Newmarket, Suffolk
■ Stewards' Enquiry : James Doyle two-day ban: careless riding (April 5, 7)

FOCUS
A decent little handicap, but the steady early pace dictates that the form should be treated with caution.

NOTEBOOK
Weightless, despite refusing to settle through the early parts, took full advatage of a drop in class and came good for connections at the fifth time of asking. He is probably flattered by this, as he was best placed when the race began in earnest, but this former Group 3 winner should at least be high on confidence now and is clearly not done with in handicaps just yet.
Mataram(USA), another to pull hard early on, finished his race strongly and would have no doubt been helped by a stronger pace. He retains a progressive profile. (op 4-1)
Tufton has to rate flattered as he very much got the run of the race out in front. He has yet to really prove his stamina for this trip, but it was still an improved effort and this lightly-raced colt is in good hands. (op 4-1)
Chicken Soup was denied a clear passage at a crucial stage and was unfortunate not to win. He remains in good form and is evidently capable of success off this mark. (op 2-1)
Baizically(IRE) would have enjoyed a stronger pace on this step back up in distance and was not beaten at all far. This was still a touch disappointing, however. (tchd 15-8)

778 KEMPTON FOR SUMMER WEDDINGS H'CAP — 5f (P)
5:20 (5:20) (Class 5) (0-70,72) 3-Y-O — **£2,914** (£867; £433; £216) **Stalls** High

Form — RPR
-124 **1** **Daddy Cool**^{34} [502] 3-9-0 **69** .... AmirQuinn$^{(3)}$ 5 — 75
(W G M Turner) *t.k.h: mde all: responded wl whn chal ins fnl f* **10/3^{2}**
-611 **2** *nk* **Sohraab**^{12} [671] 3-9-6 **72** .... SteveDrowne 3 — 77
(H Morrison) *a.p: rdn and chsd wnr ins fnl f* **6/4^{1}**
23-0 **3** *1 1/2* **Nou Camp**^{18} [636] 3-8-4 **56** oh2 .... ChrisCatlin 7 — 56
(N A Callaghan) *plld hrd: chsd wnr tl fdd and lost 2nd ins fnl f* **15/2**
1-35 **4** *hd* **Hereford Boy**^{45} [387] 3-9-4 **70** .... RobertHavlin 2 — 69
(D K Ivory) *hld up in rr: hdwy over 1f out: hdwy over 1f out: nt rch ldrs* **9/1**
0634 **5** *1 1/2* **Head To Head (IRE)**^{5} [713] 3-8-6 **58** .... AdrianMcCarthy 4 — 52
(Peter Grayson) *in tch tl rdn 2f out: nt qckn after* **16/1**
-655 **6** *nk* **Arnie's Joint (IRE)**^{15} [659] 3-8-8 **63** .... (b^{1}) JamesDoyle$^{(3)}$ 6 — 56
(N P Littmoden) *in rr: nvr on terms* **14/1**
0-42 **7** *3/4* **Temtation (IRE)**^{15} [659] 3-8-0 **57** .... WilliamBuick$^{(5)}$ 8 — 47
(J R Boyle) *chsd ldrs tl rdn and wknd over 1f out* **11/2^{3}**
0405 **8** *3* **Redflo**^{26} [574] 3-8-4 **56** oh8 .... JimmyQuinn 1 — 35
(Ms J S Doyle) *outpcd and a bhd* **66/1**

60.89 secs (0.49) **Going Correction** -0.025s/f (Stan) — **8** Ran SP% **114.3**
Speed ratings (Par 98):95,94,92,91,89 88,87,82
CSF £8.70 CT £33.16 TOTE £5.10: £1.80, £1.10, £1.50; EX 11.90 Place 6 £312.74, Place 5 £146.90.
Owner Mascalls Stud **Bred** Mascalls Stud **Trained** Sigwells, Somerset
■ Stewards' Enquiry : Amir Quinn caution: careless riding

FOCUS
Plenty raced keenly in the early stages and very few got competitive in this modest handicap. The proximity of the relatively consistent third suggests the form should be given a chance.
Sohraab Official explanation: trainer said colt was struck into
T/Plt: £256.20 to a £1 stake. Pool: £48,510.50. 138.20 winning tickets. T/Qpdt: £41.50 to a £1 stake. Pool: £3,343.90. 59.60 winning tickets. JS

CURRAGH (R-H)
Sunday, March 25

OFFICIAL GOING: Heavy

779a TALLY HO STUD EUROPEAN BREEDERS FUND MAIDEN — 5f
2:25 (2:28) 2-Y-O — **£8,797** (£2,581; £1,229; £418)

RPR
1 **Sammy The Snake (IRE)** 2-8-12 .... DJMoran$^{(5)}$ 11 — 86
(B W Duke) *rn loose bef s: led: rdn 2f out: hdd over 1f out: rallied u.p: regained ld cl home* **12/1**
2 *1/2* **Scupio** 2-9-3 .... DPMcDonogh 6 — 84+
(Kevin Prendergast, Ire) *mid-div: 3rd and hdwy 2f out: led over 1f out: strly pressed whn cocked jaw and hdd cl home* **7/1^{3}**
3 *3* **Irish Jig (IRE)** 2-9-3 .... WSupple 9 — 73
(G M Lyons, Ire) *towards rr: hdwy under 2f out: 7th over 1f out: kpt on wl clsng stages* **5/1^{2}**
4 *nk* **Porto Marmay (IRE)** 2-8-12 .... JMurtagh 1 — 67
(K J Condon, Ire) *chsd ldrs on stands rail: 2nd and chal 2f out: 3rd 1f out: kpt on same pce* **9/1**
5 *hd* **Jade Mountain** 2-9-3 .... PJSmullen 10 — 72
(D K Weld, Ire) *hld up towards rr: hdwy 2f out: 4th 1f out: kpt on same pce* **9/2^{1}**
6 *nk* **Dick Morris (IRE)** 2-8-12 .... CPGeoghegan$^{(5)}$ 15 — 71
(J G Coogan, Ire) *chsd ldrs on outer: 5th and effrt over 1f out: no ex ins fnl f* **20/1**
7 *5* **Georgebernardshaw (IRE)** 2-9-3 .... JAHeffernan 12 — 53
(A P O'Brien, Ire) *trckd ldrs: 4th 1/2-way: wknd fr 1 1/2f out* **5/1^{2}**
8 *1* **My Girl Sophie (USA)** 2-8-12 .... KJManning 5 — 44
(J S Bolger, Ire) *hld up: kpt on same pce fr 2f out* **5/1^{2}**
9 *1/2* **Darraghs Day (IRE)** 2-9-3 .... CO'Donoghue 3 — 47
(Miss Martina Anne Doran, Ire) *cl 2nd to 1/2-way: sn wknd* **33/1**
10 *3* **Sawherfirstandknew (IRE)** 2-8-12 .... NGMcCullagh 8 — 31
(Miss Martina Anne Doran, Ire) *slowly away and bhd: kpt on same pce fr 2f out* **50/1**
11 *1 3/4* **Gracious Girl (IRE)** 2-8-9 .... CDHayes$^{(3)}$ 14 — 25
(Enda Kelly, Ire) *nvr a factor* **16/1**
12 *3/4* **Lady Namid (IRE)** 2-8-9 .... RPCleary$^{(3)}$ 13 — 22
(Patrick Morris, Ire) *nvr a factor* **25/1**
13 *1* **Siamsa Sraide (IRE)** 2-9-3 .... DMGrant 2 — 24
(J S Bolger, Ire) *a bhd* **20/1**
14 *5* **Drumalee Lass (IRE)** 2-8-2 .... JPMurphy$^{(10)}$ 7 — —
(P M Mooney, Ire) *nvr a factor* **20/1**
15 *4* **Mullagh Abu (IRE)** 2-8-7 .... SMGorey$^{(5)}$ 16 — —
(M O Quigley, Ire) *v.s.a and a bhd* **33/1**
R **Iron Mola (IRE)** 2-9-3 .... WMLordan 4 — —
(M O Quigley, Ire) *ref to r* **25/1**

69.50 secs (8.20) **Going Correction** +1.50s/f (Heav) — **16** Ran SP% **134.1**
Speed ratings: 94,93,88,87,87 87,79,77,76,71 69,67,66,58,51 —
CSF £92.85 TOTE £10.50: £2.30, £2.90, £1.90, £2.50; DF 151.90.
Owner Joseph Duke **Bred** M Doyle **Trained** Lambourn, Berks

NOTEBOOK
Sammy The Snake(IRE), a raider from England, got loose before the start, but did not seem to over-exert himself and was allowed to take his chance. Soon in front, he knew his job, but looked beaten when passed by Scupio over a furlong out. However, the runner-up cocked his jaw and hung under pressure, letting him back in, and he got back up to win. It will be fascinating to see how he fares when upped in grade in the future, and equally interesting to see how much he improves on this.

782a LODGE PARK STUD EUROPEAN BREEDERS FUND PARK EXPRESS STKS (GROUP 3) (FILLIES) — 1m
3:55 (3:56) 3-Y-O+ — **£43,986** (£12,905; £6,148; £2,094)

RPR
1 **Ardbrae Lady**^{140} [6356] 4-9-10 **103** .... JMurtagh 5 — 102
(Joseph G Murphy, Ire) *trckd ldrs: 5th 1/2-way: 3rd and hdwy 2f out: 2nd and chal over 1f out: sn led: styd on wl* **7/1^{3}**
2 *1* **Danehill Music (IRE)**^{140} [6356] 4-9-13 **98** .... WMLordan 6 — 103+
(David Wachman, Ire) *trckd ldrs on inner: 4th 1/2-way: nt clr run and lost pl briefly 2f out: 4th 1f out: rdn and styd on wl* **8/1**
3 *1/2* **Truly Mine (IRE)**^{146} [6261] 3-8-9 .... PJSmullen 8 — 96
(D K Weld, Ire) *hld up in tch: nt clr run 2 1/2f out: 7th 1 1/2f out: r.o wl ins fnl f: nrest at fin* **5/1^{2}**
4 *1/2* **La Conquistadora**^{154} [6113] 3-8-9 .... KJManning 7 — 95
(J S Bolger, Ire) *settled 2nd: led 2f out: rdn and strly pressed over 1f out: sn hdd: no ex ins fnl f* **9/4^{1}**
5 *4* **Dani's Girl (IRE)**^{197} [5192] 4-9-10 **88** .... DMGrant 3 — 90
(P A Fahy, Ire) *hld up towards rr: prog on outer under 3f out: 4th under 2f out: no ex fnl f* **16/1**
6 *7* **Saricana (IRE)**^{202} [5073] 3-8-9 .... MJKinane 1 — 73
(John M Oxx, Ire) *trckd ldrs in 3rd: 2nd and rdn to chal 2f out: wknd over 1f out* **8/1**
7 *1* **Cheyenne Star (IRE)**^{140} [6356] 4-9-10 **101** .... DPMcDonogh 2 — 74
(Ms F M Crowley, Ire) *hld up in tch: 6th 1/2-way: no imp fr 2f out* **7/1^{3}**
8 *16* **Dimenticata (IRE)**^{190} [5394] 3-8-9 **102** .... CDHayes 9 — 39
(Kevin Prendergast, Ire) *s.i.s and hld up in rr: in tch 2 1/2f out: sn no ex* **7/1^{3}**
9 *4 1/2* **Gemini Gold (IRE)**^{328} [1363] 4-9-10 **94** .... JAHeffernan 4 — 33
(Joseph G Murphy, Ire) *led: hdd & wknd 2f out: eased fnl f* **20/1**

1m 55.4s (13.30) **Going Correction** +1.50s/f (Heav)
WFA 3 from 4yo 17lb — **9** Ran SP% **117.8**
Speed ratings: 93,92,91,91,87 80,79,63,58
CSF £62.80 TOTE £8.30: £2.40, £2.70, £2.00; DF 67.60.
Owner Robert G Power **Bred** Mrs M Mason **Trained** Fethard, Co Tipperary
■ First leg of an opening-day treble for Johnny Murtagh, who also won the Irish Lincolnshire on Deauville Vision.

FOCUS
Not the strongest of Group 3 races. It has been rated through the sixth.

NOTEBOOK
Ardbrae Lady, disappointing after finishing runner-up in last year's Irish 1000 Guineas, returned to winning ways on her four-year-old reappearance. She stayed on well, appreciating the testing ground, and could well be aimed at the Gladness Stakes next. She is also due to be covered by Galileo. (op 7/1 tchd 8/1)
Danehill Music(IRE), who won this race last year, was one place behind Ardbrae Lady in a Listed race on her final start of 2006, and she again found that rival too strong. She finished well, though, giving the strong impression that she will appreciate stepping up to ten furlongs this year. (op 7/1)
Truly Mine(IRE) did not get the best of runs but finished to good effect and is clearly well regarded as she came here on the back of only one previous start. A maiden should be a formality before she returns to better company. (op 9/2)
La Conquistadora, a beaten favourite on her final start of 2006 in Listed grade, ran well for a long way and only weakened out of the places inside the last, but this was still a touch disappointing. (op 7/2 tchd 2/1)
Dani's Girl(IRE) would not have found this testing ground suitable so she ran well in the circumstances.
Saricana(IRE), a Roscommon maiden winner, did not get home over this longer trip having travelled well for a long way. She will be of more interest back over seven furlongs. (op 7/1)

783 - 785a (Foreign Racing) - See Raceform Interactive

^{772}KEMPTON (A.W) (R-H)
Monday, March 26

OFFICIAL GOING: Standard
Wind: Fresh, across Weather: Sunny and mild

786 BIG JACKPOTS AT INTERCASINO.CO.UK H'CAP — 5f (P)
2:10 (2:11) (Class 6) (0-55,55) 3-Y-O — **£2,047** (£604; £302) **Stalls** High

Form — RPR
4-23 **1** **Jojesse**^{13} [671] 3-8-12 **53** .... JamieSpencer 10 — 61+
(G A Swinbank) *towards rr: hdwy on rail over 2f out: r.o to ld fnl 50 yds* **11/8^{1}**
-602 **2** *1/2* **Ioweyou**^{27} [574] 3-8-11 **52** .... (b) LPKeniry 11 — 58
(J S Moore) *led: drvn clr over 1f out: hdd and nt qckn fnl 50 yds* **7/1^{3}**
064- **3** *1 1/2* **Eastern Princess**^{100} [6839] 3-8-5 **46** oh1 .... (v^{1}) RichardThomas 8 — 47
(J A Geake) *sn chsng ldr: hrd rdn and hung lft over 1f out: kpt on same pce* **25/1**
3-06 **4** *nk* **Kilvickeon (IRE)**^{6} [713] 3-8-6 **47** oh1 ow1 .... GrahamGibbons 4 — 47
(Peter Grayson) *chsd ldrs: styd on same pce fnl 2f* **10/1**
2-32 **5** *shd* **Scarlett Heart (IRE)**^{25} [588] 3-9-0 **55** .... FergusSweeney 1 — 54+
(P J Makin) *broke wl: sn in mid-div on outside: forced v wd home turn: r.o fnl f* **9/1**
0-33 **6** *1 1/4* **Foreland Sands (IRE)**^{49} [360] 3-8-2 **46** oh1 .... StephaneBreux$^{(3)}$ 7 — 41
(J R Best) *prom tl no ex over 1f out* **7/2^{2}**
0-06 **7** *3/4* **The Power Of Phil**^{28} [567] 3-8-9 **50** .... PaulHanagan 6 — 42
(Miss Joanne Priest) *stdd s: bhd tl styd on wl fnl f* **25/1**
6-06 **8** *1/2* **Bridget's Team**^{21} [619] 3-8-11 **52** .... (b^{1}) DaleGibson 3 — 42
(D G Bridgwater) *a abt same pl* **33/1**
-203 **9** *shd* **Priceless Melody (USA)**^{27} [574] 3-8-9 **50** .... (b) JimCrowley 2 — 40
(Mrs A J Perrett) *wd: a towards rr* **10/1**
4050 **10** *nk* **Redflo**^{1} [778] 3-8-4 **48** .... JamesDoyle$^{(3)}$ 9 — 37
(Ms J S Doyle) *dwlt: bhd: sme hdwy over 1f out: sn wknd* **33/1**
000- **11** *1/2* **Golden Ribbons**^{124} [6562] 3-8-5 **46** oh1 .... JoeFanning 5 — 33
(J R Boyle) *prom 3f: wkng whn n.m.r over 1f out* **25/1**

60.56 secs (0.16) **Going Correction** 0.0s/f (Stan) — **11** Ran SP% **122.4**
Speed ratings (Par 96):98,97,94,94,94 92,90,90,90,89 88
CSF £11.39 CT £171.16 TOTE £2.20: £1.20, £2.20, £4.90; EX 14.60.

Owner S J Beard **Bred** S J Beard **Trained** Melsonby, N Yorks

FOCUS
An ordinary sprint handicap run in a time 0.77 seconds slower than the following Class 5 handicap but the form should prove reasonable. The draw played its usual part over this trip with the first three starting from three of the four highest stalls.

787 INTERCASINO.CO.UK H'CAP 5f (P)
2:40 (2:41) (Class 5) (0-70,68) 4-Y-0+ **£2,817** (£838; £418; £209) **Stalls** High

Form RPR

6421 **1** **Lady Bahia (IRE)**[13] [668] 6-8-10 **60**........................(b) GrahamGibbons 1 71+
(Peter Grayson) *prom on outside: hrd rdn over 1f out: r.o to ld fnl 75 yds* **5/1**[3]

5001 **2** *1* **Pride Of Joy**[10] [688] 4-8-10 **60**...................................... JimCrowley 9 67
(D K Ivory) *chsd ldr: led 3f out: rdn clr over 1f out: hdd and nt qckn fnl 75 yds* **11/2**

3444 **3** *1 1/2* **Kempsey**[20] [626] 5-8-7 **64** ow1..(b) RyanBird(7) 2 66
(J J Bridger) *led 2f: chsd ldr after tl over 1f out: one pce* **9/1**

-000 **4** *nk* **No Time (IRE)**[57] [276] 7-9-4 **68**.................................... SteveDrowne 4 69
(A J McCabe) *outpcd in rr tl styd on wl appr fnl f* **9/1**

6246 **5** *3/4* **Taboor (IRE)**[29] [561] 9-8-12 **62**.................................... JamieSpencer 10 60
(R M H Cowell) *hit gate and dwlt: sn in tch on rail: rdn to chse ldrs 2f out: no ex over 1f out* **9/2**[2]

50-0 **6** *shd* **Pamir (IRE)**[20] [626] 5-9-2 **66**...(b) IanMongan 6 63
(P R Chamings) *in tch: wd st: no hdwy fnl 2f* **8/1**

4000 **7** *nk* **Sands Crooner (IRE)**[20] [626] 4-9-0 **64**................(v) CatherineGannon 7 60
(D Shaw) *sn bhd: hmpd on rail over 3f out: hrd rdn over 1f out: nt pce to chal* **16/1**

16-4 **8** *1 3/4* **Sandwith**[28] [566] 4-8-13 **63**....................................... PaulHanagan 8 53
(J S Wainwright) *in tch tl outpcd fnl 2f* **4/1**[1]

010- **9** *1 1/2* **Two Acres (IRE)**[213] [4756] 4-8-6 **56**............................ FergusSweeney 3 41
(A G Newcombe) *sn rdn along: a rr div* **10/1**

59.79 secs (-0.61) **Going Correction** 0.0s/f (Stan) **9** Ran SP% **116.3**
Speed ratings (Par 103):104,102,100,99,98 98,97,94,92
CSF £32.88 CT £242.84 TOTE £4.50: £1.20, £2.10, £3.30; EX 26.50.
Owner Peter Grayson Racing Clubs Limited **Bred** Piercetown Stud **Trained** Formby, Lancs

FOCUS
A slightly better quality sprint than the opener and the winning time was 0.77 seconds quicker and the form looks solid rated through the runner-up. The draw did not have such a big effect this time, with the winner coming from the outside stall and the third starting from stall 2.

788 INTERCASINO.CO.UK MEDIAN AUCTION MAIDEN STKS 1m 2f (P)
3:10 (3:12) (Class 6) 3-4-Y-0 **£2,047** (£604; £302) **Stalls** High

Form RPR

020- **1** **Sir Liam (USA)**[167] [5893] 3-8-8 77.................................... JamieSpencer 2 60+
(P Mitchell) *t.k.h in rr: hdwy and in tch 1/2-way: rdn to ld 2f out: styd on* **1/1**[1]

5 **2** *1 1/2* **Santaverti**[21] [611] 4-10-0 .... GeorgeBaker 4 57
(G L Moore) *chsd ldr: led 3f out tl 2f out: one pce* **6/4**[2]

040- **3** *hd* **Rudry World (IRE)**[385] [604] 4-9-9 56...................... KevinGhunowa(5) 3 57
(P A Blockley) *in tch: effrt over 2f out: one pce* **16/1**

00- **4** *7* **Travelling Fox**[314] [1759] 4-10-0 .... JimmyQuinn 5 43
(Jane Chapple-Hyam) *led tl 3f out: wknd 2f out* **6/1**[3]

00 **5** *26* **Broad Town Girl**[28] [565] 4-9-2 .... KylieManser(7) 6 —
(Mrs H Sweeting) *plld hrd in 3rd early: outpcd and dropped to rr after 3f: bhd whn rn v wd home turn and c to stands' rail* **66/1**

2m 10.96s (1.96) **Going Correction** 0.0s/f (Stan)
WFA 3 from 4yo 20lb **5** Ran SP% **111.7**
Speed ratings (Par 101):92,90,90,85,64
CSF £2.82 TOTE £1.70: £2.10, £1.70; EX 3.80.
Owner Taylor And Sheldon Partners **Bred** Keene Ridge Farm **Trained** Epsom, Surrey

FOCUS
This looked a weak maiden and a moderate early pace resulted in the slowest winning time of the four races over the trip at the meeting. The form is limited by the proximity of the third.
Rudry World(IRE) Official explanation: jockey said gelding hung left
Broad Town Girl Official explanation: jockey said filly hung left

789 PLAY BLACKJACK AT INTERCASINO.CO.UK CLASSIFIED STKS 1m 2f (P)
3:40 (3:42) (Class 7) 4-Y-0+ **£1,365** (£403; £201) **Stalls** High

Form RPR

-001 **1** **War Of The Roses (IRE)**[5] [721] 4-9-6 45...................... JosedeSouza 2 61+
(R Brotherton) *t.k.h: in tch: effrt 2f out: r.o to ld jst ins fnl f: rdn out: readily* **9/2**[2]

1600 **2** *3/4* **Diktatorship (IRE)**[27] [578] 4-9-0 45............................. TonyHamilton 3 51
(G A Swinbank) *led: hdd and edgd lft jst ins fnl f: kpt on* **7/2**[1]

-060 **3** *1/2* **Kilmeena Magic**[57] [273] 5-9-0 40...................................... PatDobbs 13 50
(J C Fox) *hld up towards rr: hdwy 2f out: nt clr run and eased lft ins fnl f: styd on* **14/1**

4-54 **4** *nk* **Chalice Welcome**[50] [350] 4-9-0 43............................ StephenCarson 4 49+
(C F Wall) *lost 12l s: bhd tl gd hdwy on rail over 1f out: styd on to chse ldrs ins fnl f: no imp fnl 50 yds* **9/2**[2]

0-55 **5** *1* **Big Ralph**[57] [272] 4-9-0 43.. JamieMackay 12 47
(M Wigham) *t.k.h: a.p: one pce appr fnl f* **8/1**[3]

350- **6** *shd* **Ming Vase**[165] [5925] 5-9-0 45.. LeeEnstone 11 47
(P T Midgley) *mid-div: rdn 4f out: styd on same pce fnl 2f* **14/1**

0434 **7** *1 1/4* **Savoy Chapel**[5] [721] 5-9-0 45..............................(v) CatherineGannon 10 45
(A W Carroll) *rrd s: hld up in rr: wd st: rdn and r.o fnl 2f: nrst fin* **8/1**[3]

4100 **8** *1/2* **Simplified**[10] [558] 4-9-0 44... DavidKinsella 14 44
(N B King) *hld up towards rr: sme hdwy and wd st: no imp over 1f out* **12/1**

3004 **9** *2* **Zando**[11] [682] 5-9-0 43... PaulDoe 8 40
(E G Bevan) *prom tl wknd over 1f out* **16/1**

0-00 **10** *nk* **Tetrode (USA)**[10] [318] 5-9-0 42...................................... SamHitchcott 6 39
(M F Harris) *t.k.h in rr: rdn over 2f out: nvr trbld ldrs* **66/1**

4640 **11** *1* **Elms Schoolboy**[21] [616] 5-8-11 45..........................(b) EmmettStack(3) 5 37
(P Howling) *dwlt: sn in midfield on outside: wnt prom 1/2-way: hrd rdn 3f out: wknd and wd st* **14/1**

000- **12** *shd* **Bollywood (IRE)**[98] [6854] 4-8-11 40................................ AmirQuinn(3) 1 37
(J J Bridger) *chsd ldrs: drvn along over 3f out: sn outpcd* **33/1**

6000 **13** *shd* **Penwell Hill (USA)**[13] [666] 8-9-0 43.......................... SimonWhitworth 7 37
(Miss M E Rowland) *prom tl wknd 2f out* **40/1**

-440 **14** *3 1/2* **Colonel Bilko (IRE)**[51] [341] 5-9-0 42..................................(e[1]) LPKeniry 9 30
(Ms J S Doyle) *mid-div: wknd 3f out: hrd rdn and no ch fnl 2f* **25/1**

2m 10.27s (1.27) **Going Correction** 0.0s/f (Stan) **14** Ran SP% **125.1**
Speed ratings (Par 97):94,93,93,92,91 91,90,90,88,88 87,87,87,84
CSF £20.90 TOTE £5.80: £2.50, £2.60, £2.60; EX 21.50.
Owner P S J Croft **Bred** Mrs J Bailey **Trained** Elmley Castle, Worcs

FOCUS
A big field, but a poor race and thanks to a modest gallop the winning time was just 0.69 seconds quicker than the preceding slowly-run maiden over the same trip. The form looks sound for the level, rated around the placed horses.
Chalice Welcome Official explanation: jockey said gelding reared as stalls opened and was slow away

790 £600 FREE AT INTERCASINO.CO.UK H'CAP (DIV I) 1m 2f (P)
4:10 (4:12) (Class 6) (0-60,60) 3-Y-0 **£1,365** (£403; £201) **Stalls** High

Form RPR

6562 **1** **King Of The Beers (USA)**[4] [731] 3-8-12 **54**.............(p) PaulHanagan 12 57
(R A Harris) *chsd ldrs: led jst over 1f out: drvn to hold on fnl f* **10/3**[1]

000 **2** *nk* **A Mothers Love**[17] [649] 3-8-4 **46** oh1........................ EdwardCreighton 2 49
(P J McBride) *mid-div: grad lost pl fr 1/2-way and dropped to rr 3f out: gd hdwy over 1f out: pressed wnr fnl f: jst hld* **33/1**

-002 **3** *2* **Citrus Chief (USA)**[27] [572] 3-8-11 **58**............................ TolleyDean(5) 9 57
(R A Harris) *prom: hrd rdn 2f out: kpt on same pce* **7/1**[3]

000- **4** *shd* **Alnwick**[175] [5738] 3-9-1 **57**.. LPKeniry 1 56
(P D Cundell) *in tch: effrt over 2f out: hrd rdn over 1f out: kpt on fnl f* **10/1**

0-64 **5** *nk* **The Dagger**[19] [633] 3-9-1 **60**................................... StephaneBreux(3) 13 58
(J R Best) *hld up and bhd: rdn and r.o fnl 2f: nrst fin* **8/1**

-660 **6** *1/2* **Brean Dot Com (IRE)**[19] [636] 3-8-13 **55**....................... RobertHavlin 11 52
(Mrs P N Dutfield) *mid-div: hdwy to chse ldrs over 1f out: one pce* **11/1**

0-00 **7** *3/4* **Tranquility**[48] [373] 3-8-4 **46** oh1.. JimmyQuinn 6 42
(J Pearce) *hmpd s: towards rr: hdwy to chse ldrs over 1f out: one pce* **33/1**

00-0 **8** *1* **Night Falcon**[17] [649] 3-8-8 **50** ow2................................... SteveDrowne 7 44
(H Morrison) *sn rdn up to chse ldrs: outpcd fnl 2f* **9/1**

-561 **9** *1/2* **Muncaster Castle (IRE)**[21] [624] 3-9-0 **56**................... J-PGuillambert 3 49
(R F Fisher) *led after 2f: disp ld fr 1/2-way tl wknd over 1f out* **9/2**[2]

600 **10** *3/4* **Meadfoot**[27] [573] 3-8-7 **52**...................................... RichardKingscote(3) 4 44
(B R Millman) *led 2f: disp ld fr 1/2-way tl wknd over 1f out* **33/1**

-301 **11** *1* **It's No Problem (IRE)**[27] [572] 3-8-11 **53**................ SimonWhitworth 10 43
(M Salaman) *dwlt: towards rr: rdn 3f out: nvr trbld ldrs* **10/1**

-344 **12** *1 1/4* **Raquel White**[21] [624] 3-8-3 **52**...................................... JosephWalsh(7) 5 39
(J L Flint) *rrd s: a bhd* **8/1**

6000 **13** *3 1/2* **Elizabeth Garrett**[24] [602] 3-7-13 **46** oh1.................. DuranFentiman(5) 8 27
(M J Gingell) *t.k.h: in tch: drvn along 3f out: sn outpcd* **66/1**

2m 9.78s (0.78) **Going Correction** 0.0s/f (Stan) **13** Ran SP% **122.8**
Speed ratings (Par 96):96,95,94,94,93 93,92,92,91,91 90,89,86
CSF £131.09 CT £752.02 TOTE £4.60: £2.40, £16.50, £3.60; EX 155.60.
Owner Dr Simon Clarke **Bred** Liberation Farm, Oratis Thoroughbreds Et Al **Trained** Earlswood, Monmouths

FOCUS
A moderate handicap and the winning time was 0.91 seconds slower than the second division. The form is limited rated around the fourth, sixth and seventh.
Tranquility Official explanation: jockey said filly suffered interference as stalls opened
Muncaster Castle(IRE) Official explanation: jockey said gelding hung left

791 £600 FREE AT INTERCASINO.CO.UK H'CAP (DIV II) 1m 2f (P)
4:40 (4:42) (Class 6) (0-60,60) 3-Y-0 **£1,365** (£403; £201) **Stalls** High

Form RPR

006- **1** **Dan Tucker**[210] [4873] 3-9-2 **58**.. JamieSpencer 1 75+
(B J Meehan) *t.k.h and stdd in rr: plenty to do 4f out: hdwy over 2f out: qcknd wl to ld ins fnl f: rdn out* **2/1**[1]

0-06 **2** *1 1/4* **Cnoc Moy (IRE)**[28] [569] 3-9-4 **60**.................................. GeorgeBaker 11 67+
(C F Wall) *chsd ldrs: led over 1f out: hdd and nt pce of wnr ins fnl f* **4/1**[2]

-544 **3** *3* **Party Palace**[63] [209] 3-8-4 **46** oh1..................................... ChrisCatlin 7 48
(H S Howe) *t.k.h: prom: led 2f out tl over 1f out: one pce* **11/2**[3]

5-04 **4** *2 1/2* **Zilli**[27] [577] 3-8-3 **48**.. JamesDoyle(3) 13 45
(N P Littmoden) *chsd ldrs: rdn after 4f: wknd over 1f out* **12/1**

-000 **5** *4* **Conny Nobel (IRE)**[24] [603] 3-8-10 **59**........................ JosephWalsh(7) 12 48
(J L Flint) *sn led: rdn and hdd 2f out: wknd over 1f out* **16/1**

00-0 **6** *3/4* **Danum Diva (IRE)**[26] [583] 3-8-4 **46** oh1...................... AdrianTNicholls 2 34+
(T J Pitt) *hld up and wl bhd: pushed along and wd st: nrst fin* **25/1**

000- **7** *1 1/4* **Sadler's Hill (IRE)**[166] [5906] 3-8-10 **52**............................... LPKeniry 4 38
(M J McGrath) *t.k.h towards rr: rdn 3f out: nvr rchd ldrs* **16/1**

3-55 **8** *1/2* **Tumble Jill (IRE)**[68] [157] 3-8-6 **55** ow3.......................(p) RyanBird(7) 10 40
(J J Bridger) *in tch on rail: outpcd by ldng quartet 3f out: grad fdd* **20/1**

340- **9** *4* **Clewer**[182] [5563] 3-8-11 **58**.. KevinGhunowa(5) 9 35
(P A Blockley) *stdd s: t.k.h towards rr: hdwy into midfield 4f out: rdn and no imp fnl 3f* **9/1**

00-0 **10** *1/2* **Mum's Memories**[48] [373] 3-7-11 **46** oh1...................... DebraEngland(7) 6 22
(W J Musson) *chsd ldrs: outpcd over 3f out: eased whn btn* **33/1**

5123 **11** *hd* **Jemima Godfrey**[27] [572] 3-8-7 **54**............................ DuranFentiman(5) 8 30
(M J Gingell) *a bhd* **8/1**

06-0 **12** *8* **Deep Cover (IRE)**[75] [93] 3-8-11 **53**.................................... AdamKirby 3 14
(R M Flower) *in tch on outside: hrd rdn and wd bnd 4f out: bhd fnl 3f* **16/1**

06-0 **13** *2 1/2* **Fiona's Wonder**[47] [386] 3-8-5 **47**................................... PaulHanagan 5 3
(R A Harris) *t.k.h in midfield: rdn over 3f out: sn wknd* **12/1**

2m 8.87s (-0.13) **Going Correction** 0.0s/f (Stan) **13** Ran SP% **134.4**
Speed ratings (Par 96):100,99,96,94,91 90,89,89,86,85 85,79,77
CSF £10.59 CT £44.22 TOTE £3.80: £2.60, £1.70, £3.40; EX 15.40.
Owner Favourites Racing XXVI **Bred** N And Mrs N Nugent **Trained** Manton, Wilts

FOCUS
This looked a much stronger heat than the first division, amongst the principals at least and the form has been rated fairly positively through the third. The winning time was 0.91 seconds faster and was also the quickest of the four races over the trip on the day.
Fiona's Wonder Official explanation: jockey said colt lost its action

792 PLAY ROULETTE AT INTERCASINO.CO.UK H'CAP 2m (P)
5:10 (5:10) (Class 6) (0-50,50) 4-Y-0+ **£2,047** (£604; £302) **Stalls** High

Form RPR

3450 **1** **Lady Pilot**[35] [495] 5-8-11 **47**.. RichardThomas 11 58
(Jim Best) *t.k.h in midfield: hdwy 2f out: r.o to ld ins fnl f: rdn clr* **12/1**

2202 **2** *3* **Nod's Star**[12] [677] 6-8-13 **49**..(t) ChrisCatlin 10 56
(Mrs L C Jewell) *chsd ldr: led over 2f out tl ins fnl f: nt pce of wnr* **7/2**[1]

4552 **3** *1* **Countback (FR)**[21] [615] 8-8-10 **46**...........................(p) CatherineGannon 4 52
(A W Carroll) *t.k.h: prom: rdn to chal over 2f out: one pce appr fnl f* **12/1**

0410 **4** *shd* **Tip Toes (IRE)**[27] [578] 5-8-10 **46** oh1.............................. JimmyQuinn 12 52
(P Howling) *mid-div: effrt over 2f out: styd on u.p* **16/1**

2646 **5** *nk* **Lysander's Quest (IRE)**[24] [607] 9-8-10 **46** oh1......... FergusSweeney 6 52
(R Ingram) *hld up towards rr: hdwy 6f out: rdn and lost pl over 2f out: styd on fnl f* **8/1**

2464 **6** *shd* **Come What July (IRE)**[12] 677 6-8-5 **48**........................ PatrickHills(7) 9 — 54
(D Shaw) *hld up towards rr: gd hdwy on rail over 2f out: no imp fnl f* **5/1**[2]

54-3 **7** *¾* **Toni Alcala**[21] 618 8-9-0 **50**..(p) PaulHanagan 3 — 55
(R F Fisher) *t.k.h: a.p: rdn and no ex fnl 2f* **7/1**[3]

-464 **8** *1* **Domenico (IRE)**[34] 508 9-8-10 **46** oh1.............................. AdamKirby 1 — 49
(J R Jenkins) *t.k.h in rr: effrt and hung rt over 2f out: sme late hdwy* **14/1**

4200 **9** *1* **Iceni Warrior**[6] 716 5-8-11 **47**... JoeFanning 13 — 49
(P Howling) *hld up in tch: n.m.r over 2f out: sn rdn and btn* **20/1**

4-30 **10** *hd* **Mustakhlas (USA)**[24] 607 6-8-10 **46**...................... GrahamGibbons 14 — 48
(B P J Baugh) *led tl over 2f out: hrd rdn and wknd over 1f out* **12/1**

2-45 **11** *½* **Myrtle Bay (IRE)**[35] 495 4-8-6 **50**............................... NeilChalmers(3) 7 — 51
(J C Tuck) *chsd ldrs: hrd rdn over 2f out: sn wknd* **12/1**

306 **12** *1¾* **Finished Article (IRE)**[21] 617 10-9-0 **50**.................... J-PGuillambert 2 — 49
(K J Burke) *t.k.h in rr: mod effrt over 2f out: n.d* **10/1**

/00- **13** *4* **Mungo Jerry (GER)**[248] 3382 6-9-0 **50**.................................. JDSmith 8 — 44
(B N Pollock) *a bhd* **28/1**

60/0 **14** *31* **Saintly Thoughts (USA)**[57] 285 12-8-3 **46** oh1......(p) HaddenFrost(7) 5 — 3
(R J Hodges) *mid-div on outside: hdwy 6f out: wknd over 4f out: sn bhd* **20/1**

3m 33.25s (1.85) **Going Correction** 0.0s/f (Stan)
WFA 4 from 5yo+ 5lb **14** Ran SP% **127.9**
Speed ratings (Par 101):95,93,93,92,92 92,92,91,91,91 91,90,88,72
CSF £55.61 CT £546.21 TOTE £14.40: £5.40, £2.40, £2.60; EX 55.10.
Owner Odds On Racing **Bred** Genesis Green Stud Ltd **Trained** Lewes, E Sussex
■ Stewards' Enquiry : Chris Catlin one-day ban: careless riding (Apr 7)

FOCUS
A very weak staying handicap, in fact with the top weight rated just 50 this would at one time have been called a banded race. The form looks straightforward with the third, fourth and fifth close to recent form.

793 INTERCASINO.CO.UK APPRENTICE H'CAP — 7f (P)
5:40 (5:41) (Class 5) (0-70,70) 4-Y-0+ **£2,817** (£838; £418; £209) **Stalls** High

Form — RPR

0-45 **1** **Takitwo**[29] 560 4-8-3 **59**.. JamieHamblett(5) 5 — 72
(P D Cundell) *trckd ldrs: led over 1f out: pushed out: cheekily* **4/1**[2]

6233 **2** *½* **What Do You Know**[5] 724 4-8-8 **62**.................................. NicolPolli(3) 2 — 74
(A M Hales) *disp ld: led over 2f out: rdn and hdd over 1f out: kpt on: a hld* **7/1**

6605 **3** *2½* **Sailor King (IRE)**[21] 614 5-9-2 **70**.......................... JamesMillman(3) 12 — 75
(D K Ivory) *mid-div: rdn and hdwy 2f out: wnt 3rd over 1f out: one pce* **2/1**[1]

2562 **4** *1¾* **Imperium**[5] 724 6-8-8 **64**... SophieDoyle(5) 8 — 64
(Jean-Rene Auvray) *towards rr: rdn and styd on fnl 2f: nvr nrr* **13/2**

-066 **5** *1¼* **Just Fly**[46] 389 7-8-5 **56** oh4......................................(v) KevinGhunowa 10 — 53
(Dr J R J Naylor) *towards rr tl rdn and styd on fnl 2f* **16/1**

2300 **6** *nk* **Lucius Verrus (USA)**[5] 724 7-8-8 **62**.....................(v) PatrickHills(3) 11 — 58
(D Shaw) *s.i.s: bhd: hrd rdn and hdwy 2f out: nt rch ldrs* **12/1**

620- **7** *shd* **Digital**[143] 6326 10-8-9 **67**... MatthewDavies(7) 6 — 63
(M R Channon) *rrd s: bhd tl r.o appr fnl f* **14/1**

0103 **8** *nk* **Seneschal**[29] 561 6-8-9 **65**.. JosephWalsh(5) 4 — 60
(A B Haynes) *chsd ldrs: rdn over 2f out: sn outpcd* **6/1**[3]

3510 **9** *½* **Mystic Man (FR)**[12] 672 9-8-8 **62**..................................(b) TolleyDean(3) 9 — 56
(I W McInnes) *mid-div: effrt over 2f out: no ex over 1f out* **20/1**

3344 **10** *½* **Buzzin'Boyzee (IRE)**[3] 734 4-8-0 **56**.................... BernadetteQuinn(5) 3 — 49
(P D Evans) *dwlt: a towards rr* **25/1**

640- **11** *3* **It's Unbelievable (USA)**[168] 5879 4-8-13 **64**.................. RoryMoore 1 — 49
(P T Midgley) *disp ld tl over 2f out: wknd wl over 1f out* **25/1**

-014 **12** *shd* **H Harrison (IRE)**[2] 750 7-8-13 **64**................................ DuranFentiman 7 — 49
(I W McInnes) *prom: hrd rdn 2f out: sn wknd* **12/1**

1m 25.2s (-1.60) **Going Correction** 0.0s/f (Stan) **12** Ran SP% **133.8**
Speed ratings (Par 103):109,108,105,103,102 101,101,101,100,100 96,96
CSF £36.17 CT £77.08 TOTE £4.60: £1.60, £3.30, £1.30; EX 31.90 Place 6 £20.77, Place 5 £12.28.
Owner Miss M C Fraser **Bred** Roden House Stud **Trained** Compton, Berks

FOCUS
Probably the best race on the card - certainly the best performance against the clock - and the form looks solid with the front pair pulling clear of the heavily-backed favourite, and the form should work out.

T/Plt: £48.80 to a £1 stake. Pool: £54,134.65. 809.10 winning tickets. T/Qpdt: £12.50 to a £1 stake. Pool: £3,189.80. 187.40 winning tickets. LM

758 LINGFIELD (L-H)
Tuesday, March 27

OFFICIAL GOING: Standard
Wind: Almost nil. Weather: Sunny, mild.

794 CSG (S) STKS — 1m 2f (P)
2:10 (2:10) (Class 6) 3-Y-0 **£2,184** (£644; £322) **Stalls** Low

Form — RPR

-035 **1** **Peppin's Gold (IRE)**[8] 708 3-8-7 50........................(t) AdrianMcCarthy 7 — 49
(B R Millman) *hld up in last pair: prog over 3 out: rdn and sltly outpcd 2f out: r.o to ld last 100yds: pushed out* **13/2**

-460 **2** *1* **Best Woman**[13] 676 3-8-7 45... PaulDoe 6 — 47
(P Howling) *hld up in last pair: prog on outer over 3f out: led 2f out: rdn and idled fr over 1f out: hdd and hung rt last 100yds* **12/1**

2006 **3** *shd* **A Nod And A Wink (IRE)**[13] 676 3-8-7 48.................. PatDobbs 4 — 47
(R Hannon) *taken down early: t.k.h early: trckd ldng pair: rdn and nt qckn over 2f out: hanging over 1f out: r.o last 150yds* **7/2**[3]

2200 **4** *nk* **Bertrada (IRE)**[8] 708 3-8-7 53...................................... RobertHavlin 2 — 46
(H Morrison) *lw: trckd ldr: led over 2f out to 2f out: pressed ldr after: no ex fnl 150yds* **10/3**[2]

42-3 **5** *6* **The Slider**[13] 676 3-8-7 55.. PaulHanagan 5 — 35
(P A Blockley) *swtg: led: rdn and hdd over 2f out: sn btn* **6/5**[1]

0000 **6** *¾* **First Frost**[13] 676 3-8-4 40.. MarcHalford(3) 1 — 33
(M J Gingell) *chsd ldrs: rdn wl over 2f out: no prog and sn btn* **33/1**

0 **7** *33* **Smiling Tiger**[20] 635 3-8-12 .... HayleyTurner 3 — —
(M J Gingell) *plld hrd: trckd ldng trio: rdn and wknd over 3f out: t.o* **50/1**

2m 10.67s (2.88) **Going Correction** +0.05s/f (Slow) **7** Ran SP% **116.7**
Speed ratings (Par 96):90,89,89,88,84 83,57
CSF £79.13 TOTE £8.20: £3.30, £3.90; EX 79.50.There was no bid for the winner.
Owner C Barrett, I Hall & C Knowles **Bred** Golden Vale Stud **Trained** Kentisbeare, Devon

FOCUS
A bit of a stop-start gallop resulted in a modest winning time, even for a seller. The front four finished in a bit of a heap and the form looks moderate rated around the first two.
The Slider Official explanation: jockey said filly was on its toes in the prelminaries

795 RUDRIDGE MEDIAN AUCTION MAIDEN STKS — 1m (P)
2:40 (2:40) (Class 6) 3-4-Y-0 **£2,730** (£806; £403) **Stalls** High

Form — RPR

4- **1** **Jaady (USA)**[155] 6145 3-8-10 .... JimmyFortune 2 — 71+
(J H M Gosden) *lw: t.k.h early: trckd ldng pair: plld out and effrt over 1f out: rdn to ld last 150yds and edgd lft: sn in command* **8/15**[1]

200- **2** *1¾* **Spritza (IRE)**[189] 5464 3-8-5 70..................................... PaulHanagan 4 — 52
(M L W Bell) *lw: led: jnd 3f out: rdn 2f out: hdd and outpcd last 150yds* **9/4**[2]

5043 **3** *1½* **Simpsons Gamble (IRE)**[30] 559 4-9-13 50..........(p) AdrianMcCarthy 3 — 59
(R M Flower) *plld hrd early: trckd ldr: chal and upsides fr 3f out tl wknd fnl f* **12/1**[3]

040- **4** *8* **Sherjawy (IRE)**[143] 6332 3-8-10 58...............................(b[1]) ChrisCatlin 1 — 36
(Miss Z C Davison) *t.k.h early: hld up in last: rdn over 3f out: sn lost tch* **25/1**

1m 39.29s (-0.14) **Going Correction** +0.05s/f (Slow)
WFA 3 from 4yo 17lb **4** Ran SP% **107.5**
Speed ratings (Par 101):102,100,98,90
CSF £1.94 TOTE £1.50; EX 2.30.
Owner Hamdan Al Maktoum **Bred** Shadwell Farm LLC **Trained** Newmarket, Suffolk
■ Stewards' Enquiry : Paul Hanagan one-day ban: careless riding (Apr 7)

FOCUS
Only two mattered according to the market, but despite the small field the gallop was sound. The proximity of a 50-rated horse in third may appear to hold the form down, but that oftens happens in races like this and it is probably wise to give the winner the benefit of the doubt.

796 OYSTER PARTNERSHIP FILLIES' H'CAP — 7f (P)
3:10 (3:10) (Class 5) (0-70,62) 4-Y-0+ **£2,914** (£867; £433; £216) **Stalls** Low

Form — RPR

005- **1** **Miswadah (IRE)**[102] 6827 4-8-6 **55**............................... PatrickHills(7) 1 — 63
(D M Simcock) *fit: led after 1f: mde rest and waited in front: shkn up and in command over 1f out: kpt on wl* **11/4**[2]

0040 **2** *2* **Another Genepi (USA)**[6] 724 4-9-2 **58**...................(p) JimmyFortune 4 — 61
(K A Ryan) *lw: trckd ldrs: effrt to dispute 2nd wl over 1f out: sn hanging and fnd little* **9/4**[1]

-040 **3** *shd* **Chalentina**[36] 497 4-8-12 **54**.. IanMongan 6 — 57
(P Howling) *swtg: trckd ldrs: drvn and effrt 2f out: styd on u.p fnl f: n.d to wnr* **11/1**

023- **4** *5* **Supreme Kiss**[119] 6632 4-8-11 **56**................................. JamesDoyle(3) 5 — 46+
(Mrs N Smith) *s.s: detached in last tl gd prog on inner over 2f out: disp 2nd wl over 1f out: fnd nil and sn btn* **9/2**

100- **5** *3½* **Shinko (IRE)**[189] 5453 4-8-6 **55**..................................(p) AmyBaker(7) 7 — 36
(Miss J Feilden) *lw: dwlt: racd wd: trckd ldrs tl wknd over 2f out* **16/1**

225- **6** *1¾* **Riquewihr**[175] 5756 7-9-4 **60**..(p) PaulHanagan 2 — 36
(J S Wainwright) *plld hrd: led for 1f: pressed wnr tl wknd rapidly 2f out* **7/2**[3]

1m 25.28s (-0.61) **Going Correction** +0.05s/f (Slow) **6** Ran SP% **112.1**
Speed ratings (Par 100):105,102,102,96,92 90
CSF £9.34 TOTE £4.90: £1.90, £1.90; EX 14.30.
Owner Kevin F O'Donnell **Bred** Shadwell Estate Company Limited **Trained** Newmarket, Suffolk

FOCUS
An ordinary fillies' handicap, but they went a good pace and the winning time was a creditable one for a race like this. the runner-up looks the best guide to the level.
Supreme Kiss Official explanation: jockey said filly missed the break
Riquewihr Official explanation: jockey said mare ran too free

797 SCOTS CHALLENGE H'CAP — 6f (P)
3:40 (3:40) (Class 6) (0-55,54) 4-Y-0+ **£2,388** (£705; £352) **Stalls** Low

Form — RPR

4506 **1** **Mulberry Lad (IRE)**[3] 750 5-8-12 **53**.................................. ChrisCatlin 2 — 63
(P W Hiatt) *cl up on inner: effrt to ld wl over 1f out: hrd rdn and jnd fnl f: hld on wl* **6/1**[2]

0201 **2** *shd* **Balerno**[11] 690 8-8-12 **53**.. IanMongan 5 — 63
(Mrs L J Mongan) *hld up in midfield: swtchd to inner over 1f out: hrd rdn to chal and upsides fnl f: nt qckn nr fin* **7/1**

4002 **3** *hd* **Mind Alert**[6] 723 6-8-6 **47**...(v) AdrianMcCarthy 3 — 56
(D Shaw) *settled towards rr: prog on inner wl over 1f out: jnd wnr fnl f and looked gng best: pushed along and nt go by* **15/2**

3463 **4** *1½* **Muktasb (USA)**[11] 690 6-8-11 **52**....................................(v) DaneO'Neill 1 — 57
(D Shaw) *dwlt: hld up in last: prog over 1f out: chsd ldrs ins fnl f: kpt on but nvr able to chal* **13/2**[3]

0261 **5** *shd* **Primarily**[12] 680 5-8-7 **48**.................................. RobbieFitzpatrick 11 — 52+
(Peter Grayson) *wl in tch: rdn and nt qckn on outer 2f out: styd on same pce fnl f: nvr able to chal* **11/1**

1542 **6** *2½* **Shava**[27] 586 7-8-12 **53**... FergusSweeney 4 — 50
(H J Evans) *hld up and sn in last trio: effrt over 1f out: one pce and n.d* **4/1**[1]

41-0 **7** *½* **Davids Mark**[22] 613 7-8-6 **54**...................................... SophieDoyle(7) 9 — 49
(J R Jenkins) *hld up and sn in last trio: no prog tl kpt on fnl f: no ch* **16/1**

43-2 **8** *1¼* **Pearl Farm**[11] 687 6-8-9 **50**.. OscarUrbina 7 — 42
(C A Horgan) *b. wl in tch in midfield: lost pl and struggling in rr 2f out: n.d after* **4/1**[1]

4460 **9** *½* **The London Gang**[3] 751 4-8-9 **53**..........................(bt) JamesDoyle(3) 12 — 43
(Miss D A McHale) *drvn fr wdst draw and gd spd to ld: hdd & wknd over 1f out* **20/1**

0000 **10** *1½* **Edin Burgher (FR)**[6] 722 6-8-7 **48**...........................(p) SamHitchcott 10 — 34
(T T Clement) *chsd ldr to 1/2-way: sn btn u.p: no ch whn n.m.r 1f out and eased* **16/1**

0000 **11** *½* **Auentraum (GER)**[3] 750 7-8-1 **49**..........................(e[1]) JosephWalsh(7) 8 — 33
(Ms J S Doyle) *hld up: rapid prog on outer to press ldr 1/2-way: upsides wl over 1f out: wknd rapidly* **40/1**

1m 12.76s (-0.05) **Going Correction** +0.05s/f (Slow) **11** Ran SP% **119.2**
Speed ratings (Par 101):102,101,101,99,99 96,95,93,93,91 90
CSF £48.40 CT £324.36 TOTE £10.90: £3.20, £2.70, £2.10; EX 74.80 Trifecta £429.60 Pool £665.58. - 1.10 winning units..
Owner P W Hiatt **Bred** Mountarmstrong Stud **Trained** Hook Norton, Oxon

FOCUS
An ordinary handicap and, although the bare form is moderate, this looked a reasonable race for the grade. They seemed to go a good pace.

798 SV.TWO MAIDEN STKS 5f (P)
4:10 (4:12) (Class 5) 3-Y-0+ £2,914 (£867; £433; £216) Stalls High

Form RPR

0- 1 **Dualagi**[200] 5147 3-8-2 .... JosephWalsh(7) 7 60+
(J S Moore) *strong: taken down early: s.i.s: off the pce in last trio: rdn over 1f out: str run to ld last 100yds: won gng away* **11/1**

6022 2 1 ¼ **Ioweyou**[1] 786 3-8-9 52 ....(b) SimonWhitworth 3 55
(J S Moore) *chsd ldng pair: rdn 2f out: styd on to ld briefly ins fnl f: sn outpcd by wnr* **4/1**[2]

-405 3 2 **Inscribed (IRE)**[12] 680 4-9-7 45 ....(v[1]) PatDobbs 6 53
(G A Huffer) *chsd ldrs: rdn over 2f out: hanging over 1f out: kpt on fnl f but easily outpcd* **10/1**

6345 4 ½ **Head To Head (IRE)**[2] 778 3-9-0 58 .... RobbieFitzpatrick 1 51
(Peter Grayson) *trckd ldng pair: effrt on inner 2f out: drvn to dispute ld ins fnl f: sn outpcd* **10/1**

220- 5 shd **Castano**[179] 5645 3-8-9 75 .... JamesMillman(5) 5 51+
(B R Millman) *s.i.s: struggling in last pair: gd prog over 1f out: n.m.r and effrt petered out ins fnl f* **10/11**[1]

00- 6 ¾ **Straight Gal (IRE)**[271] 3006 4-9-4 .... JamesDoyle(3) 8 48
(Mrs N Smith) *dwlt: outpcd in last pair: no prog tl kpt on fnl f* **50/1**

0-5 7 1 ½ **Wendy's Boy**[13] 678 3-9-0 .... DaneO'Neill 9 43
(R Hannon) *taken down early: w ldr at furious pce: stl upsides ent fnl f: wknd rapidly* **8/1**[3]

34 8 hd **Royal Dagger (IRE)**[28] 574 3-9-0 .... ChrisCatlin 2 42
(Rae Guest) *led at furious pce: hdd & wknd rapidly ins fnl f* **14/1**

0500 9 3 **Redflo**[1] 786 3-8-2 48 .... SophieDoyle(7) 4 26
(Ms J S Doyle) *t.k.h: hld up bhd ldrs: wknd rapidly over 1f out* **50/1**

59.85 secs (0.07) **Going Correction** +0.05s/f (Slow)
WFA 3 from 4yo 12lb 9 Ran SP% **120.6**
Speed ratings (Par 103):101,99,95,95,94 93,91,90,86
CSF £57.18 TOTE £20.80: £2.80, £1.60, £3.00; EX 87.70 TRIFECTA Not won..
Owner Uplands Acquisitions Limited **Bred** B Burrough **Trained** Upper Lambourn, Berks

FOCUS
A very weak maiden, but the pace was strong early and the race is rated through the runner-up.
Castano Official explanation: jockey said gelding missed the break and did not face the kickback

799 PREMIER SHOWFREIGHT APPRENTICE H'CAP 1m 2f (P)
4:40 (4:40) (Class 5) (0-75,74) 4-Y-0+ £2,914 (£867; £433; £216) Stalls Low

Form RPR

23-4 1 **Dower House**[65] 205 12-9-5 74 ....(t) PatrickHills 5 80
(Andrew Turnell) *hld up in 4th: trckd ldng pair over 2f out gng wl: wd bnd 2f out: shkn up to ld jst ins fnl f: styd on wl* **3/1**[2]

3105 2 1 ¼ **King After**[4] 740 5-8-5 60 oh3 ....(v) NicolPolli 3 63
(J R Best) *s.v.s: hld up in last: effrt 2f out: rdn and kpt on same pce to take 2nd ins fnl f: no imp on wnr* **10/3**[3]

-433 3 shd **Generous Lad (IRE)**[32] 539 4-8-8 68 ....(p) JosephWalsh(5) 2 71
(A B Haynes) *t.k.h: hld up bhd ldng pair: rdn 3f out: effrt u.p over 1f out: kpt on same pce* **5/2**[1]

0400 4 1 ¼ **Makai**[4] 740 4-8-6 61 .... TolleyDean 4 61
(J J Bridger) *trckd ldr: rdn to chal 3f out: nt qckn over 1f out: one pce after* **11/1**

11-3 5 1 **Revolve**[22] 610 7-8-2 60 oh2 ....(b) JackMitchell(3) 1 58
(Mrs L J Mongan) *lw: led: kicked on 3f out: drvn 2f out: hdd & wknd jst ins fnl f* **10/3**[3]

2m 7.41s (-0.38) **Going Correction** +0.05s/f (Slow) 5 Ran SP% **108.1**
Speed ratings (Par 103):103,102,101,100,100
CSF £12.60 TOTE £3.90: £1.90, £2.90; EX 16.60 Place 6 £430.48, Place 5 £49.06..
Owner Mrs Claire Hollowood **Bred** Lord Howard De Walden **Trained** Broad Hinton, Wilts

FOCUS
Just a modest handicap for the grade rated through the runner-up, but the pace was not too bad considering the size of the field, and the winning time was 3.26 seconds quicker than the opening seller.
King After Official explanation: jockey said gelding missed the break
T/Plt: £828.70 to a £1 stake. Pool: £50,861.80. 44.80 winning tickets. T/Qpdt: £47.00 to a £1 stake. Pool: £4,383.65. 68.90 winning tickets. JN

766 WOLVERHAMPTON (A.W) (L-H)
Tuesday, March 27

OFFICIAL GOING: Standard
Wind: Light, half-against. Weather: Fine.

800 BOOK ONLINE AT WOLVERHAMPTON-RACECOURSE.CO.UK H'CAP (DIV I) 7f 32y(P)
2:00 (2:00) (Class 6) (0-50,50) 4-Y-0+ £1,535 (£453; £226) Stalls High

Form RPR

2242 1 **Over To You Bert**[11] 690 8-8-5 50 .... HaddenFrost(7) 12 57
(R J Hodges) *sn chsng ldr: led over 2f out: pushed out* **6/1**[3]

0040 2 nk **Gem Bien (USA)**[33] 519 9-8-9 47 oh1 ow1 ....(p) TomEaves 6 54
(D W Chapman) *s.i.s: in rr: rdn 2f out: hdwy 1f out: r.o* **28/1**

-003 3 1 **Laith (IRE)**[6] 722 4-8-12 50 ....(p) MickyFenton 4 54
(Miss V Haigh) *hld up and bhd: rdn and hdwy 2f out: kpt on same pce fnl f* **7/1**

4600 4 nk **Blue Knight (IRE)**[6] 721 8-8-8 46 oh1 .... TPQueally 8 49
(P Howling) *hld up in tch: rdn over 2f out: hung lft wl ins fnl f: nt qckn* **16/1**

0626 5 1 ½ **A Teen**[12] 682 9-8-10 48 .... JimmyQuinn 2 47
(P Howling) *a.p: rdn 3f out: no ex towards fin* **8/1**

3205 6 nk **Seldemosa**[6] 723 6-8-10 48 .... JimCrowley 9 47
(M S Saunders) *hld up in mid-div: hdwy over 2f out: rdn wl over 1f out: one pce* **5/1**[2]

1000 7 shd **Charlottebutterfly**[20] 637 7-8-8 46 oh1 .... BrettDoyle 10 44
(P J McBride) *hld up towards rr: rdn and sme hdwy over 2f out: no imp fnl f* **8/1**

6006 8 ½ **Tribute (IRE)**[44] 435 6-8-5 46 oh1 .... JasonEdmunds(3) 7 43
(John A Harris) *hld up and bhd: c wd st: nvr nrr* **22/1**

0-40 9 shd **Only If I Laugh**[39] 485 6-8-12 50 .... GrahamGibbons 3 47
(M J Attwater) *hld up in mid-div: rdn 4f out: lost pl over 2f out: n.d after* **4/1**[1]

2000 10 nk **Midmaar (IRE)**[21] 632 6-8-12 50 ....(b) DarryllHolland 1 46
(M Wigham) *led early: hld up in tch: rdn over 2f out: wknd ins fnl f* **13/2**

000- 11 shd **Bond Angel Eyes**[180] 5637 4-8-3 46 ....(p) DuranFentiman(5) 5 42
(G R Oldroyd) *sn led: rdn and hdd over 2f out: wknd ins fnl f* **20/1**

00-0 12 6 **Red Lantern**[27] 579 6-8-8 46 oh1 .... PaulMulrennan 11 26
(M W Easterby) *hld up and bhd: rdn and c v wd st: sn struggling* **50/1**

1m 29.47s (-0.93) **Going Correction** -0.20s/f (Stan) 12 Ran SP% **119.4**
Speed ratings (Par 101):97,96,95,95,93 93,93,92,92,91 91,85
CSF £170.39 CT £1222.80 TOTE £5.30: £1.60, £8.70, £2.20; EX 89.30.
Owner R J Hodges **Bred** J K S Cresswell **Trained** Charlton Mackrell, Somerset

FOCUS
A weak event rated around the placed horses. The winning time was 0.14 seconds faster than the second division, but still only modest form for the grade.

801 BOOK ONLINE AT WOLVERHAMPTON-RACECOURSE.CO.UK H'CAP (DIV II) 7f 32y(P)
2:30 (2:30) (Class 6) (0-50,50) 4-Y-0+ £1,535 (£453; £226) Stalls High

Form RPR

-050 1 **Union Jack Jackson (IRE)**[21] 632 5-8-9 47 ....(b) DaleGibson 4 55
(John A Harris) *hld up in mid-div: hdwy on ins over 2f out: rdn wl over 1f out: r.o to ld last strides* **20/1**

1024 2 hd **Prince Of Gold**[43] 440 7-8-12 50 ....(b) GrahamGibbons 12 58
(R Hollinshead) *hld up in rr: sn swtchd lft: nt clr run on ins over 2f out: hdwy wl over 1f out: rdn to ld wl ins fnl f: hdd last strides* **13/2**[3]

045- 3 ½ **Attacca**[180] 5636 6-8-9 47 ow1 .... DarryllHolland 2 53
(J R Weymes) *hld up in tch: rdn over 1f out: led ins fnl f: sn hdd: nt qckn* **13/2**[3]

0-06 4 ¾ **Danettie**[20] 637 6-8-12 50 .... JamieSpencer 1 55
(W M Brisbourne) *sn led: rdn wl over 1f out: hdd and no ex ins fnl f* **6/1**[2]

046 5 hd **Very Well Red**[18] 649 4-8-10 48 .... JimCrowley 5 52
(P W Hiatt) *hld up in mid-div: hdwy 3f out: c wd st: rdn over 1f out: one pce fnl f* **14/1**

-133 6 3 ½ **Wodhill Be**[33] 519 7-8-10 48 .... AdamKirby 8 43
(D Morris) *hld up and bhd: nt clr run 2f out: rdn and hdwy over 1f out: no imp fnl f* **8/1**

3063 7 1 **Fulvio (USA)**[20] 637 7-8-12 50 ....(v) TPQueally 6 42
(P Howling) *hld up and bhd: hdwy on outside over 2f out: sn rdn: wknd over 1f out* **6/1**[2]

-306 8 ½ **Task Complete**[30] 557 4-8-5 46 oh1 ....(b) NeilChalmers(3) 11 37
(Jean-Rene Auvray) *s.i.s: sn swtchd lft: rdn over 2f out: a in rr* **20/1**

4144 9 ½ **Christian Bendix**[6] 723 5-8-12 50 ....(p) JimmyQuinn 3 40
(P Howling) *led early: hld up in tch: rdn 3f out: wknd wl over 1f out* **11/2**[1]

6452 10 3 ½ **Prettilini**[8] 710 4-8-11 49 .... J-PGuillambert 7 30
(R Brotherton) *prom: wkng whn n.m.r over 2f out* **9/1**

-050 11 10 **Kissi Kissi**[44] 430 4-8-3 46 oh1 ....(v) KevinGhunowa(5) 10 —
(M J Attwater) *plld hrd: sn prom: wknd 2f out* **25/1**

2000 12 nk **Princess Arwen**[12] 686 5-8-8 46 oh1 ....(b) BrettDoyle 9 —
(Mrs Barbara Waring) *chsd ldrs tl wknd over 3f out* **40/1**

1m 29.61s (-0.79) **Going Correction** -0.20s/f (Stan) 12 Ran SP% **114.2**
Speed ratings (Par 101):96,95,95,94,94 90,88,88,87,83 72,72
CSF £134.48 CT £962.90 TOTE £21.00: £3.20, £2.30, £3.00; EX 192.10.
Owner Adrian Swingler **Bred** Tom Foley **Trained** Eastwell, Leics

FOCUS
The winning time was 0.14 seconds slower than the first division and modest for the class. The form is rated through the first and second.
Union Jack Jackson(IRE) Official explanation: trainer said, regarding the apparent improvement in form, gelding benefitted from today's longer trip and the refitting of blinkers
Wodhill Be Official explanation: jockey said mare was denied a clear run

802 RINGSIDE SUITE 700 THEATRE STYLE CONFERENCE MEDIAN AUCTION MAIDEN STKS 5f 216y(P)
3:00 (3:03) (Class 6) 3-4-Y-0 £2,218 (£654; £327) Stalls Low

Form RPR

622- 1 **Gower**[161] 6024 3-8-13 85 .... SteveDrowne 1 65+
(R Charlton) *mde all: clr fnl f: easily* **1/5**[1]

0-00 2 5 **Master Ben (IRE)**[7] 715 4-9-12 37 ....(b) PhillipMakin 4 41
(S R Bowring) *w wnr tl rdn wl over 1f out: one pce* **66/1**

0 3 2 **Bear Bottom**[26] 589 3-8-13 .... TPQueally 6 35
(W J Musson) *hld up in tch: effrt over 2f out: rdn and swtchd lft wl over 1f out: one pce* **10/1**[2]

4 4 **Just Spike** 4-9-12 .... GrahamGibbons 5 23
(B P J Baugh) *s.i.s: bhd: rdn over 2f out: no rspnse* **40/1**

60-0 5 5 **Spanish Air**[22] 624 3-8-8 57 ....(t) J-PGuillambert 3 3
(J W Hills) *chsd ldrs: rdn over 2f out: sn wknd* **20/1**

6 32 **Hughmanbean (IRE)** 4-9-12 .... DanielTudhope 2 —
(D Carroll) *bhd: lost action and eased 3f out: fin lame* **12/1**[3]

1m 15.81s **Going Correction** -0.20s/f (Stan)
WFA 3 from 4yo 13lb 6 Ran SP% **108.8**
Speed ratings (Par 101):92,85,82,77,70 28
CSF £24.63 TOTE £1.20: £1.02, £13.00; EX 15.80.
Owner D J Deer **Bred** D J And Mrs Deer **Trained** Beckhampton, Wilts

FOCUS
A hugely uncompetitive contest won as expected by Gower but the overall form is weak.
Spanish Air Official explanation: jockey said filly was never travelling
Hughmanbean(IRE) Official explanation: vet said gelding finished lame

803 SPONSOR A RACE BY CALLING 0870 22 2442 H'CAP 5f 216y(P)
3:30 (3:30) (Class 5) (0-70,67) 4-Y-0+ £3,071 (£906; £453) Stalls Low

Form RPR

1002 1 **Came Back (IRE)**[7] 717 4-8-8 64 .... MichaelJStainton(5) 1 81+
(J Mackie) *a.p: wnt 2nd 2f out: rdn to ld 1f out: r.o wl* **11/4**[1]

6-60 2 2 **Dasheena**[69] 161 4-7-11 55 ....(be[1]) MCGeran(7) 4 63+
(A J McCabe) *s.i.s: sn chsng ldrs: lost pl over 3f out: rdn whn nt clr run and swtchd rt over 1f out: r.o ins fnl f: nt trbl wnr* **50/1**

0003 3 nk **Dvinsky (USA)**[22] 621 6-9-1 66 .... DarryllHolland 5 73
(P Howling) *chsd ldrs: rdn 2f out: kpt on fnl f* **8/1**[2]

-126 4 ¾ **George The Second**[34] 513 4-8-13 67 .... RichardKingscote(3) 11 72
(Mrs H Sweeting) *w ldrs: led over 3f out: rdn and hdd 1f out: no ex towards fin* **14/1**

0-65 5 2 **Hoh Wotanite**[25] 609 4-8-9 65 ....(b[1]) RussellKennemore(5) 13 64+
(R Hollinshead) *hld up and bhd: c v wd ent st: sn hrd rdn and edgd rt: hdwy and hung lft ins fnl f: nvr trbld ldrs* **16/1**

06-0 6 1 ½ **General Feeling (IRE)**[78] 67 6-8-5 56 .... JamieMackay 8 50
(M Mullineaux) *s.i.s: nvr nrr* **40/1**

610- 7 hd **Paddywack (IRE)**[153] 6174 10-8-11 62 ....(b) TonyCulhane 6 56
(D W Chapman) *hld up in mid-div: rdn over 2f out: no hdwy* **33/1**

5000 8 ½ **Charlie Delta**[6] 724 4-9-0 65 ....(p) JamieSpencer 9 57
(J R Boyle) *hld up in mid-div: rdn and sme hdwy wl over 1f out: no further prog* **10/1**[3]

0-45 **9** *nk* **Polar Force**[60] 251 7-8-2 **58**.................... KevinGhunowa(5) 12 49
(Mrs C A Dunnett) *s.i.s: a bhd* **25/1**

000- **10** *1* **Kennington**[136] 6452 7-8-11 **62**....................(b) AdamKirby 3 50
(Mrs C A Dunnett) *led 1f: rdn over 2f out: wknd wl over 1f out* **20/1**

6-22 **11** *½* **Devon Flame**[11] 688 8-9-2 **67**.................... GeorgeBaker 10 54
(R J Hodges) *a bhd* **8/1**[2]

-062 **12** *½* **Inwaan (IRE)**[3] 751 4-8-7 **58**....................(t) TPQueally 2 43
(P R Webber) *led after 1f tl over 3f out: rdn and wknd over 1f out* **11/4**[1]

00-6 **13** *nk* **Up Tempo (IRE)**[63] 228 9-8-9 **60**....................(b) PaulMulrennan 7 44
(C R Dore) *a bhd* **25/1**

1m 13.57s (-2.24) **Going Correction** -0.20s/f (Stan) **13** Ran SP% **117.0**
Speed ratings (Par 103):106,103,102,101,99 97,97,96,95,94 93,93,92
CSF £195.08 CT £805.37 TOTE £4.70: £2.20, £10.50, £2.10; EX 173.50.
Owner W I Bloomfield **Bred** Yeomanstown Stud **Trained** Church Broughton , Derbys

FOCUS
A modest handicap. The winner did the job readily and the form looks straightforward enough rated around the third and fourth.
Hoh Wotanite Official explanation: jockey said colt had no more to give
Charlie Delta Official explanation: jockey said gelding hung right
Devon Flame Official explanation: jockey said gelding lost a shoe

804 GET MARRIED AT WOLVERHAMPTON RACECOURSE CLASSIFIED STKS 1m 4f 50y(P)
4:00 (4:02) (Class 7) 4-Y-0+ **£2,047** (£604; £302) **Stalls** Low

Form RPR

-246 **1** **Trysting Grove (IRE)**[14] 665 6-8-11 43.................... SaleemGolam(3) 1 54
(E G Bevan) *hld up in mid-div: smooth hdwy over 3f out: led over 1f out: drvn out* **7/2**[2]

2 *¾* **Colwyn Bay (IRE)**[103] 5282 5-9-0 45....................(p) JamieSpencer 3 53
(Jane Chapple-Hyam) *hld up in tch: rdn 2f out: wnt 2nd jst over 1f out: edgd rt ins fnl f: nt qckn* **15/8**[1]

-065 **3** *3½* **Silver Mont (IRE)**[12] 683 4-8-12 42....................(b) PhillipMakin 10 47
(S R Bowring) *hld up in mid-div: hdwy over 3f out: led over 2f out: rdn and hdd over 1f out: no ex fnl f* **11/2**[3]

3330 **4** *5* **Twilight Avenger (IRE)**[7] 716 4-8-7 44.................... KevinGhunowa(5) 12 39
(W M Brisbourne) *hld up and bhd: hdwy over 3f out: rdn over 2f out: wknd fnl f* **12/1**

5-00 **5** *1¾* **Flashing Floozie**[30] 558 4-8-12 41.................... DarryllHolland 7 36
(A W Carroll) *stdd s: hld up in rr: rdn and hdwy over 2f out: no further prog* **16/1**

0-60 **6** *4* **Stallone**[70] 148 10-9-0 45.................... TonyHamilton 2 30
(N Wilson) *hld up in mid-div: hdwy on ins over 2f out: sn rdn: wknd over 1f out* **12/1**

6400 **7** *¾* **Elms Schoolboy**[1] 789 5-9-0 45....................(b) JimmyQuinn 11 29
(P Howling) *s.i.s: rdn over 2f out: a bhd* **9/1**

000- **8** *6* **Don Pasquale**[119] 2141 5-9-0 40.................... MickyFenton 8 19
(J T Stimpson) *prom: wnt 2nd over 6f out: rdn and ev ch over 2f out: wknd wl over 1f out* **50/1**

354/ **9** *4* **Cottam Grange**[14] 4565 7-9-0 41.................... DanielTudhope 6 13
(I W McInnes) *hld up in mid-div: rdn 4f out: sn struggling* **14/1**

0650 **10** *1¾* **Ronnies Lad**[5] 730 5-9-0 45....................(p) PaulMulrennan 4 10
(J R Norton) *chsd ldr over 5f: wknd over 3f out* **12/1**

0005 **11** *5* **Layed Back Rocky**[7] 716 5-9-0 43.................... J-PGuillambert 9 —
(M Mullineaux) *led: rdn and hdd over 2f out: sn wknd* **16/1**

2m 39.47s (-2.95) **Going Correction** -0.20s/f (Stan)
WFA 4 from 5yo+ 2lb **11** Ran SP% **125.9**
Speed ratings (Par 97):101,100,98,94,93 91,90,86,83,82 79
CSF £11.28 TOTE £4.40: £1.20, £2.00, £2.00; EX 13.80.
Owner E G Bevan **Bred** Knocktoran Stud **Trained** Ullingswick, H'fords

FOCUS
A terrible race best assessed through the winner.
Ronnies Lad Official explanation: jockey said gelding hung left

805 HORIZONS RESTAURANT - OPENING SOON H'CAP 1m 1f 103y(P)
4:30 (4:30) (Class 6) (0-65,64) 4-Y-0+ **£2,388** (£705; £352) **Stalls** Low

Form RPR

1-46 **1** **Scamperdale**[58] 286 5-9-0 **60**.................... TPQueally 7 68+
(B P J Baugh) *hld up: sn in tch: rdn over 2f out: hung lft over 1f out: r.o to ld last strides* **5/2**[1]

1341 **2** *hd* **My Michelle**[29] 571 6-9-2 **62**.................... TonyCulhane 1 70
(B Palling) *led: rdn wl over 1f out: hdd last strides* **7/2**[2]

500- **3** *½* **Lord Of Dreams (IRE)**[141] 6382 5-9-0 **60**.................... BrettDoyle 3 67
(D W P Arbuthnot) *a.p: rdn over 1f out: ev ch ins fnl f: nt qckn* **4/1**[3]

4-55 **4** *½* **Summer Lodge**[65] 204 4-9-0 **63**....................(be) StephenDonohoe(3) 5 69
(A J McCabe) *prom: wnt 2nd 6f out: rdn 2f out: r.o one pce fnl f* **11/1**

1060 **5** *1* **Street Life (IRE)**[26] 594 9-8-11 **64**.................... AlanRutter(7) 10 68+
(W J Musson) *swtchd lft sn after s: hld up in rr: rdn over 2f out: hdwy over 1f out: nt rch ldrs* **10/1**

640- **6** *3½* **Miss Odd Sox**[353] 918 4-8-13 **59**.................... DavidAllan 6 56
(W M Brisbourne) *hld up and bhd: rdn 3f out: n.d* **40/1**

140- **7** *shd* **Topflight Wildbird**[199] 5173 4-9-2 **62**.................... J-PGuillambert 4 59
(Mrs G S Rees) *hld up towards rr: hdwy over 3f out: sn rdn: wknd wl over 1f out* **33/1**

2-30 **8** *3* **King's Spear (IRE)**[12] 685 4-8-11 **64**.................... MCGeran(7) 2 55
(P W Chapple-Hyam) *hld up in tch: wknd over 3f out* **7/1**

-660 **9** *5* **Goose Chase**[62] 235 5-8-3 **56**.................... KylieManser(7) 8 37
(P A Blockley) *a bhd* **16/1**

2200 **10** *nk* **Blackmail (USA)**[18] 651 9-8-12 **58**....................(b) DarryllHolland 9 38
(P Mitchell) *hld up in mid-div: hdwy over 5f out: rdn and wknd over 3f out* **12/1**

2m 0.52s (-2.10) **Going Correction** -0.20s/f (Stan) **10** Ran SP% **119.7**
Speed ratings (Par 101):101,100,100,99,99 95,95,93,88,88
CSF £11.47 CT £34.50 TOTE £4.60: £1.40, £1.20, £1.60; EX 14.90.
Owner Park Lane Thoroughbreds **Bred** Mrs J A Prescott **Trained** Audley, Staffs

FOCUS
A modest but competitive handicap rated around the first three but not totally solid.
Blackmail(USA) Official explanation: jockey said gelding hung right throughout

806 STAY AT THE WOLVERHAMPTON HOLIDAY INN H'CAP 7f 32y(P)
5:00 (5:00) (Class 6) (0-60,60) 4-Y-0+ **£2,388** (£705; £352) **Stalls** High

Form RPR

0-00 **1** **Motu (IRE)**[13] 673 6-9-0 **58**....................(v) DanielTudhope 11 67
(I W McInnes) *hld up in mid-div: hdwy on outside over 2f out: rdn and edgd lft over 1f out: led ins fnl f: r.o* **12/1**

4-00 **2** *1¼* **Benny The Bus**[12] 686 5-8-13 **57**.................... GrahamGibbons 10 63
(Mrs G S Rees) *led over 1f: w ldr: led over 2f out: sn rdn: hdd ins fnl f: nt qckn* **12/1**

0252 **3** *2* **Haroldini (IRE)**[12] 681 5-8-13 **60**....................(p) JasonEdmunds(3) 4 61
(J Balding) *a.p: rdn and one pce fnl f* **2/1**[1]

000- **4** *¾* **Reveur**[87] 6993 4-8-11 **55**.................... TomEaves 1 54
(M Mullineaux) *hld up and bhd: hdwy on ins over 2f out: rdn and one pce fnl f* **25/1**

3100 **5** *nk* **Mister Benji**[12] 686 8-8-5 **56**.................... SoniaEaton(7) 2 54
(B P J Baugh) *a.p: no ex fnl f* **11/1**

-052 **6** *½* **Hits Only Cash**[29] 570 5-8-12 **56**.................... J-PGuillambert 8 53
(J Pearce) *s.i.s: in rr: pushed along over 3f out: c v wd st: nvr nr ldrs* **5/1**[2]

3330 **7** *shd* **Kingsmaite**[12] 681 6-8-8 **52**....................(t) PhillipMakin 7 49
(S R Bowring) *hld up in mid-div: pushed along 3f out: rdn wl over 1f out: no hdwy* **7/1**[3]

005- **8** *1* **Iced Diamond (IRE)**[224] 4456 8-9-0 **58**.................... DavidAllan 5 52
(W M Brisbourne) *hld up and bhd: rdn and sme hdwy over 1f out: n.d* **10/1**

0-00 **9** *2* **Richelieu**[58] 286 5-9-0 **58**.................... TonyCulhane 6 47
(J J Lambe, Ire) *a bhd* **14/1**

2134 **10** *6* **Desert Lover (IRE)**[5] 729 5-8-10 **54**....................(tp) DarryllHolland 9 27
(R J Price) *prom tl rdn and wknd over 2f out* **7/1**[3]

640- **11** *1¼* **Bond Free Spirit (IRE)**[197] 5243 4-8-3 **52**.................... DuranFentiman(5) 3 22
(G R Oldroyd) *w ldr: led over 5f out tl over 2f out: wknd over 1f out* **33/1**

1m 28.43s (-1.97) **Going Correction** -0.20s/f (Stan) **11** Ran SP% **121.3**
Speed ratings (Par 101):103,101,99,98,98 97,97,96,93,87 85
CSF £152.03 CT £420.41 TOTE £17.20: £4.50, £3.20, £2.00; EX 182.50 Place 6 £53.23, Place 5 £9.93..
Owner G Parkinson **Bred** J Hanly **Trained** Catwick, E Yorks

FOCUS
A very moderate race. The form is probably sound for the grade but not many short-term winners are likely to emerge from the race, with the possible exception of the fourth.
Desert Lover(IRE) Official explanation: jockey said gelding hung left
T/Plt: £36.70 to a £1 stake. Pool: £58,025.70. 1,151.10 winning tickets. T/Qpdt: £4.60 to a £1 stake. Pool: £3,707.90. 587.00 winning tickets. KH

727 SOUTHWELL (L-H)
Wednesday, March 28

OFFICIAL GOING: Standard
Wind: virtually nil

807 BOOK TICKETS ON-LINE MEDIAN AUCTION MAIDEN STKS 7f (F)
2:10 (2:12) (Class 6) 3-4-Y-O **£2,184** (£644; £322) **Stalls** Low

Form RPR

320- **1** **Mount Hermon (IRE)**[180] 5655 3-8-12 77.................... SteveDrowne 3 64+
(H Morrison) *mde all: rdn clr over 1f out: easily* **1/2**[1]

\- **2** *5* **Acapulco Bay** 3-8-12.................... PaulMulrennan 1 51
(Miss J A Camacho) *chsd ldrs on inner: rdn along over 2f out: kpt on ins last: no ch w wnr* **20/1**

040- **3** *¾* **Storm Mission (USA)**[124] 6576 3-8-12 49.................... EdwardCreighton 4 49
(Miss V Haigh) *chsd ldng pair: rdn along wl over 2f out: kpt on same pce* **40/1**

53-3 **4** *1* **Winged Farasi**[18] 655 3-8-12 70.................... MickyFenton 7 46
(Miss J Feilden) *cl up: rdn and ev ch over 2f out: sn drvn: edgd rt and wknd* **5/2**[2]

0-04 **5** *1¼* **Cryptic Clue (USA)**[45] 429 3-8-12 47.................... JamieSpencer 10 43
(D W Chapman) *dwlt and towards rr. wd st: gd hdwy 2f out: rdn and wnt 2nd ent last: sn hung lft and wknd* **20/1**

00- **6** *1¾* **Mr Crystal (FR)**[104] 6815 3-8-12.................... PaulHanagan 8 39
(Micky Hammond) *in tch: rdn along 1/2-way: sn btn* **66/1**

-440 **7** *1½* **Chart Oak**[13] 683 4-9-13 53.................... JimmyQuinn 5 35
(P Howling) *chsd ldrs: rdn along wl over 2f out: grad wknd* **16/1**[3]

6-00 **8** *5* **Night Reveller (IRE)**[6] 728 4-9-3 28.................... RussellKennemore(5) 6 17
(M C Chapman) *dwlt: a bhd* **200/1**

00 **9** *½* **Danehill Warrior (IRE)**[5] 745 3-8-5.................... MartinGuest(7) 9 20
(R C Guest) *in tch: rdn along 1/2-way: sn wknd* **66/1**

6 **10** *58* **Feels Like Heaven**[9] 711 3-8-7.................... DavidAllan 2 —
(T D Easterby) *s.i.s: a bhd* **33/1**

1m 31.56s (0.76) **Going Correction** +0.025s/f (Slow)
WFA 3 from 4yo 15lb **10** Ran SP% **119.5**
Speed ratings (Par 101):96,90,89,88,86 84,83,77,76,10
CSF £18.56 TOTE £1.80: £1.10, £4.50, £7.60; EX 18.90 Trifecta £418.00 Part won. Pool: £588.85 - 0.10 winning units..
Owner Wood Street Syndicate III **Bred** Illumnatus Investments And Elite Bloodst **Trained** East Ilsley, Berks

FOCUS
The winner apart, this was a low-grade affair. The finishing position of the third causes some concern, but Mount Hermon was value for much more than the winning margin and he should be ignored when rating the rest of the field.
Feels Like Heaven Official explanation: jockey said filly was never travelling

808 HOSPITALITY PACKAGES AVAILABLE H'CAP 1m 6f (F)
2:45 (2:45) (Class 6) (0-65,66) 4-Y-0+ **£2,730** (£806; £403) **Stalls** Low

Form RPR

2120 **1** **Blue Hills**[3] 775 6-9-4 **65**....................(b) WilliamCarson(7) 7 77
(P W Hiatt) *trckd ldr: led over 5f out: rdn clr 3f out: styd on wl* **7/4**[1]

630- **2** *4* **Great As Gold (IRE)**[81] 6178 8-8-12 **55**.................... GregFairley(3) 9 61
(B Ellison) *chsd ldrs: rdn along over 4f out: drvn to chse wnr fnl 2f: no imp* **7/1**[3]

-156 **3** *2½* **Tioga Gold (IRE)**[22] 631 8-8-3 **48**.................... RussellKennemore(5) 1 51
(L R James) *hld up in tch: hdwy over 4f out: chsd ldrs 3f out: sn rdn and kpt on same pce* **10/1**

-150 **4** *1* **Red River Rock (IRE)**[13] 683 5-8-7 **47**....................(be) PaulMulrennan 6 49
(T J Fitzgerald) *keen: trckd ldrs: hdwy 4f out: rdn to chse ldrs 3f out: drvn and one pce fnl 2f* **9/2**[2]

-535 **5** *¾* **Scaramoushca**[26] 603 4-8-10 **54** ow1....................(be[1]) AdamKirby 8 54
(P S McEntee) *midfield: rdn along over 4f out: drvn 3f out and n.d* **12/1**

-000 **6** *6* **Monmouthshire**[8] 716 4-8-4 **50** oh2.................... EdwardCreighton 5 40
(R J Price) *chsd ldrs on inner: rdn along 4f out: drvn 3f out and sn wknd* **14/1**

0001 **7** *1½* **Bethanys Boy (IRE)**[6] 730 6-9-12 **66** 6ex.................... SimonWhitworth 2 56
(P A Blockley) *stdd s and hld up wl in rr: hdwy over 4f out: wd st: sn rdn and no imp* **10/1**

050- **8** 3/4 **Sara Mana Mou**[216] [4734] 4-8-1 **52** oh5 ow2 .... EmmettStack(3) 4 37
(J G Portman) *chsd ldrs: rdn along 6f out: sn wknd* **20/1**

0000 **9** 3 1/2 **Takes Tutu (USA)**[22] [631] 8-8-12 **52** .... JamieSpencer 3 36
(C R Dore) *in tch: rdn along 6f out: sn btn* **12/1**

10 1/2 **Rocknest Island (IRE)**[26] [3920] 4-8-8 **52** .... PaulHanagan 10 35
(P D Niven) *led: rdn along and hdd over 5f out: sn wknd* **25/1**

-000 **11** 23 **College Rebel**[13] [683] 6-8-3 **46** oh1 .... PatrickMathers(3) 11 —
(J F Coupland) *a bhd* **100/1**

3m 10.36s (0.76) **Going Correction** +0.025s/f (Slow)
WFA 4 from 5yo+ 4lb **11** Ran SP% **116.9**
Speed ratings (Par 101):98,95,94,93,93 89,89,88,86,86 73
CSF £13.69 CT £96.98 TOTE £2.90: £1.30, £2.90, £2.70; EX 17.00 Trifecta £85.40 Pool: £429.60 - 3.57 winning units..
Owner Tom Pratt **Bred** Darley **Trained** Hook Norton, Oxon

FOCUS
A very moderate staying event with no early pace. The jockey can claim plenty of credit on the winner, as he wound the pace up from the front. Blue Hills's best ever run.
Monmouthshire Official explanation: jockey said gelding had no more to give
Takes Tutu(USA) Official explanation: jockey said gelding had no more to give
College Rebel Official explanation: jockey said mare had no more to give

809 S & A FINANCE (NOTTINGHAM) LTD H'CAP 1m (F)
3:15 (3:15) (Class 5) (0-75,75) 4-Y-0+ **£3,238** (£963; £481; £240) **Stalls** Low

Form RPR

000- **1** **Future's Dream**[172] [5810] 4-9-2 **75** .... PatCosgrave 4 94+
(K R Burke) *disp ld tl led ovr 2f out: rdn clr wl over 1f out: kpt on* **4/1**[2]

5120 **2** 3 1/2 **Luckylover**[46] [427] 4-9-0 **73** .... (t) TPQueally 1 84
(M G Quinlan) *disp ld: rdn and hdd over 2f out: one pce fr wl over 1f out* **4/1**[2]

-215 **3** 1 1/4 **Majehar**[19] [650] 5-8-2 **61** oh1 .... AdrianMcCarthy 5 69
(A G Newcombe) *outpcd and pushed along towards rr: hdwy 2f out: kpt on u.p appr last* **7/2**[1]

3605 **4** 1 3/4 **Conrad**[13] [681] 4-8-3 **62** .... PaulHanagan 3 66
(R A Fahey) *chsd ldng pair: rdn along over 2f out: sn drvn and wknd* **5/1**[3]

3000 **5** 13 **Undeterred**[21] [634] 11-8-7 **66** .... (v) JimCrowley 2 40
(K J Burke) *s.i.s: a rr* **33/1**

0062 **6** 2 **Shifty**[6] [732] 8-7-10 **62** .... KellyHarrison(7) 7 32
(D Carroll) *chsd ldng pair: rdn along 3f out: sn drvn and wknd* **4/1**[2]

0606 **7** 5 **Tyzack (IRE)**[22] [629] 6-8-10 **69** .... MickyFenton 6 27
(W M Brisbourne) *dwlt: a rr* **9/1**

1m 42.94s (-1.66) **Going Correction** +0.025s/f (Slow) **7** Ran SP% **111.8**
Speed ratings (Par 103):109,105,104,102,89 87,82
CSF £19.35 TOTE £6.10: £3.30, £2.70; EX 24.10.
Owner Mrs Maura Gittins **Bred** Mrs D Du Feu **Trained** Middleham Moor, N Yorks

FOCUS
The form looks sound for the grade, and the time was far quicker than a later race over the same distance. Decent efforts from the first two.
Shifty Official explanation: jockey said gelding hung right in the straight
Tyzack(IRE) Official explanation: jockey said gelding lost its action

810 SOUTHWELL-RACECOURSE.CO.UK H'CAP 5f (F)
3:50 (3:51) (Class 4) (0-85,84) 4-Y-0+ **£5,181** (£1,541; £770; £384) **Stalls** High

Form RPR

4112 **1** **Egyptian Lord**[6] [727] 4-8-6 **72** .... (b) RobbieFitzpatrick 9 83
(Peter Grayson) *dwlt and towards rr: gd hdwy to chse ldrs 2f out: rdn and styd on to ld ins last: drvn out* **7/1**[3]

2404 **2** nk **Figaro Flyer (IRE)**[12] [692] 4-8-11 **77** .... TonyCulhane 7 87
(P Howling) *cl up: rdn along and outpcd 2f out: swtchd rt and hdwy over 1f out: drvn and styd on strly ins last: jst hld* **14/1**

-206 **3** 1 3/4 **Pieter Brueghel (USA)**[32] [554] 8-9-3 **83** .... JoeFanning 3 87
(D Nicholls) *hld up in tch: pushed along and outpcd after 2f: nt clr run over 2f out: swtchd rt and rdn: styd on strly ins last* **10/1**

1131 **4** 1/2 **Canadian Danehill (IRE)**[6] [727] 5-8-12 **81** 6ex ..... (p) JamesDoyle(3) 10 83
(R M H Cowell) *cl up: rdn and ev ch wl over 1f out: sn drvn and wknd ent last* **11/4**[1]

5036 **5** hd **Pawan (IRE)**[29] [575] 7-8-9 **80** .... (b) AnnStokell(5) 8 82
(Miss A Stokell) *led: rdn wl over 1f out: hung bdly lft ent last: sn hdd and kpt on same pce* **16/1**

-061 **6** 3/4 **Efistorm**[61] [254] 6-8-11 **77** .... PaulMulrennan 2 76
(C R Dore) *cl up on outer: effrt 2f out and ev ch tl rdn and wkng whn carried lft ins last* **12/1**

126- **7** 3 **Cape Presto (IRE)**[115] [6690] 4-8-7 **73** .... (v) AdrianMcCarthy 1 62
(Mrs C A Dunnett) *sn towards rr: rdn along 1/2-way: sn no imp* **16/1**

-500 **8** 1/2 **Glenviews Youngone (IRE)**[39] [490] 4-8-12 **78** .... GrahamGibbons 4 65
(Peter Grayson) *wnt lft s: sn chsng ldrs: rdn along over 2f out and sn wknd* **50/1**

6-33 **9** 3 **Desperate Dan**[32] [554] 6-9-4 **84** .... (b) JamieSpencer 6 61
(J A Osborne) *hld up in rr: effrt whn n.m.r over 2f out: sn rdn and no imp* **10/3**[2]

5-60 **10** 1 1/2 **Dancing Mystery**[32] [554] 13-9-0 **80** .... (b) StephenCarson 12 52
(E A Wheeler) *dwlt: sn cl up: rdn along 2f out and sn wknd* **40/1**

144- **11** 3 **Rosein**[132] [6499] 5-8-10 **76** .... J-PGuillambert 5 38
(Mrs G S Rees) *dwlt: sn rdn: outpcd and bhd fr 1/2-way* **9/1**

03-0 **12** 3 1/2 **Bold Minstrel (IRE)**[32] [554] 5-8-10 **76** .... SteveDrowne 11 26
(M Quinn) *cl up: rdn along 2f out: drvn and wknd over 1f out* **18/1**

59.95 secs (-0.35) **Going Correction** +0.075s/f (Slow) **12** Ran SP% **117.1**
Speed ratings (Par 105):105,104,101,100,100 99,94,93,89,86 81,76
CSF £99.72 CT £996.44 TOTE £6.10: £1.80, £4.20, £3.20; EX 73.30 Trifecta £433.90 Pool: £745.69 - 1.22 winning units..
Owner D & R Rhodes & Mrs S Grayson **Bred** I A N Wight And Mrs D M Wight **Trained** Formby, Lancs
■ Stewards' Enquiry : Ann Stokell one-day ban: careless riding (Apr 8)

FOCUS
A good sprint handicap. Egyptian Lord continues to progress.

811 ARENA LEISURE PLC H'CAP 1m 3f (F)
4:25 (4:25) (Class 4) (0-80,77) 4-Y-0+ **£5,181** (£1,541; £770; £384) **Stalls** Low

Form RPR

0314 **1** **Mahmjra**[22] [631] 5-8-3 **63** oh2 .... EdwardCreighton 2 77
(C N Allen) *mde all: set str pce: rdn and qcknd clr wl over 2f out: drvn over 1f out: styd on gamely fnl f* **11/2**[2]

03-2 **2** 1 **Black Falcon (IRE)**[15] [669] 7-8-10 **70** .... MickyFenton 10 82
(M A Peill) *hld up in rr: stdy hdwy 4f out: chsd ldng pair 3f out: drvn to chal over 1f out and ev ch tl no ex last 100 yds* **8/1**

4355 **3** 7 **Jackie Kiely**[15] [669] 6-8-10 **70** .... (t) J-PGuillambert 8 70
(R Brotherton) *hld up towards rr: stdy hdwy over 4f out: rdn to chse ldng pair 2f out and ev ch tl drvn and one pce appr last* **12/1**

1110 **4** 3 **Jazrawy**[12] [693] 5-9-2 **76** .... DanielTudhope 4 71
(D Carroll) *chsd wnr: rdn along over 3f out: sn drvn and outpcd fnl 2f* **6/1**[3]

0-64 **5** 1 **Torrens (IRE)**[50] [377] 5-8-12 **72** .... PaulHanagan 3 66
(R A Fahey) *hld up towards rr: hdwy 4f out: rdn along 3f out and ss no imp* **10/1**

231- **6** 1 **Bollin Derek**[172] [5815] 4-9-2 **77** .... DavidAllan 6 69
(T D Easterby) *chsd ldrs and sn rdn along: outpcd and rr over 5f out: styd on fnl 2f* **7/2**[1]

0016 **7** 6 **Kylkenny**[15] [669] 12-8-9 **74** .... (t) TravisBlock(5) 5 56
(H Morrison) *trckd ldrs: rdn along over 3f out: sn drvn and wknd* **10/1**

4-11 **8** 5 **Muntami (IRE)**[8] [631] 6-8-9 **72** .... StephenDonohoe(3) 1 45
(John A Harris) *hld up: rdn along over 4f out: wknd 3f out* **7/2**[1]

006- **9** 2 **Dance World**[53] [6941] 7-9-0 **77** .... (p) JamesDoyle(3) 9 47
(Miss J Feilden) *chsd ldng pair: rdn along over 4f out and grad wknd* **66/1**

345- **10** 10 **Stolen Glance**[113] [6716] 4-8-2 **64** oh2 .... (b[1]) DaleGibson 7 16
(M W Easterby) *sn rdn along in rr: a bhd* **16/1**

2m 26.13s (-2.77) **Going Correction** +0.025s/f (Slow)
WFA 4 from 5yo+ 1lb **10** Ran SP% **118.5**
Speed ratings (Par 105):111,110,105,103,102 101,97,93,92,84
CSF £49.87 CT £512.64 TOTE £8.70: £1.90, £2.40, £3.10; EX 84.20 Trifecta £499.30 Part won. Pool: £703.24 - 0.20 winning units..
Owner Travel Spot Ltd **Bred** Darley **Trained** Newmarket, Suffolk

FOCUS
A fair middle-distance handicap run at a very strong early pace. An improved effort from Mahmjra.
Muntami(IRE) Official explanation: jockey said gelding did not like the kickback

812 TURF RACING ON MONDAY H'CAP 1m (F)
4:55 (4:56) (Class 6) (0-50,50) 4-Y-0+ **£2,388** (£705; £352) **Stalls** Low

Form RPR

6660 **1** **Feelin Irie (IRE)**[7] [723] 4-8-11 **49** .... (p) PatCosgrave 7 59
(J R Boyle) *cl up: led after 2f: rdn wl clr over 2f out: styd on u.p fnl f* **8/1**

0145 **2** 3 **Mid Valley**[21] [637] 4-8-12 **50** .... (v) J-PGuillambert 3 54
(J R Jenkins) *rr whn sltly hmpd and swtchd rt after 2f: sn bhd: hdwy on inner over 2f out: sn rdn and styd on fnl f* **3/1**[1]

-000 **3** 1/2 **Inca Soldier (FR)**[13] [682] 4-8-8 **46** oh1 .... PaulFessey 6 49
(R C Guest) *in tch: hdwy to chse ldrs 1/2-way: rdn wl over 2f out and kpt on appr last* **16/1**

0520 **4** 3/4 **Shadow Jumper (IRE)**[22] [627] 6-8-8 **46** .... (v) MickyFenton 9 47
(J T Stimpson) *chsd ldrs: hdwy 3f out: rdn to chse wnr over 2f out: sn drvn and one pce appr last* **12/1**

4055 **5** 3 1/2 **Hometomammy**[8] [715] 5-8-5 **50** oh1 ow4 .... (p) WilliamCarson(7) 13 44
(P W Hiatt) *in tch: rdn along 3f out: sn drvn and kpt on one pce* **12/1**

0-32 **6** 1 3/4 **Bob Baileys**[13] [682] 5-8-10 **48** .... (b) JimCrowley 5 38
(P R Chamings) *in tch whn hmpd and lost pl after 2f: kpt on u.p fnl 2f: n.d* **9/2**[2]

000- **7** 1/2 **Peak Seasons (IRE)**[9] [5724] 4-8-5 **48** .... (v[1]) RussellKennemore(5) 12 37
(M C Chapman) *chsd ldrs: rdn along 3f out: sn wknd* **33/1**

15-0 **8** 16 **Cape Sydney (IRE)**[31] [557] 4-8-8 **46** oh1 .... TonyHamilton 4 —
(D W Barker) *in tch: rdn along 1/2-way: sn wknd* **28/1**

-010 **9** 6 **Government (IRE)**[6] [729] 6-8-6 **49** .... NicolPolli(5) 10 —
(M C Chapman) *led 2f: cl up tl rdn along over 3f out and sn wknd* **8/1**

10 1 1/2 **Otriad (RUS)**[158] 4-8-9 **47** .... JamieSpencer 14 —
(B J Curley) *sn rdn along and outpcd: a rr* **6/1**[3]

00-0 **11** 2 **Monashee River (IRE)**[6] [733] 4-8-12 **50** .... EdwardCreighton 1 —
(Miss V Haigh) *dwlt: a rr* **50/1**

00-4 **12** 39 **Earthling**[34] [524] 6-8-8 **46** oh1 .... (b) PaulMulrennan 8 —
(D W Chapman) *chsd ldng pair whn lost action and wknd qckly after 2f: sn bhd and virtually p.u* **8/1**

1m 45.71s (1.11) **Going Correction** +0.025s/f (Slow) **12** Ran SP% **120.4**
Speed ratings (Par 101):95,92,91,90,87 85,85,69,63,61 59,20
CSF £32.25 CT £388.34 TOTE £9.90: £2.00, £1.80, £5.60; EX 50.60 Trifecta £295.00 Part won. Pool: £415.55 - 0.51 winning units. Place 6 £162.28, Place 5 £105.49.
Owner M Khan X2 **Bred** Thomas F Brennan And Holborn Trust Co Ltd **Trained** Epsom, Surrey

FOCUS
A very moderate event. The early pace was good, but Feelin Irie was left clear on the home bend when Government dropped away and nothing could get in a blow. That may have had something to do with Earthling, who dropped right back through the field after a couple of furlongs. The winning time was 2.77 seconds slower than the earlier 61-75 handicap.
Otriad(RUS) Official explanation: jockey said colt was never travelling
Monashee River(IRE) Official explanation: jockey said filly was never travelling
Earthling Official explanation: jockey said gelding lost its action
T/Plt: £250.90 to a £1 stake. Pool: £59,304.05. 172.50 winning tickets. T/Qpdt: £156.30 to a £1 stake. Pool: £3,655.30. 17.30 winning tickets. JR

794 LINGFIELD (L-H)
Thursday, March 29

OFFICIAL GOING: Standard
Meeting transferred from Doncaster. It does not count as the start of the turf season for statistical purposes.
Wind: Moderate, across races 1-4; almost nil races 5-7 Weather: Cloudy

813 LINGFIELDPARK.CO.UK APPRENTICE H'CAP 1m 4f (P)
2:20 (2:20) (Class 5) (0-70,70) 4-Y-0+ **£2,914** (£867; £433; £216) **Stalls** Low

Form RPR

4603 **1** **Turner's Touch**[28] [587] 5-9-0 **70** .... (p) JemmaMarshall(7) 1 77
(G L Moore) *hld up in rr: hdwy over 1f out: led ins fnl f: pushed out to hold on narrowly* **9/1**

2424 **2** hd **Tresor Secret (FR)**[14] [683] 7-8-9 **58** .... JerryO'Dwyer 2 65
(J Gallagher) *chsd ldr: led briefly jst ins fnl f: kpt on* **8/1**

4333 **3** nk **Generous Lad (IRE)**[2] [799] 4-9-0 **68** .... (p) KevinGhunowa(3) 5 74
(A B Haynes) *sn led: set modest pce: hdd jst ins fnl f: kpt on* **4/1**[1]

1052 **4** 1/2 **King After**[2] [799] 5-8-8 **57** .... (v) StephaneBreux 3 62
(J R Best) *hld up in 4th: hrd rdn and nt clr run over 1f out: swtchd outside fnl 100 yds: kpt on* **11/2**[3]

1212 **5** 1 1/2 **Three Thieves (UAE)**[6] [747] 4-9-0 **70** .... TolleyDean(5) 4 73
(M S Saunders) *lw: chsd ldng pair: rdn over 3f out: one pce appr fnl f* **9/2**[2]

6-41 **6** 1 1/4 **Velvet Valley (USA)**[7] [733] 4-8-9 **67** 5ex .... JosephWalsh(7) 6 68
(C E Longsdon) *lw: wd: hld up in tch: rdn over 2f out: sn outpcd* **4/1**[1]

45-6 **7** ½ **Treetops Hotel (IRE)**[85] 23 8-8-12 **64**...................... WilliamBuick(3) 7 64
(B R Johnson) *hld up towards rr: swtchd to rail 5f out: effrt and hrd rdn 3f out: outpcd fnl 2f* **4/1**[1]

2m 33.11s (-1.28) **Going Correction** -0.05s/f (Stan)
WFA 4 from 5yo+ 2lb 7 Ran SP% **114.7**
Speed ratings (Par 103):102,101,101,101,100 99,99
CSF £76.43 TOTE £12.20: £4.30, £4.30; EX 63.50.
Owner The Wacko Partnership **Bred** Hedgeholme Stud **Trained** Woodingdean, E Sussex

FOCUS
No great pace on early as has become the norm for middle-distance contests here, especially those with small fields, and that did not suit a few of these. The race developed into a bit of a sprint from the home bend and again the middle of the track seemed the place to be in the straight. Just ordinary form, but it makes sense.

814 LINGFIELD PARK FOR WEDDINGS MAIDEN AUCTION STKS 5f (P)
2:50 (2:51) (Class 5) 2-Y-O **£3,886** (£1,156; £577; £288) **Stalls** High

Form RPR
1 **Dubai Princess (IRE)** 2-8-6 ow1............................... JamieSpencer 5 81+
(J A Osborne) *cmpt: str: lw: trckd ldrs: led 1f out: rdn clr: readily* **4/1**[1]
2 *4* **Concertmaster** 2-8-10 .... JosedeSouza 2 69
(R M Beckett) *wl grwn: lw: in tch: sltly hmpd and pushed along briefly after 1f: rdn to chal over 1f out: nt qckn fnl f* **4/1**[1]
3 *nk* **Hucking Harmony (IRE)** 2-8-2 .... StephaneBreux(3) 3 63+
(J R Best) *str: scope: lw: broke wl: led: gng wl whn rn v wd home turn: sn hdd: kpt on fnl f* **9/2**[2]
4 *shd* **Ben** 2-8-9 .... SteveDrowne 1 66
(P G Murphy) *str: bit bkwd: chsd ldng pair: lft in ld ent st: hdd and nt pce of wnr 1f out* **12/1**
5 *nk* **Southwest Star (IRE)** 2-8-9 .... LPKeniry 6 65
(J S Moore) *leggy: lw: dwlt: hld up in rr of main gp: hdwy over 1f out: styd on fnl f* **4/1**[1]
6 *nk* **Swindon Town Flyer (IRE)** 2-8-10 .... DaneO'Neill 9 65
(A B Haynes) *w'like: wd: hld up in rr of main gp: effrt 2f out: r.o fnl f* **12/1**
7 *nk* **Baytown Blaze** 2-8-4 .... HayleyTurner 4 58
(P S McEntee) *lt-f: chsd ldr: wd home turn: sn btn* **25/1**
8 *5* **In Decorum** 2-8-4 .... RichardThomas 7 38
(J A Geake) *neat: outpcd and bhd: mod effrt 2f out: nt trble ldrs* **25/1**
9 *21* **King Of Dalyan (IRE)** 2-8-10 .... AdrianTNicholls 8 —
(D Nicholls) *small: outpcd and bhd: no ch fnl 2f* **13/2**[3]

59.09 secs (-0.69) **Going Correction** -0.05s/f (Stan) 9 Ran SP% **114.6**
Speed ratings (Par 92):103,96,96,95,95 95,94,86,52
CSF £19.83 TOTE £4.00: £1.50, £1.60, £2.30; EX 19.50 Trifecta £47.80 Pool: £446.21 - 6.62 winning tickets..
Owner A F O'Callaghan **Bred** Darley **Trained** Upper Lambourn, Berks
■ The first two-year-old race of the 2007 Flat season.

FOCUS
Several of these looked as though the experience would do them good, but the form may be stronger than usual for a race of its type. The winning time was the fourth fastest of the 70 that have taken place for two-year-olds here over this trip since the Polytrack was laid.

NOTEBOOK
Dubai Princess(IRE) ◆, an 18,000euros half-sister to the smart juvenile Swiss Lake, was the paper favourite but was friendless on the track and her price doubled. Once under way however, she did everything right and showed a very impressive turn of foot to pull right away from her rivals. She has some lofty targets later in the season and although she will need to improve a good deal in order to justify her place in those contests, this was the best possible start. (op 2-1)
Concertmaster, whose dam was a sister to the top-class middle-distance performer Millkom, attracted plenty of support in the market and ran a very creditable debut even though he was blown away by the winner. He can probably be rated a little better than the margin he was beaten considering he stuck close to the disadvantaged inside. (op 7-1)
Hucking Harmony(IRE) ◆, out of a winning half-sister to Crystal Wind and Faydini, showed good early speed and looked as though she would take some catching, but she forgot to negotiate the home bend and ran extremely wide. Under the circumstances she did very well to hang on to third and although she would probably not have been able to contain the winner, she would certainly have been second. With this experience under her belt she should not take long in breaking her duck. Official explanation: jockey said filly hung badly right on final bend (op 7-1)
Ben, a relatively cheap yearling, is out of a half-sister to the smart sprinter Daring Destiny. He showed some ability on this debut and had every chance until done for foot in the home straight. His stable is not renowned for winning juvenile debutants, so this was quite encouraging. (op 16-1)
Southwest Star(IRE), whose dam was a half-sister to three winners, did not get going until the race was over and may appreciate a stiffer 5f than this with this experience under his belt. (op 3-1)
Swindon Town Flyer(IRE), whose dam is from the family of Robellino and Johannesburg, was forced to race wide from his outside draw and could never get there in time. He is another that may appreciate a less-sharp 5f.
King Of Dalyan(IRE), a brother to Desert Realm, was completely clueless. The market suggested that he was thought capable of much better than this, but he appears to need more time. (op 7-1 tchd 6-1)

815 LINGFIELD PARK FOR CONFERENCES H'CAP 7f (P)
3:20 (3:20) (Class 4) (0-85,85) 3-Y-O **£5,505** (£1,637; £818; £408) **Stalls** Low

Form RPR
6-21 **1** **Captain Jacksparra (IRE)**[16] 670 3-9-0 **75**.......................... NCallan 5 82
(K A Ryan) *dwlt: plld hrd in 4th: effrt over 2f out: r.o to ld ins fnl f: rdn out* **5/1**[3]
41-2 **2** ¾ **Vitznau (IRE)**[8] 725 3-8-5 **71**.. WilliamBuick(5) 1 76
(R Hannon) *lw: t.k.h: trckd ldng pair: effrt on rail over 1f out: squeezed through ins fnl f: r.o to snatch 2nd on line* **1/1**[1]
11 **3** *shd* **Annemasse**[8] 725 3-9-10 **85** 6ex.. JoeFanning 2 90
(M Johnston) *led and set modest pce: qcknd over 3f out: hrd rdn and hdd ins fnl f: kpt on* **6/4**[2]
431- **4** *2* **Tencendur (IRE)**[196] 5308 3-9-4 **79**............................ AdrianTNicholls 3 79
(D Nicholls) *pressed ldr: rdn over 2f out: one pce fnl f* **16/1**
40-6 **5** *6* **Ede's Dot Com (IRE)**[41] 483 3-9-4 **79**.............................. IanMongan 4 63
(P M Phelan) *hld up in rr: rdn and outpcd whn tempo increased over 3f out: n.d after* **66/1**

1m 26.89s (1.00) **Going Correction** -0.05s/f (Stan) 5 Ran SP% **114.0**
Speed ratings (Par 100):92,91,91,88,81
CSF £11.01 TOTE £5.60: £1.70, £1.20; EX 15.30.
Owner J Duddy,B McDonald,A Heeney,M McMenamin **Bred** Quay Bloodstock **Trained** Hambleton, N Yorks

FOCUS
Some progressive sorts on show in this tight little handicap, but the small field always made an unsatisfactory pace likely and that is how it proved. Even so it will be a surprise if a few of these do not find further success. The fourth limits the form, but the winner is progressive and the front three should go on from here.

816 HOLD YOUR PRODUCT LAUNCH AT LINGFIELD PARK MAIDEN STKS 1m (P)
3:50 (3:51) (Class 5) 3-Y-O **£3,886** (£1,156; £577; £288) **Stalls** High

Form RPR
032- **1** **Palamoun**[168] 5914 3-9-3 82.. MichaelHills 4 81+
(B W Hills) *h.d.w: lw: led after 2f and set modest pce: qcknd over 2f out: rdn clr over 1f out: comf* **4/9**[1]
0 **2** *3* **High Profit (IRE)**[22] 633 3-9-3 .... AntonyProcter 2 71
(D R C Elsworth) *bit bkwd: dwlt: hdwy to trck wnr after 3f: outpcd fnl 2f* **7/1**[3]
20-3 **3** *3½* **Deadline (UAE)**[13] 694 3-9-3 75.. JoeFanning 1 63
(P T Midgley) *cl up: outpcd over 2f out: sn btn* **11/4**[2]
04- **4** *shd* **Above And Below (IRE)**[167] 5941 3-8-12 .... DarryllHolland 3 58?
(M Quinn) *misbehaved bef s: racd freely early: led 2f: stdd bk to last 1f later: swtchd outside and effrt 3f out: no imp* **40/1**

1m 38.21s (-1.22) **Going Correction** -0.05s/f (Stan) 4 Ran SP% **110.9**
Speed ratings (Par 98):104,101,97,97
CSF £4.41 TOTE £1.40; EX 3.70.
Owner Palamoun Estates Limited **Bred** Mrs R J Mitchell **Trained** Lambourn, Berks

FOCUS
This looked a weak maiden on paper with just the four runners of which only three could be given any realistic chance, but although the result was as the market suggested the winning time was decent, just 0.87 seconds slower than the following Listed race. Not easy to assess, but the winner is likely to prove a bit better than the bare form.

817 DONCASTER MILE (LISTED RACE) 1m (P)
4:20 (4:20) (Class 1) 4-Y-O+
£14,762 (£5,595; £2,800; £1,396; £699; £351) **Stalls** High

Form RPR
125- **1** **Banknote**[208] 5019 5-9-0 93... DarryllHolland 5 103
(A M Balding) *lw: mde all: dictated modest pce: qcknd over 2f out: hrd rdn and jnd by runner-up ins fnl f: pushed out nr fin* **4/1**[3]
-154 **2** ½ **Chicken Soup**[4] 777 5-9-0 88... NCallan 2 102
(T J Pitt) *t.k.h: disp 2nd pl: drvn to join wnr fnl f: no ex and hld nr fin* **6/1**
4410 **3** *1½* **Orchard Supreme**[5] 761 4-9-0 101.............................. JimmyFortune 3 99
(R Hannon) *t.k.h: sn stdd in rr: effrt over 2f out: kpt on to take 3rd on line* **2/1**[1]
0123 **4** *shd* **Impeller (IRE)**[12] 701 8-9-0 99.. LPKeniry 4 98
(J S Moore) *lw: t.k.h: hld up in rr: rdn and outpcd 2f out: r.o fnl f* **11/2**
3-22 **5** *shd* **Bomber Command (USA)**[19] 658 4-9-0 95.................. MichaelHills 1 98
(J W Hills) *lw: t.k.h: in tch: rdn 3f out: one pce fnl 2f: lost 3rd pl fnl strides* **10/3**[2]
212- **6** *2* **Neardown Beauty (IRE)**[124] 6594 4-8-9 82.................... JamesDoyle 6 88
(I A Wood) *t.k.h: disp 2nd pl tl wknd 2f out* **20/1**

1m 37.34s (-2.09) **Going Correction** -0.05s/f (Stan) 6 Ran SP% **110.8**
Speed ratings (Par 111):108,107,106,105,105 103
CSF £26.47 TOTE £4.60: £2.60, £3.50; EX 25.00.
Owner The Queen **Bred** Exors Of The Late Queen Elizabeth **Trained** Kingsclere, Hants

FOCUS
Not the most strongly run of races, though a much more solid pace than when this race was run here for the first time last year. The quality of the line-up, although competitive enough, was a little below Listed class with the highest official rating just 101, and a similar field would have turned out had this been a Class 2 handicap. The form does not look solid.

NOTEBOOK
Banknote, who ran a blinder under top weight in the London Mile Final at Kempton when last seen nearly seven months ago, has won after a similar layoff in the past so the absence was not a problem. He has also won after making the running, so his rider's decision to be positive on him was a shrewd move and his attitude could not be faulted when he faced a serious challenge from the runner-up in the home straight. He can forget handicaps now, as he was badly in with the majority of his rivals at the weights, and he will find life tough in Group company, but he is now a winner at Listed level so connections will have been delighted. (op 9-2)
Chicken Soup, considered by many to have been unlucky over an extra quarter-mile at Kempton last time, was back to probably a more suitable trip but had an even stiffer task than the winner at the weights. Always in a good position, he put in a strong challenge down the home straight and looked likely to score, but his rival was in no mood to give in.
Orchard Supreme, beaten just two lengths though only eighth in the Winter Derby here last time, was back over his best trip and was best in at the weights, but he ideally needs a stronger pace than this and his finishing effort was too little too late. (op 13-8 tchd 9-4)
Impeller(IRE) does most of his racing over further these days, so the modest pace was as great an inconvenience to him as any and it was no great surprise that his finishing effort fell short. (op 13-2)
Bomber Command(USA), narrowly beaten by Orchard Supreme in the Lincoln Trial at Wolverhampton and 5lb worse off here, was another probably not helped by the ordinary pace and was safely held over the last couple of furlongs. (tchd 3-1)
Neardown Beauty(IRE), reappearing from four months off, showed up for a long way but she had a mountain to climb at the weights and eventually found it all too much. (op 25-1)

818 PLAY GOLF AT LINGFIELD PARK H'CAP 5f (P)
4:50 (4:50) (Class 2) (0-100,93) 4-Y-O+
£11,217 (£3,358; £1,679; £840; £419; £210) **Stalls** High

Form RPR
000- **1** **Merlin's Dancer**[201] 5182 7-9-3 **92**............................... AdrianTNicholls 8 103
(D Nicholls) *lw: mde all: restrained in front early: qcknd 3f out: hrd drvn over 1f out: rdn out to hold on fnl 50 yds* **12/1**
0-66 **2** ¾ **Talbot Avenue**[40] 490 9-8-10 **85**.. TPQueally 3 93
(M Blanshard) *lw: in tch: hrd rdn over 1f out: r.o to chse wnr ins fnl f: hld fnl 50 yds* **11/2**
61-4 **3** ½ **Stoneacre Lad (IRE)**[40] 490 4-8-13 **88**.................(b) GrahamGibbons 2 95
(Peter Grayson) *lw: chsd ldng pair: drvn to go 2nd over 1f out: nt qckn fnl f* **4/1**[3]
0-00 **4** *nk* **Total Impact**[13] 692 4-8-7 **82**... JamieSpencer 1 87
(C A Cyzer) *dwlt: bhd: rdn over 2f out: hdwy over 1f out: kpt on fnl f* **10/3**[2]
060- **5** ¾ **The Lord**[151] 6243 7-8-8 **86**... AmirQuinn(3) 5 89
(W G M Turner) *dwlt: bhd: rdn over 2f out: gd hdwy fnl f* **14/1**
5-62 **6** ½ **Graze On**[33] 554 5-8-7 **82**..(b) RobbieFitzpatrick 4 83
(Peter Grayson) *in tch: effrt 2f out: styd on same pce* **3/1**[1]
3-60 **7** *hd* **Classic Encounter (IRE)**[40] 490 4-9-0 **89**............... FergusSweeney 7 89
(D M Simcock) *chsd wnr tl over 1f out: no ex* **5/1**

57.86 secs (-1.92) **Going Correction** -0.05s/f (Stan) 7 Ran SP% **114.5**
Speed ratings (Par 109):113,111,111,110,109 108,108
CSF £75.21 CT £314.32 TOTE £13.30: £2.90, £2.20; EX 49.00 Trifecta £109.60 Pool: £435.48 - 2.82 winning tickets..

Owner Chalfont Foodhalls Ltd **Bred** Cheveley Park Stud Ltd **Trained** Sessay, N Yorks

FOCUS

This was a decent sprint handicap despite the absence of the probable favourite Turn On The Style. They went a good pace too and the winning time was only 0.6 of a second outside the course record. Pretty solid form.

NOTEBOOK

Merlin's Dancer, fourth in this race last year off a 2lb lower mark in his only previous outing on sand, was given a more positive ride this time, but unlike in 2006 he kept on finding enough in front to hold on. He went on to win at the big Chester meeting last year and is likely to follow a similar route this time. (op 11-1)

Talbot Avenue is being cut some slack by the Handicapper and was back down to the same mark as for his last win in July 2003. He ran a fine race in defeat and despite his long losing run he does not seem to lack a will to win, but for some reason he just cannot force his head in front where it matters. (op 9-2)

Stoneacre Lad(IRE), able to race off his correct mark this time, had every chance and ran another fair race here, but was unable to confirm recent course form with Talbot Avenue on 1lb worse terms. He does seem better suited to Southwell and Wolverhampton. (op 9-2)

Total Impact, back on his last winning mark, ran his best race for a while but may prefer the extra furlong these days. (tchd 7-2)

The Lord, reappearing from a five-month break, was very tardy at the start and could ill afford to give away that much ground against these rivals. Official explanation: jockey said gelding missed the break (tchd 16-1)

Graze On, who ran so well when second in a race run in course-record time here last month, was 1lb higher this time but after having every chance, he was never doing enough in the home straight. He is not proving very consistent these days. (tchd 10-3)

Classic Encounter(IRE), who finished behind both Talbot Avenue and Stoneacre Lad here last month, was meeting them on similar terms and though he showed up for a long way, he had nothing left in the straight and finished about the same distance behind the pair as last time. (op 7-1)

819 ARENA LEISURE PLC LADY RIDERS' H'CAP — 1m 2f (P)
5:20 (5:20) (Class 5) (0-70,70) 4-Y-0+ — £2,810 (£871; £435; £217) — Stalls Low

Form				RPR
1040	1		**Topiary Ted**[15] 675 5-10-1 **69** .... MissVCartmel(5) 7	79
			(H Morrison) *lw: lost 6l s: hld up and bhd: stdy hdwy on outside 2f out: r.o to ld fnl 100 yds: pushed out* **9/2**[3]	
3602	2	nk	**Hawk Arrow (IRE)**[6] 740 5-9-5 **59** .... MissHayleyMoore(5) 1	68
			(G L Moore) *lw: hld up towards rr: hdwy 3f out: led ins fnl f: sn hdd: kpt on* **3/1**[1]	
6044	3	4	**Augustine**[6] 740 6-10-4 **70** .... (b) MrsMarieKing(3) 5	71
			(P W Hiatt) *plld hrd: hdwy to ld after 2f: rdn over 2f out: hdd and no ex ins fnl f* **10/3**[2]	
420-	4	2 ½	**Viable**[84] 5497 5-9-8 **62** .... MissLAllan(5) 3	59
			(Mrs P Sly) *plld hrd: led 2f: sltly hmpd and restrained in 4th: rdn and one pce fnl 2f* **8/1**	
204-	5	1 ¾	**Keisha Kayleigh (IRE)**[92] 6954 4-9-7 **56** .... (v) MissLEllison 2	49
			(B Ellison) *hld up in tch: shkn up 2f out: no imp* **5/1**	
0122	6	2 ½	**Shaheer (IRE)**[20] 651 5-9-7 **56** .... MissEJJones 4	45
			(J Gallagher) *plld hrd: prom: rdn 3f out: wknd wl over 1f out* **5/1**	
020-	7	2	**Sunny Afternoon**[397] 514 7-9-2 **56** oh3 .... MissAWallace(5) 6	41
			(R Rowe) *bit bkwd: chsd ldrs tl wknd over 2f out* **50/1**	

2m 7.96s (0.17) **Going Correction** -0.05s/f (Stan) — 7 Ran SP% **112.7**

Speed ratings (Par 103):97,96,93,91,90 88,86

CSF £17.82 TOTE £6.20: £3.60, £1.80; EX 26.80 Place 6 £3,793.74, Place 5 £180.56.

Owner Ron Plant **Bred** Stowell Hill Ltd And Mrs C Van Straubenzee **Trained** East Ilsley, Berks

FOCUS

A moderate race, run at a very steady early gallop, and the track bias was especially evident with the front pair making their efforts mid-track in the home straight. Very ordinary form.

T/Plt: £653.00 to a £1 stake. Pool: £60,115.85. 67.20 winning tickets. T/Qpdt: £49.10 to a £1 stake. Pool: £4,373.90. 65.90 winning tickets. LM

820 - 824a (Foreign Racing) - See Raceform Interactive

813 LINGFIELD (L-H)

Friday, March 30

OFFICIAL GOING: Standard

825 LINGFIELDPARK.CO.UK (S) STKS — 1m 2f (P)
2:10 (2:11) (Class 5) 4-Y-0+ — £2,914 (£867; £433; £216) — Stalls Low

Form				RPR
-441	1		**Sawwaah (IRE)**[6] 768 10-9-3 50 .... (v) AdrianTNicholls 6	69
			(D Nicholls) *lw: stdd s: hld up in last: prog on wd outside 2f out: hanging over 1f out: picked up and r.o to ld last 150yds: sn clr* **11/2**[3]	
4164	2	2 ½	**Bridgewater Boys**[8] 733 6-9-3 60 .... (p) NCallan 2	64
			(K A Ryan) *t.k.h: pressed ldr: rdn to ld wl over 1f out: hung bdly rt and hdd 1f out: plugged on nr fin* **5/2**[1]	
1010	3	nk	**Competitor**[6] 753 6-9-3 63 .... (v) DaneO'Neill 3	63
			(J Akehurst) *lw: rousted along early: chsd ldrs: rdn 3f out: clsng whn lft in ld 1f out: sn hdd and one pce* **5/2**[1]	
-025	4	hd	**Rose Muwasim**[25] 620 4-8-4 48 .... (v[1]) DominicFox(3) 11	53
			(K J Burke) *hld up in rr: gng v easily over 2f out: swtchd ins and effrt over 1f out: rdn and fnd nil* **16/1**	
0205	5	1 ¾	**Casablanca Minx (IRE)**[23] 634 4-8-4 61 .... (b) JamesDoyle(3) 7	50
			(N P Littmoden) *chsd ldrs: rdn and struggling over 2f out: sn btn* **4/1**[2]	
1000	6	1	**Ellesappelle**[17] 665 4-8-5 53 .... LukeMorris(7) 10	53
			(R A Harris) *lw: t.k.h: trckd ldng pair: rdn 3f out: jinked and rdr unbalanced over 2f out: sn btn* **20/1**	
0	7	5	**Emma Gee**[13] 699 5-8-7 .... LPKeniry 8	38
			(J Akehurst) *mde most to wl over 1f out: wknd* **50/1**	
-200	8	1 ¼	**Final Esteem**[25] 620 4-8-12 63 .... DarryllHolland 9	41
			(R A Harris) *in tch tl wknd over 2f out* **11/1**	

2m 6.93s (-0.86) **Going Correction** -0.10s/f (Stan) — 8 Ran SP% **113.5**

Speed ratings (Par 103):99,97,96,96,95 94,90,89

CSF £19.35 TOTE £6.40: £1.40, £1.70, £1.60; EX 26.90 Trifecta £40.00 Pool £382.89 - 6.79 winning units..There was no bid for the winner.

Owner Mrs Alex Nicholls **Bred** Shadwell Estate Company Limited **Trained** Sessay, N Yorks

FOCUS

Not a bad seller, but it was weakened by its withdrawals and the early pace was just modest. The form has not been rated positively but does make sense.

826 LINGFIELD PARK FOR CONFERENCES MAIDEN STKS — 7f (P)
2:45 (2:45) (Class 5) 3-Y-0 — £2,914 (£867; £433; £216) — Stalls Low

Form				RPR
323-	1		**Hazzard County (USA)**[163] 6055 3-9-3 76 .... DaneO'Neill 5	84+
			(D M Simcock) *t.k.h: trckd ldr after 3f: rdn to chal 2f out: led 1f out: styd on wl* **9/4**[1]	
34	2	1 ¼	**Esteem Machine (USA)**[44] 456 3-9-0 .... MarcHalford(3) 3	78
			(D R C Elsworth) *lw: led at decent pce: kicked on over 2f out: hdd and one pce 1f out* **9/4**[1]	
06-	3	7	**Paradise Walk**[171] 5890 3-8-9 .... RichardKingscote(3) 2	55
			(R Charlton) *t.k.h: hld up: effrt 3f out: rdn and fnd little over 2f out : no ch w ldng pair after* **13/2**[3]	
64	4	1	**Pride Of Northcare (IRE)**[15] 684 3-9-0 .... EmmettStack(3) 1	58
			(G A Huffer) *awkward s: chsd ldr for 3f: rdn 3f out: sn struggling* **16/1**	
	5	11	**The Blue Stacks (USA)** 3-9-3 .... NCallan 4	29+
			(K A Ryan) *tall: str: scope: lw: stdd s: hld up in last: sn plld hrd and hrd to steer: wknd 3f out: t.o* **11/4**[2]	

1m 24.09s (-1.80) **Going Correction** -0.10s/f (Stan) — 5 Ran SP% **107.4**

Speed ratings (Par 98):106,104,96,95,82

CSF £7.18 TOTE £2.60: £1.40, £1.60; EX 6.40.

Owner Khalifa Dasmal **Bred** Cho, Llc **Trained** Newmarket, Suffolk

FOCUS

An interesting little three-year-old maiden which was run at a fair pace and the two with the best previous form duly played out the finish. A very decent winning time for a race like this, and the first two, who came clear, look improved.

The Blue Stacks(USA) Official explanation: jockey said colt hung badly right

827 LINGFIELD PARK FOR WEDDINGS H'CAP — 7f (P)
3:20 (3:20) (Class 4) (0-85,85) 4-Y-0+ — £4,857 (£1,445; £541; £541) — Stalls Low

Form				RPR
00-0	1		**Raza Cab (IRE)**[13] 699 5-8-2 **71** oh1 .... JimmyQuinn 3	81
			(Karen George) *lw: hld up bhd ldrs: clsd 2f out: shkn up to ld over 1f out: pushed out and in command fnl f* **14/1**	
10-5	2	¾	**Royal Dignitary (USA)**[24] 629 7-9-0 **83** .... AdrianTNicholls 7	91
			(D Nicholls) *led after 1f: rdn and hdd over 1f out: kpt on but no real ch w wnr fnl f* **11/4**[1]	
2503	3	1	**Garstang**[14] 692 4-8-9 **78** .... (b) BrettDoyle 5	83
			(Peter Grayson) *t.k.h early: hld up in last: effrt over 2f out: clsd on ldrs over 1f out: swtchd ins and fnd nil* **9/2**[3]	
3114	3	dht	**Danetime Lord (IRE)**[6] 757 4-8-6 **75** .... (p) CatherineGannon 1	80
			(K A Ryan) *lw: hld up in 6th: shkn up 3f out: prog 2f out: chsd ldrs jst over 1f out: sn rdn and nt qckn* **3/1**[2]	
060-	5	3	**Makabul**[212] 4922 4-8-5 **74** .... (t) JimCrowley 8	71
			(B R Millman) *trckd ldr over 5f out: rdn to chal 2f out: wknd tamely fnl f* **11/1**	
500-	6	½	**Desert Dreamer (IRE)**[137] 6461 6-8-7 **76** .... PaulDoe 4	72
			(P R Chamings) *s.i.s: t.k.h and trckd ldng pair 5f out: cl up wl over 1f out: sn wknd* **7/1**	
316-	7	nk	**Mujood**[154] 6204 4-9-2 **85** .... StephenCarson 6	80
			(Eve Johnson Houghton) *lw: led for 1f: lost pl: rdn 3f out: trying to rally whn hmpd on inner wl over 1f out: btn after* **11/2**	

1m 23.9s (-1.99) **Going Correction** -0.10s/f (Stan) — 7 Ran SP% **112.7**

Speed ratings (Par 105):107,106,105,105,101 101,100

TRI:Raza Cab/Royal Diginitary/Garstang £102.44, RC/RD/Danetime Lord £74.52; Trifecta: RC/RD/GG £154.10 (0.34 winning units), RC/RD/DL £91.70 (1.68 winning unit). CSF £50.97 CT £74.52 TOTE £19.20: £7.30, £2.40; EX 62.00.

Owner B R Phillips **Bred** Rathyork Stud **Trained** Higher Easington, Devon

■ Stewards' Enquiry : Catherine Gannon caution: careless riding

FOCUS

A fair handicap, run at a modest pace. The form looks just ordinary for grade, with the winner back to his level of a year ago.

Garstang Official explanation: jockey said gelding hung left

828 PLAY GOLF AT LINGFIELD PARK H'CAP — 6f (P)
3:55 (3:55) (Class 2) (0-100,100) 4-Y-0+ — £11,217 (£3,358; £1,679; £840; £419; £210) — Stalls Low

Form				RPR
600-	1		**Lady Livius (IRE)**[183] 5643 4-8-9 **91** .... DaneO'Neill 7	101
			(R Hannon) *lw: trckd ldng pair: effrt 2f out: led over 1f out: edgd lft but wl in command fnl f* **16/1**	
5320	2	1 ¼	**Qadar (IRE)**[6] 762 5-9-4 **100** .... (b) NCallan 8	106
			(N P Littmoden) *hld up in midfield in modly run affair: effrt 2f out: drvn to chse ldng pair 1f out: styd on: unable to chal* **5/2**[1]	
4130	3	shd	**Distinctly Game**[20] 660 5-8-2 **87** .... AndrewMullen(3) 4	93
			(K A Ryan) *lw: led at mod pce: rdn 2f out: hdd and nt qckn over 1f out: one pce after* **13/2**	
0005	4	1	**Moayed**[6] 759 8-8-4 **89** .... (b) JamesDoyle(3) 6	92
			(N P Littmoden) *s.i.s: hld up in last in modly run r: effrt 2f out: styd on: nvr rchd ldrs* **9/2**[2]	
04	5	nk	**Machinist (IRE)**[43] 474 7-8-13 **95** .... SilvestreDeSousa 2	97
			(D Nicholls) *awkward s: hld up in midfield in modly run r: effrt 2f out: kpt on same pce fr over 1f out* **9/2**[2]	
1211	6	nk	**Lucayos**[14] 692 4-8-3 **88** .... RichardKingscote(3) 1	89
			(Mrs H Sweeting) *pressed ldr: upsides over 1f out: fdd* **11/2**[3]	
030-	7	½	**Phantom Whisper**[189] 5501 4-8-5 **87** .... JimCrowley 3	87
			(B R Millman) *bit bkwd: t.k.h: hld up in 6th in modly run r: effrt 2f out: one pce* **17/2**	
020-	8	shd	**Continent**[188] 5534 10-8-5 **87** .... (t) AdrianTNicholls 5	86
			(D Nicholls) *taken down early: hld up in last pair: effrt on outer 2f out: sn nt qckn: one pce after* **14/1**	

1m 11.86s (-0.95) **Going Correction** -0.10s/f (Stan) — 8 Ran SP% **116.7**

Speed ratings (Par 109):102,100,100,98,98 98,97,97

CSF £57.38 CT £299.87 TOTE £22.20: £4.20, £1.10, £2.60; EX 135.20 TRIFECTA Not won..

Owner Mrs John Lee **Bred** W Maxwell Ervine **Trained** East Everleigh, Wilts

FOCUS

This was a decent handicap, but it was run at a muddling pace and the form should be treated with a degree of caution. A personal best from Lady Livius, with the second running to his course form with the third.

NOTEBOOK

Lady Livius(IRE) did the job on this seasonal bow and first run on the AW. She was always in the right place to strike when the race became serious turning for home, showed a turn of foot when asked to win her race and is clearly capable of running well when fresh. Looking to have grown somewhat from three to four, it is worth remembering that she won the Super Sprint at Newbury in 2005, and she could just be the sort to nick some valuable black type on turf at some stage this year. She is also entitled to improve for the run.

Qadar(IRE), down in class and with the blinkers back on, had his chance on this return to a sixth furlong yet did not really help his cause by racing keenly early on. He would have appreciated a stronger pace. (op 11-4)

Distinctly Game, whose stable won this with the progressive Mutamared last year, was given a positive ride and showed his previous effort at Wolverhampton to be all wrong. He is possibly a little flattered, but still helps to set the standard of this form. (op 7-1)

Moayed would not have really enjoyed the modest early pace and can be rated a little better than the bare form. Official explanation: jockey said gelding was denied a clear run (op 6-1)

Machinist(IRE), having his first outing since returning from Dubai, could not quicken where it mattered and never really looked like hitting the front. (tchd 11-2)

Lucayos, a winner of three of his last four outings over course and distance, was simply found out on this step up in class. He can find less competitive assignments. (op 9-2)

Phantom Whisper proved free through the early stages on this first outing since September and should benefit for the run. (op 11-1)

Continent was not really suited by being held up off the modest early pace on this AW debut and failed to get involved from off the pace. He is another who ought to benefit for this seasonal return. (op 12-1)

829 BOOK ONLINE FOR A £2 DISCOUNT CONDITIONS STKS 1m 4f (P)
4:30 (4:30) (Class 3) 4-Y-0+

£7,478 (£2,239; £1,119; £560; £279; £140) Stalls Low

Form RPR

20-3 **1** **Active Asset (IRE)**[9] 726 5-9-0 83 DarryllHolland 7 76
(M Quinn) *hld up in 5th: prog on outer 3f out: disp ld jst over 2f out: drvn to assert ent fnl f: kpt on wl* 7/1[3]

-050 **2** *1* **Hathaal (IRE)**[5] 775 8-8-7 60 (vt) SCreighton(7) 4 74
(E J Creighton) *lw: hld up in last: effrt 3f out: shkn up to chse ldng pair 2f out: styd on to take 2nd last 75yds: nt rch wnr* 50/1

6441 **3** *1 1/4* **Sgt Schultz (IRE)**[14] 693 4-8-12 83 LPKeniry 3 72
(J S Moore) *lw: trckd clr ldr: clsd to dispute ld jst over 2f out: hdd and one pce ent fnl f* 9/4[2]

1224 **4** *1 1/2* **Eva Soneva So Fast (IRE)**[13] 698 5-9-0 92 JimmyQuinn 6 70
(J L Dunlop) *settled in 3rd: lost pl as field clsd up 3f out: sn rdn: kpt on one pce fnl 2f* 5/6[1]

40-4 **5** *shd* **Boot 'n Toot**[13] 702 6-8-9 74 J-PGuillambert 2 64
(C A Cyzer) *stdd s: t.k.h: hld up in 4th: rdn over 2f out: one pce and no prog over 1f out* 10/1

15-5 **6** *9* **Flame Creek (IRE)**[14] 434 11-9-0 81 EdwardCreighton 1 55
(E J Creighton) *led and sn clr: c bk to field over 3f out: hdd jst over 2f out: sn btn* 16/1

2m 31.08s (-3.31) **Going Correction** -0.10s/f (Stan)
WFA 4 from 5yo+ 2lb 6 Ran SP% **114.8**
Speed ratings (Par 107):107,106,105,104,104 98
CSF £190.43 TOTE £8.10: £2.60, £5.70; EX 130.90.
Owner Brian Morton **Bred** Rathasker Stud **Trained** Newmarket, Suffolk

FOCUS
A fair conditions event in which the sixth went off much too fast. The race is very hard to assess accurately with the form being held down by the 60-rated runner-up.

NOTEBOOK
Active Asset(IRE) showed the benefit of his seasonal debut at Kempton nine days previously and got off the mark for his current connections at the second time of asking with a decisive success. He had adapted well to this surface, evidently stays this trip well now and his confidence should have been nicely boosted. His trainer is hoping for a return to Kempton for the valuable Rosebery Handicap next month. (op 13-2)

Hathaal(IRE) was given a patient ride and showed greatly improved form in defeat. This looks to be his trip and he could build on this, as despite looking to face a stiff task at these weights, he was well thought of when trained by Sir Michael Stoute and was rated in the 90s earlier in his career. (op 66-1 tchd 80-1)

Sgt Schultz(IRE) appeared to run his race in defeat and can have no real excuses. He may just be weighted to his best now. (op 5-2 tchd 11-4 in a place)

Eva Soneva So Fast(IRE) proved very disappointing as he held a leading chance at the weights and came into this in good form. (op 11-10 tchd 6-5 in places)

Boot 'n Toot was not disgraced at the weights having run too freely through the early stages. She may just benefit for a drop back in trip. (op 8-1)

Flame Creek(IRE) Official explanation: jockey said gelding lost its action

830 PERFECT WEDDING VENUE AT LINGFIELD PARK H'CAP 1m (P)
5:05 (5:06) (Class 5) (0-70,70) 4-Y-0+ £2,914 (£867; £433; £216) Stalls High

Form RPR

0165 **1** **Samuel Charles**[16] 674 9-9-4 **70** (p) NCallan 1 78
(C R Dore) *trckd ldng pair: rdn to chse ldr 2f out: forced into ld jst ins fnl f: kpt on wl* 6/1[3]

0532 **2** *1/2* **Magic Warrior**[5] 773 7-9-0 **66** PatDobbs 6 73
(J C Fox) *hld up in 6th: effrt on outer 2f out: r.o to press wnr ins fnl f: nt qckn and no imp last 75yds* 5/2[1]

0344 **3** *1 1/4* **Golden Spectrum (IRE)**[6] 770 8-8-1 **60** (b) LukeMorris(7) 2 64
(R A Harris) *lw: plld hrd early: trckd ldr: led over 2f out: hdd and no ex jst ins fnl f* 15/2

0/ **4** *1 3/4* **Slew Charm (FR)**[41] 6265 5-8-8 **60** (t) SamHitchcott 4 60
(Noel T Chance) *trckd ldrs: rdn wl over 2f out: nt qckn and no imp 2f out: kpt on u.p* 6/1[3]

051- **5** *3/4* **Treasure House (IRE)**[192] 5444 6-9-2 **68** DaleGibson 8 66
(M Blanshard) *lw: plld hrd early: hld up in last: effrt and rdn over 2f out: no prog tl kpt on fnl f: n.d* 13/2

004- **6** *1 1/2* **Aggravation**[179] 5734 5-9-0 **69** MarcHalford(3) 7 64
(D R C Elsworth) *hld up in last pair: sme prog and gng wl 2f out: nt clr run sn after: rdn and no rspnse over 1f out* 4/1[2]

0206 **7** *2 1/2* **Rafferty (IRE)**[15] 681 8-8-6 **58** ow1 LPKeniry 3 47
(S Dow) *led to over 2f out: wknd and eased* 12/1

4/0- **8** *9* **Mr Velocity (IRE)**[356] 915 7-8-10 **62** TPQueally 5 30
(E F Vaughan) *wl in tch: last and wkng over 2f out: t.o* 14/1

1m 38.02s (-1.41) **Going Correction** -0.10s/f (Stan) 8 Ran SP% **116.6**
Speed ratings (Par 103):103,102,101,99,98 97,94,85
CSF £21.89 CT £116.18 TOTE £6.00: £1.70, £1.50, £2.10; EX 14.20 Trifecta £69.90 Pool £769.79 - 7.81 winning units. Place 6 £199.27, Place 5 £142.57.
Owner Chris Marsh **Bred** Sheikh Mohammed Obaid Al Maktoum **Trained** West Pinchbeck, Lincs

FOCUS
An ordinary handicap, run at a sound pace. The form looks sound.

T/Plt: £166.20 to a £1 stake. Pool: £66,508.50. 292.10 winning tickets. T/Qpdt: £125.70 to a £1 stake. Pool: £3,857.80. 22.70 winning tickets. JN

800 WOLVERHAMPTON (A.W) (L-H)
Friday, March 30

OFFICIAL GOING: Standard
Wind: light across Weather: dull

831 DIGITAL PRINTS FROM BONUSPRINT.COM H'CAP 7f 32y(P)
2:00 (2:01) (Class 6) (0-65,65) 4-Y-0+ £2,730 (£806; £403) Stalls High

Form RPR

U356 **1** **Tancredi (SWE)**[15] 686 5-8-10 **62** JerryO'Dwyer(3) 9 76
(N B King) *anticipated s: sn chsng ldr: led wl over 1f out: drvn out* 25/1

2332 **2** *1 1/2* **What Do You Know**[4] 793 4-8-8 **62** WilliamBuick(5) 5 72
(A M Hales) *sn led: rdn and hdd wl over 1f out: no ex towards fin* 9/4[2]

-451 **3** *1* **Takitwo**[4] 793 4-8-3 **59** JamieHamblett(7) 4 67
(P D Cundell) *led early: a.p: rdn wl over 1f out: one pace fnl f:* 13/8[1]

4142 **4** *3/4* **Kew The Music**[8] 729 7-8-9 **58** ChrisCatlin 6 64
(M R Channon) *s.i.s: hld up in rr: pushed along over 3f out: swtchd lft wl over 1f out: hdwy on ins fnl f: nvr nrr* 8/1[3]

2024 **5** *1* **Cabourg (IRE)**[34] 549 4-8-7 **59** (b) GregFairley(3) 3 62
(R Bastiman) *t.k.h in mid-div: hdwy on outside 2f out: hung lft fr over 1f out: one pce* 10/1

-503 **6** *1* **Boy Dancer (IRE)**[33] 556 4-8-6 **55** PaulHanagan 2 55
(D W Barker) *t.k.h: prom: rdn over 2f out: wknd wl over 1f out* 11/1

320- **7** *nk* **Sedge (USA)**[167] 5974 7-8-11 **60** MickyFenton 1 60
(P T Midgley) *prom: nt clr run on ins and lost pl bnd after 1f: bhd fnl 3f* 12/1

0256 **8** *1 1/2* **Supercast (IRE)**[9] 724 4-9-2 **65** (t) GeorgeBaker 8 61
(W M Brisbourne) *hld up and bhd: hdwy over 2f out: rdn over 1f out: edgd lft and wknd ins fnl f* 12/1

1m 29.13s (-1.27) **Going Correction** -0.10s/f (Stan) 8 Ran SP% **116.6**
Speed ratings (Par 101):103,101,100,99,98 97,96,94
CSF £83.03 CT £153.13 TOTE £38.90: £4.80, £1.20, £1.10; EX 224.50.
Owner Richard S Keeley **Bred** Team Hogdala Ab **Trained** Newmarket, Suffolk
■ Stewards' Enquiry : William Buick two-day ban: careless riding (Apr 10-11)

FOCUS
An ordinary handicap in which nothing got involved from the rear. The winner was up a length on his previous best but the next two were a bit disappointing given their Kempton form. There was controversy as the winner's stall appeared to open a split second ahead of the others, but the result was allowed to stand.

832 PONTIN'S FAMILY HOLIDAYS (S) STKS 7f 32y(P)
2:35 (2:35) (Class 6) 3-Y-0 £2,047 (£604; £302) Stalls High

Form RPR

3634 **1** **Mick Is Back**[31] 572 3-8-9 54 (p) StephenDonohoe(3) 12 57
(P D Evans) *outpcd in rr: rdn and gd hdwy 1f out: r.o wl to ld cl home* 7/1

0-56 **2** *1 1/4* **Suhayl Star (IRE)**[29] 589 3-9-4 65 JDSmith 8 60+
(M Wigham) *led 1f: chsd ldr: led over 2f out: clr whn rdn over 1f out: ct cl home* 10/3[1]

2265 **3** *1* **Razzano (IRE)**[48] 417 3-8-2 52 KevinGhunowa(5) 4 46
(A M Hales) *a.p: carried lft wl over 1f out: kpt on ins fnl f* 11/2[3]

0224 **4** *1 1/4* **Ranavalona**[11] 711 3-8-2 54 (v) WilliamBuick(5) 1 43
(A M Balding) *a.p: rdn over 2f out: one pce fnl f* 4/1[2]

-656 **5** *hd* **Birdie Birdie**[17] 667 3-8-7 45 (v) PaulHanagan 5 42
(R A Fahey) *prom: rdn and lost pl over 5f out: rallied over 2f out: one pce fnl f* 25/1

0000 **6** *shd* **Haydock Express (IRE)**[49] 404 3-8-10 45 ow1 JerryO'Dwyer(3) 11 48
(Peter Grayson) *outpcd in rr: rdn and edgd rt wl over 1f out: hung lft and r.o ins fnl f: nrst fin* 40/1

6-30 **7** *3/4* **Best Option**[14] 689 3-8-7 55 ChrisCatlin 6 40
(W R Muir) *chsd ldrs: rdn over 2f out: no hdwy* 16/1

-040 **8** *shd* **Tenterhooks (IRE)**[31] 572 3-8-7 45 (be[1]) MickyFenton 7 40
(A J McCabe) *led after 1f: rdn and hdd over 2f out: edgd rt wl over 1f out: wknd ins fnl f* 25/1

6604 **9** *1* **Kings Shillings**[16] 676 3-9-4 55 (b) DanielTudhope 10 48
(D Carroll) *s.s: rdn and sme hdwy over 2f out: eased whn btn wl ins fnl f* 13/2

5-03 **10** *5* **Lady Cartuccia**[25] 619 3-8-7 48 GrahamGibbons 2 24
(J J Quinn) *mid-div: rdn over 3f out: wknd fnl f* 15/2

05-0 **11** *9* **Little Tiny Tom**[17] 667 3-8-5 39 PaulPickard(7) 9 6
(C N Kellett) *bhd fnl 2f* 200/1

00 **12** *1/2* **Inchwall**[23] 633 3-8-12 RobbieFitzpatrick 3 4
(Peter Grayson) *s.s: outpcd* 50/1

1m 30.67s (0.27) **Going Correction** -0.10s/f (Stan) 12 Ran SP% **114.5**
Speed ratings (Par 96):94,92,91,90,89 89,88,88,87,81 71,70
CSF £28.35 TOTE £8.30: £2.90, £1.60, £3.40; EX 42.80.There was no bid for the winner. Ranavalona was claimed by P Evans for £6,000. Suhayl Star was claimed by A Darke for £6,000
Owner J E Abbey, Mike Nolan **Bred** J E Abbey **Trained** Pandy, Monmouths

FOCUS
There was no hanging about and the field was soon strung out. This was just a modest claimer, but the time was decent and the form looks solid, rated through the winner and the sixth.

Birdie Birdie Official explanation: jockey said filly hung both ways down the home straight

833 PONTINSBINGO.COM CLAIMING STKS 1m 141y(P)
3:10 (3:10) (Class 5) 4-Y-0+ £3,238 (£963; £481; £240) Stalls Low

Form RPR

-621 **1** **Blue Sky Thinking (IRE)**[16] 674 8-9-3 80 PatCosgrave 2 79
(K R Burke) *hld up in mid-div: stdy hdwy over 4f out: rdn over 2f out: led ins fnl f: r.o* 5/6[1]

6006 **2** *nk* **Grimes Faith**[13] 699 4-8-11 79 (b) HaddenFrost(7) 11 79
(R Hannon) *hld up and bhd: hdwy over 3f out: ev ch ins fnl f: nt qckn* 11/4[2]

-340 **3** *1* **Namroud (USA)**[24] 629 8-8-13 67 PaulHanagan 3 72
(R A Fahey) *chsd ldr: led over 3f out: rdn wl over 1f out: hdd and no ex ins fnl f* 13/2[3]

3440 **4** *10* **Buzzin'Boyzee (IRE)**[4] 793 4-8-1 56 BernadetteQuinn(7) 5 46
(P D Evans) *prom: ev ch over 2f out: rdn and wknd wl over 1f out* 14/1

4005 **5** *2* **Spy Gun (USA)**[15] 682 7-8-9 43 (b[1]) ChrisCatlin 6 43
(T Wall) *led: rdn and hdd over 3f out: wknd over 2f out* 33/1

300- **6** *2* **Bond Diamond**[197] 5320 10-8-12 61 MickyFenton 10 42
(P T Midgley) *hld up and bhd: stdy hdwy over 3f out: wknd wl over 1f out* 14/1

0000 **7** *3 1/2* **Crusoe (IRE)**[7] 742 10-8-2 38 (b) SoniaEaton(7) 9 31
(A Sadik) *a bhd: lost tch 3f out: a bhd* 66/1

8 *42* **Tiana Bleu (IRE)** 5-7-13 .... WilliamBuick(5) 7 —
(P S Felgate) *s.i.s: a in rr: t.o fnl 3f* **33/1**

600- **U** **Katsumoto (IRE)**[232] 4304 4-8-9 45.......... StephenDonohoe(3) 1 —
(A J McCabe) *prom tl sddle slipped and lost pl over 4f out: t.o whn rdr uns 1f out* **33/1**

1m 50.62s (-1.14) **Going Correction** -0.10s/f (Stan) **9** Ran SP% **118.2**
Speed ratings (Par 103):101,100,99,90,89 87,84,46,—
CSF £63.20 TOTE £1.70: £1.02, £1.30, £2.50; EX 4.80
.Grimes Faith was claimed by K A Ryan for £14,000.\x\x
Owner Triple Trio Partnership **Bred** Thomas J Murphy **Trained** Middleham Moor, N Yorks

FOCUS
The bookmakers went 14/1 bar the first three home in this fairly uncompetitive claimer. Fair form, the right horses coming clear, but the time was modest.

834 BONUSPRINT.COM H'CAP — 1m 1f 103y(P)
3:45 (3:45) (Class 6) (0-65,65) 3-Y-O — **£2,730** (£806; £403) **Stalls** Low

Form — RPR

3052 **1** **Ella Y Rossa**[7] 744 3-8-7 **59**.......... StephenDonohoe(3) 11 — 64
(P D Evans) *hld up and bhd: hdwy over 2f out: rdn to ld ins fnl f: jst hld on* **9/2**[2]

1443 **2** *shd* **Beau Sancy**[8] 731 3-8-11 **65**.......... TolleyDean(5) 2 — 70+
(R A Harris) *hld up: sn mid-div: rdn and hdwy whn swtchd rt wl over 1f out: hung lft ins fnl f: r.o: jst failed* **7/2**[1]

3440 **3** *1 1/2* **Raquel White**[4] 790 3-8-1 **55** ow3.......... KevinGhunowa(5) 1 — 57
(J L Flint) *a.p: led over 2f out: hdd and nt qckn ins fnl f* **9/1**

020- **4** *7* **Kingsmead (USA)**[197] 5321 3-8-12 **61**.......... MickyFenton 9 — 49
(Miss J Feilden) *hld up and bhd: pushed along over 3f out: hdwy on wd outside over 2f out: hung lft over 1f out: nvr nr ldrs* **10/1**

0005 **5** *nk* **Conny Nobel (IRE)**[4] 791 3-8-4 **60** ow1.......... HaddenFrost(7) 6 — 47
(J L Flint) *prom: rdn over 3f out: wknd over 2f out* **20/1**

-650 **6** *3/4* **Silca Key**[14] 694 3-9-1 **64**.......... TonyCulhane 7 — 50
(M R Channon) *prom: led over 5f out: rdn and hdd over 2f out: wknd over 1f out* **7/1**[3]

-613 **7** *nk* **Poniard (IRE)**[17] 667 3-8-10 **59**..........(p) TonyHamilton 10 — 44
(D W Barker) *prom: rdn over 2f out: sn wknd* **12/1**

6-42 **8** *13* **Mizzle (USA)**[20] 661 3-9-2 **65**.......... JoeFanning 4 — 24
(M Johnston) *led: hdd over 5f out: wknd 3f out* **9/2**[2]

01-0 **9** *nk* **Play Straight**[35] 535 3-9-0 **63**.......... DanielTudhope 8 — 21
(I W McInnes) *mid-div: pushed along over 3f out: bhd fnl 2f* **16/1**

40-0 **10** *7* **Bathwick Breeze**[14] 694 3-8-11 **65** ow2.......... JamesMillman(5) 3 — 9
(B R Millman) *hld up in mid-div: pushed along over 4f out: bhd fnl 3f* **33/1**

000- **11** *35* **Dee Valley Boy (IRE)**[215] 4829 3-8-4 **53**.......... PaulHanagan 5 — —
(J D Bethell) *a bhd: rdn over 4f out: sn t.o* **12/1**

2m 2.85s (0.23) **Going Correction** -0.10s/f (Stan) **11** Ran SP% **119.1**
Speed ratings (Par 96):94,93,92,86,86 85,85,73,73,67 36
CSF £20.92 CT £138.54 TOTE £6.00: £1.70, £1.90, £3.10; EX 29.40.
Owner Miss D L Wisbey & R J Viney **Bred** Miss Deborah Wisbey **Trained** Pandy, Monmouths

FOCUS
There were a few lightly-raced sorts in this modest affair. The form looks sound, rated through the third, with slight steps up from the first two.
Mizzle(USA) Official explanation: trainer had no explanation for the poor form shown
Bathwick Breeze Official explanation: jockey said colt was never travelling

835 PONTIN'S - BOOK EARLY H'CAP — 5f 20y(P)
4:20 (4:22) (Class 5) (0-75,75) 4-Y-O+ — **£4,533** (£1,348; £674; £336) **Stalls** Low

Form — RPR

0-05 **1** **Fizzlephut (IRE)**[62] 269 5-8-9 **66**.......... PaulFitzsimons 6 — 79
(Miss J R Tooth) *chsd ldr: led over 2f out: clr over 1f out: r.o* **14/1**

1121 **2** *2* **Almaty Express**[32] 566 5-8-13 **75**..........(b) WilliamBuick(5) 4 — 81
(J R Weymes) *chsd ldrs: rdn over 1f out: edgd lft and wnt 2nd ins fnl f: nt trble wnr* **3/1**[2]

5431 **3** *nk* **Desert Master**[32] 567 4-9-2 **73**.......... GeorgeBaker 7 — 78
(C F Wall) *s.i.s: hdwy whn nt clr run over 2f out: swtchd rt wl over 1f out: kpt on ins fnl f* **10/3**[3]

-223 **4** *1/2* **Financial Times (USA)**[32] 566 5-9-4 **75**..........(vt) PaulHanagan 5 — 78+
(Stef Liddiard) *bhd: nt clr run over 3f out: rdn and hdwy 1f out: kpt on* **11/4**[1]

-610 **5** *1/2* **Cornus**[5] 774 5-9-1 **72**..........(b) JoeFanning 8 — 73+
(A J McCabe) *bhd: c wd and hmpd wl over 1f out: sn swtchd lft: nvr nrr* **16/1**

1-04 **6** *3/4* **Desert Opal**[62] 269 7-8-12 **72**..........(p) LiamJones(3) 10 — 70
(C R Dore) *bhd: c wd st: nvr nr ldrs* **10/1**

0-00 **7** *hd* **Coconut Moon**[32] 566 5-8-7 **64**.......... DavidAllan 2 — 62
(E J Alston) *prom: rdn over 2f out: wknd ins fnl f* **8/1**

050- **8** *1/2* **Law Maker**[197] 5309 7-9-4 **75**..........(v) MickyFenton 9 — 71
(A Bailey) *mid-div: wknd wl over 1f out* **40/1**

-000 **9** *8* **Signor Panettiere**[8] 727 6-9-4 **75**..........(tp) ChrisCatlin 1 — 42
(A D Brown) *led: hdd over 2f out: wknd over 1f out* **28/1**

62.01 secs (-0.81) **Going Correction** -0.10s/f (Stan) **9** Ran SP% **113.4**
Speed ratings (Par 103):102,98,98,97,96 95,95,94,81
CSF £54.93 CT £176.28 TOTE £15.70: £3.40, £1.30, £1.70; EX 76.60.
Owner Warwick Racing Partnership **Bred** Tally-Ho Stud **Trained** Lambourn, Berks

FOCUS
An ordinary sprint handicap. The bare form is not that solid but should work out with the next four behind the winner all of some interest.
Signor Panettiere Official explanation: trainer said gelding made a noise

836 PONTINS.COM MAIDEN FILLIES' STKS — 1m 141y(P)
4:55 (4:55) (Class 5) 3-Y-O — **£3,071** (£906; £453) **Stalls** Low

Form — RPR

224- **1** **La Spezia (IRE)**[181] 5679 3-9-0 75.......... HayleyTurner 2 — 81+
(M L W Bell) *a gng wl: shkn up to ld wl over 1f out: readily* **5/2**[2]

4-2 **2** *2* **Elyaadi**[20] 655 3-9-0.......... TonyCulhane 1 — 76
(M R Channon) *led: rdn 3f out: sn hung rt: hdd wl over 1f out: one pce* **8/15**[1]

53 **3** *6* **Ochre (IRE)**[9] 720 3-9-0..........(t) MatthewHenry 3 — 63
(M A Jarvis) *hld up in tch: pushed along over 3f out: wknd wl over 1f out* **9/1**[3]

2-43 **4** *1 1/2* **Snow Dancer (IRE)**[7] 745 3-8-10 68 ow1.......... PBradley(5) 4 — 61
(A Berry) *w ldr: rdn and ev ch over 2f out: wknd wl over 1f out* **20/1**

1m 50.64s (-1.12) **Going Correction** -0.10s/f (Stan) **4** Ran SP% **108.6**
Speed ratings (Par 95):100,98,92,91
CSF £4.30 TOTE £3.40; EX 4.90 Place 6 £27.93, Place 5 £20.16.
Owner Mark Dixon And Luke Lillingston **Bred** Mount Coote Stud And M H Dixon **Trained** Newmarket, Suffolk

FOCUS
An ordinary maiden. It is doubtful whether La Spezia had to improve much from last year, and the second and third have not progressed.
T/Plt: £27.20 to a £1 stake. Pool: £65,679.80. 1,761.35 winning tickets. T/Qpdt: £11.50 to a £1 stake. Pool: £3,100.70. 199.10 winning tickets. KH

786 KEMPTON (A.W) (R-H)
Saturday, March 31

OFFICIAL GOING: Standard
Wind: Strong, across

838 INTERCASINO.CO.UK MASAKA STKS (LISTED RACE) (FILLIES) — 1m (P)
2:25 (2:25) (Class 1) 3-Y-O
£14,762 (£5,595; £2,800; £1,396; £699; £351) **Stalls** High

Form — RPR

4-00 **1** **Precocious Star (IRE)**[44] 476 3-8-12.......... FergusSweeney 3 — 87
(K R Burke) *lw: trckd ldrs: rdn to ld jst ins f: hld on cl home* **8/1**

414- **2** *nk* **Fiumicino**[166] 6007 3-8-12 74.......... DaneO'Neill 5 — 87
(M R Channon) *trckd ldr tl jst over 1f out: rdn and kpt on to regain 2nd cl home* **20/1**

020- **3** *nk* **Mystery Ocean**[155] 6201 3-8-13 85 ow1.......... GeorgeBaker 9 — 87
(R M Beckett) *chsd ldrs: rdn to go 2nd 1f out: kpt on but lost 2nd cl home* **7/1**[3]

113- **4** *hd* **Laurentina**[154] 6217 3-8-12 94.......... SteveDrowne 6 — 85
(B J Meehan) *lw: led tl hdd jst ins fnl f: kpt on one pce* **13/8**[1]

21- **5** *1/2* **Princess Valerina**[155] 6199 3-8-12 84.......... MichaelHills 7 — 84
(B W Hills) *t.k.h: in tch but rdn over 2f out: styd on fnl f* **11/4**[2]

41- **6** *1 1/4* **Lakshmi (IRE)**[262] 3407 3-8-12 82.......... ChrisCatlin 2 — 81
(M R Channon) *bit bkwd: mid-div: rdn over 2f out: kpt on one pce* **10/1**

221- **7** *1/2* **Ronaldsay**[204] 5157 3-8-12 76.......... JimmyFortune 1 — 80
(R Hannon) *swtchd rt s: helup in rr: mde mod late hdwy on outside* **12/1**

332- **8** *shd* **Musical Beat**[98] 6927 3-8-12 71.......... EdwardCreighton 8 — 80?
(Miss V Haigh) *a in rr though mde mod late hdwy* **50/1**

130- **9** *11* **Harvest Joy (IRE)**[216] 4840 3-8-12 90.......... JimCrowley 4 — 55
(B R Millman) *a bhd* **16/1**

1m 41.35s (0.55) **Going Correction** +0.05s/f (Slow) **9** Ran SP% **117.8**
Speed ratings (Par 103):99,98,98,98,97 96,95,95,84
CSF £153.16 TOTE £13.50: £2.50, £5.40, £2.40; EX 196.50.
Owner Market Avenue Racing Club Ltd **Bred** Tom Twomey **Trained** Middleham Moor, N Yorks

FOCUS
A contest run at a very steady early pace and the time was modest for a race of its type, 1.94 seconds slower than the Easter Stakes. The proximity of a 74-rated filly in second, plus the fact that a large blanket would have covered the first five home, strongly suggests the form is substandard for the grade. It has been rated around the winner and fifth.

NOTEBOOK
Precocious Star(IRE), the only filly in the race not to be returning from a significant break, was never far away and showed a willing attitude to just come out best in a bunched finish. She had been beaten out of sight in two outings on sand in Dubai earlier this year, though form shown there can be unreliable, and whilst the way the race was run did not truly test her stamina for the trip and only just finishing ahead of a 74-rated filly does little for the form, the records will show that she is the winner of a Listed race. That is probably all that matters. (op 11-1 tchd 12-1)
Fiumicino, a beaten favourite off a mark of 73 in a Pontefract nursery when last seen in October but already a winner over this trip prior to that, was always close to the pace but did not have a lot of room to play with when still in there pitching coming to the last furlong and had to be switched inside. She ran on really well to snatch back the runner-up spot, but her proximity does not do a great deal for the form and she may not be easy to place now. (op 25-1)
Mystery Ocean, on her toes beforehand, had yet to tackle further than 6f prior to this and her rider put up 1lb overweight. She stayed on well towards the far side of the track to make the frame, but given the way the race was run the limit of her stamina is still unproven. She may yet improve, but will need to if she is to make her mark at this sort of level. (op 8-1 tchd 17-2)
Laurentina, the highest rated in the line-up and the pick of the paddock, had the best form in this field having finished third behind the Oaks favourite Passage Of Time at Newmarket on her final start at two. She very much had the run of the race out in front, but was still unable to see it out and on this evidence she is going to be extremely hard to place unless this race was badly needed. (op 9-4)
Princess Valerina, one of the least exposed in the field, was keen enough in behind but once switched wide in the home straight she had every chance and was never quite doing enough to get involved. She did not perform as though the extra two furlongs was a problem so it remains to be seen quite where she goes from here. (op 9-4)
Lakshmi(IRE), another lightly raced as a two-year-old, was also stepping up two furlongs in trip but could never land a blow. She was returning from a longer absence than all her rivals, so that does give her some hope should she come on for it. (op 15-2)
Ronaldsay looked fit enough beforehand despite having not run since September. (op 11-1 tchd 10-1)

839 INTERCASINO.CO.UK EASTER STKS (LISTED RACE) (C&G) — 1m (P)
2:55 (2:57) (Class 1) 3-Y-O
£14,762 (£5,595; £2,800; £1,396; £699; £351) **Stalls** High

Form — RPR

310- **1** **Dubai's Touch**[161] 6102 3-9-1 102.......... J-PGuillambert 4 — 109
(M Johnston) *sn led: rdn ent fnl f: styd on wl* **7/2**[2]

301- **2** *1/2* **Prime Defender**[143] 6402 3-8-12 106.......... MichaelHills 6 — 105
(B W Hills) *hld up: hdwy over 2f out: wnt 2nd over 1f out: kpt on but no imp on wnr ins fnl f* **7/4**[1]

530- **3** *2 1/2* **Danebury Hill**[183] 5653 3-8-12 100..........(t) SteveDrowne 8 — 99
(B J Meehan) *bit bkwd: in tch: hdwy on ins 2f out: kpt on but no imp on first 2 fnl f* **15/2**[3]

430- **4** *3 1/2* **Norisan**[175] 5805 3-8-12 100.......... DaneO'Neill 1 — 91
(R Hannon) *lw: broke wl sn hdd: trckd wnr tl wknd appr fnl f* **10/1**

41-2 **5** *nk* **Habalwatan (IRE)**[71] 184 3-8-12 89..........(b) JimmyFortune 3 — 90
(C E Brittain) *s.i.s: sn rdn in rr: no hdwy fnl 2f* **12/1**

1- **6** *4* **Water Mill (USA)**[210] 5020 3-8-12 90.......... LPKeniry 7 — 81
(A M Balding) *chsd ldrs tl rdn and wknd 2f out* **8/1**

02-0 **7** *3* **Valdan (IRE)**[7] 760 3-8-12 92.......... JimCrowley 5 — 74
(P D Evans) *b.hind: a in rr* **16/1**

1m 39.41s (-1.39) **Going Correction** +0.05s/f (Slow) **7** Ran SP% **104.1**
Speed ratings (Par 106):108,107,105,101,101 97,94
CSF £8.23 TOTE £4.20: £2.10, £1.70; EX 9.00.
Owner Salem Suhail **Bred** Miss S N Ralphs **Trained** Middleham Moor, N Yorks
■ St Philip was withdrawn (11/2, refused to enter stalls.) R4 applies, deduct 15p in the £.

FOCUS
A much stonger pace than for the Masaka and the winning time was 1.94 seconds quicker. The two market leaders pulled nicely clear and the form looks solid and up to scratch for the grade, if a fair way off series Guineas trial form.

NOTEBOOK
Dubai's Touch, a three-time winner in a busy campaign at two including at this level, had only once truly disappointed and that was on heavy ground in his final outing. This switch to Polytrack for the first time suited him much better though, and he was given a typically aggressive ride for a Johnston inmate. He faced a stern challenge from the favourite throughout the last furlong, but as is the norm for one from the yard he just kept on pulling out that bit more and would not be denied. He looked fit for this in the paddock and is pretty much exposed now, but with this yard you can never be quite sure how much more can be squeezed out of him. (op 3-1 tchd 9-2)
Prime Defender, who broke the all-aged course record over 6f at Wolverhampton when last seen, looked fit and was representing the Dewhurst form having finished 11th of the 15 runners behind Teofilo last October. Given a patient ride, he was produced with his effort down the outside passing the two-furlong pole and did little wrong, but the winner proved far too tough and he could never quite get to him. Given the decent pace there is no suggestion that he did not stay the trip and there should be races to be won with him this term. (op 5-2 tchd 11-4)
Danebury Hill, who showed his best form on a sound surface at two including when placed in the Solario, plugged on after switching to the inside passing the course intersection, but could never make much impression on the front pair. He probably ran close to his official mark, but may not be easy to place from now on. (op 8-1 tchd 9-1)
Norisan, placed a couple of times at this level at two, seemed to find this trip beyond him as a juvenile and unless he needed this run it looked a similar story here too. He is another for whom opportunities may not be that easy to find. (op 20-1)
Habalwatan(IRE), the most experienced in the field, had already scored three times on Polytrack this winter but in much lesser company than this and he had the lowest BHB ratings in the field. He never made any impression from off the pace and was suitably outclassed. (op 11-1)
Water Mill(USA), winner of a maiden here last September in his only outing to date, faced a stiff task and was firmly put in his place but was at least entitled to need this. (op 13-2 tchd 6-1)
Valdan(IRE) looked lean and hard fit beforehand. (op 14-1)

840 INTERCASINO.CO.UK H'CAP 7f (P)
3:30 (3:31) (Class 2) (0-100,100) 4-Y-0+

£9,971 (£2,985; £1,492; £747; £372; £187) **Stalls** High

Form RPR

1236 **1** **Waterside (IRE)**[21] 658 8-9-4 **100** .... GeorgeBaker 7 110
(G L Moore) *sn trckd ldr: shkn up to ld ins fnl f: won w smething in hand* **14/1**

02-6 **2** *1* **Cross The Line (IRE)**[7] 759 5-8-6 **88** .... LPKeniry 5 95
(A P Jarvis) *a in tch: hung rt appr fnl f: r.o to go 2nd nr fin* **10/1**

131 **3** *½* **Lethal**[7] 757 4-8-5 **87** oh1 ow1 .... JimCrowley 3 93
(D K Ivory) *led tl rdn and hdd ins fnl f: lost 2nd nr fin* **8/1**

020- **4** *hd* **High Curragh**[224] 4601 4-8-5 **90** .... AndrewMullen(3) 12 95
(K A Ryan) *bit bkwd: trckd ldrs: rdn and kpt on one pce fnl f* **16/1**

-464 **5** *1 ¼* **Marajaa (IRE)**[21] 658 5-8-6 **88** .... FergusSweeney 11 90
(W J Musson) *a.p: rdn over 1f out: kpt on one pce* **5/1**[3]

0/2- **6** *¾* **Presumptive (IRE)**[364] 828 7-8-3 **88** .... RichardKingscote(3) 10 88+
(R Charlton) *bhd tl hdwy on ins over 1f out: nvr nrr* **15/2**

11-2 **7** *½* **Ceremonial Jade (UAE)**[42] 487 4-8-13 **95** .... (t) OscarUrbina 2 94
(M Botti) *hld up: rdn and hdwy over 2f out: no ex appr fnl f* **10/3**[1]

1111 **8** *½* **Ektimaal**[21] 657 4-8-7 **89** .... (t) SteveDrowne 4 87
(E A L Dunlop) *in tch: hdwy on ins 2f out: fdd ent fnl f* **4/1**[2]

-506 **9** *nk* **Zato (IRE)**[44] 473 4-8-9 **91** .... ChrisCatlin 8 88
(M R Channon) *a in rr* **12/1**

/00- **10** *3 ½* **Moonlight Man**[346] 1086 6-8-5 **94** .... HaddenFrost(7) 9 82
(R Hannon) *bit bkwd: a towards rr* **50/1**

5030 **11** *shd* **Wessex (USA)**[21] 658 7-8-8 **90** .... J-PGuillambert 6 78
(P A Blockley) *b: mid-div: rdn 3f out: sn btn* **40/1**

4144 **12** *1 ½* **Gallantry**[7] 759 5-8-5 **87** .... NickyMackay 1 71
(D Shaw) *lw: slowly away: a bhd* **12/1**

1m 25.16s (-1.64) **Going Correction** +0.05s/f (Slow) 12 Ran SP% **124.0**
Speed ratings (Par 109):111,109,109,109,107 106,106,105,105,101 101,99
CSF £153.68 CT £1219.42 TOTE £18.80: £3.70, £4.10, £2.60; EX 173.60.
Owner Nigel Shields **Bred** Yeomanstown Stud **Trained** Woodingdean, E Sussex

FOCUS
A very competitive handicap and a decent gallop, but the first five were always prominent and it was difficult to make ground from the rear. The form looks absolutely rock solid, with another personal best from Waterside.

NOTEBOOK
Waterside(IRE) was never far from the pace and responded extremely well to pressure when brought with his effort down the outside to record a 16th career victory with a degree of comfort. He has done nothing but improve this winter and was winning this off a 16lb higher mark than when last successful in handicap company on sand, which incidentally was when he beat recent Listed winner Banknote at this track nearly a year ago. He is a credit to his trainer. (op 12-1 tchd 16-1)
Cross The Line(IRE) ◆ duly stepped up from his recent return to action and finished well to snatch second but could never get to a rival at the top of his game. His three career victories, including two here, have been over a mile and he does look better suited by that trip. He should not take long in going one better. (op 8-1)
Lethal, who was on his toes beforehand, had been raised 3lb for his victory over course and distance seven days earlier and had an extra 2lb to contend with this time thanks to a combination of being out of the handicap and his rider's overweight. He attempted the same forcing tactics that had proved successful last time, but in this better company he was just unable to see it out. This was another solid effort nonetheless. (op 10-1)
High Curragh ◆, making his sand debut, was always there or thereabouts and kept on right to the line. This was a decent effort in such a competitive handicap after seven months off and despite being on a career-high mark, he is one to keep an eye out for. Official explanation: jockey said gelding hung left in the closing stages (tchd 20-1)
Marajaa(IRE), meeting Waterside for the third race in a row, came out best when the pair met over the extended 1m in the Lincoln Trial at Wolverhampton, but over this trip he could not match the finishing pace of his old rival despite giving it his best shot. He is 8lb higher than when gaining his only victory to date over course and distance in November and the Handicapper seems to have him where he wants him. (op 6-1 tchd 13-2)
Presumptive(IRE) ◆ had been absent since finishing runner-up in this very race last year, but he looked fit enough beforehand and was noted putting in some good late work. He is one to watch out for in the coming weeks. (op 10-1)
Ceremonial Jade(UAE), held up as usual, tried to move closer soon after turning for home but his effort came to very little. He may have been 5lb higher than for his last win, but this was disappointing in view of how promising he looked last autumn. (op 3-1 tchd 11-4)
Ektimaal, bidding to extend his unbeaten record on sand to five, made his effort on the inside after crossing the intersection but never offered a threat. The 8lb rise since his last win appears to have nailed him to the floor. (op 7-2)

841 INTERCASINO.CO.UK CONDITIONS STKS 6f (P)
4:05 (4:05) (Class 3) 3-Y-0+

£6,855 (£2,052; £1,026; £513; £256; £128) **Stalls** High

Form RPR

305- **1** **Eisteddfod**[147] 6335 6-9-4 103 .... (t) JimmyFortune 5 96
(P F I Cole) *lw: a in tch: rdn to ld jst ins fnl f: r.o wl* **2/1**[2]

0050 **2** *1* **Tony James (IRE)**[35] 550 5-9-4 88 .... SteveDrowne 2 93
(K O Cunningham-Brown) *lw: trckd ldr: ev ch ent fnl f: nt pce of wnr but kpt on* **10/1**[3]

1-00 **3** *hd* **Mutamared (USA)**[50] 415 7-9-4 .... MichaelHills 6 92
(K A Ryan) *hld up in tch: effrt over 1f out: kpt on one pce* **10/11**[1]

000- **4** *3* **Cav Okay (IRE)**[242] 4026 3-8-8 96 .... DaneO'Neill 3 82
(R Hannon) *bit bkwd: led tl rdn and hdd jst ins fnl f: wknd* **12/1**

000/ **5** *1* **Bigalos Bandit**[557] 5379 5-9-1 .... AndrewMullen(3) 7 80
(D Nicholls) *trckd ldrs: rdn 2f out: hung rt and wknd fnl f* **25/1**

3422 **6** *3 ½* **Black Oval**[10] 722 6-8-10 49 ow4 .... MarkCoumbe(7) 4 69?
(S Parr) *lw: a bhd: lost tch over 1f out* **66/1**

120- **P** **Karayel (IRE)**[193] 5466 3-8-8 93 .... PatDobbs 1 —
(R Hannon) *wl bhd whn p.u bef 1/2-way* **12/1**

1m 13.11s (-0.59) **Going Correction** +0.05s/f (Slow)
WFA 3 from 5yo+ 13lb 7 Ran SP% **115.5**
Speed ratings (Par 107):105,103,103,99,98 93,—
CSF £22.54 TOTE £3.00: £1.90, £3.10; EX 22.60.
Owner Elite Racing Club **Bred** Elite Racing Club **Trained** Whatcombe, Oxon

FOCUS
A wide range of abilities in this conditions sprint, but the pace was decent enough. The race has been rated through the runner-up, with the sixth limiting the form.

NOTEBOOK
Eisteddfod, reappearing from nearly five months off and making his sand debut in his 26th race, had an obvious chance at the weights and the application of the first-time tongue tie also appeared to benefit him. Brought with his effort widest of all, he saw it out well and will now presumably head back into Pattern company.
Tony James(IRE) may have been a Gimcrack winner in his youth, but mostly modest efforts over the past two seasons meant that he had plenty on at these weights based on official ratings. He ran well though, having been close to the pace from the start, and managed to split a couple of rivals rated 15lb and 16lb higher than him, but it is always dangerous to take form in these types of races at face value and he still has to prove himself competitive off his current mark in proper handicap company. (op 12-1 tchd 14-1)
Mutamared(USA), winner of a competitive handicap over course and distance last September, came into this off the back of a couple of moderate efforts on turf in Dubai. He was brought through on the inside to hold every chance, but was never quite doing enough. He is not going to be easy to place off his current mark. (op Evens tchd 11-10)
Cav Okay(IRE), reappearing from eight months off and trying further than 5f for the first time, faced a stiff task against his elders and after making much of the running he was eventually swamped. A return to the minimum trip and his own age group should help him. (op 11-1 tchd 14-1)
Bigalos Bandit, reappearing from 18 months off and making his debut for the yard, ran well for a long way before understandably getting tired. It will be interesting to see what his talented trainer can get out of him this term. (op 33-1)
Black Oval had no chance at this level and was completely outclassed, though she did pick up £128.70 with Karayel pulling up.

842 PLAY ROULETTE AT INTERCASINO.CO.UK H'CAP (LONDON MILE QUALIFIER) 1m (P)
4:40 (4:40) (Class 4) (0-85,85) 4-Y-0+ **£4,728** (£1,406; £702; £351) **Stalls** High

Form RPR

3120 **1** **Councellor (FR)**[14] 697 5-8-12 **79** .... (t) MickyFenton 8 91
(Stef Liddiard) *t.k.h: trckd ldrs: led over 1f out: edgd bdly lft but r.o cl home* **11/1**

654- **2** *¾* **Electric Warrior (IRE)**[180] 5722 4-8-12 **79** .... FergusSweeney 9 89
(K R Burke) *lw: in tch: rdn and r.o to chse wnr ins fnl f* **6/1**

522- **3** *1 ¼* **King Of Argos**[112] 6772 4-9-3 **84** .... JimmyFortune 6 91
(E A L Dunlop) *in tch early: c wd into st: rdn and r.o wl fnl f: nvr nrr* **4/1**[3]

-212 **4** *nk* **Rapid City**[56] 340 4-9-1 **85** .... JamesDoyle(3) 4 91
(Miss J Feilden) *led tl rdn and hdd jst ins fnl f: no ex* **7/2**[2]

2420 **5** *1 ¼* **Rebellious Spirit**[21] 657 4-9-4 **85** .... JimCrowley 2 89
(P W Hiatt) *trckd ldr tl wknd ins fnl f* **16/1**

50-5 **6** *2* **Paraguay (USA)**[7] 765 4-8-9 **76** .... EdwardCreighton 3 75
(Miss V Haigh) *hld up in rr: no hdwy fnl 2f* **16/1**

2/0- **7** *nk* **King's Majesty (IRE)**[371] 728 5-9-2 **83** .... GeorgeBaker 7 81
(L A Dace) *lw: in rr: effrt on ins over 2f out: sn btn* **10/1**

2111 **8** *nk* **Lopinot (IRE)**[7] 765 4-9-2 **83** .... SteveDrowne 5 81
(P J Makin) *lw: b.hind: trckd ldrs tl wknd 2f out* **5/2**[1]

15-0 **9** *3 ½* **Hypnotic**[21] 657 5-8-5 **75** .... (t) AndrewMullen(3) 1 65
(D Nicholls) *hld up: a bhd* **25/1**

1m 40.62s (-0.18) **Going Correction** +0.05s/f (Slow) 9 Ran SP% **118.1**
Speed ratings (Par 105):102,101,100,99,98 96,96,95,92
CSF £77.05 CT £315.24 TOTE £15.30: £2.60, £2.80, £1.80; EX 102.70.
Owner D Gilbert **Bred** Janus Bloodstock & Pontchartrain Stud **Trained** Great Shefford, Berks

FOCUS
Quite a competitive handicap, but the pace was ordinary and the winning time was 1.21 seconds slower than the three-year-old colts in the Easter Stakes. The form looks pretty sound, with the principals all close to their marks.
Rapid City Official explanation: jockey said gelding hung left-handed in the home straight

843 PLAY BLACKJACK AT INTERCASINO.CO.UK H'CAP 7f (P)
5:15 (5:17) (Class 4) (0-80,78) 3-Y-0 **£4,728** (£1,406; £702; £351) **Stalls** High

Form RPR

1- **1** **Supa Sal**[263] 3385 3-9-1 **75** .... JimmyFortune 2 81
(P F I Cole) *trckd ldrs: hung bdly lft fr 2f out: stend up whn rchd stands' rail and r.o wl to ld last stride* **4/1**[3]

22-1 **2** *hd* **King's Apostle (IRE)**[14] 700 3-9-1 **78** .... LiamJones(3) 4 85+
(W J Haggas) *b.hind: lw: t.k.h: trckd ldr: led 2f out: hung rt fnl f: hdd post* **9/2**

21-3 **3** *hd* **Prince Of Charm (USA)**[8] 737 3-8-7 **67** .... (p) NickyMackay 8 72+
(P Mitchell) *hld up in rr: gd hdwy over 1f out: chsd ldr ins fnl f: lost 2nd cl home* **7/2**[2]

1- **4** *¾* **Roodolph**[194] 5417 3-9-4 **78** .... StephenCarson 6 81
(Eve Johnson Houghton) *s.i.s: in tch: rdn 2f out: styd on wl fnl f* **12/1**

-132 **5** *1* **Satyricon**[15] 694 3-9-0 **74** .... (b) OscarUrbina 9 74
(M Botti) *lw: in tch: hdwy on ins over 1f out: kpt on one pce ins fnl f* **5/2**[1]

23-0 **6** *2* **Jack Oliver**[10] 725 3-8-5 **72** .... KMay(7) 7 67
(B J Meehan) *prom tl rdn and wknd appr fnl f* **14/1**

-053 **7** *½* **Jord (IRE)**[10] 725 3-8-11 **71** .... SteveDrowne 1 65
(A J McCabe) *led tl rdn and hdd 2f out: wknd appr fnl f* **14/1**

-351 **8** *1* **Mr Loire**[29] [606] 3-9-1 **75**........ DaneO'Neill 5 66
(H J L Dunlop) *hld up in rr: rdn 3f out: sn btn* **20/1**
460- **9** *2* **Lady Lafitte (USA)**[183] [5647] 3-8-7 **67**........ MichaelHills 3 53
(B W Hills) *in tch: on outside whn rdn over 2f out: sn btn* **14/1**
1m 26.34s (-0.46) **Going Correction** +0.05s/f (Slow) **9** Ran SP% **121.4**
Speed ratings (Par 100):104,103,103,102,101 99,98,97,95
CSF £23.73 CT £71.13 TOTE £5.10: £1.90, £1.60, £1.70; EX 19.10.
Owner Ben & Sir Martyn Arbib **Bred** Arbib Bloodstock Partnership **Trained** Whatcombe, Oxon

FOCUS

A competitive little handicap and an interesting race in that the time was very respectable even though the first two home were hanging all over the track. Some of these are still unexposed and winners should emerge from this race, which has been rated around the fifth and sixth.

844 £600 FREE AT INTERCASINO.CO.UK H'CAP 2m (P)

5:50 (5:50) (Class 4) (0-85,82) 4-Y-0+ **£4,728** (£1,406; £702; £351) **Stalls** High

Form RPR
0410 **1** **Newnham (IRE)**[26] [617] 6-8-11 **70**........ JackMitchell(7) 9 82
(J R Boyle) *lw: hld up in tch: hdwy fr 2f out: led fnl 100yds: hld on wl* **13/2**
0451 **2** *nk* **Salut Saint Cloud**[6] [775] 6-9-1 **67** 6ex........(p) SimonWhitworth 5 79
(G L Moore) *t.k.h in mid-div: hdwy to ld 2f out: strly rdn: hdd fnl 100yds but pressed wnr to line* **4/1**[2]
4441 **3** *3 1/2* **Synonymy**[17] [677] 4-8-10 **67**........(b) SteveDrowne 4 75
(M Blanshard) *chsd ldrs tl lost pl over 3f out: rallied over 1f out and styd on fnl f* **5/1**[3]
001- **4** *3 1/2* **High Point (IRE)**[122] [6655] 9-9-10 **76**........ DaneO'Neill 7 80
(G P Enright) *hld up: hdwy on outside over 3f out: one pce ins fnl 2f* **7/1**
2-31 **5** *2 1/2* **Night Cruise (IRE)**[45] [457] 4-9-11 **82**........ JimCrowley 10 83
(J A Osborne) *lw: t.k.h: in tch: ev ch fr over 2f out but rdn and fnd little fr over 1f out* **2/1**[1]
0/66 **6** *2* **Red Wine**[48] [434] 8-9-6 **75**........(be) JamesDoyle(3) 3 73
(A J McCabe) *hld up: effrt on outside 2f out: one pce after* **40/1**
550- **7** *4* **Establishment**[140] [6438] 10-9-12 **78**........ JimmyFortune 2 71
(C A Cyzer) *in tch: rdn over 3f out: wknd over 1f out* **12/1**
050- **8** *5* **Cavallini (USA)**[35] [5479] 5-9-6 **72**........ GeorgeBaker 6 59
(G L Moore) *lw: trckd ldrs: led over 4f out: hdd 2f out: sn wknd* **14/1**
/04- **9** *10* **Pocketwood**[108] [6381] 5-9-6 **72**........ StephenCarson 1 47
(Jean-Rene Auvray) *trckd ldr: led 6f out to over 4f out: wknd over 2f out* **33/1**
00- **10** *26* **Freddy (ARG)**[259] [3533] 8-9-11 **77**........(t) RobertHavlin 8 21
(D K Ivory) *b: mde most tl hung rt and hdd 6f out: wknd over 3f out* **20/1**
3m 29.46s (-1.94) **Going Correction** +0.05s/f (Slow)
WFA 4 from 5yo+ 5lb **10** Ran SP% **120.3**
Speed ratings (Par 105):106,105,104,102,101 100,98,95,90,77
CSF £33.20 CT £144.58 TOTE £8.30: £1.90, £2.10, £1.70; EX 44.10 Place 6 £354.77, Place 5 £86.01.
Owner M Khan X2 **Bred** Ballygallon Stud **Trained** Epsom, Surrey

FOCUS

A solidly run staying handicap thanks to the outsiders Pocketwood and Freddy and ultimately a thrilling battle between the front pair who pulled clear of the others. Sound form, with improved efforts from the first two.

Freddy(ARG) Official explanation: jockey said horse hung left-handed throughout

T/Plt: £1,278.10 to a £1 stake. Pool: £79,580.40. 45.45 winning tickets. T/Qpdt: £92.80 to a £1 stake. Pool: £4,561.20. 36.35 winning tickets. JS

NEWCASTLE (L-H)

Saturday, March 31

OFFICIAL GOING: Good to soft (soft in places between 6f and 1m in straight)

Meeting switched from Doncaster.

Wind: Fresh, half behind

845 WILLIAMHILLPOKER.COM BROCKLESBY CONDITIONS STKS 5f

2:10 (2:10) (Class 4) 2-Y-O

£7,478 (£2,239; £1,119; £560; £279; £140) **Stalls** High

Form RPR
1 **Mister Hardy** 2-8-11........ PaulHanagan 11 85+
(R A Fahey) *cl up far side: effrt 2f out: rdn to ld ins last: kpt on wl* **11/2**[1]
2 *1 3/4* **Fol Hollow (IRE)** 2-8-11........ AdrianTNicholls 3 78
(D Nicholls) *s.i.s and rr far side: swtchd rt and gd hdwy 2f out: styd on wl fnl f* **12/1**
3 *1/2* **Portrush Storm** 2-8-6........ DanielTudhope 9 71
(D Carroll) *keen: chsd ldrs far side: effrt and ev ch 2f out tl rdn and no ex wl ins last* **20/1**
4 *nk* **Not My Choice (IRE)** 2-8-8........ GregFairley(3) 8 75
(T J Pitt) *prom far side: led 2f out: sn rdn: hdd ins last and kpt on same pce* **11/2**[1]
5 *nk* **Runswick Bay** 2-8-11........ NCallan 16 74+
(G M Moore) *led stands side gp: rdn wl over 1f out: kpt on ins last: nt rch ldrs* **7/1**[3]
6 *nk* **Turn And River (IRE)** 2-7-13........ PatrickDonaghy(7) 17 67
(M Brittain) *s.i.s and bhd stands side: hdwy 2f out: styd on ins last: nrst fin* **50/1**
7 *1* **Alpen Adventure (IRE)** 2-8-11........ DarryllHolland 4 68
(Mrs L Stubbs) *dwlt and towards rr far side: hdwy 2f out: sn rdn and edgd lft kpt on ins last* **12/1**
8 *2 1/2* **Hamish McGonagall** 2-8-11........ DavidAllan 13 58
(T D Easterby) *in tch stands side: rdn along: rn green and wknd fnl 2f* **20/1**
9 *1 1/4* **Silver Wind** 2-8-8........ StephenDonohoe(3) 1 53
(P D Evans) *outpcd and bhd far side tl some late hdwy* **11/2**[1]
10 *4* **The Magic Blanket (IRE)** 2-8-11........ TomEaves 5 37
(Mrs L Stubbs) *mid-field: rdn along whn n.m.r wl over 1f out: sn wknd* **20/1**
11 *1 3/4* **Goldhill Fair** 2-8-4........ JackDean(7) 14 30
(W G M Turner) *chsd ldrs stands side: rdn along and edgd lft over 2f out: sn wknd* **13/2**[2]
12 *3/4* **Blazing Bullet (IRE)** 2-8-11........ TonyHamilton 7 27
(N Wilson) *overall ldr far side: rdn along and hdd 2f out: sn wknd* **33/1**
13 *6* **Wizzy Izzy (IRE)** 2-8-6........ PaulMulrennan 12 —
(N Wilson) *cl up stands side: rdn along 1/2-way: sn wknd* **33/1**
14 *1 3/4* **Northgate Lodge (USA)** 2-8-11........ DeanMernagh 15 —
(M Brittain) *chsd ldrs stands side: rdn along over 2f out: sn wknd* **12/1**
15 *4* **La Belle Joannie** 2-8-1........ RoryMoore(5) 6 —
(P T Midgley) *a outpcd and rr far side* **50/1**
F **Miss Tilen** 2-8-1........ WilliamBuick(5) 2 —
(V Smith) *outpcd and towards rr far side: rdn along 2f out: hmpd and fell wl over 1f out* **25/1**
64.99 secs (3.49) **Going Correction** +0.575s/f (Yiel) **16** Ran SP% **123.0**
Speed ratings (Par 94):95,92,91,90,90 89,88,84,82,75 73,71,62,59,53 —
CSF £64.46 TOTE £6.20: £2.40, £3.90, £10.30; EX 93.00 TRIFECTA Not won..
Owner The Cosmic Cases **Bred** Mrs M Bryce **Trained** Musley Bank, N Yorks

FOCUS

An ordinary bunch on looks and the group that raced far side held the edge over those on the stands' side. The pace seemed fair. The level has been set through race averages, with the winner likely to be capable of better.

NOTEBOOK

Mister Hardy, a 30,000 Kyllachy half-brother to a triple juvenile winner, had the run of the race on the far side and showed a good attitude to win at the first time of asking. He should have no problems with six furlongs and is entitled to improve for the experience. (op 6-1)

Fol Hollow(IRE) ♦, out of a prolific winner at up to 9f, took time to grasp what was required but made up a considerable amount of ground in the closing stages. He will appreciate further in due course and appeals as the type to win races.

Portrush Storm, whose stable has done well on sand this winter, is related to several winners and showed enough on this racecourse debut to suggest a small race can be found, especially in a race confined to her own sex.

Not My Choice(IRE), who cost 40,000 euros and is related to winners abroad, showed ability on this racecourse debut and is entitled to improve for the experience. He is in good hands and is capable of better. (op 9-2 tchd 6-1)

Runswick Bay ♦, a half-brother to the useful Musicanna, looks better than the bare form of this racecourse debut suggests as he fared the best of those to race in the stands side group. He will be suited by 6f in due course and appeals as the type to win a similar event. (op 12-1)

Turn And River(IRE), related to a couple of winners abroad, was fractious in the preliminaries but showed ability on this racecourse debut and is entitled to improve for the experience.

Alpen Adventure(IRE) was far from disgraced on this racecourse debut and left the impression that a stiffer test of stamina would be in his favour. He has physical scope and may be capable of better. (op 16-1)

846 WILLIAM HILL SPRING MILE (H'CAP) 1m 3y(S)

2:40 (2:42) (Class 2) 4-Y-O+

£15,580 (£4,665; £2,332; £1,167; £582; £292) **Stalls** Centre

Form RPR
300- **1** **European Dream (IRE)**[91] [5810] 4-8-13 **77**........ DarryllHolland 14 95
(R C Guest) *hld up stands side: smooth hdwy over 2f out: rdn to ld ent last: sn clr* **12/1**
500- **2** *6* **Dancing Lyra**[15] [5512] 6-9-1 **79**........ PaulHanagan 11 83
(R A Fahey) *hld up stands side: pushed along and outpcd over 3f out: gd hdwy over 1f out: kpt on: no ch w wnr* **12/1**
00-0 **3** *2* **Shot To Fame (USA)**[14] [697] 8-9-2 **80**........(t) AdrianTNicholls 12 80
(D Nicholls) *led and sn clr stands side: rdn along 2f out: hdd ent last and sn no ex* **20/1**
205- **4** *2* **Prince Samos (IRE)**[303] [2169] 5-9-8 **86**........ SilvestreDeSousa 19 81
(D Nicholls) *in tch stands side: effrt over 2f out: sn rdn and kpt on same pce* **16/1**
013- **5** *1* **Mezuzah**[154] [6210] 7-9-7 **85**........ PaulMulrennan 10 78
(M W Easterby) *swtchd to stands side: chsd ldrs: rdn along over 2f out: drvn and no ex app last* **16/1**
32-6 **6** *1* **Vacation (IRE)**[21] [656] 4-9-6 **87**........ SaleemGolam(3) 3 77+
(V Smith) *towards rr far side: outpcd and rr 3f out: styd on u.p to ld far side gp ins last: no ch w stands side: 1st of 7 in grp* **14/1**
300- **7** *1/2* **Focus Group (USA)**[259] [3552] 6-9-8 **86**........ GrahamGibbons 17 75
(J J Quinn) *hld up stands side: rdn along over 3f out: kpt on fnl f: no imp* **13/2**[3]
106- **8** *3/4* **Daaweitza**[175] [5810] 4-8-12 **76**........ TonyHamilton 5 64+
(B Ellison) *bhd and outpcd far side: hdwy over 2f out: ev ch in that gp ins fnl f: one pce: 2nd of 7 in grp* **20/1**
-524 **9** *10* **Byron Bay**[25] [629] 5-9-3 **81**........(p) TomEaves 2 46+
(I Semple) *chsd ldr far side: led that grp over 3f out tl ins last: no ex: 3rd of 7in grp* **16/1**
2-22 **10** *1* **Resplendent Nova**[7] [757] 5-9-0 **78**........ JimmyQuinn 13 40
(P Howling) *in tch stands side: rdn along 3f out: grad wknd* **6/1**[2]
050- **11** *7* **Goodbye Mr Bond**[203] [5188] 7-9-8 **86**........ KDarley 6 32
(E J Alston) *chsd ldrs far side: rdn and wknd fr 2f out: 4th of 7 in grp* **14/1**
120- **12** *4* **Bailieborough (IRE)**[182] [5680] 8-9-5 **86**........(b[1]) GregFairley(3) 7 23
(B Ellison) *led far side tl over 3f out: sn wknd: 5th of 7 in grp* **40/1**
430- **13** *shd* **Fort Churchill (IRE)**[176] [5787] 6-9-5 **83**........(bt) PatCosgrave 4 20
(B Ellison) *hld up in tch far side: effrot over 3f out: sn rdn and wknd over 2f out: 6th of 7 in grp* **40/1**
0006 **14** *1* **Boo**[7] [761] 5-9-6 **87**........(v) AndrewElliott(3) 1 21
(K R Burke) *a outpcd far side: last of 7 in grp* **20/1**
11-0 **15** *4* **Speagle (IRE)**[10] [726] 5-9-2 **80**........ DanielTudhope 15 5
(D Carroll) *chsd ldrs stands side: rdn 3f out: sn wknd* **25/1**
12-6 **16** *29* **Neardown Beauty (IRE)**[2] [817] 4-9-4 **82**........ JoeFanning 9 —
(I A Wood) *midfield stands side: rdn and edgd lft 1/2-way: sn btn* **18/1**
6511 **17** *8* **Dichoh**[25] [629] 4-9-1 **79** 5ex........ NCallan 20 —
(M A Jarvis) *in tch stands side: rdn along 3f out: sn wknd* **10/3**[1]
300- **18** *15* **Nautical**[182] [5682] 9-8-8 **77**........ PatrickHills(5) 18 —
(A W Carroll) *dwlt and a rr stands side* **40/1**
200- **19** *22* **South Cape**[169] [5943] 4-9-10 **88**........ TonyCulhane 8 —
(M R Channon) *swtchd to r stands side: in tch tl rdn and wknd 3f out* **14/1**
1m 47.29s (5.39) **Going Correction** +0.825s/f (Soft) **19** Ran SP% **134.4**
Speed ratings (Par 109):106,100,98,96,95 94,93,92,82,81 74,70,70,69,65 36,28,13,—
CSF £148.40 CT £2895.29 TOTE £13.80: £2.90, £4.10, £4.50, £4.40; EX 152.00 TRIFECTA Not won..
Owner You Trotters **Bred** Limetree Stud Ltd **Trained** Brancepeth, Co Durham
■ Stewards' Enquiry : Silvestre De Sousa one-day ban: careless riding (Apr 11)

FOCUS

Not the strongest of handicaps and a race in which the larger stands-side group always held sway over those that raced on the far side. The pace was sound though, and the time little more than a second slower than the Lincoln. The winner impressed, and the second was back to his winning mark.

NOTEBOOK

European Dream(IRE), returned to the Flat after a three-month break, had the race run to suit and turned in his best effort yet. All his three Flat wins have been here (also won at this course over hurdles) but things panned out well for him and life is going to be much tougher after reassessment. (op 14-1)

Dancing Lyra, fit from a stint hurdling, shaped as though retaining all his ability back on the Flat and, like the winner, made up plenty of ground in the closing stages. He goes well in testing conditions and looks worth another try over a mile and a quarter. He is sure to win races this year granted a sufficient test of stamina. (op 10-1)

Shot To Fame(USA) ◆, sharpened up from a spin at Lingfield after a break last time, has slipped to a fair mark and, although he has not won for nearly three years, showed more than enough to suggest that should not be the case for too long, especially when returned to 7f in races where he is allowed to dominate.

Prince Samos(IRE), having his first run for David Nicholls, shaped well from his favourable draw over a trip that looks a bare minimum. The return to 1m2f should suit and he is sure to win a race around that trip this term.

Mezuzah, who won this race from a 15lb lower mark last year, was far from disgraced on this first run for five months. He goes particularly well in testing ground but may remain vulnerable to progressive or well handicapped types from his current mark.

Vacation(IRE), a dual Polytrack winner this winter, shaped better than the bare form as he fared the best of those to race on the unfavoured far side group. He may be the type that needs things to fall right but he looks capable of winning a race on turf, especially when returned to a bit further. (op 22-1 tchd 25-1)

Focus Group(USA) stayed on from the rear and was far from disgraced on this first run since the middle of July. He should be down in the weights for this and will be of more interest returned to 1m2f. (op 8-1)

Daaweitza was another on the far side group to shape better than the bare form on this reappearance run. He is on a fair mark and is not one to be writing off just yet.

Bailieborough(IRE) Official explanation: trainer said gelding was unsuited by the good to soft (soft in places) ground

Fort Churchill(IRE) Official explanation: trainer said gelding was unsuited by the good to soft (soft in places) ground

Dichoh, a four-time winner on artificial surfaces this winter, was well supported from a potentially favourable turf mark but he was one of the first off the bridle and proved a disappointment. This tacky ground may well have been against him and he is worth another chance on a sound surface on turf. Official explanation: jockey said gelding was unsuited by the good to soft (soft in places) ground (op 7-2 tchd 4-1 in places)

847 WILLIAMHILL.CO.UK CAMMIDGE TROPHY (LISTED RACE) 6f

3:15 (3:15) (Class 1) 3-Y-O+

£17,034 (£6,456; £3,231; £1,611; £807; £405) **Stalls** High

Form	Pos	Btn	Horse	Jockey	RPR
411-	**1**		**Rising Shadow (IRE)**^{147} [6335] 6-9-5 103	JimmyQuinn 8	115
			(T D Barron) *s.i.s and towards rr stands side: hdwy over 2f out: rdn wl over 1f out: styd on ins last to ld nr fin*	**13/2**^{3}	
013-	**2**	¾	**Sierra Vista**^{170} [5921] 7-8-11 102	PaulHanagan 11	105
			(D W Barker) *overall ldr stands side: rdn over 1f out: edgd lft ins last: hdd nr fin*	**16/1**	
020-	**3**	1 ¾	**Skhilling Spirit**^{175} [5812] 4-9-2 97	PaulFessey 12	105+
			(T D Barron) *slowly away and bhd stands side tl styd on fnl 2f: nrst fin*	**9/1**	
-415	**4**	2 ½	**Appalachian Trail (IRE)**^{37} [528] 6-9-5	(b) TomEaves 10	100
			(I Semple) *trckd ldrs gng wl stands side: rdn wl over 1f out: drvn and no ex ins last*	**9/2**^{2}	
21-1	**5**	5	**Hinton Admiral**^{7} [760] 3-8-6 103	JoeFanning 7	85
			(M Johnston) *chsd ldrs stands side tl rdn 2f out and sn wknd*	**7/2**^{1}	
005-	**6**	¾	**Steenberg (IRE)**^{182} [5682] 8-9-2 108	NCallan 3	80
			(M H Tompkins) *hld up stands side: effrt over 2f out: sn rdn and no imp*	**9/1**	
04-6	**7**	*hd*	**Angus Newz**^{35} [551] 4-9-0 90	ShaneKelly 1	77+
			(M Quinn) *racd alone far side: chsd ldrs: rdn and ch 2f out: sn wknd*	**28/1**	
016-	**8**	4	**Danum Dancer**^{175} [5809] 3-8-6 90	(b) SilvestreDeSousa 9	70
			(N Bycroft) *chsd ldrs stands side: rdn along over 2f out: sn btn*	**33/1**	
340-	**9**	½	**Pivotal Flame**^{181} [5712] 5-9-2 109	(p) GrahamGibbons 4	66
			(E S McMahon) *prom tl rdn and wknd over 2f out*	**7/2**^{1}	
514-	**10**	2	**Mecca's Mate**^{168} [5957] 6-8-11 100	TonyHamilton 6	55
			(D W Barker) *towards rr: rdn along 1/2-way: nvr on terms*	**22/1**	
100-	**11**	*hd*	**The Kiddykid (IRE)**^{175} [5812] 7-9-5 103	StephenDonohoe 5	62
			(P D Evans) *chsd ldrs: rdn 1/2-way: sn btn*	**16/1**	
4515	**12**	7	**Bahamian Pirate (USA)**^{21} [660] 12-9-2 93	AdrianTNicholls 2	38
			(D Nicholls) *dwlt: a rr*	**33/1**	

1m 16.96s (1.87) **Going Correction** +0.575s/f (Yiel)
WFA 3 from 4yo+ 13lb **12** Ran SP% **121.4**
Speed ratings (Par 111):110,109,106,103,96 95,95,90,89,86 86,77
CSF £102.80 TOTE £8.40: £2.70, £4.80, £3.20; EX 90.80 Trifecta £666.10 Part won. Pool: £938.29 - 0.10 winning units..

Owner G Morrill **Bred** 6c Stallions Ltd **Trained** Maunby, N Yorks

FOCUS

Not the strongest of Listed races and one in which the early pace was just fair. Decent enough form though among the principals, the winner continuing his late 2006 improvement and the runner-up rated to her best 6f form.

NOTEBOOK

Rising Shadow(IRE), having his first run for nearly five months, carried on the improvement that saw him notch a handicap and a Listed event last backend. As usual he forfeited ground at the start but made it up to cut down a rival that had enjoyed the run of the race. This trip and a good gallop on easy ground are his requirements and he may well be capable of better. (op 11-2)

Sierra Vista is a useful sprinter who had the run of the race under ideal conditions and confirmed she retains all her ability on this first start since last October. Equally effective over 5f, she looks the type to win a similar race this year when allowed to dominate. (op 14-1)

Skhilling Spirit ◆, who tends to lose ground at the start, ran an eyecatching race as he was beaten a similar distance to the amount of ground he lost out of the gates. He goes particularly well with cut in the ground and, although his style of racing means he needs things to pan out well for him, he appeals as the type to win again this term. (op 16-1)

Appalachian Trail(IRE), having his first start after a stint in Dubai, travelled in his customary strong fashion for much of the way but failed to pick up in the anticipated manner once asked for his effort. He may be best granted more cover in a strongly run race and is not one to write off just yet. (op 5-1 tchd 4-1)

Hinton Admiral, turned out quickly after his reappearance win over 7f on Polytrack the previous Saturday, proved a bit of a disappointment. This may have come too quickly and faster ground may have suited so, given his record, he is not one to be writing off just yet. (op 4-1 tchd 9-2)

Steenberg(IRE), a useful performer on his day, would have preferred more of an end-to-end gallop over this trip but was still a shade disappointing on this reappearance run (has gone well fresh before). He is the type that needs things to drop right and has not won as many as his ability suggests he should have done. (op 7-1)

Angus Newz, who won three times in Listed company last year, had the benefit of a recent start on Polytrack but was not at her best having raced alone on the far side. (op 18-1)

Pivotal Flame, who goes well fresh and who proved to be a model of consistency last year, had conditions to suit for this reappearance run but ran a long way his best for no apparent reason. Official explanation: jockey said horse was unsuited by the good to soft ground (op 9-2 tchd 5-1 in places)

848 WILLIAM HILL LINCOLN (HERITAGE H'CAP) 1m 3y(S)

3:55 (3:55) (Class 2) 4-Y-O+

£61,660 (£18,560; £9,280; £4,630; £2,320; £1,170) **Stalls** Centre

Form	Pos	Btn	Horse	Jockey	RPR
31P2	**1**		**Very Wise**^{14} [701] 5-8-11 **91** 5ex	JoeFanning 16	104+
			(W J Haggas) *sn led stands rail: rdn clr wl over 1f out: styd on wl*	**9/1**^{3}	
422-	**2**	1	**Rio Riva**^{154} [6219] 5-9-3 **97**	TomEaves 7	108+
			(Miss J A Camacho) *hld up stands side: hdwy over 2f out: rdn to chse wnr over 1f out: kpt on ins last*	**10/1**	
054-	**3**	4	**Mutawaffer**^{176} [5787] 6-8-8 **88**	TonyHamilton 20	90
			(R A Fahey) *midfield: effrt over 2f out: sn chsng ldrs: rdn over 1f out and kpt on same pce*	**10/1**	
445-	**4**	*nk*	**Raptor (GER)**^{162} [6093] 4-9-8 **102**	PatCosgrave 17	103
			(K R Burke) *dwlt and towards rr tl styd on wl fnl 2f: nrst fin*	**25/1**	
00-0	**5**	3 ½	**My Paris**^{21} [658] 6-9-1 **95**	NCallan 19	88
			(K A Ryan) *chsd ldrs: effrt 2f out: sn rdn and no imp*	**9/1**^{3}	
000-	**6**	1	**Audience**^{154} [6219] 7-8-9 **89**	JimmyQuinn 18	80
			(J Akehurst) *hmpd s and bhd stands side tl styd on fnl 2f: nrst fin*	**20/1**	
050-	**7**	*hd*	**Crooked Throw (IRE)**^{6} [783] 8-8-11 **94**	WJLee$^{(3)}$ 2	84+
			(C F Swan, Ire) *stdd s and swtchd rt to stands rails: hld up and bhd tl styd on fnl 2f: nrst fin*	**25/1**	
-345	**8**	2	**Bolodenka (IRE)**^{44} [473] 5-9-3 **97**	PaulHanagan 9	83+
			(R A Fahey) *midfield towards outer: rdn along over 3f out: sn no imp*	**16/1**	
30-2	**9**	*nk*	**Blythe Knight (IRE)**^{64} [255] 7-9-4 **98**	GrahamGibbons 5	83
			(J J Quinn) *prom stands side: rdn along 3f out: sn btn*	**22/1**	
000-	**10**	¾	**Blue Spinnaker (IRE)**^{147} [6337] 8-8-8 **88**	DaleGibson 8	71
			(M W Easterby) *bhd stands side tl sme late hdwy*	**33/1**	
32-0	**11**	1 ¾	**Collateral Damage (IRE)**^{21} [658] 4-8-9 **89**	DavidAllan 6	68
			(T D Easterby) *a rr stands side*	**33/1**	
230-	**12**	½	**Granston (IRE)**^{189} [5520] 6-8-10 **90**	DarryllHolland 13	68
			(J D Bethell) *prom stands side tl rdn and outpcd fr over 2f out*	**14/1**	
140-	**13**	*shd*	**Zero Tolerance (IRE)**^{147} [6336] 7-9-10 **104**	PhillipMakin 14	82
			(T D Barron) *early ldr stands side: cl up tl wknd wl over 2f out*	**12/1**	
60-5	**14**	6	**Capable Guest (IRE)**^{32} [576] 5-8-10 **90**	SamHitchcott 4	54+
			(M R Channon) *cl up far side: led that gp 3f out: no ch w stands side: 1st of 3 in grp*	**33/1**	
-111	**15**	2 ½	**Gentleman's Deal (IRE)**^{7} [761] 6-8-13 **93** 5ex	PaulMulrennan 15	51
			(M W Easterby) *midfield stands side: struggling 3f out: sn btn*	**7/2**^{1}	
216-	**16**	6	**Montpellier (IRE)**^{154} [6226] 4-8-8 **88**	TPQueally 10	33
			(E A L Dunlop) *hld up stands side: hdwy over 3f out: sn rdn and wknd*	**22/1**	
0302	**17**	5	**Yarqus**^{7} [759] 4-8-6 **93**	WilliamCarson$^{(7)}$ 12	26
			(C E Brittain) *prom stands side tl wknd wl over 2f out*	**20/1**	
50-3	**18**	10	**Tanzanite (IRE)**^{21} [658] 5-8-10 **90**	BrettDoyle 11	—
			(D W P Arbuthnot) *in tch stands side tl rdn and wknd over 2f out*	**8/1**^{2}	
30-0	**19**	9	**Rain Stops Play (IRE)**^{14} [701] 5-8-9 **89**	ShaneKelly 3	—
			(M Quinn) *led far side trio to 3f out: sn wknd: 2nd of 3 in grp*	**28/1**	
3-06	**20**	3	**St Petersburg**^{63} [259] 7-8-7 **90**	SaleemGolam$^{(3)}$ 1	—
			(M H Tompkins) *close up far side trio to 3f out: sn wknd: 3rd of 3 in grp*	**66/1**	

1m 46.18s (4.28) **Going Correction** +0.825s/f (Soft) **20** Ran SP% **131.4**
Speed ratings (Par 109):111,110,106,105,102 101,101,99,98,97 96,95,95,89,87 81,76,66,57,54
CSF £86.22 CT £968.70 TOTE £10.50: £3.20, £3.20, £3.10, £5.00; EX 122.80 Trifecta £1752.90 Pool £28,047.10, 11.36 winning units.

Owner J M Greetham **Bred** J M Greetham **Trained** Newmarket, Suffolk

■ Another temporary venue for the Lincoln, which was run at Redcar a year ago and will be back at Doncaster in 2008.

FOCUS

Mainly exposed performers but nevertheless a competitive handicap. The bulk of the runners raced stands side and a high draw was even more important than in the Spring Mile, with the top five in the draw all finishing in the first six. The pace was fair. The winner was quite impressive, and the second improved again.

NOTEBOOK

Very Wise ◆, an improved performer on artificial surfaces this winter, turned in his best effort back on turf to win the season's first big handicap with more in hand than the official margin suggests. He is a more relaxed individual these days, is effective on a sound surface and he is the type to win more races on turf this year. (op 8-1)

Rio Riva ◆, who progressed into a useful handicapper last year, fared easily the best of those drawn in single figures and did well to pull clear of the remainder. He looks at least as good as ever and appeals strongly as the type to win a decent race around this trip this year. (op 8-1)

Mutawaffer showed he retains all his ability on this first start for six months. He should not be inconvenienced by the return to further and is essentially a consistent sort but the fact that he has not won since September 2003 has to be a concern. (op 14-1)

Raptor(GER) ◆, a useful performer around a mile in Germany, had conditions to suit and showed more than enough after a tardy start on this first run for Karl Burke to suggest a similar event can be found. (op 22-1)

My Paris, fit from a recent run on Polytrack, had the run of the race from a favourable draw but seemed beaten on merit. He is likely to continue to look vulnerable against the more progressive sorts in this type of event, despite a slipping handicap mark. (op 8-1)

Audience, back on the same mark as when last successful, was not disgraced after meeting early trouble from his favourable draw on this first run after a break. He does not have the best of strike-rates and has little margin for error from his current mark, though. (op 22-1)

Crooked Throw(IRE) was anything but disgraced from this draw and looks well worth a try over a bit further than a mile. (op 20-1)

Capable Guest(IRE), an infrequent winner but who finished a very creditable third in this race last year, fared the best of the far side trio but was comprehensively outpointed by those that raced stands side.

Gentleman's Deal(IRE), who extended his unbeaten all-weather run to seven in last Saturday's Winter Derby, looked to have fair claims under a 5lb penalty from this lower turf mark but proved a disappointment in this tacky ground. He was beaten a similar distance in this race last year but, while obviously better than this, has a bit to prove now on grass. Official explanation: jockey said gelding was unsuited by the good to soft (soft in places) ground (op 5-1)

Montpellier(IRE) Official explanation: jockey said gelding was unsuited by the good to soft (soft in places) ground

Rain Stops Play(IRE) Official explanation: jockey said gelding was unsuited by the good to soft (soft in places) ground

849 WILLIAM HILL 0800 444040 MAIDEN STKS 1m 2f 32y

4:30 (4:31) (Class 5) 3-Y-O **£3,886** (£1,156; £577; £288) **Stalls** Low

Form	Pos	Btn	Horse	Jockey	RPR
5-	**1**		**Harland**^{172} [5883] 3-9-3	NCallan 9	87+
			(M A Jarvis) *trckd ldrs: hdwy 3f out: rdn to ld 1/2f out: kpt on strly*	**10/11**^{1}	

-	2	3 1/2	**Eradicate (IRE)** 3-9-3 .... JoeFanning 2 *(M Johnston) str: scope: trckd ldrs: hdwy to ld 3f out: rdn and hdd 1 1/2f out: kpt on same pce ins last* **10/3^{2}**	78+
	3	3 1/2	**Crispian (IRE)** 3-9-3 .... TonyCulhane 6 *(W J Haggas) hld up towards rr: hdwy 4f out: rdn to chse ldrs over 2f out: kpt on ins last* **10/1**	72+
6-4	4	1	**Riguez Dancer**^{46} [449] 3-9-3 .... LeeEnstone 10 *(P C Haslam) hld up towards rr: hdwy over 3f out: rdn 2f out: kpt on ins last: nrst fin* **33/1**	70
4-	5	1/2	**Top Tiger**^{175} [5814] 3-8-12 .... PatrickHills$^{(5)}$ 5 *(M H Tompkins) chsd ldrs: rdn along 3f out: drvn and wknd fnl 2f* **17/2^{3}**	69
05-	6	7	**Seteem (USA)**^{199} [5293] 3-9-3 .... KimTinkler 3 *(N Tinkler) s.i.s: a rr* **66/1**	57
6-	7	5	**Decent Proposal**^{246} [3908] 3-8-12 .... DavidAllan 7 *(T D Easterby) a rr* **50/1**	43
00-	8	1/2	**Wingsinmotion (IRE)**^{219} [4724] 3-8-12 .... PatCosgrave 4 *(Miss Tracy Waggott) in tch: rdn along over 4f out and sn wknd* **200/1**	42?
2-	9	4	**Murdoch**^{165} [6023] 3-9-3 .... GrahamGibbons 11 *(E S McMahon) keen: cl up: led after 2f: rdn along and hdd 3f out: sn wknd* **9/1**	39
40-2	10	6	**Cadwell**^{16} [684] 3-9-3 58 .... AdrianTNicholls 1 *(D Nicholls) led 2f: prom tl rdn along over 3f out and sn wknd* **20/1**	29

2m 20.75s (8.95) **Going Correction** +0.85s/f (Soft) **10** Ran SP% **116.7**

Speed ratings (Par 98):98,95,92,91,91 85,81,81,78,73

CSF £3.79 TOTE £2.00: £1.10, £1.50, £2.60; EX 4.80 Trifecta £14.00 Pool: £382.04, 19.34 winning units.

Owner Sheikh Mohammed **Bred** Darley **Trained** Newmarket, Suffolk

FOCUS

They finished well strung out here in a maiden in which the early leaders finished at the back of the field. The first three home all appeal as likely future winners and the next two will have possibilities in handicap company.

Cadwell Official explanation: jockey said colt was unsuited by the good to soft ground

850 WILLIAMHILLCASINO.COM MARCH H'CAP — 1m 2f 32y

5:05 (5:14) (Class 4) (0-85,85) 4-Y-0+ **£6,477** (£1,927; £963; £481) **Stalls** Low

Form				RPR
1-01	1		**Esthlos (FR)**^{7} [770] 4-8-6 **73** .... JoeFanning 16 *(J Jay) racd wd in midfield: smooth hdwy to ld over 2f out: edgd to far rail: kpt on strly* **7/1^{3}**	85
3-00	2	3	**Mustajed**^{42} [488] 6-8-11 **83** .... JamesMillman$^{(5)}$ 15 *(B R Millman) in tch: hdwy and ev ch over 2f out: kpt on same pce fnl f* **33/1**	89
06-0	3	nk	**Lucayan Dancer**^{7} [765] 7-9-2 **83** .... AdrianTNicholls 10 *(D Nicholls) hld up: hdwy over 2f out: kpt on fnl f: no imp* **12/1**	88
111-	4	hd	**Cleaver**^{150} [6301] 6-8-7 **77** .... AndrewElliott$^{(3)}$ 11 *(Lady Herries) hld up and bhd: plenty to do 3f out: carried hd high and styd on fr 2f out: nrst fin* **4/1^{1}**	82+
24-1	5	2	**Davenport (IRE)**^{79} [101] 5-8-9 **76** .... (p) NCallan 14 *(B R Millman) hld up: nt clr run over 2f out: hdwy over 1f out: no imp* **13/2^{2}**	85+
210-	6	hd	**Superior Star**^{234} [4257] 4-8-5 **72** .... (v) DaleGibson 9 *(R A Fahey) hld up in tch: hdwy 3f out: rdn and no ex over 1f out* **22/1**	73
311-	7	2 1/2	**Compromiznotension (IRE)**^{154} [6210] 4-8-12 **79** .... TomEaves 5 *(I Semple) led 1f: cl up: ev ch over 2f out: sn rdn and no ex* **15/2**	75
311-	8	3/4	**Dium Mac**^{166} [6008] 6-8-5 **79** .... SuzzanneFrance$^{(7)}$ 2 *(N Bycroft) hld up in tch: n.m.r and keen fr 1/2-way: edgd lft and outpcd fr 3f out* **7/1^{3}**	74
046-	9	1 1/2	**Tsaroxy (IRE)**^{196} [5396] 5-8-6 **73** .... PaulMulrennan 8 *(J Howard Johnson) hld up: no room wl over 2f out: sn btn* **20/1**	65
00-4	10	1/2	**James Caird (IRE)**^{11} [353] 7-9-1 **85** .... SaleemGolam$^{(3)}$ 7 *(M H Tompkins) hld up: effrt 3f out: nvr rchd ldrs* **16/1**	76
200-	11	4	**Sforzando**^{172} [5897] 6-7-12 **72** .... KristinStubbs$^{(7)}$ 4 *(Mrs L Stubbs) missed break: a bhd* **25/1**	55
020-	12	1 1/4	**Along The Nile**^{176} [5787] 5-9-4 **85** .... TonyCulhane 12 *(K G Reveley) hld up: nt clr run over 2f out: n.d* **20/1**	66
425-	13	7	**Faith And Reason (USA)**^{20} [3589] 4-8-13 **80** .... TPQueally 6 *(B J Curley) chsd ldrs to 3f out: sn rdn and btn* **33/1**	48
006-	14	25	**Sir Arthur (IRE)**^{244} [3984] 4-8-10 **77** .... KDarley 3 *(M Johnston) chsd ldrs to 3f out: sn rdn and btn* **12/1**	—
200-	15	shd	**Nesno (USA)**^{206} [5115] 4-8-10 **77** .... (v^{1}) DarryllHolland 1 *(J D Bethell) led after 1f to over 2f out: sn wknd* **25/1**	—
-500	16	14	**Happy As Larry (USA)**^{14} [701] 5-9-3 **84** .... RobbieFitzpatrick 17 *(T J Pitt) hld up: rdn over 4f out: nvr on terms* **16/1**	—

2m 19.21s (7.41) **Going Correction** +0.85s/f (Soft) **16** Ran SP% **124.7**

Speed ratings (Par 105):104,101,101,101,99 99,97,96,95,95 92,91,85,65,65 54

CSF £230.80 CT £2733.22 TOTE £9.20: £2.80, £7.80, £2.00, £1.80; EX 381.70 TRIFECTA Not won. Place 6 £937.61, Place 5 £234.15.

Owner Ms Medina Jessop **Bred** J Jay **Trained** Newmarket, Suffolk

FOCUS

An ordinary handicap, but sound enough form, rated around the second and third. The winner improved significantly on his all-weather win and the fourth and fifth shaped better than the bare facts indicate.

T/Jkpt: Not won. T/Plt: £899.50 to a £1 stake. Pool: £139,302.20. 113.05 winning tickets. T/Qpdt: £37.90 to a £1 stake. Pool: £8,243.50. 160.80 winning tickets. RY

851 - 857a (Foreign Racing) - See Raceform Interactive

641 NAD AL SHEBA (L-H)

Saturday, March 31

OFFICIAL GOING: Turf course - good; dirt course - fast

858a GODOLPHIN MILE (SPONSORED BY ETISALAT) (GROUP 2) (DIRT) — 1m (D)

2:40 (2:40) 3-Y-0+

£306,122 (£102,040; £51,020; £25,510; £15,306; £10,204)

			RPR
1		**Spring At Last (USA)**^{28} 4-9-0 111 .... (vt) GKGomez 12 *(Doug O'Neill, U.S.A) trckd ldr wd: rdn to ld 2 1/2f out: r.o wl: comf* **7/1^{3}**	121
2	2 3/4	**Parole Board (USA)**^{36} [543] 5-9-0 112 .... TedDurcan 16 *(S Seemar, UAE) in rr of mid-div: gng wl 4f out: smooth prog to chal 2f out: r.o wl* **16/1**	114
3	1 1/4	**Mullins Bay**^{51} [399] 6-9-0 112 .... WCMarwing 14 *(M F De Kock, South Africa) nvr far off pce: trckd wnr 3 1/2f out: ev ch fnl 2 1/2f: nt qckn fnl f* **7/1^{3}**	112
4	4 1/4	**Dixie Meister (USA)**^{84} 5-9-0 110 .... (bt) DFlores 3 *(J Canani, U.S.A) slowly away: racd in rr: r.o wl fnl 3f: nrst fin* **6/1^{2}**	102
5	3/4	**Court Masterpiece**^{37} [530] 7-9-0 119 .... KerrinMcEvoy 13 *(Saeed Bin Suroor) settled in rr of mid-div: rdn to cl 3 1/2f out: nt qckn* **8/1**	100
6	1/4	**Fusaichi Richard (JPN)**^{84} 4-9-0 115 .... CSoumillon 4 *(K Matsuda, Japan) mid-div: trckd ldrs 2 1/2f out: ev ch 2f out: one pce* **9/1**	99
7	1 3/4	**Nelore Pora (BRZ)**^{30} [599] 5-9-0 107 .... (b) ZMRosa 7 *(P Nickel Filho, Brazil) sn led: hdd 2 1/2f out: wknd* **25/1**	95
8	1	**Merlerault (USA)**^{48} [437] 4-9-0 106 .... SPasquier 5 *(P Demercastel, France) mid-div: gng wl on rail 4f out: n.m.r 3f out: one pce* **16/1**	93
9	1/2	**Gold For Sale (ARG)**^{30} [599] 5-9-0 105 .... (t) MJKinane 2 *(I Jory, Saudi Arabia) sn rdn along on rail: nvr nr to chal* **33/1**	92
10	3 1/4	**Gharir (IRE)**^{23} [642] 5-9-0 105 .... (b) MartinDwyer 8 *(E Charpy, UAE) sn rdn along: n.d* **20/1**	84
11	4 1/4	**Singing Poet (IRE)**^{30} [601] 6-9-0 104 .... (bt) TPO'Shea 9 *(E Charpy, UAE) slowly away: nvr able to chal* **22/1**	75
12	1 1/4	**Vortex**^{30} [599] 8-9-0 109 .... (t) JMurtagh 15 *(Miss Gay Kelleway) mid-div: wd: rdn 4f out: n.d after* **12/1**	72
13	1 1/4	**Killybegs (IRE)**^{37} [530] 4-9-0 115 .... LDettori 6 *(Saeed Bin Suroor) trckd ldr rail: rdn to chal 3f out: wknd* **11/2^{1}**	69
14	13	**Boston Lodge**^{30} [599] 7-9-0 109 .... (vt) EddieAhern 11 *(Doug Watson, UAE) nvr nr to chal* **9/1**	39

1m 36.16s (-1.44) **Going Correction** +0.175s/f (Slow) **14** Ran SP% **121.1**

Speed ratings: 114,111,110,105,105 104,103,102,101,98 94,92,91,78

Owner J Paul Reddam & WinStar Farm LLC **Bred** WinStar Farm Llc **Trained** USA

FOCUS

A competitive event on paper, but those drawn high dominated. The form has been rated through the third, with the winner back to his best.

NOTEBOOK

Spring At Last(USA) ultimately ran out a decisive winner. Back over his ideal trip and taking on lesser animals than the likes of Lava Man, whom he finished behind in a Grade 1 Handicap at Santa Anita last time, he travelled strongly up with the pace throughout. Although headed by Parole Board approaching the final furlong, Gomez had kept a little in reserve and he rallied to fight off that rival's challenge in style. Pulling clear in the closing stages, he looked a grade better than most of these.

Parole Board(USA) only won a handicap last time out, but he had looked a high-class prospect earlier in his career and this performance suggests that connections are well on the way to getting him back to his best. He came with what looked like a winning run in the straight, but in the end found the American colt too strong.

Mullins Bay, who completed a clean-sweep for those drawn wide, had run with promise behind Kandidate on his dirt debut here in February but had been lame subsequently and not enjoyed the ideal preparation for this assignment. It is to his credit that he ran so well in defeat, and there can be little doubt that his trainer will win Group races with this former Ballydoyle inmate.

Dixie Meister(USA) could not live with Discreet Cat in the Cigar Mile last autumn, but he has two Grade 2 successes to his name and looked a big player here. Being drawn low was perhaps not in his favour, though, and, more importantly, he missed the break and ended up being towards the rear facing kickback. He stayed on late but could never trouble the principals.

Court Masterpiece, who finished sixth in this race last year, did not run badly considering he is nowhere near as effective on this surface as he is on turf.

Fusaichi Richard(JPN) could not repeat Japan's success in this race last year. Chasing the pace throughout, he had every chance but was just not good enough.

Nelore Pora(BRZ) set the pace to the race but he was a sitting duck early in the straight.

Merlerault(USA) was not disgraced, having only previously won a Listed event on the All-Weather in France.

Singing Poet(IRE) needs further. (tchd 20/1)

Vortex may have done better had the pace been stronger and he been ridden more patiently.

Killybegs(IRE) was running on dirt for the first time and yet was still sent off favourite. A prominent racer, he tried to keep up with the pace at the head of affairs but was being cajoled along by Dettori from some way out and was eased when clearly beaten in the straight. He is another who will be happier when back on turf.

Boston Lodge has been in good form at the Carnival but could never get competitive on this occasion and simply failed to run his race.

859a UAE DERBY (SPONSORED BY S & M AL NABOODAH GROUP) (GROUP 2) (DIRT) — 1m 1f (D)

3:15 (3:16) 3-Y-0

£612,244 (£204,081; £102,040; £51,020; £30,612; £20,408)

			RPR
1		**Asiatic Boy (ARG)**^{30} [596] 4-9-4 115 .... WCMarwing 10 *(M F De Kock, South Africa) trckd front two: gng wl 3f out: forged clr 2f out: easily* **10/11^{1}**	121
2	9 1/2	**Jack Junior (USA)**^{183} [5653] 3-8-9 105 .... RHills 2 *(B J Meehan) mid-div: rdn to trck ldr 3 1/2f out: r.o: no ch w wnr* **33/1**	102
3	2 3/4	**Adil (KSA)**^{29} 3-8-9 100 .... KDesormeaux 12 *(J Gardel, Saudi Arabia) mid-div: rdn to cl 3f out: r.o: no ch w wnr* **50/1**	97
4	3 3/4	**Rallying Cry (USA)**^{30} [596] 3-8-9 105 .... TedDurcan 1 *(Saeed Bin Suroor) rdn to dispute rail: hdd 2f out: kpt on one pce* **33/1**	90
5	shd	**Victory Tetsuni (USA)**^{30} [596] 3-8-9 100 .... YTake 5 *(Hideyuki Mori, Japan) slowly away: nvr able to chal: r.o late* **16/1**	89
6	2 1/4	**Traffic Guard (USA)**^{50} [414] 3-8-9 106 .... JohnEgan 6 *(J S Moore) mid-div rail: rdn 4f out: nt qckn* **33/1**	85
7	2 1/4	**Eu Tambem (BRZ)**^{30} [601] 4-9-4 115 .... LDettori 13 *(Saeed Bin Suroor) mid-div: wd: rdn 3 1/2f out: nvr a threat after* **7/2^{2}**	82
8	2 1/2	**Joe Louis (ARG)**^{50} [414] 4-9-4 107 .... (t) MJKinane 3 *(I Jory, Saudi Arabia) nvr nr to chal* **40/1**	77
9	3/4	**Day Pass (USA)**^{30} [596] 3-8-9 107 .... (t) GKGomez 4 *(Saeed Bin Suroor) disp centre: rdn 3 1/2f out: wknd 3f out* **20/1**	75
10	1	**Folk (USA)**^{23} [647] 3-8-5 111 .... KerrinMcEvoy 11 *(Saeed Bin Suroor) mid-div wd: rdn 3 1/2f out: wd in st: nt threaten: lame* **9/2^{3}**	69
11	5 1/2	**Seal Point (USA)**^{37} [527] 3-8-9 100 .... PaulEddery 9 *(Christian Wroe) nvr bttr than mid-div* **66/1**	62
12	10	**Bartola (ARG)**^{28} 4-9-0 .... PFalero 7 *(J C Maldotti, Argentina) nvr able to chal* **33/1**	40
13	nse	**Greetings (BRZ)**^{23} [647] 4-9-0 102 .... RichardMullen 8 *(P Nickel Filho, Brazil) sn rdn in rr: nvr able to chal* **50/1**	40

1m 48.82s (-1.98) **Going Correction** +0.175s/f (Slow)

WFA 3 from 4yo 19lb **13** Ran SP% **123.0**

Speed ratings: 115,106,104,100,100 98,96,94,93,92 88,79,79

Owner Sheikh Mohammed Bin Khalifa Al Maktoum **Bred** Haras Arroyo De Luna **Trained** South Africa

■ A third UAE Derby success for trainer Mike De Kock.

FOCUS

This year's UAE Derby attracted a really smart field, and when you consider last season's renewal went the way of Discreet Cat (with Invasor fourth), it surely cannot be long before this race is upgraded to a Group 1. The likes of Asiatic Boy, Eu Tambem and Folk came into it with some high-class form to their name and, with all three looking to enhance their reputations further, it made for a mouth-watering contest. The pace was good from the start and Asiatic Boy powered home alone. He posted an RPR 7lb higher than Discreet Cat in last year's renewal.

NOTEBOOK

Asiatic Boy(ARG) ◆, one of the 'big three', easily came out on top, and he did so in quite stunning fashion. He had shown himself a very smart sort with comfortable victories on his three previous starts in Dubai, including when landing the UAE 2,000 Guineas on his penultimate outing, but this performance moved him to another level and confirmed he will be able to compete with the very best dirt horses anywhere in the world. His victory is all the more special as he became the first horse to win the UAE Triple Crown. He was unable to dominate this time, but his rider didn't panic and had him well positioned on the pace throughout. It was just a question of what he would find when asked for maximum effort at the top of the straight, and he fairly bounded clear of his 12 rivals to come home a mightily impressive winner. He has a terrific cruising speed, but his stamina was never an issue and he looked as strong at the finish as he did on the turn for home. There is every chance we will see him in the UK this year for something like the Queen Anne and it would be fascinating to see how he compares to the pick of the home-based turf performers.

Jack Junior(USA) ◆ ran a huge race in second and further enhanced Brian Meehan's reputation as an excellent international trainer. He only had two runs to his name coming into this - his sixth in a Group 3 at Newmarket being the pick - and both had come on turf, but he had clearly been well prepared for his first start in Dubai. Having travelled quite well just off the pace, he was left behind when Asiatic Boy kicked for home, but he kept on in good style to claim the runner-up's spot. He is open to any amount of improvement and could be a real money-spinner if campaigned in the US this year. Meehan is keen to run him in at least one of the US Triple Crown races, and the Kentucky Derby is a possible option.

Adil(KSA), unbeaten in three dirt starts in Saudi Arabia this year, ran very well faced with his toughest task to date. He could not quite match the early pace shown by some of his rivals, but he was still able to keep tabs on the leaders and stayed on better than most in the straight.

Rallying Cry(USA) had to be driven along early to hold his position from his inside draw, but stayed at the front end for longer than many might have expected. However, we are unlikely to see the very best of him until he returns to turf.

Victory Tetsuni(USA) was detached early after starting very slowly and could make no impression.

Traffic Guard(USA) lacked the pace of some of these and can probably do better when returned to turf. He may be aimed at the Irish Derby, with his trainer confident he will stay 1m4f.

Eu Tambem(BRZ) had been earmarked as a possible for the Dubai World Cup after winning the third round of the Maktoum challenge, but he was rerouted to this race after switching to Godolphin. Having lacked the basic speed to hold a position early on, he appeared to have to use up plenty of energy to try to race more handily and had nothing left when asked for his effort. On this evidence, he wants further.

Day Pass(USA) did not get home after showing good early speed and will surely be suited by a return to much shorter distances.

Folk(USA) created a fine impression on her debut in Dubai when landing the UAE 1,000 Guineas, and bettered that form when taking the Oaks, clocking the same time Discreet Cat recorded in this race last year in the process. However, both those wins were gained from the front and, unable to dominate this time, she was not the same filly. It later transpired she returned lame on her off-fore and, as long as that problem is not too serious, she may yet take high rank among the fillies and mares in the US.

860a DUBAI GOLDEN SHAHEEN (SPONSORED BY GULF NEWS) (GROUP 1) (DIRT) — 6f (D)

3:55 (3:55) 3-Y-O+

£612,244 (£204,081; £102,040; £51,020; £30,612; £20,408)

Pos	Dist	Horse	RPR
1		**Kelly's Landing (USA)**[56] 6-9-0 ....(t) LDettori 3 (E Kenneally, U.S.A) *trckd ldr far rail: smooth prog to ld 2f out: r.o wl* **11/1**	117
2	½	**Friendly Island (USA)**[70] 6-9-0 110.... GKGomez 8 (T Pletcher, U.S.A) *mid-div centre: rdn to cl 2f out: r.o wl: nrst fin* **7/1**[3]	115
3	1 ¼	**Salaam Dubai (AUS)**[30] 597 6-9-0 104....(v) JMurtagh 9 (A Selvaratnam, UAE) *racd centre: gng wl 4f out: rdn 3f out: r.o wl: nrst fin* **66/1**	111
4	¾	**Harvard Avenue (USA)**[42] 6-9-0 108....(vt[1]) CNakatani 13 (Doug O'Neill, U.S.A) *racd in rr: rdn 3f out: r.o fnl 2f: nrst fin* **20/1**	109
5	¾	**Bishop Court Hill (USA)**[63] 7-9-0 110.... JRVelazquez 1 (T Pletcher, U.S.A) *led far side: hdd 2f out: kpt on one pce* **12/1**	107
6	2 ¼	**Thor's Echo (USA)**[30] 597 5-9-0 120....(vt) TedDurcan 5 (S Seemar, UAE) *trckd ldrs far side: ev ch whn rdn 3f out: one pce* **7/2**[1]	100
7	¾	**Terrific Challenge (USA)**[30] 597 5-9-0 110....(bt) RichardMullen 10 (Doug Watson, UAE) *racd centre: gng wl 3f out: rdn 2f out: one pce* **8/1**	98
8	1	**Marchand D'Or (FR)**[182] 5701 4-9-0 116.... DBonilla 4 (F Head, France) *prom far side: trckd ldr whn rdn 2 1/2f out: nt qckn* **12/1**	95
9	1 ¼	**Tiza (SAF)**[23] 644 5-9-0 110....(bt) KShea 6 (H J Brown, South Africa) *trckd ldrs far side: ev ch 2f out: wknd* **33/1**	91
10	¾	**Agnes Jedi (JPN)**[30] 597 5-9-0 106....(b) YTake 7 (Hideyuki Mori, Japan) *nvr nr to chal* **50/1**	89
11	½	**Seeking The Best (IRE)**[41] 6-9-0 .... YFukunaga 14 (Hideyuki Mori, Japan) *sn rdn along nr side: nvr a threat* **33/1**	87
12	1 ¼	**Areyoutalkingtome**[35] 551 4-9-0 115.... EddieAhern 2 (C A Cyzer) *nvr able to chal* **9/1**	84
13	1	**Bounty Quest**[30] 597 5-9-0 106.... MartinDwyer 11 (Doug Watson, UAE) *prom centre: rdn 3f out: nt qckn* **33/1**	81
14	5	**Thajja (IRE)**[30] 597 6-9-0 108....(v) RHills 12 (Doug Watson, UAE) *racd centre: nvr able to chal* **40/1**	66
15	¾	**Nightmare Affair (USA)**[63] 6-9-0 ....(vt) ECastro 16 (G Marano, U.S.A) *a in rr nr side* **8/1**	63
16	shd	**National Colour (SAF)**[44] 474 5-8-9 112.... WCMarwing 15 (S Tarry, South Africa) *slowly away: nvr nr to chal nr side* **5/1**[2]	58

1m 10.34s (-0.36) **Going Correction** +0.375s/f (Slow) **16** Ran SP% **126.8**

Speed ratings: 117,116,114,113,112 109,108,107,105,104 104,102,101,94,93 93

.

Owner Summerplace Farm Llc (john Lally) **Bred** Summerplace Farm **Trained** USA

FOCUS

A race that has been dominated over the years by the Americans, and that trend continued with four of the first five home US-trained. A low draw has also been a big advantage on the straight track this season, and that bias was confirmed. The form has been rated through the winner and fourth and is not particularly strong by Group 1 standards.

NOTEBOOK

Kelly's Landing(USA) was one of four horses running in the race that had contested last year's Breeders' Cup Sprint. He had had no luck that day, being handed the widest stall of all on a day when the rail was everything, but he fared much better on this occasion. Tracking the pace on the favoured far side, he hit the front inside the final two furlongs and was always going to hold the challenge of his compatriot Friendly Island. He is a huge beast, and one would imagine that this straight track was far more to his liking than racing around a turn in the US. (op 12/1)

Friendly Island(USA), well drawn when runner-up in the Breeders' Cup Sprint last year, could not confirm form with Kelly's Landing on this straight track, but he still ran well. Challenging from off the pace, he could not quite overhaul the winner, but he beat the rest fair and square. (op 8/1)

Salaam Dubai(AUS) ran a blinder, reversing recent course form with five rivals. While the main action was taking place towards the far side, he finished strongly down the centre, and it is clear that on his day he is capable of very smart form indeed.

Harvard Avenue(USA), another American-trained contender, did best of those unfavourably drawn in double-figures, but he was no doubt aided by the fact that he raced more towards the centre of the track to halfway and then edged over to the far side. He gets further than this and stayed on well towards the finish. (op 16/1)

Bishop Court Hill(USA), a confirmed front-runner, can have no excuse as he had a great draw and was able to dictate the pace as he likes. He was just not good enough to make all in this company.

Thor's Echo(USA), last year's Breeders' Cup Sprint winner, was a shade disappointing in his prep for this, but was expected to have come on for that run. He disappointed, though, as he travelled well enough through the first half of the race but lacked the pace to trouble the main players late on. He looks to have gone backwards since leaving the US.

Terrific Challenge(USA) had several of these behind him when successful in a Group 3 race over this course and distance last month, but he was not well drawn in stall ten and ended up doing most of his racing on the slower ground centre to stands' side.

Marchand D'Or(FR), winner of last year's Group 1 Prix Maurice de Gheest, is clearly a high-class performer on turf, but this performance suggests he is a fair way below that level on dirt.

Seeking The Best(IRE) was one of several who had his chance seriously compromised by a high draw.

Areyoutalkingtome was well drawn but this was a different test to that which he normally faces on Polytrack, where his turn of foot is more effective. (op 8/1)

National Colour(SAF), another drawn in double figures, missed the break badly and simply never got into the race. A high-class mare on her day, she normally has bags of early speed, and had she got a flyer those drawn high may have enjoyed a better lead on the stands' side.

861a DUBAI SHEEMA CLASSIC (SPONSORED BY NAKHEEL) (GROUP 1) (TURF) — 1m 4f (T)

4:55 (4:55) 4-Y-O+

£1,530,612 (£510,204; £255,102; £127,551; £76,530; £51,020)

Pos	Dist	Horse	RPR
1		**Vengeance Of Rain (NZ)**[27] 7-8-11 ....(t) ADelpech 4 (D Ferraris, Hong Kong) *t.k.h on rail in 4th: gng v wl 3f out: rdn to ld 1 1/2f out: r.o wl* **9/1**	122
2	1 ¼	**Oracle West (SAF)**[30] 598 6-8-11 113.... WCMarwing 2 (M F De Kock, South Africa) *mid-div rail: trckd wnr 2 1/2f out: n.m.r 1 1/2f out: r.o wl once clr: nrest at fin* **33/1**	120
3	½	**Youmzain (IRE)**[188] 5561 4-8-11 118.... RichardHughes 13 (M R Channon) *settled in rr: gng wl 3f out: trckd runner-up 2f out: r.o: nrst fin* **13/2**[3]	121+
4	shd	**Sir Percy**[168] 5964 4-8-11 121.... MartinDwyer 7 (M P Tregoning) *short of room after 1f: nt far off pce: ev ch whn rdn 2f out: nt qckn* **4/1**[1]	121
5	1 ¼	**Sushisan (AUS)**[23] 642 5-8-11 113.... KShea 9 (H J Brown, South Africa) *a mid-div: r.o fnl 1 1/2f* **25/1**	117
6	shd	**Pop Rock (JPN)**[42] 6-8-11 119.... OPeslier 10 (Katsuhiko Sumii, Japan) *settled in rr: nvr able to chal* **9/2**[2]	117+
7	¾	**Quijano (GER)**[30] 598 5-8-11 116.... AStarke 12 (P Schiergen, Germany) *trckd ldrs: rdn to ld 2f out: hdd 1 1/2f out: wknd* **9/1**	115
8	¼	**Bellamy Cay**[21] 663 5-8-11 115.... SPasquier 1 (A Fabre, France) *mid-div: rdn 3f out: nvr able to chal* **33/1**	115
9	1	**Red Rocks (IRE)**[147] 6344 4-8-12 120 ow1.... CNakatani 5 (B J Meehan) *mid-div: dropped to rr 3f out: n.m.r 2f out: r.o late* **9/2**[2]	116
10	2 ¼	**Best Alibi (IRE)**[30] 598 4-8-11 115.... LDettori 6 (Saeed Bin Suroor) *sn led: rdn and hdd 2f out: wknd* **14/1**	112
11	2 ¾	**Honey Ryder (USA)**[35] 6-8-7 116....(b) GKGomez 14 (T Pletcher, U.S.A) *mid-div: wd: rdn 3 1/2f out: nt qckn* **20/1**	101
12	¾	**Host (CHI)**[56] 7-8-11 113.... JRVelazquez 15 (T Pletcher, U.S.A) *racd in 3rd: rdn 3f out: wknd qckly* **33/1**	104
13	shd	**Obrigado (FR)**[34] 4-8-11 115....(vt) DFlores 8 (N Drysdale, U.S.A) *racd in rr: nvr nr to chal* **25/1**	106
14	4 ¾	**Laverock (IRE)**[30] 598 5-8-11 118.... KerrinMcEvoy 3 (Saeed Bin Suroor) *settled in rr: rdn to cl 3 1/2f out: sn wknd* **14/1**	96

2m 31.03s (0.03) **Going Correction** +0.225s/f (Good)

WFA 4 from 5yo+ 2lb **14** Ran SP% **124.3**

Speed ratings: 108,107,106,106,105 105,105,105,104,103 101,100,100,97

.

Owner Raymond Gianco Chow Hon Man **Bred** K Biggs Enterprises, Porter St Inventments, R N Ru **Trained** Hong Kong

FOCUS

This had the potential to be an outstanding renewal of the Sheema Classic, with a Breeders' Cup Turf winner lining up against last year's Epsom Derby hero, as well as a Melbourne Cup runner-up and plenty of others with high-class form to their name. However, several of these, including some of the higher-profile runners, had something to prove, and the race did not work out as one might have hoped. The pace was just steady, which did not suit some. It has been rated through the Youmzain and Sir Percy, who matched his Derby form. Collier Hill missed the race with a joint problem and might not run again.

NOTEBOOK

Vengeance Of Rain(NZ) showed himself at the top of his game when winning the Group 1 Hong Kong Gold Cup at the beginning of March and was able to follow up in what looked a tougher race. His effort is all the more creditable considering that he raced very keenly off the modest tempo but, crucially, he was always well placed and had enough left when asked for his effort in the straight. To give an idea of what this horse is capable of at his best, he beat Pride a neck in the Hong Kong Cup at the end of 2005. Although seven, he is clearly as good as ever, and he has the King George at Ascot and the Melbourne Cup as possible targets later this year.

Oracle West(SAF) could manage only 11th in this race last year and, although he is obviously a much better horse than that run implies, his proximity suggests this was not as strong a Group 1 as it looked on paper. Still, he deserves plenty of credit for what was surely something like a career-best performance.

Youmzain(IRE) looks the horse to take from the race as he came from a mile back to claim third on the line. Dropped in soon after the start from his unfavourable wide draw, he was almost last for much of the way in a race run at just an ordinary gallop. The only thing that went right for him was that he enjoyed a clear passage against the inside rail in the straight, and he stayed on in the style of a high-class individual, although by that time the winner had gone beyond recall. He landed a Group 1 in Germany on his final start of last season and, on this evidence, there are more races to be won with him at the top level. His trainer is considering swtiching the colt back to 1m2f, reasoning he would be more likely to get the strong pace he prefers. (op 7/1)

Sir Percy was having just his second start since landing last year's Epsom Derby, having been off the track since flopping in the Champion Stakes in October. Having recovered from being hampered soon after the start, he kept on well in the straight, but just lacked the sharpness of some of his rivals, and a stronger pace would also have suited better. It also turned out that he had been struck into several times during the race and in the circumstances connections will no doubt be delighted with this effort. He will be off the track until Royal Ascot, with the Prince Of Wales's Stakes his likely target. (op 9/2)

Sushisan(AUS), the winner of a 1m2f handicap round here off a mark of 107 on his previous start, found himself much further back than was ideal after being badly hampered soon after the start, and he can be considered unlucky not to have finished closer.

Pop Rock(JPN), last year's Melbourne Cup runner-up, was poorly positioned towards the rear and forced wide entering the back straight, so he did well to finish so close. It almost goes without saying that he would have been seen to much better effect off a stronger pace.

Quijano(GER) is one of the success stories of this year's Carnival, having won two handicaps and a Group 3, but he failed to produce his best this time. Admittedly, this was his toughest task to date, but he had finished in front of Oracle West on his previous start and perhaps his recent exertions have just taken their toll.

Bellamy Cay is another who would have been totally unsuited by the ordinary pace.

Red Rocks(IRE), last year's Breeders' Cup Turf winner, seemed to race a little keenly and was below his best. He was short of room in the straight, but he had it all to do at that stage anyway and basically failed to fire. There will be other days for him, with next month's Tattersalls Gold Cup at the Curragh a likely target.

Best Alibi(IRE) was given every possible chance from the front, even if he was a little keen, but he weakened tamely. He has yet to reproduce the sort of form he showed for Sir Michael Stoute last year. (op 12/1)

Laverock(IRE), the other Godolphin challenger, was never seen with a chance.

862a DUBAI DUTY FREE (SPONSORED BY DUBAI DUTY FREE) (GROUP 1) (TURF) — 1m 194y(T)

5:40 (5:41) 3-Y-O+

£1,530,612 (£510,204; £255,102; £127,551; £76,530; £51,020)

			RPR
1		**Admire Moon (JPN)**[42] 4-9-0 121 ....(t) YTake 10 (H Matsuda, Japan) *mid-div: gng wl 3f out: smooth prog to chal 2f out: led 1f out: r.o wl* **11/2**[1]	127
2	1/2	**Linngari (IRE)**[37] 530 5-9-0 119 .... KShea 16 (H J Brown, South Africa) *settled in rr: n.m.r 3f out: r.o wl fnl 1 1/2f: nrest at fin* **20/1**	124
3	4 1/4	**Daiwa Major (JPN)**[97] 6-9-0 121 .... KAndo 13 (Hiroyuki Uehara, Japan) *mid-div: wd: trckd ldr 3f out: led 2f out: hdd 1 1/2f out: r.o wl* **11/2**[1]	115+
4	2	**Seihali (IRE)**[30] 600 8-9-0 115 ....(b) JMurtagh 1 (D Selvaratnam, UAE) *wl away: trckd ldr rail: led briefly 1 1/2f out: nt qckn* **20/1**	111+
5	nse	**Kapil (SAF)**[23] 646 5-9-0 118 .... RFradd 7 (M F De Kock, South Africa) *in rr of mid-div: rdn 3f out: r.o: nvr able to chal* **16/1**	111
6	2 1/4	**Flashy Wings**[203] 5191 4-8-9 113 .... RichardHughes 9 (M R Channon) *settled in rr: trckd wnr 3f out: nt qckn* **20/1**	101
7	1/2	**Formal Decree (GER)**[30] 600 4-9-0 113 .... KerrinMcEvoy 14 (Saeed Bin Suroor) *in rr of mid-div: n.m.r 3f out: nvr nr to chal* **16/1**	105
8	2 1/4	**Pompeii Ruler (AUS)**[21] 5-9-0 116 .... CNewitt 8 (Mick Price, Australia) *t.k.h: mid-div: ev ch whn rdn 2 1/2f out: nt qckn* **8/1**[3]	101
9	3/4	**Stormy River (FR)**[182] 5701 4-9-0 120 .... OPeslier 3 (N Clement, France) *mid-div: rdn 3f out: n.m.r 2f out: r.o late* **10/1**	99
10	hd	**Irridescence (SAF)**[30] 600 6-8-9 115 .... WCMarwing 4 (M F De Kock, South Africa) *sn led: hdd 2f out: wknd* **14/1**	94+
11	3/4	**Best Name**[30] 600 4-9-0 117 .... LDettori 2 (Saeed Bin Suroor) *mid-div rail: rdn 3f out: one pce* **12/1**	98
12	1	**English Channel (USA)**[37] 5-9-0 121 .... JRVelazquez 11 (T Pletcher, U.S.A) *trckd ldrs tl rdn 4f out: hmpd 3f out: wknd* **10/1**	96
13	3 1/4	**Bad Girl Runs (SAF)**[36] 547 5-8-9 111 .... MJKinane 15 (M F De Kock, South Africa) *swtchd to rail in rr: nvr able to chal* **40/1**	84
14	1 1/2	**Mystical (IND)**[23] 645 5-9-0 115 .... MartinDwyer 6 (S Ganapathy, India) *mid-div: rdn 3f out: nt qckn* **20/1**	86
15	2	**Miesque's Approval (USA)**[56] 8-9-0 120 ....(t) ECastro 12 (M D Wolfson, U.S.A) *nvr nr to chal* **14/1**	82
16	8 1/4	**Lava Man (USA)**[28] 6-9-0 122 ....(vt) CNakatani 5 (Doug O'Neill, U.S.A) *trckd ldr tl 3f out: wknd* **7/1**[2]	66+

1m 47.94s (-1.86) **Going Correction** +0.225s/f (Good) **16** Ran SP% **126.8**

Speed ratings: 117,116,112,111,110 108,108,106,105,105 105,104,101,99,98 90

.

Owner Riichi Kondo **Bred** Northern Racing **Trained** Japan

FOCUS

A very high-class renewal featuring nine individual Group 1 winners from all around the globe. A high draw has generally been a disadvantage in this race over the past few years but on this occasion the first three home were drawn in double figures, and the first two came from off the pace. They were undoubtedly helped by the decent gallop, set by Irridescence and Lava Man.

NOTEBOOK

Admire Moon(JPN), a Grade 2 winner last time out, had previously split Pride and Vengeance Of Rain in the Hong Kong Cup, form that had been given a boost by the success of the latter in the Sheema Classic earlier on the card. Held up off the pace, Yutaka Take settled his mount well and let the leaders set the race up for him. He switched him out to challenge in the straight and, once sent for home, there was only ever going to be one result. He did get the perfect trip on this occasion, but there is also no doubt that he is a high-class horse who is still improving, and he is likely to win more top prizes over distances around 1m2f later this year.

Linngari(IRE) was a disappointment in this race last year but showed his true form this time around. He came from well off the pace to chase the winner home and, although perhaps flattered to get as close as he did to the eventual winner, he is a smart performer on his day, as his easy success in Group 2 company prior to this confirms. (op 18/1)

Daiwa Major(JPN) beat his compatriot Admire Moon in a Grade 1 race at Tokyo last autumn, but was unable to confirm the form on foreign soil. In fairness, while the winner enjoyed the run of the race, he struggled from his wide draw, racing five wide into the first turn and committing too soon. Had he been ridden more patiently he might have given the winner more to do.

Seihali(IRE) ran his usual game race, tracking the decent gallop on the rail before sticking on determinedly under pressure in the straight. He really is a credit to his trainer as he appears as good as ever at the age of eight.

Kapil(SAF) impressed in winning a Listed event over a mile at the track last time out but this was a big step up in grade. He came out best of the three Mike de Kock runners, though, running on stoutly from well off the pace, but he was another for whom the race was very much run to suit.

Flashy Wings, a high-class juvenile who failed to score at three, ran a promising race on her seasonal reappearance. She followed Kapil through from off the pace, and should be able to win a Group race restricted to her own sex back in Europe.

Formal Decree(GER), who has enjoyed a successful time of it in Dubai this winter but whose stable had had precious little to shout about earlier on the card, did not get the best of luck in running when trying to make up ground from off the pace in the straight. He would have finished a bit closer with a clear run.

Pompeii Ruler(AUS), the only Australian horse to run on the night, did not settle and failed to give his running. He is a lot better than he showed here.

Stormy River(FR), last year's Prix Jean Prat winner, was another who did not get the clearest of runs in the straight. He seemed to get the trip well enough, though, as he ran on again late. (op 11/1)

Irridescence(SAF) was denied an easy lead and failed to show her best form. (op 12/1)

Best Name was another disappointment from the Saeed Bin Suroor stable, despite having the strong pace he requires.

English Channel(USA) did too much too soon, racing up with the gallop and wide of the fence from her unfavourable draw, rather than tucking in behind the pace like the first two home.

Miesque's Approval(USA), last year's Breeders' Cup Mile winner, had been disappointing on his previous start and again failed to fire.

Lava Man(USA), who is notorious for failing to give his running away from his home base of California, dropped away tamely after duelling for the lead to the straight. (op 15/2)

863a DUBAI WORLD CUP (SPONSORED BY EMIRATES AIRLINE) (GROUP 1) (DIRT) — 1m 2f (D)

6:30 (6:32) 3-Y-O+

£1,836,734 (£612,244; £306,122; £153,061; £91,836; £61,224)

			RPR
1		**Invasor (ARG)**[56] 347 5-9-0 105 .... FJara 7 (K McLaughlin, U.S.A) *mid-div: trckd ldr 4 1/2f out: gng wl 3f out: rdn 2f out: led 1 1/2f out: r.o wl* **5/4**[1]	132
2	1 3/4	**Premium Tap (USA)**[43] 5-9-0 123 ....(t) KDesormeaux 5 (J Kimmel, U.S.A) *disp rail: led 4f out: r.o strly: hdd 1 1/2f out: kpt on* **7/1**[3]	128
3	8	**Bullish Luck (USA)**[27] 8-9-0 115 ....(b) BPrebble 3 (A S Cruz, Hong Kong) *tk v t.k.h in mid-div: dropped to last 3 1/2f out: rdn and r.o fnl 3f: nvr a threat* **40/1**	114
4	5 1/4	**Vermilion (JPN)**[59] 5-9-0 115 .... C-PLemaire 2 (S Ishizaka, Japan) *mid-div rail: hrd rdn 3f out: nt qckn* **33/1**	105
5	2 1/2	**Forty Licks (ARG)**[43] 5-9-0 115 ....(t) MJKinane 6 (I Jory, Saudi Arabia) *disp wd for 5f: rdn 3 1/2f out: wknd* **18/1**	100
6	2 3/4	**Kandidate**[51] 399 5-9-0 115 ....(t) SebSanders 4 (C E Brittain) *settled in rr: rdn to cl 4 1/2f out: nvr able to chal* **22/1**	95
7	2 3/4	**Discreet Cat (USA)**[126] 6611 4-9-0 128 .... LDettori 1 (Saeed Bin Suroor) *settled in rr: wd into st and rdn: no rspnse: eased fnl f* **11/8**[2]	90

1m 59.97s (-3.33) **Going Correction** +0.175s/f (Slow) **7** Ran SP% **114.0**

Speed ratings: 120,118,112,108,106 103,101

.

Owner Hamdan Al Maktoum **Bred** Haras Clausan **Trained** USA

FOCUS

A field of just seven runners represented the smallest turnout in the Dubai World Cup's 12-year history, but this renewal was as eagerly anticipated as any in recent memory, with the two highest rated horses in the world, Discreet Cat and Invasor, clashing in the richest race on the planet. The race itself did not unfold as many might have hoped, though, with Discreet Cat running abysmally, but we still saw a top-class performance from last year's Breeders' Cup Classic winner Invasor, who clocked a very fast sub-two minute time.

NOTEBOOK

Invasor(ARG) confirmed himself the best dirt horse in the world. The clock confirms this was the performance of a true champion, for his time of 1m 59.97s has only been bettered by Dubai Millennium's 1m 59.50s in the history of this famous race. There were concerns beforehand that he would not be able to stay in touch in the early stages, but he always held a good position with the early pace perhaps not quite as strong as one might have expected and, with only Premium Tap to worry about at the top of the straight, he was always going to prove the strongest. He is not a flashy type by any means in terms of racing style, but he wins his races by being able to sustain a powerful finishing effort, and it is probably fair to say he would have won by even further had the leaders gone off quicker. Provided he stays fit, he must have a serious chance of gaining another Breeders' Cup Classic in October, and he is certainly the one they all have to beat wherever he goes.

Premium Tap(USA), who beat Forty Licks in Saudi Arabia's most prestigious race last time, deserves loads of credit for a fine run in second. He was basically beaten by a true star, but showed himself one of the best around in his own right and he could be in for a profitable season, so long as he does not bump into Invasor too often.

Bullish Luck(USA), fifth in last year's Dubai Duty Free, won the separate race for third and was in turn well clear of the remainder; a very creditable effort considering he raced keenly. This was his first start on dirt, but he seemed to cope well enough with the new surface.

Vermilion(JPN), winner of a Grade 1 in Japan at the end of January, weakened rather tamely in the straight about two furlongs out and was seemingly not up to the task.

Forty Licks(ARG) was held by Premium Tap on their recent running in Saudi Arabia and could not turn the tables. His connections were making bullish noises beforehand, so this could be considered rather disappointing.

Kandidate is at his best when able to dominate, but he was not quick enough into his stride to get to the lead and he was unable to repeat the form of his win in the second round of the Al Maktoum challenge.

Discreet Cat(USA) failed to fire. He came into this unbeaten in six career starts, and had around seven lengths to spare over Invasor on the pair's only previous meeting in last year's UAE Derby, but he failed to beat a rival this time. The Godolphin stable is badly out of form at the moment and it later transpired that he was suffering from an aggressive throat abscess, which may explain this tame effort. At the same time, though, the tactics employed probably did him few favours, as he was seemingly ridden to get the trip, having never won beyond 1m1f. Held up in last early on, he was always going to struggle to make up the lost ground on such classy performers and, considering he is such a naturally free-going type, he may have resented the new tactics. His rider reported afterwards that he did not face the kickback. It is clear that there were a number of factors that could explain the below-par showing and it will probably just be worth putting a line through this. Hopefully he can return to his best back over shorter distances in the US.

[825]LINGFIELD (L-H)

Sunday, April 1

OFFICIAL GOING: Standard

Wind: Strong against

864 FURLONGS & FAVOURITES MAIDEN STKS — 1m (P)
2:00 (2:00) (Class 5) 3-Y-O — **£2,817** (£838; £418; £209) **Stalls** High

Form — RPR

42- **1** **Dubai Twilight**[208] 5089 3-9-3 .... MichaelHills 4 — 74+
(B W Hills) *led after 1f: mde rest: rdn and drew clr over 1f out: r.o wl* **2/11**[1]

2 *1 3/4* **Easterly Breeze (IRE)** 3-9-3 .... JimmyFortune 7 — 65+
(W R Muir) *s.i.s: bhd: rdn and hdwy wl over 1f out: chsd wnr ins fnl f: r.o wl but no ch w wnr* **12/1**[3]

66 **3** *5* **County Kerry (UAE)**[11] 720 3-8-12 .... DaneO'Neill 6 — 48
(Jean-Rene Auvray) *w.w in tch: rdn and effrt over 2f out: wknd over 1f out* **33/1**

00-0 **4** *1/2* **Dawson Creek (IRE)**[57] 342 3-9-0 50 .... JamesDoyle(3) 1 — 52
(B Gubby) *w.w in tch: rdn over 2f out: wknd over 1f out* **50/1**

225- **5** *1/2* **Little Miss Tara (IRE)**[186] 5624 3-8-12 75 .... RichardHughes 2 — 46
(A B Haynes) *led for 1f: chsd ldrs: rdn to chse wnr wl over 2f out: tl jst ins fnl f: wknd* **7/1**[2]

0 **6** *2* **Miss Invincible**[16] 689 3-8-12 .... JamieSpencer 3 — 41
(A P Jarvis) *s.i.s: hdwy on outer over 2f out: no hdwy wl over 1f out* **12/1**[3]

0 **7** *15* **Parma (IRE)**[34] 569 3-8-12 .... OscarUrbina 5 — 7
(M Botti) *chsd wnr after 1f tl 3f out: sn rdn: wkng whn short of room wl over 1f out: eased ins fnl f* **50/1**

1m 38.4s (-1.03) **Going Correction** 0.0s/f (Stan) — 7 Ran SP% **119.3**
Speed ratings (Par 98):105,103,98,97,97 95,80
CSF £4.40 TOTE £1.30: £1.10, £3.50; EX 5.20.
Owner Gainsborough **Bred** Highclere Stud **Trained** Lambourn, Berks

FOCUS
An uncompetitive maiden, but a decent winning time for a race like this. The winner was a class above his rivals, with the form held down by the fourth.

865 DINNER DANCES AT LINGFIELD PARK H'CAP — 1m (P)
2:30 (2:30) (Class 4) (0-80,77) 4-Y-O+ — **£4,857** (£1,445; £722; £360) **Stalls** High

Form — RPR

0-63 **1** **Spring Goddess (IRE)**[60] 314 6-8-12 71 .... JamieSpencer 8 — 81
(A P Jarvis) *t.k.h: hld up in last: c wd and shkn up wl over 1f out: r.o to ld last 100 yds: pushed out: readily* **5/1**[2]

0-60 **2** *1 1/4* **Magic Rush**[8] 765 5-9-1 77 .... JerryO'Dwyer(3) 6 — 84
(Mrs Norma Pook) *chsd ldr: rdn and upsides 2f out: led 1f out: hdd last 100 yds : nt pce of wnr* **8/1**

00-3 **3** *nk* **Northern Desert (IRE)**[87] 38 8-8-12 71 .... ChrisCatlin 5 — 77
(P W Hiatt) *t.k.h: stdd and hld up in rr: hdwy over 2f out: kpt on u.p: onepced last 100 yds* **8/1**

2231 **4** *3/4* **Binnion Bay (IRE)**[7] 773 6-8-5 67 6ex .... (b) MarcHalford(3) 3 — 73+
(J J Bridger) *t.k.h: s.i.s: sn in midfield: rdn and effrt over 2f out: nt clr run thrght fnl f* **10/1**

0-00 **5** *hd* **Glencalvie (IRE)**[15] 697 6-9-1 74 .... (v) DaneO'Neill 4 — 78
(J Akehurst) *led: rdn over 2f out: sn hrd pressed: hdd 1f out: no ex ins fnl f* **7/1**[3]

2-34 **6** *1* **Final Tune (IRE)**[18] 672 4-9-0 73 .... AdamKirby 7 — 75
(Miss M E Rowland) *hld uo in tch: rdn and hdwy to chse ldrs over 2f out: kpt on same pce fnl f* **7/1**[3]

1126 **7** *1/2* **Spot The Subbie (IRE)**[7] 773 4-8-8 67 .... NCallan 2 — 68
(Jamie Poulton) *trckd ldrs on inner: shkn up 3f out: nt clr run over 1f out: nt rcvr* **5/1**[2]

131- **8** *1* **Reeling N' Rocking (IRE)**[127] 6595 4-8-9 68 .... MichaelHills 1 — 66
(B W Hills) *s.i.s: sn in tch in midfield: rdn 3f out: lost pl and bhd 2f out: n.d after* **10/3**[1]

1m 37.69s (-1.74) **Going Correction** 0.0s/f (Stan) — 8 Ran SP% **112.7**
Speed ratings (Par 105):108,106,106,105,105 104,104,103
CSF £42.76 CT £311.73 TOTE £3.80: £1.80, £4.50, £4.00; EX 46.60 TRIFECTA Not won..
Owner Grant & Bowman Limited **Bred** Ballyhane Stud **Trained** Twyford, Bucks

FOCUS
Quite a competitive little handicap run in a creditable time for the grade. The race has been rated at face value but the fourth lends doubts to the form.
Binnion Bay(IRE) Official explanation: jockey said gelding was denied a clear run
Reeling N' Rocking(IRE) Official explanation: jockey said filly was never travelling

866 PLAY GOLF AT LINGFIELD PARK H'CAP — 7f (P)
3:00 (3:01) (Class 6) (0-60,63) 4-Y-O+ — **£2,047** (£604; £302) **Stalls** Low

Form — RPR

64-1 **1** **Greenwood**[8] 750 9-9-7 63 .... RobertHavlin 9 — 71
(P G Murphy) *hld up in last pair: hdwy and weaved through over 1f out: r.o wl to ld nr fin* **15/2**

0050 **2** *shd* **Hand Chime**[37] 533 10-8-1 50 .... AmyBaker(7) 5 — 58
(Miss J Feilden) *t.k.h: hld up towards rr: hdwy wl over 2f out: rdn and ev ch ins fnl f: no ex nr fin* **25/1**

0023 **3** *1/2* **Mind Alert**[5] 797 6-8-9 51 ow1 .... (v) DaneO'Neill 8 — 58
(D Shaw) *t.k.h: hld up in tch: hdwy to chse ldng pair wl over 1f out: shkn up to ld 1f out: sn drvn: hdd nr fin* **9/2**[2]

0404 **4** *1 3/4* **Zazous**[11] 724 6-8-12 57 .... MarcHalford(3) 11 — 59
(J J Bridger) *t.k.h: hld up: rdn and c v wd 2f out: str run to chse ldng trio ins last: no imp last 100 yds* **6/1**[3]

2006 **5** *1 1/2* **Mine The Balance (IRE)**[8] 770 4-8-12 54 .... (b) AdamKirby 12 — 52
(H J Manners) *chsd ldr: rdn and ev ch over 2f out: wknd last 100 yds* **20/1**

5-14 **6** *hd* **Mountain Pass (USA)**[39] 516 5-9-0 59 .... (p) StephenDonohoe(3) 3 — 57
(B J Llewellyn) *s.i.s: hld up in last: swtchd rt over 1f out: rdn and r.o wl ins fnl f: nvr nrr* **4/1**[1]

5061 **7** *1* **Mulberry Lad (IRE)**[5] 797 5-9-2 58 6ex .... ChrisCatlin 4 — 53
(P W Hiatt) *chsd ldrs on inner: rdn over 2f out: kpt on same pce fnl f* **8/1**

3000 **8** *3/4* **Crafty Fox**[16] 690 4-7-12 47 .... JosephWalsh(7) 6 — 40
(A P Jarvis) *chsd ldrs: rdn over 2f out: wknd wl over 1f out* **16/1**

0005 **9** *1 1/4* **Certifiable**[9] 739 6-8-13 55 .... (p) AdrianMcCarthy 2 — 45
(Miss Z C Davison) *led: rdn over 2f out: hdd 1f out: sn wknd* **17/2**

445- **10** *nk* **Royal Senga**[209] 5055 4-8-12 54 .... FergusSweeney 7 — 43
(C A Horgan) *t.k.h: chsd ldrs: rdn and chsd ldng pair over 2f out: wknd 2f out* **22/1**

6040 **11** *shd* **Methusaleh (IRE)**[10] 729 4-8-2 49 .... PatrickHills(5) 1 — 43+
(D Shaw) *hld up towards rr on inner: effrt and rdn 2f out: nt clr run over 1f out: nvr on terms* **16/1**

-600 **12** *1 1/4* **Ten Prophets (IRE)**[40] 504 4-8-13 55 .... NCallan 10 — 41
(J J Bridger) *hld up: rdn and effrt on outer wl over 2f out: wknd wl over 1f out* **20/1**

0-60 **13** *8* **Up Tempo (IRE)**[5] 803 9-9-1 60 .... (b) LiamJones(3) 14 — 25
(C R Dore) *in tch in midfied: rdn 3f out: sn wknd* **16/1**

1m 25.13s (-0.76) **Going Correction** 0.0s/f (Stan) — 13 Ran SP% **121.2**
Speed ratings (Par 101):104,103,103,101,99 99,98,97,95,95 95,94,84
CSF £189.89 CT £952.24 TOTE £9.00: £1.90, £7.50, £1.90; EX 206.70 Trifecta £248.20 Part won. Pool: £349.63 - 0.50 winning units..
Owner The Golden Anorak Partnership **Bred** Britton House Stud And C Gregson **Trained** East Garston, Berks

FOCUS
A low-grade handicap, but a competitive one and again the time was solid. The third looks the best guide to the form.
Up Tempo(IRE) Official explanation: trainer said gelding had bled internally

867 LINGFIELDPARK.CO.UK H'CAP — 6f (P)
3:30 (3:31) (Class 2) (0-105,105) 4-Y-O+ — **£9,971** (£2,985; £1,492; £747) **Stalls** Low

Form — RPR

2224 **1** **Maltese Falcon**[8] 762 7-9-2 103 .... (t) JimmyFortune 1 — 111
(P F I Cole) *mde all: shkn up and fnd ex jst over 1f out: rdn and styd on wl fnl f* **2/1**[2]

5401 **2** *1/2* **Ajigolo**[22] 660 4-8-10 97 .... SamHitchcott 3 — 104
(M R Channon) *hld up in tch: hdwy on outer to chse wnr wl over 2f out: rdn over 1f out: kpt on but a hld by wnr* **5/2**[3]

42-0 **3** *1* **Ripples Maid**[22] 660 4-8-5 92 .... RichardThomas 4 — 96
(J A Geake) *chsd wnr tl wl over 2f out: rdn 2f out: kpt on same pce ins fnl f* **7/1**

0-10 **4** *hd* **Border Music**[8] 762 6-9-4 105 .... (b) RichardHughes 2 — 108
(A M Balding) *trckd ldrs on inner: rdn and nt qckn over 1f out: kpt on same pce ins fnl f* **15/8**[1]

1m 11.85s (-0.96) **Going Correction** 0.0s/f (Stan) — 4 Ran SP% **109.2**
Speed ratings (Par 109):106,105,104,103
CSF £7.26 TOTE £3.00; EX 6.30.
Owner Christopher Wright **Bred** Stratford Place Stud **Trained** Whatcombe, Oxon

FOCUS
A disappointing turnout for the money and something of a tactical event as a result with the winner able to dictate. The time was modest for the grade.

NOTEBOOK
Maltese Falcon was favoured by this small field and his rider held all the cards after being allowed to dominate. The gelding had done well to make the frame from a bad draw in Listed company on his previous visit here, but this time his jockey did not have to move on him until Ajigolo threw down a challenge inside the final furlong. (tchd 9-4)
Ajigolo was 7lb higher than for his win last month and that just found him out, although he did nothing wrong. (op 9-4 tchd 2-1)
Ripples Maid had it all to do with Ajigolo on recent placings but, although never looking like bridging that gap, kept on well enough to suggest she can progress up the sprinting ladder this year. (op 13-2)
Border Music proved a disappointing favourite. He really wants a bigger field, a good pace and plenty of cover, none of which was in evidence here. This 6f trip is arguably on the short side to boot. (op 2-1 tchd 9-4)

868 LINGFIELD PARK FOR WEDDINGS H'CAP — 1m 4f (P)
4:00 (4:00) (Class 3) (0-95,86) 4-Y-O+ — **£7,124** (£2,119; £1,059; £529) **Stalls** Low

Form — RPR

-031 **1** **Art Modern (IRE)**[23] 652 5-8-13 81 .... (b) FergusSweeney 3 — 88
(G L Moore) *hld up in last: rdn and effrt over 1f out: r.o wl to ld last 50 yds* **9/4**[2]

412 **2** *nk* **Lemonette (USA)**[15] 702 4-8-2 76 .... PatrickHills(5) 4 — 83
(J W Hills) *w ldr: shkn up 2f out: rdn to ld ins fnl f: hdd and no ex last 50 yds* **3/1**[3]

3216 **3** *nk* **Polish Power (GER)**[15] 698 7-9-3 85 .... LPKeniry 2 — 92
(J S Moore) *led at v slow pce: qcknd over 3f out: rdn over 2f out: hdd and no ex ins fnl f* **7/2**

00-1 **4** *1* **I Have Dreamed (IRE)**[11] 726 5-9-4 86 .... KDarley 1 — 91
(T G Mills) *trckd ldng pair: rdn and effrt 2f out: kpt on same pce fnl f* **2/1**[1]

2m 50.04s (15.65) **Going Correction** 0.0s/f (Stan)
WFA 4 from 5yo+ 1lb — 4 Ran SP% **111.3**
Speed ratings (Par 107):47,46,46,45
CSF £9.23 TOTE £2.70; EX 10.30.
Owner Matthew Green **Bred** Sir Eric Parker **Trained** Woodingdean, E Sussex

FOCUS
A very slow early pace followed by a sprint to the line resulted in a meaningless winning time, over 15 seconds slower than the following maiden over the same trip. The bare form is ordinary but should not be taken too seriously.

NOTEBOOK
Art Modern(IRE) found the best turn of foot in what was a very slowly-run affair. He challenged late and widest of all to gain a narrow verdict, and while he is building up a portfolio of wins at this track, the form of this particualr race is more or less worthless. (op 11-4)
Lemonette(USA), narrowly denied close home, would not have appreciated the way this race was run, but she has a progressive profile and remains capable of better. (op 5-2)
Polish Power(GER) is not a natural front-runner and he led on sufferance here, setting a pedestrian gallop. He tried to quicken the pace running down the hill but could not get away from his rivals and was collared inside the last.
I Have Dreamed(IRE) has made the running in the past and he might have fared better this time had he taken up the pace-making duties that no-one else wanted. (tchd 5-2)

869 LINGFIELD PARK FOR CONFERENCES MAIDEN STKS — 1m 4f (P)
4:30 (4:32) (Class 5) 3-4-Y-O — **£2,817** (£838; £418; £209) **Stalls** Low

Form — RPR

-222 **1** **Moon Empress (FR)**[37] 537 4-9-8 62 .... NCallan 6 — 69
(W R Muir) *chsd ldrs: hdwy wl over 3f out: chsd ldr and rdn over 2f out: led jst ins fnl f: drvn out* **9/4**[1]

4 **2** *3/4* **Anne Bronte**[9] 735 3-8-2 .... AdrianTNicholls 5 — 66
(M Johnston) *chsd ldr tl led 3f out: rdn over 2f out: hdd jst ins fnl f: kpt on same pce* **7/2**[3]

0-03 **3** *2* **Stringsofmyheart**[30] 603 3-7-13 66 .... LiamJones(3) 2 — 63
(W J Haggas) *s.i.s and pushed along: sn settled midfield: hdwy 3f out: rdn and wandered over 1f out: wnt 3rd ins last: nvr nrr* **11/4**[2]

/60- **4** *3/4* **Telegonus**[122] 5429 4-9-13 75 .... SamHitchcott 4 — 69?
(C E Longsdon) *chsd ldrs: 3rd and rdn over 2f out: kpt on same pce last 2f: lost 3rd ins fnl f* **10/1**

The Form Book, Raceform Ltd, Compton, RG20 6NL

52 **5** *5* **Santaverti**[6] 788 4-9-13 JimCrowley 8 61
(G L Moore) *hld up towards rr: effrt and hdwy over 3f out: no imp 2f out* **6/1**

30-0 **6** *shd* **Conservative**[23] 651 4-9-13 64 RobertHavlin 10 60
(P G Murphy) *hld up in last pair: pushed along and hdwy 3f out: no prog whn hung lft wl over 1f out: nvr nr ldrs* **10/1**

404- **7** *4* **Sagassa**[127] 6597 3-8-2 48 AdrianMcCarthy 9 47
(W De Best-Turner) *led tl 3f out: sn rdn: wknd over 2f out* **50/1**

0- **8** *5* **Wicked Lady (UAE)**[38] 6987 4-9-8 DaneO'Neill 7 41
(B R Johnson) *w.w in midfield: rdn and effrt 4f out: no prog wl over 2f out: eased ins fnl f* **16/1**

060- **9** *2 1/2* **Sterling Moll**[173] 5903 4-9-5 46 JamesDoyle(3) 1 37
(W De Best-Turner) *hld up towards rr: rdn wl over 4f out: no ch last 3f* **33/1**

-000 **10** *17* **Mo Chroi**[41] 500 4-9-1 35 RyanBird(7) 3 10
(J J Bridger) *a last: rdn and lost tch over 4f out: t.o last 2f* **50/1**

2m 35.02s (0.63) **Going Correction** 0.0s/f (Stan)
WFA 3 from 4yo 21lb **10** Ran SP% **124.9**
Speed ratings (Par 103):97,96,95,94,91 91,88,85,83,72
CSF £11.21 TOTE £2.70: £1.30, £1.40, £1.70; EX 11.20 Trifecta £32.70 Pool: £521.09, 11.29 winning units.
Owner Foursome Thoroughbreds **Bred** Eric Puerari And Oceanic Bloodstock **Trained** Lambourn, Berks

FOCUS
Another steadily run race. Modest maiden form, but it seems to make sense.

870 TIPPLES & TENSION H'CAP 1m 2f (P)
5:00 (5:00) (Class 4) (0-85,89) 4-Y-0+ £4,857 (£1,445; £722; £360) Stalls Low

Form RPR

000- **1** **Cactus King**[143] 6418 4-9-1 **80** IanMongan 7 87
(P M Phelan) *t.k.h: hld up in last pair shkn up over 1f out: str run and edgd lft ins fnl f: led on post* **15/2**

112- **2** *shd* **Evident Pride (USA)**[112] 6781 4-8-13 **78** DaneO'Neill 4 85+
(B R Johnson) *w.w in midfield: hdwy over 2f out: swtchd lft over 1f out: rdn to ld 1f out: hdd on post* **1/1**[1]

-320 **3** *1* **Jebel Ali (IRE)**[16] 693 4-8-7 **75** ow1 (b[1]) JamesDoyle(3) 5 80
(B Gubby) *chsd ldr tl led 3f out: rdn and hung rt over 1f out: hdd 1f out: kpt on same pce fnl f* **7/1**[3]

0-36 **4** *1* **Suits Me**[18] 675 4-8-4 **69** oh1 ChrisCatlin 1 72
(T P Tate) *led tl 3f out: sn rdn: kpt on same pce u.p* **9/2**[2]

040- **5** *1/2* **Barathea Blazer**[100] 6917 8-9-3 **82** RichardHughes 6 84
(K McAuliffe) *hld up in last pair: rdn and effrt 2f out: kpt on same pce* **11/1**

02-0 **6** *20* **Birkside**[8] 758 4-8-8 **73** (t) NCallan 3 37
(B G Powell) *led to post: chsd ldng pair tl 3f out: sn rdn: wknd over 2f out: eased fnl f* **9/2**[2]

2m 6.38s (-1.41) **Going Correction** 0.0s/f (Stan) **6** Ran SP% **119.0**
Speed ratings (Par 105):105,104,104,103,102 86
CSF £16.74 TOTE £11.90: £3.30, £1.40; EX 28.00 Place 6 £147.96, Place 5 £124.81.
Owner Tony Smith **Bred** Hascombe And Valiant Studs **Trained** Ashtead, Surrey

FOCUS
A fair handicap but the early pace was not that strong and once again the winner came from last to first. The form may not prove too solid. Phil Phelan's first winner since moving from Ireland.
T/Plt: £84.50 to a £1 stake. Pool: £60,879.95. 525.65 winning tickets. T/Qpdt: £24.10 to a £1 stake. Pool: £2,873.30. 88.10 winning tickets. SP

871 - 872a (Foreign Racing) - See Raceform Interactive

NAVAN (L-H)
Sunday, April 1

OFFICIAL GOING: Soft to heavy

873a NIGHTCLUB PROMOTION 18-30 CLUB H'CAP 5f
3:15 (3:15) (45-75,74) 3-Y-0+ £4,668 (£1,087; £479; £277)

RPR

1 **Controvento (IRE)**[134] 6527 5-8-12 65 (b) CDTimmons(7) 19 80
(Eamon Tyrrell, Ire) *trckd ldrs on stand's side: 4th and hdwy 1 1/2f out: led under 1f out: styd on wl* **6/1**[1]

2 *1 1/4* **Scalded Cat (IRE)**[200] 5304 4-8-10 59 WJLee(3) 13 69
(Daniel William O'Sullivan, Ire) *towards rr on stand's side: hdwy 1 1/2f out: r.o wl ins fnl f: nvr nrr* **16/1**

3 *shd* **Glencairn Star**[149] 6320 6-9-11 71 (p) PaulHanagan 14 81
(R A Fahey) *hld up towards rr: hdwy 1 1/2f out: 4th under 1f out: kpt on* **6/1**[1]

4 *1/2* **Wildwish (IRE)**[160] 6149 3-8-13 73 CDHayes(3) 4 76
(Enda Kelly, Ire) *trckd ldrs on far side: 6th 1/2-way: kpt on fnl f* **14/1**

5 *shd* **The Last Laugh**[166] 6039 3-9-3 74 PJSmullen 2 76
(M J Grassick, Ire) *prom on far rail: 2nd 2f out: led over 1f out: hdd under 1f out: kpt on* **6/1**[1]

6 *1 1/4* **Ebenholz (IRE)**[158] 6185 4-8-12 58 (b) NGMcCullagh 6 61
(Mrs John Harrington, Ire) *mid-div: sltly hmpd 1/2-way: kpt on fr over 1f out* **8/1**[2]

7 *3/4* **Miss Spirit (IRE)**[354] 994 4-8-9 55 WSupple 5 55
(Michael Mulvany, Ire) *mid-div on far rail: hmpd 1/2-way: kpt on u.p fr over 1f out* **20/1**

8 *nk* **Tango Step (IRE)**[55] 361 7-9-4 64 MCHussey 10 63
(Bernard Lawlor, Ire) *hld up: kpt on fr over 1f out* **10/1**[3]

9 *4* **Grecian Dancer**[177] 5796 4-9-10 70 FMBerry 3 55
(Charles O'Brien, Ire) *mid-div on far side: bmpd 1/2-way: effrt over 1f out: sn no ex* **8/1**[2]

10 *nk* **Wychwood Wanderer (IRE)**[160] 6150 4-9-4 64 JMurtagh 15 48
(M Halford, Ire) *nvr a factor: kpt on fr over 1f out* **8/1**[2]

11 *3/4* **Tornadodancer (IRE)**[152] 6286 4-9-3 63 KJManning 12 44
(T G McCourt, Ire) *trckd ldrs: 5th 1 1/2f out: no ex fnl f* **20/1**

12 *1 1/4* **Captain Cole (IRE)**[163] 6086 4-8-6 57 OCasey(5) 9 34
(Peter Casey, Ire) *nvr a factor* **14/1**

13 *3/4* **Palanoverre (IRE)**[160] 6152 3-8-11 71 RPCleary(3) 16 40
(Francis Ennis, Ire) *in rr: rdn over 2f out: kpt on ins fnl f* **14/1**

14 *1/2* **Dafaroun (IRE)**[160] 6150 6-10-0 74 JAHeffernan 1 46
(T Hogan, Ire) *towards rr thrght* **12/1**

15 *1/2* **Salishan (IRE)**[166] 6038 5-8-3 54 SMGorey(5) 20 24
(Adrian McGuinness, Ire) *hld up towards rr: no imp fr 2f out* **16/1**

16 *3/4* **Vintage Year (IRE)**[249] 3857 5-9-7 72 MACleere(5) 11 40
(T J O'Mara, Ire) *chsd ldrs early: no ex fr 2f out* **12/1**

17 *1 1/2* **Mother's Day**[299] 2334 4-8-13 66 AmyKathleenParsons(7) 8 28
(F J Bowles, Ire) *led: hdd over 1f out: sn wknd* **20/1**

18 *3* **Miss Modesty (IRE)**[218] 4823 4-9-3 63 FranciscoDaSilva 7 14
(Paul Magnier, Ire) *reminders early: a bhd* **20/1**

19 *hd* **Faynita (IRE)**[169] 5977 5-9-1 61 (p) DPMcDonogh 18 12
(Adrian McGuinness, Ire) *prom: 2nd 1/2-way: wknd u.p fr 2f out* **8/1**[2]

20 *8* **Stravinskaya (USA)**[166] 6038 5-8-4 50 DMGrant 17 —
(H Rogers, Ire) *chsd ldrs early: wknd fr 1/2-way* **20/1**

1m 11.7s (4.90)
WFA 3 from 4yo+ 11lb **20** Ran SP% **167.4**
CSF £130.52 CT £647.99 TOTE £10.80: £2.80, £4.00, £2.90, £4.50.
Owner Michael A O'Reilly **Bred** Mrs Ann Mooney **Trained** The Curragh, Co Kildare

NOTEBOOK
Controvento(IRE), who is generally progressive, posted her third course-and-distance win on soft ground. (op 7/1)
Scalded Cat(IRE) only had two behind her with a quarter of a mile left but came home strongly.
Glencairn Star, back to his last winning mark for this seasonal bow, came through from off the pace to have his chance and did not appear to do much wrong in defeat. It would come as little surprise to see his new trainer place him to advantage before long. (op 6/1 tchd 13/2)

875a ENNISTOWN STUD EUROPEAN BREEDERS FUND SALSABIL STKS (LISTED RACE) (FILLIES) 1m 2f
4:15 (4:16) 3-Y-0+ £32,989 (£9,679; £4,611; £1,570)

RPR

1 **Anna Pavlova**[171] 5917 4-10-0 PaulHanagan 4 113
(R A Fahey) *trckd ldrs: 5th 1/2-way: smooth hdwy early st: led over 1f out: sn rdn clr: easily* **5/4**[1]

2 *5* **Bon Nuit (IRE)**[153] 6267 5-9-11 100 NGMcCullagh 5 101
(Mrs John Harrington, Ire) *hld up in tch: 5th and hdwy 2f out: mod 2nd ins fnl f: kpt on same pce u.p* **10/1**

3 *shd* **Tartouche**[176] 5803 6-10-0 DPMcDonogh 9 104
(Mrs John Harrington, Ire) *cl up in 2nd: led appr st: rdn and hdd over 1f out: sn outpcd: kpt on u.p* **4/1**[2]

4 *5* **Glitter Baby (IRE)**[147] 6358 4-9-11 (t) MJKinane 2 92
(M G Quinlan) *hld up in rr: hdwy on outer early st: 6th 2f out: mod 4th and no imp fnl f* **16/1**

5 *nk* **Whoneedswings (IRE)**[161] 6115 5-9-11 80 WMLordan 1 91
(David Wachman, Ire) *led: hdd appr st: 4th u.p 2f out: kpt on same pce* **33/1**

6 *2 1/2* **Sacrosanct (IRE)**[147] 6356 4-9-11 94 JAHeffernan 3 87
(A P O'Brien, Ire) *towards rr: rdn and no imp st* **12/1**

7 *1 3/4* **Princess Nala (IRE)**[273] 3128 5-9-11 92 JMurtagh 6 84
(M Halford, Ire) *hld up in tch: 7th 1/2-way: no imp st* **6/1**[3]

8 *3/4* **Luminous One (IRE)**[147] 6357 3-8-7 93 DJMoran 11 83
(J S Bolger, Ire) *chsd ldrs: 6th 1/2-way: no ex early st* **10/1**

9 *7* **Galistic (IRE)**[204] 5194 4-9-11 92 DMGrant 8 70
(Patrick J Flynn, Ire) *hld up in tch: 7th appr st: sn rdn and no imp* **14/1**

10 *19* **Kapera (FR)**[306] 4-9-11 FMBerry 7 35
(Noel Lawlor, Ire) *prom: 4th 1/2-way: 3rd into st: sn rdn and wknd: trailing fnl f* **50/1**

11 *dist* **Valentina Guest (IRE)**[158] 6184 6-9-11 92 PJSmullen 10 —
(Peter Casey, Ire) *prom: 3rd 1/2-way: 2nd into st: sn wknd: eased 2f out: t.o* **16/1**

2m 26.5s (10.70)
WFA 3 from 4yo+ 19lb **11** Ran SP% **127.9**
CSF £17.46 TOTE £2.10: £1.70, £2.60, £2.80; DF 13.50.
Owner Galaxy Racing **Bred** Raymond Cowie **Trained** Musley Bank, N Yorks

FOCUS
A good renewal of this mares' Listed prize and the progressive winner is value for a little further than the winning margin. The form looks sound rated through the placed horses.

NOTEBOOK
Anna Pavlova ◆ got her season off to a perfect start and, as she looked to be idling late on, can be rated value for a little further than her winning margin. She was travelling all over her rivals into the home straight, showed a turn of foot when asked to win her race nearing the final furlong, and once again advertised her liking for the underfoot conditions. She looks capable of successfully stepping up to Group company now and her trainer later indicated that the Irish St Leger was her big target this year. (op 10/11)
Bon Nuit(IRE) ended last year with two solid placed efforts in this grade and basically ran very close to that level on this seasonal return. She has a habit of finding one too good these days, but does deserve to go one better as she appears to give her all. This run should also help bring her on. (op 8/1)
Tartouche, making her Irish debut for new connections having been purchased for 150,000gns at the December Sales, was far from disgraced under her penalty over a trip short of her best. She has clearly not lost any of her enthusiasm, is entitled to improve a deal for the outing, and is one to respect when reverting to a stiffer test. (op 4/1 tchd 9/2)
Glitter Baby(IRE), up in class on this debut for new connections, had her usual blinkers left off and was equipped with a first-time tongue tie. She ran creditably - and in keeping with her best efforts last year - so no doubt connections will be more than hopeful of gaining some valuable black type after this.
Whoneedswings(IRE) has slipped to a decent handicap mark now and, with the benefit of this run under her belt, could find another opening when her sights are lowered.

878 - 879a (Foreign Racing) - See Raceform Interactive

823 LONGCHAMP (R-H)
Sunday, April 1

OFFICIAL GOING: Heavy

880a PRIX D'HARCOURT (GROUP 2) 1m 2f
3:20 (3:22) 4-Y-0+ £50,068 (£19,324; £9,223; £6,149; £3,074)

RPR

1 **Boris De Deauville (IRE)**[22] 663 4-8-12 YBarberot 7 116
(S Wattel, France) *held up, 8th but well in touch straight, led just inside final f, ran on well* **132/10**

2 *1 1/2* **Pearl Sky (FR)**[22] 663 4-8-8 ACrastus 2 109
(Y De Nicolay, France) *always in touch, 7th straight, ran on on outside to take 2nd on line* **5/2**[1]

3 *nse* **Irish Wells (FR)**[182] 5716 4-9-1 DBoeuf 4 116
(F Rohaut, France) *led after 1 1/2f, headed just inside final 2f, driven to lead again briefly 1f out, lost 2nd on line* **5/2**[1]

4 *3/4* **Soldier Hollow**[147] 6365 7-9-1 OPeslier 6 115
(P Schiergen, Germany) *tracked leader, 2nd straight, took narrow lead just inside final 2f, headed 1f out, ran on one pace* **58/10**[3]

5 *nk* **Elasos (FR)**[22] 663 5-8-12 .... DBonilla 9 111
(D Sepulchre, France) *held up, headway to disputed 4th at half-way, 4th straight, ridden & outpaced 2f out, ran on again final 150y* **13/1**

6 *1 1/2* **Runaway**[22] 663 5-8-12 .... SPasquier 5 108
(A Fabre, France) *mid-division, 6th on inside straight, disputed 3rd over 1f out, one pace* **48/10**[2]

7 *1 1/2* **Blushing King (FR)**[22] 663 5-8-12 .... FVeron 10 106
(J-L Guillochon, France) *slowly into stride, last to straight, kept on same pace on outside, never a factor* **50/1**

8 *15* **Nordic Thunder (GER)**[168] 6001 4-8-12 .... CSoumillon 1 79
(A Fabre, France) *led for 1 1/2f, 3rd straight, beaten well over 1f out, eased* **15/2**

9 *3* **Aspectus (IRE)**[214] 4942 4-9-1 .... JVictoire 3 76
(H Blume, Germany) *prominent, 5th straight, weakened quickly 2f out, ridden & found nothing, eased* **21/1**

2m 13.4s (5.40) **Going Correction** +0.925s/f (Soft) **9** Ran SP% **121.5**
Speed ratings: 115,113,113,113,112 111,110,98,96
PARI-MUTUEL: WIN 14.20; PL 2.30, 1.40, 1.40; DF 25.20.
Owner Mme M Bryant & L Haegel **Bred** Petra Bloodstock Agency Ltd **Trained** France

NOTEBOOK
Boris De Deauville(IRE) turned around Saint-Cloud form with Pearl Sky on 4lb better terms, recording an emphatic victory. His only two successes have come in Group events and he had this one at his mercy at the furlong marker. Dropped out early on, he came with a sweeping late run and acted well on the very heavy ground. A hurdling career has been ruled out for him now and connections will now be looking at either the Prix Ganay or the Prix d'Ispahan, with the preference being for the latter.
Pearl Sky(FR) did not really start firing until towards the end of the race. Towards the tail of the field early on, she started to motor from a furlong and a half out and stole second place virtually on the line. She lost little in defeat and her trainer feels that she needs a longer trip, so the Prix d'Hedouville is now a likely target.
Irish Wells(FR) was always well up with the pace and often in the lead, but he did not pull on this occasion. He led into the straight but surrendered his advantage a furlong and a half out before staying on bravely throughout the final stages. His trainer was delighted with this seasonal debut and the next target is to be the Prix Ganay, where the extra half-furlong will be a distinct advantage.
Soldier Hollow made a promising start to the season. For a long time he followed the third, and he held a slight advantage running into the final furlong. He failed to quicken but stuck to his guns until the line, and he is another likely contender for the Ganay, when hopefully the ground will be in a better state.

COLOGNE (R-H)
Sunday, April 1

OFFICIAL GOING: Soft

881a PREIS DER TELEWETTE - FRUHJAHRS-MEILE (LISTED RACE) 1m
3:35 (3:51) 4-Y-0+ **£8,784** (£2,703; £1,351; £676)

RPR

1 **Apollo Star (GER)**[129] 6574 5-8-11 .... ASuborics 7 101
(Mario Hofer, Germany) **6/1**

2 *2 1/2* **Imonso (GER)**[252] 3776 4-8-9 .... JiriPalik 8 94
(J Hirschberger, Germany) **21/10**[1]

3 *1 3/4* **Konig Turf (GER)**[518] 6190 5-8-9 .... TMundry 9 90
(C Sprengel, Germany) **29/10**[2]

4 *hd* **Mharadono (GER)**[133] 6529 4-9-2 .... KKerekes 6 97
(P Hirschberger, Germany) **24/1**

5 *6* **Madresal (GER)**[129] 6574 8-9-0 .... AStarke 3 83
(P Schiergen, Germany) **36/10**[3]

6 *hd* **Silex (GER)**[260] 3563 4-9-2 .... FilipMinarik 5 85
(P Schiergen, Germany) **71/10**

7 *1/2* **Dream Of Gold (GER)**[335] 4-8-9 .... AHelfenbein 2 77
(D K Richardson, Germany) **22/1**

8 *11* **Proudance (GER)**[260] 3563 5-8-9 .... J-PCarvalho 1 55
(R Suerland, Germany) **84/10**

9 *3* **King Marju (IRE)**[22] 657 5-8-9 .... PatCosgrave 4 49
(K R Burke) *started slowly, last throughout, ridden 2f out, no headway* **17/1**

1m 39.8s (1.41) **9** Ran SP% **130.8**
(including 10 euro stakes): WIN 70; PL 19, 13, 16; SF 280.
Owner J Spranke **Bred** H Gerwin **Trained** Germany

NOTEBOOK
Apollo Star(GER) was twice placed at Group 3 level last backend.
King Marju(IRE) is often nervous in the stalls and a false start (when only four gates opened) and subsequent long delay did for him here. Slowly away, he was in last place throughout.

882a JAXX GRAND PRIX AUFGALOPP (GROUP 3) 1m 3f
4:10 (4:25) 4-Y-0+ **£21,622** (£6,757; £3,378; £2,027)

RPR

1 **Egerton (GER)**[112] 6782 6-9-2 .... TMundry 6 118
(P Rau, Germany) *held up, close 7th straight, brought wide, headway to lead well over 1f out, hung steadily right to 1f out, ridden out* **2/1**[2]

2 *1 1/4* **Lauro (GER)**[147] 6365 4-8-11 .... AStarke 4 111
(P Schiergen, Germany) *always close up, 4th straight, challenging when bumped & squeezed back well over 1f out, rallied final f, finished well* **6/4**[1]

3 *1 1/4* **Bussoni (GER)**[261] 3516 6-9-0 .... ASuborics 5 112
(H Blume, Germany) *tracked leader, led over 2f out to well over 1f out, hung left & bumped 2nd, kept on one pace* **57/10**[3]

4 *5* **Loup De Mer (GER)**[25] 5-8-9 .... YLerner 3 99
(W Baltromei, Germany) *held up in touch, 8th straight, kept on final 2f, never near to challenge* **71/10**

5 *8* **One Little David (GER)**[253] 7-8-9 .... AHelfenbein 2 86
(P Vovcenko, Germany) *held up in rear, headway & 6th straight, one pace final 2f* **42/1**

6 *1/2* **Akarem**[162] 6103 6-8-9 .... PatCosgrave 1 85
(K R Burke) *mid-division, headway on inside to go 3rd straight, one pace final 2f* **106/10**

7 *4* **Gandolfino (GER)**[28] 5-8-9 ....(b) ABoschert 8 79
(W Baltromei, Germany) *led to over 2f out* **22/1**

8 *12* **All Spirit (GER)**[189] 5561 5-9-2 .... FilipMinarik 5 67
(N Sauer, Germany) *always in rear, last straight* **24/1**

9 *13* **Birkspiel (GER)**[36] 552 6-9-0 .... DarryllHolland 9 44
(S Dow) *disputed 3rd on outside, 5th straight, soon weakened* **17/2**

2m 21.72s (0.92) **9** Ran SP% **130.4**
WIN 30; PL 12, 12, 15; SF 48.
Owner Stall Reckendorf **Bred** Gestut Rottgen **Trained** Germany

NOTEBOOK
Egerton(GER), who performed with credit at the highest level last season, enjoyed this drop in class and easier ground.
Akarem needs further and ran perfectly respectably on his first start for over five months. He slipped through on the inside to go third entering the home straight but was then outpaced before plugging on again in the closing stages.
Birkspiel(GER) won this race in 2006, when it was run at Bremen as the Grosser Preis der Bremer Wirtschaft, but dropped out quickly in the last quarter mile this time. The ground had dried out too much for him to be seen at his best.

864 LINGFIELD (L-H)
Monday, April 2

OFFICIAL GOING: Standard
Wind: Fresh, half against

883 LINGFIELDPARK.CO.UK MEDIAN AUCTION MAIDEN STKS 5f (P)
2:10 (2:11) (Class 6) 2-Y-0 **£2,388** (£705; £352) **Stalls High**

Form RPR

1 **Thunder Bay** 2-9-3 .... SamHitchcott 2 63+
(M R Channon) *trckd ldrs on inner: rdn over 1f out: led ins fnl f: r.o wl* **7/2**[2]

2 *1/2* **Only In Jest** 2-8-5 .... JackDean(7) 3 56
(W G M Turner) *chsd ldr for 1f: trckd ldrs after: rdn wl over 1f out: ev ch 1f out: kpt on same pce* **5/1**

3 *hd* **Grange Poppy (IRE)** 2-8-12 .... EddieAhern 5 55
(Peter Grayson) *chsd ldr after 1f tl over 1f out: rdn and kpt on same pce fnl f* **3/1**[1]

4 *shd* **Mama Leo** 2-8-12 .... JimmyQuinn 4 55
(P D Evans) *led: rdn wl over 1f out: hdd ins fnl f: kpt on same pce* **3/1**[1]

5 *nk* **New Balls Please (IRE)** 2-9-3 .... IanMongan 1 59
(P M Phelan) *t.k.h: hld up: swtchd rt wl over 3f out: hdwy and rdn wl over 1f out: kpt on same pce* **9/2**[3]

6 *2 1/2* **Miss Antropist (IRE)** 2-8-7 .... TolleyDean(5) 6 44
(R A Harris) *s.i.s: a last: hmpd and stmbld wl over 3f out: rdn over 2f out: kpt on but nt pce to trble ldrs* **14/1**

62.81 secs (3.03) **Going Correction** -0.05s/f (Stan) **6** Ran SP% **113.7**
Speed ratings (Par 90):73,72,71,71,71 67
CSF £21.31 TOTE £3.40: £1.80, £3.70; EX 17.90.
Owner The Abercrombie Partnership **Bred** A C M Spalding **Trained** West Ilsley, Berks

FOCUS
A field of newcomers and it was no surprise to see the Channon and Turner representatives come out on top. The runners finished in a heap and the level of the form is guessy.

NOTEBOOK
Thunder Bay, who is related to some pretty speedy performers, is quite a late foal, but his stable are renowned for getting their juveniles ready and having held a good early positioned, he picked up well inside the final furlong to come through and win with a bit to spare. This was not a great contest, but it was a bright start to his career and connections are likely to wait to see how he comes out of this before making any plans. (tchd 4-1)
Only In Jest, whose stable regularly make a bright start to the season with their juveniles, had their first juvenile runner of the year disappoint in the Brocklesby, but this filly knew her job and shaped really well in second. Her trainer should have little trouble finding a race with her. (tchd 9-2)
Grange Poppy(IRE), easily the oldest in the line-up, is a half-sister to fair sprinter Fast Heart and she soon held a prominent position. However, it was clear from before the final bend she was struggling for pace and she could only keep on at the same pace close home. A little improvement should see her winning. (tchd 10-3)
Mama Leo knew her job and was bounced out in front, but could not repel the principals and was run out of the places. This was a respectable first effort and she is likely to be kept busy in the coming weeks. (op 10-3)
New Balls Please(IRE) is related to plenty of winners and he shaped quite promisingly despite having taken a grip early on. He will need to improve to score, but that is entirely possible. (op 5-1)
Miss Antropist(IRE) did not enjoy the best of trips, being slowly away and then stumbling having been hampered before the turn into the straight. She did not shape too badly considering and will benefit from a bit further in time. (op 16-1)

884 ENTERTAIN AT LINGFIELD PARK MAIDEN STKS 1m 2f (P)
2:40 (2:41) (Class 5) 3-Y-0 **£2,914** (£867; £433; £216) **Stalls Low**

Form RPR

0- 1 **Mandragola**[220] 4768 3-9-3 .... DaneO'Neill 4 76+
(B W Hills) *hld up in tch: hdwy 3f out: rdn 2f out: chsd ldr 1f out: r.o wl to ld last 50 yds: readily* **9/2**[3]

00-2 2 *1/2* **Norman The Great**[12] 720 3-9-3 72 .... JohnEgan 7 73
(Jane Chapple-Hyam) *hld up in midfield: hdwy wl over 2f out: rdn and hung lft wl over 1f out: led over 1f out: hdd and no ex last 50 yds* **2/1**[1]

-252 3 *6* **Miss Saafend Plaza (IRE)**[28] 611 3-8-12 72........(b) RichardHughes 1 57
(R Hannon) *led: rdn over 2f out: hdd over 1f out: sn btn* **11/4**[2]

4 *1* **Allaire** 3-8-12 .... JoeFanning 8 55
(M Johnston) *sn chsng ldr: rdn and ev ch over 2f out: wknd over 1f out* **5/1**

0- 5 *1* **Restless Soul**[138] 6486 3-8-12 .... EddieAhern 6 53
(C A Cyzer) *chsd ldrs: rdn over 2f out: outpcd 2f out* **17/2**

00- 6 *1* **Susie May**[148] 6349 3-8-12 .... J-PGuillambert 2 51
(C A Cyzer) *chsd ldrs: rdn 3f out: outpcd over 2f out* **16/1**

7 *6* **Augustus Caeser (IRE)** 3-8-10 .... SCreighton(7) 5 45
(E J Creighton) *s.i.s: a bhd: lost tch over 2f out* **33/1**

0 8 *10* **Winforjoe (IRE)**[17] 689 3-8-9 .... AmirQuinn(3) 3 21
(J J Bridger) *t.k.h: hld up in tch: rdn over 3f out: sn bhd: t.o* **66/1**

2m 6.27s (-1.52) **Going Correction** -0.05s/f (Stan) **8** Ran SP% **115.7**
Speed ratings (Par 98):104,103,98,98,97 96,91,83
CSF £14.12 TOTE £6.70: £1.70, £1.20, £1.20; EX 18.20.
Owner Gainsborough **Bred** Gainsborough Stud Management Ltd **Trained** Lambourn, Berks
■ A winner for Barry Hills on his 70th birthday.

FOCUS
Just a fair maiden, but the front pair drew nicely clear. Sound form, rated around the sixth.

885 LINGFIELD PARK GOLF CLUB H'CAP — 6f (P)
3:10 (3:10) (Class 5) (0-75,75) 3-Y-O — **£2,914** (£867; £433; £216) **Stalls** Low

Form — RPR

640- **1** **Crystal Gazer (FR)**[198] 5372 3-9-2 **73** .... RichardHughes 4 — 80
(R Hannon) *in tch in midfield: rdn 2f out: str run fnl f to ld nr fin* **7/1**

6112 **2** ½ **Sohraab**[8] 778 3-8-10 **72** .... TravisBlock(5) 2 — 77
(H Morrison) *trckd ldr on inner: rdn to chal over 1f out: led ins fnl f: hdd and no ex nr fin* **11/8**[1]

313- **3** ½ **Blue Charm**[103] 6881 3-9-4 **75** .... LPKeniry 7 — 79
(S Kirk) *prom: pressed ldr wl over 2f out: rdn 2f out: ev ch tl no ex last 50 yds* **5/1**[2]

511- **4** 1¼ **Tipsy Prince**[175] 5860 3-9-4 **75** .... FergusSweeney 3 — 75
(David Pinder) *taken down early: s.i.s: bhd: rdn and hdwy over 1f out: r.o wl ins fnl f: nt rch ldrs* **12/1**

430- **5** ½ **Mind The Style**[195] 5442 3-9-1 **75** .... AmirQuinn(3) 6 — 74?
(W G M Turner) *led: rdn 2f out hdd ins fnl f: wknd last 50 yds* **33/1**

515 **6** 5 **Divertimenti (IRE)**[17] 694 3-9-3 **74** .... (p) EddieAhern 9 — 58
(M J Wallace) *pressed ldrs: rdn and ev ch 2f out: wknd qckly over 1f out* **13/2**[3]

505- **7** ½ **Road To Recovery**[205] 5162 3-8-7 **64** .... (v) JimmyQuinn 1 — 46
(A M Balding) *s.i.s: hld up in rr on inner: rdn over 2f out: sn outpcd and n.d after* **12/1**

5600 **8** shd **Inquisitress**[10] 737 3-8-4 **64** .... MarcHalford(3) 8 — 46
(J J Bridger) *chsd ldrs on outer: rdn over 2f out: wknd wl over 1f out* **25/1**

-526 **9** ¾ **Stoneacre Gareth (IRE)**[14] 707 3-9-2 **73** .... GeorgeBaker 5 — 52
(Peter Grayson) *rrd as stalls opened: sn in tch in midfield: rdn over 2f out: wknd wl over 1f out* **10/1**

1m 12.51s (-0.30) **Going Correction** -0.05s/f (Stan) — **9** Ran SP% **115.9**
Speed ratings (Par 98):100,99,98,97,96 89,89,88,87
CSF £17.07 CT £53.97 TOTE £9.70: £2.80, £1.10, £1.70; EX 21.70.
Owner A F Merritt **Bred** Cheik Sultan B K B Z Al Nahyan **Trained** East Everleigh, Wilts

FOCUS
Not a bad contest and it should produce winners. The runner-up was effectively 3lb well in and is rated to his mark, with the winner back to his early juvenile form.
Stoneacre Gareth(IRE) Official explanation: jockey said gelding had no more to give

886 HBLB LINGFIELD PARK LEISURE CLUB H'CAP — 7f (P)
3:40 (3:40) (Class 4) (0-85,83) 3-Y-O — **£4,857** (£1,445; £722; £360) **Stalls** Low

Form — RPR

122- **1** **Autograph Hunter**[120] 6691 3-9-1 **80** .... JoeFanning 5 — 84
(M Johnston) *dwlt: hdwy to chse ldr 5f out: ev ch and rdn 2f out: kpt on u.p ins fnl f to ld nr fin* **9/2**[3]

313- **2** nk **Ravi River (IRE)**[205] 5172 3-9-4 **83** .... RichardHughes 4 — 86
(B W Hills) *led: rdn wl over 1f out: rdn on tl hdd and no ex nr fin* **5/6**[1]

2 **3** nk **Nans Joy (IRE)**[10] 737 3-8-6 **71** .... JohnEgan 3 — 73
(E J O'Neill) *t.k.h: trckd ldrs: rdn over 1f out: swtchd lft ins fnl f: kpt on: nt quite rch ldrs* **4/1**[2]

154- **4** hd **Murrin (IRE)**[144] 6412 3-8-10 **75** .... DaneO'Neill 1 — 76
(T G Mills) *s.i.s: hld up in tch in last: hdwy to press ldng pair over 2f out: kpt on same pce u.p fnl f* **8/1**

306- **5** 3 **Urban Warrior**[169] 5989 3-7-13 **69** oh4 .... WilliamBuick(5) 2 — 63
(Mrs Norma Pook) *t.k.h: chsd ldr for 2f: chsd ldrs: rdn wl over 1f out: wknd fnl f* **16/1**

1m 25.45s (-0.44) **Going Correction** -0.05s/f (Stan) — **5** Ran SP% **109.7**
Speed ratings (Par 100):100,99,99,99,95
CSF £8.74 TOTE £4.90: £1.20, £1.40; EX 9.70.
Owner A D Spence **Bred** Barry Taylor **Trained** Middleham Moor, N Yorks

FOCUS
Despite the early pace not appearing that strong and the first four finishing in a heap, the winning time was not at all bad and the form may be alright.

887 LINGFIELD PARK FOR WEDDINGS (S) STKS — 1m (P)
4:10 (4:10) (Class 6) 3-Y-O+ — **£2,184** (£644; £322) **Stalls** High

Form — RPR

0524 **1** **King After**[4] 813 5-9-9 57 .... (v) StephaneBreux(3) 1 — 59
(J R Best) *hld up in rr: hdwy on outer over 2f out: rdn and hung lft wl over 1f out: r.o to ld last 100 yds: sn in command* **6/4**[1]

4340 **2** 1½ **Savoy Chapel**[7] 789 5-9-6 45 .... ShaneKelly 6 — 49
(A W Carroll) *s.i.s: hld up bhd: hdwy 2f out: rdn over 1f out: r.o fnl f: wnt 2nd nr fin: no ch w wnr* **15/2**

/0-0 **3** ¾ **Grand Welcome (IRE)**[21] 372 5-8-13 44 .... (bt) SCreighton(7) 3 — 48
(E J Creighton) *led and sn clr: 3l clr and pushed along 1f out: hdd last 100 yds: immediately btn* **25/1**

4045 **4** shd **Laugh 'n Cry**[16] 702 6-9-1 49 .... (b) J-PGuillambert 5 — 43
(C A Cyzer) *t.k.h: chsd ldr: rdn 2f out: hung lft and onepced ins fnl f* **9/4**[2]

000/ **5** 5 **Lady Josh**[13] 6610 4-8-8 .... JackDean(7) 7 — 31
(W G M Turner) *chsd ldrs: rdn over 4f out: kpt on tl wknd wl over 1f out* **25/1**

300- **6** 2½ **Postage (USA)**[291] 2573 4-9-6 54 .... EddieAhern 8 — 30
(K A Morgan) *chsd ldrs: wnt 3rd and rdn over 2f out: wknd wl over 1f out* **6/1**[3]

0-00 **7** ½ **Homebred Star**[16] 699 6-8-13 38 .... JemmaMarshall(7) 2 — 29
(G P Enright) *in tch on outer: hdwy on outer over 3f out: outpcd wl over 2f out* **14/1**

50/0 **8** nk **Fellow Ship**[12] 26 7-8-13 34 .... (bt) JosephWalsh(7) 4 — 28
(P Butler) *s.i.s: a wl bhd* **40/1**

302/ **9** 3½ **Keynes (JPN)**[498] 5-9-6 .... (t) JimmyQuinn 9 — 20
(E J Creighton) *a bhd* **16/1**

1m 39.17s (-0.26) **Going Correction** -0.05s/f (Stan) — **9** Ran SP% **119.5**
Speed ratings (Par 101):99,97,96,96,91 89,88,88,84
CSF £14.15 TOTE £2.60: £1.10, £1.70, £5.70; EX 9.90.The winner was bought in for 7,000gns.
Owner D S Nevison **Bred** Mrs J McCreery **Trained** Hucking, Kent

FOCUS
A weak seller with only one of the nine runners rated above 50. The first four pulled well clear and the immediate future does not look very bright for the others.

888 GOLF AND RACING DAYS OUT H'CAP — 1m (P)
4:40 (4:40) (Class 6) (0-65,65) 4-Y-O+ — **£2,388** (£705; £352) **Stalls** High

Form — RPR

300- **1** **White Bear (FR)**[264] 3404 5-9-3 **64** .... (b) JohnEgan 5 — 72
(C R Dore) *t.k.h: hld up in tch: hdwy to trck ldrs 3f out: effrt on inner over 1f out: rdn to ld ins last: r.o wl* **7/1**

5110 **2** nk **Postmaster**[10] 742 5-8-6 **53** .... RobertHavlin 6 — 61+
(R Ingram) *hld up in last: hdwy 2f out: swtchd rt 1f out: r.o stongly fnl f: nt quite rch ldr* **13/2**[3]

1144 **3** 1¼ **Our Kes (IRE)**[14] 712 5-9-4 **65** .... PaulDoe 10 — 69
(P Howling) *in tch on outer: hdwy to trck ldrs over 2f out: led over 1f out: sn rdn: hdd ins last: no ex* **11/2**[2]

0665 **4** 1½ **Just Fly**[7] 793 7-8-0 **52** .... (v) KevinGhunowa(5) 3 — 53
(Dr J R J Naylor) *chsd ldr: rdn and upsides ldr over 2f out: no ex ins fnl f* **5/1**[1]

-212 **5** nk **Wodhill Gold**[69] 228 6-8-13 **60** .... (v) HayleyTurner 7 — 60
(D Morris) *chsd ldrs: rdn wl over 3f out: no prog over 1f out* **5/1**[1]

4060 **6** ½ **Beneking**[9] 750 7-8-10 **57** .... (p) MickyFenton 2 — 56
(D Burchell) *sn led: rdn wl over 2f out: hdd over 1f out: fdd fnl f* **15/2**

0603 **7** 1¾ **Moon Bird**[24] 650 5-8-9 **56** .... EddieAhern 11 — 55+
(C A Cyzer) *hld up in last pair: hdwy 3f out: n.m.r briefly over 2f out: pushed along and keeping on same pce whn nt clr run ins last* **11/2**[2]

-305 **8** 4 **Golden Alchemist**[28] 610 4-8-11 **58** .... IanMongan 1 — 44
(M D I Usher) *sn pushed along to chse ldrs on inner: rdn and lost pl 3f out: n.d after* **7/1**

0000 **9** 2½ **Atticus Trophies (IRE)**[9] 751 4-8-4 **54** oh6 ow3 .... (vt) JamesDoyle(3) 9 — 34
(Ms J S Doyle) *chsd ldrs on outer: rdn wl over 2f out: sn wknd* **40/1**

1m 38.05s (-1.38) **Going Correction** -0.05s/f (Stan) — **9** Ran SP% **116.6**
Speed ratings (Par 101):104,103,102,100,100 100,98,94,91
CSF £52.34 CT £272.49 TOTE £10.80: £2.80, £2.40, £1.80; EX 64.80.
Owner Page, Ward, Marsh **Bred** J P Villey **Trained** West Pinchbeck, Lincs
■ Stewards' Enquiry : Kevin Ghunowa two-day ban: careless riding (Apr 13-14)
Robert Havlin two-day ban: careless riding (Apr 13-14)

FOCUS
A modest handicap and something of a rough race, but the time was fair enough, 1.12 seconds quicker than the seller. Sound form.

889 DINE IN THE TRACKSIDE CARVERY H'CAP — 1m (P)
5:10 (5:11) (Class 5) (0-75,74) 3-Y-O — **£2,914** (£867; £433; £216) **Stalls** High

Form — RPR

-621 **1** **Alfresco**[17] 694 3-9-4 **74** .... (b) PaulEddery 2 — 82+
(Pat Eddery) *stdd s: hld up in last pair on inner:gd hdwy to chse ldr over 1f out: shkn up to ld ins last: in command after: comf* **2/1**[1]

6412 **2** ½ **Ballyshane Spirit (IRE)**[28] 624 3-7-13 **60** oh3 .... WilliamBuick(5) 5 — 64
(N A Callaghan) *t.k.h: chsd ldr: rdn to ld 2f out: hdd ins fnl f: kpt on but a hld* **4/1**[3]

034- **3** 2½ **Feolin**[175] 5859 3-9-0 **70** .... RobertHavlin 1 — 68
(H Morrison) *chsd ldng pair: rdn over 2f out: outpcd over 1f out: kpt on same pce* **8/1**

-323 **4** ½ **Blue Monkey (IRE)**[35] 565 3-9-3 **73** .... HayleyTurner 6 — 70
(M L W Bell) *hld up in tch: rdn and effrt over 2f out: outpcd over 1f out: kpt on same pce fnl f* **6/1**

360- **5** nk **Stagehand (IRE)**[178] 5783 3-9-3 **73** .... JimCrowley 3 — 69
(B R Millman) *t.k.h: led: rdn and hdd 2f out: wknd fnl f* **8/1**

4-61 **6** 1½ **Hucking Heat (IRE)**[10] 738 3-9-0 **70** .... GeorgeBaker 4 — 63
(J R Best) *stdd s: hld up in last pair: hdwy on outer 3f out: rdn wl over 1f out: wknd 1f out* **5/2**[2]

1m 40.62s (1.19) **Going Correction** -0.05s/f (Stan) — **6** Ran SP% **118.4**
Speed ratings (Par 98):92,91,89,88,88 86
CSF £11.20 TOTE £3.00: £1.30, £2.60; EX 13.80 Place 6 £46.52, Place 5 £8.27.
Owner Pat Eddery Racing (Caerleon) **Bred** Usk Valley Stud **Trained** Nether Winchendon, Bucks

FOCUS
Some progressive three-year-old handicappers on show, but this race was spoilt by a lack of early pace and the winning time was by far the slowest of the three races over the trip at the meeting. The form therefore is not rock solid.
T/Plt: £9.20 to a £1 stake. Pool: £47,928.15. 3,786.05 winning tickets. T/Qpdt: £5.80 to a £1 stake. Pool: £3,072.70. 386.00 winning tickets. SP

807 SOUTHWELL (L-H)
Monday, April 2

OFFICIAL GOING: All-weather - standard; turf course - good
Wind: Virtually nil

890 GOLF AND RACING AT SOUTHWELL MAIDEN AUCTION STKS — 5f (F)
2:30 (2:30) (Class 6) 2-Y-O — **£2,184** (£644; £322) **Stalls** High

Form — RPR

0 **1** **Baytown Blaze**[4] 814 2-8-4 .... ChrisCatlin 3 — 67
(P S McEntee) *mde most rdn wl over 1f out: kpt on fnl f* **5/1**[2]

2 2 **Ballycroy Boy (IRE)** 2-8-9 .... PaulHanagan 8 — 64
(A Bailey) *sn outpcd and bhd: swtchd rt to stands rail 1/2-way: gd hdwy over 1f out: styd on strly ins last: nrst fin* **8/1**

3 ¾ **Geoffdaw** 2-9-1 .... JamieSpencer 14 — 67
(M J Wallace) *dwlt: in tch stands side: effrt 2f out: sn rdn and kpt on ins last* **4/1**[1]

4 nk **Mystickhill (IRE)** 2-8-4 .... RobbieFitzpatrick 4 — 55
(T J Pitt) *trckd ldrs: hdwy to chse wnr 2f out: sn rdn and ch tl wknd ins last* **6/1**[3]

5 shd **Redbrick Girl** 2-8-7 .... CatherineGannon 6 — 57
(K A Ryan) *cl up: rdn along 2f out: grad wknd appr last* **8/1**

6 3 **Woodford Regen** 2-8-7 .... PaulMulrennan 9 — 45
(M W Easterby) *prom: rdn along 2f out: grad wknd* **13/2**

7 1 **Paddy Rielly (IRE)** 2-8-10 ow1 .... StephenDonohoe(3) 5 — 47
(P D Evans) *outpcd and bhd tl styd on fnl 2f* **20/1**

8 1 **Pequeno Dinero (IRE)** 2-7-11 .... KellyHarrison(7) 1 — 34
(C W Fairhurst) *in tch: rdn along 1/2-way: sn hung rt and wknd* **40/1**

9 ¾ **Ocean Transit (IRE)** 2-8-1 .... LiamJones(3) 7 — 31
(W G M Turner) *a rr* **14/1**

10 2½ **Border Defence (IRE)** 2-8-12 .... SimonWhitworth 12 — 29
(P A Blockley) *prom:rdn along 2f out: sn wknd* **16/1**

11 5 **Rope Bridge (IRE)** 2-8-12 .... DavidAllan 2 — 9
(T D Easterby) *chsd ldrs: rdn along and hung rt 1/2-way: sn wknd* **20/1**

12 ¾ **Bank On Bertie** 2-8-12 .... DaleGibson 13 — 6
(M W Easterby) *in tch:rdn along and outpcd 1/2-way: sn bhd* **14/1**

13 7 **Stevie Smurnoff** 2-8-5 .... NSLawes(7) 11 — —
(M W Easterby) *s.i.s: a bhd* **66/1**

61.95 secs (1.65) **Going Correction** 0.0s/f (Stan) — **13** Ran SP% **119.2**
Speed ratings (Par 90):86,82,81,81,80 76,74,72,71,67 59,58,47
CSF £42.80 TOTE £8.20: £1.90, £3.70, £1.60; EX 66.20 TRIFECTA Not won..
Owner Eventmaker Racehorses **Bred** Ms Clare Sharp **Trained** Newmarket, Suffolk

FOCUS
This juvenile maiden will most likely prove just moderate as the season develops. Few got into it from off the pace. The winner is assessed as improving by 5lb on her debut effort.

NOTEBOOK
Baytown Blaze, seventh at Lingfield on her debut four days previously, put that previous experience to good use and got off the mark in fairly ready fashion. She also had the benefit of a low draw here, but handled the deeper surface without fuss (dam was a winner on Fibresand for this yard) and this April foal is clearly well forward for the time of year. Her trainer later indicated he has earmarked the Queen Mary in June for his filly, but that should really be regarded as overly ambitious. (op 9-2)
Ballycroy Boy(IRE), a half-brother to four winners at up to a mile, took time to find his full stride and was doing some good late work towards the finish. He should learn a deal from this debut experience, but will probably want at least another furlong in due course. (op 14-1 tchd 16-1)
Geoffdaw ◆, whose trainer took this last year with Chief Editor, is a half-brother to most notably his yard's Espartarno, who won his first two races last term and went off favourite for the Windsor Castle at Royal Ascot. He did not help his cause with a sluggish start and then by running distinctly green, but showed his worth late on by staying on in good fashion. It should also be noted he was not aided by a double-figure draw and he appears the one to take from the race with the immediate future in mind. (tchd 9-2)
Mystickhill(IRE), half-sister to a juvenile winner over this trip, knew her job for this racecourse debut and had her chance. Her yard is just struggling for winners at present and her sire does not have a great record on this surface, so she could be capable of better with experience under her belt when switching to the turf. (op 9-2)
Redbrick Girl, who pedigree on the dam's side suggests she will appreciate a stiffer test in due course, showed up nicely enough on her debut and is entitled to come on for the outing. (tchd 17-2)
Woodford Regen, from a yard with a decent record in this event, was very well backed throughout the day at bigger prices and was evidently expected to go well on her debut. She had to be rousted along from the start, and her fate was sealed from halfway, but she still showed signs of ability. Another furlong will be to her liking in due course and she does have a bit of scope. (op 15-2 tchd 6-1)

891 BOOK TICKETS ON-LINE AMATEUR RIDERS' CLAIMING STKS — 1m 4f
3:00 (3:00) (Class 6) 4-Y-0+ — **£2,109** (£648; £324) **Stalls** Low

Form — RPR
422- **1** **Court Of Appeal**[170] [5955] 10-10-11 68....................(tp) MissLEllison 11 — 72
(B Ellison) *a.p: led 1/2-way: rdn along 2f out: drvn ent last: edgd rt and hld on gamely* **13/2**[2]
515- **2** *shd* **Nero's Return (IRE)**[198] [5367] 6-11-3 82.............................. MrWHogg 6 — 78
(M Johnston) *prom: hdwy over 2f out: rdn to chal over 1f out and ev ch tl drvn and edgd lft ins last: no ex towards fin* **10/11**[1]
-626 **3** *6* **Regency Red (IRE)**[9] [767] 9-10-5 55.................. MrBenBrisbourne(5) 1 — 61
(W M Brisbourne) *hld up in rr: hdwy on inner over 3f out: swtchd rt and rdn wl over 1f out: styd on ins last: nrst fin* **18/1**
/53- **4** *1 1/2* **Supa Tramp**[31] [1216] 4-10-5 63.................................. MrDHutchison(3) 4 — 58
(G L Moore) *chsd ldrs: rdn along 4f out: drvn over 2f out and kpt on same pce* **8/1**[3]
3060 **5** *3/4* **Finished Article (IRE)**[7] [792] 10-10-7 50..................(bt[1]) MrSWalker 10 — 54
(K J Burke) *keen: prom: effrt 3f out: rdn along and ev ch 2f out: sn wknd* **20/1**
45-3 **6** *nk* **Tedstale (USA)**[11] [730] 9-10-8 67................................(b) MissARyan(5) 3 — 60
(K A Ryan) *dwlt and towards rr: hdwy over 4f out: rdn to chse ldrs 3f out: drvn and one pce fnl 2f* **10/1**
40-0 **7** *2 1/2* **Migration**[58] [220] 11-10-13 53.. MrsMMorris 5 — 56
(Mrs S Lamyman) *hld up in rr: hdwy on outer to chse ldrs 4f out: rdn along 3f out and sn wknd* **16/1**
00-0 **8** *3* **Scotty's Future (IRE)**[28] [617] 9-10-13 46....................... MrsCBartley 2 — 51
(A Berry) *bhd til sme late hdwy* **50/1**
1U-0 **9** *nk* **Bid For Fame (USA)**[28] [618] 10-11-0 65....................... MrSPearce(3) 7 — 55
(J Pearce) *a rr* **28/1**
010- **10** *5* **Lewis Island (IRE)**[4] [1931] 8-10-6 65........................ MrPCollington(5) 8 — 41
(K J Burke) *chsd ldrs: rdn along over 5f out and sn wknd* **11/1**
000/ **11** *15* **Just A Gigolo**[1403] [1955] 7-10-8 40...................(tp) MissLHaagensen(5) 9 — 19
(P D Niven) *led: hdd 1/2-way: rdn along over 4f out and sn wknd* **125/1**

2m 42.66s (2.36) **Going Correction** -0.10s/f (Good)
WFA 4 from 6yo+ 1lb — **11** Ran SP% **116.4**
Speed ratings (Par 101):88,87,83,82,82 82,80,78,78,75 65
CSF £12.24 TOTE £6.50: £1.90, £1.10, £4.40; EX 17.70 Trifecta £255.10 Part won. Pool: £359.33 - 0.78 winning units..Nero's Return was claimed by G. L. Moore for £10,000.
Owner Spring Cottage Syndicate No 2 **Bred** John And Susan Davis **Trained** Norton, N Yorks
FOCUS
A modest claimer, confined to amateur riders, which saw the two best in at the weights dominate. The runner-up was 10lb below last year's form.
Supa Tramp Official explanation: vet said gelding finished distressed

892 HOSPITALITY PACKAGES AVAILABLE H'CAP — 5f (F)
3:30 (3:30) (Class 6) (0-60,58) 4-Y-0+ — **£2,388** (£705; £352) **Stalls** High

Form — RPR
00-0 **1** **Whinhill House**[20] [668] 7-9-0 54...................(v) PatCosgrave 5 — 69
(D W Barker) *wnt rt s: mde all: rdn wl over 1f out: drvn and styd on wl fnl f* **20/1**
5430 **2** *1 1/2* **Dysonic (USA)**[11] [729] 5-8-9 49.....................................(v) DavidAllan 9 — 58
(J Balding) *trckd ldrs: hdwy to chse wnr 2f out: sn rdn and ev ch tl drvn and nt qckn ins last* **5/1**[1]
4631 **3** *3 1/2* **Triskaidekaphobia**[10] [746] 4-9-4 58.........................(t) DarryllHolland 11 — 55
(Miss J R Tooth) *a.p: rdn along 2f out: drvn and grad wknd appr last* **6/1**[2]
6233 **4** *nk* **Favouring (IRE)**[11] [729] 5-8-4 49....................(b) RussellKennemore(5) 8 — 45
(M C Chapman) *hmpd s and towards rr: hdwy 2f out: sn rdn and kpt on wl fnl f: nrst fin* **6/1**[2]
2615 **5** *1 1/4* **Primarily**[6] [797] 5-8-8 48... RobbieFitzpatrick 1 — 39
(Peter Grayson) *in tch on far side: rdn along 2f out: snd riven and kpt on same pce* **5/1**[1]
014 **6** *1/2* **Spirit Of Coniston**[20] [668] 4-8-3 48....................(b) DuranFentiman(5) 10 — 37
(C J Teague) *prominet: rdn along 2f out: sn drvn and wknd over 1f out* **16/1**
500- **7** *hd* **Gone'N'Dunnett (IRE)**[103] [6877] 8-8-12 52.......................(v) ChrisCatlin 4 — 40
(Mrs C A Dunnett) *in tch towards far side: rdn along 2f out: one pce fnl* **16/1**
125- **8** *1 3/4* **Dazzler Mac**[221] [4735] 6-8-9 56.............................. SuzzanneFrance(7) 12 — 38
(N Bycroft) *bhd til sme late hdwy* **14/1**
300- **9** *3* **Throw The Dice**[150] [6315] 5-9-4 58..............................(p) PaulHanagan 7 — 29+
(D W Barker) *badly hmpd s: a rr* **12/1**
0000 **10** *shd* **Mystery Pips**[18] [680] 7-8-10 50.......................................(v) KimTinkler 6 — 21
(N Tinkler) *hmpd s and a towards rr* **50/1**
464- **11** *1 3/4* **Compton Plume**[194] [5487] 7-9-4 58................................ DaleGibson 2 — 23
(M W Easterby) *chsd ldrs towards far side: rdn along 1/2-way: sn wknd* **20/1**
-354 **12** *nk* **Optical Seclusion (IRE)**[51] [421] 4-8-7 50...........(b) SaleemGolam(3) 13 — 14
(T J Etherington) *chsd ldrs: rdn along 1/2-way and sn wknd* **33/1**
1060 **13** *1* **Orchestration (IRE)**[17] [690] 6-8-5 48........................(v) DominicFox(3) 3 — 8
(K J Burke) *in tch far side: rdn along 1/2-way: sn outpcd* **16/1**
6233 **14** *3 1/2* **Thoughtsofstardom**[10] [746] 4-8-12 52.................(be) JamieSpencer 14 — —
(P S McEntee) *in tch towards stands side: rdn along 1/2-way: sn wandered and wknd* **17/2**[3]

59.58 secs (-0.72) **Going Correction** 0.0s/f (Stan) — **14** Ran SP% **118.9**
Speed ratings (Par 101):105,102,97,96,94 93,93,90,85,85 82,82,80,75
CSF £112.06 CT £710.80 TOTE £22.30: £7.40, £2.00, £2.20; EX 192.90 TRIFECTA Not won..
Owner D W Barker **Bred** W R And Mrs Arblaster **Trained** Scorton, N Yorks
FOCUS
A typical sprint for the class. Solid form, rated through the runner-up, with the winner taking advantage of a reduced mark.
Thoughtsofstardom Official explanation: jockey said gelding resented the kickback

893 DINE IN THE QUEEN MOTHER RESTAURANT H'CAP — 1m 3f
4:00 (4:00) (Class 6) (0-60,64) 3-Y-O — **£2,388** (£705; £352) **Stalls** Low

Form — RPR
06-1 **1** **Dan Tucker**[7] [791] 3-9-8 64 6ex.. JamieSpencer 7 — 72+
(B J Meehan) *hld up in rr: hdwy 4f out: rdn to chal on outer over 1f out: drvn to led and edgd lft jst ins last: kpt on* **8/11**[1]
3342 **2** *1 1/2* **Skye But N Ben**[19] [676] 3-8-8 50...............................(b) PaulFessey 12 — 55
(T D Barron) *trckd ldrs: hdwy 4f out: led 3f out: rdn wl over 1f out: drvn: edgd rt and hdd jst ins last: kpt on same pce* **8/1**[2]
4-50 **3** *1 1/4* **Featherlight**[34] [572] 3-8-3 48.......................................(b) LiamJones(3) 3 — 51
(J Jay) *trckd ldrs: hdwy 4f out: rdn along and ev ch 2f out: sn rdn and wkng whn n.m.r ent last* **20/1**
660- **4** *3/4* **Bollin Felix**[188] [5597] 3-8-11 53... DavidAllan 2 — 55
(T D Easterby) *in tch: hdwy to chse ldrs over 3f out: rdn wl over 2f out: kpt on u.p appr last* **8/1**[2]
600 **5** *hd* **David's Cavalier**[9] [769] 3-8-8 55................. RussellKennemore(5) 14 — 56
(R Hollinshead) *hld up and bhd: hdwy over 3f out: rdn over 2f out: kpt on u.p fnl f: nrst fin* **66/1**
3334 **6** *1 1/4* **Gold Response**[56] [370] 3-8-13 55............................. DeanMcKeown 13 — 54
(D Shaw) *stdd s: hld up and bhd: hdwy 3f out: swtchd lft and rdn wl over 1f out: kpt on ins last: nrst fin* **16/1**
5-64 **7** *1/2* **Green Day Packer (IRE)**[11] [731] 3-8-10 59............... HaddenFrost(7) 9 — 57
(P C Haslam) *keen: chsd ldrs: rdn along 3f out: wknd fnl 2f* **16/1**
6-00 **8** *3/4* **Roca Redonda (IRE)**[56] [357] 3-9-0 59.................. JerryO'Dwyer(3) 10 — 56
(V Smith) *bhd tl styd on fnl 3f* **50/1**
0513 **9** *1/2* **Muree Queen**[14] [708] 3-8-10 52.............................. EdwardCreighton 4 — 48
(Miss J S Davis) *chsd ldrs: rdn along over 3f out: drvn and wknd over 2f out* **25/1**
400- **10** *2* **Private Peachey (IRE)**[229] [4480] 3-8-13 55............... GrahamGibbons 5 — 48
(B R Millman) *cl up: led 1/2-way: rdn along and hdd 3f out: wknd over 2f out* **40/1**
0-56 **11** *3 1/2* **Intensifier (IRE)**[62] [304] 3-9-3 59.. TPO'Shea 8 — 46
(P A Blockley) *a towards rr* **16/1**
4415 **12** *2 1/2* **My Sara**[46] [469] 3-9-4 60..(v) PaulHanagan 11 — 43
(R A Fahey) *a rr* **10/1**[3]
046- **13** *2 1/2* **Miss Havisham (IRE)**[193] [5491] 3-8-6 48.................... PaulMulrennan 1 — 26
(J R Weymes) *led to 1/2-way: rdn along and wknd over 4f out* **66/1**

2m 28.33s (0.33) **Going Correction** -0.10s/f (Good) — **13** Ran SP% **122.9**
Speed ratings (Par 96):94,92,92,91,91 90,90,89,89,87 85,83,81
CSF £6.66 CT £73.63 TOTE £1.70: £1.10, £2.10, £4.20; EX 10.30 Trifecta £103.40 Pool: £432.65 - 2.97 winning units..
Owner Favourites Racing XXVI **Bred** N And Mrs N Nugent **Trained** Manton, Wilts
FOCUS
A weak three-year-old handicap, run at a modest pace. The winner did not have to improve on his Kempton form but should continue to progress.
My Sara Official explanation: trainer had no explanation for the poor form shown
Miss Havisham(IRE) Official explanation: jockey said bit slipped

894 SOUTHWELL-RACECOURSE.CO.UK H'CAP — 6f
4:30 (4:31) (Class 6) (0-60,60) 3-Y-O — **£2,388** (£705; £352) **Stalls** Low

Form — RPR
36-3 **1** **Mandurah (IRE)**[19] [679] 3-8-11 53............................. AdrianTNicholls 8 — 55
(D Nicholls) *mde all: rdn wl over 1f out: drvn ins last and kpt on gamely* **11/4**[1]
4-32 **2** *nk* **Ellablue**[40] [511] 3-9-4 60.. ChrisCatlin 10 — 62
(Rae Guest) *cl up: rdn and ev ch over 1f out tl drvn ins last and no ex last 50 ydss* **8/1**[3]
260- **3** *1 1/2* **Almora Guru**[203] [5238] 3-9-3 59.. DavidAllan 14 — 56
(W M Brisbourne) *chsd leaders tl lost pl and trdn along 1/2-way: hdwy wl over 1f out: styd on strly ins last: nrst fin* **40/1**
6-46 **4** *hd* **Suntan Lady (IRE)**[85] [65] 3-8-7 49......................... EdwardCreighton 9 — 45
(Miss V Haigh) *in tch on inner: hdwy 2f out: rdn and ev ch 1f out: drvn and one pce ins last* **22/1**
435- **5** *1/2* **Princess Ellis**[170] [5956] 3-8-12 57......................... StephenDonohoe(3) 13 — 52
(E J Alston) *cl up: rdn 2f out and ev ch tl drvn and wknd ent last* **11/1**
50-0 **6** *nk* **Esteemed Prince**[14] [711] 3-8-8 50...........................(e) DeanMcKeown 1 — 44
(D Shaw) *s.i.s and bhd on inner: hdwy 2f out: sn rdn and kpt on ins last: nrst fin* **40/1**
0-00 **7** *hd* **Chingford (IRE)**[34] [577] 3-8-11 53................................ NickyMackay 3 — 46
(J G Portman) *chsd ldrs: rdn along 2f out: drvn and wknd appr last* **10/1**
2030 **8** *1* **Priceless Melody (USA)**[7] [786] 3-8-8 50...............(b) DarryllHolland 12 — 40
(Mrs A J Perrett) *chsd ldrs: rdn along over 2f out: sn one pce* **10/1**
040- **9** *3/4* **Tomorrow's Dancer**[157] [6200] 3-8-13 55..................... JamieSpencer 11 — 43
(K A Ryan) *s.i.s and bhd tl sme late hdwy* **7/2**[2]
550- **10** *3/4* **Peggys Flower**[195] [5448] 3-9-3 59.. PatCosgrave 2 — 45
(M Wigham) *chsd ldrs: rdn over 2f out: grad wknd* **25/1**
006 **11** *3* **Fareham Creek**[34] [574] 3-8-8 50... TPQueally 6 — 27
(D K Ivory) *a towards rr* **50/1**
-465 **12** *1/2* **Glen Avon Girl (IRE)**[52] [404] 3-8-9 56.................... DuranFentiman(5) 5 — 31
(T D Easterby) *s.i.s: a rr* **14/1**
440 **13** *1/2* **Cap St Jean (IRE)**[48] [449] 3-9-2 58.................................... LeeEnstone 7 — 32
(P C Haslam) *a rr* **12/1**
40-0 **14** *1 1/4* **Clewer**[7] [791] 3-9-2 58..(p) TPO'Shea 4 — 28
(P A Blockley) *chsd ldrs: rdn along 1/2-way: sn wknd* **16/1**

1m 15.95s (-0.15) **Going Correction** -0.10s/f (Good) — **14** Ran SP% **121.8**
Speed ratings (Par 96):97,96,94,94,93 93,93,91,90,89 85,85,84,82
CSF £23.99 CT £762.94 TOTE £3.80: £1.60, £1.80, £14.90; EX 27.10 Trifecta £274.60 Part won. Pool: £386.79 - 0.68 winning units..
Owner Martin Hignett **Bred** Michael Lyons **Trained** Sessay, N Yorks
FOCUS
A moderate three-year-old sprint. There did not seem to be any real draw bias. The bare form looks pretty modest, rated through the third and fourth, with the winner not needing to improve on his Wolverhampton form.

Tomorrow's Dancer Official explanation: jockey said gelding was unsuited by the good ground

895 BUY ANNUAL MEMBERSHIP H'CAP 7f
5:00 (5:00) (Class 5) (0-70,68) 4-Y-0+ **£3,071** (£906; £453) **Stalls** Low

Form RPR
6421 **1** **Dudley Docker (IRE)**^{38} [533] 5-8-12 **62**.............................. TPQueally 3 70
(C R Dore) *hld up towards rr: hdwy 2f out: swtchd lft and qcknd to ld appr last: sn rdn and edgd lft: kpt on wl* **9/2**[1]

002- **2** 1/2 **Musicmaestroplease (IRE)**^{146} [6387] 4-8-7 **60**........... DominicFox(3) 2 67
(S Parr) *hld up towards rr: gd hdwy on inner 2f out: rdn over 1f out: chal ins last: kpt on u.p* **8/1**

1513 **3** 3/4 **Parkview Love (USA)**^{8} [773] 6-8-13 **63**..................(v) DeanMcKeown 1 68
(D Shaw) *trckd ldrs: effrt 2f out: sn rdn and kpt on u.p fnl f* **9/2**[1]

0002 **4** 1/2 **Aperitif**^{13} [718] 6-9-2 **66**.................................... AdrianTNicholls 6 70
(D Nicholls) *a.p:effrt and ev ch 2f out: sn rdn and one pce ent last* **9/1**

1151 **5** 1/2 **Louisiade (IRE)**^{13} [718] 6-8-13 **63**...........................(p) JamieSpencer 11 65
(K A Ryan) *hld up in tch: gd hdwy on outer over 2f out: ev ch over 1f out: sn rdn and one pce ent last* **5/1**[2]

0140 **6** *nk* **H Harrison (IRE)**^{7} [793] 7-9-0 **67**............................ AndrewElliott(3) 9 69
(I W McInnes) *chsd ldrs: rdn along on inner 2f out: sn drvn and kpt on same pce* **16/1**

024- **7** 1/2 **Petite Mac**^{187} [5620] 7-8-7 **64**............................ SuzzanneFrance(7) 7 64
(N Bycroft) *towards rr tl styd on fnl 2f* **33/1**

060- **8** *shd* **Corrib (IRE)**^{122} [6664] 4-9-4 **68**.................................... TonyCulhane 10 68
(B Palling) *rr and rdn along 1/2-way: sn rdn and kpt on u.p fnl 2f: nrst fin* **33/1**

0310 **9** 1/2 **Cerebus**^{12} [724] 5-8-13 **66**.................................(bt) StephenDonohoe(3) 12 65
(A J McCabe) *prom: rdn to ld wl over 1f out: drvn and hdd appr last: sn wknd* **9/1**

-011 **10** *5* **Island Green (USA)**^{11} [729] 4-8-10 **60**...................... DanielTudhope 13 46
(D Carroll) *a towards rr* **13/2**[3]

46-0 **11** *3* **Falmassim**^{13} [717] 4-9-2 **66**.. PaulMulrennan 8 44
(Miss J A Camacho) *led: rdn along over 2f out: hdd wl over 1f out and sn wknd* **50/1**

26-0 **12** 2 1/2 **Sentiero Rosso (USA)**^{76} [151] 5-9-2 **66**......................(tp) TomEaves 4 38
(B Ellison) *s.i.s: a rr* **12/1**

-000 **13** *12* **Polonius**^{9} [770] 6-8-7 **60**...(b[1]) NeilChalmers(3) 5 —
(G J Smith) *cl up: rdn along over 2f out: drvn wl over 1f out and sn wknd* **100/1**

1m 28.04s (-1.16) **Going Correction** -0.10s/f (Good) **13** Ran SP% **119.9**
Speed ratings (Par 103):102,101,100,100,99 99,98,98,97,92 88,85,72
CSF £39.95 CT £153.44 TOTE £7.10: £1.90, £2.00, £2.00; EX 69.10 Trifecta £372.90 Part won. Pool: £525.31 - 0.34 winning units..
Owner Sean J Murphy **Bred** Nuri Fuat Basak **Trained** West Pinchbeck, Lincs
■ Stewards' Enquiry : Adrian T Nicholls two-day ban: careless riding (Apr 13-14)

FOCUS
An open affair and any number was still in with a chance racing inside the final furlong. The form is modest but solid, and should prove reliable.

896 ON THE TURF ON THE 24TH H'CAP 6f
5:30 (5:31) (Class 6) (0-60,60) 4-Y-0+ **£2,388** (£705; £352) **Stalls** Low

Form RPR
050- **1** **Maison Dieu**^{197} [5401] 4-8-11 **56**......................... StephenDonohoe(3) 12 68
(E J Alston) *hld up and bhd: gd hdwy 2f out: rdn ent last: styd on to ld last 50 yds* **22/1**

-052 **2** *hd* **Bodden Bay**^{10} [743] 5-8-13 **55**...................................... DanielTudhope 6 66
(I W McInnes) *cl up: rdn to ld over 1f out:d riven and edgd lft ins last: hdd last 50 yds: kpt on* **7/1**

12-3 **3** 2 1/2 **Vegas Boys**^{86} [50] 4-9-4 **60**.. JamieMackay 5 64
(M Wigham) *hld up in midfield: hdwy 2f out: swtchd lft wl over 1f out: sn rdn and chsd ldrs ent last: kpt on same pce* **7/2**[1]

000- **4** *shd* **Rainbow Bay**^{145} [6399] 4-9-4 **60**..................................(b) ChrisCatlin 3 63
(E J O'Neill) *dwlt and towards rr: hdwy on inner over 2f out: rdn to chse ldrs over 1f out: kpt on same pce ins last* **14/1**

-240 **5** *shd* **Brut**^{20} [668] 5-8-13 **55**.. TonyHamilton 2 58
(D W Barker) *led: rdn over 2f out: drvn and hdd over 1f out: wknd ins last* **16/1**

064 **6** 3 1/2 **Winthorpe (IRE)**^{13} [717] 7-9-2 **58**..........................(p) GrahamGibbons 9 50
(J J Quinn) *in tch: hdwy to chse ldrs 2f out: sn rdn and kpt on same pce* **5/1**[3]

000- **7** 1/2 **Dunn Deal (IRE)**^{217} [4894] 7-9-1 **60**.............................. LiamJones(3) 1 51
(W M Brisbourne) *chsd ldrs on inner: rdn along over 2f out: grad wknd appr fnl f* **33/1**

3144 **8** 1/2 **Desert Light (IRE)**^{10} [743] 6-9-0 **56**.........................(v) DeanMcKeown 4 45
(D Shaw) *hld up: hdwy 2f out: sn rdn and no imp appr last* **25/1**

3452 **9** 3/4 **Monte Major (IRE)**^{10} [746] 6-9-1 **57**..........................(v) AdamKirby 13 44
(D Shaw) *dwlt: sn chsng ldrs on outer: rdn along wl over 2f out and sn wknd* **20/1**

2411 **10** *nk* **Soba Jones**^{14} [710] 10-8-12 **57**.............................. JasonEdmunds(3) 10 43
(J Balding) *chsd ldrs: rdn along wl over 2f out and sn wknd* **12/1**

056- **11** *hd* **Whitbarrow (IRE)**^{158} [6193] 8-8-11 **58** ow3.............. JamesMillman(5) 8 44
(B R Millman) *cl up: rdn along wl over 2f out: sn wknd* **16/1**

-123 **12** *shd* **Owed**^{13} [718] 5-9-2 **58**..(t) SebSanders 7 43
(R Bastiman) *cl up: rdn along over 2f out: sn wknd* **4/1**[2]

35-4 **13** *4* **Middle Eastern**^{18} [681] 5-8-13 **55**.................................... TPO'Shea 14 28
(P A Blockley) *a towards rr* **9/1**

520- **14** *7* **Mannello**^{213} [4985] 4-9-1 **57**.. TonyCulhane 11 9
(B Palling) *a rr* **66/1**

1m 14.68s (-1.42) **Going Correction** -0.10s/f (Good) **14** Ran SP% **124.9**
Speed ratings (Par 101):105,104,101,101,101 96,95,95,94,93 93,93,88,78
CSF £167.49 CT £709.31 TOTE £24.40: £6.30, £3.60, £1.50; EX 293.10 Trifecta £434.40 Part won. Pool: £611.91 - 0.50 winning units. Place 6 £16.53, Place 5 £8.63.
Owner Whitehills Racing Syndicate **Bred** Andy Miller **Trained** Longton, Lancs

FOCUS
A competitive sprint handicap. The time was the pick of the turf races and the form looks solid, rated through the runner-up. The race could work out well.
Soba Jones Official explanation: jockey said gelding was unsuited by the good ground
Owed Official explanation: jockey said gelding had no more to give
Middle Eastern Official explanation: jockey said gelding was never travelling
T/Plt: £16.20 to a £1 stake. Pool: £50,569.75. 2,271.50 winning tickets. T/Qpdt: £8.00 to a £1 stake. Pool: £3,633.70. 332.40 winning tickets. JR

748 SAINT-CLOUD (L-H)
Monday, April 2

OFFICIAL GOING: Heavy

897a PRIX EDMOND BLANC (GROUP 3) 1m
2:50 (2:53) 4-Y-0+ **£27,027** (£10,811; £8,108; £5,405; £2,703)

RPR
1 **Racinger (FR)**^{218} [4862] 4-8-12 .... DBonilla 9 116
(F Head, France) *made all, brought field wide entering straight, reached outside hedge over 1f out, soon ridden, driven out* **79/10**

2 *nk* **Turtle Bowl (IRE)**^{22} 5-8-12 .... DBoeuf 10 116
(F Rohaut, France) *racd in 5th, brought wd and reached outside headge 1 1/2f out, sn hrd rdn, stayed on to tk 2nd 100yds out, nrst fin* **24/10**[1]

3 3/4 **Passager (FR)**^{155} [6250] 4-9-0 .... C-PLemaire 2 116
(Mme C Head-Maarek, France) *tracked winner in 2nd, ridden 1f out, kept on but lost 2nd 100 yards out* **6/1**

4 *3* **Kavafi (IRE)**^{16} [706] 5-8-12 .... MBlancpain 3 107
(C Laffon-Parias, France) *raced in 4th, effort and outpaced by first three from 1 1/2f out* **53/10**[3]

5 1 1/2 **Gwenseb (FR)**^{155} [6250] 4-8-9 .... OPeslier 4 101
(C Laffon-Parias, France) *raced in 6th, oushed along towards inside 2 1/2f out, kept on same pace* **10/1**

6 3/4 **Valentino (FR)**^{16} [706] 8-8-12 .... CSoumillon 5 102
(A De Royer-Dupre, France) *missed break, last to over 1 1/2f out, never a factor* **33/10**[2]

7 *shd* **Major Grace (FR)**^{16} [706] 4-8-12 .... ACrastus 8 102
(Y De Nicolay, France) *raced in 7th, never a factor* **20/1**

8 *3* **Wiesenpfad (FR)**^{134} [6529] 4-9-0 .... JVictoire 7 97
(W Hickst, Germany) *close up in 3rd, weakened 1 1/2f out* **13/2**

1m 43.6s (-3.90) **8** Ran SP% **121.2**
PARI-MUTUEL: WIN 8.90; PL 2.70, 1.60, 2.20; DF 14.90.
Owner P Goral **Bred** Mme Rene Geffroy **Trained** France

NOTEBOOK
Racinger(FR) took control from the start and was given a highly professional ride. He quickened things up a furlong and a half out and drifted gradually across to the stands' rail before holding off the runner-up. Considered very unlucky last season, this was only his second career victory. He may well travel to the Far East next time out as both the QEII in Hong Kong and the Singapore Cup are being considered, as well as the Muguet.
Turtle Bowl(IRE), who looked extremely well in the paddock, moved away from the rail as the winner drifted towards it a furlong and half out. There was no serious interference, though, and he found a way between the winner and the third to close up well at the finish. He definitely looks like a horse that will appreciate a longer trip. He also has the Far East options, in addition to the Muguet over this course and distance.
Passager(FR) put up a good performance considering that he was giving a kilo to the winner and runner-up and was only beaten a total of a length. He followed the winner for much of the race and stuck to his task until the bitter end, only being run out of second place inside the final furlong. He probably needed the outing to bring him to his best and his trainer is now looking at the Muguet and the Lockinge Stakes.
Kavafi(IRE), who settled in fourth place, had every chance on entering the straight, but he could only run on one-paced throughout the final two furlongs and gradually dropped out of contention. He is possibly not quite in this league.

FOLKESTONE (R-H)
Tuesday, April 3

OFFICIAL GOING: Good
Wind: Strong, across Weather: Overcast

898 EUROPEAN BREEDERS' FUND MAIDEN STKS 5f
2:20 (2:20) (Class 5) 2-Y-O **£3,562** (£1,059; £529; £264) **Stalls** Low

Form RPR
1 **Nikindi (IRE)** 2-9-3 .... JohnEgan 5 77+
(J S Moore) *trckd ldng pair: effrt to ld jst over 1f out: rdn and styd on wl* **7/2**[2]

2 3/4 **Silver Guest** 2-9-3 .... SamHitchcott 1 76+
(M R Channon) *dwlt: rcvrd to chse ldrs after 2f: swtchd rt and effrt over 1f out: drvn to press wnr ins fnl f: kpt on* **2/1**[1]

3 1 3/4 **Fox's Den** 2-9-3 .... SebSanders 4 67
(R M Beckett) *trckd ldng pair: cl up over 1f out: shkn up and nt qckn jst ins fnl f: kpt on same pce* **8/1**

4 *nk* **Sauze D'Oulx** 2-8-12 .... JamesMillman(5) 6 66
(B R Millman) *uns rdr gng out on to crse: chsd ldrs on outer: rdn and green 2f out: kpt on* **25/1**

5 1/2 **Cee Bargara** 2-9-3 .... ShaneKelly 3 64
(J A Osborne) *mde most to jst over 1f out: grad fdd* **7/1**

6 2 1/2 **Shepherds Warning (IRE)** 2-8-9 .... StephenDonohoe(3) 9 49
(P D Evans) *dwlt: rn green: outpcd and wl bhd: styd on fr over 1f out: nvr nrr* **33/1**

7 *nk* **Non Sucre (USA)** 2-9-3 .... SimonWhitworth 2 53
(P A Blockley) *wnt rt s: w ldr to 2f out: wknd fnl f* **14/1**

8 *2* **Sirjoshua Reynolds** 2-9-3 .... JimmyFortune 10 45
(N A Callaghan) *wnt rt s: rn green and sn bdly outpcd: nvr on terms* **4/1**[3]

9 *6* **Korcula** 2-9-3 .... DaneO'Neill 8 21
(M J Wallace) *s.s: rcvrd to chse ldrs over 3f out: sing to weaken whn stmbld wl over 1f out* **25/1**

10 *4* **Portway Lane** 2-8-5 .... JackDean(7) 11 —
(W G M Turner) *s.s: sn t.o* **25/1**

61.26 secs (0.46) **Going Correction** -0.025s/f (Good) **10** Ran SP% **120.3**
Speed ratings (Par 92):95,93,91,90,89 85,85,82,72,66
CSF £10.81 TOTE £3.90: £1.40, £1.10, £2.40; EX 10.30 Trifecta £38.30 Pool: £336.84 - 6.24 winning units..
Owner J Wells, R S S Ambrose & H Wilson **Bred** Frank Barry **Trained** Upper Lambourn, Berks

FOCUS
A modest juvenile maiden which was run at a fair pace. The field stayed stands' side. The principals were not given hard races and the race has been rated on the positive side. The form should work out.

NOTEBOOK

Nikindi(IRE), who cost 11,000euros and is bred to make his mark early on, got his career off to a perfect start and justified strong market support in the process. He clearly knew his job as he was handy throughout and, as he looked to be idling somewhat when in front entering the final furlong, he certainly had a little up his sleeve at the finish. Evidently well regarded by his trainer, he should come on a fair bit fitness-wise for this and already has the valuable Tattersalls Sales race at the Curragh in August as his big target this term - it should be noted the stable saddled Southandwest to finish second in that event last year. (op 7-1 tchd 3-1)

Silver Guest ◆, a 42,000gns half-brother to most notably Agigolo, who was a smart 5-6f winner for this yard in 2005, forfeited his rails draw by making a very sluggish start and was then always playing catch up. He ran on well when the penny dropped from halfway and clearly has ability, so should be able to pick up something similar in the coming weeks now he has this debut experience under his belt. (op 6-4 tchd 11-8 and 9-4)

Fox's Den, a cheap purchase whose dam was a dual 5f winner on easy ground at two, did nothing wrong on his debut and left the impression he would benefit from the run. He lacks scope, but can be placed to advantage on this evidence. (op 12-1)

Sauze D'Oulx, still to reach his second birthday, unshipped his rider going out onto the course and is clearly still somewhat headstrong. However, he did show ability in the race itself, and was not given too hard a time late on, so can be expected to step up on this effort in due course.

Cee Bargara, whose stable were off the mark with their first juvenile runner at Lingfield recently, cost 30,000gns as foal and is out of a dam whose progeny to have raced have all been successful to date. He broke smartly and held every chance, before tiring at the business end of the race. (op 11-2 tchd 8-1)

Shepherds Warning(IRE), whose pedigree suggests a mix of speed and stamina, looked clueless through the early parts yet stayed on well enough when the penny dropped from halfway. She can be expected to prove a deal sharper next time.

Sirjoshua Reynolds, at 60,000gns the most expensive of these at the sales, broke well enough yet showed an awkward head carriage when restrained through the early parts and thus got himself badly outpaced. He is entitled to come on for this debut experience, but may just be one to have reservations about in the short term. (tchd 9-2)

899 BURTON AND BRADBEER MEDIAN AUCTION MAIDEN STKS — 6f

2:55 (2:55) (Class 5) 3-Y-O — **£2,914** (£867; £433; £216) **Stalls** Low

Form — RPR

62- **1** **Genki (IRE)**^{169} 6015 3-9-3 .... SteveDrowne 6 — 79+
(R Charlton) *dwlt: hld up in tch: stdy prog on outer over 2f out: led over 1f out: rdn and styd on wl* **9/4**^{2}

00- **2** *1 ¼* **Welsh Auction**^{186} 5645 3-9-0 .... EmmettStack$^{(3)}$ 1 — 73
(G A Huffer) *racd against nr side rail: disp ld tl narrow advantage after 2f: edgd rt and hdd over 1f out: one pce fnl f* **25/1**

3- **3** *1 ¾* **Spriggan**^{227} 4588 3-9-3 .... AdamKirby 9 — 68
(C G Cox) *dwlt: w ldrs on outer: stl nrly upsides over 1f out: one pce* **4/1**^{3}

300- **4** *2* **Astroangel**^{152} 6310 3-8-12 67 .... DarryllHolland 2 — 57
(M H Tompkins) *trckd ldrs and racd against nr side rail: shkn up 2f out: edgd rt over 1f out: nt qckn* **14/1**

642- **5** *¾* **Impromptu**^{193} 5509 3-9-3 78 .... SebSanders 5 — 60
(R M Beckett) *trckd ldrs: shkn up 2f out: no prog: one pce and no imp after* **5/4**^{1}

6005 **6** *3* **Rogers Lodger**^{27} 636 3-9-3 56 .... JimmyQuinn 7 — 51
(J Akehurst) *sn last: effrt on outer to chse ldrs 2f out: wknd jst over 1f out* **25/1**

000- **7** *nk* **Maeve (IRE)**^{114} 6778 3-8-5 50 .... SCreighton$^{(7)}$ 3 — 45
(E J Creighton) *dwlt: sn trckd ldrs: rdn 2f out: wknd jst over 1f out* **66/1**

20-0 **8** *1 ¼* **Merlins Quest**^{14} 713 3-9-3 58 .... GeorgeBaker 4 — 46
(J M Bradley) *reminders s: w ldrs to over 2f out: wknd wl over 1f out* **33/1**

660- **9** *5* **Mr Forthright**^{172} 5947 3-8-10 60 .... BarrySavage$^{(7)}$ 8 — 31
(J M Bradley) *w ldrs over 2f: wknd over 2f out* **50/1**

1m 13.69s (0.09) **Going Correction** -0.025s/f (Good) — **9** Ran SP% **116.0**

Speed ratings (Par 98):98,96,94,91,90 86,85,84,77

CSF £59.25 TOTE £3.00: £1.30, £5.30, £1.60; EX 84.70 Trifecta £516.10 Part won. Pool: £726.98 - 0.50 winning units..

Owner Ms Gillian Khosla **Bred** Rathbarry Stud **Trained** Beckhampton, Wilts

FOCUS

A moderate maiden, which run at a strong early pace, and the first three look potential improvers. The sixth and seventh limit the form.

Impromptu Official explanation: trainer said gelding was scoped on returning home and found to have a respiratory infection

900 COME RACING IN KENT (S) H'CAP — 7f (S)

3:30 (3:30) (Class 6) (0-65,62) 3-Y-O — **£2,388** (£705; £352) **Stalls** Low

Form — RPR

0-06 **1** **Doctor Ned**^{17} 700 3-7-13 48 oh1 .... WilliamBuick$^{(5)}$ 1 — 50
(N A Callaghan) *hanging rt thrght: pressed ldr: led over 1f out: rdn and hld on nr fin: jinked and uns rdr after* **7/2**^{1}

6341 **2** *¾* **Mick Is Back**^{4} 832 3-8-13 60 6ex .... (p) StephenDonohoe$^{(3)}$ 3 — 65+
(P D Evans) *dwlt: settled in last trio: prog 2f out: repeatedly denied clr run fr over 1f out to last 125yds: r.o strly nr fin: unlucky* **4/1**^{2}

0020 **3** *hd* **Totally Free**^{27} 636 3-9-0 58 .... (v) HayleyTurner 9 — 58
(M D I Usher) *racd towards outer: pushed along to chse ldrs 4f out: effrt u.p 2f out to chse wnr fnl f: kpt on* **12/1**

2415 **4** *1 ¼* **Strike Force**^{21} 671 3-9-4 62 .... (p) TedDurcan 10 — 59
(R A Harris) *trckd ldrs: rdn and effrt 2f out: one pce fnl f* **7/2**^{1}

0-60 **5** *2 ½* **Avery**^{27} 636 3-8-4 55 .... HaddenFrost$^{(7)}$ 4 — 45
(R J Hodges) *mde most to over 1f out: wknd ins fnl f* **12/1**

-300 **6** *¾* **Best Option**^{4} 832 3-8-11 55 .... MartinDwyer 5 — 43
(W R Muir) *dwlt: nt gng wl in last trio after 2f: kpt on fr over 1f out: n.d* **11/2**^{3}

40-4 **7** *hd* **Sherjawy (IRE)**^{7} 795 3-9-0 58 .... (b) AdrianMcCarthy 11 — 46
(Miss Z C Davison) *t.k.h: pressed ldng pair: wknd over 1f out* **25/1**

000- **8** *1 ½* **Iron Dancer (IRE)**^{183} 5735 3-8-6 50 .... TPO'Shea 7 — 34
(P A Blockley) *chsd ldrs: rdn wl over 2f out: wknd over 1f out* **28/1**

00-0 **9** *1 ½* **Mr Mini Scule**^{57} 360 3-8-12 56 .... DaneO'Neill 6 — 36
(A B Haynes) *trckd ldrs to over 2f out: sn rdn and wknd* **16/1**

0000 **10** *2 ½* **Elizabeth Garrett**^{8} 790 3-7-11 48 oh3 .... MCGeran$^{(7)}$ 2 — 21
(M J Gingell) *dwlt: a wl in rr: struggling over 2f out* **50/1**

3-64 **11** *2 ½* **Show Business (IRE)**^{73} 194 3-8-2 53 .... (tp) JosephWalsh$^{(7)}$ 8 — 20
(P Butler) *dwlt: a wl in rr: struggling fr over 2f out* **16/1**

1m 29.03s (1.13) **Going Correction** -0.025s/f (Good) — **11** Ran SP% **116.2**

Speed ratings (Par 96):92,91,90,89,86 85,85,83,82,79 76

CSF £16.82 CT £152.96 TOTE £4.80: £1.60, £1.40, £2.70; EX 21.30 Trifecta £108.10 Pool: £847.18 - 5.56 winning units..There was no bid for the winner. Mick Is Back was claimed by M. J. Gingell for £7,000.

Owner Gallagher O'Rourke **Bred** Foreneish Bloodstock **Trained** Newmarket, Suffolk

■ William Buick was knocked unconscious when unseated after the line and was unable to weigh in, but the result stood.

FOCUS

A weak handicap. The winner was the least exposed in the field and can do better. The form looks straightforward enough rated through the third, fifth and sixth.

Mick Is Back ◆ Official explanation: jockey said gelding was denied a clear run

901 INVICTA MOTORS ASHFORD MAIDEN STKS — 7f (S)

4:05 (4:11) (Class 5) 3-Y-O+ — **£2,914** (£867; £433; £216) **Stalls** Low

Form — RPR

22- **1** **Thabaat**^{211} 5067 3-8-11 .... RHills 6 — 80+
(B W Hills) *led nr side gp: overall ldr over 2f out: hung rt sn after: clr over 1f out: comf* **4/11**^{1}

3 **2** *5* **Thunderbolt Jaxon**^{17} 700 3-8-11 .... JimmyFortune 5 — 67
(P W Chapple-Hyam) *pressed wnr nr side: carried rt over 2f out: outpcd fr over 1f out* **4/1**^{2}

3 *3 ½* **Encores** 3-8-11 .... ShaneKelly 10 — 58
(N A Callaghan) *dwlt: off the pce nr side: pushed along 1/2-way: effrt 2f out: kpt on same pce* **16/1**

0- **4** *1 ½* **Astrolibra**^{167} 6050 3-8-6 .... DarryllHolland 1 — 49
(M H Tompkins) *pressed nr side ldrs tl rdn and btn 2f out* **14/1**

- **5** *1* **Everygrainofsand (IRE)** 4-9-11 .... GeorgeBaker 7 — 56
(J R Best) *racd alone far side: overall ldr to over 2f out: wknd* **10/1**^{3}

6 *7* **Simpleton** 4-9-8 .... StephaneBreux$^{(3)}$ 2 — 38
(J R Best) *s.s: bhd on nr side: prog and jst in tch over 2f out : sn wknd* **33/1**

060- **7** *11* **Charanne**^{133} 6557 4-9-3 30 .... (b^{1}) StephenDonohoe$^{(3)}$ 3 — —
(J M Bradley) *chsd nr side ldrs to 1/2-way: sn wknd and bhd* **50/1**

000- **8** *14* **Lucky Tern**^{172} 5951 4-9-4 25 .... PietroRomeo$^{(7)}$ 8 — —
(J M Bradley) *racd alone in centre: wl on terms to 1/2-way: veering bdly and wknd over 2f out: t.o* **50/1**

00-0 **9** *1 ¼* **Magical World**^{53} 403 4-8-13 30 .... (b^{1}) BarrySavage$^{(7)}$ 4 — —
(J M Bradley) *reluctant to go to post: hanging bdly: in tch for 3f: t.o* **50/1**

1m 27.65s (-0.25) **Going Correction** -0.025s/f (Good)

WFA 3 from 4yo 14lb — **9** Ran SP% **123.8**

Speed ratings (Par 103):100,94,90,88,87 79,66,50,49

CSF £2.47 TOTE £1.40: £1.10, £1.10, £3.10; EX 3.00 Trifecta £8.70 Pool: £1,111.55 - 90.51 winning units..

Owner Hamdan Al Maktoum **Bred** Shadwell Estate Company Limited **Trained** Lambourn, Berks

FOCUS

A weak and uncompetitive maiden won, as expected, by hot favourite Thabaat, who was a cut above his rivals on formand did not nned to improve to score.

Everygrainofsand(IRE) Official explanation: jockey said gelding hung left under pressure

902 KMFM WINNER TRISHA WORTHY H'CAP — 7f (S)

4:40 (4:41) (Class 5) (0-75,74) 4-Y-O+ — **£2,914** (£867; £433; £216) **Stalls** Low

Form — RPR

002- **1** **Apply Dapply**^{160} 6174 4-8-11 67 .... SteveDrowne 5 — 76+
(H Morrison) *dwlt: settled in rr: prog fr over 2f out: plld out and effrt over 1f out: styd on wl to ld last 100yds: pushed out* **5/1**^{3}

-621 **2** *¾* **His Master's Voice (IRE)**^{17} 697 4-9-4 74 .... BrettDoyle 7 — 81
(D W P Arbuthnot) *trckd ldrs: clsd 2f out: effrt to ld jst ins fnl f: hdd and one pce last 100yds* **4/1**^{1}

/000 **3** *1 ¼* **Thomas Lawrence (USA)**^{40} 524 6-8-4 60 oh15 .... TPO'Shea 3 — 64
(P A Blockley) *mde most to wl over 1f out: sn rdn and nt qckn: styd on again last 150yds* **66/1**

0033 **4** *hd* **Dvinsky (USA)**^{7} 803 6-8-10 66 .... ShaneKelly 10 — 69
(P Howling) *trckd across fr wd draw to press ldr: led wl over 1f out: hdd jst ins fnl f: folded tamely nr fin* **9/2**^{2}

000- **5** *1 ¼* **Capricho (IRE)**^{167} 6054 10-8-7 63 .... (b^{1}) PaulDoe 9 — 63
(J Akehurst) *t.k.h: cl up: poised to chal over 1f out: upsides ent fnl f: wknd* **17/2**

030- **6** *¾* **Ten Shun**^{101} 6932 4-9-0 73 .... StephenDonohoe$^{(3)}$ 8 — 71
(P D Evans) *t.k.h: hld up in tch on outer: effrt and cl up over 1f out: wknd ins fnl f* **11/2**

0-00 **7** *2 ½* **Li Shih Chen**^{45} 486 4-8-11 67 .... SebSanders 6 — 59
(A P Jarvis) *chsd ldrs: lost pl over 2f out: struggling after* **12/1**

000- **8** *½* **Danawi (IRE)**^{127} 6618 4-8-4 60 oh12 .... JimmyQuinn 4 — 50
(M R Hoad) *trckd ldrs to over 2f out: sn u.p and btn* **25/1**

020- **9** *2* **Logsdail**^{153} 6301 7-8-2 65 .... JemmaMarshall$^{(7)}$ 2 — 50
(G L Moore) *t.k.h: hld up in last trio: no prog whn sltly hmpd wl over 1f out: no ch after: eased* **14/1**

1424 **10** *3* **Kew The Music**^{4} 831 7-7-11 60 oh6 .... MatthewDavies$^{(7)}$ 1 — 37
(M R Channon) *a in last trio: drvn and no prog over 2f out* **6/1**

1m 26.63s (-1.27) **Going Correction** -0.025s/f (Good) — **10** Ran SP% **114.7**

Speed ratings (Par 103):106,105,103,103,102 101,98,97,95,92

CSF £24.88 CT £1163.82 TOTE £5.20: £2.00, £1.50, £10.40; EX 17.00 TRIFECTA Not won..

Owner L A Garfield **Bred** N R Shields And K R Burke **Trained** East Ilsley, Berks

FOCUS

They went a fair pace in this and the winning time was the fastest of the three races over the trip, though the others were a three-year-old seller and an all-aged maiden, so perhaps that was to be expected. On this occasion the whole field stayed nearside. Ordinary form, but solid enough. The winner is capable of a bit better.

903 EASTWELL MANOR FILLIES' H'CAP — 1m 4f

5:10 (5:10) (Class 5) (0-70,70) 4-Y-O+ — **£2,914** (£867; £433; £216) **Stalls** Low

Form — RPR

303- **1** **Love Always**^{188} 5628 5-9-3 68 .... DaneO'Neill 4 — 73+
(S Dow) *trckd ldrs gng wl: effrt over 2f out: rdn to ld over 1f out: in command fnl f: cosily* **4/1**^{2}

6-22 **2** *nk* **Don't Mind Me**^{15} 712 4-8-3 52 oh3 .... JimmyQuinn 5 — 59+
(T Keddy) *hld up: nt handling trck fr over 4f out in last pair and plenty to do: prog 2f out: swtchd lft and r.o to cl on eased wnr fin* **7/2**^{1}

2101 **3** *nk* **Mon Petite Amour**^{11} 742 4-8-8 60 .... BrettDoyle 3 — 63
(D W P Arbuthnot) *trckd ldrs: led 6f out to 4f out: effrt again 2f out: styd on but readily hld* **7/1**

-120 **4** *½* **Maria Antonia (IRE)**^{57} 369 4-8-5 57 .... TPO'Shea 8 — 59
(P A Blockley) *hld up: prog on outer to ld 4f out: hdd over 1f out: one pce* **4/1**^{2}

360- **5** *2 ½* **Spring Dream (IRE)**^{241} 4159 4-9-4 70 .... TedDurcan 1 — 68
(M R Channon) *led at slow pce to over 10f out: styd chsng ldrs: rdn over 2f out: no prog after* **12/1**

304- **6** *1 ½* **Pochard**^{186} 5650 4-8-7 62 .... StephenDonohoe$^{(3)}$ 6 — 58
(J M P Eustace) *t.k.h: hld up in last: plenty to do 3f out: rdn 2f out: styd on fnl f: no ch* **11/1**

0-16 **7** *½* **Evolve (USA)**^{57} 369 4-8-3 55 .... NickyMackay 2 — 50
(M Botti) *dwlt: led over 10f out and maintained modest pce: hdd 6f out: lost pl over 3f out: shkn up and no prog 2f out* **11/2**^{3}

210- **8** 3 1/2 **Sovietta (IRE)**[36] 6843 6-8-6 **57**....(t) FergusSweeney 7 47
(A G Newcombe) *hld up in tch: effrt over 3f out: rdn to chse ldrs over 2f out: wknd wl over 1f out* **12/1**

2m 49.11s (8.61) **Going Correction** -0.025s/f (Good)
WFA 4 from 5yo+ 1lb **8** Ran SP% **113.8**
Speed ratings (Par 100):70,69,69,69,67 66,66,63
CSF £18.24 CT £93.31 TOTE £4.20: £1.50, £2.00, £1.80; EX 14.60 Trifecta £58.80 Pool: £371.85 - 4.49 winning units..
Owner T Staplehurst **Bred** T Staplehurst **Trained** Epsom, Surrey

FOCUS
An extremely messy contest run at a dawdle for the most part and the lead changed hands several times. The winning time was unsurprisingly pedestrian and the form looks dubious. Love Always was entitled to win on last year's best.

904 PORT LYMPNE H'CAP 1m 1f 149y
5:40 (5:40) (Class 5) (0-70,69) 3-Y-O **£2,914** (£867; £433; £216) **Stalls** Low

Form RPR
00-3 **1** **Brave Quest (IRE)**[29] 611 3-8-9 **60**.... IanMongan 3 67
(Mrs L J Mongan) *chsd clr ldr: clsd over 2f out: hrd rdn to ld over 1f out: kpt on u.p* **10/1**
05-4 **2** 1 1/2 **Best Selection**[10] 764 3-9-0 **65**.... SebSanders 11 69
(A P Jarvis) *pushed along in midfield after 2f: effrt over 2f out: styd on u.p fr over 1f out: tk 2nd nr fin* **5/1**[2]
0-66 **3** nk **Fine Ruler (IRE)**[18] 694 3-9-0 **65**.... SamHitchcott 5 69
(M R Channon) *racd freely: led and sn clr: rdn and hdd over 1f out: edgd lft but kpt on* **15/2**
06-5 **4** 1 1/2 **Urban Warrior**[1] 886 3-8-11 **65**.... JamesDoyle(3) 12 66
(Mrs Norma Pook) *chsd clr ldrs: rdn over 2f out: plugged on but n.d* **16/1**
1 **5** 1 1/4 **Tremelo Pointe (IRE)**[19] 684 3-9-3 **68**.... SteveDrowne 4 66
(H Morrison) *chsd clr ldrs: rdn over 2f out: no real imp wl over 1f out: eased whn hld last 75yds* **3/1**[1]
000- **6** 2 1/2 **Linlithgow (IRE)**[114] 6778 3-8-4 **55** oh3.... JimmyQuinn 2 48
(J L Dunlop) *s.i.s: mostly last: pushed along 1/2-way and wl off the pce : rdn and styd on fnl 2f: no ch* **12/1**
1115 **7** shd **Global Traffic**[57] 370 3-9-1 **69**....(b) StephenDonohoe(3) 6 62
(P D Evans) *s.i.s: hld up wl in rr: plenty to do 4f out: rdn and one pce fnl 3f* **7/1**
400- **8** nk **Diggs Lane (IRE)**[147] 6385 3-8-4 **55** oh4.... HayleyTurner 9 47
(N A Callaghan) *off the pce in midfield: pushed along over 4f out: no prog fnl 3f* **10/1**
-020 **9** 2 1/2 **Diamond Light (USA)**[29] 624 3-9-1 **66**.... TPQueally 8 53
(M Botti) *hld up in midfield: effrt 4f out: drvn and no imp ldrs 2f out : hanging and wknd* **16/1**
0005 **10** nk **Woodygo**[11] 738 3-8-4 **58**.... StephaneBreux(3) 7 45
(J R Best) *t.k.h: hld up in rr: gng wl enough over 3f out: shkn up and wknd 2f out* **13/2**[3]

2m 4.94s (-0.29) **Going Correction** -0.025s/f (Good) **10** Ran SP% **116.9**
Speed ratings (Par 98):100,98,98,97,96 94,94,94,92,91
CSF £59.57 CT £402.74 TOTE £9.00: £2.70, £2.00, £2.70; EX 51.20 Trifecta £315.80 Part won. Pool: £444.91 - 0.60 winning units. Place 6 £13.56, Place 5 £9.11.
Owner The Most Welcome Partnership **Bred** Islanmore Stud **Trained** Epsom, Surrey

FOCUS
They went a decent pace in this, thanks mainly to Fine Ruler tearing off in front, but that eventually took its toll and the principals found it a struggle to get home over the last furlong or so. The form seems sound enough and should work out at a similar modest level.
Diggs Lane(IRE) Official explanation: jockey said gelding stumbled leaving stalls
T/Plt: £12.50 to a £1 stake. Pool: £54,641.00. 3,167.25 winning tickets. T/Qpdt: £3.60 to a £1 stake. Pool: £3,750.80. 754.20 winning tickets. JN

890 SOUTHWELL (L-H)
Tuesday, April 3

OFFICIAL GOING: Standard
Wind: Fresh, across Weather: Overcast

905 SOUTHWELL-RACECOURSE.CO.UK H'CAP 5f (F)
2:10 (2:13) (Class 5) (0-70,68) 4-Y-0+ **£3,238** (£963; £481; £240) **Stalls** High

Form RPR
1121 **1** **Count Cougar (USA)**[14] 717 7-8-13 **68**.... MichaelJStainton(5) 1 81+
(S P Griffiths) *sn chsng ldr: rdn to ld over 1f out: r.o: eased nr fin* **9/4**[1]
0-04 **2** 1 1/2 **Melalchrist**[29] 621 5-9-1 **65**....(p) NCallan 4 72
(K A Ryan) *chsd ldrs: rdn over 1f out: r.o* **6/1**[3]
-133 **3** shd **Gifted Lass**[71] 214 5-8-13 **63**.... DavidAllan 2 70
(J Balding) *sn led: rdn and hdd over 1f out: styd on same pce ins fnl f* **5/1**[2]
006- **4** 2 1/2 **Never Without Me**[202] 5286 7-8-8 **61**.... PatrickMathers(3) 6 59
(J F Coupland) *prom: outpcd 4f out: styd on u.p appr fnl f* **20/1**
5114 **5** 1/2 **The Fisio**[12] 727 7-9-1 **65**....(v) EddieAhern 9 61
(S Gollings) *chsd ldrs: outpcd over 3f out: styd on ins fnl f* **11/1**
55-5 **6** hd **Witchry**[12] 727 5-9-4 **68**.... LPKeniry 3 63
(A G Newcombe) *dwlt: outpcd: hdwy u.p over 1f out: one pce ins fnl f* **5/1**[2]
0220 **7** 1 **Stoneacre Boy (IRE)**[12] 727 4-9-1 **65**....(b) GrahamGibbons 5 57
(Peter Grayson) *s.i.s: outpcd: styd on ins fnl f: nvr nrr* **5/1**[2]
0600 **8** 6 **Maktavish**[40] 521 8-8-12 **62**....(b) JosedeSouza 7 32
(R Brotherton) *chsd ldrs 3f* **20/1**
0 **9** 4 **Polar Fox**[12] 727 4-8-12 **62**.... DeanMcKeown 8 18
(D Shaw) *dwlt: outpcd* **80/1**

59.96 secs (-0.34) **Going Correction** +0.025s/f (Slow) **9** Ran SP% **114.1**
Speed ratings (Par 103):103,100,100,96,95 95,93,84,77
CSF £15.47 CT £60.34 TOTE £2.60: £1.30, £1.80, £2.00; EX 18.80.
Owner M Grant **Bred** Angus Glen Farm (1996) Ltd **Trained** Easingwold, N Yorks
■ Stewards' Enquiry : Jose de Souza caution: careless riding

FOCUS
A fair race for the grade, and the pace was sound. Count Cougar came into the race in fine form and showed improvement again. The form looks solid and should work out.
Stoneacre Boy(IRE) Official explanation: jockey said gelding hung badly right

906 BOOK TICKETS ON LINE MEDIAN AUCTION MAIDEN FILLIES' STKS 6f (F)
2:45 (2:46) (Class 5) 3-4-Y-0 **£3,886** (£1,156; £577; £288) **Stalls** Low

Form RPR
00 **1** **Kadia**[12] 728 4-9-10.... MickyFenton 1 48
(P T Midgley) *disp ld over 3f: sn rdn: styd on to ld ins fnl f* **20/1**
0052 **2** 1/2 **Jember Red**[14] 714 4-9-7 **42**....(v) MarkLawson(3) 3 46
(B Smart) *disp ld tl led over 2f out: rdn over 1f out: hdd and unable qck ins fnl f* **2/1**[2]
0 **3** 3 1/2 **Caterina Ballerina (USA)**[43] 498 3-8-12.... NCallan 4 36
(K A Ryan) *disp ld tl hung rt fr over 3f out: sn rdn: styd on same pce appr fnl f* **4/5**[1]
00 **4** 6 **Clock Face (IRE)**[10] 752 3-8-12.... LPKeniry 2 31
(M D I Usher) *sn outpcd: eased whn no ch wl over 1f out* **11/2**[3]

1m 18.14s (1.24) **Going Correction** +0.10s/f (Slow)
WFA 3 from 4yo 12lb **4** Ran SP% **109.0**
Speed ratings (Par 100):95,94,89,81
CSF £57.78 TOTE £25.20; EX 57.80.
Owner Mrs M Hills **Bred** M And S Hills **Trained** Westow, N Yorks

FOCUS
A very bad race indeed and the form looks worth ignoring, especially with the favourite running poorly.
Caterina Ballerina(USA) Official explanation: jockey said filly hung badly right throughout

907 HELEN CLARKE HAPPY 40TH BIRTHDAY CLASSIFIED STKS 1m 3f (F)
3:20 (3:20) (Class 7) 3-Y-0+ **£2,388** (£705; £352) **Stalls** Low

Form RPR
0002 **1** **A Mothers Love**[8] 790 3-8-2 **42**.... EdwardCreighton 8 55+
(P J McBride) *hld up: hdwy over 2f out: styd on to ld last strides* **11/2**[3]
0426 **2** nk **Dispol Peto**[12] 579 7-9-3 **45**....(bt) DuranFentiman(5) 10 54
(R Johnson) *hld up: hdwy over 4f out: led 2f out: sn rdn: hdd last strides* **5/1**[2]
-605 **3** 2 **Color Man**[38] 553 3-8-2 **45**....(p) DaleGibson 7 48
(Mrs A J Perrett) *sn led: rdn and hdd 2f out: styd on same pce ins fnl f* **16/1**
000 **4** 5 **Danalova**[49] 449 3-8-2 **45**.... PaulHanagan 11 39
(R A Fahey) *chsd ldrs: rdn over 3f out: styd on same pce fnl 2f* **11/1**
403- **5** 3 1/2 **Queen Of Diamonds (IRE)**[17] 6302 4-9-8 **41**.... TomEaves 14 36
(Mrs K Walton) *prom: rdn over 2f out: wknd over 1f out* **25/1**
0403 **6** 1 **Montecristo**[29] 615 14-9-1 **42**.... LukeMcJannet(7) 5 34
(Rae Guest) *sn outpcd: sme late hdwy: nvr nrr* **14/1**
000- **7** hd **Arthurs Dream (IRE)**[22] 4984 5-9-8 **45**.... RichardMullen 1 34
(A W Carroll) *s.s: in rr tl sme late hdwy* **13/2**
2/00 **8** 1/2 **Fire At Will**[10] 768 5-9-1 **45**.... MarkCoumbe(7) 6 33
(A W Carroll) *chsd ldrs: rdn over 3f out: wknd over 1f out* **100/1**
-544 **9** 1 **Padre Nostro (IRE)**[14] 716 8-9-1 **43**.... ChrisGlenister(7) 3 32
(J R Holt) *hld up: racd keenly: rdn over 4f out: wknd over 2f out* **4/1**[1]
000- **10** 4 **Chookie Windsor**[183] 5733 4-9-8 **44**....(p) NCallan 9 25
(A G Juckes) *mid-div: hdwy over 7f out: rdn and wknd 3f out* **14/1**
-555 **11** 1 1/4 **Big Ralph**[8] 789 4-9-8 **43**....(b[1]) JamieMackay 13 23
(M Wigham) *chsd ldr: rdn and ev ch over 2f out: wknd over 1f out* **16/1**
3304 **12** 5 **Twilight Avenger (IRE)**[7] 804 4-9-5 **43**.... LiamJones(3) 4 14
(W M Brisbourne) *mid-div: rdn over 3f out: wknd over 2f out* **8/1**
0-00 **13** 7 **Acece**[39] 537 3-7-13 **45** ow2....(b[1]) KevinGhunowa(5) 12 —
(M Appleby) *chsd ldrs over 7f* **66/1**
0-06 **14** 3 **Danum Diva (IRE)**[8] 791 3-8-2 **43**.... CatherineGannon 2 —
(T J Pitt) *plld hrd and prom: hmpd and lost pl 9f out: rdn and wknd over 3f out* **20/1**

2m 29.2s (0.30) **Going Correction** +0.10s/f (Slow)
WFA 3 from 4yo+ 20lb **14** Ran SP% **121.0**
Speed ratings (Par 97):102,101,100,96,94 93,93,92,92,89 88,84,79,77
CSF £32.32 TOTE £7.30: £2.70, £1.70, £6.80; EX 37.60.
Owner P J McBride **Bred** Foursome Thoroughbreds **Trained** Newmarket, Suffolk

FOCUS
A very moderate race, but sound form for the grade, rated through the third and fourth. The winner is unexposed and might be capable of a bit better yet.
Padre Nostro(IRE) Official explanation: jockey said gelding was never travelling

908 PLAY GOLF COME RACING MAIDEN FILLIES' STKS 7f (F)
3:55 (3:55) (Class 5) 3-4-Y-O **£4,210** (£1,252; £625; £312) **Stalls** Low

Form RPR
1 **Viami (IRE)**[155] 6261 3-8-12.... FMBerry 4 70
(J G Burns, Ire) *chsd ldrs: outpcd 1/2-way: rallied over 1f out: styd on u.p to ld towards fin* **7/2**[2]
20-2 **2** 1/2 **Empress Olga (USA)**[18] 689 3-8-12 **70**.... JamieSpencer 2 69
(E A L Dunlop) *s.i.s: sn trcking ldrs: led over 1f out: sn hung rt: hdd towards fin* **8/13**[1]
3 2 **Verone (USA)** 3-8-12.... NCallan 7 64
(M Botti) *a.p: rdn and ev ch over 1f out: sn edgd rt: styd on same pce ins fnl f* **14/1**
442- **4** nk **Princess Palatine (IRE)**[171] 5959 3-8-12 **67**.... PatCosgrave 1 63
(K R Burke) *led: hdd over 5f out: led over 2f out: rdn and hdd over 1f out: no ex ins fnl f* **7/1**[3]
5 5 **Frisbee** 3-8-12.... DavidAllan 6 50
(T D Easterby) *dwlt: sn pushed along in rr: wknd 2f out* **25/1**
40-0 **6** 9 **Tequila Rose (IRE)**[58] 350 4-9-5 **40**.... WilliamCarson(7) 3 27
(M A Buckley) *led over 5f out: hdd over 2f out: wknd over 1f out* **100/1**
7 7 **Glenmore Lodge** 4-9-12.... MickyFenton 5 8
(P T Midgley) *s.i.s: in rr: wknd 1/2-way* **66/1**

1m 31.81s (1.01) **Going Correction** +0.10s/f (Slow)
WFA 3 from 4yo 14lb **7** Ran SP% **109.6**
Speed ratings (Par 100):98,97,95,94,89 78,70
CSF £5.49 TOTE £5.40: £1.80, £1.10; EX 6.10.
Owner Mrs Mary McDonald **Bred** Keatly Overseas Ltd **Trained** Curragh, Co Kildare

FOCUS
Modest maiden form and probably far from solid with the runner-up disappointing again. The time was 0.8 slower than the concluding 46-55 handicap.

909 RACING AGAIN ON THE 13TH H'CAP 1m 6f (F)
4:30 (4:30) (Class 6) (0-65,65) 4-Y-0+ **£3,071** (£906; £453) **Stalls** Low

Form RPR
4501 **1** **Lady Pilot**[8] 792 5-9-1 **53** 6ex.... RichardThomas 3 71+
(Jim Best) *s.i.s and hmpd s: hld up: hdwy over 4f out: led and hung rt over 1f out: rdn out* **7/1**[3]
5052 **2** 3/4 **They All Laughed**[21] 665 4-8-8 **56**.... WilliamCarson(7) 12 71
(P W Hiatt) *hld up and bhd: hdwy over 2f out: rdn to chse wnr fnl f: styd on* **15/2**
000- **3** 6 **Rare Coincidence**[65] 6321 6-9-3 **55**....(p) TomEaves 6 62
(R F Fisher) *chsd ldr: led over 4f out: rdn and hdd over 1f out: wknd ins fnl f* **16/1**

23-3 4 3½ **Eforetta (GER)**[19] 685 5-9-9 61 ChrisCatlin 2 63+
(D J Wintle) *chsd ldrs: lost pl over 10f out: rdn over 4f out: hdwy u.p over 1f out: wknd ins fnl f* **7/4**[1]

-333 5 2½ **Plenty Cried Wolf**[19] 683 5-9-3 55 PaulHanagan 5 53
(R A Fahey) *led over 9f: rdn over 2f out: wknd fnl f* **7/2**[2]

1504 6 1¾ **Red River Rock (IRE)**[6] 808 5-8-9 47 (be) PaulMulrennan 8 43
(T J Fitzgerald) *chsd ldrs: rdn over 3f out: wknd wl over 1f out* **7/1**[3]

0050 7 1¾ **Activist**[10] 767 9-8-7 52 KellyHarrison(7) 9 45
(D Carroll) *mid-div: rdn over 4f out: sn wknd* **33/1**

000- 8 4 **Piccolomini**[28] 4229 5-8-12 50 (b) TonyHamilton 10 38
(E W Tuer) *hld up in tch: rdn over 4f out: wknd over 3f out* **50/1**

/40- 9 2 **Spectested (IRE)**[23] 346 6-8-12 50 (p) RichardMullen 11 35
(A W Carroll) *sn drvn aong in rr: n.d* **33/1**

062 10 7 **Exit Fast (USA)**[12] 730 6-9-8 60 MickyFenton 7 35
(P T Midgley) *prom: rdn 1/2-way: wknd 4f out* **16/1**

0-00 11 24 **Coppington Melody (IRE)**[79] 134 4-7-13 47. KrishlovyGundowry(7) 1 —
(B W Duke) *sn outpcd* **50/1**

60-4 12 2 **Bariloche**[28] 630 4-9-10 65 (be) PatCosgrave 4 —
(J R Boyle) *prom: drvn along thrght: wkng whn hmpd over 4f out: eased* **14/1**

3m 9.49s (-0.11) **Going Correction** +0.10s/f (Slow)
WFA 4 from 5yo+ 3lb **12** Ran SP% **123.6**
Speed ratings (Par 101):104,103,100,98,96 95,94,92,91,87 73,72
CSF £59.96 CT £827.13 TOTE £8.40: £2.40, £2.90, £4.90; EX 70.80.
Owner Odds On Racing **Bred** Genesis Green Stud Ltd **Trained** Lewes, E Sussex

FOCUS
This was run at a decent pace. Sound form for the grade of race with the first two nicely clear.
Red River Rock(IRE) Official explanation: jockey said gelding hung right
Bariloche Official explanation: jockey said colt hung left

910 DINE IN THE QUEEN MOTHER RESTAURANT H'CAP 7f (F)
5:00 (5:01) (Class 6) (0-55,54) 3-Y-O **£3,238** (£963; £481; £240) **Stalls** Low

Form RPR

0-52 1 **Time For Change (IRE)**[67] 253 3-8-7 54 ChrisGlenister(7) 4 56
(B W Hills) *s.i.s: sn chsng ldrs: shkn up to ld ins fnl f: styd on* **13/2**

600- 2 nk **Ingleby Hill (IRE)**[151] 6316 3-8-10 50 PaulFessey 11 51
(T D Barron) *chsd ldrs: rdn 1/2-way: r.o nr fin* **10/1**

560 3 ¾ **Missus Molly Brown**[36] 567 3-8-5 45 PaulHanagan 6 44
(R A Fahey) *sn outpcd: r.o wl ins fnl f: nt rch ldrs* **12/1**

0410 4 shd **Mr Chocolate Drop (IRE)**[47] 469 3-9-0 54 JamieSpencer 5 53
(M J Attwater) *s.i.s: sn chsng ldrs: hmpd 2f out: rdn to ld and hung lft fr over 1f out: hdd and no ex ins fnl f* **7/2**[1]

554- 5 nk **Silly Gilly (IRE)**[122] 6679 3-8-13 53 PatCosgrave 3 51
(K R Burke) *chsd ldrs: rdn over 2f out: styd on* **4/1**[2]

0002 6 hd **Flushed**[21] 667 3-8-10 50 (be) NCallan 10 48
(A J McCabe) *led: rdn and hung rt 2f out: sn hdd: hmpd and no ex ins fnl f* **4/1**[2]

-002 7 ½ **Jousting**[15] 708 3-8-6 49 (v) SaleemGolam(3) 9 45
(V Smith) *a.p: rdn over 2f out: kpt on* **11/2**[3]

0-00 8 ½ **Mum's Memories**[8] 791 3-8-5 45 RichardMullen 7 40
(W J Musson) *outpcd: styd on u.p ins fnl f: nt rch ldrs* **66/1**

000- 9 6 **Orotund**[182] 5753 3-8-10 50 DavidAllan 8 30
(T D Easterby) *dwlt: hdwy over 4f out: rdn and wknd over 1f out* **25/1**

4000 10 2 **Emefdream**[54] 390 3-8-12 52 ChrisCatlin 1 26
(E J O'Neill) *chsd ldrs: lost pl 5f out: n.d after* **14/1**

1m 31.73s (0.93) **Going Correction** +0.10s/f (Slow) **10** Ran SP% **119.7**
Speed ratings (Par 96):98,97,96,96,96 96,95,94,88,85
CSF £71.59 CT £784.77 TOTE £7.90: £2.30, £4.90, £5.30; EX 104.50 Place 6 £2,679.87, Place 5 £1,590.52.
Owner B W Hills **Bred** Mrs A M Upsdell **Trained** Lambourn, Berks

FOCUS
A moderate handicap in which they finished in a heap, suggesting that the form is only plating class.
T/Plt: £4,440.60 to a £1 stake. Pool: £54,747.45. 9.00 winning tickets. T/Qpdt: £43.10 to a £1 stake. Pool: £4,429.50. 76.00 winning tickets. CR

CATTERICK (L-H)
Wednesday, April 4

OFFICIAL GOING: Good to firm (firm in places)
The ground had dried out and was described as 'on the quick side of good but bare and rough in places'.
Wind: light, half-behind Weather: fine, sunny and warm

912 GO RACING AT PONTEFRACT NEXT TUESDAY (S) STKS 7f
2:20 (2:22) (Class 6) 3-Y-O+ **£2,730** (£806; £403) **Stalls** Low

Form RPR

4411 1 **Sawwaah (IRE)**[5] 825 10-9-11 60 (v) AdrianTNicholls 2 69
(D Nicholls) *s.i.s: sn mid-div: hdwy to ld 2f out: drvn clr* **11/4**[1]

005- 2 3½ **Zhitomir**[155] 6273 9-9-5 61 PhillipMakin 7 54
(M Dods) *hld up: hdwy on outside over 2f out: styd on to take 2nd nr line* **13/2**

0400 3 nk **Methusaleh (IRE)**[3] 866 4-9-6 60 PatrickHills(5) 12 59
(D Shaw) *s.i.s: gd hdwy on ins 2f out: styd on strly ins last* **10/1**

100- 4 nk **Cut Ridge (IRE)**[134] 6549 8-9-0 50 (p) TonyHamilton 3 47
(J S Wainwright) *trckd ldrs: led over 4f out tl 2f out: kpt on same pce* **16/1**

3206 5 ½ **Penel (IRE)**[13] 729 6-9-11 48 (p) LeeEnstone 14 57
(P T Midgley) *chsd ldrs: sn drvn along: kpt on one pce fnl 2f* **28/1**

00-0 6 2½ **Telepathic (IRE)**[79] 135 7-9-2 45 StephenDonohoe(3) 13 44
(A Berry) *bhd: hdwy 2f out: nvr nr ldrs* **100/1**

040- 7 ½ **Woodwee**[97] 6961 4-9-2 48 MarkLawson(3) 4 43
(R E Barr) *led tl over 4f out: wknd fnl 2f* **50/1**

0-10 8 1 **Just James**[29] 629 8-9-5 68 PaulQuinn 10 40
(D Nicholls) *in rr: sme hdwy over 2f out: nvr nr ldrs* **11/2**[2]

0-12 9 shd **Wiltshire (IRE)**[11] 750 5-9-6 53 RoryMoore(5) 9 46
(P T Midgley) *mid-div: kpt on fnl 2f: nvr a threat* **7/1**

1000 10 shd **Dark Moon**[12] 743 4-9-6 50 DeanMcKeown 11 41
(D Shaw) *s.i.s: bhd tl sme hdwy fnl 2f* **33/1**

-400 11 ¾ **Flamestone**[30] 619 3-8-5 48 (b) PaulHanagan 15 38
(J D Bethell) *mid-div: kpt on fnl 2f: nvr on terms* **33/1**

0-00 12 1 **Howards Princess**[52] 430 5-9-6 48 (p) DaleGibson 8 36
(J Hetherton) *chsd ldrs: lost pl 2f out* **20/1**

5-00 13 2½ **Cape Sydney (IRE)**[7] 812 4-9-6 45 (p) CatherineGannon 5 29
(D W Barker) *trckd ldrs: rdn over 2f out: lost pl over 1f out* **20/1**

3200 14 4 **Tyrone Sam**[20] 686 5-9-11 56 (b) PatCosgrave 1 23
(K A Ryan) *mid-div: sn drvn along: hmpd on ins over 4f out: sme hdwy over 3f out: wkng whn hmpd on ins and eased 150yds out* **6/1**[3]

-450 15 5 **Legal Set (IRE)**[30] 622 11-9-0 47 (t) AnnStokell(5) 6 4
(Miss A Stokell) *sn lost pl over 2f out* **66/1**

1m 24.9s (-2.46) **Going Correction** -0.325s/f (Firm)
WFA 3 from 4yo+ 14lb **15** Ran SP% **120.4**
Speed ratings (Par 101):101,97,96,96,95 92,92,91,91,90 90,88,86,81,75
CSF £18.15 TOTE £2.70: £1.30, £2.30, £3.60; EX 20.80.There was no bid for the winner.
Owner Mrs Alex Nicholls **Bred** Shadwell Estate Company Limited **Trained** Sessay, N Yorks

FOCUS
Sawwaah completed a hat-trick in this modest seller. Overall the form at this low level looks fairly sound.
Just James Official explanation: jockey said gelding was denied a clear run
Legal Set(IRE) Official explanation: jockey said gelding had an irregular heartbeat

913 "TUESDAY 8TH MAY IS LADIES NIGHT" H'CAP 1m 7f 177y
2:50 (2:51) (Class 6) (0-65,62) 4-Y-0+ **£2,730** (£806; £403) **Stalls** Low

Form RPR

05-4 1 **I'll Do It Today**[30] 618 6-9-5 56 PaulHanagan 7 63
(J M Jefferson) *trckd ldrs: styd on fnl 2f: led last 150yds: hld on towards fin* **12/1**

4-30 2 ½ **Toni Alcala**[9] 792 8-8-13 50 (p) DeanMcKeown 6 58+
(R F Fisher) *hld up in mid-division: effrt and nt clr run over 1f out: styd on strly ins last* **12/1**

630- 3 nk **Mulligan's Pride (IRE)**[36] 4914 6-9-1 52 (b) RoystonFfrench 8 58
(James Moffatt) *s.i.s: hdwy to chse ldrs over 5f out: qcknd to ld over 2f out: hdd and no ex ins last* **25/1**

00/3 4 nk **Festive Chimes (IRE)**[19] 537 6-9-6 60 JerryO'Dwyer(3) 1 66+
(N B King) *hld up in tch: hdwy on inner and nt clr run over 2f out: keeping on wl whn n.m.r ins last: eased towards fin* **8/1**

400- 5 ½ **True (IRE)**[114] 6790 6-8-8 45 PaulFessey 12 50
(Mrs S Lamyman) *hld up in rr: hdwy over 2f out: kpt on same pce fnl f* **20/1**

64-4 6 nk **Rajayoga**[10] 775 6-8-6 48 PatrickHills(5) 5 52
(M H Tompkins) *in tch: effrt over 2f out: 3rd and keeping on same pce whn hit over hd by rival rdr's whip jst ins last* **7/1**

030- 7 3 **Just Waz (USA)**[18] 5369 5-8-6 48 MichaelJStainton(5) 2 49
(R M Whitaker) *chsd ldrs: effrt on inner over 2f out: one pce* **12/1**

050- 8 3½ **Accordello (IRE)**[60] 6178 6-9-1 57 JamieMoriarty(5) 15 54
(K G Reveley) *s.i.s: effrt and drvn on wd outside over 6f out: c wd st: nvr nr ldrs* **9/2**[2]

000- 9 1¼ **Scarrabus (IRE)**[309] 1660 6-8-10 50 GregFairley(3) 3 45
(A Crook) *rr-div: effrt on inner over 2f out: nvr nr ldrs* **100/1**

116- 10 3½ **Ostfanni (IRE)**[20] 3955 7-9-11 62 PatCosgrave 9 53
(M Todhunter) *chsd ldrs: reminders over 7f out: chal over 4f out: wknd 2f out* **4/1**[1]

020- 11 ½ **Etoile Russe (IRE)**[81] 6430 5-9-11 62 (t) JoeFanning 4 52
(P C Haslam) *mde most: hdd over 2f out: lost pl over 1f out* **20/1**

640/ 12 1 **In Dream's (IRE)**[29] 5400 5-8-5 45 AndrewElliott(3) 14 34
(G M Moore) *sn chsng ldrs: chal over 4f out: lost pl over 2f out* **5/1**[3]

00-3 13 2 **Arcangela**[29] 628 4-8-5 46 AdrianTNicholls 13 33
(Miss Tracy Waggott) *hld up in rr: effrt on outer over 2f out: sn btn* **40/1**

302/ 14 1½ **Alghaazy (IRE)**[551] 4998 6-8-8 45 DaleGibson 10 30
(Micky Hammond) *hld up in rr: effrt over 3f out: sn wknd* **40/1**

6/0- 15 2 **Water Pistol**[36] 1219 5-8-12 52 StephenDonohoe(3) 11 34
(M C Chapman) *w ldrs: lost pl over 5f out* **66/1**

3m 26.67s (-4.73) **Going Correction** -0.325s/f (Firm)
WFA 4 from 5yo+ 4lb **15** Ran SP% **123.4**
Speed ratings (Par 101):98,97,97,97,97 97,95,93,93,91 91,90,89,88,87
CSF £143.09 CT £3539.87 TOTE £13.20: £3.70, £3.90, £6.70; EX 110.40.
Owner Mr & Mrs J M Davenport **Bred** Mrs D W Davenport **Trained** Norton, N Yorks

FOCUS
A low-grade handicap, and a large blanket would have covered the first half-dozen. The gallop was very steady and the runner-up has been rated the best horse on the day.
Rajayoga Official explanation: jockey said gelding hung left in straight

914 CATTERICKBRIDGE.CO.UK H'CAP 1m 5f 175y
3:20 (3:20) (Class 4) (0-85,85) 4-Y-0+ **£5,181** (£1,541; £770; £384) **Stalls** Low

Form RPR

410- 1 **Halla San**[180] 5792 5-9-3 78 PaulHanagan 6 98+
(R A Fahey) *hld up: hdwy 7f out: effrt over 3f out: led over 2f out: clr over 1f out: heavily eased ins last* **15/8**[1]

302- 2 7 **Charlotte Vale**[44] 6275 6-8-5 66 oh1 DaleGibson 2 69
(Micky Hammond) *hld up in last: hdwy 3f out: styd on to take 2nd ins last* **15/2**

660- 3 1¼ **Aleron (IRE)**[81] 4764 9-8-7 68 (p) GrahamGibbons 9 69
(J J Quinn) *trckd ldrs: rdn and outpcd over 3f out: styd on same pce fnl 2f* **6/1**[3]

625- 4 shd **Mighty Moon**[110] 6836 4-9-7 85 (bt) DavidAllan 4 86
(J O'Reilly) *dwlt: sn trcking ldrs: effrt over 4f out: one pce fnl 2f* **6/1**[3]

550- 5 1¼ **Balyan (IRE)**[32] 2975 6-8-12 78 JamieMoriarty(5) 3 77
(J Howard Johnson) *trckd ldrs: drvn 6f out: sn outpcd: kpt on fnl 2f* **14/1**

220- 6 2½ **Oddsmaker (IRE)**[13] 5533 6-8-9 70 (t) DeanMcKeown 5 66
(M A Barnes) *led: t.k.h: hdd over 2f out: wknd appr fnl f* **9/1**

7 8 **Great Quest (IRE)**[18] 4865 5-8-6 67 RoystonFfrench 7 52
(James Moffatt) *chsd ldrs: drvn 8f out: outpcd over 4f out: n.d after: eased ins last* **25/1**

134- 8 ¾ **Baltic Princess (FR)**[256] 3748 4-8-9 73 JoeFanning 1 57
(M Johnston) *chsd ldrs: wkng whn stmbld 5f out: sn lost pl: eased and bhd fnl f* **4/1**[2]

2m 55.81s (-8.69) **Going Correction** -0.325s/f (Firm)
WFA 4 from 5yo+ 3lb **8** Ran SP% **115.6**
Speed ratings (Par 105):111,107,106,106,105 104,99,99
CSF £17.03 TOTE £2.80: £1.20, £2.20, £1.90; EX 19.30.
Owner Mrs Catherine Reynard **Bred** Hascombe And Valiant Studs **Trained** Musley Bank, N Yorks
■ Stewards' Enquiry : Dale Gibson caution: careless riding

FOCUS
A strongly-run race and in the end a one-horse race. Overall it was not strong form but the winner should go on from here.
Baltic Princess(FR) Official explanation: trainer's rep had no explanation for the poor form shown

915 GODS SOLUTION H'CAP 7f

3:50 (3:52) (Class 5) (0-75,75) 4-Y-0+ £3,238 (£963; £481; £240) Stalls Low

Form RPR

400- 1 **Sir Orpen (IRE)**[168] 6048 4-8-10 67 PaulFessey 6 76
(T D Barron) *trckd ldrs: outpcd and lost pl over 3f out: hdwy over 2f out: styd on to ld ins last: hld on towards fin* **4/1**[2]

610- 2 nk **Major Magpie (IRE)**[179] 5810 5-9-4 75 PhillipMakin 3 84
(M Dods) *hld up in tch: effrt over 2f out: edgd rt and styd on strly fnl f: jst hld* **13/2**

0111 3 1 **Kabis Amigos**[11] 771 5-8-12 69 (t) AdrianTNicholls 8 75
(D Nicholls) *led tl hdd and no ex ins last* **3/1**[1]

435- 4 2 **Ryedale Ovation (IRE)**[216] 4958 4-9-1 72 DavidAllan 5 73
(T D Easterby) *sn chsng ldrs: styd on same pce appr fnl f* **6/1**[3]

5036 5 ¾ **Boy Dancer (IRE)**[5] 831 4-8-4 61 oh1 JoeFanning 4 60+
(D W Barker) *s.s: detached in last tl styd on wl fnl 2f: fin wl* **17/2**

000- 6 ½ **Press Express (IRE)**[154] 6301 5-8-8 65 PaulHanagan 7 63
(R A Fahey) *in tch: effrt over 3f out: sn outpcd: kpt on fnl 2f* **8/1**

-000 7 7 **Kabeer**[12] 739 9-7-13 61 oh5 (t) NataliaGemelova(5) 1 40
(A J McCabe) *w ldr: wknd appr fnl f* **8/1**

500- 8 hd **Malinsa Blue (IRE)**[202] 5317 5-8-4 61 oh1 RoystonFfrench 2 40
(B Ellison) *trckd ldrs: lost pl over 1f out* **14/1**

0000 9 12 **Polish Emperor (USA)**[30] 621 7-8-6 63 (v) CatherineGannon 10 11
(D W Barker) *in tch: drvn and outpcd over 3f out: wandered 2f out: sn wknd* **33/1**

1m 24.08s (-3.28) **Going Correction** -0.325s/f (Firm) 9 Ran SP% **115.0**
Speed ratings (Par 103):105,104,103,101,100 99,91,91,77
CSF £30.04 CT £88.56 TOTE £5.60: £2.00, £2.50, £1.40; EX 39.20.
Owner Owen Boyle **Bred** Mrs Ann Stack **Trained** Maunby, N Yorks
■ Stewards' Enquiry : Adrian T Nicholls caution: used whip down the shoulder in forehand position

FOCUS
A strongly-run handicap and the form looks sound.
Kabeer Official explanation: jockey said gelding bled from the nose

916 TOYTOP MAIDEN STKS 5f 212y

4:20 (4:21) (Class 5) 3-Y-0+ £3,238 (£963; £481; £240) Stalls Low

Form RPR

23- 1 **Weekend Fling (USA)**[274] 3173 3-8-8 JoeFanning 1 66+
(M Johnston) *mde all: pushed along over 2f out: clr 1f out: unchal* **1/2**[1]

6- 2 2½ **Kyrenia Girl (IRE)**[270] 3286 3-8-8 PaulQuinn 8 54
(T D Easterby) *chsd ldrs: styd on to take 2nd ins last: no ch w wnr* **20/1**

46 3 1¼ **Modern Verse (USA)**[11] 758 4-9-11 DeanMcKeown 2 59+
(G A Swinbank) *rrd s: in rr: shkn up over 2f out: styd on ins last* **7/1**[2]

00- 4 nk **Meridian Grey (USA)**[269] 3328 3-8-10 AndrewMullen(3) 7 54
(K A Ryan) *chsd ldrs: one pce fnl 2f* **11/1**

50 5 hd **Mr Whoppit**[22] 670 3-8-13 DavidAllan 9 53
(T D Easterby) *w wnr: one pce fnl 2f* **28/1**

00- 6 1¼ **Imperial Beach (USA)**[279] 3018 3-8-13 PaulFessey 10 50
(T D Barron) *s.i.s: hld up in rr: hd over 4f out: kpt on same pce fnl 2f* **9/1**[3]

7 2½ **Pearl Valley** 3-8-8 PaulHanagan 4 37
(R A Fahey) *in rr: kpt on fnl 2f: nvr a factor* **9/1**[3]

0- 8 10 **Good Etiquette**[195] 5491 3-8-13 RoystonFfrench 6 12
(Mrs S Lamyman) *sltly hmpd s: a last: detached fnl 2f* **80/1**

1m 12.94s (-1.06) **Going Correction** -0.325s/f (Firm)
WFA 3 from 4yo 12lb 8 Ran SP% **116.9**
Speed ratings (Par 103):94,90,89,88,88 86,83,70
CSF £16.24 TOTE £1.70: £1.10, £4.50, £1.60; EX 12.10.
Owner Mr & Mrs Christopher Wright **Bred** Grapestock Llc **Trained** Middleham Moor, N Yorks

FOCUS
A weak sprint maiden, difficult to rate accurately but a very ready winner.

917 YARM H'CAP 1m 3f 214y

4:50 (4:51) (Class 5) (0-75,67) 3-Y-0 £3,238 (£963; £481) Stalls Low

Form RPR

330- 1 **Always Best**[152] 6322 3-9-3 66 JoeFanning 1 63
(M Johnston) *trckd ldr: jnd ldr over 5f out: led over 2f out: kpt on u.p: all out* **4/5**[1]

20-5 2 nk **Colditz (IRE)**[35] 582 3-9-4 67 TonyHamilton 2 64
(D W Barker) *restrained handy in last: effrt 4f out: chal 1f out: hrd rdn and jst hld* **5/1**[3]

0023 3 6 **Citrus Chief (USA)**[9] 790 3-8-9 58 PaulHanagan 3 45
(R A Harris) *led: qcknd over 4f: hdd over 2f out: wknd fnl f* **15/8**[2]

2m 36.85s (-2.15) **Going Correction** -0.325s/f (Firm) 3 Ran SP% **107.0**
Speed ratings (Par 98):94,93,89
CSF £4.51 TOTE £1.50; EX 4.50.
Owner Always Trying Partnership III **Bred** Mrs R D Peacock **Trained** Middleham Moor, N Yorks

FOCUS
A pathetic turn-out for a £5,000 added handicap. Just a steady pace and the first two look pretty exposed.

918 TOTESPORT BIG SCREEN IS HERE EVERY DAY H'CAP 5f

5:20 (5:25) (Class 6) (0-65,62) 3-Y-0 £2,730 (£806; £403) Stalls Low

Form RPR

064- 1 **Darcy's Pride (IRE)**[178] 5835 3-8-9 53 TonyHamilton 4 61
(D W Barker) *chsd ldrs: led jst ins last: hld on towards fin* **33/1**

6-31 2 ½ **Mandurah (IRE)**[2] 894 3-9-1 59 6ex AdrianTNicholls 6 65
(D Nicholls) *chsd ldrs: chal over 1f out: no ex towards fin* **2/1**[1]

3-50 3 1½ **Minimum Fuss (IRE)**[15] 713 3-8-9 56 (b) StephenDonohoe(3) 1 57
(M C Chapman) *led: hdd jst ins last: fdd* **11/1**

03-5 4 ½ **Strathmore (IRE)**[21] 679 3-9-4 62 PaulHanagan 7 61
(R A Fahey) *chsd ldrs: outpcd and lost pl after 2f: hdwy over 1f out: styd on towards fin* **4/1**[3]

0-63 5 shd **Moonlight Applause**[15] 713 3-8-8 52 DavidAllan 10 51
(T D Easterby) *chsd ldrs: outpcd after 2f: hdwy over 1f out: gng on at fin* **12/1**

150- 6 1¼ **Back In The Red (IRE)**[154] 6291 3-8-13 62 (p) MichaelJStainton(5) 3 56
(R A Harris) *chsd ldrs: one pce fnl 2f* **7/2**[2]

650- 7 5 **Seaton Snooks**[218] 4912 3-9-4 62 GrahamGibbons 2 38
(T D Easterby) *in tch: outpcd after 2f: no ch after* **9/1**

00-0 8 5 **La Esperanza**[36] 574 3-8-3 50 DominicFox(3) 8 8
(Miss A Stokell) *dwlt: lost pl after 2f: sn bhd* **50/1**

3261 9 5 **Pretty Selma**[15] 713 3-8-6 50 (b) JoeFanning 9 —
(R M H Cowell) *unruly and led rdrless to post: dwlt: hung rt and sn outpcd: no ch whn eased 1f out* **11/1**

-024 10 5 **Mangano**[43] 505 3-8-4 48 oh3 PaulQuinn 5 —
(A Berry) *dwlt: sn wl bhd* **28/1**

58.51 secs (-2.09) **Going Correction** -0.50s/f (Hard) 10 Ran SP% **118.3**
Speed ratings (Par 96):96,95,92,92,91 89,81,73,65,57
CSF £99.48 CT £846.81 TOTE £30.30: £5.10, £1.40, £3.10; EX 91.50 Place 6 £67.60, Place 5 £38.46.
Owner Ms Jenny Hanson **Bred** Leo Cox **Trained** Scorton, N Yorks

FOCUS
A low-grade three-year-old sprint handicap. There was no hanging about and the form at this level looks solid.
T/Plt: £55.80 to a £1 stake. Pool: £54,031.55. 705.75 winning tickets. T/Qpdt: £2.90 to a £1 stake. Pool: £3,504.50. 883.05 winning tickets. WG

883 LINGFIELD (L-H)

Wednesday, April 4

OFFICIAL GOING: Standard
Wind: moderate against

919 LINGFIELDPARK.CO.UK MAIDEN STKS 7f (P)

2:30 (2:31) (Class 5) 3-Y-0 £2,914 (£867; £433; £216) Stalls Low

Form RPR

54 1 **Chattan Clan**[46] 489 3-9-3 (t) DaneO'Neill 4 70
(R A Kvisla) *hld up in 5th: prog to trck ldr over 2f out: hanging lft but rdn to ld 1f out: grad gained upper hand* **11/1**[3]

366- 2 1 **Love On Sight**[234] 4400 3-8-12 100 DarryllHolland 1 62
(A P Jarvis) *led and dictated stdy pce: shkn up and hdd 1f out: nt qckn* **4/11**[1]

32-5 3 ¾ **Baltic Belle (IRE)**[14] 720 3-8-12 70 PatDobbs 5 60
(R Hannon) *trckd ldrs gng wl: rdn and fnd nil wl over 1f out: styd on ins fnl f but all too late* **6/1**[2]

- 4 1¾ **Dr Dream (IRE)** 3-9-3 LPKeniry 7 60+
(D M Simcock) *w'like: bit bkwd: s.s: rn green and sn urged along in last: no prog tl styd on fnl f* **12/1**

00- 5 1 **Metropolitan Chief**[174] 5918 3-9-3 FergusSweeney 6 58+
(D M Simcock) *lw: s.i.s: hld up in last pair: rdn over 2f out: sn btn* **25/1**

26 6 1 **Firebird Annie (IRE)**[12] 745 3-8-12 MickyFenton 2 50?
(A Bailey) *trckd ldr to over 2f out: sn btn* **25/1**

0 7 5 **Magroom**[81] 116 3-9-3 (v[1]) SamHitchcott 3 41
(B R Johnson) *t.k.h: hld up bhd ldrs: cl up whn nt clr run on inner 2f out: wknd sn after* **80/1**

1m 25.42s (-0.47) **Going Correction** -0.025s/f (Stan) 7 Ran SP% **112.6**
Speed ratings (Par 98):101,99,99,97,95 94,89
CSF £15.26 TOTE £12.40: £1.90, £1.10; EX 27.60.
Owner Investment Ab Rustningen **Bred** S J And Mrs Pembroke **Trained** Newmarket, Suffolk

FOCUS
An uncompetitive affair on paper, but it did not work out that way with hot favourite Love On Sight being turned over at 4/11. The winner is progressive but the form is not rock solid.

920 LINGFIELD PARK GOLF CLUB (S) STKS 6f (P)

3:00 (3:02) (Class 6) 3-Y-0+ £2,184 (£644; £322) Stalls Low

Form RPR

6004 1 **Blue Knight (IRE)**[8] 800 8-9-8 41 (p) ShaneKelly 11 53
(P Howling) *hld up in last trio: effrt and wd bnd 2f out: prog over 1f out: one reminder then urged along fnl f: r.o to ld nr fin* **8/1**

0000 2 hd **Midmaar (IRE)**[8] 800 6-9-13 50 (b) JamieMackay 12 57
(M Wigham) *w ldrs: led wl over 1f out: rdn over a l clr fnl f: collared nr fin* **10/1**

0-00 3 1¾ **Boisdale (IRE)**[41] 523 9-9-8 41 TonyCulhane 6 47
(P S Felgate) *hld up bhd ldrs: nt clr run over 1f out: styd on fnl f: nvr able to chal* **50/1**

-000 4 nk **Dolly**[18] 699 5-9-3 39 (p) RichardThomas 7 41
(Tom Dascombe) *settled in midfield: pushed along over 2f out: prog to dispute 2nd 1f out: styd on same pce* **12/1**

00-0 5 ¾ **Shreddy Shrimpster**[28] 636 3-8-0 50 KevinGhunowa(5) 9 39
(A B Haynes) *racd wd: trckd ldrs: effrt 2f out: rdn to dispute 2nd 1f out: one pce* **8/1**

0005 6 1½ **Hotchpotch (USA)**[12] 734 4-9-10 50 (p) StephaneBreux(3) 4 45
(J R Best) *dwlt: hld up in last trio: urged along and no rspnse wl over 1f out* **4/1**[2]

0-03 7 nk **Balian**[14] 723 4-9-8 45 (b) MickyFenton 1 39
(Mrs P Sly) *trckd ldrs on inner: cl enough over 1f out: nt qckn and sn btn* **6/1**[3]

5003 8 nk **Sham Ruby**[12] 743 5-9-3 41 (t) HayleyTurner 5 33
(M R Bosley) *disp ld to wl over 1f out: sn wknd* **8/1**

4000 9 2 **Teyaar**[14] 722 11-9-13 45 DaneO'Neill 3 37
(M Wellings) *disp ld to wl over 1f out: sn wknd* **14/1**

-060 10 ¾ **Bear Essential**[16] 708 3-8-10 53 PaulEddery 8 29
(Mrs P N Dutfield) *dwlt: hld up in last: rdn 2f out: no prog* **20/1**

4000 U **Mister Elegant**[13] 729 5-9-8 52 SamHitchcott 2 —
(J L Spearing) *wl in rr: pushed along over 3f out: 8th but styng on whn rn out of room over 1f out: stmbld and uns rdr* **7/2**[1]

1m 12.53s (-0.28) **Going Correction** -0.025s/f (Stan)
WFA 3 from 4yo+ 12lb 11 Ran SP% **120.0**
Speed ratings (Par 101):100,99,97,97,96 94,93,93,90,89 —
CSF £87.22 TOTE £6.90: £2.50, £4.40, £13.70; EX 65.50 Trifecta £211.10 Part won. Pool £297.38 - 0.51 winning units..There was no bid for the winner.
Owner Mrs J P Howling **Bred** Mrs Ann Egan **Trained** Newmarket, Suffolk

FOCUS
A typically competitive seller. The form is poorish but seems to make sense.

921 WENDY STUART'S 50TH BIRTHDAY H'CAP 1m 4f (P)

3:30 (3:30) (Class 5) (0-75,74) 4-Y-0+ £2,914 (£867; £433; £216) Stalls Low

Form RPR

3-41 1 **Dower House**[8] 799 12-9-5 74 (t) ChrisCatlin 7 81
(Andrew Turnell) *trckd ldng pair: wnt 2nd over 2f out: rdn to ld narrowly over 1f out: kpt on wl: jst hld on* **13/2**

6031 2 hd **Turner's Touch**[6] 813 5-9-1 70 (b) GeorgeBaker 2 77+
(G L Moore) *hld up in last pair: stl last whn dash sed 2f out: urged along and r.o ins fnl f: jst failed* **10/3**[2]

0104 3 nk **Red Birr (IRE)**[21] 675 6-9-2 71 EddieAhern 1 77
(P R Webber) *hld up bhd ldrs: rdn and effrt 2f out: pressed wnr over 1f out: no ex last 50yds* **6/1**

3-15 **4** *nk* **Poseidon's Secret (IRE)**[11] [753] 4-9-2 **72**........................ PaulEddery 4 78
(Pat Eddery) *lw: led: set slow pce to 1/2-way: narrowly hdd 5f out: rdn 3f out: styd on inner and n.m.r 1f out: kpt on* **3/1**[1]

-521 **5** *3/4* **Musango**[12] [740] 4-8-12 **68**........................ DaneO'Neill 3 73
(B R Johnson) *hld up bhd ldrs: rdn and effrt over 2f out: chal and upsides jst over 1f out: wknd last 75yds* **4/1**[3]

0-60 **6** *3 1/2* **Prime Powered (IRE)**[11] [753] 6-9-5 **74**........................ FergusSweeney 5 73
(R M Beckett) *dwlt: hld up in last pair: rdn on outer over 2f out: hanging and fnd nil wl over 1f out* **12/1**

50-6 **7** *2* **Capistrano**[14] [726] 4-8-13 **69**........................ MickyFenton 6 65
(Mrs P Sly) *pressed ldr: narrow ld 5f out: hdd over 1f out: wkng whn n.m.r ent fnl f* **9/1**

2m 37.78s (3.39) **Going Correction** -0.025s/f (Stan)
WFA 4 from 5yo+ 1lb 7 Ran SP% **113.4**
Speed ratings (Par 103):87,86,86,86,85 83,82
CSF £27.86 TOTE £8.40: £1.80, £2.30; EX 13.30.
Owner Mrs Claire Hollowood **Bred** Lord Howard De Walden **Trained** Broad Hinton, Wilts

FOCUS
A competitive contest and there was little over a length between the front five at the line. There was no pace on, though, and the form is far from solid.
Capistrano Official explanation: jockey said gelding hung left

922 WEATHERBYS BANK CONDITIONS STKS 7f (P)
4:00 (4:00) (Class 3) 3-Y-O **£7,570** (£2,265; £1,132) **Stalls** Low

Form RPR

131- **1** **Majuro (IRE)**[176] [5884] 3-9-0 **91**........................ DarryllHolland 2 93
(M R Channon) *led and sn 3 l clr: rdn over 2f out: narrowly hdd ins fnl f: fought bk wl to ld on line* **9/2**[3]

11-0 **2** *shd* **Cesc**[11] [760] 3-9-2 **92**........................ EddieAhern 3 95
(P J Makin) *lw: hld up in last: chsd wnr over 2f out: chal over 1f out: narrow ld ins fnl f: hdd on line* **9/4**[2]

12-6 **3** *5* **Resplendent Alpha**[19] [695] 3-9-2 **98**........................ ShaneKelly 1 82
(P Howling) *b.hind: lw: trckd wnr to over 2f out: plld out and shkn up over 1f out: carried hd awkwardly and no rspnse* **4/6**[1]

1m 26.25s (0.36) **Going Correction** -0.025s/f (Stan) 3 Ran SP% **108.9**
Speed ratings (Par 102):96,95,90
CSF £12.69 TOTE £3.40; EX 5.90.
Owner Capital **Bred** Tally-Ho Stud **Trained** West Ilsley, Berks

FOCUS
A disappointing turnout for this conditions contest, but the pace was reasonable considering the small field. The front two looked to produce a very useful level of form but it is far from solid.

NOTEBOOK
Majuro(IRE), off the track since winning a similar event on the turf at Leicester in October, was allowed the run of the race out in front and was just too strong for Cesc. He looked vulnerable when strongly challenged in the straight, but battled on most gamely. He may not prove the easiest to place from now on but, having won four of his seven career starts, he does not exactly owe his connections a great deal. (op 4-1 tchd 5-1 in a place)
Cesc never landed a blow in a course-and-distance Listed contest on his return from a break, but this was obviously much easier and he was just held. He looked the most likely winner for much of the way up the straight, but just lost out on the nod. (op 5-2)
Resplendent Alpha, well held in a French Listed race on his return from a break last time, proved a huge disappointment stepped up to his furthest trip to date. He was beaten before stamina became an issue and did not convince with his attitude. (op 8-11)

923 EXHIBITIONS AT LINGFIELD PARK H'CAP 7f (P)
4:30 (4:30) (Class 5) (0-70,70) 4-Y-O+ **£2,914** (£867; £433; £216) **Stalls** Low

Form RPR

0032 **1** **Special Place**[12] [739] 4-8-10 **62**........................ OscarUrbina 5 72
(J A R Toller) *lw: hld up in last trio: effrt on outer over 2f out: hanging and in trble over 1f out: r.o to ld last 150yds: rdn out* **7/2**[2]

3044 **2** *1* **Arctic Desert**[12] [739] 7-9-4 **70**........................(t) DarryllHolland 1 78
(Miss Gay Kelleway) *b: b.hind: dwlt: in tch: chsd ldng pair over 2f out: nt qckn wl over 1f out: styd on fnl f: outpcd by wnr* **6/1**[3]

1030 **3** *3/4* **Seneschal**[9] [793] 6-8-13 **65**........................ SamHitchcott 8 71
(A B Haynes) *pressed ldr: led over 2f out: rdn and looked in command over 1f out: idled and hdd last 150yds: no ex* **7/1**

6-06 **4** *nk* **General Feeling (IRE)**[8] [803] 6-8-4 **56**........................ HayleyTurner 3 61
(M Mullineaux) *hw: dwlt: mostly in last pair: rdn 3f out: no prog tl styd on fnl f to take 4th last stride* **16/1**

4513 **5** *1/2* **Takitwo**[5] [831] 4-8-7 **59**........................ LPKeniry 4 63
(P D Cundell) *chsd ldrs: rdn 3f out: struggling 2f out: kpt on last 100yds* **2/1**[1]

5446 **6** *1 1/2* **Hammer Of The Gods (IRE)**[13] [727] 7-9-3 **69**........................(bt) EddieAhern 6 72+
(P S McEntee) *led at decent pce: hdd over 2f out: rdn over 1f out: hld whn n.m.r ins fnl f: eased* **7/1**

4044 **7** *3 1/2* **Zazous**[3] [866] 6-8-3 **58** ow1........................ MarcHalford(3) 2 49
(J J Bridger) *dropped to last and rdn 1/2-way: sn struggling* **8/1**

1m 24.32s (-1.57) **Going Correction** -0.025s/f (Stan) 7 Ran SP% **111.8**
Speed ratings (Par 103):107,105,105,104,104 102,98
CSF £23.34 CT £135.35 TOTE £3.60: £1.80, £2.50; EX 22.40 Trifecta £90.10 Pool £558.42 - 4.40 winning units.
Owner Miss Julia Staughton **Bred** Miss J Staughton & Mrs O Staughton **Trained** Newmarket, Suffolk
■ Stewards' Enquiry : Sam Hitchcott caution: careless riding

FOCUS
A modest handicap, but the pace seemed reasonable. The form looks sound, rated through the third.

924 DINNER DANCES AT LINGFIELD PARK H'CAP 1m (P)
5:00 (5:02) (Class 6) (0-60,60) 3-Y-O **£2,388** (£705; £352) **Stalls** High

Form RPR

-062 **1** **Cnoc Moy (IRE)**[9] [791] 3-9-4 **60**........................ GeorgeBaker 10 74+
(C F Wall) *sn trckd ldr: led 2f out: drew rt away over 1f out: easily* **11/10**[1]

0000 **2** *4* **Mark Of Love (IRE)**[12] [738] 3-9-3 **59**........................ TonyCulhane 3 59
(M R Channon) *lw: prom: rdn on inner over 2f out: styd on fr over 1f out to take 2nd last 75yds: no ch w wnr* **9/1**

000- **3** *1/2* **Rosie Cross (IRE)**[184] [5738] 3-9-1 **57**........................ HayleyTurner 6 56
(Eve Johnson Houghton) *racd freely: led to 2f out: no ch w wnr after: lost 2nd last 75yds* **33/1**

0044 **4** *1 1/4* **Brave Jack (IRE)**[12] [738] 3-8-12 **57**........................ StephaneBreux(3) 7 53+
(J R Best) *lw: sn pushed along towards rr: effrt u.p over 2f out: kpt on fnl f: n.d* **5/1**[2]

50-0 **5** *nk* **Ireland Dancer (IRE)**[25] [655] 3-9-4 **60**........................ IanMongan 11 55
(P M Phelan) *t.k.h: prom: rdn over 2f out: outpcd wl over 1f out: n.d after* **25/1**

05-0 **6** *3/4* **Lancaster's Quest**[11] [758] 3-9-3 **59**........................ RobertHavlin 8 53
(R Ingram) *s.i.s: t.k.h and racd opn outer: effrt fr rr 3f out: no real prog fnl 2f* **14/1**

000- **7** *hd* **Kanonkop**[166] [6071] 3-9-1 **57**........................ ChrisCatlin 4 50
(Miss J R Gibney) *reluctant to enter stalls: s.i.s: a towards rr: n.d fnl 2f* **50/1**

0-66 **8** *hd* **Perfect Practice**[36] [577] 3-9-2 **58**........................ EddieAhern 1 51
(J A R Toller) *hld up in midfield: rdn over 2f out: no prog* **9/1**

04-2 **9** *nk* **Bathwick Fancy (IRE)**[12] [736] 3-9-1 **57**........................(t) NickyMackay 5 49
(J G Portman) *s.i.s: sn rchd midfield: rdn over 2f out: no imp over 1f out: wknd ins fnl f* **14/1**

4-04 **10** *1* **Rubilini**[12] [737] 3-9-2 **58**........................ SamHitchcott 9 48
(M R Channon) *chsd ldrs: rdn 3f out: no prog 2f out: wknd fnl f* **13/2**[3]

0-00 **11** *hd* **Poyle Ruby**[65] [293] 3-8-6 **55**........................ LauraReynolds(7) 12 44
(M Blanshard) *plld hrd on outer: bmpd after 2f and dropped to last: n.d after* **66/1**

050- **12** *27* **She Wont Wait**[266] [3409] 3-8-13 **55**........................ FergusSweeney 2 —
(T M Jones) *t.k.h early: chsd ldrs 2f: lost pl 1/2-way: wknd: t.o* **66/1**

1m 38.59s (-0.84) **Going Correction** -0.025s/f (Stan) 12 Ran SP% **122.7**
Speed ratings (Par 96):103,99,98,97,96 96,96,95,95,94 94,67
CSF £12.24 CT £229.99 TOTE £2.30: £1.10, £2.40, £8.40; EX 14.90 Trifecta £297.80 Pool £751.04 - 1.79 winning units. Place 6 £715.80, Place 5 £584.49.
Owner Peter Botham **Bred** Miss Gemma Cunningham **Trained** Newmarket, Suffolk

FOCUS
A modest handicap, but an easy winner in the form of Cnoc Moy, who is improving. The form seems to make sense.
Ireland Dancer(IRE) Official explanation: jockey said gelding hung left
T/Plt: £161.40 to a £1 stake. Pool: £60,486.75. 273.50 winning tickets. T/Qpdt: £34.60 to a £1 stake. Pool: £3,266.20. 69.80 winning tickets. JN

NOTTINGHAM (L-H)
Wednesday, April 4

OFFICIAL GOING: Good to firm
All of the races were on the inside track.
Wind: light behind

925 SHOWSEC H'CAP 5f 13y
2:10 (2:10) (Class 5) (0-70,70) 3-Y-O **£2,914** (£867; £433; £216) **Stalls** High

Form RPR

040- **1** **Pickering**[149] [6377] 3-9-2 **68**........................ KDarley 14 81+
(E J Alston) *dwlt: hld up in rr: effrt and nt clr run wl over 1f out: gd hdwy on stands rails ent last: led nr fin* **15/2**

2042 **2** *1/2* **Diminuto**[16] [707] 3-8-1 **60**........................ FrankiePickard(7) 1 65
(M D I Usher) *led far side gp: drifted rt fr 2f out: rdn and overall ldr 1f out: drvn ins last: hdd and nt qckn towards fin* **8/1**

660- **3** *1* **Windjammer**[247] [3994] 3-7-13 **56** oh1........................ DuranFentiman(5) 9 57
(T D Easterby) *a cl up: effrt 2f out: sn rdn and ev ch tl drvn and one pce ins last* **16/1**

-354 **4** *1/2* **Hereford Boy**[10] [778] 3-9-4 **70**........................ SebSanders 10 70
(D K Ivory) *rr and pushed along 1/2-way: swtchd lft: rdn and hdwy 2f out: sn drvn and hung lft: chsd ldr ins last: wknd last 100 yds* **7/1**

5-00 **5** *3/4* **Bahamian Love**[21] [679] 3-8-8 **60**........................[1] MichaelHills 11 57
(B W Hills) *chsd ldrs stands side: rdn along and edgd lft wl over 1f out: drvn and one pce fnl f* **13/2**[3]

310- **6** *1* **Picture Frame**[218] [4912] 3-8-11 **70**........................ DavidProbert(7) 5 63
(J T Stimpson) *swtchd to r stands side: towards rr tl styd on appr last: nrst fin* **16/1**

3341 **7** *shd* **Pirner's Brig**[16] [707] 3-9-2 **68**........................ PaulMulrennan 12 61
(M W Easterby) *overall ldr stands rail: rdn along 2f out: drvn: edgd lft and hdd 1f out: wknd ins last* **4/1**[1]

324- **8** *shd* **Mujart**[114] [6788] 3-8-4 **59** ow2........................ SaleemGolam(3) 4 52
(J A Pickering) *dwlt: swtchd to r stands side: effrt and sme hdwy 2f out: sn rdn and no imp* **12/1**

0545 **9** *1/2* **Perlachy**[15] [713] 3-9-2 **68**........................(v) DanielTudhope 8 59
(Mrs N Macauley) *cl up stands side: effrt and ev chance 2f out: sn rdn and wknd* **6/1**[2]

02-0 **10** *3/4* **The Geester**[15] [713] 3-8-6 **58**........................(b) AdrianMcCarthy 7 46
(S R Bowring) *chsd ldrs stands side: effrt over 2f out: sn rdn and grad wknd* **20/1**

4-06 **11** *7* **Hephaestus**[22] [671] 3-8-6 **65** ow2........................ MarkCoumbe(7) 2 28
(A J Chamberlain) *dwlt: a rr far side* **40/1**

1-15 **12** *1/2* **Sister Etienne (IRE)**[16] [707] 3-9-3 **69**........................ NCallan 3 30
(J T Stimpson) *keen: chsd ldr far side: rdn along over 2f out and sn wknd* **12/1**

60.90 secs (-0.90) **Going Correction** -0.175s/f (Firm) 12 Ran SP% **117.3**
Speed ratings (Par 98):100,99,97,96,95 94,93,93,92,91 80,79
CSF £65.65 CT £949.66 TOTE £6.80: £2.70, £3.00, £9.60; EX 88.60.
Owner The Selebians **Bred** Mrs Rosalynd Norman **Trained** Longton, Lancs

FOCUS
A modest sprint which saw those drawn high at an advantage. The form is rated through the fourth.
Pirner's Brig Official explanation: jockey said colt hung left throughout
Sister Etienne(IRE) Official explanation: jockey said filly had no more to give

926 EUROPEAN BREEDERS' FUND NOVICE STKS 5f 13y
2:40 (2:40) (Class 4) 2-Y-O **£4,533** (£1,348; £674; £336) **Stalls** High

Form RPR

1 **Fred's Lad** 2-8-12........................ PaulMulrennan 5 82
(M W Easterby) *chsd ldrs: rdn along and sltly outpcd 2f out: gd hdwy over 1f out: chal and hung lft ins last: led last 50 yds* **25/1**

2 *1* **Ten Down** 2-8-12........................ JamieSpencer 4 78
(J A Osborne) *mde most stands rail: effrt and qcknd wl over 1f out: pushed clr ins last: hdd and nt qckn last 50 yds* **9/4**[2]

3 *2* **Fast Feet** 2-8-12........................ NCallan 2 70+
(K A Ryan) *s.i.s: hdwy to join ldrs 1/2-way: rdn wl over 1f and kpt on same pce* **2/1**[1]

4 *nk* **Brassini** 2-8-12........................ JimCrowley 3 69
(B R Millman) *cl up: effrt 2f out: sn rdn and one pce appr last* **8/1**[3]

5 *4* **Tazawud** 2-8-12........................ RHills 1 53
(M Johnston) *cl up: rdn along over 2f out: sn hung lft and wknd* **9/4**[2]

6 *nk* **Varinia (IRE)** 2-8-7........................ DeanMernagh 6 47+
(M Brittain) *rrd s: a rr* **25/1**

61.46 secs (-0.34) **Going Correction** -0.175s/f (Firm) 6 Ran SP% **113.7**
Speed ratings (Par 94):95,93,90,89,83 82
CSF £82.44 TOTE £18.90: £5.60, £1.80; EX 97.40.

Owner Derek Pearson **Bred** A C M Spalding **Trained** Sheriff Hutton, N Yorks

FOCUS

This looked a fair little novice event, but it remains to be seen how it works out. It was run at a sound pace and produced a somewhat surprising winner.

NOTEBOOK

Fred's Lad, an early-foaled half-brother to two debutant winners, maintained the family tradition with a ready success at the first time of asking. He took time to get the hang of things early on, but when angled off the rail with his effort nearing the final furlong he found an extra gear and came through horses to score despite tending to hang left. Obviously he is entitled to improve for the experience and he did appear at home on the decent ground. (tchd 22-1)

Ten Down ◆, a 32,000gns purchase bred for speed, had the benefit of the stands' rail and did nothing wrong in defeat. He showed decent early dash here and, with this experience behind him, should take a lot of beating on his next assignment. (op 11-4)

Fast Feet, a 70,000gns purchase bred to make his mark as a sprinter, overcame a messy start and had his chance. He ran green on the way to the start and will no doubt benefit a great deal for this debut experience. (op 7-4)

Brassini, a brother to mile winner Don Pietro and half-brother to prolific 6-7f winner Warden Warren, showed early pace and left the impression he would be all the better for this debut outing. (tchd 9-1)

Tazawud, who well-bred dam was a six furlong winner as a juvenile, is the first juvenile to be sent out by his powerful stable and was not surprisingly popular in the betting ring. He knew his job from the gates, but hung his chance away on the outside of the pack when it mattered and clearly will need to learn from the experience. He is fully entitled to do so, however. (op 3-1)

Varinia(IRE), half-sister to two maidens, was the sole filly in the line-up and she lost her chance by rearing at the start. She did show a bit of ability, however.

927 WEATHERBYS BLOODSTOCK INSURANCE CONDITIONS STKS — 5f 13y

3:10 (3:10) (Class 4) 3-Y-O+ — **£6,477** (£1,927; £963; £481) **Stalls** High

Form			Horse	Jockey	RPR
000-	1		**Fire Up The Band**^{208} [5158] 8-9-1 95 .... SilvestreDeSousa 3 *(D Nicholls) led 2f: cl up tl led again wl over 1f out: sn rdn: drvn and hung lft ins last: kpt on wl* **9/1**		103
042-	2	¾	**Bond City (IRE)**^{174} [5921] 5-9-1 103 .... NCallan 7 *(G R Oldroyd) chsd ldrs: rdn along and sltly outpcd wl over 1f out: swtchd rt and rdn ent last: styd on wl* **7/2**^{2}		101
4/6-	3	1 ½	**Patavellian (IRE)**^{333} [1485] 9-9-1 109 ....(b) SteveDrowne 2 *(R Charlton) dwlt: sn in tch: gd hdwy on outer 2f out: rdn to chse wnr and ev ch over 1f out: wknd ins last* **9/4**^{1}		95
200-	4	1	**Terentia**^{174} [5919] 4-8-10 97 .... JimmyFortune 8 *(E S McMahon) chsd ldrs: rdn along 2f out: kpt on same pce* **7/2**^{2}		87
334-	5	1	**Charles Darwin (IRE)**^{157} [6243] 4-9-1 89 .... TedDurcan 5 *(M Blanshard) chsd ldrs: rdn along over 2f out: grad wknd* **7/1**^{3}		88
360-	6	1	**Cape Royal**^{172} [5957] 7-9-1 92 ....(bt) KDarley 4 *(J M Bradley) cl up: held after 2f: rdn and hdd wl over 1f out: wknd appr last* **20/1**		84
302-	7	1 ¼	**Turnkey**^{313} [1979] 5-8-8 98 .... AdeleRothery$^{(7)}$ 6 *(D Nicholls) s.i.s and wl bhd tl styd on wl appr last* **16/1**		80
0264	8	6	**Nepro (IRE)**^{10} [774] 5-9-1 70 ....(vt) EdwardCreighton 1 *(E J Creighton) s.i.s: a rr* **66/1**		58

59.79 secs (-2.01) **Going Correction** -0.175s/f (Firm) — **8** Ran SP% **109.9**

Speed ratings (Par 105):109,107,105,103,102 100,98,89

CSF £37.35 TOTE £10.00: £2.60, £1.20, £1.30; EX 30.00.

Owner A A Bloodstock Ltd **Bred** Miss A J Rawding And P M Crane **Trained** Sessay, N Yorks

■ Stewards' Enquiry : Silvestre De Sousa two-day ban: careless riding (Apr 16,17)

FOCUS

A decent conditions sprint which provided a back-to-form winner. The form looks fair enough.

Turnkey Official explanation: jockey said gelding missed the break

928 WEATHERBYS PRINTING H'CAP — 1m 1f 213y

3:40 (3:41) (Class 5) (0-70,69) 4-Y-O+ — **£3,238** (£963; £481; £240) **Stalls** Low

Form			Horse	Jockey	RPR
-012	1		**Shape Up (IRE)**^{13} [733] 7-9-1 **66** ....(v) NCallan 1 *(R Craggs) mde all: qcknd over 2f out: rdn clr wl over 1f out: easily* **7/2**^{1}		80
0/63	2	6	**Camille Pissarro (USA)**^{20} [681] 7-8-10 **61** .... EdwardCreighton 6 *(D J Wintle) in tch: hdwy 3f out: rdn to chse wnr 2f out: sn driven and no imp appr last* **8/1**		63
014-	3	¾	**Royal Flynn**^{33} [6301] 5-8-12 **63** .... TomEaves 10 *(M Dods) bhd: hdwy on outer 3f out: rdn 2f out: styd on wl fnl f* **7/1**^{3}		64+
6-55	4	½	**Smart Cat (IRE)**^{40} [537] 4-8-9 **60** .... TPQueally 8 *(A P Jarvis) in tch: hdwy to chse ldrs 3f out: sn rdn along and kpt on same pce* **13/2**^{2}		60
0-06	5	½	**The Pen**^{43} [242] 5-8-7 **58** .... PaulMulrennan 5 *(C W Fairhurst) prom: chsd wnr over 4f out: rdn along 3f out and grad wknd* **16/1**		57
025/	6	1 ½	**Kingscape (IRE)**^{562} [5361] 4-9-2 **67** .... JamieSpencer 7 *(J R Fanshawe) held up in rr: hdwy 3f out: n.m.r wl over 1f out: swtchd rt and no imp appr last* **8/1**		68+
-210	7	hd	**King's Ransom**^{12} [740] 4-9-0 **65** ....(b) SebSanders 9 *(W R Muir) hld up: hdwy on outer to chse wnr 3f out: rdn along over 2f out: snd riven and wknd* **12/1**		61
00-0	8	1 ¼	**King's Account (USA)**^{91} [28] 5-8-9 **60** .... SteveDrowne 3 *(S Gollings) prom: rdn along 4f out: sn wknd* **18/1**		53
1364	9	1 ¼	**Reaching Out (IRE)**^{19} [651] 5-8-11 **65** ....(b) JamesDoyle$^{(3)}$ 4 *(N P Littmoden) hld up: effrt and sme hdwy over 3f out: sn rdn along and wknd 2f out* **9/1**		56
000-	10	36	**Orpen's Astaire (IRE)**^{202} [5316] 4-7-13 **55** .... DuranFentiman$^{(5)}$ 12 *(Jedd O'Keeffe) racd wd and edgd rt thrght: rdn along over 4f out and sn wknd* **16/1**		—
460-	U		**Billy One Punch**^{176} [5904] 5-9-4 **69** .... JimmyFortune 2 *(G G Margarson) uns rdr s* **8/1**		—

2m 10.21s (0.51) **Going Correction** -0.175s/f (Firm) — **11** Ran SP% **116.1**

Speed ratings (Par 103):90,85,84,84,83 82,82,81,80,51 —

CSF £30.78 CT £186.65 TOTE £4.40: £1.60, £3.00, £3.20; EX 42.60.

Owner Ray Craggs **Bred** Gainsborough Stud Management Ltd **Trained** Sedgefield, Co Durham

FOCUS

A moderate handicap, run at an uneven pace. The winner prospered from an excellent front-running ride.

Kingscape(IRE) Official explanation: jockey said gelding was denied a clear run

Reaching Out(IRE) Official explanation: jockey said gelding lost a shoe and its action

Orpen's Astaire(IRE) Official explanation: jockey said gelding had a breathing problem

929 WEATHERBYS BANK "FURTHER FLIGHT" STKS (LISTED RACE) — 1m 6f 15y

4:10 (4:10) (Class 1) 4-Y-O+

£14,762 (£5,595; £2,800; £1,396; £699; £351) **Stalls** Low

Form			Horse	Jockey	RPR
610-	1		**Mount Kilimanjaro (IRE)**^{285} [2804] 4-8-11 88 .... JimmyFortune 1 *(J L Dunlop) a.p: led briefly wl over 2f out: sn rdn and hdd: cl up and drvn on inner: rallied to ld again wl ins last* **20/1**		103
420-	2	nk	**The Last Drop (IRE)**^{164} [6126] 4-8-11 112 ....(t) RHills 5 *(B W Hills) trckd ldrs: effrt and pushed along 3f out: outpcd and n.m.r 2f out: swtchd rt and rdn over 1f out: styd on towards fin* **5/4**^{1}		103+
536-	3	½	**Under The Rainbow**^{120} [6722] 4-8-6 100 .... KDarley 7 *(B W Hills) a.p: rdn to ld 2f out: drvn and hdd wl ins last: no ex towards fin* **14/1**		97
111-	4	nk	**Hawridge Prince**^{172} [5967] 7-9-6 111 .... JimCrowley 4 *(B R Millman) hld up in tch: effrt on outer over 3f out: rdn over 2f out: kpt on u.p ins last: nrst fin* **8/1**		107+
40-2	5	¾	**Geordieland (FR)**^{11} [756] 6-9-0 108 .... JamieSpencer 2 *(J A Osborne) hld up in tch: smooth hdwy 3f out: cl up on bit over 1f out: shkn up ent last and sn btn* **11/4**^{2}		100
4-4	6	nk	**Hovering (IRE)**^{11} [756] 4-8-7 90 ow1 .... BrettDoyle 3 *(M G Quinlan) led: rdn along 3f out: sn hdd: drvn and kpt on fr over 1f out* **66/1**		96
210-	7	1 ¼	**Group Captain**^{137} [6516] 5-9-0 107 .... RichardHughes 8 *(R Charlton) hld up: effrt and sme haedway over 2f out: sn rdn and btn* **6/1**^{3}		98
006-	8	5	**Sienna Storm (IRE)**^{188} [5641] 4-8-11 96 .... MichaelHills 6 *(M H Tompkins) hld up: a rr* **50/1**		91

3m 7.35s (0.25) **Going Correction** -0.175s/f (Firm)

WFA 4 from 5yo+ 3lb — **8** Ran SP% **111.4**

Speed ratings (Par 111):92,91,91,91,90 90,90,87

CSF £43.42 TOTE £17.50: £3.90, £1.60, £3.10; EX 59.00.

Owner L Neil Jones **Bred** Abergwaun Farms **Trained** Arundel, W Sussex

■ Stewards' Enquiry : Jimmy Fortune three-day ban: careless riding (Apr 16-18)

FOCUS

A decent field lined up, but it was disappointing that the pace was so poor. While the winner has plenty of scope for improvement, he was the lowest-rated horse in the race and should not have gone close at the weights. The form is not solid.

NOTEBOOK

Mount Kilimanjaro(IRE) ◆, not seen since breaking a bone when eighth in the Queen's Vase at Royal Ascot last season, is officially rated 88 and therefore looked to face a stiff task at these weights. However, he has always been well regarded by connections and that rating clearly underestimated him as he scored a brave success under a strong ride from Fortune. Granted he ran close to the modest early pace, but really he was one who would have enjoyed a stronger gallop and that showed as he was headed only to rally in taking fashion when asked for maximum effort. He has an abundance of scope, is clearly versatile as regards underfoot conditions, and it would not be surprising to see him take much higher rank as he matures further. His trainer later indicated that he would now step up further in class for the Group 2 Yorkshire Cup next month, a race connections won with the high-class Millenary in 2004.

The Last Drop(IRE) can certainly be called an unlucky loser, as he was given no place to go when needing some space to make an effort and was forced to come around some rivals to get a run. While the winner has scope for more improvement and put up a splendid effort in victory, it is not too difficult to argue that The Last Drop should have won and would have been better served coming down the centre of the track, where he eventually came, rather than try and take an awkward route close to the far rail and through a wall of horses. It was also slightly surprising that more use was not made of him, as he was a guaranteed stayer of the distance at the top level. He has definitely not gone backwards since last season and should make his mark in some of the best staying races in the coming season. (op 6-4)

Under The Rainbow was given every opportunity under a fine ride by her jockey but was not quite good enough. The distance did not seem to present her with any problems, although the time of the race was not particularly quick, and one suspects she will be campaigned at this sort of trip in the short-term. (op 16-1)

Hawridge Prince, who was conceding weight to all his rivals, made a highly satisfactory reappearance and looks set for another fine season. A stronger tempo would have suited him, as he stays every yard of 2m, and he should be given close attention next time wherever his trainer decides to take him. (op 7-1 tchd 9-1)

Geordieland(FR) looked like hacking all over his rivals approaching the furlong pole, but as soon as Jamie Spencer asked for a response he found nothing. He has become disappointing but you can find excuses for this effort - mainly due to the lack of pace - and it would be dangerous to write him off quite yet. (op 9-4 tchd 2-1)

Hovering(IRE), who set the modest early tempo, was easily passed when challenged and the form should not be taken at face value. All of her best Irish form came at distances at around 10f, so she would be worthy of some note if dropped back to that sort of trip. (op 80-1)

Group Captain was held up off the slow pace and never landed a blow. He looked slightly uncomfortable on the quick ground under pressure, and would have been more at home on softer ground. That said, he was not disgraced and should come on for the run. (op 15-2)

930 WEATHERBYS FINANCE H'CAP — 1m 54y

4:40 (4:43) (Class 5) (0-75,75) 4-Y-O+ — **£2,914** (£867; £433; £216) **Stalls** Centre

Form			Horse	Jockey	RPR
4120	1		**Symbol Of Peace (IRE)**^{21} [675] 4-9-0 **74** .... RichardKingscote$^{(3)}$ 1 *(J W Unett) mde all: clr over 4f out: rdn over 2f out and sn hung bdly rt to stands rail: kpt on wl u.p ins last* **6/1**^{3}		84
-631	2	hd	**Spring Goddess (IRE)**^{3} [865] 6-9-2 **73** 6ex .... JamieSpencer 2 *(A P Jarvis) hld up in rr: hdwy on inner 3f out: rdn fr wl over 1f out: drvn ins last: styd on wl: jst failed* **9/4**^{1}		83
000-	3	1 ¾	**The Osteopath (IRE)**^{159} [6206] 4-9-0 **71** .... TomEaves 3 *(M Dods) wnt rt s: trckd ldrs: hdwy 3f out: rdn to chse wnr over 2f out: sn drvn and edgd rt fr over 1f out: one pce* **7/1**		77
-346	4	½	**Final Tune (IRE)**^{3} [865] 4-8-13 **73** .... PatrickMathers$^{(3)}$ 6 *(Miss M E Rowland) in tch: hdwy to chse ldrs 3f out: sn rdn and kpt on same pce fnl 2f* **9/1**		77
000-	5	2	**Street Warrior (IRE)**^{124} [6661] 4-9-4 **75** .... KDarley 8 *(M Johnston) chsd clr ldr: rdn along 3f out: sn drvn and wknd* **7/2**^{2}		75
506-	6	3	**Flighty Fellow (IRE)**^{251} [3883] 7-8-7 **69** .... DuranFentiman$^{(5)}$ 7 *(T D Easterby) s.i.s and bhd tl styd on fnl 2f: nvr a factor* **16/1**		62
3/0-	7	2 ½	**Toparudi**^{383} [33] 6-8-8 **68** .... SaleemGolam$^{(3)}$ 4 *(M H Tompkins) hmpd s: chsd ldrs tlr idden along over 3f out and sn wknd* **11/1**		55
640-	8	17	**Alsadaa (USA)**^{171} [5986] 4-8-11 **75** .... NSLawes$^{(7)}$ 9 *(M W Easterby) chsd laders: rdn along 4f out: sn wknd* **33/1**		23
310/	9	20	**Registrar**^{564} [5313] 5-8-12 **69** .... SebSanders 5 *(Mrs C A Dunnett) hmpd s: a towards rr* **11/1**		—

1m 43.51s (-2.89) **Going Correction** -0.175s/f (Firm) — **9** Ran SP% **115.3**

Speed ratings (Par 103):107,106,105,104,102 99,97,80,60

CSF £19.84 CT £95.01 TOTE £8.40: £2.10, £1.20, £2.00; EX 31.50.

Owner John Malone **Bred** Calley House Syndicate **Trained** Preston, Shropshire
■ Stewards' Enquiry : Tom Eaves caution: careless riding
FOCUS
A fair race for the grade and the time was over two seconds quicker than the 3yo handicap later on the card. The form does, however, look messy because of the way the winner drifted under pressure.

931 WEATHERBYS MESSAGING SERVICE H'CAP — 1m 54y
5:10 (5:11) (Class 5) (0-70,70) 3-Y-O — **£2,914** (£867; £433; £216) **Stalls** Centre

Form — RPR
65-1 **1** **Ambrosiano**[12] 736 3-9-2 **68** .... AdamKirby 13 — 76
(C G Cox) *in tch: gd hdwy 3f out: led 2f out: sn rdn and styd on wl fnl f* **10/1**
305- **2** *1 1/4* **Perfect Courtesy (IRE)**[222] 4767 3-9-2 **68** .... JamieSpencer 8 — 73
(G A Swinbank) *hld up and bhd: stdy hdwy 3f out: rdn to chse wnr appr last: snd riven and no imp* **11/2**[2]
504- **3** *1* **Eager Igor (USA)**[167] 6064 3-9-4 **70** .... StephenCarson 10 — 73
(Eve Johnson Houghton) *midfield: hdwy on inenr over 3f out: nt clr run and swiyched rt 2f out: sn rdn and kpt on wl fnl f* **8/1**
40-3 **4** *3 1/2* **Storm Mission (USA)**[7] 807 3-8-6 **58** .... EdwardCreighton 12 — 53
(Miss V Haigh) *towards rr: hdwy 3f out: sn rdn and kpt on fnl 2f* **33/1**
060- **5** *nk* **Anatolian Prince**[156] 6254 3-8-13 **65** .... TedDurcan 2 — 59
(J M P Eustace) *chsd ldrs: effrt 4f out: rdn along 3f out and kpt on same pce fnl 2f* **8/1**
06-0 **6** *hd* **Beckenham's Secret**[14] 725 3-9-0 **66** .... JimCrowley 15 — 60
(B R Millman) *towards rr: hdwy on outer wl over 2f out: sn rdn and kpt on fnl 2f: nrst fin* **20/1**
200- **7** *3/4* **High Five Society**[155] 6285 3-8-13 **65** .... AdrianMcCarthy 14 — 57
(S R Bowring) *in tch: rdn along over 3f out: grad wknd* **50/1**
022- **8** *1 1/2* **Nota Liberata**[155] 6270 3-9-4 **70** .... NCallan 3 — 59
(G M Moore) *keen: chsd ldrs: hdwy to ld wl over 2f out: rdn and hdd 2f out: drvn and wknd appr last* **9/2**[1]
0016 **9** *2 1/2* **Dance Of Dreams**[12] 738 3-8-7 **62** .... JamesDoyle(3) 7 — 45
(N P Littmoden) *hld up: a towards rr* **14/1**
005 **10** *8* **Tina's Ridge (IRE)**[37] 569 3-8-8 **60** .... KDarley 6 — 24
(E J Alston) *s.i.s: a rr* **11/1**
460- **11** *6* **Bollin Fergus**[189] 5615 3-8-5 **62** .... DuranFentiman(5) 11 — 13
(T D Easterby) *prominent: rdn along over 3f out and sn wknd* **50/1**
034- **12** *2 1/2* **Just Oscar (GER)**[241] 4171 3-9-2 **68** .... PaulMulrennan 5 — 13
(W M Brisbourne) *led: rdn along 4f out: hdd wl over 2f out and sn wknd* **20/1**
410- **13** *nk* **Centenary (IRE)**[170] 6007 3-9-2 **68** .... TomEaves 4 — 12
(J J Quinn) *chsd ldrs: rdn along 4f out: sn wknd* **17/2**
000- **14** *12* **Dumas (IRE)**[186] 5681 3-9-1 **67** .... SebSanders 9 — —
(A P Jarvis) *chsd ldr: rdn along over 3f out and sn wknd* **7/1**[3]

1m 44.96s (-1.44) **Going Correction** -0.175s/f (Firm) — **14** Ran SP% **119.3**
Speed ratings (Par 98):100,98,97,94,93 93,93,91,89,81 75,72,72,60
CSF £60.00 CT £468.91 TOTE £8.80: £4.10, £2.60, £2.90; EX 58.20 Place 6 £124.13, Place 5 £17.86 .
Owner Paul G Jacobs **Bred** Whitsbury Manor Stud **Trained** Lambourn, Berks
FOCUS
A competitive handicap for 3yos probably slightly spoiled by the lack of early pace. The form could be slightly suspect, with the fourth seemingly running to his best, but the first three drew clear and would give one some enthusiasm for future races.
High Five Society Official explanation: jockey said gelding clipped heels 3f out
Dumas(IRE) Official explanation: jockey said colt stopped very quickly
T/Jkpt: Not won. T/Plt: £331.60 to a £1 stake. Pool: £61,919.30. 136.30 winning tickets. T/Qpdt: £8.70 to a £1 stake. Pool: £4,663.20. 394.30 winning tickets. JR

831 WOLVERHAMPTON (A.W) (L-H)
Thursday, April 5

OFFICIAL GOING: Standard
Wind: Light, across Weather: Sunny

932 RINGSIDE SUITE AMATEUR RIDERS' CLAIMING STKS — 1m 141y(P)
2:10 (2:10) (Class 6) 4-Y-O+ — **£2,307** (£709; £354) **Stalls** Low

Form — RPR
1515 **1** **Louisiade (IRE)**[3] 895 6-10-6 63 ....(p) MissARyan(5) 5 — 64
(K A Ryan) *hld up in tch: led jst over 2f out: edgd rt fnl f: r.o* **7/2**[1]
0240 **2** *1/2* **Machinate (USA)**[30] 625 5-10-4 49 .... MrBenBrisbourne(5) 9 — 61
(W M Brisbourne) *stdd s: hld up in mid-div: hdwy over 2f out: rdn and edgd lft over 1f out: ev ch ins fnl f: nt qckn* **14/1**
0-00 **3** *3 1/2* **Itcanbedone Again (IRE)**[21] 685 8-10-0 52 .... MrJRavenall(7) 3 — 52+
(Ian Williams) *hld up towards rr: hdwy jst over 1f out: r.o ins fnl f: nrst fin* **16/1**
4404 **4** *nk* **Buzzin'Boyzee (IRE)**[6] 833 4-9-13 55 .... MrRichardEvans(7) 1 — 50
(P D Evans) *hld up in rr: hdwy on ins over 2f out: one pce fnl f* **8/1**
0000 **5** *shd* **Capital Lass**[21] 686 4-10-4 50 .... MrSWalker 2 — 48
(A J McCabe) *s.i.s: hld up and bhd: hdwy over 2f out: no ex wl ins fnl f* **25/1**
-452 **6** *1* **Keon (IRE)**[34] 605 5-10-8 54 .... MissSSharratt(3) 10 — 53
(R Hollinshead) *t.k.h in tch: ev ch 2f out: rdn and wknd ins fnl f* **11/1**
3300 **7** *3/4* **Kingsmaite**[9] 806 6-10-0 52 ....(b) MrKApark(7) 4 — 47
(S R Bowring) *hld up in mid-div: no real prog fnl f* **20/1**
013- **8** *1/2* **Everest (IRE)**[222] 4475 10-11-1 70 ....(p) MissLEllison 6 — 54
(B Ellison) *led: hung rt and hdd jst over 2f out: wknd over 1f out* **4/1**[2]
6054 **9** *1* **Conrad**[8] 809 4-10-2 62 .... MrBMcHugh(5) 13 — 44
(R A Fahey) *prom: rdn and ev ch 2f out: wknd over 1f out* **11/2**[3]
0065 **10** *hd* **Mine The Balance (IRE)**[4] 866 4-10-7 54 ow3....(b) MrSJEdwards(5) 7 — 51
(H J Manners) *a bhd* **25/1**
0502 **11** *1 1/2* **Hand Chime**[4] 866 10-9-12 50 .... MrRBirkett(7) 11 — 38
(Miss J Feilden) *hld up towards rr: rdn and short-lived effrt on outside over 2f out* **12/1**
00-0 **12** *3 1/2* **Grandad Bill (IRE)**[22] 674 4-10-0 59...... MissEmma-JaneJenkins(7) 12 — 33
(W J Musson) *w ldrs tl wknd 3f out* **25/1**
000- **13** *2 1/2* **Sheriff's Deputy**[120] 6544 7-10-6 46 .... MrPCollington(5) 8 — 32
(C N Kellett) *w ldr tl rdn over 3f out: wknd over 2f out* **100/1**

1m 51.98s (0.22) **Going Correction** +0.025s/f (Slow) — **13** Ran SP% **114.6**
Speed ratings (Par 101):100,99,96,96,96 95,94,94,93,93 91,88,86
CSF £47.28 TOTE £4.50: £1.20, £3.60, £5.70; EX 67.80 TRIFECTA Not won..
Owner Whitestonecliffe Racing Partnership **Bred** Mrs Noelle Walsh **Trained** Hambleton, N Yorks
FOCUS
A modest claimer run at a steady pace and the winner did not need to improve to score.

933 BOOK ONLINE AT WOLVERHAMPTON-RACECOURSE.CO.UK H'CAP — 1m 141y(P)
2:40 (2:41) (Class 5) (0-70,76) 4-Y-O+ — **£3,238** (£963; £481; £240) **Stalls** Low

Form — RPR
43-1 **1** **Italian Romance**[76] 186 4-9-4 **70** .... ShaneKelly 5 — 77
(J W Unett) *sn led: rdn over 2f out: edgd lft wl ins fnl f: r.o* **5/2**[1]
-216 **2** *1* **Chia (IRE)**[54] 427 4-9-0 **66** .... RobertHavlin 2 — 71
(D Haydn Jones) *led early: chsd wnr tl over 4f out: wnt 2nd again 2f out: sn rdn: edgd rt ins fnl f: nt qckn* **10/1**
3443 **3** *1/2* **Golden Spectrum (IRE)**[6] 830 8-8-0 **59** ....(b) LukeMorris(7) 6 — 63+
(R A Harris) *hld up and bhd: rdn over 2f out: c wd st: hdwy on outside fnl f: nrst fin* **9/1**
1651 **4** *1/2* **Samuel Charles**[6] 830 9-9-10 **76** 6ex........(p) NCallan 7 — 79
(C R Dore) *a.p: chsd wnr over 4f out tl rdn 2f out: kpt on same pce fnl f* **15/2**
1443 **5** *3/4* **Our Kes (IRE)**[3] 888 5-8-13 **65** .... TonyCulhane 3 — 66
(P Howling) *hld up: swtchd lft and hdwy on ins over 1f out: no ex ins fnl f* **4/1**[2]
02-2 **6** *6* **Musicmaestroplease (IRE)**[3] 895 4-8-5 **60** .... DominicFox(3) 8 — 49
(S Parr) *hld up and bhd: hdwy over 3f out: rdn over 2f out: wknd wl over 1f out* **4/1**[2]
-563 **7** *1 1/4* **Ocean Of Dreams (FR)**[22] 672 4-9-4 **70** .... SebSanders 1 — 56
(J D Bethell) *hld up in tch: wknd over 3f out* **13/2**[3]

1m 50.86s (-0.90) **Going Correction** +0.025s/f (Slow) — **7** Ran SP% **112.8**
Speed ratings (Par 103):105,104,103,103,102 97,96
CSF £27.39 CT £191.32 TOTE £3.40: £2.00, £4.40; EX 32.80 Trifecta £54.60 Pool: £283.13 - 3.68 winning tickets..
Owner Nick Hubbard and Partners 2 **Bred** Cheveley Park Stud Ltd **Trained** Preston, Shropshire
FOCUS
A minor but competitive little handicap rated around the third and fourth to previous Lingfield form.

934 WOLVERHAMPTON-RACECOURSE.CO.UK (S) STKS — 5f 20y(P)
3:10 (3:10) (Class 6) 3-Y-O — **£2,198** (£755) **Stalls** Low

Form — RPR
00-0 **1** **Savanagh Forest (IRE)**[61] 343 3-8-7 45 .... ShaneKelly 2 — 43+
(M Quinn) *chsd ldr: led over 1f out: rdn ins fnl f: r.o* **1/1**[1]
2 *3/4* **Lula (IRE)** 3-8-7 .... RobertHavlin 4 — 37
(M Quinn) *hld up: rdn over 1f out: lft 2nd ins fnl f: r.o: nt trble wnr* **9/2**[3]
-530 **U** **Spinning Game**[23] 667 3-8-13 45 ....(b) TonyCulhane 1 — —
(D W Chapman) *led: hdd over 1f out: hung rt ins fnl f: 2nd and btn whn sn swvd rt and uns rdr* **11/8**[2]

63.76 secs (0.94) **Going Correction** +0.025s/f (Slow) — **3** Ran SP% **110.3**
Speed ratings (Par 96):93,91,—
CSF £5.14 TOTE £1.80; EX 5.60.There was no bid for the winner.
Owner B Morton & P Montgomery **Bred** Adieu Cherie Partnership **Trained** Newmarket, Suffolk
FOCUS
A dire seller with the winner rated value for two lengths over her stablemate.

935 PARADE RESTAURANT H'CAP — 7f 32y(P)
3:40 (3:43) (Class 5) (0-75,75) 3-Y-O — **£3,238** (£963; £481; £240) **Stalls** High

Form — RPR
2331 **1** **Arch Of Titus (IRE)**[17] 711 3-9-3 **74** ....(t) JamieSpencer 3 — 84
(M L W Bell) *s.i.s: hld up and bhd: hdwy whn swtchd lft over 1f out: rdn to ld ins fnl f: sn edgd rt: r.o wl* **11/2**[3]
-645 **2** *2* **Proper (IRE)**[15] 725 3-8-8 **65** .... ChrisCatlin 6 — 70
(M R Channon) *led: hdd and rdn wl over 1f out: kpt on ins fnl f* **13/2**
2201 **3** *hd* **Cherri Fosfate**[13] 744 3-9-4 **75** ....(b) DanielTudhope 2 — 79
(D Carroll) *a.p: rdn and nt qckn fnl f* **10/1**
23 **4** *1 1/4* **Nans Joy (IRE)**[3] 886 3-9-0 **71** .... GrahamGibbons 5 — 72
(E J O'Neill) *chsd ldrs: rdn wl over 1f out: one pce* **4/1**[1]
2131 **5** *1/2* **Convivial Spirit**[13] 737 3-9-1 **72** ....(t) LPKeniry 7 — 72
(E F Vaughan) *hld up in mid-div: rdn over 1f out: no real prog fnl f* **5/1**[2]
-334 **6** *1 1/2* **Hollywood George**[36] 584 3-8-13 **70** .... NCallan 1 — 66
(K A Ryan) *a.p: rdn to ld wl over 1f out: hdd & wknd ins fnl f* **11/2**[3]
-620 **7** *6* **Straight Face (IRE)**[15] 725 3-8-11 **68** .... JamieMackay 4 — 47
(M Wigham) *outpcd: nvr nr ldrs* **33/1**
20-1 **8** *1/2* **Grand Lucre**[29] 635 3-8-11 **68** .... EddieAhern 8 — 46
(J W Hills) *hld up in mid-div: nt clr run briefly over 2f out: sn bhd* **10/1**
1-35 **9** *3* **Tobago Reef**[13] 744 3-8-7 **71** ....(p) KristinStubbs(7) 10 — 41
(Mrs L Stubbs) *sn w ldr: wknd over 2f out* **12/1**
32-0 **10** *14* **Retaliate**[12] 754 3-8-13 **70** .... SebSanders 9 — 2
(M Quinn) *prom tl wknd over 2f out* **25/1**

1m 28.56s (-1.84) **Going Correction** +0.025s/f (Slow) — **10** Ran SP% **113.4**
Speed ratings (Par 98):111,108,108,107,106 104,97,97,93,77
CSF £39.92 CT £345.71 TOTE £5.10: £2.00, £2.90, £4.50; EX 54.30 Trifecta £466.40 Part won. Pool of £656.97 - 0.44 winning tickets..
Owner Mrs Maureen Buckley **Bred** J Connolly **Trained** Newmarket, Suffolk
FOCUS
A good clip resulted in a very smart winning time in this open-looking handicap where four of the field had won last time. The form seems sound rated around the third, fourth and fifth to recent efforts.
Tobago Reef Official explanation: jockey said gelding hung right-handed throughout
Retaliate Official explanation: jockey said filly had no more to give

936 NAME A RACE TO ENHANCE YOUR BRAND MAIDEN STKS — 1m 4f 50y(P)
4:10 (4:11) (Class 5) 3-Y-O+ — **£2,968** (£876; £438) **Stalls** Low

Form — RPR
1 **Rickety Bridge (IRE)**[134] 4-9-12 .... NCallan 2 — 68
(P R Chamings) *s.i.s: hld up: hdwy on outside over 2f out: rdn to ld over 1f out: wandered ins fnl f: r.o* **12/1**
2 *3/4* **Dolce Dovo**[175] 5932 4-9-7 .... JamieSpencer 5 — 61
(W J Haggas) *hld up: hdwy over 3f out: ev ch over 1f out: rdn and nt qckn ins fnl f* **11/10**[1]
006- **3** *7* **Cavendish**[146] 6421 3-8-6 42 ....(b[1]) DaleGibson 3 — 53
(J M P Eustace) *led: rdn and hdd over 1f out: wknd fnl f* **66/1**
00-3 **4** *shd* **Dana Music (USA)**[19] 703 3-8-6 74 .... TedDurcan 8 — 53
(M R Channon) *hld up in tch: rdn and wnt 2nd over 2f out: wknd wl over 1f out* **7/2**[2]
402- **5** *5* **Campbells Lad**[142] 6482 6-9-10 49 .... PatrickMathers(3) 9 — 47
(Mrs G S Rees) *stdd s: hld up and bhd: rdn over 2f out: nvr nr ldrs* **33/1**
6 *hd* **Penicuik** 3-8-1 .... RoystonFfrench 4 — 40
(M Johnston) *hld up in tch: rdn 4f out: wknd 2f out* **9/2**[3]
7 *2* **Wolds Way**[19] 5-9-13 .... DavidAllan 6 — 43
(T D Easterby) *w ldr tl rdn over 2f out: sn wknd* **10/1**

00 **8** *15* **Miss Wolf**[12] 769 7-9-8 .... PaulEddery 7 14
(G H Jones) *stdd s: hld up in rr: no ch fnl 3f* **100/1**

9 *nk* **Arthur Parker**[7] 6-9-13 .... (t) EddieAhern 1 19
(J A B Old) *t.k.h: prom tl wknd over 3f out* **28/1**

2m 41.98s (-0.44) **Going Correction** +0.025s/f (Slow)
WFA 3 from 4yo 21lb 4 from 5yo+ 1lb **9** Ran SP% **113.7**
Speed ratings (Par 103):102,101,96,96,93 93,91,81,81
CSF £25.14 TOTE £17.70: £4.60, £1.10, £10.80; EX 41.40 TRIFECTA Not won..
Owner Mrs Ann Jenkins **Bred** Jockey Hall Kriva Syndicate **Trained** Baughurst, Hants

FOCUS
A poor maiden with the third seriously limiting the form and the favourite beginning to look a perpetual bridesmaid.

937 HOTEL & CONFERENCING AT WOLVERHAMPTON H'CAP 1m 1f 103y(P)
4:40 (4:44) (Class 5) (0-75,69) 3-Y-O **£3,238** (£963; £481; £240) **Stalls** Low

Form RPR
5503 **1** **Homes By Woodford**[13] 744 3-9-2 **67** .... PaulHanagan 1 71
(R A Harris) *a.p: rdn to ld wl over 1f out: drvn out* **3/1**[2]

-532 **2** *3/4* **Dr McFab**[13] 738 3-9-4 **69** .... JamieSpencer 7 72
(J A Osborne) *hld up in tch: rdn and hung lft wl over 1f out: hung lft ins fnl f: r.o* **11/4**[1]

-101 **3** *1* **News Of The Day (IRE)**[59] 357 3-8-7 **58** .... JoeFanning 2 59
(M Johnston) *led: hdd wl over 1f out: sn rdn: no ex ins fnl f* **4/1**

3-54 **4** *shd* **Krakatau (FR)**[42] 520 3-8-6 **57** .... ChrisCatlin 5 57
(D J Wintle) *chsd ldr: ev ch over 2f out: kpt on same pce fnl f* **10/3**[3]

024- **5** *1 3/4* **Robert The Brave**[133] 6569 3-8-13 **67** .... StephenDonohoe(3) 4 64
(A J McCabe) *uns rdr and bolted bef s: hld up: rdn and no hdwy fnl 2f* **6/1**

0-00 **6** *8* **Cavallo Di Ferro (IRE)**[20] 694 3-8-7 **65** .... MCGeran(7) 6 46
(M J Gingell) *stdd s: hld up: rdn over 3f out: sn struggling* **33/1**

2m 4.93s (2.31) **Going Correction** +0.025s/f (Slow) **6** Ran SP% **112.0**
Speed ratings (Par 98):90,89,88,88,86 79
CSF £11.60 TOTE £4.70: £1.80, £1.90; EX 13.90 Place 6 £78.55, Place 5 £30.01.
Owner Mrs Ruth M Serrell **Bred** Mrs H B Raw **Trained** Earlswood, Monmouths

FOCUS
An ordinary contest and the fact they went no great pace was reflected in a moderate winning time. The placed horses were close to form but there are doubts over how solid the form is.
Dr McFab Official explanation: jockey said colt hung left home straight
T/Plt: £123.20 to a £1 stake. Pool: £69,036.25. 408.80 winning tickets. T/Qpdt: £14.20 to a £1 stake. Pool: £3,672.80. 190.30 winning tickets. KH

838 KEMPTON (A.W) (R-H)
Saturday, April 7

OFFICIAL GOING: Standard
Wind: Moderate, half-behind.

938 INTERCASINO.CO.UK SNOWDROP FILLIES' STKS (LISTED RACE) 1m (P)
2:10 (2:10) (Class 1) 4-Y-O+
£14,762 (£5,595; £2,800; £1,396; £699; £351) **Stalls** High

Form RPR
-366 **1** **Expensive**[43] 546 4-8-12 .... EddieAhern 2 101
(C F Wall) *lw: trckd ldr: led appr fnl 2f: drvn over 1f out: styd on strly ins last: readily* **7/2**[3]

3436 **2** *4* **Dont Dili Dali**[30] 648 4-8-12 .... (p) JohnEgan 3 92
(J S Moore) *rr but in tch: pushed along 4f out: drvn and styd on fr 2f out to take 2nd ins last but no ch w wnr* **10/3**[2]

141- **3** *3/4* **Rakata (USA)**[178] 5908 5-8-12 74 .... JimmyFortune 6 90
(P F I Cole) *chsd ldrs: rdn over 2f out: styd on to dispute 2nd ins last but nvr gng pce to trble wnr: wknd nr fin* **13/2**

320- **4** *1 1/4* **Highway To Glory (IRE)**[163] 6190 4-8-12 95 .... (t) JamieSpencer 4 87
(M Botti) *stdd s: hld up in rr: swtchd lft to outside over 2f out: rdn and kpt on fr over 1f out but nvr gng pce to be competitive* **5/1**

1201 **5** *1 1/2* **Symbol Of Peace (IRE)**[3] 930 4-8-12 74 .... RichardKingscote 5 84
(J W Unett) *led tl hdd appr fnl 2f: wknd fnl f* **11/1**

411- **6** *1 1/2* **Persian Express (USA)**[153] 6350 4-8-12 89 .... MichaelHills 1 80
(B W Hills) *chsd ldrs: rdn 3f out: wknd appr fnl f* **11/4**[1]

1m 38.03s (-2.77) **Going Correction** +0.025s/f (Slow) **6** Ran SP% **110.3**
Speed ratings (Par 108):114,110,109,108,106 105
CSF £14.89 TOTE £5.60: £2.40, £1.90; EX 19.70.
Owner M Tilbrook **Bred** Genesis Green Stud **Trained** Newmarket, Suffolk

FOCUS
An ordinary Listed race with none of the runners officially rated above 99, but run at a decent gallop and won in emphatic style by Expensive, who was ridden close to the pace and ran to her Dubai form. The winning time was very quick.

NOTEBOOK
Expensive, who was ridden close to the pace, always had matters under control once asked to go for home. She had struggled in better company in Dubai earlier in the year, but took to this surface well and connections may run her in a Group 3 race at Lingfield next, on Classic trials day, as they believe 7f suits her just as well. (op 5-1)
Dont Dili Dali, who was wearing cheekpieces for the first time, looks as if she needs at least 10f these days and could not reel in Expensive after being held up. Her recent runs have been over longer trips and a return to further will be in her favour. (op 11-4)
Rakata(USA), the only five-year-old in the line-up and from an in-form stable, was progressive at the end of last season in lesser company. She had a tough task based on official ratings and, although this good effort will have done her handicap mark some damage, connections will be pleased she has increased her paddock value by earning black type. (op 15-2)
Highway To Glory(IRE), who was tried in a tongue tie for the first time, was held up in the rear and never got into contention, her effort flattening out in the closing stages. Most of her best form has come on a surface with ease in it, so she might not be that easy to place.
Symbol Of Peace(IRE) made the running and did as well as could be expected considering how much she had to find on official ratings. (op 12-1)
Persian Express(USA), backed into favouritism, was disappointing, although in mitigation she had to race wide from her outside draw. (op 5-2)

939 INTERCASINO.CO.UK H'CAP (LONDON MILE QUALIFIER) 1m (P)
2:45 (2:47) (Class 3) (0-90,89) 3-Y-O
£8,724 (£2,612; £1,306; £653; £326; £163) **Stalls** High

Form RPR
21 **1** **Zaham (USA)**[29] 649 3-8-9 **80** .... RHills 2 91+
(M Johnston) *sn trcking ldr: led over 2f out: drvn along fnl f: hld on readily* **3/1**[2]

21- **2** *1* **Tybalt (USA)**[178] 5906 3-9-3 **88** .... JimmyFortune 5 97+
(J H M Gosden) *t.k.h: chsd ldrs: wnt 2nd 2f out: rdn and kpt on to chse wnr ins last: kpt on but a hld* **9/4**[1]

15-4 **3** *2 1/2* **Bed Fellow (IRE)**[14] 754 3-8-12 **83** .... SebSanders 10 86
(A P Jarvis) *chsd ldrs: rdn over 2f out: styd on to dispute 2nd 1f out: nvr gng pce to rch wnr: no ex nr fin* **8/1**

1-64 **4** *hd* **Lazy Darren**[31] 638 3-8-6 **77** .... RichardSmith 9 79+
(R Hannon) *broke wl: stdd rr: hdwy on outside fom 2f out: r.o wl fnl f but nvr gng pce to rch ldrs* **20/1**

212- **5** *shd* **Safe Investment (USA)**[220] 4928 3-9-1 **86** .... RichardHughes 11 88
(J H M Gosden) *bit bkwd: stdd s: sn in tch: hdwy 4f out: rdn to chse ldrs over 2f out: kpt on but nvr gng pce to rch chalng position* **7/1**

434- **6** *1 1/4* **Putra Square**[179] 5893 3-8-13 **84** .... NCallan 7 83
(P F I Cole) *bit bkwd: mid-div: drvn along fr 5f out: stl struggling for pce over 2f out: kpt on fnl f but nvr in contention* **6/1**[3]

154- **7** *nk* **Diysem (USA)**[189] 5665 3-8-11 **82** .... JamieSpencer 1 81
(B J Meehan) *hld up towards rr: rdn and styd on fr over 2f out: nvr gng pce to rch ldrs* **20/1**

620- **8** *3/4* **Heywood**[168] 6100 3-9-3 **88** .... TPO'Shea 8 85
(M R Channon) *lw: rr: ridden over 2f out: sme prog fnl f:nvr in contention* **20/1**

-522 **9** *1* **Eau Good**[38] 584 3-8-8 **82** .... RichardKingscote(3) 4 77
(B G Powell) *towards rr: rdn and hdwy on outside 3f out: nvr quite gng pce to trble ldrs: one pce fnl 2f* **20/1**

134- **10** *shd* **Salient**[130] 6634 3-8-10 **81** .... PaulDoe 6 75
(J Akehurst) *bit bkwd: chsd ldrs: n.m.r and lost pl ins fnl 3f: n.d after* **50/1**

412- **11** *1 1/4* **Strikeen (IRE)**[119] 6760 3-9-4 **89** .... DaneO'Neill 3 81
(T G Mills) *rr: hdwy to chse ldrs 4f out: sn rdn: wknd ins fnl 2f* **12/1**

560- **12** *6* **Dora Explora**[200] 5459 3-8-13 **87** .... StephenDonohoe(3) 12 65
(P D Evans) *sn led: hdd appr fnl 2f: wknd over 1f out* **50/1**

1m 39.21s (-1.59) **Going Correction** +0.025s/f (Slow) **12** Ran SP% **124.3**
Speed ratings (Par 102):108,107,104,104,104 102,102,101,100,100 99,93
CSF £9.66 CT £51.40 TOTE £4.80: £1.80, £1.40, £3.00; EX 14.70 Trifecta £104.90 Pool £473.05 - 3.20 winning units..
Owner Hamdan Al Maktoum **Bred** London Thoroughbred Services Ltd **Trained** Middleham Moor, N Yorks

FOCUS
A competitive three-year-old handicap with only 12lb separating the entire field on official ratings, but dominated in both the betting and the race by the two least-exposed runners. Solid form, with the unexposed front pair improving, and a race that should work out.

NOTEBOOK
Zaham(USA), who was coltish in the paddock beforehand, soon took a prominent position despite his low draw and, in the manner of many of those from the Mark Johnston stable, found plenty for pressure to hold the favourite throughout the last 2f. He should pick up more decent handicaps if as effective on turf. (op 9-2 tchd 5-1)
Tybalt(USA) was weak in the market, but travelled strongly in the race until asked for maximum effort, from which point he could not produce an extra gear. He has Classic entries, but on this evidence does not look good enough, especially as the time was over a second slower than the opening Listed race, although like the winner he should progress with time and possibly longer trips back on turf. (op 5-4)
Bed Fellow(IRE) had been well held in two previous runs on Polytrack, but was nevertheless well supported beforehand. Always close to the pace, he had every chance but was no match for the first two and just managed to hold off the fast-finishing Lazy Darren for third. The Handicapper probably just has his measure for now. (op 12-1)
Lazy Darren was last on the home turn and did well to make up so much ground, but he has already been held in lower-grade handicaps so this apparently improved effort may have to be treated with some caution. (op 33-1)
Safe Investment(USA), the lesser-fancied of the two Gosden runners, ran well on this Polytrack debut and was not given a hard race once held. (op 8-1)
Putra Square, having his first run on Polytrack, was noted making late headway but never got to the leaders. It will be little surprise to see him come on for the run and be far more competitive next time. (op 8-1 tchd 17-2)
Diysem(USA) had to race wide from his outside draw and, in the circumstances, it was no surprise his effort flattened out late on. (op 25-1)

940 INTERCASINO.CO.UK ROSEBERY STKS (HERITAGE H'CAP) 1m 3f (P)
3:20 (3:21) (Class 2) (0-105,99) 4-Y-O+
£24,928 (£7,464; £3,732; £1,868; £932; £468) **Stalls** High

Form RPR
-000 **1** **Luberon**[44] 529 4-9-9 **98** .... JoeFanning 11 109
(M Johnston) *trcked ldr: led wl over 2f out: drvn clr over 1f out and styd on strly* **16/1**

04-2 **2** *2 1/2* **Woolfall Blue (IRE)**[62] 353 4-8-5 **80** .... JimmyQuinn 1 87
(G G Margarson) *lw: chsd ldrs: rdn to go 2nd 2f out: kpt on wl u.p but nvr any ch w wnr* **20/1**

0-01 **3** *nk* **Weightless**[13] 777 7-9-1 **90** .... NCallan 15 97
(N P Littmoden) *chsd ldrs: rdn over 2f out: styd on u.p fnl f to press for 2nd but nvr any ch w wnr* **14/1**

133- **4** *1 1/4* **Celtic Spirit (IRE)**[180] 5869 4-8-8 **83** .... JosedeSouza 9 89+
(R M Beckett) *lw: chsd ldrs: rdn over 2f out: kpt on fr over 1f out: styd on cl home but nvr gng pce to be competitive* **9/1**

40-1 **5** *hd* **Tabadul (IRE)**[72] 250 6-9-6 **95** .... RHills 5 99+
(E A L Dunlop) *rr: hdwy on outside over 2f out: drvn and styd on fr over 1f out: nt pce to rch ldrs* **4/1**[1]

141- **6** *1* **All The Good (IRE)**[155] 6319 4-9-7 **96** .... KDarley 10 100+
(G A Butler) *lw: rr: rdn and stl plenty to do 2f out: r.o ins fnl f: gng on cl home but nvr a danger* **10/1**

1234 **7** *1/2* **Impeller (IRE)**[9] 817 8-9-10 **99** .... JohnEgan 8 101
(J S Moore) *rr: wnt wide bnd after 2f: rdn over 2f out: r.o fr over 1f out: nvr a danger* **9/1**

00-2 **8** *1/2* **Kings Quay**[14] 763 5-9-3 **92** .... (t) GrahamGibbons 14 93
(J J Quinn) *in tch: rdn to chse ldrs 3f out: styd on same pce fnl f* **16/1**

50-4 **9** *2 1/2* **Invention (USA)**[14] 763 4-9-0 **89** .... MartinDwyer 7 86
(W J Knight) *in tch: rdn over 3f out: wknd fnl f* **25/1**

120- **10** *hd* **Charlie Tokyo (IRE)**[154] 6337 4-8-9 **84** .... DaleGibson 4 81
(R A Fahey) *mid-div: ridde and sme hdwy 3f out: nvr rchd ldrs: wknd fnl f* **25/1**

2242 **11** *nk* **Quince (IRE)**[21] 698 4-8-13 **88** .... (v) JimmyFortune 12 84
(J Pearce) *rr: rdn over 2f out: nvr in contention* **8/1**

3-13 **12** *shd* **Royal Jet**[14] 763 5-9-5 **94** .... RichardHughes 2 90
(M R Channon) *stdd s and swtchd rt towards ins: pushed along over 2f out: nvr in contention* **13/2**[2]

00-6 **13** *1* **Dunaskin (IRE)**[22] 608 7-9-3 **92** .... SebSanders 13 86
(Karen McLintock) *led tl hdd wl over 2f out: wknd wl over 1f out* **33/1**

120- **14** *1/2* **Futun**[227] 4711 4-9-10 **99** .... NickyMackay 3 93
(L M Cumani) *bit bkwd: pushed wd bnd after 2f: a in rr* **7/1**[3]

0-31 **15** ¾ **Active Asset (IRE)**[8] [829] 5-8-11 **86** .... DarryllHolland 6 78
(M Quinn) *a towards rr* **11/1**

2m 20.94s (-1.74) **Going Correction** +0.025s/f (Slow) **15** Ran SP% **128.2**
Speed ratings (Par 109):107,105,104,104,103 103,102,102,100,100 100,100,99,99,98
CSF £319.96 CT £4566.43 TOTE £22.50: £7.80, £5.40, £5.20; EX 1079.80 Trifecta £5412.00 Pool £30,490.29 - 4.00 winning units..
Owner Brian Yeardley Continental Ltd **Bred** Card Bloodstock **Trained** Middleham Moor, N Yorks
■ The second running of this prestigious handicap on sand, and the first over 1m3f.

FOCUS
A good renewal of this traditionally competitive early-season handicap, but run over a furlong further than in previous years. Close to the pace was the place to be as the first four were in the leading five throughout and the form has not been rated quite as positively at it might have been as a result. The winning time was decent.

NOTEBOOK
Luberon gave his trainer a quick double on the card under a positive ride. The evidence of two previous efforts on an artificial surface suggested he was more effective on turf, but he stays 12f well and, once his rider kicked for home over 2f out, he never looked likely to be reeled in.
Woolfall Blue(IRE), whose liking for this track overcame the step up in class, gave the winner the briefest of scares but never looked like getting on terms. His draw would not have helped his cause either, even over this distance.
Weightless, who was trying the longest trip he has tackled to date, kept going well enough and only just failed to get the runner-up spot. (tchd 16-1)
Celtic Spirit(IRE) was always in the leading bunch and rallied to hold off Tabadul for fourth place. He looks a progressive sort and this should have put him right for a return to turf, where some cut in the ground is in his favour. (op 8-1)
Tabadul(IRE), a winner in Dubai in January, did best of those held up off the pace, but his effort flattened out late on. (op 7-2 tchd 5-1)
All The Good(IRE) was the eye-catcher, keeping on well in the closing stages over a trip that is very much on the short side for him nowadays. He is, however, slightly high in the handicap now and will need to find some more improvement. (op 12-1)
Impeller(IRE), who has been in fine form this year, got involved in a barging match with Futun and did fairly well to finish where he did. (op 12-1 tchd 8-1)
Charlie Tokyo(IRE), who was making his sand debut without any headgear, raced keenly on the outside of his field before eventually fading. He can be expected to come on for the run.
Royal Jet dwelt at the start from his outside stall and his rider soon made a bee-line for the rail. He got into mid-division on the home turn from which point he could make no further progress. (op 6-1 tchd 7-1)
Futun, who was trying the Polytrack for the first time, did not recover after some traffic problems early in the race. (op 9-1)

941 INTERCASINO.CO.UK MAGNOLIA STKS (LISTED RACE) 1m 2f (P)
3:50 (3:50) (Class 1) 4-Y-O+
£14,762 (£5,595; £2,800; £1,396; £699; £351) **Stalls** High

Form RPR

115- **1** **Imperial Star (IRE)**[261] [3681] 4-8-13 101 .... JimmyFortune 5 114+
(J H M Gosden) *swtg: trckd ldrs: drvn and qckndto ld jst over 1f out: sn in command: readily* **8/1**

-202 **2** 1 ¾ **Grand Passion (IRE)**[14] [761] 7-8-13 107 .... SteveDrowne 9 109
(G Wragg) *rr: hday 2f out: drive and qcknd fins fnl f to go 2nd nr fin but nvr a danger to wnr* **8/1**

-314 **3** ½ **Charlie Cool**[30] [642] 4-8-13 .... JamieSpencer 8 108
(W J Haggas) *b.hind: trckd ldr: chal 4f oyt: led 3f out: rdn over 2f out: hdd appr fnl f: styd on same pce* **5/2**[1]

10-1 **4** nk **Sri Diamond**[91] [57] 7-8-13 109 .... JohnEgan 10 107
(S Kirk) *in tch: drvn and hday over 2f out: styd on fnl f but nvr quite gng trble ldrs* **7/1**

1542 **5** ½ **Chicken Soup**[9] [817] 5-8-13 88 .... NCallan 6 106
(T J Pitt) *rr: rdn over 2f out: hdwy over 1f out: fin wl but nvr quite gng pce to be competitive* **14/1**

114- **6** 2 **Dansili Dancer**[203] [5374] 5-8-13 100 .... AdamKirby 2 102
(C G Cox) *chsd ldrs: rdn 3f out: one pce 2f out: wknd fnl f* **5/1**[3]

6506 **7** 1 ¼ **Cimyla (IRE)**[14] [761] 6-8-13 105 .... GeorgeBaker 4 100
(C F Wall) *lw: chsd ldrs: rdn 3f out: wknd over 1f out* **9/2**[2]

555- **8** 2 ½ **Nakheel**[162] [6203] 4-8-13 102 .... RHills 7 95
(M Johnston) *bit bkwd: a towards rr and nvr in contention* **15/2**

032- **9** 1 ¼ **Adventuress**[189] [5666] 4-8-8 87 ....(b) KDarley 3 87
(B J Meehan) *plld hrd: stdd towards rr: sme prog 1/2-way: rn wd bnd 3f out: nt rcvr* **33/1**

3600 **10** 3 ½ **Hail The Chief**[14] [759] 10-8-13 90 .... DaneO'Neill 1 85
(R Hannon) *lw: sn led: hdd 3f out: wknd fr 2f out* **50/1**

2m 7.40s (-1.60) **Going Correction** +0.025s/f (Slow) **10** Ran SP% **121.5**
Speed ratings (Par 111):107,105,105,104,104 102,101,99,98,96
CSF £73.44 TOTE £12.40: £3.00, £2.70, £1.50; EX 83.70 Trifecta £223.90 Pool £662.30 - 2.10 winning units..
Owner H R H Princess Haya Of Jordan **Bred** Deerfield Farm **Trained** Newmarket, Suffolk

FOCUS
A strong renewal of this Listed contest, but the steady early pace contributed to the race being the first of the day to be run outside the standard time. Nevertheless it produced a decisive winner in Motivator's half-brother Imperial Star. The form is fair for the grade, with the runner-up a good guide.

NOTEBOOK
Imperial Star(IRE), who was making his Polytrack debut and got on his toes before the race, tracked the leaders before picking up well to collar the favourite entering the final furlong and drawing away to win with something in hand. Twice a winner on fast turf, he has few miles on the clock and it will be a surprise if he cannot make his mark in Group company this summer, with the Earl of Sefton or the Gordon Richards Stakes next on the agenda. (op 6-1)
Grand Passion(IRE) finished runner-up in the Winter Derby last time so gives a good line to the value of the form. He kept on well for pressure, but had no chance with the winner. (op 15-2)
Charlie Cool, who has been running well in Dubai recently, was ridden positively in an attempt to take advantage of the short straight, but could not resist the finishing surge of the winner. (op 4-1 tchd 9-2 in places)
Sri Diamond had the highest official rating in the race but had to miss the recent Winter Derby, which he won in 2006, with a minor injury and was a market negative. In the circumstances he ran well to finish fourth ahead of Chicken Soup. (op 9-2)
Chicken Soup had a difficult task judged on official figures and looked to have a hard race, just missing out on a place in the final furlong.
Dansili Dancer, making his all-weather debut, looked fairly fit but ran as if the outing will put him right for a return to turf. (op 6-1)
Cimyla(IRE) paid late on for trying to hold his place on the outside of his field. (op 6-1 tchd 13-2)
Nakheel, who was bidding to give his trainer a quickfire treble, was quite keen under early restraint and did not look totally happy on the sharp track. He has a decent reputation but needs to start producing the goods on the track again. (op 13-2 tchd 8-1)
Adventuress, who is reported to be in-foal, failed to handle the home turn and did not look at ease on the track. Official explanation: jockey said filly hung left throughout

942 INTERCASINO.CO.UK E B F MAIDEN STKS 5f (P)
4:20 (4:21) (Class 4) 2-Y-O **£5,181** (£1,541; £770; £384) **Stalls** High

Form RPR

1 **Fat Boy (IRE)** 2-9-3 .... RichardHughes 10 81+
(R Hannon) *w'like: scope: str: trckd ldrs: shkn up and qcknd over 1f out: led last half f: comf* **9/4**[1]

2 1 ¼ **Artdeal** 2-9-3 .... JamieSpencer 2 76
(M J Wallace) *str: sn led: rdn over 1f out: hdd and outpcd last half f but styd on wl for clr 2nd* **6/1**

3 1 ¾ **Iamagrey (IRE)** 2-8-12 .... LPKeniry 3 64
(J S Moore) *unf: sn chsng ldr: rdn 2f out: outpcd ins fnl f* **20/1**

4 ¾ **Bella Natasha (IRE)** 2-8-12 .... NCallan 6 61+
(K A Ryan) *str: s.i.s: sn rcvrd and in tch: drvn and kpt on fr over 1f out but nvr gng pce to be competitive* **7/2**[2]

5 1 **Rio Taffeta** 2-9-3 .... TedDurcan 7 62
(M R Channon) *unf: s.i.s: hday whn rn wd bnd over 2f out: kpt on again fnl f but nvr in contention* **13/2**

6 nk **Private Code** 2-8-12 .... JohnEgan 5 56
(T J Pitt) *w'like: chsd ldrs: rdn 2f out: wknd ins fnl f* **11/2**[3]

7 nk **Splitthedifference** 2-9-3 .... TPO'Shea 8 60
(M R Channon) *w'like: leggy: s.i.s: bhd: drvn over 2f out: styd on fnl f: nvr in contention* **20/1**

8 1 **Bazguy** 2-9-0 .... StephenDonohoe(3) 4 56
(P D Evans) *s.i.s: bhd: rdn 1/2-way: kpt on ins fnl f* **14/1**

9 1 ½ **Defnikov** 2-9-3 .... EdwardCreighton 9 50
(Miss J S Davis) *leggy: b: spd 3f* **50/1**

10 ½ **Lord Deevert** 2-9-0 .... AmirQuinn(3) 1 48
(W G M Turner) *leggy: v.s.a: hung lft most of way and a towards rr* **20/1**

62.90 secs (2.50) **Going Correction** +0.025s/f (Slow) **10** Ran SP% **118.9**
Speed ratings (Par 94):81,79,76,75,73 72,72,70,68,67
CSF £15.60 TOTE £2.90: £1.70, £2.00, £6.60; EX 19.50.
Owner M Sines **Bred** Peter Mooney **Trained** East Everleigh, Wilts

FOCUS
None of these juveniles had previously had an outing, but it looked a fair maiden and market confidence in Fat Boy proved justified.

NOTEBOOK
Fat Boy(IRE), a 70,000gns son of Choisir and trainer Richard Hannon's first 2yo runner of the season, was a graduate of the breeze-up sales at the track only three weeks ago and gave his sire his first winner. He got a good lead from the runner-up and, when asked to win his race, went through a gap without hesitation and strode out really well to the line. A nice type for this early stage of the season, he looks the sort who can run up a sequence and the Lily Agnes Stakes at Chester could be one of those races. (tchd 5-2 and 11-4 in a place)
Artdeal, who is already gelded, is by a speedy sire, but his distaff pedigree did not immediately suggest he would make an early two-year-old. However, he clearly knew his job as he broke fast and got across to the rail from his low-number stall, but despite keeping on well had no answer to the winner's challenge. He should not be too long in picking up a maiden. (tchd 13-2 in places)
Iamagrey(IRE), a half-sister to sprinting winners but a late foal, showed early speed from a low draw and, although no match for the first two, she looks more than capable of finding a race against her own sex and will improve for the run. (op 16-1)
Bella Natasha(IRE), who was green and a bit on edge in the paddock, is a late April foal and looked and ran as if the experience would bring her on. The stable knows how to handle a decent juvenile, so it would be little surprise to see her improve into a fair sort. (op 6-1)
Rio Taffeta, whose stable has being doing well already this season with juveniles, is bred to appreciate longer trips and looks as if he will need a little more time. He was on his toes before the race. Official explanation: jockey said gelding hung left-handed (op 7-1)
Private Code, an early foal who carries the famous Sangster family silks, was on her toes before the race and a little keen racing just behind the leaders, so it was unsurprisingly she faded once in line for home. (op 5-1 tchd 9-2)
Splitthedifference will definitely come on a little bit for the experience.
Lord Deevert Official explanation: jockey said colt missed the break

943 PLAY BLACKJACK AT INTERCASINO.CO.UK H'CAP 6f (P)
4:55 (4:55) (Class 2) (0-105,94) 3-Y-O
£9,971 (£2,985; £1,492; £747; £372; £187) **Stalls** High

Form RPR

133- **1** **Ebn Reem**[162] [6204] 3-8-12 **85** .... NCallan 6 95+
(M A Jarvis) *lw: trckd ldr: led 2f out: drvn and r.o wl fnl f* **2/1**[1]

100- **2** 1 ½ **El Bosque (IRE)**[190] [5655] 3-9-1 **88** .... JimCrowley 8 89
(B R Millman) *lw: chsd ldrs: rdn over 2f out: styd on u.p fnl f to take 2nd but nvr gng pce of wnr* **16/1**

006- **3** ½ **Dazed And Amazed**[203] [5373] 3-9-7 **94** .... RichardHughes 3 97+
(R Hannon) *in tch: rdn and styng on whn n.m.r and swtchd lft ins fnl 2f and lost pl: rallied and r.o ins last* **13/2**

304- **4** ¾ **Reebal**[154] [6332] 3-8-9 **82** .... JamieSpencer 2 79
(B J Meehan) *s.i.s: sn pushed along: rdn and c wd bnd 3f out: styd on fnl f but nvr in contention* **7/1**

042- **5** 1 **Spoof Master (IRE)**[175] [5956] 3-8-13 **89** .... AmirQuinn(3) 7 83
(W G M Turner) *led tl hdd 2f out: wknd ins last* **14/1**

22-1 **6** 1 ¼ **Gower**[11] [802] 3-8-12 **85** .... SteveDrowne 4 76
(R Charlton) *chsd ldrs: rdn 2f out: wknd fnl f* **5/1**[3]

330- **7** hd **Bazroy (IRE)**[168] [6096] 3-9-4 **94** .... StephenDonohoe(3) 1 84
(P D Evans) *towards rr most of way* **14/1**

1-42 **8** 2 **Penny Post (IRE)**[14] [755] 3-8-12 **85** .... JoeFanning 5 69
(M Johnston) *lw: bmpd s: sn rcvrd: hdwy to chse ldrs 1/2-way: rdn 2f out: wknd fnl f* **7/2**[2]

1m 12.96s (-0.74) **Going Correction** +0.025s/f (Slow) **8** Ran SP% **117.3**
Speed ratings (Par 104):105,103,102,101,100 98,98,95
CSF £37.83 CT £183.75 TOTE £3.10: £1.50, £5.40, £1.90; EX 80.60.
Owner Sheikh Ahmed Al Maktoum **Bred** Darley **Trained** Newmarket, Suffolk

FOCUS
A tight little sprint in which two with recent Polytrack form were taken on by six making their seasonal debuts. Solid form, the winner value for a bit extra.

NOTEBOOK
Ebn Reem was allowed to go off favourite despite the fact that he had been well beaten at 1-2 on his only previous encounter with Polytrack. He raced quite keenly on the outside of the leader, but found plenty when sent about his work at the 2f pole and, in the end, scored in the style of an improved performer. There are plenty of good handicaps for him in the next couple of months. (op 5-2 tchd 11-4 and 3-1 in a place)
El Bosque(IRE) finished fourth in last year's Newbury Super Sprint and had been dropped 8lb following a moderate effort on soft ground at the backend in another valuable sales race. He handled this surface well enough and, although no match, kept on to chase home the favourite. (op 20-1)
Dazed And Amazed was the subject of market support on this All-Weather debut and better can be expected with this run under his belt. Some of his juvenile form could make him look fairly handicapped if finding his best form. (op 10-1)

Reebal, who was wearing blinkers towards the end of last season, ran quite well from his low stall having been at the rear early, and stayed on past early leader Spoof Master. (op 8-1 tchd 13-2)
Spoof Master(IRE), who was on his toes before the race, tried to make the most of a decent draw and will appreciate some ease in the ground back on turf.
Gower found this much harder than when scoring from a 37-rated rival on his Polytrack debut last time and was easily brushed aside. (op 7-2)
Penny Post(IRE) challenged early in the straight but that was short-lived and she is clearly better than this effort indicates. (tchd 3-1)

944 INTERCASINO.CO.UK QUEEN'S PRIZE (H'CAP) 2m (P)

5:30 (5:31) (Class 2) (0-105,100) 4-Y-0+

£9,971 (£2,985; £1,492; £747; £372; £187) **Stalls** High

Form				RPR
010-	1		**Odiham**[133] 6610 6-9-8 **99**..............(v) SteveDrowne 3	108
			(H Morrison) *swtg: racd in 3rd: rdn and hdwy over 2f out: str chal ins last: led cl home: all out* **10/3**[2]	
11-1	2	*nk*	**Salute (IRE)**[28] 662 8-8-6 **83** oh1 ow2.............. RobertHavlin 1	92
			(P G Murphy) *lw: chsd ldrs in 4th: rdn over 3f out: hdwy on ins fr 3f out: nt clr run over 2f out: led sn after: hdd and no ex cl home* **4/1**[3]	
250-	3	*3 1/2*	**Galient (IRE)**[210] 5185 4-9-1 **96**.............. NCallan 6	101
			(M A Jarvis) *chsd ldr tl led over 5f out: rdn 3f out: hdd 2f out: sn btn* **6/4**[1]	
434-	4	*7*	**King's Head (IRE)**[13] 4936 4-9-2 **97**.............. GeorgeBaker 2	95+
			(G L Moore) *lw: hld up in 5th but in tch: hday to chse ldrs over 3f out: sn rdn: wknd 2f out* **7/1**	
0/3-	5	*20*	**Shabernak (IRE)**[360] 991 8-9-9 **100**.............. JamieSpencer 5	72
			(M L W Bell) *sn led: hdd over 5f out: wknd 3f out* **13/2**	
360/	6	*29*	**Helvetio**[21] 5-8-7 **84**.............. JoeFanning 4	22
			(Micky Hammond) *a in rr: wl bhd fr 1/2-way* **14/1**	

3m 28.54s (-2.86) **Going Correction** +0.025s/f (Slow)
WFA 4 from 5yo+ 4lb **6** Ran SP% **115.6**
Speed ratings (Par 109):108,107,106,102,92 78
CSF £17.55 TOTE £4.90: £1.80, £2.20; EX 19.70 Place 6 £338.58, Place 5 £121.29 .
Owner D L Brooks, J F Dean, Mrs J Scott **Bred** Glebe Stud **Trained** East Ilsley, Berks
■ Stewards' Enquiry : Robert Havlin two-day ban: used whip with excessive frequency (Apr 18-19)

FOCUS
A disappointingly small turnout for this traditional staying handicap, but it produced a rousing finish with Odiham just getting the better of Salute in the dying strides. A career best from Odiham, but he and the runner-up might have been suited by the way the race was run.

NOTEBOOK
Odiham, who can go well fresh, has a good record on Polytrack, including a Listed win over course and distance last season, and he battled on to just outstay Salute in the final furlong. His future is very much in the hands of the Handicapper, and he will surely find things tough in the short-term. (op 7-2 tchd 4-1 in a place)
Salute(IRE) was a little unlucky in that he carried 2lb overweight and did not get a clear passage when trying for a run up the inside of the favourite well over 2f out. He lost nothing in defeat and, although he is 15lb higher than when scoring the first win of his hat-trick in December and will go up again for this, he has been rated as high as 82 in the past. (op 9-2 tchd 5-1 in a place)
Galient(IRE) has been gelded since last season having disappointed in two admittedly high-class races, but his Queen's Vase form entitled him to start favourite in this company. He ran well enough but could not find another gear when taken on for the lead by the principals. He might be the sort for the Chester Cup. (op 7-4 tchd 15-8)
King's Head(IRE), a former stable companion of the market leader, was fit from a recent run over hurdles but was trying this trip for the first time on the Flat. He travelled really well but appeared not to see out the last 2f, and will be interesting if dropped in trip again. (op 13-2 tchd 6-1 and 8-1)
Shabernak(IRE) has only been lightly raced of late and, after making the running, was soon on the retreat when headed at the end of the back straight. (op 6-1 tchd 11-2 and 7-1)
T/Plt: £1,236.70 to a £1 stake. Pool: £111,900.55. 66.05 winning tickets. T/Qpdt: £335.40 to a £1 stake. Pool: £4,760.10. 10.50 winning tickets. ST

LEOPARDSTOWN (L-H)

Saturday, April 7

OFFICIAL GOING: Good

946a DIMITROVA 1,000 GUINEAS TRIAL STKS (GROUP 3) (FILLIES) 7f

2:55 (2:55) 3-Y-0 **£35,189** (£10,324; £4,918; £1,675)

			RPR
1		**Arch Swing (USA)**[203] 5394 3-9-0.............. MJKinane 1	99+
		(John M Oxx, Ire) *trckd ldrs in 3rd: prog on inner early st: chal over 1f out: narrow advantage ins fnl f: kpt on u.p* **1/1**[1]	
2	*shd*	**Four Sins (GER)**[200] 5466 3-9-0 95.............. FMBerry 2	99
		(John M Oxx, Ire) *led: strly pressed ent st: narrowly hdd under 1f out: kpt on u.p: jst failed* **12/1**	
3	*3/4*	**Theann**[174] 5994 3-9-0 104.............. JAHeffernan 11	102+
		(A P O'Brien, Ire) *hld up in rr: swtchd to outer under 2f out: r.o strly fnl f: nvr nrr* **8/1**[3]	
4	*hd*	**Liscanna (IRE)**[153] 6357 3-9-0 88.............. WMLordan 10	96
		(David Wachman, Ire) *hld up towards rr: 6th and hdwy early st: styd on wl ins fnl f* **50/1**	
5	*3/4*	**Once Upon A Grace (IRE)**[13] 780 3-9-0.............. PJSmullen 8	94
		(Ms F M Crowley, Ire) *mid-div: 7th 1/2-way: 5th into st: 3rd ins fnl f: no ex cl home* **11/1**	
6	*1/2*	**La Conquistadora**[13] 782 3-9-0 97.............. KJManning 7	93
		(J S Bolger, Ire) *trckd ldrs in 4th: effrt early st: no imp fnl f: kpt on same pce* **10/1**	
7	*nk*	**Newgate Lodge (IRE)**[181] 5850 3-9-0 97.............. JMurtagh 9	92
		(M Halford, Ire) *hld up: 8th 1/2-way: kpt on same pce st* **16/1**	
8	*3/4*	**Petite Cherie (IRE)**[200] 5464 3-9-0 98.............. DPMcDonogh 3	90
		(G M Lyons, Ire) *cl up in 2nd: chal appr st: no ex fr 2f out* **25/1**	
9	*1 1/4*	**Brazilian Bride (IRE)**[223] 4853 3-9-0 107.............. CDHayes 6	87
		(Kevin Prendergast, Ire) *trckd ldrs: 5th 1/2-way: rdn and no imp st* **5/1**[2]	
10	*1 1/2*	**Nell Gwyn (IRE)**[188] 5714 3-9-0.............. CO'Donoghue 4	83
		(A P O'Brien, Ire) *hld up towards rr: no imp st* **16/1**	
11	*1/2*	**Gee Kel (IRE)**[200] 5464 3-9-0 101.............. WSupple 5	81
		(Francis Ennis, Ire) *racd keenly: stmbld after 1f: 6th 1/2-way: no ex st* **20/1**	

1m 29.3s (-2.90) **Going Correction** -0.325s/f (Firm) **11** Ran SP% **125.2**
Speed ratings: 103,102,102,101,100 100,100,99,97,96 95
CSF £16.08 TOTE £1.90: £1.10, £3.20, £2.90; DF 23.50.
Owner P Garvey **Bred** T L Folkerth **Trained** Currabeg, Co Kildare

FOCUS
A decent and competitive renewal of this Group 3 but the form is limited bu the proximity of the fourth.

NOTEBOOK
Arch Swing(USA), who had the highest official rating in the line-up, narrowly maintain her unbeaten record on her first start since September. Always close to the pace, she held every chance from the turn in but had to dig deep to make sure of victory. He trainer felt that she was fit enough but probably did get a bit tired in the closing stages, and he expected her to improve on this and added that quicker ground would show her off to best effect. She will have to improve substantially if she is to take a hand in the 1000 Guineas at Newmarket, but she should not be underestimated for next month's Classic. (op 1/1 tchd 11/10)

Four Sins(GER) ran an excellent race, making the running and keeping on strongly under pressure from the turn in. A promising juvenile last year, she disappointed in the Goffs Million when last seen in action but that run came on unsuitably soft ground and she was clearly back to her best. A step up in trip should show her off to best effect and she could have her next start in the Cheshire Oaks. (op 14/1)

Theann held her own in good company last term and made an encouraging start to her campaign. She was last turning in but came home strongly and just found the line coming too soon. Her performance here suggested that she will be well worth trying over a mile and she looks good enough to make her mark at this level.

Liscanna(IRE) showed some useful form last year in handicaps, but the 88-rated filly looked to be up against it here. However, she showed that she had done well over the winter when staying on well over the final furlong and a half. She is possibly best with an ease in the ground and, on this evidence, she should not have to wait long to pick up some valuable black type. (op 33/1)

Once Upon A Grace(IRE) looked a good prospect when winning a 6f maiden at the Curragh last month. She was encountering decidedly different ground here and was taking a major rise in class but acquitted herself well. This was only her second start and she can do better still. (op 9/1)

La Conquistadora came here off a solid fourth-place finish in last month's Park Express Stakes and probably ran to a similar level.

Brazilian Bride(IRE) was involved in some scrimmaging early on and could never work her way into a challenging position. A Group 3 winner last year, she also ran well in two Group 1 events and was well below that form here. She is capable of much better. (op 11/2)

Gee Kel(IRE), another decent juvenile from last year, also suffered in the early scrimmaging and nearly came down. This run can be forgiven.

948a LEOPARDSTOWN 2,000 GUINEAS TRIAL STKS (GROUP 3) (COLTS & GELDING) 1m

4:00 (4:01) 3-Y-0 **£30,790** (£9,033; £4,304; £1,466)

			RPR
1		**Creachadoir (IRE)**[13] 785 3-9-0 102.............. KJManning 2	111+
		(J S Bolger, Ire) *cl 2nd and disp ld: led ent st: sn qcknd clr: styd on wl: eased cl home* **12/1**	
2	*3 1/2*	**Confuchias (IRE)**[159] 6262 3-9-0 102.............. WSupple 1	103
		(Francis Ennis, Ire) *trckd ldrs in 4th: rdn st: mod 2nd fr over 1f out: kpt on u.p* **15/2**	
3	*nk*	**Summit Surge (IRE)**[218] 5005 3-9-0 99..............(t) JMurtagh 8	102
		(G M Lyons, Ire) *hld up: 6th and prog on inner early st: kpt on wl ins fnl f* **16/1**	
4	*nk*	**Consul General**[146] 6456 3-9-0.............. PJSmullen 4	101
		(D K Weld, Ire) *settled 3rd: 4th into st: kpt on u.p* **7/1**[3]	
5	*1/2*	**Yellowstone (IRE)**[160] 6249 3-9-0 115.............. CO'Donoghue 9	100
		(A P O'Brien, Ire) *hld up in rr: r.o wl fr over 1f out* **8/1**	
6	*nk*	**Alarazi (IRE)**[13] 785 3-9-0.............. MJKinane 5	99
		(John M Oxx, Ire) *trckd ldrs in 5th: rdn st: kpt on fr over 1f out* **9/2**[2]	
7	*3*	**Admiralofthefleet (USA)**[196] 5521 3-9-3 115.............. JAHeffernan 7	95
		(A P O'Brien, Ire) *sn led and disp: hdd ent st: outpcd 2f out: no ex fr over 1f out* **6/5**[1]	
8	*hd*	**Blackberry Boy (IRE)**[200] 5467 3-9-0 99.............. PShanahan 6	92
		(D K Weld, Ire) *hld up in rr: no imp st* **33/1**	
9	*3*	**Regional Counsel**[224] 4825 3-9-0 100.............. DPMcDonogh 3	85
		(Kevin Prendergast, Ire) *hld up in tch: no imp st* **12/1**	

1m 40.2s (-4.20) **Going Correction** -0.325s/f (Firm) **9** Ran SP% **123.2**
Speed ratings: 108,104,104,103,103 103,100,99,96
CSF £104.80 TOTE £12.40: £2.90, £2.40, £8.10; DF 102.70.
Owner Mrs J S Bolger **Bred** Frank Dunne **Trained** Coolcullen, Co Carlow

FOCUS
A very interesting race that brought together three previous Group winners and several promising colts. The race is rated around the runner-up, fourth and eighth.

NOTEBOOK
Creachadoir(IRE) ◆ came into this a maiden but had shown decent form at Group 2 level last year when running a good fourth in the Railway Stakes. Third to Alarazi on testing ground at the Curragh last month, he was much more at home on this surface and disputed the lead from an early stage. He quickened up impressively to move into a useful advantage with a quarter of a mile to run and was soon in full command. This was a very likeable performance and he is clearly a colt with a fine future. Jim Bolger will now decide between the Irish 2000 Guineas or the French Derby for him, and he could be a live contender for either race.

Confuchias(IRE) acquitted himself well on his first start since landing a 7f Group 3 on soft ground here last October. This was easily his toughest assignment to date but he travelled well throughout and led the chase as the winner moved clear. He could well prove capable of improving on this effort. (op 7/1 tchd 8/1)

Summit Surge(IRE) was reappearing for the first time since finishing third in a Tralee nursery last September in which the runner-up spot was filled by Finsceal Beo. Given a patient ride, he stayed on well from the turn in and would have finished closer but for meeting some trouble in running. This was an encouraging effort on his part. (op 12/1)

Consul General had a good position from early on and held every chance from the turn in but could not make any further impression from over a furlong out. He might appreciate more ease in the ground but should have a solid future at Pattern level.

Yellowstone(IRE), whose best effort last term saw him finish third to stablemate Mount Nelson in a French Group 1, fared best of the two Ballydoyle representatives. He could never land a telling blow but stayed on well from over a furlong out. He can be expected to make good progress off the back of this run. (op 7/1)

Alarazi(IRE) defeated the winner when making a successful debut at the Curragh, but was taking a major rise in class. He could never land a telling blow but was not disgraced and could improve on this if he steps up to 1m2f. (op 7/2)

Admiralofthefleet(USA), last year's Royal Lodge Stakes winner, shared the top official rating of 115 and went off favourite but did not run up to form. He made the running but was a spent force early in the straight, although recent seasons have shown that it is premature to draw firm conclusions about Ballydoyle runners on their reappearances. (op 6/4)

947 - 951a (Foreign Racing) - See Raceform Interactive

MUSSELBURGH (R-H)

Sunday, April 8

OFFICIAL GOING: Good to firm (good in places)

Wind: Moderate, against

952 TOTEPLACEPOT MAIDEN STKS 5f

2:20 (2:21) (Class 5) 2-Y-O **£3,238** (£963; £481; £240) **Stalls** Low

Form	Pos	Dist	Horse	Jockey	RPR
	1		**Primo Heights** 2-8-12	DanielTudhope 10	80
			(J S Goldie) *outpcd in rr whn checked after 1f and sn bhd: gd hdwy wl over 1f out: str run to ld jst ins last: edgd rt and styd on* **33/1**		
	2	4	**Eager Diva (USA)** 2-8-12	NCallan 7	64+
			(K A Ryan) *swtchd rt after s and in tch: pushed along and sltly outpcd 2f out: stayed on strly ins last* **11/2**[3]		
	3	nk	**Elijah Pepper (USA)** 2-9-3	PaulFessey 8	68
			(T D Barron) *chsd ldrs: hdwy to chal 2f out and ev ch whn rdn and hung rt ent last: kpt on same pce* **8/1**		
	4	1 1/2	**Howards Way** 2-9-3	TomEaves 1	62
			(I Semple) *sn outpcd in rr: hdwy wl over 1f out: styd on strly ins last: nrst fin* **10/1**		
	5	shd	**Guertino (IRE)** 2-9-3	PaulEddery 2	61+
			(B Smart) *led: rdn along and hdd wl over 1f out: edgd rt and kpt on same pce ins last* **10/3**[1]		
	6	nk	**Maracana Boy (IRE)** 2-9-3	PhillipMakin 4	60
			(M Dods) *cl up: rdn to ld wl over 1f out: hdd jst ins last and kpt on same pce* **7/2**[2]		
	7	5	**Upstanding** 2-8-5	PatrickDonaghy(7) 5	35
			(M Brittain) *cl up: rdn along and wknd wl over 1f out* **66/1**		
2	8	7	**Ballycroy Boy (IRE)**[6] [890] 2-9-3	MickyFenton 6	12
			(A Bailey) *chsd ldrs: rdn along 2f out and sn wknd* **10/3**[1]		
	9	1 1/4	**Straight (IRE)** 2-9-3	DeanMernagh 9	7
			(M Brittain) *in tch on outer: rdn along 2f out: sn wknd* **40/1**		
	10	3	**Limestone** 2-9-3	DarryllHolland 3	—
			(J R Weymes) *sn outpcd and bhd* **25/1**		

63.12 secs (2.62) **Going Correction** +0.325s/f (Good) **10** Ran SP% **114.7**

Speed ratings (Par 92):92,85,85,82,82 82,74,62,60,56

CSF £198.59 TOTE £33.30: £6.70, £2.30, £2.70; EX 238.10.

Owner The Vital Sparks **Bred** Jim Goldie **Trained** Uplawmoor, E Renfrews

■ Stewards' Enquiry : Paul Eddery four-day ban: failed to ride out for fourth place (Apr 19-22)

FOCUS

Just a modest juvenile maiden, but a nice start from the wide-margin winner and there should be future winners behind. The leaders appeared to go off too fast and set the race up for the closers.

NOTEBOOK

Primo Heights, a half-sister to Blazing Heights, a dual 5-6f winner at two and three, and Geojimali, who won the sixth race on this card, created a good impression on her racecourse debut. She struggled to go the frantic early pace, but found her feet in the latter half of the contest and came clear of her rivals under hands-and-heels riding. The bare form is probably just modest, but she looks the type to improve.

Eager Diva(USA), a $45,000 purchase, out of a sister to Grade 3 winner Sing For Free, was no match for the winner late on but still shaped with promise. She should find a similar event. (op 5-1 tchd 6-1)

Elijah Pepper(USA), a $17,000 half-brother to One Dove, a winner over 1m1f in the US, was supported at big prices and made a respectable introduction. He might have given the winner more to think about had he not hung right under pressure, but he should have learnt from this experience. (op 14-1)

Howards Way, the first foal of an unraced half-sister to Rose Of Battle, a 5f winner at two, struggled to go the early pace but stayed on nicely close home. He should improve plenty and can pick up a similar event, possibly on a stiffer track. (op 11-1 tchd 12-1)

Guertino(IRE), whose sales price dropped from 57,000gns to 14,000gns, is out of a mare who was placed over 6f as a juvenile. He probably went off a little too fast and should be capable of better. (op 2-1)

Maracana Boy(IRE), a 28,000gns half-brother to four winners, including triple 7f-1m winner Direct Reaction, and Fontanally Springs, a dual 5-6f winner at two and three, could not sustain his challenge late on. He's by Captain Rio, so easier ground may suit. (op 4-1 tchd 9-2)

Ballycroy Boy(IRE) got going late on when second on the Fibresand at Southwell on his debut and this quick 5f proved far from ideal. He gives the impression 6f on easier ground will suit better. (op 7-2 tchd 4-1 in a place)

953 TOTEPOOL H'CAP 7f 30y

2:50 (2:50) (Class 4) (0-85,85) 4-Y-O+ **£5,505** (£1,637; £818; £408) **Stalls** High

Form	Pos	Dist	Horse	Jockey	RPR
3406	1		**Stoic Leader (IRE)**[62] [371] 7-8-10 **77**	PaulHanagan 10	85
			(R F Fisher) *in tch: hdwy on inner to chse ldrs over 2f out: rdn over 1f out: swtchd lft ins last: drvn and styd on to ld nr line* **8/1**		
064-	2	shd	**Angaric (IRE)**[161] [6239] 4-8-6 **73**	RoystonFfrench 6	81
			(B Smart) *chsd ldrs: hdwy on outer 2f out: rdn ent last and ev ch tl drvn and no ex last strides* **7/1**[3]		
5-50	3	nk	**Glenbuck (IRE)**[33] [629] 4-9-3 **84**	(v) MickyFenton 8	91
			(A Bailey) *led after 1f: rdn along 2f out: drvn ent last: hdd and no ex last strides* **14/1**		
500-	4	1 1/4	**Fiefdom (IRE)**[166] [6160] 5-8-10 **77**	NCallan 12	81
			(I W McInnes) *a.p: effrt to chal over 1f out and ev ch tl drvn: edgd lft and no ex last 100 yds* **9/2**[1]		
200-	5	2 1/2	**Cool Ebony**[182] [5833] 4-8-11 **78**	PaulFessey 9	75+
			(M Dods) *dwlt and in rr: hdwy 3f out: rdn to chse ldrs over 2f out: kpt on ins last: nrst fin* **11/1**		
0-52	6	hd	**Royal Dignitary (USA)**[9] [827] 7-9-4 **85**	AdrianTNicholls 5	82
			(D Nicholls) *prom: effrt over 2f out and chance tl rdn and wknd over 1f out* **9/2**[1]		
1406	7	2 1/2	**H Harrison (IRE)**[6] [895] 7-8-1 **71** oh4	AndrewElliott(3) 7	61
			(I W McInnes) *led 1f: cl up tl rdn over 2f out and grad wknd* **12/1**		
460-	8	3 1/2	**Stellite**[143] [6499] 7-8-8 **75**	DanielTudhope 4	56
			(J S Goldie) *a towards rr* **12/1**		
534-	9	hd	**Regent's Secret (USA)**[134] [6607] 7-8-5 **79**	GaryBartley(7) 1	60+
			(J S Goldie) *stdd s: hld up and a bhd* **10/1**		
000-	10	2	**King Of The Moors (USA)**[196] [5554] 4-8-7 **74**	PhillipMakin 3	49
			(T D Barron) *towards rr: effrt 1/2-way: sn rdn along and nvr a factor* **11/2**[2]		
460-	11	5	**Campo Bueno (FR)**[143] [6499] 5-9-2 **83**	KDarley 11	45
			(A Berry) *midfield: rdn along 3f out: sn wknd* **28/1**		
500-	12	24	**Toy Top (USA)**[187] [5749] 4-8-10 **77**	TomEaves 2	—
			(M Dods) *a outpcd and bhd* **28/1**		

1m 30.77s (0.83) **Going Correction** +0.325s/f (Good) **12** Ran SP% **121.7**

Speed ratings (Par 105):108,107,107,106,103 103,100,96,95,93 87,60

CSF £64.86 CT £780.53 TOTE £8.70: £2.80, £2.60, £4.60; EX 54.10.

Owner Alan Willoughby **Bred** P J Higgins **Trained** Ulverston, Cumbria

■ Stewards' Enquiry : Royston Ffrench two-day ban: careless riding & used whip with excessive frequency (Apr 19-20)

FOCUS

A fair handicap and the winning time was 1.15 seconds quicker than the following maiden. Just ordinary form though.

King Of The Moors(USA) Official explanation: jockey said gelding hung left throughout

Campo Bueno(FR) Official explanation: jockey said gelding was unsuited by the good to firm (good in places) ground

954 TOTEQUADPOT MAIDEN STKS 7f 30y

3:20 (3:22) (Class 5) 3-Y-O+ **£3,238** (£963; £481; £240) **Stalls** High

Form	Pos	Dist	Horse	Jockey	RPR
222-	1		**Gazboolou**[202] [5431] 3-8-12 79	PatCosgrave 8	72
			(K R Burke) *trckd ldrs: hdwy 3f out: rdn to ld wl over 1f out: drvn ent last and kpt on gamely* **5/2**[2]		
03-	2	1/2	**Leon Knights**[170] [6072] 3-8-12	NickyMackay 4	71
			(G A Butler) *trckd ldrs: hdwy over 2f out: rdn to chal over 1f out and ev ch tl drvn and no ex last 100 yds* **13/2**[3]		
	3	3 1/2	**Hubble Bubble (USA)** 3-8-12	JoeFanning 5	61
			(M Johnston) *cl up: led 3f out: rdn over 2f out: hdd wl over 1f out: kpt on same pce fnl f* **13/2**[3]		
060-	4	1 1/4	**Howards Tipple**[150] [6414] 3-8-12 70	TomEaves 11	58
			(I Semple) *chsd ldrs: hdwy over 2f out: sn rdn and one pce appr last* **22/1**		
2	5	1/2	**Shot Gun**[15] [758] 3-8-12	ChrisCatlin 7	57+
			(M R Channon) *bhd: rdn along 3f out: swtchd lft and drvn wl over 1f out: styd on u.p ins last: nt rch ldrs* **13/8**[1]		
00	6	1	**Grey Light (IRE)**[64] [342] 3-8-9	GregFairley(3) 10	54+
			(L Lungo) *towards rr: hdwy 3f out: sn rdn and kpt on ins last: nrst fin* **50/1**		
050-	7	nk	**Four Kings**[216] [5063] 6-9-12 34	PaulFessey 6	59?
			(Karen McLintock) *led: rdn along and hdd 3f out: sn drvn and wknd fnl 2f* **150/1**		
46-6	8	1 3/4	**Linton Dancer (IRE)**[57] [425] 4-9-7 40	(b[1]) DarryllHolland 12	49?
			(J R Weymes) *chsd ldng pair: rdn along 3f out: wknd fnl 2f* **50/1**		
00-	9	1/2	**Amanda Carter**[199] [5495] 3-8-7	PaulHanagan 3	43
			(R A Fahey) *a towards rr* **100/1**		
0-	10	1/2	**A Big Sky Brewing (USA)**[165] [6175] 3-8-12	PhillipMakin 13	46
			(T D Barron) *a rr* **16/1**		
	11	hd	**Phreeze** 3-8-12	DeanMcKeown 1	46
			(G A Swinbank) *a rr* **11/1**		
0-06	12	3/4	**Polish Star**[25] [678] 3-8-12 57	TonyHamilton 9	44
			(J S Wainwright) *a rr* **66/1**		
40-	13	1 1/4	**Warm Tribute (USA)**[180] [5901] 3-8-12	MickyFenton 14	41
			(W G Harrison) *dwlt: keen and sn chsng ldrs on inner tl n.m.r and lost pl after 1 1/2f: sn towards rr* **100/1**		

1m 31.92s (1.98) **Going Correction** +0.325s/f (Good)

WFA 3 from 4yo+ 14lb **13** Ran SP% **120.0**

Speed ratings (Par 103):101,100,96,95,94 93,92,90,90,89 89,88,87

CSF £18.91 TOTE £4.10: £1.60, £2.50, £2.10; EX 26.90.

Owner Mrs Maura Gittins **Bred** Cheveley Park Stud Ltd **Trained** Middleham Moor, N Yorks

FOCUS

Just an ordinary maiden and the winning time was 1.15 seconds slower than the previous 71-85 handicap. It paid to be handy, and some of the hold-up horses are better than the bare form. The seventh and eighth were too close for comfort, but they raced prominently, which helps explain it.

Shot Gun Official explanation: jockey said gelding missed the break

Phreeze Official explanation: jockey said colt missed the break

955 TOTESPORT.COM MUSSELBURGH GOLD CUP (A H'CAP STKS) 1m 6f

3:50 (3:50) (Class 4) (0-85,82) 4-Y-O+

£12,464 (£3,732; £1,866; £934; £466; £234) **Stalls** High

Form	Pos	Dist	Horse	Jockey	RPR
15-0	1		**Kristensen**[33] [628] 8-8-12 **67**	(v) TonyHamilton 8	75
			(Karen McLintock) *rdn along 1f: midfield tl hdwy over 4f out: rdn to chse ldng pair over 2f out: drvn and styd on wl fnl f to ld last 50yds* **14/1**		
41/5	2	3/4	**Alrida (IRE)**[46] [515] 8-8-13 **68**	PaulHanagan 14	75
			(R A Fahey) *in tch: hdwy to chse ldr over 4f out: rdn to chal 2f out: drvn to ld over 1f out: hdd and no ex last 50 yds* **7/2**[1]		
20-6	3	1 1/2	**Oddsmaker (IRE)**[4] [914] 6-9-1 **70**	(t) DeanMcKeown 9	75
			(M A Barnes) *sn led: pushed clr over 5f out: rdn along 3f out: drvn and hdd over 1f out: ev ch tl no ex last 50 yds* **14/1**		
313-	4	3	**Grey Outlook**[156] [6321] 4-8-7 **65**	RoystonFfrench 13	66
			(Miss L A Perratt) *hld up in rr: stdy hdwy over 4f out: rdn over 2f out: styd on wl u.p appr last: nrst fin* **14/1**		
012-	5	3/4	**La Estrella (USA)**[116] [6811] 4-9-10 **82**	TPQueally 1	82
			(J G Given) *in tch: hdwy over 4f out: effrt to chse ldng pair 3f out and sn rdn along: drvn and one pce friom wl over 1f out* **10/1**		
-111	6	2	**Global Strategy**[39] [585] 4-8-12 **70**	ChrisCatlin 6	67
			(Rae Guest) *towards rr: pushed along after 4f: rdn along and hdwy over 4f out: kpt on u.p fnl 2f: nt rch ldrs* **7/2**[1]		
200-	7	1 1/4	**Touch Of Ivory (IRE)**[40] [6211] 4-8-3 **61**	(p) NickyMackay 12	56
			(P Monteith) *chsd ldrs: rdn along 4f out: drvn over 2f out and grad wknd* **33/1**		
350-	8	2 1/2	**Trance (IRE)**[163] [6205] 7-9-10 **79**	(p) PaulFessey 11	71
			(T D Barron) *hld up and bhd: sme hdwy on outer over 2f out: nvr a factor* **8/1**[3]		
3-22	9	3	**Black Falcon (IRE)**[11] [811] 7-9-5 **74**	MickyFenton 5	62
			(M A Peill) *hld up in rr: effrt and sme hdwy on outer 3f out: sn rdn along and nvr a factor* **6/1**[2]		
/515	10	10	**Positive Profile (IRE)**[53] [457] 9-9-2 **71**	GrahamGibbons 4	45
			(J J Quinn) *chsd ldrs: rdn along over 4f out and sn wknd* **12/1**		
056-	11	25	**Brigadore (USA)**[234] [4537] 4-9-3 **75**	KDarley 3	14
			(E J Alston) *trckd ldrs: pushed along 1/2-way: grad lost pl and bhd fnl 3f* **8/1**[3]		
406-	12	21	**Soho Square**[63] [3248] 4-8-11 **72**	(b[1]) GregFairley(3) 10	—
			(L Lungo) *prom: rdn along over 5f out and sn wknd* **33/1**		
/00-	13	29	**Howards Dream (IRE)**[199] [5360] 9-7-12 **53** oh8	(t) SilvestreDeSousa 7	—
			(D A Nolan) *chsd ldrs: rdn along and wknd 1/2-way: sn bhd* **200/1**		

3m 6.58s (0.88) **Going Correction** +0.325s/f (Good)

WFA 4 from 6yo+ 3lb **13** Ran SP% **124.1**

Speed ratings (Par 105):110,109,108,107,106 105,104,103,101,95 81,69,53

CSF £64.56 CT £732.72 TOTE £20.00: £5.70, £2.30, £6.10; EX 151.70 Trifecta £259.10 Part won. Pool: £365.00 - 0.10 winning tickets..

Owner Equiname Ltd **Bred** Lordship Stud Limited **Trained** Ingoe, Northumberland

FOCUS

Good prize money, but just ordinary form for the level. The pace was good though, and the form looks pretty solid.

956 TOTEEXACTA MAIDEN STKS 1m 4f
4:20 (4:20) (Class 5) 3-Y-O+ **£3,238** (£963; £481; £240) **Stalls** High

Form RPR
50- **1** **Danish Rebel (IRE)**^{120} [6757] 3-8-8 ow1 .... TomEaves 7 79
(G A Charlton) *mde all: rdn along over 2f out: styd on wl u.p fnl f* **33/1**
5-23 **2** *2* **Sowdrey**^{16} [735] 3-8-7 79 .... ChrisCatlin 1 75
(M R Channon) *chsd ldrs: hdwy 4f out: rdn along over 2f out: chsd wnr over 1f out: sn drvn and no imp* **15/2**^{2}
005- **3** *8* **Soubriquet (IRE)**^{29} [5609] 4-9-6 55 ....(t) MCGeran$^{(7)}$ 8 60+
(M A Barnes) *chsd wnr: rdn along over 4f out: drvn and hung rt 2f out: sn one pce* **20/1**^{3}
2 **4** *7* **Old Etonian (UAE)**^{15} [764] 3-8-7 .... JoeFanning 2 51
(M Johnston) *rrd and wnt bdly rt s: sn chsng ldrs: rdn along to chse wnr 3f out: drvn and hld whn hmpd 2f out and sn wknd* **1/8**^{1}
40- **5** *22* **Fleetwood Image**^{279} [3157] 3-8-8 ow1 .... DarryllHolland 6 17
(J R Weymes) *hmpd s: chsd ldrs tl rdn along and wknd over 4f out* **33/1**
00-0 **6** *19* **Ross Is Boss**^{66} [321] 5-10-0 27 .... DeanMcKeown 3 —
(C J Teague) *s.i.s: a bhd* **200/1**
660- **7** *1 1/4* **Dramatic Review (IRE)**^{17} [6213] 5-9-7 45 ....(tp) GaryBartley$^{(7)}$ 4 —
(J Barclay) *hmpd s: chsd ldrs: rdn along and wknd 1/2-way: sn wl bhd* **100/1**
0- **U** **Cinaman (IRE)**^{197} [5537] 3-8-7 .... PaulHanagan 5 —
(R F Fisher) *rrd and uns rdr stalls* **40/1**

2m 41.5s (4.60) **Going Correction** +0.325s/f (Good)
WFA 3 from 4yo 21lb 4 from 5yo 1lb **8 Ran SP% 115.2**
Speed ratings (Par 103):97,95,90,85,71 58,57,—
CSF £224.14 TOTE £38.20: £4.50, £1.40, £2.50; EX 228.30.
Owner J I A Charlton **Bred** Brendan Ferris **Trained** Stocksfield, Northumberland

FOCUS
A weak maiden and something of a turn-up with the favourite running a shocker. As a result the form is far from solid.
Old Etonian(UAE) Official explanation: trainer had no explanation for the poor form shown

957 TOTESPORT 0800 221 221 H'CAP 5f
4:50 (4:50) (Class 4) (0-85,85) 4-Y-O+ **£6,477** (£1,927; £963; £481) **Stalls** Low

Form RPR
313- **1** **Geojimali**^{174} [6009] 5-8-10 **81** .... GaryBartley$^{(7)}$ 13 88+
(J S Goldie) *stdd s and bhd: hdwy wl over 1f out: str run ent last to ld last 50 yds* **8/1**^{3}
203- **2** *nk* **Handsome Cross (IRE)**^{197} [5532] 6-9-7 **85** .... SilvestreDeSousa 9 91
(D Nicholls) *cl up: rdn to ld over 1f out: drvn ins last: hdd and nt qckn last 50 yds* **6/1**^{2}
200- **3** *nk* **Spiritual Peace (IRE)**^{162} [6212] 4-8-13 **77** ....(p) NCallan 5 82
(K A Ryan) *chsd ldrs: hdwy and cl up 2f out: rdn and ev ch over 1f out: kpt on u.p ins last* **12/1**
400- **4** *1* **High Reach**^{185} [5777] 7-8-11 **82** .... NeilBrown$^{(7)}$ 10 83
(T D Barron) *trckd ldrs: effrt 2f out: sn rdn and kpt on same pce ins last* **6/1**^{2}
205- **5** *1/2* **Ptarmigan Ridge**^{156} [6320] 11-8-12 **76** .... RoystonFfrench 11 76
(Miss L A Perratt) *chsd ldrs: hdwy on outer 2f out: sn rdn and ev ch tl drvn and wknd ins last* **16/1**
041- **6** *1/2* **Blazing Heights**^{156} [6320] 4-9-1 **79** .... DanielTudhope 3 77+
(J S Goldie) *prom: effrt to dispute ld 2f out and ev ch tl rdn and wknd ent last* **9/2**^{1}
456- **7** *3/4* **Kings College Boy**^{184} [5791] 7-8-6 **70** .... PaulFessey 12 65+
(R A Fahey) *towards rr: hdwy 2f out: sn rdn and kpt on ins last: nrst fin* **12/1**
046- **8** *1 1/2* **Bo McGinty (IRE)**^{174} [6009] 6-8-8 **77** .... JamieMoriarty$^{(5)}$ 6 67
(R A Fahey) *sn rdn along and a towards rr* **10/1**
01-0 **9** *shd* **Circuit Dancer (IRE)**^{23} [692] 7-9-7 **85** .... AdrianTNicholls 8 74
(D Nicholls) *chsd ldrs: rdn along 1/2-way: sn wknd* **10/1**
000- **10** *1 1/2* **Rare Breed**^{237} [4422] 4-9-2 **80** .... DarryllHolland 7 64
(Mrs L Stubbs) *led: rdn along and hdd wl over 1f out: sn wknd* **10/1**
030- **11** *1 3/4* **Oranmore Castle (IRE)**^{174} [6009] 5-8-7 **78** .... AdeleRothery$^{(7)}$ 2 56
(D Nicholls) *a towards rr* **10/1**
425- **12** *8* **Misphire**^{162} [6212] 4-9-0 **78** .... PhillipMakin 1 27
(M Dods) *s.i.s: a rr* **11/1**

61.75 secs (1.25) **Going Correction** +0.325s/f (Good) **12 Ran SP% 123.8**
Speed ratings (Par 105):103,102,102,100,99 98,97,95,95,92 89,77
CSF £58.04 CT £598.73 TOTE £9.20: £3.30, £2.90, £5.10; EX 73.30.
Owner Fyffees 2 **Bred** Jim Goldie **Trained** Uplawmoor, E Renfrews

FOCUS
A good sprint handicap for the grade. The winning time was 0.46 seconds faster than the following three-year-old handicap, and 1.37 seconds quicker than the juvenile maiden. The runner-up sets the standard but it is difficult to be totally confident in the strength of the form.
Rare Breed Official explanation: jockey said gelding was unsuited by the good to firm (good in places) ground
Misphire Official explanation: jockey said filly was unsuited by the good to firm (good in places) ground

958 TOTESPORTCASINO.COM H'CAP 5f
5:20 (5:20) (Class 5) (0-75,75) 3-Y-O **£3,238** (£963; £481; £240) **Stalls** Low

Form RPR
1- **1** **Valery Borzov (IRE)**^{166} [6157] 3-9-7 **75** .... AdrianTNicholls 4 88+
(D Nicholls) *hld up in tch: hdwy to trck ldrs 2f out: qcknd to ld last: comf* **7/4**^{1}
310- **2** *1 3/4* **Baileys Outshine**^{172} [6056] 3-9-3 **71** .... TPQueally 5 73
(J G Given) *led: rdn wl over 1f out: hdd and nt qckn ins last* **9/1**
06-5 **3** *3/4* **Nomoreblondes**^{15} [752] 3-8-8 **62** .... MickyFenton 6 61
(P T Midgley) *cl up: effrt and ev ch over 1f out: sn rdn and nt qckn ins last* **16/1**
0-1 **4** *1 1/2* **Dualagi**^{12} [798] 3-8-9 **63** .... LPKeniry 1 56
(J S Moore) *towards rr and pushed along 1/2-way: sn rdn: drvn and kpt on ins last: nt rch ldrs* **3/1**^{2}
-214 **5** *1* **Ronnie Howe**^{20} [707] 3-9-4 **72** .... PhillipMakin 8 61
(M Dods) *trckd ldrs gng: shkn up over 1f out: sn rdn and btn* **7/1**^{3}
311- **6** *1 1/2* **Milson's Point (IRE)**^{106} [6931] 3-9-4 **72** .... TomEaves 7 55
(I Semple) *cl up on outer: rdn along 2f out and sn wknd* **15/2**
034- **7** *shd* **Woqoodd**^{186} [5766] 3-9-0 **73** .... JamieMoriarty$^{(5)}$ 3 56
(R A Fahey) *bhd tl styd on fnl 2f* **12/1**
120- **8** *6* **Lafontaine Bleu**^{184} [5788] 3-8-12 **66** .... TonyHamilton 2 25
(R A Fahey) *chsd ldrs: rdn along 1/2-way: sn wknd* **12/1**

62.21 secs (1.71) **Going Correction** +0.325s/f (Good) **8 Ran SP% 116.9**
Speed ratings (Par 98):99,96,95,92,91 88,88,78
CSF £19.24 CT £194.21 TOTE £2.80: £1.30, £2.50, £3.00; EX 18.00 Place 6 £2,632.96, Place 5 £493.78.
Owner D Kilburn/I Hewitson/D Nicholls **Bred** Vincent Harrington **Trained** Sessay, N Yorks

FOCUS
A fair three-year-old sprint won by a progressive colt, who could rate a fair bit higher. The winning time was not great, only 0.91 seconds quicker than the earlier juvenile maiden, and 0.46 seconds slower than the older-horse handicap, but a positive view has been taken of the form.
T/Jkpt: Not won. T/Plt: £1,400.50 to a £1 stake. Pool: £69,547.45. 36.25 winning tickets. T/Qpdt: £126.70 to a £1 stake. Pool: £3,818.60. 22.30 winning tickets. JR

959 - 962a (Foreign Racing) - See Raceform Interactive

879 LONGCHAMP (R-H)
Sunday, April 8

OFFICIAL GOING: Good to soft

963a PRIX NOAILLES (GROUP 2) (C&F) 1m 2f 110y
3:20 (3:50) 3-Y-O **£50,068** (£19,324; £9,223; £6,149; £3,074)

RPR
1 **Soldier Of Fortune (IRE)**^{147} [6456] 3-9-2 .... CSoumillon 4 116
(A P O'Brien, Ire) *raced in 3rd, went 2nd 2f out, ridden to lead just inside final f, comfortably* **18/10**^{2}
2 *1 1/2* **Spirit One (FR)**^{16} [749] 3-9-2 .... DBoeuf 5 113
(P Demercastel, France) *led to just inside final f, one pace* **29/10**^{3}
3 *3* **Spycrawler (USA)**^{156} 3-9-2 .... OPeslier 1 108
(A Fabre, France) *raced in 4th, kept on at one pace to take 3rd 100 yards out, never threatened leaders* **17/10**^{1}
4 *1* **Quest For Honor**^{22} [704] 3-9-2 .... SPasquier 3 106
(A Fabre, France) *raced in 2nd to 2f out, one pace* **57/10**
5 *6* **Staraco (FR)**^{22} [704] 3-9-2 .... ASanglard 2 95
(B Goudot, France) *last throughout* **10/1**

2m 7.40s (-7.20) **Going Correction** -0.40s/f (Firm) **5 Ran SP% 122.4**
Speed ratings: 110,108,106,106,101
PARI-MUTUEL: WIN 2.80; PL 1.60, 1.90; SF 7.90.
Owner Mrs John Magnier **Bred** J S Bolger **Trained** Ballydoyle, Co Tipperary

NOTEBOOK
Soldier Of Fortune(IRE) put up a faultless winning performance in this Classic trial and he must now be a serious contender for European Classics. Settled in third position, he took a little time to find top gear and then quickened well inside the final furlong to win going away. There is plenty of scope for further improvement and he will now head for the Prix Greffulhe at Saint-Cloud on May 14. The Prix du Jockey Club is already being talked about for this son of Galileo.
Spirit One(FR) was much more at home on this good ground and was soon taking the field along at a reasonable pace. He stuck to his task when challenged and only gave ground during the last 100 yards. There is speed on his dam's side and maybe this distance is just beyond his capabilities at this level, but whatever happens he will be accompanied by a pacemaker next time out as his trainer feels he idles when in front.
Spycrawler(USA), a really decent-looking colt, was made favourite but ran a little below expectations. Fourth for much of the event, he still had plenty to do in the straight, but began to lengthen his stride from a furlong and half out and ran on well at the finish without ever threatening the first two. It was just his second race and considerable progress can be expected in the future, so it would be unwise to write him off.
Quest For Honor, smartly away, was then settled in second position where he remained for much of the race. Taken up the far rail, he stayed on throughout the final two furlongs and did not lose third place until inside the final furlong. A decent race should come his way but maybe not at this level.

952 MUSSELBURGH (R-H)
Monday, April 9

OFFICIAL GOING: Good to firm
Wind: Moderate, against

964 SETANTA.COM FILLIES' H'CAP 5f
2:20 (2:21) (Class 5) (0-70,70) 4-Y-O+ **£3,238** (£963; £481; £240) **Stalls** Low

Form RPR
121- **1** **How's She Cuttin' (IRE)**^{157} [6315] 4-9-2 **63** .... PhillipMakin 4 81
(T D Barron) *trckd ldrs: smooth hdwy to ld 11/2f out: rdn ent last and sn hung bdly right: styd on* **7/2**^{1}
32-1 **2** *1 1/4* **Hypnosis**^{53} [465] 4-9-9 **70** .... PatCosgrave 9 84+
(D W Barker) *in tch: hdwy 2f out: rdn to chse wnr ent last: ev ch whn carried bdly rt: no room on far rail whn eased nr fin* **5/1**^{2}
000- **3** *3 1/2* **Ashes (IRE)**^{157} [6315] 5-9-1 **62** .... PaulMulrennan 3 63
(K R Burke) *cl up: rdn 2f out and ev ch tl outpcd ent last* **14/1**
020- **4** *3* **Rothesay Dancer**^{133} [6622] 4-8-12 **59** ....(p) DanielTudhope 2 49
(J S Goldie) *towards rr: hdwy 1/2-way: rdn over 1f out: kpt on same pce* **8/1**
666- **5** *shd* **Champagne Cracker**^{182} [5865] 6-8-11 **58** .... TomEaves 10 47
(M Dods) *outpcd and bhd tl hdwy wl over 1f out: kpt on ins last: nrst fin* **12/1**
00-0 **6** *4* **Katie Boo (IRE)**^{57} [432] 5-8-8 **55** .... JoeFanning 6 30
(A Berry) *outpcd and bhd tl styd on fnl 2f* **25/1**
230- **7** *2* **Our Little Secret (IRE)**^{177} [5970] 5-8-13 **65** .... PBradley$^{(5)}$ 7 33
(A Berry) *cl up: rdn along 2f out and sn wknd* **13/2**^{3}
000- **8** *shd* **Mint**^{194} [5620] 4-9-1 **62** .... TonyHamilton 8 29
(D W Barker) *prom: rdn along 1/2-way: sn wknd* **16/1**
0-00 **9** *shd* **Melandre**^{73} [251] 5-8-8 **55** .... DeanMernagh 11 22
(M Brittain) *chsd ldrs on outer: rdn 1/2-way: snw eakened* **33/1**
5-50 **10** *2 1/2* **Titian Saga (IRE)**^{17} [746] 4-8-4 **51** oh1 ....(v^{1}) AdrianTNicholls 1 9
(D Nicholls) *led: rdn along 2f out: sn hdd & wknd* **14/1**

60.71 secs (0.21) **Going Correction** +0.25s/f (Good) **10 Ran SP% 97.0**
Speed ratings (Par 100):108,106,100,95,95 89,85,85,85,81
CSF £13.80 CT £111.22 TOTE £3.30: £1.20, £1.60, £3.50; EX 15.90.
Owner Chris McHale **Bred** A M Burke **Trained** Maunby, N Yorks
■ Lady Bahia was withdrawn (4/1, refused to enter stalls.) R4 applies, deduct 20p in the £.
■ Stewards' Enquiry : Dean Mernagh caution: used whip when out of contention
Phillip Makin five-day ban: careless riding (Apr 20-24)

FOCUS
This modest fillies' handicap produced a decent winning time for a race of its type. The winner remains progressive, as does the runner-up, although there are doubts over what they achieved here.
Melandre Official explanation: trainer said mare was found to be in season
Titian Saga(IRE) Official explanation: jockey said filly had no more to give

965 RACING UK PART OF SETANTA SPORTS PACK H'CAP 2m
2:55 (2:55) (Class 6) (0-65,55) 4-Y-0+ £2,590 (£770; £385; £192) Stalls Low

Form RPR
00/0 1 Kyber[20] 716 6-9-1 45 DanielTudhope 7 58
(J S Goldie) *mde all: rdn wl over 2f out: styd on strly* 5/2[1]
350- 2 2½ Hugs Destiny (IRE)[7] 5369 6-9-7 51 (t) DeanMcKeown 8 61
(M A Barnes) *trckd ldrs: hdwy 4f out: rdn to chse wnr over 2f out: drvn and no imp appr last* 7/2[2]
166- 3 15 King's Envoy (USA)[64] 3350 8-8-12 45 AndrewMullen(3) 6 37
(Mrs J C McGregor) *hld up in tch: hdwy on outer 3f out: sn rdn and kpt on same pce* 9/1
0-30 4 2½ Arcangela[5] 913 4-8-12 46 SilvestreDeSousa 1 35
(Miss Tracy Waggott) *chsd wnr: rdn along over 3f out and sn outpcd* 15/2
000/ 5 5 Vertigo Blue[41] 6697 4-8-11 45 PaulFessey 3 28
(A C Whillans) *hld up in rr: effrt and sme hdwy 3f out: sn rdn and nvr a factor* 12/1
54/0 6 3½ Cottam Grange[13] 804 7-9-1 45 RoystonFfrench 5 24
(I W McInnes) *in tch: effrt 5f out: rdn along over 3f out and sn outpcd* 7/1
410- 7 1¾ Tuscany Rose[23] 5618 4-8-11 45 PaulHanagan 9 22
(M Todhunter) *chsd ldng pair: rdn along 3f out: drvn and wknd over 2f out* 4/1[3]
000- 8 80 Taili[120] 5581 6-9-1 45 MickyFenton 4 —
(D A Nolan) *chsd ldrs 4f: sn lost pl and bhd: t.o fr 1/2-way* 100/1

3m 37.12s (3.22) **Going Correction** +0.25s/f (Good)
WFA 4 from 6yo+ 4lb 8 Ran SP% 113.7
Speed ratings (Par 101):101,99,92,91,88 86,85,45
CSF £11.19 CT £65.26 TOTE £3.10: £2.50, £1.50, £1.90; EX 10.60.
Owner Great Northern Partnership **Bred** P B Holmes **Trained** Uplawmoor, E Renfrews

FOCUS
A dire staying handicap that was run at an uneven pace, dictated by the winner. The form has been rated through the runner-up and should be treated with caution.

966 RACINGUK.TV (S) STKS 1m 4f
3:30 (3:30) (Class 6) 4-Y-0+ £1,943 (£578; £288; £144) Stalls High

Form RPR
22-1 1 Court Of Appeal[7] 891 10-9-5 68 (tp) JamieMoriarty(5) 6 63
(B Ellison) *towards rr: pushed along 5f out: gd hdwy on outer 3f out: rdn to ld 2f out: drvn and edgd rt ins last: styd on* 3/1[1]
150- 2 1¾ Just Observing[20] 3015 4-9-3 75 (p) LeeEnstone 5 54
(P C Haslam) *hld up and bhd: hdwy 3f out: rdn and hung rt ent last: sn drvn and nt rch wnr* 6/1
00-0 3 1½ Susiedil (IRE)[18] 730 6-8-13 36 (v) AdrianTNicholls 1 46
(S T Mason) *in tch: hdwy over 5f out: rdn to ld briefly over 2f out: sn hdd: drvn and edgd lft ent last: one pce* 66/1
5-36 4 ¾ Tedstale (USA)[7] 891 9-9-4 67 (b) NCallan 10 50
(K A Ryan) *in tch: hdwy over 3f out: rdn to chse ldrs 2f out: styng on whn hmpd entering last: kpt on u.p towards fin* 10/3[2]
05/0 5 shd Frith (IRE)[72] 270 5-9-4 75 PaulMulrennan 8 50
(Mrs L B Normile) *chsd ldrs: hdwy over 4f out: rdn and ev ch over 2f out: sn drvn and grad wknd* 25/1
150- 6 5 Kristalchen[244] 4227 5-8-13 38 PatCosgrave 3 37
(D W Thompson) *bhd: hdwy 4f out: rdn along 3f out: kpt on u.p fnl 2f: nt rch ldrs* 28/1
000- 7 4 Roonah (FR)[160] 6272 4-8-12 43 PaulFessey 2 31
(Karen McLintock) *bhd: hdwy over 4f out: rdn along over 3f out: nvr a factor* 66/1
3000 8 hd Second Reef[45] 538 5-9-4 53 PaulHanagan 12 35
(J R Weymes) *midfield: hdwy over 4f out: sn rdn along and nvr a factor* 11/2[3]
50-6 9 ½ Ming Vase[14] 789 5-9-4 46 JoeFanning 4 34
(P T Midgley) *in tch: hdwy to chse ldrs over 4f out: rdn over 2f out and grad wknd* 14/1
00-0 10 2½ Mayadeen (IRE)[16] 767 5-9-4 58 TomEaves 9 30
(I Semple) *midfield: rdn along 1/2-way: sn lost pl and bhd* 15/2
400- 11 1 Ho Pang Yau[183] 5840 9-8-11 43 GaryBartley(7) 13 29
(J S Goldie) *led: rdn along over 3f out: driuven and hdd over 2f out: sn wknd* 28/1
0620 12 7 Exit Fast (USA)[6] 909 6-9-4 60 MickyFenton 11 18
(P T Midgley) *prom: rdn along over 4f out and sn wknd* 10/1
000- 13 16 Fardi (IRE)[280] 3140 5-8-13 43 PBradley(5) 7 —
(K W Hogg) *midfield: effrt and in tch 4f out: sn rdn and wknd 3f out* 66/1

2m 41.48s (4.58) **Going Correction** +0.25s/f (Good)
WFA 4 from 5yo+ 1lb 13 Ran SP% 120.5
Speed ratings (Par 101):94,92,91,91,91 87,85,85,84,83 82,77,67
CSF £20.35 TOTE £3.00: £1.40, £1.80, £13.10; EX 12.00.The winner was bought in for 5,200gns. Just Observing was claimed by P. T. Midgley for £12,000.
Owner Spring Cottage Syndicate No 2 **Bred** John And Susan Davis **Trained** Norton, N Yorks

FOCUS
A very weak affair and the form is greatly limited by the third and the sixth. The winner at least came into this in good form.
Mayadeen(IRE) Official explanation: jockey said gelding never travelled
Exit Fast(USA) Official explanation: jockey said gelding lost its action

967 US PGA TOUR ONLY ON SETANTA GOLF H'CAP 7f 30y
4:05 (4:06) (Class 5) (0-70,68) 4-Y-0+ £3,238 (£963; £481; £240) Stalls High

Form RPR
032- 1 Dispol Isle (IRE)[173] 6054 5-9-2 62 PaulFessey 7 75
(T D Barron) *trckd ldrs: hdwy 3f out: swtchd lft and rdn to chse ldr wl over 1f out: styd on to ld ins last: drvn out* 6/1[2]
-001 2 1½ Motu (IRE)[13] 806 6-9-1 61 (v) RoystonFfrench 12 70
(I W McInnes) *hld up: hdwy on outer over 2f out: rdn ent last: kpt on* 7/1[3]
0402 3 2 Another Genepi (USA)[13] 796 4-8-11 57 (b) NCallan 9 61
(K A Ryan) *led: qcknd clr over 2f out and sn rdn: drvn and hdd ins last: wknd towards fin* 15/2
034- 4 1¾ Flylowflylong (IRE)[151] 6419 4-9-4 64 TonyHamilton 10 65
(I Semple) *hld up towards rr: hdwy on inner wl over 2f out: sn rdn along: kpt on appr last: nearest fin* 22/1
00-4 5 1¾ Cut Ridge (IRE)[5] 912 8-8-1 50 (p) AndrewMullen(3) 5 47
(J S Wainwright) *s.i.s and bhd: hdwy on wd outside over 2f out: kpt on wl appr last: nrst fin* 40/1
45-3 6 1½ Attacca[13] 801 6-8-4 50 PaulHanagan 6 44
(J R Weymes) *in tch: effrt and n.m.r home turn: sn rdn along and chsd ldrs over 2f out: one pce* 6/1[2]
-002 7 1¼ Local Poet[16] 771 6-8-7 58 (b) DuranFentiman(5) 13 48
(I Semple) *hld up and bhd: hdwy 3f out: swtchd lft and rdn 2f out: sn no imp* 14/1
306- 8 ½ Esoterica (IRE)[202] 5446 4-8-13 66 GaryBartley(7) 1 55
(J S Goldie) *stdd s: hld up and bhd tl styd on fnl 2f* 16/1
3101 9 2 Writ (IRE)[23] 699 5-9-4 64 TomEaves 3 48
(I Semple) *midfield whn pushed wd home turn: sn rdn and no hdwy* 11/2[1]
00-0 10 2 Baylaw Star[26] 673 6-9-8 68 JoeFanning 2 47
(I W McInnes) *prom: rdn along over 3f out: sn wknd* 16/1
40-0 11 4 It's Unbelievable (USA)[14] 793 4-9-5 65 MickyFenton 11 33
(P T Midgley) *chsd ldrs: rdn along 4f out: sn wknd* 33/1
306- 12 7 John Keats[167] 6159 4-9-6 66 DanielTudhope 4 16
(J S Goldie) *a rr* 10/1
1543 13 2½ Hamaasy[20] 717 6-8-6 52 AdrianTNicholls 8 —
(D Nicholls) *keen: chsd ldrs: rdn along 3f out: lost pl qckly and eased 2f out* 11/2[1]

1m 31.16s (1.22) **Going Correction** +0.25s/f (Good) 13 Ran SP% 120.9
Speed ratings (Par 103):103,101,99,97,96 94,93,92,90,87 83,75,72
CSF £47.40 CT £326.27 TOTE £9.10: £1.70, £1.80, £7.00; EX 54.00.
Owner W B Imison **Bred** Mrs I A Balding **Trained** Maunby, N Yorks

FOCUS
A moderate handicap, run at an decent pace. The form looks sound enough rated through the winner and runner-up.
Motu(IRE) Official explanation: jockey said gelding missed the break
Cut Ridge(IRE) Official explanation: jockey said mare missed the break
Attacca Official explanation: jockey said gelding was denied a clear run
Hamaasy Official explanation: jockey said gelding hung violently right and lost its action

968 SETANTA SPORTS PACK, DEDICATED TO LIVE SPORT MAIDEN STKS 1m 1f
4:40 (4:42) (Class 5) 3-Y-0+ £2,914 (£867; £433; £216) Stalls High

Form RPR
4- 1 Record Breaker (IRE)[255] 3892 3-8-10 JoeFanning 4 79+
(M Johnston) *trckd ldrs: pushed along 3f out: hdwy to ld 2f out: sn rdn and rn green: edgd rt ent last: styd on* 5/4[1]
-322 2 1¼ Emerald Wilderness (IRE)[17] 745 3-8-10 76 TPO'Shea 8 75
(M R Channon) *trckd ldrs on inner: led 1/2-way: rdn nd hdd 2f out: sn drvn and kpt on same pce* 15/8[2]
323- 3 ½ Bold Indian (IRE)[102] 6963 3-8-10 69 TomEaves 7 73
(I Semple) *a.p: effrt to chal and ev ch over 2f out: sn rdn and kpt on fnl f* 10/1[3]
36- 4 13 Dilwin (IRE)[208] 5289 3-8-10 AdrianTNicholls 2 47
(D Nicholls) *midfield: effrt and in tch over 3f out: sn rdn and wknd 2f out* 12/1
5 nk March Mate 3-8-10 PatCosgrave 3 46
(B Ellison) *s.i.s and bhd tl styd on fnl 3f: nvr a factor* 66/1
65- 6 ¾ Patavian (IRE)[214] 5126 3-8-10 TonyHamilton 12 44
(I Semple) *s.i.s and bhd tl styd on wl fnl 2f* 20/1
7 3 Cottam Eclipse[138] 6-9-13 DanielTudhope 11 38
(I W McInnes) *towards rr: hdwy on inner 3f out: sn rdn and no imp fnl 2f* 100/1
040- 8 4 Alavana (IRE)[206] 5334 3-8-5 52 PaulQuinn 10 25
(D W Barker) *chsd ldrs: rdn along 3f out: sn wknd* 80/1
9 2½ Malguru 3-8-10 DeanMcKeown 1 25
(G A Swinbank) *a towards rr* 25/1
00-0 10 1¾ Nimrana Fort[17] 741 4-9-13 54 (v[1]) PaulMulrennan 6 22
(J S Wainwright) *prom: rn wd bnd over 4f out and sn wknd* 33/1
060- 11 5 Dee Jay Wells[192] 5647 3-8-10 73 PaulHanagan 5 12
(R A Fahey) *midfield: rdn along over 4f out and sn wknd* 14/1
060/ 12 40 Fitasabuckstoat (IRE)[681] 2093 4-9-8 PBradley(5) 9 —
(K W Hogg) *led to 1/2-way: sn wknd* 100/1

1m 55.42s (1.56) **Going Correction** +0.25s/f (Good)
WFA 3 from 4yo+ 17lb 12 Ran SP% 118.9
Speed ratings (Par 103):103,101,101,89,89 88,86,82,80,78 74,38
CSF £3.42 TOTE £2.00: £2.80, £1.50, £1.80; EX 3.00.
Owner Leung Kai Fai & Vincent Leung **Bred** Sir E J Loder **Trained** Middleham Moor, N Yorks

FOCUS
This three-year-old maiden revolved around the two market leaders and they duly dominated the finish. The form looks solid and the promising winner can rate higher.
Alavana(IRE) Official explanation: jockey said filly was unsuited by the good to firm going

969 THEHEARTSREWARD.CO.UK H'CAP 1m
5:15 (5:16) (Class 4) (0-85,85) 4-Y-0+ £5,181 (£1,541; £770; £384) Stalls High

Form RPR
000- 1 Emerald Bay (IRE)[312] 2162 5-8-13 80 TomEaves 4 91
(I Semple) *led 3f: cl up tl led again over 2f out: rdn clr appr last: styd on* 5/1[3]
/00- 2 2½ Frank Crow[184] 5810 4-8-6 73 PaulHanagan 8 78
(J S Goldie) *keen: chsd ldrs: rdn along over 2f out: kpt on u.p fnl f* 16/1
20-0 3 nk Bailieborough (IRE)[9] 846 8-9-1 85 GregFairley(3) 6 90
(B Ellison) *hld up: hdwy wl over 2f out: rdn wl over 1f out: kpt on ins last* 8/1
03 4 2½ Quai Du Roi (IRE)[16] 765 5-8-10 77 NCallan 3 76
(K A Ryan) *v.s.a: hdwy 1/2-way: rdn to chse ldrs over 2f out: snd driven and wknd wl over 1f out* 2/1[1]
443- 5 1 Hula Ballew[206] 5337 7-8-10 77 PhillipMakin 5 74
(M Dods) *in tch: hdwy over 3f out: rdn along and wkng whn n.m.r wl over 1f out* 9/1
045- 6 1 Northern Boy (USA)[182] 5863 4-8-6 73 PaulFessey 1 67
(T D Barron) *cl up: led after 3f: rdn along and hdd over 2f out: sn drvn and wknd wl over 1f out* 4/1[2]
255- 7 6 Dark Charm (FR)[214] 5137 8-7-11 71 JamesRogers(7) 7 51
(R A Fahey) *a rr* 12/1
14-0 8 8 Choreography[26] 672 4-8-7 74 AdrianTNicholls 2 36
(D Nicholls) *chsd ldrs: rdn along wl over 2f out: sn drvn and wknd* 11/2

1m 43.78s (1.28) **Going Correction** +0.25s/f (Good) 8 Ran SP% 120.1
Speed ratings (Par 105):103,100,100,97,96 95,89,81
CSF £82.17 CT £645.19 TOTE £6.50: £2.60, £4.30, £2.00; EX 87.70.
Owner Clarke Boon **Bred** Kildaragh Stud **Trained** Carluke, S Lanarks
■ Stewards' Enquiry : Greg Fairley one-day ban: careless riding (Apr 20)

FOCUS
A fair handicap and the form looks straightforward enough with the winner running to the mark set when second in this event last year.
Quai Du Roi(IRE) Official explanation: jockey said gelding missed the break

Dark Charm(FR) Official explanation: jockey said, regarding the running and riding, his instructions were to sit handy or mid-division and give the gelding a hands and heels ride and make his best way home; he added he'd been unable to follow the instructions as he had been shuffled backwards at the start; trainer's rep added he was dissatisfied with the ride as jockey failed to ride to instructions; vet added gelding finished lame
Choreography Official explanation: jockey said gelding had no more to give

970 RACING UK SKY CHANNEL 432 H'CAP 5f

5:45 (5:45) (Class 6) (0-60,59) 3-Y-O **£2,590** (£770; £385; £192) **Stalls** Low

Form					RPR
-231	1		**Jojesse**[14] [786] 3-9-3 **57** NCallan 7 (G A Swinbank) *in tch: hdwy 1/2-way: rdn to ld ent last: sn drvn and kpt on wl* **11/4**[2]		59
-064	2	nk	**Kilvickeon (IRE)**[14] [786] 3-8-8 **48** ow3 GrahamGibbons 10 (Peter Grayson) *led: pushed along and hdd wl over 1f out: sn rdn and rallied ins last: kpt on* **10/1**		49
0-	3	½	**Beechside (IRE)**[173] [6047] 3-8-8 **48** ow1 (t) TomEaves 9 (W A Murphy, Ire) *n.m.r s: hld up: hdwy 1/2-way: rdn to ld over 1f out: sn drvn: hdd ent last: kpt on* **33/1**		47
64-1	4	½	**Darcy's Pride (IRE)**[5] [918] 3-9-5 **59** 6ex TonyHamilton 5 (D W Barker) *chsd ldrs stand rail: ridden wl over 1f out: drvn and kpt on ins last* **5/1**[3]		56
0222	5	shd	**Ioweyou**[13] [798] 3-9-3 **57** (b) LPKeniry 3 (J S Moore) *chsd ldrs: rdn along wl over 1f out: kpt on same pce ins last* **8/1**		54
605-	6	nk	**The Brat**[210] [5238] 3-8-5 **45** PaulHanagan 4 (J S Wainwright) *in tch: hdwy 2f out: sn rdn and kpt on appr last* **22/1**		41
-312	7	1¼	**Mandurah (IRE)**[5] [918] 3-9-5 **59** 6ex AdrianTNicholls 2 (D Nicholls) *towards rr: hdwy 2f out: sn rdn and no imp* **2/1**[1]		51
0240	8	5	**Mangano**[5] [918] 3-8-5 **45** JoeFanning 8 (A Berry) *hmpd after 1f: chsd ldrs on outer: rdn along 1/2-way and sn wknd* **33/1**		19
500-	9	1¼	**My Two Girls (IRE)**[210] [5238] 3-9-4 **58** MickyFenton 6 (P T Midgley) *hmpd after 1f: cl up tl rdn 2f out and sn wknd* **28/1**		27
050-	10	3½	**Blakeshall Rose**[136] [6582] 3-8-6 **46** ow1 DeanMcKeown 1 (A J Chamberlain) *s.i.s: a rr* **14/1**		2

62.27 secs (1.77) **Going Correction** +0.25s/f (Good) **10 Ran SP% 117.2**
Speed ratings (Par 96):95,94,93,92,92 92,90,82,80,74
CSF £28.95 CT £595.47 TOTE £3.30: £1.30, £3.30, £11.20; EX 46.20 Place 6 £65.54, Place 5 £42.65.
Owner S J Beard **Bred** S J Beard **Trained** Melsonby, N Yorks
■ Stewards' Enquiry : Graham Gibbons three-day ban: careless riding (Apr 20-22)

FOCUS
A moderate sprint which produced a modest winning time in relation to the opening fillies' event over the same course and distance. The first six finished in a heap and the form looks far from solid.
T/Plt: £84.20 to a £1 stake. Pool: £52,365.55. 453.90 winning tickets. T/Qpdt: £57.90 to a £1 stake. Pool: £1,870.20. 23.90 winning tickets. JR

WARWICK (L-H)

Monday, April 9

OFFICIAL GOING: Good to firm
Wind: Light, behind Weather: Fine turning overcast

971 CHERRIESRACING.COM (S) STKS 5f

2:05 (2:08) (Class 6) 2-Y-O **£2,590** (£770; £385; £192) **Stalls** Centre

Form				RPR
	1		**Nestor Protector (IRE)** 2-8-11 DaneO'Neill 1 (A B Haynes) *mde all: rdn over 1f out: hung rt ent fnl f: r.o wl and in command towards fin* **15/2**	57
6	2	1¾	**Shepherds Warning (IRE)**[6] [898] 2-8-6 ow3 StephenDonohoe(3) 4 (P D Evans) *a.p: racd 4 wd ent st over 2f out: rdn over 1f out: edgd rt ins fnl f: nt pce of wnr towards fin* **10/11**[1]	48
	3	1¾	**Miss Willoughby** 2-8-6 ChrisCatlin 6 (J Ryan) *prom: racd 5 wd ent st over 2f out: pushed along over 1f out: swtchd lft ins fnl f: kpt on same pce* **12/1**	38
	4	2	**Amazing Day** 2-8-4 JackDean(7) 3 (W G M Turner) *rdn s: prom: racd 3 wd ent st over 2f out: rdn over 1f out: wknd fnl f* **5/1**[2]	35
6	5	shd	**Miss Antropist (IRE)**[7] [883] 2-8-1 TolleyDean(5) 2 (R A Harris) *prom: racd 2 wd ent st over 2f out: rdn and edgd lft whn faltered on path over 1f out: wknd fnl f* **7/1**	30
	6	17	**Riskie Blue (IRE)** 2-8-6 JohnEgan 7 (J S Moore) *wnt rt s: rn green: a wl bhd* **6/1**[3]	—

61.70 secs (2.30) **Going Correction** -0.275s/f (Firm) **6 Ran SP% 115.3**
Speed ratings (Par 90):70,67,64,61,61 33
CSF £15.48 TOTE £9.90: £3.20, £1.30; EX 31.10.The winner was bought in for 12,600gns. Shepherds Warning was claimed by Robert Stronge for £6,000.
Owner Abacus Employment Services Ltd **Bred** Mrs C Roper **Trained** Limpley Stoke, Bath

FOCUS
An ordinary race, even by selling standards. The winning time was very slow, 2.34 seconds slower than the following fillies' maiden.

NOTEBOOK
Nestor Protector(IRE), an 8,000euros first foal of a 7f winner, overcame greenness to make a winning debut. He was fairly clueless in the straight and hung to his right, but he always looked like doing enough. This was a weak race, but he has some size about him and should leave the bare form behind. He was bought in for 12,600gns. (op 11-1 tchd 12-1)
Shepherds Warning(IRE) showed ability on her debut in maiden company at Folkestone, but she failed to produce any improvement and was well held in second. She was claimed by Robert Stronge for £6,000. (tchd 4-5 tchd evens and 11-10 in places)
Miss Willoughby, the first foal of a mare who was unplaced over 6-7f at three, never posed a threat and will probably need to improve a touch to win a similar event. (op 16-1)
Amazing Day, a 6,500euros half-brother to Tiger Hunter, a 6f winner at three, out of a triple 5-6f juvenile scorer, is another who will probably have to improve to get his head in front. (op 8-1)
Miss Antropist(IRE) was well beaten and looks flattered by her Lingfield debut effort. (op 8-1 tchd 13-2)
Riskie Blue(IRE), a 2,800gns half-sister to Notty Bitz, a dual 5-6f winner at two, and Alittleriskie, a 5f juvenile scorer, out of a mare who won four minor races over 5-6f at two and three, blew her race with a very awkward start and was too green to do herself justice. (op 10-3)

972 CHERRIESRACING.COM MAIDEN FILLIES' STKS 5f

2:40 (2:46) (Class 5) 2-Y-O **£3,238** (£963; £481; £240) **Stalls** Centre

Form				RPR
	1		**Kylayne** 2-9-0 DarryllHolland 4 (P W D'Arcy) *mde most: pushed out and rn wl ins fnl f* **6/1**[2]	81+
	2	1½	**Sinead Of Aglish (IRE)** 2-9-0 DaneO'Neill 8 (A B Haynes) *s.i.s: sn chsd ldrs: rdn to take 2nd over 1f out: ev ch ent fnl f: nt qckn* **11/2**[1]	75
4	3	5	**Mystickhill (IRE)**[7] [890] 2-9-0 RobbieFitzpatrick 1 (T J Pitt) *w wnr: rdn 2f out: wknd fnl f* **11/2**[1]	55
4	4	2½	**Mama Leo**[7] [883] 2-8-11 StephenDonohoe(3) 5 (P D Evans) *chsd ldrs: rdn 2f out: sn wknd* **11/2**[1]	45
	5	½	**Lujiana** 2-8-7 PatrickDonaghy(7) 9 (M Brittain) *midfield: pushed along 3f out: no hdwy* **33/1**	43
F	6	½	**Miss Tilen**[9] [845] 2-9-0 AdamKirby 12 (V Smith) *midfield: rdn over 2f out: nvr able to chal* **22/1**	41
	7	nk	**Ba Speedbird (IRE)** 2-9-0 ChrisCatlin 11 (M R Channon) *chsd ldrs: rdn over 2f out: wknd over 1f out* **7/1**[3]	40
	8	1½	**Zahwah** 2-9-0 NickyMackay 3 (J G Portman) *s.s: bhd: nvr trbld ldrs* **16/1**	34
	9	½	**Jane's Delight (IRE)** 2-9-0 DO'Donohoe 2 (P C Haslam) *upset in stalls: rn green: a bhd* **9/1**	32
	10	6	**Una Auroraborealis** 2-9-0 RichardMullen 10 (J Ryan) *in tch: sn pushed along: wknd wl over 1f out* **20/1**	8
	11	5	**Alto Singer (IRE)** 2-9-0 JimCrowley 13 (B R Millman) *dwlt and wnt rt s: a bhd* **9/1**	—

59.36 secs (-0.04) **Going Correction** -0.275s/f (Firm) **11 Ran SP% 110.9**
Speed ratings (Par 89):89,86,78,74,73 73,72,70,69,59 51
CSF £32.54 TOTE £5.90: £1.80, £1.30, £2.20; EX 38.30.
Owner Mrs Jan Harris **Bred** D P And Mrs J A Martin **Trained** Newmarket, Suffolk
■ Only In Jest (13/2, burst out of stalls) & Tallulah Sunrise (33/1, ref to ent stalls) were withdrawn. R4, deduct 10p in the £.

FOCUS
Just an ordinary fillies' maiden but, using the third and fourth home as a guide, the front two looked to produce fair efforts in pulling so far clear. The winning time was 2.34 seconds quicker than the opening seller.

NOTEBOOK
Kylayne ◆, a 15,000gns half-sister to Global Guardian, who was placed over 7f at two, out of a quite useful 7f juvenile winner, seemed to know her job - she was well away and showed good speed throughout - and stayed on best to make a winning debut. The front two were clear and this looked a useful enough effort. (tchd 7-1)
Sinead Of Aglish(IRE) ◆, a 14,000euros half-sister to Sister Etienne, a triple 5f winner at two and three, out of a half-sister to very smart sprinting juvenile Shindella, represented the trainer who landed the opening seller with a newcomer and was well backed. She was basically beaten by a better filly on the day, but looks well up to finding a similar event in the coming weeks. (op 12-1)
Mystickhill(IRE), whose debut fourth on the Fibresand at Southwell represented just moderate form, produced what appeared a slightly improved effort. (op 4-1)
Mama Leo, like the third home, ran in a moderate sand maiden on her debut and she basically just found a few of these too good. (op 6-1 tchd 13-2)
Lujiana, a 2,000gns half-sister to among others Mother's Day, a 5f winner at two, and Turibius, a multiple 5-6f winner, out of a 7f juvenile scorer, hails from a stable with quite a few juveniles in their care this year and showed ability. (op 40-1)
Miss Tilen was well beaten when falling in the Brocklesby on her debut, but she put that bad experience behind her. (op 25-1)

973 CHERRIESRACING.COM MAIDEN STKS 7f 26y

3:15 (3:17) (Class 5) 3-Y-O **£3,238** (£963; £481; £240) **Stalls** Low

Form				RPR
032-	1		**Shmookh (USA)**[164] [6199] 3-9-3 **79** RHills 8 (J L Dunlop) *a.p: led 2f out: hung lft over 1f out: r.o wl and wl in command ins fnl f* **1/1**[1]	76+
44-	2	3½	**Ideally (IRE)**[206] [5340] 3-9-3 MichaelHills 6 (B W Hills) *trckd ldrs: wnt 2nd over 1f out: edgd rt whn outpcd by wnr ins fnl f: no ex cl home* **3/1**[2]	67
	3	hd	**Six Of Diamonds (IRE)** 3-9-3 ShaneKelly 2 (J A Osborne) *s.i.s: midfield: pushed along 3f out: hdwy 1f out: fin wl* **14/1**	66+
64-	4	1	**Spirit Of Adjisa (IRE)**[101] [6976] 3-9-3 DaneO'Neill 1 (Pat Eddery) *in tch: rdn and nt qckn over 1f out: styd on towards fin* **7/1**[3]	64
00-	5	½	**Is It Time (IRE)**[227] [4774] 3-8-12 JimCrowley 4 (Mrs P N Dutfield) *racd keenly: led: hdd 2f out: wkng whn hung rt ins fnl f* **50/1**	57
-	6	1	**Schoenberg (USA)** 3-9-3 JohnEgan 11 (C R Egerton) *midfield: pushed along 2f out: carried rt wl ins fnl f whn no imp on ldrs* **20/1**	60+
03	7	shd	**Waqaarr**[41] [573] 3-9-3 DarryllHolland 14 (M R Channon) *trckd ldrs: rdn 2f out: one pce fnl f* **12/1**	60
	8	5	**Poppets Sweetlove** 3-8-12 SteveDrowne 7 (A B Haynes) *s.s: bhd: nvr rchd ldrs* **50/1**	42
0-	9	½	**Almondillo (IRE)**[276] [3253] 3-9-3 GeorgeBaker 3 (C F Wall) *midfield: rdn and wknd over 1f out* **33/1**	45
0	10	½	**Sixfields Flyer (IRE)**[24] [689] 3-8-12 PaulEddery 5 (Pat Eddery) *s.s: midfield: rdn 3f out: sn wknd* **25/1**	39
4	11	7	**Mandalay Prince**[33] [635] 3-9-3 RichardMullen 10 (W J Musson) *dwlt: sn rdn along: a bhd* **16/1**	26
	12	1	**Boz** 3-9-3 NickyMackay 12 (L M Cumani) *a bhd* **20/1**	23

1m 23.02s (-1.18) **Going Correction** -0.275s/f (Firm) **12 Ran SP% 128.0**
Speed ratings (Par 98):100,96,95,94,94 92,92,87,86,85 77,76
CSF £3.88 TOTE £1.70: £1.50, £1.30, £2.40; EX 5.30.
Owner Hamdan Al Maktoum **Bred** Shadwell Farm LLC **Trained** Arundel, W Sussex

FOCUS
An ordinary maiden run in a time 1.11 seconds quicker than the following 3yo 0-60 handicap. The winner did not need to improve and the proximity of the fifth seems to hold down the form.

974 DIAMOND SPORTS BETS H'CAP 7f 26y

3:50 (3:51) (Class 6) (0-60,60) 3-Y-O **£2,730** (£806; £403) **Stalls** Low

Form				RPR
-302	1		**Knapton Hill**[45] [535] 3-8-11 **58** RussellKennemore(5) 12 (R Hollinshead) *trckd ldrs: swtchd rt to chal over 2f out: edgd lft over 1f out: led ins fnl f: r.o* **11/2**[2]	64
6433	2	1¼	**Candyland (IRE)**[41] [577] 3-9-2 **58** ShaneKelly 11 (M Quinn) *led: hung rt and rdn under 2f out: hdd ins fnl f: nt qckn towards fin* **9/1**	61

6556 **3** 1 ½ **Arnie's Joint (IRE)**[15] 778 3-9-4 **60**...........................(v[1]) GeorgeBaker 2 59
(N P Littmoden) *midfield: nt clr run over 3f out: rdn and hdwy over 1f out: chsd ldrs ins fnl f: kpt on* **7/1**[3]

016- **4** nk **Forced Upon Us**[109] 6900 3-9-4 **60**.............................. RichardMullen 9 58
(P J McBride) *s.i.s and bmpd s: midfield: hdwy 2f out: styd on ins fnl f: gaining cl home* **10/1**

4366 **5** 1 **Calloff The Search**[26] 679 3-8-13 **58**..................(p) SaleemGolam[(3)] 14 53
(W G M Turner) *prom: rdn over 1f out: kpt on same pce ins fnl f* **14/1**

0-00 **6** 1 ½ **Mr Mini Scule**[6] 900 3-9-0 **56**.. DaneO'Neill 8 48
(A B Haynes) *prom: rdn over 1f out: no ex ins fnl f* **25/1**

0-00 **7** ¾ **Merlins Quest**[6] 899 3-9-2 **58**....................................... DarryllHolland 6 48
(J M Bradley) *midfield: rdn 2f out: outpcd over 1f out* **25/1**

64-3 **8** ½ **Eastern Princess**[14] 786 3-8-10 **52**.......................(v) RichardThomas 10 40
(J A Geake) *midfield: rdn and outpcd 2f out* **10/1**

06-2 **9** nk **Emma Jean Lad (IRE)**[23] 700 3-9-4 **60**............................ JohnEgan 4 48
(J S Moore) *s.i.s: bhd: rdn and hung bdly rt on bnd 3f out: hdwy over 2f out: kpt on ins fnl f* **9/4**[1]

60-0 **10** 1 ¼ **Mr Forthright**[6] 899 3-8-11 **60**...................................... BarrySavage[(7)] 3 44
(J M Bradley) *a bhd* **20/1**

200- **11** shd **Grazie Mille**[157] 6322 3-8-13 **58**............................... StephenDonohoe[(3)] 1 42
(R Brotherton) *a bhd* **18/1**

4640 **12** 2 **Jost Van Dyke**[26] 679 3-8-8 **53**........................... RichardKingscote[(3)] 5 32
(J W Unett) *midfield: rdn and wknd over 1f out* **10/1**

400- **13** 8 **Prince Noel**[177] 5958 3-9-0 **56**.. DO'Donohoe 7 14
(N Wilson) *s.i.s: a bhd* **14/1**

1m 24.13s (-0.07) **Going Correction** -0.275s/f (Firm) **13** Ran SP% **127.0**
Speed ratings (Par 96):93,91,89,89,88 86,85,85,84,83 83,81,71
CSF £56.68 CT £369.93 TOTE £5.30: £1.30, £2.80, £2.50; EX 54.90.
Owner R Hollinshead **Bred** Newsells Park Stud Limited **Trained** Upper Longdon, Staffs

FOCUS
A very modest handicap and, with the pace ordinary, it proved hard to make up ground. The winning time was 1.11 seconds slower than the previous 3yo maiden. Knapton Hill is going the right way but the runner-up had the run of the race and casts some doubt over the form.
Merlins Quest Official explanation: jockey said colt hung left-handed throughout
Emma Jean Lad(IRE) Official explanation: jockey said gelding missed the break

975 CHERRIESRACING.COM H'CAP 1m 22y
4:25 (4:28) (Class 5) (0-70,70) 4-Y-0+ **£3,886** (£1,156; £577; £288) **Stalls** Low

Form RPR
0-33 **1** **Northern Desert (IRE)**[8] 865 8-8-2 **56** oh1....................... ChrisCatlin 1 61
(P W Hiatt) *trckd ldrs: rdn 2f out: wnt 2nd over 1f out: r.o to ld last stride* **6/1**[3]

3561 **2** hd **Tancredi (SWE)**[10] 831 5-8-11 **68**.......................... JerryO'Dwyer[(3)] 11 73
(N B King) *w ldr: rdn to ld 2f out: hdd last stride* **5/1**[2]

26-6 **3** 1 **Convince (USA)**[16] 751 6-7-13 **58** oh4 ow2.........(p) KevinGhunowa[(5)] 6 61
(J M Bradley) *midfield: rdn and hdwy 2f out: chsd ldrs over 1f out: nt qckn fnl strides* **18/1**

5-60 **4** nk **Todlea (IRE)**[37] 379 7-9-0 **68**...................................(t) DaneO'Neill 5 70+
(Jean-Rene Auvray) *racd keenly: hld up: hdwy over 2f out: styng on whn swtchd rt ins fnl f: gaining towards fin* **12/1**

60-4 **5** 2 **Charlie Bear**[15] 773 6-8-3 **57**..................................... AdrianMcCarthy 12 54
(Miss Z C Davison) *midfield: rdn over 1f out: nvr able to chal* **7/1**

22-5 **6** shd **Legal Lover (IRE)**[90] 75 5-8-3 **62**....................... RussellKennemore[(5)] 9 59
(R Hollinshead) *racd keenly: led: rdn and hdd 2f out: no ex ins fnl f* **8/1**

300- **7** ¾ **Wizby**[121] 6762 4-7-9 **56** oh5.................................. BernadetteQuinn[(7)] 3 51
(P D Evans) *bhd: hdwy over 1f out: kpt on ins fnl f* **33/1**

00-5 **8** shd **The Gaikwar (IRE)**[80] 179 8-8-7 **66**.................(b) MichaelJStainton[(5)] 4 61
(R A Harris) *s.s: bhd: sme hdwy 2f out: no imp on ldrs* **8/1**

2402 **9** shd **Machinate (USA)**[4] 932 5-7-9 **56** oh7......................... LukeMorris[(7)] 10 51
(W M Brisbourne) *s.i.s: bhd: rdn and hdwy 2f out: kpt on: nvr rchd ldrs* **7/1**

0060 **10** 1 **Lady Edge (IRE)**[18] 729 5-8-4 **58**.................................. RichardMullen 8 51
(A W Carroll) *upset by unruly horse in next stall: trckd ldrs: rdn over 3f out: wknd over 1f out* **20/1**

104- **11** 4 **Jordan's Light (USA)**[103] 6946 4-9-2 **70**............................ JohnEgan 13 53
(T J Pitt) *hld up: rdn 2f out: no imp* **9/2**[1]

-220 **12** nk **Golden Square**[53] 462 5-8-2 **56**............................... CatherineGannon 14 39
(A W Carroll) *prom: rdn over 2f out: wknd over 1f out* **16/1**

-640 **13** 3 **Jools**[35] 616 9-8-2 **56**.. JamieMackay 2 32
(D K Ivory) *broke wl: racd keenly: dropped to midfield after 2f: wknd 4f out* **16/1**

1m 38.96s (-0.64) **Going Correction** -0.075s/f (Good) **13** Ran SP% **128.8**
Speed ratings (Par 103):100,99,98,98,96 96,95,95,95,94 90,90,87
CSF £39.10 CT £552.20 TOTE £5.70: £1.50, £2.50, £6.40; EX 102.30.
Owner Clive Roberts **Bred** J P Hardiman **Trained** Hook Norton, Oxon

FOCUS
A moderate handicap and, with the pace only ordinary, it proved hard to make up ground. The race has been rated through the runner-up, but the form does not look solid.
Todlea(IRE) Official explanation: jockey said gelding was hampered shortly after start

976 WIN WITH CHERRIESRACING.COM H'CAP 1m 2f 188y
5:00 (5:00) (Class 6) (0-60,60) 4-Y-0+ **£2,730** (£806; £403) **Stalls** Low

Form RPR
6354 **1** **Apex**[21] 710 6-8-4 **53**.. HaddenFrost[(7)] 9 61
(M Hill) *midfield: hdwy 3f out: rdn to ld over 1f out: edgd rt ins fnl f: pushed out towards fin: jst hld on* **16/1**

0005 **2** hd **Choristar**[16] 767 6-8-11 **58**.. MichaelJStainton[(5)] 12 69+
(J Mackie) *hld up: nt clr run over 3f out and over 2f out: stmbld and hdwy wl over 1f out: edgd lft ins fnl f: fin strly: unluc* **5/1**[1]

011- **3** 1 ½ **Scutch Mill (IRE)**[68] 6810 5-9-1 **60**...........................(t) JerryO'Dwyer[(3)] 8 65
(P C Haslam) *s.i.s: hld up: hdwy over 2f out: sn rdn: styd on ins fnl f* **13/2**[2]

140- **4** 1 ¼ **General Flumpa**[192] 5652 6-8-9 **58**............................... KirstyMilczarek[(7)] 3 61
(Miss Tor Sturgis) *hld up: hdwy 2f out: rdn to chse ldrs over 1f out: styd on ins fnl f: one pce towards fin* **12/1**

00-0 **5** 5 **Orpen Quest (IRE)**[35] 610 5-8-9 **56**............................(v) KevinGhunowa[(5)] 2 50
(M J Attwater) *led: rdn 2f out: hdd over 1f out: wknd ins fnl f* **20/1**

500- **6** shd **Foolish Groom**[159] 6300 6-8-8 **55**........................ RussellKennemore[(5)] 5 49
(R Hollinshead) *trckd ldrs: rdn over 2f out: one pce ins fnl f* **16/1**

000- **7** ¾ **Salvestro**[178] 5936 4-8-13 **55**.. RichardMullen 1 47
(A W Carroll) *trckd ldrs: rdn over 2f out: one pce fnl f* **8/1**[3]

0-40 **8** ½ **Stravara**[38] 607 4-9-4 **60**... GeorgeBaker 6 52
(R Hollinshead) *racd keenly: midfield: hdwy 4f out: rdn 2f out whn cl up: wknd ins fnl f* **14/1**

614 **9** nk **Bobering**[17] 741 7-8-3 **52**.. SoniaEaton[(7)] 14 43
(B P J Baugh) *hld up: rdn and hdwy over 1f out: kpt on: nt trble ldrs* **16/1**

000- **10** ¾ **Bob's Your Uncle**[144] 5868 4-9-4 **60**.............................. NickyMackay 10 50
(J G Portman) *midfield: hdwy 4f out: rdn over 2f out: wknd over 1f out* **8/1**[3]

54-6 **11** ½ **King Gabriel (IRE)**[71] 279 5-8-12 **54**................................. ChrisCatlin 7 43
(Andrew Turnell) *prom: rdn 3f out: wknd over 1f out* **8/1**[3]

3-10 **12** 1 ¾ **Danzare**[46] 72 5-9-3 **59**.. SteveDrowne 11 45
(J L Spearing) *midfield: hdwy 4f out: rdn over 2f out: wknd over 1f out* **17/2**

406- **13** ½ **Kristoffersen**[158] 3431 7-8-13 **55**...................................... JimCrowley 13 40
(Ian Williams) *hld up: rdn over 2f out: nvr on terms* **20/1**

50-0 **14** ¾ **Joy In The Guild (IRE)**[35] 616 4-8-12 **54**............... FergusSweeney 15 37
(W S Kittow) *stdd s: hld up: rdn 2f out: nvr on terms* **16/1**

4-46 **15** 12 **Western Roots**[45] 538 6-8-10 **52**...................................... DaneO'Neill 17 14
(M Appleby) *hld up: hdwy into midfield over 4f out: wknd over 2f out* **14/1**

0/0- **16** 13 **Be Wise Girl**[380] 733 6-8-11 **53**............................... CatherineGannon 4 —
(A W Carroll) *w ldr: rdn and wknd over 2f out* **33/1**

-060 **17** 1 ½ **Consonant (IRE)**[26] 675 10-8-12 **54**...................... RobbieFitzpatrick 16 —
(D G Bridgwater) *in tch: rdn over 3f out: sn wknd* **16/1**

2m 17.26s (-2.14) **Going Correction** -0.075s/f (Good) **17** Ran SP% **136.8**
Speed ratings (Par 101):104,103,102,101,98 98,97,97,97,96 96,94,94,93,85 75,74
CSF £102.14 CT £609.51 TOTE £29.30: £6.50, £1.60, £2.30, £7.50; EX 742.80 Place 6 £58.27, Place 5 £42.95.
Owner Martin Hill **Bred** P D And Mrs C E Player And Jonathon Jay **Trained** Broadhempston, Devon
■ Martin Hill's first winner and runner since resuming training after a break, and his first ever Flat winner.

FOCUS
A moderate handicap run at a decent pace. Apex ran his best race since last summer on his debut for this yard, and the form loos solid.
Western Roots Official explanation: jockey said gelding ran flat
T/Jkpt: Not won. T/Plt: £116.60 to a £1 stake. Pool: £56,880.75. 356.00 winning tickets. T/Qpdt: £16.00 to a £1 stake. Pool: £2,227.80. 103.00 winning tickets. DO

YARMOUTH (L-H)
Monday, April 9

OFFICIAL GOING: Good to firm
Wind: Light, half-behind Weather: Overcast

977 TOTEPLACEPOT MAIDEN STKS 1m 3y
2:25 (2:28) (Class 5) 3-Y-0+ **£2,849** (£847; £423; £211) **Stalls** High

Form RPR
5- **1** **Provost**[194] 5616 3-8-11 .... J-PGuillambert 13 89+
(M Johnston) *mde virtually all: hung lft ins fnl f: drvn out* **5/2**[1]

0- **2** 1 ½ **Apple Blossom (IRE)**[195] 5592 3-8-8 ow2.................... RobertHavlin 15 83
(G Wragg) *chsd ldrs: shkn up fnl f: styd on* **25/1**

36- **3** nk **Northern Jem**[184] 5806 3-8-11 .... EddieAhern 3 85
(G G Margarson) *a.p: chsd wnr over 2f out: sn rdn: styd on same pce ins fnl f* **5/2**[1]

30- **4** 14 **Red Current**[158] 6309 3-8-6 .... JamieSpencer 12 48+
(J R Fanshawe) *hld up: swtchd lft and hdwy over 2f out: hung lft and wknd over 1f out* **9/1**[3]

0- **5** nk **Premio Loco (USA)**[161] 6254 3-8-11 .... SebSanders 8 52+
(C F Wall) *hld up: plld hrd: effrt and hung lft over 1f out: n.d* **12/1**

6 2 **Haasem (USA)** 4-9-12 .... MartinDwyer 14 52
(E A L Dunlop) *dwlt: hld up: hdwy 1/2-way: hung lft and wknd fr over 2f out* **4/1**[2]

7 5 **Nothingtodeclaire** 3-8-8 .... EmmettStack[(3)] 4 36
(G A Huffer) *dwlt: outpcd* **33/1**

0- **8** ½ **Korty**[297] 2623 3-8-11 .... DavidKinsella 6 35
(W J Musson) *chsd wnr over 5f: sn rdn and wknd* **66/1**

9 5 **Royal Rock** 3-8-11 .... JimmyQuinn 10 23
(C F Wall) *s.i.s and hmpd s: hdwy over 6f out: wknd over 2f out* **33/1**

0- **10** 3 ½ **Gyration (IRE)**[181] 5901 3-8-11 .... TPQueally 7 15
(J G Given) *hld up: plld hrd: wknd 3f out* **40/1**

0 **11** 8 **Winds Of Kildare (IRE)**[72] 260 4-9-12 .... OscarUrbina 2 —
(C N Allen) *plld hrd and prom: rdn over 3f out: sn wknd* **33/1**

00 **12** ½ **Smiling Tiger**[13] 794 3-8-4 .... MCGeran[(7)] 11 —
(M J Gingell) *sn outpcd* **100/1**

000/ **13** 1 ½ **Romantic Gift**[910] 6113 5-9-7 53.................................. IanMongan 5 —
(Mrs C A Dunnett) *mid-div: wknd 3f out* **50/1**

14 1 **Elegans** 3-8-6 .... DMylonas 9 —
(Mrs C A Dunnett) *wnt rt s: sn outpcd* **66/1**

0432 **15** shd **Wodhill Schnaps**[47] 518 6-9-12 49...............................(v) HayleyTurner 1 —
(D Morris) *prom over 4f* **16/1**

1m 38.9s (-1.00) **Going Correction** +0.025s/f (Good)
WFA 3 from 4yo+ 15lb **15** Ran SP% **121.8**
Speed ratings (Par 103):106,104,104,90,89 87,82,82,77,73 65,65,63,62,62
CSF £76.81 TOTE £3.70: £1.10, £4.40, £1.70; EX 61.70 Trifecta £92.30 Part won. Pool: £130.14 - 0.10 winning tickets..
Owner Highclere Thoroughbred Racing XL **Bred** C G P Wyatt **Trained** Middleham Moor, N Yorks

FOCUS
Not as competitive as the size of the field might suggest, but the time was good, 2.19 seconds faster than the later fillies' handicap. The field came down the middle of the track and the front three pulled miles clear of the others, suggesting they are all above-average. The third set the standard.
Korty Official explanation: jockey said gelding had no more to give

978 TOTECOURSE TO COURSE CLAIMING STKS 6f 3y
3:00 (3:00) (Class 6) 3-Y-0+ **£1,943** (£578; £288; £144) **Stalls** High

Form RPR
0000 **1** **Charlie Delta**[13] 803 4-9-13 66...................................(b[1]) MartinDwyer 5 66
(J R Boyle) *prom: wnt centre over 4f out: swtchd stands' side and chsd ldr over 2f out: led over 1f out: shkn up and r.o* **5/2**[2]

4253 **2** 1 ¼ **Danish Blues (IRE)**[16] 751 4-9-13 55.......................(e) JamieSpencer 7 62
(D E Cantillon) *hld up: wnt centre over 4f out: hdwy and swtchd stands' side over 2f out: hrd rdn fnl f: styd on same pce* **9/4**[1]

6035 **3** 1 **Tuscan Flyer**[19] 722 9-9-4 47......................................(b) SebSanders 8 50
(R Bastiman) *led stands' side over 4f: no ex ins fnl f* **7/2**[3]

6265 **4** 3 **A Teen**[13] 800 9-9-5 47.. JimmyQuinn 6 42
(P Howling) *chsd ldr stands' side over 3f: sn rdn: styd on same pce appr fnl f* **11/1**

-400 **5** 4 **Princess Kai (IRE)**[56] 442 6-9-1 40.............................. DavidKinsella 3 26
(R Ingram) *hld up in tch: styd centre over 4f out: led that gp and hung rt fr over 2f out: wknd over 1f out* **20/1**

050- **6** 13 **Master Malarkey**[182] 5874 4-9-11 44.................................. DMylonas 4 —
(Mrs C A Dunnett) *racd centre: chsd ldrs over 3f* **25/1**

004- 7 2½ **Canary Girl**[182] 5873 4-9-4 34 .... HayleyTurner 1 —
(Mrs C A Dunnett) *racd centre: led that gp over 3f: sn wknd* **22/1**

00-5 8 9 **Renegade (IRE)**[96] 26 6-9-9 46 ....(b) IanMongan 2 —
(Mrs L J Mongan) *racd centre: chsd ldrs over 3f* **8/1**

1m 14.22s (0.52) **Going Correction** +0.025s/f (Good) **8** Ran SP% **114.0**
Speed ratings (Par 101):97,95,94,90,84 67,64,52
CSF £8.24 TOTE £4.00: £1.70, £1.10, £1.70; EX 11.80 Trifecta £37.90 Pool: £203.48 - 3.81 winning tickets..
Owner M Khan X2 **Bred** P K Gardner **Trained** Epsom, Surrey
■ Stewards' Enquiry : Ian Mongan two-day ban: used whip with excessive force (Apr 20-21)

FOCUS
A weakish claimer in which they finished very much in the sort of order that adjusted official ratings suggested they should. The winner was much better than this in the recent past, while the runner-up ran to last year's turf form. The field split into two early, with two staying against the stands' rail whilst the others raced more towards the centre, but the two groups had merged before reaching the two-furlong pole.

979 TOTESPORT.COM FILLIES' H'CAP 1m 3y
3:35 (3:36) (Class 4) (0-85,85) 4-Y-0+ **£4,731** (£1,416; £708; £354; £176) **Stalls High**

Form RPR

/52- 1 **Royal Fantasy (IRE)**[295] 2673 4-8-6 70 .... JamieSpencer 4 82+
(J R Fanshawe) *stdd and hmpd s: racd centre: hdwy over 1f out: rdn to ld last strides* **5/2**[1]

004- 2 *hd* **Inaminute (IRE)**[163] 6221 4-8-8 75 .... AndrewElliott(3) 6 81
(K R Burke) *led centre: rdn over 1f out: hung lft ins fnl f: hdd last strides* **9/2**[2]

4 3 1 **Snow Gretel (IRE)**[39] 590 4-9-4 82 ....(t) OscarUrbina 1 86
(M Botti) *hld up: racd centre: hdwy over 2f out: ev ch over 1f out: sn rdn and carried lft: no ex wl ins fnl f* **15/2**

00-5 4 1¾ **Skyelady**[26] 675 4-8-9 73 ....(p) HayleyTurner 2 73
(Miss J A Camacho) *racd centre: chsd ldrs: rdn over 1f out: styd on* **15/2**

000- 5 4 **Dancing Guest (IRE)**[191] 5666 4-9-7 85 .... EddieAhern 8 76
(G G Margarson) *racd centre: hld up: effrt and hung lft fr over 2f out: nt run on* **16/1**

000- 6 2 **Dictatrix**[189] 5722 4-8-13 77 ....(b[1]) SebSanders 7 63
(J M P Eustace) *s.i.s: racd centre: hld up: rdn over 2f out: sn wknd* **10/1**

-403 7 2 **Magical Music**[23] 702 4-8-5 69 .... JimmyQuinn 9 51
(J Pearce) *racd centre: chsd ldrs: rdn over 2f out: wknd over 1f out* **6/1**[3]

354- 8 2 **Al Rayanah**[164] 6206 4-7-13 66 oh4 .... LiamJones(3) 3 43
(G Prodromou) *racd centre: plld hrd: trckd ldr: rdn over 2f out: wknd over 1f out* **6/1**[3]

000- 9 2 **Dune Melody (IRE)**[163] 6221 4-8-8 72 .... MartinDwyer 5 44
(J S Moore) *plld hrd and prom: swtchd to r alone stands's ide over 5f out: rdn and hung lft over 2f out: sn wknd* **14/1**

1m 41.09s (1.19) **Going Correction** +0.025s/f (Good) **9** Ran SP% **120.5**
Speed ratings (Par 102):95,94,93,92,88 86,84,82,80
CSF £14.32 CT £76.92 TOTE £2.40: £1.90, £2.20, £1.40; EX 14.50 Trifecta £36.90 Pool: £240.95 - 4.63 winning tickets..
Owner Nigel & Carolyn Elwes **Bred** Aylesfield Farms Stud **Trained** Newmarket, Suffolk
■ Stewards' Enquiry : Andrew Elliott two-day ban: careless riding (Apr 20-21)

FOCUS
There was no pace on early, which resulted in a few pulling for their heads and this developed into something of a sprint. The bare form is not solid and underplays the winner's superiority. The winning time was 2.19 seconds slower than the earlier maiden over the same trip. Whilst the majority of the field raced out towards the centre of the track, one horse was brought to race alone against the stands' rail after a couple of furlongs.

980 TOTE TEXT BETTING 60021 H'CAP 7f 3y
4:10 (4:11) (Class 6) (0-65,64) 4-Y-0+ **£2,266** (£674; £337; £168) **Stalls High**

Form RPR

-620 1 **High Ambition**[16] 770 4-8-12 58 ....(v[1]) SebSanders 8 76
(P W D'Arcy) *racd stands' side: hld up: hdwy over 2f out: led ins fnl f: rdn clr: 1st of 10 in gp* **16/1**

-016 2 3½ **Million Percent**[23] 697 8-9-0 63 .... LiamJones(3) 7 71
(C R Dore) *racd stands' side: a.p: led over 2f out: hdd and no ex ins fnl f: 2nd of 10 in gp* **5/1**[2]

535- 3 4 **Mugeba**[173] 6061 6-8-9 55 ....(t) JimmyQuinn 13 52
(Miss Gay Kelleway) *racd stands' side: hld up: hdwy over 2f out: rdn over 1f out: wknd ins fnl f: 3rd of 10 in gp* **8/1**

4-00 4 ½ **Networker**[15] 773 4-8-9 55 .... EddieAhern 10 51
(P J McBride) *racd stands' side: hld up: hdwy over 2f out: sn hung lft: outpcd over 1f out: styd on ins fnl f: 4th of 10 in gp* **10/1**

2012 5 2 **Balerno**[13] 797 8-8-10 56 .... IanMongan 1 47+
(Mrs L J Mongan) *racd far side: hld up: hdwy to chse ldr over 2f out: led that side ins fnl f: no ch w stands' side: 1st of 6 in gp* **7/1**[3]

1336 6 1¾ **Wodhill Be**[13] 801 7-8-4 50 oh5 .... HayleyTurner 9 36
(D Morris) *racd stands' side: mid-div: hdwy over 2f out: hung lft and wknd over 1f out: 5th of 10 in gp* **16/1**

6001 7 1¼ **Marmooq**[17] 734 4-9-3 63 .... JamieSpencer 4 46+
(J Gallagher) *led far side: rdn over 2f out: hdd & wknd ins fnl f: 2nd of 6 in gp* **9/2**[1]

4-50 8 2½ **Jellytot (USA)**[25] 681 4-8-10 59 .... AndrewElliott(3) 16 35
(J G'Reilly) *led stands' side over 4f: wknd over 1f out: 6th of 10 in gp* **20/1**

0-00 9 ½ **She's Dunnett**[71] 274 4-8-1 50 .... DominicFox(3) 14 24
(Mrs C A Dunnett) *racd stands' side: prom over 4f: 7th of 10 in gp* **33/1**

1440 10 3½ **Christian Bendix**[13] 801 5-8-1 50 oh5 ....(p) EmmettStack(3) 15 15
(P Howling) *racd stands' side: w ldr tl rdn over 2f out: wknd over 1f out: 8th of 10 in gp* **28/1**

213- 11 4 **Panshir (FR)**[225] 4845 6-8-4 50 oh1 .... DMylonas 12 4
(Mrs C A Dunnett) *racd stands' side: chsd ldrs over 4f: 9th of 10 in gp* **12/1**

4600 12 ¾ **The London Gang**[13] 797 4-8-2 51 ow1 ....(bt) StephaneBreux(3) 2 3
(Miss D A McHale) *racd far side: hld up: wknd over 2f out: eased: 3rd of 6 in gp* **25/1**

/64- 13 ¾ **Haneen (USA)**[297] 2608 4-8-11 64 .... SCreighton(7) 11 14
(R W Price) *racd stands' side: bhd whn hung lft fnl 3f: last of 10 in gp* **16/1**

-425 14 3½ **Imperial Lucky (IRE)**[63] 358 4-9-0 60 .... MartinDwyer 6 1
(D K Ivory) *racd far side: chsd ldrs over 4f: 4th of 6 in gp* **7/1**[3]

000- 15 2 **Life's A Whirl**[151] 6419 5-8-7 53 ....(p) TPQueally 5 —
(Mrs C A Dunnett) *racd far side: chsd ldr over 3f: sn wknd: 5th of 6 in gp* **25/1**

6060 16 ½ **Cool Tiger**[19] 722 4-8-4 50 oh3 ....(p) AlanDaly 3 —
(P Howling) *racd far side: s.i.s: sn prom: wknd over 2f out: last of 6 in gp* **33/1**

1m 25.87s (-0.73) **Going Correction** +0.025s/f (Good) **16** Ran SP% **127.2**
Speed ratings (Par 101):105,101,96,95,93 91,90,87,86,82 78,77,76,72,70 69
CSF £90.40 CT £713.49 TOTE £41.80: £13.80, £2.30, £1.30, £4.60; EX 158.50 TRIFECTA Not won..
Owner Skeltools Ltd **Bred** A B Phipps **Trained** Newmarket, Suffolk

FOCUS
A low-grade handicap, but quite a competitive race due to the size of the field and the pace looked strong, resulting in a fair time and some healthy margins separating the runners at the end. The field split into two with the larger group of ten racing towards the stands' side, whilst six stayed towards the far side. With horses drifting under pressure, the two groups had merged before reaching the two-furlong pole and it was those that raced stands' side that had much the best of it. Sound-looking form.
Imperial Lucky(IRE) Official explanation: jockey said filly lost its action

981 TOTEEXACTA MEDIAN AUCTION MAIDEN STKS 1m 2f 21y
4:45 (4:45) (Class 6) 3-5-Y-0 **£2,047** (£604; £302) **Stalls Low**

Form RPR

03- 1 **Pigeon Flight**[166] 6173 3-8-8 .... JamieSpencer 3 65+
(M L W Bell) *trckd ldrs: led over 2f out: sn rdn and hung lft: styd on u.p* **6/4**[1]

40 2 1 **Wassendale**[49] 498 3-8-4 ow1 .... MartinDwyer 1 55
(J W Hills) *chsd ldr: ev ch over 2f out: hmpd sn after: rdn over 1f out: styd on* **11/4**[3]

265- 3 2½ **Longhill Tiger**[187] 5768 4-9-13 75 .... EddieAhern 4 58
(G G Margarson) *led over 7f: styd on same pce fnl f* **15/8**[2]

0- 4 75 **Lady Althea**[173] 6052 4-9-8 .... SebSanders 2 —
(Mrs C A Dunnett) *hld up: wknd over 3f out* **10/1**

2m 12.71s (4.61) **Going Correction** +0.175s/f (Good)
WFA 3 from 4yo 19lb **4** Ran SP% **110.5**
Speed ratings (Par 101):88,87,85,25
CSF £6.03 TOTE £1.60; EX 4.40.
Owner A Buxton **Bred** Major W R Paton-Smith **Trained** Newmarket, Suffolk
■ Stewards' Enquiry : Jamie Spencer one-day ban: careless riding (Apr 20)

FOCUS
A modest maiden and something of a tactical affair with just the four runners. The time was unsurprisingly slow and the form probably does not amount to much.

982 TOTESPORTCASINO.COM H'CAP 1m 3f 101y
5:20 (5:24) (Class 6) (0-65,61) 4-Y-0+ **£2,137** (£635; £317; £158) **Stalls Low**

Form RPR

02-6 1 **Royal Premier (IRE)**[77] 215 4-8-11 54 ....(v) SebSanders 9 70+
(H J Collingridge) *a.p: led over 2f out: pushed clr fr over 1f out: eased nr fin* **15/2**[3]

5-30 2 7 **Missie Baileys**[16] 767 5-8-12 55 .... IanMongan 5 57
(Mrs L J Mongan) *mid-div: outpcd over 3f out: hdwy over 2f out: rdn to chse wnr over 1f out: sn outpcd* **5/1**[1]

6-00 3 1¼ **Royal Auditon**[41] 578 6-8-12 55 ....(p) J-PGuillambert 4 55
(T T Clement) *sn pushed along and prom: led over 3f out: hdd over 2f out: outpcd over 1f out* **40/1**

4-56 4 *nk* **Garibaldi (GER)**[18] 732 5-8-8 58 ow1 ....(t) JamesO'Reilly(7) 3 58
(J O'Reilly) *hld up: hdwy over 3f out: sn rdn: styd on same pce appr fnl f* **13/2**[2]

5-00 5 ¾ **Night Groove (IRE)**[24] 315 4-8-11 57 ....(b) JamesDoyle(3) 10 55
(N P Littmoden) *prom: lost pl 6f out: hdwy and hung lft fr over 2f out: no imp appr fnl f* **33/1**

4104 6 *nk* **Tip Toes (IRE)**[14] 792 5-8-4 47 oh1 .... JimmyQuinn 8 45
(P Howling) *hld up: hdwway and nt clr run over 2f out: nt trble ldrs* **12/1**

-200 7 1½ **Magic Amigo**[48] 503 6-9-4 61 .... EddieAhern 1 56
(J R Jenkins) *hld up in tch: wknd 2f out* **9/1**

4-34 8 7 **Cragganmore Creek**[48] 503 4-8-4 47 oh2 ....(v) HayleyTurner 7 31
(D Morris) *chsd ldrs: rdn over 2f out: wknd over 1f out* **14/1**

1226 9 8 **Shaheer (IRE)**[11] 819 5-8-13 56 .... TPQueally 2 27
(J Gallagher) *led 8f: wknd 2f out* **12/1**

2m 28.95s (1.45) **Going Correction** +0.175s/f (Good) **9** Ran SP% **79.2**
Speed ratings (Par 101):101,95,95,94,94 94,92,87,82
CSF £18.58 CT £244.96 TOTE £6.40: £1.80, £1.90, £8.10; EX 26.60 TRIFECTA Not won..
Owner Maynard Durrant Partnership I **Bred** Mrs Anne Hughes **Trained** Exning, Suffolk

FOCUS
A weak race in which the market was turned on its head by the late withdrawal of the gambled-on 11-10 favourite Le Soleil (vet's advice at s, deduct 45p in the £ under Rule 4.) The form looks modest, though the winner could hardly have done it any easier, value for 9l.
T/Plt: £25.60 to a £1 stake. Pool: £50,044.80. 1,424.15 winning tickets. T/Qpdt: £23.90 to a £1 stake. Pool: £1,262.50. 39.00 winning tickets. CR

983 - 988a (Foreign Racing) - See Raceform Interactive

897 SAINT-CLOUD (L-H)
Monday, April 9

OFFICIAL GOING: Good

989a PRIX PENELOPE (GROUP 3) (FILLIES) 1m 2f 110y
2:20 (2:20) 3-Y-0 **£27,027** (£10,811; £8,108; £5,405; £2,703)

RPR

1 **Mrs Lindsay (USA)**[31] 3-9-0 .... SPasquier 6 105
(F Rohaut, France) *rcd in 2nd early, 3rd ½-way, pushed along and went 2nd 2f out, chal appr fnl f, rdn and styd on to ld fnl strides* **2/1**[1]

2 *snk* **Sismix (IRE)**[23] 705 3-9-0 .... OPeslier 9 105
(C Laffon-Parias, France) *sn led, rdn and ran on 1½f out, hdd fnl strides* **46/10**[3]

3 2 **Topka (FR)**[23] 705 3-9-0 .... TJarnet 1 101
(F Doumen, France) *rcd in 3rd early, disp cl 4th str, rdn and styd on 1½f out, tk 3rd fnl f* **10/1**

4 1½ **Fontcia (FR)**[23] 705 3-9-0 .... IMendizabal 8 99
(D Sepulchre, France) *in tch, 4th ½-way, disp cl 4th str, pushed along 2f out, styd on steadily but nvr threatened ldrs* **43/10**[2]

5 1 **Beatrix Kiddo (FR)**[18] 3-9-0 .... CSoumillon 2 97
(Robert Collet, France) *mid-division on inside, 7th straight, ridden 1 1/2f out, stayed on steadily* **83/10**

6 1½ **Empreinte Celebre (IRE)**[33] 3-9-0 .... C-PLemaire 7 94
(J-C Rouget, France) *mid-division, 6th straight, driven on outside 1 1/2f out, no headway* **58/10**

7 1 **Bold Girl (IRE)**[44] 3-9-0 ....(b) JVictoire 4 92
(H-A Pantall, France) *held up, 8th straight, ridden 2f out, no impression* **83/10**

8 2 **Claire Et Bleu (FR)**[23] 705 3-9-0 .... AlxiBadel 3 89
(Mme M Bollack-Badel, France) *towards rear, last half-way, never dangerous* **21/1**

9 2 1/2 **Prototype**[176] 6000 3-9-0 .... TThulliez 5 84
(P Bary, France) *prominent, 2nd half-way, under pressure 1 1/2f out, weakened* **15/1**

2m 17.2s (-2.40) **9** Ran SP% **126.2**
PARI-MUTUEL: WIN 3.00; PL 1.40, 1.80, 2.50; DF 8.00.
Owner Mme B Jenney **Bred** Derry Meeting Farm **Trained** Sauvagnon, France

NOTEBOOK
Mrs Lindsay(USA), third on her only start at two, did not look at her best in the paddock and was rather on her toes, but she did little wrong in the race. Tucked in just behind the leaders, she was a little caught for speed when things quickened up in the straight but then came with a persistent challenge and responded gamely to her jockey to lead 50 yards out. Her trainer thinks she will come on a lot for the outing and she will either go for the Prix Saint-Alary or the Prix de Diane, but not both.
Sismix(IRE) was asked to make all the running and put up a very game effort, sticking to her guns throughout the final furlong. She reversed form with several of the other runners and will now be aimed at a similar event. She is also engaged in the Diane.
Topka(FR) ran an honest race and was staying on at the finish. Settled on the rail and always well placed, she was another who lacked pace when things quickened up in the straight but she ran on to take third place inside the final furlong.
Fontcia(FR) was given every possible chance but she could not go with the first two in the final furlong and a half and lost third place in the final stages.

990a PRIX RIGHT ROYAL (LISTED RACE) 1m 7f 110y
3:20 (3:21) 4-Y-O+ **£17,568** (£7,027; £5,270; £3,754; £1,757)

RPR

1 **Spectaculaire**[33] 4-8-12 .... OPeslier 8 109
(A Fabre, France)

2 3/4 **Host Nation**[18] 4-8-12 .... SPasquier 7 108
(A Fabre, France)

3 5 **Daramsar (FR)**[176] 5999 4-9-4 .... CSoumillon 5 109
(A De Royer-Dupre, France)

4 nk **Macleya (GER)**[182] 5881 5-8-13 .... JVictoire 11 100
(A Fabre, France) **16/1**[1]

5 3/4 **El Tango (GER)**[135] 6610 5-9-2 .... FilipMinarik 6 102
(P Schiergen, Germany)

6 1 1/2 **Morna (FR)**[30] 663 4-8-11 .... YBarberot 3 100
(S Wattel, France)

7 3/4 **Tusculum (IRE)**[11] 823 4-9-0 ....(b) IMendizabal 1 102
(A Fabre, France)

8 nk **Soledad (IRE)**[169] 6119 7-9-2 .... RonanThomas 10 100
(G Cherel, France)

9 1 1/2 **Peppertree Lane (IRE)**[156] 6336 4-8-12 .... KDarley 9 98
(M Johnston) *in tch towards outside, 5th 1/2-way, led 4f out, pushed along appr st, hdd 2f out, rdn & wknd 1 1/2f out (SP 16-1)*

10 10 **The West's Awake (USA)**[196] 5584 4-8-12 .... TThulliez 2 88
(E Libaud, France)

11 **Tirwanako (FR)**[44] 5-9-2 .... F-XBertras 4 88
(J-L Pelletan, France)

3m 23.5s (-15.20)
WFA 4 from 5yo+ 3lb **11** Ran SP% **5.9**
PARI-MUTUEL: WIN 8.80; PL 1.90, 1.90, 1.20; DF 26.00.
Owner Wertheimer Et Frere **Bred** Wertheimer Et Frere **Trained** Chantilly, France

NOTEBOOK
Peppertree Lane(IRE) found the ground had dried up so much in the past week that it had turned against him. Given every chance, he was always well placed and took the advantage rounding the final turn before gradually dropping out of contention in the last furlong and a half. No doubt connections will wait for a softer surface next time out.

PONTEFRACT (L-H)
Tuesday, April 10

OFFICIAL GOING: Good (good to firm in places)
Wind: Moderate, behind

991 STRAWBERRY HILL MEDIAN AUCTION MAIDEN STKS 1m 2f 6y
2:20 (2:21) (Class 5) 3-Y-O **£3,886** (£1,156; £577; £288) **Stalls** Low

Form RPR

42- 1 **Salaasa (USA)**[158] 6318 3-9-3 .... RHills 5 89+
(M Johnston) *trckd ldr: hdwy to ld over 2f out: sn clr: comf* **8/11**[1]

0- 2 3 1/2 **Veracity**[190] 5730 3-9-3 .... NCallan 7 78+
(M A Jarvis) *trckd ldng pair: niggled along 3f out: rdn to chse wnr fnl 2f: kpt on u.p* **9/4**[2]

2244 3 13 **Ranavalona**[11] 832 3-8-12 51 .... RobbieFitzpatrick 1 49
(C Smith) *keen: trckd ldrs: effrt 3f out: sn rdn along and onepce fnl 2f* **33/1**

2-0 4 shd **Murdoch**[10] 849 3-9-3 .... RichardMullen 8 54
(E S McMahon) *set stdy pce: pushed along over 3f out: rdn and hdd over 2f out: sn drvn and outpcd* **14/1**

46 5 1 **John Dillon (IRE)**[56] 449 3-9-3 .... LeeEnstone 3 52
(P C Haslam) *hld up in rr: hdwy on outer over 3f out: rdn along over 2f out: kpt on same pce* **20/1**

00 6 3 **Park's Prodigy**[56] 449 3-9-3 .... AdrianTNicholls 6 46
(P C Haslam) *plld hrd: hld up: a rr* **100/1**

0- 7 7 **Lucy Rebecca**[164] 6215 3-8-12 .... JamieSpencer 9 28
(M R Channon) *dwlt. hdwy and in tch 4f out: sn rdn along and btn* **10/1**[3]

000- 8 2 1/2 **Present**[208] 5321 3-8-12 56 .... HayleyTurner 4 23
(D Morris) *chsd ldrs: rdn along 1/2-way: sn wknd* **66/1**

0- 9 6 **Me No Puppet**[162] 6257 3-8-12 .... KDarley 2 12
(E J Alston) *midefrield: rdn along 1/2-way: sn wknd* **50/1**

2m 12.86s (-1.22) **Going Correction** -0.15s/f (Firm) **9** Ran SP% **116.6**
Speed ratings (Par 98):98,95,84,84,83 81,75,73,69
CSF £2.39 TOTE £1.80: £1.10, £1.10, £6.40; EX 2.90.
Owner Hamdan Al Maktoum **Bred** Shadwell Farm LLC **Trained** Middleham Moor, N Yorks

FOCUS
A two-horse race according to the market and that is how it proved. The pace was only ordinary, but the two main contenders still stamped their class on the contest and pulled miles clear of the others. Not that easy a race to assess with doubts over the third.

992 ANNUAL BADGE HOLDERS H'CAP 6f
2:50 (2:50) (Class 6) (0-65,65) 4-Y-O+ **£3,238** (£963; £481; £240) **Stalls** Low

Form RPR

456- 1 **Brigadore**[174] 6060 8-9-2 63 .... TPQueally 1 74
(J G Given) *s.i.s and bhd: gd hdwy on inner over 2f out: swtchd rt and str run over 1f out: led ins last: kpt on* **14/1**

-042 2 1/2 **Melalchrist**[7] 905 5-9-4 65 ....(p) NCallan 2 74+
(K A Ryan) *qckly away and led: qcknd clr 2f out: rdn and hdd ins last: kpt on wl u.p* **4/1**[1]

4620 3 1 1/4 **Violent Velocity (IRE)**[21] 718 4-8-13 60 .... GrahamGibbons 16 65
(J J Quinn) *s.i.s aqnd swtchd lft s: bhd tiull gd hdwy on inner wl over 1f out: rdn and styd on wl fnl f* **16/1**

466- 4 1 3/4 **Dorn Dancer (IRE)**[188] 5765 5-9-1 62 .... TomEaves 14 62
(D W Barker) *stdd and swed lft s: bhd tl hdwy on inner wl over 1f out: sn rdn and kpt on ins last* **10/1**

000- 5 1 **Night In (IRE)**[182] 5902 4-9-1 62 ....(t) KimTinkler 3 59
(N Tinkler) *chsd ldrs on inner: hdwy over 2f out: sn rdn and kpt on samer pce appr last* **20/1**

20-0 6 1 **Digital**[15] 793 10-8-11 65 .... MatthewDavies(7) 6 63+
(M R Channon) *midfeild: hdwy 2f out: rdn and styng on whn hmpd ent last: swtchd lft and kpt on towards fin* **10/1**

-000 7 hd **Funfair Wane**[19] 727 8-8-13 60 .... AdrianTNicholls 9 53
(D Nicholls) *cl up: rdn along 2f out: drvn and wknd appr last* **18/1**

00-4 8 1 3/4 **Rainbow Bay**[8] 896 4-8-13 60 ....(b) ChrisCatlin 15 48
(E J O'Neill) *racd wd: towards rr tl styd on appr last: n.d* **9/1**

605- 9 1 1/2 **Divine Spirit**[197] 5577 6-9-1 62 .... JamieSpencer 8 46
(M Dods) *hld up towards rr tl sme late hdwy* **17/2**[3]

00-0 10 shd **Greek Secret**[98] 8 4-8-8 62 ....(b) JamesO'Reilly(7) 10 45
(J O'Reilly) *chsd ldrs, rdn along 2f out: grad wknd* **12/1**

1340 11 2 **Going Skint**[21] 717 4-9-1 62 .... DaleGibson 5 39
(M Wellings) *a towards rr* **16/1**

266- 12 1/2 **Conjecture**[138] 6572 5-8-10 62 .... NataliaGemelova(5) 11 38
(R Bastiman) *chsd ldrs: rdn along over 2f out: sn wknd* **20/1**

10-0 13 1 **Paddywack (IRE)**[14] 803 10-8-13 60 ....(b) SebSanders 4 33
(D W Chapman) *chsd ldrs: hdwy 2f out: rdn whn bmpd over 1f out and sn wknd* **18/1**

-001 14 1 3/4 **Bobby Rose**[17] 751 4-9-4 65 .... RobertHavlin 12 33
(D K Ivory) *midfield: rdn along 2f out: sn btn* **8/1**[2]

00-0 15 3/4 **Throw The Dice**[5] 892 5-8-11 58 ....(p) PaulHanagan 13 23
(D W Barker) *chsd ldrs on outer: rdn along 2f out: sn drvn and wknd* **14/1**

156- 16 2 **Apache Nation (IRE)**[165] 6206 4-9-4 65 .... PhillipMakin 7 24
(M Dods) *a towards rr* **14/1**

1m 15.36s (-2.04) **Going Correction** -0.15s/f (Firm) **16** Ran SP% **129.3**
Speed ratings (Par 101):107,106,104,102,101 99,99,97,95,94 92,91,90,87,86 84
CSF £73.03 CT £979.08 TOTE £13.60: £2.80, £1.70, £5.90, £2.40; EX 80.50.
Owner White Rose Poultry Ltd **Bred** Fulling Mill Stud **Trained** Willoughton, Lincs
■ Stewards' Enquiry : T P Queally one-day ban: careless riding (Apr 21)

FOCUS
A modest handicap run at a good pace and in a decent time for the class. It looks pretty sound with the runner-up and third running close to their recent All-Weather form.
Divine Spirit Official explanation: jockey said gelding was denied a clear run
Bobby Rose Official explanation: jockey said gelding was unsuited by the track

993 DALBY STAND H'CAP 1m 4y
3:25 (3:26) (Class 3) (0-95,95) 4-Y-O+
£9,348 (£2,799; £1,399; £700; £349; £175) **Stalls** Low

Form RPR

510- 1 **Robustian**[171] 6097 4-8-5 82 .... StephenCarson 2 91+
(Eve Johnson Houghton) *keen: trckd ldrs: swtchd lft and hdwy to chal over 1f out rdn ins last: led last 100 yds* **16/1**

120- 2 hd **Benandonner (USA)**[172] 6076 4-8-4 81 .... PaulHanagan 9 90
(R A Fahey) *chsd ldr: effrt 2f out: rdn to ld over 1f out: jnd and drvn ins last: hdd and no ex last 100 yds* **12/1**

103- 3 1 3/4 **Wind Star**[197] 5579 4-8-10 87 .... JamieSpencer 7 92
(G A Swinbank) *trckd ldrs: hdwy over 2f out: rdn over 1f out: drvn ins last and kpt on same pce* **4/1**[1]

2/02 4 1/2 **Tufton**[16] 777 4-8-13 90 ....(t) OscarUrbina 11 94
(M Botti) *keen: trckd ldrs: swtchd ins and ev ch over 1f out: sn rdn and one pce ins last* **8/1**[3]

3-15 5 hd **Fajr (IRE)**[80] 197 5-8-10 87 .... JimmyQuinn 12 90
(Miss Gay Kelleway) *hld up: hdwy over 2f out: rdn to chse ldrs over 1f out: kpt on ins last* **8/1**[3]

/04- 6 1 3/4 **Ballinteni**[164] 6226 5-8-5 82 ow1 .... MartinDwyer 5 81+
(D M Simcock) *hmpd s and bhd tl gd hdwy on inner wl over 1f out: styng on whn bmpd 1f out: fin wl* **9/1**

0060 7 nk **Hopeful Purchase (IRE)**[17] 759 4-8-11 88 ....(p) RHills 4 87
(W J Haggas) *led: rdn along over 2f out: drvn and hdd over 1f out: wknd ins last* **5/1**[2]

55-5 8 1 1/4 **Sew'N'So Character (IRE)**[81] 185 6-8-4 81 .... DaleGibson 10 77
(M Blanshard) *hld up: hdwy 2f out: rdn to chse ldrs over 1f out: drvn and edgd lft ent last: sn wknd* **14/1**

500- 9 1 1/2 **Krugerrand (USA)**[157] 6337 8-8-9 86 .... RichardMullen 6 78
(W J Musson) *wnt rt s: bhd tl styd on fnl 2f: n.d* **25/1**

0-50 10 1/2 **Capable Guest (IRE)**[10] 848 5-8-11 88 .... ChrisCatlin 3 79
(M R Channon) *a towards rr* **5/1**[2]

040- 11 2 **Go Tech**[186] 5787 7-8-5 82 .... DavidAllan 8 69
(T D Easterby) *chsd ldrs: rdn along 3f out: sn wknd* **22/1**

00- 12 26 **Major League (USA)**[319] 1340 5-8-4 81 oh2 .... HayleyTurner 15 8
(D Morris) *wnt rt s: a bhd* **80/1**

6-40 13 hd **Chief Commander (FR)**[31] 656 4-9-1 92 .... JohnEgan 13 18
(Jane Chapple-Hyam) *midfield on outer: rdn along over 3f out and sn wknd* **16/1**

1/5- 14 54 **Akram (IRE)**[283] 3091 5-9-4 95 .... FMBerry 1 —
(Jonjo O'Neill) *chsd ldrs: rdn along over 3f out and sn wknd* **16/1**

1m 42.68s (-3.02) **Going Correction** -0.15s/f (Firm) **14** Ran SP% **127.0**
Speed ratings (Par 107):109,108,107,106,106 104,104,103,101,101 99,73,72,18
CSF £203.11 CT £959.78 TOTE £24.10: £5.70, £4.10, £2.10; EX 356.30.
Owner Michael Doran & R F Johnson Houghton **Bred** T J Cooper **Trained** Blewbury, Oxon
■ A first winner as a trainer for Eve Johnson Houghton since taking over the licence from her father, Fulke.

FOCUS
Flipando was withdrawn after bolting before the start (8/1, deduct 10p in the £ from bets prior to withdrawal but not SP bets.) New market formed. A very competitive handicap run at a decent pace and the winning time was well up to scratch for the class. Those that raced close to the pace appeared to hold the advantage as few were able to make up ground from the back. Sound form.

NOTEBOOK

Robustian ◆, making his return from a six-month break, had gained his only previous win over 1m3f, but they went a decent pace in this. After having raced close to the pace throughout, this demanding track brought his stamina into play for the final dash to the line and he did it well. He will not mind a return to further and, given a sound surface, there looks to be more to come from him. (new market new market op 33-1)

Benandonner(USA) ◆, making his debut for the yard after nearly six months off, was always there or thereabouts and had every chance in the home straight, but was just run out of it. There will be other opportunities for him this term, especially when allowed his own way out in front. (new market new market)

Wind Star ◆ had conditions in his favour and the decent pace would have been a help too. He duly ran with plenty of credit having raced close to the pace from the off and just lacked a decisive turn of foot at the end. He did not see the racecourse until ten months ago, so still has a bit of scope and should come on for this first run in more than six months. (new market new market op 9-2)

Tufton was in a handy enough position throughout and was presented with enough of a gap on the inside after the field had swung for home had he been up to it, but lacked a decisive turn of foot. He did hold a fitness advantage over the trio that beat him, but having missed the whole of 2006 he still does not have many miles on the clock and gives the impression he will be suited by going back up in trip. (new market new market op 10-1)

Fajr(IRE), off for 80 days, stayed on well over the last couple of furlongs and did best of those held up in a race otherwise dominated by those that raced handily, but he is on a career-high mark now so will need to find improvement from somewhere. (new market new market op 9-1)

Ballinteni ◆, very lightly raced and off since October, soon found himself right out the back and that proved not the place to be as things turned out. Still last passing the two-furlong pole, he fairly motored up the inside rail up the final climb and was finishing best of all. Provided he can be kept sound, there are races to be won with him for his new yard this term and he is certainly one for the notebook. (new market new market op 12-1)

Hopeful Purchase(IRE), who is gradually creeping down the weights, set a decent pace but seemed to get very tired up the final climb and was swamped, which was surprising as he has won over further than this. (new market new market op 6-1 tchd 7-1)

Major League(USA) Official explanation: jockey said gelding ran too keen early

Akram(IRE) Official explanation: jockey said gelding finished lame

994 JAMAICAN FLIGHT H'CAP — 2m 1f 216y

4:00 (4:00) (Class 5) (0-75,71) 4-Y-0+ — **£3,886** (£1,156; £577; £288) **Stalls** Low

Form — RPR

554- **1** **Tribe**[307] [2357] 5-9-10 **69** ... JimmyFortune 5 — 83+
(P R Webber) *hld up in rr: stdy hdwy on outer 6f out: led wl over 2f out and sn clr: easily* **6/1**[3]

30-2 **2** *3* **Great As Gold (IRE)**[13] [808] 8-9-3 **62** ... TomEaves 13 — 70
(B Ellison) *hld up: stdy hdwy over 6f out: rdn to ld over 3f out: hdd wl over 2f out and sn drvn: kpt on: no ch w wnr* **13/2**

461- **3** *6* **Malakiya (IRE)**[38] [6027] 4-9-6 **70** ... FMBerry 4 — 71
(Jonjo O'Neill) *hld up and bhd: stdy hdwy 1/2-way: chsd ldrs 4f out: rdn along to chse ldng pair 3f out: sn drvn and no imp* **9/2**[1]

-023 **4** *1 3/4* **Capitalise (IRE)**[17] [677] 4-8-4 **54** ... ChrisCatlin 1 — 57+
(V Smith) *hld up in tch: hdwy 5f out: rdn along 3f out: styd on same pce fnl 2f* **9/1**

0141 **5** *2 1/2* **Rule For Ever**[22] [709] 5-9-12 **71** ... JoeFanning 3 — 68
(I W McInnes) *towards rr: hdwy 4f out: sn rdn along and kpt on same pce fnl 2f* **9/1**

-333 **6** *3 1/2* **Sand Repeal (IRE)**[16] [775] 5-9-3 **62** ... (v) BrettDoyle 2 — 55
(Miss J Feilden) *in tch on inner: effrt and hdwy over 4f out: rdn along 3f out: sn outpcd* **9/1**

-113 **7** *8* **Victory Quest (IRE)**[22] [709] 7-9-5 **64** ... (v) PaulFessey 6 — 48
(Mrs S Lamyman) *trckd ldrs: hdwy to ld 6f out: rdn along and hdd over 3f out and sn wknd* **14/1**

4413 **8** *2* **Synonymy**[10] [844] 4-9-2 **66** ... SteveDrowne 10 — 48
(M Blanshard) *in tch: rdn along over 4f out: wkng whn n.m.r over 3f out and sn btn* **5/1**[2]

66-0 **9** *nk* **Jamaican Flight (USA)**[67] [333] 14-8-7 **52** oh7 ... JimmyQuinn 8 — 34
(Mrs S Lamyman) *prom: rdn along over 6f out and sn wknd* **100/1**

40-0 **10** *34* **Spectested (IRE)**[7] [909] 6-8-7 **52** oh2 ... RichardMullen 9 — —
(A W Carroll) *rel to r and lost 20l s: t.o thrght* **50/1**

0-65 **11** *3* **Greyside (USA)**[22] [709] 4-9-1 **65** ... (p) PaulMulrennan 11 — 6
(C A Mulhall) *chsd ldrs: rdn along 6f out: wknd over 4f out* **33/1**

1201 **12** *16* **Blue Hills**[13] [808] 6-8-10 **62** ... (b) WilliamCarson(7) 7 — —
(P W Hiatt) *in tch: rdn along 6f out: drvn wkng whn n.m.r over 3f out: sn bhd* **13/2**

612 **13** *2 1/2* **Al Moulatham**[22] [709] 8-9-2 **61** ... (bt) SamHitchcott 12 — —
(R Ford) *sn led: clr after 3f: rdn along over 7f out: hdd 6f out and sn wknd* **14/1**

3m 56.39s (-6.61) **Going Correction** -0.15s/f (Firm) — **13** Ran SP% **125.0**

WFA 4 from 5yo+ 5lb

Speed ratings (Par 103):108,106,104,103,102 100,97,96,95,80 79,72,71

CSF £46.79 CT £199.10 TOTE £7.30: £3.00, £2.60, £1.80; EX 58.90.

Owner Iain Russell Watters **Bred** Addison Racing Ltd Inc **Trained** Mollington, Oxon

FOCUS

They went a good gallop in this staying handicap and the principals came from off the pace. The winner is unexposed as a stayer and value for further, with the second and third fair guides to the form.

995 HIGH-RISE H'CAP — 1m 2f 6y

4:35 (4:36) (Class 2) (0-100,96) 3-Y-0+

£11,217 (£3,358; £1,679; £840; £419; £210) **Stalls** Low

Form — RPR

20-0 **1** **Charlie Tokyo (IRE)**[3] [940] 4-9-2 **84** ... (b) PaulHanagan 2 — 93+
(R A Fahey) *keen: trckd ldrs: smooth hdwy on inner 2f out: rdn to ld ins last: styd on wl* **13/2**[2]

20-0 **2** *2* **Along The Nile**[10] [850] 5-9-1 **83** ... (t) KDarley 1 — 89
(K G Reveley) *trckd ldng pair: effrt 2f out: swtchd rt and rdn over 1f out: chsd wnr ins last: kpt on* **15/2**

6-03 **3** *nk* **Lucayan Dancer**[10] [850] 7-9-1 **83** ... AdrianTNicholls 11 — 88
(D Nicholls) *midfield: hdwy on outer to chal 4f out: rdn to ld wl over 2f out: drvn and edgd lft over 1f out: hdd and nt qckn ins last* **7/1**[3]

4413 **4** *1* **Sgt Schultz (IRE)**[11] [829] 4-9-0 **82** oh10 ... LPKeniry 10 — 85
(J S Moore) *in tch: hdwy 3f out: rdn wl over 1f out: kpt on u.p ins last* **8/1**

30-0 **5** *nk* **Fort Churchill (IRE)**[10] [846] 6-9-0 **82** ... (bt) PatCosgrave 4 — 85+
(B Ellison) *towards rr: hdwy 2f out: rdn and styng on whn hmpd over 1f out: kpt on strly ins last: nrst fin* **15/2**

031- **6** *3/4* **Folio (IRE)**[157] [6337] 7-9-6 **88** ... TPQueally 6 — 89
(W J Musson) *hld up towards rr: hdwy 4f out: rdn along to chse ldrs 3f out: kpt on same pce appr last* **17/2**

00-0 **7** *1/2* **Counsel's Opinion (IRE)**[24] [701] 10-9-10 **92** ... GeorgeBaker 7 — 92
(C F Wall) *dwlt: hld up in rr: hdwy 2f out: rdn over 1f out and sn no imp* **7/1**[3]

014- **8** *1/2* **Best Prospect (IRE)**[157] [6337] 5-10-0 **96** ... JamieSpencer 3 — 95+
(M Dods) *hld up in rr: hdwy 2f out: shkn up over 1f out: sn btn* **11/2**[1]

302- **9** *3/4* **Mudawin (IRE)**[150] [6438] 6-9-13 **95** ... JohnEgan 5 — 93
(Jane Chapple-Hyam) *keen: hld up: a rr* **10/1**

/46- **10** *1/2* **Tender Falcon**[338] [1517] 7-9-0 **82** ... MartinDwyer 9 — 79
(R J Hodges) *chsd ldr: rdn along 3f out: wknd fnl 2f* **33/1**

054- **11** *5* **Nelsons Column (IRE)**[173] [5758] 4-9-5 **87** ... TomEaves 8 — 74
(G M Moore) *led: rdn along and jnd 4f out: hdd wl over 2f out: sn drvn and wknd over 1f out* **16/1**

2m 13.73s (-0.35) **Going Correction** -0.15s/f (Firm) — **11** Ran SP% **116.8**

Speed ratings (Par 109):95,93,93,92,92 91,91,90,90,89 85

CSF £54.24 CT £354.20 TOTE £9.70: £2.80, £2.80, £2.00; EX 54.30.

Owner S L Tse **Bred** J Donnelly **Trained** Musley Bank, N Yorks

FOCUS

They went only a very steady pace for much of the way in this, resulting in a very moderate winning time for a race of its class, 0.87 seconds slower than the earlier three-year-old maiden. How reliable the form is because of that remains to be seen, but those that tried to come from the back looked to be up against it. The race has been rated through the second and third.

NOTEBOOK

Charlie Tokyo(IRE), who did not enjoy the run of the race in the Rosebery on the Kempton Polytrack three days earlier, had the blinkers back on for this return to turf and things panned out perfectly for him this time. He was keen early once again, but a wonderful gap appeared for him against the inside rail turning for home and he made full use of it. He has not always impressed with his attitude in a finish, but there was no sign of that here. (op 17-2 tchd 9-1)

Along The Nile, back on a more suitable surface and with the tongue-tie reapplied, was never far off the pace and kept battling right to the line. He has a fine record at this track and although still 5lb above his last winning mark, is running well enough to defy it. (op 5-1)

Lucayan Dancer, who finished a long way ahead of Along The Nile on much easier ground at Newcastle last month, was sent for home rounding the home bend but could not get clear of his field and was run out of it. (tchd 13-2 and 15-2)

Sgt Schultz(IRE), fit from the sand, would not have been helped by the steady pace on this drop in trip and, although he stayed on well down the outside over the last furlong or so, he was never quite doing enough. (op 7-1 tchd 9-1)

Fort Churchill(IRE) ◆, beaten out of sight when drawn on the wrong side on much softer ground over an inadequate trip in the Spring Mile at Newcastle last month, is the one to take from the race. He was attempting to come from well off the pace in a race where those that raced handy were at an advantage, but would have been even closer had he not met serious traffic problems up the home straight. (op 11-1)

Folio(IRE) ◆, returning from five months off and 2lb higher, made some late headway down the outside over the last couple of furlongs and can be expected to come on for this. (op 8-1)

Counsel's Opinion(IRE) is finally being given some help by the Handicapper, but his come-from-behind style was not suited to this contest and his final position was as close as he got.

Best Prospect(IRE), closely matched with Folio on their running at Windsor last November, could never get anywhere near but he was one of several that found it hard to come from off the pace in this contest. Having said that, he ran very close to form with his old rival. (op 8-1)

Mudawin(IRE) was always going to find this trip inadequate on this return to action and, with the early pace so moderate, he made the situation even worse by pulling like a train. At least this will have blown away the cobwebs. (tchd 9-1)

996 PONTEFRACT-RACES.CO.UK MAIDEN FILLIES' STKS (DIV I) — 6f

5:05 (5:06) (Class 5) 3-Y-O — **£3,238** (£963; £481; £240) **Stalls** Low

Form — RPR

6 **1** **Poppy's Rose**[17] [752] 3-9-0 ... DanielTudhope 5 — 64
(I W McInnes) *towards rr: hdwy 1/2-way: rdn to chse ldr ent last: sn drvn and edgd lft: styd on wl to ld nr fin* **14/1**

35-5 **2** *nk* **Princess Ellis**[8] [894] 3-9-0 57 ... KDarley 3 — 63
(E J Alston) *mde most: rdn clr over 1f out: drvn ins last: hdd and no ex nr fin* **17/2**

3 *2 1/2* **Blackmalkin (USA)** 3-9-0 ... SebSanders 6 — 56
(C E Brittain) *cl up: effrt 3fd out: sn rdn and ev ch tl drvn and one pce appr last* **9/1**

02- **4** *4* **Cape Velvet (IRE)**[207] [5348] 3-9-0 ... EddieAhern 8 — 44
(J W Hills) *towards rr: effrt and pushed along 3f out: sn rdn and styd on appr last: n.d* **1/1**[1]

00- **5** *1* **Compton Special**[130] [6663] 3-9-0 ... TPQueally 1 — 41
(J G Given) *prom: rdn along 1/2-way: sn one pce* **28/1**

00- **6** *8* **Miss Daawe**[188] [5764] 3-9-0 ... PaulEddery 2 — 17
(S Parr) *sn pushed along and a rr* **100/1**

43- **7** *2 1/2* **House Maiden (IRE)**[175] [6031] 3-9-0 ... MartinDwyer 10 — 9
(D M Simcock) *a rr* **5/1**[3]

30 **8** *3/4* **Spanish Needle**[17] [752] 3-9-0 ... JimmyFortune 7 — 7
(P R Webber) *prom: rdn along 3f out: drvn 2f out and sn wknd* **9/2**[2]

050- **9** *shd* **Hot Cherry**[225] [4897] 3-9-0 47 ... (b[1]) DaleGibson 9 — 6
(J M P Eustace) *chsd ldrs on outer: rdn along over 2f out and sn wknd* **50/1**

1m 16.41s (-0.99) **Going Correction** -0.15s/f (Firm) — **9** Ran SP% **118.4**

Speed ratings (Par 95):100,99,96,90,89 78,75,74,74

CSF £127.41 TOTE £19.60: £3.00, £2.60, £2.20; EX 124.80.

Owner Mrs Ann Morris **Bred** Mrs A Morris **Trained** Catwick, E Yorks

FOCUS

An ordinary maiden but a creditable winning time for a race of its type, 0.48 seconds faster than the second division. The race has been rated to the best view of the form.

997 BETFAIR.COM APPRENTICE SERIES ROUND ONE H'CAP — 1m 4f 8y

5:35 (5:35) (Class 5) (0-75,74) 4-Y-0+ — **£3,886** (£1,156; £577; £288) **Stalls** Low

Form — RPR

240- **1** **Cripsey Brook**[200] [5511] 9-9-6 **74** ... (t) DanielleMcCreery 7 — 81
(K G Reveley) *hld up: hdwy 4f out: rdn over 2f out: styd on to ld ins last: edgd lft and kpt on* **14/1**

2-53 **2** *3/4* **Wulimaster (USA)**[43] [564] 4-9-1 **70** ... JamieHamblett 2 — 76
(D W Barker) *hld up in midfield: hdwy over 3f out: rdn 2f out: styd on ins last* **5/1**[3]

10-4 **3** *1/2* **Intavac Boy**[18] [742] 6-8-1 **60** ... JamesRogers(5) 1 — 65
(R A Fahey) *chsd ldng pair: rdn along 3f out: hdwy 2f out: styd on ins last* **11/8**[1]

0443 **4** *3* **Augustine**[12] [819] 6-9-1 **69** ... WilliamCarson 3 — 69+
(P W Hiatt) *led and set stgrong pce: rdn along 3f out: drvn 2f out: hdd & wknd ins last* **10/3**[2]

2000 **5** *1* **Greenbelt**[19] [733] 6-8-4 **61** ... JosephWalsh(3) 4 — 60+
(G M Moore) *cl up: rdn 3f out and ev ch tl drvn and wknd 1f out* **9/1**

0-00 **6** *14* **Migration**[8] 891 11-8-1 **60** oh7 .... NSLawes(5) 5 36
(Mrs S Lamyman) *hld up towards rr: hdwy on outer 3f out: sn rdn and btn* **33/1**
005/ **7** *3* **Newtonian (USA)**[510] 6371 8-8-1 **60** oh4 .... PatrickDonaghy(5) 8 31
(M Brittain) *s.i.s and bhd: hdwy and in tch 4f out: sn rdn and wknd* **11/1**
-035 **8** *28* **Mister Maq**[60] 402 4-7-12 **60** oh6 .... (b) DavidProbert(7) 6 —
(A Crook) *keen: in tch: rdn along over 4f out and sn wknd* **28/1**

2m 41.24s (0.94) **Going Correction** -0.15s/f (Firm)
WFA 4 from 6yo+ 1lb **8** Ran SP% **113.2**
Speed ratings (Par 103):90,89,89,87,86 77,75,56
CSF £80.46 CT £159.65 TOTE £10.70: £2.50, £1.50, £1.20; EX 53.90.
Owner Reveley Farms **Bred** Overbury Stud And Stowell Hill Ltd **Trained** Lingdale, Redcar & Cleveland

■ Stewards' Enquiry : Danielle McCreery one-day ban: used whip in the incorrect place (Apr 21)
William Carson four-day ban: used whip with excessive frequency (Apr 21-24)
James Rogers one-day ban: used whip with excessive frequency (Apr 21)

FOCUS
The race was restricted to apprentices who had not ridden more than ten winners prior to the start of the turf season. With Augustine and Greenbelt soon taking each other on, the early gallop was very strong but they could not maintain it. The pace eventually collapsed and with it the winning time, which was very slow for the class. Weak handicap form.

998 PONTEFRACT-RACES.CO.UK MAIDEN FILLIES' STKS (DIV II) 6f
6:05 (6:07) (Class 5) 3-Y-O **£3,238** (£963; £481; £240) **Stalls** Low

Form RPR
1 **Cha Cha Cha** 3-9-0 .... NCallan 4 72+
(K A Ryan) *dwlt and wnet rt s: sn trcking ldrs: pushed along over 2f out: rdn and hdwy to ld appr last: styd on wl* **4/1**[2]
33- **2** *1 1/2* **Support Fund (IRE)**[197] 5563 3-9-0 .... StephenCarson 3 64
(Eve Johnson Houghton) *hld up towards rr: hdwy on inner wlo over 1f out: rdn to chse wnr ins last: kpt on u.p* **2/1**[1]
0- **3** *1 1/2* **Uace Mac**[246] 4196 3-8-7 .... SuzzanneFrance(7) 1 59
(N Bycroft) *led: rdn along wl over 1f out: hdd appr last: kpt on* **66/1**
U-03 **4** *1* **Comptonspirit**[27] 678 3-9-0 .... DeanMcKeown 2 56
(B P J Baugh) *chsd ldrs: rdn along 2f out: sn drvn and kpt on same pce* **12/1**
50- **5** *3 1/2* **Stormburst (IRE)**[313] 2166 3-9-0 .... PaulFessey 6 46
(M Dods) *hld up towards rr: pushed along over 2f out: swtchd outside and rdn over 1f out: sn edgd lft and no imp* **15/2**[3]
6 *1/2* **Regal Cheer** 3-9-0 .... SebSanders 9 44
(C F Wall) *s.i.s and hmpd s: rr tl sme late hdwy* **9/1**
7 *3* **Abadia** 3-9-0 .... TPQueally 5 35
(J G Given) *s.i.s and hmpd s: rn green and a rr* **8/1**
50- **8** *1/2* **Bond Casino**[211] 5237 3-8-9 .... (p) DuranFentiman(5) 7 34
(G R Oldroyd) *chsd ldrs: rdn along 1/2-way: sn wknd* **10/1**
430- **9** *shd* **Rue Soleil**[161] 6278 3-9-0 62 .... JamieSpencer 8 33
(J R Weymes) *prom: rdn along 2f out: sn wknd* **10/1**
0- **10** *2* **Rock Diva (IRE)**[147] 6481 3-9-0 .... LeeEnstone 10 27
(P C Haslam) *chsd ldrs on outer: rdn along over 2f out: sn wknd* **33/1**

1m 16.89s (-0.51) **Going Correction** -0.15s/f (Firm) **10** Ran SP% **116.5**
Speed ratings (Par 95):97,95,93,91,87 86,82,81,81,78
CSF £12.36 TOTE £4.60: £1.90, £1.30, £9.10; EX 15.20 Place 6 £262.91, Place 5 £223.43.
Owner Guy Reed **Bred** G Reed **Trained** Hambleton, N Yorks

FOCUS
The slower of the two divisions by 0.48sec and only modest form, but it was still a nice performance from the winner nevertheless. It has been rated through the runner-up to her debut form.
T/Jkpt: Not won. T/Plt: £237.30 to a £1 stake. Pool: £83,232.55. 255.95 winning tickets. T/Qpdt: £139.00 to a £1 stake. Pool: £3,307.80. 17.60 winning tickets. JR

BATH (L-H)
Wednesday, April 11

OFFICIAL GOING: Firm
Wind: Nil Weather: Overcast, warm

999 P & C MORRIS MAIDEN STKS 5f 11y
2:30 (2:32) (Class 5) 2-Y-O **£2,914** (£867; £433; £216) **Stalls** Low

Form RPR
1 **Vhujon (IRE)** 2-9-0 .... StephenDonohoe(3) 13 91
(P D Evans) *showed gd early spd and mde all: clr 1/2-way: rdn and in control fnl 2f: comf* **33/1**
2 *3* **Just A Dancer (IRE)** 2-8-12 .... MichaelHills 4 74
(B W Hills) *mid-div: rdn and hdwy 2f out: wnt 2nd over 1f out: no ch w wnr* **9/2**[2]
2 **3** *2* **Concertmaster**[13] 814 2-9-3 .... SebSanders 16 71
(R M Beckett) *hld up in midfield: effrt 2f out: styd on to take 3rd ins fnl f* **4/1**[1]
4 **4** *3/4* **Ben**[13] 814 2-9-3 .... SteveDrowne 7 68
(P G Murphy) *chsd spdy wnr tl over 1f out: no ex fnl f* **8/1**
5 **5** *1 1/2* **Southwest Star (IRE)**[13] 814 2-9-3 .... JohnEgan 5 62
(J S Moore) *in tch: hrd rdn 2f out: btn whn hung lft fnl f* **9/2**[2]
6 *hd* **Group Therapy** 2-9-3 .... JamieSpencer 11 61
(J A Osborne) *s.s: bhd tl stdy hdwy 2f out: nvr nr to chal: can do bttr* **7/1**
0 **7** *nk* **Ocean Transit (IRE)**[9] 890 2-8-5 .... JackDean(7) 8 55
(W G M Turner) *sn outpcd towards rr: styd on fnl 2f* **80/1**
8 *3* **Blue Zenith (IRE)** 2-8-12 .... LPKeniry 3 43
(J S Moore) *s.i.s: drvn along in rr: sme late hdwy* **25/1**
9 *hd* **Alfredtheordinary** 2-9-3 .... SamHitchcott 2 47
(M R Channon) *colty: rn green and rdn in rr: nvr rchd ldrs* **20/1**
0 **10** *1 1/2* **Border Defence (IRE)**[9] 890 2-8-12 .... (b[1]) KevinGhunowa(5) 10 41
(P A Blockley) *prom: hrd rdn 2f out: hung lft and wknd 1f out* **66/1**
11 *3/4* **Higgy's Boy (IRE)** 2-9-3 .... RichardHughes 15 38
(R Hannon) *s.s: a in rr* **11/2**[3]
12 *6* **Mister Cafnex (IRE)** 2-8-12 .... DJMoran(5) 6 14
(B W Duke) *in tch early: rdn and lost pl over 3f out: sn struggling towards rr* **11/1**
13 *nk* **O'Casey (IRE)** 2-9-3 .... FergusSweeney 1 13
(J G M O'Shea) *chsd ldrs over 2f* **100/1**

61.28 secs (-1.22) **Going Correction** -0.275s/f (Firm) **13** Ran SP% **119.0**
Speed ratings (Par 92):98,93,90,88,86 86,85,80,80,78 76,67,66
CSF £170.54 TOTE £35.30: £7.90, £2.20, £1.90; EX 338.80 Trifecta £376.00 Part won. Pool £529.58 - 0.10 winning units..
Owner Nick Shutts **Bred** Robert Berns **Trained** Pandy, Monmouths

FOCUS
This could prove to be a fair juvenile maiden. The speedy winner did the job well and the form looks straightforward rated through the placed horses.

NOTEBOOK
Vhujon(IRE), whose sales price increased markedly as a yearling to 23,000euros, clearly knew his job as he pinged out of the gates and eventually made all for a comfortable debut success. His early speed saw him have the race pretty much wrapped up at the two pole, he bounced off the firm surface and has to rate the fastest juvenile to have been seen out on turf to date at this early stage of the season. It was not surprising that his trainer later indicated he thought a lot of him and, with the possibility of Chester next month coming into the equation, that the Norfolk or the Windsor Castle at Royal Ascot will be his main target. (op 40-1)
Just A Dancer(IRE) ◆, by an exciting first-season sire and out of a dam who won on her debut at two, lacked the early pace to get near the winner yet kept on nicely inside the final two furlongs. This sharp filly ought to come on for this debut experience and find a race before too long. (op 4-1)
Concertmaster, runner up on his debut at Lingfield, failed to make his previous experience count in the early part of the race and was doing his best work towards the finish. He has scope, however, and is entitled to come on a bit again for the run. (op 7-2 tchd 9-2)
Ben, fourth at Lingfield on his debut, eventually paid for trying to go with the winner through the early parts yet still ran close to his previous form with the third. A small race should come his way. (op 11-1)
Southwest Star(IRE), fifth on his debut at Lingfield, broke better this time but was still unable to reverse previous form with the third and fourth. He may have found this ground a bit too firm, as he looked uneasy in the final furlong and hung left. (op 5-1)
Group Therapy, bred for speed and a half-brother to Norfolk Stakes third Classic Encounter, was never a threat after a sluggish start and being restrained early on. However, he did make headway in the home straight and left a clear impression that he would be all the better for this debut experience. (op 13-2 tchd 6-1)
Higgy's Boy(IRE), whose yard got off the mark with their first juvenile runner at Kempton five days previously, missed the break and looked pretty clueless for most of the race. He should only improve for the experience. (tchd 9-2 and 6-1)

1000 RACECOURSE VIDEO SERVICES (S) STKS 5f 11y
3:00 (3:00) (Class 6) 2-Y-O **£1,943** (£578; £288; £144) **Stalls** Low

Form RPR
1 **No Point (IRE)** 2-8-6 .... TPO'Shea 6 46
(P A Blockley) *chsd ldr: drvn to ld over 1f out: rn green: rdn out to hold on fnl 50 yds* **11/4**[3]
0 **2** *hd* **Portway Lane**[8] 898 2-8-1 .... TolleyDean(5) 5 45
(W G M Turner) *led tl over 1f out: rallied wl u.p: jst hld* **5/2**[2]
6 **3** *1 1/2* **Riskie Blue (IRE)**[2] 971 2-8-7 ow1 .... JohnEgan 3 40
(J S Moore) *a 3rd: drvn to chse ldng pair whn hung lft over 1f out: nt qckn ins fnl f* **11/4**[3]
4 *9* **Scrap N'Dust** 2-8-3 .... LiamJones(3) 2 3
(W G M Turner) *s.i.s: sn drvn along and outpcd in rr: no ch fnl 2f* **9/4**[1]

64.22 secs (1.72) **Going Correction** -0.275s/f (Firm) **4** Ran SP% **112.7**
Speed ratings (Par 90):75,74,72,57
CSF £10.07 TOTE £4.40; EX 9.70.There was no bid for the winner.
Owner Mrs Joanna Hughes **Bred** Mrs J Hughes **Trained** Lambourn, Berks

FOCUS
A very weak event, even for a seller, with a field made up of just fillies. The time was poor. The second and third were well held on their respective debuts and the form should have no real bearing outside of this class.

NOTEBOOK
No Point(IRE) defied greenness to reel in the long-time leader close home and open her account at the first time of asking. She looked to win this a little cosily, and will improve for the experience, but this was a poor event and she is probably best kept to this grade. (op 7-2 tchd 4-1)
Portway Lane, who was slow to start on her debut at Folkestone eight days previously, showed decent early dash on this drop into this lowly company and was only reeled in near the line. This was obviously a step in the right direction and her trainer can place her to go one better in this grade. (op 11-4 tchd 3-1)
Riskie Blue(IRE), last of sixth on her debut at Warwick two days previously, again ran green on this drop into the bottom level and appeared a little uneasy on the firm surface. (op 9-4)
Scrap N'Dust, a January foal who attracted no interest at the sales, proved popular in the betting ring yet was always playing catch up after missing the break. (tchd 5-2)

1001 WEATHERBYS BLOODSTOCK INSURANCE MAIDEN STKS 1m 5y
3:30 (3:31) (Class 5) 3-Y-O+ **£2,914** (£867; £433; £216) **Stalls** Low

Form RPR
022- **1** **Shake On It**[200] 5527 3-8-11 78 .... (t) StephenCarson 6 71
(Eve Johnson Houghton) *t.k.h: chsd ldrs: led over 1f out: hrd rdn and hld on wl fnl f* **7/4**[2]
30- **2** *hd* **Gunner's View**[181] 5914 3-8-11 .... JamieSpencer 9 71
(B J Meehan) *chsd ldr: led jst ins fnl 3f tl over 1f out: rallied and str chal fnl f: r.o* **6/1**[3]
4- **3** *shd* **Binocular**[201] 5508 3-8-11 .... RichardHughes 8 70
(B W Hills) *led tl jst ins fnl 3f: rallied and str chal fnl f: r.o* **13/8**[1]
0- **4** *4* **Valley Observer (FR)**[310] 2287 3-8-11 .... AdamKirby 3 61+
(W R Swinburn) *sn bhd: hdwy and edgd rt 2f out: edgd lft 1f out: hld by first 3 fnl f: should improve* **16/1**
/0 **5** *3 1/2* **Lockerley Man**[51] 498 4-9-12 .... FergusSweeney 4 57?
(W S Kittow) *mid-div: effrt over 2f out: hung lft over 1f out: no imp* **50/1**
5-60 **6** *3 1/2* **Fly By Jove (IRE)**[73] 274 4-9-12 46 .... LPKeniry 1 49?
(Jane Southcombe) *chsd ldrs: hrd rdn and outpcd over 2f out: sn btn* **100/1**
0- **7** *1/2* **Shine And Rise (IRE)**[151] 6434 3-8-11 .... MickyFenton 11 44
(C G Cox) *stdd s: plld hrd towards rr: wd bnd after 3f: n.d after: styd on steadily fnl 2f* **15/2**
3060 **8** *1/2* **Task Complete**[15] 801 4-9-4 45 .... (b) NeilChalmers(3) 5 42
(Jean-Rene Auvray) *mid-div: shkn up and outpcd fnl 3f* **80/1**
000- **9** *4* **Fun In The Sun**[257] 3895 3-8-11 40 .... SteveDrowne 10 34
(Jane Southcombe) *reluctant early: wnt rt and lost grnd after s: sn wl bhd: passed btn horses in st* **150/1**
0- **10** *7* **Just Matty**[317] 2063 4-9-12 .... DaneO'Neill 7 21
(J G M O'Shea) *t.k.h: in tch: nt handle bnd after 3f: rn green and lost pl: n.d fnl 4f* **66/1**
11 *11* **Interactive (IRE)**[33] 4-9-12 .... ChrisCatlin 2 —
(Andrew Turnell) *s.s: gd hdwy and prom after 2f: wknd 3f out* **25/1**

1m 39.3s (-1.80) **Going Correction** -0.05s/f (Good)
WFA 3 from 4yo 15lb **11** Ran SP% **116.6**
Speed ratings (Par 103):107,106,106,102,99 95,95,94,90,83 72
CSF £12.36 TOTE £3.20: £1.50, £1.70, £1.50; EX 14.10 Trifecta £19.50 Pool £519.07 - 18.83 winning units..
Owner Eden Racing (III) **Bred** Car Colston Hall Stud **Trained** Blewbury, Oxon

FOCUS
No strength in depth to this maiden, which saw the three market leaders play out a tight finish. The form is fair but the fifth and sixth hold it down.

The Form Book, Raceform Ltd, Compton, RG20 6NL

Just Matty Official explanation: jockey said gelding hung left

1002 WEATHERBYS PRINTING H'CAP 1m 2f 46y
4:00 (4:00) (Class 6) (0-65,65) 4-Y-0+ £2,266 (£674; £337; £168) Stalls Low

Form				RPR
13-0	1		**Double Spectre (IRE)**[33] 651 5-9-3 64 ... DaneO'Neill 3 (Jean-Rene Auvray) *in tch: effrt over 2f out: led ins fnl f: drvn out* 6/1[3]	72
-212	2	¾	**Can Can Star**[58] 445 4-9-4 65 ... ShaneKelly 12 (A W Carroll) *wd: hld up in midfield: rdn and hdwy 2f out: r.o to take 2nd nr fin* 10/3[1]	72
100-	3	¾	**Good Article (IRE)**[173] 6070 6-9-0 64 ... RPCleary(3) 9 (D K Ivory) *t.k.h: in tch: led 2f out tl ins fnl f: nt qckn fnl f* 6/1[3]	69
3-06	4	¾	**Russian Dream (IRE)**[50] 507 4-9-1 62 ... (p) AdamKirby 13 (W R Swinburn) *stdd s: hld up in rr: rdn and hdwy 2f out: hung lft over 1f out: styd on same pce* 11/1	66
-065	5	nk	**Odessa Star (USA)**[23] 712 4-9-4 65 ... EddieAhern 10 (J G Portman) *plld hrd: w ldrs: led 4f out tl 2f out: one pce fnl f: 4th and btn whn hmpd and snatched up fnl stride* 8/1	69+
/00-	6	¾	**Tom Bell (IRE)**[262] 2998 7-8-4 51 oh1 ... ChrisCatlin 7 (J G M O'Shea) *towards rr: rdn and styd on fnl 3f: nvr nrr* 20/1	53
3-60	7	nk	**Orphina (IRE)**[61] 402 4-8-4 51 oh6 ... (t) JimmyQuinn 1 (B G Powell) *prom: rdn over 2f out: no ex over 1f out* 14/1	52
6654	8	1	**Just Fly**[9] 888 7-8-0 52 ... (v) KevinGhunowa(5) 4 (Dr J R J Naylor) *in tch: effrt over 2f out: no imp* 9/1	52
4-00	9	1	**Hatch A Plan (IRE)**[6] 753 6-8-13 65 ... TravisBlock(5) 11 (Mouse Hamilton-Fairley) *hld up towards rr: shkn up 3f out: nvr rchd ldrs* 11/2[2]	63
	10	½	**Baileys Best**[109] 6088 5-9-1 62 ... FergusSweeney 6 (J G M O'Shea) *led tl 4f out: hrd rdn and wknd over 2f out* 12/1	59
000/	11	11	**Backlash**[667] 2539 6-8-4 51 oh6 ... HayleyTurner 2 (A W Carroll) *v.s.a: a bhd: rdn and no ch fnl 2f* 16/1	27
0060	12	6	**Miss Sudbrook (IRE)**[51] 497 5-8-4 51 oh6 ... RichardMullen 8 (A W Carroll) *t.k.h: in tch: drvn along 4f out: sn lost pl: eased whn no ch fnl f* 50/1	15

2m 10.17s (-0.83) **Going Correction** -0.05s/f (Good) 12 Ran SP% 123.4
Speed ratings (Par 101):101,100,99,99,98 98,98,97,96,96 87,82
CSF £27.41 CT £130.87 TOTE £7.70: £2.90, £1.60, £2.20; EX 33.30 Trifecta £200.00 Pool £338.15 - 1.20 winning units..
Owner The Dragon Partnership **Bred** R Bailey **Trained** Upper Lambourn, Berks

FOCUS
A moderate handicap in which there was no pace on early and a couple pulled hard as a result. Ordinary form for the grade.
Just Fly Official explanation: jockey said gelding ran too free

1003 REDCIRCLERACING.CO.UK SYNDICATE H'CAP 2m 1f 34y
4:30 (4:30) (Class 5) (0-75,74) 4-Y-0+ £3,238 (£963; £481; £240) Stalls Low

Form				RPR
026-	1		**Dark Parade (ARG)**[197] 5587 6-8-6 55 oh1 ... JamieSpencer 5 (P D Evans) *chsd ldr tl 5f out: trckd ldrs after tl led over 1f out: rdn clr: readily* 4/1[3]	66+
154-	2	2½	**Cantabilly (IRE)**[16] 6070 4-9-7 74 ... RichardHughes 4 (R J Hodges) *t.k.h: settled in rr: hdwy to press ldrs over 1f out: nt pce of wnr: kpt on to take 2nd nr fin* 4/1[3]	79
1321	3	hd	**Lorikeet**[26] 691 8-9-6 72 ... JamesDoyle(3) 6 (Noel T Chance) *hld up in 5th: hdwy 5f out: led ins fnl 3f tl over 1f out: one pce* 9/4[1]	77
0/06	4	5	**Lord Nellsson**[28] 677 11-8-6 55 oh3 ... HayleyTurner 2 (Andrew Turnell) *in tch: wnt 2nd 5f out: led briefly 3f out: wknd over 1f out* 6/1	54
522-	5	8	**Kayf Aramis**[166] 6205 5-9-11 74 ... (p) SteveDrowne 3 (J L Spearing) *led tl 3f out: wknd over 2f out* 3/1[2]	66+
0/0-	6	19	**Coustou (IRE)**[40] 5610 7-8-13 62 ... (p) JimCrowley 1 (R M Stronge) *chsd ldrs: grad lost pl fr 6f out: bhd fnl 4f* 33/1	29

3m 49.96s (0.36) **Going Correction** -0.05s/f (Good)
WFA 4 from 5yo+ 4lb 6 Ran SP% 113.0
Speed ratings (Par 103):97,95,95,93,89 80
CSF £20.34 TOTE £5.20: £2.40, £2.00; EX 16.80.
Owner N J Jones **Bred** Firmamento **Trained** Pandy, Monmouths

FOCUS
An ordinary staying handicap and with such a small field the pace was always likely to be modest. The front five were in a line across the track passing the two-furlong pole. The winner was value for further but the form is not strong.

1004 BET365.COM H'CAP 5f 11y
5:00 (5:01) (Class 5) (0-75,75) 3-Y-0+ £3,238 (£963; £481; £240) Stalls Low

Form				RPR
000-	1		**Spanish Ace**[215] 5148 6-9-10 72 ... JamieSpencer 14 (J M Bradley) *prom: led ins fnl f: rdn out* 7/1[3]	84+
060-	2	2	**Willhewiz**[234] 4629 7-9-4 66 ... JohnEgan 13 (M S Saunders) *led at gd pce tl ins fnl f: nt pce of wnr* 9/1	71
33-4	3	½	**Who's Winning (IRE)**[91] 91 6-9-7 72 ... RichardKingscote(3) 2 (B G Powell) *chsd ldrs: effrt 2f out: kpt on fnl f* 12/1	75
-051	4	hd	**Fizzlephut (IRE)**[12] 835 5-9-10 72 ... PaulFitzsimons 11 (Miss J R Tooth) *chsd ldr tl over 1f out: one pce* 6/1[2]	74
346-	5	nk	**Chatshow (USA)**[114] 6858 6-9-4 66 ... RichardMullen 4 (A W Carroll) *towards rr: r.o fnl 2f: nrst fin* 16/1	67+
000-	6	1¾	**Malapropism**[177] 6009 7-9-6 75 ... ThomasO'Brien(7) 15 (M R Channon) *chsd ldrs: hrd rdn and edgd lft 1f out: no ex* 10/1	70
2013	7	hd	**Sir Douglas**[17] 774 4-9-3 70 ... TolleyDean(5) 6 (R A Harris) *wnt rt s: rdn along towards rr: styd on u.p fnl 2f* 8/1	64
3544	8	1	**Hereford Boy**[7] 925 3-8-6 68 ... RPCleary(3) 3 (D K Ivory) *mid-div on rail: pushed along and kpt on steadily fnl 2f* 16/1	54+
3055	9	¾	**Ivory Lace**[41] 592 6-9-10 75 ... JamesDoyle(3) 16 (S Woodman) *outpcd towards rr on outside: nvr nrr* 10/1	63
400-	10	nk	**Shes Minnie**[177] 6009 4-9-12 74 ... FergusSweeney 7 (J G M O'Shea) *hmpd s: pushed along towards rr: n.d* 25/1	61
4443	11	nk	**Kempsey**[16] 787 5-8-7 62 ... (b) RyanBird(7) 5 (J J Bridger) *in tch: rdn 3f out: sn outpcd* 16/1	48
30-5	12	1	**Mind The Style**[9] 885 3-8-13 75 ... AmirQuinn(3) 1 (W G M Turner) *chsd ldrs on rail tl hrd rdn and btn 2f out* 14/1	52
56-0	13	nk	**Brandywell Boy (IRE)**[26] 692 4-9-13 75 ... JimCrowley 9 (D J S Ffrench Davis) *hmpd s: rdn along and a bhd* 14/1	56
-605	14	5	**Avery**[8] 900 3-8-2 61 oh6 ... (b[1]) JimmyQuinn 8 (R J Hodges) *hmpd s: a bhd* 50/1	19
-220	15	shd	**Devon Flame**[15] 803 8-9-1 63 ... RichardHughes 10 (R J Hodges) *mid-div tl wknd 2f out: eased whn no ch ins fnl f* 4/1[1]	26

60.63 secs (-1.87) **Going Correction** -0.275s/f (Firm)
WFA 3 from 4yo+ 11lb 15 Ran SP% 130.6
Speed ratings (Par 103):103,99,99,98,98 95,95,93,92,91 91,89,89,81,81
CSF £74.32 CT £790.57 TOTE £7.60: £2.40, £3.30, £4.30; EX 66.20 Trifecta £449.10 Pool £708.53 - 1.12 winning units. Place 6 £173.58, Place 5 £84.04..
Owner racingshares.co.uk **Bred** Farleigh Court Racing Partnership **Trained** Sedbury, Gloucs

FOCUS
A competitive, if modest sprint handicap in which the draw did not play much of a part, but the ability to race handily certainly did. The first four were always at the sharp end and it proved impossible for anything to come from the back. Spanish Ace was one of a number who went into this potentially well handicapped. Fair form for the grade.
Devon Flame Official explanation: jockey said gelding lost its action
T/Plt: £237.00 to a £1 stake. Pool: £68,839.45. 211.95 winning tickets. T/Qpdt: £12.20 to a £1 stake. Pool: £4,881.80. 295.90 winning tickets. LM

911 MAISONS-LAFFITTE (R-H)
Wednesday, April 11

OFFICIAL GOING: Good

1005a PRIX DJEBEL (LISTED RACE) (C&G) (STRAIGHT) 7f (S)
2:35 (2:36) 3-Y-0 £17,568 (£7,027; £5,270; £3,514; £1,757)

			RPR
1		**US Ranger (USA)**[122] 3-9-2 ... C-PLemaire 1 (J-C Rouget, France) 1/2[1]	118+
2	4	**Prior Warning**[26] 695 3-9-2 ... DBoeuf 6 (D Smaga, France)	104
3	1	**Stoneside (IRE)**[171] 6118 3-9-2 ... OPeslier 7 (Rod Collet, France)	101
4	3	**Carimo (IRE)**[9] 3-9-2 ... JVictoire 5 (J-P Gallorini, France)	93
5	hd	**Flyng Teapot (IRE)**[12] 3-9-2 ... CSoumillon 2 (C Boutin, France)	93
6	2	**Another True Story**[185] 5829 3-9-2 ... RKoplik 3 (Z Koplik, France)	87
7	nk	**Alaska River (GER)** 3-9-2 ... AStarke 4 (P Schiergen, Germany)	86

1m 23.7s (-6.60) **Going Correction** -0.75s/f (Hard) 7 Ran SP% 66.7
Speed ratings: 107,102,101,97,97 95,95
PARI-MUTUEL: WIN 1.50; PL 1.10, 1.30; SF 3.30.
Owner Michael Tabor **Bred** Joseph Allen **Trained** Pau, France
■ Stewards' Enquiry : R Koplik 200 fine; excessive use of the whip

NOTEBOOK
US Ranger(USA), unbeaten in three starts at the lesser tracks at two, has been partly purchased by Michael Tabor over the winter and he will no doubt have been delighted to see the son of Danzig make an impressive return to action. Expected to come on for the outing, he raced a shade keenly against the rail and was undoubtedly well placed throughout, but he showed a smart change of pace to quickly settle the outcome and won with any amount in hand, leaving a couple of previous Listed winners behind. With Ballydoyle being light on 2000 Guineas contenders this season it would come as no surprise to see him supplemented for the first Classic of the year. He was given quotes around the 12-1 mark for Newmarket.

1006a PRIX IMPRUDENCE (LISTED RACE) (FILLIES) (STRAIGHT) 7f (S)
3:05 (3:08) 3-Y-0 £17,568 (£7,027; £5,270; £3,514; £1,757)

			RPR
1		**Magic America (USA)**[165] 6228 3-9-0 ... JMurtagh 15 (Mme C Head-Maarek, France) 32/10[1]	107
2	2	**Winter Fashion (FR)**[22] 3-9-0 ... TJarnet 5 (F Head, France)	101
3	snk	**Beauty Is Truth (IRE)**[194] 5654 3-9-0 ... (b) TThulliez 3 (Robert Collet, France) 21/1[2]	101
4	½	**Galaxie Des Sables (FR)**[19] 748 3-9-0 ... RonanThomas 10 (Mme N Rossio, France)	100
5	1	**Fairy Dress (USA)**[19] 748 3-9-0 ... JAuge 17 (Robert Collet, France)	97
6	snk	**Viola Carlita (FR)**[148] 3-9-0 ... YBarberot 2 (J-P Gallorini, France)	97
7	1	**Nolas Lolly (IRE)**[180] 3-9-0 ... SPasquier 6 (U Suter, France)	94
8	hd	**Cicerole (FR)**[176] 6046 3-9-0 ... IMendizabal 7 (J-C Rouget, France)	93
9	2½	**Zut Alors (IRE)**[142] 6546 3-9-0 ... CSoumillon 11 (Robert Collet, France)	87
10	1½	**Rakiza (IRE)**[142] 3-9-0 ... DBonilla 9 (F Head, France)	83
0		**Ascot Family (IRE)**[194] 5664 3-9-0 ... ABadel 1 (A Lyon, France)	—
0		**Boccassini (GER)**[234] 4644 3-9-0 ... AStarke 14 (M Rulec, Germany)	—
0		**Ikat (IRE)**[32] 3-9-0 ... C-PLemaire 12 (D Sepulchre, France)	—
0		**Highest Height (FR)**[140] 3-9-0 ... DBoeuf 4 (D Smaga, France)	—
0		**Moquette (USA)**[160] 3-9-0 ... JVictoire 16 (H-A Pantall, France)	—
0		**Belle Aire (GER)**[26] 696 3-9-0 ... WMongil 13 (D K Richardson, Germany)	—
0		**Only Answer**[9] 3-9-0 ... OPeslier 8 (A Fabre, France)	—

1m 24.5s (-5.80) **Going Correction** -0.75s/f (Hard) 17 Ran SP% 28.4
Speed ratings: 103,100,100,99,98 98,97,97,94,92 —,—,—,—,— —,—
PARI-MUTUEL: WIN 4.20; PL 2.10, 6.60, 5.70; DF 95.60.
Owner Dr T A Ryan **Bred** Castleton Group **Trained** Chantilly, France

NOTEBOOK
Magic America(USA), who finished sixth in last year's Cheveley Park and was a winner of a Group 3 race subsequently, made a winning reappearance and is now a possible candidate for the 1000 Guineas. She picked up well in the closing stages, was going further clear at the line and will be very much suited by the step up to a mile.

LEICESTER (R-H)

Thursday, April 12

OFFICIAL GOING: Good to firm

Wind: almost nil

1007 LADBROKES.COM MEDIAN AUCTION MAIDEN STKS 5f 2y

2:10 (2:10) (Class 5) 2-Y-O **£3,238** (£963; £481; £240) **Stalls** Low

Form RPR

1 **Kersaint (IRE)** 2-9-3 .... NCallan 6 86
(K A Ryan) *in tch: rdn and hdwy 2f out: rdn to ld ins fnl f: jst hld on* **10/13**

2 2 *shd* **Silver Guest**[9] [898] 2-9-3 .... JamieSpencer 5 86
(M R Channon) *stdd s: hld up bhd: hdwy 2f out: rdn 1f out: chsd wnr ins fnl f: r.o: jst hld* **8/131**

3 *1 1/2* **Bosun Breese** 2-9-3 .... JohnEgan 2 80
(P W D'Arcy) *chsd ldr: rdn to ld jst over 1f out: hdd ins fnl f: one pced* **14/1**

4 *1 1/4* **Gaitskell** 2-9-3 .... GrahamGibbons 8 75
(R Hollinshead) *chsd ldrs: rdn over 1f out: kpt on same pce insde fnl f* **33/1**

6 5 *3 1/2* **Turn And River (IRE)**[12] [845] 2-8-5 .... PatrickDonaghy(7) 9 56
(M Brittain) *led: rdn over 2f out: hdd jst over 1f out: fdd ins fnl f* **14/1**

6 *1/2* **Avertitop** 2-9-3 .... RichardHughes 7 59
(R Hannon) *hld up in tch on outer: rdn wl over 1f out: wknd 1f out* **8/12**

7 *nk* **Little Pete (IRE)** 2-9-3 .... DaneO'Neill 4 58
(R A Farrant) *s.i.s: swtchd rt after 1f: effrt and rdn wl over 1f out: wknd 1f out* **50/1**

0 8 *7* **Silver Wind**[12] [845] 2-9-0 .... StephenDonohoe(3) 1 30
(P D Evans) *rrd in stalls: s.i.s: a outpcd and bhd* **16/1**

9 *3/4* **Kairaba** 2-9-3 .... EddieAhern 3 27
(J Pearce) *rr: in tch: rdn after 2f out: sn struggling and no ch* **12/1**

60.86 secs (-0.04) **Going Correction** -0.20s/f (Firm) **9** Ran SP% **113.9**
Speed ratings (Par 92):92,91,89,87,81 81,80,69,68
CSF £16.30 TOTE £11.30: £2.10, £1.02, £3.60; EX 20.50 Trifecta £201.70 Pool £483.01 - 1.70 winning units..
Owner Brendan P Hayes **Bred** Kilfrush Stud **Trained** Hambleton, N Yorks

FOCUS
An average juvenile event, run at a solid early pace. The first pair came clear and the form is rated through the runner-up.

NOTEBOOK
Kersaint(IRE), the first foal of a three-year-old 1m winner in France, showed a great attitude under pressure in the final furlong and just did enough to register a winning debut. He is clearly well forward, handled the quick surface well, and looks a fair prospect for connections. A sixth furlong will be to his liking in due course. (op 12-1 tchd 14-1 and 9-1)
Silver Guest, who lost out at the start on his debut nine days previously, was ridden with patience and again ran distinctly green when the gun was put to his head. He eventually hit full stride, but found the winner too resolute when it mattered and is clearly still learning his trade. No doubt he has the scope to win a race or two, however. (tchd 8-11)
Bosun Breese, a 15,000gns first foal of a triple 7f-1m winner, travelled nicely on the stands' side and showed good early pace. He got undone by his lack of experience, but his stable has made a good start with their juveniles, and he should improve enough for this experience to get closer next time out. (op 9-1)
Gaitskell, who cost 30,000gns, was another to show up well early on before finding just the same pace when asked for his effort. He will be better suited by another furlong in due course and has a future. (op 50-1 tchd 28-1)
Turn And River(IRE), sixth in the Broklesby 12 days previously, showed decent early dash yet had nothing left in the tank when pressed for the lead and was eventually well beaten. It remains to be seen which way she goes. (tchd 18-1)

1008 LADBROKES.COM (S) STKS 5f 218y

2:45 (2:45) (Class 6) 3-Y-O **£2,266** (£674; £337; £168) **Stalls** Centre

Form RPR

5156 1 **Divertimenti (IRE)**[10] [885] 3-9-5 74 .... (p) JamieSpencer 7 71+
(M J Wallace) *stdd s: hld up wl in rr: hdwy over 2f out: led over 1f out: edgd rt but sn clr: easily* **13/81**

-400 2 *5* **Pat Will (IRE)**[50] [512] 3-9-0 50 .... (v1) SteveDrowne 8 51
(P D Evans) *led tl rdn and hdd over 1f out: kpt on but no ch w wnr* **25/1**

4154 3 *shd* **Strike Force**[9] [900] 3-9-5 62 .... (p) PaulHanagan 2 56
(R A Harris) *bhd and pushed along: hdwy 2f out: styd on u.p fnl f: nvr nrr* **9/22**

6-54 4 *1* **Slipasearcher (IRE)**[50] [512] 3-8-11 59 .... (b) StephenDonohoe(3) 1 48
(P D Evans) *chsd ldrs: rdn wl over 2f out: kpt on same pce* **13/23**

0400 5 *3/4* **Tenterhooks (IRE)**[13] [832] 3-8-6 45 .... (be) PatrickMathers(3) 5 40
(A J McCabe) *chsd ldrs: rdn 1/2-way: kpt on same pce fnl f* **28/1**

0-40 6 *3* **Sherjawy (IRE)**[9] [900] 3-9-0 57 .... (b) AdrianMcCarthy 4 36
(Miss Z C Davison) *chsd ldrs: rdn 1/2-way: wknd over 1f out* **25/1**

-464 7 *1/2* **Suntan Lady (IRE)**[10] [894] 3-8-9 49 .... (b1) EdwardCreighton 3 30
(Miss V Haigh) *hld up in midfield: hdwy 3f out: rdn and wknd over 2f out* **20/1**

60-3 8 *3/4* **Almora Guru**[10] [894] 3-8-9 59 .... DavidAllan 6 28
(W M Brisbourne) *chsd ldrs: rdn over 2f out: wknd over 1f out* **8/1**

300 9 *nk* **Bahama Gold**[29] [676] 3-8-9 45 .... MickyFenton 15 27
(D G Bridgwater) *in tch: rdn and hdwy 3f out: wknd wl over 1f out* **33/1**

420- 10 *shd* **Hester Brook (IRE)**[206] [5434] 3-8-9 57 .... FergusSweeney 13 27
(J G M O'Shea) *s.i.s: sn in midfield: swtchd lft over 3f out: rdn and wknd over 2f out* **10/1**

0-00 11 *shd* **Vital Tryst**[19] [769] 3-9-0 35 .... (v1) TPQueally 9 31
(J G Given) *racd in midfield: lost pl over 3f out: no ch after* **33/1**

0- 12 *12* **Skiddaw Fox**[149] [6480] 3-9-0 .... TomEaves 10 —
(Mrs L Williamson) *hld up in midfield: hmpd and lost pl over 3f out: no ch after: t.o* **66/1**

0006 13 *2 1/2* **Haydock Express (IRE)**[13] [832] 3-8-11 45 .... JerryO'Dwyer(3) 11 —
(Peter Grayson) *chsd ldrs tl 1/2-way: sn bhd: t.o* **25/1**

06-0 14 *1 1/4* **Emerald Sky**[60] [429] 3-8-9 26 .... HayleyTurner 12 —
(R Brotherton) *chsd ldrs tl over 3f out: sn wknd: t.o* **80/1**

1m 11.91s (-1.29) **Going Correction** -0.20s/f (Firm) **14** Ran SP% **118.2**
Speed ratings (Par 96):100,93,93,91,90 86,86,85,84,84 84,68,65,63
CSF £55.28 TOTE £2.40: £1.30, £4.00, £1.50; EX 50.90 Trifecta £229.70 Part won. Pool £323.66 - 0.44 winning units..The winner bought by Conor Dore for 11,500gns
Owner Mrs Sonia Rogers **Bred** Airlie Stud **Trained** Newmarket, Suffolk
■ Stewards' Enquiry : Fergus Sweeney three-day ban; careless riding (Apr 23-25)

FOCUS
A weak seller and the winner bounced back to near his best, hence winning as he was entitled to. The runner-up sets the level for the form.

1009 LADBROKES.COM CONDITIONS STKS 5f 218y

3:20 (3:21) (Class 4) 3-Y-O

£6,232 (£1,866; £933; £467; £233; £117) **Stalls** Centre

Form RPR

153- 1 **He's A Humbug (IRE)**[205] [5455] 3-9-0 87 .... NCallan 7 88+
(K A Ryan) *t.k.h: led after 1f: mde rest: rdn wl over 1f out: flashed tail u.p: edgd lft ins fnl f: r.o wl* **11/41**

120- 2 *1* **Southandwest (IRE)**[209] [5335] 3-9-0 92 .... JohnEgan 1 85+
(J S Moore) *plld hrd: led for 1f out: hld up bhd ldrs: rdn 2f out: r.o u.p to chse wnr ins fnl f: a hld* **3/12**

310- 3 *1* **Northern Fling**[229] [4824] 3-9-0 88 .... AdrianTNicholls 2 82
(D Nicholls) *stdd s: hdwy to chse ldrs over 3f out: rdn over 2f out: kpt on same pce ins fnl f* **6/1**

132- 4 *1 1/4* **Teasing**[132] [6659] 3-8-9 77 .... JimmyQuinn 6 73
(J Pearce) *trckd ldng pair: rdn over 2f out: unable qck fnl f* **20/1**

412- 5 *shd* **Fool Me (IRE)**[248] [4200] 3-8-12 90 .... RichardMullen 4 76
(E S McMahon) *t.k.h: sn chsng ldr: rdn and ev ch wl over 1f out: wknd ins fnl f* **11/2**

145- 6 *3/4* **Dowlleh**[186] [5829] 3-9-0 78 .... JoeFanning 3 76?
(T T Clement) *t.k.h: hld up bhd: hdwy and rdn 2f out: eased whn btn ins fnl f* **16/1**

052- 7 *3 1/2* **Nina Blini**[119] [6822] 3-8-9 89 .... JamieSpencer 5 60
(B J Meehan) *hld up in tch: hdwy over 2f out: rdn over 1f out: wknd 1f out* **4/13**

1m 12.95s (-0.25) **Going Correction** -0.20s/f (Firm) **7** Ran SP% **112.0**
Speed ratings (Par 100):93,91,90,88,88 87,82
CSF £10.77 TOTE £3.80: £1.80, £2.20; EX 9.80 Trifecta £33.50 Pool £691.81 - 14.63 winning units..
Owner David Fravigar, Kathy Dixon **Bred** Denis McDonnell **Trained** Hambleton, N Yorks

FOCUS
An interesting three-year-old conditions sprint. However, the lack of early pace spoilt a few chances and the form is limited by the fourth/sixth.

1010 LADBROKES.COM KIBWORTH H'CAP 1m 1f 218y

3:55 (3:55) (Class 3) (0-95,87) 3-Y-O **£4,508** (£4,508; £1,038; £519; £258) **Stalls** High

Form RPR

-211 1 **Zar Solitario**[22] [719] 3-9-7 **87** .... JoeFanning 5 100+
(M Johnston) *led for 1f: chsd ldr tl led again over 3f out: clr over 1f out: jnd on line* **10/111**

-245 1 *dht* **New Beginning (IRE)**[43] [584] 3-8-10 **76** .... PaulHanagan 1 84
(Mrs S Lamyman) *hld up wl bhd: hdwy over 3f out: rdn over 1f out: edgd rt fnl f: styd on wl to join ldr on line* **33/1**

4-64 3 *hd* **Sahrati**[27] [694] 3-8-11 **77** .... EddieAhern 6 85
(C E Brittain) *hld up off pce in midfield: rdn over 3f out: styd on u.p wl over 1f out: kpt on ins fnl f* **10/1**

060- 4 *8* **Moonwalking**[182] [5916] 3-8-9 **75** .... DaleGibson 3 67
(Jedd O'Keeffe) *hld up wl off pce in last: rdn over 4f out: styd on past btn horses fnl f: nvr on terms* **33/1**

555- 5 *1* **King Joshua (IRE)**[175] [6066] 3-8-10 **76** .... JohnEgan 2 66
(D R C Elsworth) *t.k.h: led after 2f: hdd and rdn over 3f out: chsd wnr tl wknd over 1f out* **9/1**

321- 6 *2* **Eglevski (IRE)**[192] [5720] 3-9-0 **80** .... TedDurcan 4 66
(J L Dunlop) *t.k.h: led after 1f tl 8f out: chsd ldrs: rdn wl over 3f out: wknd 2f out* **11/23**

11-0 7 *5* **Sweeney (IRE)**[60] [436] 3-9-6 **86** .... NCallan 8 62
(M A Jarvis) *t.k.h: hld up bhd ldrs: rdn to chse ldng pair over 3f out: edgd rt over 2f out: sn wknd* **9/22**

2m 4.68s (-3.62) **Going Correction** -0.20s/f (Firm) **7** Ran SP% **110.9**
Speed ratings (Par 102): **106,106,105,99,98 97,93**WIN ZS £0.80, NB £11.50; PL ZS £1.30, NB £3.90; EX ZS/NB £24.80, NB/ZS £11.30; CSF ZS/NB £16.74, NB/ZS £30.35; TC ZS/NB/SI £91.70, NB/ZS/SI £169.08 TRIFECTA ZS/NB/SI £40.40 - 6.05 winning units. NB/ZS/SI £120.00 - 2.04 winning units. Pool £690.027 Owner.
Owner Sheikh Mohammed **Bred** Azienda Agricola Razza Del Sole Srl **Trained** Middleham Moor, N Yorks
■ Stewards' Enquiry : Joe Fanning 18-day ban: failed to ride out when he would have won outright (Apr 23-May 10)
Paul Hanagan two-day ban: careless riding (Apr 23-24)

FOCUS
A fair three-year-old handicap which was run at a strong early pace. The form looks sound enough.

NOTEBOOK
Zar Solitario, bidding for a hat-trick from a 10lb lower mark having won his last two outings on the sand, was just caught on the line having raced up with the searching early pace. His rider appeared to take things a little easy, and later received an 18-day suspension for failing to ride out fully to the line, but that looked a touch harsh as the son of Singspiel was surely tiring after his early exertions and being sent for home before the final furlong. He remains progressive, should get a little further in time, and is the type his leading trainer tends to excel with. (op 33-1)
New Beginning(IRE) relished the strong early pace and bounced back to his best by just doing enough to get up late on and share the spoils. The switch to turf was in his favour, he gets the tip well now and is open to a little more improvement, but no doubt the Handicapper will have his say for this. (op 33-1)
Sahrati has slipped to a decent mark now as a result of not taking to the All-Weather during the winter and returned to form with a solid effort in defeat. He was another to really enjoy the strong early pace. (op 11-1 tchd 14-1)
Moonwalking was doing all of his best work towards the finish on this seasonal bow and clearly got the longer trip. He can be ridden more prominently now connections know he stays and improvement is likely for the run. (op 25-1)
King Joshua(IRE), making his debut for David Elsworth, paid for refusing to settle and was well below his previous best. He looks tricky. (op 7-1 tchd 12-1)
Eglevski(IRE) proved far too keen for his own good on this return from a 192-day break and was disappointing. He has the scope to do a bit better this term and, while he will obviously need to settle better in the future, it will be disappointing if he cannot defy his current mark. (op 9-2)
Sweeney(IRE), too keen when tried in Listed company in France on his last outing 60 days previously, again lost any chance by refusing to settle and ran no sort of race. He is in real danger of going the wrong way. Official explanation: jockey said that gelding ran too free (op 4-1)

1011 LADBROKES.COM MAIDEN STKS 1m 1f 218y

4:30 (4:32) (Class 5) 3-Y-O+ **£4,533** (£1,348; £674; £336) **Stalls** High

Form RPR

052- 1 **Bergonzi (IRE)**[152] [6447] 3-8-8 78 .... RobertHavlin 10 73
(J H M Gosden) *in tch: hdwy over 3f out: chsd ldr 2f out: styd on u.p to ld ins fnl f: hld on wl nr fin* **11/23**

0- 2 *nk* **Bedizen**[334] [1674] 4-9-13 .... NickyMackay 8 73+
(Sir Michael Stoute) *t.k.h: chsd ldrs: rdn over 1f out: ev ch ins fnl f: kpt on* **7/1**

524- **3** *1 1/2* **Alpes Maritimes**[192] [5720] 3-8-8 75 .... TedDurcan 4 70
(G Wragg) *t.k.h: chsd ldrs: led and edgd rt u.p over 2f out: hdd ins fnl f: kpt on same pce* **9/2**[2]

4 *hd* **Gold Prospect** 3-8-8 .... JamieSpencer 12 69+
(M L W Bell) *s.i.s: t.k.h: hld up in rr: swtchd lft over 3f out: rn wl fnl f: nt rch ldrs* **7/2**[1]

5 *1 1/4* **Kasban**[171] [6151] 3-8-8 .... MartinDwyer 6 67+
(E A L Dunlop) *rn green early: hld up in midfield: hdwy over 3f out: rdn over 2f out: kpt on steadily: nt rch ldrs* **12/1**

6 *1/2* **Heron Bay** 3-8-8 .... SteveDrowne 17 66
(G Wragg) *s.i.s: hld up bhd: pushed along and hdwy 3f out: r.o wl ins fnl f: nrst fin* **16/1**

- **7** *shd* **Motarjm (USA)** 3-8-8 .... NCallan 14 66
(M A Jarvis) *hld up in midfield: hdwy to chse ldrs over 3f out: rdn 2f out: kpt on same pce* **7/2**[1]

06- **8** *nk* **Lady Songbird (IRE)**[257] [3946] 4-9-8 .... AdamKirby 1 60
(W R Swinburn) *hld up bhd: hdwy 3f out: chsng ldrs and rdn over 1f out: no hdwy fnl f* **25/1**

6 **9** *7* **Blue Bird's Dream**[19] [769] 4-9-13 .... JimmyQuinn 5 51
(E J Alston) *t.k.h: chsd ldr tl led over 3f out: rdn and hdd over 2f out: sn wknd* **66/1**

0- **10** *1 3/4* **Elusory**[162] [6298] 3-8-8 .... SebSanders 11 48
(J L Dunlop) *hld up in midfield: rdn over 3f out: no prog over 1f out* **16/1**

660- **11** *1* **Finnegans Rainbow**[24] [6972] 5-9-8 37 .... RussellKennemore(5) 2 46
(M C Chapman) *t.k.h: led tl rdn and hdd over 3f out: sn wknd* **250/1**

00-4 **12** *3/4* **Herninski**[44] [181] 4-9-3 42 .... NicolPolli(5) 13 39
(M C Chapman) *hld up in midfield: rdn and wknd over 3f out* **200/1**

0-0 **13** *3/4* **Sir Duke (IRE)**[19] [769] 3-8-8 .... JohnEgan 3 43
(P W D'Arcy) *in tch: rdn and wknd over 3f out* **80/1**

0-00 **14** *4* **Filliemou (IRE)**[52] [495] 6-9-8 33 .... ShaneKelly 16 30
(A W Carroll) *hld up in rr: rdn over 3f out: sn lost tch* **250/1**

15 *10* **Quite A Splash (USA)** 3-8-8 .... MickyFenton 7 15
(S Curran) *s.i.s: a bhd: t.o* **200/1**

0555 **16** *1* **Hometomammy**[15] [812] 5-9-6 44 .... WilliamCarson(7) 15 13
(P W Hiatt) *racd in midfield: rdn and lost pl wl over 3f out: t.o* **125/1**

2m 6.88s (-1.42) **Going Correction** -0.20s/f (Firm)
WFA 3 from 4yo+ 19lb **16** Ran SP% **119.1**
Speed ratings (Par 103):97,96,95,95,94 94,93,93,88,86 85,85,84,81,73 72
CSF £42.71 TOTE £7.30: £2.00, £3.90, £1.80; EX 44.50 Trifecta £148.60 Part won. Pool £209.39 - 0.60 winning units..
Owner H R H Princess Haya Of Jordan **Bred** Deerforest Stud **Trained** Newmarket, Suffolk
■ Stewards' Enquiry : Ted Durcan two-day ban: careless riding (Apr 23-24)

FOCUS
An interesting maiden, but the first and third dictate it is not a strong one and it was slowly run. Several in behind look potential improvers, however.

1012 LADBROKESCASINO.COM MAIDEN STKS 1m 3f 183y
5:05 (5:06) (Class 5) 3-4-Y-O **£4,533** (£1,348; £674; £336) **Stalls** High

Form RPR
06- **1** **Right To Play (USA)**[176] [6052] 4-9-13 .... JimmyFortune 2 85+
(J H M Gosden) *sn chsng ldr: led wl over 3f out: shkn up and hung lft 2f out: clr ins fnl f: idled nr fin* **3/1**[2]

030- **2** *1/2* **Grand Heights (IRE)**[198] [5585] 3-8-7 75 .... TedDurcan 8 75
(J L Dunlop) *t.k.h: hld up in midfield: rdn over 3f out: hdwy over 2f out: chsd wnr ins fnl f: kpt on* **7/2**[3]

3 *1 1/2* **Just Julie (USA)**[171] [6153] 3-8-2 .... ChrisCatlin 1 68
(N A Callaghan) *t.k.h: hld up: hdwy over 5f out: rdn to chse ldrs over 3f out: kpt on same pce fnl f* **22/1**

4 *hd* **Dig Gold (USA)** 3-8-8 ow1 .... NCallan 10 73+
(M A Jarvis) *s.i.s: t.k.h: sn chsng ldrs: rdn to chal 3f out: sn carried lft: kpt on one pce u.p* **11/4**[1]

03- **5** *5* **Super Cross (IRE)**[201] [5537] 3-8-7 .... JamieSpencer 6 64
(E A L Dunlop) *plld hrd: chsd ldrs: rdn over 2f out: wknd 1f out* **3/1**[2]

6- **6** *11* **Intersky Music (USA)**[94] [6019] 4-9-13 .... DeanMcKeown 3 49
(Jonjo O'Neill) *s.i.s: hld up in last: n.d* **66/1**

7 *hd* **Laughing Game** 3-8-2 .... HayleyTurner 7 41
(M L W Bell) *hld up: rdn 7f out: wknd 4f out: sn wl bhd* **33/1**

02-2 **8** *5* **Into Action**[47] [553] 3-8-7 76 .... RichardHughes 9 38
(R Hannon) *led tl hdd over 3f out: wknd over 2f out: eased ins fnl f* **10/1**

6- **9** *23* **Just Chrissie**[348] [1278] 3-8-2 .... JimmyQuinn 4 —
(G Fierro) *s.i.s: a bhd: t.o last 3f* **100/1**

00- **10** *11* **Pleasure Pursuit**[159] [6331] 3-8-7 .... (b[1]) DO'Donohoe 5 —
(K A Ryan) *racd in midfield: rdn over 5f out: lost tch 4f out: t.o last 3f* **66/1**

2m 31.46s (-3.04) **Going Correction** -0.20s/f (Firm)
WFA 3 from 4yo 21lb **10** Ran SP% **119.2**
Speed ratings (Par 103):102,101,100,100,97 89,89,86,71,63
CSF £13.93 TOTE £4.10: £1.60, £1.40, £3.80; EX 17.10 Trifecta £164.30 Pool £375.03 - 1.62 winning units..
Owner H R H Princess Haya Of Jordan **Bred** And Mrs Robert A Witt **Trained** Newmarket, Suffolk

FOCUS
Another steadily-run maiden. The winner is value for a little further than his winning margin with the runner-up setting the standard.

1013 LEVY BOARD H'CAP 7f 9y
5:40 (5:40) (Class 4) (0-85,85) 4-Y-O+ **£5,181** (£1,541; £770; £384) **Stalls** Centre

Form RPR
61- **1** **Sound Of Nature (USA)**[178] [6019] 4-8-7 73 ow1 .... RichardHughes 11 95+
(H R A Cecil) *taken down early: rrd and lost ll as stalls opened: sn trcking ldrs gng wl: wnt 2nd over 1f out: rdn to ld ins last* **7/4**[1]

-040 **2** *1* **Orpen Wide (IRE)**[27] [509] 5-8-9 76 .... (b) TPQueally 8 85
(M C Chapman) *sn led: rdn wl over 1f out: hdd ins fnl f: nt pce of wnr* **20/1**

060- **3** *2* **Phluke**[139] [6580] 6-9-3 84 .... StephenCarson 14 88
(Eve Johnson Houghton) *racd in centre: chsd ldrs: rdn over 2f out: kpt on same pce fnl f* **12/1**

063- **4** *3 1/2* **Master Pegasus**[229] [4819] 4-9-4 85 .... GeorgeBaker 4 80+
(C F Wall) *t.k.h: hld up in rr: hdwy 3f out: shkn up over 2f out: no hdwy after* **9/2**[2]

354- **5** *nk* **Matuza (IRE)**[128] [6720] 4-8-11 78 .... JimmyFortune 5 72
(W R Muir) *t.k.h: chsd ldrs: rdn 3f out: wnt 2nd over 2f out tl over 1f out: sn wknd* **8/1**

00-0 **6** *1 3/4* **Surwaki (USA)**[37] [629] 5-8-12 79 .... EddieAhern 7 68
(R M H Cowell) *chsd ldr tl over 2f out: wknd over 1f out* **28/1**

16-2 **7** *2* **Fann (USA)**[19] [765] 4-8-13 80 .... SebSanders 15 64
(C E Brittain) *racd in centre: in tch in midfield: rdn over 3f out: no ch last 2f* **12/1**

40-0 **8** *1* **Isphahan**[19] [757] 4-8-6 73 .... (v) MartinDwyer 6 55
(A M Balding) *chsd ldrs: rdn 3f out: wknd over 2f out* **20/1**

210- **9** *hd* **My Arch**[194] [5678] 5-9-4 85 .... NCallan 12 66
(K A Ryan) *racd wd: rdn 1/2-way: sn outpcd* **15/2**[3]

030- **10** *3* **Give Me The Night (IRE)**[196] [5642] 4-9-2 83 .... RoystonFfrench 1 56
(B Smart) *bhd: rdn 3f out: no prog* **33/1**

0/0- **11** *6* **Mister Minty (IRE)**[334] [1684] 5-8-4 71 oh26 .... PaulHanagan 9 29
(Mrs S Lamyman) *a outpcd in rr* **80/1**

124- **12** *1* **Spirit Of Arosa (IRE)**[314] [2205] 4-8-11 78 .... DaneO'Neill 3 33
(J Akehurst) *rr: rdn over 3f out: sn struggling and no ch* **8/1**

1m 23.78s (-2.32) **Going Correction** -0.20s/f (Firm) **12** Ran SP% **121.1**
Speed ratings (Par 105):105,103,101,97,97 95,92,91,91,88 81,80
CSF £47.75 CT £346.39 TOTE £2.00: £1.10, £5.70, £4.50; EX 51.30 Trifecta £237.50 Pool £622.42 - 1.86 winning units. Place 6 £23.43, Place 5 £18.32..
Owner K Abdulla **Bred** Juddmonte Farms Inc **Trained** Newmarket, Suffolk

FOCUS
A fair handicap and the form looks solid enough rated around the placed horses. The winner remains progressive.
Spirit Of Arosa(IRE) Official explanation: trainer said filly bled from the nose
T/Plt: £24.30 to a £1 stake. Pool: £62,920.55. 1,882.75 winning tickets. T/Qpdt: £9.30 to a £1 stake. Pool: £3,208.70. 254.80 winning tickets. SP

1014 - 1020a (Foreign Racing) - See Raceform Interactive

898 FOLKESTONE (R-H)
Friday, April 13

OFFICIAL GOING: Good to firm
Wind: Moderate across

1021 GALABINGO.CO.UK MEDIAN AUCTION MAIDEN STKS 5f
2:10 (2:11) (Class 6) 2-Y-O **£2,730** (£806; £403) **Stalls** Low

Form RPR
3 **1** **Geoffdaw**[11] [890] 2-9-3 .... JamieSpencer 1 68+
(M J Wallace) *mde all: responded wl whn chal 1f out: rdn out* **10/11**[1]

0 **2** *hd* **Non Sucre (USA)**[10] [898] 2-9-3 .... SimonWhitworth 5 67
(P A Blockley) *racd keenly: trckd keenly: chal 1f out: edgd rt u.p but r.o and only jst hld* **5/1**[3]

5 **3** *1 1/2* **Rio Taffeta**[6] [942] 2-9-3 .... TedDurcan 6 61
(M R Channon) *racd 4th: wnt 3rd over 2f out: styd on fnl f* **5/1**[3]

4 *1 3/4* **Midnite Blews (IRE)** 2-9-3 .... DaneO'Neill 4 54+
(A B Haynes) *s.i.s: bhd: effrt 2f out: kpt on fnl f* **5/2**[2]

5 *9* **Amwell House** 2-9-3 .... EddieAhern 2 18
(J R Jenkins) *chsd first 2 tl wknd sn after 1/2-way* **16/1**

61.53 secs (0.73) **Going Correction** -0.125s/f (Firm) **5** Ran SP% **120.2**
Speed ratings (Par 90):89,88,86,83,69
CSF £6.94 TOTE £1.60: £1.10, £2.50; EX 5.30.
Owner Mike & Denise Dawes **Bred** Barton Stud Partnership **Trained** Newmarket, Suffolk

FOCUS
Just the five runners and this looks like a modest juvenile, best rated through the winner. Little Big Boy (9/2) was withdrawn on vet's advice. R4 applies to bets struck at board prices prior to withdrawal, deduct 15p in the £. New market formed.

NOTEBOOK
Geoffdaw's debut third form at Southwell was let down when the runner-up that day was well beaten at Musselburgh on his next start, but this was not much of a race and he narrowly justified strong market support. It is probably fair to say he had more in hand than the official margin suggests, as Spencer did not have to go for his stick and he always looked like keeping the runner-up at bay. He is likely to find things harder in winners' races, but one suspects we have not seen the best of him yet and he appeals as the type to do well in nurseries a little further down the line. (old market op 2-1 new market tchd evens)
Non Sucre(USA)'s debut seventh over this course and distance represented just moderate form, with the sixth home that day since getting beaten in a seller, but this was a much-improved effort. His performance is all the more creditable considering the favourite had the benefit of the rail to run against, although that one did win a shade cosily. (old market op 7-1 tchd 8-1)
Rio Taffeta shaped with some promise on his debut on the Polytrack six days earlier, but it was hard to know what that form was worth and he proved very easy to back. He still looked a little green and is likely to come into his own over further, possibly in nurseries later in the season. (old market op 11-2 tchd 8-1 new market op 6-1)
Midnite Blews(IRE), a 5,000 euros half-brother to useful 5f juvenile winner Bunditten, out of a useful two-year-old sprinter in France, hails from a stable that saddled a first-time-out winner at Warwick earlier in the week. He attracted some support beforehand, but just looked in need of the experience and should know a lot more next time. (old market op 13-2 tchd 3-1 new market op 11-4)
Amwell House, the first foal of a mare who was placed over 1m6f, and later placed over hurdles, struggled to go with his four rivals when it mattered. (old market op 22-1 tchd 33-1)

1022 CORAL BACKING THE NSPCC H'CAP 6f
2:45 (2:45) (Class 5) (0-70,70) 3-Y-O **£2,914** (£867; £433; £216) **Stalls** Low

Form RPR
0-01 **1** **Nordic Light (USA)**[30] [679] 3-8-11 70 .... MCGeran(7) 3 81+
(P W Chapple-Hyam) *a.p: led over 1f out: rdn out* **5/1**[1]

251- **2** *1 1/4* **Mac Gille Eoin**[157] [6388] 3-9-4 70 .... IanMongan 5 75
(J Gallagher) *hld up in rr: hdwy over 2f out: wnt 2nd over 1f out: kpt on* **8/1**

254- **3** *3/4* **Twitch Hill**[182] [5950] 3-8-9 61 .... DaneO'Neill 11 64
(H Candy) *a.p: styd on one pce fnl f* **7/1**[3]

0043 **4** *3/4* **Realy Naughty (IRE)**[21] [738] 3-9-0 66 .... MichaelHills 6 68+
(B G Powell) *in rr: making hdwy whn swtchd lft over 1f out: r.o: nvr nrr* **7/1**[3]

222- **5** *1 1/2* **Napoleon Dynamite (IRE)**[139] [6603] 3-9-3 69 .... EddieAhern 13 65
(J W Hills) *chsd ldr on far side: hung lft over 1f out: r.o but no ch w stands' side runners* **17/2**

435- **6** *1 3/4* **Billy Red**[155] [6409] 3-9-0 66 .... [1] RichardHughes 4 57
(J R Jenkins) *led tl rdn and hdd wl over 1f out: sn btn* **14/1**

00-6 **7** *1/2* **Mid Ocean**[39] [624] 3-8-11 63 .... (t) JohnEgan 12 52
(P W D'Arcy) *led gp of 3 far side to 1/2-way: no ch w stands' side runners fr over 1f out* **11/1**

4420 **8** *2* **Charlotte Grey**[30] [679] 3-8-11 63 .... EdwardCreighton 8 46
(C N Allen) *chsd ldrs tl wknd 2f out* **20/1**

010- **9** *shd* **Stir Crazy (IRE)**[148] [6500] 3-9-1 67 .... SamHitchcott 10 50
(M R Channon) *bhd whn stmbld over 4f out: nvr on terms* **25/1**

240- **10** *2* **Queensgate**[163] [6291] 3-8-7 59 .... TedDurcan 9 36
(M Blanshard) *chsd ldrs tl wknd 2f out* **40/1**

002- **11** *3/4* **Go Imperial (IRE)**[129] [6710] 3-8-10 65 .... JerryO'Dwyer(3) 7 40
(M G Quinlan) *chsd ldr tl wknd 2f out* **16/1**

-562 **12** *4* **Suhayl Star (IRE)**[14] [832] 3-8-12 64 .... OscarUrbina 2 27
(S W Hall) *a bhd* **6/1**[2]

2500 **13** *7* **Ginger Pop**[20] 752 3-8-12 **64**......................(v[1]) SebSanders 14 6
(G G Margarson) *rear of far side gp of 3 thrght* **16/1**

000- **14** *13* **Giovanni D'Oro (IRE)**[158] 6377 3-8-9 **61**...................... JamieSpencer 1 —
(N A Callaghan) *slowly away: a bhd* **10/1**

1m 12.73s (-0.87) **Going Correction** -0.125s/f (Firm) **14** Ran SP% **124.5**
Speed ratings (Par 98):100,98,97,96,94 92,91,88,88,85 84,79,70,52
CSF £44.81 CT £296.86 TOTE £5.30: £2.30, £5.10, £2.70; EX 44.20 Trifecta £99.60 Pool: £190.95, 1.36 winning units.
Owner Times Of Wigan **Bred** L Hudson **Trained** Newmarket, Suffolk

FOCUS
Just a modest sprint handicap, but probably not bad form for the grade rated around the fourth, fifth and sixth. Three raced on the far side of the track, but the much larger group on the stands' side were at a distinct advantage. The winning time was 0.70 seconds slower than the following older-horse handicap.
Billy Red Official explanation: jockey said gelding hung both ways

1023 CORALPOKER.COM H'CAP 6f
3:20 (3:20) (Class 4) (0-85,85) 4-Y-0+ **£4,857** (£1,445; £722; £360) **Stalls** Low

Form RPR
105- **1** **Forest Dane**[159] 6352 7-8-7 **77**...................... JamesDoyle(3) 2 88+
(Mrs N Smith) *hld up in rr: hdwy on outside 2f out: qcknd to ld jst ins fnl f: rdn out* **11/1**

2116 **2** *¾* **Lucayos**[14] 828 4-8-9 **79**...................... RichardKingscote(3) 6 87
(Mrs H Sweeting) *trckd ldr: led 1/2-way: hung rt and hdd jst ins fnl f: kpt on* **6/1**[3]

16-0 **3** *¾* **Mujood**[14] 827 4-9-4 **85**......................(b) StephenCarson 3 91
(Eve Johnson Houghton) *chsd ldrs: rdn 2f out: kpt on* **10/1**

146- **4** *shd* **River Kirov (IRE)**[219] 5117 4-8-11 **78**...................... JamieSpencer 4 83
(P W Chapple-Hyam) *t.k.h: rdn to chal appr fnl f: no ex ins* **4/1**[2]

5150 **5** *nk* **Mandarin Spirit (IRE)**[27] 697 7-8-7 **74** ow1................(b) OscarUrbina 7 79
(G C H Chung) *hld up in tch: rdn to chal over 1f out: nt qckn fnl f* **8/1**

212 **6** *nk* **Rowe Park**[28] 692 4-9-0 **81**...................... LPKeniry 1 85
(Mrs L C Jewell) *hld up in rr: mde sme late hdwy* **4/1**[2]

123- **7** *1* **Diane's Choice**[163] 6292 4-9-4 **85**...................... DaneO'Neill 8 86
(J Akehurst) *chsd ldrs tl wknd fnl f* **7/2**[1]

330- **8** *1 ½* **Scarlet Flyer (USA)**[199] 5591 4-8-9 **76**...................... RichardHughes 5 72
(G L Moore) *a in rr* **11/1**

4-00 **9** *3 ½* **Azygous**[28] 692 4-8-11 **78**...................... SebSanders 9 64
(J Akehurst) *led to 1/2-way: wknd qckly sn after* **25/1**

1m 12.03s (-1.57) **Going Correction** -0.125s/f (Firm) **9** Ran SP% **117.2**
Speed ratings (Par 105):105,104,103,102,102 102,100,98,94
CSF £76.47 CT £694.89 TOTE £15.40: £3.80, £1.90, £3.40; EX 101.40 Trifecta £366.90 Pool: £527.18, 1.02 winning units.
Owner The Ember Partnership **Bred** Loan And Development Corporation **Trained** Bury, W Sussex
■ Jockey James Doyle lost his right to claim with success in this race.

FOCUS
A fair sprint, run in a time 0.70 seconds faster than the previous three-year-old handicap and rated around the third and fourth, so sound enough.
Diane's Choice Official explanation: jockey said filly was denied a clear run

1024 CORAL BET BY FREEPHONE ON 0800 242 232 MAIDEN FILLIES' STKS 1m 1f 149y
3:55 (3:56) (Class 5) 3-Y-0 **£2,914** (£867; £433; £216) **Stalls** Low

Form RPR
0- **1** **Going To Work (IRE)**[114] 6886 3-9-0...................... SebSanders 1 72+
(D R C Elsworth) *t.k.h in mid-div: rdn to ld over 1f out: sn clr* **7/1**[3]

-333 **2** *3* **Nicomedia (IRE)**[28] 689 3-9-0 **71**...................... RichardHughes 8 67
(R Hannon) *led: rdn and hung lft fr 2f out: hdd over 1f out: kpt on one pce* **15/8**[2]

04- **3** *1 ½* **Irish Dancer**[238] 4552 3-9-0...................... JamieSpencer 9 64
(J L Dunlop) *chsd ldrs: rdn 2f out: hung rt and one pce after* **1/1**[1]

0-4 **4** *1 ¾* **Astrolibra**[10] 901 3-9-0...................... MichaelHills 6 61?
(M H Tompkins) *trckd ldr: ev ch 2f out: wknd fnl f* **25/1**

5- **5** *½* **Silver Mitzva (IRE)**[118] 6840 3-9-0......................(p) OscarUrbina 3 60?
(M Botti) *hld up in tch: effrt 2f out: sn btn* **20/1**

6 *shd* **Pretty Demanding (IRE)** 3-8-11...................... JerryO'Dwyer(3) 7 60
(M G Quinlan) *hld up: no hdwy fnl 2f* **33/1**

04- **7** *1 ½* **Mirin**[118] 6840 3-9-0...................... SteveDrowne 2 57
(G Wragg) *chsd ldrs tl wknd over 3f out* **8/1**

8 *8* **Hermanita** 3-9-0...................... TedDurcan 5 43
(G Wragg) *slowly away: a bhd* **20/1**

9 *32* **Karrumba (IRE)** 3-9-0...................... AdrianMcCarthy 4 —
(B J McMath) *a bhd: lost tch 3f out: t.o* **66/1**

2m 6.49s (1.26) **Going Correction** 0.0s/f (Good) **9** Ran SP% **126.2**
Speed ratings (Par 95):94,91,90,89,88 88,87,80,55
CSF £21.52 TOTE £9.20: £2.40, £1.60, £1.02; EX 39.60 Trifecta £130.60 Pool: £735.75, 4.00 winning units.
Owner Matthew Green **Bred** Glending Bloodstock **Trained** Newmarket, Suffolk

FOCUS
This looked like a pretty ordinary fillies' maiden and the winning time was 1.51 seconds slower than the following 46-60 handicap. The form is rated around the placed horses, although the proximity of the fourth and fifth limits confidence.
Karrumba(IRE) Official explanation: trainer said filly returned with sore shins

1025 CORAL.CO.UK H'CAP 1m 1f 149y
4:30 (4:30) (Class 6) (0-60,60) 4-Y-0+ **£2,914** (£867; £433; £216) **Stalls** Low

Form RPR
3221 **1** **Norwegian**[21] 741 6-8-8 **50**......................(p) PaulEddery 14 56
(Ian Williams) *t.k.h: trckd ldrs: hdwy on ins to ld fnl 100yds* **5/1**[2]

- **2** *¾* **Near Germany (IRE)**[46] 7-9-0 **59**...................... JamesDoyle(3) 4 63+
(R Curtis) *dropped out in rr: gd hdwy fr 2f out to go 2nd cl home* **50/1**

0 **3** *shd* **Ellen's Girl (IRE)**[21] 741 4-8-7 **49**......................(p) MichaelHills 11 53
(B G Powell) *led tl rdn and hdd fnl 100yds: lost 2nd post* **28/1**

1102 **4** *½* **Postmaster**[11] 888 5-8-9 **51**...................... SteveDrowne 5 54+
(R Ingram) *t.k.h: hld up in rr: hdwy on outside over 1f out: styd on: nvr nrr* **4/1**[1]

1-35 **5** *shd* **Revolve**[17] 799 7-9-2 **58**......................(b) IanMongan 10 61
(Mrs L J Mongan) *trckd ldr tl rdn and one pce ent fnl f* **9/1**[3]

3100 **6** *1 ¾* **Comeintothespace (IRE)**[21] 742 5-8-9 **51**...................... DaneO'Neill 1 50
(R A Farrant) *mid-div: effrt on outside 2f out: one pce appr fnl f* **9/1**[3]

0-00 **7** *¾* **Wassfa**[47] 559 4-9-4 **60**......................(t) SebSanders 13 58
(C E Brittain) *mid-div: one pce fnl 2f* **12/1**

0005 **8** *¾* **Scroll**[21] 742 4-8-8 **50**......................(v) TedDurcan 6 46
(P Howling) *dropped in rr s: rdn in mid-div whn no hdwy fr over 2f out* **14/1**

4-55 **9** *1 ½* **Bentley Brook (IRE)**[95] 72 5-9-2 **58**...................... SimonWhitworth 3 51
(P A Blockley) *in rr: effrt over 2f out: nvr nr to chal* **9/1**[3]

0-00 **10** *4* **Camp Attack**[72] 315 4-8-8 **50**...................... LPKeniry 8 35
(S Dow) *trckd ldrs tl wknd 3f out* **33/1**

100- **11** *5* **By Storm**[139] 6601 4-7-13 **48**...................... KirstyMilczarek(7) 7 23
(John Berry) *trckd ldrs tl wknd 3f out* **20/1**

054- **12** *3* **Simplify**[213] 5267 5-8-6 **48**......................(p) JohnEgan 9 17
(T M Jones) *plld hrd: a in rr* **20/1**

1013 **13** *2* **Mon Petite Amour**[10] 903 4-9-4 **60**...................... BrettDoyle 2 25
(D W P Arbuthnot) *hld up: nvr got into r* **4/1**[1]

066- **14** *38* **Hang Loose**[150] 6480 4-8-13 **58**...................... JerryO'Dwyer(3) 12 —
(S W Hall) *a bhd: lost tch over 3f out: t.o* **20/1**

2m 4.98s (-0.25) **Going Correction** 0.0s/f (Good) **14** Ran SP% **123.7**
Speed ratings (Par 101):101,100,100,99,99 98,97,97,96,92 88,86,84,54
CSF £257.05 CT £6312.34 TOTE £4.20: £2.40, £15.40, £8.40; EX 268.30 TRIFECTA Not won..
Owner Robert Bee **Bred** Darley **Trained** Portway, Worcs

FOCUS
A modest but competitive handicap run in a time 1.51 seconds quicker than the preceding fillies' maiden and rated through the third, backed up by the fifth and sixth.
Revolve Official explanation: jockey said gelding was denied a clear run final stages
Mon Petite Amour Official explanation: trainer's rep said filly may have been in season

1026 CORAL - 1500 BETTING SHOPS NATIONWIDE APPRENTICE H'CAP 1m 4f
5:05 (5:05) (Class 6) (0-60,58) 4-Y-0+ **£2,730** (£806; £403) **Stalls** Low

Form RPR
00-4 **1** **Icannshift (IRE)**[39] 615 7-9-2 **50**...................... RichardKingscote 2 57+
(T M Jones) *mde all: rdn clr over 2f out: unchal* **12/1**

-304 **2** *1 ¾* **Recalcitrant**[39] 616 4-9-3 **52**...................... JamesDoyle 10 55
(S Dow) *chsd wnr thrght: no imp but kpt on fr over 2f out* **10/1**

000- **3** *nk* **Harcourt (USA)**[46] 5897 7-9-10 **58**...................... MarcHalford 3 61
(M Madgwick) *a.p: kpt on one pce ins fnl 2f* **25/1**

4242 **4** *shd* **Tresor Secret (FR)**[15] 813 7-9-10 **58**...................... StephaneBreux 7 60
(J Gallagher) *trckd ldrs: rdn over 1f out: kpt on one pce* **17/2**

-300 **5** *¾* **Ganymede**[74] 291 6-8-12 **51**...................... JackMitchell(5) 13 52
(Mrs L J Mongan) *towards rr: hdwy on outside over 1f out: nvr nrr* **12/1**

004- **6** *1 ½* **Final Bid (IRE)**[20] 6578 4-9-5 **57**...................... JerryO'Dwyer(3) 4 56
(M G Quinlan) *in tch: hdwy to go 3rd 1/2-way: rdn and wknd 2f out* **7/4**[1]

0-14 **7** *1* **Enthusius**[20] 612 4-8-10 **53**...................... JemmaMarshall(8) 1 51
(G L Moore) *trckd ldrs tl wknd 2f out* **5/1**[2]

5-60 **8** *nk* **Treetops Hotel (IRE)**[15] 813 8-9-0 **53**...................... PatrickHills(5) 8 50
(B R Johnson) *hld up in rr: mde mod late hdwy* **8/1**[3]

-010 **9** *¾* **Smoothie (IRE)**[24] 716 9-8-9 **48**...................... TolleyDean(5) 6 44
(E G Bevan) *bhd tl sme hdwy over 1f out: n.d* **25/1**

1204 **10** *½* **Maria Antonia (IRE)**[10] 903 4-9-1 **57**...................... JosephWalsh(7) 9 52
(P A Blockley) *stdd s: sn mid-div but nvr got into r* **14/1**

653- **11** *¾* **Adage**[176] 6068 4-8-12 **52**......................(t) AshleyHamblett(5) 5 46
(David Pinder) *hld up in rr: nvr on terms* **25/1**

0103 **12** *3 ½* **Competitor**[14] 825 6-9-2 **50**......................(v) LiamJones 11 39
(J Akehurst) *in rr: rdn 4f out and nvr got into r* **16/1**

-005 **13** *28* **Rowan Pursuit**[68] 349 6-8-4 **45**......................(b) DavidProbert(7) 12 —
(E A Wheeler) *in rr: lost tch 3f out: t.o* **33/1**

2m 42.81s (2.31) **Going Correction** 0.0s/f (Good)
WFA 4 from 6yo+ 1lb **13** Ran SP% **126.2**
Speed ratings (Par 101):92,90,90,90,90 89,88,88,87,87 86,84,65
CSF £128.35 CT £2979.32 TOTE £11.80: £3.50, £3.00, £10.20; EX 129.50 Trifecta £355.60 Part won. Pool: £500.93 - 0.10 winning units. Place 6 £ 834.78,. Place 5 £ 515.31.
Owner Mrs R A Jennings **Bred** Piercetown Stud **Trained** Albury Heath, Surrey

FOCUS
A modest handicap restricted to apprentices in which very few got involved and a moderate time, even for the grade. The form is rated around the third and sixth.
T/Plt: £442.30 to a £1 stake. Pool: £52,533.15. 86.70 winning tickets. T/Qpdt: £220.80 to a £1 stake. Pool: £2,865.50. 9.60 winning tickets. JS

905 SOUTHWELL (L-H)
Friday, April 13

OFFICIAL GOING: Standard
Wind: Nil Weather: Overcast

1027 SOUTHWELL-RACECOURSE.CO.UK AMATEUR RIDERS' H'CAP 1m (F)
2:20 (2:20) (Class 6) (0-60,57) 4-Y-0+ **£2,307** (£709; £354) **Stalls** Low

Form RPR
0203 **1** **Windy Prospect**[20] 768 5-10-12 **53**......................(p) MrAshleePrice(5) 5 66
(P A Blockley) *chsd ldrs: short of room and swtchd lft wl over 2f out: sn rdn: led 1f out: styd on* **6/1**[2]

0-35 **2** *1 ¼* **The Grey One (IRE)**[20] 750 4-10-10 **53**......................(p) MissHDavies(7) 13 63
(J M Bradley) *stdd after s: t.k.h: hld up bhd: hdwy on outer 2f out: rdn and edgd lft 1f out: chsd wnr ins last: hld* **14/1**

3000 **3** *2 ½* **Kingsmaite**[8] 932 6-10-7 **50**......................(bt) MrKApark(7) 10 54
(S R Bowring) *sn chsng ldrs: w ldr after 2f out: rdn over 3f out: led 2f out: hdd 1f out: no ex ins fnl f* **11/1**

-155 **4** *2 ½* **Scottish River (USA)**[75] 279 8-11-6 **56**...................... MrLeeNewnes 8 55
(M D I Usher) *v.s.a: bhd: hdwy 4f out: rdn wl over 3f out: styd on last 2f: nt rch ldrs* **10/1**

010- **5** *½* **Kirkhammerton (IRE)**[165] 6256 5-11-3 **56**...................... MrSPearce(3) 12 53
(A J McCabe) *hld up in rr: rdn and hdwy over 2f out: styd on: nt rch ldrs* **6/1**[2]

4044 **6** *hd* **Buzzin'Boyzee (IRE)**[8] 932 4-10-7 **50**...................... MrRichardEvans(7) 3 47
(P D Evans) *in tch in midfield: chsd ldrs over 3f out: rdn 2f out: kpt on same pce* **9/1**[3]

350/ **7** *nk* **Sea Mark**[1002] 2410 11-11-1 **51**...................... MissLEllison 7 47
(A D Brown) *towards rr and pushed along: styd on last 2f: nt rch ldrs* **20/1**

6601 **8** *1 ¾* **Feelin Irie (IRE)**[16] 812 4-11-6 **56**......................(p) MrSWalker 11 48
(J R Boyle) *t.k.h: led: rdn 3f out: hdd 2f out: wknd over 1f out* **5/1**[1]

1000 **9** *¾* **Paso Doble**[20] 768 9-11-0 **55**......................(b) MissRBastiman(5) 2 46
(R Bastiman) *hld up towards rr: sme hdwy over 3f out: no hdwy last 2f* **14/1**

1340 **10** *1* **Desert Lover (IRE)**[17] 806 5-10-9 **52**......................(t) MrMPrice(7) 9 40
(R J Price) *chsd ldrs: rdn 4f out: sn struggling: no ch last 3f* **10/1**

020- **11** *½* **Moon Forest (IRE)**[143] 6556 5-11-2 **57**......................(p) MissSBradley(5) 1 44
(J M Bradley) *t.k.h: chsd ldr for 2f: styd prom: ev ch 3f out : wknd over 2f out* **33/1**

0/20 **12** *½* **Mangrove Cay (IRE)**[61] 431 5-11-1 **51**...................... MissADeniel 6 37
(A J Lockwood) *racd in midfield: outpcd 4f out: n.d* **25/1**

2000 **13** *8* **Tyrone Sam**[9] 912 5-11-1 **56**........................(b) MissARyan(5) 4 24
(K A Ryan) *stdd s: bhd: rdn 5f out: no ch last 3f* **10/1**
500- **14** *5* **El Palmar**[301] 2599 6-10-9 **50**........................ MrStephenHarrison(5) 14 6
(M J Attwater) *t.k.h: chsd ldrs on outer: rdn and struggling 4f out: no ch last 3f* **14/1**
1m 44.9s (0.30) **Going Correction** +0.05s/f (Slow) **14** Ran SP% **122.4**
Speed ratings (Par 101):100,98,96,93,93 93,92,91,90,89 88,88,80,75
CSF £86.83 CT £939.82 TOTE £8.30: £2.60, £4.00, £3.40; EX 122.80.
Owner Bill Cahill **Bred** T J Cooper **Trained** Lambourn, Berks
■ Stewards' Enquiry : Mr Ashlee Price three-day ban: used whip with excessive frequency (Apr 28, May 14,21)

FOCUS
A typically moderate amateur riders' handicap but sound enough form rated through the winner.

1028 GOLF AND RACING AT SOUTHWELL (S) STKS 6f (F)
2:55 (2:55) (Class 6) 3-Y-0+ **£2,184** (£644; £322) **Stalls** Low

Form RPR
0-01 **1** **Whinhill House**[11] 892 7-9-13 54........................(v) PatCosgrave 1 64
(D W Barker) *chsd ldrs: rdn over 3f out: c wd over 2f out: chsd wnr ins fnl f: styd on u.p to ld on post* **11/4**[1]
46-5 **2** *shd* **Borzoi Maestro**[75] 287 6-9-13 46........................(p) AdamKirby 13 63
(G F Bridgwater) *led: rdn 1f out: kpt on u.p: hdd on post* **40/1**
2065 **3** *1 ¼* **Penel (IRE)**[9] 912 6-9-9 48........................(p) LeeEnstone 5 55
(P T Midgley) *sn outpcd and drvn in rr: styd on u.p over 1f out: nrst fin* **4/1**[2]
40-3 **4** *1* **Rudry World (IRE)**[18] 788 4-9-9 60........................ TPO'Shea 9 52+
(P A Blockley) *chsd ldrs: outpcd whn short of room and lost pl over 4f out: sn rdn: wl bhd: tl styd on wl ins last: nrst fin* **10/1**
4110 **5** *nk* **Soba Jones**[11] 896 10-9-10 57........................ JasonEdmunds(3) 12 55
(J Balding) *v.s.a: hdwy into midfield: over 3f out: rdn and kpt on last 2f: nt rch ldrs* **4/1**[2]
1105 **6** *shd* **Mister Incredible**[25] 710 4-9-10 51........................(v) SaleemGolam(3) 2 55
(J M Bradley) *chsd ldr: rdn and ev ch over 1f out: wknd ins fnl f* **13/2**[3]
0300 **7** *1* **Sundried Tomato**[31] 668 8-9-9 43........................(p) HayleyTurner 10 48
(D W Chapman) *chsd ldrs: rdn over 3f out: c wd over 2f out: wknd 2f out* **20/1**
0660 **8** *1 ½* **Blushing Russian (IRE)**[21] 746 5-9-6 45........................(p) BarrySavage(7) 6 48
(J M Bradley) *in tch: rdn and effrt 2f out: wknd fnl f* **28/1**
-060 **9** *¾* **Bridget's Team**[18] 786 3-8-10 50........................ DaleGibson 4 40
(D G Bridgwater) *chsd ldrs: rdn over 3f out: wknd wl over 2f out* **22/1**
0055 **10** *2 ½* **Spy Gun (USA)**[14] 833 7-9-9 43........................(b) ChrisCatlin 11 34
(T Wall) *racd wd: chsd ldrs for 2f: sn outpcd: no ch after* **16/1**
00-0 **11** *4* **Sabo Prince**[25] 710 5-9-6 42........................(p) StephenDonohoe(3) 3 22
(J M Bradley) *slowly away: a wl bhd* **33/1**
0600 **12** *23* **Drink To Me Only**[23] 721 4-9-9 42........................(b[1]) NCallan 8 —
(J R Weymes) *chsd ldrs for 2f: sn rdn and outpcd: no ch last 3f: eased: t.o* **14/1**
1m 17.44s (0.54) **Going Correction** +0.05s/f (Slow)
WFA 3 from 4yo+ 12lb **12** Ran SP% **119.6**
Speed ratings (Par 101):98,97,96,94,94 94,93,91,90,86 81,50
CSF £139.32 TOTE £3.70: £1.70, £14.90, £2.30; EX 117.10.There was no bid for the winner.
Owner D W Barker **Bred** W R And Mrs Arblaster **Trained** Scorton, N Yorks
■ Stewards' Enquiry : Adam Kirby caution: used whip with excessive frequency

FOCUS
An ordinary seller but the form looks solid enough.
Rudry World(IRE) Official explanation: jockey said gelding never travelled
Drink To Me Only Official explanation: jockey said gelding never travelled; trainer said gelding had been struck into during the race and had lost a shoe

1029 SOUTHWELL-RACECOURSE.CO.UK MAIDEN AUCTION FILLIES' STKS 5f (F)
3:30 (3:31) (Class 6) 2-Y-0 **£2,184** (£644; £322) **Stalls** High

Form RPR
1 **Well Informed** 2-8-11........................ NCallan 5 75+
(K A Ryan) *dwlt: sn pressing ldr: led over 2f out: sn pushed clr: easily* **6/4**[1]
2 *4* **Mujada** 2-7-11........................ AndrewHeffernan(7) 1 49
(M Brittain) *bhd: outpcd after 1f: kpt on over 1f: wnt 2nd nr fin: no ch w wnr* **25/1**
6 **3** *hd* **Woodford Regen**[11] 890 2-8-6........................ PaulMulrennan 4 50
(M W Easterby) *led: rdn and hdd over 2f out: sn outpcd by wnr: lost 2nd nr fin* **5/2**[2]
4 *9* **Ridgeway Jazz** 2-8-4........................ HayleyTurner 3 12
(M D I Usher) *pushed along and outpcd after 1f: no ch after* **14/1**
5 *¾* **Fitolini** 2-8-8........................ J-PGuillambert 8 13
(Mrs G S Rees) *pressed ldrs: rdn over 2f out: wknd qckly over 1f out* **10/3**[3]
6 *5* **Weet Intolerance** 2-8-4........................ ChrisCatlin 6 —
(B D Leavy) *chsd ldrs tl outpcd after2f: no ch after: t.o* **16/1**
7 *1 ½* **Mimton (IRE)** 2-7-13........................ LanceBetts(7) 9 —
(N Wilson) *s.i.s: a outpcd and wl bhd: t.o* **25/1**
60.82 secs (0.52) **Going Correction** -0.15s/f (Stan) **7** Ran SP% **111.9**
Speed ratings (Par 87):89,82,82,67,66 58,56
CSF £38.89 TOTE £1.80: £1.60, £5.40; EX 21.80.
Owner Kevin Lee & David Barlow **Bred** J A E Hobby **Trained** Hambleton, N Yorks

FOCUS
A very weak maiden with the possible exception of the winner. The winning time was 0.79 seconds slower than the later 0-60.

NOTEBOOK
Well Informed ◆, a 16,000gns half-sister to Bygone Days, a high-class multiple 6f winner, recovered well from a slow start and was basically in a different league to this lot. She deserves her chance in better company. (op 13-8 tchd 7-4)
Mujada, an 800gns half-sister to Cheney Hill, a 5f winner at three, out of a 7f winner, was well held back in second. This represents just moderate form and she will probably have to improve to win a similar event. (op 20-1)
Woodford Regen, sixth in a weak maiden over this course and distance on her debut, had every chance but was well held and is seemingly pretty moderate. (tchd 10-3)
Ridgeway Jazz, by Kalanisi, never landed a blow on her debut and should be better for the experience. (tchd 12-1)
Fitolini, a half-sister to 5f juvenile winner Crow's Nest Lad, out of a multiple 5-6f winner, attracted some support in the market but offered little. Official explanation: jockey said filly had no more to give (op 4-1 tchd 3-1)

1030 NOBBY HAMILTON RETIREMENT MEDIAN AUCTION MAIDEN STKS 1m 4f (F)
4:05 (4:05) (Class 5) 3-5-Y-0 **£2,968** (£876; £438) **Stalls** Low

Form RPR
462- **1** **Actodos (IRE)**[198] 5623 3-8-6 76 ow1........................ JimCrowley 2 82+
(B R Millman) *mde all: clr w 2nd wl over 3f out: pushed clr over 1f out: nt extended* **8/11**[1]
2 *5* **Salsadar** 3-8-0........................ DavidKinsella 1 63
(J H M Gosden) *s.i.s: hld up: hdwy 7f out: chsd wnr wl over 3f out: sn rdn: wknd over 1f out* **11/4**[2]
4400 **3** *18* **Chart Oak**[16] 807 4-9-11 50........................ J-PGuillambert 3 47+
(P Howling) *trckd ldrs: chsd ldng pair and rdn 4f out: sn no ch* **14/1**
0 **4** *1 ¼* **Wolds Way**[8] 936 5-9-12........................ DavidAllan 4 41
(T D Easterby) *chsd wnr: rdn wl over 5f out: wknd 4f out: sn no ch* **11/1**[3]
-000 **5** *8* **Orphir (IRE)**[19] 775 4-9-11 35........................(p) JimmyQuinn 7 29
(Mrs N Macauley) *bhd: rdn 7f out: lost tch 4f out: t.o last 3f* **50/1**
3-60 **6** *12* **Inflagrantedelicto (USA)**[29] 684 3-8-5 57........................(b[1]) DaleGibson 5 9
(D W Chapman) *chsd ldrs: wnt 2nd 5f out tl wl over 3f out: sn rdn and wknd: t.o last 3f* **20/1**
7 *6* **Cinnamon Girl**[35] 4-9-6........................ ChrisCatlin 8 —
(A M Hales) *in tch in midfield: rdn over 7f out: wknd wl over 4f out: t.o last 3f* **25/1**
8 *59* **Glad Star (GER)** 4-9-11........................ PhillipMakin 6 —
(D W Chapman) *dwlt: sn rdn: lost tch 7f out: wl t.o last 4f* **25/1**
2m 41.79s (-0.30) **Going Correction** +0.05s/f (Slow)
WFA 3 from 4yo 21lb 4 from 5yo 1lb **8** Ran SP% **114.0**
Speed ratings (Par 103):103,99,87,86,81 73,69,30
CSF £2.60 TOTE £1.70: £1.02, £1.70, £2.50; EX 3.30.
Owner G Jewell & S Perry **Bred** Miss Kay Skehan **Trained** Kentisbeare, Devon

FOCUS
An uncompetitive maiden but the winner was value for an eight-length success and the form is rated through the fourth.

1031 POCHIN@LONGEATONPLUMBERSCLUB H'CAP 5f (F)
4:40 (4:40) (Class 6) (0-60,58) 3-Y-0 **£2,388** (£705; £352) **Stalls** High

Form RPR
0203 **1** **Totally Free**[10] 900 3-9-4 **58**........................(v) HayleyTurner 3 62
(M D I Usher) *chsd ldrs: rdn wl over 2f out: chsd ldr ins fnl f: r.o to ld last 50 yds* **11/1**
-635 **2** *¾* **Moonlight Applause**[9] 918 3-8-12 **52**........................ DavidAllan 5 53
(T D Easterby) *led: rdn 1/2-way: hdd and no ex last 50 yds* **13/2**[3]
2-00 **3** *1 ¼* **The Geester**[9] 925 3-9-4 **58**........................(b) PhillipMakin 6 55
(S R Bowring) *s.i.s: sn in tch: hdwy over 2f out: chsd ldr 1f out: hung rt and no ex wl ins fnl f* **16/1**
5450 **4** *2* **Perlachy**[9] 925 3-8-13 **58**........................(v) DuranFentiman(5) 9 47
(Mrs N Macauley) *chsd ldrs: rdn over 2f out: kpt on same pce u.p fnl f* **11/1**
-045 **5** *1 ½* **Cryptic Clue (USA)**[16] 807 3-8-7 **47**........................ TomEaves 1 31
(D W Chapman) *s.i.s: hdwy into midfield 3f out: rdn 2f out: kpt on same pce* **10/1**
0552 **6** *nk* **The Tinker Man**[24] 713 3-8-5 **52**........................ FrankiePickard(7) 10 35+
(M D I Usher) *s.i.s: bhd and hung lft sn after s: racd on far rail: styd on ins fnl f: n.d* **13/2**[3]
3350 **7** *shd* **Pappas Image**[31] 671 3-8-7 **50**........................(be) PatrickMathers(3) 4 32
(A J McCabe) *s.i.s: hdwy to chse ldr after 2f: rdn and ev ch wl over 1f out: wknd 1f out* **14/1**
340 **8** *1* **Royal Dagger (IRE)**[17] 798 3-8-10 **50**........................ ChrisCatlin 2 29+
(Rae Guest) *chsd ldrs: rdn over 2f out: wknd wl over 1f out* **6/1**[2]
530- **9** *2 ½* **Mandriano (ITY)**[148] 6500 3-8-9 **49**........................(v[1]) PatCosgrave 7 19
(D W Barker) *sn rdn: chsd ldr for 2f: wknd wl over 1f out* **9/1**
530U **10** *nk* **Spinning Game**[8] 934 3-8-5 **45**........................(b) DaleGibson 8 14
(D W Chapman) *a bhd: n.d* **33/1**
-503 **11** *hd* **Minimum Fuss (IRE)**[9] 918 3-8-13 **56**........................ StephenDonohoe(3) 14 24
(M C Chapman) *chsd ldrs tl over 2f out: sn wknd* **14/1**
-600 **12** *1 ½* **Tizzydore (IRE)**[25] 708 3-8-9 **49**........................ FergusSweeney 11 12
(A G Newcombe) *a outpcd in rr* **25/1**
3-03 **13** *nk* **Nou Camp**[19] 778 3-9-0 **54**........................ NCallan 12 16
(N A Callaghan) *bhd: rdn over 3f out: n.d* **4/1**[1]
5000 **14** *1* **Redflo**[17] 798 3-8-5 **45**........................ JimmyQuinn 13 3
(Ms J S Doyle) *a bhd* **50/1**
60.03 secs (-0.27) **Going Correction** -0.15s/f (Stan) **14** Ran SP% **124.7**
Speed ratings (Par 96):96,94,92,89,87 86,86,84,80,80 80,77,77,75
CSF £82.62 CT £1172.89 TOTE £13.40: £3.20, £2.30, £5.90; EX 88.40.
Owner I Sheward **Bred** B Mills **Trained** Upper Lambourn, Berks

FOCUS
Moderate handicap form rated around the fourth and fifth.
The Tinker Man ◆ Official explanation: jockey said colt hung left-handed throughout
Minimum Fuss(IRE) Official explanation: jockey said filly hung left-handed throughout
Nou Camp Official explanation: jockey said gelding was unsuited by the fibre sand surface
Redflo Official explanation: jockey said filly missed the break

1032 HOSPITALITY PACKAGES AVAILABLE H'CAP 1m 6f (F)
5:15 (5:15) (Class 6) (0-65,61) 4-Y-0+ **£2,388** (£705; £352) **Stalls** Low

Form RPR
5011 **1** **Lady Pilot**[10] 909 5-9-7 **58** 6ex........................ RichardThomas 13 72
(Jim Best) *t.k.h: hld up in midfield: hdwy gng wl 5f out: rdn to ld wl over 1f out: styd on wl* **9/2**[2]
0522 **2** *¾* **They All Laughed**[10] 909 4-8-9 **56**........................ WilliamCarson(7) 8 69+
(P W Hiatt) *hld up in last: hdwy 4f out: stl modest 8th over 3f out: c wd over 2f out: rdn over 1f out: wnt 2nd ins last: nt rch wnr* **7/2**[1]
3356 **3** *5* **Bienheureux**[73] 302 6-9-3 **54**........................(t) NCallan 10 60
(Miss Gay Kelleway) *hld up towards rr: hdwy to trck ldrs wl over 3f out: rdn to chse wnr briefly 1f out: wknd ins fnl f* **11/2**
6002 **4** *1* **Diktatorship (IRE)**[18] 789 4-8-5 **45**........................ PaulHanagan 5 50
(G A Swinbank) *t.k.h: hld up in tch: hdwy over 4f out: chsd ldrs and rdn over 3f out: kpt on same pce* **5/1**[3]
2022 **5** *½* **Nod's Star**[18] 792 6-8-13 **50**........................(t) ChrisCatlin 14 54
(Mrs L C Jewell) *chsd ldrs: wnt 2nd over 4f out: rdn to ld wl over 2f out: hdd wl over 1f out: wknd ins fnl f* **7/1**
1563 **6** *3* **Tioga Gold (IRE)**[16] 808 8-8-5 **47**........................ RussellKennemore(5) 6 47
(L R James) *prom: chsd ldr over 7f out tl led 5f out: rdn and hdd wl over 2f out: wknd over 1f out* **14/1**
403- **7** *2* **Swords**[154] 6426 5-9-7 **61**........................ StephenDonohoe(3) 3 58
(Heather Dalton) *t.k.h: hld up in rr: sme hdwy 4f out: rdn and kpt on over 1f out: n.d* **8/1**

0006 **8** *11* **Monmouthshire**[16] [808] 4-8-5 **45**..............................(v) DeanMcKeown 1 27
(R J Price) *t.k.h: chsd ldrs tl lost pl 5f out: wl bhd last 3f* **25/1**

00-4 **9** *21* **Travelling Fox**[18] [788] 4-8-11 **51**.. JimmyQuinn 2 3
(Jane Chapple-Hyam) *led for 2f: chsd ldrs tl rdn 4f out: wknd qckly over 3f out: eased last 2f: t.o* **25/1**

03-5 **10** *20* **Queen Of Diamonds (IRE)**[10] [907] 4-8-2 **45**............ AndrewElliott(3) 7 —
(Mrs K Walton) *chsd ldr tl led after 2f tl after 4f: chsd ldrs tl wknd 5f out: sn wl bhd: t.o* **40/1**

0-0 **11** *2* **Saitama**[100] [23] 5-9-4 **55**.. AdamKirby 4 —
(A M Hales) *t.k.h: hld up: bhd and rdn over 7f out: lost tch over 4f out: t.o and eased last 3f* **50/1**

000/ **12** *5* **Litzinsky**[82] [4085] 9-8-8 **45**.. JimCrowley 12 —
(Mrs L J Young) *bhd: rdn 8f out: lost tch 6f out: t.o and eased last 3f* **50/1**

00-0 **13** *27* **Fardi (IRE)**[4] [966] 5-8-8 **45**... HayleyTurner 9 —
(K W Hogg) *t.k.h: chsd ldr after 2f tl led after 4f: hdd 5f out: sn wknd: t.o and eased last 3f* **66/1**

3m 8.76s (-0.84) **Going Correction** +0.05s/f (Slow)
WFA 4 from 5yo+ 3lb **13** Ran SP% **118.3**
Speed ratings (Par 101):104,103,100,100,99 98,97,90,78,67 66,63,47
CSF £19.25 CT £89.61 TOTE £3.80: £1.70, £1.70, £1.90; EX 16.50 Place 6 £ 92.83, Place 5 £ 17.00.
Owner Odds On Racing **Bred** Genesis Green Stud Ltd **Trained** Lewes, E Sussex

FOCUS
Ordinary handicap form but the first two home are in form so it looks solid enough for the grade, with the form rated around the next four home.
Saitama Official explanation: jockey said mare never travelled
T/Plt: £103.10 to a £1 stake. Pool: £45,622.40. 322.75 winning tickets. T/Qpdt: £13.20 to a £1 stake. Pool: £3,100.40. 173.50 winning tickets. SP

919 LINGFIELD (L-H)
Saturday, April 14

OFFICIAL GOING: Standard
Wind: Virtually nil

1033 BETDIRECT.COM MAIDEN AUCTION STKS 5f (P)
1:35 (1:35) (Class 5) 2-Y-O **£2,914** (£867; £433; £216) **Stalls** High

Form RPR

1 **Cake (IRE)** 2-8-6 .... RichardHughes 4 66+
(R Hannon) *cmpt: str: bit bkwd: mde all: rdn clr 2f out: in command after: rdn out* **11/8**[1]

3 **2** *1 1/4* **Hucking Harmony (IRE)**[16] [814] 2-8-3 .... StephaneBreux(3) 7 61
(J R Best) *pressed wnr: hung rt bnd 2f out: sn rdn and outpcd: kpt on again ins fnl f* **7/4**[2]

3 *3/4* **Bookiebasher Dude** 2-8-13 .... ShaneKelly 5 65
(M Quinn) *wl grwn: str: lw: v.s.a: bhd on outer: hdwy over 1f out: r.o wl ins fnl f: nrst fin* **16/1**

5 **4** *1 3/4* **New Balls Please (IRE)**[12] [883] 2-8-9 .... IanMongan 8 54
(P M Phelan) *in tch: rdn and effrt 2f out: kpt on same pce* **14/1**

5 *2 1/2* **Areweplayingout (IRE)** 2-8-6 .... RobbieFitzpatrick 1 41
(Peter Grayson) *leggy: s.i.s: in tch: hdwy on inner over 2f out: rdn 2f out: wknd over 1f out* **25/1**

6 *4* **Purple Ransom (IRE)** 2-8-10 .... JamesDoyle(3) 6 32
(I A Wood) *str: scope: bkwd: chsd ldrs tl over 2f out: sn rdn and wknd* **33/1**

7 *hd* **Replicator** 2-8-9 .... PaulEddery 3 27
(Pat Eddery) *neat: lw: v.s.a: a bhd* **11/2**[3]

61.51 secs (1.73) **Going Correction** 0.0s/f (Stan) **7** Ran SP% **113.2**
Speed ratings (Par 92):86,84,82,80,76 69,69
CSF £3.89 TOTE £2.20: £1.50, £1.60; EX 3.40.
Owner Simon Leech **Bred** Carpet Lady Partnership **Trained** East Everleigh, Wilts

FOCUS
This did not look that good a maiden, even though the winner is well regarded and a couple had already shown some promise. The winning time was modest and those that raced up with the pace held a big advantage, as the first two home held those positions throughout.

NOTEBOOK
Cake(IRE), a half-sister to a winning juvenile, is bred for speed and showed good pace from the start. Railing like a greyhound, an injection of speed off the final bend took her clear and she never looked like getting caught from then on. The market suggested she was expected to make a winning debut and, even though the form may not be great, she may be able to find another race before the better juveniles emerge. (op 13-8 tchd 5-4 after 2-1 in a place)
Hucking Harmony(IRE), promising on her debut here, was always on the winner's shoulder but, even though she did not repeat her wayward antics this time, she still looked awkward on the home bend, carrying her head to one side, and was left flat-footed when the favourite quickened away straightening up for home. There was no way back from that, but she is worth another chance on a more conventional track. (op 6-4)
Bookiebasher Dude ◆, out of a dam who scored twice at sprint trips and was a half-sister to five winners including the Middle Park-winner Hayil, did everything wrong on this debut, missing the break badly and then racing very wide around the home bend, so under the circumstances he did extremely well to finish so close. He is probably the one to take out of the race.
New Balls Please(IRE) had his chance, but lacked a turn of foot in the home straight. It is debatable whether this was an improvement on his debut effort and he may need a drop in class in order to get off the mark.
Areweplayingout(IRE), out of a dual winner over a mile, also has plenty of speed in her pedigree and showed some ability mid-race on this debut, but may be one for nurseries later on in the season.
Purple Ransom(IRE), out of a half-sister to the high-class sprinter Andreyev, showed a bit of speed until past halfway and can improve.
Replicator, a half-brother to four winners out of a dam who scored four times over 5f herself, is bred to go a bit but he completely fluffed the start and there was no way back. (op 6-1 tchd 13-2)

1034 BETDIRECT.COM GET INVOLVED CONDITIONS STKS 7f (P)
2:10 (2:11) (Class 4) 4-Y-O+ **£4,857** (£1,445; £722; £360) **Stalls** Low

Form RPR

110- **1** **Levera**[297] [2739] 4-8-12 **107**.. JamieSpencer 4 113+
(A King) *h.d.w: lw: mde all: rdn and qcknd wl over 1f out: edgd lft ins fnl f: r.o wl* **11/10**[1]

1020 **2** *3/4* **Vortex**[14] [858] 8-8-12 **108**..(t) JimmyQuinn 6 111
(Miss Gay Kelleway) *lw: hld up in rr: rdn and hdwy wl over 1f out: chsd wnr over 1f out: r.o but a hld* **11/2**

05-1 **3** *2* **Eisteddfod**[14] [841] 6-9-3 **103**..(t) JimmyFortune 3 111
(P F I Cole) *trckd ldrs: rdn 2f out: kpt on same pce* **5/1**[3]

4401 **4** *nk* **Red Cape (FR)**[21] [759] 4-8-12 **98**.. JohnEgan 7 105
(Jane Chapple-Hyam) *stdd aftr s: t.k.h: hld up in tch on outer: rdn and effrt wl over 1f out: kpt on same pce* **9/2**[2]

434- **5** *3 1/2* **Song Of Passion (IRE)**[203] [5525] 4-8-7 **90**................... RichardHughes 1 91
(R Hannon) *chsd ldr: rdn 2f out: wknd 1f out* **9/1**

6 *4* **Sensasse (IRE)**[538] [6042] 4-8-7 .... SteveDrowne 2 80?
(Mrs A J Perrett) *lengthy: bit bkwd: hld up inrr: rdn over 2f out: outpcd 2f out: no ch after* **25/1**

1m 24.61s (-1.28) **Going Correction** 0.0s/f (Stan) **6** Ran SP% **111.7**
Speed ratings (Par 105):107,106,103,103,99 94
CSF £7.55 TOTE £1.80: £1.40, £2.30; EX 7.20.
Owner Four Mile Racing **Bred** Cheveley Park Stud Ltd **Trained** Barbury Castle, Wilts

FOCUS
A decent conditions event, with three of the six runners rated 103 or higher. The pace was solid and the form should stand up, with the runner-up setting the standard.

1035 BETDIRECT.COM INTERNATIONAL TRIAL STKS (LISTED RACE) 1m (P)
2:45 (2:45) (Class 1) 3-Y-O
£14,762 (£5,595; £2,800; £1,396; £699; £351) **Stalls** High

Form RPR

2-26 **1** **Fares (IRE)**[21] [760] 3-9-0 **90**..(b) SebSanders 2 98
(C E Brittain) *lw: t.k.h: hld up in tch: rdn and hdwy over 1f out: edgd lft u.p fnl f: r.o wl to ld last 50 yds* **14/1**

113- **2** *1/2* **Champery (USA)**[232] [4775] 3-9-0 **100**................................. JoeFanning 7 97
(M Johnston) *sn led: stdd pce wl over 3f out: rdn 2f out: edgd lft u.p jst over 1f out: hdd and no ex last 50 yds* **2/1**[2]

30-4 **3** *hd* **Norisan**[14] [839] 3-9-0 **99**.. RichardHughes 6 97
(R Hannon) *swtg: hld up in tch: rdn and outpcd over 2f: r.o wl u.p fnl f: nt rch ldrs* **10/1**

025- **4** *1 1/2* **Bicoastal (USA)**[195] [5714] 3-8-9 **105**..............................(b) JamieSpencer 4 88
(B J Meehan) *h.d.w: bit bkwd: trckd ldrs: rdn over 2f out: ev ch over 1f out: wknd wl ins fnl f* **7/4**[1]

411- **5** *nk* **Solid Rock (IRE)**[131] [6699] 3-9-0 **96**.................................... DaneO'Neill 3 92
(T G Mills) *t.k.h: hld up in rr: hdwy 4f out: rdn to chse ldr over 2f: ev ch over 1f out: wknd ins fnl f* **7/1**[3]

31-1 **6** *3/4* **Majuro (IRE)**[10] [922] 3-9-0 **91**.. JohnEgan 1 94+
(M R Channon) *lw: s.i.s: t.k.h: sn chsd ldr tl over 2f out: effrt whn nt clr run and snatched up over 1f out: nt rcvr* **10/1**

14- **7** *1 1/4* **Ransom Captive (USA)**[175] [6105] 3-8-9 **91**......................... EddieAhern 5 83
(M A Magnusson) *stdd s: t.k.h: hld up in rr: rdn and effrt 2f out: wknd over 1f out* **12/1**

1m 38.04s (-1.39) **Going Correction** 0.0s/f (Stan) **7** Ran SP% **114.7**
Speed ratings (Par 106):106,105,105,103,103 102,101
CSF £42.74 TOTE £21.20: £6.30, £2.30; EX 60.10.
Owner Mohammed Rashid **Bred** Darley **Trained** Newmarket, Suffolk
■ Stewards' Enquiry : Joe Fanning two-day ban; careless riding (May 11-12)

FOCUS
An interesting race, though a little unsatisfactory thanks to a stop-start gallop, and one or two reputations took a knock. The time was reasonable enough for the grade under the circumstances, being 0.36 seconds faster than the following Class 5 handicap for older horses and the form is rated around the placed horses.

NOTEBOOK
Fares(IRE), very experienced on sand, was also fighting-fit having been kept on the go during the winter, but he had already been well held at this level in the Spring Cup here last time and had the lowest official rating of these. On this occasion, however, everything went right for him and he was produced at the ideal time down the centre of the track to record his third, and by far his biggest, victory on Polytrack. The extra furlong may have been a factor and he will no doubt be given a chance to take on even more exalted company than this.
Champery(USA), who showed good form on turf at two, was given a trademark positive ride for one from the stable and, when he kicked for home off the final bend, it looked as though he might take some catching. However, he failed to last home and showed once again how hard it is for a horse to make all the running if sticking to the inside rail in the home straight. He has obviously retained his ability and should go one better when things pan out right for him. (op 5-2 tchd 11-4 and 15-8)
Norisan, given a waiting ride, was produced with his effort widest of all down the straight and finished well, but could not get there in time. He seemed to see out the trip better on this slightly faster Polytrack, but still may be best suited by racing over shorter. (op 12-1)
Bicoastal(USA) was the highest rated of these after running with credit in lofty company at two, but despite holding every chance she found little in the run to the line. She may have needed this first run in six months, but this was still not the ideal start to her season and quite where she goes from here is anyone's guess. (op 11-8 tchd 15-8 in places)
Solid Rock(IRE), bidding for a course hat-trick after four months off, made his bid around the outside turning for home but his effort soon flattened out. He may not be easy to place from now on. (op 10-1 tchd 13-2)
Majuro(IRE), winner of an unsatisfactory three-runner contest here on his return earlier in the month, tried to squeeze through between Champery and the inside rail starting up the home straight but inevitably ran out of room and was forced to snatch up. This can basically be ignored. (op 15-2)
Ransom Captive(USA) faced a stiff task on only her third outing and return from a six-month break. Held up out the back, she tried to get involved turning for home but her effort came to little. (op 14-1 tchd 16-1)

1036 32RED.COM H'CAP 1m (P)
3:15 (3:16) (Class 5) (0-70,70) 4-Y-O+ **£2,914** (£867; £433; £216) **Stalls** High

Form RPR

2314 **1** **Binnion Bay (IRE)**[13] [865] 6-8-11 **66**..............................(b) AmirQuinn(3) 4 77
(J J Bridger) *lw: trckd ldr: led gng wl 2f out: edgd rt but r.o wl u.p fnl f* **8/1**

5133 **2** *1 3/4* **Parkview Love (USA)**[12] [895] 6-9-4 **70**..........................(v) DaneO'Neill 9 77
(D Shaw) *plld hrd: chsd ldrs: rdn 2f out: chsd wnr 1f out: no imp ins fnl f* **5/1**[2]

5322 **3** *1/2* **Magic Warrior**[15] [830] 7-9-2 **68**... PatDobbs 8 74
(J C Fox) *lw: hld up in rr: rdn and effrt over 1f out: r.o steadily fnl f: nt rch ldrs* **9/1**

5241 **4** *3/4* **King After**[12] [887] 5-8-3 **58**......................................(v) StephaneBreux(3) 7 62
(J R Best) *chsd ldrs: rdn wl over 3f out: hdwy jst over 1f out: wknd wl ins fnl f* **12/1**

4250 **5** *1 3/4* **Imperial Lucky (IRE)**[5] [980] 4-9-3 **69**.............................. JimCrowley 10 69
(D K Ivory) *t.k.h: hld up towards rr on outer: rdn 3f out no hdwy fnl f* **20/1**

5612 **6** *1/2* **Tancredi (SWE)**[5] [975] 5-8-13 **68**................................. JerryO'Dwyer(3) 2 67
(N B King) *lw: led: rdn and hdd 2f out: wknd qckly jst over 1f out: eased wl ins fnl f* **11/4**[1]

0/0- **7** *1/2* **Wild Fell Hall (IRE)**[328] [1868] 4-9-4 **70**................................ AdamKirby 6 68+
(W R Swinburn) *bit bkwd: slowly away: bhd: rdn and outpcd over 3f out: styd on fnl f: n.d* **20/1**

3446 **8** *1* **Trifti**[22] [739] 6-9-2 **68**..(b) SebSanders 3 64
(C A Cyzer) *swtg: chsd ldrs: rdn wl over 2f out: wknd over 1f out* **10/1**

0442 **9** *1/2* **Arctic Desert**[10] [923] 7-9-4 **70**...................................(t) JamieSpencer 11 64
(Miss Gay Kelleway) *swtg: stdd after s and dropped in bhd: c wd and rdn wl over 1f out: no prog* **11/2**[3]

04-6 **10** *10* **Aggravation**[15] [830] 5-9-1 **67**.. JohnEgan 5 38
(D R C Elsworth) *racd in midfield on inner: rdn wl over 3f out: wknd 2f out: eased fnl f* **6/1**

1m 38.4s (-1.03) **Going Correction** 0.0s/f (Stan) **10** Ran SP% **120.4**
Speed ratings (Par 103):105,103,102,102,100 99,99,98,97,87
CSF £49.42 CT £376.86 TOTE £11.80: £2.70, £1.90, £3.10; EX 41.60.
Owner J J Bridger **Bred** Fieldspring Ltd **Trained** Liphook, Hants

FOCUS
An ordinary if competitive handicap contested by several experienced Polytrack handicappers and rated through the fourth to his best recent form. Despite being 0.36 seconds slower than the three-year-olds in the preceding Listed race, the winning time was still very respectable for the grade.
Wild Fell Hall(IRE) ◆ Official explanation: jockey said gelding was outpaced

1037 SPORTING HIGHLIGHTS LTD MAIDEN STKS 6f (P)
3:55 (3:56) (Class 5) 3-Y-O **£2,914** (£867; £433; £216) **Stalls** Low

Form RPR
04- **1** **Rasaman (IRE)**[184] [5915] 3-9-3 .... MatthewHenry 7 78+
(M A Jarvis) *w ldr: rdn 2f out: led ins fnl f: r.o wl* **13/2**[3]

0- **2** *nk* **Express Wish**[197] [5658] 3-9-3 .... ShaneKelly 8 77+
(J Noseda) *t.k.h: led: pushed along over 1f out: hdd and rdn ins fnl f: unable qckn* **11/10**[1]

222- **3** *1 ¼* **Kyle (IRE)**[152] [6457] 3-9-3 **78**.. RichardHughes 6 73
(R Hannon) *hld up in midfield: hdwy over 2f out: rdn over 1f out: chsd ldng pair ins fnl f: kpt on: nt pce to rch ldrs* **5/2**[2]

5- **4** *1 ¼* **Bajeel (IRE)**[252] [4138] 3-9-3 .... NickyMackay 3 69
(G A Butler) *h.d.w: bit bkwd: chsd ldrs: rdn 2f out: chsd ldng pair over 1f out tl ins fnl f: kpt on same pce* **14/1**

5- **5** *3* **Pusey Street Lady**[299] [2703] 3-8-12 .... JimCrowley 9 55
(J Gallagher) *s.i.s: in tch in midfield: rdn 3f out: outpcd over 2f out: kpt on steadily fnl f* **66/1**

06- **6** *½* **Polish World (USA)**[176] [6072] 3-9-3 .... DaneO'Neill 1 59
(E A L Dunlop) *t.k.h: chsd ldrs: rdn 2f out: wknd jst over 1f out* **25/1**

7 *2* **Sugar Land** 3-8-12 .... SebSanders 5 48
(C A Cyzer) *str: bkwd: sn outpcd and rdn in rr: hdwy wl over 2f out: wknd over 1f out: nvr on terms* **50/1**

8 *1* **Mango Masher (IRE)** 3-9-3 .... JohnEgan 11 50+
(C R Egerton) *tall: scope: bit bkwd: v.s.a: outpcd in rr: sme late hdwy: nvr on terms* **33/1**

0-4 **9** *1* **Take To The Skies (IRE)**[21] [752] 3-9-3 .... JamieSpencer 10 47
(A P Jarvis) *wnt rt s: a outpcd and bhd: hung rt bnd over 2f out* **7/1**

10 *7* **Ultimate Akdov (USA)** 3-9-3 .... JimmyFortune 4 26
(P F I Cole) *wl grwn: bit bkwd: stdd s: plld hrd: hld up in tch: rdn over 3f out: sn bhd* **14/1**

1m 13.22s (0.41) **Going Correction** 0.0s/f (Stan) **10** Ran SP% **125.6**
Speed ratings (Par 98):97,96,94,93,89 88,85,84,83,73
CSF £14.97 TOTE £8.90: £2.00, £1.50, £1.20; EX 24.60.
Owner Thurloe Thoroughbreds XVII **Bred** Rasana Partnership **Trained** Newmarket, Suffolk

FOCUS
An ordinary maiden in which the the front pair forced the pace from the start and nothing else got into it. There is probably very little to get excited about outside the principals, although the form looks solid enough rated around the winner, third, fifth and sixth.
Sugar Land Official explanation: jockey said filly ran very green
Ultimate Akdov(USA) Official explanation: jockey said colt ran keen early on

1038 32RED.COM FILLIES' H'CAP 1m (P)
4:40 (4:46) (Class 6) (0-60,58) 3-Y-0+ **£2,388** (£705; £352) **Stalls** High

Form RPR
3-20 **1** **Pearl Farm**[18] [797] 6-9-2 **50**.. FergusSweeney 5 61+
(C A Horgan) *lw: hld up in midfield: hdwy 3f out: rdn wl over 1f out: chsd ldr jst over 1f out: r.o wl to ld last 100 yds* **8/1**

0336 **2** *1 ¾* **Nikki Bea (IRE)**[22] [734] 4-9-6 **54**.. PaulDoe 8 61
(Jamie Poulton) *t.k.h: trckd ldrs: chsd ldr over 2f out: rdn to ld wl over 1f out: hdd and no ex last 100 yds* **11/1**

-120 **3** *2* **Saucy**[40] [616] 6-9-2 **50**... JimCrowley 10 52
(A W Carroll) *hld up in midfield: hdwy over 2f out: rdn and chsd ldng pair ins fnl f: kpt on same pce* **7/1**[2]

060- **4** *¾* **Blue Line**[206] [5474] 5-9-5 **53**... GeorgeBaker 6 57+
(M Madgwick) *hld up bhd: hdwy 2f out: rdn wl over 1f out: r.o fnl f: nvr nrr* **8/1**

5210 **5** *hd* **Mademoiselle**[23] [732] 5-9-5 **58**....................................... TolleyDean[(5)] 9 58
(R A Harris) *led for 1f: led again over 3f out: rdn and hdd wl over 1f out: wknd fnl f* **8/1**

00-4 **6** *shd* **Reveur**[18] [806] 4-9-6 **54**... EddieAhern 7 54
(M Mullineaux) *swtg: slowly away: bhd: effrt on outer bnd over 2f out: styd on fnl f: nvr nrr* **14/1**

2055 **7** *2* **Casablanca Minx (IRE)**[15] [825] 4-9-6 **57**.................(b) JamesDoyle[(3)] 4 52
(N P Littmoden) *led after 1f tl rdn and hdd over 3f out: styd prom tl wknd jst over 1f out* **10/1**

6030 **8** *1 ¼* **Moon Bird**[12] [888] 5-9-8 **56**... SebSanders 1 57+
(C A Cyzer) *t.k.h: hld up in midfield on inner: effrt and rdn over 2f out: keeping on same pce whn nt clr run over 1f out: no ch after* **4/1**[1]

5303 **9** *1* **Solicitude**[39] [627] 4-9-2 **50**.......................................(p) HayleyTurner 3 40
(D Haydn Jones) *t.k.h: chsd ldrs: rdn 3f out: sn outpcd* **15/2**[3]

004- **10** *1 ½* **First Rhapsody (IRE)**[239] [4548] 5-9-3 **51**....................... JimmyFortune 12 38
(T J Etherington) *stdd s and dropped in bhd: rdn over 1f out: no real hdwy* **12/1**

/04- **11** *2* **Grand Court (IRE)**[247] [4287] 4-9-4 **52**............................ JamieSpencer 2 34
(M J Wallace) *lw: stdd s: hld up in rr: hdwy 3f out: rdn and wknd wl over 1f out* **8/1**

00-5 **12** *10* **Shinko (IRE)**[18] [796] 4-9-4 **52**..................................... RichardHughes 11 11
(Miss J Feilden) *chsd ldrs: rdn wl over 2f out: wknd 2f out* **20/1**

1m 39.96s (0.53) **Going Correction** 0.0s/f (Stan) **12** Ran SP% **125.3**
Speed ratings (Par 98):97,95,93,92,92 92,90,88,87,86 84,74
CSF £98.41 CT £671.08 TOTE £14.40: £4.20, £4.20, £1.90; EX 220.80.
Owner Mrs B Woodford **Bred** Steve Starkey **Trained** Uffcott, Wilts

FOCUS
A competitive fillies' handicap, if not the greatest quality. The winning time was much slower than the two earlier contests over the trip, but given the different standard of the horses involved Pearl Farm's time was perfectly respectable for the type of race and the form looks reasonable rated around the placed horses.
Blue Line Official explanation: jockey said mare suffered interference on the home bend
Casablanca Minx(IRE) Official explanation: jockey said filly hung left
Shinko(IRE) Official explanation: jockey said filly lost a shoe

1039 BETDIRECTPOKER.COM H'CAP 1m 2f (P)
5:15 (5:15) (Class 6) (0-65,67) 3-Y-O **£2,388** (£705; £352) **Stalls** Low

Form RPR
55-2 **1** **Paymaster General (IRE)**[23] [728] 3-9-4 **65**................ HayleyTurner 14 74
(M D I Usher) *h.d.w: lw: t.k.h: hld up wl off pce: hdwy over 3f out: rdn to chse ldr over 2f out: ld jst ins last: wnt rt nr fin: r.o* **10/1**

006- **2** *1 ¼* **Adversane**[143] [6561] 3-9-2 **63**.. JamieSpencer 13 70
(J L Dunlop) *lw: slowly away: hld up in rr: hdwy on outer over 3f out: chsd ldrs and rdn 2f out: wandered and flashed tail u.p: wnt 2nd nr fin* **9/2**[2]

6-54 **3** *hd* **Urban Warrior**[11] [904] 3-9-0 **64**................................... JamesDoyle[(3)] 11 71
(Mrs Norma Pook) *chsd ldrs: wnt 2nd 4f out: rdn to ld wl over 2f out: hdd jst ins fnl f: no ex last 100 yds* **14/1**

000- **4** *4* **Rustic Gold**[115] [6887] 3-9-0 **64**.................................. StephaneBreux[(3)] 5 63
(J R Best) *hld up in midfield: pushed along and hdwy over 4f out: chsd ldrs over 3f out: ev ch 2f out: wknd fnl f* **12/1**

5621 **5** *1 ¾* **King Of The Beers (USA)**[19] [790] 3-8-13 **60**.................(p) JohnEgan 3 56
(R A Harris) *racd in midfield: hdwy 5f out: rdn and outpcd over 3f out: kpt on same pce after* **11/2**[3]

42-2 **6** *1 ¼* **Right Option (IRE)**[20] [776] 3-8-12 **59**............................ SebSanders 10 52
(S Dow) *chsd ldrs tl rdn and lost pl over 3f out: n.d after* **10/1**

00-0 **7** *1 ½* **Kanonkop**[10] [924] 3-8-8 **55**.. ChrisCatlin 8 45
(Miss J R Gibney) *bhd:plld wd and rdn 4f out: kpt on last 2f: nvr on terms* **33/1**

000- **8** *nk* **Kyloe Belle (USA)**[178] [6055] 3-8-13 **60**........................ JimCrowley 9 50
(Mrs A J Perrett) *hld up in midfield: rdn and lost pl 4f out: sn bhd: kpt on u.p fnl f* **20/1**

00-4 **9** *1 ½* **Go Dancing**[58] [469] 3-8-4 **58**.. MCGeran[(7)] 4 45
(P W Chapple-Hyam) *lw: chsd clr ldr tl 5f out: wknd wl over 3f out* **10/1**

-663 **10** *2* **Fine Ruler (IRE)**[11] [904] 3-9-6 **67**................................ SamHitchcott 7 50
(M R Channon) *t.k.h: led and sn clr: hdd wl over 2f out: wknd qckly over 2f out* **9/1**

000- **11** *8* **Converti**[220] [5105] 3-8-9 **56**.. JosedeSouza 12 24
(P F I Cole) *bhd: rdn wl over 4f out: no ch last 3f: t.o* **10/1**

0-31 **12** *5* **Brave Quest (IRE)**[11] [904] 3-9-4 **65**................................ IanMongan 2 24
(Mrs L J Mongan) *lw: chsd ldrs: wnt 2nd 5f out tl 4f out: sn rdn and wknd: eased over 1f out: t.o* **7/2**[1]

606 **13** *24* **Bluecrop Boy**[28] [703] 3-8-8 **55**..................................(b[1]) AdamKirby 6 —
(D J S Ffrench Davis) *nvr gng wl: reminders after 1f: a wl bhd: lost tch 6f out: t.o and eased last 2f* **66/1**

2m 7.95s (0.16) **Going Correction** 0.0s/f (Stan) **13** Ran SP% **125.7**
Speed ratings (Par 96):99,98,97,94,93 92,91,90,89,88 81,77,58
CSF £56.66 CT £657.24 TOTE £12.90: £3.00, £2.10, £4.70; EX 95.10 Place 6 £57.03, Place 5 £44.52.
Owner The Paymasters **Bred** Miss Mary Davidson And Mrs Steffi Von Schilcher **Trained** Upper Lambourn, Berks

FOCUS
A big field and with Fine Ruler almost bolting out out in front the early pace was very strong, but they paid for that later and the finish was almost in slow motion. The field finished well spread out and the form is probably reliable enough for the grade, rated through the third.
Brave Quest(IRE) Official explanation: jockey said gelding ran flat
T/Plt: £37.90 to a £1 stake. Pool: £51,816.10. 997.40 winning tickets. T/Qpdt: £24.40 to a £1 stake. Pool: £2,300.70. 69.50 winning tickets. SP

845 NEWCASTLE (L-H)
Saturday, April 14

OFFICIAL GOING: Good (good to firm in places)
Wind: Light, half-behind

1040 BET365.COM H'CAP 1m 3y(S)
2:05 (2:05) (Class 4) (0-80,79) 4-Y-0+
£5,608 (£1,679; £839; £420; £167; £167) **Stalls** High

Form RPR
0-03 **1** **Exit Smiling**[23] [732] 5-8-8 **69**...................................... MickyFenton 17 80+
(P T Midgley) *in tch: n.m.r fr 2f out to ins fnl f: styd on wl to ld towards fin* **16/1**

5-06 **2** *¾* **Little Jimbob**[36] [651] 6-9-2 **77**.................................... PaulHanagan 10 83
(R A Fahey) *led to over 2f out: rallied to ld ins fnl f: kpt on: hdd towards fin* **20/1**

0-56 **3** *1 ½* **Paraguay (USA)**[14] [842] 4-8-12 **73**........................... EdwardCreighton 3 76
(Miss V Haigh) *hld up: stdy hdwy 1/2-way: effrt 2f out: kpt on fnl f* **25/1**

000- **4** *shd* **Fair Shake (IRE)**[12] [5961] 7-8-4 **65** oh3............................(v) PaulFessey 6 67+
(Karen McLintock) *hld up: nt clr run over 2f out: kpt on fnl f: nrst fin* **66/1**

0-03 **5** *½* **Shot To Fame (USA)**[14] [846] 8-9-4 **79**...............(t) SilvestreDeSousa 13 80
(D Nicholls) *cl up gng wl: led over 2f out to ins fnl f: sn no ex* **5/2**[1]

2-62 **5** *dht* **Cross The Line (IRE)**[14] [840] 5-9-3 **78**........................... LPKeniry 4 79
(A P Jarvis) *midfield: effrt over 2f out: kpt on same pce fnl f* **9/1**

216- **7** *shd* **Middlemarch (IRE)**[149] [6502] 7-9-0 **75**........................... PhillipMakin 12 76
(J S Goldie) *midfield: shkn up 2f out: kpt on fnl f: no imp* **20/1**

546- **8** *shd* **Mount Usher**[227] [4937] 5-8-10 **71**.................................. DeanMcKeown 5 72+
(G A Swinbank) *missed break: hld up: hdwy and swtchd wd over 1f out: sn prom: kpt on same pce ins fnl f* **14/1**

06-0 **9** *1 ¾* **Daaweitza**[14] [846] 4-9-0 **75**... TomEaves 11 72
(B Ellison) *prom: drvn over 2f out: n.m.r and outpcd over 1f out: no imp fnl f* **7/1**[3]

400- **10** *1 ¼* **Moody Tunes**[172] [6160] 4-9-1 **76**.................................. PatCosgrave 2 70
(K R Burke) *hld up: pushed along 3f out: nvr rchd ldrs* **33/1**

13-0 **11** *hd* **Everest (IRE)**[9] [932] 10-8-9 **75**.......................... JamieMoriarty[(5)] 16 68
(B Ellison) *hld up: pushed along over 4f out: n.d* **20/1**

166- **12** *½* **Ahlawy (IRE)**[280] [3301] 4-9-2 **77**.................................... PaulMulrennan 8 69
(M W Easterby) *cl up: ev ch over 1f out: wknd ins fnl f* **40/1**

001- **13** *1 ½* **Amwaal (USA)**[194] [5727] 4-9-4 **79**..................................... RHills 15 68
(J L Dunlop) *trckd ldrs: effrt and ev ch over 1f out: wknd ins fnl f* **9/2**[2]

300- **14** *shd* **Just Lille (IRE)**[212] [5320] 4-8-9 **70**........................... RoystonFfrench 7 59
(Mrs A Duffield) *racd wd in midfield: rdn over 3f out: sn btn* **50/1**

403- **15** *1 ¾* **Breaking Shadow (IRE)**[168] [6221] 5-8-5 **73**.............. DeanHeslop[(7)] 14 57
(M A Peill) *hld up: hdwy and prom 3f out: rdn and wknd over 1f out* **14/1**

40-0 **16** *1 ½* **Alsadaa (USA)**[10] [930] 4-8-9 **70**................................... DaleGibson 9 51
(M W Easterby) *chsd ldrs: drvn over 2f out: sn lost pl* **80/1**

034 **R** **Quai Du Roi (IRE)**[5] [969] 5-9-2 **77**.................................(b[1]) NCallan 1 —
(K A Ryan) *ref to r* **12/1**

1m 39.83s (-2.07) **Going Correction** -0.125s/f (Firm) **17** Ran SP% **124.4**
Speed ratings (Par 105):105,104,102,102,102 102,102,101,100,98 98,98,96,96,94 93,—
CSF £311.96 CT £7967.51 TOTE £27.60: £5.20, £2.90, £5.80, £9.10; EX 526.90 Trifecta £152.10 Part won. Pool: £214.23 - 0.10 winning tickets..

Owner Peter Mee **Bred** Mrs D O Joly **Trained** Westow, N Yorks

FOCUS

An ordinary handicap in which the whole field raced stands side. The pace was fair and the form is rated through the third.

Fair Shake(IRE) Official explanation: jockey said gelding was denied a clear run

Middlemarch(IRE) Official explanation: jockey said, regarding running and riding, his orders were to do his best but suffered interference approx 1f out

Daaweitza Official explanation: jockey said gelding was denied a clear run

1041 BET365 H'CAP 7f

2:35 (2:35) (Class 2) (0-100,100) 4-Y-O+

£9,971 (£2,985; £1,492; £747; £372; £187) Stalls High

Form RPR

000- 1 **Giganticus (USA)**[198] 5639 4-8-6 **88** MichaelHills 13 96+
(B W Hills) *trckd ldrs: rdn to ld over 1f out: kpt on wl fnl f* **4/1**[1]

610- 2 1 **Dhaular Dhar (IRE)**[167] 6243 5-8-13 **95** DanielTudhope 1 99+
(J S Goldie) *hld up: effrt whn n.m.r over 1f out: gd hdwy to chse wnr wl ins fnl f: r.o* **16/1**

13-5 3 nk **Mezuzah**[14] 846 7-8-6 **88** oh1 ow2 PaulMulrennan 7 91
(M W Easterby) *led to over 1f out: kpt on same pce fnl f* **16/1**

1-20 4 nk **Ceremonial Jade (UAE)**[14] 840 4-8-13 **95** (t) OscarUrbina 6 97
(M Botti) *hld up: hdwy on outside over 1f out: kpt on fnl f* **13/2**[3]

3-60 5 1 **Compton's Eleven**[58] 470 6-8-11 **93** TedDurcan 11 93
(M R Channon) *hld up in tch: effrt over 1f out: one pce fnl f* **15/2**

620- 6 hd **Zomerlust**[203] 5529 5-8-11 **93** GrahamGibbons 12 92+
(J J Quinn) *hld up: rdn 3f out: kpt on fnl f: no imp* **16/1**

040- 7 ¾ **Sir Xaar (IRE)**[211] 5341 4-9-2 **98** RoystonFfrench 9 95
(B Smart) *chsd ldrs tl rdn and no ex over 1f out* **12/1**

100- 8 hd **Nanton (USA)**[163] 6313 5-8-4 **86** PaulHanagan 4 86+
(N Wilson) *midfield: rdn whn n.m.r and outpcd over 1f out: kpt on ins fnl f* **22/1**

30-0 9 hd **Commando Scott (IRE)**[21] 757 6-8-3 **88** PatrickMathers(3) 5 84
(I W McInnes) *chsd ldrs: ev ch over 2f out: no ex fnl f* **16/1**

400- 10 ½ **Game Lad**[250] 4202 5-8-7 **89** DavidAllan 10 88+
(T D Easterby) *hld up: rdn over 2f out: styng on but no imp whn nt clr run fnl f* **14/1**

0-54 11 1¾ **Obe Gold**[58] 470 5-8-13 **95** NCallan 8 95+
(M R Channon) *midfield: drvn over 2f out: btn fnl f* **8/1**

000- 12 2 **Indian Trail**[189] 5812 7-8-11 **100** AdeleRothery(7) 3 85+
(D Nicholls) *plld hrd: cl up on outside tl wknd appr fnl f* **25/1**

/10- 13 2 **River Bravo (IRE)**[301] 2658 4-8-12 **94** AdrianMcCarthy 2 73
(P W Chapple-Hyam) *chsd ldrs tl hung lft and wknd wl over 1f out* **11/2**[2]

1m 26.13s (-1.89) **Going Correction** -0.125s/f (Firm) 13 Ran SP% **117.7**

Speed ratings (Par 109):105,103,103,103,102 101,100,100,100,99 97,95,93

CSF £69.58 CT £962.71 TOTE £4.70: £2.30, £5.30, £5.30; EX 79.40 TRIFECTA Not won..

Owner DM James,Cavendish Inv Ltd,Matthew Green **Bred** Gaines-Gentry Thoroughbreds Et Al **Trained** Lambourn, Berks

■ Stewards' Enquiry : Patrick Mathers caution: in breach of Rule 158, allowed gelding to coast home with no assistance

Graham Gibbons two-day ban: failed to ride out for fifth place (Apr 25-26)

FOCUS

A fair handicap but one in which the pace was only fair and the form looks solid enough rated through the fifth to eighth. The field again raced stands' side.

NOTEBOOK

Giganticus(USA) ◆, making his reappearance and, having his first start since being gelded, had the run of the race and ran right up to his best. He did not go on last year after an encouraging reappearance but it may be different this time round. (op 7-2)

Dhaular Dhar(IRE) ◆ was an improved performer last year but looks better than ever judged by this promising reappearance run. A much stronger gallop would have been in his favour and this versatile sort, who handles soft ground, is the type to win more races this term granted a decent pace. (op 18-1)

Mezuzah, dropped in trip, had the run of the race and fared much better than on his reappearance, despite being out of the handicap and carrying overweight. Although he has little margin for error from his current mark, he has always looked much more effective in softer ground. (op 20-1)

Ceremonial Jade(UAE), unexposed on turf, was not disgraced and is another that would have been suited by a stronger overall gallop. A useful performer on Polytrack up to a mile, he is high enough in the weights but may be capable of a bit better. (op 15-2)

Compton's Eleven, the type that needs things to drop right, is not a prolific winner but has dropped to a handy mark and is another that would have been better served by a decent gallop. (op 7-1)

Zomerlust shaped as though retaining much of his ability on this first start for over six months. A more strongly-run race over six furlongs with cut in the ground are his requirements but he is the type that needs things to drop right.

Game Lad Official explanation: jockey said gelding was denied a clear run

Indian Trail, a useful sprinter, failed to settle in this muddling event over this trip on his reappearance under his inexperienced rider. He will be a different proposition back over sprint distances later this season. (tchd 28-1 in a place)

River Bravo(IRE), one of the few in this field open to further improvement, ran as though feeling this ground and he will be worth another chance with more give underfoot. Official explanation: jockey said colt was unsuited by the good (good to firm in places) ground (op 4-1)

1042 BET365 CALL 08000 322 365 H'CAP 1m 4f 93y

3:05 (3:09) (Class 5) (0-70,76) 4-Y-O+ £4,533 (£1,348; £674; £336) Stalls Low

Form RPR

000- 1 **Le Soleil (GER)**[183] 5954 6-8-6 **57** TPQueally 14 73+
(B J Curley) *midfield: smooth hdwy over 2f out: led 1f out: pushed clr: readily* **11/4**[1]

0 2 1½ **Great Quest (IRE)**[10] 914 5-9-0 **65** RoystonFfrench 6 74
(James Moffatt) *hld up: hdwy outside over 1f out: chsd wnr ins fnl f: kpt on: no imp* **50/1**

040- 3 1 **Balwearie (IRE)**[172] 6158 6-8-2 **56** oh6 AndrewMullen(3) 15 64
(Miss L A Perratt) *chsd ldrs: led 3f to 1f out: kpt on same pce* **25/1**

421- 4 1¼ **Osolomio (IRE)**[159] 6382 4-8-13 **65** DaleGibson 10 71+
(G A Swinbank) *chsd ldrs: drvn and outpcd 2f out: kpt on wl fnl f* **4/1**[3]

0-43 5 nk **Intavac Boy**[4] 997 6-8-9 **60** PaulHanagan 4 65
(R A Fahey) *hld up: hdwy over 2f out: kpt on fnl f: no imp* **10/3**[2]

24-1 6 ½ **Carlton Scroop (FR)**[21] 767 4-8-9 **61** (b) MickyFenton 9 65
(J Jay) *midfield: rdn over 5f out: effrt 3f out: no imp over 1f out* **15/2**

144- 7 1 **Danzatrice**[189] 5815 5-8-0 **56** DuranFentiman(5) 13 59
(C W Thornton) *hld up: rdn 4f out: kpt on fr 2f out: nvr rchd ldrs* **14/1**

603- 8 ½ **Tranos (USA)**[28] 5452 4-8-8 **60** KDarley 16 62
(Micky Hammond) *hld up towards rr: hdwy and prom 4f out: effrt over 2f out: edgd lft and no ex over 1f out* **16/1**

540- 9 1¼ **Alfonso**[36] 5031 6-8-12 **66** MarkLawson(3) 3 66
(P Monteith) *midfield: outpcd over 5f out: sme late hdwy: n.d* **33/1**

00-0 10 nk **Sforzando**[14] 850 6-8-12 **70** KristinStubbs(7) 2 70
(Mrs L Stubbs) *missed break: bhd tl sme late hdwy: nvr on terms* **33/1**

0005 11 1 **Greenbelt**[4] 997 6-8-10 **61** TomEaves 7 59
(G M Moore) *in tch tl rdn and wknd wl over 1f out* **20/1**

064- 12 nk **Andre Chenier (IRE)**[18] 2812 6-8-9 **60** TonyHamilton 8 58
(P Monteith) *sn pushed along towards rr: nvr on terms* **12/1**

000- 13 hd **Vice Admiral**[172] 6161 4-8-6 **58** oh1 ow2 PaulMulrennan 12 56
(M W Easterby) *chsd ldrs tl wknd fr 2f out* **20/1**

603- 14 1½ **Sporting Gesture**[162] 6317 10-8-11 **69** NSLawes(7) 5 64
(M W Easterby) *hld up: nt clr run over 2f out: nvr on terms* **20/1**

0121 15 1¾ **Shape Up (IRE)**[10] 928 7-9-11 **76** (v) NCallan 11 69+
(R Craggs) *cl up: chal 3f out: wknd wl over 1f out* **8/1**

600- 16 47 **Highest Regard**[186] 5904 5-9-0 **65** PatCosgrave 1 —
(N P McCormack) *led to 3f out: sn lost pl* **40/1**

2m 40.36s (-3.19) **Going Correction** -0.125s/f (Firm)

WFA 4 from 5yo+ 1lb 16 Ran SP% **141.3**

Speed ratings (Par 103):105,104,103,102,102 101,101,100,100,99 99,99,98,97,96 65

CSF £184.57 CT £3161.17 TOTE £4.80: £1.30, £9.50, £6.30, £1.90; EX 256.60 TRIFECTA Not won..

Owner Curley Leisure **Bred** Gestut Wittekindshof **Trained** Newmarket, Suffolk

FOCUS

A run-of-the-mill handicap in which the pace seemed sound. The winner is value for around five lengths and the form looks sound.

Shape Up(IRE) Official explanation: jockey said gelding had no more to give

1043 EUROPEAN BREEDERS' FUND NOVICE STKS 5f

3:45 (3:46) (Class 4) 2-Y-O £4,533 (£1,348; £674; £336) Stalls High

Form RPR

1 1 **Mister Hardy**[14] 845 2-9-0 JamieMoriarty(5) 2 90
(R A Fahey) *hld up in tch on outside: smooth hdwy to ld over 1f out: rdn out fnl f* **8/11**[1]

1 2 1¼ **Thunder Bay**[12] 883 2-9-0 TedDurcan 5 80
(M R Channon) *dwlt: hld up in tch: hdwy to chse wnr ins fnl f: r.o* **7/1**

6 3 2½ **Varinia (IRE)**[10] 926 2-8-0 PatrickDonaghy(7) 8 63
(M Brittain) *led to over 1f out: kpt on same pce fnl f* **20/1**

4 ½ **Cayman Fox** 2-8-7 RoystonFfrench 9 61+
(James Moffatt) *dwlt: sn chsng ldrs: rdn whn n.m.r 1/2-way: rallied fnl f: kpt on* **11/2**[3]

5 1½ **Timewatch** 2-8-12 KDarley 6 60
(M Johnston) *cl up tl rdn and no ex over 1f out* **9/2**[2]

0 6 1½ **Northgate Lodge (USA)**[14] 845 2-8-12 DeanMernagh 4 54
(M Brittain) *cl up tl wknd wl over 1f out* **33/1**

7 1¾ **Little Finch (IRE)** 2-8-7 PaulFessey 1 42
(R C Guest) *s.i.s: sn outpcd: sme late hdwy: nvr on terms* **33/1**

0 8 6 **Bank On Bertie**[12] 890 2-8-5 NSLawes(7) 3 23
(M W Easterby) *cl up to 2f out: sn rdn and btn* **40/1**

9 5 **One Tou Many** 2-8-7 DeanMcKeown 7 —
(C W Fairhurst) *missed break: sn wl bhd: nvr on terms* **20/1**

60.79 secs (-0.71) **Going Correction** -0.125s/f (Firm) 9 Ran SP% **121.8**

Speed ratings (Par 94):100,98,94,93,90 88,85,76,68

CSF £6.55 TOTE £1.70: £1.10, £1.70, £3.70; EX 8.20 Trifecta £38.00 Pool: £752.45 - 14.03 winning tickets..

Owner The Cosmic Cases **Bred** Mrs M Bryce **Trained** Musley Bank, N Yorks

FOCUS

Little strength in depth but another step in the right direction for Mister Hardy, who looks the type to progress again, and the form looks sound enough.

NOTEBOOK

Mister Hardy ◆'s Brocklesby win has taken a few knocks but he turned in an improved effort under his penalty. He travelled strongly on this much quicker ground, won with more in hand than the official margin suggests and appeals as the type to progress again, especially when upped to six furlongs. The Woodcote at Epsom is reportedly the aim. (op 4-5 tchd 11-10)

Thunder Bay, who scrambled home in an ordinary event on Polytrack on his debut, turned in a much-improved effort on this first run on turf. He will have no problems with six furlongs and appeals as the type to win more races. (op 13-2)

Varinia(IRE) left her debut form behind and, although she had the run of the race next to the stands' rail, showed enough to suggest a small race can be found in due course. (tchd 22-1)

Cayman Fox, a small filly lacking in physical scope, attracted support on this racecourse debut and was not disgraced given her greenness and the fact that she did not enjoy the run of the race. She looks capable of winning a small event but, judging by her physique, there may not be too much in the way of further improvement. (op 8-1 tchd 5-1)

Timewatch, the first foal of a useful French sprinter, was arguably the nicest looker in the field as a strong sort with plenty of scope but ran as though this debut run was needed. He may well leave this bare form well behind in due course. (tchd 7-2)

Northgate Lodge(USA) fared better than on his debut on easier ground at this course last month but he is likely to continue to look vulnerable in this type of event.

1044 ST JAMES SECURITY MAIDEN STKS 1m 2f 32y

4:30 (4:42) (Class 5) 3-Y-O+ £3,562 (£1,059; £529; £264) Stalls Low

Form RPR

5- 1 **Celestial Halo (IRE)**[235] 4680 3-8-7 MichaelHills 1 82+
(B W Hills) *trckd ldrs: led over 3f out: pushed clr fnl 2f* **4/6**[1]

2 13 **Campli (IRE)**[154] 5-9-7 MichaelJStainton(5) 13 54
(Micky Hammond) *dwlt: hld up: rdn and kpt on wl fnl f: tk 2nd on line* **33/1**

030- 3 hd **El Dececy (USA)**[199] 5623 3-8-7 RHills 10 50
(J L Dunlop) *chsd ldrs: effrt and wnt 2nd over 3f out: rdn and one pce fr 2f out* **9/2**[2]

42-0 4 nk **Dechiper (IRE)**[23] 732 5-9-12 51 DanielTudhope 11 53
(R Johnson) *hld up: hdwy over 2f out: kpt on fnl f: no imp* **50/1**

-005 5 ¾ **Counterfactual (IRE)**[23] 732 4-9-9 48 MarkLawson(3) 8 52
(B Smart) *rrd s: plld hrd in midfield: effrt 3f out: sn one pce* **25/1**

6 ½ **Bernix**[53] 5-9-12 (t) DavidAllan 14 51
(T D Easterby) *hld up: styd on fr 2f out: nvr rchd ldrs* **33/1**

3 7 ½ **Bivouac (UAE)**[23] 728 3-8-7 DeanMcKeown 5 46
(G A Swinbank) *keen: prom tl outpcd fr 2f out* **12/1**

42 8 1 **Anne Bronte**[13] 869 3-8-2 RoystonFfrench 2 39
(M Johnston) *led to over 3f out: outpcd fr 2f out* **7/1**[3]

60- 9 hd **Monet's Lady (IRE)**[248] 4260 3-8-2 PaulHanagan 12 38
(R A Fahey) *hld up: rdn 3f out: n.d* **40/1**

04- 10 nk **Highland Legacy**[171] 6173 3-8-7 MickyFenton 3 43
(M L W Bell) *dwlt: hld up midfield: shkn up over 2f out: nvr nrr* **12/1**

0- 11 1½ **Fantastic Delight**[226] 4959 4-9-7 TomEaves 4 39
(G M Moore) *prom tl rdn and wknd over 2f out* **50/1**

0-34 12 1¼ **Storm Mission (USA)**[10] 931 3-8-7 56 EdwardCreighton 9 38
(Miss V Haigh) *midfield: rdn 3f out: sn no ex* **50/1**

13 14 **Our Kenny**[115] 5-9-12 J-PGuillambert 7 15
(C W Thornton) *dwlt: a bhd* **80/1**

00/ **14** *11* **Bahrall**[531] 6178 4-9-12 .... LPKeniry 6 —
(A P Jarvis) *in tch tl rdn and wknd over 3f out* **100/1**

2m 9.31s (-2.49) **Going Correction** -0.125s/f (Firm)
WFA 3 from 4yo+ 19lb **14** Ran SP% **126.3**
Speed ratings (Par 103):104,93,93,93,92 92,91,91,90,90 89,88,77,68
CSF £43.34 TOTE £1.60: £1.10, £8.70, £1.50; EX 52.80 Trifecta £431.20 Part won. Pool: £607.37 - 0.85 winning tickets..
Owner J Hanson **Bred** Roncon Churchtown Bloodstock And Lane Ltd **Trained** Lambourn, Berks

FOCUS
A race lacking anything in the way of strength, but the winner looks the sort to go on to better things and the fifth sets the level for the form.
Highland Legacy Official explanation: jockey said colt was denied a clear run

1045 SIMPSON & GREGG MAIDEN FILLIES' STKS 1m 3y(S)
5:10 (5:11) (Class 5) 3-Y-0+ **£3,562** (£1,059; £529; £264) **Stalls** High

Form RPR

323- **1** **Nadawat (USA)**[196] 5679 3-8-9 76 .... RHills 9 65
(J L Dunlop) *chsd ldrs: rdn to ld ins fnl f: hld on wl* **5/4**[1]

6 **2** *nk* **Diksie Dancer**[47] 565 3-8-9 .... NCallan 14 64
(K A Ryan) *led to ins fnl f: kpt on but a hld* **10/1**

32-0 **3** *nk* **Musical Beat**[14] 838 3-8-9 71 .... EdwardCreighton 10 64
(Miss V Haigh) *cl up: rdn over 2f out: ev ch tl ins fnl f: kpt on u.p* **6/1**[3]

5- **4** *2 1/2* **Balliasta (IRE)**[186] 5891 3-8-9 .... MichaelHills 16 58+
(B W Hills) *midfield: effrt and shkn up 2f out: kpt on fnl f: nvr nr ldrs* **9/4**[2]

5 *1 1/2* **Music Review** 3-8-6 ow2 .... JamieMoriarty[(5)] 1 56+
(R A Fahey) *dwlt: hld up: hdwy outside over 2f out: kpt on fnl f: no imp* **40/1**

0- **6** *nk* **Heart Of Glass (IRE)**[164] 6298 3-8-2 .... LukeMorris[(7)] 11 54
(M L W Bell) *dwlt: sn midfield: pushed along over 2f out: sn no imp* **20/1**

7 *hd* **Entre Chat** 3-8-9 .... (t) OscarUrbina 4 53
(M Botti) *midfield: rdn over 2f out: kpt on same pce* **20/1**

36-0 **8** *shd* **Alisdanza**[102] 12 5-9-3 40 .... SladeO'Hara[(7)] 8 57
(N Wilson) *chsd ldrs tl rdn and outpcd fr 2f out* **80/1**

333- **9** *1 1/2* **Coronation Flight**[168] 6211 4-9-10 49 .... DeanMcKeown 7 54
(F P Murtagh) *hld up: rdn 3f out: nt pce to chal* **33/1**

06- **10** *3* **On The Map**[160] 6349 3-8-9 .... LPKeniry 5 43
(A P Jarvis) *chsd ldrs: rdn over 2f out: wknd over 1f out* **33/1**

11 *nk* **Cecina Marina** 4-9-10 .... J-PGuillambert 12 46
(C W Thornton) *chsd ldrs tl wknd fr 2f out* **66/1**

5-0 **12** *1 1/4* **Celtic Memories (IRE)**[35] 655 3-8-9 .... DaleGibson 3 39
(M W Easterby) *prom: outpcd over 3f out: sn btn* **66/1**

6-0 **13** *1/2* **Decent Proposal**[14] 849 3-8-9 .... DavidAllan 6 38
(T D Easterby) *missed break: a bhd* **66/1**

14 *1/2* **Maroussies Rock** 3-8-9 .... KDarley 13 37
(P C Haslam) *s.i.s: a bhd* **16/1**

15 *2 1/2* **Miss Lightning**[70] 4-9-5 .... NataliaGemelova[(5)] 2 35
(R Bastiman) *missed break: nvr on terms* **100/1**

0 **16** *3/4* **Pickledallnuts**[23] 728 3-8-9 .... TomEaves 15 29
(Miss J A Camacho) *bhd: rdn 1/2-way: nvr on terms* **33/1**

1m 41.91s (0.01) **Going Correction** -0.125s/f (Firm)
WFA 3 from 4yo+ 15lb **16** Ran SP% **132.0**
Speed ratings (Par 100):94,93,93,90,89 89,88,88,87,84 84,82,82,81,79 78
CSF £15.97 TOTE £2.30: £1.40, £3.80, £1.80; EX 26.90 Trifecta £100.10 Pool: £358.25 - 2.54 winning tickets. Place 6 £132.63, Place 5 £11.09.
Owner Hamdan Al Maktoum **Bred** Shadwell Farm LLC **Trained** Arundel, W Sussex
■ Stewards' Enquiry : Edward Creighton one-day ban: not riding to his draw (Apr 25)

FOCUS
Not a strong race rated through the fourth but limited by the eighth and ninth, and a muddling gallop resulted in a modest winning time for the class, 2.08 seconds slower than the opening handicap over the same trip. Those racing prominently held the edge and the field again raced stands' side.
T/Plt: £713.90 to a £1 stake. Pool: £60,000.00. 61.35 winning tickets. T/Qpdt: £6.70 to a £1 stake. Pool: £3,724.00. 408.20 winning tickets. RY

1046 - (Foreign Racing) - See Raceform Interactive

[779]CURRAGH (R-H)
Sunday, April 15

OFFICIAL GOING: Good to firm

1047a VERGLAS LOUGHBROWN STKS (LISTED RACE) 7f
2:55 (2:55) 3-Y-0 **£21,993** (£6,452; £3,074; £1,047)

RPR

1 **Honoured Guest (IRE)**[15] 852 3-9-1 .... JAHeffernan 11 109+
(A P O'Brien, Ire) *trckd ldrs: 5th 1/2-way: smooth hdwy 2f out: led 1f out: drvn clr: easily* **4/1**[2]

2 *1 3/4* **Alexander Tango (IRE)**[204] 5522 3-8-12 104 .... MJKinane 5 102
(T Stack, Ire) *hld up in rr: 6th and hdwy over 1f out: kpt on wl* **7/1**

3 *1* **Howya Now Kid (IRE)**[232] 4824 3-9-1 94 .... DPMcDonogh 1 102
(G M Lyons, Ire) *led and disp: hdd 1f out: kpt on same pce* **12/1**

4 *3* **Fleeting Shadow (IRE)**[196] 5715 3-9-1 112 .... PJSmullen 2 94
(D K Weld, Ire) *hld up towards rr: 5th and prog 1 1/2f out: 4th and no imp ins fnl f* **11/2**[3]

5 *hd* **Dimenticata (IRE)**[21] 782 3-8-12 102 .... CDHayes 8 90
(Kevin Prendergast, Ire) *chsd ldrs: 6th 1/2-way: 4th and effrt 1 1/2f out: no ex fnl f* **12/1**

6 *1* **Trinity College (USA)**[196] 5715 3-9-1 103 .... DavidMcCabe 6 91
(A P O'Brien, Ire) *cl 3rd: rdn 2f out: no ex fr over 1f out* **10/1**

7 *hd* **Newgate Lodge (IRE)**[8] 946 3-8-12 99 .... JMurtagh 10 87
(M Halford, Ire) *hld up: effrt 2f out: no imp: one pce* **11/1**

8 *4* **Kingsdale Orion (IRE)**[182] 5993 3-9-1 79 .... PBBeggy 9 79
(Ms Florence Mills, Ire) *hld up in tch: rdn and wknd fr over 2f out* **100/1**

9 *9* **Bravely (IRE)** 3-9-1 .... KJManning 3 55
(J S Bolger, Ire) *cl 2nd: wknd fr 2f out* **14/1**

10 *hd* **Rabatash (USA)**[231] 4850 3-9-4 107 .... WMLordan 7 57
(David Wachman, Ire) *s.i.s: sn chsd ldrs in 4th: wknd fr 2f out* **9/4**[1]

1m 23.6s (-3.90) **Going Correction** -0.40s/f (Firm) **11** Ran SP% **119.1**
Speed ratings: 106,104,102,99,99 98,97,93,82,82
CSF £33.04 TOTE £5.30: £2.10, £2.30, £4.50; DF 42.60.
Owner Derrick Smith **Bred** King Bloodstock **Trained** Ballydoyle, Co Tipperary

FOCUS
A good bunch of three-year-olds lined up for this Listed contest. The early pace was sound and the form looks solid enough.

NOTEBOOK
Honoured Guest(IRE) ◆, off the mark at the third attempt on his seasonal debut 15 days previously, showed himself to be a progressive three-year-old with a comfortable display on this step up in grade. He still looks to be learning his trade and, while he went on the faster ground successfully, he may just be happiest with a little more ease underfoot. Connections later mooted a possible trip to France for the 2,000gns there and that is a clear indication of just how well he has done from two-to-three. He should also have little trouble with a mile in due course. (op 5/1)
Alexander Tango(IRE) ◆, who ran with credit in the face of some stiff tasks as a juvenile, found the winner gone beyond recall by the time she hit her full stride. This rates a decent comeback effort, she ought to improve a deal for the outing, and can certainly win at this level before too long.
Howya Now Kid(IRE), who signed off with a fair effort in the valuable Sales race at this track in August last term, had his chance from the front and posted personal-best effort on this three-year-old debut. His yard has made a bright start to the season and he could have more to offer over this sort of trip now.
Fleeting Shadow(IRE), fifth of nine behind Holy Roman Emperor in France on his final outing last year, had an obvious chance at these weights and has to rate disappointing on this seasonal return. However, with his yard yet to hit top form this season, he is not one to write off on the back of this display. (op 4/1)
Rabatash(USA), a Group 3 winner over six furlongs at this track on his last outing at two, was never in the hunt after a sluggish start and dropped out tamely when it mattered in the home straight. He was later reported to have finished distressed. Official explanation: jockey said colt ran very free for first 2f and found nothing thereafter; vet said colt was distressed post-race (op 2/1 tchd 5/2)

1049a CASTLEMARTIN & LA LOUVIERE STUDS GLADNESS STKS (GROUP 3) 7f
3:55 (3:57) 4-Y-0+ **£30,743** (£8,986; £4,256; £1,418)

RPR

1 **Mustameet (USA)**[126] 6784 6-9-6 117 .... DPMcDonogh 5 119+
(Kevin Prendergast, Ire) *settled 4th: 3rd and hdwy under 2f out: chal ins fnl f: r.o wl u.p to ld cl home* **5/4**[1]

2 *3/4* **An Tadh (IRE)**[211] 5393 4-9-3 109 .... JMurtagh 2 111
(G M Lyons, Ire) *attempted to make all: strly pressed fr under 2f out: kpt on wl u.p: hdd cl home* **6/1**

3 *shd* **Marcus Andronicus (USA)**[275] 3494 4-9-0 112 .... JAHeffernan 3 108
(A P O'Brien, Ire) *chsd ldr in 2nd: rdn to chal fr under 2f out: kpt on u.p fnl f* **10/3**[2]

4 *6* **Danehill Music (IRE)**[21] 782 4-9-0 100 .... WMLordan 1 92
(David Wachman, Ire) *trckd ldrs in 3rd: 4th and no ex fr under 2f out* **11/1**

5 *5* **Farinelli**[183] 5978 4-9-0 100 .... MJKinane 4 78
(John M Oxx, Ire) *reluctant to load: hld up: 5th 1/2-way: no ex fr over 2f out* **11/2**[3]

6 *12* **Senor Benny (USA)**[21] 781 8-9-0 102 .... KJManning 6 46
(M McDonagh, Ire) *a towards rr: no ex fr 2 1/2f out* **33/1**

1m 24.2s (-3.30) **Going Correction** -0.40s/f (Firm) **6** Ran SP% **108.5**
Speed ratings: 102,101,101,94,88 74
CSF £8.56 TOTE £1.90: £1.10, £2.70; DF 7.40.
Owner Hamdan Al Maktoum **Bred** Shadwell Farm LLC **Trained** Friarstown, Co Kildare

FOCUS
A fair renewal of this Group 3 prize. The winner did well to overcome the modest early pace and the form is rated through the runner up running to his best.

NOTEBOOK
Mustameet(USA), who has now made his seasonal return in this event for the last three years - winning it in 2005 and runner up in 2006, confirmed he retains all of his ability with a ready success. Considering this trip is plenty sharp enough for him these days, he deserves plenty of credit as the early pace was only modest and he went without fuss on the quick surface. This very likeable six-year-old looks set for another decent season on this evidence and his connections will be no doubt trying to find success at the top level. (op 11/10 tchd 1/1)
An Tadh(IRE), who progressed to win at this grade last year, got very much the run of the race from the front on this seasonal bow and has to rate a little flattered. This still rates a solid effort, however, and he looks capable of further improvement as a four-year-old. Somewhat of a 7f specialist, he will likely bid to win the Ballycorus Stakes at Leopardstown in June for a second consecutive year. (op 6/1 tchd 13/2)
Marcus Andronicus(USA), the French 2,000 Guineas runner up and not seen since finishing out the back in last year's July Cup, proved easy to back on this return to action and ultimately ran as though the race was needed. He has the class to win in this company and 7f could prove to be his optimum trip. (op 11/4)
Danehill Music(IRE) did not really look happy on this much quicker surface and has shown all of her best form with some cut underfoot. (op 10/1 tchd 12/1)

1050a ASCON ROHCON ALLEGED STKS (LISTED RACE) 1m 2f
4:25 (4:26) 4-Y-0+ **£21,993** (£6,452; £3,074; £1,047)

RPR

1 **Dylan Thomas (IRE)**[190] 5822 4-9-8 126 .... JAHeffernan 2 118+
(A P O'Brien, Ire) *hld up in 5th: smooth hdwy into 3rd under 2f out: led over 1f out: qcknd clr: easily* **8/15**[1]

2 *3* **Fracas (IRE)**[176] 6103 5-9-1 111 .... WMLordan 1 100
(David Wachman, Ire) *trckd ldrs on outer: 3rd 1/2-way: impr into 2nd over 1 1/2f out: kpt on same pce ins fnl f* **9/1**[3]

3 *1* **Heliostatic (IRE)**[197] 5697 4-9-6 112 .... KJManning 3 103
(J S Bolger, Ire) *led: rdn and strly pressed 2f out: hdd over 1f out: kpt on same pce u.p* **4/1**[2]

4 *1* **Nick's Nikita (IRE)**[189] 5854 4-8-12 98 .... JMurtagh 7 93
(M Halford, Ire) *2nd early: 4th 1/2-way: 5th and rdn 2f out: kpt on fr over 1f out* **10/1**

5 *3/4* **Harrington (IRE)**[15] 856 5-9-1 87 .... PShanahan 6 95
(Noel Furlong, Ire) *prom: 2nd 1/2-way: rdn to chal early st: outpcd under 2f out: sn no ex* **20/1**

6 *1/2* **Jalmira (IRE)**[161] 6360 6-8-12 87 .... WJLee 5 91
(C F Swan, Ire) *hld up: 6th into st: kpt on same pce fr 2f out* **33/1**

7 *7* **Yellow Ridge (IRE)**[50] 56 4-9-1 70 .... (t) FranciscoDaSilva 4 82?
(Luke Comer, Ire) *hld up in rr: rdn ent st: sn wknd* **100/1**

2m 12.4s (3.10) **Going Correction** +0.225s/f (Good) **7** Ran SP% **113.0**
Speed ratings: 96,93,92,92,91 91,85
CSF £6.12 TOTE £1.30: £1.10, £3.30; DF 4.10.
Owner Mrs John Magnier **Bred** Tower Bloodstock **Trained** Ballydoyle, Co Tipperary

FOCUS
An interesting Listed event which saw a winning return to action for the high-class Dylan Thomas, who is value for further than his winning margin.

NOTEBOOK
Dylan Thomas(IRE), last year's Irish Derby and Irish Champion Stakes winner, was having his first outing since failing to shine on the Dirt in the Grade 1 Belmont Gold Cup back in October. He faced a straightforward task at the weights and won pretty much as he was entitled to, proving he retains his ability. Indeed he could have won by further if he had been fully ridden out and this race should serve as a nice confidence booster for an impending return to top company. That may come next in the Prix Ganay later this month. (op 4/11)

Fracas(IRE) was firmly put in his place when the winner asserted on this seasonal debut, and is flattered by his proximity to that rival at the finish, but was not disgraced according to official figures. He has clearly had his problems, but is still a decent sort on his day and is ideally better suited by an easier surface. (op 10/1)
Heliostatic(IRE), behind the winner when failing to get home in the Irish Derby at this venue last year, enjoyed the run of the race out in front and was made to look one paced when the winner swept past. This is his trip and he is entitled to come on for the run. (op 5/1)

1051 - 1053a (Foreign Racing) - See Raceform Interactive

KREFELD (R-H)
Sunday, April 15

OFFICIAL GOING: Soft

1054a DR BUSCH-MEMORIAL (GROUP 3) 1m 110y
3:25 (3:30) 3-Y-O **£21,622** (£6,757; £3,378; £2,027)

RPR

1 **Davidoff (GER)** 3-9-2 ... AStarke 1 106
(P Schiergen, Germany) *racd in 4th, closed up fr over 3f out, 2nd on ins str, hmpd over 2f out, led and hung lft ins fnl f, driven clr* **41/10**

2 *2* **Global Dream (GER)**[182] [5998] 3-9-2 ... ABoschert 3 102
(U Ostmann, Germany) *raced in 3rd to over 3f out, 4th straight, led over 1 1/2f out to inside final furlong, one pace* **13/10**[1]

3 *2 1/2* **Kaleo**[140] 3-9-2 ... EPedroza 5 97
(A Wohler, Germany) *held up in rear, last straight, stayed on one pace final 1 1/2f* **21/10**[2]

4 *3/4* **Lowenherz (GER)** 3-9-2 ... ASuborics 2 96
(A Wohler, Germany) *tracked leader, 3rd straight, every chance 1 1/2f out, one pace* **3/1**[3]

5 *8* **Ailton (GER)**[39] 3-9-2 ...(b) ADeVries 4 80
(W Baltromei, Germany) *led to over 1 1/2f out* **72/10**

1m 45.2s (-1.40) 5 Ran SP% **132.5**
(Including 10 Euros stake): WIN 51; PL 18, 14; SF 106.
Owner Frau M Herbert **Bred** Dr K Schulte **Trained** Germany

962 LONGCHAMP (R-H)
Sunday, April 15

OFFICIAL GOING: Good

1055a PRIX DE LA GROTTE (GROUP 3) (FILLIES) 1m
2:50 (2:54) 3-Y-O **£27,027** (£10,811; £8,108; £5,405; £2,703)

RPR

1 **Darjina (FR)**[163] 3-9-0 ... CSoumillon 9 105
(A De Royer-Dupre, France) *raced in 2nd, challenged 2f out, driven to lead 100 yards out, driven out* **18/10**[1]

2 *snk* **Missvinski (USA)**[30] [696] 3-9-0 ... C-PLemaire 7 105
(J-C Rouget, France) *hld up in 8th, ran on on outside 1 1/2f out, rdn to chal fnl f, ev ch 100y out, pressed winner to line* **11/1**

3 *1* **Chinandega (FR)**[23] [748] 3-9-0 ... SPasquier 8 103
(P Demercastel, France) *hld up, disp 5th str, gd hdwy on outside 2f out to chal 1 1/2f out, led narrowly appr fnl f to 100 yards out, kept on* **11/1**

4 *1 1/2* **Legerete (USA)**[196] [5714] 3-9-0 ... OPeslier 1 100
(A Fabre, France) *prominent in 3rd, 4th straight, pushed along over 1 1/2f out, stayed on at one pace under pressure* **5/2**[2]

5 *hd* **Anabaa's Creation (IRE)**[141] [6609] 3-9-0 ... GMosse 2 100
(A De Royer-Dupre, France) *mid-division, disputing 5th straight, dropped to rear before staying on to take 5th inside final furlong* **79/10**

6 *nk* **Green Lyons (IRE)**[17] 3-9-0 ... TThulliez 3 99
(Mme C Head-Maarek, France) *held up in last, driven to chase leaders 1 1/2f out, some late headway but never dangerous* **32/1**

7 *nk* **Nuqoosh**[169] [6228] 3-9-0 ... DBonilla 4 98
(F Head, France) *raced in 4th, 3rd and pushed along straight, outpaced over 1f out* **15/2**[3]

8 *1/2* **Iron Lips**[169] [6229] 3-9-0 ... MBlancpain 5 97
(C Laffon-Parias, France) *settled towards rear, 7th straight, some headway on rail 1 1/2f out, weakened final furlong* **5/2**[2]

9 *2 1/2* **Poltava (FR)**[196] [5714] 3-9-0 ... DBoeuf 6 92
(D Smaga, France) *led, pressed 2f out, headed approaching final furlong, weakened* **89/10**

1m 38.4s (-4.00) **Going Correction** -0.325s/f (Firm) 9 Ran SP% **145.7**
Speed ratings: 107,106,105,104,104 103,103,103,100
PARI-MUTUEL: WIN 2.80; PL 1.60, 2.80, 3.10; DF 14.00.
Owner Princess Zahra Aga Khan **Bred** Princess Zahra Aga Khan **Trained** Chantilly, France

NOTEBOOK
Darjina(FR), a fine-looking filly with considerable scope for improvement, definitely looks to be Classic material. This was just her second outing and she learnt a lot. Settled in second position early, she was outpaced by fitter opponents halfway up the straight but ran on again at the finish to win narrowly. Her target is now the Poule d'Essai des Pouliches, and the one thing her trainer feels would be against her in the future is testing ground.
Missvinski(USA) looked the likely winner at the furlong pole but, try as she did, she could not hold the renewed challenge of the winner. She went down fighting and is a very consistent and versatile filly, but possibly not quite up to Group 1 standard. Nevertheless, she will be allowed to take her chance in the Pouliches.
Chinandega(FR) was brought with a very promising run from two out and still looked dangerous running into the final furlong. Her stride just began to shorten in the closing stages though, and possibly she was unsuited by the rather lively ground.
Legerete(USA), given every possible chance, never quite looked capable of finishing in the first three. Settled in third position, she was outpaced halfway up the straight and then stayed on without quickening throughout the final furlong. This outing will have done her the power of good and this daughter of Rahy will almost certainly now be raced over distances in excess of a mile. She is a possible for the Prix Vanteaux at the end of the month over an extended nine furlongs.

1056a PRIX DE FONTAINEBLEAU (GROUP 3) (COLTS) 1m
3:20 (3:26) 3-Y-O **£27,027** (£10,811; £8,108; £5,405; £2,703)

RPR

1 **Chichi Creasy (FR)**[17] 3-9-2 ... RonanThomas 10 117
(Mme N Rossio, France) *reluctant to load, racd in cl 2nd, led 2f out, pushed along and qckned 1 1/2f out, found more whn pressed ins fnl f, gamely* **15/1**

2 *1* **Battle Paint (USA)**[196] [5715] 3-9-2 ... C-PLemaire 8 115
(J-C Rouget, France) *prominent, disputing 3rd straight, ridden and went 2nd approaching final furlong, held by winner final 100 yards* **14/10**[1]

3 *1/2* **Visionario (IRE)**[196] [5715] 3-9-2 ... CSoumillon 5 113
(A Fabre, France) *held up in mid-division, disputing 6th straight, ridden and stayed on 1 1/2f out, nearest at finish* **31/10**[2]

4 *1 1/2* **Lawman (FR)**[17] 3-9-2 ... OPeslier 3 110
(J-M Beguigne, France) *held up, 8th straight, ran on final 1 1/2f to take 4th 50 yards out* **78/10**[3]

5 *3/4* **Makaan (USA)**[168] [6249] 3-9-2 ... DBonilla 2 108
(F Head, France) *prominent, disputing 3rd on rail straight, ridden to go 2nd 1 1/2f out, no extra under pressure final furlong* **14/1**

6 *hd* **Astronomer Royal (USA)**[252] [4177] 3-9-2 ... CO'Donoghue 4 108
(A P O'Brien, Ire) *mid-division, 4th and shaken up straight, no extra from over 1f out* **15/1**

7 *2* **San Domenico**[211] [5399] 3-9-2 ... TThulliez 7 103
(P Bary, France) *prominent in 3rd early, disputing 6th straight, one pace from over 1 1/2f out* **32/1**

8 *3/4* **Hurricane Fly (IRE)**[23] [749] 3-9-2 ... F-XBertras 1 101
(J-L Pelletan, France) *led, headed 2f out, soon ridden, weakened over 1f out* **87/10**

9 *1/2* **Knowledge (FR)**[26] 3-9-2 ... GMosse 6 100
(Y De Nicolay, France) *held up, 9th straight, never dangerous* **31/1**

10 *3/4* **Law Lord**[208] [5471] 3-9-2 ... SPasquier 9 99
(A Fabre, France) *held up in last, effort 2f out, no impression* **28/1**

1m 38.2s (-4.20) **Going Correction** -0.325s/f (Firm) **10** Ran SP% **116.5**
Speed ratings: 108,107,106,105,104 104,102,101,100,100
PARI-MUTUEL: WIN 16.00; PL 2.40, 1.30, 1.50; DF 18.20.
Owner Mlle B Rossio **Bred** Mme Christine Pastor & Mlle Beatrice Rossio **Trained** France

■ Stewards' Enquiry : C O'Donoghue 200 fine: careless riding

NOTEBOOK
Chichi Creasy(FR) had to dig deep to hold off the favourite throughout the final furlong. He had been given an astute ride by his unfashionable jockey, took the advantage just before the final furlong and was very courageous in the run to the line. Injury meant that no engagements were made for the colt so he would have to be supplemented into the Poulains. The Classic might be bypassed in favour of the Prix de la Jonchere and the Prix Jean Prat.
Battle Paint(USA), an imposing individual, lost little in defeat and is sure to come on a lot for the outing. Fourth on the outside running down the hill, he began a progressive effort from two out and looked dangerous at the furlong marker. He did not quite go through with his challenge and was rather one-paced during the final 100 yards, but was meeting a much fitter individual and had not been out for nearly seven months. Another valid point is that he did not let himself down properly on the firmish ground. He will strip much fitter in the Poulains.
Visionario(IRE) was given a patient ride and allowed to gallop along in mid-division during the early stages. He made a forward move from a furlong and a half out and was running on really well at the finish. Connections feel he does not enjoy the hill at Longchamp, even though he has won at the track, and they may have a valid point for, once balanced in the straight, he did quicken nicely. He will be allowed to take his chance in the Poulains and the longer Jockey-Club is now being talked about as another target.
Lawman(FR), given a waiting race, was not seen until the race was virtually over. He did not have much room when trying to make a forward move and did pass several rivals inside the final furlong. It is no surprise to learn that he will now go for the longer Prix de Guiche as part of his preparation for the Jockey-Club.

1057a PRIX LA FORCE (GROUP 3) 1m 2f
3:50 (3:55) 3-Y-O **£27,027** (£10,811; £8,108; £5,405; £2,703)

RPR

1 **Literato (FR)**[23] [749] 3-9-2 ... C-PLemaire 3 108
(J-C Rouget, France) *hld up in last, ran on down outside 2f out, chal over 1f out, ridden to lead 100 yards out, driven out* **3/1**[3]

2 *3/4* **Chinese Whisper (IRE)**[182] [6003] 3-9-2 ... CSoumillon 1 107
(A P O'Brien, Ire) *racd in 3rd, 5th halfway, disp 5th str, pushed along 2f out, led over 1f out, rdn and ran on til hdd 100 yards out* **21/10**[1]

3 *4* **Friston Forest (IRE)**[168] [6249] 3-9-2 ... SPasquier 5 100
(A Fabre, France) *raced in 3rd: 2nd half-way, pushed along and every chance over 1f out, not pace of leading pair final furlong* **5/2**[2]

4 *1 1/2* **Navio (FR)**[39] 3-9-2 ... IMendizabal 4 97
(J-C Rouget, France) *raced in 2nd, 3rd half-way, driven and lost place 1 1/2f out, ridden and ran on to take 4th final furlong* **82/10**

5 *2 1/2* **Special Day (FR)**[131] 3-9-2 ... OPeslier 2 93
(F Head, France) *raced in 5th, 4th half-way, disputing 5th straight, soon pushed along, last and outpaced over 1f out* **13/1**

6 *1 1/2* **Ombrageux (IRE)**[36] 3-9-2 ... JVictoire 6 90
(H-A Pantall, France) *led, pushed along 2f out, headed over 1f out, weakened final furlong* **63/10**

2m 4.80s (-3.20) **Going Correction** -0.325s/f (Firm) **6** Ran SP% **117.5**
Speed ratings: 99,98,95,94,92 90
PARI-MUTUEL: WIN 4.00; PL 1.70, 1.70; SF 13.10.
Owner H Morin **Bred** Bsh Of Administrativa **Trained** Pau, France

■ Stewards' Enquiry : C Soumillon 200 fine: careless riding

NOTEBOOK
Literato(FR), given a highly professional ride, won in style. Waited with in the early stages, he was brought progressively up the centre of the track to take the lead inside the final furlong. He stayed on well and a longer trip will not be a problem. This little grey colt has now won five of his six races and he will not be out again until the Jockey-Club on June 3, when he should make his presence felt at the finish.
Chinese Whisper(IRE) looked all over the winner at the furlong marker but ran out of steam with 100 yards left to run. He is definitely a bit of handful, even for his very experienced jockey, but he has plenty of ability and he streaked into the lead with a furlong and a half to run looking most unlikely to be caught. However, he did not keep up the good work until the end. It would be no surprise if cheekpieces were fitted next time out and he is still talked about as a possible for the Jockey-Club later in the season.
Friston Forest(IRE) was well backed but proved somewhat disappointing. Given every possible chance, he followed the leader for much of the ten furlongs but found very little under pressure, and just stayed on one-paced to finish a distant fourth.
Navio(FR), well placed in the early part of the race, gradually dropped out of contention in the straight and did not look up to this class. Products of his sire love to get their toe in and possibly the fastish ground played a role in his performance, which was below expectations.

WINDSOR (R-H)
Monday, April 16

OFFICIAL GOING: Good to firm
Wind: Light behind Weather: Sunny, warm

1058 READING POST MAIDEN STKS 5f 10y
2:30 (2:30) (Class 5) 2-Y-0 **£3,238** (£963; £481; £240) **Stalls** High

Form RPR
4 **1** **Sauze D'Oulx**[13] [898] 2-8-13 ow1 JamesMillman(5) 9 82
(B R Millman) *fast away: mde all: hanging lft 1/2-way: taken to nr side rail sn after: hrd pressed fnl f: pushed out and a holding on* **10/1**[3]
2 **2** ¾ **Ten Down**[12] [926] 2-9-3 JamieSpencer 6 78+
(J A Osborne) *dwlt: off the pce towards rr: prog on outer 1/2-way: chsd wnr over 1f out: drvn to chal fnl f: styd on but a hld* **5/6**[1]
3 1 ¾ **Red Expresso (IRE)** 2-9-3 EddieAhern 5 78+
(M L W Bell) *fractious to post: dwlt: outpcd in last: sme prog and swtchd to outer over 1f out: shkn up and r.o: promising* **14/1**
4 ¾ **Barraland** 2-9-3 TedDurcan 8 68
(M R Channon) *dwlt: sn chsd ldrs: effrt to dispute 2nd wl over 1f out: wl hld whn checked 1f out* **10/1**[3]
5 ½ **Regal Rhythm (IRE)** 2-9-3 SteveDrowne 7 66
(B J Meehan) *chsd ldrs: shkn up and green 2f out: disp 2nd sn after: one pce* **20/1**
0 **6** shd **Higgy's Boy (IRE)**[5] [999] 2-9-3 PatDobbs 4 66
(R Hannon) *chsd ldrs: rdn and one pce fr 2f out* **25/1**
7 3 **Enodoc** 2-9-3 MartinDwyer 10 54
(W R Muir) *in tch: effrt against nr side rail 2f out: hmpd jst over 1f out: no ch after* **12/1**
8 1 ¼ **Cracking (IRE)** 2-9-3 RichardHughes 2 49
(R Hannon) *mostly chsd wnr to wl over 1f out: wkng whn n.m.r sn after* **9/2**[2]
9 ½ **Seventh Cloud (IRE)** 2-8-12 SebSanders 3 42
(A P Jarvis) *sn outpcd: nvr on terms* **33/1**
10 ½ **Never Sold Out (IRE)** 2-9-3 PaulEddery 1 45
(Pat Eddery) *outpcd and sn struggling in last pair* **25/1**

61.87 secs (0.77) **Going Correction** -0.025s/f (Good) **10 Ran SP% 120.7**
Speed ratings (Par 92):92,90,88,86,86 85,81,79,78,77
CSF £18.68 TOTE £11.30: £1.90, £1.10, £3.80; EX 28.10 Trifecta £55.60 Pool: £494.22, 6.30 winnning units.
Owner Mrs L S Millman **Bred** Knight's Bloodstock **Trained** Kentisbeare, Devon

FOCUS
This was probably just an average juvenile. It was run at a sound pace and it saw the two with the previous best form dominate the finish. The third has been rated as finishing alongside the runner-up.

NOTEBOOK
Sauze D'Oulx showed the clear benefit of his debut at Folkestone and made all to open his account. He displayed good early speed, was helped by bagging the stands'-side rail two out, and displayed a decent attitude to fend off the runner-up at the business end of the race. No doubt his previous experience counted for a lot this time, but he remains open to improvement and should have little trouble with a sixth furlong in due course.
Ten Down, runner-up on his debut at Nottingham, was forced to race from off the pace this time after a sluggish start yet still emerged to have every chance in the home straight. He was always held late on by the winner, who it should be noted had the benefit of the stands' rail, and like that rival his previous experience was an advantage here. He can still be placed to get off the mark in the coming weeks. (tchd 4-5 and 10-11, and Evens in places)
Red Expresso(IRE) ◆, a 70,000gns first foal of an unraced half-sister to Cheveley Park winner Seazun, played up at the start and proved very green through the early parts of the race. He was noted doing some nice work towards the finish and, with this debut experience sure to bring him on, looks the one to take from the race with the future in mind. (op 11-1)
Barraland, whose sales price rose to 105,000euros as a yearling, showed ability and would have been a little closer with a better passage nearing the final furlong. He is bred for speed and should learn a deal for the experience. (op 12-1)
Regal Rhythm(IRE), who as a January foal was the oldest in this line-up, is a half-brother to a 6f juvenile winner and out of a dam who was a multiple winner in Italy. He left the impression this debut experience was needed, something his position in the betting would also indicate, and should prove sharper next time out. (op 25-1)
Higgy's Boy(IRE) showed a little more than had been the case on his Bath debut five days previously and looks the type to do a little better as he gains further experience. (op 33-1 tchd 40-1)
Cracking(IRE), yet to reach his second birthday and whose pedigree is all speed, displayed decent early pace to go with the winner before weakening out of it after passing the 2f pole and finding himself a little tight for room. He is evidently though capable of better. (op 5-1 tchd 11-2 in a place)

1059 118 118 CLAIMING STKS 1m 2f 7y
3:05 (3:06) (Class 5) 3-Y-0 **£3,238** (£963; £481; £240) **Stalls** Low

Form RPR
432 **1** **Shawhill**[22] [772] 3-8-11 67 JerryO'Dwyer(3) 8 64
(A M Hales) *hld up: prog to ld 6f out: mde rest: rdn 2f out: styd on wl and in command fnl f* **7/2**[2]
1013 **2** 1 ½ **News Of The Day (IRE)**[11] [937] 3-8-9 58 GregFairley(3) 3 59
(M Johnston) *settled in midfield: rdn over 2f out: prog on outer wl over 1f out : styd on to take 2nd ins fnl f: no imp on wnr* **13/2**
2101 **3** nk **Sweet World**[22] [776] 3-9-3 66 SebSanders 5 64
(A P Jarvis) *hld up in last trio: prog to trck ldng pair over 5f out: chsd wnr and plld out to chal over 1f out: kpt on same pce* **5/1**[3]
5322 **4** 1 ½ **Dr McFab**[11] [937] 3-9-10 71 JamieSpencer 10 68
(J A Osborne) *trckd ldrs: wnt 2nd 3f out: drvn and hanging wl over 1f out: nt qckn* **5/2**[1]
4432 **5** ¾ **Beau Sancy**[17] [834] 3-9-12 69 JohnEgan 7 68
(R A Harris) *hld up in midfield: pushed along bnd over 5f out: lost pl and n.m.r over 2f out: drvn and one pce after* **15/2**
0055 **6** 1 **Conny Nobel (IRE)**[17] [834] 3-8-3 55 (tp) KevinGhunowa(5) 4 48
(J L Flint) *t.k.h early: hld up in midfield: drvn over 2f out: no prog* **20/1**
5443 **7** 1 ½ **Party Palace**[21] [791] 3-8-7 54 AdrianTNicholls 2 45
(H S Howe) *t.k.h early: lost pl after 3f and sn in last trio: effrt on outer over 3f out: wknd over 1f out* **16/1**
50-0 **8** 2 **Mayireneyrbel**[24] [737] 3-8-5 50 SimonWhitworth 1 39
(J Akehurst) *dwlt: a in last trio and no prog wl over 2f out* **33/1**
0-04 **9** ½ **Dawson Creek (IRE)**[15] [864] 3-9-0 50 SteveDrowne 9 47
(B Gubby) *mde most to 6f out: chsd wnr to 3f out: wknd* **20/1**
6040 **10** 5 **Kings Shillings**[17] [832] 3-8-9 55 ow1 (b) DanielTudhope 6 32
(D Carroll) *dwlt: a in last trio: rdn and wknd 2f out: eased ins fnl f* **12/1**

2m 8.59s (0.29) **Going Correction** -0.025s/f (Good) **10 Ran SP% 118.6**
Speed ratings (Par 98):97,95,95,94,93 92,91,90,89,85
CSF £26.33 TOTE £5.00: £1.90, £1.90, £1.40; EX 32.50 Trifecta £176.30 Part won. Pool: £248.40, 0.60 winning units..The winner was claimed by Tom Dascombe for £17,000. Dr McFab was claimed by D W Pinder for £22,000
Owner Brick Farm Racing **Bred** Taker Bloodstock **Trained** Preston Capes, Northants

FOCUS
A reasonable claimer, with several runners in good form on sand coming into it. The form looks solid enough. However none of these look well treated for handicaps.

1060 CORAL BACKING NSPCC H'CAP 1m 67y
3:40 (3:40) (Class 4) (0-85,84) 4-Y-0+ **£5,181** (£1,541; £770; £384) **Stalls** High

Form RPR
22-3 **1** **King Of Argos**[16] [842] 4-9-4 84 JamieSpencer 3 99+
(E A L Dunlop) *hld up in last pair: scythed through fr over 3f out gng v easily: led 1f out: cruised clr* **4/1**[1]
160- **2** 3 ½ **Pure Imagination (IRE)**[152] [6301] 6-8-1 72 (b) KevinGhunowa(5) 10 79
(J M Bradley) *hld up wl in rr: effrt on inner whn nt clr run over 2f out: swtchd lft: hrd rdn and r.o to take 2nd nr fin* **33/1**
00-0 **3** ½ **Music Note (IRE)**[23] [765] 4-9-0 80 JohnEgan 12 86
(Miss Gay Kelleway) *led at fast pce: drvn 2f out: hdd 1f out: kpt on but no ch w wnr after* **16/1**
00-5 **4** shd **Street Warrior (IRE)**[12] [930] 4-8-7 73 KDarley 9 79
(M Johnston) *s.i.s: last and nt gng wl: drvn 1/2-way: styd on fr over 2f out: nrly snatched 3rd* **5/1**[2]
0-40 **5** 2 ½ **James Caird (IRE)**[16] [850] 7-9-1 81 (b) SebSanders 14 81
(M H Tompkins) *trckd ldrs: shkn up over 2f out: outpcd and btn over 1f out* **7/1**[3]
400- **6** 1 ¼ **Bonnie Prince Blue**[190] [5833] 4-9-0 80 MichaelHills 11 77
(B W Hills) *mostly chsd ldr to 2f out: wknd u.p* **4/1**[1]
-005 **7** ¾ **Glencalvie (IRE)**[15] [865] 6-8-7 73 (v) MartinDwyer 2 68
(J Akehurst) *pressed ldrs to 2f out: sn btn: eased ins fnl f* **14/1**
060- **8** hd **Glenmuir (IRE)**[173] [6176] 4-8-13 79 JimCrowley 13 74
(B R Millman) *chsd ldrs: hrd rdn over 2f out: no imp over 1f out: wknd* **12/1**
00B- **9** shd **Postgraduate (IRE)**[284] [3223] 5-9-4 84 PaulDoe 5 79
(W J Knight) *hld up towards rr: racd on wd outside fr 4f out: shuffled along over 2f out: nvr nr ldrs* **18/1**
0600 **10** nk **General Knowledge (USA)**[46] [593] 4-8-12 78 (t) TedDurcan 7 72
(B G Powell) *in tch in midfield: hrd rdn and effrt over 2f out: wknd over 1f out* **33/1**
400- **11** hd **Abwaab**[198] [5666] 4-8-13 79 StephenCarson 8 72
(Eve Johnson Houghton) *chsd ldrs: rdn 3f out: no prog: wknd over 1f out* **12/1**
005- **12** nk **Silver Blue (IRE)**[139] [6633] 4-8-12 78 PatDobbs 4 71
(R Hannon) *in tch in midfield: lost pl and struggling 3f out: no ch after* **12/1**
6000 **13** 17 **Hail The Chief**[9] [941] 10-9-2 82 RichardHughes 6 36
(R Hannon) *chsd ldrs: rdn 1/2-way: sn btn: t.o* **12/1**

1m 41.91s (-2.79) **Going Correction** -0.025s/f (Good) **13 Ran SP% 123.6**
Speed ratings (Par 105):112,108,108,107,105 104,103,103,103,102 102,102,85
CSF £150.50 CT £1994.38 TOTE £4.60: £2.40, £15.00, £4.00; EX 232.00 TRIFECTA Not won..
Owner P G Goulandris **Bred** Chippenham Lodge Stud Ltd **Trained** Newmarket, Suffolk
■ Stewards' Enquiry : Kevin GhunowaL one-day ban: careless riding (Apr 27)
Paul Doe 14-day ban: in breach of Rule 157 (Jun 19-Jul 2)

FOCUS
A very smart winning time for the grade, due to the searching early pace. The impressive winner is value for plenty further, although the placed form is not strong.
Postgraduate(IRE) Official explanation: 40-day ban: (Jun 19-Jul 28)
Hail The Chief Official explanation: vet said horse returned lame behind

1061 CORAL BET BY FREEPHONE ON 0800 242 232 H'CAP 5f 10y
4:15 (4:16) (Class 4) (0-80,80) 4-Y-0+ **£5,181** (£1,541; £770; £384) **Stalls** High

Form RPR
0616 **1** **Efistorm**[19] [810] 6-9-0 76 JohnEgan 11 83
(C R Dore) *in tch in midfield: effrt towards outer 2f out: threaded through jst over 1f out: drvn to ld last 75yds* **7/1**[3]
0-00 **2** ½ **Fromsong (IRE)**[65] [419] 9-9-4 80 RobertHavlin 4 86
(D K Ivory) *pressed ldr: drvn to ld 1f out: hdd last 75yds: kpt on* **25/1**
-000 **3** ½ **Smokin Beau**[51] [554] 10-9-1 77 TedDurcan 8 81
(N P Littmoden) *racd against nr side rail: pressed ldng pair: rdn and nt qckn 2f out: styd on wl last 150yds* **16/1**
0302 **4** hd **Nusoor (IRE)**[49] [566] 4-8-8 70 RichardMullen 2 73
(Peter Grayson) *keen and veering early: chsd ldrs on outer after 2f: drvn to try to chal 1f out: kpt on same pce* **12/1**
400- **5** nk **Our Fugitive (IRE)**[192] [5791] 5-8-10 72 RichardHughes 6 74
(A W Carroll) *sn racd against nr side rail: mde most: hdd 1f out: hanging lft and nt qckn* **7/1**[3]
4042 **6** nk **Figaro Flyer (IRE)**[19] [810] 4-9-4 80 IanMongan 3 81
(P Howling) *outpcd and wl in rr: prog on wd outside 1/2-way: chsng ldrs over 1f out: fdd fnl f* **8/1**
020- **7** shd **Calypso King**[192] [5782] 4-8-10 72 SebSanders 13 72
(R M Beckett) *in tch in midfield: rdn to chse ldrs over 1f out: no imp* **13/2**[2]
6105 **8** ½ **Cornus**[17] [835] 5-8-9 71 (be) SteveDrowne 5 70+
(A J McCabe) *dwlt: bmpd after 1f: struggling in rr after: no prog tl styd on fnl f: n.d* **18/1**
4313 **9** 1 ¼ **Desert Master**[17] [835] 4-8-11 73 EddieAhern 12 67
(C F Wall) *chsd ldrs: rdn wl over 1f out: nt qckn: wknd ins fnl f* **9/2**[1]
60-5 **10** 1 **Makabul**[17] [827] 4-8-10 72 (bt[1]) JimCrowley 10 63
(B R Millman) *s.s: outpcd and wl detached in last: no prog tl r.o last 150yds* **12/1**
060- **11** hd **Silver Prelude**[273] [3593] 6-8-5 67 oh4 ow1 MartinDwyer 1 57
(D K Ivory) *prom: hanging lft fr 1/2-way: wknd over 1f out* **33/1**
302- **12** 5 **Devine Dancer**[219] [5181] 4-8-13 75 DaneO'Neill 7 47
(H Candy) *bmpd after 1f: a struggling towards rr: wknd over 1f out* **10/1**
050- **13** 1 **Mr Rooney (IRE)**[231] [4888] 4-8-6 68 AdrianTNicholls 9 36
(D Nicholls) *hmpd after 1f: struggling in rr: no prog whn hmpd over 1f out: eased* **7/1**[3]

60.33 secs (-0.77) **Going Correction** -0.025s/f (Good) **13 Ran SP% 122.5**
Speed ratings (Par 105):105,104,103,103,102 102,101,101,99,97 97,89,87
CSF £173.26 CT £2797.95 TOTE £9.10: £3.40, £6.60, £5.80; EX 344.30 TRIFECTA Not won..
Owner Sean J Murphy **Bred** E Duggan And D Churchman **Trained** West Pinchbeck, Lincs

FOCUS
An open sprint which saw the first seven closely covered at the finish. The form seems sound enough.

Nusoor(IRE) Official explanation: jockey said gelding hung right throughout
Devine Dancer Official explanation: jockey said filly suffered interference in running
Mr Rooney(IRE) Official explanation: jockey said colt lost its action

1062 ARENA LEISURE PLC MAIDEN STKS — 1m 2f 7y
4:45 (4:49) (Class 5) 3-Y-O — **£3,238** (£963; £481; £240) **Stalls** Low

Form — RPR

3- **1** **Fort Amhurst (IRE)**[185] [5939] 3-9-3 .... JamieSpencer 9 — 81+
(E A L Dunlop) *hld up: prog to trck ldrs 6f out: effrt to ld 2f out: clr fnl f: comf* **5/2**[1]

3 **2** *1 1/2* **Guardian Of Truth (IRE)**[23] [764] 3-9-3 .... PaulDoe 10 — 74
(W J Knight) *led after 3f: tried to kick on wl over 2f out: hdd 2f out: kpt on same pce* **7/1**

3 *shd* **Haarth Sovereign (IRE)** 3-9-3 .... TedDurcan 11 — 74+
(W R Swinburn) *hld up in rr: green and hanging fr over 3f out: prog 2f out: styd on fnl f: nrst fin* **33/1**

3- **4** *2* **Common Purpose (USA)**[172] [6188] 3-9-3 .... RichardHughes 6 — 70
(J H M Gosden) *led for 3f: trckd ldr after: shkn up to chal 3f out: nt qckn and btn 2f out* **10/3**[2]

00- **5** *1* **I Predict A Riot (IRE)**[170] [6220] 3-9-3 .... KDarley 3 — 68
(J W Hills) *towards rr: urged along and struggling 4f out: kpt on fr over 1f out: n.d* **22/1**

6 *1/2* **A Little More (IRE)** 3-9-3 .... SimonWhitworth 2 — 67
(P A Blockley) *in tch in midfield: rdn over 2f out: one pce and no prog* **66/1**

062- **7** *1/2* **Radical Views**[212] [5379] 3-9-3 73 .... MichaelHills 1 — 66
(B W Hills) *sn pressed ldrs: hanging lft over 3f out: btn 2f out: fdd* **11/2**[3]

8 *1* **Cheonmado (USA)** 3-9-3 .... PaulEddery 13 — 64
(Simon Earle) *dwlt: hld up in last pair: shkn up over 3f out: kpt on but nvr on terms* **50/1**

02- **9** *nk* **Cavalry Twill (IRE)**[149] [6523] 3-9-3 .... EddieAhern 12 — 64
(P F I Cole) *hld up in midfield: effrt and hanging lft over 2f out: no prog: wknd fnl f* **10/1**

10 *15* **Kilmiston Saturn** 3-9-0 .... JerryO'Dwyer(3) 4 — 35
(A M Hales) *s.s: last pair tl sme prog over 3f out: sn wknd: t.o* **100/1**

00 **11** *1 1/2* **Magroom**[12] [919] 3-9-3 ....(p) SamHitchcott 5 — 32
(B R Johnson) *in tch tl wknd wl over 2f out: t.o* **100/1**

2m 8.72s (0.42) **Going Correction** -0.025s/f (Good) **11** Ran SP% **101.3**
Speed ratings (Par 98):97,95,95,94,93 92,92,91,91,79 78
CSF £13.53 TOTE £3.10: £1.20, £2.10, £5.70; EX 20.40 TRIFECTA Not won..
Owner Gainsborough **Bred** Gainsborough Stud Management Ltd **Trained** Newmarket, Suffolk
■ Earl Marshal was withdrawn (7/1, refused to enter stalls.) R4 applies, deduct 20p in the £.

FOCUS
A fair three-year-old maiden. The form is not entirely rock solid but makes sense around the second and fourth.

1063 AT THE RACES H'CAP — 6f
5:15 (5:19) (Class 5) (0-75,75) 4-Y-O+ — **£3,238** (£963; £361; £361) **Stalls** High

Form — RPR

-625 **1** **Saviours Spirit**[51] [550] 6-9-1 72 .... DaneO'Neill 14 — 84+
(T G Mills) *s.s: last pair tl prog on outer over 2f out: drvn and styd on wl fr over 1f out: led last 50yds* **5/1**[1]

213- **2** *hd* **Mr Cellophane**[146] [6555] 4-9-2 73 .... EddieAhern 7 — 85
(J R Jenkins) *trckd ldrs gng wl: effrt to ld over 1f out: sn drvn and idled: hdd last 50yds: kpt on* **12/1**

-404 **3** *1 1/2* **Adantino**[30] [697] 8-8-13 75 ....(b) JamesMillman(5) 4 — 82
(B R Millman) *wl in rr: prog on outer 2f out: squeezed through fnl f and styd on: unable to chal* **11/1**

110- **3** *dht* **Keyaki (IRE)**[170] [6223] 6-9-4 75 .... GeorgeBaker 15 — 82
(C F Wall) *trckd ldrs nr side: nt clr run and swtchd lft over 1f out: styd on: nt rch ldrs* **16/1**

3-43 **5** *3/4* **Who's Winning (IRE)**[5] [1004] 6-8-12 72 .... RichardKingscote(3) 12 — 77
(B G Powell) *mde most to over 1f out: no ex* **8/1**[3]

530- **6** *shd* **China Cherub**[188] [5896] 4-9-2 73 .... RichardHughes 11 — 77
(R Hannon) *in tch in midfield: effrt whn hmpd jst over 1f out: kpt on fnl f* **14/1**

1113 **7** *hd* **Kabis Amigos**[12] [915] 5-8-12 69 ....(t) AdrianTNicholls 9 — 73
(D Nicholls) *w ldr to over 1f out: one pce* **7/1**[2]

6053 **8** *3/4* **Sailor King (IRE)**[21] [793] 5-8-12 69 .... RobertHavlin 2 — 71
(D K Ivory) *racd towards outer: pressed ldrs: rdn 2f out: fdd fnl f* **14/1**

106- **9** *hd* **Linda Green**[117] [6882] 6-9-0 71 .... EdwardCreighton 8 — 72+
(M R Channon) *settled towards rr: nt clr run fr 2f out: kpt on nr fin: no ch* **16/1**

00-0 **10** *nk* **Nautical**[16] [846] 9-9-4 75 .... RichardMullen 13 — 75
(A W Carroll) *a towards rr on inner: shkn up over 2f out: keeping on but no real ch whn nt clr run ins fnl f* **9/1**

5403 **11** *1/2* **Marko Jadeo (IRE)**[23] [771] 9-8-7 69 .... TolleyDean(5) 5 — 68+
(R A Harris) *hld up in rr: nt clr run fr 2f out to 1f out: hmpd sn after: r.o but no ch* **25/1**

00-6 **12** *1/2* **Desert Dreamer (IRE)**[17] [827] 6-9-3 74 .... PaulDoe 3 — 71
(P R Chamings) *dwlt: wl in rr: effrt and sme prog on outer 2f out: no hdwy fnl f: fdd* **25/1**

2640 **13** *1* **Nepro (IRE)**[12] [927] 5-8-6 70 ....(tp) SCreighton(7) 1 — 64
(E J Creighton) *racd on outer: chsd ldrs: rdn 2f out: wkng whn n.m.r jst ins fnl f* **66/1**

340- **14** *shd* **Roman Quest**[208] [5476] 4-9-3 74 .... SteveDrowne 16 — 68
(H Morrison) *trckd ldrs: effrt 2f out: no imp over 1f out: fdd* **15/2**[3]

6263 **15** *3 1/2* **Zarzu**[24] [734] 8-9-4 75 .... JohnEgan 6 — 58+
(C R Dore) *in tch in midfield: nt clr run over 1f out: hmpd ent fnl f: eased* **20/1**

-330 **16** *7* **Desperate Dan**[19] [810] 6-9-4 75 ....(b) JamieSpencer 10 — 37+
(J A Osborne) *dwlt: hld up in last trio: stl there but gng wl enough whn bdly hmpd jst over 1f out: eased* **10/1**

1m 13.18s (-0.49) **Going Correction** -0.025s/f (Good) **16** Ran SP% **126.2**
Speed ratings (Par 103):102,101,99,99,98 98,98,97,97,96 96,95,94,93,89 79
3rd Pl: A 2.60, K 6.50; T/C SS-MC-A 339.52; SS-MC-K 480.33 CSF £64.60 TOTE £7.00: £1.80, £4.10; EX 100.80 Trifecta £131.30 Part won. Pool: £369.90 - 0.30 winning units. Place 6 £330.18, Place 5 £221.77..
Owner J E Harley **Bred** Mrs S Shaw **Trained** Headley, Surrey
■ Stewards' Enquiry : George Baker four-day ban: careless riding (Apr 27-30)

FOCUS
A fair handicap, run at a solid pace. The form should be treated with a little caution as there were some hard-luck stories in behind, although those who had clear passages did run pretty much to form.
Nautical Official explanation: jockey said gelding was denied a clear run
Marko Jadeo(IRE) Official explanation: jockey said gelding was denied a clear run
Zarzu Official explanation: jockey said gelding suffered interference in running
Desperate Dan Official explanation: jockey said gelding suffered interference in running
T/Jkpt: Not won. T/Plt: £422.00 to a £1 stake. Pool: £86,574.15. 149.75 winning tickets. T/Qpdt: £166.80 to a £1 stake. Pool: £3,856.10. 17.10 winning tickets. JN

932 WOLVERHAMPTON (A.W) (L-H)
Monday, April 16

OFFICIAL GOING: Standard to fast
Wind: Fresh across Weather: Cloudy with sunny spells

1064 WOLVERHAMPTON-RACECOURSE.CO.UK H'CAP — 7f 32y(P)
2:10 (2:11) (Class 6) (0-60,60) 4-Y-O+ — **£2,388** (£705; £352) **Stalls** High

Form — RPR

4104 **1** **Carcinetto (IRE)**[33] [673] 5-9-0 59 .... StephenDonohoe(3) 1 — 73
(P D Evans) *a.p: led over 1f out: rdn and swished tail ins fnl f: r.o* **7/1**[3]

20-0 **2** *1 3/4* **Sedge (USA)**[17] [831] 7-9-2 58 ....(p) MickyFenton 7 — 67
(P T Midgley) *sn outpcd: hdwy and hung lft over 2f out: rdn to chse wnr fnl f: r.o* **11/1**

2523 **3** *1 1/2* **Haroldini (IRE)**[20] [806] 5-9-1 60 ....(p) JasonEdmunds(3) 5 — 65+
(J Balding) *hld up: hdwy and hmpd over 2f out: sn rdn: styd on same pce fnl f* **5/1**[2]

5342 **4** *2 1/2* **Franksalot (IRE)**[75] [310] 7-9-2 58 .... RoystonFfrench 12 — 57
(I W McInnes) *sn outpcd: styd on appr fnl f: nvr trbld ldrs* **16/1**

400- **5** *1 3/4* **Indian Edge**[150] [6507] 6-9-4 60 .... FergusSweeney 10 — 54
(B Palling) *mid-div: sn pushed along: hdwy 1/2-way: rdn over 2f out: hung lft and wknd fnl f* **22/1**

0-00 **6** *2* **Ebraam (USA)**[32] [686] 4-9-4 60 .... DeanMcKeown 11 — 49
(D Shaw) *hld up: hdwy over 2f out: wknd over 1f out* **16/1**

560- **7** *1* **Regal Dream (IRE)**[203] [5573] 5-8-13 60 .... PatrickHills(5) 4 — 46
(J W Unett) *chsd ldrs: led 2f out: sn rdn and hdd: wknd fnl f* **9/1**

-002 **8** *3/4* **Benny The Bus**[20] [806] 5-9-3 59 .... J-PGuillambert 9 — 43
(Mrs G S Rees) *chsd ldrs: rdn over 2f out: sn edgd lft: wknd over 1f out* **9/1**

0003 **9** *6* **Thomas Lawrence (USA)**[13] [902] 6-9-1 57 .... TPO'Shea 8 — 26
(P A Blockley) *led 6f out: rdn and hdd 2f out: wknd over 1f out* **16/1**

0610 **10** *12* **Mulberry Lad (IRE)**[15] [866] 5-9-1 57 .... ChrisCatlin 6 — —
(P W Hiatt) *sn pushed along in rr: wknd over 2f out* **16/1**

0110 **11** *3* **Island Green (USA)**[14] [895] 4-8-11 60 .... KellyHarrison(7) 3 — —
(D Carroll) *prom: rdn 1/2-way: wknd over 2f out* **9/2**[1]

0522 **12** *1* **Bodden Bay**[14] [896] 5-9-3 59 .... NCallan 2 — —+
(I W McInnes) *led: hdd 6f out: rdn whn hmpd over 2f out: sn wknd and eased* **7/1**[3]

1m 28.34s (-2.06) **Going Correction** -0.175s/f (Stan) **12** Ran SP% **116.1**
Speed ratings (Par 101):104,102,100,97,95 93,92,91,84,70 67,66
CSF £79.96 CT £426.71 TOTE £8.80: £3.10, £2.90, £1.50; EX 53.70.
Owner Mrs Sally Edwards **Bred** M A Doyle **Trained** Pandy, Monmouths

FOCUS
A modest handicap, but run at a decent pace. The form looks pretty solid and should stand up.
Island Green(USA) Official explanation: trainer said gelding bled from the nose
Bodden Bay Official explanation: jockey said gelding suffered interference in running

1065 SPONSOR A RACE BY CALLING 0870 220 2442 (S) STKS — 5f 20y(P)
2:40 (2:41) (Class 6) 3-Y-O+ — **£2,047** (£604; £302) **Stalls** Low

Form — RPR

6-52 **1** **Borzoi Maestro**[3] [1028] 6-9-10 46 ....(p) AdamKirby 5 — 62
(G F Bridgwater) *sn led: drvn along thrght: edgd rt over 1f out: styd on* **7/1**[2]

2535 **2** *1* **Blackheath (IRE)**[24] [743] 11-9-2 60 .... AndrewMullen(3) 10 — 54
(D Nicholls) *mid-div: hdwy 1/2-way: r.o ins fnl f* **8/1**[3]

211 **3** *1/2* **Magic Amour**[23] [766] 9-9-10 62 ....(b) TPO'Shea 8 — 57
(P A Blockley) *chsd ldrs: rdn over 1f out: edgd lft ins fnl f: styd on same pce* **5/6**[1]

26-0 **4** *1/2* **Sharp Hat**[100] [46] 13-9-5 43 .... HayleyTurner 11 — 50
(D W Chapman) *sn pushed along in rr: r.o ins fnl f: nrst fin* **25/1**

4500 **5** *1 1/2* **Legal Set (IRE)**[12] [912] 11-9-0 45 ....(b) AnnStokell(5) 2 — 45
(Miss A Stokell) *s.i.s: sn outpcd: hdwy over 1f out: nt rch ldrs* **40/1**

6600 **6** *1 1/4* **Blushing Russian (IRE)**[3] [1028] 5-9-3 45 ....(p) BarrySavage(7) 13 — 45
(J M Bradley) *s.s: r.o ins fnl f: nrst fin* **40/1**

0400 **7** *nk* **Saintly Place**[41] [632] 6-9-5 40 .... ShaneKelly 9 — 39
(A W Carroll) *s.s: r.o ins fnl f: nvr nrr* **25/1**

0600 **8** *3/4* **Feminist (IRE)**[38] [653] 5-8-11 41 .... StephenDonohoe(3) 1 — 31
(J M Bradley) *chsd ldrs: rdn 1/2-way: wknd fnl f* **18/1**

6000 **9** *1 1/4* **Maktavish**[13] [905] 8-9-5 58 ....(v[1]) J-PGuillambert 4 — 32
(R Brotherton) *chsd ldrs over 3f* **12/1**

105- **10** *1 1/2* **Mynd**[159] [6399] 7-9-0 58 .... MichaelJStainton(5) 3 — 26
(B Palling) *stmbld s: outpcd* **9/1**

005- **11** *3/4* **Leah's Pride**[357] [1195] 6-8-11 45 ....(t) JamesDoyle(3) 12 — 19
(Miss D A McHale) *chsd ldrs: rdn 1/2-way: sn wknd* **20/1**

00 **12** *2* **Polar Fox**[13] [905] 4-9-5 57 ....(v[1]) DeanMcKeown 6 — 17
(D Shaw) *chsd ldrs: hung rt and wknd 1/2-way* **28/1**

5000 **13** *1 1/2* **Mind That Fox**[32] [680] 5-9-5 42 ....(b) ChrisCatlin 7 — 11
(T Wall) *chsd ldrs 3f* **40/1**

62.22 secs (-0.60) **Going Correction** -0.175s/f (Stan) **13** Ran SP% **124.3**
Speed ratings (Par 101):97,95,94,93,91 89,88,87,85,83 82,78,76
CSF £59.53 TOTE £8.10: £2.20, £2.10, £1.20; EX 40.10.There was no bid for the winner
Owner Battlefield Brook Racing **Bred** B A Beale & Bbb Computer Services Ltd **Trained** Shrewley, Warwicks
■ Six years after taking out a licence, a first winner for trainer Gary Bridgwater, son of Ken and brother of David.

FOCUS
A moderate seller, with four of the first five home aged nine or older, and with so much pace amongst those drawn low, it was no surprise that those drawn high or who tried to come from behind found it such a struggle. Not strong form, with the favourite below his best.
Legal Set(IRE) Official explanation: jockey said gelding hung right
Saintly Place Official explanation: jockey said gelding was distracted by discarded blindfold in next stall and was slowly away

1066 HORIZONS RESTAURANT - OPENING THIS SATURDAY APPRENTICE CLAIMING STKS — 1m 141y(P)
3:15 (3:18) (Class 6) 4-Y-O+ — **£2,730** (£806; £403) **Stalls** Low

Form — RPR

6211 **1** **Blue Sky Thinking (IRE)**[17] [833] 8-9-5 77 .... AndrewElliott 5 — 72
(K R Burke) *chsd ldr tl led over 3f out: clr 2f out: rdn out* **10/11**[1]

6514 **2** 2½ **Samuel Charles**[11] 933 9-9-5 75....................(p) LiamJones 6 67
(C R Dore) *a.p: rdn to chse wnr and hung lft fr over 2f out: no imp fnl f* **11/2**[2]

3403 **3** ½ **Namroud (USA)**[17] 833 8-8-10 67 ow2.................. JamieMoriarty(3) 10 60
(R A Fahey) *sn chsng ldrs: rdn over 2f out: styd on same pce fnl f* **7/1**[3]

-000 **4** ¾ **Top Jaro (FR)**[34] 669 4-9-5 69.................. SaleemGolam 4 64
(Jennie Candlish) *s.i.s: hld up: n.m.r over 7f out: hdwy over 1f out : rdn and hung lft ins fnl f: nt rch ldrs* **14/1**

0454 **5** 1 **Laugh 'n Cry**[14] 887 6-8-5 47.................. AshleyHamblett(5) 1 53
(C A Cyzer) *mid-div: rdn 1/2-way: styd on: nt pce to chal* **20/1**

0-40 **6** shd **Earthling**[19] 812 6-8-0 43..................(p) DanielleMcCreery(5) 7 48
(D W Chapman) *mid-div: rdn over 3f out: nvr trbld ldrs* **80/1**

4526 **7** hd **Keon (IRE)**[11] 932 5-8-6 53.................. RussellKennemore(5) 12 54
(R Hollinshead) *stdd s: styd on ins fnl f: nvr nrr* **16/1**

000/ **8** 1 **Honeystreet (IRE)**[9] 3412 7-8-4 .... MarcHalford 3 44
(D Burchell) *s.i.s: n.d* **66/1**

0402 **9** 6 **Gem Bien (USA)**[20] 800 9-8-2 49..................(p) KellyHarrison(5) 11 35
(D W Chapman) *hld up: n.d* **20/1**

6000 **10** nk **The London Gang**[7] 980 4-8-9 50..................(b) JamesDoyle 2 36
(Miss D A McHale) *mid-div: rdn and wknd over 2f out* **25/1**

5204 **11** 5 **Shadow Jumper (IRE)**[19] 812 6-8-12 45..................(v) DavidProbert(7) 9 36
(J T Stimpson) *led: clr over 6f out: hdd over 3f out: wknd over 2f out* **66/1**

0024 **12** 2½ **Aperitif**[14] 895 6-9-1 60.................. AndrewMullen 8 27
(D Nicholls) *hld up: stmbld over 7f out: rdn and wknd over 2f out* **10/1**

1m 49.77s (-1.99) **Going Correction** -0.175s/f (Stan) **12** Ran SP% **119.5**
Speed ratings (Par 101):101,98,98,97,96 96,96,95,90,90 85,83
CSF £5.41 TOTE £1.80: £1.02, £2.20, £2.60; EX 6.40.Namroud was claimed by Mrs B. Ramsden for £8,000
Owner Triple Trio Partnership **Bred** Thomas J Murphy **Trained** Middleham Moor, N Yorks
■ Stewards' Enquiry : David Probert one-day ban: failed to ride to draw (Apr 27); two-day ban: used whip when out of contention above shoulder height without giving gelding time to respond (Apr 28-29)

FOCUS
An uncompetitive claimer though a strong pace thanks to Shadow Jumper, but take him out of the equation and the position of the front three never changed, as they held those positions in the main group throughout. They were the 'right' trio as far as official ratings were concerned too, as they had upwards of 5lb in hand of the others. The bare form is only modest.

1067 WEATHERBYS PRINTING FILLIES' H'CAP 5f 20y(P)
3:50 (3:50) (Class 5) (0-75,75) 3-Y-0+ **£3,071** (£906; £453) **Stalls** Low

Form RPR

00-3 **1** **Ashes (IRE)**[7] 964 5-9-3 **68**.................. PaulMulrennan 10 72
(K R Burke) *a.p: rdn over 1f out: hung lft and r.o to ld wl ins fnl f* **7/1**

054- **2** nk **Overwing (IRE)**[162] 6353 4-9-9 **74**.................. BrettDoyle 7 77
(R M H Cowell) *hld up: hdwy over 1f out: ev ch ins fnl f: edgd lft: r.o* **12/1**

0-00 **3** 1½ **Cosmic Destiny (IRE)**[24] 746 5-8-10 **61** oh11.................. JoeFanning 8 59
(E F Vaughan) *s.i.s and hmpd s: hdwy over 1f out: sn rdn: hung lft ins fnl f: styd on same pce* **33/1**

1333 **4** hd **Gifted Lass**[13] 905 5-8-12 **63**.................. DavidAllan 4 60
(J Balding) *chsd ldr tl led over 1f out: hdd and unable qck wl ins fnl f* **9/2**[1]

-314 **5** ½ **Muara**[69] 376 5-8-11 **62**.................. TonyHamilton 6 57
(D W Barker) *sn outpcd: hdwy u.p fnl f: nt trble ldrs* **6/1**[3]

10-2 **6** 1 **Baileys Outshine**[8] 958 3-8-10 **71**.................. TPQueally 2 63
(J G Given) *chsd ldrs: rdn over 1f out: no ex fnl f* **9/1**

5113 **7** 1¼ **Grange Lili (IRE)**[67] 387 3-8-13 **74**.................. GrahamGibbons 1 61
(Peter Grayson) *s.i.s: outpcd: hrd rdn over 1f out: nt trble ldrs* **12/1**

424- **8** 1 **Xaluna Bay (IRE)**[181] 6035 4-9-9 **74**.................. NCallan 9 58
(W R Muir) *chsd ldrs: rdn over 1f out: wknd fnl f* **6/1**[3]

0012 **9** ¾ **Pride Of Joy**[21] 787 4-8-12 **63**.................. ChrisCatlin 3 44
(D K Ivory) *led over 3f: wknd fnl f* **5/1**[2]

5000 **10** 2½ **Glenviews Youngone (IRE)**[19] 810 4-9-10 **75**...... RobbieFitzpatrick 5 47
(Peter Grayson) *chsd ldrs: rdn 1/2-way: wknd over 1f out* **10/1**

62.05 secs (-0.77) **Going Correction** -0.175s/f (Stan)
WFA 3 from 4yo+ 10lb **10** Ran SP% **113.3**
Speed ratings (Par 100):99,98,96,95,95 93,91,89,88,84
CSF £84.87 CT £1707.73 TOTE £10.60: £2.20, £2.90, £15.30; EX 70.80.
Owner Bryce, Dower, Morgan **Bred** E Campion **Trained** Middleham Moor, N Yorks

FOCUS
A moderate fillies' sprint in which the complexion of the race changed dramatically in the home staight. Three horses came right over to the stands' side of the track, including the winner and the third, and those drawn high dominated. It did appear the faster ground was towards the nearside. The time was slower than the seller and the form is dubious, with the third a long way out of the handicap.

1068 HOTEL & CONFERENCING AT WOLVERHAMPTON MAIDEN FILLIES' STKS 1m 141y(P)
4:25 (4:26) (Class 5) 3-Y-0+ **£3,071** (£906; £453) **Stalls** Low

Form RPR

5- **1** **Silver Pivotal (IRE)**[170] 6215 3-8-8 .... NickyMackay 9 73+
(G A Butler) *hld up: hdwy over 2f out: led over 1f out: hung lft ins fnl f: r.o wl* **9/2**[2]

2 3 **Wise Little Girl** 3-8-8 .... NCallan 4 67+
(M A Jarvis) *s.i.s: hdwy over 5f out: rdn over 1f out: styd on same pce fnl f* **5/1**[3]

633- **3** 4 **Mystery River (USA)**[178] 6071 3-8-1 73.................. KMay(7) 3 62+
(B J Meehan) *chsd ldrs: nt clr run wl over 1f out: wknd fnl f* **4/1**[1]

4 1¾ **Sopran Gath (ITY)**[181] 6044 4-9-6 72.................. JamesDoyle(3) 5 59
(J W Hills) *hld up in tch: led 2f out: sn rdn and hdd: wknd fnl f* **10/1**

5 1¼ **Lady Friend** 5-9-4 .... PatrickHills(5) 7 56
(J W Hills) *hld up: hmpd over 7f out: effrt over 2f out: sn hung lft: wknd over 1f out* **20/1**

4 **6** hd **Imperial Amber**[23] 769 5-9-9 .... ChrisCatlin 13 56?
(Karen George) *chsd ldr tl led 7f out: rdn and hdd 2f out: wknd fnl f* **25/1**

7 hd **Movie Mogul** 3-8-8 .... HayleyTurner 1 52
(M L W Bell) *s.i.s: hld up: hmpd over 7f out: rdn and edgd rt over 1f out: nvr trbld ldrs* **11/1**

2- **8** 1½ **Cape Thea**[150] 6504 3-8-8 .... AdamKirby 10 48
(W R Swinburn) *hld up: effrt over 2f out: wknd over 1f out* **5/1**[3]

3 **9** 6 **Verone (USA)**[13] 908 3-8-8 .... TPQueally 8 36
(M Botti) *chsd ldrs: ev ch over 2f out: sn rdn and wknd* **10/1**

10 4 **Lady Dedlock** 3-8-8 .... JimmyQuinn 2 27
(C A Cyzer) *s.i.s: outpcd* **50/1**

-420 **11** 1 **Mizzle (USA)**[17] 834 3-8-8 63.................. JoeFanning 12 25
(M Johnston) *sn pushed along in rr: wknd over 3f out* **10/1**

0 **12** 18 **Nikinoo**[28] 711 4-9-9 .... DaleGibson 11 —
(B Palling) *plld hrd and prom: lost pl 7f out: wknd over 5f out* **100/1**

0600 **13** 13 **Miss Sudbrook (IRE)**[5] 1002 5-9-9 40..................(v) ShaneKelly 6 —
(A W Carroll) *chsd ldr: rdn 3f out: sn wknd* **100/1**

1m 49.68s (-2.08) **Going Correction** -0.175s/f (Stan)
WFA 3 from 4yo+ 15lb **13** Ran SP% **119.7**
Speed ratings (Par 100):102,99,95,94,93 92,92,91,86,82 81,65,54
CSF £26.29 TOTE £3.90: £2.60, £2.40, £1.90; EX 15.90.
Owner The Distaff Partnership **Bred** Stratford Place Stud **Trained** Blewbury, Oxon

FOCUS
Not much strength in depth in this fillies' maiden, but the pace was solid and the front pair finished clear of the rest, so they probably have futures.

1069 STAY AT WOLVERHAMPTON HOLIDAY INN H'CAP 1m 1f 103y(P)
4:55 (4:57) (Class 6) (0-65,65) 4-Y-0+ **£2,388** (£705; £352) **Stalls** Low

Form RPR

3152 **1** **Penang Cinta**[24] 741 4-8-10 **60**.................. StephenDonohoe(3) 2 71
(P D Evans) *hld up: hdwy 1/2-way: rdn to ld 1f out: edgd lft: r.o* **2/1**[1]

-461 **2** hd **Scamperdale**[20] 805 5-9-2 **63**.................. TPQueally 9 74
(B P J Baugh) *s.i.s: hld up: hdwy and hung lft over 1f out: rdn and hung rt ins fnl f: r.o* **15/2**[3]

/40- **3** 1 **Montchara (IRE)**[189] 5870 4-8-13 **60**.................. PaulHanagan 4 69
(G Wragg) *chsd ldrs: rdn to ld over 1f out: sn hdd: styd on same pce* **7/1**[2]

00-3 **4** 1¾ **Lord Of Dreams (IRE)**[20] 805 5-9-0 **61**.................. BrettDoyle 13 66
(D W P Arbuthnot) *hld up: plld hrd: hdwy over 2f out: nt clr run over 1f out: styd on same pce fnl f* **10/1**

006- **5** ½ **Bijou Dan**[119] 6863 6-8-13 **65**..................(b) DuranFentiman(5) 7 69
(D W Thompson) *hld up: hdwy over 2f out: rdn over 1f out: styd on* **28/1**

4-43 **6** ½ **Port 'n Starboard**[38] 651 6-9-3 **64**.................. JimmyQuinn 3 67
(C A Cyzer) *chsd ldrs: rdn and ev ch 1f out: no ex* **9/1**

-004 **7** 1 **Dark Planet**[23] 753 4-9-0 **61**..................(p) RichardThomas 6 62
(D Burchell) *chsd ldr 7f out: rdn to ld 2f out: hdd over 1f out: wknd ins fnl f* **16/1**

3412 **8** 2½ **My Michelle**[20] 805 6-9-3 **64**.................. DaleGibson 1 60
(B Palling) *led: rdn and hdd 2f out: wknd fnl f* **7/1**[2]

-050 **9** 8 **Piper General (IRE)**[25] 732 5-8-10 **60**.................. JasonEdmunds(3) 5 40
(J Balding) *prom: rdn 1/2-way: wknd over 2f out* **28/1**

461 **10** 1½ **Ruffie (IRE)**[25] 732 4-9-4 **65**..................(e) NCallan 10 42
(Miss Gay Kelleway) *hld up: rdn and wknd over 2f out* **11/1**

4433 **11** 1¼ **Golden Spectrum (IRE)**[11] 933 8-8-12 **59**..................(b) JoeFanning 11 34
(R A Harris) *mid-div: hdwy over 5f out: rdn and wknd over 1f out* **16/1**

U012 **12** 7 **The City Kid (IRE)**[23] 768 4-9-0 **61**..................(b) ShaneKelly 12 22
(C R Dore) *mid-div: hdwy over 5f out: rdn and wknd over 2f out* **16/1**

2m 0.49s (-2.13) **Going Correction** -0.175s/f (Stan) **12** Ran SP% **122.1**
Speed ratings (Par 101):102,101,100,99,98 98,97,95,88,86 85,79
CSF £17.44 CT £90.88 TOTE £4.00: £1.10, £2.40, £4.00; EX 24.50.
Owner Trevor Gallienne **Bred** Mrs A K H Ooi **Trained** Pandy, Monmouths

FOCUS
A routine handicap, but a competitive one as there were eight spread right across the track at the furlong pole. However, as in the fillies' sprint two races earlier, there seemed to be a big advantage to those brought over towards the stands' rail in the home straight and the first two home came widest. The form seems sound enough.
T/Plt: £95.60 to a £1 stake. Pool: £52,668.45. 402.10 winning tickets. T/Qpdt: £24.90 to a £1 stake. Pool: £3,141.30. 93.10 winning tickets. CR

1070 - 1072a (Foreign Racing) - See Raceform Interactive

925 NOTTINGHAM (L-H)
Tuesday, April 17

OFFICIAL GOING: Good to firm
All races were run on the old jump course. After 10mm water applied two days beforehand the ground was described as 'genuine good to firm'.
Wind: Light, half against Weather: Fine and sunny

1073 EUROPEAN BREEDERS' FUND MAIDEN STKS 5f 13y
2:20 (2:21) (Class 5) 2-Y-0 **£3,562** (£1,059; £529; £264) **Stalls** High

Form RPR

1 **Grand Fleet** 2-9-3 .... JoeFanning 4 79+
(M Johnston) *chsd ldr: led over 2f out: rdn and edgd lft 1f out: styd on strly: eased towards fin* **9/4**[2]

2 2 **Irving Place** 2-9-3 .... JamieSpencer 5 66
(M L W Bell) *hld up in tch: effrt and swtchd lft over 2f out: wnt 2nd over 1f out: no imp* **2/1**[1]

3 1 **Al Muheer (IRE)** 2-9-3 .... SebSanders 1 62
(C E Brittain) *chsd wnr: kpt on same pce fnl f* **7/1**[3]

4 1¾ **Dawn Light (IRE)** 2-8-9 .... AndrewMullen(3) 8 50
(Mrs A Duffield) *led tl over 2f out: fdd fnl f* **16/1**

5 1½ **Shipboard Romance (IRE)** 2-8-9 .... StephenDonohoe(3) 2 44
(P D Evans) *swvd bdly lft s: sme hdwy over 2f out: lost pl over 1f out* **9/1**

6 ½ **Dhaka Dazzle** 2-9-3 .... EdwardCreighton 7 47
(M R Channon) *dwlt: hdwy over 2f out: hung lft and lost pl over 1f out* **9/1**

7 4 **Rye Beau (IRE)** 2-9-3 .... RoystonFfrench 6 31
(Mrs A Duffield) *chsd ldrs: sn drvn along: lost pl 2f out* **11/1**

62.32 secs (0.52) **Going Correction** -0.20s/f (Firm) **7** Ran SP% **110.8**
Speed ratings (Par 92):87,83,82,79,77 76,69
CSF £6.68 TOTE £2.80: £1.60, £1.40; EX 6.40.
Owner Gainsborough **Bred** Gainsborough Stud Management Ltd **Trained** Middleham Moor, N Yorks

FOCUS
All newcomers and apart from the first two they were not that big in the paddock. It was probably a weak event with the time modest, but the winner has plenty of potential, Mark Johnston's first two-year-old success this time.

NOTEBOOK
Grand Fleet ◆, a March foal, is a half-brother to three winners including the smart Lend A Hand. With a fair amount of size and scope and a quite attractive individual, his inexperience showed once in front but in the end he ran out a most decisive winner. He will be even better suited by six and looks potentially useful. (op 5-2)
Irving Place, a January foal, was the biggest in the line-up. Dropped in, he was switched to go in pursuit of the winner but was always very much second best. This will have opened his eyes and he can surely find a race. (op 9-4 tchd 5-2)
Al Muheer(IRE), a March foal, was noisy in the paddock and green to post. Drawn on the wide outside, he showed ability on his debut and will improve for the experience. (op 4-1)
Dawn Light(IRE), a February foal, is only small but showed plenty of toe from her stands'-side draw. (op 20-1)
Shipboard Romance(IRE), a March foal, was nibbled at in the market but she lost all chance when diving badly left leaving the stalls. Official explanation: jockey said filly hung left leaving stalls (op 12-1)

Dhaka Dazzle, very backward in his coat, missed a beat at the start and hung left before dropping out. (op 11-1 tchd 17-2)

1074 DON'T MISS THE COUNTRYSIDE EVENING H'CAP 5f 13y

2:50 (2:52) (Class 5) (0-70,70) 4-Y-0+ **£3,238** (£963; £481; £240) **Stalls** High

Form RPR

-046 **1** **Desert Opal**[18] [835] 7-8-8 **63**....................(p) LiamJones(3) 1 76
(C R Dore) *chsd ldrs on outer: led 1f out: hld on towards fin* **18/1**

0004 **2** *nk* **No Time (IRE)**[22] [787] 7-7-11 **56**.................... MCGeran(7) 5 68+
(A J McCabe) *swtchd rt s: hdwy and nt clr run over 1f out: swtchd lft jst ins last: r.o: no ex nr fin* **20/1**

0422 **3** *nk* **Melalchrist**[7] [992] 5-8-13 **65**....................(p) NCallan 16 76
(K A Ryan) *led tl 1f out: no ex fnl 75yds* **15/8**[1]

0531 **4** *1* **Methaaly (IRE)**[27] [724] 4-9-1 **67**.................... JohnEgan 17 74
(Jane Chapple-Hyam) *chsd ldrs: kpt on same pce fnl f* **7/2**[2]

0-40 **5** *¾* **Russian Rocket (IRE)**[23] [774] 5-9-4 **70**.................... DMylonas 15 74
(Mrs C A Dunnett) *chsd ldr: kpt on same pce fnl f* **9/1**

05-0 **6** *shd* **Divine Spirit**[7] [992] 6-8-10 **62**.................... JamieSpencer 12 66+
(M Dods) *hood removed v late: in rr: hdwy 2f out: styd on strly ins last* **8/1**[3]

350- **7** *1* **Hotham**[175] [6159] 4-8-12 **64**.................... PatCosgrave 13 64
(N Wilson) *chsd ldrs: wknd fnl f* **28/1**

060- **8** *½* **Memphis Man**[117] [6892] 4-8-5 **57**.................... RoystonFfrench 6 56
(W M Brisbourne) *mid-div: kpt on fnl 2f: nvr trbld ldrs* **14/1**

445- **9** *hd* **Ryedane (IRE)**[165] [6315] 5-8-12 **64**.................... DavidAllan 9 62
(T D Easterby) *in tch: sn drvn along: outpcd fnl 2f* **16/1**

264- **10** *¾* **Charles Parnell (IRE)**[154] [6478] 4-9-3 **69**.................... RichardMullen 4 64
(M Dods) *sn outpcd and in rr: sme hdwy 2f out: nvr on terms* **14/1**

0-00 **11** *1* **Paddywack (IRE)**[7] [992] 10-8-1 **60**....................(b) DanielleMcCreery(7) 11 52
(D W Chapman) *sn outpcd and in rr* **33/1**

000- **12** *3* **Meikle Barfil**[190] [5878] 5-8-6 **58**....................(p) JoeFanning 10 39
(J M Bradley) *s.i.s: sme hdwy on outside over 2f out: wknd over 1f out* **25/1**

0000 **13** *hd* **Verite**[64] [442] 4-8-6 **58**....................(be) JamesDoyle 7 38
(A J McCabe) *prom: lost pl over 1f out* **66/1**

460- **14** *½* **Dutch Key Card (IRE)**[185] [5970] 6-8-4 **56** oh1..........(b) AdrianTNicholls 8 34
(C Smith) *mid-div: wknd fnl 2f* **100/1**

59.88 secs (-1.92) **Going Correction** -0.20s/f (Firm) **14** Ran SP% **120.1**
Speed ratings (Par 103):107,106,106,104,103 103,101,100,100,99 97,92,92,91
CSF £344.91 CT £1022.93 TOTE £20.80: £5.60, £5.60, £1.30; EX 212.20.
Owner Page, Ward, Marsh **Bred** Juddmonte Farms **Trained** West Pinchbeck, Lincs
■ Stewards' Enquiry : M C Geran one-day ban: careless riding (May 31)

FOCUS
A low-grade sprint handicap and the quicker ground was possibly away from the stands'-side rail. The form looks sound enough rated around the third and fourth.
Verite Official explanation: jockey said gelding hung both ways

1075 CHECK OUT OUR 2007 THEMED MEETINGS MAIDEN STKS 1m 54y

3:20 (3:21) (Class 5) 3-Y-0 **£3,238** (£963; £481; £240) **Stalls** Centre

Form RPR

6- **1** **Ea (USA)**[249] [4333] 3-9-3 .... RHills 4 85+
(Sir Michael Stoute) *trckd ldr: led 3f out: shkn up and r.o strly fnl f* **1/1**[1]

04- **2** *1* **Transcend**[171] [6220] 3-9-3 .... RobertHavlin 9 83+
(J H M Gosden) *trckd ldrs: chal 1f out: kpt on same pce* **2/1**[2]

0-22 **3** *5* **Norman The Great**[15] [884] 3-9-3 75.................... JohnEgan 6 72
(Jane Chapple-Hyam) *hld up in midfield: hdwy 4f out: hung lft over 1f out: kpt on same pce* **9/1**

00- **4** *2½* **Majestic Chief**[174] [6173] 3-9-3 .... NCallan 7 66?
(K A Ryan) *led tl 3f out: kpt on one pce* **40/1**

5 *1½* **Willow Dancer (IRE)** 3-9-3 .... AdamKirby 3 62
(W R Swinburn) *rr-div: hdwy 4f out: nvr trbld ldrs* **25/1**

32- **6** *8* **Marriaj (USA)**[174] [6173] 3-9-3 .... RoystonFfrench 1 44
(B Smart) *t.k.h: sn trcking ldrs: drvn over 4f out: wknd over 1f out* **6/1**[3]

300- **7** *5* **Barley Moon**[122] [6840] 3-8-12 67.................... TedDurcan 2 27
(T Keddy) *trckd ldrs: lost pl over 2f out* **100/1**

0-0 **8** *24* **Good Etiquette**[13] [916] 3-9-3 .... TomEaves 5 —
(Mrs S Lamyman) *unruly in stalls: drvn along in rr: bhd fnl 3f* **300/1**

1m 45.34s (-1.06) **Going Correction** -0.05s/f (Good) **8** Ran SP% **115.2**
Speed ratings (Par 98):103,102,97,94,93 85,80,56
CSF £3.17 TOTE £1.80: £1.10, £1.10, £2.10; EX 4.40.
Owner Niarchos Family **Bred** Flaxman Holdings Ltd **Trained** Newmarket, Suffolk

FOCUS
A modest pace but in the end the first two pulled clear with the third setting the standard. The winner could turn out to be quite useful, the runner-up will surely go one better in a similar event.
Marriaj(USA) Official explanation: trainer's rep said colt was unsuited by the good to firm ground

1076 SUBSCRIBE TO RACING UK ON 08700 506957 H'CAP 1m 54y

3:50 (3:52) (Class 4) (0-85,85) 3-Y-0 **£5,829** (£1,734; £866; £432) **Stalls** Centre

Form RPR

321- **1** **Kay Gee Be (IRE)**[246] [4424] 3-8-13 **80**.................... JamieSpencer 3 85+
(M J Wallace) *hld up in mid-div: effrt 2f out: led jst ins last: hld on towards fin* **7/2**[1]

3240 **2** *nk* **Copper King**[41] [638] 3-8-6 **76** ow1.................... StephenDonohoe(3) 9 80
(P D Evans) *hld up in rr: effrt over 2f out: styd on wl ins last: jst hld* **33/1**

410- **3** *1¼* **Spirit Of The Mist (IRE)**[210] [5466] 3-8-13 **80**.................... JohnEgan 4 81+
(T J Pitt) *led tl jst ins last: kpt on same pce* **17/2**

4-54 **4** *1¾* **Arena's Dream (USA)**[25] [744] 3-8-5 **72**.................... DaleGibson 8 69
(R A Fahey) *mid-div: effrt over 2f out: styd on wl ins last* **40/1**

621- **5** *nk* **Colchium (IRE)**[122] [6840] 3-8-6 **73**.................... DavidAllan 12 69
(H Morrison) *mid-div: effrt over 2f out: styd on same pce fnl f* **25/1**

050- **6** *hd* **La Roca (IRE)**[199] [5676] 3-9-4 **85**....................(t) SebSanders 7 81
(R M Beckett) *chsd ldrs: wknd ins last* **25/1**

5-11 **7** *1* **Ambrosiano**[13] [931] 3-8-7 **74**.................... AdamKirby 13 68
(C G Cox) *hld up in mid-div: hdwy on outside over 3f out: hrd rdn and hung lft over 1f out: kpt on one pce* **9/2**[2]

001- **8** *nk* **Guiseppe Verdi (USA)**[176] [6143] 3-8-8 **75**.................... RobertHavlin 14 68
(J H M Gosden) *hld up in rr: hdwy over 2f out: kpt on: nvr trbld ldrs* **9/2**[2]

103- **9** *½* **Monkey Glas (IRE)**[191] [5843] 3-8-8 **75**.................... PatCosgrave 6 67
(K R Burke) *chsd ldrs: edgd lft over 1f out: sn fdd* **12/1**

500- **10** *3* **Lap Of Honour (IRE)**[155] [6458] 3-8-5 **72**.................... SimonWhitworth 10 57
(N A Callaghan) *hld up in rr: hdwy on outside over 2f out: wknd over 1f out* **66/1**

046- **11** *3½* **Our Herbie**[155] [6458] 3-8-9 **76**.................... MichaelHills 11 53
(J W Hills) *s.i.s: swtchd lft after s: hld up in rr: nvr a factor* **20/1**

114- **12** *nk* **Steam Cuisine**[199] [5676] 3-9-2 **83**.................... BrettDoyle 1 59
(M G Quinlan) *chsd ldrs: lost pl over 1f out* **12/1**

01- **13** *1¾* **Zahour Al Yasmeen**[293] [2980] 3-8-10 **77**.................... TedDurcan 2 49
(M R Channon) *trckd ldrs: ev ch tl wknd qckly appr fnl f* **18/1**

22-1 **14** *10* **Autograph Hunter**[15] [886] 3-9-0 **81**.................... JoeFanning 5 30
(M Johnston) *mid-div: sn pushed along: sme hdwy on inner over 3f out: sn lost pl: bhd and eased fnl f* **6/1**[3]

1m 45.02s (-1.38) **Going Correction** -0.05s/f (Good) **14** Ran SP% **123.4**
Speed ratings (Par 100):104,103,102,100,100 100,99,98,98,95 91,91,89,79
CSF £139.84 CT £964.38 TOTE £4.50: £1.80, £9.60, £4.00; EX 246.40 TRIFECTA Not won..
Owner Par Jeu Partnership **Bred** Pursuit Of Truth Syndicate **Trained** Newmarket, Suffolk
■ Stewards' Enquiry : Jamie Spencer one-day ban: careless riding (Apr 28)

FOCUS
A competitive three-year-old handicap run at a fair gallop and the form looks sound.

1077 PADDOCKS CONFERENCE CENTRE NOTTINGHAM RACECOURSE MAIDEN STKS 1m 1f 213y

4:20 (4:21) (Class 5) 3-Y-0+ **£3,238** (£963; £481; £240) **Stalls** Low

Form RPR

5- **1** **Hannicean**[171] [6214] 3-8-10 .... PhilipRobinson 7 75+
(M A Jarvis) *led 1f: quite keen: rdn over 3f out: n.m.r over 2f out: rallied over 1f out: led last 100yds: r.o* **1/1**[1]

06- **2** *¾* **Inchlaggan (IRE)**[187] [5918] 3-8-10 .... MichaelHills 3 71+
(B W Hills) *led after 1f tl over 2f out: hdd over 1f out: kpt on same pce* **12/1**

52-2 **3** *4* **Maslak (IRE)**[25] [735] 3-8-10 82.................... RHills 8 63+
(E A L Dunlop) *sn trcking ldrs: led over 2f out tl over 1f out: kpt on same pce* **5/1**[3]

0- **4** *1* **Just Two Numbers**[200] [5658] 3-8-10 .... JamieSpencer 1 61+
(W Jarvis) *sn trcking ldrs: drvn over 3f out: one pce fnl 2f* **20/1**

5 *¾* **Good Cause (IRE)**[149] 6-9-13 .... TomEaves 2 59?
(Mrs S Lamyman) *s.i.s: hdwy on outer 2f out: kpt on: nvr trbld ldrs* **200/1**

04 **6** *½* **Wolds Way**[4] [1030] 5-9-13 .... DavidAllan 4 58?
(T D Easterby) *in tch: drvn over 4f out: kpt on one pce fnl 3f* **66/1**

0- **7** *10* **Elounda (IRE)**[171] [6215] 3-8-6 ow1.................... TedDurcan 5 34
(H R A Cecil) *trckd ldrs: lost pl over 2f out* **7/2**[2]

8 *18* **Officer** 3-8-10 .... JDSmith 6 —
(Sir Michael Stoute) *rn v green and sn pushed along in rr: lost pl over 3f out: sn bhd* **12/1**

2m 9.57s (-0.13) **Going Correction** -0.05s/f (Good)
WFA 3 from 5yo+ 17lb **8** Ran SP% **111.0**
Speed ratings (Par 103):98,97,94,93,92 92,84,70
CSF £13.90 TOTE £1.80: £1.10, £2.60, £1.50; EX 11.40.
Owner Magno-Pulse Ltd **Bred** Derek R Price **Trained** Newmarket, Suffolk
■ Philip Robinson's comeback ride, his first since October after undergoing hip surgery.

FOCUS
No gallop and quite a messy affair with little between the first six at the line. The proximity of the two older jumps horses at the line must be a cause for concern and it is hard to be positive about the form.

1078 RACING AGAIN ON SATURDAY NIGHT H'CAP 1m 1f 213y

4:50 (4:50) (Class 5) (0-75,75) 4-Y-0+ **£3,238** (£963; £481; £240) **Stalls** Low

Form RPR

40-1 **1** **Cripsey Brook**[7] [997] 9-8-10 **74**....................(t) DanielleMcCreery(7) 4 80
(K G Reveley) *s.i.s: hdwy and n.m.r over 1f out: styd on strly ins last: led nr fin* **6/1**[2]

615- **2** *nk* **Piper's Song (IRE)**[197] [5734] 4-8-10 **67**.................... DaneO'Neill 1 72
(H Candy) *trckd ldrs: styd on to ld over 1f out: hdd and no ex towards fin* **3/1**[1]

/632 **3** *1½* **Camille Pissarro (USA)**[13] [928] 7-8-4 **61** oh2.......... EdwardCreighton 9 64
(D J Wintle) *chsd ldrs: drvn over 3f out: hung lft over 1f out: no ex ins last* **13/2**[3]

350- **4** *nk* **The Aldbury Flyer**[179] [6076] 4-9-2 **73**.................... AdamKirby 2 75
(W R Swinburn) *t.k.h: trckd ldrs: rdn over 2f out: kpt on same pce fnl f* **20/1**

1-22 **5** *1½* **Starcross Maid**[33] [685] 5-8-2 **62** oh8 ow1.................... PatrickMathers(3) 7 61
(J F Coupland) *in rr: kpt on fnl 2f: nvr trbld ldrs* **14/1**

600- **6** *nk* **Snowed Under**[214] [5346] 6-9-4 **75**.................... PatCosgrave 5 74
(J D Bethell) *led after 2f: hdd over 2f out: one pce* **13/2**[3]

/60- **7** *½* **Darusso**[32] [6260] 4-8-8 **65**.................... JohnEgan 3 66+
(J S Moore) *hld up in rr: effrt over 3f out: styng on on inner whn nt clr run ins last: nt rcvr* **8/1**

60-U **8** *4* **Billy One Punch**[13] [928] 5-8-12 **69**.................... JamieSpencer 6 59
(G G Margarson) *led 2f: trckd ldrs: led over 2f out tl over 1f out: wknd and eased ins last* **6/1**[2]

361- **9** *1½* **Lunar River (FR)**[191] [5830] 4-8-9 **66**....................(t) FergusSweeney 8 53
(David Pinder) *trckd ldrs: rdn over 2f out: wknd fnl f* **17/2**

2m 9.57s (-0.13) **Going Correction** -0.05s/f (Good) **9** Ran SP% **113.3**
Speed ratings (Par 103):98,97,96,96,95 94,94,91,90
CSF £23.84 CT £119.85 TOTE £6.10: £1.50, £1.30, £2.50; EX 16.00 Place 6 £9.53, Place 5 £7.77.
Owner Reveley Farms **Bred** Overbury Stud And Stowell Hill Ltd **Trained** Lingdale, Redcar & Cleveland

FOCUS
A modest handicap run at just a steady pace. The winner came from last to first in the final furlong and with the third sets the level for the form.
T/Jkpt: £22,559.80 to a £1 stake. Pool: £587,827.00. 18.50 winning tickets. T/Plt: £13.40 to a £1 stake. Pool: £87,798.45. 4,777.90 winning tickets. T/Qpdt: £7.30 to a £1 stake. Pool: £2,924.10. 293.50 winning tickets. WG

971 WARWICK (L-H)

Tuesday, April 17

OFFICIAL GOING: Good to firm
Wind: Light, across Weather: Cloudy with sunny spells

1079 EUROPEAN BREEDERS' FUND MAIDEN FILLIES' STKS 5f

2:30 (2:32) (Class 5) 2-Y-0 **£3,562** (£1,059; £529; £264) **Stalls** Centre

Form RPR

1 **Piece Of My Heart** 2-9-0 .... EddieAhern 6 70+
(P F I Cole) *chsd ldrs: hung rt 3f: rdn and hung lft over 1f out: hung rt and led ins fnl f: r.o* **11/2**[3]

2 *½* **Ramatni** 2-9-0 .... KDarley 2 68
(M Johnston) *w ldrs: led 3f out: hdd 2f out: rdn and ev ch ins fnl f: styd on* **11/4**[1]

3 *1¼* **Shamrock Lady (IRE)** 2-9-0 .... PaulEddery 5 63
(Pat Eddery) *sn outpcd: hdwy over 1f out: r.o* **14/1**

4 *nk* **Andrasta** 2-9-0 .... SteveDrowne 8 62
(B J Meehan) *swvd rt s: sn chsng ldrs: hung lft over 1f out: styd on same pce ins fnl f* **11/2**[3]
5 *1/2* **Carolina Blini** 2-9-0 .... RichardHughes 4 60
(B J Meehan) *w ldrs: led 2f out: sn hung lft: hdd and no ex ins fnl f* **7/2**[2]
6 *1 1/4* **Leading Edge (IRE)** 2-9-0 .... TPO'Shea 1 55
(M R Channon) *s.i.s: outpcd: r.o ins fnl f: nt rch ldrs* **9/1**
7 *3/4* **Ephesian (IRE)** 2-9-0 .... TPQueally 3 52
(Mrs A Duffield) *led 2f: rdn whn n.m.r wl over 1f out: wknd fnl f* **11/1**
8 *1 3/4* **New Minerton (IRE)** 2-9-0 .... JimCrowley 7 45
(B R Millman) *sn outpcd* **9/1**

62.51 secs (3.11) **Going Correction** +0.275s/f (Good) **8 Ran SP% 114.7**
Speed ratings (Par 89):86,85,83,82,81 79,78,75
CSF £21.10 TOTE £8.20: £1.70, £1.40, £4.40; EX 24.80.
Owner Mr & Mrs Christopher Wright **Bred** Stratford Place Stud **Trained** Whatcombe, Oxon

FOCUS
No form to go on, but some decent stables were represented and this looked a fair juvenile maiden for fillies, although the time modest limits confidence.

NOTEBOOK
Piece Of My Heart, a half-sister to Pearl's A Singer, a dual 1m4f-1m6f who was also successful over hurdles, and 6f juvenile scorer Culture Queen, overcame greenness to make a winning debut. She hung to her right in the straight, despite her rider trying to correct her with his whip, ending up towards the stands'-side rail, but she still proved good enough. She did look quite awkward, but hopefully that can be ironed out as she matures and she deserves her chance in better company. (op 9-2 tchd 6-1)
Ramatni, a sister to Shot Gun, placed over 1m at three, out of a 7f juvenile winner, sister to high-class two-year-old Bint Allayl, showed good speed throughout but was just worn down late on. She should win her maiden next time before stepping up in class. (op 7-2 tchd 5-2)
Shamrock Lady(IRE), a half-sister to dual middle-distance winner Make My Hay, who was also successful over hurdles, out of a 5f juvenile winner, struggled to go the early pace but ran on nicely close home. She is open to plenty of improvement. (op 16-1 tchd 12-1)
Andrasta, a 14,000gns half-sister to among others Game Time, a 1m juvenile winner, out of a 1m4f at three, did not help her chance by getting wound up before the start and swerving right coming out of the stalls. She ran very well in the circumstances and could go close next time if going the right way from this. (op 10-3 tchd 13-2)
Carolina Blini, a 19,500gns half-sister to Big Snake, a dual winner at two in Italy, out of a 5f juvenile scorer, showed good speed for much of the way but could not sustain her challenge. (op 5-1)
Ephesian(IRE) Official explanation: trainer later said filly was found to be dehydrated

1080 DEREK CRUTCHLEY "LIFETIME IN RACING" H'CAP 5f
3:00 (3:01) (Class 5) (0-75,78) 4-Y-0+ **£3,071** (£906; £453) **Stalls** Centre

Form RPR
00-1 **1** **Spanish Ace**[6] 1004 6-9-8 **78** 6ex...................................... KDarley 3 90
(J M Bradley) *unruly in stalls: chsd ldrs: rdn to ld ins fnl f: r.o* **15/8**[1]
46-5 **2** *hd* **Chatshow (USA)**[6] 1004 6-8-10 **66**...................................... JimCrowley 1 78
(A W Carroll) *hld up: hdwy 2f out: rdn and ev ch ins fnl f: r.o* **7/1**[2]
0620 **3** *2 1/2* **Inwaan (IRE)**[21] 803 4-8-7 **63**......................................(t) ChrisCatlin 7 66
(P R Webber) *hld up: hdwy over 1f out: carried rt ins fnl f: nt rch ldrs* **14/1**
330- **4** *shd* **Chinalea (IRE)**[183] 6020 5-9-2 **72**......................................(p) MickyFenton 10 74
(C G Cox) *dwlt: hdwy over 3f out: rdn over 1f out: hung rt ins fnl f: styd on same pce* **12/1**
5-56 **5** *1/2* **Witchry**[14] 905 5-8-10 **66**...................................... LPKeniry 6 67
(A G Newcombe) *chsd ldrs: nt clr run over 1f out: styd on same pce ins fnl f* **10/1**
0514 **6** *nk* **Fizzlephut (IRE)**[6] 1004 5-9-2 **72**...................................... PaulFitzsimons 12 72
(Miss J R Tooth) *led: hdd 4f out: led 2f out: hdd and no ex ins fnl f* **7/1**[2]
600- **7** *2* **Welcome Approach**[175] 6159 4-8-12 **68**...................................... PhillipMakin 4 60
(J R Weymes) *hld up in tch: rdn over 1f out: wknd ins fnl f* **14/1**
216/ **8** *1* **Charming Ballet (IRE)**[477] 6662 4-8-13 **69**...................................... IanMongan 2 58
(N P Littmoden) *sn outpcd: styd on ins fnl f: nrst fin* **25/1**
0/44 **9** *hd* **Pulse**[86] 201 9-7-11 **60** oh3......................................(p) LukeMorris(7) 13 48
(Miss J R Tooth) *chsd ldrs: ev ch wl over 1f out: wknd fnl f* **50/1**
-000 **10** *shd* **Coconut Moon**[18] 835 5-9-1 **71**...................................... JimmyQuinn 5 59+
(E J Alston) *racd keenly: led 4f out: hdd 2f out: wknd and eased fnl f: sddle slipped* **16/1**
6313 **11** *3/4* **Triskaidekaphobia**[15] 892 4-8-4 **60** oh2......................................(t) RichardThomas 9 45
(Miss J R Tooth) *chsd ldrs over 3f* **8/1**[3]
3-00 **12** *2 1/2* **Bold Minstrel (IRE)**[20] 810 5-9-4 **74**...................................... ShaneKelly 8 50
(M Quinn) *s.i.s: hmpd 4f out: outpcd* **18/1**

59.60 secs (0.20) **Going Correction** +0.275s/f (Good) **12 Ran SP% 118.0**
Speed ratings (Par 103):109,108,104,104,103 103,100,98,98,97 96,92
CSF £14.43 CT £147.38 TOTE £2.60: £1.80, £2.80, £4.60; EX 12.20.
Owner racingshares.co.uk **Bred** Farleigh Court Racing Partnership **Trained** Sedbury, Gloucs

FOCUS
An ordinary handicap but the form looks solid enough rated around the principals.
Coconut Moon Official explanation: jockey said saddle slipped

1081 WATCH ALL UK RACING AT BETTER MAIDEN STKS 1m 22y
3:30 (3:31) (Class 5) 3-Y-0 **£2,914** (£867; £433; £216) **Stalls** Low

Form RPR
1 **Woodcraft** 3-9-3 .... RichardHughes 2 77+
(B W Hills) *dwlt: hdwy to ld over 6f out: rdn and hdd 1f out: sn hung rt: rallied to ld wl ins fnl f* **7/2**[2]
44- **2** *3/4* **Stark Contrast (USA)**[249] 4333 3-9-3 .... KDarley 3 74
(G A Butler) *trckd ldrs: rdn to ld 1f out: sn edgd rt: hdd wl ins fnl f* **6/4**[1]
330- **3** *1* **Kalasam**[200] 5655 3-9-3 **76**...................................... EddieAhern 1 72
(W R Muir) *hld up: hdwy over 1f out: r.o* **13/2**
242- **4** *3 1/2* **Masai Moon**[193] 5788 3-9-3 **78**...................................... JimCrowley 6 64
(B R Millman) *chsd ldrs: rdn and hung rt over 1f out: wknd ins fnl f* **4/1**[3]
06- **5** *1 1/4* **Mujma**[173] 6188 3-9-3 .... MartinDwyer 7 61
(Sir Michael Stoute) *chsd ldrs: rdn over 2f out: hung lft and wknd over 1f out* **7/1**
00 **6** *1 1/2* **Sixfields Flyer (IRE)**[8] 973 3-8-12 .... PaulEddery 8 53
(Pat Eddery) *hld up: shkn up over 1f out: nvr trbld ldrs* **100/1**
7 *nk* **Best Of Gold (IRE)** 3-9-3 .... SteveDrowne 4 57
(B J Meehan) *s.i.s: shkn up over 1f out: n.d* **20/1**
05 **8** *9* **Whodunit (UAE)**[38] 655 3-9-3 .... ChrisCatlin 5 36
(P W Hiatt) *sn led: hdd over 6f out: w wnr tl rdn over 2f out: wknd over 1f out* **50/1**

1m 40.44s (0.84) **Going Correction** 0.0s/f (Good) **8 Ran SP% 115.8**
Speed ratings (Par 98):95,94,93,89,88 87,86,77
CSF £9.20 TOTE £4.80: £1.70, £1.20, £2.20; EX 9.70.
Owner K Abdulla **Bred** Juddmonte Farms Ltd **Trained** Lambourn, Berks

FOCUS
Probably just an ordinary maiden, rated around the third, but it should produce the odd winner.

1082 BETTERBET.COM CONDITIONS STKS 1m 22y
4:00 (4:03) (Class 4) 4-Y-0+ **£6,477** (£1,927; £963; £481) **Stalls** Low

Form RPR
060- **1** **Kew Green (USA)**[32] 6516 9-8-8 **100**...................................... EddieAhern 1 99
(P R Webber) *hld up in tch: rdn over 1f out: r.o to ld post* **13/2**[3]
-153 **2** *shd* **Kalankari (IRE)**[53] 540 4-8-12 .... MartinDwyer 6 103
(A M Balding) *chsd ldr tl led 2f out: sn rdn: hdd post: fin lame* **6/4**[1]
130- **3** *3* **Dream Theme**[206] 5523 4-8-12 **100**...................................... RichardHughes 4 96
(B W Hills) *hld up and bhd: hdwy 2f out: sn rdn: no ex ins fnl f* **13/8**[2]
-055 **4** *3 1/2* **Bahar Shumaal (IRE)**[24] 756 5-8-8 **95**......................................(b) J-PGuillambert 3 84
(C E Brittain) *chsd ldrs: rdn over 2f out: wknd over 1f out* **9/1**
0-00 **5** *1* **Rain Stops Play (IRE)**[17] 848 5-8-8 **87**...................................... ShaneKelly 2 82
(M Quinn) *led 6f: wknd fnl f* **14/1**

1m 38.45s (-1.15) **Going Correction** 0.0s/f (Good) **5 Ran SP% 108.1**
Speed ratings (Par 105):105,104,101,98,97
CSF £16.21 TOTE £6.60: £2.60, £1.30; EX 18.90.
Owner Stetson Racing **Bred** Tim Foreman **Trained** Mollington, Oxon

FOCUS
A small field but a fairly competitive conditions event nevertheless and the form should prove reasonable.

1083 CASABELLE DESIGN (THE ANNE SENDALL GROUP) H'CAP 1m 2f 188y
4:30 (4:31) (Class 4) (0-80,80) 4-Y-0+ **£4,857** (£1,445; £722; £360) **Stalls** Low

Form RPR
026- **1** **Flying Clarets (IRE)**[172] 6202 4-9-0 **76**...................................... PaulHanagan 10 89
(R A Fahey) *chsd ldrs: rdn to ld and hung lft fr wl over 1f out: r.o* **9/2**[3]
5000 **2** *2* **Fantoche (BRZ)**[32] 693 5-9-4 **80**......................................(t) J-PGuillambert 8 90
(M J Wallace) *hld up: hdwy over 1f out: rdn and hung rt ins fnl f: r.o* **8/1**
203- **3** *nk* **Fregate Island (IRE)**[283] 3301 4-9-2 **78**...................................... RichardHughes 3 87
(B J Meehan) *chsd ldr: rdn whn hmpd wl over 1f out: no ex ins fnl f* **7/2**[2]
611- **4** *1 1/4* **Pagano (IRE)**[124] 6825 4-9-0 **76**...................................... EddieAhern 7 83
(A King) *prom: rdn over 1f out: styd on same pce* **10/3**[1]
1-00 **5** *5* **Speagle (IRE)**[17] 846 5-9-1 **77**...................................... DanielTudhope 4 75
(D Carroll) *led: clr 8f out: rdn and hdd over 1f out: wknd ins fnl f* **5/1**
0-60 **6** *1 3/4* **Capistrano**[13] 921 4-7-13 **68** ow2...................................... JosephWalsh(7) 9 63
(Mrs P Sly) *hld up in tch: rdn over 3f out: wknd over 1f out* **20/1**
7 *2 1/2* **Brastar Jelois (FR)**[10] 4-9-2 **78**...................................... MartinDwyer 6 68
(D E Pipe) *hld up: rdn over 2f out: n.d* **14/1**
25-0 **8** *3* **Faith And Reason (USA)**[17] 850 4-9-0 **76**...................................... TPQueally 1 61
(B J Curley) *hld up: rdn over 2f out: sn wknd and eased* **11/1**
5000 **9** *16* **Happy As Larry (USA)**[17] 850 5-9-1 **77**...................................... RobbieFitzpatrick 2 33
(T J Pitt) *hld up: rdn over 3f out: sn wknd* **10/1**

2m 18.16s (-1.24) **Going Correction** 0.0s/f (Good) **9 Ran SP% 120.1**
Speed ratings (Par 105):104,102,102,101,97 96,94,92,80
CSF £42.00 CT £142.86 TOTE £5.10: £2.10, £2.60, £1.50; EX 58.20.
Owner The Matthewman Partnership **Bred** Gabriel Bell **Trained** Musley Bank, N Yorks

FOCUS
A fair handicap run at a good pace. The winning time was 1.77 quicker than the following 61-75 and the form looks pretty sound rated around the placed horses.

1084 NEWBURY LIVE ON FRIDAY WITH BETTER H'CAP 1m 2f 188y
5:00 (5:00) (Class 5) (0-75,75) 3-Y-0 **£3,238** (£963; £481; £240) **Stalls** Low

Form RPR
2-50 **1** **Callisto Moon**[27] 719 3-8-8 **65**...................................... JimCrowley 2 72
(Ian Williams) *a.p: rdn over 1f out: r.o to ld wl ins fnl f* **10/1**
10-0 **2** *nk* **Love Brothers**[27] 719 3-9-2 **73**...................................... ChrisCatlin 5 79
(M R Channon) *led: rdn over 1f out: edgd lft and hdd wl ins fnl f* **15/2**
6-11 **3** *1 3/4* **Dan Tucker**[15] 893 3-9-1 **72**...................................... RichardHughes 8 75
(B J Meehan) *hld up in tch: rdn to chse ldr 2f out: styd on same pce ins fnl f* **7/4**[1]
511- **4** *2 1/2* **My Secrets**[145] 6569 3-9-4 **75**...................................... KDarley 4 74
(M Johnston) *chsd ldr tl rdn over 3f out: no ex fnl f* **2/1**[2]
4-13 **5** *1 1/4* **Pret A Porter (UAE)**[87] 196 3-8-12 **69**......................................(b) EddieAhern 7 65
(P D Evans) *trckd ldrs: racd keenly: wnt 2nd over 3f out: rdn and hung rt fr over 2f out: wknd fnl f* **7/1**[3]
5031 **6** *1 1/4* **Homes By Woodford**[12] 937 3-9-0 **71**...................................... PaulHanagan 6 65
(R A Harris) *hld up: rdn over 2f out: n.d* **14/1**
-236 **7** *1 1/2* **L'Oiseau De Feu (USA)**[41] 633 3-9-1 **72**...................................... VinceSlattery 3 63
(Mrs K Waldron) *hld up: rdn over 2f out: a in rr* **25/1**

2m 19.93s (0.53) **Going Correction** 0.0s/f (Good) **7 Ran SP% 113.6**
Speed ratings (Par 98):98,97,96,94,93 92,91
CSF £78.92 CT £193.00 TOTE £11.10: £5.50, £3.00; EX 64.80 Place 6 £156.92, Place 5 £71.53.

Owner B W Bedford **Bred** Barton Stud **Trained** Portway, Worcs

FOCUS
A fair handicap but it was run at a fairly modest pace and the form is not entirely convincing, with the third the best guide.
T/Plt: £489.30 to a £1 stake. Pool: £48,565.90. 72.45 winning tickets T/Qpdt: £72.70 to a £1 stake. Pool: £2,399.20. 24.40 winning tickets CR

BEVERLEY (R-H)
Wednesday, April 18

OFFICIAL GOING: Good to firm
The well watered ground was described as 'genuine good to firm, very level with a good cover of grass'.
Wind: Light, half against Weather: fine and sunny

1086 WELCOME BACK TO BEVERLEY (S) STKS 1m 100y
2:10 (2:10) (Class 5) 3-Y-0+ **£3,076** (£915; £457; £228) **Stalls** High

Form RPR
00-6 **1** **Bond Diamond**[19] 833 10-9-6 **57**...................................... MickyFenton 11 55
(P T Midgley) *hld up in midfield: stdy hdwy 3f out: rdn over 1f out: styd on to ld last 100 yds* **11/2**[2]
00-0 **2** *nk* **Danawi (IRE)**[15] 902 4-9-6 **48**...................................... ChrisCatlin 7 55
(M R Hoad) *keen: sn led: rdn wl over 1f out: edgd rt and drvn ins last: hdd and no ex last 100 yds* **25/1**
00-0 **3** *3/4* **Baby Barry**[29] 715 10-9-9 **54**......................................(p) DominicFox(3) 4 59
(K J Burke) *in tch:hdwy to chse ldrs 3f out: pushed along 2f out: swtchd lft and rdn over 1f out: kpt on* **50/1**
4111 **4** *shd* **Sawwaah (IRE)**[14] 912 10-9-12 **67**......................................(v) AdrianTNicholls 13 59
(D Nicholls) *hld up in rr: switcehd lft and hdwy wl over 1f out: sn rdn and styd on ins last: nrst fin* **1/1**[1]

0-00 **5** 1 1/4 **Pepper Road**[43] [625] 8-9-6 43 ....(t) DavidAllan 17 50
(R Bastiman) *midfield: hdwy over 2f out: rdn to cjase ldrs over 1f out: kpt on same pce ins last* **25/1**

3-10 **6** 2 **Crush On You**[34] [682] 4-9-7 47 .... GrahamGibbons 10 47
(R Hollinshead) *a.p: rdn along wl over 2f out: sn one pace* **22/1**

0242 **7** shd **Prince Of Gold**[22] [801] 7-9-12 45 ....(b) NCallan 2 52
(R Hollinshead) *hld up towards rr: hdwy over 2f out: rdn over 1f out: edgd rt and no imp ins last* **9/1**[3]

00-0 **8** 1/2 **Sheriff's Deputy**[13] [932] 7-9-1 42 .... KevinGhunowa(5) 12 45
(C N Kellett) *in tch: rdn along over 2f out: sn b eaten* **125/1**

000- **9** 1 **Airedale Lad (IRE)**[32] [5485] 6-9-1 43 .... MichaelJStainton(5) 16 43
(R M Whitaker) *towards rr tl styd on fnl 3f: nvr a factor* **10/1**

6060 **10** shd **Smart Pick**[61] [485] 4-8-12 45 .... LiamJones(3) 14 37
(Mrs L Williamson) *a towards rr* **80/1**

0-06 **11** 1/2 **Borodinsky**[83] [238] 6-9-3 43 .... MarkLawson(3) 5 41
(R E Barr) *chsd ldrs: rdn along over 2f out: sn wknd* **50/1**

5000 **12** 1 1/4 **Contra Mundum (USA)**[47] [605] 4-9-6 60 ....(p) PaulHanagan 6 39
(B S Rothwell) *cl up on inner: rdn along over 2f out and grad wknd* **16/1**

60-0 **13** 6 **Evolution Ex (USA)**[106] [12] 5-9-12 60 ....(vt) DanielTudhope 9 32
(I W McInnes) *chsd ldrs: rdn along 3f out: sn wknd* **11/1**

60-0 **14** 3/4 **Jabraan (USA)**[57] [504] 5-9-6 41 ....(b) DaleGibson 8 25
(D W Chapman) *a rr* **100/1**

15 6 **Our Flossie (IRE)**[30] 4-9-1 .... SilvestreDeSousa 15 7
(A D Brown) *s.i.s: a rr* **80/1**

0000 **16** 6 **Paso Doble**[5] [1027] 9-9-12 50 ....(b) SebSanders 1 5
(R Bastiman) *a rr* **28/1**

1m 46.53s (-0.87) **Going Correction** -0.075s/f (Good) **16** Ran SP% **122.4**
Speed ratings (Par 103):101,100,99,99,98 96,96,96,95,94 94,93,87,86,80 74
CSF £142.05 TOTE £7.30: £2.10, £6.40, £10.00; EX 168.50.There was no bid for the winner. Sawwah was claimed by Tom Dascombe for £6,000
Owner Peter Mee **Bred** Britton House Stud And R G Fuller **Trained** Westow, N Yorks
■ Stewards' Enquiry : Silvestre De Sousa one-day ban: used whip when out of contention (Apr 29)

FOCUS
A moderate seller. The form looks limited although the time suggests it should be sound.

1087 BEVERLEY-RACECOURSE.CO.UK MAIDEN AUCTION STKS 5f
2:45 (2:47) (Class 5) 2-Y-O **£3,076** (£915; £457; £228) **Stalls** High

Form RPR

2 **1** **Artdeal**[11] [942] 2-8-13 .... SebSanders 15 74
(M J Wallace) *mde all: jst hld on* **5/4**[1]

2 shd **Mission Impossible** 2-8-13 .... LeeEnstone 11 74
(P C Haslam) *chsd ldrs: sltly hmpd 3f out: styd on wl ins last: jst hld* **14/1**

5 **3** 1/2 **Runswick Bay**[18] [845] 2-8-13 .... TomEaves 14 72
(G M Moore) *chsd ldrs: kpt on wl: no ex wl ins last* **9/4**[2]

4 1/2 **Berrymead** 2-8-4 .... DaleGibson 13 61
(M W Easterby) *s.s: hdwy 2f out: kpt on wl fnl f* **40/1**

5 nk **Taurian** 2-8-9 .... MickyFenton 6 65+
(Mrs L Stubbs) *hmpd s: sn bhd: hdwy 2f out: styd on strly ins last* **100/1**

5 dht **Lady Rangali (IRE)** 2-8-6 .... RoystonFfrench 9 62
(Mrs A Duffield) *chsd ldrs on outer: edgd lft 2f out: kpt on fnl f* **20/1**

7 hd **Secret Asset (IRE)** 2-8-9 .... DavidAllan 17 64
(W M Brisbourne) *mid-div: hdwy 2f out: kpt on wl fnl f* **33/1**

00 **8** 1 1/2 **Ocean Transit (IRE)**[7] [999] 2-7-11 .... LukeMorris(7) 8 53
(W G M Turner) *mid-divsion hdwy over 2f out: one pce fnl f* **20/1**

9 3 1/2 **Fly Kiss** 2-8-4 .... RichardMullen 5 39
(C E Brittain) *sltly hmpd s: in rr: sme hdwy 2f out: nvr on terms* **33/1**

10 4 **Keeparryappy (IRE)** 2-8-11 .... PhillipMakin 12 30
(K R Burke) *hdwy over 3f out: sn chsng ldrs: wknd 1f out* **10/1**[3]

11 1 1/2 **Indecision** 2-8-2 .... NSLawes(7) 7 22
(M W Easterby) *swvd lft s: bhd tl sme hdwy fnl 2f* **100/1**

00 **12** 1 1/2 **Bank On Bertie**[4] [1043] 2-8-11 .... PaulMulrennan 4 18
(M W Easterby) *chsd ldrs 3f: sn wknd* **66/1**

13 hd **Amy Lionheart** 2-8-4 .... KimTinkler 2 10
(N Tinkler) *s.s: a bhd* **100/1**

14 1 **Chief Powderface (IRE)** 2-8-9 .... PaulHanagan 10 11
(Jedd O'Keeffe) *mid-div: nvr a factor* **33/1**

15 1/2 **Fizzy Lover** 2-8-1 .... DuranFentiman(5) 1 6
(T D Easterby) *s.i.s: a in rr* **40/1**

16 2 **Tagula King (IRE)** 2-8-9 .... DanielTudhope 3 1
(D Carroll) *hmpd s: a bhd* **50/1**

0 **17** 10 **Blazing Bullet (IRE)**[18] [845] 2-8-11 .... TonyHamilton 16 —
(N Wilson) *chsd ldrs: lost pl over 2f out: sn bhd and eased* **25/1**

64.53 secs (0.53) **Going Correction** -0.075s/f (Good) **17** Ran SP% **124.5**
Speed ratings (Par 92):92,91,91,90,89 89,89,87,81,75 72,70,69,68,67 64,48
CSF £19.18 TOTE £2.20: £1.40, £3.50, £1.40; EX 22.70.
Owner Matthew Green **Bred** Miss A Shaykhutdinova **Trained** Newmarket, Suffolk

FOCUS
A modest maiden, in which a few caught the eye. The winner and the third had a good draw and previous experience and the form looks sound enough. The race ought to produce winners.

NOTEBOOK
Artdeal franked the form of his maiden at Kempton - the winner is well regarded - after having the run of the race from a beneficial draw. It is debatable as to whether he will be the best horse to emerge from this contest. (op 6-4 tchd Evens)
Mission Impossible was really well supported in the market just before the off and only just failed to land the cash. He is sprint bred and a nice sort, so one would suspect an ordinary maiden at the very least is well within his grasp. (op 40-1)
Runswick Bay, who ran well from a poor draw in the Brocklesby, had the benefit of a good draw and helped to share the pace early. He appeared to get outpaced at one stage before staying on again, so 6f is probably going to suit him. (op 5-2 tchd 11-4)
Berrymead, from a family of winners, had a nice draw but ruined that advantage with a poor start. However, she was given time to recover and finished nicely. The experience will have done her good and she can expect to improve considerably for the run. (op 50-1)
Lady Rangali(IRE) shaped nicely down the middle of the course, although noticeably edging to her left, and should benefit from the run. She has a decent pedigree and the shrewd trainer will no doubt find her a suitable opportunity soon. (op 16-1)
Taurian found all sorts of trouble but caught the eye just behind the leaders, weaving around to find room in the latter stages. There is little chance of him going off at such huge odds next time, and he can go close if learning something from the run. Official explanation: jockey said, regarding the running and riding, his instructions had been to leave the stalls as quickly as he could, that the gelding goes well for a slap down the shoulder, and that he was to do his best; he added he had been hampered when the stalls opened, picked his way through the field, but was short of room in closing stages (op 16-1)
Fly Kiss was really green in the early stages and only got the idea late on. A sixth furlong will probably suit her and there should be more to come from her. (op 50-1)
Indecision ran much better than his finishing position suggests but may need more time to fully get the hang of things.

Chief Powderface(IRE) Official explanation: trainer said colt was unsuited by the good to firm ground

1088 MUSIC ON THE MEADOWS HERE 16 JUNE H'CAP 5f
3:20 (3:21) (Class 3) (0-95,95) 4-Y-0+ **£7,772** (£2,312; £1,155; £577) **Stalls** High

Form RPR

033- **1** **Pivotal's Princess (IRE)**[202] [5642] 5-9-4 95 .... SebSanders 13 108
(E S McMahon) *trckd ldrs: swtchd lft and hdwy over 1f out: rdn and styd on inside last to ld last 75 yds* **15/2**[3]

60-6 **2** 3/4 **Cape Royal**[14] [927] 7-8-8 90 ....(bt) KevinGhunowa(5) 18 100
(J M Bradley) *led: rdn over 1f out: hdd and no ex last 75 yds* **9/1**

040- **3** 3/4 **Green Park (IRE)**[186] [5957] 4-8-8 85 .... PaulHanagan 8 93
(R A Fahey) *midfield: effrt 2f out: sn rdn and styd on wlo fnl f: nrst fin* **16/1**

415- **4** 1 **Bluebok**[192] [5832] 6-8-7 84 ....(t) LPKeniry 16 88
(J M Bradley) *chsd ldrs: rdn wl over 1f out: kpt on u.p ins last* **16/1**

120- **5** nk **Fullandby (IRE)**[187] [5942] 5-9-4 95 .... KDarley 5 98+
(T J Etherington) *hld up towards rr: swtchd outside and gd hdwy over 1f out: fin strly* **25/1**

050- **6** 1 **Wyatt Earp (IRE)**[193] [5812] 6-8-8 90 .... JamieMoriarty(5) 12 89+
(R A Fahey) *hld up in rr:hdwy on inner 2f out: nt clr run and swtchd lft over 1f out: swtchd rt and r.o strly ins last: nrst fin* **9/1**

0-22 **7** nk **Dig Deep (IRE)**[92] [155] 5-8-7 84 .... PaulMulrennan 11 82
(W J Haggas) *hld up in midfield: effrt 2f out: sn rdn and kpt on ins last: nrst fin* **7/1**[2]

-504 **8** shd **First Order**[39] [660] 6-8-10 87 ....(v) TomEaves 4 85
(I Semple) *prom: effrt to chse ldr 2f out: sn rdn and wknd ent last* **25/1**

004- **9** 3/4 **Steel Blue**[152] [6508] 7-7-13 81 oh3 .... NataliaGemelova(5) 6 76
(R M Whitaker) *s.i.s and bhd tl styd on wl appr last* **66/1**

510/ **10** nk **Playful Dane (IRE)**[543] [6021] 10-8-0 84 ow2 .... PNolan(7) 14 78+
(K A Ryan) *stmbld s and bhd tl styd on wl appr last* **18/1**

021- **11** 1/2 **Royal Challenge**[265] [3880] 6-8-5 85 .... SaleemGolam(3) 3 77
(M H Tompkins) *nvr nr ldrs* **33/1**

100- **12** hd **Caribbean Coral**[192] [5832] 8-8-11 88 .... MickyFenton 10 80
(J J Quinn) *nvr bttr then midfield* **50/1**

000- **13** 1 **Desert Commander (IRE)**[214] [5358] 5-9-0 91 .... NCallan 19 79
(K A Ryan) *prom on inner: rdn along 2f out: sn drvn and wknd* **2/1**[1]

042- **14** 1/2 **Stonecrabstomorrow (IRE)**[191] [5877] 4-8-5 82 .... DaleGibson 7 68
(R A Fahey) *dwlt: a rr* **25/1**

000- **15** 2 1/2 **Gallery Girl (IRE)**[186] [5957] 4-8-7 84 .... DavidAllan 9 61
(T D Easterby) *midfield: hdwy and in tch wl over 1f out: sn rdn and btn over 1f out* **25/1**

350- **16** 1/2 **Blue Tomato**[200] [5667] 6-8-7 87 .... LiamJones(3) 1 62
(J M Bradley) *a rr* **80/1**

20-0 **17** 3/4 **Continent**[19] [828] 10-8-8 85 .... AdrianTNicholls 17 58
(D Nicholls) *in tch: rdn along 2f out: sn btn* **16/1**

502- **18** 1 3/4 **Grazeon Gold Blend**[231] [4922] 4-8-11 88 .... GrahamGibbons 15 54
(J J Quinn) *in tch: rdn along and wandered 2f out: sn wknd* **11/1**

62.66 secs (-1.34) **Going Correction** -0.075s/f (Good) **18** Ran SP% **131.9**
Speed ratings (Par 107):107,105,104,103,102 100,100,100,99,98 97,97,95,95,91 90,89,86
CSF £73.00 CT £1121.55 TOTE £10.30: £2.00, £2.00, £3.80, £4.20; EX 55.30.
Owner R L Bedding **Bred** George Delahunt **Trained** Lichfield, Staffs
■ Stewards' Enquiry : Adrian T Nicholls one-day ban: failed to ride out to line (Apr 29)
Micky Fenton one-day ban: careless riding (Apr 29)

FOCUS
A solid sprint which was, as ever, dominated by the draw. The form is solid and ought to work out.

NOTEBOOK
Pivotal's Princess(IRE) started the new season in great style, much in keeping with the way she finished the last one. She powered clear of her rivals in the final stages and came home a decisive winner. One suspects she will head for Chester next - she made her seasonal debut there last season - and hope to get a decent draw. (op 8-1)
Cape Royal made a bold bid to make all from a good draw and only found the strong-finishing mare too good in the final stages. His victories are few and far between, so he would not want to rise in the handicap too much for this effort. (op 7-1)
Green Park(IRE) made a highly satisfactory seasonal reappearnce from a moderate draw and position during the race. He is nicely handicapped now and should be respected next time. (op 25-1)
Bluebok tracked his stablemate throughout the race but could not pick up when asked. He is still high in the handicap and his form suggests a flatter track suits him. (op 18-1)
Fullandby(IRE), who looked like the race would bring him on, is definitely one to take from the race as long as he can keep finding some improvement. His racing style and draw would not have been suited to the track, yet he still kept on well down the centre of the track when asked to close. He might not be easy to place and will probably have to try his hand in conditions events to have a level chance. (op 28-1)
Wyatt Earp(IRE) found all kinds of trouble in running and fairly flew home when the gaps eventually opened. However, he is still a bit too high in the handicap to have an obvious chance, although you must always respect his chance if running at York. Official explanation: jockey said gelding was denied a clear run (op 12-1)
Dig Deep(IRE) did not run too badly and still has some scope for improvement, but shaped like a horse that is in the grip of the Handicapper. He does stay further, so it might be that the minimum trip is not his ideal one now. (tchd 13-2)

1089 LEVY BOARD H'CAP 1m 1f 207y
3:55 (3:55) (Class 4) (0-85,82) 3-Y-O **£4,857** (£1,445; £722; £360) **Stalls** High

Form RPR

111 **1** **Ten A Penny (USA)**[25] [754] 3-9-4 82 .... TPQueally 4 91+
(J A Osborne) *sn trcking ldrs: smooth hdwy on outside over 2f out: shkn up to ld 1f out: hld on wl* **11/4**[1]

221- **2** 3/4 **Letham Island (IRE)**[137] [6675] 3-8-10 74 .... KDarley 3 77
(M Johnston) *led: qcknd over 5f out: hdd 1f out: kpt on wl* **8/1**

1- **3** 1 **Sumi Girl (IRE)**[226] [5059] 3-8-13 77 .... PaulHanagan 6 78
(R A Fahey) *bmpd s: hld up in rr: hdwy over 4f out: nt clr run on ins over 1f out: styd on same pce fnl f* **7/1**

2-14 **4** 1 **Nassmaan (IRE)**[28] [719] 3-8-6 77 .... MCGeran(7) 7 76
(P W Chapple-Hyam) *swvd lft s: hld up in rr: effrt 3f out: kpt on: nvr trbld ldrs* **5/1**

23-3 **5** 1/2 **Bold Indian (IRE)**[9] [968] 3-8-7 71 ow2 .... TomEaves 5 69
(I Semple) *t.k.h: trckd ldr: outpcd over 1f out: kpt on same pce* **4/1**[3]

41- **6** 1 1/2 **Free Offer**[252] [4238] 3-9-3 81 .... SebSanders 2 76
(J L Dunlop) *hld up in rr: effrt over 2f out: nvr rchd ldrs* **3/1**[2]

-220 **7** 5 **Rain And Shade**[53] [553] 3-9-0 78 .... TonyHamilton 1 63
(E W Tuer) *trckd ldrs on outer: pushed along 4f out: hung rt and lost pl over 1f out* **25/1**

2m 7.88s (0.58) **Going Correction** -0.075s/f (Good) **7** Ran SP% **115.8**
Speed ratings (Par 100):94,93,92,91,91 90,86
CSF £25.66 CT £139.95 TOTE £3.30: £1.80, £2.90; EX 27.50.

The Form Book, Raceform Ltd, Compton, RG20 6NL

Owner Lord Blyth And Ten **Bred** Chesapeake Farm, Mary R Odom & W S Farish **Trained** Upper Lambourn, Berks

FOCUS
A good, competitive three-year-old handicap won by the highly-progressive and unbeaten Ten A Penny and best rated taround the fourth and fifth.
Bold Indian(IRE) Official explanation: jockey said gelding ran too freely

1090 RAPID LAD STKS (H'CAP) 1m 1f 207y
4:30 (4:31) (Class 5) (0-70,70) 4-Y-0+ **£3,238** (£963; £481; £240) **Stalls** High

Form / RPR

0052 **1** **Choristar**^{9} 976 6-8-6 **58** ... KDarley 8 — 68+
(J Mackie) *in tch: t.k.h: str run to ld 1f out: drvn out* **9/4**^{1}

541- **2** *2* **Light Sentence**^{200} 5683 4-8-5 **57** ... DeanMcKeown 2 — 63
(G A Swinbank) *stdd s: in rr: drvn over 4f out: hdwy and swtchd outside over 1f out: styd on to take 2nd last 75yds* **6/1**^{3}

-645 **3** *1* **Torrens (IRE)**^{21} 811 5-9-4 **70** ... PaulHanagan 11 — 74+
(R A Fahey) *mid-field: effrt over 2f out: n.m.r over 1f out: styd on ins last: tk 3rd nr line* **10/3**^{2}

053- **4** *shd* **Haifa (IRE)**^{112} 6947 4-8-10 **62** ... RoystonFfrench 13 — 66
(Mrs A Duffield) *trckd ldrs: led over 1f out: sn hdd and no ex* **25/1**

4434 **5** *shd* **Augustine**^{8} 997 6-9-3 **69** ... ChrisCatlin 5 — 73
(P W Hiatt) *sn trcking ldrs: kpt on same pce fnl f* **9/1**

0-63 **6** *½* **Oddsmaker (IRE)**^{10} 955 6-8-9 **68** ...(t) MCGeran$^{(7)}$ 10 — 71
(M A Barnes) *dwlt: t.k.h: sn trcking ldrs: n.m.r over 1f out: styd on same pce* **9/1**

200- **7** *½* **Sudden Impulse**^{42} 6317 6-8-9 **61** ... SilvestreDeSousa 3 — 63+
(A D Brown) *prom on outer: lost pl after 4f: hdwy: nt clr run and swtchd ins 2f out: swtchd wd ins last: r.o* **16/1**

-065 **8** *½* **The Pen**^{14} 928 5-8-1 **56** oh1 ... AndrewElliott$^{(3)}$ 14 — 57
(C W Fairhurst) *chsd ldrs: one pce whn n.m.r over 1f out* **16/1**

614- **9** *shd* **Fairy Monarch (IRE)**^{171} 6232 8-8-0 **57** oh3 ow1 ...(b) RoryMoore$^{(5)}$ 7 — 58
(P T Midgley) *hld up in rr: hdwy into midfield over 4f out: nvr rchd ldrs* **33/1**

/00- **10** *3* **Zonic Boom (FR)**^{112} 6954 7-8-4 **56** oh1 ...(tp) CatherineGannon 6 — 51
(Heather Dalton) *in rr: nvr a factor* **33/1**

200- **11** *hd* **Apache Point (IRE)**^{190} 5904 10-8-5 **57** ... KimTinkler 1 — 52
(N Tinkler) *in rr: hdwy on outer over 3f out: wknd over 1f out* **50/1**

060- **12** *½* **Dream Of Paradise (USA)**^{200} 5690 4-8-4 **59** ... LiamJones$^{(3)}$ 12 — 53
(Mrs L Williamson) *led tl over 1f out: sn lost pl* **40/1**

630- **13** *10* **Jenny Soba**^{167} 6314 4-8-3 **60** ... MichaelJStainton$^{(5)}$ 9 — 35
(R M Whitaker) *chsd ldrs: sn drvn along: lost pl over 2f out: sn bhd and eased* **66/1**

201- **14** *6* **Floodlight Fantasy**^{80} 5972 4-9-0 **66** ...(p) PaulMulrennan 4 — 29
(Jedd O'Keeffe) *in tch: lost pl 5f out: bhd fnl 3f* **33/1**

2m 4.14s (-3.16) **Going Correction** -0.075s/f (Good) **14** Ran SP% **118.5**
Speed ratings (Par 103):109,107,106,106,106 106,105,105,105,102 102,102,94,89
CSF £14.45 CT £45.22 TOTE £2.80: £1.40, £2.20, £1.90; EX 20.20.
Owner Derbyshire Racing **Bred** Coln Valley Stud **Trained** Church Broughton , Derbys

FOCUS
A moderate handicap and there were a few hard-luck stories in behind, but the time was decent and the form looks sound overall.

1091 NEW FIXTURE HERE ON WEDNESDAY 9 MAY STKS (H'CAP) 7f 100y
5:05 (5:05) (Class 5) (0-70,70) 3-Y-O **£3,238** (£963; £481; £240) **Stalls** High

Form / RPR

2131 **1** **Pietersen (IRE)**^{54} 535 3-9-0 **66** ...(b) PaulFessey 12 — 71
(T D Barron) *a.p: challenegd over 2f out: rdn to ld over 1f out: drvn and edgd rt ins last: kpt on* **7/1**^{2}

00-4 **2** *1 ¼* **Astroangel**^{15} 899 3-8-7 **64** ... PatrickHills$^{(5)}$ 10 — 66
(M H Tompkins) *in tch: hdwy to chse ldrs over 3f out: rdn along 2f out: styng on whn n.m.r 1f out: kpt on ins last* **16/1**

04-3 **3** *shd* **Eager Igor (USA)**^{14} 931 3-9-4 **70** ... StephenCarson 11 — 74+
(Eve Johnson Houghton) *in tch on inner: hdwy over 2f out: nt clr run and swtchd lft over 1f out: fin strly* **7/4**^{1}

30-0 **4** *½* **Pennyrock (IRE)**^{93} 140 3-8-10 **62** ... GrahamGibbons 9 — 62
(J J Quinn) *keen: chsd ldrs: hdwy 2f out: rdn and ch ent last: kpt on same pce towards fin* **14/1**

6-52 **5** *¾* **La Marmotte (IRE)**^{72} 357 3-8-8 **60** ... PaulHanagan 15 — 58
(R E Barr) *led: rdn along over 2f out: hdd over 1f out: drvn and wknd ins last* **10/1**

3021 **6** *1 ½* **Knapton Hill**^{9} 974 3-8-7 **64** 6ex ... RussellKennemore$^{(5)}$ 2 — 58
(R Hollinshead) *rr: hdwy 3f out: rdn along 2f out: kpt on ins last: nrst fin* **14/1**

550- **7** *1 ¼* **Beaumont Boy**^{216} 5307 3-8-8 **60** ... DeanMcKeown 6 — 51
(G A Swinbank) *hld up towards rr: hdwy over 2f out: sn rdn and kpt on ins last: nrst fin* **20/1**

030- **8** *½* **Delta Shuttle (IRE)**^{176} 6157 3-8-13 **68** ... AndrewElliott$^{(3)}$ 8 — 58
(K R Burke) *towards rr: wd 3f out: sn rdn and kpt on fnl 2f* **14/1**

22-0 **9** *½* **Nota Liberata**^{14} 931 3-9-2 **68** ... DanielTudhope 7 — 57
(G M Moore) *chsd ldrs: rdn along over 2f out and sn btn* **7/1**^{2}

00-4 **10** *1 ½* **Meridian Grey (USA)**^{14} 916 3-8-13 **65** ... NCallan 14 — 50
(K A Ryan) *prom: rdn along over 2f out: drvn and wknd over 1f out* **8/1**^{3}

642- **11** *½* **Flower Of Cork (IRE)**^{322} 2139 3-8-11 **63** ... DavidAllan 5 — 47
(T D Easterby) *a rr* **33/1**

1-00 **12** *nk* **Play Straight**^{19} 834 3-8-5 **60** ...(p) PatrickMathers$^{(3)}$ 1 — 43
(I W McInnes) *a rr* **66/1**

50-0 **13** *½* **Seaton Snooks**^{14} 918 3-8-1 **58** ... DuranFentiman$^{(5)}$ 13 — 40
(T D Easterby) *a rr* **33/1**

400- **14** *½* **Ensign's Trick**^{167} 6310 3-8-10 **65** ... LiamJones$^{(3)}$ 3 — 46
(W M Brisbourne) *bhd fr 1/2-way* **40/1**

60-0 **15** *hd* **Desert Soul**^{26} 738 3-8-12 **64** ... KDarley 4 — 44
(M Johnston) *towards rr: effrt and sme hdwy on outer over 2f out: sn rdn and wknd* **12/1**

1m 33.1s (-1.21) **Going Correction** -0.075s/f (Good) **15** Ran SP% **129.7**
Speed ratings (Par 98):103,101,101,100,100 98,96,96,95,94 93,93,92,91,91
CSF £116.69 CT £289.75 TOTE £6.80: £2.10, £4.50, £1.60; EX 105.40.
Owner Sporting Occasions No 8 **Bred** Noel Finegan **Trained** Maunby, N Yorks
■ Stewards' Enquiry : Stephen Carson caution: careless riding

FOCUS
A moderate contest and, although solid enough, unlikely to produce anything other than the occasional winner.

1092 RACING HERE AGAIN NEXT THURSDAY STKS (FILLIES' H'CAP) 1m 4f 16y
5:40 (5:40) (Class 5) (0-70,66) 3-Y-O **£3,238** (£963; £481; £240) **Stalls** High

Form / RPR

043- **1** **Its Moon (IRE)**^{235} 4788 3-9-3 **65** ... GrahamGibbons 2 — 68
(T D Walford) *trckd ldrs: led 2f out: jst hld on* **25/1**

501- **2** *shd* **Dee Cee Elle**^{162} 6385 3-8-6 **54** ... KDarley 9 — 57
(M Johnston) *chsd ldrs: hmpd 7f out: led over 2f out: sn hdd: styd on towards fin: jst hld* **7/2**^{2}

05-6 **3** *hd* **Dansimar**^{28} 719 3-9-4 **66** ... NCallan 10 — 69
(M R Channon) *mid-div: effrt over 2f out: styd on strly fnl f: jst hld* **3/1**^{1}

263- **4** *1 ½* **Red**^{162} 6385 3-9-2 **64** ... SebSanders 8 — 64
(R M Beckett) *trckd ldrs: kpt on same pce fnl f* **9/2**^{3}

160- **5** *1* **Group Force (IRE)**^{166} 6322 3-8-3 **56** ... PatrickHills$^{(5)}$ 4 — 55
(M H Tompkins) *hld up in rr: hdwy over 2f out: styd on fnl f* **16/1**

052- **6** *¾* **Summer Of Love (IRE)**^{153} 6498 3-9-4 **66** ... JosedeSouza 3 — 63
(P F I Cole) *trckd ldrs on outer: effrt over 2f out: kpt on same pce appr fnl f* **14/1**

00-0 **7** *nk* **Present**^{8} 991 3-8-5 **56** ... SaleemGolam$^{(3)}$ 11 — 53?
(D Morris) *led tl over 2f out: kpt on one pce* **66/1**

004- **8** *1 ¾* **Miami Tallyce (IRE)**^{119} 6879 3-8-12 **60** ... ChrisCatlin 6 — 54
(E J O'Neill) *mid-divsion: effrt 3f out: one pce* **16/1**

4150 **9** *4* **My Sara**^{16} 893 3-8-8 **56** ...(v) PaulHanagan 1 — 44+
(R A Fahey) *prom whn stmbld path: jinked lft and lost pl bnd after 2f: hdwy 3f out: wknd fnl f* **8/1**

-000 **10** *hd* **Roca Redonda (IRE)**^{16} 893 3-8-10 **58** ... DeanMcKeown 12 — 45
(V Smith) *trckd ldrs: t.k.h: wknd 1f out* **14/1**

600- **11** *6* **Olgarena (IRE)**^{219} 5237 3-7-13 **52** oh1 ... DuranFentiman$^{(5)}$ 5 — 30
(T D Easterby) *in rr: drvn over 4f out: bhd fnl 3f* **50/1**

004- **12** *7* **Last Flight (IRE)**^{190} 5886 3-9-1 **63** ... TPQueally 7 — 30
(J L Dunlop) *s.i.s: hmpd bnd after 2f: drvn over 5f out: bhd fnl 3f* **7/1**

2m 40.94s (0.73) **Going Correction** -0.075s/f (Good) **12** Ran SP% **121.4**
Speed ratings (Par 95):94,93,93,92,92 91,91,90,87,87 83,78
CSF £112.73 CT £355.43 TOTE £30.40: £6.30, £1.70, £2.20; EX 181.90 Place 6 £ 105.11, Place 5 £ 14.25.
Owner Jaass One Racing **Bred** Darley **Trained** Sheriff Hutton, N Yorks

FOCUS
A modest but competitive three-year-old fillies' handicap and the form seems sound but limited.
T/Plt: £103.40 to a £1 stake. Pool: £54,832.15. 386.95 winning tickets. T/Qpdt: £14.60 to a £1 stake. Pool: £4,014.80. 203.20 winning tickets. JR

NEWMARKET (ROWLEY) (R-H)
Wednesday, April 18

OFFICIAL GOING: Good to firm. The Craven meeting has been cut to two days.
Wind: Light, half-behind Weather: Sunny

1093 XPLOR MAIDEN STKS 1m 2f
2:00 (2:01) (Class 4) 3-Y-O **£5,181** (£1,541; £770; £384) **Stalls** High

Form / RPR

0- **1** **Arabian Gulf**^{172} 6214 3-9-3 ... KerrinMcEvoy 6 — 92+
(Sir Michael Stoute) *h.d.w: bit bkwd: chsd ldr: led over 1f out: rdn out* **7/1**

34-6 **2** *nk* **Putra Square**^{11} 939 3-9-3 83 ... LDettori 15 — 90
(P F I Cole) *chsd ldrs: chal over 2f out: edgd rt over 1f out: r.o* **11/1**

-2 **3** *1 ¼* **Eradicate (IRE)**^{18} 849 3-9-3 ... JoeFanning 14 — 88
(M Johnston) *lw: led over 8f: styd on same pce ins fnl f* **4/1**^{3}

2- **4** *1* **Broomielaw**^{211} 5457 3-9-3 ... JamieSpencer 4 — 86+
(E A L Dunlop) *hld up: nt clr run wl over 2f out: hdwy over 1f out: nt rch ldrs* **11/4**^{1}

2- **5** *1 ¾* **Urban Spirit**^{201} 5658 3-9-3 ... RichardHughes 10 — 83+
(B W Hills) *lw: hld up: hdwy 3f out: rdn over 1f out: styd on same pce* **3/1**^{2}

4- **6** *3 ½* **Rhaam**^{201} 5659 3-9-3 ... MartinDwyer 9 — 76
(B W Hills) *lw: chsd ldrs: rdn over 2f out: wknd over 1f out* **16/1**

7 *¾* **Spice Route** 3-9-3 ... EddieAhern 1 — 75+
(M L W Bell) *str: bkwd: hld up: styd on ins fnl f: nvr nrr* **50/1**

24- **8** *nk* **Murbek (IRE)**^{201} 5658 3-9-3 ... RHills 8 — 74
(M A Jarvis) *lw: hld up: plld hrd: hdwy over 1f out: sn edgd rt: n.d* **6/1**

L **9** *3 ½* **Rose Row**^{32} 700 3-8-12 ... VinceSlattery 12 — 62
(Mrs Mary Hambro) *leggy: unf: s.i.s and hmpd s: sn mid-div: wknd over 2f out* **125/1**

10 *½* **Two Timer (IRE)** 3-9-3 ... JohnEgan 13 — 66+
(D R C Elsworth) *gd sort: bit bkwd: plld hrd and prom: rdn over 2f out: wknd over 1f out* **33/1**

0- **11** *3* **Buckthorn**^{172} 6220 3-9-3 ... SteveDrowne 3 — 61
(G Wragg) *hld up: rdn and wknd over 2f out* **100/1**

12 *shd* **Bubbly Girl** 3-8-12 ... EdwardCreighton 7 — 56
(P J McBride) *lt-f: s.i.s: sn pushed along in rr: wknd over 2f out* **150/1**

13 *1* **Splinter Group** 3-9-3 ... OscarUrbina 2 — 59
(N A Callaghan) *w'like: scope: hld up: bhd fnl 3f* **66/1**

2m 6.55s (0.84) **Going Correction** -0.175s/f (Firm) **13** Ran SP% **121.5**
Speed ratings (Par 100):89,88,87,86,85 82,82,81,79,78 76,76,75
CSF £81.27 TOTE £9.50: £2.70, £3.00, £1.90; EX 79.70.
Owner K Abdulla **Bred** Juddmonte Farms Ltd **Trained** Newmarket, Suffolk

FOCUS
This looked like a very good maiden and it should produce some classy types. The early pace was just ordinary and, although they were racing from about four out, those who sat handy were at an advantage; the runner-up sets the standard. They all raced towards the far-side rail.
Murbek(IRE) Official explanation: jockey said colt ran too keen early on
Two Timer(IRE) Official explanation: jockey said colt ran too free

1094 NGK SPARK PLUGS/COACHMAKERS CONDITIONS STKS 5f
2:35 (2:35) (Class 3) 2-Y-O **£6,477** (£1,927; £963; £481) **Stalls** High

Form / RPR

1 **Spirit Of Sharjah (IRE)** 2-8-9 ... MJKinane 2 — 92+
(Miss J Feilden) *leggy: scope: b.nr hind: chsd ldrs: shkn up to ld over 1f out: r.o wl* **10/1**

2 *2 ½* **Dark Angel (IRE)** 2-8-9 ... MichaelHills 4 — 82
(B W Hills) *w'like: leggy: lw: hld up: hdwy over 1f out: r.o: no ch w wnr* **3/1**^{3}

3 *1 ½* **Major Eazy (IRE)** 2-8-9 ... RichardHughes 3 — 76
(B J Meehan) *gd sort: scope: bit bkwd: chsd ldr: edgd lft 2f out: sn ev ch: no ex ins fnl f* **9/4**^{1}

1 4 nk **Nikindi (IRE)**^{15} [898] 2-9-4 .... JohnEgan 5 84
(J S Moore) *w'like: led: rdn and edgd lft 2f out: sn hdd: wknd wl ins fnl f* **11/4^{2}**

5 2 **Jebel Tara** 2-8-9 .... EddieAhern 7 67
(C E Brittain) *w'like: scope: chsd ldrs: rdn 1/2-way: wknd fnl f* **12/1**

6 4 **Orpen's Art (IRE)** 2-8-9 .... JamieSpencer 1 51
(N A Callaghan) *cmpt: scope: lw: hld up: pushed along 1/2-way: wknd over 1f out* **13/2**

59.58 secs (-0.89) **Going Correction** -0.175s/f (Firm) **6** Ran SP% **112.6**
Speed ratings (Par 96):100,96,93,93,89 83
CSF £39.97 TOTE £10.90: £3.00, £2.50; EX 44.90.

Owner A Dee **Bred** Mrs Kathleen Reynolds **Trained** Exning, Suffolk

FOCUS
A race won last year by subsequent Queen Mary winner Gilded. Hard to be sure of the strength of this year's renewal, but Spirit Of Sharjah created a very good impression and Nikindi, a winner on his debut at Folkestone, looks the best guide to the strength of the form. They raced towards the far side, but the rail was by no means crucial.

NOTEBOOK
Spirit Of Sharjah(IRE) ◆, an 8,000gns half-brother to five winners, including Great Gift, champion three-year-old in Holland, out of a dual 5-7f winner at two and three, attracted some support in the market, despite the fact he was representing a stable hardly renowned for his exploits with two-year-olds, and ran out a very impressive winner. He raced a little keenly towards the outside, but was always going well and showed a very useful turn of foot to quicken clear of his five rivals. He showed signs of inexperience under pressure, looking a bit ungainly, but he will know a lot more next time and should improve. He is likely to have on more run before heading to Royal Ascot where, on this evidence, he will be well worth his place in either the Coventry, Norfolk or Windsor Castle. (op 16-1)

Dark Angel(IRE), a 61,000gns half-brother to among others, 1m4f winner Colleton River, made a pleasing debut in second. He could not match the winner's change of pace, but stayed on nicely to finish clear of the remainder and looks well up to finding a maiden. (op 11-4)

Major Eazy(IRE), a 70,000euros half-brother to top-class sprinter Carmine Lake, a triple winner at two and three, including the Prix de l'Abbaye, and to 7f winner Three Secrets, out of a 6f winner on her juvenile debut, showed good speed early on but lacked a change of pace at the business end. He already holds a Group 1 entry, so really ought to do better. (op 2-1 tchd 5-2 and 11-4 in places)

Nikindi(IRE), well backed when landing an ordinary maiden at Folkestone on his debut, had no easy task conceding 9lb all round and was well held. He seemed to run his race and helps set the standard. (op 9-4 tchd 3-1 in places)

Jebel Tara, an 18,000gns half-brother to Cream Of Esteem, who was placed over 1m4f, showed ability and should improve. (op 16-1 tchd 11-1)

Orpen's Art(IRE), a 70,000gns first foal of a 1m2f winner, did not show as much as one might have expected. (op 12-1 tchd 6-1)

1095 SPORTING INDEX EUROPEAN FREE H'CAP (LISTED RACE) 7f
3:10 (3:10) (Class 1) 3-Y-O

£17,034 (£6,456; £3,231; £1,611; £807; £405) **Stalls** High

Form RPR

01-2 **1** **Prime Defender**^{18} [839] 3-9-5 **106** .... MichaelHills 3 110
(B W Hills) *h.d.w: chsd ldr: led over 1f out: sn rdn: jst hld on* **5/2^{1}**

126- **2** shd **Tobosa**^{179} [6102] 3-9-1 **102** .... KerrinMcEvoy 7 106+
(W Jarvis) *hld up: swtchd lft over 1f out: r.o wl ins fnl f: jst failed* **3/1^{2}**

122- **3** 1 **Eddie Jock (IRE)**^{193} [5806] 3-9-3 **104** .... JamieSpencer 6 105
(M L W Bell) *chsd ldrs: rdn over 1f out: styd on* **9/1**

1-15 **4** 1 ½ **Hinton Admiral**^{18} [847] 3-9-7 **108** 5ex .... J-PGuillambert 2 106
(M Johnston) *led over 5f: no ex wl ins fnl f* **11/2**

30-3 **5** nk **Danebury Hill**^{18} [839] 3-8-13 **100** .... (t) RichardHughes 4 97
(B J Meehan) *prom: rdn over 1f out: styd on same pce ins fnl f* **9/1**

210- **6** 1 ¼ **Vital Statistics**^{201} [5654] 3-9-7 **108** .... DaneO'Neill 1 101
(D R C Elsworth) *lw: dwlt: hld up: rdn over 2f out: n.d* **20/1**

110- **7** 3 **Hamoody (USA)**^{186} [5965] 3-9-6 **107** .... LDettori 5 93
(P W Chapple-Hyam) *lw: hld up: effrt over 2f out: wknd over 1f out: eased* **4/1^{3}**

1m 23.36s (-3.14) **Going Correction** -0.175s/f (Firm) **7** Ran SP% **113.7**
Speed ratings (Par 106):110,109,108,107,106 105,101
CSF £10.10 TOTE £3.60: £1.60, £3.50; EX 17.00.

Owner S Falle, M Franklin, J Sumsion **Bred** Christopher J Mason **Trained** Lambourn, Berks

FOCUS
A competitive renewal of the Free Handicap, and the pace was fair, but this form, although solid enough, is some way short of what will be required to win the 2000 Guineas. The winning time was 1.23 seconds quicker than the Nell Gwyn, and 1.87 seconds faster than the later maiden won by Snaafy. They raced towards the far side.

NOTEBOOK
Prime Defender, runner-up in the Easter Stakes on the Polytrack at Kempton on his seasonal reappearance, was a well-backed favourite on this drop in trip and return to turf and just proved good enough. Always well positioned, he looked likely to win well when getting on top around a furlong out, but Tobosa really got going late on and he would have been beaten in another stride. His trainer has not ruled out a tilt at the 2000 Guineas, but it would be a surprise if he proved up to that class and the Jersey Stakes at Royal Ascot is probably a more suitable option. (op 9-2 tchd 5-1 in a place)

Tobosa, a most progressive juvenile last season who was sixth in the Horris Hill on his final start of the year, showed he has trained on with a fine effort in second. He took an age to pick up when switched out into the clear, but he really began to motor in the last furlong and would have won in another stride. He is not good enough to be considered a serious candidate for our 2000 Guineas, but a step up to 1m ought to suit and he could do well if given his chance in a foreign classic. (op 11-4 tchd 10-3 and 7-2 in a place)

Eddie Jock(IRE), a tough, smart juvenile last year, made a pleasing return to action back in third. He has clearly trained on from two to three and should take a lot of racing this year. (op 7-1 tchd 13-2)

Hinton Admiral, the winner of consecutive Listed races on the Polytrack but below form when only fifth in a 6f Listed race at Newcastle on his previous start, had no easy task under the 5lb penalty he picked up for his Spring Cup success and was well held. (op 6-1 tchd 5-1 and 13-2 in a place)

Danebury Hill could not reverse recent Easter Stakes form with Prime Defender and basically just seemed to find a few of these too good. (op 16-1)

Vital Statistics, the winner of a 6f Listed event at two, never posed a threat stepped up to her furthest trip to date off the back of a 201-day break. (op 16-1)

Hamoody(USA) looked to have a serious amount of talent as a juvenile - he won the Group 2 Richmond Stakes - but he also displayed signs of waywardness, almost ruining his chance of winning at Goodwood by pulling very hard. Off the track since beating only two home in the Dewhurst, he was well below form on his return to action and offered little encouragement for the future. He may turn out to be best over sprint trips, but there has to be a serious question mark over which way he will go. Official explanation: jockey said colt ran too free (op 5-2)

1096 SHADWELL NELL GWYN STKS (GROUP 3) (FILLIES) 7f
3:45 (3:46) (Class 1) 3-Y-O

£28,390 (£10,760; £5,385; £2,685; £1,345; £675) **Stalls** High

Form RPR

150- **1** **Scarlet Runner**^{201} [5654] 3-8-12 110 .... KerrinMcEvoy 9 98
(J L Dunlop) *led far side pair: overall ldr ins fnl f: r.o* **15/2^{2}**

411- **2** nk **Sander Camillo (USA)**^{280} [3415] 3-9-1 115 .... LDettori 6 100
(J Noseda) *h.d.w: overall ldr centre: hdd over 4f out: led again over 2f out: rdn and hdd ins fnl f: styd on: 1st of 8 in gp* **4/7^{1}**

120- **3** ½ **Blue Rocket (IRE)**^{201} [5654] 3-8-12 95 .... MJKinane 10 96
(T J Pitt) *lw: b.hind: chsd wnr far side: rdn over 1f out: styd on: 2nd of 2 in gp* **12/1**

10- **4** ½ **Kaseema (USA)**^{186} [5966] 3-8-12 97 .... RHills 4 95
(Sir Michael Stoute) *lw: racd centre: chsd ldrs: rdn over 1f out: styd on: 2nd of 8 in gp* **15/2^{2}**

2-1 **5** ¾ **Barshiba (IRE)**^{67} [418] 3-8-12 84 .... JohnEgan 3 93+
(D R C Elsworth) *lw: racd centre: dwlt: plld hrd: hdwy over 5f out: rdn and swvd lft over 1f out: sn outpcd: styd on nr fin: 3rd of 8 in gp* **9/1^{3}**

310- **6** nk **Pretty Majestic (IRE)**^{208} [5503] 3-8-12 90 .... JamieSpencer 7 92
(M R Channon) *racd centre: s.i.s: hld up: hdwy over 2f out: rdn over 1f out: no ex ins fnl f: 4th of 8 in gp* **25/1**

1- **7** ¾ **Fantasy Parkes**^{208} [5507] 3-8-12 78 .... DO'Donohoe 8 90
(K A Ryan) *stmbld s: racd centre: chsd ldrs: rdn over 2f out: styd on same pce appr fnl f: 5th of 8 in gp* **25/1**

143- **8** 2 **Kompete**^{161} [6402] 3-8-12 90 .... DaneO'Neill 1 85
(V Smith) *s.i.s: racd centre: hld up: rdn and hung rt fr over 2f out: hmpd over 1f out: n.d: 6th of 8 in gp* **25/1**

-001 **9** 1 **Precocious Star (IRE)**^{18} [838] 3-8-12 92 .... PatCosgrave 2 82
(K R Burke) *lw: racd centre: prom: lost pl over 5f out: in rr whn hmpd over 1f out: 7th of 8 in gp* **25/1**

52-0 **10** 2 ½ **Nina Blini**^{6} [1009] 3-8-12 89 .... (b^{1}) RichardHughes 5 76
(B J Meehan) *racd centre: chsd ldr tl led over 4f out: hdd over 2f out: wknd over 1f out: last of 8 in gp* **100/1**

1m 24.59s (-1.91) **Going Correction** -0.175s/f (Firm) **10** Ran SP% **121.3**
Speed ratings (Par 105):103,102,102,101,100 100,99,97,96,93
CSF £12.16 TOTE £9.10: £2.10, £1.10, £3.40; EX 18.80.

Owner Nicholas Jones **Bred** Coln Valley Stud **Trained** Arundel, W Sussex

FOCUS
This looked like a good renewal of the Nell Gwyn Stakes beforehand, but the race itself was highly unsatisfactory, with the field finishing in a bunch and a few of the lower-rated fillies finishing plenty close enough for comfort. The pace was just ordinary, with none of the ten runners particularly keen to set a good gallop, and the field also split into two groups. There was not enough evidence throughout the day to say one part of the track was riding quicker than another, but it has to be worth noting that both the winner and third raced towards the far-side rail, whereas the remainder raced down the middle of the track. Unsurprisingly, the winning time was 1.23 seconds slower than the Free Handicap. The form has been rated fairly negatively, with the first two well below teir two-year-old best.

NOTEBOOK
Scarlet Runner's form tailed off when faced with soft ground towards the end of last year, but nobody could argue with her record when there is 'firm' in the going description; she won her maiden, ran third to Sander Camillo in the Albany, and then won the Group 3 Princess Margaret. Returning from a near five-month break with conditions to suit, she was one of only two fillies to race towards the far-side rail and sustained her challenge to the line to reverse Royal Ascot form with Sander Camillo on 3lb better terms. This was her first try over 7f and she saw it out well; if anything a stronger pace would have seen her in an even better light. She fully deserves to take her chance in the 1000 Guineas, but that would require a significant step up in form, especially if Finsceal Beo is as good as she was last year. (op 8-1)

Sander Camillo(USA) came into this ante-post favourite for the 1000 Guineas following impressive wins in both the Albany Stakes and the Cherry Hinton during her juvenile campaign, but she had been off the track since last July having been withdrawn from the Cheveley Park on account of the soft ground. Trying 7f for the first time, she was taken towards the middle of the track, but the pace was nowhere near as quick as she would have liked and, unable to get any cover, she always looked to be doing too much in the hands of Dettori. She responded to pressure to throw down a serious challenge to the two fillies on the far side of the track, faring best of those who raced down the middle in the process, but she failed to produce a turn of foot, and that proved to be her undoing. A few of the lower rated runners finished too close for comfort, which means she has to be rated as running well below form, but that owes much to the ordinary early gallop and she also had to concede 3lb all round. While a defeat in her prep run is not ideal, a much better performance can be expected next month. For a start this will have taken the freshness out of her, giving her every chance of settling better in the big race, and also provided her with some much-needed race sharpness. Perhaps most crucially of all, she should get the race run to suit in the Guineas, and it is far too early to write her off. She was later found to have 'tied up' during the race, and perhaps that goes some way to explaining this sub-standard showing. Official explanation: trainer said filly was found to have tied up after the race (op 4-9 tchd 8-13, 4-6 in places and 8-11 in a place)

Blue Rocket(IRE), a highly-regarded sort but probably not at her best when beating only two home in the Cheveley Park on her final start as a juvenile, made a very pleasing return to action. She raced towards the far side of the track, which may or may not have put her at an advantage, but whatever the case, she does look a smart prospect. (op 16-1)

Kaseema(USA) ◆, a winner on her debut at Yarmouth before running creditably in the Rockfel, made a highly-encouraging reappearance. She travelled as well as anything for much of the way, but just lacked a change of gear at the business end and would have found the ordinary pace against her over a trip that is likely to prove plenty short enough. She looks as though she has plenty more to offer, particularly when stepped up in trip in a stronger-run race, and 25/1 for the 1000 Guineas looks a very fair price. (op 10-1)

Barshiba(IRE), who came into this off the back of just a minor success in a Polytrack maiden at Lingfield, did well to finish so close, although it is possible the steady early gallop flatters her somewhat. She was very keen and then hung quite badly to her left under pressure (she is evidently only partially sighted in one eye) before getting the hang of things late on and running on nicely to finish just off the principals. Whatever the true merit of this effort, she looks a very nice prospect and should stay further. Official explanation: jockey said filly hung left (op 14-1)

Pretty Majestic(IRE), trying her furthest trip to date off the back of a 208-day break, ran a respectable race without proving she is up to this class. (op 33-1)

Fantasy Parkes was an unknown quantity, as she had just a Haydock maiden success last September to her name, but she ran creditably enough. She stumbled at the start, but seemed to recover from that well enough. (op 33-1)

1097 CONNAUGHT ACCESS FLOORING FEILDEN STKS (LISTED RACE) 1m 1f
4:20 (4:21) (Class 1) 3-Y-O

£15,898 (£6,025; £3,015; £1,503; £753; £378) **Stalls** High

Form RPR

010- **1** **Petara Bay (IRE)**^{179} [6104] 3-8-13 91 .... DaneO'Neill 1 108+
(T G Mills) *h.d.w: hld up: edgd rt and hdwy to ld over 1f out: sn rdn: r.o* **4/1^{3}**

The Form Book, Raceform Ltd, Compton, RG20 6NL

2-1 **2** *hd* **Salford Mill (IRE)**[102] 53 3-8-13 76 .... TedDurcan 7 108+
(D R C Elsworth) *hld up: hdwy over 2f out: rdn and ev ch over 1f out: r.o* **9/1**

50-0 **3** *2 1/2* **Fishforcompliments**[25] 760 3-8-13 100 .... JamieSpencer 4 103
(R A Fahey) *chsd ldrs: led over 2f out: sn rdn and edgd rt: hdd over 1f out: no ex ins fnl f* **7/1**

01- **4** *5* **Al Shemali**[190] 5901 3-8-13 92 .... KerrinMcEvoy 2 93
(Sir Michael Stoute) *lw: chsd ldrs: rdn over 2f out: wknd over 1f out* **10/3**[1]

15- **5** *2* **Hearthstead Maison (IRE)**[193] 5805 3-8-13 97 .... JoeFanning 6 89
(M Johnston) *led: hdd 7f out: led again over 3f out: hdd over 2f out: wknd over 1f out* **7/2**[2]

220- **6** *14* **Massive (IRE)**[157] 6456 3-8-13 105 .... LDettori 8 61
(M R Channon) *chsd ldrs: rdn over 2f out: wknd over 1f out* **15/2**

410- **7** *3 1/2* **Don't Panic (IRE)**[201] 5653 3-8-13 95 .... EddieAhern 5 54
(P W Chapple-Hyam) *lw: hld up: plld hrd: hdwy to ld 7f out: hdd over 3f out: wknd wl over 1f out* **16/1**

10- **8** *132* **To The Max (IRE)**[199] 5715 3-8-13 96 .... MJKinane 3 —
(R Hannon) *hld up: plld hrd: virtually p.u fnl 7f* **8/1**

1m 49.76s (-2.19) **Going Correction** -0.175s/f (Firm) **8** Ran SP% **116.6**
Speed ratings (Par 106):102,101,99,95,93 80,77,—
CSF £40.12 TOTE £5.70: £1.70, £2.20, £2.50; EX 47.10.
Owner Mrs B Ecclestone **Bred** Swettenham Stud **Trained** Headley, Surrey

FOCUS
A fair renewal and, although the runner-up has a rating of just 76, he is well regarded and the form should not be rated lower on account of his good performance. The third is probably the best guide.

NOTEBOOK
Petara Bay(IRE) may not have coped with the heavy ground in the Racing Post Trophy last autumn, although his trainer believes it was more down to weakness, but he had looked a very useful prospect previously, and he is certainly bred for the job. Nicely backed on this reappearance, he travelled well throughout and came with a good, strong run from the back of the field to hit the front with over a furlong to run. He still showed signs of inexperience in front, but he won the battle with another well-regarded type in Salford Mill, and will undoubtedly be suited by a step up in trip. The Dante could be next on his agenda, ahead of a tilt at the Derby. (op 9-2 tchd 5-1)
Salford Mill(IRE) may have only won a Polytrack maiden but his connections shunned the potential easy pickings of a handicap off his lenient mark of 76 in favour of a crack at this better company. He did not let them down, running a screamer and only going down narrowly to an equally well-regarded type. He completed a one-two for Peintre Celebre and is likely to take on the winner again in the Dante. (op 11-2)
Fishforcompliments did not set the world alight on his reappearance on Polytrack but that outing gave him a fitness edge over the opposition, and his best two-year-old form gave him a chance in this company. He ran well, but the impression left is that he is going to remain difficult to place this season and vulnerable to less-exposed and improving rivals. (op 17-2)
Al Shemali, winner of a soft-ground maiden last autumn, was a bit too keen for his own good in the early stages and perhaps this ground was lively enough for him. He can prove better than this bare form suggests in time. (op 4-1)
Hearthstead Maison(IRE), fifth in the Group 3 Autumn Stakes last October and representing last's year's winning stable, put the pace to the race but was unable to go with the main protagonists in the closing stages. He should get further than this as the season progresses and is entitled to come on for this reappearance outing. (op 3-1)
Massive(IRE), who ran his best race at two when narrowly denied in a Group 3 race over this distance in France, probably found this ground too fast for him. Nevertheless, he might be another who proves difficult to place this season. Official explanation: jockey said colt was unsuited by the good to firm ground (op 7-1 tchd 8-1)
Don't Panic(IRE), the only runner in the field without Group entries, failed to settle in the early stages and gave himself little chance of getting home. Official explanation: jockey said colt ran too free and was unsuited by the good to firm ground
To The Max(IRE) Official explanation: jockey said colt was wrong behind

1098 ALEX SCOTT MAIDEN STKS (C&G) 7f
4:55 (4:55) (Class 4) 3-Y-O **£5,181** (£1,541; £770; £384) **Stalls** High

Form RPR

0- **1** **Snaafy (USA)**[236] 4768 3-9-0 .... RHills 3 77+
(B W Hills) *s.i.s: hdwy to chse ldr 6f out: chal over 2f out: rdn to ld ins fnl f: r.o* **7/4**[2]

30- **2** *1/2* **Wolf River (USA)**[203] 5607 3-9-0 .... RichardHughes 10 76
(D M Simcock) *led: rdn over 2f out: hdd ins fnl f: styd on* **16/1**

33- **3** *3/4* **Shevchenko (IRE)**[173] 6199 3-9-0 .... ShaneKelly 4 74+
(J Noseda) *hld up: nt clr run over 2f out: hdwy over 1f out: r.o* **13/8**[1]

30- **4** *1 1/4* **Lights Of Vegas**[242] 4592 3-9-0 .... JamieSpencer 7 71
(B J Meehan) *prom: rdn 3f out: styd on same pce fnl f* **17/2**

0- **5** *1/2* **Calculating (IRE)**[202] 5640 3-9-0 .... KerrinMcEvoy 6 70
(J H M Gosden) *h.d.w: s.s: hld up: hdwy 2f out: no ex fnl f* **15/2**[3]

6 *3/4* **Getrah** 3-9-0 .... MichaelHills 8 68+
(W J Haggas) *gd sort: hld up in tch: n.m.r and lost pl over 2f out: styd on ins fnl f* **16/1**

2340 **7** *3* **Leg Sweep**[48] 591 3-8-11 70 .... MarcHalford(3) 9 60
(D R C Elsworth) *lw: chsd ldrs: rdn over 2f out: wknd fnl f* **16/1**

8 *1 1/4* **Velocity's Gift** 3-9-0 .... PaulEddery 5 57
(Pat Eddery) *w'like: s.s: hld up: hung lft and wknd over 1f out* **33/1**

1m 25.23s (-1.27) **Going Correction** -0.175s/f (Firm) **8** Ran SP% **117.3**
Speed ratings (Par 100):100,99,98,97,96 95,92,90
CSF £30.73 TOTE £3.00: £1.20, £4.20, £1.10; EX 48.60.
Owner Hamdan Al Maktoum **Bred** Shadwell Farm LLC **Trained** Lambourn, Berks

FOCUS
Often a decent maiden, but this did not look one of the stronger renewals. A steady early pace also puts a question mark over the value of the form as the first two benefited from racing prominently throughout.
Getrah Official explanation: jockey said gelding lost its action

1099 VOUTE SALES STKS (H'CAP) 6f
5:30 (5:31) (Class 2) (0-100,98) 3-Y-O **£11,658** (£3,468; £1,733; £865) **Stalls** High

Form RPR

314- **1** **Sakhee's Secret**[193] 5806 3-9-2 93 .... SteveDrowne 11 113+
(H Morrison) *h.d.w: hld up: hdwy over 2f out: led over 1f out: hung lft: r.o wl* **9/4**[1]

23-0 **2** *5* **Aahayson**[25] 760 3-8-12 89 .... PatCosgrave 15 94
(K R Burke) *led: hdd over 3f out: rdn and ev ch over 1f out: sn outpcd* **10/1**[3]

2-11 **3** *nk* **Imprimis Tagula (IRE)**[55] 520 3-7-9 79 oh2 .... AmyBaker(7) 9 83
(A Bailey) *chsd ldrs: led briefly over 1f out: no ex ins fnl f* **25/1**

1120 **4** *2* **Si Foo (USA)**[25] 760 3-8-11 88 .... MartinDwyer 13 86
(A M Balding) *prom: rdn over 2f out: styd on same pce appr fnl f* **10/1**[3]

16-0 **5** *hd* **Danum Dancer**[18] 847 3-8-13 90 ....(b) J-PGuillambert 3 87
(N Bycroft) *b: chsd ldrs: led over 3f out: rdn and hdd over 1f out: sn hung rt: wknd ins fnl f* **16/1**

210- **6** *1 1/2* **Averticus**[192] 5843 3-8-2 79 .... PaulEddery 7 76+
(B W Hills) *lw: hld up: swtchd rt and hdwy over 1f out: nt trble ldrs* **33/1**

113- **7** *1 1/4* **Lady Lily (IRE)**[179] 6096 3-8-11 88 .... TedDurcan 2 77
(H R A Cecil) *bit bkwd: hld up: plld hrd: rdn over 1f out: n.d* **8/1**[2]

30-0 **8** *nk* **Bazroy (IRE)**[11] 943 3-9-1 95 .... StephenDonohoe(3) 6 83
(P D Evans) *chsd ldrs: rdn 2f out: wknd fnl f* **40/1**

54-0 **9** *nk* **Diysem (USA)**[11] 939 3-8-7 84 .... JamieSpencer 12 71+
(B J Meehan) *hld up: r.o ins fnl f: nvr nrr* **14/1**

000- **10** *1 1/4* **King's Bastion (IRE)**[194] 5788 3-8-6 83 .... HayleyTurner 1 66
(M L W Bell) *bkwd: s.i.s: nvr nrr* **33/1**

151- **11** *1/2* **College Scholar (GER)**[173] 6204 3-9-1 92 .... TPO'Shea 17 74
(M R Channon) *lw: hld up in tch: rdn and wknd over 1f out* **10/1**[3]

2-33 **12** *1 1/4* **Black Moma (IRE)**[42] 639 3-8-2 79 oh3 .... RichardSmith 14 57
(R Hannon) *chsd ldrs over 4f* **33/1**

2-63 **13** *hd* **Resplendent Alpha**[14] 922 3-9-7 98 .... JimmyQuinn 8 75
(P Howling) *b: s.i.s: nt clr run over 1f out: n.d* **25/1**

101- **14** *nk* **Cheap Street**[187] 5940 3-8-13 90 .... NickyMackay 16 66
(J G Portman) *hld up in tch: rdn and wknd over 1f out* **20/1**

031- **15** *hd* **Lord Theo**[275] 3591 3-8-3 80 ow1 .... JamesDoyle 4 56
(N P Littmoden) *lw: prom over 3f* **25/1**

10-3 **16** *1 1/4* **Northern Fling**[6] 1009 3-8-11 88 .... KerrinMcEvoy 10 60
(D Nicholls) *lw: s.i.s: a in rr* **12/1**

615- **17** *nk* **Disco Dan**[187] 5940 3-8-5 82 .... DeanMernagh 5 53
(D M Simcock) *hld up: rdn over 2f out: a in rr* **16/1**

23-1 **18** *7* **Weekend Fling (USA)**[14] 916 3-8-3 80 .... JoeFanning 18 30
(M Johnston) *chsd ldrs over 3f* **12/1**

1m 10.59s (-2.51) **Going Correction** -0.175s/f (Firm) **18** Ran SP% **130.5**
Speed ratings (Par 104):109,102,101,99,99 97,95,94,94,92 92,90,90,89,89 87,87,78
CSF £22.99 CT £492.41 TOTE £3.00: £2.20, £3.20, £7.60, £3.00; EX 43.80 Place 6 £ 76.98, Place 5 £ 25.72.
Owner Miss B Swire **Bred** Miss B Swire **Trained** East Ilsley, Berks

FOCUS
A competitive handicap on paper but it was won in emphatic fashion by Sakhee's Secret, who looks a Pattern-class propsect. The form behind looks solid and the time was good for the grade.

NOTEBOOK
Sakhee's Secret ◆, who disappointed when sent off at odds-on for a conditions race at Ascot last autumn, looked potentially well handicapped for this seasonal reappearance back over 6f and on faster ground. He won in terrific fashion, looking in a completely different league to the rest, and he should be able to make the grade in Listed company at the very least, although his trainer is keen to give him time between his races. (op 5-2 tchd 3-1)
Aahayson faced a stiff task on the All-Weather last time and did not settle either, but that outing meant that he had the benefit of fitness over a number of his rivals. Back over a more suitable trip, he made the running and kept on well next to the far rail, and was just unfortunate that he ran into a machine who was particularly well handicapped. (op 11-1 tchd 12-1)
Imprimis Tagula(IRE), seeking a hat-trick following a couple of wins on Fibresand in February, had been raised 6lb since, but was racing from 2lb out of the handicap here as well so he had plenty on his plate. He ran with credit though, and is clearly still improving. (op 33-1)
Si Foo(USA), who finished in mid-division in a Polytrack Listed event last time out, found this company more suitable, although the drop back to six was arguably against her. (op 12-1)
Danum Dancer, who took on older horses in the Cammidge Trophy last time out, was happier back against his own age group, but whether he has anything in hand of the Handicapper off a mark of 90 is open to debate.
Averticus, representing an in-form stable, ran alright, but he will need to improve to defy his current mark.
Lady Lily(IRE) did not settle that well and also failed to enjoy the clearest of runs. She could be a bit better than her finishing position suggests. (op 13-2)
Bazroy(IRE) looks likely to prove difficult to place this season as he appears to be not up to Listed grade while also looking vulnerable off big weights in handicap company. (tchd 50-1)
Diysem(USA), who finished one place behind Putra Square (second in the opening maiden on the card) in a decent Kempton handicap last time, was unsuited by the drop back to sprinting. He will be more effective when stepped up in trip again. (op 16-1)
King's Bastion(IRE), whose form tailed off in the second half of last year, looked very much in need of this seasonal reappearance beforehand, and in the circumstances he was not disgraced.
Resplendent Alpha Official explanation: jockey said colt missed the break and was never travelling
Cheap Street Official explanation: jockey said colt lost its action
T/Plt: £92.60 to a £1 stake. Pool: £83,270.70. 656.40 winning tickets. T/Qpdt: £6.30 to a £1 stake. Pool: £5,045.80. 587.25 winning tickets. CR

1093
NEWMARKET (ROWLEY) (R-H)
Thursday, April 19

OFFICIAL GOING: Good to firm
Wind: Light behind Weather: Fine and sunny

1100 B.A.S.I.C. INSURANCE WOOD DITTON STKS 1m
2:00 (2:01) (Class 4) UNRACED 3-Y-O **£6,477** (£1,927; £963; £481) Stalls Low

Form RPR

1 **Chantilly Tiffany** 3-8-12 .... JamieSpencer 11 75
(E A L Dunlop) *w'like: scope: chsd ldr: rdn to ld ins fnl f: r.o* **16/1**

2 *1/2* **Zifaaf (USA)** 3-8-12 .... RHills 10 74
(B W Hills) *neat: chsd ldrs: led over 1f out: rdn and hdd ins fnl f: unable qck nr fin* **11/2**[2]

3 *3/4* **King's Event (USA)** 3-9-3 .... KerrinMcEvoy 2 77+
(Sir Michael Stoute) *gd sort: chsd ldrs: nt clr run and swtchd rt over 1f out: r.o* **11/10**[1]

4 *1/2* **Hazytoo** 3-9-3 .... NCallan 6 76
(N A Callaghan) *w'like: leggy: a.p: rdn over 1f out: styd on same pce ins fnl f* **10/1**

5 *1* **Triple Beat** 3-9-3 .... RichardHughes 3 74+
(H R A Cecil) *cmpt: scope: bkwd: hld up: effrt and nt clr run over 2f out: r.o ins fnl f: nt rch ldrs* **7/1**[3]

6 *3* **Sky Masterson** 3-9-3 .... JimmyFortune 8 67+
(J H M Gosden) *cmpt: led: rdn and hdd over 1f out: wknd ins fnl f* **14/1**

7 *nk* **Imply** 3-9-3 .... KDarley 12 66
(J H M Gosden) *gd sort: scope: s.s: hld up: hdwy over 4f out: rdn over 2f out: wknd over 1f out* **9/1**

8 *3/4* **Cheeky Jack (USA)** 3-9-3 .... MichaelHills 5 64
(B J Meehan) *w'like: scope: hld up: a in rr* **16/1**

9 *1 3/4* **Natural Action** 3-9-3 .... DarryllHolland 9 60
(W Jarvis) *w'like: bkwd: hld up: effrt over 3f out: wknd 2f out* **50/1**

10 1 **Zachary Scott** 3-9-3 .... EddieAhern 4 58
(C E Brittain) *wl grwn: s.i.s: hld up: a in rr* **25/1**

1m 41.19s (1.82) **Going Correction** -0.25s/f (Firm) **10** Ran SP% **118.8**
Speed ratings (Par 100):80,79,78,78,77 74,73,73,71,70
CSF £103.53 TOTE £17.40: £3.40, £1.80, £1.10; EX 91.70.
Owner Ballygallon Stud Ltd **Bred** Ballygallon Stud **Trained** Newmarket, Suffolk

FOCUS
Hard to know what to make of this year's Wood Ditton, but it looked a reasonable enough renewal and should produce its share of winners. Interestingly, the only two fillies in the line up finished one-two. The pace was just ordinary and those who raced handy were at an advantage. The winning time was 5.64 seconds slower than the Craven.

1101 WYCK HALL STUD MAIDEN FILLIES' STKS 5f
2:35 (2:37) (Class 4) 2-Y-0 **£4,533** (£1,348; £674; £336) **Stalls** Low

Form RPR

1 **Mookhlesa** 2-9-0 .... RHills 11 80+
(B W Hills) *gd sort: hld up in tch: racd keenly: led over 1f out: rdn out* **8/1**

2 ½ **Missit (IRE)** 2-9-0 .... DarryllHolland 6 78
(M R Channon) *w'like: leggy: chsd ldrs: rdn over 1f out: r.o* **9/2**[3]

3 1¼ **Spinning Lucy (IRE)** 2-9-0 .... MichaelHills 1 73+
(B W Hills) *leggy: scope: lw: s.i.s: sn chsng ldrs: nt clr run and swtchd rt over 1f out: r.o wl ins fnl f* **10/3**[1]

4 hd **Littlemisssunshine (IRE)** 2-9-0 .... LPKeniry 7 72
(J S Moore) *neat: lw: chsd ldrs: rdn over 1f out: styd on same pce ins fnl f* **7/1**

5 nk **Alexander Nepotism (IRE)** 2-9-0 .... LDettori 8 71
(B J Meehan) *neat: scope: mid-div: rdn and hung rt over 1f out: styd on* **6/1**

2 6 shd **Eager Diva (USA)**[11] [952] 2-9-0 .... NCallan 5 71
(K A Ryan) *neat: lw: w ldr tl led 1/2-way: hdd over 1f out: no ex ins fnl f* **4/1**[2]

7 nk **Affirmatively** 2-9-0 .... JohnEgan 10 69
(D R C Elsworth) *w'like: scope: s.i.s: hld up: swtchd rt and hdwy over 1f out: styd on* **16/1**

8 2½ **Quick Sands (IRE)** 2-9-0 .... DaneO'Neill 13 59
(R Hannon) *w'like: scope: mid-div: rdn 1/2-way: wknd fnl f* **16/1**

0 9 1¾ **Una Auroraborealis**[10] [972] 2-9-0 .... BrettDoyle 4 52
(J Ryan) *led to 1/2-way: wknd fnl f* **100/1**

10 ¾ **Romany Princess (IRE)** 2-9-0 .... RichardHughes 9 49
(R Hannon) *w'like: s.s: hld up: effrt and swtchd rt over 1f out: sn wknd* **14/1**

11 2 **Crying Aloud (USA)** 2-9-0 .... TPO'Shea 3 41
(P A Blockley) *w'like: s.i.s: hld up: wknd over 1f out* **33/1**

12 2½ **Whistful Miss** 2-9-0 .... JimmyQuinn 2 31
(P Howling) *cmpt: bkwd: s.i.s: hld up: wknd over 1f out* **50/1**

13 shd **Emily's Dens Joy (IRE)** 2-9-0 .... JamesDoyle 12 31
(Miss D A McHale) *small: w ldrs 3f: wknd fnl f* **100/1**

60.21 secs (-0.26) **Going Correction** -0.25s/f (Firm) **13** Ran SP% **124.5**
Speed ratings (Par 91):92,91,89,88,88 88,87,83,80,79 76,72,72
CSF £45.49 TOTE £9.20: £2.80, £2.00, £1.70; EX 65.40.
Owner Hamdan Al Maktoum **Bred** Shadwell Estate Company Limited **Trained** Lambourn, Berks

FOCUS
Very little form to go on, but this looked like a decent fillies' contest, probably one of the best maidens to be run so far this year.

NOTEBOOK
Mookhlesa, the first foal of an unraced sister to La-Faah, a very useful triple 6-7f winner at two, including the Horris Hill, upstaged her better fancied stablemate to make a winning debut. She is clearly held in high regard in her own right, as the plan is to give her one more run before aiming at the Queen Mary. (op 7-1 tchd 13-2)
Missit(IRE) ◆, a 35,000gns half-sister to 7f juvenile winner Night Sphere, ran on nicely to claim second and shaped with plenty of promise for the future. She should improve with the benefit of this experience and will be very hard to beat in maiden company next time. (tchd 5-1, 4-1 in places and 11-2 in a place)
Spinning Lucy(IRE) ◆, whose sales price increased from 34,000euros as a foal to 130,000euros, is a half-sister to the smart Midris, a dual 6f winner at two. Representing last year's winning trainer, she was well supported in the market and would surely have justified the confidence with anything like a clear run. She only got in the clear when the race was all over, but she still had just enough time to show an impressive burst of speed and claim a place. She should win her maiden next time before stepping up in class, and it is by no means out of the question she will join Mookhlesa at Royal Ascot. Official explanation: jockey said filly was denied a clear run (op 7-2)
Littlemisssunshine(IRE), a 54,000gns half-sister to triple 6f winner Bohola Flyer, and to Slate and Cappa Blanca, both 7f winners at two, out of a useful dual 5f-1m winner, shaped very nicely on her racecourse debut. Her stable has plenty of firepower in the juvenile division this year and this one should soon be winning. (op 8-1)
Alexander Nepotism(IRE), out of an unraced half-sister to Northern Spur, a top-class 1m2f-1m7f winner in France/US, hung right and ended up widest of all, but she still showed plenty of ability. (op 7-1 tchd 15-2)
Eager Diva(USA), runner-up on her debut in a modest maiden at Musselburgh, would have found this a lot tougher. She will find things easier back on a lesser course. (tchd 5-1)
Affirmatively ◆, out of a 1m winner at three, made a very pleasing introduction. She should come on a bundle for this and is probably worth keeping on the right side of. (op 12-1)
Quick Sands(IRE), a 40,000gns first foal of a half-sister to quite useful Francis Cadell, a 6f winner at two, and to Khabfair, a triple 6f winner at two and three, offered some promise for the future. (tchd 20-1)
Una Auroraborealis, who beat only one home on her debut at Warwick, enjoyed the run of the race and is probably flattered. (op 66-1)
Romany Princess(IRE) Official explanation: jockey said filly missed the break

1102 FEDERATION OF BLOODSTOCK AGENTS ABERNANT STKS (LISTED RACE) 6f
3:10 (3:11) (Class 1) 3-Y-0+ **£15,898** (£6,025; £3,015; £1,503; £753; £378) **Stalls** Low

Form RPR

102- 1 **Asset (IRE)**[302] [2739] 4-9-4 107 .... RichardHughes 5 121+
(R Hannon) *lw: trckd ldrs: led over 1f out: r.o wl* **11/4**[1]

204- 2 2½ **Assertive**[207] [5549] 4-9-4 106 .... DaneO'Neill 10 113
(R Hannon) *bit bkwd: trckd ldrs: rdn and ev ch over 1f out: unable qckn ins fnl f* **8/1**

4-25 3 1 **Paradise Isle**[55] [547] 6-9-3 .... KDarley 12 109
(C F Wall) *racd wd: chsd ldrs: rdn and ev ch over 1f out: no ex ins fnl f* **13/2**[2]

120- 4 1½ **Baltic King**[188] [5942] 7-9-8 110 .... (t) JimmyFortune 7 110
(H Morrison) *lw: hld up: rdn over 2f out: r.o ins fnl f: nrst fin* **15/2**[3]

-003 5 ¾ **Mutamared (USA)**[19] [841] 7-9-4 98 .... NCallan 11 104
(K A Ryan) *hld up: hdwy over 2f out: rdn and edgd lft over 1f out: styd on same pce* **8/1**

4012 6 ½ **Ajigolo**[18] [867] 4-9-4 97 .... DarryllHolland 2 102
(M R Channon) *chsd ldrs: rdn and swtchd rt over 1f out: no ex* **16/1**

006- 7 nk **Quito (IRE)**[173] [6218] 10-9-8 111 .... (b) JamieSpencer 8 105
(D W Chapman) *dwlt: hld up: swtchd rt over 1f out: styd on ins fnl f: nrst fin* **20/1**

00-0 8 shd **The Kiddykid (IRE)**[19] [847] 7-9-8 100 .... StephenDonohoe 9 105
(P D Evans) *lw: chsd ldrs over 4f* **50/1**

-000 9 nk **Excusez Moi (USA)**[26] [762] 5-9-4 102 .... KerrinMcEvoy 4 100+
(C E Brittain) *s.i.s: hld up: nt clr run over 2f out: hmpd over 1f out: n.d* **8/1**

13-2 10 nk **Sierra Vista**[19] [847] 7-8-13 102 .... JohnEgan 3 94
(D W Barker) *led: rdn: edgd rt and hdd over 1f out: wknd ins fnl f* **8/1**

010- 11 1¼ **Fantasy Believer**[188] [5942] 9-9-8 104 .... JimmyQuinn 1 99
(J J Quinn) *bkwd: hld up: a in rr* **25/1**

00-1 12 3 **Fire Up The Band**[15] [927] 8-9-4 105 .... SilvestreDeSousa 6 86
(D Nicholls) *chsd ldrs: rdn 1/2-way: wknd over 1f out* **12/1**

69.64 secs (-3.46) **Going Correction** -0.25s/f (Firm) course record **12** Ran SP% **120.4**
Speed ratings (Par 111):113,109,108,106,105 104,104,104,103,103 101,97
CSF £24.59 TOTE £3.30: £1.50, £3.20, £2.50; EX 39.10.
Owner Highclere Thoroughbred Racing XXVI **Bred** Peter Gibbons And Dermot Forde **Trained** East Everleigh, Wilts

FOCUS
This looked like a reasonable renewal of the Abernant Stakes - last year's winner Paradise Isle helps give the form a solid look in third - and Asset won in the style of horse capable of competing at Group level. The winning time was a course record.

NOTEBOOK
Asset(IRE) ◆, gelded since running second in the Jersey Stakes at Royal Ascot last June, improved for the drop back to sprinting and ran out a very impressive winner, breaking the course record in the process. Always in a good position, he picked up well when asked and was in a different league to this lot. His effort is all the more creditable considering he is expected to improve for the outing. He is likely to face much tougher tasks as the season progresses, but has been compared favourably by his owners with Lake Coniston, who won both the Duke Of York Stakes and the July Cup, and he is expected to follow a similar path. (op 7-2 tchd 4-1 and 9-2 in places)
Assertive, a Listed winner at both two and three, he ran a fine race on his return from a 207-day break but was no match for his Group-class stablemate. He could well pick up a similar race at some stage this season, maybe even a Group 3, while he also has the option of being campaigned abroad. (op 9-1 tchd 10-1)
Paradise Isle, successful in this race last year, came into this season's renewal off the back of some solid efforts in Dubai and ran another good race. She raced more towards the middle of the track than most of these, but that was probably no disadvantage considering she has run very well in the past when racing on her own. (op 5-1)
Baltic King, only eighth in this race last year, made a very pleasing return to action and can be expected to come on for the run. (op 8-1 tchd 7-1)
Mutamared(USA) absolutely loves fast ground and showed enough to suggest he will be well worth campaigning at this sort of level this season. (tchd 15-2 and 17-2)
Ajigolo, who has rediscovered something like his best form on the sand this winter, was worth a try in a race like this and ran with credit. Official explanation: jockey said colt hung right
Quito(IRE), returning from a 173-day break, ran well enough considering he started very slowly and he can do better with the benefit of this outing. (op 16-1)
Excusez Moi(USA) enjoyed a terrible run and this effort is best forgotten. Official explanation: jockey said horse suffered interference in running (op 10-1)
Sierra Vista Official explanation: jockey said mare hung right

1103 BANSHAHOUSESTABLES.COM CRAVEN STKS (GROUP 3) (C&G) 1m
3:45 (3:46) (Class 1) 3-Y-0 **£28,390** (£10,760; £5,385; £2,685; £1,345; £675) **Stalls** Low

Form RPR

10- 1 **Adagio**[187] [5965] 3-8-12 113 .... KerrinMcEvoy 2 114+
(Sir Michael Stoute) *h.d.w: b.hind: s.i.s: hdwy over 6f out: nt clr run over 2f out: led and edgd lft ins fnl f: comf* **5/4**[1]

114- 2 1½ **Sonny Red (IRE)**[301] [2771] 3-8-12 99 .... JamieSpencer 1 110
(R Hannon) *lw: led: rdn and edgd rt over 1f out: edgd lft and hdd ins fnl f: styd on same pce* **16/1**

615- 3 1¾ **Thousand Words**[180] [6104] 3-8-12 112 .... RichardHughes 9 106
(B W Hills) *chsd ldr: rdn over 1f out: styd on same pce fnl f* **5/2**[2]

040- 4 shd **He's A Decoy (IRE)**[187] [5965] 3-8-12 .... WMLordan 5 106
(David Wachman, Ire) *h.d.w: prom: racd keenly: swtchd rt 1/2-way: rdn over 1f out: styd on same pce fnl f* **10/1**

213- 5 shd **Striving Storm (USA)**[180] [6102] 3-8-12 104 .... EddieAhern 3 106
(P W Chapple-Hyam) *lw: chsd ldrs: rdn over 1f out: styng on same pce whn hung lft ins fnl f* **16/1**

125- 6 nk **Big Robert**[202] [5653] 3-8-12 106 .... MartinDwyer 7 105+
(W R Muir) *lw: hld up: rdn over 2f out: nt clr run over 1f out: styng on whn n.m.r wl ins fnl f: nvr able to chal* **9/1**[3]

13- 7 6 **Broghill**[194] [5806] 3-8-12 97 .... JimmyFortune 4 92
(J H M Gosden) *hld up in tch: plld hrd: rdn: hung rt and wknd over 1f out* **10/1**

100- 8 6 **Teslin (IRE)**[172] [6249] 3-8-12 96 .... KDarley 8 78
(M Johnston) *chsd ldrs: rdn over 3f out: wknd over 2f out* **25/1**

1m 35.55s (-3.82) **Going Correction** -0.25s/f (Firm) **8** Ran SP% **116.8**
Speed ratings (Par 108):109,107,105,105,105 105,99,93
CSF £25.02 TOTE £2.30: £1.30, £2.90, £1.30; EX 23.70.
Owner D Smith, M Tabor & Mrs J Magnier **Bred** New England Stud, Myriad And Elite Bloodstock **Trained** Newmarket, Suffolk

FOCUS
Not a great renewal, but a very pleasing performance from Adagio, who won in the style of a high-class colt and is definitely short-list material for both the Guineas and the Derby. The race was run in a time 5.64sec quicker than the Wood Ditton earlier on the card and the form has been rated positively around the third and fourth.

NOTEBOOK
Adagio, who finished seventh in the Dewhurst on his final start at two, looked to have done particularly well physically and was the subject of good reports. Well backed on this reappearance, he was none too well away, still showed signs of inexperience and enjoyed anything but a clear run, but travelled strongly throughout and picked up in style when the gap finally came. He won without being given a hard race and looks a colt of immense potential. The Guineas is next for him, for which he is now best priced 5-1, and with his breeding suggesting he should get the Derby trip without much trouble he could be a Golan or Sir Percy type, capable of running big races in both Classics. He is 14-1 for Epsom and fast ground, which certainly seemed to suit him here, will be to his advantage. (op 6-4 tchd 7-4 and 15-8 in places)
Sonny Red(IRE), off the track since disappointing a little behind Dutch Art in the Norfolk Stakes last June (got jarred up), had previously looked a smart performer in the making, albeit on soft ground, and he proved he has trained on with a solid effort in second behind an impressive winner. He finished clear of the rest and could be an interesting candidate for the French Guineas, where he should get more give.

Thousand Words, whose trainer has a good record in the trials, winning this race twice in the past three years, looked the biggest threat to the favourite on his two-year-old form, having won the Somerville Tattersall Stakes and finished a creditable fifth in the Racing Post Trophy. He ran a fair race, without looking Guineas class, but this ground may well have been a bit quick for him. (tchd 11-4 and 3-1 in places)
He's A Decoy(IRE) finished one place behind Adagio in the Dewhurst but he had much more experience as a juvenile and Stoute's charge has progressed at a greater rate from two to three. He could be a difficult horse to place this season. (op 17-2 tchd 15-2 and 7-1 in places)
Striving Storm(USA), who finished third in the Horris Hill on his final start at two, hails from a stable that houses stronger Classic prospects in the shape of Dutch Art and Authorized, so his trainer will not have been disappointed with this solid effort. It would not be a surprise to see him racing on the continent in search of Group race or even Classic success, and easier ground will not go amiss. (op 20-1)
Big Robert, fifth behind Thousand Words in the Somerville Tattersall Stakes last autumn, got a bit closer to that old rival on his reappearance, keeping on well at the finish having not enjoyed the clearest of runs. He will appreciate stepping up to ten furlongs this term. (tchd 8-1)
Broghill, one of the least exposed runners in the line-up, did not settle in the early stages, hung on the fast ground and was eased when his chance had gone. A son of Selkirk, he is another who is likely to appreciate getting his toe in. (tchd 8-1 and 11-1 in a place)
Teslin(IRE) looked outclassed in this company and is likely to be difficult to place this term, unless connections opt for trips abroad. (op 28-1)

1104 WEATHERBYS EARL OF SEFTON STKS (GROUP 3) 1m 1f
4:20 (4:20) (Class 1) 4-Y-0+
£28,390 (£10,760; £5,385; £2,685; £1,345; £675) **Stalls** Low

Form RPR
232- **1** **Manduro (GER)**[201] 5704 5-8-12 .... SPasquier 5 121+
(A Fabre, France) *a.p: chsd ldr over 4f out: led over 1f out: pushed clr* **6/4**[1]
406- **2** *4* **Speciosa (IRE)**[222] 5184 4-8-9 114 .... MickyFenton 1 110
(Mrs P Sly) *led: rdn and hdd over 1f out: sn outpcd* **12/1**
610- **3** *1 3/4* **Final Verse**[173] 6218 4-8-12 109 .... KerrinMcEvoy 8 109
(Sir Michael Stoute) *bit bkwd: racd alone in centre: prom: shkn up over 1f out: edgd lft and styd on same pce* **14/1**
2-13 **4** *hd* **Illustrious Blue**[26] 761 4-8-12 105 .... PaulDoe 9 109+
(W J Knight) *hld up: rdn over 2f out: styd on ins fnl f: nrst fin* **12/1**
035- **5** *1 1/2* **Snoqualmie Boy**[187] 5968 4-8-12 108 .... JohnEgan 2 105
(D R C Elsworth) *chsd ldrs: rdn over 2f out: wknd ins fnl f* **9/1**
126- **6** *1 1/4* **Ivy Creek (USA)**[301] 2775 4-8-12 109 .... SteveDrowne 7 103
(G Wragg) *lw: hld up: racd keenly: hdwy over 2f out: rdn and wknd over 1f out* **9/1**
15- **7** *1/2* **Secret World (IRE)**[302] 2739 4-8-12 105 .... LDettori 4 102
(J Noseda) *s.i.s: hld up: rdn and wknd over 1f out* **11/2**[2]
230- **8** *2 1/2* **Dunelight (IRE)**[201] 5675 4-8-12 107 ....(b) PhilipRobinson 3 96
(C G Cox) *racd keenly: trckd ldr 5f: rdn and wknd over 1f out* **20/1**
15-1 **9** *25* **Imperial Star (IRE)**[12] 941 4-8-12 110 .... JimmyFortune 6 44
(J H M Gosden) *lw: swtg: hld up: rdn over 3f out: sn wknd* **13/2**[3]

1m 47.26s (-4.69) **Going Correction** -0.25s/f (Firm) course record 9 Ran SP% **115.5**
Speed ratings (Par 113):110,106,104,104,103 102,101,99,77
CSF £21.47 TOTE £2.30: £1.20, £2.40, £5.10; EX 18.10.
Owner Baron G Von Ullmann **Bred** Rolf Brunner **Trained** Chantilly, France

FOCUS
Sound form for Group 3 standard and a race run at a good pace and in a course-record time.

NOTEBOOK
Manduro(GER) endured a frustrating run of placed efforts last season but he boasted solid Group 1 form and ran out an impressive winner off a decent pace. He relished this quick ground, clocking a course-record time in victory and giving every indication that he will be a real threat in the big 1m2f Group 1 contests to come. His next outing is likely to be in the Prix d'Ispahan, before a return to this country for either the Queen Anne or the Prince of Wales's Stakes at Royal Ascot. (op 11-8 tchd 13-8 and 7-4 in a place)
Speciosa(IRE), unbeaten in three previous starts at this track, including in the 1000 Guineas last year, was down in the paper as only a runner in the event of suitable ground, and one could hardly describe these conditions as ideal for this soft-ground loving filly. She ran a super race in the circumstances and, while she could not live with the winner in the latter stages, she beat the rest well enough and looks set for a successful season when back racing against members of her own sex on easier ground. (op 10-1)
Final Verse, who disappointed on his return from an injury on his final start last year, was racing on quick ground for the first time since finishing a very creditable sixth in the 2000 Guineas. Kept wide of the rest, he raced alone up the centre of the track and stuck on well to hold on to third place. He clearly retains his ability and a race at Listed or Group 3 level should be within his ability this season. (op 12-1)
Illustrious Blue had a fitness edge over most of his rivals and got the fast pace he likes, but he had only ever run on ground officially described as faster than good once before in his career (on debut) and the suspicion is that he is at his best with a little cut. His record at Goodwood is particularly eye-catching and he will be one to consider if turning up for a Listed or Group 3 contest at that track.
Snoqualmie Boy, held in Group company last term, ran as though he needed this reappearance, but he may have to drop back into Listed grade for a winning opportunity. (op 10-1)
Ivy Creek(USA), last seen at Royal Ascot last year, was entitled to need this reappearance outing on ground that would have been plenty quick enough for him. He should come on a bundle for the run and it would come as no surprise to see him turn up for the Huxley Stakes at Chester, where his trainer has such a good record. (op 11-1 tchd 8-1)
Secret World(IRE), another who had been absent since running at last year's Royal meeting (stress fracture), ran as though the race would bring him on plenty. The stable's runners have been requiring an outing this term and this well-regarded colt still has the potential to develop into a Group horse. Official explanation: jockey said colt ran too free (op 8-1 tchd 10-1 in a place)
Dunelight(IRE), a progressive handicapper last term, may fall between two stools this season and could prove difficult to place, although he is better when granted an uncontested lead. (op 25-1)
Imperial Star(IRE), an impressive winner at Kempton on his reappearance, was a market drifter and proved very disappointing. Presumably something was amiss. Official explanation: trainer said colt ran too free (op 9-2)

1105 ROSSDALES MAIDEN FILLIES' STKS 7f
4:55 (4:56) (Class 4) 3-Y-0 **£5,181** (£1,541; £770; £384) **Stalls** Low

Form RPR
3- **1** **Yaqeen**[293] 3043 3-9-0 .... RHills 9 89+
(M A Jarvis) *lw: hld up: hdwy 3f out: rdn to ld over 1f out: r.o* **5/6**[1]
030- **2** *2* **Cassiara**[223] 5157 3-9-0 78 .... KDarley 6 76
(J Pearce) *lw: w ldr: rdn and ev ch over 1f out: sn outpcd: r.o ins fnl f* **50/1**
3- **3** *hd* **Costume**[299] 2867 3-9-0 .... RichardHughes 10 75+
(J H M Gosden) *hld up: rdn over 2f out: nt clr run over 1f out: r.o wl ins fnl f: nrst fin* **9/2**[2]
02- **4** *nk* **High 'n Dry (IRE)**[159] 6433 3-9-0 .... MartinDwyer 5 75
(C A Cyzer) *led over 5f: styd on same pce ins fnl f* **66/1**
26- **5** *hd* **Thunderousapplause**[180] 6098 3-9-0 .... NCallan 12 81+
(K A Ryan) *chsd ldrs: rdn and ev ch over 1f out: no ex ins fnl f* **28/1**
4- **6** *shd* **Arabian Treasure (USA)**[203] 5638 3-9-0 .... KerrinMcEvoy 8 74
(Sir Michael Stoute) *lw: chsd ldrs: rdn over 2f out: styd on same pce fnl f* **8/1**[3]
7 *2* **Soul Mountain (IRE)** 3-9-0 .... MichaelHills 2 69+
(B W Hills) *w'like: scope: hld up in tch: nt clr run over 2f out: styd on same pce appr fnl f* **25/1**
8 *nk* **Luck Be A Lady (IRE)** 3-9-0 .... MJKinane 15 68+
(J Noseda) *wl grwn: hld up: plld hrd: hdwy over 1f out: wknd ins fnl f* **14/1**
4- **9** *2 1/2* **Voice**[161] 6414 3-9-0 .... JimmyQuinn 3 61
(H R A Cecil) *hld up in tch: rdn and wknd over 1f out* **33/1**
66-2 **10** *2 1/2* **Love On Sight**[15] 919 3-9-0 90 .... JamieSpencer 4 55
(A P Jarvis) *s.i.s: hld up: nt clr run over 2f out: n.d* **11/1**
11 *shd* **Trivia (IRE)** 3-9-0 .... OscarUrbina 7 55
(N A Callaghan) *gd sort: hld up: a in rr* **100/1**
12 *2 1/2* **Wells Of Badr (IRE)** 3-9-0 .... AdrianMcCarthy 11 48
(P W Chapple-Hyam) *leggy: unf: hld up: wknd 2f out* **100/1**
13 *1* **All Began (IRE)** 3-9-0 .... SteveDrowne 1 46
(G Wragg) *w'like: scope: s.s: outpcd* **33/1**
20- **14** *1 1/2* **Danseuse**[300] 2800 3-9-0 .... LDettori 14 42
(B J Meehan) *chsd ldrs 5f* **14/1**

1m 24.57s (-1.93) **Going Correction** -0.25s/f (Firm) 14 Ran SP% **124.1**
Speed ratings (Par 97):101,98,98,98,97 97,95,95,92,89 89,86,85,83
CSF £80.78 TOTE £1.80: £1.10, £11.60, £1.90; EX 108.40.
Owner Hamdan Al Maktoum **Bred** Brookdale And Dr Ted Folkerth **Trained** Newmarket, Suffolk

FOCUS
Several of these had managed to make the frame as juveniles, but the interest revolved around the winner, who was putting her 1000 Guineas credentials on the line. The pace looked sound enough and the winning time was decent enough for a race of its type, although the overall form may not prove that strong.
Trivia(IRE) Official explanation: jockey said, regarding running and riding, his orders were to jump out, not to bustle the filly and to settle wherever it was happy, adding that from the start it had a high head carriage, was changing legs and seemed uncomfortable; vet said filly was lame on right fore and was sore in its joints

1106 THE CURRAGH "HOME OF THE IRISH CLASSICS" H'CAP 1m 2f
5:30 (5:33) (Class 3) (0-95,92) 3-Y-0 **£9,067** (£2,697; £1,348; £673) **Stalls** Low

Form RPR
1- **1** **Metaphoric (IRE)**[183] 6049 3-8-7 81 ow2 .... JamieSpencer 6 94
(M L W Bell) *h.d.w: hld up: hdwy over 2f out: rdn to ld ins fnl f: r.o* **7/1**
421- **2** *nk* **Regal Flush**[169] 6298 3-8-10 84 .... KerrinMcEvoy 3 97
(Sir Michael Stoute) *lw: led: rdn adn hung rt fr over 1f out: hdd ins fnl f: r.o* **9/2**[2]
5-1 **3** *1 3/4* **Wandle**[27] 735 3-9-4 92 .... DaneO'Neill 7 101
(T G Mills) *lw: mid-div: hdwy over 3f out: rdn and ev ch over 1f out: styd on same pce ins fnl f* **9/2**[2]
11 **4** *2 1/2* **Players Please (USA)**[53] 563 3-9-0 88 .... KDarley 11 93
(M Johnston) *w ldrs: rdn and ev ch over 1f out: no ex ins fnl f* **9/4**[1]
01- **5** *2* **Mutadarrej (IRE)**[234] 4867 3-8-13 87 .... RHills 8 88
(J L Dunlop) *lw: b: w ldr: rdn and ev ch wl over 1f out: wknd ins fnl f* **14/1**
214- **6** *1* **Amazing Request**[193] 5828 3-8-10 84 .... SteveDrowne 4 83
(R Charlton) *h.d.w: hld up: rdn over 2f out: nvr trbld ldrs* **33/1**
-644 **7** *3* **Lazy Darren**[12] 939 3-8-4 78 oh1 .... RichardSmith 1 71
(R Hannon) *hld up: hrd rdn over 1f out: n.d* **9/1**
60-0 **8** *7* **Dora Explora**[12] 939 3-8-7 84 .... StephenDonohoe(3) 10 64
(P D Evans) *hld up: hdwy and swtchd rt 1/2-way: rdn and wknd over 1f out* **66/1**
12-4 **9** *4* **Nordic Affair**[96] 113 3-8-8 82 .... JohnEgan 2 54
(D R C Elsworth) *prom: hung rt fnl 4f: rdn and wknd over 1f out* **25/1**
53-1 **10** *12* **Rabbit Fighter (IRE)**[27] 745 3-8-10 84 .... TPO'Shea 5 34
(P A Blockley) *lw: chsd ldrs over 7f* **14/1**
12-5 **11** *12* **Safe Investment (USA)**[12] 939 3-8-12 86 .... RichardHughes 9 13
(J H M Gosden) *hld up: rdn over 2f out: sn wknd and eased* **6/1**[3]
616- **12** *70* **Tastahil (IRE)**[216] 5343 3-8-6 80 .... MartinDwyer 12 —
(B W Hills) *lw: s.i.s: sn rdn to join ldrs: lost pl 1/2-way: sn bhd and eased* **25/1**

2m 2.68s (-3.03) **Going Correction** -0.25s/f (Firm) 12 Ran SP% **129.4**
Speed ratings (Par 102):102,101,100,98,96 95,93,87,84,75 65,9
CSF £41.11 CT £166.66 TOTE £8.50: £2.40, £2.10, £2.20; EX 45.40 Place 6 £7.40, Place 5 £5.30..
Owner The Royal Ascot Racing Club **Bred** Gerrardstown House Stud **Trained** Newmarket, Suffolk

FOCUS
This race has been won by some very progressive three-year-olds in recent years, such as last year's winner Papal Bull who went on to win twice in Group company. This year's renewal was run at a fair pace and even though the time was only about average for the type of contest, they finished well spread out and there should be plenty of winners emerge from this.

NOTEBOOK
Metaphoric(IRE) ◆, carrying 2lb overweight and on very different ground to his successful debut last October, was a hard horse for the Handicapper to assess after just one outing. Making his effort widest of all, he battled on in good style to just prevail and, even though the margin was only narrow, he is entitled to carry on improving with racing especially as he should appreciate stepping up in trip again. (op 11-2)
Regal Flush ◆ was quickly sent to the front against the stands' rail and tried to make every yard. However, he hung right away from the rail over the last furlong or so to join his nearest rivals and arguably lost more ground than he was beaten by. It is hard to crab this effort, but the inference is that he did not appreciate this quick ground on an undulating track and looks capable of even better back on a softer surface. (op 5-1 tchd 6-1)
Wandle ◆, making his handicap debut after winning a four-runner maiden over a longer trip on Polytrack last time, had every chance and even though he did hold a fitness advantage over the front pair, this was still a fine effort. A return to further and possibly an easier surface should see him winning again. (op 7-2 tchd 5-1 and 11-2 in places)
Players Please(USA), unbeaten in two outings on Polytrack and making his turf debut off a 9lb higher mark, was up with the pace throughout but just lacked a turn of foot where it mattered on this different terrain. He is another that may be helped by a return to further and easier ground. (op 100-30)
Mutadarrej(IRE), not seen since winning a Chepstow maiden last August which worked out well, travelled well and raced close to the pace for much off the way before dropping out as lack of a recent run took its toll. He should be a different proposition next time. (op 11-1 tchd 16-1)
Amazing Request, another making his handicap debut, never offered a threat but did not disgrace himself either and, as there is quite a bit of stamina in his pedigree, he should be capable of better when faced with a greater test.
Nordic Affair Official explanation: jockey said colt hung right
Rabbit Fighter(IRE) Official explanation: jockey said gelding stopped quickly
Safe Investment(USA) Official explanation: jockey said colt lost its action
Tastahil(IRE) Official explanation: vet said colt returned lame

T/Plt: £8.40 to a £1 stake. Pool: £96,913.40. 8,372.95 winning tickets. T/Qpdt: £4.50 to a £1 stake. Pool: £4,233.80. 691.90 winning tickets. CR

RIPON (R-H)

Thursday, April 19

OFFICIAL GOING: Good to firm

The well watered ground was described as 'genuine good to firm with an excellent cover of grass'.

Wind: Moderate across Weather: Fine and sunny at first becoming overcast and cool

1107 EBF EAT SLEEP & DRINK AT NAGS HEAD PICKHILL MAIDEN STKS 5f

2:10 (2:12) (Class 5) 2-Y-O **£4,210** (£1,252; £625; £312) **Stalls** Low

Form RPR

1 **Cristal Clear (IRE)** 2-8-12 .... DavidAllan 5 76
(T D Easterby) *trckd ldrs: hung rt rthoughout: led 2f out: r.o strly* **12/1**

5 2 *1 1/4* **Cee Bargara**[16] [898] 2-9-3 .... TPQueally 6 76
(J A Osborne) *s.s: stdy hdwy 2f out: r.o to take 2nd ins last* **9/2**[2]

3 *1* **Dan Tucket** 2-9-3 .... TedDurcan 7 72
(M R Channon) *sn outpcd and drvn along in midfield: hdwy 2f out: styd on ins last* **16/1**

4 *1 1/4* **New Jersey (IRE)** 2-9-3 .... DO'Donohoe 1 67+
(K A Ryan) *chsd ldr: led over 2f out: sn hdd and stmbld: fdd fnl f* **11/4**[1]

0 5 *1 3/4* **Upstanding**[11] [952] 2-8-5 .... PatrickDonaghy(7) 2 55
(M Brittain) *led tl over 2f out: wknd over 1f out* **50/1**

6 *nk* **Dalarossie** 2-9-3 .... SebSanders 8 59
(E J Alston) *chsd ldrs: wknd appr fnl f* **12/1**

7 *1* **Tara's Force (IRE)** 2-8-12 .... GrahamGibbons 3 50
(J J Quinn) *dwlt: sn prom: wknd over 1f out* **10/1**

8 *hd* **Complete Frontline (GER)** 2-9-3 .... PatCosgrave 11 54
(K R Burke) *sn outpcd and pushed along: kpt on fnl 2f: nvr a factor* **33/1**

5 9 *hd* **Tazawud**[15] [926] 2-9-3 .... J-PGuillambert 12 53
(M Johnston) *swvd rt s: sn chsng ldrs: hung rt and lost pl over 2f out* **9/2**[2]

10 *10* **Ingleby Star (IRE)** 2-9-3 .... PaulFessey 10 13
(T D Barron) *s.s: a detached in rr* **5/1**[3]

61.13 secs (0.93) **Going Correction** +0.025s/f (Good) **10** Ran SP% **115.0**

Speed ratings (Par 92):93,91,89,87,84 84,82,82,81,65

CSF £64.40 TOTE £17.60: £3.80, £1.80, £4.80; EX 71.10 Trifecta £102.70 Part won. Pool £144.72 - 0.10 winning units..

Owner Mrs Jennifer E Pallister **Bred** Castlefarm Stud **Trained** Great Habton, N Yorks

FOCUS

Traditionally quite a strong maiden and the winner has a fair amount of potential while the runner-up sets a reasonable standard.

NOTEBOOK

Cristal Clear(IRE), an April foal, is one of the first crop of the French 2000 Guineas winner Clodovil. Long in the back and with an awkward head carriage, in the end she ran out a most convincing winner and could prove at least useful.

Cee Bargara, with a previous outing under his belt, missed the break but finished strongly to snatch second spot near the line. (op 100-30 tchd 3-1)

Dan Tucket, a February foal is out of a mare that won up to a mile six. A smallish, close-coupled individual, he struggled to go the pace but picked up nicely late on. (op 14-1)

New Jersey(IRE), a February foal cost 88,000gns. as a yearling. A robust, strongly-made type he showed ahead hard against the stands'-side rail at halfway but had been overtaken when he stumbled on the downhill part of the track. He was carrying tons of condition and should improve a fair bit for the outing. (op 9-4 tchd 3-1)

Upstanding, with a previous outing under her belt, took them along but in the end did not get home. (op 40-1)

Dalarossie, a March foal, is out of a tough mare that won seven times over the minimum trip for this yard at up to seven. A sharp type, he showed bags of toe before tiring and he should be better for the outing and the experience. (op 14-1 tchd 16-1)

Tazawud, having his second start, is only small and drawn on the wide outside wanted to hang right before dropping right away at the halfway mark. (op 5-1)

1108 COPT HEWICK H'CAP 6f

2:45 (2:46) (Class 4) (0-85,80) 3-Y-O **£4,731** (£1,416; £708; £354; £176) **Stalls** Low

Form RPR

404- 1 **Baltimore Jack (IRE)**[170] [6271] 3-9-1 **77** .... DaleGibson 3 84
(M W Easterby) *chsd ldrs on stands' side: kpt on wl to ld nr fin* **20/1**

34-4 2 *nk* **Sparkling Eyes**[26] [755] 3-8-10 **72** .... SebSanders 12 78
(C E Brittain) *chsd ldr: ld over 1f out: hdd and no ex nr fin* **25/1**

-134 3 *3/4* **Go On Green (IRE)**[29] [725] 3-8-11 **78** .... MarkFlynn(5) 14 82
(E A L Dunlop) *mid-div: hdwy over 2f out: kpt on wl ins last* **12/1**

40-1 4 *1/2* **Pickering**[15] [925] 3-8-13 **75** .... DavidAllan 2 80+
(E J Alston) *swvd rt s: hdwy over 2f out: n.m.r over 1f out: styd on wl towards fin* **6/1**[2]

1632 5 *hd* **Fractured Foxy**[48] [606] 3-8-10 **72** .... GrahamGibbons 6 74
(J J Quinn) *chsd ldrs: kpt on same pce ins last* **16/1**

61-3 6 *3* **Majestic Cheer**[26] [755] 3-8-13 **75** .... TedDurcan 8 68
(M R Channon) *chsd ldrs: n.m.r over 1f out: wknd ins last* **20/1**

2-21 7 *1/2* **Doubtful Sound (USA)**[36] [678] 3-9-0 **76** .... PaulFessey 5 67+
(T D Barron) *dwlt: bhd: styd on strly fnl f: nrst fin* **9/1**

1-1 8 *3/4* **Valery Borzov (IRE)**[11] [958] 3-9-4 **80** 5ex.................. AdrianTNicholls 13 69
(D Nicholls) *chsd ldrs: wknd appr fnl f* **5/2**[1]

630- 9 *1 1/4* **Fathom Five (IRE)**[201] [5681] 3-9-3 **79** .... TomEaves 7 64
(B Smart) *mid-div: kpt on fnl 2f: nvr a threat* **33/1**

120- 10 *1* **Durova (IRE)**[187] [5956] 3-8-4 **71** .... DuranFentiman(5) 11 53
(T D Easterby) *chsd ldr: tl hdd & wknd over 1f out* **33/1**

11- 11 *1 3/4* **Estimator**[112] [6965] 3-9-3 **79** .... TPQueally 9 56
(Pat Eddery) *chsd ldrs: hung rt and outpcd over 2f out: sn lost pl* **15/2**[3]

400- 12 *1/2* **Eloquent Rose (IRE)**[187] [5956] 3-8-12 **77** .... SaleemGolam(3) 4 53
(Mrs A Duffield) *chsd ldrs: lost pl over 1f out* **16/1**

01- 13 *hd* **Flying Valentino**[253] [4251] 3-9-4 **80** .... DanielTudhope 15 55
(G A Swinbank) *mid-div on wd outside: wknd over 1f out* **16/1**

003- 14 *4* **Riverside Dancer (USA)**[162] [6400] 3-8-13 **75** .... DO'Donohoe 1 38
(K A Ryan) *chsd ldrs: lost pl over 2f out* **15/2**[3]

060- 15 *13* **Prince Rossi (IRE)**[215] [5366] 3-9-0 **76** .... PatCosgrave 10 —
(J D Bethell) *in rr: bhd and eased fnl f* **40/1**

1m 12.91s (-0.09) **Going Correction** +0.025s/f (Good) **15** Ran SP% **123.4**

Speed ratings (Par 100):101,100,99,98,98 94,94,93,91,90 87,87,86,81,64

CSF £431.46 CT £6250.86 TOTE £22.30: £5.20, £4.40, £3.90; EX 551.20 TRIFECTA Not won..

Owner D Swales **Bred** P Monagnan And J Collins And G Dillon **Trained** Sheriff Hutton, N Yorks

FOCUS

A competitive three-year-old sprint handicap with little to choose between the first five home in the end. Solid form with those in the frame behind the winner close to their marks.

Pickering Official explanation: jockey said colt was denied a clear run

Doubtful Sound(USA) Official explanation: jockey said colt did not handle the track

Fathom Five(IRE) Official explanation: jockey said gelding ran too free in early stages

Prince Rossi(IRE) Official explanation: trainer had no explanation for the poor form shown

1109 RIPON SILVER BOWL CONDITIONS STKS 1m 1f 170y

3:20 (3:20) (Class 3) 4-Y-O+

£6,855 (£2,052; £1,026; £513; £256; £128) **Stalls** High

Form RPR

4330 1 **Hattan (IRE)**[26] [761] 5-9-7 110 .... SebSanders 4 112
(C E Brittain) *led: qcknd 5f out: hld on wl towards fin* **2/1**[1]

0-60 2 *nk* **Championship Point (IRE)**[70] [401] 4-9-7 .... TedDurcan 3 111
(M R Channon) *trckd ldrs: effrt over 3f out: chal over 1f out: kpt on towards fin* **11/2**

55-0 3 *2* **Nakheel**[12] [941] 4-9-0 100 .... J-PGuillambert 6 100
(M Johnston) *trckd ldrs: effrt 3f out: styd on same pce fnl 2f* **4/1**[3]

500- 4 *1 1/4* **Chantaco (USA)**[215] [5374] 5-9-0 94 .... PaulHanagan 5 98
(A M Balding) *hld up in tch: effrt on outer over 2f out: kpt on: nvr nr to chal* **11/4**[2]

/00- 5 *3 1/2* **Acropolis (IRE)**[78] [3078] 6-9-0 102 ....(p) TomEaves 2 91?
(I Semple) *hld up in last but wl in tch: drvn over 3f out: nvr trbld ldrs* **16/1**

110- 6 *7* **Macorville (USA)**[194] [5804] 4-9-3 91 .... DO'Donohoe 1 80
(G M Moore) *trckd wnr: chal over 3f out: wknd 2f out* **10/1**

2m 3.03s (-1.97) **Going Correction** +0.025s/f (Good) **6** Ran SP% **110.4**

Speed ratings (Par 107):108,107,106,105,102 96

CSF £12.87 TOTE £2.60: £2.00, £1.90; EX 15.60.

Owner Saeed Manana **Bred** Darley **Trained** Newmarket, Suffolk

FOCUS

A steady gallop for the first half mile and Sanders shrewdly wound it up from the front. Overall the form makes sense with the runner-up repeating the mark he showed first time out at three.

NOTEBOOK

Hattan(IRE), who looked very fit indeed, had the best chance of official ratings. In a tactical affair, his rider started to crank up the pace leaving the back straight and his mount answered his every call but it was a close run thing in the end. (tchd 9-4 and 5-2 in a place)

Championship Point(IRE), who had 5lb to find with the winner, was back after a ten-week break after his abortive trip to Dubai. He threw down a strong challenge to the winner but, after showing a slight tendency to hang, in the end was just held at bay. He seems at his peak in the first half of the year. (op 6-1)

Nakheel looked in good order and hopefully is on the way back after suffering a pelvic injury last spring. He was a Listed winner at two. (op 3-1)

Chantaco(USA), who had 9lb to find with the winner, sat a fraction off the pace. He stuck to his guns but was never going to enter the argument. (op 3-1 tchd 10-3 in places)

Acropolis(IRE), fourth in the 2004 Arc, has lost his way since and has cut no ice over hurdles. On his first outing for this yard and fitted with cheekpieces for the first time, he was the first to come under pressure and never threatened to take a hand. He is in the right hands to stage a revival but looks to have more stamina than speed now.

Macorville(USA), much improved and a winner three-times in handicap company last year, had a stone to find and all his wins have been with give in the ground. (op 12-1)

1110 RIPON "COCK O' THE NORTH" H'CAP 1m

3:55 (3:55) (Class 3) (0-90,88) 3-Y-O

£9,348 (£2,799; £1,399; £700; £349; £175) **Stalls** High

Form RPR

1- 1 **Manaal (USA)**[182] [6063] 3-8-5 **75** .... PaulHanagan 3 83
(Sir Michael Stoute) *hld up in rr: effrt over 3f out: nt clr run and swtchd rt 2f out: styd on to ld ins last: edgd lft: jst hld on* **11/2**

21-2 2 *shd* **Mr Napper Tandy**[26] [754] 3-9-4 **88** .... TedDurcan 2 96+
(M R Channon) *trckd ldrs: led over 1f out: hdd ins last: edgd rt: r.o towards fin: jst failed* **3/1**[2]

31-4 3 *2 1/2* **Tencendur (IRE)**[21] [815] 3-8-7 **77** .... AdrianTNicholls 9 79
(D Nicholls) *led tl over 1f out: kpt on same pce* **11/1**

140- 4 *1 1/2* **Rosbay (IRE)**[187] [5958] 3-8-12 **82** .... DavidAllan 8 81
(T D Easterby) *hld up in rr: effrt and n.m.r over 2f out: kpt on fnl f* **12/1**

140- 5 *1* **Musical Mirage (USA)**[222] [5187] 3-9-1 **85** .... DeanMcKeown 6 81
(G A Swinbank) *t.k.h: trckd ldrs: effrt over 3f out: wknd fnl f* **16/1**

120- 6 *hd* **Frosty Night (IRE)**[212] [5466] 3-9-3 **87** .... JoeFanning 1 83
(M Johnston) *in rr: hdwy 4f out: sn chsng ldrs: outpcd over 1f out: kpt on ins last* **5/1**[3]

13-2 7 *1/2* **Ravi River (IRE)**[17] [886] 3-8-13 **83** .... SebSanders 5 78
(B W Hills) *trckd ldrs: effrt 3f out: fdd over 1f out* **2/1**[1]

105- 8 *7* **Chin Wag (IRE)**[215] [5373] 3-9-1 **85** .... PatCosgrave 7 64
(K R Burke) *chsd ldr: wkng whn hmpd 2f out* **14/1**

1m 41.76s (0.66) **Going Correction** +0.025s/f (Good) **8** Ran SP% **119.0**

Speed ratings (Par 102):97,96,94,92,91 91,91,84

CSF £23.39 CT £180.87 TOTE £4.80: £1.60, £1.40, £4.00; EX 18.10 Trifecta £187.10 Pool £511.41 - 1.94 winning units..

Owner Hamdan Al Maktoum **Bred** Shadwell Farm LLC **Trained** Newmarket, Suffolk

■ Stewards' Enquiry : Ted Durcan caution: careless riding

Paul Hanagan caution: careless riding; two-day ban: careless riding (Apr 30, May 1)

FOCUS

A steady gallop and in the end the first two pulled away. The winner was making it two from two and can improve again, although the runner-up maybe should have got up.

NOTEBOOK

Manaal(USA), a lengthy filly, took a maiden at Brighton in October on her sole start at two. Shut in on the rails, she stayed on in gallant fashion but in the end it was a very close call. She will have learnt plenty and a step up in trip will be in her favour. (op 3-1)

Mr Napper Tandy, beaten by a subsequent winner at Kempton, was racing from a 4lb higher mark. He worked hard to take a narrow advantage but with his rider persisting in using his whip in his left hand, he edged right and came off just second best. (op 7-2)

Tencendur(IRE), who looked very fit indeed, had his own way in front but in the end he was no match for the first two. (op 12-1)

Rosbay(IRE), 7lb higher than his nursery success, was well supported at long odds. Tightened up when trying to improve, he was never a threat though sticking on strongly at the finish. A much stronger gallop would have played more to his strengths. (op 33-1)

Musical Mirage(USA), backward in her coat, took a keen grip and did not see it out.

Frosty Night(IRE), carrying tons of condition, seemed ill at ease on this undulating track. Staying on in his own time at the finish, there is better to come. (op 6-1 tchd 9-2)

Ravi River(IRE) saw plenty of daylight and looked as though he was keen to get on with it. In the end he did not see it out and looks set for a return to seven furlongs. (op 3-1 tchd 10-3)

1111 SKELTON MAIDEN STKS 1m
4:30 (4:31) (Class 5) 3-Y-O £3,238 (£963; £481; £240) Stalls High

Form RPR
2- 1 Colorado Rapid (IRE)[224] 5125 3-9-3 JoeFanning 13 89+
(M Johnston) *s.i.s: sn chsng ldrs: wnt 2nd over 5f out: led over 2f out: hung bdly lft: styd on wl* 4/6[1]
3222 2 2 1/2 Emerald Wilderness (IRE)[10] 968 3-9-3 76 TedDurcan 8 77
(M R Channon) *trckd ldrs: wnt 2nd 2f out: kpt on: no real imp* 4/1[2]
0- 3 6 He's Mine Too[226] 5088 3-9-3 SebSanders 6 63
(J D Bethell) *t.k.h in mid-div: hdwy on outer over 2f out: kpt on to take 3rd towards fin* 20/1
4 1/2 Jentris Girl (IRE) 3-8-12 GrahamGibbons 15 57
(T D Easterby) *s.i.s: hdwy over 3f out: kpt on fnl 2f* 100/1
462- 5 hd Jawaab (IRE)[182] 6066 3-9-3 74 PaulHanagan 9 61
(M A Buckley) *s.i.s: sn trcking ldrs: kpt on steadily fnl 2f* 11/1
024- 6 shd Run Free[187] 5959 3-9-3 68 TonyHamilton 14 61
(N Wilson) *sn prom: one pce fnl 2f* 33/1
5- 7 3/4 Chip N Pin[296] 2943 3-8-7 DuranFentiman(5) 4 54+
(T D Easterby) *s.i.s: bhd whn carried wd bnd over 6f out: hdwy on outer over 3f out: nvr nrr* 100/1
00- 8 1/2 Galway Girl (IRE)[191] 5898 3-8-12 DavidAllan 7 53?
(T D Easterby) *in rr: rn wd bnd over 6f out: kpt on fnl 3f: nvr a factor* 100/1
4- 9 hd Pagan Starprincess[254] 4228 3-8-12 DanielTudhope 10 53
(G M Moore) *hld up towards rr: stdy hdwy on inner over 2f out: nvr nr to chal* 33/1
0- 10 shd Wisdom's Kiss[169] 6290 3-9-3 PatCosgrave 3 58
(J D Bethell) *t.k.h towards rr: sme hdwy 3f out: nvr nr ldrs* 100/1
0 11 4 Malguru[10] 968 3-9-3 J-PGuillambert 11 48
(G A Swinbank) *chsd ldrs: drvn 3f out: lost pl over 1f out* 50/1
4-4 12 1/2 Strabinios King[79] 304 3-9-3 DeanMcKeown 12 47
(P C Haslam) *led tl hdd & wknd over 2f out* 33/1
3- 13 nk Dark Energy[167] 6318 3-9-3 TomEaves 1 46
(B Smart) *sn trcking ldrs: lost pl over 1f out* 8/1[3]
14 hd Ja Myford 3-9-3 PaulMulrennan 5 46
(P T Midgley) *s.i.s: sn detached in rr* 66/1

1m 41.41s (0.31) **Going Correction** +0.025s/f (Good) 14 Ran SP% 120.4
Speed ratings (Par 98):99,96,90,90,89 89,88,88,88,88 84,83,83,83
CSF £3.04 TOTE £1.70: £1.10, £1.30, £5.40; EX 3.80 Trifecta £27.40 Pool £622.27 - 16.12 winning units..
Owner Luke Lillingston **Bred** Mount Coote Stud And M Johnston **Trained** Middleham Moor, N Yorks

FOCUS
A fair maiden but no strength in depth and they went 20/1 bar four. The first two finished clear with little to choose between the next seven home. The runner-up is the best guide, the winner has the potential to go on to much better things.
Galway Girl(IRE) Official explanation: jockey said filly failed to handle the bend
Pagan Starprincess Official explanation: jockey said filly was denied a clear run

1112 NEWBY APPRENTICE H'CAP 5f
5:05 (5:05) (Class 5) (0-70,69) 4-Y-0+ £3,238 (£963; £481; £240) Stalls Low

Form RPR
-000 1 Paddywack (IRE)[2] 1074 10-8-10 60 (b) DanielleMcCreery 9 66
(D W Chapman) *s.i.s: hdwy over 2f out: styd on to ld towards fin* 11/1
50-0 2 1 Mr Rooney (IRE)[3] 1061 4-8-10 68 (t) AdeleRothery(8) 5 70
(D Nicholls) *led 1f: led over 2f out: rdn and hung rt fnl f: hdd towards fin* 6/1[3]
6-04 3 1/2 Sharp Hat[3] 1065 13-8-5 55 oh8 JamieHamblett 6 56
(D W Chapman) *chsd ldrs: kpt on wl ins last* 11/1
0-30 4 1 Beamsley Beacon[77] 320 6-8-2 55 oh10 (bt) SoniaEaton(3) 1 52
(S T Mason) *chsd ldrs: kpt on same pce appr fnl f* 33/1
2556 5 hd Ceredig[34] 688 4-8-5 55 oh1 WilliamCarson 12 51
(P W Hiatt) *chsd ldrs: kpt on same pce fnl f* 9/1
340- 6 3/4 Seven No Trumps[170] 6276 10-7-10 56 oh6 ow1 PietroRomeo(10) 3 50
(J M Bradley) *mid-div: kpt on fnl 2f: nt rch ldrs* 12/1
2405 7 nk Brut[17] 896 5-7-13 56 oh1 ow1 PNolan(7) 10 49
(D W Barker) *trckd ldrs: styd on same pce fnl 2f* 7/2[1]
6006 8 3/4 Amanda's Lad (IRE)[50] 581 7-8-0 57 oh10 ow2 PaulPickard(7) 4 47
(M C Chapman) *chsd ldrs: one pce fnl 2f* 33/1
220- 9 nk Compton Classic[152] 6521 5-8-4 57 (p) GaryBartley(3) 2 46
(J S Goldie) *in rr: hdwy on ins stands' side 2f out: nvr nr ldrs* 4/1[2]
5500 10 nk The Leather Wedge (IRE)[50] 581 8-8-2 55 oh8 MCGeran(3) 7 43
(R Johnson) *led after 1f: hdd over 2f out: wknd over 1f out* 14/1
00-4 11 3/4 Ruby's Dream[27] 746 5-8-3 56 oh5 ow1 (p) MarkCoumbe(3) 13 41
(J M Bradley) *slghtly hmpd s: mid-div: hdwy on outer over 2f out: lost pl over 1f out* 16/1
060- 12 3 1/2 Colorus (IRE)[195] 5791 4-8-11 69 NSLawes(8) 14 41
(M W Easterby) *hmpd & swtchd rt s and wnt to r far side: edgd lft and join others after 2f: chsd ldrs tl wknd over 1f out* 9/1
00-4 13 1 North Fleet[26] 751 4-8-0 58 ow2 BarrySavage(8) 15 27
(J M Bradley) *swtchd rt s: chsd ldrs: lost pl over 1f out* 12/1
600- 14 4 Zimbali[224] 5131 5-8-2 55 oh10 (p) ChrisGlenister(3) 11 9
(J M Bradley) *in rr: sme hdwy on outer over 2f out: lost pl over 1f out: sn bhd* 33/1

60.93 secs (0.73) **Going Correction** +0.025s/f (Good) 14 Ran SP% 129.9
Speed ratings (Par 103):95,93,92,91,90 89,89,87,87,86 85,80,78,72
CSF £80.69 CT £766.09 TOTE £13.90: £3.20, £2.80, £4.00; EX 81.70 Trifecta £337.50 Part won. Pool £475.42 - 0.50 winning units. Place 6 £1,074.82, Place 5 £275.21..
Owner David W Chapman **Bred** C McEvoy **Trained** Stillington, N Yorks
■ Stewards' Enquiry : Barry Savage three-day ban; careless riding and not keeping straight from the stalls (Apr 30, May 1-2)

FOCUS
A low-grade apprentices' handicap won by a ten-year-old with the third three years older and very ordianry form for the grade. The winning time was also moderate for the class, just 0.2 seconds faster than the earlier two-year-old maiden.
T/Plt: £805.00 to a £1 stake. Pool: £65,008.50. 58.95 winning tickets. T/Qpdt: £19.30 to a £1 stake. Pool: £4,704.40. 180.00 winning tickets. WG

1113 - 1116a (Foreign Racing) - See Raceform Interactive

1033 LINGFIELD (L-H)
Friday, April 20

OFFICIAL GOING: Standard
There seemed a slight bias to those who raced handily.
Wind: light against

1117 LINGFIELD PARK GOLF CLUB MEDIAN AUCTION MAIDEN STKS 7f (P)
5:15 (5:18) (Class 6) 3-4-Y-O £2,730 (£806; £403) Stalls Low

Form RPR
6-3 1 Teen Ager (FR)[27] 758 3-8-13 LPKeniry 4 77+
(J S Moore) *prom: trckd ldr 3f out: rdn to ld over 1f out: styd on wl and grad drew clr* 12/1
032- 2 1 3/4 Le Singe Noir[185] 6034 3-8-13 73 J-PGuillambert 1 72
(D M Simcock) *chsd ldrs: pushed along 3f out: prog on inner to chse ldng pair over 2f out: plld out and kpt on to take 2nd nr fin* 12/1
420- 3 nk Obstructive[205] 5607 3-8-13 74 RobertHavlin 5 71
(D K Ivory) *taken down early: reluctant to enter stalls: led: gng easily over 2f out: rdn and hdd over 1f out: nt qckn* 16/1
-5 4 nk Everygrainofsand (IRE)[17] 901 4-9-12 GeorgeBaker 9 74
(J R Best) *towards rr: prog and n.m.r over 2f out: outpcd sn after: styd on wl fnl f: gaining at fin* 16/1
0- 5 2 1/2 Mutual Friend (USA)[174] 6214 3-8-10 StephenDonohoe(3) 10 64
(E A L Dunlop) *s.i.s: sn trckd ldrs: effrt to go 4th 2f out: sn outpcd: rdn and no rspnse* 11/10[1]
-423 6 1 3/4 Racing Times[27] 752 3-8-13 72 PaulDoe 7 59
(W J Knight) *taken down early: plld hrd early: hld up and wl in rr: prog on wd outside over 2f out: outpcd sn after: one pce* 5/2[2]
-255 7 nk Follow The Flag (IRE)[28] 737 3-8-13 69 JamesDoyle 2 59+
(N P Littmoden) *towards rr: effrt over 2f out: outpcd whn nt clr run wl over 1f out: n.d* 8/1[3]
-222 8 3/4 Bertie Swift[69] 423 3-8-13 68 JimCrowley 8 57
(J Gallagher) *prom tl fdd over 2f out* 16/1
634- 9 1/2 Distiller (IRE)[203] 5647 3-8-13 72 RichardMullen 11 55
(W R Muir) *a towards rr and sn pushed along: brief effrt on inner over 2f out: sn btn* 50/1
10 1 Samsons Son 3-8-10 StephaneBreux(3) 3 53
(J R Best) *dwlt: a struggling in rr* 66/1
00- 11 1 3/4 Itsawindup[138] 6689 3-8-13 AdrianMcCarthy 12 48
(W J Knight) *pressed ldr to 3f out: sn wknd* 66/1
12 nk Massams Lane 3-8-13 AdamKirby 13 47
(P S McEntee) *s.i.s and hld up fr wd draw: a bhd* 66/1
50- 13 9 Dancing Jest (IRE)[175] 6199 3-8-8 ChrisCatlin 6 19
(Rae Guest) *sn t.o* 66/1

1m 25.01s (-0.88) **Going Correction** -0.15s/f (Stan)
WFA 3 from 4yo 13lb 13 Ran SP% 128.3
Speed ratings (Par 101):99,97,96,96,93 91,91,90,89,88 86,86,75
CSF £156.30 TOTE £15.30: £6.00, £3.90, £4.20; EX 139.60.
Owner Mrs Fitri Hay **Bred** Haras De Beauvoir **Trained** Upper Lambourn, Berks

FOCUS
Just an ordinary pace in which there seemed to be a bias in favour of those that raced handily. The winning time was 0.79 seconds slower than the following 51-65 handicap and the form is best rated around the placed horses.
Follow The Flag(IRE) Official explanation: jockey said gelding was denied a clear run
Massams Lane Official explanation: jockey said gelding never travelled
Dancing Jest(IRE) Official explanation: jockey said filly did not face the kickback

1118 LINGFIELD PARK FOR CONFERENCES H'CAP 7f (P)
5:45 (5:47) (Class 6) (0-65,65) 4-Y-0+ £2,388 (£705; £352) Stalls Low

Form RPR
0-11 1 Cativo Cavallino[35] 687 4-8-3 55 NataliaGemelova(5) 10 69
(J E Long) *chsd ldng pair tl wnt 2nd after 3f: clr of rest fr 3f out: led jst over 2f out: rdn clr 1f out: tired but unchal* 7/1[3]
00-5 2 1 1/4 Capricho (IRE)[17] 902 10-8-13 60 (b) PaulDoe 6 71
(J Akehurst) *dwlt: off the pce towards rr: prog 2f out: wnt 2nd last 150yds: clsd on wnr but unable to chal* 12/1
0321 3 3 Special Place[16] 923 4-9-4 65 GeorgeBaker 14 68+
(J A R Toller) *stdd s: sn wl off the pce in rr: prog over 2f out: rdn and styd on to snatch 3rd last strides: no ch* 7/2[2]
0/0- 4 shd New Proposal (IRE)[352] 1402 5-8-8 55 DarryllHolland 12 58
(A P Jarvis) *taken down early: chsd ldrs: outpcd fr 1/2-way: kpt on fnl 2f: n.d* 33/1
0010 5 1/2 Marmooq[11] 980 4-8-6 56 JerryO'Dwyer(3) 5 57
(J Gallagher) *drvn to ld and set str pce: clr of rest whn hdd jst over 2f out: wknd fnl f* 8/1
0650 6 3 Mine The Balance (IRE)[15] 932 4-8-7 54 ow2 (b) LPKeniry 3 48
(H J Manners) *hld up and sn wl off the pce: no real prog over 2f out: plugged on fnl f* 33/1
6201 7 2 High Ambition[11] 980 4-9-3 64 6ex (v) SebSanders 13 52
(P W D'Arcy) *stdd s and sn off the pce in rr: effrt on outer over 2f out: sn no prog u.p* 3/1[1]
2414 8 1/2 King After[6] 1036 5-8-8 58 (v) StephaneBreux(3) 7 45
(J R Best) *chsd ldrs: rdn and nt on terms 1/2-way: no ch fnl 2f* 15/2
100- 9 2 Prince Valentine[189] 5937 6-8-7 54 FergusSweeney 9 36
(G L Moore) *hld up: sn wl off the pce in last pair: nvr a factor* 12/1
320- 10 2 Inka Dancer (IRE)[139] 6672 5-8-10 57 AdrianMcCarthy 4 34
(B Palling) *chsd ldr for 3f: wknd 2f out* 20/1
503- 11 1 1/2 Devonia Plains (IRE)[263] 3996 5-8-8 62 NBazeley(7) 8 35
(Mrs P N Dutfield) *dwlt: a wl in rr: u.p and struggling 1/2-way* 25/1
0303 12 1 1/4 Seneschal[16] 923 6-9-3 64 ChrisCatlin 2 34
(A B Haynes) *hld up in midfield and off the pce: gng wl enough over 2f out: wknd tamely over 1f out* 8/1
5020 13 1 Hand Chime[15] 932 10-7-12 52 AmyBaker(7) 1 19
(Miss J Feilden) *dwlt: a off the pce and wl in rr* 25/1

1m 24.22s (-1.67) **Going Correction** -0.15s/f (Stan) 13 Ran SP% 127.4
Speed ratings (Par 101):103,101,98,98,97 94,91,91,88,86 84,83,82
CSF £87.78 CT £362.13 TOTE £9.40: £2.60, £3.70, £1.60; EX 93.20.
Owner P Saxon **Bred** Miss A M Rees **Trained** Caterham, Surrey

FOCUS
A modest handicap, but reasonable form for the grade. Just as in the first race, it appeared an advantage to race handy and the winner is rated back to the level of his juvenile form. The winning time was 0.79 seconds quicker than the opening maiden.
Inka Dancer(IRE) Official explanation: jockey said mare hung right home straight

1119 HOLD YOUR PRODUCT LAUNCH HERE CLASSIFIED STKS 1m (P)
6:15 (6:16) (Class 7) 3-Y-0+ £2,184 (£644; £322) Stalls High

Form RPR
6363 **1** **Kinsman (IRE)**[30] 721 10-9-7 45..............................(p) J-PGuillambert 1 52
(T D McCarthy) *trckd ldng pair gng wl: effrt 2f out: led over 1f out: edgd rt and drvn out: hld on* **15/2**
-646 **2** *1/2* **Homecroft Boy**[74] 360 3-8-7 44 ow3................. StephenDonohoe(3) 12 50
(P D Evans) *hld up and sn last: plenty to do whn effrt over 2f out: str run on outer to go 2nd last 100yds: gaining fast but too much to do* **13/2**[3]
-336 **3** *1 1/4* **Foreland Sands (IRE)**[25] 786 3-8-4 45................ StephaneBreux(3) 11 44
(J R Best) *hld up in rr: prog over 2f out: drvn to dispute 2nd jst ins fnl f: kpt on same pce* **5/2**[1]
-000 **4** *shd* **Pajada**[52] 577 3-8-7 45.. RichardSmith 7 44
(M D I Usher) *chsd ldrs: rdn and lost pl 1/2-way: effrt and nt clr run on inner over 2f out: drvn to dispute 2nd ins fnl f: one pce* **16/1**
0002 **5** *3* **Dexileos (IRE)**[30] 721 8-9-7 45................................(t) FergusSweeney 4 41
(David Pinder) *trckd ldrs: rdn to go 2nd briefly over 2f out: wknd over 1f out* **6/1**[2]
05-0 **6** *1* **Global Achiever**[28] 743 6-9-0 45..........................(p) MarvinCheung(7) 5 39
(G C H Chung) *led for 2f: w ldr tl led again 3f out to over 1f out: bmpd along furiously and wknd* **12/1**
0-03 **7** *5* **Grand Welcome (IRE)**[18] 887 5-9-0 44....................(bt) SCreighton(7) 2 27
(E J Creighton) *led after 2f to 3f out: wknd rapidly over 2f out* **10/1**
060- **8** *2 1/2* **Batchworth Blaise**[188] 5969 4-9-7 45.......................... PaulFitzsimons 9 21
(E A Wheeler) *t.k.h: hld up in rr: sltly hmpd after 3f: no prog 2f out: wknd* **50/1**
0-06 **9** *nk* **Agnes Gift**[29] 728 4-9-7 45... JamieMackay 6 21
(Rae Guest) *chsd ldrs: u.p and struggling fr 1/2-way: wknd* **9/1**
5550 **10** *1 1/4* **Big Ralph**[17] 907 4-9-7 43...(b) JimmyQuinn 8 18
(M Wigham) *sn pushed along to chse ldrs: wknd u.p over 2f out* **8/1**
400- **11** *2* **Sahara Dawn (IRE)**[190] 5923 3-8-7 45........................ DanielTudhope 10 9
(D Carroll) *a in rr: detached in last pair over 2f out* **16/1**
00-0 **12** *2* **Golden Ribbons**[25] 786 3-8-7 44.................................. DarrylHolland 3 5
(J R Boyle) *a in rr: detached in last pair over 2f out* **33/1**

1m 39.42s (-0.01) **Going Correction** -0.15s/f (Stan)
WFA 3 from 4yo+ 14lb 12 Ran SP% **122.5**
Speed ratings (Par 97):94,93,92,92,89 88,83,80,80,79 77,75
CSF £57.64 TOTE £8.20: £2.50, £3.20, £2.40; EX 82.20.
Owner W Weeding **Bred** Elsdon Farms **Trained** Godstone, Surrey

FOCUS
A very moderate classified event, best rated through the winner.

1120 BANQUETING AT LINGFIELD PARK H'CAP 6f (P)
6:45 (6:46) (Class 6) (0-50,50) 4-Y-0+ £2,388 (£705; £352) Stalls Low

Form RPR
0501 **1** **Union Jack Jackson (IRE)**[24] 801 5-8-9 50...(b) StephenDonohoe(3) 2 61+
(John A Harris) *trckd ldrs gng wl: effrt and got through to ld jst ins fnl f: rdn out* **11/2**[3]
0002 **2** *3/4* **Midmaar (IRE)**[16] 920 6-8-12 50..................................(b) JamieMackay 4 57
(M Wigham) *pressed ldng pair: rdn to ld narrowly wl over 1f out: hdd jst ins fnl f: one pce* **9/1**
6155 **3** *1 1/4* **Primarily**[18] 892 5-8-10 48.. LPKeniry 7 51
(Peter Grayson) *pushed along in midfield over 3f out: effrt u.p on outer over 1f out: styd on fnl f: tk 3rd nr fin* **8/1**
0033 **4** *hd* **Laith (IRE)**[24] 800 4-8-12 50...(p) MickyFenton 11 53
(Miss V Haigh) *trckd ldrs: produced to chal 1f out: fnd nil* **10/1**
4634 **5** *nk* **Muktasb (USA)**[24] 797 6-8-12 50..................................(v) AdamKirby 3 52
(D Shaw) *stdd s: hld up: gng wl enough over 1f out: sn rdn and nt qckn: styd on ins fnl f* **7/1**
-003 **6** *1/2* **Cosmic Destiny (IRE)**[4] 1067 5-8-12 50...................... RichardMullen 6 50
(E F Vaughan) *plld hrd: hld up in rr: gng strly over 1f out: sn rdn and fnd nil: styd on ins fnl f* **11/2**[3]
0443 **7** *3/4* **Ask No More**[36] 680 4-8-9 50...............................(b) DominicFox(3) 1 48
(P L Gilligan) *drvn to ld on inner: hdd wl over 1f out: wknd fnl f* **9/2**[1]
4400 **8** *2 1/2* **Christian Bendix**[11] 980 5-8-10 48............................(p) JimmyQuinn 12 39
(P Howling) *w ldng pair to 2f out: wknd over 1f out* **16/1**
006/ **9** *3/4* **Juxta Pose**[538] 6150 4-8-12 50... JimCrowley 10 38
(P Winkworth) *outpcd: last and virtually t.o over 2f out: r.o fnl f* **33/1**
6541 **10** *shd* **King Of Charm (IRE)**[30] 722 4-8-11 49.................(b) FergusSweeney 8 37
(G L Moore) *racd on outer: nvr bttr than midfield: rdn over 2f out: wknd over 1f out* **5/1**[2]
000- **11** *hd* **Parthenope**[265] 3950 4-8-10 48.................................... RichardThomas 5 35
(J A Geake) *chsd ldng trio to over 2f out: sn wknd* **40/1**
00-6 **12** *1* **Straight Gal (IRE)**[24] 798 4-8-12 50................................ JamesDoyle 9 34
(Mrs N Smith) *dwlt: a in rr: struggling fr 1/2-way* **33/1**

1m 12.16s (-0.65) **Going Correction** -0.15s/f (Stan) 12 Ran SP% **122.5**
Speed ratings (Par 101):98,97,95,95,94 94,93,89,88,88 88,86
CSF £55.55 CT £410.50 TOTE £8.60: £2.50, £2.50, £4.20; EX 50.50.
Owner Adrian Swingler **Bred** Tom Foley **Trained** Eastwell, Leics

FOCUS
A moderate sprint handicap run in a time 0.68 seconds slower than the following 66-80 and rated around the principals.
King Of Charm(IRE) Official explanation: jockey said gelding hung right
Straight Gal(IRE) Official explanation: jockey said filly was hampered on leaving stalls

1121 LINGFIELD PARK FOR WEDDINGS H'CAP 6f (P)
7:15 (7:17) (Class 4) (0-80,80) 4-Y-0+ £4,857 (£1,445; £722; £360) Stalls Low

Form RPR
000- **1** **Orpsie Boy (IRE)**[237] 4807 4-9-1 77.............................. GeorgeBaker 7 87
(N P Littmoden) *stdd s: hld up in last trio: rapid prog and dream run on inner over 1f out: drvn and r.o bravely to ld nr fin* **4/1**[2]
0202 **2** *hd* **Effective**[26] 774 7-8-11 73.. DarryllHolland 5 82
(A P Jarvis) *pressed ldr: rdn to ld over 1f out: styd on fnl f: collared nr fin* **7/1**[3]
0426 **3** *2 1/2* **Figaro Flyer (IRE)**[4] 1061 4-8-13 80......................... AnnStokell(5) 4 82
(P Howling) *cl up: chsd ldng pair over 2f out: tried to chal jst over 1f out: one pce* **9/1**
160- **4** *nk* **Peter Island (FR)**[214] 5427 4-9-4 80.............................. JimCrowley 3 81
(J Gallagher) *led: kicked on over 2f out: hdd over 1f out: fading nr fin* **25/1**
500- **5** *1* **Wicked Uncle**[286] 3281 8-8-13 75...........................(v) J-PGuillambert 2 73
(S Gollings) *settled midfield: rdn and nt qckn wl over 1f out: styd on ins fnl f* **33/1**
2-11 **6** *hd* **Louphole**[74] 361 5-9-0 76... SebSanders 11 73
(P J Makin) *stdd s: hld up in last trio: effrt and sme prog over 1f out: no imp ldrs last 100yds* **3/1**[1]
5033 **7** *shd* **Garstang**[21] 827 4-9-2 78............................(b) RobbieFitzpatrick 6 77+
(Peter Grayson) *trckd ldrs: 4th over 1f out: rdn and no imp whn nt clr run ins fnl f and eased* **10/1**
-602 **8** *shd* **Magic Rush**[19] 865 5-8-12 77.................................. JerryO'Dwyer(3) 12 74
(Mrs Norma Pook) *nvr bttr than midfield: drvn over 2f out: no prog* **12/1**
500- **9** *nk* **Fast Bowler**[158] 6461 4-8-12 77........................... StephenDonohoe(3) 1 73
(J M P Eustace) *settled in midfield: effrt on inner 2f out: no prog over 1f out* **7/1**[3]
2264 **10** *1* **Katiypour (IRE)**[27] 765 10-9-2 78..........................(p) RichardThomas 8 71
(P Mitchell) *hld up in last trio: effrt on outer 2f out: sn no prog* **8/1**
50-0 **11** *3* **Law Maker**[21] 835 7-8-10 72...(v) MickyFenton 9 56
(A Bailey) *pressed ldng pair to wl over 2f out: sn struggling* **20/1**
1121 **12** *1/2* **Egyptian Lord**[23] 810 4-9-0 76............................. FrankieMcDonald 10 58
(Peter Grayson) *rrd s: chsd ldrs on outer: wknd 2f out* **14/1**

1m 11.48s (-1.33) **Going Correction** -0.15s/f (Stan) 12 Ran SP% **126.1**
Speed ratings (Par 105):102,101,98,98,96 96,96,96,95,94 90,89
CSF £33.82 CT £249.57 TOTE £3.90: £2.00, £2.00, £2.20; EX 43.20.
Owner Miss Vanessa Church **Bred** Minch Bloodstock **Trained** Newmarket, Suffolk

FOCUS
A fair sprint handicap run in a time 0.68 seconds quicker than the previous 46-50, but the form looks pretty solid, rated through the fourth.
Garstang Official explanation: jockey said gelding was denied a clear run

1122 LINGFIELDPARK.CO.UK H'CAP 1m 2f (P)
7:45 (7:47) (Class 4) (0-80,80) 3-Y-O £4,857 (£1,445; £541; £541) Stalls Low

Form RPR
1-2 **1** **Serengeti**[44] 638 3-9-4 80.. JoeFanning 13 95+
(M Johnston) *s.i.s: sn rcvrd on outer to press ldrs: effrt to ld 2f out: clr 1f out: rdn and in no real danger after* **9/4**[1]
013- **2** *2* **Mafeking (UAE)**[146] 6599 3-9-1 77................................ FergusSweeney 4 83
(M R Hoad) *edgy bef gng in stalls: hld up in rr: prog on inner wl over 1f out: styd on to take 2nd ins fnl f: no ch w wnr* **20/1**
-521 **3** *3/4* **Resplendent Ace (IRE)**[30] 720 3-9-1 77........................ JimmyQuinn 2 82
(P Howling) *trckd ldrs: n.m.r after 2f: effrt over 2f out: kpt on fr over 1f out* **16/1**
21 **3** *dht* **Warm Embraces (IRE)**[27] 758 3-8-10 75.................. MarcHalford(3) 8 80
(D R C Elsworth) *trckd ldrs: effrt to chal 2f out: brushed aside by wnr over 1f out: one pce* **9/2**[3]
20-1 **5** *1* **Sir Liam (USA)**[25] 788 3-8-8 77................................ JackMitchell(7) 1 80+
(P Mitchell) *settled in midfield: effrt whn n.m.r over 2f out and lost pl: styd on fr over 1f out: nt rch ldrs* **16/1**
333- **6** *2 1/2* **Spiderback (IRE)**[181] 6106 3-8-10 72................................ PatDobbs 10 70
(R Hannon) *hld up in last pair: outpcd 2f out: styd on fnl f: no ch* **16/1**
145- **7** *shd* **Sri Pekan Two**[213] 5459 3-9-4 80.. EddieAhern 6 78
(P F I Cole) *trckd ldrs: rdn over 2f out: no imp over 1f out: wknd* **11/4**[2]
4203 **8** *nk* **Title Deed (USA)**[26] 772 3-8-10 72................................. SebSanders 7 69
(A P Jarvis) *led for 2f: pressed ldr: led again over 2f out to 2f out: wknd rapidly fnl f* **20/1**
1- **9** *3/4* **Happy Go Lily**[166] 6349 3-9-4 80..................................... AdamKirby 12 76
(W R Swinburn) *settled in last pair: wl off the pce whn wd bnd 2f out: plugged on* **10/1**
312- **10** *nk* **Shouldntbethere (IRE)**[143] 6639 3-8-8 70...................... JimCrowley 5 65
(Mrs P N Dutfield) *settled in midfield: gng wl enough 3f out: sme prog on outer 2f out: wknd over 1f out* **66/1**
4-1 **11** *1* **Jaady (USA)**[24] 795 3-9-0 76.. RHills 11 70
(J H M Gosden) *dwlt: hld up in rr: taken v wd bnd 2f out: no prog* **9/1**
2013 **12** *6* **Cherri Fosfate**[15] 935 3-9-0 76.................................(b) DanielTudhope 3 58
(D Carroll) *chsd ldrs: rdn over 3f out: wknd over 2f out: n.m.r over 1f out* **20/1**
2216 **13** *2 1/2* **My Mirasol**[52] 572 3-8-4 66.. ChrisCatlin 9 43
(D E Cantillon) *led after 2f to over 2f out: wkng rapidly whn n.m.r over 1f out* **33/1**

2m 5.19s (-2.60) **Going Correction** -0.15s/f (Stan) 13 Ran SP% **131.1**
Speed ratings (Par 100):104,102,101,101,101 99,98,98,98,97 97,92,90
PL Resplendant Ace £2.40, Warm Embraces £0.80; TR Serengeti/Mafeking/RA £322.67, SI/MG/WE £104.61 CSF £60.20 CT £104.61 TOTE £3.70: £1.20, £9.60, £0.80; EX 98.90 Place 6 £413.57, Place 5 £56.34.
Owner Sheikh Mohammed **Bred** Darley **Trained** Middleham Moor, N Yorks

FOCUS
A fair middle-distance handicap and the form looks solid rated around the placed horses.
My Mirasol Official explanation: trainer said filly bled from the nose
T/Plt: £235.10 to a £1 stake. Pool: £60,000.80. 186.25 winning tickets. T/Qpdt: £25.10 to a £1 stake. Pool: £5,177.90. 152.10 winning tickets. JN

NEWBURY (L-H)
Friday, April 20

OFFICIAL GOING: Good to firm (good in places)
Wind: moderate across

1123 BURGES SALMON EUROPEAN BREEDERS' FUND MAIDEN STKS 5f 34y
1:40 (1:44) (Class 4) 2-Y-O £6,477 (£1,927; £963; £481) Stalls High

Form RPR
1 **Winker Watson** 2-9-3 .... JimmyFortune 9 90+
(P W Chapple-Hyam) *w'like: str: scope: towards rr but in tch: gd hdwy 2f out: drvn and qcknd to ld appr fnl f: r.o strly* **9/4**[1]
2 *2 1/2* **Legendary Guest** 2-9-3 .... DarryllHolland 10 78
(M R Channon) *w'like: scope: chsd ldrs: drvn along 2f out: styd on wl to chse wnr fnl f but no imp* **9/1**
3 *nk* **Party In The Park** 2-9-3 .... RichardHughes 7 77
(R Hannon) *unf: b.bkwd: pressed ldr tl led jst ins fnl 2f: sn rdn: hdd appr fnl f: kpt on same pce ins last* **16/1**
4 *1 1/4* **Harlech Castle** 2-9-3 .... JoeFanning 4 72
(P F I Cole) *unf: b.bkwd: disp ld 3f: styd pressing ldrs tl outpcd ins fnl f* **8/1**
5 *shd* **Mansii** 2-9-3 .... SebSanders 6 71
(C E Brittain) *w'like: scope: b.bkwd: in tch but sn pushed along: kpt on ins fnl f but nvr gng pce to rch ldrs* **33/1**
6 *1/2* **Nacho Libre** 2-9-3 .... MichaelHills 3 69
(B W Hills) *w'like: scope: b.bkwd: rr but in tch: pushed along 1/2-way: hdwy: styd on fr over 1f out: kpt on same pce fnl 100yds* **3/1**[2]
7 *1/2* **Flying Indian** 2-8-12 .... MartinDwyer 11 62
(A M Balding) *w'like: b.bkwd: s.i.s: bhd: shkn up 2f out: kpt on ins last but nvr in contention* **16/1**

6 **8** *2* **Private Code**[13] [942] 2-8-12 .... JohnEgan 1 54
(T J Pitt) *chsd ldrs: rdn 2f out: wknd fnl f* **16/1**

9 *shd* **Rough Rock (IRE)** 2-9-3 .... LDettori 2 59
(B J Meehan) *w'like: b.bkwd: rr: shkn up 1/2-way: sme prog fnl f* **12/1**

10 *6* **No Nines** 2-9-3 .... RHills 8 35
(B W Hills) *w'like: str: s.i.s: a outpcd* **9/2**[3]

0 **11** *hd* **Lord Deevert**[13] [942] 2-9-0 .... AmirQuinn(3) 5 34
(W G M Turner) *w'like: pressed ldrs: rdn over 2f out: sddle slipped and lost pl over 1f out* **100/1**

61.37 secs (-1.19) **Going Correction** -0.325s/f (Firm) **11** Ran SP% **124.3**
Speed ratings (Par 94):96,92,91,89,89 88,87,84,84,74 74
CSF £25.56 TOTE £3.30: £1.70, £2.80, £3.20; EX 34.20.

Owner The Comic Strip Heroes & Mrs J D Trotter **Bred** Mrs John Trotter **Trained** Newmarket, Suffolk

FOCUS
This looked like a very good maiden - plenty of powerful juvenile stables were represented and they looked a nice bunch in the paddock. They raced towards the stands' side, but not tight against the rail.

NOTEBOOK
Winker Watson ◆, a 56,000gns half-brother to five winners, including dual 5f two-year-old scorer Choysia, justified market confidence to make a winning debut. He clearly knew his job, as having travelled better than anything throughout, he was most professional when asked to go and win the race. He looks a very useful prospect and his trainer said afterwards he will either go for the National Stakes at Sandown, or head straight to Royal Ascot. (op 15-8 tchd 5-2 in places)
Legendary Guest, a 45,000gns half-brother to 6f two-year-old winner Mafaheem, out of a 5f juvenile winner, took the eye in the paddock and ran a nice ran in second. He probably just bumped into a very useful sort and should have little bother in winning a similar event. (op 10-1)
Party In The Park, a 62,000gns half-brother to 7f juvenile winner Hallandale, and Lindbergh, a 5f winner at three, out of a multiple 5-6f two-year-old scorer, showed good speed throughout. He could prove hard to beat in an ordinary maiden next time. (tchd 18-1)
Harlech Castle ◆, a half-brother to five winners, including useful triple 5-7f juvenile winner Brecon Beacon, and very useful sprinter Eisteddfod, out of a useful 6f-1m winner, showed signs of inexperience and can be expected to improve next time. (op 4-1)
Mansii, a 25,000gns half-brother to Chicago Nights, who was placed over 6f at two, lacked the speed of some of these but kept on well for pressure. He can be expected to do better when stepped up to 6f.
Nacho Libre ◆, a 150,000euros half-brother to among others high-class dual 5-6f juvenile winner Always Hopeful, was caught out wide and never looked like troubling the principals. He can do better. (op 4-1)
Flying Indian, a 25,000gns half-sister to In Reality, who was placed over 6f at two, later a winner in US, out of a 1m winner, was the first runner for Hawk Wing as a sire. She travelled nicely for much of the way, but just lacked the speed to go with some of these late on and gave the impression she will come into her own over slightly further at a lesser track.
Private Code showed some ability on her debut at Kempton and, even though she raced widest of all, she helps give the form a solid look.
No Nines, a 40,000gns half-brother to five sprint winners, notably Golden Nun, a very smart multiple 6f winner, out of a triple 5-6f winner at two and three, was backed down from 20/1 to 9/2 on course, but he was never seen with a chance after starting slowly. (op 20-1)
Lord Deevert Official explanation: jockey said saddle slipped

1124 DUBAI DUTY FREE FINEST SURPRISE H'CAP 7f (S)
2:10 (2:14) (Class 3) (0-95,95) 3-Y-O

£9,971 (£2,985; £1,492; £747; £372; £187) **Stalls** High

Form RPR

1- **1** **Phoenix Tower (USA)**[172] [6254] 3-8-11 **88** .... RichardHughes 12 103+
(H R A Cecil) *unf: scope: lw: trckd ldrs: qcknd to ld 1f out: sn clr: easily* **9/2**[2]

310- **2** *4* **Jaasoos (IRE)**[208] [5546] 3-8-5 **82** .... MatthewHenry 7 87
(M A Jarvis) *swtg: pressed ldrs tl led 4f out: rdn over 2f out: hdd 1f out: kpt on wl to hold 2nd but no ch w wnr* **14/1**

1- **3** *3/4* **Escape Route (USA)**[182] [6072] 3-8-11 **88** .... JimmyFortune 9 91+
(J H M Gosden) *towards rr but in tch: drvn and styd on fr 2f out: kpt on ins last: styd on cl home* **3/1**[1]

132- **4** *1/2* **Aqmaar**[205] [5624] 3-8-13 **90** .... RHills 15 92
(J L Dunlop) *w ldr: slt advantage after 2f: narrowly hdd 4f out: styd pressing ldrs: rdn 2f out: one pce fnl f* **6/1**

100- **5** *hd* **Soviet Palace (IRE)**[234] [4912] 3-8-8 **85** .... NCallan 6 86
(K A Ryan) *swtg: led 2f: styd pressing ldrs and stl wl there over 1f out: no ex ins last* **66/1**

21- **6** *3/4* **Thunder Storm Cat (USA)**[216] [5371] 3-9-1 **92** .... JoeFanning 16 91
(P F I Cole) *b.bkwd: chsd ldrs: rdn over 2f out: styd on same pce fr over 1f out* **5/1**[3]

531- **7** *nk* **Cool Box (USA)**[160] [6444] 3-8-7 **84** .... JamesDoyle 8 82
(Mrs A J Perrett) *towards rr: rdn 3f out: styd on fr over 1f out: kpt on nr fin but nvr in contention* **33/1**

604- **8** *1* **Lunces Lad (IRE)**[187] [5989] 3-8-8 **85** .... TedDurcan 2 81+
(M R Channon) *s.i.s: bhd: effrt and nt clr run 2f out: styd on ins fnl f: gng on cl home* **16/1**

1-02 **9** *shd* **Cesc**[16] [922] 3-9-1 **92** .... EddieAhern 4 87
(P J Makin) *lw: mid-div: pushed along and hday to chse ldrs 2f out: nvr quite gng pce to be competitive: wknd ins last* **12/1**

00-2 **10** *1/2* **El Bosque (IRE)**[13] [943] 3-8-13 **90** .... JimCrowley 14 84
(B R Millman) *chsd ldrs: rdn over 2f out: wkng whn hmpd over 1f out* **25/1**

004- **11** *nk* **Mubaashir (IRE)**[181] [6100] 3-9-1 **95** .... StephenDonohoe(3) 5 88
(E A L Dunlop) *rr: rdn over 2f out: kpt on fnl f but nvr in contention* **28/1**

12 *2 1/2* **Ask The Butler**[239] [4750] 3-8-7 **84** .... MickyFenton 13 71
(A W Carroll) *s.i.s: a bhd* **50/1**

230- **13** *1 1/2* **Everymanforhimself (IRE)**[195] [5806] 3-9-4 **95** .... TPQueally 11 78
(J G Given) *lw: pressed ldrs: rdn 3f out: wknd over 1f out* **25/1**

21-5 **14** *3/4* **Princess Valerina**[20] [838] 3-8-8 **85** ow1 .... MichaelHills 1 66
(B W Hills) *wnt bdly lft s: sn rcvrd to chse ldrs: wknd over 1f out* **9/1**

1m 23.35s (-3.65) **Going Correction** -0.325s/f (Firm) **14** Ran SP% **121.9**
Speed ratings (Par 102):107,102,101,101,100 99,99,98,98,97 97,94,92,91
CSF £62.06 CT £223.37 TOTE £5.10: £2.10, £4.70, £1.70; EX 114.00.

Owner K Abdulla **Bred** Juddmonte Farms Inc **Trained** Newmarket, Suffolk

FOCUS
This looked like a competitive handicap beforehand, but Phoenix Tower bolted up and looks a potential Pattern-class performer, and the form has been rated positively. The winning time was 0.95 seconds quicker than the fillies' maiden. Once again they all raced stands' side and, although nobody seemed too desperate to grab the rail, a middle to high draw was an advantage.

NOTEBOOK
Phoenix Tower(USA) ◆ only had a Wolverhampton maiden success to his name coming into this, but he has clearly done well over the winter and left that form well behind with a most impressive success. The Jersey Stakes was mentioned as a possible target, but his trainer feels he is more of a miler and the 7f trip could just be on the short side. It will be interesting to see whether he goes for a big handicap next time - races like the Silver Bowl at Haydock and the Britannia spring to mind - or is stepped up to Listed/Group company. (op 3-1 tchd 5-1 in places)
Jaasoos(IRE) had conditions to suit for his first run in 208 days and ran a pleasing race behind the potentially smart winner. He is on to keep on the right side of when the ground is quick. (op 16-1 tchd 12-1)
Escape Route(USA), the winner of a Lingfield maiden on his sole start as a juvenile, has been given a entry in both the Guineas and the Derby. He ran well, but just gave the impression this run will sharpen him and he may also benefit from a step up to 1m. (op 7-2)
Aqmaar ran well off the back of a 205-day break and is another open to improvement. (op 9-1 tchd 10-1 in places)
Soviet Palace(IRE), gelded since he was last seen, ran a big race and shaped with plenty of promise for the season ahead. (tchd 80-1)
Thunder Storm Cat(USA), off the track since winning a 6f maiden here last September, may have finished closer had his rider made more use of his rails draw. (op 7-2)
Cool Box(USA) ran a respectable race off a 9lb higher mark than when winning a 6f handicap on the Polytrack at Lingfield when last seen 160 days previously. There should be better to come. (op 40-1)
Lunces Lad(IRE), gelded since he was last seen, was denied a clear run when trying to stay on and was unlucky not to finish closer. Official explanation: jockey said gelding was denied a clear run (op 14-1 tchd 20-1)
Cesc Official explanation: jockey said colt was unsuited by the good to firm (good in places) ground
Princess Valerina ◆ had a poor draw in stall one and ended up even wider of the main pack when going left coming out of the stalls. She is much better than she was able to show and should not be underestimated next time. (op 8-1)

1125 DUBAI DUTY FREE FULL OF SURPRISES H'CAP 5f 34y
2:40 (2:42) (Class 2) (0-110,107) 4-Y-O+

£9,971 (£2,985; £1,492; £747; £372; £187) **Stalls** High

Form RPR

500- **1** **Green Manalishi**[195] [5807] 6-8-9 **98** .... NCallan 3 113+
(K A Ryan) *trckd ldrs: led travelling wl appr fnl f: drvn ins last: hld on wl* **9/2**[2]

440- **2** *hd* **River Falcon**[173] [6243] 7-8-4 **93** oh2 .... NickyMackay 2 103
(J S Goldie) *lw: towards rr: rdn 2f out: str run fr over 1f out: fin wl but a jst hld* **9/1**

060- **3** *2* **The Tatling (IRE)**[190] [5921] 10-8-11 **100** .... DarryllHolland 4 103
(J M Bradley) *rr: pushed along and hdwy fr 2f out: kpt on ins last but nvr gng pce of ldng pair* **10/1**

600- **4** *1 1/2* **Sweet Afton (IRE)**[239] [4749] 4-8-6 **95** .... MickyFenton 1 92
(M S Saunders) *slt ld in centre of crse: rdn 2f out: hdd over 1f out: wknd ins last* **50/1**

510/ **5** *hd* **Baron's Pit**[552] [5900] 7-9-4 **107** .... TedDurcan 10 104+
(E F Vaughan) *b: b.wkd: hld up in rr: shkn up and styd on steadily fnl f: gng on cl home* **12/1**

00-1 **6** *3/4* **Merlin's Dancer**[22] [818] 7-8-7 **96** .... AdrianTNicholls 6 90
(D Nicholls) *chsd ldrs: rdn 2f out: wknd ins fnl f* **12/1**

14-0 **7** *1/2* **Mecca's Mate**[20] [847] 6-8-11 **100** .... JohnEgan 12 92+
(D W Barker) *rr: hdwy on rails and hmpd ins fnl 2f: swtchd lft over 1f out: nt clr run ins last: styd on cl home but fin on bit* **16/1**

501- **8** *nk* **Woodcote (IRE)**[195] [5807] 5-8-8 **97** .... (p) PhilipRobinson 8 88
(C G Cox) *pressed ldrs: chal fr 2f out tl over 1f out: wknd ins last* **11/2**[3]

003- **9** *1 1/4* **Corridor Creeper (FR)**[188] [5957] 10-8-9 **98** .... (p) SteveDrowne 5 85
(J M Bradley) *chsd ldrs: rdn 2f out: wknd fnl f* **8/1**

/44- **10** *1* **Northern Empire (IRE)**[297] [2959] 4-8-13 **102** .... LDettori 9 85
(B J Meehan) *b.bkwd: in tch: hdwy to trck ldrs 1/2-way: nvr gng pce to be competitive: wknd fnl f* **8/1**

2241 **11** *2* **Maltese Falcon**[19] [867] 7-8-11 **100** .... (t) JimmyFortune 7 76
(P F I Cole) *lw: chsd ldrs: rdn 2f out: sn wknd* **4/1**[1]

60-5 **12** *2* **The Lord**[22] [818] 7-8-8 **100** ow3 .... AmirQuinn(3) 11 69
(W G M Turner) *chsd ldrs over 3f* **25/1**

59.69 secs (-2.87) **Going Correction** -0.325s/f (Firm) **12** Ran SP% **122.0**
Speed ratings (Par 109):109,108,105,103,102 101,100,100,98,96 93,90
CSF £46.36 CT £310.75 TOTE £4.30: £2.40, £3.20, £3.80; EX 59.00 TRIFECTA Not won..

Owner T Fawcett,S McCarthy,J Brennan&J Smith **Bred** E Aldridge **Trained** Hambleton, N Yorks

FOCUS
A very competitive renewal of this decent sprint handicap and it could produce some nice winners as the season progresses with the winner close to his best. They raced towards the stands' side, but the first four home were drawn in the bottom four stalls.

NOTEBOOK
Green Manalishi ◆ was only 3lb higher than when winning this race for David Arbuthnot last year and proved good enough to make a successful debut for Kevin Ryan, who gave 75,000gns for him at the Horses In Training sales. He only had a head to spare at the line, but he could have been called the winner two out such was the ease with which he travelled, and he was entitled to get tired late on considering he had been off the track for over six months. He will now be aimed at the Epsom Dash and appeals as a 'must back' if granted a high draw, especially considering his new stable won that race last year with a similar type in Desert Lord. (op 4-1 tchd 5-1 and 11-2 in places)
River Falcon ◆, returning from a 173-day break, was 2lb out of the handicap and racing on ground probably quick enough, so this was a decent effort. He has won in the month of May in three of the last four seasons and must be kept on the right side of in the coming weeks. (op 16-1)
The Tatling(IRE) has struggled of late - his last win came in 2005 - but the Handicapper has given him a bit of a chance and he ran very well off the back of a 190-day break. (tchd 9-1)
Sweet Afton(IRE) ◆, formerly trained in Ireland, ran a very pleasing race on her debut for new connections. She showed tremendous early speed and could do well this season for a yard that knows what it is doing with sprinters.
Baron's Pit is very smart indeed on his day, but he has had his problems over the years and was having his first start for his third trainer off the back of a 552-day absence. He shaped very nicely under his big weight and hopefully he can go the right way from this.
Merlin's Dancer was unable to dominate and failed to defy a 4lb rise in the weights for his recent Lingfield success. (op 11-1)
Mecca's Mate ◆ got no sort of a run when trying to stay on and will hardly have noticed she was in a race. She probably would not have been far away with a clear passage and will be one to look out for in the next few weeks. Official explanation: jockey said mare was denied a clear run
Woodcote(IRE) was well supported but could offer little at the business end on his first run in 195 days. (op 8-1 tchd 17-2)
Northern Empire(IRE) Official explanation: jockey said gelding hung right
Maltese Falcon has been in fine form on the sand this winter, but his best efforts tend to come when able to dominate and that was always going to be difficult in this field. (op 9-2 tchd 5-1 in a place)

1126 DUBAI DUTY FREE GOLF WORLD CUP CONDITIONS STKS 1m 2f 6y
3:15 (3:15) (Class 3) 3-Y-O

£7,478 (£2,239; £1,119; £560; £279; £140) **Stalls** Low

Form RPR

231- **1** **Light Shift (USA)**[213] 5456 3-8-8 83 .... TedDurcan 2 104
(H R A Cecil) *hld up towards rr: hdwy over 2f out: drvn and str run fr over 1f out to ld ins last: drvn out* **7/1**[3]

512- **2** *1 1/4* **Kid Mambo (USA)**[195] 5805 3-8-13 100 .... DaneO'Neill 3 106
(T G Mills) *lw: w ldr tl def advantage 4f out: rdn and styd on wl whn chal over 1f out: hdd and no ex ins last* **3/1**[2]

312- **3** *1* **Monzante (USA)**[202] 5665 3-8-13 100 .... RichardHughes 7 105
(R Charlton) *chsd ldrs: rdn over 2f out and sn wnt 2nd: no imp over 1f out: sn outpcd ins last* **7/1**[3]

211- **4** *5* **Duke Of Tuscany**[219] 5292 3-8-13 95 .... JimmyFortune 1 95
(R Hannon) *chsd ldrs: rdn 3f out: wknd ins fnl 2f* **10/1**

5 *1* **Stuart Little (DEN)**[188] 3-9-3 .... EddieAhern 4 97
(P W Chapple-Hyam) *w'like: str: slt advantage to 4f out: sn rdn: wknd appr fnl 2f* **20/1**

523- **6** *nk* **Medicine Path**[181] 6104 3-8-13 110 .... RichardMullen 6 93
(E J O'Neill) *t.k.h in rr: rdn and effrt 3f out: nvr gng pce to get into contention and sn wknd* **2/1**[1]

7 *7* **Without Excuse (USA)**[187] 3-8-13 ....(p) LDettori 5 79?
(M Botti) *w'like: rr: rdn and effrt fr 4f out: nvr gng pce to get into contention and sn btn* **16/1**

1- **8** *8* **Go On Be A Tiger (USA)**[192] 5892 3-8-13 90 .... JohnEgan 8 64
(M R Channon) *rr: hdwy on outside 4f out: sn rdn: wknd 3f out* **7/1**[3]

2m 3.91s (-4.80) **Going Correction** -0.325s/f (Firm) **8** Ran SP% **115.6**
Speed ratings (Par 102):106,105,104,100,99 99,93,87
CSF £28.66 TOTE £9.10: £2.30, £2.00, £1.80; EX 36.60.
Owner Niarchos Family **Bred** Flaxman Holdings Ltd **Trained** Newmarket, Suffolk

FOCUS
Hard to know exactly what to make of the form of this conditions contest, but they went a good pace and the first three home came clear. The winning time was 1.75 seconds quicker than the following fillies' maiden and the form could prove decent.

NOTEBOOK
Light Shift(USA), who again had two handlers and looked fit, improved for the step up to 1m when off the mark at Newmarket on her third and final starts as a juvenile and this even longer trip suited well on her reappearance. She lacks size, but showed she has trained on with a smart effort against the colts and geldings. Always going well in behind the leaders, she stayed on best of all when switched out with her effort and was well on top at the finish. She is now likely to run in an Oaks trial and that will determine whether she goes to Epsom, or to Royal Ascot for the Ribblesdale. Henry Cecil said afterwards he thinks she will improve for some give underfoot. (op 8-1 tchd 6-1)
Kid Mambo(USA), the winner of a Sandown maiden before running second to Caldra in the Autumn Stakes at Ascot, ran with credit stepped up in trip on his seasonal reappearance. He handled this fast surface well enough, but his two best efforts last season came with some cut in the ground. (op 11-4 tchd 10-3 in a place)
Monzante(USA), who showed very useful form on the Polytrack at Kempton towards the end of last year, ran well stepped up in trip and returned to turf off the back of a 202-day break. He could build on this. (op 15-2 tchd 8-1)
Duke Of Tuscany, returning from a seven-month break, failed to pose a threat to the front three and finished up well held. He probably wants easier ground and it also remains to be seen whether he has the stamina for this sort of trip. Official explanation: jockey said colt hung left (op 20-1)
Stuart Little(DEN), a triple winner in Denmark as a juvenile, ran a respectable race on his first start for new connections, especially considering he was conceding weight all round. (op 25-1)
Medicine Path was the clear form pick judged on his third in last season's Racing Post Trophy, but he had little chance of getting this trip on breeding and was nowhere near his best off the back of a six-month break. He did not look the easiest of rides, taking a grip early and then hardly convincing than his mind was 100% on the job in hand when asked for an effort in the straight. It is probably too early to write him off, though, as this should have taken the freshness out of him, and a return to shorter trips should help. Official explanation: jockey said colt was unsuited by the good to firm (good in places) ground (tchd 15-8 and 9-4)
Go On Be A Tiger(USA) looked a decent enough prospect when winning a 1m maiden here last October, but he offered nothing on his return to action and has it all to prove now. (op 5-1)

1127 ROBERT SANGSTER MEMORIAL MAIDEN FILLIES' STKS 1m 2f 6y
3:50 (3:51) (Class 4) 3-Y-O **£6,477** (£1,927; £963; £481) **Stalls** Low

Form RPR

3- **1** **Folk Opera (IRE)**[191] 5906 3-9-0 .... PhilipRobinson 6 89+
(M A Jarvis) *trckd ldrs: led over 2f out: drvn and styd on strly fnl f* **9/2**[2]

35- **2** *2* **Brisk Breeze (GER)**[238] 4765 3-9-0 .... TedDurcan 1 85
(H R A Cecil) *lw: chsd ldrs: rdn over 2f out: chsd wnr appr fnl f: kpt on same pce* **9/1**

3- **3** *2* **Eternal Path (USA)**[174] 6215 3-9-0 .... LDettori 13 81
(Sir Michael Stoute) *lw: keen hold: chsd ldr: led over 6f out: rdn and hdd over 2f out: wknd fnl f* **10/11**[1]

2- **4** *1/2* **Fidelia (IRE)**[140] 6663 3-9-0 .... EddieAhern 3 80
(G Wragg) *w'like: leggy: t.k.h: chsd ldrs: pushed along 3f out: wknd over 1f out* **14/1**

53- **5** *1 3/4* **Fascinatin Rhythm**[133] 6746 3-9-0 .... SebSanders 14 77
(V Smith) *rr: hdwy on outside over 3f out:chsd ldrs 2f out but nvr gng pce to be competitive* **100/1**

0- **6** *4* **Mirthful (USA)**[217] 5344 3-9-0 .... RichardHughes 5 69
(B W Hills) *led: hdd over 6f out: rdn 3f out: wknd sn after* **17/2**[3]

7 *1/2* **Galianna (IRE)** 3-9-0 .... DaneO'Neill 15 68+
(Pat Eddery) *w'like: b.bkwd: s.i.s: bhd: kpt on fnl 2f: styng on cl home* **33/1**

5- **8** *nk* **Tebee**[182] 6073 3-9-0 .... JimmyFortune 7 68
(J H M Gosden) *mid-div: pushed along over 3f out: nvr in contention* **14/1**

0- **9** *shd* **Ashmal (USA)**[174] 6215 3-9-0 .... RHills 4 67
(J L Dunlop) *b.bkwd: mid-div tl outpcd 4f out: styd on again ins last* **33/1**

5- **10** *3/4* **Verbatim**[222] 5209 3-9-0 .... MartinDwyer 2 66
(A M Balding) *chsd ldrs: rdn 3f out: sn wknd* **100/1**

3- **11** *3 1/2* **Composing (IRE)**[205] 5623 3-9-0 .... SteveDrowne 10 59
(H Morrison) *rr: sme hdwy 3f out but nvr in contention* **28/1**

00- **12** *1 1/2* **Iolanthe**[190] 5914 3-9-0 .... MichaelHills 8 56
(B J Meehan) *b.bkwd: s.i.s: a towards rr* **100/1**

05- **13** *hd* **Galingale (IRE)**[206] 5596 3-9-0 .... MickyFenton 11 56
(Mrs P Sly) *a in rr* **100/1**

2- **14** *8* **Beautiful Reward (FR)**[199] 5754 3-9-0 .... OscarUrbina 9 41
(J R Fanshawe) *sn towards rr* **12/1**

15 *nk* **Montrachet** 3-9-0 .... HayleyTurner 12 40
(M L W Bell) *lenghty: s.i.s: a in rr* **100/1**

2m 5.66s (-3.05) **Going Correction** -0.325s/f (Firm) **15** Ran SP% **126.4**
Speed ratings (Par 97):99,97,95,95,94 90,90,90,90,89 86,85,85,78,78
CSF £45.58 TOTE £6.00: £2.30, £3.40, £1.10; EX 62.90.
Owner Sheikh Mohammed **Bred** Abbeville & Meadow Court Partners **Trained** Newmarket, Suffolk

FOCUS
This looked like a hot maiden and it should produce plenty of winners. However, the pace was just ordinary and the winning time was 1.75 seconds slower than the 1m2f conditions contest, which limits confidence a little.
Beautiful Reward(FR) Official explanation: vet said filly was found to have an irregular heartbeat

1128 BRIDGET MAIDEN FILLIES' STKS 7f (S)
4:25 (4:26) (Class 4) UNRACED 3-Y-O **£6,477** (£1,927; £963; £481) **Stalls** High

Form RPR

1 **Promising Lead** 3-9-0 .... LDettori 15 88
(Sir Michael Stoute) *gd sort: sn in tch: shkn up to ld ins fnl 2f: kpt on wl fnl f: cosily* **10/3**[1]

2 *1/2* **Sister Act** 3-9-0 .... OscarUrbina 4 87
(J R Fanshawe) *lengthy: b.bkwd: towards rr tl hdwy 3f out: qcknd to trck ldrs over 1f out: wnt 2nd wl ins last and kpt on but a jst hld by wnr* **9/1**

3 *nk* **Graduation** 3-9-0 .... JimmyFortune 9 86
(E A L Dunlop) *leggy: hld up towards rr but nvr far away: hday 3f out: rdn to chse wnr fnl f: a jst hld: lost 2nd cl home* **7/2**[2]

4 *6* **Talk More (USA)** 3-9-0 .... TPQueally 16 70
(J Noseda) *w'like: scope: b.bwkd: sn led: shkn up and green ins fnl 3f: hdd ins fnl 2f: wknd fnl f* **20/1**

5 *1/2* **Angel Kate (IRE)** 3-9-0 .... TedDurcan 7 69+
(H R A Cecil) *leggy: chsd ldrs: drvn and outpcd 3f out: kpt on again fnl f* **16/1**

6 *1 3/4* **Azeema (IRE)** 3-9-0 .... MichaelHills 12 64+
(B W Hills) *w'like: b.bkwd: slowly into stride: bhd: effrt and nt clr run 2f out: swtchd lft over 1f out: fin strly ins last but nvr a danger* **18/1**

7 *3* **Sympatric Friendly** 3-9-0 .... JoeFanning 2 56
(W J Haggas) *w'like: chsd ldrs: rdn over 2f out: wknd over 1f out* **40/1**

8 *shd* **Razaana (USA)** 3-9-0 .... MartinDwyer 14 56
(J L Dunlop) *w'like: b.bkwd: in tch: rdn and sme hdwy 3f out: nvr in contention: wknd fr 2f out* **25/1**

9 *hd* **Spinneret** 3-9-0 .... PhilipRobinson 11 55
(M A Jarvis) *tall: unf: scope: chsd ldr over 3f: wknd over 2f out* **4/1**[3]

10 *1 1/2* **Sweet Gale (IRE)** 3-9-0 .... SebSanders 5 51
(J Noseda) *w'like: b.bkwd: towards rr tl mod prog fnl 2f* **50/1**

11 *1 1/4* **Bidding Time** 3-9-0 .... HayleyTurner 6 48
(M L W Bell) *w'like: b.bkwd: rr: drvn into mid-div 1/2-way: nvr in contention and sn wknd* **66/1**

12 *1 3/4* **Intricate Dance (USA)** 3-9-0 .... RichardHughes 10 43
(B W Hills) *w'like: swtg: chsd ldrs: pushed along 1/2-way: sn btn* **17/2**

13 *nk* **Luna Danza** 3-9-0 .... BrettDoyle 1 42
(B J Meehan) *leggy: mid-div and rdn 1/2-way: nvr in contention and sn bhd* **80/1**

14 *1* **Mabaahej (USA)** 3-9-0 .... RHills 3 39
(B W Hills) *w'like: scope: str: s.i.s: a towards rr* **11/1**

15 *5* **Kyburg** 3-9-0 .... NCallan 8 26
(P F I Cole) *leggy: unf: chsd ldrs to 1/2-way* **40/1**

- **16** *6* **Caro Mio (IRE)** 3-9-0 .... SteveDrowne 13 10
(R Charlton) *w'like: s.i.s: a in rr* **20/1**

1m 24.3s (-2.70) **Going Correction** -0.325s/f (Firm) **16** Ran SP% **128.2**
Speed ratings (Par 97):102,101,101,94,93 91,88,88,87,86 84,82,82,81,75 68
CSF £32.99 TOTE £3.50: £2.00, £2.70, £2.10; EX 44.30.
Owner K Abdulla **Bred** Juddmonte Farms Ltd **Trained** Newmarket, Suffolk
■ Stewards' Enquiry : Michael Hills one-day ban: careless riding (May 1)

FOCUS
A maiden restricted to unraced fillies, so hard to know exactly what the form is worth, but they looked a decent bunch in the paddock and plenty of winners should come out of this in the coming weeks. The pace could have been stronger, though, and the winning time was 0.95 seconds slower than the earlier handicap won by the 88-rated Phoenix Tower.
Intricate Dance(USA) Official explanation: jockey said filly ran too free

1129 PETER SMITH MEMORIAL MAIDEN STKS 1m 3f 5y
4:55 (4:57) (Class 4) 3-Y-O **£6,477** (£1,927; £963; £481) **Stalls** Low

Form RPR

2- **1** **Western Adventure (USA)**[227] 5088 3-9-3 .... JimmyFortune 1 93+
(E A L Dunlop) *w'like: scope: str: chsd ldrs: hrd drvn to led appr fnl f: rdn out* **10/11**[1]

33- **2** *3* **Tempelstern (GER)**[211] 5495 3-9-3 .... TedDurcan 2 89+
(H R A Cecil) *w'like: trckd ldrs: led over 4f out: rdn and styd on wl fr 2f out: hdd appr fnl f: styd on but a hld by wnr* **3/1**[2]

0- **3** *2* **Samuel**[174] 6220 3-9-3 .... EddieAhern 8 83
(J L Dunlop) *rr: sme prog whn hmpd 3f out: drvn and styd on fr 2f out: tk 3rd cl home but nvr gng pce to rch ldrs* **12/1**

04- **4** *nk* **Rock 'N' Roller (FR)**[205] 5623 3-9-3 .... MartinDwyer 9 82
(W R Muir) *rr: hdwy on outside fr 3f out: nvr gng pce to be competitive but tk modest 3rd briefly ins last: styd on same pce* **14/1**

0- **5** *6* **Make Haste (IRE)**[192] 5892 3-9-3 .... SteveDrowne 5 72
(R Charlton) *disp 2nd tl over 4f out: sn rdn: wknd fr 3f out* **14/1**

6 *3/4* **Philatelist (USA)** 3-9-3 .... NCallan 7 71
(M A Jarvis) *unf: scope: b.bwkd: chsd ldrs: rdn 4f out: wknd fr 3f out* **13/2**[3]

7 *6* **Mowadeh (IRE)** 3-9-3 .... JohnEgan 4 60
(M R Channon) *scope: lw: a towards rr* **40/1**

6 **8** *13* **Winter Lane**[60] 499 3-9-3 .... RichardHughes 6 38
(A M Balding) *chsd ldrs tl wknd over 4f out* **25/1**

03- **9** *hd* **Storm Path (IRE)**[199] 5759 3-9-3 .... StephenCarson 3 38
(Eve Johnson Houghton) *swtg: led tl hdd over 4f out: sn wknd* **66/1**

2m 18.79s (-3.48) **Going Correction** -0.325s/f (Firm) **9** Ran SP% **119.5**
Speed ratings (Par 100):99,96,95,95,90 90,85,76,76
CSF £3.81 TOTE £1.90: £1.10, £1.50, £3.40; EX 3.60 Place 6 £62.18, Place 5 £25.26.
Owner Gainsborough **Bred** Gainsborough Farm Llc **Trained** Newmarket, Suffolk
■ Stewards' Enquiry : Steve Drowne one-day ban: careless riding (May 1)

FOCUS
This did not look the strongest renewal of what is traditionally a decent maiden. The field came home fairly strung out behind the ready winner with the runner-up and fourth the best guides to the level for now.

T/Jkpt: Not won. T/Plt: £67.60 to a £1 stake. Pool: £87,898.15. 949.10 winning tickets. T/Qpdt: £29.20 to a £1 stake. Pool: £3,537.60. 89.50 winning tickets. ST

The Form Book, Raceform Ltd, Compton, RG20 6NL

THIRSK (L-H)

Friday, April 20

OFFICIAL GOING: Good to firm (firm in places)

Wind: virtually nil

1130 EBF HABTON NOVICE STKS 5f

2:00 (2:00) (Class 4) 2-Y-O **£5,181** (£1,541; £770; £384) **Stalls** High

Form RPR

12 **1** **Thunder Bay**[6] [1043] 2-9-0 .... SamHitchcott 2 78+
(M R Channon) *in tch: smooth hdwy 1/2-way: led wl over 1f out: pushed clr ins last: comf* **8/11**[1]

2 *3* **Geordie Girl** 2-8-7 .... PaulFessey 6 59
(R C Guest) *rr: hdwy 1/2-way: swtchd lft and effrt to chse wnr over 1f out: sn rdn and no imp* **20/1**

43 **3** *1* **Mystickhill (IRE)**[11] [972] 2-8-7 .... DavidAllan 4 55
(T J Pitt) *cl up: ev ch 2f out: sn rdn and kpt on same pce appr last* **7/1**[3]

06 **4** *3/4* **Northgate Lodge (USA)**[6] [1043] 2-8-5 .... PatrickDonaghy(7) 3 57
(M Brittain) *cl up: led after 1f: rdn along 2f out: sn hdd and grad wknd* **16/1**

000 **5** *3 1/2* **Bank On Bertie**[2] [1087] 2-8-12 .... PaulMulrennan 7 43
(M W Easterby) *led 1f: cl up tl rdn and wknd fnl 2f* **66/1**

6 *5* **Rievaulx Valentino** 2-8-12 .... DO'Donohoe 5 23
(K A Ryan) *clsd up: rdn along over 2f out and sn wknd* **5/2**[2]

60.45 secs (0.55) **Going Correction** -0.075s/f (Good) **6** Ran SP% **111.1**
Speed ratings (Par 94):92,87,85,84,78 70
CSF £17.71 TOTE £1.50: £1.10, £5.20; EX 16.80.
Owner The Abercrombie Partnership **Bred** A C M Spalding **Trained** West Ilsley, Berks

FOCUS
An ordinary novice event and the comfortable winner is value for further. The form is rated through the third.

NOTEBOOK
Thunder Bay made it two wins from three starts and did the job pretty much as he pleased. He is clearly a fair sort for the time of year, handles this sort of ground well, and deserves a crack in better company now. (op 5-6 tchd 4-6)
Geordie Girl, bred to appreciate further, took time to get the hang of things yet was noted as doing her best work from halfway. She is entitled to improve for the experience and should enjoy another furlong in due course. (op 40-1)
Mystickhill(IRE) had every chance yet was again found wanting at the business end of her race. She is clearly limited, but still helps to set the standard for this form. (op 8-1 tchd 13-2)
Northgate Lodge(USA) showed early pace until weakening out of it nearing the final furlong and ran close enough to his Newcastle form with the winner. He probably wants easier ground. (op 25-1)
Bank On Bertie Official explanation: jockey said colt lost its action closing stages
Rievaulx Valentino, bred to make his mark at two at around this trip, was popular in the betting ring for this racecourse bow yet he eventually proved most disappointing. He was beaten before halfway and something may well have been amiss, as his stable has sent out a couple of juvenile debutants to win already this term. (op 7-4 tchd 11-4)

1131 ROSEDALE H'CAP 1m

2:30 (2:31) (Class 5) (0-75,74) 3-Y-O **£3,886** (£1,156; £577; £288) **Stalls** Low

Form RPR

2-03 **1** **Musical Beat**[6] [1045] 3-9-1 **71** .... EdwardCreighton 10 78+
(Miss V Haigh) *hld up: smooth hdwy on outer over 3f out: led over 1f out: sn rdn and kpt on* **5/1**[2]

-324 **2** *1 1/2* **Grand Symphony**[51] [583] 3-8-11 **67** .... PaulHanagan 3 69
(W Jarvis) *trckd ldng pair: effrt over 2f out and sn ev ch: rdn over 1f out: kpt on same pce ins last* **6/1**[3]

0-33 **3** *2 1/2* **Deadline (UAE)**[22] [816] 3-9-4 **74** .... KDarley 7 70
(P T Midgley) *in tch: pushed along and outpcd over 3f out: rdn wl over 1f out: styd on ins last* **6/1**[3]

602- **4** *shd* **Coconut Queen (IRE)**[199] [5748] 3-9-0 **73** .... SaleemGolam(3) 2 69
(Mrs A Duffield) *led: rdn along 2f out: hdd over 1f out: hmpd ins last and sn one pce* **8/1**

0-22 **5** *3/4* **Empress Olga (USA)**[17] [908] 3-9-0 **70** .... DO'Donohoe 1 64
(E A L Dunlop) *chsd ldrs: hdwy on inner and ev ch 2f out: sn rdn and wknd* **4/1**[1]

0521 **6** *1* **Ella Y Rossa**[21] [834] 3-8-7 **63** .... CatherineGannon 6 55
(P D Evans) *rr tl styd on fnl 2f: nrst fin* **9/1**

030- **7** *hd* **Smugglers Bay (IRE)**[245] [4566] 3-8-11 **67** .... DavidAllan 8 59
(T D Easterby) *cl up: rdn along 3f out: sn wknd* **13/2**

330- **8** *2* **Espejo (IRE)**[205] [5614] 3-9-4 **74** .... PatCosgrave 9 61
(K R Burke) *in tch on inner: rdn along over 2f out and sn wknd* **8/1**

400- **9** *2 1/2* **The Mighty Ogmore**[199] [5748] 3-8-4 **60** .... PaulFessey 5 41
(R C Guest) *a rr* **18/1**

1m 39.9s (0.20) **Going Correction** -0.075s/f (Good) **9** Ran SP% **116.1**
Speed ratings (Par 98):96,94,92,91,91 90,89,87,85
CSF £35.22 CT £185.35 TOTE £5.80: £2.60, £2.60, £2.10; EX 32.70.
Owner R J Budge **Bred** Juddmonte Farms Ltd **Trained** Wiseton, Notts

FOCUS
A modest handicap featuring some unexposed three-year-olds. The form, rated through the runner-up, should work out.

1132 BILSDALE H'CAP 1m

3:05 (3:05) (Class 5) (0-70,70) 4-Y-O+ **£3,886** (£1,156; £577; £288) **Stalls** Low

Form RPR

301- **1** **Shy Glance (USA)**[168] [6323] 5-9-1 **67** .... DaleGibson 14 81+
(G A Swinbank) *towards rr and pushed along 1/2-way: gd hdwy on outer 2f out: rdn to chal and edgd lft ent last: sn led and styd on wl* **9/2**[1]

3-50 **2** *3* **Sir Bond (IRE)**[89] [200] 6-7-13 **56** oh1 .... DuranFentiman(5) 8 60
(G R Oldroyd) *chsd ldng pair: hdwy to ld 2f out: sn rdn: drvn and hdd ins last: one pce* **16/1**

056- **3** *1 1/4* **Tough Love**[213] [5444] 8-9-1 **67** .... DavidAllan 7 68
(T D Easterby) *hld up in rr: gd hdwy on inner over 2f out: rdn to chse ldrs over 1f out: kpt on ins last* **9/1**

14-0 **4** *hd* **Fairy Monarch (IRE)**[2] [1090] 8-7-13 **56** oh3 ....(b) RoryMoore(5) 3 57
(P T Midgley) *trckd ldrs: smooth hdwy over 2f out: rdn over 1f out: sn one pce* **8/1**

401- **5** *3/4* **Spinning**[221] [5241] 4-9-4 **70** .... PaulFessey 6 69
(T D Barron) *chsd ldrs: rdn along 2f out: kpt on same pce* **15/2**

440- **6** *1/2* **Champain Sands (IRE)**[207] [5579] 8-8-8 **65** .... MichaelJStainton(5) 15 63+
(E J Alston) *stdd s and bhd: hdwy on inner 2f out: styd on appr last: nrst fin* **12/1**

320- **7** *1/2* **Efidium**[178] [6160] 9-8-10 **69** .... LukeMorris(7) 2 66
(N Bycroft) *in tch: rdn along over 2f out: sn no imp* **13/2**[2]

4003 **8** *1 3/4* **Methusaleh (IRE)**[16] [912] 4-8-3 **60** .... PatrickHills(5) 11 53
(D Shaw) *towards rr tl styd on fnl 2f: nvr a factor* **7/1**[3]

260- **9** *1 1/4* **Terenzium (IRE)**[113] [4446] 5-8-5 **57** oh3 ow1 .... DeanMcKeown 1 47
(Micky Hammond) *in tch: rdn along 3f out: grad wknd* **25/1**

0003 **10** *nk* **Inca Soldier (FR)**[23] [812] 4-8-4 **59** oh10 ow3 .... SaleemGolam(3) 4 48
(R C Guest) *keen: sn led: rdn along and hdd 2f out: sn wknd* **28/1**

0365 **11** *4* **Boy Dancer (IRE)**[16] [915] 4-8-7 **59** .... TomEaves 13 39
(D W Barker) *stdd s: hld up and a rr* **9/1**

00-0 **12** *1* **Wizby**[11] [975] 4-8-4 **56** oh5 .... CatherineGannon 9 34
(P D Evans) *chsd ldrs on outer: effrt wl over 2f out: sn rdn and btn* **33/1**

/00- **13** *1 1/2* **Passionately Royal**[273] [3716] 5-8-8 **60** .... DeanMernagh 10 34
(M Brittain) *midfield: rdn along 3f out and sn wknd* **66/1**

0/00 **14** *8* **Definite Guest (IRE)**[56] [538] 9-8-8 **60** ....(b) PaulHanagan 5 16
(R A Fahey) *cl up: rdn along wl over 2f out and sn wknd* **12/1**

1m 37.91s (-1.79) **Going Correction** -0.075s/f (Good) **14** Ran SP% **119.9**
Speed ratings (Par 103):105,102,100,100,99 99,98,97,95,95 91,90,89,81
CSF £77.00 CT £647.85 TOTE £4.90: £2.10, £4.50, £3.40; EX 100.70.
Owner Walcal Property Development Ltd **Bred** R D Hubbard & Constance Sczesny **Trained** Melsonby, N Yorks

FOCUS
A moderate handicap which was run at a fair pace. The winner looks progressive and the form appears sound rated around the runner-up, fourth and fifth.
Champain Sands(IRE) Official explanation: jockey said, regarding running and riding, that his orders were to jump out, get onto the rail in rear and challenge as late as possible; trainer said the gelding is always ridden this way, including the win on the track last year, adding that it often finds nothing coming off the bridle and this was the case

1133 HAWNBY H'CAP 7f

3:40 (3:40) (Class 5) (0-75,74) 4-Y-O+ **£3,886** (£1,156; £577; £288) **Stalls** Low

Form RPR

1036 **1** **Flying Bantam (IRE)**[27] [771] 6-8-6 **62** .... PaulHanagan 2 69
(R A Fahey) *in tch: hdwy over 2f out: rdn over 1f out: styd on ins last to ld nr fin* **6/1**[3]

1130 **2** *nk* **Kabis Amigos**[4] [1063] 5-8-13 **69** ....(t) SilvestreDeSousa 1 75
(D Nicholls) *led: rdn along and hdd 2f out: rallied to ld ent last: sn hung bdly rt: hdd and no ex nr fin* **5/2**[1]

305- **3** *nk* **Il Castagno (IRE)**[282] [3395] 4-9-3 **73** .... TomEaves 5 78
(B Smart) *cl up: rdn to ld 2f out: drvn and hdd ent last: ev ch whn carried rt: no ex towards fin* **16/1**

06- **4** *1/2* **Crosby Vision**[232] [4953] 4-9-0 **70** .... KDarley 8 74
(J R Weymes) *towards rr: gd hdwy over 2f out: rdn over 1f out: kpt on ins last: nrst fin* **16/1**

-563 **5** *1/2* **Paraguay (USA)**[6] [1040] 4-9-3 **73** .... EdwardCreighton 11 75
(Miss V Haigh) *hld up in rr: gd hdwy on outer over 2f out: rdn and edgd repeatedly lft over 1f out: kpt on ins last* **9/2**[2]

0012 **6** *shd* **Motu (IRE)**[11] [967] 6-8-2 **61** ....(v) PatrickMathers(3) 7 63
(I W McInnes) *hld up: hdwy over 2f out: sn rdn and kpt on ins last: nrst fin* **6/1**[3]

022- **7** *hd* **Khetaab (IRE)**[113] [6703] 5-8-4 **60** oh10 .... DavidKinsella 4 62?
(E J Alston) *chsd ldrs: rdn along over 2f out: drvn and wknd appr last* **33/1**

060- **8** *nk* **Goodwood Spirit**[174] [6227] 5-8-2 **63** .... KevinGhunowa(5) 6 64
(J M Bradley) *bhd tl styd on fnl 2f* **33/1**

1143 **9** *3/4* **Danetime Lord (IRE)**[21] [827] 4-8-7 **63** ....(p) CatherineGannon 9 62
(K A Ryan) *chsd ldng pair: rdn along 2f out: sn wknd* **7/1**

230- **10** *3/4* **Viva Volta**[188] [5961] 4-9-0 **70** .... DavidAllan 10 67
(T D Easterby) *chsd ldrs: rdn along 2f out: wknd over 1f out* **8/1**

0/6- **11** *2* **Ocean Gift**[262] [4033] 5-9-4 **74** .... KimTinkler 3 65
(N Tinkler) *a rr* **20/1**

1m 25.25s (-1.85) **Going Correction** -0.075s/f (Good) **11** Ran SP% **121.3**
Speed ratings (Par 103):107,106,106,105,105 105,104,104,103,102 100
CSF £21.63 CT £233.49 TOTE £8.90: £2.80, £1.80, £3.40; EX 31.70.
Owner The Matthewman Partnership **Bred** Robinski Bloodstock Limited **Trained** Musley Bank, N Yorks

■ Stewards' Enquiry : Tom Eaves four-day ban: used whip with excessive force and frequency without giving gelding time to respond (May 1-4)

FOCUS
A modest handicap, run at an uneven gallop. The field fifnished in a heap and the form, rated around the third and fourth, looks worth treating with caution.
Motu(IRE) Official explanation: jockey said gelding lost its action

1134 SWAINBY H'CAP 5f

4:15 (4:16) (Class 4) (0-80,79) 4-Y-O+ **£5,181** (£1,541; £770; £384) **Stalls** High

Form RPR

141- **1** **Aegean Dancer**[248] [4453] 5-8-13 **77** .... MarkLawson(3) 11 89
(B Smart) *cl up stands side: led wl over 1f out: rdn clr ent last: kpt on* **13/2**[2]

036- **2** *1 1/4* **Mimi Mouse**[209] [5532] 5-9-1 **76** .... DavidAllan 14 83
(T D Easterby) *overall ldr stands side: rdn 2f out: sn hdd: drvn and one pce ent last* **7/1**[3]

456- **3** *hd* **Bond Boy**[168] [6320] 10-8-12 **78** ....(v) DuranFentiman(5) 13 84
(G R Oldroyd) *trckd ldrs stands side: effrt 2f out: rdn and styd on ins last* **16/1**

600- **4** *1* **River Thames**[183] [6065] 4-9-2 **77** .... DO'Donohoe 10 80+
(K A Ryan) *trckd ldrs stands side: hdwy 2f out: sn rdn and kpt on ins last* **15/2**

000- **5** *3/4* **Highland Warrior**[168] [6320] 8-8-10 **76** .... RoryMoore(5) 17 76
(P T Midgley) *s.i.s and bhd stands side: hdwy 2f out: swtchd lft and rdn over 1f out: kpt on ins last: nrst fin* **12/1**

0-11 **6** *1* **Spanish Ace**[3] [1080] 6-9-3 **78** 6ex .... KDarley 8 74+
(J M Bradley) *dwlt: in tch on outer of stands side gp: hdwy 1/2-way: rdn wl over 1f out and sn one pce* **3/1**[1]

0060 **7** *shd* **Amanda's Lad (IRE)**[1] [1112] 7-7-11 **65** oh20 .... MCGeran(7) 12 61
(M C Chapman) *cl up stands side: rdn along 2f out: grad wknd* **66/1**

-000 **8** *1/2* **Danzig River (IRE)**[49] [609] 6-8-11 **72** .... PaulQuinn 9 66
(D Nicholls) *hld up stands side: effrt and n.m.r over 1f out: kpt on ins last* **33/1**

1030 **9** *nk* **Night Prospector**[52] [575] 7-8-12 **78** ....(p) TolleyDean(5) 16 71
(R A Harris) *in tch stands side: rdn along 2f out and sn btn* **10/1**

116- **10** *3/4* **Bel Cantor**[161] [6425] 4-9-1 **79** .... RichardKingscote(3) 7 69
(W J H Ratcliffe) *cl up stands side: rdn along 2f out and sn wknd* **16/1**

010- **11** *1 1/4* **Henry Hall (IRE)**[202] [5684] 11-8-9 **70** .... KimTinkler 2 56
(N Tinkler) *prom far side: rdn along wl over 1f out: kpt on to ld that gp ent last: no ch w stands side* **20/1**

440- **12** *nk* **Ellens Academy (IRE)**[209] [5534] 12-8-12 **78**........ MichaelJStainton(5) 3 72+
(E J Alston) *rr far side: hmpd over 1f out: swtchd rt and fin wl* **16/1**

6-40 **13** *1/2* **Sandwith**[25] [787] 4-8-11 **72**..............................(p) TonyHamilton 6 55
(J S Wainwright) *prom far side: led that gp 1/2-way: rdn wl over 1f out: hdd ent last and one pce* **33/1**

600- **14** *1 3/4* **Mormeatmic**[168] [6320] 4-9-0 **75**........................ PaulMulrennan 5 52
(M W Easterby) *chsd ldrs far side: hdwy 2f out: sn rdn and one pce* **40/1**

160- **15** *1 3/4* **Smiddy Hill**[160] [6452] 5-8-7 **68**................................ TomEaves 1 38
(R Bastiman) *led far side to 1/2-way: sn rdn and wkng whn hung lft over 1f out: sn bhd* **25/1**

58.69 secs (-1.21) **Going Correction** -0.075s/f (Good) **15** Ran SP% **115.5**
Speed ratings (Par 105):106,104,103,102,100 99,99,98,97,96 94,94,93,90,87
CSF £41.09 CT £527.67 TOTE £7.70: £2.40, £2.60, £4.80; EX 34.60.
Owner Pinnacle Piccolo Partnership **Bred** Theobalds Stud **Trained** Hambleton, N Yorks
■ Soto was withdrawn (9/1, rider unseated and injured in parade ring.) R4 applies, deduct 10p in the £.

FOCUS
A high draw not surprisingly proved a must in this open sprint handicap. The form looks fair rated through the runner-up.
Ellens Academy(IRE) Official explanation: jockey said gelding was denied a clear run

1135 CARPENTERS ARMS FELIXKIRK MEDIAN AUCTION MAIDEN STKS (DIV I) 6f
4:45 (5:02) (Class 5) 3-4-Y-O **£3,238** (£963; £481; £240) **Stalls** High

Form RPR

1 **Sea Rover (IRE)** 3-9-0 .... DeanMernagh 9 76
(M Brittain) *cl up: led 2f out: rdn clr appr last: kpt on* **10/1**

054- **2** *6* **Falcon's Fire (IRE)**[158] [6466] 3-8-11 60.................... SaleemGolam(3) 11 58
(Mrs A Duffield) *sn pushed along in rr: hdwy 1/2-way: rdn to chse wnr over 1f out: no imp* **10/3**[2]

000- **3** *4* **Miss Taboo (IRE)**[161] [6421] 3-8-4 30........................ RoryMoore(5) 7 41
(P T Midgley) *sn led: rdn along 1/2-way: sn hdd and grad wknd* **20/1**

226- **4** *1* **Morristown Music (IRE)**[188] [5956] 3-8-9 70............. TonyHamilton 5 38
(J S Wainwright) *chsd ldrs: rdn along 2f out: sn drvn and btn* **3/1**[1]

30-0 **5** *10* **Mandriano (ITY)**[7] [1031] 3-9-0 49........................ PatCosgrave 8 13
(D W Barker) *cl up: rdn along 1/2-way: sn wknd and eased* **12/1**

5 **6** *8* **The Blue Stacks (USA)**[21] [826] 3-9-0 .... DO'Donohoe 3 —
(K A Ryan) *cl up on outer: rdn along 1/2-way: sn wknd and eased* **11/2**[3]

1m 12.88s (0.38) **Going Correction** -0.075s/f (Good)
WFA 3 from 4yo 11lb **6** Ran SP% **85.0**
Speed ratings (Par 103):94,86,80,79,66 55
CSF £24.42 TOTE £8.50: £2.80, £1.80; EX 24.60.
Owner Mel Brittain **Bred** Darley **Trained** Warthill, N Yorks
■ Onatopp (5/2, unruly in stalls), Whithorn (14/1, rdr uns & inj) and Orotund (33/1, injured in stalls) withdrawn. R4, deduct 25p.

FOCUS
A dire first division of the maiden, decimated by five non-runners in all, but the debut winner still did the job nicely with the runner-up setting the level for now.
The Blue Stacks(USA) Official explanation: jockey said colt hung right final 3f and lost its action

1136 CARPENTERS ARMS FELIXKIRK MEDIAN AUCTION MAIDEN STKS (DIV II) 6f
5:20 (5:28) (Class 5) 3-4-Y-O **£3,238** (£963; £481; £240) **Stalls** High

Form RPR

0-0 **1** **Northern Dare (IRE)**[38] [670] 3-8-7 .... AdeleRothery(7) 3 70
(D Nicholls) *trckd ldrs: hdwy over 2f out: led wl ins last* **20/1**

2 *nk* **Soccerjackpot (USA)** 3-9-0 .... DeanMcKeown 4 69+
(G A Swinbank) *s.i.s: sn intch on outer: hdwy and cl up 1/2-way: rdn to ld over 1f out: wandered and hdd wl ins last: no ex* **8/13**[1]

5- **3** *5* **Futuristic Dragon (IRE)**[185] [6024] 3-9-0 .... TPO'Shea 2 54
(P A Blockley) *cl up: led wl over 2f out: rdn and hdd over 1f out: sn one pce* **5/1**[2]

- **4** *nk* **Lady Valentino** 3-8-9 .... TomEaves 6 48+
(M Dods) *sn outpcd and bhd tl hdwy 2f out: styd on wl fnl f: nrst fin* **14/1**

000- **5** *5* **Mambomoon**[178] [6157] 3-9-0 37................................ DavidAllan 10 38
(T D Easterby) *cl up: rdn along wl over 2f out and sn wknd* **50/1**

00-6 **6** *6* **Miss Daawe**[10] [996] 3-8-9 .... KDarley 7 15
(S Parr) *led: rdn along 1/2-way: sn hdd & wknd fnl 2f* **50/1**

0 **7** *3* **Pearl Valley**[16] [916] 3-8-9 .... PaulHanagan 9 6
(R A Fahey) *a rr* **10/1**

40-0 **8** *7* **Bond Free Spirit (IRE)**[24] [806] 4-9-1 47................ DuranFentiman(5) 8 —
(G R Oldroyd) *cl up: rdn along 1/2-way: sn wknd* **9/1**[3]

2060 **9** *8* **Bee Magic**[36] [680] 4-9-11 45.................................. SamHitchcott 1 —
(C N Kellett) *a rr* **16/1**

1m 11.99s (-0.51) **Going Correction** -0.075s/f (Good)
WFA 3 from 4yo 11lb **9** Ran SP% **118.9**
Speed ratings (Par 103):100,99,92,92,85 77,73,64,53
CSF £33.58 TOTE £20.70: £3.30, £1.10, £1.80; EX 96.60 Place 6 £101.51, Place 5 £62.11..
Owner Jim Dale **Bred** Frank Moynihan **Trained** Sessay, N Yorks

FOCUS
This second divison of the maiden was the stronger of the pair and the first two came clear.
T/Plt: £1,244.80 to a £1 stake. Pool: £57,893.50. 33.95 winning tickets. T/Qpdt: £176.70 to a £1 stake. Pool: £2,890.30. 12.10 winning tickets. JR

1137 - 1142a (Foreign Racing) - See Raceform Interactive

[1123]NEWBURY (L-H)
Saturday, April 21

OFFICIAL GOING: Good to firm
Wind: Moderate, across

1143 DUBAI INTERNATIONAL AIRPORT MAIDEN STKS 1m (S)
1:40 (1:42) (Class 4) 3-Y-O **£6,477** (£1,927; £963; £481) **Stalls** Centre

Form RPR

2- **1** **Diamond Tycoon (USA)**[190] [5939] 3-9-3 .... JamieSpencer 2 109+
(B J Meehan) *h.d.w: rangy: mde all: c readily clr fr over 1f out: impressive* **8/1**

2 *6* **Lucarno (USA)** 3-9-3 .... RobertHavlin 3 91
(J H M Gosden) *str: lw: s.i.s: sn rcvrd: trckd ldrs 1/2-way: drvn and chsd wnr ins last but nvr any ch* **50/1**

42- **3** *1 1/4* **Black Rock (IRE)**[231] [5020] 3-9-3 .... PhilipRobinson 14 89
(M A Jarvis) *b.bkwd: front rnk: chsd wnr fr 3f out but no ch whn rdn fr 2f out: outpcd and lost 2nd fnl f* **7/4**[1]

- **4** *nk* **Yaroslav (USA)** 3-9-3 .... SteveDrowne 12 88
(R Charlton) *w'like: scope: chsd ldrs: disp 2nd over 3f out: sn rdn: outpcd fr over 1f out* **33/1**

5 *1* **Ascalon** 3-9-3 .... DaneO'Neill 18 86+
(Pat Eddery) *tall: scope: lw: s.i.s: bhd: stdy hdwy fr 2f out: styd on wl fnl f: gng on cl home* **25/1**

6 *nk* **Pipedreamer** 3-9-3 .... JimmyFortune 11 85+
(J H M Gosden) *wll grwn: lw: towards rr tl hdwy over 3f out: trckd ldrs and shkn up 2f out: sn no imp: fdd fnl f: should improve* **12/1**

2- **7** *1* **Walking Talking**[175] [6214] 3-9-3 .... RichardHughes 15 83+
(H R A Cecil) *lw: rr: styd on fr over 2f out but nvr in contention* **5/2**[2]

0- **8** *3* **Danetime Panther (IRE)**[253] [4323] 3-9-3 .... EddieAhern 7 76
(P F I Cole) *h.d.w: lw: chsd wnr over 4f: rdn 3f out: wknd fr 2f out* **33/1**

9 *5* **Stand Guard** 3-9-3 .... LDettori 16 64
(Sir Michael Stoute) *str: b.bkwd: in tch: shkn up 3f out: nvr gng pce to rch ldrs: eased whn hld fr over 1f out* **6/1**[3]

10 *2* **Give Me A Break** 3-9-3 .... AdrianMcCarthy 13 60
(P W Chapple-Hyam) *cmpt: rr: drvn and sme prog 3f out: nvr in contention* **33/1**

6- **11** *1* **Sweet Request**[215] [5425] 3-8-12 .... SebSanders 17 52
(R M Beckett) *towards rr: nvr in contention* **66/1**

0-0 **12** *shd* **Shine And Rise (IRE)**[10] [1001] 3-9-3 .... AdamKirby 8 57
(C G Cox) *h.d.w: lw: chsd ldrs to 1/2-way* **100/1**

13 *2* **Noticeable (IRE)** 3-9-3 .... EdwardCreighton 5 52
(M R Channon) *str: lw: in tch: rdn and green over 3f out: sn wknd* **66/1**

14 *2 1/2* **Jawaaneb (USA)** 3-8-12 .... RHills 4 42
(J L Dunlop) *small: s.i.s: a towards rr* **25/1**

0- **15** *1* **Yeoman Leap**[186] [6023] 3-9-3 .... LPKeniry 6 44
(A M Balding) *b.bkwd: s.i.s: sn rcvrd to chse ldrs: wknd fr 3f out* **100/1**

16 *2 1/2* **Punching** 3-9-3 .... StephenCarson 10 39
(Eve Johnson Houghton) *neat: in tch to 1/2-way* **66/1**

1m 36.14s (-4.48) **Going Correction** -0.225s/f (Firm) **16** Ran SP% **123.0**
Speed ratings (Par 100):113,107,105,105,104 104,103,100,95,93 92,92,90,87,86 84
CSF £366.01 TOTE £7.00: £2.50, £17.90, £1.10; EX 197.70.
Owner Racegoers Club Owners Group **Bred** W S Farish Et Al **Trained** Manton, Wilts
■ Stewards' Enquiry : Jimmy Fortune caution: allowed colt to coast home with no assistance

FOCUS
A very good maiden won in a very smart time and in impressive style by a Pattern-class performer in the making. The third and seventh set a fair standard and the form should work out.

1144 DUBAI TENNIS CHAMPIONSHIPS STKS (REGISTERED AS THE JOHN PORTER STAKES) (GROUP 3) 1m 4f 5y
2:10 (2:10) (Class 1) 4-Y-O+
£27,254 (£10,329; £5,169; £2,577; £1,291; £648) **Stalls** Low

Form RPR

265- **1** **Maraahel (IRE)**[132] [6782] 6-9-3 121..............................(b1) RHills 7 120
(Sir Michael Stoute) *lw: t.k.h and set modest pce tl qcknd fr 5f out: hrd drvn whn chal fr 2f out: hld on wl thrght fnl f* **9/4**[1]

1134 **2** *nk* **Mighty**[28] [761] 4-8-11 105.. JohnEgan 8 114
(Jane Chapple-Hyam) *lw: in tch: rdn and hdwy to chse wnr 3f out: hrd rdn to chal fr 2f out: upsides ins last: no ex nr fin* **11/1**

325- **3** *1 1/4* **Munsef**[182] [6103] 5-8-12 110.................................. MartinDwyer 5 112
(J L Dunlop) *chsd ldrs: rdn and outpcd over 4f out: styd on again u.p fnl f: gng on cl home* **11/4**[2]

113- **4** *1* **Sergeant Cecil**[181] [6119] 8-9-5 115.............................. LDettori 9 118
(B R Millman) *b.bkwd: hld up in rr: pushed along 3f out: swtchd rt to outside 2f out: drvn and styd on fnl f: gng on cl home* **8/1**

313- **5** *1/2* **Admiral's Cruise (USA)**[218] [5342] 5-9-1 112............(b1) JimmyFortune 3 113
(B J Meehan) *rr: hdwy 4f out: drvn to chse ldrs fr 3f out: one pce fnl 2f* **4/1**[3]

334- **6** *1 3/4* **The Whistling Teal**[182] [6103] 11-8-12 107.................... SteveDrowne 1 107
(G Wragg) *hld up in rr: rdn over 3f out: kpt on fr over 1f out but nvr gng pce to get into contention* **25/1**

50-6 **7** *nk* **Akarem**[20] [882] 6-8-12 105.................................... PatCosgrave 2 107
(K R Burke) *chsd ldr: rdn 4f out: sn one pce* **28/1**

442- **8** *3* **Bulwark (IRE)**[189] [5967] 5-8-12 104..........................(be) JimCrowley 6 102
(Mrs A J Perrett) *hld up: hdwy 5f out: rdn 4f out: wknd fr 3f out* **33/1**

111- **9** *1* **Green Room (FR)**[174] [6251] 4-8-8 101.............................. EddieAhern 4 97
(J L Dunlop) *lw: chsd ldrs: rdn over 3f out: sn wknd* **16/1**

2m 36.83s (0.84) **Going Correction** 0.0s/f (Good)
WFA 4 from 5yo+ 1lb **9** Ran SP% **113.0**
Speed ratings (Par 113):97,96,95,95,94 93,93,91,90
CSF £26.72 TOTE £3.10: £1.40, £3.50, £1.30; EX 24.60 Trifecta £186.10 Pool: £524.46 - 2.00 winning tickets..
Owner Hamdan Al Maktoum **Bred** Shadwell Estate Company Limited **Trained** Newmarket, Suffolk

FOCUS
A decent renewal but an unsatisfactory pace led to something of a sprint to the line, which did not suit the stronger stayers who were held up. The form should not be taken literally.

NOTEBOOK
Maraahel(IRE), third in this race last year, had 6lb in hand of his nearest rival on official ratings. With blinkers replacing the usual visor, he was plenty keen enough out in front, but his rider excels on front-runners and was able to slow things right down rounding the turn into the straight, before quickening things up again once in line for home. He held on well from Mighty's strong challenge and will apparently now head to Royal Ascot to try and repeat last year's success in the Hardwicke Stakes. (op 15-8 tchd 7-4)
Mighty, highly progressive on the All-Weather this winter, was always well placed in what was a tactical race, but this was still a career-best effort and he has clearly translated his improvement from the sand back to turf. (tchd 12-1)
Munsef, runner-up in this 12 months ago, failed to win a race last year and was subsequently gelded. This race was not run to suit him and, although he finished well, he was never going to get to the front two. He showed that he retains his ability though, and he may benefit from dropping back into Listed company for a confidence booster. (op 10-3)
Sergeant Cecil ◆, who made the leap from handicapper to Group 1 winner last season, had to give weight all round and made a highly encouraging return to the track over a trip well short of his best despite looking as though the race would bring him on beforehand. Held up out the back as usual, he was at a major disadvantage given the lack of pace, and he only got going late on. He did fly home to finish fourth though, and this will have set him up very nicely for the season ahead. The Yorkshire Cup is apparently next on his agenda. (op 10-1)
Admiral's Cruise(USA), blinkered for the first time, has needed his first run of the season in his previous two years of racing but won second time up both in 2005 and 2006, so it is entirely possible that he will come on a bundle for this reappearance and be difficult to beat next time. (op 9-2)
The Whistling Teal, fifth in this race last year when the ground was more suitable, will no doubt now be heading to Chester in an attempt to follow up last year's success in the Ormonde Stakes, and connections will be hoping for a spot of rain for him.
Akarem had already had a race this season when sixth in a German Group 3 earlier in the month so he had a fitness advantage over most of the field. He also raced handily in what was a tactical race. Softer ground might help him, but he looks likely to prove difficult to place this term. (op 20-1)

Bulwark(IRE), who is not straightforward, needs further and would not have been suited by this tactical race.
Green Room(FR), who looked suited to soft ground when improving from winning handicaps to taking a fillies' Listed race in Italy last backend, had more to do against the colts and up in grade. She will be happier back racing against her own sex. (op 20-1)

1145 BLOOR HOMES SPRING CUP (HERITAGE H'CAP) 1m (S)
2:40 (2:43) (Class 2) 4-Y-O+
£24,928 (£7,464; £3,732; £1,868; £932; £468) **Stalls** Centre

Form RPR

130- **1** **Pinpoint (IRE)**^{168} [6337] 5-9-8 **100** AdamKirby 11 112
(W R Swinburn) *lw: chsd ldrs: rdn: edgd lft and led 1f out: drvn out* **8/1^{2}**

150- **2** *1 1/4* **Royal Oath (USA)**^{177} [6192] 4-9-1 **93** JimmyFortune 4 102
(J H M Gosden) *lw: chsd ldrs: chal over 2f out: tl slt ld over 1f out: sn hdd: stayed on but nt pce of wnr ins last* **9/1^{3}**

613- **3** *1 1/4* **Heaven Sent**^{261} [4083] 4-8-9 **87** NickyMackay 10 93
(Sir Michael Stoute) *chsd ldrs: rdn over 2f out: styd on fnl f but nvr quite gng pce of ldng pair* **8/1^{2}**

155- **4** *hd* **Macedon**^{225} [5150] 4-8-4 **82** ow1 MartinDwyer 21 88
(J S Moore) *towards rr: rdn and hdwy over 2f out: styd on fnl f but nvr quite gng pce to chal* **12/1**

4645 **5** *shd* **Marajaa (IRE)**^{21} [840] 5-8-9 **87** BrettDoyle 7 93
(W J Musson) *in tch: rdn and hdwy over 2f out: pressed ldrs 1f out: kpt on same pce ins last* **33/1**

402- **6** *nk* **Acheekyone (IRE)**^{289} [3224] 4-8-10 **88** MichaelHills 19 93+
(B J Meehan) *hld up in rr: hdwy and nt clr run over 1f out: swtchd lft and r.o wl: gng on cl home* **8/1^{2}**

00-6 **7** *hd* **Audience**^{21} [848] 7-8-9 **87** PaulDoe 3 92
(J Akehurst) *rr: hdwy over 2f out: sn rdn to chasde ldrs: kpt on same pce ins last* **25/1**

-155 **8** *hd* **Fajr (IRE)**^{11} [993] 5-8-9 **87** JohnEgan 22 91
(Miss Gay Kelleway) *b: towards rr: hdwy over 2f out: r.o fnal f: nt pce to rch ldrs* **16/1**

0-05 **9** *1 1/2* **My Paris**^{21} [848] 6-9-1 **93** DO'Donohoe 9 94
(K A Ryan) *pressed ldrs tl slt advantage fr over 2f out tl hdd over 1f out: one pce whn hmpd sn after* **16/1**

320- **10** *hd* **Direct Debit (IRE)**^{303} [2774] 4-8-10 **88** JamieSpencer 13 88+
(M L W Bell) *chsd ldrs: rdn to chal 2f out: one pce whn hmpd 1f out: n.d after* **20/1**

00-5 **11** *nk* **Plum Pudding (IRE)**^{35} [701] 4-9-3 **95** RichardHughes 14 95
(R Hannon) *lw: rr: hdwy over 2f out: kpt on fnl f but nvr gng pce to be competitive* **10/1**

2124 **12** *hd* **Rapid City**^{21} [842] 4-8-7 **85** JamesDoyle 5 84
(Miss J Feilden) *rr: rdn and hdwy over 1f out: fin wl: nt trble ldrs* **20/1**

000- **13** *1* **Ace Of Hearts**^{190} [5945] 8-9-5 **97** SebSanders 16 94
(C F Wall) *b.bkwd: rr: hdwy fr 2f out but nvr in contention* **25/1**

3450 **14** *shd* **Bolodenka (IRE)**^{21} [848] 5-9-3 **95** PaulHanagan 12 92
(R A Fahey) *chsd ldrs: rdn 3f out: wknd over 1f out* **12/1**

00-0 **15** *1 1/2* **Nanton (USA)**^{7} [1041] 5-8-7 **85** JimmyQuinn 1 78
(N Wilson) *pressed ldrs: ev ch 2f out: wknd fnl f* **33/1**

5060 **16** *1/2* **Zato (IRE)**^{21} [840] 4-8-11 **89** TedDurcan 20 81
(M R Channon) *rr: sme prog fnl 2f: nvr rchd ldrs* **25/1**

530- **17** *1 1/2* **The Snatcher (IRE)**^{211} [5501] 4-9-1 **93** DaneO'Neill 8 82
(R Hannon) *towards rr: pushed along 1/2-way and nvr gng pce to be competitive* **50/1**

040- **18** *1/2* **Rocamadour**^{203} [5675] 5-9-6 **98** DarryllHolland 18 85
(M R Channon) *lw: pressed ldrs: ev ch over 2f out: sn rdn: wknd over 1f out* **25/1**

00-1 **19** *1/2* **European Dream (IRE)**^{21} [846] 4-8-11 **89** JoeFanning 2 75
(R C Guest) *a towards rr* **16/1**

/13- **20** *1* **Night Crescendo (USA)**^{331} [1951] 4-8-13 **91** LDettori 15 75
(Mrs A J Perrett) *lw: in tch: hdwy to chse ldrs 1/2-way: wknd fr 2f out* **15/2^{1}**

40-0 **21** *nk* **Zero Tolerance (IRE)**^{21} [848] 7-9-10 **102** PaulFessey 23 85
(T D Barron) *racd alone under stands rail and mde most tl hdd over 2f out: sn wknd* **33/1**

300- **22** *3 1/2* **Prince Of Thebes (IRE)**^{183} [6093] 6-9-4 **99** RichardKingscote$^{(3)}$ 6 74
(J Akehurst) *swtg: nvr bttr than mid-div* **50/1**

16-0 **23** *7* **Middlemarch (IRE)**^{7} [1040] 7-7-12 **76** oh1 AdrianMcCarthy 17 35
(J S Goldie) *chsd ldrs over 5f* **33/1**

1m 36.92s (-3.70) **Going Correction** -0.225s/f (Firm) **23** Ran SP% **137.8**
Speed ratings (Par 109):109,107,106,106,106 105,105,105,104,103 103,103,102,102,100 100,98,98,97,96 96,92,85
CSF £72.23 CT £634.00 TOTE £10.10: £3.20, £3.10, £2.60, £3.50; EX 633.92 Trifecta £1163.50 Part won. Pool: £1,638.80 - 0.40 winning tickets..
Owner Full Circle **Bred** Joseph Rogers **Trained** Aldbury, Herts
■ Stewards' Enquiry : Adam Kirby three-day ban: careless riding May 2-4)

FOCUS
A competitive handicap run at a fair gallop, although the time was 0.78sec slower than the maiden which opened the card. The form looks solid and should work out.

NOTEBOOK
Pinpoint(IRE), whose best effort last year came when third in the Cambridgeshire, was well supported on course from 16-1. He came with a strong run in the closing stages, as one might expect of a gelding that gets a further two furlongs, and looks Listed class at least on this evidence. Whether he will be as suited to races of fewer runners often run at a more tactical pace remains to be seen, though. The immediate plan is a decent handicap over 1m2f at Newmarket on Guineas weekend. (op 16-1)
Royal Oath(USA), missing the tongue tie he wore on all but one of his five starts last season, also saw his race out strongly. Being quite lightly raced, he remains open to further improvement. (op 10-1 tchd 11-1)
Heaven Sent, a progressive filly last summer, had been off the track since August, but she returned in fine fettle and put up a career-best effort. Even if the Handicapper puts her up a few pounds for this she will remain of interest for a similar race.
Macedon, whose connections had had plans to run him in Dubai this spring but were unable to get him rated high enough last summer to make him eligible, looked one of the more interesting runners, being still lightly raced and open to considerable improvement this term. Carrying 1lb overweight, he finished to some effect and looks set for a good season.
Marajaa(IRE), fit from an All-Weather campaign, looked one of the more exposed runners in the line-up, but he had only had three previous starts on turf in this country and so was open to a little improvement, especially on quick ground.
Acheekyone(IRE) seems to find winning difficult but he once again ran well in defeat. Representing a yard whose runners are tending to need their reappearance outings, he was staying on late after not enjoying the best of luck inside the final two furlongs. (op 9-1)
Audience, running off a 2lb lower mark than when last successful, followed up his sixth in the Lincoln last time, albeit from a good draw, with another solid effort. He looks to have returned in good form.
Fajr(IRE), who appears to be high enough in the handicap at present, might have been suited by a stronger all round pace.
My Paris finished one place in front of Audience in the Lincoln but could not confirm the form on this quicker ground.
Direct Debit(IRE) should improve for this first outing since finishing down the field in the Britannia Handicap at Royal Ascot. (op 22-1 tchd 25-1 in places)
Plum Pudding(IRE) appeared to have conditions to suit but was disappointing.
Rapid City, having his first outing on turf in this country, finished well from off the pace and will be suited by a return to 1m2f.
Night Crescendo(USA), who beat Acheekyone over this course and distance last April, looked to have a good chance on that form and was sent off favourite with Dettori aboard, but his stable has not really kicked into gear yet and he was disappointing. (op 8-1 tchd 10-1 in a place)
Zero Tolerance(IRE), who needs softer ground than this, was the only one to race down the normally favoured stands'-side rail. The rest raced up the centre of the track.

1146 DUBAI DUTY FREE STKS (REGISTERED AS THE FRED DARLING STAKES) (GROUP 3) (FILLIES) 7f (S)
3:15 (3:19) (Class 1) 3-Y-O
£27,254 (£10,329; £5,169; £2,577; £1,291; £648) **Stalls** Centre

Form RPR

01- **1** **Majestic Roi (USA)**^{317} [2375] 3-9-0 81 JamieSpencer 3 102+
(M R Channon) *lw: stdd s: t.k.h and hld up rr: stdy hdwy fr 2f out: qcknd to ld ins fnl f: drvn and hld on wl cl home* **25/1**

211- **2** *nk* **Indian Ink (IRE)**^{204} [5654] 3-9-0 111 RichardHughes 6 101
(R Hannon) *trckd ldrs: shkn up over 1f out: n.m.r 1f out: drvn and qcknd ins last: kpt on wl but a jst hld by wnr* **15/8^{1}**

160- **3** *2* **Elusive Flash (USA)**^{182} [6105] 3-9-0 82 JoeFanning 5 96
(P F I Cole) *led: rdn over 2f out: kpt slt advantage tl hdd ins last: sn one pce* **66/1**

221- **4** *2* **Cast In Gold (USA)**^{182} [6099] 3-9-0 87 LDettori 4 91
(B J Meehan) *lw: chsd ldrs: rdn and ev ch 2f out: wknd ins last* **7/1^{3}**

123- **5** *1/2* **Silca Chiave**^{204} [5654] 3-9-0 107 TedDurcan 1 89
(M R Channon) *chsd ldrs: rdn and ev chnace 2f out: wknd ins last* **8/1**

116- **6** *nk* **Sesmen**^{210} [5522] 3-9-0 105 (t) OscarUrbina 10 89
(M Botti) *chsd ldrs: rdn over 2f out: wknd fnl f* **10/1**

12-0 **7** *1/2* **Darrfonah (IRE)**^{86} [246] 3-9-0 109 SebSanders 9 87
(C E Brittain) *chsd ldrs: rdn along 3f out: stl ev ch 2f out: wknd fnl f* **16/1**

120- **8** *1 1/2* **Wid (USA)**^{204} [5654] 3-9-0 101 RHills 12 83
(J L Dunlop) *rr: rdn and sme prog 2f out: sn one pce and nvr in contention* **12/1**

130- **9** *1* **Russian Rosie (IRE)**^{211} [5503] 3-9-0 89 EddieAhern 11 81
(J G Portman) *a towards rr* **80/1**

311- **10** *1* **Wait Watcher (IRE)**^{214} [5464] 3-9-0 99 TPO'Shea 7 78
(P A Blockley) *a towards rr* **20/1**

2- **11** *nk* **Cartimandua**^{281} [3495] 3-9-0 JimmyFortune 13 77
(E S McMahon) *b.bkwd: in tch: rdn 1/2-way: sn btn* **40/1**

612- **12** *2 1/2* **Silk Blossom (IRE)**^{214} [5464] 3-9-0 112 MichaelHills 8 71
(B W Hills) *a towards rr* **4/1^{2}**

123- **13** *5* **Puggy (IRE)**^{189} [5966] 3-9-0 102 (t) DaneO'Neill 2 58
(R A Kvisla) *t.k.h: in tch: drvn to chse ldrs over 3f out: wknd 2f out* **9/1**

1m 23.67s (-3.33) **Going Correction** -0.225s/f (Firm) **13** Ran SP% **124.8**
Speed ratings (Par 105):110,109,107,105,104 104,103,101,100,99 99,96,90
CSF £73.05 TOTE £29.00: £6.30, £1.60, £14.80; EX 100.80 TRIFECTA Not won..
Owner Jaber Abdullah **Bred** Gaines-Gentry Thoroughbreds **Trained** West Ilsley, Berks
■ Stewards' Enquiry : Oscar Urbina one-day ban: used whip in incorrect place in forehand position (May 2)

FOCUS
Run in a time almost identical to that of the Greenham Stakes later on the card, this 1000 Guineas trial saw much-improved efforts from the winner, third and fourth. However, the winner is not entered at Newmarket and the form may not be totally reliable.

NOTEBOOK
Majestic Roi(USA), one of only three in the race not entered in the 1000 Guineas, was well regarded at two but had only won a maiden so came into the race officially rated just 81. She impressed in quickening up from off the pace to beat a Group 1 winner into second, so it is difficult to crab the form, and she looks likely to benefit from a step up in trip, as her Oaks entry suggests. She certainly seems to be a fast-ground filly. (op 40-1)
Indian Ink(IRE), last year's Cheveley Park winner, was given every chance and quickened up well with the winner, the pair having the race to themselves in the closing stages. As a daughter of Indian Ridge it is quite possible that conditions were plenty fast enough for her, but she still ran a very acceptable Guineas trial. Her stamina for a mile should not be a concern on pedigree, so 16-1 looks a fair each-way price for the Newmarket Classic. (op 13-8 tchd 2-1 in places)
Elusive Flash(USA) is the spanner in the works with regard to rating the form as she had looked fairly exposed at two, although it is possible that she has improved for this faster ground. She also got the run of the race out in front. Another not entered at Newmarket, she is likely to chase further black type at Bath next.
Cast In Gold(USA) is another with only a maiden win to her name but she ran into some smart fillies in defeat prior to that and looked a potential improver at three. That was reflected in the betting as she was well supported in from big prices early. Her breeding suggests she should get a mile and further this term and, coming from the stable she does, she should improve for this reappearance outing. (op 18-1)
Silca Chiave, runner-up in the Moyglare and third in the Cheveley Park, looked the stable first string on that form, but she was well and truly eclipsed by her stablemate. She seems to go on any ground but looks a sprinting prospect for the rest of the year.
Sesmen had looked a smart prospect prior to flopping in the Fillies' Mile and had a tongue tie fitted for the first time on her three-year-old reappearance. A stronger pace over this trip - she is already a winner over a mile - would probably have suited her, and she is another who can improve for the outing. (op 9-1 tchd 11-1)
Darrfonah(IRE) had the advantage of having had a previous outing this term - in Dubai - but she is a half-sister to Dilshaan and bred to be an Oaks filly so it would be unwise to discount improvement when she is stepped up in distance. (op 14-1)
Wid(USA), last in the Cheveley Park on her final start at two, should have been happier back on this faster surface but was again found wanting. She needs to drop in grade.
Silk Blossom(IRE), the Lowther winner, improved for soft ground last season and these conditions were probably just too fast for this daughter of Barathea. (op 9-2)
Puggy(IRE), who was keen off the fairly steady early gallop, failed to give the Rockfel form a boost and was most disappointing. She could prove hard to place this season. Official explanation: jockey said filly stopped very quickly (op 14-1)

1147 LANE'S END GREENHAM STKS (GROUP 3) (C&G) 7f (S)
3:55 (3:57) (Class 1) 3-Y-O
£27,254 (£10,329; £5,169; £2,577; £1,291; £648) **Stalls** Centre

Form RPR

12- **1** **Major Cadeaux**^{305} [2719] 3-9-0 106 RichardHughes 6 117
(R Hannon) *lw: b: mde all: drvn and qcknd fr over 1f out: kpt on strly thrght fnl f: readily* **10/3^{2}**

111- **2** 3½ **Dutch Art**[204] 5656 3-9-0 121 .... JimmyFortune 7 108
(P W Chapple-Hyam) *lw: t.k.h early: trckd wnr most of way: rdn and effrt over 1f out: kpt on same pce ins last* **8/11**[1]

110- **3** 1 **Halicarnassus (IRE)**[189] 5965 3-9-0 116 .... DarryllHolland 3 106
(M R Channon) *disp 2nd: rdn over 2f out: kpt on same pce fr over 1f out* **8/1**[3]

-214 **4** 2½ **Mastership (IRE)**[28] 760 3-9-0 96 ....(b) EddieAhern 1 99
(C E Brittain) *in tch: rdn and effrt over 2f out: nvr gng pce to be competitive: wknd fnl f* **33/1**

13- **5** ¾ **Tariq**[305] 2719 3-9-0 103 .... LDettori 4 97
(P W Chapple-Hyam) *chsd ldrs: rdn 3f out: wknd over 1f out* **8/1**[3]

131- **6** 23 **Captain Marvelous (IRE)**[175] 6229 3-9-0 117 .... MichaelHills 2 37
(B W Hills) *rdn along 1/2-way: nvr in contention: eased fnl f* **14/1**

1m 23.66s (-3.34) **Going Correction** -0.225s/f (Firm) **6** Ran SP% **112.8**
Speed ratings (Par 108):110,106,104,102,101 74
CSF £6.21 TOTE £4.30: £2.00, £1.30; EX 6.70.
Owner N A Woodcock, A C Pickford & David Mort **Bred** R Evain **Trained** East Everleigh, Wilts

FOCUS
An informative Guineas trial and run in a very similar time to that of the fillies' trial earlier on the card. It was something of a tactical race but the winner still impressed in pulling nicely clear.

NOTEBOOK
Major Cadeaux ◆, who was last seen finishing runner-up in the Coventry Stakes, in which he got jarred up, has always been well regarded in his stable and has been considered a Guineas horse for some time. He enjoyed the run of the race here, setting a steady gallop before quickening things up inside the final quarter mile, but he still drew stylishly clear from a dual Group 1 winner in Dutch Art, and made a very good impression. He would not be a certainty to get the mile at Newmarket on paper, but his trainer is confident that he will do so, and the bookmakers were quick to slash his odds for the 2000 Guineas to a best price of 6-1. (tchd 3-1 and 7-2)
Dutch Art, unbeaten at two including wins in the Group 1 Prix Morny and Middle Park Stakes, was a hot favourite to make a winning reappearance, but his trainer had warned that he was not 100 per cent fit for his return, in contrast with his stablemate Tariq. It was disappointing that he was unable to match the winner, who admittedly got the run of the race out in front, when that rival quickened up, but on the plus side he did not seem to be beaten by the trip and should come on for this. His trainer thought that the tactical nature of the race was all against him and that he will be a different proposition at Newmarket in a fortnight's time, and he should know, as he sent out Rodrigo de Triano to finish fourth in this race prior to winning the Guineas. There is still a doubt about his capacity to get a mile, but his trainer has always been confident on that front. His Guineas price has drifted out to 12-1 with the bookmakers and almost double that on the exchanges. (op 5-6 tchd 10-11 and 4-6 in a place)
Halicarnassus(IRE) was flattered by his win in the Superlative Stakes when the leaders fell in a heap in front of him and waltzed home for a visually-impressive success, but he was also well below form when running poorly in the Dewhurst. His true ability probably lies somewhere in between those two performances, and this effort seemed to back that view up. He could well be a difficult horse to place this season. (op 9-1 tchd 10-1)
Mastership(IRE), who was rated just 65 at the end of last season's turf campaign, improved out of all recognition on the All-Weather over the winter, and while an outsider here, he had a valuable fitness edge on his rivals. His performance is probably the best guide to the level of the form. (op 25-1)
Tariq, like Major Cadeaux, was last seen in the Coventry Stakes at Royal Ascot, where he finished third. He has not grown but looked very fit for this reappearance so his performance was a bit disappointing in the circumstances. It looks as though he will be a sprinter this season. (tchd 15-2)
Captain Marvelous(IRE), who won a Group 2 race in France last season having previously run third in the Middle Park, ran way below his best. Perhaps the ground was too fast but he has plenty to prove now. Official explanation: jockey said colt moved poorly throughout (op 12-1)

1148 PERTEMPS H'CAP — 2m
4:25 (4:28) (Class 4) (0-85,85) 4-Y-0+ **£7,772** (£2,312; £1,155; £577) **Stalls** High

Form RPR

301- **1** **Junior**[39] 6244 4-8-11 77 .... RichardHughes 4 86+
(B J Meehan) *lw: mde all: hrd rdn fr 3f out: hld on gamely thrght fnl 2f* **5/2**[1]

200- **2** hd **Ned Ludd (IRE)**[39] 6017 4-8-11 77 .... EddieAhern 12 86
(J G Portman) *chsd ldrs: rdn 3f out: chal over 2f out: kpt on wl u.p fnl 2f but nvr quite gng pce of wnr ins last* **20/1**

6-11 **3** ½ **Dundry**[63] 488 6-9-3 79 ....(p) GeorgeBaker 14 89+
(G L Moore) *hld up rr: stdy hdwy whn nt clr run 2f out:swtchd rt to outside over 1f out: str run fnl f:fin wl:nt quite get up* **17/2**

50-0 **4** shd **Trance (IRE)**[13] 955 7-9-1 77 ....(p) PaulFessey 10 85
(T D Barron) *lw: mid-div: rdn over 3f out: stayed on fr over 2f out: kpt on wl fnl f: one pce nr fin* **8/1**[3]

23/1 **5** 1½ **Mind How You Go (FR)**[45] 640 9-8-10 75 .... StephaneBreux(3) 6 81
(J R Best) *chsd ldrs: rdn and outpcd 3f out: styd on u.p fr 2f out: kpt on cl home* **12/1**

-133 **6** shd **Nawow**[51] 593 7-8-10 72 .... DaneO'Neill 9 78
(P D Cundell) *rr: hdwy on outside fr 3f out: chsd ldrs and rdn fr 2f out: kpt on same pce ins last* **16/1**

1-12 **7** ¾ **Salute (IRE)**[14] 944 8-9-9 85 .... RobertHavlin 13 90
(P G Murphy) *in tch: rdn to chse ldrs fr 3f out: one pce fr over 1f out* **10/1**

01-4 **8** 1¼ **High Point (IRE)**[21] 844 9-8-10 72 .... JimmyQuinn 1 75
(G P Enright) *chsd ldrs: rdn 3f out: wknd fnl f* **20/1**

22-5 **9** ¾ **Kayf Aramis**[10] 1003 5-8-10 72 ....(p) SteveDrowne 5 75
(J L Spearing) *chsd wnr: chal fr 4f out tl over 2f out: wknd fnl f* **14/1**

5-56 **10** 2½ **Flame Creek (IRE)**[22] 829 11-9-4 80 .... OscarUrbina 7 80
(E J Creighton) *lw: hld up in rr: hdwy 3f out: nvr in contention: wknd over 1f out* **50/1**

30-2 **11** 1 **Mister Right (IRE)**[16] 693 6-9-0 76 ....(t) JamieSpencer 3 74
(D J S Ffrench Davis) *rr: sme hdwy on ins 3f out: nvr in contention: wknd over 1f out* **8/1**[3]

166- **12** 2½ **Stoop To Conquer**[24] 5526 7-9-5 81 .... JimmyFortune 11 76
(A W Carroll) *mid-div: rdn over 3f out: sn btn* **7/2**[2]

50-0 **13** shd **Establishment**[21] 844 10-9-0 76 .... TedDurcan 2 71
(C A Cyzer) *chsd ldrs: rdn over 3f out: wknd 2f out* **25/1**

04-0 **14** 5 **Pocketwood**[21] 844 5-8-10 72 .... StephenCarson 8 61
(Jean-Rene Auvray) *a towards rr* **80/1**

3m 32.98s (-3.17) **Going Correction** 0.0s/f (Good)
WFA 4 from 5yo+ 4lb **14** Ran SP% **129.4**
Speed ratings (Par 105):107,106,106,106,105 105,105,104,104,103 102,101,101,98
CSF £65.12 CT £403.30 TOTE £3.40: £1.90, £5.90, £3.10; EX 83.30.
Owner Paul Green **Bred** P C Green **Trained** Manton, Wilts
■ Stewards' Enquiry : Paul Fessey two-day ban: careless riding (May 2-3)

FOCUS
A fair staying handicap and very competitive with the form looking sound enough. The pace was good through the early stages, but the eventual winner, Junior, slowed things up down the back straight, and a few of these would have preferred a more end-to-end gallop.
Mister Right(IRE) Official explanation: jockey said gelding was unsuited by the slow pace

1149 DUBAI DUTY FREE MILLENNIUM MILLIONAIRE H'CAP — 1m 2f 6y
4:55 (4:58) (Class 4) (0-85,86) 4-Y-0+ **£5,829** (£1,734; £866; £432) **Stalls** Low

Form RPR

221- **1** **Red Gala**[190] 5934 4-9-3 84 .... LDettori 1 100+
(Sir Michael Stoute) *lw: trckd ldrs: drvn along fr 2f out: qckd to ld last half f: readily* **7/4**[1]

326- **2** 1¼ **Samurai Way**[197] 5792 5-9-1 82 .... NickyMackay 5 91
(L M Cumani) *chsd ldrs: rdn over 2f out: styd on fnl f and tk 2nd cl home but nvr gng pce to rch wnr* **6/1**[2]

300- **3** nk **Instructor**[132] 5810 6-8-12 79 .... PaulHanagan 3 87
(R A Fahey) *led: rdn fr 3f out: styd on wl tl hdd last half f: lost 2nd cl home* **16/1**

0311 **4** 3 **Art Modern (IRE)**[20] 868 5-9-1 82 ....(b) GeorgeBaker 7 84+
(G L Moore) *towards rr: hdwy over 2f out: rdn and r.o wl fnl f: gng on nr fin: nt rch ldrs* **12/1**

10-1 **5** hd **Robustian**[11] 993 4-9-5 86 .... StephenCarson 11 88
(Eve Johnson Houghton) *chsd ldrs: hrd rdn fr 2f out: wknd fnl f* **7/1**[3]

661- **6** ½ **Brief Goodbye**[211] 5511 7-9-0 81 .... TedDurcan 14 82
(John Berry) *swtg: rr: hdwy fr 3f out: styd on fnl 2f: one pce ins last* **16/1**

0/04 **7** 3 **Prince Nureyev (IRE)**[31] 726 7-8-13 80 .... JimCrowley 4 75
(B R Millman) *lw: chsd ldrs: rdn 3f out: wknd fr 2f out* **14/1**

16-0 **8** ¾ **Montpellier (IRE)**[21] 848 4-9-4 85 .... RichardHughes 2 79
(E A L Dunlop) *hld up in tch: trckd ldrs and rdn over 2f out: wknd over 1f out* **11/1**

9 1 **Dafarabad (IRE)**[81] 3814 5-8-12 79 .... JamieSpencer 8 71
(Jonjo O'Neill) *rr tl hdwy on ins to 5f out: chsd ldrs 4f out: wknd over 1f out* **16/1**

100- **10** 1¼ **Great View (IRE)**[159] 6462 8-8-8 78 .... RichardKingscote(3) 16 68
(Mrs A L M King) *lw: rr: hdwy on outside 5f out: nvr gng pce to rch ldrs: wknd 2f out* **28/1**

21/ **11** 1¾ **Top Gear**[739] 982 5-9-4 85 .... PaulDoe 9 71?
(Mrs L J Mongan) *lw: hld up in rr: nt clr run over 2f out: taken to outside over 1f out: kpt on fnl f: nvr in contention* **25/1**

0-02 **12** ½ **Along The Nile**[11] 995 5-9-3 84 ....(t) JimmyFortune 12 69
(K G Reveley) *rr: sme hdwy and n.m.r over 2f out: nvr in contention after* **11/1**

045- **13** shd **Russian Consort (IRE)**[81] 3980 5-9-0 81 .... DaneO'Neill 10 66
(A King) *lw: chsd ldrs: rdn 3f out: sn wknd* **22/1**

116- **14** ¾ **Strawberry Lolly**[239] 4763 4-9-2 83 .... EddieAhern 15 67
(M Botti) *rr: sme hdwy whn nt clr run over 2f out: eased and n.d after* **20/1**

2m 7.38s (-1.33) **Going Correction** 0.0s/f (Good) **14** Ran SP% **128.2**
Speed ratings (Par 105):105,104,103,101,101 100,98,97,97,96 94,94,94,93
CSF £11.66 CT £141.77 TOTE £2.60: £1.60, £2.50, £3.90; EX 21.70 Place 6 £37.17, Place 5 £18.62..
Owner Cheveley Park Stud **Bred** Cheveley Park Stud Ltd **Trained** Newmarket, Suffolk
■ Stewards' Enquiry : L Dettori one-day ban: careless riding (May 2); one-day ban: second instance of careless riding (May 3)

FOCUS
A steadily-run handicap that suited those that raced fairly prominently. The form looks solid, though, rated through the third.
Robustian Official explanation: jockey said gelding hung right
Montpellier(IRE) Official explanation: jockey said gelding ran too free
T/Jkpt: Not won. T/Plt: £46.80 to a £1 stake. Pool: £129,634.90. 2,021.35 winning tickets.
T/Qpdt: £18.50 to a £1 stake. Pool: £4,779.50. 190.50 winning tickets. ST

1073 NOTTINGHAM (L-H)
Saturday, April 21

OFFICIAL GOING: Good to firm
Over the previous three days 30mm water had been put on the track. 'Good to firm with wet patches was the verdict'. All races run on inside old jump course.
Wind: light, half-against Weather: fine, sunny at first and mild

1150 WBX.COM WORLD BET EXCHANGE MAIDEN STKS — 5f 13y
5:30 (5:33) (Class 5) 2-Y-0 **£2,817** (£838; £418; £209) **Stalls** High

Form RPR

6 **1** **Group Therapy**[10] 999 2-9-3 .... MartinDwyer 8 75
(J A Osborne) *s.i.s: t.k.h: hdwy over 3f out: chal over 1f out: led ins last: hld on towards fin* **7/2**[1]

2 nk **Rebel Aclaim (IRE)** 2-8-9 .... JerryO'Dwyer(3) 6 69
(M G Quinlan) *led tl hdd ins last: kpt on wl towards fin* **11/1**

53 **3** 3½ **Rio Taffeta**[8] 1021 2-9-3 .... EdwardCreighton 10 60
(M R Channon) *sn outpcd and pushed along: hdwy 2f out: styd on to take 3rd ins last* **11/2**

4 2½ **In Honour (IRE)** 2-9-3 .... RichardMullen 11 50
(E S McMahon) *s.v.s: detached in last: hdwy over 1f out: fin wl: improve* **11/1**

5 ½ **She's Our Dream** 2-8-12 .... MickyFenton 9 43
(R C Guest) *prom: hmpd and lost pl over 3f out: kpt on fnl 2f* **17/2**

6 nk **Outside Edge (IRE)** 2-9-3 .... AdamKirby 3 47
(W R Swinburn) *trckd ldrs: lost pl 2f out* **4/1**[2]

7 1 **Jazzing About (USA)** 2-9-3 .... FergusSweeney 7 43
(P A Blockley) *dwlt: hdwy over 2f out: hung lft and lost pl over 1f out* **20/1**

8 ¾ **Rub Of The Relic (IRE)** 2-9-3 .... SimonWhitworth 2 40
(P A Blockley) *sn outpcd in rr: kpt onf inal 2f: nvr on terms* **50/1**

9 ¾ **Sonsue** 2-8-12 .... JamieMackay 4 32
(B Palling) *dwlt: sme hdwy over 2f out: wknd over 1f out* **66/1**

10 2 **Ridge Wood Dani (IRE)** 2-9-0 .... StephenDonohoe(3) 1 29
(E J Alston) *chsd ldrs: lost pl over 1f out* **20/1**

11 ¾ **Fidelias Dance** 2-8-12 .... KDarley 5 21
(M Johnston) *w ldrs: wandered and lost pl over 1f out* **9/2**[3]

62.68 secs (0.88) **Going Correction** -0.075s/f (Good) **11** Ran SP% **116.0**
Speed ratings (Par 92):89,88,82,78,78 77,76,74,73,70 69
CSF £40.33 TOTE £3.10: £1.80, £3.70, £2.00; EX 50.50.
Owner Elaine and Martyn Booth **Bred** Stratford Place Stud **Trained** Upper Lambourn, Berks

FOCUS
A fair juvenile contest rated around the third, and the first two could improve on the bare form.

NOTEBOOK
Group Therapy, a sharp type, took a keen grip after missing a beat at the start. He took a while to get on top and this is as far as he wants to get for the time being. (op 3-1)
Rebel Aclaim(IRE), a close-coupled February foal, knew her job. To her credit she fought back when headed and deserves to go one better. (op 7-1)

Rio Taffeta, the most experienced in the line-up, struggled badly to go the pace. Putting in all his best work at the finish, he already needs six furlongs. (op 7-1)

In Honour(IRE) ◆, a February foal, is an attractive, deep-bodied colt. He stood still when the gates opened and was still last with a furlong to run. He finished with a rare rattle and looks the best prospect in the line-up. (op 18-1)

She's Our Dream, a smallish, neat filly, did quite well to finish so close after being left short of room and stumbling early on. Official explanation: jockey said filly had been stumbling in the latter stages (op 12-1)

Outside Edge(IRE), a February foal, is on the small side and was noisy beforehand. He showed plenty of toe but began to struggle soon after the halfway mark. (op 9-2 tchd 5-1)

Fidelias Dance, a February foal, looks immature as yet. A lazy walker, she showed a moderate action going down and, coming off a straight line, she dropped right away. (op 4-1)

1151 JOIN WBX.COM NOW FOR £150 FREE BETS FILLIES' H'CAP 5f 13y

6:00 (6:00) (Class 5) (0-70,70) 3-Y-O **£2,817** (£838; £418; £209) **Stalls** High

Form RPR

100- **1** **Morinqua (IRE)**[189] 5956 3-9-4 **70** JamieMackay 2 81
(J G Given) *mde all on far side: overall ldr: rdn and styd on wl* **16/1**

521- **2** *2* **Aquilegia (IRE)**[171] 6295 3-9-3 **69** RichardMullen 16 75+
(E S McMahon) *led stands' side gp: hung bdly lft over 1f out: kpt on ins last* **9/2**[1]

104- **3** *1* **Cuppacocoa**[195] 5829 3-9-4 **70** AdamKirby 3 70
(C G Cox) *racd far side: in tch: styd on to take 2nd that side wl ins last* **11/2**[2]

0422 **4** *nk* **Diminuto**[17] 925 3-8-5 **64** FrankiePickard(7) 9 63
(M D I Usher) *s.s: hdwy over 2f out: kpt on same pce* **7/1**

360- **5** *hd* **Game Lady**[218] 5347 3-8-12 **67** StephenDonohoe(3) 14 65
(I A Wood) *chsd ldrs stands' side: kpt on same pce fnl f* **25/1**

260- **6** *hd* **Violet's Pride**[173] 6255 3-8-2 **57** DominicFox(3) 4 54
(S Parr) *chsd ldr far side: one pce fnl f: 3rd in that gp* **33/1**

204- **7** *nk* **Early Promise (IRE)**[186] 6032 3-8-3 **62** LukeMorris(7) 15 58
(P L Gilligan) *swvd lft s: racd stands' side: stmbld over 3f out: styd on wl ins last* **16/1**

321- **8** *nk* **Feelin Foxy**[134] 6742 3-9-4 **70** (v) KDarley 5 65
(D Shaw) *racd far side: chsd ldng pair that side: kpt on same pce fnl 2f: 4th in that gp* **8/1**

503- **9** *3* **Ocean Blaze**[186] 6025 3-9-1 **67** AdrianMcCarthy 10 52
(B R Millman) *chsd ldrs stands' side: wknd over 1f out* **16/1**

022- **10** *3* **Izabela Hannah**[186] 6025 3-9-2 **68** SebSanders 7 42
(R M Beckett) *racd stands' side: nvr nr ldrs* **9/2**[1]

006- **11** *½* **Silver Flame**[281] 3495 3-8-8 **60** FergusSweeney 1 32
(A W Carroll) *racd far side: a last in that gp of 5* **40/1**

0-60 **12** *nk* **Mid Ocean**[8] 1022 3-8-10 **62** (t) DarryllHolland 6 33
(P W D'Arcy) *dwlt: racd stands' side: nvr on terms* **13/2**[3]

0-20 **13** *2* **Descargo**[80] 311 3-8-0 **59** ow2 JackDean(7) 11 23
(W G M Turner) *in tch stands' side: edgd rt over 3f out: sn lost pl* **33/1**

0000 **14** *13* **Redflo**[8] 1031 3-8-4 **56** oh11 JamesDoyle 8 —
(Ms J S Doyle) *racd stands' side: mid-div: lost pl 3f out: sn bhd* **100/1**

61.23 secs (-0.57) **Going Correction** -0.075s/f (Good) **14** Ran SP% **119.5**

Speed ratings (Par 95):101,97,96,95,95 95,94,94,89,84 83,83,80,59

CSF £82.99 CT £473.50 TOTE £15.00: £3.70, £3.00, £2.50; EX 101.60.

Owner The Living Legend Racing Partnership **Bred** Corrin Stud **Trained** Willoughton, Lincs

FOCUS

Five went to race exclusively on the far side as the ground seemed slower against the stands' side rail after the watering. The form has a solid look about it with the third a consistent sort.

Aquilegia(IRE) Official explanation: jockey said filly hung left

Silver Flame Official explanation: jockey said filly hung right

1152 SUBSCRIBE NOW RACING UK £15 PER MONTH H'CAP 1m 6f 15y

6:30 (6:30) (Class 6) (0-65,65) 4-Y-0+ **£2,388** (£705; £352) **Stalls** Low

Form RPR

-635 **1** **Treason Trial**[64] 481 6-8-11 **52** MickyFenton 1 58
(Stef Liddiard) *hld up in rr: hdwy over 3f out: styd on to ld towards fin* **16/1**

26-1 **2** *shd* **Dark Parade (ARG)**[10] 1003 6-9-3 **61** StephenDonohoe(3) 10 66
(P D Evans) *chsd ldrs: styd on to ld ins last: hdd nr fin* **15/8**[1]

-130 **3** *nk* **Mister Completely (IRE)**[76] 354 6-8-12 **53** JamesDoyle 8 58
(Ms J S Doyle) *trckd ldrs: led over 1f out: hung lft: hdd ins last: no ex towards fin* **16/1**

345- **4** *¾* **My Legal Eagle (IRE)**[113] 5836 13-8-4 **45** DaleGibson 9 49
(E G Bevan) *in rr: hdwy over 2f out: kpt on wl fnl f* **25/1**

-144 **5** *3 ½* **Amwell Brave**[60] 507 6-9-1 **56** RichardMullen 4 55
(J R Jenkins) *mid-div: hdwy over 3f out: one pce fnl 2f* **10/1**[3]

0653 **6** *shd* **Silver Mont (IRE)**[25] 804 4-8-2 **45** (b) AdrianMcCarthy 7 44
(S R Bowring) *chsd ldrs: one pce fnl 3f* **16/1**

06-0 **7** *¾* **Kristoffersen**[12] 976 7-8-11 **52** KDarley 12 50
(Ian Williams) *mid-div: drvn 7f out: sn lost pl: kpt on fnl 2f* **18/1**

03-0 **8** *½* **Swords**[8] 1032 5-9-2 **57** CatherineGannon 2 54
(Heather Dalton) *trckd ldrs: t.k.h: effrt on outside over 2f out: one pce* **16/1**

20-5 **9** *1 ½* **Rose Bien**[27] 775 5-9-9 **64** (p) EdwardCreighton 16 59
(P J McBride) *trckd ldrs: wknd over 1f out* **6/1**[2]

2130 **10** *shd* **Reminiscent (IRE)**[50] 607 8-8-4 **45** (p) RichardThomas 13 40
(B P J Baugh) *in rr: drvn 4f out: nvr a factor* **12/1**

0/0- **11** *hd* **Highliner**[467] 73 5-8-8 **52** GregFairley(3) 6 47
(Mrs L Williamson) *trckd ldrs: wknd over 1f out* **50/1**

0-00 **12** *1* **Danceinthevalley (IRE)**[50] 605 5-8-3 **47** PatrickMathers(3) 14 40
(I W McInnes) *led: swtchd lft after s: t.k.h: hdd & wknd over 1f out* **66/1**

-330 **13** *½* **Art Investor**[66] 458 4-9-5 **62** SebSanders 11 55
(D R C Elsworth) *mid-div: hdwy 4f out: lost pl over 1f out* **10/1**[3]

-000 **14** *16* **Filliemou (IRE)**[9] 1011 6-8-4 **45** DavidKinsella 5 15
(A W Carroll) *in rr: lost pl over 2f out: sn wl bhd* **66/1**

15 *6* **Samizdat (FR)**[123] 4-9-3 **65** (b) TravisBlock(5) 15 27
(H Morrison) *hld up in mid-field: hdwy to chse ldrs 5f out: lost pl 3f out: sn bhd* **20/1**

3m 7.36s (0.26) **Going Correction** +0.075s/f (Good)

WFA 4 from 5yo+ 2lb **15** Ran SP% **117.3**

Speed ratings (Par 101):102,101,101,101,99 99,98,98,97,97 97,96,96,87,84

CSF £42.73 CT £510.80 TOTE £17.60: £5.50, £1.30, £3.90; EX 119.10.

Owner Mrs Stef Liddiard **Bred** A Pereira, Arnstein Stud **Trained** Great Shefford, Berks

FOCUS

A low-grade stayers' handicap run at a very steady pace and the first three rather getting into each others way in the closing stages. Even so the form looks sound rated through the placed horses.

1153 BET NOW AT WBX.COM MEDIAN AUCTION MAIDEN STKS 1m 1f 213y

7:00 (7:02) (Class 6) 3-Y-O **£2,388** (£705; £352) **Stalls** Low

Form RPR

35-3 **1** **Fever**[31] 719 3-9-3 75 PatDobbs 1 74
(R Hannon) *trckd ldr: forced wd over 2f out: led over 1f out: hld on towards fin* **5/4**[1]

00- **2** *hd* **Crystal Prince**[178] 6173 3-9-3 MickyFenton 8 74
(T P Tate) *led: shkn up over 4f out: ducked rt over 2f out: hdd over 1f out: rallied: jst hld* **66/1**

3 *5* **Mad Rush (USA)** 3-9-3 MartinDwyer 7 69+
(L M Cumani) *trckd ldrs: effrt whn hmpd over 2f out: kpt on to take modest 3rd last 75yds* **5/1**[3]

23- **4** *1* **Cleide Da Silva (USA)**[206] 5607 3-8-12 SebSanders 4 57
(J Noseda) *hld up: hdwy over 3f out: sn chsng ldrs: wknd fnl f* **6/4**[2]

5-5 **5** *3 ½* **Silver Mitzva (IRE)**[8] 1024 3-8-12 (p) DarryllHolland 3 53+
(M Botti) *trckd ldrs: rdn and hung lft over 3f out: wknd and eased jst ins last* **16/1**

5- **6** *¾* **The Quantum Kid**[222] 5239 3-9-0 SaleemGolam(3) 5 53
(T J Etherington) *s.i.s: outpcd over 3f out: nvr a factor* **22/1**

06- **7** *2* **Toboggan Lady**[138] 6697 3-8-12 VHalliday 2 44
(Mrs A Duffield) *mid-div: outpcd over 3f out* **100/1**

0-0 **8** *2 ½* **Lucy Rebecca**[11] 991 3-8-12 KDarley 6 39
(M R Channon) *in rr: drvn 4f out: nvr on terms* **16/1**

2m 14.39s (4.69) **Going Correction** +0.075s/f (Good) **8** Ran SP% **119.7**

Speed ratings (Par 96):84,83,79,79,76 75,74,72

CSF £99.10 TOTE £2.20: £1.10, £9.60, £1.90; EX 89.70.

Owner The Royal Ascot Racing Club **Bred** Roan Rocket Partners **Trained** East Everleigh, Wilts

FOCUS

A tactical affair and overall the form looks modest. The leader jinked away from the running rail coming to the two furlong marker, shying at a racecourse personnel with a bright, luminous bib stood hard against the running rail.

1154 VISITNOTTINGHAM.COM H'CAP 1m 1f 213y

7:30 (7:31) (Class 6) (0-60,60) 3-Y-O **£2,388** (£705; £352) **Stalls** Low

Form RPR

3422 **1** **Skye But N Ben**[19] 893 3-8-11 **53** (b) SebSanders 5 60
(T D Barron) *chsd ldrs: wnt 2nd over 2f out: led appr fnl f: styd on towards fin* **3/1**[1]

6005 **2** *1 ¼* **David's Cavalier**[19] 893 3-8-13 **55** FergusSweeney 4 60
(R Hollinshead) *trckd ldrs: led 7f out tl over 1f out: no ex ins last* **16/1**

000- **3** *2* **Sonara (IRE)**[205] 5640 3-9-4 **60** DarryllHolland 12 61
(M H Tompkins) *chsd ldrs: wnt 3rd 2f out: styd on same pce* **9/1**

065- **4** *1 ½* **Windbeneathmywings (IRE)**[161] 6449 3-9-4 **60** JamesDoyle 16 58
(J W Hills) *mid-div: hdwy 4f out: kpt on wl fnl f* **28/1**

050- **5** *1* **Isabella's Best (IRE)**[185] 6058 3-8-13 **55** ChrisCatlin 8 51
(E J O'Neill) *in rr: hdwy on wd outside over 2f out: styd on fnl f* **20/1**

0021 **6** *½* **A Mothers Love**[18] 907 3-8-11 **53** EdwardCreighton 15 49
(P J McBride) *hld up in rr: styd on fnl 2f: nvr trbld ldrs* **6/1**[2]

465 **7** *4* **Snake Hips**[29] 745 3-9-3 **59** DaleGibson 3 47
(B Palling) *tk keen grip on inner: trckd ldrs: hmpd after 1f: wknd fnl f* **20/1**

00-0 **8** *3* **Private Peachey (IRE)**[19] 893 3-8-10 **52** AdrianMcCarthy 10 34
(B R Millman) *led: hdd 7f out: wknd over 1f out* **28/1**

0444 **9** *½* **Brave Jack (IRE)**[17] 924 3-8-13 **55** RichardMullen 11 36
(J R Best) *in rr: nvr on terms* **7/1**[3]

6300 **10** *2 ½* **Lawyer To World**[29] 737 3-8-11 **53** MickyFenton 14 30
(N A Callaghan) *s.i.s: a in rr* **11/1**

062- **11** *½* **Regal Ovation**[207] 5597 3-9-3 **59** MartinDwyer 9 35
(W R Muir) *chsd ldrs: rdn over 4f out: lost pl over 2f out* **7/1**[3]

005- **12** *hd* **Clytha**[184] 6063 3-9-1 **57** HayleyTurner 1 32
(M L W Bell) *prom: rdn and lost pl 3f out* **16/1**

0050 **13** *1 ¼* **Tina's Ridge (IRE)**[17] 931 3-9-1 **57** KDarley 2 30
(E J Alston) *s.i.s: hdwy whn nt clr run 3f out: sn btn* **16/1**

050- **14** *7* **Ski For Luck (IRE)**[224] 5178 3-9-3 **59** TPO'Shea 13 18
(J L Dunlop) *t.k.h: trckd ldrs: lost pl over 2f out* **20/1**

00-0 **15** *nk* **Grazie Mille**[12] 974 3-8-10 **55** StephenDonohoe(3) 6 14
(R Brotherton) *a in rr: bhd fnl 3f* **66/1**

2m 11.5s (1.80) **Going Correction** +0.075s/f (Good) **15** Ran SP% **122.9**

Speed ratings (Par 96):95,94,92,91,90 90,86,84,84,82 81,81,80,74,74

CSF £50.53 CT £404.97 TOTE £4.10: £2.00, £7.00, £2.30; EX 48.30.

Owner Carequick Ltd-(air Conditioning) **Bred** Charles And David Hodge **Trained** Maunby, N Yorks

FOCUS

Another low-grade three-year-old handicap with the first three up there throughout in a race not run at a strong pace. The form is rated around the fourth and fifth.

Lawyer To World Official explanation: jockey said colt was denied a clear run

1155 COUNTRYSIDE RACENIGHT H'CAP 1m 54y

8:00 (8:00) (Class 6) (0-65,65) 3-Y-O **£2,388** (£705; £352) **Stalls** Centre

Form RPR

055- **1** **Graceful Steps (IRE)**[172] 6270 3-8-13 **60** RichardMullen 8 71
(E J O'Neill) *chsd ldrs: hrd drvn 4f out; swtchd rt over 1f out: styd on to ld towards fin* **20/1**

0002 **2** *¾* **Mark Of Love (IRE)**[17] 924 3-8-12 **59** KDarley 5 68
(M R Channon) *chsd ldrs: chal over 2f out: led appr fnl f: hdd and no ex towards fin* **7/1**[2]

350- **3** *1 ¼* **Grand Art (IRE)**[183] 6074 3-9-3 **64** SebSanders 16 70+
(M H Tompkins) *rr-div: hdwy on ins over 3f out: hrd rdn over 2f out: keeping on same pce whn n.m.r ins last* **11/1**

004- **4** *2* **Ask Yer Dad**[148] 6576 3-9-3 **64** MickyFenton 3 66
(Mrs P Sly) *led after 1f tl appr fnl f: wknd fnl 75yds* **7/1**[2]

640- **5** *1 ¾* **Baby Dordan (IRE)**[193] 5898 3-9-3 **64** MartinDwyer 9 62
(H J L Dunlop) *chsd ldrs: one pce fnl 2f* **12/1**

00-0 **6** *1 ½* **High Five Society**[17] 931 3-9-1 **62** AdrianMcCarthy 17 56
(S R Bowring) *mid-div: hdwy on outside over 2f out: one pce fnl 2f* **20/1**

054- **7** *shd* **Bidable**[158] 6481 3-9-4 **65** FergusSweeney 6 59
(B Palling) *trckd ldrs: wknd fnl f* **20/1**

603- **8** *shd* **Princess Zada**[199] 5764 3-9-1 **62** ChrisCatlin 2 56
(B R Millman) *t.k.h: led 1f: trckd ldrs: wknd appr fnl f* **20/1**

060- **9** *1 ¾* **Mighty Missouri (IRE)**[260] 4105 3-9-4 **65** AdamKirby 11 55
(W R Swinburn) *hld up in rr: sme hdwy over 2f out: nvr on terms* **14/1**

246- **10** *½* **Anthea**[218] 5349 3-8-13 **65** JamesMillman(5) 7 53
(B R Millman) *s.s: bhd tl kpt on fnl 2f: nvr a factor* **12/1**

4122 **11** *nk* **Ballyshane Spirit (IRE)**[19] 889 3-8-6 **60** KirstyMilczarek(7) 13 48
(N A Callaghan) *mid-div: effrt over 3f out: nvr nr ldrs* **5/1**[1]

16-4 **12** *nk* **Forced Upon Us**[12] 974 3-8-12 **59** EdwardCreighton 15 46
(P J McBride) *mid-div: nvr a factor* **9/1**

000- **13** *shd* **Extractor**[228] 5091 3-8-12 **59** .... TPO'Shea 12 46
(J L Dunlop) *mid-div: rdn over 3f out: lost pl 2f out* **20/1**
05-5 **14** *1 1/4* **Rebel Pearl (IRE)**[45] 633 3-8-10 **60** .... JerryO'Dwyer(3) 10 44
(M G Quinlan) *hld up: a in rr* **25/1**
040- **15** *5* **Lapina (IRE)**[197] 5784 3-8-13 **60** .... PatDobbs 14 32
(Pat Eddery) *in rr: bhd fnl 3f* **16/1**
405- **16** *1 3/4* **One And Gone (IRE)**[193] 5900 3-8-13 **65** .... JamieMoriarty(5) 4 33
(R A Fahey) *s.s: a bhd* **8/1**[3]

1m 46.95s (0.55) **Going Correction** +0.075s/f (Good) **16** Ran SP% **126.7**
Speed ratings (Par 96):100,99,98,96,94 92,92,92,90,90 90,89,89,88,83 81
CSF £145.85 CT £1721.04 TOTE £23.10: £7.00, £2.20, £1.90, £2.50; EX 149.10 Place 6 £86.48, Place 5 £40.49.
Owner J C Fretwell **Bred** John Davis And Newtown Stud **Trained** Averham Park, Notts

FOCUS
A third low-grade handicap carrying a mere £3,500 guaranteed prizemoney. The form though only modest has a sound look about it.
Mighty Missouri(IRE) Official explanation: jockey said gelding was never travelling
T/Plt: £69.70 to a £1 stake. Pool: £46,305.90. 484.70 winning tickets. T/Qpdt: £26.90 to a £1 stake. Pool: £3,180.80. 87.50 winning tickets. WG

1130 THIRSK (L-H)
Saturday, April 21

OFFICIAL GOING: Firm
Wind: Virtually nil

1156 SQUIRE FREDERICK BELL CLAIMING STKS 5f
2:30 (2:31) (Class 5) 2-Y-O **£3,886** (£1,156; £577; £288) **Stalls** High

Form RPR
0 **1** **Splitthedifference**[14] 942 2-8-13 .... SamHitchcott 6 66
(M R Channon) *dwlt: sn trcking ldrs: hdwy 2f out: rdn to ld appr last: sn clr* **7/4**[1]
5 **2** *3* **Redbrick Girl**[19] 890 2-9-2 .... NCallan 3 57
(K A Ryan) *led: rdn along and hdd over 1f out: kpt on sme pce* **2/1**[2]
3 *2* **Echostar** 2-8-6 .... ChrisCatlin 5 39
(E J O'Neill) *trckd ldrs tl pushed along and outpcd 1/2-way: rdn and styd on fnl f* **5/1**[3]
02 **4** *1/2* **Portway Lane**[10] 1000 2-8-1 .... LiamJones(3) 2 35
(W G M Turner) *dwlt: sn chsng ldrs: effrt on outer 2f out: sn rdn and wknd over 1f out* **10/1**
3 **5** *1* **Miss Willoughby**[12] 971 2-8-2 .... DavidKinsella 1 29
(J Ryan) *prom: rdn along 2f out: sn wknd* **10/1**
6 *2 1/2* **Mujinda** 2-8-9 .... PatrickDonaghy(7) 4 33
(M Brittain) *in tch: rdn along 1/2-way: sn wknd* **11/1**

60.21 secs (0.31) **Going Correction** -0.225s/f (Firm) **6** Ran SP% **112.9**
Speed ratings (Par 92):88,83,80,79,77 73
CSF £5.60 TOTE £2.80: £1.70, £1.80; EX 4.80.The winner was claimed by Declan Carroll for £8,000.
Owner Peter Taplin **Bred** Peter Taplin **Trained** West Ilsley, Berks

FOCUS
Not a bad juvenile claimer for the time of year; Splitthedifference certainly looks better than this level.

NOTEBOOK
Splitthedifference ◆ caught the eye running on late in a reasonable maiden on his debut at Kempton and, with the benefit of that experience, he found this a straightforward opportunity to get off the mark. He won quite nicely and looks a little bit better than this sort of level. He was claimed by Declan Carroll for £8,000 and that could turn out to be a bit of a snip. (old market op 9-4)
Redbrick Girl's debut fifth in a maiden at Southwell represented just moderate form and she proved no match for the winner. She probably ran into a reasonable sort of the level and should be up to winning a similar event. (old market op 5-2 tchd 11-4)
Echostar, the first foal of a 7f winner, ran a respectable race considering the first two home had the benefit of experience, but she is clearly only moderate. (old market op 5-1 tchd 6-1)
Portway Lane's recent second in a four-runner seller at Bath did not amount to much and she was put in her place. (old market op 9-1)
Miss Willoughby looks of very limited ability. (new market)

1157 POLAR FORD H'CAP 7f
3:05 (3:06) (Class 3) (0-90,90) 4-Y-O+ **£7,772** (£2,312; £1,155; £577) **Stalls** Low

Form RPR
004- **1** **Bustan (IRE)**[155] 6299 8-9-1 **87** .... J-PGuillambert 1 99
(G C Bravery) *in tch: hdwy 2f out: swtchd rt and rdn over 1f out: styd on to ld ins last* **14/1**
600- **2** *1* **Imperial Echo (USA)**[245] 4593 6-8-9 **81** .... TomEaves 12 90
(T D Barron) *hld up and bhd: gd hdwy on inner over 2f out: swtchd rt and effrt over 1f out: styd on strly ins last* **16/1**
010- **3** *shd* **Malcheek (IRE)**[177] 6192 5-8-11 **83** .... DavidAllan 6 92
(T D Easterby) *trckd ldr: hdwy to ld 2f out: shkn up over 1f out: rdn and hdd ins last: one pce* **11/4**[1]
522- **4** *1 1/2* **Creative Mind (IRE)**[202] 5710 4-8-11 **83** .... ChrisCatlin 3 88
(E J O'Neill) *led: rdn along and hdd 2f out: drvn and grad wknd fnl f* **7/1**[3]
0-06 **5** *1/2* **Surwaki (USA)**[9] 1013 5-8-5 **77** .... RoystonFfrench 2 80
(R M H Cowell) *prom: rdn along over 2f out and grad wknd* **20/1**
65- **6** *1/2* **Flipando (IRE)**[203] 5680 6-8-11 **90** .... NeilBrown(7) 7 92
(T D Barron) *hld up: hdwy over 2f out: rdn over 1f out: kptr on ins last: nrst fin* **5/1**[2]
4061 **7** *nk* **Stoic Leader (IRE)**[13] 953 7-8-7 **79** .... DeanMcKeown 9 80
(R F Fisher) *in tch: effrt over 2f out: sn rdn and no imp appr last* **10/1**
160- **8** *1 1/2* **Passion Fruit**[175] 6221 6-8-8 **80** .... PaulMulrennan 8 77
(C W Fairhurst) *hld up: a rr* **20/1**
0-00 **9** *hd* **Commando Scott (IRE)**[7] 1041 6-9-0 **86** .... DanielTudhope 4 83
(I W McInnes) *chsd ldrs: rdn over 2f out: sn btn* **8/1**
0402 **10** *1 1/4* **Orpen Wide (IRE)**[9] 1013 5-8-8 **80** ow2........(b) NCallan 10 73
(M C Chapman) *towards rr: effrt on outer over 2f out: sn rdn and no hdwy* **7/1**[3]
04-2 **11** *3 1/2* **Inaminute (IRE)**[12] 979 4-8-5 **77** .... DaleGibson 11 61
(K R Burke) *chsd ldrs: rdn along wl over 2f out and sn wknd* **10/1**
000- **12** *5* **Guest Connections**[182] 6094 4-8-12 **84** .... AdrianTNicholls 5 54
(D Nicholls) *hld up: a rr* **40/1**

1m 23.85s (-3.25) **Going Correction** -0.225s/f (Firm) **12** Ran SP% **122.1**
Speed ratings (Par 107):109,107,107,106,105 104,104,102,102,101 97,91
CSF £219.58 CT £820.45 TOTE £17.50: £4.70, £7.40, £1.90; EX 181.50.
Owner Mrs J Morley **Bred** Sean Twomey **Trained** Newmarket, Suffolk

FOCUS
A good handicap run at a fair pace and solid form rated through the runner-up.

NOTEBOOK
Bustan(IRE), off the track since pulling up over hurdles last November, showed he retains plenty of ability for the Flat with a very useful effort on his return to action. Surprisingly enough this was the shortest trip he has ever raced over, and the way he stayed on suggests a stiffer 7f may suit even better; a return to 1m should also pose him few problems. (op 16-1 tchd 20-1)
Imperial Echo(USA) ◆, returning from an eight-month break, was last rounding the final bend but he stayed on to good effect up the inside rail and was closing fast at the line. This should have sharpened him up and he could prove hard to beat in similar company next time. (op 14-1)
Malcheek(IRE) ◆, returning from a 177-day break, was produced with every chance but just found a couple too good on the day. He can be expected to come on for the run and ought to go close next time. (tchd 3-1 in a place)
Creative Mind(IRE) ◆, runner-up in a German Listed race on his final start last year, ran with real promise on his return to action. He just got tired late on and can be expected to come on for the run. (op 8-1 tchd 6-1)
Surwaki(USA) can have few excuses.
Flipando(IRE) was having his first run in 203 days and is another who can be expected to improve. (op 15-2)
Stoic Leader(IRE), 2lb higher than when winning at Musselburgh on his previous start, was short of room at a crucial stage and is better than he was able to show. Official explanation: jockey said gelding was denied a clear run (op 7-1)

1158 CONSTANT SECURITY H'CAP 1m 4f
3:40 (3:40) (Class 5) (0-75,72) 4-Y-O+ **£3,886** (£1,156; £577; £288) **Stalls** Low

Form RPR
21-4 **1** **Osolomio (IRE)**[7] 1042 4-8-10 **65** .... DaleGibson 4 78+
(G A Swinbank) *mde all: rdn wl over 1f out: styd on strly* **8/11**[1]
0-00 **2** *2 1/2* **Sforzando**[7] 1042 6-8-6 **67** .... KristinStubbs(7) 5 72
(Mrs L Stubbs) *in tchm hdwy over 3f out: rdn to chse wnr wl over 1f out: edgd rt ent last and sn no imp* **10/1**
50-2 **3** *1 1/4* **Just Observing**[12] 966 4-8-10 **70** ....(p) RoryMoore(5) 1 73
(P T Midgley) *in tch: hdwy 3f out: rdn over 2f out: kpt on u.p appr last* **12/1**
000- **4** *6* **Richtee (IRE)**[201] 5725 6-8-4 **58** oh3........ RoystonFfrench 2 51
(R A Fahey) *rrd and lost 10l s: bhd tl styd on fnl 4f:* **8/1**[3]
105- **5** *3/4* **Maneki Neko (IRE)**[155] 4231 5-9-4 **72** .... TonyHamilton 6 64
(E W Tuer) *hld up in rr: hdwy on outer 3f out: rdn 2f out: sn edgd lft and btn* **9/1**
60-5 **6** *3/4* **Spring Dream (IRE)**[18] 903 4-9-1 **70** .... NCallan 7 61
(M R Channon) *trckd ldrs: hdwy to chse wnr over 3f out: rdn 2f out and sn wknd* **7/1**[2]
510- **7** *nk* **Bright Sun (IRE)**[203] 5685 6-9-2 **70** ....(t) KimTinkler 3 61
(N Tinkler) *keen: chsd wnr: pushed along 4f out: rdn along 3f out and sn wknd* **14/1**

2m 34.05s (-1.15) **Going Correction** -0.225s/f (Firm)
WFA 4 from 5yo+ 1lb **7** Ran SP% **115.0**
Speed ratings (Par 103):94,92,91,87,87 86,86
CSF £9.33 TOTE £1.60: £1.10, £3.80; EX 15.20.
Owner Hokey Cokey Partnership (2) **Bred** Dr T A Ryan **Trained** Melsonby, N Yorks

FOCUS
A weak handicap won in good style by the progressive Osolomio but doubts over the current form of the placed horses.
Richtee(IRE) Official explanation: jockey said mare missed the break

1159 MICHAEL FOSTER MEMORIAL CONDITIONS STKS 6f
4:15 (4:15) (Class 3) 4-Y-O+
£7,478 (£2,239; £1,119; £560; £279; £140) **Stalls** High

Form RPR
3-40 **1** **Tax Free (IRE)**[51] 597 5-9-10 107 .... AdrianTNicholls 3 115
(D Nicholls) *hld up: hdwy on outer over 2f out: rdn to ld ent last: kpt on wl* **11/4**[2]
42-2 **2** *1 1/4* **Bond City (IRE)**[17] 927 5-9-0 103 .... ChrisCatlin 1 101
(G R Oldroyd) *hld up: gd hdwy on outer 2f out: rdn over 1f out: kpt on wl fnl f* **14/1**
435- **3** *1/2* **Fayr Jag (IRE)**[190] 5942 8-9-12 109 .... DavidAllan 2 112
(T D Easterby) *prom: effrt 2f out: rdn to ld briefly over 1f out: hdd and nt qckn ent last* **9/1**
3660 **4** *hd* **Celtic Mill**[28] 762 9-9-12 103 ....(p) TomEaves 9 111
(D W Barker) *led: rdn along 2f out: edgd lft and drvn wl over 1f out: sn hdd and one pce ins last* **10/1**
232- **5** *1/2* **Advanced**[175] 6230 4-9-0 109 .... NCallan 4 98
(K A Ryan) *prom: effrt and ev ch over 2f out: sn rdn and wkng whn n.m.r over 1f out* **10/11**[1]
000 **6** *nk* **Beckermet (IRE)**[51] 597 5-9-0 100 .... RoystonFfrench 6 97
(R F Fisher) *cl up: rdn over 2f out: sn drvn and wknd wl over 1f out* **8/1**[3]
0F0- **7** *shd* **Tabaret**[287] 3312 4-9-0 100 .... DeanMcKeown 8 96+
(R M Whitaker) *trckd ldrs on rail: effrt 2f out: nt clr run over 1f out and jst ins last: kpt on* **33/1**
0365 **8** *2 1/2* **Pawan (IRE)**[24] 810 7-8-9 78 ....(b) AnnStokell(5) 5 89?
(Miss A Stokell) *a rr* **100/1**
1/6- **9** *17* **The Bear**[344] 1633 4-9-0 93 .... TonyHamilton 7 38
(J S Wainwright) *keen: chsd ldrs to 1/2-way: sn lost pl and bhd* **50/1**

1m 10.21s (-2.29) **Going Correction** -0.225s/f (Firm) **9** Ran SP% **121.8**
Speed ratings (Par 107):106,104,103,103,102 102,102,98,76
CSF £42.35 TOTE £4.50: £1.60, £2.10, £2.60; EX 30.00.
Owner Ian Hewitson **Bred** Denis & Mrs Teresa Bergin **Trained** Sessay, N Yorks
■ Stewards' Enquiry : David Allan caution: careless riding

FOCUS
A very good conditions sprint and decent form, although not rock solid.

NOTEBOOK
Tax Free(IRE) ◆ failed to show his best form in the dirt in Dubai this winter, but a bit of sun on his back clearly did him no harm and he produced a smart effort on his return to the UK. He had a bit to find with the likes of Bond City and Advanced at the weights, but was always going well just in behind the pace and was far too good for his eight rivals at the business end. He has always promised to develop into a Group horse and, on the evidence of this success, he might just be capable of making the jump up in class this year. (op 3-1)
Bond City(IRE) could possibly be rated slightly better than the bare form, as he raced widest off all from stall one, but he was basically beaten by a better horse. He has started the season in good form and ought to pick up plenty of prizemoney as the season progresses. (op 11-1)
Fayr Jag(IRE) is not quite the force of old, but he is still pretty smart and this was a fine effort under his big weight off the back of a 190-day break. (op 8-1)
Celtic Mill took them along against the rail, but he had no easy task under joint-top weight and found a few too strong late on. (op 15-2)
Advanced looked to have everything going for him – he came into this with a progressive profile and was getting loads of weight from some of the big guns – but he proved disappointing. Having raced keenly, he offered little under pressure and might have found this ground a bit on the quick side. (op 13-8)

Tabaret ◆, having his first run in 287 days, would have been closer with a clear run and could be one to look out for. Official explanation: jockey said colt was denied a clear run

Pawan(IRE) Official explanation: jockey said gelding was unsuited by the firm ground

1160 THOMAS LORD STKS (H'CAP) 5f
4:45 (4:46) (Class 3) (0-90,90) 3-Y-O **£7,772** (£2,312; £1,155; £577) **Stalls** High

Form				RPR
1241	1		**Daddy Cool**27 778 3-8-1 **76** oh2 LiamJones(3) 11 (W G M Turner) *cl up: led 1/2-way: rdn and wandered ent last: drvn and kpt on wl towards fin* **9/2**2	82
1-51	2	1 1/2	**Rebel Duke (IRE)**72 387 3-8-9 **81** NCallan 10 (M G Quinlan) *trckd ldrs: hdwy 2f out: rdn and ev ch ent last: kpt on same pce* **5/1**3	82
313-	3	hd	**Steelcut**325 2127 3-8-13 **90** JamieMoriarty(5) 8 (R A Fahey) *hld up: hdwy 2f out: swtchd rt and rdn over 1f out: drvn and edgd rt ent last: kpt on* **5/1**3	90
130-	4	shd	**Pegasus Dancer (FR)**197 5788 3-8-1 **76** AndrewMullen(3) 12 (K A Ryan) *dwlt and bhd tl hdwy 2f out: rdn and styng on whn edgd lft ins last: kpt on* **10/1**	76
100-	5	1	**Avertuoso**240 4736 3-9-1 **90** MarkLawson(3) 9 (B Smart) *keen: chsd ldrs: effrt and ch 2f out: sn rdn and wknd over 1f out* **8/1**	86
613-	6	2 1/2	**The Nifty Fox**189 5956 3-8-7 **79** DavidAllan 1 (T D Easterby) *prom on outer: rdn wl over 1f out and grad wknd* **28/1**	66+
1-00	7	1/2	**Deserted Dane (USA)**44 641 3-9-4 **90** DeanMcKeown 3 (G A Swinbank) *cl up: rdn along over 2f out and sn wknd* **7/2**1	76+
020-	8	2 1/2	**Ice Mountain**203 5681 3-9-1 **87** RoystonFfrench 5 (B Smart) *chsd ldrs: rdn over 2f out: sn wknd* **16/1**	64
512-	9	1	**Just Joey**233 4946 3-8-13 **85** TomEaves 2 (J R Weymes) *rr fr 1/2-way* **14/1**	58
050-	10	3/4	**Pelican Key (IRE)**182 6096 3-8-9 **81** ChrisCatlin 6 (D M Simcock) *a rr* **14/1**	51
105-	11	9	**Winning Spirit (IRE)**235 4910 3-8-9 **81** AdrianTNicholls 7 (D Nicholls) *led to 1/2-way: sn wknd* **14/1**	19

58.42 secs (-1.48) **Going Correction** -0.225s/f (Firm) **11 Ran SP% 123.3**
Speed ratings (Par 102):102,99,99,99,97 93,92,88,87,85 71
CSF £28.83 CT £121.02 TOTE £6.10: £2.20, £1.70, £2.20; EX 20.90.

Owner Mascalls Stud **Bred** Mascalls Stud **Trained** Sigwells, Somerset

FOCUS
A decent enough sprint handicap, but those drawn high were at a significant advantage and the form does not look that strong. The winning time was 0.12 seconds quicker than the following maiden.

NOTEBOOK
Daddy Cool's previous six starts had come on sand, so he had to prove his effectiveness on turf, but he soon had the rail to race against from his favourable draw and, handling the surface well, he repelled all-comers for a game success. This was a good effort from 2lb out of the handicap and he is most progressive, but it is worth remembering he had everything go his way this time. (op 13-2)

Rebel Duke(IRE) ◆, like the winner, in decent form on sand this winter, showed good speed throughout, but was just unable to peg back Daddy Cool, who had the rail to run against. He gives the impression he has not stopped improving just yet. (op 11-2)

Steelcut showed useful form as a juvenile, but he had not been seen since last May and has since been gelded. He may well have finished closer with a clearer run and should have more to offer. (op 11-2 tchd 13-2)

Pegasus Dancer(FR) just lacked the sharpness of some of these on his return from a 197-day break and he should come on for the run. (tchd 9-1 and 11-1)

Avertuoso, having his first run since last August, is now a gelding and can build on this. (op 10-1)

The Nifty Fox (op 33-1 tchd 25-1)

Deserted Dane(USA), highly tried but well held in a couple of runs on the dirt in Dubai this winter, was poorly drawn on his return to the UK and could make little impression. (op 3-1)

1161 PINDER DALE MAIDEN STKS 5f
5:20 (5:20) (Class 5) 3-Y-O **£3,886** (£1,156; £577; £288) **Stalls** High

Form				RPR
224-	1		**Jack Rackham**337 1811 3-9-3 81 RoystonFfrench 2 (B Smart) *hld up in tch: effrt 2f out and sn rdn: styd on wl ins fnl f to ld nr fin* **5/4**1	72+
52-0	2	nk	**Foxy Music**89 219 3-9-3 48 DavidAllan 7 (E J Alston) *led: rdn wl over 1f out: drvn and edgd lft ins last: hdd nr fin* **12/1**	71
	3	hd	**Maia** 3-8-12 AdrianTNicholls 5 (D Nicholls) *trckd ldrs: switchd lft and effrt wl over 1f out: sn rdn and rn green: styd on strly towards fin* **8/1**3	65+
23P-	4	3	**Fast Freddie**263 4026 3-9-3 79 RobbieFitzpatrick 1 (T J Pitt) *cl up on outer: rdn along wl over 1f out and sn btn* **6/4**2	59
00-0	5	1	**My Two Girls (IRE)**12 970 3-8-7 54 (p) RoryMoore(5) 3 (P T Midgley) *cl up: rdn 2f out and grad wknd* **20/1**	51?
000-	6	2	**Baybshambles (IRE)**179 6157 3-9-0 35 MarkLawson(3) 4 (R E Barr) *a rr* **66/1**	49?
0-00	7	11	**La Esperanza**17 918 3-8-7 45 (p) AnnStokell(5) 6 (Miss A Stokell) *prom to 1/2-way: sn wknd* **66/1**	—

58.54 secs (-1.36) **Going Correction** -0.225s/f (Firm) **7 Ran SP% 111.0**
Speed ratings (Par 98):101,100,100,95,93 90,73
CSF £15.75 TOTE £2.00: £1.70, £3.90; EX 15.90 Place 6 £43.24, Place 5 £35.28..

Owner Mrs F Denniff **Bred** A S Denniff **Trained** Hambleton, N Yorks

■ Stewards' Enquiry : Royston Ffrench caution: used whip without giving gelding time to respond

FOCUS
A very difficult race to assess, as the 81-rated Jack Rackham had just a neck to spare over 48-rated Foxy Music, yet the time was only 0.12 seconds slower than the previous 76-90 handicap. The runner-up had the run of the race, whereas the eventual winner could have enjoyed a better trip.

La Esperanza Official explanation: jockey said filly was unsuited by the firm ground

T/Plt: £69.50 to a £1 stake. Pool: £56,326.55. 590.95 winning tickets. T/Qpdt: £9.40 to a £1 stake. Pool: £2,182.90. 170.10 winning tickets. JR

1064 WOLVERHAMPTON (A.W) (L-H)
Saturday, April 21

OFFICIAL GOING: Standard
Wind: light, behind Weather: Fine and sunny

1162 ASTORE-HARRISON PERFECT FURNISHINGS FOR HORIZONS APPRENTICE H'CAP 1m 141y(P)
6:45 (6:45) (Class 5) (0-70,70) 4-Y-O+ **£1,989** (£1,989; £453) **Stalls** Low

Form				RPR
000-	1		**The Bonus King**196 3947 7-8-6 **60** AshleyHamblett(3) 4 (J Jay) *led 1f: chsd ldrs: rdn to ld over 1f out: jnd post* **4/1**2	65
320-	1	dht	**Gigs Magic (USA)**175 6213 4-8-6 **57** DuranFentiman 2 (M Johnston) *prom: rdn over 1f out: r.o to join wnr post* **9/2**3	62
4330	3	nk	**Golden Spectrum (IRE)**5 1069 8-8-5 **59** (b) TolleyDean(3) 5 (R A Harris) *chsd ldr 7f out: rdn and ev ch fr over 2f out: r.o* **11/2**	63
-554	4	1/2	**Summer Lodge**25 805 4-8-7 **63** (be) MCGeran(5) 6 (A J McCabe) *led over 7f out: rdn and hdd over 1f out: styd on same pce ins fnl f* **10/1**	66
1332	5	2 1/2	**Parkview Love (USA)**7 1036 6-9-2 **70** (v) PatrickHills(3) 3 (D Shaw) *trckd ldrs: rdn over 2f out: no ex fnl f* **11/8**1	68
00-0	6	5	**Bond Angel Eyes**25 800 4-8-1 **57** oh11 ow1 (p) NSLawes(5) 1 (G R Oldroyd) *hld up: rdn 3f out: wknd over 1f out* **33/1**	44

1m 51.09s (-0.67) **Going Correction** -0.125s/f (Stan) **6 Ran SP% 107.7**
Speed ratings (Par 103):97,97,96,96,94 89
WIN BK £2.20, GM £2.80; PL BL £1.80, GM £2.00; EX BK/GM £9.90, GM/BK £7.60; CSF BK/GM £10.03, GM/BK £10.30.

Owner Mrs Mo Done & Mrs Janet Martin **Bred** Red House Stud **Trained** Newmarket, Suffolk
Owner J Barson **Bred** R McDonald **Trained** Middleham Moor, N Yorks

FOCUS
A moderate handicap, confined to apprentice riders. The pace was steady and the form should be treated with a little caution.

1163 VERSATILE KENT PERFECTLY CEILING HORIZONS CLAIMING STKS 5f 20y(P)
7:15 (7:16) (Class 6) 3-Y-O+ **£2,388** (£705; £352) **Stalls** Low

Form				RPR
4520	1		**Monte Major (IRE)**19 896 6-9-5 57 (v) PatrickHills(5) 10 (D Shaw) *mid-div: hdwy 1/2-way: rdn to ld and hung lft fr over 1f out: r.o* **9/2**3	65
-304	2	1 3/4	**Beamsley Beacon**2 1112 6-9-6 43 (bt) PaulFessey 6 (S T Mason) *led 4f out: rdn and hdd over 1f out: styd on same pce* **8/1**	55
2113	3	1 1/4	**Magic Amour**5 1065 9-8-9 62 (v) KevinGhunowa(5) 12 (P A Blockley) *chsd ldrs: chal 1/2-way: hmpd over 1f out: no ex ins fnl f* **6/4**1	45
4-60	4	2	**He's A Rocket (IRE)**85 254 6-9-0 42 LeeEnstone 2 (K R Burke) *led 1f: chsd ldrs: rdn 1/2-way: styd on same pce appr fnl f* **14/1**	37
0000	5	1/2	**Mind That Fox**5 1065 5-8-7 42 JosephWalsh(7) 3 (T Wall) *sn pushed along in rr: styd on u.p fr over 1f out: nvr nrr* **33/1**	36
-000	6	nk	**Howards Princess**17 912 5-8-13 45 (p) PaulMulrennan 8 (J Hetherton) *prom: rdn over 1f out: wknd fnl f* **20/1**	33
0300	7	2 1/2	**New Options**36 688 10-9-0 49 (b) BrettDoyle 9 (Peter Grayson) *s.i.s: outpcd* **20/1**	25
-504	8	4	**She's Our Beauty (IRE)**58 523 4-8-6 43 (p) DuranFentiman(5) 11 (S T Mason) *chsd ldrs 3f* **25/1**	8
5130	R		**Quiet Times (IRE)**28 766 8-10-0 78 (b) DO'Donohoe 4 (K A Ryan) *ref to r* **7/2**2	—
50-0	R		**Blakeshall Rose**12 970 3-8-0 42 (p) MCGeran(7) 7 (A J Chamberlain) *unruly to post: ref to r* **66/1**	—

62.15 secs (-0.67) **Going Correction** -0.125s/f (Stan)
WFA 3 from 4yo+ 10lb **10 Ran SP% 116.0**
Speed ratings (Par 101):100,97,95,92,91 90,86,80,—,—
CSF £36.45 TOTE £5.50: £1.80, £2.80, £1.20; EX 76.80.

Owner Danethorpe Racing Ltd **Bred** B Kennedy **Trained** Danethorpe, Notts

FOCUS
A poor claimer, weakened notably by the refusal to race of top-rated Quiet Times, and the form is rated around the first two.

1164 MARSHAL TYRES GREAT GRIP AND VALUE (S) STKS 7f 32y(P)
7:45 (7:45) (Class 6) 3-Y-O **£2,388** (£705; £352) **Stalls** High

Form				RPR
00	1		**Solidgoldesyaction**38 678 3-8-7 PaulHanagan 1 (P A Blockley) *chsd ldrs: rdn over 3f out: n.m.r and edgd lft ins fnl f: styd on u.p to ld towards fin* **6/1**3	46
00-0	2	nk	**Iron Dancer (IRE)**18 900 3-8-12 48 AlanDaly 4 (P A Blockley) *chsd ldrs: rdn to ld and edgd lft 1f out: hdd towards fin* **66/1**	50
350-	3	1	**Marist Madame**228 5084 3-8-7 50 RobertHavlin 12 (D K Ivory) *hld up: hdwy over 1f out: edgd lft and r.o wl ins fnl f: nt rch ldrs* **33/1**	46+
00-0	4	nk	**Giovanni D'Oro (IRE)**8 1022 3-8-12 56 JamieSpencer 2 (N A Callaghan) *s.i.s: hld up: hdwy over 2f out: sn hung lft: hrd rdn fr over 1f out: styd on* **6/1**3	47
4-20	5	shd	**Denton Hawk**74 373 3-8-12 54 PaulFessey 5 (M Dods) *hld up: hdwy over 1f out: n.m.r ins fnl f: eased nr fin* **11/2**2	47
50-0	6	1 1/4	**Peggys Flower**19 894 3-8-7 57 DO'Donohoe 9 (M Wigham) *s.i.s: hld up: plld hrd: hdwy 1/2-way: rdn over 2f out: styd on same pce fnl f* **10/1**	38
4640	7	1/2	**Suntan Lady (IRE)**9 1008 3-8-2 49 (v) DuranFentiman(5) 11 (Miss V Haigh) *hld up: rdn over 1f out: styd on ins fnl f: nvr nrr* **20/1**	37
54-5	8	1 1/4	**Silly Gilly (IRE)**18 910 3-8-7 53 PatCosgrave 3 (K R Burke) *led 1f: chsd ldr tl led over 2f out: rdn and hdd 1f out: btn whn hmpd ins fnl f* **11/2**2	34
0556	9	shd	**Conny Nobel (IRE)**5 1059 3-8-7 55 (tp) KevinGhunowa(5) 10 (J L Flint) *chsd ldrs: rdn 1/2-way: wknd ins fnl f* **7/2**1	38
6050	10	4	**Avery**10 1004 3-8-5 52 HaddenFrost(7) 6 (R J Hodges) *hld up in tch: rdn over 2f out: sn wknd* **12/1**	28
0026	11	3 1/2	**Flushed**18 910 3-8-5 49 (be) MCGeran(7) 8 (A J McCabe) *led 6f out: rdn and hdd over 2f out: sn wknd* **8/1**	19

1m 30.74s (0.34) **Going Correction** -0.125s/f (Stan) **11 Ran SP% 118.7**
Speed ratings (Par 96):93,92,91,91,91 89,89,87,87,82 78
CSF £358.38 TOTE £8.30: £2.60, £7.70, £7.50; EX 502.90.There was no bid for the winner.

Owner Market Avenue Racing Club Ltd **Bred** Templeton Stud And Sue Brendish **Trained** Lambourn, Berks

FOCUS
A very weak affair. The first pair came clear to provide a one-two for trainer Paul Blockley.

1165 FLOORS-2-GO FITTED HORIZONS PERFECTLY H'CAP 5f 216y(P)
8:15 (8:15) (Class 5) (0-70,70) 4-Y-0+ **£3,071** (£906; £453) **Stalls** Low

Form RPR

0021 **1** **Came Back (IRE)**[25] [803] 4-8-13 **70** MichaelJStainton(5) 6 84+
(J Mackie) *chsd ldr: led 2f out: rdn out* **6/4**[1]

4466 **2** *1* **Hammer Of The Gods (IRE)**[17] [923] 7-9-1 **67** (bt) BrettDoyle 2 78
(P S McEntee) *led: hdd 2f out: sn rdn: no ex towards fin* **7/2**[2]

1-02 **3** *1 1/4* **Gilded Cove**[103] [66] 7-8-8 **65** RussellKennemore(5) 1 72
(R Hollinshead) *hld up: hdwy over 1f out: nt rch ldrs* **13/2**[3]

0-00 **4** *2 1/2* **Royal Envoy (IRE)**[28] [771] 4-8-13 **65** DeanMcKeown 3 64
(D Shaw) *trckd ldrs: rdn over 1f out: styd on same pce* **33/1**

000- **5** *nk* **Namir (IRE)**[185] [6048] 5-8-8 **65** (vt) PatrickHills(5) 7 63
(D Shaw) *hld up: hdwy over 1f out: sn rdn and no imp* **20/1**

3-00 **6** *hd* **Littledodayno (IRE)**[47] [621] 4-9-2 **68** DO'Donohoe 5 65
(M Wigham) *hld up: r.o ins fnl f: nvr nrr* **18/1**

0-33 **7** *nk* **Royal Orissa**[58] [521] 5-8-7 **59** ow1 RobertHavlin 11 55
(D Haydn Jones) *s.i.s: hld up: r.o ins fnl f: nrst fin* **10/1**

2200 **8** *hd* **Devon Flame**[10] [1004] 8-8-4 **63** ow3 HaddenFrost(7) 12 59
(R J Hodges) *mid-div: rdn over 2f out: wknd over 1f out* **20/1**

6006 **9** *nk* **Regal Royale**[28] [757] 4-9-4 **70** TedDurcan 10 65
(Peter Grayson) *broke wl: lost pl 5f out: nt clr run over 1f out: hung lft ins fnl f: nvr trbld ldrs* **9/1**

6006 **10** *1 1/4* **Mambazo**[54] [566] 5-8-7 **62** (e) RichardKingscote(3) 9 53
(S C Williams) *prom: rdn over 2f out: wknd over 1f out* **9/1**

00-0 **11** *1/2* **Dunn Deal (IRE)**[19] [896] 7-8-3 **58** LiamJones(3) 4 47
(W M Brisbourne) *trckd ldrs: plld hrd: rdn and wknd over 1f out* **33/1**

1m 14.41s (-1.40) **Going Correction** -0.125s/f (Stan) 11 Ran SP% **125.3**
Speed ratings (Par 103):104,102,101,97,97 97,96,96,95,94 93
CSF £6.67 CT £28.46 TOTE £3.40: £2.20, £1.70, £1.80; EX 19.50.
Owner W I Bloomfield **Bred** Yeomanstown Stud **Trained** Church Broughton , Derbys

FOCUS
A modest sprint won by a progressive colt. The form has been rated positively and the third helps to set the level.

1166 ACP LTD ARCHITECTS WITH NEW HORIZONS MAIDEN STKS 1m 141y(P)
8:45 (8:50) (Class 5) 3-Y-0+ **£2,817** (£838; £418; £209) **Stalls** Low

Form RPR

6- **1** **Gulf Express (USA)**[325] [2144] 3-8-11 JamieSpencer 6 86+
(Sir Michael Stoute) *s.i.s: hld up: hdwy over 1f out: edgd lft and r.o to ld wl ins fnl f* **13/8**[1]

552- **2** *1/2* **Vanquisher (IRE)**[201] [5730] 3-8-11 79 TedDurcan 10 78
(W J Haggas) *s.i.s: sn chsng ldrs: led over 1f out: rdn and hdd wl ins fnl f* **7/4**[2]

4/0- **3** *3 1/2* **Ashes Regained**[187] [6021] 4-9-5 ChrisGlenister(7) 5 73
(B W Hills) *plld hrd: led: sddle slipped sn after s: hdd over 1f out: no ex ins fnl f* **14/1**

5 **4** *3 1/2* **Ganache (IRE)**[28] [758] 5-9-12 JimCrowley 2 65
(P R Chamings) *chsd ldr: ev ch over 2f out: rdn and wknd over 1f out* **9/1**[3]

5 *3/4* **Golden Wave (IRE)** 3-8-6 PaulHanagan 9 55+
(J Noseda) *hld up: r.o ins fnl f: nvr nrr* **12/1**

-4 **6** *nk* **Dr Dream (IRE)**[17] [919] 3-8-11 LPKeniry 13 60
(D M Simcock) *hld up: hdwy over 2f out: hung lft and wknd over 1f out* **14/1**

7 *1* **Adenium (IRE)** 3-8-11 PatCosgrave 12 57
(W R Swinburn) *s.i.s: hld up: swtchd lft over 2f out: nt trble ldrs* **33/1**

00- **8** *hd* **Osiris Way**[187] [6019] 5-9-12 RobertHavlin 4 60
(P R Chamings) *chsd ldrs: rdn over 2f out: sn wknd* **100/1**

46- **9** *5* **The Diamond Bond**[236] [4880] 3-8-11 TomEaves 8 45
(G R Oldroyd) *mid-div: hung rt fr 1/2-way: wknd 2f out* **66/1**

40 **10** *3/4* **Mandalay Prince**[12] [973] 3-8-11 BrettDoyle 3 44
(W J Musson) *hld up: nvr nr to chal* **33/1**

00- **11** *1 1/2* **Sew In Character**[217] [5381] 3-8-11 (b[1]) DeanMcKeown 7 40
(M Blanshard) *plld hrd and prom: wknd over 2f out* **100/1**

0 **12** *1 1/2* **Boz**[12] [973] 3-8-11 NickyMackay 11 37
(L M Cumani) *hld up: pushed along over 5f out: a in rr* **33/1**

0- **13** *18* **Three Half Crowns (IRE)**[183] [6072] 3-8-11 JimmyQuinn 1 —
(P Howling) *chsd ldrs: rdn 1/2-way: wknd over 3f out* **25/1**

1m 49.55s (-2.21) **Going Correction** -0.125s/f (Stan)
WFA 3 from 4yo+ 15lb 13 Ran SP% **121.6**
Speed ratings (Par 103):104,103,100,97,96 96,95,95,90,90 88,87,71
CSF £4.47 TOTE £2.60: £1.60, £1.60, £2.90; EX 5.10.
Owner Saeed Suhail **Bred** Gracefield And Brad Ray **Trained** Newmarket, Suffolk

FOCUS
A fair maiden for the track. The form looks sound through the 79-rated runner-up and the fourth and sixth.

1167 DERRY BUILDING SERVICES POWERING HORIZONS H'CAP 1m 1f 103y(P)
9:15 (9:18) (Class 6) (0-60,60) 4-Y-0+ **£2,388** (£705; £352) **Stalls** Low

Form RPR

1554 **1** **Scottish River (USA)**[8] [1027] 8-8-13 **55** HayleyTurner 11 71
(M D I Usher) *s.i.s: hld up: hdwy over 2f out: led and edgd lft ins fnl f: r.o* **14/1**

2211 **2** *1 1/2* **Norwegian**[8] [1025] 6-9-3 **59** (p) JimCrowley 10 72
(Ian Williams) *hld up in tch: rdn and ev ch ins fnl f: unable qckn* **11/4**[2]

3 *1 1/4* **Rio (IRE)**[327] [2090] 5-9-4 **60** PaulHanagan 3 71
(J Balding) *chsd ldrs: led over 1f out: rdn and hdd whn hmpd ins fnl f: no ex* **16/1**

616- **4** *4* **Gizmondo**[262] [4051] 4-9-4 **60** JamieSpencer 8 63
(M L W Bell) *hld up: hdwy over 2f out: rdn and hung lft fr over 1f out: styd on same pce* **5/2**[1]

-655 **5** *1 1/4* **Medieval Maiden**[68] [445] 4-9-3 **59** BrettDoyle 5 59
(W J Musson) *hld up: nt clr run wl over 1f out: hmpd ins fnl f: nvr nr to chal* **8/1**

4032 **6** *1 3/4* **Buscador (USA)**[28] [767] 8-8-12 **57** LiamJones(3) 4 54
(W M Brisbourne) *chsd ldr: disp ld fr 6f out tl led over 2f out: rdn and hdd over 1f out: wknd ins fnl f* **9/2**[3]

06-0 **7** *1 1/2* **Sweet Medicine**[38] [112] 5-9-4 **60** JimmyQuinn 13 54
(P Howling) *mid-div: rdn over 3f out: wknd over 1f out: hmpd ins fnl f* **33/1**

330- **8** *hd* **El Capitan (FR)**[194] [5868] 4-8-10 **57** PatrickHills(5) 12 50
(Miss Gay Kelleway) *prom: rdn over 2f out: wknd over 1f out: hmpd ins fnl f* **20/1**

0003 **9** *1* **Desert Hawk**[29] [742] 6-8-6 **53** (b) DuranFentiman(5) 1 44
(W M Brisbourne) *chsd ldrs: nt clr run over 2f out: wknd over 1f out* **8/1**

0-05 **10** *2* **Orpen Quest (IRE)**[12] [976] 5-8-8 **55** (v) KevinGhunowa(5) 2 42
(M J Attwater) *led: jnd 6f out: hdd over 2f out: sn wknd* **12/1**

000/ **11** *30* **New Realm (USA)**[12] [5505] 5-9-1 **57** (b[1]) RobertHavlin 9 —
(R A Farrant) *s.i.s and rel to r: bhd fnl 5f* **66/1**

12 *11* **Anything Once (USA)**[238] [4827] 4-9-3 **59** TomEaves 6 —
(B Smart) *chsd ldrs 7f* **16/1**

2m 0.40s (-2.22) **Going Correction** -0.125s/f (Stan) 12 Ran SP% **131.0**
Speed ratings (Par 101):104,102,101,98,96 95,94,93,92,91 64,54
CSF £57.27 CT £674.48 TOTE £13.30: £4.20, £2.00, £3.40; EX 38.30 Place 6 £131.03, Place 5 £46.76.
Owner M D I Usher **Bred** The Thoroughbred Corporation **Trained** Upper Lambourn, Berks
■ Stewards' Enquiry : Hayley Turner caution: careless riding

FOCUS
A moderate handicap, run at a solid pace. The form looks sound enough for the grade rated through the runner up.
T/Plt: £278.00 to a £1 stake. Pool: £59,638.40. 156.55 winning tickets. T/Qpdt: £133.40 to a £1 stake. Pool: £4,545.90. 25.20 winning tickets. CR

1168 - 1170a (Foreign Racing) - See Raceform Interactive

NAAS (L-H)
Saturday, April 21

OFFICIAL GOING: Good (good to firm in places)

1171a WOODLANDS STKS (LISTED RACE) 5f
4:00 (4:01) 3-Y-0+ **£21,993** (£6,452; £3,074; £1,047)

RPR

1 **Dandy Man (IRE)**[217] [5375] 4-9-12 115 PShanahan 6 122+
(Tracey Collins, Ire) *trckd ldrs in 3rd: smooth hdwy to ld under 2f out: clr over 1f out: eased cl home: impressive* **4/6**[1]

2 *4 1/2* **Flash McGahon (IRE)**[216] [5408] 3-9-2 100 MJKinane 8 100
(John M Oxx, Ire) *trckd ldrs on stand's side: 6th 1/2-way: impr into 3rd 1 1/2f out: mod 2nd and kpt on fnl f* **6/1**[3]

3 *2 1/2* **Absolutelyfabulous (IRE)**[217] [5393] 4-9-6 96 WMLordan 7 89
(David Wachman, Ire) *trckd ldrs: 4th 1/2-way: kpt on fr 1 1/2f out* **12/1**

4 *3/4* **Osterhase (IRE)**[195] [5849] 8-9-12 112 (b) FMBerry 5 92
(J E Mulhern, Ire) *sn led: hdd under 2f out: kpt on same pce fr over 1f out* **5/1**[2]

5 *shd* **Benwilt Breeze (IRE)**[202] [5706] 5-9-9 94 (t) JMurtagh 2 89
(G M Lyons, Ire) *chsd ldrs: 5th 1/2-way: sn rdn: kpt on u.p fr over 1f out* **16/1**

6 *2 1/2* **Drumin Orpen (IRE)**[12] [986] 4-9-6 77 PJSmullen 9 77
(Joseph Crowley, Ire) *in rr: kpt on wout threatening fr over 1 1/2f out* **50/1**

7 *2 1/2* **Inourthoughts (IRE)**[9] [1015] 3-8-10 87 RPCleary 3 64
(Francis Ennis, Ire) *chsd ldrs: 7th and rdn over 2f out: no ex fr 1 1/2f out* **20/1**

8 *nk* **Shinko Dancer (IRE)**[6] [1048] 4-9-6 73 (tp) WSupple 4 67
(H Rogers, Ire) *broke wl: settled 2nd: rdn over 2f out: sn wknd* **50/1**

9 *9* **Sling Back (IRE)**[6] [1048] 6-9-6 82 KJManning 1 34
(Eamon Tyrrell, Ire) *hld up: rdn and no imp fr 2f out: eased ins fnl f* **14/1**

59.00 secs (-3.00)
WFA 3 from 4yo+ 10lb 9 Ran SP% **119.9**
CSF £5.41 TOTE £1.50: £1.10, £2.80, £3.30; DF 7.60. Tracey Collins' first winner as a trainer.
Owner Exors of the late A McLean **Bred** Mountarmstrong Stud **Trained** The Curragh, Co Kildare

NOTEBOOK
Dandy Man(IRE) ◆ won in the style of a top-class sprinter. He showed glimpses of brilliance last season and was most unlucky to only finish fourth in last year's King's Stand, winning the race on the far side. Having reportedly strengthened up over the winter, he blew his rivals away and was still pulling under two furlongs out. This was mightily impressive and he is going to take some stopping in races such as the King's Stand and Nunthorpe this season, with a crack at the Prix De L'Abbaye later in the year highly likely. In the meantime he may turn up at Sandown for the Temple Stakes. (op 4/5 tchd 9/10)
Flash McGahon(IRE), a Listed winner at two, has clearly progressed over the winter and this effort suggested he can win again at this level, with a return to 6f likely to benefit the colt. (op 11/2 tchd 7/1)

1172 - 1174a (Foreign Racing) - See Raceform Interactive

1027 SOUTHWELL (L-H)
Sunday, April 22

OFFICIAL GOING: Standard
The surface was described as riding 'loose and light, very slow and quite deep'. It was watered between races
Wind: Light, half-behind Weather: Overcast but dry and mild

1175 ALAN MEALE MP MAIDEN FILLIES' STKS 6f (F)
2:10 (2:12) (Class 5) 3-Y-0+ **£4,533** (£1,348; £674; £336) **Stalls** Low

Form RPR

44 **1** **Gold Digger Miss (USA)**[37] [689] 3-8-12 TPQueally 11 71+
(J Noseda) *w ldrs: led over 1f out: sn wnt clr: eased towards fin* **7/2**[2]

2 *6* **Expensive Art (IRE)** 3-8-12 JamieSpencer 2 52+
(N A Callaghan) *led tl over 1f out: hung right: no ch w wnr* **11/10**[1]

000- **3** *nk* **Pappas Ruby (USA)**[272] [3785] 4-9-9 38 JosedeSouza 1 54
(R M Beckett) *sn chsng ldrs: outpcd over 4f out: hdwy on ins 3f out: kpt on same pce fnl 2f* **33/1**

0- **4** *1* **Bonnet O'Bonnie**[241] [4731] 3-8-12 DaleGibson 12 48
(J Mackie) *hmpd s: t.k.h on outer: hdwy to chse ldrs over 4f out: one pce fnl 2f* **12/1**

5 *nk* **Boleyna (USA)** 3-8-12 (e[1]) ChrisCatlin 7 47
(Rae Guest) *sn chsng ldrs: outpcd over 3f out: swtchd wd outside and hdwy over 2f out: kpt on* **12/1**

6 *3* **Bay City Stroller (IRE)** 3-8-9 StephenDonohoe(3) 6 37
(A J McCabe) *sn outpcd and wl bhd: hdwy on inner 3f out: nvr nr ldrs* **16/1**

6000 **7** *2 1/2* **Meadfoot**[27] [790] 3-8-12 50 (p) JimCrowley 13 29
(B R Millman) *swvd lft s: sn chsng ldrs: lost pl over 2f out* **40/1**

0 **8** *5* **Glenmore Lodge**[19] [908] 4-9-9 MickyFenton 3 13
(P T Midgley) *s.i.s: sn drvn along and bhd* **100/1**

The Form Book, Raceform Ltd, Compton, RG20 6NL

502- **9** *nk* **Ocean Of Champagne**[195] [5860] 3-8-7 59.........(p) MichaelJStainton(5) 8 12
(A Dickman) *s.i.s: sn bhd: hung rt over 2f out* **11/1**

6-2 **10** *1 3/4* **Kyrenia Girl (IRE)**[18] [916] 3-8-12 .... DavidAllan 4 6
(T D Easterby) *chsd ldrs: drvn and outpcd over 3f out: lost pl over 2f: eased whn bhd ins last* **7/1**[3]

0-06 **11** *25* **Tequila Rose (IRE)**[19] [908] 4-9-4 40....................(v[1]) JamieMoriarty(5) 5 —
(M A Buckley) *t.k.h: trckd ldrs: rdn and lost pl over 3f out: sn bhd: virtually p.u* **100/1**

1m 17.01s (0.11) **Going Correction** -0.025s/f (Stan)
WFA 3 from 4yo 11lb **11** Ran SP% **119.3**
Speed ratings (Par 100):98,90,89,88,87 83,80,73,73,71 37
CSF £7.71 TOTE £5.20: £1.40, £1.20, £6.80; EX 12.40 Trifecta £218.10 Part won. Pool £307.24 - 0.34 winning units..
Owner Tom Ludt **Bred** Grapestock Llc & Westwood Thoroughbreds Llc **Trained** Newmarket, Suffolk

FOCUS
A weak maiden with the third rated just 38 but the winner could hardly have done her job in better style.
Expensive Art(IRE) Official explanation: jockey said filly lost a near-fore shoe and hung right

1176 JOHN CARTER H'CAP 6f (F)
2:40 (2:41) (Class 4) (0-80,80) 3-Y-O **£5,181** (£1,541; £770; £384) **Stalls** Low

Form RPR

41- **1** **Off The Record**[160] [6463] 3-8-6 **67**.. TPQueally 5 89+
(J G Given) *s.i.s: t.k.h: sn trcking ldrs: led on bit over 2f out: shkn up and wnt clr 1f out* **5/1**[2]

-132 **2** *5* **Sheriff's Silk**[40] [671] 3-8-11 **72**..............................(b) RoystonFfrench 6 75
(B Smart) *chsd ldrs: edgd rt over 1f out: no ch w wnr* **15/8**[1]

0530 **3** *1 3/4* **Jord (IRE)**[22] [843] 3-8-8 **69**.. NCallan 4 67
(A J McCabe) *led tl over 2f out: kpt on same pce appr fnl f* **9/1**

040- **4** *1 3/4* **Chjimes (IRE)**[183] [6102] 3-9-5 **80**.. PatCosgrave 2 73+
(K R Burke) *prom: hmpd over 4f out: hung lft and kpt on same pce fnl 2f* **15/2**

532 **5** *3* **Kelamon**[39] [678] 3-8-5 **66**.. HayleyTurner 10 50
(M D I Usher) *chsd ldrs on outer: outpcd over 3f out: edgd lft and hdwy 2f out: fdd ins last* **12/1**

4-1 **6** *3/4* **My Drop (IRE)**[87] [237] 3-8-13 **74**.. ChrisCatlin 7 55
(E J O'Neill) *chsd ldrs: wknd over 1f out* **10/1**

2-21 **7** *1 3/4* **New York Oscar (IRE)**[102] [90] 3-8-9 **73**............ StephenDonohoe(3) 1 49+
(A J McCabe) *hld up: hmpd over 4f out: kpt on fnl 2f: nvr a factor* **20/1**

304- **8** *8* **Rainbow Fox**[228] [5113] 3-8-13 **74**.. PaulHanagan 3 26
(R A Fahey) *sn drvn along: outpcd and lost pl over 3f out: bhd whn eased ins last* **12/1**

150- **9** *3 1/2* **Lucky Bee (IRE)**[202] [5721] 3-8-13 **74**.............................. JamieSpencer 9 16
(G A Swinbank) *chsd ldrs on outer: lost pl over 2f out: bhd whn eased ins last* **7/1**[3]

1m 16.21s (-0.69) **Going Correction** -0.025s/f (Stan) **9** Ran SP% **115.0**
Speed ratings (Par 100):103,96,94,91,87 86,84,73,69
CSF £14.68 CT £81.46 TOTE £6.60: £2.10, £1.30, £2.40; EX 17.50 Trifecta £113.50 Pool £447.82 - 2.80 winning units..
Owner Ian Henderson **Bred** P Onslow **Trained** Willoughton, Lincs

FOCUS
Ordinary form but the winner did it really well and looks way ahead of his official 67 rating with the placed horses setting the standard.

1177 HOSPITALITY PACKAGES AVAILABLE MAIDEN STKS 1m (F)
3:10 (3:12) (Class 5) 3-4-Y-0 **£3,238** (£963; £481; £240) **Stalls** Low

Form RPR

1 **Sky More** 3-8-12 .... EddieAhern 2 72+
(M A Jarvis) *in rr: hdwy on inner 3f out: styd on to ld ins last: drvn rt out* **9/1**

0 **2** *2* **Phreeze**[14] [954] 3-8-12 .... JamieSpencer 12 67+
(G A Swinbank) *s.i.s: reminders after s: racd wd: gd hdwy over 3f out: chsng ldrs 2f out: styd on to take 2nd ins last* **14/1**

3 *1 1/4* **Gunfighter (IRE)**[29] 4-9-12 .... TonyHamilton 14 69
(J S Wainwright) *racd wd: w ldrs: led over 4f out: clr over 2f out: hdd and no ex ins last* **100/1**

3 **4** *2* **Encores**[19] [901] 3-8-12 .... ChrisCatlin 1 60
(N A Callaghan) *prom: hdwy to chse ldrs over 2f out: one pce* **12/1**

043- **5** *15* **Angel Voices (IRE)**[260] [4155] 4-9-7 70............................ PatCosgrave 7 21
(K R Burke) *chsd ldrs: wknd fnl 2f* **3/1**[2]

0 **6** *1 1/4* **Bugsy's Boy**[43] [655] 3-8-12 .... TPQueally 6 23
(P W D'Arcy) *in rr: hdwy on outer over 3f out: nvr nr ldrs* **33/1**

7 *hd* **Feeling Peckish (USA)** 3-8-7 .... RussellKennemore(5) 8 22
(M C Chapman) *chsd ldrs: one pced fnl 2f* **100/1**

30 **8** *nk* **Bivouac (UAE)**[8] [1044] 3-8-12 .... DeanMcKeown 4 21
(G A Swinbank) *led tl over 4f out: wknd 2f out* **8/1**[3]

9 *22* **Betteras Bertie**[36] 4-9-5 .... PatrickDonaghy(7) 5 —
(M Brittain) *sn outpcd and wl bhd* **100/1**

0-0 **10** *6* **Just Matty**[11] [1001] 4-9-12 .... JimCrowley 3 —
(J G M O'Shea) *trckd ldrs: lost pl over 3f out: bhd whn eased over 2f out* **100/1**

-0 **11** *22* **Motarjm (USA)**[10] [1011] 3-8-12 .... NCallan 10 —
(M A Jarvis) *chsd ldrs: drvn over 4f out: lost pl 3f out: sn heavily eased: virtually p.u* **10/11**[1]

12 *1 1/2* **Star In Our Eyes (IRE)** 3-8-0 .... KrishlovyGundowry(7) 9 —
(M C Chapman) *s.i.s: sn wl bhd: t.o 4f out* **100/1**

13 *hd* **Ebn Zahr (UAE)** 3-8-12 .... PaulMulrennan 13 —
(Miss J E Foster) *s.i.s: racd wd: sn bhd: t.o 4f out* **40/1**

1m 43.81s (-0.79) **Going Correction** -0.025s/f (Stan)
WFA 3 from 4yo 14lb **13** Ran SP% **123.2**
Speed ratings (Par 103):102,100,98,96,81 80,80,80,58,52 30,28,28
CSF £128.39 TOTE £7.70: £2.50, £4.10, £6.70; EX 152.90 Trifecta £336.30 Part won. Pool £473.69 - 0.34 winning units..
Owner Sheikh Ahmed Al Maktoum **Bred** Darley **Trained** Newmarket, Suffolk

FOCUS
With the favourite flopping this did not take a deal of winning, the first four a long way clear of the 70-rated fifth.
Motarjm(USA) Official explanation: trainer's rep had no explanation for the poor form shown; jockey said gelding never travelled

1178 T & J BUILDERS H'CAP 1m 4f (F)
3:40 (3:41) (Class 6) (0-60,60) 4-Y-0+ **£3,071** (£906; £453) **Stalls** Low

Form RPR

5222 **1** **They All Laughed**[9] [1032] 4-9-4 **60**.. ChrisCatlin 6 73
(P W Hiatt) *hld up in rr: hdwy over 4f out: led on outer over 1f out: styd on wl towards fin* **10/3**[2]

243- **2** *1 1/2* **Pee Jay's Dream**[36] [6275] 5-9-5 **60**.............................. PaulMulrennan 10 71
(M W Easterby) *led 2f: w ldrs: led over 4f out tl over 1f out: no ex ins last* **6/1**[3]

6323 **3** *3 1/2* **Camille Pissarro (USA)**[5] [1078] 7-9-0 **55**............(b) EdwardCreighton 12 60
(D J Wintle) *in tch: hdwy to chal over 2f out: styd on same pce appr fnl f* **15/2**

260- **4** *nk* **York Cliff**[211] [5531] 9-9-0 **55**.. EddieAhern 14 60
(W M Brisbourne) *sn prom: kpt on same pce fnl 2f* **16/1**

000- **5** *1 1/2* **Nabir (FR)**[72] [2286] 7-9-3 **58**.......................................(t) PaulHanagan 11 60
(P D Niven) *chsd ldrs: chal 3f out: one pce* **33/1**

3215 **6** *1 1/4* **Nimello (USA)**[31] [733] 11-9-2 **57**.................................... SamHitchcott 2 57
(A G Newcombe) *hld up in rr: effrt 3f out: sn chsng ldrs: one pce fnl 2f* **11/1**

2040 **7** *2* **Maria Antonia (IRE)**[9] [1026] 4-9-0 **56**.................................. TPO'Shea 3 53
(P A Blockley) *in rr: hdwy over 5f out: nvr rchd ldrs* **9/1**

340/ **8** *7* **Naughty Nod (IRE)**[548] [6005] 4-9-4 **60**..........................(b[1]) PatCosgrave 5 46
(K R Burke) *chsd ldrs: wknd 2f out* **20/1**

9 *11* **Off Stage (IRE)**[39] [4752] 4-9-0 **56**.................................... JamieSpencer 8 24
(Carl Llewellyn) *led fter 2f tl over 4f out: lost pl 2f out: heavily eased ins last* **25/1**

10-5 **10** *nk* **Kirkhammerton (IRE)**[9] [1027] 5-8-10 **54**............(b) StephenDonohoe(3) 1 22
(A J McCabe) *in rr: bhd fnl 3f* **12/1**

3563 **11** *1 1/4* **Bienheureux**[9] [1032] 6-8-12 **53**..(t) NCallan 13 19
(Miss Gay Kelleway) *s.i.s: sme hdwy over 3f out: rdn and no rspnse over 2f out: virtually p.u ins last* **3/1**[1]

40-0 **12** *20* **Topflight Wildbird**[26] [805] 4-9-4 **60**.............................. J-PGuillambert 7 —
(Mrs G S Rees) *chsd ldrs: drvn over 5f out: lost pl over 4f out: bhd and eased over 2f out: virtually p.u: t.o* **33/1**

2m 41.06s (-1.03) **Going Correction** -0.025s/f (Stan)
WFA 4 from 5yo+ 1lb **12** Ran SP% **120.5**
Speed ratings (Par 101):102,101,98,98,97 96,95,90,83,83 82,68
CSF £23.07 CT £141.31 TOTE £4.30: £1.70, £2.70, £2.30; EX 26.10 Trifecta £97.20 Pool £279.45 - 2.04 winning units..
Owner Clive Roberts **Bred** T G And B B Mills **Trained** Hook Norton, Oxon

FOCUS
A low-grade handicap and in the end they came home well strung out. The form looks sound and could be rated a fraction higher.
Topflight Wildbird Official explanation: jockey said filly did not face the kick-back

1179 TOTESPORT H'CAP 7f (F)
4:10 (4:10) (Class 2) (0-100,99) 4-Y-0+
£11,217 (£3,358; £1,679; £840; £419; £210) **Stalls** Low

Form RPR

040- **1** **Wise Dennis**[204] [5675] 5-8-12 **93**.. JamieSpencer 8 103
(A P Jarvis) *s.i.s: hdwy on outside over 2f out: led jst ins last: styd on strly: readily* **5/1**[3]

0300 **2** *1 1/4* **Wessex (USA)**[22] [840] 7-8-8 **89** ow1.. NCallan 6 96
(P A Blockley) *hld up in tch: effrt 3f out: sn chsng ldrs: styd on to take 2nd post* **7/2**[1]

54-5 **3** *shd* **Matuza (IRE)**[10] [1013] 4-8-4 **85** oh3.................................... JamesDoyle 1 92
(W R Muir) *t.k.h: trckd ldrs: led over 4f out: rdn and wnt rt over 1f out: hdd and no ex jst ins last* **9/1**

/01- **4** *1 3/4* **Partners In Jazz (USA)**[330] [2012] 6-9-4 **99**.............................. PaulFessey 4 101
(T D Barron) *trckd ldrs: kpt on same pce appr fnl f* **4/1**[2]

54-2 **5** *2* **Electric Warrior (IRE)**[22] [842] 4-8-4 **85** oh4.................. PaulHanagan 5 82
(K R Burke) *trckd ldrs: effrt on outer 2f out: kpt on same pce* **5/1**[3]

6-03 **6** *hd* **Mujood**[9] [1023] 4-8-4 **85** oh3..................................(b) StephenCarson 7 81
(Eve Johnson Houghton) *hld up: effrt on inner over 2f out: kpt on: nvr trbld ldrs* **16/1**

0/0- **7** *3/4* **Capricorn Run (USA)**[202] [5722] 4-8-5 **89**............. StephenDonohoe(3) 2 84
(A J McCabe) *led tl over 4f out: one pce fnl 2f* **33/1**

00-0 **8** *8* **Game Lad**[8] [1041] 5-8-6 **87**.. DavidAllan 9 61
(T D Easterby) *chsd ldrs: rdn and lost pl over 2f out* **17/2**

3-53 **9** *1 1/4* **Mezuzah**[8] [1041] 7-8-6 **87**.. PaulMulrennan 3 57
(M W Easterby) *chsd ldrs: lost pl over 2f out: bhd and eased ins last* **8/1**

1m 29.31s (-1.49) **Going Correction** -0.025s/f (Stan) **9** Ran SP% **116.0**
Speed ratings (Par 109):107,105,105,103,101 100,100,90,89
CSF £22.99 CT £154.94 TOTE £7.10: £2.60, £1.10, £3.10; EX 27.10 Trifecta £379.00 Part won. Pool £533.93 - 0.78 winning units..
Owner Allen B Pope, Andrew J King **Bred** J And Mrs Bowtell **Trained** Twyford, Bucks

FOCUS
Quite a valuable handicap and run at a sound pace. The runner-up is a Fibresand specialist and is the key to the overall value of the form.

NOTEBOOK
Wise Dennis, absent since September, recorded his last success at York in May 2005 from a 6lb higher mark. Looking a picture of health and drawn wide, he was ridden with bags of confidence and in the end ran out a most convincing winner on just his second start on the All-Weather. (op 11-2 tchd 6-1)
Wessex(USA), just 1lb higher than his last success, went down fighting, reunited with his favourite jockey. His record here is now four wins, five seconds and two thirds from 13 starts. (op 4-1)
Matuza(IRE), 3lb 'wrong', took a keen grip. He came off a straight line under pressure and in the end just missed out on second spot. (op 12-1)
Partners In Jazz(USA), 5lb higher than when taking the Victoria Cup at Ascot in May, his last public appearance, was making his All-Weather debut. Full of beans and perky beforehand, he gave a good account of himself and all his four career wins have been on a straight track. (tchd 7-2 and 9-2)
Electric Warrior(IRE) was up against it running from 4lb out of the handicap. (op 6-1)
Mujood, 3lb out of the handicap, was in effect 7lb higher than his last success. (op 10-1)

1180 SOUTHWELL-RACECOURSE.CO.UK H'CAP 1m (F)
4:40 (4:40) (Class 3) (0-90,87) 4-Y-0 **£6,939** (£2,076; £1,038; £519; £258) **Stalls** Low

Form RPR

00-1 **1** **Future's Dream**[25] [809] 4-8-13 **81**.. PatCosgrave 3 99
(K R Burke) *led: qcknd 3f out: sn rdn: styd on strly fnl f* **9/2**[3]

5110 **2** *3 1/2* **Dichoh**[22] [846] 4-9-2 **84**.. NCallan 2 94
(M A Jarvis) *trckd ldrs: rdn and edgd lft over 1f out: kpt on: no imp* **2/1**[1]

-011 **3** *1/2* **Esthlos (FR)**[22] [850] 4-8-12 **80**.. JamieSpencer 4 89
(J Jay) *trckd ldrs: rdn and hung lft 2f out: kpt on same pce* **3/1**[2]

1201 **4** *3* **Councellor (FR)**[22] [842] 5-9-1 **83**.................................(t) MickyFenton 5 85
(Stef Liddiard) *t.k.h: trckd ldrs: hung lft and outpcd over 2f out: kpt on fnl f* **17/2**

2-66 **5** *2 1/2* **Vacation (IRE)**[22] [846] 4-9-2 **87**.................................. SaleemGolam(3) 7 83
(V Smith) *trckd ldrs: drvn over 3f out: lost pl over 2f out: no threat after* **11/2**

4-15 **6** *2 1/2* **Davenport (IRE)**[22] [850] 5-8-8 **76**.................................(p) JimCrowley 6 66
(B R Millman) *s.i.s: effrt 3f out: lost pl over 1f out* **12/1**

66-0 **7** *1 1/4* **Ahlawy (IRE)**[8] [1040] 4-8-7 **75**....................................... PaulMulrennan 8 63
(M W Easterby) *s.i.s: hld up on outer: effrt 3f out: hung lft and sn lost pl* **33/1**

130- **8** *1/2* **Freeloader (IRE)**[141] [6678] 7-9-2 **84**.................................. PaulHanagan 1 70
(R A Fahey) *hld up in tch: effrt 3f out: nvr a factor* **16/1**

1m 43.03s (-1.57) **Going Correction** -0.025s/f (Stan) **8** Ran SP% **118.9**
Speed ratings (Par 107):106,102,102,99,96 94,92,92
CSF £14.58 CT £31.69 TOTE £5.60: £2.30, £1.30, £1.60; EX 16.90 Trifecta £78.30 Pool £801.89 - 7.27 winning units..
Owner Mrs Maura Gittins **Bred** Mrs D Du Feu **Trained** Middleham Moor, N Yorks

FOCUS
A tight-knit handicap resulted in a most decisive all-the-way winner. The pace was not strong but the form looks very solid and has been rated positively.

NOTEBOOK
Future's Dream, a winner first time out in 2006, was 6lb higher than when making a winning return here last month. Stepping up the pace from the front, in the end he won going away. The suspicion is that he is at his best after a short break. (op 4-1)
Dichoh, happy to be back on the All-Weather, was 6lb higher than his win here last month. He tried hard to lay it down to the winner but, edging left and ending up against the far-side rail, in the end he had to concede defeat. His four career wins have been on the artificial surfaces, connections will be hoping fast ground on turf will suit him equally well. (tchd 15-8 and 5-2)
Esthlos(FR), who looked very fit indeed, was 7lb higher than Newcastle and was dropping back in trip. In the end the winner simply outpowered him. (op 5-1)
Councellor(FR), a keen type, was racing from a 4lb higher mark. Tapped for toe when the winner injected some speed into the contest, he was staying on in his own time late on. A much stronger pace would have suited him much better. (op 8-1 tchd 9-1)
Vacation(IRE), out of luck with the draw at Newcastle, is twice a winner on Polytrack. He looked very fit but was in trouble even before the pace increased. (tchd 13-2)
Davenport(IRE) will be seen to better effect with give in the ground on turf and in a more truly-run race. (op 14-1)

1181 ARENA LEISURE PLC H'CAP — 1m 3f (F)
5:10 (5:12) (Class 5) (0-75,75) 4-Y-0+ £3,238 (£963; £481; £240) Stalls Low

Form RPR

022- **1** **William's Way**[138] [6716] 5-9-1 **72**..................................... JamieSpencer 6 81
(I A Wood) *hld up: jinked rt bnd after 2f: smooth hdwy over 3f out: shkn up and led last 50yds: edgd lft: drvn rt out* **11/2**[3]

306- **2** *1/2* **Cordier**[135] [2000] 5-9-4 **75**.. DaleGibson 3 83
(J Mackie) *w ldrs: narrow advantage 3f out: hdd and no ex towards fin* **12/1**

3141 **3** *1 1/2* **Mahmjra**[25] [811] 5-8-12 **69**... PFredericks 7 74
(C N Allen) *led after 1f tl 3f out: styd on same pce fnl f* **7/4**[1]

5220 **4** *3* **Bolckow**[31] [733] 4-8-1 **61**... PatrickMathers(3) 5 61
(J T Stimpson) *sn chsng ldrs: sn drvn along: fdd ins last* **8/1**

45-0 **5** *2 1/2* **Stolen Glance**[25] [811] 4-8-6 **63** oh1 ow2.................... PaulMulrennan 2 59
(M W Easterby) *sn chsng ldrs: chal 3f out: wknd 1f out* **25/1**

-416 **6** *2* **Velvet Valley (USA)**[24] [813] 4-8-13 **70**........................ SamHitchcott 4 63
(C E Longsdon) *in rr: drvn 5f out: hdwy to chse ldrs over 3f out: wknd over 1f out* **5/2**[2]

4/ **7** *10* **Fixateur**[82] 5-9-4 **75**.. TPQueally 1 51
(J G Given) *led 1f: rdn and lost pl 7f out: detached over 4f out* **16/1**

031- **8** *28* **Lady Romanov (IRE)**[295] [3075] 4-9-1 **72**.......................... EddieAhern 8 —
(M H Tompkins) *hld up in rr: effrt u.p over 4f out: lost pl 3f out: sn bhd: virtually p.u* **8/1**

2m 27.57s (-1.33) **Going Correction** -0.025s/f (Stan) **8** Ran SP% **120.0**
Speed ratings (Par 103):103,102,101,99,97 96,88,68
CSF £70.93 CT £163.52 TOTE £4.60: £1.60, £3.20, £1.10; EX 65.40 Trifecta £140.10 Pool £843.11 - 4.27 winning units. Place 6 £94.61, Place 5 £68.42..
Owner Lewis Caterers **Bred** Lewis Caterers **Trained** Upper Lambourn, Berks

FOCUS
A modest handicap with the winner benefiting from a vintage Spencer ride.
T/Plt: £83.00 to a £1 stake. Pool: £63,459.85. 557.75 winning tickets. T/Qpdt: £62.10 to a £1 stake. Pool: £2,763.70. 32.90 winning tickets. WG

1182 - 1183a (Foreign Racing) - See Raceform Interactive

[945] LEOPARDSTOWN (L-H)
Sunday, April 22

OFFICIAL GOING: Good to firm

1184a HERITAGE STKS (LISTED RACE) (C & G) — 1m
3:25 (3:25) 4-Y-0+ £21,993 (£6,452; £3,074; £1,047)

RPR

1 **Danak (IRE)**[258] [4213] 4-9-3 108.. MJKinane 6 112
(John M Oxx, Ire) *trckd ldrs: 5th 1/2-way: 6th early st: hdwy 1 1/2f out: disp ld ins fnl f: led on line* **9/4**[1]

2 *shd* **Heliostatic (IRE)**[7] [1050] 4-9-5 112..................................... KJManning 5 114
(J S Bolger, Ire) *trckd ldrs in 4th: rdn st: chal over 1f out: disp ld ins fnl f: edgd lft: kpt on wl: hdd on line* **6/1**

3 *hd* **Decado (IRE)**[306] [2721] 4-9-5 111.................................... DPMcDonogh 7 114+
(Kevin Prendergast, Ire) *hld up: 7th and rdn ent st: r.o wl ins fnl f: jst failed* **9/2**[3]

4 *nk* **Quinmaster (USA)**[204] [5697] 5-9-0 109.................................... JMurtagh 3 108+
(M Halford, Ire) *hld up in tch: 6th 1/2-way: 5th st: rdn to chal whn nt clr run over 1f out: kpt on u.p* **5/1**

5 *2 1/2* **Dynamo Dancer (IRE)**[245] [4640] 4-9-0 96.............................. WSupple 4 102
(G M Lyons, Ire) *chsd ldrs in 3rd: chal early st: hmpd and checked wl ins fnl f: no ex* **25/1**

6 *1 3/4* **Crooked Throw (IRE)**[22] [848] 8-9-0 94.................................... WJLee 8 98
(C F Swan, Ire) *hld up in rr: rdn st: kpt on ins fnl f* **16/1**

7 *nk* **Prince Of Light (IRE)**[204] [5682] 4-9-3 .... JoeFanning 1 100
(M Johnston) *cl 2nd: rdn st: wkng whn hmpd 1f out: no ex* **7/2**[2]

8 *hd* **Ireland's Call (IRE)**[168] [6356] 6-9-0 94.............................. PJSmullen 2 97
(Peter Casey, Ire) *led: strly pressed st: hdd 1f out: no ex* **33/1**

1m 39.4s (-5.00) **Going Correction** -0.325s/f (Firm) **8** Ran SP% **114.8**
Speed ratings: 112,111,111,111,108 107,106,106
CSF £16.44 TOTE £2.90: £1.40, £1.90, £1.70; DF 8.90.
Owner H H Aga Khan **Bred** H H The Aga Khan's Studs S C **Trained** Currabeg, Co Kildare
■ Stewards' Enquiry : K J Manning one-day ban: careless riding (May 2)

NOTEBOOK
Danak(IRE), who did not race as a juvenile, quickly established himself as a smart performer last season and ended the year unbeaten in three starts, closing out with a victory in this grade. Rightly made favourite, he could have done with a stronger gallop and found himself with plenty of ground to make up as they turned into the straight, but it was clear from a furlong out he was beginning to hit top stride and he flashed past the post with Heliostatic, just getting the better of that one on a bob of the head. He is held in quite high regard at home and there is every reason to believe he will improve significantly for a step up to 1m2f. (op 9/4 tchd 2/1)
Heliostatic(IRE), dropping back to a mile, made the favourite pull out all the stops and looked to have won as they flashed past the post, but connections will no doubt have been pleased to see him return to something like his best. He has not built on the early promise he showed, but is clearly up to winning at this level. (op 9/2)
Decado(IRE) ◆, who had not been seen since disappointing in last season's St James's Palace Stakes, had earlier placed in the Irish 2000 Guineas and connections will no doubt have been delighted to see him return with such a promising effort. He is entitled to improve a good deal for the run and should make his mark at least at Listed level this season. (op 4/1)
Quinmaster(USA), a progressive handicapper last season, ran well enough here to suggest he can make his mark at this level in 2007 and is entitled to come on for the run. (op 9/2)
Prince Of Light(IRE), a progressive three-year-old last season who proved himself up to Listed level, ran most disappointingly on this return and has a bit to prove now. (op 7/2 tchd 4/1)

1185a P.W.MCGRATH MEMORIAL BALLYSAX STKS (GROUP 3) — 1m 2f
3:55 (3:56) 3-Y-O £30,790 (£9,033; £4,304; £1,466)

RPR

1 **Mores Wells**[15] [950] 3-9-1 ....(t) DPMcDonogh 6 111
(Kevin Prendergast, Ire) *trckd ldrs: mod 5th 1/2-way: 3rd and hdwy 4f out: 2nd st: chal fr over 1f out: kpt on wl to ld cl home* **12/1**

2 *1/2* **Ferneley (IRE)**[205] [5653] 3-9-1 106.. WSupple 9 110
(Francis Ennis, Ire) *racd keenly: sn led: rdn st: strly pressed fnl f: hdd and no ex cl home* **14/1**

3 *1 1/2* **Macarthur**[179] [6182] 3-9-1 .... JAHeffernan 8 107
(A P O'Brien, Ire) *hld up: 5th under 4f out: hdwy whn edgd lft early st: 3rd and kpt on ins fnl f* **2/1**[1]

4 *nk* **Creachadoir (IRE)**[15] [948] 3-9-4 111.................................. KJManning 1 110
(J S Bolger, Ire) *hld up: 7th 4f out: hdwy st: 3rd briefly under 1f out: sn no ex: kpt on* **5/2**[2]

5 *hd* **Anton Chekhov**[168] [6357] 3-9-1 .... CO'Donoghue 2 106
(A P O'Brien, Ire) *chsd ldrs: mod 4th 1/2-way: clsr 3rd and rdn st: 5th under 1f out: kpt on* **9/2**[3]

6 *3 1/2* **Summit Surge (IRE)**[15] [948] 3-9-1 103...............................(t) JMurtagh 7 100
(G M Lyons, Ire) *towards rr: 8th 4f out: kpt on same pce st* **14/1**

7 *4* **Hasanka (IRE)**[205] [5661] 3-8-12 .... MJKinane 5 90
(John M Oxx, Ire) *towards rr: no imp st* **15/2**

8 *29* **Mister Castlefield (IRE)**[22] [852] 3-9-1 55.............................. AO'Shea 4 41
(Mrs A M O'Shea, Ire) *chsd ldrs in mod 3rd: wknd qckly 4f out: eased bef st: t.o* **100/1**

9 *1 1/4* **The Ethiopian (IRE)**[168] [6357] 3-9-1 .... DavidMcCabe 3 38
(A P O'Brien, Ire) *disp ld early: 2nd and drvn along 1/2-way: wknd appr st: eased over 1f out: t.o* **33/1**

2m 5.50s (-4.90) **Going Correction** -0.325s/f (Firm) **9** Ran SP% **116.8**
Speed ratings: 106,105,104,104,104 101,98,74,73
CSF £166.36 TOTE £13.80: £2.50, £3.80, £1.50; DF 122.90.
Owner Iona Equine Syndicate **Bred** Cliveden Stud Ltd & Ocean Bloo **Trained** Friarstown, Co Kildare

FOCUS
A race with a rich tradition of producing top-class horses such as Sinndar, High Chaparral and Galileo, but whilst there were a few several promising performances, it was perhaps not the greatest of renewals.

NOTEBOOK
Mores Wells, a promising juvenile who reappeared with a narrow win at the course earlier in the month, was taking a big rise in grade, but he is bred to be classy and it was no surprise to see him leave his previous form behind, making smooth headway to go in pursuit of the runner-up and staying on too strongly for him in the final half furlong. According to connections he actually likes this fast ground, which is unusual for a Sadler's Wells, and there is every reason to believe he can develop into a live outsider come Derby time. (op 14/1)
Ferneley(IRE), a smart two-year-old who was having his first taste of going beyond 7f, was a bit keen in the lead and as a result he deserves a fair degree of credit for keeping on as well as he did. This represented an improvement in form and he should find a race at this sort of level, with the drop back to a mile unlikely to hinder him.
Macarthur, a full-brother to 2005 Derby hero Motivator, ran out a workmanlike winner in heavy ground on his sole start at two and was tackling vastly different underfoot conditions here. Hovering around second-favouritism for the Derby coming into the race, he ran well enough without suggesting he is potentially top-class, but he is likely to improve for a step up to 1m4f and his trainer will no doubt have left a bit to work on, so he is not one to give up on just yet. (op 6/4)
Creachadoir(IRE), a ready winner of the 2000 Guineas trial on his reappearance, travelled strongly on this rise in distance and was a bit short of room before the turn into the straight, but he held every chance in the end and was unable to see this trip out as well as those around him. He is likely to prove best back at a mile. (op 9/4)
Anton Chekhov, another interesting contender from Ballydoyle, broke his maiden in a Listed race at two and it was fascinating to see how much he had progressed over the winter. A son of Montjeu, he chased the early leaders but could not quicken under pressure and just kept plugging away. He too will relish an extra quarter mile and probably softer ground, so is another likely to improve on this, but he did not have the look of a Derby winner here. (op 5/1 tchd 11/2)
Hasanka(IRE), a fascinating contender being the only filly in the line-up, won her sole start at two and came into this hoping to boost her Oaks claims, but never got out of the rear and proved to be quite disappointing. Her trainer is now likely to lower her sights and admits she probably needs more time. (op 7/1)

1186 - 1188a (Foreign Racing) - See Raceform Interactive

[881] COLOGNE (R-H)
Sunday, April 22

OFFICIAL GOING: Good

1189a CAGLIOSTRO-SPRINTPREIS (LISTED RACE) — 6f
2:05 (2:07) 3-Y-O+ £8,784 (£2,703; £1,351; £338; £338)

RPR

1 **Sacho (GER)**[189] [6005] 9-9-6 .... THellier 3 108
(W Kujath, Germany) **122/10**

2 *1 1/4* **Lucky Strike**[13] 9-9-6 .... ADeVries 7 104
(A Trybuhl, Germany) **13/10**[1]

3 *nk* **Shinko's Best (IRE)**[184] [6093] 6-9-6 .... ASuborics 5 103
(A Kleinkorres, Germany) **5/2**[2]

4 *hd* **Fulminant (IRE)**[153] 6547 6-9-2 ....(b) AHelfenbein 8 99
(W Kujath, Germany) **137/10**
4 *dht* **Santiago Atitlan**[13] 5-9-6 .... EPedroza 10 103
(A Wohler, Germany) **52/10**[3]
6 *2* **Salontiger (GER)**[273] 5-9-0 .... NRichter 4 91
(A Kleinkorres, Germany) **31/1**
7 *2* **Omasheriff (IRE)**[13] 5-9-2 .... JVictoire 2 87
(W Baltromei, Germany) **143/10**
8 *2 ½* **Solvana (IRE)**[224] 5225 5-9-2 .... FJohansson 6 79
(Wido Neuroth, Norway) **30/1**
9 *½* **Deauville (GER)**[184] 6093 4-9-2 ....(b) AStarke 9 78
(Frau E Mader, Germany) **82/10**
10 *1* **Dizzy Dreamer (IRE)**[153] 6547 4-9-2 .... RobertHavlin 1 75
(P W Chapple-Hyam) *hld up on rails in mid-div, 6th str, stying on frm 2f out but stl 6th whn n.m.r on rail 1f out, no ch after* **188/10**

1m 10.37s (-2.94) **10** Ran SP% **131.4**
(including ten euro stakes): WIN 132; PL 21, 13, 13: SF 372.
Owner Stall Zorbas **Bred** Gestut Etzean **Trained** Germany

NOTEBOOK
Dizzy Dreamer(IRE) stuck to the inside throughout and was was staying on steadily until her path was blocked. She won over 6f last summer, but probably needs 7f now, particularly on fast ground.

1190a GERLING-PREIS (GROUP 2) 1m 4f
4:15 (4:25) 4-Y-O+ **£27,027** (£10,135; £4,054; £2,703)

RPR
1 **Saddex**[201] 5762 4-8-11 .... EPedroza 3 113
(P Rau, Germany) *raced in 3rd to straight, got through on rails to lead just inside final f, driven out* **31/10**[2]
2 *hd* **Bussoni (GER)**[21] 882 6-8-11 .... ADeVries 1 112
(H Blume, Germany) *hld up towards rr, hdwy & 4th str, chal 2f out, ev ch whn hung lft 1f out, straightened & ran on, jst failed* **4/1**[3]
3 *shd* **Prince Flori (GER)**[231] 5051 4-9-4 .... FilipMinarik 2 120
(S Smrczek, Germany) *5th straight, switched to outside over 1f out, ran on final f, every chance 50yds out, unable to quicken last strides* **4/1**[3]
4 *1 ¼* **Donaldson (GER)**[168] 6365 5-9-4 .... ASuborics 7 117
(P Rau, Germany) *sweating up & reluctant to load, led after 1f until headed just inside final furlong, no extra last 100yds* **111/10**
5 *2 ½* **La Dancia (IRE)**[196] 5857 4-8-7 .... DBonilla 8 103
(P Rau, Germany) *tracked leader to straight, one pace from over 1f out* **79/10**
6 *½* **Expensive Dream (GER)**[280] 3579 8-8-11 .... APietsch 5 105
(P Vovcenko, Germany) *last to straight, kept on but never a factor* **36/1**
7 *1 ½* **Brisant (GER)**[183] 6109 5-8-11 .... AHelfenbein 6 103
(M Trybuhl, Germany) *raced in 4th to 4f out, 7th straight, soon beaten* **39/1**
8 *2* **Schiaparelli (GER)**[203] 5709 4-9-4 .... AStarke 4 108
(P Schiergen, Germany) *raced in 6th to straight, effort on outside, beaten well over 1f out* **14/10**[1]

2m 30.57s (-2.33)
WFA 4 from 5yo+ 1lb **8** Ran SP% **130.8**
WIN 41; PL 15, 16, 16: SF 272.
Owner Stall Avena **Bred** The Niarchos Family **Trained** Germany

SAN SIRO (R-H)
Sunday, April 22

OFFICIAL GOING: Good to firm

1191a PREMIO MACHERIO (MAIDEN) (C&G) 1m 2f
3:30 (3:30) 3-Y-O **£6,757** (£2,973; £1,622; £811)

RPR
1 **Rainaldino (IRE)** 3-9-0 .... YLerner 7 —
(O Pessi, Italy) **41/20**[2]
2 *1 ¾* **Diamond Peak (IRE)** 3-9-0 .... MDemuro 1 —
(L D'Auria, Italy) **17/10**[1]
3 *nk* **Carlitos Tevez (IRE)** 3-9-0 .... URispoli 6 —
(A & G Botti, Italy) **32/10**[3]
4 *1* **Signalman** 3-9-0 .... DPorcu 11 —
(M Gasparini, Italy) **23/1**
5 *1* **Plutonik Rock (IRE)** 3-9-0 .... EBotti 8 —
(A & G Botti, Italy) **32/10**[3]
6 *9* **Royal Rumble (IRE)**[316] 2474 3-9-0 .... MarcoMonteriso 2 —
(G Miliani, Italy) **92/10**
7 *2 ¼* **Beat The Odds** 3-9-0 .... DVargiu 9 —
(V Caruso, Italy) **18/1**
8 *1* **Bolero De Aighenta (ITY)** 3-9-0 .... MEsposito 5 —
(P Cadeddu, Italy) **25/1**
9 *½* **Dumas (ITY)** 3-9-0 .... SGandini 10 —
(F Contu, Italy) **74/1**
10 *4* **Sopran Bodar (ITY)** 3-9-0 .... PConvertino 3 —
(M Marcialis, Italy) **83/1**
P **Feeling (IRE)** 3-8-10 .... MTellini 4 —
(P W Chapple-Hyam) *towards rear when bit slipped through mouth on final turn well over 4f out, eased & pulled up* **9/2**

2m 5.00s (-1.70) **11** Ran SP% **161.2**
(including one euro stakes): WIN 3.05; PL 1.51, 1.48, 4.32; DF 4.33.
Owner Razza Dormello Olgiata **Bred** Razza Dormello Olgiata Di Citai Spa **Trained** Italy

NOTEBOOK
Feeling(IRE) was about seventh when the bit slipped through his mouth starting the final turn. There was nothing that Tellini could do and he allowed the colt to ease up as soon as possible.

1192a PREMIO AMBROSIANO (GROUP 3) 1m 2f
4:35 (4:40) 4-Y-O+ **£27,365** (£12,041; £6,568; £3,284)

RPR
1 **Pressing (IRE)**[13] 4-8-11 .... DPorcu 1 113
(R Feligioni, Italy) *always in touch, 3rd straight, led over 3f out, pushed clear, comfortably* **51/20**[3]
2 *3* **Exhibit One (USA)**[242] 4714 5-8-8 .... EBotti 7 104
(V Valiani, Italy) *held up, 5th straight, ran on from 2f out to take 2nd inside final f, no threat to winner* **23/10**[2]
3 *1 ¼* **Aspectus (IRE)**[21] 880 4-8-11 .... MDemuro 5 105
(H Blume, Germany) *a in tch, wnt 2nd after 4f, led over 4f out, hdd over 3f out, rdn over 1f out, found nothing & lost 2nd ins fnl f* **97/100**[1]
4 *1 ¾* **Nordhal**[190] 5982 8-8-11 .... DVargiu 4 102
(B Grizzetti, Italy) *2nd for 4f, 4th straight, one pace final 3f* **195/10**
5 *19* **One Little David (GER)**[21] 882 7-8-11 .... MTellini 2 68
(P Vovcenko, Germany) *held up, 6th straight, well behind final 3f* **33/2**
6 *4 ½* **Rainer (FR)**[28] 8-8-11 .... YLerner 3 68
(F Losani, Italy) *last straight, always behind* **17/2**
7 *dist* **Giores (IRE)** 4-8-11 .... MEsposito 8 —
(R Feligioni, Italy) *led to over 4f out, soon tailed off* **51/20**[3]

2m 1.50s (-5.20) **7** Ran SP% **158.5**
WIN: 3.55 (coupled with Giores); PL 1.74, 2.03; DF 8.26.
Owner Scuderia Zaro SRL **Bred** Azienda Agricola Del Parco **Trained** Italy

991 PONTEFRACT (L-H)
Monday, April 23

OFFICIAL GOING: Good to firm (firm in places)
Wind: Almost nil.

1193 WENT EDGE MEDIAN AUCTION MAIDEN FILLIES' STKS 5f
2:10 (2:10) (Class 5) 2-Y-O **£3,886** (£1,156; £577; £288) **Stalls** Low

Form RPR
1 **Loch Jipp (USA)** 2-9-0 .... TonyHamilton 13 71
(J S Wainwright) *chsd ldrs: led and edgd lft over 1f out: r.o* **50/1**
2 *2* **Far Gone** 2-9-0 .... HayleyTurner 10 63+
(M L W Bell) *prom: outpcd 2f out: rallied and nt clr run over 1f out: r.o* **6/1**[2]
3 *shd* **Lake Sabina** 2-9-0 .... RichardMullen 15 63
(E S McMahon) *wnt rt s: sn chsng ldrs: rdn over 1f out: styd on* **14/1**
4 *2¼* **Musical Charm (IRE)** 2-9-0 .... DavidAllan 12 62
(T D Easterby) *s.i.s: sn prom: outpcd 1/2-way: styd on ins fnl f: fin 5th 2l, shd, 2l, hd: plcd 4th* **14/1**
5 *nk* **Myriola** 2-9-0 .... TPQueally 11 61
(J G Given) *led: hdd over 3f out: rdn over 1f out: wknd ins fnl f: fin 6th: plcd 5th* **16/1**
6 *shd* **Willyn (IRE)** 2-9-0 .... TomEaves 8 60
(J R Weymes) *s.i.s: outpcd: r.o ins fnl f: nrst fin: fin 7th: plcd 6th* **66/1**
7 *nk* **Holly Golightley** 2-9-0 .... NCallan 3 65+
(K A Ryan) *hmpd start: chsd ldrs: rdn whn hmpd over 1f out: nt rcvr: fin 8th: plcd 7th* **7/2**[1]
63 8 **Varinia (IRE)**[9] 1043 2-8-7 .... PatrickDonaghy(7) 6 62
(M Brittain) *went lft start: chsd ldr: led over 3f out: rdn: hung lft and hdd over 1f out: wknd towards fin: fin 4th, 2l, shd, 2l: plcd 8th* **6/1**[2]
9 *4* **Aquarian Dancer** 2-9-0 .... PaulMulrennan 1 35
(Jedd O'Keeffe) *sn outpcd* **9/1**
4 10 *nk* **Dawn Light (IRE)**[6] 1073 2-9-0 .... RoystonFfrench 2 34
(Mrs A Duffield) *mid-div: sn drvn along: wknd over 1f out* **15/2**
11 *nk* **Teatime Lady (USA)** 2-9-0 .... PaulFessey 14 33
(T D Barron) *sn outpcd* **7/1**[3]
12 *3* **Miss Kin (IRE)** 2-9-0 .... RobbieFitzpatrick 4 21
(T J Pitt) *s.i.s: sn outpcd* **12/1**
13 *¾* **Herolds Bay** 2-9-0 .... DaleGibson 9 18
(M W Easterby) *s.i.s: outpcd* **33/1**

64.82 secs (1.02) **Going Correction** -0.075s/f (Good) **13** Ran SP% **118.4**
Speed ratings (Par 89):88,84,84,81,80 80,80,81,73,73 72,67,66
CSF £326.96 TOTE £61.90: £14.70, £2.50, £3.90; EX 571.40.
Owner I Barran **Bred** R L Quinichet And Lorraine R Quinichett **Trained** Kennythorpe, N Yorks
■ Stewards' Enquiry : Patrick Donaghy three-day ban: careless riding (May 4, 7-8); one-day ban: not keeping straight from stalls (May 9)

FOCUS
The bare form of this fillies' maiden is probably just fair, but a few of these shaped quite nicely and the race should produce winners, with hampered seventh rated as finishing second.

NOTEBOOK
Loch Jipp(USA) ◆, a half-sister to sprint winner I'm Sailing, and to Cobi Ky, a winner at around 1m, belied her big odds to make a winning debut in good style. She has plenty of size and there should be even better to come. Her trainer is eyeing a tilt at the Hilary Needler. (op 40-1)
Far Gone, a half-sister to Loupy, who was placed at two in France, did not enjoy the clearest of runs but stayed on well once in the clear. (op 11-2)
Lake Sabina, the first foal of a multiple 7f winner, made a pleasing introduction and can build on this. (op 16-1)
Musical Charm(IRE), a half-sister to multiple sprint winner Piddies Pride, should be all the better for this experience and ought to go close in similar company next time. (op 11-1)
Myriola, the first foal of a mare who was unplaced over 7f on her only start at three, showed good speed throughout and will surely be more at home on an easier track. (tchd 20-1)
Willyn(IRE) ◆, a half-sister to Denton Hawk, who was placed over 5f-7f at two and three, caught the eye running on nicely close home. She should know more next time and is one to look out for. (tchd 80-1)
Holly Golightley ◆, a 10,000gns purchase, out of a 7f two-year-old winner, would not have been far away had she not been badly hampered against the far rail over a furlong from the finish. (op 3-1 tchd 4-1)
Varinia(IRE) showed good early speed, but she hung left under strong pressure in the straight and badly hampered Holly Golightley. As a result, the Stewards' had little choice but to place her behind Holly Golightley. She can surely do better on a flatter track. (op 5-1 tchd 9-2)

1194 CORNMARKET H'CAP 1m 4f 8y
2:40 (2:40) (Class 5) (0-70,70) 3-Y-O **£3,886** (£1,156; £577; £288) **Stalls** Low

Form RPR
-033 1 **Stringsofmyheart**[22] 869 3-8-13 **65**....................(p) DarrylHolland 6 74
(W J Haggas) *dwlt: sn led: pushed along over 2f out: rdn over 1f out: hdd jst ins fnl f: rallied and sn led again: styd on wl* **8/1**
000- 2 *½* **Force Group (IRE)**[171] 6324 3-8-11 **63**.................... MichaelHills 9 71
(M H Tompkins) *hld up in rr: stdy hdwy over 4f out: chsd wnr wl over 1f out rdn to ld jst ins fnl f: sn edgd lft: hdd and no ex* **7/1**
1500 3 *9* **My Sara**[5] 1092 3-8-4 **56**.................... RoystonFfrench 2 49
(R A Fahey) *cl up: rdn along over 2f out: drvn wl over 1f out and kpt on same pce* **17/2**
6215 4 *hd* **King Of The Beers (USA)**[9] 1039 3-8-1 **60**....................(p) LukeMorris(7) 7 53
(R A Harris) *trckd ldrs: hdwy 4f out: rdn over 2f out: drvn wl over 1f out and kpt on same pce* **9/1**
30-1 5 *3* **Always Best**[19] 917 3-9-2 **68**.................... KDarley 8 56
(M Johnston) *cl up: rdn along 3f out: drvn 2f out and sn wknd* **7/2**[1]

03-1 **6** *9* **Pigeon Flight**[14] [981] 3-9-4 **70** HayleyTurner 4 44
(M L W Bell) *t.k.h: hld up in rr: hdwy on outer to chse ldrs over 4f out: rdn along 3f out: sn btn and eased* **13/2**[3]

0-52 **7** *3/4* **Colditz (IRE)**[19] [917] 3-9-2 **68** TonyHamilton 1 41
(D W Barker) *hld up: a towards rr* **11/1**

-425 **8** *1 1/2* **Greek God**[76] [373] 3-8-4 **56** oh1 JimmyQuinn 5 26
(W Jarvis) *chsd ldrs: rdn along 4f out: sn wknd* **9/2**[2]

064 **9** *34* **President Dan**[37] [703] 3-8-13 **65** NCallan 3 —
(M R Channon) *chsd ldrs: rdn along over 4f out: sn wknd* **16/1**

2m 38.6s (-1.70) **Going Correction** -0.075s/f (Good) 9 Ran SP% **112.1**
Speed ratings (Par 98):102,101,95,95,93 87,87,86,63
CSF £60.28 CT £485.48 TOTE £8.20: £2.60, £3.20, £3.00; EX 76.90.
Owner Mrs Denis Haynes **Bred** Wretham Stud **Trained** Newmarket, Suffolk
■ Stewards' Enquiry : Darryll Holland caution: used whip down shoulder in forehand position

FOCUS
Not much strength in depth in this middle-distance handicap, but the front two pulled clear and the race could rate a little better.
Pigeon Flight Official explanation: jockey said gelding ran too free

1195 FRYSTON H'CAP 6f
3:10 (3:11) (Class 2) (0-100,100) 3-Y-0+
£9,971 (£2,985; £1,492; £747; £372; £187) **Stalls** Low

Form RPR

20-0 **1** **Kostar**[30] [759] 6-9-5 **92** PhilipRobinson 7 109
(C G Cox) *chsd ldrs: led and edgd lft ins fnl f: r.o wl* **13/2**[2]

060- **2** *5* **Mr Wolf**[184] [6095] 6-9-5 **92** (p) TomEaves 13 94
(D W Barker) *led: rdn and hdd ins fnl f: sn outpcd* **16/1**

45 **3** *1/2* **Machinist (IRE)**[24] [828] 7-9-5 **92** SilvestreDeSousa 11 93
(D Nicholls) *hld up: hdwy over 1f out: edgd lft and r.o ins fnl f: nrst fin* **14/1**

322- **4** *nk* **Viking Spirit**[163] [6445] 5-9-8 **95** AdamKirby 16 95
(W R Swinburn) *chsd ldrs: rdn over 2f out: no ex fnl f* **13/2**[2]

20-6 **5** *3/4* **Zomerlust**[9] [1041] 5-9-6 **93** GrahamGibbons 14 91
(J J Quinn) *s.i.s: hld up: hdwy over 1f out: nt rch ldrs* **17/2**[3]

130- **6** *2* **Fantasy Explorer**[212] [5535] 4-9-3 **90** JimmyQuinn 12 82
(J J Quinn) *trckd ldr: racd keenly: rdn and ev ch over 1f out: wknd ins fnl f* **14/1**

00-6 **7** *1 1/4* **Coeur Courageux (FR)**[44] [660] 5-9-1 **88** (t) TonyHamilton 10 76
(D Nicholls) *hld up: styd on fnl f: nvr nrr* **33/1**

-000 **8** *nk* **Commando Scott (IRE)**[2] [1157] 6-8-13 **86** SebSanders 5 73
(I W McInnes) *mid-div: hdwy u.p over 1f out: wknd ins fnl f* **9/1**

13-1 **9** *1 1/4* **Geojimali**[15] [957] 5-8-6 **86** oh1 GaryBartley(7) 9 69
(J S Goldie) *hld up: nvr nrr* **11/2**[1]

1-66 **10** *1* **Connect**[85] [277] 10-8-7 **87** (b) AshleyMorgan(7) 2 67
(M H Tompkins) *mid-div: rdn 1/2-way: n.d* **50/1**

40-0 **11** *shd* **Sir Xaar (IRE)**[9] [1041] 4-9-9 **96** RoystonFfrench 8 76
(B Smart) *prom over 4f* **10/1**

-540 **12** *1 3/4* **Obe Gold**[9] [1041] 5-9-6 **93** DarryllHolland 15 68
(M R Channon) *mid-div: pushed along and lost pl over 4f out: n.d after* **14/1**

02-0 **13** *3* **Turnkey**[19] [927] 5-9-11 **98** AdrianTNicholls 3 64
(D Nicholls) *s.i.s: hld up: a in rr* **28/1**

040- **14** *1* **Coleorton Dancer**[198] [5812] 5-9-7 **94** NCallan 1 57
(K A Ryan) *chsd ldrs: rdn over 2f out: wknd over 1f out: eased ins fnl f* **12/1**

063- **15** *2* **Out After Dark**[198] [5812] 6-9-13 **100** (p) KDarley 4 57
(C G Cox) *chsd ldrs 4f* **9/1**

000- **16** *18* **Tara Too (IRE)**[193] [5919] 4-8-13 **86** oh1 TPQueally 6 —
(J G Portman) *hld up: rdn and wknd over 2f out: virtually p.u fnl f* **80/1**

1m 14.91s (-2.49) **Going Correction** -0.075s/f (Good) 16 Ran SP% **124.8**
Speed ratings (Par 109):113,106,105,105,104 101,99,99,97,96 96,94,90,88,86 62
CSF £106.63 CT £1435.00 TOTE £8.60: £2.30, £3.30, £4.20, £1.80; EX 208.60 TRIFECTA Not won..
Owner Mrs P Scott-Dunn And Mrs F J Ryan **Bred** Mrs P Scott-Dunn **Trained** Lambourn, Berks

FOCUS
Just an ordinary handicap for the grade and not rated too positively, but Kostar won very well and did so in a creditable time; 2.17 seconds quicker than the fillies' maiden.

NOTEBOOK
Kostar was a beaten favourite over 7f on the Polytrack on his reappearance, but that run clearly put him spot on and he bolted up. He seemed a touch keen early, but was always in a good position and blew his 15 rivals away once switched in the clear. He will obviously be deserving of his place in some of the major sprint handicaps this summer, but the assessor will hammer him for this success and that will make things a lot tougher. (op 8-1)
Mr Wolf ◆ ran a most encouraging race on his seasonal reappearance. Having shown his customary early speed, he kept on surprisingly well considering he could have been expected to need the outing and found only the impressive winner too good. This should put him just right and he appeals as one to have on-side. (op 14-1)
Machinist(IRE) fared best of the hold-up horses but just got going too late. (op 16-1)
Viking Spirit ran with credit on his return from a 163-day break and is open to improvement. (op 7-1)
Zomerlust was dropped in from his wide draw and got going too late. (op 8-1 tchd 9-1)
Geojimali looked a sprint handicapper to follow when winning at Musselburgh on his reappearance, but things did not fall into place for him this time. Official explanation: jockey said gelding was denied a clear run (op 4-1)
Coleorton Dancer Official explanation: jockey said gelding had no more to give

1196 PONTEFRACT MARATHON H'CAP 2m 5f 122y
3:40 (3:40) (Class 5) (0-75,70) 4-Y-0+ **£4,533** (£1,348; £674; £336) **Stalls** Low

Form RPR

0-22 **1** **Great As Gold (IRE)**[13] [994] 8-9-8 **65** TomEaves 12 73
(B Ellison) *hld up in rr: hdwy to chse ldrs over 5f out: rdn along 4f out: styd on to chal ent fnl f: drvn and edgd lft: led nr fin* **7/4**[1]

0-34 **2** *nk* **Noddies Way**[25] [691] 4-8-1 **53** LiamJones(3) 7 61
(J F Panvert) *trckd ldrs: hdwy 5f out: led 4f out: rdn wl over 1f out: drvn ins fnl f: hdd and no ex towards fin* **9/2**[2]

-302 **3** *5* **Toni Alcala**[19] [913] 8-8-8 **51** (p) DeanMcKeown 11 54
(R F Fisher) *trckd ldrs gng wl: smooth hdwy 4f out: rdn and ev ch over 1f out: drvn and one pce ins fnl f* **15/2**

1415 **4** *3 1/2* **Rule For Ever**[13] [994] 5-9-10 **67** DanielTudhope 4 66
(I W McInnes) *trckd ldrs: hdwy to dispute ld 4f out and ev ch tl drvn and wknd appr fnl f* **6/1**[3]

00-5 **5** *3/4* **True (IRE)**[19] [913] 6-8-8 **51** oh6 PaulFessey 1 49
(Mrs S Lamyman) *hld up in rr: hdwy over 6f out: rdn to chse ldrs 3f out: sn drvn and no imp* **12/1**

U66/ **6** *4* **Iloveturtle (IRE)**[16] [4609] 7-8-8 **51** oh6 (t) NCallan 3 45
(M C Chapman) *chsd clr ldr: rdn along over 3f out and grad wknd* **7/1**

6-00 **7** *1 1/2* **Jamaican Flight (USA)**[13] [994] 14-8-8 **51** oh6 JimmyQuinn 9 44?
(Mrs S Lamyman) *led and sn clr: rdn along 6f out: hdd 4f out and sn wknd* **80/1**

0-00 **8** *1 1/2* **Spectested (IRE)**[13] [994] 6-8-8 **51** oh6 (p) RichardMullen 2 42?
(A W Carroll) *in rr: hdwy 5f out: rdn and in tch over 3f out: drvn and no prog fnl 2f* **50/1**

0/5- **9** *7* **Columbus (IRE)**[44] [6178] 10-8-11 **54** HayleyTurner 6 38
(Jennie Candlish) *bhd: rdn along 1/2-way: nvr a factor* **28/1**

/0-0 **10** *11* **Water Pistol**[8] [913] 5-8-1 **51** oh3 PaulPickard(7) 10 24
(M C Chapman) *chsd ldrs: rdn along 6f out: sn btn* **100/1**

000- **11** *3 1/2* **Compton Commander**[184] [4960] 9-8-12 **55** RoystonFfrench 5 25
(E W Tuer) *a towards rr* **25/1**

30- **12** *100* **Liberman (IRE)**[8] [5846] 9-9-13 **70** DaleGibson 8 —
(R Curtis) *prom: rdn along 7f out: sn wknd* **25/1**

4m 55.97s (-4.83) **Going Correction** -0.075s/f (Good)
WFA 4 from 5yo+ 6lb 12 Ran SP% **116.1**
Speed ratings (Par 103):105,104,103,101,101 100,99,98,96,92 91,—
CSF £8.43 CT £46.82 TOTE £2.70: £1.40, £1.80, £1.90; EX 15.10.
Owner Keith Middleton **Bred** Rathasker Stud **Trained** Norton, N Yorks

FOCUS
Just a modest staying handicap and not that strong with several out of the handicap not beaten that far.
Spectested(IRE) Official explanation: jockey said gelding lost one of its cheekpieces
Liberman(IRE) Official explanation: trainer said gelding bled from the nose

1197 SUBSCRIBE ONLINE @ RACINGUK.TV MAIDEN STKS 6f
4:10 (4:11) (Class 5) 3-Y-0+ **£3,886** (£1,156; £577; £288) **Stalls** Low

Form RPR

0-0 **1** **A Big Sky Brewing (USA)**[15] [954] 3-9-0 PaulFessey 4 63+
(T D Barron) *towards rr: hdwy on inner 2f out: rdn ent fnl f: kpt on wl to ld last 75yds* **20/1**

2 *1/2* **Gleneagles (IRE)** 3-9-0 DarryllHolland 6 61+
(W J Haggas) *in midfield: hdwy towards inner 2f out: rdn and ev ch ent fnl f: sn drvn and kpt on* **9/2**[3]

430- **3** *shd* **Bid For Gold**[199] [5788] 3-9-0 75 PaulMulrennan 5 61
(Jedd O'Keeffe) *a prom: swtchd rt and rdn over 1f out: led and edgd lft ins fnl f: hdd and no ex last 75yds* **4/1**[2]

2-02 **4** *2 1/2* **Wolfman**[48] [632] 5-9-11 49 (p) NCallan 17 56
(D W Barker) *sn led: rdn wl over 1f out: drvn and hdd ins fnl f: kpt on same pce* **7/1**

6- **5** *3/4* **Five Wishes**[256] [4295] 3-8-9 TonyHamilton 13 46
(M Dods) *chsd ldrs: rdn along 2f out: drvn and one pce appr fnl f* **8/1**

00- **6** *2* **Aussie Blue (IRE)**[199] [5790] 3-9-0 DeanMcKeown 7 44+
(R M Whitaker) *towards rr: hdwy 2f out: styd on ins fnl f: nrst fin* **20/1**

000- **7** *1 1/2* **Eternal Legacy (IRE)**[235] [4961] 5-9-6 47 JimmyQuinn 14 37
(E J Alston) *chsd ldrs: rdn 2f out: wknd appr fnl f* **22/1**

3-32 **8** *1 1/2* **Distant Sun (USA)**[91] [208] 3-9-0 66 (p) TomEaves 9 35
(I Semple) *cl up: rdn along 2f out: wknd appr fnl f* **9/4**[1]

9 *1 1/4* **Aslan** 3-9-0 DavidAllan 15 31
(T D Easterby) *s.i.s and bhd tl styd on fnl 2f* **25/1**

-304 **10** *1/2* **Boppys Dream**[34] [714] 5-9-1 43 (p) RoryMoore(5) 11 27
(P T Midgley) *in tch: rdn along over 2f out: sn wknd* **100/1**

11 *3 1/2* **Terandeil** 3-8-9 ChrisCatlin 1 13+
(J G M O'Shea) *s.i.s: a in rr* **20/1**

00- **12** *3* **Whozart (IRE)**[135] [6771] 4-9-11 DanielTudhope 12 11
(A Dickman) *dwlt and towards rr: hdwy on outer and in tch 1/2-way: sn rdn and wknd* **100/1**

0- **13** *1 1/4* **Bunderos (IRE)**[205] [5679] 3-8-9 RoystonFfrench 16 —
(Mrs A Duffield) *chsd ldrs: rdn along over 2f out and sn wknd* **50/1**

030- **14** *1/2* **Briery Blaze**[210] [5577] 4-9-6 52 KDarley 10 —
(Mrs K Walton) *a towards rr* **25/1**

15 *nk* **Irish Mickey** 3-8-11 AndrewMullen(3) 3 5
(James Moffatt) *a in rr* **100/1**

1m 17.08s (-0.32) **Going Correction** -0.075s/f (Good)
WFA 3 from 4yo+ 11lb 15 Ran SP% **123.8**
Speed ratings (Par 103):99,98,98,94,93 91,89,87,85,84 80,76,74,73,73
CSF £102.44 TOTE £24.30: £6.60, £2.60, £2.20; EX 175.70.
Owner Trevor Boanas **Bred** Braeburn Farm Corp **Trained** Maunby, N Yorks

FOCUS
Just an ordinary sprint maiden best rated through the fourth. The winning time was 2.17 seconds slower than the 86-100 handicap.

1198 CATTERICK RACES ON THE 25TH APRIL H'CAP 1m 4y
4:40 (4:41) (Class 5) (0-75,73) 4-Y-0+ **£3,886** (£1,156; £577; £288) **Stalls** Low

Form RPR

06-6 **1** **Flighty Fellow (IRE)**[19] [930] 7-8-11 **66** (b) DavidAllan 8 74
(T D Easterby) *chsd ldrs: swtchd rt and hdwy 2f out: rdn to ld jst ins fnl f: styd on wl* **10/1**

0004 **2** *1 1/2* **Top Jaro (FR)**[7] [1066] 4-9-3 **72** HayleyTurner 10 77
(Jennie Candlish) *cl up: rdn to ld 2f out: drvn over 1f out: hdd jst ins fnl f: kpt on* **25/1**

45-6 **3** *1/2* **Northern Boy (USA)**[14] [969] 4-9-1 **70** PaulFessey 5 74+
(T D Barron) *in midfield: hdwy over 2f out: rdn to chse ldng pair over 1f out: drvn and kpt on ins fnl f* **8/1**[3]

04-0 **4** *1 3/4* **Jordan's Light (USA)**[14] [975] 4-8-13 **68** (v) RobbieFitzpatrick 3 68
(T J Pitt) *trckd ldrs: effrt 2f out: rdn and hung rt over 1f out: drvn and kpt on ins fnl f* **12/1**

040- **5** *1 3/4* **Society Music (IRE)**[219] [5384] 5-8-12 **67** TonyHamilton 1 63
(M Dods) *in midfield: hdwy and n.m.r over 1f out: kpt on ins fnl f: nrst fin* **22/1**

0-54 **6** *hd* **Skyelady**[14] [979] 4-9-2 **71** (p) TomEaves 4 66
(Miss J A Camacho) *chsd ldrs: rdn along over 2f out: grad wknd appr fnl f* **12/1**

00-0 **7** *3/4* **King Of The Moors (USA)**[15] [953] 4-8-8 **70** NeilBrown(7) 14 64
(T D Barron) *towards rr: hdwy towards inner 2f out: sn rdn and kpt on fnl f: nrst fin* **20/1**

51-5 **8** *1/2* **Treasure House (IRE)**[24] [830] 6-8-13 **68** NCallan 17 60
(M Blanshard) *hld up in rr: hdwy 2f out: sn rdn and styd on appr fnl f: nrst fin* **12/1**

2430 **9** *1* **Bay Boy**[31] [747] 5-9-4 **73** (b) KDarley 2 63
(M Johnston) *in tch: hdwy on inner 2f out: sn rdn and no imp fr over 1f out* **13/2**[1]

000- **10** *nk* **Playtotheaudience**[205] [5685] 4-8-8 **68** JamieMoriarty(5) 13 57
(R A Fahey) *s.i.s: hdwy into midfield 1/2-way: effrt and rdn 2f out: nt rch ldrs* **11/1**

40-5 **11** *shd* **She's Our Lass (IRE)**[30] 771 6-9-4 **73**...................... DanielTudhope 16 62
(D Carroll) *hld up: a towards rr* **14/1**
03-0 **12** *3 1/2* **Breaking Shadow (IRE)**[9] 1040 5-9-2 **71**....................(p) JimmyQuinn 7 52
(M A Peill) *chsd ldrs: rdn along 2f out: sn drvn and wknd appr fnl f* **14/1**
406- **13** *3/4* **Star Of The Desert (IRE)**[37] 5879 4-8-12 **67**.............. PaulMulrennan 9 46
(Mrs K Walton) *prom: rdn along over 2f out: sn wknd* **25/1**
00-2 **14** *2 1/2* **Frank Crow**[14] 969 4-9-4 **73**.. DarrylHolland 11 47
(J S Goldie) *in tch on outer: rdn along over 2f out and sn wknd* **15/2**[2]
344- **15** *nk* **Selective**[308] 2705 8-9-0 **69**.. ChrisCatlin 15 42
(A W Carroll) *a towards rr* **22/1**
0/5- **16** *3* **Brace Of Doves**[353] 1455 5-9-0 **69**............................... RoystonFfrench 6 35
(D W Whillans) *led: rdn along and hdd 2f out: sn wknd* **50/1**
150- **17** *32* **Night Cru**[213] 5504 4-9-2 **71**.. SebSanders 12 —
(C F Wall) *a in rr* **8/1**[3]

1m 44.75s (-0.95) **Going Correction** -0.075s/f (Good) **17** Ran SP% **124.3**
Speed ratings (Par 103):101,99,99,97,95 95,94,94,93,92 92,89,88,85,85 82,50
CSF £252.64 CT £2114.67 TOTE £13.60: £3.70, £6.90, £2.30, £2.70; EX 422.10.
Owner David W Armstrong **Bred** F Hinojosa **Trained** Great Habton, N Yorks

FOCUS
Very few got involved in this fair handicap and this looks like modest form rated through the runner-up.
Brace Of Doves Official explanation: jockey said gelding ran too free
Night Cru Official explanation: vet said gelding suffering from irregular heartbeat

1199 BETFAIR.COM APPRENTICE SERIES ROUND 2 H'CAP 1m 2f 6y
5:10 (5:11) (Class 5) (0-70,70) 4-Y-O+ **£3,886** (£1,156; £577; £288) **Stalls** Low

Form RPR
6453 **1** **Torrens (IRE)**[5] 1090 5-9-0 **70**..................................... JamesRogers(5) 1 77+
(R A Fahey) *hld up: hdwy over 1f out: rdn to ld wl ins fnl f: r.o* **7/4**[1]
-364 **2** *2* **Suits Me**[22] 870 4-9-2 **67**... JamieHamblett 3 70
(T P Tate) *chsd ldrs: lost pl 6f out: hdwy over 2f out: rdn and ev ch ins fnl f: styd on same pce* **9/2**[3]
4345 **3** *2* **Augustine**[5] 1090 6-9-2 **67**... WJCafferty 9 66
(P W Hiatt) *hld up in tch: racd keenly: trckd ldr 6f out: led 3f out: rdn and hdd ins fnl f: no ex* **4/1**[2]
00-0 **4** *1* **Malinsa Blue (IRE)**[19] 915 5-8-0 **56**.............................. LanceBetts(5) 2 53
(B Ellison) *trckd ldrs: racd keenly: rdn over 1f out: styd on same pce fnl f* **20/1**
316 **5** *1* **Blushing Prince (IRE)**[14] 742 9-8-0 **56** oh6......(t) PatrickDonaghy(5) 10 51
(R C Guest) *hld up: hdwy over 5f out: rdn over 1f out: wknd ins fnl f* **25/1**
40-4 **6** *5* **General Flumpa**[14] 976 6-8-2 **58**............................ AdeleRothery(5) 7 44
(Miss Tor Sturgis) *hld up: sme hdwy over 1f out: n.d* **10/1**
140- **7** *4* **Moonlight Fantasy (IRE)**[230] 5082 4-8-5 **56** oh6.. DanielleMcCreery 11 34
(N Tinkler) *led 7f: hung rt and wknd fnl f* **14/1**
130- **8** *7* **Ruby Legend**[189] 6008 9-8-5 **59**................................ FrankiePickard(3) 8 24
(K G Reveley) *hld up: a in rr* **16/1**
/0-0 **9** *1 3/4* **Toparudi**[19] 930 6-8-7 **65**.. AshleyMorgan(7) 6 27
(M H Tompkins) *dwlt: hld up: a in rr* **18/1**
0/0- **10** *1 1/2* **Pearson Glen (IRE)**[209] 1467 8-8-1 **57** oh11 ow1...(e) BradleyRoper(5) 5 16
(James Moffatt) *chsd ldrs over 7f* **50/1**
100- **11** *25* **Oh Danny Boy**[41] 5354 6-8-0 **58**.................................... PaulPickard(7) 12 —
(M C Chapman) *mid-div: hdwy 7f out: rdn and wknd 3f out: virtually p.u fnl f* **18/1**

2m 12.47s (-1.61) **Going Correction** -0.075s/f (Good) **11** Ran SP% **117.3**
Speed ratings (Par 103):103,101,99,99,98 94,91,85,84,82 62
CSF £9.02 CT £27.91 TOTE £3.00: £1.40, £1.90, £1.50; EX 9.30 Place 6 £581.62, Place 5 £128.32..
Owner Mrs Catherine Reynard **Bred** Dermot Cantillon And Forenaghts Stud **Trained** Musley Bank, N Yorks

FOCUS
A modest handicap restricted to apprentices who, at the start of the 2007 turf season, had not ridden more than ten winners. The winner looks capable of better but the fifth anchors the form.
T/Jkpt: Not won. T/Plt: £1,409.50 to a £1 stake. Pool: £69,126.65. 35.80 winning tickets. T/Qpdt: £19.30 to a £1 stake. Pool: £5,286.30. 202.55 winning tickets. JR

1058 WINDSOR (R-H)
Monday, April 23

OFFICIAL GOING: Good to firm (good in places)
Wind: Moderate, half behind Weather: Mainly overcast

1200 WELCOME BACK TO MONDAY NIGHT RACING APPRENTICE H'CAP 6f
5:25 (5:25) (Class 5) (0-75,75) 4-Y-O+ **£3,238** (£963; £481; £240) **Stalls** High

Form RPR
303- **1** **Gwilym (GER)**[122] 6913 4-8-5 **65**.............................. AshleyHamblett(3) 6 74
(D Haydn Jones) *w ldrs: led over 2f out: hld on wl u.p fnl f: in control and pushed out nr fin* **16/1**
4030 **2** *1/2* **Marko Jadeo (IRE)**[7] 1063 9-8-9 **69**............................. TolleyDean(3) 10 77
(R A Harris) *chsd ldrs: drvn to chal ins fnl 2f: kpt on: hld cl home* **11/1**
4043 **3** *3/4* **Adantino**[7] 1063 8-9-4 **75**..(b) JamesMillman 7 80
(B R Millman) *sn pushed along towards rr: r.o fnl 2f: nrst fin* **9/1**[3]
0-06 **4** *1* **Digital**[13] 992 10-7-13 **63**.. MatthewDavies(7) 4 65
(M R Channon) *s.s: towards rr: hdwy and drifted to far rail over 1f out: styd on: nt rch ldrs* **14/1**
1050 **5** *shd* **Cornus**[7] 1061 5-8-9 **71**..(be) MCGeran(5) 1 73
(A J McCabe) *s.s: hdwy 3f out: chsd ldrs 2f out: one pce fnl f* **16/1**
0010 **6** *shd* **Bobby Rose**[13] 992 4-8-5 **65**... MACleere(3) 13 67
(D K Ivory) *prom: promising chal 2f out: no ex ins fnl f* **20/1**
30-6 **7** *hd* **China Cherub**[7] 1063 4-8-11 **73**................................. HaddenFrost(5) 3 74
(R Hannon) *sn drvn along towards rr: styd on fnl 2f: nvr able to chal* **17/2**
4-11 **8** *1 1/4* **Greenwood**[22] 866 9-8-4 **66**..................................... JosephWalsh(5) 8 63
(P G Murphy) *hld up in tch: effrt over 2f out: no imp over 1f out* **10/1**
0-00 **9** *hd* **Nautical**[7] 1063 9-8-13 **75**....................................... MarkCoumbe(5) 5 72
(A W Carroll) *hld up and bhd: sme hdwy and hrd rdn over 1f out: nvr nr to chal* **11/1**
60-5 **10** *1/2* **Duke Of Milan (IRE)**[33] 724 4-8-4 **64**.......................... SCreighton(3) 15 59
(G C Bravery) *bhd: rdn over 2f out: n.d* **12/1**
000- **11** *2* **Lizarazu (GER)**[122] 6919 8-8-13 **73**...................(p) JackMitchell(3) 12 62
(R A Harris) *stdd s: sn in midfield: rdn and btn 2f out* **33/1**
212- **12** *4* **Musical Script (USA)**[166] 6395 4-8-4 **64**...................... PatrickHills(3) 14 41
(Mouse Hamilton-Fairley) *t.k.h: led tl over 2f out: sn wknd* **8/1**[3]
530- **13** *3/4* **Young Bertie**[188] 6036 4-8-10 **67**................................. TravisBlock 16 42
(H Morrison) *w ldrs to 1/2-way: sn wknd* **5/1**[2]
000- **14** *1/2* **Pachello (IRE)**[216] 5453 5-8-1 **63** ow1.......................... BarrySavage(5) 9 36
(J M Bradley) *chsd ldrs over 3f* **20/1**
63-0 **15** *15* **Kingscross**[103] 91 9-8-12 **74**................................. LauraReynolds(5) 11 2
(M Blanshard) *blindfold lft on whn stalls opened: missed break by 20l: a t.o* **20/1**

1m 12.93s (-0.74) **Going Correction** -0.05s/f (Good) **15** Ran SP% **125.6**
Speed ratings (Par 103):102,101,100,99,98 98,98,96,96,95 93,87,86,86,66
CSF £178.83 CT £944.23 TOTE £18.70: £5.90, £4.10, £2.20; EX 420.60.
Owner S Kon, D Llewelyn and J Runeckles **Bred** B Krutmann **Trained** Efail Isaf, Rhondda C Taff

FOCUS
A typically modest, but competitive, apprentice race, run at an routine pace but with the field soon strung out. The form looks solid enough rated around the principals and sixth.
Kingscross Official explanation: jockey said she had difficulty removing the blinds and gelding missed the break

1201 BETFAIR MAIDEN STKS 5f 10y
5:55 (5:55) (Class 5) 2-Y-O **£3,238** (£963; £481; £240) **Stalls** High

Form RPR
1 **Mount Pleasure (USA)** 2-9-3 .... MartinDwyer 8 79+
(J A Osborne) *stdd s: hld up towards rr: shkn up and hdwy 2f out: rn green and hung lft over 1f out: r.o to ld fnl strides* **12/1**
6 **2** *hd* **Avertitop**[11] 1007 2-9-3 .... RichardHughes 5 78
(R Hannon) *pressed ldr: rdn to ld 1f out: kpt on: hdd fnl strides* **5/1**[3]
4 **3** *1 1/2* **Brassini**[19] 926 2-9-3 .... JimCrowley 9 72
(B R Millman) *led: rdn and hdd 1f out: nt qckn fnl f* **10/3**[2]
4 *2 1/2* **Huzzah (IRE)** 2-9-3 .... LDettori 4 62
(B W Hills) *4th and rdn along most of way: styd on same pce fnl 2f* **8/1**
5 *1/2* **Balata** 2-8-12 .... JamesMillman(5) 1 60+
(B R Millman) *bmpd s: towards rr: hdwy over 2f out: 6th and hld whn hmpd over 1f out: styd on nr fin* **25/1**
0 **6** *nk* **Kairaba**[11] 1007 2-9-3 .... EddieAhern 7 59
(J Pearce) *chsd ldng pair tl no ex over 1f out* **25/1**
7 *shd* **Polish Priory (IRE)** 2-8-9 .... StephenDonohoe(3) 2 53
(P D Evans) *bmpd s: towards rr: effrt over 2f out: kpt on: nvr able to chal* **25/1**
8 *1 3/4* **Ink Spot** 2-9-3 .... JamieSpencer 6 51+
(M L W Bell) *s.s: rn green in rr: swtchd wd and effrt over 2f out: no imp: bttr for experience* **5/2**[1]
9 *2* **Abfabfong (IRE)** 2-9-3 .... JimmyFortune 3 43
(P F I Cole) *pushed along in midfield: nt pce to chal* **5/1**[3]
10 *nk* **Insured** 2-9-0 .... PatrickMathers(3) 10 42+
(A J McCabe) *pushed along in midfield: outpcd and btn whn hmpd on stands' rail and swtchd lft over 2f out: n.d* **40/1**
11 *3* **Danny Boy Blue** 2-9-3 .... IanMongan 11 30
(Mrs L J Mongan) *s.i.s: outpcd: a bhd* **33/1**

61.35 secs (0.25) **Going Correction** -0.05s/f (Good) **11** Ran SP% **120.7**
Speed ratings (Par 92):96,95,93,89,88 88,87,85,81,81 76
CSF £68.75 TOTE £15.70: £3.30, £2.30, £1.90; EX 62.30.
Owner Cavendish Star Racing **Bred** Jmr Enterprises, Usa **Trained** Upper Lambourn, Berks
■ Stewards' Enquiry : Jimmy Fortune caution: careless riding

FOCUS
Unexposed sorts, but probably a decent maiden, run at a reasonable pace and the winner can do better.

NOTEBOOK
Mount Pleasure(USA), a $42,000 son of Mt Livermore, is bred to be speedy. Though settled well of the pace, he picked up strongly when asked and, despite wandering through greenness, just managed to get up. He should come on for the experience and be sharper next time, so his future looks bright. (op 10-1)
Avertitop showed the benefit of his debut run with a bold effort which only just failed. This was probably a decent maiden, and he looks capable of getting off the mark soon. (op 13-2 tchd 8-1)
Brassini had shown promise on his debut, and this was even better, since he showed plenty of pace from the word go. There is a maiden waiting for him in the coming weeks. (tchd 11-4 and 7-2)
Huzzah(IRE) is a 36,000gns son of the speedy Acclamation, but his dam stayed a mile and a half and this five furlongs looked a bit sharper than ideal. He showed enough on this debut to give encouragement for the future, but is likely to improve when able to race over an extra furlong. (op 9-2 tchd 4-1 and 10-1 in a place)
Balata ◆, an 18,000gns son of high-class sprinter Averti, is a half-brother to winners up to a mile, and six furlongs should be no problem for him as the summer progresses. This was a promising debut, especially as he received a bump at both ends of the race, and improvement looks likely.
Kairaba, a cheaply-bought son of the top-class ten and 12-furlong performer Storming Home, is speedily bred on his dam's side, but he did not show much on his racecourse debut. This, however, was a much-improved effort which puts him in with a chance in routine maidens over the minimum trip for the time being. (tchd 33-1)
Polish Priory(IRE)'s sire was the top-class miler Polish Precedent, but her dam stayed beyond two miles, so this trip would be plenty sharp enough. That said, it was a creditable debut against a field of colts and geldings, and she will come into her own when she is able to race over longer trips. (op 20-1)
Ink Spot ◆ arrived on the course with a good reputation and was made favourite to make a winning debut. A 32,000gns son of the top-class sprinter Diktat and very speedy juvenile Good Girl, he showed none of their pace, but he was far too green to do himself justice and it was be no surprise to see a different horse next time out. (op 100-30 tchd 7-2)

1202 WILLIAM HILL 0800 44 40 40 H'CAP 1m 67y
6:25 (6:26) (Class 4) (0-85,84) 3-Y-O **£6,477** (£1,927; £963; £481) **Stalls** High

Form RPR
5220 **1** **Eau Good**[16] 939 3-8-11 **80**................................ StephenDonohoe(3) 10 89
(B G Powell) *towards rr: rdn 3f out: gd hdwy over 1f out: styd on to ld nr fin* **25/1**
331- **2** *1/2* **Hunting Tower**[186] 6066 3-9-0 **80**................................... RichardHughes 2 88+
(R Hannon) *led: rdn and edgd rt over 1f out: kpt on: hdd nr fin* **11/1**
34-0 **3** *2* **Salient**[16] 939 3-8-13 **79**... PaulDoe 8 82
(J Akehurst) *t.k.h: chsd ldng pair: rdn over 2f out: nt qckn fnl f* **66/1**
412- **4** *nk* **Count Ceprano (IRE)**[184] 6100 3-9-4 **84**........................... AdamKirby 6 86
(W R Swinburn) *dwlt: hld up towards rr: hdwy over 2f out: edgd lft and styd on fnl f* **9/2**[2]
1- **5** *hd* **Lovelace**[367] 1121 3-8-13 **82**....................................... GregFairley(3) 3 84
(M Johnston) *w ldr: hrd rdn and hung lft over 1f out: no ex fnl f* **10/1**
22-1 **6** *1/2* **Gazboolou**[15] 954 3-8-13 **79**..................................... PatCosgrave 14 80
(K R Burke) *t.k.h: chsd ldrs: one pce fnl 2f* **14/1**
21- **7** *nk* **Lacework**[143] 6663 3-8-12 **78**....................................... JamieSpencer 13 81+
(Sir Michael Stoute) *dwlt: t.k.h in midfield: effrt 2f out: hrd rdn over 1f out: no imp* **11/4**[1]
561- **8** *1 1/4* **Sam Lord**[192] 5939 3-9-2 **82**.. JimmyFortune 1 79
(J H M Gosden) *dwlt: t.k.h: sn in midfield on outside: rdn and stayed on same pce 3f* **12/1**

6211 **9** ½ **Alfresco**[21] 889 3-9-0 **80**......(b) PaulEddery 11 76
(Pat Eddery) *stdd s: hld up in rr: rdn over 2f out: nvr rchd ldrs* **9/1**

22-1 **10** 1 ¼ **Shake On It**[12] 1001 3-8-12 **78**......(t) StephenCarson 9 71
(Eve Johnson Houghton) *in tch: rdn over 2f out: btn over 1f out* **12/1**

000- **11** 2 **Fish Called Johnny**[205] 5681 3-9-3 **83**......(t) LDettori 12 72
(B J Meehan) *in tch: rdn 3f out: wknd 2f out* **15/2**

45-6 **12** 1 ½ **Dowlleh**[11] 1009 3-8-12 **78**...... SamHitchcott 5 63
(T T Clement) *dwlt: a bhd* **66/1**

13-6 **13** *hd* **My Learned Friend (IRE)**[30] 754 3-9-0 **80**...... MartinDwyer 7 65
(A M Balding) *chsd ldrs: rdn 3f out: wknd over 1f out* **13/2**[3]

1m 43.4s (-1.30) **Going Correction** -0.05s/f (Good) 13 Ran SP% **126.3**
Speed ratings (Par 100):104,103,101,101,101 100,100,98,98,97 95,93,93
CSF £291.34 CT £17066.00 TOTE £29.70: £7.30, £2.70, £9.40; EX 414.50.
Owner Sir Clement Freud **Bred** Baydon House Stud **Trained** Lambourn, Berks

FOCUS
A competitive race of its sort, with every runner having previously won, run at a fair pace dictated by the runner-up. The form makes sense rated around the third, fourth and sixth and looks solid enough.

1203 BET ONLINE @ WILLIAMHILL.CO.UK MAIDEN FILLIES' STKS 1m 67y
6:55 (6:57) (Class 5) 3-Y-O £3,238 (£963; £481; £240) **Stalls** High

Form RPR

3- **1** **Gyroscope**[175] 6254 3-9-0 ...... JamieSpencer 10 81
(Sir Michael Stoute) *trckd ldr: led 2f out: rdn to hold on whn jnd by runner-up fnl f* **5/6**[1]

2 ½ **Truly Enchanting (IRE)** 3-9-0 ...... LDettori 3 80
(J Noseda) *hld up towards rr: hdwy 3f out: jnd wnr 1f out: edgd bdly lft: r.o: jst hld* **8/1**

3 4 **Orama's Ghost** 3-9-0 ...... MartinDwyer 12 74+
(Sir Michael Stoute) *dwlt: sn in tch: rdn over 2f out: swtchd to stands' rail 1f out: fin wl* **14/1**

4 *shd* **Jacaranda Ridge** 3-9-0 ...... J-PGuillambert 13 70
(M A Jarvis) *chsd ldrs: rdn and styd on same pce fnl 2f* **28/1**

6- **5** 1 **Handset (USA)**[209] 5595 3-9-0 ...... RichardHughes 11 68
(H R A Cecil) *led tl 2f out: wknd over 1f out* **13/2**[3]

6 *nk* **Marzelline (IRE)** 3-9-0 ...... AdamKirby 4 67+
(W R Swinburn) *s.i.s: bhd: shkn up and hdwy 2f out: nt rch ldrs* **14/1**

7 *nk* **Prima Ballerina** 3-9-0 ...... RobertHavlin 6 67
(J H M Gosden) *hld up towards rr: hdwy 3f out: no imp over 1f out* **33/1**

8 5 **Labor Day (IRE)** 3-9-0 ...... JimmyFortune 2 55
(J H M Gosden) *in tch: rdn over 2f out: sn outpcd* **25/1**

63- **9** ¾ **Penny From Heaven (IRE)**[169] 6349 3-9-0 ...... DO'Donohoe 9 54
(E A L Dunlop) *t.k.h: prom tl wknd over 2f out* **16/1**

2- **10** 1 ¼ **First Bloom (USA)**[146] 6644 3-9-0 ...... EddieAhern 14 51
(P F I Cole) *prom 5f* **9/2**[2]

11 *nk* **Driving Miss Suzie** 3-9-0 ...... LPKeniry 7 50
(A M Balding) *mid-div: rdn 3f out: sn btn* **66/1**

0- **12** 3 ½ **Piano Key**[179] 6186 3-9-0 ...... RichardSmith 8 42
(M D I Usher) *dwlt: a towards rr: rdn and n.d fnl 3f* **100/1**

13 21 **Devils Desire** 3-8-9 ...... KevinGhunowa[(5)] 5 —
(J M Bradley) *a towards rr: rdn and no ch fnl 3f* **100/1**

U **Silver Surprise** 3-8-11 ...... AmirQuinn[(3)] 1 —
(J J Bridger) *v.s.a: wl bhd whn uns rdr after 150yds* **100/1**

1m 45.04s (0.34) **Going Correction** -0.05s/f (Good) 14 Ran SP% **131.1**
Speed ratings (Par 95):96,95,91,91,90 90,89,84,84,82 82,79,58,—
CSF £9.31 TOTE £2.00: £1.20, £2.10, £4.10; EX 10.10.
Owner Cheveley Park Stud **Bred** The Niarchos Family **Trained** Newmarket, Suffolk

FOCUS
Likely to be a good maiden, run at a fair if unspectacular pace but little to go on and hard to rate with confidence, although may produce winners.

1204 ARENA LEISURE PLC MAIDEN STKS 1m 2f 7y
7:25 (7:28) (Class 5) 3-Y-O £3,238 (£963; £481; £240) **Stalls** Low

Form RPR

0- **1** **Overrule (USA)**[208] 5616 3-9-3 ...... TPQueally 13 91
(J Noseda) *in tch: effrt 3f out: led wl over 1f out: rdn out* **18/1**

6- **2** ½ **Tranquil Tiger**[195] 5893 3-9-3 ...... RichardHughes 8 90+
(H R A Cecil) *prom: nt handle bnd into st and sn rdn along: swtchd wd and rallied 1f out: clsd on wnr: jst hld* **9/4**[1]

36-3 **3** 2 **Northern Jem**[14] 977 3-9-3 85...... EddieAhern 12 86
(G G Margarson) *cl up: hmpd on rail ent st: drvn to join ldrs 2f out: 2nd and hld whn rdr dropped whip ins fnl f* **5/1**

52- **4** 4 **Mystic Dancer**[185] 6072 3-9-3 ...... LDettori 1 78
(Sir Michael Stoute) *led and set str early pce: sn 4l clr: stdd tempo bnd into st: hdd wl over 1f out: sn btn* **11/4**[2]

4 **5** ½ **Gold Prospect**[11] 1011 3-9-3 ...... JamieSpencer 7 77
(M L W Bell) *s.s: t.k.h: sn chsng ldrs: rdn to dispute ld 4f out: wknd over 1f out* **3/1**[3]

4- **6** 2 **Wester Ross (IRE)**[177] 6214 3-9-3 ...... MickyFenton 6 74
(J M P Eustace) *prom: rdn whn n.m.r and swtchd lft 2f out: no ex* **5/1**

7 1 ¼ **Eastern Emperor** 3-9-3 ...... AdamKirby 2 71+
(W R Swinburn) *bhd: rdn 4f out: styd on fnl 2f* **50/1**

0- **8** *shd* **Pelleas**[188] 6023 3-9-0 ...... RichardKingscote[(3)] 3 71
(R Charlton) *in tch: rdn and no hdwy fnl 4f* **100/1**

0 **9** 5 **Quite A Splash (USA)**[11] 1011 3-9-3 ...... DaneO'Neill 14 62?
(S Curran) *mid-div: hrd rdn 4f out: n.d after* **150/1**

10 1 **Atacama King (USA)** 3-9-3 ...... RobertHavlin 5 60
(J H M Gosden) *dwlt: a towards rr* **50/1**

11 3 **Shavansky** 3-9-3 ...... JimmyFortune 4 54
(J H M Gosden) *dwlt: a towards rr* **16/1**

12 ¾ **Stafford Will (IRE)** 3-9-3 ...... VinceSlattery 10 53?
(J G M O'Shea) *a bhd* **100/1**

06- **13** 1 **Dr Light (IRE)**[143] 6658 3-9-3 ...... LPKeniry 9 51
(S Kirk) *s.s: a bhd* **100/1**

-000 **14** ½ **Tranquility**[28] 790 3-8-12 44...... PatCosgrave 11 45?
(J Pearce) *mid-div tl wknd 4f out* **100/1**

2m 8.88s (0.58) **Going Correction** -0.05s/f (Good) 14 Ran SP% **135.5**
Speed ratings (Par 98):95,94,93,89,89 87,86,86,82,81 79,78,78,77
CSF £66.55 TOTE £24.80: £6.00, £1.60, £1.90; EX 91.20.
Owner Sheikh Marwan Al Maktoum **Bred** Avalon Farms Inc **Trained** Newmarket, Suffolk

FOCUS
This looked a decent maiden on paper and, although the time was not that good, the form should prove strong for the level rated around the third and fourth.

1205 AT THE RACES H'CAP 1m 3f 135y
7:55 (7:56) (Class 5) (0-75,75) 3-Y-O £3,238 (£963; £481; £240) **Stalls** Low

Form RPR

0-25 **1** **Morning Farewell**[30] 764 3-9-2 **73**...... JimmyFortune 7 80
(P W Chapple-Hyam) *led after 2f tl 7f out: led 4f out: drvn out* **6/1**[3]

33-6 **2** *hd* **Spiderback (IRE)**[3] 1122 3-9-1 **72**......(b) RichardHughes 9 79
(R Hannon) *s.s: hld up in rr: stdy hdwy 3f out: wnt 2nd over 1f out: clsd on wnr: jst hld* **5/2**[1]

064- **3** 2 ½ **Crimson Monarch (USA)**[195] 5882 3-8-12 **69**...... JimCrowley 8 72
(Mrs A J Perrett) *hld up in midfield: hdwy to dispute 2nd ins fnl 2f: nt qckn fnl f* **16/1**

1-40 **4** 5 **Personal Column**[33] 719 3-9-0 **71**...... RobertHavlin 4 66
(T G Mills) *mid-div: hdwy in centre 3f out: hrd rdn 2f out: one pce* **20/1**

-132 **5** *shd* **Daylami Dreams**[57] 563 3-9-3 **74**...... JohnEgan 6 69
(J S Moore) *in tch: rdn to chse ldrs over 2f out: wknd over 1f out* **9/2**[2]

565- **6** *hd* **Polish Red**[221] 5321 3-9-4 **75**...... EddieAhern 3 70
(G G Margarson) *led 2f: prom tl wknd wl over 1f out* **16/1**

1150 **7** *hd* **Global Traffic**[20] 904 3-8-7 **67** ow1......(b) StephenDonohoe[(3)] 13 61
(P D Evans) *s.s: bhd: rdn and styd on fnl 3f: nt rch ldrs* **14/1**

2-20 **8** 3 ½ **Into Action**[11] 1012 3-8-13 **70**...... DaneO'Neill 2 59
(R Hannon) *towards rr: rdn over 3f out: nvr rchd ldrs* **33/1**

000- **9** 1 ½ **Lightning Queen (USA)**[188] 6023 3-8-4 **61**...... MartinDwyer 12 47
(B W Hills) *chsd ldrs tl wknd over 2f out* **16/1**

64-1 **10** ¾ **Sweetheart**[87] 258 3-9-4 **75**...... IanMongan 5 60
(Jamie Poulton) *prom tl hrd rdn and wknd 2f out* **20/1**

050- **11** *nk* **Proposal**[209] 5595 3-8-4 **61** oh2...... SimonWhitworth 14 46
(A W Carroll) *s.s: a bhd* **66/1**

0-31 **12** 20 **Petrosian**[32] 731 3-8-8 **68**......(b[1]) GregFairley[(3)] 11 21
(M Johnston) *prom: led 7f out tl 4f out: sn wknd* **13/2**

012- **13** 23 **Greyt Big Stuff (USA)**[154] 6536 3-9-4 **75**...... LDettori 10 —
(Miss Gay Kelleway) *t.k.h: w ldrs tl lost pl qckly over 5f out: sn bhd: eased whn no ch fnl f* **6/1**[3]

2m 30.13s (0.03) **Going Correction** -0.05s/f (Good) 13 Ran SP% **126.9**
Speed ratings (Par 98):97,96,95,91,91 91,91,89,88,87 87,74,58
CSF £21.85 CT £244.59 TOTE £7.50: £3.10, £1.90, £5.90; EX 41.90 Place 6 £839.88, Place 5 £253.79..
Owner Clark, Darke & Matthews **Bred** Glebe Stud And J F Dean **Trained** Newmarket, Suffolk

FOCUS
A moderate, but competitive, race. The pace was respectable, with the winner making much of the running and the runner-up coming from the rear. the first three were clear but the form is best rated around the sixth and seventh.
Greyt Big Stuff(USA) Official explanation: jockey said gelding was never travelling
T/Plt: £972.70 to a £1 stake. Pool: £68,023.30. 51.05 winning tickets. T/Qpdt: £200.90 to a £1 stake. Pool: £4,995.90. 18.40 winning tickets. LM

999 BATH (L-H)
Tuesday, April 24

OFFICIAL GOING: Firm
Wind: Moderate, across

1206 PREMIER CONSERVATORY ROOFS AND K2 ROOF SYSTEMS H'CAP 1m 2f 46y
5:35 (5:36) (Class 6) (0-50,52) 4-Y-O+ £2,733 (£813; £406; £202) **Stalls** Low

Form RPR

0060 **1** **Monmouthshire**[11] 1032 4-8-3 **46** oh1......(v) KevinGhunowa[(5)] 9 53
(R J Price) *in rr tl hdwy over 3f out: drvn to ld 1f out: kpt on wl* **14/1**

-440 **2** ½ **Jarvo**[93] 203 6-8-8 **46** oh1...... RoystonFfrench 10 52+
(I W McInnes) *in rr: rdn and hdwy fr 3f out: styd on to chse wnr ins fnl f but a jst hld* **12/1**

30-0 **3** ¾ **Ronsard (IRE)**[64] 496 5-8-6 **47** ow1...... StephenDonohoe[(3)] 14 51
(P D Evans) *in rr tl hdwy fr 3f out: r.o fr over 1f out: gng on cl home* **10/1**

-600 **4** ½ **Orphina (IRE)**[13] 1002 4-8-11 **49**......(t) JimCrowley 1 52
(B G Powell) *sn led: hdd over 6f out: styd chsng ldr tl led 2f out: hdd 1f out and sn one pce* **10/1**

03 **5** *shd* **Ellen's Girl (IRE)**[11] 1025 4-8-12 **50**......(p) MichaelHills 11 53
(B G Powell) *chsd ldrs: rdn to chal 2f out: stl ev ch over 1f out: styd on same pce* **13/2**[1]

003 **6** 1 **Itcanbedone Again (IRE)**[19] 932 8-8-8 **46** oh1...... PaulEddery 13 47+
(Ian Williams) *in rr: hmpd ins fnl 5f: drvn and styd on fnl 2f: kpt on cl home* **7/1**[2]

0 **7** 1 ¼ **Ceol Eile (IRE)**[101] 121 4-8-12 **50**...... RobertHavlin 7 49
(D Haydn Jones) *mid-div: c wd into st 3f out: styd on u.p fr over 1f out but nvr gng pce to be competitive* **20/1**

5-00 **8** 2 **Elopement (IRE)**[64] 496 5-8-11 **49**...... JohnEgan 5 44
(W M Brisbourne) *in rr: sme hdwy whn hmpd 2f out: swtchd rt over 1f out: kpt on cl home: nvr a danger* **8/1**[3]

-005 **9** ¾ **Flashing Floozie**[28] 804 4-8-8 **46** oh1...... MartinDwyer 3 40
(A W Carroll) *chsd ldrs: rdn 3f out: wknd over 1f out* **16/1**

0300 **10** *shd* **Christmas Truce (IRE)**[78] 363 8-8-7 **52** ow2...... RyanBird[(7)] 8 45
(J J Bridger) *awkward s and v.s.a: styd on fr 2f out: nvr in contention* **25/1**

5550 **11** *nk* **Hometomammy**[12] 1011 5-8-8 **46** oh1...... ChrisCatlin 2 39
(P W Hiatt) *chsd ldrs tl rdn and wknd 2f out* **33/1**

-544 **12** *nk* **Chalice Welcome**[29] 789 4-8-8 **46**...... StephenCarson 15 38
(C F Wall) *chsd ldrs: rdn 3f out: wknd form 2f out* **13/2**[1]

000- **13** 2 **Noble Calling (FR)**[106] 6132 10-8-5 **46**...... EmmettStack[(3)] 4 34
(R J Hodges) *slowly away: t.k.h and sn rcvrd to chse ldrs: wknd over 2f out* **25/1**

1452 **14** *hd* **Mid Valley**[27] 812 4-8-11 **49**......(v) KDarley 12 37
(J R Jenkins) *chsd ldrs tl wknd over 2f out* **17/2**

5052 **15** 3 **Cape Of Storms**[32] 742 4-8-10 **48**...... IanMongan 6 30
(R Brotherton) *led over 6f out: hdd & wknd 2f out* **17/2**

0-00 **16** 1 ¾ **Huxley (IRE)**[32] 742 8-8-8 **46** oh1......(t) LPKeniry 16 25
(D J Wintle) *wd bnd 5f out: a in rr* **33/1**

2m 10.1s (-0.90) **Going Correction** -0.075s/f (Good) 16 Ran SP% **128.1**
Speed ratings (Par 101):100,99,99,98,98 97,96,95,94,94 94,93,92,92,89 88
CSF £170.03 CT £1781.45 TOTE £19.50: £4.80, £2.70, £4.40, £2.50; EX 281.60.
Owner Dick's Neighbours **Bred** Usk Valley Stud **Trained** Ullingswick, H'fords

FOCUS
A very moderate handicap rated around the fourth and fifth and not a race to dwell on. The winning time was 0.77 seconds quicker than the later 56-70, but they went a steady pace in that race.
Itcanbedone Again(IRE) Official explanation: jockey said gelding slipped on bend
Christmas Truce(IRE) Official explanation: jockey said gelding missed the break
Mid Valley Official explanation: jockey said gelding ran too free
Cape Of Storms Official explanation: jockey said gelding ran too free

1207 KENT BUILDING PLASTICS AND K2 ROOF SYSTEMS MAIDEN STKS 5f 11y
6:05 (6:10) (Class 5) 3-Y-O+ **£2,914** (£867; £433; £216) **Stalls** Low

Form RPR

526- **1** **Ken's Girl**[204] 5735 3-8-9 67 IanMongan 2 76
(W S Kittow) *mde all: drvn clr fnl f* **10/1**

54- **2** *3* **Metal Guru**[211] 5563 3-8-4 RussellKennemore(5) 8 65
(R Hollinshead) *chsd ldrs: rdn and styd on to chse wnr fnl f but a hld* **14/1**

2- **3** *3/4* **Millachy**[232] 5052 3-8-9 MichaelHills 9 63
(B W Hills) *chsd ldrs: rdn and outpcd 1/2-way: styd on again fnl f* **6/4**[1]

322 **4** *1/2* **Ellablue**[22] 894 3-8-9 65 ChrisCatlin 3 61
(Rae Guest) *pressed ldrs: rdn 1/2-way: one pce fr over 1f out* **7/1**[3]

5 *3/4* **Lochstar** 3-9-0 MartinDwyer 1 63+
(A M Balding) *wnt lft s: sn rcvrd to chse ldrs: rdn 1/2-way: one pce fr over 1f out* **2/1**[2]

5565 **6** *1 1/2* **Ceredig**[5] 1112 4-9-10 54 JimCrowley 7 62
(P W Hiatt) *in rr: rdn 3f out: sme prog fnl f* **16/1**

000- **7** *3* **Georges Pride**[211] 5563 3-8-9 50 KevinGhunowa(5) 10 47
(J M Bradley) *in rr: sn rdn: sme hdwy fnl f* **100/1**

335/ **8** *shd* **Burford Lass (IRE)**[596] 4989 4-9-5 60 JohnEgan 6 45
(D K Ivory) *spd to 1/2-way* **25/1**

9 *shd* **Juce Of Hearts** 3-9-0 RichardThomas 4 46
(J L Spearing) *chsd ldrs 3f* **40/1**

10 *5* **The Carpet Man** 3-9-0 SteveDrowne 5 28
(A W Carroll) *slowly away: a in rr* **50/1**

60.69 secs (-1.81) **Going Correction** -0.275s/f (Firm)
WFA 3 from 4yo 10lb **10** Ran SP% **116.7**
Speed ratings (Par 103):103,98,97,96,95 92,87,87,87,79
CSF £133.53 TOTE £6.90: £2.40, £2.90, £1.10; EX 68.60.
Owner Midd Shire Racing **Bred** D R Tucker **Trained** Blackborough, Devon

FOCUS
A weak sprint maiden but sound-enough form rated through the fourth.

1208 WEATHERBYS PRINTING H'CAP 1m 3f 144y
6:35 (6:36) (Class 4) (0-85,84) 4-Y-O+ **£5,181** (£1,541; £770; £384) **Stalls** Low

Form RPR

210- **1** **Ollie George (IRE)**[247] 4626 4-8-13 **80** LPKeniry 2 91+
(A M Balding) *t.k.h: trckd ldrs: wnt 2nd 3f out: rdn over 2f out: styd on to ld last 110yds: in command cl home* **10/3**[1]

4-36 **2** *nk* **Baizically (IRE)**[30] 777 4-9-3 **84** MartinDwyer 3 94
(J A Osborne) *sn led: drvn and styd on fr over 2f out: hdd and one pce fnl 110yds* **9/2**[2]

014- **3** *3 1/2* **Mull Of Dubai**[171] 5935 4-8-5 **72** JohnEgan 4 76
(J S Moore) *towards rr: hdwy over 3f out: rdn over 2f out: kpt on fnl f but nvr gng pce of ldng pair* **8/1**[3]

1- **4** *hd* **Magic Moth**[435] 403 4-8-5 **72** KDarley 9 76+
(M Johnston) *chsd ldrs: drvn along fr 4f out: styd on u.p fnl 2f but nvr gng pce to be competitive* **9/2**[2]

630- **5** *5* **Takafu (USA)**[186] 6075 5-8-9 **75** IanMongan 12 71
(W S Kittow) *settled towards rr after 2f: rdn over 3f out: mod prog fnl 2f* **8/1**[3]

-154 **6** *3 1/2* **Poseidon's Secret (IRE)**[20] 921 4-8-6 **73** PaulEddery 11 63
(Pat Eddery) *sn chsng ldr: rdn over 3f out: btn sn after* **12/1**

40-0 **7** *shd* **Our Teddy (IRE)**[79] 353 7-8-10 **81** KevinGhunowa(5) 5 71
(P A Blockley) *in rr: sme hdwy 3f out: nvr in contention and wknd over 2f out* **16/1**

410- **8** *1/2* **Sualda (IRE)**[27] 4604 8-8-10 **79** StephenDonohoe(3) 10 68
(P D Evans) *a towards rr* **14/1**

200- **9** *2 1/2* **Gracechurch (IRE)**[23] 6076 4-8-6 **73** RobertHavlin 6 58
(R J Hodges) *chsd ldrs: rdn 4f out: wknd 3f out* **8/1**[3]

2m 26.41s (-3.89) **Going Correction** -0.075s/f (Good)
WFA 4 from 5yo+ 1lb **9** Ran SP% **113.0**
Speed ratings (Par 105):109,108,106,106,103 100,100,100,98
CSF £17.65 CT £108.35 TOTE £4.10: £1.40, £2.10, £2.80; EX 18.60.
Owner Peter R Grubb **Bred** Lawrence Walsh **Trained** Kingsclere, Hants

FOCUS
A decent handicap and sound form rated around the first two, who came clear.

1209 WEATHERBYS BLOODSTOCK INSURANCE H'CAP 1m 5y
7:05 (7:06) (Class 4) (0-80,80) 4-Y-O+ **£5,181** (£1,541; £770; £384) **Stalls** Low

Form RPR

0-54 **1** **Street Warrior (IRE)**[8] 1060 4-8-11 **73** KDarley 5 81
(M Johnston) *s.i.s: in rr but in tch: hdwy 3f out: rdn 2f out: styd on strly fnl f: sn edgd lft: led cl home* **3/1**[1]

444- **2** *nk* **Veiled Applause**[180] 6189 4-8-6 **68** JosedeSouza 3 75
(R M Beckett) *t.k.h: chsd ldrs: led 2f out: rdn over 1f out: kpt on wl: hdd cl home* **12/1**

026- **3** *3/4* **Carmenero (GER)**[185] 6094 4-8-13 **75** MartinDwyer 9 80+
(W R Muir) *hld up in rr: hdwy over 3f out: styng on to chse ldrs whn pushed lft ins fnl f: one pce cl home* **15/2**

453- **4** *hd* **Merrymadcap (IRE)**[176] 6259 5-8-10 **72** SteveDrowne 7 77
(M Blanshard) *in rr: rdn over 2f out: gd hdwy over 1f out: fin strly fnl f* **15/2**

210- **5** *3/4* **Personify**[198] 5833 5-8-12 **74** (p) JohnEgan 6 79+
(C G Cox) *chsd ldrs: pushed along over 2f out: styng on whn hmpd wl ins fnl f: nt rcvr* **7/2**[2]

2-60 **6** *hd* **Neardown Beauty (IRE)**[24] 846 4-8-13 **80** KevinGhunowa(5) 2 83
(I A Wood) *t.k.h in rr: rdn over 2f out: styd on on fnl f but nvr gng pce to be competitive* **16/1**

4442 **7** *1 1/2* **Grey Boy (GER)**[38] 699 6-9-2 **78** JimCrowley 10 77
(A W Carroll) *led tl hdd 2f out: wkng whn hmpd wl ins fnl f* **7/1**[3]

550- **8** *1 1/2* **Full Victory (IRE)**[196] 5896 5-8-11 **73** DaneO'Neill 1 69
(R A Farrant) *in rr: rdn and sme hdwy 3f out: nvr gng pce to trble ldrs* **9/1**

-604 **9** *1* **Todlea (IRE)**[15] 975 7-8-6 **68** (t) ChrisCatlin 4 61
(Jean-Rene Auvray) *t.k.h: chsd ldrs: rdn and wknd over 2f out* **10/1**

1m 40.89s (-0.21) **Going Correction** -0.075s/f (Good) **9** Ran SP% **115.9**
Speed ratings (Par 105):98,97,96,96,96 95,94,92,91
CSF £39.99 CT £250.71 TOTE £4.60: £1.50, £5.20, £2.90; EX 66.80.
Owner Luk King Tin **Bred** Monsieur Laurent Cottrell **Trained** Middleham Moor, N Yorks
■ Stewards' Enquiry : K Darley three-day ban: careless riding (May 7-9)

FOCUS
Just an ordinary handicap for the grade and not the most solid, with the pace ordinary and they finished in a bit of a bunch. The winning time was 0.17 seconds slower than the following 0-45.

1210 OAKLEY GREEN CONSERVATORIES AND K2 ROOF SYSTEMS CLASSIFIED STKS 1m 5y
7:35 (7:38) (Class 7) 3-Y-O+ **£1,943** (£578; £288; £144) **Stalls** Low

Form RPR

5 **1** **Mountain Climb (IRE)**[34] 721 5-9-0 42 HaddenFrost(7) 13 52
(J D Frost) *t.k.h: chsd ldrs: rdn to ld ins fnl f and hung rt: hld on all out* **7/1**[2]

033- **2** *shd* **Lady Duxyana**[204] 5733 4-9-7 40 (v) RichardSmith 7 52
(M D I Usher) *in rr: hdwy fr 3f out: rdn: swtchd lft and r.o strly fnl f: jst failed* **16/1**

0-00 **3** *3/4* **Joe Jo Star**[33] 179 5-9-7 42 PaulEddery 9 50
(B P J Baugh) *chsd ldrs: rdn to chal ins fnl f: no ex nr fin* **8/1**[3]

006- **4** *2* **Shandelight (IRE)**[209] 5615 3-8-7 45 RoystonFfrench 8 41
(Mrs A Duffield) *in rr: rdn 3f out: r.o fr over 1f out: fin wl* **7/1**[2]

336- **5** *hd* **The Jailer**[293] 3195 4-9-7 42 DaneO'Neill 2 45
(J G M O'Shea) *chsd ldr: led 2f out: hdd & wknd ins fnl f* **12/1**

6462 **6** *3/4* **Homecroft Boy**[4] 1119 3-8-7 44 SteveDrowne 15 39
(P D Evans) *in rr: rdn 3f out: styd on fr over 1f out: kpt on ins fnl f* **6/1**[1]

/000 **7** *hd* **Fire At Will**[21] 907 5-9-0 42 MarkCoumbe(7) 16 43
(A W Carroll) *in rr: rdn and hung bdly lft over 3f out: styd on fnl f: nvr in contention* **50/1**

000- **8** *nk* **Lady Ambitious**[148] 6618 4-9-7 44 RobertHavlin 11 42
(D K Ivory) *in rr: stl plenty to do 2f out: r.o fnl f* **28/1**

2160 **9** *2 1/2* **Weet Yer Tern (IRE)**[5] 571 5-9-7 44 (v) JohnEgan 6 36
(W M Brisbourne) *chsd ldrs: hung rt bnd 5f out: sn rcvrd: wknd fr ins fnl 2f* **7/1**[2]

0000 **10** *1* **Emefdream**[21] 910 3-8-7 45 ChrisCatlin 3 30
(E J O'Neill) *led tl hdd 2f out: sn wknd* **20/1**

0000 **11** *1 1/2* **Lord Chamberlain**[34] 721 14-9-2 42 (b) KevinGhunowa(5) 4 31
(J M Bradley) *a towards rr* **20/1**

3402 **12** *3 1/2* **Savoy Chapel**[13] 887 5-9-7 45 (v) JimCrowley 12 23
(A W Carroll) *a in rr*

050- **13** *1* **Frenchgate**[117] 6616 6-9-2 41 (p) NataliaGemelova(5) 1 20
(I W McInnes) *sme prog and rdn into mid-div over 3f out: sn wknd* **14/1**

-066 **14** *3* **Shannon Arms (USA)**[31] 768 6-9-4 45 (p) StephenDonohoe(3) 5 13
(R Brotherton) *chsd ldrs: rdn 3f out: wknd over 2f out* **8/1**[3]

006- **15** *3 1/2* **Gala Jackpot (USA)**[306] 2782 4-9-7 43 MartinDwyer 14 —
(W M Brisbourne) *a towards rr* **14/1**

3000 **16** *18* **Bahama Gold**[12] 1008 3-8-2 45 RoryMoore(5) 10 —
(D G Bridgwater) *chsd ldrs 5f* **66/1**

1m 40.72s (-0.38) **Going Correction** -0.075s/f (Good)
WFA 3 from 4yo+ 14lb **16** Ran SP% **125.0**
Speed ratings (Par 97):98,97,97,95,94 94,94,93,91,90 88,85,84,81,77 59
CSF £110.40 TOTE £7.30: £2.50, £3.60, £3.50; EX 33.90.
Owner Ifji Rochjobi **Bred** Michael Finn Jnr **Trained** Scorriton, Devon
■ Jimmy Frost's first training success on the Flat.

FOCUS
A very moderate classified event and, with the pace good from the start, they were soon well strung out. The winning time was 0.17 seconds quicker than the previous 66-80, although that was a steadily-run race, and the form looks sound enough.
Weet Yer Tern(IRE) Official explanation: jockey said gelding slipped on final bend
Shannon Arms(USA) Official explanation: jockey said gelding failed to handle the bend

1211 MB FRAMES AND K2 ROOF SYSTEMS H'CAP 1m 2f 46y
8:05 (8:05) (Class 5) (0-70,70) 3-Y-O **£3,238** (£963; £481; £240) **Stalls** Low

Form RPR

22-1 **1** **Fongs Gazelle**[30] 772 3-9-4 **70** KDarley 2 79+
(M Johnston) *chsd ldrs: rdn over 2f out: styd on to ld ins fnl f: drvn out* **15/8**[1]

004- **2** *1 3/4* **Bachnagairn**[210] 5585 3-9-3 **69** SteveDrowne 8 71+
(R Charlton) *hld up in rr but in tch: hdwy on outside fr 2f out: drvn to chal ins fnl f: no ex cl home* **15/8**[1]

3010 **3** *1 1/4* **It's No Problem (IRE)**[29] 790 3-8-1 **56** oh4 LiamJones(3) 6 56
(M Salaman) *in tch: chsd ldrs 3f out: rdn to take slt ld appr fnl f: hdd and one pce ins fnl f* **9/1**[3]

-135 **4** *1 1/2* **Pret A Porter (UAE)**[7] 1084 3-9-0 **69** (b) StephenDonohoe(3) 3 66+
(P D Evans) *in rr: hdwy on ins whn hmpd over 1f out: swtchd rt and kpt on fnl f: nvr in contention* **5/1**[2]

4430 **5** *1 3/4* **Party Palace**[8] 1059 3-8-4 **56** oh2 ChrisCatlin 1 50
(H S Howe) *t.k.h: sn led: rdn over 2f out: edgd lft over 2f out and hdd: wknd fnl f* **20/1**

660- **6** *2* **Kyllachy Storm**[150] 6592 3-9-0 **66** JimCrowley 7 56
(R J Hodges) *chsd ldrs: led over 2f out: hdd & wknd qckly over 1f out* **12/1**

-550 **7** *3* **Tumble Jill (IRE)**[29] 791 3-7-11 **56** oh6 (p) LukeMorris(7) 4 40
(J J Bridger) *a in rr* **40/1**

000- **8** *22* **The Grey Bam Bam**[251] 4487 3-8-1 **56** oh6 EmmettStack(3) 5 —
(R J Hodges) *stmbld after s: sn chsng ldrs: wknd qckly fr 3f out* **50/1**

2m 10.87s (-0.13) **Going Correction** -0.075s/f (Good) **8** Ran SP% **113.1**
Speed ratings (Par 98):97,95,94,93,92 90,88,70
CSF £5.03 CT £22.03 TOTE £3.40: £1.10, £1.10, £3.20; EX 5.90 Place 6 £116.73, Place 5 £24.16.
Owner Around The World Partnership **Bred** Miss S N Ralphs **Trained** Middleham Moor, N Yorks

FOCUS
A modest handicap and, with the pace steady, the winning time was 0.77 seconds slower than earlier 46-50. The form is not strong with a couple finishing close up from out od the handicap.
T/Plt: £132.10 to a £1 stake. Pool: £61,147.60. 337.80 winning tickets. T/Qpdt: £21.10 to a £1 stake. Pool: £4,406.10. 154.50 winning tickets. ST

1021 FOLKESTONE (R-H)
Tuesday, April 24

OFFICIAL GOING: Good to firm
Wind: Almost nil Weather: Sunny and warm

1212 FOLKESTONE-RACECOURSE.CO.UK APPRENTICE H'CAP 6f
2:10 (2:10) (Class 6) (0-60,60) 4-Y-O+ **£2,730** (£806; £403) **Stalls** Low

Form RPR

/00- **1** **Exponential (IRE)**[385] 864 5-8-12 **60** PietroRomeo(8) 5 72
(J M Bradley) *pressed ldng pair towards nr side: effrt over 1f out: urged along and led last 75yds: hld on wl* **50/1**

2532 **2** *hd* **Danish Blues (IRE)**[15] 978 4-8-10 **55** (p) MatthewDavies(5) 3 67
(D E Cantillon) *taken down early: w ldr and racd nr side: rdn to ld narrowly ent fnl f: fnd little and hdd last 75yds* **4/1**[1]

2255 **3** ½ **Misaro (GER)**[57] [566] 6-9-6 **60**..........(b) JackDean 1 70
(R A Harris) *racd against nr side rail: mde most: rdn and hdd ent fnl f: no ex nr fin* **4/1**[1]

004- **4** 3 ½ **Briery Lane (IRE)**[172] [6323] 6-9-3 **60**.......... BarrySavage(3) 7 60
(J M Bradley) *chsd ldrs but nvr on terms: n.d fr over 1f out: plugged on* **9/1**[3]

50-6 **5** *hd* **Montzando**[32] [746] 4-8-12 **52**..........(v) JosephWalsh 2 51
(B R Millman) *chsd ldng trio and racd nr side: rdn 1/2-way and nt on terms: one pce after* **9/1**[3]

50-1 **6** ½ **Piddies Pride (IRE)**[34] [723] 5-9-5 **59**..........(v) ChrisGlenister 12 56+
(Miss Gay Kelleway) *wl in rr: urged along 2f out: swtchd rt and kpt on fnl f: no ch* **10/1**

-000 **7** ¾ **Napoletano (GER)**[40] [686] 6-8-9 **57**.......... ThomasBubb(8) 6 52
(S Dow) *taken down early: reluctant to go bhd stalls: s.i.s: wl in rr and outpcd: kpt on fr over 1f out: no ch* **16/1**

-602 **8** 2 **Dasheena**[28] [803] 4-9-1 **55**..........(be) MCGeran 13 44+
(A J McCabe) *rrd s: racd wd: nvr on terms w ldrs* **12/1**

23-4 **9** 1 **Supreme Kiss**[28] [796] 4-9-2 **56**.......... SophieDoyle 14 42+
(Mrs N Smith) *racd wd: hld up: gng wl enough 1/2-way: effrt 2f out: nvr on terms and no real prog* **16/1**

60-5 **10** 2 ½ **Piccostar**[31] [751] 4-9-3 **57**.......... MarkCoumbe 8 36
(A B Haynes) *dwlt: nvr on terms w ldrs: struggling over 2f out* **16/1**

600- **11** *hd* **Enjoy The Buzz**[239] [4872] 8-8-4 **52**.......... JakePayne(8) 4 30
(J M Bradley) *nvr bttr than midfield and nvr on terms w ldrs: struggling over 2f out* **40/1**

05-1 **12** *nk* **Miswadah (IRE)**[28] [796] 4-9-0 **59**.......... DavidProbert(5) 10 36
(D M Simcock) *racd wd: spd to 1/2-way but nt on terms: wknd wl over 1f out* **13/2**[2]

6460 **13** 4 **Caustic Wit (IRE)**[34] [724] 9-8-12 **60**..........(p) BenjaminWishart(8) 9 25
(M S Saunders) *taken down early: racd wd: chsd ldrs but nvr on terms: wknd 2f out* **14/1**

06-0 **14** 1 **Cool Sting (IRE)**[46] [650] 4-9-4 **58**..........(b) BradleyRoper 11 20
(M G Quinlan) *dwlt: racd wd: sn wl bhd* **16/1**

1m 12.04s (-1.56) **Going Correction** -0.225s/f (Firm) **14** Ran SP% **124.7**
Speed ratings (Par 101):101,100,100,95,95 94,93,90,89,86 85,85,80,78
CSF £251.34 CT £847.55 TOTE £59.60: £17.60, £1.40, £1.60; EX 345.70 TRIFECTA Not won..
Owner Spitting Mick Partnership **Bred** Rossenarra Stud **Trained** Sedbury, Gloucs
■ Pietro Romeo's first winner.

FOCUS
A decent-size field and a competitive race on paper, but rendered less so by a massive draw and track bias. The front three, who occupied those positions throughout and pulled right away from the rest, were all drawn low. The form is modest rated through the third, but given the way the race was run it may be best not to condemn the unplaced horses too much.

1213 THE LOOKOUT RESTAURANT CLAIMING STKS 5f
2:40 (2:40) (Class 6) 3-Y-O **£2,388** (£705; £352) **Stalls** Low

Form RPR

0-50 **1** **Mind The Style**[13] [1004] 3-9-2 72.......... AmirQuinn(3) 4 59
(W G M Turner) *racd keenly against nr side rail: mde virtually all: hrd pressed fr over 1f out: hld on nr fin* **15/8**[1]

0-05 **2** *nk* **Shreddy Shrimpster**[20] [920] 3-8-0 45.......... DavidKinsella 2 39
(A B Haynes) *restless stalls: hld up and sn last: effrt jst over 1f out: swtchd rt ins fnl f: r.o nr fin: too much to do* **9/1**

-030 **3** *hd* **Nou Camp**[11] [1031] 3-8-9 54.......... OscarUrbina 6 47
(N A Callaghan) *cl up: effrt to chal over 1f out: pressed wnr fnl f: nt qckn last 75yds* **9/2**[3]

-420 **4** 1 **Temtation (IRE)**[30] [778] 3-7-7 55..........(p) MCGeran(7) 1 34
(J R Boyle) *cl up: swtchd rt and effrt over 1f out: nt qckn ins fnl f* **2/1**[2]

0-00 **5** 4 **Golden Ribbons**[4] [1119] 3-8-0 44..........(b[1]) AdrianMcCarthy 3 20
(J R Boyle) *t.k.h early: hld up bhd ldrs: rdn 2f out: wknd fnl f* **25/1**

406- **6** 1 **Autumn Storm**[217] [5448] 3-8-6 57..........(b[1]) EddieAhern 5 22
(R Ingram) *pressed wnr tl wknd over 1f out* **10/1**

60.14 secs (-0.66) **Going Correction** -0.225s/f (Firm) **6** Ran SP% **109.2**
Speed ratings (Par 96):96,95,95,93,87 85
CSF £17.60 TOTE £2.70: £1.80, £3.30; EX 19.00.
Owner Stephen Bell and Tracy Turner **Bred** N And L Warburton **Trained** Sigwells, Somerset

FOCUS
Not a great claimer and suspect form, though the time was respectable enough for the type of contest. The favourite was quick to bag the stands' rail in front and that was probably crucial in the outcome.
Nou Camp Official explanation: jockey said gelding hung right
Temtation(IRE) Official explanation: jockey said filly was unsuited by the good to firm ground

1214 LADBROKES THE NATION'S FAVOURITE H'CAP 5f
3:15 (3:15) (Class 5) (0-75,73) 4-Y-O+ **£3,238** (£963; £481; £240) **Stalls** Low

Form RPR

0042 **1** **No Time (IRE)**[7] [1074] 7-7-11 **59** oh3.......... MCGeran(7) 4 66+
(A J McCabe) *hld up off the pce: prog whn nt clr run over 1f out: swtchd rt 1f out: r.o to ld last strides* **7/2**[2]

-000 **2** *shd* **Azygous**[11] [1023] 4-9-4 **73**.......... SimonWhitworth 3 80+
(J Akehurst) *trckd ldrs: got through against nr side rail to ld jst ins fnl f: collared last strides* **12/1**

0-31 **3** 1 ½ **Ashes (IRE)**[8] [1067] 5-8-11 **66** 6ex.......... PaulMulrennan 7 67
(K R Burke) *taken to post 25 mins early: chsd ldrs and pushed along: effrt to chal jst over 1f out: one pce ins fnl f* **8/1**

60-2 **4** *hd* **Willhewiz**[13] [1004] 7-8-11 **66**.......... RichardHughes 2 67
(M S Saunders) *racd nr side: mde most: hdd jst ins fnl f: nt qckn* **5/2**[1]

220- **5** ½ **Tamino (IRE)**[191] [5987] 4-8-8 **63**.......... EddieAhern 8 62
(H Morrison) *hld up on outer and off the pce: pushed along over 1f out: kpt on steadily: nvr nr ldrs* **4/1**[3]

00-6 **6** ¾ **Malapropism**[13] [1004] 7-8-11 **73**.......... MatthewDavies(7) 6 69
(M R Channon) *pressed ldr to jst over 1f out: wknd ins fnl f* **9/1**

020- **7** 1 ¼ **Westbrook Blue**[143] [6682] 5-9-1 **73**..........(tp) AmirQuinn(3) 5 65
(W G M Turner) *s.i.s: mostly last and off the pce: no ch over 1f out: plugged on* **12/1**

6400 **P** **Nepro (IRE)**[8] [1063] 5-9-1 **70**..........(t) OscarUrbina 1 —
(E J Creighton) *mostly in last pair: no prog whn p.u over 1f out: lame* **14/1**

59.17 secs (-1.63) **Going Correction** -0.225s/f (Firm) **8** Ran SP% **114.0**
Speed ratings (Par 103):104,103,101,101,100 99,97,—
CSF £43.69 CT £314.63 TOTE £4.60: £1.60, £4.20, £1.60; EX 76.30 Trifecta £154.20 Pool: £534.39 - 2.46 winning tickets..
Owner Paul J Dixon **Bred** Tally-Ho Stud **Trained** Babworth, Notts

FOCUS
Quite a competitive little sprint handicap run at a good pace and a thrilling finish and the first two may prove better than the bare form.
Willhewiz Official explanation: jockey said gelding hung right throughout

1215 FOLKESTONE RACECOURSE FOR WEDDINGS MAIDEN STKS 7f (S)
3:50 (3:51) (Class 5) 3-Y-O+ **£2,914** (£867; £433; £216) **Stalls** Low

Form RPR

34- **1** **Subadar**[186] [6072] 3-8-13.......... RichardHughes 3 60+
(R Charlton) *rrd bef stalls opened: w ldng pair: rdn 2f out: led u.p ins fnl f: drvn out* **1/2**[1]

2 ½ **Golden Platitude (IRE)** 4-9-12.......... AdamKirby 2 63+
(W R Swinburn) *trckd ldrs: effrt over 1f out: chal ent fnl f: styd on but hld last 75yds* **7/2**[2]

0 **3** 1 ¼ **Sugar Land**[10] [1037] 3-8-8.......... SimonWhitworth 1 50
(C A Cyzer) *racd against nr side rail: w ldr: led wl over 2f out: hdd and fdd ins fnl f* **33/1**

\- **4** ½ **Spinal Tap (IRE)** 3-8-10.......... RichardKingscote(3) 5 54+
(C R Egerton) *dwlt: pushed along in last: clsd over 2f out: nt qckn and reminders over 1f out: kpt on ins fnl f* **12/1**[3]

5 ½ **Fervent** 3-8-6.......... BarrySavage(7) 6 53?
(J M Bradley) *hld up in tch: nt clr run against nr side rail 2f out to 1f out: no imp whn in the clr fnl f* **66/1**

60- **6** 4 **Chant De Guerre (USA)**[237] [4920] 3-8-8.......... EddieAhern 7 37
(H J L Dunlop) *sn in rr: rdn and effrt on outer over 2f out: chsng ldrs over 1f out: wknd* **16/1**

54-2 **7** 2 **Cantique (IRE)**[104] [90] 3-8-8 61.......... JamesDoyle 4 31
(Ms J S Doyle) *mde most towards outer to wl over 2f out: wknd wl over 1f out* **20/1**

1m 27.43s (-0.47) **Going Correction** -0.225s/f (Firm)
WFA 3 from 4yo 13lb **7** Ran SP% **111.7**
Speed ratings (Par 103):93,92,91,90,89 85,83
CSF £2.28 TOTE £1.30: £1.10, £1.60; EX 3.00.
Owner K Abdulla **Bred** Juddmonte Farms Ltd **Trained** Beckhampton, Wilts

FOCUS
An uncompetitive maiden and not a great race either, as the winning time was moderate for the class. the form is difficult to assess with those having form appearing to run below par.

1216 LADBROKES XTRA H'CAP 1m 7f 92y
4:25 (4:25) (Class 5) (0-75,72) 4-Y-O+ **£2,914** (£867; £433; £216) **Stalls** Low

Form RPR

200- **1** **Himba**[209] [5628] 4-8-7 **55**.......... OscarUrbina 5 62
(Mrs A J Perrett) *mde all: set stdy pce tl shkn up over 3f out: hrd pressed over 1f out: kpt on wl* **3/1**[2]

4-04 **2** 1 **Madiba**[32] [389] 8-8-5 **50** oh5.......... DavidKinsella 7 56?
(P Howling) *trckd ldng pair: effrt over 2f out: pressed wnr over 1f out: nt qckn and hld ins fnl f* **9/2**[3]

16 **3** ½ **Caucasienne (FR)**[56] [578] 4-9-5 **67**.......... EddieAhern 1 72
(J W Hills) *trckd wnr: rdn and nt qckn over 2f out: lost 2nd over 1f out: kpt on again last 100yds* **11/8**[1]

-000 **4** 10 **Hatch A Plan (IRE)**[13] [1002] 6-9-1 **65**.......... TravisBlock(5) 4 61+
(Mouse Hamilton-Fairley) *hld up in 4th: rdn and nt qckn over 2f out: eased whn btn fnl f* **6/1**

2-06 **5** *hd* **Birkside**[15] [870] 4-9-7 **72**.......... RichardKingscote(3) 8 64?
(B G Powell) *a last: lost tch 4f out* **9/1**

3m 28.84s (1.64) **Going Correction** +0.125s/f (Good)
WFA 4 from 6yo+ 3lb **5** Ran SP% **109.6**
Speed ratings (Par 103):100,99,99,93,93
CSF £15.99 TOTE £5.70: £1.80, £2.00; EX 13.10 Trifecta £28.40 Pool: £100.26 - 2.50 winning tickets..
Owner Martin & Valerie Slade **Bred** Hellwood Stud Farm **Trained** Pulborough, W Sussex

FOCUS
A moderate handicap made even more so by three non-runners and not strong rated around the first two. An ordinary pace and something of a tactical affair, but even though there were four still in with every chance turning for home, the actual order of the runners changed little during the contest.

1217 FOLKESTONE RACECOURSE FOR EXHIBITIONS MAIDEN FILLIES' STKS 1m 4f
5:00 (5:00) (Class 5) 3-Y-O+ **£2,914** (£867; £433; £216) **Stalls** Low

Form RPR

1 **Moraine** 3-8-7 ow1.......... RichardHughes 7 68+
(R Charlton) *trckd ldrs: effrt on inner whn nt clr run 4f out: shkn up over 2f out: clsd on inner over 1f out: drvn to ld last 100yds* **2/1**[2]

00- **2** ½ **Lindy Lou**[178] [6215] 3-8-6.......... EddieAhern 6 66
(C A Cyzer) *t.k.h: led after 2f: rdn and pressed over 2f out: hdd and nt qckn last 100yds* **7/1**[3]

3 **3** *nk* **Just Julie (USA)**[12] [1012] 3-8-7 ow1.......... OscarUrbina 3 67
(N A Callaghan) *trckd ldr after 2f: rdn to chal 2f out: wandering and nt qckn u.p fr over 1f out* **10/11**[1]

50-0 **4** 6 **Valart**[86] [283] 4-9-11 60.......... J-PGuillambert 5 56
(A J Lidderdale) *led tl rn wd bnd after 2f: chsd ldrs after tl wknd fr 2f out* **16/1**

5 ¾ **Act Three** 3-8-4 ow1.......... NeilChalmers(3) 4 56
(Mouse Hamilton-Fairley) *s.s: in tch: pushed along and outpcd over 3f out: n.d after* **33/1**

000- **6** 30 **Nahlass**[115] [6987] 4-9-11 45.......... JamesDoyle 1 7
(Ms J S Doyle) *hld up: prog to join ldrs 7f out: rdn and wknd 4f out: t.o* **66/1**

2m 42.07s (1.57) **Going Correction** +0.125s/f (Good)
WFA 3 from 4yo 20lb **6** Ran SP% **108.5**
Speed ratings (Par 100):99,98,98,94,93 73
CSF £14.84 TOTE £2.70: £1.40, £2.10; EX 13.80.
Owner K Abdulla **Bred** Juddmonte Farms Ltd **Trained** Beckhampton, Wilts

FOCUS
A weak fillies' maiden run at an ordinary pace in which only half the field could be fancied, but the winner is unexposed and may be capable of better, with the third setting the standard.
Valart Official explanation: jockey said filly hung right throughout

1218 NEXT MEETING MAY 3RD H'CAP 1m 1f 149y
5:30 (5:30) (Class 5) (0-75,74) 3-Y-O **£2,914** (£867; £433; £216) **Stalls** Low

Form RPR

4325 **1** **Beau Sancy**[8] [1059] 3-8-8 **69**.......... TolleyDean(5) 4 70
(R A Harris) *hld up in 3rd: trckd ldr over 2f out: rdn to ld over 1f out: kpt on wl* **10/1**

606- **2** ½ **Postsprofit (IRE)**[172] [6324] 3-8-12 **68**.......... OscarUrbina 5 68+
(N A Callaghan) *s.s: hld up in tch but lost tch 3f out: rdn and effrt over 1f out: r.o fnl f: too much to do* **15/2**[3]

21-2 **3** *shd* **Letham Island (IRE)**[6] 1089 3-9-4 **74**............................ J-PGuillambert 3 74
(M Johnston) *led: rdn wl over 2f out: hdd over 1f out: kpt on but nt qckn fnl f: lost 2nd last stride* **8/15**[1]

502- **4** *8* **Mud Monkey**[168] 6385 3-8-5 **64**............................ RichardKingscote(3) 1 48
(B G Powell) *chsd ldr to over 2f out: wknd* **7/2**[2]

2m 6.74s (1.51) **Going Correction** +0.125s/f (Good) **4** Ran SP% **108.3**
Speed ratings (Par 98):98,97,97,91
CSF £60.67 TOTE £9.40; EX 54.80 Place 6 £65.38, Place 5 £34.76.
Owner S & A Mares **Bred** Mrs J Keegan **Trained** Earlswood, Monmouths

FOCUS
A strange race with the two outsiders prevailing and probably weak form, but the favourite made sure the race was run at a true gallop and there is no reason to believe this was a fluke.
T/Plt: £121.30 to a £1 stake. Pool: £42,886.55. 257.90 winning tickets. T/Qpdt: £37.80 to a £1 stake. Pool: £2,473.00. 48.30 winning tickets. JN

1175 SOUTHWELL (L-H)
Tuesday, April 24

OFFICIAL GOING: Good to firm (good in places)
15mm water had been put on the track over the previous seven days. Despite the official change the ground was described as 'good to firm, firm in places'
Wind: Light, across Weather: Overcast but fine and dry

1219 PLAY POKER AT SKYPOKER.COM H'CAP 6f
2:00 (2:01) (Class 5) (0-70,70) 3-Y-O **£3,071** (£906; £453) **Stalls** Low

Form RPR
22-6 **1** **Social Rhythm**[34] 725 3-9-1 **70**............................ MarcHalford(3) 1 81+
(H J Collingridge) *hld up towards rr: gd hdwy on ins 2f out: n.m.r over 1f out: styd on wl to ld wl ins fnl f* **5/1**[2]

156- **2** *3/4* **Nobilissima (IRE)**[198] 5829 3-9-1 **67**............................ SebSanders 11 71
(J L Spearing) *trckd ldr: led 2f out: hdd and no ex towards fin* **6/1**[3]

60-4 **3** *1 1/2* **Howards Tipple**[16] 954 3-9-1 **67**............................ TomEaves 5 66
(I Semple) *prom: effrt over 2f out: styd on fnl f* **8/1**

4504 **4** *3/4* **Perlachy**[11] 1031 3-8-5 **62**............................(v) DuranFentiman(5) 3 59
(Mrs N Macauley) *prom: effrt over 2f out: kpt on same pce appr fnl f* **11/1**

5-52 **4** *dht* **Princess Ellis**[14] 996 3-8-5 **57**............................ AdrianTNicholls 14 54
(E J Alston) *sn trcking ldrs on outer: chal over 1f out: kpt on same pce ins fnl f* **7/1**

334- **6** *nk* **Multitude (IRE)**[190] 6013 3-8-13 **65**............................ DavidAllan 12 61
(T D Easterby) *in rr-div: hdwy on outer 2f out: styd on wl towards fin* **16/1**

400- **7** *1* **Lovers Kiss**[122] 6926 3-8-4 **56** oh5............................(b) DaleGibson 4 49?
(N Wilson) *swvd rt s: trckd ldrs: fdd fnl f* **50/1**

5563 **8** *1/2* **Arnie's Joint (IRE)**[15] 974 3-8-8 **60**............................(b) JamieSpencer 13 52
(N P Littmoden) *bhd and drvn along: hdwy on outer 2f out: kpt on: nvr rchd ldrs* **9/2**[1]

610- **9** *1 1/4* **Auction Oasis**[168] 6388 3-8-9 **61**............................ JamieMackay 8 49
(B Palling) *swvd bdly rt s: led: tk keen grip: hdd 2f out: wknd fnl f* **25/1**

3-20 **10** *1/2* **Vadinka**[98] 147 3-9-4 **70**............................ KimTinkler 2 56
(N Tinkler) *in tch: effrt over 2f out: one pce* **9/1**

3-50 **11** *3/4* **Minnie Mill**[81] 336 3-8-8 **60** ow2............................ GrahamGibbons 7 44
(B P J Baugh) *chsd ldrs: wknd 2f out* **33/1**

34-0 **12** *3/4* **Woqoodd**[16] 958 3-8-13 **70**............................ JamieMoriarty(5) 10 52
(R A Fahey) *hmpd s: a in rr* **12/1**

20-0 **13** *nk* **Lafontaine Bleu**[16] 958 3-8-12 **64**............................ TonyHamilton 6 45
(R A Fahey) *s.i.s: a in rr and sn drvn along* **20/1**

0-56 **14** *nk* **Wiseton Dancer (IRE)**[93] 202 3-8-4 **56** oh4............ EdwardCreighton 9 36
(Miss V Haigh) *hmpd s: a in rr* **40/1**

1m 15.44s (-0.66) **Going Correction** -0.20s/f (Firm) **14** Ran SP% **120.6**
Speed ratings (Par 98):96,95,93,92,92 91,90,89,87,87 86,85,84,84
CSF £33.13 CT £246.96 TOTE £7.20: £2.20, £1.10, £5.10; EX 42.20.
Owner A Fairfield **Bred** And Mrs A Fairfields **Trained** Exning, Suffolk

FOCUS
A modest handicap but solid enough form for the level.
Arnie's Joint(IRE) Official explanation: trainer said gelding had been unsuited by the good to firm, good in places ground

1220 PLAY MONOPOLY AT SKYBETVEGAS.COM MEDIAN AUCTION MAIDEN STKS 1m 3f
2:30 (2:30) (Class 6) 3-Y-O **£2,184** (£644; £322) **Stalls** Low

Form RPR
1 **Rumpus (GER)** 3-9-3............................ MickyFenton 4 65+
(T P Tate) *hld up in rr: hdwy on outside over 5f out: led 2f out: edgd lft: styd on wl ins fnl f* **13/2**

2 *1 1/4* **Serhaaphim** 3-8-12............................ JamieSpencer 6 58+
(M L W Bell) *chsd ldrs: sn drvn along: reminders over 5f out: chal 2f out: kpt on ins fnl f* **7/2**[2]

064- **3** *1/2* **Hatton Flight**[164] 6449 3-9-3 58............................(p) RichardMullen 7 62
(A M Balding) *chsd ldrs: effrt on ins 3f out: n.m.r 1f out: kpt on same pce* **4/1**[3]

4 *6* **Starr Flyer** 3-9-3............................ DavidAllan 8 51
(A Bailey) *s.i.s: bhd tl kpt on fnl 2f: nvr a threat* **33/1**

402 **5** *4* **Wassendale**[15] 981 3-8-12 63............................ SebSanders 3 39
(J W Hills) *gave problems s: led 1f: led over 4f out: hdd 2f out: no rspnse and sn wknd* **15/8**[1]

000- **6** *2 1/2* **Jewelled Dagger (IRE)**[117] 6963 3-9-3 33............................ TomEaves 2 39
(I Semple) *chsd ldrs: drvn and lost pl over 4f out* **50/1**

00-0 **7** *1/2* **Wingsinmotion (IRE)**[24] 849 3-8-12 44............................ SilvestreDeSousa 9 33
(Miss Tracy Waggott) *led after 1f: hdd over 4f out: wkng whn hmpd 3f out* **25/1**

\- **8** *6* **Top Rocker** 3-9-3............................ TonyHamilton 1 28
(E W Tuer) *s.s: a in rr and sn drvn along* **14/1**

2443 **9** *10* **Ranavalona**[14] 991 3-8-12 53............................ RobbieFitzpatrick 5 —
(C Smith) *hld up in tch: lost pl over 3f out: bhd whn heavily eased ins fnl f* **9/1**

2m 25.11s (-2.89) **Going Correction** -0.20s/f (Firm) **9** Ran SP% **115.8**
Speed ratings (Par 96):102,101,100,96,93 91,91,86,79
CSF £29.15 TOTE £8.90: £2.70, £1.20, £1.70; EX 34.60.
Owner T P Tate **Bred** Gestut Graditz **Trained** Tadcaster, N Yorks
■ Stewards' Enquiry : Silvestre De Sousa caution: careless riding

FOCUS
A weak maiden with the third rated just 58. The first two have size and scope and should improve; the form is rated through the third, but limited by the proximity of the sixth.
Wassendale Official explanation: jockey said filly lost her action
Ranavalona Official explanation: jockey said filly had a breathing problem

1221 PLAY SKY POKER ON DIGITAL CHANNEL 846 (S) STKS 7f
3:05 (3:06) (Class 6) 3-Y-O+ **£2,184** (£644; £322) **Stalls** Low

Form RPR
-120 **1** **Wiltshire (IRE)**[20] 912 5-9-12 53............................ MickyFenton 8 59
(P T Midgley) *restless in stalls and hood removed v late: missed break: hdwy on ins over 2f out: swtchd rt 1f out: styd on to ld nr fin* **4/1**[1]

006- **2** *shd* **Cyfrwys (IRE)**[155] 6541 6-9-2 57............................(p) JamieMackay 9 49
(B Palling) *led: edgd lft over 1f out: hdd towards fin* **9/1**

0-34 **3** *1 1/2* **Rudry World (IRE)**[11] 1028 4-9-7 57............................ AlanDaly 6 50
(P A Blockley) *s.i.s: mid-div: sn drvn along: hdwy over 2f out: styd on fnl f* **8/1**

50-0 **4** *1* **Four Kings**[16] 954 6-9-7 45............................ TonyHamilton 2 48
(Karen McLintock) *sn chsng ldrs: kpt on wl fnl f* **7/1**[3]

0-00 **5** *3/4* **Red Lantern**[28] 800 6-9-7 37............................ DaleGibson 14 46
(M W Easterby) *hld up on outer: in rr tl styd on fnl 2f: nt rch ldrs* **50/1**

60-0 **6** *nk* **Dutch Key Card (IRE)**[7] 1074 6-9-7 55............................ RobbieFitzpatrick 4 45
(C Smith) *mid-div: sn drvn along: kpt on fnl 2f: nvr a threat* **14/1**

1104 **7** *2* **Blythe Spirit**[31] 766 8-9-7 55............................ JamieMoriarty(5) 10 45
(R A Fahey) *hld up towards rr: hdwy and nt clr run over 2f out: kpt on: nvr nr to chal* **4/1**[1]

500- **8** *1 1/4* **Bold Tiger (IRE)**[256] 4057 4-9-7 45............................ SilvestreDeSousa 1 36
(Miss Tracy Waggott) *chsd ldrs: fdd fnl f* **25/1**

00-0 **9** *nk* **Tantien**[31] 431 5-8-13 33............................(p) JerryO'Dwyer(3) 3 31
(T Keddy) *chsd ldrs: drvn over 2f out: sn outpcd* **80/1**

00-0 **10** *1 3/4* **Champagne Rossini (IRE)**[15] 504 5-9-2 38............(b) MarkFlynn(5) 13 31
(M C Chapman) *chsd ldrs: wknd fnl 2f* **50/1**

0003 **11** *2* **Kingsmaite**[11] 1027 6-9-5 39............................(b) LeeTopliss(7) 7 31
(S R Bowring) *sn detached in rr: nvr a factor* **6/1**[2]

0-00 **12** *1/2* **Tapsalteerie**[31] 766 4-8-9 30............................ NSLawes(7) 5 19
(M W Easterby) *chsd ldrs: lost pl over 1f out* **50/1**

0-00 **13** *3/4* **Teddy Monty (IRE)**[89] 243 4-9-4 30............................ MarkLawson(3) 11 23
(R E Barr) *in rr: drvn 4f out* **40/1**

5450 **14** *6* **Pontefract Glory**[58] 557 4-9-7 41............................(b) TomEaves 12 7
(M Dods) *chsd ldrs: lost pl 2f out* **10/1**

1m 29.38s (0.18) **Going Correction** -0.20s/f (Firm) **14** Ran SP% **117.1**
Speed ratings (Par 101):90,89,88,87,86 85,83,82,81,79 77,76,76,69
CSF £37.85 TOTE £4.40: £2.00, £3.10, £2.40; EX 46.90.The winner was bought in for 5,500gns.
Owner David Mann **Bred** John Perotta **Trained** Westow, N Yorks

FOCUS
A moderate winning time, even for a seller, rated through the winner but limited by the proximity of the fourth and fifth.
Blythe Spirit Official explanation: jockey said gelding was denied a clear run

1222 SKYBETVEGAS.COM CASINO RACE H'CAP 2m
3:40 (3:40) (Class 6) (0-65,63) 4-Y-O+ **£2,388** (£705; £352) **Stalls** Low

Form RPR
335- **1** **Trafalgar Day**[239] 4884 4-9-4 **57**............................ RichardMullen 6 68+
(W M Brisbourne) *hld up in mid-div: smooth hdwy on outer over 2f out: qcknd to ld over 1f out: edgd lft ins fnl f: drvn out* **10/1**

3336 **2** *1 1/4* **Sand Repeal (IRE)**[14] 994 5-9-11 **60**............................(v) BrettDoyle 1 66
(Miss J Feilden) *trckd ldrs: nt clr run over 2f out: chal and hmpd over 1f out: keeping on same pce whn hmpd ins fnl f* **11/2**

3-34 **3** *nk* **Eforetta (GER)**[21] 909 5-9-10 **59**............................ EdwardCreighton 12 66+
(D J Wintle) *chsd ldrs: drvn over 4f out: styng on same pce whn hmpd ins fnl f* **7/2**[1]

200- **4** *2 1/2* **Mystified (IRE)**[28] 6509 4-8-3 **47**............................ DuranFentiman(5) 5 50
(R F Fisher) *in rr-div: hdwy and pushed along over 4f out: styd on fnl f* **14/1**

/200 **5** *hd* **Mangrove Cay (IRE)**[11] 1027 5-8-12 **47**............................ SilvestreDeSousa 4 51+
(A J Lockwood) *set mod pce: qcknd over 5f out: edgd rt and hdd over 1f out: keeping on same pce whn bdly hmpd ins fnl f: eased nr fin* **20/1**

00-0 **6** *nk* **Piccolomini**[21] 909 5-8-12 **47**............................(b) TonyHamilton 3 49
(E W Tuer) *trckd ldrs: effrt and hung lft over 1f out: one pce* **50/1**

30-3 **7** *8* **Mulligan's Pride (IRE)**[20] 913 6-8-12 **52**............(b) JamieMoriarty(5) 7 44
(James Moffatt) *hld up in rr: sme hdwy over 3f out: nvr on terms* **9/2**[3]

5-41 **8** *shd* **I'll Do It Today**[20] 913 6-9-9 **58**............................ TomEaves 13 50
(J M Jefferson) *w ldrs: wknd over 1f out* **4/1**[2]

1-00 **9** *11* **Red River Rebel**[55] 585 9-8-12 **50**............................ MarkLawson(3) 9 29
(J R Norton) *w ldrs: drvn over 4f out: lost pl over 2f out* **14/1**

04-0 **10** *13* **Watermill (IRE)**[109] 45 4-7-13 **45**............................ DanielleMcCreery(7) 11 9
(D W Chapman) *swtchd lft after s: hld up in rr: drvn over 4f out: sn bhd* **50/1**

020- **11** *1/2* **Jamaar**[364] 1219 5-9-11 **60**............................ MickyFenton 2 23
(C N Kellett) *s.i.s: hdwy to chse ldrs after 4f: drvn over 5f out: sn lost pl* **33/1**

00-0 **12** *16* **Roonah (FR)**[15] 966 4-8-6 **45**............................ DO'Donohoe 10 —
(Karen McLintock) *hld up in rr: drvn over 4f out: sn bhd: eased ins fnl f* **66/1**

0 **13** *29* **Daring Racer (GER)**[31] 753 4-9-10 **63**............................ SebSanders 8 —
(S Dow) *mid-div: effrt over 4f out: heavily eased over 2f out: virtually p.u* **10/1**

3m 36.81s (-4.69) **Going Correction** -0.20s/f (Firm)
WFA 4 from 5yo+ 4lb **13** Ran SP% **120.4**
Speed ratings (Par 101):103,102,102,100,100 100,96,96,91,84 84,76,61
CSF £62.32 CT £236.79 TOTE £15.20: £3.20, £2.40, £1.80; EX 112.20.
Owner Mrs C P Lees-Jones **Bred** Major W R Paton-Smith **Trained** Great Ness, Shropshire
■ Stewards' Enquiry : Silvestre De Sousa four-day ban: dropped hands and lost 5th place (May 7-10)
Richard Mullen five-day ban: careless riding (May 5-9)

FOCUS
A very moderate stayers' handicap run at a very steady pace and they were getting in each others' way in the final stages. The previously out-of-form sixth holds the form down.

1223 EXPERIENCE THE THRILLS OF SKYBETVEGAS.COM H'CAP 7f
4:15 (4:15) (Class 4) (0-80,80) 4-Y-O+ **£4,857** (£1,445; £722; £360) **Stalls** Low

Form RPR
041- **1** **Hiccups**[175] 6273 7-9-4 **80**............................ DarryllHolland 6 88
(M Dods) *in tch: hdwy on ins over 2f out: styd on wl to ld last 75yds* **12/1**

4060 **2** *1 1/4* **H Harrison (IRE)**[16] 953 7-8-1 **66**............................ AndrewElliott(3) 7 71
(I W McInnes) *chsd ldrs: kpt on wl fnl f* **50/1**

-035 **3** *1/2* **Shot To Fame (USA)**[10] 1040 8-9-3 **79**............................(t) AdrianTNicholls 2 83
(D Nicholls) *led tl hdd and no ex wl ins fnl f* **7/2**[1]

00-4 **4** *2 1/2* **Fiefdom (IRE)**[16] 953 5-9-0 **76**............................ DanielTudhope 3 73
(I W McInnes) *sn chsng ldrs: kpt on same pce appr fnl f* **17/2**

35-4 **5** *1 ¼* **Ryedale Ovation (IRE)**[20] 915 4-8-8 **70**......................(b[1]) DavidAllan 8 64
(T D Easterby) *mid-div: effrt over 2f out: kpt on fnl f* **16/1**

261- **6** *1* **Carnivore**[221] 5345 5-9-0 **76**.. GrahamGibbons 13 67
(T D Barron) *stdd and swtchd lft s: bhd: hdwy 2f out: n.m.r jst ins fnl f: kpt on* **5/1**[2]

00-3 **7** *¾* **The Osteopath (IRE)**[20] 930 4-8-9 **71**..................(b[1]) TonyHamilton 12 60
(M Dods) *t.k.h in rr: effrt on wd outside over 2f out: styd on fnl f* **14/1**

5340 **8** *nk* **Plateau**[50] 614 8-8-4 **69** ow1.................................... SaleemGolam[(3)] 10 58
(C R Dore) *chsd ldrs: lost pl over 1f out* **25/1**

0054 **9** *½* **Moayed**[25] 828 8-8-12 **74**...(b) SebSanders 5 61
(N P Littmoden) *s.i.s: pushed along in rr: hdwy on ins over 2f out: nvr nr ldrs* **11/2**[3]

1505 **10** *3* **Mandarin Spirit (IRE)**[11] 1023 7-8-11 **73**..................(b) JamieSpencer 4 53
(G C H Chung) *hld up: hdwy over 2f out: wknd and eased ins fnl f* **7/1**

00-4 **11** *1 ½* **Fair Shake (IRE)**[10] 1040 7-8-4 **66** oh1.........................(v) DO'Donohoe 9 42
(Karen McLintock) *in rr: bhd and drvn over 3f out* **14/1**

46-0 **12** *1* **Bo McGinty (IRE)**[16] 957 6-8-8 **75**.......................... JamieMoriarty[(5)] 11 48
(R A Fahey) *trckd ldrs on outer: rdn and lost pl 2f out* **33/1**

350- **13** *4* **Foreign Edition (IRE)**[159] 6499 5-9-2 **78**............................ TomEaves 1 41
(Miss J A Camacho) *sn chsng ldrs: rdn over 2f out: lost pl over 1f out* **10/1**

1m 27.16s (-2.04) **Going Correction** -0.20s/f (Firm) **13** Ran SP% **122.0**
Speed ratings (Par 105):103,101,101,98,96 95,94,94,93,90 88,87,82
CSF £524.43 CT £2544.82 TOTE £14.10: £3.30, £8.40, £1.90; EX 455.80.
Owner J M & Mrs E E Ranson **Bred** Mrs Susan Corbett **Trained** Denton, Co Durham

FOCUS
A competitive handicap run at a strong pace and the form looks solid enough.

1224 SKY BET FREEPHONE 08000 722 421 H'CAP 1m 3f
4:50 (4:50) (Class 6) (0-60,59) 3-Y-O **£2,388** (£705; £352) **Stalls** Low

Form RPR

01-2 **1** **Dee Cee Elle**[6] 1092 3-8-10 **54**..................................... GregFairley[(3)] 13 63+
(M Johnston) *w ldr: led 3f out: styd on strly fnl f* **7/4**[1]

00-6 **2** *1 ½* **Linlithgow (IRE)**[21] 904 3-8-11 **52**..................................... SebSanders 8 58
(J L Dunlop) *rn in snatches: sn chsng ldrs: sn drvn along: kpt on same pce fnl f* **11/2**[3]

0-00 **3** *shd* **Marju's Gold**[84] 304 3-9-0 **55**..................................... GrahamGibbons 1 61+
(E J O'Neill) *tk fierce grip in midfield: hdwy over 2f out: kpt on same pce fnl f* **10/1**

006 **4** *2* **Park's Prodigy**[14] 991 3-8-9 **50**...............................(t) AdrianTNicholls 2 53+
(P C Haslam) *t.k.h in rr: hdwy over 3f out: kpt on same pce fnl 2f* **50/1**

005- **5** *2 ½* **Francesco**[175] 6284 3-9-1 **56**..................................... JamieSpencer 4 54
(M L W Bell) *trckd ldrs gng wl: effrt 2f out: sn rdn: fdd over 1f out* **15/8**[2]

00-0 **6** *2 ½* **Dee Valley Boy (IRE)**[25] 834 3-8-9 **50**..................(v[1]) DarryllHolland 12 44
(J D Bethell) *led tl 3f out: wknd over 1f out* **66/1**

20-4 **7** *6* **Kingsmead (USA)**[25] 834 3-9-4 **59**.............................. MickyFenton 10 43
(Miss J Feilden) *chsd ldrs: wknd over 2f out* **14/1**

06-0 **8** *shd* **Currahee**[33] 728 3-8-9 **50**.. TomEaves 11 34
(Miss J A Camacho) *s.s: in rr tl sme hdwy fnl 2f: nvr on terms* **33/1**

000- **9** *1 ¼* **Salto Chico**[190] 6007 3-8-10 **51**...................................... RichardMullen 5 33
(W M Brisbourne) *sn chsng ldrs: drvn over 4f out: lost pl over 2f out* **20/1**

50-0 **10** *2* **Mujamead**[77] 373 3-8-9 **50**...(v[1]) LeeEnstone 6 28
(P C Haslam) *hmpd bnd after 2f: in rr: effrt on outer 5f out: sn btn* **50/1**

040- **11** *1* **Bellapais Boy**[259] 4228 3-9-0 **55**...................................... DavidAllan 9 31
(T D Easterby) *in rr: drvn over 5f out: nvr on terms* **33/1**

6060 **12** *nk* **Bluecrop Boy**[10] 1039 3-8-2 **50**.............................. FrankiePickard[(7)] 7 26
(D J S Ffrench Davis) *mid-div: drvn and lost pl 4f out* **100/1**

0400 **13** *1 ¾* **Kings Shillings**[8] 1059 3-9-0 **55**..............................(v[1]) DanielTudhope 14 28
(D Carroll) *s.s: hdwy on wd outside over 5f out: lost pl 4f out* **50/1**

2m 25.83s (-2.17) **Going Correction** -0.20s/f (Firm) **13** Ran SP% **121.3**
Speed ratings (Par 96):99,97,97,96,94 92,88,88,87,85 85,85,83
CSF £11.44 CT £78.92 TOTE £3.30: £1.30, £2.40, £3.10; EX 14.10.
Owner Douglas Livingston **Bred** Pollards Stables **Trained** Middleham Moor, N Yorks

FOCUS
A low-grade middle-distance three-year-old handicap but a highly-progressive winner with the next four unexposed.
Kings Shillings Official explanation: jockey said gelding had no more to give

1225 PERTEMPS PEOPLE DEVELOPMENT "HANDS AND HEELS" APPRENTICE H'CAP 1m 4f
5:25 (5:25) (Class 5) (0-70,69) 4-Y-O+ **£3,071** (£906; £453) **Stalls** Low

Form RPR

00-3 **1** **Rare Coincidence**[21] 909 6-8-2 **55** oh1............(p) PatrickDonaghy[(3)] 3 70
(R F Fisher) *led and sn wl clr: drvn 3f out: kpt on wl: unchal* **3/1**[1]

010- **2** *10* **Let It Be**[199] 5815 6-8-11 **61**................................ DanielleMcCreery 6 60
(K G Reveley) *sn trcking ldrs: kpt on to take 2nd over 1f out: nvr anywhere nr wnr* **8/1**

006- **3** *3* **Border Tale**[151] 6560 7-8-2 **55** oh3.............................(p) JamesRogers[(3)] 7 49
(James Moffatt) *hld up in last: kpt on fnl 3f: nvr nrr* **16/1**

0000 **4** *shd* **Second Reef**[15] 966 5-8-0 **55** oh4.............................(v[1]) PaulPickard[(5)] 5 49
(J R Weymes) *hld up: hdwy to chse clr ldr over 7f out: one pce fnl 2f* **16/1**

1-05 **5** *1 ¼* **Blue Hedges**[81] 332 5-8-8 **58**..................................... JamieHamblett 4 50
(H J Collingridge) *hld up in rr: kpt onf inal 3f: nvr a factor* **7/2**[2]

-300 **6** *1 ¾* **Love You Always (USA)**[64] 496 7-8-5 **55** oh2................(t) AmyBaker 1 44
(Miss J Feilden) *trckd ldrs: tk keen grip: hung rt and one pce fnl 2f* **12/1**

606/ **7** *8* **Silent Street**[580] 5408 4-8-1 **56** oh5.............................. FrankiePickard[(5)] 2 31
(K G Reveley) *staedied s: t.k.h: sn trcking ldrs: lost pl 3f out* **5/1**[3]

-113 **8** *5* **Three Boars**[33] 733 5-9-5 **69**...(b) JackMitchell 8 37
(S Gollings) *hld up in rr: hdwy on outer over 7f out: edgd rt and lost pl over 2f out: bhd whn eased ins last* **7/2**[2]

2m 37.62s (-2.68) **Going Correction** -0.20s/f (Firm)
WFA 4 from 5yo+ 1lb **8** Ran SP% **116.7**
Speed ratings (Par 103):100,93,91,91,90 89,83,80
CSF £28.25 CT £331.63 TOTE £4.10: £1.50, £3.20, £5.40; EX 32.40 Place 6 £95.27, Place 5 £33.59.
Owner A Kerr **Bred** D R Tucker **Trained** Ulverston, Cumbria

FOCUS
The first round of a new 'hands and heels' apprentice series, for jockeys yet to ride more than ten winners. The enterprisingly-ridden winner was never in any danger and is rated back to old form.
Three Boars Official explanation: jockey said gelding hung right throughout
T/Jkpt: Not won. T/Plt: £136.00 to a £1 stake. Pool: £58,875.80. 315.85 winning tickets. T/Qpdt: £23.60 to a £1 stake. Pool: £2,850.50. 89.20 winning tickets. WG

[1162] WOLVERHAMPTON (A.W) (L-H)
Tuesday, April 24

OFFICIAL GOING: Standard
Wind: Light, half-behind Weather: Fine

1226 BANK MACHINE CASH IS KING H'CAP 5f 216y(P)
2:20 (2:20) (Class 5) (0-70,76) 4-Y-O+ **£2,968** (£876; £438) **Stalls** Low

Form RPR

0646 **1** **Winthorpe (IRE)**[22] 896 7-8-4 **56**..................................... TPO'Shea 1 68
(J J Quinn) *hld up in tch on ins: led over 1f out: sn rdn: r.o wl* **15/2**

4002 **2** *1 ½* **Mistral Sky**[31] 766 8-8-11 **63**.......................................(v) HayleyTurner 3 71
(Stef Liddiard) *sn led: rdn and hdd over 1f out: nt qckn ins fnl f* **8/1**

50-1 **3** *1 ¼* **Maison Dieu**[22] 896 4-8-7 **62**.............................. StephenDonohoe[(3)] 7 66
(E J Alston) *hld up and bhd: swtchd rt wl over 1f out: rdn and hdwy fnl f: nrst fin* **6/1**[2]

-655 **4** *¾* **Hoh Wotanite**[28] 803 4-8-6 **63**.........................(b) RussellKennemore[(5)] 5 65
(R Hollinshead) *towards rr: hdwy whn nt clr run briefly 2f out: hrd rdn over 1f out: one pce fnl f* **7/1**[3]

0211 **5** *¾* **Came Back (IRE)**[3] 1165 4-9-5 **76** 6ex.................. MichaelJStainton[(5)] 8 76
(J Mackie) *led early: a.p: ev ch 2f out: sn rdn: no ex fnl f* **13/8**[1]

-006 **6** *1* **Ebraam (USA)**[8] 1064 4-8-8 **60**..................................... DeanMcKeown 9 57
(D Shaw) *s.i.s: sn chsng ldrs: rdn and edgd lft over 1f out: fdd fnl f* **6/1**[2]

206- **7** *5* **Pitbull**[234] 5031 4-8-10 **62**... JimmyQuinn 2 44
(Mrs G S Rees) *s.i.s: short-lived effrt on ins wl over 1f out* **20/1**

503- **8** *1 ½* **The History Man (IRE)**[197] 5864 4-8-13 **65**.................(b) PatCosgrave 4 42
(M Mullineaux) *w ldr: rdn and wknd 2f out* **20/1**

000- **9** *2* **Highland Song (IRE)**[152] 6572 4-8-3 **60**................ KevinGhunowa[(5)] 11 31
(R F Fisher) *mid-div on outside: bhd fnl 2f* **50/1**

5-00 **10** *13* **Pauvic (IRE)**[98] 155 4-9-4 **70**.. TPQueally 6 2
(Mrs A Duffield) *sn bhd* **33/1**

1m 14.1s (-1.71) **Going Correction** -0.10s/f (Stan) **10** Ran SP% **116.5**
Speed ratings (Par 103):107,105,103,102,101 100,93,91,88,71
CSF £62.41 CT £394.24 TOTE £9.50: £2.00, £2.90, £2.30; EX 45.90.
Owner Green Roberts Savage Whittall Williams **Bred** M Conaghan **Trained** Settrington, N Yorks

FOCUS
A modest sprint handicap but a fair time and sound enough rated through the third.

1227 RACING ALL YEAR ROUND H'CAP 1m 141y(P)
2:55 (2:55) (Class 6) (0-55,61) 4-Y-O+ **£2,047** (£604; £302) **Stalls** Low

Form RPR

5541 **1** **Scottish River (USA)**[3] 1167 8-9-6 **61** 6ex...................... HayleyTurner 4 73
(M D I Usher) *hld up in rr: hdwy on ins wl over 1f out: led ins fnl f: pushed out* **7/2**[1]

0-00 **2** *1* **Fortress**[31] 750 4-8-11 **52**.. WSupple 1 62
(E J Alston) *led early: hld up in tch: led wl over 1f out: sn rdn and edgd rt: hdd ins fnl f: kpt on* **28/1**

-064 **3** *2* **General Feeling (IRE)**[20] 923 6-8-13 **54**........................ PatCosgrave 2 60
(M Mullineaux) *hld up and bhd: hdwy on ins over 2f out: rdn over 1f out: one pce ins fnl f* **12/1**

42-6 **4** *½* **Lilac Star**[50] 612 4-8-13 **54**.. JimmyFortune 8 59
(Pat Eddery) *a.p: led over 3f out: rdn and hdd wl over 1f out: no ex ins fnl f* **11/2**[2]

5426 **5** *1 ¼* **Shava**[28] 797 7-8-11 **52**.. VinceSlattery 5 54
(H J Evans) *hld up towards rr: rdn and hdwy over 1f out: no imp fnl f* **10/1**

032- **6** *½* **Mucho Loco (IRE)**[15] 6277 4-8-11 **52**...........................(b) DaneO'Neill 6 53
(R Curtis) *hld up in tch: n.m.r and bmpd wl over 1f out: rdn and no imp fnl f* **20/1**

-265 **7** *2* **Sun Bian**[30] 773 5-8-9 **50**.. LPKeniry 13 47
(L P Grassick) *prom: ev ch over 2f out: sn rdn: wknd wl over 1f out* **33/1**

140 **8** *shd* **Bobering**[15] 976 7-8-2 **50**.. SoniaEaton[(7)] 7 47
(B P J Baugh) *hld up towards rr: racd wd fr 3f out: n.d* **7/2**[1]

0551 **9** *hd* **Fuel Cell (IRE)**[40] 682 6-8-11 **52**.................................. JimmyQuinn 9 48
(J O'Reilly) *hld up and bhd: rdn over 2f out: n.d* **16/1**

-050 **10** *2* **Orpen Quest (IRE)**[3] 1167 5-8-9 **55**..................(v) KevinGhunowa[(5)] 11 47
(M J Attwater) *hld up: hdwy 6f out: rdn 3f out: wkng whn bmpd wl over 1f out* **9/1**

40-0 **11** *¾* **Right Ted (IRE)**[7] 742 4-8-9 **50**...................................... NCallan 12 40
(T Wall) *sn led: hdd over 3f out: rdn and wknd wl over 1f out* **25/1**

0-03 **12** *¾* **Susiedil (IRE)**[15] 966 6-8-9 **50**...............................(v) PaulFessey 10 39
(S T Mason) *mid-div: rdn 3f out: bhd fnl 2f* **33/1**

-064 **13** *3 ½* **Danettie**[28] 801 6-8-5 **49**.. LiamJones[(3)] 3 44+
(W M Brisbourne) *t.k.h in mid-div: bhd whn rdn 3f out: c wd st: no ch whn nt clr run over 1f out* **8/1**[3]

1m 51.62s (-0.14) **Going Correction** -0.10s/f (Stan) **13** Ran SP% **121.5**
Speed ratings (Par 101):96,95,93,92,91 91,89,89,89,87 86,86,83
CSF £119.66 CT £800.32 TOTE £4.10: £1.90, £7.50, £4.20; EX 142.00.
Owner M D I Usher **Bred** The Thoroughbred Corporation **Trained** Upper Lambourn, Berks
■ Stewards' Enquiry : Dane O'Neill two-day ban: careless riding (May 7-8)

FOCUS
The fact they went no great gallop was reflected in a modest winning time for the class and not that solid, despite the placed horses being close to form.
Fuel Cell(IRE) Official explanation: jockey said gelding was denied a clear run
Danettie Official explanation: jockey said mare ran too freely

1228 JOHN SMITH'S EXTRA SMOOTH H'CAP 7f 32y(P)
3:25 (3:25) (Class 4) (0-80,79) 3-Y-O **£4,728** (£1,406; £702; £351) **Stalls** High

Form RPR

421- **1** **All Of Me (IRE)**[114] 6998 3-9-3 **78**.................................. DaneO'Neill 8 85+
(T G Mills) *s.i.s: hld up and bhd: hdwy on outside over 1f out: hrd rdn to ld nr fin* **18/1**

-211 **2** *½* **Captain Jacksparra (IRE)**[26] 815 3-9-3 **78**........................ NCallan 9 84
(K A Ryan) *hld up and bhd: hdwy 2f out: hung lft over 1f out: led ins fnl f: hdd nr fin* **5/1**[2]

416- **3** *nk* **Dream Lodge (IRE)**[190] 6010 3-9-1 **76**.............................. TPQueally 11 81
(J G Given) *s.i.s: hdwy on outside 2f out: edgd lft over 1f out: rdn and ev ch ins fnl f: nt qckn* **15/2**

41- **4** *shd* **Curzon Prince (IRE)**[251] 4492 3-9-4 **79**.............................. WSupple 1 88+
(C F Wall) *hld up: nt clr run on ins and swtchd rt over 1f out: rdn and r.o wl ins fnl f: nrst fin* **20/1**

316- **5** *nk* **Farley Star**[212] 5546 3-9-4 **79**.. SteveDrowne 7 83+
(R Charlton) *hld up in mid-div: lost pl 2f out: r.o ins fnl f: nt rch ldrs* **5/1**[2]

20-1 **6** *4* **Mount Hermon (IRE)**[27] 807 3-9-2 **77**.............................. JimmyFortune 6 71
(H Morrison) *prom: ev ch over 2f out: n.m.r ent st: wknd over 1f out* **7/2**[1]

621- **7** *hd* **Ghost Dancer**[198] 5843 3-8-13 **74** .... NickyMackay 10 67
(L M Cumani) *t.k.h in mid-div: hdwy to ld 2f out: sn rdn: edgd lft 1f out: hdd & wknd ins fnl f* **11/1**

41- **8** *nk* **Flores Sea (USA)**[190] 6013 3-8-11 **72** .... PaulFessey 2 64
(T D Barron) *prom: rdn 2f out: sn wknd* **6/1**[3]

0130 **9** *½* **Cherri Fosfate**[4] 1122 3-8-8 **76** .... (b) KellyHarrison(7) 4 67
(D Carroll) *hld up in tch: wknd wl over 1f out* **20/1**

322- **10** *1* **Mason Ette**[257] 4295 3-9-0 **75** .... PhilipRobinson 3 64
(C G Cox) *sn led: hdd 2f out: rdn over 1f out: wknd fnl f* **11/1**

31- **11** *16* **Kondakova (IRE)**[204] 5735 3-9-0 **75** .... HayleyTurner 5 22
(M L W Bell) *led early: w ldr: rdn over 2f out: sn wknd* **20/1**

1m 28.78s (-1.62) **Going Correction** -0.10s/f (Stan) **11** Ran SP% **117.8**
Speed ratings (Par 100):105,104,104,103,103 99,98,98,97,96 78
CSF £102.78 CT £561.29 TOTE £18.40: £6.90, £1.70, £3.70; EX 106.80.
Owner John Humphreys **Bred** Lynn Lodge Stud **Trained** Headley, Surrey

FOCUS
There were several unexposed types in this very competitive handicap won in a fair winning time and the form is rated positively and should stand up.

1229 STAY AT THE WOLVERHAMPTON HOLIDAY INN H'CAP 2m 119y(P)
4:00 (4:01) (Class 6) (0-50,49) 4-Y-0+ **£2,047** (£604; £302) **Stalls** Low

Form RPR

0 **1** **Rocknest Island (IRE)**[27] 808 4-8-8 **49** .... (p) AndrewMullen(3) 3 59
(P D Niven) *a.p: rdn to ld over 1f out: styd on wl* **16/1**

1046 **2** *3* **Tip Toes (IRE)**[15] 982 5-8-11 **45** .... JimmyQuinn 5 51
(P Howling) *hld up in mid-div: hdwy on ins over 4f out: rdn and ev ch over 1f out: one pce ins fnl f* **11/2**[2]

000/ **3** *1 ½* **Theflyingscottie**[271] 5059 5-8-11 **45** .... DeanMcKeown 9 50
(D Shaw) *hld up and bhd: hung lft fr 4f out: hdwy on ins 3f out: styd on ins fnl f* **10/1**

4-46 **4** *½* **Rajayoga**[20] 913 6-8-11 **45** .... NCallan 6 49
(M H Tompkins) *prom: led after 4f: rdn over 2f out: hdd over 1f out: no ex fnl f* **15/8**[1]

5523 **5** *2 ½* **Countback (FR)**[29] 792 8-8-12 **46** .... (p) CatherineGannon 2 47
(A W Carroll) *led after 1f tl after 4f: prom: ev ch 2f out: wknd ins fnl f* **7/1**[3]

006- **6** *½* **Aristi (IRE)**[35] 4929 6-8-4 **45** .... (p) KirstyMilczarek(7) 8 45
(R M Stronge) *hld up in mid-div: hdwy 6f out: wknd 2f out* **10/1**

4640 **7** *3 ½* **Domenico (IRE)**[16] 792 9-8-11 **45** .... JimmyFortune 1 41
(J R Jenkins) *hld up towards rr: rdn over 3f out: short-lived effrt on outside over 2f out* **7/1**[3]

-406 **8** *10* **Earthling**[8] 1066 6-8-11 **45** .... TPQueally 4 29
(D W Chapman) *led 1f: prom tl wknd over 3f out* **14/1**

000- **9** *2* **Sunny Parkes**[209] 5618 4-8-7 **45** .... HayleyTurner 10 27
(M Mullineaux) *a bhd* **33/1**

0/60 **10** *shd* **Charnwood Street (IRE)**[50] 617 8-8-8 **45** .... (v) LiamJones(3) 11 27
(D Shaw) *towards rr: pushed along 7f out: wl bhd fnl 3f* **50/1**

000- **11** *1 ¾* **Indian Chase**[34] 6857 10-8-6 **45** .... MichaelJStainton(5) 7 25
(Dr J R J Naylor) *bhd fnl 5f* **12/1**

3m 41.46s (-1.67) **Going Correction** -0.10s/f (Stan)
WFA 4 from 5yo+ 4lb **11** Ran SP% **118.5**
Speed ratings (Par 101):99,97,96,96,95 95,93,88,87,87 87
CSF £102.47 CT £943.89 TOTE £21.10: £5.20, £1.80, £3.60; EX 219.90.
Owner Mrs Kate Young **Bred** G Martin **Trained** Barton-le-Street, N Yorks

FOCUS
A weak contest with only four horses in the handicap proper, but the form appears sound rated through the runner-up.
Rocknest Island(IRE) ◆ Official explanation: trainer's rep said, regarding apparent improvement in form, that the filly was better suited by the surface

1230 JOHN SMITH'S H'CAP 1m 1f 103y(P)
4:35 (4:35) (Class 4) (0-85,85) 3-Y-O **£4,728** (£1,406; £702; £351) **Stalls** Low

Form RPR

332- **1** **Prince Sabaah (IRE)**[204] 5720 3-8-11 **78** .... PatDobbs 6 89+
(R Hannon) *a.p: carried rt briefly bnd over 7f out: rdn 3f out: led 2f out: edgd lft towards fin: r.o* **13/2**

-115 **2** *1* **Hurlingham**[31] 754 3-9-1 **85** .... AndrewMullen(3) 2 94
(M Johnston) *led 1f: prom: rdn over 2f out: ev ch whn edgd rt ins fnl f: nt qckn* **15/8**[1]

01- **3** *2 ½* **Sanbuch**[300] 2979 3-9-3 **84** .... NickyMackay 3 88+
(L M Cumani) *hld up: rdn and hdwy over 1f out: one pce fnl f* **4/1**[2]

0316 **4** *3 ½* **Homes By Woodford**[7] 1084 3-8-1 **71** .... LiamJones(3) 1 68
(R A Harris) *hld up: hdwy on ins 2f out: swtchd rt wl over 1f out: sn rdn: one pce* **14/1**

006- **5** *1 ¼* **Carson's Spirit (USA)**[209] 5624 3-8-13 **80** .... NCallan 7 75
(W S Kittow) *stdd s: t.k.h in rr: rdn 2f out: no rspnse whn hung lft 1f out* **20/1**

01- **6** *3 ½* **Maraca (IRE)**[168] 6386 3-8-9 **76** .... JimmyFortune 4 64
(J H M Gosden) *led after 1f: jinked rt bnd over 7f out: rdn and hdd 2f out: wknd 1f out* **9/2**[3]

414- **7** *14* **History Boy**[129] 6846 3-8-13 **80** .... JimmyQuinn 5 40
(D J Coakley) *plld hrd: hmpd and carried rt bnd over 7f out: hdwy 5f out: wknd over 2f out* **7/1**

2m 0.28s (-2.34) **Going Correction** -0.10s/f (Stan) **7** Ran SP% **110.2**
Speed ratings (Par 100):106,105,102,99,98 95,83
CSF £17.75 TOTE £7.30: £3.30, £2.00; EX 30.20.
Owner D Boocock **Bred** D Boocock **Trained** East Everleigh, Wilts

FOCUS
There were some unexposed types in this interesting little handicap won in a decent time. The form is best rated through the fourth and should work out.
Hurlingham Official explanation: jockey said colt hung right-handed
History Boy Official explanation: jockey said gelding ran too freely

1231 RINGSIDE SUITE 700 THEATRE STYLE MAIDEN STKS 1m 4f 50y(P)
5:05 (5:06) (Class 5) 3-5-Y-O **£2,968** (£876; £438) **Stalls** Low

Form RPR

0-2 **1** **Veracity**[14] 991 3-8-7 .... PhilipRobinson 4 73+
(M A Jarvis) *set modest pce tl cocked jaw: rn wd and hdd over 6f out: hdwy on outside to ld 2f out: rdn clr fnl f: r.o wl* **8/13**[1]

0/ **2** *5* **Grizebeck (IRE)**[963] 5264 5-9-13 .... DeanMcKeown 3 62
(R F Fisher) *hld up: hdwy and wnt 2nd over 6f out: led over 4f out: rdn and hdd 2f out: no ex fnl f* **80/1**

60-4 **3** *2* **Telegonus**[23] 869 4-9-12 72 .... SamHitchcott 1 59
(C E Longsdon) *prom: lft in ld over 6f out: hdd over 4f out: rdn over 2f out: wknd over 1f out* **10/1**[3]

3322 **4** *½* **Reciprocation (IRE)**[38] 703 3-8-8 76 ow1 .... (t) NCallan 5 57
(K McAuliffe) *chsd ldr tl carried rt and lost pl briefly bnd over 6f out: rdn 3f out: wknd wl over 1f out* **15/8**[2]

0- **5** *¾* **Gatecrasher**[344] 1741 4-9-12 .... JimmyFortune 2 57?
(Pat Eddery) *hld up: rdn and btn whn hung lft over 1f out* **28/1**

2m 42.73s (0.31) **Going Correction** -0.10s/f (Stan)
WFA 3 from 4yo 20lb 4 from 5yo 1lb **5** Ran SP% **110.5**
Speed ratings (Par 103):94,90,89,89,88
CSF £36.82 TOTE £1.60: £1.10, £16.10; EX 57.90.
Owner Sheikh Mohammed **Bred** Darley **Trained** Newmarket, Suffolk

FOCUS
A moderate winning time for this dreadful maiden and best rated through the winner to debut form.

1232 BOOK ONLINE @ WOLVERHAMPTON-RACECOURSE.CO.UK CLASSIFIED STKS 7f 32y(P)
5:40 (5:41) (Class 6) 3-Y-O+ **£1,943** (£578; £288; £144) **Stalls** High

Form RPR

-006 **1** **Hayley's Flower (IRE)**[39] 689 3-8-8 50 .... (b[1]) PatDobbs 5 57
(J C Fox) *a.p: rdn over 2f out: led wl ins fnl f: r.o* **16/1**

4020 **2** *1* **Machinate (USA)**[15] 975 5-9-4 55 .... LiamJones(3) 10 59
(W M Brisbourne) *hld up in mid-div: hdwy on outside 2f out: rdn and edgd lft 1f out: ev ch wl ins fnl f: nt qckn* **11/4**[1]

6-00 **3** *1* **Epidaurian King (IRE)**[83] 311 4-9-7 55 .... DeanMcKeown 3 59+
(D Shaw) *s.i.s: sn hld up in mid-div: hdwy whn nt clr run briefly on ins 2f out: plld out ins fnl f: r.o* **8/1**

4104 **4** *½* **Mr Chocolate Drop (IRE)**[21] 910 3-8-3 54 .....(p) MichaelJStainton(5) 7 50
(M J Attwater) *plld hrd: sn chsng ldr: rdn and ev ch over 2f out: n.m.r ins fnl f: nt qckn* **8/1**

-061 **5** *½* **Doctor Ned**[21] 900 3-8-8 51 .... WSupple 2 49
(N A Callaghan) *led: rdn over 1f out: hdd wl ins fnl f: no ex* **3/1**[2]

40-0 **6** *1* **Tomorrow's Dancer**[22] 894 3-8-8 54 .... NCallan 12 50+
(K A Ryan) *dwlt: hld up in rr: hdwy over 2f out: hmpd and nt rcvr ins fnl f* **4/1**[3]

04-4 **7** *½* **Above And Below (IRE)**[26] 816 3-8-8 52 .... JimmyQuinn 1 49+
(M Quinn) *a.p: rdn over 1f out: n.m.r ins fnl f: one pce* **11/2**

300- **8** *6* **Telling**[190] 6013 3-8-8 50 .... TPQueally 6 29
(Mrs A Duffield) *s.i.s: sn hld up in mid-div: bhd fnl 3f* **20/1**

050- **9** *1* **Fiddlers Spirit (IRE)**[231] 5094 3-8-8 51 .... SamHitchcott 4 27
(J G M O'Shea) *hld up and bhd: rdn over 3f out: sn struggling* **50/1**

0-50 **10** *1 ½* **Meathop (IRE)**[50] 619 3-8-8 45 .... CatherineGannon 8 23
(R F Fisher) *sn prom: rdn 3f out: sn wknd* **66/1**

50-0 **11** *12* **Hot Cherry**[14] 996 3-8-8 47 .... (b) HayleyTurner 9 —
(J M P Eustace) *s.i.s: rdn over 3f out: a in rr* **66/1**

1m 29.85s (-0.55) **Going Correction** -0.10s/f (Stan)
WFA 3 from 4yo+ 13lb **11** Ran SP% **124.9**
Speed ratings (Par 101):99,97,96,96,95 94,93,87,85,84 70
CSF £62.74 TOTE £19.10: £4.50, £2.00, £3.20; EX 92.20 Place 6 £361.34, Place 5 £105.69.
Owner Miss H J Flower **Bred** Clybaun Bloodstock **Trained** Collingbourne Ducis, Wilts

FOCUS
This turned out to be a messy affair in the home straight and was not much better than a seller. The placed horses set the standard.
Epidaurian King(IRE) Official explanation: jockey said gelding was denied a clear run
Above And Below(IRE) Official explanation: jockey said filly was denied a clear run
Fiddlers Spirit(IRE) Official explanation: jockey said colt suffered interference in running
T/Plt: £213.00 to a £1 stake. Pool: £47,114.65. 161.40 winning tickets. T/Qpdt: £24.40 to a £1 stake. Pool: £2,883.00. 87.10 winning tickets. KH

1233 - 1234a (Foreign Racing) - See Raceform Interactive

912

CATTERICK (L-H)
Wednesday, April 25

OFFICIAL GOING: Good to firm (firm in places)
Wind: Strong, half across

1235 WOT-IF-WE (S) STKS 5f
2:10 (2:10) (Class 6) 2-Y-O **£2,730** (£806; £403) **Stalls** Low

Form RPR

1 **My Sheilas Dream (IRE)** 2-8-9 ow3 .... NCallan 3 52
(J L Spearing) *cl up: led over 3f out: rdn and edgd lft ent fnl f: kpt on* **6/4**[1]

F6 **2** *½* **Miss Tilen**[16] 972 2-8-3 .... LiamJones(3) 2 47
(V Smith) *outpcd and towards rr: hdwy 2f out: sn rdn: styd on u.p ins fnl f* **11/4**[2]

0 **3** *½* **O'Casey (IRE)**[14] 999 2-8-8 .... StephenDonohoe(3) 1 50
(J G M O'Shea) *cl up: ev ch 2f out: sn rdn and n.m.r ent fnl f: kpt on u.p* **12/1**

4 **4** *2 ½* **Amazing Day**[16] 971 2-8-4 .... JackDean(7) 6 40
(W G M Turner) *led over 1f: sn pushed along and swtchd to ins: cl up tl rdn and n.m.r ent fnl f: wknd* **7/1**

1 **5** *2 ½* **No Point (IRE)**[14] 1000 2-8-12 .... TPO'Shea 5 31
(P A Blockley) *s.i.s: pushed along and hdwy to chse ldrs 1/2-way: sn rdn and wknd wl over 1f out* **9/2**[3]

35 **6** *1 ¼* **Miss Willoughby**[4] 1156 2-8-6 .... (v[1]) JamieMackay 4 20
(J Ryan) *sn outpcd and a in rr* **10/1**

61.96 secs (1.36) **Going Correction** -0.075s/f (Good) **6** Ran SP% **114.1**
Speed ratings (Par 90):86,85,84,80,76 74
CSF £6.00 TOTE £2.10: £1.10, £2.20; EX 5.60.The winner was sold to John McGrath for 7,000gns. O'Casey was subject to a friendly claim.
Owner J Spearing **Bred** Carrigbeg Stud And Gavan Kinch **Trained** Kinnersley, Worcs

FOCUS
A very moderate race, even by selling standards, and not solid form.

NOTEBOOK
My Sheilas Dream(IRE), a 15,000euros purchase whose dam was placed over 7f at two, knew her job and landed a gamble on her racecourse debut. This is very moderate form and she might not be open to that much improvement. (op 3-1)
Miss Tilen, dropped into selling company following her sixth in a fair fillies' maiden at Warwick, struggled to go the pace for much of the way and got going too late. A stiffer track or 6f should suit better. (op 4-1)
O'Casey(IRE) failed to beat a rival in a good maiden at Bath on his debut, but this was much easier and he ran a respectable race. (op 16-1)
Amazing Day appeared to improve slightly on the form he showed when fourth on his debut at Warwick, but was still not good enough. (op 9-2)
No Point(IRE) managed to win a four-runner seller on her debut at Bath, but that was a truly awful event and she was well beaten under her penalty. (op 9-4)

1236 PRINCE OF MY HEART MAIDEN STKS 7f
2:45 (2:46) (Class 5) 3-Y-O **£3,238** (£963; £481; £240) **Stalls** Low

Form RPR

40-0 **1** **Alavana (IRE)**[16] 968 3-8-12 50 ... PaulQuinn 4 57
(D W Barker) *bhd: n.m.r bnd after 2f: hdwy 2f out: swtchd outside and str run over 1f out: rdn and edgd lft ins fnl f: led nr fin* **50/1**

0-04 **2** ½ **Pennyrock (IRE)**[7] 1091 3-9-3 62 ... PatCosgrave 6 61
(J J Quinn) *prom: effrt over 2f out: rdn to ld over 1f out: drvn ins fnl f: hdd and no ex nr fin* **11/2**[3]

000- **3** *nk* **Sparky Vixen**[175] 6298 3-8-12 30 ... DeanMcKeown 5 55
(G A Swinbank) *towards rr whn stmbld after 1f: hdwy over 2f out: swtchd ins and rdn over 1f out: n.m.r and styd on wl fnl f* **16/1**

5-0 **4** 1 ¼ **Chip N Pin**[6] 1111 3-8-7 ... DuranFentiman(5) 1 52
(T D Easterby) *n.m.r and bhd after 1f: hdwy 2f out: sn rdn and kpt on ins fnl f: nrst fin* **12/1**

3 **5** 1 ¼ **Hubble Bubble (USA)**[17] 954 3-9-0 ... GregFairley(3) 10 53
(M Johnston) *cl up: led 1/2-way: rdn 2f out: hdd over 1f out and grad wknd* **13/8**[1]

5-4 **6** 1 ¼ **Bajeel (IRE)**[11] 1037 3-9-3 ... NCallan 11 50
(G A Butler) *prom: effrt 2f out: sn rdn and wknd appr fnl f* **2/1**[2]

046- **7** *hd* **Myfrenchconnection (IRE)**[210] 5613 3-8-12 60 ... RoryMoore(5) 7 49
(P T Midgley) *chsd ldrs: rdn along 2f out: grad wknd appr fnl f* **11/1**

8 3 **Dendor** 3-9-3 ... TonyHamilton 9 41
(D W Barker) *s.i.s: hdwy over 2f out: swtchd ins and rdn whn hmpd over 1f out: nvr a factor* **33/1**

9 3 ½ **Little Nipper** 3-9-0 ... AndrewMullen(3) 3 32
(W J H Ratcliffe) *a towards rr* **33/1**

0-05 **10** 7 **Mandriano (ITY)**[5] 1135 3-9-3 47 ... RoystonFfrench 8 13
(D W Barker) *led: hdd 1/2-way: rdn 2f out and sn wknd* **50/1**

000- **11** 3 ½ **Smirfy's Silver**[257] 4321 3-9-3 56 ... PaulMulrennan 12 —
(W M Brisbourne) *chsd ldrs on outer: rdn along 3f out: sn wknd* **33/1**

1m 27.68s (0.32) **Going Correction** -0.075s/f (Good) 11 Ran SP% **121.5**
Speed ratings (Par 98):95,94,94,92,91 89,89,86,82,74 70
CSF £309.14 TOTE £57.20: £10.90, £2.50, £4.80; EX 383.40.
Owner David T J Metcalfe **Bred** Oak Lodge Bloodstock **Trained** Scorton, N Yorks

FOCUS
A very weak maiden run in a time 1.02 seconds slower than the 51-65 handicap and modest form rated through the runner-up. The leaders may just have gone off a little too fast.

1237 RICHMOND CONDITIONS STKS 1m 3f 214y
3:20 (3:20) (Class 4) 3-Y-O **£4,985** (£1,492; £746; £373) **Stalls** Low

Form RPR

4-22 **1** **Elyaadi**[26] 836 3-8-7 72 ... SamHitchcott 2 76+
(M R Channon) *hld up: hdwy over 3f out: rdn and qcknd to ld over 1f out: sn clr* **7/4**[2]

50-1 **2** 5 **Danish Rebel (IRE)**[17] 956 3-9-4 75 ... PaulMulrennan 3 79
(G A Charlton) *led: pushed along 3f out: rdn wl over 1f out: sn hdd and kpt on same pce* **5/1**

0-02 **3** 2 **Love Brothers**[8] 1084 3-8-12 73 ... NCallan 4 70
(M R Channon) *trckd ldr: effrt over 3f out: rdn to chal 2f out: sn drvn and wknd appr fnl f* **13/8**[1]

010- **4** *shd* **Clarricien (IRE)**[179] 6216 3-9-4 78 ... TPO'Shea 1 76
(E J O'Neill) *trckd ldr: pushed along and reminders 1/2-way: rdn along over 3f out: btn over 2f out* **7/2**[3]

2m 38.31s (-0.69) **Going Correction** -0.075s/f (Good) 4 Ran SP% **113.3**
Speed ratings (Par 100):99,95,94,94
CSF £10.35 TOTE £3.10; EX 16.00.
Owner Sheikh Ahmed Al Maktoum **Bred** Darley **Trained** West Ilsley, Berks

FOCUS
This race often produces a smart type - Shanty Star (03) and Melrose Avenue (05) landed this race en-route to winning the Queen's Vase, while subsequent Group-1 winner Youmzain won last year's renewal - so the form should not be underestimated, although it is not strong but sound enough.

1238 8TH MAY IS VIRGIN VIE LADIES NIGHT H'CAP 7f
3:50 (3:51) (Class 6) (0-65,65) 3-Y-O **£2,730** (£806; £403) **Stalls** Low

Form RPR

46-3 **1** **Last Sovereign**[92] 222 3-9-2 63 ... NCallan 11 80+
(R Charlton) *trckd ldrs: smooth hdwy to ld over 1f out: sn clr* **7/4**[1]

066- **2** 5 **Ruthles Philly**[226] 5237 3-8-9 56 ... CatherineGannon 9 56
(D W Barker) *cl up: led over 2f out and sn rdn: hdd over 1f out: kpt on: no ch w wnr* **20/1**

500- **3** 2 **Josr's Magic (IRE)**[205] 5721 3-9-4 65 ... RoystonFfrench 2 60
(Mrs A Duffield) *in tch: hdwy 2f out: sn rdn: styd on ins fnl f: nrst fin* **7/1**[2]

00-6 **4** 1 ½ **Imperial Beach (USA)**[21] 916 3-9-1 62 ... PaulFessey 1 53
(T D Barron) *cl up in inner: rdn along 2f out: grad wknd appr fnl f* **12/1**

420- **5** 1 ½ **Cheshire Prince**[198] 5866 3-9-3 64 ... DavidAllan 12 51
(W M Brisbourne) *in tch: hdwy to chse ldrs 2f out: sn rdn and no imp fnl f* **14/1**

24-0 **6** *nk* **Mujart**[21] 925 3-8-4 56 ... RussellKennemore(5) 4 42
(J A Pickering) *chsd ldng pair: rdn along 2f out: drvn and wknd appr fnl f* **16/1**

-006 **7** 1 ½ **Cavallo Di Ferro (IRE)**[20] 937 3-8-8 62 ... MCGeran(7) 8 44
(M J Gingell) *towards rr tl styd on fnl 2f: nrst fin* **50/1**

-525 **8** *nk* **La Marmotte (IRE)**[7] 1091 3-8-10 60 ... MarkLawson(3) 10 41
(R E Barr) *led: rdn along and hdd over 2f out: sn drvn and wknd* **10/1**

5620 **9** 2 ½ **Suhayl Star (IRE)**[12] 1022 3-9-1 62 ... JamieMackay 5 37
(S W Hall) *dwlt: a towards rr* **10/1**

154- **10** 1 ¼ **Only A Grand**[179] 6208 3-8-11 63 ... NataliaGemelova(5) 15 34
(R Bastiman) *a towards rr* **22/1**

2112 **11** 1 **Put It On The Card**[68] 478 3-9-3 64 ... (p) PhillipMakin 14 32
(J S Wainwright) *hld up: a towards rr* **9/1**[3]

42-4 **12** *shd* **Princess Palatine (IRE)**[22] 908 3-9-4 65 ... PatCosgrave 13 33
(K R Burke) *hld up: hdwy into midfield 1/2-way: sn pushed along and nvr a factor* **11/1**

0-00 **13** 3 ½ **Seaton Snooks**[7] 1091 3-8-11 58 ... TonyHamilton 6 17
(T D Easterby) *a towards rr* **20/1**

350- **14** 1 **Superjain**[138] 6750 3-8-8 62 ... PaulPickard(7) 7 18
(J M Jefferson) *a towards rr* **25/1**

40-5 **15** 2 **Shady Green (IRE)**[41] 684 3-8-10 57 ... PaulMulrennan 3 8
(M W Easterby) *sn outpcd and wl bhd fr 1/2-way* **11/1**

1m 26.66s (-0.70) **Going Correction** -0.075s/f (Good) 15 Ran SP% **133.6**
Speed ratings (Par 96):101,95,93,91,89 89,87,87,84,82 81,81,77,76,74
CSF £50.88 CT £236.25 TOTE £2.60: £1.10, £6.00, £3.20; EX 80.40.
Owner Mountgrange Stud **Bred** Gestut Hof Ittlingen And Cheveley Park Stud Ltd **Trained** Beckhampton, Wilts

FOCUS
A modest race, but a decisive winner in the form of Last Sovereign and he could prove better still in a race that could rate higher. The winning time was 1.02 seconds quicker than the earlier three-year-old maiden, although that was a very weak race.

1239 MOONAX H'CAP 1m 3f 214y
4:25 (4:25) (Class 5) (0-70,69) 4-Y-O+ **£3,238** (£963; £481; £240) **Stalls** Low

Form RPR

350- **1** **Mister Arjay (USA)**[173] 6321 7-8-11 66 ... JamieMoriarty(5) 4 78
(B Ellison) *trckd ldrs: hdwy to ld 3f out and sn rdn clr: kpt on wl appr fnl f* **7/1**

316- **2** 5 **Bronze Dancer (IRE)**[176] 6275 5-9-5 69 ... NCallan 8 73
(G A Swinbank) *trckd ldrs: effrt over 2f out: rdn to chse wnr over 1f out: sn drvn and no imp ins fnl f* **6/4**[1]

50-2 **3** *nk* **Hugs Destiny (IRE)**[16] 965 6-8-5 55 oh1 ... (t) DeanMcKeown 9 59
(M A Barnes) *trckd ldrs: hdwy to chse wnr over 2f out: sn rdn and kpt on same pce* **5/1**[2]

504- **4** 3 **San Deng**[10] 5751 5-8-9 62 ... GregFairley(3) 3 61
(Micky Hammond) *prom: rdn along 3f out: kpt on same pce fnl 2f* **8/1**

230- **5** 3 ½ **Squirtle (IRE)**[167] 6415 4-8-11 65 ... StephenDonohoe(3) 1 59
(W M Brisbourne) *dwlt: towards rr tl styd on fnl 2f* **11/2**[3]

50-6 **6** *nk* **Kristalchen**[16] 966 5-8-5 55 oh10 ... PaulFessey 5 48?
(D W Thompson) *hld up in tch: hdwy on inner whn n.m.r over 3f out: sn rdn along and n.d* **20/1**

0000 **7** 5 **Contra Mundum (USA)**[7] 1086 4-8-4 60 ... DuranFentiman(5) 6 45
(B S Rothwell) *in tch: rdn along over 3f out: sn wknd* **33/1**

0-00 **8** 40 **Fardi (IRE)**[12] 1032 5-8-2 57 oh10 ow2 ... RoryMoore(5) 2 —
(K W Hogg) *led: rdn along and hdd 3f out: sn wknd* **50/1**

2m 36.91s (-2.09) **Going Correction** -0.075s/f (Good)
WFA 4 from 5yo+ 1lb 8 Ran SP% **105.3**
Speed ratings (Par 103):103,99,99,97,95 94,91,64
CSF £14.97 CT £42.10 TOTE £8.60: £2.20, £1.10, £1.70; EX 17.00.
Owner Keith Middleton **Bred** Barbara Hunter **Trained** Norton, N Yorks
■ Patavium (6/1) was withdrawn on vet's advice. Rule 4 applies, deduct 10p in the £.

FOCUS
An ordinary handicap run at a modest early pace and something of a tactical affair. The form is best rated through the third.
Fardi(IRE) Official explanation: jockey said gelding hung right-handed throughout

1240 WHITE MUZZLE H'CAP 5f
5:00 (5:00) (Class 6) (0-60,60) 3-Y-O **£2,730** (£806; £403) **Stalls** Low

Form RPR

60-3 **1** **Windjammer**[21] 925 3-9-1 57 ... DavidAllan 5 73+
(T D Easterby) *mde all: rdn and qcknd clr 2f out: styd on strly* **9/2**[2]

30-0 **2** 4 **Rue Soleil**[15] 998 3-8-12 59 ... JamieMoriarty(5) 4 55
(J R Weymes) *prom: pushed along and sltly outpcd 1/2-way: rdn wl over 1f out: styd on ins fnl f* **33/1**

05-6 **3** *hd* **The Brat**[16] 970 3-8-4 46 oh1 ... PaulFessey 3 41
(J S Wainwright) *towards rr: hdwy 2f out: sn rdn and styd on ins fnl f* **12/1**

4-14 **4** *hd* **Darcy's Pride (IRE)**[16] 970 3-9-2 58 ... TonyHamilton 8 53
(D W Barker) *sn chsng wnr: rdn along 2f out: sn drvn and no imp: wknd towards fin* **13/2**[3]

0-05 **5** 3 **My Two Girls (IRE)**[4] 1161 3-8-7 54 ... (p) RoryMoore(5) 2 37
(P T Midgley) *sn outpcd and bhd: rdn along 1/2-way: swtchd wd and hdwy over 1f out: kpt on u.p ins fnl f* **16/1**

2311 **6** *shd* **Jojesse**[16] 970 3-9-4 60 ... NCallan 1 43
(G A Swinbank) *broke wl: stdd to trck ldrs: pushed along and outpcd after 2f: rdn over 2f out and sn btn* **1/1**[1]

0-3 **7** ½ **Beechside (IRE)**[16] 970 3-8-6 47 ... (t) DeanMcKeown 7 29
(W A Murphy, Ire) *hld up: hdwy 2f out: rdn and edgd lft ent fnl f: n.d* **12/1**

5030 **8** 4 **Minimum Fuss (IRE)**[12] 1031 3-8-10 55 ow1 ... (b) StephenDonohoe(3) 6 21
(M C Chapman) *chsd ldrs: rdn along 2f out: sn wknd* **12/1**

66-0 **9** 6 **Esprit De Nuit (IRE)**[92] 222 3-8-4 46 oh1 ... RoystonFfrench 9 —
(Mrs A Duffield) *dwlt: a towards rr* **25/1**

60.29 secs (-0.31) **Going Correction** -0.075s/f (Good) 9 Ran SP% **117.3**
Speed ratings (Par 96):99,92,92,91,87 87,86,79,70
CSF £134.32 CT £1671.61 TOTE £5.80: £1.60, £7.40, £4.10; EX 116.30.
Owner April Fools **Bred** P E Clinton **Trained** Great Habton, N Yorks

FOCUS
A modest three-year-old sprint handicap in which all the action unfolded against the inside rail, but the winner bolted up and looks to have a future.
Jojesse Official explanation: jockey said gelding was unsuited by the track
Beechside(IRE) Official explanation: trainer said filly was found to be in season

1241 BETFAIR APPRENTICE TRAINING SERIES H'CAP 5f 212y
5:30 (5:31) (Class 6) (0-65,65) 4-Y-O+ **£2,730** (£806; £403) **Stalls** Low

Form RPR

6203 **1** **Violent Velocity (IRE)**[15] 992 4-9-0 60 ... NeilBrown 4 71
(J J Quinn) *hld up in tch: gd hdwy on outer wl over 1f out: rdn and qcknd to ld ins fnl f: sn clr* **5/2**[2]

6-52 **2** 1 ¼ **Chatshow (USA)**[8] 1080 6-9-0 65 ... MarkCoumbe(5) 3 72
(A W Carroll) *chsd ldrs: hdwy on inner 2f out: sn rdn and ev ch ent fnl f: sn drvn and one pce* **9/4**[1]

533- **3** 1 ¾ **Bahamian Duke**[216] 5493 4-9-4 64 ... LukeMorris 9 66
(K R Burke) *prom: effrt 2f out: rdn and hung lft over 1f out: kpt on same pce ins fnl f* **5/1**[3]

64-0 **4** *nk* **Compton Plume**[23] 892 7-8-7 58 ... NSLawes(5) 1 59
(M W Easterby) *led: rdn along and hdd 2f out: kpt on u.p and ev ch tl one pce ins fnl f* **12/1**

00-0 **5** 1 ¼ **Jun Fan (USA)**[99] 154 5-8-1 52 ... LanceBetts(5) 8 49
(B Ellison) *cl up: rdn to ld briefly wl over 1f out: sn drvn and one pce ent fnl f* **11/1**

0-06 **6** ½ **Katie Boo (IRE)**[16] 964 5-8-2 53 ... MCGeran(5) 5 49
(A Berry) *bhd tl styd on fnl 2f: nrst fin* **25/1**

00-0 **7** *hd* **Mint**[16] 964 4-8-10 59 ... JamieHamblett(3) 10 54
(D W Barker) *chsd ldrs on outer: rdn along 2f out: sn drvn and wknd* **33/1**

-000 **8** 1 ¾ **Melandre**[16] 964 5-8-4 55 ... PatrickDonaghy(5) 2 45
(M Brittain) *chsd ldrs: rdn along 2f out: grad wknd* **50/1**

314- **9** 4 **The Old Soldier**[260] 4233 9-8-2 53 ... DeanHeslop(5) 7 31
(A Dickman) *s.i.s: a towards rr* **8/1**

56-0 **10** *shd* **Apache Nation (IRE)**[15] [992] 4-9-0 **63**......................... GaryBartley(3) 6 41
(M Dods) *a bhd* **14/1**

1m 13.81s (-0.19) **Going Correction** -0.075s/f (Good) **10** Ran SP% **118.6**

Speed ratings (Par 101):98,96,94,93,91 91,91,88,83,83

CSF £8.58 CT £26.35 TOTE £3.90: £1.80, £1.40, £1.70; EX 10.80 Place 6 £182.82, Place 5 £148.51.

Owner Mrs S Quinn **Bred** Miss Jill Finegan **Trained** Settrington, N Yorks

FOCUS

A moderate handicap confined to apprentices who had not ridden more than ten winners. It was run at a strong early pace, which seemed to take its toll on a couple late on. The form looks sound enough but not that strong.

T/Plt: £547.90 to a £1 stake. Pool: £35,838.70. 47.75 winning tickets. T/Qpdt: £39.50 to a £1 stake. Pool: £2,110.40. 39.50 winning tickets. JR

EPSOM (L-H)

Wednesday, April 25

OFFICIAL GOING: Good to firm (good in places on round course)

Wind: Moderate, across Weather: Fine but cloudy

1242 GET EXCLUSIVE LIVE SHOW PRICES AT BLUESQ.COM STKS (H'CAP) 5f

1:50 (1:52) (Class 3) (0-95,95) 4-Y-0+

£8,101 (£2,425; £1,212; £607; £302; £152) **Stalls** High

Form RPR

0-62 **1** **Cape Royal**[7] [1088] 7-8-11 **90**.................................(bt) KevinGhunowa(5) 13 99
(J M Bradley) *racd against nr side rail: sn chsd ldrs: effrt 2f out: drvn to dispute ld fnl f: jst prevailed* **3/1**[1]

511- **2** *shd* **Kay Two (IRE)**[191] [6009] 5-8-10 **84**................................. PhilipRobinson 4 93
(R J Price) *lw: pressed ldr: led jst over 2f out: jnd fnl f: jst pipped nr fin* **9/1**

2-10 **3** *hd* **Moorhouse Lad**[81] [344] 4-9-0 **88**................................. ChrisCatlin 1 96
(B Smart) *b.hind: w ldrs fr wd draw: drvn over 1f out: r.o fnl f: jst hld* **16/1**

03-2 **4** *1/2* **Handsome Cross (IRE)**[17] [957] 6-9-0 **88**.................. AdrianTNicholls 6 94
(D Nicholls) *chsd ldrs: rdn 2f out: tried to chal fnl f: styd on but nvr quite rchd ldrs* **6/1**[3]

15-4 **5** *nk* **Bluebok**[7] [1088] 6-8-10 **84**...(t) JamieSpencer 12 89
(J M Bradley) *lw: prom 2f: lost pl and midfield after: hanging lft but styd on against nr side rail fnl f* **9/2**[2]

-600 **6** *1 3/4* **Classic Encounter (IRE)**[27] [818] 4-8-13 **87**.............. RichardHughes 7 86
(D M Simcock) *mde most to jst over 2f out: styd pressing ldrs: cl up but hld whn n.m.r ent fnl f: fdd* **14/1**

5110 **7** *1/2* **Magic Glade**[46] [660] 8-8-13 **87**.. JimCrowley 5 84
(Tom Dascombe) *warm: chsd ldrs: rdn 2f out: one pce and no imp after* **16/1**

560- **8** *1/2* **Masta Plasta (IRE)**[228] [5182] 4-8-13 **94**...................... AdeleRothery(7) 9 89
(D Nicholls) *hld up in rr: effrt 2f out: no imp on ldrs 1f out* **16/1**

000- **9** *hd* **Idle Power (IRE)**[175] [6292] 9-9-0 **91**.............................. AmirQuinn(3) 10 85
(J R Boyle) *bit bkwd: t.k.h: hld up in rr: hanging lft after 1f: sme prog and swtchd lft fnl f: nvr a factor* **25/1**

10-2 **10** *1* **Dhaular Dhar (IRE)**[11] [1041] 5-9-7 **95**........................... DanielTudhope 2 86
(J S Goldie) *lw: dwlt: outpcd and wl bhd: styd on ins fnl f* **8/1**

004- **11** *1* **Pic Up Sticks**[165] [6445] 8-8-10 **87**.......................... RichardKingscote(3) 8 74
(B G Powell) *b: bit bkwd: awkward s: wl in rr: nvr pce to rch ldrs* **20/1**

006- **12** *1/2* **Jayanjay**[127] [6865] 8-8-0 **81** ohl1.................................... JackMitchell(7) 11 66
(P Mitchell) *in tch tl fdd over 1f out* **12/1**

000- **13** *15* **Don't Tell Sue**[303] [2931] 4-8-9 **83**................................... PaulFitzsimons 3 14
(Miss J R Tooth) *bit bkwd: spd on outer to 1/2-way: wknd rapidly over 1f out: t.o* **50/1**

55.55 secs (-0.13) **Going Correction** +0.15s/f (Good) **13** Ran SP% **121.2**

Speed ratings (Par 107):107,106,106,105,105 102,101,100,100,98 97,96,72

CSF £30.20 CT £394.96 TOTE £4.40: £1.60, £3.70, £6.70; EX 41.90.

Owner E A Hayward **Bred** D R Brotherton **Trained** Sedbury, Gloucs

FOCUS

A highly-competitive sprint likely to produce its share of winners and solid enough rated through the winner and fifth.

NOTEBOOK

Cape Royal, who very nearly made all to win at Beverley last week under today's rider, had the ideal draw for a front runner, but on this occasion opted to take a lead. Hard against the rail throughout, he came through to have every chance inside the final furlong and a half and stuck his neck out willingly under pressure to narrowly prevail. A very useful sprinter on his day, he is clearly at the top of his game at the moment. (op 11-4)

Kay Two(IRE), a progressive sprinter towards the end of last season making his seasonal reappearance, was 6lb higher than when winning at Pontefract back in October and bidding for a hat-trick. Having showed good early speed, he went on two furlongs out and made the winner work hard, but was unable to hold on. There is no reason why he cannot progress further this season and develop into a top sprint handicapper, with this run expected to improve him. (op 10-1)

Moorhouse Lad ran a blinder from a bad draw. His good early speed would probably have seen him winning from a higher berth and he kept on dourly under pressure, but was never quite getting there. He too looks most progressive and can find a decent prize coming his way this season. (op 20-1 tchd 22-1)

Handsome Cross(IRE), who ran a blinder on his reappearance at Musselburgh, was up 3lb but still looked to hold major claims from a reasonable draw. He broke well, but had to sit in behind the leaders and just lacked a finishing kick to propel him into the battle for first place. There are races in him off this sort of mark. (op 11-2)

Bluebok, who shaped promisingly behind Cape Royal on his reappearance at Beverley, held a good early position, but lacked the basic speed of his stable companion and did not look overly comfortable on the course. (op 6-1 tchd 4-1)

Classic Encounter(IRE) has basically been a disappointing sort who has failed to go on from his early promise. He was on hias toes beforehand and made a lot of the early running, but was struggling when squeezed for room in the closing stages.

Dhaular Dhar(IRE) was always likely to find this trip on the short side. (tchd 10-1)

1243 WEATHERBYS BANK BLUE RIBAND TRIAL STKS (CONDITIONS RACE) 1m 2f 18y

2:20 (2:23) (Class 2) 3-Y-0 **£12,464** (£3,732; £1,866; £934) **Stalls** Low

Form RPR

1- **1** **Raincoat**[313] [2619] 3-9-1 84.. RichardHughes 2 99+
(J H M Gosden) *lw: hld up in 3rd: squeezed through 2f out: led over 1f out: shkn up and sn clr* **6/5**[1]

42-1 **2** *4* **Dubai Twilight**[24] [864] 3-9-1 91... MichaelHills 1 91
(B W Hills) *lw: led: rdn 2f out: hdd over 1f out: no ch w wnr after: tired but hld on for 2nd* **7/4**[2]

10-3 **3** *nk* **Spirit Of The Mist (IRE)**[8] [1076] 3-8-13 80.......................... JohnEgan 5 88
(T J Pitt) *scope: reluctant to enter stalls: chsd ldr to 2f out where bmpd sltly: sn outpcd: kpt on fnl f* **11/2**[3]

1-25 **4** *3 1/2* **Habalwatan (IRE)**[25] [839] 3-9-3 89.................................(b) SebSanders 3 85
(C E Brittain) *a last: hrd rdn and struggling 3f out* **7/1**

2m 8.35s (-0.69) **Going Correction** +0.225s/f (Good) **4** Ran SP% **109.7**

Speed ratings (Par 104):111,107,107,104

CSF £3.65 TOTE £2.10; EX 3.50.

Owner K Abdulla **Bred** Juddmonte Farms Ltd **Trained** Newmarket, Suffolk

FOCUS

A race that has become unfashionable over the years and this was one of the weaker renewals in memory. That said, it was a decent winning time, being just 0.12 seconds slower than the City And Suburban. The form is rated at face value through the runner-up.

NOTEBOOK

Raincoat, ready winner of an average Sandown maiden on his debut back in June, was put away afterwards with an autumn campaign in mind, but he got 'sick' and had to be kept back for the remainder of the season. This looked an ideal starting point for the son of Barathea, appearing to face only the one serious rival and, having travelled strongly thoughout, he squeezed through before going clear under a hands-and-heels ride from Hughes. This was a highlypromising reappearance that earned him quotes of 25/1 for the Derby, but he will need to prove his mettle against stiffer opposition before coming under any consideration. (op 7-4)

Dubai Twilight, ready winner of a 1m Polytrack maiden on his reappearance, attempted to make all but it was clear from two furlongs out Raincoat had his measure and in the end he just held on for second. It is possible this distance proved beyond the son of Alhaarth and he may be capable of better back at a 1m, but is not going to be easy to place off this mark. (op 5-4)

Spirit Of The Mist(IRE), winner of a course maiden last season, was beaten off this mark in a handicap on his reappearance, but seemed to show improved form for the rise in distance and very nearly got up for second. He was unfortunate to bump into the very useful winner and will find life easier back in handicaps. (op 8-1)

Habalwatan(IRE), the most exposed in the field, was always going to struggle attempting to give weight and was never going particularly well. (op 6-1)

1244 BET@BLUESQ.COM GREAT METROPOLITAN STKS (H'CAP) 1m 4f 10y

2:55 (3:00) (Class 3) (0-95,95) 4-Y-0+

£9,348 (£2,799; £1,399; £700; £349; £175) **Stalls** Centre

Form RPR

0-66 **1** **Lake Poet (IRE)**[80] [353] 4-8-11 87................................... SebSanders 12 100
(C E Brittain) *trckd ldrs: 5th st: pushed along and stdy prog 3f out: rdn to ld over 1f out: styd on strly* **11/1**

635- **2** *2 1/2* **Solent (IRE)**[207] [5678] 5-9-5 94...................................... RichardHughes 15 103
(R Hannon) *led at stdy pce: rdn over 2f out: hdd over 1f out: one pce and sn no ch w wnr* **7/2**[1]

-004 **3** *1 1/4* **Dzesmin (POL)**[40] [693] 5-8-6 81 ow1................................(p) JohnEgan 8 88+
(R C Guest) *hld up wl in rr: 12th st: prog on wd outside over 2f out: styd on to snatch 3rd last strides: no ch* **20/1**

036- **4** *shd* **Tilt**[173] [6319] 5-8-10 85.. DaneO'Neill 14 92
(B Ellison) *chsd ldrs: pushed along 5f out: 6th st: outpcd over 2f out: kpt on fr over 1f out: nvr able to chal* **11/1**

064/ **5** *hd* **Night Hour (IRE)**[672] [2831] 5-8-12 87................................ JimmyFortune 3 94
(J H M Gosden) *mostly chsd ldr to 2f out: hrd rdn and one pce* **14/1**

102- **6** *2* **Nordwind (IRE)**[271] [3888] 6-8-12 87.................................. AdamKirby 6 90
(W R Swinburn) *bit bkwd: settled in midfield: 10th st: outpcd 3f out: effrt 2f out: kpt on but nt pce to rch ldrs* **10/1**

2-33 **7** *nk* **Nawamees (IRE)**[18] [662] 9-8-7 82..............................(p) RichardMullen 5 85+
(G L Moore) *towards rr: 11th st: struggling over 2f out: no ch whn n.m.r 1f out: kpt on after* **16/1**

230- **8** *1/2* **Ti Adora (IRE)**[181] [6191] 5-9-5 94...................................... DarrylHolland 9 96
(P W D'Arcy) *swtg: edgy: n.m.r and dropped to last after 2f: sme prog 7f out: 9th st: struggling whn n.m.r and wandering 2f out: no prog* **16/1**

0-14 **9** *3/4* **I Have Dreamed (IRE)**[24] [868] 5-8-11 86........................... KDarley 13 87
(T G Mills) *warm: prom: 3rd st: rdn wl over 2f out: btn sn after: wknd fnl f* **7/1**[3]

265- **10** *3/4* **Enjoy The Moment**[253] [4459] 4-8-13 89......................... JamieSpencer 1 89
(J A Osborne) *swtg: hld up and last after 3f: wl off the pce st: taken to outer and shuffled along over 2f out: hanging lft and nvr nr ldrs* **5/1**[2]

1-53 **11** *1 1/4* **Tranquilizer**[54] [608] 5-8-6 81...(t) EddieAhern 2 79
(D J Coakley) *chsd ldrs: 4th st: pushed along and lost pl over 2f out: eased whn btn fnl f* **20/1**

245- **12** *1* **Transvestite (IRE)**[172] [6336] 5-8-5 85.......................... PatrickHills(5) 11 81
(J W Hills) *bit bkwd: chsd ldrs: 7th st: sn rdn and outpcd: n.d after: wknd and eased fnl f* **10/1**

06-0 **13** *3 1/2* **Sienna Storm (IRE)**[21] [929] 4-9-2 95........................ SaleemGolam(3) 4 85
(M H Tompkins) *a wl in rr: 13th and rdn st: sn struggling* **25/1**

-211 **14** *28* **Kames Park (IRE)**[32] [763] 5-9-5 94.................................... TomEaves 7 40
(I Semple) *s.s: rousted along to rcvr: chsd ldrs after 4f: rdn 5f out: 8th and losing pl st: hanging and t.o* **8/1**

2m 40.31s (1.58) **Going Correction** +0.225s/f (Good)

WFA 4 from 5yo+ 1lb **14** Ran SP% **129.1**

Speed ratings (Par 107):103,101,100,100,100 98,98,98,97,97 96,95,93,74

CSF £51.53 CT £806.78 TOTE £14.50: £3.50, £2.10, £7.10; EX 62.30 Trifecta £1047.70 Part won. Pool: £1,475.66 - 0.40 winning units..

Owner Mohammed Rashid **Bred** Philip And Mrs Jane Myerscough And Charles O'Brien **Trained** Newmarket, Suffolk

FOCUS

A highly-competitive contest likely to produce its share of winners with the runner-up to previous handicap form and the race could be rated higher.

NOTEBOOK

Lake Poet(IRE) has been running respectably on the All-Weather but was returning to turf off a higher mark and could have been handed a kinder draw. Having broke well though, he was able to obtain a decent position and ran on really strongly under pressure in the final quarter mile, ultimately winning with a bit to spare. This represented an improved effort and he looks to have progressed from two to three. (op 12-1)

Solent(IRE) is a solid and reliable handicapper who looked to hold every chance off this mark and was fit if slightly warm for this reappearance. The support for him throughout the day suggested he was ready and he was able to dominate at his own pace, but could do nothing when the winner went past and was made to settle for second. He is a versatile sort who should continue to pay his way. (op 9-2 tchd 11-2 and 6-1 in places)

Dzesmin(POL) hinted at better to come when a keeping-on fourth at Lingfield last month and this represented a personal best from the five-year-old. He got going too late, but is likely to stay further and may even benefit from a more positive ride in future.

Tilt, who looked fit for this seasonal debut, is not the easiest to win with, but he is rarely far away and this has to go down as a pleasing reappearance. (op 16-1)

Night Hour(IRE), having his first start for Gosden and returning from a a 22-month absence, looked fairly straight and had two handlers in the paddock. He kept finding under pressure and plugged on for fifth, but never looked like winning and will need to improve on this if he is to be winning off this mark. (op 16-1)

Nordwind(IRE), tried over 2m when last seen in July, is fully effective at this trip, but the run was almost certainly needed and as a result it has to go down as a promising effort. Official explanation: jockey said gelding hung left

Nawamees(IRE) was squeezed for room late on but it made no real difference as to where he finished. (op 14-1)

Ti Adora(IRE) got a far from ideal trip through and can be expected to leave this behind in time.

I Have Dreamed(IRE) seems to have trouble with his consistency and has generally been a disappointment.

Enjoy The Moment, although solid enough in the market, was not given the most intelligent ride and hung on the camber in the straight. He is a good deal better than this and connections are likely to step him up in trip in future. (op 6-1)

1245 BET@BLUESQ.COM CITY AND SUBURBAN STKS (HERITAGE H'CAP) — 1m 2f 18y

3:30 (3:36) (Class 2) (0-105,105) 4-Y-0+

£24,928 (£7,464; £3,732; £1,868; £932; £468) **Stalls** Low

Form — RPR

2-25 **1** **Blue Bajan (IRE)**[32] [761] 5-9-5 100 MichaelHills 5 — 111+
(Andrew Turnell) *settled in midfield: 8th st: prog sn after: rdn to chal over 1f out: led ent fnl f: styd on wl* **4/1**[1]

0-01 **2** *1 ¼* **Charlie Tokyo (IRE)**[15] [995] 4-8-8 89 (b) PaulHanagan 7 — 97
(R A Fahey) *lw; settled in midfield: n.m.r 4f out: 7th st: prog sn after: rdn to chal and upsides 1f out: nt qckn* **7/1**[2]

20-2 **3** *1 ¼* **Benandonner (USA)**[15] [993] 4-8-3 84 DaleGibson 11 — 90
(R A Fahey) *trckd ldr: led 4f out: hrd pressed fr 3f out: hdd and one pce ent fnl f* **10/1**[3]

0-15 **4** *nk* **Tabadul (IRE)**[18] [940] 6-9-0 95 RHills 16 — 100
(E A L Dunlop) *prom: trckd ldr 4f out: chal over 2f out: upsides 1f out: no ex* **7/1**[2]

2340 **5** *shd* **Impeller (IRE)**[18] [940] 8-9-3 98 JohnEgan 4 — 103+
(J S Moore) *lw: hld up in midfield: 10th st: nt clr run and swtchd rt over 2f out: styd on wl fnl f: gaining at fin* **12/1**

0-05 **6** *1* **Fort Churchill (IRE)**[15] [995] 6-8-0 81 (bt) AdrianMcCarthy 2 — 84
(B Ellison) *lw: settled wl in rr: 16th st: prog on wd outside over 2f out: clsd but hanging lft over 1f out: one pce fnl f: no ch* **14/1**

3-40 **7** *2 ½* **Langford**[74] [420] 7-8-3 87 SaleemGolam(3) 6 — 85
(M H Tompkins) *trckd ldrs: 4th st: rdn and cl up 2f out: wknd u.p fnl f* **25/1**

0-00 **8** *¾* **Counsel's Opinion (IRE)**[15] [995] 10-8-10 91 SebSanders 14 — 88
(C F Wall) *s.s: wl in rr: 14th st: shkn up and sme prog on inner 2f out: no imp fnl f* **25/1**

006- **9** *hd* **Wovoka (IRE)**[278] [3710] 4-8-6 87 MartinDwyer 8 — 84
(M R Channon) *trckd ldrs: 5th st: cl up and rdn 2f out: wknd and eased fnl f* **33/1**

-033 **10** *1 ½* **Lucayan Dancer**[15] [995] 7-8-3 84 AdrianTNicholls 13 — 78
(D Nicholls) *towards rr: 13th st: sn rdn: effrt on outer over 2f out: hanging lft and nvr on terms w ldrs* **20/1**

600- **11** *hd* **Red Lancer**[195] [5920] 6-8-2 83 SilvestreDeSousa 1 — 76
(D Nicholls) *settled midfield: 9th st: rdn wl over 2f out: outpcd sn after: eased whn no ch fnl f* **16/1**

520- **12** *6* **Zaif (IRE)**[200] [5804] 4-8-5 89 MarcHalford(3) 3 — 71
(D R C Elsworth) *towards rr: 12th and rdn st: sn struggling: lost tch over 2f out* **16/1**

00-1 **13** *½* **Cactus King**[24] [870] 4-8-2 83 ChrisCatlin 9 — 64
(P M Phelan) *lw: settled in rr: 15th st: rdn and no prog wl over 2f out: sn btn* **14/1**

0-34 **14** *2 ½* **Pagan Sword**[39] [701] 5-8-6 87 JimCrowley 18 — 63
(Mrs A J Perrett) *lw: mostly in midfield: 11th st: sn struggling: bhd fnl 2f* **14/1**

34-0 **15** *1 ¼* **Regent's Secret (USA)**[17] [953] 7-7-12 79 oh1 JimmyQuinn 15 — 53
(J S Goldie) *hld up in last: rdn 3f out: sn bhd* **40/1**

3114 **16** *3* **Art Modern (IRE)**[4] [1149] 5-8-1 82 (b) RichardMullen 12 — 50
(G L Moore) *prom: 3rd st: rdn and wknd rapidly wl over 2f out* **14/1**

0001 **17** *37* **Luberon**[18] [940] 4-9-10 105 J-PGuillambert 10 — 3
(M Johnston) *led to 4f out: 6th and wkng rapidly st: t.o* **7/1**[2]

2m 8.23s (-0.81) **Going Correction** +0.225s/f (Good) **17 Ran SP% 130.5**

Speed ratings (Par 109):112,111,110,109,109 108,106,106,106,104 104,99,99,97,96 94,64

CSF £29.94 CT £279.49 TOTE £5.00: £1.80, £2.30, £3.00, £2.40; EX 38.30 Trifecta £277.60 Pool: £821.26 - 2.10 winning units..

Owner Dr John Hollowood **Bred** Dr J Hollowood **Trained** Broad Hinton, Wilts

FOCUS

Possibly not as competitive a handicap as the numbers suggested, with a number of exposed, out-of-form performers lining up. The form looks solid enough, though, rated around the third and fifth to form.

NOTEBOOK

Blue Bajan(IRE), who ran with credit on the All-Weather over the winter and early spring, including in Listed company, finished runner-up in the Cambridgeshire on his final start on turf, form which had been given a boost when the third Pinpoint won the Spring Cup at the weekend. Racing off a 6lb higher mark than at Newmarket, he picked up well from off the pace and ran out a fairly convincing winner. He looks Listed class and connections are already eyeing the Wolferton Stakes at Royal Ascot. (op 9-2 tchd 7-2)

Charlie Tokyo(IRE), 5lb higher for his Pontefract win, led home his stablemate and clearly remains an improving type. He could well face another small hike for this performance though, which will leave him vulnerable. (op 8-1)

Benandonner(USA), up with the pace throughout, seems just as effective over 1m2f as he is over a mile, and he ran another solid race in defeat. He was racing off a 10lb higher mark than when last successful, and, like his stablemate, looks likely to remain one to be shot at. (tchd 12-1)

Tabadul(IRE), who did best of the hold-up horses in a tactical affair at Kempton last time, overcame his poor draw to race prominently. He had every chance but is another who looks high enough in the handicap at present. (op 10-1)

Impeller(IRE) has a good record at this track having won three of his previous seven starts here, but his style of running does require luck in avoiding trouble. He did not get a smooth passage this time but was staying on strongly at the finish, and would almost certainly have been third at least with a clearer run.

Fort Churchill(IRE) did not handle the track particularly well but once again he was noted putting in some good late work. Three of his four wins have come over 1m4f, and a return to that distance will be of benefit to him.

Langford ran well on a few occasions last turf season without getting his head in front, and a fruitless All-Weather campaign has seen his mark drop to a fairly attractive level, but he has always been at his best over a bit shorter.

Counsel's Opinion(IRE), whose losing run stretches back two years, was slowly away and was towards the rear for much of the race. He made some late headway though, and was not disgraced in the circumstances. Although an old boy now, he retains ability. (op 20-1)

Wovoka(IRE) looked fit enough and was given every chance but possibly needed this seasonal reappearance as he did not see it out as well as some.

Luberon, who got the run of things when successful at Kempton last time, got to the front again but he lost the advantage rounding the turn into the straight and was in trouble very quickly. Something may have been amiss. Official explanation: trainer had no explanation for the poor form shown (op 6-1)

1246 TROY O'CONNOR MEMORIAL MAIDEN STKS — 1m 114y

4:00 (4:07) (Class 5) 3-Y-0+ **£4,533** (£1,348; £674; £336) **Stalls** Low

Form — RPR

25 **1** **Shot Gun**[17] [954] 3-8-11 DarryllHolland 5 — 76+
(M R Channon) *lw: t.k.h: trckd ldr: rdn to ld 2f out: hung lft fnl f: styd on* **10/1**

3- **2** *1 ¼* **Fashion Model**[204] [5754] 3-8-6 PhilipRobinson 3 — 70+
(M A Jarvis) *hld up in 4th: effrt towards inner to chal 2f out: pressed wnr after: hld whn hmpd 150yds out: hld on for 2nd* **5/4**[1]

55-5 **3** *shd* **King Joshua (IRE)**[13] [1010] 3-8-11 74 JohnEgan 6 — 73
(D R C Elsworth) *swtg: t.k.h: trckd ldng pair: rdn and hanging lft over 2f out: nt qckn sn after: styd on ins fnl f* **14/1**

03-2 **4** *nk* **Leon Knights**[17] [954] 3-8-11 78 NickyMackay 4 — 75+
(G A Butler) *lw: hld up in 5th: rdn and struggling wl over 2f out: nt clr run and swtchd rt jst over 1f out: r.o last 150yds: gaining at fin* **8/1**[3]

2 **5** *½* **Easterly Breeze (IRE)**[24] [864] 3-8-11 MartinDwyer 2 — 72+
(W R Muir) *lw: hld up in 6th: rdn and struggling 3f out: kpt on steadily fr over 1f out* **12/1**

0- **6** *nk* **Optical Illusion (USA)**[197] [5883] 3-8-11 JamieSpencer 1 — 70
(E A L Dunlop) *bit bkwd: s.i.s: hld up in last: awkward downhill 4f out: effrt on outer over 2f out: chsng ldrs but hanging lft: one pce over 1f out* **11/4**[2]

040- **7** *2 ½* **Rock Anthem (IRE)**[194] [5939] 3-8-11 74 LDettori 7 — 65
(J L Dunlop) *lw: led at stdy pce: rdn and hdd 2f out: wknd fnl f* **10/1**

1m 50.12s (4.38) **Going Correction** +0.225s/f (Good) **7 Ran SP% 114.8**

Speed ratings (Par 103):89,87,87,87,87 86,84

CSF £23.27 TOTE £11.50: £3.60, £1.60; EX 25.00.

Owner Sheikh Ahmed Al Maktoum **Bred** Darley **Trained** West Ilsley, Berks

■ Stewards' Enquiry : Darryll Holland caution: careless riding

FOCUS

A steadily-run maiden won in a very slow time, 2.2 seconds slower than the following three-year-old handicap. The form is rated around the winner and fifth.

1247 JOHNNY & CORA MCLOUGHLIN MEMORIAL STKS (H'CAP) — 1m 114y

4:35 (4:40) (Class 5) (0-75,77) 3-Y-0 **£4,533** (£1,348; £674; £336) **Stalls** Low

Form — RPR

221- **1** **Malyana**[194] [5933] 3-9-4 75 PhilipRobinson 7 — 80+
(M A Jarvis) *lw: led for 1f: trckd ldr: led again wl over 1f out: edgd lft sn after: jnd ins fnl f: fnd ex nr fin* **9/4**[1]

21- **2** *hd* **Docofthebay (IRE)**[174] [6303] 3-9-3 74 JamieSpencer 15 — 79
(J A Osborne) *dwlt: hld up in rr: 9th st: prog on outer over 2f out: hung lft but jnd wnr 100yds out: outbattled nr fin* **9/2**[2]

-544 **3** *1 ¾* **Arena's Dream (USA)**[8] [1076] 3-9-1 72 PaulHanagan 9 — 73+
(R A Fahey) *warm: in tch in midfield: 8th st: sn rdn: hanging lft fr over 2f out: no real prog tl r.o wl fnl f: tk 3rd on line* **8/1**[3]

2-53 **4** *hd* **Baltic Belle (IRE)**[21] [919] 3-9-0 71 PatDobbs 14 — 72
(R Hannon) *chsd ldrs: 6th st: effrt towards outer over 2f out: clsd but hanging lft over 1f out: kpt on same pce* **25/1**

-031 **5** *¾* **Musical Beat**[5] [1131] 3-9-6 77 6ex MickyFenton 1 — 80+
(Miss V Haigh) *lw: prom: 4th st: cl 3rd whn hmpd on inner 2f out: nt rcvr but kpt on same pce* **8/1**[3]

54-4 **6** *¾* **Murrin (IRE)**[23] [886] 3-9-4 75 DaneO'Neill 3 — 75+
(T G Mills) *hld up in midfield: 7th st: nt clr run wl over 1f out: plld out and styd on fnl f: nt rch ldrs* **11/1**

41-4 **7** *½* **Benny The Bat**[87] [275] 3-9-4 75 SteveDrowne 4 — 71
(H Morrison) *wnt rt s: plld hrd and prom: 3rd st: hanging over 2f out: wknd jst over 1f out* **12/1**

0-40 **8** *4* **Royal Guest**[33] [738] 3-8-7 64 MartinDwyer 10 — 52
(M R Channon) *lw: led after 1f and set decent pce: hdd & wknd wl over 1f out* **33/1**

60-5 **9** *1 ¼* **Stagehand (IRE)**[23] [889] 3-8-13 70 JimCrowley 2 — 63+
(B R Millman) *chsd ldrs: 5th st: sn rdn: hanging lft over 2f out: btn whn squeezed out 1f out: eased* **20/1**

4125 **10** *1* **Professor Twinkle**[49] [638] 3-9-3 74 PaulDoe 5 — 57
(W J Knight) *hmpd s: hld up in last: gng wl enough 3f out: hanging bdly lft after and no prog* **12/1**

123- **11** *¾* **Situla (IRE)**[136] [6777] 3-9-1 72 JimmyQuinn 13 — 54
(H J L Dunlop) *settled in rr: 10th st: rdn and no prog over 2f out* **33/1**

531- **12** *1 ½* **Putra Laju (IRE)**[133] [6808] 3-9-1 72 EddieAhern 12 — 51
(J W Hills) *a wl in rr: 11th st: shkn up and no prog 3f out* **33/1**

1-33 **13** *11* **Prince Of Charm (USA)**[25] [843] 3-8-11 68 (p) BrettDoyle 11 — 23
(P Mitchell) *hld up: 12th st: sn wknd and wl bhd* **9/1**

1m 47.92s (2.18) **Going Correction** +0.225s/f (Good) **13 Ran SP% 122.3**

Speed ratings (Par 98):99,98,97,97,96 95,95,91,90,89 89,87,77

CSF £11.00 CT £71.06 TOTE £3.20: £1.50, £1.70, £3.20; EX 13.20 Place 6 £40.81, Place 5 £16.73.

Owner Sheikh Ahmed Al Maktoum **Bred** Darley **Trained** Newmarket, Suffolk

■ Stewards' Enquiry : Martin Dwyer two-day ban: careless riding (May 7-8)

FOCUS

A fair handicap in which the two of the least exposed runners in the line-up came out best, as a result of which the form is not easy to rate.

Docofthebay(IRE) ◆ Official explanation: jockey said colt hung left closing stages

Stagehand(IRE) Official explanation: jockey said gelding was denied a clear run

Professor Twinkle Official explanation: jockey said colt hung left in straight

T/Jkpt: £27,341.20 to a £1 stake. Pool: £115,526.50. 3.00 winning tickets. T/Plt: £41.90 to a £1 stake. Pool: £97,364.00. 1,693.50 winning tickets. T/Qpdt: £12.70 to a £1 stake. Pool: £4,562.60. 264.30 winning tickets. JN

[938] KEMPTON (A.W) (R-H)

Wednesday, April 25

OFFICIAL GOING: Standard

Wind: Nil Weather: Fine

1248 JYSKEBANK.COM H'CAP — 5f (P)

6:20 (6:21) (Class 6) (0-60,60) 3-Y-0 **£2,047** (£604; £302) **Stalls** High

Form — RPR

-325 **1** **Scarlett Heart (IRE)**[30] [786] 3-8-13 55 SebSanders 9 — 68+
(P J Makin) *hld up in midfield: hdwy over 2f out: rdn to ld over 1f out: sn in command: readily* **7/2**[1]

2225 **2** *3* **Ioweyou**[16] [970] 3-9-0 **56**....(b) LPKeniry 12 58
(J S Moore) *led for 1f: cl up: ev ch 2f out: rdn over 1f out: outpcd by wnr fnl f* **4/1**[2]

006- **3** *3/4* **Misaine (IRE)**[224] [5288] 3-8-13 **55**.... NickyMackay 3 54
(T J Etherington) *led after 1f: rdn and hdd over 1f out: hung bdly lft and outpcd fnl f* **25/1**

50-6 **4** *nk* **Back In The Red (IRE)**[21] [918] 3-9-4 **60**.... PaulHanagan 1 58
(R A Harris) *t.k.h: cl up: ev ch 2f out: rdn over 1f out: carried lft fnl f: kpt on same pce* **13/2**

0642 **5** *1 3/4* **Kilvickeon (IRE)**[16] [970] 3-8-7 **49**.... RichardMullen 7 41+
(Peter Grayson) *missed break and v.s.a: hdwy 1/2-way: hung lft last 2f: r.o: nvr nrr* **13/2**

4-30 **6** *1/2* **Eastern Princess**[16] [974] 3-8-4 **46** oh1....(v) RichardThomas 6 36
(J A Geake) *chsd ldrs: lost pl and rdn 1/2-way: kpt on same pce last 2f* **14/1**

0000 **7** *1/2* **Redflo**[4] [1151] 3-7-12 **47** oh1 ow1.... SophieDoyle(7) 10 35
(Ms J S Doyle) *squeezed s: hld up in midfield: hdwy wl over 1f out: no prog fnl f* **66/1**

0-36 **8** *shd* **O'Dwyer (IRE)**[86] [295] 3-8-10 **52**....(p) SilvestreDeSousa 11 40
(A D Brown) *wnt lft s: in tch: rdn 1/2-way: wknd wl over 1f out* **16/1**

5526 **9** *1/2* **The Tinker Man**[12] [1031] 3-8-3 **52**.... FrankiePickard(7) 8 38
(M D I Usher) *sn outpcd in rr: hung lft but r.o last 2f: nvr nrr* **7/1**

050- **10** *2 1/2* **Princely Royal**[199] [5829] 3-8-11 **56**.... AmirQuinn(3) 5 33
(J J Bridger) *bhd: brief effrt u.p 2f out: wknd over 1f out* **33/1**

0-50 **11** *1 1/2* **Wendy's Boy**[29] [798] 3-8-10 **52**.... DaneO'Neill 4 24
(R Hannon) *taken down early: racd wd: prom tl wknd wl over 1f out: eased ins fnl f* **11/2**[3]

61.45 secs (1.05) **Going Correction** +0.05s/f (Slow) **11** Ran SP% **117.6**
Speed ratings (Par 96):93,88,87,86,83 82,82,81,81,77 74
CSF £17.08 CT £309.06 TOTE £3.80: £1.70, £1.60, £7.30; EX 10.30.
Owner Ten Horsepower **Bred** Mrs P J Makin **Trained** Ogbourne Maisey, Wilts
■ Stewards' Enquiry : Nicky Mackay three-day ban: careless riding (May 7-9)

FOCUS
A modest sprint handicap in which the draw played its usual part. The form looks very ordinary with the runner-up the best guide and could rate fractionally higher.
Kilvickeon(IRE) Official explanation: jockey said gelding reared in stalls

1249 SURREY HERALD H'CAP 1m 2f (P)
6:50 (6:51) (Class 6) (0-65,65) 4-Y-0+ **£2,047** (£604; £302) **Stalls** High

Form RPR

000/ **1** **Charmatic (IRE)**[150] [5772] 6-9-4 **65**.... ChrisCatlin 9 72
(Andrew Turnell) *chsd ldrs: rdn wl over 1f out: kpt on u.p to ld ins fnl f: styd on wl* **16/1**

400- **2** *1/2* **Pothos Way (GR)**[192] [5992] 4-9-1 **62**.... JimCrowley 6 68
(P R Chamings) *in tch: hdwy over 3f out: chsd ldrs and rdn 2f out: kpt on u.p fnl f* **14/1**

0602 **3** *1/2* **First Friend (IRE)**[49] [634] 6-8-8 **62**.... HaddenFrost(7) 12 67
(M Hill) *chsd ldr tl 6f out: rdn wl over 1f out: led ins fnl f: sn hdd: fdd nr fin* **5/1**[3]

043- **4** *shd* **Duelling Banjos**[35] [6878] 8-9-1 **62**.... DaneO'Neill 13 67
(J Akehurst) *chsd ldrs: lost pl wl over 2f out: rdn 2f out: r.o fnl f: nt quite rch ldrs* **8/1**

050- **5** *nk* **Bold Cross (IRE)**[314] [2583] 4-8-13 **63**.... SaleemGolam(3) 8 67
(E G Bevan) *t.k.h: led: rdn wl over 1f out: hdd ins fnl f: kpt on same pce* **25/1**

6 *nk* **Tibouchina (IRE)**[207] [5698] 4-9-0 **61**.... SebSanders 4 65
(R M Beckett) *s.i.s: hld up in midfield: hdwy over 4f out: chsd ldrs over 2f out: rdn and kpt on same pce wl over 1f out* **16/1**

0605 **7** *3/4* **Street Life (IRE)**[29] [805] 9-8-9 **63**.... AlanRutter(7) 14 65+
(W J Musson) *hld up in rr: hdwy over 2f out: n.m.r and swtchd lft 1f out: r.o: nvr able to chal* **9/2**[2]

6022 **8** *nk* **Hawk Arrow (IRE)**[27] [819] 5-9-1 **62**.... GeorgeBaker 1 64
(G L Moore) *stdd s: dropped in bhd: hdwy on outer wl over 2f out: rdn 2f out: kpt on fnl f: nt rch ldrs* **3/1**[1]

20-4 **9** *2* **Viable**[27] [819] 5-8-6 **60**.... JosephWalsh(7) 10 58
(Mrs P Sly) *s.i.s: sn pushed along to chse ldrs: wnt 2nd 6f out tl wl over 1f out: sn wknd* **20/1**

-601 **10** *1* **Siena Star (IRE)**[79] [363] 9-9-2 **63**.... MickyFenton 5 59
(Stef Liddiard) *hld up in midfield: rdn and no prog over 2f out: no ch fnl f* **9/1**

300- **11** *2 1/2* **Oakley Absolute**[181] [6189] 5-9-4 **65**.... RichardHughes 2 56
(R Hannon) *hld up in rr: rdn 2f out: no hdwy* **12/1**

4004 **12** *3* **Makai**[29] [799] 4-8-9 **59** ow1.... AmirQuinn(3) 3 45
(J J Bridger) *t.k.h: hld up in midfield: rdn wl over 3f out: wknd over 2f out* **16/1**

2100 **13** *43* **King's Ransom**[21] [928] 4-9-2 **63**.... RichardMullen 7 —
(W R Muir) *hld up in rr: rdn 5f out: lost tch over 3f out: t.o* **20/1**

2m 9.10s (0.10) **Going Correction** +0.05s/f (Slow) **13** Ran SP% **126.3**
Speed ratings (Par 101):101,100,100,100,99 99,99,98,97,96 94,92,—
CSF £228.83 CT £1305.53 TOTE £27.40: £7.40, £7.60, £3.00; EX 563.00.
Owner T L Morshead **Bred** Patsy Byrne **Trained** Broad Hinton, Wilts

FOCUS
A routine handicap of its type and, with the field using the inner loop, there was not a great deal of room over the last furlong or so, hence the principals rather finishing in a heap. The form is limited overall through the fifth on last year's form.
Hawk Arrow(IRE) Official explanation: jockey said gelding never travelled
King's Ransom Official explanation: trainer's rep said gelding finished distressed

1250 JYSKE BANK PRIVATE BANKING COPENHAGEN MEDIAN AUCTION MAIDEN STKS 1m 3f (P)
7:20 (7:22) (Class 6) 3-4-Y-0 **£2,047** (£604; £302) **Stalls** High

Form RPR

622- **1** **Coeur De Lionne (IRE)**[210] [5622] 3-8-8 75.... SteveDrowne 7 73+
(R Charlton) *trckd ldng pair: swtchd lft 2f out: sn led and nudged clr: fnl f: eased nr fin* **4/9**[1]

2 *3 1/2* **Alexander Guru** 3-8-8.... TedDurcan 5 58
(M Blanshard) *led at stdy pce: rdn over 2f out: hdd 2f out: kpt on but no ch w wnr* **20/1**

023- **3** *1* **Aussie Cricket (FR)**[160] [6498] 3-8-3 68.... ChrisCatlin 6 52
(D J Coakley) *stdd after s: t.k.h: in tch: rdn and hdwy to chse ldr over 2f out tl 2f out: sn outpcd* **5/1**[2]

4 *nk* **Leander** 3-8-8.... TPQueally 2 56+
(B R Johnson) *s.i.s: hld up in last pair: hdwy 2f out: r.o u.p fnl f: nrst fin* **14/1**[3]

606- **5** *2 1/2* **The Graig**[249] [4588] 3-8-8 52.... RobertHavlin 9 52
(C Drew) *hld up in tch in midfield: rdn over 2f out: wknd over 1f out* **33/1**

6 *1 1/4* **Just An Angel (IRE)** 3-8-3.... JimmyQuinn 8 45
(A P Jarvis) *w.w in tch: rdn over 2f out: sn outpcd* **14/1**[3]

00- **7** *2* **Keagles (ITY)**[152] [6587] 4-9-8.... RichardThomas 4 41
(J E Long) *pressed ldr tl rdn over 2f out: wknd 2f out* **100/1**

0 **8** *nk* **Laughing Game**[13] [1012] 3-8-3.... HayleyTurner 1 41
(M L W Bell) *t.k.h: hld up in tch on outer: rdn 3f out: wknd over 2f out* **16/1**

9 *1* **Glentimon (IRE)** 3-8-8.... FrankieMcDonald 3 44
(S Kirk) *s.i.s: hld up in last pair: rdn over 3f out: outpcd over 2f out* **25/1**

2m 28.33s (5.65) **Going Correction** +0.05s/f (Slow)
WFA 3 from 4yo 19lb **9** Ran SP% **117.7**
Speed ratings (Par 101):81,78,77,77,75 74,73,73,72
CSF £16.54 TOTE £1.50: £1.02, £5.80, £1.30; EX 15.20.
Owner Mountgrange Stud **Bred** Hawthorn Villa Stud **Trained** Beckhampton, Wilts
■ Stewards' Enquiry : Steve Drowne one-day ban: careless riding (May 7)

FOCUS
An uncompetitive maiden run at a dawdle resulting in a pedestrian winning time for a race of its class and the form looks modest and best rated around those in the first four.

1251 JYSKE BANK PRIVATE BANKING COPENHAGEN H'CAP 1m (P)
7:50 (7:50) (Class 6) (0-65,64) 4-Y-0+ **£2,047** (£604; £302) **Stalls** High

Form RPR

3541 **1** **Apex**[16] [976] 6-8-4 **57** ow3.... HaddenFrost(7) 11 68+
(M Hill) *sn led: mde rest: rdn over 1f out and edgd rt briefly ins fnl f: r.o strly* **9/2**[1]

3030 **2** *1* **Seneschal**[5] [1118] 6-9-4 **64**.... DaneO'Neill 8 73
(A B Haynes) *t.k.h: trckd ldrs: hdwy on inner over 2f out: chsd wnr 2f out: swtchd lft ins fnl f: kpt on* **8/1**

050- **3** *2 1/2* **Princess Lavinia**[147] [6652] 4-9-0 **60**.... SteveDrowne 5 63
(G Wragg) *hld up in midfield: short of room 5f out: rdn and hdwy over 2f out: chsd ldng pair ins fnl f: kpt on* **8/1**

360- **4** *1* **Murrumbidgee (IRE)**[180] [6206] 4-8-7 **58**.... PatrickHills(5) 1 59
(J W Hills) *hld up: hdwy on outer over 3f out: kpt on over 1f out: nt trble ldrs* **8/1**

606- **5** *1/2* **Fangorn Forest (IRE)**[278] [3708] 4-8-12 **63**....(p) TolleyDean(5) 4 63
(R A Harris) *s.i.s: bhd: rdn 3f out: styd on fnl f: nvr trbld ldrs* **20/1**

2421 **6** *nk* **Over To You Bert**[29] [800] 8-8-7 **53**.... RichardHughes 6 52
(R J Hodges) *t.k.h: chsd wnr: ev ch and rdn 2f: wknd over 1f out* **6/1**[3]

-230 **7** *1 3/4* **Sedgwick**[42] [675] 5-9-3 **63**.... TPQueally 7 58
(J G Given) *hld up in tch: hdwy 4f out: chsd ldrs over 3f out: rdn and wknd over 2f out* **15/2**

0011 **8** *nk* **War Of The Roses (IRE)**[30] [789] 4-8-8 **54**.... JosedeSouza 3 48
(R Brotherton) *t.k.h: chsd ldrs: rdn 2f out: wknd over 1f out* **5/1**[2]

5-00 **9** *hd* **Baba Ghanoush**[51] [614] 5-9-0 **60**.... PaulDoe 10 54
(W Jarvis) *hld up in mdfield: hdwy over 3f out: rdn over 2f out: wknd wl over 1f out* **12/1**

240- **10** *hd* **Cove Mountain (IRE)**[120] [6942] 5-8-11 **57**.... LPKeniry 2 50
(S Kirk) *hld up in tch: hdwy on outer 4f out: rdn and wknd over 2f out* **11/1**

10/0 **11** *9* **Registrar**[21] [930] 5-9-4 **64**.... DMylonas 12 37
(Mrs C A Dunnett) *t.k.h: chsd ldrs tl wknd and hmpd 2f out* **33/1**

050/ **12** *10* **Belshazzar (USA)**[389] [4493] 6-8-2 **55**.... JosephWalsh(7) 13 5
(D C O'Brien) *slowly away: a bhd: lost tch over 3f out: t.o* **100/1**

1m 40.65s (-0.15) **Going Correction** +0.05s/f (Slow) **12** Ran SP% **119.0**
Speed ratings (Par 101):102,101,98,97,97 96,94,94,94,94 85,75
CSF £39.97 CT £288.41 TOTE £6.30: £2.30, £2.90, £3.10; EX 40.80.
Owner Martin Hill **Bred** P D And Mrs C E Player And Jonathon Jay **Trained** Broadhempston, Devon
■ Stewards' Enquiry : Hadden Frost two-day ban: careless riding (May 7-8)
Dane O'Neill two-day ban: careless riding (May 9-10)

FOCUS
A low-grade handicap, but quite a competitive one and sound form rated through the runner-up. The race only concerned the front pair from some way out though.

1252 DIGIBET POKER H'CAP 6f (P)
8:20 (8:20) (Class 5) (0-75,74) 4-Y-0+ **£3,886** (£1,156; £577; £288) **Stalls** High

Form RPR

0334 **1** **Dvinsky (USA)**[22] [902] 6-8-10 **66**.... IanMongan 9 78
(P Howling) *mde all: rdn and wnt 2l clr 2f out: in command after: eased nr fin* **8/1**

13-2 **2** *1 3/4* **Mr Cellophane**[9] [1063] 4-9-3 **73**.... EddieAhern 8 80+
(J R Jenkins) *hld up in midfield: hdwy wl over 1f out: rdn over 1f out: chsd wnr ins fnl f: kpt on but nt trble wnr* **5/2**[1]

2022 **3** *1* **Effective**[5] [1121] 7-9-3 **73**.... JamieSpencer 5 77
(A P Jarvis) *t.k.h: chsd wnr for 2f: rdn to chse wnr and ev ch 2f out: kpt on same pce fnl f* **4/1**[2]

00-5 **4** *1/2* **Norcroft**[31] [774] 5-8-8 **64**....(p) DMylonas 11 66
(Mrs C A Dunnett) *t.k.h: chsd ldrs on inner: rdn 2f out: kpt on same pce fnl f* **12/1**

0-00 **5** *1/2* **Gavarnie Beau (IRE)**[51] [621] 4-8-9 **65**.... TedDurcan 3 66+
(M Blanshard) *stdd s: hld up: hdwy and effrt on inner over 2f out: nt clr run 2f out: r.o ins fnl f: nt trble ldrs* **25/1**

00-6 **6** *hd* **Dictatrix**[16] [979] 4-9-2 **72**....(b) SebSanders 2 72
(J M P Eustace) *s.i.s: dropped in bhd: rdn over 2f out: styd on fnl f: nt rch ldrs* **20/1**

0000 **7** *1 1/4* **Anfield Dream**[50] [626] 5-8-6 **62**.... NickyMackay 7 58
(J R Jenkins) *chsd ldrs on outer: rdn 2f out: wknd ins fnl f* **33/1**

-110 **8** *shd* **Greenwood**[2] [1200] 9-8-10 **66**.... RobertHavlin 6 62+
(P G Murphy) *hld up bhd: rdn 2f out: sme late hdwy: n.d* **9/1**

0130 **9** *1 1/4* **Sir Douglas**[14] [1004] 4-9-4 **74**.... PaulHanagan 4 66
(R A Harris) *bhd: rdn over 2f out: no imp* **7/1**[3]

-236 **10** *1/2* **Morse (IRE)**[31] [774] 6-9-1 **74**.... RichardKingscote(3) 1 65
(J A Osborne) *chsd wnr after 2f tl 2f out: sn wknd* **10/1**

060 **11** *1/2* **Regal Royale**[4] [1165] 4-9-0 **70**.... RichardMullen 10 59
(Peter Grayson) *in tch: rdn 1/2-way: wknd wl over 1f out* **10/1**

1m 13.33s (-0.37) **Going Correction** +0.05s/f (Slow) **11** Ran SP% **119.6**
Speed ratings (Par 103):104,101,100,99,99 98,97,96,95,94 93
CSF £28.13 CT £95.44 TOTE £11.90: £2.90, £1.40, £1.80; EX 46.20.
Owner Richard Berenson **Bred** Eclipse Bloodstock And Tipperary Bloodstock **Trained** Newmarket, Suffolk
■ Stewards' Enquiry : Ian Mongan three-day ban: careless riding (May 7-9)

FOCUS
A fair handicap, but the winner was allowed an easy lead and this is probably not strong form for the grade, with the winner rated to last year's turf form.
Morse(IRE) Official explanation: jockey said gelding had no more to give

1253 DIGIBET SPORTS BETTING H'CAP — 2m (P)

8:50 (8:50) (Class 4) (0-80,80) 4-Y-O+ **£6,477** (£1,927; £963; £481) **Stalls** High

Form — RPR

222- **1** **Dhehdaah**^{18} [2357] 6-8-8 **63**................ MickyFenton 9 75+
(Mrs P Sly) *hld up in midfield: hdwy over 2f out: rdn to chse ldr 2f out: led over 1f out: styd on wl* **6/1**^{2}

4101 **2** *2* **Newnham (IRE)**^{25} [844] 6-8-12 **74**................ JackMitchell(7) 5 87+
(J R Boyle) *hld up bhd: effrt on inner whn stmbld over 2f out: swtchd lft ins fnl f: r.o wl to go 2nd nr fin: nvr nrr* **9/2**^{1}

20-0 **3** *nk* **Most Definitely (IRE)**^{32} [753] 7-9-2 **71**................ JimCrowley 4 79
(R M Stronge) *stdd s: hld up in last: gd hdwy 3f out: chsd ldrs 2f out: rdn and styd on steadily ins fnl f: nrst fin* **33/1**

54-2 **4** *nk* **Cantabilly (IRE)**^{14} [1003] 4-9-7 **80**................ RichardHughes 14 88
(R J Hodges) *chsd ldrs: wnt 2nd over 5f out: led over 2f out: sn rdn: hdd over 1f out: kpt on same pce: lost 2 pls nr fin* **6/1**^{2}

4130 **5** *1* **Synonymy**^{15} [994] 4-8-7 **66**................(b) SteveDrowne 6 73
(M Blanshard) *w.w bhd ldrs: hdwy 4f out: kpt on same pce u.p last 2f* **12/1**

4512 **6** *2* **Salut Saint Cloud**^{25} [844] 6-9-1 **70**................(p) SimonWhitworth 13 74
(G L Moore) *w.w in tch: hdwy to chse ldrs 3f out: rdn and kpt on same pce over 1f out* **6/1**^{2}

2125 **7** *1 3/4* **Three Thieves (UAE)**^{27} [813] 4-8-12 **71**................ TedDurcan 7 73
(M S Saunders) *w.w in midfield: hdwy 4f out: gng wl 3f out: rdn 2f out: fnd nil and sn wknd* **11/1**

2-12 **8** *6* **Arsad (IRE)**^{73} [434] 4-8-11 **70**................ EddieAhern 8 65
(C E Brittain) *hld up in rr: hdwy over 4f out: rdn over 3f out: wknd 2f out* **7/1**^{3}

10-2 **9** *nk* **Star Of Canterbury (IRE)**^{32} [753] 4-8-10 **69**................ JamieSpencer 3 64
(A P Jarvis) *t.k.h: hld up in rr: hdwy 4f out: rdn over 2f out: wknd over 1f out* **8/1**

000- **10** *7* **Our Monogram**^{212} [5564] 11-9-2 **71**................ GeorgeBaker 11 57
(R M Beckett) *chsd ldr tl rdn 5f out: wknd 3f out* **33/1**

-005 **11** *11* **Speagle (IRE)**^{8} [1083] 5-9-10 **79**................ DanielTudhope 12 52
(D Carroll) *led: clr 1/2-way tl 4f out: hdd over 2f out: sn wknd: eased ins fnl f: t.o* **25/1**

025- **12** *12* **Hiddensee (USA)**^{36} [3098] 5-9-11 **80**................ SebSanders 2 39
(M Wigham) *racd in midfield: rdn 7f out: rdn and lost pl 5f out: no ch last 3f: t.o* **20/1**

-153 **13** *1 1/4* **Theatre Groom (USA)**^{33} [747] 8-8-13 **68**................ IanMongan 1 25
(M R Bosley) *t.k.h: chsd ldrs on outer: rdn 5f out: wknd over 3f out: eased fnl f: t.o* **12/1**

3m 29.19s (-2.21) **Going Correction** +0.05s/f (Slow)
WFA 4 from 5yo+ 4lb **13** Ran SP% **122.9**
Speed ratings (Par 105):107,106,105,105,105 104,103,100,100,96 91,85,84
CSF £32.67 CT £837.89 TOTE £8.10: £2.20, £2.00, £7.60; EX 56.80.
Owner D Bayliss, T Davies, G Libson & P Sly **Bred** Wickfield Farm Partnership **Trained** Thorney, Cambs

FOCUS
A fair staying handicap and solid, reliable form.

1254 DIGIBET CASINO H'CAP — 1m 4f (P)

9:20 (9:20) (Class 6) (0-50,50) 4-Y-O+ **£2,047** (£604; £302) **Stalls** Centre

Form — RPR

1006 **1** **Comeintothespace (IRE)**^{12} [1025] 5-8-12 **50**................ DaneO'Neill 2 57
(R A Farrant) *stdd s: hld up: hdwy 5f out: rdn 2f out: led ins fnl f: r.o strly* **11/1**

1032 **2** *1/2* **Danelor (IRE)**^{36} [716] 9-8-12 **50**................(p) PaulHanagan 8 56
(D Shaw) *stdd s: t.k.h: hld up in rr: hdwy 3f out: rdn over 1f out: ev ch ins fnl f: nt pce of wnr nr fin* **11/2**^{2}

50/0 **3** *3/4* **Sea Mark**^{12} [1027] 11-8-12 **50**................ SilvestreDeSousa 1 55
(A D Brown) *bhd: hdwy over 2f out: styd on under and ev ch 1f out: unable qckn wl ins fnl f* **25/1**

/00- **4** *1/2* **Inn For The Dancer**^{36} [1204] 5-8-5 **50**................ HaddenFrost(7) 6 54
(J C Fox) *hld up in bhd: hdwy on outer over 3f out: rdn and outpcd over 2f out: r.o wl ins fnl f: nrst fin* **10/1**

53-0 **5** *nk* **Adage**^{12} [1026] 4-8-11 **50**................(t) ChrisCatlin 3 54
(David Pinder) *s.i.s: sn in tch: hdwy to chse ldrs 4f out: rdn and outpcd over 2f out: kpt on u.p ins fnl f* **20/1**

000- **6** *shd* **Shamrock Bay**^{37} [5960] 5-8-10 **48**................ EddieAhern 9 52
(C R Dore) *hld up bhd ldrs: hdwy to ld over 2f out: rdn wl over 1f out: hdd ins fnl f: wknd nr fin* **5/1**^{1}

300- **7** *3/4* **Snake Skin**^{149} [6627] 4-8-11 **50**................ JimCrowley 13 52
(J Gallagher) *trckd ldrs: rdn over 2f out: ev ch wl over 1f out tl wknd last 100yds* **33/1**

4646 **8** *3/4* **Come What July (IRE)**^{30} [792] 6-8-5 **48**................ PatrickHills(5) 12 49
(D Shaw) *hld up bhd: rdn and gd hdwy on inner over 2f out: ev ch over 1f: wknd last 100yds* **5/1**^{1}

2461 **9** *1* **Trysting Grove (IRE)**^{29} [804] 6-8-7 **48**................ SaleemGolam(3) 14 48
(E G Bevan) *t.k.h: hld up in midfield: effrt on inner over 2f out: chsd ldrs and rdn 2f out: wknd ins fnl f* **15/2**

06-2 **10** *1/2* **Bill Bennett (FR)**^{39} [71] 6-8-12 **50**................ OscarUrbina 5 49
(J Jay) *chsd ldrs: rdn 2f out: wknd 1f out: eased whn btn ins fnl f* **6/1**^{3}

100/ **11** *4* **Bretton**^{656} [3317] 6-8-5 **48**................ NataliaGemelova(5) 11 40
(J E Long) *t.k.h: chsd ldr tl led over 5f out: hdd over 2f out: sn rdn: wknd over 1f out* **25/1**

005- **12** *1/2* **Mamichor**^{275} [3804] 4-8-10 **49**................ SebSanders 4 41
(B R Johnson) *t.k.h: chsd ldrs tl wnt 2nd over 5f out tl over 2f out: wknd qckly over 1f out* **8/1**

100- **13** *dist* **Surdoue**^{399} [696] 7-8-11 **49**................ HayleyTurner 10 —
(D Morris) *led tl rdn and hdd over 5f out: sn wl bhd: virtually p.u last 3f: t.o* **25/1**

2m 37.17s (0.27) **Going Correction** +0.05s/f (Slow)
WFA 4 from 5yo+ 1lb **13** Ran SP% **122.5**
Speed ratings (Par 101):101,100,100,99,99 99,99,98,97,97 94,94,—
CSF £67.40 CT £1513.32 TOTE £14.00: £3.20, £2.20, £5.40; EX 107.10 Place 6 £54.28, Place 5 £28.06.
Owner Rodney Farrant **Bred** D And Mrs D Veitch **Trained** Upper Lambourn, Berks
■ Stewards' Enquiry : Saleem Golam four-day ban: used whip with excessive force (May 7-10)

FOCUS
A terrible race and they finished in a bunch. The form looks sound though, rated around the first two.

Bill Bennett(FR) Official explanation: jockey said gelding ran flat
T/Plt: £221.20 to a £1 stake. Pool: £48,045.70. 158.55 winning tickets. T/Qpdt: £6.80 to a £1 stake. Pool: £3,931.90. 423.70 winning tickets. SP

1086 BEVERLEY (R-H)

Thursday, April 26

OFFICIAL GOING: Good to firm (good in places)
First two races hand-timed.
Wind: Strong, across

1255 RACING AGAIN ON 9TH MAY CLAIMING STKS — 5f

2:20 (2:21) (Class 5) 2-Y-O **£2,914** (£867; £433; £216) **Stalls** High

Form — RPR

3 **1** **Echostar**^{5} [1156] 2-8-8................ ChrisCatlin 6 56
(E J O'Neill) *prom: n.m.r and swtchd lft after 1f: hdwy 2f out: rdn to ld jst ins fnl f: sn drvn and kpt on* **9/2**^{3}

62 **2** *hd* **Shepherds Warning (IRE)**^{17} [971] 2-8-8................ JamieSpencer 2 55
(R M Stronge) *wnt rt s: cl up: rdn to ld and hung rt wl over 1f out: hdd ins fnl f: sn drvn and kpt on wl* **9/4**^{2}

3 *2 1/2* **Demure Princess** 2-8-3................ LiamJones(3) 1 43+
(W G M Turner) *wnt lft s and outpcd in rr tl hdwy wl over 1f out: styd on strly ins fnl f* **12/1**

0 **4** *1 1/2* **Limestone**^{18} [952] 2-9-7................ DarryllHolland 11 52
(J R Weymes) *chsd ldrs: rdn along 1/2-way and sn one pce* **12/1**

5 *1 3/4* **Majigal** 2-8-12................ PaulMulrennan 7 36
(M W Easterby) *s.i.s and bhd tl styd on appr fnl f* **8/1**

52 **6** *4* **Redbrick Girl**^{5} [1156] 2-9-2................ NCallan 3 24+
(K A Ryan) *bmpd s and sn led: rdn along 1/2-way: hdd wl over 1f out: wkng whn n.m.r over 1f out* **7/4**^{1}

0 **7** *2* **Stevie Smurnoff**^{24} [890] 2-9-3................ DaleGibson 10 17
(M W Easterby) *s.i.s: a in rr* **25/1**

64.60 secs (0.60) **Going Correction** -0.125s/f (Firm) **7** Ran SP% **115.7**
Speed ratings (Par 92):90,89,85,83,80 74,70
CSF £15.45 TOTE £6.90: £3.00, £1.50; EX 15.00.The winner was claimed by T. R. Pearson for £8,000.
Owner P D Player **Bred** P D And Mrs Player **Trained** Averham Park, Notts

FOCUS
An ordinary claimer that produced a good finish but the form looks fairly weak.

NOTEBOOK
Echostar, who finished two lengths behind the favourite on her debut, was also 2lb worse off. However, that experience and the stiffer track enabled her to stay on after being unable to keep up with the frenetic early gallop. Claimed after the race, she is modest but showed the right attitude, which should enable her to hold her own at a similar level. (op 10-3)
Shepherds Warning(IRE), having her first run for her new trainer after being claimed out of a seller last time, took on the favourite in the early stages and, after fighting off that rival, was immediately taken on by the winner. She showed plenty of heart for the battle and only went down narrowly, so should be capable of finding a race in this grade before long. (op 11-4 tchd 10-3)
Demure Princess ◆, who has a fair amount of speed on her dam's side, was a little slowly away and could not go the early gallop, but was noted keeping on in good style in the final couple of furlongs without ever looking likely to trouble the principals. She should benefit from the experience, looks to have a bit of scope and can pick up a small race on this evidence. (op 11-1 tchd 10-1)
Limestone, with the benefit of a previous run, broke well never went the pace and merely kept on as his rivals tired. (op 14-1)
Majigal, who got loose in the parade ring beforehand, missed the break and ran green, but did hint at some ability by running on late. (op 11-1)
Redbrick Girl, who beat the winner by two lengths at Thirsk last time, was also 2lb better off. She tried to put her experience to good use, but got in a battle for the lead and once headed dropped away quite quickly. She is clearly better than this but connections may be better off trying to settle her next time, as she does not appear to be lasting home. Official explanation: trainer's rep had no explanation for the poor form shown (op 2-1 tchd 6-4)

1256 HOLTBY BUILDERS LTD H'CAP — 1m 1f 207y

2:55 (2:55) (Class 5) (0-70,70) 3-Y-O **£3,886** (£1,156; £577; £288) **Stalls** High

Form — RPR

00-3 **1** **Madaarek (USA)**^{48} [649] 3-9-4 **70**................ RHills 4 79+
(E A L Dunlop) *trckd ldrs: hdwy over 2f out: rdn to chse ldr over 1f: sn drvn and styd on to ld nr fin* **8/11**^{1}

0132 **2** *3/4* **News Of The Day (IRE)**^{10} [1059] 3-8-3 **58**................ GregFairley(3) 1 66
(M Johnston) *cl up: led 3f out: rdn wl over 1f out: drvn ins fnl f: hdd and no ex nr fin* **10/3**^{2}

0-04 **3** *4* **Falimar**^{55} [603] 3-8-12 **64**................ TomEaves 3 64
(Miss J A Camacho) *led: rdn along and hdd 3f out: kpt on same pce u.p appr fnl f* **12/1**

60-0 **4** *1 1/4* **Dee Jay Wells**^{17} [968] 3-9-4 **70**................ PaulHanagan 7 68
(R A Fahey) *trckd ldrs: pushed along 3f out: rdn over 2f out and sn one pce* **14/1**

000- **5** *2 1/2* **Jafaru**^{234} [5067] 3-8-4 **56** oh9................ NickyMackay 8 49
(G A Butler) *chsd ldrs: rdn along 3f out: sn outpcd* **11/1**^{3}

546 **6** *3 1/2* **Giddywell**^{47} [655] 3-8-6 **63**................ RussellKennemore(5) 6 49
(R Hollinshead) *a in rr* **22/1**

05-6 **7** *10* **Seteem (USA)**^{26} [849] 3-9-3 **69**................ KimTinkler 2 36
(N Tinkler) *a in rr* **33/1**

2m 5.60s (-1.70) **Going Correction** -0.125s/f (Firm) **7** Ran SP% **111.0**
Speed ratings (Par 98):101,100,97,96,94 91,83
CSF £3.04 CT £12.22 TOTE £1.80: £1.20, £1.60; EX 2.90.
Owner Hamdan Al Maktoum **Bred** Shadwell Farm LLC **Trained** Newmarket, Suffolk

FOCUS
A modest handicap with a pace to match and the form limited by the proximity of the runner-up.

1257 SUE HAS GOT HER BUS PASS STKS (H'CAP) — 7f 100y

3:25 (3:26) (Class 3) (0-90,86) 3-Y-O **£7,124** (£2,119; £1,059; £529) **Stalls** High

Form — RPR

320- **1** **Voodoo Moon**^{216} [5503] 3-9-0 **85**................ GregFairley(3) 7 91
(M Johnston) *mde all: rdn over 2f out: drvn ent fnl f and styd on gamely* **14/1**

1- **2** *1* **Fragrancy (IRE)**^{188} [6073] 3-8-7 **75**................ PhilipRobinson 2 78
(M A Jarvis) *trckd wnr: effrt 3f out: rdn: edgd rt 2f out and over 1f out: drvn and kpt on ins fnl f* **6/1**

213- **3** *1/2* **White Deer (USA)**^{222} [5359] 3-9-2 **84**................ J-PGuillambert 8 88+
(M Johnston) *trckd ldrs on inner: hdwy 2f out: rdn: n.m.r and swtchd lft 1f out: kpt on u.p ins fnl f* **5/1**^{2}

512- **4** *hd* **Artimino**^{214} [5546] 3-9-2 **84**................ JamieSpencer 6 86+
(J R Fanshawe) *trckd ldrs: effrt and n.m.r 2f out and over 1f out: rdn and nt qckn ins fnl f* **7/4**^{1}

316- **5** *2 1/2* **Majounes Song**[273] 3874 3-9-4 **86** .... KDarley 1 81
(M Johnston) *chsd ldrs on outer: rdn along 2f out: drvn and wknd appr fnl f* **22/1**

3311 **6** *3/4* **Arch Of Titus (IRE)**[21] 935 3-8-12 **80** .... (t) NCallan 3 73
(M L W Bell) *s.i.s and lost 6l s: hdwy and in tch 3f out: rdn over 2f out and sn btn* **11/2**[3]

1- **7** *3 1/2* **Handsome Falcon**[219] 5442 3-8-10 **78** .... PaulHanagan 4 63
(R A Fahey) *in tch whn n.m.r after 2f: a in rr after* **14/1**

103- **8** *1/2* **Charlie Tipple**[232] 5113 3-8-6 **74** .... DavidAllan 5 57
(T D Easterby) *hld up in rr whn hmpd and snatched up after 2f: no ch after* **16/1**

1- **9** *nk* **Trepa (USA)**[232] 5112 3-8-11 **79** .... DarryllHolland 9 62
(W Jarvis) *in tch: effrt over 2f out: sn rdn and btn* **9/1**

1m 32.2s (-2.11) **Going Correction** -0.125s/f (Firm) 9 Ran SP% **116.3**
Speed ratings (Par 102):107,105,105,105,102 101,97,96,96
CSF £95.94 CT £489.38 TOTE £17.20: £3.20, £2.20, £2.10; EX 105.40.

Owner Mrs R Dick **Bred** Angmering Park Stud **Trained** Middleham Moor, N Yorks

FOCUS
An decent and interesting handicap and a fair winning time for a race like this, 1.27sec than the later handicap for older horses, so rated positively.

NOTEBOOK
Voodoo Moon had some decent form on a sound surface as a juvenile, and showed she had trained on with a fine performance from the front on this return to action. She was faced with several challengers in the straight but fought them all off and, although she will go up in the weights for this, her enthusiasm will always stand her in good stead. (op 18-1 tchd 20-1)

Fragrancy(IRE), whose only previous experience had been when winning a Polytrack maiden in the autumn, ran really well but could not get past the battle-hardened winner. Her Oaks entry is unlikely to be taken up now, especially as a mile seems her trip, but she can pay her way in fillies' handicaps on this evidence. (op 3-1)

White Deer(USA), a stable companion of the winner, tracked that filly for most of the way but found her getting in his way and could never get a clear-enough run to make a sustained challenge. He can prove capable of better when things fall his way. (op 8-1)

Artimino, made favourite in a bid to follow up last year's win in this race for the same stable, was another to not get the best of runs, but once in the clear he had time to deliver a challenge and found less than had looked likely. He may be better than this, but has to prove that is the case. (op 2-1)

Majounes Song, the third of the Johnston runners, was always close to the pace but faded in the final quarter mile. She is bred to stay a fair bit further than this and she may be suited by a step up in trip and a return to front-running. (op 20-1)

Arch Of Titus(IRE), a dual All-Weather winner, was stepping up in grade and off a higher mark. He was reluctant to go to post and then missed the break badly, so did well to reach the heels of the leaders early in the straight, but from then on could make no further impression. He may appreciate easier ground on turf (op 8-1 tchd 5-1)

Handsome Falcon, a narrow winner over 5f here on his sole previous start in the autumn, still looked green and, after being squeezed out in the early stages, was unable to play any further active part in proceedings. He can be forgiven this. Official explanation: jockey said gelding failed to handle the bend (op 12-1)

Charlie Tipple was another to suffer in some scrimmaging at the end of the back straight. Official explanation: jockey said gelding failed to handle the bend (op 40-1)

Trepa(USA), another to have won an ordinary maiden on his sole start at two, found this more difficult off a higher mark in a better-grade race. (op 7-1 tchd 10-1)

1258 GO RACING IN YORKSHIRE FILLIES' H'CAP 1m 1f 207y
4:00 (4:00) (Class 5) (0-70,70) 4-Y-0+ **£3,400** (£1,011; £505; £252) **Stalls** High

Form RPR

0650 **1** **The Pen**[8] 1090 5-8-1 **56** oh1 .... AndrewElliott(3) 10 65
(C W Fairhurst) *trckd ldr: led 3f out: rdn wl over 1f out: drvn and wandered ins fnl f: styd on wl* **8/1**

400- **2** *nk* **Tcherina (IRE)**[50] 6202 5-8-13 **70** .... DuranFentiman(5) 8 78
(T D Easterby) *trckd ldrs: hdwy over 2f out: rdn over 1f out: drvn and ev ch whn edgd rt wl ins fnl f: kpt on* **10/1**

00-0 **3** *nk* **Sudden Impulse**[8] 1090 6-8-9 **61** .... PaulMulrennan 9 69+
(A D Brown) *trckd ldrs: hdwy on inner 2f out: nt clr run over 1f out: swtchd lft and drvn ins fnl f: hrd drvn and hung lft nr fin* **5/1**[3]

156- **4** *1 1/4* **Collette's Choice**[281] 3634 4-8-8 **60** .... PaulHanagan 7 71+
(R A Fahey) *hld up: stdy hdwy 3f out: rdn and nt clr run over 1f out: styng on whn hmpd ins fnl f and again nr fin* **10/3**[1]

212- **5** *1* **Wasalat (USA)**[145] 6684 5-9-3 **69** .... TonyHamilton 4 72+
(D W Barker) *hld up: hdwy on outer 3f out: rdn wl over 1f out: kpt on same pce fnl f* **12/1**

203/ **6** *nk* **Prelude**[577] 5511 6-8-4 **56** oh4 .... PaulQuinn 13 58
(W M Brisbourne) *t.k.h: chsd ldrs: rdn along 2f out: kpt on same pce fnl 2f* **33/1**

00-0 **7** *1* **Just Lille (IRE)**[12] 1040 4-9-2 **68** .... RoystonFfrench 5 68
(Mrs A Duffield) *midfield: hdwy 3f out: rdn 2f out and no imp appr fnl f* **25/1**

214- **8** *hd* **Bronze Star**[127] 6883 4-8-11 **63** .... JamieSpencer 1 63
(J R Fanshawe) *stdd s: hld up in midfield: hdwy on outer 3f out: rdn 2f out and sn btn* **9/2**[2]

360- **9** *1/2* **Shekan Star**[213] 5581 5-7-11 **56** oh3 .... DanielleMcCreery(7) 3 55+
(K G Reveley) *a in rr* **16/1**

-622 **10** *1/2* **Bavarica**[80] 358 5-8-10 **69** .... AmyBaker(7) 6 67
(Miss J Feilden) *chsd ldrs: hdwy 3f out: rdn 2f out: drvn and wknd over 1f out* **14/1**

500- **11** *8* **Epicurean**[154] 6571 5-8-4 **56** .... PaulFessey 11 38
(Mrs K Walton) *a in rr* **9/1**

60-0 **12** *6* **Dream Of Paradise (USA)**[8] 1090 4-8-4 **59** .... LiamJones(3) 2 29
(Mrs L Williamson) *led: rdn along and hdd 3f out: drvn and wknd 2f out* **40/1**

100- **13** *5* **Paradise Expected**[61] 6147 4-8-9 **66** .... JamieMoriarty(5) 12 26
(C Grant) *a towards rr* **50/1**

2m 5.20s (-2.10) **Going Correction** -0.125s/f (Firm) 13 Ran SP% **119.6**
Speed ratings (Par 100):103,102,102,101,100 100,99,99,99,98 92,87,83
CSF £83.06 CT £446.93 TOTE £10.90: £3.30, £3.70, £2.10; EX 114.40.

Owner William Hill **Bred** Mrs R D Peacock **Trained** Middleham Moor, N Yorks

■ Stewards' Enquiry : Paul Mulrennan three-day ban: careless riding (May 7-9)
Andrew Elliott one-day ban: careless riding (May 7)

FOCUS
A modest handicap run at a sound pace, the time being fractionally faster than the earlier three-year-old race. The winner sets the standard with the unlucky fourth rated as having won.

1259 CONSTANT SECURITY MAIDEN STKS 1m 100y
4:35 (4:36) (Class 5) 3-Y-0+ **£3,238** (£963; £481; £240) **Stalls** High

Form RPR

1 **Seleet (IRE)** 3-8-11 .... RHills 4 59+
(M A Jarvis) *hld up in rr: gd hdwy on outer over 2f out: rdn and qcknd to ld ins fnl f: sn clr* **10/1**

44-2 **2** *2 1/2* **Stark Contrast (USA)**[9] 1081 3-8-11 .... BrettDoyle 12 53
(G A Butler) *trckd ldrs: hdwy to dispute ld wl over 1f out and ev ch tl drvn and nt qckn ins fnl f* **5/2**[2]

6 **3** *1* **Bernix**[12] 1044 5-9-11 .... DavidAllan 10 55
(T D Easterby) *hld up and bhd: hdwy over 2f out: rdn and styd on wl fnl f: nrst fin* **33/1**

/0-0 **4** *1/2* **Mister Minty (IRE)**[14] 1013 5-9-8 35 .... MarkLawson(3) 8 54?
(Mrs S Lamyman) *rrd s: hld up and bhd: gd hdwy over 2f out: sn rdn and styd on ins fnl f: nrst fin* **200/1**

240- **5** *3/4* **Cavalry Guard (USA)**[198] 5883 3-8-11 72 .... JamieSpencer 1 48
(H R A Cecil) *hld up in midfield: gd hdwy to ld over 1f out: sn rdn: hdd & wknd ins fnl f* **6/1**[3]

0 **6** *5* **Cottam Eclipse**[17] 968 6-9-11 .... RoystonFfrench 5 41?
(I W McInnes) *chsd ldr: led 3f out: rdn 2f out: drvn and hdd over 1f out: grad wknd* **100/1**

30-2 **7** *1 1/4* **Gunner's View**[15] 1001 3-8-11 75 .... KDarley 2 34
(B J Meehan) *prom: effrt on outer end ev ch over 2f out: sn rdn and wknd over 1f out* **7/1**

0 **8** *1 3/4* **Betteras Bertie**[4] 1177 4-9-11 .... AdrianTNicholls 9 34
(M Brittain) *s.i.s and bhd: wd st: nvr a factor* **200/1**

0-2 **9** *1/2* **Bedizen**[14] 1011 4-9-11 .... NickyMackay 6 33
(Sir Michael Stoute) *trckd ldrs: hdwy over 3f out: effrt to dispute ld wl over 1f out: sn rdn and wknd* **6/5**[1]

10 *11* **To Sir With Love (NZ)**[333] 6-9-11 .... TonyHamilton 11 —
(J S Wainwright) *led: rdn along and hdd 3f out: sn wknd* **80/1**

11 *5* **Diplomatic Dan (IRE)** 4-9-11 .... SteveDrowne 7 —
(E J Alston) *midfield: rdn along over 3f out: sn wknd* **50/1**

005- **12** *10* **The Dandy Fox**[192] 6012 3-8-8 48 ow2 .... PaulMulrennan 3 —
(R Bastiman) *in tch: rdn along over 3f out: sn wknd* **250/1**

1m 47.51s (0.11) **Going Correction** -0.125s/f (Firm)
WFA 3 from 4yo+ 14lb 12 Ran SP% **118.4**
Speed ratings (Par 103):94,91,90,90,89 84,83,81,80,69 64,54
CSF £35.50 TOTE £17.00: £3.30, £1.80, £4.30; EX 53.10.

Owner Hamdan Al Maktoum **Bred** Keatly Overseas Ltd **Trained** Newmarket, Suffolk

FOCUS
A modest maiden limited by the proximity of the fourth and a moderate winning time for the grade.
Bedizen Official explanation: trainer's rep said gelding finished lame behind

1260 CLEVERLY RETIRES YET AGAIN H'CAP 7f 100y
5:10 (5:11) (Class 6) (0-60,60) 4-Y-0+ **£2,914** (£867; £433; £216) **Stalls** High

Form RPR

3424 **1** **Franksalot (IRE)**[10] 1064 7-9-2 **58** .... RoystonFfrench 12 67
(I W McInnes) *hld up in tch: hdwy 2f out: swtchd rt and rdr dropped whip ent fnl f: styd on wl to ld last 100yds* **10/1**[3]

0-45 **2** *1 1/4* **Charlie Bear**[17] 975 6-8-13 **55** .... AdrianMcCarthy 10 61
(Miss Z C Davison) *hld up in midfield: hdwy on outer 3f out: rdn to chse ldrs over 1f out: drvn and ev ch ins fnl f: nt qckn towards fin* **15/2**[2]

0653 **3** *1/2* **Penel (IRE)**[13] 1028 6-8-9 **51** ow1 .... (p) LeeEnstone 3 56
(P T Midgley) *a.p: effrt 2f out: sn rdn and ev ch tl drvn and no ex wl ins fnl f* **25/1**

0245 **4** *hd* **Cabourg (IRE)**[27] 831 4-9-2 **58** .... (b) PaulMulrennan 11 63
(R Bastiman) *trckd ldrs gng wl: smooth hdwy over 2f out: shkn up and ev ch ent fnl f: sn rdn and no ex last 100yds* **16/1**

-600 **5** *hd* **Blue Empire (IRE)**[57] 579 6-8-12 **57** .... LiamJones(3) 7 61+
(C R Dore) *hld up towards rr: hdwy on outer 2f out: rdn and styd on wl fnl f: nrst fin* **16/1**

22-0 **6** *3* **Khetaab (IRE)**[6] 1133 5-8-8 **50** .... KDarley 15 47
(E J Alston) *led: rdn along and hdd 3f out: drvn and one pce fnl 2f* **4/1**[1]

-502 **7** *nk* **Sir Bond (IRE)**[6] 1132 6-8-8 **55** .... DuranFentiman(5) 14 51
(G R Oldroyd) *cl up: led 3f out: rdn wl over 1f out: drvn and hdd ins fnl f: wknd* **4/1**[1]

605- **8** *1 1/4* **Making Music**[184] 6159 4-9-1 **57** .... DavidAllan 2 55+
(T D Easterby) *midfield: effrt and hdwy over 2f out: sn rdn and kpt on ins fnl f: nt rch ldrs* **33/1**

0001 **9** *3/4* **Paddywack (IRE)**[7] 1112 10-8-10 **59** .... (b) DanielleMcCreery(7) 9 50
(D W Chapman) *bhd: hdwy over 2f out: sn rdn and kpt on appr fnl f: nvr a factor* **11/1**

0000 **10** *7* **Verite**[9] 1074 4-9-2 **58** .... NeilPollard 13 31
(A J McCabe) *a towards rr* **100/1**

000- **11** *1/2* **Dancing Deano (IRE)**[142] 6719 5-9-1 **57** .... BrettDoyle 5 29
(R Hollinshead) *a towards rr* **16/1**

-100 **12** *hd* **Danzare**[17] 976 5-9-1 **57** .... SteveDrowne 4 29
(J L Spearing) *a towards rr* **16/1**

000- **13** *shd* **Crosby Hall**[248] 4666 4-9-4 **60** .... (t) KimTinkler 6 31
(N Tinkler) *a in rr* **50/1**

-500 **14** *13* **Kineta (USA)**[69] 479 4-8-10 **52** .... JamieSpencer 8 —
(W R Muir) *a towards rr* **16/1**

-301 **15** *15* **Steel Grey**[37] 715 6-8-7 **49** .... DeanMernagh 1 —
(M Brittain) *hld up: a in rr* **40/1**

1m 33.47s (-0.84) **Going Correction** -0.125s/f (Firm) 15 Ran SP% **110.8**
Speed ratings (Par 101):99,97,97,96,96 93,92,91,90,82 81,81,81,66,49
CSF £59.25 CT £997.86 TOTE £9.40: £2.50, £2.90, £6.10; EX 86.70 Place 6 £206.37, Place 5 £109.77.

Owner Stephen Hackney And Martin Higgins **Bred** J P Hardiman **Trained** Catwick, E Yorks
■ Rondo (4/1 CF) withdrawn (refused to go to post). Rule 4 applies, deduction 20p in £.

FOCUS
A moderate handicap run 1.27sec slower than the earlier three-year-old race over the trip but sound enough form, rated around the third and fourth.
Sir Bond(IRE) Official explanation: jockey said gelding ran too free early stages
Dancing Deano(IRE) Official explanation: jockey said gelding hung right-handed throughout
Kineta(USA) Official explanation: jockey said filly never travelled
Steel Grey Official explanation: jockey said gelding was unsuited by the good to firm (good in places) ground; trainer said gelding was found to be lame near-hind following morning
T/Plt: £182.20 to a £1 stake. Pool: £55,310.45. 221.60 winning tickets. T/Qpdt: £43.40 to a £1 stake. Pool: £2,330.70. 39.70 winning tickets. JR

[1219]SOUTHWELL (L-H)

Thursday, April 26

OFFICIAL GOING: Standard

After no rain the surface was again described as 'loose and light, slow and quite deep'. It was again watered between races.

Wind: Moderate, across Weather: Overcast, breezy and very cool

1261 PLAY POKER AT SKYPOKER.COM MEDIAN AUCTION MAIDEN STKS 7f (F)

5:40 (5:41) (Class 6) 3-4-Y-O **£2,184** (£644; £322) **Stalls** Low

Form RPR

3234 **1** **Blue Monkey (IRE)**[24] [889] 3-8-13 70.......................... MickyFenton 4 70
(M L W Bell) *mid-div: effrt over 3f out: hung lft and led appr fnl f: pushed out* **4/6**[1]

0465 **2** *3* **Very Well Red**[30] [801] 4-9-7 47.. ChrisCatlin 7 61
(P W Hiatt) *trckd ldr: led 2f out: hdd and no ex appr fnl f* **12/1**

2-50 **3** *1 1/4* **Bold Saxon (IRE)**[97] [184] 3-8-13 68.......................... RichardSmith 8 58
(M D I Usher) *chsd ldrs: effrt 3f out: kpt on same pce* **7/2**[2]

00- **4** *3* **Didactic**[222] [5389] 3-8-10 ....(b[1]) StephenDonohoe(3) 6 49
(A J McCabe) *led tl 2f out: wknd appr fnl f* **20/1**

-2 **5** *11* **Acapulco Bay**[29] [807] 3-8-13 .... TomEaves 1 17
(Miss J A Camacho) *dwlt: sn chsng ldrs: drvn 3f out: sn wknd* **11/2**[3]

-002 **6** *1/2* **Master Ben (IRE)**[30] [802] 4-9-5 45.............................(b) LeeTopliss(7) 5 21
(S R Bowring) *swtchd outside after 1f: sn drvn along to chse ldrs: lost pl 3f out* **33/1**

7 *8* **Miss Admiral** 3-8-8 .... DaleGibson 3 —
(S R Bowring) *s.s: sn bhd and drvn along: lost tch over 4f out: sn t.o* **33/1**

8 *16* **Sharpattack** 3-8-13 .... DeanMcKeown 2 —
(M Botti) *s.i.s: bhd: lost tch over 4f out: t.o* **16/1**

1m 30.44s (-0.36) **Going Correction** -0.025s/f (Stan)
WFA 3 from 4yo 13lb 8 Ran SP% **121.8**
Speed ratings (Par 101):101,97,96,92,80 79,70,52
CSF £11.64 TOTE £1.60: £1.10, £2.40, £2.00; EX 8.10.
Owner J A Barton And R P B Michaelson **Bred** Sweetmans Bloodstock **Trained** Newmarket, Suffolk

FOCUS
A very weak maiden with the runner-up rated just 47 and the form rated negatively as a result.
Acapulco Bay Official explanation: jockey said gelding was never travelling

1262 PLAY MONOPOLY AT SKYBETVEGAS.COM CLAIMING STKS 6f (F)

6:10 (6:13) (Class 6) 3-Y-0+ **£2,184** (£644; £322) **Stalls** Low

Form RPR

56-0 **1** **Whitbarrow (IRE)**[24] [896] 8-8-13 53 ow1.............(b) JamesMillman(5) 5 76
(B R Millman) *mde all: styd on strly* **20/1**

2630 **2** *4* **Zarzu**[10] [1063] 8-9-11 78.. EddieAhern 3 70
(C R Dore) *mid-div: hdwy on outer over 2f out: styd on to take 2nd ins fnl f* **9/2**[2]

2526 **3** *1/2* **Cleveland**[33] [766] 5-9-1 62.. RussellKennemore(5) 8 64
(R Hollinshead) *trckd wnr: t.k.h: hung bdly rt over 1f out and ended up stands' side: kpt on same pce* **11/4**[1]

1105 **4** *1 1/4* **Soba Jones**[13] [1028] 10-9-1 55..................................... ChrisCatlin 2 55
(J Balding) *hood removed v late: chsd ldrs: kpt on same pce fnl 2f* **7/1**[3]

4430 **5** *4* **Ask No More**[6] [1120] 4-8-12 50................................(b) DominicFox(3) 13 42
(P L Gilligan) *mid-div on outside: kpt on fnl 2f: nvr nr ldrs* **14/1**

5220 **6** *1/2* **Bodden Bay**[10] [1064] 5-9-5 59.................................. DanielTudhope 11 44
(I W McInnes) *mid-div: kpt on fnl 2f: nvr nr ldrs* **9/1**

3000 **7** *2* **Sundried Tomato**[13] [1028] 8-8-10 42.................(p) MichaelJStainton(5) 7 34
(D W Chapman) *bhd: hung rt and sme hdwy 2f out: nvr a factor* **33/1**

-011 **8** *1/2* **Whinhill House**[13] [1028] 7-9-4 60..............................(v) PatCosgrave 9 35
(D W Barker) *chsd ldrs: hung rt over 2f out and ended up stands' side: wknd over 1f out* **9/2**[2]

5630 **9** *1/2* **Ocean Of Dreams (FR)**[21] [933] 4-9-11 68...................... TomEaves 12 41
(J D Bethell) *mid-div: lost pl over 3f out* **15/2**

-030 **10** *5* **Balian**[22] [920] 4-9-5 45...(b) MickyFenton 1 19
(Mrs P Sly) *a bhd* **33/1**

4 **11** *4* **Just Spike**[30] [802] 4-9-4 .... DeanMcKeown 6 —
(B P J Baugh) *s.s: sn detached in rr* **50/1**

-413 **12** *8* **Best Lead**[57] [580] 8-9-5 53....................................(b) SaleemGolam(3) 4 —
(Ian Emmerson) *sn bhd* **22/1**

55-0 **13** *5* **On The Trail**[83] [339] 10-9-1 40.................................(p) DaleGibson 10 —
(D W Chapman) *chsd ldrs on outer: lost pl 3f out* **66/1**

1m 16.4s (-0.50) **Going Correction** -0.025s/f (Stan) 13 Ran SP% **122.4**
Speed ratings (Par 101):102,96,96,94,89 88,85,85,84,77 72,61,55
CSF £105.32 TOTE £16.20: £3.30, £1.10, £1.80; EX 114.20.
Owner Mrs H Brain **Bred** James Burns And A Moynan **Trained** Kentisbeare, Devon

FOCUS
A fair claimer but not easy to rate, assessed through the winner to last year's form.
Cleveland Official explanation: jockey said gelding hung right in the home straight
Sundried Tomato Official explanation: jockey said gelding had been hanging
Balian Official explanation: jockey said gelding resented the kickback

1263 PLAY SKY POKER AT SKYBETVEGAS.COM H'CAP 1m 4f (F)

6:40 (6:40) (Class 5) (0-75,72) 4-Y-0+ **£3,071** (£906; £453) **Stalls** Low

Form RPR

3553 **1** **Jackie Kiely**[29] [811] 6-9-1 68..................................(t) J-PGuillambert 6 76+
(R Brotherton) *mid-div: effrt 3f out: led over 1f out: kpt on wl* **9/2**[3]

240- **2** *1 1/4* **Ha'Penny Beacon**[183] [6178] 4-8-8 62........................ DanielTudhope 5 68
(D Carroll) *hld up in tch: hdwy over 4f out: chal over 2f out: no ex ins fnl f* **12/1**

3 *3/4* **Arafan (IRE)**[82] [1000] 5-9-0 67.. NCallan 1 72
(Dr R D P Newland) *led: set mod pce: qcknd over 5f out: hdd over 4f out: led over 3f out tl over 1f out: kpt on same pce* **4/1**[2]

600- **4** *7* **Boxhall (IRE)**[194] [5963] 5-8-9 ow1.................................... SladeO'Hara(7) 8 63
(N Wilson) *dwlt: hld up wl in tch: effrt 3f out: sn wl outpcd* **7/1**

01-0 **5** *6* **Floodlight Fantasy**[8] [1090] 4-8-12 66..........................(b[1]) PaulHanagan 7 50
(Jedd O'Keeffe) *t.k.h in rr: hdwy over 4f out: rdn and lost pl over 2f out* **20/1**

-110 **6** *nk* **Muntami (IRE)**[29] [811] 6-9-1 71..................... StephenDonohoe(3) 9 55
(John A Harris) *hld up wl in tch: hdwy on outside to chse ldrs over 6f out: lost pl over 2f out* **6/1**

0160 **7** *3 1/2* **Kylkenny**[29] [811] 12-9-0 72.......................................(t) TravisBlock(5) 4 50
(H Morrison) *w ldrs: t.k.h: led over 4f out tl over 3f out: lost pl over 2f out* **17/2**

-532 **8** *12* **Wulimaster (USA)**[16] [997] 4-9-3 71.......................... TomEaves 10 30
(D W Barker) *sn trcking ldrs: lost pl over 3f out* **10/3**[1]

5/0- **9** *2 1/2* **Don'Tcallmeginger (IRE)**[358] [1424] 4-8-8 65............ SaleemGolam(3) 3 20
(M H Tompkins) *t.k.h: w ldrs: drvn over 5f out: lost pl and n.m.r over 4f out: sn bhd* **25/1**

2m 41.92s (-0.17) **Going Correction** -0.025s/f (Stan)
WFA 4 from 5yo+ 1lb 9 Ran SP% **114.9**
Speed ratings (Par 103):99,98,97,93,89 88,86,78,76
CSF £56.40 CT £232.95 TOTE £6.30: £2.20, £2.80, £1.90; EX 41.80.
Owner P S J Croft **Bred** Mrs M Chaworth Musters **Trained** Elmley Castle, Worcs

FOCUS
A very steady gallop to halfway. The winner did well coming from off the pace and was recording his seventh course success. Overall the form looks pretty modest.
Muntami(IRE) Official explanation: jockey said gelding had no more to give

1264 SKYBETVEGAS.COM CASINO RACE H'CAP 1m (F)

7:10 (7:10) (Class 5) (0-75,74) 4-Y-0+ **£3,071** (£906; £453) **Stalls** Low

Form RPR

1202 **1** **Luckylover**[29] [809] 4-9-0 73.....................................(t) JerryO'Dwyer(3) 5 93
(M G Quinlan) *led: clr over 1f out: styd on strly: eased towards fin* **11/4**[1]

-031 **2** *5* **Exit Smiling**[12] [1040] 5-8-9 65.................................... MickyFenton 4 73
(P T Midgley) *hld up: drvn over 4f out: hdwy 3f out: styd on to take 2nd over 1f out: no ch w wnr* **9/2**[2]

010- **3** *4* **Rowan Lodge (IRE)**[183] [6176] 5-9-0 70........................ EddieAhern 1 69
(M H Tompkins) *sn trcking ldrs: rdn over 2f out: edgd rt: kpt on one pce* **12/1**

10-6 **4** *2 1/2* **Superior Star**[26] [850] 4-9-0 70.................................(v) PaulHanagan 7 63
(R A Fahey) *chsd ldrs: drvn over 4f out: hung lft 2f out: nvr nr to chal* **6/1**[3]

5-13 **5** *nk* **Call My Bluff (FR)**[104] [110] 4-9-2 72........................ ChrisCatlin 3 64
(Rae Guest) *hld up in last: effrt over 3f out: sn chsng ldrs: wknd over 1f out* **8/1**

0626 **6** *39* **Shifty**[29] [809] 8-8-11 67.. DanielTudhope 6 —
(D Carroll) *chsd ldrs: drvn 4f out: lost pl 2f out: eased and sn bhd* **8/1**

4211 **7** *7* **Dudley Docker (IRE)**[24] [895] 5-9-4 74.............................. NCallan 2 —
(C R Dore) *chsd ldrs: drvn 4f out: lost pl wl over 1f out: heavily eased ins fnl f* **11/4**[1]

1m 42.55s (-2.05) **Going Correction** -0.025s/f (Stan) 7 Ran SP% **115.7**
Speed ratings (Par 103):109,104,100,97,97 58,51
CSF £15.78 TOTE £4.00: £2.50, £3.50; EX 14.10.
Owner Roger Turner **Bred** Shutford Stud **Trained** Newmarket, Suffolk

FOCUS
A strong gallop set by the progressive winner resulting in a decent winning time for the class of race. The race is rated through the winner to recent form.
Dudley Docker(IRE) Official explanation: trainer said gelding lost its action

1265 EXPERIENCE THE THRILLS OF SKYBETVEGAS.COM H'CAP 7f (F)

7:40 (7:40) (Class 5) (0-70,69) 4-Y-0+ **£3,071** (£906; £453) **Stalls** Low

Form RPR

0-00 **1** **Alsadaa (USA)**[12] [1040] 4-8-9 60.................................. DaleGibson 5 69
(M W Easterby) *chsd ldrs: drvn over 3f out: styd on to ld nr fin* **16/1**

1230 **2** *nk* **Owed**[24] [896] 5-9-4 69..(v[1]) NCallan 4 77
(R Bastiman) *w ldrs: led over 2f out: edgd lft fnl f: hdd nr fin* **10/3**[1]

4103 **3** *3/4* **Branston Tiger**[77] [388] 8-8-11 65.........................(v) AndrewElliott(3) 8 71
(Ian Emmerson) *w ldrs on outer: kpt on same pce ins fnl f* **16/1**

0-26 **4** *3 1/2* **Tour D'Amour (IRE)**[95] [200] 4-8-6 59........................ PaulFessey 3 56
(R Craggs) *sn outpcd and in rr: hdwy on outer 2f out: styd on ins fnl f* **4/1**[2]

3100 **5** *shd* **Cerebus**[24] [895] 5-8-12 66...........................(bt) StephenDonohoe(3) 2 63
(A J McCabe) *w ldr: led over 4f out tl over 2f out: wknd fnl f* **7/1**[3]

250- **6** *2* **Contemplation**[192] [6008] 4-8-12 63.............................. PaulHanagan 10 54
(J Balding) *hld up: effrt over 2f out: kpt on: nvr nr ldrs* **10/3**[1]

4-30 **7** *6* **Tabulate**[34] [742] 4-8-6 57.. ChrisCatlin 6 33
(P L Gilligan) *s.i.s: swtchd wd after 1f: hdwy over 3f out: hrd rdn over 2f out: wknd over 1f out* **9/1**

000- **8** *5* **Indian's Feather (IRE)**[198] [5896] 6-9-3 68...............(b) KimTinkler 7 31
(N Tinkler) *s.i.s: sn drvn along: sme hdwy on ins over 2f out: sn wknd* **16/1**

0005 **9** *3/4* **Capital Lass**[21] [932] 4-7-11 55 oh6.............................. MCGeran(7) 9 16
(A J McCabe) *s.i.s: in rr whn n.m.r over 3f out* **16/1**

13/- **10** *21* **Zanjeer**[583] [5380] 7-8-10 61.. TomEaves 1 —
(N Wilson) *led tl over 4f out: lost pl over 3f out: sn bhd and eased* **14/1**

1m 30.73s (-0.07) **Going Correction** -0.025s/f (Stan) 10 Ran SP% **118.9**
Speed ratings (Par 103):99,98,97,93,93 91,84,78,77,53
CSF £70.29 CT £896.91 TOTE £17.80: £4.00, £1.20, £5.00; EX 148.80.
Owner Mrs Jean Turpin **Bred** Shadwell Farm LLC **Trained** Sheriff Hutton, N Yorks

FOCUS
A modest handicap and a much-improved effort from the unfancied winner. The form is rated at face value despite the modest time.
Cerebus Official explanation: jockey said gelding had no more to give

1266 SKY BET FREEPHONE 08000 722 421 H'CAP 1m (F)

8:10 (8:10) (Class 6) (0-60,59) 3-Y-0 **£2,388** (£705; £352) **Stalls** Low

Form RPR

544 **1** **Krakatau (FR)**[21] [937] 3-9-2 57...................................... MickyFenton 8 64
(D J Wintle) *mid-div: effrt over 3f out: edgd lft over 1f out: styd on to ld ins fnl f* **11/2**[2]

-521 **2** *1 1/4* **Time For Change (IRE)**[23] [910] 3-8-10 58.............. ChrisGlenister(7) 3 62
(B W Hills) *sn chsng ldrs: led 2f out: hdd and no ex ins fnl f* **4/1**[1]

6606 **3** *1* **Brean Dot Com (IRE)**[31] [790] 3-8-13 54..................... RobertHavlin 14 60+
(Mrs P N Dutfield) *lost pl on wd outside after 1f: hdwy whn n.m.r and swtchd rt over 1f out: styd on fnl f* **11/1**

00-0 **4** *1/2* **Prince Noel**[17] [974] 3-8-9 50.. TomEaves 5 51
(N Wilson) *led tl over 4f out: rallied and edgd lft over 1f out: kpt on same pce* **25/1**

-340 **5** *3* **Storm Mission (USA)**[12] [1044] 3-8-9 50................ EdwardCreighton 11 44
(Miss V Haigh) *hld up in rr: hdwy over 2f out: kpt on fnl f* **12/1**

000- **6** *1/2* **Cheery Cat (USA)**[177] [6285] 3-9-1 56.............................. NCallan 7 49
(D W Barker) *chsd ldrs: led and hung lft over 2f out: sn hdd: wknd and eased ins fnl f* **9/1**

1044 **7** *6* **Mr Chocolate Drop (IRE)**[2] [1232] 3-8-8 54.....(p) MichaelJStainton(5) 12 33
(M J Attwater) *mid-div: hdwy on outer over 2f out: nvr nr ldrs* **13/2**[3]

0260 **8** *1/2* **Flushed**[5] [1164] 3-8-7 51 ow2.............................(be) StephenDonohoe(3) 10 29
(A J McCabe) *w ldr: led over 4f out: hdd over 2f out: sn wknd* **18/1**

3500 **9** *3* **Pappas Image**[13] [1031] 3-8-2 **50** ow2 .... AdamCarter(7) 4 21
(A J McCabe) *s.i.s: nvr on terms* **25/1**
5130 **10** *shd* **Muree Queen**[24] [893] 3-8-7 **48** .... EddieAhern 9 19
(Miss J S Davis) *sn bhd and drvn along* **11/1**
060- **11** *3/4* **Palmetto Point**[182] [6188] 3-8-13 **54** .... SteveDrowne 2 23
(H Morrison) *s.i.s: in rr-div and reminders over 4f out: lost pl over 2f out* **8/1**
6130 **12** *11* **Poniard (IRE)**[27] [834] 3-9-4 **59** ....(p) PatCosgrave 6 3
(D W Barker) *chsd ldrs: rdn and lost pl over 3f out: eased 2f out* **12/1**
0020 **13** *8* **Jousting**[23] [910] 3-8-8 **49** ....(v) ChrisCatlin 1 —
(V Smith) *a in rr: bhd and virtually p.u* **16/1**

1m 44.97s (0.37) **Going Correction** -0.025s/f (Stan) 13 Ran SP% **120.7**
Speed ratings (Par 96):97,95,94,94,91 90,84,84,81,81 80,69,61
CSF £28.00 CT £243.71 TOTE £6.20: £1.40, £2.20, £3.20; EX 27.50 Place 6 £36.14, Place 5 £29.49.
Owner Ocean Trailers Ltd **Bred** Millsec, Ltd **Trained** Naunton, Gloucs

FOCUS
A low-grade handicap but the principals can do better with the third setting the level.
Palmetto Point Official explanation: jockey said gelding was never travelling
T/Plt: £64.50 to a £1 stake. Pool: £44,342.25. 501.80 winning tickets. T/Qpdt: £25.50 to a £1 stake. Pool: £3,181.10. 92.30 winning tickets. WG

977 YARMOUTH (L-H)
Thursday, April 26

OFFICIAL GOING: Good to firm
A strong tailwind resulted in some very quick times on the straight course, including a course record.
Wind: Fresh, behind Weather: Overcast

1267 CAPE INDUSTRIAL SERVICES MAIDEN STKS 6f 3y
5:25 (5:26) (Class 5) 3-Y-0+ **£2,849** (£847; £423; £211) **Stalls** High

Form RPR
3 **1** **Blackmalkin (USA)**[16] [996] 3-8-9 .... SebSanders 5 56+
(C E Brittain) *mde all: rdn over 1f out: styd on strly fnl f* **3/1**[3]
6- **2** *1 3/4* **Sundae**[287] [3457] 3-9-0 .... RichardHughes 3 55+
(C F Wall) *t.k.h: hld up in tch: hdwy 2f out: chsd wnr over 1f out: ev ch and rdn 1f out: fnd little and wl hld after* **11/8**[1]
3 *3/4* **He's My Best (USA)** 3-9-0 .... LDettori 6 53+
(J Noseda) *hld up in tch: rdn to chse wnr 1/2-way tl over 1f out: kpt on same pce fnl f* **13/8**[2]
0 **4** *3/4* **Massams Lane**[6] [1117] 3-9-0 .... HayleyTurner 1 50
(P S McEntee) *in tch on outer: rdn over 3f out: kpt on same pce fnl f* **50/1**
04-0 **5** *2 1/2* **Canary Girl**[17] [978] 4-9-6 34 ....(v[1]) DMylonas 4 40
(Mrs C A Dunnett) *chsd wnr tl 1/2-way: rdn over 2f out: wknd wl over 1f out* **66/1**
6 *5* **Musical Box** 3-8-6 .... MarcHalford(3) 2 21
(G Prodromou) *s.i.s: a last: lost tch over 2f out* **33/1**

1m 11.55s (-2.15) **Going Correction** -0.50s/f (Hard)
WFA 3 from 4yo 11lb 6 Ran SP% **111.6**
Speed ratings (Par 103):94,91,90,89,86 79
CSF £7.49 TOTE £2.80: £1.70, £1.40; EX 7.00.
Owner Sheikh Marwan Al Maktoum **Bred** Darley **Trained** Newmarket, Suffolk

FOCUS
A very modest maiden and with a horse rated 34 beaten less than six lengths, the form looks very ordinary. Very few ever got into this.

1268 HOWARDS GROUP & PKF H'CAP 7f 3y
5:55 (5:55) (Class 4) (0-85,84) 4-Y-0+ **£4,728** (£1,406; £702; £351) **Stalls** High

Form RPR
-503 **1** **Glenbuck (IRE)**[18] [953] 4-9-4 **84** ....(v) RichardMullen 8 94
(A Bailey) *mde all: rdn wl over 1f out: r.o strly* **20/1**
0-05 **2** *1 1/2* **Guildenstern (IRE)**[33] [757] 5-8-8 **77** .... RichardKingscote(3) 1 83
(P L Gilligan) *chsd ldrs: rdn to chse wnr over 2f out: edgd rt briefly over 1f out: kpt on same pce fnl f* **20/1**
61-1 **3** *3* **Sound Of Nature (USA)**[14] [1013] 4-9-0 **80** .... RichardHughes 4 78+
(H R A Cecil) *bmpd s: hld up: hdwy 3f out: 4l 5th and effrt whn nt clr run over 1f out: kpt on fnl f: nt trble ldrs* **4/9**[1]
14-0 **4** *1 3/4* **Mina A Salem**[33] [759] 5-8-8 **74** .... SebSanders 7 68
(C E Brittain) *chsd wnr: rdn over 3f out: wknd wl over 1f out* **7/1**[3]
-322 **5** *2* **Barney McGrew (IRE)**[68] [486] 4-8-9 **75** .... OscarUrbina 5 64
(J A R Toller) *bmpd s: towards rr: rdn and effrt 3f out: wknd 2f out* **13/2**[2]
000- **6** *shd* **Cool Panic (IRE)**[250] [4593] 5-9-0 **80** .... HayleyTurner 6 68
(M L W Bell) *wnt lft s: trckd ldrs: rdn 2f out: edgd lft over 1f out: sn wknd* **12/1**
-534 **7** *5* **Sonny Parkin**[85] [314] 5-8-8 **77** ....(v) EmmettStack(3) 3 52
(G A Huffer) *slowly away: a last and nvr gng wl: eased ins fnl f* **50/1**

1m 22.12s (-4.48) **Going Correction** -0.50s/f (Hard) course record 7 Ran SP% **114.3**
Speed ratings (Par 105):105,103,99,97,95 95,89
CSF £296.30 CT £559.00 TOTE £29.40: £5.00, £7.00; EX 247.20.
Owner Middleham Park Racing XLII **Bred** Mrs Teresa Monaghan **Trained** Newmarket, Suffolk

FOCUS
The winner made sure this was run at a true pace and took 8/100ths of a second off the course record which had stood for 19 years. Much of that would have been due to the fast ground and strong following wind though. The race is rated around the first two.

1269 EASTERN POWER SYSTEMS H'CAP 6f 3y
6:30 (6:30) (Class 6) (0-65,65) 3-Y-0 **£1,943** (£578; £288; £144) **Stalls** High

Form RPR
0-30 **1** **Almora Guru**[14] [1008] 3-8-11 **58** .... TedDurcan 2 57
(W M Brisbourne) *hld up: hdwy over 2f out: rdn to ld over 1f out: hld on nr fin* **14/1**
4002 **2** *hd* **Pat Will (IRE)**[14] [1008] 3-8-5 **52** oh1 ow1 ....(b) RichardMullen 8 50
(P D Evans) *sn led: clr tl 1/2-way: rdn wl over 1f out: hdd over 1f out: kpt on wl u.p last 100yds* **7/1**
0-14 **3** *1/2* **Dualagi**[18] [958] 3-9-1 **62** .... JohnEgan 5 59
(J S Moore) *stdd s: hdwy to chse ldng pair after 2f: rdn 2f out: ev ch over 1f out: unable qckn wl ins fnl f* **15/8**[1]
04-0 **4** *1/2* **Early Promise (IRE)**[5] [1151] 3-8-12 **62** .... RichardKingscote(3) 1 57
(P L Gilligan) *chsd ldrs tl outpcd after 2f: rdn and hdwy over 2f out: kpt on same pce fnl f* **3/1**[2]
35-6 **5** *3 1/2* **Billy Red**[13] [1022] 3-9-3 **64** ....(e[1]) DarryllHolland 6 48
(J R Jenkins) *chsd ldr tl over 2f out: hanging lft over 1f out: wknd fnl f* **4/1**[3]
2031 **6** *3 1/2* **Totally Free**[13] [1031] 3-8-13 **60** ....(v) HayleyTurner 3 33
(M D I Usher) *a bhd: rdn and outpcd 1/2-way: no ch after* **5/1**

1m 11.73s (-1.97) **Going Correction** -0.50s/f (Hard) 6 Ran SP% **115.6**
Speed ratings (Par 96):93,92,92,91,86 82
CSF £104.96 CT £270.98 TOTE £9.10: £5.20, £2.60; EX 73.40.
Owner J W Jenkins **Bred** Alpha Bloodstock Limited **Trained** Great Ness, Shropshire

FOCUS
A moderate sprint run in an ordinary time and, with little covering the first four at the line, the form looks modest but sound enough.
Almora Guru Official explanation: trainer said, regarding apparent improvement in form, that the filly settled better on a flatter track.
Early Promise(IRE) Official explanation: trainer said filly was not suited by the track
Totally Free Official explanation: trainer said gelding was unsuited by the good to firm ground

1270 NATIONWIDE PLANT HIRE H'CAP 5f 43y
7:00 (7:01) (Class 4) (0-85,82) 3-Y-0 **£3,067** (£3,067; £702; £351) **Stalls** High

Form RPR
110- **1** **Mambo Spirit (IRE)**[200] [5829] 3-9-4 **82** .... TPQueally 6 89+
(J G Given) *hmpd s: hld up: hdwy and swtchd lft 2f out: rdn and ev ch over 1f out: r.o to join ldr on line* **11/4**[2]
4-42 **1** *dht* **Sparkling Eyes**[7] [1108] 3-8-8 **72** .... SebSanders 1 79
(C E Brittain) *chsd ldrs: wnt 2nd over 2f out: sn rdn: led 1f out: kpt on u.p: jnd on line* **5/4**[1]
512- **3** *2* **Bookiesindex Boy**[167] [6427] 3-8-6 **70** ....(v[1]) StephenCarson 3 70
(J R Jenkins) *chsd ldr: led over 2f out: rdn wl over 1f out: hdd 1f out: wknd last 100yds* **9/1**
000- **4** *3* **Racing Stripes (IRE)**[173] [6332] 3-8-8 **72** .... JohnEgan 4 61
(J S Moore) *led tl rdn and hdd over 2f out: wknd over 1f out* **9/2**[3]
100- **5** *shd* **Camissa**[323] [2342] 3-8-10 **74** .... DarryllHolland 5 63
(D K Ivory) *unruly stalls: wnt rt s: outpcd in rr: brief effrt 2f out: nvr trbld ldrs* **14/1**
5260 **6** *4* **Stoneacre Gareth (IRE)**[24] [885] 3-8-7 **71** .... RichardMullen 2 45
(Peter Grayson) *wnt rt s: bhd: rdn over 3f out: n.d* **16/1**

60.26 secs (-2.54) **Going Correction** -0.50s/f (Hard) 6 Ran SP% **111.8**
Speed ratings (Par 100):100,100,96,92,91 85
WIN: Mambo Spirit £1.70, Sparkling Eyes £0.90. PL: MS £1.50, SE £1.40. EX: MS/SE £2.20, SE/MS £3.00. CSF: MS/SE £3.27, SE/MS £2.41..
Owner Jones, Jones, Clarke & O'Sullivan **Bred** R Warren **Trained** Willoughton, Lincs
Owner A J Richards **Bred** Sarl Ewar Stud Farms France **Trained** Newmarket, Suffolk

FOCUS
A fair little sprint handicap and a solid pace, but something of a rough race rated through the dead-heating favourite.
Racing Stripes(IRE) Official explanation: trainer said gelding bled from the nose
Camissa Official explanation: trainer said filly was unsuited by the good to firm ground

1271 BURGH HALL LEISURE COMPLEX CLASSIFIED STKS 1m 2f 21y
7:30 (7:30) (Class 7) 3-Y-0+ **£1,295** (£385; £192; £96) **Stalls** Low

Form RPR
4402 **1** **Jarvo**[2] [1206] 6-9-4 42 .... PatrickMathers(3) 10 57
(I W McInnes) *hld up in rr: rdn and gd hdwy over 3f out: led wl over 1f out: clr 1f out: drvn out* **13/2**[3]
6000 **2** *2 1/2* **Veba (USA)**[34] [741] 4-9-7 41 .... HayleyTurner 9 52
(M D I Usher) *s.i.s: t.k.h: hld up and bhd: stl plenty to do 3f out: rdn and hdwy 2f out: styd on to chse wnr ins fnl f: no ch w wnr* **14/1**
203- **3** *1 1/2* **Coffin Dodger**[146] [6657] 4-9-0 44 .... KirstyMilczarek(7) 15 49
(C N Allen) *taken down early: stdd s: hld up in rr: hdwy 5f out: jnd ldrs 3f out: rdn and edgd lft wl over 1f out: one pce after* **10/1**
0030 **4** *2* **Captain Bolsh**[36] [721] 4-9-7 45 .... SebSanders 16 45
(J Pearce) *stdd s: dropped in bhd: rdn and hdwy over 3f out: kpt on u.p fnl f: nt rch ldrs* **18/1**
5-10 **5** *3/4* **Dubai Sunday (JPN)**[41] [691] 6-9-7 45 .... AdamKirby 3 47+
(P S McEntee) *slowly away: hld up in midfield: hdwy over 3f out: chsng ldrs and short of room wl over 1f out: sn outpcd: kpt on fnl f* **3/1**[2]
0004 **6** *2* **Danalova**[23] [907] 3-8-4 45 .... DO'Donohoe 1 37+
(R A Fahey) *trckd ldrs: rdn 3f out: wknd wl over 1f out* **12/1**
0-00 **7** *1 1/4* **Bold Phoenix (IRE)**[89] [266] 6-9-7 45 ....(b) TPQueally 13 38
(B J Curley) *hld up in midfield on outer: hdwy 5f out: led gng wl 3f out: hdd wl over 1f out: sn btn* **11/4**[1]
60-0 **8** *hd* **Finnegans Rainbow**[14] [1011] 5-9-7 45 .... StephenCarson 14 37
(M C Chapman) *sn led: rdn and hdd 3f out: wknd wl over 1f out* **22/1**
6000 **9** *3 1/2* **Bournonville**[37] [716] 4-9-4 41 .... MarcHalford(3) 8 31
(M Wigham) *hld up and bhd: plld out and hdwy u.p 3f out: wknd wl over 1f out* **20/1**
3040 **10** *2 1/2* **Twilight Avenger (IRE)**[23] [907] 4-9-7 45 .... TedDurcan 7 26
(W M Brisbourne) *t.k.h: chsd ldrs: rdn wl over 3f out: wknd 2f out* **18/1**
0-40 **11** *hd* **Herninski**[11] [1011] 4-9-0 42 .... CharlotteKerton(7) 11 25
(M C Chapman) *racd wd: hdwy 5f out: wknd over 3f out: no ch last 2f* **50/1**
2000 **12** *1/2* **Iceni Warrior**[31] [792] 5-9-7 45 .... JimmyQuinn 5 24
(P Howling) *hld up in midfield: rdn wl over 2f out: sn wknd* **12/1**
-000 **13** *17* **She's Dunnett**[17] [980] 4-9-7 45 ....(t) DMylonas 6 —
(Mrs C A Dunnett) *t.k.h: hld up in midfield: rdn and wknd 4f out: wl bhd last 3f: t.o* **22/1**
50-0 **14** *dist* **Frenchgate**[2] [1210] 6-9-2 41 .... NataliaGemelova(5) 4 —
(I W McInnes) *chsd ldr tl wl over 3f out: sn wknd and eased* **25/1**

2m 9.02s (0.92) **Going Correction** 0.0s/f (Good)
WFA 3 from 4yo+ 17lb 14 Ran SP% **125.9**
Speed ratings (Par 97):96,94,92,91,90 89,88,87,85,83 82,82,68,—
CSF £91.48 TOTE £7.80: £2.60, £5.10, £2.90; EX 111.80.
Owner F S W Partnership **Bred** Lloyd Farm Stud **Trained** Catwick, E Yorks

FOCUS
By far the biggest field on the night for the worst race. The form appears sound for the level, but most of these will find it very hard to win another contest.
Dubai Sunday(JPN) Official explanation: jockey said gelding suffered interference in running
Frenchgate Official explanation: jockey said gelding moved poorly throughout

1272 CUSTOM KITCHENS H'CAP 1m 6f 17y
8:00 (8:00) (Class 4) (0-85,83) 4-Y-0+ **£4,728** (£1,406; £702; £351) **Stalls** High

Form RPR
051- **1** **Power Of Future (GER)**[168] [6415] 4-9-4 **80** .... TedDurcan 6 91+
(H R A Cecil) *trckd ldrs: wnt 2nd 6f out: rdn to ld over 2f out: styd on wl u.p ins fnl f* **5/1**[3]
406- **2** *1 3/4* **Whispering Death**[194] [5963] 5-9-9 **83** ....(v) DarryllHolland 3 89
(W J Haggas) *s.i.s: bustled along early: racd in midfield: plld out over 3f out: hdwy over 2f out: ev ch over 1f: no ex last 100yds* **3/1**[2]

102- **3** *hd* **Buster Hyvonen (IRE)**[12] 5946 5-9-1 **75**........................ OscarUrbina 1 80
(J R Fanshawe) *t.k.h: hld up in midfield: rdn 4f out: hung lft under over 1f out: kpt on: nt pce to rch ldrs* **11/4**[1]

403- **4** *1* **Annambo**[306] 2869 7-9-0 **74**.. RichardMullen 8 78
(D Morris) *hld up wl in tch: hdwy to chse ldrs over 3f out: rdn over 2f out: ev ch over 1f out: kpt on same pce ins fnl f* **12/1**

-054 **5** *1 1/2* **Jeepstar**[38] 709 7-8-7 **72**.. PatrickHills(5) 4 75+
(S C Williams) *led: shkn up and qcknd over 4f out: hdd over 2f out: wknd jst ins fnl f* **5/1**[3]

03-0 **6** *5* **Country Pursuit (USA)**[106] 95 5-9-8 **82**....................(p) SebSanders 2 77
(C E Brittain) *chsd ldrs tl 6f out: rdn over 2f out: sn wknd* **8/1**

06-0 **7** *nk* **Zabeel Palace**[36] 726 5-9-4 **78**.. TPQueally 5 72
(B J Curley) *hld up in last pair: outpcd 4f out: n.d* **20/1**

060- **8** *hd* **Mersey Sound (IRE)**[181] 6205 9-9-3 **77**............................ JohnEgan 7 71
(D R C Elsworth) *hld up in last: rdn and outpcd 4f out: n.d* **12/1**

3m 3.37s (-1.93) **Going Correction** 0.0s/f (Good)
WFA 4 from 5yo+ 2lb **8** Ran SP% **116.3**
Speed ratings (Par 105):105,104,103,103,102 99,99,99
CSF £20.79 CT £49.46 TOTE £5.50: £2.00, £1.10, £1.30; EX 20.00 Place 6 £6,630.66, Place 5 £3,900.86.
Owner G Schoeningh **Bred** Gestut Elite **Trained** Newmarket, Suffolk

FOCUS
A reasonable staying handicap and, thanks to Jeepstar, one run at a solid pace and the form is sound rated around the placed horses.
T/Plt: £849.00 to a £1 stake. Pool: £39,252.65. 33.75 winning tickets. T/Qpdt: £31.60 to a £1 stake. Pool: £4,492.60. 105.20 winning tickets. SP

SANDOWN (R-H)

Friday, April 27

OFFICIAL GOING: Good (good to firm in places)
Other races under Rules of jump racing
Wind: Virtually nil

1274 BETFRED GORDON RICHARDS STKS (GROUP 3) 1m 2f 7y

1:45 (1:46) (Class 1) 4-Y-0+

£28,390 (£10,760; £5,385; £2,685; £1,345; £675) **Stalls High**

Form RPR

31-0 **1** **Red Rocks (IRE)**[27] 861 4-9-7 121.. LDettori 2 126
(B J Meehan) *hld up in rr: pushed along and gd hdwy on outside fr 3f out: led ins fnl 2f: styd on strly fnl f* **11/4**[2]

134- **2** *2* **Mashaahed**[195] 5968 4-9-0 110.. RHills 6 115
(B W Hills) *chsd ldrs in 3rd: drvn to chal 2f out: kpt on wl fnl f but no imp on wnr* **10/1**

6-16 **3** *1/2* **Kandidate**[27] 863 5-9-3 114..(t) SebSanders 3 117
(C E Brittain) *lw: chsd ldr: rdn 3f out: chal 2f out: styd on same pce fnl f* **13/2**

210- **4** *1 1/4* **Notnowcato**[195] 5964 5-9-7 122.................................. JamieSpencer 5 119
(Sir Michael Stoute) *bit bkwd: b: stmbld s: in rr but in tch: drvn along over 2f out: styd on ins fnl f but nvr gng pce to rch ldrs* **7/2**[3]

222- **5** *1* **Mountain High (IRE)**[288] 3444 5-9-0 119...................... JimmyFortune 4 110
(Sir Michael Stoute) *lw: led: rdn 3f out: hdd ins fnl 2f: wknd ins fnl f* **5/2**[1]

145- **6** *17* **Art Deco (IRE)**[287] 3517 4-9-0 113.. JohnEgan 1 77
(C R Egerton) *chsd ldrs: drvn along 4f out: wknd ins fnl 3f: bbv* **7/1**

2m 9.16s (-1.08) **Going Correction** +0.10s/f (Good) **6** Ran SP% **112.4**
Speed ratings (Par 113):108,106,106,105,104 90
CSF £28.41 TOTE £3.30: £1.90, £4.70; EX 40.00.
Owner J Paul Reddam **Bred** Ballylinch Stud **Trained** Manton, Wilts

FOCUS
A good renewal of this race, with last season's Breeders' Cup Turf and Juddmonte International winners Red Rocks and Notnowcato on show, and Sir Michael Stoute's hand strengthened by Mountain High in the line-up. The form appears sound enough, rated through the third, and it was a new personal best from the winner.

NOTEBOOK
Red Rocks(IRE), although slightly disappointing when not getting the best of runs in the Sheema Classic, at least had the benefit of that outing, and as a result he looked pretty fit. This race also represented an easier assignment and, despite reservations over the trip, he stayed on strongly down the outside to win with a bit to spare. A consistent colt who showed top form on several occasions last season, it was that touch of class that saw him through and he deserves much credit for defying the 7lb Group 1 penalty. Connections are eyeing a return to that level for a tilt at the Tattersalls Gold Cup at the Curragh next month, but he will need to improve on this effort, as he is likely to face much tougher opposition and it would not be a surprise if more use is made of him. In the long-term, things are geared towards another crack at the Breeders' Cup Turf, for which Coral's quote of 5-1 makes little appeal at this stage. (op 3-1 tchd 4-1)
Mashaahed ◆, progressive at Listed and Group 3 level last season, had a bit to find with the best of these at the weights, but the return to this distance was always going to suit and his stable has been going particularly well. Settled nicely against the rail in third, he was short of room early in the straight and Hills was unable to make his move when he wanted to, but his partner stuck on willingly and has Chester's Huxley Stakes on his agenda. (op 14-1)
Kandidate is a battle-hardened performer who improved throughout last season, winning at this level on Kempton's Polytrack and again in Dubai in February. He was out of his depth in the Dubai World Cup last time, but this represented a much more realistic task and he acquitted himself well. (op 7-1 tchd 6-1)
Notnowcato, a highly-progressive four-year-old last season whose finest hour came when pipping Maraahel in the Juddmonte International, had not been seen since running disappointingly in the Champion Stakes, but this was an ideal comeback race and he looked to hold every chance despite a 7lb penalty for his Group 1 success. However, he looked short of peak fitness in the paddock and a stumble coming out of the stalls hardly did him any favours. He was being niggled before the turn into the straight and could never launch a challenge, though he was staying on nicely under just hands-and-heels riding in the final furlong. He is likely to show the benefit of this run wherever he turns up next. (op 11-4 tchd 5-2)
Mountain High(IRE) did little wrong last season after making a winning reappearance, twice finishing second at Group 2 level, including behind Maraahel in the Hardwicke Stakes. He had plenty of use made of him on this return but began to look vulnerable three furlongs out and was brushed aside by several speedier/fitter rivals. A fine, big horse, he should come on appreciably for the outing and can make his mark at a higher level. (op 11-4 tchd 3-1)
Art Deco(IRE), a smart three-year-old last season, did not have to improve much on the best of his form to play a hand, but he got a bit warm in the preliminaries and it was clear some way from home that he was not going particularly well. He dropped right out inside the final quarter-mile, but is a good deal better than this and it emerged post-race that he had bled. This was hardly the ideal start to the season. Official explanation: trainer said colt was scoped post-race and was found to have bled (op 8-1)

1275 BETFREDCASINO ESHER CUP (H'CAP) 1m 14y

2:15 (2:19) (Class 2) (0-100,94) 3-Y-0

£12,464 (£3,732; £1,866; £934; £466; £234) **Stalls High**

Form RPR

610- **1** **Desert Dew (IRE)**[188] 6102 3-9-4 **94**................................ MichaelHills 10 105+
(B W Hills) *h.d.w: in tch: hdwy 4f out: drvn to ld wl over 1f out: styd on wl: readily* **7/1**[3]

301- **2** *3* **Aegean Prince**[192] 6032 3-8-4 **80**.................................. RichardMullen 4 84
(W R Muir) *in rr: drvn and hdwy over 2f out: styd on wl to take 2nd ins fnl f but no imp on wnr* **50/1**

211 **3** *1 1/2* **Zaham (USA)**[20] 939 3-8-11 **87**.. RHills 11 88+
(M Johnston) *lw: disp ld at str pce: rdn over 2f out: hdd wl over 1f out: styd on same pce ins fnl f* **7/4**[1]

012- **4** *3/4* **Buccellati**[197] 5916 3-8-8 **84**.. MartinDwyer 2 83
(A M Balding) *t.k.h in rr: drvn 3f out: hdwy 2f out: n.m.r and swtchd rt 1f out: kpt on nr fin and gng on cl home* **14/1**

211- **5** *1* **Tredegar**[172] 6379 3-8-12 **88**.. SebSanders 1 85+
(P F I Cole) *bit bkwd: sn disputing ld at str pce: rdn 3f out: hdd wl over 1f out: wknd fnl f* **14/1**

21-2 **6** *hd* **Tybalt (USA)**[20] 939 3-9-3 **93**.. JimmyFortune 8 90
(J H M Gosden) *swtg: s.i.s and stmbld after 1f: drvn and hdwy over 3f out: styd on same pce fnl 2f* **9/4**[2]

214- **7** *1/2* **Rose Of Petra (IRE)**[189] 6074 3-8-7 **83**........................ JamieSpencer 5 78
(Sir Michael Stoute) *chsd ldrs: rdn over 2f out: wknd fnl f* **12/1**

01- **8** *6* **Mr Aviator (USA)**[138] 6778 3-8-4 **80** oh4........................ RichardSmith 3 62
(R Hannon) *in rr: rdn and sme hdwy over 2f out: nvr gng pce to be competitive* **16/1**

2-11 **9** *1/2* **Chookie Hamilton**[98] 184 3-8-7 **83**.................................. TomEaves 9 63
(I Semple) *chsd ldrs: rdn 5f out: wknd over 2f out* **33/1**

015- **10** *1 1/4* **Kilburn**[223] 5359 3-8-12 **88**.. PhilipRobinson 6 66
(C G Cox) *bit bkwd: chsd ldrs: rdn over 3f out: sn btn* **14/1**

13-4 **11** *41* **Laurentina**[27] 838 3-9-4 **94**.. LDettori 7 —
(B J Meehan) *s.i.s: bhd and stmbld after 1f: rdn over 3f out: nvr in contention: eased fnl f: t.o* **16/1**

1m 42.74s (-1.21) **Going Correction** +0.10s/f (Good) **11** Ran SP% **124.0**
Speed ratings (Par 104):110,107,105,104,103 103,103,97,96,95 54
CSF £307.48 CT £901.96 TOTE £9.70: £2.90, £12.00, £1.40; EX 591.00 TRIFECTA Not won..
Owner Gainsborough **Bred** Mrs Rebecca Philipps **Trained** Lambourn, Berks

FOCUS
A typically good three-year-old handicap for the course, with several progressive types and favourite Zaham, along with Tredegar, ensured there was a decent pace. The form looks strong and is rated fairly positively.

NOTEBOOK
Desert Dew(IRE), whose stable has won this race twice in the last ten years, had not been seen since disappointing on ground that was thought too soft for him in the Group 3 Horris Hill at Newbury. However, his earlier Newmarket maiden win showed him to be a colt of at least useful ability and he made a mockery of his mark of 94, quickening clear over a furlong out and running on strongly despite looking to idle inside the final half-furlong. The step up to 1m suited the Indian Ridge colt, who also benefited from having the early leaders coming back to him, and connections' initial thoughts were to let him take his chance in the Dee Stakes at Chester next month, as handicaps are going to be out following this. (op 10-1 tchd 13-2, 11-1 in a place)
Aegean Prince comes from a stable that has made a relatively slow start to the season and it was easy to see why he was dismissed in the betting, as the form of his 7f Lingfield maiden win last season was not good. However, he has clearly done well from two to three and finished well to claim second without looking likely to get to the winner. The extra furlong was in his favour and, although he will go up a few pounds, he looked as though he would come on for the run beforehand, and there is surely a race or two in him this season.
Zaham(USA) has been a typically progressive Mark Johnston-trained three-year-old, winning his maiden at Lingfield and gaining a battling success over Tybalt in a Kempton handicap off a 7lb lower mark. Open to improvement on this turf debut, he was strongly supported into favouritism despite being 2lb worse off with his Kempton victim and looked to have an ideal draw for a front-runner, right against the rail. He was unable to get things his own way though, as Tredegar was also intent on leading and the pair ended up going too fast. This did not stop Zaham hanging on for a place, and he rates a little better than he showed here. (op 11-4)
Buccellati ◆, having his first start since finishing second at Newmarket off a 4lb lower mark last October, looked fit beforehand but was a bit on his toes. In the race itself he was a real eyecatcher. A shade keen early on, Martin Dwyer did a good job settling him and, although it was clear the colt was not getting near the leader, he made good late headway in between runners. His yard has yet to get going and a little improvement should see him land a nice prize this season. (op 16-1)
Tredegar finished his juvenile season in good style, winning a Newmarketmaiden and supplementing that with victory in a novice stakes at Wolverhampton, but he was unable to sustain the gallop on this reappearance. (op 12-1)
Tybalt(USA) is not overly big and there was no guarantee he would improve as much on his Kempton second as expected. In rear early, he made limited headway under pressure and was basically a bit disappointing, suggesting he may find life difficult off his current mark. (op 2-1 tchd 15-8)
Rose Of Petra(IRE), who is related to Islington and Greek Dance, looked the type to have improved a good deal over the winter and she was in with every chance over two furlongs out, but could not sustain her effort. (tchd 11-1)
Mr Aviator(USA) was green and whinnying in the paddock beforehand. (op 14-1)
Kilburn was reportedly unsuited by the ground. Official explanation: trainer said colt was unsuited by the good (good to firm places) ground (op 16-1)
Laurentina looked pretty fit beforehand but she stumbled leaving the stalls and was never going thereafter. Official explanation: jockey said filly was unsettled in stalls, stumbled and never travelled thereafter

1276 TEXT "BETFRED" TO 83080 FOR MOBILE BETTING CONDITIONS STKS 1m 14y

4:00 (4:01) (Class 3) 3-Y-0

£7,478 (£2,239; £1,119; £560; £279; £140) **Stalls High**

Form RPR

2- **1** **Yeaman's Hall**[199] 5892 3-8-10.. MartinDwyer 5 103
(A M Balding) *h.d.w: led: drvn and hdd over 1f out: n.m.r on rail: green and rallied gamely ins fnl f to ld again fnl 100yds* **4/1**[3]

216- **2** *nk* **Sunshine Kid (USA)**[188] 6104 3-9-0 97........................ JimmyFortune 2 106
(J H M Gosden) *chsd ldrs: wnt 2nd over 2f out: drvn to ld over 1f out: hung rt u.p ins fnl f: hdd and one pce fnl 100yds* **6/5**[1]

1 **3** *8* **Lone Wolfe**[95] 208 3-8-10 73.. JohnEgan 3 84
(Jane Chapple-Hyam) *b.hind: in tch: rdn over 3f out: styd on to take 3rd over 1f out but nvr in contention w ldng pair* **8/1**

214- **4** *2 1/2* **Opera Music**[188] 6102 3-9-0 97.. LDettori 4 82
(S Kirk) *swtg: sn chsng ldr: rdn over 2f out: wknd over 1f out* **7/2**[2]

401- **5** *3 1/2* **Magic Mountain (IRE)**[272] 3949 3-9-0 87.................... RichardHughes 6 74
(R Hannon) *chsd ldrs: rdn 3f out: wknd appr fnl 2f* **10/1**

6 27 **Silca Elegance** 3-8-7 .... TedDurcan 1 —
(M R Channon) *w/like: scope: bit bkwd: s.i.s: in rr: rdn over 4f out: lost tch over 3f out* **20/1**

1m 43.3s (-0.65) **Going Correction** +0.10s/f (Good) **6** Ran SP% **112.6**
Speed ratings (Par 102):107,106,98,96,92 65
CSF £9.33 TOTE £5.30: £2.40, £1.30; EX 10.70.
Owner George Strawbridge **Bred** George Strawbridge **Trained** Kingsclere, Hants

FOCUS
A race that has thrown up several smart performers over the years, including Little Rock and Medicean, and the fact the front two pulled some eight lengths clear bodes well for their futures. The third's modest rated from one outing probably does not reflect his true ability.

NOTEBOOK
Yeaman's Hall ◆, a promising second at Newbury on his sole start at two, missed his engagement at Newbury last weekend and this was a more competitive heat. However, he is held in quite high regard at home and has the looks to be a smart performer. Soon in front, he strode out well in the straight and looked to have them all on the stretch, but Sunshine Kid eventually drew alongside and indeed went past him, but he rallied despite being a bit pressed for room on the rail and got back up in determined fashion. He is in the Dante and looks worth his place in a better contest, but connections are unlikely to risk him on very fast ground. (op 6-1 tchd 7-2)
Sunshine Kid(USA), who took this option as opposed to the Sandown Classic Trial, was thought good enough to run in the Racing Post Trophy on his final start at two, having won his maiden at Newbury, and the faster ground was expected to suit for this seasonal reappearance. He looked pretty fit, was rightly made favourite, and came to head the winner over a furlong out, but Yeaman's Hall proved most determined and simply stayed on too strongly for him. He will no doubt win a nice prize this season, but there is no reason why he should reverse form with his conqueror if they clash again. (op Evens tchd 7-4)
Lone Wolfe, ready winner of a 7f Kempton maiden on his debut, was tackling some classy types and third was probably as good a run as connections could have hoped for. He has ability and is likely to improve for an additional couple of furlongs. (op 5-1)
Opera Music was the main disappointment of the race. Still in the 2000 Guineas, he showed useful form to finish fourth in the Horris Hill at two and the extra yardage here was expected to suit. However, having been prominent early on, he could not race with the front pair and cannot line up for the opening Classic on this evidence. (op 4-1 tchd 3-1)
Magic Mountain(IRE), a 6f Salisbury maiden winner at two, should stay this sort of trip and it just looked a case of him being outclassed. He should improve for the run and handicaps beckon. (op 14-1)
Silca Elegance, another who missed Newbury last weekend, holds an entry in the Derby but he did not move well to post and was too inexperienced to make an impact here. It is likely that he will have to drop into maiden company to get off the mark.

1277 BETFREDCASINO H'CAP 1m 2f 7y
4:35 (4:35) (Class 3) (0-90,90) 3-Y-O
£7,478 (£2,239; £1,119; £560; £279; £140) **Stalls** High

Form RPR
12 1 **Silkwood**[37] 719 3-8-11 **83** .... PhilipRobinson 9 92+
(M A Jarvis) *lw: trckd ldrs: drvn and n.m.r 2f out: qcknd to ld appr fnl f: pushed out: readily* **2/1**[2]
52-1 2 ¾ **Bergonzi (IRE)**[15] 1011 3-8-6 **78** .... TedDurcan 3 86
(J H M Gosden) *chsd ldrs: rdn 3f out: led ins fnl 2f: hdd appr fnl f: styd on but nt pce of wnr* **16/1**
0-31 3 hd **Surrey Spinner**[53] 611 3-8-8 **80** .... JimCrowley 8 87
(Mrs A J Perrett) *str: bit bkwd: chsd ldrs: hrd drvn and one pce over 2f out: kpt on u.p fnl f to take 3rd but nvr gng pce to trble wnr* **14/1**
103- 4 ½ **Hanging On**[189] 6074 3-9-4 **90** .... AdamKirby 5 96
(W R Swinburn) *bit bkwd: hld up in rr: hdwy fr 2f out: kpt on ins fnl f and n.m.r cl home* **12/1**
410- 5 5 **Paceman (USA)**[197] 5916 3-8-10 **82** .... RichardHughes 2 79
(R Hannon) *w/like: scope: in rr tl rapid hdwy to chse ldrs 5f out: rdn to chal over 2f out: wknd over 1f out* **20/1**
001- 6 3 **Spume (IRE)**[212] 5622 3-8-5 **77** .... MartinDwyer 7 68
(Sir Michael Stoute) *lengthy: lw: chsd ldr: rdn 3f out: wknd ins fnl 2f* **6/4**[1]
0-1 7 ½ **Mandragola**[25] 884 3-8-7 **79** .... MichaelHills 1 69
(B W Hills) *in rr but in tch: sme prog over 3f out: nvr in contention and wknd fnl 2f* **12/1**
30-3 8 hd **Kalasam**[10] 1081 3-8-4 **76** .... RichardMullen 6 66
(W R Muir) *in rr: rdn and sme prog on ins 3f out: wknd 2f out* **25/1**
42-1 9 ¾ **Salaasa (USA)**[17] 991 3-9-3 **89** .... RHills 4 78
(M Johnston) *led tl hdd ins fnl 2f: wknd qckly* **13/2**[3]

2m 12.55s (2.31) **Going Correction** +0.10s/f (Good) **9** Ran SP% **123.2**
Speed ratings (Par 102):94,93,93,92,88 86,86,85,85
CSF £37.09 CT £379.86 TOTE £3.50: £1.30, £3.80, £3.10; EX 47.70 Place 6 £48.73, Place 5 £44.90.
Owner Sheikh Mohammed **Bred** Darley **Trained** Newmarket, Suffolk

FOCUS
A race with a good recent history - Hazyview and Linas Selection won two of the last three runnings - and this year's renewal, rated more positively than might have been with the placed horses fair improvers, looks likely to produce a decent handicap winner or two through the season.

NOTEBOOK
Silkwood, one of two fillies in the field, has an Oaks entry and there was no disgrace in her recent defeat by a progressive Mark Johnston three-year-old at Kempton. Making her turf debut, she took a while to get going, but was always doing enough in the final half-furlong and looks to be crying outfor another two furlongs. She is unlikely to develop into an Epsom contender, but is going the right way and remains open to improvement. (op 11-4)
Bergonzi(IRE), narrow winner of a Leicester maiden on his reappearance, has made good progress from two to three and this represented another improvement. Always well positioned, he went on inside the final quarter-mile and stuck on strongly once headed, suggesting he may stay a bit further. (op 12-1)
Surrey Spinner, winner of a Lingfield maiden over this distance, raised his game for the return to turf and it has to go down as a decent effort considering his stable has started the season slowly. He was doing his best work late and a little more improvement should enable him to win off this sort of mark.
Hanging On, a half-sister to smart stayer Barolo, was thought good enough to try her luck in the Group 3 Prestige Stakes at two and she made a highly-encouraging reappearance under top weight. She is another whose stable has yet to hit form, but she is likely to be winning when it does. (op 20-1 tchd 11-1)
Paceman(USA), held off this mark in a Newmarket handicap on his final start at two, finished a bit adrift of the front four and may need some assistance from the Handicapper before he is back winning. (op 16-1)
Spume(IRE) was most disappointing. He improved with racing at two, landing a Salisbury maiden on his final start, and looked to be on an attractive mark of 77 considering he has been working with some of his trainer's brighter three-year-old prospects. Solid at the head of the market, he held an ideal early position, but there was little response when he was asked to make his move and this effort leaves him with a bit to prove, for all that he is thought capable of much better. (op 7-4 tchd 15-8, 2-1 in a place)
Mandragola, who did not look great in his coat, found this a lot tougher than his Lingfield maiden. (op 10-1)
Salaasa(USA), who was representing the trainer responsible for the last two winners of this race, stopped very quickly under pressure and failed to build on the promise of his recent maiden success. (op 5-1)
T/Plt: £134.90 to a £1 stake. Pool: £66,288.00. 358.55 winning tickets. T/Qpdt: £34.20 to a £1 stake. Pool: £3,577.20. 77.40 winning tickets. ST

1226 WOLVERHAMPTON (A.W) (L-H)
Friday, April 27

OFFICIAL GOING: Standard
Wind: Light, against Weather: Sunny spells

1278 BETDIRECT.COM GET INVOLVED MAIDEN STKS (DIV I) 7f 32y(P)
1:40 (1:41) (Class 5) 3-Y-O
£2,266 (£674; £337; £168) **Stalls** High

Form RPR
033- 1 **Rule Of Life**[167] 6434 3-9-3 76 .... KDarley 8 79+
(B W Hills) *trckd ldr: led over 2f out: edgd lft and pushed clr fnl f* **4/9**[1]
2 7 **Six Of Hearts** 3-9-0 .... RichardKingscote(3) 1 60
(J A Osborne) *chsd ldrs: rdn 1/2-way: styd on same pce fnl 2f* **13/2**[2]
0 3 nk **Royal Rock**[18] 977 3-9-3 .... IanMongan 10 60+
(C F Wall) *hld up: swtchd rt and hdwy over 1f out: sn hung lft: nvr nr to chal* **40/1**
4 2½ **Vincenzio (IRE)** 3-9-3 .... PaulHanagan 11 53+
(C R Egerton) *hld up: r.o ins fnl f: nvr nrr* **14/1**
5 1¾ **Golden Brown (IRE)** 3-9-3 .... FergusSweeney 4 49
(David Pinder) *led: rdn and hdd over 2f out: wknd fnl f* **66/1**
3 6 1 **Singleb (IRE)**[39] 711 3-9-3 .... PaulFessey 7 46+
(T D Barron) *hld up: effrt 1/2-way: n.d* **25/1**
6 7 hd **Pretty Demanding (IRE)**[14] 1024 3-8-9 .... JerryO'Dwyer(3) 12 40
(M G Quinlan) *sn outpcd* **33/1**
0-0 8 1¼ **Gyration (IRE)**[18] 977 3-9-3 .... TPQueally 2 42
(J G Given) *prom: racd keenly: wknd over 2f out* **66/1**
30- 9 nk **Spectacular Joy (IRE)**[228] 5245 3-9-3 .... RoystonFfrench 3 41
(Mrs A Duffield) *s.i.s: sn chsng ldrs: rdn 1/2-way: wknd over 2f out* **33/1**
10 hd **Womaniser (IRE)** 3-9-3 .... NickyMackay 5 41
(L M Cumani) *s.s: outpcd* **9/1**[3]

1m 29.7s (-0.70) **Going Correction** -0.15s/f (Stan) **10** Ran SP% **114.4**
Speed ratings (Par 98):98,90,89,86,84 83,83,82,81,81
CSF £3.15 TOTE £1.50: £1.02, £2.20, £9.60; EX 4.60 Trifecta £78.10 Pool £313.72, 2.85 winning units.
Owner K Abdulla **Bred** Juddmonte Farms Ltd **Trained** Lambourn, Berks

FOCUS
Despite a convincing winner, this maiden lacked strength in depth and the winning time was 1.67 seconds slower than the second division. The winner sets the standard.
Gyration(IRE) Official explanation: trainer said colt was found to be lame the following morning

1279 BETDIRECTPOKER.COM COME AND 'AVE SOME APPRENTICE (S) STKS 1m 4f 50y(P)
2:10 (2:11) (Class 6) 4-Y-0+
£2,184 (£644; £322) **Stalls** Low

Form RPR
-343 1 **Rudry World (IRE)**[3] 1221 4-8-8 57 .... SophieDoyle(5) 3 59
(P A Blockley) *led 1f: chsd ldrs: edgd lft over 2f out: led 1f out: r.o* **6/1**[3]
0 2 1½ **Brastar Jelois (FR)**[10] 1083 4-8-8 78 .... (v[1]) HaddenFrost 5 52
(D E Pipe) *trckd ldrs: led 2f out: rdn and hdd 1f out: styd on same pce* **2/1**[1]
0010 3 shd **Bethanys Boy (IRE)**[30] 808 6-9-3 60 .... MCGeran(3) 1 62+
(P A Blockley) *s.s: hld up: plld hrd: hdwy to ld over 5f out: hdd 2f out: styd on same pce fnl f* **9/4**[2]
6263 4 1 **Regency Red (IRE)**[25] 891 9-8-10 55 .... Julie-AnneCumine(10) 6 61
(W M Brisbourne) *hld up: hdwy over 4f out: rdn over 1f out: styd on* **8/1**
4545 5 1¼ **Laugh 'n Cry**[11] 1066 6-8-6 47 .... JosephWalsh(3) 2 48+
(C A Cyzer) *hld up: plld hrd: outpcd 4f out: r.o ins fnl f: nvr nrr* **10/1**
6 ¾ **Berlin Bunker (IRE)**[31] 6-8-9 .... NSLawes(5) 8 52
(B Ellison) *led after 1f: hdd 10f out: chsd ldrs: rdn over 2f out: styd on same pce appr fnl f* **8/1**
4-54 7 1¾ **Royal Sailor (IRE)**[18] 372 5-8-7 37 .... MarvinCheung(7) 9 49?
(J Ryan) *s.i.s: sn chsng ldrs: rdn over 2f out: wknd fnl f* **40/1**
000/ 8 4 **Compton Quay**[500] 2559 5-9-0 59 .... (p) JamieHamblett 10 42
(Karen George) *hld up: rdn over 4f out: n.d* **25/1**
5/0- 9 ½ **Golden Measure**[437] 414 7-8-8 45 .... (e[1]) SoniaEaton(6) 4 42
(B P J Baugh) *led 10f out: hdd over 5f out: wkng whn hmpd over 2f out: bhd whn hmpd over 1f out* **33/1**

2m 46.34s (3.92) **Going Correction** -0.15s/f (Stan)
WFA 4 from 5yo+ 1lb **9** Ran SP% **118.9**
Speed ratings (Par 101):80,79,78,78,77 76,75,73,72
CSF £18.75 TOTE £6.60: £3.00, £1.10, £1.40; EX 26.60 Trifecta £71.60 Pool £174.59, 1.73 winning units.No bid for the winner. Berlin Bunker (IRE) was claimed by Luke Dace for £6,400. Brastar Jelois (FR) was claimed by Phil Pye for £6,400
Owner Rudry Racing Partnership **Bred** Richard Leonard **Trained** Lambourn, Berks
■ Stewards' Enquiry : Sophie Doyle one-day ban: careless riding (May 8)

FOCUS
A messy affair, run at a slow pace with most of the runners failing to settle, and the form looks weak.

1280 BETDIRECTPOKER.COM GET INVOLVED H'CAP 7f 32y(P)
2:40 (2:41) (Class 6) (0-60,60) 4-Y-0+
£2,388 (£705; £352) **Stalls** High

Form RPR
4023 1 **Another Genepi (USA)**[18] 967 4-9-1 **57** .... (b) NCallan 9 76
(K A Ryan) *mde all: rdn clr fnl 2f* **4/1**[2]
3006 2 7 **Lucius Verrus (USA)**[32] 793 7-8-13 **60** .... (v) PatrickHills(5) 4 61
(D Shaw) *mid-div: rdn 1/2-way: hdwy over 2f out: sn hung rt: hung lft and styd on fnl f: no ch w wnr* **7/1**
000- 3 1½ **Bens Georgie (IRE)**[194] 5987 5-9-1 **57** .... RobertHavlin 1 54
(D K Ivory) *prom: rdn over 2f out: sn outpcd* **12/1**
000- 4 ½ **Millfield (IRE)**[209] 5684 4-9-2 **58** .... IanMongan 3 54
(P R Chamings) *s.s: hld up: plld hrd: nt clr run over 2f out: hdwy over 1f out: n.d* **8/1**
000- 5 1 **Kirkby's Treasure**[293] 3289 9-9-1 **57** .... DeanMcKeown 12 50+
(G A Swinbank) *sn outpcd: styd on ins fnl f: nvr nrr* **9/1**
5233 6 hd **Haroldini (IRE)**[11] 1064 5-9-4 **60** .... (p) PaulHanagan 8 52
(J Balding) *mid-div: rdn over 2f out: wknd over 1f out* **10/3**[1]
0020 7 nk **Benny The Bus**[11] 1064 5-9-3 **59** .... GrahamGibbons 2 51
(Mrs G S Rees) *chsd ldrs: rdn over 2f out: wknd over 1f out* **10/1**
05-0 8 1¼ **Iced Diamond (IRE)**[31] 806 8-9-1 **57** .... FergusSweeney 6 45
(W M Brisbourne) *s.i.s: hld up: n.d* **12/1**

421- **9** *2* **Ours (IRE)**[157] 6557 4-9-4 **60**....................(b) DarryllHolland 5 43
(J D Bethell) *prom: chsd wnr 3f out: sn rdn: hung lft over 1f out: wknd fnl f* **6/1**[3]
66-0 **10** *5* **Hang Loose**[14] 1025 4-8-13 **55**.................... EddieAhern 10 25
(S W Hall) *chsd wnr 4f: wknd 2f out* **20/1**
260- **11** *1 ¼* **Jodrell Bank (IRE)**[207] 5729 4-8-12 **57**.................... MarcHalford[(3)] 7 24
(J Ryan) *s.i.s: hld up: rdn 1/2-way: sn wknd* **33/1**
000 **12** *28* **Polar Fox**[11] 1065 4-9-1 **57**....................(v) TPQueally 11 —
(D Shaw) *s.i.s: hld up: wknd 1/2-way* **50/1**

1m 28.07s (-2.33) **Going Correction** -0.15s/f (Stan) **12** Ran SP% **125.1**
Speed ratings (Par 101):107,99,97,96,95 95,95,93,91,85 84,52
CSF £33.71 CT £327.44 TOTE £5.00: £1.70, £3.00, £8.00; EX 43.30 TRIFECTA Not won..
Owner Hambleton Racing Ltd I **Bred** Joseph Lacombe Stables Inc **Trained** Hambleton, N Yorks

FOCUS
A moderate affair that did not take much winning but the time was decent for the grade and the winner is rated to earlier efforts.
Ours(IRE) Official explanation: jockey said gelding had no more to give

1281 BETDIRECTPOKER.COM $50,000 FREEROLL (S) STKS 7f 32y(P)
3:15 (3:16) (Class 6) 3-Y-O **£2,047** (£604; £302) **Stalls** High

Form RPR
3346 **1** **Hollywood George**[22] 935 3-8-12 68....................(p) NCallan 7 57+
(K A Ryan) *a.p: chsd wnr 3f out: led over 1f out: edgd lft: comf* **8/13**[1]
50-3 **2** *1 ½* **Marist Madame**[6] 1164 3-8-7 50.................... RobertHavlin 2 48
(D K Ivory) *chsd ldrs: rdn over 2f out: styd on* **14/1**
0-06 **3** *1* **Peggys Flower**[6] 1164 3-8-7 57.................... DO'Donohoe 6 45
(M Wigham) *plld hrd and prom: rdn over 1f out: kpt on ins fnl f* **14/1**
455- **4** *½* **Mickleberry (IRE)**[269] 4017 3-8-8 65 ow1.................... DarryllHolland 1 45
(J D Bethell) *led: rdn and hdd over 1f out: no ex ins fnl f* **13/2**[2]
001 **5** *2 ½* **Solidgoldesyaction**[6] 1164 3-8-12.................... PaulHanagan 8 43
(P A Blockley) *mid-div: rdn 1/2-way: no imp fnl 2f* **8/1**[3]
0-02 **6** *1 ½* **Iron Dancer (IRE)**[6] 1164 3-8-12 48.................... TPO'Shea 10 39
(P A Blockley) *hld up: rdn 1/2-way: r.o ins fnl f: nvr nrr* **14/1**
4005 **7** *4* **Tenterhooks (IRE)**[15] 1008 3-8-4 45....................(be) PatrickMathers[(3)] 9 23
(A J McCabe) *s.i.s: rdn 1/2-way: n.d* **25/1**
0060 **8** *2* **Fareham Creek**[25] 894 3-8-12 46.................... HayleyTurner 11 23
(D K Ivory) *s.i.s: a in rr* **50/1**
00 **9** *4* **Pickledallnuts**[13] 1045 3-8-8 ow1.................... PaulMulrennan 4 9
(Miss J A Camacho) *chsd ldr 4f: hung rt and wknd over 2f out* **50/1**

1m 29.89s (-0.51) **Going Correction** -0.15s/f (Stan) **9** Ran SP% **114.1**
Speed ratings (Par 96):96,94,93,92,89 88,83,81,76
CSF £10.65 TOTE £1.80: £1.02, £3.00, £5.90; EX 12.00 Trifecta £59.30 Pool: £316.99, 3.79 winning units.The winner was sold to Mandy Rowland for 13,500gns.
Owner Sunpak Potatoes **Bred** Chippenham Lodge Stud Ltd **Trained** Hambleton, N Yorks

FOCUS
The favourite was best in at the weights and made it tell against a moderate field. The form looks reasonable rated around the runner-up and fifth.

1282 BETDIRECT.COM GET INVOLVED MAIDEN STKS (DIV II) 7f 32y(P)
3:50 (3:52) (Class 5) 3-Y-O **£2,266** (£674; £337; £168) **Stalls** High

Form RPR
1 **Riggins (IRE)** 3-9-3.................... NickyMackay 7 92+
(L M Cumani) *hld up: hdwy over 2f out: led and edgd lft 1f out: sn clr* **4/1**[3]
62 **2** *7* **Diksie Dancer**[13] 1045 3-8-12.................... NCallan 3 69+
(K A Ryan) *chsd clr ldr tl led over 2f out: rdn: edgd lft and hdd 1f out: sn btn* **2/1**[1]
3 *2 ½* **Etain (IRE)** 3-8-12.................... DarryllHolland 2 63+
(W R Swinburn) *s.i.s: hdwy over 1f out: nrst fin* **14/1**
0 **4** *2 ½* **Mango Masher (IRE)**[13] 1037 3-9-3.................... PaulHanagan 5 61
(C R Egerton) *hld up: styd on ins fnl f: nvr nrr* **14/1**
5 *1 ¾* **Elusive Dreams (USA)** 3-9-3.................... RobertHavlin 8 56+
(J H M Gosden) *s.s and hmpd s: styd on ins fnl f: nvr nrr* **9/4**[2]
05 **6** *3* **Faithful Ruler (USA)**[41] 700 3-9-3....................(b[1]) EddieAhern 4 49
(M A Magnusson) *led and sn clr: hdd over 2f out: sn wknd* **11/1**
50- **7** *½* **Gallows Hill (USA)**[313] 2680 3-8-12.................... JamieMoriarty[(5)] 10 47+
(R A Fahey) *outpcd* **28/1**
0-0 **8** *nk* **Almondillo (IRE)**[18] 973 3-9-3.................... IanMongan 6 47
(C F Wall) *chsd ldrs: rdn over 2f out: sn wknd* **28/1**
0 **9** *1* **Hello Nod**[36] 728 3-9-3.................... PaulMulrennan 9 44
(Miss J A Camacho) *dwlt and wnt lft s: outpcd* **40/1**
0 **10** *3 ½* **Abadia**[17] 998 3-8-12.................... TPQueally 12 30
(J G Given) *mid-div: rdn 1/2-way: wknd over 2f out* **25/1**
5-50 **11** *2* **Brynris**[94] 224 3-9-3 36.................... GrahamGibbons 11 30
(Mrs G S Rees) *mid-div: rdn 1/2-way: sn wknd* **80/1**

1m 28.03s (-2.37) **Going Correction** -0.15s/f (Stan) **11** Ran SP% **120.2**
Speed ratings (Par 98):107,99,96,93,91 87,87,86,85,81 79
CSF £12.14 TOTE £6.30: £2.00, £1.30, £4.10; EX 14.90 Trifecta £125.90 Pool: £603.018, 3.40 winning units.
Owner Scuderia Rencati Srl **Bred** Compagnia Generale S R L **Trained** Newmarket, Suffolk

FOCUS
As in the first division, a seven-length winner, but the winning time here was 1.67 seconds faster and not an easy race to assess.
Elusive Dreams(USA) ◆ Official explanation: jockey said colt was hampered at the start

1283 BETDIRECTPOKER.COM $50,000 FREEROLL H'CAP 7f 32y(P)
4:25 (4:26) (Class 5) (0-75,75) 4-Y-O+ **£3,238** (£963; £481; £240) **Stalls** High

Form RPR
2212 **1** **Harare**[34] 770 6-8-7 **71**....................(v) WilliamCarson[(7)] 8 83
(R J Price) *racd keenly: sn trcking ldr: led 2f out: rdn out* **4/1**[2]
3464 **2** *2* **Final Tune (IRE)**[23] 930 4-8-12 **72**.................... PatrickMathers[(3)] 7 79
(Miss M E Rowland) *a.p: rdn 2f out: styd on* **10/1**
330- **3** *1* **Moves Goodenough**[156] 6564 4-8-9 **66**.................... HayleyTurner 2 70
(Andrew Turnell) *hld up: swtchd rt over 1f out: styd on ins fnl f: nt trble ldrs* **16/1**
26-0 **4** *shd* **Cape Presto (IRE)**[30] 810 4-9-1 **72**....................(v) DMylonas 4 76
(Mrs C A Dunnett) *led 5f: sn rdn: no ex ins fnl f* **16/1**
01-1 **5** *nk* **Shy Glance (USA)**[7] 1132 5-9-2 **73** 6ex.................... DaleGibson 1 76
(G A Swinbank) *chsd ldrs: rdn over 2f out: no ex fnl f* **10/11**[1]
0-01 **6** *2 ½* **Raza Cab (IRE)**[28] 827 5-9-4 **75**.................... DarryllHolland 6 71
(Karen George) *hld up: hdwy over 1f out: wknd ins fnl f* **10/1**
6126 **7** *7* **Tancredi (SWE)**[13] 1036 5-8-10 **70**.................... JerryO'Dwyer[(3)] 5 48
(N B King) *s.s: hld up: hdwy over 2f out: wknd over 1f out: eased* **9/1**[3]

1m 28.76s (-1.64) **Going Correction** -0.15s/f (Stan) **7** Ran SP% **112.3**
Speed ratings (Par 103):103,100,99,99,99 96,88
CSF £40.35 CT £568.24 TOTE £5.70: £1.90, £3.60; EX 33.00 Trifecta £282.60 Part won. Pool: £398.07, 0.50 winning units..
Owner Mrs P A Wallis **Bred** Limestone Stud **Trained** Ullingswick, H'fords

FOCUS
A fair little handicap run at a reasonable pace but ordinary form rated around the placed horses.
Shy Glance(USA) Official explanation: trainer's rep said, regarding running, that the race may have come too soon

1284 BETDIRECTCASINO.COM H'CAP 1m 141y(P)
5:00 (5:00) (Class 6) (0-65,64) 4-Y-O+ **£2,388** (£705; £352) **Stalls** Low

Form RPR
4612 **1** **Scamperdale**[11] 1069 5-9-3 **63**....................(p) TPQueally 2 71
(B P J Baugh) *chsd ldrs: nt clr run over 3f out: rdn to ld and hung lft ins fnl f: edgd rt towards fin* **15/8**[1]
5411 **2** *hd* **Scottish River (USA)**[3] 1227 8-9-1 **61** 6ex.................... HayleyTurner 8 69
(M D I Usher) *hld up: hdwy over 2f out: rdn and ev ch ins fnl f: styd on* **10/3**[2]
0526 **3** *1 ¾* **Hits Only Cash**[31] 806 5-8-10 **56**.................... DeanMcKeown 3 60
(J Pearce) *chsd ldrs: lost pl 7f out: hdwy over 1f out: hung lft ins fnl f: r.o* **13/2**[3]
4120 **4** *¾* **My Michelle**[11] 1069 6-9-4 **64**.................... DaleGibson 10 66
(B Palling) *led over 7f out: rdn over 1f out: hdd and no ex ins fnl f* **10/1**
00-5 **5** *nk* **Wally Barge**[53] 616 4-8-6 **52**.................... RobertHavlin 6 54
(D K Ivory) *chsd ldr 6f out: rdn and ev ch 1f out: styd on same pce* **20/1**
0-46 **6** *½* **Reveur**[13] 1038 4-8-7 **53**.................... RoystonFfrench 4 53
(M Mullineaux) *hld up: swtchd rt over 1f out: n.m.r and r.o ins fnl f: nt trble ldrs* **11/1**
5544 **7** *shd* **Summer Lodge**[6] 1162 4-9-0 **63**....................(be) StephenDonohoe[(3)] 9 63
(A J McCabe) *hld up: hdwy over 5f out: rdn over 1f out: styd on same pce* **10/1**
003- **8** *1* **Beautiful Summer (IRE)**[211] 5637 4-8-11 **57**.................... PaulHanagan 1 55
(R A Fahey) *led: hdd over 7f out: chsd ldrs: rdn over 2f out: wknd fnl f* **8/1**
4020 **9** *1* **Gem Bien (USA)**[11] 1066 9-7-11 **50** oh1....................(p) DanielleMcCreery[(7)] 7 46
(D W Chapman) *dwlt: hld up: rdn over 2f out: n.d* **20/1**

1m 51.71s (-0.05) **Going Correction** -0.15s/f (Stan) **9** Ran SP% **118.3**
Speed ratings (Par 101):94,93,92,91,91 90,90,89,89
CSF £8.23 CT £31.88 TOTE £2.70: £1.60, £1.60, £2.30; EX 11.40 Trifecta £12.90 Pool: £484.22 - 26.61 winning units; Place 6 £30.97, Place 5 £26.16.
Owner Park Lane Thoroughbreds **Bred** Mrs J A Prescott **Trained** Audley, Staffs

FOCUS
No great pace on in this handicap and the winning time was modest for the grade. The form is not strong and assessed through the sixth to his recent best.
T/Plt: £33.70 to a £1 stake. Pool: £41,719.00. 903.40 winning tickets. T/Qpdt: £21.30 to a £1 stake. Pool: £1,878.70. 65.00 winning tickets. CR

HAYDOCK (L-H)
Saturday, April 28

OFFICIAL GOING: Good (good to firm in places)
Wind: Light, half-behind Weather: Fine and sunny

1285 EBF LEE CAVANAGH 21ST BIRTHDAY MAIDEN FILLIES' STKS 5f
5:45 (5:47) (Class 5) 2-Y-O **£3,238** (£963; £481; £240) **Stalls** Centre

Form RPR
1 **Janina** 2-9-0.................... MartinDwyer 6 82+
(B W Hills) *in tch: led over 2f out: rdn out and rn wl ins fnl f* **3/1**[1]
4 **2** *1 ½* **Cayman Fox**[14] 1043 2-9-0.................... RoystonFfrench 4 76
(James Moffatt) *led: hdd over 2f out: rdn over 1f out: nt pce of wnr ins fnl f* **6/1**
3 *nk* **Jennifers Joy (IRE)** 2-9-0.................... DarryllHolland 7 75
(M R Channon) *in tch: pushed along 2f out: r.o and gaining towards fin* **6/1**
4 *2 ½* **Socceroo** 2-9-0.................... JohnEgan 16 65
(T J Pitt) *midfield: hdwy 2f out: rdn over 1f out: edgd lft ins fnl f: styd on* **9/2**[2]
5 *shd* **Edie Superstar (USA)** 2-9-0.................... TomEaves 9 64
(M A Magnusson) *prom: rdn over 1f out: kpt on same pce fnl f* **5/1**[3]
6 *1 ½* **Eastern Romance** 2-9-0.................... NCallan 15 58
(K A Ryan) *s.i.s: sn chsd ldrs: rdn over 1f out: edgd lft and one pce ins fnl f* **8/1**
7 *½* **Eboracum Dream** 2-9-0.................... DavidAllan 17 56
(T D Easterby) *s.s: towards rr: rdn over 2f out: styd on fr over 1f out: nvr rchd ldrs* **50/1**
44 **8** *¾* **Mama Leo**[19] 972 2-8-7.................... BernadetteQuinn[(7)] 8 53
(P D Evans) *prom: rdn 2f out: wknd fnl f* **33/1**
9 *1 ½* **Twilight Belle (IRE)** 2-9-0.................... TedDurcan 12 47
(B J Meehan) *s.s: outpcd: styd on fnl f: nvr rchd ldrs: bttr for r* **14/1**
10 *hd* **Note Perfect** 2-9-0.................... DaleGibson 2 47
(M W Easterby) *sn outpcd: nvr on terms* **66/1**
11 *1* **La Chicaluna** 2-9-0.................... JamieMackay 1 43
(J G Given) *s.i.s: in tch: rn green: lost pl over 2f out: n.d after* **33/1**
5 **12** *nk* **Areweplayingout (IRE)**[14] 1033 2-9-0.................... RichardMullen 13 41
(Peter Grayson) *midfield: pushed along 3f out: no hdwy* **50/1**
13 *1 ¾* **Caprima (IRE)** 2-9-0.................... DeanMernagh 14 34
(M Brittain) *midfield: rdn over 2f out: sn lost pl* **80/1**
14 *8* **Eighty Twenty** 2-9-0.................... DeanMcKeown 10 2
(M W Easterby) *s.s: a outpcd* **80/1**
0 **15** *2 ½* **Miss Kin (IRE)**[5] 1193 2-9-0.................... VHalliday 11 —
(T J Pitt) *s.s and rdr briefly lost iron: a bhd* **66/1**
16 *22* **Ruby's Smile** 2-9-0.................... PhillipMakin 3 —
(R Brotherton) *s.i.s: midfield: rdn and wknd over 1f out: sn eased* **66/1**

60.17 secs (-1.90) **Going Correction** -0.575s/f (Hard) **16** Ran SP% **122.9**
Speed ratings (Par 89):92,89,89,85,84 82,81,80,78,77 76,75,72,60,56 20
CSF £20.35 TOTE £3.70: £2.10, £2.20, £2.60; EX 29.10.
Owner Hamdan Al Maktoum **Bred** H G And J R Dutfield **Trained** Lambourn, Berks

FOCUS
The going was described as perfect. Not an easy race to assess, but the winner scored well and this could be a decent maiden.

NOTEBOOK
Janina ◆, a 100,000gns first foal of the useful Lady Dominatrix, was the pick of the paddock and came out best in the race too. She was not helped by having to race wide of the rest, but she picked up well when asked to go about her business and won convincingly. She will be all the better for the experience and could prove to be above average. (op 5-2)
Cayman Fox, one of a quartet with the benefit of a run, showed good pace from the outset and stuck to her task to cope with all but the winner. There ought to be a maiden in her. (op 8-1)
Jennifers Joy(IRE), a 150,000euros daughter of Green Desert, was being rousted along some way out but she responded to pressure and kept on. She can do better with this behind her. (op 7-1 tchd 8-1)

Socceroo, the first foal of the sprinter Silca Boo, raced nearest the stands' side and made a satisfactory debut. (op 11-4)
Edie Superstar(USA), a $260,000 half-sister to four winners, showed pace and gave some encouragement for the future. (op 8-1)
Eastern Romance, related to several sprinters including the smart juvenile Blue Tomato, was up there from the outset and, though one-paced when it mattered, it would be a surprise if she does not improve. (op 10-1)
Eboracum Dream, from a family that has done well for this yard in the past, was never able to get in a blow but did enough to suggest she is worth another look.
Twilight Belle(IRE), an 87,000gns half-sister to Twilight Blues, kept on after getting outpaced and will know more next time. (tchd 16-1)

1286 NORTHERN RACING CLUB H'CAP 5f
6:15 (6:17) (Class 5) (0-75,78) 3-Y-O £2,817 (£838; £418; £209) Stalls Centre

Form RPR
3120 1 **Mandurah (IRE)**[19] 970 3-8-5 **62**... AdrianTNicholls 6 70
(D Nicholls) *a.p: rdn over 1f out: r.o to ld towards fin* **8/1**
00-1 2 *nk* **Morinqua (IRE)**[7] 1151 3-9-7 **78**... TPQueally 2 85
(J G Given) *led: rdn over 1f out: hdd towards fin* **11/2**[3]
1 3 *1 1/4* **Cha Cha Cha**[18] 998 3-9-1 **72**... NCallan 9 74
(K A Ryan) *midfield: rdn over 2f out: hdwy 1f out: styd on ins fnl f: nt pce to chal ldng pair* **6/1**
10-6 4 *1 1/2* **Picture Frame**[24] 925 3-8-6 **68**... RoryMoore(5) 12 65
(J T Stimpson) *towards rr: outpcd 3f out: styd on wl fnl f: nt rch ldrs* **14/1**
-210 5 *nk* **New York Oscar (IRE)**[6] 1176 3-9-2 **73**...(be[1]) JamesDoyle 5 69
(A J McCabe) *prom: rdn and carried hd high whn edgd rt over 1f out: no ex ins fnl f* **25/1**
2145 6 *nk* **Ronnie Howe**[20] 958 3-8-13 **70**... PhillipMakin 13 65
(M Dods) *s.i.s: bhd: hdwy over 1f out: styd on same pce ins fnl f* **12/1**
665- 7 *1 1/4* **Bollin Franny**[240] 4946 3-8-10 **67**... JohnEgan 10 57
(T D Easterby) *midfield: rdn whn carried rt over 1f out: no imp on ldrs* **12/1**
0-14 8 *hd* **Pickering**[9] 1108 3-9-4 **75**... DavidAllan 4 65
(E J Alston) *towards rr: rdn and hdwy over 1f out: one pce ins fnl f* **11/4**[1]
530- 9 *1/2* **Mandy's Maestro (USA)**[210] 5681 3-8-8 **65**... DeanMcKeown 1 53
(R M Whitaker) *chsd ldrs: rdn over 2f out: outpcd over 1f out* **33/1**
21-0 10 *4* **Feelin Foxy**[7] 1151 3-8-11 **68**...(v) TomEaves 3 41
(D Shaw) *prom: rdn over 2f out: wknd over 1f out* **12/1**
1-36 11 *9* **Majestic Cheer**[9] 1108 3-9-2 **73**... DarryllHolland 11 14
(M R Channon) *s.v.s: a wl bhd* **4/1**[2]

59.51 secs (-2.56) **Going Correction** -0.575s/f (Hard) 11 Ran SP% **124.0**
Speed ratings (Par 98):97,96,94,92,91 91,89,88,88,81 67
CSF £54.57 CT £297.20 TOTE £12.00: £2.40, £2.20, £2.50; EX 40.30.
Owner Martin Hignett **Bred** Michael Lyons **Trained** Sessay, N Yorks
■ Stewards' Enquiry : James Doyle two-day ban: careless riding (May 9-10)

FOCUS
A fair handicap and sound form, although limited to some extent by the fourth and fifth.
Majestic Cheer Official explanation: jockey said gelding lost its hind legs on leaving stalls

1287 HAYDOCK PARK RAILS AND RING BOOKMAKERS H'CAP 1m 30y
6:45 (6:45) (Class 4) (0-85,85) 4-Y-O+ £6,477 (£1,927; £963; £481) Stalls Low

Form RPR
10-2 1 **Major Magpie (IRE)**[24] 915 5-8-10 **77**... DarryllHolland 14 89+
(M Dods) *dwlt: hld up: rdn and hdwy whn swtchd lft over 1f out: swtchd rt ins fnl f: str run to ld fnl stride* **5/1**[1]
00-0 2 *hd* **Moody Tunes**[14] 1040 4-8-8 **75**... PatCosgrave 5 84
(K R Burke) *midfield: hdwy 3f out: rdn over 2f out: ev ch wl ins fnl f: r.o* **8/1**[3]
0/0- 3 *shd* **Burley Flame**[387] 898 6-8-6 **73**... TPQueally 4 82
(J G Given) *in tch: rdn to chse ldr over 2f out: led wl ins fnl f: ct fnl stride* **18/1**
225- 4 *3/4* **Bold Marc (IRE)**[163] 6502 5-8-9 **79**... AndrewElliott(3) 2 86
(K R Burke) *led: shkn up over 2f out: hdd wl ins fnl f: no ex fnl strides* **8/1**[3]
32-0 5 *1* **Adventuress**[21] 941 4-8-11 **85**... KMay(7) 3 90
(B J Meehan) *midfield: stmbld on bnd over 4f out: hdwy over 2f out: styd on ins fnl f: nt pce of ldrs towards fin* **9/1**
50-0 5 *dht* **Goodbye Mr Bond**[28] 846 7-9-4 **85**... DavidAllan 8 90
(E J Alston) *midfield: rdn over 3f out: hdwy over 2f out: styd on ins fnl f: nt pce of ldrs towards fin* **7/1**[2]
20-0 7 *1 1/4* **Efidium**[8] 1132 9-7-11 **71** oh4... LukeMorris(7) 12 73
(N Bycroft) *hld up: rdn over 2f out: hdwy over 1f out: styd on ins fnl f: nt rch ldrs* **25/1**
015- 8 *2 1/2* **Shout (IRE)**[161] 6519 4-8-11 **78**... JamesDoyle 9 74
(J W Hills) *midfield: rdn 3f out: one pce fnl f* **25/1**
000- 9 *hd* **Crocodile Bay (IRE)**[141] 6744 4-8-10 **77**... BrettDoyle 15 73
(B J Meehan) *hld up: rdn 4f out: hdwy over 1f out: one pce ins fnl f* **28/1**
55-0 10 *1 1/2* **Dark Charm (FR)**[19] 969 8-8-4 **71**... DaleGibson 1 63
(R A Fahey) *s.s: bhd: rdn 2f out: plugged on fnl f: nvr trbld ldrs* **16/1**
5-50 11 *5* **Sew'N'So Character (IRE)**[18] 993 6-8-12 **79**... TedDurcan 11 60
(M Blanshard) *midfield: rdn over 2f out: wknd ins fnl f* **12/1**
413- 12 *3/4* **Nevada Desert (IRE)**[147] 6678 7-8-8 **75**... DeanMcKeown 16 54
(R M Whitaker) *in tch: wkng whn n.m.r and hmpd 2f out* **16/1**
5/5- 13 *3 1/2* **Nawaqees**[354] 1569 4-8-8 **75**... MartinDwyer 13 46
(J L Dunlop) *prom: rdn and wkng whn edgd rt 2f out* **7/1**[2]
030- 14 *1/2* **Bordello**[214] 5598 4-8-4 **71** oh1... CatherineGannon 10 41
(K A Ryan) *racd keenly: in tch: rdn over 3f out: sn wknd* **25/1**
103- 15 *2* **Regal Raider (IRE)**[118] 6999 4-8-8 **75**... TomEaves 7 40
(I Semple) *trckd ldrs: rdn over 2f out: wknd over 1f out: eased fnl f* **14/1**
43-5 16 *59* **Hula Ballew**[19] 969 7-8-9 **76**... PhillipMakin 17 —
(M Dods) *a bhd: t.o* **25/1**

1m 41.58s (-3.93) **Going Correction** -0.45s/f (Firm) 16 Ran SP% **124.1**
Speed ratings (Par 105):101,100,100,99,98 98,97,95,95,93 88,87,84,83,81 22
CSF £40.90 CT £713.10 TOTE £4.00: £1.60, £2.60, £7.20, £2.50; EX 68.00.
Owner Mrs Patsy Monk **Bred** J Hutchinson **Trained** Denton, Co Durham

FOCUS
Not that strong a gallop, but the form looks fairly sound, rated through the runner-up, fourth and fifth.
Nawaqees Official explanation: jockey said colt lost its action and hung right final 2f
Hula Ballew Official explanation: jockey said mare lost its action

1288 ANNUAL BADGEHOLDERS LES FAULKNER MEMORIAL H'CAP 1m 2f 120y
7:15 (7:17) (Class 4) (0-80,80) 4-Y-O+ £5,181 (£1,541; £770; £384) Stalls High

Form RPR
416- 1 **Forroger (CAN)**[201] 5869 4-9-1 **77**... PhilipRobinson 2 86+
(M A Jarvis) *racd keenly: a handy: led 2f out: rdn over 1f out: r.o wl* **9/4**[1]
004- 2 *1 1/4* **Greek Well (IRE)**[253] 4549 4-8-11 **73**... TomEaves 9 79+
(Sir Michael Stoute) *midfield: rdn and hdwy over 2f out: wnt 2nd ins fnl f: r.o: a hld* **8/1**[3]
311- 3 *1/2* **High Treason (USA)**[200] 5897 5-9-2 **78**... BrettDoyle 3 83
(W J Musson) *midfield: rdn and hdwy 2f out: styd on ins fnl f* **6/1**[2]
000- 4 *1* **Cruise Director**[160] 4560 7-9-4 **80**... EddieAhern 16 83
(Ian Williams) *a.p: led 3f out: rdn and hdd 2f out: no ex ins fnl f* **50/1**
51P0 5 *1* **Daring Affair**[53] 629 6-9-4 **80**... PhillipMakin 8 84+
(K R Burke) *midfield: rdn and hdwy over 1f out: styng on whn n.m.r and hmpd wl ins fnl f: nt rcvr* **28/1**
02-6 6 *nk* **Kildare Sun (IRE)**[92] 256 5-9-2 **78**... DaleGibson 6 79
(J Mackie) *hld up: rdn and hdwy over 1f out: kpt on ins fnl f* **20/1**
441- 7 *hd* **Abstract Art (USA)**[348] 1738 4-9-1 **77**... MartinDwyer 10 77
(Miss Venetia Williams) *midfield: hdwy 3f out: rdn 2f out: one pce ins fnl f* **25/1**
3/3- 8 *1 1/4* **Missoula (IRE)**[360] 1423 4-9-1 **77**... NCallan 17 76+
(M H Tompkins) *midfield: rdn over 3f out: edgd lft ins fnl f: sn eased whn no imp* **25/1**
11-0 9 *3/4* **Dium Mac**[28] 850 6-8-10 **79**... SuzzanneFrance(7) 5 82+
(N Bycroft) *racd keenly: hld up: continually denied run over 1f out: swtchd rt ent fnl f: nvr rchd ldrs* **12/1**
0-11 10 *nk* **Cripsey Brook**[11] 1078 9-8-11 **80**...(t) DanielleMcCreery(7) 7 76
(K G Reveley) *s.i.s: in rr: kpt on fnl f: nvr on terms* **12/1**
6305 11 *nk* **Tous Les Deux**[34] 777 4-8-12 **74**... RichardMullen 11 70
(Peter Grayson) *s.i.s: in rr: rdn over 2f out: nvr nr ldrs* **33/1**
56-0 12 *nk* **Brigadore (USA)**[20] 955 4-8-11 **73**... DavidAllan 15 68
(E J Alston) *midfield: pushed along over 2f out: nvr able to chal* **25/1**
200- 13 *1 3/4* **Rawdon (IRE)**[206] 5769 6-8-13 **75**...(v) HayleyTurner 13 67
(M L W Bell) *midfield: rdn over 2f out: wknd over 1f out* **20/1**
-156 14 *shd* **Davenport (IRE)**[6] 1180 5-9-0 **76**...(p) DeanMcKeown 14 68
(B R Millman) *trckd ldrs: rdn over 2f out: hung lft over 1f out: sn n.m.r whn wkng* **16/1**
6-00 15 *3* **Ahlawy (IRE)**[6] 1180 4-8-13 **75**... TPQueally 4 61
(M W Easterby) *hld up: pushed along over 2f out: n.d* **50/1**
042- 16 *2 1/2* **Manipulate**[250] 4661 4-8-12 **79**... AshleyHamblett(5) 12 61
(L M Cumani) *prom tl rdn and wknd over 2f out* **9/1**
323- 17 *2 1/2* **Greek Easter (IRE)**[291] 3373 4-8-7 **76**... KMay(7) 1 53
(B J Meehan) *led: hdd 3f out: rdn and wknd over 2f out* **14/1**

2m 13.65s (-4.08) **Going Correction** -0.45s/f (Firm) 17 Ran SP% **125.5**
Speed ratings (Par 105):96,95,94,94,93 93,92,92,91,91 91,90,89,89,87 85,83
CSF £16.96 CT £101.58 TOTE £3.20: £1.70, £2.10, £2.20, £6.80; EX 22.20.
Owner Stephen Dartnell **Bred** M C Byrne **Trained** Newmarket, Suffolk

FOCUS
They went a very steady pace in this competitive handicap which limits the form, but the first two look capable of progressing and the form is sound enough.
Daring Affair Official explanation: jockey said mare was denied a clear run
Dium Mac Official explanation: jockey said gelding was denied a clear run
Rawdon(IRE) Official explanation: jockey said gelding lost a fore shoe

1289 WARRINGTON GUARDIAN H'CAP 1m 2f 120y
7:45 (7:46) (Class 5) (0-75,74) 3-Y-O £3,238 (£963; £481; £240) Stalls High

Form RPR
-543 1 **Urban Warrior**[14] 1039 3-8-11 **67**... JamesDoyle 13 75
(Mrs Norma Pook) *led for 2f: dropped to midfield 6f out: hdwy over 2f out: led ins fnl f: r.o u.p* **20/1**
11-4 2 *hd* **My Secrets**[11] 1084 3-9-1 **74**... GregFairley(3) 10 82
(M Johnston) *a.p: rdn to ld over 1f out: hdd ins fnl f: r.o u.p* **7/1**[2]
341- 3 *1/2* **Filios (IRE)**[179] 6284 3-8-13 **74**... AshleyHamblett(5) 7 87+
(L M Cumani) *midfield: hdwy whn nt clr run over 2f out: nt clr run over 1f out: sn swtchd rt: fin strly: unlucky* **5/1**[1]
025- 4 *1 3/4* **Arctic Wings (IRE)**[161] 6523 3-8-12 **68**... DarryllHolland 3 71
(W R Muir) *s.i.s: in rr: hdwy 2f out: swtchd rt over 1f out: r.o ins fnl f* **20/1**
03-5 5 *1/2* **Super Cross (IRE)**[16] 1012 3-9-2 **72**... MartinDwyer 9 74
(E A L Dunlop) *led after 2f: rdn and hdd over 1f out: no ex ins fnl f* **7/1**[2]
006 6 *1 1/2* **Grey Light (IRE)**[20] 954 3-8-8 **64**... PaulHanagan 5 64
(L Lungo) *hld up: rdn and hdwy 3f out: styd on same pce ins fnl f* **8/1**[3]
30-0 7 *shd* **Trump Call (IRE)**[68] 498 3-8-11 **67**... JosedeSouza 14 66
(R M Beckett) *in tch: rdn 2f out: one pce ins fnl f* **9/1**
002- 8 *6* **River Deuce**[177] 6303 3-9-0 **70**... NCallan 12 58
(M H Tompkins) *midfield: rdn and hdwy over 3f out: n.m.r and swtchd rt over 1f out: fdd ins fnl f* **14/1**
166- 9 *1* **Terry Molloy (IRE)**[224] 5366 3-9-0 **70**... PatCosgrave 11 56
(K R Burke) *hld up: rdn over 2f out: no imp* **33/1**
5-42 10 *6* **Best Selection**[25] 904 3-8-11 **67**... JohnEgan 4 42
(A P Jarvis) *prom: rdn over 2f out: wknd over 1f out* **8/1**[3]
031- 11 *3* **Doubly Guest**[194] 6007 3-9-1 **71**... TomEaves 8 40
(G G Margarson) *s.i.s: in rr: rdn over 2f out: nvr trbld ldrs* **12/1**
24-5 12 *5* **Robert The Brave**[23] 937 3-8-10 **66**... TedDurcan 2 25
(A J McCabe) *hld up: rdn over 2f out: nvr on terms* **33/1**
010- 13 *29* **Maid To Believe**[182] 6217 3-8-13 **69**... EddieAhern 15 —
(J L Dunlop) *prom: wknd over 4f out* **10/1**
550- 14 *5* **Grand Diamond (IRE)**[231] 5178 3-8-10 **66** ow1... PhillipMakin 17 —
(J S Goldie) *midfield: rdn and wknd over 2f out* **16/1**
2-30 15 *17* **Bewildering (IRE)**[70] 492 3-8-10 **66**... RichardMullen 16 —
(E J O'Neill) *trckd ldrs: rdn and wknd over 2f out: dismntd after line* **9/1**

2m 14.68s (-3.05) **Going Correction** -0.45s/f (Firm) 15 Ran SP% **128.6**
Speed ratings (Par 98):93,92,92,91,90 89,89,85,84,80 78,74,53,49,37
CSF £157.52 CT £833.42 TOTE £35.80: £6.50, £2.40, £2.70; EX 250.90.
Owner A Morris **Bred** White Horse Bloodstock Ltd **Trained** Rockley, Wilts

FOCUS
Sound handicap form, rated around the winner to the best he showed as a juvenile. The third looked unlucky and should have won by a few lengths.
Maid To Believe Official explanation: jockey said filly lost its action
Bewildering(IRE) Official explanation: jockey said colt lost its action

1290 ST HELENS STAR MAIDEN STKS 1m 3f 200y
8:15 (8:17) (Class 5) 3-Y-O £2,817 (£838; £418; £209) Stalls High

Form RPR
0 1 **Spice Route**[10] 1093 3-9-3... EddieAhern 3 86+
(M L W Bell) *in tch: effrt 3f out: led wl over 1f out: r.o wl* **8/1**
234- 2 *2* **Yossi (IRE)**[192] 6058 3-9-3 78... NCallan 5 83
(M H Tompkins) *hld up: plld out and hdwy 2f out: chsd wnr over 1f out: hung lft ins fnl f: one pce cl home* **4/1**[2]
4-6 3 *1 1/4* **Rhaam**[10] 1093 3-9-3... MartinDwyer 6 81+
(B W Hills) *towards rr: rdn over 3f out: hdwy over 2f out: sn hung lft: r.o ins fnl f* **7/1**

30-2 **4** *nk* **Grand Heights (IRE)**[16] 1012 3-9-3 77 .... TedDurcan 1 81
(J L Dunlop) *chsd ldr after 2f: led 2f out: sn hdd: no ex ins fnl f* **5/1**[3]

-232 **5** *5* **Sowdrey**[20] 956 3-9-3 75 .... SamHitchcott 7 73
(M R Channon) *midfield: rdn over 4f out: no imp on ldrs* **12/1**

4 **6** *1 1/4* **Dig Gold (USA)**[16] 1012 3-9-3 .... PhilipRobinson 4 71
(M A Jarvis) *led: rdn and hdd 2f out: wkng whn hmpd ins fnl f* **3/1**[1]

02- **7** *nk* **Silmi**[157] 6561 3-9-3 .... PaulHanagan 11 70
(E A L Dunlop) *in rr: plugged on over 1f out: nvr on terms* **12/1**

5- **8** *3* **Tommy Tobougg**[176] 6318 3-9-3 .... TomEaves 2 65
(I Semple) *s.s: in rr: nvr trbld ldrs* **33/1**

24-3 **9** *3* **Alpes Maritimes**[16] 1011 3-9-3 75 .... DarryllHolland 8 60
(G Wragg) *trckd ldrs: rdn over 3f out: wknd over 1f out* **7/1**

2030 **10** *13* **Title Deed (USA)**[8] 1122 3-9-3 68 .... JohnEgan 10 40
(A P Jarvis) *prom tl wknd over 3f out* **33/1**

11 *3 1/2* **Irish Plane (IRE)** 3-9-0 .... AndrewElliott[(3)] 9 34
(K R Burke) *hung bdly rt on bnd over 5f out: a bhd* **50/1**

2m 31.18s (-3.81) **Going Correction** -0.45s/f (Firm) 11 Ran SP% **121.0**
Speed ratings (Par 98):94,92,91,91,88 87,87,85,83,74 72
CSF £40.80 TOTE £12.30: £3.30, £1.90, £2.90; EX 64.50 Place 6 £131.75, Place 5 £68.75..
Owner Mrs G Rowland-Clark and K J Mercer **Bred** Usk Valley Stud **Trained** Newmarket, Suffolk

FOCUS
A strong maiden which looked unusually well run. The form looks solid and has been rated fairly positively, with the first three still in the Derby, and it is expected to work out.
Alpes Maritimes Official explanation: jockey said gelding lost its action closing stages
Irish Plane(IRE) Official explanation: jockey said colt hung right-handed
T/Plt: £143.70 to a £1 stake. Pool: £59,328.70. 301.30 winning tickets. T/Qpdt: £69.10 to a £1 stake. Pool: £3,562.05. 38.10 winning tickets. DO

[1007]LEICESTER (R-H)
Saturday, April 28

OFFICIAL GOING: Good to firm (good in places)
Wind: Fresh against Weather: Fine

1291 JOHN SMITH'S MEDIAN AUCTION MAIDEN STKS 5f 2y
2:20 (2:24) (Class 5) 2-Y-O **£3,238** (£963; £481; £240) **Stalls** Low

Form RPR

1 **Just Sort It** 2-9-3 .... TedDurcan 8 72
(W Jarvis) *s.i.s: outpcd: hdwy: hung lft and nt clr run over 1f out: r.o to ld nr fin* **25/1**

44 **2** *nk* **Ben**[17] 999 2-9-3 .... RobertHavlin 2 71
(P G Murphy) *chsd ldrs: n.m.r over 1f out: led ins fnl f: sn edgd rt and hdd: r.o* **17/2**[2]

3 *shd* **The Real Guru** 2-9-3 .... RoystonFfrench 7 71
(Mrs A Duffield) *mid-div: sn pushed along: hdwy over 1f out: led wl ins fnl f: edgd rt and hdd nr fin* **66/1**

4 *1 1/4* **Bahama Baileys** 2-9-3 .... J-PGuillambert 3 66
(M Johnston) *led: rdn and edgd lft over 1f out: hdd and unable qckn ins fnl f* **12/1**[3]

5 **5** *1 3/4* **Regal Rhythm (IRE)**[12] 1058 2-9-3 .... SteveDrowne 9 59
(B J Meehan) *w ldrs: rdn and hung lft over 1f out: hung rt and no ex ins fnl f* **12/1**[3]

2 **6** *4* **Legendary Guest**[8] 1123 2-9-3 .... DarryllHolland 5 43
(M R Channon) *chsd ldrs: rdn 1/2-way: hung rt and wknd fnl f* **1/2**[1]

6 **7** *nk* **Dhaka Dazzle**[11] 1073 2-9-3 .... EdwardCreighton 11 41
(M R Channon) *s.i.s: outpcd: styd on ins fnl f: nvr nrr* **80/1**

433 **8** *1/2* **Mystickhill (IRE)**[8] 1130 2-8-12 .... RobbieFitzpatrick 10 34
(T J Pitt) *prom: rdn 1/2-way: wknd over 1f out* **33/1**

9 *1 3/4* **Transcendent (IRE)** 2-9-3 .... NCallan 4 32
(J D Bethell) *chsd ldrs over 3f* **20/1**

10 *34* **Valentine Blue** 2-9-3 .... RichardHughes 13 —
(A B Haynes) *s.s: outpcd* **25/1**

61.69 secs (0.79) **Going Correction** -0.025s/f (Good) 10 Ran SP% **110.7**
Speed ratings (Par 92):92,91,91,89,86 80,79,78,76,21
CSF £183.68 TOTE £21.00: £5.90, £2.00, £14.80; EX 46.00.
Owner Robert J Harriss **Bred** North Farm Stud **Trained** Newmarket, Suffolk
■ Gaitskell (12/1, vet's advice) & City Wizzard (25/1, refused to enter stalls) were withdrawn. R4 applies, deduct 5p in the £.

FOCUS
A fair maiden likely to produce its share of winners and best rated through the fifth for now.

NOTEBOOK
Just Sort It, a half-brother to several winners over further, was soon being hurried along following a slow start and appeared to be finding the pace too much, but he came strong in the final quarter mile and, despite still showing signs of greeness, he ran on strongly to prevail close home. This was a highly-pleasing first effort and, with a good deal of improvement anticipated as he steps up in distance, is one to keep on-side. (op 33-1 tchd 16-1)
Ben, who has twice shown solid form in defeat at Lingfield and Bath, was well drawn and held an ideal early position. He had to force he way through against the rail, but would have won if good enough and is likely to continue to remain vulnerable to something less exposed. (op 10-1 tchd 8-1)
The Real Guru is bred for speed and he made good heading to take it up going into the final furlong, but was unable to repel the strong late challenge of the winner and just lost out on second. This was a highly satisfactory debut and he should learn from the experience. (op 50-1)
Bahama Baileys ◆, who is bred to appreciate upwards of 6f, knew his job and was able to make the most of a decent draw, but he found himself done for speed at the business end and was run out of the placings. This was a promising first effort and, even though he will definitely benefit from a sixth furlong, he should find a race at this distance. (op 10-1)
Regal Rhythm(IRE), a one-paced fifth on his debut at Windsor, showed a little improvement in form, but it was slightly disconcerting how he hung under pressure and did not look to find much. It is possible he requires softer ground and now looks more of a nursery type. (tchd 14-1)
Legendary Guest, who made a really promising debut when second on the hottest two-year-old race of the season so far at Newbury the previous week, was understandably made a strong favourite and he soon held a prominent position. However, it was clear from well over two furlongs out he was not going as well as his rider would have liked and in the end he dropped right out. This was clearly not his running and he deserves a chance to atone, but does have a little bit to prove now. (op 8-11)
Dhaka Dazzle, as was the case on his Nottingham debut, found this distance on the sharp side and he is another who unlikely to be at his best until contesting nurseries over further. (op 66-1 tchd 50-1)

1292 JOHN SMITH'S EXTRA SMOOTH H'CAP 5f 218y
2:55 (2:55) (Class 4) (0-85,84) 4-Y-O+ **£5,047** (£1,510; £755; £377; £188) **Stalls** Centre

Form RPR

0000 **1** **Danzig River (IRE)**[8] 1134 6-7-11 **70** oh1 .... AdeleRothery[(7)] 5 82
(D Nicholls) *hld up: plld hrd: hdwy and nt clr run over 1f out: r.o to ld wl ins fnl f* **20/1**

10-2 **2** *1 1/4* **Perfect Story (IRE)**[90] 277 5-9-4 **84** .... OscarUrbina 4 92
(J A R Toller) *sn pushed along in rr: hung rt and r.o ins fnl f: nt rch wnr* **13/2**[3]

23-0 **3** *nk* **Diane's Choice**[15] 1023 4-9-4 **84** .... NCallan 9 91
(J Akehurst) *chsd ldrs: rdn over 2f out: ev ch ins fnl f: unable qckn towards fin* **6/1**[2]

160- **4** *nk* **Hoh Hoh Hoh**[178] 6292 5-9-4 **84** .... RichardHughes 1 90
(R J Price) *led: rdn and edgd rt fr over 1f out: hdd wl ins fnl f* **4/1**[1]

2063 **5** *3/4* **Pieter Brueghel (USA)**[31] 810 8-9-2 **82** .... SilvestreDeSousa 8 86
(D Nicholls) *chsd ldr: rdn over 2f out: styd on same pce ins fnl f* **4/1**[1]

005- **6** *3/4* **Angel Sprints**[191] 6065 5-8-11 **77** .... AlanDaly 7 79
(C J Down) *chsd ldrs: rdn over 2f out: no ex ins fnl f* **22/1**

00-4 **7** *3/4* **High Reach**[20] 957 7-9-1 **81** .... PhillipMakin 2 80
(T D Barron) *chsd ldrs: rdn over 2f out: no ex fnl f* **4/1**[1]

1314 **8** *2* **Canadian Danehill (IRE)**[31] 810 5-9-2 **82** ....(p) BrettDoyle 3 75
(R M H Cowell) *trckd ldrs: racd keenly: rdn over 1f out: looked hld whn nt clr run and wknd ins fnl f* **12/1**

136- **9** *4* **Paris Bell**[186] 6160 5-8-10 **76** .... PaulQuinn 6 57
(T D Easterby) *dwlt: rdn 1/2-way: wknd over 1f out* **10/1**

1m 12.12s (-1.08) **Going Correction** -0.025s/f (Good) 9 Ran SP% **113.5**
Speed ratings (Par 105):106,104,103,103,102 101,100,97,92
CSF £141.48 CT £888.72 TOTE £19.80: £5.60, £2.60, £2.60; EX 200.80.
Owner Miss Anna Graves **Bred** Orpendale **Trained** Sessay, N Yorks

FOCUS
A competitive sprint and Danzig River returned to form to run out a ready winner under a fine ride from Adele Rothery. The form looks sound with the first three close to their form.

1293 JOHN SMITH'S EXTRA COLD H'CAP 1m 3f 183y
3:30 (3:30) (Class 3) (0-95,94) 3-Y-O
£9,348 (£2,799; £1,399; £700; £349; £175) **Stalls** High

Form RPR

-221 **1** **Man Of Vision (USA)**[52] 638 3-8-8 **81** .... DarryllHolland 7 93
(M R Channon) *hld up: hdwy over 5f out: led over 2f out: drvn out* **7/2**[2]

621- **2** *1 3/4* **Gull Wing (IRE)**[181] 6242 3-8-2 **75** .... HayleyTurner 3 84
(M L W Bell) *hld up: hdwy over 2f out: chsd wnr over 1f out: styd on same pce fnl f* **10/1**

2451 **3** *3* **New Beginning (IRE)**[16] 1010 3-8-7 **80** .... RichardThomas 5 84
(Mrs S Lamyman) *chsd ldrs: lost pl 7f out: hdwy over 2f out: wknd ins fnl f* **14/1**

-643 **4** *3/4* **Sahrati**[16] 1010 3-8-8 **81** ow1 .... NCallan 2 84
(C E Brittain) *chsd ldr tl rdn over 2f out: wknd fnl f* **15/2**[3]

-21 **5** *2 1/2* **Soldiers Quest**[57] 602 3-8-13 **86** .... J-PGuillambert 1 85
(M Johnston) *s.i.s: hdwy over 7f out: rdn over 3f out: outpcd fnl 2f* **6/4**[1]

623- **6** *6* **Audit (IRE)**[192] 6058 3-8-5 **78** ....(v) NickyMackay 4 67
(Sir Michael Stoute) *led over 9f: wknd over 1f out* **8/1**

4-62 **7** *5* **Putra Square**[10] 1093 3-9-7 **94** .... RichardHughes 6 75
(P F I Cole) *chsd ldrs over 9f* **8/1**

2m 29.82s (-4.68) **Going Correction** -0.125s/f (Firm) 7 Ran SP% **112.0**
Speed ratings (Par 102):110,108,106,106,104 100,97
CSF £35.33 TOTE £4.50: £1.90, £3.50; EX 24.10.
Owner Sheikh Mohammed **Bred** Darley **Trained** West Ilsley, Berks

FOCUS
A good three-year-old handicap made-up of several progressive sorts and rated positively around those in the frame behind the winner.

NOTEBOOK
Man Of Vision(USA), off the mark on his handicap debut over 1m2f at Lingfield last month, was up 5lb and making his turf debut, but has clearly improved again and he ran out a ready winner, seeing out the trip well. Evidently on the up, there is no reason why he cannot continue to progress and defy a higher mark in future. (op 3-1)
Gull Wing(IRE), winner of a 1m1f Wolverhampton maiden back in October, had earlier shown decent form in defeat behind Shorthand at Nottingham and looked certain to be suited by this new distance. In on a potentially attractive mark, she made steady headway to give herself every chance over a furlong out, but could not get to the winner and was forced to settle for second. She will not be long in winning again if improving at all on this. (op 13-2 tchd 11-2)
New Beginning(IRE) has progressed as he has gone up in distance and came into this off the back of dead-heating in a course 1m2f handicap earlier in the month. Up 4lb and another quarter mile in trip, he looked to hold every chance two out, but was unable to see it out as well as the front pair and perhaps 1m2f is his ideal distance. (op 18-1)
Sahrati, just a head behind New Beginning at the course last time, was unable to reverse the form and also seemed to find this extra distance beyond her. (op 10-1)
Soldiers Quest, who had the look of a typically progressive sort from the yard coming in this, lost his race coming out of the stalls as he was slowly away and he to be used up early on to get a prominent position. He stopped disappointingly in the straight, but deserves another chance and may even prefer slightly slower ground. Official explanation: trainer's rep had no explanation for the poor form shown (op 2-1 tchd 9-4 in places)
Putra Square Official explanation: trainer's rep said colt had a breathing problem

1294 TOTESPORT.COM LEICESTERSHIRE STKS (LISTED RACE) 7f 9y
4:05 (4:05) (Class 1) 4-Y-O+ **£14,762** (£5,595; £2,800; £1,396; £699) **Stalls** Centre

Form RPR

010- **1** **New Seeker**[181] 6252 7-9-5 109 ....(b) TedDurcan 2 114
(P F I Cole) *mde all: drvn out* **7/4**[1]

0000 **2** *1 3/4* **Excusez Moi (USA)**[9] 1102 5-9-2 102 .... NCallan 1 106
(C E Brittain) *dwlt: sn prom: rdn to chse wnr 2f out: styd on same pce ins fnl f* **5/1**[3]

0202 **3** *1* **Vortex**[14] 1034 8-9-2 108 ....(t) RichardHughes 3 103
(Miss Gay Kelleway) *hld up in tch: rdn over 2f out: edgd lft over 1f out: no ex wl ins fnl f* **5/1**[3]

400- **4** *1/2* **Balthazaar's Gift (IRE)**[238] 5011 4-9-2 113 .... NickyMackay 5 102
(L M Cumani) *hld up: rdn over 2f out: hdwy over 1f out: no ex ins fnl f* **5/2**[2]

520- **5** *1* **Suggestive**[196] 5962 9-9-7 108 ....(b) DarryllHolland 4 105
(W J Haggas) *chsd wnr tl rdn 2f out: styd on same pce appr fnl f* **15/2**

1m 24.22s (-1.88) **Going Correction** -0.025s/f (Good) 5 Ran SP% **110.0**
Speed ratings (Par 111):109,107,105,105,104
CSF £10.68 TOTE £2.60: £1.80, £2.30; EX 12.80.
Owner Elite Racing Club **Bred** Shadwell Estate Company Limited **Trained** Whatcombe, Oxon

FOCUS
The form is not strong in a race where New Seeker was able to dominate at his own tempo.

The Form Book, Raceform Ltd, Compton, RG20 6NL

NOTEBOOK

New Seeker was always going to be dangerous if he got his own way in front and his rider carried out the tactics to perfection, taking them along at his own tempo and just having to be pushed out to score. These are his ideal conditions and, although he will find life tougher back up in grade, he is likely to remain a threat when things go his way. (op 6-4)

Excusez Moi(USA), who has been shaping as though a return to this distance may help, would have preferred a stronger pace and it was no real surprise to see him outpaced by the winner who was always dominating him. He is likely to prove best at a strongly-run 6f. (op 6-1 tchd 9-2)

Vortex ran well when second at Lingfield on his return from Dubai, but he was at a disadvantage in being held up off the slow pace and could not make any impression. (tchd 4-1)

Balthazaar's Gift(IRE), an unlucky loser in last season's Golden Jubilee at Royal Ascot, did not really go on from that effort and this return to 7f on his debut for connections did not really suit. He will be better off over a strongly-run 6f. (op 11-4 tchd 7-2)

Suggestive, who had a bit on at the weights, is past his best and could not capitalise on his good early position. (op 10-1)

1295 JOHN SMITH'S CLUB AND INSTITUTE UNION H'CAP — 1m 1f 218y

4:35 (4:35) (Class 5) (0-70,70) 4-Y-0+ — **£3,238** (£963; £481; £240) **Stalls** High

Form — RPR

2122 **1** **Can Can Star**[17] [1002] 4-9-1 **67** .... RichardHughes 1 — 76+
(A W Carroll) *s.i.s: hld up: racd keenly: hdwy over 3f out: swtchd lft over 1f out: led ins fnl f: rdn out* **15/2**[3]

3333 **2** 2 **Generous Lad (IRE)**[30] [813] 4-9-2 **68** ....(p) SteveDrowne 3 — 73
(A B Haynes) *led 9f out: rdn over 2f out: hdd and unable qckn ins fnl f* **8/1**

06-0 **3** 3/4 **Lady Songbird (IRE)**[16] [1011] 4-9-0 **66** .... AdamKirby 12 — 70
(W R Swinburn) *hld up in tch: rdn over 2f out: nt clr run over 1f out: styd on* **10/1**

530- **4** 1/2 **Theatre Royal**[244] [4838] 4-8-7 **62** .... NeilChalmers(3) 13 — 65
(Mouse Hamilton-Fairley) *hld up: hdwy over 2f out: nt clr run over 1f out: nt trble ldrs* **28/1**

-2 **5** 1/2 **Near Germany (IRE)**[15] [1025] 7-8-8 **60** .... RobertHavlin 7 — 62
(R Curtis) *hld up: hdwy and hung rt fr over 1f out: nvr trbld ldrs* **11/1**

2112 **6** nk **Norwegian**[7] [1167] 6-8-4 **56** oh1 ....(p) PaulEddery 5 — 57
(Ian Williams) *chsd ldrs: rdn over 3f out: no ex ins fnl f* **11/2**[2]

3-01 **7** nk **Double Spectre (IRE)**[17] [1002] 5-9-2 **68** .... VinceSlattery 10 — 69
(Jean-Rene Auvray) *hld up: rdn over 3f out: swtchd rt and hdwy over 1f out: nvr nrr* **14/1**

4-20 **8** 2 **Ariodante**[98] [195] 5-8-9 **64** .... StephenDonohoe(3) 9 — 61
(J M P Eustace) *hld up: rdn over 3f out: n.d* **10/1**

00-0 **9** 2 1/2 **Major League (USA)**[18] [993] 5-9-4 **70** .... IanMongan 2 — 62
(D Morris) *trckd ldrs: rdn over 2f out: nt clr run over 1f out: wkng whn hmpd ins fnl f* **40/1**

4-04 **10** 2 **Jordan's Light (USA)**[5] [1198] 4-9-2 **68** ....(v) RobbieFitzpatrick 6 — 57
(T J Pitt) *hld up: rdn over 2f out: a in rr* **9/1**

060- **11** 13 **Primitive Academy**[14] [6684] 5-9-1 **67** .... J-PGuillambert 11 — 31
(J R Holt) *chsd ldrs: stmbld over 4f out: rdn over 2f out: wknd over 1f out* **33/1**

0521 **F** **Chorister**[10] [1090] 6-8-13 **65** .... NickyMackay 4 — —
(J Mackie) *chsd ldrs: broke nr fore and fell over 7f out: dead* **9/4**[1]

2m 7.45s (-0.85) **Going Correction** -0.125s/f (Firm) — **12** Ran SP% **121.0**

Speed ratings (Par 103):98,96,95,95,95 94,94,92,90,89 78,—

CSF £66.74 CT £614.44 TOTE £11.60: £2.20, £3.40, £2.50; EX 78.60.

Owner K F Coleman **Bred** A W And I Robinson **Trained** Cropthorne, Worcs

FOCUS

A modest contest with little strength in behind, but it should produce the odd winner.

1296 JOHN SMITH'S PREMIER CLUB MAIDEN STKS — 1m 1f 218y

5:05 (5:05) (Class 5) 3-Y-0+ — **£3,886** (£1,156; £577; £288) **Stalls** High

Form — RPR

36- **1** **Many Volumes (USA)**[246] [4768] 3-8-10 .... RichardHughes 2 — 89+
(H R A Cecil) *mde all: pushed clr fr over 1f out: eased nr fin* **4/6**[1]

2 2 1/2 **Cedar Mountain (IRE)** 4-9-13 .... RobertHavlin 4 — 87
(J H M Gosden) *hld up: hdwy 3f out: rdn to chse wnr over 1f out: no imp* **4/1**[2]

3 5 **Manbar (USA)** 3-8-3 .... JamieHamblett(7) 5 — 74+
(Sir Michael Stoute) *chsd ldrs: rdn over 2f out: sn outpcd* **15/2**[3]

4 hd **Wing Express (IRE)** 3-8-10 .... NickyMackay 1 — 74
(L M Cumani) *hld up: pushed along 1/2-way: rdn over 3f out: outpcd fr over 2f out* **8/1**

0- **5** 2 1/2 **Evita**[182] [6215] 3-8-5 .... StephenCarson 7 — 64
(L M Cumani) *chsd wnr 6f: wnt 2nd again 3f out: rdn and wknd over 1f out* **20/1**

5 **6** 5 **Good Cause (IRE)**[11] [1077] 6-9-13 .... RichardThomas 6 — 62?
(Mrs S Lamyman) *plld hrd and prom: trckd wnr 6f out tl rdn 3f out: sn wknd* **28/1**

7 24 **Long Gone**[19] 4-9-5 .... StephenDonohoe(3) 8 — —
(John A Harris) *s.s: outpcd: sme hdwy over 4f out: sn wknd* **66/1**

2m 6.93s (-1.37) **Going Correction** -0.125s/f (Firm)

WFA 3 from 4yo+ 17lb — **7** Ran SP% **112.6**

Speed ratings (Par 103):100,98,94,93,91 87,68

CSF £3.41 TOTE £1.90: £1.10, £2.70; EX 5.00.

Owner K Abdulla **Bred** Juddmonte Farms Inc **Trained** Newmarket, Suffolk

FOCUS

A decent maiden that looks sound, could rate higher in time and is likely to produce winners.

1297 JOHN SMITH'S H'CAP — 1m 60y

5:35 (5:35) (Class 5) (0-70,70) 3-Y-0 — **£3,886** (£1,156; £577; £288) **Stalls** High

Form — RPR

0-26 **1** **Tetouan**[36] [737] 3-9-3 **69** .... SteveDrowne 7 — 77+
(R Charlton) *a.p: chsd ldr over 2f out: led over 1f out: r.o wl* **2/1**[1]

3412 **2** 2 1/2 **Mick Is Back**[25] [900] 3-8-4 **63** ....(p) JackMitchell(7) 5 — 65
(J R Boyle) *hld up: hdwy and hung rt fr over 3f out: rdn over 1f out: chsd wnr ins fnl f: no imp* **11/2**[3]

30-4 **3** 1 1/4 **Red Current**[19] [977] 3-8-13 **65** .... OscarUrbina 6 — 64
(J R Fanshawe) *hld up in tch: rdn over 2f out: styd on same pce fnl f* **12/1**

34-0 **4** 1 **Just Oscar (GER)**[24] [931] 3-8-10 **65** .... StephenDonohoe(3) 8 — 62
(W M Brisbourne) *s.i.s: hld up: hdwy u.p over 1f out: nt rch ldrs* **25/1**

006- **5** shd **April Fool**[178] [6298] 3-8-10 **62** .... RichardThomas 4 — 59
(J A Geake) *hld up: hdwy and hung rt over 1f out: nt trble ldrs* **12/1**

044- **6** 1 **Tenancy (IRE)**[151] [6644] 3-9-0 **69** .... RichardKingscote(3) 2 — 63
(J A Osborne) *led: rdn and hdd over 1f out: wknd ins fnl f* **7/1**

1- **7** 1 3/4 **Feeling Wonderful (IRE)**[179] [6270] 3-9-4 **70** .... J-PGuillambert 10 — 60
(M Johnston) *chsd ldrs: rdn over 2f out: wknd fnl f* **4/1**[2]

2550 **8** 1/2 **Follow The Flag (IRE)**[8] [1117] 3-9-2 **68** .... IanMongan 1 — 57
(N P Littmoden) *s.i.s: hld up: n.d* **12/1**

33-2 **9** 5 **Support Fund (IRE)**[18] [998] 3-9-1 **67** .... StephenCarson 9 — 45
(Eve Johnson Houghton) *hld up: rdn over 3f out: wknd over 1f out* **9/1**

000- **10** 25 **Iced Tango**[269] [4049] 3-7-13 **56** oh8 .... KevinGhunowa(5) 3 — —
(F Jordan) *chsd ldr tl rdn over 3f out: wknd over 2f out* **50/1**

1m 44.73s (-0.57) **Going Correction** -0.125s/f (Firm) — **10** Ran SP% **120.1**

Speed ratings (Par 98):97,94,93,92,92 91,89,88,83,58

CSF £13.60 CT £108.82 TOTE £2.80: £1.30, £2.00, £2.10; EX 20.90 Place 6 £716.41, Place 5 £96.36.

Owner Mountgrange Stud **Bred** Fittocks Stud **Trained** Beckhampton, Wilts

FOCUS

A modest event, but looks surprisingly solid for the type of race at this time of year, and Tetouan did it well.

T/Plt: £607.00 to a £1 stake. Pool: £50,057.65. 60.20 winning tickets. T/Qpdt: £21.30 to a £1 stake. Pool: £2,950.70. 102.50 winning tickets. CR

1107 RIPON (R-H)

Saturday, April 28

OFFICIAL GOING: Good to firm (good in places)

Wind: Virtually nil

1298 TOTESCOOP6 H'CAP — 6f

2:30 (2:30) (Class 3) (0-95,95) 3-Y-0

£9,348 (£2,799; £1,399; £700; £349; £175) **Stalls** Low

Form — RPR

0-30 **1** **Northern Fling**[10] [1099] 3-8-9 **86** .... AdrianTNicholls 4 — 93
(D Nicholls) *hld up in rr: hdwy wl over 1f out: swtchd outside and str run ent fnl f: led last 50yds* **18/1**

4P3- **2** 1/2 **Dickie Le Davoir**[204] [5788] 3-8-10 **87** .... PatCosgrave 6 — 93
(K R Burke) *hld up in tch: hdwy wl over 1f out: rdn to ld ins fnl f: hdd and nt qckn last 50yds* **22/1**

20-0 **3** 1 1/4 **Heywood**[21] [939] 3-8-9 **86** .... TPO'Shea 9 — 90+
(M R Channon) *dwlt and bhd: swtchd to ins and hdwy 2f out: nt clr run over 1f out: styd on wl fnl f* **28/1**

300- **4** shd **Celtic Sultan (IRE)**[203] [5809] 3-9-4 **95** .... MickyFenton 13 — 97
(T P Tate) *in tch on outer: hdwy 1/2-way: rdn to ld wl over 1f out: hdd ins fnl f: kpt on same pce* **16/1**

145- **5** 1 1/4 **Top Bid**[264] [4200] 3-8-4 **86** .... DuranFentiman(5) 5 — 84
(T D Easterby) *cl up: rdn to ld briefly 2f out: sn hdd: drvn and one pce ins fnl f* **50/1**

105- **6** nk **Ponty Rossa (IRE)**[224] [5356] 3-9-0 **91** .... DavidAllan 2 — 88
(T D Easterby) *trckd ldrs: effrt 2f out: swtchd lft and rdn ins fnl f: one pce* **12/1**

20-2 **7** 6 **Southandwest (IRE)**[16] [1009] 3-8-13 **90** .... JohnEgan 7 — 69
(J S Moore) *chsd ldrs: rdn along over 2f out: grad wknd* **7/1**[2]

14- **8** 1 1/2 **Osteopathic Remedy (IRE)**[204] [5788] 3-8-9 **86** .... TomEaves 12 — 61
(M Dods) *nvr bttr than midfield* **9/1**[3]

33-1 **9** 3/4 **Ebn Reem**[21] [943] 3-9-2 **93** .... PhilipRobinson 1 — 65
(M A Jarvis) *led: rdn along 1/2-way: hdd 2f out and sn btn* **1/1**[1]

501- **10** 3/4 **Prospect Place**[233] [5133] 3-8-5 **82** .... PaulFessey 3 — 52
(M Dods) *prom: rdn along over 2f out: sn wknd* **28/1**

30-0 **11** 2 **Everymanforhimself (IRE)**[8] [1124] 3-9-2 **93** .... TPQueally 11 — 57
(J G Given) *a towards rr* **20/1**

10-1 **12** 2 **Fontana Amorosa**[35] [755] 3-8-6 **83** .... KDarley 10 — 41
(K A Ryan) *in rr fr 1/2-way* **10/1**

210- **13** 1 1/2 **Atlantic Light**[175] [6332] 3-8-10 **90** .... GregFairley(3) 8 — 44
(M Johnston) *a towards rr* **20/1**

12-5 **14** 3 1/2 **Fool Me (IRE)**[16] [1009] 3-8-10 **87** .... RichardMullen 14 — 30
(E S McMahon) *cl up: rdn along wl over 2f out: sn wknd* **25/1**

1m 11.8s (-1.20) **Going Correction** -0.20s/f (Firm) — **14** Ran SP% **127.0**

Speed ratings (Par 102):100,99,97,97,95 95,87,85,84,83 80,78,76,71

CSF £374.83 CT £10553.42 TOTE £28.00: £7.90, £8.20, £5.80; EX 905.40 TRIFECTA Not won..

Owner Jim Dale/Jason Berry **Bred** Lady Juliet Tadgell **Trained** Sessay, N Yorks

■ Stewards' Enquiry : Pat Cosgrave caution: used whip from above shoulder height

FOCUS

A good, competitive three-year-old sprint handicap. They all raced near side in the early stages, but the rail did not look crucial and they were spread out across the track at the line. Reliable form.

NOTEBOOK

Northern Fling only beat two home in a decent handicap at Newmarket during the Craven meeting, but he left that form well behind with a useful effort. His rider claimed afterwards he did not handle the track that well early on, and he had to be switched out towards the centre of the track to get a clear run, so he could even be rated a little better than the bare form. Official explanation: trainer's rep had no explanation for the apparent improvement in form (op 16-1)

Dickie Le Davoir, gelded since he was last seen, ran a cracker off the back of a 204-day break considering this ground was probably a little bit quicker than he really cares for. (op 28-1 tchd 20-1)

Heywood ◆, dropped back from a 1m and returned to turf, was unlucky not to finish closer as he was denied a clear run when trying to stay on tight against the near-side rail. There could be a decent handicap in him this season over either 6f or 7f. (op 25-1)

Celtic Sultan(IRE) ◆ was tried in pattern company on all four of his starts after winning his maiden last year and is clearly held in very high regard. This was a fine effort carrying top weight on his reappearance, especially considering he was forced to raced widest of all in the early stages, and he looks worth keeping on the right side of this term. (op 18-1 tchd 20-1)

Top Bid, a very useful juvenile, made a pleasing return from a 264-day break. He should prove just as effective over 5f.

Ponty Rossa(IRE), who tried her hand in Group 3 company on her final start at two, finished clear of the remainder on her return to action. (op 14-1)

Southandwest(IRE) Official explanation: jockey said gelding lost its action

Ebn Reem, 8lb higher than when winning on the Polytrack at Kempton on his reappearance, showed good early speed against the near-side rail but found disappointingly little under pressure. He is obviously much better than he showed on this occasion. Official explanation: trainer had no explanation for the poor form shown (op 11-8 tchd 6-4 in places)

Fontana Amorosa Official explanation: jockey said filly was unsuited by the good to firm (good in places) ground

1299 GRAHAME STOWE BATESON SUPPORTING XIII HEROES H'CAP — 5f

3:05 (3:05) (Class 5) (0-75,75) 4-Y-0+ — **£3,238** (£963; £481; £240) **Stalls** Low

Form — RPR

60-0 **1** **Colorus (IRE)**[9] [1112] 4-8-12 **69** .... DaleGibson 13 — 76
(M W Easterby) *a cl up: qcknd to ld ent fnl f: sn rdn and kpt on* **25/1**

5-00 **2** nk **Monashee Brave (IRE)**[91] [269] 4-9-1 **72** .... GrahamGibbons 11 — 78
(J J Quinn) *cl up: effrt and ch over 1f out: rdn ins fnl f and kpt on* **9/1**

4223 **3** 1/2 **Melalchrist**[11] 1074 5-8-11 **68**......(p) DO'Donohoe 1 72
(K A Ryan) *led: rdn along over 2f out: drvn and hdd ent fnl f: kpt on under pressure* **11/4**[1]

45-0 **4** nk **Ryedane (IRE)**[11] 1074 5-8-5 **62**......DavidAllan 14 65
(T D Easterby) *chsd ldrs: rdn along 2f out: kpt on u.p fnl f* **10/1**

05-5 **5** nk **Ptarmigan Ridge**[20] 957 11-8-13 **75**......JamieMoriarty(5) 12 77
(Miss L A Perratt) *chsd ldrs: rdn along 2f out: kpt on fnl f* **16/1**

0421 **6** hd **No Time (IRE)**[4] 1214 7-8-0 **64** 5ex......MCGeran(7) 7 65
(A J McCabe) *trckd ldrs: hdwy 2f out: rdn over 1f out and kpt on same pce* **4/1**[2]

110- **7** 1 **Elkhorn**[204] 5791 5-9-1 **72**......TomEaves 10 70+
(Miss J A Camacho) *towards rr tl styd on appr fnl f: nrst fin* **6/1**[3]

10-0 **8** hd **Henry Hall (IRE)**[8] 1134 11-8-11 **68**......KimTinkler 3 65
(N Tinkler) *chsd ldrs: rdn along wl over 1f out and kpt on same pce* **10/1**

00-0 **9** 1 1/2 **Mormeatmic**[8] 1134 4-8-13 **70**......PaulMulrennan 8 62
(M W Easterby) *t.k.h: in rr tl sme late hdwy* **25/1**

-000 **10** nk **Pauvic (IRE)**[4] 1226 4-8-8 **65**......(p) CatherineGannon 4 56
(Mrs A Duffield) *chsd ldrs: rdn along 2f out: grad wknd* **33/1**

144- **11** hd **Soto**[223] 5401 4-9-1 **72**......JimmyQuinn 9 62
(M W Easterby) *a towards rr* **16/1**

06-4 **12** nk **Never Without Me**[25] 905 7-8-4 **61** oh1......AdrianTNicholls 5 50+
(J F Coupland) *a towards rr* **16/1**

014- **13** nk **George The Best (IRE)**[185] 6174 6-8-5 **62**......PaulHanagan 2 50
(Micky Hammond) *hld up: a in rr* **14/1**

000/ **14** 10 **Demolition Molly**[571] 5684 6-7-13 **61** oh16......NataliaGemelova(5) 6 13
(R F Marvin) *dwlt: t.k.h: a in rr* **100/1**

59.48 secs (-0.72) **Going Correction** -0.20s/f (Firm) **14** Ran SP% **125.1**
Speed ratings (Par 103):97,96,95,95,94 94,92,92,90,89 89,88,88,72
CSF £239.27 CT £857.13 TOTE £30.30: £6.00, £4.40, £1.70; EX 230.00 Trifecta £563.10 Part won. Pool £793.12 - 0.34 winning units..
Owner Silvano Scanu **Bred** M Ervine **Trained** Sheriff Hutton, N Yorks
■ Stewards' Enquiry : Graham Gibbons one-day ban: failed to keep straight from the stalls (May 9)

FOCUS
A modest sprint handicap, but typically competitive. They raced near side but, just as in the opener, there did not appear to be any bias towards the rail. The winning time was only 0.70 seconds quicker than the later two-year-old fillies' maiden.
Henry Hall(IRE) Official explanation: jockey said horse was denied a clear run
Mormeatmic Official explanation: jockey said gelding became unbalanced on the undulations
Never Without Me Official explanation: jockey said gelding was denied a clear run
George The Best(IRE) Official explanation: jockey said gelding was denied a clear run

1300 TOTESPORT.COM H'CAP 2m
3:40 (3:40) (Class 2) (0-100,95) 4-Y-0+
£12,464 (£3,732; £1,866; £934; £466; £234) **Stalls** Low

Form RPR

/21- **1** **Raucous (GER)**[264] 4204 4-8-6 **80**......MickyFenton 1 87+
(T P Tate) *mde all: qckned 3f out: rdn 2f out: styd on wl u.p fnl f* **7/1**[3]

10-1 **2** 3/4 **Halla San**[24] 914 5-9-9 **93**......PaulHanagan 4 99
(R A Fahey) *hld up: hdwy over 3f out: swtchd outside and rdn wl over 1f out: ev ch ent fnl f: sn drvn: edgd rt and kpt on* **3/1**[2]

40-3 **3** hd **Gee Dee Nen**[40] 316 4-8-3 **77**......JimmyQuinn 2 82
(M H Tompkins) *hld up in tch: hdwy 4f out: rdn to chal over 1f out and ev ch: drvn ins fnl f and kpt on* **14/1**

351- **4** 2 **Escayola (IRE)**[19] 6321 7-9-0 **87**......(b) MarkLawson(3) 9 90
(Grant Tuer) *chsd ldrs: rdn along and outpcd over 2f out: styd on wl fnl f* **12/1**

31-6 **5** 2 1/2 **Bollin Derek**[31] 811 4-8-2 **76**......DaleGibson 6 76
(T D Easterby) *chsd wnr: rdn along over 3f out: drvn 2f out and kpt on same pce* **7/1**[3]

10-6 **6** 1 **Macorville (USA)**[9] 1109 4-9-3 **91**......KDarley 7 90
(G M Moore) *prom: effrt 3f out and sn rdn: drvn wl over 1f out and grad wknd* **20/1**

0-04 **7** 1 1/2 **Trance (IRE)**[7] 1148 7-8-9 **79**......PaulFessey 3 76
(T D Barron) *hld up in rr: hdwy on outer 4f out: rdn along to chse ldrs over 2f out: sn drvn: edgd rt and btn* **10/1**

0- **8** 2 1/2 **Burntoakboy**[16] 4541 9-8-1 **76** oh6......DuranFentiman(5) 5 70
(Dr R D P Newland) *hld up towards rr: hdwy over 4f out: rdn along 3f out and sn btn* **11/4**[1]

031- **9** shd **Dr Sharp (IRE)**[183] 6205 7-9-3 **87**......AdrianTNicholls 10 81
(T P Tate) *trckd ldrs: rdn along 3f out: wknd fnl 2f* **8/1**

60/6 **10** 1 1/2 **Helvetio**[21] 944 5-8-10 **80**......PaulMulrennan 8 72
(Micky Hammond) *a in rr* **66/1**

3m 31.83s (-1.17) **Going Correction** +0.175s/f (Good)
WFA 4 from 5yo+ 4lb **10** Ran SP% **117.5**
Speed ratings (Par 109):109,108,108,107,106 105,105,103,103,102
CSF £28.51 CT £291.70 TOTE £7.50: £2.00, £2.00, £2.70; EX 33.50 Trifecta £456.10 Part won. Pool £642.45 - 0.10 winning units..
Owner The Ivy Syndicate **Bred** Gestut Graditz **Trained** Tadcaster, N Yorks
■ Stewards' Enquiry : Jimmy Quinn caution: careless riding

FOCUS
A good staying handicap and the pace seemed fair enough, even though Raucous made every yard.

NOTEBOOK
Raucous(GER) ◆ had not been seen since narrowly winning his maiden over 1m4f here last August, but he showed himself on a good mark on his return to action with a narrow success. Given a really positive ride, he looked beaten when strongly challenged half way up the straight, but he had saved just enough and battled on most gamely. His trainer holds him in very high regard and thinks he could develop into a Listed/Group 3 horse. He is now around a 12/1 shot for the Chester Cup, but a 3lb penalty will only put him on 7st 9lb and he would be no sure thing to make the cut. Wherever he goes next time, he looks open to plenty more improvement and will be worthy of the utmost respect. (tchd 6-1)
Halla San ◆, representing last year's winning connections, had no easy task having been raised 15lb for a runaway success in an ordinary event at Catterick on his reappearance, but he was open to more improvement stepping up to 2m for the first time and ran a cracker behind the potentially decent winner. There could be more to come and he appeals as a stayer to follow (op 11-4)
Gee Dee Nen ran very close to his best returned to the level and showed enough to suggest he can find a race off his current sort of mark. (op 16-1)
Escayola(IRE), in good form over hurdles recently, ran well off a mark 7lb higher than when winning on the Flat at Musselburgh last November. (tchd 14-1)
Bollin Derek, 2lb out of the handicap, ran much better than he did on the Fibresand at Southwell on his reappearance and should be able to go on again from this when there is some give in the ground. (op 9-1)
Macorville(USA) looks a better horse when there is some give in the ground.
Burntoakboy is much improve over hurdles since he was last seen on the Flat, as he showed when winning the Coral Cup at the Cheltenham festival, but he was well held from 6lb out of the handicap. (op 5-2 tchd 100-30)

1301 TOTEEXACTA (S) STKS 1m 1f 170y
4:10 (4:11) (Class 5) 3-4-Y-0
£2,914 (£867; £433; £216) **Stalls** High

Form RPR

04-5 **1** **Keisha Kayleigh (IRE)**[30] 819 4-9-0 54......(v) JamieMoriarty(5) 9 50
(B Ellison) *trckd ldr: hdwy 3f out: led 2f out: rdn and hung bdly rt ent fnl f: drvn and jst hld on* **2/1**[1]

0-00 **2** nk **Faversham**[54] 620 4-9-10 73......DO'Donohoe 7 54
(M Wigham) *hld up in tch: hdwy over 2f out: rdn wl over 1f out: swtchd rt and drvn ins fnl f: styd on wl towards fin* **4/1**[2]

5564 **3** 2 **Irish Relative (IRE)**[40] 708 3-8-7 43......PaulFessey 10 47
(T D Barron) *chsd ldrs: hdwy 3f out: rdn and ev ch over 1f out: swtchd rt and drvn ins fnl f: kpt on same pce* **6/1**

0- **4** 2 1/2 **Mister Pete (IRE)**[150] 1100 4-9-10......JimmyQuinn 6 45
(W Storey) *midfield: gd hdwy on outer 3f out: rdn and ev ch 2f out: sn edgd rt and wknd* **33/1**

30-0 **5** 4 **Jenny Soba**[10] 1090 4-9-0 59......MichaelJStainton(5) 2 32
(R M Whitaker) *bhd tl sme late hdwy* **17/2**

40/0 **6** 5 **Naughty Nod (IRE)**[6] 1178 4-9-10 60......PatCosgrave 1 27
(K R Burke) *bhd tl sme late hdwy* **11/2**[3]

200- **7** shd **Elite Land**[163] 4909 4-9-3 44......SuzzanneFrance(7) 8 27
(N Bycroft) *t.k.h: hld up and bhd tl sme late hdwy* **16/1**

0-00 **8** 1 3/4 **Nimrana Fort**[19] 968 4-9-10 49......(p) PaulMulrennan 5 23
(J S Wainwright) *chsd ldrs: rdn along 3f out: sn wknd* **25/1**

9 2 1/2 **Nortelco (IRE)**[13] 4-9-10......PaulHanagan 3 18
(Micky Hammond) *a in rr* **20/1**

-060 **10** 1 3/4 **Danum Diva (IRE)**[25] 907 3-7-11 39......(b[1]) DuranFentiman(5) 12 —
(T J Pitt) *t.k.h: led: rdn along 3f out: hdd 2f out and sn wknd* **22/1**

00 **11** 16 **Glenmore Lodge**[6] 1175 4-9-5......MickyFenton 11 —
(P T Midgley) *dwlt: a in rr* **33/1**

0-01 **12** 1 1/4 **Raven Rascal**[40] 708 3-8-6 47......AdrianTNicholls 4 —
(J F Coupland) *hld up: a in rr* **11/1**

2m 5.91s (0.91) **Going Correction** +0.175s/f (Good)
WFA 3 from 4yo 17lb **12** Ran SP% **126.6**
Speed ratings (Par 103):103,102,101,99,95 91,91,90,88,87 74,73
CSF £9.67 TOTE £3.50: £1.40, £2.50, £1.90; EX 10.00 Trifecta £102.80 Pool £234.68 - 1.62 winning units..There was no bid for the winner.
Owner C E Sherry **Bred** Ronnie Boland **Trained** Norton, N Yorks
■ Stewards' Enquiry : Jamie Moriarty one-day ban: used whip with excessive frequency (tbn)

FOCUS
A poor seller, although the time was creditable, 0.14 seconds faster than the later three-year-old maiden. The third and fourth look better guides to the form than the first two.
Nimrana Fort Official explanation: jockey said gelding hung left-handed
Glenmore Lodge Official explanation: jockey said filly was unsuited by the track and lost its action
Raven Rascal Official explanation: jockey said filly was unsuited by the track

1302 TOTEPOOL MAIDEN AUCTION FILLIES' STKS 5f
4:40 (4:42) (Class 5) 2-Y-0
£3,238 (£963; £481; £240) **Stalls** Low

Form RPR

1 **Tia Mia** 2-8-6......TPQueally 5 78+
(J G Given) *sn led and overall ldr stands' side: rdn clr 2f out: styd on* **4/1**[2]

2 **2** 2 **Sinead Of Aglish (IRE)**[19] 972 2-8-6......JimmyQuinn 14 70+
(A B Haynes) *led far side: rdn wl over 1f out: kpt on ins fnl f: no ch w wnr* **6/4**[1]

3 2 **La Guancha** 2-8-4......PaulFessey 2 60
(T D Barron) *chsd wnr stands' side: rdn along 2f out: kpt on same pce appr fnl f* **14/1**

4 5 **Bellas Chicas (IRE)** 2-8-6......MickyFenton 3 42
(P T Midgley) *chsd ldrs stands' side: rdn along 2f out: sn outpcd* **33/1**

05 **5** shd **Upstanding**[9] 1107 2-7-11......PatrickDonaghy(7) 9 40
(M Brittain) *in tch stands' side: rdn along 2f out: sn no imp* **20/1**

0 **6** 1 3/4 **Little Finch (IRE)**[14] 1043 2-8-6 ow2......GrahamGibbons 8 35
(R C Guest) *chsd ldng pair stands' side: rdn along 2f out: sn wknd* **20/1**

2 **7** 1 **Mujada**[15] 1029 2-7-11......AndrewHeffernan(7) 11 29
(M Brittain) *racd stands' side: a towards rr* **14/1**

0 **8** nk **Pequeno Dinero (IRE)**[26] 890 2-7-11......KellyHarrison(7) 10 27
(C W Fairhurst) *a in rr stands' side* **50/1**

9 1 **Welcome Return (IRE)** 2-8-6......KDarley 7 25
(T D Easterby) *s.i.s and a bhd stands' side* **8/1**[3]

4 **10** 3 **Bella Natasha (IRE)**[21] 942 2-8-12......DO'Donohoe 12 19
(K A Ryan) *chsd ldr far side: rdn along 1/2-way: sn outpcd and bhd* **4/1**[2]

0 **11** nk **Herolds Bay**[5] 1193 2-8-6......PaulMulrennan 1 12
(M W Easterby) *a in rr stands' side* **66/1**

P **Look Busy (IRE)** 2-8-6......AdrianMcCarthy 4 —
(A Berry) *racd stands' side: sn bhd and p.u after 1 1/2f* **33/1**

60.18 secs (-0.02) **Going Correction** -0.20s/f (Firm) **12** Ran SP% **123.3**
Speed ratings (Par 89):92,88,85,77,77 74,73,72,70,66 65,—
CSF £10.08 TOTE £6.20: £1.90, £1.10, £4.80; EX 12.90 Trifecta £143.20 Pool £552.66 - 2.74 winning units..
Owner Dachel Stud **Bred** Dachel Stud **Trained** Willoughton, Lincs

FOCUS
Just an ordinary fillies' maiden. The favourite, Sinead Of Aglish, was one of only two fillies to race far side, but the much larger group on the near side of the track appeared at an advantage. The winning time was only 0.70 seconds slower than the earlier 61-75 handicap for four-year-olds and upwards.

NOTEBOOK
Tia Mia, a 20,000gns purchase, out of a 1m2f winner in Italy, made a winning debut in emphatic fashion. She probably would have been made to work harder had Sinead Of Aglish not raced on the opposite side of the track, but this was still a very promising start to her career and she deserves her chance in a higher grade. (op 9-1 tchd 10-1)
Sinead Of Aglish(IRE) ◆, a pleasing second on her debut at Warwick, could be considered an unlucky loser as she raced on the opposite side of the track to the winner and was 14 lengths clear of the only other filly to race far side, Bella Natasha. She should soon be winning in similar company. (op 11-8 tchd 15-8 and 2-1 in places)
La Guancha, a 2,000gns purchase out of a mare who was unplaced over sprint trips at two and three, made a satisfactory introduction and is open to improvement. (op 16-1)
Bellas Chicas(IRE), a 3,200euros half-sister to among others Inch Island, a triple 7f-1m winner, showed some ability on her racecourse debut and may do even better when there is some cut in the ground.
Upstanding was well held and may need dropping into claiming or selling company, with nurseries not an option until later in the season. (op 25-1)
Bella Natasha(IRE), fourth on her debut at Kempton, raced on the far side of the track along with the eventual runner-up, but she offered nothing. (op 100-30 tchd 5-2)
Look Busy(IRE) Official explanation: jockey said filly lost its action and pulled up

1303 TOTESPORT 0800 221 221 MAIDEN STKS 1m 1f 170y
5:15 (5:18) (Class 5) 3-Y-O £3,238 (£963; £481; £240) Stalls High

Form RPR

02- **1** **Jeer (IRE)**[238] 5025 3-9-3 .... DO'Donohoe 4 60+
(E A L Dunlop) *in tch: hdwy 3f out: rdn to ld 1 1/2f out: styd on fnl f* **6/1**[3]

022- **2** 1 1/4 **Latanazul**[207] 5760 3-8-12 80............ JimmyQuinn 12 52+
(J L Dunlop) *trckd ldng pair: hdwy to ld 3f out: rdn and hdd 1 1/2f out: kpt on u.p ins fnl f* **10/11**[1]

50- **3** 3 **Spirit Of Ecstacy**[217] 5536 3-8-12 .... GrahamGibbons 2 46
(G M Moore) *led: rdn along and hdd 3f out: drvn and sltly outpcd 2f out: kpt on u.p ins fnl f* **50/1**

40-0 **4** 1 **Devilfishpoker Com**[103] 136 3-8-10 45............ PatrickDonaghy(7) 3 49
(R C Guest) *cl up: effrt and ev ch over 2f out: sn rdn and kpt on same pce fr over 1f out* **100/1**

5 hd **Honorable Love** 3-8-9 .... MarkLawson(3) 5 44+
(M Dods) *s.i.s: t.k.h in rr: hdwy over 2f out: sn rdn and kpt on ins fnl f: nrst fin* **25/1**

60- **6** shd **Grand Dream (IRE)**[200] 5886 3-9-3 .... KDarley 10 48
(J G Given) *in tch: hdwy to chse ldrs 3f out: rdn 2f out and grad wknd appr fnl f* **14/1**

7 1 3/4 **Muqadam (IRE)** 3-9-3 .... PaulHanagan 6 45+
(Sir Michael Stoute) *bhd: gd hdwy on outer over 2f out: rdn and edgd rt over 1f out: sn no imp* **11/4**[2]

4 **8** nk **Jentris Girl (IRE)**[9] 1111 3-8-7 .... DuranFentiman(5) 11 39+
(T D Easterby) *hld up in rr: styd on fnl 2f* **18/1**

00-6 **9** shd **Mr Crystal (FR)**[31] 807 3-9-3 45............ PaulMulrennan 15 44
(Micky Hammond) *in tch on inner: rdn along 3f out: kpt on same pce fnl 2f* **66/1**

4-0 **10** 2 1/2 **Pagan Starprincess**[9] 1111 3-8-12 .... DanielTudhope 7 34
(G M Moore) *nvr bttr than midfield* **18/1**

0 **11** 1 **Ja Myford**[9] 1111 3-9-3 .... MickyFenton 9 37
(P T Midgley) *chsd ldrs: rdn along over 3f out: sn wknd* **66/1**

00- **12** 7 **Blue Jet (USA)**[179] 6270 3-8-12 .... MichaelJStainton(5) 14 23
(R M Whitaker) *t.k.h: in tch tl rdn over 2f out and grad wknd* **33/1**

06- **13** nk **Caviar Heights (IRE)**[176] 6316 3-8-12 .... JamieMoriarty(5) 8 23
(Miss L A Perratt) *a in rr* **50/1**

14 4 **Piperman** 3-9-3 .... PaulFessey 1 15
(M Dods) *t.k.h: hld up: a bhd* **25/1**

000- **15** 9 **Dream On Dreamers (IRE)**[152] 6625 3-9-3 33........ AdrianMcCarthy 16 —
(R C Guest) *s.i.s: a bhd* **100/1**

2m 6.05s (1.05) **Going Correction** +0.175s/f (Good) **15 Ran SP% 130.0**
Speed ratings (Par 98):102,101,98,97,97 97,96,95,95,93 93,87,87,84,76
CSF £12.13 TOTE £9.30: £2.70, £1.10, £10.10; EX 17.40 Trifecta £349.50 Part won. Pool £492.33 - 0.50 winning units..

Owner Mohammed Jaber **Bred** Floors Farming And Side Hill Stud **Trained** Newmarket, Suffolk

FOCUS
A very ordinary maiden and the 45-rated Devilfishpoker Com does little for the form in fourth. The winning time was 0.14 seconds slower than the earlier seller, so it is hard to put a positive spin on it.

Muqadam(IRE) Official explanation: jockey said colt was green and hung left-handed

Piperman Official explanation: jockey said gelding lost its action

1304 TOTESPORTCASINO.COM CONDITIONS STKS 1m 4f 10y
5:50 (5:50) (Class 3) 4-Y-O+ £6,855 (£2,052; £1,026; £513; £256) Stalls High

Form RPR

10-0 **1** **Peppertree Lane (IRE)**[19] 990 4-8-8 105............ KDarley 2 95+
(M Johnston) *trckd ldr: led 3f out: pushed 2 l clr 1f out: kpt on:* **5/4**[1]

504- **2** nk **Lets Roll**[119] 6319 6-8-9 90............ DanielTudhope 4 92
(C W Thornton) *led: rdn along and hdd 3f out: drvn and sltly outpcd wl over 1f out: rallied wl fnl furlong* **11/2**[3]

303- **3** 1/2 **Camrose**[175] 6334 6-8-9 100............(b) JimmyQuinn 5 91
(J L Dunlop) *trckd ldrs: hdwy over 2f out: rdn and ev ch over 1f out: sn drvn and one pce ins fnl f* **5/2**[2]

403- **4** 2 1/2 **Kyoto Summit**[222] 5430 4-8-8 89............ PaulMulrennan 1 87
(M W Easterby) *hld up: hdwy over 2f out: sn rdn and kpt on same pce appr fnl f* **11/1**

660- **5** 7 **Gavroche (IRE)**[224] 5374 6-8-9 98............ MickyFenton 3 76
(J R Boyle) *in tch: hdwy 3f out: rdn to chse ldng pair wl over 1f out: sn drvn and wknd* **11/2**[3]

2m 36.82s (-0.18) **Going Correction** +0.175s/f (Good)
WFA 4 from 6yo 1lb **5 Ran SP% 112.1**
Speed ratings (Par 107):107,106,106,104,100
CSF £8.77 TOTE £2.10: £1.50, £1.80; EX 4.40 Place 6 £472.70, Place 5 £11.87.

Owner P D Savill **Bred** Gestut Wittekindshof **Trained** Middleham Moor, N Yorks

FOCUS
Quite a good conditions contest, although Peppertree Lane didn't have to be at his best to win.

NOTEBOOK
Peppertree Lane(IRE), down the field in a Listed race in France on his reappearance, looked set to win quite well when taking up the running, but this ground was quicker than he likes and, carrying his head a touch high, he only just held on. Despite winning, he was below his best and will appreciate a return to easier conditions. (op 6-4)

Lets Roll, returned to the Flat after a couple of respectable runs over hurdles towards the end of last year, ran a creditable race in defeat, very nearly taking advantage of the favourite not running up to his best. (op 13-2 tchd 7-1)

Camrose was perhaps not quite at his best on his return from a 175-day break, but he was not beaten that far and can be expected to come on for the outing. (op 2-1 tchd 11-4)

Kyoto Summit, having his first start since leaving Luca Cumani's yard, had a bit to find at the weights and was well held. This was his first run since last September and better can be expected when he is returned to a more suitable grade. (op 12-1 tchd 14-1)

Gavroche(IRE) offered little immediate promise off the back of a 224-day break. (op 9-2 tchd 4-1)

T/Plt: £650.90 to a £1 stake. Pool: £77,627.50. 87.05 winning tickets. T/Qpdt: £4.70 to a £1 stake. Pool: £3,696.00. 578.30 winning tickets. JR

1274 SANDOWN (R-H)
Saturday, April 28

OFFICIAL GOING: Good (good to firm in places)
Other races under Rules of jumps racing
Wind: Light, behind Weather: Sunny and warm

1305 BETFRED MILE (GROUP 2) 1m 14y
3:55 (4:01) (Class 1) 4-Y-O+
£48,263 (£18,292; £9,154; £4,564; £2,286; £1,147) Stalls High

Form RPR

620- **1** **Jeremy (USA)**[196] 5962 4-9-0 112............ LDettori 1 118+
(Sir Michael Stoute) *dwlt: hld up in last pair: stdy prog on outer fr 3f out: shkn up to ld jst over 1f out: styd on wl* **2/1**[1]

033- **2** 1 1/4 **Bahia Breeze**[182] 6218 5-8-11 106............ PJSmullen 2 109
(Rae Guest) *trckd ldng pair: rdn over 2f out: clsd to try to chal over 1f out: chsd wnr fnl f but readily hld* **10/1**

444- **3** nk **Take A Bow**[175] 6334 6-9-0 100............ JimCrowley 7 111
(P R Chamings) *settled in rr: rdn 3f out: no prog tl styd on fr over 1f out: clsng on runner-up at fin* **16/1**

3-00 **4** 3 1/2 **Road To Love (IRE)**[65] 531 4-9-0 .... RHills 8 103
(M Johnston) *lw: sn trckd ldr: rdn to ld wl over 2f out: hdd jst over 1f out: one pce* **10/3**[2]

10-3 **5** 2 1/2 **Final Verse**[9] 1104 4-9-0 109............ JimmyFortune 4 97
(Sir Michael Stoute) *led to wl over 2f out: hld whn n.m.r on inner over 1f out: fdd* **7/2**[3]

020- **6** 3 **Babodana**[161] 6516 7-9-0 105............ SaleemGolam 9 90
(M H Tompkins) *trckd ldng pair: hrd rdn 3f out: wknd wl over 1f out* **20/1**

000- **7** 4 **Jedburgh**[196] 5962 6-9-0 105............(b) SebSanders 6 81
(J L Dunlop) *settled in midfield: shkn up over 2f out: wknd wl over 1f out* **14/1**

-003 **8** 1 1/2 **Royal Power (IRE)**[64] 542 4-9-0 .... ChrisCatlin 3 78
(M R Channon) *hld up in tch: rdn 3f out: hanging and struggling fr over 2f out* **25/1**

1150 **9** 8 **Areyoutalkingtome**[28] 860 4-9-0 115............ EddieAhern 5 59
(C A Cyzer) *lw: a in last pair: wknd over 2f out* **14/1**

1m 41.22s (-2.73) **Going Correction** +0.05s/f (Good) **9 Ran SP% 115.5**
Speed ratings (Par 115):115,113,113,109,107 104,100,98,90
CSF £23.68 TOTE £2.70: £1.50, £2.20, £4.80; EX 24.60 Trifecta £871.10 Pool £1,226.96 - 1 winning unit..

Owner Mrs Elizabeth Moran **Bred** Brookdale **Trained** Newmarket, Suffolk

FOCUS
A fair renewal, run at a decent pace, and won in good style by last year's Jersey Stakes winner Jeremy. The form is not strong for the grade but looks sound enough rated around the placed horses.

NOTEBOOK
Jeremy(USA), who looked fit enough for his reappearance, had never been beyond 7f before but his breeding suggested it should not be a problem. Appreciating the decent gallop set by his stablemate Final Verse, he came with a powerful run from the back of the field to win in the manner of a colt who has improved from three to four. The bare form might not back that up, but he won cosily, should improve for the run and looks set for a good season. One would imagine that all the top 1m races are likely to be on his agenda, with Newbury his first stop. (op 7-4 tchd 5-2)
Bahia Breeze, who also looked fit for her reappearance, has been placed in Group company before as well as winning in Listed grade, but this was still probably close to being a personal-best effort. She will find things easier when back racing against her own sex. (op 8-1)
Take A Bow, despite having been off the track since November, looked fit for his reappearance. All his wins to date have come over distances at up to 1m, but he was racing over further for much of last season and this performance off a good gallop suggests he will again be wanting a longer trip this year. (op 25-1)
Road To Love(IRE) was the subject of a gamble from 7-1 in the morning as punters expected him to get his own way in front and make a bold bid to make all, as he did on three occasions last summer. In the event, the Stoute second-string denied him his favoured role and a strong pace ensued, which played into the hands of the other Stoute-trained colt Jeremy, who was held up. Ideally he probably wants another two furlongs, although one would imagine that he will be kept to right-handed tracks, on which he seems to excel. (op 5-1)
Final Verse, who ran with promise on his reappearance at Newmarket nine days earlier, was sent into the lead, robbing his stable companion's main market rival of his favoured front-running role, and he probably set too fast a pace for his own good. (op 4-1 tchd 9-2)
Babodana, a twilight horse for a while now, had been placed in this race the previous two years, but he lacked the benefit of a previous outing this time around and, having tracked the strong pace set by the leading duo, he got tired and weakened out of things inside the final two furlongs.
Jedburgh, a 7f specialist who had not run over a trip this far for the best part of three years, did not get home. (op 20-1)
Royal Power(IRE) won the German 2000 Guineas last year but has struggled in this country and abroad since. He probably wants easier ground than he had here. (op 20-1)
Areyoutalkingtome had the highest official rating in the race but that was awarded for performances over sprint distances on Polytrack so had little relevance to this race. Official explanation: trainer said colt was found to be jarred up after the race (op 12-1)

1306 BETFREDPOKER CLASSIC TRIAL (GROUP 3) 1m 2f 7y
4:25 (4:31) (Class 1) 3-Y-O
£28,390 (£10,760; £5,385; £2,685; £1,345; £675) Stalls High

Form RPR

120- **1** **Regime (IRE)**[189] 6104 3-9-0 108............ LDettori 4 111+
(M L W Bell) *hld up in last pair: prog 3f out: rdn to ld over 1f out: in command fnl f* **11/2**

13-5 **2** 2 **Striving Storm (USA)**[9] 1103 3-9-0 104............ EddieAhern 7 107
(P W Chapple-Hyam) *lw: sn led: jnd 1/2-way: c to centre in st: drvn and hdd over 1f out: hanging lft and nt qckn after* **17/2**

21- **3** nk **Asperity (USA)**[212] 5640 3-9-0 98............ JimmyFortune 2 106
(J H M Gosden) *hld up: quick move to trck ldr after 2f and racd wd: upsides fr 1/2-way tl hdd over 1f out: carried lft and nt qckn* **3/1**[1]

4 2 1/2 **Chariots Of Fire (IRE)**[20] 959 3-9-0 .... WMLordan 5 101
(David Wachman, Ire) *w'like: hld up in tch: effrt to chse ldrs 2f out: cl enough wl over 1f out: fdd* **5/1**[3]

33- **5** nk **Al Tharib (USA)**[211] 5658 3-9-0 .... RHills 3 101
(Sir Michael Stoute) *hld up in rr: shkn up and outpcd 3f out: plugged on fr over 1f out* **8/1**

5-1 **6** 1 3/4 **Celestial Halo (IRE)**[14] 1044 3-9-0 90............ MichaelHills 8 97
(B W Hills) *trckd ldrs: rdn wl over 2f out: sn struggling: wknd* **7/1**

10-1 **7** 1 **Petara Bay (IRE)**[10] 1097 3-9-0 91............ DaneO'Neill 1 95
(T G Mills) *lw: reluctant to enter stalls: hld up in rr: rdn and outpcd wl over 2f out: no ch after* **7/2**[2]

0-43 **8** 2½ **Norisan**[14] 1035 3-9-0 100 .... SebSanders 6 90
(R Hannon) *trckd ldr for 2f: rdn 3f out: wknd 2f out* **25/1**

2m 9.65s (-0.59) **Going Correction** +0.05s/f (Good) 8 Ran SP% **117.3**
Speed ratings (Par 108):104,102,102,100,99 98,97,95
CSF £52.14 TOTE £5.90: £2.30, £2.50, £1.80; EX 57.50.
Owner Highclere Thoroughbred Racing XL **Bred** Philip Brady **Trained** Newmarket, Suffolk

FOCUS
The early pace was not quick and the form does not look that strong, but it was a likeable effort from the winner, who should do better.

NOTEBOOK
Regime(IRE), a below-par seventh in the Racing Post Trophy on his final start last season, looked as though he would come on a bit for the run beforehand so it is encouraging that he won in such style. He did have the highest official rating in the race, though, so he was entitled to be there or thereabouts. The way he finished up the hill suggests that another two furlongs should be within his compass, and he is unlikely to race again before either the Derby or the French equivalent. His trainer, who sent out Motivator to win at Epsom two years ago, quite naturally favours the former, for which he is a best-priced 25-1 with the bookmakers. (op 17-2)
Striving Storm(USA) gave a boost to the Craven form, in which he was fifth, and stayed this longer trip well, despite hanging left under pressure. Connections are considering the Chester Vase next, but he may need to go abroad to pick up Group honours. (op 11-1)
Asperity(USA), who looked pretty fit for this reappearance, was sent off favourite despite having a bit to prove in this grade. He ran well and will benefit from this experience, so he ought to make his mark at this level. Like most in this race, he holds a Derby entry, but he did not shape as though crying out for another two furlongs. (op 4-1)
Chariots Of Fire(IRE), who is quite a good-bodied type, cost 950,000euros and is a half-brother to smart juveniles Damson and Geminiani. Given that he had only won his maiden 20 days earlier this was a good effort, especially as he is bred to stay further than this - he will improve for 1m4f - and the steady early pace would not have suited him. (op 4-1)
Al Tharib(USA), a scopey sort, ran with promise in a couple of maidens at two and it was interesting to see his trainer pitch him in at this level on his reappearance rather than take the easier pickings of a maiden somewhere. He was a bit disappointing, though, and looks to need more time. (op 7-1)
Celestial Halo(IRE), a 13-length winner of his maiden earlier in the month, looked very fit for this step up in class but, like the Irish horse, he too looks to need further, and this steadily-run contest did not suit him at all.
Petara Bay(IRE), turned out surprisingly quickly after his Feilden Stakes win ten days earlier, never got in a blow and was way below his best. He may have bounced, but it is also worth noting he was uncharacteristically reluctant to go in the stalls and may have been out of sorts for some reason. (op 11-4)
Norisan, the most exposed runner in the line-up, did not find the step up in trip helping him to bridge the class gap. (op 40-1)

1307 TEXT "BETFRED" TO 83080 FOR MOBILE BETTING H'CAP 1m 14y
4:55 (5:04) (Class 2) (0-100,97) 4-Y-0+
£12,464 (£3,732; £1,400; £1,400; £466; £234) **Stalls** High

Form RPR
-500 **1** **Capable Guest (IRE)**[18] 993 5-8-7 86 .... (v) ChrisCatlin 1 99
(M R Channon) *sn in last: nt handle bnd over 4f out: drvn 3f out: prog on outer over 2f out: led jst over 1f out: surged clr* **5/1**[3]
0-00 **2** 2½ **Humungous (IRE)**[49] 658 4-9-1 94 .... LDettori 4 101
(C R Egerton) *trckd ldrs: effrt over 2f out: rdn to ld briefly over 1f out: styd on wl fnl f but no ch w wnr* **7/2**[1]
00-0 **3** 4 **Prince Of Thebes (IRE)**[7] 1145 6-9-4 97 .... PaulDoe 2 95
(J Akehurst) *swtg: fractious paddock: dwlt and rousted along to chse ldr: led over 2f out to over 1f out: sn outpcd* **7/1**
560- **3** dht **Red Somerset (USA)**[211] 5660 4-8-8 87 .... JimCrowley 3 85
(R J Hodges) *bit bkwd: scratchy to post: hld up in tch: rdn wl over 2f out: no prog tl kpt on fnl f* **13/2**
0-03 **5** nk **Bailieborough (IRE)**[19] 969 8-8-6 85 .... EddieAhern 9 82
(B Ellison) *trckd ldrs: outpcd over 2f out: effrt wl over 1f out to chse ldrs: sn outpcd* **15/2**
-005 **6** 7 **Rain Stops Play (IRE)**[11] 1082 5-8-8 87 .... WMLordan 5 68
(M Quinn) *s.i.s: sn led: hdd over 2f out: wknd rapidly over 1f out* **20/1**
3020 **7** 3 **Yarqus**[28] 848 4-9-1 94 .... SebSanders 7 68
(C E Brittain) *hld up in rr: rdn 3f out: wknd 2f out* **9/2**[2]
4103 **8** 9 **Orchard Supreme**[30] 817 4-8-9 88 .... PatDobbs 8 41
(R Hannon) *v scratchy to post: hld up: gng wl enough over 2f out: rdn and wknd rapidly sn after* **9/2**[2]

1m 41.71s (-2.24) **Going Correction** +0.05s/f (Good) 8 Ran SP% **117.6**
Speed ratings (Par 109):113,110,106,106,106 99,96,87
WIN: £7.40. PL: £2.30, £1.60, Prince Of Thebes £1.40, Red Somerset £1.10. EX: £24.90. CSF: £23.60. TRIC: CG/H/POT £62.02. CG/H/RS £58.15..
Owner John Guest **Bred** Mountarmstrong Stud **Trained** West Ilsley, Berks

FOCUS
They went a decent gallop here and the winner came from well off the pace. The form looks sound, rated around the first two.

NOTEBOOK
Capable Guest(IRE), visored for the first time in a long while and running off a career-low mark. Held up in last in a race run at a good pace, the race fell into his lap somewhat in the straight. He finished well down the outside, drew away for a clear-cut success, and this was a welcome return to form. Whether things will fall as kindly next time remains to be seen. (op 13-2)
Humungous(IRE) has been difficult to place since his two-year-old days but his handicap mark has dropped a bit and he had a chance in this company if reproducing his effort at Bath last September. He ran well, finishing clear of the rest, but the winner, who was held up and picked up from off the strong gallop, stayed on too strongly for him. (tchd 3-1 and 4-1 in places)
Prince Of Thebes(IRE), who had two handlers in the paddock, was very much on his toes beforehand and sweated up badly. He ran well considering, especially as he chased the strong pace for most of the way. (tchd 15-2 and 9-1 in places)
Red Somerset(USA), who is quite lightly raced for a four-year-old, looked in need of the run beforehand so is entitled to come on for this seasonal reappearance. (tchd 15-2 and 9-1 in places)
Bailieborough(IRE) looks held off his current mark. (op 6-1)
Rain Stops Play(IRE), back in handicap company, did too much in front and paid the price in the latter stages. He prefers easier ground than he had here. (op 16-1)

1308 BETFREDBINGO FLAT V JUMP JOCKEYS H'CAP 1m 14y
5:30 (5:36) (Class 4) (0-80,78) 4-Y-0+ **£6,477** (£1,927; £963; £481) **Stalls** High

Form RPR
1106 **1** **Bold Diktator**[35] 765 5-11-2 76 .... APMcCoy 4 85
(Tom Dascombe) *lw: mde all: set stdy pce to 2f out: rdn over 1f out and sn 2l clr: drvn out* **8/1**
6000 **2** ½ **General Knowledge (USA)**[12] 1060 4-11-1 75 .... (t) SebSanders 8 83
(B G Powell) *cl up on inner: effrt 2f out: drvn to go 2nd ins fnl f: clsd on wnr but a hld* **20/1**
6-00 **3** ½ **Daaweitza**[14] 1040 4-11-0 74 .... DaneO'Neill 1 81+
(B Ellison) *lw: hld up wl in rr: prog on outer 2f out: drvn and r.o fnl f: nrst fin* **3/1**[1]
0-60 **4** nk **Desert Dreamer (IRE)**[12] 1063 6-10-12 72 .... ChrisCatlin 11 78+
(P R Chamings) *taken down early: s.s: hld up in last pair: prog and swtchd outside over 1f out: r.o fnl f: gaining at fin* **16/1**
600- **5** nk **Genari**[218] 5504 4-10-12 72 .... (t) BarryFenton 3 77
(P F I Cole) *mostly chsd wnr: rdn over 2f out: no imp over 1f out: lost 2nd and fdd ins fnl f* **8/1**
0-50 **6** ½ **Cape Greko**[83] 351 5-11-4 78 .... (v) TimmyMurphy 7 82
(A M Balding) *trckd ldrs: rdn and effrt 2f out: one pce fr over 1f out* **14/1**
30-0 **7** 1 **Scarlet Flyer (USA)**[15] 1023 4-10-13 73 .... PatDobbs 9 75
(G L Moore) *hld up in rr: rdn 2f out: kpt on fnl f: n.d* **16/1**
530- **8** hd **Optimus (USA)**[170] 6418 5-11-3 77 .... RichardJohnson 10 79
(B G Powell) *trckd ldrs: effrt on inner 2f out: no imp fr over 1f out* **11/1**
3-00 **9** 5 **Everest (IRE)**[14] 1040 10-11-0 74 .... TJO'Brien 6 64
(B Ellison) *a in rr: last and struggling 2f out* **20/1**
060- **10** 1¾ **Zamboozle (IRE)**[325] 2341 5-11-2 76 .... JimCrowley 5 62
(D R C Elsworth) *dwlt: sn trckd ldrs: effrt on outer over 2f out: wknd over 1f out* **14/1**
-220 **11** 2 **Resplendent Nova**[28] 846 5-11-3 77 .... MickFitzgerald 2 58
(P Howling) *trckd ldrs tl wknd 2f out* **7/1**[3]
-225 **12** 5 **Bomber Command (USA)**[30] 817 4-11-3 77 .... MichaelHills 12 47
(J W Hills) *t.k.h: hld up in midfield: wknd over 2f out* **7/2**[2]

1m 44.95s (1.00) **Going Correction** +0.05s/f (Good) 12 Ran SP% **124.9**
Speed ratings (Par 105):97,96,96,95,95 94,93,93,88,86 84,79
CSF £164.96 CT £594.03 TOTE £7.30: £2.10, £5.50, £1.80; EX 294.70 Place 6 £43.67, Place 5 £15.57.
Owner Oneway RSM Racing Club **Bred** T J And Mrs Heywood **Trained** Lambourn, Berks

FOCUS
A novelty race in which Flat jockeys take on their Jumps counterparts. The winner was allowed to dictate a steady gallop in front, while the third and fourth were given too much to do and deserve to rate better than the bare form suggests.
Bomber Command(USA) Official explanation: jockey said gelding suffered interference in running
T/Jkpt: Not won. T/Plt: £22.00 to a £1 stake. Pool: £164,116.66. 5,437.65 winning tickets. T/Qpdt: £11.60 to a £1 stake. Pool: £6,286.80. 398.95 winning tickets. JN

1278 WOLVERHAMPTON (A.W) (L-H)
Saturday, April 28

OFFICIAL GOING: Standard
Wind: Light, against Weather: Fine

1309 BETDIRECTPOKER.COM COME AND 'AVE SOME AMATEUR RIDERS' H'CAP 5f 216y(P)
7:00 (7:01) (Class 6) (0-60,65) 4-Y-0+ **£2,307** (£709; £354) **Stalls** Low

Form RPR
1440 **1** **Desert Light (IRE)**[26] 896 6-11-3 56 .... (v) MrsMMorris 5 66
(D Shaw) *hld up in tch: led and hung lft fr over 1f out: r.o* **12/1**
5011 **2** 1¼ **Union Jack Jackson (IRE)**[8] 1120 5-10-9 55 .... (b) MrCAHarris(7) 1 61
(John A Harris) *hld up and bhd: hdwy on ins 2f out: r.o to take 2nd post* **6/1**
041 **3** shd **Carcinetto (IRE)**[12] 1064 5-11-5 65 .... MrRichardEvans(7) 3 74+
(P D Evans) *led early: prom: led over 2f out: hdd and sddle slipped over 1f out: lost 2nd post* **11/2**[3]
20-0 **4** 1 **Moon Forest (IRE)**[15] 1027 5-10-9 55 .... (p) MissHDavies(7) 8 57
(J M Bradley) *hld up towards rr: hdwy fnl f: nrst fin* **40/1**
6461 **5** nk **Winthorpe (IRE)**[4] 1226 7-11-6 62 6ex .... MrMWalford(3) 2 69+
(J J Quinn) *hld up in tch on ins: rdn over 1f out: nt qckn and hld whn nt clr run on ins cl home* **9/4**[1]
0231 **6** 1¼ **Another Genepi (USA)**[1] 1280 4-11-5 63 6ex .... (b) MissARyan(5) 12 61
(K A Ryan) *racd wd: chsd ldrs: lost pl over 2f out: rdn and edgd lft wl over 1f out: no real prog fnl f* **10/3**[2]
056- **7** nk **Matterofact (IRE)**[231] 5167 4-11-7 60 .... MrSWalker 13 57
(M S Saunders) *hld up towards rr: hdwy 2f out: sn rdn: no imp fnl f* **20/1**
2465 **8** 3 **Taboor (IRE)**[33] 787 9-11-0 60 .... MrsRCaudillo(7) 10 47
(R M H Cowell) *s.i.s: nvr nr ldrs* **20/1**
00-0 **9** hd **Kennington**[32] 803 7-10-13 59 .... (b) MrLOliver(7) 4 45
(Mrs C A Dunnett) *sn led: hung rt bnd and hdd over 2f out: wknd 1f out* **20/1**
66-0 **10** hd **Conjecture**[18] 992 5-11-2 60 .... MissRBastiman(5) 6 46
(R Bastiman) *prom tl wknd 2f out* **18/1**
520- **11** 3½ **Indian Lady (IRE)**[207] 5756 4-11-1 54 .... MissLEllison 9 28
(Mrs A L M King) *s.i.s: sn chsng ldrs: wknd wl over 2f out: fin lame* **25/1**

1m 15.46s (-0.35) **Going Correction** -0.05s/f (Stan) 11 Ran SP% **117.0**
Speed ratings (Par 101):100,98,98,96,96 94,94,90,90,89 85
CSF £75.16 CT £448.05 TOTE £16.20: £2.70, £2.30, £1.90; EX 80.80.
Owner Danethorpe Racing Ltd **Bred** Anthony M Cahill **Trained** Danethorpe, Notts

FOCUS
The two at the head of the market in this modest sprint handicap had already been successful here this week. The form looks solid enough rated around the placed horses.
Carcinetto(IRE) Official explanation: jockey said saddle slipped
Indian Lady(IRE) Official explanation: trainer said filly finished lame

1310 BETDIRECTPOKER.COM GET INVOLVED FILLIES' H'CAP 1m 141y(P)
7:30 (7:30) (Class 5) (0-70,65) 3-Y-O **£2,914** (£867; £433; £216) **Stalls** Low

Form RPR
3332 **1** **Nicomedia (IRE)**[15] 1024 3-8-10 64 .... HaddenFrost(7) 5 70
(R Hannon) *hld up in rr: hdwy on outside over 3f out: rdn to ld ins fnl f: r.o wl* **9/4**[1]
440- **2** 1¾ **Susanna's Prospect (IRE)**[171] 6394 3-9-3 64 .... RichardHughes 2 66
(B J Meehan) *led: hdd over 5f out: rdn over 2f out: rallied to take 2nd nr fin* **11/2**[3]
065- **3** nk **Dansil In Distress**[158] 6558 3-9-4 65 .... LPKeniry 7 66
(S Kirk) *sn w ldr: led over 5f out: rdn wl over 1f out: hdd and no ex ins fnl f* **9/1**
650- **4** ½ **Rowan River**[224] 5380 3-8-12 64 .... PatrickHills(5) 4 64+
(M H Tompkins) *hld up in tch: lost pl 5f out: nt clr run on ins over 2f out: hdwy whn hung lft wl over 1f out: swtchd rt ins fnl f: sn hung lft: r.o* **20/1**
063- **5** 3 **Wanessa Tiger (IRE)**[215] 5580 3-8-13 60 .... TPO'Shea 6 53
(M R Channon) *hld up: hdwy over 5f out: rdn 3f out: wkng whn nt clr run briefly ins fnl f* **9/1**
4403 **6** nk **Raquel White**[29] 834 3-8-4 56 .... KevinGhunowa(5) 3 49
(J L Flint) *t.k.h: prom: lost pl over 3f out: bhd fnl 2f* **17/2**
5216 **7** 5 **Ella Y Rossa**[8] 1131 3-8-13 63 .... StephenDonohoe(3) 8 44
(P D Evans) *hld up: hdwy over 5f out: wknd over 2f out* **9/2**[2]

1m 52.02s (0.26) **Going Correction** -0.05s/f (Stan) 7 Ran SP% **99.6**
Speed ratings (Par 95):96,94,94,93,91 90,86
CSF £10.82 CT £55.88 TOTE £2.60: £1.10, £2.70; EX 11.70.

Owner Kemal Kurt **Bred** George E McMahon **Trained** East Everleigh, Wilts
■ Paradise Walk (13/2) withdrawn (arrived at start without declared cheekpieces): Rule 4 applies deduction 10p in £.
■ Stewards' Enquiry : Patrick Hills one-day ban: careless riding (May 9)

FOCUS
A modest contest in which they went no gallop and form to have reservations about.
Ella Y Rossa Official explanation: jockey said filly ran flat

1311 BETDIRECTPOKER.COM $50,000 FREEROLL (S) STKS 1m 141y(P)
7:55 (7:55) (Class 6) 3-Y-0+ £2,047 (£604; £302) Stalls Low

Form RPR
000- **1** **Hilversum**[334] [2077] 5-9-1 37 ....(p) StephenDonohoe(3) 1 48
(Miss J A Camacho) *a.p: rdn over 2f out: led ins fnl f: drvn out* **13/2**
000- **2** *nk* **Raul Sahara**[195] [4439] 5-9-6 40 .... RichardKingscote(3) 9 52
(J W Unett) *hld up and bhd: hdwy over 2f out: rdn over 1f out: kpt on ins fnl f* **12/1**
2031 **3** *3* **Windy Prospect**[15] [1027] 5-10-0 58 ....(p) TPO'Shea 10 50
(P A Blockley) *mid-div: hdwy over 5f out: led over 2f out: rdn over 1f out: hdd ins fnl f: no ex* **2/1**[1]
0550 **4** *nk* **Casablanca Minx (IRE)**[14] [1038] 4-9-4 54 ....(b) IanMongan 4 40
(N P Littmoden) *hld up and bhd: hdwy on outside 3f out: hung lft fr over 1f out: kpt on same pce* **11/4**[2]
0-00 **5** *6* **Jabraan (USA)**[10] [1086] 5-9-6 38 ....(p) LiamJones(3) 2 31
(D W Chapman) *chsd ldrs: lost pl 3f out: n.d after* **40/1**
0330 **6** *nk* **Burnley Al (IRE)**[44] [681] 5-9-9 53 ....(b) RobbieFitzpatrick 11 30
(Peter Grayson) *mid-div: hung lft on ins over 3f out: hdwy over 2f out: wknd over 1f out* **6/1**[3]
000- **7** *½* **King Of Chav's (IRE)**[13] [3785] 4-9-9 40 .... SteveDrowne 13 29
(A Bailey) *chsd ldrs tl wknd 2f out* **33/1**
0-00 **8** *5* **Tantien**[4] [1221] 5-9-1 33 ....(p) JerryO'Dwyer(3) 3 13
(T Keddy) *led: rdn and hdd over 2f out: wknd wl over 1f out* **50/1**
-030 **9** *9* **Grand Welcome (IRE)**[8] [1119] 5-9-9 43 ....(bt) EdwardCreighton 8 —
(E J Creighton) *sn w ldr: wknd over 2f out* **20/1**
000- **10** *5* **Joint Expectations (IRE)**[145] [6706] 3-8-8 45 .... DMylonas 6 —
(Mrs C A Dunnett) *bhd fnl 3f* **33/1**
0000 **11** *4* **Crusoe (IRE)**[29] [833] 10-9-6 38 ....(b) StephaneBreux(3) 12 —
(A Sadik) *a bhd* **25/1**
000- **12** *7* **Wee Ziggy**[281] [3698] 4-9-9 45 .... NickyMackay 7 —
(M Mullineaux) *a bhd: eased whn no ch fnl 3f* **33/1**
000- **13** *47* **Wolf Pack**[192] [6059] 5-9-9 40 ....(p) FergusSweeney 5 —
(R W Price) *chsd ldrs: rdn over 5f out: sn lost pl: t.o* **40/1**

1m 50.92s (-0.84) **Going Correction** -0.05s/f (Stan)
WFA 3 from 4yo+ 15lb **13** Ran SP% **119.6**
Speed ratings (Par 101):101,100,98,97,92 92,91,87,79,74 71,65,23
CSF £72.97 TOTE £8.70: £2.50, £4.60, £1.80; EX 90.40.There was no bid for the winner. Casablanca Minx was claimed by Diamond Racing Ltd for £6,000.
Owner Mrs S Camacho **Bred** Mrs S Camacho **Trained** Norton, N Yorks

FOCUS
A weak seller with the first two having shown no recent form and the form is rated negatively.
Burnley Al(IRE) Official explanation: jockey said gelding hit its head on stalls and returned with a cut above the eye

1312 BETDIRECT.COM GET INVOLVED MAIDEN FILLIES' STKS 1m 1f 103y(P)
8:25 (8:27) (Class 5) 3-Y-0+ £3,071 (£906; £453) Stalls Low

Form RPR
1 **Cosmodrome (USA)** 3-8-10 .... NickyMackay 6 75+
(L M Cumani) *a.p: led ins fnl f: r.o wl* **8/1**
2 **2** *1* **Dolce Dovo**[23] [936] 4-9-11 72 ....(b) J-PGuillambert 5 76
(W J Haggas) *wnt rt and bmpd s: hld up in mid-div: rdn and hdwy over 2f out: r.o ins fnl f: nt rch wnr* **10/3**[2]
0- **3** *1½* **Ravarino (USA)**[236] [5068] 3-8-10 .... JDSmith 3 70
(Sir Michael Stoute) *a.p: rdn over 1f out: nt qckn fnl f* **8/1**
4-0 **4** *1¼* **Voice**[9] [1105] 3-8-10 .... RichardHughes 10 68
(H R A Cecil) *led: rdn over 1f out: hdd ins fnl f: one pce* **9/2**[3]
0- **5** *¾* **Kailasha (IRE)**[182] [6215] 3-8-10 .... IanMongan 13 66+
(C F Wall) *t.k.h in rr: rdn and hdwy over 1f out: nt rch ldrs* **25/1**
5- **6** *1½* **Set The Scene (IRE)**[174] [6349] 3-8-10 .... JimmyFortune 12 63
(J H M Gosden) *chsd ldr: ev ch over 2f out: rdn and hung lft over 1f out: wknd fnl f* **11/4**[1]
7 *1½* **White Moss (IRE)** 3-8-5 .... PatrickHills(5) 2 60
(M H Tompkins) *mid-div: hung rt over 3f out: rdn and hung lft wl over 1f out: no hdwy* **33/1**
66- **8** *½* **Inchmahome**[336] [2034] 4-9-11 .... LPKeniry 1 62
(E F Vaughan) *broke wl: sn stdd into mid-div: no hdwy fnl 2f* **20/1**
9 *1½* **Selique** 3-8-7 .... StephenDonohoe(3) 4 56
(E A L Dunlop) *nvr nr ldrs* **20/1**
6- **10** *1¼* **Karmest**[217] [5536] 3-8-10 .... RobbieFitzpatrick 9 54
(E S McMahon) *wnt lft s: prom: rdn over 2f out: wknd wl over 1f out* **7/1**
11 *6* **Memorata** 3-8-10 .... SteveDrowne 8 42
(R Charlton) *bmpd s: a bhd* **12/1**
0- **12** *8* **Classic Hall (IRE)**[225] [5353] 4-9-11 .... PaulDoe 7 29
(T Keddy) *s.i.s and hmpd s: a bhd* **66/1**
0- **13** *dist* **Maiden Investor**[245] [4799] 4-9-6 .... TolleyDean(5) 11 —
(M S Saunders) *plld hrd: sn mid-div: hung rt and hdwy 6f out: hung rt and rn wd bnd over 3f out: sn lost pl: t.o* **50/1**

2m 1.78s (-0.84) **Going Correction** -0.05s/f (Stan)
WFA 3 from 4yo 15lb **13** Ran SP% **130.1**
Speed ratings (Par 100):101,100,98,97,97 95,94,93,92,91 86,79,—
CSF £35.63 TOTE £15.30: £3.40, £2.30, £3.10; EX 59.60.
Owner Fittocks Stud **Bred** Fittocks Stud **Trained** Newmarket, Suffolk
■ Stewards' Enquiry : Tolley Dean one-day ban: improper riding - struck mount with foot on pulling up (May 9)

FOCUS
There was little previous form to go on in this interesting maiden with the runner-up probably the best guide to the level.
White Moss(IRE) Official explanation: jockey said filly hung right on final bend
Maiden Investor Official explanation: jockey said filly was unsteerable

1313 SIMON & LISA STANHOPE 40TH BIRTHDAY CELEBRATION H'CAP 5f 20y(P)
8:55 (8:55) (Class 6) (0-65,65) 3-Y-0 £2,388 (£705; £352) Stalls Low

Form RPR
4200 **1** **Charlotte Grey**[15] [1022] 3-8-13 60 .... EdwardCreighton 3 67
(C N Allen) *sn led: rdn wl over 1f out: drvn out* **7/2**[3]
2252 **2** *1¼* **Ioweyou**[3] [1248] 3-8-9 56 ....(b) LPKeniry 1 58
(J S Moore) *led early: a.p: rdn wl over 1f out: kpt on same pce fnl f* **9/4**[1]
10-0 **3** *¾* **Stir Crazy (IRE)**[15] [1022] 3-9-4 65 .... TPO'Shea 5 64
(M R Channon) *hld up: rdn and hdwy wl over 1f out: sn edgd lft: nt qckn ins fnl f* **4/1**
3454 **4** *2½* **Head To Head (IRE)**[32] [798] 3-8-9 56 .... RobbieFitzpatrick 6 46
(Peter Grayson) *s.i.s: outpcd whn hit rails over 3f out: hdwy on ins wl over 1f out: one pce fnl f* **10/1**
-361 **5** *1* **Sunley Sovereign**[46] [667] 3-9-0 61 .... JimmyFortune 7 48
(D W Chapman) *prom tl rdn and wknd over 1f out* **3/1**[2]
-060 **6** *8* **Hephaestus**[24] [925] 3-8-13 60 .... DeanMcKeown 8 18
(A J Chamberlain) *chsd ldrs: rdn over 2f out: sn bhd* **16/1**

61.99 secs (-0.83) **Going Correction** -0.05s/f (Stan) **6** Ran SP% **113.0**
Speed ratings (Par 96):104,102,100,96,95 82
CSF £11.98 CT £31.18 TOTE £5.40: £3.70, £1.50; EX 17.10.
Owner Travel Spot Ltd **Bred** Finbar Kent **Trained** Newmarket, Suffolk

FOCUS
This low-grade sprint handicap did not take much winning but the form looks sound enough rated around the winner and third.

1314 BETDIRECTPOKER.COM $50,000 FREEROLL H'CAP 1m 4f 50y(P)
9:20 (9:20) (Class 6) (0-65,64) 4-Y-0+ £2,388 (£705; £352) Stalls Low

Form RPR
40-3 **1** **Montchara (IRE)**[12] [1069] 4-9-3 62 .... SteveDrowne 2 75+
(G Wragg) *chsd ldr: rdn to ld 1f out: r.o wl* **3/1**[1]
0326 **2** *2* **Buscador (USA)**[7] [1167] 8-8-9 55 .... RichardKingscote(3) 5 62
(W M Brisbourne) *led: rdn over 2f out: hdd 1f out: nt qckn* **6/1**
-311 **3** *1* **Apache Fort**[87] [309] 4-9-0 59 .... PaulDoe 1 64+
(T Keddy) *hld up towards rr: hdwy wl over 1f out: r.o one pce fnl f* **10/3**[2]
-550 **4** *1* **Bentley Brook (IRE)**[15] [1025] 5-8-11 55 .... TPO'Shea 12 59
(P A Blockley) *hld up towards rr: hdwy 1f out: nt rch ldrs* **16/1**
2634 **5** *¾* **Regency Red (IRE)**[1] [1279] 9-8-8 55 .... LiamJones(3) 10 58
(W M Brisbourne) *hld up in tch: c wd and rdn over 2f out: no real prog fnl f* **12/1**
3-00 **6** *nk* **Swords**[7] [1152] 5-9-1 59 .... CatherineGannon 9 61+
(Heather Dalton) *n.m.r s: hld up and bhd: hmpd on ins over 4f out: hdwy wl over 1f out: no further prog fnl f* **14/1**
0030 **7** *nk* **Desert Hawk**[7] [1167] 6-8-9 53 ....(v) RobbieFitzpatrick 7 55
(W M Brisbourne) *hld up in tch: hdwy over 3f out: rdn over 2f out: wknd ins fnl f* **20/1**
2-00 **8** *shd* **Key Partners (IRE)**[14] [428] 6-8-13 62 .... RussellKennemore(5) 11 63
(B D Leavy) *plld hrd: sn mid-div: rdn and hdwy over 2f out: wknd ins fnl f* **40/1**
-220 **9** *4* **Raise The Heights (IRE)**[59] [585] 4-9-5 64 .... FergusSweeney 3 59
(C Tinkler) *s.s: rdn over 2f out: a bhd* **12/1**
440- **10** *1¼* **Thorny Mandate**[264] [4205] 5-9-2 60 .... JimmyFortune 8 53
(W M Brisbourne) *prom tl wknd over 1f out* **25/1**
0004 **11** *5* **Birthday Star (IRE)**[35] [767] 5-9-0 58 .... BrettDoyle 4 43
(W J Musson) *hld up in mid-div: rdn over 3f out: sn bhd* **4/1**[3]

2m 40.69s (-1.73) **Going Correction** -0.05s/f (Stan)
WFA 4 from 5yo+ 1lb **11** Ran SP% **121.3**
Speed ratings (Par 101):103,101,101,100,99 99,99,99,96,95 92
CSF £21.66 CT £65.13 TOTE £4.20: £1.90, £2.70, £2.00; EX 32.00 Place 6 £60.29, Place 5 £13.66..
Owner Mollers Racing **Bred** Hollybank Breeders **Trained** Newmarket, Suffolk
■ Stewards' Enquiry : Brett Doyle seven-day ban: improper riding - intentional inteference (May 9-16)

FOCUS
Most of these were fully exposed in this moderate handicap run at a modest pace, but the winner looks the exception.
Raise The Heights(IRE) Official explanation: jockey said gelding was slowly away from the stalls
T/Plt: £13.70 to a £1 stake. Pool: £60,671.95. 3,221.30 winning tickets. T/Qpdt: £8.80 to a £1 stake. Pool: £3,638.70. 303.60 winning tickets. KH

BRIGHTON (L-H)
Sunday, April 29

OFFICIAL GOING: Good to firm (firm in places)
Wind: Fresh, behind Weather: Bright and mild

1315 EUROPEAN BREEDERS' FUND MAIDEN STKS 5f 59y
2:10 (2:10) (Class 4) 2-Y-0 £4,037 (£1,208; £604; £302; £150) Stalls Low

Form RPR
0 **1** **Cracking (IRE)**[13] [1058] 2-9-3 .... RichardHughes 1 76
(R Hannon) *mde all: drvn clr fnl f* **5/2**[2]
23 **2** *1¾* **Concertmaster**[18] [999] 2-9-3 .... SebSanders 2 69
(R M Beckett) *w wnr tl hrd rdn and nt qckn fnl f* **11/8**[1]
6 **3** *hd* **Swindon Town Flyer (IRE)**[31] [814] 2-9-3 .... LPKeniry 3 68
(A B Haynes) *chsd ldng pair: hung lft and hrd rdn over 1f out: kpt on fnl f* **7/2**[3]
00 **4** *1½* **Lord Deevert**[9] [1123] 2-9-3 .... AmirQuinn 4 63
(W G M Turner) *t.k.h early: sn bhd: hrd rdn and hung lft over 1f out: nvr rchd ldrs* **20/1**
533 **5** *1½* **Rio Taffeta**[8] [1150] 2-9-3 .... JHBowman 5 57
(M R Channon) *in tch: effrt and hung lft ins fnl 2f: no ex over 1f out* **15/2**

61.26 secs (-1.04) **Going Correction** -0.40s/f (Firm) **5** Ran SP% **109.4**
Speed ratings (Par 94):92,89,88,86,84
CSF £6.28 TOTE £3.70: £1.80, £1.10; EX 7.10.
Owner A C Pickford & N A Woodcock **Bred** Adieu Cherie Partnership **Trained** East Everleigh, Wilts

FOCUS
A weakly-contested race, run at a moderate tempo, with three of the field failing to act on the track, and modest form.

NOTEBOOK
Cracking(IRE), a 30,000gns half-brother to several winners up to a mile, showed the benefit of his initial outing in this weaker race. Acting on the track better than most of his rivals, he had to be hard ridden to make sure but his family background suggests more improvement should be forthcoming. (op 3-1 tchd 9-4)
Concertmaster continues to run well without success. This was a weak maiden, and therefore a good opportunity to get off the mark, but he is now qualified for nurseries and that will be an attractive alternative if he cannot find a maiden. (op 13-8 tchd 15-8)
Swindon Town Flyer(IRE) again gave the impression that a stiffer test would suit, and in addition he was ill-at-ease on the camber. Six furlongs beckons. (op 3-1 tchd 11-4)
Lord Deevert ran his best race to date and, though this was a poor race, he does seem to be improving. Nurseries will be his metier, and on breeding he is likely to be effective from five to seven furlongs. Official explanation: jockey said colt was unsuited by the good to firm (firm in places) ground (op 25-1)
Rio Taffeta, whose Australian jockey was having his first ride in Britain, did not look happy on the track, but ought to find hisr home in six and seven furlong nurseries in due course. (op 6-1)

1316 ALAMO RENT A CAR H'CAP 6f 209y
2:40 (2:41) (Class 5) (0-75,75) 3-Y-O **£2,849** (£847; £423; £211) **Stalls** Low

Form RPR
6452 **1** **Proper (IRE)**[24] 935 3-8-13 **70** ChrisCatlin 6 80
(M R Channon) *led 1f: led 3f out: hrd rdn over 1f out: hld on wl fnl f* **11/8**[1]
10- **2** ¾ **Slate (IRE)**[217] 5546 3-9-4 **75** JamieSpencer 4 83+
(J A Osborne) *stdd s: covered up in rr: smooth hdwy 2f out: pressed wnr over 1f out: hrd drvn: nt qckn fnl 50yds* **11/8**[1]
6000 **3** 6 **Inquisitress**[27] 885 3-8-3 **63** MarcHalford(3) 3 55
(J J Bridger) *chsd ldrs: hmpd on rail 3f out: one pce fnl 2f* **8/1**[2]
002 **4** ¾ **Tenement (IRE)**[78] 417 3-8-0 **62** oh3 ow1 KevinGhunowa(5) 5 53
(Jamie Poulton) *chsd ldrs: hrd rdn and hung lft fnl 2f: one pce* **12/1**[3]
000- **5** 3 **Alloro**[172] 6394 3-8-4 **61** oh1 JamesDoyle 1 44
(D J S Ffrench Davis) *led after 1f tl 3f out: wknd 2f out* **12/1**[3]

1m 20.96s (-1.74) **Going Correction** -0.40s/f (Firm) **5** Ran SP% **110.7**
Speed ratings (Par 98):93,92,85,84,81
CSF £3.41 TOTE £2.50: £1.20, £1.40; EX 4.30.
Owner Billy Parish **Bred** Sean Finnegan **Trained** West Ilsley, Berks
■ Stewards' Enquiry : James Doyle one-day ban: careless riding (May 11)
Kevin Ghunowa one-day ban: careless riding (May 10)

FOCUS
Only a moderate handicap in terms of quality and depth and best assessed through the winner, but run at a fair pace.

1317 RACECOURSE VIDEO SERVICES (S) STKS 5f 213y
3:15 (3:15) (Class 6) 3-Y-O+ **£1,943** (£578; £288; £144) **Stalls** Low

Form RPR
3505 **1** **Le Chiffre (IRE)**[36] 766 5-9-12 60 (p) SebSanders 7 67
(K R Burke) *pressed ldr: led 3f out tl over 2f out: drvn to ld again ins fnl f* **3/1**[2]
5352 **2** ½ **Blackheath (IRE)**[13] 1065 11-9-3 55 AndrewMullen(3) 3 59
(D Nicholls) *chsd ldrs on rail: rdn to ld over 2f out: hdd ins fnl f: kpt on* **9/4**[1]
0030 **3** 1¾ **Sham Ruby**[25] 920 5-9-1 41 (t) JimCrowley 11 49
(M R Bosley) *sn pushed along towards rr: gd hdwy over 1f out: r.o wl to take 3rd ins fnl f* **16/1**
00-0 **4** 2½ **Bollywood (IRE)**[34] 789 4-8-13 38 RyanBird(7) 6 47
(J J Bridger) *mid-div: pushed along and lost pl 4f out: styd on wl fnl 2f* **50/1**
100- **5** 1 **Dotty's Daughter**[165] 6491 3-8-4 57 (p) RoystonFfrench 8 36
(Mrs A Duffield) *chsd ldrs: sn rdn along: one pce fnl 2f* **8/1**
0-04 **6** shd **Giovanni D'Oro (IRE)**[8] 1164 3-8-9 53 JamieSpencer 1 40
(N A Callaghan) *sn outpcd towards rr: styd on fnl 2f* **13/2**[3]
000 **7** 3 **Magroom**[13] 1062 3-8-9 42 (v) FrankieMcDonald 13 31
(B R Johnson) *s.i.s: bhd: effrt on outside whn sltly hmpd over 2f out: no imp* **33/1**
030- **8** ¾ **Justenjoy Yourself**[356] 1534 5-9-1 41 (p) SamHitchcott 9 27
(R W Price) *in tch: rdn and no hdwy fnl 3f* **25/1**
6006 **9** nk **Blushing Russian (IRE)**[13] 1065 5-9-7 42 (p) KevinGhunowa(5) 10 37
(J M Bradley) *w ldrs tl wknd and edgd lft over 1f out* **25/1**
6000 **10** ½ **Ten Prophets (IRE)**[28] 866 4-9-6 52 AmirQuinn 4 30
(J J Bridger) *wl bhd tl r.o fnl f* **16/1**
-006 **11** ¾ **Mr Mini Scule**[20] 974 3-8-9 49 LPKeniry 12 24
(A B Haynes) *wnt rt s: sn prom: hung lft over 2f out: sn wknd* **16/1**
6000 **12** nk **Feminist (IRE)**[13] 1065 5-8-8 41 (p) BarrySavage(7) 5 21
(J M Bradley) *led tl 3f out: wknd 2f out* **33/1**
00-0 **13** 5 **Lucky Tern**[26] 901 4-9-6 25 ChrisCatlin 2 11
(J M Bradley) *outpcd: a in rr* **50/1**

68.93 secs (-1.17) **Going Correction** -0.40s/f (Firm)
WFA 3 from 4yo+ 11lb **13** Ran SP% **115.4**
Speed ratings (Par 101):91,90,88,84,83 83,79,78,77,77 76,75,69
CSF £8.93 TOTE £4.30: £2.00, £1.50, £4.70; EX 13.50 Trifecta £139.50 Part won. Pool £196.50 - 0.70 winning units..The winner was sold to Ron Harris for 5,200gns.
Owner Nigel Shields **Bred** Agricola Del Parco **Trained** Middleham Moor, N Yorks

FOCUS
A competitive seller, run at a good pace and rated around the third and fourth.
Ten Prophets(IRE) Official explanation: jockey said gelding was unsuited by the good to firm (firm in places) ground

1318 BRIGHTON JIVE 75 H'CAP 7f 214y
3:50 (3:58) (Class 5) (0-70,68) 4-Y-O+ **£2,775** (£830; £415; £207; £103) **Stalls** Low

Form RPR
-410 **1** **Night Wolf (IRE)**[55] 614 7-8-6 **56** (t) PaulDoe 9 63
(Jamie Poulton) *mde all: hrd rdn ins fnl 2f: hld on gamely fnl f* **13/2**[3]
44-2 **2** ½ **Veiled Applause**[5] 1209 4-9-4 **68** SebSanders 4 74
(R M Beckett) *hld up in rr: gd hdwy 2f out: drvn to press wnr fnl f: jst hld* **7/4**[1]
3000 **3** 2½ **Christmas Truce (IRE)**[5] 1206 8-8-2 **55** oh4 ow1 (b) MarcHalford(3) 2 55
(J J Bridger) *s.s: t.k.h in rr: hdwy and hrd rdn over 1f out: styd on fnl f* **25/1**
4140 **4** shd **King After**[9] 1118 5-8-3 **56** (b[1]) StephaneBreux(3) 7 56
(J R Best) *plld hrd: prom: hrd rdn 2f out: no ex fnl f* **11/1**
25/6 **5** nk **Kingscape (IRE)**[25] 928 4-9-3 **67** JamieSpencer 6 66+
(J R Fanshawe) *dwlt: sn trcking ldrs: hrd rdn and hung bdly lft 2f out: one pce* **7/2**[2]
00-0 **6** nk **Prince Valentine**[9] 1118 6-8-4 **54** (p) ChrisCatlin 1 52
(G L Moore) *in tch: rdn over 2f out: one pce* **8/1**
60-0 **7** 2½ **Goodwood Spirit**[9] 1133 5-8-7 **62** KevinGhunowa(5) 3 55
(J M Bradley) *chsd ldrs: hrd rdn 2f out: no ex over 1f out* **12/1**
0050 **8** 4 **Scroll**[16] 1025 4-8-4 **54** oh4 (v) AdrianMcCarthy 10 38
(P Howling) *in rr: hrd rdn over 2f out: n.d after* **16/1**
0-50 **9** 4 **The Gaikwar (IRE)**[20] 975 8-9-0 **64** (b) AmirQuinn 8 38
(R A Harris) *bhd fnl 3f* **16/1**

1m 33.52s (-1.52) **Going Correction** -0.40s/f (Firm) **9** Ran SP% **114.7**
Speed ratings (Par 103):91,90,88,87,87 87,84,80,76
CSF £18.12 CT £270.91 TOTE £8.90: £1.80, £1.40, £7.30; EX 22.60 Trifecta £303.20 Part won. Pool £427.08 - 0.50 winning units..
Owner Miss N Henton **Bred** Watership Down Stud **Trained** Whitcombe, Dorset

FOCUS
A low-grade handicap in which the winner made all and the runner-up is rated to his latest form.
The Gaikwar(IRE) Official explanation: jockey said gelding lost a front shoe

1319 GOOD LUCK SUZANNA H'CAP 1m 3f 196y
4:25 (4:27) (Class 6) (0-60,60) 4-Y-O+ **£1,943** (£578; £288; £144) **Stalls** High

Form RPR
5630 **1** **Bienheureux**[7] 1178 6-8-6 **50** (t) JerryO'Dwyer(3) 6 58
(Miss Gay Kelleway) *bhd: hrd rdn and hdwy 2f out: styd on to ld 1f out: idled in front: drvn out* **13/2**
3042 **2** 1 **Recalcitrant**[16] 1026 4-8-10 **52** JamesDoyle 1 58
(S Dow) *prom: led over 2f out: hrd rdn and hdd 1f out: kpt on* **7/2**[2]
-554 **3** nk **Liberty Run (IRE)**[53] 634 5-8-8 **52** NeilChalmers(3) 2 58
(Mouse Hamilton-Fairley) *in tch: n.m.r on rail 5f out: drvn to press ldrs fnl 2f: kpt on* **3/1**[1]
2260 **4** 1 **Shaheer (IRE)**[20] 982 5-8-11 **52** JimCrowley 5 56
(J Gallagher) *chsd ldrs: drvn along and outpcd 3f out: styd on fnl f* **10/1**
-600 **5** 3 **Treetops Hotel (IRE)**[16] 1026 8-8-3 **51** (p) JackMitchell(7) 3 50
(B R Johnson) *hld up towards rr: effrt over 2f out: nt pce to chal* **13/2**
0-41 **6** 1¼ **Icannshift (IRE)**[16] 1026 7-8-10 **54** RichardKingscote(3) 8 51
(T M Jones) *prom: led 3f out tl over 2f out: wknd over 1f out* **4/1**[3]
-000 **7** 8 **Camp Attack**[16] 1025 4-8-6 **48** PaulDoe 4 32
(S Dow) *a bhd: no ch fnl 3f* **11/1**
005- **8** 44 **Three Counties (IRE)**[275] 3905 6-9-5 **60** SebSanders 7 —
(N I M Rossiter) *led tl 3f out: wknd qckly over 2f out: bhd whn virtually p.u over 1f out* **16/1**

2m 31.92s (-0.28) **Going Correction** -0.40s/f (Firm)
WFA 4 from 5yo+ 1lb **8** Ran SP% **117.2**
Speed ratings (Par 101):84,83,83,82,80 79,74,44
CSF £30.31 CT £83.32 TOTE £8.90: £2.30, £1.80, £1.20; EX 18.40 Trifecta £185.80 Pool £549.71 - 2.10 winning units..
Owner Mr & Mrs I Henderson **Bred** N R Shields **Trained** Exning, Suffolk
■ Stewards' Enquiry : Jerry O'Dwyer one-day ban: used whip with excessive frequency (May 10)

FOCUS
A moderate contest, run at an ordinary pace for the trip and rated through the second.
Icannshift(IRE) Official explanation: jockey said gelding had no more to give
Three Counties(IRE) Official explanation: jockey said horse had no more to give

1320 RADIOREVERB H'CAP 1m 1f 209y
4:55 (4:56) (Class 6) (0-65,64) 3-Y-O **£1,943** (£578; £288; £144) **Stalls** High

Form RPR
00-0 **1** **Kyloe Belle (USA)**[15] 1039 3-8-9 **55** JimCrowley 4 63
(Mrs A J Perrett) *w ldr: led and drvn along over 2f out: hld on wl* **13/2**[3]
55-1 **2** 1¾ **Graceful Steps (IRE)**[8] 1155 3-9-4 **64** RichardMullen 5 69
(E J O'Neill) *cl up: rdn 4f out: chsd wnr over 2f out: kpt on wl: a hld* **11/10**[1]
5500 **3** 5 **Tumble Jill (IRE)**[5] 1211 3-8-2 **51** ow1 MarcHalford(3) 1 47
(J J Bridger) *led: hrd rdn and hdd over 2f out: wknd over 1f out* **10/1**
0-53 **4** nk **Hills Place**[53] 636 3-8-5 **54** StephaneBreux(3) 2 49
(J R Best) *in tch: rdn 4f out: wknd 2f out* **7/2**[2]
3000 **5** 14 **Lawyer To World**[8] 1154 3-8-4 **50** PaulEddery 3 18
(N A Callaghan) *in tch: rdn 4f out: wknd 2f out: 5th and no ch whn eased fnl f* **7/2**[2]

2m 1.69s (-0.91) **Going Correction** -0.40s/f (Firm) **5** Ran SP% **114.5**
Speed ratings (Par 96):87,85,81,81,70
CSF £14.93 TOTE £7.60: £2.30, £1.30; EX 20.40.
Owner Martin & Valerie Slade **Bred** Winning Ways Farm **Trained** Pulborough, W Sussex

FOCUS
A weak race, run at a modest pace, but the winner is a likely improver, the runner-up is rated to his recent form, but the form is limited by the third.

1321 EXPRESS CAFE H'CAP 5f 59y
5:25 (5:25) (Class 5) (0-70,68) 4-Y-O+ **£2,849** (£847; £423; £211) **Stalls** Low

Form RPR
2553 **1** **Misaro (GER)**[5] 1212 6-8-5 **60** (b) TolleyDean(5) 8 75
(R A Harris) *prom: hrd rdn over 1f out: kpt on to ld ins fnl f* **15/8**[1]
660- **2** 1¾ **Harrison's Flyer (IRE)**[120] 6990 6-8-3 **58** (p) KevinGhunowa(5) 3 67
(J M Bradley) *in tch: drvn to ld over 1f out: hdd and outpcd ins fnl f* **15/2**
234- **3** shd **One Way Ticket**[130] 6890 7-9-4 **68** (p) JamieSpencer 6 76
(J M Bradley) *led tl over 1f out: kpt on ins fnl f* **4/1**[2]
0036 **4** 1¼ **Cosmic Destiny (IRE)**[9] 1120 5-8-5 **55** JamesDoyle 9 59
(E F Vaughan) *stdd in rr s: smooth hdwy 2f out: hrd rdn over 1f out: fnd little* **9/1**
100- **5** 2½ **Multahab**[196] 5987 8-8-13 **63** (t) AdamKirby 5 58
(Miss D A McHale) *prom on outside: hung rt over 2f out: hrd rdn and wknd over 1f out* **15/2**
0-02 **6** 2½ **Mr Rooney (IRE)**[10] 1112 4-9-1 **68** (t) AndrewMullen(3) 1 54
(D Nicholls) *sn pushed along on rail: prom tl hrd rdn and wknd 2f out* **9/2**[3]
0-00 **7** 5 **Sarah's Art (IRE)**[97] 214 4-8-10 **60** (b) ChrisCatlin 4 28
(Miss D A McHale) *s.s: outpcd: a bhd* **16/1**

59.80 secs (-2.50) **Going Correction** -0.40s/f (Firm) **7** Ran SP% **112.4**
Speed ratings (Par 103):104,101,101,99,95 91,83
CSF £16.07 CT £49.42 TOTE £2.30: £1.70, £3.20; EX 35.10 Trifecta £63.30 Pool £303.50 - 3.40 winning units. Place 6 £4.58, Place 5 £3.80..
Owner Messrs Criddle Davies Dawson & Villa **Bred** Wilhelm Fasching **Trained** Earlswood, Monmouths
■ Stewards' Enquiry : Tolley Dean caution: careless riding

FOCUS
A modest but competitive sprint, despite the lack of runners, with a strong pace being set by perennial front-runner One Way Ticket. The winner sets the level in an average race for the grade.
Multahab Official explanation: jockey said gelding hung right in the straight
T/Plt: £5.60 to a £1 stake. Pool: £62,425.10. 8,049.55 winning tickets. T/Qpdt: £4.30 to a £1 stake. Pool: £3,342.60. 574.70 winning tickets. LM

1322 - 1329a (Foreign Racing) - See Raceform Interactive

[871] NAVAN (L-H)
Sunday, April 29

OFFICIAL GOING: Firm (good to firm in places)

1330a VINTAGE CROP STKS (LISTED RACE) 1m 5f
4:00 (4:02) 4-Y-O+ **£21,993** (£6,452; £3,074; £1,047)

RPR
1 **Yeats (IRE)**[173] 6392 6-9-8 121 JAHeffernan 10 124+
(A P O'Brien, Ire) *settled 3rd: hdwy ent st: led under 3f out: rdn clr fr 2f out: easily* **1/3**[1]

2 *5* **Reform Act (USA)**[176] 6369 4-9-1 106 .... PJSmullen 8 107
(D K Weld, Ire) *trckd ldrs in 5th: 4th 1/2-way: prog into 2nd 2f out: sn rdn and no imp: kpt on same u.p fnl f* **8/1**[3]

3 *1 1/4* **Cool Touch (IRE)**[211] 5697 4-9-1 105 .... OCasey 3 105
(Peter Casey, Ire) *hld up towards rr: 7th and prog 5f out: 5th 2f out: mod 3rd and kpt on fr over 1f out* **12/1**

4 *3 1/2* **Clara Allen (IRE)**[175] 6358 9-8-12 100 .... TPO'Shea 4 96
(John E Kiely, Ire) *hld up: prog 5f out: 4th into st: 3rd briefly over 2f out: sn no ex* **14/1**

5 *5 1/2* **Sacrosanct (IRE)**[28] 875 4-8-12 94 .... DavidMcCabe 5 89
(Joseph Crowley, Ire) *towards rr: last 1/2-way: kpt on st* **50/1**

6 *1* **Valentina Guest (IRE)**[28] 875 6-8-12 92 .... WSupple 2 86
(Peter Casey, Ire) *hld up: 6th 1/2-way: effrt over 4f out: no ex st* **33/1**

7 *1* **Tartouche**[28] 875 6-9-3 103 .... DPMcDonogh 6 90
(Mrs John Harrington, Ire) *led: jnd 1/2-way: led again ent st: hdd under 3f out: sn wknd* **13/2**[2]

8 *26* **Dryandra (IRE)**[36] 756 4-8-12 85 .... NGMcCullagh 1 47
(John Joseph Murphy, Ire) *prom: disp ld 1/2-way: hdd ent st: wknd qckly: t.o* **50/1**

9 *18* **Alpha Jet**[17] 1017 7-9-1 .... WMLordan 9 22
(Patrick J Flynn, Ire) *4th early: wknd 5f out: trailing st: t.o* **50/1**

2m 48.1s (-11.90)
WFA 4 from 6yo+ 1lb **10** Ran SP% **122.6**
CSF £4.36 TOTE £1.20: £1.10, £1.60, £1.80; DF 4.50.
Owner Mrs John Magnier & Mrs David Nagle **Bred** Barronstown Stud & Orpendale **Trained** Ballydoyle, Co Tipperary

NOTEBOOK
Yeats(IRE) had 7lb in hand of his nearest rival on adjusted official ratings and proved fit enough for this reappearance to run out a very comfortable winner against inferior rivals. He looks set for another good season and might take in a race at Leopardstown at the end of May before making a bid to retain the Ascot Gold Cup. (op 1/4)

1331 - 1334a (Foreign Racing) - See Raceform Interactive

CAPANNELLE (R-H)
Sunday, April 29

OFFICIAL GOING: Good

1335a PREMIO BOTTICELLI (LISTED RACE) (C&G) 1m 2f 110y
3:25 (4:26) 3-Y-O **£18,919** (£8,324; £4,541; £2,270)

RPR

1 **Zar Solitario**[17] 1010 3-8-12 .... EddieAhern 4 101
(M Johnston) *led after 1f: two l clr fr 2f out: rdn out (2.54/1)* **5/2**[2]

2 *2* **Rob's Love (ITY)**[189] 6123 3-9-2 .... CFiocchi 2 102
(R Menichetti, Italy) **4/5**[1]

3 *1 1/2* **Gimmy (IRE)**[14] 3-8-12 .... DVargiu 5 95
(B Grizzetti, Italy) **74/10**

4 *nse* **Furia Ceca**[105] 3-8-12 .... SMulas 7 95
(F & L Brogi, Italy) **17/1**

5 *2* **Saltagioo (ITY)** 3-8-12 .... EBotti 3 91
(A & G Botti, Italy) **5/1**[3]

6 *15* **Wycherley (IRE)** 3-8-12 .... MDemuro 1 64
(F & L Brogi, Italy) **86/10**

7 *3* **Ancus Martius (FR)**[14] 3-8-12 .... MTellini 6 59
(R Biondi, Italy) **49/1**

2m 12.1s (132.10) **7** Ran SP% **130.7**
TOTE (including one euro stakes): WIN 3.54: PL 1.55, 1.27: DF 2.87.
Owner Sheikh Mohammed **Bred** Azienda Agricola Razza Del Sole Srl **Trained** Middleham Moor, N Yorks

NOTEBOOK
Zar Solitario was completing a four-timer following three wins in the UK. He will have to be supplemented if he is to return for the Derby Italiano, but should he win that race, or even finish in the first four, he will earn double prize money because he is Italian-bred.
Rob's Love(ITY) tried to close the gap throughout the final quarter-mile but could not do so. However, he was attempting to concede 4lb all round so his conqueror needs to continue improving. The longer trip in the Derby should not prove a problem, though.

1336a PREMIO PARIOLI GIOCO DEL LOTTO (GROUP 3) (COLTS) 1m
5:10 (5:19) 3-Y-O **£64,611** (£28,429; £15,507; £7,753)

RPR

1 **Golden Titus (IRE)**[33] 3-9-2 .... SLandi 14 102
(A Renzoni, Italy) *sn cl up fr wd draw: 7th st: rdn 2f out: 3rd 1f out: drvn to ld 100yds out: r.o* **5/4**[1]

2 *3/4* **Freemusic (IRE)**[14] 3-9-2 .... MDemuro 7 100
(L Riccardi, Italy) *led tl hdd 100yds out: r.o* **126/10**

3 *1/2* **Amante Latino**[21] 3-9-2 .... SMulas 4 99
(V Caruso, Italy) *hld up in rr to st: gd hdwy on outside fnl 1 1/2f: nrest at fin* **38/10**[2]

4 *1 1/4* **Golden Dynamic (IRE)**[35] 3-9-2 .... MTellini 13 96
(G Di Chio, Italy) *2nd st: chal 3f out: rdn and one pce fr over 2f out* **92/10**

5 *3* **Ladak**[35] 3-9-2 .... DVargiu 2 89
(B Grizzetti, Italy) *towards rr to st: sme prog over 2f out: nvr a factor* **26/1**

6 *2* **Project Dane (IRE)** 3-9-2 .... ACorniani 3 84
(L Polito, Italy) *prom: 5th st: btn over 2f out* **32/1**

7 *3* **Fares (IRE)**[15] 1035 3-9-2 ....(b) EddieAhern 12 78
(C E Brittain) *cl up whn squeezed bk after 1 1/2f: nvr nrr than mid-div after* **44/10**

8 *nk* **Walharer**[35] 3-9-2 .... PConvertino 9 77
(B Grizzetti, Italy) *prom: 6th st: wknd 2f out* **26/1**

9 *1 1/4* **Sanripoli (IRE)** 3-9-2 .... CColombi 8 74
(V Valiani, Italy) *4th st: wknd over 2f out* **46/1**

10 *nk* **Danao (USA)**[14] 3-9-2 ....(b) GMarcelli 1 73
(R Menichetti, Italy) *prom to 1/2-way* **32/1**

11 *12* **Moriwood (ITY)**[35] 3-9-2 .... EBotti 15 46
(A Botti, Italy) *plld hrd early: 7th st: sn btn* **43/10**[3]

12 *2* **Selmis**[14] 3-9-2 ....(b) GBietolini 10 41
(V Caruso, Italy) *8th st: sn btn* **48/10**

13 *3/4* **King Etoil (ITY)**[14] 3-9-2 .... MPasquale 6 39
(S Saggiomo, Italy) *mid-div whn hmpd after 3f: nt rcvr* **21/1**

14 *12* **Pure Passion (IRE)**[14] 3-9-2 .... GTemperini 5 12
(A Maggi, Italy) *s.s: a bhd* **136/1**

15 *15* **Xenes**[21] 3-9-2 .... CFiocchi 11 —
(R Menichetti, Italy) *a bhd: t.o* **32/1**

1m 39.3s (-0.50) **15** Ran SP% **161.0**
WIN 2.25; PL 1.42, 2.38, 1.81: DF 18.45.
Owner Scuderia Millenium **Bred** Scuderia Golden Horse Srl **Trained** Italy
■ The Italian 2000 Guineas, this race has been downgraded from Group 2 status.

NOTEBOOK
Golden Titus(IRE) was speedy enough to take second in the Prix Robert Papin and fifth in the Prix Morny but his trainer believes he will stay much further this year. He had to race on the outside all the way here and lost a good position early in the straight before coming back strongly in the final 300 yards. He could take his chance in the Prix du Jockey-Club, but a more realistic programme would be to challenge the older horses in the Premio Emilio Turati, and then go to France for the Prix Jean Prat.
Freemusic(IRE) was on his own out in front for a long time, which may not have helped, but he battled on gamely. He should stay at least 1m2f.
Fares(IRE) was squeezed back in the early stages and indeed his jockey reported that he was bumped on two occasions. He never looked capable of taking a hand, however.

1337a PREMIO CARLO CHIESA (GROUP 3) (F&M) 6f
5:40 (5:58) 3-Y-O+ **£24,628** (£10,836; £5,911; £2,955)

RPR

1 **Docksil**[316] 2670 3-8-5 .... PConvertino 9 102
(B Grizzetti, Italy) *a.p: narrow ldr fr 1/2-way: drvn out* **86/10**

2 *1 1/2* **Sakhee's Song (IRE)** 3-8-5 .... SMulas 13 98
(B Grizzetti, Italy) *led to 1/2-way: ev ch 1f out: r.o* **86/10**

3 *1/2* **Solzah (IRE)**[700] 2115 4-9-2 .... EddieAhern 15 99
(L Brogi, Italy) *a cl up on outside: ev ch over 1f out: kpt on same pce* **176/10**

4 *3* **Sabasha (FR)**[28] 4-9-2 .... RMarchelli 6 90
(F Rohaut, France) *outpcd tl hdwy over 2f out: squeezed through wl over 1f out: r.o to take 4th on line* **29/10**[2]

5 *nse* **Vitamina Plus (ITY)** 3-8-5 .... SLandi 2 87
(R Giorgetti, Italy) *cl up on rails: swtchd out 2f out: r.o to rch 4th dist: lost 4th on line* **79/10**

6 *2* **Shalimar (ITY)**[514] 5-9-2 .... MDemuro 14 84
(L Brogi, Italy) *prom on outside tl wkng over 1f out* **176/10**

7 *3* **Turritella (IRE)** 6-9-2 .... GErcegovic 8 75
(P Martometti, Italy) *bhd tl hdwy on outside fr 1/2-way: no ex fr 1 1/2f out* **133/10**

8 *1/2* **Velvet Revolver (IRE)**[175] 6363 4-9-2 .... GMarcelli 1 73
(L Riccardi, Italy) *chsd ldrs on rails to wl over 1f out* **19/10**[1]

9 *nk* **Lady Marmelade (ITY)**[175] 6363 4-9-2 .... MEsposito 12 72
(D Ducci, Italy) *mid-div whn squeezed bk 2f out* **5/1**[3]

10 *3 1/2* **Bahalita (IRE)**[36] 4-9-2 .... MarcoMonteriso 11 62
(L Riccardi, Italy) *spd to over 2f out: wkng whn bmpd 1 1/2f out* **19/1**

11 *3 1/2* **Musa Golosa**[182] 6252 4-9-2 .... DVargiu 10 51
(B Grizzetti, Italy) *a outpcd* **53/10**

12 *2 1/2* **Shoshiba (IRE)**[175] 6363 4-9-2 .... MTellini 3 44
(P Martometti, Italy) *a outpcd* **133/10**

13 *1 1/2* **Hatria (IRE)** 5-9-2 .... MPasquale 5 39
(A Renzoni, Italy) *a outpcd* **40/1**

14 *3* **Armenian Heritage**[70] 4-9-2 .... GBietolini 4 30
(Gianluca Bietolini, Italy) *a outpcd* **40/1**

68.80 secs (-1.50)
WFA 3 from 4yo+ 11lb **14** Ran SP% **159.3**
WIN 9.57 (coupled with Sakhee's Song): PL 4.58, 10.29, 22.60: DF112.23.
Owner Scuderia Bogi Sas **Bred** Curtasse S N C **Trained** Italy

NOTEBOOK
Docksil

DUSSELDORF (R-H)
Sunday, April 29

OFFICIAL GOING: Good

1338a AKDOV - STUTENPREIS GERMAN 1,000 GUINEAS (GROUP 2) (FILLIES) 1m
4:00 (4:14) 3-Y-O **£67,568** (£25,676; £12,162; £6,081)

RPR

1 **Mi Emma (GER)**[21] 3-9-2 .... EPedroza 13 111
(A Wohler, Germany) *mid-div: hdwy to go 2nd 1/2-way: led jst over 2f out: sn clr: easily* **18/10**[1]

2 *9* **Mystic Lips (GER)**[21] 3-9-2 .... AHelfenbein 10 93
(Andreas Lowe, Germany) *a.p: 5th st: wnt 2nd wl over 1f out: no ch w wnr* **167/10**

3 *1 1/4* **Bahama Mama (IRE)**[21] 3-9-2 .... WPanov 9 90
(W Hickst, Germany) *6th st: styd on at one pce u.p* **20/1**

4 *nk* **Hashbrown (GER)**[21] 3-9-2 .... FilipMinarik 8 89
(C Sprengel, Germany) *uns rdr bef s: s.i.s: 9th st: styd on one pce on wd outside* **24/1**

5 *3* **Prianca (GER)**[20] 3-9-2 .... J-PCarvalho 3 83
(Mario Hofer, Germany) *in rr to st: nvr a factor* **25/1**

6 *nk* **America Nova (FR)**[37] 748 3-9-2 .... JAuge 12 83
(R Gibson, France) *sme prog fr rr fnl 1 1/2f: nvr a factor* **29/1**

7 *3/4* **Chantra (GER)**[20] 3-9-2 .... ADeVries 6 81
(P Rau, Germany) *prom: 6th st: sn btn* **41/10**[2]

8 *2 1/2* **Praia (GER)** 3-9-2 .... JBojko 2 76
(A Wohler, Germany) *prom: 4th st: wknd wl over 1f out* **33/1**

9 *3/4* **Taita (GER)**[20] 3-9-2 .... JohnEgan 4 75
(H J Groschel, Germany) *a in rr* **134/10**

10 *1/2* **Sybilia (GER)**[189] 6122 3-9-2 .... THellier 5 74
(J Hirschberger, Germany) *led to jst over 2f out: wknd qckly* **48/10**[3]

11 *1 1/4* **Laeya Star (GER)**[189] 6122 3-9-2 .... ABoschert 11 71
(U Ostmann, Germany) *pressed ldr: 3rd st: wknd wl over 1f out* **87/10**

12 *nk* **Pakama (GER)**[189] 6122 3-9-2 ....(b) ASuborics 7 71
(Mario Hofer, Germany) *bhd fnl 2f* **72/10**

13 **Kick Back (GER)**[43] 3-9-2 .... AStarke 1 71
(P Schiergen, Germany) *prom: 7th st: sn wknd* **16/1**

1m 38.16s (-3.00) **13** Ran SP% **132.4**
(Including 10 Euros stake): WIN 28; PL 19, 42, 48; SF 317.
Owner Rennstall Darboven **Bred** Gestut Idee **Trained** Germany

NOTEBOOK
Mi Emma(GER) is now unbeaten in three - all this year - and is clearly the best three-year-old female miler in Germany. The merit of her opposition is questionable, but she never gave them a chance. It is quite possible that her next race will be the Coronation Stakes at Royal Ascot.

1273 LONGCHAMP (R-H)
Sunday, April 29

OFFICIAL GOING: Good

1339a PRIX VANTEAUX (GROUP 3) (FILLIES) 1m 1f 55y
2:20 (2:24) 3-Y-O **£27,027** (£10,811; £8,108; £5,405; £2,703)

RPR
1 **Just Little (FR)**[37] [748] 3-9-0 C-PLemaire 5 103
(J-C Rouget, France) *in tch in 4th: rdn to chal appr fnl f: led narrowly 50yds out: rdn out* **3/1**[2]
2 1/2 **Elva (IRE)**[50] 3-9-0 CSoumillon 8 102
(J-C Rouget, France) *racd in 2nd: led 1 1/2f out: narrowly hdd 50yds out: kpt on* **9/4**[1]
3 1/2 **Party Girl (FR)**[28] [879] 3-9-0 THuet 3 101
(R Pritchard-Gordon, France) *towards rr: drvn & r.o 1 1/2f out: sltly crossed Diyakalanie over 1f out:wnt 3rd 150yds out:jst hld on for 3rd:disq & plcd 5th* **25/1**
4 hd **Chinandega (FR)**[14] [1055] 3-9-0 SPasquier 6 100
(P Demercastel, France) *hld up disputing last: last st: r.o on outside 1 1/2f out: jst missed 3rd: fin 4th: plcd 3rd* **4/1**[3]
5 1/2 **Diyakalanie (FR)**[33] 3-9-0 DBoeuf 7 99
(J Boisnard, France) *racd in 5th: pushed along on outside st: nvr nrr: fin 5th: plcd 4th* **25/1**
6 1 1/2 **Grande Rousse (FR)**[185] 3-9-0 TThulliez 1 97
(P Bary, France) *led: hdd 1 1/2f out: styd on u.p tl no ex fnl 150yds* **4/1**[3]
7 2 **Furusato (USA)**[26] 3-9-0 TJarnet 2 94
(M Delzangles, France) *racd in 3rd: pushed along 2f out: wknd over 1f out* **11/1**
8 shd **Une Pivoine (FR)**[28] [879] 3-9-0 OPeslier 4 93
(J E Pease, France) *hld up disputing last: 7th st: n.d* **10/1**

1m 54.0s (-1.80) **Going Correction** -0.175s/f (Firm) 8 Ran SP% **120.9**
Speed ratings: 101,100,100,99,99 98,96,96
PARI-MUTUEL: WIN 6.30; PL 1.40, 1.10, 1.40; DF 4.60.
Owner E Gann & R C Thompson **Bred** J-P J Dubois **Trained** Pau, France
■ Stewards' Enquiry : T Huet two-day ban: careless riding (May 8-9)

NOTEBOOK
Just Little(FR) was landing her fourth race on the trot and was winning at Group 3 level for the first time. On this occasion she proved her stamina and also showed courage when driven to the line. Held up in the early part of the race, she began a forward move halfway up the straight and took the advantage with 100 yards left to run. Going the right way, her programme could now consist of the Prix Saint-Alary or the Prix de Diane, or both, but she will have to be supplemented into those races.
Elva(IRE) ran well but found her more experienced stablemate too strong. Passed by her well inside the final furlong, it appeared that she did not quite get home, and it would be no surprise to see her running over a shorter distance next time out.
Party Girl(FR), dropped out last for much of the race, quickened from a furlong and a half out and stayed on well at the finish. Initially she finished fourth but she was promoted to third place by the Stewards.
Diyakalanie(FR) did not appear on the scene until the straight, being another one held up for a late run. She did well to finish fifth but was hampered by the third past the post so gained a place after a Stewards enquiry.

1340a PRIX GANAY (GROUP 1) 1m 2f 110y
3:20 (3:26) 4-Y-O+ **£115,824** (£46,338; £23,169; £11,574; £5,797)

RPR
1 **Dylan Thomas (IRE)**[14] [1050] 4-9-2 CSoumillon 3 125+
(A P O'Brien, Ire) *in tch: 4th 1/2-way: hdwy 2f out: wnt 2nd 1 1/2f out: led 150yds out: sn qcknd clr: easily* **4/9**[1]
2 2 **Irish Wells (FR)**[28] [880] 4-9-2 DBoeuf 6 119
(F Rohaut, France) *racd in 2nd: led 1 1/2f out: hdd 150yds out: nt pce of wnr* **5/1**[2]
3 3/4 **Doctor Dino (FR)**[162] 5-9-2 OPeslier 5 118
(R Gibson, France) *mid-div: 5th 1/2-way: pushed along 2f out: r.o to take 3rd cl home* **16/1**
4 hd **Boris De Deauville (IRE)**[28] [880] 4-9-2 YBarberot 2 118
(S Wattel, France) *mid-div: 6th on rail 1/2-way: hdwy and wnt 3rd 1 1/2f out: kpt on but lost pl cl home* **11/1**
5 6 **Egerton (GER)**[28] [882] 6-9-2 C-PLemaire 8 107
(P Rau, Germany) *in tch: 3rd 1/2-way: pushed along st: no ex fr over 1f out* **9/1**[3]
6 hd **Pearl Sky (FR)**[28] [880] 4-8-13 ACrastus 4 103
(Y De Nicolay, France) *hld up: 7th 1/2-way: nvr in contention* **12/1**
7 nk **Blushing King (FR)**[28] [880] 5-9-2 FVeron 1 106
(J-L Guillochon, France) *hld up: last 1/2-way: rdn 1 1/2f out: no imp* **66/1**
8 8 **Sign Of The Wolf**[28] 7-9-2 F-XBertras 7 92
(F Rohaut, France) *drvn to ld: hdd 1 1/2f out: eased* **100/1**

2m 7.90s (-6.70) **Going Correction** -0.175s/f (Firm) 8 Ran SP% **120.3**
Speed ratings: 117,115,115,114,110 110,110,104
PARI-MUTUEL: WIN 1.40; PL 1.10, 1.20, 1.60; DF 2.70.
Owner Mrs John Magnier **Bred** Tower Bloodstock **Trained** Ballydoyle, Co Tipperary

NOTEBOOK
Dylan Thomas(IRE) looked in exceptional shape in the paddock and never really looked like getting beaten, although his jockey did have to be patient early in the straight. Once in the clear to make a run, he quickened like a top-class performer to lead a furlong out and the race was over at this point. He was in a different class to the others and is going to be a force to be reckoned with wherever he goes in the future. Connections are now looking at the Tattersalls Gold Cup at the Curragh, and it would be no surprise to see him back at Longchamp for the Arc de Triomphe later in the year. Incidentally, he broke the record time for this race in victory. (op 1/2)
Irish Wells(FR) ran well up to expectations but had no chance with the winner. He reversed form with two old rivals, though, and is certainly going the right way. His pacemaker Sign Of The Wolf did a fine job before he took the advantage a furlong and a half out, but there was nothing he could do when the winner flashed past him soon after. He is better over a longer distance and connections will now be looking at races like the Coronation Cup and the Grand Prix de Saint-Cloud.
Doctor Dino(FR) delighted his connections with this run. Settled in fifth position early on, he was always going well and was asked to make his dash to the line halfway up the straight. From that point on he ran on in a very promising way, and should definitely land another Group event this season. A top-of-the-ground horse, connections are now looking towards the Singapore International Cup at Kranji next month.
Boris De Deauville(IRE) made an effort running into the final furlong and a half and for a moment he looked dangerous, but he could find only the one pace. Definitely better on a softer surface, he will probably not be seen out again until later in the year when the ground may have eased a bit. (op 10/1)

1341a PRIX DE BARBEVILLE (GROUP 3) 1m 7f 110y
3:50 (3:57) 4-Y-O+ **£27,027** (£10,811; £8,108; £5,405; £2,703)

RPR
1 **Host Nation**[20] [990] 4-8-8 SPasquier 1 108
(A Fabre, France) *racd in 3rd: 2nd st: rdn to ld appr fnl f: hdd 100yds out: led again nr fin: drvn out* **4/1**[3]
2 nk **Le Miracle (GER)**[210] [5711] 6-9-2 DBoeuf 5 112
(W Baltromei, Germany) *led after 2f: drvn over 1 1/2f out: hdd 100yds out: rallied to ld again briefly: hdd nr fin* **6/1**
3 nk **Ponte Tresa (FR)**[31] [823] 4-8-8 CSoumillon 4 108
(Y De Nicolay, France) *racd in 4th: rdn and r.o 1 1/2f out: pressing ldrs fnl f: tk 3rd on line* **6/4**[1]
4 nk **Soledad (IRE)**[20] [990] 7-9-0 RonanThomas 2 109
(G Cherel, France) *led 2f: 2nd 1/2-way: 3rd st: r.o on rail 2f out: rdn and ev ch 1 1/2f out: kpt on* **20/1**
5 1 **Spectaculaire**[20] [990] 4-8-12 OPeslier 3 110
(A Fabre, France) *racd in last: rdn 1 1/2f out: nvr in chalng position* **2/1**[2]

3m 21.5s (-5.10) **Going Correction** -0.175s/f (Firm)
WFA 4 from 6yo+ 3lb 5 Ran SP% **112.4**
Speed ratings: 105,104,104,104,104
PARI-MUTUEL: WIN 5.00; PL 2.50, 2.20; SF 21.20.
Owner K Abdulla **Bred** Juddmonte Farms Ltd **Trained** Chantilly, France

NOTEBOOK
Host Nation, never far from the front, came to take the lead a furlong and a half out and then dug deep to hold off both the runner-up and third. He is a real fighter, is improving and may well go on to better things. Connections are now looking at the Prix Vicomtesse Vigier and he has been entered in the Ascot Gold Cup.
Le Miracle(GER) ran really well considering it was his first outing of the year. After a couple of furlongs he took the lead which he did not give up until passed by the winner in the straight. He then stayed on, on ground that probably did not have enough cut in it for him. Now a six-year-old, he will definitely come on for this outing and is another marked down for the Vicomtesse Vigier. He was giving 8lb to the winner here.
Ponte Tresa(FR), a big filly, began her challenge for the lead early in the straight but never quite made it to the head of affairs. She stayed on well and lost nothing in defeat, but her trainer felt that she needs more juice in the ground to show her best. She is also likely to take her chance in the Vicomtesse Vigier, and is also entered in the Gold Cup at Royal Ascot.
Soledad(IRE), the outsider of this quintet, ran a very gallant race. Smartly away, he led for a couple of furlongs before settling in second position. Throughout the straight he fought gallantly and was finally only beaten under a length by the winner. He looks to have retained his ability.
Spectaculaire, who beat Host Nation at Saint-Cloud recently, was ridden with restraint and it did not appear to suit on this occasion. He is better than this and will be helped by a stronger gallop.

1117 LINGFIELD (L-H)
Monday, April 30

OFFICIAL GOING: Standard
Wind: fresh, half-against Weather: Sunny and warm

1342 CELEBRATE YOUR BIRTHDAY AT LINGFIELD PARK CLAIMING STKS 1m 4f (P)
2:20 (2:23) (Class 6) 4-Y-O+ **£2,184** (£644; £322) **Stalls** Low

Form RPR
0061 1 **Comeintothespace (IRE)**[5] [1254] 5-9-0 50 DaneO'Neill 8 57
(R A Farrant) *hld up in midfield: hdwy to ld 3f out: drvn out* **4/1**[2]
4-16 2 1/2 **Carlton Scroop (FR)**[16] [1042] 4-9-4 60 (b) GihanArnolda(7) 4 68
(J Jay) *s.i.s: towards rr: hdwy over 2f out: r.o to take 2nd fnl 50yds: jst hld* **8/1**
3 3/4 **Blue Eyed Eloise**[22] 5-8-8 ow1 (v[1]) SamHitchcott 1 49
(B R Johnson) *hld up in rr: hdwy to press wnr 3f out: hrd rdn and nt qckn ins fnl f* **66/1**
2424 4 3/4 **Tresor Secret (FR)**[17] [1026] 7-9-0 58 JimCrowley 3 54
(J Gallagher) *in tch: effrt 3f out: 4th and hld whn flashed tail ins fnl f* **2/1**[1]
-302 5 4 **Missie Baileys**[21] [982] 5-8-11 53 PaulDoe 7 44
(Mrs L J Mongan) *prom: outpcd 4f out: tried to rally 2f out: no imp* **8/1**
-450 6 6 **Myrtle Bay (IRE)**[35] [792] 4-8-5 48 ow1 NeilChalmers(3) 10 33
(J C Tuck) *prom: led briefly over 3f out: wknd over 2f out* **10/1**
-005 7 13 **Night Groove (IRE)**[21] [982] 4-8-9 49 (b) JamesDoyle 6 13
(N P Littmoden) *sn led: hdd & wknd over 3f out: eased when no ch fnl f* **16/1**
300- 8 3 1/2 **High Hope (FR)**[59] [4836] 9-8-12 52 (b) FergusSweeney 9 9
(G L Moore) *dwlt: sn in tch: jnd ldrs 3f out: sn hrd rdn and wknd: eased whn no ch fnl f* **11/2**[3]
9 8 **Whistling Fred**[38] 8-8-10 LPKeniry 2 —
(B De Haan) *towards rr: rdn and n.d fnl 4f: bhd whn eased fnl f* **25/1**
00-0 10 22 **Full Of Zest**[36] [278] 5-8-13 52 (b) IanMongan 5 —
(Mrs L J Mongan) *prom tl wknd qckly 5f out: wl bhd whn eased 2f out* **16/1**

2m 33.09s (-1.30) **Going Correction** 0.0s/f (Stan)
WFA 4 from 5yo+ 1lb 10 Ran SP% **117.1**
Speed ratings (Par 101):104,103,103,102,100 96,87,85,79,65
CSF £36.29 TOTE £5.40: £3.00, £2.30, £16.50; EX 25.80 Trifecta £299.00 Part won. Pool £421.24 - 0.34 winning units..The winner was claimed by K Burke for £8,000.
Owner Rodney Farrant **Bred** D And Mrs D Veitch **Trained** Upper Lambourn, Berks

FOCUS
A routine claimer, but run at a solid gallop, but despite the first two running to form, looks pretty weak.
Night Groove(IRE) Official explanation: jockey said gelding ran too free early
High Hope(FR) Official explanation: jockey said gelding had no more to give

1343 CONFERENCES AT LINGFIELD PARK MEDIAN AUCTION MAIDEN STKS 1m (P)

2:50 (2:51) (Class 5) 3-Y-O **£2,914** (£867; £433; £216) **Stalls** High

Form RPR

0-5 **1** **Premio Loco (USA)**^{21} [977] 3-9-3 .... IanMongan 3 91
(C F Wall) *w ldr: led after 2f: rdn clr fnl f* **14/1**

0- **2** *5* **Muhannak (IRE)**^{268} [4140] 3-9-3 .... NickyMackay 1 80
(G A Butler) *cl up on rail: hrd rdn 2f out: wnt 2nd ins fnl f: nt pce of wnr* **25/1**

0 **3** *1 1/4* **Sweet Gale (IRE)**^{10} [1128] 3-8-12 ....(t) SebSanders 10 72+
(J Noseda) *prom: chsd wnr over 2f out tl ins fnl f: no ex* **14/1**

3 **4** *1* **Six Of Diamonds (IRE)**^{21} [973] 3-9-3 .... MartinDwyer 2 75
(J A Osborne) *chsd ldrs: hrd rdn 2f out: one pce* **5/2**^{1}

0-5 **5** *nk* **Mutual Friend (USA)**^{10} [1117] 3-9-3 .... SteveDrowne 7 74
(E A L Dunlop) *mid-div: effrt 3f out: styd on same pce* **11/4**^{2}

6 *1 1/4* **Murtaad** 3-9-3 .... RHills 8 75+
(W J Haggas) *s.i.s: bhd: rdn and sme hdwy 3f out: nt pce to chal* **9/2**^{3}

0 **7** *7* **Samsons Son**^{10} [1117] 3-9-3 .... DaneO'Neill 4 55
(J R Best) *prom: hrd rdn 2f out: sn wknd* **50/1**

0 **8** *4* **Cheonmado (USA)**^{14} [1062] 3-9-3 .... PaulEddery 6 46
(Simon Earle) *s.s: plld hrd in rr: rdn 4f out: nvr nr ldrs* **25/1**

6- **9** *hd* **Dancewiththestars (USA)**^{156} [6591] 3-8-12 .... JamieSpencer 9 40
(J R Fanshawe) *bhd: sme hdwy over 3f out: sn wknd* **8/1**

0-0 **10** *1/2* **Yeoman Leap**^{9} [1143] 3-9-3 .... LPKeniry 11 44
(A M Balding) *led 2f: prom tl hrd rdn and wknd over 2f out* **50/1**

0-0 **11** *2* **Just A Flash (IRE)**^{106} [128] 3-9-3 .... SamHitchcott 12 40
(B R Johnson) *s.i.s: rdn 4f out: a bhd* **66/1**

55- **12** *10* **Ardmaddy (IRE)**^{189} [6145] 3-9-3 .... OscarUrbina 5 17
(J A R Toller) *in tch: outpcd over 4f out: sn lost pl* **11/1**

1m 36.99s (-2.44) **Going Correction** 0.0s/f (Stan) **12** Ran SP% **119.3**
Speed ratings (Par 98):112,107,105,104,104 103,96,92,92,91 89,79
CSF £324.74 TOTE £18.20: £5.10, £5.50, £5.00; EX 372.80 TRIFECTA Not won..
Owner Bernard Westley **Bred** Kidder, Cole & Griggs **Trained** Newmarket, Suffolk

FOCUS
This looked a modest maiden on paper, but it produced an outstanding winning time for a race of its type. The fourth and fifth are the best guides to the level, but it has been rated fairly positively in view of the time.
Mutual Friend(USA) Official explanation: jockey said colt hung left in straight
Murtaad Official explanation: jockey said colt was denied a clear run closing stages
Ardmaddy(IRE) Official explanation: trainer said gelding moved poorly

1344 PERFECT WEDDING VENUE AT LINGFIELD PARK (S) STKS 7f (P)

3:20 (3:21) (Class 6) 3-Y-O+ **£2,184** (£644; £322) **Stalls** Low

Form RPR

3362 **1** **Nikki Bea (IRE)**^{16} [1038] 4-9-2 54 .... PaulDoe 11 63
(Jamie Poulton) *in tch: effrt 3f out: led over 1f out: drvn clr and edgd lft: styd on* **11/4**^{2}

0105 **2** *3* **Marmooq**^{10} [1118] 4-9-10 55 .... JerryO'Dwyer$^{(3)}$ 9 66
(J Gallagher) *sn led and set gd pce: hdd over 1f out: nt qckn* **9/4**^{1}

0022 **3** *4* **Midmaar (IRE)**^{10} [1120] 6-9-7 52 ....(b) JamieMackay 1 50
(M Wigham) *prom: outpcd over 3f out: kpt on to take 3rd ins fnl f* **6/1**^{3}

-050 **4** *1* **Hilltop Fantasy**^{55} [625] 6-9-2 45 ....(p) DaneO'Neill 4 42
(V Smith) *prom 2f: settled in midfield: effrt and nt clr run over 2f out: styd on to take 4th ins fnl f* **10/1**

0050 **5** *3/4* **Rowan Pursuit**^{17} [1026] 6-9-2 39 ....(b) StephenCarson 3 40
(E A Wheeler) *prom tl hrd rdn and wknd over 1f out* **25/1**

-003 **6** *3/4* **Boisdale (IRE)**^{26} [920] 9-9-7 41 .... JimCrowley 12 43
(P S Felgate) *chsd ldrs: effrt on outside 3f out: hrd rdn and wknd over 1f out* **16/1**

2060 **7** *3* **Rafferty (IRE)**^{31} [830] 8-9-0 53 .... ThomasBubb$^{(7)}$ 6 36
(S Dow) *prom tl wknd over 2f out* **10/1**

0-04 **8** *3 1/2* **Bollywood (IRE)**^{1} [1317] 4-9-0 38 .... RyanBird$^{(7)}$ 10 26
(J J Bridger) *sn outpcd in rr* **10/1**

0-0 **9** *3/4* **Wicked Lady (UAE)**^{21} [869] 4-9-2 ....(v^{1}) SamHitchcott 2 19
(B R Johnson) *s.i.s: drvn along and a bhd* **33/1**

0200 **10** *2 1/2* **Hand Chime**^{10} [1118] 10-9-0 50 .... AmyBaker$^{(7)}$ 8 18
(Miss J Feilden) *s.i.s: towards rr whn hmpd on rail after 2f: n.d* **16/1**

0/00 **11** *5* **Ghaill Force**^{22} [615] 5-9-7 41 ....(p) AmirQuinn 5 5
(P Butler) *missed break by 20l: a t.o* **50/1**

1m 25.8s (-0.09) **Going Correction** 0.0s/f (Stan) **11** Ran SP% **119.5**
Speed ratings (Par 101):100,96,92,90,90 89,85,81,80,78 72
CSF £9.36 TOTE £4.80: £1.20, £1.60, £1.60; EX 11.60 Trifecta £24.60 Pool £307.87 - 8.85 winning units..The winner was bought in for 6,500gns.
Owner Nikki Beach Partnership **Bred** Dr Paschal Carmody **Trained** Whitcombe, Dorset

FOCUS
A weak non-handicap seller, with only the first two showing their form, but run at a fair gallop.
Ghaill Force Official explanation: jockey said gelding missed the break

1345 LINGFIELDPARK.CO.UK FILLIES' H'CAP 7f (P)

3:50 (3:54) (Class 5) (0-70,70) 3-Y-O **£2,914** (£867; £433; £216) **Stalls** Low

Form RPR

644- **1** **Blue Bamboo**^{195} [6024] 3-8-13 65 .... JimCrowley 6 67
(Mrs A J Perrett) *prom: led over 2f out: drvn out* **9/1**

420- **2** *1 1/2* **Whipchord (IRE)**^{224} [5419] 3-8-10 62 .... PatDobbs 11 60
(R Hannon) *chsd ldrs: hrd rdn 2f out: kpt on to take 2nd fnl 100yds* **20/1**

030- **3** *shd* **Rumbled**^{193} [6064] 3-9-4 70 .... RichardThomas 12 68
(J A Geake) *wd: hld up in midfield: hung rt and awkward on bnds: outpcd over 2f out: styd on strly fnl f* **50/1**

2521 **4** *nk* **Madrigale**^{45} [689] 3-8-13 65 .... FergusSweeney 1 62
(G L Moore) *chsd ldrs: effrt 2f out: one pce* **15/8**^{1}

3306 **5** *hd* **First Princess (IRE)**^{84} [370] 3-8-8 60 ....(p) JohnEgan 3 56
(J S Moore) *in tch: effrt 2f out: one pce fnl f* **9/1**

655- **6** *1/2* **Kashmir Lady (FR)**^{185} [6199] 3-9-1 67 .... DaneO'Neill 5 68+
(H Candy) *hld up in midfield: promising move whn nt clr run ent st: gng on at fin* **6/1**^{2}

2003 **7** *1/2* **Mutoon (IRE)**^{46} [684] 3-8-4 56 oh3 .... NickyMackay 9 55+
(S C Williams) *towards rr: rdn over 3f out: hdwy and in tch whn nt clr run on rail over 1f out: nt rcvr* **20/1**

0-10 **8** *nk* **Grand Lucre**^{25} [935] 3-9-0 66 .... RHills 2 59
(J W Hills) *led tl over 2f out: wknd and lost 2nd pl ins fnl f* **7/1**^{3}

043- **9** *1 1/4* **Nashharry (IRE)**^{217} [5570] 3-8-13 65 .... FrankieMcDonald 7 55
(S Kirk) *in tch: rdn and lost pl 1/2-way: n.d after* **20/1**

00-3 **10** *3/4* **Rosie Cross (IRE)**^{26} [924] 3-8-5 57 .... StephenCarson 8 45
(Eve Johnson Houghton) *prom tl wknd over 1f out* **11/1**

061- **11** *hd* **Dancing Duo**^{182} [6258] 3-8-10 62 .... SteveDrowne 14 49
(D Shaw) *towards rr: rdn 3f out: n.d* **16/1**

326- **12** *1 1/2* **Isobel Rose (IRE)**^{145} [6730] 3-8-13 68 .... StephenDonohoe$^{(3)}$ 10 51
(E A L Dunlop) *bhd: rdn 1/2-way: sme hdwy on rail ent st: n.d* **14/1**

004- **13** *1 1/2* **Regal Curtsy**^{157} [6575] 3-8-12 64 .... IanMongan 4 44
(P R Chamings) *sn wl bhd* **25/1**

1m 26.19s (0.30) **Going Correction** 0.0s/f (Stan) **13** Ran SP% **122.5**
Speed ratings (Par 95):98,96,96,95,95 95,94,94,92,91 91,89,88
CSF £184.37 CT £8517.57 TOTE £5.70: £3.00, £5.90, £16.10; EX 134.80 TRIFECTA Not won..
Owner D J Burke **Bred** Mountgrange Stud Ltd **Trained** Pulborough, W Sussex

FOCUS
A moderate contest for fillies only and not strong form even for the grade.
Rumbled ◆ Official explanation: jockey said filly hung right on bend
Madrigale Official explanation: trainer said filly was found to have a fracture of the off-fore
Mutoon(IRE) Official explanation: jockey said filly was denied a clear run
Dancing Duo Official explanation: jockey said filly hung left
Regal Curtsy Official explanation: jockey said filly did not appreciate the kickback

1346 LINGFIELDPARK.CO.UK H'CAP 6f (P)

4:20 (4:23) (Class 6) (0-60,60) 3-Y-O **£2,388** (£705; £352) **Stalls** Low

Form RPR

06-6 **1** **Polish World (USA)**^{16} [1037] 3-9-3 59 .... DaneO'Neill 9 74
(E A L Dunlop) *dwlt: hdwy over 3f out: led 1f out: pushed clr: easily* **3/1**^{1}

5630 **2** *5* **Arnie's Joint (IRE)**^{6} [1219] 3-9-4 60 ....(b) SteveDrowne 8 60
(N P Littmoden) *t.k.h in midfield: hdwy to ld 3f out: hrd rdn and hdd 1f out: no ch w wnr* **5/1**^{2}

530- **3** *1/2* **Oh So Saucy**^{224} [5419] 3-9-3 59 .... IanMongan 6 58+
(C F Wall) *hld up in rr: nt clr run ent st: rdn and hdwy over 1f out: r.o* **12/1**

1543 **4** *1/2* **Strike Force**^{18} [1008] 3-9-3 59 ....(p) JimCrowley 11 56
(R A Harris) *a.p: hrd rdn and one pce fnl 2f* **5/1**^{2}

645- **5** *1/2* **Wadnagin (IRE)**^{135} [6839] 3-8-10 57 .... JamieMoriarty$^{(5)}$ 2 55+
(I A Wood) *in tch on rail: dropped towards rr over 4f out: hmpd over 3f out: swtchd rt over 1f out: styd on wl fnl f* **10/1**

300- **6** *1/2* **Nabra**^{186} [6186] 3-9-4 60 .... RHills 5 54
(J H M Gosden) *in tch: rdn to chse ldrs 3f out: one pce fnl 2f* **13/2**

350- **7** *3/4* **King Of Tricks**^{180} [6296] 3-9-2 58 .... RichardSmith 7 50
(M D I Usher) *sn led: hdd after 2f: rdn and btn over 2f out* **25/1**

423 **8** *3* **Time Share (IRE)**^{79} [421] 3-9-0 56 .... MartinDwyer 12 39
(J A Osborne) *chsd ldrs: led after 2f tl 3f out: hrd rdn and wknd wl over 1f out* **6/1**^{3}

0056 **9** *hd* **Rogers Lodger**^{27} [899] 3-8-12 54 ....(b^{1}) SimonWhitworth 4 36
(J Akehurst) *t.k.h towards rr: unbalanced bnd 4f out: swtchd outside and hdwy 3f out: wd and wknd ent st* **12/1**

40-0 **10** *shd* **Queensgate**^{17} [1022] 3-9-0 56 .... FrankieMcDonald 1 38
(M Blanshard) *w ldrs 2f: sn lost pl: bhd whn hmpd 1f out* **14/1**

50-0 **11** *11* **Princely Royal**^{5} [1248] 3-9-0 56 .... AmirQuinn 3 5
(J J Bridger) *chsd ldrs 2f: sn bhd* **50/1**

1m 13.71s (0.90) **Going Correction** 0.0s/f (Stan) **11** Ran SP% **122.9**
Speed ratings (Par 96):94,87,86,86,85 84,83,79,79,79 64
CSF £18.49 CT £164.18 TOTE £4.80: £1.60, £2.80, £3.20; EX 28.50 Trifecta £275.10 Part won. Pool £387.53 - 0.34 winning units..
Owner Gainsborough **Bred** Racehorse Management, Llc **Trained** Newmarket, Suffolk

FOCUS
A modest handicap, but with an unexposed winner and sound form in behind.

1347 LINGFIELD PARK GOLF CLUB APPRENTICE H'CAP 1m 2f (P)

4:50 (4:52) (Class 6) (0-60,60) 4-Y-O+ **£2,388** (£705; £352) **Stalls** Low

Form RPR

5-00 **1** **Garrulous (UAE)**^{75} [459] 4-9-6 60 .... JemmaMarshall 8 69
(G L Moore) *trckd ldrs: led 1f out: cruised clr* **10/1**

6460 **2** *2 1/2* **Come What July (IRE)**^{5} [1254] 6-8-8 48 .... HaddenFrost 13 52
(D Shaw) *trckd ldr: rdn to chal over 1f out: nt pce of wnr* **11/2**^{3}

20-1 **3** *1 1/2* **Gigs Magic (USA)**^{9} [1162] 4-9-4 58 .... WilliamCarson 6 59
(M Johnston) *hld up in tch: rdn to chse ldrs 2f out: kpt on to take 3rd ins fnl f* **5/1**^{2}

0-00 **4** *1 1/4* **Secam (POL)**^{35} [372] 8-8-3 46 oh1 ....(e) JosephWalsh$^{(3)}$ 11 45
(Mrs P Townsley) *sn led: rdn 2f out: hdd and no ex 1f out* **50/1**

16-4 **5** *1/2* **Gizmondo**^{9} [1167] 4-8-13 58 .... ChrisHough$^{(5)}$ 4 56
(M L W Bell) *mid-div: effrt 2f out: styd on fnl f* **9/2**^{1}

2403 **6** *nk* **Kumakawa**^{41} [716] 9-8-10 50 .... MCGeran 12 47
(N P Littmoden) *chsd ldrs: hrd rdn 2f out: one pce* **16/1**

4003 **7** *3/4* **Rowan Warning**^{38} [740] 5-9-2 56 .... HarryPoulton 3 52
(J R Boyle) *prom: hrd rdn over 1f out: sn wknd* **5/1**^{2}

430 **8** *shd* **Great Man (FR)**^{60} [594] 6-9-6 60 .... JamieHamblett 7 56
(Noel T Chance) *mid-div: effrt on rail 2f out: no imp* **13/2**

-355 **9** *nk* **Revolve**^{17} [1025] 7-9-4 58 ....(p) KylieManser 5 53
(Mrs L J Mongan) *mid-div: effrt 2f out: hrd rdn and no imp over 1f out* **10/1**

40-6 **10** *1/2* **Alwariah**^{78} [431] 4-8-8 53 .... SophieDoyle$^{(5)}$ 2 47
(Ms J S Doyle) *s.s: bhd most of way: nvr rchd ldrs* **25/1**

11 *2 1/2* **Infidel (IRE)**^{44} [4857] 7-7-13 46 oh1 .... AmeliaHegarty$^{(7)}$ 9 35
(J R Best) *hrd rdn over 2f out: a towards rr* **20/1**

12 *11* **Bearna Bhui (IRE)**^{265} [4235] 4-7-13 46 oh1 .... ThomasBubb$^{(7)}$ 1 14
(S Dow) *a in rr: wl bhd fnl 5f* **33/1**

000- **13** *45* **Flying Spud**^{443} [382] 6-8-3 46 oh1 .... MarkCoumbe$^{(3)}$ 10 —
(A J Chamberlain) *a towards rr: wl bhd fnl 5f* **66/1**

2m 8.29s (0.50) **Going Correction** 0.0s/f (Stan) **13** Ran SP% **119.3**
Speed ratings (Par 101):98,96,94,93,93 93,92,92,92,91 89,81,45
CSF £61.01 CT £314.62 TOTE £12.30: £3.10, £2.00, £2.10; EX 77.30 TRIFECTA Not won. Place 6 £3474.25, Place 5 £1049.59..
Owner Dr C A Barnett **Bred** Darley **Trained** Woodingdean, E Sussex

FOCUS
A weak handicap rated through the fourth and a race that took little winning.

T/Plt: £5,872.10 to a £1 stake. Pool: £60,732.35. 7.55 winning tickets. T/Qpdt: £276.70 to a £1 stake. Pool: £4,039.50. 10.80 winning tickets. LM

[1261]SOUTHWELL (L-H)

Monday, April 30

OFFICIAL GOING: Standard

Wind: moderate half-against

1348 BETDIRECTPOKER.COM GET INVOLVED MEDIAN AUCTION MAIDEN STKS 1m (F)

5:25 (5:26) (Class 5) 3-5-Y-0 **£3,071** (£906; £453) **Stalls Low**

Form RPR

0-0 **1** **Danetime Panther (IRE)**[9] 1143 3-8-12 JosedeSouza 7 76+
(P F I Cole) *trckd ldrs on outer: hdwy over 2f out: shkn up and qcknd to ld ins fnl f: comf* **9/4**[1]

6 **2** *1 1/4* **Sky Masterson**[11] 1100 3-8-12 RobertHavlin 4 73+
(J H M Gosden) *trckd ldng pair: hdwy to ld wl over 1f out: sn rdn: drvn and hdd ins fnl f: one pce* **5/2**[2]

3-34 **3** *8* **Winged Farasi**[33] 807 3-8-12 70 MickyFenton 3 55
(Miss J Feilden) *cl up on inner: effrt 3f out: rdn and ev ch 2f: sn drvn and wknd over 1f out* **5/1**

4 *nk* **Istead Rise (IRE)** 3-8-7 KevinGhunowa(5) 5 54
(P A Blockley) *towards rr: pushed along 1/2-way: rdn and hdwy over 2f out: kpt on same pce u.p* **25/1**

5 *2 1/2* **Goldan Jess (IRE)**[288] 3577 3-8-12 75 DanielTudhope 6 49
(D Carroll) *led: rdn along 3f out: hdd wl over 1f out and sn wknd* **12/1**

6 *1/2* **Carefree Flapper** 3-8-2 PatrickHills(5) 2 42
(G A Swinbank) *in rr: pushed along 1/2-way: sn outpcd* **4/1**[3]

7 *3/4* **April The Second** 3-8-7 TolleyDean(5) 1 46
(R J Price) *a in rr* **33/1**

1m 45.42s (0.82) **Going Correction** +0.10s/f (Slow) 7 Ran SP% **110.5**

Speed ratings (Par 103):99,97,89,89,86 86,85

CSF £7.54 TOTE £3.80: £3.50, £1.10; EX 9.10.

Owner The Pink Panther Partnership **Bred** Edward Sexton **Trained** Whatcombe, Oxon

FOCUS

Despite the small field and lack of depth, this was probably a better-quality maiden than usual for the track. The two market leaders dominated, pulling a long way clear of a 70-rated performer, and the time was about what you would expect for a race of its type.

1349 SAKS, NEWARK, HAIR AND BEAUTY H'CAP 6f (F)

5:55 (5:57) (Class 6) (0-50,50) 4-Y-0+ **£2,730** (£806; £403) **Stalls Low**

Form RPR

224- **1** **Megalo Maniac**[252] 4656 4-8-9 47 TonyHamilton 11 61
(R A Fahey) *midfield: hdwy over 2f out: rdn to chse ldr and edgd lft over 1f out: drvn and styd on ent fnl f to ld last 100yds* **7/1**[3]

1056 **2** *1* **Mister Incredible**[17] 1028 4-8-7 50 (v) KevinGhunowa(5) 12 61
(J M Bradley) *trckd ldrs: hdwy 3f out: led wl over 1f out: rdn appr fnl f: drvn: hdd and no ex last 100yds* **6/1**[2]

00-4 **3** *3* **Guadaloup**[97] 225 5-8-12 50 DeanMernagh 7 52
(M Brittain) *chsd ldrs: rdn along over 2f out: drvn and kpt on same pce fnl f* **14/1**

4305 **4** *1* **Ask No More**[4] 1262 4-8-8 49 (b) DominicFox(3) 3 48
(P L Gilligan) *chsd ldrs on inner: rdn along 2f out: sn drvn and kpt on same pce* **15/2**

4000 **5** *2* **Christian Bendix**[10] 1120 5-8-10 48 (p) RobertHavlin 8 41
(P Howling) *cl up: led wl over 2f out: sn rdn: hdd wl over 1f out and grad wknd* **12/1**

2334 **6** *2 1/2* **Favouring (IRE)**[28] 892 5-8-6 49 (v) PatrickHills(5) 6 35
(M C Chapman) *outpcd towards rr and swtchd outside after 1f: rdn along 1/2-way: sme hdwy over 2f out: nvr nr ldrs* **7/2**[1]

001 **7** *3 1/2* **Kadia**[27] 906 4-8-9 47 MickyFenton 5 22
(P T Midgley) *hmpd and squeezed out s: in rr whn n.m.r bnd after 2f: swtchd outside and wd st and sme late hdwy* **16/1**

020- **8** *1/2* **Double Carpet (IRE)**[146] 6721 4-8-8 49 AndrewElliott(3) 10 23
(G Woodward) *a in midfield* **16/1**

000- **9** *nk* **Immaculate Red**[200] 5929 4-8-9 47 (b) DavidAllan 4 20
(R Bastiman) *nvr nr ldrs* **20/1**

-500 **10** *3/4* **Titian Saga (IRE)**[21] 964 4-8-9 47 AdrianTNicholls 14 17
(D Nicholls) *led: rdn along 3f out: sn hdd & wknd* **9/1**

00-0 **11** *1 1/2* **Bahamian Bay**[111] 77 5-8-5 50 AndrewHeffernan(7) 9 16
(M Brittain) *prom: pushed along after 2f: rdn and lost pl 1/2-way: sn bhd* **33/1**

2120 **12** *nk* **Astorygoeswithit**[61] 586 4-8-10 48 (be) AdamKirby 1 13
(P S McEntee) *in tch: rdn along 1/2-way and sn wknd* **12/1**

000- **13** *1 1/4* **Coalite (IRE)**[265] 4232 4-8-10 48 (p) SilvestreDeSousa 2 9
(A D Brown) *a outpcd and bhd* **33/1**

1m 17.37s (0.47) **Going Correction** +0.10s/f (Slow) 13 Ran SP% **115.2**

Speed ratings (Par 101):100,98,94,93,90 87,82,82,81,80 78,78,76

CSF £45.74 CT £567.16 TOTE £7.00: £2.30, £3.30, £3.80; EX 42.80.

Owner A Long **Bred** E R W Stanley And New England Stud Farm Ltd **Trained** Musley Bank, N Yorks

■ Mission Affirmed (20/1) was withdrawn at the start. rule 4 does not apply.

FOCUS

A big field, but a bad race with the top weights rated just 50 and featuring some iffy performers to boot. The pace was solid enough though and the principals finished well spread out with the runner-up the guide to the level.

Astorygoeswithit Official explanation: jockey said gelding stumbled leaving the stalls

1350 NEWARK ADVERTISER H'CAP 1m (F)

6:25 (6:25) (Class 6) (0-55,55) 4-Y-0+ **£2,590** (£770; £385; £192) **Stalls Low**

Form RPR

-352 **1** **The Grey One (IRE)**[17] 1027 4-8-9 55 (p) KevinGhunowa(5) 13 66
(J M Bradley) *trckd ldrs: hdwy to chal over 2f out: rdn to ld wl over 1f out: drvn clr ent fnl f: styd on* **7/2**[1]

0-50 **2** *3 1/2* **Kirkhammerton (IRE)**[8] 1178 5-8-13 54 (b) AdamKirby 4 57
(A J McCabe) *cl up: led over 4f out: rdn along over 2f out: hdd wl over 1f out: drvn and one pce ent fnl f* **9/1**

4320 **3** *2* **Wodhill Schnaps**[21] 977 6-8-8 49 (v) HayleyTurner 5 47
(D Morris) *towards rr: hdwy on inner whn hmpd bnd over 4f out: trckd ldrs 3f out: rdn and edgd lft wl over 1f out: kpt on ins fnl f* **6/1**[3]

0-60 **4** *3/4* **Ming Vase**[21] 966 5-8-7 48 oh1 ow2 MickyFenton 7 45
(P T Midgley) *prom: rdn along over 2f out: one pce fr wl over 1f out* **14/1**

5510 **5** *3* **Fuel Cell (IRE)**[6] 1227 6-8-11 52 VHalliday 11 42
(J O'Reilly) *outpcd and bhd: rdn along 1/2-way: styd on fnl 2f: nvr a factor* **13/2**

4520 **6** *nk* **Mid Valley**[6] 1206 4-8-10 51 (v) RobertHavlin 1 40
(J R Jenkins) *in rr: wd st: rdn and hdwy 2f out: no imp fr over 1f out* **9/2**[2]

500- **7** *1/2* **Simply St Lucia**[7] 3263 5-8-10 51 (b[1]) TomEaves 2 39
(J R Weymes) *sn led: hdd over 4f out and sn rdn along: wknd 3f out* **22/1**

-003 **8** *9* **Epidaurian King (IRE)**[6] 1232 4-9-0 55 DanielTudhope 9 22
(D Shaw) *in tch: rdn along 3f out and sn outpcd* **6/1**[3]

401/ **9** *6* **Red Flyer (IRE)**[330] 1446 8-8-1 47 oh1 ow1 PatrickHills(5) 10 —
(B P J Baugh) *dwlt: a in rr* **10/1**

000- **10** *6* **Woolfall King (IRE)**[244] 4909 4-8-2 46 oh1 DominicFox(3) 8 —
(G G Margarson) *in tch on inner: edgd lft bnd over 4f out: sn rdn along and outpcd* **50/1**

00/0 **11** *hd* **Bahrall**[16] 1044 4-8-2 46 oh1 AndrewElliott(3) 12 —
(A P Jarvis) *in tch on outer: rdn along 1/2-way: wkng whn wd st and sn bhd* **25/1**

1m 45.09s (0.49) **Going Correction** +0.10s/f (Slow) 11 Ran SP% **118.2**

Speed ratings (Par 101):101,97,95,94,91 91,90,81,75,69 69

CSF £35.16 CT £188.74 TOTE £5.30: £1.90, £3.00, £1.80; EX 26.00.

Owner R Miles **Bred** Blackdown Stud **Trained** Sedbury, Gloucs

FOCUS

This was not a great race, but the pace was solid and they finished well spread out. The runner-up sets the standard and the race has been rated fairly positively.

Epidaurian King(IRE) Official explanation: trainer said gelding did not handle the fibresand

Woolfall King(IRE) Official explanation: jockey said gelding lost its action

Bahrall Official explanation: jockey said gelding was never travelling

1351 BETDIRECTPOKER.COM COME AND 'AVE SOME H'CAP 5f (F)

6:55 (6:56) (Class 4) (0-80,78) 3-Y-0 **£5,019** (£1,493; £746; £372) **Stalls High**

Form RPR

41-1 **1** **Off The Record**[8] 1176 3-8-13 73 6ex TPQueally 2 89+
(J G Given) *wnt lft s: sn cl up: shkn up to ld over 1f out: pushed clr* **2/5**[1]

12-3 **2** *4* **Bookiesindex Boy**[4] 1270 3-9-3 77 (b) RobertHavlin 6 79
(J R Jenkins) *led: rdn along 2f out: hdd over 1f out and kpt on same pce* **14/1**

4224 **3** *4* **Diminuto**[9] 1151 3-7-11 64 oh1 FrankiePickard(7) 3 52
(M D I Usher) *in tch: hdwy 2f out: sn rdn and no imp* **8/1**[2]

3410 **4** *4* **Pirner's Brig**[26] 925 3-8-7 67 PaulMulrennan 4 40
(M W Easterby) *cl up: rdn along over 2f out: sn wknd* **9/1**[3]

20-0 **5** *shd* **Durova (IRE)**[11] 1108 3-8-10 70 DavidAllan 7 43
(T D Easterby) *chsd ldrs: rdn along over 2f out: sn wknd* **20/1**

1130 **6** *3/4* **Grange Lili (IRE)**[14] 1067 3-8-13 73 (b) GrahamGibbons 5 43
(Peter Grayson) *dwlt and a outpcd in rr* **18/1**

031- **7** *2 1/2* **Crow's Nest Lad**[276] 3907 3-8-8 73 DuranFentiman(5) 8 34
(T D Easterby) *in tch: rdn along and bhd fr 1/2-way* **14/1**

60.27 secs (-0.03) **Going Correction** 0.0s/f (Stan) 7 Ran SP% **115.9**

Speed ratings (Par 100):100,93,87,80,80 79,75

CSF £8.20 CT £23.65 TOTE £1.20: £1.10, £4.00; EX 7.60.

Owner Ian Henderson **Bred** P Onslow **Trained** Willoughton, Lincs

FOCUS

This race looked a match on paper, but after the withdrawal of Morinqua who would have been a clear second-favourite, this was reduced to a straightforward task for Off The Record and he made no mistake.

1352 BETDIRECTCASINO.COM FILLIES' H'CAP 1m (F)

7:25 (7:25) (Class 5) (0-75,72) 4-Y-0+ **£5,019** (£1,493; £746; £372) **Stalls Low**

Form RPR

00-0 **1** **Indian's Feather (IRE)**[4] 1265 6-9-0 68 TomEaves 4 73
(N Tinkler) *trckd ldng pair: outpcd and swtchd outside over 4f out: gd hdwy over 2f out: rdn to ld and edgd lft 1 1/2f out: drvn out* **20/1**

-264 **2** *nk* **Tour D'Amour (IRE)**[4] 1265 4-8-5 59 PaulFessey 7 63
(R Craggs) *led 1f: cl up tl led again over 3f out: rdn and hdd over 2f out: sn drvn and ev ch tl no ex wl ins fnl f* **3/1**[1]

4610 **3** *1/2* **Ruffie (IRE)**[14] 1069 4-8-10 64 (e) JimmyQuinn 8 67
(Miss Gay Kelleway) *trckd ldrs: hdwy 3f out: rdn to chal wl over 1f out and ev ch tl drvn and no ex wl ins fnl f* **7/2**[2]

4 **4** *1 1/2* **Sopran Gath (ITY)**[14] 1068 4-8-13 72 PatrickHills(5) 2 72
(J W Hills) *t.k.h: trckd ldrs on inner: n.m.r and hmpd over 3f out: hdwy over 2f out: sn rdn and kpt on u.p ins fnl f* **9/1**

5-05 **5** *2* **Stolen Glance**[8] 1181 4-8-6 60 PaulMulrennan 3 55
(M W Easterby) *dwlt: sn rdn along: hdwy and cl up 1/2-way: rdn to ld over 2f out: drvn and hdd 1 1/2f out: wknd and n.m.r ent fnl f* **7/2**[2]

06-5 **6** *15* **Fangorn Forest (IRE)**[5] 1251 4-8-4 63 (p) TolleyDean(5) 1 23
(R A Harris) *a in rr* **8/1**

250- **7** *38* **Scotch Pancake**[153] 6633 4-9-4 72 (t) DO'Donohoe 6 —
(E A L Dunlop) *led after 1f: rdn along and hdd over 3f out: wknd qckly* **5/1**[3]

1m 44.75s (0.15) **Going Correction** +0.10s/f (Slow) 7 Ran SP% **112.0**

Speed ratings (Par 100):103,102,102,100,98 83,45

CSF £75.95 CT £265.41 TOTE £17.30: £4.30, £2.20; EX 227.70.

Owner James Marshall & Mrs Susan Marshall **Bred** The Duke Of Roxburghe's Stud, Beckhampton House St **Trained** Langton, N Yorks

FOCUS

A modest fillies' handicap, won by the complete outsider, and there was little separating the front three at the line. The pace seemed solid and the time was 0.67 seconds faster than the opening maiden, and the form appears reasonable rated around the runner-up and fourth.

1353 AMBITIONS PERSONNEL H'CAP 1m 3f (F)

7:55 (7:57) (Class 6) (0-65,63) 3-Y-0 **£3,071** (£906; £453) **Stalls Low**

Form RPR

1-21 **1** **Dee Cee Elle**[6] 1224 3-9-4 63 6ex GregFairley(3) 7 76
(M Johnston) *trckd ldrs: hdwy and cl up 1/2-way: led 3f out: rdn over 2f out: drvn appr fnl f and styd on wl* **5/4**[1]

2154 **2** *3* **King Of The Beers (USA)**[7] 1194 3-8-13 60 (p) TolleyDean(5) 2 68
(R A Harris) *hld up in tch: hdwy on inner 4f out: rdn to chal 2f out: sn drvn and ev ch tl no ex ins fnl f* **5/2**[2]

-560 **3** *5* **Intensifier (IRE)**[28] 893 3-9-0 56 (b[1]) TPO'Shea 4 56
(P A Blockley) *chsd ldng pair: rdn along and outpcd over 4f out: styd on again fnl 2f* **7/1**[3]

0046 **4** *3* **Danalova**[4] 1271 3-8-4 46 oh1 DO'Donohoe 6 40
(R A Fahey) *cl up: rdn along over 4f out: drvn along over 2f out and grad wknd* **9/1**

0-00 **5** *5* **Night Falcon**[35] 790 3-8-5 47 (v[1]) JimmyQuinn 5 33
(H Morrison) *led: rdn along over 4f out: hdd 3f out and sn wknd* **15/2**

5-00 **6** *47* **Celtic Memories (IRE)**[16] 1045 3-8-11 53 DaleGibson 1 —
(M W Easterby) *sn rdn along and outpcd in rr: t.o fr 1/2-way* **18/1**

000 **7** *66* **Smiling Tiger**[21] 977 3-7-13 **46** oh1 DuranFentiman(5) 3 —
(M J Gingell) *in tch: rdn along and outpcd 7f out: t.o fnl 4f* **80/1**

2m 28.83s (-0.07) **Going Correction** +0.10s/f (Slow) **7** Ran SP% **113.8**
Speed ratings (Par 96):104,101,98,96,92 58,10
CSF £4.46 TOTE £1.60: £1.10, £2.60; EX 3.40 Place 6 £24.81, Place 5 £17.40..
Owner Douglas Livingston **Bred** Pollards Stables **Trained** Middleham Moor, N Yorks

FOCUS
This looked a weak handicap, especially as the two outsiders were out of it from an early stage and the race became a match between the two market leaders, but the time was decent for a race of its type so it may be best to take a more positive view of the form which is rated slightly above average for the grade.
T/Plt: £26.40 to a £1 stake. Pool: £47,201.45. 1,302.80 winning tickets. T/Qpdt: £5.50 to a £1 stake. Pool: £3,994.20. 528.20 winning tickets. JR

1200 WINDSOR (R-H)
Monday, April 30

OFFICIAL GOING: Good to firm
Wind: moderate against

1354 VC CASINO.COM MAIDEN AUCTION FILLIES' STKS 5f 10y
5:40 (5:41) (Class 5) 2-Y-0 **£3,238** (£963; £481; £240) **Stalls** High

Form RPR

0 **1** **Affirmatively**[11] 1101 2-8-6 JohnEgan 2 72
(D R C Elsworth) *fast away fr wd draw: led and sn crossed to nr side rail: hanging lft fr 1/2-way: rdn over 1f out: hung lft fnl f: styd on* **9/4**[1]

2 *1 1/2* **Miss Versatile (IRE)** 2-8-6 LPKeniry 3 66
(J S Moore) *dwlt: sn rcvrd to chse ldrs: effrt 2f out: rn green after: styd on to chse wnr ins fnl f* **20/1**

3 *1* **Tan Bonita (USA)** 2-8-10 DarryllHolland 13 66
(M J Wallace) *racd against nr side rail: mostly chsd wnr to over 1f out: kpt on again ins fnl f* **10/1**

0 **4** *hd* **Zahwah**[21] 972 2-8-3 EmmettStack(3) 1 61
(J G Portman) *dwlt: gd spd fr wd draw: chsd wnr over 1f out to ins fnl f: one pce* **50/1**

5 *1* **Perfect Flight** 2-8-8 JamieSpencer 12 59
(M Blanshard) *n.m.r after 1f and off the pce in midfield: effrt 2f out: nt clr run over 1f out: styd on steadily* **8/1**

6 *shd* **Tamrai Dancer** 2-8-4 JamesDoyle 4 55
(R M Beckett) *s.i.s: racd on outer: chsd ldrs: effrt over 1f out: one pce fnl f* **33/1**

0 **7** *shd* **Seventh Cloud (IRE)**[14] 1058 2-8-10 SebSanders 9 60
(A P Jarvis) *chsd ldrs: nt clr run over 1f out tl ent fnl f: kpt on* **33/1**

8 *1 3/4* **Talk Of Saafend (IRE)** 2-8-8 RichardHughes 8 51
(R Hannon) *outpcd and wl off the pce: green but sme prog 2f out: styng on whn nt clr run jst over 1f out* **13/2**[3]

9 *2* **Stand In Flames** 2-8-4 PaulEddery 7 39
(Pat Eddery) *s.s: outpcd and wl in rr: nvr nrr* **33/1**

5 **10** *hd* **Carolina Blini**[13] 1079 2-8-10 LDettori 11 45
(B J Meehan) *prom: rdn 2f out: n.m.r and wknd jst over 1f out* **7/2**[2]

0 **11** *1* **Polish Priory (IRE)**[7] 1201 2-8-7 ow4 StephenDonohoe(3) 14 41
(P D Evans) *off the pce in midfield: rdn and no prog 2f out* **11/1**

12 *1 3/4* **Ponder Anew (IRE)** 2-8-13 PhillipMakin 5 37
(K R Burke) *a outpcd and struggling* **16/1**

13 *nk* **Bantham Bay** 2-7-13 KMay(7) 6 28
(B J Meehan) *a wl outpcd* **33/1**

14 *5* **Bold Diva** 2-8-4 RichardThomas 10 6
(A W Carroll) *s.s: a bhd* **66/1**

62.98 secs (1.88) **Going Correction** +0.20s/f (Good) **14** Ran SP% **120.7**
Speed ratings (Par 89):92,89,88,87,86 85,85,82,79,79 77,75,74,66
CSF £55.36 TOTE £3.70: £1.70, £4.20, £2.40; EX 69.60.
Owner Wyck Hall Stud **Bred** Wyck Hall Stud Ltd **Trained** Newmarket, Suffolk

FOCUS
A reasonable fillies' maiden that should produce a few winners.

NOTEBOOK
Affirmatively ◆ confirmed the promise she showed on her debut in a hot Newmarket maiden with a straightforward success. She was a lot sharper this time, but she still showed signs of inexperience and can improve again. She deserves her chance in a higher grade and could well be competitive in Listed company in time. (op 5-2 tchd 11-4 in a place)
Miss Versatile(IRE), a 10,000euros sister to Khetaab, who was placed over 7f at three, shaped nicely on her racecourse debut behind the potentially useful winner. She should know more next time and looks capable of winning a similar event.
Tan Bonita(USA), a 20,000gns first foal of an unraced half-sister to Wildmanstan, a multiple winner at two to five over 6f-1m1f in the US, showed plenty of ability back in third. She looks capable of winning a similar event, but knew her job better than some of these and others may be open to more improvement.
Zahwah improved significantly on the form she showed on her debut at Warwick and is coming along nicely. (op 40-1)
Perfect Flight, out of a useful multiple winner in Norway and Sweden who was champion Scandinavian two-year-old filly, was a shade unlucky not to finish closer and should be able to build on this.
Tamrai Dancer, the first foal of an unraced half-sister to Queen Zenobia, a 1m winner at three, can be rated slightly better than the bare form as she raced widest of all in the straight.
Seventh Cloud(IRE) ◆ improved on the form she showed on her debut over this course and distance and would have been even closer with a clearer run. Official explanation: jockey said filly was denied a clear run
Talk Of Saafend(IRE) ◆, a 14,000gns half-sister to 6f juvenile winner and useful 1m1f winner in Hong Kong Millenium Princess, and to two winners at four in the US, out of a dual winner at in Italy, was not given a hard time once her chance had gone. She should show much-improved form next time. (op 15-2)
Carolina Blini showed good speed on her debut at Warwick, but she was beaten some way out this time and proved disappointing. Official explanation: jockey said filly never travelled and hung right under pressure (op 10-3)

1355 VC CASINO.COM H'CAP 1m 3f 135y
6:10 (6:11) (Class 5) (0-70,70) 3-Y-O **£3,238** (£963; £481; £240) **Stalls** Low

Form RPR

04-0 **1** **Highland Legacy**[16] 1044 3-8-11 **63** JamieSpencer 8 74
(M L W Bell) *hld up in last pair: rdn and prog on outer fr wl over 2f out: sustained effrt to ld ins fnl f: styd on wl* **5/1**[2]

4321 **2** *1 1/4* **Shawhill**[14] 1059 3-9-1 **67** SteveDrowne 6 76
(Tom Dascombe) *trckd ldrs: effrt over 2f out: rdn to ld wl over 1f out: hdd ins fnl f: styd on* **9/2**[1]

643- **3** *1* **Coyote Creek**[199] 5947 3-9-1 **67** MartinDwyer 13 75
(E F Vaughan) *settled towards rr: prog on outer over 2f out: edgd rt u.p fr over 1f out: styd on but unable to chal* **6/1**[3]

64-3 **4** *5* **Crimson Monarch (USA)**[7] 1205 3-9-3 **69** (b[1]) JimCrowley 7 72+
(Mrs A J Perrett) *trbld passage fr 4f out: swtchd lft over 1f out: styd on fnl f but no ch of rching ldrs* **9/2**[1]

1500 **5** *1/2* **Global Traffic**[7] 1205 3-8-11 **66** (b) StephenDonohoe(3) 1 65
(P D Evans) *hld up in rr: prog on outer over 2f out: hrd rdn and no imp over 1f out* **10/1**

52-6 **6** *nk* **Summer Of Love (IRE)**[12] 1092 3-8-12 **64** SebSanders 5 63
(P F I Cole) *trckd ldrs: rdn and cl enough 2f out: wknd jst over 1f out* **16/1**

5-63 **7** *5* **Dansimar**[12] 1092 3-9-2 **68** DarryllHolland 10 59
(M R Channon) *t.k.h early: hld up bhd ldrs: rdn and n.m.r on inner over 2f out: sn wknd* **6/1**[3]

00-0 **8** *nk* **Iolanthe**[10] 1127 3-9-0 **66** LDettori 14 56
(B J Meehan) *led after 1f: hrd rdn over 2f out: hdd & wknd rapidly wl over 1f out* **25/1**

000- **9** *2 1/2* **Muffett's Dream**[176] 6349 3-8-8 **60** RichardThomas 11 46
(J A Geake) *t.k.h: hld up bhd ldrs: pushed along 5f out: wknd rapidly 2f out* **66/1**

430- **10** *5* **Revisionist (IRE)**[178] 6322 3-8-12 **64** DaneO'Neill 4 42
(R Hannon) *led for 1f: prom tl wknd rapidly over 2f out* **14/1**

2523 **11** *5* **Miss Saafend Plaza (IRE)**[28] 884 3-9-4 **70** (b) RichardHughes 12 40
(R Hannon) *hld up in last pair: brief effrt over 2f out: nt clr run over 1f out: heavily eased* **14/1**

0050 **12** *6* **Woodygo**[27] 904 3-8-1 **56** StephaneBreux(3) 3 16
(J R Best) *s.i.s: sn in midfield: rdn over 3f out: struggling whn hmpd on inner over 2f out: wknd* **20/1**

643- **13** *8* **Hemispear**[152] 6650 3-8-13 **65** PaulFitzsimons 2 13
(Miss J R Tooth) *w ldrs tl wknd rapidly and bmpd abt fr 3f out* **40/1**

2m 27.87s (-2.23) **Going Correction** -0.05s/f (Good) **13** Ran SP% **122.4**
Speed ratings (Par 98):105,104,103,100,99 99,96,96,94,91 87,83,78
CSF £27.51 CT £142.69 TOTE £6.60: £2.10, £2.90, £3.20; EX 46.70.
Owner B J Warren **Bred** Deerfield Farm **Trained** Newmarket, Suffolk

FOCUS
A reasonable middle-distance handicap featuring a few unexposed types and the pace was fair. The form looks solid rated around the fifth and sixth.
Crimson Monarch(USA) Official explanation: jockey said gelding was denied a clear run
Global Traffic Official explanation: jockey said colt failed to handle the bend
Miss Saafend Plaza(IRE) Official explanation: jockey said filly was never travelling and lost her action
Hemispear Official explanation: jockey said filly had been hampered

1356 PLAY BLACKJACK AT VC CASINO.COM H'CAP 1m 2f 7y
6:40 (6:40) (Class 4) (0-85,85) 4-Y-0+ **£6,477** (£1,927; £963; £481) **Stalls** Low

Form RPR

4-22 **1** **Woolfall Blue (IRE)**[23] 940 4-8-10 **77** SebSanders 14 86+
(G G Margarson) *pushed up to ld after 1f: mde rest: hrd rdn fnl 2f: styd on wl* **11/2**[2]

-120 **2** *1 1/4* **Blacktoft (USA)**[83] 377 4-8-6 **76** (e) SaleemGolam(3) 1 82
(S C Williams) *v s.i.s: hld up in rr: hdwy into midfield 1/2-way: prog on outer over 2f out: chsd wnr over 1f out: kpt on* **25/1**

-002 **3** *3/4* **Mustajed**[30] 850 6-8-12 **84** JamesMillman(5) 9 89+
(B R Millman) *settled wl in rr: effrt on inner 3f out: nt clr run and swtchd lft to outer wl over 1f out: styd on: nt rch ldng pair* **6/1**[3]

002- **4** *1 1/2* **Del Mar Sunset**[172] 6418 8-8-7 **77** LiamJones(3) 7 79
(W J Haggas) *t.k.h: hld up in rr: effrt whn nt clr run over 2f out: prog over 1f out: styd on: nvr rchd ldrs* **10/1**

4465 **5** *shd* **Prince Charlemagne (IRE)**[40] 726 4-8-10 **77** IanMongan 12 79
(N P Littmoden) *hld up in midfield: effrt over 2f out: sn rdn and one pce* **6/1**[3]

-310 **6** *nk* **Active Asset (IRE)**[23] 940 5-9-4 **85** DarryllHolland 4 86
(M Quinn) *prom: chsd wnr 1/2-way to wl over 1f out: fdd* **12/1**

00/0 **7** *shd* **Prize Fighter (IRE)**[77] 444 5-8-10 **77** TedDurcan 3 78
(H R A Cecil) *t.k.h: hld up bhd ldrs: effrt over 2f out: disp 2nd wl over 1f out: sn fdd u.p* **8/1**

21 **8** *1 3/4* **Multicultural**[37] 769 4-8-5 **72** MartinDwyer 10 70
(D M Simcock) *hld up towards rr: shkn up on inner over 2f out: swtchd lft wl over 1f out: shuffled along and no prog* **5/1**[1]

000- **9** *1/2* **Cortesia (IRE)**[203] 5869 4-8-11 **78** AdrianMcCarthy 13 75
(P W Chapple-Hyam) *chsd wnr after 2f to 1/2-way: wknd u.p wl over 1f out* **16/1**

00-0 **10** *3/4* **Krugerrand (USA)**[20] 993 8-8-11 **85** AlanRutter(7) 8 81
(W J Musson) *dwlt: hld up in last: stl last whn rn into trble on inner over 2f out: shuffled along and styd on: nvr nr ldrs* **16/1**

626- **11** *6* **Mustamad**[327] 2366 4-8-9 **76** FergusSweeney 6 60
(Miss A M Newton-Smith) *prom 3f: lost pl: rdn in midfield 1/2-way: sn struggling* **50/1**

036- **12** *5* **Punta Galera (IRE)**[156] 6600 4-9-2 **83** RichardHughes 5 58
(R Hannon) *led for 1f: chsd wnr to 1/2-way: btn over 2f out: eased* **9/1**

0 **13** *7* **Dafarabad (IRE)**[9] 1149 5-8-8 **75** JamieSpencer 2 36
(Jonjo O'Neill) *prom and racd wd: rdn over 4f out: wknd 3f out: sn bhd* **16/1**

2m 6.63s (-1.67) **Going Correction** -0.05s/f (Good) **13** Ran SP% **122.0**
Speed ratings (Par 105):104,103,102,101,101 100,100,99,99,98 93,89,84
CSF £137.70 CT £867.45 TOTE £7.20: £2.30, £6.20, £2.50; EX 314.20.
Owner J F Bower **Bred** Calley House Syndicate **Trained** Newmarket, Suffolk
■ Stewards' Enquiry : James Millman one-day ban: careless riding (May 11)

FOCUS
A fair handicap run in a time 1.64 seconds quicker than the later maiden. The form is rated around the winner and third and looks sound enough.
Multicultural Official explanation: jockey said colt did not handle the good to firm ground
Punta Galera(IRE) Official explanation: jockey said gelding did not handle the good to firm ground

1357 PLAY AT VC CASINO.COM H'CAP 6f
7:10 (7:10) (Class 4) (0-80,80) 4-Y-0+ **£6,477** (£1,927; £963; £481) **Stalls** High

Form RPR

000- **1** **Roman Maze**[203] 5877 7-9-2 **78** TedDurcan 16 90
(W M Brisbourne) *hld up in rr and a gng wl: prog fr 2f out: threaded through to ld jst ins fnl f: r.o and hld on wl* **20/1**

46-4 **2** *shd* **River Kirov (IRE)**[17] 1023 4-9-1 **77** JamieSpencer 13 89+
(P W Chapple-Hyam) *dwlt: hld up in rr: prog and nt clr run twice fr 2f out: got through to press wnr ins fnl f: r.o but nt go past* **4/1**[1]

06-0 **3** *1 1/2* **Linda Green**[14] 1063 6-8-8 **70** EdwardCreighton 1 77+
(M R Channon) *settled in rr: prog on outer fr 2f out: rdn to dispute ld 1f out: nt qckn* **14/1**

0-50 **4** *3* **Makabul**[14] 1061 4-8-8 **70**.......... JimCrowley 14 68
(B R Millman) *settled in rr and sn towards outer: prog wl over 2f out: rdn to chal over 1f out: outpcd fnl f* **20/1**

5314 **5** *½* **Methaaly (IRE)**[13] 1074 4-8-5 **67**.......... JohnEgan 7 64+
(Jane Chapple-Hyam) *trckd ldrs: effrt to ld 2f out: hdd & wknd jst ins fnl f* **11/2**[3]

-116 **6** *1* **Louphole**[10] 1121 5-9-0 **76**.......... SebSanders 11 70
(P J Makin) *rrd s: hld up in last trio: pushed along and stdy prog fr 2f out: nvr rchd ldrs* **9/2**[2]

4263 **7** *3½* **Figaro Flyer (IRE)**[10] 1121 4-9-3 **79**.......... IanMongan 15 62
(P Howling) *hld up in midfield on inner: steadily taken towards outer fr over 2f out: n.m.r over 1f out: u.p and btn after* **9/1**

00-0 **8** *1¾* **Fast Bowler**[10] 1121 4-9-0 **79**.......... StephenDonohoe(3) 9 57
(J M P Eustace) *hld up in last pair: shkn up wl over 1f out: kpt on: nvr nr ldrs* **14/1**

1162 **9** *½* **Lucayos**[17] 1023 4-9-1 **80**.......... RichardKingscote(3) 2 56
(Mrs H Sweeting) *pressed ldrs: nrly upsides over 1f out: sn wknd* **10/1**

100- **10** *2* **Blue Aura (IRE)**[215] 5627 4-9-0 **76**.......... JamesDoyle 5 46
(R M Beckett) *mde most to 2f out: wknd over 1f out* **33/1**

60-4 **11** *½* **Peter Island (FR)**[10] 1121 4-9-3 **79**..........(v) RichardHughes 3 48
(J Gallagher) *w ldr to 2f out: wknd over 1f out* **20/1**

30-4 **12** *1½* **Chinalea (IRE)**[13] 1080 5-8-8 **70**..........(p) PhilipRobinson 6 34
(C G Cox) *chsd ldrs: losing pl whn n.m.r on inner 2f out: no ch after* **7/1**

00-0 **13** *4* **Dune Melody (IRE)**[21] 979 4-8-7 **69** ow2.......... LPKeniry 10 21
(J S Moore) *pushed along in midfield: wknd 2f out* **50/1**

24-0 **P** **Xaluna Bay (IRE)**[14] 1067 4-8-10 **72**.......... MartinDwyer 12 —
(W R Muir) *nvr beyond midfield: bhd whn p.u over 1f out: b.b.v* **20/1**

1m 14.12s (0.45) **Going Correction** +0.20s/f (Good) **14** Ran SP% **122.4**
Speed ratings (Par 105):105,104,102,98,98 96,92,89,89,86 85,83,78,—
CSF £92.90 CT £1233.04 TOTE £13.50: £5.00, £2.70, £2.70; EX 108.20.
Owner The Jenko and Thomo Partnership **Bred** Juddmonte Farms **Trained** Great Ness, Shropshire
■ Stewards' Enquiry : James Doyle caution: careless riding

FOCUS
A fair sprint handicap and typically competitive. A high draw proved to be an advantage and the first four came from off the pace.
Loughole ◆ Official explanation: jockey said gelding fly-jumped on leaving the stalls
Lucayos Official explanation: jockey said gelding had no more to give
Chinalea(IRE) Official explanation: jockey said gelding was denied a clear run
Xaluna Bay(IRE) Official explanation: jockey said filly had bled from the nose

1358 VC CASINO.COM MAIDEN STKS 1m 2f 7y
7:40 (7:41) (Class 5) 3-Y-O **£3,238** (£963; £481; £240) **Stalls** Low

Form RPR

1 **Dansant** 3-9-3.......... NickyMackay 7 86
(G A Butler) *trckd ldrs gng wl: effrt to ld over 1f out: rdn and styd on strly* **28/1**

2 *1¾* **Secret Tune** 3-9-3.......... RichardHughes 6 82
(Pat Eddery) *w ldrs: rousted along bnd over 6f out to over 5f out: disp ld 4f out to over 1f out: outpcd* **14/1**

3 *2½* **Master Halling** 3-9-3.......... SteveDrowne 2 77+
(R Charlton) *settled wl in rr: prog over 2f out: rn green and edgd lft: rdn and styd on: nrst fin* **16/1**

352- **4** *¾* **Castara Bay**[156] 6599 3-9-3 79.......... DaneO'Neill 12 76
(R Hannon) *led after 3f: jnd over 4f out: hdd over 2f out: sn btn: kpt on again ins fnl f* **3/1**[1]

5 *¾* **Gone Gold (USA)** 3-9-3.......... LDettori 8 75
(J Noseda) *w ldrs: disp ld over 4f out to over 1f out: fdd* **9/2**[3]

6 *½* **Ancient Culture** 3-9-3.......... KerrinMcEvoy 13 74+
(Sir Michael Stoute) *s.s: hld up towards rr: sme prog on inner 3f out: shkn up and no imp fnl 2f* **4/1**[2]

7 *1¼* **Russian Epic** 3-9-3.......... PhilipRobinson 1 71
(M A Jarvis) *led for 3f: wd bnd after and lost pl: effrt again on outer 3f out: chsd ldrs 2f out: wknd fnl f* **4/1**[2]

0-0 **8** *1½* **Buckthorn**[12] 1093 3-9-3.......... TedDurcan 4 68+
(G Wragg) *settled wl in rr: pushed along whn nt clr run briefly 2f out: kpt on same pce* **50/1**

04-6 **9** *½* **Becharm**[105] 141 3-8-12 65.......... FergusSweeney 9 62?
(A G Newcombe) *trckd ldrs: cl up 3f out: wknd over 1f out* **66/1**

6 **10** *nk* **A Little More (IRE)**[14] 1062 3-9-3.......... SimonWhitworth 5 67
(P A Blockley) *settled towards rr: rdn and one pce fr over 2f out* **33/1**

50- **11** *3½* **Marquee (IRE)**[202] 5883 3-9-3.......... AlanDaly 11 60
(P A Blockley) *chsd ldrs: rdn 3f out: wknd 2f out* **100/1**

\- **12** *9* **Shine Like A Star** 3-8-12.......... IanMongan 10 38
(J L Dunlop) *a wl in rr: rdn over 4f out: sn bhd* **25/1**

2m 8.27s (-0.03) **Going Correction** -0.05s/f (Good) **12** Ran SP% **110.4**
Speed ratings (Par 98):98,96,94,94,93 93,92,90,90,90 87,80
CSF £299.60 TOTE £30.40: £10.20, £3.40, £3.10; EX 303.60.
Owner Damiano Drago **Bred** Mrs Cino Del Duca **Trained** Blewbury, Oxon

FOCUS
The bare form of this maiden is just ordinary, but is should still produce some winners with the fourth the best guide. There was not that much pace on early and the winning time was 1.64 seconds slower than the earlier 71-85 handicap.
Russian Epic Official explanation: jockey said colt hung left-handed

1359 MONDAY NIGHT RACING WITH VC CASINO.COM H'CAP 1m 67y
8:10 (8:10) (Class 5) (0-75,75) 3-Y-O **£3,238** (£963; £481; £240) **Stalls** High

Form RPR

600- **1** **Rudry Dragon (IRE)**[204] 5841 3-9-2 **73**.......... SimonWhitworth 1 83
(P A Blockley) *trckd ldrs: prog to ld wl over 1f out: hung lft whn rdn but r.o fnl f* **25/1**

21-2 **2** *1¼* **Docofthebay (IRE)**[5] 1247 3-9-3 **74**.......... JamieSpencer 10 81
(J A Osborne) *hld up in midfield: prog 2f out: chsd wnr jst over 1f out: veered bdly whn rdn: styd on but no real imp* **6/4**[1]

4-33 **3** *4* **Eager Igor (USA)**[12] 1091 3-9-1 **72**.......... StephenCarson 9 70
(Eve Johnson Houghton) *hld up in midfield: prog 2f out: disp 2nd over 1f out: sn outpcd* **13/2**[2]

-616 **4** *½* **Hucking Heat (IRE)**[28] 889 3-8-10 **70**.......... StephaneBreux(3) 7 67
(J R Best) *hld up in midfield: prog over 2f out: disp 2nd over 1f out: sn outpcd* **25/1**

001- **5** *1* **Our Ruby**[243] 4920 3-8-9 **73**.......... MCGeran(7) 14 68
(P W Chapple-Hyam) *hld up towards rr: sme prog fr over 2f out: rdn and outpcd fr over 1f out* **14/1**

450- **6** *hd* **Loch Tay**[200] 5916 3-9-1 **72**.......... RichardHughes 12 66
(M L W Bell) *hld up wl in rr: shkn up over 2f out: nvr on terms* **7/1**[3]

03-0 **7** *shd* **Goose Green (IRE)**[56] 624 3-8-8 **65**.......... SteveDrowne 2 59
(R J Hodges) *w ldr: led over 2f out to wl over 1f out: wknd* **50/1**

214- **8** *1* **Event Music (IRE)**[192] 6092 3-9-2 **73**.......... DarryllHolland 5 65
(M R Channon) *trckd ldng pair tl wknd 2f out* **9/1**

12-0 **9** *¾* **Shouldntbethere (IRE)**[10] 1122 3-8-9 **66**.......... AlanDaly 11 56
(Mrs P N Dutfield) *s.i.s: wl in rr: effrt on outer 3f out: no prog over 1f out: wknd* **25/1**

541 **10** *½* **Chattan Clan**[26] 919 3-9-4 **75**..........(t) DaneO'Neill 4 64
(R A Kvisla) *mde most to over 2f out: wknd* **20/1**

60-5 **11** *1¼* **Anatolian Prince**[26] 931 3-8-6 **63**.......... TedDurcan 3 49
(J M P Eustace) *t.k.h: prom tl wknd over 2f out* **16/1**

-233 **12** *21* **Henry The Seventh**[82] 382 3-8-12 **69**.......... MartinDwyer 6 7
(J W Hills) *a struggling in last pair* **20/1**

30-4 **P** **Lights Of Vegas**[12] 1098 3-9-4 **75**.......... LDettori 13 —
(B J Meehan) *stirrup broke sn after s: sn t.o: p.u 1f out* **8/1**

1m 45.9s (1.20) **Going Correction** -0.05s/f (Good) **13** Ran SP% **122.5**
Speed ratings (Par 98):92,90,86,86,85 85,84,83,83,82 81,60,—
CSF £60.13 CT £311.81 TOTE £37.80: £7.20, £1.30, £2.40; EX 100.50 Place 6 £711.14, Place 5 £308.89..
Owner J McCarthy H Downs & B Allen **Bred** Kilnamoragh Stud **Trained** Lambourn, Berks

FOCUS
A modest handicap and a very ordinary time for a race of its type but the form looks sound rated through the runner-up.
Event Music(IRE) Official explanation: jockey said filly had run too free
Anatolian Prince Official explanation: jockey said colt had been unsuited by the good to firm ground
T/Jkpt: Not won. T/Plt: £6,466.00 to a £1 stake. Pool: £83,704.45. 9.45 winning tickets. T/Qpdt: £144.20 to a £1 stake. Pool: £6,785.30. 34.80 winning tickets. JN

1309 WOLVERHAMPTON (A.W) (L-H)
Monday, April 30

OFFICIAL GOING: Standard
Wind: fresh against

1360 BETDIRECTPOKER.COM COME AND 'AVE SOME H'CAP 7f 32y(P)
2:00 (2:00) (Class 6) (0-50,50) 4-Y-O+ **£2,047** (£604; £302) **Stalls** High

Form RPR

0030 **1** **Inca Soldier (FR)**[10] 1132 4-8-8 **46**.......... PaulMulrennan 7 56
(R C Guest) *hld up and bhd: rdn and hdwy on outside 2f out: edgd lft fr jst over 1f out: led wl ins fnl f: r.o* **10/1**

0030 **2** *1* **Methusaleh (IRE)**[10] 1132 4-8-3 **46**.......... PatrickHills(5) 2 53
(D Shaw) *hld up in mid-div: rdn and hdwy on ins over 2f out: ev ch fnl f: kpt on* **5/1**[2]

0041 **3** *½* **Blue Knight (IRE)**[26] 920 8-8-8 **46**.......... JimmyQuinn 5 52
(P Howling) *chsd ldrs: rdn over 3f out: edgd lft and led jst over 1f out: hdd wl ins fnl f: nt qckn* **8/1**

400- **4** *¾* **Seesawmilu (IRE)**[200] 5928 4-8-9 **47**.......... DavidAllan 11 51
(E J Alston) *hld up and bhd: rdn and hdwy on ins wl over 1f out: sn swtchd rt: carried sltly lft ent fnl f: one pce* **14/1**

5-36 **5** *¾* **Attacca**[21] 967 6-8-10 **48**.......... DarryllHolland 3 50
(J R Weymes) *a.p: rdn over 1f out: one pce* **11/4**[1]

0630 **6** *¾* **Fulvio (USA)**[34] 801 7-8-12 **50**..........(v) J-PGuillambert 9 50
(P Howling) *hld up towards rr: rdn and sme hdwy over 2f out: no further prog* **9/1**

-106 **7** *2½* **Crush On You**[12] 1086 4-8-9 **47**.......... GrahamGibbons 12 40
(R Hollinshead) *in rr: pushed along over 3f out: nvr nrr* **14/1**

0/62 **8** *nk* **Aphrodelta**[98] 207 5-8-8 **46** oh1.......... ChrisCatlin 6 39
(P D Cundell) *hld up towards rr: rdn 3f out: n.d* **11/2**[3]

13-0 **9** *2½* **Panshir (FR)**[21] 980 6-8-11 **49**.......... TPQueally 4 35
(Mrs C A Dunnett) *chsd ldr: ev ch 2f out: sn rdn: wknd over 1f out* **12/1**

000/ **10** *nk* **Miss Lovat**[504] 6562 4-8-12 **50**.......... RichardMullen 8 35
(W M Brisbourne) *prom: rdn over 3f out: wknd over 2f out* **25/1**

0250 **11** *1½* **Alistair John**[38] 746 4-8-8 **46** oh1.......... DeanMcKeown 1 27
(Mrs G S Rees) *led: rdn and hdd jst over 1f out: wknd fnl f* **12/1**

460- **12** *31* **Mytton's Pride**[261] 4354 4-8-9 **47**.......... NCallan 10 —
(A Bailey) *sn stdd into mid-div: bhd fnl 3f: t.o* **25/1**

1m 29.09s (-1.31) **Going Correction** -0.175s/f (Stan) **12** Ran SP% **125.3**
Speed ratings (Par 101):100,98,98,97,96 95,92,92,89,89 87,52
CSF £62.90 CT £437.62 TOTE £14.30: £4.20, £1.90, £1.80; EX 111.80.
Owner Philip Pinnington **Bred** Sheikh Sultan B K B Z Al Nahyan **Trained** Brancepeth, Co Durham

FOCUS
A tightly-knit banded handicap and sound form rated around the placed horses.
Crush On You Official explanation: jockey said filly never travelled

1361 BETDIRECTPOKER.COM GET INVOLVED H'CAP 1m 4f 50y(P)
2:30 (2:35) (Class 6) (0-60,60) 3-Y-O **£2,218** (£654; £327) **Stalls** Low

Form RPR

000- **1** **Credit Slip**[180] 6297 3-8-11 **53**.......... JimmyFortune 9 61
(J L Dunlop) *hld up towards rr: hdwy over 5f out: rdn over 3f out: r.o u.p to ld last stride* **5/1**[2]

006- **2** *shd* **Distant Sunset (IRE)**[222] 5482 3-9-0 **56**.......... MichaelHills 8 64
(B W Hills) *hld up in tch: rdn over 3f out: led jst over 1f out: hrd rdn and hdd last stride* **9/2**[1]

000- **3** *hd* **Chiff Chaff**[176] 6349 3-9-4 **60**.......... NCallan 6 68
(M L W Bell) *hld up in tch: rdn 3f out: swtchd rt jst over 1f out: r.o ins fnl f* **5/1**[2]

06-3 **4** *2½* **Cavendish**[25] 936 3-8-13 **55**..........(b) TedDurcan 7 59
(J M P Eustace) *chsd ldr: led wl over 2f out: rdn and hdd jst over 1f out: one pce* **11/1**

60-0 **5** *4* **Monet's Lady (IRE)**[16] 1044 3-8-4 **46**.......... DO'Donohoe 2 43
(R A Fahey) *hld up and bhd: rdn and swtchd rt over 1f out: styd on fnl f: n.d* **8/1**

3346 **6** *¾* **Gold Response**[28] 893 3-8-13 **55**.......... DeanMcKeown 3 51
(D Shaw) *uns rdr and loose bef s: hld up and bhd: sme hdwy over 3f out: sn rdn: no imp fnl f* **7/1**[3]

0233 **7** *2* **Citrus Chief (USA)**[26] 917 3-8-9 **58**..........(p) LukeMorris(7) 5 51
(R A Harris) *prom: rdn over 3f out: wknd 2f out* **8/1**

000- **8** *7* **Double Precedent**[246] 4829 3-8-4 **46** oh1.......... RoystonFfrench 1 28
(M Johnston) *led: rdn and hdd wl over 2f out: wknd wl over 1f out* **9/1**

4650 **9** *5* **Snake Hips**[9] 1154 3-9-1 **57**.......... DaleGibson 11 31
(B Palling) *pushed along over 4f out: a bhd* **20/1**

00-0 **10** *9* **Sadler's Hill (IRE)**[35] 791 3-8-9 **51** ow1.......... DarryllHolland 4 10
(M J McGrath) *bhd fnl 4f* **33/1**

The Form Book, Raceform Ltd, Compton, RG20 6NL

50-5 **11** *3* **Isabella's Best (IRE)**[9] 1154 3-8-12 **54**............................ ChrisCatlin 12 8
(E J O'Neill) *hld up in mid-div: rdn over 4f out: sn bhd* **9/1**

2m 39.71s (-2.71) **Going Correction** -0.175s/f (Stan) **11** Ran SP% **122.3**
Speed ratings (Par 96):102,101,101,100,97 96,95,90,87,81 79
CSF £29.03 CT £122.22 TOTE £7.70: £2.20, £1.80, £2.60; EX 26.60.
Owner Hesmonds Stud **Bred** Hesmonds Stud Ltd **Trained** Arundel, W Sussex

FOCUS
A competitive if modest handicap won in a respectable time with the finish fought out by a trio of unexposed types who could all do better.

1362 BETDIRECTPOKER.COM $50,000 FREEROLL CLASSIFIED STKS 1m 4f 50y(P)
3:00 (3:00) (Class 7) 4-Y-0+ **£1,706** (£503; £252) **Stalls** Low

Form RPR
-206 **1** **Experimental (IRE)**[22] 372 13-9-1 45............................... DaleGibson 4 56
(John A Harris) *a.p: pushed along over 6f out: wnt 2nd over 3f out: led ins fnl f: drvn out* **8/1**[3]
0024 **2** *nk* **Diktatorship (IRE)**[17] 1032 4-9-0 44............................ TonyHamilton 3 56
(G A Swinbank) *led: hdd 9f out: chsd ldr: led over 4f out: rdn over 1f out: hdd ins fnl f: nt qckn* **5/4**[1]
0400 **3** *5* **Twilight Avenger (IRE)**[4] 1271 4-9-0 41..........................(v[1]) TedDurcan 10 48
(W M Brisbourne) *hld up and bhd: rdn and hdwy on outside 3f out: one pce fnl f* **14/1**
0500 **4** *shd* **Activist**[27] 909 9-8-8 45...(p) KellyHarrison(7) 12 47
(D Carroll) *hld up in mid-div: hdwy over 3f out: rdn over 2f out: one pce fnl f* **14/1**
4036 **5** *1 ½* **Montecristo**[27] 907 14-9-1 41.. NCallan 5 45
(Rae Guest) *hld up in mid-div: rdn over 2f out: nt clr run briefly over 1f out: no real prog* **14/1**
4060 **6** *1* **Earthling**[6] 1229 6-9-1 45...(b) TomEaves 1 43
(D W Chapman) *t.k.h early: prom: swtchd rt over 3f out: rdn whn hung lft over 1f out: sn btn* **16/1**
00-0 **7** *1 ¼* **Arthurs Dream (IRE)**[8] 907 5-9-1 43.......................... DarryllHolland 2 41
(A W Carroll) *dwlt and wnt rt s: hld up and bhd: rdn and hdwy on outside over 2f out: edgd lft over 1f out: no imp* **15/2**[2]
0000 **8** *5* **Iceni Warrior**[4] 1271 5-9-1 45.. JimmyQuinn 11 33
(P Howling) *hld up in tch: stmbld over 5f out: rdn over 3f out: wknd over 1f out* **16/1**
4000 **9** *3 ½* **Elms Schoolboy**[34] 804 5-9-1 42...........................(b) J-PGuillambert 7 28
(P Howling) *t.k.h in mid-div: rdn over 3f out: bhd fnl 2f* **20/1**
626- **10** *2 ½* **Blue Opal**[122] 6972 5-8-10 40...................................(p) DuranFentiman(5) 6 24
(Miss S E Hall) *a bhd* **12/1**
-004 **11** *1 ½* **Welsh Whisper**[56] 620 8-9-1 43............................... EdwardCreighton 8 21
(S A Brookshaw) *t.k.h early: rdn 3f out: a bhd* **25/1**
-000 **12** *12* **Danceinthevalley (IRE)**[9] 1152 5-9-1 43.................. RoystonFfrench 9 2
(I W McInnes) *t.k.h: prom: led 9f out tl over 4f out: rdn and wknd 3f out* **12/1**

2m 41.52s (-0.90) **Going Correction** -0.175s/f (Stan)
WFA 4 from 5yo+ 1lb **12** Ran SP% **123.1**
Speed ratings (Par 97):96,95,92,92,91 90,89,86,84,82 81,73
CSF £18.95 TOTE £11.40: £3.70, £1.10, £3.70; EX 38.30.
Owner Mrs A E Harris **Bred** Noel Broderick **Trained** Eastwell, Leics

FOCUS
A dire affair but sound enough form rated around the first three.
Montecristo Official explanation: trainer's rep said gelding lost a near-hind shoe
Arthurs Dream(IRE) Official explanation: jockey said gelding hung in home straight
Danceinthevalley(IRE) Official explanation: jockey said gelding ran too freely

1363 BETDIRECT.COM H'CAP 5f 20y(P)
3:30 (3:30) (Class 4) (0-85,85) 4-Y-0+ **£4,857** (£1,445; £722; £360) **Stalls** Low

Form RPR
-220 **1** **Dig Deep (IRE)**[12] 1088 5-9-2 **83**.................................... PaulMulrennan 6 104+
(W J Haggas) *a gng wl: led ins fnl f: pushed out* **7/2**[1]
2234 **2** *2 ½* **Financial Times (USA)**[31] 835 5-8-8 **75**.....................(t) HayleyTurner 1 82+
(Stef Liddiard) *sn led: rdn over 1f out: hdd ins fnl f: nt qckn* **8/1**[3]
30-0 **3** *hd* **Phantom Whisper**[31] 828 4-9-4 **85**................................... TedDurcan 7 91
(B R Millman) *sn outpcd and bhd: hdwy on outside over 1f out: sn hung lft: r.o ins fnl f* **16/1**
0461 **4** *1* **Desert Opal**[13] 1074 7-8-2 **72**...(p) MarcHalford(3) 3 75
(C R Dore) *hld up in mid-div: hdwy on ins whn swtchd rt 2f out: rdn over 1f out: one pce* **11/1**
602- **5** *nk* **Westport**[178] 6320 4-8-9 **76**... NCallan 5 78
(K A Ryan) *bhd: rdn whn n.m.r 2f out: hdwy on ins wl over 1f out: one pce fnl f* **9/2**[2]
6161 **6** *2* **Efistorm**[14] 1061 6-8-10 **80**.. LiamJones(3) 13 74
(C R Dore) *bhd: hdwy whn swtchd lft over 1f out: no further prog fnl f* **10/1**
000- **7** *4* **Cashel Mead**[204] 5832 7-8-13 **85**...................................... TravisBlock(5) 9 65
(J L Spearing) *outpcd* **33/1**
-004 **8** *1 ¼* **Total Impact**[32] 818 4-9-1 **82**... EddieAhern 12 58
(C A Cyzer) *prom tl wknd over 1f out* **11/1**
1212 **9** *shd* **Almaty Express**[31] 835 5-8-3 **75**..............................(b) WilliamBuick(5) 8 50
(J R Weymes) *prom tl rdn and wknd over 1f out* **9/1**
650- **10** *hd* **Prince Namid**[180] 6292 5-9-4 **85**................................ RoystonFfrench 10 59
(Mrs A Duffield) *outpcd* **20/1**
00-0 **11** *10* **Rare Breed**[22] 957 4-8-11 **78**.. TomEaves 4 16
(Mrs L Stubbs) *prom 3f* **25/1**
-626 **P** **Graze On**[32] 818 5-9-1 **82**..(b) GrahamGibbons 2 —
(Peter Grayson) *led early: chsd ldrs tl broke down and p.u 2f out: dead* **9/2**[2]

61.35 secs (-1.47) **Going Correction** -0.175s/f (Stan) **12** Ran SP% **122.9**
Speed ratings (Par 105):104,100,99,98,97 94,88,86,85,85 69,—
CSF £32.36 CT £416.74 TOTE £4.40: £1.70, £3.20, £4.40; EX 48.80.
Owner G Roberts/F Green/Tessona Racing **Bred** Sir Eric Parker **Trained** Newmarket, Suffolk

FOCUS
A competitive-looking handicap run at a good pace and rated through the runner-up.
Westport Official explanation: jockey said gelding suffered interference 1/2f after start
Prince Namid Official explanation: jockey said gelding reared as stalls opened

1364 BETDIRECTPOKER.COM $50,000 FREEROLL MAIDEN FILLIES' STKS 1m 4f 50y(P)
4:00 (4:00) (Class 5) 3-4-Y-0 **£2,968** (£876; £438) **Stalls** Low

Form RPR
1 **Pentasilea**[220] 5518 4-9-12 .... JimmyQuinn 4 70
(H J L Dunlop) *chsd ldr: led 2f out: rdn over 1f out: drvn out* **12/1**
0- **2** *2 ½* **Super Sifted (GER)**[160] 6558 3-8-7 .... TPQueally 7 64+
(H R A Cecil) *hld up in tch: lost pl 4f out: hdwy on ins over 2f out: styd on to take 2nd last strides: bttr for r* **33/1**
4- **3** *nk* **Teodora Adivina**[194] 6049 3-8-7 .... TedDurcan 5 64
(H R A Cecil) *led: rdn and hdd 2f out: no ex ins fnl f: lost 2nd last strides* **4/6**[1]
0- **4** *5* **Snow Ballerina**[242] 4964 3-8-7 .... DO'Donohoe 6 56
(E A L Dunlop) *hld up in tch: rdn and outpcd over 3f out: no imp fnl 2f* **6/1**[2]
000- **5** *¾* **Sky Beam (USA)**[202] 5886 3-8-7 48.. TPO'Shea 9 55
(J L Dunlop) *hld up and bhd: pushed along over 1f out: nt clr run and swtchd rt ins fnl f: nvr nr ldrs* **40/1**
5-06 **6** *1* **Khyberie**[59] 603 4-9-12 48.. DeanMcKeown 3 55
(G Wragg) *hld up and bhd: sme hdwy on outside over 1f out: n.d* **20/1**
0-5 **7** *1 ½* **Restless Soul**[28] 884 3-8-7 .... EddieAhern 8 51
(C A Cyzer) *hld up towards rr: rdn and hdwy over 4f out: outpcd over 3f out: wknd over 1f out* **16/1**
60- **8** *shd* **Lady Traill**[176] 6349 3-8-7 .... MichaelHills 2 50
(B W Hills) *hld up in mid-div: pushed along over 3f out: sn bhd: carried rt ins fnl f* **14/1**
2-0 **9** *8* **First Bloom (USA)**[7] 1203 3-8-8 ow1.. NCallan 1 39
(P F I Cole) *prom tl wknd 3f out* **7/1**[3]
0 **10** *21* **Lady Dedlock**[14] 1068 3-8-7 .... J-PGuillambert 10 4
(C A Cyzer) *a towards rr: eased whn no ch over 2f out* **100/1**

2m 41.95s (-0.47) **Going Correction** -0.175s/f (Stan)
WFA 3 from 4yo 20lb **10** Ran SP% **118.1**
Speed ratings (Par 100):94,92,92,88,88 87,86,86,81,67
CSF £345.01 TOTE £11.40: £2.80, £7.00, £1.10; EX 568.90.
Owner Cyril Humphris **Bred** Cyril Humphris **Trained** Lambourn, Berks
■ Stewards' Enq: T P Queally 20-day ban: breach of Rule 158 (insufficient effort) (Jun 13-Jul 2)

FOCUS
Only time will show the value of this form in what looked an ordinary maiden, but at present it looks limited.
Super Sifted(GER) ◆ Official explanation: jockey said, regarding running and riding, his orders were to jump the filly out, get it balanced and in rhythm and finish as close as he could, adding that he met interference on the final bend, it only became apparent inside the final furlong that he might catch the third horse, making his final effort to pass with no expectation of catching the winner
Teodora Adivina Official explanation: trainer said filly had tied up during the race
Lady Traill Official explanation: jockey said filly was never on the bridle
First Bloom(USA) Official explanation: jockey said filly had no more to give

1365 BETDIRECTCASINO.COM H'CAP 1m 141y(P)
4:30 (4:30) (Class 4) (0-80,80) 3-Y-0 **£3,151** (£3,151; £722; £360) **Stalls** Low

Form RPR
2222 **1** **Emerald Wilderness (IRE)**[11] 1111 3-8-13 **75**................. JHBowman 2 80+
(M R Channon) *hld up: hdwy on ins whn nt clr run 2f out: led jst ins fnl f: edgd rt and jnd post* **13/2**
01-0 **1** *dht* **Guiseppe Verdi (USA)**[13] 1076 3-8-13 **75**...................... JimmyFortune 1 79
(J H M Gosden) *hld up: hdwy over 3f out: led jst over 2f out: rdn and hdd wl over 1f out: r.o u.p to join ldr on post* **9/2**[3]
06-2 **3** *nk* **Postsprofit (IRE)**[6] 1218 3-8-6 **68**...................................... ChrisCatlin 4 71?
(N A Callaghan) *hung rt thrght: led after 1f: hdd jst over 2f out: rdn to ld jst over 1f out: hdd jst ins fnl f: kpt on* **10/1**
310- **4** *2 ½* **Plane Painter (IRE)**[191] 6100 3-9-3 **79**......................... J-PGuillambert 3 77
(M Johnston) *prom: lft 2nd 5f out: rdn and ev ch 2f out: wknd over 1f out* **7/1**
1 **5** *hd* **Tutor (IRE)**[63] 565 3-9-4 **80**... EddieAhern 5 77
(W J Haggas) *hld up in tch: ev ch on outside 2f out: rdn and wknd over 1f out* **6/4**[1]
45-0 **P** **Sri Pekan Two**[10] 1122 3-9-1 **77**.. NCallan 6 —
(P F I Cole) *chsd ldr over 6f out tl p.u lame 5f out* **7/2**[2]

1m 50.18s (-1.58) **Going Correction** -0.175s/f (Stan) **6** Ran SP% **115.3**
Speed ratings (Par 100):100,100,99,97,97 —
WIN: GV £2.20, EW £3.60; PL: GV £2.20, EW £2.30; EX: GV/EW £22.30, EW/GV £6.20; CSF: GV/EW £16.72, EW/GV £18.06..
Owner Mohammed Jaber **Bred** Mrs Joan Murphy **Trained** West Ilsley, Berks
Owner H R H Princess Haya Of Jordan **Bred** Runnymede Farm Inc And Catesby W Clay
■ **Trained** Newmarket, Suffolk

■ The first winner in Britain, albeit a dead-heat, for Australian jockey Hugh Bowman.

FOCUS
A competitive little handicap but ordinary form, rated through the winner.
Sri Pekan Two Official explanation: vet said gelding pulled up lame behind

1366 BETDIRECTPOKER.COM $50,000 FREEROLL H'CAP 1m 141y(P)
5:00 (5:00) (Class 6) (0-60,60) 4-Y-0+ **£2,218** (£654; £327) **Stalls** Low

Form RPR
00-5 **1** **Indian Edge**[14] 1064 6-9-2 **58**.. NCallan 6 69
(B Palling) *sn led: rdn and edgd rt wl over 1f out: hld on wl* **10/3**[2]
5263 **2** *hd* **Hits Only Cash**[3] 1284 5-9-0 **56**.................................... DeanMcKeown 2 67
(J Pearce) *hld up and bhd: rdn and hdwy wl over 1f out: ev ch ins fnl f: r.o* **3/1**[1]
-460 **3** *1 ¼* **Western Roots**[21] 976 6-9-4 **60**.. ChrisCatlin 3 68
(M Appleby) *stdd s: hld up in rr: hdwy on outside over 2f out: rdn and ev ch ins fnl f: nt qckn* **11/2**[3]
3303 **4** *1 ¼* **Golden Spectrum (IRE)**[9] 1162 8-8-10 **59**................(b) LukeMorris(7) 5 64
(R A Harris) *hld up in mid-div: hdwy over 3f out: rdn over 1f out: one pce* **11/2**[3]
-406 **5** *3* **Pelham Crescent (IRE)**[38] 741 4-8-13 **55**...............(b) J-PGuillambert 8 53
(B Palling) *prom: ev ch over 2f out: sn rdn: wknd wl over 1f out* **9/1**
106- **6** *hd* **Mr Belvedere**[342] 1915 6-8-4 **46**...................................(p) RichardMullen 1 43
(A J Lidderdale) *led early: prom: rdn over 3f out: wknd ins fnl f* **12/1**
00-0 **7** *1* **Life's A Whirl**[21] 980 5-8-7 **49**...(p) DMylonas 7 44
(Mrs C A Dunnett) *sn chsng ldr: lost 2nd and rdn over 2f out: wknd 1f out* **25/1**
0202 **8** *shd* **Machinate (USA)**[6] 1232 5-8-13 **55**..........................(v[1]) EddieAhern 10 50
(W M Brisbourne) *hld up in rr: c wd and rdn wl over 1f out: no rspnse* **8/1**
600- **9** *3 ½* **Smart Cassie**[231] 5250 4-8-13 **55**.. VinceSlattery 4 42
(H J Evans) *broke wl: sn stdd into mid-div: lost pl over 3f out: sn bhd* **25/1**

1m 50.09s (-1.67) **Going Correction** -0.175s/f (Stan) **9** Ran SP% **115.3**
Speed ratings (Par 101):100,99,98,97,94 94,93,93,90
CSF £13.77 CT £51.37 TOTE £4.60: £1.60, £1.70, £2.80; EX 16.60 Place 6 £106.03, Place 5 £24.96.
Owner Nigel Thomas and Christopher Mason **Bred** Christopher J Mason **Trained** Tredodridge, Vale Of Glamorgan

FOCUS
A moderate handicap but straightforward form rated around those in the frame.

T/Plt: £146.50 to a £1 stake. Pool: £52,046.40. 259.20 winning tickets. T/Qpdt: £22.40 to a £1 stake. Pool: £2,996.70. 98.60 winning tickets. KH

1206 BATH (L-H)

Tuesday, May 1

OFFICIAL GOING: Firm

Wind: Brisk, behind

1367 M J CHURCH MAIDEN AUCTION STKS — 5f 11y

2:10 (2:10) (Class 6) 2-Y-O — **£2,072** (£616; £308; £153) **Stalls** Low

Form — RPR

1 **In Uniform** 2-8-11 .... RichardMullen 9 — 81+
(E S McMahon) *in tch: pushed along and hdwy 1/2-way: qckend to ld jst ins fnl f: comf* **12/1**[3]

5 2 1 ¾ **Alexander Nepotism (IRE)**[12] 1101 2-8-11 .... JamieSpencer 3 — 74
(B J Meehan) *sn led: shkn up over 1f out: hdd jst ins fnl f: sn outpcd* **8/11**[1]

3 2 **Shatter Resistant (IRE)** 2-8-11 .... JHBowman 4 — 66
(M R Channon) *chsd ldrs: drvn along 2f out: styd on same pce fnl f* **28/1**

0 4 2 ½ **Alfredtheordinary**[20] 999 2-8-9 .... SamHitchcott 8 — 54
(M R Channon) *in tch: rdn along 1/2-way: kpt on same pce fr over 1f out* **66/1**

62 5 nk **Avertitop**[8] 1201 2-8-11 .... RichardHughes 6 — 55
(R Hannon) *sn chsng ldrs: rdn 1/2-way: wknd ins fnl 2f* **2/1**[2]

6 3 ½ **Happy Hacker (IRE)** 2-7-11 .... BernadetteQuinn(7) 11 — 34
(P D Evans) *slowly away and bhd: styd on fr over 1f out but nvr in contention* **66/1**

5 7 shd **Shipboard Romance (IRE)**[14] 1073 2-8-4 ....(v[1]) JimmyQuinn 5 — 33
(P D Evans) *chsd ldrs: rdn 1/2-way: wknd ins fnl 2f* **40/1**

8 6 **Lord Of The Wing** 2-9-2 .... SebSanders 7 — 21
(R M Beckett) *s.i.s: a outpcd* **25/1**

9 8 **Virtual Paddy** 2-8-9 .... TedDurcan 1 — —
(M Blanshard) *a bdly outpcd* **66/1**

61.19 secs (-1.31) **Going Correction** -0.35s/f (Firm) — 9 Ran SP% **113.1**

Speed ratings (Par 91):96,93,90,86,85 79,79,70,57

CSF £20.76 TOTE £14.50: £3.40, £1.02, £4.70; EX 27.80 Trifecta £30.60 Pool: £516.43 - 11.98 winning units..

Owner J C Fretwell **Bred** Mrs H B Raw **Trained** Lichfield, Staffs

FOCUS

A fair juvenile maiden, although there was not a great deal of strength in depth and not an easy race to assess.

NOTEBOOK

In Uniform ◆, a 25,000gns half-brother to multiple middle-distance winner Green Room, 6f two-year-old scorer Scarlet Ribbons, and Scarlet Invader, a 7f winner at three, out of a high-class 1m winner at two in Italy, is entered in the Group 1 Phoenix Stakes. Having just about managed to stay in touch in the early stages, he really got the hang of things late on and found much more under pressure than the strong-travelling favourite. He should have little trouble in staying 6f and deserves to take his chance in better company. (op 9-1)

Alexander Nepotism(IRE) probably ran into quite a nice type, but she still failed to build on the promise she showed when fifth in a good Newmarket maiden on her debut and was a shade disappointing. Soon showing good speed and travelling strongly, she looked the most likely winner for much of the way, but failed to pick up when asked for her effort. Perhaps she will benefit from a more patient ride in future. (tchd 4-5)

Shatter Resistant(IRE), a 25,000euros half-brother to 1m scorer Gane Marie, and prolific 1m winner in Italy Prioloso, is already a gelding but this was a pleasing introduction. He is open to improvement and should be up to winning a similar race before the nursery season kicks in. (op 25-1)

Alfredtheordinary, a stablemate of the third, built on the form he showed when down the field in a good course-and-distance maiden on his debut and could be a reasonable type for nurseries later in the season.

Avertitop was soon about three lengths down on the favourite and was in trouble a long way out. He had previously shown plenty of ability when second at Windsor and can be given another chance. (op 5-2)

1368 SALTWELL SIGNS (S) STKS — 1m 2f 46y

2:40 (2:41) (Class 6) 3-Y-O+ — **£1,943** (£578; £288; £144) **Stalls** Low

Form — RPR

0-00 1 **Mayireneyrbel**[15] 1059 3-8-3 47 .... NickyMackay 3 — 57
(J Akehurst) *clsd on ldrs 1/2-way: rdn to ld and veered bdly lft over 1f out: styd on wl* **9/1**

0 2 2 **Prince Des Neiges (FR)**[37] 564 4-9-4 70 ....(p) WilliamBuick(5) 6 — 61+
(Ian Williams) *chsd ldr: rdn whn bdly hmpd over 1f out: rallied to retake 2nd last strides but a hld by wnr* **9/1**

-065 3 hd **Birkside**[7] 1216 4-9-9 72 .... GeorgeBaker 10 — 59
(B G Powell) *in tch: hdwy over 3f out: n.m.r whn chalng over 1f out: chsd wnr fnl f: no imp* **10/3**[1]

0103 4 7 **Bethanys Boy (IRE)**[4] 1279 6-10-0 50 .... SimonWhitworth 7 — 56+
(P A Blockley) *sn led: rdn: bdly hmpd and hdd over 1f out: nt rcvr* **6/1**

0005 5 9 **Undeterred**[34] 809 11-9-6 68 ....(b) StephenDonohoe(3) 2 — 28
(K J Burke) *towards rr: drvn and styd on fr over 2f out: nvr in contention* **9/2**[2]

00/5 6 ¾ **Lady Josh**[29] 887 4-8-11 38 .... JackDean(7) 8 — 22
(W G M Turner) *chsd ldrs: rdn 3f out: sn wknd* **33/1**

-000 7 3 **Homebred Star**[29] 887 6-9-9 36 .... AdamKirby 5 — 21
(G P Enright) *towards rr tl drvn and mod prog fnl 2f* **28/1**

0000 8 1 ¾ **Filliemou (IRE)**[10] 1152 6-9-4 33 .... RichardHughes 9 — 13
(A W Carroll) *a towards rr* **16/1**

0-03 9 8 **Baby Barry**[13] 1086 10-9-6 52 ....(p) DominicFox(3) 4 — 3
(S Parr) *chsd ldrs 6f* **15/2**

1030 10 6 **Competitor**[18] 1026 6-10-0 47 ....(v) DaneO'Neill 11 — —
(J Akehurst) *in tch: rdn 3f out: sn btn* **11/2**[3]

000- 11 45 **Bellini Star**[262] 4350 4-9-9 50 .... JimmyQuinn 1 — —
(G A Ham) *prom early: t.o* **25/1**

00/ 12 22 **Little Miss Lili**[944] 5867 6-9-4 .... AdrianMcCarthy 12 — —
(Miss Z C Davison) *prom early: t.o* **100/1**

2m 8.96s (-2.04) **Going Correction** -0.15s/f (Firm)

WFA 3 from 4yo+ 15lb — 12 Ran SP% **119.8**

Speed ratings (Par 101):102,100,100,94,87 86,84,83,76,71 35,18

CSF £85.70 TOTE £18.10: £3.80, £2.30, £1.70; EX 177.90 TRIFECTA Not won..The winner was bought in for 3,800gns. Birkside was claimed by Simon Dow for £6,000.

Owner The Hullhunter Partnership **Bred** M H D Madden And Partners **Trained** Epsom, Surrey

■ Stewards' Enquiry : Nicky Mackay two-day ban: careless riding (May 12,14)

FOCUS

A run-of-the-mill seller and not that convincing form-wise, although the winning time was 0.24 seconds faster than the following maiden, and 0.93 seconds quicker than later 56-70 handicap.

Undeterred Official explanation: jockey said gelding was hampered at start

Baby Barry Official explanation: jockey said gelding felt wrong behind

Competitor Official explanation: trainer said horse was unsuited by the firm ground

Bellini Star Official explanation: jockey said gelding ran too free

Little Miss Lili Official explanation: jockey said mare lost its action

1369 WESTERN DAILY PRESS MAIDEN STKS — 1m 2f 46y

3:10 (3:13) (Class 5) 3-Y-O — **£2,849** (£847; £423; £211) **Stalls** Low

Form — RPR

-23 1 **Eradicate (IRE)**[13] 1093 3-9-3 .... KDarley 1 — 82+
(M Johnston) *led over 1m out: pushed clr fr 2f out: easily* **1/3**[1]

3 2 4 **Haarth Sovereign (IRE)**[15] 1062 3-9-3 .... AdamKirby 4 — 74
(W R Swinburn) *led tl over 1m out: styd chsng wnr: drvn and hung lft 3f out: kpt on to hold 2nd fr over 1f out but no ch w wnr* **3/1**[2]

3 ½ **Compton Falcon** 3-9-3 .... NickyMackay 2 — 73
(G A Butler) *trckd ldrs in 3rd: drvn to dispute 2nd fr 2f out but nvr any ch w wnr: one pce and dropped to 3rd fnl f* **12/1**[3]

5- 4 15 **Boogie Board**[325] 2461 3-8-9 .... DominicFox(3) 3 — 40
(S Parr) *a in rr: no ch fnl 4f* **66/1**

2m 9.20s (-1.80) **Going Correction** -0.15s/f (Firm) — 4 Ran SP% **109.2**

Speed ratings (Par 99):101,97,97,85

CSF £1.66 TOTE £1.40; EX 1.70.

Owner A D Spence **Bred** Sir Eric Parker **Trained** Middleham Moor, N Yorks

FOCUS

An uncompetitive maiden best rated through the runner-up. The winning time was 0.24 seconds slower than the earlier seller, but 0.69 seconds faster than the following 56-70 handicap.

1370 GIFT WITH A DIFFERENCE AT SPORTINGSPIRITS.CO.UK H'CAP — 1m 2f 46y

3:40 (3:41) (Class 5) (0-70,76) 3-Y-O — **£3,238** (£963; £481; £240) **Stalls** Low

Form — RPR

40-0 1 **Lapina (IRE)**[10] 1155 3-8-4 **56** oh1 ....(b[1]) RichardMullen 2 — 59
(Pat Eddery) *t.k.h to go 3rd over 6f out: rdn to chse ldr over 1f out: kpt on u.p to ld fnl 100yds* **25/1**

04-2 2 1 ¼ **Bachnagairn**[7] 1211 3-9-3 **69** .... JamieSpencer 5 — 70
(R Charlton) *led reminders over 3f out: rdn over 2f out: hdd and fnd no ex fnl 100yds* **4/6**[1]

3242 3 9 **Grand Symphony**[11] 1131 3-9-2 **68** .... KerrinMcEvoy 1 — 52
(W Jarvis) *trckd ldr: rdn over 2f out: no imp: lost 2nd and wknd qckly over 1f out* **9/4**[2]

3251 4 5 **Beau Sancy**[7] 1218 3-9-5 **76** 6ex .... TolleyDean(5) 4 — 50
(R A Harris) *a in 4th: pushed along over 3f out: sn no ch* **6/1**[3]

2m 9.89s (-1.11) **Going Correction** -0.15s/f (Firm) — 4 Ran SP% **108.9**

Speed ratings (Par 99):98,97,89,85

CSF £44.16 TOTE £19.20; EX 45.30.

Owner Aitken, Anderson, Phillips & Vanner **Bred** W Maxwell Ervine **Trained** Nether Winchendon, Bucks

FOCUS

Very weak form for the grade and the winning time was slower than both the earlier seller and maiden. The runner-up is the best guide to the level.

Lapina(IRE) Official explanation: trainer said, regarding apparent improvement in form, that the filly was suited by the first time blinkers

1371 M J CHURCH FILLIES' H'CAP — 1m 3f 144y

4:10 (4:10) (Class 5) (0-75,74) 4-Y-O+ **£3,785** (£1,132; £566; £283; £141) **Stalls** Low

Form — RPR

116- 1 **Hanella (IRE)**[249] 4778 4-9-4 **74** .... SebSanders 1 — 83+
(R M Beckett) *trckd ldr: drvn to ld appr fnl f: styd on wl to go clr cl home* **2/1**[1]

03-1 2 2 **Love Always**[28] 903 5-9-2 **72** .... DaneO'Neill 2 — 78
(S Dow) *led: rdn over 2f out: hdd appr fnl f: sn outpcd* **9/4**[2]

0-45 3 4 **Boot 'n Toot**[32] 829 6-9-3 **73** .... JamieSpencer 7 — 73
(C A Cyzer) *hld up in rr: rdn and styd on to go 3rd over 2f out but nvr gng pce to rch ldng pair* **10/3**[3]

-002 4 nk **Sforzando**[10] 1158 6-8-6 **69** .... KristinStubbs(7) 6 — 68
(Mrs L Stubbs) *racd in 3rd tl dropped to rr and pushed along 4f out: n.d after but kpt on fnl f* **9/2**

0254 5 8 **Rose Muwasim**[32] 825 4-8-1 **60** oh12 ....(p) DominicFox(3) 3 — 46?
(S Parr) *racd in 4th tl drvn and sme prog into 3rd 4f out: nvr in contention and wknd over 2f out* **22/1**

2m 29.9s (-0.40) **Going Correction** -0.15s/f (Firm) — 5 Ran SP% **109.7**

Speed ratings (Par 100):95,93,91,90,85

CSF £6.77 TOTE £2.90: £1.70, £1.50; EX 5.50.

Owner Frank Brady **Bred** Cathal Ryan **Trained** Whitsbury, Hants

FOCUS

A modest fillies' handicap thatwas steadily run with the runner-up setting the standard.

Boot 'n Toot Official explanation: jockey said mare hung right going up straight

1372 EUROPEAN BREEDERS' FUND LANSDOWN FILLIES' STKS (LISTED RACE) — 5f 11y

4:40 (4:42) (Class 1) 3-Y-O+

£15,330 (£5,810; £2,907; £1,449; £726; £364) **Stalls** Low

Form — RPR

103- 1 **Enticing (IRE)**[206] 5802 3-8-12 105 .... JamieSpencer 6 — 115+
(W J Haggas) *trckd ldrs gng wl: led appr fnl f: drvn and sn qcknd clr: impressive* **9/4**[1]

000- 2 5 **Folga**[254] 4633 5-9-0 94 .... TPQueally 4 — 94
(J G Given) *pressed ldrs: drvn to chal fr 2f out: kpt on fnl f but no ch w wnr* **15/2**

000- 3 1 ¾ **Empress Jain**[201] 5921 4-9-0 92 .... PhilipRobinson 2 — 88
(M A Jarvis) *chsd ldrs: rdn over 2f out: styd on same pce fnl f* **13/2**[3]

1206 4 ½ **Woodnook**[38] 762 4-9-0 90 .... RichardHughes 10 — 86
(J A R Toller) *towards rr: hdwy over 2f out: kpt on fnl f but nvr gng pce to trble ldrs* **8/1**

13-0 5 ½ **Lady Lily (IRE)**[13] 1099 3-8-6 86 ow1 .... TedDurcan 12 — 81
(H R A Cecil) *s.i.s: bhd: hdwy on outside over 1f out: fin wl but nvr in contention* **9/1**

435- 6 shd **Leopoldine**[201] 5919 4-9-0 89 .... JimmyQuinn 7 — 84
(H Morrison) *in tch: pushed along 1/2-way: kpt on fnl f but nvr gng pce to be competitive* **11/1**

00-4 7 ¾ **Sweet Afton (IRE)**[11] 1125 4-9-0 93 .... MickyFenton 1 — 81
(M S Saunders) *slt ld: rdn over 2f out: hdd over 1f out and sn wknd* **12/1**

104- 8 ¾ **Mango Music**[201] 5919 4-9-0 86 .... JHBowman 5 — 78
(M R Channon) *chsd ldrs: rdn over 2f out: wknd fnl f* **14/1**

00-1 9 1 **Lady Livius (IRE)**[32] 828 4-9-0 96 .... DaneO'Neill 9 — 75
(R Hannon) *outpcd most of way* **5/1**[2]

455- **10** *2* **Bridge It Jo**[228] [5335] 3-8-5 88 .... JamesDoyle 8 64
(Miss J Feilden) *a outpcd* **50/1**

625- **11** *22* **Musical Romance (IRE)**[234] [5181] 4-9-0 73 ....(b) KDarley 3 —
(B J Meehan) *slowly away: nvr travelling and sn lost tch* **50/1**

58.75 secs (-3.75) **Going Correction** -0.35s/f (Firm) course record
WFA 3 from 4yo+ 9lb **11** Ran SP% **120.3**
Speed ratings (Par 108):116,108,105,104,103 103,102,101,99,96 61
CSF £20.03 TOTE £2.90: £1.60, £3.00, £2.50; EX 24.90 Trifecta £29.50 Pool: £791.89 - 19.04 winning units..
Owner Lael Stable **Bred** Lael Stables **Trained** Newmarket, Suffolk

FOCUS
Just an ordinary Listed contest, but Enticing was a hugely-impressive winner and broke the track record by over a second. This is rated well above average for the grade.

NOTEBOOK
Enticing(IRE) ◆ was no sure thing to train on considering she was such a precocious type last season and her dam, Superstar Leo, failed to make a three-year-old, but her trainer describes her as a "bigger, stronger sort" than her mother and she produced a stunning effort on her reappearance. Admittedly this was not a strong race, but she was shouldering 7lb penalty for last season's Molecomb success and could not have been any more impressive. Always travelling very strongly just off the furious early pace, she fairly bounded clear of her ten rivals when asked for an effort and took over a second off the track record in the process. She is sure to be aimed at many of the big sprints this season and races like the Temple Stakes and King's Stand could be on the agenda in the coming weeks. (op 3-1)
Folga, quite a progressive type, picked up some valuable back type on her return from a 254-day break, but was literally blown away by Enticing. She will not always come up against such smart rivals at this level and she could well nick a similar event at some stage this season. (op 7-1)
Empress Jain, having her first run since last October, ran right up to something like her best to pick up some black type. Like the runner-up, she should continue to go well at this sort of level. (op 9-2)
Woodnook, a much-improved performer on the All-Weather this winter, showed herself just as effective on turf with a solid effort. (op 9-1)
Lady Lily(IRE), carrying 1lb overweight, struggled to land a blow after starting slowly and might be better over 6f. (op 12-1)
Leopoldine ran a respectable race without quite proving she is up to this level. (op 12-1 tchd 14-1 and 10-1)
Sweet Afton(IRE) showed terrific early speed but could not sustain her challenge. Official explanation: jockey said filly hung right (op 10-1)
Lady Livius(IRE) could not repeat the form she showed when winning a 6f handicap on the Polytrack off a mark of 91 on her previous start and the drop in trip appeared to find her out. (tchd 6-1)
Musical Romance(IRE) Official explanation: jockey said filly bolted to post

1373 PREMPO RACING H'CAP 5f 11y
5:10 (5:11) (Class 5) (0-70,69) 3-Y-O **£3,238** (£963; £481; £240) **Stalls** Low

Form RPR

04-3 **1** **Cuppacocoa**[10] [1151] 3-9-4 **69** .... PhilipRobinson 2 76
(C G Cox) *trckd ldr: led jst ins fnl f: drvn out* **10/11**[1]

5440 **2** *1 1/2* **Hereford Boy**[20] [1004] 3-9-3 **68** .... RobertHavlin 1 69
(D K Ivory) *led: rdn 2f out: hdd jst ins fnl f: kpt on same pce* **8/1**

03-0 **3** *3/4* **Ocean Blaze**[10] [1151] 3-8-13 **64** .... AdrianMcCarthy 6 62
(B R Millman) *chsd ldrs in 3rd thrght: effrt to chal over 1f out: sn one pce* **12/1**

-544 **4** *3/4* **Slipasearcher (IRE)**[19] [1008] 3-8-6 **60** ow3........(b) StephenDonohoe(3) 3 55
(P D Evans) *towards rr: rdn 1/2-way: hdwy over 1f out: kpt on cl home: nt rch ldrs* **8/1**

-143 **5** *2 1/2* **Dualagi**[5] [1269] 3-8-11 **62** ....(p) LPKeniry 8 47
(J S Moore) *chsd ldrs: rdn 1/2-way and sn btn* **5/1**[2]

00-0 **6** *5* **Georges Pride**[7] [1207] 3-8-3 **57** oh5 ow2........(t) GregFairley(3) 7 23
(J M Bradley) *sn chsng ldrs: wknd 2f out* **20/1**

0-00 **7** *5* **Buzbury Rings**[38] [752] 3-8-9 **60** ....(p) JamieSpencer 5 6
(A M Balding) *a outpcd* **13/2**[3]

60.86 secs (-1.64) **Going Correction** -0.35s/f (Firm) **7** Ran SP% **117.1**
Speed ratings (Par 99):99,96,95,94,90 82,74
CSF £9.64 CT £56.47 TOTE £1.70: £1.20, £3.40; EX 5.60 Trifecta £26.50 Pool: £438.45 - 11.72 winning units. Place 6 £213.89, Place 5 £141.24.
Owner John And Anne Soul **Bred** A J Coleing **Trained** Lambourn, Berks

FOCUS
A modest handicap and sound but weak form for the level.
T/Plt: £1,033.70 to a £1 stake. Pool: £54,165.20. 38.25 winning tickets. T/Qpdt: £344.10 to a £1 stake. Pool: £2,511.50. 5.40 winning tickets. ST

1348 SOUTHWELL (L-H)
Tuesday, May 1

OFFICIAL GOING: Standard
Wind: Moderate, half against

1374 BETDIRECTPOKER.COM $50,000 FREEROLL CLAIMING STKS 1m (F)
2:30 (2:30) (Class 6) 4-Y-O+ **£2,184** (£644; £322) **Stalls** Low

Form RPR

-100 **1** **Just James**[27] [912] 8-8-11 64 .... AdrianTNicholls 3 62
(D Nicholls) *dwlt: reminders after 3f: hdwy over 3f out: rdn to ld wl over 1f out: drvn out* **2/1**[2]

360- **2** *hd* **Thunderwing (IRE)**[213] [5689] 5-9-5 66 .... PatCosgrave 2 70
(K R Burke) *trckd ldr: hdwy to ld wl over 2f out: rdn: hung lft and hdd wl over 1f out: drvn and kpt on wl fnl f* **11/10**[1]

00-0 **3** *12* **El Palmar**[18] [1027] 6-8-0 48 ....(v[1]) KevinGhunowa(5) 5 28
(M J Attwater) *led: rdn along 3f out: sn hdd and outpcd fnl 2f* **7/1**[3]

0-0 **4** *6* **Clear Picture**[93] [272] 4-8-10 .... NCallan 4 19
(A P Jarvis) *chsd ldng pair: rdn along over 3f out and sn wknd* **12/1**

5 *17* **Hewaar (IRE)**[676] [2898] 4-8-6 .... JamesO'Reilly(7) 6 —
(J O'Reilly) *sn outpcd and rdn along in rr: a bhd* **12/1**

1m 44.65s (0.05) **Going Correction** +0.05s/f (Slow) **5** Ran SP% **108.8**
Speed ratings (Par 101):101,100,88,82,65
CSF £4.46 TOTE £2.90: £2.40, £1.10; EX 4.30.
Owner G G N Bloodstock Ltd **Bred** Miss S N Ralphs **Trained** Sessay, N Yorks

FOCUS
A moderate bunch in this claimer. The two market leaders came well clear and the form is straightforward rated through the winner.

1375 JOHN WHITE ASSOCIATES LLP MAIDEN STKS 1m (F)
3:00 (3:00) (Class 5) 3-Y-O **£2,968** (£876; £438) **Stalls** Low

Form RPR

1 **Idle No More (USA)** 3-9-3 .... JimmyFortune 7 92+
(J H M Gosden) *chsd ldrs: smooth hdwy to ld over 2f out: pushed clr over 1f out: easily* **8/1**

52-2 **2** *8* **Vanquisher (IRE)**[10] [1166] 3-9-3 79 .... DarryllHolland 1 73
(W J Haggas) *led: rdn along 3f out: sn hdd: drvn and one pce fnl 2f* **1/1**[1]

3 *4* **Collioure (USA)** 3-8-12 .... JosedeSouza 4 59
(P F I Cole) *pushed along towards rr: hdwy over 2f out: sn rdn and kpt on appr fnl f* **14/1**

32 **4** *4* **Thunderbolt Jaxon**[28] [901] 3-8-10 .... MCGeran(7) 2 55
(P W Chapple-Hyam) *cl up: rdn along 3f out: sn wknd* **9/2**[3]

0-0 **5** *shd* **Lindhoven (USA)**[38] [764] 3-9-3 .... HayleyTurner 6 55
(C E Brittain) *bhd tl sme late hdwy* **20/1**

0 **6** *5* **Cheeky Jack (USA)**[12] [1100] 3-9-3 .... NCallan 3 43
(B J Meehan) *chsd ldng pair: rdn along over 3f out: sn wknd* **4/1**[2]

00- **7** *3* **Finlay's Footsteps**[255] [4608] 3-9-3 .... DanielTudhope 5 36
(G M Moore) *outpcd and bhd fr 1/2-way* **66/1**

P **Graham Two (IRE)** 3-9-3 .... DaleGibson 8 —
(G P Kelly) *dwlt: sn rdn along and outpcd: t.o and p.u after 2f* **100/1**

1m 42.64s (-1.96) **Going Correction** +0.05s/f (Slow) **8** Ran SP% **113.2**
Speed ratings (Par 99):111,103,99,95,94 89,86,—
CSF £16.19 TOTE £11.80: £2.40, £1.10, £2.10; EX 21.00.
Owner Stonerside Stable Llc **Bred** Stonerside Stable **Trained** Newmarket, Suffolk

FOCUS
A modest maiden, but the debutant winner impressed in easily pulling clear of the 79-rated runner-up and the winning time was outstanding for a race of its type. He is value for further than his winning margin and looks useful despite the form having been rated negatively through the runner-up.

1376 BETDIRECT.COM GET INVOLVED (S) STKS 1m 4f (F)
3:30 (3:30) (Class 6) 4-Y-O+ **£2,184** (£644; £322) **Stalls** Low

Form RPR

22/2 **1** **Mr Mischief**[56] [628] 7-8-12 80 .... LeeEnstone 13 61+
(P C Haslam) *hld up in midfield: hdwy to trck ldrs 1/2-way: effrt 3f out: led wl over 1f out: sn rdn and edgd lft: clr ent fnl f* **3/1**[1]

-364 **2** *7* **Tedstale (USA)**[22] [966] 9-8-12 60 ....(b) NCallan 8 50
(K A Ryan) *chsd ldrs: hdwy to ld over 3f out: sn rdn and hdd wl over 1f out: drvn and one pce appr fnl f* **6/1**[2]

053- **3** *2* **Orchard House (FR)**[42] [6973] 4-8-6 39 ow1........(b) GihanArnolda(7) 10 48
(J Jay) *towards rr: hdwy over 3f out: styd on fnl 2f: tk 3rd nr fin* **25/1**

05/0 **4** *1 1/4* **Newtonian (USA)**[21] [997] 8-8-12 62 .... DavidAllan 12 45
(M Brittain) *chsd ldrs: hdwy and cl up 3f out: sn rdn and ev ch tl drvn and wknd wl over 1f out* **10/1**

3431 **5** *5* **Rudry World (IRE)**[4] [1279] 4-8-12 57 .... AlanDaly 6 37
(P A Blockley) *midfield: rdn along over 4f out: drvn and no imp fnl 3f* **7/1**[3]

400- **6** *5* **Asbury Park**[38] [5770] 4-8-12 57 ....(t) HayleyTurner 4 29
(M R Bosley) *a in rr* **28/1**

354/ **7** *9* **Selkirk Grace**[910] [6524] 7-8-12 54 .... PaulMulrennan 5 15
(K A Morgan) *chsd ldrs: rdn along over 3f out: sn wknd* **6/1**[2]

-225 **8** *hd* **Starcross Maid**[14] [1078] 5-8-7 55 .... AdrianTNicholls 9 9
(J F Coupland) *hld up in rr: hdwy 5f out: rdn along and in tch 4f out: rdn over 3f out and sn btn* **3/1**[1]

0 **9** *16* **Ettrbee (IRE)**[84] [374] 5-8-7 .... RoystonFfrench 1 —
(H Alexander) *led: rdn along 5f out: hdd over 3f out and sn wknd* **150/1**

05-0 **10** *2* **Gavanello**[16] [630] 4-8-7 33 .... RussellKennemore(5) 7 —
(M C Chapman) *chsd ldrs 4f: sn lost pl and bhd* **100/1**

030/ **11** *6* **Strong Will**[43] [4105] 7-8-12 .... GrahamGibbons 3 —
(J R Holt) *prom: rdn along 1/2-way: sn wknd* **25/1**

300/ **12** *5* **Maunby Roller (IRE)**[138] [4343] 8-8-12 ....(v) JosedeSouza 2 —
(K A Morgan) *chsd ldrs: rdn along 1/2-way: sn wknd* **50/1**

0 **13** *47* **Our Flossie (IRE)**[13] [1086] 4-8-7 ....(b[1]) SilvestreDeSousa 11 —
(A D Brown) *a bhd* **100/1**

2m 41.8s (-0.29) **Going Correction** +0.05s/f (Slow) **13** Ran SP% **115.9**
Speed ratings (Par 101):102,97,96,95,91 88,82,82,71,70 66,63,31
CSF £19.67 TOTE £4.10: £1.60, £2.00, £3.00; EX 20.40.The winner was sold to M. C. Chapman for 15,200gns.
Owner Middleham Park Racing I **Bred** Mrs Maureen Barbara Walsh **Trained** Middleham Moor, N Yorks

FOCUS
A very weak affair. The winner was clear best-in at the weights and won accordingly but is rated well below his official mark.

1377 BETDIRECTPOKER.COM COME AND 'AVE SOME H'CAP 6f (F)
4:00 (4:00) (Class 5) (0-70,70) 4-Y-O+ **£3,071** (£906; £453) **Stalls** Low

Form RPR

2302 **1** **Owed**[5] [1265] 5-9-3 **69** ....(p) NCallan 6 79
(R Bastiman) *mde all: rdn and hung lft wl over 1f out: drvn ent fnl f and kpt on gamely* **7/4**[1]

1315 **2** *3/4* **Sweet Pickle**[65] [561] 6-9-2 **68** ....(e) PatCosgrave 5 76
(J R Boyle) *dwlt: hdwy 1/2-way: chsd wnr wl over 1f out and sn rdn: drvn and styd on wl fnl f* **7/1**[3]

260- **3** *4* **Word Perfect**[185] [6212] 5-9-2 **68** ....(b) DaleGibson 7 64
(M W Easterby) *cl up: rdn along over 2f out: sn drvn and one pce fr over 1f out* **8/1**

35-3 **4** *1* **Mugeba**[22] [980] 6-8-4 **56** oh1 ....(t) SilvestreDeSousa 4 49
(Miss Gay Kelleway) *towards rr: hdwy to chse ldrs over 2f out: sn rdn and no imp* **15/2**

1005 **5** *6* **Cerebus**[5] [1265] 5-9-0 **66** ....(bt) JimmyFortune 2 41
(A J McCabe) *chsd ldng pair: rdn along wl over 2f out and sn btn* **7/1**[3]

-330 **6** *2 1/2* **Royal Orissa**[10] [1165] 5-8-4 **56** .... HayleyTurner 3 24
(D Haydn Jones) *sn rdn along: a in rr* **9/2**[2]

300- **7** *5* **Joy And Pain**[174] [6396] 6-8-6 **63** ....(v) KevinGhunowa(5) 8 16
(M J Attwater) *stmbld s: hdwy on outer to chse ldrs over 3f out: rdn wl over 2f out and sn btn* **16/1**

0000 **8** *shd* **Pauvic (IRE)**[3] [1299] 4-9-4 **70** ....(v) RoystonFfrench 1 22
(Mrs A Duffield) *stmbld s: a bhd* **25/1**

1m 17.43s (0.53) **Going Correction** +0.05s/f (Slow) **8** Ran SP% **112.1**
Speed ratings (Par 103):98,97,91,90,82 79,72,72
CSF £13.89 CT £75.49 TOTE £1.90: £1.30, £1.90, £2.20; EX 7.10.
Owner Naughty Diesel Ltd **Bred** Helshaw Grange Stud, N Kent And H Phillips **Trained** Cowthorpe, N Yorks

FOCUS
A moderate handicap, run at a sound pace. The first two came clear and the form looks straightforward rated around that pair.

Joy And Pain Official explanation: jockey said gelding had stumbled leaving the stalls
Pauvic(IRE) Official explanation: jockey said gelding had stumbled leaving the stalls

1378 BETDIRECTPOKER.COM $50,000 FREEROLL H'CAP — 1m 3f (F)
4:30 (4:30) (Class 5) (0-70,70) 4-Y-0+ — **£3,071** (£906; £453) **Stalls** Low

Form — RPR

140- **1** **Sugitani (USA)**[392] [881] 5-9-1 **70**.....(b) JerryO'Dwyer(3) 4 — 82
(N B King) *rr: pushed along 1/2-way: rdn and hdwy 4f out: drvn to chse ldr over 1f out: styng on whn hmpd nr fin: jst hld: fin 2nd, shd: awrdd r* **7/1**

5411 **2** *shd* **Apex**[6] [1251] 6-8-4 **63** 6ex ow3..... HaddenFrost(7) 7 — 75+
(M Hill) *trckd ldrs: hdwy over 3f out: led over 2f out: rdn over 1f out: edgd lft nr fin: jst hld on: fin 1st, shd: disq: plcd 2nd* **4/1**[2]

1413 **3** *2½* **Mahmjra**[9] [1181] 5-9-3 **69**..... EdwardCreighton 9 — 77
(C N Allen) *led: rdn along over 3f out: hdd wl over 2f out: sn drvn and kpt on same pce* **2/1**[1]

-040 **4** *6* **Jordan's Light (USA)**[3] [1295] 4-9-4 **70**.....(v) NCallan 6 — 68
(T J Pitt) *trckd ldrs: smooth hdwy 4f out: led briefly wl over 2f out: sn rdn and hdd: wknd wl over 1f out* **9/2**[3]

0/0- **5** *3* **Rust En Vrede**[20] [4511] 8-8-8 **60**..... GrahamGibbons 5 — 54
(J J Quinn) *chsd ldrs: rdn along 4f out: sn driv en and outpcd 3f out* **20/1**

0/0- **6** *¾* **Scott**[438] [443] 6-8-3 **58**..... LiamJones(3) 3 — 50
(J Jay) *rr: hdwy and in tch 1/2-way: rdn along 4f out and sn wknd* **12/1**

000- **7** *17* **Catherines Cafe (IRE)**[190] [6128] 4-8-1 **56** oh9..... AndrewMullen(3) 1 — 21
(A C Whillans) *chsd ldr: rdn along over 4f out and sn wknd* **50/1**

8 *2½* **Investment Pearl (IRE)**[97] [6156] 4-8-10 **62**..... DarryllHolland 2 — 23
(D R Gandolfo) *a in rr* **40/1**

3-04 **9** *63* **Broughtons Folly**[76] [459] 4-9-1 **67**..... BrettDoyle 8 — —
(W J Musson) *a in rr: bhd 1/2-way: t.o fnl 3f* **15/2**

2m 28.36s (-0.54) **Going Correction** +0.05s/f (Slow) — **9** Ran SP% **112.6**
Speed ratings (Par 103):102,103,101,96,94 94,81,79,34
CSF £30.43 CT £70.20 TOTE £3.80: £1.70, £1.70, £1.20; EX 31.40.
Owner Martin Bailey **Bred** Jayeff 'B' Stables **Trained** Newmarket, Suffolk
■ Stewards' Enquiry : Hadden Frost two-day ban: careless riding (May 12,14)
Edward Creighton three-day ban: careless riding (May 12,14-15)

FOCUS
A poor handicap, run at a fair gallop but sound form rated through the third. The original placings of the first two were later reversed by the Stewards.
Scott Official explanation: jockey said gelding suffered interference shortly after the start
Broughtons Folly Official explanation: vet said filly finished lame

1379 BETDIRECTPOKER.COM GET INVOLVED APPRENTICE H'CAP — 7f (F)
5:00 (5:00) (Class 6) (0-60,60) 4-Y-0+ — **£2,388** (£705; £352) **Stalls** Low

Form — RPR

5-40 **1** **Middle Eastern**[29] [896] 5-8-8 **54**.....(p) SophieDoyle(5) 11 — 63
(P A Blockley) *in tch: hdwy whn clipped heels and stmbld bdly wl over 2f out: rcvrd to ld 2f out: sn rdn: edgd lft and kpt on fnl f* **5/1**[1]

0001 **2** *1½* **Charlie Delta**[22] [978] 4-9-2 **60**.....(b) JackMitchell(3) 3 — 65
(J R Boyle) *towards rr: rdn along 1/2-way: gd hdwy 2f out: styd on wl u.p fnl f: nt rch wnr* **11/2**[2]

026- **3** *¾* **Divine White**[263] [4329] 4-8-9 **53**.....(p) AshleyHamblett(3) 9 — 56
(P Bowen) *chsd ldrs: rdn along 2f out: sn drvn and one pce fr over 1f out* **10/1**

0100 **4** *3½* **Government (IRE)**[34] [812] 6-8-3 **47**..... NicolPolli(3) 7 — 41
(M C Chapman) *led: rdn along and hdd wl over 2f out: grad wknd* **14/1**

-000 **5** *hd* **Wassfa**[18] [1025] 4-8-9 **55**..... WilliamCarson(5) 6 — 48
(C E Brittain) *towards rr tl styd on fnl 2f: nrst fin* **9/1**

-500 **6** *5* **Jellytot (USA)**[22] [980] 4-8-13 **57**..... JamesO'Reilly(3) 4 — 37
(J O'Reilly) *cl up: rdn and ev ch over 2f out: sn drvn and wknd* **10/1**

001- **7** *nk* **Prospect Court**[239] [5062] 5-8-13 **57**..... NeilBrown(3) 2 — 37
(A C Whillans) *cl up on inner: led briefly wl over 2f out: sn hdd & wknd* **15/2**[3]

0030 **8** *2½* **Kingsmaite**[7] [1221] 6-8-1 **49**.....(bt) LeeTopliss(7) 10 — 22
(S R Bowring) *a towards rr* **11/1**

5656 **9** *2½* **Ceredig**[7] [1207] 4-8-9 **53**..... LukeMorris(3) 8 — 20
(P W Hiatt) *chsd ldrs: rdn along 1/2-way: wknd over 2f out* **10/1**

0-06 **10** *hd* **Sowerby**[42] [715] 5-8-0 **46** oh1.....(b) PatrickDonaghy(5) 12 — 12
(M Brittain) *stdd s: hld up: a in rr* **33/1**

-005 **11** *1* **Barzak (IRE)**[56] [627] 7-8-3 **47** oh1 ow1.....(b) RussellKennemore(3) 5 — 10
(S R Bowring) *s.i.s: a bhd* **12/1**

0050 **12** *23* **Capital Lass**[5] [1265] 4-8-3 **49**..... MCGeran(5) 1 — —
(A J McCabe) *lost many lengths at s: a wl bhd* **14/1**

1m 31.32s (0.52) **Going Correction** +0.05s/f (Slow) — **12** Ran SP% **113.4**
Speed ratings (Par 101):99,97,96,92,92 86,86,83,80,80 79,52
CSF £30.09 CT £265.78 TOTE £4.90: £2.30, £1.60, £3.40; EX 24.70 Place 6 £9.10, Place 5 £7.97.
Owner Isla & Colin Cage **Bred** Mrs L A Sadler **Trained** Lambourn, Berks

FOCUS
A weak handicap, confined to apprentice riders, but fairly sound. The winner did very well to score considering he clipped heels on the final bend.
T/Plt: £4.90 to a £1 stake. Pool: £48,441.30. 7,184.00 winning tickets. T/Qpdt: £3.20 to a £1 stake. Pool: £2,479.00. 561.60 winning tickets. JR

1360 WOLVERHAMPTON (A.W) (L-H)
Tuesday, May 1

OFFICIAL GOING: Standard
Wind: Fresh, half against Weather: Fine

1380 PERTEMPS PEOPLE DEVELOPMENT HANDS & HEELS APPRENTICE SERIES H'CAP — 1m 1f 103y(P)
6:30 (6:31) (Class 6) (0-50,51) 4-Y-0+ — **£2,388** (£705; £352) **Stalls** Low

Form — RPR

4021 **1** **Jarvo**[5] [1271] 6-8-8 **51** 6ex..... SamuelDrury(5) 1 — 58
(I W McInnes) *a.p: led jst over 2f out: clr wl over 1f out: jst hld on* **5/1**[2]

0002 **2** *hd* **Veba (USA)**[5] [1271] 4-8-5 **46** oh1..... LauraReynolds(3) 4 — 54+
(M D I Usher) *hld up and bhd: nt clr run over 2f out: hdwy wl over 1f out: r.o wl ins fnl f: jst failed* **9/2**[1]

00-0 **3** *1¾* **Don Pasquale**[35] [804] 5-8-8 **46** oh1..... SoniaEaton 8 — 49
(J T Stimpson) *hld up in tch: ev ch 2f out: one pce fnl f* **40/1**

0000 **4** *2* **Fire At Will**[7] [1210] 5-8-8 **46** oh1..... JamieHamblett 10 — 45
(A W Carroll) *hld up in mid-div: hdwy 3f out: swtchd lft wl over 1f out: no ex wl ins fnl f* **10/1**

0603 **5** *2* **Kilmeena Magic**[36] [789] 5-8-3 **46** oh1..... Julie-AnneCumine(5) 3 — 41
(J C Fox) *hld up and bhd: hdwy on ins 2f out: wknd fnl f* **9/2**[1]

33-2 **6** *¾* **Lady Duxyana**[7] [1210] 4-8-8 **46** oh1.....(v) FrankiePickard 7 — 40
(M D I Usher) *hld up and bhd: stdy hdwy 5f out: wknd wl over 1f out* **8/1**[3]

/0-0 **7** *7* **Be Wise Girl**[22] [976] 6-8-9 **50**..... MarkCoumbe(3) 9 — 30
(A W Carroll) *led 1f: chsd ldr: led over 4f out tl jst over 2f out: wknd wl over 1f out* **20/1**

33-0 **8** *2½* **Coronation Flight**[17] [1045] 4-8-8 **49**..... JamesRogers(3) 6 — 24
(F P Murtagh) *s.i.s: hld up in rr: hdwy on wd outside 3f out: sn wknd* **10/1**

0000 **9** *1½* **Crusoe (IRE)**[3] [1311] 10-8-5 **46** oh1.....(b) AdeleRothery(3) 11 — 18
(A Sadik) *prom: pushed along over 5f out: wknd over 3f out* **40/1**

530- **10** *1¼* **Boucheen**[140] [6799] 4-8-5 **46** oh1..... JohnCavanagh(3) 12 — 15
(Ms Deborah J Evans) *half-rrd s: rcvrd to ld after 1f: hdd over 4f out: sn rdn: wknd 2f out* **16/1**

0-03 **11** *1* **Ronsard (IRE)**[7] [1206] 5-8-5 **46**..... BernadetteQuinn(3) 5 — 13
(P D Evans) *a bhd* **9/2**[1]

00/0 **12** *8* **Backlash**[20] [1002] 6-8-8 **46** oh1..... JosephWalsh 2 — —
(A W Carroll) *bhd fnl 4f* **33/1**

2m 0.75s (-1.87) **Going Correction** -0.25s/f (Stan) — **12** Ran SP% **119.0**
Speed ratings (Par 101):98,97,96,94,92 92,85,83,82,81 80,73
CSF £26.85 CT £810.13 TOTE £6.00: £1.20, £2.80, £12.80; EX 34.40.
Owner F S W Partnership **Bred** Lloyd Farm Stud **Trained** Catwick, E Yorks
■ Sam Drury's first winner.
■ Stewards' Enquiry : Mark Coumbe one-day ban: failed to ride to draw (May 12)

FOCUS
Plating-class form and a repeat one-two from Yarmouth five days earlier, form that sets the level.
Boucheen Official explanation: jockey said gelding missed the break

1381 BETDIRECT.COM CLASSIFIED STKS — 1m 141y(P)
7:00 (7:00) (Class 7) 3-Y-0+ — **£2,047** (£604; £302) **Stalls** Low

Form — RPR

6400 **1** **Jools**[22] [975] 9-9-7 44..... HayleyTurner 8 — 53
(D K Ivory) *hld up and bhd: hdwy whn swtchd lft wl over 1f out: r.o to ld nr fin* **8/1**

0660 **2** *nk* **Shannon Arms (USA)**[7] [1210] 6-9-4 45..... AndrewMullen(3) 2 — 53
(R Brotherton) *led: clr over 6f out: rdn 1f out: ct nr fin* **13/2**[3]

0025 **3** *½* **Dexileos (IRE)**[11] [1119] 8-9-7 45.....(t) FergusSweeney 11 — 51
(David Pinder) *a.p: rdn 2f out: kpt on ins fnl f* **14/1**

0004 **4** *1¾* **Pajada**[11] [1119] 3-8-7 45..... RichardSmith 12 — 45
(M D I Usher) *a.p: rdn 3f out: kpt on same pce fnl 2f* **10/1**

4-04 **5** *1* **Fairy Monarch (IRE)**[11] [1132] 8-9-2 44.....(b) RoryMoore(5) 13 — 45
(P T Midgley) *hld up and bhd: hdwy over 3f out: sn rdn: one pce fnl 2f* **5/2**[1]

-005 **6** *½* **Lady's Law**[40] [728] 4-9-7 43..... ChrisCatlin 1 — 44
(Rae Guest) *hld up in tch: rdn and no real prog fnl 2f* **15/2**

400 **7** *2* **Jonny Behave**[52] [661] 3-8-7 45..... JamesDoyle 4 — 37
(I A Wood) *prom: rdn over 2f out: wknd 1f out* **22/1**

6-00 **8** *2½* **Alisdanza**[17] [1045] 5-9-0 45..... SladeO'Hara(7) 9 — 34
(N Wilson) *a towards rr* **10/1**

000- **9** *6* **Hesaguru (IRE)**[222] [5495] 3-8-7 45..... VHalliday 6 — 18
(J O'Reilly) *prom: rdn over 3f out: sn wknd* **40/1**

-000 **10** *1* **Mum's Memories**[28] [910] 3-8-7 43..... TPQueally 10 — 16
(W J Musson) *a bhd* **10/1**

-500 **11** *¾* **Meathop (IRE)**[7] [1232] 3-8-7 45..... CatherineGannon 5 — 14
(R F Fisher) *bhd fnl 3f* **33/1**

00-0 **12** *15* **Wee Ziggy**[3] [1311] 4-9-7 45..... SebSanders 3 — —
(M Mullineaux) *hld up in mid-div: clipped heels after 1f: pushed along whn nt clr run on ins over 3f out: sn bhd* **20/1**

5400 **13** *10* **Hill Of Almhuim (IRE)**[38] [751] 4-9-7 43.....(v) RobbieFitzpatrick 7 — —
(Peter Grayson) *s.s: t.o fnl 4f* **6/1**[2]

1m 50.45s (-1.31) **Going Correction** -0.25s/f (Stan)
WFA 3 from 4yo+ 14lb — **13** Ran SP% **127.5**
Speed ratings (Par 97):95,94,94,92,91 91,89,87,82,81 80,67,58
CSF £60.91 TOTE £8.10: £2.90, £2.50, £5.20; EX 74.30.
Owner Dean Ivory **Bred** Tsarina Stud **Trained** Radlett, Herts
■ Stewards' Enquiry : Catherine Gannon one-day ban: careless riding (May 12)

FOCUS
Another weak race but it was run at a good gallop thanks to Shannon Arms and the form looks sound rated around the third and fourth.
Meathop(IRE) Official explanation: jockey said gelding hung left-handed throughout

1382 BETDIRECTPOKER.COM COME AND AVE SOME H'CAP — 7f 32y(P)
7:30 (7:30) (Class 5) (0-70,70) 4-Y-0+ — **£3,238** (£963; £481; £240) **Stalls** High

Form — RPR

0530 **1** **Sailor King (IRE)**[15] [1063] 5-9-1 **67**..... JimCrowley 6 — 82+
(D K Ivory) *hld up in mid-div: hdwy 2f out: shkn up to ld jst over 1f out: pushed clr ins fnl f* **4/1**[1]

3325 **2** *3* **Parkview Love (USA)**[10] [1162] 6-9-4 **70**.....(v) DeanMcKeown 3 — 74
(D Shaw) *hld up and bhd: hdwy on ins whn nt clr run wl over 1f out: rdn and r.o to take 2nd wl ins fnl f: no ch w wnr* **7/1**[3]

0-54 **3** *1½* **Norcroft**[6] [1252] 5-8-12 **64**.....(p) DMylonas 2 — 64
(Mrs C A Dunnett) *led early: a.p: rdn to ld wl over 1f out: sn hdd: one pce* **9/1**

0110 **4** *1* **Doctor's Cave**[47] [681] 5-8-10 **62**.....(b) SebSanders 9 — 60
(K O Cunningham-Brown) *sn led: rdn and hdd wl over 1f out: no ex ins fnl f* **12/1**

0643 **5** *shd* **General Feeling (IRE)**[7] [1227] 6-8-4 **56** oh2..... SilvestreDeSousa 4 — 53
(M Mullineaux) *s.s: rdn and hdwy over 1f out: one pce fnl f* **17/2**

1100 **6** *shd* **Lii Najma**[38] [757] 4-9-2 **68**..... TedDurcan 7 — 65
(C E Brittain) *prom: ev ch over 2f out: rdn over 1f out: wknd fnl f* **10/1**

0610 **7** *¾* **Stoic Leader (IRE)**[10] [1157] 7-9-1 **67**..... J-PGuillambert 8 — 62
(R F Fisher) *hld up in mid-div: rdn over 2f out: btn whn nt clr run ins fnl f* **7/1**[3]

31-0 **8** *½* **Reeling N' Rocking (IRE)**[30] [865] 4-8-11 **68**..... PatrickHills(5) 1 — 62
(B W Hills) *hld up and bhd: short-lived effrt on ins wl over 1f out* **9/2**[2]

0022 **9** *¾* **Mistral Sky**[7] [1226] 8-8-11 **63**.....(v) HayleyTurner 10 — 55
(Stef Liddiard) *chsd ldr tl over 3f out: wknd wl over 1f out* **10/1**

220- **10** *2* **Snow Bunting**[130] [6919] 9-8-6 **58**..... TPQueally 5 — 45
(Jedd O'Keeffe) *a bhd* **14/1**

1m 27.81s (-2.59) **Going Correction** -0.25s/f (Stan) — **10** Ran SP% **116.2**
Speed ratings (Par 103):104,100,98,97,97 97,96,96,95,92
CSF £31.91 CT £238.38 TOTE £4.60: £1.50, £2.00, £2.70; EX 56.30.
Owner John Stocker **Bred** Janus Bloodstock **Trained** Radlett, Herts

FOCUS
A modest handicap but it was won in good style by Sailor King, who travelled strongly. The winner and the fairly reliable runner-up give a good guide to the level of the form.

The Form Book, Raceform Ltd, Compton, RG20 6NL

1383 BETDIRECTPOKER.COM GET INVOLVED H'CAP 5f 216y(P)

7:55 (7:55) (Class 5) (0-75,75) 3-Y-O £3,154 (£944; £472; £236; £117) Stalls Low

Form RPR

60-5 **1** **Game Lady**[10] 1151 3-8-9 **66** SebSanders 3 70
(I A Wood) *mde all: rdn over 1f out: drvn out* **9/1**

22-5 **2** *nk* **Napoleon Dynamite (IRE)**[18] 1022 3-8-6 **68** PatrickHills(5) 4 71
(J W Hills) *chsd wnr: rdn and hung lft over 1f out: nt qckn ins fnl f* **5/2**[2]

6325 **3** *3* **Fractured Foxy**[12] 1108 3-8-10 **72** NataliaGemelova(5) 2 66
(J J Quinn) *chsd ldrs: rdn and one pce fnl 2f* **3/1**[3]

50-2 **4** *1* **Tracer**[38] 752 3-9-1 **72** PatDobbs 1 63
(R Hannon) *hld up in tch: rdn over 2f out: one pce* **2/1**[1]

11-4 **5** *3* **Tipsy Prince**[29] 885 3-9-4 **75** FergusSweeney 6 57
(David Pinder) *s.i.s: a bhd* **13/2**

010- **6** *6* **Smash N'Grab (IRE)**[210] 5747 3-8-4 **61** DO'Donohoe 5 25
(K A Ryan) *prom: rdn over 2f out: wknd wl over 1f out* **14/1**

1m 14.48s (-1.33) **Going Correction** -0.25s/f (Stan) 6 Ran SP% **116.9**
Speed ratings (Par 99):98,97,93,92,88 80
CSF £33.27 TOTE £9.50: £5.20, £1.60; EX 71.40.
Owner C S Tateson **Bred** The Hon E J Wills **Trained** Upper Lambourn, Berks

FOCUS
A competitive little handicap run at a good pace and rated through the reliable third.

1384 BETDIRECTPOKER.COM $50,000 FREEROLL H'CAP 5f 20y(P)

8:25 (8:25) (Class 6) (0-50,50) 4-Y-O+ £2,388 (£705; £352) Stalls Low

Form RPR

0146 **1** **Spirit Of Coniston**[29] 892 4-8-4 **47** (b) DuranFentiman(5) 5 57
(C J Teague) *hld up in mid-div: hdwy over 1f out: rdn to ld wl ins fnl f: r.o* **16/1**

060- **2** *¾* **Miss Mujahid Times**[182] 6274 4-8-12 **50** (p) SilvestreDeSousa 6 57
(A D Brown) *a.p: rdn over 1f out: r.o to take 2nd towards fin* **20/1**

35-4 **3** *1 ½* **Desert Dust**[89] 317 4-8-12 **50** BrettDoyle 13 52
(R M H Cowell) *chsd ldr: led 2f out: rdn and hdd wl ins fnl f: no ex* **11/1**

3042 **4** *1 ¼* **Beamsley Beacon**[10] 1163 6-8-12 **50** (bt) PaulFessey 11 47
(S T Mason) *chsd ldrs: rdn wl over 1f out: one pce fnl f* **12/1**

0555 **5** *shd* **Lady Hopeful (IRE)**[39] 746 5-8-9 **47** (b) RobbieFitzpatrick 12 44
(Peter Grayson) *s.s: rdn over 1f out: kpt on ins fnl f* **16/1**

6345 **6** *shd* **Muktasb (USA)**[11] 1120 6-8-12 **50** (v) DeanMcKeown 9 46
(D Shaw) *s.s: hld up: stdy hdwy on outside over 2f out: rdn over 1f out: one pce fnl f* **5/1**[2]

0-40 **7** *shd* **Ruby's Dream**[12] 1112 5-8-7 **50** (p) KevinGhunowa(5) 4 46
(J M Bradley) *a.p: rdn and no ex ins fnl f* **14/1**

40-6 **8** *shd* **Seven No Trumps**[12] 1112 10-8-12 **50** HayleyTurner 3 46
(J M Bradley) *bhd: sme hdwy over 1f out: one pce fnl f* **20/1**

4302 **9** *nk* **Dysonic (USA)**[29] 892 5-8-12 **50** (v) TedDurcan 1 45
(J Balding) *hld up in tch: rdn whn nt clr run briefly on ins jst over 1f out: one pce* **11/8**[1]

0-24 **10** *4* **Navigation (IRE)**[78] 441 5-8-6 **47** (b) SaleemGolam(3) 8 27
(T J Etherington) *s.s: a in rr* **7/1**[3]

036- **11** *2* **Miacarla**[243] 4948 4-8-8 **46** ChrisCatlin 10 19
(A Berry) *led: hdd 2f out: wknd ins fnl f: eased* **33/1**

61.71 secs (-1.11) **Going Correction** -0.25s/f (Stan) 11 Ran SP% **118.2**
Speed ratings (Par 101):98,96,94,92,92 92,91,91,91,84 81
CSF £300.27 CT £3701.24 TOTE £20.00: £3.80, £8.80, £4.20; EX 583.00.
Owner Richardson Kelly O'Gara Partnership **Bred** Green Square Racing **Trained** Station Town, Co Durham

FOCUS
This looked more open than the betting suggested and the pace was not that strong, resulting in the hold-up horses being at a bit of a disadvantage. However, the form looks sound if modest.
Muktasb(USA) Official explanation: jockey said gelding missed the break

1385 BETDIRECTCASINO.COM H'CAP 1m 1f 103y(P)

8:55 (8:55) (Class 5) (0-75,78) 4-Y-O+ £3,238 (£963; £481; £240) Stalls Low

Form RPR

22-1 **1** **William's Way**[9] 1181 5-9-7 **78** 6ex SebSanders 8 89
(I A Wood) *hld up and bhd: hdwy on outside 2f out: rdn to ld jst over 1f out: rdn out* **7/1**[3]

045- **2** *2 ½* **Oscillator**[237] 5109 4-9-2 **73** NickyMackay 1 79
(G A Butler) *hld up in mid-div: hdwy 2f out: rdn and ev ch jst over 1f out: nt qckn* **4/1**[2]

53-4 **3** *1 ½* **Merrymadcap (IRE)**[7] 1209 5-9-4 **75** TedDurcan 6 78
(M Blanshard) *hld up towards rr: smooth hdwy over 2f out: rdn over 1f out: one pce fnl f* **4/1**[2]

1260 **4** *hd* **Pop Music (IRE)**[48] 675 4-8-11 **68** (p) JamesDoyle 3 71
(Miss J Feilden) *chsd ldr: led 3f out: rdn 2f out: hdd jst over 1f out: no ex* **7/1**[3]

100- **5** *1* **Luna Landing**[179] 6319 4-9-2 **73** DaleGibson 4 74
(Jedd O'Keeffe) *hld up in mid-div: pushed along over 3f out: nt clr run and lost pl over 2f out: styd on ins fnl f* **9/1**

3 **6** *1 ½* **Rio (IRE)**[10] 1167 5-8-2 **62** AndrewElliott(3) 2 60
(J Balding) *led early: prom: nt clr run and lost pl over 2f out: n.d after* **7/2**[1]

210- **7** *1* **Pactolos Way**[207] 5786 4-9-1 **72** JimCrowley 5 68
(P R Chamings) *hld up in tch: rdn and wnt 2nd 2f out: wknd over 1f out* **16/1**

-500 **8** *4* **Fantasy Ride**[41] 726 5-9-1 **72** JimmyQuinn 7 60
(J Pearce) *s.i.s: hld up and bhd: nt clr run on ins fr 2f out tl swtchd rt over 1f out: nt rcvr* **10/1**

00-0 **9** *6* **Highest Regard**[17] 1042 5-8-8 **70** (p) JamieMoriarty(5) 9 46
(N P McCormack) *sn led: hdd 3f out: rdn and wknd 2f out* **33/1**

1m 59.72s (-2.90) **Going Correction** -0.25s/f (Stan) 9 Ran SP% **115.1**
Speed ratings (Par 103):102,99,98,98,97 96,95,91,86
CSF £35.02 CT £127.91 TOTE £7.80: £1.30, £1.40, £1.50; EX 48.70.
Owner Lewis Caterers **Bred** Lewis Caterers **Trained** Upper Lambourn, Berks

FOCUS
Not a bad handicap and quite competitive. The first two look capable of better and the form appears sound.
Rio(IRE) Official explanation: jockey said gelding was denied a clear run
Fantasy Ride Official explanation: jockey said gelding was denied a clear run

1386 BETDIRECTPOKER.COM $50,000 FREEROLL MEDIAN AUCTION MAIDEN FILLIES' STKS 7f 32y(P)

9:20 (9:21) (Class 6) 3-4-Y-O £2,184 (£644; £322) Stalls High

Form RPR

0- **1** **Fuschia**[187] 6187 3-8-9 SebSanders 4 76
(R Charlton) *sn led: edgd rt wl over 1f out: rdn out* **7/2**[2]

30-2 **2** *1 ½* **Cassiara**[12] 1105 3-8-9 **78** KDarley 5 72
(J Pearce) *sn prom: chsd wnr over 2f out: sn rdn: nt qckn ins fnl f* **1/3**[1]

43-0 **3** *5* **House Maiden (IRE)**[21] 996 3-8-9 **60** TedDurcan 1 59
(D M Simcock) *led early: lost pl over 3f out: wnt 3rd over 1f out: no ch w ldng pair* **14/1**

0-4 **4** *2* **Bonnet O'Bonnie**[9] 1175 3-8-9 DaleGibson 6 54
(J Mackie) *hld up: rdn and short-lived effrt on outside 2f out* **12/1**[3]

0- **5** *7* **Zameliana**[343] 1912 3-8-4 KevinGhunowa(5) 3 36
(Dr J R J Naylor) *w ldr tl rdn 3f out: wknd 2f out* **100/1**

6 *1 ¼* **Yurchenko** 3-8-9 TPQueally 2 32
(M Wellings) *t.k.h: hdwy over 3f out: rdn and wknd wl over 1f out* **40/1**

1m 28.38s (-2.02) **Going Correction** -0.25s/f (Stan) 6 Ran SP% **115.0**
Speed ratings (Par 98):101,99,93,91,83 81
CSF £5.19 TOTE £6.40: £1.20, £1.10; EX 7.40 Place 6 £1,187.08, Place 5 £406.21.
Owner D J Deer **Bred** D J And Mrs Deer **Trained** Beckhampton, Wilts

FOCUS
An ordinary maiden best rated through the 60-rated third with the runner-up not appearing to run to previous turf form.
House Maiden(IRE) Official explanation: jockey said saddle slipped
T/Plt: £5,383.90 to a £1 stake. Pool: £58,633.25. 7.95 winning tickets. T/Qpdt: £460.30 to a £1 stake. Pool: £4,105.90. 6.60 winning tickets. KH

FRANKFURT (L-H)

Tuesday, May 1

OFFICIAL GOING: Good

1387a FRUHJAHRSPREIS DES BANKHAUS METZLER (GROUP 3) 1m 2f

4:10 (4:20) 3-Y-O £21,622 (£6,757; £3,378; £2,027)

RPR

1 **Shrek (GER)** 3-9-0 EPedroza 5 97
(A Wohler, Germany) *racd in 4th: r.o fr over 1f out to ld cl home* **6/5**[1]

2 *¾* **Axxos (GER)**[177] 3-9-0 AStarke 9 96
(P Schiergen, Germany) *trckd ldr: 3rd st: led wl over 1f out: hrd rdn fnl f: unable qck and ct cl home* **115/10**

3 *2 ½* **Allanit (GER)** 3-9-0 THellier 1 91
(J Hirschberger, Germany) *set gd pce: led to wl over 1f out: r.o at one pce* **38/10**[2]

4 *1* **Appel Au Maitre (FR)**[198] 3-9-0 EddieAhern 8 90
(Wido Neuroth, Norway) *a.p: 2nd st: kpt on at one pce fr over 1f out* **11/2**[3]

5 *1 ¼* **Lord Hill (GER)**[193] 6092 3-9-0 HGrewe 3 87
(C Zeitz) *towards rr tl sme prog fnl 1 1/2f: nvr nr to chal* **154/10**

6 *hd* **Global Champion**[198] 5998 3-9-0 J-PCarvalho 6 87
(Mario Hofer, Germany) *hdwy 4f out: 6th st: one pce fnl 2f* **124/10**

7 *1 ½* **Montalembert (USA)**[157] 6599 3-9-0 JohnEgan 2 84
(J S Moore) *plld hrd early: 5th st: sn wknd* **106/10**

8 *6* **Marzipan (GER)**[254] 3-9-0 FilipMinarik 10 74
(P Schiergen, Germany) *a bhd* **98/10**

9 *4* **Perdono (USA)**[170] 6456 3-9-0 KKerekes 4 66
(A Wohler, Germany) *a bhd* **104/10**

10 *3* **Classic Caro (GER)** 3-9-0 MSuerland 7 61
(Frau Marion Rotering, Germany) *a bhd* **39/1**

2m 7.03s (-1.54) 10 Ran SP% **132.4**
(including 10 Euro stake): WIN 22; PL 14, 25, 19; SF 134.
Owner Frau C Ostermann-Richter **Bred** Frau C Ostermann-Richter **Trained** Germany

NOTEBOOK
Montalembert(USA), who won a conditions race on Polytrack on his final start at two, was taking a step up in grade and ruined his chance by failing to settle in the early stages.

1085 SAINT-CLOUD (L-H)

Tuesday, May 1

OFFICIAL GOING: Soft

1388a PRIX CLEOPATRE (GROUP 3) 1m 2f 110y

1:20 (1:20) 3-Y-O+ Fillies £27,027 (£10,811; £8,108; £5,405; £2,703)

RPR

1 **Vadapolina (FR)**[23] 3-8-9 CSoumillon 1 111+
(A Fabre, France) *racd in 3rd: smooth hdwy to ld 2 1/2f out: sn clr: easily* **7/10**[1]

2 *2 ½* **Chill (FR)**[30] 879 3-8-9 C-PLemaire 3 102
(J-C Rouget, France) *hld up in 6th: styd on to take 2nd ins fnl f: no ch w wnr* **54/10**[3]

3 *1 ½* **Terra Incognita**[23] 3-8-9 JMurtagh 5 99
(Y De Nicolay, France) *racd in 4th: rdn and ev ch briefly 2 1/2f out: one pce: lost 2nd ins fnl f* **79/10**

4 *1 ½* **Fontcia (FR)**[22] 989 3-8-9 SPasquier 4 96
(D Sepulchre, France) *racd in 5th: rdn to dispute 3rd briefly over 1 1/2f out: sn btn: lft 4th 100yds out* **12/1**

5 *6* **Sismix (IRE)**[22] 989 3-8-9 OPeslier 2 86
(C Laffon-Parias, France) *led: jnd 1/2-way: led again 3f out: hdd 2 1/2f out: wknd* **41/10**[2]

6 *10* **Posamina (FR)**[14] 3-8-9 MSautjeau 6 68
(A Fabre, France) *pressed ldr tl disp ld 1/2-way: hdd 3f out: wknd* **7/10**[1]

P **Bold Girl (IRE)**[22] 989 3-8-9 (b) TJarnet 7 —
(H-A Pantall, France) *hld up in last: btn but styng on at one pce in 4th whn broke leg 100yds out: dead* **25/1**

2m 10.3s (-9.30) 7 Ran SP% **175.7**
PARI-MUTUEL: WIN 1.70 (coupled with Posamina); PL 1.20, 1.90; DF 4.30.
Owner H H Aga Khan **Bred** Snc Lagardere Elevage **Trained** Chantilly, France

NOTEBOOK
Vadapolina(FR) swept her six rivals aside in this truly-run race and could have won by at least five lengths but for being eased inside the final furlong. Cerainly Classic material, she has done well since her seasonal debut and will now go for the Prix de Diane, providing the going is good.
Chill(FR) put up a decent effort in the straight and took second place well inside the final furlong, but she never had a chance of catching the winner. The trip might have been a little long and the going a little on the lively side for her.
Terra Incognita, given every possible chance, could not go with the winner when things quickened up in the straight. She stayed on one-paced and tired inside the final furlong.
Fontcia(FR), held up for much of the race, made some late progress in the straight but never looked like troubling the first three past the post.

1389a PRIX DU MUGUET (GROUP 2) 1m

3:05 (3:04) 4-Y-0+ **£50,068** (£19,324; £9,223; £6,149; £3,074)

RPR

1 **Racinger (FR)**[29] [897] 4-8-11 .... LDettori 5 118
(F Head, France) *disp ld tl hdd over 4f out: disp ld again jst over 1 1/2f out tl narrowly hdd over 1f out: rallied to ld fnl 80yds* **37/10**[2]

2 *nk* **Turtle Bowl (IRE)**[29] [897] 5-8-11 .... DBoeuf 8 117
(F Rohaut, France) *hld up in rr: hdwy on ins to go 6th st: disp ld jst over 1 1/2f out tl led narrowly over 1f out: hdd 80yds out: no ex* **5/1**[3]

3 *1 1/2* **Passager (FR)**[29] [897] 4-8-11 .... C-PLemaire 6 114
(Mme C Head-Maarek, France) *racd in 5th: 7th st: kpt on wl fr over 1f out* **59/10**

4 *1 1/2* **Gwenseb (FR)**[29] [897] 4-8-8 .... OPeslier 4 108
(C Laffon-Parias, France) *hld up in 7th: 4th st: ev ch briefly jst over 1 1/2f out: one pce* **21/1**

5 *1 1/2* **Lateral**[220] [5543] 4-9-1 .... SPasquier 9 112
(P Schiergen, Germany) *hld up in 9th: last st: effrt on outside fr 2f out: kpt on clsng stages* **64/10**

6 *1 1/2* **Krataios (FR)**[184] [6250] 7-9-1 .... MBlancpain 7 109
(C Laffon-Parias, France) *racd in 6th: 8th st: rdn and one pce fnl 1 1/2f* **16/1**

7 *2 1/2* **Kentucky Dynamite (USA)**[240] [5049] 4-8-11 .... CSoumillon 3 100
(A De Royer-Dupre, France) *racd in 4th: 5th st: sn pushed along and outpcd: modest late hdwy* **28/10**[1]

8 *3/4* **Marchand D'Or (FR)**[31] [860] 4-9-4 .... DBonilla 10 106
(F Head, France) *hld up in last: 9th st: hdwy on ins to dispute 4th briefly over 1f out: wknd* **9/1**

9 *1 1/2* **New Girlfriend (IRE)**[185] [6230] 4-8-8 .... TThulliez 2 93
(Robert Collet, France) *racd in 3rd: wknd 1 1/2f out* **21/1**

10 *10* **Fastmambo (USA)**[16] 4-8-11 .... AMalenfant 1 76
(F Head, France) *disp ld tl led over 4f out: hdd jst over 1 1/2f out: wknd and eased* **9/1**

1m 39.1s (-8.40) **10** Ran SP% **127.2**
PARI-MUTUEL: WIN 4.70; PL 1.60, 1.70, 1.80; DF 9.00.
Owner P Goral **Bred** Mme Rene Geffroy **Trained** France

NOTEBOOK

Racinger(FR) never ceases to progress and is gradually going up a scale which could end with a Group 1 victory by the end of the season. Always perfectly placed and handy, he hit the front at the two-furlong marker and then ran on bravely hold the runner-up. This was his second Group success of the season and connections may be tempted by the Lockinge Stakes, but a more likely target now is the Queen Anne Stakes at Royal Ascot.
Turtle Bowl(IRE), held up out the back, was given an awful lot to do in the straight. He began to make rapid progress from a furlong and a half out to challenge the winner, but he was never able to take the lead. He has now had four runs this season and is likely to be given a little rest, before returning for the Prix Jacques-Le-Marois at Deauville in August.
Passager(FR) did not appear on the scene until the final furlong and a half. In mid-division early on, he put in his best work at the finish but was once again beaten by two old rivals. Possibly a longer trip might be an advantage in future.
Gwenseb(FR), a Group winner at two, has been running well in good class company since, but she is always beaten by the three who finished ahead of her on this occasion. She was putting in her best work at the finish but was run out of third place in the final stages.

15 ASCOT (R-H)

Wednesday, May 2

OFFICIAL GOING: Good to firm
Wind: brisk behind

1390 WATERHOMES.COM GARTER CONDITIONS STKS 5f

2:10 (2:10) (Class 3) 2-Y-0
£7,478 (£2,239; £1,119; £560; £279; £140) **Stalls** Low

Form RPR

1 **1** **Mount Pleasure (USA)**[9] [1201] 2-9-1 .... JimmyFortune 6 92
(J A Osborne) *lw: towards rr: drvn and hdwy on outside fr 2f out: str run fnl f to ld cl home* **6/1**[3]

4 **2** *nk* **Littlemisssunshine (IRE)**[13] [1101] 2-8-7 ow1.............. JohnEgan 8 83
(J S Moore) *lw: chsd ldrs: edgd rt over 2f out: drvn to ld jst ins fnl f: edgd rt and lft: kpt on wl: hdd cl home* **9/1**

1 **3** *nk* **Kersaint (IRE)**[20] [1007] 2-8-11 .... NCallan 7 87+
(K A Ryan) *lw: pressed ldrs: slt advantage ins fnl 2f: hdd jst ins fnl f: styd on wl u.p: gng on again cl home* **13/2**

3 **4** *1* **Major Eazy (IRE)**[14] [1094] 2-8-11 .... JamieSpencer 4 87+
(B J Meehan) *lw: in rr: effrt on rails and n.m.rover 2f out and lost position: pushed along and gd hdwy fnl f: fin wl: gng on cl home* **5/1**[2]

121 **5** *hd* **Thunder Bay**[12] [1130] 2-9-1 .... DarryllHolland 5 85
(M R Channon) *chsd ldrs: drvn along 1/2-way: kpt on fnl f but nt pce to chal ins fnl f* **8/1**

41 **6** *1 1/4* **Sauze D'Oulx**[16] [1058] 2-8-11 ow1.......................... JamesMillman(5) 2 81
(B R Millman) *sn slt ld: rdn 1/2-way: hdd ins fnl 2f: wknd ins fnl f* **20/1**

1 **7** *1 1/4* **Fat Boy (IRE)**[25] [942] 2-9-1 .... RichardHughes 1 75
(R Hannon) *lw: pressed ldr: rdn 1/2-way: wknd fnl f* **2/1**[1]

8 *13* **Battlecruiser (IRE)** 2-8-11 .... J-PGuillambert 3 19
(M Johnston) *cmpt: bit bkwd: sn rdn and outpcd* **9/1**

60.89 secs (-0.51) **Going Correction** -0.125s/f (Firm) **8** Ran SP% **113.5**
Speed ratings (Par 97):99,98,98,96,96 94,92,71
CSF £56.95 TOTE £7.60: £2.40, £1.90, £2.60; EX 81.20 Trifecta £476.40 Part won. Pool £671.12 - 0.20 winning units..
Owner Cavendish Star Racing **Bred** Jmr Enterprises, Usa **Trained** Upper Lambourn, Berks

FOCUS

The best two-year-old race of the season so far in terms of quality, featuring five previous winners. A couple did not enjoy the clearest of runs, but the time was about what would be expected for a race like this and the form looks reliable enough.

NOTEBOOK

Mount Pleasure(USA), more the finished article than when winning narrowly on his Windsor debut, may have only won this narrowly but he is value for further as he met a bit of interference at the start and had to circle the field down the wide outside to make his effort. The way he finished suggests an extra furlong will be well within his range and the yard can do little wrong with their juveniles at present. (op 5-1)
Littlemisssunshine(IRE) ◆, fourth in a Newmarket maiden on her debut that is starting to work out, was always up with the pace and, after switching wide to hit the front, kept battling right to the line. Some may argue that her rider's 1lb overweight made the different, but it was also notable that she was inclined to run about over the last furlong or so on these undulations and perhaps easier ground will suit her better. A maiden should be hers sooner rather than later. (tchd 10-1)
Kersaint(IRE) ◆ was always up with the pace and stayed on again after looking like dropping away. This effort confirmed what had been evident on his Leicester debut, that he will relish another furlong. (op 6-1 tchd 7-1)
Major Eazy(IRE) ◆, third behind a potentially smart juvenile on his Newmarket debut, had to wait for a gap against the stands' rail in order to get a run and by the time he got through it was much too late. Although he has a sprinter's pedigree, he will have no problem getting a bit further than this and a maiden is a formality. (op 11-2)
Thunder Bay, the most experienced in the field, had every chance and kept on trying but this better company proved too much for him. There are still races to be won with him at a slightly easier level. (op 9-1)
Sauze D'Oulx attempted the same forcing tactics that proved effective at Windsor, but he could not dominate these rivals in the same way and eventually found it all too much.
Fat Boy(IRE), successful from the plum draw on his Kempton Polytrack debut, was in a good position in the early stages, but found little off the bridle and was well held. The different surface gives him an obvious excuse, but either he is not as good as his debut victory suggested or he needs easier ground on grass. Official explanation: jockey said colt stopped very quickly (tchd 9-4 and 5-2 in places)
Battlecruiser(IRE) faced a stiff task as the only newcomer in the field despite his connections, and he was struggling to go the pace from the off. A glance at his stamina-laden pedigree on the dam's side helps explain why he had such difficulty staying in touch and he will surely leave this debut effort behind over further. (op 11-1)

1391 X FACTOR SWINLEY CONDITIONS STKS 1m (R)

2:45 (2:47) (Class 2) 3-Y-O **£12,464** (£3,732; £1,866; £934; £466) **Stalls** High

Form RPR

154- **1** **Italian Girl**[214] [5672] 3-9-1 95.................................. JamieSpencer 1 103+
(A P Jarvis) *h.d.w: lw: racd in cl 4th tl hdwy over 3f out: led ins fnl 2f: sn clr: easily* **9/4**[1]

5-1 **2** *3* **Silver Pivotal (IRE)**[16] [1068] 3-9-1 85.......................... NickyMackay 4 99+
(G A Butler) *lw: chsd ldrs: n.m.r and hmpd on rail ins fnl 2f: rallied and r.o wl to take 2nd ins fnl f: no ch w wnr* **11/4**[2]

3 *1 1/2* **Jaleela (USA)** 3-8-9 .... RHills 2 84
(W J Haggas) *neat: bit bkwd: racd in last pl but in tch: hdwy over 2f out to chse wnr appr fnl f: nvr any ch: one pce and lost 2nd nr fin* **9/2**

223- **4** *4* **Fretwork**[218] [5595] 3-8-12 78.................................. DaneO'Neill 3 78
(R Hannon) *chsd ldr: led ins fnl 3f: hdd ins fnl 2f: wknd over 1f out* **7/2**[3]

140- **5** *36* **Alovera (IRE)**[214] [5672] 3-9-1 97.......................... DarryllHolland 5 —
(M R Channon) *led tl hdd ins fnl 3f: wkng whn hmpd over 2f out: eased fnl f: t.o* **7/1**

1m 40.68s (-1.42) **Going Correction** -0.125s/f (Firm) **5** Ran SP% **110.3**
Speed ratings (Par 105):102,99,97,93,57
CSF £8.72 TOTE £2.90: £1.60, £2.00; EX 9.40.
Owner Michael Tabor **Bred** Barton Stud **Trained** Twyford, Bucks
■ Stewards' Enquiry : Dane O'Neill two-day ban: careless riding (May 14-15)
Nicky Mackay one-day ban: careless riding (May 15)

FOCUS

Some fair fillies on show but, despite an easy winner who looks Listed class, and the five runners finishing well spread out, this was rather an unsatisfactory race.

NOTEBOOK

Italian Girl, who did show some form in Pattern company last term after making a winning debut at this track, proved well suited by this drop in class on this first start in seven months. Her jockey rode a shrewd race too, making sure her main danger was locked away before she made her race-winning move once in line for home. She ended up winning this easily, but the margin would have been much less had the runner-up got a run and she may not be the easiest to place from now on. (tchd 15-8 and 5-2)
Silver Pivotal(IRE) had the advantage of race-fitness over her rivals having landed a Wolverhampton Polytrack maiden last month, but can still be rated much better than the bare form. She had nowhere to go straightening up for home and went for an audacious run up the inside of Fretwork that was never going to come off, and she paid the penalty. The way she powered home after finally extricating herself suggests she would have given the favourite a lot more to think about with a clear run and she remains a filly of potential. (tchd 7-2)
Jaleela(USA), out of a sister to the top-class miler Aljabr, faced a stiff task on this belated debut but did show some ability and was very much third-best. She should have little trouble gaining that all-important maiden victory with her long-term future in the paddocks in mind. (op 5-1)
Fretwork, placed in decent maidens in all three of her starts as a juvenile, had every chance but did not get home. She may have needed it, but she is yet to confirm the promise of her narrow defeat by the current Oaks favourite Passage Of Time on soft ground on her debut, though she has not encountered the same sort of ground since either. Official explanation: jockey said filly hung right (op 4-1)
Alovera(IRE), more than five lengths behind Italian Girl in a Newmarket Listed event when last seen seven months ago, made much of the running but had already blown up when hampered against the rail by the runner-up soon after turning in. (op 5-1)

1392 BRITAIN'S GOT TALENT PARADISE STKS (LISTED RACE) 1m (S)

3:20 (3:26) (Class 1) 4-Y-0+ **£17,034** (£6,456; £3,231; £1,611; £807) **Stalls** Low

Form RPR

015- **1** **Cesare**[229] [5341] 6-9-0 109.................................. JamieSpencer 2 121+
(J R Fanshawe) *lw: hld up last pl but in tch: smooth hdwy over 2f out to ld appr fnl f: sn clr: eased cl home: v easily* **2/1**[1]

-134 **2** *4* **Illustrious Blue**[13] [1104] 4-9-0 107.................................. PaulDoe 6 108
(W J Knight) *lw: pressed ldrs: rdn and one pce 3f out: kpt on again fnl f to take 2nd cl home but nvr any ch w easy wnr* **4/1**[3]

30-0 **3** *nk* **Dunelight (IRE)**[13] [1104] 4-9-0 105..........................(v) DaneO'Neill 4 107
(C G Cox) *lw: trckd ldr: led 3f out: rdn and hdd over 1f out: sn no ch w wnr: lost 2nd cl home* **7/1**

35-5 **4** *11* **Snoqualmie Boy**[13] [1104] 4-9-3 106.......................... JohnEgan 1 85
(D R C Elsworth) *lw: chsd ldrs: rdn over 2f out: wknd over 1f out* **8/1**

-004 **5** *12* **Road To Love (IRE)**[4] [1305] 4-9-0 .... RHills 3 54
(M Johnston) *lw: led: rdn along 1/2-way: hdd 3f out: sn btn* **5/2**[2]

1m 37.86s (-3.94) **Going Correction** -0.125s/f (Firm) course record **5** Ran SP% **105.5**
Speed ratings (Par 111):114,110,109,98,86
CSF £9.24 TOTE £2.50: £1.50, £2.00; EX 7.20.
Owner Cheveley Park Stud **Bred** Cheveley Park Stud Ltd **Trained** Newmarket, Suffolk

FOCUS

A competitive little Listed race run at a good gallop and fair form for the grade, with the winner value for a little further. The winner looked impressive but was certainly suited by the way the race was run.

NOTEBOOK

Cesare, last year's Hunt Cup winner, made a very impressive return to action, travelling strongly off the good gallop set by Dunelight and Road To Love, before quickening up easily to go on and win in style. He clearly had the race run to suit on this occasion, and might not be seen to such good effect off a steadier early pace, but on this evidence he is certainly Group class, and may well be capable of competing against the best over a mile later in the season. He is not in the Queen Anne, but could be supplemented. (op 9-4)
Illustrious Blue could not get cover in this small field and ran a fair race in the circumstances. He also stays further, and at the moment he looks an ideal candidate for the Festival Stakes at Goodwood on 25th May. (op 9-2 tchd 5-1 and 3-1 in places)

Dunelight(IRE) likes to make the running but with Road To Love in the field he had competition for that role. He is on a stiff enough mark for handicaps at present but might be able to win a Listed contest when granted an uncontested lead. (op 6-1)
Snoqualmie Boy has run his best races over further but this was still a bit disappointing. He is another who is probably more at home in a bigger field where he can get cover. (op 13-2)
Road To Love(IRE), who was denied the lead in a stronger contest at Sandown four days earlier, was once again taken on for pacemaking duties, and ended up setting too strong a gallop for his own good. He wants another two furlongs really, and is another who looks a candidate for the Festival Stakes at Goodwood later in the month. (op 11-4)

1393 WOODCOTE STUD SAGARO STKS (GROUP 3) 2m
3:55 (3:56) (Class 1) 4-Y-0+
£28,390 (£10,760; £5,385; £2,685; £1,345; £675) **Stalls** Low

Form RPR
300- **1** **Tungsten Strike (USA)**[236] 5156 6-9-0 110 DarryllHolland 4 115
(Mrs A J Perrett) *lw: mde virtually all: drvn and styd on strly fr over 2f out* **9/2**[3]
300- **2** 1 1/2 **Baddam**[200] 5963 5-9-0 105 IanMongan 2 113
(M R Channon) *lw: in rr: rdn and hdwy on outside over 4f out to chse wnr fr 3f out: kpt on u.p but a hld fnl 2f* **9/1**
20-2 **3** 3 1/2 **The Last Drop (IRE)**[28] 929 4-8-11 112 (t) RHills 1 111+
(B W Hills) *lw: hld up in rr: hdwy whn n.m.r bnd 3f: lost improving position hdwy over 2f out: hung rt: chsd ldrs and one pce sn after* **11/8**[1]
11-4 **4** 8 **Hawridge Prince**[28] 929 7-9-3 111 JimCrowley 3 102
(B R Millman) *s.i.s: sn in tch: hdwy to chse ldrs 6f out: sn rdn: wknd over 2f out* **5/2**[2]
10-1 **5** 4 **Odiham**[25] 944 6-9-0 92 (v) JimmyFortune 5 94
(H Morrison) *chsd wnr fr 10f out: hrd rdn fr 6f out: wknd fr 3f out* **12/1**
-013 **6** 26 **Weightless**[25] 940 7-9-0 99 NCallan 6 63
(N P Littmoden) *chsd ldr to 10f out: wknd fr 3f out* **25/1**

3m 25.52s (-4.64) **Going Correction** -0.125s/f (Firm)
WFA 4 from 5yo+ 3lb **6** Ran SP% **110.4**
Speed ratings (Par 113):106,105,103,99,97 84
CSF £39.98 TOTE £5.40: £2.20, £3.20; EX 45.20.
Owner John Connolly **Bred** Minster Stud **Trained** Pulborough, W Sussex

FOCUS
Not the strongest Group 3 race ever run and rated around the principals. With Hawridge Prince failing to run to his best and, to a lesser extent, The Last Drop disappointing, it probably did not take much winning.

NOTEBOOK
Tungsten Strike(USA), narrowly beaten in this race last year when it was run at Lingfield, was not strongly hassled for the lead and took full advantage. It is possible that he has improved a bit over the winter, but he did get the run of things here. The Henry II Stakes at Sandown next month, a race which he won last year, will be his next stop. (op 4-1)
Baddam, who won twice at the Royal Meeting here last year, wants further than this, so in the circumstances he ran well to chase home the winner, who got the run of the race. (op 10-1 tchd 11-1 in a place)
The Last Drop(IRE), who has a habit of finding trouble in running, was short of room rounding the bend into the straight and then showed a less-than-attractive tendency to hang towards the rail once in line for home. He has only won once in ten starts, which is a poor return for a horse of his class, and he looks one to swerve. (op 7-4)
Hawridge Prince, saddled with a 3lb penalty for winning a Group 3 race last year, probably found this ground too fast - he has never won on ground officially described as quicker than good. (op 2-1)
Odiham, whose only win to date on turf came back in 2004, has since recorded three wins from five starts on Polytrack. He is clearly a superior horse on the artificial surface and had plenty on his plate in this company.
Weightless, taking a big step up in distance, did not get home. He is another happier on softer ground.

1394 WATERHOMES.COM PAVILION STKS (LISTED RACE) 6f
4:30 (4:30) (Class 1) 3-Y-0
£17,034 (£6,456; £3,231; £1,611; £807; £405) **Stalls** Low

Form RPR
362- **1** **Hoh Mike (IRE)**[207] 5802 3-8-11 110 JamieSpencer 5 103+
(M L W Bell) *h.d.w: bit bkwd: hld up in rr: edgd rt over 2f out: smooth hdwy over 1f out: drvn and styd on wl to ld nr fin: won readily* **2/1**[1]
-154 **2** 1/2 **Hinton Admiral**[14] 1095 3-9-1 105 J-PGuillambert 2 105
(M Johnston) *lw: led: rdn over 1f out: hdd and no ex nr fin* **2/1**[1]
241- **3** 1 3/4 **Medley**[292] 3495 3-8-6 95 RHills 3 91
(R Hannon) *chsd ldr: rdn over 2f out: one pce ins fnl f* **7/1**[3]
11-5 **4** 1/2 **Solid Rock (IRE)**[18] 1035 3-8-11 96 DaneO'Neill 1 94
(T G Mills) *chsd ldrs: rdn over 2f out: one pce fnl f* **12/1**
06-3 **5** nk **Dazed And Amazed**[25] 943 3-9-1 95 JimmyFortune 6 97
(R Hannon) *lw: towards rr but in tch: pushed rt over 2f out: styd on to briefly chse ldr appr fnl f but no imp: sn one pce* **16/1**
455- **6** 1 **Elhamri**[207] 5802 3-9-1 105 DPMcDonogh 4 94
(S Kirk) *lw: chsd ldrs: rdn over 2f out: wknd ins fnl f* **5/1**[2]

1m 13.41s (-1.49) **Going Correction** -0.125s/f (Firm) **6** Ran SP% **109.4**
Speed ratings (Par 107):104,103,101,100,99 98
CSF £5.60 TOTE £2.80: £1.60, £1.90; EX 6.90.
Owner M Lynch & the late D Allport **Bred** John Malone **Trained** Newmarket, Suffolk

FOCUS
Solid Listed form rated around the runner-up and backed up by the third and fifth.

NOTEBOOK
Hoh Mike(IRE), who had to settle for second in the Norfolk Stakes and Cornwallis Stakes at this track last year, had 9lb in hand of his nearest rival based on adjusted official ratings, and that gave him a strong chance in this lesser company. He won easier than the winning margin suggests, overcoming a less than clear run, and he got the 6f well, but his season will be judged on how he gets on when taking on his elders. (tchd 9-4 in a place and 85-40 in places)
Hinton Admiral, unlike the winner, was race-fit, having already had two starts this season. He enjoyed the run of the race next to the stands' rail and beat the rest well enough, but the winner proved just too classy. He remains steadily progressive and it would not come as a surprise to see him win again at this level. (op 5-2 tchd 11-4 in a place)
Medley, fourth in the Albany Stakes before winning her maiden on her third start last year, was entitled to need this reappearance outing. She is open to improvement this year and might get a bit further. (op 6-1)
Solid Rock(IRE), progressive on the All-Weather over the winter when winning over 7f and a mile, had work on his plate in this company down in distance. This performance only went to confirm the view that he is likely to be difficult to place this season. (op 14-1 tchd 20-1 in a place)
Dazed And Amazed, another who is likely to continue to be difficult to place, has struggled since winning a Listed race at Newbury over this trip last June.
Elhamri had a good juvenile campaign but he was a real speedball last year and he will appreciate a drop back to the minimum trip. (op 4-1)

1395 KELTBRAY H'CAP 1m (S)
5:05 (5:09) (Class 4) (0-85,85) 4-Y-0+ **£6,477** (£1,927; £963; £481) **Stalls** Low

Form RPR
121- **1** **Hassaad**[161] 6564 4-8-13 80 RHills 16 92+
(W J Haggas) *h.d.w: lw: wnt rt s: hld up in rr: gd hdwy fr 2f out: drvn and qcknd fnl f to ld fnl 50yds: readily* **7/2**[2]
-625 **2** 1/2 **Cross The Line (IRE)**[18] 1040 5-8-11 78 NCallan 12 89
(A P Jarvis) *lw: towards rr: drvn and hdwy fr 2f out: styd on to ld ins fnl f: hdd and no ex fnl 50yds* **11/2**[3]
-606 **3** 1 1/2 **Neardown Beauty (IRE)**[8] 1209 4-8-13 80 JamesDoyle 7 88
(I A Wood) *mid-div: hdwy over 2f out: styd on wl fnl f but nvr quite gng pce to rch ldrs* **25/1**
0-03 **4** 1 1/4 **Music Note (IRE)**[16] 1060 4-8-13 80 JohnEgan 8 85
(Miss Gay Kelleway) *b: b.hind: lw: led: rdn and kpt on fr over 2f out: hdd ins fnl f and sn outpcd* **9/1**
000- **5** nk **It's A Dream (FR)**[212] 5732 4-8-10 80 MarcHalford(3) 9 84+
(D R C Elsworth) *lw: in rr: sitched rt and hdwy fr 2f out: kpt on wl fnl f but nvr gng pce to be competitive* **16/1**
200- **6** 1 1/4 **Binanti**[235] 5175 7-9-4 85 GeorgeBaker 10 86
(P R Chamings) *in rr: rdn over 2f out: r.o wl thrght fnl f but nvr in contention* **20/1**
-241 **7** 1 1/2 **Samarinda (USA)**[61] 604 4-8-9 76 MickyFenton 14 74
(Mrs P Sly) *mid-div: hdwy fr 3f out: chsd ldrs fr 2f out: wknd ins fnl f* **12/1**
002- **8** nk **Bee Stinger**[155] 6635 5-9-2 83 DPMcDonogh 3 80
(I A Wood) *lw: towards rr after 3f: rdn over 2f out: nvr gng pce to rch ldrs* **12/1**
651- **9** 1 **Rubenstar (IRE)**[193] 6094 4-8-8 80 PatrickHills(5) 15 75
(M H Tompkins) *sn chsng ldrs: rdn over 2f out: wknd fnl f* **20/1**
600- **10** 1 1/2 **Habshan (USA)**[216] 5639 7-9-2 83 DarryllHolland 6 75
(C F Wall) *chsd ldrs: pushed along fr 3f out: wknd over 1f out* **25/1**
01-0 **11** 2 **Amwaal (USA)**[18] 1040 4-8-10 77 IanMongan 1 64
(J L Dunlop) *swtg: chsd ldrs: rdn over 2f out: wknd sn after* **16/1**
52-1 **12** 3/4 **Royal Fantasy (IRE)**[23] 979 4-8-6 73 JamieSpencer 2 58
(J R Fanshawe) *in rr: rdn over 2f out and nvr in contention* **10/3**[1]
/0-0 **13** 3/4 **King's Majesty (IRE)**[32] 842 5-8-13 80 PaulDoe 4 63
(L A Dace) *lw: s.i.s: a towards rr* **28/1**
05-0 **14** 1 3/4 **Silver Blue (IRE)**[16] 1060 4-8-8 75 DaneO'Neill 11 54
(R Hannon) *nvr in contention* **25/1**
236- **15** 3/4 **First Show**[324] 2510 5-8-8 75 RichardMullen 13 53
(R A Harris) *chsd ldrs over 5f* **25/1**
124- **16** 1/2 **Press The Button (GER)**[238] 5107 4-9-1 82 NickyMackay 5 59
(J R Boyle) *chsd ldrs over 5f* **12/1**

1m 39.44s (-2.36) **Going Correction** -0.125s/f (Firm) **16** Ran SP% **133.9**
Speed ratings (Par 105):106,105,104,102,102 101,99,99,98,96 94,94,93,91,90 90
CSF £23.14 CT £470.69 TOTE £5.00: £1.70, £2.10, £5.40, £2.10; EX 28.70 Trifecta £736.70 Pool £1,390.50 - 1.34 winning units. Place 6 £128.26, Place 5 £39.57..
Owner Hamdan Al Maktoum **Bred** Shadwell Estate Company Limited **Trained** Newmarket, Suffolk

FOCUS
A decent handicap with by far the biggest field of the day and the runners were inclined to shun the stands' rail and come down the centre. The winning time was 1.58 seconds slower than the earlier Listed event, which is about what would be expected, and the form looks solid rated around the third, fourth and fifth.
Royal Fantasy(IRE) Official explanation: jockey said filly never travelled
Press The Button(GER) Official explanation: jockey said gelding stopped quickly
T/Plt: £140.60 to a £1 stake. Pool: £76,161.95. 395.25 winning tickets. T/Qpdt: £27.60 to a £1 stake. Pool: £5,186.10. 138.55 winning tickets. ST

1248 KEMPTON (A.W) (R-H)
Wednesday, May 2

OFFICIAL GOING: Standard
Wind: fresh across

1396 DIGIBET MEDIAN AUCTION MAIDEN STKS 1m 4f (P)
5:45 (5:46) (Class 5) 3-5-Y-0 **£3,238** (£963; £481; £240) **Stalls** Centre

Form RPR
3-62 **1** **Spiderback (IRE)**[9] 1205 3-8-9 70 ow1 (b) JimmyFortune 9 71+
(R Hannon) *trckd ldrs: shkn up to ld over 1f out: sn clr: easily* **4/6**[1]
00 **2** 5 **Laughing Game**[7] 1250 3-8-3 FrankieMcDonald 4 57
(M L W Bell) *hld up in tch: hdwy over 3f out: ev ch 2f out: kpt on but nt pce of wnr* **33/1**
04- **3** 3/4 **Generous Jem**[204] 5903 4-9-8 J-PGuillambert 3 57
(G G Margarson) *trckd ldr: led over 2f out: rdn and hdd over 1f out: one pce after* **12/1**[3]
0-5 **4** 5 **Gatecrasher**[8] 1231 4-9-13 PaulEddery 1 54
(Pat Eddery) *trckd ldrs: rdn over 3f out: one pce fnl 2f* **20/1**
2350 **5** nk **Compton Express**[38] 775 4-9-8 44 SimonWhitworth 11 49
(Jamie Poulton) *in rr: mde sme late hdwy* **20/1**
/00- **6** 3 **Lady Diktat**[372] 1222 5-9-3 64 TravisBlock(5) 10 44
(Mouse Hamilton-Fairley) *hld up: a towards rr* **25/1**
000/ **7** shd **Silver Dreamer (IRE)**[517] 6034 5-9-8 33 JDSmith 2 44
(H S Howe) *slowly away: a bhd* **66/1**
6 **8** 4 **Just An Angel (IRE)**[7] 1250 3-7-10 JosephWalsh(7) 7 36
(A P Jarvis) *trckd ldrs: wknd 3f out* **33/1**
2 **9** 2 **Salsadar**[19] 1030 3-8-3 DavidKinsella 5 34
(J H M Gosden) *led tl hdd over 2f out: wknd qckly* **11/4**[2]

2m 37.28s (0.38) **Going Correction** 0.0s/f (Stan)
WFA 3 from 4yo+ 19lb **9** Ran SP% **115.1**
Speed ratings (Par 103):98,94,94,90,90 88,88,85,84
CSF £38.08 TOTE £1.70: £1.02, £15.10, £2.90; EX 44.90.
Owner John Manley **Bred** Roger And Henry O'Callaghan **Trained** East Everleigh, Wilts

FOCUS
This modest maiden did not take a lot of winning with the winner not needing to be at his best to score.

1397 DIGIBET CASINO CLAIMING STKS 1m 3f (P)
6:20 (6:20) (Class 6) 3-Y-0 **£2,047** (£604; £302) **Stalls** High

Form RPR
-503 **1** **Featherlight**[30] 893 3-8-8 51 (b) JamieSpencer 2 61+
(J Jay) *hld up in rr: hdwy to trck ldrs over 3f out: led on bit ins fnl f: v easily* **9/2**[2]
6053 **2** 1 1/2 **Color Man**[29] 907 3-9-1 49 (p) JimCrowley 6 57
(Mrs A J Perrett) *led: rdn and hung lft fr over 1f out: hdd ins fnl f: kpt on but no ch w easy wnr* **3/1**[1]

2-26 **3** *3* **Right Option (IRE)**[18] 1039 3-8-11 57 DarrylIHolland 3 48
(S Dow) *trckd ldr: ev ch 2f out: one pce after* **3/1**[1]
4305 **4** *2* **Party Palace**[8] 1211 3-7-13 45 MCGeran(7) 1 39
(H S Howe) *mid-div: rdn over 3f out: kpt on one pce ins fnl 2f* **15/2**[3]
5003 **5** *3 ½* **Tumble Jill (IRE)**[3] 1320 3-8-4 50 ow3 MarcHalford(3) 4 34
(J J Bridger) *trckd ldrs tl wknd ins fnl 2f* **12/1**
4626 **6** *8* **Homecroft Boy**[8] 1210 3-8-11 50 JimmyFortune 7 24
(P D Evans) *broke wl: chsd ldrs tl wknd 2f out* **3/1**[1]
004- **7** *34* **Grand Officer (IRE)**[151] 6670 3-8-9 43 (b) DaneO'Neill 5 —
(D J S Ffrench Davis) *bhd: lost tch 4f out: t.o* **25/1**

2m 24.0s (1.32) **Going Correction** 0.0s/f (Stan) **7** Ran SP% **116.5**
Speed ratings (Par 97):95,93,91,90,87 81,57
CSF £19.03 TOTE £5.90: £3.10, £1.90; EX 10.90.The winner was claimed by Jamie Poulton for £9,000.
Owner Keith Wills **Bred** Keith Wills **Trained** Newmarket, Suffolk

FOCUS
A very moderate race but they went a fair gallop from the off, although only one horse was going to win from a long way out. The form is rated at face value for the moment.

1398 DIGIBET POKER MAIDEN STKS 7f (P)
6:55 (6:58) (Class 5) 3-Y-0 **£3,238** (£963; £481; £240) **Stalls** High

Form RPR
53- **1** **Mutanaseb (USA)**[186] 6220 3-9-3 RHills 9 89+
(M A Jarvis) *mde all: edgd lft over 1f out: rdn out* **11/8**[1]
3- **2** *1 ¼* **Ballroom Dancer (IRE)**[188] 6186 3-8-12 DarrylHolland 14 81
(J Noseda) *chsd wnr thrght: hung lft u.p over 1f out: kpt on but no imp on wnr ins fnl f* **11/2**[3]
4 **3** *4* **Hazytoo**[13] 1100 3-9-3 JamieSpencer 10 76
(N A Callaghan) *chsd ldrs: nt qckn ins fnl 2f* **4/1**[2]
4 *¾* **Pivotal Truth** 3-8-12 MichaelHills 11 69
(B W Hills) *chsd ldrs: rdn over 2f out: one pce after* **25/1**
5 *5* **Up The Chimney** 3-9-3 NCallan 1 61+
(A P Jarvis) *towards rr: mde sme late hdwy but nvr nr to chal* **25/1**
36- **6** *1 ½* **The King And I (IRE)**[222] 5508 3-9-3 LPKeniry 5 57
(J S Moore) *in tch: rdn over 2f out: sn btn* **33/1**
7 *1* **Medicea Sidera** 3-8-12 FergusSweeney 8 49
(E F Vaughan) *towards rr tl stdy late hdwy* **66/1**
8 *1 ½* **Fraternal** 3-9-3 DaneO'Neill 13 50
(R Charlton) *s.i.s: nvr rchd ldrs* **14/1**
9 *nk* **Conbextra** 3-9-3 JohnEgan 2 49
(J S Moore) *towards rr: rdn over 3f out: sn btn* **7/1**
10 *3* **Red Brick Road (IRE)** 3-9-3 StephenDonohoe 12 42
(A J Lidderdale) *s.i.s: outpcd and a bhd* **100/1**
11 *¾* **Practical Joke (IRE)** 3-9-3 PaulDoe 4 40
(W J Knight) *chsd ldrs tl wknd over 2f out* **33/1**
12 *2 ½* **Confide In Me** 3-9-3 NickyMackay 3 33
(G A Butler) *a towards rr* **14/1**
03 **13** *3* **Bear Bottom**[36] 802 3-9-3 RichardMullen 7 25
(W J Musson) *mid-div tl wknd over 2f out* **40/1**
14 *18* **Egregius Max** 3-9-3 GeorgeBaker 6 —
(C F Wall) *slowly away: sn wl bhd and styd there* **50/1**

1m 26.28s (-0.52) **Going Correction** 0.0s/f (Stan) **14** Ran SP% **123.8**
Speed ratings (Par 99):102,100,96,95,89 87,86,84,84,81 80,77,73,53
CSF £8.60 TOTE £2.30: £1.30, £1.60, £2.20; EX 7.50.
Owner Hamdan Al Maktoum **Bred** Spendthrift Farm Llc **Trained** Newmarket, Suffolk

FOCUS
This looked a decent maiden, considering the performances of those who came into the race with a run under their belts. It was also given some extra spice with a few unraced runners who had some decent pedigrees. The pace was good and plenty of winners should emerge from the race.
Egregius Max Official explanation: jockey said colt did not face the kickback

1399 DIGIBET SPORTS BETTING H'CAP 1m (P)
7:30 (7:31) (Class 6) (0-65,69) 3-Y-0 **£2,047** (£604; £302) **Stalls** High

Form RPR
0022 **1** **Mark Of Love (IRE)**[11] 1155 3-9-0 61 DarrylHolland 11 76
(M R Channon) *racd keenly: trckd ldr: led over 3f out: pushed out fnl f* **6/1**[2]
6-31 **2** *2* **Last Sovereign**[7] 1238 3-9-5 69 6ex RichardKingscote(3) 14 79
(R Charlton) *trckd ldrs: wnt 2nd over 2f out: no imp ins fnl f* **4/7**[1]
533 **3** *9* **Ochre (IRE)**[33] 836 3-9-4 65 (b[1]) NCallan 8 54
(M A Jarvis) *chsd ldrs: rdn 2f out: no ch w first 2 after* **8/1**[3]
060- **4** *shd* **Marlyn Ridge**[215] 5655 3-9-2 63 RobertHavlin 6 52
(D K Ivory) *bhd: hdwy over 2f out: no ch w first 3* **33/1**
-356 **5** *¾* **Here's Blue Chip (IRE)**[41] 731 3-9-3 64 JohnEgan 10 51
(P W D'Arcy) *prom tl rdn and no prog fr over 2f out* **25/1**
050- **6** *1* **Art Gallery**[161] 6561 3-8-9 56 (b[1]) RichardMullen 9 41
(G L Moore) *mid-div: sme prog fr over 2f out but nvr on terms* **20/1**
005- **7** *2* **Brouhaha**[187] 6200 3-9-0 64 EmmettStack(3) 3 44
(Miss Diana Weeden) *nvr bttr than mid-div* **40/1**
656- **8** *1 ¼* **Amazing King (IRE)**[201] 5933 3-8-9 63 JackDean(7) 12 41
(W G M Turner) *led tl hdd over 3f out: wknd over 2f out* **66/1**
050 **9** *nk* **Whodunit (UAE)**[15] 1081 3-9-2 63 JimCrowley 4 40
(P W Hiatt) *in tch tl wknd qckly 2f out* **66/1**
6-50 **10** *9* **Hard As Iron**[40] 738 3-8-10 57 FergusSweeney 5 13
(M Blanshard) *in rr: rdn 3f out: nvr on terms* **28/1**
064- **11** *3 ½* **Doonigan (IRE)**[169] 6475 3-8-9 56 LPKeniry 13 4
(A M Balding) *slowly away: a bhd* **33/1**
06-0 **12** *½* **On The Map**[18] 1045 3-9-2 63 JamieSpencer 7 10
(A P Jarvis) *a bhd* **25/1**
0 **13** *2 ½* **King Canute (IRE)**[56] 633 3-8-13 60 MichaelHills 2 1
(M J Wallace) *a bhd* **40/1**
053- **14** *3 ½* **Compton Charlie**[169] 6475 3-9-4 65 GeorgeBaker 1 —
(J G Portman) *in tch on outside tl wknd over 3f out* **25/1**

1m 40.61s (-0.19) **Going Correction** 0.0s/f (Stan) **14** Ran SP% **122.5**
Speed ratings (Par 97):100,98,89,88,88 87,85,83,83,74 71,70,68,64
CSF £8.82 CT £31.90 TOTE £7.00: £2.10, £1.02, £1.80; EX 13.50.
Owner Box 41 **Bred** G Swift **Trained** West Ilsley, Berks

FOCUS
A modest but interesting handicap with the first two finishing well clear and the form could rate higher.
Doonigan(IRE) Official explanation: jockey said gelding missed the break
Compton Charlie Official explanation: jockey said gelding did not face the kickback

1400 DIGIBET.COM H'CAP 6f (P)
8:05 (8:05) (Class 6) (0-50,50) 3-Y-0+ **£2,047** (£604; £302) **Stalls** High

Form RPR
0005 **1** **Christian Bendix**[2] 1349 5-9-3 48 (p) IanMongan 1 59
(P Howling) *mde all: rdn out fnl f* **10/1**
0-40 **2** *1 ½* **North Fleet**[13] 1112 4-9-5 50 LPKeniry 8 56
(J M Bradley) *chsd wnr thrght: no imp fnl f* **10/1**
0334 **3** *¾* **Laith (IRE)**[12] 1120 4-9-5 50 (p) MickyFenton 11 54
(Miss V Haigh) *t.k.h: mid-div tl hdwy over 2f out to chse ldrs over 2f out* **9/2**[2]
1553 **4** *nk* **Primarily**[12] 1120 5-9-3 48 GeorgeBaker 3 51
(Peter Grayson) *chsd ldrs: rdn and no ex fr over 1f out* **13/2**[3]
0-16 **5** *hd* **Piddies Pride (IRE)**[8] 1212 5-9-4 49 (v) JohnEgan 5 51+
(Miss Gay Kelleway) *in rr tl hdwy over 2f out: nvr nr to chal* **10/3**[1]
5410 **6** *1 ½* **King Of Charm (IRE)**[12] 1120 4-9-4 49 (b) FergusSweeney 7 47
(G L Moore) *in tch on outside tl one pce fnl 2f* **9/1**
0433 **7** *1 ¼* **Simpsons Gamble (IRE)**[36] 795 4-9-5 50 (b) AdrianMcCarthy 9 44
(R M Flower) *hld up: nvr on terms* **8/1**
00/0 **8** *2 ½* **Romantic Gift**[23] 977 5-9-3 48 RichardMullen 6 35
(Mrs C A Dunnett) *a bhd* **66/1**
0600 **9** *shd* **Orchestration (IRE)**[30] 892 6-9-0 48 oh1 (v) DominicFox(3) 12 34
(S Parr) *hld up: hdwy on ins 3f out: wknd over 1f out* **20/1**
000- **10** *hd* **Buckle And Hyde**[185] 6235 4-9-0 48 RichardKingscote(3) 10 34
(Mrs A L M King) *s.i.s: a bhd* **33/1**
041- **11** *2* **Megalala (IRE)**[219] 5573 6-9-2 50 MarcHalford(3) 4 30
(J J Bridger) *rrd up leaving stalls: a bhd* **14/1**
6610 **12** *2* **Grand View**[47] 687 11-9-3 48 oh1 (p) DarrylHolland 2 22
(J R Weymes) *setttled in rr and a bhd* **12/1**

1m 13.82s (0.12) **Going Correction** 0.0s/f (Stan) **12** Ran SP% **117.4**
Speed ratings (Par 101):99,97,96,95,95 93,91,88,88,87 85,82
CSF £103.26 CT £525.33 TOTE £9.60: £4.50, £4.50, £1.30; EX 179.70.
Owner Mrs A K Petersen **Bred** C B Petersen **Trained** Newmarket, Suffolk
■ Stewards' Enquiry : Ian Mongan one-day ban: careless riding (May 14)

FOCUS
This was a moderate sprint where, as usual, everything unfolded down the home straight. The form appears sound enough rated around the first two.
Piddies Pride(IRE) Official explanation: jockey said mare was denied a clear run closing stages

1401 DIGITOTE H'CAP 7f (P)
8:35 (8:35) (Class 4) (0-80,78) 4-Y-0+ **£5,181** (£1,541; £770; £384) **Stalls** High

Form RPR
00-6 **1** **Bonnie Prince Blue**[16] 1060 4-9-4 78 MichaelHills 7 88
(B W Hills) *hld up in tch: hdwy to ld wl over 1f out: r.o wl* **5/2**[1]
-016 **2** *¾* **Raza Cab (IRE)**[5] 1283 5-8-12 75 JerryO'Dwyer(3) 9 83
(Karen George) *hld up: over 1f out: r.o to go 2nd ins fnl f* **8/1**
100- **3** *¾* **Torquemada (IRE)**[168] 6489 6-8-5 64 oh1 ow1 PaulDoe 6 71
(W Jarvis) *chsd ldrs: ev ch 2f out: nt qckn ins fnl f* **20/1**
460- **4** *shd* **Seamus Shindig**[236] 5148 5-9-3 77 DaneO'Neill 10 83
(H Candy) *prom: nt clr run over 2f out: kpt on but nt qckn fnl f* **7/1**[3]
043- **5** *1 ¾* **Lavenham (IRE)**[231] 5294 4-9-0 74 JimmyFortune 2 75
(R Hannon) *in rr: hdwy ins fnl 2f: nvr nr to chal* **12/1**
2015 **6** *1* **Symbol Of Peace (IRE)**[25] 938 4-9-1 78 RichardKingscote(3) 8 77
(J W Unett) *led tl hdd & wknd over 1f out* **11/2**[2]
1000 **7** *nk* **Hollow Jo**[70] 513 7-9-0 74 MickyFenton 1 72
(J R Jenkins) *in tch on outside: rdn over 1f out: nvr nr to chal* **20/1**
3141 **8** *2* **Binnion Bay (IRE)**[18] 1036 6-8-11 71 (b) AmirQuinn 4 64
(J J Bridger) *chsd ldrs: rdn over 2f out: wknd over 1f out* **7/1**[3]
0330 **9** *1 ½* **Garstang**[12] 1121 4-9-3 77 (b) GeorgeBaker 11 66
(Peter Grayson) *slowly away: a bhd* **9/1**
50-0 **10** *5* **Full Victory (IRE)**[8] 1209 5-8-13 73 RobertHavlin 5 49
(R A Farrant) *trckd ldr tl rdn and wknd over 2f out* **12/1**
600- **11** *19* **Kavachi (IRE)**[182] 6301 4-8-6 66 FergusSweeney 3 —
(G L Moore) *a bhd* **25/1**

1m 25.55s (-1.25) **Going Correction** 0.0s/f (Stan) **11** Ran SP% **118.8**
Speed ratings (Par 105):107,106,105,105,103 102,101,99,97,91 70
CSF £22.31 CT £334.22 TOTE £3.90: £1.60, £2.60, £4.80; EX 54.40.
Owner G J Hicks **Bred** George Joseph Hicks **Trained** Lambourn, Berks

FOCUS
A fair handicap run at a good gallop and solid form rated around the placed horses.
Symbol Of Peace(IRE) Official explanation: jockey said filly had no more to give

1402 DIGIBET BUYBACK H'CAP 2m (P)
9:05 (9:06) (Class 6) (0-50,50) 4-Y-0+ **£2,047** (£604; £302) **Stalls** High

Form RPR
2 **1** **Colwyn Bay (IRE)**[36] 804 5-8-10 47 (p) JamieSpencer 3 58+
(Jane Chapple-Hyam) *in rr tl hdwy 6f out: led 2f out: rdn out* **2/1**[1]
/05- **2** *1 ¼* **Gaelic Roulette (IRE)**[160] 891 7-8-9 46 NCallan 1 55
(J Jay) *in tch: chsd wnr over 1f out: no imp ins fnl f* **13/2**
-340 **3** *7* **Cragganmore Creek**[23] 982 4-8-5 48 oh1 (v) SaleemGolam(3) 8 49
(D Morris) *in rr: rdn and hdwy over 2f out: styd on: no ch w first 2 ins fnl f* **11/1**
4460 **4** *1* **Scuzme (IRE)**[75] 481 4-8-3 50 (p) JemmaMarshall(7) 7 49
(Miss Sheena West) *in rr: hdwy to go 2nd 7f out: led over 3f out: hdd 2f out: sn outpcd* **16/1**
0462 **5** *6* **Tip Toes (IRE)**[8] 1229 5-8-9 46 oh1 JimmyQuinn 10 38
(P Howling) *chsd ldrs tl rdn and wknd 2f out* **9/2**[3]
5046 **6** *3 ½* **Red River Rock (IRE)**[29] 909 5-8-9 46 oh1 (be) JimmyFortune 11 34
(T J Fitzgerald) *mid-div: no hdwy fnl 2f* **7/2**[2]
00-6 **7** *2 ½* **Nahlass**[8] 1217 4-8-0 47 oh2 SophieDoyle(7) 4 32
(Ms J S Doyle) *a in rr* **40/1**
60-0 **8** *6* **Sterling Moll**[31] 869 4-8-6 46 oh4 AdrianMcCarthy 2 24
(W De Best-Turner) *chsd ldr to 7f out: wknd 3f out* **66/1**
5500 **9** *13* **Hometomammy**[8] 1206 5-8-9 46 oh1 JimCrowley 5 8
(P W Hiatt) *a bhd* **25/1**
430- **10** *5* **Royal Axminster**[275] 3998 12-8-6 50 NBazeley(7) 12 6
(Mrs P N Dutfield) *led tl hdd over 3f out: sn wknd* **33/1**
00/0 **11** *5* **Litzinsky**[19] 1032 9-8-6 46 oh1 EmmettStack(3) 13 —
(Mrs L J Young) *chsd ldrs: rdn over 3f out: sn wknd* **66/1**
000/ **U** **Jahash**[18] 5346 9-8-9 46 oh1 PaulEddery 9 —
(Simon Earle) *uns rdr in stalls* **11/1**
000- **U** **Beaufort**[162] 6551 5-8-9 46 FergusSweeney 6 —
(Mike Murphy) *uns rdr leaving stalls* **25/1**

3m 32.14s (0.74) **Going Correction** 0.0s/f (Stan)
WFA 4 from 5yo+ 3lb **13** Ran SP% **125.7**
Speed ratings (Par 101):98,97,93,93,90 88,87,84,77,75 72,—,—
CSF £15.65 CT £123.25 TOTE £3.50: £1.40, £2.50, £2.60; EX 23.30 Place 6 £20.19, Place 5 £13.67..

The Form Book, Raceform Ltd, Compton, RG20 6NL

Owner Philip M Hickey **Bred** Tower Bloodstock **Trained** Newmarket, Suffolk

FOCUS

Eleven of the 13 runners finished outside the first four last time, so the form is not to be taken too seriously, although it appears sound enough. There was drama before the race even got going, as Beaufort and Jahash decided it better to run without their jockeys. Those who were left did not go that fast.

T/Plt: £75.50 to a £1 stake. Pool: £45,635.05. 441.10 winning tickets. T/Qpdt: £34.30 to a £1 stake. Pool: £3,486.20. 75.00 winning tickets. JS

1150 NOTTINGHAM (L-H)

Wednesday, May 2

OFFICIAL GOING: Good to firm (firm in back straight)

30mm water had been put on the track over the previous ten days. The going was described as 'just on the fast side of good with an excellent cover'.

Wind: fresh, half-behind Weather: fine and sunny

1403 RACING UK ON CHANNEL 432 MAIDEN STKS — 6f 15y

2:00 (2:02) (Class 5) 3-Y-O — **£2,914** (£867; £433; £216) **Stalls** High

Form — RPR

450- **1** **Tombi (USA)**214 [5681] 3-9-3 **84** ... EddieAhern 11 — 85+
(J Howard Johnson) *chsd ldr: rdn to ld over 1f out: r.o wl: eased nr fin* **5/4**1

00-2 **2** 4 **Welsh Auction**29 [899] 3-9-0 **70** ... EmmettStack(3) 12 — 73
(G A Huffer) *led: rdn and hdd over 1f out: styd on same pce* **11/1**

2 **3** 2 **Expensive Art (IRE)**10 [1175] 3-8-12 ... SebSanders 13 — 62
(N A Callaghan) *chsd ldrs: rdn over 1f out: sn outpcd* **10/1**3

62- **4** 3 1/2 **Inspainagain (USA)**244 [4956] 3-8-10 ... NeilBrown(7) 1 — 59+
(T D Barron) *hld up: hdwy over 2f out: rdn and edgd rt over 1f out: wknd fnl f* **16/1**

44- **5** 1 3/4 **Celtic Change (IRE)**247 [4880] 3-9-3 ... PhillipMakin 2 — 51+
(M Dods) *s.i.s: styd on ins fnl f: nvr nrr* **14/1**

5 **6** shd **Fervent**8 [1215] 3-8-12 ... KevinGhunowa(5) 5 — 51
(J M Bradley) *prom 4f* **50/1**

60- **7** 3 **Miss Capricorn**270 [4151] 3-8-9 ... AndrewMullen(3) 10 — 37
(K A Ryan) *mid-div: rdn 1/2-way: wknd 2f out* **66/1**

8 1 3/4 **Mix N Match** 3-9-0 ... LiamJones(3) 9 — 37
(W J Haggas) *trckd ldrs: racd keenly: rdn and wknd over 2f out* **10/1**3

05- **9** 2 **Baarrij**257 [4566] 3-8-12 ... SteveDrowne 6 — 26
(T J Pitt) *s.i.s: outpcd* **16/1**

00- **10** hd **Neon**229 [5352] 3-8-12 ... ChrisCatlin 7 — 25
(J W Hills) *sn outpcd* **33/1**

2220 **11** 2 1/2 **Bertie Swift**12 [1117] 3-9-0 **67** ... JerryO'Dwyer(3) 4 — 23
(J Gallagher) *s.i.s: outpcd* **20/1**

12 2 1/2 **Arithmatix (USA)** 3-9-3 ... BrettDoyle 8 — 15
(G A Butler) *mid-div: wknd 1/2-way* **4/1**2

0-0 **13** 1 1/4 **Skiddaw Fox**20 [1008] 3-9-3 ... SilvestreDeSousa 3 — 11
(Mrs L Williamson) *chsd ldrs over 3f* **100/1**

1m 12.37s (-2.63) **Going Correction** -0.525s/f (Hard) — **13** Ran SP% **121.5**

Speed ratings (Par 99):96,90,88,83,81 80,76,74,71,71 68,64,63

CSF £16.40 TOTE £2.30: £1.30, £3.00, £2.30; EX 14.20.

Owner Transcend Bloodstock LLP **Bred** Sun Valley Farm **Trained** Billy Row, Co Durham

■ Stewards' Enquiry : Kevin Ghunowa caution: allowed gelding to coast home with no assistance

FOCUS

A fair maiden which saw those drawn high at an advantage. The easy winner is value for further and the form looks sound.

Arithmatix(USA) Official explanation: trainer's rep said colt was unsuited by the fast ground

1404 NOTTINGHAMSHIRE CHAMBER OF COMMERCE AND INDUSTRY FILLIES' H'CAP — 6f 15y

2:35 (2:35) (Class 5) (0-70,67) 3-Y-O+ — **£3,238** (£963; £481; £240) **Stalls** High

Form — RPR

5444 **1** **Slipasearcher (IRE)**1 [1373] 3-8-7 **58** ow1 ... (b) StephenDonohoe 5 — 63
(P D Evans) *swvd lft s: swtchd stands' side rail after 1f: hrd rdn and hdwy on ins 2f out: styd on to ld nr fin* **6/1**

0604 **2** hd **Glamaraazi (IRE)**48 [686] 4-8-13 **54** ... TonyHamilton 10 — 61
(R A Fahey) *led 1f: hung lft and led over 1f out: hdd and no ex towards fin* **11/4**1

56-2 **3** 2 **Nobilissima (IRE)**8 [1219] 3-9-2 **67** ... SebSanders 2 — 65+
(J L Spearing) *sn chsng ldrs: kpt on same pce fnl f* **4/1**2

3145 **4** 3 1/2 **Muara**16 [1067] 5-9-0 **62** ... NeilBrown(7) 7 — 53
(D W Barker) *w ldrs: wknd jst ins fnl f* **5/1**3

0/25 **5** 5 **Ellcon (IRE)**74 [489] 4-9-12 **67** ... EddieAhern 4 — 43
(J A Osborne) *chsd ldrs: wknd over 1f out* **9/1**

150- **6** shd **Tilsworth Charlie**180 [6325] 4-8-9 **53** ... (v) PatrickMathers(3) 8 — 29
(J R Jenkins) *sltly hmpd s: w ldrs: wknd over 1f out* **16/1**

20-0 **7** 1/2 **Mannello**30 [896] 4-9-0 **55** ... JamieMackay 3 — 29
(B Palling) *s.i.s: nvr nr ldrs* **33/1**

66-5 **8** 1 1/2 **Champagne Cracker**23 [964] 6-9-0 **55** ... PhillipMakin 1 — 25
(M Dods) *trckd ldrs: outpcd over 2f out: hmpd and swtchd lft over 1f out* **8/1**

0-00 **9** nk **Mint**7 [1241] 4-9-4 **59** ... PatCosgrave 9 — 28
(D W Barker) *swvd lft s: led after 1f: hung lft hdd & wknd over 1f out* **10/1**

1m 12.93s (-2.07) **Going Correction** -0.525s/f (Hard)

WFA 3 from 4yo+ 10lb — **9** Ran SP% **116.6**

Speed ratings (Par 100):92,91,89,84,77 77,76,74,74

CSF £23.12 CT £75.17 TOTE £7.50: £2.50, £1.40, £1.20; EX 21.70.

Owner Barry McCabe **Bred** Hugo Merry And Theo Waddington **Trained** Pandy, Monmouths

FOCUS

A moderate sprint handicap and a modest time for the grade, 0.56 seconds slower than the preceding maiden but the form appears sound enough.

Glamaraazi(IRE) Official explanation: jockey said filly hung left throughout

Mint Official explanation: jockey said filly hung left throughout

1405 PADDOCKSNOTTINGHAM.CO.UK H'CAP — 5f 13y

3:10 (3:11) (Class 6) (0-60,60) 4-Y-O+ — **£2,388** (£705; £352) **Stalls** High

Form — RPR

006- **1** **Raccoon (IRE)**230 [5309] 7-8-13 **55** ... SebSanders 13 — 79+
(D W Chapman) *tubed: mde all: rdn clr fnl f* **12/1**

000- **2** 2 1/2 **Brunelleschi**206 [5842] 4-8-11 **60** ... (b1) LukeMorris(7) 17 — 75
(P L Gilligan) *hld up: rdn 2f out: sn edgd lft: styd on ins fnl f: nvr nrr* **12/1**

5-06 **3** 2 **Divine Spirit**15 [1074] 6-9-4 **60** ... SteveDrowne 16 — 68
(M Dods) *mid-div: hdwy over 2f out: sn rdn and edgd lft: styd on same pce fnl f* **7/2**1

60-2 **4** 1 1/4 **Harrison's Flyer (IRE)**3 [1321] 6-8-11 **58** ... (p) KevinGhunowa(5) 15 — 61+
(J M Bradley) *chsd ldrs: rdn and hung lft fr over 2f out: wknd ins fnl f* **9/2**3

1-00 **5** 1 1/4 **Davids Mark**36 [797] 7-8-8 **53** ... PatrickMathers(3) 8 — 52
(J R Jenkins) *chsd ldrs: rdn over 1f out: sn wknd* **33/1**

4050 **6** 1/2 **Brut**13 [1112] 5-8-12 **54** ... TonyHamilton 10 — 51+
(D W Barker) *mid-div: hdwy and hung lft over 2f out: n.d* **8/1**

00-0 **7** nk **Meikle Barfil**15 [1074] 5-8-13 **55** ... (p) TedDurcan 11 — 51
(J M Bradley) *s.i.s: hdwy and hung lft over 1f out: n.d* **22/1**

00-1 **8** 2 1/2 **Exponential (IRE)**8 [1212] 5-9-4 **60** ... BrettDoyle 2 — 47
(J M Bradley) *chsd ldrs over 4f* **4/1**2

00-0 **9** 1/2 **Enjoy The Buzz**8 [1212] 8-8-10 **52** ... ChrisCatlin 14 — 37
(J M Bradley) *chsd ldrs: rdn over 2f out: hung lft and wknd over 1f out* **28/1**

2000 **10** 1/2 **City For Conquest (IRE)**47 [688] 4-8-12 **54** ... (b) StephenDonohoe 4 — 37
(John A Harris) *chsd ldrs 4f* **25/1**

3130 **11** 1 1/2 **Triskaidekaphobia**15 [1080] 4-9-2 **58** ... (t) EddieAhern 6 — 36
(Miss J R Tooth) *chsd ldrs over 4f* **14/1**

/440 **12** 1 **Pulse**15 [1080] 9-9-1 **57** ... (p) StephenCarson 5 — 31
(Miss J R Tooth) *chsd ldrs over 4f* **50/1**

-043 **13** 1 3/4 **Sharp Hat**13 [1112] 13-8-5 **54** ... JamieHamblett(7) 1 — 22
(D W Chapman) *unruly to post: s.s: outpcd* **20/1**

000- **14** 1/2 **Whistler**223 [5493] 10-8-13 **55** ... (b) PaulFitzsimons 9 — 21
(Miss J R Tooth) *sn outpcd* **28/1**

4600 **15** 3/4 **Sir Loin**65 [566] 6-8-5 **54** ... (v) DanielleMcCreery(7) 3 — 18
(N Tinkler) *chsd ldrs over 4f* **33/1**

58.98 secs (-2.82) **Going Correction** -0.525s/f (Hard) — **15** Ran SP% **121.3**

Speed ratings (Par 101):101,97,93,91,89 89,88,84,83,82 80,78,76,75,74

CSF £132.63 CT £481.38 TOTE £15.80: £3.90, £3.40, £2.20; EX 174.40.

Owner P D Savill **Bred** P D Savill **Trained** Stillington, N Yorks

FOCUS

A moderate sprint in which it again paid to be drawn high. The form is rated through the third and looks solid enough.

1406 NOTTINGHAMRACECOURSE.CO.UK H'CAP — 1m 6f 15y

3:45 (3:45) (Class 6) (0-60,60) 4-Y-O+ — **£2,047** (£604; £302) **Stalls** Low

Form — RPR

0-31 **1** **Rare Coincidence**8 [1225] 6-8-12 **54** ... (p) EddieAhern 2 — 64
(R F Fisher) *led: qcknd over 4f out: styd on wl: unchal* **5/2**1

-030 **2** 2 **Ronsard (IRE)**1 [1380] 5-8-6 **48** ow2 ... RobertHavlin 3 — 55
(P D Evans) *s.i.s: hdwy 4f out: wnt 2nd over 2f out: no imp* **16/1**

45-4 **3** 1 1/2 **My Legal Eagle (IRE)**11 [1152] 13-8-1 **46** ... LiamJones(3) 1 — 51
(E G Bevan) *hld up in rr: hdwy on outer over 2f out: kpt on wl to take 3rd towards fin* **10/1**

6351 **4** 1/2 **Treason Trial**11 [1152] 6-8-13 **55** ... AmirQuinn 13 — 59
(Stef Liddiard) *hld up in rr: hdwy over 3f out: styd on wl fnl f* **5/1**2

2010 **5** 1/2 **Blue Hills**22 [994] 6-8-11 **60** ... (b) WilliamCarson(7) 9 — 63
(P W Hiatt) *hld up in midfield: effrt on inner over 3f out: kpt on wl fnl 2f* **16/1**

00/3 **6** 1 1/2 **Theflyingscottie**8 [1229] 5-8-4 **46** oh1 ... CatherineGannon 4 — 47
(D Shaw) *bhd: styd on fnl 2f: nt rch ldrs* **16/1**

320- **7** 1 1/4 **Knight Valliant**239 [5082] 4-8-12 **55** ... TonyHamilton 8 — 54
(J Howard Johnson) *chsd ldrs: one pce fnl 2f* **9/1**

30-0 **8** 1/2 **El Capitan (FR)**11 [1167] 4-8-11 **54** ... PatDobbs 12 — 53
(Miss Gay Kelleway) *mid-div: effrt over 3f out: hung lft over 1f out: nvr rchd ldrs* **33/1**

00-0 **9** 1/2 **Zonic Boom (FR)**14 [1090] 7-8-10 **52** ... (t) JamieMackay 11 — 50
(Heather Dalton) *s.i.s: hld up in rr: kpt on fnl 3f: nvr on terms* **25/1**

0-23 **10** 1 3/4 **Hugs Destiny (IRE)**7 [1239] 6-8-12 **54** ... (t) SebSanders 15 — 50
(M A Barnes) *chsd ldrs: hung lft and wknd over 1f out* **8/1**3

0-46 **11** 4 **General Flumpa**9 [1199] 6-9-2 **58** ... TedDurcan 10 — 48
(Miss Tor Sturgis) *mid-div: wknd over 2f out* **12/1**

101- **12** 1 3/4 **Guadiana (GER)**191 [6133] 5-8-4 **46** ... ChrisCatlin 5 — 34
(A W Carroll) *in rr: drvn over 3f out: nvr on terms* **22/1**

500- **13** shd **Phone In**145 [6748] 4-8-13 **56** ... PhillipMakin 14 — 43
(R Brotherton) *sn trcking wnr: wknd 2f out* **12/1**

220- **14** 13 **Alqaayid**185 [6238] 6-8-9 **54** ... StephaneBreux(3) 16 — 23
(P W Hiatt) *t.k.h in mid-div: hdwy on outer 7f out: lost pl 3f out* **50/1**

0-00 **15** 1/2 **Water Pistol**9 [1196] 5-8-6 **48** ... StephenCarson 6 — 17
(M C Chapman) *chsd ldrs: drvn 5f out: lost pl over 3f out* **100/1**

3m 6.16s (-0.94) **Going Correction** +0.10s/f (Good)

WFA 4 from 5yo+ 1lb — **15** Ran SP% **122.6**

Speed ratings (Par 101):106,104,104,103,103 102,101,101,101,100 98,97,96,89,89

CSF £44.90 CT £360.30 TOTE £3.20: £1.40, £5.80, £3.00; EX 83.60.

Owner A Kerr **Bred** D R Tucker **Trained** Ulverston, Cumbria

FOCUS

A poor staying handicap rated around the third and fourth and the form looks pretty ordinary.

1407 VERSION ONE PAPERLESS OFFICE FILLIES' H'CAP — 1m 1f 213y

4:20 (4:21) (Class 4) (0-85,82) 3-Y-O — **£6,477** (£1,927; £963; £481) **Stalls** Low

Form — RPR

1-0 **1** **Happy Go Lily**12 [1122] 3-9-1 **79** ... TedDurcan 5 — 84
(W R Swinburn) *a.p: chsd ldr over 6f out: rdn to ld over 1f out: jst hld on* **8/1**

21-0 **2** hd **Ronaldsay**32 [838] 3-8-12 **76** ... PatDobbs 11 — 80+
(R Hannon) *s.i.s: hld up: hdwy on ins 2f out: rdn and ev ch ins fnl f: r.o* **15/2**3

0-1 **3** 1 **Going To Work (IRE)**19 [1024] 3-8-9 **73** ... SebSanders 1 — 77+
(D R C Elsworth) *plld hrd and prom: lost pl 7f out: hdwy over 2f out: nt clr run over 1f out and ins fnl f: r.o* **5/2**1

234 **4** nk **Nans Joy (IRE)**27 [935] 3-8-7 **71** ... ChrisCatlin 9 — 73
(E J O'Neill) *hld up: racd keenly: hdwy over 2f out: rdn and ev ch whn edgd lft ins fnl f: styd on same pce* **8/1**

01- **5** 2 **Sell Out**172 [6433] 3-9-0 **78** ... SteveDrowne 6 — 76
(G Wragg) *s.i.s: hdwy 7f out: rdn over 1f out: hung lft and no ex ins fnl f* **16/1**

1- **6** 2 1/2 **Flower Of Kent (USA)**168 [6486] 3-8-12 **76** ... RichardHughes 2 — 69+
(J H M Gosden) *racd keenly: sn led: hdd over 7f out: chsd ldrs: rdn over 2f out: wkng whn n.m.r ins fnl f* **10/3**2

41-1 **7** 1/2 **Hostage**119 [21] 3-9-1 **79** ... EddieAhern 3 — 72
(M L W Bell) *prom: racd keenly: rdn over 2f out: wkng whn hmpd 1f out* **9/1**

41-6 **8** 6 **Lakshmi (IRE)**32 [838] 3-9-4 **82** ... JHBowman 4 — 75+
(M R Channon) *chsd ldr tl led over 7f out: rdn and hdd over 1f out: wkng whn hmpd sn after: eased* **12/1**

00-0 **9** 16 **Cavort (IRE)**42 [725] 3-8-3 **72** ... WilliamBuick(5) 7 — 23
(Pat Eddery) *trckd ldrs: plld hrd: hung lft and wknd over 3f out* **25/1**

34-3 **10** *31* **Feolin**[30] [889] 3-8-6 **70** ow1 .... RobertHavlin 10 —
(H Morrison) *bhd fnl 7f* **20/1**
2m 12.08s (2.38) **Going Correction** +0.10s/f (Good) **10** Ran SP% **117.8**
Speed ratings (Par 98):94,93,93,92,91 89,88,84,71,46
CSF £67.40 CT £195.29 TOTE £15.20: £2.90, £2.60, £1.40; EX 104.80.
Owner Donal Cunningham **Bred** Razza Pallorsi **Trained** Aldbury, Herts
FOCUS
An interesting fillies' handicap for three-year-olds. It was run at just a modest early pace, however, and the form, rated through the fourth, should be treated with a degree of caution.
Feolin Official explanation: jockey said filly was in season

1408 SUBSCRIBE TO RACING UK MAIDEN FILLIES' STKS (DIV I) 1m 54y
4:55 (4:55) (Class 5) 3-Y-O **£2,590** (£770; £385; £192) **Stalls** Centre

Form RPR
4-6 **1** **Arabian Treasure (USA)**[13] [1105] 3-9-0 .... KerrinMcEvoy 7 81+
(Sir Michael Stoute) *mde all: qcknd 3f out: edgd rt fnl f: hld on wl* **6/4**[1]
2 *½* **Classira (IRE)** 3-9-0 .... PhilipRobinson 6 77
(M A Jarvis) *trckd wnr: chal over 1f out: no ex ins fnl f* **4/1**[3]
3 *1 ¼* **Blackberry Pie (USA)** 3-9-0 .... SteveDrowne 3 74+
(R Charlton) *dwlt: in rr: hdwy 2f out: styd on ins fnl f* **14/1**
2- **4** *shd* **Cut The Cake (USA)**[207] [5814] 3-9-0 .... TPQueally 5 73
(J Noseda) *hld up in tch: effrt 2f out: styd on ins fnl f* **11/4**[2]
063- **5** *1 ½* **Naughty Thoughts (IRE)**[205] [5859] 3-8-11 70 .... AndrewMullen(3) 11 70
(K A Ryan) *rrd s: sn prom: one pce fnl 2f* **16/1**
6 *1 ¼* **Sweet Clover** 3-9-0 .... PatCosgrave 1 67
(K R Burke) *chsd ldrs: drvn over 3f out: wknd fnl f* **25/1**
0 **7** *2* **All Began (IRE)**[13] [1105] 3-9-0 .... TedDurcan 9 63
(G Wragg) *s.i.s: kpt on fnl 2f: nvr a factor* **25/1**
0- **8** *½* **Miss Marvellous (USA)**[239] [5095] 3-9-0 .... ChrisCatlin 8 61
(J R Fanshawe) *sn trcking ldrs: wknd 2f out* **33/1**
0-6 **9** *7* **Heart Of Glass (IRE)**[18] [1045] 3-9-0 .... HayleyTurner 10 45
(M L W Bell) *in rr whn rn bnd after 1f: nvr a factor* **40/1**
652- **10** *¾* **Aaron's Way**[210] [5764] 3-9-0 65 .... SebSanders 4 44
(A W Carroll) *t.k.h in rr: hdwy on ins 4f out: lost pl over 2f out* **25/1**
1m 47.25s (0.85) **Going Correction** +0.10s/f (Good) **10** Ran SP% **116.1**
Speed ratings (Par 96):99,98,97,97,95 94,92,91,84,84
CSF £7.08 TOTE £2.70: £1.20, £1.90, £2.60; EX 10.30.
Owner Saeed Suhail **Bred** Calumet Farm **Trained** Newmarket, Suffolk
FOCUS
Probably the stronger of the two divisions and a solid maiden, best rated around the fourth and fifth.
Aaron's Way Official explanation: jockey said filly ran too freely

1409 SUBSCRIBE TO RACING UK MAIDEN FILLIES' STKS (DIV II) 1m 54y
5:30 (5:31) (Class 5) 3-Y-O **£2,590** (£770; £385; £192) **Stalls** Centre

Form RPR
3- **1** **Small Fortune**[285] [3700] 3-9-0 .... SteveDrowne 5 75
(R Charlton) *hld up in tch: swtchd rt over 3f out: rdn to chse ldr over 1f out: hung lft: styd on to ld wl ins fnl f* **6/4**[1]
5 **2** *½* **Angel Kate (IRE)**[12] [1128] 3-9-0 .... TedDurcan 9 74
(H R A Cecil) *s.i.s: sn rcvrd to ld: rdn over 1f out: hdd wl ins fnl f* **3/1**[3]
3 *1 ½* **Jamboretta (IRE)** 3-9-0 .... KerrinMcEvoy 1 74+
(Sir Michael Stoute) *hld up in tch: swtchd rt over 1f out: styd on* **9/4**[2]
545- **4** *3* **Satin Braid**[181] [6309] 3-9-0 70 .... SebSanders 2 64
(A W Carroll) *trckd ldrs: plld hrd: rdn over 2f out: wknd fnl f* **16/1**
00- **5** *1 ¼* **Split The Wind (USA)**[208] [5780] 3-9-0 .... StephenCarson 6 61
(Eve Johnson Houghton) *hld up: rdn over 3f out: nvr trbld ldrs* **66/1**
0- **6** *¾* **Anthill**[269] [4177] 3-8-9 .... KevinGhunowa(5) 8 59
(I A Wood) *plld hrd and prom: rdn over 2f out: wknd over 1f out* **50/1**
7 *9* **Petite Arvine (USA)** 3-9-0 .... HayleyTurner 3 38
(M L W Bell) *s.i.s: rdn over 4f out: a in rr* **20/1**
8 *6* **Highbourne Lady** 3-9-0 .... VinceSlattery 7 25
(B N Pollock) *prom: lost pl 6f out: bhd fnl 5f* **100/1**
00 **9** *¾* **Tia Jade**[81] [418] 3-9-0 .... AntonyProcter 10 23
(M J Gingell) *hld up: rdn and wknd over 3f out* **200/1**
1m 47.67s (1.27) **Going Correction** +0.10s/f (Good) **9** Ran SP% **111.4**
Speed ratings (Par 96):97,96,95,92,90 90,81,75,74
CSF £5.86 TOTE £2.30: £1.10, £1.80, £1.20; EX 7.90.
Owner The Queen **Bred** The Queen **Trained** Beckhampton, Wilts
FOCUS
This second division of the fillies' maiden has been rated slightly the lesser of the pair. The early pace was only average and the form does not look as solid.
Anthill Official explanation: jockey said filly ran too freely

1410 GREAT HOSPITALITY PACKAGES AVAILABLE NOW H'CAP 1m 54y
6:00 (6:02) (Class 5) (0-70,70) 3-Y-O **£2,914** (£867; £433; £216) **Stalls** Centre

Form RPR
236- **1** **Keidas (FR)**[183] [6285] 3-9-4 **70** .... EddieAhern 1 75+
(C F Wall) *mde all: rdn and kpt on gamely fnl f* **10/3**[2]
60-0 **2** *½* **Mighty Missouri (IRE)**[11] [1155] 3-8-10 **62** ....(p) TedDurcan 4 66
(W R Swinburn) *trckd ldrs: rdn to chal over 1f out: no ex wl ins fnl f* **11/1**
54-0 **3** *1 ¼* **Bidable**[11] [1155] 3-8-10 **62** .... JamieMackay 8 63
(B Palling) *chsd ldrs: effrt over 3f out: kpt on same pce appr fnl f* **16/1**
1311 **4** *1 ¾* **Pietersen (IRE)**[14] [1091] 3-8-11 **70** ....(b) NeilBrown(7) 2 67+
(T D Barron) *hld up in tch: effrt over 3f out: kpt on same pce fnl 2f* **9/4**[1]
30-0 **5** *2 ½* **Delta Shuttle (IRE)**[14] [1091] 3-9-0 **66** .... PatCosgrave 5 57
(K R Burke) *trckd ldrs: rdn over 3f out: one pce* **9/1**
5610 **6** *¾* **Muncaster Castle (IRE)**[37] [790] 3-8-4 **56** .... AdrianTNicholls 3 45
(R F Fisher) *trckd wnr: hrd drvn over 3f out: wknd over 1f out* **6/1**[3]
0-01 **7** *shd* **Alavana (IRE)**[7] [1236] 3-8-4 **56** 6ex .... PaulQuinn 7 45
(D W Barker) *in rr: hrd drvn over 4f out: nvr nr to chal* **14/1**
050- **8** *1* **Kings Art (IRE)**[212] [5738] 3-8-11 **63** .... DavidAllan 9 50
(W M Brisbourne) *in rr: drvn over 3f out: nvr nr ldrs* **14/1**
036- **9** *14* **Woodland Traveller (USA)**[231] [5283] 3-9-2 **68** ......(t) StephenCarson 10 23
(N Tinkler) *hld up in rr: hdwy to chse ldrs over 4f out: wknd over 2f out* **25/1**
2000 **10** *2 ½* **Not Too Taxing**[47] [694] 3-8-10 **62** .... PatDobbs 6 11
(R Hannon) *in rr: bhd fnl 3f* **16/1**
1m 47.08s (0.68) **Going Correction** +0.10s/f (Good) **10** Ran SP% **115.4**
Speed ratings (Par 99):100,99,98,96,94 93,93,92,78,75
CSF £39.49 CT £524.80 TOTE £4.50: £2.10, £3.80, £2.10; EX 50.40 Place 6 £16.65, Place 5 £10.09..
Owner M Tilbrook **Bred** B Fassbender **Trained** Newmarket, Suffolk
FOCUS
Modest stuff, but the race looks solid enough rated around the winner and third and should produce the odd winner at a similar level.

T/Plt: £19.90 to a £1 stake. Pool: £47,315.70. 1,735.60 winning tickets. T/Qpdt: £10.80 to a £1 stake. Pool: £1,827.90. 124.20 winning tickets. CR

1193 PONTEFRACT (L-H)
Wednesday, May 2

OFFICIAL GOING: Good to firm (firm in places)
Wind: virtually nil

1411 EUROPEAN BREEDERS' FUND BETFRED.COM MAIDEN STKS 5f
2:20 (2:22) (Class 4) 2-Y-O **£4,533** (£1,348; £674; £336) **Stalls** Low

Form RPR
52 **1** **Cee Bargara**[13] [1107] 2-9-3 .... TPQueally 8 78
(J A Osborne) *dwlt: sn trcking ldrs: hdwy on inner 2f out: swtchd rt and effrt over 1f out: rdn to ld jst ins fnl f: kpt on wl* **9/4**[1]
2 **2** *1 ½* **Irving Place**[15] [1073] 2-9-3 .... HayleyTurner 1 72
(M L W Bell) *wnt rt s: led: rdn along 2f out: drvn and hdd jst ins fnl f: kpt on same pce* **3/1**[2]
4 **3** *shd* **Barraland**[16] [1058] 2-9-3 .... SamHitchcott 7 72
(M R Channon) *cl up: effrt 2f out: rdn and edgd lft appr fnl f: sn drvn and kpt on same pce* **9/2**[3]
4 *nk* **Atabaas Pride** 2-9-3 .... KDarley 3 70+
(M Johnston) *hmpd s and bhd tl gd hdwy on outer wl over 1f out: styd on strly ins fnl f: nrst fin* **13/2**
5 *¾* **Natural Rhythm (IRE)** 2-9-3 .... RoystonFfrench 9 67
(Mrs A Duffield) *in tch: pushed along and sltly outpcd 1/2-way: styd on wl appr fnl f: nrst fin* **33/1**
6 *4* **Fyodorovich (USA)** 2-9-3 .... DeanMcKeown 5 51+
(J S Wainwright) *t.k.h: cl up: rdn along and wkng whn n.m.r over 1f out* **11/1**
7 *¾* **Smileforawhile (IRE)** 2-9-3 .... DO'Donohoe 4 48
(K A Ryan) *hmpd s: bhd tl sme late hdwy* **8/1**
8 *½* **Thomas Malory (IRE)** 2-9-3 .... EdwardCreighton 6 46
(Miss V Haigh) *prom: rdn along 1/2-way: sn wknd* **33/1**
9 *½* **Zaplamation (IRE)** 2-9-3 .... PaulHanagan 2 44
(D W Barker) *trckd ldrs on inner: rdn along over 2f out: sn wknd* **11/1**
63.77 secs (-0.03) **Going Correction** -0.275s/f (Firm) **9** Ran SP% **120.9**
Speed ratings (Par 95):89,86,86,85,84 78,77,76,75
CSF £9.58 TOTE £3.30: £1.20, £1.40, £1.90; EX 8.90.
Owner A Taylor **Bred** Mrs R Pease **Trained** Upper Lambourn, Berks
FOCUS
A reasonable maiden that should produce winners, with the winner setting a fair standard.
NOTEBOOK
Cee Bargara confirmed the promise of his two previous efforts with a decisive success. He had to wait for a gap, but picked up well once in the clear and deserves to take his chance in better company. (op 11-4 tchd 3-1 in places)
Irving Place, runner-up on is debut at Nottingham, had every chance was was basically beaten by a better horse. (tchd 10-3 and 4-1 in a place)
Barraland, fourth on his debut at Windsor, showed good early speed and gave the impression a less-testing track may suit better. (op 7-1)
Atabaas Pride ◆, out of a smart dual 1m winner at three in France, has been given an entry in the Group 1 Phoenix Stakes. He was a real eyecatcher, staying on strongly in the straight having lost several lengths when hampered soon after the start. He should win next time, but is unlikely to be much value as he will have gone into many a notebook following this display. (op 9-2 tchd 7-1)
Natural Rhythm(IRE), a 16,000gns brother to three-year-old winers Ballyshane Sprit (1m) and Northern Chorus (5f), kept on nicely and should be better for the experience.
Fyodorovich(USA) Official explanation: jockey said colt hung badly right

1412 TOTESPORT.COM MAIDEN STKS 1m 2f 6y
2:55 (2:56) (Class 5) 3-Y-O **£4,533** (£1,348; £674; £336) **Stalls** Low

Form RPR
30-3 **1** **El Dececy (USA)**[18] [1044] 3-9-3 75 .... MartinDwyer 9 81
(J L Dunlop) *mde most: rdn clr 2f out: styd on wl* **9/2**[2]
0 **2** *5* **Officer**[15] [1077] 3-9-3 .... PaulHanagan 1 71
(Sir Michael Stoute) *cl up: rdn along over 2f out: sn drvn and kpt on same pce* **7/1**[3]
4-3 **3** *1 ¼* **Binocular**[21] [1001] 3-9-3 .... KDarley 4 69
(B W Hills) *chsd ldrs: rdn along over 4f out: drvn 2f out: kpt on same pce* **4/5**[1]
4 *2 ½* **Intersky Charm (USA)** 3-9-3 .... DeanMcKeown 10 64
(R M Whitaker) *dwlt: hdwy to trck ldrs 1/2-way: rdn along over 2f out: sn no imp* **14/1**
5 *2* **Day Of Days (IRE)** 3-9-3 .... JimmyQuinn 5 60+
(M H Tompkins) *s.i.s and bhd tl sme late hdwy* **20/1**
00 **6** *2* **Malguru**[13] [1111] 3-9-3 .... DaleGibson 8 56
(G A Swinbank) *chsd ldrs: rdn along 4f out: outpcd 3f out* **33/1**
0 **7** *2 ½* **Zachary Scott**[13] [1100] 3-9-3 .... AdrianTNicholls 2 52
(C E Brittain) *chsd ldrs: effrt over 4f out: sn rdn along and wknd over 3f out* **12/1**
00- **8** *20* **Fairy Slipper**[223] [5495] 3-8-12 .... PaulMulrennan 6 9
(Jedd O'Keeffe) *a in rr* **100/1**
4430 **9** *14* **Ranavalona**[8] [1220] 3-8-12 53 .... RobbieFitzpatrick 3 —
(C Smith) *t.k.h: chsd ldrs on inner 3f: sn lost pl and bhd fr 1/2-way* **40/1**
2m 10.79s (-3.29) **Going Correction** -0.275s/f (Firm) **9** Ran SP% **111.7**
Speed ratings (Par 99):102,98,97,95,93 91,89,73,62
CSF £32.97 TOTE £5.50: £1.40, £1.70, £1.10; EX 23.50.
Owner Hamdan Al Maktoum **Bred** Shadwell Farm LLC **Trained** Arundel, W Sussex
■ Stewards' Enquiry : Robbie Fitzpatrick one-day ban: used whip in incorrect place (May 14)
FOCUS
An ordinary maiden and the form does not look that solid.
Intersky Charm(USA) Official explanation: jockey said colt hung right on first bend
Ranavalona Official explanation: jockey said filly hung right throughout

1413 SKYBET.COM H'CAP 1m 4y
3:30 (3:30) (Class 5) (0-70,70) 4-Y-O+ **£4,533** (£1,348; £674; £336) **Stalls** Low

Form RPR
0-04 **1** **Malinsa Blue (IRE)**[9] [1199] 5-8-4 **56** .... RoystonFfrench 2 69
(B Ellison) *a.p: hdwy to ld 2f out: rdn ent fnl f: styd on wl* **10/1**
-255 **2** *1* **Pab Special (IRE)**[61] [604] 4-9-1 **70** .... AndrewElliott(3) 12 81
(K R Burke) *cl up: effrt and ev ch 2f out: sn rdn: drvn ins fnl f and kpt on* **13/2**[3]
406- **3** *1 ¼* **Joshua's Gold (IRE)**[200] [5974] 6-8-11 **63** .... DanielTudhope 3 71
(D Carroll) *trckd ldrs: hdwy 2f out: rdn to chse ldng pair over 1f out: drvn and kpt on ins fnl f* **9/1**

40-6 **4** *2* **Champain Sands (IRE)**[12] [1132] 8-8-13 **65**........................ KDarley 10 69
(E J Alston) *hld up in rr: hdwy on outer wl over 1f out: rdn and kpt on ins fnl f: nrst fin* **12/1**

5-63 **5** *shd* **Northern Boy (USA)**[9] [1198] 4-9-4 **70**........................ DeanMcKeown 5 73
(T D Barron) *dwlt: sn in tch: effrt 3f out: sn rdn and kpt on same pce fnl 2f* **7/2**[2]

00-6 **6** *shd* **Press Express (IRE)**[28] [915] 5-8-10 **62**........................ PaulHanagan 11 65
(R A Fahey) *bmpd after 1f: in tch: effrt and sme hdwy over 2f out: sn rdn and no imp fr over 1f out* **9/4**[1]

000- **7** *3* **Boreana**[230] [5320] 4-8-11 **63**........................ PaulMulrennan 1 59
(Jedd O'Keeffe) *chsd ldrs on inner: rdn along 3f out: sn btn* **22/1**

-045 **8** *1/2* **Fairy Monarch (IRE)**[1] [1381] 8-8-0 **57** oh3 ow1..........(b) RoryMoore(5) 4 52
(P T Midgley) *a in rr* **14/1**

-012 **9** *1 3/4* **Holiday Cocktail**[49] [675] 5-8-8 **60**..........................(v) GrahamGibbons 6 51
(J J Quinn) *a in rr* **15/2**

305- **10** *15* **Apsara**[211] [5751] 6-8-13 **65**........................ DO'Donohoe 7 21
(G M Moore) *led: rdn along 3f out: hdd 2f out and sn wknd* **16/1**

000- **11** *25* **Nell Tupp**[126] [6944] 4-7-13 **56** oh6..........................(b[1]) DuranFentiman(5) 8 —
(G Woodward) *a bhd* **125/1**

1m 43.31s (-2.39) **Going Correction** -0.275s/f (Firm) **11** Ran SP% **122.6**
Speed ratings (Par 103):100,99,97,95,95 95,92,92,90,75 50
CSF £76.84 CT £633.47 TOTE £13.90: £2.80, £2.60, £3.10; EX 83.50.
Owner Mrs Andrea M Mallinson **Bred** Martin Donovan **Trained** Norton, N Yorks

FOCUS
A modest handicap in which those who raced handy appeared to be at an advantage, but the form looks sound enough.
Press Express(IRE) Official explanation: trainer had no explanation for the poor form shown

1414 LADBROKES FILLIES' H'CAP 1m 2f 6y
4:05 (4:05) (Class 3) (0-90,83) 3-Y-0+
£9,348 (£2,799; £1,399; £700; £349; £175) **Stalls** Low

Form RPR

211- **1** **Abandon (USA)**[130] [6929] 4-9-10 **77**........................ PaulHanagan 4 88+
(W J Haggas) *led to 1/2-way: cl up tl led again over 2f out and sn rdn: drvn ent fnl f: styd on gamely* **4/1**[2]

26-1 **2** *shd* **Flying Clarets (IRE)**[15] [1083] 4-9-9 **81**........................ JamieMoriarty(5) 2 92
(R A Fahey) *cl up: slt ld 1/2-way: rdn and hdd over 2f out: sn drvn and ev ch: kpt on wl fnl f: jst hld* **6/1**[3]

4-11 **3** *1/2* **Lisathedaddy**[46] [702] 5-9-10 **77**........................ DaleGibson 3 87+
(B G Powell) *hld up in rr: pushed along and outpcd over 2f out: rdn over 1f out: styd on strly ins fnl f: nrst fin* **8/1**

1-1 **4** *2* **Manaal (USA)**[13] [1110] 3-8-12 **80**........................ MartinDwyer 5 85
(Sir Michael Stoute) *trckd ldrs: effrt 3f out: rdn 2f out: kpt on same pce* **11/10**[1]

1P05 **5** *6* **Daring Affair**[4] [1288] 6-9-13 **80**........................ PaulMulrennan 1 74
(K R Burke) *in tch: effrt over 3f out: sn rdn along and no imp fnl 2f* **11/1**

40-5 **6** *1 1/4* **Musical Mirage (USA)**[13] [1110] 3-9-1 **83**........................ DeanMcKeown 8 74
(G A Swinbank) *in rr: hdwy on outer to chse ldrs 3f out: sn rdn and btn* **20/1**

120- **7** *2 1/2* **Jane Of Arc (FR)**[236] [5157] 3-8-8 **76**........................ JimmyQuinn 6 62
(M H Tompkins) *a in rr* **14/1**

16-0 **8** *32* **Strawberry Lolly**[11] [1149] 4-9-13 **80**........................ KDarley 7 2
(M Botti) *chsd ldrs: rdn along over 3f out: sn wknd* **20/1**

2m 9.96s (-4.12) **Going Correction** -0.275s/f (Firm)
WFA 3 from 4yo+ 15lb **8** Ran SP% **117.5**
Speed ratings (Par 104):105,104,104,102,98 97,95,69
CSF £29.01 CT £180.25 TOTE £5.00: £1.50, £1.70, £1.90; EX 28.10.
Owner Cheveley Park Stud **Bred** 6 C Stallions Limited **Trained** Newmarket, Suffolk
■ Stewards' Enquiry : Jamie Moriarty one-day ban: used whip in incorrect place (May 14)

FOCUS
A decent fillies' handicap run significantly faster than the two other races over the trip on the day and sound form.

NOTEBOOK
Abandon(USA), a lightly-raced half-sister to Tawqeet, was making her debut on turf having won two of her three runs on sand before Christmas. Dropping a quarter mile in trip, she was ridden positively and showed plenty of courage to hold after the runner-up looked to have taken her measure halfway up the straight. She can continue to progress if none the worse for this hard race. (op 9-2 tchd 5-1)
Flying Clarets(IRE), who returned to winning ways dropped back to this trip and returned to fast ground on her seasonal return last time, was racing off her highest mark to date as a result. She looked the most likely winner halfway up the straight and gave her all in the finish, only just losing out. She sets the standard for the form and if not raised again for this effort, can gain compensation in similar company. (op 8-1)
Lisathedaddy, four times a winner around Lingfield's Polytrack, was having only her third outing on turf but was racing from a 10lb lower mark than on sand. She ran with credit and was closing on the first two near the line, suggesting that she is capable of winning similar races on turf. (op 15-2)
Manaal(USA), a three-year-old who had been raised 5lb for her narrow win at Ripon, was stepping up in trip and, after having been close enough turning in, had nothing left in the closing stages. She may be better off back at a mile against her own age group for the time being. (op 5-4 tchd Evens)
Daring Affair, a useful filly on sand but also a winner on fast turf, had looked unlucky at the weekend but was left behind in this slightly better-class race, having been close enough on the run to the straight. (op 10-1 tchd 8-1)
Strawberry Lolly Official explanation: jockey said filly was unsuited by the good to firm ground

1415 32RED PLC H'CAP 1m 4f 8y
4:40 (4:40) (Class 5) (0-75,74) 3-Y-O **£4,533** (£1,348; £674; £336) **Stalls** Low

Form RPR

00-3 **1** **Sonara (IRE)**[11] [1154] 3-8-4 **60**........................ JimmyQuinn 8 68+
(M H Tompkins) *trckd ldrs on inner: hdwy 3f out: effrt over 1f out: rdn to ld ins fnl f: styd on wl* **9/2**[2]

1-42 **2** *hd* **My Secrets**[4] [1289] 3-9-4 **74**........................ KDarley 1 82
(M Johnston) *a.p: hdwy to ld 3f out: rdn wl over 1f out: drvn and hdd ins fnl f: rallied wl towards fin* **1/1**[1]

60-4 **3** *5* **Moonwalking**[20] [1010] 3-9-4 **74**........................ DaleGibson 3 74
(Jedd O'Keeffe) *in tch: hdwy over 3f out: rdn wl over 1f out: kpt on same pce appr fnl f* **15/2**[3]

305- **4** *7* **Monsieur Dumas (IRE)**[186] [6224] 3-8-11 **67**.............. RoystonFfrench 7 56
(T P Tate) *cl up: effrt 3f out: rdn 2f out and grad wknd* **10/1**

0-34 **5** *3 1/2* **Dana Music (USA)**[27] [936] 3-9-0 **70**........................ SamHitchcott 4 53
(M R Channon) *in rr tl styd on fnl 2f* **14/1**

546- **6** *2* **Sendali (FR)**[217] [5616] 3-8-6 **65**........................ AndrewElliott(3) 6 45
(J D Bethell) *chsd ldrs: rdn along 3f out: sn wknd* **12/1**

00-4 **7** *16* **Majestic Chief**[15] [1075] 3-8-13 **69**........................ DO'Donohoe 5 23
(K A Ryan) *led: rdn along and hdd 3f out: sn wknd* **33/1**

2200 **8** *18* **Rain And Shade**[14] [1089] 3-8-10 **71**..........................(t) JamieMoriarty(5) 2 —
(E W Tuer) *in tch: rdn along 5f out and sn wknd* **14/1**

2m 37.09s (-3.21) **Going Correction** -0.275s/f (Firm) **8** Ran SP% **113.0**
Speed ratings (Par 99):99,98,95,90,88 87,76,64
CSF £9.12 CT £31.12 TOTE £5.50: £1.90, £1.10, £1.70; EX 9.50.
Owner Mrs Beryl Lockey **Bred** Kevin Gaffney **Trained** Newmarket, Suffolk
■ Stewards' Enquiry : Jimmy Quinn caution: used whip without giving gelding time to respond

FOCUS
A fair handicap in which the first two came clear and, with the form rated positively, both look capable of winning more races.

1416 FRIENDS OF THE NORTHERN RACING COLLEGE H'CAP 1m 2f 6y
5:15 (5:18) (Class 5) (0-75,75) 4-Y-0+ **£4,533** (£1,348; £674; £336) **Stalls** Low

Form RPR

0-23 **1** **Just Observing**[11] [1158] 4-8-8 **70**..........................(p) RoryMoore(5) 1 81
(P T Midgley) *trckd ldrs: hdwy 2f out: rdn to ld over 1f out: drvn ins fnl f: hld on gamely* **12/1**

/55- **2** *shd* **Sin City**[292] [3502] 4-9-1 **72**........................ PaulHanagan 9 83+
(R A Fahey) *hld up in tch: hdwy on outer 2f out: rdn to chal and hung lft ent fnl f: sn drvn: jst failed* **9/2**[3]

/0-0 **3** *1 3/4* **Wild Fell Hall (IRE)**[18] [1036] 4-8-11 **68**........................ DO'Donohoe 5 76
(W R Swinburn) *trckd ldrs: effrt 2f out: sn rdn and kpt on fnl f* **12/1**

443- **4** *2 1/2* **Stargazer Jim (FR)**[133] [6888] 5-8-13 **70**........................ MartinDwyer 8 73
(W J Haggas) *led: rdn along 3f out: drvn and hdd over 1f out: wknd ins fnl f* **3/1**[2]

12-5 **5** *1 3/4* **Wasalat (USA)**[6] [1258] 5-8-12 **69**........................ JimmyQuinn 7 69
(D W Barker) *hld up in rr: hdwy on inner over 2f out: rdn to chse ldrs over 1f out: sn no imp* **9/1**

3642 **6** *2* **Suits Me**[9] [1199] 4-8-10 **67**........................ RoystonFfrench 4 63
(T P Tate) *hld up towards rr: pushed along 4f out: rdn 3f out and sn no hdwy* **11/4**[1]

00-6 **7** *1 1/4* **Snowed Under**[15] [1078] 6-8-13 **73**........................ AndrewElliott(3) 10 66
(J D Bethell) *cl up: ev ch 3f out: sn rdn and wknd wl over 1f out* **9/1**

044- **8** *3 1/2* **Colton**[184] [6259] 4-9-2 **73**........................ DaleGibson 13 60
(J M P Eustace) *a in rr* **10/1**

30-0 **9** *hd* **Ruby Legend**[9] [1199] 9-7-11 **61** oh2........................ FrankiePickard(7) 11 47
(K G Reveley) *a bhd* **33/1**

200- **10** *3* **Dakota Rain (IRE)**[230] [5320] 5-9-0 **71**........................ EdwardCreighton 12 52
(Jennie Candlish) *t.k.h: cl up on outer: rdn along 3f out: drvn 2f out and sn wknd* **40/1**

2m 10.85s (-3.23) **Going Correction** -0.275s/f (Firm) **10** Ran SP% **119.7**
Speed ratings (Par 103):101,100,99,97,96 94,93,90,90,88
CSF £67.11 CT £679.77 TOTE £14.50: £3.00, £1.80, £2.70; EX 87.40 Place 6 £57.89, Place 5 £44.72.
Owner O R Dukes **Bred** Stratford Place Stud **Trained** Westow, N Yorks

FOCUS
A fair handicap and a close finish, but the slowest of the three races over the trip on the day and best rated through the fifth.
T/Jkpt: Not won. T/Plt: £39.80 to a £1 stake. Pool: £63,170.85. 1,156.30 winning tickets. T/Qpdt: £30.70 to a £1 stake. Pool: £2,225.80. 53.60 winning tickets. JR

1417 - 1420a (Foreign Racing) - See Raceform Interactive

1233 CHANTILLY (R-H)
Wednesday, May 2

OFFICIAL GOING: Good

1421a PRIX ALLEZ FRANCE (GROUP 3) (F&M) 1m 2f
3:05 (3:06) 4-Y-0+ **£27,027** (£10,811; £8,108; £5,405; £2,703)

RPR

1 **Macleya (GER)**[23] [990] 5-8-7........................ SPasquier 9 108
(A Fabre, France) *prom: sn racing in 2nd: pushed along to chal 2f out: led 1 1/2f out: r.o wl fnl 100yds: drvn out* **169/10**

2 *1* **Satwa Queen (FR)**[143] [6785] 5-9-2........................ TThulliez 12 115
(J De Roualle, France) *hld up towards rr: disputing 9th st: pushed along and r.o over 1 1/2f out: wnt 3rd and fin wl fr 1f out: nrst at fin* **17/10**[1]

3 *nk* **Nickelle (FR)**[24] [962] 4-8-7........................ RonanThomas 7 106
(J-P Gallorini, France) *sn led: pushed along st: hdd 1 1/2f out: kpt on* **9/2**[2]

4 *2 1/2* **Sureyya (GER)**[24] [962] 4-8-7........................ OPeslier 5 101
(E Lellouche, France) *prom: 4th st: rdn 1 1/2f out: nt pce of ldrs* **11/1**

5 *1/2* **Fair Breeze (GER)**[156] 4-8-7........................ ASuborics 2 100
(Mario Hofer, Germany) *mid-div: disputing 6th st: drvn 1 1/2f out: styd on u.p fnl f* **15/1**

6 *1* **Tonic Star (FR)**[24] [962] 4-8-7........................ GFaucon 10 98
(E Lellouche, France) *mid-div: 8th st: nvr in contention* **26/1**

7 *1 1/2* **Princess Jones**[31] 7-8-7........................ FVeron 4 96
(J-L Guillochon, France) *hld up: disputing 9th st: r.o fnl f but n.d* **36/1**

8 *nk* **Kankakee (USA)**[33] [837] 4-8-7........................ TGillet 1 95
(J E Pease, France) *hld up: 11th st: effrt 2f out: n.d* **11/1**

9 *nk* **Mussoorie (FR)**[192] [6120] 4-8-7........................ C-PLemaire 3 95
(R Gibson, France) *prom on rail: 3rd st: wknd over 1f out* **12/1**

10 *8* **Kibaar (USA)**[188] 4-8-7........................ CSoumillon 6 80
(J E Hammond, France) *prom early: disputing 6th st: sn outpcd* **88/10**[3]

11 *1/2* **Quezon Sun (GER)**[24] [962] 4-8-7........................ YBarberot 11 79
(S Wattel, France) *in tch towards outside: 5th st: sn pushed along: no imp* **24/1**

12 *1/2* **Quelle Amore (GER)**[220] [5561] 4-9-2........................ EPedroza 8 87
(A Wohler, Germany) *towards rr: last st: nvr a factor* **24/1**

2m 1.60s (-5.20) **12** Ran SP% **116.0**
PARI-MUTUEL: WIN 17.90; PL 3.50, 1.50, 2.00; DF 22.00.
Owner R C Thompson **Bred** Gestut Schlenderhan **Trained** Chantilly, France

NOTEBOOK
Macleya(GER), back in trip, did a workmanlike job to win this Group 3 contest. Now a five-year-old, she was always handy and went to the head of affairs halfway up the straight. She was then challenged by the favourite but had enough in hand during the final stages. She will almost certainly next turn out for the Prix Corrida, which is over slightly further, and that should be an advantage.
Satwa Queen(FR) had a wide outside draw and never really got into this race until the final furlong and a half. Putting in her best work at the finish, she was conceding four kilos to the winner, who had had the advantage of a previous race this season, so it was a fine effort, and she looks sure to have another successful season. Her main target is the Prix de L'Opera in October but, in the shorter term, she may be sent to Ascot for the Queen Anne Stakes.
Nickelle(FR), as usual, was asked to make all the running, and she set a fairly decent pace. Although passed in the straight, she never gave up and only lost second place in the final few strides.

Sureyya(GER), never far from the leaders, began her run from two furlongs out but never really looked like worrying the first three past the post. This daughter of Monsun might prefer more juice in the ground.

[1235]CATTERICK (L-H)
Thursday, May 3

OFFICIAL GOING: Good to firm (firm in places)
This meeting was transferred from Redcar where the newly aligned bend was not fit for racing.
Wind: moderate across

1422 CATTERICKBRIDGE.CO.UK MAIDEN AUCTION STKS 5f
2:20 (2:21) (Class 5) 2-Y-O £2,817 (£838; £418; £209) **Stalls** Low

Form RPR
5 **1** **Lady Rangali (IRE)**[15] 1087 2-8-7 .... RoystonFfrench 5 69
(Mrs A Duffield) *cl up: led 1/2-way: rdn over 1f out: kpt on wl* **5/2**[2]
2 *shd* **Lady Benjamin** 2-8-7 .... KDarley 4 69
(P C Haslam) *led to 1/2-way: cl up and rdn over 1f out: ev ch ins fnl f: kpt on* **11/1**[3]
3 *3/4* **Select Committee** 2-8-12 .... GrahamGibbons 7 71
(J J Quinn) *chsd ldrs: swtchd rt and hdwy over 1f out: sn rdn and styd on wl fnl f: nrst fin* **12/1**
4 *2 1/2* **Maid In Bloom** 2-8-4 .... ChrisCatlin 3 53
(B Smart) *sn rdn along and outpcd in rr: hdwy 2f out: styd on wl appr fnl f: nrst fin* **22/1**
0 **5** *1 3/4* **Complete Frontline (GER)**[14] 1107 2-8-12 .... PatCosgrave 8 54
(K R Burke) *prom on outer: rdn along 2f out: grad wknd* **12/1**
0 **6** *3/4* **Holly Golightley**[10] 1193 2-8-7 .... NCallan 6 46
(K A Ryan) *chsd ldrs: rdn along over 2f out: sn btn* **11/8**[1]
7 *1 1/2* **Grudge** 2-8-9 .... TonyHamilton 1 42
(D W Barker) *sn outpcd and rdn along in rr: sme hdwy and in tch 2f out: sn wknd* **12/1**
8 *1 1/4* **Moonlight Gambler (IRE)** 2-9-2 .... DavidAllan 2 44
(T D Easterby) *sn outpcd and bhd tl sme late hdwy* **12/1**
06 **9** *6* **Little Finch (IRE)**[5] 1302 2-7-13 .... RoryMoore(5) 9 8
(R C Guest) *a towards rr* **40/1**

59.60 secs (-1.00) **Going Correction** -0.30s/f (Firm) **9 Ran SP% 116.6**
Speed ratings (Par 93):96,95,94,90,87 86,84,82,72
CSF £30.62 TOTE £2.80: £1.50, £2.70, £4.60; EX 23.70.
Owner Mrs Sarah E Woodhead **Bred** Mrs C Hartery **Trained** Constable Burton, N Yorks

FOCUS
This was an average juvenile contest best assessed using the winner and fifth.

NOTEBOOK
Lady Rangali(IRE) hung left on her debut at Beverley, so going the other way round would have suited and she ran out a game winner. There could be better to come again. (op 11-4 tchd 9-4)
Lady Benjamin, a 16,000gns half-sister to among others Tuscarora, a multiple 6f-1m winner, out a winner over 1m3f, showed good pace from the outset and saw her race out well. With this race under her belt, she should be even better equipped next time. (op 17-2 tchd 8-1)
Select Committee, a 14,000gns half-brother to dual 6f winner Dematraf, out of a 6f-7f two-year-old scorer, was not as well drawn as the first two, but still shaped well and did some particularly good work in the closing stages. He finished clear of the remainder and should find a race.
Maid In Bloom, a 2,000gns first foal whose dam was placed over 5f at two, was a little way off the front three but still showed ability. (op 20-1)
Complete Frontline(GER) did not really improve a great deal on his debut. (tchd 14-1)
Holly Golightley, who had a luckless run first time out at Pontefract, faced a totally different track here and may not have been suited by it. (op 13-8 tchd 7-4)

1423 GO RACING AT THIRSK THIS SATURDAY (S) STKS 7f
2:50 (2:50) (Class 6) 3-Y-O+ £2,047 (£604; £302) **Stalls** Low

Form RPR
-500 **1** **King Marju (IRE)**[32] 881 5-9-4 74 ....(v) NCallan 5 59
(K R Burke) *trckd ldrs on inner: smooth hdwy to ld wl over 1f out: rdn and edgd lft ent fnl f: styd on* **5/6**[1]
1001 **2** *1 1/2* **Just James**[2] 1374 8-9-10 64 .... AdrianTNicholls 7 61
(D Nicholls) *midfield: hdwy 2f out: swtchd ins and rdn to chse wnr whn n.m.r ent fnl f: swtchd rt and rdn: kpt on* **3/1**[2]
240- **3** *2* **Chairman Bobby**[218] 5620 9-9-4 53 .... CatherineGannon 13 50
(D W Barker) *led: rdn along 2f out: sn hdd and kpt on same pce appr fnl f* **10/1**[3]
000- **4** *1 1/4* **Andorran (GER)**[10] 4734 4-9-4 47 ....(tp) DanielTudhope 15 47
(A Dickman) *s.i.s and bhd: hdwy 2f out: sn rdn and styd on wl fnl f: nrst fin* **20/1**
-060 **5** *1/2* **Borodinsky**[15] 1086 6-9-1 40 .... MarkLawson(3) 10 46
(R E Barr) *in tch: hdwy to chse ldrs 3f out and sn rdn: drvn and one pce fnl 2f* **16/1**
0-06 **6** *shd* **Telepathic (IRE)**[29] 912 7-9-4 45 .... StephenDonohoe 9 45
(A Berry) *towards rr: hdwy on outer over 2f out: sn rdn and kpt on same pce* **25/1**
00-0 **7** *1* **Filey Buoy**[5] 682 5-8-13 40 ....(p) MichaelJStainton(5) 6 43
(R M Whitaker) *chsd ldrs: rdn along over 2f out: sn btn* **40/1**
006- **8** *1 1/4* **World At My Feet**[225] 5485 5-8-6 42 .... SuzzanneFrance(7) 3 35
(N Bycroft) *chsd ldrs: rdn along over 2f out: sn wknd* **22/1**
0-06 **9** *3* **Bond Angel Eyes**[12] 1162 4-8-8 44 ....(p) DuranFentiman(5) 8 27
(G R Oldroyd) *a towards rr* **25/1**
060- **10** *nk* **Instinct**[126] 6962 6-9-4 39 .... MickyFenton 2 31
(Micky Hammond) *a in rr* **40/1**
30-0 **11** *nk* **Fairgame Man**[41] 743 9-8-11 44 ....(p) DanielleMcCreery(7) 4 30
(J S Wainwright) *a towards rr* **50/1**
00-0 **12** *7* **Bold Tiger (IRE)**[9] 1221 4-9-4 45 .... SilvestreDeSousa 1 12
(Miss Tracy Waggott) *prom: rdn along over 2f out and sn wknd* **33/1**
00- **13** *5* **Smart Angus**[232] 5288 3-8-7 ow6 .... JamieMoriarty(5) 12 5
(R A Fahey) *a bhd* **28/1**
14 *3/4* **The Social Drinker**[10] 5-9-4 ....(t) RoystonFfrench 11 —
(F P Murtagh) *s.i.s: a bhd* **50/1**
0600 **15** *3* **Danum Diva (IRE)**[5] 1301 3-8-1 39 ....(b) ChrisCatlin 14 —
(T J Pitt) *bhd fr 1/2-way* **40/1**

1m 26.4s (-0.96) **Going Correction** -0.05s/f (Good)
WFA 3 from 4yo+ 12lb **15 Ran SP% 129.0**
Speed ratings (Par 101):103,101,99,97,97 96,95,94,90,90 90,82,76,75,72
CSF £2.85 TOTE £1.60: £1.10, £1.40, £3.50; EX 5.30.The winner was bought in for 13,000gns.
Owner Mrs Maura Gittins **Bred** T Stewart **Trained** Middleham Moor, N Yorks

FOCUS
A typical seller and the form is sound but poor. The winning time was 0.52 seconds slower than the following 61-75, but 1.10 seconds faster than the later maiden.

1424 CATTERICK LADIES' NIGHT TUESDAY 8TH MAY H'CAP 7f
3:20 (3:21) (Class 5) (0-75,76) 3-Y-O £2,817 (£838; £418; £209) **Stalls** Low

Form RPR
4521 **1** **Proper (IRE)**[4] 1316 3-9-8 76 6ex .... ChrisCatlin 7 79
(M R Channon) *cl up: rdn to ld ent fnl f: kpt on wl* **15/8**[1]
2-00 **2** *1* **Nota Liberata**[15] 1091 3-8-12 66 .... NCallan 6 66
(G M Moore) *trckd ldrs: hdwy 2f out: effrt and nt clr run over 1f out: swtchd rt and rdn ent fnl f: styd on* **3/1**[2]
66-2 **3** *shd* **Ruthles Philly**[8] 1238 3-8-4 58 oh2 .... CatherineGannon 2 58
(D W Barker) *sn led: rdn 2f out: drvn and hdd ent fnl f: kpt on same pce* **5/1**
02-4 **4** *nk* **Coconut Queen (IRE)**[13] 1131 3-9-4 72 .... RoystonFfrench 4 71
(Mrs A Duffield) *dwlt: in rr tl hdwy wl over 1f out: sn rdn and styd on strly ins fnl f* **4/1**[3]
503- **5** *3 1/2* **Stepaside (IRE)**[332] 2281 3-9-4 72 .... KDarley 5 62
(M Johnston) *chsd ldng pair: pushed along and outpcd 1/2-way: sn rdn and btn* **8/1**
055- **6** *1 1/2* **Crosby Millie**[206] 5859 3-8-8 62 .... PhillipMakin 1 48
(J R Weymes) *chsd ldrs: rdn along over 2f out: sn wknd* **25/1**

1m 25.88s (-1.48) **Going Correction** -0.05s/f (Good) **6 Ran SP% 111.4**
Speed ratings (Par 99):106,104,104,104,100 98
CSF £7.59 TOTE £2.80: £1.70, £2.00; EX 8.30.
Owner Billy Parish **Bred** Sean Finnegan **Trained** West Ilsley, Berks
■ Stewards' Enquiry : Catherine Gannon ten-day ban: failed to ride out for 2nd place (May 14-23)

FOCUS
A fair handicap in which the winning time was 0.52 seconds quicker than the previous seller, and 1.62 seconds faster than the later maiden. The fourth represents the best guide to the level.

1425 REETH MEDIAN AUCTION MAIDEN STKS 7f
3:50 (3:50) (Class 5) 3-Y-O £2,817 (£838; £418; £209) **Stalls** Low

Form RPR
54-2 **1** **Falcon's Fire (IRE)**[13] 1135 3-9-3 56 .... RoystonFfrench 3 60
(Mrs A Duffield) *a.p: rdn along 2f out: styd on u.p ins fnl f to ld last 75yds* **8/1**[3]
0-22 **2** *2* **Welsh Auction**[1] 1403 3-9-3 70 .... NCallan 7 55
(G A Huffer) *led: rdn along wl over 1f out: drvn ins fnl f: hdd & wknd last 75yds* **4/6**[1]
00- **3** *2* **Tullythered (IRE)**[270] 4171 3-9-3 .... PatCosgrave 1 49
(K R Burke) *a.p: rdn along on inner over 2f out: sn drvn and kpt on same pce appr fnl f* **80/1**
46-0 **4** *hd* **Myfrenchconnection (IRE)**[8] 1236 3-9-3 60 .... MickyFenton 4 49
(P T Midgley) *chsd ldrs: rdn along 2f out: sn one pce* **12/1**
0 **5** *nk* **Dendor**[8] 1236 3-9-3 .... TonyHamilton 2 48
(D W Barker) *in tch: n.m.r on inner 1/2-way: rdn along and kpt on appr fnl f: nrst fin* **25/1**
0 **6** *5* **Intricate Dance (USA)**[13] 1128 3-8-12 .... KDarley 9 29
(B W Hills) *sn rdn along in rr: a bhd* **4/1**[2]
00-6 **7** *2* **Baybshambles (IRE)**[12] 1161 3-9-0 45 .... MarkLawson(3) 5 29
(R E Barr) *chsd ldrs: rdn along over 2f out: sn drvn and wknd* **66/1**
-4 **8** *1/2* **Lady Valentino**[13] 1136 3-8-12 .... PhillipMakin 6 23
(M Dods) *a towards rr* **8/1**[3]

1m 27.5s (0.14) **Going Correction** -0.05s/f (Good) **8 Ran SP% 116.5**
Speed ratings (Par 99):97,94,92,92,91 86,83,83
CSF £14.05 TOTE £8.10: £1.80, £1.10, £11.10; EX 18.10.
Owner BDC Racing Club **Bred** E Balbo Di Vinadio **Trained** Constable Burton, N Yorks

FOCUS
A moderate maiden in which the winning time was 1.62 seconds slower than the earlier 61-75 handicap, and 1.10 seconds slower than the seller. the form has been rated negatively through the fourth.
Intricate Dance(USA) Official explanation: jockey said filly lost its action
Lady Valentino Official explanation: jockey said filly finished distressed

1426 DON'T MISS TOTESPORT SATURDAY 26TH MAY APPRENTICE CLAIMING STKS 5f 212y
4:20 (4:20) (Class 6) 3-4-Y-O £2,047 (£604; £302) **Stalls** Low

Form RPR
0-40 **1** **Rainbow Bay**[23] 992 4-9-3 58 ....(b) MCGeran(5) 1 59+
(E J O'Neill) *dwlt and towards rr: smooth hdwy 1/2-way: led wl over 1f out and sn clr* **5/6**[1]
-000 **2** *3* **Cape Sydney (IRE)**[29] 912 4-9-2 41 ....(p) JamieMoriarty(3) 11 47
(D W Barker) *chsd ldrs: rdn along 2f out: kpt on u.p appr fnl f* **12/1**
0050 **3** *1/2* **Tenterhooks (IRE)**[6] 1281 3-8-3 45 ....(be) PatrickMathers 3 37
(A J McCabe) *in tch: hdwy 2f out: sn rdn and kpt on same pce appr fnl f* **11/1**
566- **4** *1 3/4* **Ishibee (IRE)**[170] 6472 3-8-5 55 .... SaleemGolam 10 33
(Mrs A Duffield) *towards rr: hdwy 2f out: sn rdn and kpt on fnl f* **8/1**[3]
5 *nk* **Whithorn** 4-9-9 .... GaryBartley(5) 2 48+
(J Balding) *s.i.s and bhd tl styd on wl appr fnl f: nrst fin* **25/1**
40-0 **6** *1* **The Salwick Flyer (IRE)**[81] 430 4-9-7 50 .... StephenDonohoe 7 38
(A Berry) *prom: rdn along 2f out: sn drvn and grad wknd* **14/1**
066- **7** *shd* **Seriously Lucky (IRE)**[290] 3581 3-8-9 50 .... HMuya(5) 8 41+
(D Nicholls) *bhd tl sme late hdwy* **18/1**
400- **8** *1 1/4* **Musette (IRE)**[240] 5077 4-8-10 35 .... MichaelJStainton(3) 4 26
(R E Barr) *chsd ldrs: rdn along 1/2-way: sn wknd* **40/1**
-055 **9** *hd* **My Two Girls (IRE)**[8] 1240 3-8-2 54 .... RoryMoore(5) 6 25
(P T Midgley) *in tch: effrt over 2f out: sn rdn and nvr a factor* **13/2**[2]
6-00 **10** *3 1/2* **Esprit De Nuit (IRE)**[8] 1240 3-8-5 45 ....(v[1]) DuranFentiman(3) 9 17
(Mrs A Duffield) *led: rdn along over 2f out: hdd wl over 1f out and sn wknd* **40/1**
B-50 **11** *5* **Polly Rocket**[84] 390 3-8-3 .... AndrewMullen 5 —
(P D Niven) *a bhd* **40/1**

1m 14.1s (0.10) **Going Correction** -0.05s/f (Good)
WFA 3 from 4yo 10lb **11 Ran SP% 118.1**
Speed ratings (Par 101):97,93,92,90,89 88,88,86,86,81 74
CSF £11.89 TOTE £1.80: £1.30, £3.40, £2.80; EX 16.90.The winner was claimed by P D Evans for £7,000. Cape Sydney was claimed by M G Quinlan for £8,000.
Owner Kevin Lee & David Barlow **Bred** Ms R A Myatt **Trained** Averham Park, Notts

FOCUS
An ordinary race, but a fast and furious early gallop. The form is poor and not solid.
Seriously Lucky(IRE) Official explanation: jockey said gelding was denied a clear run
Polly Rocket Official explanation: jockey said filly hung right-handed throughout

1427 CALL 01748 810165 FOR RACEDAY HOSPITALITY FILLIES' H'CAP 5f

4:50 (4:50) (Class 4) (0-85,77) 3-Y-0+ **£4,728** (£1,406; £702; £351) **Stalls** Low

Form RPR

2-12 **1** **Hypnosis**[24] 964 4-9-9 73 PatCosgrave 2 85+
(D W Barker) *trckd ldrs: hdwy over 1f out: rdn ent fnl f: led last 100yds* **11/10**[1]

0000 **2** *1* **Coconut Moon**[16] 1080 5-9-6 70 KDarley 3 78
(E J Alston) *led: rdn along 2f out: drvn ins fnl f: hdd and no ex last 100yds* **7/1**

36-2 **3** *1½* **Mimi Mouse**[13] 1134 5-9-13 77 DavidAllan 1 80
(T D Easterby) *trckd ldng pair: effrt 2f out: swtchd ins and rdn to chal ent fnl f: sn drvn and nt qckn* **5/2**[2]

-313 **4** *2½* **Ashes (IRE)**[9] 1214 5-8-13 63 oh3 PaulMulrennan 4 57
(K R Burke) *cl up: rdn 2f out: drvn and wknd appr fnl f* **7/2**[3]

58.91 secs (-1.69) **Going Correction** -0.30s/f (Firm)
WFA 3 from 4yo+ 9lb **4** Ran SP% **110.9**
Speed ratings (Par 102):101,99,97,93
CSF £8.88 TOTE £1.90; EX 13.90 Place 6 £2.51, Place 5 £2.38..
Owner J P Rider R Snowden **Bred** Mrs V E Hughes **Trained** Scorton, N Yorks

FOCUS
Just the four runners, but a tight little fillies' handicap with the runner-up back to something like her best.
T/Plt: £31.40 to a £1 stake. Pool: £41,691.20. 967.20 winning tickets. T/Qpdt: £5.00 to a £1 stake. Pool: £2,450.10. 358.40 winning tickets. JR

1212 FOLKESTONE (R-H)

Thursday, May 3

OFFICIAL GOING: Good to firm
It proved very difficult to make up ground from off the pace in all seven races, while it also paid to race near the stands'-side rail on the straight track.
Wind: very light across

1428 JOHN SMITH'S MAIDEN AUCTION STKS 5f

2:30 (2:30) (Class 5) 2-Y-0 **£2,914** (£867; £433; £216) **Stalls** Low

Form RPR

3 **1** **Dan Tucket**[14] 1107 2-8-13 TPO'Shea 3 74+
(M R Channon) *trckd ldng pair: chal over 1f out: pushed along to ld 100yds out: r.o* **5/6**[1]

2 *nk* **Hobson** 2-8-10 StephenCarson 2 70
(Eve Johnson Houghton) *t.k.h: pressed ldr tl led wl over 1f out: hdd and rdr dropped whip 100yds out: hld after* **6/4**[2]

3 *2½* **Sheik'N'Knotsterd** 2-8-10 SebSanders 1 60
(J Akehurst) *sn led: hdd wl over 1f out: rdn over 1f out: no ex ins fnl f* **10/1**[3]

4 *6* **Secret Meaning** 2-8-1 LiamJones(3) 5 30
(W G M Turner) *wnt rt s: sn outpcd: nvr on terms* **20/1**

0 **5** *11* **Danny Boy Blue**[10] 1201 2-8-9 IanMongan 4 —
(Mrs L J Mongan) *sn outpcd: no ch fr 1/2-way: t.o* **33/1**

60.60 secs (-0.20) **Going Correction** -0.10s/f (Good) **5** Ran SP% **111.3**
Speed ratings (Par 93):97,96,92,82,65
CSF £2.36 TOTE £1.80: £1.20, £1.40; EX 2.80.
Owner Box 41 **Bred** Grasshopper 2000 Ltd **Trained** West Ilsley, Berks

FOCUS
An ordinary juvenile maiden, but fair efforts from the front pair with the winner to Ripon form. The winning time was 0.67 seconds slower than the following older-horse maiden.

NOTEBOOK
Dan Tucket confirmed the promise he showed when third on his debut at Ripon to get off the mark. He was made to work hard and things may have been even closer had Hobson's rider not dropped his whip close home, although that one did have the benefit of the rail to run against late on. (op evens tchd 5-4 and 11-8 in a place)
Hobson, the first foal of a 5f winner at three, was very solid in the market and only just failed to make a winning debut. He could even be considered a little unlucky as his rider dropped his whip just over half a furlong from the finish. He looks well up to finding a similar race. (op 13-8 tchd 11-10)
Sheik'N'Knotsterd, a 7,000gns first foal of a 7f winner, had the benefit of the rail to run against for much of the way and may be flattered by his proximity to the front pair. Still, this was a pleasing introduction and he clearly has ability. (op 15-2)
Secret Meaning's dam was placed over 6f on her juvenile debut, but she offered very little. (op 14-1)

1429 JOHN SMITH'S SNOWDOWN COLLIERY WELFARE CLUB MAIDEN STKS 5f

3:00 (3:00) (Class 5) 3-Y-0+ **£2,914** (£867; £433; £216) **Stalls** Low

Form RPR

220- **1** **Pretty Miss**[234] 5234 3-8-9 73 DaneO'Neill 6 69
(H Candy) *chsd ldrs: hdwy to chse ldr 2f out: rdn to ld over 1f out: r.o wl* **10/11**[1]

60-0 **2** *½* **Lady Lafitte (USA)**[33] 843 3-8-9 64 MartinDwyer 2 67
(B W Hills) *led tl hdd over 1f out: kpt on same pce after* **11/2**[3]

03- **3** *7* **Come What May**[190] 6175 3-8-9 SebSanders 4 42
(Rae Guest) *pressed ldr: rdn 1/2-way: lost 2nd 2f out: sn wknd* **11/4**[2]

0 **4** *3½* **Juce Of Hearts**[9] 1207 3-9-0 RichardThomas 3 34
(J L Spearing) *taken down early: chsd ldrs: rdn 1/2-way: sn wknd* **33/1**

0300 **5** *nk* **Priceless Melody (USA)**[31] 894 3-9-0 47 (b) JimCrowley 1 33
(Mrs A J Perrett) *s.i.s: bhd: rdn after 2f out: no ch fr 1/2-way* **12/1**

6 *8* **Hello Nemo** 3-9-0 JohnEgan 5 4
(T E Powell) *wnt rt s and s.i.s: sn outpcd: t.o* **25/1**

59.93 secs (-0.87) **Going Correction** -0.10s/f (Good) **6** Ran SP% **108.9**
Speed ratings (Par 103):102,101,90,84,83 71
CSF £6.01 TOTE £1.90: £1.40, £2.30; EX 7.90.
Owner Mrs J E L Wright **Bred** Wheelersland Stud **Trained** Kingston Warren, Oxon

FOCUS
A weak maiden and the winning time was 0.67 seconds quicker than the previous juvenile contest. The runner-up sets the standard.

1430 JOHN SMITH'S WHITSTABLE LABOUR CLUB FILLIES' H'CAP 6f

3:30 (3:30) (Class 5) (0-70,64) 3-Y-0 **£2,914** (£867; £433; £216) **Stalls** Low

Form RPR

54-3 **1** **Twitch Hill**[20] 1022 3-9-1 61 DaneO'Neill 2 67+
(H Candy) *t.k.h: chsd ldr: led over 1f out: rdn and r.o wl fnl f: readily* **8/11**[1]

363- **2** *1¾* **My Tiger Lilly**[227] 5419 3-8-9 55 MartinDwyer 1 56
(W J Knight) *led tl hdd over 1f out: edgd rt and kpt on same pce fnl f* **4/1**[2]

00-0 **3** *2* **Ensign's Trick**[15] 1091 3-8-11 60 LiamJones(3) 3 55
(W M Brisbourne) *taken down early: t.k.h: chsd ldrs: ev ch 2f out: sn rdn: wknd ins fnl f* **14/1**

4230 **4** *nk* **Time Share (IRE)**[3] 1346 3-8-10 56 FergusSweeney 6 50
(J A Osborne) *hld up bhd: rdn and effrt 2f out: hung rt over 1f out: kpt on but nvr trbld ldrs* **7/1**[3]

040- **5** *6* **Blue Mistral (IRE)**[212] 5747 3-9-4 64 PaulDoe 5 40
(W J Knight) *chsd ldrs on outer: lost pl 1/2-way: bhd last 2f* **8/1**

-000 **6** *1½* **Chingford (IRE)**[31] 894 3-8-2 51 EmmettStack(3) 4 23
(J G Portman) *s.i.s: sn chsng ldrs: rdn 1/2-way: wknd 2f out: no ch fnl f* **16/1**

1m 13.72s (0.12) **Going Correction** -0.10s/f (Good) **6** Ran SP% **114.1**
Speed ratings (Par 96):95,92,90,89,81 79
CSF £4.09 TOTE £1.60: £1.10, £1.80; EX 4.20.
Owner Manor Farm Stud & Miss S Hoare **Bred** Manor Farm Stud & Miss S Hoare **Trained** Kingston Warren, Oxon

FOCUS
A moderate fillies' handicap that took little winning. The time was 1.27 seconds slower than the following 61-75.
Time Share(IRE) Official explanation: jockey said filly hung right

1431 JOHN SMITH'S EXTRA SMOOTH H'CAP 6f

4:00 (4:00) (Class 5) (0-75,75) 4-Y-0+ **£2,914** (£867; £433; £216) **Stalls** Low

Form RPR

-435 **1** **Who's Winning (IRE)**[17] 1063 6-8-10 70 RichardKingscote(3) 4 81
(B G Powell) *chsd ldng pair: hdwy to press ldr wl over 1f out: pushed ahd nr fin* **7/2**[2]

3341 **2** *hd* **Dvinsky (USA)**[8] 1252 6-9-0 71 6ex IanMongan 2 81
(P Howling) *chsd ldr tl led and edgd rt 2f out: sn rdn and carried hd awkwardly: hdd and no ex nr fin* **11/4**[1]

10-3 **3** *1½* **Keyaki (IRE)**[17] 1063 6-9-4 75 GeorgeBaker 5 81+
(C F Wall) *s.i.s: hdwy and swtchd to rail over 1f out: sn rdn: swtchd rt ins fnl f: kpt on same pce last 100yds* **11/4**[1]

0550 **4** *nk* **Ivory Lace**[22] 1004 6-8-9 73 HaddenFrost(7) 3 78
(S Woodman) *hld up bhd: swtchd to outer and hdwy over 2f out: rdn 2f out: kpt on same pce ins fnl f* **7/1**[3]

3-00 **5** *2½* **Purus (IRE)**[103] 191 5-8-11 68 JimmyQuinn 8 65
(R A Teal) *chsd ldrs on outer: rdn over 1f out: wknd ins fnl f* **16/1**

3300 **6** *1½* **Desperate Dan**[17] 1063 6-9-2 73 (b) MartinDwyer 7 66
(J A Osborne) *stdd s: t.k.h: swtchd to rail and hld up bhd: swtchd rt and rdn over 2f out: sn no imp* **7/1**[3]

0300 **7** *1¾* **Night Prospector**[13] 1134 7-9-4 75 (p) JimCrowley 6 62
(R A Harris) *led tl 2f out: sn dropped out* **11/1**

-300 **8** *nk* **Campbeltown (IRE)**[59] 613 4-8-7 64 ow1 (b[1]) FergusSweeney 1 50
(M R Hoad) *chsd ldrs tl 1/2-way: sn rdn and struggling* **33/1**

1m 12.45s (-1.15) **Going Correction** -0.10s/f (Good) **8** Ran SP% **117.7**
Speed ratings (Par 103):103,102,100,100,97 95,92,92
CSF £14.06 CT £30.01 TOTE £6.10: £1.40, £1.40, £1.20; EX 15.40 Trifecta £32.40 Pool £431.94 9.45 winning units..
Owner Tony Head and Caroline Andrus **Bred** Colin Kennedy **Trained** Lambourn, Berks

FOCUS
Just an ordinary sprint handicap. The winning time was 1.27 seconds quicker than the previous 56-70 and the form looks sound and should prove reliable.

1432 JOHN SMITH'S PARKWOOD CLUB H'CAP 7f (S)

4:30 (4:34) (Class 6) (0-60,65) 3-Y-0 **£2,730** (£806; £403) **Stalls** Low

Form RPR

0-00 **1** **Private Peachey (IRE)**[12] 1154 3-8-6 48 TPO'Shea 10 57
(B R Millman) *mde all: rdn over 2f out: clr over 1f out: in command fnl f: comf* **16/1**

6-61 **2** *2* **Polish World (USA)**[3] 1346 3-9-9 65 6ex MartinDwyer 8 69
(E A L Dunlop) *reluctant to enter stalls: t.k.h: chsd ldrs wnt 2nd wl over 2f out: rdn and hung lft 2f out: no imp on wnr* **4/6**[1]

4-40 **3** *1¼* **Ice Box (IRE)**[88] 348 3-9-0 56 JohnEgan 1 57
(M Johnston) *racd in midfield: rdn 1/2-way: outpcd over 2f out: kpt on u.p fnl f: wnt 3rd nr fin* **15/2**[3]

600- **4** *nk* **Red Flare (IRE)**[328] 2402 3-8-12 54 JHBowman 12 54
(M R Channon) *chsd ldrs: rdn over 2f out: kpt on same pce* **18/1**

00-5 **5** *hd* **Metropolitan Chief**[29] 919 3-9-4 60 FergusSweeney 4 60+
(D M Simcock) *s.i.s: t.k.h: hld up in rr: hdwy over 2f out: rdn wl over 1f out: kpt on: nrst fin* **12/1**

5603 **6** *shd* **Missus Molly Brown**[30] 910 3-8-4 46 PaulHanagan 14 45
(R A Fahey) *chsd ldrs on outer: rdn over 2f out: kpt on same pce* **7/1**[2]

4-20 **7** *5* **Bathwick Fancy (IRE)**[29] 924 3-8-13 55 (t) SebSanders 11 41
(J G Portman) *hld up in rr on outer: hdwy over 2f out: rdn and wknd over 1f out: eased whn no ch ins fnl f* **12/1**

000- **8** *7* **Musical Affair**[183] 6296 3-8-6 48 JimmyQuinn 6 16
(F Jordan) *chsd ldrs on rail: rdn over 2f out: sn struggling: no ch 1f out* **40/1**

300- **9** *shd* **Valeesha**[235] 5209 3-8-2 51 JackDean(7) 7 19
(W G M Turner) *chsd wnr tl over 2f out: sn wknd: no ch over 1f out* **50/1**

0-05 **10** *5* **Spanish Air**[37] 802 3-8-13 55 SteveDrowne 9 10
(J W Hills) *sn bhd: lost tch 1/2-way: t.o* **33/1**

1m 27.65s (-0.25) **Going Correction** -0.10s/f (Good) **10** Ran SP% **118.1**
Speed ratings (Par 97):97,94,93,92,92 92,86,78,78,73
CSF £27.36 CT £104.78 TOTE £21.30: £5.20, £1.10, £2.20; EX 59.60 Trifecta £366.10 Part won. Pool £515.64 - 0.10 winning units..
Owner The Peachey Syndicate **Bred** Paradime Ltd **Trained** Kentisbeare, Devon

FOCUS
A moderate handicap but sound enough rated around the winner, third and fourth.
Private Peachey(IRE) ◆ Official explanation: trainer said, regarding apparent improvement in form, that the gelding was better suited by being dropped back in trip

1433 JOHN SMITH'S EXTRA COLD MEDIAN AUCTION MAIDEN STKS 1m 1f 149y

5:00 (5:03) (Class 6) 3-4-Y-0 **£2,730** (£806; £403) **Stalls** Low

Form RPR

0 **1** **Noticeable (IRE)**[12] 1143 3-8-9 JHBowman 5 78
(M R Channon) *chsd ldng pair: plld out and rdn wl over 1f out: chsd ldr over 1f out: r.o wl to ld nr fin* **14/1**

255- **2** *hd* **Snake's Head**[248] 4866 3-8-4 77 JimmyQuinn 4 73
(J L Dunlop) *led: rdn 2f out: kpt on: hdd nr fin* **11/10**[1]

4 **3** *6* **Crown Office (USA)**[43] 720 3-8-4 FrancisNorton 2 61
(H Morrison) *in tch: pushed along 1/2-way: rdn wl over 2f out: outpcd 2f out: kpt on to go modest 3rd ins fnl f* **11/2**[3]

00 **4** ½ **Cheonmado (USA)**[3] 1343 3-8-9 .... MartinDwyer 3 65
(Simon Earle) *dwlt: racd in last: clsd 4f out: rdn and outpcd over 2f out: wnt modest 4th ins fnl f* **20/1**

0- **5** 3 **Far Seeking**[203] 5914 3-8-9 .... (t) JimCrowley 1 59
(Mrs A J Perrett) *s.i.s: sn chsng ldr: rdn over 2f out: lost 2nd over 1f out: sn wknd* **2/1**[2]

2m 6.20s (0.97) **Going Correction** +0.075s/f (Good) 5 Ran SP% **107.8**
Speed ratings (Par 101):99,98,94,93,91
CSF £29.21 TOTE £14.80: £6.80, £1.10; EX 29.20.
Owner Tareq Al-Mazeedi **Bred** Tareq Al Mazeedi **Trained** West Ilsley, Berks

FOCUS
A very ordinary maiden run in a time 1.95 seconds slower than the following 66-80 handicap. The third and fourth are the best guides to the level.

1434 JOHN SMITH'S H'CAP 1m 1f 149y
5:30 (5:30) (Class 4) (0-80,77) 4-Y-0+ **£4,857** (£1,445; £722; £360) **Stalls** Low

Form RPR

0002 **1** **General Knowledge (USA)**[5] 1308 4-9-2 **75** .... (t) SebSanders 2 87
(B G Powell) *mde all: sn clr: kicked 5l clr 2f out: kpt on: unchal but all out* **11/4**[2]

4531 **2** 1½ **Torrens (IRE)**[10] 1199 5-8-11 **70** .... PaulHanagan 1 79+
(R A Fahey) *w.w: hdwy 4f out: chsd wnr wl over 2f out: rdn wl over 1f out: kpt on: nt rch wnr* **10/11**[1]

605- **3** 7 **Coup D'Etat**[230] 5346 5-9-4 **77** .... (p) JimCrowley 5 72
(R A Harris) *hld up bhd: hdwy 3f out: rdn to chse ldng pair 2f out: no imp* **15/2**[3]

2604 **4** 3 **Pop Music (IRE)**[2] 1385 4-8-9 **68** .... (p) JimmyQuinn 6 57
(Miss J Feilden) *chsd wnr: rdn 3f out: sn lost 2nd: wknd wl over 1f out* **16/1**

261- **5** 5 **And Again (USA)**[202] 5935 4-9-3 **76** .... SteveDrowne 3 55
(R A Teal) *chsd ldng pair: rdn and wknd over 2f out* **16/1**

-560 **6** 1½ **Prime Contender**[43] 726 5-9-3 **76** .... GeorgeBaker 4 52
(G L Moore) *a last: nvr on terms* **12/1**

2m 4.25s (-0.98) **Going Correction** +0.075s/f (Good) 6 Ran SP% **110.3**
Speed ratings (Par 105):106,104,99,96,92 91
CSF £5.40 TOTE £3.60: £2.10, £1.30; EX 5.40 Place 6 £9.93, Place 5 £3.14..
Owner I S Smith **Bred** Juddmonte Farms Inc **Trained** Lambourn, Berks

FOCUS
A fair handicap and ordinary form for the grade, but the pace was good and the winning time was 1.95 seconds quicker than the previous maiden.
T/Plt: £3.30 to a £1 stake. Pool: £48,855.50. 10,549.75 winning tickets. T/Qpdt: £2.60 to a £1 stake. Pool: £2,152.90. 609.50 winning tickets. SP

1380 WOLVERHAMPTON (A.W) (L-H)
Thursday, May 3

OFFICIAL GOING: Standard to fast
Wind: Fresh, half-against

1435 BETDIRECTPOKER.COM COME AND 'AVE SOME H'CAP 1m 141y(P)
6:35 (6:35) (Class 6) (0-50,50) 4-Y-0+ **£2,266** (£674; £337; £168) **Stalls** Low

Form RPR

4652 **1** **Very Well Red**[7] 1261 4-8-9 **47** .... RobertHavlin 2 57+
(P W Hiatt) *trckd ldrs: led wl over 1f out: sn hung rt but in command after* **3/1**[1]

-000 **2** 2 **Bold Phoenix (IRE)**[7] 1271 6-8-8 **46** oh1 .... (b) TPQueally 9 52+
(B J Curley) *hld up: hdwy wl over 1f out: styd on to chse wnr ins fnl f* **5/1**[3]

2650 **3** ¾ **Sun Bian**[9] 1227 5-8-12 **50** .... LPKeniry 6 54
(L P Grassick) *mid-div: rdn and hdwy 3f out: kpt on fnl f* **11/1**

0-00 **4** 2 **Soviet Threat (IRE)**[82] 425 6-8-10 **48** .... (b[1]) VinceSlattery 1 47
(A G Juckes) *in tch: nt clr run on ins over 2f out and again over 1f out: kpt on one pce* **20/1**

0640 **5** 3 **Danettie**[9] 1227 6-8-11 **49** .... EddieAhern 3 42
(W M Brisbourne) *chsd ldrs: rdn 1/2-way: wknd ins fnl f* **8/1**

0520 **6** ¾ **Cape Of Storms**[9] 1206 4-8-10 **48** .... J-PGuillambert 10 39
(R Brotherton) *led tl rdn and hdd wl over 1f out: wknd fnl f* **9/1**

400 **7** 3 **Bobering**[9] 1227 7-8-5 **50** .... SoniaEaton[(7)] 7 34
(B P J Baugh) *a towards rr* **9/2**[2]

40-0 **8** 1 **Moonlight Fantasy (IRE)**[10] 1199 4-8-12 **50** .... KimTinkler 12 32
(N Tinkler) *chsd ldr to 2f out: wknd appr fnl f* **12/1**

00-0 **9** ½ **Salvestro**[24] 976 4-8-7 **50** .... WilliamBuick[(5)] 11 30
(A W Carroll) *racd wd: a bhd* **6/1**

0-00 **10** 3 **Right Ted (IRE)**[9] 1227 4-8-5 **50** .... JosephWalsh[(7)] 4 24
(T Wall) *a bhd* **25/1**

06/0 **11** 10 **Juxta Pose**[13] 1120 4-8-10 **48** .... MatthewHenry 5 —
(P Winkworth) *a in rr* **33/1**

300- **12** ½ **Hill Of Clare (IRE)**[157] 6621 5-8-8 **46** oh1 .... PaulEddery 8 —
(G H Jones) *slowly away: a bhd* **50/1**

1m 48.93s (-2.83) **Going Correction** -0.375s/f (Stan) 12 Ran SP% **124.8**
Speed ratings (Par 101):97,95,94,92,90 89,86,85,85,82 73,73
CSF £18.03 CT £155.02 TOTE £3.90: £1.80, £2.30, £3.80; EX 24.80.
Owner P W Hiatt **Bred** Butts Enterprises Limited **Trained** Hook Norton, Oxon
■ Stewards' Enquiry : Kim Tinkler two-day ban: careless riding (May 14-15)

FOCUS
A moderate handicap but the winner looks progressive at a modest level.

1436 BETDIRECTPOKER.COM GET INVOLVED H'CAP 5f 216y(P)
7:05 (7:05) (Class 6) (0-55,59) 4-Y-0+ **£2,266** (£674; £337; £168) **Stalls** Low

Form RPR

6-01 **1** **Whitbarrow (IRE)**[7] 1262 8-8-13 **59** 6ex .... (b) JamesMillman[(5)] 1 73+
(B R Millman) *trckd ldr: led over 2f out: rdn clr over 1f out: kpt up to work* **7/2**[1]

6020 **2** 2 **Dasheena**[9] 1212 4-9-0 **55** .... (be) JamesDoyle 4 63
(A J McCabe) *in tch: rdn to chse wnr 1f out: no imp* **13/2**

0223 **3** nk **Midmaar (IRE)**[3] 1344 6-8-11 **52** .... (b) JamieMackay 12 59
(M Wigham) *in tch tl outpcd 1/2-way: rdn and r.o strly fnl f: nvr nrr* **17/2**

0606 **4** 1 **Beneking**[31] 888 7-9-0 **55** .... (p) LPKeniry 3 59
(D Burchell) *mid-div: hdwy over 1f out: kpt on: nvr nrr* **12/1**

0-00 **5** ½ **Smile For Us**[87] 367 4-8-12 **53** .... (b) RobertHavlin 2 56
(C Drew) *in tch: rdn over 2f out: kpt on one pce fnl f* **20/1**

3263 **6** ¾ **Garlogs**[51] 668 4-8-12 **53** .... JamieSpencer 9 53
(R Hollinshead) *chsd ldrs: rdn and edgd lft over 1f out: sn btn* **5/1**[2]

-450 **7** 1¼ **Polar Force**[37] 803 7-9-0 **55** .... DMylonas 13 52
(Mrs C A Dunnett) *racd on outside: chsd ldrs tl wknd ins fnl f* **20/1**

-413 **8** ¾ **Kahlua Bear**[96] 268 5-8-13 **54** .... (v) DarryllHolland 7 48
(Miss K B Boutflower) *outpcd: rdn 1/2-way: nvr nr to chal* **11/2**[3]

000- **9** ½ **Stamford Blue**[212] 5755 6-8-7 **53** .... TolleyDean[(5)] 10 46
(R A Harris) *outpcd: sn rdn and a bhd* **16/1**

0-00 **10** nk **Dunn Deal (IRE)**[12] 1165 7-8-13 **54** .... EddieAhern 11 46
(W M Brisbourne) *a in rr* **22/1**

601- **11** 1 **Laphonic (USA)**[292] 3526 4-8-13 **54** .... (t) RichardHughes 6 43
(T J Etherington) *mid-div tl rdn and wknd over 2f out* **20/1**

3460 **12** nk **Blakeshall Quest**[64] 586 7-8-11 **52** .... (b) J-PGuillambert 8 40
(R Brotherton) *a struggling in rr* **33/1**

-521 **13** 4 **Borzoi Maestro**[17] 1065 6-9-0 **55** .... (p) TPQueally 5 31
(G F Bridgwater) *sn led: hdd over 2f out: wknd qckly over 1f out* **10/1**

1m 13.28s (-2.53) **Going Correction** -0.375s/f (Stan) 13 Ran SP% **122.4**
Speed ratings (Par 101):101,98,97,96,95 94,93,92,91,91 89,89,84
CSF £24.15 CT £191.53 TOTE £5.40: £2.00, £1.90, £3.10; EX 35.70.
Owner Mrs H Brain **Bred** James Burns And A Moynan **Trained** Kentisbeare, Devon

FOCUS
A moderate handicap but run 1.29sec faster than the following three-year-old contest. The form looks solid rated around the placed horses.

1437 M & J DRILLING SERVICES CELEBRATION H'CAP 5f 216y(P)
7:35 (7:35) (Class 5) (0-70,69) 3-Y-0 **£3,562** (£1,059; £529; £264) **Stalls** Low

Form RPR

5303 **1** **Jord (IRE)**[11] 1176 3-8-13 **69** .... WilliamBuick[(5)] 2 75
(A J McCabe) *hld up: hdwy 1/2-way: sustained run on outside to ld wl ins fnl f* **3/1**[2]

2-52 **2** 1 **Napoleon Dynamite (IRE)**[2] 1383 3-8-12 **68** .... PatrickHills[(5)] 6 71
(J W Hills) *trckd ldr: hung lft over 1f out: led briefly ins fnl f: nt qckn* **2/1**[1]

-005 **3** ½ **Bahamian Love**[29] 925 3-8-8 **59** .... MichaelHills 4 60
(B W Hills) *led tl rdn and hdd ins fnl f: nt qckn* **5/1**[3]

02-4 **4** shd **Kassuta**[50] 678 3-8-13 **64** .... JamieSpencer 1 65
(S C Williams) *trckd ldrs: rdn over 1f out: kpt on one pce fnl f* **11/2**

0-64 **5** ¾ **Back In The Red (IRE)**[8] 1248 3-8-4 **60** .... TolleyDean[(5)] 5 59
(R A Harris) *chsd ldrs: rdn 1/2-way: nt qckn fnl f* **11/2**

-034 **6** hd **Comptonspirit**[23] 998 3-8-9 **60** .... DeanMcKeown 7 58
(B P J Baugh) *racd on outside: kpt on fnl stages but nvr nr to chal* **14/1**

-500 **7** 1 **Minnie Mill**[9] 1219 3-8-7 **58** .... PaulEddery 3 53
(B P J Baugh) *hld up: a bhd* **28/1**

1m 14.57s (-1.24) **Going Correction** -0.375s/f (Stan) 7 Ran SP% **115.9**
Speed ratings (Par 99):93,91,91,90,89 89,88
CSF £9.73 TOTE £3.70: £1.70, £1.70; EX 12.50.
Owner Paul J Dixon And Mrs P A Barratt **Bred** M Channon **Trained** Babworth, Notts
■ Stewards' Enquiry : William Buick one-day ban: used whip with excessive frequency without giving filly time to respond (May 14)

FOCUS
A modest handicap but run 1.29sec slower than the preceding race for older horses. The form is limited by the proximity of the fifth and sixth.
Back In The Red(IRE) Official explanation: jockey said colt was struck into

1438 BETDIRECTPOKER.COM $50,000 FREEROLL H'CAP 1m 4f 50y(P)
8:05 (8:05) (Class 4) (0-85,85) 4-Y-0+ **£5,181** (£1,541; £770; £384) **Stalls** Low

Form RPR

0002 **1** **Fantoche (BRZ)**[16] 1083 5-8-13 **80** .... (t) JamieSpencer 5 93+
(M J Wallace) *mid-div: hdwy over 3f out: rdn over 1f out: led nr fin* **9/2**[3]

06-1 **2** hd **Right To Play (USA)**[21] 1012 4-9-0 **81** .... JimmyFortune 1 94+
(J H M Gosden) *trckd ldrs: led wl over 1f out: rdn and hung lft: hdd nr fin* **4/1**[2]

1-4 **3** 2½ **Magic Moth**[9] 1208 4-8-2 **72** .... GregFairley[(3)] 2 81
(M Johnston) *led for 2f: rdn over 3f out: led again over 2f out: hdd wl over 1f out: one pce fnl f* **2/1**[1]

-512 **4** ½ **Pass The Port**[54] 662 6-8-11 **78** .... RobertHavlin 7 86
(D Haydn Jones) *hld up: hdwy over 2f out: rdn and one pce fnl f* **15/2**

12-5 **5** 2½ **La Estrella (USA)**[25] 955 4-9-0 **81** .... TPQueally 8 85
(J G Given) *in tch: rdn 2f out: wknd over 1f out* **13/2**

0110 **6** 1 **Wild Pitch**[54] 662 6-8-7 **81** .... (b) JackMitchell[(7)] 4 83
(P Mitchell) *hld up in rr: hdwy over 2f out: one pce ins fnl 2f* **8/1**

1546 **7** 1½ **Poseidon's Secret (IRE)**[9] 1208 4-8-6 **73** .... (b[1]) PaulEddery 6 73
(Pat Eddery) *led after 2f: hdd over 2f out: wknd over 1f out* **20/1**

/21- **8** 8 **Mulaazem**[266] 4300 4-9-4 **85** .... DaleGibson 9 72
(J Mackie) *hld up: pushed along 4f out: wknd over 2f out* **25/1**

00/ **9** 38 **Another Choice (IRE)**[580] 5594 6-8-12 **79** .... JamesDoyle 3 5
(N P Littmoden) *a bhd: t.o* **50/1**

2m 34.75s (-7.67) **Going Correction** -0.375s/f (Stan) 9 Ran SP% **118.3**
Speed ratings (Par 105):110,109,108,107,106 105,104,99,73
CSF £22.98 CT £47.28 TOTE £5.60: £1.30, £1.10, £2.00; EX 14.10.
Owner Mrs H Wallace **Bred** Stud Raca **Trained** Newmarket, Suffolk

FOCUS
A decent handicap run in a course-record time; the form looks solid and should work out.

1439 M & J DRILLING SERVICES SILVER ANNIVERSARY H'CAP 1m 141y(P)
8:35 (8:35) (Class 4) (0-85,84) 3-Y-0 **£5,829** (£1,734; £866; £432) **Stalls** Low

Form RPR

21-1 **1** **Kay Gee Be (IRE)**[16] 1076 3-9-4 **84** .... JamieSpencer 1 91+
(M J Wallace) *hld up: hdwy whn forced wd ent st: r.o u.p to ld ins fnl f: won gng away* **7/4**[1]

16-3 **2** 1½ **Dream Lodge (IRE)**[9] 1228 3-8-10 **76** .... TPQueally 6 79
(J G Given) *in tch: chsd ldr over 5f out: sn rdn: ev ch 1f out: nt qckn ins fnl f* **10/3**[3]

12-4 **3** ½ **Count Ceprano (IRE)**[10] 1202 3-9-4 **84** .... TedDurcan 2 86
(W R Swinburn) *hld up: hung rt and c wd into st: r.o wl fnl f: nvr nrr* **5/2**[2]

33-3 **4** 1 **Mystery River (USA)**[17] 1068 3-8-7 **73** .... RichardHughes 5 73
(B J Meehan) *led tl rdn, wknd and hdd ins fnl f* **20/1**

64-4 **5** 3 **Spirit Of Adjisa (IRE)**[24] 973 3-8-4 **70** oh2 .... PaulEddery 4 63
(Pat Eddery) *chsd ldr to over 5f out: rdn over 3f out: wknd over 1f out* **16/1**

21-1 **6** 5 **All Of Me (IRE)**[9] 1228 3-9-4 **84** 6ex .... DaneO'Neill 3 66
(T G Mills) *hld up in rr: rdn over 2f out: sn btn* **11/2**

1m 48.27s (-3.49) **Going Correction** -0.375s/f (Stan) 6 Ran SP% **114.0**
Speed ratings (Par 101):100,98,98,97,94 90
CSF £8.17 TOTE £2.40: £1.80, £1.30; EX 8.90.
Owner Par Jeu Partnership **Bred** Pursuit Of Truth Syndicate **Trained** Newmarket, Suffolk

FOCUS
A decent little race and fastest of the three over the trip on the night. The form looks fairly sound rated around the placed horses.
Count Ceprano(IRE) Official explanation: jockey said colt hung right

The Form Book, Raceform Ltd, Compton, RG20 6NL

1440 **BETDIRECTCASINO.COM MEDIAN AUCTION MAIDEN STKS** **1m 141y(P)**
9:05 (9:06) (Class 6) 3-4-Y-O **£2,266** (£674; £337; £168) **Stalls** Low

Form RPR
0 **1** **Imply**[14] [1100] 3-8-13 ..... RichardHughes 13 80+
(J H M Gosden) *led early: hdd over 6f out: led over 2f out: rdn clr ent fnl f* **10/3**[2]
062- **2** *5* **Royal Rationale (IRE)**[185] [6257] 3-8-13 79 ..... JamieSpencer 9 68+
(W J Haggas) *t.k.h: hld up in mid-div: hdwy over 2f out: chsd wnr fnl f but no imp* **2/1**[1]
0 **3** *hd* **Adenium (IRE)**[12] [1166] 3-8-13 ..... PatCosgrave 11 68
(W R Swinburn) *hld up in rr: rdn 2f out: styd on fnl f: nvr nrr* **25/1**
0 **4** *nk* **Natural Action**[14] [1100] 3-8-13 ..... DarryllHolland 6 71+
(W Jarvis) *mid-div: n.m.r over 2f out and again over 1f out: styd on fnl f* **25/1**
002- **5** *1 1/4* **King Of Rhythm (IRE)**[226] [5446] 4-9-13 62 ..... DanielTudhope 7 66
(D Carroll) *hld up: mde hdwy appr fnl f: nvr nr to chal* **33/1**
523- **6** *shd* **Aegis (IRE)**[209] [5783] 3-8-13 75 ..... MichaelHills 8 64
(B W Hills) *mid-div: nt clr run over 1f out: styd on fnl f* **7/2**[3]
0 **7** *2 1/2* **Bubbly Girl**[15] [1093] 3-8-1 ..... SCreighton(7) 12 53
(P J McBride) *in rr: hdwy on outside over 2f out: wknd ins fnl f* **100/1**
50- **8** *shd* **Traditionalist (IRE)**[243] [5020] 3-8-13 ..... NickyMackay 5 58
(G A Butler) *prom: chsd ldr over 1f out tl ent fnl f: wknd* **14/1**
02- **9** *1 1/4* **Kings Confession (IRE)**[311] [2940] 4-9-13 ..... EddieAhern 10 57
(D Carroll) *hld up: nvr on terms* **33/1**
34 **10** *1/2* **Encores**[11] [1177] 3-8-13 ..... PaulEddery 1 54
(N A Callaghan) *mid-div: rdn 1/2-way: wknd over 2f out* **20/1**
11 *1/2* **Fizzy Bella** 3-8-7 ow2 ..... JerryO'Dwyer(3) 3 50
(M G Quinlan) *a bhd* **66/1**
0- **12** *4* **Henry Bernstein (USA)**[203] [5918] 3-8-13 ..... TedDurcan 2 43
(H R A Cecil) *chsd ldrs tl wknd qckly wl over 1f out* **8/1**
2-04 **13** *4* **Murdoch**[23] [991] 3-8-13 68 ..... RichardMullen 4 34
(E S McMahon) *led over 6f out: hdd over 2f out: wknd qckly* **16/1**

1m 49.21s (-2.55) **Going Correction** -0.375s/f (Stan)
WFA 3 from 4yo 14lb **13** Ran SP% **123.1**
Speed ratings (Par 101):96,91,91,91,90 89,87,87,86,86 85,82,78
CSF £10.00 TOTE £4.00: £1.50, £1.30, £7.70; EX 13.60 Place 6 £9.75, Place 5 £5.12.
Owner K Abdulla **Bred** Juddmonte Farms Ltd **Trained** Newmarket, Suffolk
■ Stewards' Enq: Tudhope 14-day ban: breach of Rule 157 (May 22-Jun 4); Carroll fined £6,000

FOCUS
An ordinary maiden run slowest of the three races over the trip on the nighta dn difficult to rate positively with the fifth and seventh holding the form down.
King Of Rhythm(IRE) Official explanation: jockey said, regarding running and riding, his orders were to jump out, sit mid-division and ride a race, adding that he got shuffled to the back, did not have a clear run round final bend and then made an effort in home straight but the gelding hung right and he therefore had to hold on to its head; trainer confirmed, adding that the gelding got jarred up on firm ground last season and he was therefore reluctant to run it on turf; 40-day suspension (May 22-Jun 30)
T/Jkpt: £10,051.10 to a £1 stake. Pool: £431,773.00. 30.50 winning tickets. T/Plt: £13.20 to a £1 stake. Pool: £88,208.45. 4,863.85 winning tickets. T/Qpdt: £4.30 to a £1 stake. Pool: £4,231.70. 717.90 winning tickets. JS

1441 - 1444a (Foreign Racing) - See Raceform Interactive

[1342]LINGFIELD (L-H)
Friday, May 4

OFFICIAL GOING: Standard
Wind: Moderate, against Weather: Fine

1445 **BETDIRECTPOKER.COM $50,000 FREEROLL MAIDEN FILLIES' STKS** **5f (P)**
2:00 (2:03) (Class 5) 2-Y-O **£3,886** (£1,156; £577; £288) **Stalls** High

Form RPR
1 **Feeling Proud (USA)** 2-9-0 ..... JimmyQuinn 9 70
(Jane Chapple-Hyam) *w'like: lw: scope: trckd ldrs gng wl: sltly wd bnd 2f out: rdn and r.o fr over 1f out: led fnl 100yds: kpt on* **16/1**
2 *nk* **Carolina Belle (USA)** 2-9-0 ..... JamieSpencer 5 69
(M J Wallace) *str: lw: trckd ldrs: effrt 2f out: rdn and got through to dispute ld ins fnl f: hdd fnl 100yds: styd on* **11/10**[1]
3 *nk* **Waveline (USA)** 2-9-0 ..... LDettori 3 67
(B J Meehan) *leggy: lw: cl up: effrt on inner to join ldr over 1f out: green and hanging after: hdd and no ex fnl 100yds* **4/1**[2]
4 *shd* **Deal Flipper** 2-9-0 ..... JimCrowley 2 67
(P Winkworth) *lt-f: s.i.s: midfield on inner: rdn 1/2-way: prog over 1f out to dispute ld ins fnl f: one pce fnl 100yds* **11/1**
4 **5** *1 3/4* **Andrasta**[17] [1079] 2-9-0 ..... SteveDrowne 7 60
(B J Meehan) *lw: led w tail swishing: jnd over 1f out: fdd ins fnl f* **15/2**[3]
6 *1* **Bellalatino (IRE)** 2-9-0 ..... JamesDoyle 4 56
(Mrs Norma Pook) *str: bit bkwd: s.i.s: nvr bttr than midfield: shkn up and one pce over 1f out* **50/1**
7 *shd* **A Wish For You** 2-9-0 ..... RobertHavlin 8 56
(D K Ivory) *gd sort: str: bkwd: sn pressed ldr: cl enough stl over 1f out: wknd fnl f* **25/1**
8 *hd* **Pixie's Blue (IRE)** 2-9-0 ..... JimmyFortune 10 55
(J H M Gosden) *leggy: lw: t.k.h and hld up on outer: pushed along and rn green over 1f out: kpt on one pce* **9/1**
9 *3 1/2* **Rubytwosox (IRE)** 2-9-0 ..... MartinDwyer 1 41
(W R Muir) *neat: scope: lw: sn outpcd and rdn: a in rr* **25/1**
10 *1 1/2* **Ballyhealy Lady** 2-9-0 ..... HayleyTurner 6 35
(D K Ivory) *wl grwn: lw: s.s: a wl in rr and sn outpcd* **33/1**

62.23 secs (2.45) **Going Correction** +0.05s/f (Slow) **10** Ran SP% **116.2**
Speed ratings (Par 90):82,81,81,80,78 76,76,76,70,68
CSF £33.13 TOTE £16.30: £3.90, £1.10, £2.10; EX 61.00 Trifecta £309.60 Part won. Pool: £436.07, 0.10 winning units..
Owner Hunters Green Partnership **Bred** Winchester Farm **Trained** Newmarket, Suffolk

FOCUS
Only Andrasta among these ten fillies had previous racecourse experience and that was on turf. The slow winning time and the fact that the first four home finished in a heap does not suggest the form is anything special.

NOTEBOOK
Feeling Proud(USA) deserves extra credit as she was forced to make her effort widest of all off the final bend and showed a very willing attitude to just get up in the closing stages. She was one of the youngest in the field and can only improve from this. (op 14-1)
Carolina Belle(USA), a $160,000 yearling, certainly knew her job and was in an ideal position just behind the leaders throughout. She had every chance had she been good enough and there did not appear to be any real excuses, but the market support suggests she is thought a bit of and it would be no surprise to see her build on this. (op 6-4 after 7-4 in places tchd 13-8 in places)
Waveline(USA) fared best of the Meehan pair and this speedily-bred 140,000euro filly showed more than enough to suggest she can win races. (op 7-2 tchd 9-2)
Deal Flipper, who took a good hold, tried to make her effort tight against the inside rail, which is never an easy thing to do here, and she did well to get so close. A half-sister to a couple of winning juveniles, there should be a race in her too. (tchd 12-1)
Andrasta showed the benefit of her previous experience by breaking well and making most of the running, but she was swamped in the home straight and did not really step forward from her debut effort. (op 6-1)

1446 **BETDIRECTPOKER.COM $50,000 FREEROLL H'CAP** **1m (P)**
2:30 (2:31) (Class 5) (0-75,75) 4-Y-0+ **£3,238** (£963; £481; £240) **Stalls** High

Form RPR
1410 **1** **Binnion Bay (IRE)**[2] [1401] 6-9-0 71 ..... (b) AmirQuinn 11 82
(J J Bridger) *lw: hld up in rr: prog on outer over 3f out: drvn to chse ldr 1f out: r.o wl u.p to ld fnl 50yds* **12/1**
2403 **2** *nk* **Sun Catcher (IRE)**[41] [757] 4-9-4 75 ..... (b) RichardHughes 12 85
(R Hannon) *lw: t.k.h: trckd ldr over 4f out: gng easily over 2f out: led wl over 1f out: sn rdn: r.o but collared fnl 50yds* **13/2**[2]
2640 **3** *2 1/2* **Katiypour (IRE)**[14] [1121] 10-9-4 75 ..... SebSanders 7 80
(P Mitchell) *lw: hld up: prog on outer fr 1/2-way: drvn to press ldng pair over 2f out: nt qckn wl over 1f out: plugged on* **10/1**
1-50 **4** *1* **Treasure House (IRE)**[11] [1198] 6-8-11 68 ..... TedDurcan 6 70+
(M Blanshard) *awkward s: hld up in last pair: effrt towards outer fr 3f out: outpcd 2f out: hrd rdn and styd on fnl f* **20/1**
500- **5** *3/4* **Barathea Dreams (IRE)**[252] [4782] 6-8-10 67 ..... JohnEgan 8 68
(J S Moore) *lw: mde most to wl over 1f out: wknd fnl f* **9/1**[3]
3213 **6** *nk* **Special Place**[14] [1118] 4-8-8 65 ..... OscarUrbina 3 67+
(J A R Toller) *lw: hld up in rr: lft bhd fr over 2f out: shkn up and styd on fr over 1f out: no ch* **13/2**[2]
0050 **7** *3/4* **Glencalvie (IRE)**[18] [1060] 6-9-0 71 ..... (v) DaneO'Neill 2 72+
(J Akehurst) *lw: hld up in midfield: plenty to do whn hmpd wl over 1f out: kpt on: no ch* **9/1**[3]
0-52 **8** *1/2* **Capricho (IRE)**[14] [1118] 10-8-5 62 ..... (b) PaulDoe 4 59
(J Akehurst) *s.i.s: racd on inner in rr: effrt whn nt clr run over 2f out to wl over 1f out: one pce* **10/1**
-331 **9** *1/2* **Northern Desert (IRE)**[25] [975] 8-9-0 71 ..... ChrisCatlin 5 67
(P W Hiatt) *a towards rr: rdn and no prog 2f out* **13/2**[2]
662- **10** *1 1/4* **Titus Lumpus (IRE)**[243] [5046] 4-8-4 61 ..... FrancisNorton 1 54
(R M Flower) *swtg: chsd ldr to over 4f out: rdn over 3f out: wknd over 2f out* **14/1**
252- **11** *8* **Dan Buoy (FR)**[214] [5734] 4-8-12 69 ..... JamieSpencer 9 44
(A King) *trckd ldrs: lost pl 3f out: struggling 2f out: eased whn no ch fnl f* **9/2**[1]
/06- **12** *5* **Power Broker**[340] [2069] 4-8-11 68 ..... (bt[1]) JimmyFortune 10 31
(P F I Cole) *bit bkwd: plld hrd early: prom: wknd rapidly over 2f out* **33/1**

1m 37.36s (-2.07) **Going Correction** +0.05s/f (Slow) **12** Ran SP% **118.4**
Speed ratings (Par 103):112,111,109,108,107 107,106,105,105,104 96,91
CSF £87.93 CT £832.66 TOTE £16.80: £5.40, £2.70, £3.60; EX 113.80 TRIFECTA Not won..
Owner J J Bridger **Bred** Fieldspring Ltd **Trained** Liphook, Hants

FOCUS
An ordinary handicap containing several Polytrack regulars, but a strong pace resulted in a decent winning time for the class.
Power Broker Official explanation: jockey said gelding ran too free

1447 **BETDIRECTPOKER.COM $50,000 FREEROLL MAIDEN STKS (DIV I)** **7f (P)**
3:00 (3:01) (Class 5) 3-4-Y-0 **£3,238** (£963; £481; £240) **Stalls** Low

Form RPR
-4 **1** **Yaroslav (USA)**[13] [1143] 3-8-12 ..... SteveDrowne 6 81+
(R Charlton) *lw: trckd ldr: effrt to chal 2f out: drvn to ld ins fnl f: grad gained upper hand* **10/11**[1]
33-3 **2** *3/4* **Shevchenko (IRE)**[16] [1098] 3-8-12 79 ..... SebSanders 5 79
(J Noseda) *led: kicked on fr 3f out: hdd ins fnl f: styd on* **7/4**[2]
-54 **3** *3 1/2* **Everygrainofsand (IRE)**[14] [1117] 4-9-10 ..... GeorgeBaker 2 74
(J R Best) *lw: trckd ldng pair: rdn over 2f out: outpcd fr over 1f out* **16/1**
4 *nk* **Zach's Harmoney (USA)** 3-8-12 ..... LDettori 11 69+
(B J Meehan) *tall: str: lw: wl in rr: gd prog on outer fr 1/2-way to chse ldrs 2f out: green and outpcd sn after: kpt on* **14/1**[3]
0- **5** *1 1/4* **First To Call**[260] [4525] 3-8-12 ..... EddieAhern 1 65
(P J Makin) *bkwd: dwlt: t.k.h: sn in midfield: rdn and in tch 2f out: outpcd wl over 1f out* **25/1**
00- **6** *nk* **Convallaria (FR)**[356] [1674] 4-9-5 ..... TedDurcan 7 64+
(G Wragg) *bit bkwd: towards rr: pushed along and struggling bef 1/2-way: kpt on fr over 1f out: n.d* **66/1**
7 *shd* **Appleby** 3-8-7 ..... RobertHavlin 9 59+
(J H M Gosden) *lengthy: str: scope: dwlt: settled wl in rr: shkn up 2f out: hanging lft and green: kpt on* **25/1**
-4 **8** *3 1/2* **Spinal Tap (IRE)**[10] [1215] 3-8-12 ..... JohnEgan 8 55
(C R Egerton) *dwlt: sn pushed along in last: a struggling: kpt on fnl f* **20/1**
0-0 **9** *1 1/2* **Korty**[25] [977] 3-8-12 ..... (t) BrettDoyle 10 51
(W J Musson) *bit bkwd: t.k.h: trckd ldrs: stl cl enough 2f out: wknd rapidly* **66/1**
0- **10** *3 1/2* **Puissant Princess (IRE)**[220] [5595] 3-8-7 ..... MichaelHills 4 36
(J W Hills) *t.k.h: hld up: wknd over 2f out* **50/1**

1m 24.82s (-1.07) **Going Correction** +0.05s/f (Slow)
WFA 3 from 4yo 12lb **10** Ran SP% **118.7**
Speed ratings (Par 103):108,107,103,102,101 101,100,96,95,91
CSF £2.45 TOTE £2.20: £1.40, £1.10, £2.90; EX 3.60 Trifecta £19.60 Pool: £480.68, 17.35 winning units..
Owner B E Nielsen **Bred** Gainsborough Farm Llc **Trained** Beckhampton, Wilts

FOCUS
The stronger of the two divisions, and fair maiden form. The two three-year-olds who dominated both the market and the race itself are decent enough, and there was definite promise from the third and fourth and improvement from the fifth and sixth.

1448 **BETDIRECTPOKER.COM COME AND 'AVE SOME H'CAP** **7f (P)**
3:30 (3:39) (Class 2) (0-105,104) 4-Y-0+
£11,840 (£3,545; £1,772; £887; £442; £222) **Stalls** Low

Form RPR
/2-6 **1** **Presumptive (IRE)**[34] [840] 7-8-4 90 oh2 ..... ChrisCatlin 10 99
(R Charlton) *hld up in last trio: prog 1/2-way to chse ldrs: drvn over 1f out: r.o wl to ld fnl 75yds* **14/1**
-204 **2** *nk* **Ceremonial Jade (UAE)**[20] [1041] 4-8-8 94 ..... (t) KerrinMcEvoy 5 102
(M Botti) *swtg: hld up in midfield: trckd ldrs over 1f out: hanging lft but got through to dispute ld ins fnl f: outpcd nr fin* **4/1**[1]

106- **3** ½ **Racer Forever (USA)**^{271} [4174] 4-9-4 **104**...................... JimmyFortune 4 111
(J H M Gosden) *swtg: dwlt: sn prom: effrt on inner wl over 1f out: led briefly jst ins fnl f: hung rt and outpcd fnl 100yds* **13/2**^{3}

104- **4** ¾ **Zidane**^{243} [5044] 5-8-4 **90** oh1.. MartinDwyer 9 95+
(J R Fanshawe) *t.k.h: hld up towards rr: effrt 2f out: styd on fr over 1f out: nrst fin* **9/2**^{2}

30-0 **5** nk **The Snatcher (IRE)**^{13} [1145] 4-8-7 **93** ow1................ RichardHughes 12 97
(R Hannon) *prog to trck ldr after 2f: rdn to chal over 1f out: upsides ent fnl f: sn outpcd* **25/1**

61-1 **6** ½ **Bobski (IRE)**^{97} [259] 5-7-13 **90** oh3............................ WilliamBuick$^{(5)}$ 8 92
(G A Huffer) *lw: dwlt: t.k.h and hld up in last pair: effrt on wd outside over 2f out: nt qckn over 1f out: kpt on* **8/1**

4-01 **7** ½ **Wavertree Warrior (IRE)**^{69} [550] 5-8-6 **92**.................... JamesDoyle 7 93
(N P Littmoden) *lw: hld up in midfield: effrt 2f out: kpt on one pce fr over 1f out: no real imp* **11/1**

2361 **8** shd **Waterside (IRE)**^{34} [840] 8-9-4 **104**.................................. GeorgeBaker 6 105
(G L Moore) *lw: trckd ldr for 2f: styd prom: rdn to chal 2f out: fdd fnl f* **9/1**

1140 **9** nk **Party Boss**^{55} [656] 5-9-4 **104**.. SebSanders 3 107+
(C E Brittain) *bit bkwd: led and dictated stdy pce: kicked on 2f out: hdd jst ins fnl f: btn whn hmpd fnl 100yds* **10/1**

/00- **10** ½ **Captain Hurricane**^{363} [1485] 5-8-1 **94**.................................. KMay$^{(7)}$ 11 93
(B J Meehan) *taken down early: restrained s: plld hrd and hld up in detached last: nvr on terms: kpt on fr over 1f out* **66/1**

0540 **11** 7 **Moayed**^{10} [1223] 8-8-4 **90** oh3....................................(b) RichardThomas 2 70
(N P Littmoden) *s.s: in tch in rr tl nt keen and wknd 2f out* **25/1**

1m 25.55s (-0.34) **Going Correction** +0.05s/f (Slow) **11** Ran SP% **105.9**
Speed ratings (Par 109):103,102,102,101,100 100,99,99,99,98 90
CSF £55.84 CT £305.72 TOTE £14.70: £3.90, £1.50, £1.70; EX 74.40 Trifecta £222.50 Pool: £313.45, 1.00 winning units.
Owner Beckhampton Stables Ltd **Bred** Dr T A Ryan **Trained** Beckhampton, Wilts
■ Eisteddfod was withdrawn (15/2, broke out of stalls). Rule 4, deduct 10p in the £.
■ Stewards' Enquiry : Jimmy Fortune two-day ban: careless riding (May 15-16)

FOCUS
Despite the late withdrawal of Eisteddfod, a very decent handicap, featuring several with smart Polytrack form, including at this track. However, the early pace was ordinary which would not have suited some of those that like to come late off a strong gallop. In the circumstances it would be hard to rate it that positively.

NOTEBOOK
Presumptive(IRE) probably did well to win, having come from well off the pace in a steadily run race, and been produced wide and late to just get up near the line. Obviously all the better for his eye-catching return from a year off at Kempton just over a month ago, he has not been the easiest to train but is a decent performer when he does make it to the track. (op 12-1)
Ceremonial Jade(UAE) ◆, who got warm beforehand, looked as though he had been produced at just the right time, but the winner was finishing just that bit stronger on his outside. He still reversed recent form with both Party Boss and Waterside and looks ready to strike. (op 9-2)
Racer Forever(USA) was up there the whole way and kept on well for third. Making his sand debut and gelded since last seen nine months ago, this was an encouraging return to action. (op 7-1)
Zidane was finishing well, but could never get there in time. The trip did not seem to be a problem though, and he should come on for this first run in eight months.
The Snatcher(IRE) was up there for most of the way and ran better than in the Newbury Spring Cup on his return from seven months off last month. (op 33-1)
Bobski(IRE) has a fine record here but was taking on better company this time and was not quite up to it.
Wavertree Warrior(IRE) Official explanation: jockey said gelding was denied a clear run

1449 BETDIRECTPOKER.COM GET INVOLVED H'CAP 1m 2f (P)
4:00 (4:04) (Class 2) (0-105,101) 4-Y-0+
£11,840 (£3,545; £1,772; £887; £442; £222) **Stalls** Low

Form RPR

-154 **1** **Tabadul (IRE)**^{9} [1245] 6-8-12 **95**.. RHills 1 106+
(E A L Dunlop) *lw: trckd ldr: led wl over 1f out: rdn and wl in command fnl f* **7/4**^{1}

-665 **2** 1¼ **Vacation (IRE)**^{12} [1180] 4-7-13 **87**................................. WilliamBuick$^{(5)}$ 2 94
(V Smith) *lw: settled in 4th: effrt on inner over 2f out: drvn to chse wnr 1f out: swtchd rt and styd on: nvr able to chal* **9/1**

210- **3** nk **Queen's Best**^{210} [5789] 4-8-4 **87**...................................... KerrinMcEvoy 3 93
(Sir Michael Stoute) *bit bkwd: trckd ldng pair: shkn up and hanging wl over 1f out: nt qckn: styd on ins fnl f* **7/2**^{2}

/024 **4** 3 **Tufton**^{24} [993] 4-8-7 **90**...(t) EddieAhern 7 91
(M Botti) *sn led and set gd pce: breather over 3f out: hdd wl over 1f out: wknd fnl f* **14/1**

1030 **5** 3½ **Orchard Supreme**^{6} [1307] 4-9-4 **101**........................... RichardHughes 6 95
(R Hannon) *hld up in rr: effrt 3f out: outpcd 2f out: no ch after* **9/1**

123- **6** shd **Ofaraby**^{181} [6337] 7-9-3 **100**... PhilipRobinson 4 94
(M A Jarvis) *swtg: hld up in rr: brief effrt 3f out: shuffled along and n.d fnl 2f* **8/1**^{3}

14-0 **7** 8 **Best Prospect (IRE)**^{24} [995] 5-8-12 **95**........................ JamieSpencer 8 74
(M Dods) *lw: hld up in last: plenty to do over 2f out: brief effrt over 1f out: nvr nr ldrs* **8/1**^{3}

00-6 **8** 9 **Tiger Tiger (FR)**^{48} [701] 6-8-6 **89**.. JohnEgan 5 51
(Jamie Poulton) *racd in 5th: rdn 1/2-way: wknd over 3f out: t.o* **11/1**

2m 5.30s (-2.49) **Going Correction** +0.05s/f (Slow) **8** Ran SP% **115.8**
Speed ratings (Par 109):111,110,110,109,107,104 104,98,90
CSF £18.96 CT £50.90 TOTE £2.60: £1.30, £3.60, £1.80; EX 25.40 Trifecta £165.20 Pool: £821.61, 3.53 winning units.
Owner Hamdan Al Maktoum **Bred** Shadwell Estate Co Ltd **Trained** Newmarket, Suffolk

FOCUS
Perhaps not as competitive as the preceding Class 2 handicap, but this race still featured some smart performers. The pace was moderate for the first couple of furlongs, but Tufton then quickened things up considerably and it developed into a fair test.

NOTEBOOK
Tabadul(IRE) always in the leader's slipstream, was asked for his effort entering the home straight and found more than enough. He had already shown decent form in three starts at Kempton, so the surface was never going to be a problem, and he should continue to go well in handicaps at around this trip. (op 9-4 tchd 5-2 in a place)
Vacation(IRE) tried to make his challenge up the inside rail and kept on well. This was his best effort of the year so far and, although his best form has come over shorter, he seemed to just about get the trip. (op 10-1)
Queen's Best, making her sand debut and upped in trip, was very keen early and did well to battle on for third on this first start in seven months. Her wins on turf came on soft ground, but she seemed to handle the surface well enough. (op 11-4)
Tufton was responsible for the decent pace, but dropped away in the home straight and may have paid for his earlier exertions. He remains lightly raced though, and is not completely without hope. (op 12-1)
Orchard Supreme has had a very busy winter and is still to convince over this trip. (op 8-1)
Ofaraby was off a 5lb higher mark than when last seen on sand and is entitled to come on for this first run in six months.
Best Prospect(IRE) was ridden with plenty of confidence out the back, but never managed to get involved.

1450 BETDIRECTCASINO.COM H'CAP 6f (P)
4:30 (4:33) (Class 4) (0-85,85) 3-Y-0 **£6,477** (£1,927; £963; £481) **Stalls** Low

Form RPR

04-1 **1** **Rasaman (IRE)**^{20} [1037] 3-8-11 **78**................................ PhilipRobinson 7 83+
(M A Jarvis) *lw: w ldr: led gng easily wl over 1f out: in command whn hung rt and shkn up ins fnl f* **7/4**^{1}

201- **2** 1 **Golden Desert (IRE)**^{176} [6414] 3-9-1 **82**.............................. DaneO'Neill 8 81
(T G Mills) *lw: hld up bhd ldrs: rdn over 1f out: chsd wnr fnl f: styd on and clsd but nvr able to chal* **6/1**^{3}

614- **3** shd **Non Compliant**^{193} [6146] 3-9-4 **85**... EddieAhern 5 84
(J W Hills) *lw: hld up in last: effrt over 1f out: r.o fnl f and nrly snatched 2nd: nvr nrr* **10/1**

01- **4** 2½ **Roshanak (IRE)**^{275} [4053] 3-9-1 **82**... LDettori 9 73
(B J Meehan) *bit bkwd: trckd ldng pair: nt qckn 2f out: reminder 1f out: styd on same pce* **6/1**^{3}

2-21 **5** 1 **Telltime (IRE)**^{100} [231] 3-8-0 **72**.................................. WilliamBuick$^{(5)}$ 1 60
(A M Balding) *mde most at gd pce: hdd wl over 1f out: wknd fnl f* **10/1**

000- **6** nk **Hythe Bay**^{205} [5909] 3-8-6 **76**....................................... StephaneBreux$^{(3)}$ 4 63
(J R Best) *hld up towards rr: rdn and no real prog fnl 2f* **50/1**

3510 **7** nk **Mr Loire**^{34} [843] 3-8-8 **75**.. JimmyQuinn 2 61
(H J L Dunlop) *t.k.h: trckd ldrs: rdn 2f out: fdd fnl f* **22/1**

10-6 **8** nk **Averticus**^{16} [1099] 3-8-10 **77**.. MichaelHills 3 63
(B W Hills) *settled towards rr: rdn and no prog 2f out* **7/2**^{2}

1- **9** 1½ **Galaxy Stars**^{133} [6905] 3-8-5 **72**..(t) MartinDwyer 6 53
(P J Makin) *lw: stdd s: plld hrd and hld up: racd wd and hanging rt 1/2-way: v wd bnd 2f out: no ch after* **16/1**

1m 12.6s (-0.21) **Going Correction** +0.05s/f (Slow) **9** Ran SP% **117.5**
Speed ratings (Par 101):103,101,101,98,96 96,96,95,93
CSF £13.03 CT £83.20 TOTE £2.80: £1.30, £2.10, £2.70; EX 20.80 Trifecta £216.40 Pool: £877.87, 2.88 winning units.
Owner Thurloe Thoroughbreds XVII **Bred** Rasana Partnership **Trained** Newmarket, Suffolk

FOCUS
A decent three-year-old sprint, featuring several unexposed sorts. Sound form, and the impressive winner can rate higher again off a stronger pace.
Galaxy Stars Official explanation: jockey said gelding hung right

1451 BETDIRECTPOKER.COM H'CAP 1m 4f (P)
5:00 (5:00) (Class 5) (0-70,70) 4-Y-0+ **£3,238** (£963; £481; £240) **Stalls** Low

Form RPR

6-10 **1** **Sunset Boulevard (IRE)**^{64} [594] 4-9-2 **68**......................... ChrisCatlin 4 75
(Miss Tor Sturgis) *lw: wl plcd in slowly run r: effrt 2f out: drvn to ld jst over 1f out: styd on* **12/1**

0226 **2** ½ **Ross Moor**^{42} [747] 5-9-4 **70**.. JamesDoyle 6 76
(Mike Murphy) *cl up: rdn to ld over 2f out: hdd jst over 1f out: styd on but hld last 100yds* **9/1**

5215 **3** ½ **Musango**^{30} [921] 4-9-2 **68**... DaneO'Neill 14 73
(B R Johnson) *swtg: hld up on outer in midifeld: clsd 2f out: drvn and styd on fnl f to take 3rd nr fin* **6/1**^{2}

1445 **4** shd **Amwell Brave**^{13} [1152] 6-9-0 **66**.. EddieAhern 13 71
(J R Jenkins) *lw: dwlt: hld up in last trio in slowly run r: prog on outer over 2f out: r.o fnl f: nrst fin* **10/1**

-014 **5** shd **Wait For The Will (USA)**^{91} [332] 11-9-3 **69**...............(b) GeorgeBaker 7 74
(G L Moore) *hld up towards rr: prog 2f out: styd on fr over 1f out: nvr able to chal* **7/1**^{3}

-162 **6** hd **Carlton Scroop (FR)**^{4} [1342] 4-8-5 **60**.......................(b) LiamJones$^{(3)}$ 11 66+
(J Jay) *lw: hld up in rr: prog and weaved through fr over 1f out: styng on whn rdr unbalanced fnl 75yds* **9/4**^{1}

16-5 **7** 1½ **Burgundy**^{104} [195] 10-8-11 **70**..................................(b) JackMitchell$^{(7)}$ 12 72
(P Mitchell) *hld up in rr: effrt over 2f out: trying to cl but no real ch whn hmpd jst over 1f out: kpt on nr fin* **16/1**

6240 **8** ½ **Hallings Overture (USA)**^{42} [740] 8-8-8 **60**...................... PaulEddery 8 61
(C A Horgan) *taken down early: dwlt: hld up in last trio: hanging lft and plugged on same pce fr over 1f out* **10/1**

3005 **9** nk **Ganymede**^{21} [1026] 6-7-13 **56** oh5................................ WilliamBuick$^{(5)}$ 3 57
(Mrs L J Mongan) *dwlt: wl in rr: rdn 3f out: kpt on fr over 1f out* **12/1**

0040 **10** 1 **Dark Planet**^{18} [1069] 4-8-8 **60**....................................(p) RichardThomas 5 59
(D Burchell) *mde most at sedate pce to over 2f out: wknd fnl f* **25/1**

130- **11** nk **Mae Cigan (FR)**^{212} [5769] 4-9-1 **67**...................................... TedDurcan 10 66
(M Blanshard) *trckd ldrs: outpcd whn n.m.r wl over 1f out: n.d after* **33/1**

00-3 **12** 1½ **Harcourt (USA)**^{21} [1026] 7-8-6 **58**..................................... MartinDwyer 2 54
(M Madgwick) *trckd ldrs: lost pl and struggling over 2f out* **16/1**

650- **13** ½ **Sonny Mac**^{250} [4842] 4-9-2 **68**.................................(vt^{1}) RichardHughes 9 64
(M J McGrath) *swtg: w ldr: nrly upsides over 2f out: wknd over 1f out* **25/1**

2000 **14** shd **Blackmail (USA)**^{26} [805] 9-8-5 **57**...........................(b) KerrinMcEvoy 1 52
(P Mitchell) *a in rr: outpcd and struggling over 2f out* **14/1**

2m 34.27s (-0.12) **Going Correction** +0.05s/f (Slow) **14** Ran SP% **130.2**
Speed ratings (Par 103):102,101,101,101,101 101,100,99,99,98 98,97,97,97
CSF £123.13 CT £737.19 TOTE £24.20: £6.90, £4.60, £2.00; EX 290.50 TRIFECTA Not won..
Owner Exors of the Late Gordon Hopkins **Bred** A J Martin **Trained** Lambourn, Berks

FOCUS
An ordinary handicap despite a decent-sized field. As has become the norm with middle-distance handicaps here, the early pace was moderate and the race developed into a sprint over the last half-mile.
Dark Planet Official explanation: jockey said gelding hung right

1452 BETDIRECTPOKER.COM $50,000 FREEROLL MAIDEN STKS (DIV II) 7f (P)
5:30 (5:31) (Class 5) 3-4-Y-0 **£3,238** (£963; £481; £240) **Stalls** Low

Form RPR

34- **1** **Fabine**^{168} [6505] 3-8-7 .... RichardHughes 5 68
(B J Meehan) *h.d.w: lw: prom: trckd ldr wl over 2f out: rdn to ld 1f out: sn clr* **7/2**^{2}

2 2½ **Arabian Gleam** 3-8-12 .... SebSanders 7 71+
(J Noseda) *str: bit bkwd: dwlt: towards rr: stdy prog over 2f out: nt clr run over 1f out: pushed along and styd on to take 2nd nr fin* **14/1**

6- **3** nk **Mia's Boy**^{227} [5458] 3-8-12 .... AdrianMcCarthy 3 65+
(P W Chapple-Hyam) *lw: s.s: last and pushed along over 4f out: stl last and nt gng wl over 2f out: r.o fr over 1f out: fin wl* **10/11**^{1}

04 **4** shd **Mango Masher (IRE)**^{7} [1282] 3-8-12 .... TedDurcan 11 65
(C R Egerton) *bit bkwd: chsd ldrs: drvn in 3rd over 2f out: kpt on same pce* **20/1**

0-6 **5** *shd* **Optical Illusion (USA)**^{9} 1246 3-8-12 .... JamieSpencer 4 64
(E A L Dunlop) *lw: led: over 2 l clr 2f out: brought wd in st: hdd 1f out: wknd fnl 100yds* **9/2**^{3}

000- **6** *½* **Krikket**^{220} 5592 3-8-4 .... LiamJones$^{(3)}$ 2 58
(W J Haggas) *bit bkwd: dwlt: rn in snatches: drvn up to chse ldng trio over 2f out: one pce after* **50/1**

7 *2 ½* **Mr Grand Lodge (FR)** 3-8-12 .... MartinDwyer 9 56+
(L M Cumani) *str: bkwd: hld up in midfield: outpcd fr over 2f out: n.d after* **20/1**

8 *7* **Ships Watch (IRE)** 3-8-7 .... SteveDrowne 1 32
(R Charlton) *wl grwn: bit bkwd: s.s: a in rr: wl outpcd fr over 2f out: shuffled along and no ch after* **25/1**

9 *2 ½* **Ridgeway Place** 3-8-7 .... DavidKinsella 6 26
(A B Haynes) *lw: dwlt: a in rr: racd on outer 1/2-way: wl outpcd fr 3f out* **66/1**

10 *4* **Rosemary And Thyme** 3-8-7 .... MichaelHills 10 15
(J W Hills) *a towards rr: brief effrt on outer 3f out: wknd over 2f out* **66/1**

0-0 **11** *15* **Brief Engagement (IRE)**^{107} 160 4-9-5 .... RobertHavlin 8 —
(T D McCarthy) *plld hrd: mostly chsd ldr to 3f out: wknd rapidly: t.o* **100/1**

1m 26.57s (0.68) **Going Correction** +0.05s/f (Slow)
WFA 3 from 4yo 12lb **11** Ran SP% **118.8**
Speed ratings (Par 103):98,95,94,94,94 94,91,83,80,75 58
CSF £46.35 TOTE £4.60: £1.60, £3.30, £1.10; EX 51.70 Trifecta £232.40 Pool £510.78, 1.56 winning units. Place 6 £19.91, Place 5 £15.01.
Owner Clipper Logistics **Bred** Mrs P A Reditt And M J Reditt **Trained** Manton, Wilts
■ Stewards' Enquiry : Adrian McCarthy 14-day ban: in breach of Rule 158 (b) (May 15-28)

FOCUS
This looked the weaker of the two divisions, with only a couple of those that had run before having shown any real signs of ability. A moderate early pace also contributed to the winning time being a lot slower than for division one.
Mia's Boy Official explanation: jockey said, regarding running and riding, that his orders were to have the colt prominent, but he missed the break by five lengths, colt did not travel well early stages and thought it had lost its action at the top of the hill, but then stayed on up the straight.
Mango Masher(IRE) Official explanation: jockey said colt hung left-handed in home straight
Brief Engagement(IRE) Official explanation: jockey said filly finished distressed
T/Jkpt: Not won. T/Plt: £30.10 to a £1 stake. Pool: £69,773.00. 1,692.00 winning tickets. T/Qpdt: £4.30 to a £1 stake. Pool: £3,948.20. 668.60 winning tickets. JN

964 MUSSELBURGH (R-H)

Friday, May 4

OFFICIAL GOING: Good to firm
Wind: Virtually nil

1453 GILBERTS H'CAP — 5f
2:20 (2:20) (Class 5) (0-70,68) 3-Y-O **£3,238** (£963; £481; £240) **Stalls** Low

Form RPR

0-31 **1** **Windjammer**^{9} 1240 3-9-2 **63** 6ex .... DavidAllan 7 74+
(T D Easterby) *cl up: led 1/2-way: rdn over 1f out: styd on* **4/6**^{1}

005- **2** *2* **Smirfys Gold (IRE)**^{212} 5766 3-8-9 **56** .... (v^{1}) GrahamGibbons 5 59
(E S McMahon) *chsd ldrs: hdwy 2f out: rdn to chse wnr wl over 1f out: drvn and one pce ins fnl f* **22/1**

0-01 **3** *nk* **Northern Dare (IRE)**^{14} 1136 3-9-2 **63** .... AdrianTNicholls 4 65+
(D Nicholls) *chsd ldrs: rdn along 1/2-way: swtchd rt and drvn over 1f out: kpt on ins fnl f* **3/1**^{2}

-53 **4** *1 ½* **Nomoreblondes**^{26} 958 3-9-1 **62** .... MickyFenton 1 59
(P T Midgley) *led: hdd 1/2-way: sn rdn and wknd wl over 1f out* **14/1**

4204 **5** *3 ½* **Temtation (IRE)**^{10} 1213 3-8-8 **55** .... RichardMullen 2 39
(Peter Grayson) *a in rr* **33/1**

0-30 **6** *1 ¾* **Beechside (IRE)**^{9} 1240 3-8-2 **49** oh1 .... PaulHanagan 6 27
(W A Murphy, Ire) *in tch: effrt and hdwy on outer over 2f out: sn rdn and btn* **28/1**

314- **7** *3 ½* **Davaye**^{207} 5860 3-9-7 **68** .... PatCosgrave 3 34
(K R Burke) *a outpcd and bhd* **12/1**^{3}

59.02 secs (-1.48) **Going Correction** -0.175s/f (Firm) **7** Ran SP% **110.1**
Speed ratings (Par 99):104,100,100,97,92 89,83
CSF £19.37 TOTE £1.70: £1.20, £5.50; EX 22.20.
Owner April Fools **Bred** P E Clinton **Trained** Great Habton, N Yorks
■ Stewards' Enquiry : Adrian T Nicholls one-day ban: careless riding (May 15)

FOCUS
Only a very modest affair. Apart from Windjammer, it would be surprising if many winners emerged from the race.

1454 E B F / EDMONDS.CO.UK MEDIAN AUCTION MAIDEN STKS — 5f
2:50 (2:50) (Class 5) 2-Y-O **£3,886** (£1,156; £577; £288) **Stalls** Low

Form RPR

0 **1** **Ingleby Star (IRE)**^{15} 1107 2-9-3 .... PaulFessey 3 80
(T D Barron) *mde virtually all: rdn over 1f out: styd on strly ins fnl f* **12/1**

3 **2** *nk* **Fast Feet**^{30} 926 2-9-3 .... NCallan 4 79
(K A Ryan) *chsd ldng pair: hdwy 2f out: rdn to chal ent fnl f and ev ch: drvn: edgd rt: rdr lost iron: no ex fnl 50yds* **11/8**^{1}

4 **3** *1 ¾* **In Honour (IRE)**^{13} 1150 2-9-3 .... RichardMullen 5 72
(E S McMahon) *s.i.s and bhd: hdwy 1/2-way: rdn wl over 1f out: kpt on ins fnl f: nrst fin* **7/4**^{2}

5 **4** *2* **Timewatch**^{20} 1043 2-9-3 .... KDarley 1 64
(M Johnston) *cl up: rdn along 2f out: grad wknd* **11/2**^{3}

5 *3* **Quarrymaster (IRE)** 2-9-3 .... PaulMulrennan 2 52
(J Howard Johnson) *chsd ldrs: rdn along and outpcd fr 1/2-way* **14/1**

59.63 secs (-0.87) **Going Correction** -0.175s/f (Firm) **5** Ran SP% **108.2**
Speed ratings (Par 93):99,98,95,92,87
CSF £28.32 TOTE £15.70: £4.60, £1.40; EX 39.50.
Owner Dave Scott **Bred** P Cosgrove **Trained** Maunby, N Yorks

FOCUS
A decent juvenile maiden for the track. The first three should hold their own in the coming months.

NOTEBOOK
Ingleby Star(IRE), who was well backed on his debut, fairly flew out of the stalls this time and showed a good attitude to hold off the favourite under pressure. He will find things tougher now when faced with other winners, but looks a speedy and tough sort and should hold his own when raised in grade. (op 14-1)
Fast Feet was a sustained challenger to the winner in the final furlong, but did seem held when his jockey lost an iron for a few strides. A fair sort, he certainly looks capable of landed a race in the next month. (op 5-4)
In Honour(IRE) was slowly away again and gave away any chance he had at the start. Experience should see him break from the stalls much quicker, but a sixth furlong will definitely help. He could be a useful sort. (op 2-1 tchd 9-4 in a place)
Timewatch was not far away in the early stages but could not keep tabs on the winner once that rival quickened. His pedigree suggests that he will get further. (op 4-1 tchd 6-1)
Quarrymaster(IRE), the only newcomer in the field and yet to reach his second birthday, only showed a bit of promise but will benefit for the experience. (op 20-1)

1455 CRUDENS GROUP H'CAP — 1m
3:20 (3:20) (Class 5) (0-75,75) 4-Y-O+ **£3,238** (£963; £481; £240) **Stalls** High

Form RPR

0-20 **1** **Frank Crow**^{11} 1198 4-9-2 **73** .... PaulHanagan 1 78
(J S Goldie) *sn led: qcknd 3f out: rdn over 2f out: hdd wl over 1f out: drvn and rallied ins fnl f to ld fnl 50yds* **9/2**^{3}

46-0 **2** *hd* **Mount Usher**^{20} 1040 5-9-0 **71** .... DeanMcKeown 7 76
(G A Swinbank) *hld up: hdwy on outer 3f out: rdn to ld wl over 1f out and sn hung bdly rt: hdd fnl 50yds* **13/8**^{1}

01-5 **3** *1 ½* **Spinning**^{14} 1132 4-8-11 **68** .... PaulFessey 6 70
(T D Barron) *trckd ldrs: effrt over 2f out: sn rdn: kpt on u.p ins fnl f* **5/2**^{2}

566- **4** *3 ½* **Musical Giant (USA)**^{290} 3620 4-8-4 **61** oh10 .... RoystonFfrench 4 55
(J Howard Johnson) *chsd wnr: rdn along over 2f out: grad wknd* **28/1**

006- **5** *shd* **Psychic Star**^{19} 5732 4-8-13 **75** .... KevinGhunowa$^{(5)}$ 5 68
(Miss Lucinda V Russell) *chsd ldrs on outer: rdn along over 2f out: grad wknd* **20/1**

455- **6** *3* **Bolton Hall (IRE)**^{232} 5320 5-8-9 **66** .... TonyHamilton 3 52
(R A Fahey) *stdd s: hld up: a in rr* **5/1**

1m 41.74s (-0.76) **Going Correction** -0.175s/f (Firm) **6** Ran SP% **109.7**
Speed ratings (Par 103):96,95,94,90,90 87
CSF £11.71 TOTE £5.20: £2.00, £1.70; EX 23.10.
Owner Mrs Janis Macpherson **Bred** Southill Stud **Trained** Uplawmoor, E Renfrews

FOCUS
A fair handicap, but the early gallop looked modest, as was the winning time. Mount Usher should have won but hung away his chance when taking the lead.

1456 DM HALL CONDITIONS STKS — 5f
3:50 (3:50) (Class 2) 3-Y-O+
£12,464 (£3,732; £1,866; £934; £466; £234) **Stalls** Low

Form RPR

60-3 **1** **The Tatling (IRE)**^{14} 1125 10-8-12 **99** .... DarryllHolland 5 105
(J M Bradley) *dwlt: sn trcking ldrs: smooth hdwy 2f out: cl up ins fnl f: led fnl 50yds: cheekily* **5/2**^{1}

40-2 **2** *hd* **River Falcon**^{14} 1125 7-8-12 **98** .... DanielTudhope 8 104
(J S Goldie) *trckd ldrs on outer: smooth hdwy 2f out: led over 1f out: rdn ins fnl f: hdd and nt qckn fnl 50yds* **11/4**^{2}

00-4 **3** *2* **Terentia**^{30} 927 4-8-7 **97** .... RichardMullen 1 92
(E S McMahon) *chsd ldrs: rdn along 2f out: drvn and kpt on ins fnl f* **5/1**^{3}

0-10 **4** *1 ½* **Fire Up The Band**^{15} 1102 8-9-2 **102** .... SilvestreDeSousa 2 95
(D Nicholls) *trckd ldrs: hdwy 2f out: sn rdn and no imp ins fnl f* **5/1**^{3}

0-16 **5** *½* **Merlin's Dancer**^{14} 1125 7-8-12 **96** .... AdrianTNicholls 4 90
(D Nicholls) *led: rdn along 2f out: hdd over 1f out: wknd* **13/2**

00/5 **6** *nk* **Bigalos Bandit**^{34} 841 5-8-12 **90** .... AndrewMullen 3 89
(D Nicholls) *hld up in rr tl styd on appr fnl f: nrst fin* **33/1**

-000 **7** *1 ¼* **Tournedos (IRE)**^{78} 474 5-9-9 **100** .... PaulHanagan 7 95
(D Nicholls) *prom: rdn along 2f out: wkng whn n.m.r over 1f out* **14/1**

600- **8** *3* **Sokoke**^{182} 6320 6-8-12 **45** .... MickyFenton 6 73?
(D A Nolan) *cl up to 1/2-way: sn rdn along and wknd* **500/1**

58.45 secs (-2.05) **Going Correction** -0.175s/f (Firm) **8** Ran SP% **111.7**
Speed ratings (Par 109):109,108,105,103,102 101,99,95
CSF £9.12 TOTE £4.60: £1.30, £1.10, £1.60; EX 9.80.
Owner Dab Hand Racing **Bred** Patrick J Power **Trained** Sedbury, Gloucs

FOCUS
A very solid conditions stakes. The form looks sounds and should work out.

NOTEBOOK
The Tatling(IRE) came back to his form under a very cool ride. This should do his confidence the world of good and he is still capable of running well at the age of 10. Connections plan to try him in back up Group company again. (tchd 7-2)
River Falcon, who finished in front of The Tatling last time, was doing his best to make him work hard for victory but had no chance once that rival loomed upsides him. It was a sound effort, however, and he has returned in great form this season. (op 4-1 tchd 9-2 in a place)
Terentia tried her best to get involved but found two old stagers in no mood to let a younger rival upstage them. Time may show this was a sound effort and she can be given another chance in a similar race. (op 9-2 tchd 4-1)
Fire Up The Band led home the four Dandy Nicholls' horses after chasing the pace. He had no easy task giving weight away to the first two, so this was probably a fair effort. (op 9-2)
Merlin's Dancer made the early running as usual and kept on reasonably well once joined. His handicap mark is quite high now and he will need to come down the weights to have an obvious chance. (op 11-2)
Bigalos Bandit ◆ is still feeling his way back after a long layoff and will be of more interest next time if given a realistic task. He really caught the eye with the way he stayed on. (op 25-1)
Sokoke appeared to run a blinder, and there seemed no fluke about the effort. Connections would be well served to get him out as quickly as possible, in case the Handicapper takes a dim view of the effort, but history does show him to be a disappointing sort and he is no good thing to go on from this effort. (op 250-1)

1457 BANK OF SCOTLAND CORPORATE H'CAP — 1m 6f
4:20 (4:20) (Class 5) (0-70,72) 4-Y-O+ **£3,238** (£963; £481; £240) **Stalls** High

Form RPR

5-01 **1** **Kristensen**^{26} 955 8-9-8 **70** .... (v) TonyHamilton 7 79
(Karen McLintock) *trckd ldrs: effrt over 2f out and sn rdn: swtchd rt and hdwy on inner to ld ent fnl f: styd on wl u.p* **4/1**^{2}

44-0 **2** *2* **Danzatrice**^{20} 1042 5-8-8 **56** .... KDarley 6 62
(C W Thornton) *hld up in rr: stdy hdwy on outer 3f out: rdn to dispute ld and ev ch 1f out: sn drvn and kpt on same pce towards fin* **3/1**^{1}

0/01 **3** *½* **Kyber**^{25} 965 6-8-0 **53** .... DuranFentiman$^{(5)}$ 4 58
(J S Goldie) *led: rdn along and hdd over 2f out: drvn and rallied appr fnl f: one pce* **4/1**^{2}

50-1 **4** *1 ¼* **Mister Arjay (USA)**^{9} 1239 7-9-5 **72** 6ex .... JamieMoriarty$^{(5)}$ 2 76
(B Ellison) *hld up in tch: effrt 3f out and sn rdn along: drvn fnl 2f and no imp* **4/1**^{2}

13-4 **5** *shd* **Grey Outlook**^{26} 955 4-9-2 **65** .... RoystonFfrench 5 68
(Miss L A Perratt) *a.p: hdwy to ld over 2f out and sn rdn: drvn and hdd 1f out: wknd* **12/1**

3023 **6** *hd* **Toni Alcala**^{11} 1196 8-8-3 **51** .... (p) PaulFessey 1 54
(R F Fisher) *chsd ldrs: hdwy on outer 3f out: rdn to chal and ev ch 2f out: sn drvn and grad wknd* **8/1**^{3}

560- **7** *10* **Kyle Of Lochalsh**^{25} 6526 7-8-1 **54** .... (t) KevinGhunowa$^{(5)}$ 3 43
(Miss Lucinda V Russell) *a in rr* **25/1**

506- **8** *10* **Ransom Strip (USA)**[187] 6244 4-9-0 **63**.......................... PaulHanagan 8 38
(R A Fahey) *a towards rr* **10/1**

3m 7.66s (1.96) **Going Correction** -0.175s/f (Firm)
WFA 4 from 5yo+ 1lb **8** Ran SP% **116.7**
Speed ratings (Par 103):87,85,85,84,84 84,78,73
CSF £16.85 CT £50.92 TOTE £5.40: £1.90, £1.70, £1.60; EX 14.90.
Owner Equiname Ltd **Bred** Lordship Stud Limited **Trained** Ingoe, Northumberland

FOCUS
A range of abilities on show. The early pace looked sound enough, but the final time was slow and the form is still questionable, as some are high in the weights while others just don't win very often.

1458 FORTH ONE H'CAP 7f 30y
4:50 (4:51) (Class 3) (0-90,84) 4-Y-0+
£8,413 (£2,519; £1,259; £630; £314; £157) **Stalls** High

Form RPR

-003 **1** **Daaweitza**[6] 1308 4-8-6 **74**.......................... JamieMoriarty(5) 3 85
(B Ellison) *in tch: hdwy over 2f out: rdn to ld ent fnl f: sn drvn and edgd rt: kpt on* **11/2**[2]

310- **2** *nk* **Stonehaugh (IRE)**[241] 5079 4-9-0 **77**..........................(t) TonyHamilton 5 87
(J Howard Johnson) *prom: hdwy 3f out: rdn to chal 2f out and ev ch tl drvn and no ex wl ins fnl f* **28/1**

-526 **3** *1/2* **Royal Dignitary (USA)**[26] 953 7-9-7 **84**.............. SilvestreDeSousa 13 93
(D Nicholls) *cl up on inner: effrt 2f out and ev ch: sn rdn and kpt on u.p ins fnl f* **13/2**

0602 **4** *3/4* **H Harrison (IRE)**[10] 1223 7-8-0 **66**.......................... AndrewElliott(3) 7 73
(I W McInnes) *cl up: rdn to ld 2f out: drvn over 1f out: hdd ent fnl f and no ex* **12/1**

650- **5** *nk* **Zennerman (IRE)**[195] 6094 4-8-12 **75**.......................... NCallan 8 81
(K A Ryan) *hld up: hdwy over 2f out: rdn to chse ldrs over 1f out: kpt on ins fnl f: nrst fin* **12/1**

0361 **6** *1* **Flying Bantam (IRE)**[14] 1133 6-8-2 **65** oh1.................. PaulHanagan 11 69
(R A Fahey) *hld up: hdwy over 2f out: rdn and ev ch whn n.m.r ent fnl f: sn wknd* **15/2**

60-0 **7** *1* **Stellite**[26] 953 7-8-11 **74**.......................... DanielTudhope 4 75
(J S Goldie) *hld up: stdy hdwy on outer over 2f out: rdn and ev ch over 1f out: drvn and wknd ins fnl f* **50/1**

00-2 **8** *1/2* **Imperial Echo (USA)**[13] 1157 6-9-6 **83**.......................... PaulFessey 1 83
(T D Barron) *hld up: gd hdwy over 2f out: rdn and styng on whn n.m.r ent fnl f: kpt on same pce* **6/1**[3]

0-44 **9** *1/2* **Fiefdom (IRE)**[10] 1223 5-8-13 **76**.......................... RoystonFfrench 9 74
(I W McInnes) *midfield: hdwy to chse ldrs over 2f out: sn rdn and no imp appr fnl f* **10/1**

6100 **10** *3/4* **Stoic Leader (IRE)**[3] 1382 7-9-2 **79**.......................... PaulMulrennan 2 76
(R F Fisher) *a towards rr* **16/1**

030- **11** *1* **King Harson**[185] 6273 8-9-1 **78**.......................... PatCosgrave 10 72
(J D Bethell) *led: rdn along and hdd 2f out: sn drvn and wknd* **25/1**

50-0 **12** *3 1/2* **Blue Tomato**[16] 1088 6-9-7 **84**.......................... DarryllHolland 6 69
(J M Bradley) *towards rr fr 1/2-way* **20/1**

3-32 **13** *2* **Fremen (USA)**[48] 697 7-9-4 **81**.......................... AdrianTNicholls 14 61
(D Nicholls) *chsd ldrs on inner: effrt over 2f out: sn rdn: n.m.r and wknd* **3/1**[1]

003- **14** *6* **Choysia**[192] 6159 4-8-2 **68**.......................... AndrewMullen(3) 12 32
(D W Barker) *a in rr* **33/1**

1m 27.67s (-2.27) **Going Correction** -0.175s/f (Firm) **14** Ran SP% **127.1**
Speed ratings (Par 107):105,104,104,103,102 101,100,100,99,98 97,93,91,84
CSF £166.07 CT £1077.13 TOTE £7.20: £2.40, £7.80, £2.60; EX 271.70.
Owner Mrs Andrea M Mallinson **Bred** C Mallinson **Trained** Norton, N Yorks
■ Stewards' Enquiry : Tony Hamilton one-day ban: used whip with excessive force (May 15)
Jamie Moriarty one-day ban: used whip with excessive frequency (May 15)

FOCUS
A solid-looking handicap run at a sound pace. The form should work out.

NOTEBOOK
Daaweitza, given too much to do at Sandown last time, finally got his slice of luck and gained a well-deserved success. He stays a bit further than 7f and can make his presence felt again next time while in such good form. (op 6-1)
Stonehaugh(IRE) shaped really nicely on his seasonal debut - he won first time out last year - but would not want to go up in the weights too much for this effort. (op 33-1)
Royal Dignitary(USA) has a good record at the course and ran a fine race under a big weight. He will always be worth considering when racing at Musselburgh. (op 9-1)
H Harrison(IRE) tracked the decent tempo and was only just run out of the places close to the line. He is capable of going close off his current handicap mark.
Zennerman(IRE) came with his effort up the centre of the track, but was never quite getting there. Having his first start for a new trainer, it was a decent effort after a long break and he is well handicapped on his best form.
Flying Bantam(IRE) had every chance but could not get to the leaders. (op 7-1)
Blue Tomato ran much better than his final position would suggest, as he did not get home. He is better over shorter and is approaching a more realistic handicap mark again after his successful spell last summer. Official explanation: jockey said gelding ran too free early stages
Fremen(USA) was very disappointing and had no real excuses. Official explanation: vet said gelding returned distressed (op 5-1)

1459 TURF TV H'CAP 7f 30y
5:20 (5:25) (Class 6) (0-65,64) 4-Y-0+ **£2,590** (£770; £385; £192) **Stalls** High

Form RPR

2031 **1** **Violent Velocity (IRE)**[9] 1241 4-9-0 **60**.......................... GrahamGibbons 14 72
(J J Quinn) *trckd ldrs: hdwy to ld 1f out: sn rdn and kpt on wl* **9/4**[1]

0126 **2** *3/4* **Motu (IRE)**[14] 1133 6-9-3 **63**..........................(v) DanielTudhope 6 73
(I W McInnes) *chsd ldrs: hdwy over 2f out: rdn over 1f out: styd on u.p ins fnl f* **9/1**

66-4 **3** *1 3/4* **Dorn Dancer (IRE)**[24] 992 5-9-0 **60**.......................... TonyHamilton 4 65
(D W Barker) *towards rr: hdwy on outer 2f out: sn rdn and styd on wl fnl f: nrst fin* **12/1**

040- **4** *1* **Riverhill (IRE)**[175] 6425 4-8-6 **52** ow2.......................... PaulMulrennan 9 55
(J Howard Johnson) *hmpd s: midfield: hdwy 2f out: sn rdn and styd on ins fnl f: nrst fin* **25/1**

1201 **5** *nk* **Wiltshire (IRE)**[10] 1221 5-8-13 **59** 6ex.......................... MickyFenton 7 61
(P T Midgley) *midfield: hdwy over 2f out: rdn and styd on fnl f: nrst fin* **16/1**

0-00 **6** *1/2* **Baylaw Star**[25] 967 6-9-3 **63**.......................... RoystonFfrench 13 64
(I W McInnes) *led: rdn along and hdd 2f out: grad wknd* **7/1**[3]

032- **7** *2 1/2* **Walnut Grove**[230] 5370 4-8-10 **56**.......................... PaulFessey 8 50
(T D Barron) *wnt bdly rt s: cl up: led 2f out: sn rdn and hdd 1f out: sn wknd and eased* **6/1**[2]

000- **8** *nk* **Oeuf A La Neige**[207] 5865 7-7-13 **50** oh2.................. DuranFentiman(5) 1 43
(Miss L A Perratt) *a towards rr* **50/1**

06-0 **9** *1/2* **Esoterica (IRE)**[25] 967 4-8-11 **64**.......................... GaryBartley(7) 3 56
(J S Goldie) *a in rr* **14/1**

34-4 **10** *2 1/2* **Flylowflylong (IRE)**[25] 967 4-9-2 **62**.......................... PaulHanagan 12 48
(I Semple) *a in rr* **8/1**

-365 **11** *1 1/2* **Attacca**[4] 1360 6-8-6 **52** oh2 ow2..........................(v) KDarley 5 34
(J R Weymes) *prom: rdn along over 2f out: sn drvn and wknd* **7/1**[3]

00-0 **12** *2* **Pachello (IRE)**[11] 1200 5-8-11 **62**.......................... KevinGhunowa(5) 2 39
(J M Bradley) *chsd ldrs: rdn 2f out: wknd over 1f out* **66/1**

300- **13** *10* **Jordans Spark**[181] 6213 6-8-8 **54** ow1.......................... PhillipMakin 11 5
(P Monteith) *hmpd s: a bhd* **20/1**

000- **14** *16* **City Miss**[230] 5368 4-8-1 **50** oh5.......................... AndrewMullen(3) 10 —
(Miss L A Perratt) *hmpd s: a bhd* **100/1**

1m 27.94s (-2.00) **Going Correction** -0.175s/f (Firm) **14** Ran SP% **124.5**
Speed ratings (Par 101):104,103,101,100,99 99,96,95,95,92 90,88,77,58
CSF £23.14 CT £218.90 TOTE £3.20: £1.40, £3.10, £2.50; EX 33.00 Place 6 £22.30, Place 5 £14.73.
Owner Mrs S Quinn **Bred** Miss Jill Finegan **Trained** Settrington, N Yorks

FOCUS
A moderate event won by an in-form, and possibly well-treated, horse. It seems unlikely that many winners will emerge from the race.
Riverhill(IRE) Official explanation: jockey said gelding suffered interference at start
Flylowflylong(IRE) Official explanation: jockey said filly suffered interference at start
Attacca Official explanation: jockey said gelding ran too free early stages
T/Plt: £51.60 to a £1 stake. Pool: £52,599.60. 743.40 winning tickets. T/Qpdt: £23.60 to a £1 stake. Pool: £2,901.00. 90.70 winning tickets. JR

1460 - (Foreign Racing) - See Raceform Interactive

983

CORK (R-H)
Friday, May 4

OFFICIAL GOING: Firm (good to firm in places on sprint course)

1461a CORK STKS (LISTED RACE) 6f
5:50 (5:46) 3-Y-0+ **£21,993** (£6,452; £3,074; £1,047)

RPR

1 **Absolutelyfabulous (IRE)**[13] 1171 4-9-4 96.......................... WMLordan 5 106
(David Wachman, Ire) *sn 2nd: rdn and outpcd briefly 1 1/2f out: hdwy to ld ins fnl f: styd on wl cl home* **11/4**[2]

2 *1/2* **That's Hot (IRE)**[25] 986 4-9-4 100.......................... JMurtagh 3 104
(G M Lyons, Ire) *hld up in rr: hdwy under 2f out: 3rd travelling wl whn nt clr run over 1f out: swtchd ins fnl f: r.o wl cl home* **9/2**[3]

3 *2 1/2* **Facchetti (USA)**[22] 1015 3-8-11 100.......................... JAHeffernan 1 97
(A P O'Brien, Ire) *attempted to make all: rdn clr 1 1/2f out: hdd ins fnl f: no ex cl home* **10/1**

4 *1 3/4* **Speed Dream (IRE)**[22] 1015 3-8-11 96.......................... DPMcDonogh 6 91
(David Wachman, Ire) *trckd ldrs in 3rd: rdn and outpcd 1 1/2f out: no imp fnl f* **6/1**

5 *nk* **Flash McGahon (IRE)**[13] 1171 3-9-0 100.......................... MJKinane 4 93
(John M Oxx, Ire) *hld up in tch: 4th and prog on outer 2f out: sn rdn: no ex fnl f* **13/8**[1]

6 *4* **Ireland's Call (IRE)**[12] 1184 6-9-7 94.......................... PJSmullen 2 81
(Peter Casey, Ire) *chsd ldrs early: wknd fr 2f out* **14/1**

1m 10.5s (-2.10)
WFA 3 from 4yo+ 10lb **6** Ran SP% **113.0**
CSF £15.56 TOTE £5.00: £2.30, £5.60; DF 46.80.
Owner Mrs John Magnier **Bred** Barouche Stud Ireland Ltd **Trained** Goolds Cross, Co Tipperary

NOTEBOOK
Absolutelyfabulous(IRE), in the frame at this level and in Group 3 company last season when she also won two handicaps over this trip, ran out a comfortable winner. Always close up, she wore down the front-running Facchetti about 150 yards from the finish and ran on. (op 4/1 tchd 5/2)
That's Hot(IRE), who defied a big weight when scoring over this course and distance last month, confirmed her improvement with a solid effort. She had only one rival behind here under two furlongs out but ran on steadily when she got room and was closing all the way to the line. (op 7/2 tchd 5/1)
Facchetti(USA), a winner over 5f on heavy ground at the Curragh in October, showed improvement from his first run of the season. In front on settling down, he only gave best inside the final furlong.
Speed Dream(IRE), winner of a 5f conditions event at Tipperary last month, was the least experienced in the line-up. Soon close up, he could make little impression from over a furlong out and failed to confirm placings with Facchetti who had finished sixth in the Tipperary race. (op 9/2)
Flash McGahon(IRE), a Listed winner over 5f at Tipperary last season, had made an encouraging start to the campaign when chasing home Dandy Man at Naas last month. He proved disappointing here, though, racing on the outside of his rivals and finding very little for pressure from a furlong and a half out. Official explanation: vet said colt pulled a shoe on its right fore during the race (op 6/4 tchd 2/1)
Ireland's Call(IRE), much improved last year when he won five handicaps on the bounce, is more effective over 7f or a mile and was struggling from halfway. (op 12/1)

GOODWOOD (R-H)
Saturday, May 5

OFFICIAL GOING: Straight course - good; round course - good to firm
Wind: Moderate, behind.

1464 BEGBIES-TRAYNOR STKS (H'CAP) 5f
2:30 (2:30) (Class 3) (0-90,88) 4-Y-0+ **£10,201** (£3,035; £1,516; £757) **Stalls** Low

Form RPR

6006 **1** **Classic Encounter (IRE)**[10] 1242 4-9-1 **85**.............. FergusSweeney 8 98
(D M Simcock) *lw: mde all: drvn along 2f out: styd on strly thrght fnl f: won gng away* **12/1**

5-45 **2** *1 1/4* **Bluebok**[10] 1242 6-8-8 **83**..........................(t) KevinGhunowa(5) 10 91
(J M Bradley) *lw: chsd ldrs: wnt 2nd ins fnl 2f: drvn to chal 1f out: kpt on same pce fnl f* **10/3**[1]

04-0 **3** *1/2* **Pic Up Sticks**[10] 1242 8-8-11 **84**.......................... RichardKingscote(3) 9 90
(B G Powell) *lw: in tch: rdn and styd on to chse ldrs over 1f out: kpt on cl home but nvr gng pce to chal* **10/1**

355- **4** *hd* **Holbeck Ghyll (IRE)**[235] 5275 5-8-7 **77**.......................... MartinDwyer 2 82+
(A M Balding) *n.m.r s and s.i.s: effrt on rails and n.m.r 2f out: drvn and kpt on fnl f: fin wl* **7/2**[2]

202- **5** *nk* **Matsunosuke**[239] 5148 5-8-0 **77**.......................... LukeMorris(7) 11 81
(A B Coogan) *chsd ldrs: rdn and ev ch 2f out: one pce ins fnl f* **5/1**[3]

560- **6** 2 1/2 **Puskas (IRE)**[343] [2014] 4-8-8 **85**.................................... BarrySavage[(7)] 7 80
(J M Bradley) *bit bkwd: towards rr: pushed along 1/2-way: kpt on ins fnl f but nvr in contention* **16/1**

005- **7** 1 **Peopleton Brook**[175] [6446] 5-8-8 **78**.................................... TedDurcan 3 70
(J M Bradley) *chsd ldrs: rdn 1/2-way: wknd ins fnl f* **8/1**

000- **8** 1 **Golden Dixie (USA)**[209] [5832] 8-9-3 **87**.............................. SebSanders 4 75
(R A Harris) *in tch: rdn 1/2-way and sn outpcd* **10/1**

-002 **9** 2 1/2 **Fromsong (IRE)**[19] [1061] 9-8-11 **81**.................................... RobertHavlin 1 60
(D K Ivory) *lw: spd 3f* **6/1**

000/ **10** 1 **Mornin Reserves**[750] [1024] 8-9-4 **88**..................................(t) AdamKirby 6 64
(W G Harrison) *swtg: b: b.hind: spd to 1/2-way* **33/1**

57.31 secs (-1.74) **Going Correction** -0.30s/f (Firm) **10** Ran SP% **122.1**
Speed ratings (Par 107):101,99,98,97,97 93,91,90,86,84
CSF £54.41 CT £354.91 TOTE £14.60: £3.20, £1.70, £2.50; EX 82.00 Trifecta £459.90 Pool: £647.80 - 1.00 winning units..

Owner Khalifa Dasmal **Bred** Stratford Place Stud **Trained** Newmarket, Suffolk

FOCUS

A tight little sprint handicap and although the pace looked solid, the final time was ordinary when compared to the other races on the straight course. There looked to be a track bias, for those drawn high coming down the centre of the track appeared to hold the advantage throughout.

NOTEBOOK

Classic Encounter(IRE), basically disappointing since his two-year-old days, was racing off his lowest-ever mark and that helped do the trick. One of three highest-drawn who came down the centre, he made every yard and always seemed to have matters under control. The switch to forcing tactics looks to have rejuvenated him. (op 14-1)

Bluebok, half a length in front of Classic Encounter at Epsom last time and 1lb worse off, kept his old rival company down the centre of the track and had every chance, but the winner was not for passing. This was another solid effort, but he remains 3lb above his last winning mark. (op 4-1)

Pic Up Sticks ◆, from a yard in decent form just now but well behind the front pair at Epsom last time, was content to sit behind the pace-setters down the centre of the track, but he took a while to pick up when switched for his effort and although he was gaining at the line, he was not doing it quickly enough. He probably needs a stiffer track than this and is 3lb below his last winning mark, so is worth keeping in mind. (op 11-1 tchd 12-1)

Holbeck Ghyll(IRE) finished in good style against the stands' rail and did much the best of those held up and those drawn low. He is still 6lb above his last winning mark, but he is entitled to come on for this first run in eight months (op 4-1)

Matsunosuke, another returning from eight months off, ran fast for a long way down the centre of the track. He may have been helped by racing on the faster strip of ground, but this was still a decent comeback under his optimum conditions. (op 8-1)

Puskas(IRE) ◆, making his debut for the yard, is entitled to come on a good deal from this first run in almost a year. He looks just the type of horse that his trainer consistently does so well with.

Fromsong(IRE) was a bit disappointing following his encouraging effort at Windsor last time, but as things turned out he may not have been done any favours by his draw. (op 5-1 tchd 13-2)

1465 ROYAL SUSSEX REGIMENT STKS (H'CAP) 6f

3:05 (3:05) (Class 4) (0-85,84) 3-Y-0+ **£7,772** (£2,312; £1,155; £577) **Stalls** Low

Form RPR

-036 **1** **Mujood**[13] [1179] 4-9-10 **84**..(v[1]) StephenCarson 8 96
(Eve Johnson Houghton) *stmbld stalls: sn led: drvn over 1f out and styd on strly fnl f* **7/1**

6251 **2** 1 3/4 **Saviours Spirit**[19] [1063] 6-9-3 **77**.................................... RobertHavlin 2 84
(T G Mills) *hld up in rr but in tch: rdn and hdwy over 1f out to chse wnr ins fnl f but no imp* **11/4[1]**

0302 **3** 2 **Marko Jadeo (IRE)**[12] [1200] 9-8-7 **72**.............................. TolleyDean[(5)] 1 73
(R A Harris) *lw: b: hld up towards rr: hdwy fr 2f out edgd rt over 1f out: hung rt ins fnl f: kpt on fnl f but nvr gng pce to chal* **14/1**

0-40 **4** nk **Chinalea (IRE)**[5] [1357] 5-8-10 **70**......................................(p) AdamKirby 4 70
(C G Cox) *lw: chsd ldrs: rdn over 2f out: styd on same pce fr over 1f out* **8/1**

02-0 **5** 2 **Devine Dancer**[19] [1061] 4-9-0 **74**.................................... DaneO'Neill 5 68
(H Candy) *in tch: hdwy 1/2-way: chsd ldrs 2f out: sn rdn: wknd ins fnl f* **12/1**

20-0 **6** 3 1/2 **Calypso King**[19] [1061] 4-8-11 **71**.................................... SebSanders 7 55
(R M Beckett) *lw: stmbld s: chsd ldrs: rdn 2f out: wknd fnl f* **13/2**

00-4 **7** 5 **River Thames**[15] [1134] 4-9-2 **76**......................................(p) MartinDwyer 6 45
(K A Ryan) *lw: t.k.h: chsd ldrs: rdn 1/2-way: sn btn* **3/1[2]**

0003 **8** 5 **Smokin Beau**[19] [1061] 10-9-3 **77**.................................... TedDurcan 3 31
(N P Littmoden) *lw: stmbld stalls: pressed ldrs to 1/2-way: sn wknd* **6/1[3]**

69.90 secs (-2.95) **Going Correction** -0.30s/f (Firm) **8** Ran SP% **117.3**
Speed ratings (Par 105):107,104,102,101,98 94,87,80
CSF £27.35 CT £268.72 TOTE £8.80: £2.40, £1.40, £3.10; EX 39.40.

Owner Eden Racing **Bred** Bloomsbury Stud And The Hon Sir David Sieff **Trained** Blewbury, Oxon

FOCUS

As in the previous race there was a big bias towards those that raced up with the pace and who came down the middle of the track. All bar Smokin Beau gave the stands' rail a wide berth and again the winner made all.

1466 E B F BEGBIES-TRAYNOR CONQUEROR STKS (LISTED RACE) (FILLES & MARES) 1m

3:40 (3:44) (Class 1) 3-Y-0+ **£14,762** (£5,595; £2,800; £1,396; £699) **Stalls** High

Form RPR

045- **1** **Harvest Queen (IRE)**[189] [6219] 4-9-4 92.............................. SebSanders 4 107+
(P J Makin) *hld up in rr but in tch: qcknd fr 3f out to ld 2f out: drvn clr fnl f* **11/8[1]**

3661 **2** 4 **Expensive**[28] [938] 4-9-7 100.................................... TedDurcan 2 101
(C F Wall) *lw: led: rdn and hdd 2f out: outpcd fnl f but kpt on wl for clr 2nd* **7/4[2]**

3-40 **3** 4 **Laurentina**[8] [1275] 3-8-6 94 ow1.................................... BrettDoyle 5 87
(B J Meehan) *chsd ldrs: rdn 3f out: btn ins fnl 2f* **9/1**

1 **4** 3/4 **Chantilly Tiffany**[16] [1100] 3-8-5.................................... MartinDwyer 1 84
(E A L Dunlop) *lw: t.k.h: chsd ldrs: rdn 3f out: wknd fr 2f out* **11/2[3]**

0/0- **5** 4 **Chatila (USA)**[234] [5300] 4-9-4 95.............................. RobertHavlin 3 78
(J H M Gosden) *bit bkwd: s.i.s: sn rcvrd to chse ldr: rdn 3f out: wknd 2f out* **12/1**

1m 38.79s (-1.48) **Going Correction** +0.025s/f (Good)
WFA 3 from 4yo 13lb **5** Ran SP% **111.5**
Speed ratings (Par 111):108,104,100,99,95
CSF £4.14 TOTE £2.60: £1.30, £1.50; EX 3.70.

Owner Bakewell Bloodstock Ltd **Bred** Bakewell Bloodstock **Trained** Ogbourne Maisey, Wilts

FOCUS

Despite the small field this was run at a very solid pace and with the five runners finishing well spread out, the form looks reliable. The runner-up looks the best guide to it, but the winner could easily rate higher.

NOTEBOOK

Harvest Queen(IRE), returning from six months off, was successful following an even longer absence on her return to action last term, so the layoff was never going to be a problem. Ridden with plenty of confidence off the pace early, once switched out for her effort she showed a very impressive turn of foot to run past her market rival as though she was standing still and win going away. She appears to still be improving and is well worth a crack at Group company against her own sex. (op 7-4 tchd 15-8)

Expensive, back on turf following her success in a similar event on Polytrack, very much enjoyed the run of the race out in front and it looked as though she would take some passing. However, once the favourite engaged the afterburner it proved no contest and she was very much second best. She may prefer a stiffer mile than this, but in truth she would not have beaten the winner on any sort of track. (tchd 15-8)

Laurentina showed up for a long way and had every chance, but found the two older filles much too classy. Easier ground would have suited her, but she will remain hard to place. (op 10-1)

Chantilly Tiffany, taking a big step up in class after her debut victory in the Wood Ditton, was comfortably seen off and the form of the Newmarket race is beginning to looks modest. She is another for whom further winning opportunities will not be easy to find. (op 9-2 tchd 6-1)

Chatila(USA), who has only managed to make the track once in the past 19 months, understandably appeared to blow up. Although she was well beaten in the end, it is interesting that her stable have decided to persevere with her. (op 10-1 tchd 9-1)

1467 MCINNES H'CAP 1m 1f 192y

4:15 (4:15) (Class 3) (0-90,87) 3-Y-0 **£9,715** (£2,890; £1,444; £721) **Stalls** High

Form RPR

1-21 **1** **Serengeti**[15] [1122] 3-9-4 **87**.. SebSanders 5 104+
(M Johnston) *lw: trckd ldr: niggled along fr 6f out: drvn to ld ins fnl 3f forged clr thrght fnl f* **4/7[1]**

613- **2** 7 **Oakley Heffert (IRE)**[173] [6458] 3-8-9 **78**.............................. RichardSmith 1 80
(R Hannon) *bkwd: chsd ldrs: rdn and one pce over 2f out: styd on ins fnl f to take mod 2nd cl home* **12/1**

302- **3** 3/4 **Bajan Pride**[173] [6458] 3-8-4 **73**.................................... MartinDwyer 3 74
(R Hannon) *lw: led: rdn 3f out: sn hdd: styd chsng wnr but no ch fr ins fnl 2f: lost mod 2nd cl home* **8/1[3]**

111- **4** 1/2 **King Charles**[228] [5459] 3-9-4 **87**.................................... DaneO'Neill 6 87
(E A L Dunlop) *chsd ldrs: rdn 3f out: styd on same pce fr over 2f out* **4/1[2]**

160- **5** 2 1/2 **Monachello (USA)**[197] [6074] 3-8-11 **80**.............................. JimCrowley 4 75
(Mrs A J Perrett) *lw: hld up in rr: hdwy over 3f out: nvr rchd ldrs: wknd ins fnl 2f* **16/1**

0 **6** 14 **Without Excuse (USA)**[15] [1126] 3-9-3 **86**..........................(p) TedDurcan 2 53
(M Botti) *s.i.s: in rr: mod prog 3f out: hung rt and wknd fr 2f out* **16/1**

2m 6.94s (-0.81) **Going Correction** +0.025s/f (Good) **6** Ran SP% **114.2**
Speed ratings (Par 103):104,98,97,97,95 84
CSF £9.32 TOTE £1.60: £1.20, £3.50; EX 12.60.

Owner Sheikh Mohammed **Bred** Darley **Trained** Middleham Moor, N Yorks

FOCUS

A race run at just an even pace and the result was very much as the market predicted. The form amongst the beaten horses looks quite sound, and the winner is probably better than even this victory might suggest.

NOTEBOOK

Serengeti ◆, making his turf debut after three runs on Polytrack, was not travelling all that well during the course of the contest, just needing to be niggled along for a few strides early and again when asked to go after the leader, but it was a different story over the last couple of furlongs as he was striding majestically clear whilst his rivals were having their own private battle for second place. This sharp, undulating track and quick ground was probably not an ideal combination for him, so he can be rated even better than the bare form. It will take a huge hike up the handicap to stop him following up, and given his trainer's record at Royal Ascot, it would be no surprise to see him turn out for a race like the King George V Handicap, where the longer trip and galloping track would be right up his street. (op 4-5 tchd 5-6)

Oakley Heffert(IRE), returning from six months off and stepping up in trip, was off the bridle a long way out and only snatched second place because others fell in a hole. That said, he is entitled to come on for it and will not always bump into a potentially smart performer like the winner. (op 14-1 tchd 16-1 and 11-1)

Bajan Pride, making his handicap debut off the back of a seven-month absence and another upped in trip, made a brave bid to make all the running and did his best to keep tabs on the favourite after he ranged alongside, but it proved an unequal struggle and his efforts eventually cost him second place. There should be an ordinary handicap to be won with him.

King Charles, returning from eight months off and bidding for a four-timer off a 5lb higher mark, never managed to get involved over this longer trip and perhaps the outing was needed. (op 3-1)

Monachello(USA) never looked like landing a blow, but this first run in seven months should have helped put him right. (op 12-1)

Without Excuse(USA), having only his second start in this country and his first in handicap company, was struggling as soon as he exited the stalls and things did not really get any better for him. (op 12-1)

1468 BEGBIES-TRAYNOR MAIDEN STKS 7f

4:50 (4:51) (Class 5) 3-Y-0 **£3,562** (£1,059; £529; £264) **Stalls** High

Form RPR

023- **1** **Bold Abbott (USA)**[260] [4572] 3-9-3 83.............................. JimCrowley 7 78+
(Mrs A J Perrett) *trckd ldrs: drvn to go 2nd over 2f out: led jst ins fnl f: drvn out* **15/8[1]**

3-3 **2** 1/2 **Spriggan**[32] [899] 3-9-3 .... AdamKirby 5 77
(C G Cox) *lw: led: rdn 2f out: hdd jst ins fnl f: kpt on wl but no ex cl home* **7/1**

43- **3** 2 **Laish Ya Hajar (IRE)**[266] [4366] 3-9-3 .... TPO'Shea 6 72
(M R Channon) *bit bkwd: chsd ldr: rdn 3f out: lost 2nd over 2f out: outpcd fnl f* **4/1[2]**

4 1 3/4 **Destour (IRE)** 3-9-3 .... SebSanders 2 67+
(J Noseda) *gd sort: str: scope: towards rr: sltly hmpd bnd 4f out: hdwy on outside and shkn up over 2f out: kpt on fnl f but nvr gng pce to be competitive* **4/1[2]**

0-5 **5** 1 **Calculating (IRE)**[17] [1098] 3-9-3 .... RobertHavlin 1 65
(J H M Gosden) *s.i.s: towards rr tl hdwy 4f out: chsd ldrs 3f out: sn pushed along: wknd over 1f out* **7/1**

00- **6** 1 1/2 **Affiliation (IRE)**[231] [5371] 3-8-12 .... PatDobbs 3 56
(R Hannon) *bit bkwd: chsd ldrs: rdn over 3f out: wknd ins fnl 2f* **33/1**

7 2 1/2 **Emperor Court (IRE)** 3-9-3.................................... MartinDwyer 4 54+
(P J Makin) *tall: s.i.s: bhd: hdwy to chse ldrs ins fnl 3f: sn rdn: wknd ins fnl 2f* **5/1[3]**

1m 27.4s (-0.64) **Going Correction** +0.025s/f (Good) **7** Ran SP% **119.4**
Speed ratings (Par 99):104,103,101,99,98 96,93
CSF £17.10 TOTE £2.70: £1.80, £3.50; EX 24.60.

Owner Mrs Priscilla Graham **Bred** M E Grimm Trust **Trained** Pulborough, W Sussex

FOCUS

Not the most competitive of maidens on paper, but a couple had already shown ability and with the winning time looking solid, so there should be a winner or two to come out of it. It has been rated through the runner-up.

1469 GOLDRING SECURITY SERVICES MEDIAN AUCTION MAIDEN STKS 5f

5:20 (5:20) (Class 5) 2-Y-O **£3,886** (£1,156; £577; £288) **Stalls** Low

Form RPR

0 **1** **Enodoc**[19] 1058 2-9-3 .... SebSanders 7 84
(W R Muir) *lw: trckd ldrs: qcknd to ld appr fnl f: r.o strly ins fnl f* **20/1**

3 **2** *1 ½* **Spinning Lucy (IRE)**[16] 1101 2-8-12 .... MartinDwyer 6 73
(B W Hills) *sn slt ld: drvn along 2f out: hdd appr fnl f: kpt on but nt pce of wnr* **4/9**[1]

3 *3 ½* **Advertisement** 2-9-3 .... DaneO'Neill 5 64
(C G Cox) *str: swtg: bit bkwd: chsd ldrs: pushed along 2f out: kpt on fnl f but nt pce of ldng pair* **12/1**

4 *1 ¼* **Aaim To Storm (USA)** 2-9-3 .... TPO'Shea 8 59
(M R Channon) *tall: str: scope: chsd ldrs: rdn over 2f out: wknd fnl f* **9/1**[2]

6 **5** *1 ¾* **Outside Edge (IRE)**[14] 1150 2-9-3 .... AdamKirby 1 52
(W R Swinburn) *chsd ldrs: pushed along whn n.m.r on rails ins fnl 2f: wknd over 1f out* **16/1**

6 *1* **Diamond Soles (IRE)** 2-8-12 .... TedDurcan 4 43
(B J Meehan) *small: s.i.s: bhd: hung rt 3f out: effrt 2f out: nvr gng pce to be competitive: sn wknd* **10/1**[3]

7 *1 ¼* **Observatory Ridge** 2-8-12 .... RichardSmith 2 38
(M D I Usher) *neat: chsd ldrs 3f* **50/1**

8 *1* **Ballinskelligs Boy** 2-9-3 .... PatDobbs 3 39
(R Hannon) *lw: wl grwn: bit bkwd: s.i.s: outpcd and nvr in contention* **12/1**

59.17 secs (0.12) **Going Correction** -0.30s/f (Firm) **8** Ran SP% **116.3**
Speed ratings (Par 93):87,84,79,77,74 72,70,69
CSF £30.25 TOTE £24.50: £4.50, £1.02, £3.20; EX 49.00.
Owner Mrs D Edginton **Bred** Fonthill Stud **Trained** Lambourn, Berks

FOCUS
A bit of a turn up and the front pair, who were two of just three horses with previous experience, pulled a long way clear of the others. The winning time was nothing special though, and the form is probably ordinary outside the first two.

NOTEBOOK
Enodoc, all the better for his Windsor debut where he probably ran better than his finishing position might suggest, put up a thoroughly professional performance here. Racing on what seemed to be the faster strip down the middle of the track, he and the favourite had the race to themselves a long way out and he saw his race out much the better. This may not have been the strongest of Goodwood maidens, but he is obviously going the right way and there should be more to come from him.
Spinning Lucy(IRE), an unlucky third on her debut in a Newmarket maiden that is starting to work out, like the winner utilised her previous experience to good effect and tried to make every yard. However, the colt would not go away and although she pulled right away from the others, she could not cope with her rival inside the last furlong. The evidence of the earlier sprint races was that the stands' rail was a major disadvantage, whilst the course taken by the winner down the centre was certainly the place to be, so she may have an excuse, but she will need to break her maiden sooner rather than later in order to justify the promise of her debut effort. (op 2-5 tchd 1-2 in places)
Advertisement, who fetched £52,000 as a two-year-old, could not live with the front pair but still emerged best of the newcomers. He has a speedy pedigree so will probably always be best suited by sprint distances. (op 10-1)
Aaim To Storm(USA), a 205,000euros yearling, showed some ability on this debut and may be suited by an extra furlong or two in due course. (op 12-1)
Outside Edge(IRE), the only other with previous experience outside the front pair, had the form of his debut effort boosted by the subsequent success of the winner at another meeting earlier in the afternoon. He did not really step up from his debut performance himself, though to be fair the rails draw was probably not in his favour. Official explanation: jockey said colt became unbalanced approaching final furlong
Diamond Soles(IRE), a 30,000gns sister to Prince Of Denmark and half-sister to Star Of Canterbury, looked as though the experience would do her a lot of good and the yard's representatives usually come on from their debuts. Her pedigree also suggests she will improve for a bit further. (op 14-1)

1470 GOODWOOD PARK HOTEL STKS (H'CAP) 1m 3f

5:50 (5:51) (Class 4) (0-80,79) 4-Y-0+ **£6,800** (£2,023; £1,011; £505) **Stalls** Low

Form RPR

03-3 **1** **Fregate Island (IRE)**[18] 1083 4-9-3 **78** .... BrettDoyle 12 85+
(B J Meehan) *trckd ldrs: drvn over 2f out: styd on u.p to ld wl ins fnl f: hld on wl* **3/1**[1]

4122 **2** *½* **Lemonette (USA)**[34] 868 4-9-1 **76** .... MartinDwyer 4 82+
(J W Hills) *rr: hdwy fr 3f out: sn rdn: str run fr over 1f out: kpt on wl fnl f to go 2nd cl home but a jst hld* **8/1**

50-4 **3** *nk* **The Aldbury Flyer**[18] 1078 4-8-12 **73** .... AdamKirby 5 78
(W R Swinburn) *led: rdn over 2f out: hdd wl ins fnl f: ct for 2nd cl home* **12/1**

-606 **4** *½* **Prime Powered (IRE)**[31] 921 6-8-11 **72** .... SebSanders 2 77
(R M Beckett) *lw: chsd ldr: rdn over 2f out: styd on same pce fnl f* **16/1**

50-5 **5** *¾* **Eldorado**[42] 578 6-8-6 **67** .... StephenCarson 13 70
(G L Moore) *sn chsng ldrs: rdn 3f out: one pce fnl 2f* **9/1**

15-2 **6** *8* **Nero's Return (IRE)**[33] 891 6-9-4 **79** .... TedDurcan 1 69
(G L Moore) *s.i.s: bhd: rdn over 3f out: sme prog fnl 2f but nvr gng pce to be competitive* **7/2**[2]

00-0 **7** *½* **Great View (IRE)**[14] 1149 8-8-11 **75** .... (p) RichardKingscote(3) 8 64
(Mrs A L M King) *lw: chsd ldrs: rdn over 3f out: wknd over 2f out* **10/1**

0312 **8** *½* **Turner's Touch**[31] 921 5-8-10 **71** .... RobertHavlin 10 59
(G L Moore) *a towards rr: mod late prog* **9/1**

60-0 **9** *shd* **Darusso**[18] 1078 4-8-4 **65** .... PaulDoe 11 53
(J S Moore) *sn pushed along: a towards rr* **10/1**

460- **10** *nk* **Imperial Harry**[175] 6432 4-8-7 **68** .... SimonWhitworth 7 55
(V Smith) *lw: b: slowly away: a towards rr* **40/1**

646- **11** *nk* **Trans Sonic**[181] 6351 4-8-6 **67** .... FergusSweeney 6 54
(A P Jarvis) *chsd ldrs: rdn 3f out: sn wknd* **15/2**[3]

510- **12** *2* **Pagan Crest**[251] 4838 4-8-12 **73** .... JimCrowley 9 56
(Mrs A J Perrett) *lw: mid-div: rdn over 3f out: sn wknd* **9/1**

2m 26.51s (-0.70) **Going Correction** +0.025s/f (Good) **12** Ran SP% **131.1**
Speed ratings (Par 105):103,102,102,102,101 95,95,94,94,94 94,93
CSF £31.07 CT £274.08 TOTE £4.20: £1.60, £2.10, £5.10; EX 31.70 Place 6 £15.73, Place 5 £5.31.
Owner Mr & Mrs G Middlebrook **Bred** G And Mrs Middlebrook **Trained** Manton, Wilts

FOCUS
Quite a competitive little handicap, run at an even pace. The front five pulled miles clear of the others and this was a race where it was crucial to race up with the pace, as apart from the runner-up all the other principals were handy.
T/Plt: £25.20 to a £1 stake. Pool: £70,223.20. 2,033.55 winning tickets. T/Qpdt: £3.50 to a £1 stake. Pool: £2,791.10. 578.70 winning tickets. ST

1100

NEWMARKET (ROWLEY) (R-H)

Saturday, May 5

OFFICIAL GOING: Good to firm
Wind: Fresh behind, becoming light behind from the 4th race onwards Weather: Cloud giving way to sunny spells

1471 STANJAMESUK.COM H'CAP 1m

2:10 (2:10) (Class 2) (0-105,101) 3-Y-O **£19,431** (£5,781; £2,889; £1,443) **Stalls** Low

Form RPR

32-4 **1** **Aqmaar**[15] 1124 3-8-10 **90** .... RHills 7 95
(J L Dunlop) *lw: trckd ldrs: racd keenly: led and edgd lft over 1f out: sn rdn: r.o* **11/2**[3]

202- **2** *½* **We'll Come**[205] 5918 3-8-2 **82** oh2 .... PaulHanagan 2 86+
(M A Jarvis) *h.d.w: bit bkwd: chsd ldrs: nt clr run fr over 1f out tl r.o wl ins fnl f* **7/4**[1]

21-6 **3** *¾* **Thunder Storm Cat (USA)**[15] 1124 3-8-12 **92** .... JosedeSouza 1 94+
(P F I Cole) *swtg: up: outpcd over 2f out: nt clr run over 1f out: r.o wl ins fnl f: nt rch ldrs* **5/1**[2]

21- **4** *hd* **Farleigh House (USA)**[242] 5091 3-8-7 **87** .... MichaelHills 6 89
(M H Tompkins) *hld up: hdwy and n.m.r over 2f out: rdn and ev ch over 1f out: unable qck ins fnl f* **8/1**

20-1 **5** *shd* **Voodoo Moon**[9] 1257 3-8-6 **89** .... GregFairley(3) 5 91
(M Johnston) *lw: sn led: hdd over 5f out: led again over 2f out: rdn: edgd rt and hdd over 1f out: styd on same pce ins fnl f* **6/1**

110- **6** *nk* **The Illies (IRE)**[205] 5916 3-8-2 **82** .... ChrisCatlin 8 83
(B W Hills) *hld up: plld hrd: hdwy over 3f out: rdn and ev ch over 1f out: no ex wl ins fnl f* **16/1**

0-35 **7** *1 ½* **Danebury Hill**[17] 1095 3-9-5 **99** .... (t) LDettori 3 101+
(B J Meehan) *chsd ldrs: rdn over 1f out: styng on same pce whn n.m.r ins fnl f* **8/1**

210- **8** *19* **Zafonical Storm (USA)**[201] 6010 3-9-2 **101** .... DJMoran(5) 4 55
(B W Duke) *chsd ldrs: led over 5f out: hdd over 2f out: wkng whn hmpd over 1f out: eased* **40/1**

1m 37.78s (-1.59) **Going Correction** -0.075s/f (Good) **8** Ran SP% **113.2**
Speed ratings (Par 105):104,103,102,102,102 102,100,81
CSF £15.24 CT £50.62 TOTE £6.60: £2.00, £1.20, £2.10; EX 21.50 Trifecta £84.10 Pool: £806.10 - 6.80 winning units..
Owner Hamdan Al Maktoum **Bred** Shadwell Estate Company Limited **Trained** Arundel, W Sussex
■ Stewards' Enquiry : Paul Hanagan two-day ban: careless riding; further three-day ban: careless riding (May 16-18,20,21)

FOCUS
A good three-year-old handicap, although the pace was just ordinary through the first couple of furlongs or so and the winning time was 2.50 seconds slower than the 2000 Guineas. The form has been rated around the more exposed fifth and sixth, but more can be expected from all of the first four.

NOTEBOOK
Aqmaar shaped nicely when fourth in a good 7f handicap at Newbury on his reappearance and confirmed that promise with a narrow success. He could be considered slightly fortunate, as both the runner-up and the third were denied clear runs, but he did well to stay on so strongly considering he had raced quite keenly through the first two furlongs. The Britannia Handicap at Royal Ascot is the obvious target, but he is no sure thing to confirm form with We'll Come and Thunder Storm Cat the next time they meet. (op 6-1 tchd 13-2)
We'll Come ◆, gelded since he was last seen 205 days previously, appeared to have done well physically but still gave the impression the run would bring him on. Stepped up in trip on his handicap debut, he can be considered a little unlucky as he was denied a clear run when trying to stay on and was also 2lb out of the weights. He just lacked the tactical pace to take the necessary gaps and ultimately got going too late, but this should sharpen him up. He will be interesting if taking his chance in something like the Silver Bowl at Haydock, and is definitely one to keep in mind for the Britannia at Royal Ascot. (op 15-8 tchd 2-1, 13-8 in a place)
Thunder Storm Cat(USA) ◆ should have finished closer when behind Aqmaar at Newbury on his reappearance and he can again be considered unlucky. Just like at Newbury he was drawn against the rail, but he again failed to use it to his advantage, racing towards the rear early and then meeting trouble when trying to stay on. Like the runner-up, he is another to keep in mind for races like Silver Bowl at Haydock and the Britannia at Royal Ascot. (tchd 4-1, 11-2 in a place)
Farleigh House(USA), the winner of a 7f maiden at Lingfield on his final start as a juvenile last September, made a pleasing reappearance and is open to improvement. (tchd 9-1 in a place)
Voodoo Moon, 4lb higher than when winning over an extended 7f at Beverley on her previous start, became outpaced at the business end and may have been better suited by setting a stronger gallop. (op 5-1)
The Illies(IRE) ran a respectable race off the back of a 205-day break. (tchd 20-1)
Danebury Hill may have finished around a length closer had he not received a bump from We'll Come inside the final furlong.
Zafonical Storm(USA) Official explanation: jockey said colt lost its action

1472 STANJAMESUK.COM DAHLIA STKS (GROUP 3) (F&M) 1m 1f

2:45 (2:48) (Class 1) 4-Y-0+
£28,390 (£10,760; £5,385; £2,685; £1,345; £675) **Stalls** Low

Form RPR

125- **1** **Echelon**[273] 4127 5-9-1 **109** .... KerrinMcEvoy 6 109+
(Sir Michael Stoute) *hld up in tch: nt clr run 2f out: led over 1f out: rdn out* **8/11**[1]

220- **2** *nk* **Topatoo**[205] 5917 5-8-12 **93** .... MichaelHills 4 105
(M H Tompkins) *hld up: hdwy over 1f out: sn rdn and ev ch: r.o* **14/1**

4362 **3** *1 ½* **Dont Dili Dali**[28] 938 4-8-12 **99** .... (p) JimmyQuinn 2 102
(J S Moore) *hld up: racd keenly: swtchd rt over 2f out: nt clr run wl over 1f out: r.o ins fnl f: nt trble ldrs* **10/1**[3]

14-2 **4** *2 ½* **Abhisheka (IRE)**[71] 546 4-8-12 **101** .... LDettori 5 97
(Saeed Bin Suroor) *lw: chsd ldr: led over 2f out: rdn and hdd over 1f out: wknd ins fnl f* **5/2**[2]

035- **5** *1* **Mrs Snow**[181] 6366 4-8-12 .... MJKinane 8 95
(Mario Hofer, Germany) *w'like: swtg: hld up: hdwy over 2f out: rdn and ev ch whn edgd lft over 1f out: wknd ins fnl f* **20/1**

6 *shd* **Enforce (USA)**[22] 4-8-12 **91** .... JamieSpencer 1 95
(E A L Dunlop) *lw: chsd ldrs: rdn 2f out: wknd fnl f* **25/1**

41-3 **7** *7* **Rakata (USA)**[28] 938 5-8-12 **86** .... JimmyFortune 7 81
(P F I Cole) *trckd ldrs: rdn over 2f out: wkng whn hmpd over 1f out* **25/1**

0- **8** *8* **Arrivee (FR)**[199] 4-8-12 .... MickyFenton 3 65
(Mrs P Sly) *lw: led: hung rt and hdd over 2f out: wknd over 1f out* **33/1**

1m 49.98s (-1.97) **Going Correction** -0.075s/f (Good) **8** Ran SP% **117.6**
Speed ratings (Par 113):105,104,103,101,100 100,93,86
CSF £12.87 TOTE £1.70: £1.10, £3.10, £2.20; EX 13.80 Trifecta £58.40 Pool: £1,143.86 - 13.90 winning units..

Owner Cheveley Park Stud **Bred** Cheveley Park Stud Ltd **Trained** Newmarket, Suffolk

■ Stewards' Enquiry : Michael Hills caution: used whip without giving mare time to respond

FOCUS

Only Echelon had previously won at this level and this looked like an ordinary fillies & mares Group 3. The pace was just ordinary through the early stages and the time was modest for the grade.

NOTEBOOK

Echelon was the clear form pick, having won twice at this level last year before running well in both the Windsor Forest Stakes and the Nassau, but she only scraped home on her seasonal reappearance and was not quite at her best, although she was conceding 3lb all round. Having tracked the leaders for much of the way, she was initially denied a clear run and her rider had to bide his time. Once finally in the clear, she was made to work to see off Topatoo, but ultimately looked to win a shade cosily. She was unproven over a trip this far and, although she stayed well enough, she just gives the impression she may be better suited to shorter distances. She should leave the bare form behind next time and will apparently now try and improve on last season's second in the Windsor Forest Stakes at Royal Ascot. (tchd 4-5, 4-6 in a place)

Topatoo progressed into a very useful handicapper last season and she has clearly improved again over the winter. Trying her hand in Group company for the first time, she ran a stormer, picking up well towards the outside to push Echelon all the way to the line. On this evidence, she may well be up to finding a similar race at some stage this season and will apparently be aimed at the Group 3 Middleton Stakes at York, the scene of all three of her career wins.

Dont Dili Dali looked unlucky not to finish even closer as she was denied a clear run when trying to switch round the entire field. She gives the impression a step back up to 1m2f will suit and she should continue to go well in similar company. (op 11-1)

Abhisheka(IRE), off the track since running second in a Listed race in Dubai in February, offered disappointingly little under pressure and finished a well-beaten fourth. She is probably better suited by easier ground. (op 3-1 tchd 10-3, 7-2 in places)

Mrs Snow, a German challenger, would probably have preferred softer ground, but she is basically not up to this level. (tchd 18-1)

Enforce(USA), an ex-French trained performer who was successful over hurdles for Lucy Wadham in March, ran a respectable race on her return to the level and first start for Ed Dunlop.

1473 STAN JAMES 2000 GUINEAS STKS (GROUP 1) (ENTIRE COLTS & FILLIES) 1m

3:25 (3:29) (Class 1) 3-Y-O

£211,352 (£80,103; £40,089; £19,988; £10,012; £5,025) **Stalls** Centre

Form RPR

123- **1** **Cockney Rebel (IRE)**^{238} [5183] 3-9-0 115.......... OPeslier 15 124+
(G A Huffer) *swtchd to r stands' side 7f out: hld up: hdwy over 2f out: rdn to ld and hung lft ins fnl f: r.o*
25/1

350- **2** *1½* **Vital Equine (IRE)**^{188} [6249] 3-9-0 116.......... ChrisCatlin 6 120
(E J O'Neill) *racd stands' side: overall ldr: rdn over 1f out: hdd and unable qck ins fnl f: 2nd of 14 in gp*
33/1

11-2 **3** *¾* **Dutch Art**^{14} [1147] 3-9-0 121.......... JimmyFortune 18 118+
(P W Chapple-Hyam) *lw: racd far side: hld up: hdwy 2f out: rdn to ld that side ins fnl f: r.o: 1st of 10 in gp*
14/1

2- **4** *shd* **Duke Of Marmalade (IRE)**^{276} [4037] 3-9-0 .... MJKinane 11 118
(A P O'Brien, Ire) *racd stands' side: chsd ldrs: rdn over 2f out: styd on: 3rd of 14 in gp*
14/1

214- **5** *½* **Eagle Mountain**^{196} [6104] 3-9-0 .... CSoumillon 13 117
(A P O'Brien, Ire) *racd stands' side: hld up: hdwy u.p and hung lft over 1f out: nt rch ldrs: 4th of 14 in gp*
14/1

12-1 **6** *hd* **Major Cadeaux**^{14} [1147] 3-9-0 117.......... RichardHughes 7 117
(R Hannon) *lw: b: trckd ldr stands' side: rdn over 1f out: styd on same pce: 5th of 14 in gp*
10/1

1 **7** *½* **US Ranger (USA)**^{24} [1005] 3-9-0 .... C-PLemaire 16 115+
(J-C Rouget, France) *nice colt: lw: racd far side: hld up: hdwy over 2f out: edgd lft & led that gp 1f out: hdd & unable qck ins fnl f: 2nd of 10 in gp*
5/1^{2}

113- **8** *1¼* **Strategic Prince**^{203} [5965] 3-9-0 117.......... EddieAhern 14 113
(P F I Cole) *h.d.w: racd far side: hld up in tch: led that gp over 1f out: rdn and hdd 1f out: no ex: 3rd of 10 in gp*
8/1

2-1 **9** *1* **Diamond Tycoon (USA)**^{14} [1143] 3-9-0 105.......... JamieSpencer 2 110
(B J Meehan) *racd stands' side: hld up in tch: rdn over 2f out: no ex fnl f: 6th of 14 in gp*
15/2

4- **10** *¾* **Haatef (USA)**^{203} [5965] 3-9-0 .... DPMcDonogh 17 108
(Kevin Prendergast, Ire) *lw: racd far side: hld up: hdwy over 3f out: rdn and ev ch that side over 1f out: no ex ins fnl f: 4th of 10 in gp*
7/1^{3}

03-5 **11** *hd* **Yellowstone (IRE)**^{28} [948] 3-9-0 .... JMurtagh 24 108
(A P O'Brien, Ire) *h.d.w: racd far side: hld up: rdn over 1f out: hung rt ins fnl f: nvr trbld ldrs: 5th of 10 in gp*
50/1

10-1 **12** *hd* **Adagio**^{16} [1103] 3-9-0 115.......... KerrinMcEvoy 3 108+
(Sir Michael Stoute) *lw: racd stands' side: hld up: hdwy over 2f out: sn swtchd lft: nt trble ldrs: 7th of 14 in gp*
4/1^{1}

01-4 **13** *2* **Al Shemali**^{17} [1097] 3-9-0 92.......... RHills 12 103+
(Sir Michael Stoute) *racd stands' side: hld up: nvr trbld ldrs: 8th of 14 in gp*
200/1

26-2 **14** *nk* **Tobosa**^{17} [1095] 3-9-0 104.......... PhilipRobinson 22 102
(W Jarvis) *lw: racd far side: chsd ldrs: led that gp over 2f out: rdn and hdd over 1f out: wknd ins fnl f: 6th of 10 in gp*
28/1

14-2 **15** *1* **Sonny Red (IRE)**^{16} [1103] 3-9-0 109.......... SteveDrowne 10 100
(R Hannon) *racd stands' side: chsd ldrs: rdn over 2f out: wknd fnl f: 9th of 14 in gp*
66/1

103- **16** *nk* **Jo'Burg (USA)**^{196} [6100] 3-9-0 97.......... KDarley 1 99
(Mrs A J Perrett) *swtg: racd stands' side: s.i.s: hld up: rdn over 2f out: sn wknd: 11th of 14 in gp*
200/1

10-3 **17** *½* **Halicarnassus (IRE)**^{14} [1147] 3-9-0 116.......... DarryllHolland 9 98
(M R Channon) *lw: racd stands' side: mid-div: hdwy over 3f out: rdn over 2f out: sn wknd: 11th of 14 in gp*
66/1

0-03 **18** *½* **Fishforcompliments**^{17} [1097] 3-9-0 100.......... PaulHanagan 5 97
(R A Fahey) *racd stands' side: chsd ldrs: rdn over 2f out: wknd over 1f out: 12th of 14 in gp*
200/1

1-2 **19** *3½* **Truly Royal**^{58} [641] 3-9-0 104.......... (t) LDettori 20 89+
(Saeed Bin Suroor) *lw: racd far side: chsd ldrs: rdn over 3f out: wknd over 1f out: 7th of 10 in gp*
33/1

1-21 **20** *1½* **Prime Defender**^{17} [1095] 3-9-0 109.......... MichaelHills 23 85
(B W Hills) *racd far side: hld up: effrt over 2f out: wknd over 1f out: 8th of 10 in gp*
66/1

55-4 **21** *nk* **Drayton (IRE)**^{58} [644] 3-9-0 .... WCMarwing 21 85
(M F De Kock, South Africa) *str: cmpt: racd far side: trckd ldr: plld hrd: led that gp over 3f out: hdd over 2f out: sn wknd: 9th of 10 in gp*
100/1

6-05 **22** *nk* **Danum Dancer**^{17} [1099] 3-9-0 88.......... (b) SilvestreDeSousa 19 84
(N Bycroft) *b: b.hind: led far side over 4f: wknd over 2f out: last of 10 in gp*
250/1

04-3 **23** *½* **Evens And Odds (IRE)**^{42} [760] 3-9-0 97.......... NCallan 8 83
(K A Ryan) *lw: racd stands' side: hld up in tch: rdn over 2f out: wknd over 1f out: 13th of 14 in gp*
33/1

1-32 **24** *2½* **Hurricane Spirit (IRE)**^{42} [760] 3-9-0 102.......... GeorgeBaker 4 77
(J R Best) *racd stands' side: hld up: wknd over 2f out: last of 14 in gp*
100/1

1m 35.28s (-4.09) **Going Correction** -0.075s/f (Good) **24** Ran SP% **127.6**

Speed ratings (Par 113):117,115,114,114,114 113,113,112,111,110 110,110,108,107,106 106,105,105,101,100 100,99,99,96

CSF £692.93 CT £11518.71 TOTE £33.60: £8.30, £21.20, £4.20; EX 1831.20 Trifecta £15706.00 Part won. Pool: £22,121.14 - 0.30 winning units..

Owner Phil Cunningham **Bred** Oak Lodge Bloodstock **Trained** Newmarket, Suffolk

■ Cockney Rebel was the longest-priced winner of the 2000 Guineas since 1978. Geoff Huffer's first Classic winner.

FOCUS

The mouthwatering re-match between last year's Dewhurst one-two, Teofilo and Holy Roman Emperor, failed to materialise, with Jim Bolger's star colt not declared because of a recurrence of the heat behind his off-fore knee, and the latter packed off to stud early. The final field was also missing Authorized and Mount Nelson, who are both seen as more Derby types, so four of the first seven horses in the ante-post betting at the beginning of the year failed to line up. Therefore this was obviously not the race it might have been, and the way it unfolded was also unsatisfactory, with the field splitting into two groups. The larger group of 14 on the near side had the call and may have had an advantage over the ten who raced on the far side of the track. Despite all that, this still looked like a good renewal of the 2000 Guineas, with plenty of solid yardsticks seemingly running to something like their best form. The winning time was 2.50 seconds quicker than the earlier 86-105 three-year-old handicap.

NOTEBOOK

Cockney Rebel(IRE) showed himself a very smart juvenile when third behind Vital Equine and Eagle Mountain in the Champagne Stakes, and while that form obviously needed improving upon, it stood up remarkably well here. He missed his intended prep run in the Craven Stakes, but apparently impressed in a racecourse gallop at Lingfield ten days previously. Drawn in the middle, he was the last to switch towards the stands' side and he was not helped in that respect by the horse in stall 14, Strategic Prince, opting to go far side. He was soon well off the pace on his side, but was always travelling very strongly towards the outer and picked up smartly to reel in long-time leader Vital Equine and win decisively. It is impossible to know whether he would have beaten third-placed Dutch Art had they both raced on the same side of the track, but the pair are set for a re-match in the St James's Palace at Royal Ascot, with both at this stage set to give the Irish Guineas a miss. He has clearly improved significantly from two to three and, although this result will have come as a surprise to many, there was certainly no fluke about it. (tchd 28-1)

Vital Equine(IRE) appeared to be exposed in better company after beating both Cockney Rebel and Eagle Mountain in the Champagne Stakes at York last season, but he has clearly done very well over the winter. He showed terrific speed for much of the way, taking the stands'-side group along at a very strong pace against the rail, and kept on surprisingly well, finding only one too good late on. He will now be aimed at the Irish Guineas, where his connections are hoping the ground will be a little more forgiving, and he must have an outstanding chance if Cockney Rebel and Dutch Art stick their original plans of going straight to Royal Ascot. (tchd 40-1)

Dutch Art, last year's Middle Park winner, was turned over at odds on in the Greenham on his reappearance, but his trainer was convinced we would see a different horse this time, and he was proved right in no uncertain terms. Held up on the far side in the early stages, he eased into contention before pulling clear of the nine horses in his group, only to be denied by two rivals racing on the opposite side of the track. He will now be aimed at the St James's Palace Stakes at Royal Ascot, before embarking on an audacious campaign that could see him running in the July Cup over 6f and the Champion Stakes over 1m2f. (tchd 16-1, 20-1 in a place)

Duke Of Marmalade(IRE), off the track since running second to Strategic Prince in the Vintage Stakes at Goodwood last August, ran a fine race on his reappearance, faring best of the O'Brien trio. It would be no surprise to see him take his chance in the Irish Guineas. (tchd 16-1, 20-1 in places)

Eagle Mountain, a high-class juvenile who split Vital Equine and Cockney Rebel in last season's Champagne Stakes, shaped very encouragingly on his seasonal bow. He did not quite have the pace of some of these, but stayed on nicely under pressure, giving the impression he can go on again when stepped up in trip. His stable do not have a stand-out Derby hope at this stage, so it would be no surprise to see him take his chance at Epsom. (op 22-1 tchd 20-1 in a place)

Major Cadeaux could not confirm Greenham form with Dutch Art, despite racing on the possibly favoured side of the track, and did not quite perform up to expectations. However, his participation had been in doubt afer he spread a plate in the morning, and he was reportedly sore afterwards. That was possibly a factor, but equally the trip may well have stretched his stamina. He has plenty of options, and connections do not rule out dropping back to 6f for something like the July Cup. (tchd 12-1)

US Ranger(USA) ◆, supplemented following his impressive success in the Prix Djebel, really filled the eye in the paddock, but things didn't fall right for him. He was carried to the far side of the course by Strategic Prince against his rider's wishes and found himself rather isolated towards the middle of the track when hitting the front of his group. He could not sustain his challenge late on, but gave the impression there will be better to come. His rider is confident he can win at the top level over 1m. (tchd 11-2, 6-1 in places)

Strategic Prince failed to run up to the form he showed when third to Teofilo and Holy Roman Emperor in the Dewhurst last season, despite having conditions to suit. There is plenty of stamina in his pedigree and he might just require further these days, so the Derby would seem the logical target. His stable saddled Generous to finish fourth in the Guineas in 1991 before winning the Derby on his next start.

Diamond Tycoon(USA) ◆, a seriously impressive winner of a very hot Newbury maiden on his seasonal reappearance, ran a respectable race, but this probably just came a little too soon in his development. He may now be stepped up in trip and dropped in grade for the Fairway Stakes at Newmarket, a race his stable won in 2005 with David Junior, who also ran down the field in the Guineas.

Haatef(USA) was entitled to go very close judged on the form of his fourth in last season's Dewhurst, but the 1m trip was a big question mark and he seemingly failed to stay. (op 13-2 tchd 6-1)

Yellowstone(IRE), only fifth in the Leopardstown 2000 Guineas Trial, ran a respectable race but basically wasn't good enough.

Adagio was a hugely impressive winner of the Craven on his reappearance, but this was disappointing. He did not travel all that strongly and basically just seemed to lack the tactical speed of a few of these. He was stopped in his run when trying to stay on, but the race was all over by that point and he was in no way unlucky. A step up in trip is almost sure to suit - his dam won over 2m - and the Derby will surely have to be considered, although this was obviously not an ideal preparation. (op 7-2 tchd 9-2)

Al Shemali left behind the form of his Fielden fourth, but was still nowhere near good enough. He is likely to come into his own over 1m2f and upwards when there is some cut in the ground. (op 150-1)

Tobosa failed to build on his unlucky second in the Free Handicap and is another who may be better suited to something like the Jersey Stakes. (tchd 33-1)

Sonny Red(IRE) failed to reverse Craven form with Adagio, even though that one ran below form, and he was basically not up to the task. (op 80-1)

Jo'Burg(USA), rated just 97, was the slowest into his stride and was never competitive.

Halicarnassus(IRE) was nowhere near good enough and has yet to prove his Superlative Stakes win was not a fluke.

Fishforcompliments did not confirm Fielden form with Al Shemali and found this company a bit hot.

Truly Royal had plenty to find, but he was still quite disappointing. His yard have not started the season very well at all.

Prime Defender ran nowhere near the form he showed when winning the Free Handicap. The trip may have been a factor, and he could bounce back in the Jersey Stakes at Royal Ascot. (op 80-1)

Drayton(IRE) showed good speed, but he was soon put in his place and is an out and out sprinter. Official explanation: jockey said colt ran too free early

Danum Dancer was nowhere near good enough and had little chance of seeing out this trip either.

Evens And Odds(IRE) attracted support at big odds, but he never featured and it remains to be seen if he is anywhere near this level.

Hurricane Spirit(IRE) progressed well over this winter over 6f-7f on Polytrack, but this provided a totally different test.

1474 STANJAMESUK.COM STKS (HERITAGE H'CAP) 6f

4:00 (4:03) (Class 2) 3-Y-O+

£31,160 (£9,330; £4,665; £2,335; £1,165; £585) **Stalls** Low

Form RPR

065- **1** **Beaver Patrol (IRE)**[191] [6192] 5-8-10 **90**............................ MJKinane 23 100
(Eve Johnson Houghton) *racd far side: chsd ldrs: rdn to ld wl ins fnl f* **20/1**

0035 **2** ¾ **Mutamared (USA)**[16] [1102] 7-9-4 **98**...................................... NCallan 26 106
(K A Ryan) *racd far side: hld up in tch: rdn to ld that side ins fnl f: sn hdd and unable qck: 2nd of 11 in gp* **11/1**

414 **3** *nk* **Grantley Adams**[72] [528] 4-9-8 **102**.................................... JHBowman 4 109
(M R Channon) *racd stands' side: chsd ldrs: rdn to ld that side ins fnl f: r.o: 1st of 18 in gp* **25/1**

100- **4** *hd* **Dark Missile**[231] [5358] 4-8-9 **94**...................................... WilliamBuick(5) 7 101
(A M Balding) *bit bkwd: racd stands' side: chsd ldrs: rdn over 1f out: styd on: 2nd of 18 in gp* **33/1**

300 **5** ¾ **Bahiano (IRE)**[86] [396] 6-8-11 **91** ow1.......................... JimmyFortune 15 95
(C E Brittain) *racd stands' side: hld up: rdn over 1f out: r.o wl ins fnl f: nt rch ldrs: 3rd of 18 in gp* **25/1**

60-4 **6** *shd* **Hoh Hoh Hoh**[7] [1292] 5-8-1 **84**.. LiamJones(3) 1 88
(R J Price) *led stands' side: rdn and hung rt fr over 1f out: hdd and no ex ins fnl f: 4th of 18 in gp* **20/1**

5033 **7** *shd* **One More Round (USA)**[42] [759] 9-9-1 **95**................(b) JamesDoyle 19 99
(N P Littmoden) *swtchd lft sn after s to r stands' side: hld up: hdwy under presure and hung lft over 1f out: nrst fin: 5th of 18 in gp* **33/1**

2-03 **8** *shd* **Ripples Maid**[34] [867] 4-8-12 **92**................................ RichardThomas 21 95
(J A Geake) *racd far side: chsd ldrs: led that gp over 2f out: rdn over 1f out: hdd and no ex ins fnl f: 3rd of 11 in gp* **16/1**

00-0 **9** ½ **Idle Power (IRE)**[10] [1242] 9-8-9 **89**.................................... AmirQuinn 16 91
(J R Boyle) *racd stands' side: hld up: hdwy u.p over 1f out: styd on same pce ins fnl f: 6th of 18 in gp* **40/1**

100- **10** *nk* **Bentong (IRE)**[259] [4601] 4-9-6 **100**....................................(t) EddieAhern 8 101
(P F I Cole) *racd stands' side: hld up in tch: rdn over 1f out: kpt on: 7th of 18 in gp* **12/1**

0-00 **11** *hd* **The Kiddykid (IRE)**[16] [1102] 7-9-6 **100**.................. StephenDonohoe 13 100+
(P D Evans) *racd stands' side: chsd ldrs: outpcd over 2f out: styd on ins fnl f: 8th of 18 in gp* **40/1**

20-5 **12** *hd* **Fullandby (IRE)**[17] [1088] 5-9-0 **94**... KDarley 30 94
(T J Etherington) *lw: racd far side: hld up in tch: rdn over 2f out: one pce fnl f: 4th of 11 in gp* **8/1**[3]

5031 **13** ½ **Glenbuck (IRE)**[9] [1268] 4-8-8 **88**..................................(v) MickyFenton 12 86
(A Bailey) *racd stands' side: chsd ldrs: rdn over 2f out: wknd ins fnl f: 9th of 18 in gp* **28/1**

0320 **14** *nk* **Secret Night**[42] [759] 4-7-13 **79**...................................... HayleyTurner 25 76
(J A R Toller) *lw: racd far side: hld up: hdwy over 1f out: nt rch ldrs: 5th of 11 in gp* **66/1**

436- **15** *hd* **Ice Planet**[231] [5355] 6-8-10 **90**.. KerrinMcEvoy 14 95+
(D Nicholls) *racd stands' side: hld up: nt clr run over 1f out: nt trble ldrs: 10th of 18 in gp* **16/1**

313 **16** *hd* **Lethal**[35] [840] 4-8-7 **87**... JohnEgan 5 83
(D K Ivory) *lw: racd stands' side: chsd ldrs: rdn and hung rt over 2f out: wknd fnl f: 11th of 18 in gp* **33/1**

102- **17** *hd* **Burning Incense (IRE)**[225] [5501] 4-9-2 **96**................... SteveDrowne 17 92
(R Charlton) *racd stands' side: hld up: rdn over 2f out: nt trble ldrs: 12th of 18 in gp* **6/1**[1]

01-0 **18** *nk* **Woodcote (IRE)**[15] [1125] 5-9-2 **96**...........................(p) PhilipRobinson 29 91
(C G Cox) *led far side over 3f: wknd fnl f: 6th of 11 in gp* **20/1**

605 **19** *nk* **Compton's Eleven**[21] [1041] 6-8-11 **91**.......................... DarryllHolland 9 85+
(M R Channon) *lw: racd stands' side: hld up: nt clr run over 1f out: nt rch ldrs: 13th of 18 in gp* **33/1**

-660 **20** *1* **Connect**[12] [1195] 10-8-3 **86** ow2..............................(b) SaleemGolam(3) 28 77
(M H Tompkins) *lw: racd far side: hld up: n.d: 7th of 11 in gp* **80/1**

10-0 **21** *shd* **Fantasy Believer**[16] [1102] 9-9-10 **104**.............................. JimmyQuinn 2 94
(J J Quinn) *racd stands' side: hld up: nt clr run over 2f out: n.d: 14th of 18 in gp* **33/1**

20-3 **22** *1* **Skhilling Spirit**[35] [847] 4-9-6 **100**...................................... PaulFessey 22 87
(T D Barron) *racd far side: hld up: effrt over 2f out: n.d: 9th of 11 in gp* **16/1**

40-3 **23** *shd* **Green Park (IRE)**[17] [1088] 4-8-5 **85**.................................... DaleGibson 6 72
(R A Fahey) *racd stands' side: hld up: rdn over 1f out: wknd fnl f: 15th of 18 in gp* **20/1**

50-6 **24** *1* **Wyatt Earp (IRE)**[17] [1088] 6-8-9 **89**.............................. PaulHanagan 18 73
(R A Fahey) *lw: racd far side: chsd ldrs: rdn over 2f out: wknd over 1f out: 9th of 11 in gp* **15/2**[2]

00-0 **25** 1¾ **Indian Trail**[21] [1041] 7-9-4 **98**.. RichardHughes 10 77
(D Nicholls) *racd stands' side: hld up in tch: rdn over 1f out: sn wknd: 16th of 18 in gp* **9/1**

34-5 **26** ½ **Charles Darwin (IRE)**[31] [927] 4-8-10 **90**...................... FrancisNorton 3 67
(M Blanshard) *racd stands' side: chsd ldrs: rdr lost iron over 3f out: wknd over 1f out: 17th of 18 in gp* **50/1**

40-0 **27** 1¼ **Coleorton Dancer**[12] [1195] 5-8-9 **92**.....................(p) AndrewMullen(3) 20 66
(K A Ryan) *racd far side: chsd ldrs: rdn over 2f out: wknd over 1f out: 10th of 11 in gp* **50/1**

4-00 **28** *6* **Mecca's Mate**[15] [1125] 6-9-6 **100**.. LDettori 11 56
(D W Barker) *racd stands' side: s.i.s: a in rr: last of 18 in gp* **20/1**

050- **29** *4* **Fictional**[210] [5812] 6-8-11 **91**.. GrahamGibbons 24 35
(E J O'Neill) *racd far side: sn pushed along in rr: wknd over 2f out: last of 11 in gp* **20/1**

1m 11.47s (-1.63) **Going Correction** -0.075s/f (Good) **29** Ran SP% **146.8**
Speed ratings (Par 109):107,106,105,105,104 104,104,103,103,102 102,102,101,101,101 100,100,100,99,98 98,96,96,95,93
CSF £205.48 CT £5598.80 TOTE £24.10: £4.50, £3.50, £7.50, £8.80; EX 327.20 Trifecta £2541.00 Part won. Pool: £3,579.00 - 0.10 winning units..

Owner G C Stevens **Bred** Kevin B Lynch **Trained** Blewbury, Oxon

FOCUS

The field split into two but, while the first and second raced in the smaller far-side group, there seemed no real bias. A strong handicap, the form of which looks solid and should prove reliable.

NOTEBOOK

Beaver Patrol(IRE), who has a decent record when fresh, was just a pound higher than when gaining his most recent victory at last year's Derby meeting. Well suited by the quick conditions, he did it a shade readily and should continue to give a good account in similar events.

Mutamared(USA), who shaped well in a Listed event here on his return, landed this event last year but was 6lb higher this time. Well at home in big-field handicaps, he found only one too good for him and this was a smart effort at the weights. (tchd 12-1)

Grantley Adams, a winner in Dubai in February, came out on top in the 18-strong group which raced on the stands' side. This was an excellent performance at the weights and he looks well up to a crack in Listed company at least. (tchd 22-1)

Dark Missile, well suited by the fast ground, ran a solid race and was keeping on well at the end. She was progressive last year before her form tailed off on her last two starts and looke to have returned better than ever.

Bahiano(IRE), third in this event a year ago, was 9lb lower here. Held up towards the rear on the stands' side, he ran on well in the final furlong. (tchd 33-1 in a place)

Hoh Hoh Hoh, who was keen going to post, made good use of his draw alongside the stands' rail and was only cut down inside the final furlong.

One More Round(USA) had a fruitless campaign on Polytrack. Coming over from stall 19 to race in the stands'-side group, he worked his way right over to the rail and finished strongly. This was encouraging, but a record of one win from his last 51 starts sets the alarm bells ringing.

Ripples Maid, back on turf, showed ahead on the far side with over two to run but was eventually mastered by the winner and second. This was a decent effort but she does look held by the handicapper.

Idle Power(IRE) was by no means disgraced, but may be most effective on easier ground these days.

Bentong(IRE), tried in a tongue tie, was outpaced by the leaders before keeping on again. He has been gelded since his last appearance back in the autumn and is entitled to come on for the run.

The Kiddykid(IRE), winner of the Group 2 Duke of York Stakes two years ago, is finally down to a winning mark and he shaped quite well on the outer of the near-side group. (op 33-1)

Ice Planet ◆, runner-up to Mutamared in this race a year ago, did not get the best of runs in the latter stages and his rider did not pursue a lost cause. He remains 10lb higher than when last tasting success in the 2005 Great St Wilfrid at Ripon, but this was a most encouraging reappearance. (op 14-1)

Lethal Official explanation: jockey said gelding hung right

Burning Incense(IRE), gelded since last season, was without the blinkers he wore on his final three starts. He never looked like enhancing his trainer's fine recent record. (op 8-1)

Wyatt Earp(IRE), who caught the eye on his reappearance over 5f at Beverley, was a pound lower here but never threatened to take advantage. (op 8-1)

Indian Trail, winner of this two years ago, travelled quite well following a slightly slow start but weakened tamely in the final furlong. (op 14-1)

Charles Darwin(IRE) Official explanation: jockey said he lost his irons

Coleorton Dancer Official explanation: jockey said gelding was unsuited by the good to firm ground

1475 STANSPOKER.CO.UK NEWMARKET STKS (LISTED RACE) (COLTS) 1m 2f

4:35 (4:37) (Class 1) 3-Y-O

£17,034 (£6,456; £3,231; £1,611; £807; £405) **Stalls** Low

Form RPR

2-12 **1** **Salford Mill (IRE)**[17] [1097] 3-8-12 104............................ KerrinMcEvoy 6 106+
(D R C Elsworth) *lw: hld up: hdwy over 2f out: rdn to ld 1f out: edgd lft: r.o* **2/1**[2]

2 1¼ **Acapulco (IRE)**[34] [878] 3-8-12 .... CSoumillon 2 104
(A P O'Brien, Ire) *gd sort: a.p: rdn and ev ch over 1f out: edgd lft: styd on same pce ins fnl f* **5/4**[1]

1- **3** *1* **Eastern Anthem (IRE)**[199] [6050] 3-8-12 90.............................. LDettori 1 103+
(Saeed Bin Suroor) *lw: chsd ldrs: rdn and nt clr run over 1f out: styng on same pce whn n.m.r towards fin* **4/1**[3]

13-0 **4** 2½ **Broghill**[16] [1103] 3-8-12 97..(b[1]) JimmyFortune 5 97
(J H M Gosden) *led: rdn and hdd 1f out: no ex* **20/1**

00-0 **5** *1* **Teslin (IRE)**[16] [1103] 3-8-12 96.. KDarley 3 95
(M Johnston) *chsd ldr: rdn over 2f out: edgd rt and ev ch over 1f out: no ex ins fnl f* **33/1**

6 1¾ **Lepido (ITY)**[192] 3-8-12 .... JamieSpencer 4 92
(L M Cumani) *lw: gd sort: leggy: hld up: reminders over 3f out: rdn and wknd over 1f out* **14/1**

2m 3.15s (-2.56) **Going Correction** -0.075s/f (Good) **6** Ran SP% **112.1**
Speed ratings (Par 107):107,106,105,103,102 101
CSF £4.86 TOTE £3.20: £1.60, £1.50; EX 5.60.

Owner A J Thompson **Bred** Mrs H D McCalmont **Trained** Newmarket, Suffolk

■ Stewards' Enquiry : C Soumillon two-day ban; careless riding (May 16-17)

FOCUS

This is decent form, but the pace was not strong and the last three home do hold it down to an extent. Salford Mill is open to improvement, as are the next two, who were both having just their second start.

NOTEBOOK

Salford Mill(IRE) was second in the Feilden Stakes here last time behind Petara Bay, whose subsequent Sandown flop was attibuted to a bacterial infection. Held up in a steadily-run race, he took a little time to find his full stride down the outside but came through to win decisively in the end. He should have no problem with the Derby trip but will need to find a good deal of improvement to figure at Epsom. (tchd 9-4, 5-2 in places)

Acapulco(IRE) won by nine lengths on his debut last month in a four-runner conditions event in testing ground at Navan. He possibly found underfoot conditions here too lively, but was staying on at the end and confirmed himself a smart colt. The step up to 12f will suit on this evidence and he should have further improvement in him. (op 7-4 tchd 11-10 in places)

Eastern Anthem(IRE), successful on his only start at two, reportedly wintered well in Dubai. He did not get the best of runs in the latter stages but that should not be put forward as an excuse. A step up to 1m4f should suit him and he ought to come on for the run. (op 3-1)

Broghill, tried in blinkers after a disappointing effort in the Craven Stakes, settled better allowed to stride on but was still a little free in the early stages. He had nothing more to offer when headed with a furlong to run. (op 16-1)

Teslin(IRE) was right in the firing line approaching the final furlong but was already weakening when slightly short of room inside the last. He was the most exposed in this line-up and could prove tricky to place successfully.

Lepido(ITY) won both his starts for Bruno Grizzetti at San Siro in the autumn but was disappointing on this British debut, receiving reminders with just under half a mile to run and failing to pick up. He might need easier ground but has a bit to prove.

1476 STAN JAMES H'CAP 1m 2f
5:10 (5:11) (Class 2) (0-100,100) 3-Y-O
£12,464 (£3,732; £1,866; £934; £466; £234) **Stalls** Low

Form				RPR
15-5	1		**Hearthstead Maison (IRE)**[17] 1097 3-8-10 **95**............ GregFairley(3) 1 (M Johnston) *chsd ldrs: swtchd rt 1f out: r.o to ld towards fin* **9/1**	102+
1-11	2	*hd*	**Boscobel**[78] 483 3-8-10 **92**............ KDarley 7 (M Johnston) *chsd ldr: rdn over 2f out: led and edgd lft over 1f out: hdd towards fin* **2/1**[1]	99
11-4	3	*1 1/2*	**Duke Of Tuscany**[15] 1126 3-8-13 **95**............ RichardHughes 5 (R Hannon) *lw: led: rdn and hdd over 1f out: styng on same pce whn n.m.r ins fnl f* **15/2**	99
1111	4	*3/4*	**Ten A Penny (USA)**[17] 1089 3-8-6 **88**............ MJKinane 3 (J A Osborne) *lw: hld up: swtchd rt and hdwy over 1f out: rdn and no ex ins fnl f* **9/4**[2]	91
0-1	5	*5*	**Overrule (USA)**[12] 1204 3-8-9 **91** ow1............ CSoumillon 6 (J Noseda) *chsd ldrs: rdn over 1f out: sn wknd* **9/2**[3]	84
10-0	6	*6*	**Stevie Gee (IRE)**[42] 760 3-9-4 **100**............ NCallan 2 (G A Swinbank) *hld up: rdn over 2f out: wknd over 1f out* **12/1**	82
125-	7	*10*	**Hart Of Gold**[231] 5366 3-8-5 **87**............ ChrisCatlin 4 (M J Wallace) *hld up: wknd over 2f out* **20/1**	50

2m 3.56s (-2.15) **Going Correction** -0.075s/f (Good) 7 Ran SP% **116.5**
Speed ratings (Par 105):105,104,103,103,99 94,86
CSF £28.38 TOTE £13.50: £5.00, £1.80; EX 30.90.
Owner Hearthstead Homes Ltd **Bred** T Nakata **Trained** Middleham Moor, N Yorks

FOCUS
The eventual third set only a steady pace but this is very useful handicap form and the first two, both trained by Mark Johnston, look capable of better.

NOTEBOOK
Hearthstead Maison(IRE) was dropping in grade after finishing fifth in the Feilden Stakes here, three places behind Salford Mill who won the previous race on this card. After being switched around the leading pair at the furlong pole, he knuckled down well to catch his stablemate near the line. There looks to be improvement to come from him. (op 7-1)
Boscobel, unbeaten in three previous starts, one on each of the three Polytrack courses, came close to retaining his unbeaten record. After having to fight to get past the pacesetter, he could not repel his stable companion late on. It could be that he will appreciate slightly easier ground. (op 15-8 tchd 9-4 in a place)
Duke Of Tuscany dictated the pace and battled on well when challenged until fading in the final furlong. This trip does appear to stretch his stamina. (op 12-1)
Ten A Penny(USA), bidding for a five-timer off a 6lb higher mark, had his chance and the only real excuse is that the lack of a true gallop possibly counted against him. (op 5-2 tchd 11-4, 3-1 in a place)
Overrule(USA), a maiden winner on his previous start, travelled quite well but soon began to struggle once coming under pressure. (tchd 4-1, 5-1 in a place)
Stevie Gee(IRE) was taking a marked step up in trip. He was supported in the market but never gave his backers much hope. (op 16-1)
Hart Of Gold, having his first start since September, was held up over this longer trip and appeared not to stay.

1477 STAN JAMES TELEBETTING H'CAP 1m 4f
5:45 (5:46) (Class 2) (0-100,99) 4-Y-O+ **£12,954** (£3,854; £1,926; £962) **Stalls** High

Form				RPR
222-	1		**Wannabe Posh (IRE)**[190] 6202 4-8-6 **87** ow1............ EddieAhern 11 (J L Dunlop) *chsd ldrs: hmpd over 10f out: rdn over 1f out: r.o to ld wl ins fnl f* **9/2**[2]	98+
5-03	2	*1 1/4*	**Nakheel**[16] 1109 4-9-0 **95**............ RHills 3 (M Johnston) *lw: led: rdn over 1f out: edgd lft and hdd wl ins fnl f* **8/1**	104
010-	3	*3/4*	**Finalmente**[203] 5963 5-9-3 **98**............ LDettori 1 (N A Callaghan) *a.p: chsd ldr 1/2-way: rdn over 2f out: styd on same pce fnl f* **8/1**	106
265-	4	*2*	**Bandama (IRE)**[219] 5641 4-9-1 **96**............ MJKinane 4 (Mrs A J Perrett) *bit bkwd: chsd ldr to 1/2-way: rdn over 2f out: no ex fnl f* **8/1**	101
010-	5	*3/4*	**Florimund**[196] 6097 4-8-5 **86**............ PaulHanagan 9 (Sir Michael Stoute) *bit bkwd: hld up in tch: rdn over 4f out: styd on same pce appr fnl f* **7/1**[3]	89+
02-0	6	*3/4*	**Mudawin (IRE)**[25] 995 6-8-13 **94**............ JMurtagh 10 (Jane Chapple-Hyam) *b: unruly in stalls: hld up: hdwy over 1f out: nt trble ldrs* **14/1**	96
2420	7	*1/2*	**Quince (IRE)**[28] 940 4-8-6 **87**............(v) JimmyQuinn 7 (J Pearce) *prom: rdn and hung rt over 1f out: wknd ins fnl f* **28/1**	88
3405	8	*5*	**Impeller (IRE)**[10] 1245 8-9-4 **99**............ JohnEgan 6 (J S Moore) *lw: hld up: plld hrd: effrt over 2f out: rdn and hung rt over 1f out: sn wknd* **12/1**	92
110-	9	*3*	**Ogee**[316] 2804 4-8-10 **91**............ KerrinMcEvoy 5 (Sir Michael Stoute) *lw: hld up: hung rt and wknd over 1f out* **3/1**[1]	80
20-0	10	*1 1/2*	**Futun**[28] 940 4-9-4 **99**............ NCallan 8 (L M Cumani) *plld hrd and prom: wknd wl over 1f out: eased* **18/1**	85
213	11	*6*	**Paktolos (FR)**[49] 698 4-8-9 **90**............ JamieSpencer 2 (A King) *hld up: hdwy over 3f out: rdn and wkng whn hung rt and slipped wl over 1f out* **9/1**	67

2m 29.93s (-3.57) **Going Correction** -0.075s/f (Good) 11 Ran SP% **122.1**
Speed ratings (Par 109):108,107,106,105,104 104,104,100,98,97 93
CSF £42.25 CT £287.84 TOTE £5.20: £2.00, £2.90, £2.90; EX 43.50 Place 6 £991.70, Place 5 £731.65.
Owner Nicholas Cooper **Bred** Vizcaya Ag **Trained** Arundel, W Sussex

FOCUS
A very competitive middle-distance handicap and the form should work out.

NOTEBOOK
Wannabe Posh(IRE) ◆, a very progressive type last year, showed she is still improving with a convincing success on her first run in 190 days, and she landed a gamble in the process. She raced a little keenly early on and was hampered when rounding the bend after a couple of furlongs, but it clearly didn't take much out of her and she showed a smart change of pace to peg back long-time leader Nakheel. She looks capable of developing into a pattern-class filly and may be aimed at a Listed race at Baden-Baden on May 19. (op 8-1)
Nakheel, trying 1m4f for the first time, was given every chance from the front and can have no excuses. He seemed to stay the trip well enough, but perhaps 1m2f will prove his optimum distance.
Finalmente ◆ finds a 1m4f his bare minimum, so this was a terrific effort on his return from a 203-day break. He may not be too far off a Group horse back over a staying trip. (op 12-1)
Bandama(IRE) ran with credit for his in-form yard off the back of a 219-day break, but this trip probably just stretches him. (tchd 15-2)
Florimund ◆ was strongly supported in the market, despite his stable also saddling the favourite, and he ran well on his return from a 196-day break. He came under pressure a fair way out, but kept responding and finished to good effect. This should sharpen him up no end and he gives the impression he will stay further. (op 8-1 tchd 11-2)
Mudawin(IRE) requires a stiffer test of stamian, so this was not too bad an effort.
Ogee, off the track since beating only one home in the Queen's Vase last June, was a solid favourite dropped in trip and returned to handicap company, but he proved disappointing. He didn't really travel with that much fluency and was beaten a fair way out. He has been kept in training for a reason, but has plenty to prove now. (op 5-2 tchd 7-2)
Futun raced far too keenly. (op 16-1 tchd 20-1)
Paktolos(FR) travelled quite nicely, but he appeared to slip inside the final quarter mile and it is probably best to forgive him this. Official explanation: jockey said gelding faltered approx 1 1/2f out (op 8-1)
T/Jkpt: Not won. T/Plt: £516.50 to a £1 stake. Pool: £177,285.30. 250.55 winning tickets. T/Qpdt: £200.80 to a £1 stake. Pool: £6,839.60. 25.20 winning tickets. CR

1156 THIRSK (L-H)
Saturday, May 5

OFFICIAL GOING: Good to firm (firm in places)
Wind: Virtually nil

1478 TOTEPLACEPOT EUROPEAN BREEDERS' FUND NOVICE STKS 5f
1:55 (1:56) (Class 4) 2-Y-O **£5,181** (£1,541; £770; £384) **Stalls** High

Form				RPR
61	1		**Group Therapy**[14] 1150 2-9-5............ TPQueally 6 (J A Osborne) *mde all: pushed clr over 1f out: easily* **7/4**[1]	93+
4	2	*5*	**New Jersey (IRE)**[16] 1107 2-8-12............ DO'Donohoe 1 (K A Ryan) *cl up: pushed along 1/2-way: rdn and hung bdly lft over 1f out: one pce* **2/1**[2]	66
	3	*1 1/2*	**Pay Parade** 2-8-7............ DavidAllan 4 (T D Easterby) *dwlt: sn chsng ldng pair: rdn along 2f out and kpt on same pce* **14/1**	55
	4	*3 1/2*	**Choisette** 2-8-7............ RoystonFfrench 2 (B Smart) *sn outpcd and edging lft in rr* **4/1**[3]	41
	5	*2 1/2*	**Gulf Coast** 2-8-12............ J-PGuillambert 3 (M Johnston) *dwlt: sn rdn along and edging lft: outpcd and bhd fr 1/2-way* **11/2**	36

58.41 secs (-1.49) **Going Correction** -0.25s/f (Firm) 5 Ran SP% **111.7**
Speed ratings (Par 95):101,93,90,85,81
CSF £5.69 TOTE £2.40: £1.60, £1.30; EX 4.80.
Owner Elaine and Martyn Booth **Bred** Stratford Place Stud **Trained** Upper Lambourn, Berks

FOCUS
Jamie Osborne has his juveniles in flying form and Group Therapy landed a quick double with ease. He looks a fair sort for this time of the season and the runner-up is rated close to his previous mark.

NOTEBOOK
Group Therapy, who played up before going into the stalls, always had things in control and won with any amount in hand. The stable's juveniles have been running really well so far this season, and he looks up with the best of them, especially as he is an early-May foal. (tchd 2-1)
New Jersey(IRE) threatened the winner briefly but was not in the same league when Group Therapy went for home. Hanging to the centre of the course under pressure did not help his cause either. He will find easier assignments in the future, even though he was getting weight. (tchd 15-8)
Pay Parade, who was said not to have come in her coat yet, did not get away too quickly but shaped with a modicum of promise once straightened out. Her dam has produced some decent sorts and she is entitled to improve for the run. (tchd 12-1)
Choisette, a Choisir filly making her debut, did not show any immediate promise and will need to improve for the effort to have any chance next time. (op 11-2)
Gulf Coast, a well-bred Dubai Destination colt, must be considered a little disappointing on his debut and will need to come on a lot for the effort to hold his own in a similar race. The stable has not been hitting the target recently with their juveniles, so he can be given another chance. (op 9-2 tchd 7-1)

1479 TOTECOURSE TO COURSE MAIDEN STKS 1m 4f
2:25 (2:27) (Class 5) 3-Y-O+ **£3,886** (£1,156; £577; £288) **Stalls** Low

Form				RPR
	1		**Secret Ploy**[22] 7-9-8............ TravisBlock(5) 1 (H Morrison) *sn pushed along and in tch: hdwy 1/2-way: rdn to chal over 3f out: slt ld wl over 1f out: styd on ins fnl f* **9/4**[2]	73+
63	2	*1*	**Bernix**[9] 1259 5-9-13............ DavidAllan 4 (T D Easterby) *trckd ldrs: hdwy over 3f out: effrt 2f out: sn rdn and ev ch tl drvn and one pce ins fnl f* **13/2**[3]	71
03-	3	*2 1/2*	**Monsoon Wedding**[224] 5536 3-8-3............ RoystonFfrench 5 (M Johnston) *led: pushed along over 4f out: rdn 3f out: drvn and hdd wl over 1f out: sn btn* **8/11**[1]	60
500/	4	*18*	**Verification**[179] 6002 4-9-13 63............ TomEaves 3 (J Howard Johnson) *t.k.h: chsd ldrs: rdn along 5f out: sn outpcd* **16/1**	38
00-0	5	*8*	**Scarrabus (IRE)**[6] 913 6-9-8 48............ PJMcDonald(5) 6 (A Crook) *chsd ldr to 1/2-way: sn rdn along and wknd: bhd fnl 4f* **33/1**	25

2m 35.43s (0.23) **Going Correction** -0.15s/f (Firm)
WFA 3 from 4yo+ 19lb 5 Ran SP% **110.8**
Speed ratings (Par 103):93,92,90,78,73
CSF £16.23 TOTE £3.00: £1.20, £2.20; EX 20.20.
Owner A M Carding **Bred** Coln Valley Stud **Trained** East Ilsley, Berks

FOCUS
A very modest event. The winner is probably the only one to take from the race and the third may prove the best guide to the level of the form.

1480 TOTESPORT.COM THIRSK HUNT CUP (H'CAP) 1m
3:00 (3:00) (Class 2) (0-100,95) 3-Y-O+ **£11,658** (£3,468; £1,733; £865) **Stalls** Low

Form				RPR
-050	1		**My Paris**[14] 1145 6-9-7 **91**............ DO'Donohoe 9 (K A Ryan) *cl up: led after 2f: rdn along over 2f out: drvn and styd on gamely fnl f* **13/2**	100
04-1	2	*nk*	**Bustan (IRE)**[14] 1157 8-9-7 **91**............ J-PGuillambert 8 (G C Bravery) *trckd ldrs: hdwy to chse wnr over 2f out: rdn to chal wl over 1f out: ev ch tl drvn and no ex wl ins fnl f* **6/1**[3]	99
300-	3	*1*	**Minority Report**[204] 5943 7-9-9 **93**............ NickyMackay 12 (L M Cumani) *hld up: hdwy on outer over 2f out: rdn wl over 1f out: styd on ins fnl f: nrst fin* **7/2**[1]	99+
0000	4	*shd*	**Kings Point (IRE)**[71] 540 6-9-6 **95**............(p) JamieMoriarty(5) 2 (R A Fahey) *chsd ldrs: effrt over 2f out: sn rdn and kpt on wl fnl f* **33/1**	100
020-	5	*shd*	**El Coto**[125] 6999 7-9-3 **87**............(p) PatCosgrave 4 (K A Ryan) *in tch: hdwy over 2f out: sn rdn and styd on appr fnl f* **40/1**	92
0600	6	*1/2*	**Zato (IRE)**[14] 1145 4-9-2 **86**............ SamHitchcott 3 (M R Channon) *s.i.s and towards rr: hdwy 2f out: n.m.r over 1f out and ins fnl f: styd on wl towards fin* **12/1**	92+

13-0 **7** *hd* **Nevada Desert (IRE)**[7] 1287 7-8-6 **81** oh7........... MichaelJStainton(5) 7 85
(R M Whitaker) *led 2f: cl up tl rdn along over 2f out and grad wknd* **66/1**
0330 **8** *shd* **Lucayan Dancer**[10] 1245 7-9-0 **84**........................ PhillipMakin 13 87
(D Nicholls) *hld up in rr: hdwy over 2f out: swtchd outside and rdn over 1f out: kpt on ins fnl f: nrst fin* **20/1**
00-0 **9** *hd* **Red Lancer**[10] 1245 6-8-11 **81** oh2........................ PaulQuinn 14 84+
(D Nicholls) *in rr tl hdwy over 2f out: sn rdn and styd on ins fnl f: nrst fin* **33/1**
03-3 **10** *½* **Wind Star**[25] 993 4-9-3 **87**........................ DeanMcKeown 6 89
(G A Swinbank) *chsd ldrs: rdn along over 2f out: drvn and no imp over 1f out* **5/1**[2]
0-00 **11** *hd* **Game Lad**[13] 1179 5-9-0 **84**........................ DavidAllan 1 85
(T D Easterby) *stdd s and hld up in rr: gd hdwy on inner 2f out: sn rdn and nt rch ldrs* **11/1**
5-6 **12** *hd* **Flipando (IRE)**[14] 1157 6-9-6 **90**........................ TomEaves 5 91
(T D Barron) *hld up in midfield: effrt 2f out: swtchd rt and rdn over 1f out: sn no imp* **6/1**[3]
1440 **13** *nk* **Gallantry**[35] 840 5-9-3 **87**........................ RoystonFfrench 15 87
(D Shaw) *towards rr: swtchd outside and effrt wl over 1f out: sn rdn and no imp* **33/1**
/60- **14** *2* **Obezyana (USA)**[202] 5990 5-9-1 **85**........................(bt) TPQueally 10 81
(A Bailey) *chsd ldrs: rdn along over 2f out: sn drvn and wknd* **66/1**
05-4 **15** *11* **Prince Samos (IRE)**[35] 846 5-9-2 **86**........................ AdrianTNicholls 11 56
(D Nicholls) *chsd ldrs: rdn along over 2f out and sn wknd* **8/1**

1m 37.15s (-2.55) **Going Correction** -0.15s/f (Firm) **15** Ran SP% **126.9**
Speed ratings (Par 109):106,105,104,104,104 104,103,103,103,103 102,102,102,100,89
CSF £45.07 CT £164.55 TOTE £9.60: £2.70, £2.30, £2.10; EX 59.60 Trifecta £111.90 Pool: £536.30 - 3.40 winning units..
Owner J D Spensley & Mrs M A Spensley **Bred** J And A Spensley **Trained** Hambleton, N Yorks

FOCUS
A good-quality handicap but a messy finish with the fourth to 11th finishing in a heap. The form is best assessed around the fifth, seventh and eighth.

NOTEBOOK
My Paris managed to get to the lead after a couple of furlongs and showed plenty of determination in the latter stages to fend off all the challengers. He is not badly handicapped and should be competitive next time. (op 9-1)
Bustan(IRE) has really rediscovered his form this season and made the winner work for his victory all the way to the line. He is really well handicapped on the best of his early-career form and has every chance to go one better next time. (tchd 11-2 and 13-2 in a place)
Minority Report, last year's winner, was brought to make a challenge down the middle of the course but could never bridge the gap, despite having every chance. He is still slightly high in the weights and could do with coming down a couple of pounds at least. (op 4-1)
Kings Point(IRE), who really seemed to struggle out in Dubai, gave his all but just could not get on terms. He has had plenty of tough assignments in the last year and might well benefit from a confidence booster, if one could be found for him.
El Coto, a stablemate of the winner, ran like a horse who was not enjoying something in the final stages, as his ears went back under pressure and he edged to the middle of the course. (op 33-1)
Zato(IRE) ◆ was really unlucky in-running and may well have been third, at least, with a clear run. He is certainly nicely handicapped on th best of his form. Official explanation: jockey said gelding was denied a clear run (op 16-1)
Red Lancer ◆ was given far too much to do and caught the eye in a big way, finishing strongly after not being given a hard time at all by his jockey. He has a history of disappointing for other trainers, but there is no disputing the promise he showed and is one to keep on-side wherever he runs next time.
Wind Star never really threatened and failed to find much for pressure. (tchd 11-2)
Game Lad Official explanation: jockey said gelding was denied a clear run
Flipando(IRE) ◆ did not run as badly as his finishing position suggests and is coming down to a handicap mark he will have every chance off. (op 5-1)

1481 TOTEEXACTA H'CAP 7f
3:35 (3:35) (Class 4) (0-85,85) 4-Y-0+ **£5,181** (£1,541; £770; £384) **Stalls** Low

Form RPR
10-3 **1** **Malcheek (IRE)**[14] 1157 5-9-4 **85**........................ DavidAllan 8 94+
(T D Easterby) *t.k.h: trckd ldrs: swtchd rt and hdwy over 2f out out: rdn to chal over 1f out: styd on strly to ld ins fnl f* **11/8**[1]
64-2 **2** *1 ¼* **Angaric (IRE)**[27] 953 4-8-7 **74**........................ RoystonFfrench 9 80
(B Smart) *a.p: hdwy to ld wl over 1f out: sn rdn: drvn and hdd ins fnl f: kpt on* **5/1**[3]
413- **3** *1 ½* **Countdown**[186] 6273 5-8-7 **79**........................ DuranFentiman(5) 1 81
(T D Easterby) *towards rr: hdwy 2f out: sn rdn: styd on ins fnl f: nrst fin* **18/1**
331- **4** *½* **Grand Opera (IRE)**[288] 3698 4-8-7 **74**........................ TomEaves 2 75
(J Howard Johnson) *dwlt: in rr tl hdwy on outer wl over 2f out: rdn and styd on ins fnl f: nrst fin* **20/1**
25-4 **5** *nk* **Bold Marc (IRE)**[7] 1287 5-8-9 **79**........................ AndrewElliott(3) 5 79
(K R Burke) *cl up on inner: effrt 2f out and ev ch tl rdn and wknd ent fnl f* **9/2**[2]
00-5 **6** *¾* **Cool Ebony**[27] 953 4-8-10 **77**........................ PhillipMakin 3 75
(M Dods) *hld up: effrt 2f out: sn rdn and kpt on same pce* **12/1**
-065 **7** *1* **Surwaki (USA)**[14] 1157 5-8-3 **75**........................ MichaelJStainton(5) 4 70
(R M H Cowell) *in tch: rdn along over 2f out: sn btn* **12/1**
16-0 **8** *nk* **Bel Cantor**[15] 1134 4-8-9 **76**........................ PaulMulrennan 7 71
(W J H Ratcliffe) *chsd ldr: rdn along over 2f out and sn wknd* **33/1**
1302 **9** *2* **Kabis Amigos**[15] 1133 5-8-4 **71** oh1........................(t) AdrianTNicholls 6 60
(D Nicholls) *led: rdn along over 2f out: sn hdd & wknd* **6/1**

1m 24.52s (-2.58) **Going Correction** -0.15s/f (Firm) **9** Ran SP% **119.6**
Speed ratings (Par 105):108,106,104,104,103 103,101,101,99
CSF £8.84 CT £89.70 TOTE £2.20: £1.10, £2.10, £3.60; EX 10.30.
Owner Mrs Susie Dicker **Bred** Carrigbeg Stud **Trained** Great Habton, N Yorks
■ Stewards' Enquiry : Adrian T Nicholls caution: used whip down shoulder in forehand position

FOCUS
A fair handicap lacking any real depth. The first three may progress, with the runner-up setting the standard, but the rest do not appeal in the short-term.

1482 TOTESPORT 0800 221 221 MAIDEN STKS 7f
4:05 (4:09) (Class 4) 3-Y-0 **£5,181** (£1,541; £770; £384) **Stalls** Low

Form RPR
0 **1** **Ragheed (USA)**[108] 160 3-9-3........................ TPQueally 5 81+
(W J Haggas) *chsd ldr: led over 2f out: sn rdn: drvn and edgd lft ins fnl f and nr fin: hld on* **3/1**[2]
2 **2** *hd* **Soccerjackpot (USA)**[15] 1136 3-9-3........................ DeanMcKeown 1 80+
(G A Swinbank) *trckd ldng pair: hdwy on inner to chal wl over 1f out: sn rdn and ev ch tl bmpd and no ex nr fin* **15/8**[1]
3 *8* **Incoming Call (USA)** 3-8-12........................ TomEaves 3 53
(Sir Michael Stoute) *hld up in tch: hdwy 3f out: rdn along 2f out: sn one pce* **15/8**[1]
0-0 **4** *shd* **Wisdom's Kiss**[16] 1111 3-9-3........................ PatCosgrave 2 58
(J D Bethell) *chsd ldrs: rdn along 3f out: sn outpcd* **66/1**
36- **5** *3* **Eltanin (IRE)**[211] 5790 3-9-3........................ TonyHamilton 4 50
(J Howard Johnson) *led: rdn along and hdd over 2f out: sn wknd* **8/1**[3]
506- **6** *7* **Cape Dancer (IRE)**[235] 5271 3-8-12 **66**........................ PaulMulrennan 7 26
(J S Wainwright) *a towards rr* **12/1**
0 **7** *3 ½* **Aslan**[12] 1197 3-9-3........................ DavidAllan 10 22
(T D Easterby) *unruly s: t.k.h: chsd ldrs to 1/2-way: sn wknd* **28/1**
0- **8** *16* **Nellie**[185] 6295 3-8-7........................ MichaelJStainton(5) 6 —
(R M Whitaker) *a towards rr* **66/1**

1m 25.27s (-1.83) **Going Correction** -0.15s/f (Firm) **8** Ran SP% **119.8**
Speed ratings (Par 101):104,103,94,94,91 83,79,60
CSF £9.53 TOTE £5.10: £1.80, £1.10, £1.10; EX 17.40.
Owner Hamdan Al Maktoum **Bred** Swordlestown Stud **Trained** Newmarket, Suffolk

FOCUS
A very modest maiden on all the evidence of the form book. The first two finished clear and the form is rated at face value through the fourth.

1483 TOTETEXT BETTING 60021 H'CAP 5f
4:40 (4:40) (Class 4) (0-80,79) 4-Y-0+ **£5,181** (£1,541; £770; £384) **Stalls** High

Form RPR
30-0 **1** **Oranmore Castle (IRE)**[27] 957 5-9-1 **76**........................ AdrianTNicholls 4 84
(D Nicholls) *led and sn swtchd rt to stands' rail: pushed along and hdd 2f out: rdn ent fnl f and styd on to ld last 100yds* **4/1**[2]
250- **2** *nk* **Jakeini (IRE)**[257] 4659 4-8-11 **72**........................ RoystonFfrench 5 79
(E S McMahon) *prom and hmpd after 1f: sn swtchd lft and cl up: rdn to ld 2f out: drvn ent fnl f: hdd and no ex last 100yds* **9/1**
3024 **3** *1* **Nusoor (IRE)**[19] 1061 4-8-9 **70**........................ RobbieFitzpatrick 6 73
(Peter Grayson) *dwlt: sn chsng ldrs: rdn to chal wl over 1f out and ev ch tl drvn and one pce ins fnl f* **4/1**[2]
/6-0 **4** *½* **Ocean Gift**[15] 1133 5-8-9 **70**........................ KimTinkler 8 72
(N Tinkler) *towards rr: hdwy 2f out: sn rdn and kpt on ins fnl f: nrst fin* **16/1**
44-0 **5** *¾* **Soto**[7] 1299 4-8-9 **70**........................ PaulMulrennan 3 69
(M W Easterby) *towards rr: hdwy 2f out: sn rdn and kpt on ins fnl f: nrst fin* **10/1**
0001 **6** *nk* **Danzig River (IRE)**[7] 1292 6-8-8 **76**........................ AdeleRothery(7) 2 74
(D Nicholls) *chsd ldrs: rdn along over 2f out and grad wknd* **6/1**[3]
00-5 **7** *shd* **Highland Warrior**[15] 1134 8-8-8 **74**........................ RoryMoore(5) 1 71
(P T Midgley) *towards rr: hdwy wl over 1f out: rdn and kpt on ins fnl f: nvr a factor* **7/1**
00-3 **8** *5* **Spiritual Peace (IRE)**[27] 957 4-9-4 **79**........................(p) DO'Donohoe 7 58
(K A Ryan) *in tch: pushed along over 2f out: sn rdn and btn* **11/4**[1]

58.78 secs (-1.12) **Going Correction** -0.25s/f (Firm) **8** Ran SP% **118.4**
Speed ratings (Par 105):98,97,95,95,93 93,93,85
CSF £40.83 CT £155.06 TOTE £5.30: £2.10, £2.30, £1.70; EX 58.60.
Owner The Knavesmire Alliance **Bred** Gigginstown House Stud **Trained** Sessay, N Yorks
■ Stewards' Enquiry : Adrian T Nicholls two-day ban: careless riding (May 16-17)

FOCUS
A fair handicap and the form seems sound enough rated through the runner-up to his best three-year-old efforts.
Oranmore Castle(IRE) Official explanation: trainer had no explanation for the apparent improvement in form
Highland Warrior Official explanation: trainer said gelding was unsuited by the good to firm (firm in places) ground
Spiritual Peace(IRE) Official explanation: jockey said gelding lost its action after suffering slight interference after 1f out

1484 TOTESPORTCASINO.COM H'CAP 6f
5:15 (5:17) (Class 5) (0-75,75) 3-Y-0 **£3,886** (£1,156; £577; £288) **Stalls** High

Form RPR
41-0 **1** **Flores Sea (USA)**[11] 1228 3-8-13 **70**........................ PhillipMakin 8 80+
(T D Barron) *dwlt: sn trcking ldrs: hdwy over 1f out: rdn ent fnl f and qcknd wl to ld last 100yds* **9/4**[1]
306- **2** *1 ½* **Valley Of The Moon (IRE)**[240] 5133 3-8-10 **72**........ JamieMoriarty(5) 4 77
(R A Fahey) *cl up: rdn to ld 1f out: sn edgd lft and drvn: hdd and no ex last 100yds* **6/1**
0-26 **3** *2* **Baileys Outshine**[19] 1067 3-9-0 **71**........................ J-PGuillambert 7 70
(J G Given) *led: rdn along 2f out: drvn and hdd 1f out: kpt on same pce* **13/2**
-360 **4** *¾* **Majestic Cheer**[7] 1286 3-9-2 **73**........................ SamHitchcott 5 70
(M R Channon) *hld up: hdwy over 2f out: rdn to chse ldrs over 1f out: sn one pce* **4/1**[2]
53-3 **5** *¾* **Billy Ruffian**[97] 280 3-8-10 **67**........................ DavidAllan 2 62
(T D Easterby) *cl up: rdn along over 2f out and sn wknd* **8/1**
00-3 **6** *nk* **Josr's Magic (IRE)**[10] 1238 3-8-8 **65**........................(b) RoystonFfrench 3 59
(Mrs A Duffield) *in rr: effrt and sme hdwy over 2f out: sn rdn and btn* **15/2**
616 **7** *9* **Fantastic Cee (IRE)**[43] 744 3-9-1 **72**........................ TPQueally 1 39
(J Noseda) *wnt lft s: sn chsng ldrs on outer: pushed along 1/2-way and sn btn* **11/2**[3]

1m 11.5s (-1.00) **Going Correction** -0.25s/f (Firm) **7** Ran SP% **116.6**
Speed ratings (Par 99):96,94,91,90,89 88,76
CSF £16.84 CT £77.08 TOTE £2.90: £2.60, £2.70; EX 24.80 Place 6 £20.91, Place 5 £16.87.
Owner Clive Washbourn **Bred** Mrs B McLay-Irons **Trained** Maunby, N Yorks

FOCUS
A modest-looking contest won by an improver and fair form for the grade rated through the third.
Majestic Cheer Official explanation: jockey said gelding was unsuited by the good to firm (firm in places) ground
T/Plt: £48.70 to a £1 stake. Pool: £47,252.70. 707.65 winning tickets. T/Qpdt: £12.20 to a £1 stake. Pool: £2,469.80. 149.60 winning tickets. JR

1191 SAN SIRO (R-H)
Saturday, May 5

OFFICIAL GOING: Soft

1485a PREMIO ACQUASERIA (MAIDEN) (FILLIES) 5f
3:35 (12:00) 2-Y-0 **£6,757** (£2,973; £1,622; £811)

RPR
1 **Mujadil Draw (IRE)** 2-8-10........................ DVargiu 7 —
(B Grizzetti, Italy) **2/1**[1]
2 *2 ½* **Blumire (ITY)** 2-8-10........................ MDemuro 5 —
(A & G Botti, Italy) **5/2**[2]

3 *1* **Desert Showa (IRE)** 2-8-10 .... SMulas 2 —
(P Paciello, Italy) **59/10**

4 *2 1/4* **Starviet (IRE)** 2-8-10 .... FJovine 4 —
(M Ciciarelli, Italy) **74/10**

5 *1* **Hi Me** 2-8-10 .... GBietolini 3 —
(M G Quinlan) *s.i.s and lost 2 l: sn in tch: 5th and rdn over 2f out: one pce* **282/100[3]**

6 *2 1/2* **Casiluca (ITY)** 2-8-10 .... PConvertino 1 —
(M Marcialis, Italy) **22/1**

7 *2* **Suzy Spitfire (FR)** 2-8-10 .... WGambarota 6 —
(J Heloury, Italy) **74/10**

8 *5 1/2* **Sedara (ITY)** 2-8-10 .... LManiezzi 8 —
(R Menichetti, Italy) **34/1**

61.50 secs (2.30) **8** Ran SP% **133.6**
(including one euro stakes): WIN 2.98; PL 1.52, 1.45, 1.99; DF 4.35.
Owner Scuderia Blueberry **Bred** Scuderia Blueberry **Trained** Italy

NOTEBOOK
Hi Me lost a couple of lengths at the start and was in trouble soon after halfway. None of her rivals had raced before and there is no telling if the form is any good.

CHURCHILL DOWNS (L-H)

Saturday, May 5

OFFICIAL GOING: Dirt course - fast; turf course - yielding

1486a KENTUCKY DERBY (GRADE 1) (DIRT) 1m 2f (D)

11:04 (11:16) 3-Y-O **£632,653** (£204,082; £102,041; £51,020; £30,612)

RPR

1 **Street Sense (USA)**[21] 3-9-0 .... CHBorel 7 126
(C Nafzger, U.S.A) *hld up, 19th after 2f, rapid hdwy on ins fr 4f out, 3rd str, driven to ld dist, driven clear, ran on well* **49/10[1]**

2 *2 1/4* **Hard Spun (USA)**[42] 3-9-0 .... MPino 8 122
(J Larry Jones, U.S.A) *led to distance, ran on* **10/1**

3 *5 3/4* **Curlin (USA)**[21] 3-9-0 .... RAlbarado 2 111
(S Asmussen, U.S.A) *squeezed back early, raced in midfield, hdwy & 7th str, rdn 1 1/2f out, stayed on to take 3rd well ins fnl f* **5/1[2]**

4 *1/2* **Imawildandcrazyguy (USA)**[35] 3-9-0 ....(b) MGuidry 5 110
(W Kaplan, U.S.A) *last to halfway, 15th on outside straight, steady progress, nearest at finish* **29/1**

5 *1/2* **Sedgefield (USA)**[29] 3-9-0 ....(b) JRLeparoux 1 109
(Darrin Miller, U.S.A) *raced in 5th, went 2nd over 3f out, 2nd straight, still 3rd inside final f, one pace* **59/1**

6 *nk* **Circular Quay (USA)**[56] 3-9-0 .... JRVelazquez 16 109
(T Pletcher, U.S.A) *allowed to settle in rear, behind to 3f out, hard ridden on outside straight, nearest at finish* **114/10**

7 *3/4* **Tiago (USA)**[28] 3-9-0 .... MESmith 15 107
(J Shirreffs, U.S.A) *in rear til headway on inside from 3f out, stayed on final 1 1/2f, never a factor* **148/10**

8 *1/2* **Any Given Saturday (USA)**[28] 3-9-0 .... GKGomez 18 106
(T Pletcher, U.S.A) *headway 3f out, 4th straight, hard ridden and no extra from over 1f out* **136/10**

9 *2 1/2* **Sam P. (USA)**[28] 3-9-0 .... RADominguez 13 102
(T Pletcher, U.S.A) *never nearer than midfield* **44/1**

10 *1 3/4* **Nobiz Like Shobiz (USA)**[28] 3-9-0 ....(b) CVelasquez 12 99
(B Tagg, U.S.A) *in touch, 6th after 4f, 5th straight, weakened approaching final f* **104/10**

11 *3* **Dominican (USA)**[21] 3-9-0 .... RBejarano 19 93
(Darrin Miller, U.S.A) *never nearer than midfield* **25/1**

12 *nk* **Zanjero (USA)**[21] 3-9-0 .... SBridgmohan 3 93
(S Asmussen, U.S.A) *towards rear til headway 3f out, 6th on inside straight, weakened over 1f out* **36/1**

13 *2 3/4* **Great Hunter (USA)**[21] 3-9-0 ....(b) CNakatani 20 88
(Doug O'Neill, U.S.A) *never nearer than midfield* **25/1**

14 *1 3/4* **Liquidity (USA)**[28] 3-9-0 .... DFlores 9 85
(Doug O'Neill, U.S.A) *in touch, 8th straight, soon weakened* **40/1**

15 *3/4* **Bwana Bull (USA)**[28] 3-9-0 ....(b) JCastellano 11 83
(J Hollendorfer, U.S.A) *always towards rear* **50/1**

16 *1* **Storm In May (USA)**[21] 3-9-0 .... JCLeyva 4 82
(W Kaplan, U.S.A) *broke well, hampered after 1f and pushed onto Curlin, 14th after 2f, always behind* **27/1**

17 *11 1/2* **Teuflesberg (USA)**[21] 3-9-0 .... StewartElliott 10 62
(Jamie Sanders, U.S.A) *pressed leaders, went 2nd over 3f out, weakened quickly over 2f out* **52/1**

18 *2 3/4* **Scat Daddy (USA)**[35] 3-9-0 .... EPrado 14 57
(T Pletcher, U.S.A) *raced in 6th, beaten when squeezed out over 2f out, dropped back quickly* **72/10[3]**

19 *6 1/4* **Stormello (USA)**[35] 3-9-0 ....(b) KDesormeaux 17 46
(W Currin, U.S.A) *rushed up on outside fr 17 draw to race in 4th, 4th 3f out, sn outpcd, wkng when hampered over 2f out* **45/1**

20 *7 1/4* **Cowtown Cat (USA)**[28] 3-9-0 .... FJara 6 33
(T Pletcher, U.S.A) *chased leader, disputing 2nd over 3f out, weakened steadily, behind final 2f* **198/10**

2m 2.17s (0.98) **20** Ran SP% **119.4**
PARI-MUTUEL (including $2 stake): WIN 11.80; PL (1-2) 6.40, 9.80; SHOW (1-2-3) 4.60, 7.00, 5.60; SF 101.80.
Owner J B Tafel **Bred** James B Tafel **Trained** USA
■ A second Kentucky Derby success for trainer Carl Nafzger, who sent out Unbridled to win in 1990, and a first for Calvin Borel.

FOCUS
A cracking renewal of the first leg of the Triple Crown and, thanks to Hard Spun, the race was run at a strong pace. Street Sense ran out a sensational winner and in doing so became the first horse to complete the Breeders' Cup Juvenile-Kentucky Derby double.

NOTEBOOK
Street Sense(USA), a quite sensational winner of last season's Breeders' Cup Juvenile when routing the opposition - including many of today's rivals - by ten lengths, is ridden by a jockey who likes to hug the rail and the strong early gallop was always likely to suit. Dropped in early, he only had one behind him after a couple of furlongs, but lit up the place with a staggering sustained burst that carried him into a stalking position turning for home. The race worked out just as the Breeders' Cup Juvenile had for him, only having to switch out to pass a rival early in the straight before powering clear. He made history by becoming the first colt to do the Breeders' Cup Juvenile-Kentucky Derby double and talk will now inevitably switch to the possibility of him completing the Triple Crown. He should have little trouble getting the longer trip in the Belmont Stakes, but the biggest stumbling block could be the Preakness next time, as Hard Spun is likely to be tougher to pass over the shorter 1m1f trip at Pimlico.
Hard Spun(USA) set strong fractions and ran an incredible race in the circumstances to keep on and finish second, well clear of the rest. It must be a worry that this race will have taken a lot out of him and that he bounces next time, but a repeat of this performance will make him hard to beat over the furlong shorter distance of the Preakness at Pimlico on the 20th May.
Curlin(USA) had no chance according to the stats as no horse unraced at two had won the Derby since the late 1800s, and he came into the race as the least experienced horse in the line-up. He had been impressive in winning three from three earlier this year, though, including a ten-length success in the Arkansas Derby last time out, and unsurprisingly he was one of the market principals. He ran well, just lacking the knowhow of some of those around him, and looks the type to go on and improve as the season progresses.
Imawildandcrazyguy(USA), who has been getting beaten by most of today's rivals on a regular basis, was stone last at halfway and appeared to be going nowhere, but he made good headway through the field in the final half mile and was finishing better than most. A similarly strong pace in the Belmont Stakes may see another good effort, but he would be an unlikely winner.
Sedgefield(USA) recorded a career-best effort back in fifth, keeping on really well having held a prominent position throughout and giving every indication that he too will be suited by the demands of the Preakness Stakes.
Circular Quay(USA) did best of those drawn in double figures and was the first home from the Todd Pletcher barn, which had five runners in the race. He was actually going on quite well close home, but it may have been a case of him just staying on past beaten horses.
Tiago(USA), fresh into this off the back of a victory in the Santa Anita Derby, got shuffled back early on and did well to make some late ground, suggesting he could be a player in the Belmont.
Nobiz Like Shobiz(USA), winner of the Wood Memorial, has had his temperament questioned on several occasions and whether the hurly burly of this race would suit looked doubtful. He was rushed up early on having been a bit slowly away and as a result had nothing left when it mattered.
Scat Daddy(USA), ready winner of the Florida Derby, was already in trouble when being squeezed out rounding for home and was not given a hard time from then on.

HAMILTON (R-H)

Sunday, May 6

OFFICIAL GOING: Good to firm (good in places)
Wind: Fresh, across

1487 WELCOME BACK MAIDEN AUCTION STKS 5f 4y

2:05 (2:05) (Class 5) 2-Y-O **£3,238** (£963; £481; £240) **Stalls** Low

Form RPR

5 **1** **Taurian**[18] [1087] 2-8-10 .... TomEaves 5 75
(Mrs L Stubbs) *w ldr: led over 1f out: edgd rt ins fnl f: hld on wl* **7/4[1]**

5 **2** *hd* **Guertino (IRE)**[28] [952] 2-9-0 .... PaulEddery 6 78
(B Smart) *chsd ldrs: effrt and ev ch ins fnl f: kpt on: jst hld* **3/1[3]**

3 *1 1/4* **Fitzroy Crossing (USA)** 2-9-0 .... GregFairley(3) 2 76
(M Johnston) *led to over 1f out: kpt on same pce ins fnl f* **9/4[2]**

0 **4** *2 1/2* **Willyn (IRE)**[13] [1193] 2-8-1 .... AndrewElliott(3) 4 53
(J R Weymes) *trckd ldrs: rdn 1/2-way: nt qckn over 1f out* **10/1**

5 *3* **Countrywide Comet (IRE)** 2-8-12 .... DO'Donohoe 1 49
(K A Ryan) *dwlt: sn prom: shkn up 1/2-way: wknd over 1f out* **9/1**

6 *3* **Next Best** 2-8-5 .... RoystonFfrench 7 30
(A Berry) *s.i.s: nvr on terms* **50/1**

61.72 secs (0.52) **Going Correction** -0.025s/f (Good) **6** Ran SP% **113.2**
Speed ratings (Par 93):94,93,91,87,82 78
CSF £7.51 TOTE £3.10: £1.70, £2.30; EX 9.10.
Owner Tyme Partnership **Bred** Angmering Park Stud **Trained** Norton, N. Yorks
■ Stewards' Enquiry : Paul Eddery one-day ban: used whip with excessive frequency without giving colt time to respond (May 17)
Tom Eaves one-day ban: used whip with excessive frequency (May 17)

FOCUS
Not a strong maiden but the pace seemed sound throughout and this form should prove reliable, rated through the winner.

NOTEBOOK
Taurian, who shaped well when just in front of a subsequent winner from a modest draw at Beverley on his debut, travelled strongly and fully confirmed that promise. Life will be tougher under a penalty but he may be capable of better. (op 2-1 tchd 9-4, 5-2 in places)
Guertino(IRE), who appeared to go off too quickly at Musselburgh on his debut, was ridden with a bit more restraint this time and turned in a much-improved effort. On this evidence he is capable of winning a similar event. (op 7-2 tchd 4-1)
Fitzroy Crossing(USA) ◆ attracted support and shaped well on this racecourse debut against two more experienced rivals. The step up to six furlongs will be in his favour and he looks sure to win a similar event. (op 6-4)
Willyn(IRE) jumped out much better this time but failed to build on her fair debut effort at Pontefract. She is likely to remain vulnerable to the more progressive sorts in this grade. (op 12-1)
Countrywide Comet(IRE), the first foal of a half-sister to a multiple winner around a mile and a quarter in Italy, was easy to back but hinted at ability on this racecourse debut. This form is only modest but he looks the sort to do better in due course. (op 10-1)
Next Best, a cheap purchase, showed no promise after a sluggish start.

1488 SUNDAY MAIL ANNUAL JUMP JOCKEYS H'CAP (TO BE RIDDEN BY NH JOCKEYS) (SERIES QUALIFIER) 1m 65y

2:40 (2:40) (Class 5) (0-70,68) 4-Y-0+ **£3,238** (£963; £481; £240) **Stalls** High

Form RPR

0-00 **1** **Just Lille (IRE)**[10] [1258] 4-11-2 **66** ....(p) GLee 7 75
(Mrs A Duffield) *in tch: effrt over 2f out: edgd rt: styd on wl fnl f to ld nr fin* **7/1[3]**

1262 **2** *nk* **Motu (IRE)**[2] [1459] 6-10-13 **63** ....(v) FergusKing 14 71
(I W McInnes) *prom: effrt over 2f out: ev ch wl ins fnl f: jst hld* **9/2[2]**

-006 **3** *1/2* **Baylaw Star**[2] [1459] 6-10-13 **63** .... PeterBuchanan 10 70
(I W McInnes) *led: rdn over 2f out: kpt on: hdd cl home* **8/1**

000- **4** *3* **Jordans Elect**[189] [6240] 7-10-13 **63** .... PadgeWhelan 15 63
(P Monteith) *prom: effrt over 2f out: kpt on same pce over 1f out* **14/1**

521- **5** *1 1/2* **Anthemion (IRE)**[262] [4518] 10-10-10 **60** .... MarkBradburne 4 57
(Mrs J C McGregor) *chsd ldrs tl rdn and no ex over 1f out* **22/1**

030- **6** *3/4* **Mystical Ayr (IRE)**[194] [6158] 5-10-6 **56** .... AdrianScholes 16 51
(Miss L A Perratt) *midfield: rdn whn n.m.r over 2f out: sn no imp* **20/1**

00-0 **7** *hd* **Touch Of Ivory (IRE)**[13] [955] 4-10-9 **59** ....(p) WilsonRenwick 11 53
(P Monteith) *towards rr: rdn 1/2-way: sme late hdwy: n.d* **12/1**

560- **8** *hd* **Thistle**[27] [4154] 6-10-11 **61** .... PJBrennan 6 55
(J Howard Johnson) *chsd ldrs tl outpcd fr 2f out* **10/1**

3650 **9** *1/2* **Boy Dancer (IRE)**[16] [1132] 4-10-6 **56** ....(p) PaddyAspell 9 49
(D W Barker) *missed break: bhd tl sme late hdwy: nvr on terms* **12/1**

455- **10** *1* **Bayberry King (USA)**[270] [4261] 4-10-5 **55** .... RichardMcGrath 13 45
(J S Goldie) *bhd: rdn 4f out: nvr on terms* **16/1**

32-1 **11** *1 1/4* **Dispol Isle (IRE)**[27] [967] 5-11-4 **68** .... TonyDobbin 12 56
(T D Barron) *hld up: rdn over 2f out: btn over 1f out* **4/1[1]**

06-0 **12** ¾ **Soho Square**[28] [955] 4-11-1 **65** .... KeithMercer 2 51
(L Lungo) *midfield: rdn 1/2-way: sn lost pl* **33/1**

01- **13** *hd* **Neil's Legacy (IRE)**[231] [5403] 5-10-8 **58** .... GerrySupple 3 43
(Miss L A Perratt) *hld up: sme hdwy over 2f out: nvr nrr* **16/1**

2-04 **14** 6 **Dechiper (IRE)**[22] [1044] 5-10-5 **55** .... KennyJohnson 1 27
(R Johnson) *a bhd* **12/1**

030- **15** *hd* **Emotive**[81] [5621] 4-10-10 **60** .... BrianHarding 5 31
(F P Murtagh) *sn bhd: rdn and no ch fr 1/2-way* **66/1**

000- **16** 3 ½ **Royal Citadel (IRE)**[209] [5874] 4-10-7 **57** .... LarryMcGrath 8 20
(Mrs L B Normile) *a bhd: edgd rt and wknd fr 3f out* **33/1**

1m 49.61s (0.31) **Going Correction** -0.025s/f (Good) **16** Ran SP% **128.9**
Speed ratings (Par 103):96,96,96,93,91 90,90,90,90,89 87,87,86,80,80 77
CSF £38.50 CT £282.48 TOTE £6.70: £1.60, £2.60, £3.80, £3.00; EX 167.00.
Owner Granville J Harper **Bred** Sweetmans Bloodstock **Trained** Constable Burton, N Yorks
■ The first Flat success for Grand National-winning rider Graham Lee.
■ Stewards' Enquiry : Fergus King one-day ban: careless riding (May 17)
Kenny Johnson three-day ban: used whip with excessive force when out of contention (May 17-19)

FOCUS
A low-grade novelty handicap which has been rated through the runner-up.

1489 SANDRA MCWILLIAMS MEMORIAL (S) STKS 1m 65y
3:20 (3:21) (Class 6) 3-Y-O **£1,943** (£578; £288; £144) **Stalls** High

Form RPR

1 **Silent Lucidity (IRE)**[212] [5798] 3-8-7 .... JamieMoriarty(5) 7 64
(P D Niven) *prom: rdn over 3f out: led over 1f out: styd on wl* **2/1**[2]

00-6 **2** 1 ½ **Jewelled Dagger (IRE)**[12] [1220] 3-8-12 45 ....(b[1]) TomEaves 6 60
(I Semple) *t.k.h: led: clr 3f out: hdd over 1f out: no ex* **10/1**

-205 **3** 14 **Denton Hawk**[15] [1164] 3-8-12 54 .... PhillipMakin 5 28
(M Dods) *hld up: effrt 3f out: nvr rchd ldrs* **7/2**[3]

50-0 **4** ½ **Beaumont Boy**[18] [1091] 3-8-12 59 .... TonyHamilton 3 27
(G A Swinbank) *hld up in tch: rdn over 3f out: btn over 1f out* **7/4**[1]

-050 **5** 6 **Mandriano (ITY)**[11] [1236] 3-8-12 40 .... RoystonFfrench 2 13
(D W Barker) *chsd ldrs tl wknd over 2f out* **18/1**

-010 **6** 9 **Raven Rascal**[8] [1301] 3-8-12 47 .... TPQueally 4 —
(J F Coupland) *hld up: rdn whn n.m.r 3f out: nvr on terms* **12/1**

00-0 **7** 14 **Olgarena (IRE)**[18] [1092] 3-8-7 48 ....(b[1]) DavidAllan 1 —
(T D Easterby) *chsd ldrs to 3f out: sn rdn and wknd* **10/1**

1m 47.53s (-1.77) **Going Correction** -0.025s/f (Good) **7** Ran SP% **123.1**
Speed ratings (Par 97):107,105,91,91,85 76,62
CSF £24.46 TOTE £7.70: £3.50, £2.30; EX 56.50.The winner was bought in for £7,000.
Owner Mrs K Egan **Bred** Mrs Jacqueline Donnelly **Trained** Barton-le-Street, N Yorks

FOCUS
A weak race, even for this grade but the winner, who landed a touch, may be capable of a bit better. The first two finished clear and the race has been rated around the runner-up.

1490 COLLIER HILL H'CAP 1m 5f 9y
3:55 (3:55) (Class 4) (0-80,80) 4-Y-O+ **£6,477** (£1,927; £963; £481) **Stalls** High

Form RPR

100- **1** **Monolith**[15] [5963] 9-9-4 **80** .... GregFairley(3) 9 91
(L Lungo) *chsd ldrs: effrt 3f out: hung lft over 1f out: rallied to ld ins fnl f: styd on wl* **4/1**[2]

50-5 **2** 1 ¼ **Balyan (IRE)**[32] [914] 6-9-3 **76** .... PaulMulrennan 5 85
(J Howard Johnson) *cl up: led 3f out to ins fnl f: no ex* **12/1**

1-41 **3** ¾ **Osolomio (IRE)**[15] [1158] 4-9-0 **73** .... DaleGibson 3 81
(G A Swinbank) *t.k.h: cl up: led briefly over 3f out: rallied: no ex ins fnl f* **6/4**[1]

-110 **4** 4 **Cripsey Brook**[8] [1288] 9-9-0 **80** ....(t) JamesReveley(7) 8 82
(K G Reveley) *hld up: rdn 3f out: styd on fnl f: nvr rchd ldrs* **14/1**

3-45 **5** 7 **Grey Outlook**[2] [1457] 4-8-3 **65** .... AndrewMullen(3) 1 57
(Miss L A Perratt) *dwlt: hld up: rdn over 3f out: n.d* **9/1**

32-4 **6** 1 **Primo Way**[100] [256] 6-9-1 **74** .... TomEaves 2 64
(I Semple) *hld up: rdn 4f out: nvr on terms* **14/1**

400- **7** ½ **Best Of The Lot (USA)**[211] [5815] 5-8-3 **62** .... RoystonFfrench 4 51
(R A Fahey) *t.k.h: hld up in tch: rdn and edgd rt 3f out: sn btn* **9/2**[3]

560/ **8** 3 ½ **Kid'Z'Play (IRE)**[304] [6236] 11-8-0 **62** oh7 ow1 .... AndrewElliott(3) 10 46
(J S Goldie) *chsd ldrs: lost pl over 5f out: n.d after* **50/1**

05-5 **9** 3 ½ **Maneki Neko (IRE)**[15] [1158] 5-8-12 **71** .... TonyHamilton 3 50
(E W Tuer) *led to over 3f out: wknd over 2f out* **12/1**

2m 50.35s (-3.05) **Going Correction** -0.025s/f (Good) **9** Ran SP% **118.9**
Speed ratings (Par 105):108,107,106,104,100 99,99,96,94
CSF £52.38 CT £103.64 TOTE £5.10: £1.70, £2.90, £2.00; EX 33.50.
Owner Elite Racing Club **Bred** Juddmonte Farms **Trained** Carrutherstown, D'fries & G'way

FOCUS
A fair handicap in which a steady early gallop suited those ridden closest to the pace. Sound form, rated through the second and third.

1491 RACING POST MEDIAN AUCTION MAIDEN STKS 1m 3f 16y
4:30 (4:30) (Class 6) 3-5-Y-O **£2,730** (£806; £403) **Stalls** High

Form RPR

65-6 **1** **Patavian (IRE)**[27] [968] 3-8-9 68 .... TomEaves 7 59
(I Semple) *chsd ldrs: rdn 3f out: led 1f out: styd on wl* **3/1**[3]

4- **2** 1 **Inasus (GER)**[263] [4466] 3-8-6 .... GregFairley(3) 5 57
(M Johnston) *led: edgd lft and hdd 1f out: no ex ins fnl f* **7/4**[1]

300/ **3** 1 ¾ **Roman Army (IRE)**[75] [5603] 5-9-12 50 ....(p) RoystonFfrench 4 55
(James Moffatt) *hld up: outpcd 1/2-way: styd on wl fnl 2f: nrst at fin* **8/1**

463 **4** ½ **Modern Verse (USA)**[32] [916] 4-9-12 .... TonyHamilton 3 54
(G A Swinbank) *t.k.h: hld up: drvn over 4f out: sn outpcd: rallied 2f out: no ex wl ins fnl f* **2/1**[2]

-0 **5** 1 **Top Rocker**[12] [1220] 3-8-9 .... PaulMulrennan 6 51
(E W Tuer) *chsd ldrs tl rdn and no ex fr 2f out* **22/1**

06-0 **6** 1 ¼ **Caviar Heights (IRE)**[8] [1303] 3-8-9 53 .... PhillipMakin 2 49
(Miss L A Perratt) *hld up in tch: smooth hdwy and cl up 4f out: rdn and outpcd fnl 2f* **33/1**

7 1 **Asrar**[109] 5-9-2 .... PJMcDonald(5) 1 43
(Miss Lucinda V Russell) *cl up tl wknd over 2f out* **33/1**

0600 **8** 13 **Smart Pick**[18] [1086] 4-9-2 40 .... JamieMoriarty(5) 8 20
(Mrs L Williamson) *hld up: struggling 1/2-way: nvr on terms* **50/1**

2m 26.7s (0.44) **Going Correction** -0.025s/f (Good)
WFA 3 from 4yo+ 17lb **8** Ran SP% **118.0**
Speed ratings (Par 101):97,96,95,94,93 93,92,82
CSF £8.75 TOTE £3.90: £1.10, £1.90, £2.10; EX 7.00.
Owner R Hyndman **Bred** Ralph And Helen O'Brien **Trained** Carluke, S Lanarks

FOCUS
A very modest event, little better than a seller, in which the pace seemed fair. The form is limited by the third, who has been rated to last season's Irish form. The winner did not need to run to his best.

1492 BERNADETTE MURPHY ESTATES H'CAP 6f 5y
5:05 (5:14) (Class 5) (0-70,67) 3-Y-O+ **£3,238** (£963; £481; £240) **Stalls** Low

Form RPR

4241 **1** **Franksalot (IRE)**[10] [1260] 7-9-7 **62** .... RoystonFfrench 3 71
(I W McInnes) *midfield: rdn 1/2-way: hdwy wl over 1f out: styd on wl to ld cl home* **4/1**[2]

0-00 **2** *nk* **Throw The Dice**[26] [992] 5-9-0 **55** ....(v[1]) TonyHamilton 10 63
(D W Barker) *led and clr: rdn 2f out: kpt on fnl f: hdd cl home* **5/1**[3]

2-43 **3** *hd* **Cross Of Lorraine (IRE)**[45] [727] 4-9-10 **65** ....(b) TomEaves 4 72
(I Semple) *midfield: outpcd 1/2-way: swtchd rt and hdwy over 1f out: edgd rt: kpt on fnl f* **4/1**[2]

56-1 **4** 3 ½ **Brigadore**[26] [992] 8-9-12 **67** .... TPQueally 9 64
(J G Given) *hld up outside: smooth hdwy over 2f out: rdn over 1f out: sn one pce* **3/1**[1]

64-0 **5** 1 ¾ **Charles Parnell (IRE)**[19] [1074] 4-9-12 **67** ....(p) PhillipMakin 1 58
(M Dods) *hung rt thrght: prom tl rdn and no ex wl over 1f out* **6/1**

-000 **6** 1 ¼ **Dunn Deal (IRE)**[3] [1436] 7-8-10 **54** .... LiamJones(3) 12 42
(W M Brisbourne) *hld up: hdwy outside over 2f out: rdn and no imp over 1f out* **11/2**

003- **7** *nk* **John O'Groats (IRE)**[210] [5840] 9-8-5 **53** oh8 ....(p) CharlotteKerton(7) 11 40
(W G Harrison) *prom tl wknd fr 2f out* **33/1**

200- **8** 4 **Obe One**[234] [5309] 7-8-12 **53** oh1 .... PaulMulrennan 2 28
(A Berry) *outpcd and bhd: nvr rchd ldrs* **12/1**

000- **9** ½ **Alexia Rose (IRE)**[187] [6274] 5-8-7 **53** oh3 .... JamieMoriarty(5) 7 26
(A Berry) *cl up tl wknd fr 2f out* **50/1**

650- **10** 2 ½ **Danni Di Guerra (IRE)**[233] [5332] 3-8-1 **55** oh8 ow2 .... AndrewMullen(3) 6 18
(J Barclay) *bhd: struggling fr 1/2-way* **50/1**

000- **11** 16 **Mister Marmaduke**[300] [3356] 6-8-12 **53** oh8 ....(t) PaulFessey 5 —
(D A Nolan) *a outpcd* **66/1**

1m 12.8s (-0.30) **Going Correction** -0.025s/f (Good)
WFA 3 from 4yo+ 10lb **11** Ran SP% **127.4**
Speed ratings (Par 103):101,100,100,95,93 91,91,85,85,81 60
CSF £26.35 CT £90.82 TOTE £4.40: £2.00, £2.10, £1.40; EX 43.00.
Owner Stephen Hackney And Martin Higgins **Bred** J P Hardiman **Trained** Catwick, E Yorks
■ Stewards' Enquiry : Charlotte Kerton one-day ban: used whip with excessive frequency (May 17)
Tony Hamilton two-day ban: used whip with excessive force (May 17-18)

FOCUS
A run-of-the-mill sprint but one run at a sound pace throughout, and those near the stands' rail held the edge. Modest form. The front pair were both rated higher last year.

1493 HOWARD MCDOWALL MEMORIAL H'CAP 5f 4y
5:40 (5:44) (Class 6) (0-60,60) 4-Y-O+ **£2,388** (£705; £352) **Stalls** Low

Form RPR

0506 **1** **Brut**[4] [1405] 5-8-12 **54** ....(p) TonyHamilton 2 67
(D W Barker) *mde all stands' rail: rdn 2f out: hrd pressed fnl f: hld on wl* **7/2**[1]

6-40 **2** ½ **Never Without Me**[8] [1299] 7-9-3 **59** .... TPQueally 1 70
(J F Coupland) *in tch stands' side: effrt and chsd wnr appr fnl f: ev ch ins fnl f: hld cl home* **12/1**

60-0 **3** 2 ½ **Memphis Man**[19] [1074] 4-8-9 **54** .... LiamJones(3) 4 56
(W M Brisbourne) *outpcd: hdwy stands' side over 1f out: kpt on wl fnl f: nt rch first two* **4/1**[2]

00-0 **4** 1 ¼ **Oeuf A La Neige**[2] [1459] 7-8-4 **49** ow1 .... GregFairley(3) 5 46+
(Miss L A Perratt) *sn drvn along in midfield: outpcd over 2f out: kpt on fnl f* **14/1**

-600 **5** ¾ **Soldiers Romance**[52] [681] 4-8-6 **48** .... DavidAllan 3 42
(T D Easterby) *cl up stands' side tl rdn and wknd over 1f out* **17/2**

0-05 **6** 1 **Jun Fan (USA)**[11] [1241] 5-8-7 **54** ow4 .... JamieMoriarty(5) 8 44
(B Ellison) *prom towards stands' side: effrt over 2f out: btn ins fnl f* **4/1**[2]

0424 **7** 1 ¼ **Beamsley Beacon**[5] [1384] 6-8-8 **50** ....(bt) PaulFessey 13 35+
(S T Mason) *prom centre tl rdn and wknd over 1f out* **15/2**[3]

6-50 **8** 1 ¼ **Champagne Cracker**[4] [1404] 6-8-13 **55** ....(p) PhillipMakin 10 36+
(M Dods) *prom centre tl wknd fr 2f out* **12/1**

36-0 **9** 4 **Miacarla**[5] [1384] 4-8-1 **46** .... AndrewElliott(3) 6 11
(A Berry) *prom towards stands' side: rdn and wknd over 1f out* **33/1**

400- **10** ¾ **Howards Prince**[237] [5250] 4-8-10 **52** .... TomEaves 12 15
(I Semple) *outpcd centre 1/2-way: nvr on terms* **14/1**

100- **11** 1 ¼ **Signor Whippee**[126] [6994] 4-8-10 **52** ....(b) PaulMulrennan 11 10
(A Berry) *outpcd centre: nvr on terms* **33/1**

34/- **12** ½ **Seafield Towers**[634] [4252] 7-9-4 **60** .... RoystonFfrench 9 16
(Miss L A Perratt) *prom centre tl wknd fr 2f out* **14/1**

0/5- **13** 9 **Lady Tilly**[311] [3002] 10-7-11 **46** oh1 .... CharlotteKerton(7) 7 —
(W G Harrison) *sn wl bhd* **100/1**

60.68 secs (-0.52) **Going Correction** -0.025s/f (Good) **13** Ran SP% **126.8**
Speed ratings (Par 101):103,102,98,96,95 93,91,89,83,81 79,79,64
CSF £49.79 CT £166.34 TOTE £5.10: £1.90, £4.90, £2.10; EX 65.40 Place 6 £39.76, Place 5 £22.91..
Owner D W Barker **Bred** Mrs Deborah O'Brien **Trained** Scorton, N Yorks

FOCUS
A modest but truly-run handicap in which things again unfolded next to the stands' rail. Fair form for the grade despite the draw bias. The first two had slipped to good marks and the winner is rated to last summer's form.
T/Plt: £175.40 to a £1 stake. Pool: £54,367.40. 226.20 winning tickets. T/Qpdt: £34.50 to a £1 stake. Pool: £2,399.60. 51.40 winning tickets. RY

1471 NEWMARKET (ROWLEY) (R-H)
Sunday, May 6

OFFICIAL GOING: Good to firm
Wind: Fresh behind Weather: Overcast

1494 STANJAMESUK.COM SUFFOLK STKS (HERITAGE H'CAP) 1m 1f
1:55 (1:59) (Class 2) 3-Y-O+
£31,160 (£9,330; £4,665; £2,335; £1,165; £585) **Stalls** Low

Form RPR

150- **1** **Supaseus**[190] [6219] 4-8-10 **92** .... JohnEgan 10 102
(H Morrison) *chsd ldr tl led over 6f out: hdd over 4f out: led and edgd rt fr over 2f out: rdn over 1f out: hung rt nr fin: all out* **10/1**

30-1 **2** *shd* **Pinpoint (IRE)**[15] [1145] 5-9-10 **106** .... AdamKirby 13 116+
(W R Swinburn) *lw: hld up in tch: rdn over 2f out: ev ch and hung lft ins fnl f: r.o* **10/3**[1]

13-0 **3** 3 **Night Crescendo (USA)**[15] [1145] 4-8-8 **90** .... MJKinane 1 94+
(Mrs A J Perrett) *lw: hld up: outpcd 1/2-way: swtchd lft over 2f out: swtchd rt over 1f out: r.o wl ins fnl f: nt rch ldrs* **12/1**

00-3 **4** 1/2 **Instructor**[15] 1149 6-8-1 **83** PaulHanagan 8 86
(R A Fahey) *led: hdd over 6f out: rdn over 2f out: kpt on u.p* **33/1**
00-0 **5** *shd* **Ace Of Hearts**[15] 1145 8-8-13 **95** EddieAhern 15 98+
(C F Wall) *hld up: swtchd rt and hdwy over 1f out: styd on same pce wl ins fnl f* **14/1**
-400 **6** *shd* **Langford**[11] 1245 7-8-1 **83** JimmyQuinn 6 86
(M H Tompkins) *hld up: hdwy over 3f out: rdn and ev ch 1f out: no ex* **16/1**
60-0 **7** *shd* **Prince Of Light (IRE)**[14] 1184 4-9-8 **104** KDarley 12 106
(M Johnston) *chsd ldrs: rdn over 2f out: hung lft and no ex ins fnl f* **14/1**
4-30 **8** 1 1/2 **Fortunate Isle (USA)**[65] 608 5-8-1 **83** JamieMackay 2 82
(R A Fahey) *swtg: chsd ldrs: nt clr run: stmbld and outpcd over 1f out: styd on ins fnl f* **33/1**
0200 **9** 1 1/4 **Yarqus**[8] 1307 4-8-10 **92** RichardHughes 5 89
(C E Brittain) *hld up: nt clr run over 2f out: sn rdn over 2f out: n.d* **40/1**
11-6 **10** 1/2 **Persian Express (USA)**[29] 938 4-8-7 **89** MichaelHills 16 85
(B W Hills) *lw: chsd ldrs: led over 4f out: rdn and hdd over 2f out: wknd fnl f* **25/1**
14-6 **11** *hd* **Dansili Dancer**[29] 941 5-9-4 **100** KerrinMcEvoy 3 99+
(C G Cox) *hld up in tch: rdn over 1f out: wkng whn hmpd ins fnl f* **7/1**[3]
50-2 **12** 1 1/2 **Royal Oath (USA)**[15] 1145 4-9-0 **96** JimmyFortune 18 89
(J H M Gosden) *lw: hld up: hdwy over 3f out: wknd fnl f* **5/1**[2]
40-0 **13** 6 **Rocamadour**[15] 1145 5-8-13 **95** DarrylHolland 4 76
(M R Channon) *lw: chsd ldrs: rdn over 2f out: sn wknd* **25/1**
00-1 **14** 3/4 **Emerald Bay (IRE)**[27] 969 5-7-12 **85** DuranFentiman(5) 9 64
(I Semple) *chsd ldrs over 6f* **16/1**
1202 **15** 24 **Blacktoft (USA)**[6] 1356 4-7-7 **80** oh4 (e) WilliamBuick(5) 7 11
(S C Williams) *s.s: outpcd* **20/1**
3143 **16** 82 **Charlie Cool**[29] 941 4-9-10 **106** JamieSpencer 14 —
(W J Haggas) *prom: lost pl over 4f out: sn bhd* **15/2**

1m 49.1s (-2.85) **Going Correction** -0.15s/f (Firm) **16** Ran SP% **126.7**
Speed ratings (Par 109): 106,105,103,102,102 102,102,101,100,99 99,98,92,92,70 —
CSF £41.41 CT £443.56 TOTE £11.70: £2.90, £1.60, £3.30, £6.30; EX 74.90 Trifecta £1007.20 Part won. Pool £1,418.68. - 0.20 winning units..
Owner Ben & Sir Martyn Arbib **Bred** Arbib Bloodstock Partnership **Trained** East Ilsley, Berks
■ Stewards' Enquiry : K Darley two-day ban: careless riding (May 17-18)

FOCUS
Decent enough handicap form, but perhaps not quite as strong as first impressions might suggest.

NOTEBOOK
Supaseus ◆ got his season off to a perfect start with a brave success under a strong ride. He did well to get across early to the stands' side, and this confirms his versatility as regards underfoot conditions, but he was hanging at a couple of stages and is probably at his happiest on a slightly easier surface. While he has been something of an in-and-out performer to date, it could be that this year he will reach greater heights and he does not have too many miles on the clock for a four-year-old. (op 12-1)
Pinpoint(IRE), 6lb higher than when winning the Spring Cup at Newbury last time, posted another improved effort and was only just denied under top weight. This display confirms him a most progressive five-year-old and he should be capable of handling the step up into Listed company at least this term. However, he is ideally suited by an easier surface and so may have to wait until later in the year. (op 4-1 tchd 9-2 in a place)
Night Crescendo(USA), whose stable has hit top form now, showed his true colours and finished a lot closer to the runner-up than he had been the case when disappointing on his seasonal return at Newbury last time. He can be rated a little better than the bare form as he did not get the best of passages and, on this evidence, he could well bag a decent handicap at some stage this season.
Instructor was given his usual positive ride and turned in another solid effort in defeat. He is in good heart at present, loves this sort of ground, and helps to set the standard of this form. (op 25-1)
Ace Of Hearts showed the benefit of his seasonal debut behind Pinpoint at Newbury and deserves a little extra credit as he saw plenty of daylight from his double-figure draw. He has begun this term in good form. (op 12-1)
Langford emerged from off the pace to have his chance and appreciated the slight drop back in trip. He is now back to his last winning mark, but is not that easy to catch right. (op 20-1)
Prince Of Light(IRE) had his chance, but he failed to raise his game for the drop in class. He is not proving that simple to place at present. (tchd 16-1 in a place)
Fortunate Isle(USA) ran better than his finishing position indicates as he did not handle the dip and must be rated better than the bare form. He also ideally needs softer ground. (tchd 40-1)
Dansili Dancer, popular in the betting on this return to turf, had his chance yet lacked the pace to stay with the principals when it mattered. (op 15-2 tchd 8-1 in places)
Royal Oath(USA), easy to back, failed to build on the promise of his run behind Pinpoint last time and was beaten too far out for this to be his true running. He now has something to prove. (op 9-2)
Charlie Cool dropped out quickly at the halfway and something was clearly amiss. Official explanation: jockey said colt never travelled (op 7-1 tchd 8-1)

1495 STANJAMESUK.COM JOCKEY CLUB STKS (GROUP 2) 1m 4f
2:30 (2:30) (Class 1) 4-Y-0+ **£51,102** (£19,368; £9,693; £4,833; £2,421) **Stalls** High

Form RPR
110- **1** **Sixties Icon**[217] 5716 4-9-3 117 LDettori 2 124+
(J Noseda) *h.d.w: a.p: chsd ldr 8f out: led 2f out: styd on strly* **5/2**[2]
13-5 **2** 3 **Admiral's Cruise (USA)**[15] 1144 5-8-12 112 (b) JimmyFortune 4 114
(B J Meehan) *lw: hld up: hdwy over 3f: rdn to chse wnr over 1f out: edgd rt and no ex ins fnl f* **4/1**
1342 **3** *nk* **Mighty**[15] 1144 4-8-12 105 JohnEgan 1 114
(Jane Chapple-Hyam) *b: b.hind: led: rdn and hdd 2f out: styng on same pce whn n.m.r ins fnl f* **9/1**
105- **4** 2 1/2 **Papal Bull**[238] 5221 4-9-1 115 KerrinMcEvoy 5 113
(Sir Michael Stoute) *h.d.w: bit bkwd: chsd ldr 4f: rdn and wknd over 1f out* **9/4**[1]
103- **5** *nk* **Linda's Lad**[287] 3778 4-8-12 SPasquier 3 110
(A Fabre, France) *lw: hld up: rdn over 2f out: wknd over 1f out* **7/2**[3]

2m 33.52s (0.02) **Going Correction** -0.15s/f (Firm) **5** Ran SP% **111.6**
Speed ratings (Par 115): 93,91,90,89,88
CSF £12.74 TOTE £2.90: £2.00, £2.30; EX 12.90.
Owner Mrs Susan Roy **Bred** Lordship Stud **Trained** Newmarket, Suffolk

FOCUS
An interesting renewal but it was run at a steady early pace and won in a very slow winning time for a race of this stature. The form might not be that solid, but it was hard not to be impressed with the winner.

NOTEBOOK
Sixties Icon ◆, last year's St Leger winner but disappointing in the Arc subsequently, made an impressive return to action, travelling well throughout and showing a smart turn of foot off a fairly steady gallop. While he stays further, he is clearly not short of speed either, and defying a Group 1 penalty in such style marks him down as a colt to follow in the big middle-distance races this season. Shirocco won this race by a similar distance last season under a Group 1 penalty, before going on to win the Coronation Cup at Epsom, and this lad is likely to take plenty of beating when he tries to follow suit. He was lightly raced and inexperienced when a highly creditable seventh in the Derby last year but is much more the finished article now. (op 2-1 tchd 11-4 in a place)
Admiral's Cruise(USA) had more to do than on his reappearance in the John Porter, but he ran as though needing the outing that day and his performance here suggests he improved a little for that race. He reversed form with Mighty on 4lb better terms, but found the winner was in a different league to him. He might find a little Listed or Group 3 race this season, but he does not look up to this level. Although entered in the Hardwicke Stakes, his trainer believes the five-year-old has the speed to drop back to 1m2f. (op 7-2)
Mighty, who put up a career-best effort in the John Porter last time, ran to a similar level here, although he once again enjoyed the run of the race, this time in front. He set a steady early pace and kept on after being headed, and he certainly looks up to winning a minor Pattern contest somewhere. The Melbourne Cup could be his long-term aim. (op 8-1)
Papal Bull, from a stable that traditionally does well with its older horses, has progressed physically over the winter, but whether he has gone the right way mentally is another question. His season tailed off somewhat after he won the King Edward VII Stakes last season, and he looked less than enthusiastic under pressure on this reappearance. He has the talent, and should come on for this run, but whether he can be trusted remains to be seen. (tchd 11-4 in a place)
Linda's Lad did not really go on after winning the Lingfield Derby Trial last season but was representing last year's winning stable and looked to have a fine chance at the weights on his best form. He was well supported on course, but was disappointing, and perhaps the steady early pace and/or quick ground were against him. (op 6-1)

1496 STAN JAMES 1000 GUINEAS STKS (GROUP 1) (FILLIES) 1m
3:10 (3:16) (Class 1) 3-Y-O
£198,730 (£75,320; £37,695; £18,795; £9,415; £4,725) **Stalls** Centre

Form RPR
611- **1** **Finsceal Beo (IRE)**[204] 5966 3-9-0 KJManning 8 121+
(J S Bolger, Ire) *lw: racd stands' side: chsd ldrs: led over 2f out: rdn out* **5/4**[1]
1-1 **2** 2 1/2 **Arch Swing (USA)**[29] 946 3-9-0 MJKinane 19 114+
(John M Oxx, Ire) *gd sort: lw: racd centre: chsd ldr: jnd stands' side over 4f out: rdn to chse wnr over 1f out: hung lft: no imp* **10/1**
011- **3** 1 1/4 **Simply Perfect**[225] 5522 3-9-0 112 JMurtagh 10 112
(J Noseda) *lw: s.i.s: hdwy and bmpd over 6f out: rdn and swtchd lft over 2f out: styd on same pce ins fnl f* **9/1**[3]
012- **4** 1 1/2 **Treat**[225] 5522 3-9-0 109 JamieSpencer 14 108
(M R Channon) *racd stands' side: trckd ldrs: rdn over 2f out: no ex fnl f* **14/1**
11-2 **5** *nk* **Indian Ink (IRE)**[15] 1146 3-9-0 111 RichardHughes 13 109+
(R Hannon) *racd stands' side: hld up: hdwy over 2f out: nt clr run over 1f out: sn rdn: styd on same pce* **17/2**[2]
3-1 **6** 1 **Yaqeen**[17] 1105 3-9-0 87 RHills 3 107+
(M A Jarvis) *lw: racd stands' side: hld up: hdwy over 3f out: hmpd and lost pl over 2f out: swtchd rt over 1f out: styd on ins fnl f* **12/1**
50-1 **7** 1/2 **Scarlet Runner**[18] 1096 3-9-0 110 KerrinMcEvoy 9 105+
(J L Dunlop) *racd stands' side: chsd ldr: led over 6f out: rdn and hdd over 2f out: wknd ins fnl f* **14/1**
23-0 **8** 1 **Puggy (IRE)**[15] 1146 3-9-0 102 (t) SPasquier 5 102+
(R A Kvisla) *racd stands' side: hld up: hmpd 6f out: swtchd rt and hdwy over 2f out: rdn whn stmbld wl over 1f out: no imp fnl f* **150/1**
0-20 **9** 3/4 **Satulagi (USA)**[80] 476 3-9-0 StephenDonohoe 1 100
(J S Moore) *racd stands' side: hld up: nt clr run over 2f out: styd on ins fnl f: nvr nrr* **200/1**
52-3 **10** 1 **Theann**[29] 946 3-9-0 CSoumillon 12 98
(A P O'Brien, Ire) *neat: s.i.s: hld up: hdwy over 2f out: sn rdn: wknd ins fnl f* **20/1**
2-0 **11** 1 3/4 **Cartimandua**[15] 1146 3-9-0 JimmyFortune 2 94
(E S McMahon) *hld up in tch: swtchd rt and hdwy over 3f out: wknd over 1f out* **200/1**
141- **12** 3 1/2 **Sweet Lilly**[202] 6010 3-9-0 102 DarrylHolland 21 86
(M R Channon) *lw: racd centre: chsd ldrs: jnd stands' side over 4f out: rdn over 2f out: hung lft and wknd over 1f out* **33/1**
10-6 **13** 2 1/2 **Vital Statistics**[18] 1095 3-9-0 106 KDarley 22 80
(D R C Elsworth) *lw: racd centre: hld up: rdn over 2f out: n.d* **100/1**
1-50 **14** 2 1/2 **Princess Valerina**[16] 1124 3-9-0 84 MichaelHills 18 74
(B W Hills) *lw: racd centre: led that gp tl merged w stands' side gp over 4f out: rdn over 2f out: wknd over 1f out* **250/1**
2-15 **15** 1 1/2 **Barshiba (IRE)**[18] 1096 3-9-0 95 JohnEgan 15 71
(D R C Elsworth) *racd stands' side: hld up: hmpd over 6f out: hdwy over 4f out: wknd over 2f out* **40/1**
2-00 **16** *nk* **Darrfonah (IRE)**[15] 1146 3-9-0 106 (b[1]) C-PLemaire 23 70
(C E Brittain) *racd centre: hld up: jnd centre gp over 4f out: rdn over 2f out: n.d* **100/1**
1-0 **17** 2 1/2 **Fantasy Parkes**[18] 1096 3-9-0 90 NCallan 4 64+
(K A Ryan) *led stands' side: hdd over 6f out: hmpd and wknd over 2f out* **150/1**
311- **18** 1/2 **Miss Beatrix (IRE)**[229] 5466 3-9-0 DPMcDonogh 7 63
(Kevin Prendergast, Ire) *neat: racd stands' side: hld up: a in rr* **12/1**
10-4 **19** 2 1/2 **Kaseema (USA)**[18] 1096 3-9-0 97 MartinDwyer 17 57
(Sir Michael Stoute) *racd centre: chsd ldrs: jnd stands' side over 4f out: rdn and wknd 3f out* **20/1**
20-3 **20** *nk* **Blue Rocket (IRE)**[18] 1096 3-9-0 98 OPeslier 11 57
(T J Pitt) *b.hind: racd stands' side: chsd ldrs over 5f* **33/1**
311- **21** 1 1/4 **Selinka**[218] 5672 3-9-0 98 EddieAhern 16 54
(R Hannon) *racd stands' side: hld up: hmpd over 6f out: hdwy over 4f out: wknd and eased over 2f out* **100/1**

1m 34.94s (-4.43) **Going Correction** -0.15s/f (Firm) **21** Ran SP% **126.3**
Speed ratings (Par 110): 116,113,112,110,110 109,108,107,107,106 104,100,98,95,94 94,91,91,88,88 87
CSF £13.13 CT £94.23 TOTE £3.10: £2.00, £2.80, £3.70; EX 18.20 Trifecta £140.00 Pool £2,754.19. - 13.96 winning units..
Owner M A Ryan **Bred** Rathberry Stud **Trained** Coolcullen, Co Carlow
■ Jim Bolger's second British Classic, after Jet Ski Lady in the 1991 Oaks, and Kevin Manning's first.
■ Stewards' Enquiry : J Murtagh three-day ban: careless riding (May 17-18,20)

FOCUS
A very strong Guineas featuring four individual Group 1 winners and missing only Sander Camillo (in season) from the main ante-post fancies. The winning time was 0.34 seconds faster than the previous day's 2000 Guineas and, although the wind was behind and the ground looked a shade quicker, this was still a very decent time for the fillies' Classic. Finsceal Beo has been rated much the best 1000 Guineas winner since Cape Verdi and the form looks bombproof based on the performances of those that followed her home.

NOTEBOOK

Finsceal Beo(IRE), last year's Champion two-year-old filly, had an outstanding chance on the form of her autumn successes at Longchamp and at this track, and this performance confirmed that she has retained that ability and developed into a top-class three-year-old. Always travelling well close to the pace on the stands' side, her rider never had a moment's worry and she drew clear to win easily. She recorded the fastest time in the history of both the 1000 and 2000 Guineas, and it was all the more remarkable as she appeared to do it without having a hard race. Her immediate programme is likely to take her to the Irish Guineas and Coronation Stakes, while a run in the Pretty Polly Stakes will see her step up in trip to 1m2f. This run suggests she should not have too much trouble getting that distance in time. (op 6-4)

Arch Swing(USA) ◆, who has always been well regarded, did not come to this race on the back of an ideal preparation, having had a setback after her workmanlike reappearance in the Guineas trial at Leopardstown last month. In the circumstances, she deserves plenty of credit for finishing second to a genuine champion, especially as she was drawn out wide and raced up the centre of the track for most of the way, while the winner had the rail to help. She got the trip well, clearly loves fast ground and is well up to winning at this level. A rematch with the winner in the Irish 1000 at the Curragh is likely. (op 12-1)

Simply Perfect, the Fillies' Mile winner, has always been considered a notch below Sander Camillo in her yard, but has the form in the book in contrast to her absent stablemate. A tough, consistent two-year-old, she has not grown much over the winter, but she clearly retains her ability. Cut to 10-1 for the Oaks, her breeding suggests that she may well struggle to get 1m4f, and the French equivalent over a furlong and a half shorter might be a more suitable target. (tchd 17-2)

Treat, who finished a length and a half behind Simply Perfect in the Fillies' Mile, ran to the pound against her old rival. Now around 16-1 for the Oaks, she is another who has stamina question marks hanging over her based on her pedigree, but her trainer has always seen her as a middle-distance filly in the making and, being by Barathea, softer ground ought to suit her. As a result the Prix de Diane may be a tempting alternative. (op 16-1)

Indian Ink(IRE), last year's Cheveley Park winner, had run a very respectable trial in the Fred Darling but there was both a slight stamina query and a worry that another race on fast ground would not suit her. In the event she got the mile well and ran a solid race, but it would not be a surprise at all to see her do better in the Irish Guineas if the ground has a bit of cut in it. (op 9-1)

Yaqeen ◆ had only won a maiden over 7f here 17 days earlier, but her trainer clearly holds her in high regard and Richard Hills preferred her to the more experienced Kaseema. She ran a blinder for one so inexperienced despite not getting the run of the race, and should improve for running in Group 1 company for the first time. The Coronation Stakes looks an ideal target for her. (tchd 14-1)

Scarlet Runner, the Nell Gwyn winner, seemed to confirm worries beforehand that she would struggle to see out the extra furlong. While she obviously gets 7f the bigger prizes are mainly over 6f and a mile so it is likely that she will have to go down the sprinting route now. (op 16-1)

Puggy(IRE) had an excuse in the Fred Darling as she was found to have an allergy infection in her throat, and on her form from last autumn when a six-and-a-half-length third to Finsceal Beo in the Rockfel, albeit in receipt of 4lb, she was fully deserving of her place in this line-up. Her price suggested she was a no-hoper but, in being beaten eight lengths by the Irish filly, this time at level weights, her performance is actually another that helps give the form a solid look. Not that happy on this quick ground, she will prefer a little cut in future. (op 100-1)

Satulagi(USA) could only finish in mid-division in the UAE 1000 Guineas and looked up against it in this company, so she was not disgraced in the circumstances. Despite not getting the clearest of runs, she stayed on well in the closing stages, albeit on the favoured stands' rail, and she might yet make her mark at minor Pattern level this season. (op 150-1)

Theann only has a maiden win to her name but she mixed it in good company on a number of occasions last year and had shaped with promise on her reappearance in the Guineas trial at Leopardstown. She stayed on well that day in a slowly-run race, but her pedigree - she is out of Temple Stakes/King's Stand Stakes winner Cassandra Go - suggested she might struggle to get the mile. That worry seemed to be borne out.

Cartimandua, whose Fred Darling performance suggested that she had plenty to find in this company, was outclassed but did not run badly. She is still a maiden and should not have too much trouble finding a race at a lower level. (op 250-1)

Sweet Lilly, who won a Listed race at Pontefract on her final start at two, was poorly drawn and ended up racing more or less widest of all for much of the way. She is not up to this grade, but should be competitive back in Listed company.

Vital Statistics is not bred to get a mile and is likely to appreciate dropping back to 6f this term.

Princess Valerina made the running up the centre of the track for much of the way, but did not see the trip out. She came into the race with a rating of 84 and sprint handicaps could be her game. (op 200-1)

Barshiba(IRE) found this all too much at this stage of her career. (tchd 33-1)

Darrfonah(IRE), who had blinkers on for the first time, was runner-up to Finsceal Beo in the Marcel Boussac last year but has not shown a great deal since. She is a middle-distance filly on pedigree, though, and it would be folly to discount improvement when she steps up to a mile and a half. It would not be a surprise if her next start is in the Oaks, and she could well run a better race there than she did here.

Fantasy Parkes got hampered after being headed, accentuating her beaten distance, but she looks like a sprinter.

Miss Beatrix(IRE), who won at Group 1 level last term, does not appear to have grown much from two to three and there must be a major doubt as to whether she has trained on.

Kaseema(USA), who sweated up beforehand, reared and was slowly away from the stalls. Her rider later suggested that she may have hurt herself in the incident, and she certainly failed to confirm the promise of either her Rockfel or Nell Gwyn runs. She was being ridden along from halfway and disappointed, but the worry beforehand had been that she needed more time, and that may well be the case. She is likely to prove better in due course and will get 1m2f later in the season. (op 16-1)

Blue Rocket(IRE), a half-sister to Halmahera, is another who is likely to do better back over sprint distances.

Selinka, who won a Listed race here last autumn, may have preferred easier ground, like many of her sire's progeny.

1497 STAN JAMES PALACE HOUSE STKS (GROUP 3) 5f

3:45 (3:48) (Class 1) 3-Y-O+

£28,390 (£10,760; £5,385; £2,685; £1,345; £675) **Stalls** Low

Form				RPR
-401	**1**		**Tax Free (IRE)**[15] 1159 5-8-13 110 ..... AdrianTNicholls 4 (D Nicholls) *sn pushed along in rr: hdwy over 3f out: rdn to chse ldr over 1f out: sn hung rt: styd on to ld post* **11/8**[1]	113
210-	**2**	*shd*	**Peace Offering (IRE)**[196] 6127 7-8-13 103 ..... PaulHanagan 9 (D Nicholls) *led: swtchd to stands' rail over 3f out: rdn over 1f out: hdd post* **14/1**	113
2-22	**3**	½	**Bond City (IRE)**[15] 1159 5-8-13 101 ..... LDettori 8 (G R Oldroyd) *hld up: rdn 1/2-way: hdwy over 1f out: ev ch ins fnl f: unable qck nr fin* **9/1**	111
062-	**4**	¾	**Presto Shinko (IRE)**[183] 6335 6-9-2 108 ..... (p) RichardHughes 6 (R Hannon) *lw: hld up: swtchd rt over 1f out: r.o wl ins fnl f: nrst fin* **7/1**[3]	111
6604	**5**	¾	**Celtic Mill**[15] 1159 9-8-13 103 ..... NCallan 7 (D W Barker) *lw: chsd ldrs: rdn 1/2-way: styd on same pce ins fnl f* **12/1**	106
F0-0	**6**	¾	**Tabaret**[15] 1159 4-8-13 98 ..... DeanMcKeown 5 (R M Whitaker) *lw: chsd ldrs: rdn and nt clr run over 1f out: styd on same pce* **20/1**	103
-302	**7**	5	**Bonus (IRE)**[43] 762 7-8-13 96 ..... (t) NickyMackay 1 (G A Butler) *hld up: plld hrd: nt clr run fr over 1f out: nvr able to chal: b.b.v* **12/1**	98+
-253	**8**	*nk*	**Paradise Isle**[17] 1102 6-8-10 104 ..... KDarley 3 (C F Wall) *s.i.s: sn chsng ldrs: hmpd over 3f out: rdn and ev ch over 1f out: sn hmpd and wknd* **5/1**[2]	81+
4-60	**9**	*nk*	**Angus Newz**[36] 847 4-8-10 90 ..... (v) FrancisNorton 2 (M Quinn) *chsd ldrs over 3f* **33/1**	80
634-	**10**	4	**Biniou (IRE)**[217] 5712 4-8-13 110 ..... EddieAhern 10 (R M H Cowell) *h.d.w: bit bkwd: s.i.s: hld up: wknd wl over 1f out* **10/1**	68

58.29 secs (-2.18) **Going Correction** -0.15s/f (Firm) **10** Ran SP% **120.1**

Speed ratings (Par 113):111,110,110,108,107 106,98,97,97,91

CSF £24.60 TOTE £2.10: £1.20, £5.30, £2.00; EX 30.00 Trifecta £571.40 Pool £804.88. - 1.00 winning unit..

Owner Ian Hewitson **Bred** Denis & Mrs Teresa Bergin **Trained** Sessay, N Yorks

■ A 1-2 for David Nicholls.

■ Stewards' Enquiry : Paul Hanagan two-day ban: careless riding (May 22-23)

FOCUS

Not a strong Group 3, and the winner has been rated a length off his best. The form looks sound enough though, rated through the second, third and sixth.

NOTEBOOK

Tax Free(IRE), who was beaten by the draw in this race last year on his seasonal reappearance, had the benefit of previous outings this time around and had a fine chance at the weights to boot. He did not win as easily as the figures suggested he should, but nevertheless he responded well to pressure, albeit edging right while doing so, to get up narrowly and record his first Group-race victory. He needs a stiff finish at this trip and he will get that in the Temple Stakes at Sandown, his next intended start, but ultimately he looks to be crying out for a return to 6f, and the Golden Jubilee and July Cup are likely to be on his agenda later in the season. (op 7-4 tchd 15-8 in a place)

Peace Offering(IRE), who showed great early speed to get over from his wide draw to the stands' side and make the running, is a real 5f specialist and made his stablemate, who gets further, pull out all the stops to get by him. He may well have improved over the winter and is entitled to come on for this reappearance. He will go to France next in search of Pattern-race success. (op 16-1)

Bond City(IRE), who has quite a poor strike-rate for a gelding of his class, finished runner-up to Tax Free at Thirsk last time when in receipt of 10lb, so he did not run badly at the revised weights even if, as looks likely, the winner was not quite at his best. He has a good record at Epsom, having won once and placed twice in four outings over the minimum trip there, and the Dash on Derby day, a race in which he was second at a big price last year, looks a likely target again. (op 12-1)

Presto Shinko(IRE) had plenty on his plate as he was the only penalised runner in the line-up, he was making his seasonal reappearance and he was running over a trip short of his best. He ran creditably in the end, staying on at the finish as one would expect of a 6f specialist, and could be in for a good season. (op 13-2 tchd 6-1)

Celtic Mill, missing the usual headgear, could not get to the front with Peace Offering in the field, but he kept on well for a respectable fifth, and showed he still has the ability to pick up a little conditions race or Listed race somewhere when he is allowed to dictate.

Tabaret, who chased home Tax Free on the 'wrong' side in this race last year, had run with promise on his reappearance at Thirsk behind his old rival when not getting a clear run, but he was another who was 10lb worse off at the weights this time. He got unbalanced in the dip and once again failed to get a clear run, but he is the type who will pop up at a price one day. (op 16-1)

Bonus(IRE) did not settle and bled during the race, so he had his excuses. Official explanation: trainer said gelding bled from the nose (op 14-1)

Paradise Isle, denied the lead by Peace Offering, was hampered in the closing stages by the eventual winner, but she was beating a retreat at the time. She needs 6f to be seen at her best, and will be a bigger threat when back racing against her own sex. (op 11-2)

Angus Newz, who had the lowest official rating in the field, is another who will be more effective racing in weaker fillies-only Pattern races.

Biniou(IRE), who has joined a new stable, was fourth in the Abbaye on his final start last year and looked to hold a leading chance on that performance. His form before that was not as strong, though, and he had not run on ground this fast before, so it was understandable when he was fairly weak in the market beforehand. Held up and towards the outside throughout, he was not given a hard ride by Ahern in a lost cause, and could well do better in time. (op 9-1 tchd 11-1)

1498 STAN JAMES MAIDEN STKS 5f

4:20 (4:22) (Class 2) 2-Y-O

£9,715 (£2,890; £1,444; £721) **Stalls** Low

Form				RPR
	1		**Achilles Of Troy (IRE)**[15] 1170 2-9-3 ..... CSoumillon 5 (A P O'Brien, Ire) *w'like: mde all: shkn up over 1f out: r.o wl* **7/4**[1]	99+
3	**2**	5	**Party In The Park**[16] 1123 2-9-3 ..... RichardHughes 6 (R Hannon) *lw: chsd wnr: rdn and hung rt over 1f out: sn outpcd* **11/4**[2]	79
5	**3**	½	**Mansii**[16] 1123 2-9-3 ..... EddieAhern 2 (C E Brittain) *chsd ldrs: rdn over 1f out: styng on same pce whn edgd rt ins fnl f* **12/1**	77
	4	¾	**Major Willy** 2-9-3 ..... KerrinMcEvoy 3 (W Jarvis) *gd sort: bit bkwd: chsd ldrs over 3f* **8/1**	74
	5	1½	**Kinout (IRE)** 2-9-3 ..... NCallan 7 (K A Ryan) *cmpt: chsd ldrs: rdn over 1f out: wknd fnl f* **6/1**[3]	68
	6	7	**American Art (IRE)** 2-9-3 ..... MichaelHills 4 (B W Hills) *w'like: leggy: s.i.s and wnt rt s: outpcd* **11/1**	40
	7	10	**Arab League (IRE)** 2-9-3 ..... KDarley 11 (M Johnston) *cmpt: scope: chsd ldrs: rdn over 3f out: sn outpcd* **14/1**	—
	8	¾	**Black Duke** 2-9-3 ..... JimmyFortune 8 (M G Quinlan) *w'like: scope: sn outpcd: bhd whn hung rt over 1f out* **25/1**	—
	9	5	**Patsymartin** 2-9-3 ..... BrettDoyle 10 (J Ryan) *w'like: str: bit bkwd: s.s: outpcd* **50/1**	—

59.14 secs (-1.33) **Going Correction** -0.15s/f (Firm) **9** Ran SP% **116.9**

Speed ratings (Par 99):104,96,95,94,91 80,64,63,55

CSF £6.62 TOTE £2.40: £1.60, £1.60, £2.90; EX 5.90.

Owner M Tabor, D Smith & Mrs John Magnier **Bred** Gigginstown House Stud **Trained** Ballydoyle, Co Tipperary

FOCUS

A decent time for a race of its type and a massively impressive winner, who put up easily the best 2-y-o performance of the season so far.

NOTEBOOK

Achilles Of Troy(IRE) ◆, who ran distinctly green on his debut at Naas in April, was all the rage in the betting ring and duly rewarded his supporters with a most taking display. He was smartly into his stride, showing plenty of speed, and it was clear from halfway that he was not going to be headed at any stage. Value for further than the winning margin, he looked right at home on the quick surface and left the impression he would have little trouble with an extra furlong in due course. His powerful connections later reported that he is a likely candidate for the Coventry Stakes at Royal Ascot next month and, at this stage, he looks the one to beat there, for this was easily the best juvenile performance of the season so far. (op 9-4 tchd 6-4 and 5-2 in places)

The Form Book, Raceform Ltd, Compton, RG20 6NL

Party In The Park, third on debut at Newbury last time, was representing a stable with a decent past record in this event. He confirmed the promise of his debut run and did little wrong in defeat, but was never a serious threat to the impressive winner. He should soon be winning and helps to set the level of this form. (op 5-2 tchd 3-1)
Mansii showed the benefit of his Newbury debut when behind the runner-up and finished a lot closer to that rival this time around. He left the impression he will appreciate another furlong in due course and has a future. (tchd 14-1)
Major Willy ♦, a 60,000euros purchase, fared best of the newcomers and caught the eye doing his best work from halfway. He ought to learn a deal from this debut experience and really should appreciate a stiffer test in due course. (op 7-1)
Kinout(IRE), who cost £62,000 and whose pedigree suggests a mix of speed and stamina, proved popular in the betting ring and showed up well enough before tiring on the climb for home. He should only learn for this experience and is presumably well thought-of by his yard. (op 12-1)
American Art(IRE), a half-brother to six winners at up to 1m4f, proved easy to back and lost any chance with a very sluggish start. He should leave this debut form behind him in time and already looks in need of further. (tchd 10-1)
Black Duke Official explanation: jockey said colt lost its action

1499 STANSPOKER.CO.UK PRETTY POLLY STKS (LISTED RACE) (FILLIES) 1m 2f

4:55 (4:55) (Class 1) 3-Y-O

£17,034 (£6,456; £3,231; £1,611; £807; £405) **Stalls** Low

Form RPR
1- **1** **Dalvina**[192] [6186] 3-8-12 90 JamieSpencer 8 107+
(E A L Dunlop) *racd centre: hld up: jnd stands' side 4f out: sn chsng ldr: rdn to ld over 1f out: edgd lft: styd on wl* **5/2**[1]
150- **2** *6* **Sudoor**[204] [5966] 3-9-3 102 RHills 1 101
(J L Dunlop) *lw: led stands' side: rdn and hdd over 1f out: styd on same pce* **5/2**[1]
24-1 **3** *1 1/4* **La Spezia (IRE)**[37] [836] 3-8-12 75 HayleyTurner 3 93
(M L W Bell) *racd stands' side: chsd ldr tl rdn over 3f out: swtchd rt over 1f out: styd on same pce* **11/1**
2- **4** *5* **Loulwa (IRE)**[197] [6099] 3-8-12 (t) LDettori 4 84
(J Noseda) *racd stands' side: hld up: rdn over 2f out: sn wknd* **9/2**[2]
14-2 **5** *2 1/2* **Fiumicino**[36] [838] 3-8-12 86 DarryllHolland 5 79
(M R Channon) *led centre trio: rdn over 3f out: wknd over 2f out* **8/1**
53-5 **6** *3 1/2* **Fascinatin Rhythm**[16] [1127] 3-8-12 82 KDarley 7 72
(V Smith) *chsd ldr centre tl wknd over 2f out* **25/1**
02- **7** *47* **Silk Dress (IRE)**[232] [5394] 3-8-12 RichardHughes 2 —
(John Joseph Murphy, Ire) *lt-f: neat: racd stands' side: hld up: wknd fnl 3f: eased: fin lame* **5/1**[3]

2m 3.27s (-2.44) **Going Correction** -0.15s/f (Firm) 7 Ran SP% **115.3**
Speed ratings (Par 104):103,98,97,93,91 88,50
CSF £8.86 TOTE £3.00: £2.50, £2.10; EX 9.90.
Owner St Albans Bloodstock LLP **Bred** Normandie Stud Ltd **Trained** Newmarket, Suffolk

FOCUS
Difficult form to assess accurately, with much depending upon how good the third turns out to be, but it has provisionally been taken at face value. Dalvina put up a very taking performance and looks well worth her place in the Oaks.

NOTEBOOK
Dalvina ♦, a cosy winner on her debut at Lingfield last October, showed she has wintered very well and ran out an impressive scorer on this big step up in class - emulating her stable's dual Oaks winner Ouija Board, who won this race by the same margin back in 2004. Having been patiently ridden early on, she moved up to the leaders full of running nearing the 2f marker and once her rider put the gun to her head she responded by coming right away from her rivals inside the final furlong. Not surprisingly she was immediately promoted to near the top of the betting in the ante-post lists for the Oaks next month, and on this evidence that is fully justified, as this late-developing filly is clearly still open to a lot of further improvement and looked better the further she went. She is now likely to take the Ouija Board route and head straight to Epsom, where her trainer does not anticipate any problems with the undulating course. (op 11-4 tchd 9-4)
Sudoor, who appeared unsuited by the soft ground in the Rockfel on her final outing last term, proved solid in the betting ring despite not looking to have quite come to herself yet this term and having to shoulder a 5lb penalty for her Listed success. She was positively ridden on this step up in trip and had her chance, but was eventually put firmly in her place by the clear-cut winner. She is entitled to improve for this seasonal return and was not disgraced at the weights. (op 11-4)
La Spezia(IRE), off the mark on her seasonal debut at Wolverhampton in March, posted a clear personal-best effort and an official rating of 75 clearly underestimates her. While her proximity at the finish does raise a slight doubt over this form, she is a well-bred filly and looks an improver over this sort of trip on fast ground. (op 14-1)
Loulwa(IRE), a promising runner-up over 7f at Lingfield on her sole outing last year, was on edge in the preliminaries ahead this three-year-old and turf debut yet still met support in the betting ring. She eventually proved disappointing, dropping out without posing a threat from off the pace and this must dent any hopes her connections held that she may have been potentially Oaks class. It should also be noted that despite being by Montjeu there is plenty of speed on her dam's side and her stamina is also yet to be proven. No doubt she will benefit for the outing, however, and is a very good-looking filly, so it is too soon to write her off just yet. (op 6-1 tchd 7-1)
Fiumicino, the Masaka second, was positively ridden and ran below that form, appearing a non-stayer on this step up in trip. (op 10-1)
Fascinatin Rhythm, a maiden having her first outing in this grade, was never really in the hunt and needs her sights lowering again. She ought to win her maiden on one of the smaller tracks.
Silk Dress(IRE), second to Arch Swing at the Curragh in Group 3 company on her final outing at two, was eased right off shortly after being asked for her effort from off the pace and was later found to have finished lame. Official explanation: vet said filly finished lame (op 7-2)

1500 STAN JAMES TELEBETTING H'CAP 7f

5:30 (5:30) (Class 2) (0-100,93) 3-Y-O **£12,954** (£3,854; £1,926; £962) **Stalls** Low

Form RPR
11 **1** **Regal Parade**[67] [584] 3-8-11 **86** KDarley 1 97+
(M Johnston) *chsd ldrs: rdn to ld 1f out: r.o* **4/1**[1]
31- **2** *2* **Miss Lucifer (FR)**[191] [6200] 3-8-10 **85** MichaelHills 2 91
(B W Hills) *lw: sn led: rdn and hdd 1f out: styd on same pce* **5/1**[3]
103- **3** *1/2* **Furnace (IRE)**[221] [5624] 3-9-1 **90** JamieSpencer 3 94
(M L W Bell) *lw: dwlt: hld up: rdn and hung rt fr 1/2-way: hdwy over 2f out: styd on u.p* **4/1**[1]
23-1 **4** *hd* **Hazzard County (USA)**[37] [826] 3-8-4 **79** MartinDwyer 7 83
(D M Simcock) *chsd ldrs: rdn over 1f out: styd on same pce ins fnl f* **7/1**
3-02 **5** *nk* **Aahayson**[18] [1099] 3-9-1 **90** PatCosgrave 9 93
(K R Burke) *chsd ldrs: rdn over 2f out: styd on same pce fnl f* **9/2**[2]
04-0 **6** *1 1/2* **Lunces Lad (IRE)**[16] [1124] 3-8-9 **84** DarryllHolland 6 83
(M R Channon) *hld up in tch: racd keenly: outpcd 1/2-way: hdwy over 1f out: nt trble ldrs* **8/1**
421- **7** *4* **Whazzis**[173] [6481] 3-8-10 **85** KerrinMcEvoy 10 73
(W J Haggas) *b.hind: chsd ldrs over 5f* **13/2**
04-0 **8** *1/2* **Mubaashir (IRE)**[16] [1124] 3-9-4 **93** StephenDonohoe 5 80
(E A L Dunlop) *chsd ldrs 5f* **33/1**
10-0 **9** *15* **Don't Panic (IRE)**[18] [1097] 3-9-1 **90** EddieAhern 4 36
(P W Chapple-Hyam) *s.i.s: hld up: wknd over 2f out* **11/1**
315- **10** *4* **Apollo Five**[297] [3455] 3-8-3 **83** WilliamBuick(5) 8 19
(D J Coakley) *bhd fnl 4f* **33/1**

1m 24.1s (-2.40) **Going Correction** -0.15s/f (Firm) **10** Ran SP% **126.0**
Speed ratings (Par 105):107,104,104,103,103 101,97,96,79,75
CSF £26.36 CT £85.52 TOTE £4.10: £2.20, £1.90, £1.80; EX 14.30 Place 6 £23.16, Place 5 £8.36..
Owner Sheikh Mohammed **Bred** Highclere Stud And Harry Herbert **Trained** Middleham Moor, N Yorks

FOCUS
This is usually a strong handicap and is expected to prove good form. The front four were all unexposed and the winner looked potentially Group class.

NOTEBOOK
Regal Parade ♦, 7lb higher than when scoring at Southwell, made it three wins from as many starts with a ready effort on this turf debut. He still looked green through most of the contest, but he relished the rising finish and had little trouble with the quick surface. A typically progressive colt from his leading stable, he promises to do even better as he steps up to a mile and it would not be a surprise to see him at Royal Ascot next month, where the Britannia Handicap looks a likely option. In the long term, he could well turn out to be a lot better than a handicapper. (op 7-2 tchd 9-2)
Miss Lucifer(FR), off the mark at this course on her second and final outing last year, had her chance from the front yet could not stay with the winner when it mattered. She kept to her task gamely once headed, however, and had no trouble with the extra furlong or the quick surface. She remains progressive. (op 9-2)
Furnace(IRE) ultimately shaped as though this seasonal bow was needed and he was doing all of his best work towards the finish. He looks to be crying out for the step up to a mile now and it is unlikely that we have yet to see the best of him. It may also be that he prefers an easier surface. (op 7-2 tchd 3-1)
Hazzard County(USA), popular in the betting ring for this handicap debut, is a consistent sort yet he did not help his cause by racing too freely through the early parts. He can do better yet, but can expect a rise in the weights again after this. (op 12-1)
Aahayson, up in trip, came into this in good heart and again ran his race, just leaving the impression he is held by the Handicapper now. He is a decent benchmark for the form. (op 9-1)
Whazzis, the subject of market support, looked uneasy on the quick ground on this three-year-old debut and failed to find any more from the 2f pole. (op 14-1)
T/Jkpt: £2,718.90 to a £1 stake. Pool: £26,807.00. 7.00 winning tickets. T/Plt: £19.50 to a £1 stake. Pool: £156,221.75. 5,823.35 winning tickets. T/Qpdt: £3.20 to a £1 stake. Pool: £7,944.10. 1,796.65 winning tickets. CR

SALISBURY (R-H)

Sunday, May 6

OFFICIAL GOING: Good to firm (good in places)
Wind: Virtually nil

1501 TOTEPLACEPOT MAIDEN STKS 6f

1:45 (1:45) (Class 4) 3-Y-O+ **£4,857** (£1,445; £722; £360) **Stalls** High

Form RPR
22-3 **1** **Kyle (IRE)**[22] [1037] 3-9-0 75 PatDobbs 7 81
(R Hannon) *a.p: led over 2f out: sn rdn: hdd over 1f out: rallied gamely ins fnl f: led fnl 50yds* **2/1**[2]
24- **2** *3/4* **Prince Of Delphi**[330] [2458] 4-9-10 DaneO'Neill 6 82
(H Candy) *trckd ldrs: rdn to ld narrowly over 1f out: no ex whn hdd fnl 50yds* **11/8**[1]
65- **3** *3* **Zeeuw (IRE)**[315] [2899] 3-9-0 TPO'Shea 2 69+
(D J Coakley) *in tch: rdn over 2f out: kpt on ins fnl f* **13/2**[3]
0 **4** *1/2* **Punching**[15] [1143] 3-9-0 StephenCarson 9 67
(Eve Johnson Houghton) *trckd ldrs: rdn over 3f out: kpt on same pce fnl f* **14/1**
5 *1 1/4* **Spiffing (IRE)**[195] [6151] 3-9-0 SebSanders 10 63
(R M Beckett) *led tl over 2f out: sn rdn: fdd ins fnl f* **8/1**
04 **6** *nk* **Massams Lane**[10] [1267] 3-9-0 JamesDoyle 8 62
(P S McEntee) *towards rr: rdn over 3f out: sme late prog: n.d* **25/1**
7 *6* **Abtak (IRE)**[643] [4012] 7-9-2 NeilChalmers(3) 4 41
(P Burgoyne) *towards rr: rdn and no imp fr 3f out* **100/1**
8 *1/2* **Lithaam (IRE)** 3-8-7 BarrySavage(7) 5 42
(J M Bradley) *a towards rr* **50/1**
0- **9** *2* **My Silver Monarch (IRE)**[213] [5773] 3-8-9 MickyFenton 1 30
(H S Howe) *s.i.s: hung lft and a in rr* **80/1**

1m 14.2s (-0.78) **Going Correction** -0.075s/f (Good)
WFA 3 from 4yo+ 10lb **9** Ran SP% **114.6**
Speed ratings (Par 105):102,101,97,96,94 94,86,85,82
CSF £4.97 TOTE £2.70: £1.10, £1.30, £2.50; EX 4.40.
Owner Noodles Racing **Bred** John Cullinan **Trained** East Everleigh, Wilts

FOCUS
Just an ordinary maiden, but the time compared favourably to that of the following 6f handicap. The winner is the best guide, with the second up 13lb on his previous form.
My Silver Monarch(IRE) Official explanation: jockey said filly hung left-handed

1502 TOTESPORT.COM H'CAP 6f

2:15 (2:16) (Class 2) (0-100,97) 3-Y-O

£12,464 (£3,732; £1,866; £934; £466; £234) **Stalls** High

Form RPR
160- **1** **Lipocco**[232] [5372] 3-8-12 **91** SebSanders 2 102
(R M Beckett) *mde all: kpt on gamely: drvn out* **5/1**[3]
211- **2** *1* **Oldjoesaid**[216] [5731] 3-8-12 **91** DaneO'Neill 4 99
(H Candy) *racd keenly trcking wnr: rdn to chal 2f out: kpt on but a hld ins fnl f* **11/4**[1]
0-20 **3** *nk* **El Bosque (IRE)**[16] [1124] 3-8-10 **89** JimCrowley 6 96
(B R Millman) *chsd ldrs: rdn over 2f out: styd on ins fnl f* **13/2**
6-35 **4** *3* **Dazed And Amazed**[4] [1394] 3-8-9 **95** HaddenFrost(7) 1 92
(R Hannon) *trckd wnr: rdn for effrt over 2f out: kpt on same pce fr over 1f out* **13/2**
150- **5** *1/2* **Alderney (USA)**[218] [5672] 3-9-4 **97** PhilipRobinson 5 93+
(M A Jarvis) *hld up bhd ldrs: n.m.r and snatched up over 4f out: rdn over 2f out: sn one pce* **3/1**[2]
00-4 **6** *2 1/2* **Cav Okay (IRE)**[36] [841] 3-9-2 **95** PatDobbs 3 83
(R Hannon) *hld up bhd ldrs: effrt 2f out: wknd ins fnl f* **16/1**
51-0 **7** *3* **College Scholar (GER)**[18] [1099] 3-8-13 **92** TPO'Shea 7 70
(M R Channon) *a in rr* **6/1**

1m 14.12s (-0.86) **Going Correction** -0.075s/f (Good) **7** Ran SP% **115.2**
Speed ratings (Par 105):102,100,100,96,95 92,88
CSF £19.44 TOTE £6.90: £2.90, £2.50; EX 31.10.

Owner The Anagram Partnership **Bred** C Scott And T Leigh **Trained** Whitsbury, Hants

FOCUS

A decent three-year-old sprint handicap likely to produce its share of winners. The winner dictated and and the third looks the best guide to the form.

NOTEBOOK

Lipocco, 8lb higher than when winning on his handicap debut at two, found the competition a bit too hot on his final couple of outings as a juvenile, but this looked more realistic and he received a fine front-running ride from Sanders to make every yard of the running. He found plenty under pressure when asked for maximum effort and, with connections expecting him to improve for this outing, it would not surprise to see further progress. He may now head for the William Hill Handicap at York. (op 8-1)

Oldjoesaid, who signed-off his juvenile season with a ready victory in a 5f Windsor nursery, had earlier proved his stamina for this distance and looked the one to beat despite the 7lb rise. A shade keen early on, he had every chance, but was never getting past the winner and in the end just held on for second. It is probable he will come on for this and there is every chance he can develop into one of the leading three-year-old sprinters. (op 9-4)

El Bosque(IRE), who found a seventh furlong beyond him in a decent handicap at Newbury recently, had earlier shaped well when second to Ebn Reem at Kempton and this was much more his form. He may need to progress to win off this mark, but there is nothing to suggest he will not be able to. (op 9-1)

Dazed And Amazed has clearly trained on from two to three and this was yet another decent effort by the colt. He gives the impression though that he is a little too high in the weights to be winning at the moment. (op 6-1 tchd 7-1)

Alderney(USA), tried unsuccessfully in Group 2 and then Listed company having won her maiden as a juvenile, was short of room at quite an early stage and then found herself unable to quicken under pressure. She is not going to find things easy off this mark, but rates a little better than the bare result. Official explanation: jockey said filly ran too free (op 9-4)

Cav Okay(IRE), a very speedy juvenile early last season, returned with a reasonable effort over 6f at Kempton but this was not so good and he will probably be of more interest later in the season once he is down in the weights. (op 20-1)

College Scholar(GER), a three-time winner as a juvenile, is believed to need softer ground than this and was always struggling in rear. (op 9-1)

1503 TOTEQUADPOT FILLIES' CONDITIONS STKS — 5f

2:55 (2:55) (Class 3) 2-Y-O — **£6,477** (£1,927; £963; £481) **Stalls** High

Form					RPR
1	**1**		**Cake (IRE)**[22] [1033] 2-8-9 ... PatDobbs 6 (R Hannon) *racd keenly: trckd ldrs: edgd lft and led wl over 1f out: pushed out* **6/5**[1]		82
	2	*1*	**Presto Levanter** 2-8-7 ow1 ... SteveDrowne 3 (R Hannon) *in tch: swtchd lft and hdwy over 1f out: kpt on to go 2nd jst ins fnl f* **10/1**		76+
01	**3**	*¾*	**Baytown Blaze**[34] [890] 2-8-9 ... TPO'Shea 5 (P S McEntee) *sn led: rdn and hdd wl over 1f out: kpt on same pce* **9/1**		75
	4	*2*	**Structura (USA)** 2-8-6 ... PaulDoe 4 (J S Moore) *slowly away: outpcd early in rr: styd on ins fnl f: nvr trbld ldrs* **7/1**[3]		64+
0	**5**	*hd*	**Flying Indian**[16] [1123] 2-8-9 ... LPKeniry 2 (A M Balding) *trckd ldr: rdn and ev ch over 2f out: one pce fnl f* **5/2**[2]		66
	6	*¾*	**Tamara Moon (IRE)** 2-8-6 ... SamHitchcott 1 (M R Channon) *chsd ldrs: rdn and effrt 2f out: wknd 1f out* **14/1**		60

62.55 secs (0.96) **Going Correction** -0.075s/f (Good) — **6** Ran SP% **112.3**

Speed ratings (Par 94):89,87,86,83,82 81

CSF £14.25 TOTE £1.80: £1.90, £2.40; EX 10.20.

Owner Simon Leech **Bred** Carpet Lady Partnership **Trained** East Everleigh, Wilts

FOCUS

Not a race to get overexcited about, but there were one or two nice performances and the race should produce winners. Cake improved on her debut effort, and the runner-up seems sure to come on for this.

NOTEBOOK

Cake(IRE), a ready winner on her debut at Lingfield, looked to have the beating of those who had already raced and it was always likely to be the debutants who posed the biggest threat. Always well positioned, she went on over a furlong out and stuck on strongly, with her stablemate chasing her home best. She is now likely to head to the Queen Mary and goes there as a progressive filly, but stands little realistic chance. (op 6-4)

Presto Levanter, a daughter of Rock Of Gibraltar, is bred to be effective at this sort of distance at this stage and she really got motoring in the final furlong, running on without being able to reel in her stablemate. She is clearly useful and would have to be fancied to reverse form with the winner were the pair to meet again. (tchd 12-1)

Baytown Blaze, ready winner of a 5f maiden at Southwell, was soon in front and held every chance, but could not race on inside the final furlong. This is as good as she is and she should continue to pay her way in similar contests for the time being. (op 10-1 tchd 8-1)

Structura(USA), who may prefer a little further in time, overcame a slow start to shape quite pleasingly in fourth and should prove capable of winning an ordinary maiden. (op 4-1)

Flying Indian, who shaped quite well in what is turning out to be an ordinary race on her debut at Newbury, showed the benefit of that experience, but could not quicken under pressure and in the end proved disappointing. (op 11-4)

Tamara Moon(IRE), who is entered in a couple of the big sales races later in the season, was a negative in the market for this racecourse debut and shaped as though the experience was needed, eventually fading away inside the final furlong. (op 16-1)

1504 TOTESPORT 0800 221 221 H'CAP — 1m 1f 198y

3:30 (3:31) (Class 4) (0-80,80) 3-Y-O — **£5,181** (£1,541; £770; £384) **Stalls** High

Form					RPR
223-	**1**		**Gremlin**[254] [4766] 3-9-0 **76** ... SebSanders 6 (A King) *chsd ldrs: rdn 3f out: drifted lft but led 1f out: styd on strly: rdn out* **5/2**[2]		87+
0-20	**2**	*5*	**Gunner's View**[10] [1259] 3-8-11 **73** ...(t) IanMongan 2 (B J Meehan) *trckd ldr: carried wd and led on bnd 6f out: qcknd clr 3f out: rdn and hdd 1f out: no ex* **20/1**		73
200-	**3**	*nk*	**Colonel Flay**[208] [5892] 3-8-6 **68** ow1 ... RobertHavlin 8 (Mrs P N Dutfield) *hld up: hdwy over 2f out: sn rdn: styd on* **12/1**		67
0	**4**	*nk*	**Ask The Butler**[16] [1124] 3-9-4 **80** ... MickyFenton 5 (A W Carroll) *mid-div: pushed along 5f out: outpcd 3f out: styd on ins fnl f* **16/1**		78
4-10	**5**	*½*	**Sweetheart**[13] [1205] 3-8-10 **72** ... SteveDrowne 7 (Jamie Poulton) *hld up: outpcd 3f out: styd on ins fnl f* **25/1**		69
100-	**6**	*½*	**Opera Crown (IRE)**[197] [6106] 3-9-1 **77** ... JosedeSouza 4 (P F I Cole) *chsd ldrs: rdn 3f out: one pce fnl 2f* **8/1**[3]		73
5-1	**7**	*1 ½*	**Hannicean**[19] [1077] 3-9-4 **80** ... PhilipRobinson 9 (M A Jarvis) *led tl rn wd and hdd 6f out: chsd ldr: rdn over 2f out: wknd ins fnl f* **10/11**[1]		73

2m 8.75s (0.29) **Going Correction** -0.075s/f (Good) — **7** Ran SP% **114.2**

Speed ratings (Par 101):95,91,90,90,90 89,88

CSF £47.22 CT £506.54 TOTE £3.70: £2.10, £4.40; EX 76.00.

Owner Mrs J K Powell **Bred** Catridge Farm Stud Ltd **Trained** Barbury Castle, Wilts

FOCUS

Not a strong renewal of what is often a decent handicap, with the favourite below par. The pace was not strong. The clear-cut winner is a shade better than the bare form and improved by 6lb on his juvenile figure, but the form behind is not strong.

Hannicean Official explanation: trainer's rep said colt failed to handle track and was struck into

1505 TOTEEXACTA MAIDEN STKS — 1m 4f

4:05 (4:06) (Class 4) 3-Y-O — **£4,857** (£1,445; £722; £360) **Stalls** High

Form					RPR
60-	**1**		**Intiquilla (IRE)**[186] [6297] 3-8-12 ... JimCrowley 2 (Mrs A J Perrett) *trckd ldr: nudged along 5f out: rdn to chal 4f out: led jst ins fnl f: drvn out* **10/1**		70+
4	**2**	*½*	**Leander**[11] [1250] 3-9-3 ... SteveDrowne 5 (B R Johnson) *trckd ldrs: rdn and nt clr run briefly on rails 4f out: steadily swtchd lft: styd strly ins fnl f* **7/1**		74
32	**3**	*½*	**Guardian Of Truth (IRE)**[20] [1062] 3-9-3 ... PaulDoe 4 (W J Knight) *led: rdn and hrd pressed over 3f out: hdd over 1f out: battled on but no ex ins fnl f* **5/4**[1]		73
0	**4**	*hd*	**Mowadeh (IRE)**[16] [1129] 3-9-3 ... JHBowman 6 (M R Channon) *cl up: rdn 3f out: led and hung rt over 1f out: hdd jst ins fnl f: no ex* **11/2**[3]		73
02-3	**5**	*1 ¾*	**Bajan Pride**[1] [1467] 3-9-3 73 ... DaneO'Neill 1 (R Hannon) *cl up: ev ch 2f out: sn rdn: cl 4th but hld whn n.m.r wl ins fnl f* **7/4**[2]		72+

2m 41.03s (4.67) **Going Correction** -0.075s/f (Good) — **5** Ran SP% **117.8**

Speed ratings (Par 101):81,80,80,80,79

CSF £72.56 TOTE £9.70: £2.10, £2.20; EX 34.00.

Owner Lady Clague **Bred** Newberry Stud Farm Ltd **Trained** Pulborough, W Sussex

FOCUS

A pedestrian winning time for a race like this and the runners were separated by three lengths at the line. The race has been rated through the third, with the winner a big improver, but the overall form is suspect.

1506 TOTESPORTCASINO.COM H'CAP — 1m 6f 21y

4:40 (4:40) (Class 2) (0-105,101) 4-Y-O+

£9,971 (£2,985; £1,492; £747; £372; £187)

Form					RPR
110-	**1**		**Cape Secret (IRE)**[255] [4742] 4-8-7 **86** ow1 ... SebSanders 1 (R M Beckett) *led after 2f: hrd pressed fr 3f out: rdn 2f out: battled on bravely: all out* **11/4**[1]		93
10-1	**2**	*shd*	**Ollie George (IRE)**[12] [1208] 4-8-8 **87** ... LPKeniry 6 (A M Balding) *trckd ldrs: rdn to chal 2f out: ev ch 1f out: kpt on cl home: jst hld* **10/3**[2]		93
322-	**3**	*nk*	**Gower Song**[226] [5502] 4-9-5 **101** ... MarcHalford[(3)] 4 (D R C Elsworth) *hld up: smooth hdwy 3f out: jnd ldrs and travelling wl 2f out: sn rdn: ev ch thrght fnl f: no ex nr fin* **11/2**		107
130-	**4**	*2*	**Peppertree**[211] [5803] 4-8-6 **85** ... OscarUrbina 3 (J R Fanshawe) *cl up: rdn over 2f out: kpt on same pce* **9/2**		88
-120	**5**	*6*	**Salute (IRE)**[15] [1148] 8-8-7 **85** ... RobertHavlin 2 (P G Murphy) *cl up: rdn over 3f out: one pce fnl 2f* **11/1**		80
35-2	**6**	*16*	**Solent (IRE)**[11] [1244] 5-9-5 **97** ... DaneO'Neill 5 (R Hannon) *led for 2f: trckd wnr: rdn to chal 3f out: wknd 2f out* **7/2**[3]		69

3m 1.00s (-6.00) **Going Correction** -0.075s/f (Good)

WFA 4 from 5yo+ 1lb — **6** Ran SP% **113.9**

Speed ratings (Par 109):109,108,108,107,104 95

CSF £12.45 TOTE £3.50: £1.80, £2.60; EX 12.60.

Owner Larkin, Legge And Milner **Bred** Declan And Catherine Macpartlin **Trained** Whitsbury, Hants

■ Stewards' Enquiry : L P Keniry caution: used whip without giving gelding time to respond

Seb Sanders two-day ban: used whip with excessive frequency (May 17-18)

FOCUS

A decent staying handicap made up of several progressive handicappers and it produced a cracking finish with the front three being separated by just a short head and a neck. The race should work out well.

NOTEBOOK

Cape Secret(IRE), a highly progressive handicapper last season who ended on a low note when trounced in very soft ground at York - connections blamed it on the travelling - has clearly progressed again from three to four and he returned with a fine winning effort, showing a great willingness under pressure and nosing out Ollie George. A tough sort, he looks capable of further progress and deserves a crack at a decent contest now, with 2m unlikely to prove a problem. (op 9-2)

Ollie George(IRE), another tough and progressive sort at three, returned with a game winning effort at Bath and looked to hold major claims with the rise in distance expected to suit. He did not get in the clear as early as his rider wanted, but picked up well close home and may have won in another stride or two. There should be more to come from him and he looks one to keep on side. (op 11-4 tchd 7-2)

Gower Song progressed from handicapper to Listed/Group 3-placed filly last season and she returned to the handicap scene here with a fine effort in defeat, just losing out as they dashed for the line. A strong traveller throughout, there is no reason why she cannot gain some more black type this season and possibly win a decent race. (op 5-1 tchd 9-2)

Peppertree, slightly unlucky on her handicap debut at Ascot last season, floundered in soft ground on her final start but this was much more like it and she ran a pleasing race, just flattening out in the final furlong. She should have no trouble finding a race off this mark and is one to keep on side this season. (op 4-1 tchd 5-1)

Salute(IRE), dropping in trip, was close enough if good enough and simply found himself done for speed when the tempo lifted. (op 10-1)

Solent(IRE), who ran a cracker in a competitive handicap on his reappearance at Epsom, was up 3lb and tackling a quarter of a mile extra, but that was no excuse for such a poor effort and there was presumably something amiss. (op 4-1 tchd 9-2)

1507 BATHWICK TYRES LADY RIDERS' SERIES H'CAP — 6f 212y

5:15 (5:15) (Class 6) (0-65,65) 4-Y-O+ — **£3,123** (£968; £484; £242) **Stalls** High

Form					RPR
0440	**1**		**Zazous**[32] [923] 6-10-0 **56** ... MissLEllison 5 (J J Bridger) *mid-div: hdwy over 2f out: hung lft and led over 1f out: all out* **16/1**		63
63-0	**2**	*nk*	**Gracie's Gift (IRE)**[112] [130] 5-10-5 **61** ...(p) MissCHannaford 3 (A G Newcombe) *towards rr: drifted lft and hdwy over 2f out: ev ch ins fnl f: hld cl home* **9/1**		67
000-	**3**	*½*	**Dr Synn**[200] [6060] 6-10-1 **62** ... MissZoeLilly[(5)] 1 (J Akehurst) *bhd: rdn and hdwy over 2f out: styd on ins fnl f* **25/1**		67
3-26	**4**	*½*	**Lady Duxyana**[5] [1380] 4-9-2 **51** oh6 ...(v) MissCNosworthy[(7)] 11 (M D I Usher) *slowly away: towards rr: styd on wl fr over 1f out: nrst fin* **20/1**		54
3521	**5**	*shd*	**The Grey One (IRE)**[6] [1350] 4-9-12 **61** 6ex ...(p) MissHDavies[(7)] 9 (J M Bradley) *hld up bhd: hdwy 2f out: styd on fnl f* **11/2**[3]		64

The Form Book, Raceform Ltd, Compton, RG20 6NL

413 **6** 1 1/4 **Carcinetto (IRE)**[8] 1309 5-10-6 **65**................................ MissEFolkes(3) 2 65
(P D Evans) *in tch: rdn over 2f out: kpt on same pce ins fnl f* **17/2**

0000 **7** 3/4 **Napoletano (GER)**[12] 1212 6-9-5 **54**................ MissHarrietCarroll(7) 17 52
(S Dow) *sltly hmpd s: towards rr: hdwy fr 4f out: nt clr run 2f out: styd on ins fnl f* **20/1**

06-6 **8** 1 1/4 **Stagnite**[100] 252 7-9-4 **51** oh2.. MissARyan(5) 7 45
(Karen George) *towards rr: styd on fr over 1f out: nvr trbld ldrs* **25/1**

0-00 **9** 1 3/4 **Goodwood Spirit**[7] 1318 5-10-1 **62**........................ MissSBradley(5) 18 52
(J M Bradley) *wnt lft s: nvr bttr than mid-div* **14/1**

6506 **10** 1 **Mine The Balance (IRE)**[16] 1118 4-9-8 **57** oh1 ow6(b) MissJGeeson(7) 10 44
(H J Manners) *chsd ldr tl over 2f out* **40/1**

400- **11** 1 **Roman Quintet (IRE)**[201] 6036 7-10-4 **65**.................... MissABevan(5) 4 49+
(R J Price) *racd alone on stands' side and led: rdn and hdd over 1f out: fdd* **20/1**

4-60 **12** hd **Aggravation**[22] 1036 5-10-8 **64**... MrsSMoore 13 48
(D R C Elsworth) *nvr bttr than mid-div* **7/1**

-452 **13** 2 1/2 **Charlie Bear**[10] 1260 6-9-9 **56**.................... MissGDGracey-Davison(5) 15 33
(Miss Z C Davison) *chsd ldrs: effrt over 2f out: wknd over 1f out* **7/2**[1]

0162 **14** 3/4 **Million Percent**[27] 980 8-10-7 **63**................................ MissEJJones 16 38
(C R Dore) *chsd ldrs tl 2f out* **4/1**[2]

20-0 **15** 1 1/4 **Sunny Afternoon**[38] 819 7-9-6 **53**......................... MissAWallace(5) 12 24
(R Rowe) *mid-div tl wknd over 2f out* **50/1**

004- **16** shd **Antigoni (IRE)**[230] 5418 4-10-8 **64**................................ MrsSBosley 8 35
(A M Balding) *mid-div tl wknd over 2f out* **12/1**

00-0 **17** 3 **Parthenope**[16] 1120 4-9-2 **51** oh6........................ MissJHannaford(7) 6 14
(J A Geake) *mid-div for over 4f* **50/1**

03-0 **18** 6 **Devonia Plains (IRE)**[16] 1118 5-9-12 **59**.................. MissKHobbs(5) 14 6
(Mrs P N Dutfield) *chsd ldrs for 4f* **40/1**

1m 30.11s (1.05) **Going Correction** -0.075s/f (Good) **18** Ran SP% **141.7**
Speed ratings (Par 101):91,90,90,89,89 87,87,85,83,82 81,81,78,77,76 75,72,65
CSF £158.57 CT £2103.30 TOTE £31.30: £4.50, £2.50, £5.30, £9.20; EX 233.80 Place 6 £227.93, Place 5 £202.66..
Owner J J Bridger **Bred** Lordship Stud **Trained** Liphook, Hants

FOCUS
A competitive lady riders' handicap. Modest form, held down by the proximity of the fourth from out of the weights.
T/Plt: £239.70 to a £1 stake. Pool: £49,531.30. 150.80 winning tickets. T/Qpdt: £384.90 to a £1 stake. Pool: £2,341.10. 4.50 winning tickets. TM

1322 GOWRAN PARK (R-H)
Sunday, May 6

OFFICIAL GOING: Good to firm

1508a IRISH STALLION FARMS EUROPEAN BREEDERS FUND MAIDEN 7f
2:00 (2:00) 2-Y-O **£7,937** (£1,849; £815; £470)

RPR

1 **Henrythenavigator (USA)** 2-9-3 .... JAHeffernan 1 95+
(A P O'Brien, Ire) *led after 2f: qcknd clr early st: styd on strly: impressive* **4/5**[1]

2 7 **Dick Morris (IRE)**[42] 779 2-8-12 .... CPGeoghegan(5) 10 75
(J G Coogan, Ire) *led early: hdd after 2f: 3rd 1/2-way: mod 2nd fr 1 1/2f out: kpt on* **9/1**

3 1 3/4 **Hawk Wood (IRE)** 2-9-3 .... WSupple 11 70
(G M Lyons, Ire) *chsd ldrs: 5th 1/2-way: hdwy early st: mod 3rd over 1f out: kpt on* **7/1**[3]

4 3 **Slaney Rock (IRE)** 2-8-12 .... DJMoran(5) 4 63
(J S Bolger, Ire) *chsd ldrs in 4th: rdn and no imp st: kpt on same pce fr over 1f out* **10/1**

5 1 3/4 **Soaring Falcon (IRE)** 2-9-3 .... PShanahan 6 58
(D K Weld, Ire) *chsd ldrs in 6th: effrt on outer early st: 5th and no imp fr over 1f out* **14/1**

6 2 1/2 **Final Flashback (IRE)** 2-9-3 .... PJSmullen 3 52
(D K Weld, Ire) *prom: 2nd 1/2-way: rdn and outpcd early st: sn no ex: eased fnl f* **13/2**[2]

7 1 1/4 **Whiskey And Rye (IRE)** 2-9-3 ....(t) RPCleary 5 48
(John J Walsh, Ire) *hld up: mod 7th 2f out: kpt on fnl f* **33/1**

8 6 **Brazilian Star (IRE)** 2-9-0 .... CDHayes(3) 2 33
(Kevin Prendergast, Ire) *a bhd: last and trailing ent st: rdn and no imp* **7/1**[3]

9 4 **Stone Bridge (IRE)**[24] 1014 2-9-3 .... NGMcCullagh 9 22
(Adrian Sexton, Ire) *a bhd* **25/1**

1m 26.1s (-4.60) **11** Ran SP% **126.4**
CSF £10.76 TOTE £1.50: £1.10, £3.50, £2.60; DF 10.10.
Owner Mrs John Magnier **Bred** Westrn Bloodstock **Trained** Ballydoyle, Co Tipperary

NOTEBOOK
Henrythenavigator(USA) put his rivals to the sword in style and announced himself a two-year-old of some potential. A full-brother to the Group 3 winner and Classic-placed Queen Cleopatra, the Kingmambo colt went to the front early on, had his rivals toiling in his wake from over two furlongs out and needed only minimal encouragement to draw clear for an emphatic success. He is one to watch with the closest attention and looks a potentially top-class prospect. (op 4/6 tchd 9/10)

1509 - 1514a (Foreign Racing) - See Raceform Interactive

1189 COLOGNE (R-H)
Sunday, May 6

OFFICIAL GOING: Good

1515a SCHWARZGOLD-RENNEN (GROUP 2) (FILLIES) 1m 3f
3:10 (3:20) 3-Y-O **£27,027** (£10,135; £4,054; £2,703)

RPR

1 **Scatina (IRE)**[28] 3-9-0 .... ASuborics 6 101
(Mario Hofer, Germany) *mde virtually all: set slow pce: rdn 2f out: narrowly hdd 1f out: styd on gamely u.p to ld again 100yds out: drvn out* **36/10**

2 1/2 **Scoubidou (GER)**[27] 3-9-0 .... ADeVries 5 100
(H Blume, Germany) *hld up: 4th st: hdwy to ld narrowly 1f out: hdd and no ex 100yds out* **1/1**[1]

3 2 1/2 **Meridia (GER)**[27] 3-9-0 .... THellier 4 96
(J Hirschberger, Germany) *hld up in 5th: effrt and no imp 2f out: styd on strly fnl f* **34/10**[3]

4 2 **Zuckerpuppe (GER)** 3-9-0 .... AStarke 7 93
(Frau E Mader, Germany) *wnt 2nd on outside after 2f: rdn to chal 2f out: sn btn* **26/10**[2]

5 dist **Elata** 3-9-0 .... J-LSilverio 3 —
(N Sauer, Germany) *last thrght: t.o fnl 1 1/2f* **36/1**

F **Waldliebe (GER)**[27] 3-9-0 .... ABoschert 2 —
(P Rau, Germany) *plld v hrd early disputing ld: restrained in 3rd: effrt 2f out: btn in 5th whn broke leg and fell cl home: dead* **17/1**

2m 24.31s (3.51) **6** Ran SP% **130.5**
(including 10 Euro stake): WIN 46; PL 15, 13; SF 86.
Owner Gestut Ittlingen **Bred** Gestut Hof Ittlingen **Trained** Germany

1516a MEHL-MUHLENS-RENNEN (GERMAN 2,000 GUINEAS) (GROUP 2) (C&F) 1m
4:15 (4:34) 3-Y-O **£67,568** (£25,676; £12,162; £6,081)

RPR

1 **Aviso (GER)**[12] 3-9-2 .... THellier 3 108
(J Hirschberger, Germany) *hld up in 7th: hdwy but hung bdly lft fr wl over 1f out: str run to ld post: fin against outside rail* **34/10**[3]

2 nse **Molly Max (GER)**[28] 3-9-2 .... FilipMinarik 2 108
(Frau K Haustein, Germany) *racd in 3rd: slipped through on ins to ld 2f out: 2 l clr ins fnl f: ct on line* **88/10**

3 1 **Champery (USA)**[22] 1035 3-9-2 .... J-PGuillambert 7 106
(M Johnston) *racd in 5th: styd on steadily u.p fr over 1 1/2f out* **91/10**

4 1 1/4 **Davidoff (GER)**[21] 1054 3-9-2 .... AStarke 6 104
(P Schiergen, Germany) *8th early: 4th st: effrt and n.m.r towards ins over 1f out: kpt on* **21/10**[1]

5 2 1/2 **Smokejumper (GER)**[198] 6092 3-9-2 .... ADeVries 5 99
(Frau E Mader, Germany) *pressed ldr: 2nd st: one pce fnl 2f* **36/1**

6 1 1/4 **Majuro (IRE)**[22] 1035 3-9-2 .... ChrisCatlin 4 96
(M R Channon) *led tl hung bdly lft on home turn and dropped bk to 6th: kpt on at one pce fnl 2f but n.d* **212/10**

7 1 1/2 **Montalembert (USA)**[5] 1387 3-9-2 .... ASuborics 8 93
(J S Moore) *last early: 8th st: nvr a factor* **286/10**

8 1 1/2 **Global Dream (GER)**[21] 1054 3-9-2 .... ABoschert 9 90
(U Ostmann, Germany) *hld up in 6th: last st: nvr a factor* **44/10**

9 1/2 **Rolling Home (GER)**[28] 3-9-2 .... EPedroza 1 89
(A Wohler, Germany) *cl up in 4th: slipped through on ins to ld 3f out: hdd over 2f out: wknd* **28/10**[2]

1m 36.68s (-1.71) **9** Ran SP% **130.5**
WIN 44; PL 21, 29, 31; SF 380.
Owner Gestut Schlenderhan **Bred** Gestut Schlenderhan **Trained** Germany

NOTEBOOK
Aviso(GER) remains unbeaten after three races, including one win at Chantilly, but he looked ill at ease on the fast ground, continually hanging sharply left inside the final two furlongs despite his rider pulling his whip through to try and correct him. He will carry on at this trip and should win more races.
Champery(USA) broke out of his stall but was quickly reloaded. Always close up, he was three wide on the turn but handled it better than several of his rivals. He should stay further.
Majuro(IRE) was unlucky at Lingfield and was entitled to finish closer to Champery this time, but he spoilt his chance by running wide. He needs easier ground.
Montalembert(USA), running for the second time in five days, was always struggling.

HANOVER (L-H)
Sunday, May 6

OFFICIAL GOING: Good

1517a GROSSER PREIS DER VGH - VERSICHERUNGEN HANNOVERSCHER STUTENPREIS (LISTED RACE) (F&M) 1m
4:00 (4:11) 4-Y-O+ **£8,108** (£2,973; £1,622; £811)

RPR

1 **Snow Gretel (IRE)**[27] 979 4-9-0 .... J-PCarvalho 6 101
(M Botti) *racd in 5th: 4th st: led over 1f out: wnt 1 1/2 l clr: drvn out: jst hld on* **74/10**

2 nk **Jalta (GER)**[202] 6022 4-8-9 .... AHelfenbein 7 95
(H Steinmetz, Germany) **68/10**

3 3/4 **Waleria (GER)**[215] 5762 4-9-4 .... KKerekes 1 103
(H J Groschel, Germany) **7/2**[3]

4 3 **Fairyland (GER)** 4-8-9 .... JLermyte 5 88
(S Wegner, Germany) **155/10**

5 1 **Lafalda Saint Mar (GER)**[266] 5-8-9 .... WPanov 8 86
(P Bradik, Germany) **166/10**

6 3/4 **Amateis (GER)**[240] 5160 4-9-4 .... DBonilla 4 93
(P Rau, Germany) **14/10**[1]

7 1 **Rovana Jowe (GER)**[344] 2043 4-9-0 .... JBojko 2 87
(A Wohler, Germany) **5/2**[2]

8 1 1/2 **Amy Storm (GER)**[189] 6248 4-9-0 .... APietsch 3 84
(P Vovcenko, Germany) **18/1**

1m 39.33s (99.33) **8** Ran SP% **134.2**
(including 10 Euro stake): WIN 84; PL 20, 17, 18; SF 734.
Owner Mrs R J Jacobs **Bred** Newsells Park Stud Limited **Trained** Newmarket, Suffolk

NOTEBOOK
Snow Gretel(IRE) took the lead in plenty of time and stayed on well to hold the late runs of her two closest pursuers, who had filled the last two places early in the straight. She had a fitness advantage, but this was still a smart effort. She is also a valuable broodmare prospect, being a half-sister to the Royal Lodge winner Snow Ridge.

1485 SAN SIRO (R-H)
Sunday, May 6

OFFICIAL GOING: Heavy

1518a COPPA D'ORO (LISTED RACE) 1m 7f
4:00 (4:18) 4-Y-O+ **£18,919** (£8,324; £4,541; £2,270)

RPR

1 **Montalegre (IRE)**[42] 5-8-11 .... DVargiu 4 102
(A & G Botti, Italy)

2 *shd* **Biff Tannen (ITY)**[379] 5-8-11 .... MarcoMonteriso 7 102
(L D'Auria, Italy)
3 *2* **Sandro Chia (IRE)**[21] 5-8-11 ....(b) DPerovic 1 100
(M Colombi, Italy)
4 *8* **Hovering (IRE)**[32] 929 4-8-8 .... JerryO'Dwyer 3 91
(M G Quinlan) *racd in 3rd to wl over 4f out: 5th st: btn over 2f out (2.76/1)*
11/4[1]
5 *16* **West Nile (IRE)** 5-8-11 ....(b) WGambarota 6 76
(A & G Botti, Italy)
6 *1/2* **Vicveris (ITY)**[574] 5-8-11 .... SMulas 2 76
(S Billeri, France)
7 *7* **Fa A Mezz**[46] 4-8-11 .... EBotti 5 71
(A & G Botti, Italy)
3m 17.4s (1.00)
WFA 4 from 5yo 2lb 7 Ran SP% **26.7**
(including 1 Euro stake): WIN 2.84; PL 1.68, 2.96; DF 12.54.
Owner Scuderia Siba **Bred** Azienda Agricola Antezzate Srl **Trained** Italy

NOTEBOOK
Hovering(IRE) broke first but soon dashed local hopes that she would take them along. The change of tactics brought no improvement but the heavy going may have been at fault.

1396 KEMPTON (A.W) (R-H)
Monday, May 7

OFFICIAL GOING: Standard
Wind: Fresh, across Weather: Heavy rain before racing, becoming sunny later

1519 BETRESCUE ANTEPOSTMAG.COM E B F MAIDEN STKS 5f (P)
2:00 (2:00) (Class 4) 2-Y-O **£4,533** (£1,348; £674; £336) **Stalls** High

Form RPR
1 **Rescue Me** 2-8-12 .... TedDurcan 4 62+
(R Hannon) *dwlt: hld up in 4th: effrt over 1f out: rn to ld fnl 50yds: readily*
11/2
2 *nk* **Valhillen** 2-9-3 .... JamieSpencer 2 66
(M J Wallace) *pressed ldr: hrd rdn and str chal fnl f: nt pce of wnr but kpt on to take 2nd nr fin*
13/2
50 3 *hd* **Carolina Blini**[7] 1354 2-8-12 .... BrettDoyle 6 60
(B J Meehan) *led: hrd rdn fnl f: hdd and nt qckn fnl 50yds*
5/1[3]
0 4 *1/2* **Replicator**[23] 1033 2-9-3 .... PaulEddery 7 63+
(Pat Eddery) *dwlt: trckd ldrs: nt clr run and swtchd lft over 1f out: kpt on wl fnl 100yds*
15/2
0 5 *2 1/2* **Abfabfong (IRE)**[14] 1201 2-9-3 .... JosedeSouza 3 53
(P F I Cole) *5th most of way: rdn 1/2-way: no imp*
10/1
0 6 *4* **No Nines**[17] 1123 2-9-3 .... MichaelHills 1 37
(B W Hills) *wnt lft s: a bhd*
4/1[2]
0 7 *1/2* **Sirjoshua Reynolds**[34] 898 2-9-3 .... FrancisNorton 5 35
(N A Callaghan) *t.k.h and nt handle bnds: dropped to rr after 2f: n.d after*
3/1[1]
63.37 secs (2.97) **Going Correction** +0.125s/f (Slow) 7 Ran SP% **111.2**
Speed ratings (Par 95):81,80,80,79,75 69,68
CSF £37.96 TOTE £5.90: £2.20, £2.90; EX 24.80.
Owner A F Merritt **Bred** Raimon Bloodstock **Trained** East Everleigh, Wilts

FOCUS
Some fairly expensive animals on display here, but the form of those that had already run was modest, and the time was very slow. Probably a weak race.

NOTEBOOK
Rescue Me, a 38,000gns yearling, is bred to come into her own over a mile to ten furlongs in due course. Soon travelling comfortably despite missing the break, she quickened well to score with a bit in hand, and looks capable of making her mark in better races than this. (op 5-1)
Valhillen, a 9,000gns yearling, was later re-sold for just 3,600gns, which is hardly encouraging, but this speedily-bred gelding made a promising debut. Though no match for the winner, he battled well under pressure and would again have every chance in a similar contest. (op 7-1)
Carolina Blini had shown ability in two races on turf, and made a satisfactory switch to the All-Weather. She is now qualified for nurseries when they begin and, though capable of winning a weak maiden, that is where her future lies. (op 11-2)
Replicator should go into the notebook after an unlucky run in which he met trouble on the inside rail. He ought to stay up to 1m in due course, so 6f will certainly suit before long. (tchd 8-1)
Abfabfong(IRE) has made little impact in his two races to date, but this 55,000gns Dr Fong colt should improve over longer trips. (op 8-1)
No Nines, a 40,000gns Noverre colt, is bred to be fast but has shown no sign of that in his two outings so far. He looks to be heading for nurseries after one more run. (op 3-1)
Sirjoshua Reynolds was hanging outwards on the bends, a considerable problem on this sharp-turning track. He has been green in both races to date, but this speedily-bred Kyllachy colt cost 60,000gns as a yearling, and had plenty of support here, so ought to do much better when the penny drops. Official explanation: jockey said colt ran very green (op 7-2)

1520 DAY TIME, NIGHT TIME, GREAT TIME H'CAP 5f (P)
2:30 (2:30) (Class 4) (0-85,85) 3-Y-O **£4,728** (£1,406; £702; £351) **Stalls** High

Form RPR
215- 1 **Goodbye Cash (IRE)**[184] 6332 3-8-0 **74** .... BernadetteQuinn(7) 7 78
(P D Evans) *hld up towards rr: hdwy over 1f out: qcknd through gap on rail to ld fnl 100yds: edgd lft nr fin*
12/1
040- 2 *1* **Whiskey Junction**[283] 3917 3-8-5 **72** ....(p) FrancisNorton 5 72
(A M Balding) *pressed ldrs: drvn to ld jst ins fnl f: hdd and nt pce of wnr fnl 100yds*
11/1
342- 3 *shd* **Fairfield Princess**[217] 5731 3-9-0 **81** .... TedDurcan 8 81
(M S Saunders) *cl up and gng wl: drvn to press ldrs over 1f out: nt qckn ins fnl f*
10/1
631- 4 *1* **Frisky Talk (IRE)**[219] 5668 3-9-2 **83** .... MichaelHills 1 79
(B W Hills) *in tch: rdn over 2f out: styd on fnl f*
10/3[3]
15- 5 *3* **Tobermory (IRE)**[217] 5731 3-9-4 **85** .... PhilipRobinson 6 69
(M A Jarvis) *led at gd pce tl wknd jst ins fnl f*
3/1[2]
-501 6 *1 1/2* **Mind The Style**[13] 1213 3-8-1 **71** oh1 ....(p) LiamJones(3) 4 50
(W G M Turner) *pressed ldr tl wknd and edgd lft over 1f out*
8/1
04-4 7 *1 1/4* **Reebal**[30] 943 3-9-1 **82** ....(b) JamieSpencer 3 56
(B J Meehan) *s.i.s: drvn along and a bhd*
11/4[1]
61.54 secs (1.14) **Going Correction** +0.125s/f (Slow) 7 Ran SP% **111.0**
Speed ratings (Par 101):95,93,93,91,86 84,82
CSF £121.38 CT £1321.57 TOTE £15.80: £6.20, £2.40; EX 85.70.
Owner D Healy **Bred** Mrs A C Peters **Trained** Pandy, Monmouths
■ Bernadette Quinn's only previous winner came in Ireland.

FOCUS
A fair handicap, run at a good gallop although the time was modest. It did not take much winning with the fifth and seventh running poorly, although the runner-up, third and fourth were close to form.

Frisky Talk(IRE) Official explanation: jockey said bit slipped through filly's mouth

1521 HARRY & PHYLLIS ASHTON RUBY ANNIVERSARY H'CAP 1m 2f (P)
3:00 (3:00) (Class 6) (0-65,65) 4-Y-O+ **£2,590** (£770; £385; £192) **Stalls** High

Form RPR
50-3 1 **Princess Lavinia**[12] 1251 4-8-13 **60** .... TedDurcan 10 71+
(G Wragg) *chsd ldrs: rdn to go 2nd over 1f out: led fnl 100yds: drvn out*
11/2[2]
3550 2 *1 1/4* **Revolve**[7] 1347 7-8-11 **58** ....(b) PaulDoe 13 66
(Mrs L J Mongan) *led 1f: chsd ldr: led 2f out: hdd and nt qckn fnl 100yds*
11/1
0-53 3 *1* **Broughtons Revival**[44] 769 5-9-4 **65** .... HayleyTurner 3 71
(W J Musson) *chsd ldrs: rdn 2f out: styd on same pce*
9/1
0030 4 *1/2* **Rowan Warning**[7] 1347 5-8-9 **56** ....(b[1]) RHills 9 61
(J R Boyle) *stdd s: hld up in rr of midfield: rdn and styd on fnl 2f: nvr nrr*
15/2[3]
00-2 5 *3/4* **Pothos Way (GR)**[12] 1249 4-9-2 **63** .... FrancisNorton 14 67
(P R Chamings) *t.k.h: chsd ldrs: rdn and one pce fnl 2f*
4/1[1]
600- 6 *5* **Uig**[151] 4040 6-8-10 **57** .... JDSmith 4 52
(H S Howe) *towards rr: rdn over 2f out: sme late hdwy*
33/1
0130 7 *1 1/2* **Mon Petite Amour**[24] 1025 4-9-0 **61** .... BrettDoyle 12 53
(D W P Arbuthnot) *hld up in midfield: rdn and no hdwy fnl 2f*
9/1
50-5 8 *3* **Bold Cross (IRE)**[12] 1249 4-9-2 **63** .... DO'Donohoe 1 49
(E G Bevan) *led after 1f: set gd gallop: hdd 2f out: sn wknd*
25/1
61-0 9 *hd* **Lunar River (FR)**[20] 1078 4-9-2 **63** ....(t) ChrisCatlin 7 49
(David Pinder) *wd in midfield: outpcd fnl 2f*
14/1
00-0 10 *2 1/2* **Oakley Absolute**[12] 1249 5-9-1 **62** .... MichaelHills 11 43
(R Hannon) *prom tl wknd over 2f out*
16/1
0/ 11 *4* **Fancy (IRE)**[227] 5516 4-8-9 **56** .... RobertHavlin 8 29
(R A Farrant) *t.k.h early: rdn over 3f out: a bhd*
14/1
43-4 12 *5* **Duelling Banjos**[12] 1249 8-9-1 **62** .... JamieSpencer 2 26
(J Akehurst) *dwlt and hmpd s: rdn 3f out: a bhd*
4/1[1]
2m 8.69s (-0.31) **Going Correction** +0.125s/f (Slow) 12 Ran SP% **121.5**
Speed ratings (Par 101):106,105,104,103,103 99,98,95,95,93 90,86
CSF £66.60 CT £546.91 TOTE £6.30: £2.00, £4.00, £2.70; EX 83.90.
Owner D R Hunnisett **Bred** Mrs E Y Hunnisett **Trained** Newmarket, Suffolk

FOCUS
A moderate handicap, but run at a decent pace. The form looks solid and reliable for the grade, with the winner and third improvers.
Duelling Banjos Official explanation: jockey said gelding never travelled

1522 DIGIBET MAIDEN STKS (DIV I) 1m (P)
3:30 (3:32) (Class 4) 3-Y-O **£4,080** (£1,214; £606; £303) **Stalls** High

Form RPR
2 1 **Lucarno (USA)**[16] 1143 3-9-3 .... JimmyFortune 4 89+
(J H M Gosden) *mde all at gd pce: pushed clr 1f out: easily*
1/2[1]
6- 2 *7* **Cape Hawk (IRE)**[220] 5659 3-9-3 .... MichaelHills 3 73
(R Hannon) *in tch: rdn 4f out: styd on to take 2nd 1f out: no ch w wnr* **8/1**[2]
0 3 *2 1/2* **Mabaahej (USA)**[17] 1128 3-8-12 .... RHills 2 62
(B W Hills) *w wnr: outpcd and lost 2nd pl 1f out: no ex*
20/1
00- 4 *1* **The Wily Woodcock**[166] 6561 3-9-3 .... RobertHavlin 5 65
(G Wragg) *t.k.h: chsd ldrs: rdn and one pce fnl 2f*
33/1
5 *1 3/4* **Dream Of Fortune (IRE)** 3-9-3 .... TPQueally 12 61+
(J Noseda) *bhd: shkn up over 3f out: styd on fnl 2f: nvr nrr*
9/1[3]
6 *2 1/2* **Central Force** 3-8-12 .... DO'Donohoe 9 50+
(E A L Dunlop) *towards rr: rdn over 3f out: sme late hdwy*
25/1
50- 7 *1 3/4* **Black Mogul**[255] 4774 3-9-3 .... PaulDoe 8 51
(W R Muir) *in tch: rdn 1/2-way: sn outpcd*
66/1
0- 8 *nk* **Soldier Field**[157] 6658 3-9-3 .... FrancisNorton 11 50
(A M Balding) *prom tl wknd 2f out*
66/1
9 *2 1/2* **Hartmann (USA)** 3-9-3 .... JamieSpencer 7 45
(B J Meehan) *s.s: sn chsng ldrs: wknd over 2f out*
9/1[3]
00 10 *hd* **Boz**[16] 1166 3-9-3 .... ChrisCatlin 13 44
(L M Cumani) *mid-div: rdn and no hdwy fnl 3f*
66/1
11 *3/4* **Beau Michael** 3-9-3 .... AdamKirby 1 43
(W R Swinburn) *mid-div: rdn and outpcd fnl 3f*
16/1
12 *1 1/2* **Look So** 3-8-12 .... TedDurcan 6 34
(R M Beckett) *mid-div: wknd 3f out: sn bhd*
50/1
U 13 *nk* **Silver Surprise**[14] 1203 3-8-7 .... TravisBlock(5) 10 33
(J J Bridger) *s.s: a bhd*
100/1
5 14 *47* **Master Jobs**[51] 703 3-9-3 .... HayleyTurner 14 —
(S C Williams) *a towards rr: no ch whn eased fnl 3f*
66/1
1m 40.59s (-0.21) **Going Correction** +0.125s/f (Slow) 14 Ran SP% **124.1**
Speed ratings (Par 101):106,99,96,95,93 91,89,89,86,86 85,84,83,36
CSF £4.77 TOTE £1.50: £1.10, £1.90, £3.90; EX 5.90.
Owner George Strawbridge **Bred** Augustin Stable **Trained** Newmarket, Suffolk

FOCUS
A mixed bunch, but with an impressive winner who made all at a good gallop. The runner-up was up 5lb on his debut. The winning time was 0.62 seconds faster than the second division.
Beau Michael Official explanation: jockey said colt ran green
Master Jobs Official explanation: jockey said saddle slipped

1523 DIGIBET MAIDEN STKS (DIV II) 1m (P)
4:00 (4:03) (Class 4) 3-Y-O **£4,080** (£1,214; £606; £303) **Stalls** High

Form RPR
1 **Padlocked (IRE)** 3-9-3 .... TPQueally 13 77+
(J Noseda) *led after 1f: hrd rdn and hld on gamely fnl f*
7/1
2- 2 *nk* **Waymark (IRE)**[209] 5882 3-9-3 .... PhilipRobinson 9 76
(M A Jarvis) *in tch: rdn over 2f out: r.o to take 2nd fnl 50yds*
7/2[3]
3-4 3 *1 1/2* **Common Purpose (USA)**[21] 1062 3-9-3 .... JimmyFortune 6 73
(J H M Gosden) *prom: drvn to chal over 1f out: nt qckn fnl 100yds* **11/4**[2]
0-4 4 *1/2* **Valley Observer (FR)**[26] 1001 3-9-3 .... AdamKirby 12 72
(W R Swinburn) *cl up: jnd wnr 2f out: no ex fnl 100yds*
16/1
2 5 *2 1/2* **Zifaaf (USA)**[18] 1100 3-8-12 .... RHills 2 61
(B W Hills) *chsd ldrs on outside: jinked lft and c wd 2f out: one pce* **2/1**[1]
0 6 *5* **Dark Druid (IRE)**[47] 720 3-9-0 .... LiamJones(3) 1 55
(I A Wood) *mid-div: effrt and drvn along 3f out: nt pce to chal*
66/1
0- 7 *3 1/2* **Dawn Mystery**[157] 6658 3-8-12 .... ChrisCatlin 3 42
(Rae Guest) *stdd s: hld up in rr: shkn up 3f out: sme late hdwy*
66/1
06 8 *1/2* **Bugsy's Boy**[15] 1177 3-9-3 .... FrancisNorton 5 45
(P W D'Arcy) *sn bhd: pushed along 3f out: nvr rchd ldrs*
66/1
0 9 *hd* **Womaniser (IRE)**[10] 1278 3-9-3 .... BrettDoyle 8 45
(L M Cumani) *s.s: sn in midfield: outpcd fr 1/2-way*
33/1
0 10 *5* **Kyburg**[17] 1128 3-8-12 .... JosedeSouza 11 28
(P F I Cole) *pressed ldrs tl wknd over 2f out*
66/1

11 *1* **Belinda Rose (IRE)** 3-8-12 .... JamieSpencer 7 26
(B J Meehan) *s.s: a bhd* **14/1**

12 *1 1/2* **African Pursuits (USA)** 3-8-12 .... TravisBlock(5) 4 28
(H Morrison) *wd: sn drvn along: bhd fr 1/2-way* **33/1**

13 *9* **Garden Party** 3-9-3 .... JDSmith 10 7
(Sir Michael Stoute) *s.s: sn chsng ldrs: wknd over 2f out* **11/1**

14 *3* **Nelly's Glen** 3-8-12 .... MichaelHills 14 —
(R Hannon) *s.s: a bhd: no ch fnl 3f* **33/1**

1m 41.21s (0.41) **Going Correction** +0.125s/f (Slow) **14** Ran SP% **130.4**
Speed ratings (Par 101):102,101,100,99,97 92,88,88,88,83 82,80,71,68
CSF £33.61 TOTE £8.80: £2.30, £2.10, £1.70; EX 76.80.
Owner Saif Misfer **Bred** Patrick F Kelly **Trained** Newmarket, Suffolk

FOCUS
Hard to weigh up, but potentially some above-average maidens on show. The winner did it nicely and the third looks the best gyuide. The winning time was 0.62 seconds slower than the first division.

Zifaaf(USA) Official explanation: jockey said filly hung left from 2f out

1524 DIGIBET SPORTS BETTING JUBILEE H'CAP (LONDON MILE QUALIFIER) 1m (P)
4:30 (4:32) (Class 3) (0-90,90) 4-Y-0+
£9,348 (£2,799; £1,399; £700; £349; £175) **Stalls** High

Form RPR

6-00 **1** **Montpellier (IRE)**[16] 1149 4-8-10 **82** .... JimmyFortune 10 96+
(E A L Dunlop) *hld up in tch: eased out over 2f out: rdn to ld ins fnl f* **12/1**

060- **2** *1 1/4* **Unshakable (IRE)**[191] 6219 8-8-12 **84** .... PaulEddery 3 95+
(Bob Jones) *hld up in tch: n.m.r and lost several pls bnd into st: rdn and rallied 2f out: r.o to take 2nd fnl 100yds* **33/1**

30-0 **3** *nk* **Granston (IRE)**[37] 848 6-9-3 **89** .... TedDurcan 11 99
(J D Bethell) *pressed ldr: hrd rdn 2f out: kpt on again fnl f* **7/1**

106- **4** *1* **Killena Boy (IRE)**[204] 5990 5-8-13 **85** .... AdamKirby 12 93
(W Jarvis) *prom: rdn to press ldr over 1f out: one pce fnl f* **10/1**

2212 **5** *nk* **Top Mark**[84] 444 5-8-6 **78** .... RobertHavlin 4 85
(J R Boyle) *led: hrd rdn over 1f out: hdd and no ex ins fnl f* **14/1**

02-6 **6** *1* **Acheekyone (IRE)**[16] 1145 4-9-2 **88** .... MichaelHills 1 93+
(B J Meehan) *wd in midfield: effrt 3f out: styd on same pce* **9/2**[2]

6455 **7** *hd* **Marajaa (IRE)**[16] 1145 5-9-1 **87** .... BrettDoyle 13 93+
(W J Musson) *hld up towards rr: rdn and sme hdwy 2f out: no imp fnl f* **5/1**[3]

4030 **8** *1 1/4* **Magical Music**[28] 979 4-8-11 **83** .... TPQueally 2 84+
(J Pearce) *towards rr: rdn over 2f out: nvr rchd ldrs* **25/1**

0-30 **9** *hd* **Tanzanite (IRE)**[37] 848 5-9-4 **90** .... SimonWhitworth 6 91
(D W P Arbuthnot) *t.k.h: in tch: effrt 3f out: rdn and btn 2f out* **14/1**

120- **10** *3* **Kingsholm**[119] 6337 5-8-12 **84** .... FrancisNorton 8 78
(A M Balding) *bhd: rdn over 2f out: n.d* **20/1**

20-0 **11** *1 1/2* **Direct Debit (IRE)**[16] 1145 4-9-0 **86** .... HayleyTurner 9 77
(M L W Bell) *t.k.h: prom tl wknd over 2f out* **12/1**

1- **12** *2 1/2* **Lady Stardust**[262] 4563 4-8-13 **85** .... JamieSpencer 14 70
(J R Fanshawe) *dwlt: sn in midfield: rdn over 2f out: sn btn* **3/1**[1]

36-0 **13** *2 1/2* **Punta Galera (IRE)**[7] 1356 4-8-11 **83** ....(b) RHills 5 62
(R Hannon) *rdn 3f out: a bhd* **33/1**

36/0 **14** *38* **Mafaheem**[72] 550 5-8-10 **82** .... ChrisCatlin 7 —
(S Dow) *a in rr: wl bhd fnl 3f* **66/1**

1m 39.59s (-1.21) **Going Correction** +0.125s/f (Slow) **14** Ran SP% **126.1**
Speed ratings (Par 107):111,109,109,108,108 107,106,105,105,102 101,98,96,58
CSF £379.39 CT £3056.58 TOTE £15.30: £5.10, £8.50, £3.10; EX 453.10.
Owner Gainsborough **Bred** M H Ings **Trained** Newmarket, Suffolk

FOCUS
The Jubilee is not the race it was, but this was still a well-contested handicap, with an ordinary early tempo stepping up at halfway. Solid form. The winner was up 3lb and can rate higher.

NOTEBOOK
Montpellier(IRE) had been given a chance by the Handicapper this time, and had no problem handling the drop in trip. Probably better suited by this track than Wolverhampton on his only previous attempt on Polytrack, he travelled smoothly and found a decent turn of foot to clinch it.
Unshakable(IRE) has been dropped to a pound below his lowest winning mark after a dip in form last year. Shuffled back on the turn into the straight, he came back strongly to show he is still capable of landing a good prize at the age of eight.
Granston(IRE), down the field in the Lincoln, lasted longer this time over a course and distance that suits, and battled gamely in the home straight. He can usually be relied upon to give his supporters a run for their money, and looked as good as ever here. (op 8-1)
Killena Boy(IRE) won over course and distance last September, and begins this season just 3lb higher. This was a solid start to the season, and he is also useful on turf, so should have a good campaign. (op 11-1)
Top Mark came into the race in fine form on Polytrack, but this was a better race than he usually runs in, and he ended up just setting the race up for stronger rivals. Nonetheless, he deserves credit for only going under in the final furlong. (op 16-1)
Acheekyone(IRE) has given the impression that he would be suited by a bit farther than 1m these days, so a step up in trip should be noted with interest. (op 5-1)
Marajaa(IRE) continues to run creditably without getting into the first three, but any leniency from the Handicapper might tilt things his way. (op 11-2 tchd 6-1)
Kingsholm Official explanation: jockey said gelding suffered interference on leaving stalls
Lady Stardust, comfortable winner of a Newbury maiden on her only previous start last August, was well beaten on this Polytrack and handicap debut. (tchd 11-4 and 7-2)

1525 DIGIBET UK FILLIES' H'CAP 6f (P)
5:00 (5:02) (Class 4) (0-85,84) 4-Y-0+ **£4,728** (£1,406; £702; £351) **Stalls** High

Form RPR

0-33 **1** **Keyaki (IRE)**[4] 1431 6-8-9 **75** .... TedDurcan 7 83+
(C F Wall) *cl up: rdn to chse ldr over 1f out: r.o to ld nr fin* **7/4**[1]

00-0 **2** *1/2* **Shes Minnie**[26] 1004 4-8-6 **72** .... RobertHavlin 5 78
(J G M O'Shea) *stdd s: hld up and bhd: rapid hdwy to ld wl over 1f out: kpt on u.p fnl f: hdd nr fin* **10/1**

3152 **3** *nk* **Sweet Pickle**[6] 1377 6-8-4 **70** oh2..........(e) ChrisCatlin 6 75
(J R Boyle) *t.k.h: hld up towards rr: nt clr run and swtchd lft over 2f out: styd on wl u.p fnl f* **4/1**[2]

00-0 **4** *1 1/4* **Tara Too (IRE)**[14] 1195 4-8-11 **80** .... EmmettStack(3) 8 81
(J G Portman) *in tch: effrt whn hmpd and swtchd rt over 1f out: kpt on fnl f* **20/1**

0-60 **5** *3/4* **China Cherub**[14] 1200 4-8-5 **71** .... FrancisNorton 9 70
(R Hannon) *chsd ldrs: drvn to ld over 2f out: hdd wl over 1f out: edgd lft: one pce* **4/1**[2]

54-2 **6** *4* **Overwing (IRE)**[21] 1067 4-8-9 **75** .... JamieSpencer 1 61
(R M H Cowell) *t.k.h: pressed ldr tl wknd over 2f out: btn whn n.m.r wl over 1f out* **5/1**[3]

500- **7** *6* **Hello Roberto**[224] 5575 6-8-1 **70** oh3..........(p) LiamJones(3) 3 37
(R A Harris) *led tl over 2f out: sn wknd* **20/1**

1m 13.98s (0.28) **Going Correction** +0.125s/f (Slow) **7** Ran SP% **111.6**
Speed ratings (Par 102):103,102,101,100,99 93,85
CSF £19.64 CT £59.88 TOTE £2.80: £1.60, £4.20; EX 35.20.
Owner S Oldroyd **Bred** Rathbarry Stud **Trained** Newmarket, Suffolk

FOCUS
A fair sprint, but the pace was just a medium one for the trip, and several of the runners suffered interference as they attempted to make their moves in the home straight. Not an easy race to assess, it has been rated around the third.

1526 DIGITOTE H'CAP 2m (P)
5:30 (5:32) (Class 5) (0-75,75) 4-Y-0+ **£2,914** (£867; £433; £216) **Stalls** High

Form RPR

402/ **1** **Gala Evening**[66] 1861 5-9-10 **75** .... AdamKirby 7 84+
(J A B Old) *stdd s: hld up in rr: hdwy on outside 3f out: hrd rdn over 2f out: led over 1f out: styd on wl* **12/1**

3-02 **2** *1 1/4* **Tavalu (USA)**[29] 691 5-8-13 **64** .... JimmyFortune 6 72
(G L Moore) *prom: drvn to press wnr over 1f out: nt qckn ins fnl f* **5/1**[3]

-433 **3** *3/4* **Follow On**[62] 458 5-9-0 **65** .... BrettDoyle 3 72+
(A P Jarvis) *towards rr: hdwy 3f out: rdn and styd on wl fnl 2f: wnt 3rd nr fin* **9/2**[2]

6-12 **4** *nk* **Dark Parade (ARG)**[16] 1152 6-9-1 **66** .... JamieSpencer 10 73
(P D Evans) *mid-div: effrt 3f out: rdn to chse ldrs over 1f out: styd on same pce* **9/4**[1]

-343 **5** *3/4* **Eforetta (GER)**[13] 1222 5-8-10 **61** .... EdwardCreighton 9 67
(D J Wintle) *chsd ldrs: led over 4f out tl over 1f out: no ex fnl f* **9/1**

50-0 **6** *5* **Bobsleigh**[30] 213 8-8-5 **56** oh8.......... RichardThomas 1 56
(H S Howe) *mid-div: effrt 3f out: nt pce to chal* **50/1**

7 *1* **Toryt (POL)**[68] 8-8-5 **56** oh4.......... HayleyTurner 12 55
(Carl Llewellyn) *in tch: rdn and lost pl 3f out: kept on fnl f* **20/1**

0-56 **8** *1* **Spring Dream (IRE)**[16] 1158 4-8-12 **66** .... TedDurcan 2 63
(M R Channon) *stdd s: hld up in rr: rdn 3f out: nvr rchd ldrs* **16/1**

65-3 **9** *nk* **Longhill Tiger**[28] 981 4-8-13 **67** .... TPQueally 14 64
(G G Margarson) *t.k.h: prom tl wknd over 2f out* **20/1**

222- **10** *1/2* **Acknowledgement**[47] 6108 5-9-4 **69** ....(b) FrancisNorton 4 65
(Carl Llewellyn) *stdd s: hld up towards rr: rdn over 2f out: n.d* **12/1**

/00- **11** *1/2* **Veverka**[22] 2186 6-8-5 **56** oh4..........(p) RichardSmith 5 52
(J C Fox) *in tch tl wknd over 4f out: sn bhd and drvn along* **50/1**

011- **12** *1/2* **Rehearsed (IRE)**[186] 6312 4-8-9 **68** .... TravisBlock(5) 11 63
(H Morrison) *prom tl wknd over 3f out* **13/2**

0220 **13** *8* **Teorban (POL)**[22] 677 8-8-7 **58** .... RobertHavlin 8 44
(Mrs N S Evans) *led tl over 4f out: wknd qckly over 2f out: bhd and eased fnl f* **25/1**

3m 32.95s (1.55) **Going Correction** +0.125s/f (Slow)
WFA 4 from 5yo+ 3lb **13** Ran SP% **127.5**
Speed ratings (Par 103):101,100,100,99,99 96,96,95,95,95 95,95,91
CSF £71.87 CT £324.14 TOTE £11.00: £4.00, £2.00, £2.60; EX 72.40 Place 6 £8,818.32, Place 5 £1,339.17.
Owner W E Sturt **Bred** Juddmonte Farms **Trained** Barbury Castle, Wilts

FOCUS
A moderate but competitive staying race. The decent early tempo steadied a bit in mid-race. Solid form, with the second to the fifth all within a pound of their pre-race marks. The winner is unexposed on the Flat.
T/Plt: £7,162.50 to a £1 stake. Pool: £53,964.10. 5.50 winning tickets. T/Qpdt: £47.70 to a £1 stake. Pool: £3,991.70. 61.80 winning tickets. LM

1040 NEWCASTLE (L-H)
Monday, May 7

OFFICIAL GOING: Good to firm (firm in places)
Wind: Fresh across

1527 DRUMMOND CENTRAL APPRENTICE CLAIMING STKS 7f
2:35 (2:36) (Class 6) 4-Y-0+ **£2,266** (£674; £337; £168) **Stalls** Centre

Form RPR

0012 **1** **Just James**[4] 1423 8-8-11 64 .... AdeleRothery(5) 12 62+
(D Nicholls) *hld up stands' side: n.m.r over 2f out: hdwy over 1f out: led ins fnl f: r.o wl* **15/8**[1]

634- **2** *nk* **Queen's Echo**[191] 6211 6-8-9 51 .... DuranFentiman 8 54
(M Dods) *swtchd to stands' rail sn after s and sn drvn along: hdwy 2f out: ev ch ins fnl f: kpt on nr fin* **4/1**[2]

000- **3** *2 1/2* **Frimley's Mattery**[211] 5839 7-8-7 47 .... NeilBrown(3) 10 48
(R E Barr) *chsd stands' side ldrs: led over 2f out: edgd lft and hdd ins fnl f: no ex* **20/1**

-005 **4** *2* **Red Lantern**[13] 1221 6-8-11 42 .... NSLawes(5) 9 49
(M W Easterby) *hld up stands' side: hdwy over 1f out: kpt on fnl f: nrst fin* **20/1**

060- **5** *2 1/2* **Cashema (IRE)**[22] 3139 6-8-2 36 ....(t) JamesRogers(5) 2 33
(James Moffatt) *sn bhd and outpcd far side: hdwy centre 2f out: kpt on wl fnl f: nrst fin* **40/1**

0200 **6** *2 1/2* **Nevinstown (IRE)**[74] 519 7-9-2 43 .... MichaelJStainton 13 35
(C Grant) *missed break: bhd stands' side tl hdwy over 1f out: nrst fin* **12/1**

0-00 **7** *shd* **Bold Tiger (IRE)**[4] 1423 4-8-7 44 ....(t) SamuelDrury(5) 14 31
(Miss Tracy Waggott) *prom stands' side gp tl rdn and no ex fr 2f out* **33/1**

0-04 **8** *1* **Four Kings**[13] 1221 6-9-2 45 .... JamieMoriarty 3 32
(Karen McLintock) *led smaller far side gp to ins fnl f: no ex* **12/1**

00-0 **9** *1 3/4* **Ho Pang Yau**[28] 966 9-8-9 42 .... GaryBartley(5) 15 26
(J S Goldie) *chsd stands' side ldrs tl wknd fr 2f out* **20/1**

000- **10** *1 3/4* **Time Marches On**[159] 4954 9-9-5 44 .... JamesReveley(3) 1 29
(K G Reveley) *sn wl bhd far side: nvr on terms* **20/1**

-500 **11** *2* **Suffolk House**[73] 533 5-8-7 40 ....(b) JemmaMarshall(5) 7 13
(M Brittain) *prom on outside of stands' side gp: rdn and wknd over 2f out* **25/1**

00-0 **12** *3/4* **Passionately Royal**[17] 1132 5-8-7 52 ....(b[1]) AndrewHeffernan(7) 11 13
(M Brittain) *led stands' side gp to over 2f out: sn btn* **18/1**

1100 **13** *1 1/4* **Island Green (USA)**[21] 1064 4-8-7 57 .... KellyHarrison(3) 4 6
(D Carroll) *cl up far side tl wknd over 2f out* **11/2**[3]

-000 **14** *4* **Teddy Monty (IRE)**[13] 1221 4-8-7 30 ....(b) DanielleMcCreery(3) 5 —
(R E Barr) *chsd far side ldrs: sn rdn along: struggling fr 3f out* **100/1**

1m 30.57s (2.55) **Going Correction** +0.10s/f (Good) **14** Ran SP% **120.1**
Speed ratings (Par 101):89,88,85,83,80 77,77,76,74,72 70,69,67,63
CSF £7.36 TOTE £2.20: £1.10, £1.90, £4.90; EX 11.50.Queen's Echo was claimed by E Nesbitt for £7,000

Owner G G N Bloodstock Ltd **Bred** Miss S N Ralphs **Trained** Sessay, N Yorks

FOCUS

A weak claimer. The field split into two groups and those on the stands' side were at an advantage. The winning time was moderate, even for a race like this.

1528 E.B.F./GRANGE INTERIORS MEDIAN AUCTION MAIDEN STKS 5f

3:05 (3:05) (Class 6) 2-Y-O **£2,914** (£867; £433; £216) **Stalls** Centre

Form				RPR
4	1		**Bahama Baileys**[9] 1291 2-9-3 J-PGuillambert 2 (M Johnston) *mde all: rdn 2f out: kpt on strly fnl f* **4/1**[2]	78+
	2	3	**Pelican Prince** 2-9-3 PatCosgrave 3 (K R Burke) *trckd ldrs: effrt 2f out: chsd wnr ins fnl f: kpt on* **7/2**[1]	66
3	3	2	**Shatter Resistant (IRE)**[6] 1367 2-9-3 SamHitchcott 1 (M R Channon) *trckd ldrs: effrt and edgd lft over 1f out: one pce fnl f* **7/2**[1]	58
	4	shd	**Gain Share** 2-9-3 PaulFessey 8 (T D Barron) *plld hrd: chsd ldrs: effrt over 1f out: no ex* **9/2**[3]	58
	5	5	**Sandies Choice** 2-8-12 DeanMernagh 11 (M Brittain) *cl up tl rdn and wknd over 1f out* **33/1**	33
	6	1 ½	**Tikinheart (IRE)** 2-9-3 DavidAllan 5 (T D Easterby) *missed break and outpcd: hdwy 1/2-way: no imp wl over 1f out* **8/1**	32
	7	shd	**Lucky Stream** 2-8-5 AndrewHeffernan(7) 6 (M Brittain) *sn outpcd in rr: nvr on terms* **80/1**	26
	8	3 ½	**Firenza Bond** 2-8-12 DuranFentiman(5) 10 (G R Oldroyd) *hld up: hmpd over 3f out: sn btn* **12/1**	17+
	9	nk	**Latin Dancer** 2-9-3 PaulHanagan 9 (B S Rothwell) *hld up in tch: blkd and hmpd over 3f out: sn btn* **33/1**	16+
	F		**Emma's Secrets** 2-8-9 PatrickMathers(3) 7 (Miss M E Rowland) *in tch: n.m.r and fell over 3f out* **8/1**	—

62.61 secs (1.11) **Going Correction** +0.10s/f (Good) **10 Ran SP% 119.7**

Speed ratings (Par 91):95,90,87,86,78 76,76,70,70,—

CSF £18.80 TOTE £4.70: £1.40, £1.80, £1.60; EX 23.60.

Owner G R Bailey Ltd (Baileys Horse Feeds) **Bred** P And Mrs A G Venner **Trained** Middleham Moor, N Yorks

■ Stewards' Enquiry : J-P Guillambert two-day ban: careless riding (Jun 4-5)

FOCUS

Just an ordinary maiden, but a useful winner who was much improved from his debut and should have further improvement in him. They all raced near side.

NOTEBOOK

Bahama Baileys ◆ improved significantly on the form he showed on his debut at Leicester to run out a most convincing winner. He deserves to take his chance in better company. (op 3-1)

Pelican Prince, a 41,000gns brother to dual 6f two-year-old winner Lindus Atenor, half-brother to 5f juvenile winner Ishi Adiva, out of a multiple sprint scorer, shaped nicely on his racecourse debut behind the useful winner. (op 10-3)

Shatter Resistant(IRE) failed to build on the form he showed when third on his debut in a reasonable maiden at Bath. (op 10-3 tchd 3-1)

Gain Share, a brother to Zylig, a 1m winner at three in Italy, half-brother to very smart juvenile Caesar Beware, out of a winner over 1m-1m3f in Italy, was quite solid in the market but he raced keenly. This was a respectable debut and there should be better to come. (tchd 5-1)

Sandies Choice, a 5,000gns first foal of a mare who was unplaced over 6f-1m3f, hails from a stable who have made little impact with their two-year-olds so far this year and she was beaten a fair way.

Firenza Bond was hampered by the faller three out and is a little better than he was able to show. (op 14-1)

Latin Dancer was also hampered by the faller three out. (tchd 28-1)

Emma's Secrets, a 34,000gns purchase, out of a smart dual 5f juvenile winner, was really well backed but her race came to a premature end when she took a nasty fall over three furlongs out. (op 28-1 tchd 33-1 in a place)

1529 SOLEX MAIDEN STKS 1m 2f 32y

3:35 (3:36) (Class 5) 3-Y-O+ **£3,238** (£963; £481; £240) **Stalls** Low

Form				RPR
/35-	1		**Dan Dare (USA)**[323] 2682 4-9-12 87 KerrinMcEvoy 6 (Sir Michael Stoute) *pressed ldr: led over 2f out: comf* **2/5**[1]	78+
-333	2	1 ½	**Deadline (UAE)**[17] 1131 3-8-11 73 PaulFessey 9 (P T Midgley) *hld up in tch: effrt over 2f out: chsd wnr over 1f out: kpt on fnl f: nt rch wnr* **5/1**[2]	71
	3	6	**Modarab**[82] 5-9-7 JamieMoriarty(5) 8 (Mrs L B Normile) *bhd: rdn 1/2-way: styd on fnl 2f: no ch w first two* **66/1**	61
5-	4	2 ½	**Livalex**[283] 3908 3-8-7 ow1 PhillipMakin 3 (M Dods) *trckd ldrs: smooth hdwy to chse wnr over 2f out: sn rdn: wknd over 1f out* **16/1**	51
226-	5	1 ½	**Musical Land (IRE)**[185] 6318 3-8-11 71 PaulHanagan 7 (J R Weymes) *prom tl rdn and wknd over 2f out* **10/1**[3]	52
	6	½	**Flagstone (USA)** 3-8-11 DaleGibson 4 (G A Swinbank) *hld up: shkn up 3f out: n.d* **10/1**[3]	51+
060-	7	hd	**Loch Awe**[276] 4111 4-9-7 46 DavidAllan 1 (R E Barr) *towards rr on ins: drvn 1/2-way: nvr on terms* **66/1**	47
0-0	8	1 ¼	**Fantastic Delight**[23] 1044 4-9-7 DanielTudhope 2 (G M Moore) *prom: rdn whn n.m.r over 2f out: sn btn* **33/1**	44
600-	9	8	**Stormingmichaelori**[166] 5363 4-9-5 43 LanceBetts(7) 5 (N Wilson) *led to over 2f out: wknd* **80/1**	34

2m 11.71s (-0.09) **Going Correction** +0.10s/f (Good)

WFA 3 from 4yo+ 15lb **9 Ran SP% 119.3**

Speed ratings (Par 103):104,102,98,96,94 94,94,93,86

CSF £2.99 TOTE £1.40: £1.02, £1.50, £16.20; EX 3.20.

Owner Philip Newton **Bred** Mill Ridge Farm Ltd **Trained** Newmarket, Suffolk

FOCUS

A weak and uncompetitive maiden in which Dan Dare was a class above. The runner-up probably ran only to a similar mark to his latest handicap run despite finishing clear of the third.

1530 KNIGHT FRANK H'CAP 6f

4:05 (4:05) (Class 5) (0-70,70) 3-Y-O **£3,562** (£1,059; £529; £264) **Stalls** Centre

Form				RPR
34-6	1		**Multitude (IRE)**[13] 1219 3-8-11 63 DavidAllan 13 (T D Easterby) *towards rr stands' side: hdwy to ld that gp ins fnl f: styd on wl to catch far side ldr nr fin* **15/2**	68
1	2	1	**Sea Rover (IRE)**[17] 1135 3-9-1 67 DeanMernagh 4 (M Brittain) *led far side quintet: rdn clr of that gp 2f out: styd on wl but ct by stands' side wnr nr fin: promising* **4/1**[2]	73+
50-0	3	1 ½	**Bond Casino**[27] 998 3-7-13 56 oh1 DuranFentiman(5) 11 (G R Oldroyd) *hld up stands' side: hdwy over 1f out: kpt on fnl f: nrst fin* **33/1**	54
3-54	4	nk	**Strathmore (IRE)**[33] 918 3-8-10 62 PaulHanagan 14 (R A Fahey) *in tch stands' side: effrt over 1f out: kpt on same pce fnl f* **9/2**[3]	59
0-01	5	¾	**A Big Sky Brewing (USA)**[14] 1197 3-8-8 60 PaulFessey 6 (T D Barron) *towards rr stands' side: hdwy over 1f out: kpt on fnl f: nvr rchd ldrs* **7/2**[1]	55
50-5	6	1 ¼	**Stormburst (IRE)**[27] 998 3-8-8 60 ow2 PhillipMakin 3 (M Dods) *hld up in tch far side: effrt over 2f out: no imp fnl f* **33/1**	55+
-144	7	¾	**Darcy's Pride (IRE)**[12] 1240 3-8-5 57 PaulQuinn 16 (D W Barker) *w stands' side ldrs tl rdn and no ex wl over 1f out* **12/1**	46
0-43	8	hd	**Howards Tipple**[13] 1219 3-8-13 65 (p) TomEaves 8 (I Semple) *w stands' side ldrs: led over 1f out to ins fnl f: no ex* **9/1**	53
4-50	9	1 ½	**Silly Gilly (IRE)**[16] 1164 3-8-4 56 oh4 AdrianTNicholls 5 (K R Burke) *dwlt: sn chsng far side ldr: rdn and wknd over 1f out* **25/1**	44+
005-	10	3 ½	**Soviet Sound (IRE)**[210] 5860 3-8-4 56 oh3 DaleGibson 9 (Jedd O'Keeffe) *bhd: sme hdwy over 1f out: n.d* **33/1**	29
50-0	11	2 ½	**Lucky Bee (IRE)**[15] 1176 3-8-13 70 JamieMoriarty(5) 2 (G A Swinbank) *chsd far side ldrs to 1/2-way: sn rdn and wknd* **18/1**	40+
0-02	12	½	**Rue Soleil**[12] 1240 3-8-4 59 AndrewMullen(3) 12 (J R Weymes) *prom stands' side: effrt over 2f out: wknd over 1f out* **33/1**	23
466-	13	1 ¼	**Nufoudh (IRE)**[249] 4955 3-8-8 60 PatCosgrave 7 (Miss Tracy Waggott) *prom on outside of stands' side gp: rdn over 2f out: wknd over 1f out* **40/1**	20
2105	14	1 ¾	**New York Oscar (IRE)**[9] 1286 3-9-4 70 (be) DanielTudhope 15 (A J McCabe) *slt ld stands' side to over 1f out: sn btn* **14/1**	25
10-0	15	5	**Centenary (IRE)**[33] 931 3-9-0 66 GrahamGibbons 1 (J J Quinn) *prom far side to 1/2-way: sn wknd* **14/1**	10+

1m 15.59s (0.50) **Going Correction** +0.10s/f (Good) **15 Ran SP% 126.5**

Speed ratings (Par 99):100,98,96,96,95 93,92,92,90,85 82,81,80,77,71

CSF £36.81 CT £996.51 TOTE £9.10: £2.60, £2.50, £8.50; EX 63.50.

Owner The Senators **Bred** R Goodwin **Trained** Great Habton, N Yorks

FOCUS

The field split into two groups, but there did not seem to be the same bias towards those on the stands' side as there had been in the first race, with Sea Rover emerging from a group of just five to claim second on the far side. Modest handicap form, and sound enough with the fourth the best guide.

1531 DUNELM HOMES EMFIELD SQUARE H'CAP 1m 3y(S)

4:35 (4:36) (Class 5) (0-70,70) 3-Y-O **£4,857** (£1,445; £722; £360) **Stalls** Centre

Form				RPR
420-	1		**Packers Hill (IRE)**[222] 5614 3-9-1 67 DeanMcKeown 7 (G A Swinbank) *stdd in midfield: hdwy to ld appr fnl f: pushed clr ins fnl f* **10/1**	74+
440-	2	3 ½	**Judge Neptune**[209] 5900 3-8-9 61 DanielTudhope 12 (J S Goldie) *midfield: effrt and swtchd lft over 2f out: ev ch over 1f out: kpt on: nt pce of wnr* **16/1**	60
0221	3	½	**Mark Of Love (IRE)**[5] 1399 3-9-1 61 6ex SamHitchcott 8 (M R Channon) *t.k.h: w ldr: led over 2f out to appr fnl f: nt qckn* **11/8**[1]	65
0-06	4	½	**Tomorrow's Dancer**[13] 1232 3-8-1 56 oh2 AndrewMullen(3) 14 (K A Ryan) *t.k.h: hld up: hdwy over 1f out: nvr rchd ldrs* **7/1**[3]	53+
04-0	5	1 ¼	**Kindlelight Blue (IRE)**[58] 655 3-9-2 68 GrahamGibbons 2 (N P Littmoden) *stdd s: effrt over 2f out: hung lft over 1f out: no imp* **20/1**	62
46-0	6	3 ½	**The Diamond Bond**[16] 1166 3-8-4 56 oh1 PaulQuinn 9 (G R Oldroyd) *hld up: effrt over 1f out: n.d* **25/1**	42
0-64	7	1 ¼	**Imperial Beach (USA)**[12] 1238 3-8-8 60 PaulFessey 3 (T D Barron) *towards rr: rdn over 2f out: no imp* **12/1**	43
3-35	8	hd	**Bold Indian (IRE)**[19] 1089 3-9-4 70 (p) TomEaves 10 (I Semple) *chsd ldrs tl wknd over 1f out* **5/1**[2]	53
00-0	9	½	**Galway Girl (IRE)**[18] 1111 3-7-13 56 oh1 (b[1]) DuranFentiman(5) 6 (T D Easterby) *prom: effrt over 2f out: wknd over 1f out* **18/1**	38
6-30	10	5	**Foxxy**[100] 267 3-9-1 67 PaddyAspell 13 (J R Norton) *prom tl rdn and wknd 2f out* **25/1**	37
1-0	11	3 ½	**Feeling Wonderful (IRE)**[9] 1297 3-9-2 68 J-PGuillambert 4 (M Johnston) *led to over 2f out: wknd over 1f out* **8/1**	30
05-0	12	18	**One And Gone (IRE)**[16] 1155 3-8-8 60 PaulHanagan 1 (R A Fahey) *hld up on outside: drvn 3f out: sn btn* **14/1**	—

1m 43.69s (1.79) **Going Correction** +0.10s/f (Good) **12 Ran SP% 129.4**

Speed ratings (Par 99):95,91,91,90,89 85,84,84,83,78 75,57

CSF £168.90 CT £362.41 TOTE £15.10: £3.80, £7.60, £1.30; EX 547.60.

Owner B Valentine **Bred** G J King **Trained** Melsonby, N Yorks

FOCUS

A modest handicap but a clear-cut winner, up 10lb. The form does not seem all that stong with the well-in third not running up to that form.

1532 NEW HOMES MORTGAGE SERVICES H'CAP 1m 4f 93y

5:05 (5:07) (Class 5) (0-70,70) 4-Y-O+ **£4,210** (£1,252; £625; £312) **Stalls** Low

Form				RPR
0-03	1		**Sudden Impulse**[11] 1258 6-8-11 63 TomEaves 1 (A D Brown) *hld up: hdwy centre 2f out: led ins fnl f: pushed out* **5/1**[2]	74
41-2	2	¾	**Light Sentence**[19] 1090 4-8-6 58 DeanMcKeown 4 (G A Swinbank) *hld up: hdwy centre to ld over 1f out: hdd ins fnl f: r.o* **2/1**[1]	68
3113	3	3 ½	**Apache Fort**[9] 1314 4-8-8 60 J-PGuillambert 3 (T Keddy) *hld up in midfield: hdwy to press ldrs over 1f out: nt qckn fnl f* **8/1**[3]	64
10-2	4	1 ¼	**Let It Be**[13] 1225 6-8-2 61 DanielleMcCreery(7) 11 (K G Reveley) *chsd ldrs: effrt over 2f out: one pce over 1f out* **11/1**	63
6501	5	2	**The Pen**[11] 1258 5-8-2 59 DuranFentiman(5) 5 (C W Fairhurst) *prom: rdn over 2f out: sn one pce* **10/1**	58
03-0	6	¾	**Tranos (USA)**[23] 1042 4-8-6 58 DaleGibson 13 (Micky Hammond) *t.k.h: cl up: led briefly 3f out: wknd over 1f out* **14/1**	56
-435	7	hd	**Intavac Boy**[23] 1042 6-8-8 60 PaulHanagan 2 (R A Fahey) *in tch: nt clr run 3f out: effrt 2f out: no imp* **5/1**[2]	57
60-3	8	½	**Aleron (IRE)**[16] 914 9-9-2 68 (p) GrahamGibbons 12 (J J Quinn) *cl up: chal over 3f out to over 1f out: wknd* **8/1**[3]	64
046	9	2 ½	**Wolds Way**[20] 1077 5-8-13 65 (b) DavidAllan 7 (T D Easterby) *hld up: hdwy to ld over 2f out: hdd & wknd over 1f out* **33/1**	57
06-3	10	4	**Border Tale**[13] 1225 7-7-13 58 oh4 ow2 (p) JamesRogers(7) 8 (James Moffatt) *bhd: outpcd over 4f out: n.d* **25/1**	44
5/05	11	13	**Frith (IRE)**[28] 966 5-8-8 65 JamieMoriarty(5) 6 (Mrs L B Normile) *led to 3f out: sn rdn and btn* **28/1**	30

2m 43.6s (0.05) **Going Correction** +0.10s/f (Good) **11 Ran SP% 123.2**

Speed ratings (Par 103):103,102,100,99,98 97,97,97,95,92 84

CSF £15.86 CT £83.22 TOTE £6.30: £1.90, £1.30, £3.70; EX 14.20 Place 6 £14.78, Place 5 £9.68.

Owner Mrs Glen E Salt **Bred** Sagittarius Bloodstock Associates Ltd **Trained** Pickering, York

FOCUS

A modest handicap run at just an ordinary pace. The first two are on the upgrade.

The Form Book, Raceform Ltd, Compton, RG20 6NL

T/Jkpt: Part won. £7,100.00 to a £1 stake. Pool: £10,000.00. 0.50 winning tickets. T/Plt: £7.20 to a £1 stake. Pool: £85,207.20. 8,613.40 winning tickets. T/Qpdt: £6.60 to a £1 stake. Pool: £3,087.10. 344.50 winning tickets. RY

1079 WARWICK (L-H)

Monday, May 7

OFFICIAL GOING: Good to firm

Wind: fresh, half-behind

1533 EUROPEAN BREEDERS' FUND PRIMROSE MAIDEN FILLIES' STKS 5f

2:10 (2:12) (Class 5) 2-Y-O **£3,562** (£1,059; £529; £264) **Stalls** Centre

Form RPR

3 **1** **Jennifers Joy (IRE)**[9] [1285] 2-9-0 .... JHBowman 3 78
(M R Channon) *led: hdd wl over 1f out: led jst ins fnl f: rdn and r.o wl* **5/2**[2]

2 **2** *1 1/4* **Ramatni**[20] [1079] 2-8-11 .... GregFairley(3) 9 73
(M Johnston) *a.p: led wl over 1f out: sn hung rt: hdd jst ins fnl f: rdn and nt qckn* **8/1**

22 **3** *shd* **Sinead Of Aglish (IRE)**[9] [1302] 2-9-0 .... JimmyQuinn 7 73+
(A B Haynes) *hld up in tch: n.m.r and lost pl 3f out: swtchd lft and hdwy 2f out: rdn and nt qckn ins fnl f* **9/4**[1]

4 *1 1/4* **Aide Memoir (IRE)** 2-9-0 .... FrankieMcDonald 11 68
(S Kirk) *chsd ldrs on outside: rdn and hung lft whn carried rt over 1f out: swtchd lft wl ins fnl f: kpt on* **40/1**

0 **5** *2* **Quick Sands (IRE)**[18] [1101] 2-9-0 .... PatDobbs 8 60
(R Hannon) *chsd ldrs: rdn over 2f out: one pce* **7/2**[3]

6 *nk* **Fabuleux Cherie** 2-9-0 .... EddieAhern 4 59
(W R Muir) *w ldr 2f: wknd wl over 1f out* **28/1**

7 *1* **Longoria (IRE)** 2-8-11 .... JerryO'Dwyer(3) 5 55
(M G Quinlan) *s.i.s: hdwy on ins over 2f out: rdn and wknd over 1f out* **11/1**

8 *nk* **Alexander Monarchy (IRE)** 2-9-0 .... NCallan 6 54
(K A Ryan) *hld up: rdn and short-lived effrt on ins 2f out* **16/1**

9 *2 1/2* **Madam Superior** 2-9-0 .... StephenDonohoe 10 44
(D J S Ffrench Davis) *prom: rdn over 2f out: wknd wl over 1f out* **100/1**

0 **10** *nk* **Bold Diva**[7] [1354] 2-9-0 .... DavidKinsella 1 42
(A W Carroll) *s.i.s: outpcd* **100/1**

11 *nk* **Marmite (IRE)** 2-9-0 .... LPKeniry 2 41
(E F Vaughan) *s.i.s: outpcd* **33/1**

59.70 secs (0.30) **Going Correction** -0.075s/f (Good) 11 Ran SP% **117.7**

Speed ratings (Par 90):94,92,91,89,86 86,84,84,80,79 79

CSF £22.17 TOTE £3.40: £1.20, £2.00, £1.40; EX 23.70.

Owner Liam Mulryan **Bred** Forenaghts Partnership No 1 **Trained** West Ilsley, Berks

■ Stewards' Enquiry : Greg Fairley three-day ban: careless riding (May 18,20-21)

FOCUS

This looked an ordinary fillies' maiden and the ability to race handily and previous experience proved crucial, with the front three all having had run at least once before. The winner and third set the standard and the form looks solid.

NOTEBOOK

Jennifers Joy(IRE), showing the benefit of her Haydock debut, was at the sharp end throughout and showed a decent attitude when challenged on both sides. She should continue to improve and an extra furlong should not be a problem. (op 85-40)

Ramatni was always up with the pace from her high draw, but once into the straight she was inclined to hang away to her right and was never doing enough. She has now finished runner-up twice over course and distance and the form of her debut is not really working out. (op 6-1)

Sinead Of Aglish(IRE) eventually did best of those held up after getting herself into all sorts of trouble throughout the contest. She may have been a bit unlucky, but she was the most experienced filly in the field so does not possess as much scope as a few of these. (op 5-2)

Aide Memoir(IRE), a cheap foal, was always up with the pace from the outside stall and may have finished even closer had she not been hampered against the stands' rail by the hanging Ramatni. She still did much the best of the newcomers and her pedigree suggests she will be suited by a bit further. (op 33-1)

Quick Sands(IRE), well backed to improve from her Newmarket debut, had every chance but did not have the speed to trouble the leaders and probably needs a step up in trip. (op 6-1)

Alexander Monarchy(IRE), a half-sister to Petardias Magic and Capable Guest, did not perform as badly as her finishing position might suggest on this debut and was probably not helped by taking a broadside from the eventual third passing the two-furlong pole. (op 12-1)

1534 RACING UK FILLIES' H'CAP 7f 26y

2:40 (2:40) (Class 5) (0-70,67) 3-Y-0+ **£3,238** (£963; £481; £240) **Stalls** Low

Form RPR

6-34 **1** **Tender The Great (IRE)**[105] [211] 4-9-9 **65**........ RichardKingscote(3) 4 76+
(B G Powell) *hld up towards rr: rdn and hdwy on ins over 2f out: r.o u.p to ld last strides* **7/1**[3]

2316 **2** *hd* **Another Genepi (USA)**[9] [1309] 4-9-9 **62**........(b) NCallan 12 72
(K A Ryan) *led: clr whn rdn over 1f out: ct last strides* **5/1**[2]

0-50 **3** *1* **Piccostar**[13] [1212] 4-9-1 **54**........ LPKeniry 6 61
(A B Haynes) *a.p: rdn over 1f out: kpt on ins fnl f* **20/1**

40-5 **4** *hd* **Baby Dordan (IRE)**[16] [1155] 3-8-11 **62**........ JimmyQuinn 1 65
(H J L Dunlop) *chsd ldrs: rdn wl over 1f out: kpt on ins fnl f* **7/1**[3]

060- **5** *2 1/2* **Safranine (IRE)**[229] [5487] 10-8-11 **55** oh1 ow2........ AnnStokell(5) 7 55
(Miss A Stokell) *s.i.s: sn chsng ldrs: rdn and no hdwy fnl 2f* **50/1**

355- **6** *1 1/2* **Miss Wedge**[327] [2554] 4-9-6 **59**........ TPO'Shea 13 55
(Tom Dascombe) *prom: ev ch over 2f out: rdn and wknd over 1f out* **14/1**

05-0 **7** *nk* **Making Music**[11] [1260] 4-9-2 **55**........ TonyHamilton 2 51
(T D Easterby) *mid-div: rdn and no hdwy fnl 2f* **8/1**

6405 **8** *1 1/2* **Danettie**[4] [1435] 6-8-9 **53** oh5........ WilliamBuick(5) 9 45
(W M Brisbourne) *hld up in mid-div: c wd bnd 3f out: no imp fnl 2f* **20/1**

6-56 **9** *1 3/4* **Fangorn Forest (IRE)**[7] [1352] 4-9-9 **67**........(p) TolleyDean(5) 14 54
(R A Harris) *bhd: rdn over 2f out: nvr nr ldrs* **25/1**

205- **10** *1 1/4* **Zell (IRE)**[224] [5583] 4-9-2 **55**........ DavidKinsella 8 39
(E J Alston) *s.i.s: a bhd* **50/1**

460- **11** *1* **Limonia (GER)**[216] [5752] 5-9-0 **53** oh1........ JamesDoyle 11 34
(Mike Murphy) *a bhd* **28/1**

066- **12** *3/4* **Ignition**[129] [6980] 5-8-11 **53** oh1........ GregFairley(3) 3 32
(W M Brisbourne) *s.i.s: a bhd* **10/1**

212- **13** *2 1/2* **Welsh Cake**[224] [5568] 4-9-13 **66**........(bt) EddieAhern 5 39
(Mrs A J Perrett) *t.k.h: prom: rdn 2f out: sn wknd: eased ins fnl f* **9/4**[1]

6U0- **P** **Reflecting (IRE)**[237] [5270] 4-9-7 **60**........ StephenDonohoe 10 —
(A W Carroll) *plld hrd: sddle sn slipped: bhd whn p.u 4f out* **66/1**

1m 23.17s (-1.03) **Going Correction** -0.075s/f (Good)

WFA 3 from 4yo+ 12lb 14 Ran SP% **121.5**

Speed ratings (Par 100):102,101,100,100,97 95,95,93,91,90 89,88,85,—

CSF £39.26 CT £699.27 TOTE £8.60: £2.90, £2.00, £7.70; EX 57.30.

Owner Miss Kwok-Mei Ada Yip **Bred** Y Wai Kwan **Trained** Lambourn, Berks

FOCUS

A competitive if modest fillies' handicap and, apart from the winner, all the principals raced close to the strong pace. Solid-looking form.

Fangorn Forest(IRE) Official explanation: jockey said filly was unsuited by the fast ground

Limonia(GER) Official explanation: jockey said mare lost its hind legs on final bend

Welsh Cake Official explanation: jockey said filly was unsuited by the loose ground

Reflecting(IRE) Official explanation: jockey said saddle slipped

1535 JOHN SMITH'S H'CAP (FOR THE COVENTRY CUP) 7f 26y

3:10 (3:12) (Class 4) (0-80,80) 3-Y-0 **£6,477** (£1,927; £963; £481) **Stalls** Low

Form RPR

31-0 **1** **Lord Theo**[19] [1099] 3-9-2 **78**........ JamesDoyle 1 80
(N P Littmoden) *mde all: hrd rdn over 1f out: r.o* **10/1**

2112 **2** *nk* **Captain Jacksparra (IRE)**[13] [1228] 3-9-4 **80**........ NCallan 8 81+
(K A Ryan) *t.k.h in rr: nt clr run and swtchd rt over 5f out: hdwy on ins 2f out: hrd rdn and r.o ins fnl f* **15/8**[1]

040- **3** *1/2* **Okikoki**[206] [5940] 3-9-3 **79**........ EddieAhern 5 79
(W R Muir) *sn w wnr: rdn over 2f out: kpt on ins fnl f* **10/1**

1-4 **4** *1* **Roodolph**[37] [843] 3-9-2 **78**........ StephenCarson 6 75
(Eve Johnson Houghton) *hld up in mid-div: rdn and carried hd high over 1f out: kpt on ins fnl f: nt rch ldrs* **5/2**[2]

01-0 **5** *shd* **Zahour Al Yasmeen**[20] [1076] 3-8-13 **75**........ JHBowman 2 72
(M R Channon) *a.p: rdn wl over 1f out: sn edgd rt: one pce fnl f* **7/1**[3]

32-4 **6** *1 1/2* **Teasing**[25] [1009] 3-9-0 **76**........ JimmyQuinn 4 69
(J Pearce) *s.i.s: hdwy on ins over 5f out: hrd rdn wl over 1f out: one pce* **11/1**

04-0 **7** *3* **Rainbow Fox**[15] [1176] 3-8-10 **72**........ RoystonFfrench 3 57
(R A Fahey) *prom: hmpd and lost pl over 5f out: rdn over 2f out: no imp fnl f* **14/1**

210- **8** *1 1/2* **Victory Spirit**[220] [5647] 3-8-12 **74**........ TPO'Shea 7 55
(H J L Dunlop) *hld up: hdwy on ins 3f out: rdn 2f out: wknd over 1f out* **25/1**

20-0 **9** *7* **Danseuse**[18] [1105] 3-9-0 **76**........ LPKeniry 9 38
(B J Meehan) *a in rr* **25/1**

1m 23.22s (-0.98) **Going Correction** -0.075s/f (Good) 9 Ran SP% **116.7**

Speed ratings (Par 101):102,101,101,99,99 98,94,92,84

CSF £29.47 CT £196.73 TOTE £12.70: £2.80, £1.20, £3.10; EX 45.50.

Owner R D Hartshorn **Bred** M J Perkins **Trained** Newmarket, Suffolk

FOCUS

Another race where it seemed an advantage to be close to the pace and only the runner-up came from the back. The winning time was marginally slower than the preceding handicap for older fillies. An improved effort from the winner, but the runner-up was unlucky.

Captain Jacksparra(IRE) Official explanation: jockey said colt was hampered on the back straight

Rainbow Fox Official explanation: jockey said gelding was hampered on the back straight

1536 EDGECOTE H'CAP 1m 4f 134y

3:40 (3:40) (Class 5) (0-70,69) 3-Y-0 **£3,238** (£963; £481; £240) **Stalls** Low

Form RPR

1354 **1** **Pret A Porter (UAE)**[13] [1211] 3-9-1 **66**........ StephenDonohoe 10 71
(P D Evans) *hld up in rr: rdn and hdwy on ins 2f out: led ins fnl f: drvn out* **9/1**

00-3 **2** *1* **Chiff Chaff**[7] [1361] 3-8-9 **60**........ StephenCarson 3 64
(M L W Bell) *a.p: rdn over 2f out: led briefly ins fnl f: nt qckn* **9/2**[1]

-003 **3** *1/2* **Marju's Gold**[13] [1224] 3-8-7 **58**........ TPO'Shea 1 61
(E J O'Neill) *t.k.h early towards rr: rdn and hdwy 2f out: ev ch ins fnl f: nt qckn* **9/2**[1]

0-00 **4** *1 3/4* **Bathwick Breeze**[38] [834] 3-8-9 **60**........ JimmyQuinn 7 60
(A B Haynes) *prom: wnt 2nd after 2f: led 3f out: rdn over 1f out: hdd and no ex ins fnl f* **40/1**

04-3 **5** *3/4* **Irish Dancer**[24] [1024] 3-9-2 **67**........ EddieAhern 9 66
(J L Dunlop) *hld up towards rr: rdn 2f out: styd on ins fnl f: nvr nrr* **6/1**[3]

-501 **6** *3/4* **Callisto Moon**[20] [1084] 3-8-13 **69**........ WilliamBuick(5) 8 67
(Ian Williams) *hld up and bhd: hdwy over 6f out: rdn over 3f out: no imp fnl 2f* **6/1**[3]

0-15 **7** *1 1/4* **Always Best**[14] [1194] 3-8-12 **66**........(b[1]) GregFairley(3) 2 62
(M Johnston) *led: rdn and hdd 3f out: wknd fnl f* **5/1**[2]

000- **8** *3/4* **Abbotts Account (USA)**[221] [5640] 3-8-6 **57**........ JamesDoyle 5 52
(Mrs A J Perrett) *hld up in tch: rdn over 3f out: wknd 2f out* **11/1**

20-5 **9** *1/2* **Cheshire Prince**[12] [1238] 3-8-11 **62**........ NCallan 4 56
(W M Brisbourne) *t.k.h in tch: rdn 2f out: wknd over 1f out* **25/1**

0-52 **10** *53* **Royal Tender (IRE)**[91] [370] 3-8-7 **61**........ RichardKingscote(3) 6 —
(B G Powell) *a bhd: rdn 5f out: lost tch 3f out: eased fnl 2f* **20/1**

2m 43.18s (-0.42) **Going Correction** -0.075s/f (Good) 10 Ran SP% **116.2**

Speed ratings (Par 99):98,97,97,96,95 95,94,93,93,60

CSF £49.12 CT £209.28 TOTE £12.80: £3.10, £2.00, £1.70; EX 45.80.

Owner John P Jones **Bred** Darley **Trained** Pandy, Monmouths

FOCUS

A routine middle-distance handicap for three-year-olds run at an ordinary pace. The winner was one of the more exposed members of the field and the overall form is nothing special.

Royal Tender(IRE) Official explanation: jockey said filly was unsuited by the undulating track

1537 WARWICKRACECOURSE.CO.UK MEDIAN AUCTION MAIDEN FILLIES' STKS 1m 22y

4:10 (4:11) (Class 5) 3-5-Y-0 **£3,238** (£963; £481; £240) **Stalls** Low

Form RPR

3 **1** **Graduation**[17] [1128] 3-8-12 .... NCallan 8 68+
(E A L Dunlop) *hld up: sn in mid-div: hdwy over 3f out: led on bit over 1f out: shkn up and qcknd clr ins fnl f: easily* **1/3**[1]

2 *3 1/2* **Pendulum Star** 3-8-12 .... StephenDonohoe 2 54
(W R Swinburn) *t.k.h in rr: hdwy 4f out: hung rt over 1f out: r.o to take 2nd nr fin: no ch w wnr* **8/1**[3]

553- **3** *hd* **Lady Alize (USA)**[170] [6520] 3-8-12 86........(t) EddieAhern 11 54
(R A Kvisla) *led: rdn and hdd over 1f out: one pce* **11/2**[2]

000- **4** *1 3/4* **Cadi May**[274] [4171] 3-8-12 40........ RoystonFfrench 10 50
(W M Brisbourne) *plld hrd early: sn w ldr: rdn 2f out: one pce* **100/1**

600- **5** *5* **Musical Chimes**[168] [6542] 4-9-11 40........ RobbieFitzpatrick 6 41
(W M Brisbourne) *prom: rdn over 1f out: wknd fnl f* **100/1**

00- **6** *1 1/2* **Lady Shirley Hunt**[233] [5389] 3-8-12 .... JimmyQuinn 4 35
(A D Smith) *t.k.h towards rr: sme hdwy whn rdn and hung lft jst over 1f out: no further prog* **100/1**

0-00 **7** *2* **Lady Lucas (IRE)**[106] [204] 4-9-4 30........(t) SCreighton(7) 9 33
(E J Creighton) *prom tl wknd wl over 1f out* **200/1**

60 **8** *hd* **Pretty Demanding (IRE)**[10] [1278] 3-8-10 ow1........(t) JerryO'Dwyer(3) 1 30
(M G Quinlan) *a bhd* **28/1**

9 *1* **Jaffna**[43] 5-9-11 .... JamesDoyle 7 30
(R T Phillips) *hld up in mid-div: rdn over 2f out: no rspnse* **80/1**

10 *2* **Storm Obsession (IRE)**[220] [5661] 3-8-12 68 .... AmirQuinn 3 23
(P J Makin) *a bhd* **25/1**

50-0 11 *3* **All Talk**[110] [162] 3-8-5 45 .... MCGeran(7) 5 16
(M J Gingell) *plld v hrd: a bhd* **100/1**

1m 39.8s (0.20) **Going Correction** -0.075s/f (Good)
WFA 3 from 4yo+ 13lb **11** Ran SP% **114.5**
Speed ratings (Par 100):96,92,92,90,85 84,82,81,80,78 75
CSF £3.34 TOTE £1.20: £1.02, £1.70, £1.20; EX 4.40.
Owner Cheveley Park Stud **Bred** Cheveley Park Stud Ltd **Trained** Newmarket, Suffolk

FOCUS
An extremely uncompetitive fillies' maiden with only three of the 11 runners starting at under 25-1, and they happened to be the first three. The winner had nothing to beat and the form looks very weak.
Cadi May Official explanation: jockey said filly hung right throughout
Lady Shirley Hunt Official explanation: jockey said filly was hampered on leaving stalls
Pretty Demanding(IRE) Official explanation: jockey said filly hung left

1538 ENTERTAIN CLIENTS AT WARWICK RACECOURSE H'CAP 1m 22y
4:40 (4:41) (Class 6) (0-60,62) 3-Y-O **£2,388** (£705; £352) **Stalls** Low

Form RPR

050- **1** **Golden Prospect**[177] [6441] 3-9-2 58 .... EddieAhern 16 66+
(J W Hills) *hld up towards rr: hdwy on outside 2f out: rdn and hung lft over 1f out: r.o to ld last strides* **16/1**

-001 **2** *nk* **Private Peachey (IRE)**[4] [1432] 3-8-12 54 6ex .... TPO'Shea 8 62
(B R Millman) *led: rdn over 1f out: edgd lft ins fnl f: hdd last strides* **4/1**[1]

006 **3** *1 1/4* **Sixfields Flyer (IRE)**[20] [1081] 3-8-8 57 .... KMay(7) 17 62+
(Pat Eddery) *hld up and bhd: rdn and hdwy fnl 2f: r.o* **25/1**

0035 **4** *1 1/4* **Gee Ceffyl Bach**[46] [731] 3-8-13 55 .... JHBowman 9 57
(M R Channon) *hld up in tch: swtchd lft over 1f out: rdn and one pce fnl f* **20/1**

0030 **5** *2* **Mutoon (IRE)**[7] [1345] 3-8-6 53 .... WilliamBuick(5) 11 50
(S C Williams) *hld up in mid-div: rdn and hdwy over 1f out: one pce fnl f* **6/1**[3]

3405 **6** *1/2* **Storm Mission (USA)**[11] [1266] 3-8-1 50 .... SCreighton(7) 10 46
(Miss V Haigh) *prom: rdn wl over 1f out: sn carried rt: one pce fnl f* **6/1**[3]

460- **7** *1/2* **The Skerret**[231] [5417] 3-9-3 59 .... MatthewHenry 7 54
(P Winkworth) *w ldr: rdn and hung lft over 1f out: hung lft and wknd ins fnl f* **16/1**

5260 **8** *3/4* **The Tinker Man**[12] [1248] 3-8-1 50 .... FrankiePickard(7) 1 43+
(M D I Usher) *hld up and bhd: rdn and hdwy whn swtchd lft over 1f out: n.d* **16/1**

4-21 **9** *nk* **Falcon's Fire (IRE)**[4] [1425] 3-9-6 62 6ex .... RoystonFfrench 2 55
(Mrs A Duffield) *hld up in tch: rdn over 3f out: wknd over 1f out* **9/2**[2]

05-0 **10** *nk* **Clytha**[16] [1154] 3-8-13 55 .... StephenCarson 6 47
(M L W Bell) *hld up in mid-div: rdn 3f out: wknd wl over 1f out* **40/1**

6200 **11** *nk* **Suhayl Star (IRE)**[12] [1238] 3-9-4 60 .... JamieMackay 13 51+
(S W Hall) *s.v.s: nvr nrr* **28/1**

0500 **12** *3/4* **Tina's Ridge (IRE)**[16] [1154] 3-8-13 55 .... (b[1]) JimmyQuinn 4 45
(E J Alston) *s.i.s: a bhd* **33/1**

055- **13** *nk* **Flying Grey (IRE)**[175] [6466] 3-8-13 55 .... FrankieMcDonald 15 44+
(P A Blockley) *a bhd* **33/1**

600- **14** *2 1/2* **Katie Kingfisher**[136] [6912] 3-8-8 50 .... JamesDoyle 5 33
(R M Beckett) *prom: rdn over 2f out: hung lft and wknd over 1f out* **20/1**

4-06 **15** *7* **Mujart**[12] [1238] 3-8-7 54 .... RussellKennemore(5) 14 21
(J A Pickering) *a bhd* **33/1**

42-0 **16** *26* **Flower Of Cork (IRE)**[19] [1091] 3-9-4 60 .... TonyHamilton 3 —
(T D Easterby) *mid-div: pushed along over 3f out: bhd fnl 2f: eased whn no ch fnl f* **28/1**

1m 39.04s (-0.56) **Going Correction** -0.075s/f (Good) **16** Ran SP% **115.9**
Speed ratings (Par 97):99,98,97,96,94 93,93,92,92,91 91,90,90,88,81 55
CSF £56.42 CT £1093.82 TOTE £13.60: £3.40, £1.90, £6.20, £5.00; EX 100.40.
Owner Michael Wauchope And Partners **Bred** D E And Mrs J Cash **Trained** Upper Lambourn, Berks

FOCUS
A low-grade affair, but a competitive handicap despite the late withdrawal of the 9/2 second-favourite The Bronx (jockey unhappy with the horse, deduct 15p in the £ under Rule 4). The winning time was 0.76 seconds faster than the preceding fillies' maiden over the same trip, but was still only ordinary for the grade. Little solid form to go on, but the race could easily be rated higher and the winner and third in particular should be capable of better.
Tina's Ridge(IRE) Official explanation: jockey said colt was denied a clear run on final bend

1539 KNOWLE APPRENTICE H'CAP 1m 22y
5:10 (5:13) (Class 6) (0-60,59) 4-Y-O+ **£2,047** (£604; £302) **Stalls** Low

Form RPR

120- **1** **Jill Dawson (IRE)**[290] [3695] 4-9-0 57 .... KirstyMilczarek(3) 5 65+
(John Berry) *led: hdd 5f out: w ldr: led 2f out: edgd lft ins fnl f: r.o* **12/1**

60-4 **2** *1 1/2* **Murrumbidgee (IRE)**[12] [1251] 4-9-1 58 .... PatrickHills(3) 10 66+
(J W Hills) *hld up and bhd: hdwy on wd outside whn rdn and hung lft over 1f out: r.o wl ins fnl f: nt rch wnr* **8/1**[3]

-000 **3** *nk* **Music Celebre (IRE)**[63] [610] 7-9-0 59 .... (b) WilliamCarson(5) 4 63
(S Curran) *chsd ldrs: ev ch 2f out: sn rdn: kpt on ins fnl f* **16/1**

00-6 **4** *shd* **Foolish Groom**[28] [976] 6-8-10 53 .... RussellKennemore(3) 11 57
(R Hollinshead) *t.k.h in tch: hrd rdn over 1f out: kpt on ins fnl f* **12/1**

000- **5** *nk* **Adobe**[190] [6232] 12-8-3 50 .... Julie-AnneCumine(7) 2 53
(W M Brisbourne) *hld up and bhd: hdwy over 1f out: nt qckn ins fnl f* **25/1**

-466 **6** *nk* **Reveur**[10] [1284] 4-8-9 52 .... SCreighton(3) 14 54
(M Mullineaux) *hld up in mid-div: hdwy over 1f out: one pce fnl f* **25/1**

6005 **7** *hd* **Blue Empire (IRE)**[11] [1260] 6-9-0 57 .... TolleyDean(3) 7 59
(C R Dore) *n.m.r s: sn mid-div: rdn and hdwy wl over 1f out: one pce fnl f* **9/1**

00-2 **8** *nk* **Raul Sahara**[9] [1311] 5-8-8 51 .... JackMitchell(3) 17 52
(J W Unett) *hld up and bhd: rdn over 2f out: hdwy over 1f out: no ex ins fnl f* **33/1**

0-00 **9** *nk* **Salvestro**[4] [1435] 4-8-8 53 .... MarkCoumbe(5) 12 54+
(A W Carroll) *hld up and bhd: nt clr run and swtchd lft 1f out: nvr trble ldrs* **16/1**

035 **10** *hd* **Ellen's Girl (IRE)**[13] [1206] 4-8-7 50 .... (p) AshleyHamblett(3) 3 54+
(B G Powell) *hld up in mid-div: nt clr run on ins and lost pl ent st: rdn and hdwy on ins 1f out: n.d* **17/2**

1126 **11** *1/2* **Norwegian**[9] [1295] 6-8-10 55 .... (p) MCGeran(5) 13 54+
(Ian Williams) *hld up towards rr: rdn over 2f out: nt clr run and swtchd rt ins fnl f: n.d* **9/2**[1]

000- **12** *1 1/4* **Sands Of Barra (IRE)**[131] [6952] 4-9-5 59 .... PJMcDonald 16 55
(I W McInnes) *prom tl wknd over 2f out* **16/1**

0600 **13** *shd* **Consonant (IRE)**[28] [976] 10-8-11 51 .... RoryMoore 1 47
(D G Bridgwater) *chsd ldr: led 5f out to 2f out: sn rdn: wknd 1f out* **14/1**

0-60 **14** *hd* **Alwariah**[7] [1347] 4-8-8 53 .... SophieDoyle(5) 8 48
(Ms J S Doyle) *a bhd* **33/1**

2-06 **15** *1/2* **Khetaab (IRE)**[11] [1260] 5-8-13 53 .... MarkFlynn 15 47
(E J Alston) *prom tl rdn and wknd wl over 1f out* **9/1**

06-0 **16** *1/2* **Komreyev Star**[48] [716] 5-8-8 53 .... JamieHamblett(5) 6 46
(R E Peacock) *prom tl rdn and wknd over 1f out* **33/1**

00-1 **17** *14* **The Bonus King**[16] [1162] 7-9-0 54 .... WilliamBuick 9 15
(J Jay) *in tch: lost pl after 2f: bhd fnl 3f* **5/1**[2]

1m 38.95s (-0.65) **Going Correction** -0.075s/f (Good) **17** Ran SP% **132.7**
Speed ratings (Par 101):100,98,98,98,97 97,97,97,96,96 96,94,94,94,93 93,79
CSF £107.70 CT £1578.50 TOTE £14.70: £3.00, £2.10, £6.90, £3.80; EX 104.10 Place 6 £27.15, Place 5 £19.07.
Owner Joe McCarthy & Friends **Bred** Sean Burke **Trained** Newmarket, Suffolk

FOCUS
A modest handicap run at an ordinary pace and the winning time was 9/100ths of a second quicker than the preceding handicap of the same grade for three-year-olds. Ordinary for for the grade.
Salvestro Official explanation: jockey said gelding was denied a clear run
Ellen's Girl(IRE) Official explanation: jockey said filly lost its action on final bend
Consonant(IRE) Official explanation: jockey said gelding hung right in home straight
The Bonus King Official explanation: jockey said gelding lost its action
T/Plt: £31.40 to a £1 stake. Pool: £65,740.70. 1,527.60 winning tickets. T/Qpdt: £7.60 to a £1 stake. Pool: £2,375.80. 229.45 winning tickets. KH

1354 WINDSOR (R-H)
Monday, May 7

OFFICIAL GOING: Good
Wind: Brisk, behind

1540 AT THE RACES MAIDEN STKS 5f 10y
2:20 (2:22) (Class 5) 2-Y-O **£3,886** (£1,156; £577; £288) **Stalls** High

Form RPR

22 **1** **Ten Down**[21] [1058] 2-9-3 .... TPQueally 11 81+
(J A Osborne) *mde all: sn clr: comf* **5/2**[1]

2 *1* **Magical Speedfit (IRE)** 2-9-3 .... JohnEgan 13 77
(G G Margarson) *chsd ldrs: rdn and styd on to chse wnr fnl f: kpt on cl home but a readily hld* **10/1**

3 *1/2* **Coasting** 2-9-3 .... JimCrowley 8 75
(Mrs A J Perrett) *in tch: hdwy fr 2f out: chsd wnr over 1f out but nvr a threat: one pce ins fnl f* **11/1**

0 **4** *3* **Rough Rock (IRE)**[17] [1123] 2-8-10 .... KMay(7) 5 63
(B J Meehan) *chsd ldrs: rdn over 1f out: sn outpcd* **16/1**

5 *2* **Master Chef (IRE)** 2-9-3 .... JimmyFortune 14 55+
(J H M Gosden) *in tch: sme prog on rails whn n.m.r over 1f out: nvr a danger after* **7/1**[3]

6 *1 1/2* **Stage Acclaim (IRE)** 2-9-3 .... GeorgeBaker 12 49
(B R Millman) *s.i.s: styng on whn hmpd over 1f out: nvr in contention after* **12/1**

7 *shd* **Luscious Lips** 2-8-12 .... RichardHughes 7 44
(R Hannon) *s.i.s: bhd: hdwy on outside over 2f out: nvr gng pce to be competitive* **12/1**

3 **8** *2 1/2* **Red Expresso (IRE)**[21] [1058] 2-9-3 .... LDettori 2 47+
(M L W Bell) *sn in mid-div: pushed along over 2f out: one pce whn hung sharply rt over 1f out: n.d after* **11/4**[2]

9 *shd* **Ramblin Bob** 2-9-3 .... SebSanders 15 38
(R M Beckett) *in tch: pushed along 1/2-way: styd on fnl f but nvr in contention* **10/1**

10 *2 1/2* **Brixworth Scribe** 2-9-3 .... MickyFenton 1 28
(B Smart) *s.i.s: bhd: sme prog 1/2-way: nvr in contention* **33/1**

11 *1 1/2* **Lightning Lad** 2-9-3 .... FergusSweeney 6 22
(J R Jenkins) *sn in tch: drvn to chse ldrs whn hmpd over 1f out: nvr in contention after* **66/1**

12 *hd* **Mums The Best** 2-8-5 .... LukeMorris(7) 3 16
(A B Coogan) *s.i.s: outpcd* **33/1**

13 *5* **Sailing By** 2-9-3 .... OscarUrbina 4 —
(B R Millman) *a outpcd* **50/1**

14 *3/4* **Smokeyourpipe (IRE)** 2-9-3 .... RichardThomas 9 —
(J L Spearing) *s.i.s: a outpcd* **50/1**

15 *4* **Nathan Dee** 2-9-3 .... RichardSmith 10 —
(R Hannon) *a in rr* **50/1**

60.90 secs (-0.20) **Going Correction** -0.20s/f (Firm) **15** Ran SP% **128.8**
Speed ratings (Par 93):93,91,90,85,82 80,80,76,75,71 69,69,61,59,53
CSF £29.57 TOTE £3.30: £2.00, £4.00, £4.80; EX 45.00 TRIFECTA Not won..
Owner P J D Pottinger **Bred** Baydon House Stud **Trained** Upper Lambourn, Berks

FOCUS
A decent juvenile maiden likely to produce its share of winners, and the form looks very solid. High numbers were favoured.

NOTEBOOK
Ten Down, who missed the break over course and distance when turned over at odds on latest, had shown more than enough to suggest he could take a race of this nature and looked to have most to fear from the newcomers. Quickly into stride on this occasion, he had them all in trouble before they began to straighten for home and always looked in control. He is in a Listed contest at Goodwood later in the week and connections will consider a quick reappearance. (tchd 9-4 and 11-4)
Magical Speedfit(IRE) ◆, a 36,000gns half-brother to last season's smart juvenile Hoh Mike, had one of the better draws and seemed to know his job, but just lacked the raw speed of the winner. He was keeping on well close home and a similar maiden should be his for the taking. (op 8-1)
Coasting, who is bred to stay a bit further later on, made good headway out wide and certainly gave the impression he is up to winning a maiden. His trainer's juveniles usually come on a good deal for their initial outing and he will eventually benefit from a sixth furlong. (op 14-1)
Rough Rock(IRE), ninth in a race that is not working out on his debut at Newbury, shaped a lot better on this occasion and has clearly learned from the experience. He could be of interest a bit later in the season once qualified for nurseries and/or tackling 6f. (tchd 20-1)
Master Chef(IRE) ◆, who is likely to benefit from a bit further in time, is with a good stable and very much shaped as though this initial outing was needed. Natural progression should see him winning a maiden, especially once being able to tackle 6f. Official explanation: jockey said colt hung left-handed (op 11-2 tchd 15-2)
Stage Acclaim(IRE), who was not the quickest away, put in some good late work and was arguably unlucky not to finish a little closer, getting squeezed for room a furlong out. (op 50-1)
Luscious Lips, one of only two fillies in the line-up, was not the quickest away but showed she has the speed for this trip and should come on for the experience. (op 11-1)

Red Expresso(IRE), one place behind Ten Down on his debut, failed to build on that and never really looked a threat. It is probable he needs a sixth furlong, but he should still have done better. (op 5-2 tchd 3-1)
Ramblin Bob, nibbled at in the market beforehand, was always struggling to go the pace, but could be of interest in a similar contest now he has gained some experience. (op 12-1)
Lightning Lad Official explanation: jockey said colt suffered interference in running

1541 FRENCH BROTHERS MEDIAN AUCTION MAIDEN STKS 6f
2:50 (2:50) (Class 5) 3-4-Y-O **£3,238** (£963; £481; £240) **Stalls** High

Form RPR
5-5 **1** **Pusey Street Lady**[23] 1037 3-8-11 .... JimCrowley 1 73+
(J Gallagher) *sn chsng ldr: drvn to ld appr fnl f: kpt on wl* **16/1**
-543 **2** *1* **Everygrainofsand (IRE)**[3] 1447 4-9-12 .... GeorgeBaker 10 78
(J R Best) *led: drvn 2f out: hdd appr fnl f: one pce ins fnl f but kpt on wl for clr 2nd* **5/2**[1]
3 *6* **Steeley Fox** 4-9-7 .... KevinGhunowa(5) 15 59
(J M Bradley) *sn chsng ldrs: kpt on fnl 2f but nvr gng pce to be competitive w ldng pair* **66/1**
4 *nk* **Glencal** 3-8-11 .... EdwardCreighton 14 50
(H Morrison) *sn in tch: drvn along 1/2-way: kpt on fr over 1f out but nvr in contention* **14/1**
05-0 **5** *5* **Road To Recovery**[35] 885 3-9-2 62......................(v) FergusSweeney 13 39
(A M Balding) *chsd ldrs: rdn 1/2-way: wknd fr 2f out* **7/1**
6 *nk* **Tubby Isaacs** 3-9-2 .... SebSanders 6 38+
(P J Makin) *s.i.s: bhd: kpt on fr over 1f out: nvr in contention* **10/1**
60-0 **7** *nk* **Batchworth Blaise**[17] 1119 4-9-12 42...............(b) PaulFitzsimons 11 41
(E A Wheeler) *t.k.h: chsd ldrs: rdn over 2f out and sn btn* **100/1**
00- **8** *3* **Little Carmela**[184] 6330 3-8-11 .... OscarUrbina 5 23
(S C Williams) *s.i.s: bhd: mod prog fr over 1f out* **33/1**
5000 **9** *1* **Ginger Pop**[24] 1022 3-9-2 62.. NeilPollard 7 25
(G G Margarson) *a towards rr* **14/1**
04 **10** *½* **Juce Of Hearts**[4] 1429 3-9-2 .... RichardThomas 4 23
(J L Spearing) *nvr bttr than mid-div: outpcd most of way* **33/1**
0 **11** *3½* **The Carpet Man**[13] 1207 3-9-2 .... SimonWhitworth 2 12
(A W Carroll) *pressed ldrs over 3f* **66/1**
12 *2* **Princess Flavia (IRE)** 3-8-11 .... MickyFenton 8 1
(M Quinn) *s.i.s: a bhd* **33/1**
13 *5* **Well Placed** 3-9-2 .... JohnEgan 12 —
(W J Haggas) *pressed ldrs: rdn over 3f out: sn btn* **7/2**[2]
0-0 **14** *1¾* **Piano Key**[14] 1203 3-8-11 .... RichardSmith 9 —
(M D I Usher) *a in rr* **66/1**
0- **15** *2½* **Contentious (IRE)**[255] 4754 3-8-11 .... RichardHughes 3 —
(D M Simcock) *chsd ldrs over 3f* **5/1**[3]
1m 11.91s (-1.76) **Going Correction** -0.20s/f (Firm)
WFA 3 from 4yo 10lb **15** Ran SP% **122.6**
Speed ratings (Par 103):103,101,93,93,86 86,85,81,80,79 75,72,65,63,60
CSF £55.12 TOTE £18.70: £4.00, £1.40, £9.20; EX 59.80 TRIFECTA Not won..
Owner C R Marks (banbury) **Bred** S R Hope **Trained** Moreton-in-Marsh, Gloucs

FOCUS
Everything points to this having been just a modest sprint maiden, with the exception of the time which was surprisingly good. The race has been rated around the runner-up
Contentious(IRE) Official explanation: jockey said filly lost its action

1542 ARENA LEISURE PLC H'CAP 1m 3f 135y
3:20 (3:20) (Class 4) (0-85,85) 4-Y-0+ **£4,857** (£1,445; £722; £360) **Stalls** Low

Form RPR
/31- **1** **Nosferatu (IRE)**[210] 5870 4-9-3 **84**.. JimCrowley 4 90
(Mrs A J Perrett) *chsd ldrs: wnt 2nd 6f out: led appr fnl 3f: hrd drvn and hld on wl fnl f* **4/1**[1]
3106 **2** *¾* **Active Asset (IRE)**[7] 1356 5-9-4 **85**................................... SebSanders 2 90
(M Quinn) *in tch: hdwy and swtchd lft to outside over 2f out: chsd wnr fr over 1f out but a jst hld* **9/1**
222- **3** *1½* **Whatizzit**[243] 5109 4-9-0 **81**.. LDettori 3 83
(E A L Dunlop) *in tch: hdwy fr 4f out to chse wnr 3f out: nvr quite gng pce to chal: no ex fnl f* **5/1**[2]
414/ **4** *1¼* **Misty Dancer**[37] 3035 8-8-13 **80**.. RichardHughes 5 80
(Miss Venetia Williams) *in tch: outpcd 3f out: styd on again fr 2f out but nvr gng pce to chal* **15/2**[3]
30-0 **5** *nk* **Optimus (USA)**[9] 1308 5-8-8 **75**...................................... FergusSweeney 1 74
(B G Powell) *in rr: hdwy 3f out: drvn to chse ldrs over 2f out: one pce fr over 1f out* **12/1**
0023 **6** *nk* **Mustajed**[7] 1356 6-8-12 **84**... JamesMillman(5) 10 85+
(B R Millman) *in rr: hdwy on rails to chse ldrs over 2f out: rdn: hung lft and one pce fr over 1f out* **4/1**[1]
00-3 **7** *5* **Ocean Avenue (IRE)**[44] 753 8-8-6 **73** ow1........................ JohnEgan 7 63
(C A Horgan) *chsd ldrs: rdn 3f out: wknd 2f out* **4/1**[1]
/60- **8** *5* **Kuster**[260] 4626 11-8-9 **83**... MJMurphy(7) 8 65
(L M Cumani) *in rr: swtchd lft to outside and sme prog over 2f out: sn wknd* **33/1**
20-0 **9** *3½* **Zaif (IRE)**[12] 1245 4-9-0 **84**... MarcHalford(3) 6 60
(D R C Elsworth) *chsd ldr to 6f out: rdn 3f out: sn btn* **10/1**
21/0 **10** *35* **Top Gear**[15] 1149 5-9-0 **81**... GeorgeBaker 9 —
(Mrs L J Mongan) *s.i.s: sn drvn to ld: hdd over 3f out: sn wknd: t.o* **20/1**
2m 29.49s (-0.61) **Going Correction** +0.075s/f (Good) **10** Ran SP% **122.9**
Speed ratings (Par 105):105,104,103,102,102 102,98,95,93,69
CSF £43.44 CT £189.74 TOTE £6.10: £2.20, £4.00, £2.00; EX 56.80 Trifecta £225.30 Pool: £349.08 - 1.10 winning units..
Owner Lady Clague **Bred** Newberry Stud Company **Trained** Pulborough, W Sussex
■ Stewards' Enquiry : James MillmanE two-day ban: careless riding (May 18,20)

FOCUS
A decent handicap won by an unexposed and progressive four-year-old, but the time was modest and the second and third are weighted to their best, which does limit the form.

1543 WINDSOR-RACECOURSE.CO.UK H'CAP 1m 2f 7y
3:50 (3:51) (Class 3) (0-90,88) 4-Y-0+ **£8,096** (£2,408; £1,203; £601) **Stalls** Low

Form RPR
04-6 **1** **Ballinteni**[27] 993 5-8-11 **81**.. RichardHughes 5 91
(D M Simcock) *chsd ldrs: drvn along fr 3f out: led over 1f out: drvn out* **9/2**[2]
/040 **2** *1¼* **Prince Nureyev (IRE)**[16] 1149 7-8-8 **78**.......................... OscarUrbina 6 86
(B R Millman) *mid-div: sme hdwy whn n.m.r over 2f out: swtchd lft and hdwy sn after: chsd wnr thrght fnl f: no imp* **16/1**
430- **3** *1* **John Terry (IRE)**[201] 6051 4-9-3 **87**................................. JimCrowley 8 93
(Mrs A J Perrett) *chsd ldrs: rdn to chal 2f out: one pce fr over 1f out* **7/1**[3]
-221 **4** *1¼* **Woolfall Blue (IRE)**[7] 1356 4-8-13 **83** 6ex....................... SebSanders 10 87
(G G Margarson) *led after 1f: rdn 3f out: hdd over 1f out: wknd ins fnl f* **5/2**[1]
/21- **5** *2* **Very Agreeable**[283] 3901 4-9-2 **86**............................... FergusSweeney 1 86
(W R Swinburn) *in tch: hdwy 3f out: drvn to press ldrs 2f out: wknd fnl f* **12/1**
0-15 **6** *2½* **Robustian**[16] 1149 4-9-2 **86**.. LDettori 7 83+
(Eve Johnson Houghton) *chsd ldrs: rdn 3f out: styd in tch tl wknd appr fnl f* **9/2**[2]
5635 **7** *3* **Paraguay (USA)**[17] 1133 4-8-4 **74** oh1.................... EdwardCreighton 11 63
(Miss V Haigh) *in rr: rdn 3f out: nvr gng pce to get into contention* **14/1**
61-6 **8** *1¾* **Brief Goodbye**[16] 1149 7-8-11 **81**....................................... MickyFenton 4 67
(John Berry) *in rr: swtchd to outside fr 3f out: sn pushed along: nvr in contention* **12/1**
31-6 **9** *4* **Folio (IRE)**[27] 995 7-9-4 **88**.. JohnEgan 3 77+
(W J Musson) *in rr: hdwy fr 3f out to chse ldrs over 2f out: sn rdn and wknd* **8/1**
3050 **10** *2* **Tous Les Deux**[9] 1288 4-8-4 **74** oh3.............................. AdrianMcCarthy 9 49
(Peter Grayson) *t.k.h early: a towards rr* **33/1**
4205 **11** *16* **Rebellious Spirit**[37] 842 4-9-0 **84**................................... GeorgeBaker 2 28
(P W Hiatt) *led 1f: styd chsng ldr tl over 3f out: sn btn* **25/1**
2m 8.36s (0.06) **Going Correction** +0.075s/f (Good) **11** Ran SP% **123.3**
Speed ratings (Par 107):102,101,100,99,97 95,93,91,88,87 74
CSF £78.12 CT £512.05 TOTE £6.00: £2.10, £5.30, £3.10; EX 92.70 TRIFECTA Not won..
Owner David Cohen **Bred** Gainsborough Stud Management Ltd **Trained** Newmarket, Suffolk
■ Stewards' Enquiry : Oscar Urbina caution: careless riding

FOCUS
A good handicap likely to produce its share of future winners, with the winner capable of better. The form looks sound.

NOTEBOOK
Ballinteni ◆, formerly in the hands of Godolphin, made a pleasing reappearance/debut for connections when a keeping-on sixth over 1m at Pontefract and this extra distance looked almost certain to suit. Ideally positioned, he responded well to pressure to go into the lead over a furlong out and was always doing enough. A promising handicapper, he looks capable of further progress and could feature in some of the better handicaps at around this distance in 2007. (tchd 11-2)
Prince Nureyev(IRE), without a win in almost four years, has run some good races in defeat and as a result was racing here off just a 15lb lower mark than when last successful. He again ran well considering he was short of room at a vital stage, but got no reward and the losing run is likely to continue. (op 14-1)
John Terry(IRE) ◆, below his best in soft ground on his final start at three, looks to have done well over the winter and he made a pleasing reappearance over what is an inadequate trip. His stable are going really well at the moment and the son of Grand Lodge looks a ready-made winner once stepping back up to 1m4f. (op 13-2)
Woolfall Blue(IRE), whose trainer willingly admitted he thought he was the new Young Mick after his win over course and distance last month, again attempted to make most of the running, but was readily brushed aside a furlong out and was not up to it under the penalty. He may be worth another chance, but looks no Young Mick on this evidence. (op 3-1 tchd 100-30)
Very Agreeable ◆, a promising maiden winner at Newmarket last summer, was returning from a lengthy absence and was particularly weak on Betfair before the race. Evidently expected to need this, she travelled up like a decent filly, but tired under pressure and can be expected to come on a good deal for the outing. A return to 1m4f should see her winning and she is most definitely one to keep on side. (op 11-1)
Robustian, although again running well, gives the impression he is going to struggle to win off this mark. (op 6-1)

1544 ROYAL WINDSOR RACECOURSE CONFERENCE CENTRE CONDITIONS STKS 1m 67y
4:20 (4:20) (Class 3) 3-Y-0 **£8,724** (£2,612; £1,306; £653) **Stalls** High

Form RPR
1-1 **1** **Phoenix Tower (USA)**[17] 1124 3-9-0 100.................... RichardHughes 2 96+
(H R A Cecil) *trckd ldr: chal gng wl 2f out: led over 1f out: clr ins fnl f: easily* **8/13**[1]
-100 **2** *2½* **Highland Harvest**[61] 638 3-8-9 77............................... MarcHalford(3) 1 85
(D R C Elsworth) *led: rdn fr 3f out: hdd over 1f out: sn outpcd by wnr: kpt on same pce for 2nd* **28/1**
22-3 **3** *1½* **Eddie Jock (IRE)**[19] 1095 3-8-11 104.............................. LukeMorris(7) 5 88
(M L W Bell) *racd in 3rd thrght: rdn 3f out: nvr quite gng pce to chal: outpcd fr 2f out* **6/1**[3]
2-1 **4** *10* **Mofarij**[67] 595 3-9-0 .... LDettori 4 75+
(Saeed Bin Suroor) *racd in 4th: drvn and hdwy 3f out: nvr quite gng pce to be competitive: dropped away tamely over 1f out* **5/2**[2]
1m 43.45s (-1.25) **Going Correction** +0.075s/f (Good) **4** Ran SP% **108.2**
Speed ratings (Par 103):109,106,105,95
CSF £14.69 TOTE £1.50; EX 20.50.
Owner K Abdulla **Bred** Juddmonte Farms Inc **Trained** Newmarket, Suffolk

FOCUS
With Highland Harvest finishing so close and Mofarij running a shocker this was something of a non-event. The winner did not need to improve on his strong Newbury form, and the runner-up is rated as having improved.

NOTEBOOK
Phoenix Tower(USA), whose impressive Newbury handicap win is working out quite well - the fourth Aqmaar won a decent handicap at Newmarket over the weekend - was well supported in his bid to keep the winning run going on what was a rise in grade and he won readily, although not as easily as had once looked. He is clearly up to Listed standard and Sandown's Heron Stakes, in that grade, is next on the agenda before a possible tilt at the St James's Palace Stakes. He would need to progress an awful long way very quickly if he were to play any part in the latter. (tchd 8-11)
Highland Harvest, a 77-rated handicapper, got the run of the race from the front and appeared to run above himself in splitting the front pair. He was not going away at the line though and does little for the form, but this was at least a step in the right direction. (op 33-1 tchd 25-1)
Eddie Jock(IRE), who developed into a smart juvenile, reappeared with a sound effort in the Free Handicap, but failed to build on it and, although perhaps unsuited by the nature of the race, should still have been expected to do a little better. (op 11-2 tchd 5-1)
Mofarij, a highly promising second to Spanish Moon on his debut at two, confirmed that promise when easily winning in Dubai back in March and looked a huge danger to the favourite. However, as has been the case for the last two seasons, his stable have started the season very slowly and this run was too bad to be true, dropping out as though something was amiss. He has it all to prove now, but had already shown himself to be better than this and may prove a different proposition later in the season. Official explanation: jockey said colt was unsuited by the track

1545 COME RACING HERE EVERY MONDAY EVENING H'CAP 6f
4:50 (4:50) (Class 4) (0-85,84) 4-Y-0+ **£4,857** (£1,445; £722; £360) **Stalls** High

Form RPR
00-0 **1** **Abwaab**[21] 1060 4-8-11 **77**...(b[1]) MickyFenton 10 85
(Eve Johnson Houghton) *mde virtually all: hrd rdn whn strly chal thrght fnl f: hld on all out* **9/1**

0433 **2** *nk* **Adantino**[14] [1200] 8-8-10 **76**................(b) JimCrowley 1 83
(B R Millman) *in rr: hdwy on outside fr 2f out: hrd rdn and edgd rt ins fnl f: str chal cl home: nt quite get up* **9/2**[3]
6-04 **3** *shd* **Cape Presto (IRE)**[10] [1283] 4-8-4 **70**................(v) DMylonas 3 77
(Mrs C A Dunnett) *pressed wnr: rdn over 2f out: stl chalng ins fnl f: no ex last strides* **16/1**
1166 **4** *1 1/4* **Louphole**[7] [1357] 5-8-10 **76**................ SebSanders 5 79
(P J Makin) *s.i.s: in rr but in tch: hdwy fr 2f out: chsd ldrs and rdn over 1f out: one pce ins fnl f* **3/1**[2]
303- **5** *3/4* **High Ridge**[213] [5782] 8-8-1 **72**................(p) KevinGhunowa(5) 2 73
(J M Bradley) *s.i.s: sn in tch: hdwy to chse ldrs 2f out: pushed rt ins fnl f: one pce* **15/2**
0600 **6** *nk* **Regal Royale**[12] [1252] 4-8-6 **72**................ AdrianMcCarthy 6 72
(Peter Grayson) *chsd ldrs: rdn over 2f out: outpcd ins fnl f* **20/1**
010 **7** *nk* **Romany Nights (IRE)**[43] [774] 7-9-4 **84**................(b) JohnEgan 9 85+
(Miss Gay Kelleway) *chsd ldrs: rdn and bmpd over 1f out: hmpd jst ins fnl f: nt rcvr* **12/1**
000- **8** *1 1/4* **Russian Symphony (USA)**[283] [3904] 6-9-1 **81**................ FergusSweeney 4 82+
(C R Egerton) *chsd ldrs: styng on u.p whn n.m.r ins fnl f: nt rcvr and eased cl home* **20/1**
3-22 **9** *1 1/2* **Mr Cellophane**[12] [1252] 4-8-9 **75**................ RichardHughes 8 66+
(J R Jenkins) *flyj. s: hld up in rr: hdwy whn edgd rt ins fnl 2f: bmpd over 1f out: nt rcvr* **5/2**[1]

1m 12.36s (-1.31) **Going Correction** -0.20s/f (Firm) **9** Ran SP% **116.6**
Speed ratings (Par 105):100,99,99,97,96 96,96,94,92
CSF £49.73 CT £638.94 TOTE £11.20: £3.60, £2.00, £3.80; EX 54.30 Trifecta £359.50 Pool: £506.40 - 1.00 winning unit. Place 6 £235.25, Place 5 £106.86.
Owner Anthony Pye-Jeary And Mel Smith **Bred** R T And Mrs Watson **Trained** Blewbury, Oxon

FOCUS
A fair sprint handicap in which runners finished well bunched, and something of a messy race. The form is sound among the principals but not that strong.
High Ridge Official explanation: jockey said gelding was short of room inside final furlong
T/Plt: £284.30 to a £1 stake. Pool: £93,276.75. 239.50 winning tickets. T/Qpdt: £67.20 to a £1 stake. Pool: £4,160.50. 45.75 winning tickets. ST

1046 CURRAGH (R-H)
Monday, May 7

OFFICIAL GOING: Round course - good to firm; straight course - good

1546a COOLMORE STKS (LISTED RACE) 5f
2:15 (2:15) 2-Y-O **£24,192** (£7,097; £3,381; £1,152)

RPR
1 **Warsaw (IRE)**[15] [1182] 2-9-1 .... JAHeffernan 4 100+
(A P O'Brien, Ire) *mde all: edgd clr over 1f out: drvn out and r.o wl: easily* **8/13**[1]
2 *1 1/2* **The Loan Express (IRE)**[16] [1170] 2-8-12 .... WMLordan 3 91
(T Stack, Ire) *trckd ldrs in 3rd: rdn to go 2nd 1f out: no imp: kpt on same pce* **5/2**[2]
3 *3/4* **Silver Guest**[25] [1007] 2-9-1 .... DarryllHolland 1 91
(M R Channon) *chsd ldrs in 4th: last after 1/2-way: kpt on fr over 1f out* **8/1**[3]
4 *1 3/4* **Inzone (IRE)**[16] [1170] 2-8-12 .... DPMcDonogh 5 81
(K J Condon, Ire) *chsd ldr in 2nd: rdn over 2f out: no ex ins fnl f* **33/1**
5 *4* **Let Me Shine (USA)**[8] [1328] 2-8-12 .... KJManning 2 65
(J S Bolger, Ire) *hld up in rr: rdn and sme prog after 1/2-way: no ex and wknd fr under 2f out* **16/1**

59.20 secs (-2.10) **Going Correction** -0.30s/f (Firm) **5** Ran SP% **110.4**
Speed ratings: 104,101,100,97,91
CSF £2.39 TOTE £1.50: £1.10, £1.80; DF 2.20.
Owner Derrick Smith **Bred** Redpender Stud Ltd **Trained** Ballydoyle, Co Tipperary

FOCUS
A solid-looking Listed contest, and the winner is likely to be seen at Royal Ascot.

NOTEBOOK
Warsaw(IRE), successful over 6f around Leopardstown on his debut, had no problem dropping down to the minimum trip and ran out a convincing winner, making virtually all and winning in good style in a very respectable time. One of the 5f juvenile races at Royal Ascot, probably the Norfolk Stakes, is on the agenda next. (op 8/11)
The Loan Express(IRE), who beat subsequent Newmarket winner Achilles Of Troy at Naas on his debut, ran a good race despite being unable to make much impression on the winner. (op 9/4)
Silver Guest, runner-up over this trip at Folkestone and Leicester last month and the only maiden in the line-up, ran on from over one furlong out having dropped to last at halfway, and he helps link the British and Irish form. (op 8/1 tchd 9/1)
Inzone(IRE), having her fourth run, had been beaten two and a half lengths by The Loan Express at Naas, and she matched that effort, although she was 5lb better off this time.
Let Me Shine(USA) had previously been beaten eight lengths by Warsaw at Leopardstown and finished the same distance behind him here. (op 14/1)

1547a AUSSIE RULES EUROPEAN BREEDERS FUND TETRARCH STKS (GROUP 3) (ENTIRE COLTS & FILLIES) 7f
2:45 (2:46) 3-Y-O **£39,587** (£11,614; £5,533; £1,885)

RPR
1 **Creachadoir (IRE)**[15] [1185] 3-9-1 111................ KJManning 10 117+
(J S Bolger, Ire) *chsd ldrs: 5th and drvn along under 3f out: 3rd and hdwy 2f out: led under 1f out: sn clr: comf* **11/4**[1]
2 *3* **Mr Napper Tandy**[18] [1110] 3-9-1 .... DarryllHolland 5 108
(M R Channon) *cl up and disp: led 2f out: hdd under 1f out: kpt on same pce* **16/1**
3 *1* **Eyshal (IRE)**[8] [1322] 3-9-1 98................ FMBerry 2 105
(John M Oxx, Ire) *chsd ldrs on stands' side: 6th 1/2-way: 5th and rdn 2f out: 3rd and styd on ins fnl f* **20/1**
4 *nk* **Alexander Tango (IRE)**[22] [1047] 3-8-12 104................ WMLordan 1 101
(T Stack, Ire) *hld up towards rr: rdn 1 1/2f out: 9th 1f out: r.o wl cl home* **6/1**
5 *1/2* **Confuchias (IRE)**[30] [948] 3-9-1 104................ WSupple 4 103
(Francis Ennis, Ire) *settled 3rd: 4th and rdn 2f out: kpt on ins fnl f* **11/1**
6 *nk* **Chariots Of Fire (IRE)**[9] [1306] 3-9-1 ....(t) PJSmullen 11 102
(David Wachman, Ire) *hld up towards rr: prog on far rail under 2f out: no imp fnl f* **7/2**[2]
7 *1 3/4* **Top Class (USA)**[16] [1174] 3-9-1 .... JAHeffernan 3 97
(A P O'Brien, Ire) *cl up on stands' side: 4th and drvn along 1/2-way: 5th 1f out: no ex* **5/1**[3]
8 *nk* **Lucky Kyllachy (USA)**[43] [784] 3-9-1 97................ DMGrant 8 96
(David Wachman, Ire) *led and disp: hdd 2f out: sn no ex* **40/1**
9 *1/2* **Angelonmyshoulder**[240] [5195] 3-9-1 .... MJKinane 7 95
(John M Oxx, Ire) *in tch: 7th 1/2-way: rdn and no imp fr over 2f out* **8/1**
10 *hd* **Spanish Harlem (IRE)**[196] [6151] 3-9-1 .... CO'Donoghue 6 94
(A P O'Brien, Ire) *hld up: no imp fr 2f out* **14/1**
11 *17* **Warriors Key (IRE)**[30] [947] 3-9-1 95................ DPMcDonogh 9 49
(Kevin Prendergast, Ire) *hld up in tch: 8th 1/2-way: sn wknd: eased 2f out* **16/1**

1m 22.5s (-5.00) **Going Correction** -0.30s/f (Firm) **11** Ran SP% **124.9**
Speed ratings: 116,112,111,111,110 110,108,107,107,107 87
CSF £53.55 TOTE £3.60: £1.20, £4.00, £3.80; DF 76.50.
Owner Mrs J S Bolger **Bred** Frank Dunne **Trained** Coolcullen, Co Carlow
■ Stewards' Enquiry : D M Grant 200 euro fine: failed to keep straight from stalls
Darryll Holland four-day ban: careless riding (May 16-18,20); 200 euro fine: failed to keep straight from stalls

FOCUS
A fair Group Three rated around the fourth, fifth and sixth.

NOTEBOOK
Creachadoir(IRE) winner of the 2000 Guineas Trial at Leopardstown, had seemed not to stay when stepped up to 1m2f in the Ballysax Stakes. Dropped in trip, he won in good style and is now likely to see Classic action, possibly in France on Sunday, before returning to the Curragh for the 2000 Guineas on May 27. (op 3/1 tchd 100/30)
Mr Napper Tandy, a maiden winner over this trip at Newmarket in October, had finished a short-head second in two handicaps this year and was taking on some higher-rated rivals on this drop back in trip. Soon disputing the lead, he went on two furlongs out but had no answer when taken on by the winner. This was a good effort, though, and it is likely to have blown his handicap mark for the near future. (op 20/1)
Eyshal(IRE), who had a busy season last year, came good in a 1m maiden at Gowran Park last month and ran a pleasing race back up in grade. (op 16/1)
Alexander Tango(IRE), successful over the course and distance on her debut in July, had run quite well in the Moyglare Stud Stakes, and finished second on her reappearance last month. The only filly in the line-up, she was again held up in rear before running on quite well in the final furlong. (op 11/2 tchd 13/2)
Confuchias(IRE), twice a winner on easy ground last year, had been beaten three and a half lengths when second to Creachadoir at Leopardstown last month, and ran close enough to that form over this shorter trip. (op 10/1)
Chariots Of Fire(IRE), a maiden winner over just short of 1m1f on his debut at Cork last month, had finished fourth at this level when upped to 1m2f at Sandown on his previous start. Involved in the incident soon after the start, he was possibly the worst sufferer, but his performance was still a bit disappointing. (op 11/2)

1548a ORATORIO EUROPEAN BREEDERS FUND ATHASI STKS (GROUP 3) (F&M) 7f
3:15 (3:15) 3-Y-O+ **£39,527** (£11,554; £5,472; £1,824)

RPR
1 **Eastern Appeal (IRE)**[43] [781] 4-9-9 97................ RPCleary 6 103
(M Halford, Ire) *cl 2nd: rdn and dropped to 3rd over 2f out: sn outpcd: r.o wl ins fnl f to ld nr fin* **10/1**
2 *nk* **Modeeroch (IRE)**[183] [6356] 4-9-9 106................ KJManning 3 102
(J S Bolger, Ire) *settled 3rd: 2nd and hdd over 2f out: rdn to ld under 1f out: kpt on wl: hdd nr fin* **13/8**[1]
3 *1/2* **Deauville Vision (IRE)**[43] [783] 4-9-9 104................ JMurtagh 2 101+
(M Halford, Ire) *trckd ldrs on outer: 4th 1/2-way: rdn and outpcd 2f out: styd on ins fnl f* **11/4**[2]
4 *3/4* **Ardbrae Lady**[43] [782] 4-9-12 103................ FMBerry 4 102
(Joseph G Murphy, Ire) *s.i.s and hld up in rr: rdn and kpt on wl fr over 1f out* **15/2**
5 *shd* **Gaudeamus (USA)**[226] [5522] 3-9-2 102................ DJMoran 1 99
(J S Bolger, Ire) *led: rdn and strly pressed 2f out: hdd under 1f out: 3rd and no ex cl home: eased nr fin* **10/1**
6 *1/2* **Offbeat Fashion (IRE)**[183] [6354] 3-8-11 .... PJSmullen 8 93
(D K Weld, Ire) *chsd ldrs: 5th 1/2-way: 4th briefly 2f out: kpt on same pce* **13/2**[3]
7 *1 1/2* **Dani's Girl (IRE)**[43] [782] 4-9-9 88................ DPMcDonogh 5 93
(P A Fahy, Ire) *chsd ldrs: 5th and rdn over 2f out: sn no ex* **16/1**
8 *5 1/2* **Sharapova (IRE)**[22] [1048] 4-9-9 79................ JAHeffernan 7 78
(M J Grassick, Ire) *a towards rr: no imp fr 2f out* **50/1**

1m 23.8s (-3.70) **Going Correction** -0.30s/f (Firm)
WFA 3 from 4yo 12lb **8** Ran SP% **115.9**
Speed ratings: 109,108,108,107,107 106,104,98
CSF £27.14 TOTE £12.60: £2.60, £1.10, £1.60; DF 53.80.
Owner Fair Is Fair Syndicate **Bred** Glashare House Stud **Trained** the Curragh, Co Kildare

FOCUS
This renewal looked well up to scratch with the winner and fourth close to previous form.

NOTEBOOK
Eastern Appeal(IRE) produced easily the best effort of her career to record her third victory, having won a maiden and Tralee handicap last term. A genuine and likeable sort, she can continue to make her presence felt at this level.
Modeeroch(IRE) lost nothing in defeat and seemed to run right up to last season's form on this seasonal debut. She held every chance from two furlongs out and led just inside the distance, but could not fend off the winner's charge. She can be expected to improve on this and can win more races. (op 2/1)
Deauville Vision(IRE) was encountering different ground from that she faced when winning the Irish Lincoln in March. She seemed outpaced around the quater-mile pole, but was keeping on well towards the finish and should do better back over 1m. She can make her mark at this level. (op 3/1)
Ardbrae Lady ran a sound race, doing her best work at the finish. She will continue to be a force to be reckoned with at this level. (op 7/1 tchd 8/1)
Gaudeamus(USA) ran creditably on her first start since finishing fifth in the Fillies' Mile. She made most of the running and had most of her rivals in trouble from two furlongs out before fading. Eased down when beaten, reportedly due to a slipping saddle, she can be expected to do better next time. Official explanation: jockey said saddle slipped approx 2f out and he was unable to ride out properly from that point (op 8/1)
Offbeat Fashion(IRE) was taking a step up in class and was not beaten far. She should be all the better for this experience as this was only her second start. (op 5/1)

1550a HIGH CHAPARRAL EUROPEAN BREEDERS FUND MOORESBRIDGE STKS (GROUP 3) 1m 2f
4:15 (4:16) 4-Y-O+ **£39,527** (£11,554; £5,472; £1,824)

RPR
1 **Septimus (IRE)**[338] [2228] 4-9-6 116................ JAHeffernan 6 119+
(A P O'Brien, Ire) *settled 2nd: impr to dispute ld appr st: sn rdn: led over 1f out: styd on wl* **4/1**[2]
2 *1 1/2* **Fracas (IRE)**[22] [1050] 5-9-1 111................ WMLordan 2 111
(David Wachman, Ire) *trckd ldrs in 3rd: prog 1 1/2f out: 2nd and kpt on wl ins fnl f* **9/2**[3]

3 ¾ **Championship Point (IRE)**[18] 1109 4-9-1 .... DarryllHolland 3 110
(M R Channon) *sn led: jnd appr st: rdn over 2f out: hdd over 1f out: kpt on same pce* **9/1**

4 1 **Grand Passion (IRE)**[30] 941 7-9-1 .... PJSmullen 7 108
(G Wragg) *trckd ldrs in 4th: rdn early st: kpt on same pce fr over 1f out* **16/1**

5 ¾ **Bon Nuit (IRE)**[36] 875 5-8-12 100.................. NGMcCullagh 4 103
(Mrs John Harrington, Ire) *racd in 5th: rdn st: kpt on same pce fr over 1f out* **25/1**

6 2 ½ **Mustameet (USA)**[22] 1049 6-9-6 117.................. DPMcDonogh 1 106
(Kevin Prendergast, Ire) *hld up in tch: 6th into st: sn rdn: no imp fr 1 1/2f out: eased ins fnl f* **1/1**[1]

7 1 **King In Waiting (IRE)**[344] 2055 4-9-1 .... MJKinane 5 99
(John M Oxx, Ire) *hld up in rr: rdn and no imp st* **12/1**

2m 10.7s (1.40) **Going Correction** +0.475s/f (Yiel) **7 Ran SP% 115.6**
Speed ratings: 113,111,111,110,109 107,107
CSF £22.73 TOTE £5.90: £3.20, £1.90; DF 29.30.
Owner D Smith, Mrs J Magnier, M Tabor **Bred** Barronstown Stud & Orpendale **Trained** Ballydoyle, Co Tipperary

FOCUS
A good Group 3 rated through the fifth, with the third and fourth close to their marks.

NOTEBOOK
Septimus(IRE), last season's Dante winner, made a successful return on his first start since finishing unplaced in last year's Epsom Derby. Always close to the pace, he stayed on well once in front, and with this run under his belt he can fulfil the considerable promise of last season's truncated campaign. (op 7/2 tchd 9/2)
Fracas(IRE), a former winner of the Derrinstown Derby Trial, had finished second to the winner's stable companion Dylan Thomas last time and posted another good effort in defeat. There are more races to be won with him if he can avoid potential top-notchers. (op 9/2 tchd 5/1)
Championship Point(IRE) turned in a sound effort from the front with the benefit of his recent run behind him. He seemed to lose his way after winning at Goodwood a year ago, but is clearly on the way back. (op 7/1)
Grand Passion(IRE), who has been in good form on the All-Weather, ran an honest race but seems to find one or two too strong at this level. (op 12/1)
Bon Nuit(IRE) has shown a good level of form since coming to Ireland, but this was probably a tougher task than she has faced recently.
Mustameet(USA) looked to have an excellent chance, but posted a very rare below-par effort. He was subsequently found to have had a nasal discharge. Official explanation: vet said horse was found to have a nasal discharge post-race (op 5/4 tchd 9/10)

1551 - 1552a (Foreign Racing) - See Raceform Interactive

[1422]CATTERICK (L-H)
Tuesday, May 8

OFFICIAL GOING: Firm (good to firm in places)
Just 7mm water had been put on the track since the previous meeting six days ago. 'Very quick, like a road' was the verdict.
Wind: Moderate, half-against Weather: Overcast, cool, blustery at times

1553 CATTERICKBRIDGE.CO.UK MAIDEN AUCTION STKS 5f
6:05 (6:05) (Class 6) 2-Y-O **£2,730** (£806; £403) **Stalls** Low

Form RPR

3 1 **Tan Bonita (USA)**[8] 1354 2-8-10 .... PatCosgrave 4 76+
(M J Wallace) *mde all: qcknd clr over 1f out: heavily eased towards fin* **4/5**[1]

2 2 ½ **Speedy Senorita (IRE)** 2-8-1 .... AndrewElliott(3) 1 58+
(K R Burke) *s.i.s: hdwy and hmpd over 1f out: styd on wl ins fnl f: tk 2nd nr line* **14/1**

3 ½ **Style Award** 2-8-1 .... AndrewMullen(3) 7 52
(W J H Ratcliffe) *s.s: hdwy on outer over 2f out: hung violently lft: kpt on fnl f* **66/1**

4 2 **Destinys Dream (IRE)** 2-8-8 .... RoystonFfrench 2 48
(Mrs A Duffield) *sn chsng ldrs: sn drvn along: styd on ins fnl f* **10/1**[3]

055 5 shd **Upstanding**[10] 1302 2-8-4 .... DeanMernagh 5 52+
(M Brittain) *chsd wnr: bdly hmpd ins fnl f: nt rcvr* **16/1**

04 6 2 **Limestone**[12] 1255 2-8-9 .... PhillipMakin 3 41
(J R Weymes) *chsd wnr: outpcd over 2f out: lost pl over 1f out* **28/1**

6 7 3 **Myriola**[15] 1193 2-8-6 .... TPQueally 8 26+
(J G Given) *w ldrs: wkng and hung rt whn sltly hmpd over 1f out* **3/1**[2]

8 5 **Amazing Spirit** 2-8-7 ow1.................. MickyFenton 6 7
(Miss V Haigh) *s.i.s: sn chsng ldrs on wd outside: lost pl over 1f out* **12/1**

61.66 secs (1.06) **Going Correction** -0.15s/f (Firm) **8 Ran SP% 114.8**
Speed ratings (Par 91):85,81,80,77,76 73,68,60
CSF £14.79 TOTE £1.50: £1.10, £2.60, £10.20; EX 9.90.
Owner Pedro Rosas **Bred** F Diaz-Valdes **Trained** Newmarket, Suffolk
■ Stewards' Enquiry : Andrew Mullen two-day ban: careless riding (May 20-21)

FOCUS
A very modest event and a moderate time, 2.96 seconds slower than the later handicap but a facile winner, although not an easy race to rate.

NOTEBOOK
Tan Bonita(USA) went clear in a matter of strides and was value for at least double the official margin. She looks all speed. (op 5-6 tchd 8-11, 10-11 in places and evens in a place)
Speedy Senorita(IRE), an April foal, looked to be carrying a fair bit of condition. She did not look at home on the track but stayed on in encouraging fashion to snatch second spot near the line. (op 20-1)
Style Award, an April foal, had two handlers in the paddock and went to post at a rate of knots. After missing the break she hung violently left causing mayhem. She is not without some ability and a more orthodox track will surely aid her cause. Official explanation: jockey said filly hung left
Destinys Dream(IRE), a rather small February foal, is bred for stamina rather than speed on her dam's side. She kept on after being tapped for toe and will be wiser as a result.
Upstanding, having her fourth start already, was knocked from pillar to post by the errant third. This will hardly have done her confidence much good. (op 14-1 tchd 18-1)
Limestone, fourth in a claimer on her second start, is a poor walker and in the end dropped right away. (op 33-1)
Myriola, who went to post well, hung right and her chance had gone when she was knocked over by the third. This must go down as a most disappointing effort after showing plenty of dash on her debut. Official explanation: jockey said filly hung right-handed (tchd 10-3 in a place)

1554 BOOK RACEDAY HOSPITALITY ON 01748 810165 CLAIMING STKS 1m 3f 214y
6:35 (6:35) (Class 6) 4-Y-O+ **£2,730** (£806; £403) **Stalls** Low

Form RPR

2-11 1 **Court Of Appeal**[29] 966 10-8-10 73.................. (tp) JamieMoriarty(5) 4 65+
(B Ellison) *s.i.s: in rr: effrt on outer over 3f out: styd on to ld fnl 50yds* **4/5**[1]

660- 2 ½ **Eijaaz (IRE)**[301] 3386 6-8-7 47.................. RoystonFfrench 3 56
(G A Harker) *hld up in tch: effrt over 2f out: led 1f out: hdd and no ex wl ins fnl f* **25/1**

3642 3 2 **Tedstale (USA)**[7] 1376 9-8-11 60.................. (b) DO'Donohoe 9 57
(K A Ryan) *hld up: hdwy over 6f out: led over 3f out: hdd 1f out: kpt on same pce* **7/2**[2]

0-00 4 3 **Roonah (FR)**[14] 1222 4-8-2 40.................. PaulFessey 6 43
(Karen McLintock) *in rr: drvn and detached over 3f out: styd on fnl 2f* **100/1**

60-2 5 ½ **Thunderwing (IRE)**[7] 1374 5-9-9 68.................. PatCosgrave 10 63
(K R Burke) *trckd ldrs: effrt 3f out: wknd appr fnl f* **13/2**[3]

000/ 6 7 **Perfect Picture**[710] 2472 8-8-2 .... (p) RoryMoore(5) 1 36
(P T Midgley) *led: hdd over 3f out: wknd over 1f out* **80/1**

0004 7 nk **Second Reef**[14] 1225 5-8-9 51.................. (v) PhillipMakin 5 38
(J R Weymes) *trckd ldrs: effrt 3f out: lost pl over 1f out* **16/1**

0-66 8 7 **Kristalchen**[13] 1239 5-8-5 45.................. GregFairley(3) 8 25
(D W Thompson) *chsd ldrs: pushed along 7f out: wknd over 2f out* **12/1**

6200 9 3 **Exit Fast (USA)**[15] 966 6-9-3 55.................. MickyFenton 7 30
(P T Midgley) *chsd ldrs: lost pl over 2f out* **50/1**

400- 10 1 **Matinee Idol**[58] 6957 4-8-12 42.................. (p) TomEaves 2 23
(Mrs S Lamyman) *chsd ldrs: lost pl 5f out: sn bhd* **40/1**

2m 36.64s (-2.36) **Going Correction** -0.125s/f (Firm) **10 Ran SP% 115.2**
Speed ratings (Par 101):102,101,100,98,98 93,93,88,86,85
CSF £31.01 TOTE £1.80: £1.02, £8.20, £1.10; EX 23.60.
Owner Spring Cottage Syndicate No 2 **Bred** John And Susan Davis **Trained** Norton, N Yorks

FOCUS
A fairly weak claimer with the winner rated 10lb off his recent best.
Matinee Idol Official explanation: trainer said filly was unsuited by the firm (good to firm places) ground

1555 "BE THE BEST DRESSED LADY" H'CAP 7f
7:05 (7:05) (Class 4) (0-80,79) 4-Y-O+ **£5,181** (£1,541; £770; £384) **Stalls** Low

Form RPR

6024 1 **H Harrison (IRE)**[4] 1458 7-8-3 67.................. AndrewElliott(3) 12 77
(I W McInnes) *chsd ldrs: hung lft and led 1f out: carried hd awkwardly: hld on towards fin* **6/1**[3]

05-3 2 hd **Il Castagno (IRE)**[18] 1133 4-8-12 73.................. TomEaves 10 82
(B Smart) *led after 1f tl 1f out: kpt on wl: jst hld* **8/1**

56-3 3 1 **Tough Love**[18] 1132 8-8-6 67.................. DavidAllan 11 73
(T D Easterby) *in rr: hdwy over 2f out: hung lft: kpt on wl fnl f* **9/1**

0353 4 2 **Shot To Fame (USA)**[14] 1223 8-9-4 79.................. (t) AdrianTNicholls 3 80
(D Nicholls) *led 1f: chsd ldrs: edgd lft over 1f out: kpt on same pce* **11/4**[1]

00-1 5 1 **Sir Orpen (IRE)**[34] 915 4-8-9 70.................. PaulFessey 8 68
(T D Barron) *chsd ldrs: kpt on same pce fnl 2f* **3/1**[2]

30-0 6 1 ¼ **Viva Volta**[18] 1133 4-8-8 69.................. PaulQuinn 4 64
(T D Easterby) *chsd ldrs: lost pl over 3f out: kpt on fnl f* **25/1**

4P0- 7 nk **Heureux (USA)**[226] 5554 4-8-6 72.................. JamieMoriarty(5) 2 66
(J Howard Johnson) *s.i.s: in rr whn checked 4f out: styd on fnl f* **12/1**

4-00 8 1 ¾ **Choreography**[29] 969 4-8-8 72.................. AndrewMullen(3) 7 61
(D Nicholls) *stdd s: hdwy on ins over 3f out: sn chsng ldrs: one pce fnl 2f: rdr lost whip over 1f out: one pce* **20/1**

0042 9 5 **Top Jaro (FR)**[15] 1198 4-8-12 73.................. HayleyTurner 1 49
(Jennie Candlish) *chsd ldrs: rdn 3f out: lost pl over 1f out* **8/1**

650- 10 12 **Titinius (IRE)**[189] 6273 7-8-6 67.................. PaulHanagan 6 10
(Micky Hammond) *in rr: bhd and hung lft fnl 2f: eased* **20/1**

1m 24.53s (-2.83) **Going Correction** -0.125s/f (Firm) **10 Ran SP% 119.2**
Speed ratings (Par 105):111,110,109,107,106 104,104,102,96,83
CSF £52.75 CT £339.16 TOTE £8.30: £2.70, £1.60, £3.20; EX 58.50.
Owner David Lees **Bred** Margaret Conlon **Trained** Catwick, E Yorks

FOCUS
A very strongly-run race with four of the runners trying to take them along resulting in a smart winning time for a race of its class, 2.73 seconds faster than the later maiden and the form looks quite solid.
Titinius(IRE) Official explanation: jockey said gelding hung left-handed throughout

1556 GORACING.CO.UK H'CAP 1m 7f 177y
7:35 (7:35) (Class 6) (0-65,65) 4-Y-O+ **£2,730** (£806; £403) **Stalls** Low

Form RPR

00-0 1 **Vice Admiral**[24] 1042 4-8-10 54.................. DaleGibson 5 59
(M W Easterby) *led 2f: w ldr: led over 4f out: crowded over 1f out: hld on towards fin* **11/2**[2]

4154 2 hd **Rule For Ever**[15] 1196 5-9-10 65.................. DanielTudhope 13 70
(I W McInnes) *mid-div: effrt 3f out: sn chsng ldrs: styd on wl ins fnl f: jst hld* **9/2**[1]

0-55 3 ½ **True (IRE)**[15] 1196 6-8-5 46.................. PaulFessey 9 50
(Mrs S Lamyman) *hld up in mid-div: effrt on outer over 2f out: kpt on wl ins fnl f* **6/1**[3]

506- 4 shd **Next Flight (IRE)**[212] 5836 8-8-6 47 oh1 ow1.................. DavidAllan 10 51
(R E Barr) *hld up in rr: hdwy over 3f out: styd on wl down outside fnl 2f: kpt on wl ins fnl f* **25/1**

01 5 nk **Rocknest Island (IRE)**[14] 1229 4-8-7 54.................. (p) AndrewMullen(3) 2 57
(P D Niven) *sn chsng ldrs: outpcd over 3f out: kpt on wl fnl f* **11/2**[2]

0-06 6 ½ **Piccolomini**[14] 1222 5-8-3 47.................. (b) GregFairley(3) 6 50
(E W Tuer) *trckd ldrs: chal over 2f out: hung lft: one pce appr fnl f* **20/1**

0-30 7 ½ **Mulligan's Pride (IRE)**[14] 1222 6-8-10 51.................. (b) RoystonFfrench 7 53
(James Moffatt) *s.i.s: in rr: hdwy over 3f out: styd on wl on outside fnl 2f* **13/2**

2005 8 3 **Mangrove Cay (IRE)**[14] 1222 5-8-6 47.................. PaulHanagan 8 45
(A J Lockwood) *chsd ldrs: drvn over 3f out: fdd over 1f out* **7/1**

000- 9 hd **Zeydnaa (IRE)**[217] 5750 7-8-5 46 oh1.................. CatherineGannon 15 44
(C R Wilson) *hld up in rr: effrt over 3f out: nvr nr ldrs* **25/1**

040- 10 2 **High Frequency (IRE)**[35] 6305 6-8-2 46 oh1.................. (p) AndrewElliott(3) 12 41
(A Crook) *w ldr: led after 2f: hdd over 4f out: lost pl over 1f out* **25/1**

00-0 11 3 ½ **Compton Commander**[15] 1196 9-8-11 52.................. TonyHamilton 3 43
(E W Tuer) *sn chsng ldrs: lost pl over 2f out* **50/1**

/64- 12 17 **Gala Casino King (IRE)**[344] 2082 4-9-0 58.................. SebSanders 1 27
(Jennie Candlish) *chsd ldrs: lost pl over 1f out: heavily eased ins fnl f* **8/1**

/5-0 13 34 **Columbus (IRE)**[15] 1196 10-8-7 48.................. HayleyTurner 14 —
(Jennie Candlish) *in rr: t.o 4f out: lame* **33/1**

3m 29.88s (-1.52) **Going Correction** -0.125s/f (Firm)
WFA 4 from 5yo+ 3lb **13 Ran SP% 121.4**
Speed ratings (Par 101):98,97,97,97,97 96,96,95,95,94 92,84,67
CSF £28.27 CT £158.01 TOTE £5.40: £3.10, £2.10, £2.60; EX 36.90.
Owner A C R Stubbs **Bred** Barry Minty **Trained** Sheriff Hutton, N Yorks

FOCUS
A moderate contest and quite a tactical affair with Dale Gibson saving just enough in front. There was only a couple of lengths between the first seven at the line and the form does not look reliable.

Columbus(IRE) Official explanation: vet said gelding was found to be lame right-fore

1557 "VIRGIN VIE AT HOME LADIES NIGHT" H'CAP 5f
8:05 (8:05) (Class 5) (0-70,68) 4-Y-0+ £3,412 (£1,007; £504) Stalls Low

Form RPR

06-1 1 **Raccoon (IRE)**[6] 1405 7-8-11 **61** 6ex.................................. SebSanders 3 86+
(D W Chapman) *mde all: clr over 1f out: heavily eased towards fin* **2/1**[1]

4216 2 5 **No Time (IRE)**[10] 1299 7-8-6 **63**.. MCGeran(7) 5 69+
(A J McCabe) *in rr: hdwy on wd outside 2f out: styd on wl to take 2nd ins fnl f* **10/1**

0-00 3 1 **Law Maker**[18] 1121 7-8-0 **57**..(v) AmyBaker(7) 11 56
(A Bailey) *mid-div: hdwy 2f out: styd on ins fnl f* **40/1**

0110 4 ½ **Whinhill House**[12] 1262 7-8-8 **58**...................................... PatCosgrave 9 55
(D W Barker) *chsd ldrs: kpt on same pce fnl 2f* **14/1**

5-04 5 nk **Ryedane (IRE)**[10] 1299 5-8-11 **61**..................................(b[1]) DavidAllan 10 57+
(T D Easterby) *sn pushed along in rr: hdwy on outside 2f out: styd on wl ins fnl f* **13/2**[3]

50-0 6 ½ **Hotham**[21] 1074 4-8-12 **62**.. TonyHamilton 14 56
(N Wilson) *chsd ldrs: kpt on same pce fnl 2f* **18/1**

36-6 7 nk **Jilly Why (IRE)**[126] 8 6-9-0 **64**...................................... PhillipMakin 7 57
(Paul Green) *chsd ldrs: one pce fnl 2f* **16/1**

430- 8 1 ¾ **Strensall**[220] 5684 10-9-1 **65**... PaulHanagan 2 51
(R E Barr) *chsd ldrs: fdd appr fnl f* **20/1**

15-0 9 shd **Northern Chorus (IRE)**[86] 432 4-8-11 **68**...........(v) JamesO'Reilly(7) 13 54
(J O'Reilly) *s.i.s: in rr: kpt on fnl 2f: nvr on terms* **50/1**

0430 10 ½ **Sharp Hat**[6] 1405 13-8-4 **54**.. DaleGibson 6 38
(D W Chapman) *s.i.s: sme hdwy 2f out: nvr a factor* **40/1**

34-3 11 nk **One Way Ticket**[9] 1321 7-9-4 **68**..................................(p) MickyFenton 4 51
(J M Bradley) *chsd wnr: wknd appr fnl f* **8/1**

5061 12 ½ **Brut**[2] 1493 5-8-10 **60** 6ex..(p) RoystonFfrench 15 41
(D W Barker) *nvr nr ldrs* **6/1**[2]

20-4 13 ½ **Rothesay Dancer**[29] 964 4-8-6 **56**.....................................(p) PaulFessey 12 35
(J S Goldie) *chsd ldrs: lost pl over 1f out* **16/1**

133- 14 2 ½ **Rudi's Pet (IRE)**[286] 3833 13-9-2 **66**............................ AdrianTNicholls 1 36
(D Nicholls) *dwlt: a in rr* **16/1**

60-0 15 ½ **Smiddy Hill**[18] 1134 5-9-1 **65**... TomEaves 8 33
(R Bastiman) *hld up: a in rr* **22/1**

58.70 secs (-1.90) **Going Correction** -0.15s/f (Firm) **15 Ran SP% 126.7**
Speed ratings (Par 103):109,101,99,98,98 97,96,94,93,93 92,91,91,87,86
CSF £22.51 CT £673.50 TOTE £3.50: £1.80, £3.00, £6.60; EX 30.90.
Owner P D Savill **Bred** P D Savill **Trained** Stillington, N Yorks

FOCUS
Amodest handicap but a decent winning time for the grade and a contest that should work out at a similar level.

1558 SPONSOR A RACE AT CATTERICK MAIDEN STKS 7f
8:35 (8:36) (Class 5) 3-Y-O £3,238 (£963; £481; £240) Stalls Low

Form RPR

-042 1 **Pennyrock (IRE)**[13] 1236 3-9-3 62.............................. GrahamGibbons 5 57+
(J J Quinn) *led: shkn up over 1f out: edgd lft: readily* **4/6**[1]

006- 2 1 ¾ **Crosby Jemma**[229] 5495 3-8-12 48................................... PhillipMakin 2 45
(J R Weymes) *w ldr: shkn up over 4f out: kpt on same pce fnl f* **14/1**

200- 3 1 ¾ **Leprechaun's Gold (IRE)**[137] 6920 3-9-0 65............... GregFairley(3) 3 45
(M Johnston) *chsd ldrs: rdn and hung lft 2f out: one pce* **3/1**[2]

4 1 **Suspender (IRE)** 3-8-7 .... HMuya(5) 8 38
(D Nicholls) *hld up: hdwy on ins over 2f out: sn swtchd outside: hung lft 1f out: kpt on ins fnl f* **25/1**

00- 5 nk **Mystic**[290] 3745 3-8-12 .... PaulQuinn 6 37
(D W Barker) *t.k.h: trckd ldrs: stmbld after 1f: fdd fnl f* **25/1**

6 ¾ **Distant Pleasure** 3-8-12 .... TomEaves 9 35
(M Dods) *s.s: in rr tl kpt on fnl 2f* **10/1**[3]

00 7 6 **Abadia**[11] 1282 3-8-12 .... TPQueally 10 19
(J G Given) *chsd ldrs: outpcd over 3f out: lost pl 2f out* **20/1**

1m 27.26s (-0.10) **Going Correction** -0.125s/f (Firm) **7 Ran SP% 113.2**
Speed ratings (Par 99):95,93,91,89,89 88,81
CSF £11.44 TOTE £1.50: £1.40, £4.70; EX 11.10 Place 6 £25.09, Place 5 £14.82.
Owner Colm McEvoy **Bred** Colm McEvoy **Trained** Settrington, N Yorks

FOCUS
A weak maiden with the runner-up, who sets the standard, rated just 48.
T/Plt: £24.40 to a £1 stake. Pool: £57,574.00. 1,718.30 winning tickets. T/Qpdt: £17.70 to a £1 stake. Pool: £3,349.10. 140.00 winning tickets. WG

CHEPSTOW (L-H)
Tuesday, May 8

OFFICIAL GOING: Good to firm (good in places)
Wind: Strong across

1559 BETDAQ FIRST FOR MULTIPLES CLAIMING STKS 1m 2f 36y
2:10 (2:10) (Class 6) 4-Y-0+ £2,072 (£616; £308; £153) Stalls Low

Form RPR

106- 1 **Nuit Sombre (IRE)**[188] 4001 7-9-5 73.........................(p) DarryllHolland 5 69
(J G M O'Shea) *led: sn clr: hrd drvn over 1f out: styd on strly and in command fnl f* **11/2**

1114 2 1 ¼ **Sawwaah (IRE)**[20] 1086 10-8-6 65.............................(p) TravisBlock(5) 2 59
(Tom Dascombe) *s.i.s: bhd: hdwy 3f out: chsd wnr appr fnl f: kpt on same pce ins fnl f* **7/4**[1]

0653 3 2 **Birkside**[7] 1368 4-8-11 70.. SteveDrowne 6 55
(S Dow) *chsd ldrs: wnt 2nd 4f out: rdn 2f out: no imp on wnr fr 2f out: lost 2nd appr fnl f* **5/1**[3]

/00- 4 2 **Celticello (IRE)**[33] 5512 5-8-12 79...................................... AlanRutter(7) 3 59
(Heather Dalton) *in rr: drvn and sme hdwy fr 3f out: nvr gng pce to get into contention* **8/1**

3233 5 nk **Camille Pissarro (USA)**[16] 1178 7-9-11 61............. EdwardCreighton 7 64
(D J Wintle) *in rr: hdwy 4f out: rdn and no imp on ldrs fnl 2f* **7/2**[2]

-606 6 6 **Fly By Jove (IRE)**[27] 1001 4-8-9 46.................................... LPKeniry 4 37
(Jane Southcombe) *in tch: rdn and sme hdwy fr 4f out: nvr gng pce to get into contention: wknd 2f out* **66/1**

326- 7 2 ½ **Dante's Diamond (IRE)**[146] 6810 5-8-13 57..................... ChrisCatlin 8 36
(D Burchell) *in tch: hdwy to chse ldrs 4f out: wknd 3f out* **9/1**

01-0 8 8 **Missouri (USA)**[9] 278 4-7-12 47.................................. LukeMorris(7) 1 13
(W G M Turner) *chsd wnr tl wknd 4f out* **33/1**

2m 10.63s (0.73) **Going Correction** +0.075s/f (Good) **8 Ran SP% 116.2**
Speed ratings (Par 101):100,99,97,95,95 90,88,82
CSF £15.84 TOTE £7.50: £2.40, £1.10, £2.30; EX 17.70 Trifecta £79.80 Pool: £298.18, 2.65 winning units.

Owner Pete Smith Car Sales **Bred** M P B Bloodstock Ltd **Trained** Elton, Gloucs

FOCUS
Not a bad claimer, featuring three horses rated in the 70s but modest form best rated through the fifth.
Camille Pissarro(USA) Official explanation: trainer said gelding returned lame

1560 BETDAQ MULTIPLES VALUE MAIDEN STKS 1m 2f 36y
2:40 (2:41) (Class 5) 3-Y-0+ £3,108 (£924; £462; £230) Stalls Low

Form RPR

0- 1 **Venerable**[192] 6220 3-8-12 .... RichardHughes 16 76
(J H M Gosden) *trckd ldrs: led 4f out: hrd drvn fr over 1f out: rdn out* **2/1**[2]

0 2 1 **Shavansky**[15] 1204 3-8-12 .... RobertHavlin 12 74+
(J H M Gosden) *in tch: hdwy to trck ldrs 3f out: wnt 2nd ins fnl 2f: hand rdn fnl f and a jst hld by wnr: should improve* **20/1**

3 3 ½ **Torba (IRE)** 3-8-10 ow3.. SamHitchcott 1 65
(Evan Williams) *s.i.s: bhd: hdwy fr 4f out: chsd wnr over 2f out but no imp: wknd fnl f* **25/1**

4 2 ½ **Candy Mountain** 3-8-7 .... EddieAhern 11 58+
(L M Cumani) *chsd ldrs: pushed along 3f out: styd on same pce fnl 2f* **8/1**[3]

3-0 5 3 ½ **Composing (IRE)**[18] 1127 3-8-7 .... SteveDrowne 4 51+
(H Morrison) *sn chsng ldrs: rdn 3f out: wknd 2f out* **7/1**[3]

5 6 1 ¾ **Willow Dancer (IRE)**[21] 1075 3-8-12 .... AdamKirby 3 53
(W R Swinburn) *mid-div: rdn over 4f out: nvr gng pce to be competitive* **14/1**

0- 7 ¾ **Queens Quay**[235] 5344 3-8-7 .... PatDobbs 10 46
(R Hannon) *in rr: sme prog fnl 2f* **40/1**

8 shd **Princess Aimee**[730] 7-9-8 .... ChrisCatlin 8 47
(D Burchell) *s.i.s: bhd: sme prog fnl 2f* **50/1**

5 9 2 ½ **Kasban**[26] 1011 3-8-12 .... RHills 7 46
(E A L Dunlop) *in rr: rdn and mod progrss 3f out: nvr gng pce to be competitive* **15/8**[1]

00 10 2 ½ **Quite A Splash (USA)**[15] 1204 3-8-12 .... JamesDoyle 2 42
(S Curran) *hmpd bnd over 6f out: a towards rr* **100/1**

0 11 1 **Stafford Will (IRE)**[15] 1204 3-8-12 .... StephenDonohoe 9 40
(J G M O'Shea) *nvr bttr than mid-div* **125/1**

0- 12 3 **Polish Prospect (IRE)**[203] 6023 3-8-7 .... FrancisNorton 14 29
(H S Howe) *t.k.h: mode most tl hdd 4f out: wknd qckly* **100/1**

/05 13 1 ½ **Lockerley Man**[27] 1001 4-9-13 .... FergusSweeney 15 32
(W S Kittow) *disp ld tl over 4f out: sn wknd* **28/1**

14 6 **Burnley (IRE)**[174] 4-9-10 .... RichardKingscote(3) 5 21
(Mrs A L M King) *in rr: brief effrt into mid-div 1/2-way* **33/1**

15 5 **Arabiyah** 3-8-7 .... TedDurcan 13 5
(L M Cumani) *mid-div tl wknd over 4f out* **16/1**

2m 9.65s (-0.25) **Going Correction** +0.075s/f (Good)
WFA 3 from 4yo+ 15lb **15 Ran SP% 126.4**
Speed ratings (Par 103):104,103,100,98,95 94,93,93,91,89 88,86,85,80,76
CSF £51.55 TOTE £2.90: £1.30, £4.70, £8.20; EX 51.10 TRIFECTA Not won..
Owner K Abdulla **Bred** Juddmonte Farms Ltd **Trained** Newmarket, Suffolk

FOCUS
A modest maiden but the first two finished clear and look likely to improve again.
Willow Dancer(IRE) Official explanation: jockey said colt never travelled
Kasban Official explanation: jockey said colt never travelled
Quite A Splash(USA) Official explanation: jockey said gelding failed to handle the bend
Polish Prospect(IRE) Official explanation: jockey said filly ran too freely
Lockerley Man Official explanation: jockey said gelding hung left
Burnley(IRE) Official explanation: jockey said gelding was unsuited by the track

1561 WESTCOUNTRYRACING.COM AFFORDABLE RACING SYNDICATES H'CAP 6f 16y
3:15 (3:15) (Class 6) (0-65,63) 3-Y-O £2,266 (£674; £337; £168) Stalls High

Form RPR

0-03 1 **Ensign's Trick**[5] 1430 3-8-8 **60**.................................... LukeMorris(7) 10 68+
(W M Brisbourne) *pressed ldrs: led ins fnl 2f: rdn ins fnl f: rdr dropped reins and lost momentum but hld on wl* **14/1**

000- 2 ½ **Tibinta**[165] 6576 3-8-7 **52** ow1................................... StephenDonohoe 13 57
(P D Evans) *chsd ldrs: rdn and styd on u.p ins fnl f but a jst hld by wnr* **7/1**[3]

504- 3 shd **The Jay Factor (IRE)**[167] 6562 3-9-3 **62**...................... RichardHughes 8 67
(Pat Eddery) *in tch: hdwy over 2f out: disp 2nd u.p ins fnl f but nvr quite gng pce to rch wnr* **6/1**[2]

5434 4 2 ½ **Strike Force**[8] 1346 3-9-0 **59**..(p) GeorgeBaker 2 57
(R A Harris) *sn in mid-div: rdn and hdwy 2f out: styd on same pce ins fnl f* **9/1**

4441 5 1 **Slipasearcher (IRE)**[6] 1404 3-8-11 **63** 6ex..........(b) BernadetteQuinn(7) 6 58+
(P D Evans) *hld up in rr: stdy hdwy fnl 2f: gng on cl home but nt rch ldrs* **10/1**

020- 6 nk **Swiftly Addicted (IRE)**[220] 5668 3-9-3 **62**........................ EddieAhern 5 56
(A King) *in tch: hdwy 2f out: styd on same pce fnl f* **7/1**[3]

0615 7 1 ¼ **Doctor Ned**[14] 1232 3-8-1 **51**...................................... WilliamBuick(5) 15 41
(N A Callaghan) *pressed ldrs: rdn 2f out: wknd fnl f* **5/1**[1]

4-20 8 hd **Cantique (IRE)**[14] 1215 3-9-1 **60**.. JamesDoyle 1 49
(Ms J S Doyle) *in rr: sme prog towards outside over 2f out: nvr gng pce to be competitive* **40/1**

-000 9 1 ¾ **Merlins Quest**[29] 974 3-8-5 **55**.................................. KevinGhunowa(5) 9 39
(J M Bradley) *chsd ldrs: rdn 1/2-way: wknd fr 2f out* **40/1**

-000 10 hd **Da Schadenfreude (USA)**[83] 460 3-8-8 **53**.............(p) SteveDrowne 7 36
(W G M Turner) *in rr: rdn 1/2-way and brief effrt: nvr gng pce to get beyond mid-div* **14/1**

0-03 11 ¾ **Stir Crazy (IRE)**[10] 1313 3-9-4 **63**............................ EdwardCreighton 11 44
(M R Channon) *slt ld tl hdd ins fnl 2f: wknd fnl f* **8/1**

0-00 12 shd **Mr Forthright**[29] 974 3-8-10 **55**.................................... DarryllHolland 3 36
(J M Bradley) *towards rr tl mod prog fnl f* **33/1**

-301 13 1 **Almora Guru**[12] 1269 3-9-3 **62**.. TedDurcan 4 40
(W M Brisbourne) *a towards rr* **16/1**

600- 14 4 **Festive Tipple (IRE)**[223] 5608 3-9-1 **60**.................... StephenCarson 14 26
(P Winkworth) *a towards rr* **16/1**

060- 15 2 ½ **Spirit Rising**[261] 4624 3-8-7 **52**.. LPKeniry 16 10
(J M Bradley) *s.i.s: outpcd* **66/1**

10-0 16 15 **Auction Oasis**[14] 1219 3-8-13 **58**.................................... JamieMackay 12 —
(B Palling) *s.i.s: outpcd* **16/1**

1m 11.45s (-0.95) **Going Correction** -0.20s/f (Firm) **16 Ran SP% 126.4**
Speed ratings (Par 97):98,97,97,93,92 92,90,90,87,87 86,86,85,79,76 56
CSF £110.77 CT £672.99 TOTE £16.80: £4.10, £2.50, £1.50, £2.70; EX 223.10 TRIFECTA Not won..
Owner Mrs Mary Brisbourne **Bred** W M Brisbourne **Trained** Great Ness, Shropshire
■ Stewards' Enq: Quinn ten-day ban: breach of R 158 (May 19-28)P Evans fined £1,000 R 155(ii)

FOCUS
Modest handicap form but the winner was back to her juvenile form and the performance of the fourth gives it a solid feel.
Slipasearcher(IRE) Official explanation: jockey said, regarding running and riding, her orders were to get the filly across and get it travelling, adding that she tried to keep it sweet and get the best out of it without hitting her; trainer confirmed adding that he was satisfied with the ride and that the filly had a hard race previously
Merlins Quest Official explanation: jockey said colt hung
Da Schadenfreude(USA) Official explanation: jockey said gelding did not handle the track
Mr Forthright Official explanation: jockey said colt hung right

1562 FREESMSALERTSATBETDAQEXCHANGEVIEWS.COM H'CAP 1m 14y
3:50 (3:51) (Class 6) (0-65,62) 4-Y-0+ **£2,266** (£674; £337; £168) **Stalls High**

Form RPR
0302 **1** **Seneschal**[13] 1251 6-9-4 **62** .... SamHitchcott 9 71
(A B Haynes) *trckd ldrs: led wl over 1f out: pushed out* **13/2**[3]
4065 **2** *3/4* **Pelham Crescent (IRE)**[8] 1366 4-8-11 **55** ....(b) JamieMackay 8 62
(B Palling) *w ldrs: stl upsides and rdn fr 2f out: kpt on fnl f but a hld by wnr* **14/1**
561- **3** *hd* **Wind Chime (IRE)**[141] 6852 10-8-10 **54** .... RichardThomas 5 61
(A G Newcombe) *in rr: drvn and hdwy fr 2f out: kpt on ins fnl f: gng on cl home* **14/1**
060- **4** *2* **Chapter (IRE)**[240] 5205 5-8-11 **55** .... RichardHughes 14 57
(Mrs A L M King) *pressed ldrs and possible slt advantage tl hdd wl over 1f out: one pce ins fnl f* **5/1**[1]
6-63 **5** *1 1/2* **Convince (USA)**[29] 975 6-8-9 **58** ....(p) KevinGhunowa(5) 4 57
(J M Bradley) *chsd ldrs: rdn over 3f out: styd on same pce u.p fnl 2f* **7/1**
150- **6** *nk* **Trevian**[165] 6577 6-8-10 **54** .... DarryllHolland 3 52
(J M Bradley) *towards rr: rdn and hdwy over 2f out: kpt on fnl f but nvr gng pce to rch ldrs* **6/1**[2]
06-0 **7** *2 1/2* **Gala Jackpot (USA)**[14] 1210 4-7-11 **48** oh3 .... LukeMorris(7) 12 41
(W M Brisbourne) *in rr: pushed along over 2f out: kpt on fnl f but nvr in contention* **40/1**
04-0 **8** *3/4* **Grand Court (IRE)**[24] 1038 4-8-5 **49** .... ChrisCatlin 10 40
(M J Wallace) *in rr: pushed along and sme hdwy fnl 2f: n.d* **20/1**
6004 **9** *3/4* **Orphina (IRE)**[14] 1206 4-8-5 **49** ....(tp) EdwardCreighton 1 38
(B G Powell) *disp ld: rdn 3f out: wknd ins fnl 2f* **10/1**
3400 **10** *hd* **Going Skint**[28] 992 4-9-1 **59** .... AdamKirby 15 48
(M Wellings) *chsd ldrs 1/2-way: rdn over 2f out: sn btn* **14/1**
5504 **11** *shd* **Casablanca Minx (IRE)**[10] 1311 4-8-7 **51** ....(b) StephenDonohoe 2 39
(P D Evans) *a towards rr* **10/1**
6600 **12** *2 1/2* **Goose Chase**[7] 805 5-8-10 **54** .... RobertHavlin 13 37
(B J Llewellyn) *stdd s: t.k.h and sn disputing ld: hmpd and lost pl over 3f out: nvr in contention after* **25/1**
-000 **13** *5* **Lockstock (IRE)**[46] 741 9-8-12 **56** .... TedDurcan 6 27
(M S Saunders) *a towards rr* **20/1**
5360 **14** *10* **Mouseen (IRE)**[9] 430 4-8-9 **53** ....(t) JamesDoyle 7 1
(R J Price) *v.s.a: a out of tch* **8/1**

1m 34.86s (-1.14) **Going Correction** -0.20s/f (Firm) **14** Ran SP% **121.9**
Speed ratings (Par 101):97,96,96,94,92 92,89,89,88,88 87,85,80,70
CSF £90.60 CT £1248.83 TOTE £9.20: £3.30, £4.50, £4.00; EX 126.00 TRIFECTA Not won..
Owner P Cook **Bred** Michael E Broughton **Trained** Limpley Stoke, Bath

FOCUS
A moderate heat run in a time 0.95sec slower than the following three-year-old 66-80 handicap, but the form looks fairly sound rated around the placed horses.
Trevian Official explanation: jockey said gelding hung right from halfway
Going Skint Official explanation: jockey said gelding became unbalanced
Goose Chase Official explanation: jockey said gelding hung badly left throughout
Mouseen(IRE) Official explanation: jockey said gelding reared as stalls opened

1563 TOTESPORT.COM H'CAP 1m 14y
4:20 (4:21) (Class 4) (0-80,79) 3-Y-O **£4,857** (£1,445; £722; £360) **Stalls High**

Form RPR
6440 **1** **Lazy Darren**[19] 1106 3-9-2 **77** .... RichardHughes 8 87+
(R Hannon) *sn trcking ldrs: chal and edgd lft fr 2f out: led wl over 1f out: r.o strly* **11/4**[1]
00-0 **2** *3 1/2* **Lap Of Honour (IRE)**[21] 1076 3-8-6 **67** .... ChrisCatlin 1 69
(N A Callaghan) *sn chsng ldr: rdn over 2f out: chsd wnr fnl f but a comf hld* **9/1**
214- **3** *nk* **Beverly Hill Billy**[214] 5783 3-9-1 **76** .... EddieAhern 7 77
(A King) *t.k.h: chsd ldrs: drvn along 2f out: kpt on u.p fnl f: keeping on cl home* **3/1**[2]
06-5 **4** *shd* **Carson's Spirit (USA)**[14] 1230 3-9-2 **77** .... FergusSweeney 2 78
(W S Kittow) *slt ld: rdn over 2f out: hdd wl over 1f out: styd on same pce u.p* **16/1**
0-50 **5** *1* **Stagehand (IRE)**[13] 1247 3-8-7 **68** .... AdrianMcCarthy 5 67
(B R Millman) *chsd ldrs: drvn along fr 3f out: styd on fnl f but nvr gng pce to be competitive* **11/1**
2402 **6** *1/2* **Copper King**[21] 1076 3-9-4 **79** .... StephenDonohoe 9 77
(P D Evans) *in rr: pushed along and hdwy 3f out: kpt on fr over 1f out but nvr gng pce to rch ldrs* **11/2**
2110 **7** *3/4* **Alfresco**[15] 1202 3-9-3 **78** ....(b) PaulEddery 6 74
(Pat Eddery) *stdd s: hld up in rr: pushed along over 2f out: styd on same pce* **9/2**[3]
400- **8** *3 1/2* **Up In Arms (IRE)**[224] 5585 3-8-10 **71** .... StephenCarson 4 59
(P Winkworth) *chsd ldrs: rdn over 3f out: sn outpcd* **25/1**

1m 33.91s (-2.09) **Going Correction** -0.20s/f (Firm) **8** Ran SP% **113.3**
Speed ratings (Par 101):102,98,98,98,97 96,95,92
CSF £27.41 CT £78.23 TOTE £3.70: £1.60, £2.10, £1.60; EX 45.50 Trifecta £216.40 Pool: £561.00 - 1.84 winning units..
Owner J B R Leisure Ltd **Bred** Henry And Mrs Rosemary Moszkowicz **Trained** East Everleigh, Wilts

FOCUS
A fair handicap but just ordinary for the grade, although the winning time was 0.95 seconds quicker than previous older-horse 51-65 and the form appears solid.

1564 LETHEBY & CHRISTOPHER H'CAP 7f 16y
4:50 (4:50) (Class 5) (0-70,70) 4-Y-0+ **£3,238** (£963; £481; £240) **Stalls High**

Form RPR
5624 **1** **Imperium**[43] 793 6-8-7 **59** ow2 .... PatDobbs 10 68
(Jean-Rene Auvray) *hld up in rr but in tch: gd hdwy fr 2f out: str run to ld wl ins fnl f: hld on readily* **7/1**[2]
4136 **2** *nk* **Carcinetto (IRE)**[2] 1507 5-8-13 **65** .... StephenDonohoe 9 73
(P D Evans) *chsd ldrs: drvn to ld appr fnl f: hdd and nt qckn wl ins fnl f* **9/2**[1]
0-04 **3** *3* **Moon Forest (IRE)**[10] 1309 5-8-0 **57** oh3 ow1....(p) KevinGhunowa(5) 11 57
(J M Bradley) *led: rdn over 2f out: hdd appr fnl f: kpt on same pce ins fnl f* **8/1**[3]
-064 **4** *3/4* **Digital**[15] 1200 10-8-3 **62** .... ThomasO'Brien(7) 5 60+
(M R Channon) *sn towards rr: drvn and hdwy over 1f out: kpt on ins fnl f but nvr gng pce to rch ldrs* **9/2**[1]
-146 **5** *nk* **Mountain Pass (USA)**[37] 866 5-8-6 **58** ....(p) RobertHavlin 8 55
(B J Llewellyn) *in rr: hdwy fr 2f out: drvn and no imp on ldrs fnl f* **9/2**[1]
00-0 **6** *4* **Lizarazu (GER)**[15] 1200 8-8-11 **70** ....(p) LukeMorris(7) 1 57
(R A Harris) *chsd ldrs: rdn over 2f out: sn wknd* **16/1**
60-0 **7** *1* **Corrib (IRE)**[36] 895 4-9-0 **66** .... JamieMackay 4 50
(B Palling) *chsd ldr: rdn 3f out: wknd ins fnl 2f* **14/1**
00-0 **8** *3/4* **Stamford Blue**[5] 1436 6-8-5 **62** ....(b) TolleyDean(5) 2 45
(R A Harris) *in rr: sme hdwy and rdn 3f out: nvr gng pce to be competitive: wknd fr 2f out* **12/1**
530- **9** *shd* **Turkish Sultan (IRE)**[207] 5953 4-8-6 **65** .... BarrySavage(7) 6 47
(J M Bradley) *outpcd most of way* **20/1**
000- **10** *3/4* **Wrighty Almighty (IRE)**[197] 6147 5-8-8 **60** ....(p) FrancisNorton 7 40
(P R Chamings) *stmbld in rr after 1f: nvr bttr than mid-div* **11/1**
0-00 **11** *3/4* **Wizby**[18] 1132 4-7-11 **56** oh5 .... BernadetteQuinn(7) 3 34
(P D Evans) *chsd ldrs over 4f* **33/1**

1m 22.17s (-1.13) **Going Correction** -0.20s/f (Firm) **11** Ran SP% **114.4**
Speed ratings (Par 103):98,97,94,93,93 88,87,86,86,85 84
CSF £37.41 CT £214.72 TOTE £7.30: £1.80, £2.10, £3.10; EX 31.00 Trifecta £225.40 Part won. Pool: £317.55, 0.85 winning units. Place 6 £154.01, Place 5 £100.08.
Owner The Cross Keys Racing Club **Bred** Mrs H B Raw **Trained** Upper Lambourn, Berks

FOCUS
A modest handicap best rated around the placed horses.
T/Jkpt: Not won. T/Plt: £363.50 to a £1 stake. Pool: £59,784.80. 120.05 winning tickets. T/Qpdt: £48.80 to a £1 stake. Pool: £4,113.10. 62.30 winning tickets. ST

1374 SOUTHWELL (L-H)
Tuesday, May 8

OFFICIAL GOING: Standard
Wind: Fresh, behind Weather: Mainly sunny apart from a heavy shower prior to the 3rd race

1565 BETDIRECTPOKER.COM $50,000 FREEROLL H'CAP 5f (F)
2:00 (2:01) (Class 5) (0-75,75) 4-Y-0+ **£3,562** (£1,059; £529; £264) **Stalls High**

Form RPR
135- **1** **Steel City Boy (IRE)**[178] 6452 4-8-12 **69** .... DanielTudhope 4 82
(D Carroll) *chsd ldrs: led 2f out: rdn out* **17/2**
1211 **2** *1 1/2* **Count Cougar (USA)**[35] 905 7-9-3 **74** .... AdrianTNicholls 1 82
(S P Griffiths) *chsd ldrs: led over 3f out: hdd 2f out: sn rdn: styd on same pce ins fnl f* **11/4**[1]
401- **3** *shd* **Tender Process (IRE)**[211] 5864 4-9-4 **75** .... GrahamGibbons 5 83+
(E S McMahon) *s.i.s: outpcd: hdwy u.p 2f out: sn edgd lft: styd on* **4/1**[2]
56-0 **4** *1* **Kings College Boy**[30] 957 7-8-11 **68** ....(b) PaulHanagan 7 72
(R A Fahey) *chsd ldrs: rdn 1/2-way: styd on same pce ins fnl f* **10/1**
0000 **5** *4* **Glenviews Youngone (IRE)**[22] 1067 4-8-10 **72**(b) RussellKennemore(5) 11 62
(Peter Grayson) *mid-div: outpcd 1/2-way: n.d after* **66/1**
2233 **6** *1/2* **Melalchrist**[10] 1299 5-8-11 **68** ....(p) NCallan 9 56
(K A Ryan) *chsd ldrs 3f* **6/1**[3]
0-01 **7** *2* **Colorus (IRE)**[10] 1299 4-9-2 **73** .... DaleGibson 12 54
(M W Easterby) *chsd ldrs: hung lft: rdn 1/2-way: sn outpcd* **10/1**
026- **8** *1 1/4* **Pick A Nice Name**[296] 3567 5-8-8 **70** .... MichaelJStainton(5) 10 46
(R M Whitaker) *s.s: outpcd* **12/1**
0-00 **9** *3 1/2* **Mormeatmic**[10] 1299 4-8-5 **69** .... NSLawes(7) 2 33
(M W Easterby) *sn outpcd* **20/1**
234- **10** *9* **Lake Chini (IRE)**[354] 1820 5-9-4 **75** ....(p) TomEaves 8 6
(M W Easterby) *s.i.s: outpcd* **10/1**
2200 **11** *7* **Stoneacre Boy (IRE)**[35] 905 4-8-8 **65** ow1 ....(b) RobbieFitzpatrick 6 —
(Peter Grayson) *sn outpcd: eased fnl 2f* **14/1**

58.36 secs (-1.94) **Going Correction** -0.30s/f (Stan) **11** Ran SP% **119.4**
Speed ratings (Par 103):103,100,100,98,92 91,88,86,80,66 55
CSF £32.56 CT £108.88 TOTE £14.50: £3.90, £1.20, £2.00; EX 52.60.
Owner Ninerus **Bred** Mrs A B McDonnell **Trained** Sledmere, E Yorks

FOCUS
A routine Fibresand sprint handicap, as usual dominated by those that raced handily and came down the centre. The form looks solid rated around the placed horses, and could rate higher.
Melalchrist Official explanation: jockey said gelding had no more to give

1566 BETDIRECT.COM GET INVOLVED MAIDEN STKS 1m 3f (F)
2:30 (2:31) (Class 5) 3-Y-0+ **£3,238** (£963; £481; £240) **Stalls Low**

Form RPR
2 **1** **Cedar Mountain (IRE)**[10] 1296 4-9-13 .... JimmyFortune 11 86+
(J H M Gosden) *hld up: hdwy over 4f out: led wl over 1f out: sn hung rt and clr: eased ins fnl f* **8/13**[1]
02/ **2** *7* **Move Over Darling (IRE)**[566] 5987 4-9-8 .... NCallan 9 64
(P F I Cole) *chsd ldrs: led 2f out: sn rdn and hdd: no ex* **12/1**
5 **3** *1* **Force Celebre (IRE)**[90] 386 3-8-10 .... JimmyQuinn 12 66
(M H Tompkins) *s.i.s: hld up: hdwy over 3f out: sn rdn and outpcd* **10/1**
2 **4** *3* **Ninetyninetreble (IRE)**[45] 769 4-9-13 .... AdrianTNicholls 8 62
(D Nicholls) *plld hrd: led for 1f: chsd ldr: led over 3f out: rdn and hdd 2f out: sn wknd* **11/2**[2]
4-0 **5** *2 1/2* **Barton Belle**[14] 229 5-9-5 .... NeilChalmers(3) 4 52
(C N Kellett) *led 10f out: rdn and hdd over 3f out: wknd over 2f out* **50/1**
00- **6** *nk* **Lady Pickpocket**[220] 5679 3-8-4 ow4 .... PatrickHills(5) 5 55
(M H Tompkins) *prom over 8f* **50/1**
7 *9* **Blue Denim** 3-8-5 .... MatthewHenry 1 35
(M A Jarvis) *dwlt: hld up: effrt over 3f out: wknd over 2f out* **7/1**[3]
00 **8** *7* **Winds Of Kildare (IRE)**[29] 977 4-9-13 .... PFredericks 10 29
(C N Allen) *hld up: wknd over 4f out* **100/1**
0- **9** *5* **Sven (SWE)**[202] 6050 3-8-10 .... JimCrowley 3 19
(B I Case) *prom over 6f* **100/1**
000- **10** *3* **Best Warning**[227] 5527 3-8-2 53 .... MarcHalford(3) 2 9
(J Ryan) *chsd ldrs: rdn over 3f out: sn wknd* **100/1**
06-5 **11** *10* **The Graig**[13] 1250 3-8-10 60 .... TPQueally 13 —
(C Drew) *hld up: sme hdwy over 3f out: sn wknd* **66/1**
4 **12** *17* **Starr Flyer**[14] 1220 3-8-10 .... DavidAllan 7 —
(A Bailey) *hld up: rdn 1/2-way: sn wknd* **33/1**

0 **13** *15* **Irish Secret (CZE)**[45] 769 3-8-10 .... JosedeSouza 6 —
(G J Smith) *s.i.s: sn mid-div: wknd 1/2-way* **100/1**

2m 30.11s (1.21) **Going Correction** -0.10s/f (Stan)
WFA 3 from 4yo+ 17lb **13** Ran SP% **118.9**
Speed ratings (Par 103):91,85,85,83,81 80,74,69,65,63 56,43,32
CSF £9.51 TOTE £1.80: £1.10, £2.70, £2.80; EX 10.70.
Owner George Strawbridge **Bred** George Strawbridge **Trained** Newmarket, Suffolk

FOCUS
Nothing like as competitive a maiden as the size of the field would suggest, best rated around the third and fourth, and the favourite was in a different league. The early pace looked strong and they finished well spread out, but several struggled to get home and, though the winning time was quicker than the following fillies' handicap, it was around a second slower than the later Class 7 classified event.

1567 BETDIRECTPOKER.COM COME AND 'AVE SOME FILLIES' H'CAP 1m 3f (F)
3:05 (3:05) (Class 4) (0-80,72) 4-Y-O+ **£4,857** (£1,445; £722; £360) **Stalls** Low

Form RPR
030- **1** **Jeu D'Esprit (IRE)**[173] 6503 4-8-12 **66** .... TPQueally 2 72
(J G Given) *mde all: qcknd over 2f out: drvn out* **12/1**
02 **2** *1* **Brastar Jelois (FR)**[11] 1279 4-8-5 **64** .... RussellKennemore(5) 4 68
(R Hollinshead) *hld up: hdwy over 3f out: rdn to chse wnr over 1f out: styd on* **9/1**
40-2 **3** *¾* **Ha'Penny Beacon**[12] 1263 4-8-12 **66** .... DanielTudhope 1 69
(D Carroll) *chsd wnr 3f: outpcd over 2f out: styd on u.p fnl f* **85/40**[1]
600- **4** *1½* **Vale De Lobo**[178] 6432 5-9-4 **72** .... JimCrowley 5 72
(B R Millman) *prom: chsd wnr 8f out: rdn over 1f out: no ex ins fnl f* **5/2**[2]
6103 **5** *3½* **Ruffie (IRE)**[8] 1352 4-8-10 **64** ....(e) NCallan 3 59
(Miss Gay Kelleway) *prom: rdn over 2f out: wknd fnl f* **9/2**[3]
6220 **5** *dht* **Bavarica**[12] 1258 5-8-8 **69** .... AmyBaker(7) 6 64
(Miss J Feilden) *hld up: rdn and hung rt over 1f out: n.d* **6/1**

2m 31.23s (2.33) **Going Correction** -0.10s/f (Stan) **6** Ran SP% **110.7**
Speed ratings (Par 102):87,86,85,84,82 82
CSF £102.59 TOTE £16.00: £6.40, £3.60; EX 101.90.
Owner Paul Moulton **Bred** Pat Garvey **Trained** Willoughton, Lincs
■ Stewards' Enquiry : Russell Kennemore one-day ban: used whip above shoulder height (May 20)

FOCUS
A race run at a crawl that developed into a three-furlong sprint and that very much played into the hands of the winner. Not surprisingly the winning time was comfortably the slowest of the three races over the trip at the meeting and the form is unlikely to work out.

1568 JOHN SAVAGE AND JAYNE DRAPER WEDDING DAY H'CAP 1m (F)
3:40 (3:40) (Class 4) (0-80,80) 4-Y-O+ **£4,857** (£1,445; £722; £360) **Stalls** Low

Form RPR
2021 **1** **Luckylover**[12] 1264 4-9-1 **80** ....(t) JerryO'Dwyer(3) 7 96+
(M G Quinlan) *sn drvn to ld: rdn over 1f out: eased towards fin* **5/4**[1]
4020 **2** *1¾* **Orpen Wide (IRE)**[17] 1157 5-8-11 **78** ....(b) RussellKennemore(5) 8 87
(M C Chapman) *hld up: hdwy to chse wnr over 2f out: rdn and hung rt over 1f out: no imp fnl f* **10/1**
0-01 **3** *9* **Indian's Feather (IRE)**[8] 1352 6-8-7 **69** 6ex .... TomEaves 3 57
(N Tinkler) *sn pushed along in rr: bhd tl mod late prog* **25/1**
2125 **4** *nk* **Wodhill Gold**[36] 888 6-8-4 **66** oh6 ....(v) HayleyTurner 5 54
(D Morris) *chsd ldrs: rdn 1/2-way: outpcd fnl 3f* **16/1**
10-3 **5** *2½* **Rowan Lodge (IRE)**[12] 1264 5-8-6 **68** .... JimmyQuinn 4 50
(M H Tompkins) *trckd ldrs: rdn over 2f out: sn hung lft and wknd* **7/1**[3]
6-00 **6** *1¼* **Sentiero Rosso (USA)**[36] 895 5-8-4 **66** oh3 .... PaulHanagan 6 45
(B Ellison) *chsd ldrs over 5f* **16/1**
12-2 **7** *13* **Evident Pride (USA)**[37] 870 4-9-3 **79** .... SebSanders 1 28
(B R Johnson) *prom over 5f* **5/2**[2]
314- **8** *143* **Lincolneurocruiser**[272] 4253 5-8-12 **74** .... NCallan 2 —
(Mrs N Macauley) *prom: rdn 1/2-way: sn wknd and eased* **16/1**

1m 42.79s (-1.81) **Going Correction** -0.10s/f (Stan) **8** Ran SP% **116.1**
Speed ratings (Par 105):105,103,94,93,91 90,77,—
CSF £15.72 CT £214.91 TOTE £2.20: £1.20, £2.40, £4.90; EX 16.20.
Owner Roger Turner **Bred** Shutford Stud **Trained** Newmarket, Suffolk

FOCUS
Thanks to the favourite, a race run at a strong pace and the front pair pulled miles clear. The form looks rock solid rated through the runner-up.
Evident Pride(USA) Official explanation: trainer had no explanation for poor form shown
Lincolneurocruiser Official explanation: jockey said gelding lost its action

1569 BETDIRECTPOKER.COM GET INVOLVED H'CAP 7f (F)
4:10 (4:10) (Class 6) (0-50,53) 4-Y-O+ **£3,071** (£906; £453) **Stalls** Low

Form RPR
24-1 **1** **Megalo Maniac**[8] 1349 4-9-1 **53** 6ex .... PaulHanagan 1 73+
(R A Fahey) *a.p: led over 1f out: rdn clr fnl f: eased nr fin* **2/1**[1]
1004 **2** *3½* **Government (IRE)**[7] 1379 6-8-4 **47** .... NicolPolli(5) 10 53
(M C Chapman) *chsd ldr: led 3f out: sn rdn and hdd: styd on same pce appr fnl f* **14/1**
3366 **3** *1¼* **Wodhill Be**[29] 980 7-8-9 **47** .... HayleyTurner 9 50
(D Morris) *hld up: plld hrd: hdwy over 1f out: nt rch ldrs* **7/1**
3600 **4** *1¼* **Piccleyes**[54] 680 6-8-1 **46** oh1 ....(be) MCGeran(7) 6 46
(A J McCabe) *chsd ldrs: led over 2f out: rdn and hdd over 1f out: wknd ins fnl f* **16/1**
3650 **5** *2* **Attacca**[4] 1459 6-8-10 **48** .... NCallan 4 42
(J R Weymes) *mid-div: rdn 1/2-way: no imp fnl 2f* **4/1**[2]
1200 **6** *2½* **Astorygoeswithit**[8] 1349 4-8-7 **48** ....(be) JerryO'Dwyer(3) 11 36
(P S McEntee) *sn led: hdd 3f out: rdn and wknd over 1f out* **20/1**
0004 **7** *shd* **Savile's Delight (IRE)**[49] 715 8-8-8 **46** oh1 ....(t) DeanMcKeown 2 34
(Miss Joanne Priest) *hld up: hdwy 1/2-way: wknd over 1f out* **25/1**
00-0 **8** *7* **Preskani**[103] 243 5-8-3 **46** .... DuranFentiman(5) 3 15
(Mrs N Macauley) *s.i.s: n.d* **20/1**
260- **9** *7* **Fadansil**[222] 5637 4-8-11 **49** .... TonyHamilton 12 —
(J Wade) *s.i.s: outpcd* **66/1**
0500 **10** *¾* **Capital Lass**[7] 1379 4-8-11 **49** ....(be[1]) JimmyQuinn 5 —
(A J McCabe) *s.i.s: hld up: sme hdwy 3f out: eased fnl 2f* **25/1**
00-3 **11** *3* **Pappas Ruby (USA)**[16] 1175 4-8-12 **50** .... SebSanders 7 —
(R M Beckett) *mid-div: sn drvn along: wknd 1/2-way* **11/2**[3]
0-03 **12** *76* **El Palmar**[7] 1374 6-8-10 **48** ....(v) GrahamGibbons 8 —
(M J Attwater) *s.i.s: hdwy over 5f out: wknd 1/2-way* **16/1**

1m 32.14s (1.34) **Going Correction** -0.10s/f (Stan) **12** Ran SP% **118.4**
Speed ratings (Par 101):88,84,82,81,78 76,75,67,59,59 55,—
CSF £30.35 CT £173.20 TOTE £2.60: £1.20, £6.30, £2.10; EX 44.00.
Owner A Long **Bred** E R W Stanley And New England Stud Farm Ltd **Trained** Musley Bank, N Yorks

FOCUS
A large field, but not a very competitive contest and barely better than a seller. The favourite scored easily but the winning time was moderate, even for a race like this, and the runner-up looks the best guide to the form.
Capital Lass Official explanation: jockey said filly missed the break
Pappas Ruby(USA) Official explanation: trainer's rep said filly would not face kickback
El Palmar Official explanation: jockey said saddle slipped

1570 BETDIRECTPOKER.COM $50,000 FREEROLL CLASSIFIED STKS 1m 3f (F)
4:40 (4:40) (Class 7) 4-Y-O+ **£1,876** (£554; £277) **Stalls** Low

Form RPR
0242 **1** **Diktatorship (IRE)**[8] 1362 4-8-12 44 .... NCallan 10 60
(G A Swinbank) *chsd ldrs: rdn to ld 2f out: sn edgd rt: styd on wl* **7/4**[1]
5004 **2** *5* **Activist**[8] 1362 9-8-5 45 ....(p) KellyHarrison(7) 3 52
(D Carroll) *chsd ldrs: led over 3f out: rdn and hdd 2f out: styd on same pce* **14/1**
13-0 **3** *8* **Kentucky Bullet (USA)**[77] 503 11-8-12 41 .... SimonWhitworth 5 39
(A G Newcombe) *hld up: hdwy over 3f out: wknd over 1f out* **14/1**
-330 **4** *6* **Moyne Pleasure (IRE)**[37] 585 9-8-7 44 .... DuranFentiman(5) 12 30
(R Johnson) *mid-div: hdwy 1/2-way: rdn over 3f out: sn wknd* **11/1**
4003 **5** *1¾* **Twilight Avenger (IRE)**[8] 1362 4-8-9 40 ....(b) LiamJones(3) 8 27
(W M Brisbourne) *hld up: sme hdwy over 3f out: sn rdn and wknd* **25/1**
0000 **6** *¾* **Bournonville**[12] 1271 4-8-9 41 .... DominicFox(3) 14 26
(M Wigham) *hld up: rn wd bnd 10f out: effrt over 3f out: sn wknd* **33/1**
5440 **7** *7* **Padre Nostro (IRE)**[35] 907 8-8-5 42 .... ChrisGlenister(7) 2 14
(J R Holt) *mid-div: rdn over 4f out: sn wknd* **14/1**
4610 **8** *hd* **Trysting Grove (IRE)**[13] 1254 6-8-12 45 .... DaleGibson 7 14
(E G Bevan) *prom over 7f* **6/1**[3]
0-00 **9** *hd* **Sheriff's Deputy**[20] 1086 7-8-9 44 .... NeilChalmers(3) 13 14
(C N Kellett) *chsd ldr: led over 4f out: rdn and hdd over 3f out: sn wknd* **50/1**
03-3 **10** *¾* **Coffin Dodger**[12] 1271 4-8-5 44 .... KirstyMilczarek(7) 11 13
(C N Allen) *s.s: hld up: effrt 4f out: sn wknd* **12/1**
51/0 **11** *nk* **Rood Boy (IRE)**[103] 242 6-8-12 45 .... JimCrowley 6 12
(Simon Earle) *hld up: sme hdwy 4f out: sn wknd* **6/1**[3]
00-0 **12** *11* **First Boy (GER)**[75] 524 8-8-12 42 .... VinceSlattery 1 —
(D J Wintle) *chsd ldrs: rdn 8f out: sn lost pl* **4/1**[2]
00-0 **13** *5* **Peak Seasons (IRE)**[23] 812 4-8-7 45 ....(b) RussellKennemore(5) 9 —
(M C Chapman) *rdn to ld: hdd over 4f out: wknd qckly* **33/1**
1/0- **14** *12* **Ally Makbul**[147] 6798 7-8-12 45 .... DanielTudhope 4 —
(Ian Emmerson) *prom: hmpd and lost pl 7f out: bhd fnl 5f* **80/1**

2m 29.09s (0.19) **Going Correction** -0.10s/f (Stan) **14** Ran SP% **133.9**
Speed ratings (Par 97):95,91,85,81,79 79,74,74,73,73 73,65,61,52
CSF £33.73 TOTE £3.10: £1.30, £5.80, £3.10; EX 28.40 Place 6 £216.73, Place 5 £151.12.
Owner Miss Sarah Kelleway **Bred** Allevamento Il Crognolo **Trained** Melsonby, N Yorks

FOCUS
A bad race despite the size of the field, but although a solid pace resulted in the fastest of the three races over the trip on the day, not too much should be read into that and the form is assessed around the first two. With some healthy margins separating the front four, the future does not look too rosy for the others.
Coffin Dodger Official explanation: trainer said filly never travelled
T/Plt: £86.00 to a £1 stake. Pool: £49,033.10. 416.05 winning tickets. T/Qpdt: £52.20 to a £1 stake. Pool: £2,211.80. 31.30 winning tickets. CR

1339 LONGCHAMP (R-H)
Tuesday, May 8

OFFICIAL GOING: Soft

1571a PRIX D'HEDOUVILLE (GROUP 3) 1m 4f
1:20 (1:21) 4-Y-O+ **£27,027** (£10,811; £8,108; £5,405; £2,703)

RPR
1 **Champs Elysees**[234] 5400 4-8-11 .... SPasquier 6 113
(A Fabre, France) *racd in 3rd: led narrowly 1 1/2f out tl drew away last 100yds* **26/10**[2]
2 *1½* **Mister Conway (FR)**[21] 1085 6-8-9 .... RonanThomas 8 109
(P Van De Poele, France) *racd in 2nd: rdn and ev ch 1 1/2f out: styng on and only a nk bhd 100yds out: no ex clsng stages* **44/10**[3]
3 *2* **Group Captain**[34] 929 5-8-9 .... CSoumillon 5 106
(R Charlton) *racd in 5th: wnt 3rd 1f out: styd on* **11/1**
4 *2½* **Mary Louhana**[30] 962 4-8-8 .... TJarnet 3 101
(M Delzangles, France) *hld up in last: 8th st: hdwy towards ins to go 4th 100yds out: one pce* **25/1**
5 *nk* **Sudan (IRE)**[40] 823 4-8-11 .... OPeslier 9 104
(E Lellouche, France) *hld up in 6th: rdn and unable qckn fr 1 1/2f out* **22/10**[1]
6 *nk* **Elasos (FR)**[37] 880 5-8-11 .... DBonilla 2 103
(D Sepulchre, France) *hld up in 7th: effrt on outside over 1 1/2f out: styd on clsng stages: nvr nr ldrs* **84/10**
7 *½* **Petrograd (IRE)**[40] 823 6-8-9 .... GFaucon 7 101
(E Lellouche, France) *set gd pce: hdd 1 1/2f out: one pce* **22/10**[1]
8 *2* **Princesse Dansante (IRE)**[30] 962 4-8-6 .... TThulliez 4 95
(F Doumen, France) *racd in 4th on ins: effrt 1 1/2f out: wknd 1f out* **87/10**
9 *10* **Kiton (GER)**[21] 1085 6-8-11 .... C-PLemaire 1 85
(P Rau, Germany) *hld up in 8th: rdn 3f out: t.o fnl 1 1/2f* **15/1**

2m 30.8s (-4.20) **9** Ran SP% **148.2**
PARI-MUTUEL: WIN 3.60; PL 2.00, 2.00, 3.20; DF 9.90.
Owner K Abdulla **Bred** Juddmonte Farms Ltd **Trained** Chantilly, France

NOTEBOOK
Champs Elysees could well turn into a very useful middle-distance horse this year judging by the way he won his first Group race. Making his seasonal debut and running over a mile and a half for the first time, he was always well placed and took command a furlong and a half out, eventually winning with something in hand. This beautifully-bred individual may well now go for the Grand Prix de Chantilly, and is likely to be entered in the Arc de Triomphe.
Mister Conway(FR), a very brave individual, never let his connections down. With a pacemaker in the field, he was allowed to gallop in second position and tried in ernest to peg back the winner throughout the final furlong, but he was a little one-paced. There are no plans for this six-year-old at the moment, but he deserves to win a race of this calibre.
Group Captain, racing in Group company for the first time, lost nothing in defeat. He quickened from a furlong and a half and then just stayed on to be an easy third without being put under any unnecessary pressure. The soft ground suited him and his trainer will now be looking for a Listed race over a similar distance. He should have another successful season.

Mary Louhana, held up in last, made her challenge up the far rail. She never looked liked troubling the first three past the post but it was still a decent effort.

1572a PRIX HOCQUART MITSUBISHI MOTORS (GROUP 2) (C&F) 1m 3f
2:50 (2:50) 3-Y-O **£50,068** (£19,324; £9,233; £6,149; £3,074)

RPR

1 **Anton Chekhov**[16] [1185] 3-9-2 .... JMurtagh 5 108
(A P O'Brien, Ire) *set stdy pce: reminders and qcknd 3f out: jnd over 2f out: hdd narrowly 1 1/2f out: rallied u.p to ld 1f out: drvn out* **73/10**[3]

2 *hd* **Royal And Regal (IRE)**[191] 3-9-2 .... SPasquier 1 107
(A Fabre, France) *racd in 2nd: disp ld over 2f out tl led narrowly 1 1/2f out: hdd 1f out: r.o under pressure clsng stages* **36/10**[2]

3 *1 1/2* **Shujoon**[40] [824] 3-9-2 .... LDettori 3 105
(A Fabre, France) *racd in 3rd: rdn 2f out: lost 3rd 1f out: rallied to regain 3rd cl home* **16/10**[1]

4 *snk* **Serabad (FR)**[52] [704] 3-9-2 .... CSoumillon 2 105
(J-C Rouget, France) *hld up in 4th: rdn 2f out: hdwy on ins to go 3rd and n.m.r 1f out: no ex and lost 3rd cl home* **16/10**[1]

5 *6* **Special Day (FR)**[23] [1057] 3-9-2 .... OPeslier 4 95
(F Head, France) *last thrght: outpcd fr 3f out* **12/1**

2m 23.0s (3.10) **5** Ran SP% **118.4**
PARI-MUTUEL: WIN 8.30; PL 2.90, 2.40; SF 27.70.
Owner Michael Tabor **Bred** W & R Barnett Ltd **Trained** Ballydoyle, Co Tipperary
■ Stewards' Enquiry : J Murtagh 100 fine: whip abuse

NOTEBOOK
Anton Chekhov was given a highly professional ride by his jockey. Setting only a moderate pace until the straight, he held on well to fend off the runner-up, who was at his side throughout the last furlong and a half. A longer distance will certainly be no problem and connections are looking at either the Derby Italiano or the English Derby.
Royal And Regal(IRE) is definitely one for the notebook. Racing for the first time since last October, he looked the likely winner when shaken up at the furlong marker, but he just tied up as the race came to an end. Considerable progress can now be expected and he is entered in all the top races. The Prix du Jockey-Club is on the cards, but one has the feeling that his trainer would like to go for the Grand Prix de Paris via the Prix du Lys. He is an exciting prospect for the rest of the season.
Shujoon, who was not suited by the lack of pace, was in third place throughout and outpaced when the winner and runner-up quickened early in the straight. He did stay on well to hold third place by a narrow margin, though.
Serabad(FR), fourth from start to finish, looked dangerous halfway up the straight when just behind the leaders, but he could not go through with his challenge. He stayed on near the rail but was rather one-paced inside the final furlong.

[1255] BEVERLEY (R-H)
Wednesday, May 9

OFFICIAL GOING: Good to firm
Wind: Virtually nil

1573 TURF TV MEDIAN AUCTION MAIDEN STKS 1m 4f 16y
2:00 (2:00) (Class 5) 3-5-Y-O **£3,238** (£963; £481; £240) **Stalls** High

Form RPR

4- 1 **Market Forces**[185] [6349] 3-8-2 .... JimmyQuinn 7 77+
(H R A Cecil) *trckd ldrs: hdwy and cl up 1/2-way: led 2f out: sn clr: v easily* **1/7**[1]

5000 2 *11* **Arabellas Homer**[75] [534] 3-7-11 40 .... DuranFentiman(5) 4 46
(Mrs N Macauley) *s.i.s: hld up in tch: hdwy over 2f out: sn rdn: kpt on fnl f: no ch w wnr* **66/1**

0-04 3 *2 1/2* **Devilfishpoker Com**[11] [1303] 3-8-7 60 .... (b) PaulFessey 1 47
(R C Guest) *prom: led after 4f: rdn along 3f out: hdd 2f out and sn btn* **16/1**[3]

3- 4 *7* **Lucky Find (IRE)**[235] [5365] 4-9-4 .... GregFairley(3) 5 31
(M Mullineaux) *cl up: lft in ld after 1f: hdd after 4f: rdn along over 3f out: sn wknd* **10/1**[2]

0- 5 *1 1/2* **Lisselan Dancer (USA)**[259] [4705] 3-8-2 .... RoystonFfrench 3 28
(J R Weymes) *prom: rdn along over 3f out: sn btn* **25/1**

00-0 6 *37* **Keep A Welcome**[122] [60] 4-9-9 35 .... (b[1]) DominicFox(3) 6 —
(S Parr) *led tl m wd bnd after 1f: a bhd after* **100/1**

2m 37.74s (-2.47) **Going Correction** -0.05s/f (Good)
WFA 3 from 4yo 19lb **6** Ran SP% **108.8**
Speed ratings (Par 103):106,98,97,92,91 66
CSF £19.70 TOTE £1.10: £1.02, £14.90; EX 19.20.
Owner K Abdulla **Bred** Juddmonte Farms Ltd **Trained** Newmarket, Suffolk

FOCUS
A complete non-event and Market Forces readily defied odds of 1/7 as he was entitled to. The opposition was only banded-class, with the third's Offical rating flattering him.
Keep A Welcome Official explanation: jockey said gelding hung left-handed and bit slipped through its mouth

1574 RBS INVOICE FINANCE H'CAP 5f
2:30 (2:30) (Class 4) (0-85,85) 4-Y-0+ **£6,477** (£1,927; £963; £481) **Stalls** High

Form RPR

150- 1 **Wanchai Lad**[193] [6212] 6-8-12 79 .... DavidAllan 14 89
(T D Easterby) *dwlt: hdwy on inner wl over 1f out: rdn ent fnl f: str run to ld on post* **7/1**[3]

6-00 2 *shd* **Bo McGinty (IRE)**[15] [1223] 6-8-6 73 .... (b) TonyHamilton 15 83
(R A Fahey) *cl up: led wl over 1f out: sn rdn: hdd on post* **4/1**[1]

41-1 3 *1 1/2* **Aegean Dancer**[19] [1134] 5-8-12 82 .... MarkLawson(3) 3 86+
(B Smart) *hdwy on outer 1/2-way: rdn to chal ent fnl f and ev ch tl drvn: edgd rt and nt qckn last 100yds* **10/1**

0-40 4 *shd* **High Reach**[11] [1292] 7-8-5 79 .... DeanHeslop(7) 11 83
(T D Barron) *led: rdn along 2f out: sn hdd and kpt on same pce* **8/1**

100- 5 *3/4* **Glasshoughton**[278] [4102] 4-8-11 78 .... PhillipMakin 13 79
(M Dods) *chsd ldrs: rdn wl over 1f out: kpt on same pce ins fnl f* **16/1**

10/0 6 *1/2* **Playful Dane (IRE)**[21] [1088] 10-8-7 81 .... PNolan(7) 12 81
(K A Ryan) *towards rr: hdwy 2f out: kpt on ins fnl f: nrst fin* **8/1**

3650 7 *1/2* **Pawan (IRE)**[18] [1159] 7-8-6 78 .... (b) AnnStokell(5) 7 76
(Miss A Stokell) *towards rr: rdn along 2f out: swtchd lft and styd on wl fnl f: nrst fin* **12/1**

310- 8 *nk* **Sunrise Safari (IRE)**[326] [2658] 4-8-13 80 .... (v) TomEaves 10 77
(I Semple) *chsd ldrs: rdn along wl over 2f out: grad wknd* **16/1**

56-3 9 *1 1/2* **Bond Boy**[19] [1134] 10-8-7 79 .... (v) DuranFentiman(5) 6 70
(G R Oldroyd) *towards rr tl styd on appr fnl f: nrst fin* **20/1**

21-0 10 *3/4* **Royal Challenge**[21] [1088] 6-9-3 84 .... SebSanders 4 73
(M H Tompkins) *prom: rdn along 2f out: grad wknd* **11/1**

453- 11 *3/4* **Balakiref**[193] [6212] 8-8-7 74 .... JimmyQuinn 5 60
(M Dods) *sn outpcd and bhd tl styd on appr fnl f* **25/1**

352- 12 *shd* **Bahamian Ballet**[230] [5493] 5-8-6 73 .... RoystonFfrench 8 58+
(E S McMahon) *chsd ldrs: rdn along 2f out: sn wknd* **10/1**

-002 13 *2* **Monashee Brave (IRE)**[11] [1299] 4-8-7 74 .... PatCosgrave 9 52
(J J Quinn) *chsd ldrs: rdn along 2f out: sn wknd* **6/1**[2]

62.53 secs (-1.47) **Going Correction** -0.15s/f (Firm) **13** Ran SP% **123.6**
Speed ratings (Par 105):105,104,102,102,101 100,99,99,96,95 94,94,90
CSF £36.31 CT £300.19 TOTE £10.90: £2.50, £2.50, £4.40; EX 21.10.
Owner Ambrose Turnbull **Bred** G T Lucas **Trained** Great Habton, N Yorks

FOCUS
A fair handicap but a draw-bores' paradise with the top two stalls fighting out the finish. The form looks solid enough rated through the fourth.
Pawan(IRE) Official explanation: jockey said gelding was unsuited by the good to frim going
Balakiref Official explanation: jockey said gelding dwelt in the stalls

1575 MARTIN SHAW WINS WITH THE YORKSHIRE POST H'CAP 1m 4f 16y
3:00 (3:00) (Class 3) (0-90,87) 4-Y-0+ **£9,067** (£2,697; £1,348; £673) **Stalls** High

Form RPR

-131 1 **Kilimandscharo (USA)**[72] [568] 5-8-0 74 .... DuranFentiman(5) 4 81+
(P J McBride) *hld up in tch: hdwy over 2f out: swtchd lft and rdn to chal over 1f out: drvn ins fnl f: led last 100yds* **10/3**[2]

2110 2 *nk* **Kames Park (IRE)**[14] [1244] 5-9-4 87 .... TomEaves 5 93
(I Semple) *hld up in tch: hdwy on outer 2f out: rdn over 1f out: styd on to ld jst ins fnl f: drvn: wandered and hdd last 100yds* **8/1**

36-4 3 *3/4* **Tilt**[14] [1244] 5-8-12 86 .... JamieMoriarty(5) 3 91
(B Ellison) *trckd ldr: effrt 3f out: rdn over 2f out: drvn to ld briefly 1f out: sn hdd and one pce* **7/4**[1]

14-3 4 *1/2* **Mull Of Dubai**[15] [1208] 4-8-4 73 oh1 .... JimmyQuinn 6 77
(J S Moore) *hld up in tch: effrt 2f out: swtchd lft and rdn over 1f out: styd on ins fnl f: nrst fin* **7/1**

00-0 5 *1/2* **Focus Group (USA)**[39] [846] 6-9-1 84 .... PatCosgrave 2 87
(J J Quinn) *chsd ldng pair: rdn along 2f out: sn drvn and one pce over 1f out* **4/1**[3]

54-0 6 *3* **Nelsons Column (IRE)**[29] [995] 4-9-3 86 .... SebSanders 1 85
(G M Moore) *led: rdn along 3f out: drvn 2f out: hdd 1f out and no ex ent fnl f* **11/1**

2m 40.14s (-0.07) **Going Correction** -0.05s/f (Good) **6** Ran SP% **111.4**
Speed ratings (Par 107):98,97,97,96,96 94
CSF £28.06 TOTE £5.40: £2.20, £3.30; EX 28.20.
Owner The Macca & Growler Partnership **Bred** Ron Dufficy **Trained** Newmarket, Suffolk
■ Stewards' Enquiry : Jamie Moriarty one-day ban: used whip with excessive frequency (May 20)

FOCUS
A decent contest but a modest winning time for a race like this, 2.4 seconds slower than the earlier maiden. The form is hard to rate and is limited by the proximity of the fourth.

NOTEBOOK
Kilimandscharo(USA), a progressive sort on the All-Weather having his first turf start of the season, was ridden confidently and moved into contention racing into the final quarter mile before sticking on gamely under pressure to prevail close home. This represented an improved effort and this fine, attractive gelding looks capable of further progress, with an extra couple of furlongs likely to suit. He should eventually make a hurdler. (op 7-2 tchd 11-4)
Kames Park(IRE), on a hat-trick when running as though something was amiss at Epsom recently, showed that running to be all wrong and recorded a fine effort considering he was conceding 18lb to the winner. (op 7-1 tchd 13-2)
Tilt is not the quickest and ideally prefers a bit further. He shaped well on his reappearance at Epsom, but tends to disappoint more often than not and found himself outpaced inside the final furlong here. (op 2-1 tchd 9-4)
Mull Of Dubai ◆, who returned with a promising effort at Bath last month, was rather unlucky as he did not get the run when his rider wanted it and by the time he reached top stride the race was all over. He would have been at least third and looks a ready-made winner off this mark. (op 13-2 tchd 15-2)
Focus Group(USA), stepping back up in trip, proved a little disappointing and does not look to be progressing. (op 5-1)
Nelsons Column(IRE) usually finds this trip stretching him and that was again the case here. (op 8-1)

1576 WOMEN IN BUSINESS FILLIES' H'CAP 1m 1f 207y
3:35 (3:35) (Class 4) (0-80,75) 3-Y-0+ **£6,477** (£1,927; £963; £481) **Stalls** High

Form RPR

2-11 1 **Fongs Gazelle**[15] [1211] 3-9-2 75 .... GregFairley(3) 4 87
(M Johnston) *trckd ldrs: hdwy 3f out: led over 2f out: sn pushed clr* **11/8**[2]

43-1 2 *5* **Its Moon (IRE)**[21] [1092] 3-8-12 68 .... ChrisCatlin 3 70
(T D Walford) *cl up: led after 2f: rdn along 3f out: hdd over 2f out: kpt on same pce* **8/1**[3]

-546 3 *1 1/4* **Skyelady**[16] [1198] 4-9-9 69 .... (p) DuranFentiman(5) 2 69
(Miss J A Camacho) *t.k.h: hld up in rr: hdwy over 2f out: rdn over 1f out: kpt on same pce* **14/1**

05-0 4 *8* **Galingale (IRE)**[19] [1127] 3-8-10 66 .... RoystonFfrench 5 49
(Mrs P Sly) *led 2f: cl up tl rdn along and edgd out 3f out: sn drvn and wknd* **33/1**

56-4 U **Collette's Choice**[13] [1258] 4-9-1 61 .... JamieMoriarty(5) 1 —
(R A Fahey) *trckd ldrs: effrt and hdwy whn sltly hmpd: stmbld and uns rdr 3f out* **5/4**[1]

2m 4.91s (-2.39) **Going Correction** -0.05s/f (Good)
WFA 3 from 4yo 15lb **5** Ran SP% **107.3**
Speed ratings (Par 102):107,103,102,95,—
CSF £11.39 TOTE £2.20: £1.30, £2.20; EX 9.20.
Owner Around The World Partnership **Bred** Miss S N Ralphs **Trained** Middleham Moor, N Yorks

FOCUS
A modest handicap but a fair time for a race like this and the fastest of the three over the trip at the meeting. The favourite failed to finish which tends to weaken the form but it may be a mistake to underestimate the race.

1577 RACING AGAIN ON 22 MAY H'CAP 5f
4:10 (4:11) (Class 4) (0-85,84) 3-Y-O **£6,477** (£1,927; £963; £481) **Stalls** High

Form RPR

24-1 1 **Jack Rackham**[18] [1161] 3-8-12 78 .... RoystonFfrench 5 88+
(B Smart) *bdly hmpd s: rdn along and detached at 1/2-way: swtchd lft and hdwy wl over 1f out: str run to ld ins fnl f: r.o* **9/1**[3]

505- 2 *2 1/2* **Mundo's Magic**[236] [5334] 3-8-7 73 .... TomEaves 10 76+
(G M Moore) *midfield: hdwy on inner whn n.m.r over 1f out: swtchd lft ent fnl f: fin strly* **12/1**

12-0 3 *shd* **Just Joey**[18] [1160] 3-9-4 84 .... PhillipMakin 1 85+
(J R Weymes) *a.p: effrt on outer and ev ch over 1f out tl rdn and nt qckn ins fnl f* **40/1**

0-05 **4** 3/4 **Durova (IRE)**[9] 1351 3-7-13 **70**................................ DuranFentiman(5) 12 68
(T D Easterby) *led: rdn along 2f out: drvn over 1f out: hdd and no ex ins fnl f* **10/1**

61- **5** *nk* **Sunnyside Tom (IRE)**[267] 4452 3-8-8 **79**.................. JamieMoriarty(5) 2 76+
(R A Fahey) *outpcd and rdn along towards rr tl styd on wl appr fnl f: nrst fin* **11/1**

4-16 **6** 1/2 **My Drop (IRE)**[17] 1176 3-8-6 **72**.. ChrisCatlin 6 67
(E J O'Neill) *wnt lft s: in tch towards outer: rdn along wl over 1f out: kpt on u.p ins fnl f* **14/1**

01-0 **7** *nk* **Prospect Place**[11] 1298 3-9-0 **80**....................................... PaulFessey 4 74+
(M Dods) *hmpd s: in tch: rdn along 2f out and sn one pce* **12/1**

4-31 **8** *shd* **Cuppacocoa**[8] 1373 3-8-2 **75** 6ex................................ JosephWalsh(7) 9 69
(C G Cox) *cl up: rdn along 2f out: grad wknd appr fnl f* **3/1**[2]

16- **9** 1 1/4 **Now Look Out**[186] 6332 3-8-9 **75**.............................. SebSanders 11 64
(E S McMahon) *trckd ldrs on inner: effrt over 2f out: sn rdn and btn* **15/8**[1]

2606 **10** *nk* **Stoneacre Gareth (IRE)**[13] 1270 3-8-7 **73** oh2 ow3 RobbieFitzpatrick 8 58
(Peter Grayson) *midfield: rdn along 1/2-way: nvr a factor* **20/1**

00-0 **11** *hd* **Eloquent Rose (IRE)**[20] 1108 3-8-8 **74**.................... CatherineGannon 3 61
(Mrs A Duffield) *a towards rr* **20/1**

130- **12** *10* **Russian Silk**[203] 6056 3-8-9 **75**... PatCosgrave 7 26
(Jedd O'Keeffe) *prom: rdn along 2f out: sn wknd* **14/1**

63.14 secs (-0.86) **Going Correction** -0.15s/f (Firm) **12 Ran SP% 127.9**
Speed ratings (Par 101):100,96,95,94,94 93,92,92,90,90 89,73
CSF £118.19 CT £4184.72 TOTE £9.60: £2.20, £4.20, £7.30; EX 203.60.
Owner Mrs F Denniff **Bred** A S Denniff **Trained** Hambleton, N Yorks

FOCUS
An extraordinary race in which the winning time was 0.62 seconds slower than the earlier handicap for older horses. The usual draw bias looked as though it would apply for most of the race until the winner's dramatic arrival and, although it could rate higher, a difficult race to assess with confidence.

1578 WHITE RABBIT H'CAP — 1m 1f 207y
4:45 (4:45) (Class 5) (0-70,70) 4-Y-0+ **£3,238** (£963; £481; £240) **Stalls** High

Form RPR

-041 **1** **Malinsa Blue (IRE)**[7] 1413 5-8-7 **59** 6ex..................... RoystonFfrench 1 70
(B Ellison) *hld up in tch: hdwy 3f out: led wl over 1f out: sn rdn and edgd rt: r.o wl fnl furlong* **3/1**[2]

040- **2** 1 1/2 **Im Spartacus**[31] 5511 5-9-4 **70**...................................... JamieSpencer 3 78
(Evan Williams) *hld up in rr: hdwy over 2f out and sn rdn: drvn to chse wnr ins fnl f: no imp* **8/13**[1]

130- **3** 1 1/2 **William John**[38] 4845 4-8-6 **58**..(t) DaleGibson 8 63
(P C Haslam) *prom: rdn along over 2f out: drvn and kpt on same pce appr fnl f* **33/1**

3300 **4** 1/2 **Art Investor**[18] 1152 4-8-8 **60**..(b[1]) SebSanders 4 64
(D R C Elsworth) *trckd ldrs: effrt over 2f out: rdn whn nt clr run and swtchd lft over 1f out: sn drvn and no imp* **8/1**[3]

50-6 **5** *4* **Contemplation**[13] 1265 4-8-10 **62**....................................... DavidAllan 5 58
(J Balding) *prom: effrt to chal 3f out: sn rdn and ev ch 2f out tl wkng whn n.m.r over 1f out* **16/1**

604- **6** *8* **Splodger Mac (IRE)**[238] 5285 8-7-12 **57** oh8 ow1(b) SuzzanneFrance(7) 7 37
(N Bycroft) *led: rdn along 3f out: drvn and hdd wl over 1f out: sn wknd* **50/1**

2m 6.63s (-0.67) **Going Correction** -0.05s/f (Good) **6 Ran SP% 108.8**
Speed ratings (Par 103):100,98,97,97,94 87
CSF £4.84 CT £31.22 TOTE £3.30: £1.90, £1.10; EX 7.10.
Owner Mrs Andrea M Mallinson **Bred** Martin Donovan **Trained** Norton, N Yorks

FOCUS
A very uncompetitive handicap, especially with the odds-on favourite a little disappointing, and that left the winner with a straightforward task and she sets the standard.

1579 LADYGATE CLASSIFIED STKS — 1m 1f 207y
5:15 (5:17) (Class 6) 3-Y-0+ **£2,730** (£806; £403) **Stalls** High

Form RPR

000- **1** **Potentiale (IRE)**[179] 6434 3-8-6 55...................................... ChrisCatlin 3 59+
(J W Hills) *towards rr: swtchd outside and hdwy wl over 1f out: str run ins fnl f: led fnl 75yds* **20/1**

5-04 **2** *1* **Chip N Pin**[14] 1236 3-8-1 55..................................... DuranFentiman(5) 14 57+
(T D Easterby) *t.k.h: in tch: pushed along over 2f out: gd hdwy on inner over 1f out: swtchd lft and rdn ent fnl f: ev ch tl no ex nr fin* **7/2**[2]

504- **3** 3/4 **Patavium (IRE)**[30] 6275 4-9-2 55................................ PJMcDonald(5) 12 56
(E W Tuer) *sn led: rdn clr over 2f out: drvn over 1f out: hdd and no ex wl ins fnl f* **10/1**[3]

-564 **4** 1/2 **Garibaldi (GER)**[30] 982 5-9-0 55..........................(b[1]) JamesO'Reilly(7) 15 55
(J O'Reilly) *hld up towards rr: gd hdwy on outer over 2f out: rdn and ev ch over 1f out: sn drvn and one pce ins fnl f* **3/1**[1]

0-05 **5** *shd* **Jenny Soba**[11] 1301 4-9-2 55................................. MichaelJStainton(5) 16 55
(R M Whitaker) *prom on inner: rdn along over 2f out: drvn over 1f out and kpt on same pce* **20/1**

500 **6** *shd* **Sadler's Kingdom (IRE)**[72] 569 3-8-6 55................. TonyHamilton 13 54+
(R A Fahey) *in tch: pushed along and sltly outpcd over 2f out: rdn over 1f out and styd on wl fnl f: nrst fin* **16/1**

00-2 **7** 1 3/4 **Ingleby Hill (IRE)**[36] 910 3-8-6 52...................................... PaulFessey 8 50
(T D Barron) *cl up: rdn along wl over 2f out: drvn over 1f out and grad wknd* **11/1**

P02- **8** *shd* **Royal Master**[207] 5497 5-9-7 55.. DaleGibson 2 51
(P C Haslam) *prom: rdn along over 2f out and grad wknd appr fnl f* **12/1**

0000 **9** *2* **Roca Redonda (IRE)**[21] 1092 3-7-13 55..................... JosephWalsh(7) 9 46
(V Smith) *s.i.s and bhd: hdwy 2f out: sn rdn and styd on ins fnl f: nrst fin* **50/1**

0216 **10** 1/2 **A Mothers Love**[18] 1154 3-8-7 53 ow1................................ TomEaves 1 46
(P J McBride) *chsd ldrs: hdwy over 2f out: sn rdn and wknd wl over 1f out* **12/1**

06-0 **11** *2* **Toboggan Lady**[18] 1153 3-8-6 49................................. RoystonFfrench 5 41
(Mrs A Duffield) *nvr bttr than midfield* **50/1**

0-04 **12** 3/4 **Mister Minty (IRE)**[13] 1259 5-9-4 55.............................. MarkLawson(3) 10 40
(Mrs S Lamyman) *a towards rr* **16/1**

000- **13** 2 1/2 **Hopeful Isabella (IRE)**[229] 5507 3-8-7 53 ow1.............. SebSanders 4 35
(Sir Mark Prescott) *hld up: a towards rr* **3/1**[1]

06/0 **14** *4* **Silent Street**[15] 1225 4-9-7 48.. PatCosgrave 6 27
(K G Reveley) *dwlt: a in rr* **50/1**

40-0 **15** *5* **Bellapais Boy**[15] 1224 3-8-6 52.......................................(b[1]) DavidAllan 17 16
(T D Easterby) *s.i.s: a in rr* **66/1**

00-0 **16** 1/2 **Telling**[15] 1232 3-8-6 48.. CatherineGannon 11 15
(Mrs A Duffield) *prom: rdn along over 3f out: wknd over 2f out* **80/1**

2m 6.56s (-0.74) **Going Correction** -0.05s/f (Good)
WFA 3 from 4yo+ 15lb **16 Ran SP% 134.9**
Speed ratings (Par 101):100,99,98,98,98 98,96,96,94,94 92,92,90,87,83 82
CSF £94.77 TOTE £25.70: £8.70, £2.40, £4.30; EX 211.50 Place 6 £95.65, Place 5 £83.77.
Owner J W Hills **Bred** Copperhead Stable **Trained** Upper Lambourn, Berks

FOCUS
A bad race, though run at a fair pace, and the form, although sound rated around the third, fourth and fifth, is unlikely to add up to much. The winner's route down the wide outside, together with the amazing performance by Jack Rackham two races earlier, suggested the centre of the track was perhaps the faster strip.
Roca Redonda(IRE) Official explanation: jockey said filly reared leaving the stalls
T/Plt: £35.30 to a £1 stake. Pool: £40,296.55. 833.30 winning tickets. T/Qpdt: £22.40 to a £1 stake. Pool: £1,625.90. 53.50 winning tickets. JR

CHESTER (L-H)
Wednesday, May 9

OFFICIAL GOING: Good to firm (good in places)
The going description seemed accurate for the first four races, but it rained during the afternoon and the ground was probably more 'good' for the last two.
Wind: Light, behind Weather: Raining

1580 JOSEPH HELER CHEESE 50TH ANNIVERSARY LILY AGNES CONDITIONS STKS — 5f 16y
1:50 (1:51) (Class 2) 2-Y-0
£13,087 (£3,918; £1,959; £980; £489; £245) **Stalls** Low

Form RPR

01 **1** **Cracking (IRE)**[10] 1315 2-9-1 .... RichardHughes 3 95
(R Hannon) *lw: mde all: rdn over 1f out: edgd rt ins fnl f: r.o gamely* **7/2**[2]

32 **2** *hd* **Fast Feet**[5] 1454 2-8-12 .... NCallan 1 91
(K A Ryan) *trckd ldrs after 1f: wnt 2nd wl over 1f out: rdn and ev ch ins fnl f: r.o* **5/2**[1]

223 **3** 2 1/2 **Sinead Of Aglish (IRE)**[2] 1533 2-8-7 .... SteveDrowne 5 76
(A B Haynes) *trckd ldrs: rdn and nt qckn on outside wl over 1f out: kpt on towards fin: nt pce of front pair* **8/1**

1 **4** *nk* **Primo Heights**[31] 952 2-8-10 .... DanielTudhope 7 78
(J S Goldie) *sn towards rr: rdn over 1f out: styd on ins fnl f: nt pce to chal* **7/1**

4 **5** *hd* **Not My Choice (IRE)**[39] 845 2-8-12 .... JohnEgan 4 79
(T J Pitt) *lw: pushed along early: sn in tch: rdn wl over 1f out: kpt on ins fnl f* **4/1**[3]

013 **6** 1/2 **Baytown Blaze**[3] 1503 2-8-7 .... HayleyTurner 8 72
(P S McEntee) *sn in rr: stmbld wl over 3f out: pushed along 2f out: nvr able to chal* **33/1**

21 **7** *2* **Artdeal**[21] 1087 2-8-12 .... JamieSpencer 6 69+
(M J Wallace) *w wnr: racd keenly and hung rt most of way: wknd ins fnl f: sn eased* **5/1**

60.44 secs (-1.61) **Going Correction** -0.325s/f (Firm) **7 Ran SP% 114.0**
Speed ratings (Par 99):99,98,94,94,93 93,89
CSF £12.62 TOTE £3.80: £2.50, £1.60; EX 6.10 Trifecta £94.90 Pool: £468.04 - 3.50 winning tickets..
Owner A C Pickford & N A Woodcock **Bred** Adieu Cherie Partnership **Trained** East Everleigh, Wilts

FOCUS
Just an ordinary renewal of the Lily Agnes with the third the best guide to the level. The winning time was 1.14 seconds quicker than the later juvenile maiden, but it would be unwise to draw too many conclusions from that as the ground deteriorated through the course of the afternoon.

NOTEBOOK
Cracking(IRE)'s Brighton maiden success represented just fair form, but he has bags of pace and always promised to be suited by Chester. Quicker into his stride than Fast Feet, the only horse drawn closer to the rail, he soon led at a good clip and kept on strongly when joined in the straight by the favourite. There can be no doubting he enjoyed the run of the race, but he is clearly one to have on-side when the emphisis is on speed. He is now likely to be aimed at the Norfolk Stakes at Royal Ascot. (op 11-4)
Fast Feet, a beaten favourite on both his starts in maiden company, including at Musselburgh just five days earlier, failed to break quickly enough to take advantage of his inside stall and forfeited the rail to Cracking. He recovered to track the pace and drew upsides the Hannon horse in the straight, but that rival had covered less ground and ultimately just proved too strong. He has proved expensive to follow so far, but really should be winning before too much longer. (op 11-4)
Sinead Of Aglish(IRE) has not had much go her way in maiden company, including when enduring a luckless passage at Warwick just two days earlier, but she still showed plenty of ability. Far from ideally drawn in stall five, she was soon playing catch-up and could make little impression on the front two when it mattered. She should win her maiden before too much longer and gives the impression she will stay 6f. (op 10-1 tchd 11-1)
Primo Heights came from well off the pace to win on her debut at Musselburgh, but that sort of running style is not ideally suited to this course and she failed to make an impression. A stiffer track or 6f should suit better. (tchd 8-1)
Not My Choice(IRE), fourth in an ordinary renewal of the Brocklesby on his only previous start, responded well to early encouragement to take up a good position just off the pace, but basically found a few of these too good late on. (op 5-1 tchd 11-2 in places)
Baytown Blaze had a bit to find in this company, but she stumbled three out and might be a little better than she showed. (op 40-1)
Artdeal did not look at all happy on the track and was below the form he showed when winning at Beverley on his previous start. He should benefit from a return to going left-handed track, or a straight course. Official explanation: jockey said bit slipped through gelding's mouth (op 6-1)

1581 WEATHERBYS BANK CHESHIRE OAKS (FOR THE ROBERT SANGSTER MEMORIAL CUP) (LISTED RACE) (FILLIES) — 1m 3f 79y
2:20 (2:21) (Class 1) 3-Y-0
£22,712 (£8,608; £4,308; £2,148; £1,076; £540) **Stalls** Low

Form RPR

31-1 **1** **Light Shift (USA)**[19] 1126 3-8-12 102................................... TedDurcan 4 107+
(H R A Cecil) *lw: hld up: hdwy 2f out: shkn up over 1f out: qcknd to ld ins fnl f: comf* **11/8**[1]

2 3/4 **All My Loving (IRE)**[32] 945 3-8-12 .... MJKinane 6 103
(A P O'Brien, Ire) *w'like: strong: in tch: effrt to ld briefly and hung lft over 1f out: styd on ins fnl f: nt pce of wnr towards fin* **9/4**[2]

413- **3** *nk* **Fashion Statement**[193] 6216 3-8-12 87......................... JamieSpencer 11 103
(M A Jarvis) *midfield: hdwy over 2f out: led and edgd lft over 1f out: hdd ins fnl f: kpt on but hld towards fin* **14/1**

110- **4** *6* **So Sweet (IRE)**^{232} 5464 3-8-12 88........ JHBowman 1 93
(M R Channon) *led: rdn whn hdd and hmpd over 1f out: wknd ins fnl f* **25/1**

03-4 **5** *1 1/4* **Hanging On**^{12} 1277 3-8-12 92........ AdamKirby 2 90
(W R Swinburn) *in tch: rdn over 2f out: sn outpcd: no imp after* **12/1**

12- **6** *1 3/4* **Hollow Ridge**^{200} 6105 3-8-12 93........ RichardHughes 12 88+
(B W Hills) *plld hrd: hdwy to chse ldr after 2f: rdn and hung rt 3f out: lost 2nd 2f out: wknd over 1f out* **10/1**^{3}

2-4 **7** *nk* **Fidelia (IRE)**^{19} 1127 3-8-12 .... SteveDrowne 9 87
(G Wragg) *racd keenly: hld up: rdn over 2f out: no imp* **18/1**

033- **8** *1 1/2* **Usk Melody**^{192} 6242 3-8-12 74........ EddieAhern 8 84?
(G A Huffer) *prom: rdn over 2f out: wknd over 1f out* **66/1**

166- **9** *1/2* **Golden Dagger (IRE)**^{221} 5672 3-8-12 90........ NCallan 5 84
(K A Ryan) *lw: hld up: rdn over 2f out: nvr on terms* **50/1**

30-0 **10** *2* **Harvest Joy (IRE)**^{39} 838 3-8-12 90........ JimCrowley 10 80
(B R Millman) *n.m.r jst after s: a bhd* **100/1**

010- **11** *1/2* **Lost In Wonder (USA)**^{228} 5522 3-8-12 86........ KerrinMcEvoy 7 79
(Sir Michael Stoute) *a bhd* **12/1**

2m 22.99s (-2.80) **Going Correction** -0.175s/f (Firm) **11** Ran SP% **117.6**
Speed ratings (Par 104):103,102,102,97,96 95,95,94,94,92 92
CSF £4.29 TOTE £2.30: £1.20, £1.50, £3.80; EX 4.40 Trifecta £229.10 Pool: £806.70 - 2.50 winning tickets..
Owner Niarchos Family **Bred** Flaxman Holdings Ltd **Trained** Newmarket, Suffolk

FOCUS
This looked a stronger renewal than recent years of this fillies' Listed prize and it was run at a sound early pace. The form appears solid with the first three coming clear and it would not be a surprise to see the progressive winner show up well if going onto the Epsom Oaks next month.

NOTEBOOK
Light Shift(USA), a ready winner against colts and geldings on her seasonal return at Newbury 19 days previously, proved very popular in the betting ring for this step up in trip and class and followed up with another improved display. She had to wait to make her effort from off the pace, and she had to come a little wider than ideal off the final bend, but her rider deserves plenty of credit for not panicking and she showed a smart turn of foot to settle the issue in the home straight. Considering the placed horses came clear of the rest and got first run on her, this must rate an impressive effort and she is value for a bit further than her winning margin. The longer trip also proved no problem and, the way she coped with this tight turning track, one would have to think that the undulations of Epsom should not pose her too many problems should she take a further step up in class for the Oaks next month. Her trainer has the current ante-post favourite for that event in Passage Of Time, but this highly-progressive daughter of Galileo looks well worthy of her place too and her potent turn of foot should stand her in good stead there. (op 13-8 tchd 7-4)
All My Loving(IRE), a sister to high-class fillies Quarter Moon and Yesterday, who were both second in the Oaks, was unraced at two and had comfortably won a 10f Leopardstown maiden on her debut in April. She was ultimately given every chance on this step up in class, getting the extra furlong without fuss, but lacked the pace of the more experienced winner inside the final furlong. This was still a clear step in the right direction, she looks the type to relish another furlong or so and, considering her pedigree, it would not come as a surprise to see her at Epsom for the Oaks next month. However, she will need to improve again a good deal for this experience to figure there. (tchd 2-1 and 5-2)
Fashion Statement, officially rated 87 after four runs as a juvenile, had signed off last season by finishing third over ten furlongs on soft ground in the Zetland Stakes at Newmarket. She has clearly wintered very well as she ran a big race on this seasonal return, especially considering she had a poor draw, and her official rating evidently underestimates her. This ground would have also been plenty quick enough for her, so she looks the type to improve further this term and is probably going to be better suited by another furlong in due course. Her trainer later reported she could now head to the Italian Oaks. (tchd 12-1)
So Sweet(IRE), who came unstuck on soft ground on her final outing last season in the Goffs Fillies' Five Hundred at the Curragh, had the run of the race out in front yet was not done any favours by the runner-up in the home straight and still put in a career-best effort in defeat on this step up in distance. She looked fit for this, but a sound surface looks the key to her and a drop back to 10f could see her resume winning ways. (op 33-1 tchd 22-1)
Hanging On, up in trip and class, showed the benefit of her seasonal bow 12 days previously and did little wrong in defeat. She has still not come in her coat and shaped as though she really now needs 1m4f.
Hollow Ridge, representing a yard with a decent past record in this Listed contest, did not help her cause by refusing to settle on this three-year-old bow and not surprisingly paid the price before the final bend. She was not at all helped by her outside stall, however, and this was the fastest surface she has raced on to date. Therefore it is too soon to be writing off this daughter of the Irish Oaks and Ribblesdale winner Bolas and it would not be a surprise to see her leave this form behind as the season progresses. (op 8-1)
Fidelia(IRE), whose trainer had won this race twice in the past six years, was stepping up from maiden company and her lack of experience cost her as she raced far too freely through the early parts. She is evidently well regarded and should have little trouble winning her maiden before no doubt stepping back up in grade. (op 20-1)
Golden Dagger(IRE) Official explanation: jockey said filly suffered interference in running
Lost In Wonder(USA) Official explanation: jockey said filly was unsuited by the track

1582 TOTESPORT CHESTER CUP HERITAGE H'CAP 2m 2f 147y

2:50 (2:51) (Class 2) 4-Y-0+
£74,784 (£22,392; £11,196; £5,604; £2,796; £1,404) **Stalls** High

Form RPR

305- **1** **Greenwich Meantime**^{243} 5153 7-9-2 **93**........ PaulHanagan 16 105
(R A Fahey) *midfield: hdwy over 3f out: led 1f out: r.o wl and in command ins fnl f* **14/1**

114- **2** *1 1/2* **Fair Along (GER)**^{25} 5526 5-8-8 **85**........ JamieSpencer 13 95
(P J Hobbs) *reminders after s: midfield: hdwy over 5f out: led 3f out: sn rdn: hdd 1f out: styd on same pce after* **11/2**^{1}

65-0 **3** *shd* **Enjoy The Moment**^{14} 1244 4-8-8 **89**........ MartinDwyer 11 99
(J A Osborne) *hld up: hdwy over 3f out: rdn and hung lft over 1f out: r.o and clsd towards fin* **14/1**

36-3 **4** *3* **Under The Rainbow**^{35} 929 4-9-5 **100**........ JimmyFortune 8 107
(B W Hills) *a.p: rdn over 1f out: one pce fnl f* **25/1**

116- **5** *1 1/2* **Som Tala**^{214} 5811 4-8-4 **85**........ TPO'Shea 2 90+
(M R Channon) *lw: midfield: rdn over 7f out: hmpd over 5f out: hdwy over 4f out: led over 3f out: sn hdd: hmpd over 1f out: one pce after* **7/1**^{3}

06-2 **6** *1 3/4* **Whispering Death**^{13} 1272 5-8-6 **83**........(b^{1}) KerrinMcEvoy 15 86
(W J Haggas) *lw: in rr: rdn and hdwy over 2f out: hung lft over 1f out: kpt on: nt trble ldrs* **15/2**

0043 **7** *5* **Dzesmin (POL)**^{14} 1244 5-8-3 **80**........ FrancisNorton 12 78
(R C Guest) *hld up: hdwy over 4f out: rdn to chse ldrs 3f out: hung lft over 1f out: sn wknd* **22/1**

0-15 **8** *3* **Odiham**^{7} 1393 6-9-1 **92**........ SteveDrowne 10 86
(H Morrison) *midfield: rdn and hmpd 4f out: wknd over 2f out* **16/1**

200- **9** *5* **Corum (IRE)**^{10} 6337 4-8-7 **88** ow4........(p) StephenDonohoe 18 77
(Mrs K Waldron) *in rr: rdn over 3f out: nvr rchd ldrs* **100/1**

31-0 **10** *8* **Dr Sharp (IRE)**^{11} 1300 7-8-10 **87**........ MickyFenton 14 67
(T P Tate) *prom: wnt 2nd over 9f out: led 8f out: hdd over 3f out: rdn and wknd over 2f out* **33/1**

50-3 **11** *4* **Galient (IRE)**^{32} 944 4-9-1 **96**........ PhilipRobinson 17 72
(M A Jarvis) *lw: in tch: rdn 4f out: wknd 3f out* **6/1**^{2}

02-6 **12** *3 1/2* **Nordwind (IRE)**^{14} 1244 6-8-10 **87**........ AdamKirby 6 59
(W R Swinburn) *stdd s: hld up: rdn 3f out: no imp* **10/1**

460- **13** *24* **Dancing Bay**^{67} 3533 10-9-10 **101**........ EddieAhern 1 46
(N J Henderson) *in tch: rdn and wknd over 3f out: eased whn btn fnl f* **20/1**

003- **14** *nk* **Winged D'Argent (IRE)**^{228} 5526 6-9-2 **93**........(p) NCallan 9 38
(B J Llewellyn) *midfield: rdn over 7f out: hdwy over 5f out: wknd over 3f out: eased whn btn fnl f* **16/1**

160- **15** *5* **Admiral (IRE)**^{323} 2723 6-8-10 **87**........ JohnEgan 4 26
(T J Pitt) *led: hdd 8f out: rdn and wknd over 4f out: eased whn btn fnl f* **10/1**

0/0- **16** *15* **Afrad (FR)**^{38} 2723 6-9-1 **92**........ RichardHughes 5 15
(N J Henderson) *prom: rdn 5f out: hmpd whn wkng sn after: eased whn btn fnl f* **20/1**

17 *36* **Flare Star**^{27} 1017 4-8-6 **87**........ WMLordan 3 —
(T Hogan, Ire) *trckd ldrs: rdn and wknd over 5f out: eased whn btn fnl f: t.o* **16/1**

3m 58.89s (-6.68) **Going Correction** -0.175s/f (Firm) course record
WFA 4 from 5yo+ 4lb **18** Ran SP% **124.7**
Speed ratings (Par 109):107,106,106,105,104 103,101,100,98,94 93,91,81,81,79 73,57
CSF £83.06 CT £1133.43 TOTE £15.50: £3.10, £1.70, £3.90, £4.60; EX 138.30 Trifecta £1825.10 Part won. Pool: £2,570.60 - 0.90 winning tickets..
Owner K Lee D Barlow B Crumbley & L Rutherford **Bred** Juddmonte Farms **Trained** Musley Bank, N Yorks
■ Stewards' Enquiry : Paul Hanagan one-day ban: careless riding (May 24)

FOCUS
A typically competitive renewal of this unique staying handicap. It was run at a frantic early pace, helping those drawn wide and racing from off the pace, resulting in a new course record. The form looks solid enough and, suprisingly, the first three were all drawn in double figures.

NOTEBOOK
Greenwich Meantime, an unfortunate third from a wide draw in this event last season when rated officially 10lb lower, was again housed wide for this seasonal return and did not help his chances again by breaking awkwardly from the gates. That cost him any chance of racing handily, but it ultimately worked out ideally as the frantic early pace proved right up his street and he eventually came home to score with a bit left up his sleeve. He is clearly well suited by this sort of unique test, a fast surface is key to him, and he is clearly still progressing as a stayer. Connections later indicated his next big target is the Northumberland Plate at Newcastle in July - a race in which he finished third last term from a 3lb lower mark. (op 12-1)
Fair Along(GER), much better known for his exploits as a novice chaser, had previously shown progressive form as a front-runner on the Flat last season and was having his first outing in this sphere since September last year. He was unable to race on the early pace as a result of his wide berth, and actually needed a few reminders soon after the gates opened, but he got a peach of a ride from Spencer and eventually came through to have every chance. No doubt he will go up in the weights for this, but he still has time on his side and on this evidence could still bag a decent handicap before going back over fences in the autumn. (op 8-1 tchd 5-1)
Enjoy The Moment showed the benefit of his seasonal debut at Epsom a fortnight previously and posted a career-best effort in defeat on this big step up in trip. Despite being another to prosper from a patient ride, he does look a big improver over longer trips this term and should be seen to even better effect when reverting to a more galloping track in due course. It would not be a surprise to see him renew rivalry with the winner in the Northumberland Plate.
Under The Rainbow fared by far the best of those to race up with the strong early gallop and ran a gallant race in defeat, especially considering she gave away weight to the principals. She got the longer trip without a fuss and really deserves to get her head back in front, but opportunities are not going to prove that simple to find.
Som Tala, having his first outing since October last year, had been progressive last season when stepped up to this sort of trip and not surprisingly proved popular in the betting ring from his low draw. He did not get the best of passages as it transpired, but still emerged to lead nearing the final bend and eventually had his chance. Considering improvement is likely for this seasonal bow he is not one to abandon on the back of this effort and, with the return to a more conventional track sure to be more to his liking, something like the Ascot Stakes at the Royal Meeting next month could be right up his street (the stable won that event last year). (op 8-1)
Whispering Death, well backed on this return to a suitably longer distance and with blinkers replacing the usual visor, kept on without seriously threatening and was not disgraced. He really looks to need a more galloping circuit and can do better, but his season will most probably be geared around another crack at the Cesarewitch in the autumn, a race in which he finished sixth last term. (op 8-1)
Galient(IRE), whose trainer sent out Anak Pekan to register back-to-back win in this event in 2004 and 2005, had finished third in his prep for this event on his seasonal bow at Kempton last month and was the ante-post favourite prior to the draw being made. It was his wide berth that ultimately proved his undoing and he was a long way below his best here, but he is another who cannot be written off just yet. (op 5-1)
Nordwind(IRE), markedly back up in trip, was hampered on the inside when trying to make up his ground from off the pace and is better than the bare form would suggest. Official explanation: jockey said gelding hung left (op 11-1)
Admiral(IRE), last season's winner of this event from a 2lb lower mark, was well drawn for one that front runs yet he was having his first outing since sustaining injury in the Ascot Stakes last year and his preparation for this follow-up bid had reportedly not been the smoothest. He was unable to dominate as he prefers, but was still beaten too far out for this to be his true running and it remains to be seen just how much racing this fragile six-year-old has left in him now. Official explanation: vet said gelding finished lame (op 9-1)
Flare Star Official explanation: trainer said filly scoped dirty post race

1583 BREITLING WATCHES & WALTONS OF CHESTER H'CAP 1m 2f 75y

3:20 (3:20) (Class 2) (0-100,100) 4-Y-O+ **£13,248** (£3,964; £1,982; £991; £493) **Stalls** High

Form RPR

/00- **1** **Temple Place (IRE)**^{23} 2848 6-8-6 **88** ow1........(t) EddieAhern 6 98
(D McCain Jnr) *midfield: hdwy over 4f out: led ins fnl f: r.o* **50/1**

110- **2** *3/4* **Stotsfold**^{214} 5804 4-9-4 **100**........ AdamKirby 5 108+
(W R Swinburn) *lw: racd keenly: a.p: led 2f out: hdd ins fnl f: nt qckn* **15/8**^{1}

0-20 **3** *1 3/4* **Blythe Knight (IRE)**^{26} 848 7-9-0 **96**........ DarryllHolland 8 101
(J J Quinn) *lw: racd keenly: a.p: led 6f out: rdn and hdd 2f out: styd on same pce ins fnl f* **13/2**

-012 **4** *1/2* **Charlie Tokyo (IRE)**^{14} 1245 4-8-10 **92**........(b) PaulHanagan 4 96
(R A Fahey) *racd keenly: midfield: hdwy over 3f out: rdn over 2f out: kpt on same pce fnl f* **4/1**^{2}

2-00 **5** *shd* **Collateral Damage (IRE)**^{39} 848 4-8-5 **87**........ KerrinMcEvoy 10 91
(T D Easterby) *midfield: rdn and hdwy over 1f out: styd on ins fnl f: nt pce to rch ldrs* **12/1**

0-10 **6** *1* **European Dream (IRE)**[18] 1145 4-8-6 **88**............................ JohnEgan 7 90
(R C Guest) *towards rr: rdn and hdwy over 1f out: kpt on ins fnl f: nvr able to chal* **14/1**

7 *hd* **Bazart**[284] 3969 5-8-11 **96**... AndrewElliott(3) 3 98
(K R Burke) *trckd ldrs: rdn 2f out: btn over 1f out* **33/1**

00-0 **8** *shd* **Blue Spinnaker (IRE)**[39] 848 8-8-4 **86**........................ MartinDwyer 11 87+
(M W Easterby) *in rr: rdn over 1f out: kpt on ins fnl f: nvr nr ldrs* **12/1**

5-40 **9** *nk* **Prince Samos (IRE)**[4] 1480 5-8-4 **86**............................ FrancisNorton 2 87
(D Nicholls) *in rr: niggled along 6f out: nvr trbld ldrs* **16/1**

3300 **10** *½* **Lucayan Dancer**[4] 1480 7-8-4 **86** oh2.......................... AdrianTNicholls 1 86+
(D Nicholls) *midfield: rdn over 4f out: lost pl over 3f out: n.d after* **6/1**[3]

200- **11** *3½* **Realism (FR)**[389] 1017 7-9-1 **97**... NCallan 9 90
(R A Fahey) *led: hdd 6f out: hmpd 5f out and wl over 4f out: stl ev ch 2f out: wknd over 1f out: eased whn btn ins fnl f* **28/1**

2m 8.87s (-4.27) **Going Correction** -0.175s/f (Firm) **11** Ran SP% **118.7**
Speed ratings (Par 109):110,109,108,107,107 106,106,106,106,105 103
CSF £143.60 CT £744.79 TOTE £64.10: £9.00, £1.50, £1.90; EX 349.70 Trifecta £746.90 Part won. Pool: £1,051.98 - 0.40 winning tickets..
Owner Brendan Richardson and Jon Glews **Bred** Swettenham Stud **Trained** Cholmondeley, Cheshire
■ Stewards' Enquiry : Darryll Holland two-day ban: careless riding (May 20-21)

FOCUS
A decent handicap, run at a strong pace. The form looks solid rated through the third and fourth, despite the surprise winner.

NOTEBOOK
Temple Place(IRE), who had lost his way over hurdles during the last jumps season, showed his true colours on this first outing on the Flat since running at Royal Ascot last year and ran out a somewhat surprising winner. The switch to this discipline brought about renewed enthusiasm as he travelled kindly through the race and showed a good attitude to peg back the runner-up inside the final furlong. It should be remembered that he did finish third in the Vase at this track in 2004 when trained by Michael Bell, so clearly enjoys this unique course and was obviously well treated on that form if consenting to put his best foot forward. Whether he will build on this now remains to be seen, however.
Stotsfold, a most progressive handicapper at three, was all the rage in the betting for this seasonal return despite having the burden of top weight. He did come through to have every chance when it mattered, but the fact he refused to settle though the early parts eventually proved his undoing and he could offer no more when challenged by the winner late on. This was still a decent comeback effort, he should settle a little better with this outing under his belt, and he does still look to be on an upward curve. (op 2-1 tchd 9-4 in places)
Blythe Knight(IRE), last seen winning a Grade 2 novice hurdle with plenty to spare at Aintree 26 days previously, deserves extra credit on this return to the Flat as he pulled his way to the front early on and that put paid to any plans his rider may have had to come from off the pace as he often prefers. He clearly remains in good form. (op 6-1 tchd 11-2)
Charlie Tokyo(IRE) has begun this term in great form and put up another solid effort in defeat, despite being another to race freely though the early parts. He is weighted to around his best at present, however. (op 7-2)
Collateral Damage(IRE) showed up well from his unfavourable draw and stayed the longer trip well enough. This was by far his best effort of the current campaign. (op 16-1)
European Dream(IRE), another stepping up in trip, ran on late but never got into contention having been at the back early on. (op 20-1)
Bazart, bought for 70,000gns and gelded since joining his new connections, did little to convince he wants this sort of trip on this British debut. He should come on a deal for the run and is one to bear in mind when reverting to around a mile on an easier surface. (tchd 40-1)
Blue Spinnaker(IRE) ◆ was unable to get seriously competitive from his outside berth and can be rated better than the bare form. His last win came at York's Dante Meeting last year from a 4lb higher mark and he should not be ignored if bidding to repeat the feat at that track later this month. Official explanation: jockey said gelding was denied a clear run
Lucayan Dancer has a decent record at this venue plus has the real benefit of stall 1 here, but he was racing from 2lb out of the handicap and simply looked to find things too hot. (op 7-1)

1584 WALKER SMITH WAY H'CAP — 1m 4f 66y
4:00 (4:00) (Class 3) (0-95,86) 3-Y-O **£10,039** (£2,986; £1,492; £745) **Stalls** Low

Form RPR

431- **1** **Swiss Act**[226] 5580 3-9-3 **82**.. J-PGuillambert 1 89+
(M Johnston) *fit: trckd ldrs: wnt 2nd 2f out: swtchd rt over 1f out: led jst ins fnl f: r.o wl and in command after* **5/1**

2-12 **2** *1¾* **Bergonzi (IRE)**[12] 1277 3-9-2 **81**.................................... JimmyFortune 8 85
(J H M Gosden) *lw: hld up: rdn and hdwy over 1f out: sn hung lft: styd on to take 2nd wl ins fnl f: nt trble wnr* **11/4**[2]

62-1 **3** *nk* **Actodos (IRE)**[26] 1030 3-9-3 **82**... JimCrowley 3 86
(B R Millman) *led: rdn over 1f out: hdd jst ins fnl f: kpt on same pce* **12/1**

0-10 **4** *3* **Mandragola**[12] 1277 3-8-12 **77**.. MichaelHills 7 76
(B W Hills) *lw: trckd ldrs: rdn over 1f out: wknd ins fnl f* **16/1**

-251 **5** *1* **Morning Farewell**[16] 1205 3-8-13 **78**............................. KerrinMcEvoy 4 75
(P W Chapple-Hyam) *prom tl rdn and wknd over 1f out* **9/2**[3]

3511 **6** *6* **Six Day War (IRE)**[70] 582 3-9-7 **86**................................ MartinDwyer 5 74
(J A Osborne) *hld up: niggled along over 5f out: rdn 3f out: nvr on terms* **7/1**

14-6 **P** **Amazing Request**[20] 1106 3-9-3 **82**.............................. RichardHughes 6 —
(R Charlton) *hld up in rr: rdn over 3f out: no rspnse: eased 2f out: t.o whn p.u and dismntd wl ins fnl f* **5/2**[1]

2m 36.56s (-4.09) **Going Correction** -0.175s/f (Firm) **7** Ran SP% **116.2**
Speed ratings (Par 103):106,104,104,102,101 97,—
CSF £19.75 CT £156.99 TOTE £6.20: £2.90, £2.10; EX 17.80.
Owner Markus Graff **Bred** Highclere Stud Ltd **Trained** Middleham Moor, N Yorks

FOCUS
A good three-year-old handicap run at a fair pace and rated through the fourth to his maiden form.

NOTEBOOK
Swiss Act ◆ improved significantly on the form he showed when winning a 1m maiden at Musselburgh on his final start as a juvenile, benefiting greatly from the step up in trip. Not as quickly into his stride as a couple of his rivals, he was unable to make full use of his rails draw, but he was never too far away and would have appreciated the even pace. A gap came at just the right time on the turn into the straight and he picked up in good style, galloping on impressively to the line to give the impression he would have won by even further had he been able to dominate throughout. He still displayed distinct signs of greenness during the race and looks capable of progressing to a smart level. The King George V handicap at Royal Ascot is the obvious target. (op 7-1)
Bergonzi(IRE), trying an extra two furlongs, had to come from further back than the eventual winner, and he made his move four wide off the home bend, but he was basically just beaten by a better horse. A return to a more galloping track may suit better. (op 3-1 tchd 10-3)
Actodos(IRE), off the mark in a Fibresand maiden over this trip on his previous start, ran very well considering Morning Farewell kept hassling him up front. He gives the impression he has plenty more to offer. (op 14-1)
Mandragola was trying this trip for the first time and did not see it out as well as the front three. (op 14-1 tchd 12-1)
Morning Farewell would have found this tougher than the Windsor handicap he won off a 5lb lower mark on his previous start, and offered little at the business end having raced a little wide near the front for much of the way. (op 4-1 tchd 5-1)
Six Day War(IRE), making his debut of turf, was never going and did not look happy on the track. (op 5-1)
Amazing Request, who was edgy beforehand, failed to run a race and something was seemingly amiss. Official explanation: vet said colt finished distressed (op 3-1 tchd 10-3)

1585 TURFTV.CO.UK EBF MAIDEN STKS — 5f 16y
4:35 (4:35) (Class 2) 2-Y-O **£8,420** (£2,505; £1,251; £625) **Stalls** Low

Form RPR

2 **1** **Dark Angel (IRE)**[21] 1094 2-9-3 .... MichaelHills 2 85+
(B W Hills) *lw: dwlt: rcvrd qckly to trck ldr: led wl over 1f out: sn qcknd clr: pushed out* **2/5**[1]

2 *2* **Eileen's Violet (IRE)** 2-8-12 .... StephenDonohoe 5 72
(P D Evans) *lengthy: in rr: rn green: pushed along 2f out: styd on to take 2nd ins fnl f: no imp on wnr* **16/1**

3 *2½* **Elusive Deal (USA)** 2-8-12 .... PaulHanagan 1 62+
(R A Fahey) *w'like: s.s: chsd ldrs: rdn over 1f out: wknd fnl f* **7/1**[3]

6 **4** *hd* **Maracana Boy (IRE)**[31] 952 2-9-3 .... DarryllHolland 3 66
(M Dods) **13/2**[2]

3 **5** *6* **Bookiebasher Dude**[25] 1033 2-9-3 .... FrancisNorton 7 42
(M Quinn) *s.i.s: pushed along and outpcd over 3f out: clsd to chse ldrs 2f out: rdn and wknd over 1f out* **9/1**

61.58 secs (-0.47) **Going Correction** -0.175s/f (Firm) **5** Ran SP% **113.1**
Speed ratings (Par 99):96,92,88,88,78
CSF £8.86 TOTE £1.40: £1.10, £3.00; EX 11.50 Place 6 £27.32, Place 5 £18.07.
Owner The Hon Mrs J M Corbett & C Wright **Bred** Yeomanstown Stud **Trained** Lambourn, Berks

FOCUS
This maiden did not get the turnout the prizemoney deserved, but Dark Angel set a useful standard and is rated in line with his Newmarket debut form. The winning time was 1.14 seconds slower than the Lily Agnes, but this lot raced on slower ground so that is probably best ignored.

NOTEBOOK
Dark Angel(IRE) ◆ showed plenty of ability when second in a good race at Newmarket on his debut and confirmed that promise without too much fuss, providing his trainer with his third straight win in this race. He looks useful and deserves to take his chance in better company. (op 4-9 tchd 1-2 in places)
Eileen's Violet(IRE), a half-sister to multiple Italian 5f-1m winner Revovegas, was last for much of the way, but she got the hang of things late on and offered plenty of encouragement in second. She should have learnt plenty from this and ought to go close next time. (tchd 18-1)
Elusive Deal(USA), a $30,000 first foal of a quite useful 7f winner France, was left behind in the straight and should know more next time. (op 11-2)
Maracana Boy(IRE) showed bright speed but finished up well held and did not really improve a great deal on his Musselburgh debut. (op 10-1 tchd 11-1)
Bookiebasher Dude shaped nicely on his debut on the Polytrack at Lingfield, but this was disappointing. (op 7-1)
T/Jkpt: Not won. T/Plt: £23.50 to a £1 stake. Pool: £152,129.00. 4,712.85 winning tickets.
T/Qpdt: £11.40 to a £1 stake. Pool: £5,899.90. 381.95 winning tickets. DO

1519 KEMPTON (A.W) (R-H)
Wednesday, May 9

OFFICIAL GOING: Standard
Wind: Moderate, half-behind Weather: Overcast

1586 2E2 MAIDEN AUCTION STKS — 5f (P)
6:20 (6:21) (Class 6) 2-Y-O **£2,047** (£604; £302) **Stalls** High

Form RPR

0 **1** **Little Pete (IRE)**[27] 1007 2-8-10 .... LPKeniry 8 70
(R A Farrant) *mde all: rdn and pressed 1f out: styd on wl* **10/1**

2 *1½* **Marias Buddy**[6] 1441 2-8-4 .... DO'Donohoe 3 58
(Eamon Tyrrell, Ire) *trckd ldng pair: rdn to press wnr 1f out: nt qckn and wl hld last 100yds* **5/2**[1]

00 **3** *½* **Seventh Cloud (IRE)**[9] 1354 2-8-1 .... WilliamBuick(5) 5 58
(A P Jarvis) *w wnr to wl over 1f out: one pce after* **5/1**

4 *1¼* **Straight And Level (CAN)** 2-8-10 .... RHills 10 57+
(J W Hills) *chsd ldng trio: awkward bnd 3f out and rdn: outpcd wl over 1f out: plugged on* **3/1**[2]

0 **5** *nk* **Talk Of Saafend (IRE)**[9] 1354 2-8-6 .... PatDobbs 4 52+
(R Hannon) *chsd ldrs but nvr on terms: rdn 1/2-way: struggling wl over 1f out: kpt on* **7/2**[3]

6 *7* **Charlie Be (IRE)** 2-8-9 .... RobertHavlin 7 27
(Mrs P N Dutfield) *outpcd and bhd after 2f* **33/1**

7 *1¼* **Rannoch** 2-8-10 .... FergusSweeney 2 23
(Miss D A McHale) *chsd ldrs: rdn and struggling bef 1/2-way: wknd over 1f out* **33/1**

0 **8** *2½* **Mister Cafnex (IRE)**[28] 999 2-8-8 .... JerryO'Dwyer(3) 9 14
(B W Duke) *sn outpcd and rdn: a bhd* **16/1**

9 *9* **Redbackcappuchino (IRE)** 2-8-4 .... RichardThomas 6 —
(J L Spearing) *s.s: a t.o* **20/1**

61.59 secs (1.19) **Going Correction** +0.025s/f (Slow) **9** Ran SP% **118.1**
Speed ratings (Par 91):91,88,87,85,85 74,72,68,53
CSF £35.49 TOTE £13.90: £4.20, £1.10, £1.90; EX 48.30.
Owner Friends of Saunton Sands **Bred** Larry Ryan **Trained** Upper Lambourn, Berks

FOCUS
An ordinary maiden in which few ever got into it and the order hardly changed during the contest. The form is rated through the runner-up and seems sound.

NOTEBOOK
Little Pete(IRE) was much more organised than on his Leicester debut and the key to this victory was quickly bagging the rail in front from his high draw. He did look likely to be swallowed up by his two nearest challengers a furlong from home, but found a bit more from somewhere and was well on top at the line. A half-brother to the stable's dual-winner Full Victory, he should continue to progress. (tchd 9-1)
Marias Buddy, asked to travel abroad just six days after finishing third on her Tipperary debut, had every chance in the home straight, but lacked a decisive turn of foot. Despite her speedy pedigree, she shapes as though she could do with a bit further. (op 15-8 tchd 3-1)
Seventh Cloud(IRE), unplaced in two Windsor maidens though she ran better than her finishing position might suggest last time, had every chance and was always safe in third, but it is debatable whether this represented much of a step forward. She may need a drop in class if she is to break her duck.
Straight And Level(CAN), a half-brother to eight winners and with very much an American pedigree, had the plum draw and was always about the same distance behind the principals. His stable is not noted for winning debutants, so he should improve a bit from this. (op 11-2)
Talk Of Saafend(IRE), just behind Seventh Cloud on her Windsor debut, ran to a similar level of form on a line through that rival and does not look amongst the stable's leading lights. (op 4-1 tchd 3-1)

Redbackcappuchino(IRE) Official explanation: jockey said filly missed the break

1587 KEMPTON.CO.UK MEDIAN AUCTION MAIDEN STKS 7f (P)
6:50 (6:52) (Class 5) 3-4-Y-O £2,914 (£867; £433; £216) Stalls High

Form RPR
5- **1** **Cherie's Dream**[225] 5592 3-8-9 .... LPKeniry 9 65
(A M Balding) *racd freely: mde all: rdn and hrd pressed fnl 2f: hld on gamely nr fin* **6/1**[3]

04- **2** *nk* **Doyles Lodge**[212] 5867 3-9-0 .... JohnEgan 4 69
(H Candy) *cl up: wnt 2nd 2f out: drvn and nrly upsides fnl f: nt qckn last 75yds* **7/2**[2]

46- **3** *2 1/2* **Geordie's Pool**[182] 6393 3-9-0 .... RHills 7 63
(J W Hills) *cl up: shkn up 2f out: nt qckn over 1f out: kpt on to take 3rd ins fnl f* **6/1**[3]

0- **4** *1* **Gold Flame**[354] 1844 4-9-12 .... FergusSweeney 12 64
(H Candy) *t.k.h: cl up: effrt on inner to chal 2f out: nt qckn over 1f out: one pce after* **11/4**[1]

6 **5** *5* **Musical Box**[13] 1267 3-8-9 .... AdrianMcCarthy 8 42
(G Prodromou) *trckd wnr to 2f out: wknd* **100/1**

04 **6** *3* **Witchingham**[103] 257 3-8-7 .... HaddenFrost(7) 1 39
(R Hannon) *dropped in fr wd draw and wl in rr: outpcd over 2f out: sme prog over 1f out: no ch* **8/1**

0 **7** *1* **Sharpattack**[13] 1261 3-8-9 .... (t) NicolPolli(5) 5 37
(M Botti) *dwlt: sn chsd ldrs: outpcd over 2f out: hanging after and no imp* **40/1**

8 *hd* **Qatar Way (GR)** 3-8-9 .... RobertHavlin 2 31
(P R Chamings) *towards rr: outpcd over 2f out: no ch after: plugged on* **28/1**

9 *1* **Nouveau (GER)** 3-9-0 .... PatDobbs 6 33
(R Hannon) *dwlt: a in rr: wl outpcd fr over 2f out* **15/2**

10 *shd* **My Mentor (IRE)** 3-9-0 .... JamieMackay 10 33
(Sir Mark Prescott) *dwlt: a wl in rr: outpcd fr over 2f out* **11/1**

0- **11** *2 1/2* **Twenty Percent**[265] 4525 3-9-0 .... TPQueally 11 27
(P R Chamings) *s.s: t.k.h early and hld up in last: already wl outpcd whn hmpd over 2f out* **40/1**

12 *1 3/4* **Charley Fox** 3-9-0 .... SimonWhitworth 13 22
(D C O'Brien) *nvr beyond midfield: wknd over 2f out* **33/1**

13 *19* **Apocalypto (IRE)** 3-9-0 .... EdwardCreighton 14 —
(E J Creighton) *hld up in midfield: wknd rapidly over 2f out: t.o* **40/1**

1m 28.35s (1.55) **Going Correction** +0.025s/f (Slow)
WFA 3 from 4yo 12lb 13 Ran SP% 123.4
Speed ratings (Par 103):92,91,88,87,81 78,77,77,76,75 73,71,49
CSF £27.04 TOTE £7.00: £2.30, £2.10, £1.80; EX 36.10.
Owner W V & Mrs E S Robins **Bred** Mrs Shirley Robins **Trained** Kingsclere, Hants
■ Stewards' Enquiry : L P Keniry caution: used whip without allowing sufficient time to respond

FOCUS
Not a great maiden and, with the early pace modest, this developed into a three-furlong sprint. The winning time was moderate, 1.3 seconds slower than the following fillies' handicap and the form is rated around the placed horses. They finished well spread out though and a couple are entitled to improve.

1588 CREATING BUSINESS ADVANTAGE FILLIES' H'CAP 7f (P)
7:20 (7:21) (Class 4) (0-80,80) 3-Y-O+ £4,728 (£1,406; £702; £351) Stalls High

Form RPR
40-1 **1** **Crystal Gazer (FR)**[37] 885 3-8-12 78 .... PatDobbs 3 86+
(R Hannon) *hld up in last but wl in tch: prog to chse ldr 2f out: edgd lft u.p over 1f out: r.o to ld last 100yds* **3/1**[2]

500- **2** *1/2* **Rydal Mount (IRE)**[205] 6020 4-9-4 72 .... FergusSweeney 6 79
(W S Kittow) *led: kicked 2l clr 2f out: kpt on u.p: worn down last 100yds* **9/1**

2505 **3** *3* **Imperial Lucky (IRE)**[25] 1036 4-8-13 67 .... DeanMernagh 5 66
(D K Ivory) *hld up in cl tch: effrt on inner over 2f out: nt qckn u.p wl over 1f out* **7/1**[3]

6 **4** *shd* **Sensasse (IRE)**[25] 1034 4-9-12 80 .... OscarUrbina 4 79
(Mrs A J Perrett) *chsd ldr to 2f out: sn btn u.p* **15/2**

00-5 **5** *3 1/2* **Dancing Guest (IRE)**[30] 979 4-9-12 80 .... TPQueally 2 70
(G G Margarson) *cl up: hanging and nt qckn over 2f out: sn btn* **3/1**[2]

054- **6** *10* **Joyful Tears (IRE)**[218] 5754 3-8-5 71 .... DO'Donohoe 1 31
(E A L Dunlop) *cl up but trapped on outer: wknd bdly over 2f out: t.o* **5/2**[1]

1m 27.05s (0.25) **Going Correction** +0.025s/f (Slow)
WFA 3 from 4yo 12lb 6 Ran SP% 112.8
Speed ratings (Par 102):99,98,95,94,90 79
CSF £28.62 CT £171.74 TOTE £2.90: £1.80, £3.50; EX 38.50.
Owner A F Merritt **Bred** Cheik Sultan B K B Z Al Nahyan **Trained** East Everleigh, Wilts
■ Stewards' Enquiry : Pat Dobbs caution: used whip in the wrong place

FOCUS
They finished quite well spread out despite the small field, but the winning time was ordinary despite being 1.3 seconds faster than the preceding maiden. The fourth to her previous run is possibly the best guide.

1589 AUTOTRADER H'CAP 6f (P)
7:50 (7:52) (Class 5) (0-70,70) 4-Y-O+ £2,914 (£867; £433; £216) Stalls High

Form RPR
046- **1** **Guilded Warrior**[249] 5036 4-8-13 65 .... FergusSweeney 8 78
(W S Kittow) *chsd ldng trio: rdn and r.o to ld over 1f out: drvn out and styd on wl* **11/1**

2-33 **2** *1* **Vegas Boys**[37] 896 4-9-0 66 .... DO'Donohoe 1 76
(M Wigham) *dwlt: sn in midfield: prog over 2f out: chsd wnr ins fnl f: no imp nr fin* **5/1**[2]

-004 **3** *1 1/2* **Royal Envoy (IRE)**[18] 1165 4-8-11 63 .... DeanMcKeown 7 69
(D Shaw) *dwlt: hld up in last: n.m.r after 2f and plenty to do: pushed along over 2f out: styd on wl after: nrst fin* **10/1**

0-24 **4** *1* **Willhewiz**[15] 1214 7-8-13 65 .... NCallan 10 68
(M S Saunders) *led at fast pce: hdd over 1f out: fdd* **10/1**

4662 **5** *1/2* **Hammer Of The Gods (IRE)**[18] 1165 7-9-1 70 .... (bt) JerryO'Dwyer(3) 9 71
(P S McEntee) *disp 2nd: drvn to chal 2f out: one pce over 1f out* **13/2**[3]

-405 **6** *1 3/4* **Russian Rocket (IRE)**[22] 1074 5-9-4 70 .... DMylonas 3 66
(Mrs C A Dunnett) *chsd ldrs: wd and urged along over 2f out: sn outpcd: plugged on fnl f* **14/1**

0106 **7** *hd* **Bobby Rose**[16] 1200 4-8-12 64 .... RobertHavlin 6 59
(D K Ivory) *hld up in midfield: gng wl enough on inner over 2f out: rdn and no rspnse wl over 1f out* **10/1**

3145 **8** *4* **Methaaly (IRE)**[9] 1357 4-9-1 67 .... JohnEgan 11 50
(Jane Chapple-Hyam) *disp 2nd: rdn whn n.m.r 2f out: sn wknd* **2/1**[1]

16/0 **9** *1/2* **Charming Ballet (IRE)**[22] 1080 4-9-0 66 .... GeorgeBaker 4 48
(N P Littmoden) *chsd ldrs: u.p and no prog over 2f out: wknd over 1f out* **16/1**

0-66 **10** *2* **Dictatrix**[14] 1252 4-9-4 70 .... (b) MickyFenton 2 46
(J M P Eustace) *dwlt: a in last trio: rdn and struggling over 2f out* **11/1**

000- **11** *4* **Bold Argument (IRE)**[212] 5872 4-8-7 66 .... NBazeley(7) 5 30
(Mrs P N Dutfield) *a in rr: sddle slipped over 2f out* **33/1**

1m 12.82s (-0.88) **Going Correction** +0.025s/f (Slow) 11 Ran SP% 122.8
Speed ratings (Par 103):106,104,102,101,100 98,98,92,92,89 84
CSF £68.17 CT £594.31 TOTE £17.10: £4.00, £1.90, £6.70; EX 193.30.
Owner The Racing Guild **Bred** Manor Farm Packers Ltd **Trained** Blackborough, Devon

FOCUS
There was a fierce pace on right from the start in this sprint handicap. Perhaps the leaders went off too quick, as those that helped force it failed to make the first three but the form looks solid enough.
Bold Argument(IRE) Official explanation: jockey said saddle slipped

1590 DIGIBET H'CAP 2m (P)
8:20 (8:22) (Class 6) (0-50,50) 4-Y-O+ £2,047 (£604; £302) Stalls High

Form RPR
05-2 **1** **Gaelic Roulette (IRE)**[7] 1402 7-8-8 46 .... NCallan 13 57+
(J Jay) *hld up in midfield: clsd on ldrs 4f out: rdn to ld over 2f out: kpt on wl and clr over 1f out* **13/8**[1]

0/36 **2** *5* **Theflyingscottie**[7] 1406 5-8-8 46 oh1 .... DeanMcKeown 10 51
(D Shaw) *hld up wl in rr: stdy prog fr 5f out: rdn to chse wnr wl over 1f out: no imp* **11/2**[2]

00-6 **3** *1 1/4* **Shamrock Bay**[14] 1254 5-8-10 48 .... TPQueally 7 51
(C R Dore) *hld up wl in rr: smooth prog over 4f out: cl up and poised to chal over 2f out: sn rdn: wknd over 1f out* **15/2**

560/ **4** *5* **Voir Dire**[571] 3279 5-8-12 50 .... RobertHavlin 8 47
(Mrs P N Dutfield) *hld up in midfield: prog to chse ldrs 4f out: outpcd and hrd rdn 2f out: plugged on* **20/1**

435- **5** *1/2* **Glory Be (ITY)**[163] 6620 5-8-8 46 oh1 .... (p) SamHitchcott 6 42
(J L Spearing) *trckd ldng pair after 6f: clsd to ld over 3f out: hdd over 2f out: sn wknd* **9/1**

560/ **6** *7* **Honour High**[728] 1620 5-8-9 47 .... SebSanders 1 35
(Lady Herries) *wl in tch: rdn over 3f out: wknd over 2f out* **10/1**

4604 **7** *1 1/4* **Sczume (IRE)**[7] 1402 4-8-2 50 .... (p) JemmaMarshall(7) 12 37
(Miss Sheena West) *hld up: prog on outer 6f out: nt on terms and wd over 2f out: sn wknd* **14/1**

-416 **8** *10* **Icannshift (IRE)**[10] 1319 7-8-5 46 oh1 .... NeilChalmers(3) 5 21
(T M Jones) *disp ld at str pce: led 4f out to over 3f out: sn wknd* **16/1**

0/ **9** *20* **Mac Lough (USA)**[275] 3691 5-8-8 46 oh1 .... MickyFenton 9 —
(Eamon Tyrrell, Ire) *disp ld at str pce to 4f out: wknd v rapidly: t.o* **25/1**

/0-0 **10** *1 1/2* **Golden Measure**[12] 1279 7-8-8 46 oh1 .... (p) PaulEddery 11 —
(B P J Baugh) *chsd ldrs: pushed along after 6f: lost pl 1/2-way: sn wknd: t.o* **50/1**

0-00 **11** *5* **The Rip**[119] 87 6-8-8 46 oh1 .... EdwardCreighton 4 —
(R M Stronge) *s.s: a in rr: wknd over 4f out: t.o* **66/1**

3403 **12** *7* **Cragganmore Creek**[7] 1402 4-8-7 48 .... (v) HayleyTurner 2 —
(D Morris) *a in rr: hrd rdn and struggling over 6f out: wknd: t.o* **6/1**[3]

0-60 **13** *53* **Nahlass**[7] 1402 4-8-0 46 oh1 .... NataliaGemelova(5) 14 —
(Ms J S Doyle) *prom for 6f: sn wknd and hopelessly t.o* **50/1**

3m 30.89s (-0.51) **Going Correction** +0.025s/f (Slow)
WFA 4 from 5yo+ 3lb 13 Ran SP% 125.2
Speed ratings (Par 101):102,99,98,96,96 92,92,87,77,76 73,70,43
CSF £10.34 CT £57.79 TOTE £2.50: £1.40, £2.50, £2.40; EX 16.00.
Owner Graham & Lynn Knight **Bred** J F Tuthill **Trained** Newmarket, Suffolk
■ Stewards' Enquiry : Sam Hitchcott three-day ban: improper riding - used whip with excessive force on a mare that was not responding (May 20-22)

FOCUS
A very modest handicap, run at a good pace which suited the hold-up runners. Solid form for the grade rated around the placed horses.
Cragganmore Creek Official explanation: jockey said gelding lost its action

1591 DIGIBET SPORTS BETTING H'CAP 1m 4f (P)
8:50 (8:54) (Class 4) (0-80,78) 4-Y-O+ £4,728 (£1,406; £702; £351) Stalls Centre

Form RPR
155- **1** **Hernando Royal**[223] 5644 4-8-13 78 .... TravisBlock(5) 5 90+
(H Morrison) *trckd ldng trio: effrt to chal 4f out: led 3f out: rdn clr 2f out: in n.d after* **15/2**

50-0 **2** *3* **Cavallini (USA)**[39] 844 5-8-10 70 .... FergusSweeney 12 77
(G L Moore) *chsd ldrs: outpcd and rdn 4f out: nt look too keen but styd on to chse wnr over 1f out: no imp* **16/1**

1 **3** *2 1/2* **Rickety Bridge (IRE)**[34] 936 4-8-12 72 .... NCallan 11 75
(P R Chamings) *dwlt: sn in midfield: rdn and prog on inner fr over 3f out: kpt on same pce fnl 2f* **10/1**

11-4 **4** *1/2* **Cleaver**[39] 850 6-9-4 78 .... SebSanders 9 80+
(Lady Herries) *hld up in rr: nvr gng that wl: last of main gp and rdn 4f out: styd on fnl 2f: no ch* **3/1**[1]

011- **5** *2 1/2* **Captain General**[206] 5991 5-8-13 73 .... JohnEgan 13 71
(J A R Toller) *settled in last pair: rdn and prog 4f out: no imp on ldrs over 2f out: eased fnl f* **9/2**[2]

0-20 **6** *hd* **Star Of Canterbury (IRE)**[14] 1253 4-8-4 69 .... WilliamBuick(5) 7 68+
(A P Jarvis) *led: kicked on over 4f out: hdd 3f out: hrd rdn to chse wnr after: wknd over 1f out* **13/2**

400- **7** *1/2* **Zirkel (IRE)**[217] 5770 4-8-11 71 .... DO'Donohoe 4 68
(Mrs A L M King) *trckd ldr: chal 4f out to 3f out: wknd 2f out* **50/1**

4655 **8** *16* **Prince Charlemagne (IRE)**[9] 1356 4-9-3 77 .... GeorgeBaker 10 48
(N P Littmoden) *towards rr: brief effrt 4f out: no prog 3f out: wknd: t.o* **7/1**

6-31 **9** *14* **Tromp**[46] 753 6-9-2 76 .... JimmyQuinn 6 25
(D J Coakley) *chsd ldrs: outpcd and rdn 4f out: wknd over 2f out: t.o* **11/2**[3]

6-50 **10** *1/2* **Burgundy**[5] 1451 10-8-3 70 .... (b) JackMitchell(7) 3 18
(P Mitchell) *dwlt: settled in last: wd and rdn bnd 3f out: sn wknd: t.o* **14/1**

610- **P** **Fear To Tread (USA)**[194] 6202 4-9-3 77 .... MickyFenton 14 —
(Mrs P Sly) *chsd ldng pair to 5f out: wknd rapidly: t.o whn p.u 2f out* **25/1**

2m 33.54s (-3.36) **Going Correction** +0.025s/f (Slow) 11 Ran SP% 123.6
Speed ratings (Par 105):112,110,108,108,106 106,105,95,85,85 —
CSF £126.77 CT £1225.58 TOTE £12.00: £3.00, £5.10, £3.60; EX 105.70.
Owner A N Solomons **Bred** The White's Farmers **Trained** East Ilsley, Berks

FOCUS
A fair handicap and a smart winning time for the class of contest. Solid form, with an improved effort from Hernando Royal.
Tromp Official explanation: trainer said gelding had a breathing problem and had since undergone epiglottic entrapment surgery
Fear To Tread(USA) Official explanation: jockey said filly lost her action

1592 DIGITOTE H'CAP — 1m 3f (P)
9:20 (9:21) (Class 6) (0-50,50) 4-Y-0+ — £2,047 (£604; £302) Stalls High

Form — RPR

1 **Raydan (IRE)**[50] [2770] 5-8-12 **50**.....(b[1]) MickyFenton 3 — 60
(D R Gandolfo) *hld up in midfield: prog on outer 6f out: chsd ldr 3f out: led 2f out and sn kicked clr: in no real danger fnl f* **20/1**

0211 2 1 1/4 **Jarvo**[8] [1380] 6-8-11 **49**..... DanielTudhope 11 — 57
(I W McInnes) *hld up in midfield: effrt 3f out: nt clr run over 2f out: prog to chse wnr over 1f out: styd on but readily hld* **11/4**[1]

00-0 3 1/2 **Snake Skin**[14] [1254] 4-8-11 **49**..... JimCrowley 12 — 56
(J Gallagher) *hld up towards rr: effrt whn nt clr run over 2f out: styd on to take 3rd over 1f out: nrst fin* **12/1**

4602 4 1 1/2 **Come What July (IRE)**[9] [1347] 6-8-8 **46**..... DeanMcKeown 7 — 50
(D Shaw) *hld up towards rr: sme prog on outer 3f out: sn outpcd: pushed along and kpt on fnl 2f: n.d* **11/2**[2]

0601 5 3 **Monmouthshire**[15] [1206] 4-8-6 **49**.....(v) KevinGhunowa(5) 1 — 48
(R J Price) *settled in rr: effrt on wd outside over 3f out: sn outpcd: sme prog 2f out: no imp over 1f out* **8/1**

00-4 6 1 **Inn For The Dancer**[14] [1254] 5-8-12 **50**..... PatDobbs 9 — 48
(J C Fox) *prom: rdn over 2f out: nt qckn and hld sn after: fdd fnl f* **7/1**[3]

625- 7 1/2 **Hansomelle (IRE)**[193] [6211] 5-8-12 **50**..... JimmyQuinn 6 — 47
(Miss Sheena West) *settled in last pair of main gp: nt clr run and swtchd ins over 2f out: reminder over 1f out: styd on: nvr nr ldrs* **9/1**

54-0 8 1 1/4 **Cool Isle**[120] [78] 4-8-12 **50**.....(b) OscarUrbina 10 — 45
(P Howling) *chsd ldrs: rdn over 3f out: no imp over 2f out: fdd* **33/1**

00-0 9 8 **Rawaabet (IRE)**[48] [732] 5-8-12 **50**..... HayleyTurner 5 — 31
(P W Hiatt) *racd freely: led after 2f: clr 6f out: hdd & wknd rapidly 2f out* **33/1**

3-00 10 2 **Panshir (FR)**[9] [1360] 6-8-11 **49**..... TPQueally 2 — 27
(Mrs C A Dunnett) *dwlt: t.k.h: hld up in rr: brief effrt 3f out: sn wknd* **16/1**

4036 11 3/4 **Kumakawa**[9] [1347] 9-8-12 **50**..... SebSanders 13 — 26
(N P Littmoden) *led for 2f: chsd ldr to 3f out: sn wknd* **14/1**

-326 12 7 **Bob Baileys**[16] [812] 5-8-10 **48**.....(b) NCallan 4 — 13
(P R Chamings) *prom tl wknd over 3f out: eased fnl 2f* **14/1**

5426 13 14 **War Feather**[88] [416] 5-8-10 **48**..... RobertHavlin 8 — —
(T D McCarthy) *a in rr: wknd 3f out: t.o* **12/1**

50/0 14 70 **Belshazzar (USA)**[14] [1251] 6-8-12 **50**..... SimonWhitworth 14 — —
(D C O'Brien) *s.v.s: a last: wl t.o 1/2-way* **100/1**

2m 22.18s (-0.50) **Going Correction** +0.025s/f (Slow) — **14** Ran SP% **121.9**
Speed ratings (Par 101):102,101,100,99,97 96,96,95,89,88 87,82,72,21
CSF £73.72 CT £727.92 TOTE £19.30: £5.00, £1.80, £4.20; EX 120.70 Place 6 £523.17, Place 5 £245.58..
Owner B R K Pain **Bred** His Highness The Aga Khan's Studs S C **Trained** Charlton Adam, Somerset
■ Stewards' Enquiry : Daniel Tudhope caution: careless riding
Oscar Urbina one-day ban: careless riding (May 20)

FOCUS
A very modest handicap in which just 4lb separated the whole field. The form looks solid with both the second and third close to their best, and the winner not far off last year's best form in Ireland.
T/Plt: £208.00 to a £1 stake. Pool: £55,562.40. 195.00 winning tickets. T/Qpdt: £50.70 to a £1 stake. Pool: £3,035.30. 44.30 winning tickets. JN

[1420]CHANTILLY (R-H)
Wednesday, May 9

OFFICIAL GOING: Good to soft

1593a PRIX DE GUICHE (GROUP 3) (COLTS) — 1m 1f
2:35 (2:42) 3-Y-0 — £27,027 (£10,811; £8,108; £5,405; £2,703)

RPR

1 **Lawman (FR)**[24] [1056] 3-9-2..... OPeslier 6 — 112
(J-M Beguigne, France) *mde all: qcknd 2f out: 2 l clr 1f out: pushed out: easily* **54/10**[3]

2 2 1/2 **Holocene (USA)**[41] [824] 3-9-2..... C-PLemaire 3 — 107
(P Bary, France) *racd in 4th: rdn and wnt 2nd 1 1/2f out: jnd for 2nd and carried rt 100yds out: regained 2nd on line* **11/1**

3 shd **Chinese Whisper (IRE)**[24] [1057] 3-9-2..... JMurtagh 7 — 107
(A P O'Brien, Ire) *racd in 6th: rdn on outside over 1 1/2f out: edgd rt: disp 2nd 100yds out: lost 2nd on line* **23/10**[2]

4 snk **Hurricane Fly (IRE)**[24] [1056] 3-9-2..... F-XBertras 1 — 107
(J-L Pelletan, France) *trckd ldr on ins in 3rd: effrt and dropped bk to 5th over 1f out: rallied on ins clsng stages* **12/1**

5 1 1/2 **Russian Desert (IRE)**[215] [5801] 3-9-2..... SPasquier 4 — 104
(A Fabre, France) *racd in 2nd: rdn 2f out: one pce: hld in 5th whn hmpd 70yds out* **68/10**

6 2 **Lowenherz (GER)**[24] [1054] 3-9-2..... EPedroza 2 — 99
(A Wohler, Germany) *racd in 5th: rdn 2f out: sn btn* **27/1**

7 1 1/2 **Mandali (FR)**[24] 3-9-2..... CSoumillon 5 — 96
(A De Royer-Dupre, France) *ref to canter to post: dismntd and led to s: last thrght* **16/10**[1]

1m 52.5s (0.30) — **7** Ran SP% **116.8**
PARI-MUTUEL: WIN 6.40; PL 2.60, 4.50; SF 43.50.
Owner C Marzocco **Bred** Petra Bloodstock Agency **Trained** France

NOTEBOOK
Lawman(FR) can now be considered a Classic prospect following this victory. Smartly into his stride, he soon led, steadied the pace rounding the final turn and picked up in good style in the straight. All being well his next race will be the Prix du Jockey Club, and there is no reason why he should not stay the extra furlong and a half.
Holocene(USA), always well placed behind the leaders, was sqeezed a little at the furlong marker but rallied again and took second place in the final few strides. He is going the right way and should make it at this level before the end of the season.
Chinese Whisper(IRE), held up in fifth place for most of the race, made his move up the centre of the track, but hung to his right a furlong out and lost second near the finish. He gives the impression that he will be suited by further.
Hurricane Fly(IRE), settled in third place early, was outpaced in the straight before running on well up the far rail inside the final furlong.

AYR (L-H)
Thursday, May 10

OFFICIAL GOING: Good (good to soft in places)
The races on the round course were run on the hurdles track.
Wind: Almost nil

1594 LADIES NIGHT AT AYR CLASSIFIED STKS — 5f
6:20 (6:22) (Class 7) 4-Y-0+ — £2,266 (£674; £337; £168) Stalls Low

Form — RPR

0000 1 **Mystery Pips**[38] [892] 7-9-0 45.....(v) KimTinkler 1 — 56
(N Tinkler) *prom: led over 1f out: pushed out fnl f* **20/1**

5040 2 1 1/2 **She's Our Beauty (IRE)**[19] [1163] 4-8-9 41.....(p) DuranFentiman(5) 8 — 51
(S T Mason) *led to over 1f out: no ex ins fnl f* **25/1**

00-0 3 1 3/4 **Whozart (IRE)**[17] [1197] 4-9-0 41..... DaleGibson 6 — 45
(A Dickman) *dwlt: t.k.h and hdwy into midfield after 2f: effrt over 1f out: kpt on ins fnl f* **25/1**

5005 4 nk **Legal Set (IRE)**[24] [1065] 11-8-9 45.....(b) AnnStokell(5) 13 — 44+
(Miss A Stokell) *in tch in centre: effrt 2f out: kpt on fnl f: no imp* **20/1**

3550 5 1 **Danethorpe (IRE)**[65] [632] 4-9-0 42.....(v) CatherineGannon 17 — 40+
(D Shaw) *dwlt: bhd in centre: hdwy over 1f out: nrst fin* **9/1**[2]

6 1/2 **Knight Of Kintyre (IRE)**[202] [6084] 4-9-0 42..... RoystonFfrench 2 — 38
(Barry Potts, Ire) *prom: effrt over 1f out: kpt on same pce* **12/1**

2000 7 hd **Beverley Beau**[74] [557] 5-8-7 42..... KristinStubbs(7) 18 — 38
(Mrs L Stubbs) *bhd in centre tl hdwy over 1f out: nvr rchd ldrs* **8/1**[1]

000- 8 1 1/4 **Tombalina**[275] [4232] 4-9-0 45..... DavidAllan 4 — 33
(C J Teague) *pressed ldrs: ev ch over 1f out: wknd ins fnl f* **50/1**

0522 9 hd **Jember Red**[37] [906] 4-8-11 45.....(v) MarkLawson(3) 3 — 32
(B Smart) *dwlt: hdwy and in tch 1/2-way: effrt over 1f out: sn no ex* **8/1**[1]

0204 10 nk **Alucica**[50] [722] 4-8-9 43.....(v) JamieMoriarty(5) 15 — 31
(D Shaw) *bhd and sn pushed along: sme late hdwy: nvr on terms* **8/1**[1]

-604 11 1/2 **He's A Rocket (IRE)**[19] [1163] 6-9-0 42.....(v) PhillipMakin 11 — 29
(K R Burke) *in tch tl rdn and wknd over 1f out* **9/1**[2]

026- 12 3/4 **Mister Jingles**[176] [6490] 4-8-9 45.....(p) MichaelJStainton(5) 9 — 27
(R M Whitaker) *sn outpcd: no ch fr 1/2-way* **16/1**

-066 13 nk **Telepathic (IRE)**[7] [1423] 7-9-0 45..... TonyHamilton 16 — 26
(A Berry) *sn outpcd centre: struggling fr 1/2-way* **16/1**

03-0 14 nk **John O'Groats (IRE)**[4] [1492] 9-8-7 45.....(b) CharlotteKerton(7) 14 — 25
(W G Harrison) *bhd: hung lft thrght: nvr on terms* **10/1**[3]

60-0 15 2 **Mytton's Pride**[10] [1360] 4-9-0 45..... PaulHanagan 5 — 17
(A Bailey) *prom to 1/2-way: sn rdn and wknd* **14/1**

00-0 16 3 **Sokoke**[6] [1456] 6-9-0 45..... PaulMulrennan 10 — 7
(D A Nolan) *in tch tl wknd fr wl over 1f out* **10/1**[3]

0006 17 1 **Howards Princess**[19] [1163] 5-9-0 43.....(p) TomEaves 12 — 3
(J Hetherton) *bhd: rdn 1/2-way: nvr on terms* **12/1**

000- 18 15 **Compton Lad**[214] [5834] 4-9-0 44..... PaulFessey 7 — —
(D A Nolan) *w ldr tl wknd wl over 1f out* **50/1**

60.36 secs (-0.08) **Going Correction** -0.025s/f (Good) — **18** Ran SP% **126.5**
Speed ratings (Par 97):99,96,93,93,91 90,90,88,88,87 87,85,85,84,81 76,75,51
CSF £437.94 TOTE £24.50: £5.80, £6.20, £11.30; EX 567.00.
Owner K Venning,M Haymes,S Perkins,G Darling **Bred** Michael Worton **Trained** Langton, N Yorks

FOCUS
A big event and a stronger race than most of this type. Th pace was sound and the whole field raced centre to far side. The form looks generally sound, rated through the runner-up. The winner will still be well in on the form she showed this time last year.
Danethorpe(IRE) Official explanation: jockey said gelding missed the break
Jember Red Official explanation: jockey said filly was unsuited by the good (good to soft places) ground

1595 BLACK BOTTLE MAIDEN H'CAP — 5f
6:50 (6:51) (Class 5) (0-70,65) 3-Y-0+ — £3,886 (£1,156; £577; £288) Stalls Low

Form — RPR

-524 1 **Princess Ellis**[16] [1219] 3-8-7 **55**..... KDarley 7 — 55
(E J Alston) *plld hrd: chsd ldrs: led 2f out: rdn fnl f: jst hld on* **4/1**[2]

2400 2 shd **Mangano**[31] [970] 3-7-12 **46** oh1..... PaulHanagan 5 — 45
(A Berry) *led to 2f out: sn drvn: kpt on wl fnl f: jst hld* **50/1**

-530 3 1/2 **Newkeylets**[58] [668] 4-8-10 **49**.....(p) PhillipMakin 6 — 51
(I Semple) *chsd ldrs: effrt and shkn up over 1f out: kpt on ins fnl f* **5/1**[3]

6-00 4 1 **Miacarla**[4] [1493] 4-8-7 **46**..... TonyHamilton 9 — 44
(A Berry) *chsd ldrs: effrt 2f out: kpt on same pce fnl f* **33/1**

6352 5 shd **Moonlight Applause**[27] [1031] 3-7-13 **52**..... DuranFentiman(5) 1 — 49+
(T D Easterby) *outpcd tl hdwy over 1f out: nrst fin* **6/1**

-024 6 2 1/2 **Wolfman**[17] [1197] 5-8-11 **50**.....(p) TomEaves 4 — 39
(D W Barker) *chsd ldrs tl rdn and no ex over 1f out* **3/1**[1]

5-63 7 1 3/4 **The Brat**[15] [1240] 3-7-13 **47** ow1..... PaulFessey 11 — 25
(J S Wainwright) *w ldrs to 2f out: sn wknd* **16/1**

00-0 8 2 1/2 **City Miss**[6] [1459] 4-8-4 **46** oh1..... GregFairley(3) 3 — 19
(Miss L A Perratt) *sn outpcd: no imp fr 2f out* **50/1**

660- 9 1/2 **Mandarin Rocket (IRE)**[304] [3355] 4-9-0 **53**..... RoystonFfrench 10 — 25
(Miss L A Perratt) *in tch tl wknd 2f out* **12/1**

/44- 10 3/4 **Keelings Donabate**[421] [645] 4-9-12 **65**..... PaulMulrennan 2 — 34
(K R Burke) *in tch to 1/2-way: sn rdn and btn* **16/1**

30-0 11 6 **Mandy's Maestro (USA)**[12] [1286] 3-8-7 **60**..... MichaelJStainton(5) 12 — 3
(R M Whitaker) *prom: drvn 1/2-way: sn wknd* **8/1**

/5-0 12 10 **Lady Tilly**[4] [1493] 10-8-0 **46** oh1.....(t) CharlotteKerton(7) 8 — —
(W G Harrison) *s.i.s: nvr on terms* **100/1**

60.13 secs (-0.31) **Going Correction** -0.025s/f (Good)
WFA 3 from 4yo+ 9lb — **12** Ran SP% **114.4**
Speed ratings (Par 103):101,100,100,98,98 94,91,87,86,85 75,59
CSF £195.52 CT £1016.13 TOTE £4.60: £1.90, £11.70, £2.00; EX 112.80.
Owner John Jackson **Bred** J E Jackson **Trained** Longton, Lancs

FOCUS
Another low-grade event but one in which the pace was sound. The field raced far side. The winenr and the third travelled best but neither found as much as expected, and the second and fourth had previously shown very little.

1596 MARTI PELLOW AT AYR RACECOURSE 27 MAY H'CAP — 6f
7:20 (7:25) (Class 6) (0-50,50) 4-Y-0+ — £2,914 (£867; £433; £216) Stalls Low

Form — RPR

00-0 1 **Coalite (IRE)**[10] [1349] 4-8-10 **48**.....(p) PhillipMakin 2 — 59
(A D Brown) *prom: effrt over 1f out: led ins fnl f: rdn and r.o wl* **50/1**

0-04 2 1/2 **Oeuf A La Neige**[4] [1493] 7-8-10 **48**.....(p) RoystonFfrench 14 — 57
(Miss L A Perratt) *midfield: hdwy to ld over 1f out: hdd ins fnl f: hld towards fin* **6/1**[1]

552- **3** 1 **Quicks The Word**[290] [3786] 7-8-5 **46** GregFairley(3) 1 52
(T A K Cuthbert) *prom: effrt over 1f out: kpt on ins fnl f* **9/1**

00-0 **4** 2 **Eternal Legacy (IRE)**[17] [1197] 5-8-8 **46** oh1 PaulHanagan 13 46
(E J Alston) *cl up tl rdn and nt qckn fnl f* **20/1**

-066 **5** 1 ¾ **Katie Boo (IRE)**[15] [1241] 5-8-12 **50** TonyHamilton 4 45
(A Berry) *cl up: ev ch over 1f out: no ex ins fnl f* **16/1**

0-43 **6** 1 ½ **Guadaloup**[10] [1349] 5-8-12 **50** DeanMernagh 15 40
(M Brittain) *cl up: effrt and ev ch over 1f out: no ex fnl f* **9/1**

3343 **7** ½ **Laith (IRE)**[8] [1400] 4-8-7 **50** (p) DuranFentiman(5) 7 39
(Miss V Haigh) *slt ld to over 1f out: sn outpcd* **7/1**[2]

230- **8** nk **Newsround**[170] [6549] 5-8-6 **49** (b) MichaelJStainton(5) 3 37+
(D W Chapman) *s.s: hdwy 1/2-way: rdn and no imp over 1f out* **12/1**

405- **9** 1 ¾ **Drum Dance (IRE)**[212] [5885] 5-8-10 **48** KimTinkler 11 31
(N Tinkler) *bhd tl sme late hdwy: nvr on terms* **8/1**[3]

040- **10** hd **Never Say Deya**[176] [6497] 4-8-9 **47** PaulMulrennan 5 29
(M J Wallace) *prom: drvn 1/2-way: btn fnl f* **10/1**

6000 **11** ¾ **Drury Lane (IRE)**[84] [463] 7-8-9 **47** (p) DaleGibson 9 27
(D W Chapman) *towards rr: rdn 1/2-way: n.d* **33/1**

0010 **12** 1 **Kadia**[10] [1349] 4-8-4 **47** RoryMoore(5) 12 24
(P T Midgley) *w ldr tl wknd fr 2f out* **16/1**

0000 **13** 1 ½ **Sundried Tomato**[14] [1262] 8-8-8 **46** oh1 (p) CatherineGannon 10 18
(D W Chapman) *bhd and sn pushed along: n.d* **25/1**

14 nk **Clew Bay (IRE)**[709] [2172] 8-8-7 **48** (p) AndrewMullen(3) 16 19
(Barry Potts, Ire) *bhd: rdn 1/2-way: nvr on terms* **33/1**

-240 **15** 1 ¼ **Navigation (IRE)**[9] [1384] 5-8-9 **47** (b) KDarley 18 15
(T J Etherington) *prom tl rdn and wknd fr wl over 1f out* **8/1**[3]

00/0 **16** 1 ½ **Miss Lovat**[10] [1360] 4-8-12 **50** DavidAllan 6 13
(W M Brisbourne) *midfield: drvn 1/2-way: sn outpcd* **66/1**

60-2 **17** ¾ **Miss Mujahid Times**[9] [1384] 4-8-12 **50** (b) TomEaves 8 11
(A D Brown) *prom: rdn whn n.m.r 2f out: sn btn* **10/1**

000- **18** 4 **Pays D'Amour (IRE)**[364] [1607] 10-8-8 **46** oh1 (t) PaulFessey 17 —
(D A Nolan) *bhd: no ch fr 1/2-way* **100/1**

1m 13.24s (-0.43) **Going Correction** -0.025s/f (Good) **18** Ran SP% **125.6**
Speed ratings (Par 101):101,100,99,96,94 92,91,90,88,88 87,86,84,83,81 79,78,73
CSF £325.82 CT £3096.69 TOTE £67.20: £15.40, £2.00, £2.60, £4.30; EX 332.10.
Owner R G Fell **Bred** M A Doyle **Trained** Pickering, York
■ Stewards' Enquiry : Royston Ffrench caution: careless riding

FOCUS
Another poor sprint. The pace was sound and the field again raced centre to far side. Regulation form for a banded-grade handicap. The winner was back to last year's best.

1597 SEE DEACON BLUE 26 MAY H'CAP 6f
7:50 (7:52) (Class 6) (0-65,68) 4-Y-O+ **£2,914** (£867; £433; £216) **Stalls** Low

Form RPR

600- **1** **Hit's Only Money (IRE)**[232] [5474] 7-8-0 **52** DuranFentiman(5) 14 62
(J S Goldie) *hld up: hdwy over 1f out: styd on to ld nr fin* **33/1**

-002 **2** ¾ **Throw The Dice**[4] [1492] 5-8-8 **55** (v) TonyHamilton 5 63
(D W Barker) *sn led: clr 2f out: hdd cl home* **5/1**[1]

0-03 **3** ½ **Memphis Man**[4] [1493] 4-8-7 **54** DavidAllan 2 60
(W M Brisbourne) *sn drvn in midfield: hdwy over 1f out: kpt on fnl f: nrst fin* **5/1**[1]

0100 **4** 1 ¼ **Mozakhraf (USA)**[78] [513] 5-9-0 **64** AndrewMullen(3) 15 66
(K A Ryan) *stall opened fractionally early: prom tl rdn and nt qckn over 1f out* **14/1**

0020 **5** 1 **Local Poet**[31] [967] 6-8-8 **55** (b) PhillipMakin 9 54+
(I Semple) *missed break: bhd tl styd on over 1f out: n.d* **16/1**

-063 **6** 2 **Divine Spirit**[8] [1405] 6-8-13 **60** (p) PaulFessey 17 53
(M Dods) *stall opened fractionally early: hld up: rdn 2f out: kpt on fnl f: no imp* **8/1**

-433 **7** ½ **Cross Of Lorraine (IRE)**[4] [1492] 4-9-4 **65** (b) TomEaves 16 57
(I Semple) *stall opened fractionally early: sn prom: rdn 2f out: wknd fnl f* **6/1**[2]

01-0 **8** ¾ **Prospect Court**[9] [1379] 5-8-7 **57** GregFairley(3) 4 47
(A C Whillans) *stall opened fractionally early: chsd ldrs tl wknd over 1f out* **14/1**

411 **9** ¾ **Franksalot (IRE)**[4] [1492] 7-9-7 **68** 6ex RoystonFfrench 1 55
(I W McInnes) *midfield: sn pushed along: no imp fr 1/2-way* **7/1**[3]

6042 **10** ¾ **Glamaraazi (IRE)**[8] [1404] 4-8-7 **54** PaulHanagan 8 39
(R A Fahey) *sn prom: rdn and wknd over 1f out* **7/1**[3]

06-0 **11** 1 ¼ **John Keats**[31] [967] 4-8-8 **62** GaryBartley(7) 18 43
(J S Goldie) *stall opened fractionally early: racd alone stands' side: no ch fr 2f out* **16/1**

6-00 **12** 6 **Falmassim**[38] [895] 4-9-1 **62** (b[1]) PaulMulrennan 11 25
(Miss J A Camacho) *midfield: drvn over 2f out: btn over 1f out* **40/1**

00-0 **13** ¾ **Highland Song (IRE)**[16] [1226] 4-8-8 **55** CatherineGannon 6 16
(R F Fisher) *chsd ldrs tl wknd over 2f out* **33/1**

1m 13.33s (-0.34) **Going Correction** -0.025s/f (Good) **13** Ran SP% **117.1**
Speed ratings (Par 101):101,100,99,97,96 93,93,92,91,90 88,80,79
CSF £186.36 CT £1019.72 TOTE £27.70: £6.30, £2.30, £2.40; EX 469.60.
Owner Mrs M Craig **Bred** T G Mooney **Trained** Uplawmoor, E Renfrews

FOCUS
A modest sprint in which the stalls of five of the field appeared to open fractionally early. The pace was sound. The race has been rated through the runner-up, with the winner running to last year's best.

1598 BLACK BOTTLE H'CAP 1m 5f 13y
8:20 (8:20) (Class 5) (0-75,72) 4-Y-O+ **£3,238** (£963; £481; £240) **Stalls** Low

Form RPR

40-0 **1** **Alfonso**[26] [1042] 6-8-7 **64** MarkLawson(3) 8 72
(P Monteith) *t.k.h: led: rdn over 2f out: hdd ins fnl f: styd on wl to regain ld post* **16/1**

4-02 **2** shd **Danzatrice**[6] [1457] 5-7-13 **58** oh2 DuranFentiman(5) 7 66
(C W Thornton) *hld up and bhd: gd hdwy over 2f out: led ins fnl f: kpt on: hdd post* **4/1**[2]

102/ **3** 5 **Princess Kiotto**[686] [2851] 6-8-13 **67** DavidAllan 3 68
(W M Brisbourne) *prom: effrt over 2f out: outpcd over 1f out* **16/1**

200- **4** 6 **Brabazon (IRE)**[11] [1326] 4-9-2 **70** (v[1]) RoystonFfrench 2 62
(Barry Potts, Ire) *hld up in tch: rdn 3f out: no imp fnl 2f* **33/1**

6-00 **5** 1 ¼ **Brigadore (USA)**[12] [1288] 4-9-3 **71** (p) KDarley 4 61
(E J Alston) *prom: effrt over 2f out: wknd over 1f out* **16/1**

230- **6** 1 ½ **Karlani (IRE)**[230] [5513] 4-8-12 **66** PaulHanagan 9 53
(G A Swinbank) *hld up: rdn over 3f out: n.d* **6/1**[3]

1-43 **7** 1 ¼ **Magic Moth**[7] [1438] 4-9-1 **72** GregFairley(3) 10 58
(M Johnston) *pressed wnr: rdn 3f out: edgd lft: wknd fr 2f out* **8/11**[1]

006- **8** 2 **Vicious Prince (IRE)**[61] [4469] 8-8-8 **67** MichaelJStainton(5) 1 50
(Mrs J C McGregor) *bhd: struggling 3f out: nvr on terms* **33/1**

2m 53.55s (-3.06) **Going Correction** -0.15s/f (Firm) **8** Ran SP% **115.7**
Speed ratings (Par 103):103,102,99,96,95 94,93,92
CSF £79.79 CT £1050.78 TOTE £19.50: £3.00, £1.60, £4.20; EX 107.90.
Owner D Irvine **Bred** G Reed **Trained** Rosewell, Midlothian

FOCUS
An ordinary event in which the early pace was not overly strong. The first two were close to the form they showed at Newcastle last month (race 1042) but the form is not strong with the favourite running poorly.

1599 SEE THE SAW DOCTORS 26 MAY H'CAP 1m 1f 20y
8:50 (8:51) (Class 4) (0-85,85) 4-Y-O+ **£5,019** (£1,493; £746; £372) **Stalls** Low

Form RPR

0-05 **1** **Goodbye Mr Bond**[12] [1287] 7-9-4 **85** DavidAllan 6 94
(E J Alston) *hld up in tch: effrt over 2f out: led ins fnl f: kpt on wl* **11/4**[2]

-035 **2** ½ **Bailieborough (IRE)**[12] [1307] 8-8-11 **83** JamieMoriarty(5) 11 91
(B Ellison) *hld up: hdwy over 1f out: chsd wnr wl ins fnl f: kpt on* **7/1**

0-10 **3** 1 **Emerald Bay (IRE)**[4] [1494] 5-9-4 **85** TomEaves 1 91
(I Semple) *t.k.h: pressed ldr: led over 2f out to ins fnl f: nt qckn* **9/2**[3]

-541 **4** nk **Street Warrior (IRE)**[16] [1209] 4-8-8 **75** KDarley 3 80
(M Johnston) *prom: effrt over 2f out: nt qckn fnl f* **2/1**[1]

245- **5** ½ **Trouble Mountain (USA)**[190] [6301] 10-8-4 **71** (t) DaleGibson 2 75
(M W Easterby) *hld up in tch: effrt over 2f out: kpt on fnl f: no imp* **14/1**

156- **6** ½ **Thumpers Dream**[212] [5895] 4-9-0 **81** RoystonFfrench 8 84?
(I W McInnes) *cl up tl rdn and no ex over 1f out* **14/1**

60-0 **7** shd **Obezyana (USA)**[5] [1480] 5-9-4 **85** (bt) PaulHanagan 5 88?
(A Bailey) *led to over 2f out: sn no ex* **20/1**

4-00 **8** 1 ¼ **Regent's Secret (USA)**[15] [1245] 7-8-6 **73** PaulFessey 10 74
(J S Goldie) *hld up: rdn 3f out: nvr on terms* **16/1**

1m 58.32s (-1.68) **Going Correction** -0.15s/f (Firm) **8** Ran SP% **114.7**
Speed ratings (Par 105):101,100,99,99,98 98,98,97
CSF £22.42 CT £83.35 TOTE £2.90: £1.30, £1.70, £2.60; EX 17.50 Place 6 £2,107.67, Place 5 £124.10.
Owner Peter J Davies **Bred** Michael Ng **Trained** Longton, Lancs

FOCUS
A fair handicap in which the gallop was only ordinary in the early stages. They finished in a bunch which limits the form. The winner has slipped to a good mark and was a length off last year's best.
T/Plt: £7,700.00 to a £1 stake. Pool: £65,925.45. 6.25 winning tickets. T/Qpdt: £69.40 to a £1 stake. Pool: £5,984.50. 63.80 winning tickets. RY

1580 CHESTER (L-H)
Thursday, May 10

OFFICIAL GOING: Good
Wind: Fresh, across Weather: Overcast

1600 AKKROBALL HUXLEY STKS (FOR THE TRADESMAN'S CUP) (GROUP 3) 1m 2f 75y
1:50 (1:50) (Class 1) 4-Y-O+ **£36,907** (£13,988; £7,000; £3,490) **Stalls** High

Form RPR

65-1 **1** **Maraahel (IRE)**[19] [1144] 6-9-5 120 (b) RHills 1 118
(Sir Michael Stoute) *s.i.s: sn led: rdn over 1f out: sn edgd lft: hdd narrowly ins fnl f: rallied to regain ld towards fin* **4/6**[1]

-251 **2** hd **Blue Bajan (IRE)**[15] [1245] 5-9-0 105 MichaelHills 4 113
(Andrew Turnell) *hld up in rr: effrt and hdwy over 1f out: led narrowly ins fnl f: hdd towards fin* **6/1**[3]

26-6 **3** 1 ½ **Ivy Creek (USA)**[21] [1104] 4-9-0 109 SteveDrowne 2 110
(G Wragg) *lw: broke wl: trckd ldrs: pushed along over 3f out: abt 2l down whn n.m.r ent fnl f: no imp after* **9/2**[2]

3301 **4** 1 ¾ **Hattan (IRE)**[21] [1109] 5-9-0 109 KerrinMcEvoy 3 107
(C E Brittain) *broke wl: chsd wnr tl rdn over 1f out: outpcd after* **13/2**

2m 8.88s (-4.26) **Going Correction** -0.175s/f (Firm) **4** Ran SP% **105.8**
Speed ratings (Par 113):110,109,108,107
CSF £4.70 TOTE £1.40; EX 4.20.
Owner Hamdan Al Maktoum **Bred** Shadwell Estate Company Limited **Trained** Newmarket, Suffolk
■ Stewards' Enquiry : Michael Hills caution: used whip without giving gelding time to respond

FOCUS
A small field for this Group 3 prize but a pleasing result, with course favourite Maraahel recording his third consecutive success in this race but rated 7lb below his best in doing so.

NOTEBOOK
Maraahel(IRE), winner of this race now for the last three years, is a perfect example of a horse with a class ceiling. At Group 3 and Group 2 level his form reads 1512331111, while his figures in Group 1 races read a less attractive 4833365265. Coming here at the top of his game, he set out to make all, but Blue Bajan loomed up as a big danger in the straight. He was headed briefly inside the final furlong but battled back well to defy his 5lb penalty. He will now go to Royal Ascot in a bid to repeat last year's success in the Hardwicke Stakes. (op 8-13 tchd 8-11 in places)
Blue Bajan(IRE) headed the winner briefly inside the final furlong but Maraahel responded well and rallied. Perhaps if he had his time again his rider would have delayed his challenge a bit longer. Nevertheless, this performance confirmed that he continues to progress - this was a career-best effort - and his turn of foot will be a valuable asset as he chases Pattern-class success in the coming months. (op 11-2)
Ivy Creek(USA), unlucky in defeat in the Dee Stakes over this course and distance last year, had run with promise on his reappearance at Newmarket and better was expected this time. He duly stepped up on his HQ run, but found the first two just that bit sharper, and a drop back to Listed company should help. (tchd 4-1 and 5-1 in a place)
Hattan(IRE), winner of a little conditions race at Ripon last time, was running here for the first time since he won the Chester Vase in 2005. Regularly held in Group company, he is a difficult horse to place off his rating. (op 7-1)

1601 ALEXANDER EVENTS H'CAP 5f 16y
2:20 (2:22) (Class 2) (0-100,100) 4-Y-O+ **£13,248** (£3,964; £1,982; £991; £493) **Stalls** Low

Form RPR

00-0 **1** **Caribbean Coral**[22] [1088] 8-8-4 **86** GrahamGibbons 6 96+
(J J Quinn) *stdd s: midfield: hdwy over 1f out: burst through gap to ld wl ins fnl f: r.o* **16/1**

03-0 **2** ½ **Corridor Creeper (FR)**[20] [1125] 10-8-6 **95** (p) BarrySavage(7) 7 103
(J M Bradley) *in tch: rdn whn swtchd rt over 1f out: led briefly ins fnl f: hld fnl strides* **16/1**

11-2 **3** ½ **Kay Two (IRE)**[15] [1242] 5-8-4 **86** KerrinMcEvoy 4 93
(R J Price) *lw: a.p: led briefly ins fnl f: nt qckn towards fin* **7/2**[2]

0000 **4** 1 ¼ **Tournedos (IRE)**[6] [1456] 5-9-4 **100** RichardHughes 13 102+
(D Nicholls) *midfield: pushed along and hdwy 2f out: nt qckn ent fnl f: styd on towards fin: nt pce of ldrs* **28/1**

-111 **5** ¾ **Turn On The Style**[82] 490 5-8-8 **93**..........................(b) AndrewElliott(3) 8 92+
(J Balding) *prom on outside: rdn and ev ch whn hung lft over 1f out: fdd ins fnl f* **8/1**

0/56 **6** *shd* **Bigalos Bandit**[6] 1456 5-8-8 **90**.................................... AdrianTNicholls 3 89
(D Nicholls) *led: rdn 2f out: hdd ins fnl f: fdd* **15/2**[3]

0-20 **7** *hd* **Dhaular Dhar (IRE)**[15] 1242 5-8-12 **94**........................ DanielTudhope 12 92+
(J S Goldie) *lw: bhd: hung lft over 1f out: styd on ins fnl f: nt pce to rch ldrs* **14/1**

60-2 **8** ½ **Mr Wolf**[17] 1195 6-8-10 **92** ow2......................................(p) DarryllHolland 1 88
(D W Barker) *prom: sn niggled along: rdn over 1f out: one pce ins fnl f* **5/2**[1]

0/4- **9** ½ **Overstayed (IRE)**[358] 1783 4-8-7 **89**.................................... ChrisCatlin 2 84
(I Semple) *racd keenly: hld up: carried hd awkwardly fr over 1f out: kpt on: nvr able to chal* **16/1**

0-50 **10** 2 **The Lord**[20] 1125 7-8-13 **95**.. AmirQuinn 9 82
(W G M Turner) *bmpd sltly sn after s: towards rr: rdn over 1f out: no imp fnl f* **33/1**

300- **11** 3½ **Mine Behind**[279] 4101 7-8-1 **86** oh1.......................... StephaneBreux(3) 14 61
(J R Best) *stdd s: sn swtchd lft: a bhd* **80/1**

-621 **12** 2½ **Cape Royal**[15] 1242 7-8-11 **93**..................................(bt) JamieSpencer 10 59
(J M Bradley) *s.s: a bhd: eased whn no ch ins fnl f* **11/1**

006- **13** 6 **Guto**[260] 4717 4-8-10 **92**.. NCallan 5 36
(K A Ryan) *s.i.s: chsd ldrs: rdn and hung rt over 2f out: sn wknd: eased whn btn over 1f out* **10/1**

59.94 secs (-2.11) **Going Correction** -0.175s/f (Firm) 13 Ran SP% **123.0**
Speed ratings (Par 109):109,108,107,105,104 104,103,102,102,98 93,89,79
CSF £253.58 CT £1114.35 TOTE £23.60: £5.00, £5.70, £1.60; EX 218.30 Trifecta £782.10 Pool: £1,542.32 - 1.40 winning tickets..
Owner Dawson And Quinn **Bred** P And C Scott **Trained** Settrington, N Yorks

FOCUS
A competitive handicap in which the leaders went off too fast and set it up for a closer. The winner is rated to last year's course form.

NOTEBOOK
Caribbean Coral, who won over this course and distance in September off a 3lb lower mark, had not shown much at Beverley on his seasonal reappearance, but that run had clearly put an edge on him, and he got a dream run through to pick up the pieces when the leaders hit the wall. He had a three-figure rating earlier in his career, so could still remain competitive after reassessment, but it has to be said that everything did fall right on this occasion. He heads for the Epsom Dash next, a race he won in 2004, and will have to race under a 4lb penalty there. (op 14-1)
Corridor Creeper(FR) may be in the veteran stage of his career, but he clearly retains plenty of speed, and he likes it around here, having run well on a number of occasions, including when successful back in 2002. He is on a mark he can win off and could well re-oppose the winner in the Dash at Epsom, a race in which he has finished sixth, third and seventh in the last three years.
Kay Two(IRE) did best of those who raced up with the strong pace from the start. He has returned this season in great form, continuing the improvement shown at the end of last year, and he remains on a mark he can win off. (op 3-1 tchd 4-1 in a place)
Tournedos(IRE), despite being drawn out wide, soon got into a nice position in midfield, off the scorching pace but within striking distance for a late swoop, but he was unable to pick up like the first two in the closing stages. He had won his previous two starts at this track, in the Listed Chester City Wall Stakes, and will no doubt return here to bid for a hat-trick of wins in that race in July. (op 25-1)
Turn On The Style, off the track since February but on a four-timer following a hat-trick of successes on the All-Weather, was one of those who helped set a fierce pace up front. It was not a great surprise to see him fail to get home, although he did not run badly in the circumstances. (tchd 9-1)
Bigalos Bandit, for whom there was some market support, had shaped with a bit of promise at Musselburgh last time when ridden patiently, but he was given an altogether different ride on this occasion, forcing things from the start. He showed good pace but was denied an uncontested lead and the result was that those at the head of affairs all cut each other's throats. (op 10-1)
Dhaular Dhar(IRE) has won over this trip, but that was on soft ground, and given that he has 7f-stamina it was always likely that he would find things happening too quickly this time. Drawn out wide, he stayed on late, and will be of more interest when stepped back up in trip. (tchd 16-1)
Mr Wolf ran well at Pontefract on his reappearance, but then he always runs well there - his record reads 1110112 at the Yorkshire track - and this represented a tougher test, as he was always going to find it harder dominating these speedier types around this sharp track. His rider putting up 2lb overweight was a surprise, but made no difference in the event. (op 10-3 tchd 7-2 and 4-1 in places)
Cape Royal, poorly drawn, came out of the stalls slowly and never got in a blow. His rider eased him down when he had no chance. Official explanation: jockey said gelding missed the break (op 12-1)
Guto Official explanation: jockey said gelding hung right

1602 MBNA CHESTER VASE (GROUP 3) (C&G) 1m 4f 66y
2:50 (2:50) (Class 1) 3-Y-O **£36,907** (£13,988; £7,000; £3,490) **Stalls** Low

Form RPR

2-1 **1** **Soldier Of Fortune (IRE)**[32] 963 3-9-2 .... MJKinane 1 111+
(A P O'Brien, Ire) *w'like: hld up bhd ldrs and racd keenly: clsd to take 2nd over 1f out: sn rdn: str chal ins fnl f: r.o to ld post* **4/9**[1]

0-1 **2** *shd* **Arabian Gulf**[22] 1093 3-8-12 95....................................... KerrinMcEvoy 3 107
(Sir Michael Stoute) *lw: chsd ldr: led over 2f out: rdn over 1f out: pressed ins fnl f: hdd post* **13/2**[3]

5-16 **3** 5 **Celestial Halo (IRE)**[12] 1306 3-8-12 98............................ MichaelHills 2 99
(B W Hills) *led: hdd over 2f out: rdn over 1f out: wknd ins fnl f* **14/1**

1-1 **4** 3 **Metaphoric (IRE)**[21] 1106 3-8-12 90.............................. JamieSpencer 4 97+
(M L W Bell) *lw: hld up bhd ldrs: rdn 3f out: no imp: eased whn btn wl ins fnl f* **4/1**[2]

2m 35.24s (-5.41) **Going Correction** -0.175s/f (Firm) 4 Ran SP% **109.3**
Speed ratings (Par 109):111,110,107,105
CSF £3.91 TOTE £1.50; EX 3.80.
Owner Mrs John Magnier **Bred** J S Bolger **Trained** Ballydoyle, Co Tipperary

FOCUS
A good performance from the winner to defy his penalty but the form looks a long way short of what will be required at Epsom, with the third setting the level.

NOTEBOOK
Soldier Of Fortune(IRE), who won the Group 2 Prix Noailles on his seasonal reappearance, had a 4lb penalty to carry and only just defied it. Keen in a fairly steadily-run race, it looked at one stage as though Arabian Gulf, who got first run on him, had stolen the race, but he wore him down late on and just got up on the line. This proved his stamina - his brother Heliostatic has found 1m2f to be his limit - but whether he is good enough for the Derby is open to question. A foreign Derby might be a better option, especially as his trainer seems to have a raft of other possibles for Epsom. (op 4-7 tchd 8-13 in a place)
Arabian Gulf is well bred and won a decent maiden at Newmarket at the Craven meeting, but this was a step up in class for him. He ran well, looking the likely winner until worn down late on, and appears likely to stay further in time. The King Edward VII at Royal Ascot looks a suitable short-term target, before the Voltigeur and St Leger later in the season. (op 4-1)
Celestial Halo(IRE), sixth in the Classic Trial at Sandown last time out, was allowed his own way in front and enjoyed the run of the race. He can have few excuses and looks likely to be difficult to place off his current mark. (op 12-1)
Metaphoric(IRE), previously unbeaten, had only won a handicap off 81 last time so had much more to do in this class. He looked to be found out by the rise in grade but should remain competitive back in handicap company off his current mark. (op 9-2 tchd 5-1 in a place)

1603 HALIFAX H'CAP 7f 122y
3:20 (3:23) (Class 2) (0-100,87) 3-Y-O **£13,248** (£3,964; £1,982; £991; £493) **Stalls** Low

Form RPR

113 **1** **Annemasse**[42] 815 3-9-3 **86**... J-PGuillambert 7 87+
(M Johnston) *trckd ldrs: rdn over 2f out: led ins fnl f: r.o* **4/1**[2]

6-1 **2** *nk* **Gulf Express (USA)**[19] 1166 3-9-1 **84**.......................... JamieSpencer 10 84+
(Sir Michael Stoute) *lw: s.i.s: hld up: rdn and hdwy over 1f out: r.o and gaining towards fin* **11/2**[3]

4026 **3** ½ **Copper King**[2] 1563 3-8-10 **79**.................................... StephenDonohoe 2 78
(P D Evans) *trckd ldrs: rdn and ev ch ins fnl f: nt qckn towards fin* **12/1**

0-00 **4** 1¼ **Dora Explora**[21] 1106 3-8-9 **78**... NCallan 3 74
(P D Evans) *midfield: rdn over 1f out: styd on same pce ins fnl f: nvr able to chal* **14/1**

01-5 **5** *shd* **Magic Mountain (IRE)**[13] 1276 3-9-4 **87**..................... RichardHughes 6 82
(R Hannon) *led: hdd over 5f out: remained prom: regained ld 2f out: sn rdn: hdd ins fnl f: one pce towards fin* **16/1**

40-4 **6** ½ **Chjimes (IRE)**[18] 1176 3-8-6 **75**.................................. FrancisNorton 9 69
(K R Burke) *dwlt: midfield: rdn over 1f out: no imp* **20/1**

31-0 **7** *hd* **Cool Box (USA)**[20] 1124 3-9-0 **83**................................. KerrinMcEvoy 1 77+
(Mrs A J Perrett) *lw: midfield: nt clr run over 1f out and ins fnl f: sn rdn briefly: nvr trbld ldrs* **7/2**[1]

5211 **8** *shd* **Proper (IRE)**[7] 1424 3-8-13 **82** 12ex....................................... ChrisCatlin 8 75
(M R Channon) *prom: led over 5f out: hdd 2f out: sn rdn: no ex ins fnl f* **14/1**

22-1 **9** 2 **Thabaat**[37] 901 3-9-0 **83**.. RHills 4 71
(B W Hills) *lw: fly-jmpd leaving stalls: hld up: nt clr run over 1f out and ins fnl f: sn eased* **4/1**[2]

1m 33.84s (-0.91) **Going Correction** -0.175s/f (Firm) 9 Ran SP% **109.3**
Speed ratings (Par 105):97,96,96,94,94 94,94,94,92
CSF £23.68 CT £206.24 TOTE £5.30: £1.80, £2.00, £3.60; EX 24.70 Trifecta £330.60 Pool: £651.92 - 1.40 winning tickets..
Owner Brian Yeardley Continental Ltd **Bred** Newsells Park Stud Limited **Trained** Middleham Moor, N Yorks

FOCUS
A fairly decent handicap but they finished in something of a heap and the form is limited by the proximity of the third and fourth.

NOTEBOOK
Annemasse had won two of his previous three starts, but those successes came on the All-Weather, and he had to prove that he would be as effective on turf. He responded well to pressure and looks a typically progressive animal from his stable. He should get a mile and the Britannia Handicap could be on the cards by the time Royal Ascot comes around. (op 11-2 tchd 6-1 in a place)
Gulf Express(USA) ◆ was not aided by the drop back in distance or his wide draw on his handicap debut. He was finishing strongly as the line approached but was never quite going to get there, and he will be suited by a return to a mile plus. He is another who has the ability to improve on his current mark. (op 9-2 tchd 6-1)
Copper King looked a lot more exposed than one or two in this field, but he was well drawn and was well placed throughout. It is probably wise to use his performance as a guide to the level of the form. (tchd 11-1)
Dora Explora, highly tried on a couple of occasions at two, has been given some slack by the Handicapper this spring and ran a better race. She seemed to appreciate the drop back in trip. (op 25-1)
Magic Mountain(IRE) looks to have started life in handicap company on a stiff enough mark, and he could do with being eased a little. (tchd 14-1)
Chjimes(IRE), who has not won since his debut over a year ago, has yet to convince that he stays this far. (op 18-1)
Cool Box(USA) did not get the clearest of runs but found little under pressure when he got to the inside in the straight anyway. This was a bit disappointing. (op 4-1 tchd 5-1 in a place)
Thabaat did not have much go her way and this run can probably be forgotten. Official explanation: jockey said colt was denied a clear run (op 3-1)

1604 SENIOR WRIGHT H'CAP 6f 18y
4:00 (4:02) (Class 3) (0-90,90) 3-Y-O **£10,363** (£3,083; £1,540; £769) **Stalls** Low

Form RPR

0-03 **1** **Heywood**[12] 1298 3-9-0 **86**... TPO'Shea 6 93
(M R Channon) *lw: midfield: pushed along and hdwy over 2f out: r.o ins fnl f to ld towards fin* **7/2**[1]

-421 **2** ½ **Sparkling Eyes**[14] 1270 3-8-5 **77**................................ KerrinMcEvoy 8 82
(C E Brittain) *trckd ldrs: rdn to ld over 1f out: hdd towards fin* **15/2**

-420 **3** 3 **Penny Post (IRE)**[33] 943 3-8-13 **85**............................ J-PGuillambert 1 81
(M Johnston) *broke wl: led early: chsd ldrs after: rdn over 1f out: kpt on ins fnl f* **13/2**[3]

P3-2 **4** *hd* **Dickie Le Davoir**[12] 1298 3-9-4 **90**................................... PatCosgrave 4 85
(K R Burke) *midfield: pushed along 3f out: styd on ins fnl f: nt pce of ldrs* **9/2**[2]

51-2 **5** ¾ **Mac Gille Eoin**[27] 1022 3-8-4 **76** oh4.................................... ChrisCatlin 5 69
(J Gallagher) *lw: prom: led over 4f out: rdn and hdd over 1f out: no ex ins fnl f* **8/1**

516- **6** 1½ **Yerevan**[242] 5207 3-8-4 **76** oh1.. FrancisNorton 3 65
(R T Phillips) *sn led: hdd over 4f out: remained prom: rdn over 1f out: wknd ins fnl f* **16/1**

15-1 **7** *shd* **Goodbye Cash (IRE)**[3] 1520 3-8-11 **83** 6ex............. StephenDonohoe 2 71
(P D Evans) *sn outpcd: nvr rchd ldrs* **9/2**[2]

42-5 **8** 2½ **Spoof Master (IRE)**[33] 943 3-9-0 **86**.................................. AmirQuinn 7 67
(W G M Turner) *w ldr: rdn over 1f out: sn wknd* **20/1**

002- **9** 15 **Espartano**[199] 6146 3-9-2 **88**.. JamieSpencer 9 24
(M J Wallace) *a bhd: eased whn n.d over 1f out* **8/1**

05-0 **10** 5 **Winning Spirit (IRE)**[19] 1160 3-8-4 **76**........................ AdrianTNicholls 10 —
(D Nicholls) *towards rr: pushed along over 2f out: last over 1f out* **20/1**

1m 14.0s (-1.65) **Going Correction** -0.175s/f (Firm) 10 Ran SP% **121.3**
Speed ratings (Par 103):104,103,99,99,98 96,95,92,72,65
CSF £31.65 CT £168.37 TOTE £5.30: £2.00, £1.80, £2.50; EX 39.90.
Owner Sheikh Mohammed **Bred** R F And S D Knipe **Trained** West Ilsley, Berks

FOCUS
A competitive little handicap and sound enough form rated around the second and third.

NOTEBOOK
Heywood showed he had the pace for 6f at Ripon last time, but the fact that he stays seven helped him wear down the eventual runner-up close home. He challenged widest of all around the bend into the straight, but that meant he kept his momentum and he looks the sort that will do well in decent, strongly-run handicaps over both this trip and 7f this season. (op 9-2 tchd 5-1 in a place)

Sparkling Eyes, who had to share the spoils at Yarmouth last time, looked set to notch another win when sent for home entering the straight, but she was eventually worn down by a stronger stayer close home. Clear of the third, she is in cracking form at present, and will not mind dropping back to 5f, as she is just as effective over that distance. (op 9-1 tchd 7-1)
Penny Post(IRE) was having her seventh career start but her first on turf. Well drawn in a good position throughout, she had every chance but came up short. (op 6-1 tchd 7-1)
Dickie Le Davoir, who finished one place in front of Heywood at Ripon on his seasonal reappearance, was unable to confirm that form on this very different track, but he was staying on at the finish and might need easier ground. (op 10-3)
Mac Gille Eoin, who ran well on his reappearance at Folkestone but had to race from 4lb out of the handicap, made much of the running but the task was too great in this class. He can do better in lower grade. (op 10-1)
Yerevan was racing from 1lb out of the handicap so was effectively racing off a career-high mark, and she was also making her seasonal reappearance against race-fit rivals. She should come on for the run.
Espartano Official explanation: jockey said saddle slipped
Winning Spirit(IRE) Official explanation: jockey said gelding had no more to give

1605 BOODLES DIAMOND MAIDEN STKS — 1m 2f 75y
4:35 (4:37) (Class 3) 3-Y-O — £7,124 (£2,119; £1,059; £529) Stalls High

Form — RPR
33-5 **1** **Al Tharib (USA)**[12] 1306 3-9-3 101 ... RHills 4 — 93+
(Sir Michael Stoute) *lw: mde all: rdn clr over 1f out: r.o wl* **2/1[1]**
6 **2** *3* **Heron Bay**[28] 1011 3-9-3 ... SteveDrowne 10 — 88+
(G Wragg) *lw: w'like: strong: midfield: pushed along to cl on ldng quartet over 3f out: styd on ins fnl f: tk 2nd fnl strides: nt trble wnr* **17/2**
6 **3** *shd* **Philatelist (USA)**[20] 1129 3-9-3 ... PhilipRobinson 1 — 88
(M A Jarvis) *trckd ldrs: rdn over 2f out: chsd wnr over 1f out but no imp: lost 2nd fnl strides* **11/2[3]**
-620 **4** *nk* **Putra Square**[12] 1293 3-9-3 92 ... (t) NCallan 6 — 87
(P F I Cole) *lw: trckd ldrs: rdn over 3f out: styd on and edgd lft ins fnl f: nt qckn fnl strides* **15/2**
2-5 **5** *4* **Urban Spirit**[22] 1093 3-9-3 ... RichardHughes 11 — 79
(B W Hills) *prom: rdn over 2f out: wknd ins fnl f* **5/2[2]**
6 *9* **Tri Chara (IRE)** 3-9-3 ... GrahamGibbons 3 — 62
(R Hollinshead) *lw: s.i.s: racd keenly: hld up: pushed along and hdwy into midfield 4f out: nvr on terms w ldrs* **25/1**
7 *3/4* **Martinet (IRE)** 3-9-3 ... (t) StephenDonohoe 9 — 61
(P D Evans) *w'like: unf: stdd s: hld up: rdn over 3f out: nvr on terms* **66/1**
5-60 **8** *4* **Seteem (USA)**[14] 1256 3-9-3 65 ... AdrianTNicholls 8 — 53
(N Tinkler) *stdd s: racd keenly: hld up: n.d* **100/1**
9 *5* **New Star (UAE)** 3-9-3 ... ChrisCatlin 2 — 44
(W M Brisbourne) *w'like: midfield: pushed along and outpcd over 5f out* **16/1**
02 **10** *16* **Phreeze**[18] 1177 3-9-3 ... JamieSpencer 5 — 13
(G A Swinbank) *hmpd sn after s: hdwy into midfield after 2f: rdn and lost pl over 6f out: n.d after* **14/1**
11 *1* **Van Ruymbeke (IRE)** 3-9-3 ... MJKinane 7 — 11
(T J Pitt) *b.bkwd: racd keenly: hld up: rdn over 4f out: nvr on terms* **16/1**

2m 10.44s (-2.70) **Going Correction** -0.175s/f (Firm) — **11 Ran SP% 124.3**
Speed ratings (Par 103):103,100,100,100,97 89,89,86,82,69 68
CSF £21.57 TOTE £2.90: £1.30, £2.50, £2.30; EX 25.20 Place 6 £60.88, Place 5 £41.78.
Owner Hamdan Al Maktoum **Bred** Phillips Racing Partnership **Trained** Newmarket, Suffolk

FOCUS
A strong maiden and solid form rated around the fourth. A race which should produce winners.

NOTEBOOK
Al Tharib(USA), who had solid maiden form at two and had finished fifth in the Sandown Classic Trial, looked to hold a strong chance back in this company, but the market turned against him and he drifted badly beforehand. He was always in control in the race itself though, making every yard and going on to win in good style, and could be another from the stable that could go for the King Edward VII at Royal Ascot. (op 11-8 tchd 9-4)
Heron Bay ran with promise on his debut at Leicester and improved on that to chase home a more experienced and already proven smart performer. He looks very useful in his own right and should have no problem going one better soon, possibly over another two furlongs. (op 14-1)
Philatelist(USA) did not run badly at Newbury on his debut and was another to build on that intial promise. He can also win his maiden and has the makings of a decent handicapper in time. (op 15-2)
Putra Square disappointed at Leicester last time but had a breathing problem that day and a tongue tie was fitted for the first time. He has an official rating of 92 and it is difficult to say he ran a million miles away from that mark in defeat, as this was a strong maiden. He can win a maiden but might struggle in handicap company unless the Handicapper cuts him some slack. (op 10-1)
Urban Spirit finished four lengths behind Putra Square on his seasonal reappearance at Newmarket, and the betting suggested that plenty of people thought he would reverse the form with that run under his belt, but the margin between the two ended up the same again. He should make a useful handicapper. (tchd 9-4 and 11-4)
Tri Chara(IRE), whose dam is a half-sister to high-class middle distance performer Ebaziya, dam of Irish Oaks winner Ebadiyla, top-class stayer Enzeli, and top-class juvenile Edabiya, was beaten a long way, but this was a strong maiden in which to make his debut and he can improve for the run. (op 100-1)
Martinet(IRE) Official explanation: trainer said gelding ran without the declared tongue-strap because it had become adrift at the start and could not be re-fitted
T/Jkpt: £6,472.60 to a £1 stake. Pool: £72,931.50. 8.00 winning tickets. T/Plt: £47.00 to a £1 stake. Pool: £132,776.55. 2,061.90 winning tickets. T/Qpdt: £11.10 to a £1 stake. Pool: £4,836.30. 320.90 winning tickets. DO

1464 GOODWOOD (R-H)
Thursday, May 10

OFFICIAL GOING: Good
Wind: Moderate, half-against Weather: Overcast with heavy mist Races 5-6

1606 TURF TV MAIDEN STKS — 1m
2:10 (2:11) (Class 5) 3-Y-O+ — £3,238 (£963; £481; £240) Stalls High

Form — RPR
6 **1** **Pipedreamer**[19] 1143 3-9-0 ... JimmyFortune 6 — 85+
(J H M Gosden) *prom: trckd ldr 1/2-way: rdn to ld wl over 1f out: wandered after: nrly jnd ins fnl f: hld on wl* **4/6[1]**
24-0 **2** *nk* **Murbek (IRE)**[22] 1093 3-9-0 84 ... MartinDwyer 7 — 78
(M A Jarvis) *lw: settled in last trio and wl off the pce: gd prog on outer fr over 2f out: nrly jnd wnr last 100yds: no ex* **11/2[2]**
5- **3** *3* **Run For Ede'S**[236] 5380 3-8-9 ... IanMongan 3 — 66
(P M Phelan) *w'like: t.k.h: trckd ldrs: effrt over 2f out: kpt on to take 3rd ins fnl f* **66/1**
4 *1 1/4* **Elegant Hawk** 3-8-9 ... JimmyQuinn 5 — 63+
(W J Knight) *athletic: settled wl in rr: shkn up 2f out: styd on wl fr over 1f out: nrst fin* **66/1**
342 **5** *hd* **Esteem Machine (USA)**[41] 826 3-8-11 74 ... MarcHalford(3) 11 — 68
(D R C Elsworth) *lw: racd freely and hanging lft: led to wl over 1f out: wknd fnl f* **11/1**
0- **6** *2 1/2* **Seeking The Buck (USA)**[272] 4333 3-9-0 ... EddieAhern 1 — 62
(M A Magnusson) *t.k.h: trckd ldr to 1/2-way: steadily fdd fnl 2f* **50/1**
04- **7** *nk* **Effigy**[187] 6331 3-9-0 ... FergusSweeney 12 — 61
(H Candy) *b.bkwd: t.k.h early: trckd ldrs: shkn up over 2f out: no prog: fdd fnl f* **25/1**
2 **8** *1* **Golden Platitude (IRE)**[16] 1215 4-9-13 ... AdamKirby 8 — 59
(W R Swinburn) *w'like: hld up in midfield: hanging rt fr 3f out: no prog* **12/1**
6-0 **9** *4* **Sweet Request**[19] 1143 3-8-9 ... SebSanders 9 — 45
(R M Beckett) *a towards rr: pushed along and struggling 3f out* **50/1**
0 **10** *1 1/2* **Fraamtastic Too**[80] 498 3-8-9 ... SimonWhitworth 2 — 41
(Jamie Poulton) *t.k.h: hld up in midfield: wknd over 2f out* **100/1**
11 *nk* **Shirley A Star (USA)** 3-8-9 ... TPQueally 4 — 41
(B J Meehan) *unf: b.bkwd: dwlt: rn green in last: nvr a factor* **10/1[3]**
0 **12** *3/4* **Luna Danza**[20] 1128 3-8-9 ... TedDurcan 10 — 39
(B J Meehan) *s.i.s: sn in midfield: wknd over 2f out* **66/1**
13 *1 1/4* **Novikov** 3-9-0 ... RobertHavlin 13 — 41
(J H M Gosden) *w'like: b.bkwd: s.v.s: a wl in rr* **20/1**

1m 40.69s (0.42) **Going Correction** +0.15s/f (Good)
WFA 3 from 4yo 13lb — **13 Ran SP% 118.5**
Speed ratings (Par 103):103,102,99,98,98 95,95,94,90,88 88,87,86
CSF £3.95 TOTE £1.70: £1.10, £1.60, £10.20; EX 5.00.
Owner Cheveley Park Stud **Bred** Cheveley Park Stud Ltd **Trained** Newmarket, Suffolk

FOCUS
This looked like quite a good maiden, and the form, although limited, makes some sense and it should certainly produce some winners. The winning time was 0.40 seconds slower than the later handicap won by 77-rated Lacework.

1607 TURFTV.CO.UK STKS (H'CAP) — 6f
2:40 (2:41) (Class 4) (0-80,79) 4-Y-O+ — £6,477 (£1,927; £963; £481) Stalls Low

Form — RPR
4351 **1** **Who's Winning (IRE)**[7] 1431 6-8-12 76 6ex ... RichardKingscote(3) 2 — 83
(B G Powell) *trckd ldr: shkn up to ld over 1f out: rdn and a holding on fnl f* **9/1**
011- **2** *1/2* **The Cayterers**[233] 5453 5-8-6 74 ... LukeMorris(7) 9 — 80
(J M Bradley) *lw: chsd ldrs: rdn and clsd 2f out: chsd wnr fnl f: styd on but nvr really able to chal* **7/1[3]**
0-40 **3** *1/2* **Peter Island (FR)**[10] 1357 4-9-4 79 ... JimCrowley 4 — 83
(J Gallagher) *rrd s: chsd ldrs: rdn 2f out: styd on ins fnl f: nvr able to chal* **25/1**
0-02 **4** *nk* **Shes Minnie**[3] 1525 4-8-11 72 ... RobertHavlin 1 — 75
(J G M O'Shea) *settled in rr: pushed along over 2f out: no prog tl styd on wl last 150yds: nrst fin* **12/1**
-005 **5** *1 1/2* **Gavarnie Beau (IRE)**[15] 1252 4-8-13 74 ... TedDurcan 5 — 73
(M Blanshard) *chsd ldng pair: rdn over 2f out: fdd fnl f* **8/1**
000- **6** *hd* **Calabaza**[197] 6174 5-8-4 65 oh3 ... (b) DavidKinsella 3 — 63
(W Jarvis) *led to over 1f out: wknd fnl f* **25/1**
3023 **7** *3/4* **Marko Jadeo (IRE)**[5] 1465 9-8-6 72 ... TolleyDean(5) 10 — 68
(R A Harris) *dwlt: racd on outer and hld up: prog over 2f out: no imp over 1f out: wknd* **9/1**
2630 **8** *shd* **Figaro Flyer (IRE)**[10] 1357 4-9-4 79 ... IanMongan 7 — 74
(P Howling) *hld up in last: shuffled along fnl 2f: nvr nr ldrs* **12/1**
6-42 **9** *3 1/2* **River Kirov (IRE)**[10] 1357 4-9-2 77 ... JimmyFortune 8 — 62
(P W Chapple-Hyam) *lw: dwlt: a in rr: rdn and no prog 2f out: moving bdly and wknd ins fnl f* **15/8[1]**
5-36 **10** *1 3/4* **Small Stakes (IRE)**[66] 614 5-8-8 69 ow1 ... (vt) SebSanders 6 — 49
(P J Makin) *nvr gng wl: a in last trio: struggling over 2f out* **9/2[2]**

1m 11.93s (-0.92) **Going Correction** -0.025s/f (Good) — **10 Ran SP% 119.7**
Speed ratings (Par 105):105,104,103,103,101 101,100,99,95,92
CSF £72.48 CT £1556.49 TOTE £11.60: £2.60, £2.60, £7.20; EX 54.80.
Owner Tony Head and Caroline Andrus **Bred** Colin Kennedy **Trained** Lambourn, Berks

FOCUS
The front two in the betting flopped and this was just a fair sprint handicap. They all raced stands' side, but avoided the rail for the first five furlongs.
River Kirov(IRE) Official explanation: jockey said gelding hung left
Small Stakes(IRE) Official explanation: trainer said gelding never travelled

1608 TURF TV AUBIGNY STKS (LISTED RACE) — 5f
3:10 (3:12) (Class 1) 2-Y-O — £12,491 (£4,734; £2,369; £1,181; £591) Stalls Low

Form — RPR
1 **1** **Spirit Of Sharjah (IRE)**[22] 1094 2-9-3 ... JimmyFortune 5 — 94+
(Miss J Feilden) *hld up bhd ldrs gng wl: shkn up to ld jst over 1f out: sn in command: readily* **4/7[1]**
0136 **2** *2 1/2* **Baytown Blaze**[1] 1580 2-8-9 ... HayleyTurner 4 — 76
(P S McEntee) *pressed ldr: rdn and hanging rt fr 2f out: chsd wnr fnl f: no ch* **40/1**
0 **3** *1 1/4* **Romany Princess (IRE)**[21] 1101 2-8-9 ... MartinDwyer 1 — 71
(R Hannon) *lw: s.i.s: outpcd in last after 2f: styd on against nr side rail fnl f: nrst fin* **20/1**
01 **4** *nk* **Affirmatively**[10] 1354 2-8-9 ... JohnEgan 2 — 70
(D R C Elsworth) *lw: chsd ldrs: rdn 1/2-way: outpcd over 1f out: n.d after* **13/2[3]**
221 **5** *nk* **Ten Down**[3] 1540 2-9-0 ... TPQueally 6 — 74+
(J A Osborne) *led: hanging bdly rt fr 1/2-way: hdd & wknd jst over 1f out* **3/1[2]**

59.81 secs (0.76) **Going Correction** -0.025s/f (Good) — **5 Ran SP% 109.2**
Speed ratings (Par 101):92,88,86,85,85
CSF £22.95 TOTE £1.50: £1.10, £5.20; EX 20.40.
Owner A Dee **Bred** Mrs Kathleen Reynolds **Trained** Exning, Suffolk

FOCUS
No strength in depth, but a very useful winner in the form of Spirit Of Sharjah, who is value for further, with the runner-up setting the level.

NOTEBOOK

Spirit Of Sharjah(IRE) ◆ was the clear form pick judged on his impressive win in a good conditions event at Newmarket on his debut and duly followed up. He did not have much to beat, but there was plenty to like about the manner of his success as, having raced keenly, he was carried out towards the centre of the track by Ten Down, and then drifted back to his left once in the clear, still showing distinct signs of greenness. However, it will have to be hoped he can mature in the right manner, as he very nearly got rid of his rider when veering out at the entrance to the course after the line, and has already displayed a tendency to race keenly. Provided he does go the right way mentally, his connections look to have a serious sprint prospect on their hands and the plan is apparently to go for the Norfolk Stakes at Royal Ascot, That makes sense because he is all speed and he must go there with a big chance. (op 8-13 tchd 4-6 in places)

Baytown Blaze ran a fine race in second turned out just a day after running down the field in the Lily Agnes, picking up some valuable black type. She is clearly very tough and will no doubt be campaigned hard. (op 33-1)

Romany Princess(IRE), down the field in a good fillies' maiden on her debut at Newmarket, struggled to go the frantic early pace but gradually got the hang of things and kept on for third. Her connections will be delighted she has managed to pick up some black type so early in her career, but the sensible option would be for her return to maiden company next time. (tchd 25-1)

Affirmatively failed to build on the form she showed when winning an ordinary maiden at Windsor on her debut. (tchd 7-1)

Ten Down tried to burn off his field, just as he had when winning his maiden at Windsor three days earlier, but he blew his chance by hanging right when seriously challenged. Official explanation: jockey said gelding hung right (tchd 11-4 and 10-3 in a place)

1609 TURF TV BETTING SHOP SERVICE STKS (H'CAP) 1m 3f
3:45 (3:47) (Class 5) (0-70,70) 4-Y-O+ **£4,857** (£1,445; £722; £360) **Stalls** Low

Form				RPR
2-61	**1**		**Royal Premier (IRE)**[31] [982] 4-8-10 **64**.........................(v) SebSanders 7 (H J Collingridge) *trckd ldrs: wnt 2nd 3f out: rdn to ld 2f out: kpt on wl u.p fnl f* **4/1**[2]	73
60-0	**2**	½	**Imperial Harry**[5] [1470] 4-9-0 **68**.......................... MickyFenton 8 (V Smith) *hld up wl in rr: prog fr 4f out: drvn 2f out: chsd wnr 1f out: kpt on but a hld* **40/1**	76
00-0	**3**	2½	**Bob's Your Uncle**[31] [976] 4-8-0 **57**............................ EmmettStack(3) 2 (J G Portman) *racd on outer in midfield: prog over 3f out: tried to chal over 1f out: wknd ins fnl f* **20/1**	61
-010	**4**	nk	**Double Spectre (IRE)**[12] [1295] 5-8-13 **67**...................... MartinDwyer 6 (Jean-Rene Auvray) *led: drvn and hdd 2f out: styd pressing ldrs tl wknd jst ins fnl f* **12/1**	70
-002	**5**	1	**Faversham**[12] [1301] 4-8-9 **63**.......................... DO'Donohoe 10 (M Wigham) *prom: chsd ldr 6f out to 3f out: tried to rally over 1f out: wknd fnl f* **14/1**	64
30-4	**6**	nk	**Theatre Royal**[12] [1295] 4-8-8 **62**.......................... TPQueally 14 (Mouse Hamilton-Fairley) *settled in midfield: rdn to chse ldrs over 2f out: one pce and no imp wl over 1f out* **16/1**	63
532-	**7**	4	**Cormorant Wharf (IRE)**[178] [6462] 7-9-0 **68**...................... JohnEgan 12 (T E Powell) *b.bkwd: hld up wl in rr: prog on outer 3f out: nt on terms and hanging rt fnl 2f* **12/1**	62
10/	**8**	1	**Moon Star (GER)**[18] 6-8-11 **65**.......................... JimmyFortune 13 (A M Hales) *towards rr: rdn 7f out: u.p and struggling over 3f out: kpt on fnl 2f* **5/1**[3]	57
-001	**9**	1½	**Garrulous (UAE)**[10] [1347] 4-8-6 **60**.......................... FergusSweeney 3 (G L Moore) *lw: trckd ldrs: rdn 3f out: wknd 2f out* **7/2**[1]	50
0040	**10**	2½	**Makai**[15] [1249] 4-7-13 **56** oh4.......................... LiamJones(3) 5 (J J Bridger) *a towards rr: n.m.r 4f out: sn rdn and struggling: hung rt fnl 2f* **33/1**	41
000-	**11**	3	**Klassen (USA)**[276] [4210] 4-8-3 **57**.......................... DavidKinsella 4 (A King) *dwlt: racd on outer in midfield: rdn and wknd over 2f out* **33/1**	37
001-	**12**	26	**Alekhine (IRE)**[190] [6289] 6-8-13 **67**..........................(p) EddieAhern 11 (J R Boyle) *b.bkwd: nvr bttr than midfield: wknd wl over 2f out: t.o* **9/1**	3
320-	**13**	4	**And I**[295] [3646] 4-9-2 **70**..........................(b[1]) GeorgeBaker 16 (C A Horgan) *t.k.h: hld up in last: lost tch 4f out: t.o* **33/1**	—
4166	**14**	3	**Velvet Valley (USA)**[18] [1181] 4-9-0 **68**..........................(b[1]) SamHitchcott 9 (C E Longsdon) *t.k.h: trckd ldrs tl wknd over 3f out: t.o* **16/1**	—
525	**15**	90	**Santaverti**[39] [869] 4-8-2 **56**.......................... JimmyQuinn 1 (G L Moore) *chsd ldr to 6f out: wknd v rapidly: sn wl t.o* **20/1**	—

2m 28.28s (1.07) **Going Correction** +0.15s/f (Good) **15** Ran SP% **123.5**

Speed ratings (Par 103):102,101,99,99,98 98,95,95,93,92 89,71,68,65,—

CSF £174.93 CT £2910.86 TOTE £5.50: £1.90, £15.00, £5.60; EX 346.30.

Owner Maynard Durrant Partnership I **Bred** Mrs Anne Hughes **Trained** Exning, Suffolk

■ Stewards' Enquiry : Martin Dwyer four-day ban: improper riding (May 21-24)

FOCUS

A modest handicap, run at a fair pace and the form looks ordinary. The first two came clear.

And I Official explanation: jockey said filly suffered interference in running

Santaverti Official explanation: jockey said gelding pulled itself up

1610 TURF TV FILLIES' H'CAP 1m
4:20 (4:22) (Class 4) (0-85,83) 3-Y-O **£6,477** (£1,927; £963; £481) **Stalls** High

Form				RPR
21-0	**1**		**Lacework**[17] [1202] 3-8-12 **77**.......................... JohnEgan 10 (Sir Michael Stoute) *lw: 8th and pushed along 1/2-way: r.o to ld last 100yds: sn clr* **7/2**[1]	85+
21-5	**2**	1¾	**Colchium (IRE)**[23] [1076] 3-8-7 **72**.......................... RobertHavlin 6 (H Morrison) *cl 6th 1/2-way: in ld ins fnl f: sn hdd and outpcd* **12/1**	76
531-	**3**	½	**Diamond Diva**[205] [6031] 3-9-4 **83**.......................... EddieAhern 3 (J W Hills) *lw: 9th and wl in tch 1/2-way: cl 4th ins fnl f: styd on same pce* **11/2**[2]	86
0315	**4**	¾	**Musical Beat**[15] [1247] 3-8-12 **77**.......................... MickyFenton 9 (Miss V Haigh) *cl 4th 1/2-way: 5th and outpcd ins fnl f: kpt on* **17/2**	78
1-	**5**	nk	**Les Fazzani (IRE)**[157] [6697] 3-9-1 **80**.......................... DO'Donohoe 1 (M J Wallace) *hld up in last 1/2-way: 6th and running on ins fnl f: nrst fin* **12/1**	80+
21-1	**6**	shd	**Malyana**[15] [1247] 3-9-0 **79**.......................... MatthewHenry 2 (M A Jarvis) *lw: cl 3rd 1/2-way: cl 3rd ins fnl f: wknd* **11/2**[2]	79
1-60	**7**	2½	**Lakshmi (IRE)**[8] [1407] 3-9-3 **82**.......................... JHBowman 5 (M R Channon) *hld up in 11th 1/2-way: nt on terms ins fnl f* **50/1**	76
130-	**8**	1¼	**Veenwouden**[223] [5655] 3-8-12 **77**.......................... AdamKirby 7 (J R Fanshawe) *hld up in 10th 1/2-way: nt on terms ins fnl f* **10/1**	69
23-1	**9**	½	**Nadawat (USA)**[26] [1045] 3-8-13 **78**.......................... MartinDwyer 11 (J L Dunlop) *cl 5th 1/2-way: nt on terms ins fnl f* **6/1**[3]	68
240-	**10**	9	**Tarkamara (IRE)**[323] [2743] 3-9-1 **80**.......................... JimmyFortune 12 (P F I Cole) *b.bkwd: in ld 1/2-way: wl bhd ins fnl f* **16/1**	50
50-6	**11**	1¼	**La Roca (IRE)**[23] [1076] 3-9-4 **83**..........................(t) SebSanders 4 (R M Beckett) *pressing ldr 1/2-way: wl bhd ins fnl f* **16/1**	50
501-	**12**	11	**Miss Ippolita**[226] [5592] 3-9-1 **80**.......................... TedDurcan 8 (J R Jenkins) *7th and wl in tch 1/2-way: t.o ins fnl f* **33/1**	22

1m 40.29s (0.02) **Going Correction** +0.15s/f (Good) **12** Ran SP% **118.9**

Speed ratings (Par 98):105,103,102,102,101 101,99,97,97,88 87,76

CSF £47.70 CT £233.68 TOTE £3.30: £1.70, £4.70, £2.40; EX 63.20.

Owner Cheveley Park Stud **Bred** Cheveley Park Stud Ltd **Trained** Newmarket, Suffolk

FOCUS

A good fillies' handicap during which the thick mist meant the runners were not visible for most of the race. The winning time was 0.40 seconds quicker than the opening maiden and the form, rated through the runner-up, does look sound.

1611 GET TURF TV IN YOUR BETTING SHOP MAIDEN STKS 1m 4f
4:55 (4:55) (Class 5) 3-Y-O **£3,238** (£963; £481; £240) **Stalls** Low

Form				RPR
3	**1**		**Manbar (USA)**[12] [1296] 3-9-3.......................... MartinDwyer 5 (Sir Michael Stoute) *w'like: mde all: rdn and pressed 2f out: rn green but styd on strly* **10/11**[1]	85+
2325	**2**	3½	**Sowdrey**[12] [1290] 3-9-3 73.......................... JHBowman 4 (M R Channon) *hld up in last: rdn and prog on outer to chse wnr over 2f out: sn chalng: wl hld over 1f out* **7/4**[2]	73
00-5	**3**	4	**I Predict A Riot (IRE)**[24] [1062] 3-9-3 70.......................... EddieAhern 1 (J W Hills) *hld up: prog to trck wnr 1/2-way: rdn 3f out: sn lost 2nd and btn* **8/1**[3]	67
0-0	**4**	2½	**Elusory**[28] [1011] 3-9-3.......................... SebSanders 2 (J L Dunlop) *trckd wnr to 1/2-way: rdn over 3f out: sn struggling* **14/1**	63
0-4	**5**	7	**Snow Ballerina**[10] [1364] 3-8-12.......................... DO'Donohoe 3 (E A L Dunlop) *in tch: rdn over 3f out: sn struggling* **14/1**	56

2m 44.01s (5.09) **Going Correction** +0.15s/f (Good) **5** Ran SP% **113.2**

Speed ratings (Par 99):89,86,84,82,81

CSF £2.86 TOTE £1.50: £1.10, £1.70; EX 3.40.

Owner Hamdan Al Maktoum **Bred** Domino Stud Of Lexington Llc **Trained** Newmarket, Suffolk

FOCUS

A fair little three-year-old maiden. The winner is value for a little further and the form looks sound rated through the runner-up and third.

1612 TURF TV FOR YOUR BETTING SHOP STKS (H'CAP) 1m 1f
5:30 (5:30) (Class 6) (0-65,63) 4-Y-O+

£2,679 (£802; £401; £200; £100; £50) **Stalls** High

Form				RPR
20-0	**1**		**Logsdail**[37] [902] 7-9-4 **63**..........................(p) GeorgeBaker 14 (G L Moore) *trckd ldrs: smooth prog over 2f out: narrow ld over 1f out: r.o and hld on wl fnl f* **6/1**	75+
0-42	**2**	shd	**Murrumbidgee (IRE)**[3] [1539] 4-8-8 **58**.......................... PatrickHills(5) 3 (J W Hills) *hld up in midfield: prog on outer over 2f out: rdn to chal over 1f out: pressed wnr fnl f: r.o: jst hld* **7/2**[1]	69
5502	**3**	3	**Revolve**[3] [1521] 7-8-13 **58**..........................(b) IanMongan 9 (Mrs L J Mongan) *mostly trckd ldr: rdn to chal 2f out: upsides over 1f out: nt qckn fnl f* **9/2**[2]	63
1024	**4**	¾	**Postmaster**[27] [1025] 5-8-7 **52**.......................... RobertHavlin 7 (R Ingram) *hld up in midfield: effrt over 2f out: nt pce to rch ldrs fr over 1f out* **7/1**	55
0000	**5**	3½	**Napoletano (GER)**[4] [1507] 6-8-9 **54**.......................... JimmyQuinn 5 (S Dow) *sn rel ldr: 2l clr 3f out: hdd over 1f out: hanging and wknd fnl f* **8/1**	50
3223	**6**	1	**Magic Warrior**[26] [1036] 7-8-12 **57**.......................... PatDobbs 1 (J C Fox) *hld up: last 4f out: effrt over 2f out: sn outpcd and btn: plugged on* **5/1**[3]	51
0003	**7**	4	**Christmas Truce (IRE)**[11] [1318] 8-8-2 **50**..........................(b) MarcHalford(3) 12 (J J Bridger) *dwlt: hld up in rr: effrt on outer 3f out: edgd rt and no imp fnl 2f* **16/1**	36
41-0	**8**	2	**Megalala (IRE)**[8] [1400] 6-8-7 **52**.......................... FrankieMcDonald 11 (J J Bridger) *plld hrd: restrained fr prom pl: dropped to rr 1/2-way: effrt on inner 3f out: no prog 2f out* **33/1**	33
060-	**9**	5	**Mixing**[190] [6300] 5-8-5 **50**.......................... DavidKinsella 4 (W Jarvis) *a wl in rr: no prog and btn 3f out* **10/1**	21
4330	**10**	½	**Simpsons Gamble (IRE)**[8] [1400] 4-8-5 **50**..........................(b) AdrianMcCarthy 13 (R M Flower) *plld hrd: hld up in midfield: wknd 3f out* **25/1**	20
/00-	**11**	13	**Salisbury Plain**[358] [1772] 6-9-1 **60**.......................... EddieAhern 2 (N I M Rossiter) *disp 2nd pl to over 3f out: sn wknd: t.o* **40/1**	3

1m 58.08s (1.22) **Going Correction** +0.15s/f (Good) **11** Ran SP% **119.2**

Speed ratings (Par 101):100,99,97,96,93 92,89,87,82,82 70

CSF £27.22 CT £107.76 TOTE £8.00: £2.00, £1.60, £2.10; EX 29.60 Place 6 £62.42, Place 5 £49.27.

Owner D T L Limited **Bred** Stetchworth Park Stud Ltd **Trained** Woodingdean, E Sussex

FOCUS

A moderate handicap that was run at a sedate early pace. The first two came clear and the form appears ordinary but sound, rated around those in the frame behind the winner.

Megalala(IRE) Official explanation: jockey said gelding ran too free

T/Plt: £132.80 to a £1 stake. Pool: £58,377.05. 320.70 winning tickets. T/Qpdt: £18.20 to a £1 stake. Pool: £2,744.90. 111.50 winning tickets. JN

1613 - 1615a (Foreign Racing) - See Raceform Interactive

1600 CHESTER (L-H)
Friday, May 11

OFFICIAL GOING: Good

Wind: Fresh, across Weather: Rain from race 3

1616 EDWARDS HOMES H'CAP 5f 16y
1:50 (1:50) (Class 2) (0-100,100) 3-Y-O **£13,248** (£3,964; £1,982; £991; £493) **Stalls** Low

Form				RPR
045-	**1**		**City Of Tribes (IRE)**[29] [1015] 3-9-5 **98**.......................... EddieAhern 3 (G M Lyons, Ire) *lw: hld up: hdwy over 1f out: rdn and str run on rail ins fnl f: led post* **9/2**[2]	102
0-12	**2**	shd	**Morinqua (IRE)**[13] [1286] 3-8-2 **81**.......................... JamieMackay 6 (J G Given) *sn led: rdn over 1f out: edgd lft ins fnl f: ct post* **9/2**[2]	85
2-02	**3**	1	**Foxy Music**[20] [1161] 3-8-2 **81** oh22.......................... MatthewHenry 1 (E J Alston) *racd keenly: a.p: rdn over 1f out: swtchd rt ins fnl f: nt qckn towards fin* **16/1**	81
511-	**4**	½	**Luscivious**[209] [5956] 3-8-12 **91**..........................(b) StephenDonohoe 2 (A J McCabe) *hld up in rr: rdn and hdwy over 1f out: swtchd rt ins fnl f: sn forced wd: r.o towards fin* **9/2**[2]	90+
2-16	**5**	¾	**Gower**[34] [943] 3-8-3 **82**.......................... JimmyQuinn 7 (R Charlton) *hld up: rdn 2f out: swtchd rt over 1f out: styd on wl fnl f: nrst fin* **8/1**	78

2411 **6** *1 ¼* **Daddy Cool**[20] [1160] 3-7-13 **81**.. LiamJones(3) 8 72
(W G M Turner) *lw: prom: rdn over 1f out: edgd rt whn no ex ins fnl f* **7/1**[3]
13-3 **7** *2* **Steelcut**[20] [1160] 3-8-10 **89**.. PaulHanagan 5 73
(R A Fahey) *chsd ldrs: pushed along 2f out: wknd 1f out* **7/2**[1]
121- **8** *1 ¾* **Yungaburra (IRE)**[156] [6732] 3-9-7 **100**.........................(b[1]) FrancisNorton 4 78
(T J Pitt) *lw: chsd ldrs: rdn 2f out: wknd 1f out: eased whn btn ins fnl f* **8/1**

60.70 secs (-1.35) **Going Correction** -0.025s/f (Good) **8** Ran SP% **117.4**
Speed ratings (Par 105):109,108,107,106,105 103,100,97
CSF £25.78 CT £301.93 TOTE £5.80: £2.00, £2.10, £2.20; EX 35.10 Trifecta £266.80 Pool: £714.02 - 1.90 winning tickets..
Owner Glenview House Stud & Shane Connolly **Bred** Mrs Mary Coonan **Trained** Dunsany, Co. Meath

■ The first winner as a trainer in Britain for former jump jockey Ger Lyons.

FOCUS
A decent sprint handicap rated through the runner-up and the performance of the well-drawn third from a long way out of the handicap should not reduce the level of the form.

NOTEBOOK
City Of Tribes(IRE), an Irish raider contesting a handicap for the first time, got a great run through on the inside in the straight and stayed on strongly to win for the first time since his debut at two at Tipperary. He was fairly highly tried after that initial win and this success will inevitably push his rating up to three figures, which means he may have to take his chance in Listed company again. Life will be more difficult in that company. (op 6-1)
Morinqua(IRE) has plenty of pace and she was able to cross over from her average draw to get to the front and try and make all. She almost did so, but was just worn down on the line. She clearly remains progressive and must be kept in mind when it is likely that she will get her own way in front. (op 11-2)
Foxy Music was only plating class on Polytrack so when he ran the 81-rated Jack Rackham to a neck in a maiden at Thirsk on his turf debut most people quite reasonably wrote it off as a fluke. However, this performance from 22lb out of the handicap, albeit from the best draw, suggests that he is either a much better horse on turf than on sand and/or he has improved out of all recognition for a change of stable. He has clearly blown a good mark here though, and connections will probably be searching for an opportunity in the coming days for him to race off his current rating. (tchd 14-1)
Luscivious, who did not look right in his coat, ideally wants softer ground than this, but he still ran a very solid race on what was his seasonal reappearance. Despite being on a mark 10lb higher than when last successful, he could still be improving. (op 7-2)
Gower tried to stay on late down the outside but was rather one paced. He will appreciate a step back up to 6f. (op 10-1)
Daddy Cool, chasing a hat-trick, had the worst of the draw and found his 5lb higher mark holding him back.
Steelcut, who shaped with promise at Thirsk on his reappearance, might not have been at home around this unique track. (tchd 4-1)

1617 AKTIV KAPITAL UK LTD DEE STKS (GROUP 3) (C&G) 1m 2f 75y
2:20 (2:20) (Class 1) 3-Y-O
£36,907 (£13,988; £7,000; £3,490; £1,748; £877) **Stalls** High

Form RPR
31-0 **1** **Admiralofthefleet (USA)**[34] [948] 3-9-3 .... MJKinane 5 115
(A P O'Brien, Ire) *lw: in tch: effrt over 2f out: led over 1f out: sn rdn: r.o wl and in command wl ins fnl f* **7/2**[3]
10-1 **2** *2* **Desert Dew (IRE)**[14] [1275] 3-8-12 103.............................. MichaelHills 7 106
(B W Hills) *lw: stdd s: racd keenly: hld up: hdwy wl over 2f out: chsd wnr over 1f out: sn lugged lft: no imp wl ins fnl f* **2/1**[1]
-254 **3** *1 ½* **Habalwatan (IRE)**[16] [1243] 3-8-12 83.................................(b) JohnEgan 4 103
(C E Brittain) *cl up: nt clr run wl over 1f out: sn rdn: styd on same pce fnl f* **25/1**
12-3 **4** *1 ¾* **Monzante (USA)**[21] [1126] 3-8-12 102........................... RichardHughes 6 100
(R Charlton) *rdn to sn ld: rdn 2f out: hdd over 1f out: wknd ins fnl f* **15/2**
11- **5** *1 ½* **Yazamaan**[253] [4963] 3-8-12 100.. RHills 2 97
(J H M Gosden) *b.hind: stdd s: racd keenly: hld up: lft bhd wl over 2f out: nvr a danger* **10/3**[2]
6-1 **6** *shd* **Ea (USA)**[24] [1075] 3-8-12 90... KerrinMcEvoy 3 97
(Sir Michael Stoute) *w'like: strong: prom: rdn and lost pl wl over 1f out: n.d after* **9/2**

2m 9.82s (-3.32) **Going Correction** -0.025s/f (Good) **6** Ran SP% **112.4**
Speed ratings (Par 109):112,110,109,107,106 106
CSF £10.99 TOTE £3.80: £2.10, £1.60; EX 8.40.
Owner Michael Tabor **Bred** Quaybloodstock Niarchos Family **Trained** Ballydoyle, Co Tipperary

FOCUS
Not a bad Derby trial in recent times, with Oath and Kris Kin going on to Epsom success in the last ten years. The performance of the third probably does not do a lot for the form but the winner outclassed the rest and the race has been rated positively.

NOTEBOOK
Admiralofthefleet(USA), disappointing when a beaten favourite in the 2000 Guineas Trial at Leopardstown on his seasonal reappearance, bounced back to his best with a convincing success. Carrying a 5lb penalty for his Royal Lodge win, he took a while to hit top gear, but once into the straight he drew clear and outclassed the rest, appreciating every yard of this longer trip. Another Derby possible for a yard with many cards to play in that department, he is a very likeable type, and will have little trouble getting another two furlongs. (op 9-4 tchd 4-1 in places)
Desert Dew(IRE) won the Esher Cup in great style last time out and was made favourite on his return to Group 3 company. He still seemed to be travelling well when he rounded the turn into the straight, but in the end the winner outclassed him. It was still a solid effort, but he may have to drop back to Listed company to return to winning ways. (op 9-4 tchd 5-2 in places)
Habalwatan(IRE), who got a bit warm beforehand, is exposed and finished last of four in the Blue Riband Trial at Epsom last time, so his performance in finishing third probably does not do a lot for the value of the form. His rating is also likely to get a bump from this, making handicaps a tougher option, but Pattern races abroad are more likely to be on his agenda anyway. (op 33-1)
Monzante(USA), whose third at Newbury last time had been given a boost when the winner won the Cheshire Oaks earlier in the week, set out to make every yard and went a fair pace in front. He was easily brushed aside by the first two though, and might appreciate dropping back in trip. (op 7-1 tchd 8-1)
Yazamaan, unbeaten in two starts as a juvenile, was disappointing on his reappearance. Keen out the back, he never threatened to land a blow, but perhaps he needed this and will be more effective on a more conventional track. (op 7-2 tchd 3-1, 4-1 in a place)
Ea(USA), winner of a Nottingham maiden last month, had a lot more on his plate in this company and could not bridge the class gap on his first attempt in Pattern grade. He was one of the least experienced in the line-up though, and can improve. (op 7-1)

1618 BLUE SQUARE ORMONDE STKS (GROUP 3) 1m 5f 89y
2:50 (2:50) (Class 1) 4-Y-O+
£42,585 (£16,140; £8,077; £4,027; £2,017; £1,012) **Stalls** Low

Form RPR
024- **1** **Ask**[244] [5185] 4-9-0 111.. KerrinMcEvoy 4 119+
(Sir Michael Stoute) *lw: racd in 2nd tl led over 2f out: qcknd impressively ins fnl f: comf* **5/2**[2]
250- **2** *2* **Scorpion (IRE)**[152] [6782] 5-9-0 .... MJKinane 7 114
(A P O'Brien, Ire) *edgy and sweating bef r: in tch: wnt 2nd over 2f out: rdn and ev ch wl over 1f out: nt pce of wnr ins fnl f* **1/1**[1]
14-1 **3** *1 ¾* **Steppe Dancer (IRE)**[48] [756] 4-9-0 101........................... EddieAhern 2 111
(D J Coakley) *lw: hld up: nt clr run over 2f out: hdwy over 1f out: kpt on same pce fnl f* **9/1**
0-01 **4** *2* **Peppertree Lane (IRE)**[13] [1304] 4-9-0 105.............................. KDarley 6 108
(M Johnston) *chsd ldrs: rdn over 1f out: wknd fnl f* **6/1**[3]
34-6 **5** *3* **The Whistling Teal**[20] [1144] 11-9-0 106.......................... SteveDrowne 1 104
(G Wragg) *in rr: niggled along 3f out: effrt wl over 1f out: no imp on ldrs: wknd fnl f* **9/1**
336- **6** *31* **Litalia (IRE)**[267] [4543] 4-8-11 .... RichardHughes 5 54
(P W Chapple-Hyam) *fit: led: rdn 3f out: hdd over 2f out: sn n.m.r and hmpd whn wkng: t.o* **25/1**

2m 52.33s (-3.09) **Going Correction** -0.025s/f (Good) **6** Ran SP% **116.7**
Speed ratings (Par 113):108,106,105,104,102 83
CSF £5.69 TOTE £3.60: £2.00, £1.30; EX 6.60.
Owner Patrick J Fahey **Bred** Side Hill Stud **Trained** Newmarket, Suffolk

■ Stewards' Enquiry : Richard Hughes caution: careless riding

FOCUS
A good-looking renewal and a very smart performance from the winner, who looks to have improved from three to four. The form is probably sound with the runner-up to last year's best.

NOTEBOOK
Ask ◆, fourth in the St Leger on his final start at three, was well supported on his seasonal reappearance and was always well placed in a race not run at a strong gallop. He quickened up well entering the straight, and did so again when strongly challenged by Scorpion inside the last. He looks a high-class prospect on this evidence and will not have many problems dropping back to a mile and a half, while also having the stamina for 1m6f, so connections have plenty of options open to them. The Hardwicke Stakes looks an ideal short-term target. (op 11-4 tchd 7-2, 4-1 in a place)
Scorpion(IRE), who sweated up badly beforehand, came to have every chance in the straight but the winner quickened away from him in the closing stages. He has not tried to make the running since winning the St Leger in 2005, but those tactics may suit him. He stays well, and will be interesting in the Cup races, even though his stable has Yeats as well for those events. (op 6-5 tchd 10-11, 5-4 in a place)
Steppe Dancer(IRE), a progressive type who won a Listed race on Polytrack last time out, did not find things going his way, as the long-time leader weakened in front of him near the rail rounding the turn into the straight, which delayed his challenge. By the time he got going the first two were away and gone, but he kept on well for third and looks capable of better. (op 12-1)
Peppertree Lane(IRE), who made a winning reappearance in a fairly weak affair at Ripon, ideally wants some decent cut in the ground, so he was up against it in this grade without his optimum conditions. (op 5-1)
The Whistling Teal won this race last year but that was a weaker renewal and he has deteriorated a little since, which is only to be expected at his age. He would have preferred much softer ground. (op 11-1)
Litalia(IRE), formerly trained in Germany where she finished third in a couple of Group races, was bought for 220,000gns in November and was making her debut for her new stable. She made much of the running, at a steady pace, but weakened with over two furlongs to run, and it looked as though the run was very much needed. (op 20-1)

1619 WARWICK INTERNATIONAL H'CAP 7f 122y
3:20 (3:20) (Class 2) (0-100,100) 4-Y-0+ £13,248 (£3,964; £1,982; £991; £493) **Stalls** Low

Form RPR
-200 **1** **Dhaular Dhar (IRE)**[1] [1601] 5-8-12 **94**........................... DanielTudhope 5 105+
(J S Goldie) *lw: hld up: hdwy 2f out: burst through to ld and lugged lft wl ins fnl f: r.o* **10/3**[1]
006 **2** *nk* **Beckermet (IRE)**[20] [1159] 5-9-2 **98**...................................... EddieAhern 6 108
(R F Fisher) *midfield: hdwy 2f out: led over 1f out: sn rdn: hdd wl ins fnl f: hld fnl strides* **14/1**
34-5 **3** *1 ½* **Song Of Passion (IRE)**[27] [1034] 4-8-8 **90**.................... RichardHughes 3 96
(R Hannon) *lw: led: hdd over 6f out: continued to chse ldr: led briefly wl over 1f out: nt qckn towards fin* **7/1**
00-1 **4** *½* **Giganticus (USA)**[27] [1041] 4-8-10 **92**................................. MichaelHills 1 100+
(B W Hills) *chsd ldrs: nt clr run over 1f out: rdn and tail flashed ins fnl f: kpt on: nt pce of ldrs towards fin* **7/2**[2]
546- **5** *shd* **Joseph Henry**[210] [5945] 5-7-11 **86** oh1........................ AdeleRothery(7) 2 91
(D Nicholls) *hld up: hdwy over 2f out: rdn and ev ch over 1f out: kpt on same pce wl ins fnl f* **10/1**
0310 **6** *3 ½* **Glenbuck (IRE)**[6] [1474] 4-8-6 **88**.....................................(v) PaulHanagan 4 84+
(A Bailey) *hung rt most of way: led over 6f out: hdd wl over 1f out: wknd ins fnl f* **5/1**[3]
-000 **7** *3 ½* **The Kiddykid (IRE)**[6] [1474] 7-9-4 **100**........................ StephenDonohoe 8 87
(P D Evans) *midfield: rdn over 2f out: outpcd after* **9/1**
60-3 **8** *½* **Red Somerset (USA)**[13] [1307] 4-8-4 **86** oh1................. FrancisNorton 7 72
(R J Hodges) *pushed along early: midfield: rdn and wknd wl over 1f out* **12/1**
0000 **9** *½* **Commando Scott (IRE)**[18] [1195] 6-8-1 **86** oh3............ LiamJones(3) 10 71
(I W McInnes) *chsd ldrs: rdn 2f out: wknd over 1f out* **16/1**
60-0 **10** *8* **Campo Bueno (FR)**[33] [953] 5-8-4 **86** oh6............................. PaulQuinn 9 51
(A Berry) *s.s: a bhd* **66/1**
00-0 **11** *½* **Mine Behind**[1] [1601] 7-8-1 **86** oh1.............................. StephaneBreux(3) 11 49
(J R Best) *bhd: rdn and hung lft wl over 1f out: nvr on terms* **33/1**
-400 **12** *68* **Chief Commander (FR)**[31] [993] 4-8-5 **87**......................... JohnEgan 12 —
(Jane Chapple-Hyam) *prom on outside: rdn and lost pl 4f out: eased whn btn over 2f out: t.o* **20/1**

1m 33.35s (-1.40) **Going Correction** -0.025s/f (Good) **12** Ran SP% **123.0**
Speed ratings (Par 109):106,105,104,103,103 100,96,96,95,87 87,19
CSF £52.15 CT £319.86 TOTE £4.70: £1.70, £3.80, £2.40; EX 77.30 Trifecta £776.40 Pool: £1,202.88 - 1.10 winning tickets..
Owner J S Goldie **Bred** Gainsborough Stud Management Ltd **Trained** Uplawmoor, E Renfrews

FOCUS
A strongly-run handicap which fell into the lap of those held up off the pace. The form looks sound rated around the third and fourth.

NOTEBOOK
Dhaular Dhar(IRE) has proven in the past, indeed at this track, that he can run well on consecutive days, and it was no surprise to see him popular in the market over this longer distance having found 5f on the sharp side the previous day. Held up out the back, the leaders set the race up nicely for him, going a good gallop, and the gaps opened up for him in the straight. Apparently his trainer is keen to run in the Golden Jubilee next, but he should be outclassed in that contest. (op 4-1 tchd 9-2 in places)
Beckermet(IRE) was not sure to stay this trip but if ever he was going to get it it was around here, a track where he has always run well. Perfectly positioned off the pace most of the way, he travelled strongly throughout and had every chance. He just found the winner staying on just too strongly at the finish.
Song Of Passion(IRE), who won over this course and distance at this meeting last year, chased the fast pace set by Glenbuck for most of the way so did quite well to hold on for third in the closing stages. She goes well on a turning track. (op 6-1)

Giganticus(USA) was a bit disappointing as he looked to have plenty in his favour off a 4lb higher mark than when successful on his reappearance at Newcastle. He had every chance and it was a little disconcerting to see him flash his tail when put under pressure in the closing stages. (op 11-4)

Joseph Henry has gone well fresh in the past, was well drawn and was another who benefited from the strong gallop. He stayed on well in the latter stages, being presented with a gap on the inside in the straight, and if he can build on this he will be one to note in the coming weeks.

Glenbuck(IRE) likes to make the running and his rider was very keen to get him to the front around this sharp track, but he did too much too soon and simply set it up for those coming from behind. Official explanation: jockey said gelding hung right throughout (op 7-1 tchd 15-2)

1620 BOODLES CHESHIRE REGIMENT MAIDEN FILLIES' STKS — 7f 2y

4:00 (4:01) (Class 3) 3-Y-O — **£7,124** (£2,119; £1,059; £529) **Stalls** Low

Form — RPR

6 **1** **Azeema (IRE)**[21] [1128] 3-9-0 .... MichaelHills 4 — 78+
(B W Hills) *lw: midfield: hdwy 2f out: r.o to ld ins fnl f: pushed out* **7/4**[1]

0 **2** *1 1/4* **Medicea Sidera**[9] [1398] 3-9-0 .... TPQueally 5 — 74
(E F Vaughan) *led: rdn over 1f out: hdd ins fnl f: sn hld* **66/1**

5- **3** *3 1/2* **Passing Hour (USA)**[287] [3893] 3-9-0 .... RichardHughes 13 — 65+
(G A Butler) *lw: a.p: rdn briefly 4f out: rdn over 1f out: one pce ins fnl f* **6/1**[3]

3 **4** *2* **Medici Pearl**[59] [670] 3-9-0 .... DavidAllan 6 — 59
(T D Easterby) *w'like: midfield: pushed along over 3f out: hdwy over 1f out: nt rch ldrs* **16/1**

05- **5** *1 1/4* **Danehill Kikin (IRE)**[207] [6014] 3-9-0 .... RHills 3 — 56
(B W Hills) *lw: racd keenly: trckd ldrs: wnt 2nd briefly 2f out: wknd ins fnl f* **9/1**

560- **6** *2* **Grethel (IRE)**[189] [6318] 3-9-0 50 .... FrancisNorton 2 — 51
(A Berry) *midfield: rdn and sme hdwy over 1f out: nt trble ldrs* **66/1**

7 *nk* **Caluba** 3-9-0 .... LeeEnstone 7 — 53+
(K R Burke) *w'like: s.i.s: towards rr: rdn whn nt clr run over 1f out: sn swtchd rt: kpt on: nvr trbld ldrs* **40/1**

0-2 **8** *3/4* **Apple Blossom (IRE)**[32] [977] 3-9-0 .... SteveDrowne 12 — 48
(G Wragg) *in tch: rdn 2f out: wknd wl over 1f out* **11/4**[2]

9 *1* **Lady Zia (IRE)** 3-9-0 .... PaulHanagan 11 — 45
(J G Burns, Ire) *w'like: s.i.s: in rr: rdn over 1f out: n.d* **25/1**

245- **10** *2 1/2* **To Party (IRE)**[243] [5206] 3-9-0 71 .... StephenDonohoe 8 — 38
(P D Evans) *fit: prom: rdn 2f out: wknd over 1f out: eased whn btn ins fnl f* **16/1**

11 *1* **Celeb Style (IRE)** 3-9-0 .... DeanMernagh 1 — 36
(D Nicholls) *w'like: in tch: rdn over 2f out: wknd over 1f out: eased whn btn ins fnl f* **7/1**

3 **12** *1/2* **Maia**[20] [1161] 3-9-0 .... PaulQuinn 14 — 34
(D Nicholls) *midfield: rdn and hung bdly rt over 2f out: sn wknd: eased whn btn ins fnl f* **20/1**

13 *3/4* **Pixie Princess (IRE)** 3-9-0 .... EddieAhern 10 — 32
(Miss V Haigh) *unf: s.i.s: a bhd: eased whn btn ins fnl f* **25/1**

1m 27.51s (-0.96) **Going Correction** -0.025s/f (Good) — **13** Ran SP% **129.5**

Speed ratings (Par 100):104,102,98,96,94 92,92,91,90,87 86,85,84

CSF £179.61 TOTE £2.90: £1.30, £17.40, £2.60; EX 224.20.

Owner D J Deer **Bred** D J And Mrs Deer **Trained** Lambourn, Berks

FOCUS

Probably not a great maiden, with the plating-class sixth the best guide and also the limit to the form.

NOTEBOOK

Azeema(IRE) ran with promise in a decent Newbury maiden on her debut and this took a lot less winning. She did not always look as though she would win as easily as she eventually did, but is clearly going the right way and it will be interesting to see what sort of mark the Handicapper gives her. (tchd 13-8 and 9-4)

Medicea Sidera was far from disgraced on her debut at Kempton none days earlier and clearly knew more about the job this time. Her rider set out to make every yard on her and she made a bold fist of it, setting a good pace and only finding the favourite too strong, but finishing well clear of the rest. She is bred to get further than this in time and should progress again. (op 50-1)

Passing Hour(USA) made her debut in a very good Ascot maiden last season but was not seen after that race in July, so she was entitled to need this run. Drawn out in the car park, she did well to get into a prominent position from there, although she was left behind in the straight. There should be improvement to come. (op 4-1 tchd 7-1)

Medici Pearl was under pressure from a long way out but responded and kept on well. She shapes as though she wants further, and she will be eligible for handicaps after one more run.

Danehill Kikin(IRE) is bred to want middle distances and is now eligible for a handicap mark based on performances over shorter trips. She could improve a good deal when sent over further. (op 12-1)

Grethel(IRE), the most experienced filly in the line-up, only showed moderate ability at two, but she is by Fruits Of Love so one is entitled to expect that she might do a bit better this season, especially as she steps up in distance. Her performance helps set the standard of the form, but she was carrying virtually no condition and it is debatable just how much improvement she is open to. (tchd 50-1)

Apple Blossom(IRE) was poorly drawn and raced towards the outside throughout, but even so this was a step backwards. She does now qualify for a handicap mark though, and might do better back on a more conventional track. (op 3-1 tchd 9-4)

Maia Official explanation: jockey said filly hung right throughout

1621 MANOR HOUSE STABLES LLP H'CAP — 1m 4f 66y

4:35 (4:35) (Class 4) (0-85,85) 4-Y-O+ — **£7,772** (£2,312; £1,155; £577) **Stalls** Low

Form — RPR

450- **1** **Stretton (IRE)**[192] [6287] 9-8-12 79 .... SteveDrowne 1 — 86
(J D Bethell) *in tch: rdn over 1f out: sn led: r.o: pushed out towards fin* **11/2**[2]

-222 **2** *nk* **Augustus John (IRE)**[71] [594] 4-8-6 73 .... JohnEgan 5 — 79
(T J Pitt) *chsd ldrs: wnt 2nd over 2f out: rdn to ld over 1f out: sn hdd: ev ch thrght fnl f: styd on* **8/1**

3-31 **3** *1* **Heathyards Pride**[70] [608] 7-8-2 74 .... WilliamBuick(5) 3 — 79
(R Hollinshead) *lw: hld up: pushed along over 2f out: hdwy over 1f out: r.o ins fnl f: nrst fin* **7/1**

5320 **4** *1/2* **Wulimaster (USA)**[15] [1263] 4-8-4 71 oh1 .... FrancisNorton 4 — 75
(D W Barker) *s.i.s: midfield: hdwy over 2f out: swtchd rt to chse ldrs over 1f out: r.o towards fin* **22/1**

25-4 **5** *3* **Mighty Moon**[37] [914] 4-8-10 84 .... (bt) JamesO'Reilly(7) 8 — 83
(J O'Reilly) *s.i.s: in rr: rdn 2f out: hdwy over 1f out: styd on: nt rch ldrs* **14/1**

120- **6** *3/4* **Kerriemuir Lass (IRE)**[196] [6202] 4-9-4 85 .... PhilipRobinson 2 — 83
(M A Jarvis) *led: hdd over 1f out: sn rdn: wknd ins fnl f* **6/1**[3]

132- **7** *1 1/2* **South O'The Border**[15] [5625] 5-8-11 78 .... RichardHughes 7 — 74
(Miss Venetia Williams) *midfield: nt clr run over 2f out: sn rdn and one pce* **11/2**[2]

00-4 **8** *1 1/4* **Cruise Director**[13] [1288] 7-9-1 82 .... EddieAhern 9 — 76
(Ian Williams) *hld up: hdwy over 3f out: rdn over 2f out whn in midfield: no imp fr over 1f out* **10/1**

10-0 **9** *2 1/2* **My Arch**[29] [1013] 5-9-2 83 .... DO'Donohoe 6 — 73
(K A Ryan) *chsd ldrs: pushed along over 7f out: wknd over 1f out: eased whn btn ins fnl f* **7/1**

10-0 **10** *1 3/4* **Bright Sun (IRE)**[20] [1158] 6-8-4 71 oh2 .... (t) KimTinkler 11 — 58
(N Tinkler) *chsd ldr tl rdn over 2f out: wkng whn n.m.r wl over 1f out* **50/1**

606- **11** *3/4* **Doctor Scott**[237] [5361] 4-8-13 80 .... RHills 12 — 66
(M Johnston) *hld up: rdn over 2f out: no imp* **5/1**[1]

46-0 **12** *1 1/4* **Tender Falcon**[31] [995] 7-8-12 79 .... PaulHanagan 10 — 63
(R J Hodges) *lw: midfield: rdn and lost pl 4f out: n.d after* **20/1**

2m 39.36s (-1.29) **Going Correction** -0.025s/f (Good) — **12** Ran SP% **124.7**

Speed ratings (Par 105):103,102,102,101,99 99,98,97,95,94 94,93

CSF £50.76 CT £322.60 TOTE £4.60: £2.40, £3.00, £2.90; EX 59.00 Place 6 £56.88, Place 5 £17.61.

Owner M J Dawson **Bred** Burton Agnes Stud Co Ltd **Trained** Middleham Moor, N Yorks

■ Stewards' Enquiry : James O'Reilly one-day ban: used whip from above shoulder height (May 22)

FOCUS

A competitive heat but full of exposed sorts and the form is ordinary but sound, rated around the placed horses.

T/Jkpt: £7,696.40 to a £1 stake. Pool: £10,840.00. 1.00 winning ticket. T/Plt: £66.20 to a £1 stake. Pool: £145,518.00. 1,604.65 winning tickets. T/Qpdt: £11.10 to a £1 stake. Pool: £6,692.90. 442.80 winning tickets. DO

1487 HAMILTON (R-H)

Friday, May 11

OFFICIAL GOING: Good

Wind: light across

1622 MITIE TWO-YEAR-OLD MAIDEN STKS — 5f 4y

6:20 (6:21) (Class 5) 2-Y-O — **£2,914** (£867; £433; £216) **Stalls** Low

Form — RPR

1 **Meeriss (IRE)** 2-9-3 .... JHBowman 7 — 77+
(M R Channon) *in tch: smooth hdwy 2f out: led ent fnl f: comf* **11/2**

0 **2** *1/2* **Smileforawhile (IRE)**[9] [1411] 2-9-3 .... PaulFessey 5 — 75
(K A Ryan) *s.i.s: outpcd tl hdwy over 1f out: chsd wnr ins fnl f: r.o* **14/1**

5 **3** *2* **Natural Rhythm (IRE)**[9] [1411] 2-9-3 .... RoystonFfrench 1 — 67
(Mrs A Duffield) *hung rt thrght: sn outpcd: hdwy over 1f out: kpt on: nrst fin* **8/1**

0 **4** *1 3/4* **Alpen Adventure (IRE)**[41] [845] 2-9-3 .... TomEaves 2 — 60
(Mrs L Stubbs) *s.i.s and outpcd: hdwy over 1f out: kpt on ins fnl f* **5/1**[3]

65 **5** *1/2* **Turn And River (IRE)**[29] [1007] 2-8-5 .... PatrickDonaghy(7) 6 — 53
(M Brittain) *w ldrs: led 2f out to ent fnl f: sn outpcd* **14/1**

6 *1/2* **Royal Sovereign (IRE)** 2-8-12 .... JamieMoriarty(5) 9 — 56
(J Howard Johnson) *w ldrs tl wknd ins fnl f* **20/1**

7 *1* **New Colossus** 2-9-3 .... RichardMullen 4 — 52
(E J O'Neill) *led to 2f out: sn rdn and btn* **11/4**[1]

8 *1* **Gin Genereux** 2-9-3 .... J-PGuillambert 8 — 48
(M Johnston) *cl up: rdn and hung rt 2f out: sn wknd* **9/2**[2]

9 *1/2* **Johnny Friendly** 2-9-3 .... PatCosgrave 3 — 46
(K R Burke) *chsd ldrs: drvn 1/2-way: wknd wl over 1f out* **16/1**

61.35 secs (0.15) **Going Correction** -0.20s/f (Firm) — **9** Ran SP% **112.0**

Speed ratings (Par 93):90,89,86,83,82 81,80,78,77

CSF £75.15 TOTE £6.60: £2.40, £3.60, £1.80; EX 98.90.

Owner Sheikh Ahmed Al Maktoum **Bred** Hugo Lascelles **Trained** West Ilsley, Berks

FOCUS

A couple of interesting runners but the leaders looked to go off plenty quick enough and, although the fourth and fifth suggest that the form is at least as good as rated, it may not prove entirely reliable.

NOTEBOOK

Meeriss(IRE) ◆, from a stable that has a good record in this race, took the eye in the paddock and beat a couple of more experienced rivals with more in hand than the official margin suggests. He is open to plenty of improvement, should be equally effective over six furlongs and looks sure to win more races. (op 4-1)

Smileforawhile(IRE) left his debut form a fair way behind and, although this race was run to suit those coming from off the pace, he is in good hands, will stay six furlongs and is sure to be placed to best advantage. (op 12-1)

Natural Rhythm(IRE), a fair way in front of the runner-up on their respective debuts at Pontefract, failed to confirm placings with that rival but nonetheless ran creditably and again shaped as though an extra furlong would be very much to his liking. (tchd 17-2)

Alpen Adventure(IRE), having his first run since the end of March, again lost ground at the start but again showed ability in a race that was run to suit. His stable is among the winners and he is capable of winning a minor event over further in due course. (op 11-2 tchd 13-2)

Turn And River(IRE) may be a bit better than the bare form given she fared the best of those up with the strong pace throughout. However, she has had a few chances and is likely to remain vulnerable to the more progressive sorts in this type of event. (op 11-1)

Royal Sovereign(IRE), a half-brother to a couple of winners from seven furlongs to a mile and a quarter, showed ability having raced close to the strong pace. He is open to improvement. (op 14-1)

New Colossus, a strong, sturdy type, represented connections that took this race last year but, although failing to justify favouritism, almost certainly did too much too soon and is capable of making amends in ordinary company. (op 3-1 tchd 5-2, 7-2 in places)

Gin Genereux, a workmanlike, lengthy type, is related to a couple of smart sprinters in the States but, as is the case with many inexperienced types at this course, looked ill at ease on the downhill gradients. He is likely to fare better in time. (op 11-2 tchd 6-1)

1623 MITIE CONDITIONS STKS — 6f 5y

6:50 (6:50) (Class 3) 3-Y-O

£8,724 (£2,612; £1,306; £653; £326; £163) **Stalls** Low

Form — RPR

-025 **1** **Aahayson**[5] [1500] 3-8-12 90 .... PatCosgrave 3 — 104
(K R Burke) *mde all: qcknd over 1f out: unchal* **5/4**[1]

-301 **2** *3 1/2* **Northern Fling**[13] [1298] 3-8-12 92 .... AdrianTNicholls 4 — 93
(D Nicholls) *hld up in tch: hdwy to chse wnr over 1f out: kpt on fnl f: no imp* **4/1**[3]

123- **3** *7* **Valiance (USA)**[181] [6443] 3-8-9 96 .... RobertHavlin 7 — 69
(J H M Gosden) *cl up tl rdn and outpcd fr 2f out* **7/2**[2]

460- **4** *5* **Adaptation**[172] [6546] 3-8-7 87 .... J-PGuillambert 2 — 52
(M Johnston) *chsd ldrs tl wknd wl over 1f out* **4/1**[3]

300- **5** 1½ **Tom Tower (IRE)**[231] 5509 3-8-9 70 AndrewMullen(3) 1 53
(A C Whillans) *prom tl rdn and wknd over 2f out* **50/1**
6 14 **Bovered (IRE)** 3-8-1 JimmyQuinn 6 —
(A Berry) *sn outpcd: lost tch fr 1/2-way* **150/1**
1m 10.81s (-2.29) **Going Correction** -0.20s/f (Firm) **6** Ran SP% **109.3**
Speed ratings (Par 103):107,102,93,86,84 65
CSF £6.27 TOTE £2.20: £1.30, £2.10; EX 6.70.
Owner Philip Richards **Bred** Whitsbury Manor Stud And Mrs M E Slade **Trained** Middleham Moor, N Yorks

FOCUS
Only a couple of serious contenders and a race in which the winner was allowed his own way in front. The form looks decent with a personal best for the runner-up.

NOTEBOOK
Aahayson had been running well in competitive handicaps and, after attracting substantial market support, won with plenty in hand after being allowed an uncontested lead. Things will be tougher from a higher mark back in handicaps after reassessment but he will be of interest in similar contests when it looks as though he may get another easy time of it in front. (op 9-4 tchd 6-5)
Northern Fling, who had turned in a career-best effort at Ripon on his previous start, ran creditably against a useful rival who was very much allowed his own way in front. A more end-to-end gallop would have suited but he has little margin for error from his 92 mark back in handicaps. (op 7-2 tchd 10-3)
Valiance(USA), the highest rated of these and a one-time Derby entry, was easy to back and was soundly beaten on this first run for over five months and on this first attempt over sprint distances. The return to seven furlongs and beyond would suit but, given he was turned over at long odds-on for his previous start, he looks one to have reservations about at present. (op 5-2)
Adaptation, a dual course and distance winner as a juvenile, was a long way below her best on this first run of the year and she is going to be difficult to place unless she steps up considerably on this run this term. (op 7-2 tchd 9-2)
Tom Tower(IRE) had a stiff task at these weights on this first start for new connections and first run since September, and not surprisingly finished well beaten. (op 40-1 tchd 33-1)
Bovered(IRE), a half-sister to a multiple winning miler in France, faced a very stiff task but showed nothing on this racecourse debut.

1624 MITIE SCOTTISH H'CAP 1m 4f 17y
7:20 (7:20) (Class 5) (0-70,70) 3-Y-O **£3,238** (£963; £481; £240) **Stalls** High

Form RPR
00-5 **1** **Jafaru**[15] 1256 3-8-2 51 oh3 (b[1]) RoystonFfrench 1 61
(G A Butler) *cl up: led 3f out: edgd lft: hld on gamely fnl f* **20/1**
551- **2** *shd* **Bayonyx (IRE)**[195] 6207 3-9-2 70 JamieMoriarty(5) 3 79
(J Howard Johnson) *prom: effrt and ev ch fr 3f out: kpt on u.p fnl f: jst hld* **3/1**[3]
4-01 **3** *nk* **Highland Legacy**[11] 1355 3-9-3 69 6ex AndrewElliott(3) 5 78
(M L W Bell) *hld up in midfield: hdwy and cl up over 3f out: drvn and outpcd over 2f out: hrd rdn and styd on fnl f* **11/4**[2]
0-31 **4** 5 **Sonara (IRE)**[9] 1415 3-9-3 66 6ex JimmyQuinn 6 67+
(M H Tompkins) *hld up: hdwy and prom 3f out: rdn and no imp fr 2f out* **5/2**[1]
-310 **5** 1¼ **Petrosian**[18] 1205 3-9-4 67 J-PGuillambert 7 66
(M Johnston) *t.k.h: in tch: drvn and outpcd over 3f out: rallied 2f out: no imp* **9/1**
-630 **6** 6 **Dansimar**[11] 1355 3-9-5 68 JHBowman 2 57
(M R Channon) *led to 3f out: rdn and wknd fr 2f out* **14/1**
0066 **7** 2 **Grey Light (IRE)**[13] 1289 3-8-13 62 TomEaves 4 48
(L Lungo) *chsd ldrs tl wknd fr 3f out* **8/1**
035- **8** 1¾ **Bret Maverick (IRE)**[228] 5580 3-8-11 60 TonyHamilton 9 43
(J R Weymes) *plld hrd in rr: struggling fnl 4f* **100/1**
50-0 **9** 11 **Grand Diamond (IRE)**[13] 1289 3-8-7 63 GaryBartley(7) 8 29
(J S Goldie) *hld up in tch: struggling over 3f out: sn btn* **50/1**
2m 38.3s (-0.88) **Going Correction** -0.05s/f (Good) **9** Ran SP% **115.7**
Speed ratings (Par 99):100,99,99,96,95 91,90,89,81
CSF £79.05 CT £224.21 TOTE £21.30: £3.40, £1.80, £1.70; EX 125.10.
Owner C McFadden **Bred** Nawara Stud Co Ltd **Trained** Blewbury, Oxon
■ Stewards' Enquiry : Jamie Moriarty three-day ban: used whip with excessive frequency (May 22-24)

FOCUS
A run-of-the-mill handicap in which the pace was just fair and the form is not that strong.

1625 MITIE MAIDEN STKS 6f 5y
7:50 (7:52) (Class 5) 3-5-Y-O **£2,914** (£867; £433; £216) **Stalls** Low

Form RPR
20- **1** **Maysarah (IRE)**[234] 5464 3-8-9 JHBowman 2 52+
(G A Butler) *t.k.h: prom stands' side: led over 2f out: rdn out fnl f* **1/1**[1]
0-04 **2** ¾ **Eternal Legacy (IRE)**[1] 1596 5-9-5 44 DavidAllan 5 53
(E J Alston) *prom: effrt over 2f out: chsd wnr fnl f: kpt on* **12/1**
6-5 **3** ¾ **Five Wishes**[18] 1197 3-8-9 PaulFessey 10 48
(M Dods) *in tch far side: effrt and edgd into centre 2f out: kpt on fnl f: nrst fin* **10/1**
-320 **4** *hd* **Distant Sun (USA)**[18] 1197 3-9-0 65 TomEaves 14 55+
(I Semple) *chsd ldrs far side: effrt over 2f out: kpt on same pce fnl f* **13/2**[2]
060- **5** ¾ **Takanewa (IRE)**[237] 5370 4-9-0 50 JamieMoriarty(5) 4 48
(J Howard Johnson) *w stands' side ldrs to 2f out: sn rdn and nt qckn* **20/1**
6 1¼ **Harts In Mo Shun (IRE)** 3-9-0 RobertHavlin 1 46
(A Berry) *s.i.s: outpcd stands' side: hdwy and hung rt over 2f out: sn no imp* **50/1**
542- **7** 1 **Hansomis (IRE)**[195] 6208 3-8-9 69 RoystonFfrench 6 38
(B Mactaggart) *in tch stands' side: rdn over 2f out: one pce over 1f out* **7/1**[3]
03-5 **8** 1¾ **Stepaside (IRE)**[8] 1424 3-9-0 72 J-PGuillambert 12 38
(M Johnston) *chsd far side ldrs: ev ch that gp wl over 1f out: sn wknd* **9/1**
00- **9** ½ **Alone It Stands (IRE)**[265] 4611 4-9-10 AdrianTNicholls 8 39
(D Nicholls) *led far side gp to ins fnl f: sn btn* **12/1**
063- **10** ½ **Forzarzi (IRE)**[226] 5615 3-8-12 61 ow3 PBradley(5) 13 38
(A Berry) *s.i.s: outpcd far side: nvr on terms* **40/1**
11 4 **Mary From Maryhill (IRE)** 3-8-9 TonyHamilton 7 18
(Miss L A Perratt) *s.i.s: a outpcd far side* **50/1**
200- **12** 7 **Graceful Flight**[273] 4324 5-9-0 35 RoryMoore(5) 11 —
(P T Midgley) *w far side ldr to 1/2-way: sn rdn and wknd* **100/1**
00- **13** 28 **Scottish Spirit (IRE)**[226] 5615 3-9-0 DaleGibson 3 —
(J S Haldane) *slt ld stands' side to over 2f out: sn btn* **200/1**
1m 12.63s (-0.47) **Going Correction** -0.20s/f (Firm)
WFA 3 from 4yo+ 10lb **13** Ran SP% **122.9**
Speed ratings (Par 103):95,94,93,92,91 90,88,86,85,85 79,70,33
CSF £14.94 TOTE £2.20: £1.40, £5.10, £2.80; EX 38.90.
Owner Fawzi Abdulla Nass **Bred** Miss Deirdre Barry **Trained** Blewbury, Oxon

FOCUS
An uncompetitive maiden in which there did not look to be too much between the sides. The pace was fair but the form is limited by the runner-up.
Graceful Flight Official explanation: jockey said mare was unsuited by the good ground

1626 MITIE MILE FILLIES' STKS (H'CAP) 1m 65y
8:20 (8:20) (Class 4) (0-80,79) 4-Y-0+ **£7,772** (£2,312; £1,155; £577) **Stalls** High

Form RPR
4-40 **1** **Flylowflylong (IRE)**[7] 1459 4-8-1 62 AndrewMullen(3) 7 66
(I Semple) *hld up: effrt over 2f out: styd on to ld towards fin* **7/2**[1]
-002 **2** ½ **Fortress**[17] 1227 4-8-2 60 oh5 JimmyQuinn 4 63
(E J Alston) *prom: effrt over 1f out: led ins fnl f: hdd towards fin* **6/1**
60-0 **3** ½ **Passion Fruit**[20] 1157 6-9-7 79 DeanMcKeown 6 81
(C W Fairhurst) *hld up: smooth hdwy over 2f out: effrt and ev ch ins fnl f: hld towards fin* **4/1**[2]
2642 **4** 1 **Tour D'Amour (IRE)**[11] 1352 4-8-4 62 PaulFessey 3 62
(R Craggs) *chsd ldrs: effrt and rdn whn n.m.r appr fnl f: kpt on ins fnl f* **9/2**[3]
024- **5** 1½ **Vanilla Delight (IRE)**[191] 5961 4-9-0 72 TomEaves 5 68
(J Howard Johnson) *led: rdn 3f out: edgd lft over 1f out: hdd and no ex ins fnl f* **4/1**[2]
06-5 **6** 3½ **Psychic Star**[7] 1455 4-8-12 75 JamieMoriarty(5) 1 63
(Miss Lucinda V Russell) *hld up in tch: drvn over 2f out: wknd wl over 1f out* **12/1**
03-0 **7** 3½ **Beautiful Summer (IRE)**[14] 1284 4-8-2 60 oh5 RoystonFfrench 2 40
(R A Fahey) *chsd ldrs tl wknd over 2f out: sn wknd* **15/2**
1m 48.68s (-0.62) **Going Correction** -0.05s/f (Good) **7** Ran SP% **114.1**
Speed ratings (Par 102):101,100,100,99,97 94,90
CSF £24.53 TOTE £4.40: £2.30, £2.50; EX 21.80.
Owner G L S Partnership **Bred** Mrs A C Peters **Trained** Carluke, S Lanarks
■ Stewards' Enquiry : Tom Eaves two-day ban: careless riding (May 22-23)

FOCUS
An ordinary handicap in which the pace was only fair and the form is weak rated through through the runner-up, despite being 5lb out of the handicap.

1627 MITIE H'CAP STKS (A QUALIFIER FOR THE HAMILTON PARK TOTEPOOL HANDICAP SERIES FINAL) 1m 1f 36y
8:50 (8:50) (Class 5) (0-70,70) 4-Y-0+ **£3,238** (£963; £481; £240) **Stalls** High

Form RPR
46-0 **1** **Tsaroxy (IRE)**[41] 850 5-8-13 70 JamieMoriarty(5) 3 79
(J Howard Johnson) *hld up towards rr: hdwy 4f out: led over 1f out: hld on wl fnl f* **5/1**[2]
30-6 **2** ½ **Mystical Ayr (IRE)**[5] 1488 5-8-4 56 JimmyQuinn 14 64
(Miss L A Perratt) *in tch: effrt over 2f out: chsd wnr ins fnl f: r.o* **10/1**
0-00 **3** 1 **Topflight Wildbird**[19] 1178 4-8-5 60 AndrewElliott(3) 9 66
(Mrs G S Rees) *midfield: effrt and ch 2f out: one pce fnl f* **25/1**
050- **4** 2½ **Dispol Veleta**[191] 6289 6-8-10 62 DeanMcKeown 8 63+
(Miss T Spearing) *hld up: hdwy whn nt clr run over 2f out: kpt on fnl f: nrst fin* **12/1**
154- **5** 1¼ **Qualitair Wings**[153] 6767 8-8-8 60 DavidAllan 5 59
(J Hetherton) *hld up: hdwy whn n.m.r over 2f out: kpt on fnl f: no imp* **12/1**
0-00 **6** 1 **Mayadeen (IRE)**[32] 966 5-8-4 56 oh1 (b[1]) PaulFessey 10 53
(I Semple) *prom: effrt and ev ch over 2f out: no ex over 1f out* **14/1**
53-4 **7** 2 **Haifa (IRE)**[23] 1090 4-8-9 61 RoystonFfrench 12 54
(Mrs A Duffield) *cl up: rdn 3f out: wknd over 1f out* **3/1**[1]
406- **8** *nk* **Toshi (USA)**[194] 6241 5-9-0 66 J-PGuillambert 7 58
(P Monteith) *hld up: hdwy over 2f out: nvr able to chal* **7/1**[3]
01-0 **9** 1 **Neil's Legacy (IRE)**[5] 1488 5-8-7 59 ow1 TonyHamilton 2 49
(Miss L A Perratt) *hld up: rdn 3f out: n.d* **25/1**
21-5 **10** 5 **Anthemion (IRE)**[5] 1488 10-8-5 60 AndrewMullen(3) 13 40
(Mrs J C McGregor) *led to over 1f out: sn btn* **12/1**
6504 **11** ½ **Following Flow (USA)**[48] 768 5-8-4 56 oh4 AdrianTNicholls 6 35
(R Allan) *hld up: rdn 3f out: n.d* **18/1**
003- **12** ¾ **Hawkit (USA)**[195] 6209 6-9-0 66 DaleGibson 1 43
(P Monteith) *bhd: rdn 4f out: nvr on terms* **16/1**
505- **13** 1½ **Entranced**[157] 6718 4-8-9 61 TomEaves 4 35
(L Lungo) *in tch: hdwy and ev ch over 3f out: wknd 2f out* **10/1**
14 33 **Besi**[33] 5-8-8 60 PatCosgrave 11 —
(P Monteith) *chsd ldrs tl wknd qckly over 2f out* **25/1**
1m 58.32s (-1.34) **Going Correction** -0.05s/f (Good) **14** Ran SP% **124.8**
Speed ratings (Par 103):103,102,101,99,98 97,95,95,94,90 89,88,87,58
CSF £55.34 CT £1142.23 TOTE £7.10: £2.50, £3.70, £10.00; EX 110.70 Place 6 £199.81, Place 5 £45.87 .
Owner Transcend Bloodstock LLP **Bred** E O'Leary **Trained** Billy Row, Co Durham

FOCUS
An ordinary handicap in which the pace was sound throughout and the form looks solid with the first three close to their 2006 marks.
Dispol Veleta Official explanation: jockey said mare was denied a clear run
T/Plt: £255.30 to a £1 stake. Pool: £65,318.05. 186.75 winning tickets. T/Qpdt: £62.40 to a £1 stake. Pool: £4,129.80. 48.90 winning tickets. RY

1445 LINGFIELD (L-H)
Friday, May 11

OFFICIAL GOING: Turf course - good (good to firm in places); all-weather - standard
Wind: Fresh, behind Weather: Changeable

1628 M & E CIVIL ENGINEERING & GROUNDWORKS FILLIES' H'CAP 1m 2f (P)
1:40 (1:41) (Class 5) (0-70,68) 3-Y-0+ **£2,914** (£867; £433; £216) **Stalls** Low

Form RPR
3321 **1** **Nicomedia (IRE)**[13] 1310 3-8-10 68 HaddenFrost(7) 5 75
(R Hannon) *s.i.s: hld up towards rr: prog over 2f out: rdn and r.o to ld nr fin: shade cosily* **4/1**[2]
0-00 **2** *hd* **Iolanthe**[11] 1355 3-9-1 66 IanMongan 2 72
(B J Meehan) *chsd ldr 2f: styd prom: rdn to go 3rd over 2f out: sn outpcd: rallied over 1f out: chal fnl f: jst hld* **25/1**
00-2 **3** *shd* **Spritza (IRE)**[45] 795 3-9-0 65 DarryllHolland 8 71
(M L W Bell) *t.k.h: trckd ldr after 2f: led over 3f out: hrd pressed over 1f out: hdd nr fin* **11/2**[3]
1-00 **4** 1¼ **Lunar River (FR)**[4] 1521 4-9-10 63 NeilChalmers(3) 1 68
(David Pinder) *hld up in midfield: prog gng wl enough over 2f out: sn outpcd: rdn and styd on fr over 1f out: nt rch ldrs* **25/1**
1300 **5** 1 **Mon Petite Amour**[4] 1521 4-9-11 61 TedDurcan 10 63
(D W P Arbuthnot) *prom: trckd ldr 3f out: chal and upsides over 1f out: wknd ins fnl f* **8/1**

641- **6** 1 1/4 **Pairumani Princess (IRE)**[200] 6145 3-8-13 **64**.............. MartinDwyer 4 63
(E A L Dunlop) *chsd ldrs: pushed along after 4f: effrt u.p over 2f out: sn struggling* **9/4**[1]

6 **7** 3 **Tibouchina (IRE)**[16] 1249 4-9-11 **61**.............................. GeorgeBaker 12 56
(R M Beckett) *dwlt: hld up in last pair: shkn up and outpcd over 2f out: no ch after* **8/1**

04-0 **8** 1 3/4 **Miami Tallyce (IRE)**[23] 1092 3-8-6 **57**................................ ChrisCatlin 6 47
(E J O'Neill) *mistimed s and v s.i.s: wl in rr: hrd rdn and no ch over 1f out* **25/1**

65-4 **9** hd **Windbeneathmywings (IRE)**[20] 1154 3-8-3 **59**........... PatrickHills(5) 7 49
(J W Hills) *hld up in rr: rdn on wd outside 3f out: sn btn* **12/1**

2160 **10** 1 **My Mirasol**[21] 1122 3-8-13 **64**..................................... RobbieFitzpatrick 9 52
(D E Cantillon) *led to over 3f out: wknd over 2f out* **20/1**

0-04 **11** 3 1/2 **Valart**[17] 1217 4-9-10 **60**.. AlanDaly 11 42
(A J Lidderdale) *chsd ldrs: drvn over 3f out: sn wknd* **50/1**

2m 5.43s (-2.36) **Going Correction** -0.175s/f (Stan)
WFA 3 from 4yo 15lb 11 Ran SP% **114.3**
Speed ratings (Par 100):102,101,101,100,99 98,96,95,95,94 91
CSF £104.36 CT £550.63 TOTE £4.70: £1.60, £10.30, £1.80; EX 76.00 TRIFECTA Not won..
Owner Kemal Kurt **Bred** George E McMahon **Trained** East Everleigh, Wilts

FOCUS
A modest fillies' handicap run at just an ordinary pace and rated through the fourth and fifth.
Windbeneathmywings(IRE) Official explanation: jockey said filly was unsuited by the surface

1629 RICHARDSON H'CAP 1m (P)
2:10 (2:10) (Class 5) (0-70,73) 4-Y-0+ **£2,914** (£867; £433; £216) **Stalls** High

Form RPR

60-4 **1** **Blue Line**[27] 1038 5-8-1 **56** oh3.. MarcHalford(3) 6 64
(M Madgwick) *hld up bhd ldrs: effrt on inner 2f out: hrd rdn fnl f: hung rt and bmpd runner-up as led last 75yds* **33/1**

5301 **2** 3/4 **Sailor King (IRE)**[10] 1382 5-9-7 **73** 6ex............................. JimCrowley 8 80
(D K Ivory) *trckd ldrs: drvn to ld jst over 1f out: edgd lft: hdd and c off worse in bump w wnr last 75yds: nt qckn* **1/1**[1]

62-0 **3** 2 **Titus Lumpus (IRE)**[7] 1446 4-8-9 **61**............................. DarryllHolland 7 65+
(R M Flower) *prom: led jst over 2f out: drvn and hdd jst over 1f out: hld whn squeezed out last 75yds* **16/1**

-504 **4** 1 3/4 **Treasure House (IRE)**[7] 1446 6-9-1 **67**............................. TedDurcan 9 65
(M Blanshard) *s.s: wl in rr: rdn over 3f out: sn no ch: styd on fnl f* **7/1**[2]

3621 **5** shd **Nikki Bea (IRE)**[11] 1344 4-8-8 **60** 6ex......................... SimonWhitworth 3 58
(Jamie Poulton) *wl in rr: rdn 3f out: sme prog over 1f out but nvr on terms* **12/1**

140- **6** 3/4 **High Class Problem (IRE)**[245] 5152 4-9-2 **68**.................. LPKeniry 2 64
(P F I Cole) *hld up in rr: rdn over 2f out: sn outpcd and btn* **14/1**

30-3 **7** 1 1/2 **Moves Goodenough**[14] 1283 4-8-13 **65**........................... ChrisCatlin 4 58
(Andrew Turnell) *trckd ldrs: rdn over 2f out: wknd over 1f out* **9/1**[3]

620- **8** hd **James Street (IRE)**[23] 6781 4-9-4 **70**.........................(b) GeorgeBaker 10 62
(J R Best) *t.k.h: led after 2f to over 2f out: wknd* **14/1**

03-4 **9** 3/4 **Chief Exec**[126] 44 5-9-4 **70**.. MartinDwyer 5 60
(C A Cyzer) *awkward s: sn led: hdd after 2f: led briefly over 2f out: wknd wl over 1f out* **10/1**

600- **10** shd **Da Bookie (IRE)**[155] 6741 7-9-3 **69**.........................(t) EdwardCreighton 1 59
(E J Creighton) *awkward s: hld up in last pair: shuffled along and no prog 2f out* **33/1**

1m 37.15s (-2.28) **Going Correction** -0.175s/f (Stan) 10 Ran SP% **114.4**
Speed ratings (Par 103):104,103,101,99,99 98,97,96,96,96
CSF £65.67 CT £592.63 TOTE £37.80: £8.40, £1.30, £4.90; EX 80.80 TRIFECTA Not won..
Owner Miss E M L Coller **Bred** Miss E M L Coller **Trained** Denmead, Hants
■ Stewards' Enquiry : Marc Halford one-day ban: careless riding (May 22)
Jim Crowley one-day ban: careless riding (May 22)

FOCUS
A modest handicap and weak form for the grade, rated through the third. Nobody was that keen to lead early on and the opening pace was just steady.

1630 WEATHERBYS BLOODSTOCK INSURANCE H'CAP 5f
2:40 (2:43) (Class 4) (0-85,85) 4-Y-0+ **£4,857** (£1,445; £722; £360) **Stalls** High

Form RPR

2126 **1** **Rowe Park**[28] 1023 4-9-0 **81**.. LPKeniry 10 93+
(Mrs L C Jewell) *racd against nr side rail: trckd ldrs: got through ent fnl f to ld last 100yds: won gng away* **3/1**[1]

-000 **2** 1 **Bold Minstrel (IRE)**[24] 1080 5-8-5 **72**................................ ChrisCatlin 8 81
(M Quinn) *mde most and racd towards nr side rail: drvn over 1f out: hdd and outpcd last 100yds* **14/1**

1100 **3** shd **Magic Glade**[16] 1242 8-9-4 **85**... JimCrowley 1 93
(Tom Dascombe) *racd on outer: pressed ldrs: rdn to chal wl over 1f out: upsides ins fnl f: outpcd last 100yds* **8/1**

0002 **4** 1 1/4 **Azygous**[17] 1214 4-8-9 **76**.. SimonWhitworth 2 80
(J Akehurst) *w ldr to jst over 1f out: one pce* **12/1**

0243 **5** shd **Nusoor (IRE)**[6] 1483 4-8-6 **73** oh1 ow2..................(b) RobbieFitzpatrick 7 76
(Peter Grayson) *wl in rr: urged along over 1f out: limited repsonse tl str burst last 100yds: fin wl* **11/2**[3]

6/00 **6** shd **Mafaheem**[4] 1524 5-9-1 **82**... IanMongan 3 85
(S Dow) *pressed ldrs: cl enough ent fnl f: fdd* **50/1**

6-00 **7** nk **Brandywell Boy (IRE)**[30] 1004 4-8-5 **72**................ FrankieMcDonald 11 74
(D J S Ffrench Davis) *wl in rr against nr side rail: struggling 2f out: styd on ins fnl f* **16/1**

00-0 **8** nk **Cashel Mead**[11] 1363 7-9-4 **85**.. SamHitchcott 5 86
(J L Spearing) *lost pl after 1f: effrt u.p over 1f out: no imp fnl f* **20/1**

06-0 **9** 1 **Jayanjay**[16] 1242 8-8-8 **75**... DarryllHolland 4 72
(P Mitchell) *racd on outer: nvr bttr than midfield: no prog over 1f out* **16/1**

05-0 **10** shd **Peopleton Brook**[6] 1464 5-8-11 **78**................................... TedDurcan 9 75+
(J M Bradley) *s.s: rcvrd into midfield after 2f: rdn whn n.m.r over 1f out: no ch* **5/1**[2]

24-6 **11** 1 **Heavens Walk**[114] 163 6-8-5 **72**.....................................(t) MartinDwyer 6 65+
(P J Makin) *chsd ldrs: lost pl wl over 1f out: wknd fnl f* **6/1**

00-0 **12** 2 1/2 **Don't Tell Sue**[16] 1242 4-8-11 **78**................................. PaulFitzsimons 12 62
(Miss J R Tooth) *rrd and v.s.a: a toiling in rr* **28/1**

57.06 secs (-1.88) **Going Correction** -0.25s/f (Firm) 12 Ran SP% **118.7**
Speed ratings (Par 105):105,103,103,101,101 100,100,99,98,98 96,92
CSF £47.33 CT £316.57 TOTE £4.80: £1.60, £5.20, £3.40; EX 65.90 TRIFECTA Not won..
Owner Mrs Sue Ashdown And Mrs Lesley Hammond **Bred** J Baker **Trained** Sutton Valence, Kent

FOCUS
A fair sprint handicap rated around the fourth and fifth to recent marks. They all raced towards the stands'-side rail and a high draw, although not essential, was a help. The winning time was 1.12 seconds faster than the following juvenile maiden.
Nusoor(IRE) Official explanation: jockey said gelding suffered interference in running

1631 EUROPEAN BREEDERS' FUND MAIDEN STKS 5f
3:10 (3:11) (Class 5) 2-Y-O **£3,562** (£1,059; £529; £264) **Stalls** High

Form RPR

43 **1** **Barraland**[9] 1411 2-9-3 .... ChrisCatlin 2 75
(M R Channon) *fast away: mde all: shkn up 2f out: clr whn hung lft fnl f: drvn out* **5/6**[1]

2 1 1/2 **Adab (IRE)** 2-9-3 .... MartinDwyer 4 69+
(J H M Gosden) *off the pce in 5th and rn green: prog to chse wnr 1f out: kpt on but nvr able to chal* **11/4**[2]

0 **3** 2 1/2 **Ballinskelligs Boy**[6] 1469 2-9-3 .... PatDobbs 7 59
(R Hannon) *pressed wnr to 2f out: fdd over 1f out* **6/1**[3]

0 **4** 1/2 **Lord Of The Wing**[10] 1367 2-9-3 .... GeorgeBaker 1 57
(R M Beckett) *chsd ldng pair but nt on terms: rn green and no prog fnl 2f* **33/1**

5 3 **Primed And Poised (USA)** 2-8-12 .... DarryllHolland 6 40
(J W Hills) *rn green: chsd ldrs to 1/2-way: wknd wl over 1f out* **16/1**

6 1 1/4 **King Bathwick (IRE)** 2-9-3 .... JimCrowley 3 40
(B R Millman) *v green and sn bdly outpcd: nvr a factor* **9/1**

58.18 secs (-0.76) **Going Correction** -0.25s/f (Firm) 6 Ran SP% **114.3**
Speed ratings (Par 93):96,93,89,88,84 82
CSF £3.46 TOTE £1.50: £1.10, £1.50; EX 3.50.
Owner Box 41 **Bred** Tattersalls Scoundrels & Trickledown Stud **Trained** West Ilsley, Berks

FOCUS
An uncompetitive juvenile maiden, but the winner set a fair standard. The winning time was 1.12 seconds slower than the previous 71-85 handicap.

NOTEBOOK
Barraland is all speed, so this track would have suited much better than Pontefract, and he confirmed the promise shown on both his previous start with a straightforward success, despite hanging to his left inside the final furlong. He looks capable of winning more races this season. (op 11-10)
Adab(IRE), a 70,000gns half-brother to three winners in Italy, including multiple 6f-1m winner Sri Rose, struggled to lay up in the early stages and looked badly in need of the experience, but he kept on nicely enough late on to take second behind the convincing winner. He should improve plenty and ought to find a similar race. (op 5-2 tchd 7-2)
Ballinskelligs Boy, last of eight in a reasonable Goodwood maiden on his debut just six days earlier, showed good speed but was put in his place late on. He is still learning and should be capable of better in time. (op 8-1)
Lord Of The Wing improved on the form he showed on his debut at Bath, but was never a threat. He is another who may need a little more time.
Primed And Poised(USA), a 23,000euros half-sister to some prolific winners in the US, including Shivley, successful 11 times over sprint trips, was the only filly in the line up and needed the experience. (op 12-1)
King Bathwick(IRE), a 23,000gns purchase, closely related to 1m1f winner Prince Sabaah, out of a 6f juvenile winner, looked far too green to do himself justice. (op 15-2 tchd 10-1)

1632 GENCO CONSTRUCTION LTD MAIDEN STKS (DIV I) 7f
3:45 (3:46) (Class 5) 3-Y-O **£2,590** (£770; £385; £192) **Stalls** High

Form RPR

03 **1** **Royal Rock**[14] 1278 3-9-3 .... IanMongan 4 81+
(C F Wall) *trckd ldr: led over 2f out: shkn up and drew clr over 1f out: comf* **12/1**[3]

2 2 1/2 **Duchess Royale (IRE)** 3-8-5 .... JamieHamblett(7) 6 66+
(Sir Michael Stoute) *s.s: detached in last tl prog over 2f out: reminders over 1f out: r.o to take 2nd last strides: encouraging debut* **12/1**[3]

00 **3** hd **Samsons Son**[11] 1343 3-9-3 .... GeorgeBaker 2 70
(J R Best) *chsd ldrs: clsd 2f out: rdn to chse wnr ins fnl f: no imp: lost 2nd last strides* **33/1**

34 **4** 1/2 **Six Of Diamonds (IRE)**[11] 1343 3-9-0 .... RichardKingscote(3) 9 69
(J A Osborne) *trckd ldrs: outpcd and pushed along over 2f out: styd on wl again ins fnl f* **9/2**[2]

5- **5** 1/2 **Galipette**[213] 5894 3-8-12 .... TedDurcan 8 63
(H R A Cecil) *t.k.h: hld up bhd ldng pair: effrt to chal wl over 1f out: sn rdn and btn: wknd ins fnl f* **4/9**[1]

0 **6** 3 1/2 **Jawaaneb (USA)**[20] 1143 3-8-12 .... MartinDwyer 3 54
(J L Dunlop) *wl in rr: shkn up 3f out: outpcd fnl 2f* **14/1**

0- **7** 3 1/2 **Hamilton House**[224] 5659 3-9-0 .... SaleemGolam(3) 10 50
(M H Tompkins) *dwlt: a in rr: rdn and struggling 3f out* **50/1**

8 3/4 **Dairy Maid** 3-8-12 .... DarryllHolland 7 43
(W J Knight) *t.k.h: led to over 2f out: wknd rapidly* **25/1**

00- **9** 1 1/4 **Kiss Chase (IRE)**[184] 6393 3-9-3 .... NickyMackay 1 44
(P Mitchell) *racd wd: nvr on terms w ldrs: wknd 2f out* **50/1**

1m 22.8s (-1.41) **Going Correction** -0.25s/f (Firm) 9 Ran SP% **120.2**
Speed ratings (Par 99):98,95,94,94,93 89,85,84,83
CSF £140.29 TOTE £13.40: £3.20, £4.60, £14.80; EX 98.80 TRIFECTA Not won..
Owner S Fustok **Bred** Deerfield Farm **Trained** Newmarket, Suffolk

FOCUS
The favourite failed to run her race and this was a weak maiden although the winner is value for further. The winning time was the slowest of the three 7f races on the card; 0.08 seconds slower than the second division, and 0.44 seconds off the concluding 56-70 handicap.
Galipette Official explanation: trainer said filly got a little tired after long lay-off
Dairy Maid Official explanation: jockey said filly ran too free

1633 GENCO CONSTRUCTION LTD MAIDEN STKS (DIV II) 7f
4:20 (4:20) (Class 5) 3-Y-O **£2,590** (£770; £385; £192) **Stalls** High

Form RPR

33- **1** **Monte Alto (IRE)**[213] 5883 3-9-3 .... NickyMackay 2 81+
(L M Cumani) *dwlt: sn trckd ldrs: pushed into ld over 1f out: rdn out cl home* **1/3**[1]

0- **2** 1 1/2 **Buxton**[247] 5106 3-9-3 .... RichardThomas 5 77
(R Ingram) *racd against nr side rail: led: rdn and hdd over 1f out: no ch w wnr but kpt on wl* **66/1**

3 2 **One Giant Leap (IRE)** 3-8-12 .... EdwardCreighton 7 67+
(H Morrison) *s.s: wl bhd in last tl stdy prog fr 1/2-way: shkn up to take 3rd ins fnl f: fair debut* **12/1**

5 **4** 3 1/2 **Golden Brown (IRE)**[14] 1278 3-9-0 .... NeilChalmers(3) 1 63
(David Pinder) *pressed ldr to 2f out: wknd jst over 1f out* **33/1**

2-0 **5** 2 **Cape Thea**[25] 1068 3-8-12 .... ChrisCatlin 8 53
(W R Swinburn) *chsd ldrs but nvr on terms: no ch fr over 2f out* **11/1**[3]

-00 **6** 4 **Adabi**[90] 418 3-9-3 .... MartinDwyer 6 47
(M P Tregoning) *s.s: nvr gng wl and a wl in rr* **5/1**[2]

000- **7** nk **Acosta**[226] 5622 3-8-12 **50**... KevinGhunowa(5) 4 47?
(Dr J R J Naylor) *chsd ldng pair to 1/2-way: sn wknd u.p* **66/1**

0- **8** 3 **Fluters House**[188] 6330 3-9-3 .... JimCrowley 9 39
(S Woodman) *a struggling and wl in rr* **66/1**

0 **9** *2* **Ridgeway Place**[7] 1452 3-8-12 .... LPKeniry 3 29
(A B Haynes) *dwlt: a wl in rr* **50/1**

1m 22.72s (-1.49) **Going Correction** -0.25s/f (Firm) **9** Ran SP% **117.1**
Speed ratings (Par 99):98,96,94,90,87 83,82,79,77
CSF £54.17 TOTE £1.30: £1.02, £14.30, £2.70; EX 41.50 Trifecta £83.10 Pool: £617.37 - 5.27 winning tickets..
Owner Timothy Steel **Bred** C H Wacker Iii **Trained** Newmarket, Suffolk

FOCUS
Like the first division, an uncompetitive maiden and the bare form looks modest but reliable. The winning time was 0.08 seconds faster than the first division, but 0.36 seconds slower than the following 56-70 handicap.

1634 TARMAC SOUTHERN H'CAP 7f
4:55 (4:55) (Class 5) (0-70,70) 3-Y-O **£2,914** (£867; £433; £216) **Stalls** High

Form RPR

3-06 **1** **Jack Oliver**[41] 843 3-9-4 **70** .... IanMongan 13 77
(B J Meehan) *hld up wl in rr: gd prog fr over 2f out in centre: clsd on ldrs 1f out: r.o u.p to ld last 75yds: jst hld on* **10/1**

40-5 **2** *nk* **Cavalry Guard (USA)**[15] 1259 3-9-4 **70** .... TedDurcan 14 76
(H R A Cecil) *dwlt: wl in rr: brought to nr side rail 1/2-way: prog 2f out: r.o wl fnl f: jst failed* **5/1**[3]

000- **3** *1 1/4* **Oscarshall (IRE)**[192] 6285 3-8-7 **62** .... SaleemGolam(3) 18 65
(M H Tompkins) *s.s: racd against nr side rail and wl in rr: prog over 2f out: drvn and styd on fr over 1f out: nrst fin* **25/1**

44-6 **4** *hd* **Tenancy (IRE)**[13] 1297 3-9-1 **67** .... MartinDwyer 11 69
(J A Osborne) *racd in centre: mde most: def advantage ent fnl f: hung lft and hdd last 75yds* **11/1**

2341 **5** *nk* **Blue Monkey (IRE)**[15] 1261 3-9-4 **70** .... DarryllHolland 15 71
(M L W Bell) *pressed ldrs: rdn over 2f out: nt look keen and nt qckn fnl f* **4/1**[2]

00-0 **6** *5* **Extractor**[20] 1155 3-8-4 **56** oh1 .... StephenCarson 16 44
(J L Dunlop) *racd against nr side rail: wl on terms tl wknd jst over 1f out* **25/1**

45-5 **7** *nk* **Wadnagin (IRE)**[11] 1346 3-8-0 **57** .... KevinGhunowa(5) 7 44
(I A Wood) *racd in centre and wl on terms w ldrs: wknd over 1f out* **14/1**

61 **8** *3/4* **Poppy's Rose**[31] 996 3-8-10 **62** .... JimCrowley 8 47
(I W McInnes) *racd centre: chsd ldrs: hanging lft and wknd over 1f out* **7/1**

20-2 **9** *2* **Whipchord (IRE)**[11] 1345 3-8-10 **62** .... PatDobbs 5 42
(R Hannon) *racd centre and chsd ldrs: wknd over 1f out* **16/1**

0024 **10** *nk* **Tenement (IRE)**[12] 1316 3-8-6 **58** .... SimonWhitworth 9 38
(Jamie Poulton) *wl in rr: rdn and no prog fnl 2f* **50/1**

0003 **11** *3* **Inquisitress**[12] 1316 3-8-8 **63** .... MarcHalford(3) 10 35
(J J Bridger) *wnt rt s: nvr bttr than midfield: no ch over 1f out* **33/1**

0434 **12** *1 1/2* **Realy Naughty (IRE)**[28] 1022 3-8-8 **65** .... PatrickHills(5) 17 33
(B G Powell) *racd nr side: chsd ldr there tl wknd rapidly 2f out* **10/3**[1]

60-6 **13** *1 3/4* **Kyllachy Storm**[17] 1211 3-8-5 **64** .... HaddenFrost(7) 2 27
(R J Hodges) *racd on outer: nvr on terms: wknd 2f out* **25/1**

-330 **14** *shd* **Prince Of Charm (USA)**[16] 1247 3-8-12 **64** .... NickyMackay 1 27
(R A Teal) *s.i.s: racd on outer in midfield: drvn and chsng ldrs 2f out: wknd and heavily eased over 1f out* **16/1**

00-0 **15** *nk* **Itsawindup**[21] 1117 3-8-6 **58** .... AdrianMcCarthy 12 20
(W J Knight) *s.s: u.p in last trio bef 1/2-way* **33/1**

00-0 **16** *3* **A Peaceful Man**[97] 342 3-8-5 **57** .... ChrisCatlin 6 11
(Mrs L C Jewell) *chsd ldrs to 1/2-way: sn wknd* **50/1**

6164 **17** *1* **Hucking Heat (IRE)**[11] 1359 3-9-4 **70** .... GeorgeBaker 3 22
(J R Best) *a wl in rr: struggling fr 1/2-way* **16/1**

05-0 **18** *1 1/2* **Brouhaha**[9] 1399 3-8-12 **64** .... LPKeniry 4 12
(Miss Diana Weeden) *wl bhd fr 1/2-way* **33/1**

1m 22.36s (-1.85) **Going Correction** -0.25s/f (Firm) **18** Ran SP% **138.3**
Speed ratings (Par 99):100,99,98,98,97 91,91,90,88,88 84,82,80,80,80 77,75,74
CSF £61.88 CT £874.34 TOTE £13.20: £2.40, £1.80, £6.40, £3.00; EX 75.30 TRIFECTA Not won. Place 6 £76.39, Place 5 £23.81.
Owner Alan Merritt&Aldridge Racing Partnership **Bred** R And Mrs Mitchell And Natton House Thoroughbreds **Trained** Manton, Wilts

FOCUS
Lots of runners and they were well spread out, with several racing towards the centre and a few trying their luck stands' side, but there did not appear to be any particular bias. Those drawn high dominated, but there did not seem to be any reason for that. A competitive heat and the form, although only modest, looks solid for the grade. The winning time was the quickest of the three 7f races on the card; 0.44 seconds quicker than the first division of the maiden, and 0.36 seconds faster than the second division.
T/Plt: £267.60 to a £1 stake. Pool: £45,149.85. 123.15 winning tickets. T/Qpdt: £61.00 to a £1 stake. Pool: £2,815.30. 34.10 winning tickets. JN

1403 NOTTINGHAM (L-H)
Friday, May 11

OFFICIAL GOING: Good (good to soft in places)
Wind: Light, half-against Weather: Cloudy with sunny spells

1635 GET TURFTV IN YOUR BETTING SHOP MEDIAN AUCTION MAIDEN STKS 6f 15y
2:00 (2:01) (Class 5) 3-Y-O **£2,914** (£867; £433; £216) **Stalls** High

Form RPR

6-2 **1** **Sundae**[15] 1267 3-9-3 .... NCallan 4 67+
(C F Wall) *hld up in tch: rdn to ld ins fnl f: r.o* **11/2**[3]

34- **2** *shd* **Excessive**[198] 6175 3-8-12 .... DaneO'Neill 12 62
(W Jarvis) *chsd ldr tl led 1/2-way: sn rdn: hdd 2f out: r.o u.p* **5/2**[1]

3 *nk* **Twosheetstothewind** 3-8-12 .... PhillipMakin 14 61+
(M Dods) *prom: nt clr run over 1f out: swtchd lft and r.o ins fnl f* **11/1**

-222 **4** *1 3/4* **Welsh Auction**[8] 1425 3-9-0 70 .... EmmettStack(3) 13 60
(G A Huffer) *led to 1/2-way: led 2f out: rdn and edgd lft over 1f out: hdd and no ex ins fnl f* **11/4**[2]

5-3 **5** *3/4* **Futuristic Dragon (IRE)**[21] 1136 3-9-3 .... TPO'Shea 10 58
(P A Blockley) *hld up: swtchd lft and hdwy over 1f out: nt trble ldrs* **14/1**

0-60 **6** *2* **Avoncreek**[79] 512 3-9-3 47 .... FergusSweeney 8 51?
(B P J Baugh) *mid-div: lost pl 1/2-way: hung lft and styd on ins fnl f* **100/1**

7 *7* **Brackenridge** 3-9-3 .... MickyFenton 1 29
(Miss E C Lavelle) *chsd ldrs 4f* **33/1**

8 *2* **Officer Material (IRE)** 3-9-3 .... AdamKirby 11 22
(C G Cox) *dwlt: outpcd* **16/1**

5- **9** *3* **Mootamaress (IRE)**[208] 5993 3-9-3 79 .... JimmyFortune 6 13
(Mrs A L M King) *chsd ldrs over 3f* **7/1**

00- **10** *3/4* **Silent Beauty (IRE)**[188] 6331 3-8-12 .... OscarUrbina 3 5
(S C Williams) *s.i.s: sme hdwy 2f out: sn wknd* **50/1**

-003 **11** *nk* **The Geester**[28] 1031 3-9-3 52 .... (b) PaulEddery 9 9
(S R Bowring) *chsd ldrs 4f* **33/1**

0- **12** *1/2* **Siesta (IRE)**[242] 5231 3-8-12 .... (e[1]) JamieSpencer 5 3
(J R Fanshawe) *hld up: sme hdwy 1/2-way: sn wknd* **14/1**

00- **13** *3/4* **Croeso Bach**[206] 6024 3-8-12 .... VinceSlattery 2 —
(J L Spearing) *prom: hung rt and wknd over 2f out* **100/1**

14 *5* **The Cube** 3-9-3 .... PaulMulrennan 7 —
(J Balding) *hld up: bhd fr 1/2-way* **50/1**

1m 17.0s (2.00) **Going Correction** +0.175s/f (Good) **14** Ran SP% **122.5**
Speed ratings (Par 99):93,92,92,90,89 86,77,74,70,69 69,68,67,60
CSF £19.41 TOTE £5.20: £2.10, £1.70, £4.10; EX 22.60.
Owner Peter Gregory **Bred** Jeremy Green And Sons **Trained** Newmarket, Suffolk

FOCUS
Modest maiden form rated through the runner-up with the 47-rated sixth finishing too close for comfort.
Silent Beauty(IRE) Official explanation: jockey said filly hung right

1636 EUROPEAN BREEDERS' FUND MEDIAN AUCTION MAIDEN FILLIES' STKS 5f 13y
2:30 (2:31) (Class 5) 2-Y-O **£3,562** (£1,059; £529; £264) **Stalls** High

Form RPR

1 **Alizadora** 2-9-0 .... SebSanders 9 78+
(Sir Mark Prescott) *racd stands' side: mde all: clr of that gp over 1f out: r.o wl* **33/1**

2 **2** *2* **Far Gone**[18] 1193 2-9-0 .... HayleyTurner 1 70
(M L W Bell) *racd far side: chsd ldr tl led that gp over 1f out: sn rdn: r.o: 1st of 7 in gp* **5/1**[2]

2 **3** *1 3/4* **Rebel Aclaim (IRE)**[20] 1150 2-8-11 .... JerryO'Dwyer(3) 3 63
(M G Quinlan) *wnt rt s: racd far side: sn led: rdn and hdd over 1f out: styd on same pce: 2nd of 7 in gp* **10/11**[1]

4 *1* **Lady Sandicliffe (IRE)** 2-9-0 .... JimmyFortune 6 59
(B W Hills) *s.i.s and hmpd s: racd far side: sn pushed along in rr: r.o ins fnl f: nvr nrr: 3rd of 7 in gp* **6/1**[3]

5 *1/2* **Monday Morning (IRE)** 2-9-0 .... JamieSpencer 5 57
(M J Wallace) *racd far side: edgd rt s: sn chsng ldrs: styd on same pce fnl f: 4th of 7 in gp* **15/2**

6 *2* **Johar Jamal (IRE)** 2-9-0 .... TPO'Shea 7 49
(M R Channon) *racd far side: hmpd s: hdwy over 3f out: rdn over 1f out: wknd ins fnl f: 5th of 7 in gp* **20/1**

7 *2* **Altercation** 2-9-0 .... NCallan 8 41
(W Jarvis) *wnt lft s: racd far side: chsd ldrs over 3f: 6th of 7 in gp* **16/1**

5 **8** *1/2* **Majigal**[15] 1255 2-9-0 .... PaulMulrennan 12 39
(M W Easterby) *racd stands' side: chsng wnr whn hmpd sn after s: lost pl over 3f out: n.d after: 2nd of 4 in gp* **33/1**

9 *1 3/4* **Validity** 2-9-0 .... (t) AdamKirby 11 32
(A J McCabe) *racd stands' side: dwlt: hdwy over 3f out: chsd wnr over 2f out tl rdn and wknd over 1f out: 3rd of 4 in gp* **80/1**

10 *2 1/2* **Jolly Tipsy** 2-8-7 .... NSLawes(7) 4 22
(M W Easterby) *racd far side: s.i.s and hmpd s: outpcd: last of 7 in gp* **33/1**

00 **11** *9* **Herolds Bay**[13] 1302 2-8-11 .... GregFairley(3) 10 —
(M W Easterby) *racd stands' side: chsd ldrs: hung lft fnl 3f: wknd 1/2-way: last of 4 in gp* **100/1**

64.18 secs (2.38) **Going Correction** +0.175s/f (Good) **11** Ran SP% **116.8**
Speed ratings (Par 90):87,83,81,79,78 75,72,71,68,64 50
CSF £182.83 TOTE £35.10: £10.30, £1.70, £1.20; EX 121.20.
Owner Miss K Rausing **Bred** Miss K Rausing **Trained** Newmarket, Suffolk

FOCUS
The field split, with four racing stands' side and the majority tacking over to race on the far side. The form is difficult to assess with confidence at this stage.

NOTEBOOK
Alizadora ◆, a half-sister to Coat Of Honour, a multiple 9-13f winner and also a winner over hurdles and fences, is bred to stay well and the market suggested little was expected on her debut, but she showed surprising speed, making every yard on the stands' side and having two lengths in hand of the far-side group at the line. She looks sure to progress and is one to keep on-side.
Far Gone shaped with promise on her debut at Pontefract and improved on that to win the race on her side, beating her nearest pursuer by almost two lengths. She should be able to go one better in similarly modest company soon. (op 6-1)
Rebel Aclaim(IRE), runner-up over this course and distance last month, was well fancied to go one better this time, but she was disappointing, even failing to win the race on her side. She was possibly unsuited by the easier ground. (op 5-6 tchd Evens and 11-10 in places)
Lady Sandicliffe(IRE), a half-sister to Mac Leader, a multiple winner in Italy at up to 1m4f, ran on late but is likely to need further than this and will welcome another furlong. Official explanation: jockey said filly was hampered at start (op 17-2)
Monday Morning(IRE), a half-sister to high-class sprinter Balthazaar's Gift, travelled well but did not find a great deal under pressure. She should improve for this debut experience, though. (op 13-2)
Johar Jamal(IRE) hails from a stable whose juveniles usually improve for their debut runs. She is bred to get a bit further, too. (op 22-1)

1637 STORA ENSO / REEL PAPER COMPANY H'CAP 1m 6f 15y
3:00 (3:16) (Class 5) (0-75,74) 3-Y-O **£3,886** (£1,156; £577; £288) **Stalls** Low

Form RPR

60-4 **1** **Bollin Felix**[39] 893 3-7-11 **55** .... (b[1]) DuranFentiman(5) 3 63+
(T D Easterby) *a.p: rdn over 2f out: nt clr run and swtchd rt wl over 1f out: styd on u.p to ld ins fnl f* **10/1**

14 **2** *2* **Serpentaria**[102] 294 3-9-6 **73** .... SebSanders 8 78+
(Sir Mark Prescott) *hld up: hdwy over 4f out: led 3f out: sn rdn and hung lft: hdd and no ex ins fnl f* **11/2**[3]

0103 **3** *1 3/4* **It's No Problem (IRE)**[17] 1211 3-8-2 **55** .... DavidKinsella 1 58
(M Salaman) *plld hrd and prom: rdn and ev ch over 1f out: no ex ins fnl f* **25/1**

-211 **4** *3/4* **Dee Cee Elle**[11] 1353 3-8-11 67 6ex .... GregFairley(3) 6 69
(M Johnston) *chsd ldrs: rdn over 3f out: styd on same pce appr fnl f* **3/1**[1]

1325 **5** *6* **Daylami Dreams**[18] 1205 3-9-5 **72** .... JamieSpencer 7 66
(J S Moore) *hld up: hdwy over 3f out: sn rdn and hung lft: wknd wl over 1f out* **11/2**[3]

0-00 **6** *8* **Present**[23] 1092 3-8-2 **55** oh2 .... HayleyTurner 2 37
(D Morris) *hld up: rdn over 3f out: n.d* **50/1**

1 **7** *nk* **Rumpus (GER)**[17] 1220 3-9-7 **74** .... MickyFenton 10 56
(T P Tate) *chsd ldr: rdn and ev ch over 3f out: wknd over 2f out* **8/1**

4-34 **8** *nk* **Crimson Monarch (USA)**[11] 1355 3-9-3 **70** .... JimmyFortune 11 52
(Mrs A J Perrett) *hld up: hdwy over 8f out: led over 4f out: hdd 3f out: rdn and wknd 2f out* **10/3**[2]

0-00 9 14 **Lucy Rebecca**[20] 1153 3-8-2 **55** TPO'Shea 5 17
(M R Channon) *hld up: pushed along 1/2-way: wknd 4f out* **40/1**

63-4 10 7 **Red**[23] 1092 3-8-11 **64** AdamKirby 4 16
(R M Beckett) *sn led: rdn and hdd over 4f out: wknd over 2f out* **10/1**

3m 8.83s (1.73) **Going Correction** +0.175s/f (Good) **10** Ran SP% **116.4**
Speed ratings (Par 99):102,100,99,99,96 91,91,91,83,79
CSF £63.10 CT £1345.37 TOTE £12.70: £3.50, £3.00, £4.60; EX 67.80.
Owner Sir Neil Westbrook **Bred** Sir & Exors Of Late Lady Westbrook **Trained** Great Habton, N Yorks

FOCUS
A modest handicap featuring three-year-olds who were untested at this sort of distance and although the first two are unexposed the bare form looks ordinary.
Crimson Monarch(USA) Official explanation: jockey said colt never travelled
Red Official explanation: jockey said filly had no more to give

1638 TURFTV.CO.UK H'CAP — 1m 1f 213y
3:35 (3:40) (Class 5) (0-75,75) 4-Y-0+ **£3,238** (£963; £481; £240) **Stalls** Low

Form RPR

0-2 1 **Im Spartacus**[2] 1578 5-8-13 **70** JamieSpencer 5 79+
(Evan Williams) *hld up in tch: led over 2f out: rdn and hung lft fr over 1f out: r.o* **7/4**[1]

30-0 2 2 **Mae Cigan (FR)**[7] 1451 4-8-10 **67** NCallan 8 71
(M Blanshard) *hld up: hdwy over 1f out: r.o: nt rch wnr* **16/1**

6050 3 hd **Street Life (IRE)**[16] 1249 9-8-7 **64** ow1 MickyFenton 10 68
(W J Musson) *hld up: hdwy and hung lft fr over 1f out: styd on* **16/1**

000- 4 hd **Gallego**[159] 6693 5-7-12 **62** MCGeran(7) 9 65
(R J Price) *s.s: hld up: racd keenly: hdwy 3f out: chsd wnr and rdn over 1f out: no ex ins fnl f* **40/1**

00-0 5 1 ¾ **Rawdon (IRE)**[13] 1288 6-9-3 **74** (v) HayleyTurner 1 74
(M L W Bell) *chsd ldrs: rdn and nt clr run 3f out: styd on same pce fnl f* **12/1**

5-00 6 ¾ **Faith And Reason (USA)**[24] 1083 4-9-2 **73** PaulMulrennan 3 71
(B J Curley) *chsd ldrs: nt clr run and lost pl 3f out: styd on ins fnl f* **16/1**

15-2 7 1 ¼ **Piper's Song (IRE)**[24] 1078 4-8-13 **70** DaneO'Neill 6 66
(H Candy) *hld up: hdwy and hung lft fr over 2f out: wknd fnl f* **2/1**[2]

104- 8 2 ½ **Dove Cottage (IRE)**[240] 5295 5-9-0 **71** FergusSweeney 7 62
(W S Kittow) *led over 7f: rdn and wknd over 1f out* **8/1**[3]

6-46 9 3 ½ **Xpres Maite**[85] 468 4-8-8 **65** PaulEddery 4 50
(S R Bowring) *hld up: n.d* **66/1**

00-0 10 7 **Nesno (USA)**[41] 850 4-9-4 **75** LDettori 2 46
(J D Bethell) *chsd ldr 4f: rdn over 2f out: sn wknd* **22/1**

5142 11 2 ½ **Samuel Charles**[25] 1066 9-9-3 **74** (p) SebSanders 11 41
(C R Dore) *hdwy over 8f out: rdn and wknd over 2f out* **16/1**

2m 10.61s (0.91) **Going Correction** +0.175s/f (Good) **11** Ran SP% **120.3**
Speed ratings (Par 103):103,101,101,101,99 99,98,96,93,87 85
CSF £32.59 CT £359.35 TOTE £2.20: £1.60, £4.30, £2.90; EX 42.50.
Owner The Regulate Partnership **Bred** John Purcell **Trained** Llancarfan, Vale Of Glamorgan

FOCUS
A modest handicap won by a well-handicapped performer but the form is not that solid, despite the placed horses being close to their marks.
Street Life(IRE) Official explanation: jockey said gelding hung left

1639 TURFTV A MATTER OF COURSE MAIDEN FILLIES' STKS — 1m 54y
4:10 (4:12) (Class 5) 3-Y-O **£3,238** (£963; £481; £240) **Stalls** Centre

Form RPR

4- 1 **In Safe Hands (IRE)**[224] 5661 3-9-0 DaneO'Neill 4 83
(C G Cox) *hld up: hdwy 1/2-way: rdn to ld wl ins fnl f* **4/1**[2]

2 2 1 **Truly Enchanting (IRE)**[18] 1203 3-9-0 LDettori 12 81
(J Noseda) *hld up in tch: plld hrd: rdn to chse ldr and hung lft over 1f out: ev ch ins fnl f: no ex towards fin* **4/6**[1]

4 3 nk **Jacaranda Ridge**[18] 1203 3-9-0 NCallan 6 80
(M A Jarvis) *led: rdn over 1f out: hdd wl ins fnl f* **11/1**[3]

4 3 **Fondled** 3-9-0 JamieSpencer 3 73+
(J R Fanshawe) *s.s: hld up: hdwy 2f out: edgd lft over 1f out: nt trble ldrs* **14/1**

0- 5 ¾ **Expedience (USA)**[197] 6186 3-9-0 SebSanders 1 72
(Sir Michael Stoute) *prom: rdn to chse ldr 3f out: wknd ins fnl f* **12/1**

40- 6 2 ½ **Vallemeldee (IRE)**[210] 5947 3-9-0 MickyFenton 16 66
(P W D'Arcy) *broke wl: sn stdd and lost pl: hung lft and styd on fr over 1f out: nt trble ldrs* **80/1**

3 7 nk **Etain (IRE)**[14] 1282 3-9-0 AdamKirby 17 65+
(W R Swinburn) *s.i.s: hld up: nt clr run 3f out: styd on appr fnl f: nvr nrr* **40/1**

0- 8 3 **Cat Six (USA)**[227] 5592 3-8-7 KMay(7) 13 58
(B J Meehan) *prom: racd keenly: hung lft and wknd 2f out* **80/1**

02- 9 nk **Peintre's Wonder (IRE)**[214] 5859 3-9-0 TPO'Shea 15 58
(E J O'Neill) *hld up: rdn over 3f out: n.d* **33/1**

0 10 shd **Movie Mogul**[25] 1068 3-9-0 HayleyTurner 10 57
(M L W Bell) *in rr: rdn 1/2-way: n.d* **100/1**

4- 11 2 ½ **Sofia Royale**[188] 6330 3-8-9 MichaelJStainton(5) 14 52
(B Palling) *a in rr* **50/1**

12 ¾ **Devon House (USA)** 3-9-0 DavidKinsella 2 50+
(J H M Gosden) *dwlt: hld up: nt clr run 3f out: a in rr* **40/1**

0 13 2 ½ **Prima Ballerina**[18] 1203 3-9-0 JimmyFortune 11 44
(J H M Gosden) *hld up: racd keenly: rdn and wknd over 2f out* **16/1**

5-4 14 5 **Boogie Board**[10] 1369 3-9-0 PaulEddery 7 33
(S Parr) *chsd ldr 5f: sn rdn and wknd* **200/1**

0-66 15 3 **Miss Daawe**[21] 1136 3-8-11 40 DominicFox(3) 5 26
(S Parr) *chsd ldrs over 5f* **200/1**

0 16 1 ¼ **Entre Chat**[27] 1045 3-9-0 (t) OscarUrbina 9 23
(M Botti) *chsd ldrs over 5f* **50/1**

1m 47.28s (0.88) **Going Correction** +0.175s/f (Good) **16** Ran SP% **124.8**
Speed ratings (Par 96):102,101,100,97,96 94,94,91,90,90 88,87,85,80,77 75
CSF £6.90 TOTE £5.60: £1.70, £1.10, £3.10; EX 9.30.
Owner Ms Elaine Flynn **Bred** Tommy Burns **Trained** Lambourn, Berks

FOCUS
Not a bad maiden on paper but they went no pace early and it turned into something of a sprint and improved form of those behind limits confidence.
Fondled Official explanation: jockey said filly was slowly away

1640 RACING AGAIN TOMORROW APPRENTICE H'CAP — 6f 15y
4:45 (4:45) (Class 6) (0-60,67) 4-Y-0+ **£2,457** (£725; £362) **Stalls** High

Form RPR

00-2 1 **Brunelleschi**[9] 1405 4-9-2 **60** (b) LukeMorris(3) 9 79+
(P L Gilligan) *s.i.s: hld up: hdwy over 2f out: rdn to ld and hung lft over 1f out: sn clr* **13/2**[2]

5006 2 5 **Jellytot (USA)**[10] 1379 4-8-11 **57** (b[1]) MCGeran(5) 17 64+
(J O'Reilly) *s.s: hld up: hmpd over 2f out: swtchd lft and hdwy over 1f out: no ch w wnr* **14/1**

030- 3 1 ¼ **Butterfly Bud (IRE)**[205] 6061 4-8-13 **57** RussellKennemore(3) 13 52
(J O'Reilly) *chsd ldrs: rdn over 2f out: hung lft and no ex fr over 1f out* **22/1**

04-4 4 hd **Briery Lane (IRE)**[17] 1212 6-9-0 **58** AshleyHamblett(3) 1 52+
(J M Bradley) *mid-div: hdwy over 2f out: sn rdn: no ex fr over 1f out* **12/1**

6560 5 1 ¾ **Ceredig**[10] 1379 4-8-7 **53** WilliamCarson(5) 10 42
(P W Hiatt) *s.i.s: hld up: swtchd lft and hdwy over 2f out: no ch whn nt clr run 1f out* **28/1**

06-2 6 6 **Cyfrwys (IRE)**[17] 1221 6-8-13 **54** (p) MichaelJStainton 15 24
(B Palling) *chsd ldr: rdn over 3f out: wknd over 1f out* **10/1**

060- 7 ½ **Ruman (IRE)**[315] 3052 5-8-10 **56** JosephWalsh(5) 5 24
(M J Attwater) *s.i.s: sn outpcd: nvr nrr* **22/1**

6000 8 ½ **Sir Loin**[9] 1405 6-8-10 **54** DanielleMcCreery(3) 12 20
(N Tinkler) *mid-div: hdwy over 2f out: rdn and wknd over 1f out* **33/1**

004- 9 1 **Full Spate**[228] 5569 12-8-6 **52** PietroRomeo(5) 8 15
(J M Bradley) *s.s: outpcd* **66/1**

-402 10 shd **North Fleet**[9] 1400 4-8-9 **55** BarrySavage(5) 16 18
(J M Bradley) *chsd ldrs over 4f* **16/1**

435- 11 1 **Turn Me On (IRE)**[277] 4201 4-9-0 **55** DuranFentiman 6 15
(T D Walford) *hld up: wknd wl over 1f out* **16/1**

6-11 12 nk **Raccoon (IRE)**[3] 1557 7-9-12 **67** 12ex PJMcDonald 4 26
(D W Chapman) *led: rdn and hdd over 1f out: sn wknd: stmbld and rdr lost iron nr fin* **6/4**[1]

00-0 13 ½ **Gone'N'Dunnett (IRE)**[39] 892 8-8-7 **51** (v) KirstyMilczarek(3) 11 8
(Mrs C A Dunnett) *chsd ldrs: stmbld 4f out: wknd over 2f out* **25/1**

6-40 14 ¾ **Scuba (IRE)**[51] 724 5-9-5 **60** (b) TravisBlock 3 15
(H Morrison) *sn outpcd* **15/2**[3]

0-00 15 9 **Kennington**[13] 1309 7-8-12 **56** (b) TolleyDean(3) 7 —
(Mrs C A Dunnett) *chsd ldrs to 1/2-way* **25/1**

00-0 16 nk **Smart Cassie**[11] 1366 4-8-11 **55** (p) ThomasO'Brien(3) 2 —
(H J Evans) *chsd ldrs: rdn 1/2-way: sn wknd* **40/1**

1m 15.64s (0.64) **Going Correction** +0.175s/f (Good) **16** Ran SP% **127.0**
Speed ratings (Par 101):102,95,93,93,91 83,82,81,80,80 78,78,77,76,64 64
CSF £88.47 CT £2000.15 TOTE £9.10: £1.60, £3.60, £5.60, £2.80; EX 94.30 Place 6 £86.64, Place 5 £45.94.
Owner Dr Susan Barnes **Bred** Dr Susan Barnes **Trained** Newmarket, Suffolk

FOCUS
A moderate sprint handicap in which there were few in-form contenders and the form is not strong. They all came stands' side.
Full Spate Official explanation: jockey said gelding missed the break
Kennington Official explanation: jockey said gelding lost its action
Smart Cassie Official explanation: jockey said filly lost its action
T/Plt: £136.00 to a £1 stake. Pool: £47,988.65. 257.45 winning tickets. T/Qpdt: £57.90 to a £1 stake. Pool: £2,605.90. 33.30 winning tickets. CR

1641 - 1646a (Foreign Racing) - See Raceform Interactive

JAGERSRO (R-H)
Friday, May 11

OFFICIAL GOING: Wet (fast)

1647a JAGERSRO SPRINT (LISTED RACE) — 6f (D)
7:36 (7:37) 3-Y-0+ **£17,924** (£5,975; £2,987; £1,867; £1,120)

RPR

1 **Maxim's (ARG)**[97] 344 6-9-4 (b) MSantos 5 —
(L Reuterskiold, Sweden) **86/10**

2 1 ½ **Media Hora (CHI)**[85] 474 7-9-4 (b) RVaras 8 —
(F Castro, Sweden) **9/2**[3]

3 1 **Zoogina Zaid (SWE)**[224] 5-9-0 EPedroza 1 —
(Vanja Sandrup, Sweden) **168/10**

4 1 ½ **Pipoldchap (CHI)**[92] 396 7-9-4 (b) NCordrey 3 —
(F Castro, Sweden) **9/10**[1]

5 hd **Relampago Plus (ARG)** 7-9-4 P-AGraberg 6 —
(B Bo, Sweden) **104/10**

6 4 **Qadar (IRE)**[42] 828 5-9-4 (b) KAndersen 7 —
(N P Littmoden) *rear early, went midfield halfway, ridden 2f out, no impression* **36/10**[2]

7 1 **Hardy Norseman (IRE)**[461] 298 4-9-4 (b) MadeleineSmith 2 —
(Madeleine Smith, Sweden) **27/1**

8 5 **Berri Chis (ARG)**[243] 5225 5-9-4 JJohansen 4 —
(Vanja Sandrup, Sweden) **183/10**

1m 13.4s (73.40) **8** Ran SP% **126.1**
(including 1Kr stake): WIN 9.63; PL 3.56, 2.24, 3.06; DF 82.17.
Owner Stall Gransater **Bred** Miguel Angel Vallina **Trained** Sweden

NOTEBOOK
Qadar(IRE) does best when covered up. However, the only horse drawn outside him was Media Hora, who went straight to the front. He saw too much daylight all the way.

1648a PRAMMS MEMORIAL (LISTED RACE) — 1m 133y
8:00 (8:02) 4-Y-0+ **£44,810** (£14,937; £7,468; £4,481; £2,987)

RPR

1 **Salt Track (ARG)**[32] 7-9-4 ESki 3 100
(Niels Petersen, Norway) **176/10**

2 4 **Maybach**[174] 6516 6-9-4 P-AGraberg 2 92
(B Bo, Sweden) **104/10**

3 2 ½ **Ancient Egypt**[943] 6077 5-9-4 ILopez 6 87
(Annelie Larsson, Sweden) **34/1**

4 1 ½ **Highway (IRE)**[224] 4-9-4 (b) MSantos 11 84
(F Castro, Sweden) **152/10**

5 3 ½ **Icaros (SWE)**[19] 4-9-4 FJohansson 8 78
(Wido Neuroth, Norway) **47/10**[3]

6 3 ½ **Pecoiquen (CHI)**[92] 400 6-9-4 (b) RVaras 1 71
(F Castro, Sweden) **109/10**

7 ½ **Vortex**[13] 1294 8-9-4 (b) NCordrey 9 70
(Miss Gay Kelleway) *midfield, ridden to take 4th 2f out, soon beaten* **18/10**[1]

8 1 ½ **Halfsong (SWE)**[180] 7-9-0 DinaDanekilde 12 63
(K P Andersen, Sweden) **52/1**

9 ½ **Miyasaki (CHI)**[327] 5-9-4 LTorres 7 66
(Rune Haugen, Norway) **149/10**

10 *1* **Be Alert (SWE)**[239] 5-9-4 ....(b) KAndersen 10 64
(L Reuterskiold, Sweden) **26/1**
11 *8* **Wazir (USA)**[442] 495 5-9-4 ....(b) YvonneDurant 4 49
(L Reuterskiold, Sweden) **87/10**
12 *7* **Albany Hall (IRE)**[382] 1202 5-9-4 .... MLarsen 5 36
(F Poulsen, France) **42/10**[2]
1m 48.3s (108.30) **12** Ran SP% **126.3**
WIN 18.64; PL 6.01, 4.06, 3.16; DF 161.32.
Owner Oslo Racing Stables AS **Bred** Arturo Vargas Lerena **Trained** Norway

NOTEBOOK
Vortex had a perfect run throughtout, as he had when winning this under the same jockey two years ago, but never looked capable of gaining a repeat. Although the track was still wet fast, it had less water in it than earlier in the evening and the kickback was less pronounced. It was his 15th race in the last eight months and he may be due for another rest.

[1390]ASCOT (R-H)
Saturday, May 12

OFFICIAL GOING: Straight course - good to soft changing to soft after race 4 (3.00); round course - soft (good to soft in places)
Weather: rain Wind: Moderate, against

1649 JOHN DOYLE FILLIES' HERITAGE H'CAP 1m (S)
1:10 (1:13) (Class 2) 3-Y-0+ **£25,908** (£7,708; £3,852; £1,924) **Stalls** Low

Form RPR
13-3 **1** **Heaven Sent**[21] 1145 4-9-8 **87** .... KerrinMcEvoy 2 103+
(Sir Michael Stoute) *lw: hld up in mid-div: smooth hdwy 3f out: led over 1f out: styd on strly: readily* **7/4**[1]
02-1 **2** *2* **Apply Dapply**[39] 902 4-8-5 **70** .... JohnEgan 8 81
(H Morrison) *lw: slowly away: towards rr: hdwy over 3f out: led over 2f out: sn rdn: hdd over 1f out: kpt on but readily hld by wnr* **6/1**[2]
2-05 **3** *3* **Adventuress**[14] 1287 4-9-6 **85** .... KDarley 6 89
(B J Meehan) *lw: mid-div: rdn over 2f out: styd on fr over 1f out: wnt 3rd nr fin* **16/1**
40-1 **4** *nk* **Mcnairobi**[72] 590 4-9-4 **83** .... JamieSpencer 9 86
(P D Cundell) *slowly away: bhd: hdwy 3f out: rdn to chse ldng pair over 1f out: kpt on same pce ins fnl f* **10/1**
133- **5** *3* **Gaelic Princess**[152] 6791 7-9-2 **81** .... ChrisCatlin 4 77+
(A G Newcombe) *bmpd s: mid-div: clsng and nt clr run 3f out: sn swtchd rt and rdn: styd on ins fnl f* **25/1**
6-20 **6** *1 ½* **Fann (USA)**[30] 1013 4-8-13 **78** .... KJManning 10 71
(C E Brittain) *chsd ldrs: led briefly 3f out: sn rdn: fdd ins fnl f* **25/1**
P055 **7** *2* **Daring Affair**[10] 1414 6-9-1 **80** .... PhillipMakin 1 68
(K R Burke) *lw: prom: rdn 3f out: one pce fnl 2f* **50/1**
3154 **8** *6* **Musical Beat**[2] 1610 3-8-2 **80** ow3.................... AdrianTNicholls 5 54
(Miss V Haigh) *led: rdn and hdd 3f out: grad fdd* **16/1**
0-13 **9** *nk* **Going To Work (IRE)**[10] 1407 3-7-7 **76** oh1.......... WilliamBuick(5) 3 50
(D R C Elsworth) *wnt rt s: prom: rdn 3f out: struggling whn n.m.r sn after* **6/1**[2]
1-60 **10** *11* **Persian Express (USA)**[6] 1494 4-9-10 **89**.................... MichaelHills 12 37
(B W Hills) *mid-div tl wknd 2f out: eased fnl f* **25/1**
321- **11** *3* **Jewaar (USA)**[259] 4814 4-9-6 **85**.................... MartinDwyer 13 26
(M A Jarvis) *prom: rdn 3f out: sn btn* **7/1**[3]
1-30 **12** *18* **Rakata (USA)**[7] 1472 5-9-5 **84**.................... JimmyFortune 7 —
(P F I Cole) *prom: rdn 3f out: sn hung rt and wknd* **20/1**
0/0- **13** *29* **Mistress Bailey (IRE)**[187] 6384 4-9-1 **85**.................... PatrickHills(5) 11 —
(D Shaw) *b.bkwd: wnt rt s: bhd fnl 4f* **66/1**
1m 44.2s (2.40) **Going Correction** +0.475s/f (Yiel)
WFA 3 from 4yo+ 13lb **13** Ran SP% **118.0**
Speed ratings (Par 96):107,105,102,101,98 97,95,89,88,77 74,56,27
CSF £10.45 CT £133.29 TOTE £2.40: £1.30, £1.60, £5.70; EX 10.20 Trifecta £172.20 Pool: £985.10 - 4.06 winning units..
Owner Cheveley Park Stud **Bred** Cheveley Park Stud Ltd **Trained** Newmarket, Suffolk

FOCUS
They came up the centre of the track in this handicap, and it was dominated by well-handicapped fillies. The form is solid although not the strongest for the grade and should work out.

NOTEBOOK
Heaven Sent, third in the Spring Cup last time out, had less to do off the same mark in a weaker event, and the softer ground was never likely to be a problem for this daughter of Pivotal. Travelling well throughout, she quickened up well to take it up inside the final two furlongs and won more easily than the winning margin suggests. She looked a Pattern-class filly in the making here and should be kept on-side. (op 15-8 tchd 13-8)
Apply Dapply, who won cleverly at Folkestone on her reappearance, was only 3lb higher here and was unlucky to run into an even better handicapped rival. She was the only one to give the winner a race and is clearly progressive, but she blew a good mark in defeat. (op 9-2 tchd 7-1 in places)
Adventuress has been fairly consistent when dropped back into handicap company, and her performance is probably the best guide to the form. She stayed on well, as a winner over 1m2f should be expected to. (tchd 14-1)
Mcnairobi has done all her winning on the Polytrack but she is unexposed on turf. Held up out the back, she stayed on well in the closing stages and it is likely that she will not mind quicker ground. (op 12-1)
Gaelic Princess, the most experienced runner in the line-up, was always likely to find some of her less-exposed rivals too strong on her first outing since December and on ground that would have been too soft for her. In the circumstances she ran well.
Fann(USA) probably needs further than this ideally but she showed up well for a long way on ground that suits.
Going To Work(IRE), the least experienced runner in the race, was racing from 1lb out of the handicap and had a tough task taking on older fillies this early in the season. She still looked green. (op 8-1)
Persian Express(USA) Official explanation: jockey said filly lost a front shoe
Jewaar(USA) took a long time to get off the mark last year but looked on a fair mark for her reappearance. This ground might not have suited her though, and she deserves another chance back on a firmer surface. (tchd 8-1)
Mistress Bailey(IRE) Official explanation: jockey said filly lost a front shoe

1650 BOVIS HOMES BUCKHOUNDS STKS (LISTED RACE) 1m 4f
1:45 (1:45) (Class 1) 4-Y-0+
£22,712 (£8,608; £4,308; £2,148; £1,076; £540) **Stalls** High

Form RPR
22-5 **1** **Mountain High (IRE)**[15] 1274 5-8-12 119.................... KerrinMcEvoy 3 114+
(Sir Michael Stoute) *lw: mde all: rdn and drifted to centre of crse over 2f out: styd on strly to assert fnl 100yds* **8/13**[1]
0-60 **2** *4* **Akarem**[21] 1144 6-8-12 105.................... PatCosgrave 5 108
(K R Burke) *chsd wnr: rdn to chal over 2f out and styd on far side rails: ev ch 1f out: hld fnl 100yds* **7/1**[2]
203- **3** *nk* **Balkan Knight**[210] 5967 7-8-12 106.................... JohnEgan 6 108
(D R C Elsworth) *b.bkwd: in tch: pushed along 4f out: swtchd to centre of crse and rdn over 2f out: styd on fnl f* **10/1**
300- **4** *5* **Star Of Light**[273] 4359 6-8-12 99.................... MartinDwyer 2 101
(B J Meehan) *t.k.h in tch: swtchd to centre of crse and rdn over 2f out: kpt on same pce* **25/1**
424- **5** *4* **Mango Mischief (IRE)**[171] 6567 6-8-7 101.................... JHBowman 1 90
(M R Channon) *plld hrd towards rr: effrt over 2f out jst off far side rails over 2f out: sn one pce* **16/1**
444/ **6** *3 ½* **Kong (IRE)**[293] 5-8-12 .... JimmyFortune 4 89
(J L Dunlop) *chsd ldrs: swtchd lft to centre of crse for effrt over 2f out: wknd over 1f out* **8/1**[3]
341- **7** *1 ½* **High Heel Sneakers**[198] 6191 4-8-10 105.................... JamieSpencer 7 85
(P F I Cole) *lw: hld up last: nt clr run briefly 3f out: sn rdn and sme hdwy jst off far side rails over 2f out: wknd over 1f out* **10/1**
2m 42.05s (9.05) **Going Correction** +1.00s/f (Soft) **7** Ran SP% **113.4**
Speed ratings (Par 111):109,106,106,102,100 97,96
CSF £5.44 TOTE £1.70: £1.30, £3.50; EX 5.90.
Owner Mrs John Magnier & M Tabor **Bred** Ballymacoll Stud Farm Ltd **Trained** Newmarket, Suffolk
■ Stewards' Enquiry : Jamie Spencer two-day ban: dropped hands and lost sixth place (May 23-24)

FOCUS
Run in teeming rain, this Listed race was run at a steady early gallop but the form looks reasonable with the placed horses pretty much to form.

NOTEBOOK
Mountain High(IRE) had presumably needed the run at Sandown more than the market suggested that day, but this was a much less competitive affair as he had 12lb in hand of his nearest rival on adjusted official ratings. In addition, McEvoy was allowed to dictate a steady pace. Coming up the centre of the track in the straight, while his closest pursuer went towards the far side, he pulled clear for a comfortable enough success which should have done his confidence some good. He looks a possible for the Hardwicke Stakes, although his powerful stable has a number of other candidates for that particular race. (op 4-6 tchd 8-11)
Akarem ran well considering he had 14lb to find with the winner on official ratings and stayed towards the possibly unfavoured far side rail in the straight. He is a proven mud-lover, though, so did have conditions very much to suit. (tchd 15-2)
Balkan Knight did not get to race on easy ground very often last year but showed here that he does appreciate a bit of dig. Performing best of those making their seasonal reappearance, he stays further than this, but is quite a difficult horse to place, and his best chance of success is likely to come in a minor conditions race somewhere.
Star Of Light, who looked as though the run would improve, had a mountain to climb on the ratings and did not help his cause by racing keenly off the steady early gallop. He looks high enough in the handicap at present but also short of Listed class. (op 20-1)
Mango Mischief(IRE), who has not won since July 2005, has joined a new stable and was entitled to need this seasonal reappearance. Another who failed to settle in the early stages, she will be more effective when she goes back to racing in fillies-only races. (op 25-1)
Kong(IRE), restricted to just two races last term, looked fit enough but ran as though the race would just put an edge on him. He should be sharper next time. (op 10-1)
High Heel Sneakers, who won a Listed race on Polytrack on her final start last season, needs to be held up in her races, but off this steady pace she pulled hard and gave herself little chance of getting home. (op 8-1)

1651 TOTESPORT.COM VICTORIA CUP (HERITAGE H'CAP) 7f
2:20 (2:24) (Class 2) 4-Y-0+
£52,972 (£15,861; £7,930; £3,969; £1,980; £994) **Stalls** Low

Form RPR
40-1 **1** **Wise Dennis**[20] 1179 5-8-12 **96**.................... JHBowman 14 113
(A P Jarvis) *hld up towards rr on stands' side: smooth hdwy over 2f out: led wl over 1f out: drew clr ins fnl f: comf* **14/1**
0-30 **2** *4* **Skhilling Spirit**[7] 1474 4-8-13 **97**.................... PhillipMakin 3 103+
(T D Barron) *lw: mid-div on stands' side: rdn and hdwy over 1f out: r.o but hung rt ins fnl f: wnt 2nd nr fin* **16/1**
0-50 **3** *¾* **Fullandby (IRE)**[7] 1474 5-8-9 **93**.................... KDarley 27 97
(T J Etherington) *mid-div in centre: hdwy 3f out: rdn and ev ch over 1f out: kpt on: lost 2nd nr fin* **10/1**[3]
01-4 **4** *hd* **Partners In Jazz (USA)**[20] 1179 6-9-1 **99**.................... PaulFessey 28 102
(T D Barron) *hld up towards rr in centre: hdwy over 2f out: sn rdn: ev ch over 1f out: kpt on* **14/1**
65-1 **5** *1 ¾* **Beaver Patrol (IRE)**[7] 1474 5-8-12 **96**.................... StephenCarson 16 95
(Eve Johnson Houghton) *mid-div on stands' side: rdn and hdwy 3f out: styd on ins fnl f* **20/1**
6-40 **6** *nk* **Pentecost**[100] 325 8-8-8 **97**.................... WilliamBuick(5) 18 95+
(A M Balding) *sn swtchd to centre gp: towards rr: rdn whn swtchd rt 2f out: styd on fnl f* **50/1**
051- **7** *1 ¼* **Ordnance Row**[259] 4790 4-8-9 **93**.................... SilvestreDeSousa 11 88
(R Hannon) *chsd ldrs on stands' side: led 3f out: rdn whn hung lft and hdd wl over 1f out: kpt on same pce fnl f* **33/1**
0-31 **8** *nk* **Malcheek (IRE)**[7] 1481 5-8-5 **89**.................... DavidAllan 17 83+
(T D Easterby) *hld up towards rr on stands' side: rdn over 2f out: styd on fr over 1f out: nt rch ldrs* **66/1**
211- **9** *¾* **Trimlestown (IRE)**[196] 6221 4-7-13 **83**.................... FrankieMcDonald 4 75+
(H Candy) *prom on stands' side: ev ch 2f out: wknd ins fnl f* **11/1**
0-03 **10** *½* **Prince Of Thebes (IRE)**[14] 1307 6-8-11 **95**.................... AmirQuinn 2 85
(J Akehurst) *chsd ldrs on stands' side: swtchd rt whn nt clr run over 2f out: kpt on same pce* **40/1**
0-00 **11** *1 ½* **Coleorton Dancer**[7] 1474 5-8-3 **90**.................... AndrewMullen(3) 9 76
(K A Ryan) *in tch on stands' side: rdn 3f out: kpt on same pce fnl 2f* **40/1**
5001 **12** *1* **Capable Guest (IRE)**[14] 1307 5-8-8 **92**....................(v) ChrisCatlin 8 76
(M R Channon) *a in mid-div on stands' side* **25/1**
0-65 **13** *½* **Zomerlust**[19] 1195 5-8-6 **90**.................... GrahamGibbons 29 72
(J J Quinn) *chsd ldrs in centre: rdn 3f out: wknd ins fnl f* **16/1**
241- **14** *1 ½* **Edaara (IRE)**[221] 5761 4-8-2 **86** ow1.................... MartinDwyer 25 64
(W J Haggas) *lw: prom in centre: ev ch 2f out: wknd over 1f out* **10/1**[3]
00-0 **15** *1 ½* **South Cape**[42] 846 4-8-2 **86**.................... TPO'Shea 26 60
(M R Channon) *chsd ldrs in centre: rdn over 2f out: sn one pce* **33/1**
453 **16** *2 ½* **Machinist (IRE)**[19] 1195 7-8-6 **90**.................... KerrinMcEvoy 6 57
(D Nicholls) *chsd ldrs on stands' side: rdn over 2f out: grad fdd* **20/1**
0-00 **17** *2 ½* **Fantasy Believer**[7] 1474 9-9-4 **102**.................... LPKeniry 10 63
(J J Quinn) *mid-div on stands' side: hdwy over 2f out: sn rdn: wknd over 1f out* **50/1**
153- **18** *nk* **Dabbers Ridge (IRE)**[247] 5135 5-9-4 **102**.................... MichaelHills 12 62
(B W Hills) *chsd ldrs on stands' side: rdn and ev ch 2f out: sn wknd* **9/1**[2]
5263 **19** *2 ½* **Royal Dignitary (USA)**[8] 1458 7-8-2 **86** ow1.......... AdrianTNicholls 5 39
(D Nicholls) *prom on stands' side: rdn over 2f out: sn wknd* **100/1**

0-11 **20** *2* **Future's Dream**[20] [1180] 4-8-2 **89** ow1 SaleemGolam(3) 1 37
(K R Burke) *led stands' side gp tl 3f out: grad fdd* **14/1**

2-31 **21** *5* **King Of Argos**[26] [1060] 4-8-11 **95** JamieSpencer 21 29
(E A L Dunlop) *lw: hld up towards rr in centre: hdwy 3f out: sn rdn: wknd 2f out: eased fnl f* **5/1**[1]

0-60 **22** *hd* **Coeur Courageux (FR)**[19] [1195] 5-8-1 **85** (t) AdrianMcCarthy 7 19
(D Nicholls) *mid-div on stands' side tl 2f out* **16/1**

0330 **23** *½* **One More Round (USA)**[7] [1474] 9-8-11 **95** (b) IanMongan 15 27
(N P Littmoden) *a bhd on stands' side* **33/1**

-010 **24** *½* **Wavertree Warrior (IRE)**[8] [1448] 5-8-8 **92** JamesDoyle 24 23
(N P Littmoden) *mid-div in centre gp tl 2f out* **66/1**

20-4 **25** *nk* **High Curragh**[42] [840] 4-8-6 **90** DO'Donohoe 20 20
(K A Ryan) *lw: mid-div on stands' side tl over 2f out* **33/1**

60-1 **26** *14* **Kew Green (USA)**[25] [1082] 9-9-2 **100** KJManning 19 —
(P R Webber) *nvr bttr than mid-div in centre* **20/1**

5-13 **27** *5* **Eisteddfod**[28] [1034] 6-9-6 **104** (t) JimmyFortune 23 —
(P F I Cole) *a towards rr in centre* **20/1**

20-5 **28** *3 ½* **Suggestive**[14] [1294] 9-9-10 **108** (b) JohnEgan 22 —
(W J Haggas) *led centre gp for 4f: sn wknd* **50/1**

1m 29.55s (1.45) **Going Correction** +0.475s/f (Yiel) **28** Ran SP% **140.2**
Speed ratings (Par 109):110,105,104,104,102 102,100,100,99,98 97,95,95,93,91 89,86,85,83,80 75,74,74,73,73 57,51,47
CSF £191.64 CT £2095.03 TOTE £15.50: £3.90, £5.30, £3.80, £4.30; EX 307.80 Trifecta £5210.80 Pool: £53,576.01 - 7.30 winning units..
Owner Allen B Pope, Andrew J King **Bred** J And Mrs Bowtell **Trained** Twyford, Bucks
■ Presumptive was withdrawn (14/1, bridle broke at start). R4, deduct 5p in the £.

FOCUS
A naturally competitive big-field handicap run at a good gallop. The form looks solid.

NOTEBOOK
Wise Dennis, who had run well on his previous two starts at this track, winning on one occasion, needs a good pace in his races as he likes to challenge from off the pace. Coming here on the back of a cosy win on Fibresand last month, he smoothly got himself into contention two furlongs out and then drew clear for a decisive win. Something of a 7f specialist, he has now won four of his nine starts over the trip, and the obvious summer targets must be the Buckingham Palace Stakes, Bunbury Cup and Totesport International Handicap.
Skhilling Spirit, who won a Listed race last year on heavy ground, has shown on more than one occasion that he likes to get his toe in, and he was the only horse from a single-figure stall to make the top eight. He finished strongly to take second place, has now filled that position on each of the three occasions he has run over 7f, and will be worth bearing in mind for a similar contest when conditions are suitable.
Fullandby(IRE), runner-up in the totesport.com Handicap over this course and distance in September, looked to hold strong claims on that form with the ground to suit, and it was no surprise to see him run well. Just as effective over 6f, he is likely to pop up in one of these valuable handicaps at some point. (op 9-1)
Partners In Jazz(USA), fourth behind Wise Dennis on Fibresand on his seasonal reappearance last month, was unable to reverse that form back on turf. Winner of this race last year off a 5lb lower mark, he stayed on well widest of all but the Handicapper may just have his measure for the time being. (op 12-1)
Beaver Patrol(IRE), who won a big-field handicap at Newmarket a week earlier, had another furlong on softer ground to deal with this time. He ran well in the circumstances, displaying his versatility, but a 6lb higher mark held him back.
Pentecost has run a number of good races here in the past and this was another creditable effort. He has slipped 8lb in the handicap since this time last year and ideally needs another furlong, but he probably still needs a little more leniency before he starts winning again.
Ordnance Row ◆ ran well as he had been off the track since last August and was never far off the pace in a race dominated in the closing stages by hold-up performers. Very much suited by give in the ground, he should come on for this and should be able to win off this sort of mark, especially in a race where he is given an uncontested lead. (op 40-1)
Malcheek(IRE), 4lb higher than when successful at Thirsk last time, needs it like a road so hardly had conditions to suit. He showed his current wellbeing with a sound effort, though.
Trimlestown(IRE) won his last two starts at three and so as a result he began this season's campaign on a career-high mark. He did a lot of work in the early stages and paid for that in the final two furlongs, but this run looked in need of it on beforehand and so he can be expected to improve for it. Official explanation: jockey said gelding had no more to give (op 10-1)
Prince Of Thebes(IRE), who has run well at this track on more than one occasion in the past, needs quicker ground.
Zomerlust, who is better over 6f, remains high enough in the weights. Official explanation: jockey said gelding was unsuited by the good to soft ground (op 20-1)
Edaara(IRE) proved expensive to follow last season but did win a Leicester maiden over this trip on soft ground on her final start. Her rider put up 1lb overweight and she was fairly weak in the market beforehand, but this was still a disappointing effort. Official explanation: jockey said filly had no more to give (tchd 12-1 in places)
Machinist(IRE) went well to two furlongs out but then got tired. He is more effective over sprint distances and is edging back down the weights.
Dabbers Ridge(IRE), who won over this course and distance at the Royal meeting last year, looked as though he would come on for the run beforehand. He did too much in the early stages of the race itself and got tired in the final furlong and a half, but can be expected to do much better next time. (op 10-1)
King Of Argos, who won in great style at Windsor last time out but was 9lb higher here, was a well-backed favourite but never threatened to land a blow. It was reasonable to expect this son of Sadler's Wells to appreciate the softish ground, but perhaps he is an exception as he looked all at sea on it. He can be given another chance back on a sound surface. Official explanation: jockey said gelding had no more to give (op 7-1)
One More Round(USA) Official explanation: jockey said gelding lost a shoe
Eisteddfod Official explanation: trainer said gelding had been struck into during the race

1652 MCGEE GROUP MAIDEN STKS 5f
3:00 (3:03) (Class 4) 2-Y-O **£6,477** (£1,927; £963; £481) **Stalls** Low

Form RPR

1 **Yem Kinn** 2-9-3 JHBowman 9 85
(M R Channon) *athletic: a.p: led wl over 1f out: kpt on wl* **11/2**

3 **2** *½* **Fitzroy Crossing (USA)**[6] [1487] 2-9-3 KDarley 4 83
(M Johnston) *unf: s.i.s: sn chsng ldrs: rdn and ev ch over 1f out: kpt on* **10/3**[1]

3 *½* **Swiss Franc** 2-9-3 KerrinMcEvoy 1 81
(D R C Elsworth) *w'like: hld up: swtchd rt and gd hdwy over 1f out: r.o: nrst fin* **9/2**[2]

4 *2* **Ruff Diamond (USA)** 2-9-0 StephaneBreux(3) 11 73
(J R Best) *str: chsd ldrs: rdn over 2f out: kpt on same pce* **25/1**

5 *shd* **Paveroc** 2-9-3 JohnEgan 5 73
(J S Moore) *w'like: prom: rdn and edgd rt fr over 1f out: kpt on same pce* **14/1**

6 *nk* **Drawnfromthepast (IRE)** 2-9-3 MartinDwyer 8 71
(J A Osborne) *leggy: mid-div: rdn over 2f out: styd on ins fnl f* **8/1**

7 *3* **Mister Fips (IRE)** 2-9-3 JamieSpencer 2 59
(Jane Chapple-Hyam) *w'like: prom: rdn and ev ch whn n.m.r on rails and snatched up 1f out: nt rcvr* **5/1**[3]

8 *shd* **Hold That Call (USA)** 2-9-3 JimmyFortune 7 59
(R Hannon) *w'like: s.i.s: bhd: hdwy over 2f out: hmpd 1f out: wknd* **6/1**

9 *shd* **Shannersburg (IRE)** 2-9-3 ChrisCatlin 6 59
(E J O'Neill) *unf: chsd ldrs: rdn over 2f out: wknd over 1f out* **16/1**

10 *3* **Victory Shout (USA)** 2-9-3 GrahamGibbons 3 47
(J R Best) *w'like: s.i.s: a towards rr* **66/1**

11 *1 ¾* **Lady Vibeeka** 2-8-8 ow3 KylieManser(7) 10 38
(Mrs H Sweeting) *unf: plld hrd: led tl wl over 1f out: sn wknd* **100/1**

65.06 secs (3.66) **Going Correction** +0.475s/f (Yiel) **11** Ran SP% **117.6**
Speed ratings (Par 95):89,88,87,84,84 83,78,78,78,73 70
CSF £23.96 TOTE £7.50: £2.50, £1.60, £1.90; EX 34.00 Trifecta £95.90 Pool: £890.79 - 6.59 winning units..
Owner Sheikh Ahmed Al Maktoum **Bred** L Dettori **Trained** West Ilsley, Berks
■ Stewards' Enquiry : Kerrin McEvoy two-day ban: careless riding (May 23-24)
John Egan three-day ban: careless riding (May 23-25)

FOCUS
An interesting maiden in which only the runner-up had previous racing experience. The race has been rated positively and it should produce plenty of winners.

NOTEBOOK
Yem Kinn, an attractive colt out of an unraced half-sister to the dam of Shiva, Limnos and Light Shift, was quietly backed and certainly knew his job first time out. He picked up well when asked to go and win his race and was always holding the more experienced runner-up close home, and has the look of a Royal Ascot horse, with the Coventry looking the best option, as another furlong ought not to cause him any problems. (op 7-1)
Fitzroy Crossing(USA), the only runner in the race with previous experience, lacked the pace of the winner when that one struck for home, but he stayed on well to take second and once again shaped as though crying out for another furlong. This looked a decent maiden and he should soon be off the mark. (op 4-1)
Swiss Franc, whose dam was a speedy two-year-old, ran with distinct promise. His rider was waiting for a gap that never came next to the rail and eventually had to switch him around horses to be brought with his run. He picked up in good style once in the clear but the first two had got first run on him and were not for catching. It is difficult to know whether he would have won with a clear run, but he would certainly have been second, and he will not have to improve much to win most maidens. (op 4-1 tchd 5-1)
Ruff Diamond(USA), whose dam twice won over 1m2f; is a half-brother to a two-year-old winner in the US and is bred to want a good deal further than this in time. He had clearly been showing plenty of speed at home though, and ran a cracker on his debut, keeping on well widest of all. He should improve for the run. (op 33-1)
Paveroc, whose dam was placed in Pattern company at up to 1m2f, is entered in the Group 1 Phoenix Stakes. He boxed on well next to the rail, shaping with promise, but might be suited by a sounder surface. (tchd 12-1)
Drawnfromthepast(IRE), who is a half-brother to Aldiruos, a 1m4f winner in France and later a multiple winner over hurdles, and Sir Axel, a multiple winner in Greece, travelled strongly but found less than had looked likely off the bridle. Perhaps he too found the ground more testing than he would care for and is another who should improve. (op 6-1)
Mister Fips(IRE), whose dam was a multiple winning sprinter, albeit at a modest level, is a half-brother to Suzieblue, who won a 5f seller at two. His sales price increased considerably at the breeze-ups and he was clearly quite well fancied as Spencer had been booked. He was hampered next to the rail by the eventual fifth a furlong out but looked to be just weakening out of contention at the time, however an ordinary maiden should come his way in the coming weeks. (op 4-1 tchd 11-2)
Hold That Call(USA), who is closely related to Rain Boots, a prolific winning sprinter in the US, may well have found the ground against him. He was hampered by Swiss Franc a furlong out but was beaten at the time. (op 9-1 tchd 11-2)
Shannersburg(IRE), a half-brother to five winners, is bred to get further in time.

1653 ALFRED FRANKS & BARTLETT SUNGLASSES H'CAP 6f
3:35 (3:38) (Class 3) (0-95,95) 4-Y-0+ **£9,067** (£2,697; £1,348; £673) **Stalls** Low

Form RPR

04-4 **1** **Zidane**[8] [1448] 5-8-12 **89** JamieSpencer 24 107+
(J R Fanshawe) *lw: hld up in mid-div: smooth hdwy fr over 2f out: led over 1f out: r.o wl: comf* **7/2**[1]

5150 **2** *2 ½* **Bahamian Pirate (USA)**[42] [847] 12-8-13 **90** AdrianTNicholls 23 101
(D Nicholls) *hld up bhd: swtchd rt and stdy hdwy fr over 2f out: rdn to chse wnr over 1f out: kpt on but no further imp* **16/1**

330- **3** *2 ½* **Come Out Fighting**[232] [5501] 4-9-4 **95** TPO'Shea 13 98
(P A Blockley) *mid-div: rdn over 2f out: styd on and edgd rt ins fnl f* **40/1**

500- **4** *hd* **King's Gait**[266] [4609] 5-8-13 **90** (b) DavidAllan 26 92+
(T D Easterby) *mid-div: nt clr run and swtchd rt 2f out: sn rdn: styd on* **16/1**

650- **5** *¾* **Trafalgar Bay (IRE)**[211] [5943] 4-8-13 **90** PatCosgrave 19 90
(K R Burke) *hld up towards rr: rdn 2f out: styd on fr over 1f out: nrst fin* **16/1**

0361 **6** *½* **Mujood**[7] [1465] 4-8-13 **90** (v) StephenCarson 21 89
(Eve Johnson Houghton) *led main gp in centre: rdn and hdd over 1f out: kpt on same pce* **12/1**

0-03 **7** *½* **Phantom Whisper**[12] [1363] 4-8-10 **87** AdrianMcCarthy 15 84
(B R Millman) *lw: chsd ldrs: rdn 2f out: kpt on same pce* **33/1**

05-1 **8** *hd* **Forest Dane**[29] [1023] 7-8-5 **82** JamesDoyle 18 79
(Mrs N Smith) *mid-div: hdwy over 2f out: sn rdn: one pce fnl f* **25/1**

050- **9** *1* **Kenmore**[211] [5943] 5-8-8 **85** GrahamGibbons 17 79
(D Nicholls) *a in mid-div* **20/1**

36-0 **10** *hd* **Ice Planet**[7] [1474] 6-8-13 **90** KerrinMcEvoy 10 83
(D Nicholls) *hld up towards rr: rdn over 2f out: sme late prog: nvr a danger* **6/1**[2]

605- **11** *nk* **Loyal Royal (IRE)**[251] [5044] 4-8-11 **88** LPKeniry 22 80
(A M Balding) *chsd ldrs: rdn over 2f out: wknd fnl f* **25/1**

4-50 **12** *1 ½* **Charles Darwin (IRE)**[7] [1474] 4-8-12 **89** KJManning 16 77
(M Blanshard) *chsd ldrs: rdn over 2f out: wknd fnl f* **12/1**

041- **13** *shd* **Yorkshire Blue**[196] [6212] 8-8-4 **81** RichardThomas 5 68
(J S Goldie) *a towards rr* **20/1**

-052 **14** *shd* **Guildenstern (IRE)**[16] [1268] 5-8-1 **81** oh4 (v[1]) DominicFox(3) 14 68
(P L Gilligan) *nvr bttr than mid-div* **25/1**

005 **15** *shd* **Bahiano (IRE)**[7] [1474] 6-9-0 **91** JimmyFortune 20 78
(C E Brittain) *mid-div: rdn over 2f out: sn wknd* **10/1**

3-10 **16** *1* **Geojimali**[19] [1195] 5-8-5 **85** SaleemGolam(3) 4 69
(J S Goldie) *a towards rr* **9/1**[3]

5400 **17** *3 ½* **Obe Gold**[19] [1195] 5-8-13 **90** (v) JHBowman 9 63
(M R Channon) *mid-div tl wknd over 1f out* **25/1**

0-00 **18** *6* **Idle Power (IRE)**[7] [1474] 9-8-12 **89** AmirQuinn 25 44
(J R Boyle) *lw: chsd ldrs: rdn 3f out: wknd over 1f out* **25/1**

The Form Book, Raceform Ltd, Compton, RG20 6NL

4-53 **19** *4* **Matuza (IRE)**[20] 1179 4-8-4 **81** oh4 FrankieMcDonald 1 24
(*W R Muir*) *racd w one other on stands' side and no ch w main gp fr over 2f out* **16/1**

3-03 **20** *nk* **Diane's Choice**[14] 1292 4-8-7 **84** MartinDwyer 3 26
(*J Akehurst*) *rrd s: racd w one other on stands' side and no ch w main gp fr over 2f out* **25/1**

152- **21** *1* **Third Set (IRE)**[286] 3970 4-8-9 **86** ChrisCatlin 2 25
(*R Charlton*) *a in rr* **11/1**

1m 15.6s (0.70) **Going Correction** +0.475s/f (Yiel) **21** Ran SP% **140.8**
Speed ratings (Par 107):114,110,107,107,106 105,104,104,103,102 102,100,100,100,100 98,94,86,80,80 79
CSF £60.67 CT £2121.46 TOTE £4.10: £1.50, £4.40, £7.80, £5.60; EX 59.40 Trifecta £899.90 Part won. Pool: £1,267.56 - 0.10 winning units..
Owner Jan and Peter Hopper **Bred** Mrs J P Hopper And Mrs E M Grundy **Trained** Newmarket, Suffolk

FOCUS
Another big-field handicap run at a good pace and the form looks solid with the third close to last year's best form. Only two horses stayed on the stands' side (finished in rear) while the rest of the field came up the centre.

NOTEBOOK
Zidane, sharper for his reappearance at Lingfield eight days earlier, has plenty of good form under quicker conditions, but he seemed to relish the give underfoot here and ran out an authoritative winner. He is likely to come back here for the Wokingham next month and, although he will have more on his plate off a higher mark, the race will no doubt again be run to suit his come-from-behind style. (op 5-1 tchd 11-2 in places)
Bahamian Pirate(USA), third in the Wokingham off a 7lb higher mark last year, likes these big-field handicaps as he is usually guaranteed a decent pace. He showed there is still life in the old dog yet with a good effort to finish on his own in second, and will no doubt be back here at the Royal meeting next month.
Come Out Fighting appeared to have plenty on his plate under top weight on his seasonal reappearance, but he looked quite fit beforehand and stayed on well for third. He looks to have progressed from three to four. (op 33-1)
King's Gait has gone well fresh in the past and is very much at home in soft ground, so it should not have been a total surprise to see him run a decent race. He was held last season off marks in the mid-90s and, although he has dropped a few pounds, remains 3lb above his last winning mark.
Trafalgar Bay(IRE) has won second time out in his two previous seasons of racing so there should be plenty of encouragement to take from this seasonal reappearance. A return to 7f will be in his favour on the evidence of this performance.
Mujood, whose stable remains in good form, was 6lb higher than when successful in a lesser event at Goodwood a week earlier. He found dominating this big field a lot more difficult but was far from disgraced. (tchd 11-1)
Phantom Whisper was never far off the pace and confirmed that he is jusst as effective ove 6f as he is over the minimum trip.
Forest Dane, coming off a career-best performance at Folkestone, had never before run in a race of this class, but he is improving at the age of seven and ran a sound race.
Kenmore looked a possible contender two furlongs out but was soon one-paced. He will be better for the run and is not badly handicapped at present.
Ice Planet, who ran a number of good races in defeat last term off this sort of mark, failed to build on the promise of his reappearance run at Newmarket. (op 13-2 tchd 7-1)
Bahiano(IRE), who has a poor strike-rate, would have preferred faster ground.

1654 MITSUBISHI ELECTRIC H'CAP 2m
4:10 (4:12) (Class 3) (0-90,89) 4-Y-0+
£10,594 (£3,172; £1,586; £793; £396; £198) **Stalls** High

Form RPR

431/ **1** **Princelet (IRE)**[28] 5699 5-9-3 **80** MichaelHills 9 90+
(*N J Henderson*) *hld up towards rr: racd wd over 6f out: hdwy and jnd main gp over 3f out: led 2f out and edgd rt: styd on wl* **5/1**[3]

00-2 **2** *1* **Ned Ludd (IRE)**[21] 1148 4-8-11 **80** EmmettStack(3) 1 89+
(*J G Portman*) *mid-div: hdwy over 2f out: rdn to chal whn squeezed out 2f out: sn swtchd rt: styd on again ins fnl f* **8/1**

01-1 **3** *3/4* **Junior**[21] 1148 4-9-1 **81** JamieSpencer 10 87
(*B J Meehan*) *lw: prom: racd wd over 6f out: jnd main gp over 3f out: rdn and ev ch whn edgd sltly lft 2f out: styd on* **5/2**[1]

064/ **4** *1/2* **Mith Hill**[24] 6012 6-9-2 **79** TPO'Shea 11 84
(*Ian Williams*) *cl up: rdn to chal 3f out: kpt on u.p fnl 2f: no ex nr fin* **8/1**

1-40 **5** *hd* **High Point (IRE)**[21] 1148 9-8-8 **71** ChrisCatlin 12 76
(*G P Enright*) *plld hrd: hld up: hdwy into mid-div over 6f out: rdn 3f out: styd on ins fnl f* **16/1**

3/15 **6** *3/4* **Mind How You Go (FR)**[21] 1148 9-8-9 **75** StephaneBreux(3) 3 79
(*J R Best*) *cl up: rdn over 3f out: no imp tl styd on ins fnl f* **7/1**

211- **7** *6* **Desert Sea (IRE)**[252] 5022 4-9-3 **83** KerrinMcEvoy 5 80
(*D W P Arbuthnot*) *led: rdn and hdd 2f out: wknd fnl f* **9/2**[2]

51-4 **8** *2 1/2* **Escayola (IRE)**[14] 1300 7-9-10 **87** (b) AdrianTNicholls 2 81
(*Grant Tuer*) *hld up and a towards rr* **10/1**

000/ **9** *4* **Green Ideal**[17] 1668 9-9-2 **79** PatCosgrave 15 68
(*Ferdy Murphy*) *cl up: rdn 4f out: wknd over 2f out* **28/1**

/06- **10** *29* **Sworn In (USA)**[374] 1409 6-9-0 **80** SaleemGolam(3) 14 34
(*N I M Rossiter*) *a in rr: lost tch 4f out* **25/1**

3m 42.76s (12.60) **Going Correction** +1.00s/f (Soft)
WFA 4 from 5yo+ 3lb **10** Ran SP% **120.4**
Speed ratings (Par 107):108,107,107,106,106 106,103,102,100,85
CSF £46.33 CT £125.22 TOTE £6.90: £2.30, £2.90, £1.50; EX 52.10 Trifecta £212.00 Pool: £1,200.86 - 4.02 winning units. Place 6 £40.90, Place 5 £26.02.
Owner John P McManus **Bred** Kilfrush Stud **Trained** Upper Lambourn, Berks

FOCUS
Not a strongly-run staying handicap, but the form looks sound enough rated around the fourth, fifth and sixth. Both the winner and third went the Bahri route under the trees running away from Swinley Bottom.

NOTEBOOK
Princelet(IRE), last seen running over hurdles at Aintree, is unexposed on the Flat and showed here that he is ahead of the Handicapper. He idled once he hit the front and is likely to rate higher later this season, with the Ascot Stakes and/or the Queen Alexandra looking likely Royal meeting targets at this stage. (op 9-2 tchd 6-1)
Ned Ludd(IRE), narrowly beaten by Junior at Newbury last time, reversed that form on this easier ground with a 1lb pull in the weights. He was the meat in the sandwich when the eventual winner and Junior squeezed him out with two furlongs to run, and he did well to rally and take second. He is still a maiden on the Flat but will surely not remain so for too long. (tchd 10-1)
Junior was perhaps not entirely happy on this softer ground but he showed he remains progressive with a solid effort off a 4lb higher mark than at Newbury. (op 2-1)
Mith Hill, who developed into a fair hurdler this last jumps season, remains on a stiff enough mark based on his performances on the Flat back in 2005. (op 14-1)
High Point(IRE), who is not quite as good on turf as he is on Polytrack, did not settle off the fairly steady early gallop, and he might have done better in a more strongly-run race. (op 20-1)
Mind How You Go(FR) should be able to win a race off this sort of mark but he too was unsuited by the steady early gallop. He was held up out the back in a race run at a good pace when successful on Polytrack in March. (op 8-1)
Desert Sea(IRE) was able to dictate his own pace so can have no excuse on that front, but he did not pick up in the straight and the conclusion has to be that the ground was far too soft for him. He can be given another chance to build on last year's successful season on Polytrack when back on a sound surface. (op 11-2 tchd 6-1)
Sworn In(USA) Official explanation: jockey said horse did not handle the track
T/Jkpt: Not won. T/Plt: £27.60 to a £1 stake. Pool: £131,834.16. 3,476.30 winning tickets. T/Qpdt: £22.40 to a £1 stake. Pool: £5,217.30. 172.00 winning tickets. TM

1285 HAYDOCK (L-H)
Saturday, May 12

OFFICIAL GOING: Good (good to soft in places on hurdle course)
Other races under Rules of jumps racing. A slightly later date than usual for this mixed meeting.
Wind: Light against Weather: Showers

1655 BETFREDCASINO FLAT V JUMP JOCKEYS H'CAP 1m 30y
2:35 (2:36) (Class 5) (0-70,72) 4-Y-0+ **£4,857** (£1,445; £722; £360) **Stalls** Low

Form RPR

060- **1** **Harvest Warrior**[247] 5136 5-11-1 **64** NoelFehily 4 78
(*T D Easterby*) *hld up: swtchd rt over 2f out: hdwy over 1f out: edgd lft and r.o to ld wl ins fnl f: won gng away* **9/1**

23-0 **2** *1 3/4* **Azreme**[50] 741 7-10-13 **62** SteveDrowne 11 72
(*P Howling*) *trckd ldrs: rdn over 1f out: ev ch ins fnl f: nt qckn towards fin* **12/1**

2552 **3** *1/2* **Pab Special (IRE)**[10] 1413 4-11-9 **72** GLee 12 81
(*K R Burke*) *a.p: rdn to ld 1f out: hdd wl ins fnl f: no ex cl home* **4/1**[1]

0-00 **4** *1* **King Of The Moors (USA)**[19] 1198 4-11-5 **68** FrancisNorton 1 75
(*T D Barron*) *trckd ldrs: rdn over 1f out: styd on same pce ins fnl f* **15/2**[3]

6121 **5** *shd* **Scamperdale**[15] 1284 5-11-5 **68** (p) DeanMcKeown 5 74
(*B P J Baugh*) *racd keenly: hld up: rdn and hdwy over 2f out: kpt on ins fnl f* **8/1**

00-0 **6** *1* **Dakota Rain (IRE)**[10] 1416 5-11-5 **68** GeorgeBaker 10 72
(*Jennie Candlish*) *led: rdn 2f out: hdd 1f out: fdd ins fnl f* **25/1**

00-1 **7** *1/2* **White Bear (FR)**[40] 888 5-11-4 **67** (b) TimmyMurphy 6 72+
(*C R Dore*) *racd keenly in midfield: n.m.r and hmpd over 2f out: sn lost pl: kpt on one pce fnl f: no imp on ldrs* **8/1**

00-0 **8** *2* **Kavachi (IRE)**[10] 1401 4-11-0 **63** APMcCoy 7 61
(*G L Moore*) *hld up: effrt over 2f out: no imp* **13/2**[2]

-006 **9** *nk* **Sentiero Rosso (USA)**[4] 1568 5-11-0 **63** PaulHanagan 3 61
(*B Ellison*) *midfield: rdn over 2f out: wknd over 1f out* **13/2**[2]

0403 **10** *4* **Chalentina**[46] 796 4-11-1 **64** SebSanders 8 53
(*P Howling*) *midfield: hdwy on outside 5f out: rdn and wknd over 1f out* **16/1**

000- **11** *3/4* **Makfly**[157] 6735 4-11-1 **64** MickFitzgerald 9 51
(*R Hollinshead*) *in tch: wknd over 2f out* **25/1**

5-00 **12** *6* **Dark Charm (FR)**[14] 1287 8-11-6 **69** RichardJohnson 2 42
(*R A Fahey*) *rdn over 2f out: a bhd* **8/1**

1m 46.4s (0.89) **Going Correction** +0.15s/f (Good) **12** Ran SP% **123.0**
Speed ratings (Par 103):101,99,98,97,97 96,96,94,93,89 89,83
CSF £116.63 CT £506.03 TOTE £13.20: £3.90, £4.10, £1.60; EX 215.80.
Owner Swanland Racing **Bred** Campbell Stud **Trained** Great Habton, N Yorks
■ Stewards' Enquiry : G Lee caution: careless riding

FOCUS
A 56-70 handicap in which the jump jockeys took on their counterparts from the Flat. It has been rated through the third, fifth and seventh, and the form looks sound.

1656 BETFREDPOKER SPRING TROPHY STKS (LISTED RACE) 7f 30y
3:05 (3:07) (Class 1) 3-Y-0+
£19,873 (£7,532; £3,769; £1,879; £941; £472) **Stalls** Low

Form RPR

-112 **1** **Munaddam (USA)**[65] 644 5-9-7 RoystonFfrench 6 114+
(*E A L Dunlop*) *a.p: led over 1f out: r.o wl and in command towards fin* **11/2**[2]

0002 **2** *1 1/4* **Excusez Moi (USA)**[14] 1294 5-9-7 102 SebSanders 3 111
(*C E Brittain*) *midfield: hdwy 2f out: chsd wnr ins fnl f: styd on but a hld* **8/1**[3]

-254 **3** *1 3/4* **Mac Love**[78] 547 6-9-7 SteveDrowne 9 110+
(*J Noseda*) *hld up: hdwy 2f out: nt clr run ins fnl f: kpt on: n.d to front pair towards fin* **14/1**

200- **4** *shd* **Vanderlin**[237] 5416 8-9-7 112 FrancisNorton 1 106
(*A M Balding*) *racd keenly: trckd ldrs: rdn and carried hd high over 1f out: hung lft ins fnl f: kpt on: nt pce to chal* **14/1**

10-1 **5** *1* **Levera**[28] 1034 4-9-7 107 MickyFenton 7 107+
(*A King*) *led: rdn and hdd over 1f out: hld whn n.m.r and hmpd towards fin* **5/4**[1]

06-0 **6** *1 1/4* **Quito (IRE)**[23] 1102 10-9-11 111 (b) PaulHanagan 5 104
(*D W Chapman*) *s.i.s: hld up: rdn 2f out: kpt on fnl f: nvr able to chal* **11/2**[2]

00-4 **7** *3/4* **Balthazaar's Gift (IRE)**[14] 1294 4-9-7 110 GeorgeBaker 2 98
(*L M Cumani*) *racd keenly: trckd ldrs: rdn over 1f out: wknd ins fnl f* **11/1**

4154 **8** *3/4* **Appalachian Trail (IRE)**[42] 847 6-9-11 109 (b) TomEaves 8 100
(*I Semple*) *hld up: rdn 2f out: no imp* **14/1**

220- **9** *5* **Invincible Force (IRE)**[217] 5802 3-8-9 107 DeanMcKeown 4 79
(*Paul Green*) *midfield: rdn and wknd over 1f out* **33/1**

1m 31.3s (-0.76) **Going Correction** +0.15s/f (Good)
WFA 3 from 4yo+ 12lb **9** Ran SP% **117.6**
Speed ratings (Par 111):110,108,106,106,105 103,103,102,96
CSF £49.71 TOTE £5.70: £2.00, £2.60, £3.10; EX 43.70 Trifecta £241.00 Part won. Pool: £339.50 - 0.70 winning units..
Owner Hamdan Al Maktoum **Bred** Shadwell Farm LLC **Trained** Newmarket, Suffolk

FOCUS
Several spoilt their chances by racing too keenly in this event, in which the pace was not strong and those who raced prominently were favoured. A good race for the grade, won impressively by Munaddam.

NOTEBOOK
Munaddam(USA), who did so well in Dubai earlier in the year, was always going well close to the pace and, quickening up a furlong out, never looked in any danger. He had the run of the race, but he is an improved performer who is effective at 6f and 7f and is going the right way. He could well win again and is likely to have a say in some of the bigger sprints. (op 7-2)
Excusez Moi(USA) is not easy to win with, but he is in form and ran a sound enough race in second if never troubling the winner. (op 10-1)

Mac Love wasn't ideally suited by the way the race panned out and didn't get the best of runs either, so this was a creditable effort. (tchd 16-1)

Vanderlin, who picked up an injury in Dubai earlier in the year, was making a belated reappearance. He raced in touch, but was keen and then inclined to edge left and lacked the pace to challenge. (op 10-1)

Levera had the run of the race in front, but dropped away in the last furlong and was well held when he met trouble close home. (op 6-4 tchd 15-8)

Quito(IRE) was unsuited by the way the race was run and never featured. (op 15-2)

1657 TEXT "BETFRED" TO 83080 FOR MOBILE BETTING CONDITIONS STKS — 6f

3:40 (3:40) (Class 2) 3-Y-0+

£10,906 (£3,265; £1,632; £817; £407; £204) **Stalls** Centre

Form				RPR
3-20	**1**		**Sierra Vista**[23] 1102 7-8-9 100 ... TomEaves 7 (D W Barker) *mde all: rdn over 1f out: r.o* **8/1**	107
262-	**2**	½	**Borderlescott**[211] 5942 5-9-0 109 ... SebSanders 3 (R Bastiman) *racd keenly: a.p: rdn over 1f out: ev ch ins fnl f: nt qckn towards fin* **6/5**[1]	110
125-	**3**	*hd*	**Fonthill Road (IRE)**[212] 5921 7-9-0 102 ... PaulHanagan 8 (R A Fahey) *in rr: outpcd 1/2-way: effrt and swtchd rt 1f out: fin strly* **7/1**[3]	109+
-326	**4**	*nk*	**Ashdown Express (IRE)**[65] 644 8-9-0 ... GeorgeBaker 2 (C F Wall) *hld up: rdn and hdwy over 1f out: ev ch ins fnl f: no ex fnl strides* **8/1**	109
/6-3	**5**	½	**Patavellian (IRE)**[38] 927 9-9-0 104 ...(b) SteveDrowne 5 (R Charlton) *in tch: rdn over 1f out: kpt on: nt pce of ldrs* **7/1**[3]	107
1/	**6**	¾	**Prince Woodman (USA)**[568] 6011 4-9-0 ... DeanMcKeown 1 (B J Meehan) *s.i.s: plld hrd in rr: rdn over 1f out: kpt on: nt pce to chal* **33/1**	105
10/5	**7**	*1*	**Baron's Pit**[22] 1125 7-9-0 104 ... RoystonFfrench 4 (E F Vaughan) *prom: rdn 2f out: wknd ins fnl f* **11/1**	102
0-01	**8**	*1 ½*	**Kostar**[19] 1195 6-9-0 102 ... MickyFenton 6 (C G Cox) *in tch: rdn and hung lft over 1f out: wknd ins fnl f* **6/1**[2]	97

1m 14.31s (-0.59) **Going Correction** +0.15s/f (Good) **8** Ran SP% **118.2**
Speed ratings (Par 109):109,108,108,107,107 106,104,102
CSF £18.74 TOTE £9.90: £2.40, £1.10, £2.10; EX 16.20.
Owner David T J Metcalfe **Bred** Mrs M Beddis **Trained** Scorton, N Yorks
■ Stewards' Enquiry : Tom Eaves three-day ban: used whip with excessive force and frequency (May 24-26)

FOCUS
Quite an interesting conditions sprint that makes sense despite the runner-up being below par. The form is rated around the winner and fourth, but the proximity of the sixth is a concern.

NOTEBOOK
Sierra Vista gained her third course success and her first outside maiden or handicap company. Making all on ground that suited her, she ran on with great gusto when challenged in the final furlong. She has been a fine servant over the years, and this confirmed that she is as good as ever. She may now go for a handicap at York with a penalty. (tchd 10-1 in places)

Borderlescott ran a sound race on his seasonal reappearance, as he raced too keenly. To his credit, he ran on well enough and has clearly come back as well as ever. (op 11-8 tchd 13-8 in places)

Fonthill Road(IRE), who was switched to get a run after being held up, ran on well on what was his first race of the campaign. He will be interesting when he gets some give in the ground. (op 10-1)

Ashdown Express(IRE) is hard to win with these days, and although he came there on the bridle on the outside two furlongs out, he did not find a great deal. (op 15-2)

Patavellian(IRE), although not beaten far, never landed a blow and may need time to regain his form after missing most of 2006. (op 11-2)

Prince Woodman(USA), returning from a long break, was too keen and not surprisingly his effort flattened out in the last furlong. (op 25-1)

Kostar, up in grade, has been raised 10lb for his Pontefract win and will find life more difficult in the short term. (op 15-2)

1658 BETFRED "THE BONUS KING" H'CAP — 6f

4:15 (4:18) (Class 4) (0-85,82) 3-Y-0 **£5,505** (£1,637; £818; £408) **Stalls** Centre

Form				RPR
310-	**1**		**Makshoof (IRE)**[216] 5829 3-9-1 **79** ... GeorgeBaker 6 (M A Jarvis) *hld up: hdwy 2f out: rdn over 1f out: r.o to ld towards fin* **6/1**[3]	88+
62-1	**2**	*nk*	**Genki (IRE)**[39] 899 3-8-13 **77** ... SteveDrowne 11 (R Charlton) *racd keenly: in tch: chalng whn struck by rival's whip over 1f out and sn carried lft: led ent fnl f: hdd towards fin* **4/1**[2]	85
1-	**3**	*1*	**Special Day**[330] 2617 3-8-13 **77** ... SebSanders 2 (B W Hills) *hld up: hdwy 2f out: rdn whn carried lft over 1f out: ev ch ins fnl f: nt qckn towards fin* **3/1**[1]	81
126-	**4**	*nk*	**Ingleby Princess**[221] 5748 3-8-12 **76** ... FrancisNorton 10 (T D Barron) *hld up: edgd lft and hdwy 2f out: styd on ins fnl f: nt pce of ldrs* **17/2**	79
-011	**5**	*2*	**Nordic Light (USA)**[29] 1022 3-8-7 **78** ... MCGeran(7) 12 (P W Chapple-Hyam) *led: rdn and hung lft over 1f out: hdd ent fnl f: fdd towards fin* **4/1**[2]	75
4-00	**6**	*7*	**Diysem (USA)**[24] 1099 3-8-11 **82** ... KMay(7) 4 (B J Meehan) *prom tl rdn and wknd 2f out* **16/1**	57
11-6	**7**	*1 ¼*	**Milson's Point (IRE)**[34] 958 3-8-8 **72** ... TomEaves 8 (I Semple) *bhd: nvr trbld ldrs* **25/1**	43
1-0	**8**	½	**Handsome Falcon**[16] 1257 3-8-13 **77** ... PaulHanagan 7 (R A Fahey) *prom tl rdn and wknd 2f out* **11/1**	46
1315	**9**	*nk*	**Convivial Spirit**[37] 935 3-8-8 **72** ...(t) RoystonFfrench 5 (E F Vaughan) *chsd ldrs tl rdn and wknd over 2f out* **12/1**	40
251-	**10**	*4*	**Buckie Massa**[155] 6749 3-9-1 **79** ... JDSmith 3 (S Kirk) *prom tl rdn and wknd 2f out* **25/1**	34
3615	**11**	*1 ¾*	**Sunley Sovereign**[14] 1313 3-8-4 **68** oh2 ... DavidKinsella 1 (D W Chapman) *midfield: rdn over 2f out: wknd over 1f out* **50/1**	18

1m 15.49s (0.59) **Going Correction** +0.15s/f (Good) **11** Ran SP% **121.4**
Speed ratings (Par 101):102,101,100,99,97 87,86,85,85,79 77
CSF £30.75 CT £90.02 TOTE £7.50: £2.20, £1.80, £1.50; EX 33.50.
Owner Hamdan Al Maktoum **Bred** J Egan **Trained** Newmarket, Suffolk

FOCUS
An interesting three-year-old handicap featuring several unexposed types, that looked above-average for the grade and should throw up some winners.

Ingleby Princess Official explanation: jockey said filly suffered interference in running

Nordic Light(USA) Official explanation: jockey said gelding hung left throughout

1659 BETFRED OVER 660 SHOPS NATIONWIDE MAIDEN STKS — 1m 2f 120y

4:45 (4:46) (Class 5) 3-Y-0 **£2,817** (£838; £418; £209) **Stalls** High

Form				RPR
3	**1**		**Mad Rush (USA)**[21] 1153 3-9-3 ... GeorgeBaker 9 (L M Cumani) *hld up: rdn and hdwy over 2f out: led over 1f out: edgd lft ins fnl f: r.o wl* **2/1**[1]	80+
4-	**2**	*3 ½*	**Coastal Command**[148] 6826 3-9-3 ... SteveDrowne 10 (R Charlton) *racd keenly: midfield: hdwy 3f out: hung lft fr over 2f out: ev ch over 1f out: eased whn no ex towards fin* **8/1**[3]	73
5	**3**	½	**Honorable Love**[14] 1303 3-8-7 ... JamieMoriarty(5) 7 (M Dods) *hld up: hdwy over 3f out: rdn and cl up 2f out: n.m.r over 1f out: sn swtchd rt: r.o towards fin* **22/1**	69+
06-2	**4**	½	**Inchlaggan (IRE)**[25] 1077 3-9-3 79 ... DeanMcKeown 4 (B W Hills) *led: hdd 7f out: styd prom: regained ld over 3f out: rdn and hdd over 1f out: n.m.r ent fnl f: one pce after* **5/1**[2]	71
	5	*5*	**Flavius (IRE)** 3-9-3 ... PaulHanagan 6 (Sir Michael Stoute) *hld up: hdwy 3f out: n.m.r over 2f out: rn green: no imp fnl f* **2/1**[1]	61+
0	**6**	*1 ½*	**Driving Miss Suzie**[19] 1203 3-8-12 ... FrancisNorton 3 (A M Balding) *midfield: pushed along 5f out: losing pl whn hmpd over 2f out: n.d after* **40/1**	53
P	**7**	*1 ¾*	**Feeling (IRE)**[20] 1191 3-8-10 ... MCGeran(7) 11 (P W Chapple-Hyam) *hld up: n.m.r over 3f out: sn rdn: no imp* **20/1**	55
540-	**8**	½	**Firestorm (IRE)**[208] 6007 3-8-10 55 ... KellyHarrison(7) 5 (C W Fairhurst) *in tch: rdn over 2f out: sn wknd* **40/1**	54
052-	**9**	*6*	**Macaroni Gin (IRE)**[227] 5616 3-9-3 66 ... DavidKinsella 1 (J Howard Johnson) *prom: led 7f out: hdd over 3f out: rdn and wknd 2f out* **16/1**	42
	10	*2*	**Beseech (IRE)** 3-8-5 ... KMay(7) 8 (B J Meehan) *prom: hung rt on bnd over 5f out: rdn over 3f out: wknd over 2f out* **20/1**	33
	11	*25*	**Demisemiquaver** 3-8-12 ... SebSanders 2 (J Noseda) *trckd ldrs tl hung lft and wknd over 3f out: t.o* **9/1**	—

2m 19.07s (1.34) **Going Correction** +0.15s/f (Good) **11** Ran SP% **129.1**
Speed ratings (Par 99):101,98,98,97,94 93,91,91,87,85 67
CSF £21.10 TOTE £3.90: £1.50, £2.40, £5.70; EX 26.80 Place 6 £300.78, Place 5 £115.43.
Owner Earle I Mack **Bred** Avalon Farm **Trained** Newmarket, Suffolk

FOCUS
This looked quite an interesting maiden, but there was a bit of trouble and the form, best rated around the winner and fourth, may not prove to be a totally reliable

Demisemiquaver Official explanation: jockey said filly was unsuited by the good ground
T/Plt: £140.70 to a £1 stake. Pool: £96,901.65. 502.70 winning tickets. T/Qpdt: £22.40 to a £1 stake. Pool: £3,220.80. 106.15 winning tickets. DO

1628 LINGFIELD (L-H)

Saturday, May 12

OFFICIAL GOING: Good to soft (good in places)

A strong tailwind behind the runners produced some fast times on the straight course despite the good to soft ground.
Wind: Strong, behind Weather: Overcast

1660 TOTESCOOP6 H'CAP — 6f

2:10 (2:10) (Class 4) (0-80,80) 3-Y-0 **£6,477** (£1,927; £963; £481) **Stalls** High

Form				RPR
401-	**1**		**Sandrey (IRE)**[208] 6014 3-9-3 **79** ... TedDurcan 3 (P W Chapple-Hyam) *lw: prom: rdn to ld wl over 1f out: clr 1f out: pushed out: easily* **9/4**[1]	92+
00-0	**2**	*1 ½*	**King's Bastion (IRE)**[24] 1099 3-9-4 **80** ... LDettori 1 (M L W Bell) *w.w in midfield: hdwy 1/2-way: rdn and outpcd 2f out: kpt on ins fnl f: wnt 2nd wl ins fnl f: no ch w wnr* **9/1**	84
42-4	**3**	½	**Masai Moon**[25] 1081 3-9-0 **76** ... JimCrowley 8 (B R Millman) *swtg: chsd ldr tl led 2f out: sn hdd and rdn: outpcd by wnr over 1f out: lost 2nd ins fnl f* **15/2**	78
1343	**4**	¾	**Go On Green (IRE)**[23] 1108 3-8-12 **79** ... MarkFlynn(5) 9 (E A L Dunlop) *hld up bhd: rdn and effrt 2f out: swtchd lft ins fnl f: r.o: nrst fin* **11/4**[2]	79+
5-60	**5**	½	**Dowlleh**[19] 1202 3-8-13 **75** ... AdamKirby 7 (T T Clement) *lw: racd in midfield: rdn over 2f out: kpt on same pce u.p fnl f* **20/1**	73
102-	**6**	½	**Bertoliver**[189] 6332 3-9-1 **77** ... PhilipRobinson 10 (D K Ivory) *lw: led tl 2f out: sn outpcd by wnr: wknd ins fnl f* **7/2**[3]	74
6060	**7**	*3 ½*	**Stoneacre Gareth (IRE)**[3] 1577 3-8-6 **68** ... RobbieFitzpatrick 4 (Peter Grayson) *prom whn j. path after 1f: rdn and lost pl 1/2-way: bhd and no ch last 2f* **25/1**	54
11-0	**8**	*nk*	**Estimator**[23] 1108 3-9-3 **79** ... DaneO'Neill 2 (Pat Eddery) *lw: s.i.s: hld up bhd: rdn after 2f: wknd over 2f out* **25/1**	64
1-0	**9**	*4*	**Trepa (USA)**[16] 1257 3-9-1 **77** ... DarryllHolland 6 (W Jarvis) *s.i.s: a bhd: no ch last 2f* **16/1**	50

1m 10.21s (-1.46) **Going Correction** -0.025s/f (Good) **9** Ran SP% **119.8**
Speed ratings (Par 101):108,106,105,104,103 103,98,97,92
CSF £23.91 CT £131.77 TOTE £2.40: £1.60, £3.10, £1.60; EX 30.60 Trifecta £118.30 Pool: £213.36 - 1.28 winning units..
Owner Nizar Anwar **Bred** Mohammad Al-Qatami **Trained** Newmarket, Suffolk
■ Blue Charm (10/1) was withdrawn on vet's advice. Rule 4 applies, deduct 5p in the £. New market formed.

FOCUS
A fair sprint, run at a decent pace, and solid form with a progressive winner and the placed horses to their marks.

1661 TOTEPOOL CHARTWELL FILLIES' STKS (GROUP 3) — 7f

2:40 (2:40) (Class 1) 3-Y-0+

£28,390 (£10,760; £5,385; £2,685; £1,345; £675) **Stalls** High

Form				RPR
022-	**1**		**Wake Up Maggie (IRE)**[246] 5159 4-9-3 106 ... RichardHughes 6 (C F Wall) *lw: w.w in tch: smooth hdwy to join ldrs on bit over 1f out: pushed into ld ins fnl f: qcknd clr: v easily* **15/8**[2]	109+
35-6	**2**	*3 ½*	**Leopoldine**[11] 1372 4-9-3 89 ... PhilipRobinson 5 (H Morrison) *lw: led in centre: hrd pressed and rdn over 1f out: hdd ins fnl f: kpt on but no ch w wnr* **25/1**	94
22-4	**3**	*1*	**Creative Mind (IRE)**[21] 1157 4-9-3 82 ...(p) DaneO'Neill 7 (E J O'Neill) *chsd ldr: rdn and ev ch over 1f out: wknd wl ins fnl f* **25/1**	92

113- **4** 3/4 **Wasseema (USA)**[245] 5184 4-9-3 109 RHills 4 90
(Sir Michael Stoute) *trckd ldrs in centre: ev ch and rdn over 1f out: sn btn: wknd ins fnl f* **4/5**[1]

20-4 **5** 3 **Highway To Glory (IRE)**[35] 938 4-9-3 100 (t) LDettori 2 82
(M Botti) *stdd s: racd in midfield: rdn over 2f out: sn outpcd* **12/1**

000- **6** 1/2 **Chantilly Beauty (FR)**[188] 6363 5-9-3 (b) TJarnet 8 81
(R Pritchard-Gordon, France) *lw: hld up bhd: rdn wl over 2f out: sn outpcd* **9/1**[3]

310- **7** 12 **Pleasing**[189] 6333 4-9-3 76 TedDurcan 3 50
(C E Brittain) *stdd s: a bhd: rdn 3f out: sn lost tch: t.o* **40/1**

0-0 **8** 22 **Arrivee (FR)**[7] 1472 4-9-3 DarryllHolland 1 —
(Mrs P Sly) *a bhd: rdn and lost tch 1/2-way: t.o last 2f* **50/1**

1m 22.42s (-1.79) **Going Correction** -0.025s/f (Good) **8** Ran SP% **120.1**
Speed ratings (Par 110):109,105,103,103,99 99,85,60
CSF £50.49 TOTE £2.80: £1.10, £5.40, £4.70; EX 64.60 Trifecta £67.60 Pool: £285.88 - 3.00 winning units..
Owner J G Lambton **Bred** Rathmoyle Exports Ltd **Trained** Newmarket, Suffolk

FOCUS
A modest Group 3, weakened by the below-par run of the favourite, but run at a decent gallop and although the winner was impressive it is questionable whether she has improved.

NOTEBOOK
Wake Up Maggie(IRE) had little to beat with Wasseema running below her best, but could not have been more impressive. She was given some tough assignments last year, but her enthusiasm has not been dimmed and she should have a good season. Her trainer regrets not entering her for the Group 2 Windsor Castle Stakes at Royal Ascot, but should find a decent alternative. (tchd 7-4)
Leopoldine battled on gamely when headed, and appears to stay this trip, which gives connections the option of both six and seven furlongs this season. However, the winner had 18lb in hand on official ratings and proved to be in a different league.
Creative Mind(IRE) has become a regular at this trip, and again ran respectably in race apparently dominated by the two favourites. The fact that she finished in front of Wassema should not be treated with some caution, since that filly was below her best, but it was still a good effort. (op 33-1)
Wasseema(USA) was having her first race since splitting a pastern last season, and faded disappointingly after showing speed for six furlongs. Assuming she has fully recovered from the injury, this classy filly can do much better on faster ground. (tchd Evens)
Highway To Glory(IRE)'s two victories were both on soft ground, and her rating going into the race was higher than both Leopoldine's and Creative Mind's, so this was a disppointing effort. (op 16-1)
Chantilly Beauty(FR) was, according to official ratings, third-best on merit, but put in a lack-lustre display despite having previous form on soft ground. Lightly-raced last season, she has not won since September 2005, but other efforts in Group company suggest she is capable of much better than this. (op 12-1)
Arrivee(FR) Official explanation: jockey said filly hung right throughout

1662 TOTESPORT DERBY TRIAL STKS (GROUP 3) (C&G) 1m 3f 106y
3:15 (3:17) (Class 1) 3-Y-O

£34,068 (£12,912; £6,462; £3,222; £1,614; £810) **Stalls** High

Form RPR

32- **1** **Aqaleem**[239] 5343 3-8-12 RHills 6 114
(M P Tregoning) *lw: in tch: rdn and outpcd over 3f out: hdwy 2f out: carried rt briefly over 1f out: led 1f out: styd on strly* **12/1**

5-51 **2** 4 **Hearthstead Maison (IRE)**[7] 1476 3-8-12 99 J-PGuillambert 7 107+
(M Johnston) *hld up in last: rdn over 3f out: styng on whn sltly hmpd over 1f out: kpt on u.p: wnt 2nd on line: no ch w wnr* **4/1**[2]

12-2 **3** shd **Kid Mambo (USA)**[22] 1126 3-8-12 104 DaneO'Neill 4 106
(T G Mills) *lw: pressed ldr tl 8f out: jnd ldr 4f out: rdn to ld narrowly 3f out: wandered over 1f out: hdd 1f out: lost 2nd post* **9/4**[1]

36-1 **4** 3 **Many Volumes (USA)**[14] 1296 3-8-12 90 RichardHughes 1 101+
(H R A Cecil) *led tl rdn and narrowly hdd 3f out: ev ch u.p after tl wknd ins fnl f* **9/2**[3]

12- **5** 3/4 **Mythical Kid (USA)**[203] 6102 3-8-12 106 LDettori 5 100
(Saeed Bin Suroor) *hld up in last pair: rdn over 3f out: hdwy to chse ldrs wl over 1f out: btn and nt pushed fnl f* **9/4**[1]

10-3 **6** 17 **Karoo Blue (IRE)**[49] 754 3-8-12 85 TedDurcan 3 71
(C E Brittain) *t.k.h: prom: jnd ldr 8f out tl over 3f out: wknd qckly over 2f out* **50/1**

1-0 **7** shd **Go On Be A Tiger (USA)**[22] 1126 3-8-12 90 DarryllHolland 2 71
(M R Channon) *trckd ldrs: rdn and outpcd over 3f out: no ch last 2f* **25/1**

2m 31.46s (1.54) **Going Correction** +0.375s/f (Good) **7** Ran SP% **113.2**
Speed ratings (Par 109):109,106,106,103,103 90,90
CSF £57.83 TOTE £12.30: £3.70, £2.40; EX 64.70.
Owner Hamdan Al Maktoum **Bred** Shadwell Estate Company Limited **Trained** Lambourn, Berks

FOCUS
An unexceptional Derby Trial on paper, but the winner looks progressive and the form is rated around the placed horses. The pace was poor for the first three furlongs, and just ordinary after that until stepping up half a mile from home.

NOTEBOOK
Aqaleem sprang a surprise to land his first victory at the third attempt, but he had shown plenty as a juvenile, and this son of Sinndar was always likely to come into his own at a mile and a quarter and beyond. Despite being held up in a modestly-run race, he stayed on to win convincingly and is now as low as 12-1 for the Derby, for which he would have to be given consideration if lining up. His participation there has not been confirmed, and he will have to improve again to win the Blue Riband, but there are other good prizes to be won with him if connections decide he is not quite ready for Epsom. (op 8-1)
Hearthstead Maison(IRE) is bred for this trip, and would not have been ideally suited by being held up in race run at a moderate early tempo. Staying on in the centre of the track when pushed even wider in a domino movement on the run to the final furlong, he was second best on merit, and can do even better with a stronger gallop. (op 9-2)
Kid Mambo(USA)'s trainer was unhappy that O'Neill chose to track the poor early pace rather than grasp the nettle and set a decent one for himself. Though trying to kick for home in the straight, he was never able to get away, with his relentless galloping style making him vulnerable to Aqaleem's better finishing acceleration. (op 7-2 tchd 4-1 in places)
Many Volumes(USA), a son of Oaks winner Reams Of Verse, should be suited by this trip as a three-year-old, but faded late on despite Hughes being able to dictate at his own tempo. This was a big step up in class, but the ground was probably the main problem, since he disappointed on soft ground last season. (op 4-1 tchd 5-1)
Mythical Kid(USA) was not ideally placed turning for home, in race where the early pace had been slack, leaving him with a bit too much to do as the tempo increased. He was a high-class juvenile with Sir Michael Stoute last season, but his new connections believe he may be best at ten furlongs this year. (op 2-1 tchd 5-2)
Karoo Blue(IRE), the only runner not entered for the Derby, was out of his depth and not certain to stay anyway. However, his last run showed he has trained on, so he can continue to make his mark over shorter trips at a more realistic level.
Go On Be A Tiger(USA) has won on soft ground, but this trip was stretching his stamina. Ten furlongs looks to be his limit at present. (tchd 33-1)

1663 TOTESPORT.COM OAKS TRIAL (LISTED RACE) (FILLIES) 1m 3f 106y
3:45 (3:46) (Class 1) 3-Y-O

£28,390 (£10,760; £5,385; £2,685; £1,345; £675) **Stalls** High

Form RPR

1- **1** **Kayah**[228] 5596 3-8-12 77 RichardHughes 6 94
(R M Beckett) *hld up: reminders 5f out: hdwy over 3f out: styd on u.p last 2f: led wl ins fnl f* **20/1**

35-2 **2** 3/4 **Brisk Breeze (GER)**[22] 1127 3-8-12 89 TedDurcan 4 92
(H R A Cecil) *in tch: rdn over 5f out: hdwy over 3f out: led narrowly over 2f out tl over 1f out: ev ch tl no ex nr fin* **9/2**[3]

3-1 **3** shd **Folk Opera (IRE)**[22] 1127 3-8-12 94 LDettori 3 92
(Saeed Bin Suroor) *chsd ldr tl led 3f out: rdn and hdd over 2f out: led again jst over 1f out tl hdd and no ex: nr fin* **11/4**[2]

01- **4** 3 1/2 **Shimoni**[206] 6058 3-8-12 78 RHills 5 86
(W J Knight) *lw: h.d.w: slowly away: bhd: rdn over 3f out: kpt on fnl f: nvr trbld ldrs* **20/1**

-221 **5** 2 1/2 **Elyaadi**[17] 1237 3-8-12 81 DarryllHolland 1 82
(M R Channon) *lw: trckd ldrs: rdn and effrt over 2f out: wknd over 1f out* **7/1**

21-2 **6** 10 **Gull Wing (IRE)**[14] 1293 3-8-12 79 DaneO'Neill 7 65
(M L W Bell) *cl up: rdn over 3f out: sn wknd: no ch last 2f* **7/1**

21- **7** 7 **Sunlight (IRE)**[204] 6071 3-8-12 83 PhilipRobinson 2 53
(M A Jarvis) *led tl 3f out: sn btn: no ch last 2f* **15/8**[1]

2m 31.52s (1.60) **Going Correction** +0.375s/f (Good) **7** Ran SP% **114.2**
Speed ratings (Par 104):109,108,108,105,104 96,91
CSF £105.75 TOTE £20.70: £5.90, £2.20; EX 80.90.
Owner J H Richmond-Watson **Bred** Lawn Stud **Trained** Whitsbury, Hants
■ Stewards' Enquiry : Richard Hughes two-day ban: used whip with excessive frequency (May 23-24)

FOCUS
A modestly-contested Oaks trial, run at a medium gallop and pretty ordinary rated around the fifth.

NOTEBOOK
Kayah was the only runner not in the Oaks, and connections must now decide whether or not to supplement her after watching this stoutly-bred filly staying on to snatch victory in the last 50 yards. A daughter of Derby winner Kahyasi, who also won the Lingfield Derby Trial, she is proving to be rather better than her trainer thought she was. The Epsom Classic is a big step up, but few top-class fillies excel over the trip, so they must be tempted to let her take her chance. (op 14-1)
Brisk Breeze(GER) got the better of Folk Opera this time, over a longer trip, only for the winner to mow them both down near the finish. The Oaks looks beyond reach, with Cecil already represented there by Passage Of Time and Light Shift. However, she may well go to Royal Ascot, with the Park Hill a possible long-term target, and should be placed to win a decent prize. (op 5-1 tchd 4-1)
Folk Opera(IRE) just about stayed the extra two furlongs, but Brisk Breeze finished in front of her this time, and her pedigree suggests that ten furlongs suits her ideally. There are good races to be won with her, but Measured Tempo looks a better Oaks option for Godolphin. (op 5-2 tchd 3-1)
Shimoni also missed the break in both her races last season, a habit that she needs to correct. That said, she stayed on well from an unpromising position and should be a live contender in decent middle-distance races from now on.
Elyaadi had already proved her abilty to stay this trip, so it was either the softer ground or better-class opponents that proved her undoing. (op 9-1 tchd 10-1)
Gull Wing(IRE), bred to stay a mile and a half and beyond, dropped out quickly in the home straight. She would be worth another chance in lower grade and on ground with less cut in it. (op 15-2)
Sunlight(IRE), a daughter of Sinndar, has winners in the family at this trip, but folded tamely when headed. Though she has yet to prove that she does stay this far, it is unlikely that the extra distance was fully to blame. (op 9-4 tchd 5-2)

1664 CPG 21ST ANNIVERSARY CONDITIONS STKS 1m 2f
4:20 (4:20) (Class 2) 4-Y-O+ **£12,464** (£3,732; £1,866; £934; £466) **Stalls** Low

Form RPR

211- **1** **Blue Ksar (FR)**[196] 6218 4-9-2 115 (t) LDettori 1 113+
(Saeed Bin Suroor) *lw: t.k.h: trckd ldr: led wl over 2f out: rdn wl over 1f out: hrd drvn fnl f: forged ahd nr fin* **6/4**[2]

554- **2** 1 1/4 **Hard Top (IRE)**[315] 3085 5-8-12 112 RHills 2 106+
(Sir Michael Stoute) *plld hrd: hld up in tch: trckd ldng pair 6f out: rdn over 2f out: kpt on same pce u.p: wnt 2nd last strides* **6/5**[1]

140- **3** hd **Foxhaven**[203] 6103 5-9-2 105 JimCrowley 4 110
(P R Chamings) *led tl hdd and rdn over 2f out: kpt on wl u.p tl no ex wl ins fnl f* **5/1**[3]

4134 **4** 13 **Sgt Schultz (IRE)**[32] 995 4-8-12 81 TedDurcan 3 80
(J S Moore) *lw: stdd s: t.k.h: hld up in tch: rdn over 3f out: sn outpcd* **16/1**

0055 **5** 12 **Undeterred**[11] 1368 11-8-12 68 J-PGuillambert 5 56
(K J Burke) *in tch: rdn wl over 3f out: sn wl bhd: t.o* **66/1**

2m 11.15s (1.43) **Going Correction** +0.375s/f (Good) **5** Ran SP% **109.5**
Speed ratings (Par 109):109,108,107,97,87
CSF £3.60 TOTE £1.90: £1.50, £1.40; EX 3.60.
Owner Godolphin **Bred** Meridan Stud And Haras Du Mezeray **Trained** Newmarket, Suffolk

FOCUS
Lacking in numbers, but the first two home made this a decent race in terms of quality, although the winner did not need to be at his best. However, the tempo was steady for the first six furlongs.

NOTEBOOK
Blue Ksar(FR) had to work hard to hold off his two pursuers, but he stays well, having been tried over two miles as a three-year-old. He has now won his last three races and, though not top-class, can probably improve again. (op 11-8 tchd 7-4 and 15-8 in a place)
Hard Top(IRE), largely disappointing last season, was gelded after his final outing. Too headstrong off a pedestrian gallop, he needs a stronger pace and an extra two furlongs to bring out the best in him. (op 5-4 tchd 11-10 and 11-8 in a place)
Foxhaven, who put up a good effort at the weights, was left to dictate his own tempo. However, he rallied well when headed, and is even more effective at a mile and a half. (op 11-2)
Sgt Schultz(IRE) has been in good form of late, on both turf and sand, but had an impossible task at the weights here. A tough sort, he can find more suitable races from ten furlongs upwards.
Undeterred had around four stones to find at the weights, so the presence in the line-up of this grand veteran was something of a mystery. (op 100-1)

1665 LINGFIELDPARK.CO.UK MAIDEN STKS 1m 2f
4:50 (4:52) (Class 5) 3-Y-O+ **£3,238** (£963; £481; £240) **Stalls** Low

Form RPR

2-0 **1** **Calabash Cove (USA)**[79] 527 3-8-11 LDettori 7 80+
(Saeed Bin Suroor) *lw: chsd ldr tl led 3f out: rdn over 1f out: drew clr ins fnl f: readily* **5/2**[1]

- **2** 2 1/2 **Hazarayna** 3-8-7 ow1 PhilipRobinson 11 68
(H R A Cecil) *rangy: scope: w'like: chsd ldrs: rdn wl over 2f out: chsd ldng pair wl over 1f out: kpt on to go 2nd on line* **12/1**

00- **3** *shd* **Chord**[206] 6049 3-8-11 .... RHills 6 72
(Sir Michael Stoute) *led tl 3f out: kpt on u.p tl nt pce of wnr ins fnl f: lost 2nd on post* **5/1**[3]
4 *2* **Marieschi (USA)** 3-8-11 .... TedDurcan 3 68+
(H R A Cecil) *w'like: lw: hld up in midfield: hdwy on inner 4f out: rdn and outpcd over 3f out: kpt on fnl f* **8/1**
00 **5** *nk* **Yes One (IRE)**[49] 764 3-8-11 .... DaneO'Neill 9 67+
(J W Hills) *hld up bhd: hdwy on rail over 2f out: styd on wl ins fnl f: nt trble ldrs* **33/1**
35 **6** *3* **Hubble Bubble (USA)**[17] 1236 3-8-11 .... J-PGuillambert 1 61
(M Johnston) *chsd ldrs: rdn 3f out: wknd over 1f out* **11/4**[2]
6-0 **7** *nk* **Dancewiththestars (USA)**[12] 1343 3-8-6 .... SimonWhitworth 5 55
(J R Fanshawe) *towards rr: outpcd wl over 3f out: hdwy over 2f out: kpt on: nt trble ldrs* **33/1**
8 *nk* **Rainbow Flame** 3-8-11 .... AdamKirby 10 60+
(W R Swinburn) *lw: tall: t.k.h: hld up in rr: outpcd wl over 3f out: hdwy 2f out: kpt on fnl f: nvr nrr* **16/1**
9 *2* **Muraco** 3-8-11 .... JosedeSouza 2 56
(R M Beckett) *w'like: scope: s.i.s: hld up in rr: outpcd over 4f out: sme late hdwy: n.d* **33/1**
-0 **10** *nk* **Shine Like A Star**[12] 1358 3-8-6 .... MatthewHenry 12 50
(J L Dunlop) *in tch in midfield: lost pl over 3f out: sn bhd* **33/1**
5- **11** *7* **Full Of Promise (USA)**[204] 6071 3-8-6 .... JimCrowley 4 36
(Mrs A J Perrett) *lw: t.k.h: chsd ldrs: rdn and wknd qckly over 3f out: no ch last 2f* **5/1**[3]
0 **12** *6* **Arthur Parker**[37] 936 6-9-12 .... (t) VinceSlattery 8 29
(J A B Old) *plld hrd: hld up in midfield: rdn over 3f out: sn wknd* **66/1**

2m 14.63s (4.91) **Going Correction** +0.375s/f (Good)
WFA 3 from 6yo 15lb **12** Ran SP% **126.5**
Speed ratings (Par 103):95,93,92,91,91 88,88,88,86,86 80,75
CSF £35.14 TOTE £4.20: £1.60, £2.40, £2.30; EX 59.90.
Owner Godolphin **Bred** Gainsborough Farm Llc **Trained** Newmarket, Suffolk

FOCUS
Some good stables represented here, but it looked an ordinary maiden, and the pace was modest for the first half-mile, so not form to be confident about.
Full Of Promise(USA) Official explanation: trainer said filly was unsuited by the good to soft (good in places) ground

1666 OCS GROUP LADIES STKS (H'CAP) (LADY AMATEUR RIDERS) 7f
5:20 (5:21) (Class 5) (0-75,75) 4-Y-0+ **£3,123** (£968; £484; £242) **Stalls** High

Form RPR
4101 **1** **Binnion Bay (IRE)**[8] 1446 6-9-12 **66** .... (b) MissLEllison 2 75
(J J Bridger) *lw: in tch: rdn and hdwy over 2f out: styd on wl u.p fnl f: led nr fin* **11/2**[2]
-000 **2** *shd* **Quantum Leap**[68] 614 10-9-3 **64** .... (p) MissHarrietCarroll(7) 9 73
(S Dow) *racd in midfield: hdwy over 2f out: ev ch 1f out: kpt on under jst hands and heels: jst hld* **14/1**
3322 **3** *¾* **What Do You Know**[43] 831 4-9-6 **65** .... (p) MissZoeLilly(5) 5 72
(A M Hales) *pressed ldrs: rdn to ld over 2f out: kpt on wl u.p tl hdd and no ex nr fin* **11/2**[2]
033- **4** *¾* **Kasumi**[188] 6350 4-10-1 **74** .... MissVCartmel(5) 12 79+
(H Morrison) *lw: h.d.w: bhd: hdwy on stands' rail over 1f out: r.o wl fnl f: nt rch ldrs* **11/2**[2]
663- **5** *2* **Outer Hebrides**[159] 6696 6-10-0 **75** .... (vt) MissHDavies(7) 11 75
(J M Bradley) *chsd ldr: rdn over 2f out: ev ch tl wknd last 100yds* **14/1**
1100 **6** *1 ¼* **Greenwood**[17] 1252 9-9-11 **65** .... MrsSMoore 6 62+
(P G Murphy) *broke wl: stdd to trck ldrs: nt clr run over 1f out tl ins fnl f: no hdwy after* **7/1**[3]
3252 **7** *½* **Parkview Love (USA)**[11] 1382 6-9-10 **64** .... (v) MrsMMorris 8 59
(D Shaw) *stdd and wnt lft s: rdn and effrt over 2f out: nt trble ldrs* **5/1**[1]
0056 **8** *½* **Lady's Law**[11] 1381 4-9-2 **63** oh16 ow2 .... MissEmma-JaneJenkins(7) 4 57?
(Rae Guest) *bhd: hdwy wl over 2f out: rdn and no hdwy wl over 1f out* **66/1**
0-00 **9** *hd* **Scarlet Flyer (USA)**[14] 1308 4-9-12 **71** .... MissHayleyMoore(5) 3 65
(G L Moore) *bhd: rdn and effrt over 2f out: kpt on same pce fnl f* **7/1**[3]
-000 **10** *5* **Li Shih Chen**[39] 902 4-9-3 **62** .... (v[1]) MissKellyBurke(5) 10 43
(A P Jarvis) *led tl over 2f out: sn wknd: uns rdr after fin* **16/1**
0652 **11** *6* **Pelham Crescent (IRE)**[4] 1562 4-9-0 **61** oh9 .... (b) MrsJMBerry(7) 1 26
(B Palling) *wnt bdly lft s: a bhd: no ch last 2f* **7/1**[3]

1m 23.36s (-0.85) **Going Correction** -0.025s/f (Good) **11** Ran SP% **121.0**
Speed ratings (Par 103):103,102,102,101,98 97,96,96,96,90 83
CSF £82.34 CT £460.29 TOTE £5.30: £2.50, £3.60, £2.90; EX 124.50 Place 6 £350.80, Place 5 £160.44.
Owner J J Bridger **Bred** Fieldspring Ltd **Trained** Liphook, Hants

FOCUS
A modest but competitive race for lady riders, run at a decent gallop and solid form rated around the second and fourth.
T/Plt: £230.10 to a £1 stake. Pool: £74,456.45. 236.15 winning tickets. T/Qpdt: £139.50 to a £1 stake. Pool: £3,317.90. 17.60 winning tickets. SP

1635 NOTTINGHAM (L-H)
Saturday, May 12

OFFICIAL GOING: Good to soft (soft in places) changing to soft after race 4 (3.30)
After 6mm overnight the persistent heavy showers soon turned the ground from'easy side of good' to 'genuine soft'.
Wind: Fresh, half-against Weather: Cloudy, turning showery from the 3rd race onwards

1667 TOTEPLACEPOT H'CAP 6f 15y
1:55 (1:56) (Class 3) (0-95,96) 3-Y-0 **£11,658** (£3,468; £1,733; £865) **Stalls** High

Form RPR
3-24 **1** **Dickie Le Davoir**[2] 1604 3-9-2 **90** .... RichardMullen 4 94
(K R Burke) *hld up: pushed along 4f out: hdwy over 2f out: led over 1f out: drvn out* **9/4**[1]
0-20 **2** *¾* **Southandwest (IRE)**[14] 1298 3-9-0 **88** .... EddieAhern 2 90
(J S Moore) *trckd ldrs: plld hrd: rdn over 2f out: ev ch over 1f out: styd on* **4/1**[3]
0-60 **3** *nk* **Averticus**[8] 1450 3-8-4 **78** oh1 .... JimmyQuinn 6 79
(B W Hills) *dwlt: hld up: hdwy over 1f out: sn rdn: styd on* **5/1**
04-1 **4** *½* **Baltimore Jack (IRE)**[23] 1108 3-8-7 **81** .... DaleGibson 8 81
(M W Easterby) *led: hung lft and hdd over 3f out: rdn over 1f out: styd on same pce ins fnl f* **11/4**[2]
0-00 **5** *2 ½* **Everymanforhimself (IRE)**[14] 1298 3-9-2 **90** .... TPQueally 3 82
(J G Given) *s.i.s: sn chsng ldrs: led over 3f out: rdn and hdd over 1f out: wkng whn n.m.r ins fnl f* **6/1**

1m 18.0s (3.00) **Going Correction** +0.575s/f (Yiel) **5** Ran SP% **108.4**
Speed ratings (Par 103):103,102,101,100,97
CSF £10.98 TOTE £2.50: £1.10, £3.40; EX 10.80.
Owner Bigwigs Bloodstock II **Bred** P And Mrs A G Venner **Trained** Middleham Moor, N Yorks
■ Stewards' Enquiry : Eddie Ahern caution: careless riding

FOCUS
A fair sprint handicap, run in an ordinary time. The form looks sound enough, rated through the runner-up.

NOTEBOOK
Dickie Le Davoir has returned in decent form and ran well to finish fourth at Chester earlier in the week. This was a lesser contest and he looked to hold strong claims with the softer ground of no inconvenience. Held up early, he made good headway around runners to lead over a furlong out and was always doing enough to hold the runner-up. He holds an entry at Hamilton next week and it would not surprise to see him take his chance there. (op 15-8)
Southandwest(IRE) was able to get a lot closer to the winner than he had done at Ripon last month and saw it out really well considering how keenly he raced. A return to faster ground is likely to suit. (op 9-2 tchd 5-1)
Averticus, a bit disappointing at Lingfield the other day having made a pleasing reappearance, appreciated the return to turf and ran really well considering he would no doubt have found this ground on the slow side. He remains capable of better off this mark. (op 13-2 tchd 7-1)
Baltimore Jack(IRE), who made a winning return off a mark of 77 at Ripon, was up 4lb and proved rather disappointing in this softer ground, hanging under pressure and not looking comfortable. He is clearly a fast-ground performer. (op 9-4)
Everymanforhimself(IRE) hinted a return to form may not be too far off, although he could ideally do with dropping a few pounds in the handicap. (op 8-1)

1668 TOTETRIFECTA H'CAP 1m 6f 15y
2:25 (2:25) (Class 4) (0-80,80) 4-Y-0+ **£6,477** (£1,927; £963; £481) **Stalls** Low

Form RPR
1336 **1** **Nawow**[21] 1148 7-9-1 **73** .... NCallan 4 83+
(P D Cundell) *sn led: set modest pce: qcknd over 4f out: styd on wl: 4l clr whn heavily eased towards fin* **5/1**[3]
11-4 **2** *1 ¾* **Pagano (IRE)**[25] 1083 4-9-2 **75** .... EddieAhern 9 80
(A King) *sn trcking ldr: rdn and n.m.r 3f out: kpt on wl fnl f* **9/4**[2]
1106 **3** *½* **Muntami (IRE)**[16] 1263 6-8-6 **67** .... AndrewElliott(3) 3 71
(John A Harris) *led early: trckd ldrs: outpcd 4f out: styd on wl fnl 2f* **14/1**
1104 **4** *¾* **Cripsey Brook**[6] 1490 9-9-1 **80** .... (t) JamesReveley(7) 6 83
(K G Reveley) *trckd ldrs: outpcd over 3f out: kpt on fnl 2f* **11/1**
6-00 **5** *shd* **Zabeel Palace**[16] 1272 5-9-4 **76** .... TPQueally 2 79
(B J Curley) *hld up in rr: effrt over 3f out: hung bdly rt over 1f out: styd on wl ins fnl f* **16/1**
221- **6** *2 ½* **Height Of Fury (IRE)**[193] 6272 4-9-3 **76** .... JimmyQuinn 5 75
(J L Dunlop) *tk fierce hold in last: effrt 4f out: hung lft over 1f out: nvr a threat* **6/4**[1]
666 **7** *5* **Red Wine**[42] 844 8-8-12 **70** .... (be) StephenDonohoe 8 65+
(A J McCabe) *hld up in rr: hdwy to chse ldrs 5f out: chal over 3f out: wknd over 1f out: eased ins fnl f* **14/1**

3m 16.55s (9.45) **Going Correction** +0.475s/f (Yiel)
WFA 4 from 5yo+ 1lb **7** Ran SP% **115.0**
Speed ratings (Par 105):92,91,90,90,90 88,85
CSF £16.90 CT £146.86 TOTE £7.10: £3.70, £1.30; EX 26.30 Trifecta £102.80 Pool: £144.90 - 1.00 winning units..
Owner Ian M Brown **Bred** Kirtlington Stud Ltd **Trained** Compton, Berks
■ Stewards' Enquiry : T P Queally 28-day ban (increased from 21 after an appeal): breach of Rule 157 (Jun 5-12, Jul 3-22); B J Curley fined £3,000 under Rules 155 (ii).

FOCUS
A decent staying handicap on paper in which Neil Callan dictated on Nawow who was value double the winning margin.
Zabeel Palace Official explanation: 40-day ban: (Jun 5-Jul 14)

1669 TOTESPORT 0800 221 221 H'CAP 5f 13y
2:55 (2:55) (Class 5) (0-70,70) 4-Y-0+ **£3,238** (£963; £481; £240) **Stalls** High

Form RPR
00-5 **1** **Namir (IRE)**[21] 1165 5-8-10 **62** .... (vt) TPQueally 17 76
(D Shaw) *racd stands' side: mde all: rdn over 1f out: styd on* **10/1**[3]
2162 **2** *2* **No Time (IRE)**[4] 1557 7-8-11 **63** .... StephenDonohoe 1 69+
(A J McCabe) *racd far side: chsd ldrs: lost pl over 3f out: hdwy over 1f out: r.o to ld that side wl ins fnl f: 1st of 11 in gp* **7/1**[2]
5201 **3** *½* **Monte Major (IRE)**[21] 1163 6-8-4 **56** oh2 .... (v) HayleyTurner 4 60
(D Shaw) *racd far side: chsd ldrs: led that side 1/2-way: rdn and hdd wl ins fnl f: 2nd of 11 in gp* **12/1**
0000 **4** *¾* **Sands Crooner (IRE)**[47] 787 4-8-10 **62** .... (v) DanielTudhope 16 63
(D Shaw) *racd stands' side: s.i.s: chsd wnr: rdn over 1f out: styd on same pce ins fnl f: last of 2 in gp* **25/1**
4650 **5** *¾* **Taboor (IRE)**[14] 1309 9-8-5 **57** .... RichardMullen 8 55
(R M H Cowell) *racd far side: s.s: hld up: r.o ins fnl f: nvr nrr: 3rd of 11 in gp* **20/1**
-000 **6** *3 ½* **Mormeatmic**[4] 1565 4-9-3 **69** .... PaulMulrennan 9 54
(M W Easterby) *racd far side: s.i.s: sn prom: lost pl 1/2-way: styd on ins fnl f: 4th of 11 in gp* **10/1**[3]
211- **7** *½* **Decider (USA)**[143] 6877 4-8-3 **60** .... KevinGhunowa(5) 13 43
(J M Bradley) *racd far side: hld up: hdwy and hung lft over 1f out: wknd ins fnl f: 5th of 11 in gp* **10/1**[3]
4560 **8** *½* **Trinculo (IRE)**[75] 566 10-8-4 **63** .... LukeMorris(7) 14 44
(R A Harris) *s.s: racd far side: outpcd: 6th of 11 in gp* **7/1**[2]
20-5 **9** *¾* **Tamino (IRE)**[18] 1214 4-8-9 **61** .... EddieAhern 6 39+
(H Morrison) *racd far side: chsd ldrs: rdn over 1f out: wknd fnl f: 7th of 11 in gp* **9/2**[1]
00-5 **10** *2 ½* **Our Fugitive (IRE)**[26] 1061 5-9-4 **70** .... NCallan 10 39+
(A W Carroll) *racd far side: plld hrd and prom: rdn over 1f out: wkng whn hmpd ins fnl f: 8th of 11 in gp* **9/2**[1]
5-00 **11** *shd* **Northern Chorus (IRE)**[4] 1557 4-8-9 **68** .... (v) JamesO'Reilly(7) 5 36
(J O'Reilly) *led far side to 1/2-way: wknd fnl f: 9th of 11 in gp* **50/1**
60-0 **12** *¾* **Silver Prelude**[26] 1061 6-8-11 **63** ow1 .... PatDobbs 7 29
(D K Ivory) *racd far side: chsd ldrs: rdn 1/2-way: wknd over 1f out: 10th of 11 in gp* **22/1**
0364 **13** *3 ½* **Cosmic Destiny (IRE)**[13] 1321 5-8-4 **56** oh2 .... JamieMackay 3 8
(E F Vaughan) *s.s: racd far side: hld up: plld hrd: bhd whn hung rt fr 1/2-way* **12/1**

63.61 secs (1.81) **Going Correction** +0.575s/f (Yiel) **13** Ran SP% **118.9**
Speed ratings (Par 103):108,104,104,102,101 96,95,94,93,89 89,87,82
CSF £74.47 CT £886.55 TOTE £11.70: £2.60, £2.10, £5.10; EX 90.70 Trifecta £204.40 Part won. Pool: £287.90 - 0.10 winning units..

Owner ownaracehorse.co.uk (Shakespeare) **Bred** B Kennedy **Trained** Danethorpe, Notts

FOCUS
A slight surprise with one of the two who opted to stay stands' side prevailing, the other finishing fourth. That said, any bias was not definite. Pretty sound form overall.

Decider(USA) Official explanation: jockey said colt was hanging left

1670 TOTESPORTCASINO.COM KILVINGTON FILLIES' STKS (LISTED RACE) 6f 15y
3:30 (3:31) (Class 1) 3-Y-0+ £17,188 (£6,498; £3,248; £1,624) Stalls High

Form RPR
301- 1 **Firenze**[212] 5919 6-9-7 99 OscarUrbina 11 105+
(J R Fanshawe) *hld up: hdwy over 2f out: wnt 2nd over 1f out: led jst ins fnl f: edgd lft: readily* 7/2[1]
0-22 2 2 **Perfect Story (IRE)**[14] 1292 5-9-3 85 HayleyTurner 12 95
(J A R Toller) *hld up: effrt over 2f out: wnt 2nd ins fnl f: no imp* 14/1
131- 3 3 **Blue Echo**[197] 6201 3-8-11 95 NCallan 4 86+
(M A Jarvis) *swtchd rt after s: led tl hdd & wknd jst ins fnl f* 6/1[3]
0-10 4 2 **Lady Livius (IRE)**[11] 1372 4-9-3 96 PatDobbs 10 79
(R Hannon) *chsd ldrs: rdn over 2f out: one pce* 16/1
563- 5 3 **Sunderland Echo (IRE)**[259] 4803 4-9-3 90 TonyHamilton 13 69
(B Ellison) *mid-div: rdn over 2f out: styd on fnl f* 6/1[3]
300- 6 2 1/2 **Bowness**[269] 4468 5-9-3 83 JamieMackay 14 61
(J G Given) *in rr: rdn over 2f out: kpt on fnl f: nvr a factor* 33/1
51- 7 3/4 **Sacre Coeur**[283] 4041 3-8-7 EddieAhern 1 56
(J L Dunlop) *swtchd lft s and trckd one other far side: led that side ins fnl f: no ch w stands' side* 9/1
-600 8 1 1/2 **Angus Newz**[6] 1497 4-9-7 90 RichardMullen 2 58
(M Quinn) *swtchd lft s and led one other far side: wknd ins fnl f* 11/1
0/1- 9 hd **Riotous Applause**[242] 5274 4-9-3 97 JimmyQuinn 3 54
(J R Fanshawe) *rrd s: sn trcking ldrs: wknd 2f out* 5/1[2]
14-0 10 4 **Golden Asha**[77] 551 5-9-3 85 DaleGibson 8 41
(G G Margarson) *in rr: rdn over 2f out: nvr on terms* 28/1
00-2 11 1 1/2 **Folga**[11] 1372 5-9-3 94 TPQueally 7 36
(J G Given) *sn chsng ldr: wknd over 1f out* 8/1

1m 16.9s (1.90) **Going Correction** +0.575s/f (Yiel)
WFA 3 from 4yo+ 10lb 11 Ran SP% **115.8**
Speed ratings (Par 108):110,107,103,100,96 93,92,90,90,84 82
CSF £54.05 TOTE £3.80: £1.50, £4.30, £2.30; EX 42.10 Trifecta £244.50 Pool: £413.26 - 1.20 winning units..

Owner Jan and Peter Hopper **Bred** Mrs J P Hopper **Trained** Newmarket, Suffolk

FOCUS
The field elected to stay stands' side for this and the classy Firenze made an impressive winning return. However she did not need to be at her best as not many showed their form. High numbers dominated, although the winner raced on the outer.

NOTEBOOK
Firenze, a progressive mare in this division last season who was recently withdrawn at Newmarket due to the fast ground, reportedly does not want it too soft either, but she coped well and defied her drift in the market with a cosy victory. Ridden confidently, it was apparent from a furlong out she was going best and simply outclassed her rivals. Connections are planning on campaigning her in all the top sprints and, whilst she is obviously going to have to raise her game, it is not a strong particularly strong division and she will always be a threat when conditions are in her favour. (op 7-4 tchd 4-1)
Perfect Story(IRE), a useful handicapper who has been in decent form, had very stiff task at the weights, but does not mind a bit of cut and she recorded a personal best, simply being outclassed by the winner. This is as good as it is likely to get for her, but she has gained some black-type. (op 25-1 tchd 12-1)
Blue Echo, a useful sprinting juvenile, had the beating of Firenze at the weights, but this was no easy task for a three-year-old in the telling conditions and she failed to last home. A pleasing reappearance effort, she has clearly trained on and can win more races this season, for all that she is not going to be the easiest to place. (op 3-1)
Lady Livius(IRE), who found 5f on firm ground too speedy for her reappearance at Bath, is not quite up to this level, but this test suited her better and she ran well enough. Another who is not going to be easy to win with this season. (op 20-1)
Sunderland Echo(IRE), a progressive handicapper last season who likes soft ground, was the gamble of the race but failed to live up to expectation and may have needed this first outing since August. (op 14-1)
Riotous Applause, a stablemate to the winner, could have been expected to fare better on this reappearance, but this ground was no good to her and she deserves another chance. (op 8-1)
Folga Official explanation: jockey said mare was unsuited by the soft ground

1671 TOTECOURSE TO COURSE MAIDEN H'CAP 1m 1f 213y
4:00 (4:03) (Class 6) (0-60,60) 4-Y-0+ £3,071 (£906; £453) Stalls Low

Form RPR
2300 1 **Sedgwick**[17] 1251 5-9-4 60 TPQueally 9 70
(J G Given) *chsd ldrs: led over 2f out: sn rdn: styd on* 11/2[2]
000- 2 2 1/2 **Moonshine Creek**[343] 2220 5-8-8 50 JamieMackay 3 55
(P W Hiatt) *led: hdd over 8f out: chsd ldr: rdn and ev ch over 2f out: edgd lft and no ex ins fnl f* 12/1
053- 3 1 1/2 **Inchdhuaig (IRE)**[147] 5240 4-8-10 52 (p) LeeEnstone 10 54
(P C Haslam) *chsd ldrs: rdn over 2f out: styd on same pce fnl f* 12/1
-055 4 3/4 **Jenny Soba**[3] 1579 4-8-8 55 MichaelJStainton(5) 12 56
(R M Whitaker) *hld up: hdwy u.p over 1f out: nt trble ldrs* 6/1[3]
-000 5 shd **Salvestro**[5] 1539 4-8-11 53 NCallan 7 53
(A W Carroll) *hld up in tch: plld hrd: rdn and hung lft over 1f out: styd on same pce* 11/2[2]
00-0 6 3 **Phone In**[10] 1406 4-8-6 53 KevinGhunowa(5) 16 48
(R Brotherton) *w ldr: led over 8f out: rdn and hdd over 2f out: wknd over 1f out* 9/1
0-00 7 3/4 **El Capitan (FR)**[10] 1406 4-8-9 51 (b) EddieAhern 11 44
(Miss Gay Kelleway) *hld up: hdwy over 2f out: rdn and hung lft over 1f out: wknd fnl f* 5/1[1]
0000 8 3 1/2 **Contra Mundum (USA)**[17] 1239 4-8-8 50 (p) StephenDonohoe 5 37
(B S Rothwell) *hld up: rdn over 3f out: n.d* 28/1
000/ 9 1/2 **Dance Sauvage**[621] 4816 4-8-9 51 ow1 DanielTudhope 13 37
(C W Thornton) *s.i.s: hld up: rdn over 3f out: n.d* 20/1
0/0 10 2 1/2 **Fancy (IRE)**[5] 1521 4-9-0 56 FergusSweeney 1 37
(R A Farrant) *chsd ldrs over 7f* 22/1
000- 11 3/4 **Dream Master (IRE)**[206] 6052 4-8-7 52 MarcHalford(3) 4 31
(J Ryan) *hld up: rdn over 3f out: a in rr* 25/1
0-55 12 1 **Wally Barge**[15] 1284 4-8-9 51 RobertHavlin 14 29
(D K Ivory) *hld up: hdwy 1/2-way: wknd over 2f out* 12/1
-300 13 23 **Tabulate**[16] 1265 4-8-6 55 LukeMorris(7) 2 —
(P L Gilligan) *hld up: effrt over 3f out: sn wknd* 15/2

2m 14.35s (4.65) **Going Correction** +0.475s/f (Yiel) 13 Ran SP% **123.0**
Speed ratings (Par 101):100,98,96,96,96 93,93,90,89,87 87,86,68
CSF £68.20 CT £777.91 TOTE £6.50: £3.00, £3.60, £4.60; EX 108.60.

Owner Mr & Mrs G Middlebrook **Bred** G And Mrs Middlebrook **Trained** Willoughton, Lincs

FOCUS
A poor handicap in which the first two were less exposed than the others. The form seems sound enough for the low level.

1672 TOTEEXACTA H'CAP 1m 54y
4:35 (4:36) (Class 5) (0-75,75) 3-Y-0 £3,238 (£963; £481; £240) Stalls Centre

Form RPR
1 1 **Sky More**[20] 1177 3-8-13 70 NCallan 7 91+
(M A Jarvis) *trckd ldrs: effrt over 3f out: led over 1f out: drew wl clr: heavily eased nr fin* 2/1[1]
31 2 6 **Lady Gloria**[79] 522 3-9-4 75 TPQueally 6 79
(J G Given) *w ldrs: led over 3f out: hdd over 1f out: no ch w wnr* 7/1
16- 3 1 1/4 **Magic Echo**[203] 6106 3-9-1 72 TonyHamilton 8 73
(M Dods) *in rr: drvn over 5f out: hdwy on wd outside over 2f out: kpt on* 11/2[3]
3565 4 4 **Here's Blue Chip (IRE)**[10] 1399 3-8-0 62 (v[1]) RoryMoore(5) 9 54
(P W D'Arcy) *in rr: hdwy on wd outside over 2f out: nvr nr ldrs* 16/1
441 5 8 **Krakatau (FR)**[16] 1266 3-8-0 62 KevinGhunowa(5) 14 35
(D J Wintle) *trckd ldrs: hung lft over 2f out: one pce* 12/1
1300 6 4 **Cherri Fosfate**[18] 1228 3-9-4 75 (b) DanielTudhope 10 39
(D Carroll) *s.i.s: hdwy on ins 4f out: wknd over 2f out* 16/1
600- 7 6 **Redcliff (GER)**[189] 6332 3-8-3 67 NSLawes(7) 4 17
(M W Easterby) *unruly in stalls: s.s: detached in rr: nvr on terms* 33/1
2213 8 11 **Mark Of Love (IRE)**[5] 1531 3-9-1 72 SamHitchcott 2 —
(M R Channon) *t.k.h: trckd ldrs: lost pl over 2f out* 7/2[2]
450- 9 nk **Majestas (IRE)**[216] 5828 3-8-8 65 StephenDonohoe 5 —
(Evan Williams) *led 2f: w ldrs: lost pl over 2f out: sn bhd* 16/1
10 10 hd **Rich Lord**[50] 744 3-8-13 73 AndrewElliott(3) 3 —
(J D Bethell) *chsd ldrs: led after 2f: hdd over 3f out: sn wknd* 25/1
1-5 F **Stravita**[85] 483 3-8-13 75 RussellKennemore(5) 15 —
(R Hollinshead) *hld up: hdwy and in midfield whn fell over 3f out* 33/1

1m 48.53s (2.13) **Going Correction** +0.475s/f (Yiel) 11 Ran SP% **118.5**
Speed ratings (Par 99):108,102,100,96,88 84,78,67,67,67 —
CSF £16.31 CT £66.97 TOTE £2.10: £1.40, £1.90, £1.80; EX 12.90.

Owner Sheikh Ahmed Al Maktoum **Bred** Darley **Trained** Newmarket, Suffolk

FOCUS
An authoritative display by Sky More, who relished the testing conditions and won in the style of a very useful performer. They finished strung out and not many handled the conditions. The runner-up's maiden win has not really worked out and the third looks the best guide.

Krakatau(FR) Official explanation: jockey said colt was unbalanced by the soft ground
Mark Of Love(IRE) Official explanation: jockey said gelding was unsuited by the soft ground
Majestas(IRE) Official explanation: jockey said gelding was unsuited by the soft ground

1673 TOTE TEXT BETTING 60021 APPRENTICE H'CAP 1m 54y
5:10 (5:11) (Class 6) (0-60,60) 4-Y-0+ £2,914 (£867; £433; £216) Stalls Centre

Form RPR
6521 1 **Very Well Red**[9] 1435 4-8-6 52 WilliamCarson(5) 2 69+
(P W Hiatt) *mde all: rdn clr over 2f out: eased ins fnl f* 5/2[1]
052- 2 4 **Casual Affair**[156] 6738 4-9-5 60 AndrewElliott 5 65+
(J D Bethell) *hld up: swtchd rt over 2f out: hdwy over 1f out: sn hung lft: no ch w wnr* 9/1
0-64 3 1 3/4 **Foolish Groom**[5] 1539 6-8-9 53 RoryMoore(3) 17 54
(R Hollinshead) *hld up: hdwy over 3f out: rdn to chse wnr over 1f out: edgd lft and no imp* 15/2[2]
-264 4 5 **Lady Duxyana**[6] 1507 4-7-12 46 oh1 (v) FrankiePickard(7) 14 35
(M D I Usher) *s.i.s: hld up: racd keenly: styd on appr fnl f: nvr nrr* 8/1[3]
0302 5 nk **Methusaleh (IRE)**[12] 1360 4-8-11 57 PatrickHills(5) 11 45
(D Shaw) *hld up: hdwy over 2f out: wknd over 1f out* 15/2[2]
036 6 6 **Itcanbedone Again (IRE)**[18] 1206 8-7-12 46 oh1 JosephWalsh(7) 8 21
(Ian Williams) *s.i.s: hld up and bhd: nvr nr to chal* 9/1
000- 7 1 1/2 **Top Dirham**[215] 5861 9-8-10 58 NSLawes(7) 12 29
(M W Easterby) *chsd ldrs tl wknd over 1f out* 20/1
0-00 8 1 **Gone'N'Dunnett (IRE)**[1] 1640 8-8-5 51 (v) KirstyMilczarek(5) 4 20
(Mrs C A Dunnett) *chsd ldrs over 5f* 22/1
3034 9 4 **Golden Spectrum (IRE)**[12] 1366 8-8-13 59 (b) LukeMorris(5) 6 19
(R A Harris) *trckd ldrs: racd keenly: wknd over 2f out* 16/1
10 1 1/2 **Minstrel Flyer (IRE)**[426] 5-8-2 48 SCreighton(5) 7 4
(E J Creighton) *s.i.s: hld up: a in rr* 50/1
4000 11 shd **Going Skint**[4] 1562 4-9-1 59 (v[1]) MichaelJStainton(3) 9 15
(M Wellings) *hld up: rdn over 4f out: wkng whn hmpd over 2f out* 22/1
0200 12 1 **Benny The Bus**[15] 1280 5-8-13 57 TravisBlock(3) 1 11
(Mrs G S Rees) *chsd ldrs: rdn over 2f out: sn wknd* 8/1[3]
0-00 13 3 **Life's A Whirl**[12] 1366 5-8-5 46 oh1 (p) MarcHalford 3 —
(Mrs C A Dunnett) *prom 5f* 33/1
000- 14 17 **Alujawill (IRE)**[206] 6053 4-8-1 47 NicolPolli(5) 15 —
(Evan Williams) *hld up: wknd 1/2-way* 16/1
2200 15 23 **Golden Square**[33] 975 5-8-7 53 AshleyHamblett(5) 13 —
(A W Carroll) *hld up: rdn over 3f out: sn hung lft and wknd* 12/1

1m 49.8s (3.40) **Going Correction** +0.475s/f (Yiel) 15 Ran SP% **132.1**
Speed ratings (Par 101):102,98,96,91,90 84,83,82,78,76 76,75,72,55,32
CSF £26.03 CT £167.92 TOTE £3.10: £1.60, £3.60, £3.70; EX 40.80 Place 6 £169.63, Place 5 £91.60.

Owner P W Hiatt **Bred** Butts Enterprises Limited **Trained** Hook Norton, Oxon

FOCUS
Just a moderate contest, but Very Well Red is progressing and should win again at a modest level. The runner-up was the only one to make any real headway in the bad ground and the third looks the best guide.

Itcanbedone Again(IRE) Official explanation: jockey said gelding was hampered leaving stalls
Golden Spectrum(IRE) Official explanation: jockey said gelding was unsuited by the soft ground
Life's A Whirl Official explanation: jockey said mare was unsuited by the soft ground
Golden Square Official explanation: jockey said gelding lost its action

T/Plt: £128.80 to a £1 stake. Pool: £60,566.65. 343.15 winning tickets. T/Qpdt: £38.50 to a £1 stake. Pool: £2,016.40. 38.70 winning tickets. CR

[1478]THIRSK (L-H)

Saturday, May 12

OFFICIAL GOING: Good to firm (firm in places)

Wind: Virtually nil

1674 TURF TV CLAIMING STKS 5f

6:15 (6:16) (Class 5) 2-Y-O **£3,886** (£1,156; £577; £288) **Stalls** High

Form RPR

622 **1** **Shepherds Warning (IRE)**[16] 1255 2-8-0 .... DuranFentiman(5) 4 58
(R M Stronge) *cl up: rdn and ev ch whn carried lft and bmpd over 1f out: led jst ins fnl f and kpt on gamely* **10/3**[3]

2 *1* **Vixens Daughter** 2-8-7 .... PaulMulrennan 7 56
(K A Ryan) *led: rdn 2f out and sn hung lft: drvn and hdd jst ins fnl f: kpt on* **8/1**

3 *1 1/4* **Seein'Red (IRE)** 2-9-3 .... MickyFenton 1 61
(P T Midgley) *v green and wnt bdly lft s: hanging thrght: hdwy over 1f out: hung rt and kpt on ins fnl f: nrst fin* **28/1**

31 **4** *hd* **Echostar**[16] 1255 2-8-5 .... JimmyQuinn 6 48
(W R Muir) *trckd ldng pair: shkn up over 2f out: sn rdn and no imp appr fnl f* **6/4**[1]

5 *nk* **Prigsnov Dancer (IRE)** 2-9-0 .... WJCafferty(7) 2 63
(P C Haslam) *sn outpcd and bhd: hdwy whn hung lft wl over 1f out: kpt on ins fnl f: nrst fin* **8/1**

6 *1 3/4* **Featherstone** 2-8-12 .... KimTinkler 5 47
(N Tinkler) *chsd ldrs: rdn and hung lft wl over 1f out: sn one pce* **20/1**

1 **U** **My Sheilas Dream (IRE)**[17] 1235 2-8-6 .... LiamJones(3) 3 —
(W G M Turner) *rrd, uns rdr and fell s* **3/1**[2]

60.70 secs (0.80) **Going Correction** 0.0s/f (Good) **7** Ran SP% **118.5**

Speed ratings (Par 93):93,91,89,89,88 85,—

CSF £31.07 TOTE £4.50: £1.70, £3.70; EX 26.40.Shepherds Warning was claimed by N. J. Vaughan for £8,000. Vixens Daughter was claimed by Richard Phillips £10,000.

Owner Tim Whiting **Bred** T M Jennings **Trained** Beedon Common, Berks

FOCUS

A competitive contest rated around the winner and fourth.

NOTEBOOK

Shepherds Warning(IRE), narrowly touched off in this grade at Beverley last time, was quickly into stride and made plenty of use of on a track that favours speedier types. She overcame being bumped into to score with a bit in hand and saw it out really well. She was claimed afterwards for £8,000. (op 4-1 tchd 3-1)

Vixens Daughter, bred to appreciate further in time, was making her debut at a lowly level but was able to show plenty. She certainly knew her job and showed good early speed, but her inexperience betrayed her late on. A little progression should see her winning a small race and she will benefit from a sixth furlong in time. (op 13-2)

Seein'Red(IRE), who cost just 900gns, made a highly encouraging debut considering how green and inexperienced he ran. Hanging throughout, he did well to finish as close as he did and should know a lot more next time. (op 25-1)

Echostar, who narrowly denied the winner at Beverley last time, was making her debut for connections and looked to hold a solid chance despite being 5lb worse off at the weights. However, she found disappointingly little for pressure and was not good enough on the day. (op 5-2)

Prigsnov Dancer(IRE), a 16,000gns son of Namid, found this too sharp a test first time up, but was putting in some good late work and should know a lot more next time. (tchd 10-1)

My Sheilas Dream(IRE) was involved in a nasty incident as the stalls opened, rearing backwards, and it remains to be seen what effect this has on her confidence. (op 5-2)

1675 BAYSDALE H'CAP 7f

6:45 (6:45) (Class 6) (0-60,60) 4-Y-O+ **£2,590** (£770; £385; £192) **Stalls** Low

Form RPR

0-02 **1** **Sedge (USA)**[26] 1064 7-9-4 **60** .... (p) MickyFenton 3 69
(P T Midgley) *trckd ldrs: hdwy 2f out: rdn to ld ins fnl f: sn drvn and kpt on wl* **4/1**[1]

5020 **2** *1/2* **Sir Bond (IRE)**[16] 1260 6-8-11 **56** .... GregFairley(3) 11 63
(G R Oldroyd) *in tch: smooth hdwy on outer 3f out: rdn to ld briefly ent fnl f: sn drvn and kpt on wl* **8/1**

4-04 **3** *shd* **Compton Plume**[17] 1241 7-9-2 **58** .... DaleGibson 6 65
(M W Easterby) *cl up: effrt to ld over 1f out: sn rdn and hdd ent fnl f: kpt on wl u.p* **14/1**

2454 **4** *1 3/4* **Cabourg (IRE)**[16] 1260 4-9-2 **58** .... (b) PaulMulrennan 10 60+
(R Bastiman) *bhd: hdwy over 2f out: swtchd outside and rdn wl over 1f out: styd on ins fnl f: nrst fin* **10/1**

5322 **5** *hd* **Danish Blues (IRE)**[18] 1212 4-8-10 **59** .... (p) MatthewDavies(7) 1 61
(D E Cantillon) *plld hrd: in tch on inner: pushed along 3f out: rdn 2f out: styd on ins fnl f: nrst fin* **6/1**[2]

1010 **6** *nk* **Writ (IRE)**[33] 967 5-9-4 **60** .... TomEaves 8 61+
(I Semple) *s.i.s and bhd: hdwy 2f out: sn rdn and kpt on ins fnl f: nrst fin* **6/1**[2]

32-0 **7** *hd* **Walnut Grove**[8] 1459 4-9-0 **56** .... PaulFessey 5 56
(T D Barron) *trckd ldrs: hdwy 3f out: rdn and ch wl over 1f out: sn drvn and btn* **15/2**[3]

00-5 **8** *nk* **Night In (IRE)**[32] 992 4-9-4 **60** .... (t) KimTinkler 9 60
(N Tinkler) *prom: hdwy to ld over 2f out: sn rdn: hdd & wknd over 1f out* **10/1**

00-0 **9** *1 3/4* **Sands Of Barra (IRE)**[5] 1539 4-9-3 **59** .... DanielTudhope 4 54
(I W McInnes) *led: rdn along and hdd over 2f out: sn wknd* **14/1**

0/00 **10** *shd* **Registrar**[17] 1251 5-9-4 **60** .... DMylonas 13 55
(Mrs C A Dunnett) *towards rr: hdwy over 2f out: sn rdn: edgd lft and btn* **50/1**

000- **11** *2 1/2* **Royal Composer (IRE)**[235] 5446 4-8-13 **60** .... DuranFentiman(5) 7 48
(T D Easterby) *nvr bttr than midfield* **9/1**

00-0 **12** *1 1/2* **Crosby Hall**[16] 1260 4-8-6 **55** .... (t) DanielleMcCreery(7) 2 39
(N Tinkler) *a towards rr* **40/1**

6-00 **13** *5* **Apache Nation (IRE)**[17] 1241 4-9-4 **60** .... PhillipMakin 15 30
(M Dods) *a towards rr* **20/1**

000- **14** *3* **Jaassey**[173] 6531 4-8-12 **57** .... MarkLawson(3) 12 19
(A Crook) *a towards rr* **33/1**

0-00 **15** *1* **Greek Secret**[32] 992 4-9-4 **60** .... DO'Donohoe 14 19
(J O'Reilly) *a towards rr* **25/1**

1m 26.14s (-0.96) **Going Correction** 0.0s/f (Good) **15** Ran SP% **128.9**

Speed ratings (Par 101):105,104,104,102,102 101,101,101,99,99 96,94,88,85,84

CSF £36.13 CT £440.82 TOTE £5.30: £2.30, £2.50, £3.40; EX 66.90.

Owner Peter Mee **Bred** Twin Creeks Farm **Trained** Westow, N Yorks

FOCUS

A modest handicap and a race where it paid to be prominent. The form looks sound rated around the winner and third.

Writ(IRE) Official explanation: jockey said gelding missed the break

1676 ARMY BENEVOLENT FUND MAIDEN STKS 1m

7:15 (7:15) (Class 5) 3-Y-O+ **£3,886** (£1,156; £577; £288) **Stalls** Low

Form RPR

52- **1** **Gold Hush (USA)**[204] 6071 3-8-8 .... SebSanders 10 71+
(Sir Michael Stoute) *trckd ldrs: smooth hdwy to ld over 2f out: pushed clr over 1f out: easily* **8/11**[1]

5443 **2** *4* **Arena's Dream (USA)**[17] 1247 3-8-13 71 .... PaulHanagan 6 61
(R A Fahey) *prom: effrt and ch 2f out: sn rdn and kpt on same pce* **2/1**[2]

0-5 **3** *shd* **Hint Of Spring**[79] 527 3-8-8 .... DO'Donohoe 8 56
(Saeed Bin Suroor) *in touch: hdwy over 2f out: rdn to chse wnr over 1f out: sn drvn and one pce* **9/2**[3]

553- **4** *2* **Sangreal**[161] 6679 3-8-5 66 .... AndrewElliott(3) 11 51
(K R Burke) *towards rr: hdwy on outer 2f out: sn rdn and kpt on ins fnl f: nrst fin* **16/1**

-060 **5** *1 3/4* **Polish Star**[34] 954 3-8-13 52 .... TonyHamilton 12 52?
(J S Wainwright) *hld up in rr: hdwy 3f out: sn rdn and kpt on same pce* **100/1**

06 **6** *1 1/2* **Cottam Eclipse**[16] 1259 6-9-12 .... DanielTudhope 5 52?
(I W McInnes) *chsd ldr: rdn along over 2f out: sn wknd* **50/1**

00 **7** *7* **Ja Myford**[14] 1303 3-8-13 .... MickyFenton 9 33
(P T Midgley) *a towards rr* **100/1**

00- **8** *2 1/2* **Two Dreamers**[231] 5536 3-8-8 .... PaulMulrennan 2 22
(A Crook) *chsd ldrs: rdn along 3f out: sn wknd* **100/1**

00- **9** *2* **Skodger (IRE)**[257] 4891 4-9-12 .... PaulFessey 7 26
(G Woodward) *led: rdn along 3f out: sn hdd & wknd* **150/1**

0-06 **10** *dist* **Ross Is Boss**[34] 956 5-9-7 25 .... DuranFentiman(5) 1 —
(C J Teague) *v.s.a: t.o and v wd bnd after 3f and home turn: virtually p.u fnl 2f* **200/1**

1m 39.16s (-0.54) **Going Correction** 0.0s/f (Good)

WFA 3 from 4yo+ 13lb **10** Ran SP% **121.4**

Speed ratings (Par 103):102,98,97,95,94 92,85,83,81,—

CSF £2.63 TOTE £1.60: £1.02, £1.10, £1.70; EX 2.70.

Owner Gainsborough **Bred** Gainsborough Farm Llc **Trained** Newmarket, Suffolk

■ Stewards' Enquiry : D O'Donohoe caution: used whip with excessive frequency

FOCUS

An uncompetitive contest and hot favourite Gold Hush ran out a ready winner. The form is modest amd limited by the fifth and sixth.

Polish Star Official explanation: jockey said gelding was unsuited by the good to firm (firm in places) ground

Ross Is Boss Official explanation: jockey said gelding missed the break and hung violently right

1677 HYGIVAC H'CAP 2m

7:45 (7:45) (Class 4) (0-85,79) 4-Y-O+ **£5,181** (£1,541; £770; £384) **Stalls** Low

Form RPR

0-33 **1** **Gee Dee Nen**[14] 1300 4-9-7 **79** .... JimmyQuinn 4 87
(M H Tompkins) *trckd ldrs: hdwy 3f out: led 2f out: rdn clr ent fnl f: styd on* **5/2**[2]

00-4 **2** *5* **Boxhall (IRE)**[16] 1263 5-8-11 **66** .... DanielTudhope 1 68
(N Wilson) *led: rdn along 3f out: hdd 2f out and sn drvn: kpt on u.p ins fnl f* **7/1**[3]

16-2 **3** *shd* **Bronze Dancer (IRE)**[17] 1239 5-9-0 **69** .... PaulHanagan 2 71
(G A Swinbank) *trckd ldrs: pushed along over 4f out: rdn to chal over 2f out and ev ch tl drvn and hung lft over 1f out: sn btn* **2/1**[1]

-040 **4** *3/4* **Trance (IRE)**[14] 1300 7-9-10 **79** .... (p) PhillipMakin 5 80
(T D Barron) *chsd ldr: hdwy to chal 3f out: sn rdn and kpt on same pce fnl 2f* **7/1**[3]

0-03 **5** *1 1/4* **Most Definitely (IRE)**[17] 1253 7-9-3 **72** .... SebSanders 3 73+
(R M Stronge) *hld up in rr: hdwy 3f out: rdn to chse ldrs whn hmpd over 1f out: sn btn* **5/2**[2]

3m 30.16s (-1.04) **Going Correction** 0.0s/f (Good)

WFA 4 from 5yo+ 3lb **5** Ran SP% **115.5**

Speed ratings (Par 105):102,99,99,99,98

CSF £19.69 TOTE £3.00: £1.90, £2.70; EX 31.50.

Owner David P Noblett **Bred** Kingwood Bloodstock **Trained** Newmarket, Suffolk

■ Stewards' Enquiry : Paul Hanagan four-day ban: careless riding (May 25-28)

FOCUS

A competitive race on paper rated through the fourth to his recent level, but it probably did not take much winning.

1678 DICK PEACOCK SPRINT H'CAP 6f

8:15 (8:17) (Class 5) (0-75,75) 4-Y-O+ **£3,886** (£1,156; £577; £288) **Stalls** High

Form RPR

160- **1** **Trojan Flight**[200] 6160 6-9-2 **73** .... PaulHanagan 6 84
(R A Fahey) *chsd ldrs: hdwy 2f out: rdn over 1f out: styd on to ld last 100yds* **11/2**[3]

03-0 **2** *1/2* **Choysia**[8] 1458 4-8-7 **64** .... (p) TomEaves 10 74
(D W Barker) *led: rdn wl over 1f out: drvn ins fnl f: hdd and no ex last 100yds* **9/1**

40-0 **3** *3* **Ellens Academy (IRE)**[22] 1134 12-9-4 **75** .... JimmyQuinn 9 76+
(E J Alston) *dwlt and towards rr: hdwy 1/2-way: nt clr run on rails over 1f out: swtchd lft and rdn ent fnl f: kpt on* **5/1**[2]

-543 **4** *1* **Norcroft**[11] 1382 5-8-5 **62** .... (p) DO'Donohoe 12 60
(Mrs C A Dunnett) *cl up: rdn wl over 1f out: drvn and wknd ent fnl f* **3/1**[1]

-043 **5** *hd* **Cape Presto (IRE)**[5] 1545 4-8-13 **70** .... DMylonas 8 67
(Mrs C A Dunnett) *prom: rdn along 2f out: drvn and one pce appr fnl f* **13/2**

6-04 **6** *1 1/4* **Ocean Gift**[7] 1483 5-8-12 **69** .... SebSanders 1 62
(N Tinkler) *stdd s: hld up towards rr: hdwy over 2f out: sn rdn and no imp appr fnl f* **6/1**

4-05 **7** *1 1/4* **Soto**[7] 1483 4-8-11 **68** .... PaulMulrennan 3 57+
(M W Easterby) *racd wd: a in midfield* **17/2**

4-05 **8** *1/2* **Charles Parnell (IRE)**[6] 1492 4-8-10 **67** .... (v[1]) DanielTudhope 5 55
(M Dods) *s.i.s: a in rr* **11/1**

00-0 **9** *3* **Toy Top (USA)**[34] 953 4-9-4 **75** .... (b) PhillipMakin 7 54
(M Dods) *chsd ldrs: rdn along over 2f out: sn wknd* **33/1**

36-0 **10** *3/4* **Paris Bell**[14] 1292 5-9-2 **73** .... PaulQuinn 2 50
(T D Easterby) *s.i.s: a towards rr* **14/1**

500- **11** *3 1/2* **Silidan**[287] 3937 4-9-2 **73** .... DeanMernagh 11 39
(M Brittain) *chsd ldrs to 1/2-way: sn wknd* **28/1**

1m 11.5s (-1.00) **Going Correction** 0.0s/f (Good) **11** Ran SP% **126.6**

Speed ratings (Par 103):106,105,101,100,99 98,96,95,91,90 86

CSF £58.87 CT £273.58 TOTE £6.80: £2.00, £3.20, £2.40; EX 84.00.

Owner Timothy O'Gram **Bred** L C And Mrs A E Sigsworth **Trained** Musley Bank, N Yorks

■ Stewards' Enquiry : Paul Hanagan two-day ban: used whip with excessive frequency (May 29-30)

Dean Mernagh two-day ban: improper riding - struck gelding on dismounting (May 23-24)

FOCUS

A modest sprint in which the front pair drew three-lengths clear of a slightly unlucky Ellens Academy. The time was good and the form looks solid.

1679 TURFTV.CO.UK MAIDEN STKS 6f

8:45 (8:47) (Class 5) 3-Y-O+ **£3,886** (£1,156; £577; £288) **Stalls** High

Form RPR

320- **1** **Expensive Detour (IRE)**[225] [5655] 3-9-2 86 TomEaves 4 59+
(Mrs L Stubbs) *hmpd s: in touch on wd outside: hdwy over 2f out: rdn to ld over 1f out: edgd rt ins fnl f: drvn out* **1/3**[1]

00-3 **2** *nk* **Miss Taboo (IRE)**[22] [1135] 3-8-11 36 MickyFenton 12 53
(P T Midgley) *in tch on stands' rail: hdwy 2f out: rdn over 1f out: styd on strly ins fnl f* **25/1**

0- **3** *1 1/4* **Swift Princess (IRE)**[220] [5764] 3-8-11 (v[1]) PhillipMakin 6 49
(K R Burke) *trckd ldrs: n.m.r over 2f out: swtchd rt and rdn over 1f out: styd on ins fnl f* **16/1**

-000 **4** *3* **Seaton Snooks**[17] [1238] 3-8-11 53 (b[1]) DuranFentiman(5) 2 44
(T D Easterby) *prom: effrt and ev ch 2f out: sn rdn and wknd over 1f out* **33/1**

200 **5** *nk* **Vadinka**[18] [1219] 3-9-2 68 KimTinkler 8 43
(N Tinkler) *chsd ldrs: rdn along 2f out: sn one pce* **6/1**[3]

6 *shd* **Musical Parkes** 3-8-8 AndrewMullen(3) 11 38+
(W J H Ratcliffe) *towards rr: hdwy and n.m.r wl over 1f out: kpt on ins fnl f: nrst fin* **25/1**

00-5 **7** *nk* **Mambomoon**[22] [1136] 3-9-2 40 (b[1]) PaulQuinn 3 42
(T D Easterby) *cl up: rdn along 2f out: wkng whn rdr dropped whip wl over 1f out* **50/1**

300- **8** *nk* **Rose Of Inchinor**[214] [5902] 4-9-7 57 PaulHanagan 10 39
(R E Barr) *led: rdn along 2f out: drvn and hdd over 1f out: sn wknd* **20/1**

60 **9** *3/4* **Blue Bird's Dream**[30] [1011] 4-9-12 JimmyQuinn 9 45+
(E J Alston) *towards rr tl styd on appr fnl f* **10/1**

0-3 **10** *5* **Uace Mac**[32] [998] 3-8-4 SuzzanneFrance(7) 13 18
(N Bycroft) *prom: rdn along over 2f out: sn wknd* **9/2**[2]

00-0 **11** *1 1/2* **Musette (IRE)**[9] [1426] 4-9-2 35 MichaelJStainton(5) 14 16
(R E Barr) *a towards rr* **100/1**

050- **12** *1 1/4* **The Keep**[178] [6492] 5-9-2 38 (v) NataliaGemelova(5) 5 12
(R E Barr) *sn outpcd and bhd* **100/1**

1m 13.28s (0.78) **Going Correction** 0.0s/f (Good)
WFA 3 from 4yo+ 10lb **12** Ran SP% **141.8**
Speed ratings (Par 103):94,93,91,87,87 87,87,86,85,78 76,75
CSF £25.41 TOTE £1.50: £1.10, £4.40, £4.50; EX 22.10 Place 6 £143.39, Place 5 £27.14.
Owner Des Thurlby **Bred** Rathbarry Stud **Trained** Norton, N. Yorks

FOCUS

A typically weak sprint maiden and the hot favourite made hard work of winning, but the form is not solid.

Vadinka Official explanation: jockey said gelding was unsuited by the good to firm (firm in places) ground

T/Plt: £104.30 to a £1 stake. Pool: £55,424.55. 387.85 winning tickets. T/Qpdt: £13.50 to a £1 stake. Pool: £3,070.30. 167.50 winning tickets. JR

1533 WARWICK (L-H)

Saturday, May 12

OFFICIAL GOING: Good to soft

Wind: Moderate, half behind Weather: Fine

1680 PCA LONG SERVICE AWARDS PRESENTATION MAIDEN AUCTION STKS 5f 110y

6:00 (6:00) (Class 5) 2-Y-O **£3,412** (£1,007; £504) **Stalls** Centre

Form RPR

1 **Spitfire** 2-9-2 StephenCarson 4 83
(J R Jenkins) *s.i.s and wnt rt: swtchd lft and hdwy over 1f out: rdn and squeezed through on ins to ld cl home* **14/1**

2 *1* **Diademas (USA)** 2-9-2 MartinDwyer 1 79
(J A Osborne) *hld up in tch: rdn over 1f out: edgd lft and led wl ins fnl f: hdd cl home* **4/1**[2]

442 **3** *nk* **Ben**[14] [1291] 2-8-9 RobertHavlin 2 71
(P G Murphy) *led: hdd over 3f out: led over 2f out: rdn over 1f out: edgd lft and hdd wl ins fnl f: sn bmpd: nt qckn* **15/8**[1]

4 *2* **Tuanku (IRE)** 2-8-6 ThomasO'Brien(7) 3 68
(M R Channon) *towards rr: hdwy on ins 2f out: sn rdn: one pce fnl f* **16/1**

5 *hd* **Dubai Dynamo** 2-8-9 LPKeniry 8 63
(J S Moore) *dwlt: hdwy 2f out: sn edgd lft: one pce fnl f* **8/1**

6 **6** *1/2* **Leading Edge (IRE)**[25] [1079] 2-8-11 JHBowman 9 64
(M R Channon) *w ldrs tl wknd wl over 1f out: btn whn rdn and edgd lft 1f out* **9/1**

7 *hd* **Supermassive Muse (IRE)** 2-8-9 GrahamGibbons 7 61
(E S McMahon) *chsd ldrs: rdn and one pce fnl 2f* **15/2**[3]

8 *2 1/2* **Khana Ras (IRE)** 2-8-13 RichardMullen 11 56
(E J O'Neill) *hung rt most of way: mid-div: rdn over 2f out: no hdwy* **11/1**

0 **9** *2 1/2* **Fly Kiss**[24] [1087] 2-8-4 HayleyTurner 10 38
(C E Brittain) *hld up in tch: rdn 2f out: sn wknd* **28/1**

0 **10** *3 1/2* **Madam Superior**[5] [1533] 2-8-4 JamesDoyle 5 26
(D J S Ffrench Davis) *w ldr: led over 3f out: hung rt and hdd over 2f out: sn rdn: wknd over 1f out* **40/1**

11 *1* **Got Green (FR)** 2-8-11 RichardSmith 12 30
(R Hannon) *s.i.s: outpcd* **25/1**

0 **12** *3* **Never Sold Out (IRE)**[26] [1058] 2-8-13 PaulEddery 13 21
(Pat Eddery) *a bhd* **50/1**

13 *9* **Days Of Thunder (IRE)** 2-8-11 RichardThomas 6 —
(G F Bridgwater) *s.i.s: sn in tch: wknd over 2f out* **66/1**

66.98 secs (1.09) **Going Correction** +0.025s/f (Good) **13** Ran SP% **121.7**
Speed ratings (Par 93):91,89,89,86,86 85,85,82,78,74 72,68,56
CSF £68.27 TOTE £17.90: £3.40, £2.00, £1.30; EX 96.60.
Owner M Francis **Bred** R B Hill **Trained** Royston, Herts
■ Stewards' Enquiry : Robert Havlin one-day ban: careless riding (May 23)

FOCUS

There were some interesting newcomers in this low-grade affair where there was not much previous form to go on and the third is the best guide to the form for now.

NOTEBOOK

Spitfire is a half-brother to several winners including six-furlong Listed scorer Fruit Of Glory. He did well to overcome a poor start and then thread his way through the eye of a needle. (op 11-1)

Diademas(USA) ◆ looked a decent early type in the paddock and should soon go one better in this sort of company. (op 7-2)

Ben, already having his fourth race, set the standard but could not repel the two newcomers in the closing stages. (op 5-2)

Tuanku(IRE) is out of a winner over jumps in France who has already produced a winning hurdler there. Not unduly knocked about by his young apprentice, he is likely to do better over further in due course.

Dubai Dynamo is a brother to Woodcote Stakes winner Sadeek. He tried to get into it after missing the break and should be better for the experience. (op 9-1)

Leading Edge(IRE) raced up with the pace this time after a better start but the end result was much the same as a debut. (op 12-1)

1681 BANBURY H'CAP 5f 110y

6:30 (6:31) (Class 6) (0-65,66) 3-Y-O+ **£2,590** (£770; £385; £192) **Stalls** Centre

Form RPR

5531 **1** **Misaro (GER)**[13] [1321] 6-9-7 66 (b) TolleyDean(5) 10 82
(R A Harris) *mde all: rdn clr wl over 1f out: r.o wl* **6/1**[2]

0636 **2** *3* **Divine Spirit**[2] [1597] 6-9-5 59 (p) JamieSpencer 1 65
(M Dods) *hld up in mid-div: hdwy on ins over 2f out: rdn and chsd wnr fnl f: no imp* **10/3**[1]

6203 **3** *2* **Inwaan (IRE)**[25] [1080] 4-9-8 62 (t) ChrisCatlin 2 62
(P R Webber) *chsd ldrs: rdn over 2f out: kpt on same pce fnl f: tk 3rd post* **6/1**[2]

4615 **4** *shd* **Winthorpe (IRE)**[14] [1309] 7-9-8 62 GrahamGibbons 4 61
(J J Quinn) *chsd wnr tl rdn 1f out: no ex* **8/1**

12-0 **5** *1 1/4* **Musical Script (USA)**[19] [1200] 4-9-8 62 RichardHughes 7 57
(Mouse Hamilton-Fairley) *prom: rdn and c wd 2f out: one pce fnl f* **12/1**

0-24 **6** *1/2* **Harrison's Flyer (IRE)**[10] [1405] 6-9-1 58 (p) RichardKingscote(3) 17 51+
(J M Bradley) *hld up in mid-div: rdn and hdwy on wd outside 2f out: no further prog fnl f* **7/1**[3]

000- **7** *2 1/2* **Colonel Cotton (IRE)**[182] [6442] 8-9-5 59 (v) JimmyFortune 3 44
(W J Knight) *dwlt: hld up: rdn and hdwy over 1f out: no imp fnl f* **9/1**

600- **8** *shd* **Currency**[251] [5042] 10-9-6 60 LPKeniry 9 45
(J M Bradley) *prom: rdn and carried wd 2f out: eased whn btn towards fin* **33/1**

-006 **9** *2 1/2* **Littledodayno (IRE)**[21] [1165] 4-9-11 65 PaulEddery 16 42
(M Wigham) *dwlt and wnt rt s: sn swtchd lft: a bhd* **22/1**

410- **10** *3/4* **Endless Summer**[215] [5872] 10-9-11 65 JamesDoyle 13 39
(A W Carroll) *a bhd* **12/1**

0000 **11** *hd* **Anfield Dream**[17] [1252] 5-9-5 59 EddieAhern 5 32
(J R Jenkins) *hld up in mid-div: rdn wl over 1f out: no rspnse: eased whn btn wl ins fnl f* **14/1**

600/ **12** *7* **Avoca Dancer (IRE)**[224] [5693] 4-9-8 62 JamieMackay 15 12
(M Wigham) *s.i.s: outpcd* **33/1**

-003 **U** **Law Maker**[4] [1557] 7-8-10 57 (v) AmyBaker(7) 14 —
(A Bailey) *sat down in stalls and uns rdr s* **22/1**

65.17 secs (-0.72) **Going Correction** +0.025s/f (Good) **13** Ran SP% **121.9**
Speed ratings (Par 101):103,99,96,96,94 93,90,90,87,86 85,76,—
CSF £25.62 CT £131.97 TOTE £7.50: £2.90, £1.80, £1.90; EX 26.60.
Owner Messrs Criddle Davies Dawson & Villa **Bred** Wilhelm Fasching **Trained** Earlswood, Monmouths

FOCUS

A tightly-knit low-grade sprint handicap but solid form rated through the winner.

Musical Script(USA) Official explanation: jockey said gelding hung right-handed throughout

Avoca Dancer(IRE) Official explanation: vet said filly lost right-fore shoe

1682 ENTERTAIN CLIENTS AT WARWICK H'CAP 7f 26y

7:00 (7:00) (Class 4) (0-85,85) 4-Y-O+ **£6,477** (£1,927; £963; £481) **Stalls** Low

Form RPR

60-3 **1** **Phluke**[30] [1013] 6-9-3 84 StephenCarson 7 95
(Eve Johnson Houghton) *w ldr: led wl over 1f out: sn rdn: r.o* **7/1**

1/5- **2** *1* **Mr Garston**[192] [6292] 4-9-2 83 MartinDwyer 2 91
(M P Tregoning) *hld up and bhd: hdwy on ins wl over 1f out: hrd rdn and kpt on ins fnl f* **5/1**[3]

41-1 **3** *1 1/4* **Hiccups**[18] [1223] 7-9-3 84 DarryllHolland 3 89
(M Dods) *hld up and bhd: hdwy over 1f out: rdn and nt qckn ins fnl f* **2/1**[1]

00-1 **4** *nk* **Roman Maze**[12] [1357] 7-9-2 83 DavidAllan 5 87+
(W M Brisbourne) *hld up and bhd: hdwy on outside wl over 1f out: sn rdn: edgd lft ins fnl f: nt rch ldrs* **7/1**

410- **5** *shd* **Jubilee Street (IRE)**[224] [5680] 8-9-2 83 RoystonFfrench 11 87
(Mrs A Duffield) *led: rdn and hdd wl over 1f out: edgd rt ins fnl f: one pce* **20/1**

4032 **6** *nk* **Sun Catcher (IRE)**[8] [1446] 4-8-11 78 (b) RichardHughes 6 81
(R Hannon) *hld up in tch: rdn over 1f out: one pce ins fnl f* **4/1**[2]

4-25 **7** *1* **Electric Warrior (IRE)**[20] [1179] 4-9-0 81 PatCosgrave 10 82
(K R Burke) *hld up in tch: rdn over 1f out: wknd towards fin* **15/2**

4420 **8** *2* **Grey Boy (GER)**[18] [1209] 6-8-8 75 FrancisNorton 9 71
(A W Carroll) *prom: rdn over 1f out: wkng whn sltly hmpd wl ins fnl f* **11/1**

1m 24.92s (0.72) **Going Correction** +0.20s/f (Good) **8** Ran SP% **119.9**
Speed ratings (Par 105):103,101,100,100,99 99,98,96
CSF £43.84 CT £98.31 TOTE £9.40: £2.90, £1.80, £1.10; EX 72.00.
Owner Mrs R F Johnson Houghton **Bred** Mrs R F Johnson Houghton **Trained** Blewbury, Oxon
■ Stewards' Enquiry : Pat Cosgrave caution: used whip with whip arm above shoulder height

FOCUS

Despite six non-runners this good handicap still turned out to be very competitive and the form is rated at face value.

1683 HBG CONSTRUCTION LTD H'CAP 1m 6f 213y

7:30 (7:31) (Class 5) (0-75,74) 4-Y-O+ **£3,886** (£1,156; £577; £288) **Stalls** Low

Form RPR

30-5 **1** **Takafu (USA)**[18] [1208] 5-9-9 74 JHBowman 6 86+
(W S Kittow) *a.p: nt clr run on ins wl over 1f out: sn rdn and swtchd rt: squeezed through ins fnl f: led nr fin: r.o* **7/1**

0545 **2** *shd* **Jeepstar**[16] [1272] 7-9-6 71 (p) RoystonFfrench 11 81
(S C Williams) *led: rdn and edgd lft wl over 1f out: hdd 1f out: led wl ins fnl f: hdd nr fin* **12/1**

2221 **3** *1* **They All Laughed**[20] [1178] 4-8-2 55 ChrisCatlin 14 64
(P W Hiatt) *hld up and bhd: hdwy on outside over 4f out: sn rdn: hung lft and led 1f out: hdd wl ins fnl f: nt qckn* **11/2**[2]

35-1 **4** *5* **Trafalgar Day**[18] [1222] 4-8-8 61 RichardMullen 7 63
(W M Brisbourne) *hld up towards rr: hdwy over 4f out: rdn 2f out: wknd 1f out* **5/1**[1]

30-5 **5** *nk* **Squirtle (IRE)**[17] [1239] 4-8-11 64 StephenDonohoe 8 65
(W M Brisbourne) *hld up in rr: rdn and hdwy on ins wl over 1f out: swtchd rt 1f out: wknd ins fnl f* **12/1**

0-00 **6** *1 3/4* **Darusso**[7] [1470] 4-8-8 61 LPKeniry 2 60
(J S Moore) *hld up in tch: rdn over 5f out: swtchd rt jst over 1f out: hung rt and wknd ins fnl f* **16/1**

1305 **7** ¾ **Synonymy**[17] 1253 4-8-7 **60**...(b) SteveDrowne 13 58
(M Blanshard) *prom: rdn 3f out: wknd over 1f out* **6/1**[3]
00-1 **8** 2½ **Himba**[18] 1216 4-8-4 **57**... MartinDwyer 5 51
(Mrs A J Perrett) *chsd ldr: rdn 3f out: wknd fnl f* **6/1**[3]
3 **9** 3 **Arafan (IRE)**[16] 1263 5-9-5 **70**... JamieSpencer 1 60
(Dr R D P Newland) *hld up towards rr: hdwy 4f out: rdn and swtchd rt 3f out: wknd wl over 1f out* **5/1**[1]
0105 **10** 3½ **Blue Hills**[10] 1406 6-8-3 **61** ow3...(b) WilliamCarson(7) 10 46
(P W Hiatt) *hld up in mid-div: hdwy 6f out: rdn over 4f out: wknd over 3f out* **14/1**
260- **11** 8 **Jayer Gilles**[199] 6178 7-8-0 **56** ow1... KevinGhunowa(5) 9 30
(Dr J R J Naylor) *t.k.h in mid-div: lost pl over 4f out* **40/1**

3m 19.29s (3.39) **Going Correction** +0.375s/f (Good)
WFA 4 from 5yo+ 2lb **11** Ran SP% **120.2**
Speed ratings (Par 103):105,104,104,101,101 100,100,98,97,95 91
CSF £89.92 CT £502.83 TOTE £9.80: £2.60, £4.00, £1.80; EX 93.20.
Owner Midd Shire Racing **Bred** G W Humphrey Jr **Trained** Blackborough, Devon
■ Stewards' Enquiry : Chris Catlin caution: careless riding
FOCUS
A tight finish to this wide-open minor handicap and the winner was back to last year's course form.

1684 WARWICKRACECOURSE.CO.UK H'CAP 7f 26y
8:00 (8:03) (Class 5) (0-75,80) 3-Y-O **£3,238** (£963; £481; £240) **Stalls** Low

Form RPR
10-2 **1** **Slate (IRE)**[13] 1316 3-9-9 **80**... JamieSpencer 2 88+
(J A Osborne) *chsd ldr: led over 4f out: rdn over 1f out: drvn out* **5/2**[2]
3-00 **2** 1½ **Goose Green (IRE)**[12] 1359 3-8-7 **64** ow1... SteveDrowne 3 68
(R J Hodges) *a.p: rdn to chse wnr jst over 1f out: one pce* **18/1**
21-0 **3** ½ **Ghost Dancer**[18] 1228 3-9-3 **74**... EddieAhern 7 77
(L M Cumani) *hld up and bhd: hdwy 2f out: sn rdn and hung lft: kpt on one pce fnl f* **7/1**
14-0 **4** 4 **Event Music (IRE)**[12] 1359 3-8-13 **70**... JHBowman 10 62
(M R Channon) *hld up and bhd: rdn and sme hdwy over 1f out: nvr trbld ldrs* **18/1**
6-1 **5** 1¼ **Tifernati**[49] 752 3-9-0 **71**... JimmyFortune 6 60+
(W J Haggas) *hld up in mid-div: hung rt 3f out: c wd st: no hdwy fnl 2f* **3/1**[3]
1- **6** 1¼ **Malaath (IRE)**[203] 6098 3-9-1 **72**... KerrinMcEvoy 8 58
(Saeed Bin Suroor) *led: hdd over 4f out: chsd wnr tl rdn jst over 1f out: wknd fnl f* **15/8**[1]
335- **7** 4 **Karma Llama (IRE)**[273] 4377 3-8-13 **70**... PaulEddery 9 45
(B Smart) *sn prom: rdn over 3f out: wknd over 2f out* **33/1**
30-0 **8** ½ **Espejo (IRE)**[22] 1131 3-8-13 **70**...(v[1]) PatCosgrave 4 44
(K R Burke) *hld up: hdwy on ins 3f out: sn rdn: wknd wl over 1f out* **40/1**
000- **9** 3 **Lordship (IRE)**[245] 5178 3-8-5 **62**... FrancisNorton 1 28
(A W Carroll) *a in rr* **33/1**

1m 25.56s (1.36) **Going Correction** +0.20s/f (Good) **9** Ran SP% **119.7**
Speed ratings (Par 99):100,98,97,93,91 90,85,85,81
CSF £46.59 CT £291.81 TOTE £3.60: £1.20, £4.20, £1.90; EX 60.40.
Owner Mountgrange Stud **Bred** Swordlestown Stud **Trained** Upper Lambourn, Berks
FOCUS
A moderate handicap but solid form best rated through the runner-up.

1685 RACING UK MAIDEN FILLIES' STKS 1m 2f 188y
8:30 (8:32) (Class 5) 3-Y-O **£3,238** (£963; £481; £240) **Stalls** Low

Form RPR
02- **1** **Toccata (IRE)**[206] 6049 3-9-0... MartinDwyer 2 78
(D M Simcock) *mde all: rdn fnl f: r.o wl* **15/2**[3]
5-6 **2** 1½ **Set The Scene (IRE)**[14] 1312 3-9-0... JimmyFortune 1 75
(J H M Gosden) *a.p: rdn to chse wnr wl over 1f out: nt qckn ins fnl f* **12/1**
3 **3** 1 **Orama's Ghost**[19] 1203 3-9-0... KerrinMcEvoy 4 73
(Sir Michael Stoute) *in tch: rdn 2f out: edgd lft ins fnl f: one pce* **1/2**[1]
0-5 **4** 8 **Evita**[14] 1296 3-9-0... EddieAhern 6 59
(L M Cumani) *chsd wnr tl rdn wl over 1f out: wknd ent fnl f* **20/1**
5 2 **Royal Secrets (IRE)** 3-9-0... JamieSpencer 7 55
(E A L Dunlop) *s.i.s: t.k.h in rr: pushed along and c wd st: hung lft over 1f out: n.d* **33/1**
6-5 **6** 14 **Handset (USA)**[19] 1203 3-9-0... RichardHughes 8 30
(H R A Cecil) *hld up and bhd: hdwy over 3f out: rdn over 2f out: wknd wl over 1f out: eased ins fnl f* **4/1**[2]
0 **7** 3½ **Memorata**[14] 1312 3-9-0... SteveDrowne 3 24
(R Charlton) *bhd fnl 4f* **33/1**

2m 24.17s (4.77) **Going Correction** +0.375s/f (Good) **7** Ran SP% **116.8**
Speed ratings (Par 96):97,95,95,89,87 77,75
CSF £84.20 TOTE £8.50: £2.80, £4.30; EX 99.50 Place 6 £308.94, Place 5 £197.84.
Owner Fawzi Abdulla Nass **Bred** Michael Dalton **Trained** Newmarket, Suffolk
FOCUS
An ordinary-looking maiden but not that solid and form that is hard to be confident about.
T/Plt: £130.70 to a £1 stake. Pool: £55,288.65. 308.60 winning tickets. T/Qpdt: £111.10 to a £1 stake. Pool: £2,929.30. 19.50 winning tickets. KH

1686 - 1688a (Foreign Racing) - See Raceform Interactive

BADEN-BADEN (L-H)
Saturday, May 12

OFFICIAL GOING: Good

1689a BETTY BARCLAY-RENNEN (GROUP 3) 2m
4:00 (4:01) 4-Y-0+ **£20,270** (£8,446; £3,378; £1,689)

RPR
1 **Bussoni (GER)**[20] 1190 6-9-0... ADeVries 9 112
(H Blume, Germany) *racd in 6th: hdwy over 2f out: 3rd st: led wl over 1 1/2f out: rdn out* **1/1**[1]
2 1½ **Bergo (GER)**[18] 4-8-11... J-PCarvalho 3 111
(W Hefter, Germany) *racd in 3rd: chsd wnr on ins fr over 1f out: kpt on* **96/10**
3 1¾ **Stephenson (FR)**[20] 6-8-11... DBoeuf 11 106
(Frau C Barsig, Germany) *midfield: hdwy over 1f out: r.o strly clsng stages: nrst fin* **28/1**
4 1½ **Darsalam (IRE)**[636] 4411 6-8-9... FilipMinarik 2 103
(A Shavuyev, Czech Republic) *racd in 2nd: led briefly 2f out: sn hdd and one pce* **84/10**
5 ½ **Dragon Fly (GER)**[11] 5-8-9... ASchikora 7 102
(Frau Jutta Mayer, Germany) *hld up in last: hdwy over 2f out: styd on wl fnl f: nrst fin* **68/10**[3]

6 nse **El Tango (GER)**[33] 990 5-8-11... AStarke 6 104
(P Schiergen, Germany) *hld up in 11th: fin wl* **41/10**[2]
7 4 **Morna (FR)**[33] 990 4-8-7... DBonilla 1 99
(S Wattel, France) *hld up towards rr: sme late hdwy* **14/1**
8 10 **Brisant (GER)**[20] 1190 5-8-9... MSuerland 5 88
(M Trybuhl, Germany) *nvr bttr than midfield* **36/1**
9 ¾ **Limatus (GER)**[20] 6-8-9... EPedroza 10 87
(P Vovcenko, Germany) *racd in 4th: wknd 2f out* **139/10**
10 16 **Swordsman (GER)**[34] 5-8-9... JBojko 8 71
(C Von Der Recke, Germany) *led to 2f out: wknd* **60/1**
11 12 **Carus (GER)**[20] 8-8-11... AHelfenbein 12 61
(D K Richardson, Germany) *prom on outside in 5th tl wknd over 2 1/2f out* **39/1**
12 5 **All Spirit (GER)**[41] 882 5-9-2... ASuborics 4 61
(N Sauer, Germany) *wl bhd fr 4f out* **22/1**

3m 23.52s (-0.07)
WFA 4 from 5yo+ 3lb **12** Ran SP% **130.5**
WIN 20; PL 13, 20, 44; SF 139.
Owner Stall Kaiserberg **Bred** Gestut Karlshof **Trained** Germany

1690 - 1692a (Foreign Racing) - See Raceform Interactive

1182
LEOPARDSTOWN (L-H)
Sunday, May 13

OFFICIAL GOING: Good to firm

1693a DERRINSTOWN STUD DERBY TRIAL STKS (GROUP 2) 1m 2f
3:55 (3:56) 3-Y-O **£54,898** (£16,047; £7,601; £2,533)

RPR
1 **Archipenko (USA)**[195] 6263 3-9-1 100... MJKinane 1 114+
(A P O'Brien, Ire) *hld up in 4th: 3rd st: 2nd and hdwy 1 1/2f out: led over 1f out: r.o wl: comf* **8/1**[3]
2 ¾ **Yellowstone (IRE)**[8] 1473 3-9-1 109... JMurtagh 4 112
(A P O'Brien, Ire) *hld up in rr: 4th ent st: sn drvn along: hdwy over 1f out: 2nd and r.o wl ins fnl f* **10/1**
3 2 **Macarthur**[21] 1185 3-9-1... JAHeffernan 5 108
(A P O'Brien, Ire) *led: edgd clr appr st: rdn and hdd over 1f out: no ex* **8/11**[1]
4 1¼ **Mores Wells**[21] 1185 3-9-1 110...(t) DPMcDonogh 6 106
(Kevin Prendergast, Ire) *cl 2nd: racd keenly: outpcd ent st: sn rdn and no imp* **2/1**[2]
5 22 **Hernando Cortes**[226] 5662 3-9-1... DavidMcCabe 3 67
(A P O'Brien, Ire) *dwlt: sn chsd ldrs: cl 3rd bef 1/2-way: drvn along and wknd fr over 3f out: trailing fr 2f out* **50/1**

2m 7.90s (-2.50) **Going Correction** -0.375s/f (Firm) **6** Ran SP% **113.4**
Speed ratings: 95,94,92,91,74
CSF £71.81 TOTE £6.40: £2.60, £2.30; DF 22.90.
Owner M Tabor & Mrs John Magnier **Bred** Eagle Holdings **Trained** Ballydoyle, Co Tipperary
FOCUS
A trial that has over the last seven years been an outstanding guide to both the English and Irish Derbies. Sinndar, Galileo and High Chaparral won at both Epsom and the Curragh, while Alamshar and Dylan Thomas both went on to win the Irish Derby following placed efforts at Epsom. Only five runners went to post for this and four of them were supplied by Aidan O'Brien.
NOTEBOOK
Archipenko(USA), on his first start of the season, looked a horse with a big future when scoring impressively in a 7f maiden here last October, defeating Honoured Guest by six lengths. Settled in a close fourth on the inner, he was still going quite well turning for home,e made his way past Macarthur with a furlong to run and kept on well towards the finish, winning with something to spare. Having reportedly taken time to get fit, he can be expected to make good progress from this and it would be most unwise to underestimate his chances at Epsom. He has stamina to prove over 1m4f but is undeniably a very promising colt. (op 6/1)
Yellowstone(IRE) vindicated connections' decision to step him up in trip following his respectable run in the previous weekend's Stan James 2000 Guineas. After settling towards the rear, he came under pressure with two furlongs to run but the winner got first run on him before he came home well and seemed suited by this trip. He certainly has the ability to win a good prize, but it is worth recalling that he had a definite fitness advantage over the winner having had two previous runs this season. (op 6/1)
Macarthur completed the placings to give Aidan O'Brien a 1-2-3. He was sent off an odds-on favourite to build on his promising Ballysax Stakes run but had suffered from a muscle twinge since that contest. He set out to make all and opened up a useful lead nearing the turn in, but could do no more when headed with over a furlong to run. On this evidence his stable would appear to have stronger Derby candidates, athough there may be more improvement to come. (op 1/1)
Mores Wells, last month's Ballysax Stakes winner, came here on the back of two course and distance victories. After racing in second, he was in trouble heading into the final quarter of a mile and was soon done with. This was not his true form. (op 7/4 tchd 9/4)

1694a DERRINSTOWN STUD 1,000 GUINEAS TRIAL (GROUP 3) (FILLIES) 1m
4:25 (4:25) 3-Y-O **£37,388** (£10,969; £5,226; £1,780)

RPR
1 **Alexander Tango (IRE)**[6] 1547 3-9-0 102... WMLordan 7 105+
(T Stack, Ire) *trckd ldrs: 6th 3f out: 4th and hdwy 2f out: led over 1f out: styd on wl: easily* **9/4**[1]
2 3 **Nell Gwyn (IRE)**[36] 946 3-9-0 90... JAHeffernan 9 94
(A P O'Brien, Ire) *hld up in rr: hdwy on outer ent st: 3rd over 1f out: kpt on wout troubling wnr* **14/1**
3 ¾ **Divine Night (IRE)**[217] 5850 3-9-0 88... NGMcCullagh 2 92
(David Wachman, Ire) *trckd ldrs in 3rd: cl up whn nt clr run on inner early st: kpt on fnl f* **50/1**
4 1¼ **Ela Enta**[14] 1332 3-9-0 96... DPMcDonogh 11 89
(Kevin Prendergast, Ire) *sn trckd ldrs in 4th: impr to chal early st: led over 1 1/2f out: hdd over 1f out: no ex* **13/2**
5 ¾ **Liscanna (IRE)**[36] 946 3-9-0 100... DMGrant 5 87
(David Wachman, Ire) *hld up: kpt on wout threatening st* **10/1**
6 ½ **Majestic Eviction (IRE)**[208] 6041 3-9-0... JMurtagh 8 86
(M Halford, Ire) *hld up: no imp st* **16/1**
7 2½ **Xinji (IRE)**[270] 4498 3-9-0... MJKinane 4 80
(John M Oxx, Ire) *trckd ldrs in 5th: effrt early st: no ex fr over 1f out* **9/1**
8 shd **Thiella (USA)**[219] 5794 3-9-0... PJSmullen 3 80
(D K Weld, Ire) *towards rr: no imp st* **6/1**[3]
9 1½ **Rock Lily**[189] 6357 3-9-0... WSupple 10 77
(Charles O'Brien, Ire) *towards rr: effrt on outer early st: no ex fr over 1f out* **25/1**

The Form Book, Raceform Ltd, Compton, RG20 6NL

10 ½ **Gaudeamus (USA)**^{6} [1548] 3-9-3 103 .... DJMoran 1 79
(J S Bolger, Ire) *led: rdn and strly pressed ent st: hdd & wknd over 1 1/2f out* **5/1**^{2}

11 7 **Navajo Moon (IRE)**^{7} [1513] 3-9-0 .... FMBerry 12 59
(David Wachman, Ire) *racd keenly: settled 2nd: rdn to chal ent st: wknd fr 2f out: eased ins fnl f* **8/1**

S **Impetious**^{211} [5966] 3-9-0 102 .... CDHayes 6 —
(Eamon Tyrrell, Ire) *chsd ldrs: 7th and rdn appr st: no ex whn sltly hmpd 2f out: sn slipped up* **33/1**

1m 39.3s (-5.10) **Going Correction** -0.375s/f (Firm) 12 Ran SP% **126.6**
Speed ratings: 110,107,106,105,104 103,101,101,99,99 92,—
CSF £40.51 TOTE £3.10: £1.40, £5.90, £15.70; DF 67.90.
Owner Noel O'Callaghan **Bred** Philip Brady **Trained** Golden, Co Tipperary
■ Stewards' Enquiry : D M Grant seven-day ban: careless riding

FOCUS
An open and competitive renewal of this 1000 Guineas trial.

NOTEBOOK
Alexander Tango(IRE) produced a commanding display and booked her place at the Curragh in two weeks' time. Having her third run of the season, she seemed to appreciate the step up to a mile following her staying-on fourth to Creachadoir in the Tetrarch Stakes. She travelled noticeably well and was still going quite easily on the heels of the leaders early in the straight and ran out an easy winner. She will now take her chance in the Irish 1000 Guineas and a good run there would not surprise. (op 100/30)
Nell Gwyn(IRE) was patiently ridden and came home strongly on the outer in the straight. She has struggled to make an impact in good company since winning at Tralee last August, but this was much more encouraging. She could be worth a try over further. (op 10/1)
Divine Night(IRE) was another to run well above her rating. She raced up with the pace and might have finished a bit closer but for meeting some trouble early in the straight. She has clearly made good progress over the winter.
Ela Enta struck the front with over a furlong to run but could not respond when the winner swept past. She probably performed to a similar level as when running second to La Conquistadora at Navan two weeks ago and looks quite capable of earning black type. (op 11/2 tchd 7/1)
Liscanna(IRE)p was putting in her best work towards the closing stages and confirmed the promise of her reappearance fourth behind Arch Swing.
Majestic Eviction(IRE) ran creditably without being able to land a telling blow. This was her first start since she won a maiden at Navan last October and there should be better to come from her. (op 14/1)
Xinji(IRE) threatened to get involved early in the straight but was fighting a losing battle from over a furlong out. The form of her maiden win last year has worked out reasonably well and she can do better in time. (op 8/1)
Thiella(USA) was a promising winner of a Gowran maiden last October but failed to land a blow on this seasonal debut and step up in class. She reportedly had a hold up a month ago and it would be unwise to hold this run against her. (op 4/1)
Gaudeamus(USA), a Group 2 winner, ran with plenty of promise in the Athasi Stakes six days previously but was way below that form here and possibly found this race coming too soon.

1696a AMETHYST STKS (GROUP 3) 1m
5:25 (5:25) 3-Y-0+ **£30,743** (£8,986; £4,256; £1,418)

RPR

1 **Danak (IRE)**^{21} [1184] 4-9-9 108 .... MJKinane 4 118+
(John M Oxx, Ire) *hld up in rr: drvn along ent st: 3rd and hdwy 1 1/2f out: 2nd ins fnl f: qcknd to ld 100yds out: r.o strly* **9/10**^{1}

2 2 **Lord Admiral (USA)**^{66} [646] 6-9-9 109 ....(b) PJSmullen 1 111
(Charles O'Brien, Ire) *sn led: rdn and strly pressed ent st: sn edgd clr: hdd 100yds out: one pce* **12/1**

3 1 **Decado (IRE)**^{21} [1184] 4-9-12 111 .... DPMcDonogh 2 112
(Kevin Prendergast, Ire) *cl 2nd: rdn to chal ent st: no imp fr over 1 1/2f out: kpt on same pce* **5/2**^{2}

4 ½ **Quinmaster (USA)**^{21} [1184] 5-9-9 109 .... JMurtagh 3 108
(M Halford, Ire) *trckd ldrs in 3rd: rdn and no imp st: kpt on same pce* **4/1**^{3}

1m 38.8s (-5.60) **Going Correction** -0.375s/f (Firm) 4 Ran SP% **108.9**
Speed ratings: 113,111,110,109
CSF £10.91 TOTE £1.90; DF 11.00.
Owner H H Aga Khan **Bred** H H The Aga Khan's Studs S C **Trained** Currabeg, Co Kildare

FOCUS
Upgraded to Group 3 status this year, this race attracted an interesting four runner field. There was little to choose between Danak, Decado and Quinmaster on their running over this course and distance last month and the trio finished in that order once again

NOTEBOOK
Danak(IRE) ◆ showed that he had made good progress from his reappearance run and confirmed last month's form with the third and fourth. He retained his unbeaten record on his debut at this level and will be worth a further step up in class. Settled towards the rear, he came under pressure nearing the straight but picked up well to get on top in the closing stages. He gave every indication here that he might do even better when he steps up to 1m2f. John Oxx has yet to decide on future plans but this progressive and likeable individual might prove capable of holding his own at the highest level. (op 6/5)
Lord Admiral(USA) came into this following a spell in Dubai . He set out to make all and had his rivals hard at work early in the straight, but was unable to withstand the winner's charge. However, this still represented a good effort in defeat and he should enjoy another good campaign. (op 8/1)
Decado(IRE), who was a fast-finishing third behind Danak last time, raced in second for much of the race, but he was starting to struggle with over a furlong to run and possibly needs easier ground to be seen at his best. (op 2/1)
Quinmaster(USA) was unable to pick up the front pair when coming under pressure in the straight but still was not beaten all that far and could well be able to make his mark at Listed level at some stage this season. (op 7/2)
T/Jkpt: @11,250.00. Pool of @15,000.00 - 1 winning unit. T/Plt: @226.10. Pool of @10,867.72. II

1695 - 1698a (Foreign Racing) - See Raceform Interactive

1689 BADEN-BADEN (L-H)
Sunday, May 13

OFFICIAL GOING: Good

1699a BADENER MEILE (GROUP 3) 1m
4:00 (4:12) 3-Y-0+ **£20,270** (£8,446; £3,378; £1,689)

RPR

1 **Banknote**^{45} [817] 5-9-4 .... FrancisNorton 1 109
(A M Balding) *racd in 2nd: rdn over 1 1/2f out: led 1f out: r.o wl* **44/10**

2 1 **Aspectus (IRE)**^{21} [1192] 4-9-8 ....(b) ADeVries 4 111
(H Blume, Germany) *led: rdn and strly pressed fr over 1 1/2f out: hdd 1f out: kpt on* **3/1**^{2}

3 nk **King Jock (USA)**^{66} [646] 6-9-6 .... PShanahan 2 108
(R J Osborne, Ire) *racd in 4th: wnt 3rd on ins over 3f out: rdn 1 1/2f out: kpt on* **19/10**^{1}

4 2 **Konig Turf (GER)**^{21} 5-9-4 .... ASuborics 8 102
(C Sprengel, Germany) *racd in 5th: kpt on at same pce fnl 2f* **58/10**

5 1 ¾ **Wiesenpfad (FR)**^{41} [897] 4-9-6 .... THellier 3 101
(W Hickst, Germany) *racd in 6th: nvr a factor* **38/10**^{3}

6 2 ½ **Madresal (GER)**^{21} 8-9-2 .... FilipMinarik 7 92
(P Schiergen, Germany) *last to 2f out: a in rr* **15/1**

7 ¾ **Silex (GER)**^{17} [1273] 4-9-4 .... WMongil 5 92
(P Schiergen, Germany) *7th st: a in rr* **21/1**

8 8 **Willingly (GER)**^{21} 8-9-4 .... AHelfenbein 6 76
(M Trybuhl, Germany) *racd in 3rd: 4th over 3f out: wknd 1 1/2f out* **15/1**

1m 37.09s (-2.02) 8 Ran SP% **130.6**
WIN 54; PL 16, 18, 17: SF 282.
Owner The Queen **Bred** Exors Of The Late Queen Elizabeth **Trained** Kingsclere, Hants

NOTEBOOK
Banknote is on the upgrade. His trainer reported that he does best when his races are well spaced. He had the best of the weights here but can win again at this level.

1335 CAPANNELLE (R-H)
Sunday, May 13

OFFICIAL GOING: Good

1700a PREMIO PRESIDENTE DELLA REPUBBLICA AT THE RACES (GROUP 1) 1m 2f
3:20 (3:37) 4-Y-0+ **£121,622** (£53,514; £28,189; £14,595)

RPR

1 **Distant Way (USA)**^{189} [6365] 6-9-2 .... MDemuro 4 118
(L Brogi, Italy) *hld up: last st: hdwy wl over 2f out: drvn to ld ins fnl f: r.o wl* **21/10**^{2}

2 ½ **Pressing (IRE)**^{21} [1192] 4-9-2 .... DPorcu 1 117
(R Feligioni, Italy) *first to show: settled in 3rd: 3rd st: led over 2f out to ins fnl f: r.o* **33/10**^{3}

3 1 **Soldier Hollow**^{42} [880] 7-9-2 .... AStarke 6 115
(P Schiergen, Germany) *hld up in 5th: hdwy over 3f out: ev ch 1 1/2f out: one pce* **41/10**

4 7 **Cherry Mix (FR)**^{189} [6365] 6-9-2 .... KerrinMcEvoy 3 103
(Saeed Bin Suroor) *trckd ldr: led wl over 3f out to over 2f out: wknd wl over 1f out* **9/10**^{1}

5 dist **Urgente**^{357} [1870] 5-9-2 .... MPasquale 2 —
(L Brogi, Italy) *sn led: hdd 3f out: wknd* **21/10**^{2}

6 1 **Mr Darec (IRE)**^{28} 4-9-2 .... CFiocchi 5 —
(M Grassi, Italy) *disp 3rd: 4th st: wknd wl over 2f out* **69/1**

2m 0.40s (-2.90) 6 Ran SP% **161.4**
(including 1 Euro stake): WIN 3.12 (coupled with Urgente); PL 1.81, 2.17; DF 6.21.
Owner Allevamento La Nuova Sbarra **Bred** Grundy Bloodstock **Trained** Italy

NOTEBOOK
Distant Way(USA) used the same tactics as when winning this race last year, when he beat Soldier Hollow by one length. He missed last summer but could try his luck at Deauville this time. The problem is that he is so much better at this course, where he has gained 13 of his 17 wins, than at any other.
Pressing(IRE) was close up all the way and fought on well when headed. He has been bought by Gary Tanaka but raced in his former colours here. If everything goes to plan, he should be moving to England shortly.
Soldier Hollow ran his usual game race and should be winning as soon as he finds easier ground.
Cherry Mix(FR) was the first to make his move but folded quickly once headed. He had beaten Distant Way and Soldier Hollow with some comfort in the Premio Roma over the course and distance last November but there was no sign of that brilliance on this occasion. Easier ground will probably help.

1701a PREMIO REGINA ELENA EMIRATES AIRLINE (GROUP 3) (FILLIES) 1m
4:30 (4:59) 3-Y-0 **£64,611** (£28,429; £15,507; £7,753)

RPR

1 **Lokaloka**^{21} 3-8-11 .... DVargiu 4 105
(B Grizzetti, Italy) *midfield: 6th over 3f out: hdwy to chal 1 1/2f out: qcknd to ld 1f out: rdn and swished tail: r.o* **15/2**

2 2 **Miss Annaleo (IRE)**^{47} 3-8-11 .... CFiocchi 12 101
(I Bugattella, Italy) *10th st: hdwy on outside over 2f out: hrd rdn over 1f out: 5th 1f out: tk 2nd 100yds out* **76/10**

3 ½ **Turfrose (GER)** 3-8-11 .... SLandi 14 100
(P Giannotti, Italy) *racd in 3rd: led 2f out to 1f out: one pce* **51/10**^{3}

4 1 **Penthouse Serenade (IRE)**^{14} 3-8-11 .... MDemuro 11 98
(M Massimi Jr, Italy) *midfield: styd on wl fr over 1f out: nrst fin* **183/10**

5 1 ½ **Samya**^{14} 3-8-11 .... MarcoMonteriso 6 95
(E Borromeo, Italy) *in tch: 4th st: nt clr run over 2f out: 4th whn squeezed up over 1f out: one pce fnl f* **2/1**^{2}

6 1 **Biz Bar**^{182} 3-8-11 .... MEsposito 10 93
(M Guarnieri, Italy) *styd on fnl 2f: nvr nr to chal* **128/10**

7 3 **Vitamina Plus (ITY)**^{14} [1337] 3-8-11 .... CColombi 7 87
(R Giorgetti, Italy) *nvr nrr* **118/1**

8 nse **Cuprea (IRE)** 3-8-11 ....(b) OFancera 8 87
(E Polito, Italy) *a midfield* **240/1**

9 1 ¾ **Donoma (IRE)**^{217} [5858] 3-8-11 .... EBotti 1 83
(A Botti, Italy) *led after 2f: hdd 2f out: wknd qckly* **14/10**^{1}

10 1 **Lasciatelapassare (IRE)** 3-8-11 .... GBietolini 2 81
(R Brogi, Italy) *6th st: btn 2f out* **83/1**

11 nk **Sweet Wind Music**^{14} 3-8-11 .... SMulas 13 81
(B Grizzetti, Italy) *last 1/2-way: sme hdwy over 3f out: btn 2f out* **52/1**

12 7 **Sopran Slam (IRE)**^{225} [5705] 3-8-11 .... MPasquale 5 67
(B Grizzetti, Italy) *midfield: bhd fnl 2f* **84/1**

13 3 **Docksil**^{14} [1337] 3-8-11 .... PConvertino 9 61
(B Grizzetti, Italy) *5th st: wknd over 2f out* **23/1**

14 10 **Leghila (ITY)**^{56} 3-8-11 .... MSanna 3 41
(P Giannotti, Italy) *led 2f: 2nd st: wknd over 2f out* **51/10**^{3}

1m 35.8s (-4.00) 14 Ran SP% **153.3**
WIN 8.51; PL 2.79, 2.77, 2.65; DF 24.72.
Owner Razza Del Terminillo **Bred** Azienda Agricola Rosati Colarieti **Trained** Italy
■ The Italian 1000 Guineas, this race has been downgraded from Group 2 status.

[1571]LONGCHAMP (R-H)

Sunday, May 13

OFFICIAL GOING: Good

1702a POULE D'ESSAI DES POULICHES (GROUP 1) (FILLIES) 1m

2:20 (2:26) 3-Y-O **£154,432** (£61,784; £30,892; £15,432; £7,730)

RPR

1 **Darjina (FR)**[28] [1055] 3-9-0 .... CSoumillon 5 117
(A De Royer-Dupre, France) *hld up: 11th st: hdwy down outside to go 2nd over 1f out: str run to ld last strides* **13/2**[2]

2 *hd* **Finsceal Beo (IRE)**[7] [1496] 3-9-0 .... KJManning 4 116
(J S Bolger, Ire) *cl up on ins: 5th st: got through on ins to ld over 1 1/2f out: hdd last strides* **4/11**[1]

3 *1 ½* **Rahiyah (USA)**[211] [5966] 3-9-0 .... TedDurcan 11 113
(J Noseda) *missed break: last early: 12th st: styd on strly fr over 1f out: nrst fin* **14/1**

4 *2 ½* **Costume**[24] [1105] 3-9-0 .... RichardHughes 3 107
(J H M Gosden) *hld up towards rr: 8th st: hdwy towards ins 2f out: kpt on fr over 1f out* **25/1**

5 *1 ½* **Peace Dream (FR)**[45] 3-9-0 .... IMendizabal 8 104
(J-C Rouget, France) *a cl up: 4th st: rdn 2f out: kpt on at same pce* **10/1**

6 *¾* **Sesmen**[22] [1146] 3-9-0 .... TJarnet 6 102
(M Botti) *racd in 2nd st: led 2f out: led over 1 1/2f out: one pce* **50/1**

7 *nse* **Bicoastal (USA)**[29] [1035] 3-9-0 ....(b) JimmyFortune 7 102
(B J Meehan) *hld up in rr: last st: styd on down outside fnl 2f* **50/1**

8 *10* **Sander Camillo (USA)**[25] [1096] 3-9-0 .... LDettori 12 79
(J Noseda) *in tch: 6th st on outside: rdn to dispute 4th briefly over 1 1/2f out: sn btn: eased clsng stages* **8/1**[3]

9 *½* **Fairy Dress (USA)**[32] [1006] 3-9-0 .... JAuge 2 78
(Robert Collet, France) *midfield: 9th st: effrt and n.m.r 2f out: unable qck* **100/1**

10 *1* **Zut Alors (IRE)**[32] [1006] 3-9-0 .... TThulliez 13 76
(Robert Collet, France) *cl up: 3rd st: sn wknd* **66/1**

11 *½* **Iron Lips**[28] [1055] 3-9-0 .... OPeslier 1 74
(C Laffon-Parias, France) *midfield on ins: 7th st: angling out for a run whn no room and hmpd 2f out: nt rcvr* **66/1**

12 *2* **I Should Care (FR)**[31] 3-9-0 .... SPasquier 10 70
(F Rodriguez Puertas, Spain) *hld up: 10th st: nvr a factor* **100/1**

13 *6* **Galaxie Des Sables (FR)**[11] [1420] 3-9-0 .... RonanThomas 9 56
(Mme N Rossio, France) *led to 2f out: wknd* **100/1**

1m 37.2s (-5.20) **Going Correction** -0.325s/f (Firm) 13 Ran SP% **127.2**
Speed ratings: 113,112,111,108,107 106,106,96,96,95 94,92,86
PARI-MUTUEL: WIN 5.00; PL 1.40, 1.20, 3.10; DF 4.40.
Owner Princess Zahra Aga Khan **Bred** Princess Zahra Aga Khan **Trained** Chantilly, France
■ Stewards' Enquiry : Richard Hughes two-day ban: carless riding (May 22-23)
C Soumillon 200euros fine: whip abuse

FOCUS

Two top-class fillies and another potentially high-class one in Rahiyah drew away from the rest in what looked a good renewal of the French 1000 Guineas. Hot favourite Finsceal Beo was unable to make it two Guineas in a week and lost her 'superstar' status, but Darjina herself deserves credit, and this unbeaten filly may go on to complete the French Guineas-Oaks double.

NOTEBOOK

Darjina(FR), who has always been highly regarded, prevailed narrowly on her reappearance in a Group 3 over course and distance and needed to have progressed significantly if she was to take this. Held up early on under a typically confident ride from Soumillon, who is a class act around this course, he launched his challenge on the filly well over a furlong out and she eventually wore down the hot favourite in the dying strides. Connections had been hugely concerned by the downpour the course had seen earlier in the day as she reportedly needs a decent surface to be at her best, so the fact she was still able to claw back 'superstar' filly Finsceal Beo underlines her talents. Connections now have the decision of whether to stick to this distance in the Coronation Stakes or up her to 1m2f in the Prix De Diane. She shapes as though she will stay, but either way she is likely to take the beating in whichever race she turns up in.

Finsceal Beo(IRE), a top-class two-year-old filly who gained superstar status with her impressive 1000 Guineas victory over a quality field just seven days ago, had reportedly come out of that run in top shape, and connections allowed her to take her chance in a bid to keep the dream alive of completing a unique English, French and Irish 1000 Guineas treble. A hot favourite, she was rousted along to obtain a good early position and made good headway on the inner to lead well over a furlong out, but she never quite got away from her rivals like she did at Newmarket and was eventually reeled in by the unexposed winner. Connections were quick to blame the 'easy' ground, but she had bolted up in the Rockfel in much worse conditions and, to be honest, there was no excuse really required as it was still a fine effort. The one note of caution for the future is that if people thought she had an easy time of it at Newmarket, the opposite could be said here, and she now heads to the Curragh looking more vulnerable than she did a week ago.

Rahiyah(USA), runner-up to Finsceal Beo in last season's Rockfel, missed Newmarket with this race in mind and was clearly ready to roll on this first start of the season. Done no favours by the draw, things worsened when she missed the break, but she showed herself to be a classy filly by running on strongly around runners and claiming third. She looked as though she may win a furlong out, but bumped into two top-class fillies with a fitness edge. She herself could progres into one of the best around if going the right way from this, and the Coronation Stakes is likely to be her next stop.

Costume, a twice-raced maiden, ran a remarkable race and emerges from the contest with much credit. In rear early on, she made relentless progress under pressure and found only three quality fillies too good. She should have no trouble shedding her maiden tag.

Peace Dream(FR), three times a winner in the Provinces, handled a step up in class when winning over the course and distance back in March, but could not take this extra step into the top level.

Sesmen, a disappointment in the Fred Darling on her reappearance, showed that run to be all wrong and kept on pretty well once headed, suggesting to she can get back to winning ways once having her sights lowered.

Bicoastal(USA), a beaten favourite on the Polytrack on her reappearance, made some late progress past beaten horses and is another who needs her sights lowering.

Sander Camillo(USA), a top sprinting juvenile who reappeared with a slightly disappointing effort in the Nell Gwyn, was forced to miss the English Guineas and instead waited for this. The supposed Noseda first string, she briefly threatened to get involved, but soon looked beaten over a furlong out and was eased off close home. At this stage she has it all to prove, but the ground would not have been entirely suitable and she deserves another chance on a quick surface.

1703a POULE D'ESSAI DES POULAINS (GROUP 1) (COLTS) 1m

2:50 (3:03) 3-Y-O **£154,432** (£61,784; £30,892; £15,432; £7,730)

RPR

1 **Astronomer Royal (USA)**[28] [1056] 3-9-2 .... CO'Donoghue 9 118
(A P O'Brien, Ire) *last 1/2-way: 12th st: c to outside: hdwy fr 2f out: drvn to ld 100yds out: drvn out: r.o wl* **33/1**

2 *½* **Creachadoir (IRE)**[6] [1547] 3-9-2 .... KJManning 4 117
(J S Bolger, Ire) *a in tch: 6th on outside st: led wl over 1f out: sn rdn: ct 100yds out: r.o* **13/2**

3 *1 ½* **Honoured Guest (IRE)**[28] [1047] 3-9-2 .... GMosse 3 113
(A P O'Brien, Ire) *9th st: r.o steadily fr over 1f out* **9/2**[2]

4 *¾* **Excellent Art**[239] [5373] 3-9-2 .... JamieSpencer 13 119+
(A P O'Brien, Ire) *in rr to st: gd hdwy wl over 1f out: swtchd sharply towards rails 1 1/2f out: nt clr run appr fnl f: fin wl* **6/1**

5 *½* **Thousand Words**[24] [1103] 3-9-2 .... RichardHughes 14 110
(B W Hills) *towards rr to st: styd on steadily fnl 2f: nrst fin* **16/1**

6 *snk* **Followmyfootsteps (USA)**[31] [1019] 3-9-2 .... SPasquier 2 110
(David Wachman, Ire) *racd in 3rd to st: disp 2nd 1f out: one pce* **33/1**

7 *1 ½* **Spirit One (FR)**[35] [963] 3-9-2 .... DBoeuf 12 107+
(P Demercastel, France) *sn trcking ldr: 2nd to 1 1/2f out: one pce* **14/1**

8 *1 ½* **Visionario (IRE)**[28] [1056] 3-9-2 .... CSoumillon 1 103+
(A Fabre, France) *5th st: keeping on steadily whn n.m.r appr fnl f: one pce* **5/1**[3]

9 *1 ½* **Battle Paint (USA)**[28] [1056] 3-9-2 .... OPeslier 5 100
(J-C Rouget, France) *led after 1 1/2f: hdd wl over 1f out: wknd qckly* **7/2**[1]

10 *1* **Stoneside (IRE)**[32] [1005] 3-9-2 .... TGillet 6 97
(Rod Collet, France) *last st: nvr a factor* **50/1**

11 *snk* **Dijeerr (USA)**[204] [6102] 3-9-2 .... LDettori 8 97
(Saeed Bin Suroor) *racd in 4th: btn 2f out* **9/1**

12 *2 ½* **Brave Tin Soldier (USA)**[226] [5656] 3-9-2 .... TThulliez 7 91+
(A P O'Brien, Ire) *first to show: sn in midfield: towards rr on outside st: hmpd 2f out: no ch after* **25/1**

13 *1 ½* **Tariq**[22] [1147] 3-9-2 .... JimmyFortune 10 88+
(P W Chapple-Hyam) *8th st: keeping on at one pce whn hmpd 1 1/2f out* **40/1**

14 *6* **Mastership (IRE)**[22] [1147] 3-9-2 ....(b) EddieAhern 11 74+
(C E Brittain) *7th st: btn whn hmpd 1 1/2f out* **100/1**

1m 37.1s (-5.30) **Going Correction** -0.325s/f (Firm) 14 Ran SP% **122.4**
Speed ratings: 113,112,111,110,109 109,108,106,105,104 103,101,99,93
PARI-MUTUEL: WIN 4.40 (coupled with Honoured Guest & Excellent Art & Brave Tin Soldier & Folowmyfootsteps); PL 13.80, 3,10, 4.40; DF 161.30.
Owner Derrick Smith **Bred** ClassicStar **Trained** Ballydoyle, Co Tipperary
■ Stewards' Enquiry : Jamie Spencer ten-day ban: two counts of causing interference (May 25 - Jun 3)

FOCUS

Hardly a vintage renewal and Ireland claimed the first four places, with O'Brien being responsible for the winner, second and fourth. Astronomer Royal improved on all his previous efforts and, along with his unlucky stablemate Excellent Art, is now bound for the St James's Palace Stakes. Creachadoir ran a blinder and continues to progress, while Honoured Guest may be better off being ridden more prominently in future.

NOTEBOOK

Astronomer Royal(USA), a 6f maiden winner at Newbury at two, shaped as though the run was needed behind a couple of these in the Prix Fontainebleau over course and distance last month and, like so many from the stable this season, he showed significantly improved form from that first run. Restrained in rear early on, he worked his way to the outside of the field in the straight and received an excellent ride from O'Donoghue to get up and deny his compatriot Creachadoir in the closing stages. This was not a strong renewal, though, and the fact that he appeared to be the O'Brien fourth-string is slightly disconcerting, but he could do no more than win and is now likely to head for the St James's Palace Stakes at Royal Ascot, and he should hold major claims in a year in which the miling colts look an unexceptional bunch.

Creachadoir(IRE), a dual Group 3 winner this season, looks to be progressing with every run and he looked to hold strong claims in a relatively modest renewal of this contest. Kept towards the outer, he produced a fine change of pace to lead over a furlong out, but as was the case with the yard's Finsceal Beo half an hour earlier, he was nailed late on. He may well have won had his rider been able to wait a bit longer and he now heads for the Irish 2000 Guineas, a race in which he is likely to have strong claims.

Honoured Guest(IRE), supplemented for this following two smooth wins in lesser grade this spring, progressed again for the extra furlong and ran on well up the straight having been poorly positioned turning in. He is likely to benefit from a more positive ride in future.

Excellent Art, one of the better sprinting two-year-olds, was purchased over the winter by Coolmore and provided O'Brien with yet another player in an open race. However, as can sometimes be the case with Spencer, he tried to be too clever and got the colt into all sorts of trouble, eventually flying home to finish a never-nearer fourth. He may well have been the best horse on the day and is another likely St James's Palace contender.

Thousand Words, who had the worst draw of all, left his Craven running behind and made some good late progress into a never-nearer fifth. He is likely to continue to fall short at this level, but should be placed to win a decent race.

Followmyfootsteps(USA), fresh into this off the back of a maiden win at Tipperary, showed greatly improved form for the extra furlong and is another who is likely to be capable of winning a small Group race back in Ireland.

Visionario(IRE), who is not the biggest, was running a decent race when squeezed for room as they approached the furlong pole. He should be rated a bit better than the bare form suggests.

Battle Paint(USA) proved most disappointing, failing to build on his Fontainebleau second and dropping right out under pressure once headed.

Dijeerr(USA), a smart juvenile for Michael Jarvis, dropped away disappointingly in the final quarter mile and is not the first Godolphin horse to disappoint this season.

Brave Tin Soldier(USA) has had his limitations exposed since stepping up in grade.

Tariq, only fifth in the Greenham on his reappearance, was in the process of bettering that effort when getting hampered and he could be worth another chance back down in grade.

Mastership(IRE) was always likely to struggle and was beaten when hampered.

1704a PRIX DE SAINT-GEORGES (GROUP 3) 5f (S)

3:30 (3:32) 3-Y-O+ **£27,027** (£10,811; £8,108; £5,405; £2,703)

RPR

1 **Peace Offering (IRE)**[7] [1497] 7-9-2 .... AdrianTNicholls 5 113
(D Nicholls) *sn chsng ldr: rdn 1/2-way: 1/2 l down 2f out: led over 1f out: r.o wl* **13/8**[1]

2 *½* **Beauty Is Truth (IRE)**[32] [1006] 3-8-8 ....(b) TThulliez 10 109
(Robert Collet, France) *led: strly pressed 1/2-way tl hdd over 1f out: r.o* **9/1**[3]

3 *1 ½* **Kourka (FR)**[19] [1234] 5-8-10 .... RonanThomas 1 100
(J-M Beguigne, France) *towards rr early: hdwy to go distant 3rd wl over 1f out: kpt on but nvr nr first two* **18/1**

4 *2* **Tycoon's Hill (IRE)**[19] [1234] 8-9-2 .... CSoumillon 3 99
(Robert Collet, France) *midfield: rdn 1/2-way: styd on to take 4th ins fnl f* **12/1**

5 *½* **Numerieus (FR)**[216] [5880] 3-8-2 .... ACrastus 7 89
(Y De Nicolay, France) *in rr tl styd on fnl f: nvr a factor* **20/1**

6 *½* **Manzila (FR)**[19] [1234] 4-8-10 .... DBonilla 4 89
(F Head, France) *nvr bttr than midfield* **10/1**

7 *1* **New Girlfriend (IRE)**[12] [1389] 4-9-3 .... OPeslier 8 92
(Robert Collet, France) *a towards rr* **3/1**[2]

8 hd **Dizzy Dreamer (IRE)**[21] [1189] 4-8-10 ....(b) RobertHavlin 9 85
(P W Chapple-Hyam) *prom early: 4th 1/2-way: wknd 2f out* **20/1**

9 2 **Biniou (IRE)**[7] [1497] 4-9-2 .... SPasquier 6 83
(R M H Cowell) *in tch: 3rd 1/2-way: wknd qckly over 1f out* **14/1**

10 4 **Matrix (GER)**[19] [1234] 6-9-2 .... DBoeuf 2 69
(W Baltromei, Germany) *immediately outpcd: last thrght* **9/1**[3]

55.20 secs (-3.60) **Going Correction** -0.325s/f (Firm)
WFA 3 from 4yo+ 9lb **10** Ran SP% **121.3**
Speed ratings: 115,114,111,108,107 107,105,105,101,95
PARI-MUTUEL: WIN 2.80; PL 1.40, 3.10, 2.90; DF 14.10.
Owner Lady O'Reilly **Bred** Chevington Stud **Trained** Sessay, N Yorks

NOTEBOOK
Peace Offering(IRE), who reappeared with a fine effort in defeat at Newmarket the previous weekend, soon held a prominent position and, although it took him a while to master Beauty Is Truth, he always looked to be holding on once edging ahead. He may well go for the Dash at Epsom next, or could come back for the Prix du Gros Chene at Chantilly next month. He should go well in whichever race he ends up in.
Beauty Is Truth(IRE) was quickly into her stride and made the winner go hard all the way, but she could not hold on from her more experienced rival. It was a smart effort from this three-year-old filly and she should definitely have it within her powers to win another sprint at this level.
Kourka(FR), outpaced from an early stage, began to run on inside the final quarter mile, but was never going to get to the front pair. She may benefit from a return to further.
Tycoon's Hill(IRE), settled towards the tail of the field early on, found the pace a little on the hot side, but was another putting in some good late work.
New Girlfriend(IRE) was the disappointment of the race, never getting involved.
Dizzy Dreamer(IRE) started well and was with the eventual runner-up until the two-furlong marker, but she then began to tie up a little next to the rail. She was wearing blinkers for the first time and certainly showed plenty of zip, but found this company too hot.
Biniou(IRE), an ex-French sprinter, was well away and in third position for the first half of the race, but he could not follow the winner and runner-up from then on and gradually dropped out of contention.

1453 MUSSELBURGH (R-H)
Monday, May 14

OFFICIAL GOING: Good (8.5)
Meeting transferred from Redcar where the reworked bends were unfit for racing.
Wind: Virtually nil

1706 TURF TV BETTING SHOP SERVICE MEDIAN AUCTION MAIDEN STKS 5f
2:10 (2:11) (Class 6) 2-Y-O **£2,047** (£604; £302) **Stalls** Low

Form RPR

4 **1** **Aaim To Storm (USA)**[9] [1469] 2-9-3 .... JHBowman 3 78
(M R Channon) *chsd ldrs: outpcd and pushed along 1/2-way: swtchd rt and rdn to chal ent fnl f: led fnl 100yds: jst hld on* **11/4**[3]

2 **2** shd **Fol Hollow (IRE)**[44] [845] 2-9-3 .... AdrianTNicholls 1 78
(D Nicholls) *chsd ldrs: swtchd rt and hdwy to ld 2f out: rdn over 1f out: drvn and hdd fnl 100yds: rallied wl nr fin* **6/4**[1]

0 **3** 2 **Keeparryappy (IRE)**[26] [1087] 2-9-3 .... PhillipMakin 5 71
(K R Burke) *prom: effrt 2f out and ev ch tl rdn and one pce ent fnl f* **22/1**

4 1 **Celeberry (IRE)**[32] [1014] 2-9-3 .... TomEaves 4 67
(J G Burns, Ire) *cl up: rdn along 2f out and grad wknd* **5/2**[2]

0 **5** 3 **Grudge**[11] [1422] 2-9-3 .... TonyHamilton 6 56
(D W Barker) *led: rdn and hdd 2f out: sn wknd* **33/1**

6 hd **Glenluji** 2-8-10 .... GaryBartley(7) 2 56
(J S Goldie) *s.i.s: a in rr* **50/1**

7 8 **Glamoroso (IRE)** 2-9-3 .... PaulHanagan 7 27
(D W Barker) *v.s.a: a bhd* **40/1**

60.73 secs (0.23) **Going Correction** +0.05s/f (Good) **7** Ran SP% **106.9**
Speed ratings (Par 91): 100,99,96,95,90 89,77
CSF £6.23 TOTE £3.40: £1.70, £1.10; EX 6.80.
Owner Stuart Le Gassick **Bred** Claiborne Farm **Trained** West Ilsley, Berks

FOCUS
A fair little maiden, with the runner-up to form. It was a good time for a race like this, slightly slower than the all-aged seller, but over a second quicker than the older-horse fillies' maiden.

NOTEBOOK
Aaim To Storm(USA) showed the clear benefit of his Goodwood debut effort nine days previously and just did enough to get off the mark at the second time of asking. He was given time to find his feet and picked up nicely when asked for his effort, eventually narrowly edging it under a hands-and-heels ride. Another furlong will be to his liking before too long and he clearly has a future. (op 3-1 tchd 5-2)
Fol Hollow(IRE), the Brocklesby second, was given every chance and, just failing, proved game in defeat. He may already need a sixth furlong, but can be considered a winner without a penalty ahead of his next assignment and really ought to go one better soon. (op 5-4)
Keeparryappy(IRE) stepped up considerably on the level of his Beverley debut and is clearly going the right way. (op 33-1)
Celeberry(IRE), a close second on his debut at Tipperary in April, had his chance yet failed to really build on that form. He gives this form a fair look. (op 9-4)

1707 RACING UK CHANNEL 432 (S) STKS 5f
2:40 (2:40) (Class 6) 3-Y-O+ **£2,047** (£604; £302) **Stalls** Low

Form RPR

330- **1** **Maromito (IRE)**[356] [1909] 10-9-7 50 .... TomEaves 7 55+
(R Bastiman) *mde all: rdn over 1f out: drvn ins fnl f: kpt on wl* **16/1**

20-0 **2** shd **Compton Classic**[25] [1112] 5-9-0 55 ....(p) GaryBartley(7) 4 55
(J S Goldie) *towards rr: hdwy 2f out: swtchd rt and rdn ent fnl f: styd on wl: jst hld* **9/2**[3]

1104 **3** 3 **Whinhill House**[6] [1557] 7-9-7 58 ....(v) PaulHanagan 2 44
(D W Barker) *cl up: rdn along wl over 1f out: kpt on same pce* **6/4**[1]

0000 **4** shd **Beverley Beau**[4] [1594] 5-9-0 42 .... KristinStubbs(7) 6 44
(Mrs L Stubbs) *chsd ldrs: rdn along wl over 1f out: kpt on same pce* **10/1**

0054 **5** nk **Legal Set (IRE)**[4] [1594] 11-9-2 45 ....(b) AnnStokell(5) 5 43
(Miss A Stokell) *chsd ldrs: rdn along wl over 1f out: sn one pce* **16/1**

33-0 **6** 1/2 **Rudi's Pet (IRE)**[6] [1557] 13-9-7 66 ....(v) AdrianTNicholls 3 41
(D Nicholls) *cl up: rdn along wl over 1f out: wknd ent fnl f* **7/2**[2]

00-5 **7** 3 1/2 **Dotty's Daughter**[15] [1317] 3-8-7 55 ....(p) RoystonFfrench 1 23
(Mrs A Duffield) *dwlt: sn outpcd in rr* **15/2**

000- **8** 5 **Alfie Lee (IRE)**[294] [3781] 10-9-4 33 ....(t) GregFairley(3) 8 10
(D A Nolan) *s.i.s: a in rr* **150/1**

00-0 **9** 22 **Alexia Rose (IRE)**[8] [1492] 5-9-2 50 .... TonyHamilton 9 —
(A Berry) *dwlt: sn outpcd in rr* **33/1**

60.37 secs (-0.13) **Going Correction** +0.05s/f (Good)
WFA 3 from 5yo+ 9lb **9** Ran SP% **116.6**
Speed ratings (Par 101): 103,102,98,97,97 96,91,83,47
CSF £87.38 TOTE £21.40: £4.60, £1.70, £1.10; EX 116.80.There was no bid for the winner.
Owner Mrs C B Bastiman **Bred** Joseph Finnegan **Trained** Cowthorpe, N Yorks

FOCUS
A typical seller. The first pair came clear, with the winner putting up his best performance for nearly a year.
Alexia Rose(IRE) Official explanation: jockey said mare lost its action

1708 SCOTTISH RACING "YOUR BEST BET" H'CAP 1m 1f
3:10 (3:10) (Class 5) (0-75,72) 3-Y-O **£2,817** (£838; £418; £209) **Stalls** High

Form RPR

5-12 **1** **Graceful Steps (IRE)**[15] [1320] 3-8-11 **65** .... JHBowman 2 74+
(E J O'Neill) *a.p: effrt to ld over 2f out: rdn over 1f out: kpt on wl fnl f* **5/2**[1]

3-55 **2** 1 3/4 **Super Cross (IRE)**[16] [1289] 3-9-4 **72** .... RoystonFfrench 4 77
(E A L Dunlop) *led: rdn along over 2f out and sn hdd: drvn and rallied ent fnl f: sn no ex* **11/4**[2]

0-04 **3** 6 **Dee Jay Wells**[18] [1256] 3-8-13 **67** ....(b[1]) PaulHanagan 1 60
(R A Fahey) *hld up in rr: effrt 2f out: swtchd lft and rdn over 1f out: kpt on ins fnl f: nrst fin* **12/1**

-520 **4** 3 **Colditz (IRE)**[21] [1194] 3-8-12 **66** .... TonyHamilton 5 53
(D W Barker) *chsd ldrs: rdn along over 2fout: sn btn* **14/1**

4221 **5** 1 **Skye But N Ben**[23] [1154] 3-8-4 **58** ....(b) PaulFessey 6 43
(T D Barron) *t.k.h: chsd ldrs: rdn along over 2f out: sn btn* **3/1**[3]

0-05 **6** nk **Delta Shuttle (IRE)**[12] [1410] 3-8-9 **63** ....(v[1]) TomEaves 3 47
(K R Burke) *chsd ldrs: rdn along 2f out: sn wknd* **8/1**

26-5 **7** 3 1/2 **Musical Land (IRE)**[7] [1529] 3-9-3 **71** .... PhillipMakin 7 48
(J R Weymes) *a in rr* **16/1**

1m 54.35s (0.49) **Going Correction** +0.05s/f (Good) **7** Ran SP% **111.6**
Speed ratings (Par 99): 99,97,92,89,88 88,85
CSF £9.14 TOTE £3.20: £1.70, £1.50; EX 11.60.
Owner J C Fretwell **Bred** John Davis And Newtown Stud **Trained** Averham Park, Notts

FOCUS
A modest handicap, but the first pair came clear and both look progressive.

1709 TURFTV.CO.UK MAIDEN FILLIES' STKS 5f
3:40 (3:42) (Class 5) 3-Y-O+ **£2,817** (£838; £418; £209) **Stalls** Low

Form RPR

3 **1** **Twosheetstothewind**[3] [1635] 3-8-12 .... PhillipMakin 6 59+
(M Dods) *dwlt: sn trcking ldrs and t.k.h: hdwy to ld over 1f out: pushed clr ins fnl f* **8/11**[1]

2045 **2** 1 3/4 **Temtation (IRE)**[10] [1453] 3-8-12 52 .... JHBowman 5 51
(Peter Grayson) *led: rdn along 2f out: hdd over 1f out: kpt on u.p fnl f* **9/1**[2]

-020 **3** 3/4 **Rue Soleil**[7] [1530] 3-8-12 59 .... PaulHanagan 4 48
(J R Weymes) *chsd ldrs: rdn along 2f out: kpt on ins fnl f* **12/1**[3]

000- **4** 2 1/2 **Cranworth Blaze**[223] [5746] 3-8-12 50 .... RoystonFfrench 7 39
(T J Etherington) *prom on outer: rdn along 2f out: sn wknd* **40/1**

040- **5** 18 **Perfect Reflection**[294] [3780] 3-8-12 25 .... TonyHamilton 3 —
(A Berry) *sn outpcd and bhd fr 1/2-way* **100/1**

61.76 secs (1.26) **Going Correction** +0.05s/f (Good) **5** Ran SP% **79.0**
Speed ratings (Par 100): 91,88,87,83,54
CSF £2.44 TOTE £1.20: £1.10, £2.50; EX 2.90.
Owner Andrew Page **Bred** Mrs R D Peacock **Trained** Denton, Co Durham
■ Mazin Lady was withdrawn (9/4, unruly in stalls.) Rule 4 applies, deduct 30p in the £.

FOCUS
This fillies' maiden was weakened by the withdrawal of Mazin Lady and the form is very ordinary. It was a moderate time even for a race like this, slower than both the juvenile maiden and the seller.

1710 RACINGUK.TV FILLIES' H'CAP 7f 30y
4:10 (4:10) (Class 4) (0-85,85) 3-Y-O+ **£4,728** (£1,406; £702; £351) **Stalls** High

Form RPR

361- **1** **La Matanza**[239] [5401] 4-9-6 **73** .... PhillipMakin 3 81
(T D Barron) *hld up in tch: hdwy over 2f out: rdn to ld wl over 1f out: drvn and edgd lft ins fnl f: hld on wl* **7/2**[2]

6063 **2** nk **Neardown Beauty (IRE)**[12] [1395] 4-10-0 **81** .... PaulHanagan 4 88
(I A Wood) *dwlt: sn in tch: hdwy whn nt clr run 2f out: swtchd ins and effrt over 1f out: sn rdn and styd on wl fnl f* **3/1**[1]

2-10 **3** nk **Dispol Isle (IRE)**[8] [1488] 5-9-1 **68** .... PaulFessey 1 74
(T D Barron) *trckd ldng pair: hdwy over 2f out: rdn and ev ch over 1f out: sn drvn and kpt on fnl f* **5/1**

4203 **4** 6 **Penny Post (IRE)**[4] [1604] 3-9-3 **85** .... GregFairley(3) 2 71
(M Johnston) *trckd ldng pair: hdwy to ld briefly and bmpd 2f out: sn rdn and hdd: wknd ent fnl f* **3/1**[1]

3253 **5** hd **Fractured Foxy**[13] [1383] 3-8-1 **71** .... NataliaGemelova(5) 6 56+
(J J Quinn) *cl up: led after 2f: rdn along 3f out: bmpd and hdd 2f out: sn wknd* **4/1**[3]

60-5 **6** 1 1/4 **Safranine (IRE)**[7] [1534] 10-8-9 **67** oh15 .... AnnStokell(5) 7 53
(Miss A Stokell) *led 2f: rdn along 3f out: hung lft over 2f out: sn wandered and wknd* **66/1**

1m 32.11s (2.17) **Going Correction** +0.05s/f (Good)
WFA 3 from 4yo+ 12lb **6** Ran SP% **110.4**
Speed ratings (Par 102): 89,88,88,81,81 79
CSF £13.84 TOTE £5.00: £3.20, £1.60; EX 16.00.
Owner J G Brown **Bred** A C M Spalding **Trained** Maunby, N Yorks

FOCUS
A modest handicap and the bare form is not up to much. It was a very moderate winning time for a race like this, 1.48 seconds slower than the following claimer, due to the lack of early pace.

1711 REDCAR CLAIMING STKS 7f 30y
4:40 (4:40) (Class 6) 3-Y-O+ **£2,047** (£604; £302) **Stalls** High

Form RPR

0063 **1** **Baylaw Star**[8] [1488] 6-9-12 61 .... RoystonFfrench 10 70+
(I W McInnes) *sn led: rdn clr 2f out: styd on wl* **5/4**[1]

34-2 **2** 2 **Queen's Echo**[7] [1527] 6-9-2 51 .... MarkLawson(3) 11 58+
(P Monteith) *dwlt: sn in tch on inner: hdwy and n.m.r 2f out: swtchd lft and rdn to chse wnr ins fnl f: kpt on* **4/1**[3]

-042 **3** 1 1/4 **Oeuf A La Neige**[4] [1596] 7-9-4 48 .... AndrewMullen(3) 6 57
(Miss L A Perratt) *bhd: hdwy wl over 2f out: sn rdn and styd on fnl f: nrst fin* **10/1**

20-0 **4** nk **Snow Bunting**[13] [1382] 9-9-8 56 .... PaulHanagan 4 57
(Jedd O'Keeffe) *midfield: hdwy 3f out: rdn to chse wnr over 1f out: sn drvn and wknd ins fnl f* **18/1**

40-3 **5** *4* **Chairman Bobby**[11] 1423 9-9-8 53............................(p) TonyHamilton 5 47
(D W Barker) *prom: rdn along over 2f out: sn edgd lft and grad wknd* **20/1**

-360 **6** *4* **O'Dwyer (IRE)**[19] 1248 3-8-8 50............................(p) PhillipMakin 1 30
(A D Brown) *in tch: rdn along wl over 2f out: sn no imp* **40/1**

0-00 **7** *2* **City Miss**[4] 1595 4-8-13 36.. GregFairley(3) 2 25
(Miss L A Perratt) *a in rr* **125/1**

50-0 **8** *1 1/2* **Danni Di Guerra (IRE)**[8] 1492 3-8-3 40...................... AndrewElliott(3) 8 19
(J Barclay) *s.i.s: a in rr* **200/1**

-040 **9** *5* **Four Kings**[7] 1527 6-9-6 45.. PaulFessey 3 12
(Karen McLintock) *chsd ldrs: rdn along 3f out: sn wknd* **80/1**

00-0 **10** *4* **Obe One**[8] 1492 7-9-8 52.. TomEaves 9 4
(A Berry) *dwlt: a in rr* **50/1**

0121 **11** *15* **Just James**[7] 1527 8-9-10 64... AdrianTNicholls 7 —
(D Nicholls) *chsd ldrs: rdn along over 2f out: wknd wl over 1f and sn eased* **3/1**[2]

1m 30.63s (0.69) **Going Correction** +0.05s/f (Good)
WFA 3 from 4yo+ 12lb 11 Ran SP% **115.5**
Speed ratings (Par 97):98,95,94,93,89 84,82,80,75,70 53
CSF £6.09 TOTE £2.50: £1.50, £1.70, £2.30; EX 9.80.
Owner Stephen Hackney And Martin Higgins **Bred** John Wilkinson Bloodstock **Trained** Catwick, E Yorks

FOCUS
A modest claimer in which the winner probably did not need to improve on his recent form. The form is rated through the third.
Just James Official explanation: vet said gelding bled from the nose

1712 JOHN SMITH'S REDCAR STRAIGHT-MILE CHAMPIONSHIP (HANDICAP QUALIFIER) 1m

5:10 (5:10) (Class 6) (0-60,58) 3-Y-0 **£2,047** (£604; £302) **Stalls** High

Form RPR

0-62 **1** **Jewelled Dagger (IRE)**[8] 1489 3-8-7 **47** ow2..................(b) TomEaves 7 61
(I Semple) *prom: trckd ldr after 3f: effrt to ld over 2f out: rdn clr appr fnl f: styd on wl* **7/2**[1]

0-04 **2** *3 1/2* **Prince Noel**[18] 1266 3-8-9 **49**....................................... AdrianTNicholls 6 55
(N Wilson) *sn led: rdn along and hdd over 2f out: drvn over 1f out and kpt on same pce* **12/1**

06-0 **3** *3* **Pegasus Prince (USA)**[61] 678 3-8-10 **50**....................... PhillipMakin 9 49
(Miss J A Camacho) *towards rr: hdwy 3f out: rdn wl over 1f out: kpt on ins fnl f: nrst fin* **16/1**

00-4 **4** *1* **Red Flare (IRE)**[11] 1432 3-8-13 **53**................................... JHBowman 1 50
(M R Channon) *hld up and bhd: hdwy 3f out: rdn over 1f out: kpt on appr fnl f: nt rch ldrs* **7/1**

1300 **5** *1 1/2* **Poniard (IRE)**[18] 1266 3-8-10 **57**..............................(p) NeilBrown(7) 12 50
(D W Barker) *chsd ldrs: rdn along wl over 2f out: sn one pce* **20/1**

050- **6** *hd* **Zain (IRE)**[144] 6900 3-8-5 **48**.......................................(t) AndrewElliott(3) 3 41
(J G Given) *prom: rdn along 3f out: drvn and one pce fnl 2f* **12/1**

-064 **7** *3/4* **Tomorrow's Dancer**[7] 1531 3-8-11 **54**...................... AndrewMullen(3) 2 45
(K A Ryan) *dwlt: hdwy 3f out: rdn to chse ldrs over 2f out: sn drvn and edgd rt wl over 1f out: sn wknd* **4/1**[2]

600- **8** *5* **Fistral**[196] 6258 3-8-7 **50**... MarkLawson(3) 11 30+
(J Hetherton) *towards rr: hdwy and pushed along 3f out: styng on whn hmpd wl over 1f out: nt rcvr* **40/1**

50-0 **9** *1 1/4* **Gallows Hill (USA)**[17] 1282 3-8-13 **53**............................ PaulHanagan 10 30+
(R A Fahey) *chsd ldrs on inner: rdn along 3f out: wkng whn hmpd wl over 1f out* **12/1**

00-6 **10** *1 3/4* **Cheery Cat (USA)**[18] 1266 3-9-0 **54**............................. TonyHamilton 14 27
(D W Barker) *in tch: rdn along wl over 2f out: sn btn* **11/1**

-400 **11** *3 1/2* **Fire Alarm**[61] 676 3-8-4 **47** ow2.................................... GregFairley(3) 4 12
(Miss Lucinda V Russell) *a in rr* **33/1**

30-0 **12** *3* **Spectacular Joy (IRE)**[7] 1278 3-9-4 **58**.................... RoystonFfrench 5 16
(Mrs A Duffield) *a towards rr* **33/1**

5643 **13** *dist* **Irish Relative (IRE)**[16] 1301 3-9-1 **55**.............................. PaulFessey 13 —
(T D Barron) *in rr: eased after 2f and bhd: virtually p.u 1/2-way* **11/2**[3]

1m 42.14s (-0.36) **Going Correction** +0.05s/f (Good) 13 Ran SP% **120.5**
Speed ratings (Par 97):103,99,96,95,94 93,93,88,86,85 81,78,—
CSF £45.06 CT £608.12 TOTE £3.90: £1.60, £4.40, £5.70; EX 54.30 Place 6 £ 4.17, Place 5 £ 2.79.
Owner A R M Galbraith **Bred** Ballyhane Stud **Trained** Carluke, S Lanarks

FOCUS
A moderate handicap, run at a sound pace. The winner confirmed the improvement shown at Hamilton and the form can be rated through the runner-up.
Irish Relative(IRE) Official explanation: jockey said saddle slipped
T/Plt: £7.00 to a £1 stake. Pool: £43,310.45. 4,511.95 winning tickets. T/Qpdt: £3.50 to a £1 stake. Pool: £2,095.90. 442.30 winning tickets. JR

1565 SOUTHWELL (L-H)
Monday, May 14

OFFICIAL GOING: Standard
The surface was very wet and patchy at first but during the afternoon it dried out and for the final three races was reckoned to be riding as normal.
Wind: Moderate, half behind Weather: Overcast and breezy at first, turning to bright and sunny.

1713 BETDIRECTPOKER.COM $50,000 FREEROLL MAIDEN AUCTION STKS 5f (F)

1:30 (1:31) (Class 5) 2-Y-0 **£3,238** (£963; £481; £240) **Stalls** High

Form RPR

20 **1** **Ballycroy Boy (IRE)**[36] 952 2-8-10............................. MickyFenton 12 70
(A Bailey) *w ldr: led over 2f out: styd on strly fnl f* **10/1**

0 **2** *1 1/4* **Rub Of The Relic (IRE)**[23] 1150 2-8-12.................... SimonWhitworth 7 68
(P A Blockley) *led over 2f: kpt on same pce fnl f* **25/1**

3 *2* **Carrickmacross (IRE)** 2-9-1.. RichardMullen 10 63+
(E S McMahon) *dwlt: bhd tl hdwy on stands' side over 1f out: fin strly* **7/1**

4 **4** *shd* **Berrymead**[26] 1087 2-8-4 .... DaleGibson 6 52
(M W Easterby) *chsd ldrs: styd on same pce appr fnl f* **9/4**[2]

2 **5** *1 1/4* **Valhillen**[7] 1519 2-8-10... JamieSpencer 3 53
(M J Wallace) *w ldrs: kpt on same pce fnl 2f* **15/8**[1]

20 **6** *nk* **Mujada**[16] 1302 2-7-11 .... AndrewHeffernan(7) 4 46
(M Brittain) *chsd ldrs on outside: one pce fnl 2f* **25/1**

7 *2 1/2* **Discanti (IRE)** 2-9-1 .... DavidAllan 8 48
(T D Easterby) *s.i.s: kpt on fnl 2f: nvr nr ldrs* **5/1**[3]

8 *7* **Lady Aviator** 2-8-8 .... PaulQuinn 11 16
(T D Easterby) *swvd rt s: nvr wnt pce* **50/1**

0 **9** *hd* **Chief Powderface (IRE)**[26] 1087 2-8-11 .... JoeFanning 9 18
(Jedd O'Keeffe) *chsd ldrs: lost pl over 1f out* **66/1**

10 *3 1/2* **Peltre** 2-7-12 ow1 .... PatrickDonaghy(7) 5 —
(M Brittain) *sn outpcd and bhd* **50/1**

0 **11** *nk* **Indecision**[26] 1087 2-8-2 .... NSLawes(7) 2 —
(M W Easterby) *swvd lft s: outpcd and lost pl after 2f* **50/1**

60.08 secs (-0.22) **Going Correction** -0.20s/f (Stan) 11 Ran SP% **118.9**
Speed ratings (Par 93):93,91,87,87,85 85,81,69,69,64 63
CSF £228.87 TOTE £13.60: £2.30, £7.10, £2.60; EX 196.50 TRIFECTA Not won..
Owner R T Collins **Bred** Paraic Fox **Trained** Newmarket, Suffolk

FOCUS
A fair maiden auction race with the third the likely big improver. The far side was not the place to be. With the favourite nearly a stone off his debut form, the level is guessy.

NOTEBOOK
Ballycroy Boy(IRE), unsuited by the firm when making a quick reappearance at Musselburgh, really buckled down. (tchd 11-1 in places)
Rub Of The Relic(IRE) had clearly learnt plenty from his debut run and pushed the winner hard all the way to the line.
Carrickmacross(IRE) ◆, a February foal, is a good-bodied individual. He missed a beat at the start and soon found himself towards the rear. Hard against the stands'-side rail, he was eating up ground at the finish and should soon be winning. (op 8-1)
Berrymead found herself rather detached towards the far side and was probably on the slower part of the track. (op 5-2)
Valhillen was in the thick of the action from the off but seemed to have no valid excuse. (op 13-8 tchd 2-1)
Mujada, having her third outing, was racing on the slower ground on the far side. She had a tough race.
Discanti(IRE), a February foal, is very much on the leg. She was getting the hang of things late on and this will have opened her eyes. (op 7-1)

1714 BETDIRECTPOKER.COM COME AND 'AVE SOME MAIDEN STKS (DIV I) 1m (F)

2:00 (2:01) (Class 5) 3-Y-0+ **£2,590** (£770; £385; £192) **Stalls** Low

Form RPR

1 **Laa Rayb (USA)** 3-9-0 .... JoeFanning 10 87+
(M Johnston) *w ldr: led 5f out: hung lft over 2f out: drvn out* **4/1**[2]

23-6 **2** *3/4* **Audit (IRE)**[16] 1293 3-9-0 ....(b[1]) EddieAhern 4 80
(Sir Michael Stoute) *hld up: hdwy to chse ldrs over 2f out: swtchd lft over 1f out: hrd rdn and put hd in air: no ex ins fnl f* **7/2**[1]

3 *6* **Artless (USA)** 4-9-8 .... JamieMackay 2 64
(Sir Mark Prescott) *s.i.s: in rr tl styd on fnl 2f: tk modest 3rd nr line* **16/1**

3 **4** *hd* **Gunfighter (IRE)**[22] 1177 4-9-13 .... PaulMulrennan 9 69
(J S Wainwright) *led tl 5f out: edgd rt over 1f out: sn wknd* **5/1**[3]

2 **5** *13* **Six Of Hearts**[17] 1278 3-9-0 .... JamieSpencer 1 36
(J A Osborne) *trckd ldrs: effrt over 2f out: sn wknd* **4/1**[2]

3 **6** *2* **Collioure (USA)**[13] 1375 3-8-9 .... JosedeSouza 8 26
(P F I Cole) *mid-div on outer: outpcd over 3f out: sn lost pl* **17/2**

54 **7** *1 3/4* **Ganache (IRE)**[23] 1166 5-9-8 .... TravisBlock(5) 6 30
(P R Chamings) *trckd ldrs: drvn over 4f out: lost pl 3f out* **10/1**

02 **P** **Ammeyrr**[56] 711 3-9-0 .... MickyFenton 5 —
(A Crook) *prom: rdn and hung rt over 3f out: sn detached: p.u over 2f out: dismntd* **12/1**

1m 41.3s (-3.30) **Going Correction** -0.275s/f (Stan)
WFA 3 from 4yo+ 13lb 8 Ran SP% **112.1**
Speed ratings (Par 103):105,104,98,98,85 83,81,—
CSF £17.63 TOTE £3.90: £2.10, £1.10, £6.50; EX 14.20 Trifecta £138.30 Pool: £315.60 - 1.62 winning units..
Owner Sheikh Ahmed Al Maktoum **Bred** Darley **Trained** Middleham Moor, N Yorks

FOCUS
A fair time for a race like this and 2.49 seconds faster than the second division. The winner won more easily than the bare form, with the somewhat quirky second probably giving his running.

1715 BETDIRECT.COM GET INVOLVED H'CAP 1m (F)

2:30 (2:31) (Class 6) (0-50,50) 4-Y-0+ **£2,730** (£806; £403) **Stalls** Low

Form RPR

0042 **1** **Government (IRE)**[6] 1569 6-8-3 **46**................................ NicolPolli(5) 13 53
(M C Chapman) *w ldr: led over 6f out: hrd rdn and kpt on wl fnl 2f* **11/2**[2]

00- **2** *1* **Tipsy Lad**[9] 3390 5-8-11 **49**..(bt) SimonWhitworth 4 54
(H J Manners) *led over 1f: w wnr: no ex ins fnl f* **40/1**

0550 **3** *2* **Spy Gun (USA)**[31] 1028 7-8-1 **46** oh1.............................. JosephWalsh(7) 1 46+
(T Wall) *prom on ins: hmpd and lost pl bnd over 4f out: hdwy on ins over 2f out: styd on wl* **20/1**

0-03 **4** *1 3/4* **Don Pasquale**[13] 1380 5-8-8 **46** oh1.................................... MickyFenton 5 42
(J T Stimpson) *mid-div: hdwy over 2f out: sn chsng ldrs: one pce* **12/1**

0200 **5** *3 1/2* **Gem Bien (USA)**[17] 1284 9-8-9 **47**.................................(p) DaleGibson 6 35
(D W Chapman) *s.i.s: bhd tl styd on fnl 2f* **14/1**

3203 **6** *shd* **Wodhill Schnaps**[14] 1350 6-8-6 **47**...........................(v) SaleemGolam(3) 12 35
(D Morris) *in rr: hdwy on outside over 2f out: kpt on: nvr nr ldrs* **4/1**[1]

-040 **7** *1* **Dechiper (IRE)**[8] 1488 5-8-12 **50**....................................... JosedeSouza 8 35
(R Johnson) *chsd ldrs: one pce fnl 2f* **9/1**

0-00 **8** *1* **Filey Buoy**[11] 1423 5-8-5 **48** oh1 ow2........................... MichaelJStainton(5) 2 31
(R M Whitaker) *prom: hmpd and lost pl on inner over 3f out: kpt on fnl 2f* **20/1**

00-0 **9** *1 3/4* **Stormingmichaelori**[7] 1529 4-8-8 **46** oh1...............(p) MatthewHenry 11 25
(N Wilson) *chsd ldrs: wknd 2f out* **25/1**

400- **10** *2 1/2* **Dandys Hurricane**[187] 6403 4-8-5 **50**........................ AdeleRothery(7) 14 23
(D Nicholls) *a in rr* **33/1**

-004 **11** *1 1/4* **Soviet Threat (IRE)**[11] 1435 6-8-8 **46**...........................(b) ChrisCatlin 7 17
(A G Juckes) *mid-div: lost pl 3f out* **7/1**

0500 **12** *1* **Orpen Quest (IRE)**[20] 1227 5-8-12 **50**..........................(v) EddieAhern 10 18
(M J Attwater) *a towards rr* **6/1**[3]

0 **13** *6* **To Sir With Love (NZ)**[18] 1259 6-8-8 **46** oh1............... PaulMulrennan 3 —
(J S Wainwright) *chsd ldrs: outpcd over 3f out: sn lost pl: eased ins fnl f* **33/1**

2056 **14** *3* **Seldemosa**[48] 800 6-8-8 **46**.......................................(v) RobertHavlin 9 —
(M S Saunders) *chsd ldrs: lost pl over 2f out: eased ins fnl f* **7/1**

1m 43.83s (-0.77) **Going Correction** -0.275s/f (Stan) 14 Ran SP% **120.7**
Speed ratings (Par 101):92,91,89,87,83 83,82,81,79,77 76,75,69,66
CSF £225.09 CT £4188.87 TOTE £9.30: £2.30, £13.80, £7.40; EX 299.50 TRIFECTA Not won..
Owner James Gordon-Hall **Bred** C H Wacker Iii **Trained** Market Rasen, Lincs

FOCUS
A moderate winning time and the slowest of the four races over the trip. A rock-bottom handicap which only the first two got into, and the form looks suspect and very weak.
Spy Gun(USA) Official explanation: jockey said gelding was denied a clear run
Orpen Quest(IRE) Official explanation: jockey said gelding never travelled
Seldemosa Official explanation: jockey said mare had no more to give

1716 BETDIRECTPOKER.COM COME AND 'AVE SOME MAIDEN STKS (DIV II) 1m (F)

3:00 (3:02) (Class 5) 3-Y-0+ £2,590 (£770; £385; £192) Stalls Low

Form				RPR
23-6	1		**Aegis (IRE)**[11] 1440 3-9-0 73 MichaelHills 5 (B W Hills) *w ldrs: led over 4f out: styd on wl fnl f* 2/1[2]	70
62	2	3	**Sky Masterson**[14] 1348 3-9-0 RobertHavlin 10 (J H M Gosden) *tracked leaders, effort on outer over 2f out, ridden and kept on same pace final furlong* 8/11[1]	63
0	3	½	**Fizzy Bella**[11] 1440 3-8-10 ow4 JerryO'Dwyer(3) 9 (M G Quinlan) *trckd ldrs: chal 3f out: kpt on same pce fnl f* 50/1	61
	4	3½	**Almost Married (IRE)** 3-9-0 JoeFanning 3 (J D Bethell) *sn chsng ldrs: wknd fnl f* 20/1	54
266	5	3	**Firebird Annie (IRE)**[40] 919 3-8-9 51 MickyFenton 2 (A Bailey) *unruly s: mde most tl over 4f out: wknd fnl 2f* 66/1	42?
0	6	1	**Little Nipper**[19] 1236 3-8-11 RichardKingscote(3) 4 (W J H Ratcliffe) *chsd ldrs: outpcd over 4f out: no threat after* 100/1	45
	7	1	**Cosmic Apollo** 5-9-13 ChrisCatlin 7 (Rae Guest) *hld up in rr: nvr nr ldrs* 25/1	42
	8	1¾	**Holiday Rock** 3-8-11 PatrickMathers(3) 6 (A J McCabe) *s.i.s: nvr nr ldrs* 100/1	38
24	9	shd	**Ninetyninetreble (IRE)**[6] 1566 4-9-6 AdeleRothery(7) 1 (D Nicholls) *dwlt: in rr: shkn up over 2f out: nvr a factor* 10/1[3]	38
0	10	12	**Miss Lightning**[30] 1045 4-9-8 DavidAllan 8 (R Bastiman) *s.i.s: sn drvn along on outer: lost pl over 3f out: sn bhd* 100/1	6

1m 43.79s (-0.81) **Going Correction** -0.275s/f (Stan)
WFA 3 from 4yo+ 13lb **10** Ran SP% **115.4**
Speed ratings (Par 103):93,90,89,86,83 82,81,79,79,67
CSF £3.56 TOTE £2.80: £1.20, £1.10, £7.80; EX 4.30 Trifecta £58.40 Pool: £393.57 - 4.78 winning units..
Owner Steve and John Jenkins & Deln Ltd **Bred** Don Commins **Trained** Lambourn, Berks
■ Stewards' Enquiry : Adele Rothery ten-day ban: failed to take all reasonable and permissable measures (May 25-Jun 3)

FOCUS
A modest winning time, 2.49 seconds slower than the first division. A weak race, with the form looking suspect.
Ninetyninetreble(IRE) Official explanation: jockey said, regarding running and riding, her orders were to make the running and to finish as close as she could, adding that the gelding missed the break which she admitted was not reported on returning to scale, stating however that the gelding is big, weak and gangly, was outpaced and was difficult to keep balanced; trainer expressed dissatisfaction with rider's efforts, adding that she did not ride to her instructions

1717 BETDIRECTPOKER.COM GET INVOLVED H'CAP 1m 3f (F)

3:30 (3:30) (Class 6) (0-65,64) 4-Y-0+ £3,238 (£963; £481; £240) Stalls Low

Form				RPR
2250	1		**Starcross Maid**[13] 1376 5-8-7 53 ChrisCatlin 5 (J F Coupland) *sn chsng ldrs: led jst ins fnl f: hld on towards fin* 11/2	61
00-0	2	nk	**Surdoue**[19] 1254 7-8-4 50 oh1 RichardMullen 6 (D Morris) *sn trcking ldrs: led 3f out: hdd jst ins fnl f: no ex towards fin* 20/1	58
5-03	3	5	**Wee Charlie Castle (IRE)**[102] 319 4-9-4 64 OscarUrbina 1 (G C H Chung) *dwlt: sn trcking ldrs: effrt over 4f out: kpt on same pce: tk 3rd wl ins fnl f* 7/2[2]	64
5/04	4	½	**Newtonian (USA)**[13] 1376 8-9-0 60 DavidAllan 4 (M Brittain) *trckd ldrs: led over 4f out: hdd 3f out: wknd appr fnl f* 5/1[3]	59
-661	5	9	**Boppys Dancer**[55] 716 4-8-7 53 ow3 (p) MickyFenton 7 (P T Midgley) *in rr: drvn over 5f out: sn lost pl: eased ins fnl f* 3/1[1]	38
-502	6	4	**Kirkhammerton (IRE)**[14] 1350 5-8-6 52 (b) JoeFanning 3 (A J McCabe) *led: hdd over 4f out: wknd over 2f out: eased ins fnl f* 3/1[1]	30
00-0	7	11	**Oh Danny Boy**[21] 1199 6-8-5 58 CharlotteKerton(7) 2 (M C Chapman) *chsd ldrs: lost pl over 4f out: sn bhd and eased* 25/1	19

2m 25.09s (-3.81) **Going Correction** -0.275s/f (Stan) **7** Ran SP% **112.9**
Speed ratings (Par 101):102,101,98,97,91 88,80
CSF £94.74 TOTE £5.60: £2.10, £7.70; EX 130.00.
Owner J F Coupland **Bred** D M Beresford **Trained** Grimsby, Lincs

FOCUS
A modest handicap run at a sound pace, in the end the first two clear. The winner has been rated to her best.

1718 BETDIRECTPOKER.COM $50,000 FREEROLL H'CAP 6f (F)

4:00 (4:01) (Class 5) (0-70,69) 4-Y-0+ £3,886 (£1,156; £577; £288) Stalls Low

Form				RPR
-011	1		**Whitbarrow (IRE)**[11] 1436 8-8-13 69 ow2 (b) JamesMillman(5) 4 (B R Millman) *mde virtually all: clr over 1f out: styd on strly* 7/2[1]	89
4-50	2	6	**Wainwright (IRE)**[78] 556 7-8-4 55 oh3 (t) AlanDaly 2 (P A Blockley) *reminders after s: mid-div: hdwy on ins 3f out: wnt 2nd over 1f out* 22/1	55
6302	3	1½	**Zarzu**[18] 1262 8-9-1 69 (p) LiamJones(3) 7 (C R Dore) *s.i.s: hdwy over 2f out: kpt on wl fnl f* 11/2[2]	65+
2336	4	hd	**Melalchrist**[6] 1565 5-9-3 68 (p) PaulMulrennan 5 (K A Ryan) *chsd ldrs: edgd rt 2f out: kpt on same pce* 10/1	63
6-00	5	shd	**Bel Cantor**[9] 1481 4-8-12 66 RichardKingscote(3) 10 (W J H Ratcliffe) *mid-div: hdwy over 2f out: kpt on wl fnl f* 6/1[3]	61
141-	6	5	**Siraj**[150] 6827 8-8-9 63 MarcHalford(3) 13 (J Ryan) *racd wd: in rr div and drvn over 4f out: kpt on fnl 2f: nvr on terms* 12/1	42
-654	7	¾	**Formidable Will (FR)**[88] 466 5-8-5 59 ow1 (vt) SaleemGolam(3) 6 (D Shaw) *w ldrs: drvn 3f out: wknd over 1f out* 14/1	35
60-3	8	shd	**Word Perfect**[13] 1377 5-9-2 67 (b) DaleGibson 8 (M W Easterby) *w ldrs: lost pl 2f out* 12/1	43
0/0-	9	nk	**Berti Bertolini**[410] 807 4-8-7 58 JamieMackay 11 (Rae Guest) *s.i.s: nvr on terms* 50/1	33
-402	10	2½	**Never Without Me**[8] 1493 7-8-8 59 ChrisCatlin 1 (J F Coupland) *rrd s: sn mid-div: wknd over 2f out* 10/1	26
166-	11	1½	**Kansas Gold**[260] 4841 4-8-11 67 MichaelJStainton(5) 14 (J Mackie) *racd wd: bhd and drvn over 4f out* 16/1	29
3-00	12	¾	**Breaking Shadow (IRE)**[21] 1198 5-9-3 68 (b) JoeFanning 3 (M A Peill) *stdd s: sn prom: t.k.h: lost pl 3f out* 12/1	28
02-0	13	5	**Tag Team (IRE)**[133] 3 6-9-2 67 StephenDonohoe 9 (John A Harris) *chsd ldrs: lost pl 3f out* 16/1	11
40-5	14	1¼	**Princess Cleo**[69] 626 4-9-0 65 DavidAllan 12 (T D Easterby) *w ldrs on outer: lost pl over 3f out: sn bhd* 16/1	5

1m 14.43s (-2.47) **Going Correction** -0.275s/f (Stan) **14** Ran SP% **123.8**
Speed ratings (Par 103):105,97,95,94,94 87,86,86,86,83 81,80,73,71
CSF £91.14 CT £432.71 TOTE £3.30: £1.40, £6.20, £2.20; EX 69.50 Trifecta £297.90 Part won. Pool: £419.64 - 0.90 winning units..
Owner Mrs H Brain **Bred** James Burns And A Moynan **Trained** Kentisbeare, Devon

FOCUS
What looked a competitive sprint handicap beforehand was turned into a procession by the revitalised Whitbarrow who was full value for his winning margin, putting up his best performance since late 2004.

1719 SOUTHWELL-RACECOURSE.CO.UK CLASSIFIED STKS 6f (F)

4:30 (4:30) (Class 7) 4-Y-0+ £1,876 (£554; £277) Stalls Low

Form				RPR
0000	1		**Crafty Fox**[43] 866 4-9-0 45 (v) RichardMullen 4 (A P Jarvis) *s.i.s: hdwy over 2f out: styd on to ld jst ins fnl f: readily* 5/1[2]	58
6000	2	2	**Orchestration (IRE)**[12] 1400 6-8-11 45 (v) DominicFox(3) 3 (S Parr) *hld up in midfield: hdwy over 2f out: chal 1f out: no ex* 16/1	52
5000	3	¾	**Titian Saga (IRE)**[14] 1349 4-8-7 45 AdeleRothery(7) 5 (D Nicholls) *trckd ldrs: effrt on outside and chal over 1f out: kpt on same pce ins fnl f* 16/1	49+
6004	4	3½	**Piccleyes**[6] 1569 6-9-0 44 (be) StephenDonohoe 7 (A J McCabe) *led tl jst ins fnl f: fdd* 10/3[1]	38
2-55	5	nk	**Bold Love**[119] 138 4-9-0 45 DavidAllan 2 (J Balding) *dwlt: sn chsng ldrs: kpt on same pce fnl 2f* 12/1	37
600	6	nk	**Hillbilly Cat (USA)**[54] 722 4-9-0 45 DavidKinsella 1 (R Ingram) *s.i.s: hdwy over 2f out: nvr trbld ldrs* 10/1	36
0300	7	1	**Piccolo Prince**[87] 479 6-9-0 45 PaulQuinn 11 (Mrs Marjorie Fife) *hmpd s: detached in last: hdwy over 2f out: nvr a factor* 25/1	33
00-4	8	2½	**Newcastles Owen (IRE)**[53] 728 4-9-0 45 DanielTudhope 8 (R Johnson) *trckd ldrs: effrt over 2f out: wknd over 1f out* 8/1[3]	25
00-0	9	nk	**Immaculate Red**[14] 1349 4-9-0 45 PaulMulrennan 9 (R Bastiman) *chsd ldrs on outer: lost pl over 2f out* 16/1	24
5-06	10	7	**Global Achiever**[24] 1119 6-8-7 43 (b) MarvinCheung(7) 12 (G C H Chung) *swvd lft s: a in rr* 16/1	2
406-	11	7	**She Whispers (IRE)**[218] 5839 4-8-11 45 RichardKingscote(3) 6 (R Hollinshead) *mid-div: lost pl over 4f out* 17/2	—
0501	12	3½	**Left Nostril (IRE)**[55] 714 4-8-11 45 (bt) JerryO'Dwyer(3) 13 (P S McEntee) *w ldrs on outer: lost pl over 2f out: sn bhd* 5/1[2]	—

1m 15.48s (-1.42) **Going Correction** -0.275s/f (Stan) **12** Ran SP% **122.2**
Speed ratings (Par 97):98,95,94,89,89 88,87,84,83,74 65,60
CSF £85.21 TOTE £7.80: £2.40, £4.60, £8.30; EX 125.40 TRIFECTA Not won..
Owner A P Jarvis **Bred** Bearstone Stud **Trained** Twyford, Bucks

FOCUS
A banded race in all but name and the form is very weak. Sound form for the grade, with the winner on a going day.
Piccolo Prince Official explanation: jockey said gelding suffered interference leaving stalls

1720 BETDIRECTCASINO.COM H'CAP 1m (F)

5:00 (5:00) (Class 5) (0-70,70) 4-Y-0+ £3,238 (£963; £481; £240) Stalls Low

Form				RPR
-055	1		**Stolen Glance**[14] 1352 4-8-6 58 ow1 PaulMulrennan 5 (M W Easterby) *chsd ldrs: effrt on outer over 2f out: led jst ins fnl f: all out* 6/1	66
0-13	2	shd	**Gigs Magic (USA)**[14] 1347 4-8-6 58 JoeFanning 1 (M Johnston) *chsd ldrs: effrt over 2f out: upsides 1f out: edgd rt: jst hld* 4/1[2]	66
-000	3	1¼	**Key Partners (IRE)**[16] 1314 6-8-7 59 ChrisCatlin 6 (J T Stimpson) *hld up in mid-div: effrt over 3f out: chsng ldrs over 1f out: edgd lft and kpt on same pce ins fnl f* 10/1	64
1254	4	1½	**Wodhill Gold**[6] 1568 6-8-5 60 (v) SaleemGolam(3) 4 (D Morris) *hld up in rr: hdwy over 2f out: kpt on fnl 2f: nvr able to chal* 3/1[1]	61
0420	5	¾	**Top Jaro (FR)**[6] 1555 4-9-3 69 MatthewHenry 3 (Jennie Candlish) *led tl hdd jst ins fnl f: fdd* 8/1	69
0060	6	1	**Sentiero Rosso (USA)**[2] 1655 5-8-11 63 StephenDonohoe 7 (B Ellison) *hld up in tch: hdwy over 4f out: effrt on wd outside over 2f out: kpt on: nvr rchd ldrs* 5/1[3]	60
0600	7	3	**Rafferty (IRE)**[14] 1344 8-7-11 56 oh6 ThomasBubb(7) 2 (S Dow) *trckd ldrs: t.k.h: effrt on inner over 2f out: lost pl over 1f out* 25/1	47
0-50	8	6	**She's Our Lass (IRE)**[21] 1198 6-9-4 70 DanielTudhope 8 (D Carroll) *hld up in last: effrt on inner 3f out: lost pl over 1f out* 6/1	47

1m 41.71s (-2.89) **Going Correction** -0.275s/f (Stan) **8** Ran SP% **114.3**
Speed ratings (Par 103):103,102,101,100,99 98,95,89
CSF £30.15 CT £237.90 TOTE £8.80: £2.10, £1.30, £2.70; EX 22.30 Trifecta £195.30 Pool: £558.52 - 2.03 winning units. Place 6 £2047.22, Place 5 £ 256.58.
Owner R S Cockerill (Farms) Ltd **Bred** R S Cockerill (farms) Ltd **Trained** Sheriff Hutton, N Yorks

FOCUS
Nothing between the first six in this very ordinary handicap, in which the pace was not that strong.
She's Our Lass(IRE) Official explanation: jockey said mare never travelled
T/Plt: £2,999.90 to a £1 stake. Pool: £41,506.75. 10.10 winning tickets. T/Qpdt: £93.80 to a £1 stake. Pool: £3,882.70. 30.60 winning tickets. WG

1540 WINDSOR (R-H)

Monday, May 14

OFFICIAL GOING: Good to soft (soft in places)
They all tended to race middle to far side in the straight, as they usually do at Windsor when the ground is on the easy side.
Wind: Almost nil Weather: Mostly fine

1721 VC CASINO.COM NOVICE STKS 5f 10y

6:00 (6:00) (Class 4) 2-Y-0 £4,533 (£1,348; £674; £336) Stalls High

Form				RPR
	1		**Carleton** 2-8-12 DarryllHolland 4 (M R Channon) *mde virtually all: drvn over 1f out: hld on wl* 8/1	80
2	2	nk	**Magical Speedfit (IRE)**[7] 1540 2-8-12 SebSanders 1 (G G Margarson) *hld up in last: rdn to chse wnr over 1f out: nt qckn and a jst hld* 4/5[1]	79
1	3	1¼	**Piece Of My Heart**[27] 1079 2-9-0 EddieAhern 3 (P F I Cole) *w wnr to 2f out: hanging and nt qckn after* 5/1[3]	77

4 11 **Cordell (IRE)** 2-8-12 .... RichardHughes 2 35+
(R Hannon) *w ldrs to 1/2-way: wknd over 1f out: eased* **11/4[2]**
63.98 secs (2.88) **Going Correction** +0.375s/f (Good) **4** Ran SP% **110.0**
Speed ratings (Par 95):91,90,88,70
CSF £15.53 TOTE £5.80; EX 19.20.
Owner Capital **Bred** Peter Taplin **Trained** West Ilsley, Berks

FOCUS
A disappointing turnout numerically for this novice contest, but this is usually quite a good race and the form has been rated positively with that in mind. They headed towards the far side in the straight.

NOTEBOOK
Carleton, a brother to Pyscho Cat, dual 6f-7f winner at 2, also successful over hurdles at three, out of a 5f-7f winner at two and three, knew his job and proved good enough to make a winning debut. This was obviously a pleasing introduction, but the form is perhaps not as strong as it might have been with the favourite looking ill at ease on the ground. His jockey thinks he will be worth his place at Royal Ascot. (op 7-1 tchd 9-1 in a place)
Magical Speedfit(IRE) never looked happy on the easy ground and failed to build on the promise he showed when runner-up in a course-and-distance maiden on his debut under faster conditions. He probably did well to finish so close and can definitely be given another chance on a quicker surface. (op 6-5)
Piece Of My Heart failed to convince with her attitude despite winning on her debut at Warwick, and she never posed a threat this time, hardly helping her chance by hanging once again. In her defence, she was shouldering a 7lb penalty against the boys, and probably got bogged down somewhat in the soft ground. (op 3-1)
Cordell(IRE), a 50,000euros purchase, out of a smart multiple winner at around 1m at two and three in France, seemingly failed to handle the ground at the business end and ran below market expectations. He can be given another chance. (op 10-3 tchd 5-2)

1722 VC CASINO.COM H'CAP 1m 2f 7y
6:30 (6:31) (Class 5) (0-75,75) 3-Y-O **£2,101** (£2,101; £481; £240) **Stalls** Low

Form RPR
5-31 1 **Fever**[23] 1153 3-9-4 **75** .... RichardHughes 3 82
(R Hannon) *cl up: grabbed far side rail and led over 2f out: styd on u.p fnl f: jnd post* **9/2[1]**
10-0 1 *dht* **Maid To Believe**[16] 1289 3-8-10 **67** .... EddieAhern 10 74
(J L Dunlop) *hld up towards rr: stdy prog over 2f out: chsd ldr over 1f out: r.o to dead-heat last stride* **14/1**
435- 3 4 **Fairly Honest**[172] 6570 3-9-1 **72** .... AntonyProcter 15 71
(D R C Elsworth) *hld up in rr: prog over 2f out: hanging lft and styd on same pce over 1f out* **16/1**
-300 4 *hd* **Bewildering (IRE)**[16] 1289 3-8-8 **65** ....(v[1]) RichardMullen 8 64
(E J O'Neill) *mde most tl hung lft bnd over 4f out: rallied 2f out: one pce* **8/1[3]**
0-00 5 *hd* **Buckthorn**[14] 1358 3-9-0 **71** .... SteveDrowne 11 70
(G Wragg) *prom: w ldrs over 3f out: one pce fnl 2f* **12/1**
1250 6 *shd* **Professor Twinkle**[19] 1247 3-9-1 **72** .... MartinDwyer 6 70
(W J Knight) *pressed ldrs: narrow ld over 4f out to over 2f out: fdd* **15/2[2]**
625- 7 *2 1/2* **Heights Of Golan**[187] 6393 3-8-10 **67** .... JamesDoyle 9 61
(I A Wood) *t.k.h: cl up: w ldrs over 3f out: wknd over 1f out* **11/1**
031- 8 *nk* **Encircled**[158] 6737 3-9-2 **73** .... RobertHavlin 5 66
(D Haydn Jones) *lost pl 6f out: effrt over 2f out: btn whn hmpd over 1f out* **20/1**
31-0 9 *1/2* **Doubly Guest**[16] 1289 3-9-0 **71** .... SebSanders 14 63
(G G Margarson) *in tch: prog to chal over 3f out: wknd over 1f out* **8/1[3]**
62-5 10 *1 3/4* **Jawaab (IRE)**[25] 1111 3-9-1 **72** .... TedDurcan 7 61
(M A Buckley) *restless stalls: trckd ldrs: cl up 2f out: wknd* **9/1**
002- 11 *1/2* **Venir Rouge**[187] 6394 3-8-13 **70** .... TPO'Shea 12 58
(M Salaman) *towards rr: hrd rdn and struggling 3f out* **16/1**
2514 12 *1 1/2* **Beau Sancy**[13] 1370 3-8-10 **72** .... TolleyDean[(5)] 2 57
(R A Harris) *racd wd in midfield: hrd rdn and btn over 2f out* **25/1**
5-21 13 *3/4* **Paymaster General (IRE)**[30] 1039 3-9-2 **73** .... HayleyTurner 1 57
(M D I Usher) *t.k.h: hld up in rr: no prog u.p 3f out* **9/2[1]**
134- 14 6 **Aypeeyes (IRE)**[151] 6824 3-9-0 **71** .... FrankieMcDonald 13 43
(S Kirk) *dwlt: a last: bhd fnl 2f* **16/1**
2m 11.66s (3.36) **Going Correction** +0.375s/f (Good) **14** Ran SP% **129.3**
Speed ratings (Par 99):101,101,97,97,97 97,95,95,94,93 92,91,91,86
TRIFECTA Tote Win F 2.90, MTB 7.50; Pl F 2.50, M 3.70, FH 6.60; Ex F-M 63.00, M-F 46.70;CSF F-M 38.34; M-F 40.74; TC F-M-F 484.50, M-F-F 534.
Owner The Royal Ascot Racing Club **Bred** Roan Rocket Partners **Trained** East Everleigh, Wilts
Owner Normandie Stud Ltd **Bred** Normandie Stud Ltd **Trained** Arundel, W Sussex

FOCUS
Just a modest handicap and, with the pace only ordinary for much of the way, any number of these still had a shout about 2f out. They raced middle to far side in the straight. The winning time was 1.48 seconds quicker than the later maiden. The dead-heaters came clear, with Fever up 5lb and Maid To Believe a bigger improver.
Bewildering(IRE) Official explanation: jockey said colt hung left throughout
Paymaster General(IRE) Official explanation: jockey had no explanation for the poor form shown

1723 VC CASINO.COM STKS (REGISTERED AS THE ROYAL WINDSOR STAKES) (LISTED RACE) (C&G) 1m 67y
7:00 (7:00) (Class 1) 3-Y-O+ **£15,410** (£5,826; £2,912; £1,456) **Stalls** High

Form RPR
12-6 1 **Army Of Angels (IRE)**[67] 646 5-9-2 110 .... LDettori 4 114
(Saeed Bin Suroor) *hld up in 4th: prog to ld jst over 2f out: sn edgd rt: drvn and hld on wl fnl f* **1/1[1]**
44-3 2 *nk* **Take A Bow**[16] 1305 6-9-2 107 .... JimCrowley 5 113
(P R Chamings) *trckd ldng pair: chal 3f out: sn rdn: rallied fnl f: a jst hld* **9/2[3]**
0-15 3 *1 1/4* **Levera**[2] 1656 4-9-2 107 .... JamieSpencer 2 110
(A King) *hld up in last: gng easily over 2f out: prog to chal over 1f out: rdn and nt qckn: wknd nr fin* **6/1**
0-35 4 8 **Final Verse**[16] 1305 4-9-2 107 .... KerrinMcEvoy 3 92
(Sir Michael Stoute) *racd freely: pressed ldr tl 3f out: wknd rapidly over 1f out* **4/1[2]**
10-1 5 *3/4* **New Seeker**[16] 1294 7-9-7 109 ....(b) TedDurcan 1 95
(P F I Cole) *led at str pce: hdd jst over 2f out: flashed tail and wknd rapidly* **12/1**
1m 45.59s (0.89) **Going Correction** +0.375s/f (Good) **5** Ran SP% **110.2**
Speed ratings (Par 111):110,109,108,100,99
CSF £5.85 TOTE £1.90: £1.10, £2.10; EX 4.80.
Owner Godolphin **Bred** Gerard Callanan **Trained** Newmarket, Suffolk

FOCUS
It was disappointing only five horses turned out for this Listed contest, but an interesting race nonetheless and, with the pace good, the form looks sound enough, although the winner was 3lb off his best. The first two home raced down the middle of the track early in the straight, but ended up close to the far rail. The winning time was 2.05 seconds faster than the later 56-70 handicap.

NOTEBOOK
Army Of Angels(IRE) was not at his best on his sole start in Dubai earlier in the year, but he was at the top of his game this time and narrowly gained his first Listed-race success. The eventual runner-up kept him up to his work all the way to the line, but he gave the impression he was always going to hold on. This looks to be his level for the time being. (op 11-8 tchd 10-11, 6-4 in places)
Take A Bow, third in the Group 2 Betfred Mile on his previous start, ran another fine race in defeat, adding to his second in this race in 2005, and his third in 2006. He is an honest type, but is always vulnerable to something less exposed. (op 4-1 tchd 5-1)
Levera was always going to struggle to dominate with New Seeker in the line-up and he was ridden with patience this time. The new tactics did not seem to have a negative effect and he appeared to run to the same sort of form he showed when fifth in this grade at Haydock two days earlier. It might just be that 7f suits best. (op 13-2 tchd 7-1)
Final Verse had conditions to suit, but he completely boiled over in the paddock and looked to have run his race before the start. He looks best avoided for the time being. Official explanation: jockey said colt ran too free (op 3-1 tchd 9-2)
New Seeker was unsuited by the soft ground and failed to follow up his recent success in this grade at Leicester under his 5lb penalty. Official explanation: jockey said gelding was unsuited by the good to soft (soft in places) ground (op 9-1 tchd 14-1)

1724 PLAY AT VC CASINO.COM H'CAP 1m 3f 135y
7:30 (7:30) (Class 5) (0-75,75) 3-Y-O **£3,238** (£963; £481; £240) **Stalls** Low

Form RPR
25-4 1 **Arctic Wings (IRE)**[16] 1289 3-8-12 **69** .... MartinDwyer 9 75+
(W R Muir) *trckd ldrs: narrow ld over 2f out: hung rt over 1f out: drvn and styd on wl* **7/1[3]**
3212 2 *1/2* **Shawhill**[14] 1355 3-9-1 **72** .... SteveDrowne 11 77
(Tom Dascombe) *hld up in midfield: smooth prog 3f out: rdn to chal over 1f out: styd on* **5/1[1]**
534- 3 *1 1/4* **Sunley Peace**[205] 6106 3-9-0 **74** .... MarcHalford[(3)] 13 77
(D R C Elsworth) *hld up towards rr: prog 3f out: styd on u.p to take 3rd nr fin* **11/2[2]**
-404 4 *hd* **Personal Column**[21] 1205 3-8-12 **69** .... RobertHavlin 8 72
(T G Mills) *led to over 2f out: pressed wnr tl over 1f out: one pce* **20/1**
035- 5 *nk* **Squadron**[158] 6737 3-8-10 **67** .... LDettori 5 69
(Mrs A J Perrett) *pressed ldr tl over 2f out: stl cl up 1f out: one pce* **8/1**
5431 6 *hd* **Urban Warrior**[16] 1289 3-9-2 **73** .... JamesDoyle 15 75
(Mrs Norma Pook) *trckd ldrs: rdn and cl up over 1f out: nt qckn* **12/1**
-113 7 *hd* **Dan Tucker**[27] 1084 3-9-1 **72** .... JamieSpencer 2 74
(B J Meehan) *hld up in rr: prog 3f out: kpt on u.p fnl 2f: nt rch ldrs* **5/1[1]**
065- 8 5 **Disintegration (IRE)**[216] 5886 3-8-7 **64** .... FergusSweeney 1 57+
(A King) *dwlt: hld up in last pair: prog to chse ldrs 2f out: wknd fnl f* **16/1**
-012 9 6 **Red Petal**[75] 582 3-9-4 **75** .... SebSanders 10 58
(Sir Mark Prescott) *t.k.h: hld up in midfield: effrt 3f out: floundering and wkng over 1f out* **8/1**
02-4 10 *nk* **Mud Monkey**[20] 1218 3-8-5 **62** .... FrankieMcDonald 12 44
(B G Powell) *s.i.s: hld up in last pair: hmpd bnd 6f out: nt clr run 3f out: no ch* **25/1**
30-0 11 10 **Revisionist (IRE)**[14] 1355 3-8-4 **61** .... RichardSmith 14 26
(R Hannon) *hld up in midfield: stmbld bdly bnd 6f out: struggling fnl 3f* **25/1**
533- 12 *nk* **Spartan Dance**[163] 6676 3-8-7 **64** .... RichardThomas 7 29
(J A Geake) *plld hrd: prom tl wknd 3f out* **20/1**
001- 13 4 **Sularno**[182] 6466 3-8-11 **73** .... TravisBlock[(5)] 4 31
(H Morrison) *prom tl wknd rapidly 3f out* **16/1**
044- 14 22 **Astral Charmer**[166] 6650 3-8-12 **69** .... JimmyQuinn 3 —
(M H Tompkins) *rdn in midfield 1/2-way: sn btn: t.o* **40/1**
2m 33.66s (3.56) **Going Correction** +0.375s/f (Good) **14** Ran SP% **122.6**
Speed ratings (Par 99):103,102,101,101,101 101,101,97,93,93 87,86,84,69
CSF £39.53 CT £213.32 TOTE £8.30: £2.10, £2.10, £3.00; EX 66.30.
Owner P Milsom **Bred** Round Hill Stud **Trained** Lambourn, Berks

FOCUS
Just a modest handicap, but very competitive and several of these finished in a heap behind the front two. Once again, they all raced far side in the straight. The form looks nothing special but should prove reliable.
Spartan Dance Official explanation: jockey said gelding ran a bit too free

1725 RENAULT TRAFIC MEDIAN AUCTION MAIDEN STKS 1m 2f 7y
8:00 (8:03) (Class 5) 3-Y-O **£3,238** (£963; £481; £240) **Stalls** Low

Form RPR
4-6 1 **Wester Ross (IRE)**[21] 1204 3-9-3 .... MickyFenton 11 75
(J M P Eustace) *led after 1f: mde rest: kpt on wl fnl 2f* **10/3[1]**
2 *3/4* **Commandment (IRE)** 3-9-3 .... JamieSpencer 3 74+
(E A L Dunlop) *hld up bhd ldrs: awkward bnd 6f out to 5f out: smooth prog over 2f out: rdn over 1f out: clsd on wnr nr fin* **9/2[3]**
0-5 3 *3/4* **Kailasha (IRE)**[16] 1312 3-8-12 .... SebSanders 2 67
(C F Wall) *trckd ldng pair: chsd wnr over 2f out: hld fnl f: lost 2nd nr fin* **4/1[2]**
4 5 **Meon Mix** 3-8-12 .... OscarUrbina 4 58
(J R Fanshawe) *dwlt: hld up in rr: prog to chse ldrs 2f out: hung lft after: fdd* **12/1**
5 *shd* **Kadouchski (FR)**[85] 3-9-3 .... PatDobbs 8 62
(Miss E C Lavelle) *chsd ldrs: outpcd over 2f out: kpt on fnl f* **13/2**
0 6 *nk* **Belinda Rose (IRE)**[7] 1523 3-8-12 .... RichardHughes 15 57
(B J Meehan) *chsd ldrs: rdn over 2f out: no imp* **20/1**
7 *1/2* **Condi (IRE)** 3-8-12 .... EddieAhern 10 56
(A J Lidderdale) *dwlt: hld up wl in rr: reminder 3f out and 2f out: styd on steadily: nrst fin* **25/1**
2 8 6 **Alexander Guru**[19] 1250 3-9-3 .... TedDurcan 7 50
(M Blanshard) *chsd ldng trio tl wknd 2f out* **16/1**
9 1 **Almahaza (IRE)** 3-9-3 .... JimCrowley 5 48
(Mrs A J Perrett) *dwlt and squeezed out s: wl in rr: u.p 4f out: no ch* **5/1**
5 10 1 **Day Of Days (IRE)**[12] 1412 3-9-3 .... JimmyQuinn 12 46
(M H Tompkins) *hld up in midfield: m green: wknd 2f out* **14/1**
11 *1 3/4* **Surprise Act** 3-9-3 .... GeorgeBaker 14 42
(P R Chamings) *dwlt: a wl in rr* **16/1**
0- 12 *1 3/4* **Time Upon Time**[206] 6073 3-8-12 .... MartinDwyer 9 34
(W J Knight) *plld hrd early: chsd ldrs tl wknd 3f out* **33/1**
0- 13 1 **Kastan**[322] 2938 3-9-3 .... JamieMackay 6 37
(B Palling) *led 1f: chsd ldr tl over 2f out: wknd rapidly* **100/1**
14 1 **Sister Agnes (IRE)** 3-8-12 .... AdamKirby 1 30
(J R Fanshawe) *a wl in rr* **20/1**
0 15 16 **Glentimon (IRE)**[19] 1250 3-9-3 .... FrankieMcDonald 16 5
(S Kirk) *a bhd: hrd rdn and no prog 4f out: t.o* **50/1**

R **16** *dist* **Supercraft (IRE)**[108] [257] 3-9-0 ow4................(v[1]) ChrisCavanagh[(7)] 13 —
(M Quinn) *dwlt: sn t.o* **100/1**

2m 13.14s (4.84) **Going Correction** +0.375s/f (Good) **16** Ran SP% **137.6**
Speed ratings (Par 99):95,94,93,89,89 89,89,84,83,82 81,79,79,78,65 —
CSF £19.58 TOTE £5.10: £2.00, £2.10, £2.50; EX 23.80.
Owner Peter Hillman **Bred** Farmers Hill Stud **Trained** Newmarket, Suffolk

FOCUS
A weak maiden by Windsor standards and the winning time was 1.48 seconds slower than the earlier 61-75 handicap. Again, they all wanted to be far side in the straight. The race has been rated through the winner.
Glentimon(IRE) Official explanation: jockey said gelding was hampered on the bend

1726 RENAULT MASTER H'CAP 1m 67y
8:30 (8:32) (Class 5) (0-70,70) 3-Y-O **£3,238** (£963; £481; £240) **Stalls** High

Form RPR
504- **1** **Leptis Magna**[235] [5496] 3-9-2 **68**.. SebSanders 14 82+
(D R C Elsworth) *dwlt: hld up wl in rr: smooth prog over 2f out: led 1f out: r.o wl* **7/1**[3]
40-0 **2** *2* **Rock Anthem (IRE)**[19] [1246] 3-9-4 **70**................................ EddieAhern 7 78+
(J L Dunlop) *hld up wl in rr: hrd rdn over 2f out: r.o to take 2nd ins fnl f: no ch w wnr* **12/1**
021- **3** *1 1/2* **World Spirit**[166] [6651] 3-9-4 **70**... ChrisCatlin 10 75
(Rae Guest) *hld up towards rr: prog over 2f out: styd on one pce fr over 1f out* **10/1**
55-6 **4** *1* **Kashmir Lady (FR)**[14] [1345] 3-9-1 **67**.......................... FergusSweeney 2 70
(H Candy) *t.k.h: sn hld up: prog 3f out: led 2f out to 1f out: outpcd* **7/1**[3]
00-6 **5** *4* **Affiliation (IRE)**[9] [1468] 3-8-9 **61**.............................. RichardHughes 1 55
(R Hannon) *prom: rdn 3f out: wknd over 1f out* **25/1**
04-4 **6** *shd* **Ask Yer Dad**[23] [1155] 3-8-10 **62**....................................... MickyFenton 11 57+
(Mrs P Sly) *led after 1f to 3f out: hanging lft over 1f out: wknd rapidly fnl f* **12/1**
6-06 **7** *shd* **Beckenham's Secret**[40] [931] 3-8-12 **64**............................ JimCrowley 4 57
(B R Millman) *led 1f: pressed ldr: led 3f out to 2f out: wkng whn bmpd over 1f out* **12/1**
05-2 **8** *1/2* **Perfect Courtesy (IRE)**[40] [931] 3-9-4 **70**...................... JamieSpencer 6 62+
(G A Swinbank) *hld up in rr: stdy prog 3f out: rdn and btn whn bmpd over 1f out* **11/4**[1]
06-3 **9** *3/4* **Paradise Walk**[45] [826] 3-9-1 **67**.. SteveDrowne 5 60+
(R Charlton) *chsd ldrs: wkng whn bdly bmpd over 1f out* **10/1**
43-0 **10** *3/4* **Nashharry (IRE)**[14] [1345] 3-8-11 **63**....................................... LPKeniry 13 51
(S Kirk) *cl up tl wknd u.p 2f out* **33/1**
53-0 **11** *nk* **Compton Charlie**[12] [1399] 3-8-11 **66**........................... EmmettStack[(3)] 9 54
(J G Portman) *chsd ldrs: awkward on bnd over 5f out: rdn over 3f out: fdd* **50/1**
4-04 **12** *shd* **Just Oscar (GER)**[16] [1297] 3-8-11 **63**...................... StephenDonohoe 12 51
(W M Brisbourne) *s.v.s: a bhd* **16/1**
06-5 **13** *nk* **April Fool**[16] [1297] 3-8-8 **60**... RobertHavlin 8 47
(J A Geake) *rdn in midfield 1/2-way: sn btn* **5/1**[2]

1m 47.64s (2.94) **Going Correction** +0.375s/f (Good) **13** Ran SP% **124.2**
Speed ratings (Par 99):100,98,96,95,91 91,91,90,90,89 89,88,88
CSF £90.57 CT £883.88 TOTE £10.00: £2.70, £3.40, £4.20; EX 78.90 Place 6 £796.99, Place 5 £47.41.
Owner Charles Green **Bred** Mrs M Gutkin **Trained** Newmarket, Suffolk

FOCUS
This looked like quite a good handicap for the grade. The winner should do better and the form ought to work out. The early pace seemed just ordinary and the winning time was 2.05 seconds slower than the earlier Listed contest. They all raced towards the far side in the straight.
Just Oscar(GER) Official explanation: jockey said gelding missed the break
T/Jkpt: Not won. T/Plt: £559.50 to a £1 stake. Pool of £75,878.60, 99.00 winning tickets T/Qpdt: £17.90 to a £1 stake. Pool of £5,693.90. 234.15 winning tickets JN

[1435]WOLVERHAMPTON (A.W) (L-H)
Monday, May 14

OFFICIAL GOING: Standard
Wind: Moderate across Weather: Fine

1727 BOOK ONLINE AT WOLVERHAMPTON-RACECOURSE.CO.UK MAIDEN AUCTION FILLIES' STKS 5f 20y(P)
2:20 (2:25) (Class 5) 2-Y-O **£2,914** (£867; £433; £216) **Stalls** Low

Form RPR
5 **1** **Fitolini**[31] [1029] 2-8-10 .... J-PGuillambert 9 72
(Mrs G S Rees) *hld up in mid-div: rdn and hdwy 2f out: swtchd rt over 1f out: r.o to ld last strides* **33/1**
2 **2** *hd* **Speedy Senorita (IRE)**[6] [1553] 2-8-6 .... FrancisNorton 2 67
(K R Burke) *a.p: rdn over 2f out: led jst ins fnl f: edgd rt: hdd last strides* **4/1**[2]
04 **3** *2 1/2* **Zahwah**[14] [1354] 2-8-4 .... EmmettStack[(3)] 5 59
(J G Portman) *outpcd and bhd: gd hdwy on outside fnl f: fin wl* **9/2**[3]
2 **4** *1/2* **Lady Benjamin**[11] [1422] 2-8-11 .... KDarley 12 61
(P C Haslam) *chsd ldrs: rdn and outpcd over 2f out: kpt on towards fin* **9/2**[3]
0 **5** *shd* **Crying Aloud (USA)**[25] [1101] 2-8-11 .... TPO'Shea 8 61
(P A Blockley) *a.p: rdn and ev ch over 1f out: one pce ins fnl f* **10/1**
3 **6** *shd* **Lake Sabina**[21] [1193] 2-8-9 .... GrahamGibbons 4 59
(E S McMahon) *a.p: rdn and ev ch over 1f out: one pce ins fnl f* **7/2**[1]
2 **7** *2* **Only In Jest**[42] [883] 2-7-12 .... LukeMorris[(7)] 3 48
(W G M Turner) *led: rdn 2f out: hdd jst ins fnl f: wknd towards fin* **11/1**
8 *1 1/2* **Orbital Orchid** 2-8-7 .... FergusSweeney 7 44
(W S Kittow) *s.i.s: outpcd: nvr nrr* **33/1**
0 **9** *1 3/4* **Bantham Bay**[14] [1354] 2-8-8 .... JohnEgan 13 39
(B J Meehan) *a bhd* **40/1**
10 *3* **Linnet Park** 2-8-11 .... TPQueally 11 31
(J G Given) *a bhd* **8/1**
0 **11** *1* **Ephesian (IRE)**[27] [1079] 2-8-10 .... NCallan 6 26
(Mrs A Duffield) *chsd ldrs: rdn over 2f out: sn wknd* **16/1**
12 *1/2* **Planet Paradise (IRE)** 2-8-7 ow2.......................... DeanMcKeown 10 22
(D Shaw) *s.i.s: a bhd* **50/1**
13 *3/4* **Last Angel (IRE)** 2-8-10 .... PaulEddery 1 22
(M Wigham) *s.i.s: outpcd* **28/1**

62.60 secs (-0.22) **Going Correction** -0.20s/f (Stan) **13** Ran SP% **126.7**
Speed ratings (Par 90):93,92,88,87,87 87,84,81,79,74 72,71,70
CSF £166.09 TOTE £34.10: £5.30, £1.70, £3.00; EX 207.40.
Owner The Top Banana Partnership **Bred** Capt J H Wilson **Trained** Sollom, Lancs

FOCUS
Not a great maiden on paper, but the pace was strong and a few of these are probably capable of a little improvement.

NOTEBOOK
Fitolini, disappointing when well backed on her Southwell debut, was friendless this time but proved much better suited by this surface. Once switched around the pace-setters a furlong out, she stayed on well, and she might be the type to do well in nurseries later in the season. (op 25-1)
Speedy Senorita(IRE) was presented with a lovely gap on the inside of the three leaders in the home straight, but once through she was inclined to edge away from the rail and was just mugged. There should be a race like this in her and she may benefit from an extra furlong. (op 10-3)
Zahwah ran an extraordinary race, failing to go the early pace before flying home down the outside from an impossible position to snatch an unlikely third. This was not the strongest of maidens and it would be wrong to get too carried away by this effort, but an extra furlong should help her and she may be able to find an opportunity before the better juveniles emerge in greater numbers. (op 8-1 tchd 9-1)
Lady Benjamin, unlike on her Catterick debut, could not get to the front this time from her wide draw and did not take the bend too well, so it is to her credit that she managed to finish so close. There should be a race like this for her back on a straight track. (op 3-1)
Crying Aloud(USA), down in grade after contesting a decent Newmarket maiden on her debut, did best of the trio that were at it hammer and tongs from a long away out. If she can avoid another speed war there should be a small race or two in her. (op 8-1)
Lake Sabina got caught up in a fierce battle for the lead and that took its toll late on. She is bred to appreciate further and there will be another day. (op 9-2 tchd 3-1)
Only In Jest showed good speed from the gate once again, but was given no peace by a couple of rivals and that eventually found her out. (op 10-1)
Linnet Park ◆, a half-sister to the dual juvenile winner Mimi Mouse, is bred to go a bit but she had a difficult draw and failed to negotiate the bend at all. She is probably capable of rather better than this. (tchd 9-1)

1728 STAY AT THE WOLVERHAMPTON HOLIDAY INN CLAIMING STKS 5f 20y(P)
2:50 (2:52) (Class 6) 2-Y-O **£2,730** (£806; £403) **Stalls** Low

Form RPR
0 **1** **Alexander Monarchy (IRE)**[7] [1533] 2-8-9 .... NCallan 1 59
(K A Ryan) *trckd ldrs: swtchd rt wl over 1f out: sn rdn: edgd rt ins fnl f: r.o to ld last strides* **15/8**[2]
5335 **2** *hd* **Rio Taffeta**[15] [1315] 2-9-0 .... SamHitchcott 2 63
(M R Channon) *w ldrs: rdn to ld wl over 1f out: hdd last strides* **13/8**[1]
44 **3** *2 1/2* **Amazing Day**[19] [1235] 2-8-1 ow1.. JackDean[(7)] 4 48
(W G M Turner) *led: hdd wl over 1f out: sn rdn: no ex ins fnl f* **16/1**
0 **4** *3/4* **Jane's Delight (IRE)**[35] [972] 2-8-9 .... LeeEnstone 9 46
(P C Haslam) *hld up in tch: rdn wl over 1f out: sn hung lft: one pce* **16/1**
65 **5** *shd* **Miss Antropist (IRE)**[35] [971] 2-8-1 .... TolleyDean[(5)] 8 43
(R A Harris) *wnt lft s: bhd: hrd rdn and hdwy over 1f out: one pce ins fnl f* **20/1**
6 *nk* **Weet A Surprise** 2-8-11 .... GrahamGibbons 6 47
(R Hollinshead) *w ldr: ev ch 2f out: rdn over 1f out: wknd ins fnl f* **16/1**
024 **7** *5* **Portway Lane**[23] [1156] 2-7-9 .... LukeMorris[(7)] 3 20
(W G M Turner) *sn pushed along: bhd whn rdn 3f out: no ch whn hung rt ins fnl f* **14/1**[3]
0 **8** *2* **Rye Beau (IRE)**[27] [1073] 2-8-8 .... J-PGuillambert 10 19
(Mrs A Duffield) *chsd ldrs on outside: rdn and wknd 2f out* **16/1**
9 *1 3/4* **Hi High** 2-8-4 .... AdrianMcCarthy 5 8
(D K Ivory) *s.i.s and sn n.m.r: outpcd* **14/1**[3]

63.22 secs (0.40) **Going Correction** -0.20s/f (Stan) **9** Ran SP% **114.5**
Speed ratings (Par 91):88,87,83,82,82 81,73,70,67
CSF £5.21 TOTE £2.90: £1.10, £1.20, £3.40; EX 5.10.The winner was the subject of a friendly claim
Owner Noel O'Callaghan **Bred** Mountarmstrong Stud **Trained** Hambleton, N Yorks

FOCUS
A moderate claimer in which the winning time was 0.62 seconds slower than the preceding fillies' maiden. Not many got into it and the form probably amounts to little.

NOTEBOOK
Alexander Monarchy(IRE), dropped in class following her Warwick debut, rather had to force her way through between Amazing Day and Weet A Surprise and then had a fair amount of ground to make up on the leader, but she responded well to driving to get up near the line. This was not a great race though and she will struggle outside this level, at least until the nurseries start. (op 2-1)
Rio Taffeta, the most experienced in the field, put that to good use and railed like a greyhound up with the pace. He looked to have the race in the bag for much of the home straight, but the winner's late surge down the middle of the track snatched the race from him. He looks very much exposed now and will not find too many better opportunities than this. (op 11-8)
Amazing Day, fourth in a couple of sellers, was given a positive ride on this sand debut but was just not good enough and will not find too many weaker races than this. (op 14-1)
Jane's Delight(IRE), down in class from her recent Warwick debut, showed up for a fair way but she is bred to be better than this level and her 20,000gns price tag is already looking expensive. (op 12-1)
Miss Antropist(IRE) did best of those held up, but she has already been beaten in a seller and probably did not achieve much.
Weet A Surprise, out of a winning juvenile from a speedy family, failed to reach her reserve as a yearling. She did show a bit of early speed before fading and to be fair she does not come from a yard noted for winning debutants. She may be nothing special, but the very best of her is likely to be seen much further down the line. Official explanation: jockey said filly lost its action

1729 HORIZONS RESTAURANT CLAIMING STKS 5f 20y(P)
3:20 (3:20) (Class 6) 3-Y-O+ **£2,388** (£705; £352) **Stalls** Low

Form RPR
3522 **1** **Blackheath (IRE)**[15] [1317] 11-9-0 55......................... SilvestreDeSousa 3 63
(D Nicholls) *chsd ldrs: rdn to ld over 1f out: r.o wl* **9/2**[2]
0000 **2** *2 1/2* **City For Conquest (IRE)**[12] [1405] 4-8-10 52............(b) FrancisNorton 12 50
(John A Harris) *towards rr: rdn and hdwy over 1f out: r.o to take 2nd cl home* **14/1**
-400 **3** *nk* **Ruby's Dream**[13] [1384] 5-8-4 48...........................(p) KevinGhunowa[(5)] 11 48
(J M Bradley) *chsd ldrs: rdn over 1f out: kpt on same pce fnl f* **33/1**
1050 **4** *nk* **New York Oscar (IRE)**[7] [1530] 3-8-11 70.................................. NCallan 9 54
(A J McCabe) *chsd ldrs: rdn over 1f out: kpt on on outside towards fin* **7/1**[3]
0120 **5** *nk* **Pride Of Joy**[28] [1067] 4-9-3 62... JimCrowley 7 54
(D K Ivory) *hld up in mid-div: hdwy over 2f out: swtchd lft ins fnl f: rdn and no ex towards fin* **7/1**[3]
2636 **6** *1 1/4* **Garlogs**[11] [1436] 4-9-8 52.. FergusSweeney 13 54
(R Hollinshead) *chsd ldr: led briefly wl over 1f out: sn rdn: wknd wl ins fnl f* **10/1**
3456 **7** *nk* **Muktasb (USA)**[13] [1384] 6-9-2 48...............................(v) DeanMcKeown 8 47+
(D Shaw) *stdd s: in rr tl sme hdwy on ins over 1f out: one pce fnl f* **9/1**
600- **8** *1* **African Concerto (IRE)**[150] [6829] 4-8-12 45......................... LPKeniry 2 40
(S Kirk) *towards rr: rdn over 3f out: nvr nr ldrs* **25/1**

5051 **9** *shd* **Le Chiffre (IRE)**[15] [1317] 5-8-11 60..............................(b) LukeMorris(7) 5 45+
(R A Harris) *outpcd: edgd lft 1f out: nvr nrr* **7/2**[1]
0-60 **10** *1/2* **Seven No Trumps**[13] [1384] 10-8-5 48.......................... BarrySavage(7) 6 38
(J M Bradley) *rdn over 2f out: a bhd* **16/1**
3000 **11** *3/4* **New Options**[23] [1163] 10-8-12 47..............................(b) GrahamGibbons 1 35
(Peter Grayson) *mid-div: rdn over 2f out: wknd ins fnl f* **33/1**
5210 **12** *1* **Borzoi Maestro**[11] [1436] 6-8-12 55..............................(p) AdamKirby 10 31
(G F Bridgwater) *led: rdn over 2f out: hdd wl over 1f out: eased whn btn ins fnl f* **9/1**

61.58 secs (-1.24) **Going Correction** -0.20s/f (Stan)
WFA 3 from 4yo+ 9lb 12 Ran SP% **116.8**
Speed ratings (Par 101):101,97,96,96,95 93,93,91,91,90 89,87
CSF £63.57 TOTE £5.50: £1.20, £7.00, £9.10; EX 80.00.
Owner Middleham Park Racing XX **Bred** John McKay **Trained** Sessay, N Yorks

FOCUS
A routine claimer run at a frantic early pace and very few ever got into it. It has been rated around the second and third. The winning time was faster than the two earlier juvenile events, but only by about as much as would be expected.
Le Chiffre(IRE) Official explanation: jockey said gelding never travelled
Borzoi Maestro Official explanation: jockey said gelding lost its action

1730 BARRY MICHAEL DYLAN THOMAS MEMORIAL H'CAP 1m 5f 194y(P)
3:50 (3:51) (Class 6) (0-65,61) 4-Y-0+ **£2,730** (£806; £403) **Stalls** Low

Form RPR
3-05 **1** **Adage**[19] [1254] 4-8-11 50..............................(t) FergusSweeney 5 64
(David Pinder) *hld up in mid-div: hdwy over 3f out: rdn over 2f out: led wl over 1f out: drvn out* **16/1**
1-22 **2** *3/4* **Light Sentence**[7] [1532] 4-9-5 58.............................. DeanMcKeown 4 71
(G A Swinbank) *hld up and bhd: pushed along over 4f out: rdn and hdwy over 2f out: styd on ins fnl f* **11/10**[1]
-006 **3** *5* **Swords**[16] [1314] 5-9-5 57.............................. J-PGuillambert 8 63
(Heather Dalton) *hld up in tch: wnt 2nd over 3f out: rdn over 2f out: one pce fnl f* **8/1**[3]
1626 **4** *2 1/2* **Carlton Scroop (FR)**[10] [1451] 4-9-8 61..........................(b) PaulEddery 2 63
(J Jay) *hld up in mid-div: outpcd 3f out: styd on fnl f* **5/1**[2]
0042 **5** *1* **Activist**[6] [1570] 9-8-0 45..............................(p) KellyHarrison(7) 10 46
(D Carroll) *t.k.h: led: clr after 4f: rdn and hdd wl over 1f out: wknd ins fnl f* **14/1**
3025 **6** *1 1/4* **Missie Baileys**[14] [1342] 5-8-13 51.............................. AmirQuinn 3 50
(Mrs L J Mongan) *led early: prom: rdn 4f out: wknd over 2f out* **12/1**
2061 **7** *nk* **Experimental (IRE)**[14] [1362] 13-8-6 49.................... DuranFentiman(5) 7 48
(John A Harris) *chsd ldr: rdn over 3f out: wknd over 2f out* **16/1**
1300 **8** *3* **Reminiscent (IRE)**[23] [1152] 8-9-3 55..............................(p) TPQueally 9 50
(B P J Baugh) *c wd st: a bhd* **14/1**
-055 **9** *6* **Blue Hedges**[20] [1225] 5-9-7 59..............................(p) NCallan 6 45
(H J Collingridge) *stdd s: c wd st: a bhd: eased whn no ch ins fnl f* **9/1**
00/0 **10** *6* **Silver Dreamer (IRE)**[12] [1396] 5-8-7 45....................(v[1]) FrancisNorton 1 23
(H S Howe) *a bhd* **33/1**

3m 3.20s (-4.17) **Going Correction** -0.20s/f (Stan)
WFA 4 from 5yo+ 1lb 10 Ran SP% **121.1**
Speed ratings (Par 101):103,102,99,98,97 97,96,95,91,88
CSF £35.40 CT £170.59 TOTE £23.00: £6.60, £1.10, £2.90; EX 68.20.
Owner Ms L Burns **Bred** Side Hill Stud **Trained** Kingston Lisle, Oxon

FOCUS
A modest staying handicap, but with Activist taking a keen hold in front at least there was a good pace on and they finished well strung out. Ordinary but sound form rated around the second and third.

1731 NAME A RACE TO ENHANCE YOUR BRAND FILLIES' H'CAP 1m 141y(P)
4:20 (4:20) (Class 5) (0-70,67) 3-Y-0 **£3,238** (£963; £481; £240) **Stalls** Low

Form RPR
0-00 **1** **Cavort (IRE)**[12] [1407] 3-9-4 67.............................. NCallan 3 73
(Pat Eddery) *a.p: rdn to ld wl over 1f out: hung rt ent fnl f: r.o* **10/1**
3065 **2** *1* **First Princess (IRE)**[14] [1345] 3-8-11 60..........................(p) JohnEgan 6 64
(J S Moore) *plld hrd towards rr: hdwy over 2f out: rdn over 1f out: ev ch wl ins fnl f: nt qckn* **14/1**
23-3 **3** *1* **Aussie Cricket (FR)**[19] [1250] 3-9-3 66.............................. TPQueally 5 68
(D J Coakley) *s.i.s: hld up and bhd: hdwy on ins 2f out: sn rdn: kpt on ins fnl f* **8/1**[3]
65-3 **4** *1/2* **Dansil In Distress**[16] [1310] 3-9-2 65.............................. LPKeniry 10 66
(S Kirk) *chsd ldr: rdn and ev ch whn bmpd jst ins fnl f: one pce* **8/1**[3]
-534 **5** *hd* **Baltic Belle (IRE)**[19] [1247] 3-9-2 65.............................. PatDobbs 12 65
(R Hannon) *hld up in tch: rdn over 3f out: kpt on ins fnl f* **9/2**[1]
60-6 **6** *3* **Chant De Guerre (USA)**[20] [1215] 3-8-11 60.................... KDarley 13 53
(H J L Dunlop) *s.i.s: hld up towards rr: rdn 3f out: sme late hdwy: nvr trbld ldrs* **16/1**
40-2 **7** *1/2* **Susanna's Prospect (IRE)**[16] [1310] 3-8-8 64.................... KMay(7) 4 56
(B J Meehan) *led: rdn and hdd wl over 1f out: wknd ins fnl f* **5/1**[2]
46-0 **8** *1 1/4* **Anthea**[23] [1155] 3-8-13 62.............................. AdrianMcCarthy 7 51
(B R Millman) *hld up and bhd: rdn over 3f out: c wd st: n.d* **14/1**
5466 **9** *1/2* **Giddywell**[18] [1256] 3-8-11 60.............................. GrahamGibbons 8 48
(R Hollinshead) *hld up in tch: lost pl 4f out: n.d after* **10/1**
61-0 **10** *1* **Dancing Duo**[14] [1345] 3-8-11 60..............................(v[1]) DeanMcKeown 2 46
(D Shaw) *prom tl rdn and wknd wl over 1f out* **14/1**
005- **11** *hd* **Inimical**[223] [5760] 3-8-8 57.............................. FergusSweeney 9 42
(W S Kittow) *a bhd* **20/1**
3-20 **12** *1 3/4* **Support Fund (IRE)**[16] [1297] 3-9-4 67.............................. StephenCarson 11 48
(Eve Johnson Houghton) *prom: rdn over 3f out: wknd over 2f out* **12/1**
63-5 **13** *13* **Wanessa Tiger (IRE)**[16] [1310] 3-8-9 58.............................. SamHitchcott 1 9
(M R Channon) *prom tl hmpd on ins and lost pl after 1f: mid-div whn rdn 4f out: bhd fnl 2f* **20/1**

1m 50.22s (-1.54) **Going Correction** -0.20s/f (Stan) 13 Ran SP% **118.4**
Speed ratings (Par 96):98,97,96,95,95 92,92,91,90,90 89,88,76
CSF £141.17 CT £1170.66 TOTE £15.50: £4.70, £4.00, £1.40; EX 202.30.
Owner Pat Eddery Racing (Lady Carla) **Bred** Tally-Ho Stud **Trained** Nether Winchendon, Bucks
■ Stewards' Enquiry : K May three-day ban: careless riding (May 25-27)

FOCUS
An ordinary fillies' handicap run at just a fair pace and the front five pulled clear of the others. The winner took advantage of a sliding mark and the form makes sense.

1732 HOTEL & CONFERENCING AT WOLVERHAMPTON RACECOURSE AMATEUR RIDERS' H'CAP 1m 4f 50y(P)
4:50 (4:51) (Class 6) (0-55,55) 4-Y-0+ **£2,307** (£709; £354) **Stalls** Low

Form RPR
-230 **1** **Hugs Destiny (IRE)**[5] [1406] 6-10-13 52............(t) MissAngelaBarnes(5) 6 64
(M A Barnes) *mde all: rdn over 1f out: r.o* **16/1**
2421 **2** *3/4* **Diktatorship (IRE)**[6] [1570] 4-11-6 54 6ex.............................. MrSWalker 9 65
(G A Swinbank) *a.p: chsd wnr 3f out: sn rdn: styd on ins fnl f* **5/2**[1]
1 **3** *5* **Dream River (USA)**[106] [285] 6-11-4 52.............................. MissNCarberry 2 55
(Patrick Martin, Ire) *hld up in tch: hung lft fr over 3f out: one pce fnl 2f* **7/2**[2]
60-4 **4** *3* **York Cliff**[22] [1178] 9-11-1 54.............................. MrBenBrisbourne(5) 1 52
(W M Brisbourne) *hld up in mid-div: rdn over 3f out: no hdwy fnl 2f* **7/1**[3]
0223 **5** *3* **Khanjar (USA)**[104] [302] 7-11-4 55.............................. MrSPearce(3) 12 48
(J Pearce) *s.i.s: t.k.h in rr: hdwy 2f out: nvr nr ldrs* **11/1**
005/ **6** *6* **Benedict Bay**[54] [3910] 5-10-11 52..............................(v) MrDHannig(7) 4 36
(J A Geake) *s.i.s: bhd: rdn 5f out: nvr nr ldrs* **50/1**
0050 **7** *5* **Ganymede**[10] [1451] 6-10-10 51.............................. MissHWarbrick(7) 11 27
(Mrs L J Mongan) *dwlt: a bhd* **20/1**
8 *1/2* **Callitquits (IRE)**[258] [5080] 5-11-1 52.............................. MrWBiddick(3) 5 27
(Jennie Candlish) *chsd wnr tl 3f out: sn wknd* **100/1**
3305 **9** *2 1/2* **Beau Torero (FR)**[61] [677] 9-11-2 55.............................. MrAMerriam(5) 7 26
(B N Pollock) *bhd after 3f: rdn 4f out: sn struggling* **20/1**
0322 **10** *3* **Danelor (IRE)**[19] [1254] 9-11-4 52..............................(p) MrsMMorris 10 18
(D Shaw) *s.i.s: sddle sn slipped: a in rr* **8/1**
4-40 **11** *11* **Lord Laing (USA)**[107] [265] 4-11-2 55..........(v[1]) MissALHutchinson(5) 3 4
(H J Collingridge) *plld hrd in tch: wknd over 3f out* **7/1**[3]
0/0- **R** **Alphun (IRE)**[137] [6959] 5-11-2 50.............................. MrJOwen 8 —
(N B King) *ref to r: tk no part* **14/1**

2m 41.14s (-1.28) **Going Correction** -0.20s/f (Stan) 12 Ran SP% **120.3**
Speed ratings (Par 101):96,95,92,90,88 84,80,80,78,76 69,—
CSF £55.13 CT £181.59 TOTE £26.30: £4.90, £1.60, £2.00; EX 107.10 Place 6 £ 140.89, Place 5 £ 50.47.
Owner J G White **Bred** Matt Gleeson **Trained** Farlam, Cumbria
■ Angela Barnes's first winner on the Flat on only her second ride.
■ Stewards' Enquiry : Mr W Biddick one-day ban: failed to ride to draw (May 29)

FOCUS
A very moderate amateur riders' handicap in which it was crucial to race up with the pace, as the winner made all and the runner-up was always in the leading trio. The winner was rated to his best post-3yo form with the second running his best race for a long time.
T/Plt: £71.10 to a £1 stake. Pool: £49,937.30. 512.15 winning tickets. T/Qpdt: £26.20 to a £1 stake. Pool: £2,875.00. 80.90 winning tickets. KH

1733 - 1735a (Foreign Racing) - See Raceform Interactive

1388 SAINT-CLOUD (L-H)
Monday, May 14

OFFICIAL GOING: Good to soft

1736a PRIX GREFFULHE MITSUBISHI MOTORS (GROUP 2) (C&F) 1m 2f
2:50 (2:50) 3-Y-O **£50,068** (£19,324; £9,223; £6,149; £3,074)

RPR
1 **Quest For Honor**[36] [963] 3-9-2.............................. CSoumillon 2 106
(A Fabre, France) *racd in 4th to st: hrd rdn and styd on fr over 1f out: drvn to ld last strides* **34/10**[2]
2 *snk* **Sagara (USA)**[14] 3-9-2.............................. TGillet 1 105
(J E Pease, France) *dwlt: last to 2f out: r.o steadily to take 2nd last stride* **7/2**[3]
3 *hd* **Sunshine Kid (USA)**[17] [1276] 3-9-2.............................. JimmyFortune 3 105
(J H M Gosden) *a cl up: disp 2nd after 4f: 2nd st: led 1 1/2f out: sn hrd rdn: ct last strides* **4/1**
4 *2 1/2* **Not Just Swing (IRE)**[36] 3-9-2.............................. SPasquier 5 101
(A Fabre, France) *led to 1 1/2f out: one pce* **6/5**[1]
5 *1 1/2* **Hight Blue Sails (FR)**[20] [1233] 3-9-2.............................. ACrastus 4 98
(P Demercastel, France) *first to show then trckd ldr: cl 3rd st: btn 1 1/2f out* **14/1**

2m 9.90s (-6.10) 5 Ran SP% **117.1**
PARI-MUTUEL: WIN 4.40; PL 2.10, 2.10; SF 16.40.
Owner De Moussac Family **Bred** Ship Commodities International **Trained** Chantilly, France

NOTEBOOK
Quest For Honor produced a bold performance under a terrific ride by Soumillon, who timed his challenge to perfection. Fourth in the early stages, he was asked for an effort half way up the straight and, having taken the lead with half a furlong left to run, he just held on from the fast-finishing runner-up.He should make his presence felt in some big races, provided there is a little cut in the ground, and the Jockey Club is a possibility.
Sagara(USA) seemed half asleep when the gates opened and was slowly away. He was being niggled along in the early stages and his jockey was still at work rounding the final turn but, with a furlong left to run, he finally realised what was expected of him, picking up impressively to close the gap on the eventual winner. He should be suited by 1m4f, but is still likely to take his chance in the Jockey Club.
Sunshine Kid(USA) looked the most likely winner when taking control at the furlong marker, but he was just reeled in late on. This looks to be the limit of his stamina.
Not Just Swing(IRE), asked to make all the running, appeared to be going easily down the back straight and rounding the final turn but suddenly ran out of steam soon after entering the straight. This below-par performance is a bit of a mystery.

1315 BRIGHTON (L-H)
Tuesday, May 15

OFFICIAL GOING: Good
Comments restricted owing to poor visibility (sea fret). The runners came towards the stands' rail in all races.
Wind: Fresh, against Weather: Rain

1737 FRIDAY-AD.CO.UK MAIDEN STKS 5f 213y
2:10 (2:11) (Class 5) 3-Y-0+ **£2,817** (£838; £418; £209) **Stalls** Low

Form RPR
0-2 **1** **Express Wish**[31] [1037] 3-9-0 0.............................. LDettori 3 88+
(J Noseda) *mde all: brought field to stands' rail 1/2-way: drew clr fnl 2f: eased fnl 50yds* **4/9**[1]
5 **2** *5* **Spiffing (IRE)**[9] [1501] 3-9-0 0.............................. GeorgeBaker 4 66
(R M Beckett) *3rd 2f out: chsd wnr fnl f: no imp* **22/1**
322- **3** *1 1/2* **Emaara**[224] [5746] 3-8-9 74.............................. MartinDwyer 6 57
(J L Dunlop) *2 l 2nd 2f out: wknd fnl f* **4/1**[2]
23 **4** *1 1/2* **Expensive Art (IRE)**[13] [1403] 3-8-4 0.............................. WilliamBuick(5) 5 52
(N A Callaghan) *5th 2f out: one pce* **12/1**[3]
5 *6* **Western Point (IRE)** 3-9-0 0.............................. JamieMackay 1 39
(Sir Mark Prescott) *n.d fnl f* **16/1**

The Form Book, Raceform Ltd, Compton, RG20 6NL

000- **6** *nk* **Madam Patti**[162] [6702] 4-9-5 38 .... RobertHavlin 7 36
(R Ingram) *4th 2f out: sn wknd* **100/1**
7 *11* **Iron Ruler (IRE)** 3-9-0 0 .... FrankieMcDonald 8 5
(P A Blockley) *s.s* **80/1**
0-00 **8** *15* **Batchworth Blaise**[8] [1541] 4-9-10 42 .... (b) StephenCarson 2 —
(E A Wheeler) *last and no ch whn eased fnl f* **100/1**
1m 11.99s (1.89) **Going Correction** +0.45s/f (Yiel)
WFA 3 from 4yo 10lb **8** Ran SP% **110.4**
Speed ratings (Par 103):105,98,96,94,86 85,71,51
CSF £15.17 TOTE £1.30: £1.02, £3.10, £1.30; EX 11.40.
Owner Peter Mitchell **Bred** Cranford Stud **Trained** Newmarket, Suffolk

FOCUS
Visibility was down to 150 yards, and riders came back in reporting conditions to be unraceable, although they did improve a little. This was a routine Brighton maiden, but the winner looks above-average for the track although he did not need to improve on his bare form. The runner-up was up 5lb on the form of his seasonal bow.
Batchworth Blaise Official explanation: jockey said gelding hung right

1738 WEATHERBYS BLOODSTOCK INSURANCE H'CAP 5f 59y
2:40 (2:49) (Class 5) (0-75,72) 3-Y-O **£2,775** (£830; £415; £207; £103) **Stalls** Low

Form RPR
4402 **1** **Hereford Boy**[14] [1373] 3-9-0 68 .... RobertHavlin 1 73
(D K Ivory) *in ld over 2f out: rdn out* **3/1**[2]
-210 **2** *1 1/4* **Comrade Cotton**[102] [336] 3-8-5 66 .... BradleyRoper(7) 5 66
(N A Callaghan) *4th over 2f out: pushed along and styd on to take 2nd ins fnl f* **11/1**
1-00 **3** *1/2* **Feelin Foxy**[17] [1286] 3-8-7 66 .... (v) PatrickHills(5) 4 64
(D Shaw) *3rd over 2f out: hrd rdn and wnt lft over 1f out: edgd rt fnl f: one pce: eased nr fin* **7/1**
-166 **4** *1/2* **My Drop (IRE)**[6] [1577] 3-9-4 72 .... ChrisCatlin 3 68
(E J O'Neill) *2nd over 2f out: hrd rdn over 1f out: no ex and lost 2nd ins fnl f* **3/1**[2]
2522 **5** *1* **Ioweyou**[17] [1313] 3-7-13 58 oh2 .... (b) WilliamBuick(5) 2 51
(J S Moore) *6th over 2f out: rdn and unable to chal* **11/4**[1]
560- **6** *3* **Shantina's Dream (USA)**[245] [5264] 3-8-7 61 .... SteveDrowne 6 43
(H Morrison) *5th over 2f out: hrd rdn and wknd over 1f out* **6/1**[3]
64.60 secs (2.30) **Going Correction** +0.45s/f (Yiel) **6** Ran SP% **111.8**
Speed ratings (Par 99):99,97,96,95,93 89
CSF £32.74 TOTE £3.80: £1.50, £4.60; EX 38.10.
Owner T G N Burrage **Bred** Mrs L R Burrage **Trained** Radlett, Herts

FOCUS
Visibility restricted to the last two and a half furlongs. A modest handicap, with Hereford Boy up 3lb and the second and third close to their winter sand form.

1739 HARDINGS BAR & CATERING SERVICES LTD (S) STKS 6f 209y
3:10 (3:19) (Class 6) 3-Y-O+ **£1,943** (£578; £288; £144) **Stalls** Low

Form RPR
0000 **1** **Magroom**[16] [1317] 3-8-3 42 .... (v) RichardSmith 12 54
(B R Johnson) *mid-div early: in ld over 1f out: drvn out* **40/1**
0313 **2** *2* **Windy Prospect**[17] [1311] 5-9-7 58 .... (p) FrankieMcDonald 10 59
(P A Blockley) *5th early and over 1f out: styd on take 2nd nr fin* **11/2**[2]
1052 **3** *shd* **Marmooq**[15] [1344] 4-9-7 60 .... ChrisCatlin 5 58
(J Gallagher) *in ld early: 2nd over 1f out: nt qckn fnl f* **5/2**[1]
0-32 **4** *nk* **Marist Madame**[18] [1281] 3-7-12 45 .... DavidKinsella 2 43
(D K Ivory) *3rd early and over 1f out: one pce fnl f* **9/1**
00-0 **5** *1 1/4* **Dancing Deano (IRE)**[19] [1260] 5-9-1 55 .... (v) FergusSweeney 4 48
(R Hollinshead) *6th early and over 1f out: no imp fnl f* **15/2**
-040 **6** *1/2* **Bollywood (IRE)**[15] [1344] 4-8-9 44 ow1 .... RyanBird(7) 1 48
(J J Bridger) *2nd early: 4th over 1f out: hrd rdn: no ex* **33/1**
030- **7** *shd* **Start Of Authority**[176] [6545] 6-9-1 47 .... JimCrowley 15 47
(J Gallagher) *4th early: 7th and btn over 1f out* **7/1**[3]
6000 **8** *3* **Goose Chase**[7] [1562] 5-9-1 54 .... (p) RobertHavlin 13 39
(B J Llewellyn) *towards rr early: 8th and btn over 1f out* **14/1**
5-00 **9** *1 3/4* **Iced Diamond (IRE)**[18] [1280] 8-9-1 52 .... GeorgeBaker 6 34
(W M Brisbourne) *s.s and last early: 10th and n.d over 1f out* **7/1**[3]
0506 **10** *1/2* **Mill By The Stream**[57] [710] 5-9-0 43 .... JackMitchell(7) 16 39
(A M Hales) *7th early: 9th and btn over 1f out* **14/1**
000- **11** *2* **Yorkie**[190] [6372] 8-9-1 43 .... SteveDrowne 14 28
(J Pearce) *mid-div early: n.d over 1f out* **20/1**
-640 **12** *shd* **Show Business (IRE)**[42] [900] 3-7-12 50 ow2 .... (t) JosephWalsh(7) 11 26
(P Butler) *dwlt and in rr early: n.d over 1f out* **50/1**
00 **13** *11* **Nikinoo**[29] [1068] 4-8-10 0 .... JamieMackay 8 —
(B Palling) *dwlt and in rr early: n.d over 1f out* **100/1**
-005 **14** *3/4* **Golden Ribbons**[21] [1213] 3-7-7 40 .... (p) WilliamBuick(5) 7 —
(J R Boyle) *in rr early: n.d over 1f out* **33/1**
1m 25.74s (3.04) **Going Correction** +0.45s/f (Yiel)
WFA 3 from 4yo+ 12lb **14** Ran SP% **120.1**
Speed ratings (Par 101):100,97,97,97,95 95,95,91,89,89 86,86,74,73
CSF £240.40 TOTE £63.40: £17.30, £2.10, £1.60; EX 668.60.The winner was bought in for 6,100gns. Marmooq (no.1) was claimed by M. J Attwater for £5,558.44. Windy Prospect (no.3) was claimed by Mrs L. J. Mongan for £6,017.82.
Owner Tann Racing **Bred** Mrs M Chaworth-Musters **Trained** Ashtead, Surrey

FOCUS
Visibility restricted to the last two and a half furlongs. A competitive non-handicap seller. A shock winner, but the overall form seems sound.
Iced Diamond(IRE) Official explanation: jockey said gelding missed the break

1740 WEATHERBYS PRINTING H'CAP 7f 214y
3:40 (3:48) (Class 6) (0-60,60) 4-Y-O+ **£2,849** (£847; £423; £211) **Stalls** Low

Form RPR
2-56 **1** **Legal Lover (IRE)**[36] [975] 5-8-11 60 .... JackMitchell(7) 4 68
(R Hollinshead) *t.k.h: prom: drvn along and led wl over 1f out: hld on u.p fnl f: all out* **10/1**
0-02 **2** *nk* **Danawi (IRE)**[27] [1086] 4-8-6 48 .... ChrisCatlin 7 56
(M R Hoad) *prom: led 5f out tl wl over 1f out: hrd rdn and rallied wl fnl f: jst hld* **10/1**
25-0 **3** *1 1/2* **Hansomelle (IRE)**[6] [1592] 5-8-5 50 .... NeilChalmers(3) 12 54
(Miss Sheena West) *bhd: hdwy over 2f out: styd on to take 3rd nr fin* **8/1**
4001 **4** *hd* **Jools**[14] [1381] 9-8-11 53 .... SteveDrowne 9 57
(D K Ivory) *in tch: rdn to chse ldrs 2f out: nt qckn fnl f* **16/1**
0350 **5** *nk* **Ellen's Girl (IRE)**[8] [1539] 4-8-5 50 .... (p) RichardKingscote(3) 11 53
(B G Powell) *chsd ldrs: rdn and edgd lft over 1f out: one pce* **10/1**
0030 **6** *1 1/4* **Christmas Truce (IRE)**[5] [1612] 8-8-8 53 .... (b) MarcHalford(3) 15 53
(J J Bridger) *bhd: styd on u.p fnl 2f: nt rch ldrs* **14/1**
3025 **7** *1* **Methusaleh (IRE)**[3] [1673] 4-8-10 57 .... PatrickHills(5) 5 55
(D Shaw) *mid-div: hdwy over 2f out: hrd rdn over 1f out: no ex* **9/2**[1]
0005 **8** *3/4* **Napoletano (GER)**[5] [1612] 6-8-12 54 .... JimCrowley 8 50
(S Dow) *prom tl rdn and btn over 2f out* **11/2**[2]
0-06 **9** *7* **Prince Valentine**[16] [1318] 6-8-10 52 .... (p) FergusSweeney 13 32
(G L Moore) *mid-div: rdn and btn 2f out* **10/1**
3005 **10** *shd* **Shrine Mountain (USA)**[101] [341] 5-8-6 48 .... (v) FrankieMcDonald 14 28
(Miss J S Davis) *t.k.h: led 3f: rdn and qckly lost pl over 3f out* **16/1**
1035 **11** *2* **Ruffie (IRE)**[7] [1567] 4-8-12 59 .... WilliamBuick(5) 1 34
(Miss Gay Kelleway) *towards rr: mod effrt 3f out: wknd wl over 1f out* **16/1**
-600 **12** *5* **Alwariah**[8] [1539] 4-8-8 50 .... JamesDoyle 3 14
(Ms J S Doyle) *mid-div: effrt and hrd rdn 2f out: sn btn: eased whn no ch fnl f* **33/1**
-602 **13** *5* **Green Pirate**[104] [313] 5-9-1 57 .... GeorgeBaker 2 9
(W M Brisbourne) *mid-div tl wknd over 2f out* **7/1**[3]
0-50 **14** *12* **Shinko (IRE)**[31] [1038] 4-8-13 55 .... MartinDwyer 10 —
(Miss J Feilden) *chsd ldrs 5f: eased whn no ch fnl f* **33/1**
1m 38.6s (3.56) **Going Correction** +0.45s/f (Yiel) **14** Ran SP% **123.7**
Speed ratings (Par 101):100,99,98,98,97 96,95,94,87,87 85,80,75,63
CSF £109.43 CT £872.93 TOTE £10.80: £2.80, £3.70, £3.60; EX 137.70.
Owner Tim Leadbeater **Bred** Ballyhane Stud **Trained** Upper Longdon, Staffs

FOCUS
Visibility restricted to the last 3f. A modest but well-contested handicap. Sound but limited form.
Alwariah Official explanation: jockey said filly was not suited by the good ground and trip

1741 BET365 BEST ODDS GUARANTEED ON EVERY RACE H'CAP 1m 3f 196y
4:10 (4:17) (Class 5) (0-70,68) 4-Y-O+ **£2,775** (£830; £415; £207; £103) **Stalls** High

Form RPR
163 **1** **Caucasienne (FR)**[21] [1216] 4-9-2 66 .... MartinDwyer 5 75
(J W Hills) *2nd 4f out and 2f out: drvn to chal fnl f: forged ahd fnl 50yds* **5/2**[1]
-540 **2** *1/2* **Flying Spirit (IRE)**[26] [640] 8-9-4 68 .... (b) GeorgeBaker 3 76
(G L Moore) *in ld 4f out and 2f out: hrd rdn and hung lft fnl f: hdd and nt qckn fnl 50yds* **13/2**
0400 **3** *6* **Makai**[5] [1609] 4-8-4 54 oh2 .... (b) MatthewHenry 7 52
(J J Bridger) *4th 2f out: one pce* **11/1**
6301 **4** *2 1/2* **Bienheureux**[16] [1319] 6-7-13 54 oh1 .... (t) WilliamBuick(5) 2 48
(Miss Gay Kelleway) *3rd 2f out: wknd over 1f out* **3/1**[2]
3120 **5** *8* **Turner's Touch**[10] [1470] 5-9-3 67 .... RobertHavlin 6 49
(G L Moore) *modest 5th and btn over 1f out* **6/1**
6345 **6** *9* **Regency Red (IRE)**[17] [1314] 9-8-1 54 oh1 .... LiamJones(3) 4 21
(W M Brisbourne) *6th and no ch over 1f out* **11/2**[3]
00-0 **7** *6* **Klassen (USA)**[5] [1609] 4-8-7 57 .... (b[1]) FergusSweeney 1 15
(A King) *7th and no ch over 1f out* **12/1**
2m 36.97s (4.77) **Going Correction** +0.45s/f (Yiel) **7** Ran SP% **112.6**
Speed ratings (Par 103):102,101,97,96,90 84,80
CSF £18.50 TOTE £3.00: £1.80, £3.30; EX 13.50.
Owner Jerry Jamgotchian **Bred** Dayton Investments Ltd **Trained** Upper Lambourn, Berks

FOCUS
Visibility was down to 150 yards. A moderate handicap, rated around the runner-up. Not much solid form to go on, but the first two finished clear.

1742 PERTEMPS PEOPLE DEVELOPMENT "HANDS AND HEELS" APPRENTICE H'CAP 1m 1f 209y
4:40 (4:44) (Class 6) (0-60,57) 4-Y-O+ **£1,943** (£578; £288; £144) **Stalls** High

Form RPR
5543 **1** **Liberty Run (IRE)**[16] [1319] 5-9-1 52 .... JamieHamblett 5 61
(Mouse Hamilton-Fairley) *in ld 2f out: pushed out to hold on fnl f* **7/4**[1]
0005 **2** *1/2* **Wassfa**[14] [1379] 4-9-3 57 .... WilliamCarson(3) 7 65
(C E Brittain) *in ld 4f out: 2nd 2f out: pressed wnr fnl f: jst hld* **4/1**[3]
05-0 **3** *9* **Mamichor**[20] [1254] 4-8-10 47 .... JemmaMarshall 2 38
(B R Johnson) *4th 2f out: nt pce of ldng pair* **8/1**
6-00 **4** *1 1/4* **Gala Jackpot (USA)**[7] [1562] 4-8-0 45 .... Julie-AnneCumine(8) 3 34
(W M Brisbourne) *5th 2f out: no imp* **12/1**
3006 **5** *5* **Love You Always (USA)**[21] [1225] 7-8-12 52 .... (t) AmyBaker(3) 9 31
(Miss J Feilden) *6th and btn 2f out* **8/1**
000- **6** *3 1/2* **Zingring**[148] [6852] 8-8-9 49 ow4 .... (b) RyanBird(3) 11 21
(J J Bridger) *2nd 4f out: 3rd 2f out: wknd qckly over 1f out* **16/1**
0022 **7** *3 1/2* **Veba (USA)**[14] [1380] 4-8-10 47 .... LauraReynolds 10 13
(M D I Usher) *7th and no ch fnl 2f* **7/2**[2]
000- **8** *82* **Lucefer (IRE)**[295] [3797] 9-8-0 45 .... (p) MarvinCheung(8) 6 —
(G C H Chung) *wl bhd fnl 2f: sddle slipped* **16/1**
2m 11.2s (8.60) **Going Correction** +0.45s/f (Yiel) **8** Ran SP% **120.3**
Speed ratings (Par 101):83,82,75,74,70 67,64,—
CSF £9.53 CT £45.87 TOTE £3.10: £1.40, £1.70, £2.00; EX 11.70 Place 6 £97.35, Place 5 £86.34.
Owner Fairley Risky **Bred** Mrs Amanda Brudenell And Mr & Mrs R A Simmons **Trained** Bramshill, Hants

FOCUS
Visibility restricted to 2f. A weak hands-and-heels only race run in a very slow time. Course specialist Liberty Run saw off Wassfa, who has slipped a long way in the weights, the pair well clear.
Mamichor Official explanation: jockey said gelding hung left
Lucefer(IRE) Official explanation: jockey said saddle slipped
T/Plt: £56.60 to a £1 stake. Pool: £52,449.00. 676.10 winning tickets. T/Qpdt: £25.90 to a £1 stake. Pool: £2,374.80. 67.70 winning tickets. LM

[1527]NEWCASTLE (L-H)
Tuesday, May 15

OFFICIAL GOING: Good to soft (good in places, 7.5)
Race times suggest that the ground was softer on the round course and the further down the straight course you went.
Wind: Almost nil

1743 HENRY COLBECK FISH & CHIPS NOVICE STKS 6f
2:20 (2:20) (Class 4) 2-Y-O **£3,886** (£1,156; £577; £288) **Stalls** Low

Form RPR
1 **Burnwynd Boy** 2-8-12 .... TomEaves 10 77
(I Semple) *chsd ldrs: rdn and outpcd over 1f out: styd on to ld wl ins fnl f: r.o* **50/1**
2 *1/2* **Abolition (USA)** 2-8-12 .... KDarley 6 76
(M Johnston) *prom: pushed along 1/2-way: hdwy and swtchd lft over 1f out: led briefly ins fnl f: no ex nr fin* **5/2**[1]
53 **3** *1/2* **Runswick Bay**[27] [1087] 2-8-12 .... NCallan 4 74
(G M Moore) *led to ins fnl f: nt qckn* **7/2**[2]

4 1 1/2 **Nine Stories (IRE)** 2-8-12 .... PaulMulrennan 1 70
(J Howard Johnson) *prom: rdn and outpcd whn n.m.r briefly 2f out: kpt on fnl f* **25/1**

31 5 1 **Dan Tucket**[12] [1428] 2-9-2 .... TPO'Shea 7 71
(M R Channon) *cl up gng wl: ev ch over 1f out: rdn and wknd ins fnl f* **7/2**[2]

6 3 **Dream Express (IRE)** 2-8-12 .... PhillipMakin 9 58
(M Dods) *s.i.s: outpcd: hdwy over 1f out: nvr rchd ldrs* **18/1**

7 1 1/4 **Always Ready** 2-8-12 .... RichardHughes 5 54
(C E Brittain) *hld up in tch: rdn 1/2-way: sn no ex* **16/1**

8 1 3/4 **Tharaya** 2-8-7 .... DavidAllan 11 44
(T D Easterby) *s.i.s: outpcd tl sme hdwy over 1f out: nvr on terms* **25/1**

9 28 **Tintorero** 2-8-12 .... JamieSpencer 8 —
(M J Wallace) *hld up in tch: rdn over 2f out: sn wknd* **4/1**[3]

1m 16.93s (1.84) **Going Correction** +0.20s/f (Good) 9 Ran SP% **113.8**
Speed ratings (Par 95):95,94,93,91,90 86,84,82,45
CSF £168.52 TOTE £50.30: £12.50, £1.40, £1.30; EX 325.30 TRIFECTA Not won..
Owner Robert Reid **Bred** Mrs A F Tullie **Trained** Carluke, S Lanarks

FOCUS
Not a strong maiden but a fair pace throughout and a race in which the field raced on the far side. The form is rated through the third and fifth.

NOTEBOOK
Burnwynd Boy, the first foal of a half-sister to winners from 6f to middle-distances, is a medium-sized sort with scope. He is not from a stable normally associated with debut winners in this grade but he showed a good attitude to get off the mark first time. He will stay 7f and may be capable of a bit better.
Abolition(USA) ◆, related to three winners in America, took the eye in the paddock as a rangy sort with plenty of scope and he shaped well, despite his apparent greenness on this racecourse debut. He should stay 7f and appeals strongly as the type to win a similar event with this experience behind him. (op 2-1 tchd 11-4 and 3-1 in a place)
Runswick Bay had run to a similar level in defeat on easy ground at this course and on a quick surface at Beverley last time and seemed to run his race over this longer trip. He is likely to remain vulnerable to the more progressive sorts in this grade but is capable of winning a minor event. (op 3-1 tchd 4-1)
Nine Stories(IRE), out of a 10f winner, looked plenty fit enough on this racecourse debut but was very easy to back and shaped as though a longer trip would see him in a better light. He may do better in due course. (tchd 22-1)
Dan Tucket, who bettered his debut effort when winning over 5f on fast ground on his previous start, travelled like the best horse in the race for much of the way but failed to get home over this trip in the conditions. The return to 5f and a quick surface should see him in a better light. (op 4-1 tchd 10-3)
Dream Express(IRE), a leggy, unfurnished type, was not totally disgraced on this racecourse debut. He should be suited by further in due course but may continue to look vulnerable in this type of event.
Tintorero Official explanation: jockey said colt never travelled

1744 WRIGHT'S PIES CLAIMING STKS 1m 3y(S)
2:50 (2:50) (Class 6) 4-Y-0+ **£1,943** (£578; £288; £144) **Stalls** Low

Form RPR

2111 1 **Blue Sky Thinking (IRE)**[29] [1066] 8-9-7 74 .... PatCosgrave 17 71
(K R Burke) *mde all stands' side: drvn and hung lft over 2f out: hld on wl fnl f* **13/8**[1]

6533 2 1/2 **Penel (IRE)**[19] [1260] 6-8-7 51 .... (p) MickyFenton 10 56
(P T Midgley) *hld up stands' side: hdwy over 2f out: chsd wnr ins fnl f: r.o: hld towards fin* **15/2**[3]

00-0 3 2 1/2 **Procrastinate (IRE)**[99] [364] 5-8-6 42 .... AndrewMullen(3) 16 52
(R F Fisher) *prom stands' side: effrt over 2f out: one pce fnl f* **100/1**

2-46 4 1 1/4 **Primo Way**[9] [1490] 6-9-1 74 .... TomEaves 12 55
(I Semple) *prom stands' side: effrt over 2f out: no ex fnl f* **4/1**[2]

2006 5 hd **Nevinstown (IRE)**[8] [1527] 7-8-11 43 .... RichardHughes 7 51
(C Grant) *s.i.s: bhd stands' side tl styd on fnl 2f: nvr rchd ldrs* **22/1**

3-00 6 12 **Coronation Flight**[14] [1380] 4-8-3 46 .... GregFairley(3) 4 18
(F P Murtagh) *chsd far side ldr: led that gp 3f out: no ch w stands' side* **20/1**

-000 7 3 **Everest (IRE)**[17] [1308] 10-9-1 70 .... DO'Donohoe 5 20
(B Ellison) *in tch far side: outpcd 1/2-way: sme late hdwy to go 2nd in that gp ins fnl f: nvr on terms* **4/1**[2]

000- 8 2 1/2 **Bottomless Wallet**[59] [4405] 6-8-4 35 .... PaulFessey 8 4
(F Watson) *led far side to 3f out: sn btn* **100/1**

0000 9 nk **Contra Mundum (USA)**[3] [1671] 4-8-11 50 .... (p) PaulMulrennan 14 10
(B S Rothwell) *towards rr stands' side: drvn 1/2-way: nvr on terms* **40/1**

60-5 10 3 **Cashema (IRE)**[8] [1527] 6-8-3 36 .... (t) JamesRogers(7) 1 2
(James Moffatt) *towards rr far side: struggling 1/2-way: nvr on terms* **33/1**

00-0 11 2 1/2 **Time Marches On**[8] [1527] 9-9-0 44 .... JamesReveley(7) 2 7
(K G Reveley) *in tch far side tl wknd over 3f out* **25/1**

100- 12 5 **Lewis Lloyd (IRE)**[238] [5445] 4-9-5 50 .... DavidAllan 15 —
(R E Barr) *cl up stands' side: rdn 3f out: sn btn* **25/1**

000- 13 9 **Noble Edge**[186] [5445] 4-9-7 46 .... FTahir 11 —
(Karen McLintock) *towards rr stands' side: struggling 1/2-way: sn btn* **40/1**

-000 14 21 **Bold Tiger (IRE)**[8] [1527] 4-8-0 41 .... (tp) SamuelDrury(7) 13 —
(Miss Tracy Waggott) *in tch stands' side to 1/2-way: sn rdn and wknd* **50/1**

1m 46.42s (4.52) **Going Correction** +0.60s/f (Yiel) 14 Ran SP% **118.4**
Speed ratings (Par 101):101,100,98,96,96 84,81,79,78,75 73,68,59,38
CSF £12.70 TOTE £2.80: £1.10, £1.80, £8.90; EX 15.80 TRIFECTA Not won..
Owner Triple Trio Partnership **Bred** Thomas J Murphy **Trained** Middleham Moor, N Yorks

FOCUS
A run-of-the-mill event in which the larger stands'-side group held a clear edge over the quintet that raced far side. Poor form overall, although it makes some sense through the third and the fifth. Blue Sky Thinking was 8lb off his recent sand form.

1745 GOLDENSHEAF/HENRY JONES/DINAISH & CHIPS H'CAP 2m 19y
3:20 (3:20) (Class 5) (0-70,70) 4-Y-0+ **£3,562** (£1,059; £529; £264) **Stalls** Low

Form RPR

015 1 **Rocknest Island (IRE)**[7] [1556] 4-8-1 53 .... (p) AndrewMullen(3) 6 61
(P D Niven) *in tch: hdwy over 4f out: sn drvn along: effrt and ev ch over 1f out: led wl ins fnl f: r.o* **13/2**

0-00 2 1/2 **Toparudi**[22] [1199] 6-9-0 60 .... JimmyQuinn 9 70
(M H Tompkins) *stdd s: hld up: swtchd lft and hdwy to ld over 1f out: hdd and no ex wl ins fnl f* **12/1**

-042 3 1/2 **Madiba**[21] [1216] 8-8-5 51 oh1 .... FrancisNorton 3 54
(P Howling) *chsd ldrs: lost pl 5f out: outpcd over 2f out: kpt on fnl f: no imp: fin 4th: plcd 3rd* **4/1**[2]

0236 4 1 1/2 **Toni Alcala**[11] [1457] 8-8-5 51 oh2 .... (p) PaulFessey 5 52
(R F Fisher) *cl up: ev ch over 2f out: wknd over 1f out: fin 5th: plcd 4th* **6/1**[3]

0-24 5 hd **Let It Be**[8] [1532] 6-8-8 61 .... DanielleMcCreery(7) 7 62
(K G Reveley) *t.k.h: cl up: led 7f out to over 1f out: sn wknd: fin 6th: plcd 5th* **10/1**

/61- 6 5 **Aston Lad**[19] [6161] 6-8-6 52 oh4 ow1 .... KDarley 10 47
(Micky Hammond) *s.i.s: hld up: pushed along 3f out: sn btn: fin 7th: plcd 6th* **3/1**[1]

4/0 7 19 **Fixateur**[23] [1181] 5-9-10 70 .... JamieSpencer 4 42
(J G Given) *hld up in tch: rdn 4f out: sn btn: fin 8th: plcd 7th* **12/1**

0-05 8 1 3/4 **Scarrabus (IRE)**[10] [1479] 6-8-3 52 oh6 ow1 .... (p) GregFairley(3) 2 22
(A Crook) *set stdy pce: hdd 7f out: wknd fr over 3f out: fin 9th: plcd 8th* **50/1**

225- D 7 **Onyergo (IRE)**[193] [6321] 5-9-0 60 .... PhillipMakin 8 63
(J R Weymes) *hld up in tch: hdwy and prom over 1f out: outpcd fnl f: fin 3rd, 1/2l & 1/2l: disq and plcd last - rdr failed to weigh-in* **6/1**[3]

3m 48.75s (13.55) **Going Correction** +0.55s/f (Yiel)
WFA 4 from 5yo+ 3lb 9 Ran SP% **113.3**
Speed ratings (Par 103):88,87,84,83,83 80,71,70,84
CSF £79.02 CT £349.91 TOTE £8.40: £2.50, £3.20, £1.30; EX 86.40 TRIFECTA Not won..
Owner Mrs Kate Young **Bred** G Martin **Trained** Barton-le-Street, N Yorks
■ Stewards' Enquiry : Phillip Makin seven-day ban: failed to weigh in (May 26-Jun 1)
Andrew Mullen caution: used whip in the incorrect place

FOCUS
A run-of-the-mill event in which the pace was on the steady side and this bare form does not look reliable. The winner is unexposed as a stayer and the original third looks the best guide.
Aston Lad Official explanation: jockey said gelding was unsuited by the slow early pace

1746 CAPE HADDIE FISH & CHIPS MEDIAN AUCTION MAIDEN STKS 1m 2f 32y
3:50 (3:50) (Class 6) 3-Y-O **£1,943** (£578; £288; £144) **Stalls** Low

Form RPR

2 1 **Secret Tune**[15] [1358] 3-9-3 .... RichardHughes 9 83+
(Pat Eddery) *pressed ldr: led 3f out: rdn and r.o wl fnl f* **11/10**[1]

633- 2 1 1/2 **Four Miracles**[194] [6303] 3-8-12 63 .... JimmyQuinn 8 69
(M H Tompkins) *hld up in tch: hdwy over 2f out: edgd lft and ev ch over 1f out: one pce ins fnl f* **7/2**[2]

3 5 **Ducal Pip Squeak** 3-8-12 .... PhillipMakin 3 59
(M Dods) *s.i.s: hld up: hdwy and prom wl over 1f out: sn rdn and nt qckn* **33/1**

2 4 1 1/4 **Serhaaphim**[21] [1220] 3-8-12 .... HayleyTurner 5 57
(M L W Bell) *chsd ldrs tl rdn and no ex fr 2f out* **11/2**[3]

6 5 2 1/2 **Carefree Flapper**[15] [1348] 3-8-12 .... JamieSpencer 4 52
(G A Swinbank) *hld up: rdn 4f out: hung lft over 2f out: nvr rchd ldrs* **14/1**

-25 6 8 **Acapulco Bay**[19] [1261] 3-9-3 .... TomEaves 10 41
(Miss J A Camacho) *t.k.h: hld up in tch: drvn over 3f out: sn btn* **16/1**

00-0 7 1/2 **Blue Jet (USA)**[17] [1303] 3-9-3 50 .... VHalliday 6 40
(R M Whitaker) *chsd ldrs tl rdn and wknd over 2f out* **100/1**

50-3 8 10 **Spirit Of Ecstacy**[17] [1303] 3-8-12 62 .... NCallan 7 15
(G M Moore) *led to 3f out: wknd over 1f out* **8/1**

2m 17.85s (6.05) **Going Correction** +0.55s/f (Yiel) 8 Ran SP% **112.8**
Speed ratings (Par 97):97,95,91,90,88 82,82,74
CSF £4.84 TOTE £1.80: £1.10, £1.50, £5.50; EX 5.80 Trifecta £115.40 Pool: £338.11 - 2.08 winning tickets..
Owner K Abdulla **Bred** Juddmonte Farms Ltd **Trained** Nether Winchendon, Bucks
■ Pat Eddery's first winner for Khalid Abdullah, for whom he rode with so much success.

FOCUS
Not a competitive event and one in which the pace was just fair. The winner looks better than the bare form and can improve but but he did not beat much.
Acapulco Bay Official explanation: jockey said gelding ran too free early
Spirit Of Ecstacy Official explanation: jockey said filly had a breathing problem

1747 HEINZ SQUEEZEME FISH & CHIPS H'CAP 7f
4:20 (4:22) (Class 5) (0-75,75) 4-Y-O+ **£3,886** (£1,156; £577; £288) **Stalls** Low

Form RPR

11- 1 **Braddock (IRE)**[388] [1141] 4-9-0 71 .... PaulFessey 5 87+
(T D Barron) *mde all in centre: hrd pressed over 1f out: kpt on wl fnl f* **5/1**[1]

30-0 2 2 **King Harson**[11] [1458] 8-9-4 75 .... PatCosgrave 6 85
(J D Bethell) *pressed wnr in centre: ev ch over 1f out: no ex ins fnl f* **14/1**

000- 3 1 1/2 **Neon Blue**[179] [6507] 6-8-7 69 .... MichaelJStainton(5) 4 75
(R M Whitaker) *prom in centre: effrt over 2f out: one pce fnl f* **50/1**

0-06 4 hd **Viva Volta**[7] [1555] 4-8-12 69 .... DavidAllan 3 75
(T D Easterby) *chsd centre ldrs: drvn over 2f out: kpt on same pce fnl f* **16/1**

6-00 5 1 1/2 **Middlemarch (IRE)**[24] [1145] 7-9-3 74 .... (b) PhillipMakin 15 76
(J S Goldie) *led stands' side gp: rdn and kpt on u.p fr over 1f out* **12/1**

0-30 6 1 **The Osteopath (IRE)**[21] [1223] 4-8-13 70 .... (b) FrancisNorton 9 69+
(M Dods) *hld up stands' side: shkn up and hdwy over 1f out: nvr nrr* **6/1**[2]

0-00 7 nk **Stellite**[11] [1458] 7-8-8 72 .... GaryBartley(7) 11 71
(J S Goldie) *prom stands' side: effrt 2f out: no ex fnl f* **9/1**

6-4 8 nk **Crosby Vision**[25] [1133] 4-8-13 70 .... NCallan 7 68
(J R Weymes) *hld up in tch in centre: effrt over 2f out: no imp fnl f* **25/1**

0-00 9 nk **Efidium**[17] [1287] 9-8-5 67 .... LukeMorris(5) 8 64
(N Bycroft) *bhd in centre: drvn 3f out: nvr rchd ldrs* **22/1**

000- 10 1 1/2 **Marshman (IRE)**[188] [6397] 8-9-1 75 .... SaleemGolam(3) 2 68
(M H Tompkins) *hld up in centre: rdn over 2f out: n.d* **9/1**

000- 11 2 1/2 **Looks Could Kill (USA)**[242] [5336] 5-9-1 72 .... KDarley 14 69+
(E J Alston) *hld up stands' side: effrt and rdn over 2f out: nvr rchd ldrs* **10/1**

03-0 12 shd **Regal Raider (IRE)**[17] [1287] 4-9-1 72 .... TomEaves 1 58
(I Semple) *hld up in tch in centre: effrt on outside of that gp over 2f out: wknd fnl f* **40/1**

0-40 13 3 **Fair Shake (IRE)**[21] [1223] 7-8-8 65 .... (v) PaulMulrennan 12 44
(Karen McLintock) *hld up stands' side: drvn over 3f out: n.d* **20/1**

0-15 14 3 1/2 **Sir Orpen (IRE)**[7] [1555] 4-8-13 70 .... JimmyQuinn 13 40
(T D Barron) *prom stands' side tl wknd over 2f out* **9/1**

00-5 15 1 3/4 **Kirkby's Treasure**[18] [1280] 9-8-8 65 .... JamieSpencer 17 30
(G A Swinbank) *hld up stands' side: rdn over 2f out: n.d* **8/1**[3]

1006 16 9 **Lii Najma**[14] [1382] 4-8-10 67 ow1 .... RichardHughes 16 9
(C E Brittain) *chsd stands' side ldrs tl rdn and wknd over 2f out* **16/1**

The Form Book, Raceform Ltd, Compton, RG20 6NL

330- **17** *3 1/2* **Queen's Composer (IRE)**[283] 4153 4-9-1 **75**........... MarkLawson(3) 10 7
(B Smart) *midfield on outside of stands' side gp: rdn and wknd fr 3f out* **22/1**

1m 29.17s (1.15) **Going Correction** +0.25s/f (Good) **17** Ran SP% **129.0**
Speed ratings (Par 103):103,100,99,98,97 95,95,95,94,93 90,90,86,82,80 70,66
CSF £72.58 CT £2057.26 TOTE £4.50: £2.10, £4.50, £8.90, £3.80; EX 99.80 TRIFECTA Not won..
Owner James M Egan **Bred** Corduff Stud And J Corcoran **Trained** Maunby, N Yorks

FOCUS
A competitive event in which the two groups that raced centre to stands'-side merged in the last half of the contest. The pace was fair and, although the first four home raced centrally, this form looks sound and should prove reliable. There is more to come from the unexposed winner.
The Osteopath(IRE) Official explanation: jockey said gelding missed the break
Kirkby's Treasure Official explanation: jockey said gelding never travelled

1748 Q PLATINUM & Q SILVER A.A.K. FISH & CHIPS FILLIES' H'CAP 5f
4:50 (4:50) (Class 6) (0-65,64) 3-Y-O+ **£2,590** (£770; £385; £192) **Stalls** Low

Form RPR
-500 **1** **Champagne Cracker**[9] 1493 6-9-0 **52**............................ PhillipMakin 5 65
(M Dods) *mde all: rdn over 1f out: edgd rt and r.o strly* **11/1**
0665 **2** *2 1/2* **Katie Boo (IRE)**[5] 1596 5-8-12 **50**................................ FrancisNorton 13 54
(A Berry) *cl up: effrt and chsd wnr over 1f out: kpt on same pce fnl f* **12/1**
0-40 **3** *2* **Rothesay Dancer**[7] 1557 4-9-4 **56**................................ JamieSpencer 10 53
(J S Goldie) *hld up: hdwy over 1f out: kpt on fnl f: no imp* **8/1**
6-43 **4** *1 3/4* **Dorn Dancer (IRE)**[11] 1459 5-9-7 **59**............................ PatCosgrave 2 50
(D W Barker) *prom: effrt over 2f out: no ex over 1f out* **7/4**[1]
230- **5** *1/2* **Princess Ileana (IRE)**[234] 5528 3-9-3 **64**.................. PaulMulrennan 14 53
(K R Burke) *prom: drvn 1/2-way: no ex over 1f out* **14/1**
24-0 **6** *3/4* **Petite Mac**[43] 895 7-9-4 **63**................................... SuzzanneFrance(7) 7 49
(N Bycroft) *bhd and rdn: hdwy 2f out: no imp fnl f* **7/1**[3]
454 **7** *3 1/2* **Muara**[13] 1404 5-9-8 **60**.. TomEaves 8 33
(D W Barker) *chsd wnr: rdn 1/2-way: wknd over 1f out* **10/1**
0626 **8** *1 1/4* **Jabbara (IRE)**[76] 586 4-8-11 **49** oh1....................(b) RichardHughes 11 18
(C E Brittain) *prom tl rdn and wknd fr 2f out* **5/1**[2]
54-0 **9** *1/2* **Only A Grand**[20] 1238 3-8-8 **60**............................. NataliaGemelova(5) 4 27
(R Bastiman) *towards rr: drvn 1/2-way: sn outpcd* **25/1**
3040 **10** *3* **Boppys Dream**[22] 1197 5-8-11 **49** oh4.............................(p) MickyFenton 1 5
(P T Midgley) *sn pushed along in rr: no imp fr 1/2-way* **33/1**
50-0 **11** *1 1/2* **Superjain**[20] 1238 3-8-12 **59**.. NCallan 6 10
(J M Jefferson) *dwlt: sn rdn in rr: nvr on terms* **40/1**
-410 **12** *22* **Tajjree**[109] 251 4-8-10 **53**...............................(tp) MichaelJStainton(5) 3 —
(Miss K B Boutflower) *dwlt: n.d* **16/1**

61.58 secs (0.08) **Going Correction** -0.025s/f (Good)
WFA 3 from 4yo+ 9lb **12** Ran SP% **123.5**
Speed ratings (Par 98):98,94,90,88,87 86,80,78,77,72 70,35
CSF £139.31 CT £1146.31 TOTE £16.20: £3.30, £2.70, £3.70; EX 140.50 Trifecta £234.40 Part won. Pool: £330.27 - 0.80 winning tickets. Place 6 £294.99, Place 5 £164.04.
Owner Jim McLaren **Bred** P Baugh **Trained** Denton, Co Durham
■ Stewards' Enquiry : Phillip Makin one-day ban: failed to ride to draw (May 26)

FOCUS
A modest handicap in which the winner got a flyer from the stalls and never looked like being pegged back. The field raced in the centre and the pace was sound. The winner is rated back to last year's best and the form looks sound.
Tajjree Official explanation: jockey said filly was unsuited by the good to soft (good in places) ground; trainer said, following examination, filly was found to have pulled muscles in hindquarters
T/Jkpt: Not won. T/Plt: £387.90 to a £1 stake. Pool: £61,379.50. 115.50 winning tickets. T/Qpdt: £72.70 to a £1 stake. Pool: £3,224.70. 32.80 winning tickets. RY

[1713] SOUTHWELL (L-H)
Tuesday, May 15

OFFICIAL GOING: Standard
Wind: Almost nil Weather: Overcast

1749 BETDIRECTPOKER.COM $50,000 FREEROLL MEDIAN AUCTION MAIDEN STKS 7f (F)
2:00 (2:00) (Class 5) 3-5-Y-O **£3,238** (£963; £481; £240) **Stalls** Low

Form RPR
03 **1** **Sweet Gale (IRE)**[15] 1343 3-8-7 ....(t) TPQueally 11 82+
(J Noseda) *hld up: hdwy over 4f out: led on bit over 2f out: clr over 1f out: eased fnl f* **1/1**[1]
460- **2** *2 1/2* **Kunte Kinteh**[243] 5307 3-8-12 68.......................... SilvestreDeSousa 7 67
(D Nicholls) *prom: racd keenly: rdn 1/2-way: styd on same pce fnl 2f: flattered by proximity to wnr* **9/2**[2]
6-0 **3** *1 3/4* **Karmest**[17] 1312 3-8-8 ow1................................... RobbieFitzpatrick 13 58
(E S McMahon) *chsd ldr tl led 3f out: sn rdn: hdd and outpcd* **10/1**
00 **4** *11* **Kyburg**[8] 1523 3-8-7 .... EddieAhern 5 28+
(P F I Cole) *prom: lost pl 6f out: n.d after* **28/1**
00 **5** *1 3/4* **Pearl Valley**[25] 1136 3-8-7 ....(e[1]) PaulHanagan 6 24
(R A Fahey) *prom: rdn over 4f out: wknd 1/2-way* **40/1**
5 **6** *nk* **Goldan Jess (IRE)**[15] 1348 3-8-12 67......................... DanielTudhope 3 28
(D Carroll) *mid-div: rdn 1/2-way: sn wknd* **11/1**
0- **7** *nk* **Tora Warning**[299] 3677 3-8-12 .... StephenDonohoe 8 27
(John A Harris) *sn outpcd* **100/1**
0 **8** *3* **My Mentor (IRE)**[6] 1587 3-8-12 .... SebSanders 12 19
(Sir Mark Prescott) *sn outpcd* **7/1**[3]
0/ **9** *shd* **Dark Chapel**[603] 5356 4-9-3 .... HaddenFrost(7) 10 19
(W J H Ratcliffe) *sn outpcd* **100/1**
5 **10** *1 1/2* **Whithorn**[12] 1426 4-9-7 .... AndrewElliott(3) 1 15
(J Balding) *s.s: outpcd* **22/1**
0-0 **11** *3/4* **Maiden Investor**[17] 1312 4-9-5 .... DeanMcKeown 9 8
(M S Saunders) *sn led: hdd 3f out: wknd 2f out* **100/1**
65 **12** *1* **Musical Box**[6] 1587 3-8-7 .... AdrianMcCarthy 4 6
(G Prodromou) *s.i.s: outpcd* **33/1**
0 **13** *6* **Jaffna**[8] 1537 5-9-5 .... J-PGuillambert 14 —
(R T Phillips) *chsd ldrs: rdn over 4f out: wknd 1/2-way* **66/1**

1m 29.47s (-1.33) **Going Correction** -0.225s/f (Stan)
WFA 3 from 4yo+ 12lb **13** Ran SP% **115.7**
Speed ratings (Par 103):98,95,93,80,78 78,77,74,74,72 71,70,63
CSF £4.68 TOTE £1.70: £1.10, £1.60, £3.20; EX 5.90.
Owner Vimal Khosla **Bred** Rozelle Bloodstock **Trained** Newmarket, Suffolk

FOCUS
A maiden lacking strength in depth despite the size of the field. The winner won pulling a cart, rated value for 8l, and with the front three pulling miles clear, the others are going to have to improve a ton in order to win a race.
Whithorn Official explanation: jockey said gelding was slowly away and failed to travel thereafter

1750 BETDIRECT.COM GET INVOLVED CLASSIFIED STKS 1m (F)
2:30 (2:30) (Class 7) 3-Y-O+ **£2,047** (£604; £302) **Stalls** Low

Form RPR
06-4 **1** **Shandelight (IRE)**[21] 1210 3-8-7 45.........................(p) RoystonFfrench 3 52
(Mrs A Duffield) *chsd ldrs: led over 2f out: rdn and hung rt fr over 1f out: styd on* **6/1**[3]
-034 **2** *1* **Don Pasquale**[1] 1715 5-8-13 44.. SoniaEaton(7) 8 53
(J T Stimpson) *sn pushed along in rr: hdwy over 2f out: rdn over 1f out: hung rt and ev ch ins fnl f: unable qck nr fin* **9/2**[1]
6565 **3** *2 1/2* **Birdie Birdie**[46] 832 3-8-7 45.......................................(v) PaulHanagan 14 44
(R A Fahey) *mid-div: hdwy over 4f out: rdn and ev ch 2f out: edgd lft over 1f out: styd on same pce* **13/2**
-604 **4** *3* **Ming Vase**[15] 1350 5-9-6 44.. LeeEnstone 7 40
(P T Midgley) *prom: rdn 1/2-way: wknd fnl f* **5/1**[2]
0050 **5** *3 1/2* **Barzak (IRE)**[14] 1379 7-9-6 43......................................(bt) DaleGibson 5 32
(S R Bowring) *sn outpcd: r.o ins fnl f: nrst fin* **6/1**[3]
6 *1* **Faiths Perfection (IRE)**[215] 5930 4-9-3 44............... JerryO'Dwyer(3) 10 30
(John Rafferty, Ire) *mid-div: hdwy u.p 1/2-way: nt run on fnl 2f* **10/1**
4000 **7** *3* **Flamestone**[41] 912 3-8-8 45 ow1..................................(b) DarryllHolland 2 21
(J D Bethell) *led over 5f: rdn and wknd over 1f out: eased ins fnl f* **14/1**
0-00 **8** *2* **Peak Seasons (IRE)**[5] 1570 4-9-6 45.......................(b) AdrianMcCarthy 9 19
(M C Chapman) *sn pushed along in rr: n.d* **33/1**
00-U **9** *nk* **Katsumoto (IRE)**[46] 833 4-9-3 45........................ PatrickMathers(3) 13 18
(A J McCabe) *hld up: a in rr* **33/1**
060- **10** *3 1/2* **Elle's Angel (IRE)**[231] 5596 3-8-7 45.. EddieAhern 6 7
(E J O'Neill) *chsd ldrs over 5f* **9/1**
0-00 **11** *3 1/2* **Bond Free Spirit (IRE)**[25] 1136 4-9-3 45............... DuranFentiman(3) 11 —
(G R Oldroyd) *s.i.s: outpcd* **20/1**
-650 **12** *nk* **Always A Story**[55] 721 5-9-6 45... PaulEddery 4 —
(Miss D Mountain) *chsd ldrs over 4f* **16/1**
0600 **13** *5* **Fareham Creek**[18] 1281 3-8-7 44...................................(p) JohnEgan 12 —
(D K Ivory) *prom to 1/2-way* **33/1**

1m 44.51s (-0.09) **Going Correction** -0.225s/f (Stan)
WFA 3 from 4yo+ 13lb **13** Ran SP% **122.0**
Speed ratings (Par 97):91,90,87,84,81 80,77,75,74,71 67,67,62
CSF £32.54 TOTE £6.60: £1.70, £2.20, £1.50; EX 41.50.
Owner Lee Bolingbroke David Andrew Rod Jordan **Bred** Limestone And Tara Studs **Trained** Constable Burton, N Yorks

FOCUS
A poor contest and a moderate time, even for a race like this. The winner is going the right way at a lowly level.

1751 BETDIRECTPOKER.COM COME AND 'AVE SOME H'CAP 1m (F)
3:00 (3:02) (Class 4) (0-85,86) 4-Y-O+ **£5,181** (£1,541; £770; £384) **Stalls** Low

Form RPR
00-5 **1** **Genari**[17] 1308 4-8-4 **71** oh1.. JoeFanning 5 90
(P F I Cole) *chsd ldr: led over 2f out: rdn out* **6/1**[3]
0211 **2** *3* **Luckylover**[7] 1568 4-9-2 **86** 6ex..............................(t) JerryO'Dwyer(3) 1 98
(M G Quinlan) *led: rdn and hdd over 2f out: styd on same pce fnl f* **11/10**[1]
4642 **3** *6* **Final Tune (IRE)**[18] 1283 4-8-2 **72**................................ PatrickMathers(3) 8 70
(Miss M E Rowland) *hld up: hdwy u.p fnl 2f: nvr trbld ldrs* **8/1**
020- **4** *hd* **Yakimov (USA)**[312] 3255 8-8-13 **80**.. VinceSlattery 7 78
(D J Wintle) *hld up: rdn over 3f out: styng on whn hung rt ins fnl f: nvr trbld ldrs* **20/1**
110- **5** *4* **Sotik Star (IRE)**[147] 6868 4-9-0 **81**......................................(t) EddieAhern 4 70
(P J Makin) *s.i.s: sn chsng ldrs: rdn and wknd 2f out* **5/1**[2]
06-5 **6** *2* **Bijou Dan**[29] 1069 6-8-1 **71** oh6.................................(b) DuranFentiman(3) 2 55
(D W Thompson) *hld up: rdn over 3f out: sn wknd* **33/1**
120- **7** *4* **Advancement**[268] 4634 4-8-5 **72**... PaulHanagan 6 47
(R A Fahey) *prom: rdn 1/2-way: sn wknd* **6/1**[3]
/0-0 **8** *2 1/2* **Mistress Bailey (IRE)**[3] 1649 4-9-4 **85**.................................. DeanMcKeown 3 54
(D Shaw) *chsd ldrs 5f* **40/1**

1m 40.56s (-4.04) **Going Correction** -0.225s/f (Stan) **8** Ran SP% **114.1**
Speed ratings (Par 105):111,108,102,101,97 95,91,89
CSF £12.81 CT £53.36 TOTE £7.70: £2.10, £1.10, £1.60; EX 13.30.
Owner R A Instone **Bred** R A Instone **Trained** Whatcombe, Oxon

FOCUS
A decent handicap and with Luckylover in the field there was never going to be any hanging about. Apart from the front pair nothing else ever got into it and the form looks rock solid.

1752 ROSELAND GROUP SUPPORTING THE NSPCC H'CAP 1m 6f (F)
3:30 (3:30) (Class 5) (0-70,70) 4-Y-O+ **£3,886** (£1,156; £577; £288) **Stalls** Low

Form RPR
3435 **1** **Eforetta (GER)**[8] 1526 5-8-12 **61**.................................... SamHitchcott 2 71
(D J Wintle) *chsd ldrs: led over 3f out: drvn out* **5/1**[2]
-120 **2** *2* **Arsad (IRE)**[20] 1253 4-9-6 **70**.. SebSanders 4 77
(C E Brittain) *a.p: rdn over 3f out: chsd wnr fnl f: styd on same pce* **5/1**[2]
1250 **3** *1/2* **Three Thieves (UAE)**[20] 1253 4-9-6 **70**................................ JohnEgan 6 76
(M S Saunders) *hld up: hdwy over 3f out: sn rdn: styd on* **7/1**[3]
455- **4** *1 3/4* **Cotton Eyed Joe (IRE)**[258] 4935 6-9-3 **66**.................. DeanMcKeown 7 70
(G A Swinbank) *hld up: hdwy over 4f out: rdn over 2f out: no ex fnl f* **3/1**[1]
30 **5** *5* **Arafan (IRE)**[3] 1683 5-9-7 **70**..................................(b) DarryllHolland 1 67
(Dr R D P Newland) *s.i.s: sn drvn along and prom: led over 11f out: hdd 8f out: rn in snatches after: rdn over 2f out: nt run on* **7/1**[3]
050- **6** *5* **Gifted Musician**[220] 5815 5-9-6 **69**..................................... EddieAhern 5 59+
(H Morrison) *sn led: hdd over 11f out: led 8f out: hdd over 3f out: rdn and wknd over 1f out* **8/1**
1130 **7** *27* **Victory Quest (IRE)**[35] 994 7-9-0 **63**..............................(v) PaulHanagan 8 15
(Mrs S Lamyman) *hld up: hdwy over 4f out: wknd 3f out* **9/1**
/0-6 **8** *21* **Scott**[14] 1378 6-8-7 **56**.. JoeFanning 3 —
(J Jay) *prom over 9f* **16/1**

3m 6.93s (-2.67) **Going Correction** -0.225s/f (Stan)
WFA 4 from 5yo+ 1lb **8** Ran SP% **110.3**
Speed ratings (Par 103):98,96,96,95,92 89,74,62
CSF £27.90 CT £163.00 TOTE £3.30: £1.10, £1.80, £2.90; EX 18.10.
Owner John W Egan **Bred** Gestut Rietberg **Trained** Naunton, Gloucs

FOCUS
A routine staying handicap in which the pace was modest. Sound form, rated through the second and third.

1753 BETDIRECTPOKER.COM $50,000 FREEROLL H'CAP — 6f (F)

4:00 (4:01) (Class 6) (0-55,55) 4-Y-0+ £3,241 (£957; £478) Stalls Low

Form RPR

0112 **1** **Union Jack Jackson (IRE)**[17] 1309 5-9-3 **55**.......(b) StephenDonohoe 5 66+
(John A Harris) *chsd ldrs: rdn to ld over 1f out: hung rt ins fnl f: drvn out* **8/1**[3]

3346 **2** *2* **Favouring (IRE)**[15] 1349 5-8-10 **48**................................(b) SebSanders 7 53
(M C Chapman) *chsd ldrs: led over 4f out: rdn and hdd over 1f out: styd on same pce* **6/1**[1]

0562 **3** *nk* **Mister Incredible**[15] 1349 4-8-9 **52**.......................(v) KevinGhunowa(5) 11 56
(J M Bradley) *w ldrs: rdn and ev ch over 1f out: no ex ins fnl f* **13/2**[2]

-502 **4** *nk* **Wainwright (IRE)**[1] 1718 7-9-0 **52**..........................(t) SimonWhitworth 8 55
(P A Blockley) *mid-div: hdwy u.p over 2f out: nt rch ldrs* **6/1**[1]

0051 **5** *nk* **Christian Bendix**[13] 1400 5-9-0 **52**..............................(p) IanMongan 9 54
(P Howling) *led: hdd over 4f out: sn rdn: outpcd over 2f out: styd on ins fnl f* **11/1**

1040 **6** *1 3/4* **Blythe Spirit**[21] 1221 8-9-3 **55**..(v) PaulHanagan 6 52
(R A Fahey) *mid-div: rdn 1/2-way: nvr trbld ldrs* **11/1**

4600 **7** *3/4* **Blakeshall Quest**[12] 1436 7-8-12 **50**.......................(b) J-PGuillambert 10 44
(R Brotherton) *sn pushed along in rr: swtchd rt over 2f out: styd on ins fnl f: nvr nrr* **40/1**

4265 **8** *shd* **Shava**[21] 1227 7-8-13 **51**.. VinceSlattery 14 45
(H J Evans) *chsd ldrs: rdn over 2f out: wknd fnl f* **16/1**

0233 **9** *3/4* **Mind Alert**[44] 866 6-9-0 **52**.......................................(v) DeanMcKeown 13 43
(D Shaw) *swtchd lft sn after s: hld up: sme hdwy over 1f out: n.d* **16/1**

1054 **10** *1/2* **Soba Jones**[19] 1262 10-9-1 **53**... EddieAhern 12 43
(J Balding) *mid-div: hung rt 3f out: n.d* **12/1**

600- **11** *2 1/2* **Rondo**[218] 5865 4-9-0 **52**..(be) RoystonFfrench 2 34
(T D Barron) *s.i.s: sn pushed along: a in rr* **8/1**[3]

4130 **12** *3* **Best Lead**[19] 1262 8-8-11 **52**......................................(b) AndrewElliott(3) 4 24
(Ian Emmerson) *sn outpcd* **40/1**

60-0 **13** *6* **Jodrell Bank (IRE)**[18] 1280 4-9-1 **53**................................. AdamKirby 3 6
(J Ryan) *sn outpcd* **66/1**

/0-4 **14** *14* **New Proposal (IRE)**[25] 1118 5-9-2 **54**.......................... DarryllHolland 1 —
(A P Jarvis) *s.i.s: hld up: bhd fr 1/2-way: eased fnl 2f* **13/2**[2]

1m 15.64s (-1.26) **Going Correction** -0.225s/f (Stan) **14** Ran SP% **120.0**
Speed ratings (Par 101):99,96,95,95,95 92,91,91,90,90 86,82,74,56
CSF £54.74 CT £346.92 TOTE £6.50: £2.10, £2.80, £2.50; EX 57.30.
Owner Adrian Swingler **Bred** Tom Foley **Trained** Eastwell, Leics

FOCUS
A moderate sprint handicap but the form looks solid and should prove reliable. There could be more to come from the winner.
New Proposal(IRE) Official explanation: jockey said saddle slipped

1754 NSPCC H'CAP — 5f (F)

4:30 (4:31) (Class 3) (0-90,88) 3-Y-0+ £10,363 (£3,083; £1,540; £769) Stalls High

Form RPR

1-11 **1** **Off The Record**[15] 1351 3-8-8 **82**.. TPQueally 6 92+
(J G Given) *mde virtually all: rdn over 1f out: edgd lft ins fnl f: r.o* **7/4**[1]

140 **2** *3/4* **Canadian Danehill (IRE)**[17] 1292 5-9-3 **82**....................(p) EddieAhern 5 92
(R M H Cowell) *trckd ldrs: rdn over 1f out: r.o* **12/1**

1-43 **3** *1* **Stoneacre Lad (IRE)**[47] 818 4-9-9 **88**...........(b) RobbieFitzpatrick 10 94
(Peter Grayson) *chsd ldr: chal 1/2-way: rdn over 1f out: edgd lft and no ex ins fnl f* **8/1**[2]

-002 **4** *3* **Bo McGinty (IRE)**[6] 1574 6-8-9 **74** oh3........................(b) PaulHanagan 9 69
(R A Fahey) *chsd ldrs: rdn 1/2-way: wknd ins fnl f* **17/2**[3]

1210 **5** *1 1/2* **Egyptian Lord**[25] 1121 4-8-11 **76**.............................(b) GrahamGibbons 7 66
(Peter Grayson) *s.i.s: plld hrd and hdwy over 3f out: hmpd 1/2-way: sn rdn and outpcd* **12/1**

1616 **6** *hd* **Efistorm**[15] 1363 6-9-0 **79**.. JohnEgan 4 68
(C R Dore) *prom: outpcd over 3f out: swtchd rt over 1f out: n.d after* **14/1**

6500 **7** *2* **Pawan (IRE)**[6] 1574 7-8-8 **78**...(b) AnnStokell(5) 2 60
(Miss A Stokell) *sn outpcd: nvr nrr* **12/1**

6-04 **8** *nk* **Kings College Boy**[7] 1565 7-8-9 **74** oh6........................(b) DaleGibson 3 55
(R A Fahey) *chsd ldrs: rdn 1/2-way: wknd over 1f out* **16/1**

6-30 **9** *nk* **Bond Boy**[6] 1574 10-9-0 **79**... DanielTudhope 1 59
(G R Oldroyd) *mid-div: outpcd over 3f out: n.d after* **16/1**

60-6 **10** *2 1/2* **Puskas (IRE)**[10] 1464 4-8-11 **83**................................... BarrySavage(7) 8 54
(J M Bradley) *sn outpcd* **50/1**

0635 **11** *1/2* **Pieter Brueghel (USA)**[17] 1292 8-9-3 **82**........................... JoeFanning 11 51
(D Nicholls) *s.i.s: sme hdwy 1/2-way: sn wknd* **10/1**

-116 **12** *7* **Spanish Ace**[25] 1134 6-9-1 **85**.............................. KevinGhunowa(5) 12 29
(J M Bradley) *sn outpcd* **33/1**

/6-0 **13** *5* **The Bear**[24] 1159 4-9-6 **85**.. LeeEnstone 13 11
(J S Wainwright) *sn outpcd* **33/1**

58.42 secs (-1.88) **Going Correction** -0.20s/f (Stan)
WFA 3 from 4yo+ 9lb **13** Ran SP% **116.4**
Speed ratings (Par 107):107,105,104,99,97 96,93,93,92,88 87,76,68
CSF £22.66 CT £137.50 TOTE £2.50: £1.80, £3.80, £1.90; EX 31.80.
Owner Ian Henderson **Bred** P Onslow **Trained** Willoughton, Lincs

FOCUS
A strong sprint handicap and this is good form, with another step up from the progressive Off The Record.

NOTEBOOK
Off The Record ◆, the only three-year-old in the line-up, is hugely progressive and defied a 9lb rise in the weights for his recent course-and-distance success to complete the four-timer. He ultimately looked to win a shade cosily and looks capable of even better again, although he does have to prove himself away from Southwell. His trainer feels he will need cut in the ground when switching to turf. (op 9-4)
Canadian Danehill(IRE) appreciated the return to sand and ran a fine race in second behind the progressive winner. (op 11-1)
Stoneacre Lad(IRE) benefited from the return to Southwell and fared best of the Grayson pair, running a solid race in third. (op 11-2)
Bo McGinty(IRE), having a rare outing on sand, ran a respectable race considering he was 3lb out of the handicap and will be one to look out for when returned to turf. (op 8-1 tchd 9-1)
Egyptian Lord would have appreciated the return to Fibresand and ran better than at Lingfield on his previous start, but he was still not quite at his best. Official explanation: jockey said gelding hung right (op 11-1 tchd 14-1)
The Bear Official explanation: jockey said gelding hung right

1755 SEE "JOURNEY SOUTH" LIVE ON 30TH MAY H'CAP — 7f (F)

5:00 (5:00) (Class 6) (0-65,65) 4-Y-0+ £3,241 (£957; £478) Stalls Low

Form RPR

1104 **1** **Doctor's Cave**[14] 1382 5-8-13 **60**....................................(b) EddieAhern 7 74
(K O Cunningham-Brown) *led: rdn and hdd over 1f out: styd on u.p to ld nr fin* **7/1**[3]

5263 **2** *nk* **Cleveland**[19] 1262 5-8-13 **60**.. GrahamGibbons 4 73
(R Hollinshead) *chsd wnr tl led over 1f out: sn rdn: edgd lft ins fnl f: hdd nr fin* **11/2**[2]

4-11 **3** *2 1/2* **Megalo Maniac**[7] 1569 4-8-12 **59** 6ex............................ PaulHanagan 12 69+
(R A Fahey) *prom: lost pl over 4f out: hdwy u.p over 1f out: nt rch ldrs* **11/10**[1]

5215 **4** *3/4* **The Grey One (IRE)**[9] 1507 4-8-8 **60**..................(p) KevinGhunowa(5) 13 65
(J M Bradley) *mid-div: hdwy 1/2-way: rdn over 2f out: styd on* **10/1**

1033 **5** *hd* **Branston Tiger**[19] 1265 8-9-1 **65**..........................(v) AndrewElliott(3) 3 69
(Ian Emmerson) *chsd ldrs: rdn over 2f out: no ex fnl f* **28/1**

06-3 **6** *1 1/4* **Joshua's Gold (IRE)**[13] 1413 6-9-2 **63**....................... DanielTudhope 11 64
(D Carroll) *chsd ldrs: rdn over 2f out: no ex fnl f* **10/1**

0062 **7** *3* **Lucius Verrus (USA)**[18] 1280 7-8-13 **60**.............................(v) TPQueally 8 53
(D Shaw) *mid-div: dropped to rr 5f out: n.d after* **16/1**

-001 **8** *8* **Alsadaa (USA)**[19] 1265 4-9-1 **62**... DaleGibson 1 34
(M W Easterby) *s.i.s: sme hdwy u.p over 2f out: sn wknd* **11/1**

13-0 **9** *1 1/4* **Larky's Lob**[105] 306 8-8-11 **65**.................................... JamesO'Reilly(7) 6 34
(J O'Reilly) *chsd ldrs: rdn 1/2-way: wknd 2f out* **25/1**

544/ **10** *3 1/2* **Lytham (IRE)**[576] 1640 6-9-1 **62**.. VinceSlattery 5 22
(D J Wintle) *sn outpcd* **33/1**

6300 **11** *1 1/4* **Ocean Of Dreams (FR)**[19] 1262 4-9-4 **65**..............(v[1]) DarryllHolland 14 22
(J D Bethell) *chsd ldrs over 4f* **20/1**

00-0 **12** *2 1/2* **Joy And Pain**[14] 1377 6-8-13 **60**.......................................(v) IanMongan 9 10
(M J Attwater) *s.i.s: hdwy 1/2-way: wknd over 2f out* **40/1**

6- **13** *18* **Dukestreet**[467] 271 6-8-13 **60**....................................... DeanMcKeown 2 —
(D Shaw) *sn outpcd* **50/1**

1m 27.94s (-2.86) **Going Correction** -0.225s/f (Stan) **13** Ran SP% **127.3**
Speed ratings (Par 101):107,106,103,102,102 101,97,88,87,83 81,79,58
CSF £45.10 CT £79.07 TOTE £12.50: £2.50, £2.10, £1.40; EX 86.10 Place 6 £17.58, Place 5 £14.15.
Owner A J Richards & Michael A Richards **Bred** Tweenhills Stud And Genesis Green Stud **Trained** Nether Wallop, Hants

FOCUS
A fair handicap for the grade, dominated by the front pair. The winner put up his best run for a couple of years.
Ocean Of Dreams(FR) Official explanation: jockey said gelding lost its action on bend
Joy And Pain Official explanation: jockey said gelding never travelled
T/Plt: £8.80 to a £1 stake. Pool: £49,734.70. 4,107.50 winning tickets. T/Qpdt: £5.10 to a £1 stake. Pool: £2,474.80. 355.70 winning tickets. CR

1756 - 1759a (Foreign Racing) - See Raceform Interactive

1733 KILLARNEY (L-H)

Tuesday, May 15

OFFICIAL GOING: Good

1760a KILLARNEY RACEGOERS CLUB RACE — 1m 6f

8:50 (8:52) 4-Y-0+ £5,135 (£1,196; £527; £304) Stalls Far side

RPR

1 **Souvenance**[249] 5156 4-9-2 .... DPMcDonogh 2 74+
(Sir Mark Prescott) *a.p: pushed along bef st: led 2 1/2f out: qckly clr: styd on wl u.p* **2/9**[1]

2 *2 1/2* **Oscar Night (IRE)**[38] 1611 8-9-0 .... CDTimmons(7) 14 73
(Adrian Maguire, Ire) *mid-div: clsr in 5th fr 5f out: no imp fr under 3f out: rdn to go mod 2nd under 2f out: kpt on wout troubling wnr* **25/1**

3 *1/2* **Mise En Place**[164] 6090 6-9-2 .... RPCleary 12 67
(J Morrison, Ire) *in rr of mid-div: clsr in 7th over 4f out: rdn and wnt mod 3rd fr over 1f out: kpt on wout threatening* **25/1**

4 *5* **Mill House Girl (IRE)**[1] 5100 6-9-4 ....(p) CPGeoghegan(5) 1 68
(S Donohoe, Ire) *chsd ldrs: 3rd bef st: 2nd 2 1/2f out: sn no imp u.p: kpt on same pce* **8/1**[2]

5 *1/2* **Our Monty (IRE)**[3] 1687 4-9-7 60...................................(b) WSupple 7 66
(K F O'Brien, Ire) *led: strly pressed and hdd 2 1/2f out: sn no imp: kpt on same pce* **20/1**

6 *4* **Kalamkar (IRE)**[13] 1418 5-9-7 90..................................(p) WMLordan 4 60
(S Donohoe, Ire) *chsd ldrs: 4th bef st: no imp fr under 3f out: kpt on same pce u.p* **10/1**[3]

7 *4 1/2* **Zalongo**[137] 5848 5-9-7 .... NPMadden 9 54
(C Byrnes, Ire) *mid-div: 6th over 4f out: no imp u.p and kpt on same pce fr bef st* **20/1**

8 *5* **Old Kippin (IRE)**[9] 6-9-2 .... NGMcCullagh 3 42
(V T O'Brien, Ire) *chsd ldrs: 8th over 4f out: sn no imp u.p* **100/1**

9 *3* **Oscar Pride (IRE)**[30] 8-9-2 ....(t) CO'Donoghue 6 39
(V T O'Brien, Ire) *mid-div best: nvr a factor* **66/1**

10 *14* **Saddlers' Queen (IRE)**[42] 5-8-11 .... SMGorey(5) 13 20
(J J Lennon, Ire) *a towards rr* **66/1**

11 *16* **Dance Of Moonlight (FR)** 4-8-13 .... WJLee(3) 11 —
(Miss Susan A Finn, Ire) *mid-div best: nvr a factor* **50/1**

12 *12* **Fantastic Star**[207] 6090 5-9-2 .... DMGrant 5 —
(Michael P Hourigan, Ire) *a bhd* **33/1**

3m 9.70s (-6.80)
WFA 4 from 5yo+ 1lb **12** Ran SP% **128.1**
CSF £16.87 TOTE £1.20: £1.10, £3.60, £3.20; DF 19.20.
Owner Miss K Rausing **Bred** Miss K Rausing **Trained** Newmarket, Suffolk

FOCUS
Sir Mark Prescott has successfully found opportunities away from the Irish tracks usually targetted by his fellow British trainers over the years and this was another example with the much-travelled filly Souvenance.

NOTEBOOK
Souvenance, who has been placed at Group 1, 2 and 3 level and in Listed company around Europe, stood out here without a penalty for her only previous win which was achieved as a two year old. The opposition here was mainly a mish mash of bumper horses and hurdlers and she won as she was entitled to. Always close up, she went to the front well over 2f out and quickly went clear to win readily. (op 1/4)
T/Jkpt: @306.90. Pool of @18,006.00 - 44 winning units. T/Plt: @403.70. Pool of @1,154.00. II

[1367]BATH (L-H)

Wednesday, May 16

OFFICIAL GOING: Good (8.2)
Wind: Moderate, ahead

1761 GROSVENOR CASINO ANCHOR ROAD BRISTOL H'CAP 1m 2f 46y
6:15 (6:15) (Class 6) (0-65,65) 4-Y-0+ **£2,184** (£644; £322) **Stalls** Low

Form RPR
-000 **1** **Elopement (IRE)**[22] 1206 5-8-1 **51** oh4 LiamJones(3) 7 60
(W M Brisbourne) *chsd ldrs: wnt 2nd over 3f out: led wl over 2f out: drvn and r.o wl fnl f* **12/1**

/60- **2** *1* **Piano Man**[291] 3948 5-8-5 **55** RichardKingscote(3) 3 62
(B G Powell) *towards rr tl hdwy and hmpd bnd 5f out: styd on again fr over 2f out: kpt on to chse wnr cl home but a hld* **10/1**

-560 **3** *2* **Fangorn Forest (IRE)**[9] 1534 4-8-13 **65** (p) TolleyDean(5) 5 68
(R A Harris) *towards rr: hdwy fr 3f out: chsd wnr and hrd drvn appr fnl f: wknd and lost 2nd cl home* **25/1**

0-02 **4** *¾* **Mae Cigan (FR)**[5] 1638 4-9-4 **65** FrancisNorton 6 67
(M Blanshard) *mid-div: hdwy whn hmpd bnd 5f out: rdn and effrt 3f out: styd on fr over 1f out: nvr gng pce to rch ldrs* **13/8**[1]

053- **5** *2* **Over Ice**[233] 5567 4-9-1 **65** JerryO'Dwyer(3) 8 63
(Karen George) *chsd ldrs: wnt wd bnd 5f out: styd front rnk: rdn over 2f out: wknd fnl f* **20/1**

6015 **6** *5* **Monmouthshire**[7] 1592 4-8-0 **52** oh2 ow1 (v) KevinGhunowa(5) 2 40
(R J Price) *towards rr: hmpd bnd 5f out: hdwy over 3f out: sn rdn: wknd fnl f* **8/1**

3-02 **7** *1 ½* **Azreme**[4] 1655 7-9-1 **62** IanMongan 9 47
(P Howling) *chsd ldrs tl over 3f out: wknd 2f out* **5/1**[3]

6023 **8** *½* **First Friend (IRE)**[21] 1249 6-8-8 **62** HaddenFrost(7) 10 46
(M Hill) *led tl hdd wl over 2f out: sn btn* **7/2**[2]

-000 **9** *29* **Lady Lucas (IRE)**[9] 1537 4-8-4 **51** oh6 (t) EdwardCreighton 1 —
(E J Creighton) *chsd ldrs: rdn 3f out: sn wknd* **100/1**

50-0 **10** *8* **Sonny Mac**[12] 1451 4-9-4 **65** (vt) ChrisCatlin 4 —
(M J McGrath) *chsd ldrs tl wknd over 3f out* **25/1**

2m 12.85s (1.85) **Going Correction** +0.125s/f (Good) **10** Ran SP% **118.3**
Speed ratings (Par 101):97,96,94,94,92 88,87,86,63,57
CSF £120.62 CT £2940.36 TOTE £15.50: £3.60, £2.90, £5.80; EX 224.10.
Owner Stratford Bards Racing **Bred** Haras Du Mezeray **Trained** Great Ness, Shropshire

FOCUS
Just a modest handicap. The leaders went off too quickly and there was some trouble in behind when the pace finally slowed just before the turn into the straight.
Mae Cigan(FR) Official explanation: jockey said gelding suffered interference in running
Monmouthshire Official explanation: jockey said gelding suffered interference in running
Azreme Official explanation: jockey said gelding ran too free
First Friend(IRE) Official explanation: vet said horse had a breathing problem
Lady Lucas(IRE) Official explanation: jockey said filly had no more to give

1762 EUROPEAN BREEDERS' FUND AND WINNING POST BOOKMAKERS MEDIAN AUCTION MAIDEN STKS 5f 11y
6:45 (6:52) (Class 5) 2-Y-0 **£3,497** (£1,040; £520; £259) **Stalls** Low

Form RPR
55 **1** **Regal Rhythm (IRE)**[18] 1291 2-9-3 SteveDrowne 2 73
(B J Meehan) *in tch: hdwy over 2f out: wnt rt jst ins fnl f: kpt on strly to ld nr fin* **11/1**

33 **2** *¾* **Shatter Resistant (IRE)**[9] 1528 2-9-3 ChrisCatlin 1 70
(M R Channon) *led: rdn 2f out: kpt on wl tl ct cl home* **8/1**

3 *1 ¾* **Elna Bright** 2-9-3 PatDobbs 9 63
(R Hannon) *chsd ldrs: chal ins fnl 2f: outpcd ins fnl f* **25/1**

4 *1 ¾* **L'Art Du Silence (IRE)** 2-9-3 FergusSweeney 5 56
(J R Boyle) *s.i.s: in rr: hdwy fr 2f out: edgd rt 1f out: kpt on strly cl home* **33/1**

2 **5** *1 ½* **Hobson**[13] 1428 2-9-3 StephenCarson 10 50+
(Eve Johnson Houghton) *chsd ldrs: rdn 2f out: btn whn sltly hmpd jst ins fnl f* **7/4**[1]

4 **6** *shd* **Aide Memoir (IRE)**[9] 1533 2-8-12 FrankieMcDonald 11 45
(S Kirk) *chsd ldrs: rdn 2f out: wknd ins fnl f* **5/2**[2]

6 **7** *nk* **Tamrai Dancer**[16] 1354 2-8-12 JamesDoyle 8 43
(R M Beckett) *mid-div on outside: rdn over 2f out: kpt on ins fnl f: nvr gng pce to rch ldrs* **11/2**[3]

45 **8** *shd* **Andrasta**[12] 1445 2-8-5 KMay(7) 4 43
(B J Meehan) *mid-div: rdn and effrt oer 2f out: nvr gng pce to be competitive* **25/1**

9 *2* **Titfer (IRE)** 2-9-3 TPO'Shea 6 40
(P A Blockley) *a outpcd* **50/1**

10 *1* **Choisky (IRE)** 2-9-3 SimonWhitworth 12 36
(J Akehurst) *chsd ldrs to 1/2-way* **16/1**

11 *2 ½* **Mairead's Boy (IRE)** 2-9-3 LPKeniry 3 26
(J S Moore) *s.i.s: outpcd* **28/1**

64.59 secs (2.09) **Going Correction** +0.35s/f (Good) **11** Ran SP% **121.7**
Speed ratings (Par 93):97,95,93,90,87 87,87,87,83,82 78
CSF £93.13 TOTE £14.80: £3.20, £1.90, £4.40; EX 55.80.
Owner N Attenborough,Mrs L Mann,Mrs L Way **Bred** Hugo Merry **Trained** Manton, Wilts
■ Stewards' Enquiry : Steve Drowne one-day ban: careless riding (May 27)

FOCUS
Just an ordinary juvenile maiden.

NOTEBOOK
Regal Rhythm(IRE)'s two previous efforts represented just modest form, but he improved for the switch to easier ground. He looks the type who could do well later in the season in nursery company when getting his preferred conditions. (op 16-1)
Shatter Resistant(IRE) did not mind the easier ground and ran a good race under a positive ride.
Elna Bright, a 27,000gns half-sister to dual 5f-6f juvenile winner Raphoola, out of a winning sprinter at two, fared best of the newcomers back in third and is open to some improvement. Official explanation: jockey said colt never travelled
L'Art Du Silence(IRE), a 26,000gns first foal of a mare who was placed over 7f-1m1f, ran on nicely in the closing stages and should improve for a step up to 6f.
Hobson could not confirm the promise he showed when a close second on his debut at Folkestone, appearing unsuited by the easier ground. (op 15-8 tchd 2-1)
Aide Memoir(IRE) looked the form pick of those who had run judged on her encouraging debut effort at Warwick, but she failed to go on from that and was disappointing, even allowing for the softer ground. She looks the type who might not progress and has plenty to prove now. (op 11-4 tchd 3-1 and 9-4)
Tamrai Dancer's debut effort at Windsor did not amount to much and she struggled to get involved. (op 10-1 tchd 11-1)

1763 GROSVENOR CASINOS GREAT NIGHTS' ENTERTAINMENT CLAIMING STKS 5f 161y
7:15 (7:19) (Class 6) 3-Y-0 **£1,943** (£578; £288; £144) **Stalls** Low

Form RPR
345- **1** **No Worries Yet (IRE)**[236] 5509 3-8-2 67 FrancisNorton 9 54
(J L Spearing) *pressed ldrs: slt ld over 3f out: styd on wl fnl f: readily* **2/1**[1]

4344 **2** *¾* **Strike Force**[8] 1561 3-8-11 57 (p) JimCrowley 10 61
(R A Harris) *towards rr: rdn 1/2-way: hdwy over 2f out: qcknd to chse wnr ins fnl f but a hld* **5/1**[2]

04U- **3** *3 ½* **Fly Time**[156] 6789 3-8-7 48 GregFairley(3) 7 48
(Mrs L Williamson) *s.i.s: sn rcvrd and chsd ldrs 1/2-way: ev ch 2f out: chsd wnr over 1f out: no imp: sn one pce* **50/1**

5016 **4** *1 ¼* **Mind The Style**[9] 1520 3-9-1 70 VinceSlattery 1 49
(W G M Turner) *slt ld tl hdd over 3f out: sn rdn: one pce fr over 1f out* **12/1**

0022 **5** *1* **Pat Will (IRE)**[20] 1269 3-7-11 55 (v) BernadetteQuinn(7) 12 35
(P D Evans) *racd wd bnd over 3f out: sn pressing wnr and ev ch: fdd ins fnl f* **11/1**

00-0 **6** *¾* **Maeve (IRE)**[43] 899 3-8-2 48 EdwardCreighton 16 31
(E J Creighton) *towards rr: pushed along 3f out: rdn 2f out: r.o ins fnl f but nvr gng pce to be competitive* **50/1**

-030 **7** *½* **Stir Crazy (IRE)**[8] 1561 3-8-2 63 ThomasO'Brien(7) 6 36
(M R Channon) *chsd ldrs: rdn to chal 2f out: wknd ins fnl f* **11/2**[3]

50-0 **8** *½* **She Wont Wait**[42] 924 3-8-5 48 ow2 (b[1]) NeilChalmers(3) 11 33
(T M Jones) *chsd ldrs and racd wd fr bnd over 3f out: ev ch over 2f out: wknd fnl f* **66/1**

0-60 **9** *¾* **Kyllachy Storm**[5] 1634 3-9-5 64 SteveDrowne 3 42
(R J Hodges) *chsd ldrs: drvn along 1/2-way: wknd appr fnl f* **10/1**

0316 **10** *shd* **Totally Free**[20] 1269 3-8-13 60 (v) HayleyTurner 8 35
(M D I Usher) *towards rr: sn pushed along: hdwy fnl f: nvr in contention* **16/1**

00- **11** *nk* **Good Luck Chip (IRE)**[200] 6222 3-7-11 LiamJones(3) 13 21
(I A Wood) *in tch: racd wd bnd over 3f out: nvr gng pce to be competitive* **50/1**

00 **12** *nk* **The Carpet Man**[9] 1541 3-9-1 SimonWhitworth 14 35
(A W Carroll) *slowly away: towards rr: pushed along 1/2-way: kpt on fnl f: nvr in contention* **80/1**

0060 **13** *½* **Mr Mini Scule**[17] 1317 3-8-0 49 KevinGhunowa(5) 2 24
(A B Haynes) *chsd ldrs: rdn over 3f out: wknd 2f out* **33/1**

-406 **14** *nk* **Sherjawy (IRE)**[34] 1008 3-8-11 52 (b) AdrianMcCarthy 4 29
(Miss Z C Davison) *chsd ldrs: rdn 1/2-way: wknd fr 2f out* **40/1**

2304 **15** *2 ½* **Time Share (IRE)**[13] 1430 3-8-4 54 ChrisCatlin 15 14
(J A Osborne) *slowly away: wd bnd over 3f out: a in rr* **6/1**

1m 13.62s (2.42) **Going Correction** +0.35s/f (Good) **15** Ran SP% **124.7**
Speed ratings (Par 97):97,96,91,89,88 87,86,86,85,84 84,84,83,83,79
CSF £11.33 TOTE £3.00: £1.60, £2.70, £8.50; EX 23.30.No Worries Yet and Strike Force were both subject to friendly claims.
Owner J Spearing **Bred** Mark Donohoe **Trained** Kinnersley, Worcs

FOCUS
A weak claimer with most of the field out of form or on the downgrade. The winner was 9lb off last year's selling win here.
Good Luck Chip(IRE) Official explanation: jockey said filly suffered interference in running
Sherjawy(IRE) Official explanation: jockey said gelding hung right

1764 GROSVENOR CASINOS DISCOVER THE GREAT TASTES H'CAP 1m 3f 144y
7:45 (7:46) (Class 6) (0-65,63) 4-Y-0+ **£2,072** (£616; £308; £153) **Stalls** Low

Form RPR
0422 **1** **Recalcitrant**[17] 1319 4-8-2 **52** WilliamBuick(5) 2 61
(S Dow) *mde all: pushed along over 2f out: c clr fnl f: unchal* **15/8**[1]

2 *3* **Power Again (GER)**[623] 6-8-8 **53** JimCrowley 3 57
(P R Chamings) *chsd wnr most of way: rdn 3f out: styd on same pce to hold 2nd fnl 2f but a easily hld* **12/1**

00-6 **3** *nk* **Lady Diktat**[14] 1396 5-8-11 **61** TravisBlock(5) 7 65
(Mouse Hamilton-Fairley) *chsd ldrs: rdn to dispute 2nd fr over 2f out but nvr gng pce to be competitive w wnr* **28/1**

14-0 **4** *½* **Bronze Star**[20] 1258 4-9-3 **62** OscarUrbina 8 65
(J R Fanshawe) *wnt rt s: sn in tch: rdn and hdwy over 2f out: disp 2nd over 1f out but nvr trbld wnr: styd on same pce* **10/3**[2]

060- **5** *hd* **Star Berry**[233] 5574 4-8-7 **52** SteveDrowne 10 55
(B J Meehan) *carried rt s: sn chsng ldrs: rdn and outpcd over 3f out: kpt on again fnl 2f but nvr gng pce to trble wnr* **10/1**

1000 **6** *1 ½* **King's Ransom**[21] 1249 4-9-4 **63** RichardMullen 9 63
(W R Muir) *carried rt s: bhd: rdn over 2f out: styd on fnl f: nt rch ldrs* **20/1**

000- **7** *½* **Squiffy**[233] 5574 4-8-9 **54** ChrisCatlin 6 53
(P D Cundell) *in tch: pushed along over 3f out: sn one pce* **12/1**

0302 **8** *13* **Ronsard (IRE)**[14] 1406 5-7-11 **49** BernadetteQuinn(7) 4 28
(P D Evans) *a towards rr* **9/2**[3]

64-0 **9** *12* **Gala Casino King (IRE)**[8] 1556 4-8-13 **58** FrancisNorton 5 17
(Jennie Candlish) *plld hrd: towards rr but in tch tl wknd fr 4f out* **16/1**

2m 31.47s (1.17) **Going Correction** +0.125s/f (Good) **9** Ran SP% **114.6**
Speed ratings (Par 101):101,99,98,98,98 97,97,88,80
CSF £26.28 CT £474.38 TOTE £2.80: £1.20, £2.50, £5.70; EX 35.40.
Owner T Staplehurst **Bred** T Staplehurst **Trained** Epsom, Surrey
■ Stewards' Enquiry : Oscar Urbina four-day ban: used whip with excessive frequency and down the shoulder in the forehand position (May 27-30)

FOCUS
It paid to be on the pace in this weak handicap. The winner is rated to her best, but there are doubts over the strength of the form.

1765 CHARLES SAUNDERS FOOD SERVICE BE HOPEFUL H'CAP 1m 5y
8:15 (8:16) (Class 5) (0-75,75) 4-Y-0+ **£4,857** (£1,445; £722; £360) **Stalls** Low

Form RPR
4111 **1** **Apex**[15] 1378 6-8-4 **68** HaddenFrost(7) 9 82
(M Hill) *trckd ldrs: qcknd to ld 2f out: nudged clr fnl f: easily* **7/2**[1]

336- **2** *3* **Barons Spy (IRE)**[203] 6176 6-9-1 **72** JamesDoyle 2 79
(R J Price) *chsd ldrs: rdn and styd on to chse wnr fnl 2f but a easily hld* **14/1**

0-00 **3** *½* **Full Victory (IRE)**[14] 1401 5-8-13 **70** LPKeniry 11 76
(R A Farrant) *in tch: rdn to chse ldrs 3f out: styd on same pce ins fnal f* **12/1**

3-43 **4** *2* **Merrymadcap (IRE)**[15] 1385 5-9-0 **71** FrancisNorton 3 72+
(M Blanshard) *towards rr: rdn 3f out: styd on fr over 1f out: gng on cl home but nvr in contention* **13/2**[2]

6533 **5** *nk* **Birkside**[8] 1559 4-8-6 **63** ow1 .... PaulDoe 7 — 64
(S Dow) *towards rr: pushed along fr 3f out: kpt on fnl f but nt rch ldrs* **14/1**

0-51 **6** *shd* **Indian Edge**[16] 1366 6-8-13 **70** .... FergusSweeney 1 — 70
(B Palling) *led tl hdd 2f out: sn btn* **7/1**[3]

26-3 **7** *2* **Carmenero (GER)**[22] 1209 4-9-4 **75** .... RichardMullen 8 — 71
(W R Muir) *chsd ldrs: rdn 3f out: wknd over 1f out* **10/1**

-604 **8** *2 ½* **Desert Dreamer (IRE)**[18] 1308 6-9-1 **72** .... JimCrowley 4 — 62
(P R Chamings) *s.i.s: bhd: sme hdwy on outside fr over 2f out: nvr rchd ldrs* **7/1**[3]

05-3 **9** *shd* **Coup D'Etat**[13] 1434 5-9-3 **74** ....(p) GeorgeBaker 5 — 64
(R A Harris) *t.k.h: sn chsng ldr: wknd over 2f out* **9/1**

00-0 **10** *2* **Gracechurch (IRE)**[6] 1208 4-8-13 **70** .... SteveDrowne 10 — 55
(R J Hodges) *chsd ldrs: rdn 3f out: sn wknd* **10/1**

1204 **11** *½* **My Michelle**[19] 1284 6-8-5 **62** .... JamieMackay 13 — 46
(B Palling) *chsd ldrs: rdn 3f out: sn wknd* **25/1**

00-0 **12** *shd* **Crocodile Bay (IRE)**[18] 1287 4-8-10 **74** .... KMay(7) 14 — 58
(B J Meehan) *towards rr: hdwy on outside and hung lft ins fnl 3f: wknd qckly fr 2f out* **14/1**

500- **13** *¾* **Golden Applause (FR)**[220] 5833 5-9-0 **71** .... SamHitchcott 12 — 53
(Mrs A L M King) *towards rr: hdwy 4f out: rdn: hmpd and wknd ins fnl 3f* **33/1**

/00- **14** *13* **Bouzouki (USA)**[301] 3644 4-8-8 **68** .... JerryO'Dwyer(3) 6 — 20
(Karen George) *s.i.s: a bhd* **50/1**

1m 41.37s (0.27) **Going Correction** +0.125s/f (Good) **14** Ran SP% **125.2**
Speed ratings (Par 103):103,100,99,97,97 97,95,92,92,90 90,89,89,76
CSF £57.46 CT £567.95 TOTE £5.20: £1.90, £5.20, £3.20; EX 97.90.
Owner Martin Hill **Bred** P D And Mrs C E Player And Jonathon Jay **Trained** Broadhempston, Devon
■ Stewards' Enquiry : K May one-day ban: careless riding (May 28)

FOCUS
A modest handicap run at a good pace. The revitalised Apex is still 11lb off his best form and should still be hard to beat in the short term. Sound form.

1766 BET NOW AT WBX.COM FILLIES' H'CAP — 5f 161y
8:45 (8:46) (Class 5) (0-70,70) 3-Y-O+ — £3,108 (£924; £462; £230) Stalls Low

Form — RPR

6-03 **1** **Linda Green**[16] 1357 6-9-4 **70** .... ThomasO'Brien(7) 14 — 82
(M R Channon) *towards rr: stl plenty to do 2f out: hdwy over 1f out: str run ins fnl f to ld cl home* **3/1**[2]

56-0 **2** *¾* **Matterofact (IRE)**[18] 1309 4-8-12 **57** .... RobertHavlin 9 — 67
(M S Saunders) *chsd ldrs: rdn to ld ins fnl f: ct cl home* **14/1**

2243 **3** *3* **Diminuto**[16] 1351 3-8-1 **62** .... FrankiePickard(7) 16 — 59
(M D I Usher) *in tch: rapid hdwy to ld 2f out: rdn and hdd ins fnl f: sn btn* **16/1**

21-2 **4** *shd* **Aquilegia (IRE)**[25] 1151 3-9-2 **70** .... RichardMullen 5 — 67+
(E S McMahon) *s.i.s: drvn to chse ldrs over 3f out: one pce fr over 1f out* **5/2**[1]

4415 **5** *1 ¼* **Slipasearcher (IRE)**[8] 1561 3-8-8 **62** ....(b) JimCrowley 12 — 55+
(P D Evans) *towards rr: rdn over 2f out: hdwy fnl f kpt on cl home* **17/2**

6-26 **6** *4* **Cyfrwys (IRE)**[5] 1640 6-8-11 **56** oh2 ....(p) JamieMackay 2 — 38
(B Palling) *slt ld tl hdd 2f out: wknd over 1f out* **33/1**

031- **7** *¾* **Efisio Princess**[215] 5951 4-8-11 **56** oh1 .... RichardThomas 1 — 36
(J E Long) *chsd ldrs: rdn 3f out: wknd over 1f out* **16/1**

100- **8** *½* **Jucebabe**[242] 5378 4-8-12 **57** .... FrancisNorton 4 — 35
(J L Spearing) *chsd ldrs: rdn 1/2-way: wknd ins fnl 2f* **16/1**

-031 **9** *2 ½* **Ensign's Trick**[8] 1561 3-8-7 **64** 6ex .... LiamJones(3) 3 — 31
(W M Brisbourne) *chsd ldrs: stmbld 4f out: sn lost position and n.d fr 1/2-way* **10/1**

0-51 **10** *4* **Game Lady**[15] 1383 3-9-1 **69** .... PaulDoe 10 — 23
(I A Wood) *chsd ldrs: chal fr 3f out to 2f out: sn wknd* **8/1**[3]

-660 **11** *½* **Dictatrix**[7] 1589 4-9-8 **70** ....(b) JerryO'Dwyer(3) 11 — 25
(J M P Eustace) *reluctant to go to s: s.i.s: a towards rr* **18/1**

00-0 **12** *8* **Hello Roberto**[9] 1525 6-9-3 **67** ....(p) TolleyDean(5) 15 — —
(R A Harris) *outpcd fr 1/2-way* **33/1**

0-00 **13** *2 ½* **Queensgate**[16] 1346 3-8-2 **56** oh3 .... ChrisCatlin 13 — —
(M Blanshard) *chsd ldrs to 1/2-way* **50/1**

1m 13.08s (1.88) **Going Correction** +0.35s/f (Good)
WFA 3 from 4yo+ 9lb **13** Ran SP% **121.7**
Speed ratings (Par 100):101,100,96,95,94 88,87,87,83,78 77,67,63
CSF £45.54 CT £615.94 TOTE £4.00: £1.90, £3.00, £5.90; EX 55.70 Place 6 £3,051.35, Place 5 £217.99.
Owner Stephen Roots **Bred** Colin Tinkler **Trained** West Ilsley, Berks

FOCUS
A modest fillies' handicap run at a good clip which suited those that were held up. A career best from Linda Green with the runner-up rated to last year's form.
Efisio Princess Official explanation: trainer later said filly was found to have an infection
Ensign's Trick Official explanation: jockey said filly stumbled badly 3f out
T/Plt: £6,284.20 to a £1 stake. Pool: £67,147.20. 7.80 winning tickets. T/Qpdt: £53.40 to a £1 stake. Pool: £5,996.50. 83.00 winning tickets. ST

YORK (L-H)
Wednesday, May 16

OFFICIAL GOING: Good (good to soft in places) changing to good to soft after race 5 (3.50)
After virtually no rain in April and 40mm so far in May the ground was described after race two as 'genuine soft'. The times suggested otherwise.
Wind: Moderate, half-behind Weather: Overcast with light rain most of the afternoon

1767 SIXTY YEARS OF TIMEFORM STKS (H'CAP) — 1m 2f 88y
1:45 (1:47) (Class 2) (0-100,97) 4-Y-O+ **£16,516** (£4,913; £2,455; £1,226) Stalls Low

Form — RPR

/23- **1** **Emirates Skyline (USA)**[221] 5813 4-9-4 **97** .... LDettori 16 — 107+
(Saeed Bin Suroor) *lw: sn trcking ldrs on outer: smooth hdwy over 3f out: led ent fnl f: sn rdn and kpt on: comf* **11/2**[1]

6-12 **2** *½* **Flying Clarets (IRE)**[14] 1414 4-8-6 **85** .... TonyHamilton 8 — 94
(R A Fahey) *a.p: hdwy to ld 2f out: sn rdn and edgd lft: hdd ent fnl f and kpt on wl u.p* **11/1**

0352 **3** *1* **Bailieborough (IRE)**[6] 1599 8-8-4 **83** .... RoystonFfrench 11 — 90
(B Ellison) *midfield: hdwy over 3f out: rdn along 2f out: kpt on u.p fnl f* **20/1**

5-60 **4** *hd* **Flipando (IRE)**[11] 1480 6-8-9 **88** .... NCallan 14 — 95
(T D Barron) *hld up towards rr: hdwy and nt clr run 3f out: sn swtchd rt and rdn: kpt on ins fnl f* **25/1**

0-00 **5** *2 ½* **Futun**[11] 1477 4-9-3 **96** .... NickyMackay 10 — 98+
(L M Cumani) *t.k.h: hld up in midfield: hdwy 4f out: rdn along and outpcd 3f out swtchd rt and rdn wl over 1f out: kpt on ins fnl f* **20/1**

0-60 **6** *½* **Dunaskin (IRE)**[39] 940 7-8-10 **89** .... SebSanders 6 — 90
(Karen McLintock) *led: rdn along 3f out: sn hung rt: hdd and bmpd 2f out: sn wknd* **12/1**

30-0 **7** *hd* **Freeloader (IRE)**[24] 1180 7-8-4 **83** oh1 .... DaleGibson 7 — 84
(R A Fahey) *in tch: hdwy to chse ldrs 4f out: rdn along over 2f out: drvn and no imp fr wl over 1f out* **33/1**

6652 **8** *1* **Vacation (IRE)**[12] 1449 4-8-4 **88** .... WilliamBuick(5) 5 — 87
(V Smith) *lw: midfield: hdwy over 3f out: rdn along 2f out: kpt on same pce appr fnl f* **12/1**

235- **9** *2 ½* **Spell Casting (USA)**[244] 5319 4-8-3 **85** .... SaleemGolam(3) 1 — 79+
(M H Tompkins) *lw: chsd ldrs: rdn along over 3f out: drvn 2f out and sn btn* **28/1**

0-00 **10** *shd* **Blue Spinnaker (IRE)**[7] 1583 8-8-7 **86** .... PaulMulrennan 4 — 80
(M W Easterby) *in tch: swtchd lft and hdwy over 3f out: rdn along 2f out and sn btn* **6/1**[2]

-005 **11** *½* **Collateral Damage (IRE)**[7] 1583 4-8-8 **87** .... DavidAllan 2 — 80+
(T D Easterby) *s.i.s and bhd: hdwy 3f out: sn rdn and n.d* **9/1**[3]

165- **12** *1 ¾* **Pevensey (IRE)**[88] 6097 5-8-11 **90** .... GrahamGibbons 3 — 80+
(J J Quinn) *s.i.s and bhd tl sme late hdwy* **6/1**[2]

4-00 **13** *shd* **Best Prospect (IRE)**[12] 1449 5-9-1 **94** .... JamieSpencer 13 — 83
(M Dods) *stdd s: hld up and bhd: hdwy 3f out: n.m.r 2f out: sn rdn and no hdwy* **11/1**

1-00 **14** *1* **Dium Mac**[18] 1288 6-7-13 **85** oh4 ow2 .... SuzzanneFrance(7) 12 — 72
(N Bycroft) *s.i.s: a towards rr* **25/1**

0-60 **15** *11* **Tiger Tiger (FR)**[12] 1449 6-8-5 **84** .... JohnEgan 15 — 51
(Jamie Poulton) *sn pushed along: a in rr* **25/1**

2214 **16** *12* **Woolfall Blue (IRE)**[9] 1543 4-8-4 **83** .... JimmyQuinn 17 — 27
(G G Margarson) *chsd ldng pair: rdn along 3f out: sn wknd* **20/1**

00-1 **17** *6* **Temple Place (IRE)**[7] 1583 6-9-0 **93** 6ex ....(t) EddieAhern 9 — 25
(D McCain Jnr) *in tch: hdwy to chse ldrs 4f out: sn rdn along and wknd over 2f out* **16/1**

2m 9.92s (-2.58) **Going Correction** +0.20s/f (Good) **17** Ran SP% **124.1**
Speed ratings (Par 109):110,109,108,108,106 106,106,105,103,103 102,101,101,100,91 82,77
CSF £56.87 CT £1154.30 TOTE £5.50: £2.00, £2.10, £5.20, £7.00; EX 53.90 Trifecta £748.00 Pool: £1,053.66 - 1.00 winning ticket..
Owner Godolphin **Bred** Darley **Trained** Newmarket, Suffolk
■ Stewards' Enquiry : Paul Mulrennan one-day ban: careless riding (May 27)
N Callan two-day ban: careless riding (May 27-28)

FOCUS
A very competitive handicap run at a decent pace and the winning time was 1.86 seconds faster than the Musidora. The bulk of the field came down the middle and the front pair were up with the pace throughout. The form looks right up to scratch for a race like this and should prove reliable. Emirates Skyline was more dominant than the bare form.

NOTEBOOK
Emirates Skyline(USA), making his handicap debut in a somewhat abbreviated career, was also returning from seven months off but he has gone well fresh in the past and there was just about enough give in the ground for him. Sat behind the leading trio for most of the journey, he was brought with his effort more towards the nearside of the track and showed an admirable attitude to get the better of the runner-up. This was a decent effort under top weight and no doubt connections will be looking for something better for him now. (op 6-1 tchd 13-2)
Flying Clarets(IRE), raised 4lb for her narrow defeat at Pontefract, travelled particularly well up with the pace and again did nothing wrong, only just losing out to a rival with a touch of class. She does handle cut, but her very best form has been on quicker ground and given her liking for this course and distance the John Smith's Cup back here in July would seem a perfect target. (tchd 12-1)
Bailieborough(IRE), still 6lb above his highest winning mark, did best of those that tried to come from off the pace and was still closing at the line. He is yet to win over this far, but stamina did not seem to be an issue here.
Flipando(IRE) ♦, trying this trip for the first time, got warm beforehand. He had to weave his way through the field to get into contention, but he was staying on well at the line and certainly stayed the distance well enough. He is now 1lb below his last winning mark and the fact that the trip did not appear to be a problem opens up more options for him, so he is very much one to keep onside.
Futun continues to do himself few favours by taking a hold and it is to his credit that he managed to finish as close as he did. A return to further looks required, but he will not be able to demonstrate his true ability as long as he refuses to settle.
Dunaskin(IRE), a regular around here and back on a winning mark, ran his usual race from the front and enjoyed an uncontested lead, but could not see it out on this occasion.
Freeloader(IRE), who has been racing over hurdles and on sand since winning on his last turf outing last September, was off an 8lb higher mark than for that victory including being 1lb wrong. He had every chance and there seemed no real excuses.
Spell Casting(USA) ♦, a maiden after seven attempts coming into this, found a tough race to make his return from an eight-month absence and for his handicap debut. He did not run badly having racing close to the pace from the start, but he was the only one to stick to the inside rail in the home straight and the evidence of the meeting was that it was not an advantage. He does not looks thrown in off this mark based on what he has achieved, but his stable do not normally rush their horses so he may well be capable of a bit more. (op 33-1)
Blue Spinnaker(IRE), winner of this race last year off a 4lb higher mark, has been disappointing since for the most part and was one of the first beaten here. (op 11-2)
Collateral Damage(IRE) got into a state in the stalls and blew his chance by rearing badly as the gates opened, finding himself several lengths adrift as a result. Under the circumstances, his finishing position was as much as could be hoped for. Official explanation: jockey said colt reared as stalls opened (op 11-1)
Pevensey(IRE) was another to effectively end his chance by walking out of the gates. (op 8-1)
Best Prospect(IRE) ♦, given his usual patient ride, found himself behind a wall of horses up the home straight and was not knocked about when it was obvious he had no chance of getting near the leaders. He is still high enough in the handicap just now, but gives the impression he is capable of much more than he has shown so far this year and it would be especially interesting to see what happens if the tongue-tie goes back on. (tchd 12-1 in a place)
Temple Place(IRE) got a little bit warm beforehand. (op 14-1)

1768 BLUE SQUARE EXCLUSIVE LIVE SHOW PRICES STKS (H'CAP) — 7f
2:15 (2:17) (Class 2) (0-100,98) 3-Y-O **£16,192** (£4,817; £2,407; £1,202) Stalls Low

Form — RPR

32-1 **1** **Shmookh (USA)**[37] 973 3-8-4 **84** oh2 .... MartinDwyer 7 — 94+
(J L Dunlop) *hld up in tch: smooth hdwy 3f out: nt clr run wl over 1f out: qcknd to ld appr last: sn rdn and kpt on* **4/1**[2]

05-6 **2** ½ **Ponty Rossa (IRE)**[18] 1298 3-8-9 **89** DavidAllan 5 97+
(T D Easterby) *lw: squeezed out s: in rr but in tch tl hdwy over 2f out: nt clr run wl over 1f out and swtchd rt: rdn and kpt on wl fnl f* **10/1**

21- **3** 2 **Musca (IRE)**[214] 5959 3-8-4 **84** oh2 RoystonFfrench 11 84
(J Howard Johnson) *lw: sn led: rdn along and hdd 2f out: drvn and hung bdly rt over 1f out: kpt on ins fnl f* **8/1**[3]

113- **4** hd **Smart Instinct (USA)**[266] 4715 3-8-13 **98** JamieMoriarty(5) 9 97
(R A Fahey) *lw: hld up in rr: hdwy wl over 1f out: kpt on ins fnl f: nrst fin* **8/1**[3]

104- **5** ¾ **Billy Dane (IRE)**[220] 5843 3-8-8 **88** TonyHamilton 10 86
(R A Fahey) *lw: cl up: rdn along and ev ch 2f out: sn drvn and grad wknd* **20/1**

14-0 **6** hd **Osteopathic Remedy (IRE)**[18] 1298 3-8-4 **84** PaulFessey 3 81
(M Dods) *chsd ldrs: effrt over 2f out: sn rdn and kpt on same pce appr fnl f* **14/1**

20-3 **7** 2 **Mystery Ocean**[46] 838 3-8-6 **86** KerrinMcEvoy 6 78
(R M Beckett) *chsd ldrs: rdn along 2f out: grad wknd* **9/1**

100- **8** 1 **Smokey Oakey (IRE)**[207] 6100 3-8-5 **85** JimmyQuinn 4 74
(M H Tompkins) *bit bkwd: a towards rr* **33/1**

315- **9** hd **Heroes**[207] 6102 3-8-9 **92** EmmettStack(3) 1 81
(G A Huffer) *cl up on inner: rdn to ld 2f out: sn drvn: hdd & wknd appr fnl f* **8/1**[3]

2-16 **10** ½ **Gazboolou**[23] 1202 3-8-1 **84** oh7 AndrewElliott(3) 12 71
(K R Burke) *cl up on outer: pushed along 1/2-way: sn rdn and wknd wl over 2f out* **22/1**

11-5 **11** hd **Tredegar**[19] 1275 3-8-8 **88** SebSanders 8 75
(P F I Cole) *t.k.h: in tch on outer: effrt 3f out: sn rdn along and wknd 2f out* **11/4**[1]

1m 23.74s (-1.66) **Going Correction** -0.10s/f (Good) **11** Ran SP% **117.8**
Speed ratings (Par 105):105,104,102,101,101 100,98,97,97,96 96
CSF £42.60 CT £316.20 TOTE £4.40: £2.10, £3.10, £3.10; EX 56.70 Trifecta £524.90 Pool: £887.20 - 1.20 winning tickets..

Owner Hamdan Al Maktoum **Bred** Shadwell Farm LLC **Trained** Arundel, W Sussex

■ Stewards' Enquiry : Tony Hamilton one-day ban: used whip with excessive force (May 27)
David Allan caution: used whip with excessive frequency

FOCUS
A strong three-year-old handicap, run at a sound pace. The form looks solid and should work out.

NOTEBOOK
Shmookh(USA), off the mark on his seasonal bow in a modest maiden at Warwick, was given a patient ride and followed up in fairly ready fashion on this handicap debut. He is clearly coming good now, seems versatile as regards underfoot conditions, and looks sure to improve again for this experience. It should be noted that he was idling when in front, so can be rated value for a little further than the winning margin, and a further step up in class now looks warranted. His connections later reported they would prefer to keep him to this sort of trip for the short term.

Ponty Rossa(IRE) showed the clear benefit of her seasonal bow at Ripon and, having been ridden patiently, eventually finished her race with purpose over this extra furlong on ground she enjoys. She can be rated better than the bare form as she was messed about at the start and met a little trouble when trying to make up her ground nearing the final furlong. Her yard has not hit top form and she looks one to keep on side, as she remains open to improvement over this trip. (op 12-1)

Musca(IRE), 2lb out of the handicap, was given a positive ride and posted a pleasing effort on this seasonal and handicap bow. He did hang markedly right when under pressure nearing the final furlong, but that was most likely down to his inexperience and the manner in which he kept on thereafter would suggest he is ready to tackle a mile now. (tchd 15-2 and 9-1)

Smart Instinct(USA), who showed very useful form in three outings at up to 6f as a juvenile, looked well beforehand but still gave the impression the run would bring him on a little. He was far from disgraced under top weight on this seasonal return and got the longer trip well. He can be ridden more prominently now connections can be confident he stays and he looks set for another good year. (op 15-2)

Billy Dane(IRE), making his seasonal debut for new connections, eventually paid for running freely through the early parts yet did not shape without promise. He should come on for this. (tchd 25-1)

Osteopathic Remedy(IRE) finished closer to the runner-up than had been the case at Ripon on his seasonal debut and seemed to appreciate the easier surface. He is still lightly-raced and should enjoy the step up to a mile in due course. Official explanation: jockey said gelding hung left-handed in home straight

Tredegar spoilt his chances by refusing to really settle early on and was done with before the 2f pole. He is better than this. Official explanation: jockey said colt hung left-handed in home straight (tchd 3-1)

1769 TATTERSALLS MUSIDORA STKS (GROUP 3) (FILLIES) 1m 2f 88y
2:45 (2:45) (Class 1) 3-Y-O **£34,068** (£12,912; £6,462; £3,222; £1,614) **Stalls** Low

Form RPR

111- **1** **Passage Of Time**[185] 6456 3-9-1 110 RichardHughes 4 108+
(H R A Cecil) *trckd ldr: hdwy on bit and cl up 2f out: shkn up to ld 1f out: rdn ins fnl f and styd on* **5/6**[1]

41-0 **2** nk **Sweet Lilly**[10] 1496 3-8-12 102 JamieSpencer 3 104
(M R Channon) *hld up: hdwy on bit 2f out: rdn to chal ent fnl f and ev ch tl no ex towards fin* **15/2**[3]

42- **3** 1 ¾ **Sues Surprise (IRE)**[200] 6217 3-8-12 MichaelHills 2 101
(B W Hills) *lw: led: rdn along and jnd 2f out: sn edgd rt and hdd 1f out: one pce* **8/1**

14- **4** ½ **Shorthand**[214] 5966 3-8-12 101 KerrinMcEvoy 5 100
(Sir Michael Stoute) *swtg: hld up: effrt 3f out and sn pushed along: styd on and ch over 1f out: sn rdn and one pce* **9/4**[2]

060- **5** 15 **Bobansheil (IRE)**[226] 5720 3-8-12 55 TonyHamilton 1 72?
(J S Wainwright) *in tch: rdn along and hdwy 3f out: drvn 2f out and sn outpcd* **250/1**

2m 11.78s (-0.72) **Going Correction** +0.20s/f (Good) **5** Ran SP% **108.6**
Speed ratings (Par 106):102,101,100,99,87
CSF £7.61 TOTE £1.70: £1.10, £2.30; EX 6.30.

Owner K Abdulla **Bred** Juddmonte Farms Ltd **Trained** Newmarket, Suffolk
■ Passage Of Time gave trainer Henry Cecil his eighth victory in this contest.

FOCUS
Tradionally the major domestic trial for the Oaks which rarely attracts a much bigger field than this. The early pace was ordinary, as can be seen from the fact that the 250-1 shot Bobansheil was still within a couple of lengths of the principals passing the 2f pole, and the winning time was 1.86 seconds slower than the earlier handicap. Even so this race provided a pointer to the Epsom Classic thanks to the victory of the odds-on favourite, who was 4lb off her bare juvenile form but is bound to do better.

NOTEBOOK
Passage Of Time, favourite for the Oaks since beating the previous week's Chester Vase winner Soldier Of Fortune in the Criterium de Saint-Cloud last November, came into this with a couple of major question marks hanging over her. Apart from suffering from a throat abscess, she had reportedly just come into season and was conceding 3lb to her four rivals. Content to take a lead from Sues Surprise for most of the way, she travelled well until sent for home over a furlong out, but was given a fright by the runner-up late on and was never able to take things easy. She never really looked like being passed though, and was by no means beaten up. This race served its purpose as a trial and, with the outing likely to have put her just right, she remains the one they all have to beat at Epsom. (op 4-5 tchd Evens and 10-11 in places)

Sweet Lilly, 12th in the 1,000 Guineas and by far the most experienced filly in the line-up, was given a patient ride on this step up in trip and slipstreamed the favourite throughout. Pulled out for her effort a furlong out, she put in a determined effort despite a couple of swishes of the tail, but could never quite get on top of the favourite. The way the race was run did not test her stamina completely and she is unlikely to stay further than this, and she may not be the easiest to place this season. (op 9-1 tchd 7-1)

Sues Surprise(IRE), beaten five lengths by Passage Of Time when last seen at Newmarket last October, was rather keen in front and set just an ordinary pace. That enabled her to keep a little bit in reserve and she kept going after being joined, but eventually had to concede defeat. It may be best to try for a confidence-boosting victory in a maiden before asking her to tackle Pattern company again. (op 10-1)

Shorthand seemed fit enough, but she was sweating and did not look great in her coat. A sister to the previous year's winner Short Skirt and representing the same connections, she was racing for the first time since finishing fourth behind Finsceal Beo in the Rockfel last October. Content to sit out the back and keen enough, she was asked to take closer order halfway up the home straight and was close enough if good enough over a furlong out, but she never really looked like getting to the front and this has to go down as a little disappointing. She will need to find a lot of improvement from somewhere in order to trouble Passage Of Time in the Oaks and it might be better to wait a little longer and aim her at the Ribblesdale. (tchd 5-2)

Bobansheil(IRE), unplaced in all four of her starts at two including when totally out of her depth in the May Hill, managed to stay in touch for longer than might have been expected here thanks to the modest gallop. She picked up £1,614 for her little jaunt round. (op 200-1)

1770 DUKE OF YORK HEARTHSTEAD HOMES STKS (GROUP 2) 6f
3:15 (3:17) (Class 1) 3-Y-O+
£56,780 (£21,520; £10,770; £5,370; £2,690; £1,350) **Stalls** Centre

Form RPR

235- **1** **Amadeus Wolf**[227] 5712 4-9-2 114 NCallan 4 120+
(K A Ryan) *lw: a.p: effrt 2f out: rdn to ld ent fnl f: kpt on strly* **3/1**[1]

510- **2** 1 ¼ **Red Clubs (IRE)**[227] 5712 4-9-6 113 MichaelHills 1 120
(B W Hills) *trckd ldrs: hdwy on outer over 2f out: rdn to ld over 1f out: drvn and hdd ent fnl f: kpt on same pce* **16/1**

114/ **3** ¾ **Soldier's Tale (USA)**[678] 3271 6-9-2 LDettori 13 114+
(J Noseda) *lw: towards rr: hdwy 2f out: sn rdn and styd on ins fnl f: nrst fin* **5/1**[3]

11-1 **4** ½ **Rising Shadow (IRE)**[46] 847 6-9-2 110 JimmyQuinn 8 112
(T D Barron) *dwlt and bhd: hdwy 2f out: sn rdn and swtchd rt over 1f out: styd on wl u.p ins fnl f: nrst fin* **8/1**

04-2 **5** nk **Assertive**[27] 1102 4-9-2 106 DaneO'Neill 15 111+
(R Hannon) *lw: in tch: effrt and n.m.r 2f out: swtchd rt and rdn over 1f out: kpt on same pce* **14/1**

211- **6** shd **Al Qasi (IRE)**[236] 5501 4-9-2 107 KerrinMcEvoy 3 111+
(P W Chapple-Hyam) *lw: towards rr: hdwy over 2f out: swtchd lft and rdn wl over 1f out: kpt on same pce fnl f* **9/2**[2]

25-3 **7** hd **Fonthill Road (IRE)**[4] 1657 7-9-2 102 JamieSpencer 5 110
(R A Fahey) *in rr: rdn along 2f out: swtchd lft and hdwy over 1f out: kpt on ins fnl f: nrst fin* **10/1**

35-3 **8** 2 **Fayr Jag (IRE)**[25] 1159 8-9-2 109 DavidAllan 11 104
(T D Easterby) *prom: rdn along over 2f out and grad wknd* **33/1**

020- **9** 1 ¼ **Welsh Emperor (IRE)**[214] 5962 8-9-6 113 MickyFenton 9 104
(T P Tate) *led: rdn along and wandered 1/2-way: sn hdd and grad wknd fnl 2f* **33/1**

035- **10** hd **Moss Vale (IRE)**[206] 6127 6-9-6 116 MartinDwyer 16 103
(D Nicholls) *cl up: led wl over 2f out: rdn and hdd over 1f out: sn wknd* **25/1**

6-06 **11** ½ **Quito (IRE)**[4] 1656 10-9-2 111 (b) TomEaves 6 97
(D W Chapman) *in tch: rdn along over 2f out: grad wknd* **22/1**

000- **12** ½ **Gift Horse**[227] 5712 7-9-2 104 EddieAhern 10 96
(D Nicholls) *bit bkwd: trckd ldrs: effrt over 2f out: sn rdn and btn* **20/1**

110- **13** 1 ¼ **Les Arcs (USA)**[227] 5717 7-9-9 118 JohnEgan 12 99
(T J Pitt) *chsd ldrs: effrt and n.m.r 2f out: sn rdn and btn* **14/1**

-223 **14** ¾ **Bond City (IRE)**[10] 1497 5-9-2 101 TedDurcan 7 89
(G R Oldroyd) *a towards rr* **66/1**

0-06 **15** 1 ¼ **Tabaret**[10] 1497 4-9-2 98 DeanMcKeown 17 85
(R M Whitaker) *prom: rdn along wl over 2f out and sn wknd* **100/1**

05-6 **16** ½ **Steenberg (IRE)**[46] 847 8-9-2 105 RHills 2 84
(M H Tompkins) *in tch: rdn along wl over 2f out and sn wknd* **16/1**

116- **17** 3 ½ **Conquest (IRE)**[229] 5656 3-8-11 114 (b) JHBowman 14 77
(W J Haggas) *hld up: hdwy whn swtchd lft 2f out: sn rdn and btn* **25/1**

1m 10.2s (-2.36) **Going Correction** 0.0s/f (Good)
WFA 3 from 4yo+ 9lb **17** Ran SP% **130.3**
Speed ratings (Par 115):115,113,112,111,111 111,110,108,106,106 105,104,103,102,100 99,95
CSF £53.34 TOTE £3.70: £1.90, £4.90, £2.60; EX 50.20 Trifecta £429.70 Pool: £2,602.70 - 4.30 winning tickets..

Owner Duddy McDonald Heeney IrishNationalStud **Bred** Ascagnano S P A **Trained** Hambleton, N Yorks

FOCUS
A strong renewal of this Group 2 sprint which resulted in a decent winning time. Solid form, with career bests from the first two and the fourth to seventh all within a pound of their marks. The form should work out.

NOTEBOOK
Amadeus Wolf, who posted a series of excellent efforts in defeat in some of the top sprint races last term, got his season off to a perfect start and ran out a much-deserved winner. He was always up with the pace, showed a potent turn of foot to settle the issue entering the final furlong, and can be rated value for a little further than the winning margin as he looked to idle a touch late on. The fact that he failed to win last term meant he did not have a penalty here, and that had a bearing on the result, yet he certainly looks the type to improve as a four-year-old this term and this will have done his confidence the world of good. A return to Group 1 company is now rightly on the cards, with his trainer mapping out the Golden Jubilee, the July Cup and then Haydock for the Betfred Sprint Cup as a likely path for him to follow. (op 4-1)

Red Clubs(IRE), the Group 2 Diadem winner last season, turned in a sterling effort in defeat under his penalty and, like the winner, looks set for another decent year. He emerges as the best horse at the weights and looks worthy of his place back at the highest level again now. (tchd 14-1)

Soldier's Tale(USA), last seen finishing fourth in the 2005 July Cup, looked big and well in the paddock and was noted finishing his race with gusto, showing he clearly retains all of his ability. He has very few miles on the clock, possesses a neat turn of foot, and it is hoped that he comes out of this without a hitch and can finally have a full season's racing. (op 11-2 tchd 6-1)
Rising Shadow(IRE), who took the Cammidge Trophy on his seasonal bow 46 days previously, again gave himself plenty to do from off the pace yet was noted finishing his race with real purpose on this debut in Group company. His style of running will always dictate he needs things to fall just right, but he is no doubt in the form of his life at present and has a Group prize well within his compass this term when the ground is on the easy side.
Assertive, second to Asset in the Abernant Stakes on his reappearance, gave a boost to the form of his stable companion and ran right up to his best in this higher grade. He deserves to find another opening and can gain reward when dropping to a slightly lower level again. (op 16-1)
Al Qasi(IRE), a highly progressive handicapper at three, deserves to be rated better than the bare form on this return to action and debut in Group company. He would have been closer had he not missed a beat at the start and, with improvement assured for this experience, still looks capable of making his mark in Group races this season. (op 11-2 tchd 6-1)
Fonthill Road(IRE) took time to hit full stride and ran with credit in defeat on this big step up in class. He ideally needs a stiffer track and looks capable of Listed success at the least this season. (tchd 11-1 in places)
Fayr Jag(IRE) ran another sound race and, while not quite matching the level of his seasonal bow at Thirsk, is still a decent benchmark for this form. (op 50-1)
Les Arcs(USA), last year's Golden Jubilee and July Cup hero, can be rated a little better than the bare form and should come on plenty for the outing. He will also relish the return to a faster surface in due course. (tchd 16-1)

1771 40% BETTER VALUE FROM BLUE SQUARE STKS (H'CAP) 1m 4f
3:50 (3:51) (Class 4) (0-85,85) 4-Y-0+ **£7,772** (£2,312; £1,155; £577) **Stalls** Centre

Form RPR
00-2 **1** **Tcherina (IRE)**[20] [1258] 5-8-2 **72** DuranFentiman(3) 3 85
(T D Easterby) *in tch: hdwy 4f out: led over 2f out: hld on wl* **11/2**[3]
11-3 **2** *1 1/4* **High Treason (USA)**[18] [1288] 5-9-0 **81** TedDurcan 11 92
(W J Musson) *hld up in rr: hdwy and nt clr run over 2f out: styd on fnl f: nt trble wnr* **7/1**
4-34 **3** *nk* **Mull Of Dubai**[7] [1575] 4-8-5 **72** JohnEgan 4 83
(J S Moore) *t.k.h in rr: snatched up over 6f out: hdwy 3f out: chal over 1f out: kpt on same pce* **12/1**
2-55 **4** *nk* **La Estrella (USA)**[13] [1438] 4-8-12 **79** TPQueally 2 90
(J G Given) *chsd ldrs: kpt on same pce appr fnl f* **14/1**
0-40 **5** *2* **Cruise Director**[5] [1621] 7-9-1 **82** EddieAhern 10 89
(Ian Williams) *trckd ldrs: rdn and edgd rt over 2f out: kpt on same pce* **20/1**
04-2 **6** *2 1/2* **Greek Well (IRE)**[18] [1288] 4-8-10 **77** KerrinMcEvoy 9 80
(Sir Michael Stoute) *lw: w ldrs: chal over 2f out: fdd over 1f out* **10/3**[2]
45-0 **7** *1* **Transvestite (IRE)**[21] [1244] 5-8-10 **82** PatrickHills(5) 1 84
(J W Hills) *s.i.s: in rr: hdwy on wd outside over 2f out: nvr rchd ldrs* **20/1**
/3-0 **8** *2* **Missoula (IRE)**[18] [1288] 4-8-9 **76** JimmyQuinn 5 75
(M H Tompkins) *hld up in rr: hdwy over 3f out: sn chsng ldrs: one pce fnl 2f* **20/1**
-031 **9** *1 3/4* **Sudden Impulse**[9] [1532] 6-8-1 **71** 6ex oh2 AndrewElliott(3) 7 67
(A D Brown) *chsd ldrs: one pce fnl 3f* **14/1**
16-1 **10** *2 1/2* **Forroger (CAN)**[18] [1288] 4-9-3 **84** PhilipRobinson 13 76+
(M A Jarvis) *t.k.h towards rr: effrt whn bdly hmpd 2f out: no ch after* **5/2**[1]
00-5 **11** *nk* **Luna Landing**[15] [1385] 4-9-0 **81** DaleGibson 14 72
(Jedd O'Keeffe) *led 2f: chsd ldrs: outpcd fnl 3f* **66/1**
2-00 **12** *6* **Peruvian Prince (USA)**[68] [652] 5-8-10 **77** TonyHamilton 6 59+
(R A Fahey) *mid-div: effrt whn bdly hmpd 2f out: lost pl: eased ins fnl f* **50/1**
41-0 **13** *18* **Abstract Art (USA)**[18] [1288] 4-8-10 **77** MartinDwyer 12 30
(Miss Venetia Williams) *led after 2f: shkn up over 4f out: hdd over 2f out: wkng whn sn hmpd and lost pl: eased ins fnl f* **40/1**
2163 **14** *3 1/2* **Polish Power (GER)**[45] [868] 7-8-13 **85** JamesMillman(5) 8 32
(J S Moore) *s.s: a in rr: eased fnl f* **33/1**
163- **15** *1 3/4* **Fossgate**[197] [6287] 6-8-9 **76** NCallan 15 20
(J D Bethell) *mid-div: hung rt and lost pl over 2f out: bhd whn eased ins fnl f* **33/1**

2m 33.39s (-1.21) **Going Correction** +0.20s/f (Good) **15** Ran SP% **126.6**
Speed ratings (Par 105):104,103,102,102,101 99,99,97,96,94 94,90,78,76,75
CSF £41.60 CT £462.11 TOTE £7.10: £2.50, £2.70, £2.90; EX 76.20.
Owner Mr & Mrs W J Williams **Bred** Ken Carroll **Trained** Great Habton, N Yorks

FOCUS
Just a steady gallop until turning in and a pretty rough race. The second and third did well to come from off the pace. The form looks very sound overall.
Forroger(CAN) Official explanation: jockey said colt suffered interference in running
Peruvian Prince(USA) Official explanation: jockey said gelding suffered interference in running
Abstract Art(USA) Official explanation: jockey said gelding had no more to give
Polish Power(GER) Official explanation: jockey said horse missed the break

1772 BET@BLUESQ.COM E B F NOVICE STKS 5f
4:25 (4:26) (Class 3) 2-Y-0 **£8,420** (£2,505; £1,251; £625) **Stalls** Centre

Form RPR
42 **1** **New Jersey (IRE)**[11] [1478] 2-8-12 NCallan 7 89
(K A Ryan) *w'like: str: lw: trckd ldrs: effrt over 1f out: styd on to ld last 75yds* **5/1**[3]
2 *1/2* **Art Advisor (IRE)** 2-8-12 SebSanders 2 87
(J Howard Johnson) *w'like: athletic: w ldr: led over 1f out: hdd and no ex wl ins fnl f* **12/1**
1 **3** *2* **Fred's Lad**[42] [926] 2-9-5 PaulMulrennan 10 87
(M W Easterby) *w'like: chsd ldrs stands' side: hung lft over 1f out: kpt on same pce* **11/2**
41 **4** *2* **Bahama Baileys**[9] [1528] 2-9-0 J-PGuillambert 8 75
(M Johnston) *athletic: led tl over 1f out: hung lft and kpt on same pce* **7/2**[1]
5 *1 1/4* **Angle Of Attack (IRE)** 2-8-12 TonyHamilton 6 68
(R A Fahey) *w'like: lengthy: chsd ldrs: outpcd after 2f: edgd rt and styd on strly fnl f: improve* **12/1**
6 **6** *1/2* **Tikinheart (IRE)**[9] [1528] 2-8-12 DavidAllan 5 67
(T D Easterby) *str: lw: s.i.s: sn chsng ldrs: kpt on same pce fnl 2f* **20/1**
01 **7** *3 1/2* **Ingleby Star (IRE)**[12] [1454] 2-9-2 PaulFessey 9 58
(T D Barron) *str: w ldrs: edgd lft and wknd over 1f out* **7/1**
1215 **8** *2* **Thunder Bay**[14] [1390] 2-9-0 MatthewDavies(7) 3 56
(M R Channon) *chsd ldrs: edgd lft and wknd over 1f out* **7/1**
0 **9** *1/2* **Caprima (IRE)**[18] [1285] 2-8-0 PatrickDonaghy(7) 4 40
(M Brittain) *w'like: s.i.s: outpcd and detached in last: kpt on fnl f* **100/1**
1 **10** *3 1/2* **Just Sort It**[18] [1291] 2-9-2 TedDurcan 1 36
(W Jarvis) *w'like: lw: unruly in stalls: s.i.s: bhd fnl 2f* **4/1**[2]

58.99 secs (-0.33) **Going Correction** 0.0s/f (Good) **10** Ran SP% **120.4**
Speed ratings (Par 97):102,101,98,94,92 92,86,83,82,76
CSF £65.59 TOTE £7.00: £2.40, £3.30, £2.20; EX 94.20.
Owner Clipper Logistics **Bred** Mark Commins **Trained** Hambleton, N Yorks
■ Stewards' Enquiry : J-P Guillambert two-day ban: careless riding (Jun 4-5)

FOCUS
Solid form, and the race should produce winners. New Jersey improved for the easier ground and the runner-up made a taking debut.

NOTEBOOK
New Jersey(IRE) still has some growing up to do. Appreciating the rain, he travelled strongly and really knuckled down to outgun the runner-up in the closing stages. (op 8-1 tchd 9-1 in a place)
Art Advisor(IRE) ◆, an April foal, is well-made type who stands over a fair amount of ground. He travelled strongly upsides and was only edged out by the much more experienced winner near the line. He will surely go one better. (op 14-1)
Fred's Lad, who looked backward in his coat, showed plenty of toe but again showed a marked tendency to lug left. (tchd 6-1)
Bahama Baileys, quite a tall individual, made the running but had no rail to help this time and he wandered towards the centre under pressure. He still has something to learn and will be better suited by six furlongs. (op 3-1 tchd 9-2)
Angle Of Attack(IRE) ◆, a March foal, is quite a lengthy type. Tapped for toe at halfway, he made his way to the stands' side and finished to some effect. This will have taught him plenty. (op 20-1)
Tikinheart(IRE) again forfeited ground at the start. He ran respectably and should improve again for the outing. (op 33-1)
Ingleby Star(IRE), carrying tons of condition, did not impress going to post and, edging left under pressure, dropped right away. He will bounce back in due course. (op 9-2)
Just Sort It, who looked very fit indeed, was very restless in the stalls and ended up with his head under the front gate. He never went a yard and this should be ignored. Official explanation: jockey said colt was upset in stalls and never travelled (op 9-2)

1773 CHRIS WRIGHT "STILL NOT TOO OLD TO ROCK'N'ROLL" STKS (H'CAP) 1m 2f 88y
5:00 (5:01) (Class 3) (0-90,87) 3-Y-0 **£8,096** (£2,408; £1,203; £601) **Stalls** Low

Form RPR
01 **1** **Spice Route**[18] [1290] 3-9-4 **87** JamieSpencer 1 99
(M L W Bell) *lw: trckd ldrs: led over 2f out: edgd rt: styd on wl ins fnl f* **6/1**[2]
02-1 **2** *1 3/4* **Jeer (IRE)**[18] [1303] 3-8-13 **82** NCallan 2 91
(E A L Dunlop) *hld up in tch: effrt 3f out: wnt 2nd 1f out: kpt on wl* **16/1**
40-4 **3** *2 1/2* **Rosbay (IRE)**[27] [1110] 3-8-12 **81** DavidAllan 3 86
(T D Easterby) *lw: hld up in rr: hdwy over 3f out: styd on same pce fnl f* **9/1**
1 **4** *nk* **Woodcraft**[29] [1081] 3-8-11 **80** RichardHughes 5 84
(B W Hills) *chsd ldrs: effrt over 3f out: styd on same pce fnl 2f* **10/1**
13- **5** *1 1/4* **Wheels In Motion (IRE)**[244] [5308] 3-8-12 **81** MickyFenton 6 83
(T P Tate) *lw: led: hung rt fr over 5f out: hdd over 2f out: kpt on same pce* **14/1**
13-3 **6** *1 1/4* **White Deer (USA)**[20] [1257] 3-9-1 **84** KDarley 8 83
(M Johnston) *chsd ldrs: effrt 4f out: sltly hmpd and swtchd lft over 1f out: kpt on same pce* **12/1**
31-2 **7** *nk* **Hunting Tower**[23] [1202] 3-9-1 **84** DaneO'Neill 7 83
(R Hannon) *mid-div: effrt 4f out: hung rt over 1f out: kpt on: nvr rchd ldrs* **6/1**[2]
4513 **8** *1 1/2* **New Beginning (IRE)**[18] [1293] 3-8-11 **80** PatCosgrave 13 76
(Mrs S Lamyman) *in rr: hdwy over 3f out: one pce fnl 2f* **33/1**
5-43 **9** *1/2* **Bed Fellow (IRE)**[39] [939] 3-9-0 **83** JHBowman 10 78
(A P Jarvis) *hld up in last: hdwy over 3f out: one pce fnl 2f* **12/1**
51- **10** *3* **Fushe Jo**[243] [5332] 3-8-9 **78** TomEaves 4 68
(J Howard Johnson) *chsd ldrs: sn pushed along: lost pl 2f out* **6/1**[2]
01-5 **11** *1 3/4* **Mutadarrej (IRE)**[27] [1106] 3-9-3 **86** RHills 14 73
(J L Dunlop) *s.i.s: sme hdwy over 3f out: nvr nr ldrs* **5/1**[1]
0-01 **12** *3/4* **Danetime Panther (IRE)**[16] [1348] 3-8-11 **80** JosedeSouza 12 65
(P F I Cole) *s.i.s: effrt 3f out: nvr nr ldrs* **33/1**
0-33 **13** *8* **Spirit Of The Mist (IRE)**[21] [1243] 3-9-0 **83** JohnEgan 11 54
(T J Pitt) *chsd ldr: lost pl over 2f out: eased ins fnl f* **20/1**
01-6 **14** *10* **Spume (IRE)**[19] [1277] 3-8-8 **77** KerrinMcEvoy 9 30
(Sir Michael Stoute) *mid-div: effrt 3f out: lost pl 2f out: bhd whn eased ins fnl f* **8/1**[3]

2m 11.58s (-0.92) **Going Correction** +0.20s/f (Good) **14** Ran SP% **128.3**
Speed ratings (Par 103):103,101,99,99,98 97,97,95,95,93 91,91,84,76
CSF £103.19 CT £881.05 TOTE £6.50: £2.40, £4.80, £4.10; EX 85.40 Place 6 £283.05, Place 5 £82.83.
Owner Mrs G Rowland-Clark and K J Mercer **Bred** Usk Valley Stud **Trained** Newmarket, Suffolk
■ Stewards' Enquiry : Jamie Spencer one-day ban: careless riding (Jun 4)

FOCUS
Just a steady gallop with almost the whole field strung across the track at the 2f marker. Plenty of unexposed types and the form looks strong and should work out well.

NOTEBOOK
Spice Route is that not big but clearly has a good engine. Dropping back in trip, he edged right in front and ended up under the stands'-side rail. He was firmly in command at the finish and the King George V Handicap looks the sensible Royal Ascot option, although he could still take his chance in the Derby. (op 5-1)
Jeer(IRE), not the best of walkers, stayed on in determined fashion to chase home the winner. He is progressing nicely and will be suited by a step up to 12f. (op 20-1)
Rosbay(IRE), a lot more exposed than most, proved well suited by the step up in trip. (op 12-1 tchd 20-1 in a place early)
Woodcraft, having just his second start, gave a good account of himself and should continue on the upward learning curve. (tchd 9-1)
Wheels In Motion(IRE), who has grown and filled out over the winter, made the running but he was hanging right going into the home turn and ended up under the stands'-side rail. In the end he failed to truly see out the trip. (op 16-1)
White Deer(USA) was still in the firing line when the winner went across his bows. The suspicion was that he was going nowhere at the time and a drop back to a mile might be the answer. (op 10-1)
Hunting Tower, 4lb higher, lacks substance and showed a marked tendency to hang. Even so he kept going all the way to the line and this extended trip suited him. (op 15-2)
Fushe Jo, an immature type, did not lack market support. Winner of his second and final outing at two, he still looked very inexperienced and was soon being driven along. He can do a fair bit better in time. (op 7-1 tchd 15-2 and 5-1)
Mutadarrej(IRE), who lacks substance, missed a beat at the start and never got competitive. (op 8-1)
Spirit Of The Mist(IRE) Official explanation: jockey said colt lost its action
Spume(IRE) again ran well below expectations and after this has an awaful lot to prove. (op 7-1 tchd 13-2)
T/Jkpt: Not won. T/Plt: £327.30 to a £1 stake. Pool: £166,021.60. 370.25 winning tickets. T/Qpdt: £41.00 to a £1 stake. Pool: £6,521.75. 117.50 winning tickets. JR

1774 - 1776a (Foreign Racing) - See Raceform Interactive

1168 NAAS (L-H)

Wednesday, May 16

OFFICIAL GOING: Good changing to good to yielding after race 4 (7.05)

1777a BLUE WIND STKS (GROUP 3) 1m 2f
7:05 (7:10) 3-Y-O+ £39,527 (£11,554; £5,472; £1,824)

RPR

1 **Four Sins (GER)**39 [946] 3-8-9 102 MJKinane 1 110+
(John M Oxx, Ire) *trckd ldrs in 4th: hdwy early st: led under 2f out: sn rdn clr: eased nr fin* **3/1**1

2 2 1/2 **Cherry Hinton**17 [1332] 3-8-9 JAHeffernan 2 102
(A P O'Brien, Ire) *mid-div: 7th 1/2-way: 4th and prog early st: 2nd and kpt on ins fnl f* **13/2**3

3 shd **Nick's Nikita (IRE)**10 [1511] 4-9-9 98 JMurtagh 3 102
(M Halford, Ire) *hld up towards rr: rdn and hdwy on inner early st: 4th over 1f out: kpt on u.p* **8/1**

4 3/4 **Blessyourpinksox (IRE)**10 [1511] 6-9-9 101 DPMcDonogh 11 101
(Peter Casey, Ire) *mid-div: 5th on outer ent st: swtchd under 2f out: kpt on u.p* **7/1**

5 hd **Reform Act (USA)**17 [1330] 4-9-9 106 PJSmullen 5 100
(D K Weld, Ire) *led: jnd 1/2-way: regained ld early st: hdd under 2f out: kpt on same pce u.p* **4/1**2

6 3 1/2 **Akua'Ba (IRE)**24 [1186] 3-8-9 (p) KJManning 14 94
(J S Bolger, Ire) *settled 2nd: 3rd appr st: sn chal: no ex fr over 1f out: eased* **8/1**

7 1 1/4 **Mount Eliza (IRE)**81 5-9-9 PShanahan 13 92
(Charles O'Brien, Ire) *towards rr: prog 2f out: 7th 1f out: no ex* **50/1**

8 nk **Bring Back Matron (IRE)**17 [1333] 3-8-9 78 DJMoran 10 91?
(J S Bolger, Ire) *chsd ldrs: 6th 1/2-way: no imp st* **25/1**

9 3 1/2 **Diamond Necklace (USA)**10 [1511] 3-8-9 100 CO'Donoghue 6 85
(A P O'Brien, Ire) *in rr of mid-div: no imp st* **7/1**

10 3 1/2 **Amusing (IRE)**37 [987] 3-8-9 86 DMGrant 4 79
(John Joseph Murphy, Ire) *a towards rr* **50/1**

11 2 1/2 **Dont Dili Dali**11 [1472] 4-9-9 (p) FMBerry 8 74
(J S Moore) *hld up: 9th 1/2-way: rdn and no imp st: sltly hmpd over 1f out* **7/1**

12 1 1/4 **Sacrosanct (IRE)**10 [1511] 4-9-9 90 WSupple 7 72
(Joseph Crowley, Ire) *a bhd* **50/1**

13 1/2 **Sakkara Star (IRE)**229 [5663] 4-9-9 87 RPCleary 9 71
(M Halford, Ire) *sn prom: disp ld 1/2-way: hdd early st: sn wknd* **50/1**

U **You're Beautiful (USA)**244 [5329] 3-8-9 94 WMLordan 12 —
(David Wachman, Ire) *rrd up and uns rdr as stalls opened* **20/1**

2m 11.6s (-4.00)
WFA 3 from 4yo+ 14lb 14 Ran SP% **134.5**
CSF £24.71 TOTE £2.90: £1.90, £3.30, £3.80; DF 13.80.
Owner H H Aga Khan **Bred** Graf U Grafin V Stauffenberg **Trained** Currabeg, Co Kildare
■ Stewards' Enquiry : D P McDonogh two-day ban: careless riding (May 25,28)

FOCUS
A solid renewal of this Group 3 that attracted four previous stakes winners and several promising and unexposed sorts.

NOTEBOOK
Four Sins(GER) confirmed the promise of her second to Arch Swing in a 7f Group 3 at Leopardstown last month with a decisive victory. After challenging for the lead early in the straight, she went to the front under two furlongs out and stayed on strongly in the closing stages to record a clear cut success. A step up to 1m 4f will not present her with any problems and she looks well worth a shot at the top middle-distance three-year-old fillies' events. Her trainer stressed that she was far from a definite starter at Epsom, but she does appeal as the type to run a big race in the Irish Oaks. (op 3/1 tchd 7/2)
Cherry Hinton, one of several maidens, ran a cracking race in defeat and made good progress from her debut third to La Conquistadora at Navan last month. She struck to her task well in the straight and seemed to cope well with the step up in trip. She will have no trouble shedding her maiden tag and looks quite capable of making her mark at stakes level. (op 5/1)
Nick's Nikita(IRE) was towards the rear off the final bend, but stayed on well and improved on her effort in a Listed race at Gowran earlier this month. She appeals as one that could pick up a Listed event and could well do better for a step up to 1m 4f. (op 10/1)
Blessyourpinksox(IRE), one place behind Nick's Nikita on her reappearance at Gowran, improved on that performance and there could well be more to come from her. Already a dual Listed winner, she could well prove capable of further stakes-race success. (op 10/1)
Reform Act(USA), who chased home Yeats on her reappearance, made much of the running and was in front early in the straight but she was unable to raise her effort inside the final quarter of a mile. Possibly quicker ground and a longer trip would show her off to best effect. (op 9/2 tchd 5/1)
Akua'Ba(IRE) could do no more from over a furlong out, but this maiden still ran a good race and showed enough to suggest that she can pick up black type. She has run into some above-average sorts in both her starts this season and will not have any trouble opening her account. (op 6/1)
Mount Eliza(IRE) was not disgraced and should be able to improve on her first run since February.
Bring Back Matron(IRE) was taking a marked rise in class having contested a Navan handicap last time. Her effort here suggests that she can pick up maiden.
Diamond Necklace(USA) failed to deliver on the promise of her third in a Gowran Listed event and was not at her best. (op 8/1 tchd 9/1)
Dont Dili Dali came here off a good run behind Echelon at Newmarket, but was unable to land a blow in a race where she looked to have a good chance. This was not her true form.

1778 - 1780a (Foreign Racing) - See Raceform Interactive

1501 SALISBURY (R-H)

Thursday, May 17

OFFICIAL GOING: Good to soft (good in places, 7.6)
The ground was changed to simply 'good to soft', with no 'good' in places after the second race.
Wind: Virtually nil

1781 AVONBRIDGE AT WHITSBURY STUD MAIDEN STKS 5f
1:55 (1:56) (Class 4) 2-Y-O £4,210 (£1,252; £625; £312) **Stalls Centre**

Form RPR

1 **Sweepstake (IRE)** 2-8-12 JimmyQuinn 13 84
(R Hannon) *racd far side and trckd lone opponent tl led 3f out: tk overall ld 1f out: kpt on wl* **14/1**

2 1 1/4 **King's General (USA)** 2-9-3 JimCrowley 9 84+
(Mrs A J Perrett) *hmpd s: bhd: hdwy fr 2f out to ld stands' side gp 1f out but 2nd to wnr on far side: kpt on wl but a hld* **12/1**

32 3 1 1/2 **Party In The Park**11 [1498] 2-9-3 PatDobbs 4 79
(R Hannon) *chsd ldrs stands' side and led overall over 2f out: hdd 1f out: sn one pce* **15/8**1

4 3 **Lowry's Art** 2-8-12 JamesDoyle 16 63
(R M Beckett) *sn chsng ldrs on stands' side: rdn and styd on same pce fr over 1f out* **33/1**

04 5 shd **Rough Rock (IRE)**10 [1540] 2-9-3 BrettDoyle 8 68
(B J Meehan) *wnt rt s: sn rcvrd to chse ldrs: effrt 2f out: wknd fnl f* **9/1**

6 1 1/2 **What Katie Did (IRE)** 2-9-0 RichardKingscote(3) 12 62
(J A Osborne) *chsd ldrs: shkn up 1/2-way: wknd appr fnl f* **6/1**3

7 shd **The Name Is Frank** 2-9-3 RichardThomas 5 62
(J W Mullins) *chsd ldrs: rdn 1/2-way: wknd fnl f* **50/1**

6 8 1/2 **Charlie Be (IRE)**8 [1586] 2-9-3 RobertHavlin 15 60
(Mrs P N Dutfield) *racd w wnr far side and led for 2f: wknd ins fnl 2f* **100/1**

9 shd **Tayarat (IRE)** 2-9-3 MartinDwyer 7 60+
(M P Tregoning) *slowly away: in rr and sn nudged along: styd on fr over 1f out: gng on cl home* **8/1**

10 nk **Spanish Bounty** 2-9-3 TPQueally 10 59
(J G Portman) *hmpd s: sn chsng ldrs: wknd over 1f out* **33/1**

54 11 1 1/2 **New Balls Please (IRE)**33 [1033] 2-9-3 IanMongan 2 53
(P M Phelan) *outpcd fr 1/2-way* **33/1**

12 3/4 **Ledgerwood** 2-9-3 J-PGuillambert 14 51
(J W Hills) *a outpcd* **33/1**

13 3/4 **Tiger's Rocket (IRE)** 2-9-3 RichardSmith 11 48
(R Hannon) *hmpd s: a bhd* **50/1**

14 shd **Hadaf (IRE)** 2-9-3 RHills 1 48
(M P Tregoning) *led stands' side tl hdd over 2f out: wknd wl over 1f out* **5/2**2

00 15 5 **Mister Cafnex (IRE)**8 [1586] 2-9-0 JerryO'Dwyer(3) 3 30
(B W Duke) *a in rr* **100/1**

63.53 secs (1.94) **Going Correction** +0.325s/f (Good) 15 Ran SP% **130.8**
Speed ratings (Par 95):97,95,92,87,87 85,85,84,84,83 81,80,78,78,70
CSF £176.78 TOTE £55.00: £11.70, £4.30, £1.40; EX 891.90.
Owner B Bull **Bred** Calley House Uk **Trained** East Everleigh, Wilts

FOCUS
The stands' side is often the place to be at Salisbury when the ground is on the soft side, and 13 of the 15-strong field duly headed in that direction but, somewhat surprisingly, the winner was one of only two who raced far side, suggesting that was in fact the place to be. Some decent yards were represented and this looked like a maiden that should produce some winners. The form makes sense through the third and the fifth.

NOTEBOOK
Sweepstake(IRE), by promising first-season sire Acclamation, cost 65,000euros and is the first foal of a sister to a smart 7f-1m6f winner. This was a fine effort on her racecourse debut but, seeing as she was one of only two horses who raced far side – the other being Charlie Be, who showed little on his debut – it is very hard to know what exactly she achieved. Only time will tell how good she is, but the chances are she will turn out to be quite useful, especially considering this victory was achieved against mainly colts and geldings. (op 33-1)
King's General(USA) ◆, a $150,000 half-brother to three winners, including a multiple sprint winner in the US, won the race on the near side in pretty good style and looks a useful prospect.
Party In The Park ran behind the well-regarded Winker Watson on his debut at Newbury, before finding only the potentially smart Achilles Of Troy too good at Newmarket, but he did little to boost the form of those two races, managing only third. This easier ground might not have been ideal, and he is clearly up to winning a maiden, but he is obviously vulnerable to something above average. (op 13-8 tchd 6-4)
Lowry's Art, a half-sister to a couple of 7f scorers, out of a 7f winner, was one of only two fillies in the race and made a pleasing debut, producing an effort towards the outer of the near-side group before flattening out. She ought to be suited by a step up in trip and should find a race.
Rough Rock(IRE) had shown some ability on his two previous starts and helps give the form a solid look. (op 12-1 tchd 14-1)
What Katie Did(IRE), an 80,000euros half-brother to juvenile winners between 5f-7f, out of a 5f two-year-old scorer, showed ability on his racecourse debut and could improve. (op 7-1 tchd 11-2)
Tayarat(IRE) ◆, a 110,000gns first foal of a 1m4f winner, was passed over by Richard Hills, but made a very promising debut, keeping on nicely in the closing stages having missed the break. He should have learnt plenty from this and ought to go close next time. (op 16-1)
Hadaf(IRE), a half-brother to 6f two-year-old winner Katheer, out of a 6f juvenile scorer, dropped away rather tamely after showing good early speed and may want better ground. (tchd 10-3)

1782 BEGBIES TRAYNOR CLAIMING STKS 6f 212y
2:25 (2:27) (Class 5) 3-Y-O £3,238 (£963; £481; £240) **Stalls Centre**

Form RPR

0354 1 **Gee Ceffyl Bach**10 [1538] 3-8-4 55 MartinDwyer 3 59+
(M R Channon) *trckd ldrs: n.m.r over 2f out: drvn to ld over 1f out: hld on wl* **7/2**2

00-0 2 1 1/2 **Fun In The Sun**36 [1001] 3-8-5 40 EdwardCreighton 5 56
(Jane Southcombe) *in rr: hdwy fr 2f out to chse wnr fnl f: kpt on wl but a hld* **100/1**

00-0 3 3 **Fish Called Johnny**24 [1202] 3-9-5 80 BrettDoyle 4 62
(B J Meehan) *in tch: pushed along and hdwy over 2f out: chsd ldrs over 1f out: styd on same pce* **5/4**1

20-0 4 hd **Hester Brook (IRE)**35 [1008] 3-8-6 54 FergusSweeney 9 48
(J G M O'Shea) *in rr: hdwy fr 2f out: kpt on fnl f but nvr gng pce to rch ldrs* **20/1**

-200 5 1 **Cantique (IRE)**9 [1561] 3-8-5 60 ow1 JamesDoyle 10 45
(Ms J S Doyle) *in tch: rdn and styd on same pce fr over 2f out* **14/1**

000- 6 3/4 **La Cuvee**189 [6409] 3-8-5 46 TravisBlock(5) 12 48
(R M Beckett) *sn bhd: pushed along over 2f out: kpt on fnl f but nvr in contention* **14/1**

6000 7 5 **Tizzydore (IRE)**34 [1031] 3-8-6 49 LPKeniry 15 30
(A G Newcombe) *in rr: hdwy 3f out: nvr rchd ldrs and one pce fnl 2f* **40/1**

343 8 nk **Musical Locket (IRE)**55 [736] 3-8-2 55 RichardSmith 16 25
(R Hannon) *chsd ldrs: rdn 3f out: wknd over 1f out* **7/1**3

3665 9 hd **Calloff The Search**38 [974] 3-8-12 56 (p) SaleemGolam(3) 13 38
(W G M Turner) *pressed ldrs: led wl over 2f out: hdd over 1f out and wknd qckly* **10/1**

0000 10 6 **Meadfoot**25 [1175] 3-8-8 50 JimCrowley 1 15
(B R Millman) *sn chsd ldrs: rdn over 2f out: wknd over 1f out* **40/1**

50-0 11 2 1/2 **Fiddlers Spirit (IRE)**23 [1232] 3-8-13 47 (b1) StephenDonohoe 8 13
(J G M O'Shea) *sn led: hdd wl over 2f out: sn wknd* **66/1**

0-00 12 1 1/2 **Princely Royal**17 [1346] 3-8-7 50 (b1) MatthewHenry 6 3
(J J Bridger) *chsd ldrs: rdn 3f out: wknd 2f out* **50/1**

0-5 13 3 1/2 **Zameliana**16 [1386] 3-8-5 AlanDaly 11 —
(Dr J R J Naylor) *prom early: bhd fr 1/2-way* **66/1**

0000 14 4 **Bahama Gold**23 [1210] 3-8-6 40 (p) RichardThomas 7 —
(D G Bridgwater) *early spd: bhd fr 1/2-way* **66/1**

6-00 **15** *1* **Fiona's Wonder**^{52} [791] 3-9-5 47 ....(p) PatDobbs 17 —
(R A Harris) *chsd ldrs: wknd 3f out* **66/1**

46-0 **16** *30* **Dispol Truly (IRE)**^{79} [577] 3-8-2 45 .... JimmyQuinn 2 —
(A G Newcombe) *racd alone stands' side: nvr on terms* **33/1**

1m 30.6s (1.54) **Going Correction** +0.325s/f (Good) **16** Ran SP% **123.1**
Speed ratings (Par 99):104,102,98,98,97 96,90,90,90,83 80,78,74,70,69 34
CSF £347.43 TOTE £5.00: £1.60, £17.20, £1.40; EX 388.40.The winner was claimed by Adrian Swingler for £7,000. Fish Called Johnny was claimed by Richard Teatum for £12,000. Fun In The Sun was claimed by P. D. Evans for £5,000. La Cuvee was claimed by B. G. Powell for £10,000.
Owner Phil Jen Racing **Bred** Phil Jen Racing **Trained** West Ilsley, Berks

FOCUS
A moderate contest, but plenty of action afterwards, with four horses claimed. Only Dispol Truly raced stands'side this time and she was beaten out of sight. The winner could do a bit better but the form is not rock solid with a lot of the field disappointing.
Zameliana Official explanation: trainer said filly finished distressed

1783 BATHWICK TYRES FILLIES' H'CAP — 1m 4f
2:55 (2:55) (Class 4) (0-85,84) 4-Y-0+ **£7,772** (£2,312; £1,155; £577) **Stalls** High

Form RPR

2221 **1** **Moon Empress (FR)**^{46} [869] 4-8-5 **71** .... MartinDwyer 4 79
(W R Muir) *in rr: pushed along 3f out: hdwy fr 2f out to ld 1f out: hrd drvn and r.o strly whn chal cl home* **10/1**

210- **2** *nk* **Swan Queen**^{258} [4997] 4-9-1 **81** .... JimmyQuinn 7 88
(J L Dunlop) *chsd ldrs: led 3f out: narrowly hdd 2f out: styd pressing ldrs and str chal thrght fnl f: no ex cl home* **7/1**

020- **3** *1 1/2* **Candle**^{202} [6202] 4-9-0 **80** .... FergusSweeney 8 85
(H Candy) *in tch: pressed ldrs fr 2f out tl slt ld over 1f out: sn hdd: styd on same pce* **9/2**^{3}

-530 **4** *1 3/4* **Tranquilizer**^{22} [1244] 5-8-9 **75** ....(t) TPQueally 6 77
(D J Coakley) *hld up in tch: drvn and sme hdwy over 2f out: kpt on same pce fr over 1f out* **12/1**

-113 **5** *1/2* **Lisathedaddy**^{15} [1414] 5-8-11 **80** .... RichardKingscote$^{(3)}$ 3 81+
(B G Powell) *hld up towards rr: hdwy over 3f out: led 2f out: hdd over 1f out: sn btn* **5/2**^{1}

61-5 **6** *13* **And Again (USA)**^{14} [1434] 4-8-10 **76** .... IanMongan 5 57
(R A Teal) *led tl hdd 3f out: wknd 2f out* **20/1**

300- **7** *2* **Island Odyssey**^{202} [6202] 4-9-4 **84** .... DO'Donohoe 2 61
(E A L Dunlop) *chsd ldrs: rdn 3f out: sn wknd* **9/1**

3-12 **8** *2* **Love Always**^{16} [1371] 5-8-3 **74** .... WilliamBuick$^{(5)}$ 1 48
(S Dow) *in tch: chsd ldr 6f out tl over 3f out: sn btn* **7/2**^{2}

2m 40.72s (4.36) **Going Correction** +0.325s/f (Good) **8** Ran SP% **113.0**
Speed ratings (Par 102):98,97,96,95,95 86,85,83
CSF £75.39 CT £359.57 TOTE £9.60: £2.40, £2.10, £1.70; EX 43.90.
Owner Foursome Thoroughbreds **Bred** Eric Puerari And Oceanic Bloodstock **Trained** Lambourn, Berks

FOCUS
The official going was changed to simply 'good to soft', with no 'good' in places before this race.A fair fillies' handicap in which the early pace was ordinary at best. The form is unconvincing overall with the winner seemingly on a harsh mark. It has been rated through the third, to last year's course-and-distance form.

1784 MYDDELTON & MAJOR MAIDEN FILLIES' STKS (DIV I) — 1m 1f 198y
3:25 (3:28) (Class 4) 3-Y-0+ **£4,210** (£1,252; £625; £312) **Stalls** High

Form RPR

5- **1** **Dance Of Light (USA)**^{216} [5939] 3-8-12 .... MartinDwyer 5 73+
(Sir Michael Stoute) *trckd ldr: led over 3f out: rdn and edgd lft jst ins fnl f: readily* **4/7**^{1}

2 *2 1/2* **Pugnacious Lady** 3-8-12 .... JamesDoyle 6 66
(J W Hills) *in rr but in tch: hdwy 2f out: rdn and styd on strly fnl f to take 2nd cl home: no ch w wnr* **66/1**

3 *hd* **Djalalabad (FR)** 3-8-12 .... PhilipRobinson 7 65
(M A Jarvis) *chsd ldrs: rdn over 2f out: chsd wnr ins fnl f: one pce and ct for 2nd cl home* **8/1**^{3}

0- **4** *nk* **Dangerous Dancer (IRE)**^{244} [5344] 3-8-9 .... RichardKingscote$^{(3)}$ 3 65
(R Charlton) *chsd ldrs: pushed along and one pce over 2f out: kpt on again ins fnl f: gng on cl home* **20/1**

4- **5** *3/4* **Ommadawn (IRE)**^{243} [5380] 3-8-12 .... OscarUrbina 8 63+
(J R Fanshawe) *chsd ldrs: rdn to chse wnr 2f out: no imp: wknd fnl f* **8/1**^{3}

6 *nk* **Hayward's Heath** 3-8-12 .... LPKeniry 10 62?
(B W Duke) *in tch: hdwy over 2f out: chsd ldrs over 1f out: kpt on but nvr gng pce to be competitive* **66/1**

7 *1 1/2* **Moonfinder (IRE)** 3-8-12 .... IanMongan 1 59
(J L Dunlop) *stdd s: in rr: drvn along 3f out: kpt on fnl 2f: nvr gng pce to rch ldrs* **20/1**

0 **8** *1/2* **Hermanita**^{34} [1024] 3-8-12 .... RobertHavlin 9 58
(G Wragg) *in rr but in tch: pushed along over 2f out: mod prog fnl f* **40/1**

0-0 **9** *3 1/2* **Queens Quay**^{9} [1560] 3-8-12 .... PatDobbs 4 51
(R Hannon) *a towards rr* **66/1**

53-3 **10** *5* **Lady Alize (USA)**^{10} [1537] 3-8-7 86 ....(t) WilliamBuick$^{(5)}$ 2 41
(R A Kvisla) *in rr: racd on outside: shkn up 3f out: nvr in contention* **6/1**^{2}

056- **11** *2 1/2* **Elmasong**^{160} [6745] 3-8-12 50 .... MatthewHenry 11 36
(J J Bridger) *led tl hdd over 3f out: sn btn* **100/1**

2m 14.49s (6.03) **Going Correction** +0.325s/f (Good) **11** Ran SP% **117.6**
Speed ratings (Par 102):88,86,85,85,85 84,83,83,80,76 74
CSF £77.87 TOTE £1.40: £1.10, £11.80, £2.00; EX 41.60.
Owner Mr & Mrs G Middlebrook **Bred** Stonewall Farm **Trained** Newmarket, Suffolk

FOCUS
A reasonable fillies' maiden, although they went a steady pace early on and the winning time was no less than 3.35 seconds slower than the second division. Rtaed around the fifth, the form is hard to rate positively given the time but the winner is sure to do a lot better than the bare form.

1785 MYDDELTON & MAJOR MAIDEN FILLIES' STKS (DIV II) — 1m 1f 198y
4:00 (4:00) (Class 4) 3-Y-0+ **£4,210** (£1,252; £625; £312) **Stalls** High

Form RPR

23-4 **1** **Fretwork**^{15} [1391] 3-8-12 78 .... PatDobbs 3 77+
(R Hannon) *mde most tl hdd 6f out: styd w ldr and led again 4f out: shkn up 2f out: sn forged clr: comf* **5/2**^{2}

2 *4* **Mercury Blue** 3-8-12 .... LPKeniry 6 69
(S Kirk) *in tch: rdn and one pce 3f out: styd on fr over 1f out: str run ins fnl f to take 2nd last stride: no ch w wnr* **33/1**

0-0 **3** *shd* **Ashmal (USA)**^{27} [1127] 3-8-12 .... RHills 9 69
(J L Dunlop) *chsd ldrs: rdn over 2f out: chsd wnr ins fnl f but no imp: ct for 2nd on line* **12/1**

3-3 **4** *1 1/4* **Eternal Path (USA)**^{27} [1127] 3-8-12 .... MartinDwyer 5 66
(Sir Michael Stoute) *t.k.h early: chsd ldrs: wnt 2nd ins fnl 3f: rdn and no imprssion on wnr fr 2f out: wknd and lost 2nd ins fnl f* **8/11**^{1}

33-0 **5** *3* **Usk Melody**^{8} [1581] 3-8-9 74 .... EmmettStack$^{(3)}$ 1 60
(G A Huffer) *sn chsng ldrs: rdn and hung rt 2f out: sn btn* **8/1**^{3}

6 **6** *3/4* **Central Force**^{10} [1522] 3-8-12 .... StephenDonohoe 8 59
(E A L Dunlop) *in rr but in tch: sme prog fnl 2f: nvr gng pce to be competitive* **25/1**

0- **7** *1 1/2* **On Watch**^{244} [5352] 3-8-12 .... FergusSweeney 7 56
(H Candy) *in rr tl mod prog fnl 2f* **50/1**

8 *1/2* **Esclarmonde (IRE)** 3-8-12 .... StephenCarson 4 55
(L M Cumani) *in rr tl mod prog fnl 2f* **25/1**

00- **9** *7* **Atlantic Dame (USA)**^{209} [6073] 3-8-12 .... JimCrowley 10 41
(Mrs A J Perrett) *w wnr: led 6f out to 4f out: wknd qckly 3f out* **66/1**

00-0 **10** *3/4* **Muffett's Dream**^{17} [1355] 3-8-12 57 .... RichardThomas 2 39
(J A Geake) *pressed ldrs to 3f out: sn wknd* **66/1**

2m 11.14s (2.68) **Going Correction** +0.325s/f (Good) **10** Ran SP% **120.9**
Speed ratings (Par 102):102,98,98,97,95 94,93,93,87,86
CSF £87.64 TOTE £3.70: £1.40, £6.80, £2.60; EX 112.90.
Owner The Queen **Bred** The Queen **Trained** East Everleigh, Wilts

FOCUS
The bare form looks of a similar standard to the first division, but the pace was better and the winning time was a massive 3.35 seconds faster. The form is more solid than division one, although with the favourite disappointing the winner probably did not need to improve on her juvenile form.
Eternal Path(USA) Official explanation: jockey said filly ran too free

1786 JORDAN BROOKES CHARTERED ACCOUNTANTS H'CAP — 6f
4:35 (4:35) (Class 5) (0-75,75) 3-Y-O **£3,238** (£963; £481; £240) **Stalls** Centre

Form RPR

22-0 **1** **Mason Ette**^{23} [1228] 3-9-2 **73** .... PhilipRobinson 5 82+
(C G Cox) *trckd ldrs: led over 1f out: rdn out fnl f* **2/1**^{1}

13 **2** *2 1/2* **Cha Cha Cha**^{19} [1286] 3-9-1 **72** .... DO'Donohoe 2 74
(K A Ryan) *chsd ldrs: ev ch 2f out: chsd wnr thrght fnl f but nvr any ch* **7/2**^{2}

300- **3** *1 1/2* **Pango's Legacy**^{220} [5871] 3-8-12 **74** .... TravisBlock$^{(5)}$ 1 71+
(H Morrison) *hld up in rr: pushed along over 2f out: styd on fr over 1f out: kpt on cl home but nvr gng pce to rch ldng pair* **11/1**

1- **4** *shd* **My Love Thomas (IRE)**^{185} [6457] 3-9-2 **73** .... MartinDwyer 3 70
(E A L Dunlop) *s.i.s: sn chsng ldrs: edgd lft 3f out: kpt on fr 2f out but nvr quite gng pce to chal: one pce ins fnl f* **4/1**^{3}

1-05 **5** *2 1/2* **Zahour Al Yasmeen**^{10} [1535] 3-9-4 **75** .... IanMongan 7 64
(M R Channon) *disp ld tl led 2f out: hdd over 1f out and sn btn* **7/2**^{2}

000- **6** *5* **Divalini**^{213} [6014] 3-8-4 **61** oh12 .... JimmyQuinn 10 35
(J Akehurst) *sn slt ld: hdd 2f out: wknd qckly* **50/1**

04-0 **7** *7* **Stargazy**^{64} [679] 3-8-2 **66** .... AshtonByles$^{(7)}$ 8 19
(R Charlton) *chsd ldrs to 1/2-way* **16/1**

36-6 **8** *10* **The King And I (IRE)**^{15} [1398] 3-8-13 **70** .... LPKeniry 9 —
(J S Moore) *chsng ldrs whn sltly hmpd 3f out: sn lost tch* **12/1**

1m 16.7s (1.72) **Going Correction** +0.325s/f (Good) **8** Ran SP% **121.6**
Speed ratings (Par 99):101,97,95,95,92 85,76,62
CSF £9.96 CT £63.89 TOTE £3.20: £1.10, £1.90, £3.20; EX 12.00.
Owner Brighthelm Racing **Bred** Barry Walters Catering **Trained** Lambourn, Berks

FOCUS
Just an ordinary three-year-old sprint handicap for the grade, run at a strong pace. They raced towards the far side, although the winner made her move up the middle. She looked well in on her second 2yo start and is rated back to that level, with the second running to her latest mark.

1787 AXMINSTER CARPETS APPRENTICE H'CAP — 6f 212y
5:05 (5:05) (Class 5) (0-70,70) 4-Y-0+ **£2,101** (£2,101; £481; £240) **Stalls** Centre

Form RPR

0002 **1** **Quantum Leap**^{5} [1666] 10-8-6 **64** ....(p) ThomasBubb$^{(7)}$ 6 73+
(S Dow) *hmpd s: in rr: swtchd to outside and hdwy fr 2f out: styd on strly fnl f to force dead heat* **5/1**^{2}

0-00 **1** *dht* **Stamford Blue**^{9} [1564] 6-8-9 **60** ....(b) LukeMorris 14 69
(R A Harris) *in rr: rdn along 3f out: hdwy fr 2f out to ld 1f out: ct on line for dead heat* **5/1**^{2}

0644 **3** *2* **Digital**^{9} [1564] 10-8-4 **62** .... MatthewDavies$^{(7)}$ 10 66
(M R Channon) *t.k.h: led tl hdd 1f out: sn one pce* **3/1**^{1}

00-0 **4** *1/2* **Bold Argument (IRE)**^{8} [1589] 4-8-10 **66** .... NBazeley$^{(5)}$ 2 69
(Mrs P N Dutfield) *wnt rt s: stdd towards rr: rdn 2f out: hdwy fnl f: nt rch ldrs* **20/1**

00-3 **5** *1 1/4* **Dr Synn**^{11} [1507] 6-8-6 **62** .... JosephWalsh$^{(5)}$ 3 61
(J Akehurst) *hmpd s: in rr: pushed along 1/2-way: kpt on fnl f but nvr in contention* **3/1**^{1}

0-00 **6** *shd* **Isphahan**^{35} [1013] 4-8-12 **70** .... DavidProbert$^{(7)}$ 12 69
(A M Balding) *chsd ldrs: drvn along 1/2-way: kpt on fnl f but nvr a danger* **11/1**

0-00 **7** *1 1/4* **Corrib (IRE)**^{9} [1564] 4-8-12 **66** .... WilliamCarson$^{(3)}$ 7 62
(B Palling) *chsd ldrs: drvn to chal over 1f out: eased whn hld ins fnl f* **10/1**

00-0 **8** *1* **Salisbury Plain**^{7} [1612] 6-8-6 **60** .... KylieManser$^{(3)}$ 11 53
(N I M Rossiter) *a towards rr* **33/1**

0-06 **9** *10* **Lizarazu (GER)**^{9} [1564] 8-9-5 **70** ....(p) JackMitchell 8 37
(R A Harris) *chsd ldrs 4f* **9/1**^{3}

1m 30.32s (1.26) **Going Correction** +0.325s/f (Good) **9** Ran SP% **118.5**
Speed ratings (Par 103):105,105,102,102,100 100,99,98,86
WIN: Quantum Leap £2.80, Stamford Blue £3.20. PL: QL £1.80, SB £2.00, Digital £1.80. EX: QL/SB £20.80, SB/QL £20.70. CSF: QL/SB £15.54, SB/QL £15.54. TRIC: QL/SB/D £44.72, SB/QL/D £44.72. Place 6 £61.90, Place 5 £25.28.
Owner Mrs M E O'Shea **Bred** L C And Mrs A E Sigsworth **Trained** Epsom, Surrey
■
Owner Brian Hicks **Bred** Mrs Wendy Miller **Trained** Earlswood, Monmouths
■ A first winner for apprentice Thomas Bubb, albeit he had to share the honours.
■ Stewards' Enquiry : William Carson caution: allowed filly to coast home
N Bazeley one-day ban: failed to ride to draw (May 28); one-day ban: careless riding (May 29)

FOCUS
A modest handicap restricted to apprentices who had not ridden more than 25 winners. They raced towards the far side, but tended to avoid the rail in the closing stages. The pace was not strong. Quantum Leap was perhaps unlucky not to win outright from Stamford Blue, who is rated to his best.

T/Plt: £86.60 to a £1 stake. Pool: £37,603.10. 316.85 winning tickets. T/Qpdt: £30.80 to a £1 stake. Pool: £2,119.30. 50.80 winning tickets. ST

1767 YORK (L-H)

Thursday, May 17

OFFICIAL GOING: Good to soft

After 4mm overnight rain the going was described as 'just on the easy side of good' though once again the times suggested otherwise.

Wind: Light, half-against Weather: Mainly overcast with light rain late on

1788 TOTESPORT 0800 221 221 STKS (H'CAP) 5f

1:45 (1:46) (Class 2) (0-100,99) 3-Y-O+ **£16,516** (£4,913; £2,455; £1,226) **Stalls** Centre

Form RPR

0-43 **1** **Terentia**13 1456 4-9-6 **95** RichardMullen 3 108
(E S McMahon) *chsd ldr: led wl over 1f out: sn rdn and styd on wl* **12/1**

3-02 **2** *¾* **Corridor Creeper (FR)**7 1601 10-8-13 **95** (p) BarrySavage(7) 9 105
(J M Bradley) *trckd ldrs: hdwy over 2f out: rdn to chse wnr ins fnl f: kpt on* **17/2**3

300- **3** *1 ¼* **Hogmaneigh (IRE)**222 5812 4-9-10 **99** JamieSpencer 8 105+
(S C Williams) *hld up in rr: swtchd rt over 2f out: styd on strly ins fnl f* **9/1**

50-0 **4** *hd* **Prince Namid**17 1363 5-8-10 **85** oh2 RoystonFfrench 12 90
(Mrs A Duffield) *hld up: hdwy on outer 2f out: rdn over 1f out: styd on wl fnl f: nrst fin* **16/1**

0-30 **5** *shd* **Green Park (IRE)**12 1474 4-8-10 **85** LDettori 6 89
(R A Fahey) *chsd ldrs: rdn along 2f out: kpt on ins fnl f* **7/1**2

522- **6** *shd* **Knot In Wood (IRE)**222 5812 5-9-1 **95** JamieMoriarty(5) 1 99+
(R A Fahey) *lw: hld up towards rr: hdwy wl over 1f out: swtchd rt and styd on wl fnl f: nrst fin* **7/1**2

460- **7** *1* **Pacific Pride**222 5812 4-9-6 **95** GrahamGibbons 2 95
(J J Quinn) *chsd ldrs: rdn along and sltly outpcd 2f out: kpt on appr fnl f* **25/1**

06-0 **8** *½* **Guto**7 1601 4-9-3 **92** (b1) NCallan 5 91
(K A Ryan) *led: rdn along 2f out: hdd wl over 1f out: sn drvn and wknd ins fnl f* **20/1**

0004 **9** *hd* **Tournedos (IRE)**7 1601 5-9-10 **99** RichardHughes 11 97
(D Nicholls) *towards rr: hdwy 2f out: sn rdn and styd on ins fnl f* **11/1**

/566 **10** *1* **Bigalos Bandit**7 1601 5-9-0 **89** JoeFanning 13 83
(D Nicholls) *prom: rdn along 2f out: edgd lft and grad wknd* **14/1**

1-23 **11** *1 ½* **Kay Two (IRE)**7 1601 5-8-11 **86** KerrinMcEvoy 16 75
(R J Price) *lw: hld up: effrt and sme hdwy 2f out: sn rdn: n.m.r and btn over 1f out* **9/2**1

6600 **12** *2* **Connect**12 1474 10-8-5 **85** oh3 (b) PatrickHills(5) 4 67
(M H Tompkins) *dwlt: sn outpcd and a in rr* **33/1**

6210 **13** *shd* **Cape Royal**7 1601 7-8-13 **93** (bt) KevinGhunowa(5) 14 74
(J M Bradley) *chsd ldrs: rdn along 2f out: sn wknd* **20/1**

-104 **14** *¾* **Fire Up The Band**13 1456 8-9-8 **97** SilvestreDeSousa 10 76
(D Nicholls) *chsd ldrs: rdn along 2f out: sn wknd* **14/1**

60-0 **15** *1 ¾* **Masta Plasta (IRE)**22 1242 4-9-3 **92** FrancisNorton 7 64
(D Nicholls) *midfield: effrt over 2f out: sn rdn and btn* **14/1**

44-0 **16** *5* **Northern Empire (IRE)**27 1125 4-9-8 **97** JimmyFortune 15 51
(B J Meehan) *s.i.s: a bhd* **20/1**

59.05 secs (-0.27) **Going Correction** +0.15s/f (Good) **16** Ran SP% **126.7**
Speed ratings (Par 109):108,106,104,104,104 104,102,101,101,99 97,94,94,92,90 82
CSF £105.97 CT £988.36 TOTE £17.00: £3.60, £2.30, £2.90, £4.80; EX 136.20 Trifecta £1344.10 Part won. Pool: £1,893.10 - 0.70 winning tickets..

Owner Dr Hugh Jones **Bred** Mrs F S Williams **Trained** Lichfield, Staffs

■ Stewards' Enquiry : Jamie Spencer one-day ban: careless riding (Jun 5)

FOCUS

A competitive sprint handicap in which most of the principals came up the centre of the track, as usual. Solid form, and better to come from the third and sixth in particular.

NOTEBOOK

Terentia, a progressive handicapper last term, had not run badly in a couple of small-field conditions races earlier this season, and was probably suited by the easier ground on this return to handicap compnay. She showed good pace throughout and clearly remains progressive. The Dash at Epsom would be a suitable race for her, but it would be understandable if connections turned their attention to trying to capture some black type with her.

Corridor Creeper(FR) ran well at Chester a week earlier and confirmed that form with five rivals. He is a marvellous old servant to the stable and deserves to go one better in the coming weeks, but he will be 4lb higher in future. (op 15-2)

Hogmaneigh(IRE) ◆, who was third in the Portland here off this mark last September, made a promising return to action, running on strongly at the finish having not enjoyed the clearest of runs. His style of running is not really suited to this track, which generally favours pace horses, and he certainly looks to be on a mark he can win off.

Prince Namid likes a good bit of dig and could have done with even softer ground, but he ran well anyway from 2lb out of the handicap. The only horse drawn in double figures to make the first eight, he finished well alongside the unfavoured stands'-side rail and is another who could soon be winning on a more suitable track, as he is currently on a mark 1lb lower than when last successful. (tchd 18-1)

Green Park(IRE) ran poorly over 6f at Newmarket last time but had shaped with plenty of promise over this trip from an average draw at Beverley previously. Backed in from 12-1 in the morning, he was always being chased along on this speed-favouring track and might be better suited by a stiffer 5f. (op 9-1)

Knot In Wood(IRE) ◆ has never won over a trip this short so this was a highly satisfactory return to action. He stayed on well from off the pace and still looks handicapped to win off his current mark when returned to 6f, a trip over which he is able to race handier. (op 8-1)

Pacific Pride, debuting for a new yard, has run well at this track on more than one occasion in the past, but he is another whose form is over further. He ran well in the circumstances and is entitled to come on for this seasonal reappearance.

Guto did not run much of a race at Chester on his seasonal reappearance, but he was lit up by the first-time blinkers here and showed plenty of speed from the off. He could not sustain it to the finish, though, and might need further help from the Handicapper. (tchd 25-1)

Tournedos(IRE) ran well at Chester (his favourite track) a week earlier but failed to reproduce that form. He probably needs quicker ground to be seen at his best.

Bigalos Bandit went too fast at Chester last week but on this occasion he could not even get to the lead. (op 16-1)

Kay Two(IRE) was not well drawn and raced towards the stands' side of the main group, but he was still disappointing. The ground ought to have suited him, but he never really looked like troubling the judge. (op 5-1)

Cape Royal, as at Chester, was compromised by a poor draw. (op 22-1 tchd 25-1)

Northern Empire(IRE) Official explanation: jockey said gelding never travelled

1789 TOTEPOOL MIDDLETON STKS (GROUP 3) (F&M) 1m 2f 88y

2:15 (2:15) (Class 1) 4-Y-O+

£28,390 (£10,760; £5,385; £2,685; £1,345; £675) **Stalls** Low

Form RPR

20-2 **1** **Topatoo**12 1472 5-8-12 103 MichaelHills 2 108
(M H Tompkins) *hld up in rr: hdwy over 2f out: rdn over 1f out: styd on wl fnl f: led nr fin* **7/2**2

12-1 **2** *nk* **Anna Pavlova**46 875 4-8-12 110 LDettori 4 107
(R A Fahey) *trckd ldrs: hdwy 3f out: swtchd to stands' rail and effrt 2f out: sn led: rdn ins fnl f: hdd and no ex nr fin* **4/6**1

315- **3** *hd* **Portal**217 5917 4-8-12 100 JamieSpencer 3 107
(J R Fanshawe) *trckd ldrs: hdwy 3f out: rdn to ld briefly 2f out: sn hdd and drvn: kpt on same pce wl ins fnl f* **8/1**3

314- **4** *6* **Maroussies Wings (IRE)**251 5155 4-9-0 105 JoeFanning 1 97
(P C Haslam) *led: rdn along and hdd 3f out: rallied u.p and ch tl drvn and wknd over 1f out* **11/1**

263- **5** *3* **Summer's Eve**217 5917 4-8-12 100 DaneO'Neill 6 90
(H Candy) *cl up: led 3f out: rdn along and hdd 2f out: sn drvn and wknd over 1f out* **20/1**

102- **6** *5* **Ivory Gala (FR)**240 5472 4-8-12 95 JimmyFortune 5 80
(B J Meehan) *hld up: rdn along 4f out: a in rr* **40/1**

-300 **7** *9* **Tanzanite (IRE)**10 1524 5-8-12 88 EddieAhern 7 63
(D W P Arbuthnot) *trckd ldrs: hdwy 3f out: rdn along over 3f out: sn wknd* **66/1**

2m 13.83s (1.33) **Going Correction** +0.325s/f (Good) **7** Ran SP% **110.3**
Speed ratings (Par 113):99,98,98,93,91 87,80
CSF £5.74 TOTE £4.60: £2.00, £1.20; EX 6.70 Trifecta £41.00 Pool: £590.24 - 10.20 winning tickets..

Owner Mrs P R Bowring **Bred** M P Bowring **Trained** Newmarket, Suffolk

FOCUS

A fair Group 3, despite the absence of Echelon, but they went a steady early pace before sprinting up the straight, and the time was very moderate for a race of its status, 2.29 seconds slower than the Dante. The favourite probably wasn not quite at her best under conditions faster than ideal for her.

NOTEBOOK

Topatoo, runner-up to Echelon at Newmarket on her reappearance, looked the main danger to the favourite on that piece of form and, being something of a course specialist, she could be expected to improve a bit for the return to Yorkshire. She stayed on strongly to edge the result close home, taking her form figures at this track to an impressive 213511221, and should continue to hold her own at this level. (tchd 4-1)

Anna Pavlova, who won a Listed event at Navan easily on her reappearance, stays further than this, so the steady early pace would not have suited her, but she was sent for home with a fair way to go in an attempt to stretch the opposition. Edging over to the unfavoured stands'-side rail would not have helped her, though, and she was caught close home. She will leave this form behind when stepped back up in distance and/or when getting a better pace. (tchd 8-13)

Portal ◆, a progressive filly last year, looks to have improved again over the winter as she had a bit to find with the first two on the ratings but ran them close, albeit in a tactical race. She probably wants quicker ground than she had here, too, so can be expected to improve on the bare form and win at this level this summer. (op 10-1)

Maroussies Wings(IRE), winner of a Group 3 race at Deauville last summer, had a 2lb penalty to carry for that success. After setting a steady pace, she was seen off by the first three in the closing stages, and was well held at the finish. She should come on for this seasonal reappearance, though, and will be suited by a return to a mile and a half. (op 10-1)

Summer's Eve, who had Portal and Topatoo behind her but Anna Pavlova in front when third in a backend Listed race at Newmarket last term, likes a bit of give but she ran very much as though this seasonal reappearance was needed. She is entitled to come on for it.

Ivory Gala(FR), who went abroad in search of black type last term, was out of her depth on her seasonal reappearance and could well be on her travels again this season. Official explanation: jockey said filly was hanging left-handed (op 33-1)

1790 TOTESPORT.COM DANTE STKS (GROUP 2) 1m 2f 88y

2:45 (2:45) (Class 1) 3-Y-O

£85,170 (£32,280; £16,155; £8,055; £4,035; £2,025) **Stalls** Low

Form RPR

31- **1** **Authorized (IRE)**208 6104 3-9-0 116 LDettori 3 121+
(P W Chapple-Hyam) *h.d.w: str: lw: trckd ldrs: hdwy on bit and cl up 2f out: led over 1f out and sn qcknd clr: impressive* **10/11**1

1-1 **2** *4* **Raincoat**22 1243 3-9-0 84 RichardHughes 1 113
(J H M Gosden) *lw: hld up in tch: hdwy over 3f out and sn pushed along: swtchd rt and rdn over 1f out: styd on to chse wnr ins fnl f* **8/1**

1-40 **3** *1* **Al Shemali**12 1473 3-9-0 92 MJKinane 2 111
(Sir Michael Stoute) *trckd ldng pair: hdwy 3f out: cl up 2f out: sn rdn and kpt on same pce u.p appr fnl f* **18/1**

0-10 **4** *2 ½* **Adagio**12 1473 3-9-0 115 KerrinMcEvoy 4 106
(Sir Michael Stoute) *led: qcknd over 3f out: rdn over 2f out: hdd over 1f out and sn wknd* **5/2**2

11- **5** *16* **Proponent (IRE)**216 5941 3-9-0 94 JimmyFortune 6 76
(R Charlton) *chsd ldr: rdn along 3f out: drvn 2f out and sn outpcd* **7/1**3

000- **6** *20* **Prince Golan (IRE)**208 6104 3-9-0 90 NCallan 5 38
(K A Ryan) *a in rr: outpcd and bhd fnl 3f* **100/1**

2m 11.54s (-0.96) **Going Correction** +0.325s/f (Good) **6** Ran SP% **110.8**
Speed ratings (Par 111):108,104,104,102,89 73
CSF £8.97 TOTE £1.80: £1.30, £2.30; EX 8.00.

Owner Saleh Al Homeizi & Imad Al Sagar **Bred** Marengo Investments And Knighton House Ltd And M **Trained** Newmarket, Suffolk

FOCUS

Traditionally the most significant Derby trial in Britain and, although it is hard to know exactly what the form is worth, Authorized won in the style of a worthy short-priced favourite for Epsom. The winning time was 2.29 seconds faster than the older fillies took in the Middleton Stakes, but still only ordinary for a race of its type.

NOTEBOOK

Authorized(IRE), cosy winner of the Racing Post Trophy on only his second start at two, returned to the track with an impressive success in the principal Derby trial. He travelled well and quickened, winning without being knocked about. It is fair to assume that his trainer has left a bit to work on, and that he can improve again between now and June 2nd. His pedigree suggests he will stay the extra two furlongs at Epsom, so it is easy to see why he is at such short odds now for the Derby. The only slight worry is that he has not yet proved his ability on fast ground, but one would be surprised if the course executive allowed conditions to be too quick. All in all he holds very strong claims of giving his trainer his second Derby winner, following Dr Devious in 1992. Dettori, looking for his first Derby winner, will keep the ride at Epsom. (op Evens tchd 11-10 in places)

Raincoat was unbeaten coming into the race and won the Blue Riband Trial at Epsom last time out, so he was still unexposed. Running on well for second behind the impressive winner, he is certainly Group class, and gives the impression that another two furlongs will be right up his street. He would have to be supplemented to run at Epsom, though, and he might end up in the French Derby instead, although the shorter distance at Chantilly is unlikely to be in his favour.

Al Shemali, who finished in mid-division in the Guineas when a 200-1 shot, reversed form with his stablemate Adagio over this longer trip. He seems to appreciate a bit of give in the ground and might be up to winning a Listed race somewhere. (op 20-1 tchd 16-1)
Adagio, disappointing when sent off favourite for the Guineas, had the chance to prove that he needs further than a mile to be seen at his best, but he again let his supporters down, racing keenly enough in front before failing to get home. His trainer was inclined to think that he is a miler, and he was certainly impressive when he won the Craven over that trip, and perhaps he is just the type that is best caught fresh. (op 3-1 tchd 7-2, 4-1 in a place)
Proponent(IRE) won a minor conditions race at Newmarket in easy fashion last autumn and was another who fell into the 'could be anything' category entering the race, but he was seemingly exposed on this step up in class. He is surely better than this form suggests, and has grown during the off-season, but has it all to prove now. (op 9-2)
Prince Golan(IRE) must have suffered a bout of déjà vu, as he was also a 100-1 shot when last behind Authorized in the Racing Post Trophy on his final start at two.

1791 BANK OF SCOTLAND CORPORATE HAMBLETON STKS (H'CAP) (LISTED RACE) 1m

3:15 (3:17) (Class 1) (0-110,108) 4-Y-0+**£20,744** (£7,843; £3,920; £1,960) **Stalls** Low

Form RPR
-203 **1** **Blythe Knight (IRE)**[8] [1583] 7-8-9 **96** GrahamGibbons 4 111
(J J Quinn) *lw: trckd ldrs gng wl: hdwy over 2f out: swtchd rt and rdn to ld over 1f out: kpt on wl fnl f* **9/1**
0-11 **2** *1* **Wise Dennis**[5] [1651] 5-8-12 **99** 3ex JHBowman 11 112+
(A P Jarvis) *in rr: sltly hmpd over 3f out and sn pushed along: effrt 2f out: sn rdn and styd on ent fnl f: nt rch wnr* **2/1**[1]
103- **3** *¾* **Pride Of Nation (IRE)**[266] [4739] 5-8-10 **97** NickyMackay 7 108+
(L M Cumani) *lw: in tch: hdwy 3f out: rdn to chse ldrs over 1f out: kpt on same pce ins fnl f* **7/2**[2]
0-00 **4** *1 ¾* **Zero Tolerance (IRE)**[26] [1145] 7-8-13 **100** JamieSpencer 2 107
(T D Barron) *led: qcknd over 3f out: jnd and rdn over 2f out: sn drvn and hdd over 1f out: wknd ins fnl f* **7/1**
600- **5** *1* **Black Charmer (IRE)**[203] [6192] 4-8-7 **94** oh2 JoeFanning 5 99
(M Johnston) *trckd ldr: smooth hdwy and cl up over 2f out: sn rdn and ev ch tl drvn and wknd ent fnl f* **40/1**
1P21 **6** *1* **Very Wise**[47] [848] 5-8-11 **98** KerrinMcEvoy 3 100
(W J Haggas) *hld up: hdwy wl over 2f out: sn rdn and no imp fr over 1f out* **11/2**[3]
3610 **7** *1 ¼* **Waterside (IRE)**[13] [1448] 8-8-7 **94** ChrisCatlin 6 94
(G L Moore) *trckd ldng pair: pushed along 3f out: rdn over 2f out and grad wknd* **25/1**
0004 **8** *3 ½* **Kings Point (IRE)**[12] [1480] 6-8-8 **95** (p) RichardHughes 13 86
(R A Fahey) *hld up: a towards rr* **20/1**
020- **9** *1 ¼* **Mine (IRE)**[236] [5523] 9-9-7 **108** (v) MJKinane 9 97
(J D Bethell) *s.i.s: a in rr* **25/1**
20-6 **10** *2 ½* **Babodana**[19] [1305] 7-9-2 **103** MichaelHills 12 86
(M H Tompkins) *in tch: effrt and hdwy over 3f out: sn rdn and btn over 2f out* **12/1**
0-10 **11** *7* **Kew Green (USA)**[5] [1651] 9-8-13 **100** EddieAhern 1 67
(P R Webber) *in tch: hdwy to trck ldrs over 3f out: rdn over 2f out and sn btn* **33/1**
20-0 **12** *14* **Kingsholm**[10] [1524] 5-8-7 **94** oh10 FrancisNorton 10 29
(A M Balding) *b.hind: chsd ldrs: rdn along 3f out: sn wknd* **100/1**

1m 38.77s (-0.73) **Going Correction** +0.325s/f (Good) **12** Ran SP% **120.0**
Speed ratings (Par 111):116,115,114,112,111 110,109,105,104,102 95,81
CSF £25.93 CT £79.99 TOTE £10.40: £2.50, £1.50, £1.70; EX 38.20 Trifecta £119.80 Pool: £2,463.50 - 14.60 winning tickets..
Owner Maxilead Limited **Bred** Gainsborough Stud Management Ltd **Trained** Settrington, N Yorks
■ Stewards' Enquiry : J H Bowman two-day ban: used whip with excessive frequency (May 28-29)

FOCUS
A competitive Listed handicap run at a fair pace. The form looks solid and should work out.

NOTEBOOK
Blythe Knight(IRE) ran well at Chester last time out when things did not go his way and the ground was more suitable here. More importantly, he got a lead this time and his rider was able to settle him just behind the pace. Produced with over a furlong to run, he won quite comfortably in the end and connections are now planning to send him abroad in search of black type. Longer term, his trainer plans to give him a Champion Hurdle campaign. (op 17-2 tchd 8-1)
Wise Dennis was impressive in winning the Victoria Cup last time out and looked the one to beat under a 3lb penalty. His style of running is to be held up out the back and come with a late run, though, and he was racing at a track where those tactics are usually hard to pull off. He ran on strongly at the finish and got the longer trip without any problem, but while he may return to winning ways back on a more suitable track, he will be 5lb higher in future. (op 9-4 tchd 5-2 in a place)
Pride Of Nation(IRE), a progressive handicapper in the first half of last year, had not been seen since August, but he returned with a highly promising performance. He likes this sort of ground and will be interesting in the Royal Hunt Cup if getting his conditions - the ground was too fast and he was poorly drawn when a beaten favourite in the race last year. (op 5-1)
Zero Tolerance(IRE), running off a 2lb lower mark than when successful in this race last year, can have no excuse as he had the bit of give in the ground which is essential to him and, moreover, he enjoyed the run of the race out in front. (op 13-2 tchd 15-2)
Black Charmer(IRE), who was placed in Group company at two, struggled in his four starts last year but has dropped a fair way in the handicap as a result, and been gelded to boot. This was a promising reappearance from 2lb out of the handicap and he should improve for the run. (op 33-1)
Very Wise, flattered by the draw when he won the Lincoln, had a 7lb higher mark to overcome here and was well held. He did not help his chances by proving very free to post. (tchd 6-1 in a place)
Waterside(IRE) is rated 10lb lower on turf than he is on the All-Weather but needs dropping further and prefers quicker ground.
Kew Green(USA) Official explanation: jockey said gelding was unsuited by the good to soft ground

1792 CONSTANT SECURITY E B F MAIDEN STKS 6f

3:50 (3:52) (Class 3) 2-Y-0 **£7,837** (£2,331; £1,165; £582) **Stalls** Centre

Form RPR
1 **Feared In Flight (IRE)** 2-9-3 MJKinane 6 92+
(B W Hills) *unf: s.s: gd hdwy 2f out: r.o strly to ld last 75yds* **6/1**[3]
2 *1 ½* **Nawaaff** 2-9-3 JHBowman 3 85+
(M R Channon) *w'like: trckd ldrs: c to chal 100yds out: no ex* **7/2**[2]
3 *½* **Montaquila** 2-9-3 EddieAhern 5 83+
(J Howard Johnson) *w'like: s.i.s: bhd tl hdwy 2f out: styd on strly ins fnl f* **14/1**
2 **4** *2 ½* **Mission Impossible**[29] [1087] 2-9-3 JimmyFortune 9 76
(P C Haslam) *w'like: w ldrs: led over 1f out: hdd and no ex wl ins fnl f* **10/3**[1]
5 *2 ½* **The Last Bottle (IRE)** 2-9-3 MickyFenton 8 68
(T P Tate) *unf: s.i.s: bhd: hdwy over 1f out: kpt on wl towards fin* **16/1**
6 *¾* **Captain Gerrard (IRE)** 2-9-3 TedDurcan 10 66
(B Smart) *leggy: t.k.h: w ldrs: led over 3f out: hung lft and hdd over 1f out: wknd ins fnl f* **6/1**[3]
7 *nk* **Captain Dunne (IRE)** 2-9-3 DavidAllan 7 65
(T D Easterby) *unf: t.k.h in midfield: edgd rt over 1f out: kpt on* **10/1**
8 *1 ¼* **Lecanvey** 2-8-12 JamieMoriarty[(5)] 11 61
(R A Fahey) *tall: leggy: in rr-div: hdwy over 2f out: nvr nr ldrs* **16/1**
9 *1 ¾* **Fulford** 2-8-10 PatrickDonaghy[(7)] 13 56
(M Brittain) *leggy: s.i.s: sn w ldrs: wknd appr fnl f* **100/1**
0 **10** *1 ½* **Zaplamation (IRE)**[15] [1411] 2-9-3 PatCosgrave 4 51
(D W Barker) *w'like: w ldrs: wknd over 1f out* **33/1**
11 *8* **Big Slick (IRE)** 2-9-3 DeanMernagh 12 27
(M Brittain) *w'like: s.i.s: sn chsng ldrs and drvn along: lost pl 2f out* **66/1**
12 *1 ½* **Hawaass (USA)** 2-9-3 JoeFanning 1 23
(M Johnston) *w'like: s.s: sn chsng ldrs: lost pl over 2f out: sn bhd* **8/1**
13 *½* **Banus Flyer (IRE)** 2-9-3 KimTinkler 2 21
(N Tinkler) *w'like: led tl over 3f out: lost pl over 1f out* **66/1**

1m 13.8s (1.24) **Going Correction** +0.15s/f (Good) **13** Ran SP% **119.4**
Speed ratings (Par 97):97,95,94,91,87 86,86,84,82,80 69,67,66
CSF £26.96 TOTE £7.30: £2.30, £1.90, £4.20; EX 25.90.
Owner J Hanson, Cavendish Inv Ltd, A Patrick **Bred** T W Bloodstock Ltd **Trained** Lambourn, Berks

FOCUS
A decent two-year-old maiden race that should throw up quite a few winners. The winner impressed, looking Royal Ascot material, and it was a pleasing start from the second and third too.

NOTEBOOK
Feared In Flight(IRE), an April foal and on the leg still, was on his toes beforehand but came from last to first, showing a nice turn of foot. He was firmly in command at the line and may now head for the Chesham at Royal Ascot, but his foreleg suggests he would not appreciate fast ground. (op 5-1 tchd 13-2, 7-1 in places)
Nawaaff ♦, a February foal, cost 120,000gns as a yearling. Bred purely for speed and a nice type, he was very green to post and continually bucking. He came with what looked a winning challenge inside the last only to find the winner too strong near the line. He is sure to go one better. (op 10-3 tchd 4-1 in places)
Montaquila ♦, an April foal, is a tall type and was very keen to post. He picked up in fine style late on and is sure to improve and make his mark. (op 16-1)
Mission Impossible, one of just two to have had a previous outing, showed plenty of speed but in the end did not see out the sixth furlong anywhere near as well as the first three. A drop back to five looks on the cards. (op 4-1 tchd 9-2)
The Last Bottle(IRE), a February foal, is like the winner and third a son of first-season sire Hawk Wing. After a tardy start and taking time to find his feet he finished in pleasing style. There should be a fair bit better to come, especially over seven.
Captain Gerrard(IRE), a February foal, cost 130,000gns as a yearling. An attractive good-bodied colt, he tended to do too much and in the end did not see it out. Hopefully this will have taught him plenty. (tchd 11-2)
Captain Dunne(IRE), a January foal, has size and scope. Not the best of walkers, he took some settling but kept on nicely when brought to the stands' side. He is sure to have learnt plenty from this. (op 12-1)
Lecanvey, a March foal, is a close-coupled individual. He stayed on in his own time and there should be better in the pipeline.
Hawaass(USA), an April foal, is an attractive, good-bodied colt. He was noisy in the paddock and after a slow start dropped right away soon after the halfway mark. He can surely do an awaful lot better than he showed here. (op 7-1)

1793 ROBERT PRATT MEMORIAL STKS (H'CAP) 2m 2f

4:25 (4:37) (Class 4) (0-80,80) 4-Y-0+ **£7,772** (£2,312; £1,155; £577) **Stalls** Low

Form RPR
2-50 **1** **Kayf Aramis**[26] [1148] 5-8-9 **70** MarcHalford[(3)] 6 79+
(J L Spearing) *chsd ldrs: led over 4f out: edgd rt over 1f out: styd on wl* **7/1**[3]
-221 **2** *1 ¼* **Great As Gold (IRE)**[24] [1196] 8-8-11 **69** JimmyFortune 17 76
(B Ellison) *chsd ldrs: effrt on wd outside over 3f out: styd on to take 2nd ins fnl f: hrd rdn and no real imp* **11/1**
0404 **3** *1* **Trance (IRE)**[5] [1677] 7-9-7 **79** (p) PaulFessey 7 85
(T D Barron) *bhd and drvn along: hdwy on inner over 3f out: styd on same pce fnl f* **16/1**
0-50 **4** *nk* **Rose Bien**[26] [1152] 5-8-1 **62** (p) DuranFentiman[(3)] 12 68
(P J McBride) *swtg: hld up in rr: hdwy on inner over 3f out: kpt on same pce fnl f* **33/1**
332- **5** *hd* **At The Money**[83] [6495] 4-8-7 **68** RichardHughes 16 74
(J M P Eustace) *trckd ldr: led after 3f: hdd over 4f out: edgd rt over 2f out: kpt on same pce* **13/2**[2]
116 **6** *7* **Global Strategy**[39] [955] 4-8-5 **66** ChrisCatlin 1 64
(Rae Guest) *chsd ldrs: drvn 6f out: wknd over 1f out* **10/1**
/156 **7** *¾* **Mind How You Go (FR)**[5] [1654] 9-9-3 **75** JHBowman 4 72
(J R Best) *led 3f: chsd ldrs: wknd over 1f out* **9/1**
5126 **8** *3* **Salut Saint Cloud**[12] [1253] 6-8-12 **70** (p) SimonWhitworth 9 64
(G L Moore) *swtg: unruly in stalls: mid-div: effrt over 3f out: wknd over 1f out* **16/1**
22-1 **9** *6* **Dhehdaah**[22] [1253] 6-8-9 **67** MickyFenton 18 54
(Mrs P Sly) *hld up in rr: hdwy 7f out: rdn over 3f out: sn btn* **7/1**[3]
-011 **10** *6* **Kristensen**[13] [1457] 8-9-3 **75** (v) NCallan 15 56
(Karen McLintock) *in tch: hdwy over 3f out: hung rt over 1f out: sn wknd and eased* **20/1**
2/21 **11** *shd* **Mr Mischief**[16] [1376] 7-8-7 **70** NicolPolli[(5)] 10 51
(M C Chapman) *hld up in rr: nvr on terms* **25/1**
-455 **12** *3* **Grey Outlook**[11] [1490] 4-8-3 **64** RoystonFfrench 5 41
(Miss L A Perratt) *trckd ldrs: rdn and lost pl over 3f out* **50/1**
220- **13** *12* **Nimra (USA)**[230] [5650] 4-9-2 **77** NickyMackay 3 41
(G A Butler) *hld up in rr: drvn along 6f out: nvr on terms* **33/1**
4333 **14** *¾* **Follow On**[10] [1526] 5-8-7 **65** JamieSpencer 8 28
(A P Jarvis) *bhd: sme hdwy u.p over 4f out: sn wknd* **4/1**[1]
1/52 **15** *9* **Alrida (IRE)**[39] [955] 8-8-7 **70** JamieMoriarty[(5)] 14 23
(R A Fahey) *chsd ldrs: lost pl over 3f out: sn bhd* **13/2**[2]
346- **16** *shd* **Riodan (IRE)**[244] [5338] 5-8-12 **70** GrahamGibbons 2 23
(J J Quinn) *swtg: chsd ldrs: lost pl over 3f out* **33/1**
06-0 **17** *37* **Sworn In (USA)**[5] [1654] 6-9-8 **80** EddieAhern 11 —
(N I M Rossiter) *b: bhd: t.o 3f out: virtually p.u* **80/1**

4m 2.17s (3.87) **Going Correction** +0.325s/f (Good)
WFA 4 from 5yo+ 3lb **17** Ran SP% **131.5**
Speed ratings (Par 105):104,103,103,102,102 99,99,98,95,92 92,91,85,85,81 81,65
CSF £82.77 CT £1234.80 TOTE £9.80: £2.30, £2.40, £4.20, £8.10; EX 71.90.
Owner Mrs Isobel Phipps Coltman **Bred** Mrs Isobel Phipps Coltman **Trained** Kinnersley, Worcs
■ The race was twelve minutes late off after the stalls were originally positioned about 100 yards further back.
■ Stewards' Enquiry : Jimmy Fortune six-day ban: improper riding - used whip with excessive force and frequency (May 28-Jun 2)

FOCUS
A sound gallop and in the end a true test of stamina. The first two ended up under the stands' side, while the third and fourth remained on the far side. The first five finished clear and the form looks sound.
Kristensen Official explanation: jockey said gelding had no more to give
Follow On Official explanation: jockey said horse was unsuited by the good to soft ground
Alrida(IRE) Official explanation: trainer had no explanation for the poor form shown

1794 TOTEEXACTA STKS (H'CAP) 1m 6f
5:00 (5:10) (Class 4) (0-85,85) 4-Y-0+ **£7,772** (£2,312; £1,155; £577) **Stalls** Low

Form				RPR
1-65	**1**		**Bollin Derek**[19] 1300 4-8-12 **76** ... DavidAllan 4 (T D Easterby) *trckd ldrs: led over 4f out: clr and edgd lft over 1f out: eased towards fin* **9/4**[1]	92+
14P-	**2**	5	**Sphinx (FR)**[272] 4560 9-9-5 **83** ... (b) FrancisNorton 2 (Jamie Poulton) *hld up: hdwy over 4f out: wnt 2nd 3f out: kpt on: no ch w wnr* **14/1**	90
-113	**3**	2	**Dundry**[26] 1148 6-9-4 **82** ... (p) GeorgeBaker 13 (G L Moore) *hld up: hdwy over 3f out: styd on same pce fnl 2f* **7/2**[2]	86
0-14	**4**	¾	**Mister Arjay (USA)**[13] 1457 7-8-6 **75** ow3 ... JamieMoriarty(5) 7 (B Ellison) *chsd ldrs: swtchd rt and racd stands' side over 3f out: kpt on same pce fnl 2f* **9/1**	78+
5-50	**5**	2	**Maneki Neko (IRE)**[11] 1490 5-8-4 **71** ... DuranFentiman(3) 9 (E W Tuer) *missed break and swtchd lft s: hld up in last: hdwy over 3f out: nvr trbld ldrs* **20/1**	71
5-45	**6**	1 ¼	**Mighty Moon**[6] 1621 4-8-13 **84** ... (bt) JamesO'Reilly(7) 11 (J O'Reilly) *chsd ldrs: sltly hmpd over 3f out: one pce fnl 2f* **18/1**	83
51-1	**7**	*shd*	**Power Of Future (GER)**[21] 1272 4-9-6 **84** ... TedDurcan 6 (H R A Cecil) *swtg: led tl over 4f out: wknd fnl 2f* **5/1**[3]	82
6-23	**8**	6	**Bronze Dancer (IRE)**[5] 1677 5-8-5 **69** ... PaulQuinn 8 (G A Swinbank) *mid-div: effrt over 3f out: sn btn* **11/1**	59
02/1	**9**	1 ¾	**Gala Evening**[10] 1526 5-9-3 **81** 6ex ... AdamKirby 3 (J A B Old) *swtg: hld up: effrt on outer 4f out: sn chsng ldrs: lost pl over 1f out* **17/2**	69
002-	**10**	¾	**Inchnadamph**[215] 5963 7-9-7 **85** ... (t) RichardMullen 10 (T J Fitzgerald) *hld up: effrt and hung rt 3f out: sn wknd* **25/1**	72
31-0	**11**	2	**Lady Romanov (IRE)**[25] 1181 4-8-8 **72** ... EddieAhern 12 (M H Tompkins) *awkward in stalls: sn trcking ldrs: drvn over 4f out: wknd 3f out* **22/1**	56
0-23	**12**	1	**Ha'Penny Beacon**[9] 1567 4-8-2 **66** ... DaleGibson 5 (D Carroll) *trckd ldrs: drvn 6f out: lost pl 3f out* **50/1**	48

3m 4.41s (4.91) **Going Correction** +0.325s/f (Good) **12** Ran SP% **125.4**
Speed ratings (Par 105):98,95,94,93,92 91,91,88,87,86 85,85
CSF £37.59 CT £116.06 TOTE £3.30: £1.70, £4.80, £2.10; EX 46.20 Place 6 £76.08, Place 5 £22.31.
Owner Sir Neil Westbrook **Bred** Sir Neil And Lady Westbrook **Trained** Great Habton, N Yorks
■ Stewards' Enquiry : Jamie Moriarty three-day ban: careless riding (May 28-30)
FOCUS
Just a steady pace and a moderate winning time. The form has not been rated as positively as it might have been, but Bollin Derek was a wide-margin and very progressive winner.
Maneki Neko(IRE) Official explanation: jockey said gelding missed the break
T/Jkpt: Part won. £51,416.40 to a £1 stake. Pool: £72,417.50. 0.50 winning tickets. T/Plt: £80.40 to a £1 stake. Pool: £174,799.35. 1,585.80 winning tickets. T/Qpdt: £21.50 to a £1 stake. Pool: £6,913.90. 237.40 winning tickets. JR

1795 - 1799a (Foreign Racing) - See Raceform Interactive

1698 BADEN-BADEN (L-H)
Thursday, May 17

OFFICIAL GOING: Soft

1800a US LANDBANKING CUP (36TH BENAZET-RENNEN) (GROUP 3) 6f
4:00 (4:04) 3-Y-0+ **£20,270** (£8,446; £3,378; £1,689)

			RPR
1		**Lucky Strike**[25] 1189 9-9-6 ... ADeVries 6 (A Trybuhl, Germany) *sn prom: led on stands' rail wl over 1f out: drvn out* **21/10**[2]	112
2	*nk*	**Donatello (GER)**[178] 6547 6-9-6 ... JAuge 5 (W Baltromei, Germany) *hdwy 2f out: rdn to take 2nd 100yds out: kpt on wl* **19/10**[1]	111
3	½	**Shinko's Best (IRE)**[25] 1189 6-9-6 ... NRichter 10 (A Kleinkorres, Germany) *a.p: led over 4f out to wl over 1f out: kpt on one pce and lost 2nd 100yds out* **68/10**[3]	110
4	2	**Arc De Triomphe (GER)**[23] 1234 5-9-6 ... FForesi 11 (D Fechner, Germany) *mid-div: trckd wnr through on stands' rail: styd on: nrest at fin* **71/10**	104
5	½	**Slade (GER)**[228] 5710 5-9-2 ... MSuerland 9 (M Trybuhl, Germany) *a in tch: one pce fr wl over 1f out* **45/2**	98
6	1	**Diable (GER)**[25] 8-9-6 ... RMarchelli 12 (H Hesse, Germany) *mid-divison: one pce fnl 2f* **22/1**	99
7	1 ¾	**Polish Magic**[44] 911 7-9-6 ... RKoplik 7 (Z Koplik, France) *led over 1f: wknd over 2f out* **24/1**	94
8	2 ½	**Signum (GER)**[38] 4-9-6 ... JiriPalik 1 (Frau A Glodde, Germany) *spd over 3f* **79/10**	86
9	1 ¾	**Stormiano (GER)**[16] 5-9-6 ... MEsposito 2 (Dr A Bolte, Germany) *w ldrs on outside tl wknd wl over 1f out* **20/1**	81
10	2 ½	**Omasheriff (IRE)**[25] 1189 5-9-6 ... DBoeuf 8 (W Baltromei, Germany) *w ldrs tl wknd qckly 1/2-way* **94/10**	74

1m 11.35s (1.06) **10** Ran SP% **130.1**
WIN 31: PL 13, 13, 17: SF 61.
Owner Stall Lucky Stables International **Bred** Red House Stud **Trained** Germany

1622 HAMILTON (R-H)
Friday, May 18

OFFICIAL GOING: Good (7.5)
Wind: strong, half-behind

1801 CHARD CONSTRUCTION E B F MAIDEN STKS 5f 4y
6:30 (6:30) (Class 5) 2-Y-O **£3,886** (£1,156; £577; £288) **Stalls** Low

Form				RPR
	1		**Lieutenant Pigeon** 2-9-3 ... RoystonFfrench 3 (B Smart) *chsd ldrs: sn pushed along: hdwy over 1f out: led ins fnl f: pushed out* **9/4**[2]	78+
	2	2	**Latin Class (USA)** 2-8-12 ... JoeFanning 1 (M Johnston) *led to ins fnl f: kpt on same pce* **6/5**[1]	66+
	3	8	**Rocheport** 2-9-3 ... TomEaves 4 (J Howard Johnson) *w ldr tl rdn and wknd wl over 1f out* **11/4**[3]	42+
	4	6	**Kingstyle (IRE)** 2-8-10 ... PatrickDonaghy(7) 2 (M Brittain) *sn outpcd and drvn along: no ch fr 1/2-way* **16/1**	20

61.36 secs (0.16) **Going Correction** -0.125s/f (Firm) **4** Ran SP% **108.8**
Speed ratings (Par 93):93,89,77,67
CSF £5.40 TOTE £3.40; EX 5.10.
Owner Dale And Ann Wilsdon **Bred** P A Mason **Trained** Hambleton, N Yorks
FOCUS
Not a strong event but the winner won with a bit to spare and is the type to win more races.
NOTEBOOK
Lieutenant Pigeon, the first foal of an ordinary, but multiple winning sprinter, took a while to grasp what was required but came through well to win with a fair bit in hand. He has physical scope for further imrpovement and should do better. (op 3-1)
Latin Class(USA) ◆, whose dam was a close fourth in the 2001 Queen Mary, looked and ran as though the race was just needed. Although on the leg at present, she has scope for further improvement and is sure to pick up a similar event. (op 5-6 tchd 5-4)
Rocheport, a half-brother to a fair winner over seven and a mile, looked and ran as though this debut run was needed. He should improve for this experience and is likely to be placed to best advantage. (op 3-1 tchd 9-4)
Kingstyle(IRE), a leggy sort lacking in physical substance, was easy to back and soundly beaten on this racecourse debut. (op 25-1)

1802 WILLIAM WALLACE H'CAP 6f 5y
7:00 (7:00) (Class 3) (0-90,96) 3-Y-O **£11,658** (£3,468; £1,733; £865) **Stalls** Low

Form				RPR
0251	**1**		**Aahayson**[7] 1623 3-9-13 **96** 6ex ... PatCosgrave 5 (K R Burke) *mde all: rdn over 1f out: r.o strly* **10/11**[1]	104+
06-2	**2**	1 ½	**Valley Of The Moon (IRE)**[13] 1484 3-8-5 **74** ... DaleGibson 4 (R A Fahey) *trckd ldrs: effrt 2f out: chsd wnr ins fnl f: r.o* **9/1**	76
05-2	**3**	*nk*	**Mundo's Magic**[9] 1577 3-8-4 **73** ... RoystonFfrench 6 (G M Moore) *cl up: rdn 2f out: one pce ins fnl f* **8/1**[3]	74
1-01	**4**	2 ½	**Flores Sea (USA)**[13] 1484 3-8-8 **77** ... PhillipMakin 2 (T D Barron) *s.i.s: outpcd: hdwy and prom over 2f out: sn rdn: no ex ins fnl f* **11/4**[2]	70
30-4	**5**	6	**Pegasus Dancer (FR)**[27] 1160 3-8-6 **75** ... DO'Donohoe 1 (K A Ryan) *prom tl rdn and wknd fr 2f* **12/1**	49
00-5	**6**	4	**Tom Tower (IRE)**[7] 1623 3-8-4 **73** oh1 ow2 ... JoeFanning 3 (A C Whillans) *t.k.h: cl up tl wknd fr 2f out* **28/1**	34

1m 12.75s (-0.35) **Going Correction** -0.125s/f (Firm) **6** Ran SP% **111.3**
Speed ratings (Par 103):97,95,94,91,83 77
CSF £10.01 TOTE £1.90: £1.60, £3.50; EX 11.10.
Owner Philip Richards **Bred** Whitsbury Manor Stud And Mrs M E Slade **Trained** Middleham Moor, N Yorks
FOCUS
A fair handicap and an improved effort from the winner, who remains at the top of his game. The pace was sound and this form should stand up.
NOTEBOOK
Aahayson, allowed the run of the race in a conditions event over course and distance the previous week, had to work much harder under a penalty back in a handicap but showed plenty of determination to run to a similar level. Life is going to be tougher after reassessment in the more competitive handicaps but he looks worth a place in Listed company. (op Evens tchd 11-10)
Valley Of The Moon(IRE) is an improved performer judged on the evidence of her two starts of this year and she ran right up to her best against an in-form rival. The return to a lesser grade should suit and she should continue to give a good account. (op 8-1 tchd 12-1)
Mundo's Magic, who turned in an improved effort on his reappearance, ran creditably in this stronger event. The return to a lesser grade may help and he is another that should continue to give a good account away from progressive sorts. (op 9-1 tchd 10-1 and 7-1)
Flores Sea(USA) looked an improved performer judged on his Thirsk defeat of Valley Of The Moon but he proved disappointing this time and did not look totally happy at this course. He is only lightly raced and would not be one to write off just yet, though.
Pegasus Dancer(FR) had run as well as he ever has done on his reappearance but he proved disappointing this time. He did not progress after winning on his debut last year and may be one to tread carefully with in the near future. (tchd 11-1)
Tom Tower(IRE), back in handicap company, was again well beaten and is one to watch at present. (tchd 25-1)

1803 GLASGOW STKS (LISTED RACE) (C&G) 1m 3f 16y
7:30 (7:30) (Class 1) 3-Y-O **£19,873** (£7,532; £3,769; £1,879) **Stalls** High

Form				RPR
-112	**1**		**Boscobel**[13] 1476 3-9-0 95 ... JoeFanning 4 (M Johnston) *mde all: qcknd clr over 2f out: unchal* **6/4**[1]	103+
1	**2**	6	**Dansant**[18] 1358 3-9-0 90 ... RoystonFfrench 3 (G A Butler) *prom: outpcd over 3f out: kpt on fnl f to go 2nd cl home* **9/2**[3]	93
2-1	**3**	*shd*	**Western Adventure (USA)**[28] 1129 3-9-0 88 ... JimmyFortune 2 (E A L Dunlop) *in tch: hdwy over 4f out: rdn over 3f out: edgd lft and one pce fnl 2f* **2/1**[2]	93
0-05	**4**	6	**Teslin (IRE)**[13] 1475 3-9-0 96 ... KerrinMcEvoy 5 (M Johnston) *chsd wnr: rdn over 3f out: wknd over 1f out* **9/2**[3]	82

2m 25.77s (-0.49) **Going Correction** +0.225s/f (Good) **4** Ran SP% **109.7**
Speed ratings (Par 107):110,105,105,101
CSF £8.26 TOTE £2.00; EX 7.40.
Owner Sheikh Mohammed **Bred** Darley **Trained** Middleham Moor, N Yorks
FOCUS
An interesting field, despite another small turnout and, although the pace was steady, this was a useful performance from Boscobel, who may be capable of better still.
NOTEBOOK
Boscobel ◆ had the run of the race at a course that suits this style of racing but, although tending to hang onto the inside rail, he showed useful form to pull clear of the remainder in the last quarter mile. His record is one of steady improvement and he looks worth a try in stronger company. (op Evens)

Dansant, who created a favourable impression when beating a subsequent winner on his debut in a Windsor maiden, bettered that effort in this stronger event. A more truly-run race would have been in his favour, he should stay a mile and a half and appeals as the type to win again. (op 5-1 tchd 11-2 and 4-1)

Western Adventure(USA), who took the eye in the paddock as a good sort with scope, failed to justify the market support but nevertheless ran his best race upped a fair way in grade. A flatter course and a stronger gallop will be more to his liking and he is also the sort to win more races. (op 9-4 tchd 15-8)

Teslin(IRE), who took the eye in the paddock, had run creditably at Newmarket but proved a disappointment, even allowing for the fact that this race was not really run to suit. He will have to show more before he is worth a bet. (op 8-1)

1804 LUDDON CONSTRUCTION MAIDEN STKS — 1m 1f 36y

8:00 (8:05) (Class 5) 3-Y-O+ — **£3,238** (£963; £481; £240) **Stalls** High

Form — RPR

2344 **1** **Nans Joy (IRE)**[16] 1407 3-8-8 73 ... KerrinMcEvoy 15 — 73
(E J O'Neill) *cl up: led gng wl over 2f out: clr over 1f out: comf* **11/4**[1]

0- **2** *2 1/2* **Freya Tricks**[196] 6318 3-8-3 ... TolleyDean(5) 5 — 68+
(I Semple) *hld up: hdwy over 2f out: chsd wnr ins fnl f: r.o* **33/1**

2-23 **3** *1* **Maslak (IRE)**[31] 1077 3-8-13 78 ... JimmyFortune 9 — 71
(E A L Dunlop) *hld up in midfield: hdwy to chse wnr over 1f out: no ex and lost 2nd ins fnl f* **11/4**[1]

4 *3* **Lochiel** 3-8-6 ... NeilBrown(7) 7 — 64
(Mrs S C Bradburne) *s.i.s: bhd tl styd on fnl 2f: n.d* **18/1**

623- **5** *nk* **Apache Dawn**[222] 5841 3-8-13 77 ... DO'Donohoe 12 — 64
(K A Ryan) *chsd ldrs: effrt over 2f out: no ex over 1f out* **9/2**[2]

425- **6** *2 1/2* **Moonhawk**[284] 4197 4-9-12 68 ... JoeFanning 4 — 60
(J Howard Johnson) *prom tl rdn and outpcd fr 2f out* **13/2**[3]

3-0 **7** *nk* **Dark Energy**[29] 1111 3-8-13 ... RoystonFfrench 2 — 58
(B Smart) *s.i.s: bhd tl styd on fnl 2f: n.d* **12/1**

5-0 **8** *3/4* **Tommy Tobougg**[20] 1290 3-8-13 ... TomEaves 14 — 56
(I Semple) *prom tl rdn and wknd fr over 1f out* **9/1**

453- **9** *6* **Snowflight**[285] 4171 3-8-8 71 ... JamieMoriarty(5) 11 — 44
(R A Fahey) *midfield: rdn 1/2-way: no imp fnl 3f* **14/1**

0 **10** *6* **Irish Plane (IRE)**[20] 1290 3-8-13 ... PhillipMakin 1 — 31
(K R Burke) *led: faltered after 2f: hdd over 2f out: sn wknd* **50/1**

- **11** *4* **Roll Em Over**[48] 4-9-7 ... LeeEnstone 13 — 20
(C W Thornton) *midfield: rdn over 3f out: sn btn* **100/1**

0 **12** *2 1/2* **Asrar**[12] 1491 5-9-4 ... MarkLawson(3) 3 — 14
(Miss Lucinda V Russell) *towards rr: drvn 1/2-way: sn btn* **80/1**

13 *2* **Shoot Out**[103] 4-9-12 ... DaleGibson 6 — 15
(C W Thornton) *towards rr: rdn 1/2-way: sn wknd* **100/1**

14 *61* **Ardent Number**[425] 7-9-5 ... PatrickDonaghy(7) 8 — —
(D A Nolan) *missed break: nvr on terms* **200/1**

2m 0.93s (1.27) **Going Correction** +0.225s/f (Good)
WFA 3 from 4yo+ 13lb — **14** Ran SP% **123.1**
Speed ratings (Par 103):103,100,99,97,96 94,94,93,88,83 79,77,75,21
CSF £112.61 TOTE £3.40: £1.50, £6.60, £1.60; EX 205.20.
Owner Frank Cosgrove **Bred** Mrs Brid Cosgrove **Trained** Averham Park, Notts

FOCUS
Not a strong maiden but one in which the pace was fair and rated to the winner's best previous form.

1805 MCGRATTAN PILING BRAVEHEART STKS (H'CAP) (LISTED RACE) — 1m 4f 17y

8:35 (8:35) (Class 1) (0-110,105) 4-Y-O+

£17,034 (£6,456; £3,231; £1,611; £807; £405) **Stalls** High

Form — RPR

/10- **1** **Scriptwriter (IRE)**[195] 6336 5-8-10 97 ... KerrinMcEvoy 6 — 109+
(Saeed Bin Suroor) *hld up in tch: stdy hdwy over 2f out: effrt and edgd lft over 1f out: styd on wl fnl f to ld post* **8/11**[1]

03-3 **2** *shd* **Camrose**[20] 1304 6-8-12 99 ... (b) JimmyFortune 8 — 106
(J L Dunlop) *hld up in tch: smooth hdwy to ld over 2f out: kpt on fnl f: hdd post* **10/1**[3]

00-5 **3** *2* **Acropolis (IRE)**[29] 1109 6-8-7 94 ow1 ... TomEaves 3 — 98
(I Semple) *hld up in tch: hdwy and cl up over 3f out: rdn and edgd rt over 1f out: one pce fnl f* **16/1**

-602 **4** *3 1/2* **Akarem**[6] 1650 6-9-4 105 ... PatCosgrave 4 — 103
(K R Burke) *prom: effrt and ev ch over 2f out: no ex over 1f out* **10/3**[2]

1102 **5** *1* **Kames Park (IRE)**[9] 1575 5-8-4 91 oh4 ... RoystonFfrench 5 — 88
(I Semple) *hld up: effrt over 3f out: hung lft 2f out: sn no imp* **12/1**

04-2 **6** *2 1/2* **Lets Roll**[20] 1304 6-8-5 92 ... DaleGibson 7 — 85
(C W Thornton) *led to over 2f out: wknd over 1f out* **12/1**

4 **7** *5* **Glitter Baby (IRE)**[47] 875 4-8-4 91 ... (t) DO'Donohoe 2 — 76
(M G Quinlan) *hld up: effrt over 3f out: sn wknd* **33/1**

0010 **8** *10* **Luberon**[23] 1245 4-9-4 105 ... JoeFanning 9 — 74
(M Johnston) *w ldr tl wknd over 2f out* **16/1**

2m 39.35s (0.17) **Going Correction** +0.225s/f (Good) — **8** Ran SP% **120.2**
Speed ratings (Par 111):108,107,106,104,103 101,98,91
CSF £10.41 CT £74.05 TOTE £1.80: £1.20, £2.10, £3.30; EX 10.80.
Owner Godolphin **Bred** Newgate Stud Co **Trained** Newmarket, Suffolk
■ Stewards' Enquiry : Kerrin McEvoy one-day ban: used whip with excessive frequency (May 29)

FOCUS
A useful contest but a muddling gallop means this bare form may not prove entirely reliable, although the runner-up is the best guide. Scriptwriter left the impression he is a lot better than the bare form.

NOTEBOOK

Scriptwriter(IRE) ◆ is a lightly-raced sort but seems to go particularly well fresh and ran up to his best to win his fourth race from his last five starts. Effective on both quicker and easier ground, he looks a bit better than the bare form and may be capable of a bit more this term. (op 11-10 tchd 5-4 in places)

Camrose does not find winning very easy and has often found less than expected off the bridle but did nothing wrong on this occasion, finding plenty after travelling well only to be mugged on the post. This shows he has a similar race in him but he would not be one to be lumping on at shortish odds next time. (op 8-1)

Acropolis(IRE), largely a disappointing type, ran creditably and left the impression that a stiffer overall test of stamina would have been in his favour on this second start for current connections. He is not going to be the easiest to place successfully, though. (tchd 14-1)

Akarem, who won this race a year ago, had run well at Ascot on his previous start but proved a shade disappointing this time. He may be suited by more give in the ground and is not one to write off yet. (op 3-1 tchd 7-2 and 4-1 in a place)

Kames Park(IRE), an improved performer on turf and sand this year, was not disgraced from 4lb out of the handicap in a race that was not really run to suit. A stronger gallop would have suited but he is the type that needs things to drop right. (op 14-1)

Lets Roll, who shaped as though retaining all his ability on his reappearance, looked to have conditions to suit and was allowed the run of the race but he proved a bit of a disappointment. His last three wins have been over a mile and five at Ayr and he will be of more interest back at that course. (op 11-1)

1806 BRANDON HOMES H'CAP — 5f 4y

9:10 (9:10) (Class 5) (0-75,72) 4-Y-O+ — **£3,886** (£1,156; £577; £288) **Stalls** Low

Form — RPR

5311 **1** **Misaro (GER)**[6] 1681 6-9-2 72 6ex ... (b) TolleyDean(5) 2 — 88
(R A Harris) *trckd ldrs: led over 1f out: rdn and r.o strly* **7/2**[1]

10-0 **2** *1 1/2* **Elkhorn**[20] 1299 5-9-5 70 ... (b) TomEaves 11 — 84+
(Miss J A Camacho) *hld up: hdwy over 1f out: chsd wnr ins fnl f: r.o* **11/2**

0423 **3** *2* **Oeuf A La Neige**[4] 1711 7-8-2 53 oh5 ... DO'Donohoe 4 — 56
(Miss L A Perratt) *sn outpcd: hdwy centre 2f out: kpt on fnl f: no imp* **10/1**

0022 **4** *1 1/4* **Throw The Dice**[8] 1597 5-8-4 55 ... (v) RoystonFfrench 9 — 54
(D W Barker) *cl up tl rdn and nt qckn over 1f out* **5/1**[3]

-110 **5** *1 3/4* **Raccoon (IRE)**[7] 1640 7-9-5 70 6ex ... JimmyFortune 8 — 63
(D W Chapman) *led to over 1f out: no ex* **5/1**[3]

00-0 **6** *1 3/4* **Welcome Approach**[31] 1080 4-9-0 65 ... PhillipMakin 5 — 51
(J R Weymes) *midfield: drvn 1/2-way: no imp over 1f out* **25/1**

-040 **7** *1/2* **Kings College Boy**[3] 1754 7-8-12 68 ... (b) JamieMoriarty(5) 3 — 53
(R A Fahey) *in tch: n.m.r over 2f out: rdn and outpcd over 1f out* **9/2**[2]

-400 **8** *1* **Sandwith**[28] 1134 4-9-3 68 ... (p) PatCosgrave 7 — 49
(J S Wainwright) *chsd ldrs tl wknd over 1f out* **33/1**

00-1 **9** *nk* **Controvento (IRE)**[47] 873 5-9-7 72 ... (b) MO'Reilly 12 — 52
(Eamon Tyrrell, Ire) *prom on outside tl wknd fr 2f out* **14/1**

000- **10** *1/2* **Strawberry Patch (IRE)**[196] 6315 8-8-3 57 ... AndrewElliott(3) 14 — 35
(J S Goldie) *in tch in centre tl wknd fr 1/2-way* **20/1**

3134 **11** *1 1/2* **Ashes (IRE)**[15] 1427 5-8-12 63 ... PaulMulrennan 13 — 36
(K R Burke) *cl up on outside tl rdn and wknd fr 2f out* **14/1**

0-00 **12** *6* **Sokoke**[8] 1594 6-7-13 57 oh8 ow4 ... PatrickDonaghy(7) 1 — 8
(D A Nolan) *sn outpcd: no ch fr 1/2-way* **100/1**

59.96 secs (-1.24) **Going Correction** -0.125s/f (Firm) — **12** Ran SP% **124.1**
Speed ratings (Par 103):104,101,98,96,93 90,90,88,87,87 84,75
CSF £23.11 CT £186.30 TOTE £5.20: £2.20, £2.70, £3.60; EX 31.10 Place 6 £55.96, Place 5 £11.45.
Owner Messrs Criddle Davies Dawson & Villa **Bred** Wilhelm Fasching **Trained** Earlswood, Monmouths

FOCUS
An ordinary handicap but a decent gallop throughout and this form looks solid and should prove reliable.
T/Plt: £27.90 to a £1 stake. Pool: £59,066.85. 1,542.90 winning tickets. T/Qpdt: £3.70 to a £1 stake. Pool: £4,478.80. 892.60 winning tickets. RY

1143 NEWBURY (L-H)

Friday, May 18

OFFICIAL GOING: Good to soft (good in places, 6.3)
Wind: strong ahead

1807 BET AT LADBROKES NOW ON 0800 777 888 FILLIES' CONDITIONS STKS — 5f 34y

1:55 (1:58) (Class 3) 2-Y-O

£6,855 (£2,052; £1,026; £513; £256; £128) **Stalls** High

Form — RPR

1 **Polar Circle (USA)** 2-8-7 ... AdrianMcCarthy 1 — 81+
(P W Chapple-Hyam) *unf: trckd ldr: led jst ins fnl 2f: drvn and r.o wl fnl f* **11/8**[1]

2 *1 1/2* **Nijoom Dubai** 2-8-7 ... JamieSpencer 3 — 70+
(M R Channon) *leggy: athletic: s.i.s sn rcvrd to chse ldrs: rdn and kpt on to chse wnr ins fnl f but a hld* **9/4**[2]

3 *2* **Rio Princess (IRE)** 2-8-7 ... SteveDrowne 7 — 62
(T G Mills) *w'like: leggy: in tch: chsd ldrs and pushed along 2f out: kpt on ins fnl f but nvr gng pce to chal* **7/1**[3]

4 *3/4* **Pantherii (USA)** 2-8-7 ... JimmyQuinn 6 — 60+
(P F I Cole) *w'like: leggy: s.i.s: hld up in rr but in tch: nudged along over 1f out: kpt on ins fnl f but nvr gng pce to be competitive* **8/1**

4 **5** *hd* **Structura (USA)**[12] 1503 2-8-10 ... LPKeniry 5 — 62
(J S Moore) *unf: led tl hdd ins fnl 2f: wknd ins fnl f* **11/1**

6 *nk* **Star In The East** 2-8-7 ... MartinDwyer 4 — 58
(A M Balding) *leggy: t.k.h in rr: n.m.r 2f out: shkn up and kpt on nr fin: nvr in contention* **22/1**

7 *7* **Maddie's Pearl (IRE)** 2-8-0 ... ThomasO'Brien(7) 2 — 33
(M R Channon) *leggy: t.k.h: chsd ldrs to 1/2-way: sn wknd* **33/1**

65.22 secs (2.66) **Going Correction** +0.20s/f (Good) — **7** Ran SP% **112.1**
Speed ratings (Par 94):86,83,80,79,78 78,67
CSF £4.39 TOTE £2.40: £1.80, £1.70; EX 4.60.
Owner Sangster Family **Bred** Swettenham Stud **Trained** Newmarket, Suffolk

FOCUS
An interesting maiden that in the past has gone to fillies of the calibre of Flashy Wings and Queen's Logic. Although the time was nothing special, a strong headwind undoubtedly affected it. Polar Circle looks a good prospect and Nijoom Dubai is a ready-made maiden winner.

NOTEBOOK

Polar Circle(USA) ◆, out of a Group-class sprinter and related to several sprinters, including Ocean Ridge, who won on her debut here before taking the Prix Robert Papin. A well-supported favourite, she knew her job and, always close to the pace, she picked up well when asked and was in control in the final furlong. She looks the sort who could make up into a Queen Mary filly and that is where connections are heading next. (op 11-10 tchd 6-4)

Nijoom Dubai ◆, out of an unraced mare and bred to appreciate a little further, showed plenty of ability despite having to race on the outside of her field. She chased home the winner and should come on for the outing. (op 11-4 tchd 3-1 in places)

Rio Princess(IRE), bought at the breeze-ups for £41,000, is bred to be speedy and was supported in the market. She was well held by the principals but showed enough to suggest she will be winning her maiden before too long, with another furlong. (op 6-1 tchd 11-2)

Pantherii(USA), who has a fair amount of scope, was doing her best work late on and the experience will have not been lost on her. (op 14-1)

Structura(USA) , the only runner with previous experience, set the pace but was brushed aside by the principals in the last furlong and a half. She can win her maiden but will need to drop in grade. (op 10-1 tchd 9-1)

Star In The East was noisy and played up badly in the paddock, twice getting rid of her rider. She was too keen in the race, but hopefully the outing will settle her down. (op 25-1)

1808 ULTIMATE TRAVEL STKS (REGISTERED AS THE CARNARVON STAKES) (LISTED RACE) 6f 8y

2:25 (2:27) (Class 1) 3-Y-O **£14,762** (£5,595; £2,800; £1,396; £699) **Stalls** High

Form RPR

14-1 **1** **Sakhee's Secret**[30] 1099 3-9-0 107 SteveDrowne 3 110+
(H Morrison) *trckd ldrs: shkn up and qckd to ld appr fnl f: pushed out: comf* **1/4**[1]

0-10 **2** *3* **Fontana Amorosa**[20] 1298 3-8-9 83 JamieSpencer 1 96
(K A Ryan) *lw: wnt lft s: sn rcvrd to press ldr: rdn to ld ins fnl 2f: hdd appr fnl f: no ch w wnr ins fnl f* **20/1**

35-3 **3** *3* **Howya Now Kid (IRE)**[33] 1047 3-9-0 RichardHughes 2 92
(G M Lyons, Ire) *w'like: leggy: chsd ldrs: drvn along fr 2f out: sn outpcd* **15/2**[2]

160- **4** *1 3/4* **Abby Road (IRE)**[223] 5802 3-8-13 99 LDettori 5 86
(B J Meehan) *slt ld tl hdd ins fnl 2f: wknd over 1f out* **8/1**[3]

4212 **5** *5* **Sparkling Eyes**[8] 1604 3-8-9 77 AdamKirby 4 67
(C E Brittain) *s.i.s: in rr but in tch: rdn over 2f out: wknd over 1f out* **25/1**

1m 14.34s (0.02) **Going Correction** +0.20s/f (Good) **5** Ran SP% **111.5**
Speed ratings (Par 107):107,103,99,96,90
CSF £7.53 TOTE £1.30: £1.10, £6.40; EX 8.00.
Owner Miss B Swire **Bred** Miss B Swire **Trained** East Ilsley, Berks

FOCUS
An uncompetitive Listed race on paper with only the potentially exciting winner rated above 100. Difficult form to assess, but unlikely that the winner needed to improve to win comfortably.

NOTEBOOK
Sakhee's Secret ◆ had plenty in hand on official ratings and the race worked out as such, with the long odds-on shot travelling well throughout and cruising up to the leaders on the bridle before coming away to score as he pleased. He seemed to handle the cut in the ground well enough, as his dam and many of the family have done in the past, although his rider felt he ran a little flat. He is clearly very progressive and is entered in the Group 1 Golden Jubilee at Royal Ascot and the July Cup, but will need to step up again if he is to figure in those races, and connections may opt for another Listed contest next. Already proven on fast ground, there is every reason to believe that he will be capable of making the step up to Group company before long and there is plenty of room at the top among the current crop of sprinters. (op 3-10)
Fontana Amorosa gained her only previous win on turf on soft ground and, despite the fact she had plenty to find with the winner on official ratings, ran her race and earned black type in the process. However, she may have destroyed her handicap mark for the time being and her trainer may choose to contest similar races against her own sex from now on.
Howya Now Kid(IRE), an Irish raider who was third in this grade over an extra furlong last time, could not go with the first two and ran as if he will appreciate a return to that trip. (op 7-1 tchd 8-1)
Abby Road(IRE)set the pace before fading and looks better suited by the minimum trip over which she won in this grade here last season. (op 9-1 tchd 10-1)
Sparkling Eyes had a mountain to climb on official figures and unsurprisingly failed to land a blow.

1809 SWETTENHAM STUD FILLIES' TRIAL STKS (LISTED RACE) 1m 2f 6y

2:55 (2:55) (Class 1) 3-Y-O **£14,762** (£5,595; £2,800; £1,396; £699) **Stalls** Low

Form RPR

1- **1** **Measured Tempo**[202] 6215 3-8-12 98 LDettori 5 101+
(Saeed Bin Suroor) *lw: sn trcking ldrs: wnt 2nd over 2f out: shaken up to ld over 1f out: pushed out fnl f: comf* **4/11**[1]

4-1 **2** *1 1/2* **In Safe Hands (IRE)**[7] 1639 3-8-12 JamieSpencer 2 94
(C G Cox) *chsd ldrs: drvn along fr 3f out: styd on wl fnl f to take 2nd last strides but no ch w wnr* **12/1**[3]

14-0 **3** *nk* **Ransom Captive (USA)**[34] 1035 3-8-12 91 SteveDrowne 1 93
(M A Magnusson) *lw: led: rdn and kpt on fr over 2f out: hdd over 1f out: sn one pce: lost 2nd last strides* **20/1**

4-25 **4** *3* **Fiumicino**[12] 1499 3-8-12 86 EdwardCreighton 6 87
(M R Channon) *in rr but in tch: rdn and one pce fnl 3f* **33/1**

21-4 **5** *8* **Cast In Gold (USA)**[27] 1146 3-8-12 98 RichardHughes 3 71
(B J Meehan) *lw: chsd ldr: rdn and lost 2nd over 2f out: wknd over 1f out* **4/1**[2]

2m 8.46s (-0.25) **Going Correction** +0.20s/f (Good) **5** Ran SP% **108.7**
Speed ratings (Par 104):109,107,107,105,98
CSF £5.68 TOTE £1.40: £1.10, £2.00; EX 5.10.
Owner Godolphin **Bred** Darley **Trained** Newmarket, Suffolk

FOCUS
This Oaks trial has produced subsequent Epsom winners Eswarah and Circus Plume in the past. The time was decent for the grade and 0.91sec faster than the quicker of the other two races over the trip on the day and Measured Tempo won with a bit more authority than the bare facts suggest, although the bare form still leaves her around a stone off the level that will be required to win at Epsom.

NOTEBOOK
Measured Tempo was long odds on largely because of her connections and reputation, but she was less impressive than expected. A good winner of a decent maiden at Newmarket on her only start last year, she moved upsides looking poised for a stylish success. However, she failed to get away from them, and although she was just pushed out in the end for a comfortable enough win, the bare form of her defeat of two 91-rated rivals leaves her plenty to find still if she is to trouble Passage Of Time and Dalvina at Epsom. However, she has the excuse of inexperience and with improvement likely she is well worth her place in a line-up that looks to lack strength in depth. (op 4-9 tchd 1-2 in places)
In Safe Hands(IRE) has no big-race entries, but she is going the right way and almost certainly improved for the step up to 1m2f, for she was doing her best in the final furlong and only took second in the last strides. (op 10-1)
Ransom Captive(USA) seemed to appreciate the return to turf and making the running more than when held up on Polytrack on her reappearance. She did not fold when headed and could well come on again. (op 14-1)
Fiumicino had been beaten the best part of 15 lengths by Dalvina at Newmarket but finished a lot closer this time. She is the first filly to emerge from that race, and the form line will give Dalvina's supporters plenty of encouragement. (op 25-1)
Cast In Gold(USA) was stepping up three furlongs, and although there is plenty of stamina on the dam's side she did not seem to stay, although she did have an excuse. Official explanation: vet said filly was distressed.

1810 TOTESPORT.COM H'CAP 1m 3f 5y

3:30 (3:30) (Class 4) (0-80,82) 3-Y-O **£7,124** (£2,119; £1,059; £529) **Stalls** Low

Form RPR

063- **1** **Mujahaz (IRE)**[211] 6066 3-8-6 67 StephenCarson 8 70
(J L Dunlop) *trckd ldr: str chal over 3f out tl led appr fnl 2f: kpt on gamely whn strly chal fr over 1f out: hld on all out* **15/2**

23-1 **2** *3/4* **Gremlin**[12] 1504 3-9-7 82 6ex JamieSpencer 9 84
(A King) *lw: chsd ldrs: drvn to chal over 1f out: upsides u.p ins fnl f: one pce cl home* **3/1**[2]

-105 **3** *nk* **Sweetheart**[12] 1504 3-8-11 72 IanMongan 1 73
(Jamie Poulton) *chsd ldrs: rdn fr 3f out: styd on wl fr over 1f out: gng on cl home but a jst hld by ldng pair* **33/1**

0-31 **4** *shd* **Madaarek (USA)**[22] 1256 3-9-2 77 GeorgeBaker 5 78+
(E A L Dunlop) *hld up in rr: n.m.r over 2f out: swtchd lft to rail over 1f out and squeezed through ins fnl f: fin wl* **11/4**[1]

12-5 **5** *1/2* **Troialini**[58] 719 3-9-4 79 AdamKirby 6 79
(S W Hall) *lw: hld up in rr: hdwy over 2f out: chsd ldrs over 1f out: kpt on ins fnl f but nvr quite gng pce to chal* **8/1**

06-2 **6** *nk* **Adversane**[34] 1039 3-8-8 69 JimmyQuinn 7 68
(J L Dunlop) *chsd ldrs: shkn up and n.m.r fr 3f out: swtchd rt 2f out: kpt on fnl f but nvr gng pce to rch ldrs* **12/1**

02-0 **7** *nk* **Cavalry Twill (IRE)**[32] 1062 3-8-9 70 SteveDrowne 3 69
(P F I Cole) *led: tl hdd over 2f out: styd front rank tl wknd wl ins fnl f* **16/1**

6-01 **8** *5* **Cry Presto (USA)**[62] 703 3-9-1 76 (t) RichardHughes 2 66
(R Hannon) *lw: in rr: hdwy 3f out: drvn to chse ldrs 2f out: wknd over 1f out* **16/1**

60-5 **9** *1 3/4* **Monachello (USA)**[13] 1467 3-9-3 78 LDettori 4 65
(Mrs A J Perrett) *in tch: chsd ldrs 3f out: sn rdn: wknd ins fnl 2f* **9/1**

06-5 **10** *1 1/4* **Mujma**[31] 1081 3-8-5 66 AdrianMcCarthy 10 51
(Sir Michael Stoute) *in tch: chsd ldrs 3f out: wknd 2f out* **7/1**[3]

2m 25.13s (2.86) **Going Correction** +0.20s/f (Good) **10** Ran SP% **119.4**
Speed ratings (Par 101):97,96,96,96,95 95,95,91,90,89
CSF £31.05 CT £719.29 TOTE £9.30: £2.70, £1.40, £6.90; EX 26.20.
Owner Hamdan Al Maktoum **Bred** Shadwell Estate Company Limited **Trained** Arundel, W Sussex

FOCUS
Quite a tight little handicap, but the early pace was modest and they finished in a heap, so it was a somewhat unsatisfactory contest. The principals were in the first three from the start.
Madaarek(USA) ◆ Official explanation: jockey said colt was denied a clear run.
Cavalry Twill(IRE) Official explanation: jockey said colt hung right-handed from 3f out, and he was concerned that if he kept riding out close home he would have clipped the heels of a rival

1811 BETFAIR H'CAP 1m 2f 6y

4:05 (4:05) (Class 5) (0-70,70) 4-Y-O+ **£3,886** (£1,156; £577; £288) **Stalls** Low

Form RPR

550- **1** **Nightspot**[286] 4160 6-9-2 68 StephenCarson 13 74+
(Eve Johnson Houghton) *trckd ldr: led over 3f out: hrd drvn and kpt on wl thrght fnl f* **7/1**[3]

46-0 **2** *1/2* **Trans Sonic**[13] 1470 4-8-13 65 (v) LDettori 8 70
(A P Jarvis) *chsd ldrs: rdn 3f out: chsd wnr fr 2f out: kpt on u.p ins fnl f but a jst hld* **7/2**[1]

0004 **3** *hd* **Hatch A Plan (IRE)**[24] 1216 6-8-8 65 TravisBlock(5) 12 70
(Mouse Hamilton-Fairley) *in rr: hdwy over 2f out: styng on but hanging lft thrght fnl f: no ex nr fin* **25/1**

150- **4** *1* **Parnassian**[198] 6301 7-9-2 68 RichardThomas 2 71+
(J A Geake) *lw: in rr: drvn along fr 4f out: hdwy fr 2f out: styd on fnl f but nvr gng pce to rch ldrs* **12/1**

4112 **5** *1/2* **Scottish River (USA)**[21] 1284 8-9-0 66 JamieSpencer 10 68
(M D I Usher) *in rr: hdwy over 2f out: rdn and effrt over 1f out: nvr gng pce to chal and one pce ins fnl f* **5/1**[2]

/06- **6** *1/2* **Jamaahir (USA)**[377] 1476 4-8-13 65 RichardHughes 4 66
(S Lycett) *led tl hdd over 3f out: styd chsng ldrs tl wknd ins fnl f* **16/1**

44 **7** *hd* **Sopran Gath (ITY)**[18] 1352 4-9-4 70 JamesDoyle 14 71
(J W Hills) *in tch: rdn and effrt fr 3f out: nvr gng pce to trble ldrs and one pce fnl 2f* **25/1**

406- **8** *1 1/4* **The Composer**[108] 5889 5-8-13 65 SteveDrowne 9 63
(M Blanshard) *lw: mid-div: rdn and kpt on fr over 2f out but nvr gng pce to be competitive* **8/1**

1 **9** *1 1/4* **Pentasilea**[18] 1364 4-9-0 66 JimmyQuinn 15 62
(H J L Dunlop) *towards rr and rdn along 3f out: no prog tl sme hdwy ins fnl f* **10/1**

10-0 **10** *1 1/2* **Pactolos Way**[17] 1385 4-9-4 70 VinceSlattery 7 63
(P R Chamings) *chsd ldrs: rdn 3f out: wknd ins fnl 2f* **33/1**

00 **11** *1 1/4* **Dafarabad (IRE)**[18] 1356 5-9-3 69 GeorgeBaker 3 59
(Jonjo O'Neill) *chsd ldrs: rdn over 3f out: wknd 2f out* **20/1**

4-46 **12** *hd* **Snark (IRE)**[81] 568 4-9-4 70 AmirQuinn 5 60
(P J Makin) *prom tl rdn and wknd fr 2f out: sddle slipped* **15/2**

-400 **13** *3/4* **Stravara**[39] 976 4-7-12 57 MCGeran(7) 16 45
(R Hollinshead) *a towards rr* **18/1**

3004 **14** *5* **Art Investor**[9] 1578 4-8-8 60 (b) LPKeniry 1 38
(D R C Elsworth) *a towards rr* **11/1**

2m 9.37s (0.66) **Going Correction** +0.20s/f (Good) **14** Ran SP% **125.9**
Speed ratings (Par 103):105,104,104,103,103 102,102,101,100,99 98,98,97,93
CSF £31.64 CT £608.99 TOTE £10.20: £3.20, £2.10, £9.00; EX 45.80.
Owner D J Deer **Bred** D J And Mrs Deer **Trained** Blewbury, Oxon
■ Stewards' Enquiry : Stephen Carson two-day ban: used whip with excessive frequency (May 29-30)

FOCUS
A low-grade handicap for the track. It paid to race handily, and the first two at the finish raced in the first three virtually throughout. The time was 0.91 sec slower than the earlier fillies' Listed race.
Hatch A Plan(IRE) Official explanation: jockey said gelding hung left-handed.
Snark(IRE) Official explanation: jockey said saddle slipped.
Stravara Official explanation: jockey said gelding hung right-handed.

1812 PENINSULA BUSINESS SERVICES MAIDEN STKS 1m 2f 6y

4:40 (4:41) (Class 4) 3-Y-O **£6,477** (£1,927; £963; £481) **Stalls** Low

Form RPR

222- **1** **Ajhar (USA)**[220] 5893 3-9-3 82 PatDobbs 4 88
(M P Tregoning) *trckd ldrs: rdn over 2f out: led appr fnl f: hld on wl* **7/4**[2]

6- **2** *1/2* **Jalil (USA)**[217] 5939 3-9-3 LDettori 8 87
(Saeed Bin Suroor) *lw: sn led: pushed along whn chal fr over 3f out: hdd appr fnl f: no ex nr fin* **6/4**[1]

0 **3** *4* **Galianna (IRE)**[28] 1127 3-8-12 RichardHughes 9 74
(Pat Eddery) *lw: chsd ldr: chal fr over 4f out tl over 2f out: wknd ins fnl f* **12/1**

6 **4** *1/2* **Ancient Culture**[18] 1358 3-9-3 JamieSpencer 13 78
(Sir Michael Stoute) *w'like: scope: trckd ldrs: pushed along fr over 2f out: styd on same pce* **13/2**[3]

25 **5** *nk* **Easterly Breeze (IRE)**[23] 1246 3-9-3 SamHitchcott 3 77
(W R Muir) *chsd ldrs: hrd rdn 2f out: styd on u.p ins fnl f: kpt on cl home* **33/1**

6 *3* **Praxiteles (IRE)** 3-9-3 JDSmith 7 72
(Sir Michael Stoute) *w'like: leggy: in tch: pushed along over 2f out: kpt on fnl f but nvr in contention* **12/1**

0-5 **7** 2 1/2 **Make Haste (IRE)**[28] 1129 3-9-3 .... SteveDrowne 1 67+
(R Charlton) *in rr: drvn along over 3f out: kpt on fnl f but nvr in contention* **16/1**

8 1 1/2 **Kings Story (IRE)** 3-9-3 .... AdamKirby 2 64+
(W R Swinburn) *w'like: bhd: shkn up over 3f out: styd on fr over 1f out: gng on cl home* **66/1**

0 **9** 1/2 **Fraternal**[16] 1398 3-9-0 .... RichardKingscote(3) 16 63+
(R Charlton) *in rr: drvn along over 3f out: sme prog fnl 2f* **66/1**

10 4 **Espoir De Lumiere** 3-8-12 .... IanMongan 12 51
(C F Wall) *leggy: b.bkwd: a towards rr* **100/1**

11 shd **Beauchamp Viking** 3-9-3 .... StephenCarson 5 55
(G A Butler) *athletic: chsd ldrs: rdn 3f out: wknd over 2f out* **66/1**

60 **12** 4 **Just An Angel (IRE)**[16] 1396 3-8-12 .... FergusSweeney 15 43
(A P Jarvis) *in tch: rdn to chse ldrs fr 3f out: wknd over 2f out* **100/1**

13 10 **Grand Vizier (IRE)** 3-9-3 .... GeorgeBaker 11 29
(C F Wall) *unf: w'like: chsd ldrs 7f* **100/1**

0 **14** 13 **Best Of Gold (IRE)**[31] 1081 3-9-3 .... PaulEddery 14 4
(B J Meehan) *w'like: a in rr* **100/1**

00- **15** 3 1/2 **Mazoran (FR)**[245] 5347 3-9-3 .... VinceSlattery 6 —
(D G Bridgwater) *s.i.s: sn drvn into mid-div: bhd fnl 4f* **150/1**

2m 9.39s (0.68) **Going Correction** +0.20s/f (Good) **15** Ran SP% **123.0**
Speed ratings (Par 101):105,104,101,101,100 98,96,95,94,91 91,88,80,69,67
CSF £4.75 TOTE £3.00: £1.30, £1.40, £2.70; EX 6.20.
Owner Hamdan Al Maktoum **Bred** Shadwell Farm LLC **Trained** Lambourn, Berks

FOCUS
An interesting maiden featuring the reappearance of the $9.7m yearling Jalil and several other well-bred sorts. The time was fractionally slower than the preceding older-horse handicap and the form has some depth to it.

1813 STAN JAMES SUPPORTS CANCERBACKUP STKS (H'CAP) 1m 4f 5y
5:15 (5:16) (Class 5) (0-75,75) 4-Y-0+ **£3,562** (£1,059; £529; £264) **Stalls** Low

Form RPR

6-03 **1** **Lady Songbird (IRE)**[20] 1295 4-8-9 **66** .... AdamKirby 7 78+
(W R Swinburn) *hld up in rr: nt clr run fr over 2f out tl gd hdwy appr fnl f: str run ins fnl f to ld fnl strides* **15/2**[3]

4-00 **2** hd **Pocketwood**[27] 1148 5-8-11 **68** .... StephenCarson 16 75
(Jean-Rene Auvray) *chsd ldr: led jst ins fnl 3f: hrd rdn and kpt on wl fr over 1f out: ct last strides* **18/1**

430- **3** 1 **True Companion**[224] 5786 8-9-1 **72** .... SamHitchcott 11 78+
(Miss E C Lavelle) *in rr: drvn and hdwy over 2f out: strayed on u.p ins fnl f: kpt on cl home* **12/1**

606- **4** 3 **Strong Survivor (USA)**[253] 5138 4-8-8 **65** .... PatDobbs 6 66
(P R Webber) *mid-div: hdwy and rdn 3f out: styd on to chse ldrs 2f out: kpt on same pce ins fnl f* **20/1**

00-0 **5** hd **Cortesia (IRE)**[18] 1356 4-8-11 **75** .... MCGeran(7) 14 76
(P W Chapple-Hyam) *chsd ldrs: drvn to chal fr 3f out: wknd fnl f* **25/1**

0621 **6** nk **Jack Rolfe**[56] 747 5-9-2 **73** .... GeorgeBaker 1 73
(G L Moore) *lw: in tch: chsd ldrs fr over 4f out: stl wl there 2f out: wknd fnl f* **7/2**[1]

0-02 **7** 1/2 **Imperial Harry**[8] 1609 4-8-11 **68** .... SimonWhitworth 9 67
(V Smith) *s.i.s: bhd: hdwy on outside over 3f out: chsd ldrs ins fnl 2f: wknd fnl f* **11/1**

0-31 **8** 3 **Montchara (IRE)**[20] 1314 4-9-0 **71** .... SteveDrowne 10 66
(G Wragg) *lw: in tch: rdn and one pce fnl 3f* **7/2**[1]

1530 **9** 2 1/2 **Theatre Groom (USA)**[23] 1253 8-8-11 **68** ....(p) FergusSweeney 13 59
(M R Bosley) *towards rr: rdn and styd on into mid-div 3f out: no further prog* **33/1**

23-0 **10** 2 1/2 **Greek Easter (IRE)**[20] 1288 4-9-0 **71** .... LDettori 15 58
(B J Meehan) *chsd ldrs: rdn over 2f out: sn btn* **12/1**

506- **11** nk **Olimpo (FR)**[125] 4900 6-9-2 **73** .... JamesDoyle 3 59
(B R Millman) *chsd ldrs: rdn 3f out: wknd over 2f out* **16/1**

06-2 **12** 38 **Cordier**[26] 1181 5-8-11 **68** .... JimmyQuinn 12 —
(J Mackie) *led tl hdd ins fnl 3f: sn wknd: t.o* **11/1**

6064 **13** 19 **Prime Powered (IRE)**[13] 1470 6-9-2 **73** .... RichardHughes 2 —
(R M Beckett) *bhd fr 1/2-way: t.o* **4/1**[2]

00-0 **14** 64 **Freddy (ARG)**[48] 844 8-9-2 **73** .... AmirQuinn 5 —
(D K Ivory) *a struggling in rr* **50/1**

2m 38.18s (2.19) **Going Correction** +0.20s/f (Good) **14** Ran SP% **132.9**
Speed ratings (Par 103):100,99,99,97,97 96,96,94,92,91 91,65,53,10
CSF £143.70 CT £1653.58 TOTE £10.00: £2.00, £7.70, £4.10; EX 336.40 Place 6 £8.41, Place 5 £7.25.
Owner Clark, Dhariwal, Godfrey & Harris **Bred** Airlie Stud And Sir Thomas Pilkington **Trained** Aldbury, Herts

FOCUS
A tight little handicap, run in driving rain. It produced a good finish in which both the winner and third did better than the bare facts indicate.
Olimpo(FR) Official explanation: jockey said gelding hung right-handed.
Prime Powered(IRE) Official explanation: jockey said gelding stopped quickly.
T/Plt: £21.70 to a £1 stake. Pool: £51,849.10. 1,740.00 winning tickets. T/Qpdt: £15.10 to a £1 stake. Pool: £1,820.30. 88.90 winning tickets. ST

1494 NEWMARKET (ROWLEY) (R-H)
Friday, May 18

OFFICIAL GOING: Good
Wind: fresh across Weather: Cloudy with sunny spells

1814 EUROPEAN BREEDERS' FUND MAIDEN FILLIES' STKS 6f
2:05 (2:07) (Class 4) 2-Y-O **£4,533** (£1,348; £674; £336) **Stalls** High

Form RPR

1 **Festoso (IRE)** 2-9-0 .... PhilipRobinson 5 79
(H J L Dunlop) *neat: s.i.s: sn trcking ldrs: rdn over 1f out: r.o to ld wl ins fnl f* **13/2**

0 **2** hd **Pixie's Blue (IRE)**[14] 1445 2-9-0 .... RobertHavlin 1 78
(J H M Gosden) *lw: chsd ldrs: hung lft and outpcd over 1f out: r.o wl ins fnl f* **13/2**

0 **3** 1 3/4 **Luscious Lips**[11] 1540 2-9-0 .... DaneO'Neill 4 73+
(R Hannon) *chsd ldr 4f out: rdn to ld 1f out: hdd wl ins fnl f* **7/2**[2]

4 nk **Miss Emma May (IRE)** 2-9-0 .... JohnEgan 6 72
(D R C Elsworth) *gd sort: leggy: lw: s.i.s: hdwy over 4f out: rdn and hung lft over 1f out: styd on* **4/1**[3]

0 **5** 1 1/4 **Fidelias Dance**[27] 1150 2-9-0 .... MichaelHills 9 68+
(M Johnston) *led: rdn and hdd 1f out: styd on same pce* **10/1**

6 3 **Lady Aquitaine (USA)** 2-9-0 .... NCallan 3 59
(B J Meehan) *w'like: scope: bit bkwd: s.i.s: hdwy 1/2-way: hung lft wl over 1f out: sn edgd rt and wknd* **3/1**[1]

7 3/4 **Loveinanelevator** 2-9-0 .... HayleyTurner 2 57
(M L W Bell) *gd sort: leggy: lw: sn outpcd* **8/1**

0 **8** 22 **Mums The Best**[11] 1540 2-8-9 .... LukeMorris(5) 8 —
(A B Coogan) *chsd ldr 2f: sn rdn and wknd* **66/1**

1m 13.72s (0.62) **Going Correction** -0.05s/f (Good) **8** Ran SP% **115.6**
Speed ratings (Par 92):93,92,90,90,88 84,83,54
CSF £48.44 TOTE £8.50: £2.70, £2.00, £1.70; EX 54.30.
Owner Prince A A Faisal **Bred** Nawara Stud Co Ltd **Trained** Lambourn, Berks
■ Harry Dunlop's first winner on turf, with his first two-year-old runner.

FOCUS
A fair fillies' juvenile maiden. The form looks sound with the first pair coming clear and the winner should rate higher.

NOTEBOOK
Festoso(IRE), the eighth foal of a dam that has produced numerous winners, most notably top-class miler Olden Times, got her career off to a perfect start with a narrow success. She took time to find her stride, but seemed to relish the climbing finish and showed a likeable attitude when asked to win her race. Open to plenty of improvement, she will get further before the season's end, and looks one to keep on-side. This was also a first juvenile runner, and winner on the turf, for her rookie trainer. (tchd 8-1)
Pixie's Blue(IRE), eighth on debut in a muddling race at Lingfield a fortnight previously, has clearly improved a deal for that experience and only just missed out on this switch to the turf. She enjoyed this extra furlong and should not be too long in going one better. (op 9-2)
Luscious Lips, well backed, showed the benefit of her debut experience at Windsor 11 days previously and posted an improved effort in defeat. She got the extra furlong well enough. (op 9-2)
Miss Emma May(IRE), the most expensive of these at the sales, is bred to make her mark over a longer trip in due course and proved too green to do herself justice on this racecourse bow. She will learn plenty from this. (tchd 5-1)
Fidelias Dance showed early dash from her rails draw, but did not look to handle the dip all that well and lacked the tactical speed when it mattered late on. She got all of this longer trip. (op 8-1 tchd 12-1)
Lady Aquitaine(USA), whose stable won this with the smart Biocoastal last year, had support in the betting ring yet she ultimately looked much in need of this debut experience, hanging left when put under pressure. Her stable's juveniles normally all come on for their first outings however, and she is presumably thought capable of better. (op 9-2 tchd 11-4)

1815 BETDIRECT.COM GET INVOLVED H'CAP 1m
2:35 (2:37) (Class 5) (0-75,75) 3-Y-O **£3,886** (£1,156; £577; £288) **Stalls** High

Form RPR

510- **1** **Oceana Gold**[221] 5866 3-8-11 **68** .... FrancisNorton 4 78
(A M Balding) *lw: chsd ldrs: led over 2f out: rdn out* **8/1**[3]

201- **2** nk **Giant Slalom**[182] 6504 3-8-10 **70** .... LiamJones(3) 6 79+
(W J Haggas) *s.i.s: hld up: hdwy over 3f out: rdn over 1f out: r.o* **11/1**

0-00 **3** 1 1/2 **Trump Call (IRE)**[20] 1289 3-8-9 **66** .... JohnEgan 1 72
(R M Beckett) *hld up: hdwy over 2f out: rdn and hung rt over 1f out: styd on* **12/1**

032- **4** 1 3/4 **Sister Maria (USA)**[154] 6832 3-9-4 **75** .... NCallan 13 77
(E A L Dunlop) *h.d.w: hld up in tch: rdn over 1f out: styd on same pce* **6/1**[2]

030- **5** 3 **Bluebelle Dancer (IRE)**[197] 6310 3-8-13 **70** .... PhilipRobinson 16 65
(W R Muir) *chsd ldrs: rdn and ev ch over 2f out: wknd ins fnl f* **20/1**

6506 **6** nk **Silca Key**[49] 834 3-8-11 **68** .... ChrisCatlin 17 67+
(M R Channon) *hld up: nt clr run over 2f out: hdwy over 1f out: nvr trbld ldrs* **16/1**

401- **7** 1 1/4 **Summer Dancer (IRE)**[161] 6745 3-8-8 **68** .... MarcHalford(3) 14 67+
(D R C Elsworth) *hld up: hmpd over 3f out: nt clr run fr over 2f out: tl styd on appr fnl f: nvr nrr* **4/1**[1]

-343 **8** 2 **Winged Farasi**[18] 1348 3-8-7 **67** .... JerryO'Dwyer(3) 15 54
(Miss J Feilden) *hld up: nt clr run over 2f out: n.d* **25/1**

1325 **9** 3/4 **Satyricon**[48] 843 3-9-2 **73** ....(b) OscarUrbina 10 58
(M Botti) *hld up: rdn over 2f out: n.d* **12/1**

3-34 **10** 1 1/4 **Mystery River (USA)**[15] 1439 3-9-0 **71** .... BrettDoyle 9 53
(B J Meehan) *chsd ldr: rdn and ev ch over 2f out: wknd fnl f* **16/1**

0-55 **11** 4 **Calculating (IRE)**[13] 1468 3-9-3 **74** .... RobertHavlin 11 47
(J H M Gosden) *mid-div: lost pl 3f out: n.d after* **16/1**

43-3 **12** nk **Laish Ya Hajar (IRE)**[13] 1468 3-9-4 **75** .... TPO'Shea 8 47
(M R Channon) *chsd ldrs: rdn over 3f out: wknd 2f out* **16/1**

00-0 **13** 1 **Barley Moon**[31] 1075 3-8-4 **61** oh1 .... HayleyTurner 12 31
(T Keddy) *led: rdn and hdd over 2f out: wknd over 1f out* **66/1**

46-0 **14** 1 3/4 **Our Herbie**[31] 1076 3-9-3 **74** .... MichaelHills 2 40
(J W Hills) *hld up: sme hdwy over 2f out: sn wknd* **22/1**

01-5 **15** 4 **Our Ruby**[18] 1359 3-9-1 **72** .... TedDurcan 3 29
(P W Chapple-Hyam) *mid-div: rdn and wknd over 2f out* **25/1**

6-23 **16** 4 **Postsprofit (IRE)**[18] 1365 3-8-12 **69** .... DaneO'Neill 7 17
(N A Callaghan) *lw: hld up: wkng whn hmpd wl over 1f out* **12/1**

321- **17** 8 **Stanley George (IRE)**[148] 6891 3-9-3 **74** .... MatthewHenry 5 3
(M A Jarvis) *lw: chsd ldrs over 6f* **8/1**[3]

1m 38.03s (-1.34) **Going Correction** -0.05s/f (Good) **17** Ran SP% **129.7**
Speed ratings (Par 99):104,103,102,100,97 97,95,93,93,91 87,87,86,84,80 76,68
CSF £92.46 CT £714.36 TOTE £10.00: £2.40, £2.50, £4.40, £2.40; EX 236.50.
Owner The C H F Partnership **Bred** The C H F Partnership **Trained** Kingsclere, Hants

FOCUS
Only a modest three-year-old handicap, run at a solid pace. The first pair look progressive, however.

1816 BETDIRECTPOKER.COM $50,000 FREEROLL THIS SUNDAY MAIDEN FILLIES' STKS 1m 4f
3:05 (3:12) (Class 4) 3-Y-O **£5,181** (£1,541; £770; £384) **Stalls** High

Form RPR

22-2 **1** **Latanazul**[20] 1303 3-9-0 **77** .... TedDurcan 3 81+
(J L Dunlop) *lw: mde all: rdn clr fnl f* **1/1**[1]

0- **2** 5 **Hypoteneuse (IRE)**[202] 6215 3-9-0 .... NCallan 7 70+
(Sir Michael Stoute) *h.d.w: a.p: chsd wnr over 5f out: rdn and ev ch over 2f out: hung rt and no ex fr over 1f out* **13/8**[2]

0 **3** 6 **White Moss (IRE)**[20] 1312 3-9-0 .... MichaelHills 9 60
(M H Tompkins) *hld up: nvr nr to chal* **20/1**

0- **4** 1 1/2 **Wild Gardenia**[184] 6486 3-9-0 .... JohnEgan 8 58
(J H M Gosden) *h.d.w: chsd ldrs: rdn over 3f out: sn wknd* **12/1**

5 3 **Last Dance** 3-9-0 .... RobertHavlin 1 53
(J H M Gosden) *s.i.s: hld up: hdwy over 3f out: sn wknd* **10/1**[3]

0 **6** 34 **Blue Denim**[10] 1566 3-9-0 .... PhilipRobinson 2 —
(M A Jarvis) *hld up: hdwy 4f out: rdn and wknd 3f out* **25/1**

0 **7** nk **Highbourne Lady**[16] 1409 3-9-0 .... StephenDonohoe 6 —
(B N Pollock) *chsd wnr over 8f: wknd over 3f out* **100/1**

The Form Book, Raceform Ltd, Compton, RG20 6NL

0- **8** ½ **Astarte**[184] 6486 3-9-0 .... PaulDoe 5 —
(P R Chamings) *hld up: wknd 5f out* **66/1**

0- **9** ½ **Fancy Woman**[202] 6215 3-9-0 .... TPO'Shea 4 —
(J L Dunlop) *bit bkwd: hld up: hdwy 8f out: wknd over 5f out* **33/1**

2m 32.94s (-0.56) **Going Correction** -0.05s/f (Good) **9** Ran SP% **122.8**
Speed ratings (Par 98):99,95,91,90,88 66,65,65,65
CSF £2.97 TOTE £2.10: £1.10, £1.10, £4.10; EX 3.60.

Owner Hamdan Al Maktoum **Bred** Shadwell Estate Company Limited **Trained** Arundel, W Sussex

FOCUS
Just a fair fillies' maiden which saw the field finish fairly strung out behind the comfortable winner. The form makes sense with those in the frame behind the winner close to previous form.
Astarte Official explanation: jockey said filly had no more to give

1817 ANIMAL HEALTH TRUST H'CAP 6f
3:40 (3:41) (Class 3) (0-95,93) 3-Y-O **£9,067** (£2,697; £1,348; £673) **Stalls** High

Form RPR

210- **1** **Longquan (IRE)**[230] 5681 3-8-13 **88** .... TedDurcan 7 102+
(P J Makin) *lw: chsd ldrs: rdn to ld over 1f out: r.o: eased nr fin* **11/2**[3]

11-4 **2** 3 **Luscivious**[7] 1616 3-9-2 **91** ....(b) StephenDonohoe 1 94
(A J McCabe) *led 5f out: rdn and hdd over 1f out: styd on same pce* **11/2**[3]

1-5 **3** 1 ¼ **Lovelace**[25] 1202 3-8-7 **82** .... JohnEgan 2 81
(M Johnston) *chsd ldrs: rdn over 1f out: styd on same pce* **11/4**[1]

3-10 **4** 2 **Ebn Reem**[20] 1298 3-9-4 **93** .... PhilipRobinson 5 86
(M A Jarvis) *led 1f: chsd ldrs: styng on same pce whn hung rt fr over 1f out* **9/2**[2]

01-0 **5** ¾ **Cheap Street**[30] 1099 3-9-1 **90** .... NCallan 4 81
(J G Portman) *lw: hld up: rdn over 2f out: sn hung rt: n.d* **12/1**

01-2 **6** 7 **Golden Desert (IRE)**[14] 1450 3-8-9 **84** .... DaneO'Neill 3 52
(T G Mills) *lw: s.i.s: hld up: rdn over 2f out: sn wknd* **13/2**

14-3 **7** 10 **Non Compliant**[14] 1450 3-8-12 **87** .... MichaelHills 6 23
(J W Hills) *s.i.s: sn pushed along in rr: wknd over 2f out* **11/2**[3]

1m 12.09s (-1.01) **Going Correction** -0.05s/f (Good) **7** Ran SP% **112.0**
Speed ratings (Par 103):104,100,98,95,94 85,72
CSF £33.76 TOTE £8.30: £3.50, £2.50; EX 74.30.

Owner R & G Marchant D M Ahier J P Carrington **Bred** J F Tuthill **Trained** Ogbourne Maisey, Wilts

FOCUS
A good little three-year-old sprint handicap. The winner is value for double his winning margin and the form looks sound with the placed horses close to form.

NOTEBOOK
Longquan(IRE) ◆, last seen finishing midfield in the Redcar Two-Year-old Trophy in 2006, showed he has wintered well and ran out a comfortable winner on this seasonal debut. He has clearly begun handicap life on a decent mark, is value for at least double his winning margin, and looks capable of reaching greater heights as the season progresses. (op 7-1)
Luscivious showed plenty of early dash this time and had his chance, yet was eventually put firmly in his place by the eased winner. He just looks weighted to his best at present, but sets the standard of this form and will enjoy an easier surface in due course. (op 7-2)
Lovelace, well backed, failed to really improve as might have been expected for the drop back to this trip and really looks to need a seventh furlong. He is not one to write off just yet. Official explanation: jockey said colt was struck into (op 7-2)
Ebn Reem was beaten before hanging when entering the dip and looks held by the Handicapper now. (op 7-2)
Non Compliant Official explanation: jockey said colt was never travelling

1818 NGK SPARK PLUGS H'CAP 7f
4:15 (4:16) (Class 3) (0-95,93) 4-Y-O+ **£9,067** (£2,697; £1,348; £673) **Stalls** High

Form RPR

000- **1** **Trafalgar Square**[237] 5523 5-8-9 **84** .... PaulDoe 12 96
(J Akehurst) *lw: chsd ldrs: led over 1f out: rdn out* **16/1**

1550 **2** hd **Fajr (IRE)**[27] 1145 5-8-11 **86** .... JohnEgan 5 97
(Miss Gay Kelleway) *hld up: hdwy 1/2-way: edgd rt over 1f out: sn ev ch: r.o* **12/1**

51-0 **3** 3 **Ordnance Row**[6] 1651 4-9-4 **93** .... SilvestreDeSousa 9 102+
(R Hannon) *chsd ldrs: lost pl over 4f out: outpcd and bhd over 2f out: r.o wl ins fnl f* **5/1**[2]

052- **4** ¾ **Irony (IRE)**[265] 4790 8-9-0 **89** .... FrancisNorton 10 91
(A M Balding) *led to 1/2-way: outpcd over 1f out: styd on ins fnl f* **40/1**

13-3 **5** shd **Countdown**[13] 1481 5-8-1 **79** .... DuranFentiman(3) 4 80
(T D Easterby) *lw: prom: outpcd over 2f out: hdwy and hung rt over 1f out: styd on same pce ins fnl f* **12/1**

316- **6** nk **Signor Peltro**[217] 5943 4-8-12 **87** .... DaneO'Neill 3 88
(H Candy) *hld up: hdwy over 1f out: styd on same pce ins fnl f* **7/1**[3]

4-12 **7** 1 **Bustan (IRE)**[13] 1480 8-9-4 **93** .... PhilipRobinson 7 91
(G C Bravery) *chsd ldrs: hmpd over 1f out: sn hung rt: styd on same pce* **8/1**

0-61 **8** ½ **Bonnie Prince Blue**[16] 1401 4-8-7 **82** .... MichaelHills 11 79+
(B W Hills) *chsd ldr: led 1/2-way: rdn and hdd over 1f out: wknd ins fnl f* **9/2**[1]

-000 **9** shd **Game Lad**[13] 1480 5-8-7 **82** .... RobertHavlin 13 79
(T D Easterby) *chsd ldrs: rdn over 1f out: no ex* **9/2**[1]

102- **10** 1 ¼ **Woodcote Place**[217] 5943 4-9-1 **90** .... TedDurcan 1 83
(P R Chamings) *hld up: effrt over 2f out: nvr trbld ldrs* **25/1**

4400 **11** 1 ¼ **Gallantry**[13] 1480 5-8-10 **85** .... DeanMcKeown 6 75
(D Shaw) *hld up: hdwy 1/2-way: wknd over 1f out* **22/1**

1-16 **12** ½ **Bobski (IRE)**[14] 1448 5-8-9 **87** .... EmmettStack(3) 14 76
(G A Huffer) *lw: prom: plld hrd: rdn and wknd over 1f out* **25/1**

13 **13** 1 ¾ **Zam Zammah**[80] 576 4-8-10 **85** .... NCallan 8 69
(Sir Michael Stoute) *b.hind: s.i.s: hld up: plld hrd: wknd over 1f out* **7/1**[3]

1m 25.65s (-0.85) **Going Correction** -0.05s/f (Good) **13** Ran SP% **124.9**
Speed ratings (Par 107):102,101,98,97,97 97,95,95,95,93 92,91,89
CSF £195.44 CT £1158.22 TOTE £27.80: £6.70, £4.40, £2.70; EX 320.80.

Owner Canisbay Bloodstock **Bred** Matthews Breeding And Racing Ltd **Trained** Epsom, Surrey

FOCUS
A competitive handicap that saw the first pair come clear late on. The first two showed improvement and the form looks sound enough rated through the fourth.

NOTEBOOK
Trafalgar Square, who has often needed his seasonal bow in the past, ran out a determined winner on this return from a 237-day break and this has to rate as a career-best effort. It will be interesting to see whether he can build on this, as he has always had an engine, but consistency has never been his strong suit.
Fajr(IRE), not beaten far in eighth in the Spring Cup last time, was produced to have every chance on this drop back in trip yet eventually found the winner too resolute at the business end. He deserves to go one better. (op 16-1)
Ordnance Row hit a flat spot at a crucial stage before taking off when meeting the rising ground and ran a funny sort of race. The suspicion is that he can defy this mark when things go more his way and this effort would suggest he may not have to dominate to be at his best. A return to a flatter track will be to his liking and another furlong should now also be well within his compass. (op 11-2)
Irony(IRE), having his first run for 265 days, was another who got outpaced before keeping on again and he rates a decent enough benchmark for this form. This run should be to his benefit. (op 50-1)
Countdown may not have been too happy on this track and was not at all disgraced. He is consistent and can find a race while his yard remains in such good form, despite the fact he is likely to go up a pound or two for this.
Signor Peltro, like many from his yard so far this term, left the impression he would improve a deal for this first run of the season. (op 14-1)
Bonnie Prince Blue, back to winning ways at Kempton last time, did not look to have many excuses and proved a little disappointing from his 4lb higher mark. (op 4-1 tchd 5-1)
Game Lad, 2lb lower than his last winning mark, could not find a change of pace when it mattered and has a little to prove at present. (op 5-1)
Zam Zammah was slow to break and then spoilt his chances by running far too freely under restraint. (op 6-1 tchd 15-2)

1819 BETDIRECT.COM H'CAP 1m 2f
4:50 (4:52) (Class 5) (0-75,75) 4-Y-O+ **£3,886** (£1,156; £577; £288) **Stalls** High

Form RPR

0503 **1** **Street Life (IRE)**[7] 1638 9-8-6 **63** .... DavidKinsella 1 73
(W J Musson) *hld up: hdwy over 2f out: rdn over 1f out: styd on to ld towards fin* **10/1**

0-43 **2** shd **The Aldbury Flyer**[13] 1470 4-9-4 **75** .... DaneO'Neill 7 85
(W R Swinburn) *lw: chsd ldrs: rdn to ld and edgd lft over 1f out: hdd towards fin* **6/1**[3]

210 **3** ½ **Multicultural**[18] 1356 4-9-0 **71** .... NCallan 15 80
(D M Simcock) *lw: chsd ldrs: led and edgd lft over 2f out: sn rdn: hdd over 1f out: unable qckn towards fin* **9/2**[2]

1133 **4** 3 ½ **Apache Fort**[11] 1532 4-8-4 **61** oh1 .... FrancisNorton 9 65+
(T Keddy) *prom: rdn 1/2-way: no ex fnl f* **12/1**

54-5 **5** 6 **Qualitair Wings**[7] 1627 8-8-4 **61** oh1 .... HayleyTurner 5 52
(J Hetherton) *hld up: hdwy over 1f out: nt trble ldrs* **25/1**

43-4 **6** ¾ **Stargazer Jim (FR)**[16] 1416 5-8-12 **69** .... TedDurcan 12 59
(W J Haggas) *hld up: hdwy over 3f out: rdn and wknd over 1f out* **7/2**[1]

5/65 **7** ½ **Kingscape (IRE)**[19] 1318 4-8-8 **65** .... OscarUrbina 10 54
(J R Fanshawe) *hld up: hdwy over 2f out: rdn and hung lft over 1f out: nt run on* **12/1**

00-5 **8** 7 **Barathea Dreams (IRE)**[14] 1446 6-9-2 **73** .... JohnEgan 6 48
(J S Moore) *hld up: rdn and edgd rt wl over 1f out: n.d* **12/1**

1560 **9** 1 **Davenport (IRE)**[20] 1288 5-9-4 **75** ....(p) RobertHavlin 2 48
(B R Millman) *hld up: rdn over 2f out: n.d* **14/1**

0050 **10** ½ **Speagle (IRE)**[23] 1253 5-9-4 **75** .... DanielTudhope 13 47
(D Carroll) *led over 7f: wknd over 1f out* **33/1**

4133 **11** 4 **Mahmjra**[17] 1378 5-8-13 **70** .... ChrisCatlin 11 35
(C N Allen) *chsd ldrs over 7f* **8/1**

1/00 **12** 1 ¾ **Economic (IRE)**[58] 726 4-9-4 **75** ....(b[1]) PaulDoe 8 37
(M Botti) *lw: hld up: wknd over 2f out* **33/1**

5000 **13** 8 **Fantasy Ride**[17] 1385 5-9-1 **72** .... DeanMcKeown 4 18
(J Pearce) *b: s.s: rdn 1/2-way: a bhd* **16/1**

64-0 **14** 8 **Vanadium**[135] 28 5-9-1 **72** .... PhilipRobinson 14 —
(J G Given) *chsd ldrs: wkng whn hmpd wl over 2f out* **16/1**

/14- **15** ½ **Where's Broughton**[151] 6862 4-9-3 **74** .... BrettDoyle 3 4
(W J Musson) *s.i.s: hld up: a in rr* **12/1**

2m 5.00s (-0.71) **Going Correction** -0.05s/f (Good) **15** Ran SP% **133.8**
Speed ratings (Par 103):100,99,99,96,91 91,90,85,84,84 80,79,73,66,66
CSF £75.03 CT £323.23 TOTE £11.50: £3.40, £3.10, £1.90; EX 59.40.

Owner W J Musson **Bred** Derek Veitch **Trained** Newmarket, Suffolk

FOCUS
An ordinary handicap for the grade which saw the first three closely covered at the finish. The form is rated through the consistent fourth.
Fantasy Ride Official explanation: jockey said gelding was never travelling

1820 BETDIRECT.COM FREEROLL PASSWORD WHEN YOU BET H'CAP 5f
5:25 (5:26) (Class 4) (0-80,80) 3-Y-O **£5,181** (£1,541; £770; £384) **Stalls** High

Form RPR

30-0 **1** **Fathom Five (IRE)**[29] 1108 3-9-1 **77** .... PhilipRobinson 3 90
(B Smart) *racd in centre: led that gp: edgd rt over 1f out: rdn to be overall ldr wl ins fnl f: r.o* **9/2**[3]

2-32 **2** 1 ¼ **Bookiesindex Boy**[18] 1351 3-8-8 **70** ....(b) RobertHavlin 8 78
(J R Jenkins) *lw: racd far side: chsd ldrs: overall ldr 1/2-way: rdn and edgd lft over 1f out: hdd wl ins fnl f: 1st of 6 in gp* **10/1**

1201 **3** 3 ½ **Mandurah (IRE)**[20] 1286 3-8-2 **67** .... EmmettStack(3) 1 62
(D Nicholls) *lw: s.i.s: racd in centre and sn chsng wnr: rdn and hung rt over 1f out: no ex fnl f: 2nd of 5 in gp* **9/2**[3]

-003 **4** 1 ½ **Feelin Foxy**[3] 1738 3-8-1 **66** ....(v) LiamJones(3) 9 56
(D Shaw) *racd far side: s.i.s: hld up: hdwy over 1f out: nvr trbld ldrs: 2nd of 6 in gp* **18/1**

0-02 **5** ¾ **King's Bastion (IRE)**[6] 1660 3-9-4 **80** .... NCallan 5 67+
(M L W Bell) *lw: racd incentre: s.i.s: sn in tch: outpcd 1/2-way: styd on ins fnl f: 3rd of 5 in gp* **4/1**[2]

2001 **6** nk **Charlotte Grey**[20] 1313 3-8-4 **66** oh1 .... ChrisCatlin 10 52
(C N Allen) *led far side to 1/2-way: wknd over 1f out: 3rd of 6 in gp* **20/1**

0-00 **7** 1 ¾ **Eloquent Rose (IRE)**[9] 1577 3-8-12 **74** .... TPO'Shea 2 54
(Mrs A Duffield) *racd centre: sn outpcd: 4th of 5 in gp* **20/1**

010- **8** 2 ½ **Loves Bidding**[280] 4321 3-8-13 **75** .... DaneO'Neill 6 46
(R Ingram) *racd far side: hld up: a in rr: 4th of 6 in gp* **33/1**

-512 **9** 1 **Rebel Duke (IRE)**[27] 1160 3-9-1 **80** ....(b[1]) JerryO'Dwyer(3) 4 47
(M G Quinlan) *lw: racd in centre: s.i.s: sn prom: hung rt and wknd over 1f out: last of 5 in gp* **11/1**

-311 **10** 2 ½ **Windjammer**[14] 1453 3-8-5 **70** .... DuranFentiman(3) 11 28
(T D Easterby) *racd far side: disp ld to 1/2-way: wknd over 1f out: 5th of 6 in gp* **9/4**[1]

2-00 **11** 2 **Retaliate**[43] 935 3-8-8 **70** .... FrancisNorton 7 21
(M Quinn) *racd far side: sn pushed along in rr: rdn and wknd 1/2-way: last of 6 in gp* **20/1**

59.48 secs (-0.99) **Going Correction** -0.05s/f (Good) **11** Ran SP% **127.0**
Speed ratings (Par 101):105,103,97,95,93 93,90,86,84,80 77
CSF £50.09 CT £226.86 TOTE £6.80: £2.30, £3.10, £2.10; EX 79.20 Place 6 £201.69, Place 5 £95.44.

Owner Hintlesham Racing **Bred** Eamonn Connolly **Trained** Hambleton, N Yorks

FOCUS
A fair three-year-old sprint handicap which the field split into two groups. The form looks sound rated through the runner-up and is rated fairly positively.

Windjammer Official explanation: jockey said gelding was never travelling
T/Plt: £238.50 to a £1 stake. Pool: £54,286.70. 166.15 winning tickets. T/Qpdt: £74.90 to a £1 stake. Pool: £3,150.20. 31.10 winning tickets. CR

[1788]YORK (L-H)

Friday, May 18

OFFICIAL GOING: Good (good to soft in places, 7.4)

The ground was reckoned to have dried out a touch for the meeting's final day, and some jockeys thought the going was a shade tacky.

Wind: strong, half-across

1821 LANGLEYS SOLICITORS E B F MARYGATE STKS (LISTED RACE) (FILLIES) 5f

1:45 (1:45) (Class 1) 2-Y-O **£14,817** (£5,602; £2,800; £1,400) **Stalls** Centre

Form RPR

1 **1** **Janina**[20] [1285] 2-8-12 .... RHills 9 95+
(B W Hills) *str: lw: trckd ldrs: hdwy 2f out: rdn to ld wl ins fnl f: kpt on strly* **5/2**[1]

1 **2** *1* **Tia Mia**[20] [1302] 2-8-12 .... TPQueally 6 91
(J G Given) *str: lw: led: rdn along wl over 1f out: drvn and hdd wl ins fnl f: kpt on* **8/1**

1 **3** *hd* **Cristal Clear (IRE)**[29] [1107] 2-8-12 .... DavidAllan 1 91
(T D Easterby) *lengthy: unf: cl up: rdn wl over 1f out and ev ch tl drvn and no ex wl ins fnl f* **11/2**

1 **4** *1 1/4* **Dubai Princess (IRE)**[50] [814] 2-8-12 .... EddieAhern 3 86
(J A Osborne) *in tch: hdwy 1/2-way: rdn wl over 1f out and kpt on same pce* **4/1**[2]

5 *3/4* **Liberty Belle (IRE)** 2-8-12 .... StephaneBreux 4 83
(J R Best) *w'like: bhd tl styd on wl appr fnl f: nrst fin* **100/1**

1 **6** *3/4* **Loch Jipp (USA)**[25] [1193] 2-8-12 .... TomEaves 11 81
(J S Wainwright) *leggy: unf: wnt rt s: chsd ldrs: rdn along 2f out and kpt on same pce* **33/1**

7 *shd* **Shivering**[29] [1113] 2-8-12 .... WJLee 2 80
(T Stack, Ire) *unf: chsd ldrs: rdn along 2f out: sn wknd* **5/1**[3]

1 **8** *1 1/2* **Feeling Proud (USA)**[14] [1445] 2-8-12 .... KerrinMcEvoy 5 75
(Jane Chapple-Hyam) *in rr tl sme late hdwy* **25/1**

31 **9** *nk* **Jennifers Joy (IRE)**[11] [1533] 2-8-12 .... JHBowman 10 74
(M R Channon) *prom: rdn along 1/2-way: sn wknd* **10/1**

2 **10** *4* **Presto Levanter**[12] [1503] 2-8-12 .... JimmyFortune 7 60
(R Hannon) *cmpt: a in rr* **11/1**

58.73 secs (-0.59) **Going Correction** +0.025s/f (Good) **10** Ran SP% **116.9**
Speed ratings (Par 98):105,103,103,101,99 98,98,96,95,89
CSF £23.23 TOTE £3.30: £1.40, £2.80, £2.30; EX 25.30 Trifecta £254.70 Pool £574.00 - 1.60 winning units..
Owner Hamdan Al Maktoum **Bred** H G And J R Dutfield **Trained** Lambourn, Berks
■ Stewards' Enquiry : David Allan one-day ban: used whip down the shoulder in forehand position (May 29)
W J Lee one-day ban: used whip with excessive frequency (May 29)

FOCUS
Eight of the nine to have run were winners, six of them unbeaten, in this decent Listed event. All the principals showed improvement and the race should work out.

NOTEBOOK
Janina ◆, a convincing winer on her Haydock debut, followed up nicely on this step up in grade. After travelling well behind the leaders, she took a little time to pick up but came through to win quite comfortably in the end. She looks an Ascot filly, with connections reportedly leaning more towards the 6f Albany Stakes than the Queen Mary. (op 9-4)
Tia Mia, a little speedball, led the field down the centre and stuck her neck out willingly when challenged. She could not hold the favourite, but deserves plenty of credit for this performance. (op 10-1)
Cristal Clear(IRE) had three subsequent winners behind her at Ripon. She showed plenty of pace and had every chance but, as on her debut, she carried her head a little high, possibly through greenness, and she was just held in the final furlong. (op 7-1)
Dubai Princess(IRE), impressive on her debut in a Polytrack maiden back in March, stepped up on that form but would probably have preferred faster ground. (op 9-2 tchd 5-1)
Liberty Belle(IRE) ◆ is a half-sister to winners at 6-7f out of a half-sister to high-class miler Jabr. Outpaced in rear following a slightly tardy start, she found her feet going to the final furlong and was nearest at the end. This was a promising debut in such warm company and she should have no problem getting off the mark, perhaps over a little further. (op 66-1)
Loch Jipp(USA), a surprise winner at Pontefract, went right leaving the stalls and flashed her tail more than once. Recovering to chase the leaders, she could not go with them in the final quarter-mile.
Shivering, a half-sister to smart sprinter The Trader who made all at Tipperary on her second start, had her limitations exposed in this better grade.
Jennifers Joy(IRE), third to Janina on their respective debuts at Haydock, and a winner since, showed bright early pace but was already starting to feel the pinch by halfway. (op 9-1)

1822 RELAND JORVIK STKS (HERITAGE H'CAP) 1m 4f

2:15 (2:16) (Class 2) (0-105,97) 4-Y-O+

£31,160 (£9,330; £4,665; £2,335; £1,165; £292) **Stalls** Centre

Form RPR

1-32 **1** **High Treason (USA)**[2] [1771] 5-8-8 **81** .... TPQueally 9 92+
(W J Musson) *hld up in rr: stdy hdwy 4f out: trckd ldrs 2f out: rdn and hit in face w whip ent fnl f: styd on gamely to ld nr fin* **5/1**[1]

54-3 **2** *1/2* **Mutawaffer**[48] [848] 6-9-1 **88** .... RoystonFfrench 1 96
(R A Fahey) *chsd ldrs: hdwy 3f out: rdn to ld wl over 1f out: drvn ins fnl f: hdd and no ex nr fin* **14/1**

1311 **3** *1* **Kilimandscharo (USA)**[9] [1575] 5-8-7 **80** 6ex .... MJKinane 7 86
(P J McBride) *hld up: smooth hdwy 4f out: rdn to chal wl over 1f out and ev ch tl drvn and no ex wl ins fnl f* **16/1**

-032 **4** *2* **Nakheel**[13] [1477] 4-9-10 **97** .... RHills 8 100
(M Johnston) *lw: dwlt: sn prom: led wl over 3f out: rdn 2f out: drvn and hdd appr fnl f: one pce* **15/2**[3]

/30- **5** *1 1/2* **Motive (FR)**[41] [3552] 6-9-5 **92** .... TomEaves 14 93
(J Howard Johnson) *hld up: hdwy over 3f out: rdn to chse ldrs 2f out: sn drvn and kpt on same pce* **66/1**

4454 **6** *shd* **Amwell Brave**[14] [1451] 6-7-7 **71** oh17 .... WilliamBuick(5) 17 72?
(J R Jenkins) *dwlt and bhd: hdwy 3f out: rdn over 2f out: styd on wl: nrst fin* **100/1**

0-66 **6** *dht* **Macorville (USA)**[20] [1300] 4-9-3 **90** .... KerrinMcEvoy 11 91
(G M Moore) *prom: effrt to chse ldr 3f out: rdn along 2f out and grad wknd* **10/1**

131- **7** *3/4* **Bauer (IRE)**[245] [5346] 4-9-3 **90** .... NickyMackay 18 89
(L M Cumani) *b.bkwd: hld up in midfield: effrt and hdwy 3f out: rdn along 2f out and sn one pce* **10/1**

-056 **8** *shd* **Fort Churchill (IRE)**[23] [1245] 6-8-8 **81** .... (bt) PatCosgrave 2 80
(B Ellison) *lw: in tch: effrt over 3f out: sn rdn along and no imp fnl 2f* **8/1**

4-61 **9** *nk* **Ballinteni**[11] [1543] 5-9-0 **87** 6ex .... EddieAhern 12 86
(D M Simcock) *hld up in rr: hdwy 3f out: rdn along over 2f out and sn no imp* **10/1**

41-6 **10** *1/2* **All The Good (IRE)**[41] [940] 4-9-9 **96** .... JHBowman 10 94
(G A Butler) *chsd ldrs: rdn along 3f out: sn drvn and wknd fnl 2f* **15/2**[3]

03-4 **11** *8* **Kyoto Summit**[20] [1304] 4-9-2 **89** .... PaulMulrennan 6 74
(M W Easterby) *a towards rr* **25/1**

1/0- **12** *1 1/4* **Dont Call Me Derek**[216] [5963] 6-9-3 **90** .... GrahamGibbons 4 73
(J J Quinn) *b.bkwd: led: rdn along and hdd over 3f out: sn wknd* **28/1**

002- **13** *15* **Simondiun**[276] [4459] 4-9-3 **90** .... JimmyFortune 3 49
(W J Haggas) *chsd ldrs: rdn along 3f out: drvn 2f out and sn wknd* **12/1**

0-12 **14** *9* **Halla San**[20] [1300] 5-9-3 **95** .... JamieMoriarty(5) 13 40
(R A Fahey) *lw: in tch: effrt 4f out: sn rdn along and wknd 3f out* **13/2**[2]

2m 32.79s (-1.81) **Going Correction** +0.30s/f (Good) **15** Ran SP% **121.9**
Speed ratings (Par 109):110,109,109,107,106 106,106,106,106,105 105,100,99,89,83
CSF £75.08 CT £1062.84 TOTE £7.20: £2.50, £3.70, £5.60; EX 82.70 Trifecta £1041.30 Part won. Pool £1,466.70 - 0.20 winning units..
Owner S Rudolf **Bred** Helmut Von Finck **Trained** Newmarket, Suffolk
■ Stewards' Enquiry : Royston Ffrench two-day ban: used whip with excessive frequency and not allowing gelding time to respond (May 29-30)

FOCUS
A decent and competitive handicap, rated through the second to last year's best and the third to his sand form. The runners came down the centre of the track in the straight. It is doubtful if High Treason had to improve on the form he showed here earlier in the week.

NOTEBOOK
High Treason(USA) ◆, a slightly unlucky runner-up to Tcherina on the opening day of the meeting, gained compensation on this quick reappearance. Travelling well before steadily picking his way through the field in the straight, he got a crack across the face when challenging inside the last but did not flinch and won a shade more easily than the margin suggests. There could be more to come. (op 6-1)
Mutawaffer, third in the Lincoln on his reappearance seven weeks ago, is proven over 1m2f but was having his first run over this far. Always prominent, he battled his way to the front but could not resist the favourite's challenge close home. This was a sound effort, and he stayed the trip, but he remains winless since his juvenile season. (op 20-1)
Kilimandscharo(USA), a progressive performer, ran another big race but, after making smooth progress down the outside to challenge, he was just held in the last 50 yards. He was 3lb badly in under the penalty he picked up at Beverley and it would be no surprise to see him adding to his tally before long.
Nakheel, raised 2lb after his good effort at Newmarket, ran another sound race, but after being headed going to the final furlong, it appeared he did not quite get home. A return to 1m2f will suit him but he might not be easy to place. (op 7-1)
Motive(FR), a lightly-raced gelding who was last in action over hurdles, ran promisingly and there could be a race in him in less competitive company.
Macorville(USA), whose last win came off this mark, had more suitable underfoot conditions than for his first two runs of the season. After chasing the leading pair, he faded out of contention in the last two furlongs. (op 8-1)
Amwell Brave, reverting to turf after a busy campaign on sand, was staying on past toiling rivals at the end. No less than 17lb out of the handicap, this was as good a run as he has ever put in and he can expect a rise in the weights for this. (op 8-1)
Bauer(IRE) was 10lb higher than for the last of his four wins in 2006 and no less than 30lb higher than the first of them. Not well drawn for this reappearance, he made a bit of late progress without ever getting into the action and should come on for the outing. (op 8-1)
All The Good(IRE) had caught the eye on his reappearance at Kempton and was reportedly targeted at this race. He was disappointing and probably needs further. (op 9-1 tchd 7-1)
Halla San was probably unsuited by the drop back from 2m but should still have run better than he did. Official explanation: trainer had no explanation for the poor form shown (op 11-2)

1823 EMIRATES AIRLINE YORKSHIRE CUP (GROUP 2) 1m 6f

2:45 (2:49) (Class 1) 4-Y-O+

£79,492 (£30,128; £15,078; £7,518; £3,766; £1,890) **Stalls** Low

Form RPR

13-4 **1** **Sergeant Cecil**[27] [1144] 8-9-3 117 .... JimmyFortune 5 119
(B R Millman) *hld up in rr: smooth hdwy 3f out: rdn to chal over 1f out: styd on to ld ins fnl f: drvn out* **10/3**[1]

0-25 **2** *3/4* **Geordieland (FR)**[44] [929] 6-8-12 105 .... TPQueally 9 113
(J A Osborne) *hld up in rr: hdwy 3f out: led on bit wl over 1f out: rdn and hdd ins fnl f: kpt on wl u.p* **17/2**

42-0 **3** *2* **Bulwark (IRE)**[27] [1144] 5-8-12 104 .... (be) JimCrowley 7 110
(Mrs A J Perrett) *hld up towards rr: hdwy over 3f out: rdn along 2f out: kpt on u.p fnl f* **40/1**

/10- **4** *nk* **Percussionist (IRE)**[76] [5395] 6-8-12 115 .... EddieAhern 3 110
(J Howard Johnson) *trckd ldrs: hdwy 3f out: rdn to chal over 2f out and ev ch tl drvn and on same pce appr fnl f* **10/1**

133- **5** *6* **Allegretto (IRE)**[252] [5155] 4-8-12 108 .... KerrinMcEvoy 6 101
(Sir Michael Stoute) *chsd ldrs: hdwy 4f out: rdn along and ch over 2f out: sn drvn and wknd* **13/2**[3]

25-3 **6** *2 1/2* **Munsef**[27] [1144] 5-8-12 111 .... RHills 1 98
(J L Dunlop) *lw: trckd ldrs: hdwy 4f out: rdn and ch over 2f out: sn wknd* **7/2**[2]

155- **7** *shd* **Rising Cross**[208] [6119] 4-8-12 110 .... JoeFanning 4 98
(J R Best) *prom: hdwy to ld 3f out: sn rdn along and hdd 2f out: sn wknd* **14/1**

320- **8** *21* **Orcadian**[34] [6515] 6-8-12 107 .... JHBowman 2 68
(J M P Eustace) *led: rdn along and hdd 3f out: sn wknd* **16/1**

040- **9** *12* **Kasthari (IRE)**[35] [5967] 8-8-12 105 .... TomEaves 10 52
(J Howard Johnson) *prom: rdn along over 4f out and sn wknd* **100/1**

0-23 **P** **The Last Drop (IRE)**[16] [1393] 4-8-12 112 .... (t) MJKinane 8 —
(B W Hills) *lw: in tch: effrt over 4f out: sn rdn along: wknd qckly 3f out: lost action and p.u 2f out* **7/2**[2]

2m 59.63s (0.13) **Going Correction** +0.30s/f (Good) **10** Ran SP% **116.5**
Speed ratings (Par 115):111,110,109,109,105 104,104,92,85,—
CSF £32.22 TOTE £3.40: £1.50, £2.70, £10.30; EX 37.80 Trifecta £1342.30 Part won. Pool £1,890.58 - 0.20 winning units..
Owner Terry Cooper **Bred** D E Hazzard **Trained** Kentisbeare, Devon

FOCUS
A good renewal of the Yorkshire Cup. The pace was sound and the three principals all came from the back of the field. Sergeant Cecil showed himself to be better than ever and Geordieland was back to last season's Goodwood Cup and Ebor form.

NOTEBOOK

Sergeant Cecil loves it here and his only defeat in five visits came in this race last year. Held up at the back before improving in the straight, he picked up really well to cut down Geordieland before holding that rival's renewed challenge. Under the Group 1 penalty for his Prix du Cadran win, this was a career-best performance and he looks the principal danger to Yeats in the Gold Cup. (op 3-1 tchd 7-2)

Geordieland(FR) disappointed on his reappearance at Nottingham but this was more like it. After making smooth progress to take it up on the bridle, he was soon headed by the winner but to his credit he battled back. There is a big race in him but he may need to be produced later. (op 9-1 tchd 8-1)

Bulwark(IRE), suited by a strongly-run race on the return to this trip, came from the rear like the two that beat him. This was a good performance, up 5lb on his previous best, but he is going to need everything to drop just right if he is to add to his five career victories. (op 33-1)

Percussionist(IRE), a winner over fences in the latest season, beat Sergeant Cecil in last year's renewal but this was only his second run on the Flat since. The ground was not quite soft enough for him but this was still a fine effort, especially as he was up with the pace all the way. (op 8-1)

Allegretto(IRE), who looked fit for this seasonal bow, ran a reasonable race against hardened stayers but was not a threat in the last two furlongs. It would not surprise to see her progress from this. (op 7-1 tchd 15-2)

Munsef, one place in front of Sergeant Cecil at Newbury and 2lb worse off here, was close enough at the two pole but did not see out this longer trip. (op 9-2 tchd 5-1)

Rising Cross, winner of the Park Hill Stakes over course and distance last September, has not grown during the off-season. She showed briefly ahead in the straight but was soon left toiling. (op 12-1)

The Last Drop(IRE) weakened quickly with three to run. He was pulled up as if something was amiss, but seemed sound afterwards. Official explanation: jockey said colt lost its action. (op 4-1 tchd 3-1)

1824 MICHAEL SEELY MEMORIAL FILLIES' STKS (LISTED RACE) 1m

3:15 (3:16) (Class 1) 3-Y-O **£17,034** (£6,456; £3,231; £1,611; £807) **Stalls** Low

Form				RPR
5-12	**1**		**Silver Pivotal (IRE)**^{16} [1391] 3-8-12 **95**........ NickyMackay 2 (G A Butler) *gd sort: lw: hld up: hdwy 2f out: rdn over 1f out: styd on strly ins fnl f to ld nr fin* **4/1**^{2}	100+
1	**2**	*nk*	**Promising Lead**^{28} [1128] 3-8-12........ KerrinMcEvoy 5 (Sir Michael Stoute) *lw: trckd ldr: hdwy and cl up 2f out: rdn to ld ent fnl f: hdd and no ex towards fin* **10/11**^{1}	100+
31	**3**	*2*	**Graduation**^{11} [1537] 3-8-12........ JimmyFortune 1 (E A L Dunlop) *trckd ldrs: hdwy to ld 2f out: rdn and hdd ent fnl f: wknd* **5/1**^{3}	95
30-0	**4**	*1*	**Russian Rosie (IRE)**^{27} [1146] 3-8-12 **89**........ TPQueally 3 (J G Portman) *led: rdn along and hdd 2f out: sn wknd* **22/1**	93
-200	**5**	*12*	**Satulagi (USA)**^{12} [1496] 3-9-1........ EddieAhern 4 (J S Moore) *trckd ldrs: rdn along wl over 2f out and sn btn* **11/2**	68

1m 40.86s (1.36) **Going Correction** +0.30s/f (Good) **5** Ran SP% **108.8**

Speed ratings (Par 104):105,104,102,101,89

CSF £7.95 TOTE £5.30: £2.20, £1.30.

Owner The Distaff Partnership **Bred** Stratford Place Stud **Trained** Blewbury, Oxon

FOCUS

This Listed event was run at only a steady pace and the runners again came down the centre in the home straight. It is hard to rate the bare form highly with the fourth not beaten far, but Silver Pivotal looks sure to improve over further.

NOTEBOOK

Silver Pivotal(IRE) ◆, an unlucky loser at Ascot, did not need to improve on that form to land this Listed event. A big filly, she became slightly outpaced when the gallop quickened but really found her stride in the final furlong to cut down the favourite. There is plenty of improvement in her over longer trips and she will be an interesting candidate for something like the Ribblesdale at Royal Ascot. (op 5-1)

Promising Lead is superbly bred, being out of a half-sister to Dansili (sire of Rail Link), Banks Hill and Intercontinental. Sent in search of some black type, she got past her old rival Graduation entering the final furlong but could not hold off the winner. She travelled well for a long way and should find a race at this level. (op 4-5 tchd evens in a place)

Graduation, who barely broke sweat when landing the odds at Warwick, came through to lead with a quarter-mile to run but was soon collared by the runner-up, finishing further behind that rival than she had at Newbury. (op 9-2 tchd 4-1)

Russian Rosie(IRE), well beaten in the Fred Darling on her reappearance, cut out only a steady pace on this first try over a mile and had no answers when headed. There was no disgrace in this but she is likely to prove difficult to place. (op 25-1)

Satulagi(USA), a staying-on ninth in the 1000 Guineas and with entries in three forthcoming Group 1 events, was well below form, but the lack of pace and easier ground did not help her. Official explanation: jockey said filly ran flat. (op 6-1 tchd 7-1)

1825 AXIS INTERMODAL STKS (H'CAP) 5f

3:50 (3:50) (Class 3) (0-90,88) 3-Y-O **£9,715** (£2,890; £1,444; £721) **Stalls** Centre

Form				RPR
-122	**1**		**Morinqua (IRE)**^{7} [1616] 3-9-0 **81**........ TPQueally 12 (J G Given) *lw: qckly away on stands rail: mde all: rdn appr fnl f and kpt on strly* **6/1**	94
50-1	**2**	*1 3/4*	**Tombi (USA)**^{16} [1403] 3-9-3 **84**........ EddieAhern 3 (J Howard Johnson) *in tch centre: hdwy 1/2-way: rdn to chse wnr ins fnl f: kpt on u.p* **4/1**^{2}	91+
00-5	**3**	*1 3/4*	**Avertuoso**^{27} [1160] 3-9-4 **88**........ MarkLawson$^{(3)}$ 10 (B Smart) *lw: dwlt: sn chsng wnr: rdn along 2f out: drvn and kpt on same pce appr fnl f* **33/1**	89
13-6	**4**	*shd*	**The Nifty Fox**^{27} [1160] 3-8-10 **77**........ MJKinane 6 (T D Easterby) *chsd ldrs: rdn along 2f out: drvn over 1f out and kpt on same pce* **7/1**	77
12	**5**	*hd*	**Sea Rover (IRE)**^{11} [1530] 3-8-2 **69** oh2........ DeanMernagh 1 (M Brittain) *a.p centre: rdn along 2f out: drvn and one pce fr over 1f out* **7/2**^{1}	69+
-050	**6**	*1/2*	**Danum Dancer**^{13} [1473] 3-9-7 **88**........(b) JHBowman 7 (N Bycroft) *b: towards rr: swtchd lft and rdn wl over 1f out: kpt on ins fnl f: nrst fin* **8/1**	86
320-	**7**	*nk*	**All You Need (IRE)**^{231} [5645] 3-8-3 **75**........ WilliamBuick$^{(5)}$ 4 (R Hollinshead) *bkwd: outpcd and bhd tl styd on appr fnl f* **20/1**	72
1306	**8**	*2 1/2*	**Grange Lili (IRE)**^{18} [1351] 3-8-2 **72**........ PatrickMathers$^{(3)}$ 8 (Peter Grayson) *s.i.s: a in rr* **100/1**	60
31-4	**9**	*3 1/2*	**Frisky Talk (IRE)**^{11} [1520] 3-9-2 **83**........ RHills 2 (B W Hills) *swtg: prom centre: rdn along 2f out: sn wknd* **14/1**	58
45-5	**9**	*dht*	**Top Bid**^{20} [1298] 3-9-3 **84**........ DavidAllan 5 (T D Easterby) *chsd ldrs: rdn along over 2f out: sn wknd* **5/1**^{3}	59
2-50	**11**	*13*	**Fool Me (IRE)**^{20} [1298] 3-9-2 **83**........ RichardMullen 9 (E S McMahon) *lw: chsd ldrs: rdn along 1/2-way: sn wknd* **20/1**	11

59.01 secs (-0.31) **Going Correction** +0.025s/f (Good) **11** Ran SP% **116.9**

Speed ratings (Par 103):103,100,97,97,96 96,95,91,86,86 65

CSF £28.83 CT £750.31 TOTE £7.40: £2.30, £2.00, £6.70; EX 19.30.

Owner The Living Legend Racing Partnership **Bred** Corrin Stud **Trained** Willoughton, Lincs

FOCUS

A fair handicap in which Morinqua improved by 7lb on her Chester form, helped by a stands' side draw, and the runner-up also put up a personal best. The form looks solid and should work out.

NOTEBOOK

Morinqua(IRE) ◆, racing from the same mark as when pipped by City Of Tribes at Chester, made all the running near the stands' rail and was never seriously threatened. She was already due to go up 4lb before this, but she is lightning fast and she can win more races even when re-assessed. (op 4-1)

Tombi(USA) came through to finish best of the rest, giving the impression that a return to 6f will suit him. He holds a Group 1 entry in the Golden Jubilee Stakes at Ascot but a more realistic assignment might be the William Hill Trophy here next month. (op 5-1)

Avertuoso, who ran his best race at two over this course and distance, has been dropped 2lb since his reappearance. Chasing the speedy winner towards the stands' side, he stuck on willingly for third.

The Nifty Fox ran a sound race and finished closer to Avertuoso than he did at Thirsk. (op 14-1)

Sea Rover(IRE), drawn one, was not helped by racing out towards the centre without much company and ran well in the circumstances. He will be suited by the return to 6f. (op 10-3 tchd 4-1 in places)

Danum Dancer, back at a more realistic level after beating just two home in the Guineas, was doing his best work at the end and needs 6f now. (op 11-1)

All You Need(IRE), having his first start since September, was running on at the end and will be suited by an extra furlong, as well as faster ground. (op 25-1)

Top Bid had made a pleasing return at Ripon but was well below-par over this furlong shorter and on easier ground. Official explanation: jockey said colt was never travelling. (op 9-2)

1826 SPORTING INDEX STKS (H'CAP) 6f

4:25 (4:25) (Class 2) (0-100,98) 4-Y-O+ **£12,954** (£3,854; £1,926; £962) **Stalls** Centre

Form				RPR
0-60	**1**		**Wyatt Earp (IRE)**^{13} [1474] 6-8-8 **88**........ TPQueally 13 (R A Fahey) *lw: hld up: hdwy whn n.m.r 2f out: sn rdn and styd on to ld ent fnl f: drvn out* **13/2**	100+
-650	**2**	*1/2*	**Zomerlust**^{6} [1651] 5-8-10 **90**........ GrahamGibbons 7 (J J Quinn) *sn pushed along towards rr: hdwy 2f out: switchd lft and drvn over 1f out: styd on wl fnl f* **11/2**^{2}	100+
062	**3**	*1 1/2*	**Beckermet (IRE)**^{7} [1619] 5-9-4 **98**........ EddieAhern 12 (R F Fisher) *lw: hld up: hdwy on rail whn hmpd 2f out: sn rdn and styd on fnl f* **7/1**	104
216-	**4**	*3/4*	**Buachaill Dona (IRE)**^{238} [5501] 4-9-4 **98**........ AdrianTNicholls 9 (D Nicholls) *trckd ldrs: edgd rt 2f out: effrt to dispute ld over 1f out and ev ch tl rdn wknd ins fnl f* **6/1**^{3}	101+
000-	**5**	*1/2*	**Ingleby Arch (USA)**^{223} [5812] 4-8-9 **89**........ PaulFessey 3 (T D Barron) *b.bkwd: trckd ldrs: pushed along and sltly outpcd 1/2-way: rdn and edgd rt 2f out: sn drvn and kpt on same pce* **8/1**	91
0000	**6**	*hd*	**Commando Scott (IRE)**^{7} [1619] 6-8-1 **84** oh1........ PatrickMathers$^{(3)}$ 10 (I W McInnes) *lw: chsd ldrs: rdn along whn hmpd 2f out: styd on u.p fnl f* **25/1**	85+
0-46	**7**	*nk*	**Hoh Hoh Hoh**^{13} [1474] 5-7-13 **84**........ WilliamBuick$^{(5)}$ 2 (R J Price) *led: rdn along wl over 1f out: hdd & wknd ent fnl f* **7/2**^{1}	84
00-4	**8**	*hd*	**King's Gait**^{6} [1653] 5-8-10 **90**........(b) DavidAllan 1 (T D Easterby) *lw: cl up: rdn along 2f out: ev ch tl drvn and wknd appr fnl f* **7/1**	90
-530	**9**	*3/4*	**Mezuzah**^{26} [1179] 7-8-7 **87**........ PaulMulrennan 6 (M W Easterby) *in rr tl styd on appr fnl f* **50/1**	84
0-00	**10**	*3/4*	**Indian Trail**^{13} [1474] 7-9-1 **95**........ MickyFenton 8 (D Nicholls) *trckd ldng pair: rdn along over 2f out: sn wknd* **33/1**	90
1-00	**11**	*nk*	**Royal Challenge**^{9} [1574] 6-8-3 **86** ow2........ SaleemGolam$^{(3)}$ 11 (M H Tompkins) *a in rr* **16/1**	80
00-0	**12**	*3/4*	**Desert Commander (IRE)**^{30} [1088] 5-8-5 **88**........(t) AndrewMullen$^{(3)}$ 4 (K A Ryan) *lw: a in rr* **12/1**	80
2-00	**13**	*1 1/4*	**Turnkey**^{25} [1195] 5-9-1 **95**........ PaulQuinn 5 (D Nicholls) *a in rr* **33/1**	83

1m 12.01s (-0.55) **Going Correction** +0.025s/f (Good) **13** Ran SP% **126.6**

Speed ratings (Par 109):104,103,101,100,99 99,99,98,97,96 96,95,93

CSF £43.58 CT £276.88 TOTE £5.30: £1.90, £2.60, £2.90; EX 51.00.

Owner Los Bandidos Racing **Bred** J W Parker And Keith Wills **Trained** Musley Bank, N Yorks

■ Stewards' Enquiry : William Buick one-day ban: failed to keep straight from stalls (May 29)

FOCUS

A good handicap, and form which should work out. Wyatt Earp enhanced his good record here, with the runner-up rated to his late 2006 form.

NOTEBOOK

Wyatt Earp(IRE), well drawn against the stands' rail, recorded his third success over course and distance. Involved in a bit of scrimmaging when improving with two to run, he looked set to win by a greater margin when striking the front but idled a little as the runner-up came home strongly. Official explanation: trainer had no explanation for the improved form shown other than that gelding possibly saw too much daylight at Newmarket last time out, and it has run well at York in the past (op 7-1)

Zomerlust ◆, reverting to a more suitable trip, had to switch for a run but came home in good style when in the clear. A stiffer track is ideal and he is capable of finding a race before long. (op 6-1 tchd 13-2)

Beckermet(IRE), down in trip after a solid effort at Chester, was caught up in a bit of trouble near the stands' rail before finishing to some effect. While he is running well at present, he is on a losing run of 25 dating back to July 2005.

Buachaill Dona(IRE) ◆, making his seasonal reapearance, took a narrow lead over a furlong from home but could not hold on. The drop back to 5f should see him return to winning ways. (op 11-2)

Ingleby Arch(USA) did not get the best of runs but was keeping on at the finish. He is on a fair mark now and will be suited by faster ground.

Commando Scott(IRE), whose last win a year ago came from a 2lb higher mark, was keeping on late against the rail after finding himself short of room. (tchd 28-1)

Hoh Hoh Hoh again showed bags of pace to lead, coming over from his low stall, but he faded once headed entering the final furlong. His turn should come when he is better drawn. (op 5-1 tchd 11-2)

King's Gait, who could have done without the ground drying out, ran a fair race from an unfavourable draw.

Desert Commander(IRE) Official explanation: jockey said gelding was never travelling.

1827 RIPLEYCOLLECTION.COM STKS (H'CAP) 1m 4f

5:00 (5:01) (Class 4) (0-80,81) 3-Y-O **£7,772** (£2,312; £1,155; £577) **Stalls** Centre

Form				RPR
41-3	**1**		**Filios (IRE)**^{20} [1289] 3-9-3 **79**........ NickyMackay 13 (L M Cumani) *hld up towards rr: stdy hdwy 3f out: swtchd lft 2f out: rdn over 1f out: styd on wl fnl f to ld last 100yds* **15/8**^{1}	92+
21-6	**2**	*1*	**Eglevski (IRE)**^{36} [1010] 3-9-3 **79**........ EddieAhern 1 (J L Dunlop) *lw: trckd ldrs gng wl: smooth hdwy over 3f out: sn cl up: rdn to ld ent fnl f: hdd and no ex last 100yds* **9/1**	88

0-43 **3** 2 ½ **Moonwalking**[16] 1415 3-8-11 **73** JimCrowley 9 78
(Jedd O'Keeffe) *hld up in rr: gd hdwy on outer 3f out: rdn to ld wl over 1f out: drvn and hdd ent fnl f: one pce* **33/1**

221- **4** 2 **Persian Peril**[289] 4055 3-8-12 **77** AndrewElliott(3) 3 79
(G A Swinbank) *in tch: hdwy 3f out: rdn to chse ldrs wl over 1f out: sn drvn and one pce* **12/1**

-111 **5** shd **Fongs Gazelle**[9] 1576 3-9-5 **81** 6ex J-PGuillambert 2 83
(M Johnston) *lw: trckd ldrs: hdwy over 3f out: rdn along 2f out: kpt on same pce* **4/1**[2]

00-2 **6** 1 ½ **Force Group (IRE)**[25] 1194 3-8-3 **68** SaleemGolam(3) 8 67+
(M H Tompkins) *hld up in rr: stdy hdwy whn hmpd and forced lft 2f out: kpt on u.p fnl f* **8/1**

020- **7** 3 **Lemon Silk (IRE)**[216] 5958 3-9-0 **76** MickyFenton 16 70
(T P Tate) *t.k.h: prom: led 3f out: sn rdn along: hdd wl over 1f out and grad wknd* **50/1**

3-12 **8** ¾ **Its Moon (IRE)**[9] 1576 3-8-6 **68** GrahamGibbons 15 61
(T D Walford) *in tch: effrt 3f out: sn rdn along and no imp* **20/1**

142 **9** 2 ½ **Serpentaria**[7] 1637 3-8-11 **73** JamieMackay 12 62
(Sir Mark Prescott) *hld up in rr: hdwy 3f out: swtchd rt and rdn wl over 1f out: sn no imp* **7/1**[3]

1-23 **10** 3 ½ **Letham Island (IRE)**[24] 1218 3-8-11 **76** AndrewMullen(3) 7 60
(M Johnston) *a in midfield* **20/1**

0-12 **11** nk **Danish Rebel (IRE)**[23] 1237 3-9-4 **80** PaulMulrennan 6 63
(G A Charlton) *led: rdn along and hdd 3f out: sn wknd* **33/1**

01- **12** 1 **Act Sirius (IRE)**[236] 5552 3-9-0 **76** PaulFessey 5 58
(J Howard Johnson) *hld up towards rr: hdwy 3f out: sn rdn and no imp* **33/1**

332- **13** 1 ¾ **Sivota (IRE)**[198] 6297 3-8-8 **70** TPQueally 11 49
(T P Tate) *in tch: hdwy to chse ldrs 3f out: rdn along over 2f out and grad wknd* **12/1**

30-0 **14** 1 **Smugglers Bay (IRE)**[28] 1131 3-8-4 **66** oh2 PaulQuinn 4 43
(T D Easterby) *t.k.h: chsd ldrs tl wknd over 4f out* **80/1**

-023 **15** 2 **Love Brothers**[23] 1237 3-9-0 **76** JHBowman 14 50
(M R Channon) *chsd ldrs: rdn along and wkng whn bmpd 2f out: sn bhd* **20/1**

10-4 **16** 37 **Clarricien (IRE)**[23] 1237 3-9-2 **78** RichardMullen 10 —
(E J O'Neill) *s.i.s: a bhd* **40/1**

2m 34.6s **Going Correction** +0.30s/f (Good) **16** Ran SP% **132.5**
Speed ratings (Par 101):104,103,101,100,100 99,97,96,95,92 92,91,90,90,88 64
CSF £19.36 CT £476.35 TOTE £3.00: £1.10, £3.40, £5.40, £2.30; EX 34.70 Place 6 £158.49, Place 5 £81.65.
Owner L Marinopoulos **Bred** Bluegate Stud **Trained** Newmarket, Suffolk

FOCUS
The pace did not look that strong, but the time compared favourably with the race over this trip for older horses. Solid form which should work out, although the third limits it somewhat. The winner, second and fourth were all improvers.
Its Moon(IRE) Official explanation: jockey said filly hung left-handed in the final 3f.
Danish Rebel(IRE) Official explanation: jockey said colt hung right-handed throughout.
Sivota(IRE) Official explanation: jockey said gelding hung right-handed in the straight.
T/Jkpt: £18,968.20 to a £1 stake. Pool: £53,431.74. 2.00 winning tickets. T/Plt: £136.60 to a £1 stake. Pool: £162,380.75. 867.70 winning tickets. T/Qpdt: £17.60 to a £1 stake. Pool: £7,014.40. 294.50 winning tickets. JR

1828 - 1831a (Foreign Racing) - See Raceform Interactive

1807 NEWBURY (L-H)

Saturday, May 19

OFFICIAL GOING: Good to soft (good in places, 5.6)
Wind: Brisk, ahead.

1832 SANDERSON WEATHERALL MAIDEN STKS 6f 8y
1:35 (1:38) (Class 3) 2-Y-O **£6,477** (£1,927; £963; £481) **Stalls** Centre

Form RPR

3 **1** **Coasting**[12] 1540 2-9-3 MJKinane 19 84+
(Mrs A J Perrett) *w'like: trckd ldrs: pushed along to ld jst ins fnl f: kpt on strly* **4/1**[2]

2 ½ **Masaalek** 2-9-3 RHills 12 83+
(M P Tregoning) *unf: str: b.bkwd: stdd in rr: hdwy and swtchd lft 2f out: qcknd to chal jst ins fnl f: kpt on but nt pce of wnr cl home* **16/1**

3 1 ½ **Greek Mythology (USA)** 2-9-3 JHBowman 17 78
(A P O'Brien, Ire) *unf: scope: lw: trckd ldrs: drvn along fr 2f out: str chal 1f out: styd on same pce ins fnl f* **11/4**[1]

6 **4** shd **American Art (IRE)**[13] 1498 2-9-3 MichaelHills 3 78
(B W Hills) *chsd ldrs: drvn to chal over 1f out tl ins fnl f: kpt on same pce* **18/1**

5 1 **First Trim (IRE)** 2-9-3 LDettori 18 75
(B J Meehan) *w'like: b.bkwd: slt advantage: rdn 2f out: hdd jst ins fnl f: wknd last half f* **14/1**

6 ¾ **Il Warrd (IRE)** 2-9-3 JamieMackay 6 72+
(M P Tregoning) *unf: scope: lw: in rr: hdwy on outside over 2f out: kpt on wl fnl f but nvr gng pce to rch ldrs* **8/1**[3]

4 **7** shd **Huzzah (IRE)**[26] 1201 2-9-3 JamieSpencer 9 72+
(B W Hills) *in rr: stdy hdwy over 1f out: kpt on cl home but nvr gng pce to be competitive* **12/1**

8 ½ **Polygraph (IRE)** 2-9-3 FrancisNorton 16 71+
(A M Balding) *cmpt: b.bkwd: towards rr: hdwy whn hmpd 2f out: kpt on wl fnl f: gng on cl home* **25/1**

9 nk **Redesignation (IRE)** 2-9-3 RichardHughes 2 70
(R Hannon) *unf: leggy: b.bkwd: in tch: chsd ldrs and pushed along 2f out: one pce ins fnl f* **12/1**

10 1 ½ **Revivalism** 2-9-3 KDarley 15 65
(J H M Gosden) *w'like: str: b.bkwd: s.i.s: towards rr and pushed along 1/2-way: kpt on fnl f but nvr gng pce to be competitive* **11/1**

5 **11** hd **Dubai Dynamo**[7] 1680 2-9-3 EddieAhern 4 65+
(J S Moore) *w'like: in rr: hdwy into mid-div 1/2-way: styd on fnl f but nvr in contention* **25/1**

12 ¾ **Conquisto** 2-9-3 DaneO'Neill 10 62
(C G Cox) *cmpt: b.bkwd: pressed ldrs: rdn 2f out: wknd fnl f* **18/1**

13 1 **Thought Is Free** 2-8-12 ChrisCatlin 5 54
(J S Moore) *w'like: s.i.s: sn prom: rdn over 2f out: wknd fnl f* **50/1**

14 ½ **Golden Penny** 2-9-3 SteveDrowne 8 58+
(H Morrison) *w'like: scope: s.i.s: hdwy into mid-div and pushed along 1/2-way: styd on again ins fnl f* **66/1**

15 hd **Vigano (IRE)** 2-9-3 GeorgeBaker 14 57+
(S Kirk) *w'like: b.bkwd: s.i.s: hdwy into mid-div 1/2-way: wknd over 1f out* **25/1**

0 **16** 1 **Thomas Malory (IRE)**[17] 1411 2-9-3 EdwardCreighton 20 54
(Miss V Haigh) *w'like: pressed ldrs: rdn over 2f out: wknd over 1f out* **100/1**

17 1 ¾ **Grylls (USA)** 2-9-3 PatDobbs 11 49
(R Hannon) *unf: pressed ldrs: rdn 2f out: wknd over 1f out* **33/1**

18 4 **Ostinata (IRE)** 2-8-12 MickyFenton 7 32
(B W Duke) *w'like: chsd ldrs: rdn over 2f out: sn btn* **100/1**

19 8 **Adam Eterno (IRE)** 2-9-3 KerrinMcEvoy 1 13
(B J Meehan) *w'like: leggy: sn rdn and bhd* **50/1**

1m 16.35s (2.03) **Going Correction** +0.20s/f (Good) **19** Ran SP% **126.4**
Speed ratings (Par 97):94,93,91,91,89 88,88,88,87,85 85,84,83,82,82 80,78,73,62
CSF £62.96 TOTE £5.30: £2.10, £4.80, £1.50; EX 97.10.
Owner Sir John Ritblat,David & Jennifer Sieff **Bred** Mrs Dare Wigan **Trained** Pulborough, W Sussex
■ Stewards' Enquiry : R Hills two-day ban: careless riding (May 30-31)

FOCUS
Usually a decent maiden, and a race that should produce its share of winners, although the principals will need to improve considerably on the bare form to play leading roles at Royal Ascot..

NOTEBOOK
Coasting ◆ showed plenty of promise on his debut in an ordinary Windsor maiden, but had clearly come on a fair amount for that experience and put it to good use to score in decent fashion. This half-brother to Watching among others looks just the type for a race such as the Coventry at Royal Ascot. (tchd 7-2)
Masaalek ◆, the first foal of a Cheshire Oaks winner but from the family of the useful juvenile Josr Algarhoud made a very promising start to his career, coming from off the pace to challenge, having raced slightly keenly early on. He could well improve past the winner and could re-oppose that rival in the Coventry Stakes.
Greek Mythology(USA), an $800,000 yearling with a good American pedigree, was made favourite despite having presumably been rejected by Kinane in favour of the winner. He ran well enough though and the experience should not be lost on him. (op 3-1 tchd 10-3)
American Art(IRE), who missed the break on his debut in what looked a decent Newmarket maiden, had learnt from that and ran much better. He was forced to race on the outside of his field from his low draw and deserves credit for managing to hold his place all the way. (op 20-1)
First Trim(IRE), by a sire who has made a good start to his career but related to 1m to 1m2f winners from the family of Bireme, knew his job and made the running until inside the last, but he could not sustain it. This was a decent performance and he should win his maiden before long.
Il Warrd(IRE), a 240,000gns yearling from the family of Diffident, was better backed than his stable companion, the runner-up, and ran creditably having had to race to the outside of the field. (tchd 17-2)
Huzzah(IRE), who ran well on his debut in a Windsor maiden, had an extra furlong and easier ground to contend with and did not perform badly. He may be better off at a lower level for the time being.
Polygraph(IRE) ◆, a 72,000gns breeze-up purchase from the family of Sleepytime, showed plenty of promise despite suffering as the runner-up made his move. He stayed on at the end without being unduly punished and looks open to a fair bit of improvement with this outing behind him.
Redesignation(IRE), a 75,000euros half-brother to the multiple 6f winner Miss Emma, was running on at the finish and this outing should have put an edge on him. (op 10-1)
Golden Penny Official explanation: jockey said colt was hampered.
Adam Eterno(IRE) Official explanation: jockey said gelding ran green

1833 PADDYPOWER.COM STKS (REGISTERED AS THE ASTON PARK STAKES) (LISTED RACE) 1m 5f 61y
2:10 (2:11) (Class 1) 4-Y-O+ **£17,034** (£6,456; £3,231; £1,611; £807) **Stalls** Centre

Form RPR

-014 **1** **Peppertree Lane (IRE)**[8] 1618 4-8-12 105 KDarley 1 111
(M Johnston) *trckd ldr: led over 4f out: hrd drvn whn chal fr over 2f out: kpt on gamely thrght fnl f* **9/2**[2]

124- **2** ¾ **Day Flight**[329] 2845 6-8-12 115 RichardHughes 5 110
(J H M Gosden) *lw: hld up in 4th: hdwy to cl on ldrs over 3f out: swtchd rt and qcknd over 1f out: r.o u.p ins fnl f: nt rch wnr* **1/2**[1]

0-03 **3** hd **Group Captain**[11] 1571 5-8-12 106 SteveDrowne 2 110
(R Charlton) *chsd ldrs in 3rd: hdwy into 2nd over 2f out: rdn to chal over 2f out: no ex u.p ins fnl f: ct for 2nd last stride* **8/1**[3]

4-65 **4** 23 **The Whistling Teal**[8] 1618 11-8-12 106 EddieAhern 4 75
(G Wragg) *racd in 5th tl hdwy to cl on ldrs 4f out: rdn over 3f out sn wknd* **16/1**

102- **5** 13 **Foreign Affairs**[272] 4639 9-9-1 111 JamieMackay 3 59
(Sir Mark Prescott) *set str pce: hdd over 4f out: sn wknd* **14/1**

2m 52.03s (1.04) **Going Correction** +0.20s/f (Good) **5** Ran SP% **108.5**
Speed ratings (Par 111):104,103,103,89,81
CSF £7.06 TOTE £4.60: £2.30, £1.10; EX 10.00.
Owner P D Savill **Bred** Gestut Wittekindshof **Trained** Middleham Moor, N Yorks

FOCUS
Not a strong race. The pace steadied after 3f and the overall time was ordinary for the grade. With the runner-up disappointing the form has been rated through the winner and the third.

NOTEBOOK
Peppertree Lane(IRE) has continued to progress this season and, with the ease in the ground in his favour, gained his first Listed success with a resolute performance typical of runners from his stable. Having taken the lead early in the straight, he kept finding extra for pressure and refused to surrender the advantage. His trainer may have to look abroad for him now, as although he handles fast ground he is considerably better when it is on the soft side, and he is more likely to get his ground on the continent. (op 5-1 tchd 11-2)
Day Flight had a fair bit in hand on official ratings and had scored first time out in each of the three previous seasons he had raced, so was unsurprisingly long odds-on. However, after travelling well he appeared to hit a flat spot halfway up the straight before staying on in the last furlong to be never nearer than at the line. His rider received some criticism for his ride and he may have preferred to make his run between horses, which was not possible, but he has something to prove now as he has still to score above Group 3 level and should have won this. (op 8-15 tchd 4-7)
Group Captain, winner of the November Handicap last autumn, has been held in three subsequent tries at Listed and Group 3 level and, after looking the most likely winner halfway up the straight, found his effort flattening out in the last furlong. It may be that this trip stretches his stamina, and a return to shorter could help. (tchd 15-2)
The Whistling Teal, who won this in 2004, has looked in recent outings as if age has caught up with him.
Foreign Affairs set off in front at a good clip before steadying the pace at the end of the back straight, but he was soon in trouble once in line for home and finished well beaten. He seems to save his best efforts for his trips abroad, as he has won seven times on the continent and in Ireland since he last scored in Britain back in 2002. (op 12-1)

1834 JUDDMONTE LOCKINGE STKS (GROUP 1) 1m (S)
2:45 (2:46) (Class 1) 4-Y-O+
£113,560 (£43,040; £21,540; £10,740; £5,380; £2,700) **Stalls** Centre

Form RPR

115- **1** **Red Evie (IRE)**[231] 5674 4-8-11 115 JamieSpencer 7 115+
(M L W Bell) *lw: hld up in rr but in tch: stdy hdwy fr 2f out: hrd drvn and qcknd to ld ins fnl f: hld on gamely cl home* **8/1**[3]

113- **2** *hd* **Ramonti (FR)**[160] 6784 5-9-0 116...(t) LDettori 8 118
(Saeed Bin Suroor) *str: lw: t.k.h early: trckd ldrs: drvn to chal ins fnl f: kpt on strly cl home: nt quite get up* **4/1**[2]

1-33 **3** *hd* **Passager (FR)**[18] 1389 4-9-0 .... RichardHughes 2 117
(Mme C Head-Maarek, France) *unf: t.k.h early: trckd ldr: led ins fnl 2f: hrd rdn and hdd ins fnl f: kpt on wl: no ex last strides* **20/1**

15-0 **4** *2 1/2* **Secret World (IRE)**[30] 1104 4-9-0 105............................... EddieAhern 5 111
(J Noseda) *hld up in rr: hdwy over 2f out: rdn and kpt on thrght fnl f but nvr gng pce to rch ldrs* **40/1**

20-1 **5** *3/4* **Jeremy (USA)**[21] 1305 4-9-0 112................................... MJKinane 1 110
(Sir Michael Stoute) *lw: hld up in rr: hdwy over 2f out: sn drvn to chse ldrs but no imp: styd on same pce ins fnl f* **4/1**[2]

432- **6** *1 1/2* **Peeress**[252] 5191 6-8-11 117............................ KerrinMcEvoy 6 103
(Sir Michael Stoute) *lw: trckd ldrs: drvn to chal ins fnl 2f: wknd u.p fnl f* **11/8**[1]

06-2 **7** *2 1/2* **Speciosa (IRE)**[30] 1104 4-8-11 110.................................. MickyFenton 4 97
(Mrs P Sly) *led tl hdd ins fnl 2f: btn over 1f out* **10/1**

40-3 **8** *20* **Marcus Andronicus (USA)**[34] 1049 4-9-0 .... RHills 3 54
(A P O'Brien, Ire) *chsd ldrs: rdn over 2f out: wknd rapidly* **16/1**

1m 40.43s (-0.19) **Going Correction** +0.20s/f (Good) **8** Ran SP% **115.4**
Speed ratings (Par 117):108,107,107,105,104 102,100,80
CSF £40.36 TOTE £8.80: £3.00, £1.40, £2.00; EX 34.90 Trifecta £216.90 Pool £3,513.21 - 11.50 winning units..
Owner Terry Neill **Bred** Dermot Cantillon & Forenaghts **Trained** Newmarket, Suffolk
■ Stewards' Enquiry : Richard Hughes one-day ban: used whip with excessive frequency (May 30)

FOCUS
Just a fair renewal of this Group 1 and the time was modest for the grade. Unsatisfactory form, but the winner is the type to do just enough and the third and fourth both appeared to improve.

NOTEBOOK
Red Evie(IRE) ◆, who won the fillies' handicap on this card last season off a mark of 83, resumed her progress into a top-class miler with a brave success, holding off the challenges of the colts on either side of her. She proved her defeat of Peeress at Leopardstown last season was no fluke and she looks sure to be a credible contender for the top mile events this season, with the Queen Anne next on the agenda, while a race like the Falmouth Stakes looks hers for the taking.
Ramonti(FR), winner of the Italian 2000 Guineas in 2005 and a three time winner at Group 1 and 2 level in his home country in 2006 before finishing third in the Hong Kong Mile, was making his first start for Godolphin. He was quite keen early on and raced wide of the others but, after looking as if he might fade at one point, rallied well and was closing down the winner near the line. He should come on for this and, best suited by a sounder surface, is likely to reoppose the winner in the Queen Anne, and it would be no surprise if he turned the tables on her there. (tchd 9-2 in places)
Passager(FR) is a consistent Group-class miler in his native France, and put up arguably a career-best effort in finishing a close third, but his proximity supports the impression that this was not the strongest renewal of this contest.
Secret World(IRE) has always been thought a lot of but has had his problems and this was just his fourth outing. He never really got into contention, but did run on past beaten rivals to be nearest at the finish. His only win was in last year's Wood Ditton, so he could well pick up several races at a lower level if connections can keep him in one piece and feel so inclined. (op 33-1)
Jeremy(USA), who finished three lengths ahead of Secret World when winning last year's Jersey, was held up as usual but, after moving on to the heels of the leaders, failed to pick up from that point. Along with his stable companion, his performance adds credence to the recent impression that his stable is not firing on all cylinders at present. (op 9-2 tchd 5-1)
Peeress, winner of this race last year, was well backed to repeat the feat. She moved up to have every chance, but untypically she then faded out of contention to finish out of the frame for the first time in her career. With her stable companion also failing to run to his best, it is difficult to avoid the impression that the stable's runners are performing a little below par at present. Official explanation: vet said mare was distressed (op 13-8)
Speciosa(IRE) seemed to have everything in her favour, easy ground and an uncontested lead, but she found very little once challenged and does not look nearly as effective away from Newmarket's Rowley Mile. She has never run on the July Course, but it may be worth her taking her chance in the Falmouth Stakes there next month. Official explanation: trainer said filly was found to be in season. (tchd 11-1, 12-1 in places)
Marcus Andronicus(USA), who has been lightly campaigned since finishing runner-up to his stable companion Aussie Rules in the French 2000 Guineas in 2006, should have appreciated the conditions here but dropped away tamely as if something was amiss.

1835 LONDON PADDY POWER GOLD CUP (HERITAGE H'CAP) 1m 2f 6y
3:15 (3:16) (Class 2) (0-105,97) 3-Y-O
£38,638 (£11,569; £5,784; £2,895; £1,444; £725) **Stalls** Centre

Form RPR

2113 **1** **Zaham (USA)**[22] 1275 3-8-11 87.. RHills 6 94+
(M Johnston) *lw: in tch: hdwy over 2f out: led 1f out: drvn and r.o strly fnl f* **4/1**[2]

1-43 **2** *3/4* **Duke Of Tuscany**[14] 1476 3-9-5 95................................ SteveDrowne 11 99
(R Hannon) *led after 1f: rdn and kpt on gamely fr over 2f out tl hdd 1f out: kpt on wl but a hld by wnr* **20/1**

2-12 **3** *1/2* **Dubai Twilight**[24] 1243 3-9-0 90................................... MichaelHills 13 93
(B W Hills) *in rr: stdy hdwy on outside fr 3f out: chsd ldrs over 1f out: kpt on wl fnl f but nvr quite gng pce to chal* **16/1**

2221 **4** *nk* **Emerald Wilderness (IRE)**[19] 1365 3-8-0 76................. ChrisCatlin 12 78
(M R Channon) *in rr: hdwy over 2f out: styd on wl u.p fr over 1f out: gng on cl home* **33/1**

12-4 **5** *shd* **Buccellati**[22] 1275 3-8-8 84...................................... FrancisNorton 2 92+
(A M Balding) *in rr: hdwy whn nt clr run over 2f out: swtchd rt and hdwy over 1f out: fin strly* **13/2**[3]

21-2 **6** *1/2* **Regal Flush**[30] 1106 3-9-1 91.................................. KerrinMcEvoy 4 96+
(Sir Michael Stoute) *lw: mid-div: n.m.r over 2f out: rdn and kpt on fr over 1f out: fin wl* **2/1**[1]

-350 **7** *6* **Danebury Hill**[14] 1471 3-9-7 97...(t) LDettori 7 87
(B J Meehan) *in rr: hdwy fr 3f out to chse ldrs 2f out: wknd fnl f* **25/1**

66-0 **8** *1/2* **Golden Dagger (IRE)**[10] 1581 3-8-11 87........................ JamieSpencer 5 76+
(K A Ryan) *in rr: hdwy whn hmpd 2f out and over 1f out: styd on ins fnl f but nvr in contention* **50/1**

115- **9** *1* **Gold Option**[238] 5521 3-9-0 90....................................... RichardHughes 3 77+
(J H M Gosden) *lw: in tch: pushed along to chse ldrs 3f out: wknd fr 2f out* **12/1**

32-1 **10** *nk* **Prince Sabaah (IRE)**[25] 1230 3-8-7 83................................. PatDobbs 9 70
(R Hannon) *chsd ldrs: rdn 3f out: wknd 2f out* **12/1**

114 **11** *1* **Players Please (USA)**[30] 1106 3-8-12 88............................. KDarley 10 73
(M Johnston) *lw: chsd ldrs: rdn 3f out: wknd 2f out* **7/1**

-210 **12** *1 1/4* **Paymaster General (IRE)**[5] 1722 3-7-12 74 oh1............ HayleyTurner 8 56
(M D I Usher) *t.k.h: chsd ldr after 2f: rdn 3f out: wknd 2f out* **100/1**

2-12 **13** *1 3/4* **Soft Morning**[111] 275 3-8-7 83.................................. JamieMackay 1 62
(Sir Mark Prescott) *led 1f: rdn 4f out: wknd fr 3f out* **16/1**

2m 9.01s (0.30) **Going Correction** +0.20s/f (Good) **13** Ran SP% **120.8**
Speed ratings (Par 105):106,105,105,104,104 104,99,99,98,98 97,96,94
CSF £89.48 CT £1177.94 TOTE £5.40: £2.00, £4.80, £3.90; EX 131.50 Trifecta £624.00 Part won. Pool £879.00 - 0.50 winning units..
Owner Hamdan Al Maktoum **Bred** London Thoroughbred Services Ltd **Trained** Middleham Moor, N Yorks

FOCUS
A competitive handicap featuring promising three-year-olds from leading stables, but it was run at a steady gallop until the runner-up went on and the finish was a bit messy, with the fifth and sixth the chief sufferers. The form overall has not been rated as positively as it might have been, but the winner looks very much the type to do better.

NOTEBOOK
Zaham(USA) ◆, who was stepping up in trip on only his second turf start, was ridden close to the pace and, after asserting entering the final furlong, was always holding the runner-up's renewed effort. He looks progressive and will take some beating against his own age group at this level in the short term. (op 5-1 tchd 11-2)
Duke Of Tuscany, who has been performing well at this trip this season, will want to avoid Johnston runners in future as he has only been beaten by horses from that yard in his last two outings. He looks high enough in the handicap, but is continuing to perform well and gives the impression that another quarter-mile will not be beyond him. (tchd 22-1)
Dubai Twilight, a Polytrack winner who had come up against Listed and Group-class performers on his three turf runs, did best of those to race from off the pace. His effort flattened out slightly and he may be worth dropping back to a mile in a race where a strong gallop is likely.
Emerald Wilderness(IRE), who got off the mark when dead-heat on Polytrack last time after a series of seconds, was another to run well from off the pace. The step up in trip seemed to suit and he may be able to add to his score at a slightly lower level.
Buccellati, another stepping up in trip, finished slightly further behind the winner despite meeting that rival on the same terms as in the Esher Cup. However, he finished well after failing to enjoy the best of runs and is well worth another chance. (op 11-2)
Regal Flush was made favourite but did not really fire, although he did not get the clearest of runs, and can be given a chance to atone once his yard returns to form. Official explanation: jockey said colt was denied a clear run. (op 5-2)
Golden Dagger(IRE) Official explanation: jockey said filly was denied a clear run.
Players Please(USA), a stable companion of the winner, finished a lot closer to the favourite at Newmarket than he did here. After racing close to the pace he went out like a damp cigarette, so the easy ground may have been a factor. (op 8-1)
Paymaster General(IRE) Official explanation: jockey said gelding ran too freely.

1836 PADDYPOWER.COM H'CAP 6f 8y
3:50 (3:51) (Class 2) (0-100,100) 4-Y-O+
£12,464 (£3,732; £1,866; £934; £466; £234) **Stalls** Centre

Form RPR

-030 **1** **Ripples Maid**[14] 1474 4-8-10 92.............................. JamieSpencer 14 106
(J A Geake) *lw: trckd ldrs: chal 2f out: led sn after: drvn and r.o strly fnl f* **11/2**[2]

125- **2** *1 3/4* **Intrepid Jack**[202] 6243 5-9-4 100...................................... SteveDrowne 2 108+
(H Morrison) *chsd ldrs: rdn over 2f out: kpt on wl to chse wnr fnl f but no imp* **15/2**[3]

63-0 **3** *3/4* **Out After Dark**[26] 1195 6-9-2 98..(p) KDarley 5 104
(C G Cox) *lw: pressed ldrs: drvn to chal 2f out: kpt on same pce ins fnl f* **8/1**

223- **4** *3/4* **Gloved Hand**[237] 5550 5-8-10 92...................................... JamesDoyle 16 96
(R M Beckett) *lw: stmbld s: sn rcvrd into mid-div: hdwy over 1f out: kpt on fnl f but nvr gng pce to rch ldrs* **12/1**

044- **5** *2 1/2* **Swinbrook (USA)**[225] 5785 6-8-4 86 oh1....................(v) HayleyTurner 10 82
(J A R Toller) *t.k.h in mid-div: drvn to chse ldrs over 1f out: kpt on same pce ins fnl f* **20/1**

0-05 **6** *1/2* **The Snatcher (IRE)**[15] 1448 4-8-9 91.......................... RichardHughes 8 86
(R Hannon) *pressed ldr: rdn and stl upsides fr 2f out: wknd ins fnl f* **12/1**

300- **7** *1* **Greenslades**[189] 6445 8-9-1 97.. EddieAhern 13 89
(P J Makin) *lw: slt ld tl hdd ins fnl 2f: wknd ins fnl f* **33/1**

6050 **8** *shd* **Compton's Eleven**[14] 1474 6-8-7 89................................ ChrisCatlin 11 80
(M R Channon) *chsd ldrs: rdn 2f out: wknd ins fnl f* **14/1**

050- **9** *2* **Dingaan (IRE)**[239] 5501 4-8-4 86 oh1.......................... FrancisNorton 15 71+
(A M Balding) *in rr: hdwy on ins whn nt clr run 2f out and over 1f out: nt rcvr but styd on wl cl home* **33/1**

00-0 **10** *1/2* **Captain Hurricane**[15] 1448 5-8-1 90.............................. KMay[(7)] 6 74
(B J Meehan) *in rr: rdn and outpcd 1/2-way: kpt on wl fnl f but nvr in contention* **50/1**

600- **11** *1/2* **Art Market (CAN)**[254] 5143 4-8-4 86 oh1....................... StephenCarson 9 68+
(G L Moore) *hld up in rr: nvr in contention* **33/1**

30-3 **12** *3* **Come Out Fighting**[7] 1653 4-8-13 95................................ MJKinane 12 68
(P A Blockley) *chsd ldrs: rdn over 2f out: wknd over 1f out: b.b.v* **7/2**[1]

000- **13** *1* **Musadif (USA)**[264] 4875 9-9-4 100.......................................(t) DaneO'Neill 7 70
(R A Kvisla) *b.bkwd: s.i.s: outpcd most of way* **80/1**

300- **14** *1* **Zowington**[185] 6496 5-8-5 87.. JamieMackay 1 54
(C F Wall) *b.bkwd: pressed ldrs on outside: ev ch 2f out: sn wknd* **15/2**[3]

460- **15** *3* **Andronikos**[167] 6692 5-9-3 99.. KerrinMcEvoy 4 57
(P F I Cole) *chsd ldrs: rdn 2f out: sn wknd* **11/2**[2]

0502 **16** *5* **Tony James (IRE)**[49] 841 5-9-4 100................................ MichaelHills 3 43
(K O Cunningham-Brown) *pressed ldrs: ev ch 2f out: sn btn* **25/1**

1m 13.63s (-0.69) **Going Correction** +0.20s/f (Good) **16** Ran SP% **130.3**
Speed ratings (Par 109):112,109,108,107,104 103,102,102,99,98 98,94,92,91,87 80
CSF £46.90 CT £358.07 TOTE £7.20: £1.90, £1.80, £2.30, £2.90; EX 46.80 Trifecta £854.20 Pool £15,957.27 - 11.60 winning units..
Owner Rex Mead & David Mead **Bred** Compton Down Stud **Trained** Kimpton, Hants

FOCUS
A good, competitive sprint run at a good pace. The winner may have been favoured by coming up the rail, but she was impressive nevertheless.

NOTEBOOK
Ripples Maid ◆, who is already a winner and placed in Listed company against her own sex, is pretty consistent as the fact that her official rating has remained constant in her last eight outings testifies. She got a good pitch on the rail, and when asked for her effort picked up in good style to win with something in hand. She is likely to go up a few pounds for this, but looks a credible contender for the Wokingham if she maintains this sort of form. (op 6-1)
Intrepid Jack, having his first outing since October, has clearly returned in good heart judged on this performance. He ran a terrific race from his outside draw and only lost out to the winner, who had a good run up the rail. He is likely to re-oppose the winner in the Wokingham and, from a yard that has some useful sprinters, could get much closer with this outing under his belt and the likelihood of more suitable, faster ground there. (op 8-1)
Out After Dark has not won since taking the Portland back in 2005, but the Handicapper has only just dropped him below that winning mark. He was another to run well from an outside draw but is arguably most effective over a stiff 5f on fast ground, so a race like the Gosforth Park Cup at the end of next month may be a reasonable option, with possibly a trip to Sandown or Beverley in between.
Gloved Hand, who was raised 4lb for finishing third in Listed company last autumn, followed the winner up the rail and ran well on this seasonal debut and first outing for her trainer, despite stumbling at the start. She will be suited by a return to 7f on this evidence (tchd 14-1)
Swinbrook(USA), another making his reappearance, ran well enough on ground that suits. He is still 6lb above his last winning mark but is likely to come on for this effort.

The Snatcher(IRE), dropping back another furlong in trip, was given a positive ride but faded late on. He is probably better over 7f on faster ground.
Greenslades likes some give in the ground and raced prominently before tiring on this seasonal debut. His only wins in recent years have been at Newmarket.
Compton's Eleven has dropped 9lb in the weights since around this time last year but may be in need of another furlong nowadays.
Dingaan(IRE) Official explanation: jockey said gelding was denied a clear run
Come Out Fighting was on the heels of the leaders travelling well but dropped out tamely and was eased as he reportedly broke a blood-vessel. Official explanation: vet said colt bled from the nose. (op 11-2)
Andronikos was well supported on this return to action but dropped away quickly, having raced close to the early pace. (op 9-1)
Tony James(IRE) Official explanation: jockey said horse had a breathing problem.

1837 CATRIDGE FARM STUD & MANOR FARM PACKERS FILLIES' H'CAP — 7f (S)

4:25 (4:28) (Class 4) (0-85,83) 3-Y-O — **£6,477** (£1,927; £963; £481) **Stalls** Centre

Form				RPR
010-	1		**Folly Lodge**^{231} [5672] 3-8-12 77 ... MichaelHills 1 (B W Hills) *stdd in rr and brought to stands' side: smooth hdwy fr 2f out to ld last half f: comf* **28/1**	92+
21-0	2	1 1/2	**Whazzis**^{13} [1500] 3-9-0 82 ... LiamJones$^{(3)}$ 5 (W J Haggas) *chsd ldrs: led ins fnl 2f: rdn over 1f out: hdd and outpcd by wnr fnl half f but kpt on wl for clr 2nd* **12/1**	91
3-1	3	2	**Gyroscope**^{26} [1203] 3-9-1 80 ... KerrinMcEvoy 8 (Sir Michael Stoute) *lw: in tch: rdn and one pce 2f out: kpt on ins fnl f: nt rch ldrs* **9/2**^{3}	84+
0-1	4	1	**Fuschia**^{18} [1386] 3-8-11 76 ... SteveDrowne 14 (R Charlton) *lw: towards rr early: hdwy over 3f out: chsd ldrs 2f out: kpt on same pce ins fnl f* **12/1**	78
31-3	5	1/2	**Diamond Diva**^{9} [1610] 3-9-4 83 ... JamieSpencer 4 (J W Hills) *lw: s.i.s: bhd: gd hdwy over 2f out: chsd ldrs over 1f out: one pce ins fnl f* **7/2**^{1}	83+
143-	6	shd	**Ficoma**^{228} [5748] 3-8-13 78 ... DaneO'Neill 6 (C G Cox) *chsd ldrs: rdn and effrt 2f out: one pce fr over 1f out* **16/1**	78
1-1	7	3/4	**Supa Sal**^{49} [843] 3-8-13 78 ... KDarley 7 (P F I Cole) *led tl hdd ins fnl 2f: wknd fnl f* **4/1**^{2}	76
01-	8	3 1/2	**Ravinia (USA)**^{182} [6520] 3-8-4 69 ... ChrisCatlin 11 (B J Meehan) *mid-div: pushed along 1/2-way: kpt on ins fnl f but nvr in contention* **25/1**	58
0-11	9	1/2	**Crystal Gazer (FR)**^{10} [1588] 3-9-2 81 ... RichardHughes 10 (R Hannon) *s.i.s: bhd tl hdwy over 2f out: sn pushed along: nvr in contention and fdd fnl f* **11/1**	69
010-	10	nk	**Sylvan (IRE)**^{245} [5372] 3-8-11 76 ... PatDobbs 9 (S Kirk) *in tch: rdn over 2f out: sn btn* **25/1**	63
01-4	11	1	**Roshanak (IRE)**^{15} [1450] 3-9-3 82 ... LDettori 13 (B J Meehan) *lw: in rr: hdwy into mid-div 3f out: shkn up 2f out: sn wknd* **7/1**	66
31-0	12	shd	**Kondakova (IRE)**^{25} [1228] 3-8-9 74 ... HayleyTurner 2 (M L W Bell) *s.i.s: bhd: sme hdwy over 2f out: sn hung lft wknd* **50/1**	58
130-	13	2	**Tender Moments**^{245} [5359] 3-9-1 80 ... GeorgeBaker 3 (C F Wall) *a towards rr and nvr in contention* **25/1**	59
44-1	14	12	**Blue Bamboo**^{19} [1345] 3-8-4 69 ... JamesDoyle 12 (Mrs A J Perrett) *chsd ldr tl over 2f out: sn wknd* **14/1**	17

1m 26.39s (-0.61) **Going Correction** +0.20s/f (Good) — **14** Ran SP% **126.1**
Speed ratings (Par 98):111,109,107,105,105 105,104,100,99,99 98,98,95,82
CSF £332.81 CT £1871.87 TOTE £39.40: £8.40, £4.90, £2.30; EX 593.90.
Owner O F Waller & T D Rootes **Bred** Shutford Stud **Trained** Lambourn, Berks

FOCUS
A competitive fillies' handicap won in 2006 by Red Evie and featuring a number of unexposed sorts. The pace was sound and the time was 1.51sec faster than the quicker of the two divisions of the maiden that followed. The winner, though drawn far side, raced closest to the stands' rail, which may have been an advantage. Solid form.
Diamond Diva Official explanation: jockey said filly ran flat.
Crystal Gazer(FR) Official explanation: jockey said filly stopped quickly
Blue Bamboo Official explanation: jockey said filly lost its action.

1838 OLYMPIC COACH BUILDERS / HENDY VAN AND TRUCK MAIDEN STKS (DIV I) — 7f (S)

4:55 (4:59) (Class 4) 3-Y-O — **£5,829** (£1,734; £866; £432) **Stalls** Centre

Form				RPR
0-	1		**Zaahid (IRE)**^{311} [3417] 3-9-3 ... RHills 8 (B W Hills) *str: b.bkwd: trckd ldrs: led over 1f out: sn in command: easily* **7/2**^{2}	77+
0	2	3 1/2	**Velocity's Gift**^{31} [1098] 3-9-3 ... PaulEddery 6 (Pat Eddery) *b.bkwd: str: awkward leaving stalls: sn in tch: hdwy 2f out: styd on u.p to chse wnr ins fnl f but nvr any ch* **11/1**	68
0-	3	1	**El Toreador (USA)**^{322} [3084] 3-8-12 ... HayleyTurner 2 (G A Butler) *lw: in tch: hdwy to chse ldrs over 2f out: hrd rdn and hung lft over 1f out: kpt on same pce ins fnl f* **4/1**^{3}	60
5-	4	hd	**Nice To Know (FR)**^{248} [5297] 3-8-12 ... JamieSpencer 1 (E A L Dunlop) *lw: w ldrs: led 4f out: rdn and hdd over 1f out: one pce ins fnl f* **7/4**^{1}	59
6	5	4	**Silca Elegance**^{22} [1276] 3-9-3 ... JHBowman 9 (M R Channon) *lw: led 3f: styd chsng ldrs: rdn over 2f out: wknd over 1f out* **7/1**	54
0	6	nk	**Officer Material (IRE)**^{8} [1635] 3-9-3 ... KDarley 5 (C G Cox) *in rr: pshd along over 2f out: rdn over 1f out: kpt on ins fnl f but nvr in contention* **20/1**	53
0	7	1 3/4	**Red Brick Road (IRE)**^{17} [1398] 3-9-3 ... FrancisNorton 4 (A J Lidderdale) *w'like: in tch: rdn and no imp on ldrs fnl 3f* **33/1**	48
0-6	8	hd	**Anthill**^{17} [1409] 3-8-12 ... JamesDoyle 7 (I A Wood) *awkward leaving stalls: in rr tl rdn and mod prog ins fnl f* **25/1**	43
0	9	1	**Egregius Max**^{17} [1398] 3-9-3 ... GeorgeBaker 11 (C F Wall) *leggy: unf: chsd ldrs 5f* **40/1**	45
60-	10	2 1/2	**Oh Gracious Me (IRE)**^{217} [5959] 3-9-3 ... SimonWhitworth 10 (P A Blockley) *w'like: str: hdwy to chse ldrs 4f out: rdn over 2f out: wknd over 1f out* **20/1**	38

1m 27.9s (0.90) **Going Correction** +0.20s/f (Good) — **10** Ran SP% **118.2**
Speed ratings (Par 101):102,98,96,96,92 91,89,89,88,85
CSF £37.71 TOTE £5.00: £1.40, £2.80, £2.00; EX 39.40.
Owner Hamdan Al Maktoum **Bred** Shadwell Estate Company Limited **Trained** Lambourn, Berks

FOCUS
Just an ordinary contest and run 1.51sec slower than the preceding fillies' handicap. However, the first four came clear and the winner looks a nice type.
Nice To Know(FR) Official explanation: jockey said filly ran too freely and hung right-handed.

1839 OLYMPIC COACH BUILDERS / HENDY VAN AND TRUCK MAIDEN STKS (DIV II) — 7f (S)

5:25 (5:30) (Class 4) 3-Y-O — **£5,829** (£1,734; £866; £432) **Stalls** Centre

Form				RPR
0	1		**Look So**^{12} [1522] 3-8-12 ... JamesDoyle 9 (R M Beckett) *trckd ldrs: drvn to ld last half f: kpt on wl u.p* **100/1**	79
6-2	2	nk	**Cape Hawk (IRE)**^{12} [1522] 3-9-3 ... RichardHughes 7 (R Hannon) *lw: trckd ldrs: led ins fnl 2f: sn rdn: hdd and no ex last half f* **3/1**^{2}	83
0-	3	8	**Parisian Dream**^{260} [4987] 3-9-3 ... MichaelHills 3 (B W Hills) *w'like: b.bkwd: s.i.s: sn rcvrd to chse ldrs: rdn 2f out: wknd fnl f* **10/1**	61
	4	3/4	**Held Captive (USA)** 3-8-12 ... JamieSpencer 5 (E A L Dunlop) *s.i.s: in rr: mod prog fr 2f out: nvr nr ldrs* **10/1**	54
42-	5	6	**Kirk Michael**^{232} [5659] 3-9-3 ... DaneO'Neill 8 (H Candy) *t.k.h: led after 2f: rdn and hdd ins fnl 2f: sn btn* **11/10**^{1}	43
	6	1 3/4	**Rustic Flame (IRE)** 3-8-12 ... KerrinMcEvoy 4 (C R Egerton) *str: lw: pressed ldrs: rdn 3f out: wknd fr 2f out* **25/1**	33
	7	1 3/4	**Cactus Rose** 3-9-3 ... SteveDrowne 10 (R Charlton) *lw: b.bkwd: wnt rt s: a towards rr* **12/1**	34
-	8	5	**Woodins Way** 3-9-3 ... AmirQuinn 2 (P J Makin) *str: b.bkwd: in rr: sme prog 1/2-way: wknd over 2f out* **9/2**^{3}	20
000-	9	2 1/2	**Cosimo Primo**^{196} [6330] 3-9-3 49 ... FrancisNorton 1 (J A Geake) *w'like: led 2f: wknd rapidly 3f out* **66/1**	13

1m 28.11s (1.11) **Going Correction** +0.20s/f (Good) — **9** Ran SP% **123.0**
Speed ratings (Par 101):101,100,91,90,83 81,79,74,71
CSF £405.17 TOTE £64.10: £8.00, £1.40, £2.50; EX 692.80 Place 6 £217.50, Place 5 £116.47..
Owner J H Richmond-Watson **Bred** Lawn Stud **Trained** Whitsbury, Hants

FOCUS
The slowest of the three races run over the trip on the day and a shock winner. The first two came well clear.
T/Jkpt: Not won. T/Plt: £192.60 to a £1 stake. Pool: £115,113.45. 436.10 winning tickets. T/Qpdt: £113.10 to a £1 stake. Pool: £5,244.10. 34.30 winning tickets. ST

1814

NEWMARKET (ROWLEY) (R-H)

Saturday, May 19

OFFICIAL GOING: Good (7.5)
Wind: fresh across Weather: cloudy

1840 BETDIRECT.COM MAIDEN STKS (DIV I) — 1m

1:20 (1:20) (Class 4) 3-Y-O — **£4,533** (£1,348; £674; £336) **Stalls** High

Form				RPR
	1		**Champfleurie** 3-8-12 ... DeanMcKeown 9 (G A Swinbank) *cmpt: hld up: hdwy over 1f out: r.o to ld wl ins fnl f* **16/1**	75
0	2	hd	**Russian Epic**^{19} [1358] 3-9-3 ... PhilipRobinson 4 (M A Jarvis) *led: rdn and edgd lft fr over 2f out: hdd wl ins fnl f* **11/8**^{1}	80
0	3	3/4	**Trivia (IRE)**^{30} [1105] 3-8-12 ... SimonWhitworth 7 (N A Callaghan) *hld up: swtchd rt and hdwy over 1f out: styd on* **15/2**	73+
	4	1 1/4	**Axiom** 3-9-3 ... DO'Donohoe 12 (E A L Dunlop) *w'like: scope: hld up in tch: rdn and ev ch over 1f out: hung lft and no ex ins fnl f* **13/2**^{2}	75
0	5	1 1/2	**Novikov**^{9} [1606] 3-9-3 ... JimmyFortune 10 (J H M Gosden) *bit bkwd: chsd ldrs: rdn over 1f out: no ex fnl f* **12/1**	72
	6	3	**Hot Diamond** 3-9-3 ... JohnEgan 3 (D R C Elsworth) *w'like: s.s: hld up: hdwy over 3f out: rdn over 2f out: sn outpcd: hung lft over 1f out: kpt on ins fnl f* **9/1**	65
	7	nk	**Pagan Belief** 3-9-0 ... MarcHalford$^{(3)}$ 8 (J A R Toller) *w'like: leggy: prom: chsd ldr over 4f out: rdn over 1f out: sn wknd* **25/1**	64
00-	8	2 1/2	**Chunky's Choice (IRE)**^{203} [6214] 3-9-3 ... DarryllHolland 1 (J Noseda) *chsd ldrs over 5f* **7/1**^{3}	59
00	9	2 1/2	**Zachary Scott**^{17} [1412] 3-9-3 ... OscarUrbina 11 (C E Brittain) *hld up in tch: rdn over 3f out: wknd 2f out* **25/1**	53
	10	nk	**Navene (IRE)** 3-8-12 ... IanMongan 13 (C F Wall) *w'like: hld up: plld hrd: hdwy over 3f out: rdn and wknd 2f out* **20/1**	47
0-	11	3/4	**Super Nebula**^{223} [5841] 3-9-0 ... DominicFox$^{(3)}$ 2 (P L Gilligan) *chsd ldr over 3f: sn rdn: wknd over 2f out* **100/1**	50
	12	49	**Formidable Guest** 3-8-12 ... JimmyQuinn 5 (J Pearce) *w'like: leggy: s.s: hld up: wknd 1/2-way* **40/1**	—

1m 39.79s (0.42) **Going Correction** -0.05s/f (Good) — **12** Ran SP% **119.2**
Speed ratings (Par 101):95,94,94,92,91 88,88,85,83,82 81,32
CSF £36.83 TOTE £18.50: £4.10, £1.10, £2.70; EX 75.40.
Owner Guy Reed **Bred** G Reed **Trained** Melsonby, N Yorks

FOCUS
This looked a fair first division of the this three-year-old maiden but possibly weaker than the second leg. The form should work out rated through the runner-up.
Trivia(IRE) Official explanation: jockey said filly suffered interference in running
Formidable Guest Official explanation: jockey said filly moved poorly

1841 BETDIRECT.COM MAIDEN STKS (DIV II) — 1m

1:50 (1:52) (Class 4) 3-Y-O — **£4,533** (£1,348; £674; £336) **Stalls** High

Form				RPR
5	1		**Ascalon**^{28} [1143] 3-9-3 ... WSupple 13 (Pat Eddery) *hld up: hdwy over 3f out: rdn and hung lft ins fnl f: r.o to ld towards fin* **5/2**^{2}	84+
2	2	3/4	**Classira (IRE)**^{17} [1408] 3-8-12 ... PhilipRobinson 5 (M A Jarvis) *hld up in tch: racd keenly: led over 1f out: sn rdn: hdd towards fin* **11/2**^{3}	77
04-2	3	3	**Transcend**^{32} [1075] 3-9-3 87 ... JimmyFortune 11 (J H M Gosden) *chsd ldrs: rdn and ev ch over 1f out: no ex ins fnl f* **10/11**^{1}	75
0-	4	hd	**Goodbye**^{274} [4559] 3-8-12 ... DeanMcKeown 3 (G A Swinbank) *hld up: plld hrd: hdwy over 1f out: nt trble ldrs* **40/1**	70
6	5	2	**Getrah**^{31} [1098] 3-9-3 ... PaulDoe 2 (W J Haggas) *hld up: shkn up over 2f out: sn hung rt: styd on ins fnl f: nvr nr to chal* **20/1**	70+
0-0	6	shd	**Henry Bernstein (USA)**^{16} [1440] 3-9-3 ... RoystonFfrench 12 (H R A Cecil) *led over 6f: wknd ins fnl f* **50/1**	70
0-0	7	3 1/2	**Hamilton House**^{8} [1632] 3-8-12 ... PatrickHills$^{(5)}$ 6 (M H Tompkins) *hld up: hdwy over 3f out: rdn and wknd over 1f out* **100/1**	62
00	8	1 1/4	**Bubbly Girl**^{16} [1440] 3-8-5 ... SCreighton$^{(7)}$ 4 (P J McBride) *chsd ldrs: rdn over 2f out: wknd over 1f out* **100/1**	54

9 2 ½ **Willie Ever** 3-9-3 .... BrettDoyle 9 53
(W J Musson) *lw: hld up: n.d* **66/1**

10 shd **Silver Suitor (IRE)** 3-9-3 .... JohnEgan 8 53
(D R C Elsworth) *wl grwn: s.s: a in rr* **33/1**

11 hd **Bee Sting** 3-9-3 .... AdamKirby 7 52
(W R Swinburn) *gd sort: s.s: a in rr* **16/1**

12 1 ½ **Roxie Princess (IRE)** 3-8-12 .... OscarUrbina 10 44
(J A R Toller) *w'like: mid-div: lost pl over 4f out: sn bhd* **66/1**

0 13 11 **Pugnacity**[117] [208] 3-8-9 .... SaleemGolam(3) 1 19
(S C Williams) *lw: plld hrd: trckd ldr: rdn and wknd over 2f out* **100/1**

1m 38.67s (-0.70) **Going Correction** -0.05s/f (Good) **13** Ran SP% **120.3**
Speed ratings (Par 101):101,100,97,97,95 94,91,90,87,87 87,85,74
CSF £15.91 TOTE £3.80: £1.60, £2.00, £1.10; EX 22.40.
Owner P J J Eddery **Bred** Patrick Eddery Ltd **Trained** Nether Winchendon, Bucks

FOCUS
This looked the slightly stronger of the two divisions. The form is rated through the 87-rated third and looks solid despite some longshots finishing close up.
Bee Sting Official explanation: jockey said colt had run too freely to post

1842 BETDIRECT.COM H'CAP 1m
2:25 (2:26) (Class 3) (0-95,93) 4-Y-0+ **£9,067** (£2,697; £1,348; £673) **Stalls** High

Form RPR

0-50 1 **Plum Pudding (IRE)**[28] [1145] 4-8-11 **93** .... HaddenFrost(7) 4 101
(R Hannon) *lw: racd in centre: chsd ldrs: led that gp over 2f out: overall ldr ins fnl f: drvn out* **7/1**[2]

-051 2 nk **Goodbye Mr Bond**[9] [1599] 7-9-0 **89** .... WSupple 1 96
(E J Alston) *racd in centre: chsd ldrs: rdn over 2f out: r.o: 2nd of 9 in gp* **12/1**

/23- 3 1 ¼ **Font**[227] [5768] 4-9-0 **89** .... OscarUrbina 13 93+
(J R Fanshawe) *lw: racd far side: hld up: hdwy over 2f out: led overall over 1f out: hdd ins fnl f: styd on: 1st of 4 in gp* **9/2**[1]

0-60 4 1 **Audience**[28] [1145] 7-8-11 **86** .... PaulDoe 10 88
(J Akehurst) *racd in centre: trckd ldrs: rdn over 2f out: styd on: 3rd of 9 in gp* **7/1**[2]

00-5 5 ½ **It's A Dream (FR)**[17] [1395] 4-8-2 **80** .... MarcHalford(3) 15 81+
(D R C Elsworth) *racd far side: s.i.s: hld up and bhd: hdwy over 2f out: rdn and hung lft over 1f out: styd on: 2nd of 4 in gp* **11/1**

000- 6 3 **Spanish Don**[268] [4739] 9-8-13 **88** .... NeilPollard 7 82
(D R C Elsworth) *b: racd in centre: hld up: rdn over 2f out: styd on fnl f: nvr nrr: 4th of 9 in gp* **33/1**

100- 7 nk **Jamieson Gold (IRE)**[231] [5677] 4-9-1 **90** .... PhilipRobinson 5 83
(B W Hills) *racd in centre: chsd ldrs: rdn over 2f out: wknd over 1f out: 5th of 9 in gp* **20/1**

0056 8 hd **Rain Stops Play (IRE)**[21] [1307] 5-8-10 **85** .... RichardMullen 8 78+
(M Quinn) *racd far side: chsd ldr tl led overall over 2f out: rdn and hdd over 1f out: wknd ins fnl f: 3rd of 4 in gp* **20/1**

6006 9 nk **Zato (IRE)**[14] [1480] 4-8-11 **86** .... DarryllHolland 9 78
(M R Channon) *lw: racd in centre: hld up: rdn over 2f out: n.d: 6th of 9 in gp* **15/2**[3]

0021 10 2 ½ **General Knowledge (USA)**[16] [1434] 4-8-4 **82**(t) RichardKingscote(3) 12 68+
(B G Powell) *racd far side: overall ldr over 5f: wknd over 1f out: last of 4 in gp* **12/1**

164- 11 nk **Tumbleweed Glory (IRE)**[285] [4209] 4-8-5 **80** .... RobertHavlin 2 65
(B J Meehan) *racd in centre: s.i.s: hld up: rdn over 2f out: sn wknd: 7th of 9 in gp* **33/1**

2-66 12 17 **Acheekyone (IRE)**[12] [1524] 4-8-12 **87** .... BrettDoyle 11 33
(B J Meehan) *racd in centre: hld up: rdn and wknd over 2f out: 8th of 9 in gp* **9/2**[1]

-034 13 3 ½ **Music Note (IRE)**[17] [1395] 4-8-5 **80** .... JohnEgan 3 18
(Miss Gay Kelleway) *lw: led centre over 5f: sn wknd and eased: last of 9 in gp: b.b.v* **9/1**

1m 37.39s (-1.98) **Going Correction** -0.05s/f (Good) **13** Ran SP% **122.3**
Speed ratings (Par 107):107,106,105,104,103 100,100,100,100,97 97,80,76
CSF £85.87 CT £436.81 TOTE £7.10: £2.40, £3.20, £1.90; EX 71.40 Trifecta £398.00 Pool £616.70 - 1.10 winning units..
Owner Hyde Sporting Promotions Limited **Bred** Tom Deane **Trained** East Everleigh, Wilts

FOCUS
A decent and competitive handicap run at a sound gallop. The form can be rated through the runner-up and looks solid.

NOTEBOOK
Plum Pudding(IRE) bounced back to his previous best and scored in game fashion. He enjoys this track and has developed into a likeable handicapper, but how he will cope with a future weight rise now remains to be seen.
Goodbye Mr Bond, 4lb higher than when scoring at Ayr last time, went down all guns blazing and had every chance on this drop in trip. He is clearly still in good heart. (op 9-1)
Font ◆, well backed, has to rate a little unfortunate as he emerged as a clear-cut winner of those who raced on the far side. He looks an obvious improver this term. (op 8-1)
Audience posted another respectable effort and has begun this season in fair form, but he does look held by the Handicapper all the same. (tchd 13-2)
It's A Dream(FR) may have benefited from a more prominent ride as he finished his race well, if anything suggesting he may prefer a stiffer test again. (op 8-1)
Acheekyone(IRE) failed to finish his race with any real purpose and is in danger of going the wrong way at present. Official explanation: trainer said gelding finished distressed (op 5-1 tchd 11-2, 6-1 in a place)
Music Note(IRE) showed his customary early dash, but was continually wanting to hang left and was eventually eased right off when headed. He was later found to have burst a blood-vessel. Official explanation: jockey said colt hung right throughout; trainer said colt had bled from the nose (op 10-1)

1843 32RED.COM 3-Y-O H'CAP 1m 4f
3:00 (3:01) (Class 2) (0-100,90) 3-Y-0 **£12,954** (£3,854; £1,926; £962) **Stalls** High

Form RPR

0-21 1 **Veracity**[25] [1231] 3-8-11 **80** .... PhilipRobinson 8 87+
(M A Jarvis) *lw: hld up: hung rt over 2f out: hdwy over 1f out: styd on to ld wl ins fnl f* **9/2**[2]

04 2 2 **Ask The Butler**[13] [1504] 3-8-9 **78** .... DarryllHolland 1 82
(A W Carroll) *chsd ldrs: rdn over 2f out: styd on* **16/1**

0-31 3 1 **El Dececy (USA)**[17] [1412] 3-8-11 **80** .... IanMongan 3 82+
(J L Dunlop) *led: rdn over 1f out: hdd wl ins fnl f* **8/1**

-621 4 ½ **Spiderback (IRE)**[17] [1396] 3-8-11 **80** ....(b) JimmyFortune 6 82
(R Hannon) *lw: s.i.s: hld up: hdwy over 3f out: rdn over 1f out: styd on same pce ins fnl f* **13/2**

331 5 2 **Stringsofmyheart**[26] [1194] 3-8-4 **73** ....(p) RoystonFfrench 4 71
(W J Haggas) *prom: chsd ldr 4f out: rdn over 2f out: no ex fnl f* **7/1**

34-2 6 4 **Yossi (IRE)**[21] [1290] 3-8-13 **82** .... JimmyQuinn 2 74
(M H Tompkins) *hld up: hdwy over 2f out: sn rdn: wknd fnl f* **7/4**[1]

5116 7 28 **Six Day War (IRE)**[10] [1584] 3-8-13 **82** .... JimCrowley 7 29
(J A Osborne) *prom: rdn 1/2-way: wknd over 4f out* **14/1**

110- 8 2 ½ **Philanthropy**[203] [6216] 3-9-4 **90** .... GregFairley(3) 5 33
(M Johnston) *chsd ldr tl rdn over 4f out: wknd over 3f out* **11/2**[3]

2m 31.3s (-2.20) **Going Correction** -0.05s/f (Good) **8** Ran SP% **119.4**
Speed ratings (Par 105):105,103,103,102,101 98,80,78
CSF £74.08 CT £568.27 TOTE £6.90: £1.80, £3.50, £2.50; EX 89.70 TRIFECTA Not won..
Owner Sheikh Mohammed **Bred** Darley **Trained** Newmarket, Suffolk

FOCUS
A decent little three-year-old handicap that is best rated through the third.

NOTEBOOK
Veracity, off the mark in a modest Wolverhampton maiden last time, followed up in ready fashion on this handicap debut and is clearly progressive. A likely weight rise may not be enough to scupper his bid for the hat-trick and he looks one to follow. (tchd 11-2)
Ask The Butler kept on to post his best effort of the current campaign and got the longer trip without any fuss. He did little wrong in defeat and helps to set the standard of this form.
El Dececy(USA) made a bold bid from the front and only dropped out inside the final furlong. He remains on an upward curve, but this goes some way to confirming his limitations. (op 13-2 tchd 6-1)
Spiderback(IRE), popular in the betting ring, was never really in the hunt from off the pace and looks held by the Handicapper now. (op 10-1)
Stringsofmyheart, raised 8lb for his Pontefract sucsess, was given a positive ride and did not look to have any excuses. (op 9-2 tchd 15-2)
Yossi(IRE), making his handicap debut, was all the rage in the betting ring beforehand and can have no real excuses. He is surely capable of better on his day, but has it to prove now all the same. (op 11-4 tchd 3-1 in places)

1844 BETDIRECT.COM STKS (HERITAGE H'CAP) 1m 6f
3:35 (3:39) (Class 2) 4-Y-0+
£24,928 (£7,464; £3,732; £1,868; £932; £468) **Stalls** High

Form RPR

456- 1 **Sentry Duty (FR)**[56] [6786] 5-9-3 **93** .... BrettDoyle 14 104
(N J Henderson) *chsd ldrs: led over 1f out: rdn out* **14/1**

310- 2 2 ½ **Mikao (IRE)**[219] [5920] 6-8-10 **89** .... SaleemGolam(3) 20 96
(M H Tompkins) *chsd ldr tl led 3f out: rdn and hdd over 1f out: styd on same pce ins fnl f* **14/1**

2-06 3 hd **Mudawin (IRE)**[14] [1477] 6-9-3 **93** .... JohnEgan 1 100
(Jane Chapple-Hyam) *b.hind: hld up: hdwy over 2f out: rdn and hung lft over 1f out: styd on: nt rch ldrs* **16/1**

10-3 4 nk **Finalmente**[14] [1477] 5-9-9 **99** .... OscarUrbina 3 106+
(N A Callaghan) *lw: hld up: n.m.r 7f out: hdwy over 2f out: swtchd rt ins fnl f: nrst fin* **7/1**[2]

0-12 5 1 ¾ **Ollie George (IRE)**[13] [1506] 4-8-11 **87** .... LPKeniry 19 91
(A M Balding) *chsd ldrs: rdn over 2f out: styd on same pce fnl f* **11/1**

21-1 6 ½ **Raucous (GER)**[21] [1300] 4-8-8 **84** .... WSupple 18 87
(T P Tate) *led 11f: rdn over 1f out: no ex* **5/1**[1]

250- 7 3 **River Alhaarth (IRE)**[259] [5010] 5-9-0 **90** .... JimmyFortune 9 89+
(P W Chapple-Hyam) *lw: hld up: styd on appr fnl f: nvr trbld ldrs* **11/1**

211- 8 1 ¼ **Juniper Girl (IRE)**[224] [5811] 4-8-13 **94** .... LukeMorris(5) 6 91
(M L W Bell) *prom: rdn over 4f out: edgd rt 2f out: sn wknd* **12/1**

2244 9 1 ½ **Eva Soneva So Fast (IRE)**[50] [829] 5-9-0 **90** .... JimmyQuinn 15 85
(J L Dunlop) *s.i.s: hld up: hdwy 8f out: rdn and wknd over 1f out* **33/1**

2-60 10 1 ½ **Nordwind (IRE)**[10] [1582] 6-8-9 **85** .... AdamKirby 8 78
(W R Swinburn) *lw: s.i.s: hld up: hdwy over 3f out: rdn and wknd over 1f out* **16/1**

3-31 11 3 ½ **Fregate Island (IRE)**[14] [1470] 4-8-7 **83** .... RobertHavlin 5 71
(B J Meehan) *hld up: hdwy over 3f out: rdn and wknd over 2f out* **14/1**

260- 12 1 **Colloquial**[204] [6205] 6-8-13 **89** .... FergusSweeney 13 76
(H Candy) *chsd ldrs: lost pl 6f out: n.d after* **33/1**

/3-5 13 2 **Shabernak (IRE)**[42] [944] 8-9-5 **95** .... DarryllHolland 2 79
(M L W Bell) *chsd ldrs: lost pl 5f out: sn bhd* **33/1**

113- 14 6 **Velvet Heights (IRE)**[155] [6836] 5-8-11 **87** .... IanMongan 16 63
(J L Dunlop) *hld up: hdwy 1/2-way: rdn over 2f out: sn wknd* **11/1**

0-30 15 6 **Galient (IRE)**[10] [1582] 4-9-5 **95** ....(p) PhilipRobinson 4 62
(M A Jarvis) *prom: hmpd 7f out: wknd 3f out* **5/1**[1]

650- 16 nk **Saint Alebe**[217] [5963] 8-9-5 **95** .... AntonyProcter 12 62
(D R C Elsworth) *bkwd: hld up: sme hdwy and hung rt 6f out: wknd 4f out* **33/1**

014/ 17 1 **Sea Wall**[193] [4514] 5-9-0 **90** .... JimCrowley 17 56
(Jonjo O'Neill) *chsd ldrs over 10f* **50/1**

10-5 18 ¾ **Florimund**[14] [1477] 4-8-9 **85** .... RoystonFfrench 11 50
(Sir Michael Stoute) *s.i.s: hld up: bhd fnl 3f* **10/1**[3]

6-00 19 ½ **Sienna Storm (IRE)**[24] [1244] 4-8-9 **90** .... PatrickHills(5) 10 54
(M H Tompkins) *s.i.s: hld up: hdwy 6f out: rdn and wknd over 2f out* **66/1**

434- 20 18 **Cresta Gold**[205] [6191] 4-9-10 **100** .... RichardMullen 7 39
(A Bailey) *prom: lost pl 7f out: bhd fnl 4f* **33/1**

2m 56.29s (-3.84) **Going Correction** -0.05s/f (Good) **20** Ran SP% **137.5**
Speed ratings (Par 109):108,106,106,106,105 105,103,102,101,100 98,98,97,93,90 90,89,89,88,78
CSF £207.55 CT £3224.08 TOTE £18.10: £4.00, £6.30, £3.30, £1.80; EX 308.80 Trifecta £1007.90 Part won. Pool £1,419.60 - 0.10 winning units..
Owner Peter Spiller **Bred** P Spiller And Mme Henri Devin **Trained** Upper Lambourn, Berks

FOCUS
A decent staying handicap, run at a sound enough gallop and solid form with the third and fourth close to recent form.

NOTEBOOK
Sentry Duty(FR), last seen running a respectable race on his hurdling and British bow at Newbury in March, showed his true colours with a comfortable sucess and rates full value for the winning margin. He is open to a deal of further improvement in this sphere and is the type his trainer excels with. (op 12-1)
Mikao(IRE) failed to find as much as seemed likely when under pressure and was eventually well held. He has begun this term on a high-enough mark, but a drop back to 12f may well pay dividends. (op 16-1)
Mudawin(IRE), last season's Ebor winner, lacked the required change of gears when it mattered yet ran a pleasing race in defeat over this suitably longer trip. He looks to be coming good again now. (op 14-1)
Finalmente was noted finishing his race with gusto on this step back up in trip. He remains in good form and can be placed to strike in this sort of company before long. (op 15-2 tchd 8-1)
Ollie George(IRE), just denied from this mark at Salisbury last time, ran a sound race in defeat and can have no excuses. (tchd 12-1)
Raucous(GER) was not surprisingly ridden positively on this drop in trip. He does not have many miles on the clock, but looks a proper stayer and really needs all of 2m now.
River Alhaarth(IRE) Official explanation: jockey said he was unable to ride out due to being hit on the arm by a loose shoe
Galient(IRE), who failed to shine from a poor draw in the Chester Cup last time, failed to run up to expectations in the first-time cheekpieces and is in danger of going the wrong way at present. (op 10-1)

Florimund Official explanation: jockey said gelding was never travelling

1845 32RED.COM H'CAP 7f
4:05 (4:12) (Class 4) (0-80,80) 4-Y-0+ **£5,181** (£1,541; £770; £384) **Stalls** High

Form RPR

000- **1** **Grizedale (IRE)**^{203} [6221] 8-8-10 **72**........(t) PaulDoe 5 83
(J Akehurst) *lw: chsd ldrs: led over 2f out: rdn and hung rt 1f out: styd on* **25/1**

00-3 **2** *1* **Neon Blue**^{4} [1747] 6-8-3 **70** ow1........ MichaelJStainton$^{(5)}$ 9 78
(R M Whitaker) *chsd ldrs: rdn over 2f out: styd on* **12/1**

3400 **3** *1 ¾* **Plateau**^{25} [1223] 8-8-5 **67**........ JohnEgan 12 70+
(C R Dore) *hld up: nt clr run over 1f out: r.o wl ins fnl f: nt rch ldrs* **33/1**

50-5 **4** *½* **Zennerman (IRE)**^{15} [1458] 4-8-13 **75**........ DO'Donohoe 1 77+
(K A Ryan) *s.i.s: hld up: nt clr run over 1f out: r.o wl ins fnl f: nvr nrr* **12/1**

51-0 **5** *hd* **Rubenstar (IRE)**^{17} [1395] 4-9-3 **79**........ DarryllHolland 2 80
(M H Tompkins) *hld up: hdwy and edgd lft over 1f out: styd on* **14/1**

0-03 **6** *nk* **Passion Fruit**^{8} [1626] 6-9-3 **79**........ DeanMcKeown 14 80
(C W Fairhurst) *s.i.s: hld up: hdwy over 2f out: rdn over 1f out: edgd lft and no ex ins fnl f* **13/2**^{2}

3012 **7** *½* **Sailor King (IRE)**^{8} [1629] 5-8-13 **75**........ JimCrowley 8 74
(D K Ivory) *lw: prom: rdn over 2f out: styd on same pce fnl f* **10/1**

61-6 **8** *nk* **Carnivore**^{25} [1223] 5-9-0 **76**........ BrettDoyle 13 74
(T D Barron) *lw: mid-div: rdn over 2f out: styd on same pce fnl f* **4/1**^{1}

2200 **9** *1 ½* **Resplendent Nova**^{21} [1308] 5-8-12 **74**........ JimmyQuinn 7 73+
(P Howling) *hld up in tch: rdn over 1f out: btn whn hmpd whn n.m.r ins fnl f* **8/1**^{3}

2136 **10** *shd* **Special Place**^{15} [1446] 4-8-4 **66** oh2........ RoystonFfrench 11 60
(J A R Toller) *lw: hld up: nt clr run over 2f out: n.d* **16/1**

0-05 **11** *shd* **Finsbury**^{104} [351] 4-8-6 **75**........ AmyBaker$^{(7)}$ 4 69
(Miss J Feilden) *s.i.s: hld up: rdn over 2f out: nt clr run over 1f out: n.d* **66/1**

255- **12** *1 ¼* **Sake (IRE)**^{271} [4653] 5-8-11 **73**........ KimTinkler 10 63
(N Tinkler) *led: hdd over 2f out: wknd fnl f* **25/1**

-005 **13** *2 ½* **Purus (IRE)**^{16} [1431] 5-8-4 **66** oh1........ RichardSmith 16 50
(R A Teal) *chsd ldrs: rdn over 2f out: wknd fnl f* **33/1**

220- **14** *½* **Blues In The Night (IRE)**^{203} [6221] 4-9-4 **80**........ FergusSweeney 15 62
(P J Makin) *prom over 4f* **14/1**

1-00 **15** *nk* **Amwaal (USA)**^{17} [1395] 4-8-12 **74**........ IanMongan 3 56
(J L Dunlop) *lw: mid-div: hdwy and hung rt over 2f out: wknd over 1f out* **16/1**

2250 **16** *1* **Bomber Command (USA)**^{21} [1308] 4-8-7 **74**........ PatrickHills$^{(5)}$ 18 53
(J W Hills) *s.i.s: hdwy over 5f out: rdn and wknd fnl f* **12/1**

00-6 **17** *nk* **Cool Panic (IRE)**^{23} [1268] 5-9-1 **77**........ RichardMullen 17 55
(M L W Bell) *lw: w ldr to 1/2-way: wknd over 1f out* **16/1**

000- **18** *3* **Our Putra**^{239} [5512] 4-9-2 **78**........ PhilipRobinson 6 48
(M A Jarvis) *b: chsd ldrs over 4f* **14/1**

1m 25.05s (-1.45) **Going Correction** -0.05s/f (Good) **18** Ran SP% **129.3**
Speed ratings (Par 105):106,104,102,102,102 101,101,100,99,98 98,97,94,94,93 92,92,88
CSF £303.32 CT £9845.55 TOTE £39.40: £7.10, £3.60, £9.60, £2.90; EX 534.80 TRIFECTA Not won..
Owner Canisbay Bloodstock **Bred** Minch Bloodstock **Trained** Epsom, Surrey
■ Stewards' Enquiry : John Egan caution: careless riding

FOCUS
A fair handicap and an open one for the grade. The form appears sound rated around the first two with the third and fourth not getting the best of runs.
Plateau Official explanation: jockey said gelding had been denied a clear run

1846 BETDIRECTPOKER.COM $50K FREEROLL TOMORROW NOVICE STKS 6f
4:40 (4:41) (Class 4) 2-Y-O **£5,181** (£1,541; £770; £384) **Stalls** High

Form RPR

1 **Declaration Of War (IRE)** 2-8-12........ RobertHavlin 4 87
(P W Chapple-Hyam) *w'like: chsd ldrs: led over 2f out: hdd 1f out: rallied to ld wl ins fnl f* **5/1**^{3}

223 **2** *½* **Silver Guest**^{12} [1546] 2-8-12........ DarryllHolland 2 86
(M R Channon) *hld up in tch: rdn to ld 1f out: hdd and unable qckn wl ins fnl f* **11/8**^{1}

5 **3** *3* **Master Chef (IRE)**^{12} [1540] 2-8-12........ WSupple 5 77
(J H M Gosden) *lw: chsd ldrs: rdn and ev ch over 1f out: no ex ins fnl f* **10/3**^{2}

4 *1 ¾* **Rockfield Tiger (IRE)** 2-8-12........ PhilipRobinson 8 71
(J A Osborne) *cmpt: scope: s.i.s: hld up: hdwy over 1f out: wknd ins fnl f* **14/1**

00 **5** *shd* **Sirjoshua Reynolds**^{12} [1519] 2-8-5........ KirstyMilczarek$^{(7)}$ 6 71
(N A Callaghan) *sn outpcd: r.o ins fnl f: nvr nrr* **33/1**

6 *5* **Liberty Island (IRE)** 2-8-12........ BrettDoyle 1 56
(B J Meehan) *neat: chsd ldrs: edgd lft and wknd over 1f out* **16/1**

7 *3* **Rimrock (IRE)** 2-8-12........ JohnEgan 7 47
(J Noseda) *w'like: s.i.s: hdwy and hung rt 4f out: rdn and wknd over 2f out* **7/1**

8 *nk* **Insomnitas** 2-8-12........ RichardMullen 3 46
(M G Quinlan) *cmpt: racd keenly: sn led: hdd over 2f out: hung lft and wknd over 1f out* **25/1**

1m 13.47s (0.37) **Going Correction** -0.05s/f (Good) **8** Ran SP% **113.7**
Speed ratings (Par 95):95,94,90,88,87 81,77,76
CSF £12.13 TOTE £8.80: £1.80, £1.10, £1.50; EX 19.50.
Owner Mrs Violet Mercer **Bred** St Simon Foundation **Trained** Newmarket, Suffolk

FOCUS
An interesting novice event. The first pair came clear but the form has question marks over it, with doubts about the runner-up.

NOTEBOOK
Declaration Of War(IRE), who cost 25,000gns, made it three winners from as many juvenile runners for his stable to date this term and got off the mark at the first time of asking. He showed a very likeable attitude to fend off the more experienced runner-up late on and, entitled to come on for the experience, may well line up in the Coventry at Royal Ascot next month. (op 4-1 tchd 7-2 and 11-2, 6-1 in a place)
Silver Guest had every chance yet found the winner too resolute at the business end of the race. He again did not appear to do much wrong in defeat, but he has now become expensive to follow and has developed a habit of finding one too good. (op 6-4 tchd 13-8 and 5-4, 7-4 in places)
Master Chef(IRE) ◆ built on the level of his Windsor debut 21 days previously and had his chance. He again looked green and should not be long in winning his maiden en-route to better things. (op 4-1)
Rockfield Tiger(IRE), an 80,000euros purchase whose dam was a 7f winner at two, did himself no favours with a sluggish start and eventually got left behind when the principals quickened for home. He should come on a fair deal for this debut experience. (op 11-1)

1847 32RED.COM SPRINT H'CAP 6f
5:15 (5:16) (Class 5) (0-75,80) 4-Y-0+ **£3,886** (£1,156; £577; £288) **Stalls** High

Form RPR

0-21 **1** **Brunelleschi**^{8} [1640] 4-8-5 **67**........(b) LukeMorris$^{(5)}$ 7 82
(P L Gilligan) *racd stands' side hld up in tch: led and hung lft over 1f out: r.o to ld overall nr fin* **10/3**^{1}

-331 **2** *¾* **Keyaki (IRE)**^{12} [1525] 6-9-7 **78**........ IanMongan 19 91+
(C F Wall) *oevrall ldr far side: rdn over 1f out: hdd nr fin: 1st of 2 that side* **9/1**

0505 **3** *1 ¼* **Cornus**^{26} [1200] 5-8-13 **70**........(be) AdamKirby 1 79
(A J McCabe) *lw: racd stands' side: hld up: hdwy over 1f out: r.o: nrst fin: 2nd of 16 in gp* **20/1**

3511 **4** *2 ½* **Who's Winning (IRE)**^{9} [1607] 6-9-6 **80**........ RichardKingscote$^{(3)}$ 10 81
(B G Powell) *racd stands' side: chsd ldrs: rdn over 1f out: styd on same pce: 3rd of 16 in gp* **6/1**^{2}

02-5 **5** *hd* **Westport**^{19} [1363] 4-9-4 **75**........ DO'Donohoe 14 75
(K A Ryan) *racd stands' side: mid-div: hdwy over 2f out: rdn over 1f out: styd on same pce: 4th of 16 in gp* **7/1**^{3}

0055 **6** *1 ¾* **Gavarnie Beau (IRE)**^{9} [1607] 4-9-1 **72**........(b^{1}) OscarUrbina 18 67+
(M Blanshard) *chsd ldr far side: rdn over 2f out: no imp fnl f: last of 2 that side* **25/1**

-005 **7** *hd* **Bel Cantor**^{5} [1718] 4-8-9 **73**........ HaddenFrost$^{(7)}$ 9 67
(W J H Ratcliffe) *racd stands' side: led that gp over 4f: no ex: 5th of 16 in gp* **16/1**

2520 **8** *nk* **Parkview Love (USA)**^{7} [1666] 6-8-3 **65** ow2........(v) PatrickHills$^{(5)}$ 4 58
(D Shaw) *racd stands' side: s.s: bhd: swtchd rt 2f out: r.o ins fnl f: nvr nrr: 6th of 16 in gp* **16/1**

66-0 **9** *1 ¼* **Kansas Gold**^{5} [1718] 4-8-10 **67**........ RoystonFfrench 8 56
(J Mackie) *racd stands' side: mid-div: rdn over 2f out: wknd over 1f out: 7th of 16 in gp* **28/1**

00-6 **10** *shd* **Calabaza**^{9} [1607] 5-8-5 **62**........(b) PaulDoe 17 51
(W Jarvis) *lw: racd stands' side: chsd ldrs: rdn and ev ch over 1f out: sn wknd: 8th of 16 in gp* **16/1**

50-0 **11** *1* **Foreign Edition (IRE)**^{25} [1223] 5-9-4 **75**........(p) PhilipRobinson 12 61
(Miss J A Camacho) *racd stands' side: hld up: rdn over 2f out: n.d: 9th of 16 in gp* **10/1**

26-0 **12** *nk* **Pick A Nice Name**^{11} [1565] 5-8-6 **68**........ MichaelJStainton$^{(5)}$ 3 53
(R M Whitaker) *lw: racd stands' side: s.i.s: hdwy over 4f out: rdn and wknd over 1f out: 10th of 16 in gp* **14/1**

6/00 **13** *1 ¾* **Charming Ballet (IRE)**^{10} [1589] 4-8-6 **63**........(e^{1}) RichardMullen 11 42
(N P Littmoden) *racd stands' side: s.i.s: hld up: a in rr: 11th of 16 in gp* **28/1**

-452 **14** *shd* **Border Artist**^{84} [549] 8-8-7 **64**........ JimmyQuinn 15 43
(J Pearce) *racd stands' side: hld up: n.d: 12th of 16 in gp* **25/1**

000- **15** *¾* **Goodenough Mover**^{234} [5627] 11-9-1 **72**........ RobertHavlin 2 48
(Andrew Turnell) *racd stands' side: chsd ldrs over 4f: 13th of 16 in gp* **33/1**

0043 **16** *½* **Royal Envoy (IRE)**^{10} [1589] 4-8-5 **62**........ DeanMcKeown 20 37
(D Shaw) *racd stands' side: s.s: hld up: a in rr: 14th of 16 in gp* **12/1**

0-03 **17** *hd* **Ellens Academy (IRE)**^{7} [1678] 12-9-3 **74**........ WSupple 13 48
(E J Alston) *lw: racd stands' side: s.i.s: hld up: hdwy 2f out: sn rdn and wknd: 15th of 16 in gp* **8/1**

1260 **18** *4* **Tancredi (SWE)**^{22} [1283] 5-8-8 **68**........ JerryO'Dwyer$^{(3)}$ 6 29
(N B King) *racd stands' side: chsd ldrs: rdn 1/2-way: wknd 2f out: last of 16 in gp* **33/1**

1m 12.32s (-0.78) **Going Correction** -0.05s/f (Good) **18** Ran SP% **137.3**
Speed ratings (Par 103):103,102,100,97,96 94,94,93,92,91 90,90,87,87,86 86,85,80
CSF £33.85 CT £581.23 TOTE £4.60: £1.70, £2.60, £5.40, £2.10; EX 55.20 Place 6 £360.62, Place 5 £215.10.
Owner Dr Susan Barnes **Bred** Dr Susan Barnes **Trained** Newmarket, Suffolk

FOCUS
A modest sprint handicap which saw the field spread wide across the track. The form is straightforward enough rated around the principals.
T/Plt: £252.10 to a £1 stake. Pool: £87,260.05. 252.60 winning tickets. T/Qpdt: £125.70 to a £1 stake. Pool: £5,114.15. 30.10 winning tickets. CR

^{1674}THIRSK (L-H)
Saturday, May 19

OFFICIAL GOING: Good
Wind: Strong, half-behind.

1848 EUROPEAN BREEDERS' FUND SUNMAID MAIDEN FILLIES' STKS 5f
2:05 (2:06) (Class 4) 2-Y-O **£5,181** (£1,541; £770; £384) **Stalls** High

Form RPR

1 **Starlit Sands** 2-9-0........ SebSanders 15 82
(Sir Mark Prescott) *mde virtually all: rdn along 2f out and sn edgd lft: kpt on wl fnl f* **4/1**^{3}

2 *hd* **Charlotti Carlotti (IRE)** 2-9-0........ PaulFessey 11 81
(T D Barron) *chsd ldrs: rdn wl over 1f out: styd on to chal ins fnl f: ev ch tl no ex towards fin* **11/2**

3 *nk* **Sudden Impact (IRE)** 2-9-0........ PhillipMakin 8 80
(Paul Green) *chsd ldrs: hdwy 2f out: rdn: rn green and hung lft 1 1/2f out: ev ch ins fnl f: no ex towards fin* **66/1**

5 **4** *3* **Musical Charm (IRE)**^{26} [1193] 2-9-0........ DavidAllan 7 69
(T D Easterby) *towards rr: hdwy 1/2-way: styd on wl appr fnl f: nrst fin* **12/1**

22 **5** *5* **Ramatni**^{12} [1533] 2-9-0........ JoeFanning 14 51
(M Johnston) *cl up: rdn along 2f out: wknd over 1f out* **2/1**^{1}

42 **6** *½* **Cayman Fox**^{21} [1285] 2-9-0........ PaulHanagan 6 50+
(James Moffatt) *cl up on outer: rdn along 2f out: bmpd 1 1/2f out and sn btn* **3/1**^{2}

0 **7** *¾* **Longoria (IRE)**^{12} [1533] 2-9-0........ TPQueally 9 47
(M G Quinlan) *dwlt: pushed along in midfield 1/2-way: sn rdn and no imp* **22/1**

8 *1* **Invincible Rose (IRE)** 2-9-0........ DeanMernagh 13 43
(M Brittain) *towards rr: hdwy 2f out: sn rdn and kpt on appr fnl f* **100/1**

4 **9** *2* **Destinys Dream (IRE)**^{11} [1553] 2-9-0........ PaulMulrennan 12 36
(Mrs A Duffield) *a towards rr* **40/1**

0 **10** *nk* **Redbackcappuchino (IRE)**^{10} [1586] 2-9-0........ RichardThomas 3 35
(J L Spearing) *a in rr* **150/1**

11 *shd* **Steph The Ref** 2-8-9........ NataliaGemelova$^{(5)}$ 10 35
(R M Whitaker) *s.i.s: a in rr* **100/1**

0 **12** 3/4 **Eboracum Dream**[21] 1285 2-8-11 .... DuranFentiman(3) 5 32
(T D Easterby) *in midfield: rdn along 1/2-way: sn outpcd* **25/1**
06 **13** 3 1/2 **Holly Golightley**[16] 1422 2-9-0 .... NCallan 4 19
(K A Ryan) *chsd ldrs towards outer: rdn along 1/2-way: sn wknd* **16/1**
14 3/4 **Foxies Bychance** 2-9-0 .... TomEaves 2 17
(R D E Woodhouse) *wnt lft s: a bhd* **150/1**
58.49 secs (-1.41) **Going Correction** -0.225s/f (Firm) **14** Ran SP% **122.7**
Speed ratings (Par 92):102,101,101,96,88 87,86,84,81,81 80,79,74,72
CSF £25.96 TOTE £5.40: £2.30, £2.60, £16.20; EX 33.40.
Owner Miss K Rausing **Bred** Miss K Rausing **Trained** Newmarket, Suffolk
■ Stewards' Enquiry : David Allan £130 fine: arrived in Parade Ring late
N Callan caution: allowed filly to coast home with no assistance from saddle

FOCUS
A modest fillies' juvenile maiden which saw three debutantes play out the finish. A high draw was an advantage but the form looks strong for the track.

NOTEBOOK
Starlit Sands, a half-sister to the smart sprinter Sea Dane among others, took full advantage of her stands'-rail draw and made just about every yard to make a winning start to her career. She is not typical of many of her trainer's juveniles in that she is bred to make her mark this year over short distances, and a mile will probably be the limit of her stamina range as she matures further. It will be very interesting to see where she is pitched in next. (op 7-2 tchd 5-1 in a place)
Charlotti Carlotti(IRE) ◆, a half-sister to numerous winners at around this distance, proved popular in the betting ring for this racecourse bow and justified each-way support with a pleasing effort. She was doing her best work towards the finish and looks capable of going one better with this experience under her belt. (tchd 5-1 and 6-1)
Sudden Impact(IRE), related to winners from 6f to 1m, was a first two-year-old runner from her first-season trainer and ran a big race in defeat. Entitled to improve plenty for this debut experience, she looks to have a future. (op 50-1)
Musical Charm(IRE), fourth at Pontefract on debut 26 days previously, hails from a stable in recent form at present and fared best of those with any previous experience. She still looked green here and was doing her best work late on, suggesting she would enjoy another furlong. (op 14-1)
Ramatni showed early dash, but her fate was apparent on passing the 2f pole and she has to rate disappointing. (op 9-4 tchd 5-2)
Cayman Fox probably used up too much energy in tracking across early from her low draw and was in trouble before the final furlong. (op 7-2 tchd 4-1 in a place)

1849 VICTORIA MAIDEN STKS 1m 4f
2:35 (2:35) (Class 5) 3-Y-O+ **£3,886** (£1,156; £577; £288) **Stalls** Low

Form RPR
26-2 **1** **Samurai Way**[28] 1149 5-9-13 87 .... NickyMackay 6 86+
(L M Cumani) *trckd ldrs: smooth hdwy 3f out: led 2f out and sn clr: easily* **4/5**[1]
04 **2** 6 **Mowadeh (IRE)**[13] 1505 3-8-10 .... TPO'Shea 11 71
(M R Channon) *hld up: hdwy 4f out: rdn to chse wnr wl over 1f out: sn drvn and no imp* **18/1**
2 **3** 2 **Campli (IRE)**[18] 1044 5-9-13 .... PaulMulrennan 13 68
(Micky Hammond) *hld up in rr: stdy hdwy over 4f out: rdn along 2f out: styd on appr fnl f: nrst fin* **33/1**
/25- **4** nk **White Lightening (IRE)**[106] 5063 4-9-13 79 .... TomEaves 7 68
(J Howard Johnson) *towards rr: pushed along and hdwy over 4f out: rdn wl over 2f out kpt on appr fnl f: nrst fin* **25/1**
632 **5** 2 **Bernix**[14] 1479 5-9-13 72 .... DavidAllan 2 65
(T D Easterby) *led 2f: cl up tl lft in ld bnd over 4f out: rdn along 3f out: hdd 2f out and grad wknd* **10/1**[3]
6 3 **Square Dealer**[67] 6-9-13 .... PaddyAspell 14 60?
(J R Norton) *bhd tl sme late hdwy* **100/1**
33-2 **7** 3/4 **Tempelstern (GER)**[29] 1129 3-8-10 80 .... TedDurcan 8 59+
(H R A Cecil) *t.k.h: prom on outer: led after 2f: bit slipped and rn wd bnd after 3f: rn v wd and hdd bnd over 4f out: sn no ch and eased* **6/4**[2]
40 **8** 9 **Jentris Girl (IRE)**[21] 1303 3-8-2 .... DuranFentiman(3) 3 39
(T D Easterby) *chsd ldrs: rdn along 4f out: sn wknd* **66/1**
0-0 **9** 5 **Niza D'Alm (FR)**[20] 365 6-9-3 .... PJMcDonald(5) 9 31
(A Crook) *a in rr* **200/1**
5 **10** 9 **Hewaar (IRE)**[18] 1374 4-9-6 .... JamesO'Reilly(7) 4 22
(J O'Reilly) *prom tl rdn along 4f out and sn wknd* **125/1**
300/ **11** dist **Pre Eminance (IRE)**[406] 5972 6-9-13 64 .... (t) TonyHamilton 5 —
(J S Wainwright) *prom: rdn along 4f out: sn wknd* **100/1**
0- **12** dist **Young Emma**[186] 6482 4-9-8 .... SebSanders 1 —
(G G Margarson) *chsd ldrs: rdn along over 5f out: sn wknd* **80/1**
2m 35.53s (0.33) **Going Correction** +0.025s/f (Good)
WFA 3 from 4yo+ 17lb **12** Ran SP% **122.7**
Speed ratings (Par 103):99,95,93,93,92 90,89,83,80,74 —,—
CSF £20.24 TOTE £2.00: £1.10, £3.10, £5.50; EX 17.30.
Owner K Bailey, P Booth, D Boorer **Bred** Darley **Trained** Newmarket, Suffolk

FOCUS
A fairly weak maiden and the winner is value for plenty further than the winning margin. He did not have to be at his best to win with his market rival having steering problems and the third and sixth hold down the form.
Tempelstern(GER) Official explanation: jockey said bit slipped through the colt's mouth.
Young Emma Official explanation: trainer later said filly was found to be in season

1850 LYME REGIS H'CAP 1m
3:05 (3:05) (Class 6) (0-65,65) 3-Y-O **£2,590** (£770; £385; £192) **Stalls** Low

Form RPR
50-1 **1** **Golden Prospect**[12] 1538 3-9-3 64 .... SebSanders 7 73+
(J W Hills) *hld up: gd hdwy on outer 3f out: rdn to ld over 1f out: drvn ins fnl f and styd on wl* **4/1**[1]
24-6 **2** 1 1/4 **Run Free**[30] 1111 3-9-4 65 .... DanielTudhope 13 71
(N Wilson) *in tch on outer: hdwy 3f out: led 2f out: sn rdn and hdd over 1f out: rallied u.p ins fnl f: no ex last 100yds* **8/1**
034- **3** 3 1/2 **Chasing Memories (IRE)**[142] 6963 3-8-11 61 .... MarkLawson(3) 18 59
(B Smart) *hld up towards rr: hdwy wl over 2f out: rdn wl over 1f out: kpt on ins fnl f* **25/1**
00-3 **4** 3/4 **Leprechaun's Gold (IRE)**[11] 1558 3-8-13 60 .... JoeFanning 16 56
(M Johnston) *in rr: hdwy 2f out: sn rdn and styd on wl fnl f* **12/1**
006- **5** 1 1/4 **Exit Strategy (IRE)**[187] 6466 3-8-11 58 .... PaulMulrennan 3 51+
(W J Haggas) *in tch on inner: hdwy over 2f out: sn rdn and kpt on same pce fr wl over 1f out* **12/1**
064- **6** 1 1/4 **Spice Bar**[180] 6536 3-8-11 63 .... (p) WilliamBuick(5) 10 54+
(A M Balding) *bhd: effrt 3f out and sn pushed along: swtchd to outside and rdn wl over 1f out: styd on ins fnl f: nrst fin* **11/2**[3]
5250 **7** 1 **La Marmotte (IRE)**[24] 1238 3-8-7 59 ow1 .... JamieMoriarty(5) 6 47
(R E Barr) *cl up: led briefly over 2f out: sn rdn and hdd: grad wknd* **22/1**
030- **8** 2 **Xaar Too Busy**[228] 5748 3-8-12 59 .... (p) PaulHanagan 4 43
(Mrs A Duffield) *chsd ldrs: rdn along over 2f out and grad wknd* **33/1**
0605 **9** 3/4 **Polish Star**[7] 1676 3-8-8 55 .... TonyHamilton 2 37
(J S Wainwright) *prom on inner: rdn along 3f out: wknd over 2f out* **11/1**
-042 **10** 1/2 **Chip N Pin**[10] 1579 3-8-7 57 .... DuranFentiman(3) 12 38
(T D Easterby) *chsd ldrs: rdn along 3f out: sn btn* **9/2**[2]
500- **11** 1 1/4 **Go Red**[241] 5482 3-8-8 55 .... DaleGibson 14 33
(M W Easterby) *s.i.s: a in rr* **33/1**
0-06 **12** 1/2 **High Five Society**[28] 1155 3-8-12 59 .... PhillipMakin 8 36
(S R Bowring) *a towards rr* **10/1**
60-0 **13** 2 **Bold Nevison (IRE)**[126] 122 3-8-7 54 .... TomEaves 1 26
(B Smart) *in midfield: rdn along 3f out: sn outpcd* **33/1**
0-40 **14** shd **Meridian Grey (USA)**[31] 1091 3-9-1 62 .... NCallan 9 34
(K A Ryan) *cl up: rdn along over 3f out: wknd over 2f out* **14/1**
400- **15** 2 1/2 **Shotley Mac**[268] 4731 3-8-7 61 .... SuzzanneFrance(7) 11 27
(N Bycroft) *a in rr* **50/1**
6-23 **16** 1 1/2 **Ruthles Philly**[16] 1424 3-8-11 58 .... PatCosgrave 5 21
(D W Barker) *led: rdn along 3f out: sn hdd & wknd* **10/1**
1m 40.12s (0.42) **Going Correction** +0.025s/f (Good) **16** Ran SP% **132.2**
Speed ratings (Par 97):98,96,93,92,91 90,89,87,86,85 84,84,82,81,79 77
CSF £36.62 CT £788.02 TOTE £4.90: £1.90, £2.50, £5.60, £1.60; EX 59.30.
Owner Michael Wauchope And Partners **Bred** D E And Mrs J Cash **Trained** Upper Lambourn, Berks

FOCUS
A modest three-year-old handicap but the winner is progressive and the form could prove solid.

1851 HALO FOODS H'CAP 1m
3:40 (3:40) (Class 4) (0-85,85) 3-Y-O **£5,181** (£1,541; £770; £384) **Stalls** Low

Form RPR
1-22 **1** **Docofthebay (IRE)**[19] 1359 3-8-11 78 .... StephenDonohoe 13 86
(J A Osborne) *hld up: gd hdwy on outer over 2f out: rdn over 1f out: hung lft ins fnl f: led nr fin* **14/1**
1122 **2** nk **Captain Jacksparra (IRE)**[12] 1535 3-9-0 81 .... NCallan 6 89
(K A Ryan) *a.p: hdwy to chse ldr 3f out: rdn to chal 2f out: drvn to ld ent fnl f: hdd and no ex nr fin* **9/2**[2]
2-1 **3** 1 3/4 **Colorado Rapid (IRE)**[30] 1111 3-9-3 84 .... JoeFanning 4 88+
(M Johnston) *cl up: led over 4f out: jnd and rdn along 2f out: drvn and hdd ent fnl f: kpt on same pce* **10/11**[1]
150- **4** 2 1/2 **Domino Dancer (IRE)**[268] 4736 3-8-13 85 .... JamieMoriarty(5) 12 83
(J Howard Johnson) *stdd s: hld up in rr: swtchd outside and hdwy over 2f out: sn rdn and kpt on ins fnl f: nrst fin* **66/1**
013- **5** hd **Practicallyperfect (IRE)**[223] 5828 3-8-10 77 .... TedDurcan 11 75
(H R A Cecil) *hld up in tch: hdwy on outer over 2f out: rdn and edgd lft over 1f out: sn one pce* **20/1**
51- **6** 1/2 **Cat De Mille (USA)**[218] 5947 3-8-13 80 .... AdrianMcCarthy 9 76
(P W Chapple-Hyam) *chsd ldrs on inner: rdn along over 2f out and sn one pce* **12/1**
03-0 **7** 3 1/2 **Monkey Glas (IRE)**[32] 1076 3-8-7 74 ow1 .... PatCosgrave 8 62
(K R Burke) *hld up in rr: hdwy over 2f out: rdn over 1f out: kpt on ins fnl f: nrst fin* **33/1**
601- **8** nk **Milliegait**[234] 5613 3-8-11 78 .... DavidAllan 15 66+
(T D Easterby) *hld up in rr: hdwy over 2f out: styd on ins fnl f: nrst fin* **50/1**
3332 **9** 5 **Deadline (UAE)**[12] 1529 3-8-6 73 .... PaulFessey 14 49
(P T Midgley) *chsd ldrs on outer: rdn along 3f out: grad wknd* **33/1**
0-56 **10** 3/4 **Musical Mirage (USA)**[17] 1414 3-8-12 79 .... DanielTudhope 7 53
(G A Swinbank) *hld up: hdwy 3f out: sn rdn along and btn 2f out* **25/1**
05-0 **11** 2 **Chin Wag (IRE)**[30] 1110 3-8-13 83 .... AndrewElliott(3) 2 53
(K R Burke) *cl up: rdn along over 3f out: drvn and wknd over 2f out* **40/1**
235- **12** 1 **Blue Madeira**[266] 4813 3-8-10 77 .... TonyHamilton 3 45+
(Mrs L Stubbs) *s.i.s: in rr whn hmpd bnd after 3f: a bhd* **40/1**
-110 **13** 1 **Chookie Hamilton**[22] 1275 3-8-11 78 .... TomEaves 1 43
(I Semple) *chsd ldrs: rdn along 3f out: wknd fnl 2f* **25/1**
52-4 **14** 21 **Mystic Dancer**[26] 1204 3-8-12 79 .... SebSanders 10 —
(Sir Michael Stoute) *led over 3f: prom tl rdn along and wknd wl over 2f out* **17/2**[3]
2-12 **15** 1 **King's Apostle (IRE)**[49] 843 3-8-12 79 .... PaulHanagan 5 —
(W J Haggas) *t.k.h: in tch: lost pl 1/2-way and sn bhd* **12/1**
1m 39.62s (-0.08) **Going Correction** +0.025s/f (Good) **15** Ran SP% **129.8**
Speed ratings (Par 101):101,100,98,96,96 95,92,91,86,86 84,83,82,61,60
CSF £74.80 CT £123.18 TOTE £22.00: £4.50, £1.90, £1.20; EX 50.60.
Owner Paul J Dixon **Bred** G And Mrs Middlebrook **Trained** Upper Lambourn, Berks

FOCUS
A good three-year-old handicap for the track. The first pair came clear late on and the form looks solid rated through the consistent second.
Mystic Dancer Official explanation: trainer's rep had no explanation for the poor form shown
King's Apostle(IRE) Official explanation: jockey said colt pulled hard and failed to handle the bend; trainer's rep said colt had returned with its tongue over the bit

1852 P K F H'CAP 6f
4:15 (4:16) (Class 3) (0-90,93) 4-Y-O+ **£7,772** (£2,312; £1,155; £577) **Stalls** High

Form RPR
653- **1** **My Gacho (IRE)**[243] 5420 5-8-11 83 .... (b) PhillipMakin 1 88
(T D Barron) *trckd ldrs: hdwy 2f out: rdn to ld ent fnl f: sn drvn and hld on wl* **8/1**
1502 **2** hd **Bahamian Pirate (USA)**[7] 1653 12-9-7 93 .... AdrianTNicholls 6 97
(D Nicholls) *hld up: hdwy on outer over 2f out: rdn wl over 1f out: styd on to chal ent fnl f: ev ch tl nt qckn nr fin* **5/1**[2]
34-0 **3** shd **Lake Chini (IRE)**[11] 1565 5-8-4 76 oh1 .... (b) DaleGibson 10 80
(M W Easterby) *led 2f: cl up: rdn to ld again wl over 1f out: drvn and hdd ent fnl f: ev ch tl nt qckn towards fin* **28/1**
04-0 **4** shd **Steel Blue**[31] 1088 7-8-6 78 .... PaulMulrennan 16 81
(R M Whitaker) *cl up on stands' rail: effrt 2f out and ev ch tl rdn and nt qckn ins fnl f* **11/2**[3]
0-40 **5** 3/4 **High Curragh**[7] 1651 4-9-3 89 .... NCallan 3 90+
(K A Ryan) *trckd ldrs: effrt and nt clr run over 1f out and again ins fnl f kpt on* **11/2**[3]
0-00 **6** shd **Blue Tomato**[15] 1458 6-8-3 80 .... KevinGhunowa(5) 4 81
(J M Bradley) *chsd ldrs: rdn along wl over 1f out: kpt on same pce ent fnl f* **14/1**
0016 **7** shd **Danzig River (IRE)**[14] 1483 6-7-11 76 .... AdeleRothery(7) 12 77+
(D Nicholls) *hld up towards rr: hdwy 2f out: nt clr run over 1f out: swtchd wd outside and rdn: kpt on wl fnl f* **14/1**
4-50 **8** nk **Curtail (IRE)**[70] 656 4-8-13 85 .... TomEaves 14 85+
(I Semple) *trckd ldrs on stands' rail: effrt whn nt clr run over 1f out: kpt on ins fnl f* **15/2**
6350 **9** 2 **Pieter Brueghel (USA)**[4] 1754 8-8-10 82 .... JoeFanning 9 76
(D Nicholls) *cl up: led after 2f: rdn along 2f out: sn drvn and hdd wl over 1f out: wkng whn n.m.r ins fnl f* **11/1**

460- **10** ½ **Bajan Parkes**[315] 3296 4-8-10 82 .... DavidAllan 5 74
(E J Alston) *in midfield: rdn along over 2f out and sn btn* **25/1**

42-0 **11** 1½ **Stonecrabstomorrow (IRE)**[31] 1088 4-8-8 80 .... PaulHanagan 15 68
(R A Fahey) *a towards rr* **9/2**[1]

00-0 **12** 1¼ **Guest Connections**[28] 1157 4-8-10 82 .... SilvestreDeSousa 13 66
(D Nicholls) *a in rr* **25/1**

/006 **13** ¾ **Mafaheem**[8] 1630 5-8-3 80 .... WilliamBuick(5) 11 62
(S Dow) *a in rr* **18/1**

1m 11.08s (-1.42) **Going Correction** -0.225s/f (Firm) **13** Ran SP% **126.6**

Speed ratings (Par 107):100,99,99,99,98 98,98,97,95,94 92,90,89

CSF £49.66 CT £1138.59 TOTE £6.70: £1.90, £2.60, £11.40; EX 51.00.

Owner Grant Mercer **Bred** Mount Coote Stud **Trained** Maunby, N Yorks

■ Stewards' Enquiry : Paul Mulrennan two-day ban: used whip with excessive frequency (May 30-31)

FOCUS

A tight sprint for the class and the first eight were very closely bunched at the finish. The form is not totally straightforward with several in behind meeting trouble in running.

NOTEBOOK

My Gacho(IRE) dug deep under maximum pressure after hitting the front 1f out and eventually held off his pursuers in game fashion. This was an especially decent effort considering he was drawn on the outside and it was a much-deserved success for the consistent five-year-old. He has also been successful on both his outings at this track now.

Bahamian Pirate(USA) came through to have every chance and only just failed under top weight. He is clearly back in good heart again now. (op 11-2 tchd 9-2)

Lake Chini(IRE), very well backed when flopping over 5f at Southwell on his debut for connections last time and with the blinkers back on, showed that effort to be all wrong on this switch back to the turf with a solid effort in defeat. He looked to need all of this extra furlong and the sounder surface was evidently much more in his favour.

Steel Blue was ridden positively from his decent draw and was not beaten at all far. This was much more like his true form, the step back up to this extra furlong helped, and his turn does not appear to be too far off. (op 7-1)

High Curragh had nowhere to go inside the final furlong when still full of running and has to rate as unlucky. This was a much more encouraging effort and he does look best kept to this trip. (op 6-1 tchd 13-2)

Blue Tomato posted by far his best effort for some time and was another who was not beaten far. He is evidently creeping back into form and is now back on a more favourable mark. (op 12-1)

Danzig River(IRE) was another who met a little trouble when trying to make up his ground from off the pace and is a little better than the bare form. (op 16-1)

Curtail(IRE) showed improved form on this switch back to turf and looks to have benefited from his recent break. He would have been closer with a better run on the rail nearing the final furlong. (op 8-1 tchd 6-1 in a place)

Stonecrabstomorrow(IRE) met support in the betting ring yet he never looked like taking advantage of his high draw and proved disappointing. (op 7-1)

1853 GLISTEN H'CAP 5f

4:45 (4:46) (Class 2) (0-100,93) 4-Y-0+ **£11,658** (£3,468; £1,733; £865) **Stalls** High

Form RPR

1003 **1** **Magic Glade**[8] 1630 8-8-11 86 .... RichardThomas 8 93
(Tom Dascombe) *trckd ldrs: hdwy over 1f out: nt clr run ent fnl f: swtchd rt and rdn: qckndto ld nr fin* **9/1**

-103 **2** *shd* **Moorhouse Lad**[24] 1242 4-9-1 90 .... TomEaves 3 97
(B Smart) *cl up: rdn to ld over 1f out: drvn and edgd rt ins fnl f: hdd nr fin* **5/1**[3]

-305 **3** *shd* **Green Park (IRE)**[2] 1788 4-8-10 85 .... PaulHanagan 2 92
(R A Fahey) *in tch: hdwy wl over 1f out: sn rdn and styd on wl fnl f* **11/4**[2]

-500 **4** *1* **The Lord**[9] 1601 7-9-3 92 .... MatthewHenry 6 95
(W G M Turner) *trckd ldrs on stands' rail: effrt over 1f out: rdn and kpt on same pce ins fnl f* **25/1**

2100 **5** ½ **Cape Royal**[2] 1788 7-8-13 93 ....(bt) KevinGhunowa(5) 4 97+
(J M Bradley) *prom: rdn to chal wl over 1f out and ev ch tl drvn and wknd ins fnl f* **16/1**

-410 **6** 1½ **Harry Up**[105] 344 6-9-0 89 .... NCallan 7 85
(K A Ryan) *led: rdn along and hdd over 1f out: wkng whn hmpd and eased ins fnl f* **16/1**

2201 **7** ¾ **Dig Deep (IRE)**[19] 1363 5-8-13 88 .... PaulMulrennan 1 81
(W J Haggas) *wnt lft s: hld up in rr: effrt 2f out: sn rdn and nvr a factor* **2/1**[1]

02-0 **8** ¾ **Grazeon Gold Blend**[31] 1088 4-8-11 86 .... GrahamGibbons 9 76
(J J Quinn) *sn rdn along and a in rr* **16/1**

0-01 **9** *6* **Oranmore Castle (IRE)**[14] 1483 5-8-5 80 .... AdrianTNicholls 5 49
(D Nicholls) *prom: rdn along 2f out: sn wknd* **8/1**

57.99 secs (-1.91) **Going Correction** -0.225s/f (Firm) **9** Ran SP% **119.3**

Speed ratings (Par 109):106,105,105,104,103 100,99,98,88

CSF £55.32 CT £160.79 TOTE £11.10: £2.90, £1.90, £1.10; EX 45.40.

Owner Alan Solomon **Bred** Juddmonte Farms **Trained** Lambourn, Berks

■ Stewards' Enquiry : Tom Eaves one-day ban: careless riding (May 30th)

FOCUS

A decent little sprint in which the first three came clear in a blanket finish. The form appears solid enough with all three close to their marks.

NOTEBOOK

Magic Glade showed a neat turn of foot when switched to make his challenge and eventually just got up where it mattered. His rider deserves the plaudits and this was the eight-year-old's highest winning mark to date. (op 8-1)

Moorhouse Lad had every chance under a positive ride and was only mugged by the winner at the line. He ran very close to his recent level and deserves to find another race after this. (op 9-2)

Green Park(IRE), fifth in a hotter sprint at York two days previously, gave his all in defeat and did nothing wrong. His last success came on his only previous outing over course and distance last year and, while he not the easiest to place successfully, he left the impression here that he could get his head back in front when faced with a stiffer test once more. (op 7-2)

The Lord, back to his last winning mark again now, was not disgraced under top weight and this was his most encouraging effort for a while. (op 16-1)

Dig Deep(IRE), 5lb higher than when scoring at Wolverhampton in April, did not look happy on this different surface and was never really in the hunt. He seems a much happier horse on the All-Weather now. (op 5-2 tchd 11-4 in places)

Oranmore Castle(IRE) Official explanation: jockey said gelding hung right-handed in the last 3f.

1854 REAL GOOD FOOD H'CAP 5f

5:20 (5:21) (Class 4) (0-85,85) 4-Y-0+ **£5,181** (£1,541; £770; £384) **Stalls** High

Form RPR

-010 **1** **Colorus (IRE)**[11] 1565 4-8-5 72 .... DaleGibson 8 85+
(M W Easterby) *trckd ldng pair far side: smooth hdwy to ld that gp wl over 1f out: overall ldr ent fnl f: sn rdn and styd on strly* **33/1**

0-00 **2** 1¼ **Continent**[31] 1088 10-9-1 82 .... SilvestreDeSousa 16 90
(D Nicholls) *chsd ldrs stands' side: rdn wl over 1f out: kpt on wl towards fin* **25/1**

0-00 **3** *shd* **Cashel Mead**[8] 1630 7-8-11 83 .... TravisBlock(5) 5 91
(J L Spearing) *in tch far side: hdwy 2f out: sn rdn and styd on wl fnl f: 2nd in gp* **33/1**

1160 **4** ½ **Spanish Ace**[4] 1754 6-8-13 85 .... KevinGhunowa(5) 10 91
(J M Bradley) *cl up stands' side: rdn wl over 1f out and ev ch: drvn and one pce ins fnl f: 2nd in gp* **40/1**

6-23 **5** *nk* **Mimi Mouse**[16] 1427 5-8-9 76 .... DavidAllan 7 81
(T D Easterby) *cl up far side: led that gp 1/2-way: rdn and hdd wl over 1f out: kpt on same pce: 3rd in gp* **14/1**

5-00 **6** *hd* **Peopleton Brook**[8] 1630 5-8-1 75 .... BarrySavage(7) 9 79
(J M Bradley) *overall ldr stands' side: rdn along wl over 1f out: hdd ent fnl f and kpt on same pce: 3rd in gp* **33/1**

55-4 **7** *hd* **Holbeck Ghyll (IRE)**[14] 1464 5-8-5 77 .... WilliamBuick(5) 19 80
(A M Balding) *chsd ldrs stands' side: rdn along wl over 1f out: kpt on same pce: 4th in gp* **3/1**[1]

1-13 **8** *hd* **Aegean Dancer**[10] 1574 5-8-12 82 .... MarkLawson(3) 15 85
(B Smart) *a.p stands' side: rdn wl over 1f out and kpt on same pce: 5th in gp* **7/2**[2]

5040 **9** ½ **First Order**[31] 1088 6-9-4 85 ....(v) TomEaves 4 86
(I Semple) *in tch far side: rdn and hdwy wl over 1f out: kpt on ins fnl f: 4th in gp* **16/1**

-121 **10** ½ **Hypnosis**[16] 1427 4-8-10 77 .... PatCosgrave 13 76
(D W Barker) *in tch stands' side: rdn along 2f out: drvn and no imp fnl f: 6th in gp* **7/1**[3]

01-3 **11** 1¾ **Tender Process (IRE)**[11] 1565 4-8-8 75 .... PaulHanagan 14 68
(E S McMahon) *towards rr stands' side: hdwy 2f out: sn rdn and no imp appr fnl f: 7th in gp* **8/1**

-404 **12** ½ **High Reach**[10] 1574 7-8-5 79 .... DeanHeslop(7) 17 70
(T D Barron) *chsd ldrs stands' side: rdn along 2f out: sn drvn and btn: 8th in gp* **14/1**

00-5 **13** *nk* **Glasshoughton**[10] 1574 4-8-10 77 .... PhillipMakin 20 67
(M Dods) *chsd ldrs stands' side: rdn along 2f out: sn wknd: 9th in gp* **11/1**

20-0 **14** *nk* **Westbrook Blue**[25] 1214 5-8-4 71 oh1 ....(tp) MatthewHenry 6 60
(W G M Turner) *in tch far side: rdn along over 2f out and sn outpcd: 5th in gp* **66/1**

2120 **15** *nk* **Almaty Express**[19] 1363 5-8-7 74 ....(b) JoeFanning 1 62
(J R Weymes) *led far side gp to 1/2-way: rdn along and wknd fnl 2f: 6th in gp* **40/1**

500- **16** ¾ **Matty Tun**[215] 6009 8-8-7 74 .... TedDurcan 18 59
(J Balding) *in midfield stands' side: rdn along 1/2-way: n.d* **40/1**

0-40 **17** *1* **River Thames**[14] 1465 4-8-8 75 .... NCallan 11 57
(K A Ryan) *a in rr stands' side* **10/1**

200- **18** *3* **Danjet (IRE)**[195] 6353 4-8-2 72 .... DuranFentiman(3) 2 43
(J M Bradley) *a towards rr far side: 7th in gp* **66/1**

1-00 **19** 1½ **Circuit Dancer (IRE)**[41] 957 7-9-2 83 .... AdrianTNicholls 12 48
(D Nicholls) *dwlt: a in rr stands' side* **33/1**

0-00 **20** *4* **Toy Top (USA)**[7] 1678 4-8-5 72 ....(b) PaulFessey 3 23
(M Dods) *a in rr far side* **66/1**

57.98 secs (-1.92) **Going Correction** -0.225s/f (Firm) **20** Ran SP% **134.9**

Speed ratings (Par 105):106,104,103,103,102 102,101,101,100,100 97,96,95,95,94 93,92,87,84,78

CSF £716.42 CT £24250.39 TOTE £62.20: £9.50, £6.40, £7.30, £6.60; EX 1496.10 Place 6 £143.56, Place 5 £47.04..

Owner Silvano Scanu **Bred** M Ervine **Trained** Sheriff Hutton, N Yorks

FOCUS

A typically open sprint for the class in which the field split into two groups. There did not seem to be much advantage on either side and the level is set by the fourth.

Colorus(IRE) Official explanation: trainer had no explanation for the improved form shown

River Thames Official explanation: jockey said colt suffered interference at the start.

Circuit Dancer(IRE) Official explanation: jockey said gelding hung left-handed throughout.

Toy Top(USA) Official explanation: jockey said filly moved poorly throughout.

T/Plt: £207.90 to a £1 stake. Pool: £63,396.55. 222.55 winning tickets. T/Qpdt: £11.00 to a £1 stake. Pool: £3,188.90. 214.20 winning tickets. JR

1800 BADEN-BADEN (L-H)

Saturday, May 19

OFFICIAL GOING: Good

1855a FESTA-RENNEN (LISTED) (FILLIES) 1m 1f

4:35 (4:36) 3-Y-0 **£10,135** (£4,054; £1,689; £1,014)

RPR

1 **Naomia (GER)**[40] 3-9-0 .... TMundry 9 90
(P Rau, Germany) **53/10**

2 *hd* **Laeya Star (GER)**[20] 1338 3-9-0 .... AStarke 6 89
(U Ostmann, Germany) **12/1**

3 1¾ **Majounes Song**[23] 1257 3-9-0 .... J-PGuillambert 5 86
(M Johnston) *racd keenly: wnt up to dispute 2nd after 2f: 2nd st: kpt on same pce fr over 1f out: jst hld 3rd* **29/10**[2]

4 *shd* **Red Diva**[34] 3-9-0 .... ASuborics 1 86
(Mario Hofer, Germany) **6/4**[1]

5 *1* **Waky Love (GER)** 3-9-0 .... ASchikora 8 84
(Frau J Meyer, Germany) **23/2**

6 *3* **Boccassini (GER)**[38] 1006 3-9-4 .... ADeVries 4 82
(M Rulec, Germany) **74/10**

7 1¼ **La Blue Hill** 3-9-0 .... AHelfenbein 3 76
(H Steinmetz, Germany) **9/2**[3]

8 *nk* **Sweet Montana (GER)** 3-9-0 .... GHind 7 75
(A Kleinkorres, Germany) **29/1**

1m 55.43s (2.76) **8** Ran SP% **130.6**

(including ten euro stakes): WIN 63; PL 23, 32, 20; SF 866.

Owner Gestut Rottgen **Bred** Gestut Rottgen **Trained** Germany

NOTEBOOK

Majounes Song was no match for the front-running winner in the straight but kept on just well enough to achieve her other aim, the earning of black type. She will stay further.

1856 - (Foreign Racing) - See Raceform Interactive

1298 RIPON (R-H)

Sunday, May 20

OFFICIAL GOING: Good (7.8)
Wind: Virtually nil

1857 SKYBET.COM WOODEN SPOON CHARITY (S) STKS — 6f

2:10 (2:11) (Class 6) 2-Y-O — **£2,590** (£770; £385; £192) **Stalls** Low

Form				RPR
443	**1**		**Amazing Day**[6] [1728] 2-8-7 .... JackDean(7) 3 (W G M Turner) *chsd ldrs: hdwy on outer 2f out: rdn to ld ins fnl f: kpt on wl* **20/1**	63
3352	**2**	*shd*	**Rio Taffeta**[6] [1728] 2-9-0 .... JHBowman 5 (M R Channon) *led: rdn and hung bdly right ent fnl f: sn hdd: rallied and kpt on wl towards fin* **11/8**[1]	63
00	**3**	*6*	**Indecision**[6] [1713] 2-9-0 .... PaulMulrennan 4 (M W Easterby) *chsd ldrs: pushed along and wandered 1/2-way: hdwy over 1f out: styd on ent fnl f* **33/1**	45
15	**4**	*4*	**No Point (IRE)**[25] [1235] 2-9-0 .... J-PGuillambert 8 (P A Blockley) *chsd ldrs: rdn along over 2f out: drvn and wknd wl over 1f out* **33/1**	33
	5	*nk*	**Caught In Paradise (IRE)** 2-9-0 .... AdrianTNicholls 1 (D Nicholls) *s.i.s and bhd tl styd on fnl 2f* **11/1**	32
03	**6**	*1 1/2*	**O'Casey (IRE)**[25] [1235] 2-9-0 .... NCallan 10 (J G M O'Shea) *cl up: rdn and ev ch 2f out: sn drvn and wknd* **11/1**	28
6	**7**	*9*	**Featherstone**[8] [1674] 2-9-0 .... KimTinkler 9 (N Tinkler) *prom: rdn along after 2f: wknd fr 1/2-way* **28/1**	—
01	**8**	*10*	**Splitthedifference**[29] [1156] 2-9-5 .... DanielTudhope 7 (D Carroll) *v.s.a: rdn along 1/2-way: no imp* **9/4**[2]	—
0	**9**	*5*	**Korcula**[47] [898] 2-9-0 .... PatCosgrave 6 (M J Wallace) *s.i.s: rdn along and sme hdwy 1/2-way: sn wknd* **7/1**[3]	—
	10	*nk*	**Welcome Inn** 2-8-9 .... (t) TomEaves 2 (M E Sowersby) *s.i.s: a outpcd and bhd* **66/1**	—

1m 15.86s (2.86) **Going Correction** +0.225s/f (Good) **10** Ran SP% **117.6**
Speed ratings (Par 91):89,88,80,75,75 73,61,47,41,40
CSF £46.93 TOTE £13.50: £3.00, £1.20, £4.30; EX 58.20 Trifecta £445.40 Part won. Pool £627.34 - 0.34 winning units..There was no bid for the winner. Rio Taffeta was claimed by Richard Teatum for £6,000.
Owner Hong Kong Breeders Club **Bred** Hong Kong Breeders Club **Trained** Sigwells, Somerset

FOCUS
A very weak juvenile seller best rated through the runner-up. They raced towards the near-side rail through the early stages, but the first two home made their challenges up the centre of the track. The winning time was 1.31 seconds slower than the first division of the two-year-old maiden, but only 0.38 seconds off the time recorded in the second division.

NOTEBOOK
Amazing Day benefited from the step up to 6f and just managed to reverse recent Wolverhampton form with Rio Taffeta to gain his first success at the fourth attempt. A penalty in this grade will make things tougher. (tchd 25-1)
Rio Taffeta could not confirm Wolverhampton form from six days earlier with Amazing Day over this longer trip and was below his best. He looks sure to win a similar race eventually, but he is clearly not one to be taking short prices about. (op 6-4 tchd 7-4, 15-8 in a place)
Indecision would have appreciated the drop into selling company, but he was still well held. (op 50-1)
No Point(IRE) is very moderate and is struggling under her penalty. (op 28-1)
Caught In Paradise(IRE), a 5,000gns first foal of a sister to 1m1f winner Beamish Prince, also a dual winner over hurdles, ran to a very moderate level of form on his racecourse debut, but is at least open to some improvement. (op 10-1 tchd 9-1)
O'Casey(IRE) Official explanation: jockey said colt hung right throughout
Featherstone Official explanation: jockey said gelding hung left throughout
Splitthedifference, claimed out of Mick Channon's yard after winning over 5f at Thirsk on his previous start, lost his race at the start on his debut for new connections, missing the break by around ten lengths. Official explanation: jockey said gelding missed the break (op 5-2)
Korcula Official explanation: jockey said gelding reared as the stalls opened
Welcome Inn Official explanation: jockey said filly missed the break

1858 DESTINY RACING CLUB MAIDEN STKS (DIV I) — 6f

2:40 (2:41) (Class 5) 2-Y-O — **£2,914** (£867; £433; £216) **Stalls** Low

Form				RPR
	1		**Bespoke Boy** 2-9-3 .... LeeEnstone 1 (P C Haslam) *mde virtually all: rdn wl over 1f out and styd on strly* **9/2**[2]	85
	2	*2*	**Nickel Silver** 2-9-3 .... RoystonFfrench 4 (B Smart) *trckd ldrs: hdwy to chse wnr over 2f out: rdn along wl over 1f out: no imp ins fnl f* **8/1**	79
	3	*3*	**Prunes** 2-8-12 .... SebSanders 2 (Sir Mark Prescott) *cl up: pushed along over 2f out: sn rdn and kpt on same pce* **7/2**[1]	65
3	**4**	*3*	**Demure Princess**[24] [1255] 2-8-5 .... JackDean(7) 6 (W G M Turner) *prom: rdn along wl over 2f out and sn one pce* **20/1**	56
634	**5**	*7*	**Varinia (IRE)**[27] [1193] 2-8-12 .... DeanMernagh 8 (M Brittain) *in rr tl sme late hdwy* **14/1**	35
04	**6**	*nk*	**Alfredtheordinary**[19] [1367] 2-9-3 .... JHBowman 7 (M R Channon) *a towards rr* **11/2**	39
	7	*1 1/2*	**Motherwell** 2-8-5 .... PatrickDonaghy(7) 11 (M Brittain) *dwlt: a in rr* **100/1**	30
	8	*1/2*	**Singer Of Songs (IRE)** 2-9-3 .... SimonWhitworth 10 (P A Blockley) *a in rr* **25/1**	33
	9	*1*	**Mafioso** 2-9-3 .... JoeFanning 12 (M Johnston) *wnt rt s: chsd ldrs: rdn along 1/2-way: sn lost pl and bhd* **9/2**[2]	30
	10	*1*	**Noplace For A Lady** 2-8-12 .... KimTinkler 3 (N Tinkler) *in rr: effrt and sme hdwy 1/2-way: sn rdn and wknd* **25/1**	22
	11	*5*	**Merchant Navy** 2-9-3 .... NCallan 9 (E A L Dunlop) *dwlt: sn chsng ldrs: rdn along 1/2-way: sn wknd* **5/1**[3]	12
	12	*13*	**Misk Hills** 2-9-3 .... MickyFenton 5 (P T Midgley) *sn outpcd and a bhd* **100/1**	—

1m 14.55s (1.55) **Going Correction** +0.225s/f (Good) **12** Ran SP% **122.8**
Speed ratings (Par 93):98,95,91,87,78 77,75,74,73,72 65,48
CSF £39.93 TOTE £7.00: £1.90, £2.40, £2.00; EX 61.20 Trifecta £397.90 Part won. Pool £560.49 - 0.94 winning units..
Owner Mrs Wendy Lucas **Bred** Mrs L J Mills **Trained** Middleham Moor, N Yorks

FOCUS
A reasonable maiden and the winning time was the quicker of the three 6f juvenile races; 0.93 seconds faster than the second division, and 1.31 seconds quicker than the previous seller. The form look strong for the track and likely to work out.

NOTEBOOK
Bespoke Boy ◆, a 45,000gns first foal of a 6f winner at three, justified strong market support with quite an impressive performance. He was allowed to stride on in the early stages, showing bags of natural speed, but he didn't help his chance by taking a keen grip, and a lesser horse would have weakened out of contention. He had these beat about two furlongs out, though, and sustained his challenge to the line to win in decisive fashion. He will need to learn to settle better if he is to make it at a higher level, but the raw ability is most certainly there and a drop back to 5f may suit. He is one to keep on side and could be Royal Ascot material; he certainly deserves his chance in better company. (op 8-1 tchd 10-1 in a place)
Nickel Silver, out of a dual 6f winner at two, chased the winner to the line but was always being held. He might just have bumped into an above-average type and, with the benefit of this outing, he should be capable of finding a similar race. (op 9-1)
Prunes, out of a dual 5f-6f winner at two, hails from a stable whose first two juvenile runners were winners. She showed some early speed, but finished up well held and can be expected to improve for the outing. (op 9-2 tchd 5-1)
Demure Princess, who caught the eye when running on into third in a claimer at Beverley on her debut, would have found this tougher but ran with credit. (op 16-1)
Varinia(IRE) never posed a threat and was below form. (op 11-1)
Alfredtheordinary could not build on his recent fourth at Bath. (op 5-1)
Mafioso, a half-brother to quite useful dual 1m2f winner La Mouline, was very green indeed and appears to need more time. The Johnston two-year-olds are proving hard to predict this season. (op 4-1)
Merchant Navy, a 60,000gns first foal of a 1m winner, was well beaten and is another who may need a little bit more time. (op 9-2 tchd 4-1)

1859 DESTINY RACING CLUB MAIDEN STKS (DIV II) — 6f

3:10 (3:10) (Class 5) 2-Y-O — **£2,914** (£867; £433; £216) **Stalls** Low

Form				RPR
	1		**Rubirosa (IRE)** 2-9-3 .... PhillipMakin 7 (M Dods) *midfield: hdwy over 2f out: swtchd rt and rdn to ld appr fnl f: styd on wl* **5/1**[2]	77
	2	*3*	**Montiboli (IRE)** 2-8-12 .... NCallan 11 (K A Ryan) *in tch: hdwy on outer to chse ldrs over 2f out: sn rdn and kpt on wl fnl f* **7/1**	63
5	**3**	*shd*	**Gulf Coast**[15] [1478] 2-9-3 .... JoeFanning 2 (M Johnston) *led: rdn along over 2f out: drvn and hdd appr fnl f: kpt on same pce* **5/2**[1]	68
	4	*hd*	**Apollo Shark (IRE)** 2-9-3 .... TomEaves 5 (J Howard Johnson) *cl up: effrt 2f out: sn rdn and ev ch tl drvn and no ex ins fnl f* **6/1**[3]	67
	5	*1 1/2*	**Prince's Decree** 2-9-3 .... DanielTudhope 3 (G M Moore) *trckd ldrs: hdwy 2f out: swtchd rt and rdn over 1f out: kpt on same pce* **16/1**	63
	6	*6*	**Rich James (IRE)** 2-9-3 .... PatCosgrave 4 (J D Bethell) *cl up: rdn along 2f out: sn wknd* **9/1**	45
	7	*1 1/2*	**Lady Grantley** 2-8-12 .... PaulMulrennan 8 (M W Easterby) *dwlt and a towards rr* **20/1**	35
	8	*nk*	**Bollin Guil** 2-9-3 .... DavidAllan 6 (T D Easterby) *sn pushed along: a in rr* **10/1**	39
5	**9**	*2 1/2*	**Sandies Choice**[13] [1528] 2-8-12 .... DeanMernagh 9 (M Brittain) *chsd ldrs: rdn along over 2f out: sn wknd* **14/1**	27
	10	*5*	**Carlton Mac** 2-8-10 .... SuzzanneFrance(7) 1 (N Bycroft) *sn outpcd and a bhd* **33/1**	17
0	**11**	*1/2*	**Lucky Stream**[13] [1528] 2-8-5 .... PatrickDonaghy(7) 10 (M Brittain) *a in rr* **50/1**	10
	R		**Toto Skyllachy** 2-9-3 .... MickyFenton 12 (T P Tate) *ref to r* **10/1**	—

1m 15.48s (2.48) **Going Correction** +0.225s/f (Good) **12** Ran SP% **122.4**
Speed ratings (Par 93):92,88,87,87,85 77,75,75,71,65 64,—
CSF £40.69 TOTE £6.00: £2.10, £2.70, £1.70; EX 49.70 Trifecta £211.00 Pool £555.86 - 1.87 winning units..
Owner Pedro Rosas **Bred** Bendis Partnership **Trained** Denton, Co Durham

FOCUS
This looked a fair maiden, although the time was 0.93 seconds slower than the first division, and only 0.38 seconds faster than the juvenile seller. The form is not easy to rate but should be this good.

NOTEBOOK
Rubirosa(IRE), 19,500gns half-brother to Golden Jess, who was placed over 5f at two, out of a 7f winner in Germany, made a winning debut in pretty good style. He was given a patient ride, but always looked to be going quite well, and he sprinted clear when a gap came around a furlong out. The winning time was slower than the first division, but he looks a fair prospect.
Montiboli(IRE), a 28,000gns half-sister to Shaydreambeliever, a dual 7f-1m winner at two, also successful over hurdles, was easy to back but she found only one too good. She would have given the winner more to think about had she not been inclined to edge to her right and she looks capable of winning a similar event provided she goes the right way from this. (op 4-1 tchd 15-2)
Gulf Coast, well beaten in a good race over 5f on his debut at Thirsk, produced an improved effort over this longer trip, but he still finished up well held. He already looks in need of another step up in trip. (op 7-2)
Apollo Shark(IRE), a 52,000gns half-brother to among others smart Lykios, a triple sprint winner at two in France, showed some early speed but was never a serious threat. (op 8-1 tchd 9-1 in a place)
Prince's Decree, a 7,500gns half-brother to quite useful Sheer Face, a multiple 7f-1m2f winner, out of a middle-distance winner, could not pick up after tracking the pace early on. He can be expected to be sharper next time. (op 22-1)

1860 RIPON, YORKSHIRE'S GARDEN RACECOURSE H'CAP — 1m

3:40 (3:40) (Class 2) (0-100,100) 4-Y-O+ **£10,094** (£3,020; £1,510; £755; £376) **Stalls** High

Form				RPR
-106	**1**		**European Dream (IRE)**[11] [1583] 4-8-5 **87** .... (p) JoeFanning 2 (R C Guest) *hld up in rr: swtchd outside and gd hdwy over 2f out: cl up on bit over 1f out: shkn up and qcknd to ld ent fnl f: cleverly* **16/1**	97+
0501	**2**	*1 1/4*	**My Paris**[15] [1480] 6-8-12 **94** .... NCallan 1 (K A Ryan) *cl up on outer: hdwy to ld over 3f out: rdn 2f out: drvn and hdd ent fnl f: kpt on u.p* **7/2**[2]	101
0-03	**3**	*2 1/2*	**Granston (IRE)**[13] [1524] 6-8-6 **88** .... TedDurcan 4 (J D Bethell) *in tch: hdwy 4f out: rdn to chse ldrs 2f out: sn drvn and one pce appr fnl f* **4/1**[3]	90
-400	**4**	*nk*	**Prince Samos (IRE)**[11] [1583] 5-8-4 **86** oh2 .... (v[1]) AdrianTNicholls 5 (D Nicholls) *dwlt: hld up in rr: hdwy on inner whn nt clr run 2f out: sn swtchd lft and rdn: kpt on ins fnl f* **33/1**	90+
22-2	**5**	*2 1/2*	**Rio Riva**[50] [848] 5-9-4 **100** .... TomEaves 8 (Miss J A Camacho) *trckd ldrs: hdwy 4f out: rdn to chse ldrs whn n.m.r over 2f out: sn drvn and btn* **6/5**[1]	95
030-	**6**	*1 1/2*	**St Andrews (IRE)**[218] [5968] 7-8-11 **100** .... MartinGuest(7) 7 (M A Jarvis) *hld up in tch: effrt on outer 3f out: rdn along 2f out and sn btn* **20/1**	92

5300 7 1 3/4 **Mezuzah**[2] 1826 7-8-5 87 PaulMulrennan 6 75
(M W Easterby) *led: pushed along and hdd over 3f out: rdn wl over 2f out and sn wknd* **16/1**

0-00 8 46 **Rocamadour**[14] 1494 5-8-10 92 ow2 JHBowman 3 —
(M R Channon) *prom: rdn along 4f out and sn wknd* **12/1**

1m 39.99s (-1.11) **Going Correction** +0.10s/f (Good) **8** Ran SP% **114.8**
Speed ratings (Par 109):109,107,105,104,102 100,99,53
CSF £71.71 CT £273.84 TOTE £16.70: £3.50, £1.30, £1.50; EX 46.00 Trifecta £186.90 Pool £840.11 - 3.19 winning units..
Owner You Trotters **Bred** Limetree Stud Ltd **Trained** Brancepeth, Co Durham

FOCUS
A decent race for the track and this looks like strong handicap form rated around the runner-up and fourth.

NOTEBOOK
European Dream(IRE), with the cheekpieces re-fitted, benefited from both the drop back in trip and return to easier ground and returned to the sort of form he showed when winning the Spring Mile earlier in the season.
My Paris was only raised 3lb for his win in the Thirsk Hunt Cup, but he found European Dream too strong late on. He should continue to run well in decent handicap company in the coming months. (op 100-30 tchd 4-1 in places)
Granston(IRE), returned to turf, was produced with every chance and appeared to run his race. (op 9-2 tchd 5-1)
Prince Samos(IRE), 2lb out of the handicap, improved on his two most recent efforts in a first-time visor.
Rio Riva was a little short of room when initially looking to produce a challenge, but he was basically well below the form he showed when second in the Lincoln on his previous start. Official explanation: trainer had no explanation for the poor form shown (op 11-8)

1861 C. B. HUTCHINSON MEMORIAL CHALLENGE CUP (FILLIES' H'CAP) 6f
4:10 (4:11) (Class 3) (0-95,88) 3-Y-0+
£9,348 (£2,799; £1,399; £700; £349; £175) **Stalls** Low

Form RPR

6000 1 **Angus Newz**[8] 1670 4-9-11 88 (v) FrancisNorton 1 98
(M Quinn) *mde all: rdn wl over 1f out: styd on strly* **4/1**[2]

00-0 2 1 **Gallery Girl (IRE)**[32] 1088 4-9-3 80 DavidAllan 6 87
(T D Easterby) *trckd ldrs: hdwy to chse wnr wl over 1f out and sn rdn: drvn and edgd lft and rt ins fnl f: kpt on same pce* **9/2**[3]

1210 3 1 1/4 **Hypnosis**[1] 1854 4-9-0 77 PatCosgrave 3 80
(D W Barker) *hld up: hdwy 2f out: rdn and n.m.r ins fnl f: swtchd rt and kpt on* **9/2**[3]

30-0 4 1/2 **Give Me The Night (IRE)**[38] 1013 4-9-3 80 RoystonFfrench 5 82
(B Smart) *sn chsd along in rr: hdwy on outer 2f out: sn rdn and kpt on same pce appr fnl f* **12/1**

04-0 5 1 1/2 **Mango Music**[19] 1372 4-9-9 86 JHBowman 4 83
(M R Channon) *cl up: rdn and ev ch 2f out: drvn and wknd over 1f out* **5/1**

011- 6 nk **Amy Louise (IRE)**[204] 6211 4-9-1 78 NCallan 2 74
(T D Barron) *trckd ldrs: effrt over 2f out: sn rdn and btn wl over 1f out* **7/2**[1]

4-00 7 2 1/2 **Golden Asha**[8] 1670 5-9-6 83 SebSanders 7 72
(G G Margarson) *sn pushed along in rr: rdn 1/2-way and nvr a factor* **8/1**

1m 13.26s (0.26) **Going Correction** +0.225s/f (Good) **7** Ran SP% **114.1**
Speed ratings (Par 104):107,105,104,103,101 100,97
CSF £22.08 TOTE £5.20: £2.40, £3.30; EX 28.90.
Owner J G Dooley **Bred** Henry And Mrs Rosemary Moszkowicz **Trained** Newmarket, Suffolk

FOCUS
A good fillies' handicap run at decent pace and rated through the winner back to last year's form.

NOTEBOOK
Angus Newz had contested Listed/Group 3 races on her last four starts, so this represented a drop in class and she took advantage. She was well drawn against the near-side rail and, allowed the run of the race, she ran on strongly to the line. (op 9-2)
Gallery Girl(IRE) ◆, upped a furlong in trip, improved significantly on the form she showed on her reappearance at Beverley. She looks capable of winning off this sort of mark. (op 5-1 tchd 11-2)
Hypnosis, seemingly ridden to get the trip, might have finished a little closer had she not been short of room inside the final furlong. (tchd 4-1)
Give Me The Night(IRE) stepped up on the form she showed on her reappearance at Leicester. (op 16-1)
Mango Music looks high enough in the weights. (op 4-1 tchd 11-2)
Amy Louise(IRE), returning from a 204-day break, did not pick up as one might have expected and was a touch disappointing. A return to 7f may suit. (op 4-1)

1862 MIDDLEHAM TRAINERS ASSOCIATION H'CAP 1m 1f 170y
4:40 (4:40) (Class 4) (0-85,84) 4-Y-0+ **£5,678** (£1,699; £849; £424; £211) **Stalls** High

Form RPR

0-00 1 **My Arch**[9] 1621 5-9-1 81 (b[1]) NCallan 13 89
(K A Ryan) *led 2f: cl up tl led again 2f out: sn rdn: drvn and hung rt ins fnl f: kpt on* **13/2**[2]

-300 2 hd **Fortunate Isle (USA)**[14] 1494 5-9-2 82 TonyHamilton 11 90
(R A Fahey) *trckd ldrs: hdwy on inner 3f out: cl up 2f out: shkn up and ev ch over 1f out: rdn and bmpd ins fnl f: styd on* **2/1**[1]

0-00 3 3/4 **Nanton (USA)**[29] 1145 5-9-3 83 DanielTudhope 12 91+
(N Wilson) *in tch: hdwy 3f out: rdn over 1f out: styng on and ev ch whn hmpd ins fnl f: kpt on* **12/1**

-000 4 2 1/2 **Ahlawy (IRE)**[22] 1288 4-8-6 72 PaulMulrennan 5 73+
(M W Easterby) *hld up in rr: hdwy on inner over 2f out: sn rdn and kpt on: nrst fin* **33/1**

2-66 5 2 1/2 **Kildare Sun (IRE)**[22] 1288 5-8-12 78 DaleGibson 6 74
(J Mackie) *chsd ldrs: rdn along over 2f out: sn one pce* **10/1**

0-00 6 1 3/4 **Krugerrand (USA)**[20] 1356 8-9-4 84 BrettDoyle 1 77+
(W J Musson) *s.i.s and sn pushed along: hdwy and in tch 1/2-way: rdn wl over 2f out and kpt on same pce* **9/1**

3000 7 1/2 **Lucayan Dancer**[11] 1583 7-9-3 83 AdrianTNicholls 10 75
(D Nicholls) *dwlt: in rr tl hdwy wl over 2f out: sn rdn and no imp* **10/1**

0/00 8 4 **Prize Fighter (IRE)**[20] 1356 5-8-11 77 TedDurcan 7 61
(H R A Cecil) *midfield: hdwy on outer 3f out: rdn over 2f out and sn btn* **10/1**

56-6 9 6 **Thumpers Dream**[10] 1599 4-9-0 80 RoystonFfrench 9 52
(I W McInnes) *hld up: hdwy on outer wl over 2f out: sn rdn and btn* **14/1**

-135 10 3/4 **Call My Bluff (FR)**[24] 1264 4-8-6 72 ChrisCatlin 4 42
(Rae Guest) *a in rr* **16/1**

06-0 11 1 1/2 **Wovoka (IRE)**[25] 1245 4-9-2 82 JHBowman 3 49
(M R Channon) *led after 2f: rdn along over 3f out: hdd wl over 2f out: grad wknd* **15/2**[3]

600- 12 10 **Kingdom Of Dreams (IRE)**[34] 4047 5-8-11 77 TomEaves 8 24
(J Mackie) *midfield: rdn along over 4f out: sn lost pl and bhd* **50/1**

400- 13 7 **The Thrifty Bear**[224] 5839 4-8-1 70 oh25 AndrewElliott[(3)] 2 3
(C W Fairhurst) *chsd ldrs: rdn along 4f out: sn wknd* **100/1**

2m 4.87s (-0.13) **Going Correction** +0.10s/f (Good) **13** Ran SP% **121.8**
Speed ratings (Par 105):104,103,103,101,99 97,97,94,89,88 87,79,74
CSF £20.02 CT £160.63 TOTE £9.30: £2.50, £1.80, £4.40; EX 21.60 Trifecta £297.00 Pool £560.54 - 1.34 winning units..
Owner J D Spensley & Mrs M A Spensley **Bred** J And A Spensley **Trained** Hambleton, N Yorks
■ Stewards' Enquiry : J H Bowman caution: eased gelding prematurely
N Callan two-day ban: careless riding (May 31, Jun 3)

FOCUS
A fair handicap run at a sound gallop and producing a close finish. The form makes sense rated around the placed horses.

1863 RIPON-RACES.CO.UK MAIDEN STKS 1m 1f
5:10 (5:12) (Class 5) 3-Y-0 **£3,562** (£1,059; £529; £264) **Stalls** High

Form RPR

6-33 1 **Northern Jem**[27] 1204 3-9-3 85 SebSanders 14 84+
(G G Margarson) *midfield: hdwy 3f out: swtchd outside and rdn to ld over 1f out: edgd rt: rdn and hung bdly lft ins fnl f: sn clr* **6/4**[1]

0-3 2 2 1/2 **Ravarino (USA)**[22] 1312 3-8-12 JDSmith 13 74
(Sir Michael Stoute) *t.k.h: trckd ldrs: effrt over 2f out: swtchd lft over 1f out: kpt on nicely ins fnl f* **12/1**[3]

5 3 3/4 **Triple Beat**[31] 1100 3-9-3 RichardHughes 4 77
(H R A Cecil) *led: hdd 3f out: led again 2f out: sn rdn and hdd: drvn and one pce ent fnl f* **6/4**[1]

0- 4 hd **Hope Road**[222] 5883 3-9-3 JoeFanning 11 77
(J R Fanshawe) *trckd ldrs gng wl: smooth hdwy 3f out: ev ch 2f out: sn rdn and wknd ent fnl f* **13/2**[2]

4 5 2 1/2 **Intersky Charm (USA)**[18] 1412 3-9-3 DeanMcKeown 9 72
(R M Whitaker) *trckd ldrs: rdn along over 2f out and grad wknd* **33/1**

60 6 5 **A Little More (IRE)**[20] 1358 3-9-3 SimonWhitworth 12 61
(P A Blockley) *hld up: hdwy over 2f out: kpt on appr fnl f: nt rch ldrs* **100/1**

6- 7 3 1/2 **Topazleo (IRE)**[225] 5814 3-9-3 TomEaves 15 54+
(J Howard Johnson) *s.i.s and bhd: pushed along 3f out: swtchd outside 2f out and styd on appr fnl f* **20/1**

-00 8 1 **Motarjm (USA)**[28] 1177 3-9-3 NCallan 1 58+
(M A Jarvis) *cl up: led 3f out: rdn and hdd 2f out: sn wknd: eased fnl f* **25/1**

0 9 nk **Petite Arvine (USA)**[18] 1409 3-8-5 ChrisHough[(7)] 5 46+
(M L W Bell) *a in rr* **100/1**

0 10 1 1/4 **Mr Grand Lodge (FR)**[16] 1452 3-8-10 MJMurphy[(7)] 3 49
(L M Cumani) *midfield: rdn along 3f out: sn wknd* **50/1**

-434 11 3/4 **Snow Dancer (IRE)**[51] 836 3-8-10 63 ow3 PBradley[(5)] 7 45
(A Berry) *a in rr* **66/1**

046- 12 6 **Sonar Sound (GER)**[245] 5402 3-9-3 76 MickyFenton 6 34
(T P Tate) *chsd ldrs: rdn along over 3f out: sn wknd* **28/1**

13 28 **Miss Poland** 3-8-12 TedDurcan 2 —
(J G Given) *a in rr* **50/1**

1m 54.9s (1.05) **Going Correction** +0.10s/f (Good) **13** Ran SP% **123.4**
Speed ratings (Par 99):99,96,96,95,93 89,86,85,85,83 83,77,53
CSF £23.75 TOTE £2.60: £1.10, £3.10, £1.30; EX 31.50 Trifecta £56.00 Pool £443.52 - 5.62 winning units. Place 6 £55.20, Place 5 £24.45..
Owner Norcroft Park Stud **Bred** Norcroft Park Stud **Trained** Newmarket, Suffolk

FOCUS
A fair maiden for the track and more solid than most, although the winner did need to be at his best to score on the face of things.
Topazleo(IRE) Official explanation: jockey said gelding missing the break and was denied a clear run
Motarjm(USA) Official explanation: jockey said gelding had a breathing problem
T/Jkpt: Not won. T/Plt: £101.50 to a £1 stake. Pool: £72,226.80. 519.45 winning tickets. T/Qpdt: £20.00 to a £1 stake. Pool: £4,202.00. 154.90 winning tickets. JR

1871 - (Foreign Racing) - See Raceform Interactive

1855 BADEN-BADEN (L-H)
Sunday, May 20

OFFICIAL GOING: Soft

1872a GROSSER MERCEDES-BENZ-PREIS (GROUP 2) 1m 3f
4:05 (4:23) 4-Y-0+ **£37,162** (£13,514; £6,757; £3,378)

RPR

1 **Prince Flori (GER)**[28] 1190 4-9-4 ADeVries 3 122
(S Smrczek, Germany) *racd in 4th bhd slow pce: swtchd outside and effrt over 1 1/2f out: str run down outside rail to ld 100yds out: rdn out* **9/5**[1]

2 1/2 **Egerton (GER)**[21] 1340 6-9-1 TMundry 7 118
(P Rau, Germany) *racd in 3rd: brought to centre ent st: led 1 1/2f out: hdd 100yds out: no ex* **23/10**[2]

3 1 1/2 **Schiaparelli (GER)**[28] 1190 4-9-4 AStarke 8 119
(P Schiergen, Germany) *set slow pce: hdd 2f out: kpt on* **9/2**[3]

4 1/2 **Donaldson (GER)**[28] 1190 5-9-4 ASuborics 4 118
(P Rau, Germany) *racd in 2nd: led narrowly on ins 2f out to 1 1/2f out: one pce* **114/10**

5 1/2 **Mohandas (FR)**[182] 6529 6-8-11 (b) J-PCarvalho 1 110
(W Hefter, Germany) *hld up towards rr: nvr a factor* **113/10**

6 nk **Arcadio (GER)**[218] 5982 5-9-1 THellier 2 114
(J Hirschberger, Germany) *hld up in last bhd slow pce: nvr a factor* **46/10**

7 2 **Expensive Dream (GER)**[28] 1190 8-8-11 RJuracek 5 106
(P Vovcenko, Germany) *a towards rr* **29/1**

8 1 1/4 **Poseidon Adventure (IRE)**[378] 1522 4-8-11 BClos 6 104
(W Figge, Germany) *5th early: nvr a factor* **102/10**

2m 21.95s (2.68) **8** Ran SP% **130.5**
(including ten euro stakes): WIN 28; PL 14, 13, 17; SF 68.
Owner Stall Reni **Bred** H A Wacek **Trained** Germany

NOTEBOOK
Prince Flori(GER) was not best suited by the slow pace but quickened up well to he did very well to give weight and a beating to the battle-hardened Egerton. He has an ambitious programme mapped out for him, including the Grand Prix de Saint-Cloud and a possible crack at the King George but further progress is by no means out of the question.

1700 CAPANNELLE (R-H)

Sunday, May 20

OFFICIAL GOING: Good to firm

1873a PREMIO TULLIO RIGHETTI (LISTED RACE) 1m

2:55 (2:56) 3-Y-O £18,919 (£8,324; £4,541; £2,270)

RPR

1 **Champery (USA)**^{14} 1516 3-8-9 .... LDettori 3 106
(M Johnston) *mde all: pushed out: easily* **13/20**^{1}

2 4 **Baylani De S'Ena (IRE)** 3-8-9 .... SMulas 2 98
(B Grizzetti, Italy)

3 *nse* **Moriwood (ITY)**^{21} 1336 3-8-9 .... MDemuro 5 98
(A & G Botti, Italy)

4 *nse* **Ladak**^{21} 1336 3-8-9 .... DVargiu 1 98
(B Grizzetti, Italy)

5 *8* **Danao (USA)**^{21} 1336 3-8-9 ....(b) CFiocchi 7 82
(R Menichetti, Italy)

6 *8* **Golden Trophy (IRE)** 3-8-9 .... GMarcelli 6 66
(L Ficuciello, Italy)

7 *3* **King Etoil (ITY)**^{21} 1336 3-8-12 .... MarcoMonteriso 4 63
(S Saggiomo, Italy)

1m 37.8s (-2.00) 7 Ran SP% **60.6**
(including one euro stakes); WIN 1.65; PL 1.41, 3.06; DF 8.36.
Owner Sheikh Mohammed **Bred** Darley **Trained** Middleham Moor, N Yorks

NOTEBOOK
Champery(USA) was entitled to start odds-on after his close third in the German 2000 Guineas and won well. He looks capable of winning a Group 3 on the Continent, if not at home.

1874a PREMIO CARLO D'ALESSIO (GROUP 3) 1m 4f

3:25 (3:27) 4-Y-O+ £38,767 (£17,057; £9,304; £4,652)

RPR

1 **Exhibit One (USA)**^{28} 1192 5-8-6 .... DVargiu 7 108
(V Valiani, Italy) *a cl up: 4th st: hdwy over 2f out: styd on to ld 100yds out: rdn and r.o* **23/20**^{2}

2 *nk* **Vol De Nuit**^{21} 6-8-9 .... MDemuro 2 111
(L Brogi, Italy) *a cl up: tk narrow ld over 5f out: hrd rdn over 1f out: hdd 100yds out: r.o* **9/10**^{1}

3 *nk* **Jack Aubrey**^{85} 5-8-9 .... PConvertino 8 111
(F Folco, Italy) *clsoe 5th st: styd on u.p fnl 2f: nrest at fin* **49/1**

4 *2* **Place In Line**^{35} 5-8-9 .... GBietolini 1 108
(Gianluca Bietolini, Italy) *a cl up: 3rd st: kpt on one pce fnl 2f* **77/10**

5 *nk* **El Biba D'Or (IRE)**^{231} 5718 8-8-9 .... MEsposito 5 107
(P Giannotti, Italy) *led to over 5f out: pressed ldr to over 2f out: wknd over 1f out* **74/10**^{3}

6 *5* **Harar (GER)**^{182} 6529 5-8-9 .... EPedroza 6 100
(Andreas Lowe, Germany) *6th st: btn 2f out* **16/1**

7 *3/4* **Graft Versus Host (IRE)** 4-8-9 .... GMarcelli 4 98
(L Ficuciello, Italy) *last thrght* **74/1**

2m 30.9s (3.70) 7 Ran SP% **131.8**
WIN 2.15; PL 1.22, 1.22; DF 1.76.
Owner Scuderia Diamante **Bred** Juddmonte Farms Inc **Trained** Italy

1875a DERBY ITALIANO ANTONVENETA ABN AMRO (GROUP 1) (C&F) 1m 4f

4:35 (4:37) 3-Y-O £218,919 (£96,324; £52,541; £26,270)

RPR

1 **Awelmarduk (IRE)**^{19} 3-9-2 ....(b) EBotti 10 105
(A & G Botti, Italy) *hld up: 13th st: hdwy on outside over 2f out: hung rt appr fnl f: led ins fnl f: drvn out* **151/4**

2 *1/2* **Shrek (GER)**^{19} 1387 3-9-2 .... EPedroza 3 104
(A Wohler, Germany) *a.p: 5th st: 3rd and rdn over 2f out: ev ch ins fnl f: r.o same pce* **21/10**^{1}

3 *nk* **Rob's Love (ITY)**^{21} 1335 3-9-2 .... CFiocchi 11 104
(R Menichetti, Italy) *a.p: 2nd st: drvn to ld appr fnl f: hdd 100yds out: one pce* **128/10**

4 *2* **Sopran Promo (IRE)**^{19} 3-9-2 .... DVargiu 4 101
(B Grizzetti, Italy) *9th st: hdwy over 2f out: n.m.r appr fnl f: kpt on same pce* **17/2**

5 *1* **Il Cadetto**^{210} 6123 3-9-2 .... GMarcelli 9 100
(L Di Dio, Italy) *6th st: styng on one pce whn squeezed up over 1f out: nvr nr to chal* **72/10**

6 *1 1/2* **Elleno (IRE)** 3-9-2 ....(b) PConvertino 1 97
(F & L Camici, Italy) *12th st: hdwy over 2f out: outpcd wl over 1f out: kpt on fnl f: nvr nrr* **104/1**

7 *1/2* **Lucky Choice (ITY)**^{210} 6123 3-9-2 .... OFancera 8 97
(A Candi, Italy) *10th st: hdwy over 3f out: kpt on one pce fnl 2f* **112/1**

8 *3/4* **Furia Ceca**^{21} 1335 3-9-2 ....(b) MPasquale 6 95
(L Brogi, Italy) *8th st: nvr a factor* **73/1**

9 *hd* **Fighting Johan (GER)**^{19} 3-9-2 ....(b) GBietolini 14 95
(H Blume, Germany) *3rd st: rdn and btn 2f out* **14/1**

10 *6* **Zar Solitario**^{21} 1335 3-9-2 .... LDettori 12 86
(M Johnston) *led to appr fnl f: wknd qckly* **21/10**^{1}

11 *1 1/2* **Depp (ITY)**^{217} 6003 3-9-2 .... MDemuro 5 84
(L D'Auria, Italy) *a bhd* **58/10**^{3}

12 *1 1/2* **Habalwatan (IRE)**^{9} 1617 3-9-2 ....(b) JohnEgan 7 82
(C E Brittain) *prom: 4th st: wknd over 2f out* **53/10**^{2}

13 *snk* **Sidereus (IRE)**^{29} 3-9-2 .... SLandi 2 81
(F & L Camici, Italy) *mid-div tl wknd over 2f out* **58/10**^{3}

14 *8* **Eternity Boy (IRE)** 3-9-2 .... CColombi 13 69
(G Colella, Italy) *6th st: wknd 3f out* **110/1**

2m 28.9s (1.70) 14 Ran SP% **153.1**
WIN 38.75; PL 6.25, 1.63, 3.01; DF 79.59.
Owner Scuderia Effevi **Bred** Effevi Snc **Trained** Italy

NOTEBOOK
Awelmarduk(IRE), a surprise winner, came with a strong run down the outside in the straight, squeezing up the fourth and fifth when hanging right, before getting up on the last 100 yards.
Zar Solitario stopped very quickly once headed and something may have been amiss. He had beaten Rob's Love by two lengths, with Furia Ceca fourth, here three weeks ago, and that form entitled him to be involved in the finish.
Habalwatan(IRE) was one of the first beaten and should have lasted a bit longer.

1876a PREMIO TUDINI (GROUP 3) 6f

5:10 (5:15) 3-Y-O+ £27,365 (£12,041; £6,568; £3,284)

RPR

1 **Per Incanto (USA)**^{42} 3-8-8 .... GBietolini 7 118
(R Brogi, Italy) *mde all on stands' side: narrow ldr tl rdn clr ins fnl f: drvn out* **87/100**^{1}

2 *2* **Sakhee's Song (IRE)**^{21} 1337 3-8-5 .... DVargiu 4 109
(B Grizzetti, Italy) *pressed wnr on stands' rail tl one pce ins fnl f* **69/10**^{3}

3 *4* **Ricine (IRE)**^{26} 1234 5-9-0 .... F-XBertras 9 99
(F Rohaut, France) *prom towards centre: rdn wl over 2f out: styd on at one pce* **17/2**

4 *1* **Dream Impact (USA)**^{19} 6-9-3 .... GMarcelli 11 99
(L Riccardi, Italy) *a.p in centre: kpt on at one pce fnl 2f* **69/10**^{3}

5 *hd* **Santiago Atitlan**^{28} 1189 5-9-3 .... EPedroza 10 98
(A Wohler, Germany) *hld up in centre: kpt on at same pce fnl 2f* **133/10**

6 *hd* **Lady Marmelade (ITY)**^{21} 1337 4-9-0 .... MEsposito 3 95
(D Ducci, Italy) *towards rr: kpt on fnl 2f* **26/1**

7 *2* **Krisman (IRE)**^{19} 8-9-3 .... SMulas 2 92
(M Ciciarelli, Italy) *nvr a factor* **29/1**

8 *1* **Thinking Robins (IRE)**^{196} 6363 4-9-3 .... GErcegovic 6 89
(P Martometti, Italy) *chsd ldrs to 1/2-way* **50/1**

9 *1/2* **Gesture**^{188} 5-9-3 .... GTemperini 12 87
(F Bruni, Germany) *hld up: racd wdst of all: nvr a factor* **64/1**

10 *2* **Hinton Admiral**^{18} 1394 3-8-8 .... LDettori 8 79
(M Johnston) *chsd ldrs: pushed along 1/2-way: rdn and btn 2f out: eased fnl f* **15/4**^{2}

11 *8* **Great Uncle Ted (USA)**^{196} 6363 4-9-3 ....(b) SLandi 1 57
(A Renzoni, Italy) *hld up: wknd over 2f out* **46/1**

12 *10* **Solzah (IRE)**^{21} 1337 4-9-0 .... MDemuro 5 24
(L Brogi, Italy) *chsd ldrs: rdn 1/2-way: wknd qckly over 2f out* **129/10**

68.60 secs (-1.70)
WFA 3 from 4yo+ 9lb 12 Ran SP% **137.2**
WIN 1.87; PL 1.25, 1.82, 2.13; DF 8.11.
Owner Scuderia Archi Romani **Bred** Scuderia Archi Romani **Trained** Italy

NOTEBOOK
Per Incanto(USA) had won two conditions events - his only races this year - by wide margins. He had a long fight with the lightly-raced second, who was racing alongside him on the rails, before establishing his superiority. He should continue to improve.
Hinton Admiral faced a tough task and was struggling to go the pace soon after half-way.

KRANJI (L-H)

Sunday, May 20

OFFICIAL GOING: Yielding

1877a SINGAPORE AIRLINES INTERNATIONAL CUP (GROUP 1) 1m 2f

1:35 (1:37) 3-Y-O+
£530,000 (£200,000; £100,000; £50,000; £15,000; £10,000)

RPR

1 **Shadow Gate (JPN)**^{49} 5-9-0 .... KatsuharuTanaka 10 121
(Y Kato, Japan) *a cl up on outside: led 2f out: drvn out: hld on wl* **6/1**

2 *1 1/4* **Cosmo Bulk (JPN)**^{49} 6-9-0 .... FIgarashi 9 119
(K Tabe, Japan) *pressed ldr on outside: disp ld 3f out to 2f out: styd on gamely u.p once hdd* **9/4**^{1}

3 *shd* **Doctor Dino (FR)**^{21} 1340 5-9-0 .... JMurtagh 11 119
(R Gibson, France) *racd in 7th: 5th st: styd on u.p fnl 2f* **9/2**^{3}

4 *3/4* **Setembro Chove (BRZ)**^{14} 6-9-0 .... RFradd 7 117
(P Shaw, Singapore) *hld up towards rr: hdwy over 2f out: 6th st: kpt on wl fnl f: nrest at fin* **33/1**

5 *1 3/4* **Kandidate**^{23} 1274 5-9-0 .... EddieAhern 1 114
(C E Brittain) *trckd ldr in 4th or 5th on ins: disp ld briefly jst over 2f out: sn rdn: lost 2nd and wknd 120yds out* **10/1**

6 *2 3/4* **Oracle West (SAF)**^{21} 6-9-0 .... WCMarwing 5 109
(M F De Kock, South Africa) *pressed ldr: disp ld 3f out to 2f out: stl ev ch on ins 1f out: wknd* **5/2**^{2}

7 *2 1/2* **Royal Admiral (NZ)**^{35} 5-9-0 ....(b) NCallow 13 105
(L Laxon, Singapore) *racd in 8th: 7th st: a midfield* **20/1**

8 *nk* **Big Easy (NZ)**^{14} 6-9-0 .... DBeadman 12 104
(L Laxon, Singapore) *hld up in 12th: nvr a factor* **100/1**

9 *1 1/4* **King And King (AUS)**^{35} 6-9-0 .... GBoss 6 102
(S Burridge, Singapore) *hld up in last: 10th st: nvr a factor* **25/1**

10 *5* **War Horn (ARG)**^{14} 5-9-0 .... BVorster 8 93
(P Shaw, Singapore) *hld up: 11th st: nvr a factor* **50/1**

11 *nk* **Dezigna (NZ)**^{36} 7-9-0 .... VColgan 2 93
(Wayne & Vanessa Hillis, New Zealand) *in rr: pushed along and outpcd over 3f out: n.d after* **33/1**

12 *9* **Crusoe (NZ)**^{35} 5-9-0 .... ACalder 3 76
(L Laxon, Singapore) *led narrowly to 3f out: wknd over 2f out* **33/1**

13 *3 1/4* **Ruwi**^{23} 5-9-0 .... KBSoo 4 70
(D Koh, Singapore) *midfield: 8th st: wknd qckly* **40/1**

2m 4.01s (124.01) 13 Ran SP% **123.7**
(including $SIN 5 stakes): WIN 19.00; PL 9.00, 17.00, 11.00; DF 60.00.
Owner T Iizuka **Bred** Shadai Farm **Trained** Japan

NOTEBOOK
Shadow Gate(JPN), settled but racing wide rather than setting the pace on this occasion, scored in good style from his compatriot to complete another international-race one-two for Japan. The son of White Muzzle is likely to return to defend the title next year.
Cosmo Bulk(JPN), who took this race in 2006, was very much in the shadow of Deep Impact last year and has now come across another better compatriot. He is a genuine and consistent sort and should contine to feature in similar events.
Doctor Dino(FR), a French challenger, ran a fine race and was just touched of for the runner-up spot. His target later in the year will be the Canadian International at Woodbine.
Kandidate had a good pitch on the rail and got to the front nearing the quarter-mile pole. However, as soon as he hit the front he was taken on by the eventual winner and, after putting up a fight, paid for his exertions in the final half-furlong. this weas a decent effort but he would have preferred faster turf or an artificial surface.

1702 LONGCHAMP (R-H)

Sunday, May 20

OFFICIAL GOING: Very soft

1879a PRIX D'ISPAHAN (GROUP 1) 1m 1f 55y

2:50 (2:55) 4-Y-O+ **£96,520** (£38,615; £19,307; £9,645; £4,831)

RPR

1 **Manduro (GER)**[31] 1104 5-9-2 SPasquier 4 128+
(A Fabre, France) *racd in 3rd: pushed along to ld 1 1/2f out: 3 l clr ent fnl f: easily* **8/13**[1]

2 5 **Turtle Bowl (IRE)**[19] 1389 5-9-2 OPeslier 3 117
(F Rohaut, France) *racd in 4th: drvn to chse ldr 2f out: wnt 2nd 1 1/2f out: no ch w wnr* **9/2**[3]

3 5 **Stormy River (FR)**[50] 862 4-9-2 TThulliez 5 107
(N Clement, France) *hld up in last: pushed along 1 1/2f out to chse ldrs: wnt 3rd 1f out: nvr in chalng position* **11/4**[2]

4 3 **Willywell (FR)**[24] 1273 5-9-2 CSoumillon 1 101
(J-P Gauvin, France) *racd in 2nd: outpcd and lost pl 1 1/2f out* **20/1**

5 4 **Palafamix (FR)**[55] 4-9-2 J-MBreux 2 93
(N Clement, France) *led to 1 1/2f out: drvn and styd on at one pce u.p tl eased fnl 100yds* **100/1**

1m 58.0s (2.20) **Going Correction** +0.625s/f (Yiel) **5** Ran SP% **112.5**
Speed ratings: 115,110,106,103,99
PARI-MUTUEL: WIN 1.90; PL 1.10, 1.40; SF 3.20.
Owner Baron G Von Ullmann **Bred** Rolf Brunner **Trained** Chantilly, France

FOCUS
Easy for Manduro. Turtle Bowl was below par in this race last year and Stormy River is not at his best first time out, so the form has been rated through the third and fourth.

NOTEBOOK
Manduro(GER), a highly consistent gelding at the top level last season, was most impressive in the Earl Of Sefton on his reappearance at Newmarket and finally landed that first Group 1 success. Despite not having the ground in his favour, he readily came clear and merely had to be ridden out to score, confirming himself as one of the leading 1m-1m2f performers in Europe. The race for first place was over in a matter of strides and he streaked past the post on his own. This horse now looks at a peak and he goes to Royal Ascot either for the Queen Anne or the Prince of Wales Stakes. This was undoubtedly the most impressive performance put up in France so far this season and he goes to Ascot with a big chance.
Turtle Bowl(IRE) was given every possible chance, but he could not go with the winner when things quickened up half way up the straight. This five-year-old was beautifully positioned throughout and was not hard ridden once the writing was on the wall. The testing ground was not in his favour and the distance was further than his best, so it is no surprise that he will now be prepared for the Queen Anne Stakes at Ascot.
Stormy River(FR), a high-class three-year-old, did not look in great shape in the paddock and was a little disappointing in the race. He was dropped out last until the two furlong marker when he flattered briefly before staying on at the one pace. He was a well beaten third and the outing will have done him a lot of good. Connections now feel sure that 1m is his best distance and he is another for the Queen Anne Stakes at Royal Ascot. It was his first race since an unlucky run in the Dubai Duty Free at Nad al Sheba in March.
Willywell(FR) was out of his class. Just behind the pacemaker early on, he was under pressure early in the straight and stayed on one paced to the line. This improved five-year-old should be capable of taking a Group 3 event some time in the future.

1880a MONTJEU COOLMORE PRIX SAINT-ALARY (GROUP 1) (FILLIES) 1m 2f

3:25 (3:28) 3-Y-O **£96,520** (£38,615; £19,307; £9,645; £4,831)

RPR

1 **Coquerelle (IRE)**[35] 3-9-0 C-PLemaire 1 113
(J-C Rouget, France) *mde all: drvn and r.o 1 1/2f out: kpt on wl to hold runner-up in fnl 100yds* **7/4**[1]

2 ½ **Believe Me (IRE)**[21] 3-9-0 OPeslier 7 112
(J-M Beguigne, France) *hld up in last: 5th st: pushed along and r.o down outside 1 1/2f out: wnt 2nd 1 1/2f out: rdn 1f out: styd on: nrest at fin* **9/2**[2]

3 5 **Anabaa's Creation (IRE)**[35] 1055 3-9-0 CSoumillon 3 103
(A De Royer-Dupre, France) *disp 2nd early: 2nd 1/2-way: pushed along st: lost pl 1 1/2f out: kpt on at one pce u.p* **7/4**[1]

4 8 **Chinandega (FR)**[21] 1339 3-9-0 SPasquier 2 89
(P Demercastel, France) *disp 2nd early: 3rd 1/2-way: pushed along st: rdn 2f out: unable qck* **15/2**[3]

5 ½ **Topka (FR)**[41] 989 3-9-0 TJarnet 4 88
(F Doumen, France) *racd in 4th: pushed along 2f out: sn rdn: no imp* **14/1**

6 shd **America Nova (FR)**[21] 1338 3-9-0 TThulliez 5 88
(R Gibson, France) *hld up in 5th: last st: drvn 2f out: unable qck* **25/1**

2m 11.1s (3.10) **Going Correction** +0.625s/f (Yiel) **6** Ran SP% **113.2**
Speed ratings: 112,111,107,101,100 100
PARI-MUTUEL: WIN 2.60; PL 1.80, 2.70; SF 10.20.
Owner Ecurie Des Monceaux **Bred** Haras Du Mezeray **Trained** Pau, France

NOTEBOOK
Coquerelle(IRE), unbeaten in three starts coming into this, including latterly over course and distance, gained her first group success with a battling victory. Leading throughout, she was able to make all and gradually built up momentum in the straight from the two furlong marker. The filly acted pretty well on the very soft ground and she now heads for the Prix de Diane at Chantilly next month. There is plenty of stamina on the dam's side so the extra half furlong will not be a problem and, although this was not a vintage Group 1, she remains capable of further improvement.
Believe Me(IRE), who has had her share of problems this winter, gave a very fair performance and she can only improve for the race. Dropped out last during the early stages, she was at least five lengths behind the winner at the beginning of the straight, but ran on really well in the final stages. Her trainer is convinced there is room for considerable further improvement and she is another who will line up for the Diane.
Anabaa's Creation(IRE), who recorded a pleasing effort behind Darjina on her reappearance, was expected to relish this new distance, but looked paceless under pressure and was readily held back in third.
Chinandega(FR), a progressive filly at a slightly lower level, did not prove up to Group 1 company and needs her sights lowering.

1881a PRIX VICOMTESSE VIGIER (GROUP 2) 1m 7f 110y

3:55 (3:59) 4-Y-O+ **£50,068** (£19,324; £9,223; £6,149; £3,074)

RPR

1 **Lord Du Sud (FR)**[85] 6-9-0 C-PLemaire 2 118
(J-C Rouget, France) *mde all: pushed along and r.o 2f out: drvn out* **7/2**[3]

2 2½ **Ponte Tresa (FR)**[21] 1341 4-8-8 ACrastus 4 111
(Y De Nicolay, France) *racd in 5th: disputing 4th st: pushed along and hdwy on ins fr 2f out: rdn and wnt 2nd over 1f out: kpt on* **10/1**

3 shd **Montare (IRE)**[71] 663 5-8-13 SPasquier 5 114
(J E Pease, France) *racd in 4th: disputing 4th and pushed along st: styd on on outside fnl f: jst missed 2nd* **5/2**[1]

4 8 **Le Miracle (GER)**[21] 1341 6-8-12 DBoeuf 3 105
(W Baltromei, Germany) *racd in 3rd: 2nd 1/2-way: pushed along st: unable qck: fin 5th: plcd 4th* **9/2**

5 20 **Daramsar (FR)**[41] 990 4-9-0 CSoumillon 6 89
(A De Royer-Dupre, France) *hld up in last: pushed along on ins st: stmbld 1 1/2f out and nrly fell whn gng for gap between Spectaculaire and Ponte Tresa: eased: fin 6th: plcd 5th* **11/4**[2]

6 2½ **Spectaculaire**[21] 1341 4-8-12 OPeslier 1 84
(A Fabre, France) *racd in 2nd: 3rd 1/2-way: pushed along st: rdn to chse ldr 1 1 1/2f out: kpt on same pce: fin 4th, 2½l, shd & 8l: plcd last of 6* **9/1**

3m 33.6s (7.00) **Going Correction** +0.625s/f (Yiel)
WFA 4 from 5yo+ 1lb **6** Ran SP% **114.7**
Speed ratings: 107,105,105,100,90 104
PARI-MUTUEL: WIN 3.70; PL 1.90, 3.10; SF 19.40.
Owner Mme B Hermelin **Bred** Alexandre Guerini **Trained** Pau, France

NOTEBOOK
Lord Du Sud(FR), one of last seasons's top French stayers, had conditions in his favour and left behind a disappointing reappearance, this trip proving much more suitable. Off since February, he has a fine record fresh and, having been allowed to bowl along in front from the very start, he appeared to thoroughly enjoy himself. He will now be allowed to take his chance in the Ascot Gold Cup providing the ground does not become too firm, but unless it comes up soft it is hard to see him featuring prominently.
Ponte Tresa(FR), supplemented into this, put up a fine performance and is another who loves to get her toes in. She is a fine looking grey mare and was held up for much of the race before producing her challenge on the far rail. Try as she did, the four-year-old could never get to the girths of the winner and she pinched second place in the final few strides. Her likely target now is the shorter Prix Corrida and a tilt at the Ascot Gold Cup has not been ruled out.
Montare(IRE), winner of last season's Prix Royal Oak, was always likely to struggle for speed on her reappearance over 1m2f and this was a significant step back in the right direction. Although unable to get there, she was coming home well and further improvement can certainly be expected. This super-consistent mare was carrying a Group 1 penalty and it would be no surprise to see her go close in the Ascot Gold Cup, where a stiffer test on better ground should see her in her element.
Le Miracle(GER), third in last season's Prix Du Cadran, put up a rather disappointing performance following a decent seasonal reappearance in a similar race at Longchamp last month. He seemed to be going well in second place early on, but could not quicken and ended up being well beaten. He may well go to Ascot for the Gold Cup and on good or firm ground the gelding is an extremely useful stayer.
Daramsar(FR), who looked a fascinating acquisition to the staying division at the start of the season, was slightly disappointing on his reappearance behind Spectaculaire at Saint-Cloud and was held here when nearly coming down having gone for a gap well over a furlong out. He has a bit to prove at present.
Spectaculaire has gone the wrong way from his Saint-Cloud win and was held when causing some interference. As a result he was placed last.

PIMLICO (L-H)

Saturday, May 19

OFFICIAL GOING: Fast

1882a PREAKNESS STKS (GRADE 1) (DIRT) 1m 1f 110y(D)

11:09 (11:18) 3-Y-O **£306,122** (£102,041; £56,122; £30,612; £15,306)

RPR

1 **Curlin (USA)**[14] 1486 3-9-0 RAlbarado 4 124
(S Asmussen, U.S.A) *stmbld sltly s, hdwy on outside 3f out, cl 4th st, rdn over 1f out, r.o steadily under drving to ld last stride* **34/10**[2]

2 hd **Street Sense (USA)**[14] 1486 3-9-0 CHBorel 8 124
(C Nafzger, U.S.A) *hld up in 8th til gd hdwy fr 3f out, tk 3rd ent st, led over 1f out, all out, ct last stride* **13/10**[1]

3 4 **Hard Spun (USA)**[14] 1486 3-9-0 MPino 7 117
(J Larry Jones, U.S.A) *rcd in 3rd, rapid hdwy to ld 4f out, hdd over 1f out, one pce* **41/10**[3]

4 1½ **C P West (USA)**[21] 3-9-0 EPrado 9 114
(N Zito, U.S.A) *rcd in 4th, hdwy to go 2nd 3f out, 2nd st, sn one pce* **249/10**

5 1¼ **Circular Quay (USA)**[14] 1486 3-9-0 JRVelazquez 3 112
(T Pletcher, U.S.A) *last to over 2f out, 8th and rdn st, nvr nr to chal* **6/1**

6 3¾ **King Of The Roxy (USA)**[42] 3-9-0 (b) GKGomez 5 105
(T Pletcher, U.S.A) *rcd in 5th, 6th st, sn btn* **142/10**

7 6½ **Mint Slewlep (USA)**[21] 3-9-0 (b) AGarcia 1 93
(W Robert Bailes, U.S.A) *a towards rr, 7th st, no hdwy* **401/10**

8 8½ **Xchanger (USA)**[28] 3-9-0 (b) RADominguez 2 78
(M Shuman, U.S.A) *led to 4f out, wknd fr 3f out, 5th & btn st* **23/1**

9 4¼ **Flying First Class (USA)**[21] 3-9-0 (b) MGuidry 6 70
(D Wayne Lukas, U.S.A) *pressed ldr, wknd over 3f out, last st* **166/10**

1m 53.46s (-2.13) **9** Ran SP% **122.8**
PARI-MUTUEL (Including $2 stake): WIN 8.80; PL (1-2) 3.80, 3.00;SHOW (1-2-3) 2.80, 2.40, 3.00; SF 23.20.
Owner Stonestreet, Padua, Midnight Cry Stables, G Bolton **Bred** Fares Farm Inc **Trained** USA
■ Curlin equalled the track record in winning this second leg of the Triple Crown.

NOTEBOOK
Curlin(USA), who only made his racecourse debut in February, was beaten eight lengths by today's runner-up in the Kentucky Derby. He had clearly learnt a lot from that experience and, despite stumbling leaving the gate, wore down his rival to get in front in the shadow of the post. He is clearly improving with racing and heads for the Belmont Stakes next, a contest that should suit him.
Street Sense(USA) had been an impressive winner of the Kentucky Derby and looked set to take this second leg of the Triple Crown when bursting clear early in the straight. However, he then appeared to weaken - his rider reported he was looking at the crowd and pulling himself up - and he was collared on the wire. With the Triple Crown no longer possible, his trainer reported that he is unlikely to reoppose the winner in the Belmont.
Hard Spun(USA), who tried to make all before finishing third in the Kentucky Derby, was held up close to the pace before kicking for home on the turn. However, he was swept aside by the eventual runner-up and finished further behind that rival than at Churchill Downs.

[1761] BATH (L-H)

Monday, May 21

OFFICIAL GOING: Good to firm (9.0)

Wind: Brisk, across

1882 E.B.F./ DAWN REED HEN PARTY NOVICE STKS 5f 11y

2:00 (2:01) (Class 5) 2-Y-0 **£3,141** (£934; £467; £233) **Stalls** Low

Form RPR

3 **1** **Waveline (USA)**[17] [1445] 2-8-0 .... KMay(7) 3 77
(B J Meehan) *in tch: hdwy to trck ldrs 2f out: drvn and qcknd fnl f to ld cl home* **5/1**[3]

01 **2** 1/2 **Little Pete (IRE)**[12] [1586] 2-9-0 .... LPKeniry 4 82
(R A Farrant) *disp ld tl slt advantage ins fnl 2f: rdn and kpt on ins fnl f: hdd and no ex cl home* **11/1**

3 3/4 **Midnight Fling** 2-8-7 .... SteveDrowne 5 72
(R Charlton) *s.i.s: bhd: pushed along 2f out: hdwy over 1f out: styd on wl fnl f: gng on cl home* **12/1**

416 **4** 1 **Sauze D'Oulx**[19] [1390] 2-9-0 .... JamesMillman(5) 6 81
(B R Millman) *sn disputing ld tl dropped to cl 2nd ins fnl 2f: wknd wl ins fnl f* **7/2**[2]

3 **5** 2 **Fox's Den**[48] [898] 2-8-12 .... SebSanders 1 67
(R M Beckett) *chsd ldrs: rdn over 2f out: wknd fnl f* **5/2**[1]

04 **6** hd **Replicator**[14] [1519] 2-8-12 .... NCallan 7 66
(Pat Eddery) *chsd ldrs: rdn 1/2-way: wknd fnl f* **5/1**[3]

7 2 1/2 **Hyper Viper (IRE)** 2-8-12 .... JohnEgan 8 57
(J S Moore) *s.i.s: bhd: pushed along 1/2-way: hdwy fnl f but nvr gng pce to be competitive* **16/1**

1 **8** 2 **Nestor Protector (IRE)**[42] [971] 2-8-12 .... DaneO'Neill 2 50
(A B Haynes) *s.i.s: sn outpcd* **16/1**

9 7 **Gillans Inn** 2-8-7 .... KevinGhunowa(5) 9 24
(J M Bradley) *s.i.s: sn rcvrd to mid-div: wknd 1/2-way* **66/1**

61.84 secs (-0.66) **Going Correction** -0.15s/f (Firm) 9 Ran SP% **113.4**

Speed ratings (Par 93):99,98,97,95,92 91,87,84,73

CSF £57.11 TOTE £7.30: £2.30, £2.90, £3.90; EX 72.00 Trifecta £265.50 Part won. Pool £374.06 - 0.34 winning units..

Owner J Paul Reddam **Bred** J Paul Reddam **Trained** Manton, Wilts

■ Stewards' Enquiry : L P Keniry two-day ban: used whip with excessive frequency (Jun 3-4)

FOCUS

Nothing more than a fair juvenile event, but it should produce the occasional future winner. The second and fourth help set the standard and the form seems pretty sound. The winning time was creditable.

NOTEBOOK

Waveline(USA), a 140,000euros purchase who shaped pleasingly on her debut at Lingfield, had a curious jockey booking given she was already receiving weight, but the pair seemed to get on well together and she came through in the final furlong to win a shade comfortably. She is nothing special and highly unlikely to warrant her Group 1 entry, but can win more races. (tchd 11-2)

Little Pete(IRE), who made all to win at Kempton last month, was trying to concede 14lb to the winner and gave it a good go, but was claimed close home. He has plenty of speed and is clearly progressive. (op 12-1 tchd 9-1)

Midnight Fling, who is bred to appreciate at least another furlong, comes from a stable whose juveniles usually benefit from a run and she shaped most pleasingly back in third. In rear early, she made good headway wide, but her lack of experience prevented her from going all the way. She should have little trouble finding a maiden on this evidence. (op 15-2)

Sauze D'Oulx, winner of a decent Windsor maiden last month, struggled in a warm contest at Ascot last time and he again fell short against improvers. He is likely to remain vulnerable. (op 4-1)

Fox's Den, a promising third on his Folkestone debut, failed to build on that and was in trouble from a relatively early stage. He is clearly better than this, but has something to prove now and may be more of a nursery type later on in the year. (tchd 11-4)

Replicator has shown enough to suggest he can win races, but it is more likely to be in nurseries later on. Official explanation: jockey said colt stumbled furlong after start (op 13-2 tchd 7-1 in places)

Hyper Viper(IRE), who is bred to appreciate further later on, was always struggling for pace and should improve for the experience. He will be capable of winning races once granted a stiffer test. (op 14-1)

1883 JOHN SMITH'S EXTRA SMOOTH MEDIAN AUCTION MAIDEN STKS 5f 11y

2:30 (2:31) (Class 6) 3-4-Y-O **£2,266** (£674; £337; £168) **Stalls** Low

Form RPR

-000 **1** **Mr Forthright**[13] [1561] 3-8-9 50 .... KevinGhunowa(5) 2 56
(J M Bradley) *in rr: rdn and hdwy over 2f out: styd on u.p to ld wl ins fnl f: drvn out* **28/1**

2 1/2 **Oystermouth** 3-8-9 .... SteveDrowne 8 49
(R Charlton) *in tch: hdwy to chse ldrs 1/2-way: led wl over 1f out: shkn up hung lft and hdd wl ins fnl f: kpt on same pce* **5/2**[1]

-660 **3** 1 1/4 **Nawayea**[82] [580] 4-8-10 45 .... KirstyMilczarek(7) 3 48
(C N Allen) *chsd ldr to 1/2-way: rdn 2f out: chal on ins and n.m.r wl ins fnl f: sn one pce* **20/1**

004- **4** 1 **Damhsoir (IRE)**[200] [6311] 3-8-9 52 .... DaneO'Neill 4 41
(H S Howe) *sn led: rdn and hdd wl over 1f out: wkng whn n.m.r ins fnl f* **14/1**[3]

6- **5** 3 **Millsini**[216] [6024] 3-8-9 .... SebSanders 1 30
(Rae Guest) *chsd ldrs: rdn 1/2-way: sn btn* **15/2**[2]

0006 **6** 9 **Chingford (IRE)**[18] [1430] 3-8-6 49 .... EmmettStack(3) 7 —
(J G Portman) *s.i.s: a struggling in rr* **16/1**

000 **7** shd **The Carpet Man**[5] [1763] 3-9-0 .... SimonWhitworth 5 3
(A W Carroll) *in rr: sme progs 1/2-way: sn wknd* **50/1**

61.56 secs (-0.94) **Going Correction** -0.15s/f (Firm)

WFA 3 from 4yo 8lb 7 Ran SP% **63.1**

Speed ratings (Par 101):101,100,98,96,91 77,77

CSF £29.16 TOTE £22.60: £7.00, £1.60; EX 41.20 TRIFECTA Not won..

Owner E A Hayward **Bred** C D Shore **Trained** Sedbury, Gloucs

FOCUS

A poor sprint maiden, weakened further by the late withdrawal of favourite Whiskey Junction (11/10, unruly in stalls. Deduct 45p in the £ under Rule 4.) The winner is rated to his maiden form here last year.

The Carpet Man Official explanation: jockey said gelding stumbled inside final furlong

1884 CATERING SERVICES INTERNATIONAL FILLIES' H'CAP 1m 5f 22y

3:00 (3:00) (Class 5) (0-70,72) 4-Y-0+ **£3,238** (£963; £481; £240) **Stalls** High

Form RPR

-560 **1** **Spring Dream (IRE)**[14] [1526] 4-8-12 63 .... JHBowman 1 68
(M R Channon) *trckd ldrs in 3rd: hdwy over 2f out: sn pressing ldr: slt ld 1f out: hld on wl* **13/2**

0-46 **2** 1/2 **Theatre Royal**[11] [1609] 4-8-9 60 .... SteveDrowne 3 64
(Mouse Hamilton-Fairley) *led: rdn 2f out: hdd 1f out: styd on ins fnl f but a hld by wnr* **7/2**[2]

1631 **3** nk **Caucasienne (FR)**[6] [1741] 4-9-7 72 6ex .... SebSanders 4 76
(J W Hills) *chsd ldrs: rdn 3f out: kpt on fr over 1f out and gng on nr fin but a hld* **15/8**[1]

0-55 **4** 2 **Squirtle (IRE)**[9] [1683] 4-8-10 61 ....(v) StephenDonohoe 2 62
(W M Brisbourne) *in rr but in tch: hdwy 3f out: rdn to chse ldrs over 2f out: kpt on same pce* **11/2**[3]

00/1 **5** 3/4 **Charmatic (IRE)**[26] [1249] 6-9-2 67 .... ChrisCatlin 6 66
(Andrew Turnell) *in rr but in tch: drvn along 3f out: nvr gng pce to be competitive and no imp on ldrs fnl 2f* **11/2**[3]

02/2 **6** 7 **Move Over Darling (IRE)**[13] [1566] 4-9-4 69 .... NCallan 7 58
(P F I Cole) *chsd ldrs tl over 2f out: wknd sn after* **9/1**

0000 **7** 6 **Lady Lucas (IRE)**[5] [1761] 4-8-4 55 oh10 ....(t) EdwardCreighton 5 35?
(E J Creighton) *a towards rr: no ch fnl 3f* **66/1**

2m 54.14s (2.64) **Going Correction** +0.025s/f (Good) 7 Ran SP% **112.6**

Speed ratings (Par 100):92,91,91,90,89 85,81

CSF £28.46 TOTE £10.60: £3.90, £3.00; EX 45.10.

Owner W H Ponsonby **Bred** R N Auld **Trained** West Ilsley, Berks

FOCUS

A modest but competitive-enough fillies' handicap. The winning time was modest. The winner had slipped to a good mark and was up a length on this year's best.

1885 GRACE SERVICES H'CAP 5f 161y

3:30 (3:32) (Class 5) (0-70,70) 3-Y-0+ **£3,238** (£963; £481; £240) **Stalls** Low

Form RPR

-246 **1** **Harrison's Flyer (IRE)**[9] [1681] 6-8-11 56 ....(p) JimCrowley 7 65
(J M Bradley) *chsd ldrs: rdn 2f out: styd on to ld last 110yds: drvn out* **13/2**

-244 **2** 1/2 **Willhewiz**[12] [1589] 7-9-4 63 .... NCallan 8 71
(M S Saunders) *pressed ldrs tl led 1f out: hdd and no ex last 110yds* **11/2**[2]

216- **3** hd **Safari Mischief**[238] [5575] 4-9-8 70 .... LiamTreadwell(3) 2 77
(P Winkworth) *slt ld tl hdd 1f out: kpt on same pce u.p* **16/1**

6-14 **4** shd **Brigadore**[15] [1492] 8-9-8 67 .... TPQueally 1 74+
(J G Given) *s.i.s: sn in tch: rdn to chse ldrs fr 2f out: kpt on ins fnl f* **6/1**[3]

040- **5** 1/2 **Drumming Party (USA)**[254] [5167] 5-9-1 60 ....(t) LPKeniry 9 65
(A M Balding) *in tch: rdn and hdwy fr 2f out: kpt on fnl f but nvr quite gng pce to rch ldrs* **16/1**

-522 **6** 3/4 **Chatshow (USA)**[26] [1241] 6-9-11 70 .... FrancisNorton 16 72
(A W Carroll) *prom towards outside: outpcd 3f out: hdwy fr 2f out: kpt on fnl f but nvr quite gng pce to rch ldrs* **4/1**[1]

-000 **7** 3/4 **Brandywell Boy (IRE)**[10] [1630] 4-9-6 70 .... JamesMillman(5) 5 70
(D J S Ffrench Davis) *in tch on ins: kpt on fr over 1f out but nvr gng pce to chal* **10/1**

11-0 **8** hd **Decider (USA)**[9] [1669] 4-8-9 59 .... KevinGhunowa(5) 3 58
(J M Bradley) *chsd ldrs: drvn to chal fr 2f out: wknd wl ins fnl f* **14/1**

3306 **9** hd **Royal Orissa**[20] [1377] 5-8-11 56 oh3 .... HayleyTurner 12 55+
(D Haydn Jones) *s.i.s: bhd: stl plenty to do 2f out: str run fnl f: fin wl* **18/1**

00/0 **10** hd **Avoca Dancer (IRE)**[9] [1681] 4-9-0 59 .... JimmyQuinn 10 57
(M Wigham) *in rr: hdwy over 1f out: kpt on ins fnl f: nvr gng pce to be competitive* **33/1**

660- **11** hd **Hard To Catch (IRE)**[349] [2331] 9-8-11 56 .... ChrisCatlin 13 53
(Mike Murphy) *in rr: hdwy to chse ldrs over 2f out: sn one pce* **40/1**

0060 **12** 1 **Littledodayno (IRE)**[9] [1681] 4-9-1 60 .... BrettDoyle 4 57+
(M Wigham) *s.i.s: hld up in rr: stdy hdwy over 1f out: nvr in contention* **10/1**

05-0 **13** 1 **Fateful Attraction**[131] [91] 4-8-11 56 oh2 ....(b) SebSanders 15 46
(I A Wood) *a towards rr: sme late prog* **18/1**

1300 **14** 3/4 **Triskaidekaphobia**[19] [1405] 4-8-11 56 ....(t) SteveDrowne 11 44
(Miss J R Tooth) *outpcd most of way* **25/1**

5605 **15** 1 1/4 **Ceredig**[10] [1640] 4-8-8 56 oh6 .... SaleemGolam(3) 6 40
(P W Hiatt) *in tch over 3f* **33/1**

4400 **16** 2 1/2 **Pulse**[19] [1405] 9-8-11 56 oh2 ....(b[1]) PaulFitzsimons 14 31
(Miss J R Tooth) *s.i.s: outpcd most of way* **50/1**

1m 10.75s (-0.45) **Going Correction** -0.15s/f (Firm) 16 Ran SP% **124.3**

Speed ratings (Par 103):97,96,96,95,95 94,93,93,92,92 92,90,89,88,86 83

CSF £40.97 CT £567.42 TOTE £8.80: £1.80, £2.20, £3.20, £2.00; EX 34.70 Trifecta £227.80 Part won. Pool £320.96 - 0.30 winning units..

Owner racingshares.co.uk **Bred** Geoff Mulcahy **Trained** Sedbury, Gloucs

FOCUS

A typically competitive sprint handicap with a bunch finish. The form is sound, rated through the second and third. The winner took advantage of a career-low mark.

Littledodayno(IRE) Official explanation: jockey said, regarding running and riding, his orders were to get the filly settled and to get it to finish, adding that he dropped it out to get it relaxed and was off the bridle about 3 1/2f out, tending to run in snatches; he added filly was denied a clear run inside 2f mark and finished on the bridle

1886 WBX.COM WORLD BET EXCHANGE H'CAP 1m 5y

4:00 (4:01) (Class 5) (0-70,74) 4-Y-0+ **£3,238** (£963; £481; £240) **Stalls** Low

Form RPR

1111 **1** **Apex**[5] [1765] 6-9-3 74 6ex .... HaddenFrost(7) 9 90
(M Hill) *hld up in mid-div: stdy hdwy over 2f out: sn trcking ldr: led appr fnl f: sn clr: easily* **6/5**[1]

00-0 **2** 5 **Wrighty Almighty (IRE)**[13] [1564] 5-8-5 55 .... PaulDoe 14 59
(P R Chamings) *chsd ldrs: wnt 2nd over 3f out: rdn 2f out: kpt on to chse wnr ins fnl f but no ch* **16/1**

0340 **3** 1 **Golden Spectrum (IRE)**[9] [1673] 8-8-3 58 ....(b) LukeMorris(5) 5 60+
(R A Harris) *t.k.h and set str pce: 5 l clr over 3f out: rdn 2f out: hdd appr fnl f: wknd and lost 2nd ins fnl f* **20/1**

0-50 **4** 1 1/2 **Bold Cross (IRE)**[14] [1521] 4-8-10 60 .... PaulFitzsimons 10 58
(E G Bevan) *in rr: hdwy and rdn fr 3f out: styd on fr over 1f out but nvr gng pce to rch ldrs* **25/1**

3030 **5** 1/2 **Voice Mail**[77] [610] 8-8-0 57 ....(v) DavidProbert(7) 8 54
(A M Balding) *hld up in rr: hdwy on ins fr 2f out: kpt on ins fnl f but nvr in contention* **9/1**[3]

000- 6 shd **Ile Michel**[169] 6693 10-8-10 **60** SebSanders 2 57
(Lady Herries) *chsd ldrs tl drvn and one pce over 3f out: styd on fnl f but nvr in contention* **16/1**
045- 7 ½ **Border Edge**[174] 6635 9-8-8 **65** ow1 RyanBird(7) 3 61
(J J Bridger) *chsd ldrs: rdn and outpcd over 3f out: kpt on again ins fnl f* **20/1**
-060 8 1 **Lizarazu (GER)**[4] 1787 8-8-12 **67** (b) TolleyDean(5) 6 60
(R A Harris) *s.i.s: bhd: hdwy fr 2f out: kpt on ins fnl f: n.d* **25/1**
606- 9 4 **Merchant Bankes**[231] 5741 4-8-9 **62** SaleemGolam(3) 1 46
(W G M Turner) *chsd ldrs: rdn 3f out: wknd 2f out* **33/1**
0-30 10 1¼ **Moves Goodenough**[10] 1629 4-9-0 **64** HayleyTurner 7 45
(Andrew Turnell) *sn towards rr: mod prog fnl 2f* **14/1**
U0-P 11 2½ **Reflecting (IRE)**[14] 1534 4-8-10 **60** FrancisNorton 15 36
(A W Carroll) *chsd clr ldr to 3f out: wknd 2f out* **66/1**
10-0 12 2 **Katie Lawson (IRE)**[89] 516 4-8-6 **56** (p) SimonWhitworth 12 27
(D Haydn Jones) *reminders in rr sn after s: a towards rr* **33/1**
500- 13 2 **Vampyrus**[208] 6177 4-8-5 **55** FrankieMcDonald 16 21
(H Candy) *in tch 5f* **20/1**
41-5 14 10 **Alexian**[77] 623 4-9-4 **68** BrettDoyle 11 11
(D W P Arbuthnot) *a towards rr* **16/1**
3021 15 1¾ **Seneschal**[13] 1562 6-9-2 **66** SteveDrowne 13 5
(A B Haynes) *a towards rr: eased over 1f out* **9/2**[2]

1m 39.65s (-1.45) **Going Correction** +0.025s/f (Good) **15** Ran SP% **127.3**
Speed ratings (Par 103):108,103,102,100,100 99,99,98,94,93 90,88,86,76,74
CSF £21.72 CT £308.57 TOTE £1.80: £1.30, £5.40, £5.20; EX 31.30 Trifecta £309.50 Pool £449.02 - 1.03 winning units..
Owner Martin Hill **Bred** P D And Mrs C E Player And Jonathon Jay **Trained** Broadhempston, Devon

FOCUS
Another rampant victory for the bang in-form Apex, who had little to beat but was impressive all the same. He could defy another rise. The placed form is not rock solid but makes sense on paper.
Reflecting(IRE) Official explanation: jockey said filly ran too free
Seneschal Official explanation: jockey said gelding slipped on turn and never travelled after

1887 BET NOW AT WBX.COM H'CAP 1m 2f 46y
4:30 (4:33) (Class 5) (0-75,75) 3-Y-O **£3,562** (£1,059; £529; £264) **Stalls** Low

Form RPR
344 1 **Six Of Diamonds (IRE)**[10] 1632 3-8-10 **70** RichardKingscote(3) 3 77+
(J A Osborne) *in tch: hdwy 3f out: led over 1f out: drvn and hld on wl fnl f* **13/2**[3]
00-0 2 1 **Up In Arms (IRE)**[13] 1563 3-8-10 **67** StephenCarson 6 72
(P Winkworth) *lost tch and detached after 3f: hdwy on outside fr 3f out: styd on strly fr over 1f out: clsng on wnr nr fin but a hld* **50/1**
43-3 3 ½ **Coyote Creek**[21] 1355 3-8-13 **70** TedDurcan 13 74
(E F Vaughan) *in rr: hdwy on outside fr 3f out: drvn and kpt on to chse ldrs ins fnl f but nvr quite gng pce to chal* **3/1**[1]
3211 4 1 **Nicomedia (IRE)**[10] 1628 3-8-7 **71** HaddenFrost(7) 5 73
(R Hannon) *trckd ldrs: led ins fnl 3f: rdn and hdd over 1f out: wknd nr fin* **11/2**[2]
5-40 5 1 **Windbeneathmywings (IRE)**[10] 1628 3-8-4 **61** oh2 JamesDoyle 2 61
(J W Hills) *s.i.s: sn mid-div: rdn and hdwy on outside fr 2f out: kpt on but nvr gng pce to rch ldrs fnl f* **33/1**
065- 6 nk **Mystical Moon**[236] 5622 3-8-8 **65** PatDobbs 8 64+
(Lady Herries) *chsd ldrs: rdn over 2f out: styd wl there tl wknd ins fnl f* **10/1**
-505 7 4 **Stagehand (IRE)**[13] 1563 3-8-9 **66** AdrianMcCarthy 9 57
(B R Millman) *towards rr after 2f: rdn 3f out: sme prog fr over 1f out: nvr in contention* **14/1**
4-45 8 2½ **Spirit Of Adjisa (IRE)**[18] 1439 3-8-4 **68** KMay(7) 1 54
(Pat Eddery) *chsd ldrs: rdn 3f out: sn btn* **14/1**
-002 9 1 **Iolanthe**[10] 1628 3-8-11 **68** BrettDoyle 7 52
(B J Meehan) *in rr tl hdwy to cl on ldrs 3f out: wknd fr 2f out* **14/1**
00-6 10 2 **Opera Crown (IRE)**[15] 1504 3-9-4 **75** NCallan 10 55
(P F I Cole) *chsd ldrs: rdn over 3f out: styd wl there tl wknd 2f out* **8/1**
450- 11 2 **Nothing Is Forever (IRE)**[215] 6058 3-8-10 **67** JimCrowley 12 43
(Mrs A J Perrett) *sn bhd* **16/1**
-030 12 1 **Leonard Charles**[81] 591 3-9-3 **74** SebSanders 4 48
(Sir Mark Prescott) *sn slt ld: hdd ins fnl 3f: wknd qckly 2f out* **8/1**
23-0 13 24 **Situla (IRE)**[26] 1247 3-8-12 **69** JimmyQuinn 11 —
(H J L Dunlop) *chsd ldrs over 6f* **25/1**

2m 9.79s (-1.21) **Going Correction** +0.025s/f (Good) **13** Ran SP% **119.7**
Speed ratings (Par 99):105,104,103,103,102 101,98,96,95,94 92,91,72
CSF £305.44 CT £1180.20 TOTE £6.50: £2.10, £8.50, £1.80; EX 188.60 TRIFECTA Not won..
Owner Booth,Durkan,Mountgrange&Wood Hall Studs **Bred** Tally-Ho Stud **Trained** Upper Lambourn, Berks

FOCUS
An ordinary handicap, but it should produce the odd winner at a similar level. The pace was strong. The runner-up is rated back to his 2yo form with the third and fourth close to their recent level. The winner improved as expected on this handicap debut.
Windbeneathmywings(IRE) Official explanation: jockey said filly missed the break and never travelled after

1888 AMATEUR JOCKEYS' ASSOCIATION H'CAP (FOR AMATEUR RIDERS) 2m 1f 34y
5:00 (5:04) (Class 6) (0-65,63) 4-Y-0+ **£2,307** (£709; £354) **Stalls** Low

Form RPR
3020 1 **Ronsard (IRE)**[5] 1764 5-11-1 **49** MrRichardEvans 6 59
(P D Evans) *in tch: stdy hdwy to ld on bit ins fnl 3f: shkn up fnl f: pushed out and hld on wl* **9/1**
60/4 2 1 **Voir Dire**[12] 1590 5-11-0 **48** MissFayeBramley 17 57
(Mrs P N Dutfield) *in rr tl hdwy over 3f out: styd on to chse wnr ins fnl f but a jst hld* **25/1**
050/ 3 1½ **Silencio (IRE)**[16] 3572 6-11-9 **57** MrCPHuxley 9 64
(A King) *chsd ldrs: led over 3f out: hdd ins fnl 3f: styd pressing wnr tl outpcd ins fnl f* **3/1**[1]
036/ 4 3 **Prince Among Men**[16] 5383 10-11-6 **54** MissJRRichards 14 57
(N G Richards) *in rr tl gd hdwy on outside over 3f out: drvn to chse ldrs 2f out: one pce u.p fnl f* **12/1**
202 5 shd **Galantos (GER)**[57] 775 6-11-6 **54** (b) MrDHutchison 12 57
(G L Moore) *chsd ldrs: rdn to chse wnr over 2f out: sn no imp: wknd fnl f* **9/2**[2]
065- 6 2½ **Top Trees**[253] 5201 9-10-12 **46** MrPCollington 1 46
(W S Kittow) *in rr: hdwy over 3f out: chsd ldrs and rdn over 2f out: sn one pce* **11/1**
5/0- 7 16 **Wavertree One Off**[502] 32 5-11-4 **52** MrSPearce 4 33
(J Ryan) *in tch: drvn along 4f out: wknd 3f out* **50/1**
-006 8 1 **Darusso**[9] 1683 4-11-8 **58** (p) MrsSMoore 2 38
(J S Moore) *chsd ldrs tl wknd 3f out* **20/1**
/064 9 1¼ **Lord Nellsson**[26] 1003 11-11-3 **51** MrCTPritchard 3 29
(Andrew Turnell) *chsd ldrs tl wknd over 3f out* **14/1**
1050 10 6 **Blue Hills**[9] 1683 6-11-9 **57** (b) MrsMarieKing 7 28
(P W Hiatt) *chsd ldrs: led 9f out tl over 3f out: sn wknd* **25/1**
232- 11 2 **Coda Agency**[174] 6630 4-11-7 **57** MrLeeNewnes 5 26
(D W P Arbuthnot) *chsd ldrs tl wknd 3f out* **12/1**
/00- 12 shd **Uncle Max (IRE)**[126] 1745 7-11-4 **52** (p) MrRPFlint 16 21
(R A Harris) *in tch: rdn over 4f out: wknd over 3f out* **40/1**
5-00 13 4 **Love Angel (USA)**[23] 775 5-11-4 **52** MissLEllison 10 16
(J J Bridger) *chsd ldrs tl wknd fr 4f out* **7/1**[3]
-540 14 13 **Royal Sailor (IRE)**[24] 1279 5-10-11 **45** MrDavidMcMinn 15 —
(J Ryan) *slowly away: bhd most of way* **50/1**
6-02 15 12 **Fondness**[11] 1615 4-11-10 **63** (bt) MrSWalker 13 —
(J P Broderick, Ire) *chsd ldrs tl wknd 4f out* **16/1**
0050 16 69 **Flashing Floozie**[14] 4-10-9 **45** MrMJJSmith 11 —
(A W Carroll) *led tl hdd 9f out: sn wknd: t.o* **50/1**
000- 17 22 **Hope's Eternal**[143] 3017 4-11-4 **54** (b) MrIPopham 8 —
(C L Popham) *a bhd: t.o* **66/1**

3m 51.89s (2.29) **Going Correction** +0.025s/f (Good)
WFA 4 from 5yo+ 2lb **17** Ran SP% **124.2**
Speed ratings (Par 101):95,94,93,92,92 91,83,83,82,79 78,78,76,70,65 32,22
CSF £227.60 CT £846.61 TOTE £12.20: £2.90, £4.90, £1.40, £2.30; EX 254.00 TRIFECTA Not won. Place 6 £171.82, Place 5 £44.66..
Owner Mrs I M Folkes **Bred** Liscannor Stud Ltd **Trained** Pandy, Monmouths
■ The first winner for Richard Evans.

FOCUS
A modest but competitive-enough handicap. The pace was strong and the race has been rated fairly positively, with the winner producing his best turf effort since late 2005, the second rated back to his old form, and the third and fourth on potentially good marks based on their Flat form.
Voir Dire Official explanation: jockey said saddle slipped
T/Jkpt: Not won. T/Plt: £265.70 to a £1 stake. Pool: £53,166.05. 146.05 winning tickets. T/Qpdt: £42.70 to a £1 stake. Pool: £3,723.40. 64.50 winning tickets. ST

1706 MUSSELBURGH (R-H)
Monday, May 21

OFFICIAL GOING: Good to firm (10.1)
Wind: Slight, across

1889 TURF TV MAIDEN AUCTION STKS 5f
2:10 (2:10) (Class 5) 2-Y-O **£2,590** (£770; £385; £192) **Stalls** Low

Form RPR
1 **Rose Siog** 2-8-7 TonyHamilton 3 74
(R A Fahey) *led 1f: cl up: rdn along and sltly outpcd 2f out: styd on u.p ent fnl f: led nr fin* **5/2**[2]
52 2 shd **Guertino (IRE)**[15] 1487 2-9-0 PaulEddery 2 81
(B Smart) *trckd ldrs: hdwy wl over 1f out: rdn to ld ins fnl f: sn drvn and edgd rt: hdd nr fin* **2/1**[1]
0 3 ½ **Secret Asset (IRE)**[33] 1087 2-8-10 DavidAllan 6 75
(W M Brisbourne) *cl up: led wl over 1f out and sn rdn: drvn and hdd ins fnl f: no ex last 100yds* **13/2**
5 4 6 **Countrywide Comet (IRE)**[15] 1487 2-8-12 PaulMulrennan 8 56
(K A Ryan) *in tch: pushed along 1/2-way: rdn wl over 1f out: sn no imp* **28/1**
3 5 nk **La Guancha**[23] 1302 2-8-5 PaulFessey 5 48
(T D Barron) *dwlt: hdwy and in tch 1/2-way: sn rdn along and wknd* **7/2**[3]
6 1¾ **Atephobia** 2-9-2 PatCosgrave 1 52
(K R Burke) *a in rr* **22/1**
50 7 hd **Areweplayingout (IRE)**[23] 1285 2-8-6 PatrickMathers(3) 4 45
(Peter Grayson) *a in rr* **66/1**
0 8 5 **Gin Genereux**[10] 1622 2-9-2 JoeFanning 7 34
(M Johnston) *cl up: led after 1f: rdn along 2f out: sn hdd & wknd qckly* **12/1**

59.82 secs (-0.68) **Going Correction** -0.25s/f (Firm) **8** Ran SP% **114.4**
Speed ratings (Par 93):95,94,94,84,83 81,80,72
CSF £7.78 TOTE £4.00: £1.90, £1.10, £1.80; EX 10.40.
Owner The Mick Sweeney Syndicate **Bred** D R Tucker **Trained** Musley Bank, N Yorks
■ Stewards' Enquiry : Paul Eddery caution: used whip with excessive frequency

FOCUS
A modest juvenile maiden which saw the first three come clear. The form is sound enough, rated through the runner-up.

NOTEBOOK
Rose Siog, a sister to 5f winners Treasure Cay and Bahamian Duke, clearly knew her job for this debut assignment and got off the mark with a very narrow success. She was well backed so is clearly well thought of by connections and showed a likeable attitude when under maximum pressure on the rail late on. Granted she had a fairly hard race for a debutante, but she is entitled to improve for the experience and looks all speed. Her trainer later indicated she may now head to the Listed Hilary Needler Stakes at Beverley at the end of this month. (op 11-4 tchd 3-1)
Guertino(IRE), whose stable had been successful with both its previous runners in the event, was just touched off at the finish and still looked green when asked for his effort, changing his legs entering the final furlong. He is well up to going one better in due course and should come on again for this experience. (op 5-2)
Secret Asset(IRE) stepped up markedly on his debut form and was not beaten at all far. He is clearly going the right way, is entitled to come on again for the run, and was nicely clear of the remainder at the finish. (tchd 6-1)
Countrywide Comet(IRE) ran close to the level of his debut form at Hamilton when behind Guertino and looks the type who needs more time. (op 25-1)
La Guancha was never in the hunt after a sluggish start and failed to build on the level of her encouraging debut display at Ripon 23 days previously. This has to be considered disappointing. (op 5-2 tchd 4-1 in places)

1890 JOHN SMITH'S EXTRA SMOOTH H'CAP 1m 4f
2:40 (2:40) (Class 5) (0-75,72) 4-Y-O+ **£3,238** (£963; £481; £240) **Stalls** High

Form RPR
06-0 1 **Toshi (USA)**[10] 1627 5-8-10 **64** MarkLawson(3) 3 71
(P Monteith) *t.k.h: hld up: hdwy on outer and cl up 1/2-way: effrt 3f out: rdn to ld 2f out: drvn out* **12/1**
-505 2 1½ **Maneki Neko (IRE)**[4] 1794 5-9-3 **68** PaulMulrennan 4 73
(E W Tuer) *trckd ldrs: hdwy over 2f out: sn rdn: chsd wnr ins fnl f: sn drvn and no imp towards fin* **5/1**[2]
06-0 3 nk **Sir Arthur (IRE)**[51] 850 4-9-7 **72** JoeFanning 2 76
(M Johnston) *led: rdn along and hdd 2f out: sn drvn and kpt on u.p* **11/1**

005- **4** *nk* **Categorical**[35] [6275] 4-9-4 **69** .... PatCosgrave 1 73
(K G Reveley) *chsd ldrs: rdn along 3f out: drvn and edgd lft wl over 1f out and again ent fnl f: one pce* **11/1**

6-4U **5** *1 1/2* **Collette's Choice**[12] [1576] 4-8-10 **61** .... TonyHamilton 5 65+
(R A Fahey) *hld up in tch: hdwy on inner 3f out: sn pushed along: rdn and nt clr run wl over 1f out: drvn and hmpd ent fnl f: sn btn* **4/5**[1]

044- **6** *1/2* **Platinum Charmer (IRE)**[199] [6317] 7-8-0 **54** oh3 ow1(p) AndrewElliott(3) 7 55
(K R Burke) *hld up in rr: hdwy to chse ldrs 1/2-way: rdn along 3f out and wknd over 2f out* **10/1**[3]

6-56 **7** *1* **Psychic Star**[10] [1626] 4-9-0 **70** .... PJMcDonald(5) 6 69
(Miss Lucinda V Russell) *hld up: a in rr* **33/1**

600- **8** *38* **Zabeel Tower**[306] [3634] 4-8-5 **56** .... RoystonFfrench 9 —
(R Allan) *a in rr* **33/1**

2m 37.79s (0.89) **Going Correction** -0.125s/f (Firm) **8** Ran SP% **111.6**
Speed ratings (Par 103):92,91,90,90,89 89,88,63
CSF £67.16 CT £671.29 TOTE £15.30: £3.60, £1.30, £2.50; EX 77.20.
Owner E Nisbet & Miss L McFadzean **Bred** T Wilson **Trained** Rosewell, Midlothian
■ Stewards' Enquiry : Pat Cosgrave two-day ban: careless riding (Jun 3-4)

FOCUS
A modest handicap which produced a moderate winning time. Ordinary form, the winner still a stone off last summer's best figures.

1891 EDINBURGH HOLIDAY CLAIMING STKS 5f
3:10 (3:10) (Class 6) 3-Y-0+ **£1,943** (£578; £288; £144) **Stalls** Low

Form RPR

1043 **1** **Whinhill House**[7] [1707] 7-9-8 56 ....(v) PatCosgrave 7 69+
(D W Barker) *mde all: rdn clr ent fnl f: kpt on strly* **7/2**[2]

026- **2** *3* **Dematraf (IRE)**[278] [4473] 5-8-5 41 .... PatrickMathers(3) 8 44
(Peter Grayson) *midfield: hdwy on outer 2f out: sn rdn and chsd wnr ins fnl f: no imp* **33/1**

-403 **3** *1 3/4* **Rothesay Dancer**[6] [1748] 4-9-9 53 .... DanielTudhope 4 53
(J S Goldie) *trckd ldrs: hdwy to chse wnr over 1f out: sn rdn and one pce* **5/1**[3]

5221 **4** *1 1/2* **Blackheath (IRE)**[7] [1729] 11-9-2 55 .... AdrianTNicholls 5 40
(D Nicholls) *towards rr: hdwy 2f out: sn rdn and kpt on ins fnl f: nrst fin* **7/4**[1]

0545 **5** *1 3/4* **Legal Set (IRE)**[7] [1707] 11-8-11 44 ....(b) AnnStokell(5) 3 34
(Miss A Stokell) *prom: rdn along 1/2-way: edgd lft 2f out and sn btn* **25/1**

3-06 **6** *1 1/4* **Rudi's Pet (IRE)**[7] [1707] 13-9-2 60 ....(v) SilvestreDeSousa 1 30
(D Nicholls) *dwlt: hdwy on inner whn n.m.r 2f out: sn rdn and btn* **6/1**

0-02 **7** *nk* **Compton Classic**[7] [1707] 5-9-7 55 .... GaryBartley(7) 2 40
(J S Goldie) *in rr tl sme late hdwy* **15/2**

00-0 **8** *hd* **Alfie Lee (IRE)**[7] [1707] 10-9-0 33 ....(t) PaulMulrennan 9 26
(D A Nolan) *prom: rdn along over 2f out: grad wknd* **250/1**

00-0 **9** *6* **Howards Prince**[15] [1493] 4-8-12 50 ....(p) PaulFessey 10 2
(I Semple) *chsd ldrs on outer: rdn along over 2f out and sn wknd* **16/1**

59.48 secs (-1.02) **Going Correction** -0.25s/f (Firm)
WFA 3 from 4yo+ 8lb **9** Ran SP% **114.4**
Speed ratings (Par 101):98,93,90,88,85 83,82,82,72
CSF £107.73 TOTE £5.70: £1.40, £7.10, £1.90; EX 107.70.Whinhill House was the subject of a friendly claim.
Owner D W Barker **Bred** W R And Mrs Arblaster **Trained** Scorton, N Yorks

FOCUS
A typically weak seller. The winner is full value for the winning margin.

1892 GET TURF TV IN YOUR BETTING SHOP H'CAP 7f 30y
3:40 (3:40) (Class 5) (0-70,71) 4-Y-0+ **£3,238** (£963; £481; £240) **Stalls** High

Form RPR

-103 **1** **Dispol Isle (IRE)**[7] [1710] 5-8-9 **68** .... NeilBrown(7) 8 78
(T D Barron) *trckd ldrs: hdwy over 2f out: swtchd lft and rdn over 1f out: led ent fnl f and styd on wl* **10/3**[1]

0631 **2** *3/4* **Baylaw Star**[7] [1711] 6-9-5 **71** 6ex .... RoystonFfrench 6 79
(I W McInnes) *cl up: rdn along over 2f out and ev ch tl drvn ins fnl f and no ex last 100yds* **6/1**[3]

3616 **3** *nk* **Flying Bantam (IRE)**[17] [1458] 6-8-12 **64** .... TonyHamilton 14 71
(R A Fahey) *trckd ldrs on inner: hdwy 3f out: swtchd lft and rdn over 1f out: drvn and kpt on wl fnl f* **9/2**[2]

0606 **4** *1* **Sentiero Rosso (USA)**[7] [1720] 5-8-8 **60** ....(t) PatCosgrave 12 64
(B Ellison) *in tch: hdwy 3f out: rdn along 2f out: drvn and kpt on ins fnl f* **12/1**

0-04 **5** *3/4* **Snow Bunting**[7] [1711] 9-8-1 **56** .... AndrewElliott(3) 13 58+
(Jedd O'Keeffe) *s.i.s and bhd: hdwy wl over 2f out: rdn and styd on ins fnl f: nrst fin* **7/1**

00-0 **6** *shd* **Redwood Rocks (IRE)**[133] [70] 6-8-9 **64** .... MarkLawson(3) 7 66
(B Smart) *led: rdn along 3f out: drvn wl over 1f out: hdd ent fnl f: wknd last 150yds* **14/1**

6-40 **7** *3/4* **Crosby Vision**[6] [1747] 4-9-4 **70** .... JoeFanning 2 70
(J R Weymes) *hld up: hdwy 3f out: rdn along 2f out: kpt on same pce appr fnl f* **14/1**

05-0 **8** *1 1/2* **Entranced**[10] [1627] 4-8-7 **59** .... PhillipMakin 9 58+
(L Lungo) *in rr tl sme late hdwy* **20/1**

100- **9** *hd* **Hazelhurst (IRE)**[276] [4567] 4-9-4 **70** .... PaulMulrennan 5 65
(J Howard Johnson) *midfield: hdwy on outer 3f out: rdn to chse ldrs 2f out: sn drvn and btn* **28/1**

6-00 **10** *1 1/2* **Esoterica (IRE)**[17] [1459] 4-8-10 **62** .... DanielTudhope 4 53
(J S Goldie) *a in rr* **16/1**

01-0 **11** *3 1/2* **Laphonic (USA)**[18] [1436] 4-8-4 **56** oh4 .... JamieMackay 3 38
(T J Etherington) *a towards rr* **50/1**

/-0 **12** *2 1/2* **Seafield Towers**[15] [1493] 7-8-4 **56** oh1 .... PaulFessey 1 31
(Miss L A Perratt) *chsd ldrs: rdn along over 3f out: sn wknd* **33/1**

2-26 **13** *shd* **Musicmaestroplease (IRE)**[46] [933] 4-8-10 **62** .... PaulEddery 10 37
(S Parr) *a in rr* **11/1**

1m 28.94s (-1.00) **Going Correction** -0.125s/f (Firm) **13** Ran SP% **116.4**
Speed ratings (Par 103):100,99,98,97,96 96,95,94,93,92 88,85,85
CSF £21.08 CT £94.20 TOTE £3.20: £1.80, £1.70, £1.90; EX 18.20.
Owner W B Imison **Bred** Mrs I A Balding **Trained** Maunby, N Yorks
■ Stewards' Enquiry : Mark Lawson caution: allowed gelding to coast home with no assistance

FOCUS
A modest handicap, run at a sound pace. The form looks straightforward with the winner and second, both of whom have good records here, being rated positively.

1893 TURFTV.CO.UK (S) STKS 1m
4:10 (4:10) (Class 6) 4-Y-0+ **£1,943** (£578; £288; £144) **Stalls** High

Form RPR

000- **1** **Sam's Secret**[202] [6273] 5-8-7 62 .... DeanMcKeown 3 53
(G A Swinbank) *trckd ldrs: hdwy 3f out: led 2f out: rdn clr over 1f out: drvn ins fnl f and kpt on* **7/1**[3]

0065 **2** *3/4* **Nevinstown (IRE)**[6] [1744] 7-8-12 43 .... JoeFanning 2 58+
(C Grant) *midfield: hdwy and nt clr run 2f out and again over 1f out: swtchd lft and rdn ent fnl f: fin wl* **14/1**

-006 **3** *hd* **Mayadeen (IRE)**[10] [1627] 5-8-12 52 ....(b) PaulFessey 5 56
(I Semple) *bhd: rdn along 4f out: gd hdwy on outer 2f out: rdn and styd on strly ins fnl f* **9/1**

500/ **4** *nk* **Tizzy May (FR)**[813] [6354] 7-8-12 75 .... TonyHamilton 10 55
(B Ellison) *trckd ldrs: hdwy 3f out: rdn to chse wnr wl over 1f out: drvn and kpt on same pce fnl f* **5/2**[1]

60-0 **5** *1 3/4* **Thistle**[15] [1488] 6-8-12 59 .... PaulMulrennan 8 51
(J Howard Johnson) *in tch: hdwy 3f out: rdn to chse ldrs 2f out: drvn and one pce appr fnl f* **7/1**[3]

0-25 **6** *nk* **Thunderwing (IRE)**[13] [1554] 5-8-12 66 ....(v) PatCosgrave 4 50
(K R Burke) *cl up: led 3f out: rdn and hdd 2f out: sn drvn and grad wknd appr fnl f* **10/3**[2]

0-00 **7** *1* **Ho Pang Yau**[14] [1527] 9-8-5 40 .... GaryBartley(7) 12 51+
(J S Goldie) *bhd: gd hdwy on inner whn nt clr run 2f out: swtchd lft: rdn and styng on whn nt clr run ins fnl f: nt rcvr* **50/1**

000- **8** *1 1/2* **Sparkbridge (IRE)**[178] [5836] 4-8-12 45 ....(b) AdrianTNicholls 1 44
(R F Fisher) *s.i.s: t.k.h and sn into midfield: effrt 3f out: sn rdn along and kpt on same pce fnl 2f* **66/1**

0450 **9** *hd* **Fairy Monarch (IRE)**[19] [1413] 8-8-7 53 ....(b) RoryMoore(5) 9 44
(P T Midgley) *towards rr: hdwy 3f out: rdn to chse ldrs 2f out: wknd appr fnl f* **8/1**

5040 **10** *1/2* **Following Flow (USA)**[10] [1627] 5-8-12 52 .... PhillipMakin 11 43
(R Allan) *s.i.s: a in rr* **25/1**

-000 **11** *2* **Alisdanza**[20] [1381] 5-8-7 43 .... DavidAllan 7 33
(N Wilson) *led: rdn along and hdd 3f out: sn wknd* **25/1**

0000 **12** *2 1/2* **Drury Lane (IRE)**[11] [1596] 7-8-7 44 ....(b) AnnStokell(5) 6 32
(Miss A Stokell) *chsd ldrs: rdn along over 2f out: sn drvn and wknd* **100/1**

1m 40.62s (-1.88) **Going Correction** -0.125s/f (Firm) **12** Ran SP% **116.6**
Speed ratings (Par 101):104,103,103,102,101 100,99,98,98,97 95,93
CSF £93.78 TOTE £8.90: £2.50, £3.80, £2.30; EX 85.70.There was no bid for the winner.
Owner Copskam Partnership **Bred** Dandy's Farm **Trained** Melsonby, N Yorks

FOCUS
A moderate seller, run at a solid pace. The winner was 20lb off last year's form with the fourth and fifth also once capable of better, and it is unlikely the second and third are any better than this at present.

1894 TURF TV BETTING SHOP SERVICE H'CAP 1m
4:40 (4:40) (Class 6) (0-65,61) 3-Y-0 **£2,590** (£770; £385; £192) **Stalls** High

Form RPR

-621 **1** **Jewelled Dagger (IRE)**[7] [1712] 3-9-8 **61** 6ex ....(b) PhillipMakin 6 70+
(I Semple) *mde all: rdn 2f out: qcknd clr over 1f out: styd on strly* **7/4**[1]

0-00 **2** *2 1/2* **Desert Soul**[33] [1091] 3-9-7 **60** .... JoeFanning 1 62
(M Johnston) *cl up: rdn to chal over 2f out and ev ch tl drvn and nt pce of wnr fr over 1f out* **9/1**

50-0 **3** *3/4* **Marquee (IRE)**[21] [1358] 3-9-2 **55** .... GrahamGibbons 10 55
(P A Blockley) *in tch: hdwy 3f out: swtchd lft and rdn 2f out: kpt on ins fnl f* **10/1**

00-3 **4** *nk* **Sparky Vixen**[26] [1236] 3-9-3 **56** .... DeanMcKeown 8 56
(G A Swinbank) *chsd ldrs: hdwy on outer over 2f out: sn rdn and kpt on appr fnl f* **5/1**[2]

450- **5** *1 1/2* **Alberts Story (USA)**[285] [4260] 3-8-13 **52** .... TonyHamilton 13 48
(R A Fahey) *chsd ldng pair: rdn along wl over 2f out: drvn wl over 1f out and sn one pce* **8/1**

00-0 **6** *1/2* **Hopeful Isabella (IRE)**[12] [1579] 3-8-6 **45** .... JamieMackay 4 40
(Sir Mark Prescott) *chsd ldrs: rdn along 3f out: drvn 2f out and sn wknd* **11/2**[3]

6-04 **7** *1/2* **Myfrenchconnection (IRE)**[18] [1425] 3-8-10 **54** .... RoryMoore(5) 12 48
(P T Midgley) *stdd s and bhd tl sme late hdwy* **14/1**

3005 **8** *3 1/2* **Poniard (IRE)**[7] [1712] 3-9-4 **57** ....(p) RoystonFfrench 7 43
(D W Barker) *in tch: rdn along 1/2-way: sn wknd* **25/1**

06-2 **9** *nk* **Crosby Jemma**[13] [1558] 3-8-11 **53** .... AndrewElliott(3) 5 38
(J R Weymes) *a in rr* **25/1**

-000 **10** *11* **Play Straight**[33] [1091] 3-9-4 **57** ....(p) DanielTudhope 2 17
(I W McInnes) *bhd fr 1/2-way* **33/1**

1m 41.33s (-1.17) **Going Correction** -0.125s/f (Firm) **10** Ran SP% **115.9**
Speed ratings (Par 97):100,97,96,96,94 94,93,90,90,79
CSF £17.95 CT £128.06 TOTE £1.80: £1.30, £4.00, £3.30; EX 21.80.
Owner A R M Galbraith **Bred** Ballyhane Stud **Trained** Carluke, S Lanarks
■ Stewards' Enquiry : Daniel Tudhope one-day ban: careless riding (Jun 5)

FOCUS
A moderate three-year-old handicap, run at an uneven pace. The winner remains progressive and the form looks pretty solid.
Poniard(IRE) Official explanation: jockey said gelding hung left-handed from start

1895 TURF TV A MATTER OF COURSE APPRENTICE H'CAP 2m
5:10 (5:10) (Class 6) (0-65,60) 4-Y-0+ **£2,590** (£770; £385; £192) **Stalls** Low

Form RPR

006- **1** **Singhalongtasveer**[50] [5061] 5-9-2 **45** ....(vt) AndrewElliott 8 50
(W Storey) *in tch: pushed along and hdwy 4f out: rdn over 2f out: styd on u.p to ld appr fnl f: drvn out* **7/1**

00-4 **2** *5* **Mystified (IRE)**[27] [1222] 4-9-1 **46** ....(b) MarkLawson 1 45+
(R F Fisher) *led and sn clr: rdn along 3f out: jnd 2f out and sn drvn: hdd appr fnl f and kpt on same pce* **5/1**[3]

0151 **3** *1/2* **Rocknest Island (IRE)**[6] [1745] 4-9-12 **60** 6ex ....(p) PJMcDonald(3) 4 58
(P D Niven) *chsd ldng pair: effrt and hdwy 3f out: sn rdn: drvn wl over 1f out: kpt on ins fnl f* **4/1**[2]

-066 **4** *3/4* **Piccolomini**[13] [1556] 5-8-12 **46** ....(b) NeilBrown(5) 7 44
(E W Tuer) *hld up in midfield: hdwy 3f out: sn rdn and kpt on same pce u.p fnl 2f* **7/1**

000- **5** *1 1/4* **Borsch (IRE)**[282] [4350] 5-8-9 **45** .... JamesRogers(7) 2 41
(Miss L A Perratt) *chsd ldrs: rdn along and outpcd over 5f out: plugged on u.p fnl 3f* **66/1**

013 **6** *shd* **Kyber**[17] [1457] 6-9-5 **53** .... GaryBartley(5) 9 49
(J S Goldie) *chsd clr ldr: hdwy 3f out: rdn to chal 2f out and ev ch: drvn and wknd wl over 1f out* **15/8**[1]

0-00 **7** ½ **Time Marches On**[6] [1744] 9-8-11 **45**.......................... JamesReveley(5) 6 40
(K G Reveley) *hld up and bhd tl styd on fnl 2f* **9/1**

/06- **8** 3 ½ **Compton Dragon (USA)**[232] [3037] 8-9-5 **55**.......... PatrickDonaghy(7) 3 46
(W M Brisbourne) *a in rr* **20/1**

0-06 **9** 69 **Keep A Welcome**[12] [1573] 4-8-7 **45**..........................(p) GaryEdwards(7) 5 —
(S Parr) *chsd ldrs: pushed along and lost pl 1/2-way: sn bhd* **80/1**

3m 32.21s (-1.69) **Going Correction** -0.125s/f (Firm)
WFA 4 from 5yo+ 2lb **9** Ran SP% **113.9**
Speed ratings (Par 101):99,96,96,95,95 95,94,93,58
CSF £40.69 CT £158.89 TOTE £12.20: £2.50, £1.40, £1.70; EX 52.20 Place 6 £153.49, Place 5 £110.51..
Owner W Storey **Bred** J O'Mulloy **Trained** Muggleswick, Co Durham

FOCUS
A poor staying handicap which was run at a strong early gallop. The winner rates full value for the winning margin and is entitled to rate this high on jumps form, but this was a weak race.
T/Plt: £296.60 to a £1 stake. Pool: £43,152.00. 106.20 winning tickets. T/Qpdt: £43.50 to a £1 stake. Pool: £3,117.40. 53.00 winning tickets. JR

1721 WINDSOR (R-H)
Monday, May 21

OFFICIAL GOING: Good (8.5)
Wind: Almost nil Weather: Overcast, drizzly

1896 COUNTRYSIDE ALLIANCE EBF MAIDEN FILLIES' STKS 5f 10y
6:10 (6:12) (Class 5) 2-Y-O **£4,533** (£1,348; £674; £336) **Stalls** High

Form RPR

1 **Lady Avenger (IRE)** 2-9-0 0.. KerrinMcEvoy 3 83
(J M P Eustace) *towards rr: prog on outer bef 1/2-way: led over 1f out: rdn clr fnl f: readily* **10/1**

3 **2** 3 **Shamrock Lady (IRE)**[34] [1079] 2-9-0 0..................... RichardThomas 10 72
(Pat Eddery) *mde most: hdd over 1f out: edgd lft after: no ch w wnr* **6/1**

3 ½ **May Day Queen (IRE)** 2-9-0 0....................................... DaneO'Neill 14 70
(R Hannon) *awkward s: sn pressed ldrs: hanging lft and nt qckn 2f out: n.m.r 1f out: kpt on* **7/2**[1]

4 1 ½ **Shabnaam** 2-9-0 0.. DO'Donohoe 11 65
(K A Ryan) *dwlt: rn green towards rr: rdn and styd on fr over 1f out: nrst fin* **9/1**

5 hd **Xtravaganza (IRE)** 2-9-0 0.. KDarley 4 64
(J W Hills) *s.i.s: wl in rr: taken to wd outside 2f out: styd on fnl f: nrst fin* **28/1**

6 nk **Cocabana** 2-9-0 0.. AdamKirby 6 63
(J G Portman) *w ldr to 2f out: wknd fnl f* **33/1**

7 ½ **Poppy Dean (IRE)** 2-8-11 0...............................(t) EmmettStack(3) 15 61
(J G Portman) *racd against nr side rail: midfield: no imp over 1f out: kpt on* **40/1**

8 1 ¼ **Evenstorm (USA)** 2-8-11 0 ow2............................... JamesMillman(5) 2 59
(B Gubby) *uns rdr in paddock: midfield: outpcd 2f out: kpt on same pce fnl f* **50/1**

9 1 ¾ **Don't Tell Anna (IRE)** 2-9-0 0..................................... RichardHughes 1 50
(R Hannon) *spd on outer for 3f: wknd over 1f out* **15/2**

2 **10** 2 ½ **Vixens Daughter**[9] [1674] 2-9-0 0................................ MickyFenton 5 41+
(R T Phillips) *spd to press ldrs to 1/2-way: wknd and eased over 1f out* **12/1**

11 1 ¼ **Lella Beya** 2-9-0 0... LDettori 16 37
(S Kirk) *dwlt: a struggling in rr* **5/1**[2]

12 ¾ **Beyabi** 2-9-0 0.. JohnEgan 7 34
(J R Jenkins) *nvr bttr than midfield: wknd wl over 1f out: eased fnl f* **28/1**

13 2 **Naked Spark (IRE)** 2-8-7 0..................................... JackDean(7) 9 27
(W G M Turner) *a towards rr: u.p and wkng 2f out* **50/1**

14 1 ½ **Theebah** 2-8-7 .... ThomasO'Brien(7) 13 22
(M R Channon) *s.s: a struggling and last* **11/2**[3]

62.34 secs (1.24) **Going Correction** +0.225s/f (Good) **14** Ran SP% **123.3**
Speed ratings (Par 90):99,94,93,91,90 90,89,87,84,80 78,77,74,71
CSF £67.04 TOTE £13.10: £3.80, £2.50, £1.50; EX 96.90.
Owner J C Smith **Bred** Herbertstown Stud Ltd **Trained** Newmarket, Suffolk

FOCUS
A reasonable fillies' maiden run in a very decent time for a race of its type; just 0.22 seconds slower than the following juvenile conditions event. A nice start from Lady Avenger, but the level of the form is guessy.

NOTEBOOK
Lady Avenger(IRE) ◆, a 45,000euros first foal of a sister to Lulua, a dual winner in the US, overcame her low draw to make a winning debut in good style. She was forced to make her move widest of all, but she was always travelling very smoothly and drew nicely clear when asked. Her connections think she will benefit from some cut in the ground, but whatever the case, she looks above average and deserves her chance in better company. (op 12-1)
Shamrock Lady(IRE) was given every chance against the often favoured near-side rail and improved on the form she showed when third on her debut at Warwick. She should be placed to advantage at some stage this season, but is likely to be vulnerable to a decent type. (op 11-2 tchd 13-2)
May Day Queen(IRE), a 28,000gns half-sister to Russian Gift, who was unplaced over 5f-6f at two, looked a nice type in the paddock and made a pleasing debut. She was a little short of room about a furlong out, but recovered her momentum to take third and should have benefited from the experience. (op 5-1 tchd 11-2)
Shabnaam, a half-sister to Silver Hotspur, who was placed over 5f-1m at two and three, took a very keen grip when first beginning to head down to the start, but she was fine in the race itself. She kept on nicely to the line and should improve plenty for the outing. (op 8-1)
Xtravaganza(IRE), an 11,000gns half-sister to Queen Of Diamonds, who was placed over 1m3f, out of a winner over 1m1f, never posed a threat but was noted staying on towards the outside of the main pack in the closing stages. (op 33-1)
Cocabana, a 14,000gns purchase, out of a 5f three-year-old winner, showed bags of speed before just getting tired inside the final furlong. She is entitled to come on for the run and could find a small race, possibly when there is a bit of cut in the ground. (op 40-1)
Don't Tell Anna(IRE) ◆, a 40,000euros half-sister to dual sprint winner Don't Tell Mum, stood out in the paddock. She finished up well held, but better can be expected in time. (op 6-1)
Lella Beya, a half-sister to the stable's high-class sprinting juvenile Elhamri, out of a 7f winner at two, was significantly supported in the market, which probably had something to do with Frankie Dettori being announced as a late jockey change. She was never going and offered little immediate promise. Official explanation: jockey said filly missed the break and ran green (op 15-2)
Theebah, a 60,000gns half-sister to several winners, including Gimcrack winner Bannister, was not unfancied in the market but was the subject of a jockey change, with a 7lb claimer taking over from Hugh Bowman. She was never seen with a chance after starting slowly, but is surely better than this. (op 9-2)

1897 WEATHERBYS BANK CONDITIONS STKS 5f 10y
6:40 (6:40) (Class 2) 2-Y-O
£12,464 (£3,732; £1,866; £934; £466; £234) **Stalls** High

Form RPR

2 **1** **Eileen's Violet (IRE)**[12] [1585] 2-8-6 0.................................. JohnEgan 5 88
(P D Evans) *pushed along in last pair over 3f out: taken to outer and effrt 2f out: edgd lft over 1f out: drvn and r.o to ld last strides* **14/1**

611 **2** shd **Group Therapy**[16] [1478] 2-9-3 0... LDettori 4 98
(J A Osborne) *sn led and grabbed nr side rail: hrd pressed fnl f: hdd last strides* **4/5**[1]

11 **3** nk **Cake (IRE)**[15] [1503] 2-8-12 0.. RichardHughes 6 94+
(R Hannon) *t.k.h: hld up bhd ldrs: nt clr run over 1f out: got through and drvn fnl f: nt quite rch ldrs* **5/1**[3]

4 ¾ **Perfect Paula (USA)** 2-8-3 0.. KerrinMcEvoy 1 81
(B J Meehan) *cl up: rdn to chal 1f out: no ex last 75yds* **16/1**

01 **5** 3 ½ **Enodoc**[16] [1469] 2-8-11 0.. DO'Donohoe 2 76
(W R Muir) *pressed ldr over 3f out to over 1f out: wknd fnl f* **7/2**[2]

6 5 **Really Really Wish** 2-8-8 0.. DaneO'Neill 3 55+
(J R Best) *dwlt: a in last pair: lft bhd fnl 2f* **66/1**

201 **7** 8 **Ballycroy Boy (IRE)**[7] [1713] 2-8-11 0................................ MickyFenton 7 29+
(A Bailey) *rousted along to be prom against rail: lost pl after 2f: jinked 2f out: sn wknd* **25/1**

62.12 secs (1.02) **Going Correction** +0.225s/f (Good) **7** Ran SP% **112.3**
Speed ratings (Par 99):100,99,99,98,92 84,71
CSF £25.03 TOTE £18.10: £3.30, £1.40; EX 26.30.
Owner Derek Buckley **Bred** Tom Radley **Trained** Pandy, Monmouths

FOCUS
A good, competitive conditions contest in which the winner and third showed improved form. The winning time was 0.22 seconds quicker than the previous maiden.

NOTEBOOK
Eileen's Violet(IRE) built on the promise she showed when second on her debut at Chester with a narrow success. She struggled to go the early gallop, but stayed on well widest of all and got up on the line. She is crying out for 6f and deserves to take her chance in the Albany Stakes at Royal Ascot. (op 16-1 tchd 12-1)
Group Therapy has already shown himself a very useful performer and he looked to run to something like his best, only just failing to concede 11lb to a decent type. A return to even faster ground should suit better. (op 5-6 tchd 8-11, 10-11 in a place)
Cake(IRE)'s two previous wins represented just ordinary form, but this was a good effort in defeat. She could even be considered a little unlucky, as she only got in the clear inside the final furlong and was gaining at the finish. (op 4-1 tchd 13-2)
Perfect Paula(USA) ◆, a $145,000 sister to the stable's high-class Jack Junior, placed over 1m1f on the dirt at three, out of a winner on turf in the US, made a very pleasing introduction. She only gave way late on and ought to win her maiden next time before stepping back up in class. (op 20-1)
Enodoc ran well below the form he showed when causing a surprise at Goodwood on his previous start and was disappointing. (op 4-1)
Really Really Wish, a 20,000euros purchase, out of a prolific 6f-1m4f winner, showed some ability and can be expected to improve for the outing.
Ballycroy Boy(IRE) Official explanation: jockey said colt was denied a clear run; vet said colt had been struck into

1898 SMITH AND WILLIAMSON H'CAP 1m 3f 135y
7:10 (7:10) (Class 4) (0-85,83) 3-Y-O **£6,477** (£1,927; £963; £481) **Stalls** Low

Form RPR

-122 **1** **Bergonzi (IRE)**[12] [1584] 3-9-4 **83**.. SteveDrowne 6 87+
(J H M Gosden) *pressed ldr: led 1/2-way: drvn and pressed fnl 2f: styd on wl last 100yds* **7/4**[1]

13-2 **2** ¾ **Oakley Heffert (IRE)**[16] [1467] 3-8-13 **78**....................... RichardHughes 2 81
(R Hannon) *trckd ldrs: rdn over 2f out: styd on fnl f to take 2nd last stride* **9/2**[3]

5-53 **3** shd **King Joshua (IRE)**[26] [1246] 3-8-9 **74**.................................... JohnEgan 5 77
(D R C Elsworth) *t.k.h: hld up in last pair: prog on outer over 3f out and hanging lft: wnt 2nd 2f out: sn chalng: nt qckn and hld last 100yds* **12/1**

61- **4** shd **Wait For The Light**[203] [6257] 3-9-2 **81**.. LDettori 7 84
(E A L Dunlop) *trckd ldrs: effrt over 2f out: carried hd high and hanging lft over 1f out: styd on ins fnl f* **9/1**

010- **5** 5 **Hi Calypso (IRE)**[205] [6217] 3-8-11 **76**............................ KerrinMcEvoy 3 71
(Sir Michael Stoute) *hld up in last: awkward bnd over 5f out: pushed along 4f out: brief effrt over 2f out: sn btn* **6/1**

20-0 **6** 7 **Jane Of Arc (FR)**[19] [1414] 3-8-4 **72** ow3...................... EmmettStack(3) 4 56
(M H Tompkins) *in tch tl wknd over 2f out* **33/1**

-422 **7** 8 **My Secrets**[19] [1415] 3-9-0 **79**.. KDarley 1 50
(M Johnston) *led to 1/2-way: chsd wnr: rdn 4f out: btn 2f out: wknd rapidly over 1f out* **3/1**[2]

2m 32.23s (2.13) **Going Correction** +0.225s/f (Good) **7** Ran SP% **114.5**
Speed ratings (Par 101):101,100,100,100,97 92,87
CSF £10.06 TOTE £2.80: £2.20, £2.20; EX 11.90.
Owner H R H Princess Haya Of Jordan **Bred** Deerforest Stud **Trained** Newmarket, Suffolk
■ Stewards' Enquiry : Steve Drowne three-day ban: used whip with excessive frequency (Jun 3-5)

FOCUS
Ordinary handicap form for the grade and the early pace was just steady. Bergonzi is progressive and likely to do better, although he might not have needed to improve to win this.

1899 COUNTRYSIDE ALLIANCE CLAIMING STKS 6f
7:40 (7:40) (Class 5) 3-Y-O+ **£3,238** (£963; £481; £240) **Stalls** High

Form RPR

-504 **1** **Makabul**[21] [1357] 4-9-3 68.................................... JamesMillman(5) 14 62
(B R Millman) *s.s: wl in rr nr side tl prog on outer 1/2-way: led gp over 1f out: drvn and styd on to ld wl ins fnl f* **2/1**[1]

230- **2** ½ **Princely Vale (IRE)**[238] [5569] 5-8-9 48..........................(p) JackDean(7) 11 54
(W G M Turner) *trckd nr side ldrs: lost pl 2f out: swtchd lft and effrt over 1f out: r.o wl fnl f: nt quite rch wnr* **10/1**

0000 **3** ½ **Going Skint**[9] [1673] 4-9-4 56...(v) AdamKirby 1 54
(M Wellings) *racd towards far side: overall ldr: hrd rdn fnl 2f: wknd and hdd wl ins fnl f* **16/1**

0220 **4** shd **Mistral Sky**[20] [1382] 8-9-4 63...(v) MickyFenton 4 54
(Stef Liddiard) *chsd ldr towards far side: rdn over 2f out: styd on fnl f: jst hld* **9/2**[2]

5060 **5** 2 **Mine The Balance (IRE)**[15] [1507] 4-9-4 50.........(b) SimonWhitworth 10 48
(H J Manners) *towards rr nr side: rdn over 2f out: styd on fr over 1f out: nt pce to rch ldrs* **33/1**

00-0 **6** nk **Festive Tipple (IRE)**[13] [1561] 3-8-5 55......................... MatthewHenry 16 43
(P Winkworth) *trckd nr side ldrs: led gp briefly wl over 1f out: wknd* **20/1**

0063 **7** nk **Arfinnit (IRE)**[58] [750] 6-9-2 45..............................(p) RichardHughes 8 44
(Mrs A L M King) *chsd nr side ldrs: nt qckn 2f out: one pce after* **15/2**

0600 **8** 1 3/4 **Task Complete**[40] [1001] 4-8-9 45..............................(b) StephenCarson 6 31
(Jean-Rene Auvray) *wl bhd in last tl styd on fr over 1f out: n.d* **33/1**

0-65 **9** 3/4 **Montzando**[27] [1212] 4-9-2 50..............................(v) JimCrowley 13 36
(B R Millman) *w nr side ldr: led gp over 2f out to wl over 1f out: wknd* **6/1**[3]

00-0 **10** 1 **African Concerto (IRE)**[7] [1729] 4-9-0 45.............. FrankieMcDonald 12 31
(S Kirk) *t.k.h: hld up in rr nr side: no prog fnl 2f* **22/1**

3000 **11** 1 1/2 **Campbeltown (IRE)**[18] [1431] 4-9-8 58..............................(b) DaneO'Neill 15 34
(M R Hoad) *mde most nr side to over 2f out: wknd* **16/1**

0225 **12** 2 **Pat Will (IRE)**[5] [1763] 3-8-4 55 ow2..............................(b) JohnEgan 2 18
(P D Evans) *w nr side ldrs: wnt towards far side 1/2-way: sn wknd and eased* **10/1**

1m 15.28s (1.61) **Going Correction** +0.225s/f (Good)
WFA 3 from 4yo+ 9lb **12 Ran SP% 122.5**
Speed ratings (Par 103):98,97,96,96,93 93,93,90,89,88 86,83
CSF £23.18 TOTE £3.60: £1.60, £2.60, £4.30; EX 31.90.
Owner M S T Partnership **Bred** D Lowe **Trained** Kentisbeare, Devon

FOCUS
A moderate claimer. The majority of these raced near side, as one would have expected, but Going Skint tried his luck towards the far side, and both Mistral Sky and Pat Will came up the middle in the straight. The runner-up is the best guide and the winner did not need to run to his mark.
Pat Will(IRE) Official explanation: jockey said filly hung both ways

1900 SUNLEY H'CAP — 5f 10y
8:10 (8:10) (Class 4) (0-85,84) 3-Y-O **£6,477** (£1,927; £963; £481) **Stalls High**

Form RPR

02-6 **1** **Bertoliver**[9] [1660] 3-8-11 **77**.............................. KerrinMcEvoy 9 84
(D K Ivory) *racd against nr side rail: mde all: hld on u.p fnl f* **8/1**

1122 **2** *shd* **Sohraab**[49] [885] 3-8-9 **75**.............................. RichardHughes 10 85+
(H Morrison) *hld up bhd ldrs: gng easily whn nt clr run and swtchd lft over 1f out: r.o fnl f: jst failed: too much to do* **11/2**[3]

201- **3** 3/4 **Ishi Adiva**[216] [6024] 3-9-3 **83**.............................. RichardThomas 2 87
(Tom Dascombe) *trckd ldrs: plld out and effrt wl over 1f out: tried to chal ins fnl f: styd on same pce* **6/1**

-165 **4** 1 1/4 **Gower**[10] [1616] 3-9-0 **80**.............................. SteveDrowne 5 80
(R Charlton) *pushed along towards rr: prog on outer 1/2-way: chsd ldrs over 1f out: kpt on same pce* **9/2**[2]

2-50 **5** 1/2 **Spoof Master (IRE)**[11] [1604] 3-9-3 **83**.............................. AmirQuinn 7 81
(W G M Turner) *mostly chsd wnr to over 1f out: one pce u.p* **12/1**

51-0 **6** 1 1/2 **Buckie Massa**[9] [1658] 3-8-8 **74**.............................. FrankieMcDonald 8 66
(S Kirk) *hld up in last trio: styd on steadily fnl 2f: nvr nr ldrs* **40/1**

20-1 **7** 1 **Pretty Miss**[18] [1429] 3-8-7 **73** ow1.............................. DaneO'Neill 4 62
(H Candy) *prom: gng wl 2f out: rdn to dispute 2nd sn after: wknd tamely* **9/1**

4-40 **8** 1 **Reebal**[14] [1520] 3-9-1 **81**.............................. LDettori 12 66
(B J Meehan) *pushed along in last trio: hanging lft whn asked for effrt 1/2-way: modest late prog* **12/1**

2-03 **9** *shd* **Just Joey**[12] [1577] 3-9-4 **84**.............................. KDarley 11 69
(J R Weymes) *sn rdn to chse ldrs: struggling fr 2f out: wknd* **10/1**

61- **10** *nk* **Dramatic Turn**[208] [6175] 3-9-0 **80**.............................. JimCrowley 6 64
(Mrs A J Perrett) *pressed ldng pair: hrd rdn 2f out: sn wknd* **4/1**[1]

42-3 **11** 4 **Fairfield Princess**[14] [1520] 3-9-2 **82**.............................. SebSanders 3 51
(M S Saunders) *dwlt: a struggling in last pair* **16/1**

61.50 secs (0.40) **Going Correction** +0.225s/f (Good) **11 Ran SP% 121.8**
Speed ratings (Par 101):105,104,103,101,100 98,96,95,95,94 88
CSF £53.55 CT £295.42 TOTE £8.20: £2.00, £2.20, £2.60; EX 41.90.
Owner Mrs A Shone **Bred** Pillar To Post Racing **Trained** Radlett, Herts

FOCUS
A fair sprint handicap and pretty solid form, rated through the winner and third. The runner-up probably should have won.
Dramatic Turn Official explanation: jockey said filly lost a shoe

1901 VC CASINO.COM MAIDEN FILLIES' STKS — 1m 67y
8:40 (8:41) (Class 5) 3-Y-0+ **£3,886** (£1,156; £577; £288) **Stalls High**

Form RPR

433- **1** **Cliche (IRE)**[244] [5464] 3-8-9 0.............................. KerrinMcEvoy 3 70+
(Sir Michael Stoute) *mde virtually all: pressed and edgd lft over 1f out: styd on wl last 150yds* **11/10**[1]

322- **2** 1 3/4 **Siamese Cat (IRE)**[205] [6215] 3-8-9 102.............................. LDettori 1 66+
(B J Meehan) *pressed wnr: rdn to chal over 1f out: readily hld last 100yds* **13/8**[2]

50- **3** 3/4 **Asturias**[233] [5679] 3-8-9 0.............................. MatthewHenry 10 64
(J W Hills) *t.k.h: hld up in rr: prog over 3f out: chsd ldng pair wl over 2f out: styd on but nvr able to chal* **66/1**

0 **4** 3/4 **Labor Day (IRE)**[28] [1203] 3-8-9 0.............................. SteveDrowne 4 62
(J H M Gosden) *hld up in midfeld: prog over 2f out: drvn and styd on fr over 1f out: nvr rchd ldrs* **12/1**[3]

3- **5** 1 1/4 **Scar Tissue**[164] [6745] 3-8-9 0.............................. RichardThomas 8 59
(Tom Dascombe) *prom: rdn over 2f out: one pce after* **50/1**

2 **6** *nk* **Pendulum Star**[14] [1537] 3-8-9 0.............................. AdamKirby 2 59+
(W R Swinburn) *s.i.s: hld up in rr: rn green but gng wl 3f out: nudged along and styd on steadily* **14/1**

4-0 **7** 3/4 **Sofia Royale**[10] [1639] 3-8-9 0.............................. KDarley 12 57
(B Palling) *pressed ldng pair to 3f out: steadily fdd* **66/1**

0- **8** 2 **Aphrodisia**[244] [5456] 3-8-6 0.............................. SaleemGolam(3) 6 52
(S C Williams) *s.s: t.k.h: sme prog into midfield 1/2-way: pushed along over 2f out: hanging lft and one pce* **66/1**

9 1 1/4 **Susanna's Dance** 3-8-9 0.............................. SebSanders 7 50
(Sir Michael Stoute) *hld up in midfield: pushed along and no prog fnl 3f* **20/1**

0 **10** 1 1/2 **Condi (IRE)**[7] [1725] 3-8-9 0.............................. JohnEgan 13 46
(A J Lidderdale) *hld up in rr: prog and cl up 3f out: sn rdn and wknd* **50/1**

11 3 1/2 **Regal Estate** 3-8-9 0.............................. PhilipRobinson 5 38
(M A Jarvis) *dwlt: last and nt handle bnd 5f out: nvr a factor* **12/1**[3]

36 **12** 4 **Collioure (USA)**[7] [1714] 3-8-9 0.............................. JHBowman 11 29
(P F I Cole) *hld up bhd ldrs: wknd 3f out* **33/1**

0 **13** 5 **Vive La Chasse (IRE)**[85] [559] 4-9-7 0.............................. StephenCarson 9 17
(Eve Johnson Houghton) *chsd ldrs to 1/2-way: sn wknd and bhd* **66/1**

1m 47.8s (3.10) **Going Correction** +0.225s/f (Good)
WFA 3 from 4yo 12lb **13 Ran SP% 125.4**
Speed ratings (Par 100):93,91,90,89,88 88,87,85,84,82 79,75,70
CSF £2.98 TOTE £2.30: £1.10, £1.20, £20.30; EX 3.20 Place 6 £25.78, Place 5 £10.96..
Owner Highclere Thoroughbred Racing XXXIX **Bred** Declan Hyland And Lillian Montgomery **Trained** Newmarket, Suffolk

FOCUS
A couple of classy fillies contested this fillies' maiden, but the pace was steady for much of the way and a few of these look flattered. The winning time was modest for a race like this and the bare form cannot be taken seriously, but the first two are a class above the remainder.
Condi(IRE) Official explanation: jockey said filly hung left
Regal Estate Official explanation: jockey said filly ran green
T/Plt: £58.30 to a £1 stake. Pool: £80,977.55. 1,013.80 winning tickets. T/Qpdt: £13.20 to a £1 stake. Pool: £5,027.40. 281.00 winning tickets. JN

1727 WOLVERHAMPTON (A.W) (L-H)
Monday, May 21

OFFICIAL GOING: Standard
Wind: Light, half-against Weather: Fine

1902 RINGSIDE SUITE CONFERENCE FACILITY H'CAP — 5f 20y(P)
6:50 (6:50) (Class 6) (0-50,50) 4-Y-0+ **£2,388** (£705; £352) **Stalls Low**

Form RPR

4000 **1** **Majestical (IRE)**[61] [722] 5-8-4 **47**.............................. (p) WilliamBuick(5) 10 61
(V Smith) *sn outpcd: rdn and hung lft ins fnl f: r.o to ld nr fin* **8/1**

1461 **2** 3/4 **Spirit Of Coniston**[20] [1384] 4-8-9 **50**.............................. (b) DuranFentiman(3) 7 61
(C J Teague) *mid-div: hdwy over 1f out: sn rdn: r.o* **7/1**[3]

5534 **3** 1/2 **Primarily**[19] [1400] 5-8-10 **48**.............................. DaleGibson 1 57
(Peter Grayson) *chsd ldrs: rdn to ld ins fnl f: hdd nr fin* **11/2**[2]

006- **4** 1 1/4 **Trombone Tom**[202] [6276] 4-8-9 **47**.............................. TomEaves 4 52
(J R Norton) *led: rdn over 1f out: hdd and unable qck ins fnl f* **16/1**

3020 **5** *shd* **Dysonic (USA)**[20] [1384] 5-8-12 **50**.............................. (v) RichardMullen 6 54
(J Balding) *chsd ldr: rdn over 1f out: styd on same pce ins fnl f* **4/1**[1]

4520 **6** 1 **Prettilini**[55] [801] 4-8-10 **48**.............................. RobertHavlin 13 49
(A W Carroll) *mid-div: rdn over 1f out: nt trble ldrs* **14/1**

6005 **7** 1/2 **Soldiers Romance**[15] [1493] 4-8-8 **46** oh1.............................. J-PGuillambert 12 45
(T D Easterby) *prom: rdn 1/2-way: no ex fnl f* **14/1**

0000 **8** *shd* **New Options**[7] [1729] 10-8-9 **47**.............................. (b) TPO'Shea 2 45
(Peter Grayson) *s.i.s: hld up: nt clr run over 1f out: nt trble ldrs* **50/1**

0-20 **9** 1 1/2 **Miss Mujahid Times**[11] [1596] 4-8-12 **50**.............................. (p) FergusSweeney 8 43
(A D Brown) *sn outpcd* **16/1**

0-14 **10** 1 **Elvina**[67] [680] 6-8-7 **48**.............................. NeilChalmers(3) 9 37
(A G Newcombe) *mid-div: rdn 1/2-way: wknd over 1f out* **10/1**

5-43 **11** *nk* **Desert Dust**[20] [1384] 4-8-11 **49**.............................. NickyMackay 5 37
(R M H Cowell) *chsd ldrs: rdn over 1f out: wknd fnl f* **4/1**[1]

0001 **12** *nk* **Mystery Pips**[11] [1594] 7-8-12 **50**.............................. (v) KimTinkler 11 37
(N Tinkler) *chsd ldrs: rdn 1/2-way: wknd fnl f* **14/1**

62.61 secs (-0.21) **Going Correction** -0.025s/f (Stan) **12 Ran SP% 121.8**
Speed ratings (Par 101):100,98,98,96,95 94,93,93,90,89 88,88
CSF £64.90 CT £347.31 TOTE £10.20: £2.50, £3.20, £2.60; EX 166.40.
Owner Raymond Tooth **Bred** Sean Beston **Trained** Exning, Suffolk

FOCUS
A routine sprint handicap of its type and the complexion of the race changed several times in the final furlong. The winning time was about what you would expect for a modest race like this. The winner was back to his late 2006 form, with the second and third running to recent form.

1903 FORESTHOLIDAYS.CO.UK FIRST ANNIVERSARY H'CAP — 7f 32y(P)
7:20 (7:20) (Class 6) (0-65,65) 3-Y-0 **£2,730** (£806; £403) **Stalls High**

Form RPR

34-6 **1** **Fealeview Lady (USA)**[90] [510] 3-8-13 **65**.............................. TravisBlock(5) 2 68+
(H Morrison) *s.i.s: hld up: hmpd over 2f out: hdwy over 1f out: r.o to ld wl ins fnl f* **5/1**[2]

1-00 **2** 3/4 **Dancing Duo**[7] [1731] 3-8-13 **60**.............................. (v) FrancisNorton 10 61
(D Shaw) *chsd ldrs: rdn to ld 1f out: hdd wl ins fnl f* **28/1**

4-04 **3** 3/4 **Early Promise (IRE)**[25] [1269] 3-8-12 **62**.............................. DominicFox(3) 7 61+
(P L Gilligan) *broke wl: stdd and lost pl sn after s: nt clr run over 2f out: hdwy over 1f out: hung lft and r.o ins fnl f* **20/1**

0216 **4** 3/4 **Knapton Hill**[33] [1091] 3-8-11 **63**.............................. WilliamBuick(5) 11 60
(R Hollinshead) *chsd ldrs: lost pl over 5f out: outpcd over 3f out: r.o ins fnl f* **8/1**

5333 **5** *nk* **Ochre (IRE)**[19] [1399] 3-9-4 **65**.............................. (p) JamieSpencer 9 61
(M A Jarvis) *s.i.s: hld up: hdwy over 1f out: sn rdn: hung lft and nt run on ins fnl f* **8/1**

4122 **6** 1 1/2 **Mick Is Back**[23] [1297] 3-8-10 **64**.............................. (p) JackMitchell(7) 4 56
(J R Boyle) *mid-div: n.m.r over 2f out: sn rdn: styd on same pce appr fnl f* **9/2**[1]

3204 **7** *hd* **Distant Sun (USA)**[10] [1625] 3-9-1 **62**.............................. TomEaves 1 54
(I Semple) *led early: chsd ldr tl led over 2f out: rdn and hdd 1f out: wknd towards fin* **5/1**[2]

-040 **8** 1 1/4 **Just Oscar (GER)**[7] [1726] 3-9-2 **63**.............................. RichardMullen 5 51
(W M Brisbourne) *hld up: rdn 1/2-way: hdwy over 2f out: wknd fnl f* **16/1**

5212 **9** 1/2 **Time For Change (IRE)**[25] [1266] 3-8-6 **60**.............................. ChrisGlenister(7) 3 47
(B W Hills) *mid-div: hdwy 1/2-way: wknd fnl f* **5/1**[2]

324 **10** 14 **Thunderbolt Jaxon**[20] [1375] 3-9-1 **62**.............................. (b[1]) RobertHavlin 6 11
(P W Chapple-Hyam) *sn led: rdn and hdd over 2f out: sn wknd* **7/1**[3]

1m 30.55s (0.15) **Going Correction** -0.025s/f (Stan) **10 Ran SP% 117.0**
Speed ratings (Par 97):98,97,96,95,95 93,93,91,91,75
CSF £131.71 CT £2617.22 TOTE £7.10: £2.00, £6.80, £7.50; EX 187.20.
Owner J J Byrne **Bred** Budget Stable **Trained** East Ilsley, Berks

FOCUS
Another modest handicap and with Thunderbolt Jaxon virtually bolting the early pace was strong, but they paid for it later and the final time was only around par for the grade. The form is pretty ordinary, rated through the runner-up.

1904 HORIZONS RESTAURANT MAIDEN STKS — 7f 32y(P)
7:50 (7:53) (Class 5) 3-Y-0+ **£3,071** (£906; £453) **Stalls High**

Form RPR

0-2 **1** **Buxton**[10] [1633] 3-8-13.............................. RobertHavlin 11 71
(R Ingram) *chsd ldrs: led over 1f out: hung lft ins fnl f: rdn out* **10/1**

4 **2** 1 3/4 **Zach's Harmoney (USA)**[17] [1447] 3-8-13.............................. JamieSpencer 10 66
(B J Meehan) *trckd ldr: rdn and ev ch over 1f out: sn edgd rt: hung lft and no ex ins fnl f* **7/4**[1]

3 *nk* **Ionian** 4-9-10.............................. NCallan 7 69
(Pat Eddery) *led: rdn over 2f out: hdd over 1f out: styd on same pce* **20/1**

03 **4** 1 1/4 **Adenium (IRE)**[18] [1440] 3-8-13.............................. TedDurcan 8 62
(W R Swinburn) *hld up in tch: rdn over 1f out: edgd lft and styd on same pce* **7/1**[3]

2 **5** *hd* **Gleneagles (IRE)**[28] 1197 3-8-13 .... MichaelHills 3 61
(W J Haggas) *chsd ldrs: rdn over 2f out: styd on same pce appr fnl f* **2/1**[2]

40 **6** *2 1/2* **Just Spike**[25] 1262 4-9-3 .... SoniaEaton(7) 2 59
(B P J Baugh) *hld up: hdwy 1/2-way: rdn and wknd over 1f out* **200/1**

00 **7** *3 1/2* **My Mentor (IRE)**[6] 1749 3-8-13 .... J-PGuillambert 4 46
(Sir Mark Prescott) *sn pushed along in rr: effrt over 2f out: sn edgd lft and wknd* **50/1**

8 *hd* **Altos Reales** 3-8-8 .... FrancisNorton 12 40
(D Shaw) *s.s: outpcd: nvr nrr* **66/1**

03 **9** *hd* **Fizzy Bella**[7] 1716 3-8-8 .... BrettDoyle 9 40
(M G Quinlan) *hld up: sme hdwy 2f out: sn wknd* **20/1**

-46 **10** *shd* **Dr Dream (IRE)**[30] 1166 3-8-13 .... FergusSweeney 6 45
(D M Simcock) *s.i.s: hld up: effrt over 2f out: sn hung lft and wknd* **14/1**

11 *1* **Capping (IRE)** 3-8-13 .... LPKeniry 1 42
(W R Swinburn) *mid-div: rdn 1/2-way: wknd over 2f out* **16/1**

12 *26* **Millers Jewel**[81] 4-9-2 .... (t) NeilChalmers(3) 5 —
(K G Wingrove) *s.s: outpcd* **200/1**

1m 30.67s (0.27) **Going Correction** -0.025s/f (Stan)
WFA 3 from 4yo 11lb **12** Ran SP% **117.8**
Speed ratings (Par 103):97,95,94,93,93 90,86,85,85,85 84,54
CSF £26.76 TOTE £13.70: £2.20, £1.60, £4.50; EX 48.50.
Owner Michael Joy **Bred** Mrs S Ingram **Trained** Epsom, Surrey
■ Stewards' Enquiry : Jamie Spencer one-day ban: used whip with excessive force (Jun 6)

FOCUS
Not a great maiden and the winning time was 0.12 seconds slower than the preceding Class 6 handicap. However, the market was fascinating with the favourite completely friendless and the five closest to him in the betting all shortening, a couple of them significantly, including the eventual winner. The field well spread out and those that raced up with the pace very much held the advantage. Ordinary form, which makes sense amongst the principals.

1905 KNOW PAINT GET GLIDDEN H'CAP 1m 141y(P)
8:20 (8:21) (Class 4) (0-80,80) 4-Y-O+ **£4,857** (£1,445; £722; £360) **Stalls** Low

Form RPR
/0-3 **1** **Ashes Regained**[30] 1166 4-9-1 **77** .... JamieSpencer 10 87+
(B W Hills) *hld up: hdwy over 2f out: rdn and hung lft fr over 1f out: led and rdr dropped whip ins fnl f: r.o* **3/1**[1]

160- **2** *1 1/4* **United Nations**[226] 5810 6-8-12 **74** .... NCallan 2 81
(N Wilson) *hld up in tch: rdn and hmpd over 1f out: styd on same pce ins fnl f* **10/1**

0500 **3** *shd* **Tous Les Deux**[14] 1543 4-8-9 **71** .... LPKeniry 7 78
(Peter Grayson) *s.i.s: hld up: hdwy over 1f out: r.o* **20/1**

000- **4** *2* **Tempsford Flyer (IRE)**[186] 6502 4-9-2 **78** .... MichaelHills 11 80
(J W Hills) *hld up: hdwy 1/2-way: rdn to chse ldr 2f out: sn hung lft: no ex ins fnl f* **6/1**[3]

3225 **5** *1* **Barney McGrew (IRE)**[25] 1268 4-8-13 **75** .... OscarUrbina 9 75
(J A R Toller) *chsd ldr tl led over 6f out: rdn and hung rt over 2f out: hdd and n.m.r ins fnl f: no ex* **8/1**

6044 **6** *1 1/2* **Pop Music (IRE)**[18] 1434 4-8-5 **67** .... (tp) JamesDoyle 4 74+
(Miss J Feilden) *chsd ldrs: hung lft over 1f out: styng on whn hmpd ins fnl f: nt rcvr* **14/1**

2121 **7** *1 1/4* **Harare**[24] 1283 6-8-7 **76** .... (v) WilliamCarson(7) 3 70
(R J Price) *hld up in tch: rdn whn hmpd over 1f out: wknd ins fnl f* **5/1**[2]

0156 **8** *hd* **Symbol Of Peace (IRE)**[19] 1401 4-8-13 **78** .... RichardKingscote(3) 1 71
(J W Unett) *led: hdd over 6f out: chsd ldrs: rdn over 2f out: wknd fnl f* **8/1**

42-0 **9** *3/4* **Manipulate**[23] 1288 4-9-0 **76** .... NickyMackay 5 67
(L M Cumani) *hld up: outpcd over 3f out: hung lft over 1f out: n.d after* **9/1**

650- **10** *3/4* **Damelza (IRE)**[244] 5446 4-8-3 **68** .... DuranFentiman(3) 6 58
(T D Easterby) *s.i.s: hld up: rdn over 2f out: n.d* **33/1**

0106 **11** *2* **Writ (IRE)**[9] 1675 5-9-4 **80** .... TomEaves 8 65
(I Semple) *chsd ldr 6f out: rdn whn hmpd over 2f out: sn wknd* **12/1**

1m 49.8s (-1.96) **Going Correction** -0.025s/f (Stan) **11** Ran SP% **119.3**
Speed ratings (Par 105):107,105,105,104,103 101,100,100,99,99 97
CSF £34.74 CT £527.70 TOTE £3.00: £2.40, £2.30, £6.10; EX 51.20.
Owner W J Gredley **Bred** Middle Park Stud Ltd **Trained** Lambourn, Berks
■ Stewards' Enquiry : Oscar Urbina caution: careless riding

FOCUS
A decent handicap run at a good clip, but even so there were several still in with a chance starting up the home straight and one or two did not see much daylight, notably the sixth. The bare form is nothing special, rated through the runner-up.

1906 CARLSBERG SUPPORTING MACMILLAN CHARITY H'CAP 1m 1f 103y(P)
8:50 (8:50) (Class 6) (0-50,52) 4-Y-O+ **£2,388** (£705; £352) **Stalls** Low

Form RPR
-000 **1** **El Capitan (FR)**[9] 1671 4-8-10 **48** .... NCallan 4 61+
(Miss Gay Kelleway) *mid-div: hdwy over 3f out: led over 1f out: sn rdn and hung lft: styd on* **5/2**[1]

105- **2** *3/4* **Rock Haven (IRE)**[243] 5485 5-8-9 **50** .... DuranFentiman(3) 13 59
(G F Bridgwater) *trckd ldrs: rdn and ev ch over 1f out: sn hung lft: styd on same pce ins fnl f* **8/1**[3]

2545 **3** *2* **Rose Muwasim**[20] 1371 4-8-6 **47** .... DominicFox(3) 3 52
(S Parr) *hld up: hdwy over 2f out: rdn and hung lft over 1f out: styd on* **12/1**

0220 **4** *3/4* **Veba (USA)**[6] 1742 4-8-9 **47** .... HayleyTurner 2 51
(M D I Usher) *hld up: hdwy over 3f out: sn rdn: styd on same pce appr fnl f* **4/1**[2]

5105 **5** *1* **Fuel Cell (IRE)**[21] 1350 6-8-7 **52** ow2 .... JamesO'Reilly(7) 1 54+
(J O'Reilly) *chsd ldrs: lost pl over 7f out: in rr whn hmpd 4f out: styd on appr fnl f* **12/1**

6602 **6** *1/2* **Shannon Arms (USA)**[20] 1381 6-8-5 **48** .... KevinGhunowa(5) 12 49
(R Brotherton) *led over 8f out: clr 6f out: rdn and hdd over 1f out: wknd fnl f* **11/1**

2005 **7** *nk* **Gem Bien (USA)**[7] 1715 9-8-9 **47** .... (b) TomEaves 6 47
(D W Chapman) *hld up: hdwy over 2f out: sn rdn and edgd lft: n.d* **16/1**

0-00 **8** *2* **Hits Only Life (USA)**[22] 503 4-8-9 **47** .... BrettDoyle 5 43
(J Pearce) *s.i.s: outpcd: nrst fin* **20/1**

-550 **9** *1 1/4* **Wally Barge**[9] 1671 4-8-12 **50** .... RobertHavlin 10 43
(D K Ivory) *hld up: rdn over 2f out: n.d* **16/1**

6306 **10** *1/2* **Fulvio (USA)**[21] 1360 7-8-10 **48** .... (v) J-PGuillambert 9 40
(P Howling) *hld up: effrt and nt clr run over 1f out: n.d* **11/1**

32-6 **11** *5* **Mucho Loco (IRE)**[27] 1227 4-8-12 **50** .... (b) DaleGibson 11 32
(R Curtis) *trckd ldrs: racd keenly: rdn and wknd over 1f out* **20/1**

0-00 **12** *13* **Dream Of Paradise (USA)**[25] 1258 4-8-7 **48** .... LiamJones(3) 7 4
(Mrs L Williamson) *chsd ldrs: rdn and wknd 1/2-way* **20/1**

600- **13** *dist* **Height Of Esteem**[200] 6308 4-8-10 **48** .... TedDurcan 8 —
(W M Brisbourne) *chsd ldrs: wknd and eased fnl 3f* **12/1**

2m 2.53s (-0.09) **Going Correction** -0.025s/f (Stan) **13** Ran SP% **125.5**
Speed ratings (Par 101):99,98,96,95,95 94,94,92,91,90 86,74,—
CSF £23.18 CT £202.84 TOTE £3.20: £2.30, £4.10, £3.70; EX 25.10.
Owner Aggbag Ltd Deauville Daze Partnership **Bred** Thierry Storme **Trained** Exning, Suffolk

FOCUS
A weak handicap in which the early pace was very strong, but those that showed up early eventually fell away and the way the race was run suited closers. The winner took advantage of a career-low mark, with the form fairly sound through the third and fourth.
Height Of Esteem Official explanation: jockey said gelding had a chronic breathing problem

1907 SPONSOR A RACE BY CALLING 0870 220 2442 H'CAP 1m 4f 50y(P)
9:20 (9:20) (Class 6) (0-60,59) 4-Y-O+ **£2,730** (£806; £403) **Stalls** Low

Form RPR
6555 **1** **Medieval Maiden**[30] 1167 4-9-0 **57** .... BrettDoyle 2 70+
(W J Musson) *hld up: hdwy over 3f out: led over 1f out: rdn clr: eased nr fin* **5/1**[2]

2301 **2** *4* **Mighty Kitchener (USA)**[114] 270 4-9-2 **59** .... IanMongan 5 66
(P Howling) *chsd ldrs: led over 2f out: rdn and hdd over 1f out: no ex ins fnl f* **20/1**

4244 **3** *1 1/4* **Tresor Secret (FR)**[21] 1342 7-8-11 **57** .... JerryO'Dwyer(3) 7 62
(J Gallagher) *led 1f: chsd ldrs: outpcd over 3f out: rallied over 1f out: styd on* **5/1**[2]

0611 **4** *2* **Comeintothespace (IRE)**[21] 1342 5-8-10 **53** ow1 .... NCallan 1 55
(K J Burke) *hld up: hdwy 1/2-way: rdn over 1f out: hung lft and wknd fnl f* **5/1**[2]

5504 **5** *1 3/4* **Bentley Brook (IRE)**[23] 1314 5-8-11 **54** .... TPO'Shea 6 53
(P A Blockley) *chsd ldrs: outpcd over 3f out: rallied over 1f out: sn hung lft and wknd* **10/3**[1]

00-0 **6** *8* **Lady Ambitious**[27] 1210 4-8-2 **45** .... HayleyTurner 3 31
(D K Ivory) *hld up: n.d* **33/1**

3456 **7** *3/4* **Regency Red (IRE)**[6] 1741 9-8-7 **53** .... LiamJones(3) 8 38
(W M Brisbourne) *hld up: hdwy over 3f out: wknd over 2f out* **20/1**

00-4 **8** *3/4* **Richtee (IRE)**[30] 1158 6-8-12 **55** .... DaleGibson 11 39
(R A Fahey) *hld up: hdwy over 2f out: sn wknd* **10/1**[3]

02-5 **9** *2* **Campbells Lad**[46] 936 6-8-1 **49** .... WilliamBuick(5) 9 30
(Mrs G S Rees) *prom: racd keenly: trckd ldr over 8f out: rdn and wknd over 2f out* **22/1**

3262 **10** *1* **Buscador (USA)**[23] 1314 8-8-11 **57** .... RichardKingscote(3) 10 36
(W M Brisbourne) *rdn to ld after 1f: hdd over 2f out: wknd over 1f out: eased* **5/1**[2]

3050 **11** *21* **Beau Torero (FR)**[7] 1732 9-8-12 **55** .... VinceSlattery 12 —
(B N Pollock) *s.i.s: sn chsng ldrs: rdn and wknd 4f out* **40/1**

2m 39.97s (-2.45) **Going Correction** -0.025s/f (Stan) **11** Ran SP% **118.1**
Speed ratings (Par 101):107,104,103,102,101 95,95,94,93,92 78
CSF £104.88 CT £530.35 TOTE £9.00: £3.50, £3.70, £1.90; EX 99.70 Place 6 £377.02, Place 5 £130.96..
Owner K L West **Bred** Eclipse Bloodstock Ltd **Trained** Newmarket, Suffolk

FOCUS
This proved a proper test of stamina thanks to Buscador and several were on and off the bridle and/or ran in snatches. The time was good and the form looks solid for the grade.
Buscador(USA) Official explanation: jockey said gelding had no more to give
T/Plt: £644.40 to a £1 stake. Pool: £67,751.80. 76.75 winning tickets. T/Qpdt: £78.30 to a £1 stake. Pool: £5,418.60. 51.20 winning tickets. CR

1908 - 1911a (Foreign Racing) - See Raceform Interactive

1573 BEVERLEY (R-H)
Tuesday, May 22

OFFICIAL GOING: Good (good to firm in places)
Wind: Slight, behind

1912 TURF TV (S) STKS 5f
2:20 (2:21) (Class 5) 3-Y-O **£2,914** (£867; £433; £216) **Stalls** High

Form RPR
45-1 **1** **No Worries Yet (IRE)**[6] 1763 3-8-11 67 .... FrancisNorton 9 67
(J L Spearing) *mde all: rdn and kpt on strly fnl f* **15/8**[1]

0-36 **2** *1* **Josr's Magic (IRE)**[17] 1484 3-8-11 63 .... (b) RoystonFfrench 14 63
(Mrs A Duffield) *trckd ldrs: hdwy to chse wnr 1/2-way: sn rdn: styd on u.p fnl f* **2/1**[2]

00-0 **3** *7* **Valeesha**[19] 1432 3-8-1 47 .... LukeMorris(5) 16 33
(W G M Turner) *in tch: hdwy 2f out: sn rdn and kpt on same pce* **16/1**

-500 **4** *nk* **Polly Rocket**[19] 1426 3-8-3 41 .... (p) GregFairley(3) 10 32
(P D Niven) *midfield: rdn along over 2f out: styd on appr fnl f* **66/1**

0503 **5** *1 1/4* **Tenterhooks (IRE)**[19] 1426 3-8-6 43 .... (be) DavidAllan 11 32+
(A J McCabe) *in tch: effrt whn nt clr run and hmpd over 1f out: nt rcvr* **18/1**

0-00 **6** *1 1/4* **Superjain**[7] 1748 3-8-2 59 ow3 .... PaulPickard(7) 15 26
(J M Jefferson) *chsd ldrs: rdn 2f out: swtchd lft and drvn over 1f out: sn one pce* **16/1**

66-0 **7** *2* **Seriously Lucky (IRE)**[19] 1426 3-8-11 45 .... AdrianTNicholls 5 21
(D Nicholls) *a towards rr* **33/1**

-500 **8** *shd* **Silly Gilly (IRE)**[15] 1530 3-8-6 52 .... PaulMulrennan 13 15
(K R Burke) *prom: rdn along 2f out: sn wknd* **8/1**[3]

00-0 **9** *3* **Shotley Mac**[3] 1850 3-8-4 61 .... SuzzanneFrance(7) 8 9
(N Bycroft) *a towards rr* **33/1**

640- **10** *1 3/4* **Afric Star**[337] 2709 3-8-6 40 .... (p) DaleGibson 7 —
(John A Harris) *a bhd* **66/1**

0300 **11** *1 1/2* **Stir Crazy (IRE)**[6] 1763 3-8-11 62 .... ChrisCatlin 2 —
(M R Channon) *cl up on outer: rdn along 1/2-way: sn wknd* **8/1**[3]

00-0 **12** *hd* **Littlemadgebob**[61] 728 3-8-3 40 .... DuranFentiman(3) 3 —
(J R Norton) *a bhd* **100/1**

000- **13** *shd* **A Foot In Front**[237] 5614 3-8-11 30 .... (v) KimTinkler 12 —
(N Tinkler) *dwlt: a bhd* **100/1**

64.15 secs (0.15) **Going Correction** +0.05s/f (Good) **13** Ran SP% **118.2**
Speed ratings (Par 99):100,98,87,86,84 82,79,79,74,71 69,69,68
CSF £5.50 TOTE £2.60: £1.10, £1.30, £5.10; EX 5.40.The winner was bought in for 10,200gns. Josr's Magic was claimed by Robert Stronge for £6,000.
Owner J Spearing **Bred** Mark Donohoe **Trained** Kinnersley, Worcs

FOCUS
This looked a match on paper and the pair drew seven-lengths clear of a bad bunch. The form is not bad for the grade.
Tenterhooks(IRE) Official explanation: jockey said filly was denied a clear run
Littlemadgebob Official explanation: trainer said filly bled from the nose

1913 JOCKEYS LOFT FOR GREAT FOOD MAIDEN STKS 7f 100y
2:50 (2:53) (Class 5) 3-Y-O £3,238 (£963; £481; £240) Stalls High

Form RPR

22 1 **Soccerjackpot (USA)**[17] 1482 3-9-3 DeanMcKeown 5 85+
(G A Swinbank) *t.k.h: cl up: led 2f out: sn clr: pushed out fnl f* **8/11**[1]

34 2 5 **Medici Pearl**[11] 1620 3-8-12 DavidAllan 1 67
(T D Easterby) *sn in tch: effrt and chsd wnr over 1f out: kpt on fnl f: no imp* **11/1**

0-3 3 1¼ **He's Mine Too**[33] 1111 3-9-3 FrancisNorton 8 69
(J D Bethell) *midfield: shkn up over 2f out: kpt on fnl f: nrst fin* **8/1**[3]

4 ½ **Jibajaba (USA)** 3-9-3 TonyHamilton 3 68+
(R A Fahey) *unruly s: bhd and green: styd on fr 2f out: nrst fin* **33/1**

0-6 5 2½ **Seeking The Buck (USA)**[12] 1606 3-9-3 (t) ChrisCatlin 15 62+
(M A Magnusson) *s.i.s: bhd: shkn up over 2f out: kpt on fnl f: nvr nr ldrs* **15/2**[2]

0- 6 hd **Lilac Moon (GER)**[253] 5237 3-8-12 RoystonFfrench 6 56
(Mrs A Duffield) *midfield: rdn and outpcd 3f out: n.d after* **100/1**

0 7 1½ **Mix N Match**[20] 1403 3-9-3 JamieSpencer 2 57+
(W J Haggas) *stdd s: hld up: shkn up outside over 2f out: nvr nrr* **20/1**

66 8 hd **I Will If You Will**[73] 661 3-8-12 PaulMulrennan 12 52
(K A Ryan) *bhd: rdn over 3f out: nvr on terms* **50/1**

0 9 2 **Poppets Sweetlove**[43] 973 3-8-12 KDarley 9 47
(A B Haynes) *dwlt: a bhd* **33/1**

6 10 nk **Distant Pleasure**[14] 1558 3-8-12 PaulFessey 11 46
(M Dods) *s.i.s: a bhd* **66/1**

00-4 11 1¼ **Didactic**[26] 1261 3-9-3 49 (b) StephenDonohoe 4 48
(A J McCabe) *chsd ldrs tl wknd over 2f out* **100/1**

0 12 ½ **Western Land**[61] 728 3-9-0 MarkLawson(3) 14 47
(B Smart) *unruly bef s: t.k.h: chsd ldrs tl wandered and wknd over 2f out* **18/1**

5-4 13 4 **Livalex**[15] 1529 3-8-12 PhillipMakin 13 32
(M Dods) *hld up in tch: rdn over 2f out: sn wknd* **14/1**

4 14 3 **Suspender (IRE)**[14] 1558 3-8-12 AdrianTNicholls 10 24
(D Nicholls) *t.k.h: led to 2f out: sn btn* **33/1**

0- 15 15 **Hillside Smoki (IRE)**[243] 5496 3-8-12 PaulQuinn 7 —
(A Berry) *bhd: lost tch 1/2-way: t.o* **125/1**

1m 32.93s (-1.38) **Going Correction** -0.075s/f (Good) **15** Ran SP% **120.9**
Speed ratings (Par 99):104,98,96,96,93 93,91,91,88,88 87,86,82,78,61
CSF £8.73 TOTE £1.80: £1.10, £2.60, £1.60; EX 11.40.
Owner sportaracing.com & George Houghton **Bred** G Chervenell **Trained** Melsonby, N Yorks
■ Stewards' Enquiry : Chris Catlin three-day ban: careless riding (Jun 3-5)

FOCUS
A fair winning time for the type of race. The form of this maiden looks solid enoughwith the winner slightly improving on previous form.
Suspender(IRE) Official explanation: jockey said filly was too free early stages

1914 WESTWOOD H'CAP 5f
3:20 (3:21) (Class 5) (0-70,70) 4-Y-O+ £3,562 (£1,059; £529; £264) Stalls High

Form RPR

4614 1 **Desert Opal**[22] 1363 7-9-1 67 (p) JamieSpencer 3 77
(C R Dore) *sn in tch: hdwy to trck ldrs 2f out: rdn: hung lft and led wl ins fnl f: hdd towards fin: rallied to ld on post* **12/1**

0-06 2 shd **Welcome Approach**[4] 1806 4-8-13 65 PhillipMakin 8 75
(J R Weymes) *chsd ldrs: led over 1f out: sn rdn and edgd rt: drvn hmpd and hdd wl ins fnl f: rallied to ld nr fin: hdd post* **50/1**

1622 3 1½ **No Time (IRE)**[10] 1669 7-8-11 63 StephenDonohoe 9 68+
(A J McCabe) *in tch: hdwy whn n.m.r over 1f out: sn rdn and kpt on ins fnl f* **7/1**[2]

0-00 4 1¼ **Henry Hall (IRE)**[24] 1299 11-9-0 66 KimTinkler 15 66
(N Tinkler) *prom: rdn along whn n.m.r and swtchd lft over 1f out: kpt on same pce* **11/1**

400- 5 ¾ **Mulligan's Gold (IRE)**[247] 5401 4-8-13 65 DavidAllan 5 62+
(T D Easterby) *towards rr: hdwy on outer 2f out: sn rdn and styd on ins fnl f* **50/1**

0-51 6 nk **Namir (IRE)**[10] 1669 5-9-0 69 (vt) SaleemGolam(3) 4 65
(D Shaw) *chsd ldrs: rdn along 2f out: kpt on same pce* **20/1**

6154 7 hd **Winthorpe (IRE)**[10] 1681 7-8-10 62 GrahamGibbons 11 58
(J J Quinn) *prom: rdn along whn n.m.r over 1f out: kpt on same pce* **8/1**

0010 8 shd **Paddywack (IRE)**[26] 1260 10-8-8 63 (b) MarkLawson(3) 13 58
(D W Chapman) *towarsd rr: hdwy wl over 1f out: sn rdn and nrst fin* **15/2**[3]

3-02 9 1½ **Choysia**[10] 1678 4-9-1 67 (p) TonyHamilton 6 57
(D W Barker) *midfield: rdn along over 2f out: no hdwy* **14/1**

0-00 10 hd **Smiddy Hill**[14] 1557 5-8-3 60 NataliaGemelova(5) 12 49
(R Bastiman) *chsd ldrs: rdn along whn n.m.r over 1f out: sn no imp* **33/1**

050 11 shd **Soto**[10] 1678 4-9-0 66 PaulMulrennan 17 55
(M W Easterby) *in tch on inner: rdn along whn n.m.r wl over 1f out: sn swtchd lft and no imp* **6/1**[1]

-144 12 hd **Brigadore**[1] 1885 8-9-1 67 KDarley 7 55
(J G Given) *dwlt: a towards rr* **6/1**[1]

1145 13 1½ **The Fisio**[49] 905 7-8-12 64 (v) ChrisCatlin 16 47
(S Gollings) *a bhd* **7/1**[2]

/01- 14 1¼ **That's Blue Chip**[290] 4164 4-8-8 60 FrancisNorton 10 38
(P W D'Arcy) *t.k.h: hld up in rr: effrt and nt clr run on inner over 2f out: no ch after* **17/2**

0-00 15 6 **Rare Breed**[22] 1363 4-8-11 70 (t) KristinStubbs(7) 1 27
(Mrs L Stubbs) *qckly away: led and swtchd rt: rdn along and edgd rt 2f out: sn hdd & wknd* **100/1**

63.99 secs (-0.01) **Going Correction** +0.05s/f (Good) **15** Ran SP% **122.3**
Speed ratings (Par 103):102,101,99,97,96 95,95,95,92,92 92,92,89,87,78
CSF £537.15 CT £4575.11 TOTE £16.30: £4.20, £13.20, £2.60; EX 593.30.
Owner Page, Ward, Marsh **Bred** Juddmonte Farms **Trained** West Pinchbeck, Lincs
■ Stewards' Enquiry : Kristin Stubbs one-day ban: careless riding (Jun 3)

FOCUS
A typically competitive sprint handicap that produced a cracking finish but there was trouble in running.

1915 SIEMENS IN PROCESS H'CAP 1m 100y
3:50 (3:52) (Class 3) (0-90,88) 4-Y-O+ £7,124 (£2,119; £1,059; £529) Stalls High

Form RPR

-604 1 **Flipando (IRE)**[6] 1767 6-9-4 88 JamieSpencer 8 99
(T D Barron) *trckd ldrs gng wl: led ent fnl f: rdn out* **6/4**[1]

4006 2 2½ **Langford**[16] 1494 7-8-9 82 SaleemGolam(3) 4 87
(M H Tompkins) *hld up in tch: effrt over 2f out: edgd rt and styd on fnl f: wnt 2nd cl home* **9/2**[3]

3-50 3 nk **Hula Ballew**[24] 1287 7-8-6 76 PaulFessey 1 81
(M Dods) *led: rdn over 2f out: hdd ent fnl f: nt qckn* **33/1**

3-00 4 1 **Nevada Desert (IRE)**[17] 1480 7-8-4 79 MichaelJStainton(5) 7 81
(R M Whitaker) *chsd ldrs: effrt over 2f out: nt qckn fnl f* **10/1**

0031 5 ½ **Daaweitza**[18] 1458 4-8-7 77 TonyHamilton 5 78
(B Ellison) *sn niggled along towards rr: hdwy ins wl over 1f out: no imp fnl f* **10/3**[2]

10-5 6 ¾ **Jubilee Street (IRE)**[10] 1682 8-8-12 82 RoystonFfrench 3 81
(Mrs A Duffield) *unruly bef s: towards rr: drvn over 3f out: kpt on fnl f: n.d* **7/1**

006- 7 ¾ **Lago D'Orta (IRE)**[312] 3500 7-8-7 77 AdrianTNicholls 6 75
(D Nicholls) *s.i.s: hld up: effrt whn nt clr run wl over 1f out: no imp fnl f* **18/1**

8 3 **Kaballero (GER)**[178] 6-8-12 82 ChrisCatlin 2 73
(S Gollings) *bhd: drvn 1/2-way: nvr on terms* **40/1**

/0-0 9 8 **Capricorn Run (USA)**[30] 1179 4-9-1 85 KDarley 9 57
(A J McCabe) *cl up tl rdn and wknd over 1f out* **22/1**

1m 45.46s (-1.94) **Going Correction** -0.075s/f (Good) **9** Ran SP% **117.8**
Speed ratings (Par 107):106,103,103,102,101 100,100,97,89
CSF £8.54 CT £157.30 TOTE £2.30: £1.10, £1.90, £4.40; EX 10.80.
Owner Mrs J Hazell **Bred** Denis McDonnell **Trained** Maunby, N Yorks

FOCUS
A fair handicap with the winner rated to his best, but not totally rock-solid.

NOTEBOOK
Flipando(IRE), fresh into this off the back of a good fourth over 1m2f at York last week, readily defied favouritism and Spencer always had things under control. He is clearly in cracking form at the minute, but will need to progress to follow up off a higher mark. (op 15-8 tchd 2-1 in places)
Langford is beginning to return to something like his best and seems to have been suited by being ridden with restraint the last twice. He could soon be of interest off this sort of mark. (op 4-1 tchd 5-1)
Hula Ballew, who ran as though something was amiss at Haydock last time, returned to something like her best back and seemed to be suited by the change in tactics. She is very capable on her day.
Nevada Desert(IRE), not beaten far in the Thirsk Hunt Cup last time, was well positioned and held every chance, but could not quicken up under pressure and is likely to remain vulnerable off this mark. (tchd 11-1)
Daaweitza was being niggled away at from quite an early stage, but kept plugging away and did not run too badly in the end. (op 4-1)
Lago D'Orta(IRE) Official explanation: trainer's rep said gelding returned lame

1916 BEST UK RACECOURSES ON TURF TV H'CAP 1m 1f 207y
4:20 (4:23) (Class 5) (0-75,74) 3-Y-O £3,886 (£1,156; £577; £288) Stalls High

Form RPR

1-01 1 **Guiseppe Verdi (USA)**[22] 1365 3-9-4 74 FrancisNorton 4 83+
(J H M Gosden) *trckd ldrs: hdwy over 2f out: rdn to ld over 1f out: kpt on* **13/8**[1]

-345 2 1½ **Dana Music (USA)**[20] 1415 3-8-12 68 ChrisCatlin 5 71
(M R Channon) *stdd s and hld up in rr: hdwy over 3f out: swtchd lft and rdn wl over 1f out: kpt on ins fnl f* **20/1**

16-3 3 1½ **Magic Echo**[10] 1672 3-9-2 72 PhillipMakin 8 72
(M Dods) *chsd ldrs: rdn along and sltly outpcd over 2f out: kpt on u.p ins fnl f* **7/2**[2]

3-16 4 1¼ **Pigeon Flight**[29] 1194 3-8-12 68 JamieSpencer 3 65
(M L W Bell) *hld up towards rr: hdwy 3f out: rdn to chse ldrs wl over 1f out: sn one pce* **13/2**[3]

-150 5 ¾ **Always Best**[15] 1536 3-8-8 64 (b) KDarley 2 60
(M Johnston) *cl up: rdn along over 2f out: drvn and ev ch over 1f out: wknd ins fnl f* **15/2**

2-44 6 3½ **Coconut Queen (IRE)**[19] 1424 3-9-1 71 RoystonFfrench 7 60
(Mrs A Duffield) *chsd ldng pair: rdn along over 2f out: drvn and wknd over 1f out* **11/1**

356 7 4 **Hubble Bubble (USA)**[10] 1665 3-8-10 66 JoeFanning 6 47
(M Johnston) *led: rdn along over 2f out: hdd & wknd over 1f out* **15/2**

06-6 8 ½ **Cape Dancer (IRE)**[17] 1482 3-8-7 63 ow1 TonyHamilton 1 43
(J S Wainwright) *in tch: effrt 3f out: sn rdn along and wknd fnl 2f* **40/1**

55-6 9 35 **Crosby Millie**[19] 1424 3-8-1 60 oh1 DuranFentiman(3) 9 —
(J R Weymes) *t.k.h early: a towards rr* **80/1**

2m 6.21s (-1.09) **Going Correction** -0.075s/f (Good) **9** Ran SP% **113.9**
Speed ratings (Par 99):101,99,98,97,97 94,91,90,62
CSF £38.78 CT £103.00 TOTE £2.40: £1.10, £2.20, £1.80; EX 33.60.
Owner H R H Princess Haya Of Jordan **Bred** Runnymede Farm Inc And Catesby W Clay **Trained** Newmarket, Suffolk

FOCUS
Not the most competitive of handicaps and the pace set by the Johnston pair was only fair. The favourite did it nicely though and is value for more than the official margin with the form is rated around the fourth to recent marks.
Crosby Millie Official explanation: jockey said filly lost its action

1917 RACING AGAIN HERE THIS SATURDAY H'CAP 1m 4f 16y
4:50 (4:50) (Class 6) (0-60,60) 3-Y-O £3,076 (£915; £457; £228) Stalls High

Form RPR

5006 1 **Sadler's Kingdom (IRE)**[13] 1579 3-8-13 55 TonyHamilton 3 62+
(R A Fahey) *trckd ldrs: pushed along 3f out: hdwy wl over 1f out and sn rdn: led ins fnl f and styd on wl* **8/1**

00-1 2 1½ **Potentiale (IRE)**[13] 1579 3-9-4 60 ChrisCatlin 1 65
(J W Hills) *hld up in rr: hdwy on outer 4f out: rdn to ld over 1f out: hdd and nt qckn ins fnl f* **7/1**[3]

0-41 3 ½ **Bollin Felix**[11] 1637 3-9-1 60 (b) DuranFentiman(3) 10 66+
(T D Easterby) *in tch: hdwy over 2f out: effrt whn nt clr run and hmpd over 1f out: kpt on ins fnl f* **15/8**[1]

06-2 4 ½ **Distant Sunset (IRE)**[22] 1361 3-9-3 59 KDarley 5 62
(B W Hills) *trckd ldrs: hdwy to chse ldr 5f out: rdn along and ev ch 2f out: sn drvn and kpt on same pce* **9/2**[2]

-006 5 ¾ **Celtic Memories (IRE)**[22] 1353 3-8-13 55 (b[1]) PaulMulrennan 11 57
(M W Easterby) *led: rdn along 3f out: drvn and hdd over 1f out: kpt on same pce* **66/1**

0-60 6 ¾ **Mr Crystal (FR)**[24] 1303 3-8-10 55 GregFairley(3) 7 56
(Micky Hammond) *in rr tl styd on fnl 2f: nrst fin* **50/1**

-004 7 shd **Bathwick Breeze**[15] 1536 3-9-2 58 GrahamGibbons 9 59
(A B Haynes) *chsd ldr: rdn along 4f out: drvn and grad wknd fnl 2f* **20/1**

0-44 8 2½ **Astrolibra**[39] 1024 3-9-1 60 SaleemGolam(3) 2 57
(M H Tompkins) *chsd ldrs: rdn along 3f out: sn wknd* **25/1**

6-00 9 1½ **Dancewiththestars (USA)**[10] 1665 3-8-13 55 JamieSpencer 8 55+
(J R Fanshawe) *a towards rr* **7/1**[3]

6-34 10 7 **Cavendish**[22] 1361 3-8-13 55 (b) FrancisNorton 4 38
(J M P Eustace) *a towards rr* **12/1**

40-0 **11** *3* **Firestorm (IRE)**[10] [1659] 3-8-13 **55** DeanMcKeown 12 33
(C W Fairhurst) *a towards rr* **16/1**
0-60 **12** *15* **Heart Of Glass (IRE)**[20] [1408] 3-8-11 **58** LukeMorris(5) 6 12
(M L W Bell) *a towards rr* **25/1**
2m 40.28s (0.07) **Going Correction** -0.075s/f (Good) **12** Ran SP% **118.6**
Speed ratings (Par 97):96,95,94,94,93 93,93,91,90,85 83,73
CSF £59.41 CT £150.17 TOTE £12.30: £2.70, £2.80, £1.10; EX 101.40.
Owner J J Staunton **Bred** Tower Bloodstock **Trained** Musley Bank, N Yorks

FOCUS
Quite a competitive if modest handicap but not the most solid race. The early pace was frenetic, but eventually settled down and the final time was about right for a race like this.
Dancewiththestars(USA) Official explanation: jockey said filly was unsuited by the good (good to firm places) ground

1918 TURF TV BETTING SHOP SERVICE H'CAP — 1m 100y
5:20 (5:22) (Class 6) (0-60,60) 4-Y-0+ **£3,241** (£957; £478) **Stalls** High

Form RPR
-004 **1** **Networker**[43] [980] 4-8-11 **53** JamieSpencer 2 65+
(P J McBride) *hld up and bhd: gd hdwy outside over 1f out: qcknd to ld ins fnl f: comf* **7/1**[3]
2632 **2** *1 1/4* **Hits Only Cash**[22] [1366] 5-9-3 **59** DeanMcKeown 12 68
(J Pearce) *prom: led appr fnl f to ins fnl f: nt pce of wnr* **8/1**
60-0 **3** *3* **Terenzium (IRE)**[32] [1132] 5-8-8 **53** GregFairley(3) 3 55
(Micky Hammond) *bhd tl styd on fr over 1f out: nrst fin* **25/1**
-132 **4** *nk* **Gigs Magic (USA)**[8] [1720] 4-8-11 **53** KDarley 7 54
(M Johnston) *hld up on outside: rdn over 3f out: styd on fnl 2f: nrst fin* **3/1**[1]
0050 **5** *3/4* **Blue Empire (IRE)**[15] [1539] 6-9-1 **57** PaulMulrennan 11 57
(C R Dore) *prom on outside: rdn and outpcd wl over 1f out: kpt on fnl f: no imp* **8/1**
0120 **6** *nk* **The City Kid (IRE)**[36] [1069] 4-8-13 **60** (b) PJMcDonald(5) 17 59
(C R Dore) *in tch: effrt 2f out: kpt on same pce fnl f* **18/1**
0055 **7** *shd* **Counterfactual (IRE)**[38] [1044] 4-8-9 **54** MarkLawson(3) 13 53
(B Smart) *midfield: outpcd over 2f out: rallying u.p whn hmpd appr fnl f: kpt on: nvr rchd ldrs* **14/1**
00-0 **8** *hd* **Apache Point (IRE)**[34] [1090] 10-8-13 **55** KimTinkler 15 53
(N Tinkler) *t.k.h: chsd ldrs: effrt 2f out: outpcd fnl f* **12/1**
0/00 **9** *shd* **Fancy (IRE)**[10] [1671] 4-8-5 **52** MichaelJStainton(5) 8 50
(R A Farrant) *cl up: rdn and ev ch tl outpcd fnl f* **33/1**
04-0 **10** *1 1/2* **First Rhapsody (IRE)**[38] [1038] 5-8-8 **53** SaleemGolam(3) 10 48
(T J Etherington) *bhd: rdn 3f out: sme hdwy over 1f out: n.d* **20/1**
1000 **11** *hd* **Danzare**[26] [1260] 5-8-12 **54** FrancisNorton 1 48
(J L Spearing) *midfield on outside: drvn over 2f out: sn no ex* **20/1**
0202 **12** *2* **Sir Bond (IRE)**[10] [1675] 6-8-12 **57** DuranFentiman(3) 4 47
(G R Oldroyd) *stdd s: hld up: pushed along over 2f out: n.d* **5/1**[2]
066 **13** *shd* **Cottam Eclipse**[10] [1676] 6-8-12 **54** RoystonFfrench 14 43
(I W McInnes) *set stdy pce: rdn over 2f out: hdd appr fnl f: sn btn* **12/1**
0-65 **14** *hd* **Contemplation**[13] [1578] 4-9-1 **57** DavidAllan 6 46
(J Balding) *cl up tl rdn and wknd appr fnl f* **16/1**
00-0 **15** *4* **Makfly**[10] [1655] 4-9-4 **60** (b1) GrahamGibbons 5 40
(R Hollinshead) *rrd s: a bhd* **33/1**
544- **16** *5* **Electron Pulse**[309] [3582] 4-9-2 **58** (p) PhillipMakin 9 26
(M Dods) *t.k.h in midfield: lost pl over 3f out: n.d after* **18/1**
1m 47.82s (0.42) **Going Correction** -0.075s/f (Good) **16** Ran SP% **134.1**
Speed ratings (Par 101):94,92,89,89,88 88,88,88,88,86 86,84,84,84,80 75
CSF £64.15 CT £1430.66 TOTE £9.30: £3.30, £2.40, £9.00, £1.10; EX 90.90 Place 6 £21.74, Place 5 £15.94.
Owner P J McBride **Bred** T S And Mrs M E Child **Trained** Newmarket, Suffolk

FOCUS
A modest handicap and they only went a steady early pace which resulted in a moderate winning time for the grade, 2.36 seconds slower than the earlier Class 3 handicap over the same trip. The form is sound enough rated through the runner-up.
Counterfactual(IRE) Official explanation: jockey said gelding raced too freely
Apache Point(IRE) Official explanation: jockey said gelding was denied a clear run
T/Jkpt: Part won. £20,482.00 to a £1 stake. Pool: £28,848.00. 0.50 winning tickets. T/Plt: £26.40 to a £1 stake. Pool: £59,781.20. 1,647.90 winning tickets. T/Qpdt: £25.80 to a £1 stake. Pool: £2,736.10. 78.30 winning tickets. JR

1291 LEICESTER (R-H)
Tuesday, May 22
OFFICIAL GOING: Good to firm (good in places, 8.5)
Wind: Light, behind Weather: Cloudy

1919 DANIEL AND EMILY MAIDEN STKS — 5f 2y
6:00 (6:01) (Class 5) 2-Y-0 **£3,238** (£963; £481; £240) **Stalls** Low

Form RPR
20 **1** **Only In Jest**[8] [1727] 2-8-7 TolleyDean(5) 13 77
(W G M Turner) *mde all: rdn over 1f out: styd on* **50/1**
2 *3/4* **Western Art (USA)** 2-9-3 SebSanders 12 80+
(P W Chapple-Hyam) *chsd wnr: rdn over 1f out: r.o* **11/8**[1]
43 **3** *hd* **Brassini**[29] [1201] 2-9-3 TedDurcan 1 79
(B R Millman) *chsd ldrs: rdn and hung rt over 1f out: r.o* **7/2**[2]
4 *nk* **Mazzanti** 2-9-3 NCallan 11 78+
(K A Ryan) *chsd ldrs: rdn 1/2-way: styd on* **6/1**
5 *nk* **Hatta Fort** 2-9-3 JHBowman 2 77+
(M R Channon) *s.i.s: hld up: hdwy and hung rt over 1f out: r.o: nrst fin* **4/1**[3]
6 *1 1/4* **Dome Rock (IRE)** 2-9-3 NickyMackay 5 72+
(L M Cumani) *hld up: hdwy and hung rt over 1f out: nt rch ldrs* **14/1**
7 *3* **Gambling Jack** 2-9-3 FergusSweeney 9 62
(A W Carroll) *s.i.s: hdwy 3f out: rdn over 1f out: wknd fnl f* **100/1**
00 **8** *6* **Madam Superior**[10] [1680] 2-8-12 SimonWhitworth 3 35
(D J S Ffrench Davis) *s.i.s: sn prom: wknd 1/2-way* **150/1**
9 *2* **An Scaribh** 2-9-3 TPQueally 6 33
(P D Evans) *dwlt: outpcd* **100/1**
5 **10** *3/4* **Amwell House**[39] [1021] 2-9-3 StephenCarson 10 30
(J R Jenkins) *prom: rdn 1/2-way: sn hung rt and wknd* **125/1**
6 **11** *hd* **Orpen's Art (IRE)**[34] [1094] 2-8-10 BradleyRoper(7) 4 29
(N A Callaghan) *s.i.s: hld up: wknd 1/2-way* **25/1**
12 *5* **Pussycat Bow** 2-8-12 DaleGibson 7 6
(M W Easterby) *s.i.s: outpcd* **50/1**
60.58 secs (-0.32) **Going Correction** -0.125s/f (Firm) **12** Ran SP% **116.5**
Speed ratings (Par 93):97,95,95,95,94 92,87,78,74,73 73,65
CSF £118.22 TOTE £40.90: £11.00, £1.10, £1.40; EX 154.50.
Owner Paul Thorman **Bred** J P Coggan **Trained** Sigwells, Somerset

FOCUS
A fair maiden that should produce winners. The third is probably the solid marker to the form.

NOTEBOOK
Only In Jest, who reportedly has plenty of temperament, made her experience count with a determined display of front running. She is clearly very quick and will take some catching at a course where the emphasis is on speed. One suspects she will not stay another furlong, so it would be no surprise if she ran in the Queen Mary at Royal Ascot.
Western Art(USA), whose trainer was 3 from 3 with his juveniles this season coming into the race, always seemed to find the pace a stride too quick for him early, although he was never far away, and only really got going in the last 50 yards. It should not be long before he emulates the rest of his stable companions who have already raced this season. (op Evens)
Brassini came down the stands' side early, but hung into the middle of the course when the tempo quickened. He was finishing really well and should easily stay another furlong. (op 4-1)
Mazzanti, who was a bit green in the early stages, picked up nicely towards the end and ran a race full of promise. He will come on plenty for the experience and will be much wiser next time, so a similar contest is well within his scope. (op 10-1)
Hatta Fort was given a really nice introductory ride and could easily turn out to be the best horse to emerge from the race. (op 7-2)
Dome Rock(IRE) was another in the field not to be given a hard time under pressure, and should be all the better for the experience. (op 40-1)
Orpen's Art(IRE) was not given an overly aggressive ride and will surely prove much better than he showed here. One suspects connections have one eye on nurseries already. (op 33-1)

1920 POMPADOURS H'CAP — 7f 9y
6:30 (6:30) (Class 4) (0-80,80) 3-Y-0 **£5,047** (£1,510; £755; £377; £188) **Stalls** Centre

Form RPR
2-43 **1** **Masai Moon**[10] [1660] 3-9-0 **76** JHBowman 13 84
(B R Millman) *mde all: rdn and hung lft over 1f out: styd on wl* **12/1**
41-4 **2** *2* **Curzon Prince (IRE)**[28] [1228] 3-9-4 **80** EddieAhern 3 83
(C F Wall) *hld up in tch: rdn over 2f out: styd on ins fnl f: nt rch wnr* **11/4**[2]
33-1 **3** *3/4* **Monte Alto (IRE)**[11] [1633] 3-9-1 **77** NickyMackay 6 78
(L M Cumani) *hmpd s: hld up: hdwy over 2f out: sn rdn: styd on ins fnl f: nrst fin* **2/1**[1]
45-4 **4** *3/4* **Satin Braid**[20] [1409] 3-8-8 **70** ow1 SebSanders 9 69
(A W Carroll) *prom: rdn over 2f out: styd on same pce ins fnl f* **33/1**
03-0 **5** *nk* **Riverside Dancer (USA)**[33] [1108] 3-8-10 **72** NCallan 4 70
(K A Ryan) *wnt rt s: plld hrd and sn trcking ldrs: rdn over 2f out: styd on same pce ins fnl f* **33/1**
1-45 **6** *shd* **Tipsy Prince**[21] [1383] 3-8-11 **73** DaneO'Neill 8 71
(David Pinder) *chsd wnr: rdn over 1f out: styd on same pce* **50/1**
33-1 **7** *5* **Rule Of Life**[25] [1278] 3-9-0 **76** RichardHughes 7 61
(B W Hills) *dwlt: hld up: rdn 1/2-way: hdwy over 1f out: wknd fnl f* **5/1**[3]
1 **8** *2* **Seleet (IRE)**[26] [1259] 3-9-4 **80** RHills 12 60
(M A Jarvis) *s.i.s: hld up: hdwy over 2f out: rdn and wknd over 1f out* **7/1**
32-2 **9** *2* **Le Singe Noir**[32] [1117] 3-8-11 **73** TPQueally 1 48
(D M Simcock) *sn pushed along in rr: wknd over 2f out* **33/1**
-004 **10** *hd* **Dora Explora**[12] [1603] 3-9-1 **77** StephenDonohoe 11 51
(P D Evans) *mid-div: sn drvn along: wknd over 2f out* **20/1**
6-54 **11** *nk* **Carson's Spirit (USA)**[14] [1563] 3-9-0 **76** FergusSweeney 10 49
(W S Kittow) *prom: rdn and wknd over 2f out* **16/1**
1m 24.44s (-1.66) **Going Correction** -0.125s/f (Firm) **11** Ran SP% **118.3**
Speed ratings (Par 101):104,101,100,100,99 99,93,91,89,89 88
CSF £43.35 CT £98.46 TOTE £14.90: £2.10, £1.70, £1.70; EX 83.20.
Owner C Roper **Bred** Mrs B A Matthews **Trained** Kentisbeare, Devon
■ Stewards' Enquiry : Eddie Ahern two-day ban: used whip with excessive frequency (Jun 3-4)

FOCUS
A decent three-year-old handicap for the track won in good style while the runner-up and third did not get on terms until late in the day and, although they set the standard, both might be suited by further.

1921 HOLLINGSHEAD (S) STKS — 7f 9y
7:00 (7:01) (Class 6) 3-Y-0+ **£2,590** (£770; £385; £192) **Stalls** Centre

Form RPR
-635 **1** **Convince (USA)**[14] [1562] 6-9-2 58 (p) KevinGhunowa(5) 9 61
(J M Bradley) *prom: rdn over 2f out: led 1f out: styd on* **13/2**
000- **2** *1/2* **Drawback (IRE)**[189] [6473] 4-9-2 55 (p) TolleyDean(5) 11 60
(R A Harris) *chsd ldrs: rdn 1/2-way: outpcd 2f out: hung rt and r.o ins fnl f* **33/1**
3R1- **3** *nk* **Sad Times (IRE)**[298] [3915] 3-8-2 60 LiamJones(3) 6 50
(W G M Turner) *outpcd: hdwy 2f out: r.o ins fnl f* **20/1**
26-0 **4** *nk* **Dante's Diamond (IRE)**[14] [1559] 5-9-7 55 (p) MickyFenton 3 58
(D Burchell) *bhd: hdwy over 2f out: rdn and ev ch over 1f out: styd on same pce ins fnl f* **20/1**
0050 **5** *1 1/4* **Napoletano (GER)**[7] [1740] 6-9-7 50 (p) SebSanders 17 55
(S Dow) *chsd ldrs: rdn over 2f out: no ex ins fnl f* **13/2**
0523 **6** *1/2* **Marmooq**[7] [1739] 4-9-12 60 DaneO'Neill 13 59
(M J Attwater) *hld up in tch: led 2f out: rdn and hdd 1f out: no ex* **9/2**[2]
300- **7** *5* **Meru Camp (IRE)**[250] [5323] 3-8-10 54 StephenCarson 4 40
(P Winkworth) *hld up: rdn and hung rt over 1f out: n.d* **33/1**
-266 **8** *9* **Cyfrwys (IRE)**[6] [1766] 6-9-2 50 (p) NCallan 18 11
(B Palling) *led: rdn and hdd 2f out: wknd fnl f* **5/1**[3]
0-05 **9** *nk* **Dancing Deano (IRE)**[7] [1739] 5-9-7 55 (v) FergusSweeney 12 15
(R Hollinshead) *hld up: hdwy u.p over 3f out: sn hung rt: wknd over 1f out* **14/1**
4000 **10** *4* **Kings Shillings**[28] [1224] 3-9-1 52 (v) StephenDonohoe 2 9
(D Carroll) *sn outpcd* **50/1**
50 **11** *2* **Whithorn**[7] [1749] 4-9-4 AndrewElliott(3) 10 —
(J Balding) *prom: racd keenly: wknd over 2f out* **66/1**
00-0 **12** *10* **Looks Could Kill (USA)**[7] [1747] 5-9-7 72 (t) EddieAhern 15 —
(E J Alston) *s.s: hdwy over 3f out: sn rdn: wknd 2f out: eased* **9/4**[1]
000 **13** *5* **Nikinoo**[7] [1739] 4-9-2 (b1) JamieMackay 7 —
(B Palling) *swvd lft s: outpcd* **100/1**
3/-0 **14** *16* **Zanjeer**[26] [1265] 7-9-7 64 JHBowman 1 —
(N Wilson) *hmpd s: chsd ldrs to 1/2-way* **12/1**
1m 25.79s (-0.31) **Going Correction** -0.125s/f (Firm)
WFA 3 from 4yo+ 11lb **14** Ran SP% **126.5**
Speed ratings (Par 101):96,95,95,94,93 92,87,76,76,71 69,58,52,34
CSF £217.47 TOTE £7.70: £1.60, £14.10, £2.20; EX 156.50.There was no bid for the winner.
Owner The Lovely Jubbly's **Bred** Juddmonte Farms Inc **Trained** Sedbury, Gloucs

FOCUS
A really poor event that will have little bearing on any future races with the fifth the best guide to the level.
Cyfrwys(IRE) Official explanation: jockey said mare never travelled
Looks Could Kill(USA) Official explanation: vet said gelding returned lame
Zanjeer Official explanation: vet said gelding was found to have an irregular heartbeat

1922 **DISPLAY LOGISTICS 10TH ANNIVERSARY H'CAP** **1m 1f 218y**
7:30 (7:30) (Class 4) (0-80,80) 4-Y-0+ **£5,047** (£1,510; £755; £377; £188) **Stalls High**

Form RPR
1-13 **1** **Sound Of Nature (USA)**[26] 1268 4-9-4 **80** RichardHughes 7 99+
(H R A Cecil) *a.p: trckd ldr over 5f out: shkn up to ld ins fnl f: r.o wl* **11/8**[1]
15-0 **2** *1 1/4* **Shout (IRE)**[24] 1287 4-9-0 **76** RHills 8 83
(J W Hills) *led: rdn over 1f out: hdd and unable qckn ins fnl f* **16/1**
0-60 **3** *1/2* **Snowed Under**[20] 1416 6-8-10 **72** PatCosgrave 9 78
(J D Bethell) *chsd ldrs: rdn over 1f out: styd on* **9/1**
1221 **4** *nk* **Can Can Star**[24] 1295 4-8-4 **73** ow1 HaddenFrost(7) 2 78
(A W Carroll) *hld up in tch: racd keenly: hung rt over 3f out: rdn over 1f out: styd on same pce fnl f* **7/1**[2]
0-00 **5** *3/4* **Red Lancer**[17] 1480 6-9-3 **79** SilvestreDeSousa 12 83
(D Nicholls) *hld up in tch: outpcd over 2f out: styd on ins fnl f* **15/2**[3]
5312 **6** *1/2* **Torrens (IRE)**[19] 1434 5-8-6 **75** JamesRogers(7) 6 78
(R A Fahey) *s.i.s: hld up: hdwy over 1f out: no ex ins fnl f* **8/1**
521- **7** *3/4* **Pentatonic**[239] 5567 4-9-2 **78** NickyMackay 4 79+
(L M Cumani) *trckd ldrs: racd keenly: rdn over 1f out: no ex fnl f* **15/2**[3]
-506 **8** *1 3/4* **Cape Greko**[24] 1308 5-9-0 **76** SebSanders 10 74
(B G Powell) *hld up: plld hrd: nt clr run over 2f out: hung rt over 1f out: nt trble ldrs* **14/1**
5531 **9** *nk* **Jackie Kiely**[26] 1263 6-8-12 **74** (t) J-PGuillambert 5 71
(R Brotherton) *hld up: rdn over 2f out: n.d* **33/1**
010- **10** *3* **Fabrian**[206] 6221 9-8-12 **77** LiamJones(3) 3 68
(R J Price) *hld up: plld hrd: rdn over 2f out: n.d* **33/1**
45-5 **11** *1/2* **Trouble Mountain (USA)**[12] 1599 10-8-9 **71** (t) DaleGibson 11 61
(M W Easterby) *chsd ldr over 4f: remained handy tl rdn and wknd over 1f out* **33/1**
131- **12** *27* **Urban Tiger (GER)**[25] 4160 4-9-4 **80** NCallan 1 16
(Carl Llewellyn) *s.i.s: hld up: wknd over 2f out* **25/1**

2m 6.70s (-1.60) **Going Correction** -0.125s/f (Firm) 12 Ran SP% **124.5**
Speed ratings (Par 105):101,100,99,99,98 98,97,96,96,93 93,71
CSF £28.02 CT £154.94 TOTE £2.50: £1.10, £8.50, £1.70; EX 41.90.
Owner K Abdulla **Bred** Juddmonte Farms Inc **Trained** Newmarket, Suffolk

FOCUS
A fair handicap won with ridiculous ease by Group 1 entered Sound Of Nature. The form is not that solid with several close up looking high enough in the handicap.
Cape Greko Official explanation: jockey said gelding did not let himself down
Fabrian Official explanation: jockey said gelding ran too free early

1923 **DENNIS JACQUES MAIDEN STKS** **5f 218y**
8:00 (8:01) (Class 5) 3-Y-O **£3,886** (£1,156; £577; £288) **Stalls Centre**

Form RPR
0- **1** **Double Bill (USA)**[272] 4716 3-9-3 JHBowman 5 74+
(P F I Cole) *racd centre: chsd ldr: rdn over 1f out: r.o to ld nr fin* **2/1**[1]
005- **2** *nk* **Gilded Youth**[224] 5890 3-9-3 77 DaneO'Neill 2 73
(H Candy) *hld up: swtchd centre over 4f out: hdwy over 2f out: r.o wl: 2nd of 14 in gp* **9/1**
622 **3** *nk* **Diksie Dancer**[25] 1282 3-8-12 72 NCallan 11 67
(K A Ryan) *overall ldr centre: rdn over 1f out: hdd nr fin: 3rd of 14 in gp* **7/2**[2]
00- **4** *2* **Kind Of Fizzy**[207] 6200 3-8-12 JamieMackay 18 61+
(Rae Guest) *s.i.s: racd centre: hld up: hdwy over 1f out: nt rch ldrs: 4th of 14 in gp* **100/1**
0- **5** *4* **Land's End (IRE)**[222] 5915 3-9-3 TPQueally 9 53+
(J Noseda) *hmpd s: racd centre: hld up: hdwy u.p and hung rt over 1f out: nvr nrr: 5th of 14 in gp* **8/1**
000- **6** *1 1/2* **Silver Appraisal**[193] 6422 3-8-12 60 PaulEddery 12 43
(Pat Eddery) *racd centre: s.i.s: hld up: styd on ins fnl f: nvr nrr: 6th of 14 in gp* **100/1**
56 **7** *shd* **Fervent**[20] 1403 3-8-12 KevinGhunowa(5) 1 48
(J M Bradley) *racd centre: outpcd: styd on ins fnl f: nrst fin: 7th of 14 in gp* **50/1**
65- **8** *1* **Give Her A Whirl**[206] 6222 3-8-12 DeanMcKeown 4 40
(G A Swinbank) *racd stands' side: chsd ldr tl led that duo 1/2-way: wknd over 1f out: 1st of 2 in gp* **11/1**
2-3 **9** *hd* **Millachy**[28] 1207 3-8-12 MichaelHills 14 39
(B W Hills) *racd centre: chsd ldrs: rdn over 2f out: wknd over 1f out: 8th of 14 in gp* **5/1**[3]
10 *1 1/4* **Tamarack (IRE)** 3-9-3 EddieAhern 8 40+
(W R Muir) *s.i.s: racd centre: hld up: n.d: 9th of 14 in gp* **33/1**
0- **11** *hd* **She's A Softie (IRE)**[199] 6331 3-8-12 TedDurcan 17 34
(C F Wall) *racd centre: hld up: n.d: 10th of 14 in gp* **66/1**
12 *1/2* **Archimage (USA)** 3-9-3 PaulFessey 6 38
(T D Barron) *s.i.s: racd centre and sn prom: rdn over 2f out: wkng whn n.m.r over 1f out: 11th of 14 in gp* **33/1**
04 **13** *2 1/2* **Punching**[16] 1501 3-9-3 StephenCarson 15 30
(Eve Johnson Houghton) *racd centre: chsd ldrs over 4f: 12th of 14 in gp* **16/1**
6 **14** *9* **Yurchenko**[21] 1386 3-8-12 AdamKirby 10 —
(M Wellings) *racd centre: wnt lft s: chsd ldrs over 3f: 13th of 14 in gp* **100/1**
5-0 **15** *3* **Mootamaress (IRE)**[11] 1635 3-9-3 74 RichardHughes 3 —
(Mrs A L M King) *led stands' side to 1/2-way: sn wknd: last of 2 that side* **40/1**
5 **16** *1 3/4* **Western Point (IRE)**[7] 1737 3-9-3 SebSanders 7 —
(Sir Mark Prescott) *racd centre: sn pushed along in rr: bhd fr 1/2-way: last of 14 in gp* **8/1**

1m 12.53s (-0.67) **Going Correction** -0.125s/f (Firm) 16 Ran SP% **133.4**
Speed ratings (Par 99):99,98,98,95,90 88,88,86,86,84 84,83,80,68,64 62
CSF £23.44 TOTE £3.70: £2.80, £3.90, £1.70; EX 40.90.
Owner Mrs Stephanie Smith **Bred** ClassicStar **Trained** Whatcombe, Oxon

FOCUS
An ordinary maiden with some promising performances. The overall level looks solid enough, with the placed horses to pre-race marks.
Fervent Official explanation: jockey said gelding did not come down the hill well

1924 **STONESTREET H'CAP** **1m 3f 183y**
8:30 (8:30) (Class 5) (0-70,70) 4-Y-0+ **£3,886** (£1,156; £577; £288) **Stalls High**

Form RPR
1521 **1** **Penang Cinta**[36] 1069 4-8-13 **65** StephenDonohoe 6 80+
(P D Evans) *hld up: hdwy to ld over 2f out: drvn out* **4/1**[2]
0-03 **2** *1 3/4* **Wild Fell Hall (IRE)**[20] 1416 4-9-4 **70** AdamKirby 8 80
(W R Swinburn) *chsd ldr: led wl over 2f out: sn hdd: styd on same pce fnl f* **9/4**[1]
-101 **3** *3* **Sunset Boulevard (IRE)**[18] 1451 4-9-4 **70** ChrisCatlin 4 75
(Miss Tor Sturgis) *chsd ldrs: rdn over 2f out: styd on same pce appr fnl f* **11/2**[3]
-460 **4** *3 1/2* **General Flumpa**[20] 1406 6-7-13 **56** NataliaGemelova(5) 2 55
(Miss Tor Sturgis) *s.i.s: hld up: hdwy over 3f out: wknd over 1f out* **10/1**
0/0- **5** *1/2* **Raffish**[63] 2585 5-8-9 **61** FergusSweeney 5 60
(M Scudamore) *hld up: hdwy over 3f out: wknd over 1f out* **33/1**
3001 **6** *1 1/4* **Sedgwick**[10] 1671 5-9-0 **66** TPQueally 3 63
(J G Given) *chsd ldrs: rdn over 3f out: wknd over 1f out* **4/1**[2]
500- **7** *8* **Monsignor Fred**[246] 5436 5-8-3 **62** AmyScott(7) 1 46
(H Candy) *hld up: racd keenly: wknd 3f out* **40/1**
5-30 **8** *12* **Longhill Tiger**[15] 1526 4-8-10 **62** SebSanders 9 27
(G G Margarson) *led: hdd wl over 2f out: sn wknd* **15/2**

2m 32.14s (-2.36) **Going Correction** -0.125s/f (Firm) 8 Ran SP% **112.4**
Speed ratings (Par 103):102,100,98,96,96 95,90,82
CSF £12.93 CT £47.60 TOTE £4.80: £1.80, £1.40, £1.60; EX 18.00 Place 6 £137.81, Place 5 £60.24..
Owner Trevor Gallienne **Bred** Mrs A K H Ooi **Trained** Pandy, Monmouths

FOCUS
A modest handicap won by an in-form sort. Overall, the form, rated around the placed horses, does not look anything special.
Longhill Tiger Official explanation: trainer said colt was found to be dehydrated on returning to the yard
T/Plt: £58.70 to a £1 stake. Pool: £61,051.10. 759.10 winning tickets. T/Qpdt: £25.00 to a £1 stake. Pool: £4,070.20. 120.40 winning tickets. CR

1660 LINGFIELD (L-H)
Tuesday, May 22

OFFICIAL GOING: Turf course - good to firm; all-weather - standard
Wind: Light, behind Weather: Sunny and warm

1925 **GO WEST LIVE AT LINGFIELD PARK H'CAP** **2m**
2:10 (2:10) (Class 6) (0-50,55) 4-Y-0+ **£2,730** (£806; £403) **Stalls Low**

Form RPR
5-21 **1** **Gaelic Roulette (IRE)**[13] 1590 7-8-12 **50** JimmyFortune 8 57+
(J Jay) *lw: hld up in midfield: prog over 5f out: trckd ldr over 4f out: led 3f out: hrd rdn fnl 2f: kpt on* **6/4**[1]
0201 **2** *1 1/2* **Ronsard (IRE)**[1] 1888 5-9-3 **55** 6ex RichardMullen 11 61
(P D Evans) *s.s: hld up in last trio: prog 6f out: wnt 3rd 4f out: drvn to chse wnr 2f out: no imp over 1f out* **5/1**[2]
4625 **3** *1 1/4* **Tip Toes (IRE)**[20] 1402 5-8-3 **46** oh1 WilliamBuick(5) 5 50
(P Howling) *hld up in last: pushed along and prog 5f out: wd bnd over 3f out: rdn and hdwy after: disp 2nd 1f out: fnd nil* **8/1**
0-06 **4** *3/4* **Bobsleigh**[6] 1526 8-8-10 **48** (b) JimmyQuinn 2 51
(H S Howe) *rn in snatches: outpcd 4f out: n.d after: r.o fnl f* **10/1**
6005 **5** *nk* **Treetops Hotel (IRE)**[23] 1319 8-8-11 **49** RichardSmith 1 52
(B R Johnson) *hld up in midfield: outpcd 4f out: effrt over 2f out: kpt on same pce and no real imp* **7/1**[3]
033- **6** *1 3/4* **Delorain (IRE)**[26] 5324 4-8-6 **49** ow1 (b) JerryO'Dwyer(3) 9 50
(N B King) *trckd ldr: led over 4f out to 3f out: wknd over 1f out* **20/1**
0-00 **7** *7* **Sterling Moll**[20] 1402 4-8-6 **46** oh1 AdrianMcCarthy 6 38
(W De Best-Turner) *hld up in rr: prog to chse ldng trio 4f out: sn rdn: wknd over 2f out* **66/1**
-135 **8** *1 1/2* **Moon Emperor**[67] 691 10-8-12 **50** (b) EddieAhern 3 40
(J R Jenkins) *lw: trckd ldrs: lost pl over 4f out: struggling in rr fnl 3f* **7/1**[3]
0 **9** *14* **Infidel (IRE)**[22] 1347 7-8-8 **46** oh1 (b[1]) JohnEgan 10 20
(J R Best) *lw: led at decent pce: hdd over 4f out: sn wknd and eased: t.o* **33/1**
4260 **10** *2* **War Feather**[13] 1592 5-8-10 **48** EdwardCreighton 7 19
(T D McCarthy) *chsd ldrs tl lost pl qckly 5f out: sn bhd: t.o* **25/1**
000- **11** *5* **Liameliss**[28] 4239 5-8-1 **46** oh1 SCreighton(7) 4 11
(M A Allen) *t.k.h: prom tl lost pl rapidly 6f out: sn bhd: t.o* **66/1**

3m 34.73s (1.47) **Going Correction** +0.075s/f (Good)
WFA 4 from 5yo+ 2lb 11 Ran SP% **116.4**
Speed ratings (Par 101):99,98,97,97,97 96,92,91,84,83 81
CSF £8.19 CT £44.60 TOTE £2.20: £1.10, £2.10, £2.80; EX 10.90 Trifecta £63.30 Pool: £423.73 - 4.75 winning units..
Owner Graham & Lynn Knight **Bred** J F Tuthill **Trained** Newmarket, Suffolk

FOCUS
A moderate staying handicap run at a fair gallop and dominated by hold-up horses. The form looks sound enough rated around the first three.

1926 **PROSPECT DISTRIBUTORS FILLIES' H'CAP** **1m 3f 106y**
2:40 (2:42) (Class 6) (0-65,65) 4-Y-0+ **£2,590** (£770; £385; £192) **Stalls High**

Form RPR
66-0 **1** **Inchmahome**[24] 1312 4-9-2 **63** LPKeniry 1 67+
(E F Vaughan) *swtg: settled in last pair: rdn 4f out: stl only 7th over 2f out: prog on inner as ldrs faltered over 1f out: led last 150yds: sn clr* **7/1**
04-3 **2** *1 1/2* **Generous Jem**[20] 1396 4-8-13 **60** JohnEgan 2 62+
(G G Margarson) *trckd ldrs: rdn and struggling over 3f out: plld out and styd on fr 2f out: bmpd 1f out: kpt on to take 2nd last 100yds* **5/2**[1]
60-5 **3** *1/2* **Star Berry**[6] 1764 4-7-12 **52** KMay(7) 3 52
(B J Meehan) *chsd ldr 3f: 3rd after: rdn 4f out: wnt 2nd again wl over 1f out: clsd and edgd rt 1f out: kpt on same pce* **7/2**[2]
-040 **4** *1/2* **Valart**[11] 1628 4-8-11 **58** (tp) EddieAhern 9 57
(A J Lidderdale) *led at decent pce: kicked on 4f out and had rest in trble: drvn over 2f out: hdd & wknd last 150yds* **12/1**
03/6 **5** *1 1/4* **Prelude**[26] 1258 6-8-7 **54** RichardMullen 5 51
(W M Brisbourne) *lw: hld up in tch: rdn 4f out: nt look keen and no prog over 2f out: kpt on fnl f* **4/1**[3]
-003 **6** *2* **Royal Audition**[43] 982 6-8-4 **51** oh1 (p) DO'Donohoe 10 45
(T T Clement) *wnt 2nd after 3f: drvn 4f out: lost pl wl over 1f out: stl cl up whn hmpd jst over 1f out: bdly hmpd sn after: eased* **11/2**
3505 **7** *5* **Compton Express**[20] 1396 4-8-4 **51** oh3 JimmyQuinn 11 37
(Jamie Poulton) *hld up in last: effrt 5f out: rdn and struggling 3f out: no prog* **13/2**
00-0 **8** *21* **Keagles (ITY)**[27] 1250 4-8-4 **51** oh1 RichardThomas 7 3
(J E Long) *in tch tl wknd over 4f out: t.o* **33/1**

2m 31.37s (1.45) **Going Correction** +0.075s/f (Good) 8 Ran SP% **122.6**
Speed ratings (Par 98):97,95,95,95,94 92,89,73
CSF £26.85 CT £75.25 TOTE £10.10: £2.60, £1.30, £1.60; EX 41.90 Trifecta £163.20 Part won. Pool: £229.92 - 0.44 winning units..
Owner A E Oppenheimer **Bred** Hascombe And Valiant Studs **Trained** Newmarket, Suffolk
■ Broughtons Revival (11/4) was withdrawn because of unsuitable ground. Rule 4 applies, deduct 25p in the £.

FOCUS
A moderate handicap run at a good gallop fought out by the less-exposed sorts. The fourth is the best guide to the level but the form appears very ordinary.
Generous Jem Official explanation: jockey said filly hung left throughout
Keagles(ITY) Official explanation: trainer later said filly was found to have an infection

1927 RENAULT MASTER H'CAP — 1m 2f
3:10 (3:11) (Class 6) (0-65,71) 3-Y-0 — **£3,238** (£963; £481; £240) **Stalls** Low

Form — RPR
-121 **1** **Graceful Steps (IRE)**[8] [1708] 3-9-3 **71** 6ex .... MCGeran(7) 1 — 79+
(E J O'Neill) *lw: s.i.s: sn prom: rdn to chse ldr 2f out: narrow ld jst over 1f out: hld on wl* **7/4**[1]
005 **2** *nk* **Yes One (IRE)**[10] [1665] 3-9-4 **65** .... EddieAhern 6 — 72
(J W Hills) *hld up wl in rr: prog fr over 2f out: drvn to chal and nrly upsides ins fnl f: jst hld* **6/1**[2]
2-66 **3** *hd* **Summer Of Love (IRE)**[22] [1355] 3-9-1 **62** .... JimmyFortune 3 — 69
(P F I Cole) *lw: hld up in midfield: drvn and effrt over 2f out: styd on to chal fnl f: nt qckn and a jst hld* **7/1**[3]
50-4 **4** *¾* **Rowan River**[24] [1310] 3-9-3 **64** .... JimmyQuinn 2 — 71+
(M H Tompkins) *hld up towards rr: stdy prog on inner over 2f out: rdn whn nt clr run 1f out: swtchd rt and styd on fnl 100yds* **12/1**
1600 **5** *1* **My Mirasol**[11] [1628] 3-9-1 **62** .... (p) JohnEgan 14 — 65
(D E Cantillon) *sn led and set str pce: hdd jst over 1f out: fdd* **33/1**
0-00 **6** *nk* **Shine And Rise (IRE)**[31] [1143] 3-9-1 **62** .... KerrinMcEvoy 5 — 64
(C G Cox) *lw: trckd ldrs: effrt and cl up 2f out: no imp 1f out: fdd* **6/1**[2]
000- **7** *1 ½* **She's So Pretty (IRE)**[249] [5352] 3-9-3 **64** .... AdamKirby 4 — 63+
(W R Swinburn) *settled in last trio: plenty to do 4f out: drvn and prog fr over 2f out: kpt on: nt rch ldrs* **12/1**
3164 **8** *3* **Homes By Woodford**[28] [1230] 3-9-4 **65** .... SteveDrowne 8 — 58
(R A Harris) *t.k.h: hld up in midfield: effrt to chse ldrs 2f out: no imp 1f out: wknd* **16/1**
00-4 **9** *2 ½* **Rustic Gold**[38] [1039] 3-8-13 **63** .... StephaneBreux(3) 10 — 51
(J R Best) *hld up in midfield and racd wd: no prog over 2f out: wknd over 1f out* **16/1**
540- **10** *shd* **The Fifth Member (IRE)**[174] [6651] 3-9-4 **65** .... PaulDoe 12 — 53
(R M Flower) *h.d.w: bit bkwd: mostly chsd ldr to 2f out: wknd* **66/1**
0 **11** *4* **Storm Obsession (IRE)**[15] [1537] 3-9-1 **62** .... (p) AmirQuinn 11 — 42
(P J Makin) *t.k.h early: pressed ldrs to over 2f out: wknd* **66/1**
2-40 **12** *¾* **Mud Monkey**[8] [1724] 3-9-1 **62** .... GeorgeBaker 9 — 41
(B G Powell) *s.s: a in last pair: wl bhd 4f out* **16/1**
5005 **13** *2 ½* **Global Traffic**[22] [1355] 3-9-3 **64** .... (b) RichardMullen 13 — 38
(P D Evans) *s.v.s: last pair tl brief effrt over 4f out: wknd 3f out* **11/1**

2m 9.70s (-0.02) **Going Correction** +0.075s/f (Good) — **13** Ran SP% **124.7**
Speed ratings (Par 97):103,102,102,102,101 100,99,97,95,95 92,91,89
CSF £12.38 CT £63.93 TOTE £2.50: £1.30, £2.30, £2.40; EX 17.90 Trifecta £180.90 Part won. Pool: £254.92 - 0.40 winning units..
Owner J C Fretwell **Bred** John Davis And Newtown Stud **Trained** Averham Park, Notts

FOCUS
A modest handicap but there were a few unexposed performers in the line-up and the form is rated fairly positively.
Homes By Woodford Official explanation: jockey said gelding was unsuited by the good to firm ground
Mud Monkey Official explanation: jockey said colt never travelled
Global Traffic Official explanation: jockey and trainer said colt was unsuited by the good to firm ground

1928 GARY THE AMAZING MEMORY MAN AYRIS MEDIAN AUCTION MAIDEN STKS — 1m 1f
3:40 (3:42) (Class 5) 3-4-Y-0 — **£3,108** (£924; £462; £230) **Stalls** Low

Form — RPR
62-2 **1** **Royal Rationale (IRE)**[19] [1440] 3-9-0 76 .... JimmyFortune 1 — 77+
(W J Haggas) *lw: trckd ldrs: wnt 2nd over 2f out: led gng easily over 1f out: shkn up and sn clr* **11/4**[2]
55-2 **2** *2* **Snake's Head**[19] [1433] 3-8-9 77 .... JimmyQuinn 7 — 66
(J L Dunlop) *led: rdn 2f out: hdd and outpcd by wnr over 1f out* **5/2**[1]
04 **3** *2 ½* **Natural Action**[19] [1440] 3-9-0 .... KerrinMcEvoy 10 — 65
(W Jarvis) *lw: unruly stalls: prom: cl up 3f out: rdn and kpt on same pce fnl 2f* **11/4**[2]
4 *1 ¾* **Anna Towkaska** 3-8-9 .... AdamKirby 4 — 56+
(W R Swinburn) *lw: settled wl in rr: shkn up 3f out: styd on steadily after: r.o to take 4th on post* **14/1**
2653 **5** *shd* **Razzano (IRE)**[30] 3-8-6 56 .... JerryO'Dwyer(3) 14 — 56?
(A M Hales) *settled towards rr: effrt on wd outside 3f out: rdn and kpt on same pce: no ch w ldrs* **16/1**
24 **6** *2 ½* **Serhaaphim**[7] [1746] 3-8-9 .... EddieAhern 8 — 51+
(M L W Bell) *lw: settled wl in rr: stl there over 3f out: pushed along over 2f out: styd on ins fnl f: nvr nr ldrs* **7/1**[3]
0-0 **7** *hd* **Twenty Percent**[13] [1587] 3-9-0 .... PaulDoe 6 — 55
(P R Chamings) *lw: reminder in rr after 2f: prog 5f out: rdn to try to cl on ldrs 2f out: one pce: fdd fnl f* **66/1**
000- **8** *1 ¼* **Ma Ridge**[254] [5206] 3-9-0 42 .... EdwardCreighton 5 — 52?
(T D McCarthy) *lw: t.k.h: mostly chsd ldr to over 2f out: wknd* **100/1**
9 *5* **River Hunter (IRE)** 3-8-9 .... LPKeniry 11 — 36
(S Kirk) *green to post: chsd ldrs tl wknd jst over 2f out* **25/1**
0/0 **10** *4* **Kolibre**[114] [272] 4-9-13 .... GeorgeBaker 2 — 33
(T T Clement) *dwlt and wl rt s: a wl in rr: no ch over 2f out* **100/1**
00- **11** *4* **Port Luanda (IRE)**[300] [3843] 3-9-0 .... PatDobbs 3 — 24
(R M Flower) *dwlt: a wl in rr: rdn and hanging lft over 2f out* **100/1**
6 **12** *hd* **Simpleton**[49] [901] 4-9-10 .... StephaneBreux(3) 12 — 23
(J R Best) *swtg: lft 20l s: latched on to bk of field after 3f: no ch fnl 3f* **66/1**
4-35 **13** *6* **Three No Trumps**[127] [139] 3-8-9 47 .... SteveDrowne 9 — 5
(P S Felgate) *nvr bttr than midfield: wknd 3f out* **50/1**
0 **14** *26* **Charley Fox**[13] [1587] 3-8-7 .... JosephWalsh(7) 13 — —
(D C O'Brien) *chsd ldrs 5f: wknd rapidly: t.o* **100/1**

1m 56.49s (1.20) **Going Correction** +0.075s/f (Good)
WFA 3 from 4yo 13lb — **14** Ran SP% **119.7**
Speed ratings (Par 103):97,95,93,91,91 89,88,87,83,79 76,76,70,47
CSF £9.75 TOTE £4.20: £1.50, £1.20, £1.70; EX 11.80 Trifecta £18.90 Pool: £505.25 - 18.98 winning units..
Owner W J Gredley **Bred** Middle Park Stud Ltd **Trained** Newmarket, Suffolk

FOCUS
A fair maiden dominated by the market leaders. The form looks modest and is limited by the proximity of the fifth, seventh and eighth.

1929 RENAULT KANGOO H'CAP — 1m 1f
4:10 (4:11) (Class 4) (0-85,85) 3-Y-0 — **£6,477** (£1,927; £963; £481) **Stalls** Low

Form — RPR
1 **1** **Padlocked (IRE)**[15] [1523] 3-8-10 **77** .... JohnEgan 4 — 92+
(J Noseda) *lw: chsd ldr over 3f out: rdn over 2f out: clsd over 1f out: led last 100yds: styd on wl* **15/8**[1]
-261 **2** *1* **Tetouan**[24] [1297] 3-8-9 **76** .... SteveDrowne 6 — 88
(R Charlton) *lw: led at str pce: rdn and hdd over 2f out: pressed ldr after: upsides ins fnl f: nt qckn* **11/4**[2]
10-5 **3** *shd* **Paceman (USA)**[25] [1277] 3-8-13 **80** .... JimmyFortune 5 — 92
(R Hannon) *lw: trckd ldng pair: wnt 2nd on inner over 3f out: led over 2f out: hrd rdn over 1f out: hdd and one pce last 100yds* **14/1**
14-0 **4** *6* **Rose Of Petra (IRE)**[25] [1275] 3-9-1 **82** .... KerrinMcEvoy 7 — 81
(Sir Michael Stoute) *lw: trckd ldrs: rdn and no imp over 2f out: wl btn over 1f out* **7/1**[3]
0-44 **5** *1 ½* **Valley Observer (FR)**[15] [1523] 3-8-4 **71** .... RichardMullen 2 — 67
(W R Swinburn) *swtg: settled in last pair: pushed along 1/2-way: rdn and effrt on outer 3f out: kpt on one pce* **12/1**
0-30 **6** *½* **Kalasam**[25] [1277] 3-8-7 **74** .... JamesDoyle 1 — 69
(W R Muir) *t.k.h: hld up in tch: rdn and struggling wl over 2f out* **33/1**
2-50 **7** *hd* **Safe Investment (USA)**[33] [1106] 3-9-4 **85** .... PatDobbs 9 — 79
(J H M Gosden) *dwlt: hld up in last: pushed along and lft bhd fr 3f out* **7/1**[3]
10- **8** *2* **Emulate**[234] [5672] 3-8-12 **79** .... OscarUrbina 8 — 69
(B W Hills) *bit bkwd: hld up towards rr: shkn up and wandered wl over 2f out: no ch after* **16/1**
41-6 **9** *2 ½* **Free Offer**[34] [1089] 3-8-13 **80** .... EddieAhern 3 — 64
(J L Dunlop) *a towards rr: green and struggling wl over 2f out* **20/1**

1m 54.09s (-1.20) **Going Correction** +0.075s/f (Good) — **9** Ran SP% **114.4**
Speed ratings (Par 101):108,107,107,101,100 99,99,97,95
CSF £6.87 CT £52.08 TOTE £3.10: £1.20, £1.30, £4.20; EX 8.40 Trifecta £75.20 Pool: £448.55 - 4.23 winning units..
Owner Saif Misfer **Bred** Patrick F Kelly **Trained** Newmarket, Suffolk

FOCUS
An interesting handicap run at a good gallop and in a very decent time for a race of its type, 2.4 seconds faster than the preceding all-aged maiden. This looks a strong race and the form should work out.
Valley Observer(FR) Official explanation: jockey said colt hung left
Emulate Official explanation: jockey said filly moved poorly

1930 RENAULT VANS H'CAP — 7f (P)
4:40 (4:46) (Class 3) (0-90,89) 3-Y-0
£9,348 (£2,799; £1,399; £700; £349; £175) **Stalls** Low

Form — RPR
-203 **1** **El Bosque (IRE)**[16] [1502] 3-8-13 **89** .... JamesMillman(5) 7 — 94
(B R Millman) *lw: cl up: trckd ldr 1/2-way: rdn to ld 2f out: 2l clr ins fnl f: jst hld on* **14/1**
1-00 **2** *shd* **Cool Box (USA)**[12] [1603] 3-8-12 **83** .... KerrinMcEvoy 4 — 88
(Mrs A J Perrett) *lw: hld up in last pair: effrt on outer over 2f out: drvn and r.o to chse wnr ins fnl f: clsd fin: jst failed* **9/2**[2]
1-3 **3** *1 ½* **Escape Route (USA)**[32] [1124] 3-9-4 **89** .... JimmyFortune 8 — 98+
(J H M Gosden) *lw: awkward s: hld up in last: effrt 2f out: rn into wall of trble 1f out: plld arnd and r.o last 100yds: no ch* **8/15**[1]
6-31 **4** *¾* **Teen Ager (FR)**[32] [1117] 3-8-7 **78** .... JohnEgan 3 — 77
(J S Moore) *lw: fractious bef s: plld hrd: hld up bhd ldrs: rdn over 2f out: one pce* **10/1**[3]
4-00 **5** *1* **Mubaashir (IRE)**[16] [1500] 3-9-4 **89** .... DO'Donohoe 1 — 85
(E A L Dunlop) *trckd ldr to 1/2-way: styd cl up on inner: fdd fnl f* **12/1**
1-01 **6** *nk* **Lord Theo**[15] [1535] 3-8-9 **80** .... JamesDoyle 2 — 76
(N P Littmoden) *led to 2f out: hung rt and wknd 1f out* **16/1**
15-0 **7** *7* **Disco Dan**[34] [1099] 3-8-9 **80** .... RichardMullen 5 — 57
(D M Simcock) *in tch tl wknd u.p 2f out: t.o* **25/1**

1m 24.34s (-1.55) **Going Correction** -0.10s/f (Stan) — **7** Ran SP% **116.6**
Speed ratings (Par 103):104,103,102,101,100 99,91
CSF £77.31 CT £93.83 TOTE £21.70: £6.10, £1.90; EX 117.80 Trifecta £239.30 Pool: £802.21 - 2.38 winning units..
Owner Wessex Racing **Bred** Mrs M Campbell-Andenaes **Trained** Kentisbeare, Devon
■ Stewards' Enquiry : James Doyle four-day ban: careless riding (Jun 3-6)

FOCUS
A decent handicap run at a fair pace, but there was trouble in running for the favourite and the runner-up would have got there in another yard. the form makes sense however, rated around the runner-up and fourth.

NOTEBOOK
El Bosque(IRE), in what became a bit of a messy race, was always well positioned and just held on from the fast-finishing Cool Box at the line. He got the 7f this time, just, but once again gave the impression that he will be happy dropping back to six. (op 12-1 tchd 16-1)
Cool Box(USA) did not get the best of luck in running at Chester last time and on this occasion he needed one more stride to win. He has not enjoyed the rub of things of late but is clearly in form and, if the Handicapper does not put him up too much, he should remain capable of winning in the coming weeks. (tchd 5-1)
Escape Route(USA), third and in front of Cool Box in a hot Newbury handicap last time out, was a well-supported favourite and travelled well in the race itself. He found his path blocked with a furlong and a half to run though, and by the time he was switched the race was all but over. He finished well and will gain compensation soon, but will no doubt be a short price to do so. (op 8-13 tchd 1-2 and 4-6 in places)
Teen Ager(FR), winner of a maiden over this course and distance last time out, failed to settle in the early stages and gave himself little chance of seeing his race out strongly. (op 9-1 tchd 8-1)
Mubaashir(IRE) has come down a fair way in the handicap but remains vulnerable to more progressive and lighter-raced rivals. (op 16-1)
Lord Theo, who made all to win last time out, was only 2lb higher here. He set a fair pace but was there to be shot at in the straight and failed to run up to his Warwick form. (op 14-1)

1931 RENAULT TRAFIC H'CAP — 7f (P)
5:10 (5:13) (Class 5) (0-75,74) 4-Y-0+ — **£3,238** (£963; £481; £240) **Stalls** Low

Form — RPR
0500 **1** **Glencalvie (IRE)**[18] [1446] 6-8-13 **69** .... (v) JimmyQuinn 11 — 75
(J Akehurst) *led: set stdy pce to 1/2-way: drvn 2f out: 2l clr fnl f: jst lasted* **11/1**
212 **2** *½* **His Master's Voice (IRE)**[49] [902] 4-9-4 **74** .... BrettDoyle 8 — 79+
(D W P Arbuthnot) *wl plcd bhd ldrs: gng easily 2f out: effrt over 1f out: r.o to chse wnr ins fnl f: clsng fin: too much to do* **4/1**[1]
0050 **3** *shd* **Purus (IRE)**[3] [1845] 5-8-9 **65** .... LPKeniry 9 — 70
(R A Teal) *lw: sn in tch on outer: prog over 2f out: drvn and r.o fr over 1f out: clsng at fin* **25/1**

5432 **4** 1 **Everygrainofsand (IRE)**[15] 1541 4-9-2 **72**..................... GeorgeBaker 6 — 74
(J R Best) *lw: cl up on inner: drvn 2f out: disp 2nd 1f out: nt qckn u.p: one pce after* **5/1**[2]

100 **5** 1 **Romany Nights (IRE)**[15] 1545 7-9-1 **71**...........................(bt) JohnEgan 5 — 70+
(Miss Gay Kelleway) *b. t.k.h: hld up in rr in steadily run r: rdn 2f out: r.o wl last 150yds: nvr nrr* **16/1**

0021 **6** shd **Quantum Leap**[5] 1787 10-8-4 **65**...............................(v) WilliamBuick(5) 1 — 64+
(S Dow) *hld up wl in rr on inner in steadily run r: hrd rdn wl over 1f out: r.o ins fnl f: nrst fin* **15/2**[3]

-360 **7** nk **Small Stakes (IRE)**[12] 1607 5-8-11 **67**...........................(vt) PatDobbs 10 — 65
(P J Makin) *nvr beyond midfield in steadily run r: styd on fnl f: no ch w ldrs* **10/1**

00-3 **8** 3/4 **Torquemada (IRE)**[20] 1401 6-8-9 **65**............................... PaulDoe 13 — 61
(W Jarvis) *prom: drvn 2f out: disp 2nd 1f out: wknd* **8/1**

5001 **9** hd **King Marju (IRE)**[19] 1423 5-9-4 **74**...........................(v) RichardMullen 12 — 70
(K R Burke) *plld hrd: trckd wnr to 1f out: wknd* **16/1**

1006 **10** 1/2 **Greenwood**[10] 1666 9-8-8 **64**............................... DO'Donohoe 14 — 58
(P G Murphy) *hld up wl in rr in steadily run r: struggling whn pce lifted fr 3f out: nvr a factor* **16/1**

346- **11** 1/2 **Zabeel House**[175] 6635 4-9-3 **73**............................... JimmyFortune 7 — 66
(J A R Toller) *hld up wl in rr in steadily run r: nvr a factor* **12/1**

0000 **12** 1 3/4 **Hollow Jo**[20] 1401 7-9-3 **73**............................... KerrinMcEvoy 4 — 61
(J R Jenkins) *lw: hld up towards rr in steadily run r: rdn 3f out: no prog* **12/1**

30-0 **13** 1 1/4 **Young Bertie**[29] 1200 4-8-9 **65**...............................(v) SteveDrowne 3 — 50
(H Morrison) *nvr bttr than midfield: drvn wl over 2f out: sn struggling* **8/1**

604- **14** 13 **Bonnie Belle**[218] 6021 4-8-6 **62**............................... MatthewHenry 2 — 12
(J R Boyle) *a last and nvr gng wl: t.o* **50/1**

1m 24.95s (-0.94) **Going Correction** -0.10s/f (Stan) **14** Ran SP% **126.9**
Speed ratings (Par 103):101,100,100,99,98 97,97,96,96,95 95,93,91,77
CSF £57.52 CT £1126.14 TOTE £13.60: £4.10, £1.50, £10.30; EX 65.70 TRIFECTA Not won. Place 6 £19.03, Place 5 £13.01.
Owner Tattenham Corner Racing **Bred** Top Of The Form Syndicate **Trained** Epsom, Surrey

FOCUS
A steadily-run handicap and questionable whether the form is reliable as the winner enjoyed an easy lead.
Hollow Jo Official explanation: jockey said gelding ran too free early
T/Plt: £34.30 to a £1 stake. Pool: £50,756.00. 1,077.85 winning tickets. T/Qpdt: £18.90 to a £1 stake. Pool: £2,785.50. 108.70 winning tickets. JN

1749 SOUTHWELL (L-H)
Tuesday, May 22

OFFICIAL GOING: Standard
After the recent dry spell the surface was reckoned to be riding 'slower than standard'.
Wind: Light, half behind Weather: Fine

1932 JOURNEY SOUTH PLAY ON 30TH H'CAP — 5f (F)
2:30 (2:31) (Class 5) (0-70,70) 3-Y-O — **£3,562** (£1,059; £529; £264) Stalls High

Form — RPR

2433 **1** **Diminuto**[6] 1766 3-8-5 **62**............................... PatrickHills(5) 7 — 67
(M D I Usher) *trckd ldrs: shkn up to ld 1f out: r.o strly: readily* **11/2**[2]

-263 **2** 1 **Baileys Outshine**[17] 1484 3-9-4 **70**............................... TPQueally 9 — 71
(J G Given) *w ldr: led over 2f out tl 1f out: no ex* **7/1**

55-4 **3** 1 3/4 **Mickleberry (IRE)**[25] 1281 3-8-7 **59** ow2............................... PatCosgrave 1 — 54
(J D Bethell) *led tl over 2f out: edgd lft 1f out: kpt on same pce* **12/1**

5-65 **4** 1 **Billy Red**[26] 1269 3-8-10 **62**............................... NCallan 4 — 54
(J R Jenkins) *sltly hmpd s: sn trcking ldrs: hung lft and kpt on same pce appr fnl f* **13/2**

0030 **5** 1/2 **The Geester**[11] 1635 3-8-4 **56**...............................(b) PaulEddery 2 — 46
(S R Bowring) *swvd rt s: sn trcking ldrs: kpt on same pce fnl 2f* **14/1**

05-2 **6** 1 **Smirfys Gold (IRE)**[18] 1453 3-8-4 **56**...............................(v) NickyMackay 5 — 42
(E S McMahon) *chsd ldrs: one pce fnl 2f* **4/1**[1]

0053 **7** 2 1/2 **Bahamian Love**[19] 1437 3-8-7 **59**............................... MichaelHills 8 — 36
(B W Hills) *sn outpcd: kpt on fnl 2f: nvr on terms* **6/1**[3]

6150 **8** hd **Sunley Sovereign**[10] 1658 3-8-5 **60**............................... AndrewElliott(3) 3 — 36
(D W Chapman) *bmpd s: mid-div: drvn 3f out: sn outpcd* **11/1**

4104 **9** 3/4 **Pirner's Brig**[22] 1351 3-8-7 **66**............................... NSLawes(7) 6 — 40
(M W Easterby) *hmpd s: sme hdwy 2f out: nvr on terms* **7/1**

50-0 **10** 4 **King Of Tricks**[22] 1346 3-8-4 **56** oh1............................... HayleyTurner 10 — 15
(M D I Usher) *sn wl outpcd and bhd* **20/1**

59.34 secs (-0.96) **Going Correction** -0.20s/f (Stan) **10** Ran SP% **115.5**
Speed ratings (Par 99):99,97,94,93,92 90,86,86,85,78
CSF £43.31 CT £455.16 TOTE £6.70: £1.70, £2.50, £4.00; EX 30.00.
Owner R H Brookes **Bred** B Minty **Trained** Upper Lambourn, Berks

FOCUS
A modest handicap but a decisive winner in Diminuto, who stepped up slightly on her best form, with the second rated to her recent level.
Billy Red Official explanation: jockey said gelding hung left
The Geester Official explanation: jockey said gelding was hampered leaving stalls

1933 FAMILY FUN DAY ON 3RD JUNE H'CAP — 7f (F)
3:00 (3:01) (Class 6) (0-50,54) 4-Y-0+ — **£2,388** (£705; £352) Stalls Low

Form — RPR

0-30 **1** **Pappas Ruby (USA)**[14] 1569 4-8-12 **50**...............................(b1) SebSanders 14 — 61
(R M Beckett) *w ldrs: led over 1f out: kpt on wl* **16/1**

500- **2** 1 1/2 **Nan Jan**[269] 4820 5-8-11 **49**...............................(t) RobertHavlin 8 — 57+
(R Ingram) *in rr: effrt and swtchd outside over 2f out: styd on wl to take 2nd towards fin* **14/1**

2006 **3** 1 1/4 **Astorygoeswithit**[14] 1569 4-8-9 **47** ow1...............................(p) NCallan 13 — 51
(P S McEntee) *w ldrs: led 3f out tl over 1f out: hung rt and no ex* **12/1**

6000 **4** 1/2 **Rafferty (IRE)**[8] 1720 8-8-12 **50**...............................(p) TPQueally 12 — 53
(S Dow) *sn trcking ldrs: effrt over 2f out: hmpd jst ins fnl f: kpt on same pce* **14/1**

3663 **5** 3/4 **Wodhill Be**[14] 1569 7-8-9 **47**............................... HayleyTurner 5 — 48
(D Morris) *hld up in mid-div: effrt over 2f out: kpt on wl fnl f* **6/1**[2]

-436 **6** 1/2 **Guadaloup**[12] 1596 5-8-10 **48**............................... DeanMernagh 1 — 48
(M Brittain) *chsd ldrs: stuck to far side in home st: kpt on same pce appr fnl f* **12/1**

0421 **7** 1/2 **Government (IRE)**[8] 1715 6-8-11 **54** 6ex............................... NicolPolli(5) 7 — 52
(M C Chapman) *led tl 3f out: kpt on one pce appr fnl f* **13/2**[3]

0250 **8** 1/2 **Methusaleh (IRE)**[7] 1740 4-8-9 **47**............................... DaneO'Neill 6 — 44
(D Shaw) *in rr and sn drvn along: hung rt and styd on fnl 2f: nvr nr ldrs* **13/2**[3]

0-2 **9** 2 **Tipsy Lad**[8] 1715 5-8-11 **49**...............................(bt) SimonWhitworth 3 — 41
(H J Manners) *sn chsng ldrs: drvn over 4f out: wknd fnl f* **8/1**

0301 **10** 4 **Inca Soldier (FR)**[22] 1360 4-8-12 **50**............................... JHBowman 9 — 32
(R C Guest) *in rr: drvn 4f out: wknd and eased 1f out* **11/4**[1]

5160 **11** 3 1/2 **Must Be Keen**[109] 337 8-8-8 **46**...............................(v) FergusSweeney 4 — 18
(P S McEntee) *in rr: nvr a factor* **25/1**

0100 **12** 8 **Kadia**[12] 1596 4-8-9 **47**............................... MickyFenton 11 — —
(P T Midgley) *s.i.s: a in rr: bhd fnl 2f* **25/1**

06-0 **13** 5 **She Whispers (IRE)**[8] 1719 4-8-5 **46** oh1............................... LiamJones(3) 2 — —
(R Hollinshead) *mid-div: lost pl over 2f out: sn bhd* **50/1**

000- **14** 9 **My Rascal (IRE)**[287] 4232 5-8-5 **46**...............................(b) AndrewElliott(3) 10 — —
(J Balding) *t.k.h: w ldrs: lost pl 3f out: sn bhd* **28/1**

1m 30.34s (-0.46) **Going Correction** -0.075s/f (Stan) **14** Ran SP% **126.4**
Speed ratings (Par 101):99,97,95,95,94 93,93,92,90,85 81,72,67,56
CSF £226.00 CT £2888.08 TOTE £20.60: £5.20, £8.20, £4.00; EX 303.20.
Owner Frank Brady **Bred** Scuderia Archi Romani **Trained** Whitsbury, Hants

FOCUS
A very moderate handicap, little better than a low-grade classified race. Not much recent form to go on, with the runner-up returning from a long absence. The winner showed improvement in the blinkers.
Astorygoeswithit Official explanation: jockey said gelding hung badly right
Methusaleh(IRE) Official explanation: jockey said gelding hung badly right

1934 PARTY IN THE PADDOCK ON THURSDAY CLASSIFIED STKS — 1m 4f (F)
3:30 (3:31) (Class 7) 4-Y-0+ — **£1,876** (£554; £277) Stalls Low

Form — RPR

6536 **1** **Silver Mont (IRE)**[31] 1152 4-8-12 43...............................(b) PaulEddery 1 — 57
(S R Bowring) *hld up in mid-div: hdwy over 4f out: styd on to ld over 1f out: hld on towards fin* **4/1**[2]

0050 **2** 3/4 **Mangrove Cay (IRE)**[14] 1556 5-8-12 45............................... PatCosgrave 7 — 56
(A J Lockwood) *chsd ldrs: chal over 2f out: hung lft and kpt on wl towards fin* **13/2**

4030 **3** 1 1/4 **Cragganmore Creek**[13] 1590 4-8-12 45...............................(v) NCallan 14 — 54
(D Morris) *hld up in mid-div: stdy hdwy over 4f out: led 3f out tl over 1f out: kpt on same pce* **11/4**[1]

3304 **4** 3 1/2 **Moyne Pleasure (IRE)**[14] 1570 9-8-9 42............................... AndrewElliott(3) 11 — 48
(R Johnson) *sn prom: styd on one pce fnl 2f* **9/1**

512/ **5** 6 **Toledo Sun**[41] 2385 7-8-12 45............................... AlanDaly 2 — 39
(S Curran) *chsd ldrs: wknd fnl 2f* **20/1**

0-00 **6** 1/2 **Be Wise Girl**[21] 1380 6-8-12 45............................... J-PGuillambert 6 — 38
(A W Carroll) *trckd ldrs: led over 4f out: hdd 3f out: swished tail: wknd over 1f out* **16/1**

0006 **7** 1 1/2 **Bournonville**[14] 1570 4-8-12 38............................... NickyMackay 12 — 35
(M Wigham) *in rr: hdwy on outer over 5f out: sn chsng ldrs: wknd over 2f out* **20/1**

3-03 **8** 7 **Kentucky Bullet (USA)**[14] 1570 11-8-12 41............................... SimonWhitworth 8 — 24
(A G Newcombe) *in rr: nvr on terms* **6/1**[3]

0400 **9** 28 **Mi Odds**[70] 665 11-8-12 40............................... JHBowman 9 — —
(Mrs N Macauley) *in rr: drvn 6f out: sn bhd* **20/1**

300- **10** 3 **On Every Street**[277] 4544 6-8-12 42...............................(v) SebSanders 10 — —
(R Bastiman) *mid-div: rdn 6f out: lost pl over 4f out: bhd and eased 3f out* **12/1**

6440 **11** 1 3/4 **Futoo (IRE)**[37] 508 6-8-12 42...............................(b) HayleyTurner 5 — —
(D W Chapman) *t.k.h: trckd ldrs: lost pl over 4f out: sn bhd* **22/1**

0-U0 **12** 25 **Katsumoto (IRE)**[7] 1750 4-8-9 45............................... PatrickMathers(3) 13 — —
(A J McCabe) *dwlt: swtchd lft after s: tk fierce hold in rr: drvn 6f out: sn wl bhd* **25/1**

0/0- **13** hd **Muqarrar (IRE)**[488] 147 8-8-12 42...............................(vt) MickyFenton 4 — —
(T J Fitzgerald) *led tl over 4f out: wknd qckly: sn wl bhd* **33/1**

2m 40.82s (-1.27) **Going Correction** -0.075s/f (Stan) **13** Ran SP% **123.3**
Speed ratings (Par 97):101,100,99,97,93 93,92,87,68,66 65,48,48
CSF £27.60 TOTE £4.80: £1.70, £3.70, £1.30; EX 35.90.
Owner Clark Industrial Services Partnership **Bred** Clark Industrial Services Partnership **Trained** Edwinstowe, Notts
■ Stewards' Enquiry : Paul Eddery caution: used whip with excessive frequency

FOCUS
An ordinary classified contest in which the first four came clear. The form is a bit more solid than the average race of this type, with the winner and third fair for the grade and the second running to his turf form here.
Mangrove Cay(IRE) Official explanation: jockey said gelding was hanging left
Muqarrar(IRE) Official explanation: jockey said gelding had no more to give

1935 OWED RUNS FOR VIKINGRACING.CO.UK H'CAP — 6f (F)
4:00 (4:02) (Class 4) (0-80,77) 4-Y-0+ — **£5,181** (£1,541; £770; £384) Stalls Low

Form — RPR

1551 **1** **Cool Sands (IRE)**[58] 774 5-8-11 **70**...............................(v) DaneO'Neill 2 — 77
(D Shaw) *sn drvn along: hdwy over 2f out: hung lft over 1f out: wandered: led towards fin: jst hld on* **7/2**[2]

6040 **2** shd **Desert Dreamer (IRE)**[6] 1765 6-8-13 **72**............................... RobertHavlin 4 — 79+
(P R Chamings) *stl had hood on whn stalls opened: s.s: bhd tl hdwy on wd outside 2f out: hung lft and styd on wl ins fnl f: jst failed* **10/1**

1523 **3** 1/2 **Sweet Pickle**[15] 1525 6-8-11 **70**...............................(e) PatCosgrave 1 — 76
(J R Boyle) *sn drvn along: hdwy to chse ldrs over 3f out: led on ins over 1f out: hdd and no ex wl ins fnl f* **7/2**[2]

3021 **4** 9 **Owed**[21] 1377 5-9-0 **73**...............................(p) NCallan 3 — 52
(R Bastiman) *led tl over 4f out: led over 2f out tl over 1f out: sn wknd* **9/4**[1]

2115 **5** 1 3/4 **Came Back (IRE)**[28] 1226 4-9-4 **77**............................... TPQueally 5 — 50
(J Mackie) *w ldrs: rdn over 2f out: lost pl over 1f out* **5/1**[3]

0-06 **6** 5 **Calypso King**[17] 1465 4-8-11 **70**...............................(b1) SebSanders 6 — 28
(R M Beckett) *t.k.h: w ldrs on outer: led over 4f out tl over 2f out: lost pl over 1f out* **8/1**

1m 17.14s (0.24) **Going Correction** -0.075s/f (Stan) **6** Ran SP% **112.1**
Speed ratings (Par 105):95,94,94,82,79 73
CSF £35.29 TOTE £6.10: £2.40, £2.70; EX 36.60.
Owner Peter Swann **Bred** Rathasker Stud **Trained** Danethorpe, Notts

FOCUS
A modest winning time for the class. The three clear leaders occupied the final three placings and the suspicion was that they went off much too fast. The runner-up was probably unlucky.
Desert Dreamer(IRE) Official explanation: jockey said, regarding running and riding, that his orders were to remove the blindfold at the last possible moment hoping to rectify the problem of the gelding being slowly away but the blindfold got stuck when he attempted to remove it with the result being slowly away again.

1936 GET THE BEST BETTING INFO AT CARLHARRIS.CO.UK H'CAP 1m (F)
4:30 (4:30) (Class 4) (0-80,71) 3-Y-O **£5,181** (£1,541; £770; £384) **Stalls** Low

Form RPR
0-10 **1** **Tilapia (IRE)**[120] 216 3-9-3 **70**.................................. SebSanders 3 80+
(Sir Mark Prescott) *led: rdn over 2f out: edgd rt 1f out: hld on towards fin* **2/1**[2]
01-2 **2** ½ **Giant Slalom**[4] 1815 3-9-0 **70**.................................. LiamJones(3) 5 79+
(W J Haggas) *hld up wl in tch: wnt cl 2nd over 3f out: rdn 2f out: swtchd lft jst ins fnl f: kpt on: no ex towards fin* **8/13**[1]
-002 **3** 5 **Nota Liberata**[19] 1424 3-8-13 **66**.................................. NickyMackay 4 64
(G M Moore) *chsd ldrs: rdn and outpcd over 4f out: tk modest 3rd 3f out: hung lft: kpt on one pce* **9/1**[3]
044 **4** 8 **Mango Masher (IRE)**[18] 1452 3-9-4 **71**.................................. RobertHavlin 1 50
(C R Egerton) *s.i.s: drvn and lost pl over 4f out: nvr on terms* **20/1**
100 **5** shd **Rich Lord**[10] 1672 3-9-3 **70**..................................(b[1]) PatCosgrave 6 49
(J D Bethell) *t.k.h: w ldrs on outer: rdn and lost pl over 3f out* **25/1**
0-40 **6** 15 **Majestic Chief**[20] 1415 3-8-10 **66**.................................. AndrewMullen(3) 2 10
(K A Ryan) *chsd ldrs: drvn and lost pl over 4f out: bhd whn eased ins fnl f* **25/1**

1m 44.27s (-0.33) **Going Correction** -0.075s/f (Stan) **6** Ran SP% **117.7**
Speed ratings (Par 101):98,97,92,84,84 69
CSF £3.73 TOTE £3.00: £1.10, £1.10; EX 4.70.
Owner G D Waters **Bred** G D Waters **Trained** Newmarket, Suffolk

FOCUS
A fair handicap dominated by the market leaders. The front pair probably had little to beat, but both are progressive and the runner-up along with the third are the best guides to the level.

1937 COME EVENING RACING ON THURSDAY MAIDEN STKS 1m 3f (F)
5:00 (5:00) (Class 5) 3-4-Y-O **£3,412** (£1,007; £504) **Stalls** Low

Form RPR
3-62 **1** **Audit (IRE)**[8] 1714 3-8-11 77..................................(b) J-PGuillambert 9 82
(Sir Michael Stoute) *trckd ldrs: wnt 2nd over 2f out: drvn and put hd in air: persuaded to do enough to ld towards fin* **15/8**[1]
3 **2** 1 **Artless (USA)**[8] 1714 4-9-7.................................. SebSanders 11 75
(Sir Mark Prescott) *trckd ldrs: led 3f out: hdd and no ex towards fin* **4/1**[3]
020 **3** 4 **Phreeze**[12] 1605 3-8-11.................................. TPO'Shea 6 73+
(G A Swinbank) *mid-div: reminders after 3f: drvn over 5f out: outpcd over 3f out: styd on fnl 2f: tk 3rd nr line* **15/2**
2-22 **4** hd **Vanquisher (IRE)**[21] 1375 3-8-8 77.................................. LiamJones(3) 1 73
(W J Haggas) *in tch: drvn over 3f out: one pce fnl 2f* **11/4**[2]
53 **5** 1 ¼ **Force Celebre (IRE)**[14] 1566 3-8-6.................................. PatrickHills(5) 8 71
(M H Tompkins) *in tch: effrt on outer over 2f out: hung lft: one pce* **8/1**
4250 **6** 22 **Greek God**[29] 1194 3-8-11 52.................................. MickyFenton 13 33
(W Jarvis) *swtchd lft after s: led tl 3f out: sn lost pl* **14/1**
00 **7** 5 **Petite Arvine (USA)**[2] 1863 3-7-13.................................. ChrisHough(7) 14 20
(M L W Bell) *s.s: sme hdwy over 4f out: lost pl over 2f out* **33/1**
0 **8** 8 **April The Second**[22] 1348 3-8-4.................................. WilliamCarson(7) 4 11
(R J Price) *in rr: t.o 3f out* **40/1**
0 **9** nk **Holiday Rock**[8] 1716 3-8-8.................................. PatrickMathers(3) 10 11
(A J McCabe) *sn drvn along: mid-div: rdn 6f out: lost pl over 3f out* **66/1**
0 **10** 2 ½ **Feeling Peckish (USA)**[30] 1177 3-8-6.................................. NicolPolli(5) 2 7
(M C Chapman) *chsd ldrs: wknd 3f out* **50/1**
0-5 **11** 2 ½ **Lisselan Dancer (USA)**[13] 1573 3-8-3.................................. AndrewElliott(3) 12 —
(J R Weymes) *mid-div: reminders over 5f out: lost pl over 3f out* **100/1**
0 **12** 29 **Glad Star (GER)**[39] 1030 4-9-12.................................. HayleyTurner 7 —
(D W Chapman) *s.s: lost pl 7f out: t.o 3f out: virtually p.u* **100/1**
50 **13** nk **Hewaar (IRE)**[3] 1849 4-9-9.................................. AndrewMullen(3) 3 —
(J O'Reilly) *sn drvn along and bhd: t.o 3f out: virtually p.u* **100/1**

2m 25.37s (-3.53) **Going Correction** -0.075s/f (Stan)
WFA 3 from 4yo 15lb **13** Ran SP% **122.8**
Speed ratings (Par 103):109,108,105,105,104 88,84,78,78,76 75,53,53
CSF £9.75 TOTE £3.00: £1.60, £1.70, £2.00; EX 14.00 Place 6 £242.27, Place 5 £75.72.
Owner Highclere Thoroughbred Racing XXXVIII **Bred** Barronstown Stud And Pacelco S A **Trained** Newmarket, Suffolk

FOCUS
A fair maiden for the track and a decent winning time for a race of its type. The first two finished clear, with winner Audit looking reluctant again.
Hewaar(IRE) Official explanation: jockey said gelding had no more to give
T/Plt: £441.30 to a £1 stake. Pool: £43,591.90. 72.10 winning tickets. T/Qpdt: £16.80 to a £1 stake. Pool: £3,337.70. 146.50 winning tickets. WG

1594 AYR (L-H)
Wednesday, May 23

OFFICIAL GOING: Good to soft
Wind: almost nil

1938 EUROPEAN BREEDERS' FUND MAIDEN STKS 6f
2:20 (2:23) (Class 4) 2-Y-O **£4,533** (£1,348; £674; £336) **Stalls** Low

Form RPR
4 **1** **Nine Stories (IRE)**[8] 1743 2-9-3.................................. PaulMulrennan 6 84
(J Howard Johnson) *chsd ldrs: drvn to ld over 1f out: styd on strly* **8/1**
0 **2** 2 ½ **Ink Spot**[30] 1201 2-9-3.................................. HayleyTurner 1 77
(M L W Bell) *s.i.s: bhd tl hdwy over 1f out: chsd wnr ins fnl f: kpt on: nt rch wnr* **7/1**[3]
3 1 ½ **Russian Reel** 2-9-3.................................. NCallan 2 72+
(K A Ryan) *t.k.h: led tl hung rt and hdd over 1f out: kpt on same pce* **4/1**[2]
04 **4** 4 **Alpen Adventure (IRE)**[12] 1622 2-9-3.................................. DavidAllan 8 60
(Mrs L Stubbs) *prom tl rdn and outpcd fr 2f out* **10/1**
5 1 **Carnival Dream** 2-8-12..................................(b[1]) RoystonFfrench 11 52
(A Berry) *dwlt: sn in tch: rdn and no ex fr over 2f out* **100/1**
6 **6** 1 **Glenluji**[9] 1706 2-8-10.................................. GaryBartley(7) 4 54
(J S Goldie) *s.i.s and outpcd: nvr rchd ldrs* **100/1**
32 **7** hd **Fitzroy Crossing (USA)**[11] 1652 2-9-3.................................. JoeFanning 7 53
(M Johnston) *w ldrs tl wknd over 1f out* **4/5**[1]
8 1 **Bourbon Highball (IRE)** 2-9-3.................................. LeeEnstone 9 50
(P C Haslam) *w ldrs tl wknd over 1f out* **50/1**

1m 14.44s (0.77) **Going Correction** +0.025s/f (Good) **8** Ran SP% **112.2**
Speed ratings (Par 95):95,91,89,84,83 81,81,80
CSF £58.93 TOTE £9.70: £1.60, £1.90, £1.70; EX 59.70.
Owner Transcend Bloodstock LLP **Bred** Stefano Stivali **Trained** Billy Row, Co Durham
■ Bere Davis (25/1, unruly in stalls) & Duke Of Touraine (50/1, vet's advice) were withdrawn.

FOCUS
A fair juvenile maiden despite the favourite disappointing. The winner stepped up on his debut form and the overall level seems pretty solid.

NOTEBOOK
Nine Stories(IRE), fourth in a novice event at Newcastle on his recent debut, got off the mark at the second attempt with a clear-cut display. He had the race in the bag passing the 2f marker, handled the ground without fuss, and looks the type who will enjoy another furlong before long. (op 10-1)
Ink Spot, who met support in the betting ring prior to disappointing on his debut at Windsor a month ago, proved easy to back here and is clearly still very much learning his trade. He got a reminder not long after missing the break and ran distinctly green, but the penny dropped nearing two out and he was noted doing his best work towards the finish over the extra furlong. While he may not be straightforward, he has ability and will no doubt come on again for this experience. (op 6-1)
Russian Reel, a half-brother to 6f winning juvenile debutant Josh among others, was well touted ahead of this racecourse bow and met support in the ring. He ultimately threw his chance away by hanging badly right when in front passing the furlong marker and will need to settle better in the future, but he should only learn for the experience and has a future. (op 11-2)
Alpen Adventure(IRE), up in trip, showed up well early on yet got himself outpaced when it mattered and was well beaten. He can find easier assignments, on this evidence will get further in time, and helps to set the level of this form.
Fitzroy Crossing(USA), all the rage in the betting ring beforehand, started to tread water soon after passing the 2f pole and has to rate as very disappointing. On pedigree he should have handled the step up to this trip and it now remains to be seen just which way he goes. (op 8-11 tchd 10-11)

1939 BURNS AN' A' THAT! FESTIVAL H'CAP 1m 1f 20y
2:50 (2:50) (Class 4) (0-85,85) 4-Y-O+ **£5,181** (£1,541; £770; £384) **Stalls** Low

Form RPR
-464 **1** **Primo Way**[8] 1744 6-8-1 71..................................(b) DuranFentiman(3) 1 76
(I Semple) *hld up in tch: stdy hdwy 2f out: rdn to ld wl ins fnl f: all out* **15/2**
4300 **2** shd **Bay Boy**[30] 1198 5-8-4 71..................................(b) JoeFanning 5 76
(M Johnston) *cl up: rdn and outpcd over 2f out: edgd lft and rallied over 1f out: kpt on fnl f: jst hld* **9/2**[3]
-103 **3** ¾ **Emerald Bay (IRE)**[13] 1599 5-9-4 **85**.................................. PhillipMakin 4 88
(I Semple) *in tch: smooth hdwy over 1f out: rdn ins fnl f: no ex towards fin* **15/8**[1]
3534 **4** nk **Shot To Fame (USA)**[15] 1555 8-8-12 **79**..................................(t) AdrianTNicholls 6 82
(D Nicholls) *led 1f: cl up: led over 3f out: rdn 2f out: hdd and no ex wl ins fnl f* **10/3**[2]
-201 **5** ½ **Frank Crow**[19] 1455 4-8-10 **77** ow2.................................. NCallan 3 79
(J S Goldie) *chsd ldrs: effrt over 2f out: one pce fnl f* **6/1**
100- **6** 13 **Abbondanza (IRE)**[221] 4711 4-9-1 **82**.................................. PaulMulrennan 2 58
(J Howard Johnson) *led after 1f: hdd over 3f out: wknd 2f out* **14/1**

1m 57.46s (-2.54) **Going Correction** -0.25s/f (Firm) **6** Ran SP% **108.8**
Speed ratings (Par 105):101,100,100,99,99 87
CSF £37.63 TOTE £8.10: £3.80, £2.10; EX 35.20.
Owner Gordon McDowall **Bred** Mrs P A Reditt And M J Reditt **Trained** Carluke, S Lanarks
■ Stewards' Enquiry : Joe Fanning caution: careless riding

FOCUS
A fair little handicap, but it was run at a muddling pace and the field finished in a heap. It is form to treat with caution.

1940 TOAST TO THE LASSIES FILLIES' H'CAP 6f
3:20 (3:20) (Class 5) (0-75,73) 4-Y-O+ **£4,533** (£1,348; £674; £336) **Stalls** Low

Form RPR
-434 **1** **Dorn Dancer (IRE)**[8] 1748 5-8-4 **59**.................................. RoystonFfrench 3 67
(D W Barker) *hld up in tch: swtchd rt 1/2-way: led over 1f out: hung rt ins fnl f: kpt on* **15/8**[1]
-024 **2** 1 ¼ **Shes Minnie**[13] 1607 4-9-4 **73**.................................. NCallan 4 77
(J G M O'Shea) *prom: effrt over 1f out: chsd wnr ins fnl f: r.o* **4/1**[3]
6652 **3** 2 **Katie Boo (IRE)**[8] 1748 5-8-1 **59** oh11.................................. AndrewMullen(3) 1 57+
(A Berry) *chsd ldrs: drvn whn no room 2f out: rallied ins fnl f: nt rch first two* **12/1**
0-50 **4** 1 ½ **Princess Cleo**[9] 1718 4-8-10 **65**.................................. DavidAllan 6 59
(T D Easterby) *t.k.h: led to over 1f out: no ex* **7/1**
25-0 **5** 1 ¾ **Misphire**[45] 957 4-9-4 **73**.................................. PhillipMakin 5 61
(M Dods) *chsd ldrs: effrt and ev ch over 1f out: sn btn* **5/2**[2]
5303 **6** 6 **Newkeylets**[13] 1595 4-8-1 **59** oh10..................................(p) DuranFentiman(3) 2 29
(I Semple) *w ldr tl wknd wl over 1f out* **12/1**

1m 13.54s (-0.13) **Going Correction** +0.025s/f (Good) **6** Ran SP% **111.2**
Speed ratings (Par 100):101,99,96,94,92 84
CSF £9.53 TOTE £2.70: £2.00, £2.10; EX 11.20.
Owner The Ebor Partnership **Bred** Timothy Coughlan **Trained** Scorton, N Yorks

FOCUS
A moderate fillies' sprint handicap. There was little strength in depth with the second favourite running poorly, and the race has been rated through the runner-up.

1941 DM HALL H'CAP 5f
3:50 (3:51) (Class 4) (0-90,88) 4-Y-O+ **£7,124** (£2,119; £1,059; £529) **Stalls** Low

Form RPR
10-0 **1** **Sunrise Safari (IRE)**[14] 1574 4-8-11 **78**..................................(v) PhillipMakin 4 92+
(I Semple) *prom: rdn whn n.m.r wl over 1f out: styd on wl fnl f to ld towards fin* **11/1**
3-24 **2** 1 **Handsome Cross (IRE)**[28] 1242 6-9-7 **88**.................................. AdrianTNicholls 1 94
(D Nicholls) *w ldrs: drvn 2f out: kpt on fnl f* **15/2**
41-6 **3** nk **Blazing Heights**[45] 957 4-8-5 **79**.................................. GaryBartley(7) 8 84
(J S Goldie) *trckd ldrs on outside: led over 1f out: edgd lft ins fnl f: hdd towards fin* **4/1**[2]
50-0 **4** shd **Kenmore**[11] 1653 5-9-2 **83**.................................. GrahamGibbons 3 88
(D Nicholls) *prom: outpcd after 2f: rallied over 1f out: kpt on fnl f* **3/1**[1]
2435 **5** ½ **Nusoor (IRE)**[12] 1630 4-8-0 **70**..................................(b) PatrickMathers(3) 2 73
(Peter Grayson) *awkward s: bhd tl hdwy over 1f out: r.o ins fnl f* **12/1**
1402 **6** nk **Canadian Danehill (IRE)**[8] 1754 5-8-12 **79**..................................(p) TPQueally 6 81
(R M H Cowell) *cl up: rdn 2f out: kpt on u.p fnl f* **9/2**[3]
5-55 **7** 1 ¼ **Ptarmigan Ridge**[25] 1299 11-8-7 **74**.................................. RoystonFfrench 7 71
(Miss L A Perratt) *t.k.h: chsd ldrs: outpcd over 1f out: kpt on ins fnl f: no imp* **6/1**
0-30 **8** nk **Spiritual Peace (IRE)**[18] 1483 4-8-12 **79**..................................(b[1]) NCallan 5 75
(K A Ryan) *led to over 1f out: wknd ins fnl f* **12/1**

59.93 secs (-0.51) **Going Correction** +0.025s/f (Good) **8** Ran SP% **113.0**
Speed ratings (Par 105):105,103,102,102,101 101,99,99
CSF £87.33 CT £389.70 TOTE £13.80: £4.30, £2.30, £2.00; EX 132.60.
Owner Mrs J Penman **Bred** Mervyn Stewkesbury **Trained** Carluke, S Lanarks

FOCUS
A fair sprint for the class. The form looks sound rated through the runner-up.

1942 ROBERT BURNS H'CAP 1m 7f
4:20 (4:20) (Class 6) (0-60,59) 4-Y-O+ £2,590 (£770; £385; £192) Stalls Low

Form RPR
0-44 1 **York Cliff**[9] 1732 9-8-11 54 LiamJones(3) 11 64
(W M Brisbourne) *hld up in midfield: stdy hdwy over 3f out: led appr fnl f: r.o wl* 10/1
006- 2 2 1/2 **Kristiansand**[6] 6209 7-8-6 49 MarkLawson(3) 9 56
(P Monteith) *hld up: hdwy and prom 5f out: led over 3f out to appr fnl f: kpt on same pce ins fnl f* 10/1
21 3 shd **Colwyn Bay (IRE)**[21] 1402 5-8-8 53 (p) MichaelJStainton(5) 4 60
(Jane Chapple-Hyam) *hld up: pushed along 1/2-way: rallied u.p over 2f out: wandered fr over 1f out: kpt on fnl f* 5/4[1]
0/06 4 1/2 **Naughty Nod (IRE)**[25] 1301 4-8-9 50 PatCosgrave 3 56
(K R Burke) *bhd: rdn over 3f out: styd on wl fr 2f out: nrst fin* 33/1
030/ 5 7 **Brave Vision**[28] 1154 11-8-2 45 AndrewMullen(3) 1 43
(A C Whillans) *in tch tl rdn and outpcd fr 2f out* 16/1
660/ 6 1 3/4 **Gardasee (GER)**[15] 3119 5-8-10 50 MickyFenton 10 46
(T P Tate) *t.k.h: cl up tl outpcd over 2f out: btn and eased fnl 2f* 9/2[2]
-660 7 3 **Kristalchen**[15] 1554 5-8-5 45 (p) PaulFessey 13 37
(D W Thompson) *prom: led after 5f: hdd over 3f out: wknd fr 2f out* 40/1
000/ 8 hd **Allez Mousson**[473] 6571 9-8-6 46 ow1 (v[1]) DavidAllan 6 38
(A Bailey) *dwlt: rdn in rr 5f out: nvr on terms* 28/1
00-0 9 1/2 **Best Of The Lot (USA)**[17] 1490 5-9-5 59 TonyHamilton 12 50
(R A Fahey) *t.k.h: cl up: ev ch over 3f out: wknd over 2f out* 6/1[3]
05-0 10 1 1/2 **Celtic Empire (IRE)**[15] 585 4-8-4 45 DaleGibson 2 35
(Jedd O'Keeffe) *in tch 5f: sn lost pl: n.d after* 20/1
066- 11 1 1/4 **The Dunion**[265] 4954 4-8-4 45 RoystonFfrench 7 33
(Miss L A Perratt) *prom tl wknd 3f out* 50/1
4-00 12 28 **Watermill (IRE)**[29] 1222 4-8-4 45 (b[1]) AdrianTNicholls 8 —
(D W Chapman) *led 5f: prom tl wknd over 3f out* 100/1

3m 20.38s (-2.09) **Going Correction** -0.25s/f (Firm)
WFA 4 from 5yo+ 1lb 12 Ran SP% **117.5**
Speed ratings (Par 101):95,93,93,93,89 88,87,86,86,85 85,70
CSF £97.14 CT £212.20 TOTE £12.60: £2.20, £2.50, £1.10; EX 65.30.
Owner P Wright-Bevans **Bred** F Hinojosa **Trained** Great Ness, Shropshire

FOCUS
A moderate race in which the front four drew clear. The form looks particularly solid, with the winner and second rated to last year's best.
Best Of The Lot(USA) Official explanation: jockey said gelding had no more to give

1943 TAM O' SHANTER H'CAP 6f
4:50 (4:52) (Class 6) (0-60,60) 3-Y-O £2,590 (£770; £385; £192) Stalls Low

Form RPR
650- 1 **Ishetoo**[238] 5613 3-8-11 58 MichaelJStainton(5) 3 64
(A Dickman) *mde all: rdn and edgd rt 2f out: hld on wl fnl f* 28/1
6-53 2 1 **Five Wishes**[12] 1625 3-8-13 55 PaulFessey 17 58+
(M Dods) *sn outpcd: plenty to do 1/2-way: gd hdwy over 1f out: kpt on wl fnl f: nt rch wnr* 5/1[1]
6036 3 1/2 **Missus Molly Brown**[20] 1432 3-8-4 46 oh1 DaleGibson 8 47
(R A Fahey) *dwlt: sn in midfield: effrt u.p over 2f out: kpt on fnl f* 16/1
5241 4 nk **Princess Ellis**[13] 1595 3-9-1 57 KDarley 10 57
(E J Alston) *cl up: effrt and hung lft over 1f out: kpt on same pce fnl f* 6/1[3]
05-0 5 1 1/4 **Soviet Sound (IRE)**[16] 1530 3-8-11 53 PaulMulrennan 15 49
(Jedd O'Keeffe) *prom: drvn 1/2-way: kpt on same pce fnl f* 33/1
000 6 1 1/4 **Abadia**[15] 1558 3-8-4 46 oh1 RoystonFfrench 7 38
(J G Given) *bhd and outpcd: hdwy over 1f out: nrst fin* 33/1
4002 7 3/4 **Mangano**[13] 1595 3-8-5 47 PaulQuinn 2 37
(A Berry) *midfield: effrt over 2f out: no imp over 1f out* 25/1
0452 8 5 **Temtation (IRE)**[9] 1709 3-8-5 52 RussellKennemore(5) 12 26
(Peter Grayson) *midfield: drvn 1/2-way: no imp wl over 1f out* 14/1
3525 9 3/4 **Moonlight Applause**[13] 1595 3-8-10 52 DavidAllan 9 24
(T D Easterby) *chsd ldrs tl rdn and no ex over 1f out* 9/1
00-5 10 1 1/2 **Compton Special**[43] 996 3-8-11 53 TPQueally 4 20
(J G Given) *chsd ldrs: drvn and edgd lft 2f out: sn btn* 16/1
06-0 11 1 1/2 **La Vecchia Scuola (IRE)**[70] 679 3-9-4 60 AdrianTNicholls 6 22
(D Nicholls) *prom: drvn over 2f out: sn btn* 28/1
00-2 12 3 **Tibinta**[15] 1561 3-8-11 53 (v[1]) NCallan 14 5
(P D Evans) *chsd ldrs tl wknd over 2f out* 5/1[1]
30U0 13 hd **Spinning Game**[40] 1031 3-8-1 46 oh1 LiamJones(3) 1 —
(D W Chapman) *outpcd and bhd: nvr on terms* 66/1
-640 14 2 **Imperial Beach (USA)**[16] 1531 3-9-1 57 PhillipMakin 13 2
(T D Barron) *a bhd* 10/1
2665 15 2 1/2 **Firebird Annie (IRE)**[9] 1716 3-8-9 51 MickyFenton 16 —
(A Bailey) *sn bhd: no ch fr 1/2-way* 22/1
03-3 16 6 **Come What May**[20] 1429 3-9-4 60 JoeFanning 18 —
(Rae Guest) *in tch to 1/2-way: sn rdn and btn* 11/2[2]
060- 17 6 **Senora Lenorah**[201] 6316 3-8-4 46 oh1 SilvestreDeSousa 5 —
(D A Nolan) *in tch tl rdn and wknd over 2f out* 100/1

1m 13.95s (0.28) **Going Correction** +0.025s/f (Good) 17 Ran SP% **124.0**
Speed ratings (Par 97):99,97,97,96,94 93,92,85,84,82 80,76,76,73,70 62,54
CSF £156.17 CT £2459.00 TOTE £33.10: £4.30, £2.30, £4.10, £1.40; EX 412.90.
Owner John H Sissons **Bred** Longdon Stud Ltd **Trained** Sandhutton, N Yorks

FOCUS
A moderate contest in which there was little solid form to go on. The winner was up 12lb, with the next five close to form. There were one or two promising performances and the race should produce winners.
Tibinta Official explanation: trainer said filly may have been unsuited by the good to soft ground
Come What May Official explanation: trainer said filly had been kicking in stalls and never travelled

1944 GILES INSURANCE CONSTRUCTION SPECIALISTS H'CAP 1m 1f 20y
5:20 (5:21) (Class 6) (0-60,60) 4-Y-O+ £2,590 (£770; £385; £192) Stalls Low

Form RPR
6-56 1 **Bijou Dan**[8] 1751 6-8-10 52 (p) TonyHamilton 11 65
(D W Thompson) *hld up: hdwy 2f out: led ins fnl f: sn clr* 25/1
05-0 2 4 **Zell (IRE)**[16] 1534 4-8-8 50 DavidAllan 4 55
(E J Alston) *led: rdn over 2f out: hdd ins fnl f: kpt on same pce* 18/1
4-22 3 nk **Queen's Echo**[9] 1711 6-8-9 51 NCallan 3 55
(P Monteith) *midfield: effrt and prom 2f out: one pce fnl f* 11/4[1]
6-00 4 1 **Komreyev Star**[16] 1539 5-8-8 50 (p) SilvestreDeSousa 8 52
(R E Peacock) *cl up tl rdn and no ex over 1f out* 20/1
0001 5 shd **Elopement (IRE)**[7] 1761 5-8-8 53 6ex LiamJones(3) 12 55
(W M Brisbourne) *chsd ldrs: rdn over 2f out: kpt on fnl f: no imp* 9/1
306- 6 2 1/2 **Little Bob**[14] 6301 6-9-4 60 (b) PatCosgrave 9 57
(J D Bethell) *chsd ldrs: early reminders: rdn and no ex fr 2f out* 10/1
-000 7 3/4 **Apache Nation (IRE)**[11] 1675 4-9-1 57 PhillipMakin 1 52
(M Dods) *chsd ldrs tl rdn and wknd wl over 1f out* 6/1[3]
0022 8 shd **Fortress**[12] 1626 4-9-4 60 KDarley 7 55
(E J Alston) *hld up: effrt over 2f out: sn no imp* 8/1
1-00 9 nk **Neil's Legacy (IRE)**[12] 1627 5-8-10 55 GregFairley(3) 10 49
(Miss L A Perratt) *hld up: shortlived effrt over 2f out: btn over 1f out* 14/1
0-62 10 3/4 **Mystical Ayr (IRE)**[12] 1627 5-9-3 59 RoystonFfrench 2 52
(Miss L A Perratt) *midfield: drvn 3f out: btn over 1f out* 10/3[2]
00-0 11 shd **Jordans Spark**[19] 1459 6-8-8 53 MarkLawson(3) 6 46
(P Monteith) *hld up: rdn and hung lft 2f out: nvr on terms* 20/1
020- 12 8 **Barataria**[207] 6213 5-8-8 50 PaulMulrennan 5 26
(R Bastiman) *dwlt: a bhd* 20/1

1m 56.14s (-3.86) **Going Correction** -0.25s/f (Firm) 12 Ran SP% **124.3**
Speed ratings (Par 101):107,103,103,102,102 99,99,99,98,98 98,91
CSF £411.88 CT £1651.45 TOTE £30.70: £6.70, £7.20, £1.40; EX 458.20 Place 6 £216.89, Place 5 £86.53.
Owner Bert Markey **Bred** James Thom And Sons **Trained** Bolam, Co Durham

FOCUS
A decent winning time for the grade, 1.32 seconds faster than the earlier Class 6 handicap. A modest event, with the winner up 4lb on his previous turf best.
Little Bob Official explanation: jockey said gelding never travelled
T/Plt: £190.40 to a £1 stake. Pool: £55,507.65. 212.80 winning tickets. T/Qpdt: £6.90 to a £1 stake. Pool: £4,298.10. 458.30 winning tickets. RY

1925 LINGFIELD (L-H)
Wednesday, May 23

OFFICIAL GOING: Standard
Wind: almost nil Weather: sunny and warm

1945 WILLIAM HILL 0800 44 40 40 MAIDEN FILLIES' STKS 6f (P)
2:10 (2:10) (Class 5) 2-Y-O £3,108 (£924; £462; £230) Stalls Low

Form RPR
1 **Baffled (USA)** 2-9-0 LDettori 7 82+
(J Noseda) *w.w in midfield: hdwy 3f out: sn chsng ldrs: rdn and ev ch over 1f out: r.o gamely to ld on line* 5/4[1]
2 shd **Bastakiya (IRE)** 2-9-0 JimmyFortune 3 82+
(J H M Gosden) *dwlt: sn in midfield: c wd bnd over 2f out: str run to ld ins fnl f: edgd lft u.p: hdd on line* 9/1
5 3 1 1/2 **Primed And Poised (USA)**[12] 1631 2-9-0 EddieAhern 6 78
(J W Hills) *chsd ldrs: rdn to ld wl over 1f out: hdd ins fnl f: kpt on same pce* 33/1
4 1 1/2 **Petit Parc** 2-9-0 IanMongan 2 73
(R A Teal) *s.i.s: bhd and short of room after 2f: hdwy 3f out: rdn over 2f out: chsd ldrs 1f out: outpcd last 100yds* 50/1
26 5 3 **Eager Diva (USA)**[34] 1101 2-9-0 DO'Donohoe 1 64
(K A Ryan) *chsd ldrs on inner: rdn over 2f out: wknd 1f out* 7/2[2]
05 6 2 **Talk Of Saafend (IRE)**[14] 1586 2-9-0 SteveDrowne 10 58
(R Hannon) *in tch in midfield on outer: rdn 3f out: sn outpcd: kpt on ins fnl f* 16/1
7 3/4 **Tell Me What (FR)** 2-9-0 PatDobbs 5 56
(R Hannon) *w ldr: rdn over 2f out: wknd qckly over 1f out* 25/1
8 1/2 **Little Angel (IRE)** 2-9-0 EdwardCreighton 9 54
(Miss V Haigh) *chsd ldrs tl 3f out: sn rdn and struggling: no ch last 2f* 66/1
9 1 3/4 **Cosenza** 2-9-0 DaneO'Neill 4 49
(H J L Dunlop) *led: rdn 2f out: sn hdd: wknd qckly over 1f out* 8/1[3]
10 3 **China Pink** 2-9-0 SebSanders 8 40
(Sir Mark Prescott) *slowly away: rn green and a outpcd in last* 9/1

1m 14.24s (1.43) **Going Correction** -0.05s/f (Stan) 10 Ran SP% **113.9**
Speed ratings (Par 90):88,87,85,83,79 77,76,75,73,69
CSF £12.83 TOTE £1.60: £1.10, £2.70, £4.90; EX 12.20 Trifecta £99.30 Pool £588.85 - 4.21 winning units..
Owner Tom Ludt **Bred** International Equities Holding, Inc **Trained** Newmarket, Suffolk

FOCUS
The bare form of this fillies' maiden looks just ordinary, with the fifth and sixth setting the level for now, but the the first two home appear quite nice types.

NOTEBOOK
Baffled(USA), a $350,000 purchase, out of a multiple winner at around 6f-1m1f in the US at two to four, looked held when Bastakiya went on inside the final furlong, but she knew her job and responded to pressure to get up literally on the line. She deserves to take her chance in better company. (op 11-8 tchd 6-5 and 6-4 in a place)
Bastakiya(IRE) ◆, a 70,000euros purchase, out of a high-class multiple winner in Argentina at two to five, looked all over the winner when hitting the front inside the final furlong, but she edged left under pressure and was just reeled in. This was still a fine effort considering she was forced to come widest of all into the straight and she looks ready-made winner. (op 8-1 tchd 10-1)
Primed And Poised(USA) improved significantly on the form she showed in a 5f maiden on the turf course here on her debut and probably just ran into a couple of nice types.
Petit Parc, a £20,000 half-sister to 7f winner Kali, and 6f juvenile scorer Emefdream, out of a 1m winner, made a pleasing debut and is open to some improvement. Official explanation: jockey said filly was denied a clear run (op 66-1)
Eager Diva(USA) ran below the form she showed in a good maiden at Newmarket on her previous start and appeared unsuited by the step up in trip. (tchd 10-3)

1946 BET ONLINE @ WILLIAMHILL.CO.UK H'CAP 6f (P)
2:40 (2:40) (Class 6) (0-60,60) 4-Y-O+ £3,238 (£963; £481; £240) Stalls Low

Form RPR
00-0 1 **Osiris Way**[32] 1166 5-9-2 58 JimCrowley 8 71+
(P R Chamings) *chsd ldr tl led over 1f out: in command and pushed out fnl f* 14/1
0012 2 1 1/4 **Charlie Delta**[22] 1379 4-9-4 60 (b) LDettori 6 66
(J R Boyle) *chsd ldrs: rdn over 2f out: chsd wnr 1f out: kpt on u.p* 4/1[1]
0060 3 3/4 **Mambazo**[32] 1165 5-9-4 60 (e) AdamKirby 4 64
(S C Williams) *taken down early: t.k.h: hld up in bhd ldrs: hdwy over 2f out: hrd rdn over 1f out: kpt on same pce fnl f* 8/1
00-3 4 2 1/2 **Bens Georgie (IRE)**[26] 1280 5-9-1 57 DaneO'Neill 3 53
(D K Ivory) *s.i.s: bhd: hdwy 3f out: rdn over 2f out: chsd ldrs fnl f: nvr able to chal* 12/1
5-10 5 1 **Miswadah (IRE)**[29] 1212 4-8-12 59 PatrickHills(5) 9 52
(D M Simcock) *chsd ldrs: rdn and c wd bnd over 2f out: wknd over 1f out* 8/1
0004 6 hd **Sands Crooner (IRE)**[11] 1669 4-9-4 60 (v) DeanMcKeown 11 53
(D Shaw) *stdd s: dropped in bhd: t.k.h: rdn and hdwy 2f out: kpt on u.p: nvr able to chal* 14/1

410- 7 1/2 **Polish Index**[239] 5593 5-9-1 57 EddieAhern 7 48
(J R Jenkins) *led tl rdn and hdd over 1f out: wknd fnl f* **16/1**

-401 8 nk **Rainbow Bay**[20] 1426 4-9-2 58 (b) StephenDonohoe 1 48
(P D Evans) *s.i.s: hld up bhd: hdwy on inner over 3f out: rdn over 2f out: nvr threatened ldrs* **5/1**[2]

0202 9 shd **Dasheena**[20] 1436 4-8-13 55 (be) SebSanders 12 45
(A J McCabe) *t.k.h: hld up in rr: rdn over 2f out: n.d* **8/1**

2033 10 3/4 **Inwaan (IRE)**[11] 1681 4-9-4 60 (t) ChrisCatlin 2 48
(P R Webber) *racd in midfield: rdn and hdwy 3f out: wknd wl over 1f out* **11/2**[3]

6-00 11 1/2 **Jayanjay**[12] 1630 8-9-4 60 RichardThomas 10 46
(P Mitchell) *towards rr on outer: bhd and rdn wl over 2f out: no ch last 2f* **16/1**

6-0 12 3 **Dukestreet**[8] 1755 6-9-4 60 SteveDrowne 5 37
(D Shaw) *slowly away: towards rr: rdn and struggling over 2f out: no ch after* **100/1**

1m 12.09s (-0.72) **Going Correction** -0.05s/f (Stan) 12 Ran SP% **119.2**
Speed ratings (Par 101):102,100,99,96,94 94,93,93,93,92 91,87
CSF £69.62 CT £493.64 TOTE £21.10: £4.50, £1.20, £2.80; EX 136.80 Trifecta £188.60 Part won. Pool £265.77 - 0.10 winning units..
Owner Mrs Alexandra J Chandris **Bred** Whitsbury Manor Stud **Trained** Baughurst, Hants

FOCUS
A moderate sprint handicap. Solid form, rated through the runner-up, with the winner value for extra.

1947 CHIPS @ WILLIAMHILLCASINO.COM H'CAP 7f (P)
3:10 (3:10) (Class 6) (0-60,61) 4-Y-0+ £3,238 (£963; £481; £240) Stalls Low

Form RPR

6215 1 **Nikki Bea (IRE)**[12] 1629 4-9-1 57 PaulDoe 7 69+
(Jamie Poulton) *chsd ldrs: wnt 2nd over 2f out: led 2f out: sn rdn clr: easily* **10/1**

35/0 2 3 1/2 **Burford Lass (IRE)**[29] 1207 4-8-13 55 DaneO'Neill 5 58
(D K Ivory) *in tch: rdn and effrt over 2f out: kpt on u.p to chse wnr over 1f out: no imp* **50/1**

-201 3 1 1/2 **Pearl Farm**[39] 1038 6-9-0 56 FergusSweeney 13 55
(C A Horgan) *racd in midfield: rdn and hdwy over 2f out: hung lft briefly wl over 1f out: kpt on u.p: no ch w wnr* **11/1**

6064 4 1/2 **Beneking**[20] 1436 7-8-12 54 (p) ChrisCatlin 4 52
(D Burchell) *chsd ldrs: rdn and hdwy 3f out: kpt on u.p fnl f: no ch w wnr* **12/1**

1121 5 1 **Union Jack Jackson (IRE)**[8] 1753 5-9-5 61 6ex..(b) StephenDonohoe 3 56
(John A Harris) *hld up towards rr: hdwy and rdn 3f out: kpt on u.p fnl f: n.d* **11/4**[1]

-503 6 shd **Piccostar**[16] 1534 4-8-12 54 LPKeniry 9 49
(A B Haynes) *racd in midfield: rdn and hdwy on outer bnd over 2f out: no hdwy over 1f out* **11/1**

55-6 7 1 **Miss Wedge**[16] 1534 4-9-0 56 SteveDrowne 2 48
(Tom Dascombe) *hld up in midfield: rdn 3f out: kpt on same pced last 2f* **8/1**[3]

00-4 8 hd **Millfield (IRE)**[26] 1280 4-9-1 57 JimCrowley 6 48
(P R Chamings) *t.k.h: hld up in rr: n.d* **9/1**

0620 9 nk **Lucius Verrus (USA)**[8] 1755 7-9-4 60 (v) DeanMcKeown 10 51
(D Shaw) *a bhd: n.d* **25/1**

3225 10 3/4 **Danish Blues (IRE)**[11] 1675 4-9-2 58 (p) EddieAhern 14 47
(D E Cantillon) *w ldr tl led after 2f: rdn and hdd 2f out: sn outpcd by wnr: lost 2nd over 1f out: fdd qckly fnl f* **8/1**[3]

0-40 11 1 1/4 **New Proposal (IRE)**[8] 1753 5-8-12 54 JimmyFortune 12 39
(A P Jarvis) *taken down early: sn led: hdd after 2f: chsd ldr tl over 2f out: sn rdn and wknd* **13/2**[2]

5060 12 3 **Mill By The Stream**[8] 1739 5-8-11 56 (b[1]) JerryO'Dwyer(3) 11 33
(A M Hales) *chsd ldrs: rdn over 2f out: wknd qckly wl over 1f out* **33/1**

0/0- 13 7 **Accent (IRE)**[59] 5574 4-8-13 55 TedDurcan 8 13
(Miss Tor Sturgis) *a bhd: rdn and lost tch over 3f out: no ch last 2f* **66/1**

0050 14 18 **Shrine Mountain (USA)**[8] 1740 5-8-13 55 (b) EdwardCreighton 1 —
(Miss J S Davis) *bolted to s: stdd s: sn detached and rdn in last: eased and t.o over 1f out* **33/1**

1m 24.78s (-1.11) **Going Correction** -0.05s/f (Stan) 14 Ran SP% **118.9**
Speed ratings (Par 101):104,100,98,97,96 96,95,95,94,93 92,89,81,60
CSF £453.15 CT £5619.61 TOTE £14.40: £2.90, £12.00, £3.40; EX 409.90 TRIFECTA Not won..
Owner Glendale Partnership Ltd **Bred** Dr Paschal Carmody **Trained** Whitcombe, Dorset

FOCUS
A moderate handicap. The winner has improved by a stone on a line through the third but the exact level is hard to pin down.
Union Jack Jackson(IRE) Official explanation: jockey said gelding ran flat
Danish Blues(IRE) Official explanation: jockey said gelding hung left
New Proposal(IRE) Official explanation: jockey said gelding ran too free
Shrine Mountain(USA) Official explanation: jockey said gelding bolted to post

1948 HEADS-UP @ WILLIAMHILLPOKER.COM H'CAP 5f (P)
3:40 (3:41) (Class 4) (0-80,77) 3-Y-0 £6,477 (£1,927; £963; £481) Stalls High

Form RPR

0504 1 **New York Oscar (IRE)**[9] 1729 3-8-8 67 (b) StephenDonohoe 6 72
(A J McCabe) *pressed ldr: rdn 2f out: led wl ins fnl f: r.o wl* **10/1**

-421 2 3/4 **Drifting Gold**[91] 511 3-8-10 69 (b) PhilipRobinson 3 71
(C G Cox) *led at gd pce: rdn over 2f out: kpt on tl hdd and no ex wl ins fnl f* **9/4**[1]

1-25 3 shd **Mac Gille Eoin**[13] 1604 3-9-2 75 JimCrowley 5 77+
(J Gallagher) *chsd ldrs: rdn and outpcd 3f out: c wd wl over 1f out: r.o strly ins fnl f: nt rch wnr* **9/2**[2]

4021 4 1 **Hereford Boy**[8] 1738 3-9-1 74 6ex DarryllHolland 1 72
(D K Ivory) *s.i.s: sn rcvrd and in tch: rdn over 3f out: chsd ldng pair over 1f out: kpt on same pce* **8/1**

0600 5 nk **Stoneacre Gareth (IRE)**[11] 1660 3-8-7 66 (b) LPKeniry 8 63
(Peter Grayson) *chsd ldrs: hdwy over 2f out: rdn 2f out: no hdwy tl kpt on u.p last 100yds* **16/1**

3251 6 nk **Scarlett Heart (IRE)**[28] 1248 3-8-6 65 EddieAhern 7 61
(P J Makin) *sn outpcd in rr: hdwy on inner over 2f out: rdn over 1f out: kpt on same pce ins fnl f* **6/1**

00-5 7 1 3/4 **Camissa**[27] 1270 3-8-13 72 DaneO'Neill 2 62
(D K Ivory) *s.i.s: bhd: some hdwy over 2f out: nvr trbld ldrs* **8/1**

300- 8 1 1/4 **Land Ahoy**[271] 4779 3-9-4 77 BrettDoyle 9 62
(D W P Arbuthnot) *racd wd: a bhd: n.d* **20/1**

2102 9 1 **Comrade Cotton**[8] 1738 3-8-2 66 WilliamBuick(5) 4 47
(N A Callaghan) *a outpcd in rr* **5/1**[3]

59.38 secs (-0.40) **Going Correction** -0.05s/f (Stan) 9 Ran SP% **121.9**
Speed ratings (Par 101):101,99,99,98,97 97,94,92,90
CSF £34.74 CT £122.39 TOTE £13.60: £4.20, £1.60, £1.70; EX 43.00 Trifecta £344.10 Part won. Pool £484.72 - 0.64 winning units..
Owner Paul J Dixon and James Kennerley **Bred** Corduff Stud And J Judd **Trained** Babworth, Notts

FOCUS
A fair sprint handicap run at a decent pace and the front pair dominated throughout, doing well to finish first and second. A slight career best from the winner.
Hereford Boy Official explanation: jockey said gelding missed the break

1949 PLAY BACKGAMMON AT WILLHILL.COM H'CAP 1m 4f (P)
4:10 (4:10) (Class 4) (0-80,80) 4-Y-0+ £6,477 (£1,927; £963; £481) Stalls Low

Form RPR

1106 1 **Wild Pitch**[20] 1438 6-8-11 80 (b) JackMitchell(7) 8 87
(P Mitchell) *hld up in rr: swtchd rt and hdwy bnd over 2f out: rdn wl over 1f out: led last 100yds: hld on* **10/1**

1222 2 hd **Lemonette (USA)**[18] 1470 4-9-3 79 EddieAhern 4 86+
(J W Hills) *hld up in midfield: hdwy over 2f out: plld out over 1f out: rdn over 1f out: r.o fnl f: jst hld* **7/2**[2]

1-44 3 1/2 **Cleaver**[14] 1591 6-9-0 76 SebSanders 5 82
(Lady Herries) *w.w in bhd ldrs: hdwy over 2f out: rdn to ld wl over 1f out: hdd last 100yds: no ex* **9/2**[3]

2262 4 1/2 **Ross Moor**[19] 1451 5-8-9 71 (b) JamesDoyle 6 76
(Mike Murphy) *hld up in tch: hdwy over 2f out: rdn wl over 1f out: kpt on same pce* **14/1**

5452 5 3 1/2 **Jeepstar**[11] 1683 7-8-13 75 (p) JimCrowley 1 74
(S C Williams) *led: rdn over 3f out: hdd wl over 1f out: wknd fnl f* **10/1**

5-26 6 3/4 **Nero's Return (IRE)**[18] 1470 6-9-3 79 GeorgeBaker 7 77
(G L Moore) *stdd s: hld up in last: reminders over 4f out: rdn and effrt over 2f out: sn struggling* **13/2**

11-5 7 1/2 **Captain General**[14] 1591 5-8-9 71 LDettori 2 68
(J A R Toller) *trckd ldrs on inner: rdn 3f out: wknd wl over 1f out* **2/1**[1]

061- 8 2 1/2 **Montosari**[176] 6630 8-8-6 68 NickyMackay 3 61
(P Mitchell) *s.i.s: sn chsng ldr: rdn and ev ch 2f out: sn wknd* **25/1**

2m 32.53s (-1.86) **Going Correction** -0.05s/f (Stan) 8 Ran SP% **115.8**
Speed ratings (Par 105):104,103,103,103,100 100,100,98
CSF £45.56 CT £182.90 TOTE £12.60: £2.60, £1.80, £1.40; EX 55.20 Trifecta £293.00 Pool £594.31 - 1.44 winning units..
Owner Mrs Julie Auletta **Bred** Wyck Hall Stud Ltd **Trained** Epsom, Surrey

FOCUS
A more strongly-run race over the trip than is usually the case here thanks to Jeepstar, but despite that all bar Nero's Return were within a length of each other a furlong out and the front four finished in a heap. Ordinary form, the fourth the best guide.

1950 CALL HOUSE @ WILLIAMHILLBINGO.COM MAIDEN STKS 1m 4f (P)
4:40 (4:42) (Class 5) 3-4-Y-0 £3,238 (£963; £481; £240) Stalls Low

Form RPR

63 1 **Philatelist (USA)**[13] 1605 3-8-9 PhilipRobinson 5 76+
(M A Jarvis) *pressed ldr tl led 2f out: sn rdn clr: eased nr fin* **4/11**[1]

-066 2 3 **Khyberie**[23] 1364 4-9-7 48 SteveDrowne 11 65
(G Wragg) *hld up in midfield: hdwy over 4f out: chsd ldng pair and rdn over 2f out: wnt 2nd 1f out: kpt on but nt trble wnr* **33/1**

3224 3 1 3/4 **Reciprocation (IRE)**[29] 1231 3-8-9 75 DaneO'Neill 2 66
(K McAuliffe) *led tl rdn and hdd 2f out: sn outpcd by wnr: lost 2nd 1f out: kpt on one pce* **12/1**

33 4 5 **Just Julie (USA)**[29] 1217 3-8-4 70 ChrisCatlin 8 53
(N A Callaghan) *wnt rt s: sn prom: rdn 3f out: wknd over 2f out* **10/1**[3]

0-2 5 1 1/2 **Super Sifted (GER)**[23] 1364 3-8-6 ow2 TedDurcan 1 53
(H R A Cecil) *chsd ldrs: rdn over 3f out: wknd over 2f out* **5/1**[2]

0 6 1/2 **Rainbow Flame**[11] 1665 3-8-9 (b[1]) AdamKirby 4 55
(W R Swinburn) *stdd s: w.w in midfield on inner: rdn wl over 4f out: 6th and no ch 2f out: plugged on* **20/1**

7 9 **Wightgar** 3-8-9 (t) FergusSweeney 3 41
(R A Kvisla) *stdd s: hld up in tch in rr: rdn over 4f out: sn lost tch: poor 7th last 3f* **66/1**

0- 8 3/4 **Agent Eleven (IRE)**[385] 1421 4-9-12 EddieAhern 6 40
(A J Lidderdale) *wl in tch: rdn 4f out: sn wl bhd: t.o last 2f* **66/1**

0-0 9 3 **Classic Hall (IRE)**[25] 1312 4-9-7 PaulDoe 12 31
(T Keddy) *t.k.h: hld up in tch on outer: rdn and lost tch over 4f out: t.o last 2f* **100/1**

0 10 hd **Kilmiston Saturn**[37] 1062 3-8-6 JerryO'Dwyer(3) 9 34
(A M Hales) *s.i.s: a bhd: rdn wl over 4f out: sn wl bhd: t.o last 2f* **100/1**

0-0 11 18 **Sven (SWE)**[15] 1566 3-8-4 ow2 HaddenFrost(7) 7 7
(B I Case) *hld up in tch in rr: rdn and wknd over 4f: wl t.o last 2f* **100/1**

50 12 14 **Master Jobs**[16] 1522 3-8-6 SaleemGolam(3) 10 —
(S C Williams) *hld up towards rr: rdn and dropped to last 8f out: t.o last 3f* **66/1**

2m 32.87s (-1.52) **Going Correction** -0.05s/f (Stan)
WFA 3 from 4yo 17lb 12 Ran SP% **121.9**
Speed ratings (Par 103):103,101,99,96,95 95,89,88,86,86 74,65
CSF £28.71 TOTE £1.40: £1.02, £7.80, £2.10; EX 19.00 Trifecta £98.40 Pool £668.13 - 4.82 winning units.
Owner Sheikh Mohammed **Bred** Darley **Trained** Newmarket, Suffolk

FOCUS
Plenty of dead wood in this maiden and the early pace was modest, but things quickened up appreciably in the second half of the race and the time was only 0.34 seconds slower than the preceding Class 4 handicap. The contest was also dominated by those that raced up with the pace, but as they included all those at the head of the market that may not be particularly significant. The winner proved a class above despite running a stone off his Chester form, based on the time.

1951 PLAY GAMES @ WILLIAMHILLARCADE.COM FILLIES' H'CAP 1m 2f (P)
5:10 (5:10) (Class 6) (0-65,65) 4-Y-0+ £3,238 (£963; £481; £240) Stalls Low

Form RPR

-004 1 **Lunar River (FR)**[12] 1628 4-9-2 63 FergusSweeney 9 71
(David Pinder) *hld up wl off the pce: gd hdwy 3f out: ev ch 2f out: rdn to ld narrowly over 1f out: edgd lft and bmpd ins fnl f: all out* **8/1**

00-6 2 hd **Uig**[16] 1521 6-8-8 55 TedDurcan 8 63
(H S Howe) *chsd ldng pair: clsd over 3f out: rdn to ld 2f out: hdd over 1f out: edgd rt and bmpd wl ins fnl f: a jst hld* **16/1**

0-41 3 2 **Blue Line**[12] 1629 5-8-10 60 MarcHalford(3) 2 64
(M Madgwick) *hld up in midfield: wl off the pce: hdwy over 3f out: rdn to chse ldrs 2f out: ev ch over 1f out: no ex last 100yds* **7/1**

3005 **4** *2* **Mon Petite Amour**[12] 1628 4-8-5 59............................ HaddenFrost(7) 1 59+
(D W P Arbuthnot) *hld up off pce in last: nt clr run over 2f out: rdn and hdwy on inner over 1f out: chsd ldrs 1f out: no hdwy ins fnl f* **6/1**
-554 **5** *½* **Smart Cat (IRE)**[49] 928 4-7-13 51 oh3....................... WilliamBuick(5) 7 50
(A P Jarvis) *s.i.s: hld up wl off the pce: hdwy over 3f out: rdn whn short of room briefly over 2f out: no hdwy tl styd on ins fnl f* **9/4**[1]
0256 **6** *3* **Missie Baileys**[9] 1730 5-8-4 51..(b[1]) PaulDoe 3 44
(Mrs L J Mongan) *led at gd pce tl hdd after 2f: chsd ldr clr of rivals: rdn over 3f out: wknd 2f out* **5/1**[2]
4050 **7** *2 ½* **Danettie**[16] 1534 6-7-13 51 oh4... LukeMorris(5) 4 39
(W M Brisbourne) *s.i.s: t.k.h and hanging rt: led after 2f tl rdn and hdd 2f out: wknd qckly over 1f out* **12/1**
022 **8** *1 ¾* **Brastar Jelois (FR)**[15] 1567 4-8-11 65......................... JackMitchell(7) 5 49
(R Hollinshead) *bhd and rdn briefly early: effrt u.p on outer over 4f out: no prog over 2f out* **11/2**[3]
6-06 **9** *nk* **Beautiful Mover (USA)**[130] 115 5-7-13 51 oh6... NataliaGemelova(5) 6 35
(J E Long) *s.i.s: sn chsng ldrs: rdn 4f out: wknd wl over 2f out: no ch over 1f out* **33/1**

2m 7.46s (-0.33) **Going Correction** -0.05s/f (Stan) **9** Ran SP% **117.2**
Speed ratings (Par 98):99,98,97,95,95 92,90,89,89
CSF £126.87 CT £943.46 TOTE £11.40: £3.80, £3.40, £2.80; EX 122.50 TRIFECTA Not won. Place 6 £195.98, Place 5 £107.50.
Owner The Little Farm Partnership **Bred** M Daguzan-Garros & Rolling Hills Farm **Trained** Kingston Lisle, Oxon

FOCUS
A very ordinary fillies' handicap, but with Danettie and Missie Baileys setting each other alight at least the early pace was strong, though that did rather set things up for the closers. Lunar River is rated back to her best but this took little winning.
Danettie Official explanation: jockey said mare hung right
Beautiful Mover(USA) Official explanation: trainer later said mare was found to have an infection
T/Jkpt: Not won. T/Plt: £161.20 to a £1 stake. Pool: £58,297.45. 263.95 winning tickets. T/Qpdt: £39.00 to a £1 stake. Pool: £3,351.90. 63.60 winning tickets. SP

1952 - 1955a (Foreign Racing) - See Raceform Interactive

1606 GOODWOOD (R-H)
Thursday, May 24

OFFICIAL GOING: Good (7.8)
Wind: virtually nil Weather: overcast, warm

1956 NATIONAL BOAT SHOWS AT EXCEL STKS (H'CAP) 1m 1f
2:00 (2:02) (Class 4) (0-85,83) 3-Y-O
£7,478 (£2,239; £1,119; £560; £279; £140) **Stalls** High

Form RPR
01-0 **1** **Mr Aviator (USA)**[27] 1275 3-8-11 **76**.............................. JimmyFortune 8 86+
(R Hannon) *trckd ldng pair: swtchd lft over 1f out: squeezed through to chal 1f out: led and edgd lft ins fnl f: r.o wl* **8/1**
015- **2** *1 ¼* **Al Khaleej (IRE)**[230] 5788 3-9-2 **81**.................................... SebSanders 6 88
(E A L Dunlop) *lw: t.k.h: hld up towards rr: hdwy over 2f out: rdn to ld and edgd rt jst over 1f out: hdd and carried lft ins fnl f: nt pce of wnr* **12/1**
-333 **3** *1 ½* **Eager Igor (USA)**[24] 1359 3-8-6 71............................... StephenCarson 7 75+
(Eve Johnson Houghton) *hld up in midfield: gng wl and nt clr run over 2f out: swtchd lft 2f out: r.o wl fnl f: nt rch ldrs* **20/1**
21- **4** *¾* **Cabinet (IRE)**[210] 6188 3-9-3 **82**.. LDettori 5 84
(Sir Michael Stoute) *strong: swtg: chsd ldr: rdn to ld 2f out: hdd jst over 1f out: kpt on same pce fnl f* **7/4**[1]
1-2 **5** *½* **Fragrancy (IRE)**[28] 1257 3-8-11 **76**............................... PhilipRobinson 3 77
(M A Jarvis) *led tl rdn and hdd 2f out: wknd fnl f* **11/2**[3]
251 **6** *nk* **Shot Gun**[29] 1246 3-8-13 **78**.. DarryllHolland 10 80+
(M R Channon) *swtg: s.i.s: t.k.h and sn in midfield: nt clr run and sltly hmpd 2f out: swtchd rt over 1f out: kpt on* **10/1**
1- **7** *1 ¼* **Samorra (IRE)**[363] 1980 3-8-13 **78**.. RHills 11 76
(M P Tregoning) *v.s.a: bhd: rdn and effrt on rail 3f out: nvr able to chalenge* **10/1**
01-2 **8** *½* **Aegean Prince**[27] 1275 3-9-4 **83**... EddieAhern 9 80
(W R Muir) *lw: trckd ldrs gng wl: rdn and btn whn short of room over 1f out* **9/2**[2]
5213 **9** *3 ½* **Resplendent Ace (IRE)**[34] 1122 3-8-12 **77**...................... TedDurcan 4 67
(P Howling) *trckd ldrs: rdn over 3f out: wknd over 2f out* **16/1**
1-0 **10** *7* **Alfredian Park**[125] 184 3-8-11 **76**.. LPKeniry 1 51
(S Kirk) *dropped in bhd sn after s: rdn 3f out: sn lost tch* **50/1**
25-0 **11** *1 ¼* **Hart Of Gold**[19] 1476 3-9-3 **82**.. KDarley 2 54
(M J Wallace) *racd in midfield on outer: rdn wl over 2f out: sn lost tch* **66/1**

1m 55.69s (-1.17) **Going Correction** 0.0s/f (Good) **11** Ran SP% **121.0**
Speed ratings (Par 101):105,103,102,101,101 101,100,99,96,90 89
CSF £101.02 CT £1867.53 TOTE £11.40: £2.60, £4.90, £6.10; EX 254.00.
Owner Mrs Sue Brendish **Bred** Dr T Keenan & Dr H G White Jr **Trained** East Everleigh, Wilts
■ Stewards' Enquiry : Seb Sanders caution: careless riding

FOCUS
A decent handicap field of largely unexposed three-year-olds. The form looks fairly solid based around the more experienced third, and the winner should be capbale of rating higher.
Alfredian Park Official explanation: jockey said gelding stumbled shortly after start

1957 PETERS OPAL STKS (REGISTERED AS THE COCKED HAT STAKES) (LISTED RACE) (C&G) 1m 3f
2:35 (2:36) (Class 1) 3-Y-O **£14,762** (£5,595; £2,800) **Stalls** Low

Form RPR
0-30 **1** **Halicarnassus (IRE)**[19] 1473 3-9-5 110......................... DarryllHolland 3 109
(M R Channon) *hld up in last: rdn over 2f out: qcknd to ld ins fnl f: eased nr fin* **7/2**[2]
1-3 **2** *1 ¼* **Eastern Anthem (IRE)**[19] 1475 3-9-0 101................................ LDettori 2 102
(Saeed Bin Suroor) *lw: trckd ldr: upsides 3f out: rdn to ld 2f out: hdd ins fnl f: nt pce of wnr* **30/100**[1]
3-04 **3** *4* **Broghill**[19] 1475 3-9-0 97... JimmyFortune 1 97+
(J H M Gosden) *led: hrd pressed and rdn 3f out: hdd 2f out: eased whn btn ins fnl f* **10/1**[3]

2m 29.88s (2.67) **Going Correction** 0.0s/f (Good) **3** Ran SP% **108.2**
Speed ratings (Par 107):90,89,86
CSF £5.31 TOTE £3.60; EX 5.50.
Owner Box 41 **Bred** Yeomanstown Lodge Stud **Trained** West Ilsley, Berks

FOCUS
In effect the Predominate Stakes with a new identity, and a disappointingly poor turnout. It was run at a steady early pace and the winner, who quickened up best, clocked a very moderate time for a race like this. The runner-up disappointed but basically reproduced Newmarket form with the third, although the winner could be better than this.

NOTEBOOK
Halicarnassus(IRE), down the field in the 2000 Guineas, has a good turn of foot on his day as we saw in the Superlative Stakes last year, and in a race not run at a strong pace he was able to outspeed the more stoutly-bred favourite. It was a good effort to defy his 5lb penalty, but the form is probably not worth a great deal. He is entered in the St James's Palace Stakes and Irish Derby, and the latter race would now look the more suitable option. (op 11-4 tchd 4-1)
Eastern Anthem(IRE), third to Salford Mill on his reappearance, was sent off a short price but disappointed badly, failing to draw clear after mastering Broghill, and succumbing to the winner's turn of foot. It is probably fair to assume that he will be more effective in a stronger-run race and over a longer trip. (op 2-5 tchd 4-9 in places)
Broghill, one place behind Eastern Anthem at Newmarket last time, made the running at a steady gallop in an attempt to preserve his suspect stamina. In the end he looked to be simply outclassed. (tchd 12-1)

1958 RAYMARINE STKS (REGISTERED AS THE HEIGHT OF FASHION STAKES) (LISTED RACE) (FILLIES) 1m 1f 192y
3:10 (3:11) (Class 1) 3-Y-O **£15,410** (£5,826; £2,912; £1,456) **Stalls** High

Form RPR
1 **1** **Cosmodrome (USA)**[26] 1312 3-9-0 78........................... NickyMackay 6 102
(L M Cumani) *w'like: w.w in tch: hdwy over 3f out: chsd ldr over 2f out: led over 1f out: styd on wl* **10/1**
50-2 **2** *1 ½* **Sudoor**[18] 1499 3-9-3 102... RHills 3 102
(J L Dunlop) *led: rdn 2f out: hdd over 1f out: kpt on same pce* **15/8**[1]
00-S **3** *4* **Impetious**[11] 1694 3-9-0 0.. PatDobbs 7 91
(Eamon Tyrrell, Ire) *hld up bhd: rdn 3f out: swtchd lft 2f out: styd on u.p: wnt 3rd ins fnl f* **20/1**
10-0 **4** *nk* **Lost In Wonder (USA)**[15] 1581 3-9-0 86................................ KDarley 4 90
(Sir Michael Stoute) *chsd ldrs tl lost pl and dropped to rr after 3f: last and pushed along wl over 3f out: swtchd lft over 2f out: styd on fnl f:* **20/1**
5-40 **5** *3* **Bicoastal (USA)**[11] 1702 3-9-0 105..(b) LDettori 5 84
(B J Meehan) *lw: hld up in tch: hdwy 6f out: chsd ldng pair 4f out: rdn over 3f out: wknd tamely wl over 1f out* **5/2**[2]
01-4 **6** *2 ½* **Shimoni**[12] 1663 3-9-0 89.. PaulDoe 8 79
(W J Knight) *s.i.s: hdwy on outer to chse ldr over 6f out: rdn 4f out: sn lost pl: no ch whn hung rt 2f out* **16/1**
10-4 **7** *nk* **So Sweet (IRE)**[15] 1581 3-9-0 94.. JHBowman 2 79
(M R Channon) *lw: t.k.h: chsd ldr: rdn over 3f out: lost 2nd over 2f out: sn wknd* **6/1**[3]
1-5 **8** *3* **Les Fazzani (IRE)**[14] 1610 3-9-0 80................................... EddieAhern 1 73
(M J Wallace) *lw: hld up bhd: rdn over 4f out: no ch last 2f* **7/1**

2m 7.52s (-0.23) **Going Correction** 0.0s/f (Good) **8** Ran SP% **114.6**
Speed ratings (Par 104):100,98,95,95,92 90,90,88
CSF £29.31 TOTE £11.40: £3.00, £1.40, £3.30; EX 36.40.
Owner Fittocks Stud **Bred** Fittocks Stud **Trained** Newmarket, Suffolk

FOCUS
The equivalent of the old Lupe Stakes. The winning time was modest but the first two came nicely clear and the form looks sound enough for the grade, albeit nothing special.

NOTEBOOK
Cosmodrome(USA), having only won a Wolverhampton maiden, came into the race rated just 78, but her trainer knows his swans from his geese and she was clearly thought to be a lot better than that. She put up a taking performance in success, beating a solid yardstick in Sudoor, and races like the Ribblesdale and Lancashire Oaks now look ideal targets for her. (op 8-1)
Sudoor, runner-up to Oaks hopeful Dalvina in the Pretty Polly on her seasonal reappearance, again had to give weight away all round. Allowed to dictate her own pace in front, her rider set a fairly steady gallop and gave her every chance in the straight. It could be said that her penalty beat her and she should be able to win at this level somewhere. (op 2-1 tchd 13-8)
Impetious, who only has a maiden win to her name, had an unfortunate experience when coming down on her reappearance at Leopardstown 11 days earlier. She kept on well enough to grab some valuable black type but is not up to this class really and is likely to remain difficult to place. (op 16-1)
Lost In Wonder(USA), last in the Cheshire Oaks on her reappearance when apparently in season, reversed form with the fourth (So Sweet) from Chester, and looks to be crying out for another two furlongs. (op 16-1)
Bicoastal(USA), seventh in the French 1000 Guineas last time out, was the highest-rated filly in the line-up, but she had her stamina to prove over this longer trip. Keen early, she simply did not get home. (op 2-1 tchd 11-4 and 3-1 in places)
Shimoni, fourth in the Oaks Trial at Lingfield last time out, looked all over the place in the straight. She is better than this, but needs a longer trip. (op 14-1)
So Sweet(IRE), fourth in the Cheshire Oaks when getting the run of the race out in front, should have appreciated the drop back in trip, but she took too much out of herself by racing keenly. (op 8-1)
Les Fazzani(IRE) Official explanation: jockey said filly was unsuited by the good ground

1959 DE NOVO STKS (H'CAP) 2m
3:45 (3:46) (Class 4) (0-85,84) 4-Y-0+ **£7,772** (£2,312; £1,155; £577) **Stalls** Low

Form RPR
140- **1** **Full House (IRE)**[26] 5963 8-9-5 **78**.................................. JimmyFortune 1 87
(P R Webber) *chsd ldrs: hdwy on outer over 4f out: led over 2f out: drifted rt but sn rdn clr: rdn out* **20/1**
-511 **2** *4* **Noble Minstrel**[109] 354 4-8-8 **69**...................................(t) OscarUrbina 15 78+
(S C Williams) *hld up bhd: hdwy on inner 6f out: nt clr run over 2f out tl over 1f out: prog and r.o to chse wnr ins fnl f: nvr able to chal* **11/2**[2]
-342 **3** *1* **Noddies Way**[31] 1196 4-7-13 **63** oh7............................ LiamJones(3) 10 66
(J F Panvert) *chsd ldr: rdn and ev ch 3f out: chsd wnr over 2f out: kpt on same pce: lost 2nd ins fnl f* **28/1**
-331 **4** *1 ½* **Gee Dee Nen**[12] 1677 4-9-9 **84**.. JimmyQuinn 12 86+
(M H Tompkins) *lw: w.w in midfield: hdwy on inner over 4f out: chsd ldrs and rdn 3f out: kpt on same pce* **9/2**[1]
-035 **5** *¾* **Most Definitely (IRE)**[12] 1677 7-8-13 **72**............................ JimCrowley 8 72
(R M Stronge) *hld up bhd: hdwy gng wl 4f out: swtchd lft over 2f out: sn rdn and no imp* **20/1**
0-51 **6** *3 ½* **Takafu (USA)**[12] 1683 5-9-6 **79**... JHBowman 3 75
(W S Kittow) *lw: t.k.h: settled in midfield: hdwy to chse ldrs over 3f out: wkng whn short of room over 2f out* **10/1**
-405 **7** *1* **High Point (IRE)**[12] 1654 9-8-12 **71**.................................... AdamKirby 7 66
(G P Enright) *hld up bhd: hdwy over 6f out: ev ch and rdn over 3f out: btn whn short of room over 1f out* **20/1**
650- **8** *1* **Diego Cao (IRE)**[40] 5804 6-9-7 **80**...................................... SebSanders 5 74+
(N J Gifford) *hld up wl bhd: hdwy on inner over 4f out: rdn 3f out: nt clr run 2f out tl over 1f out: no hdwy and eased ins fnl f* **10/1**
0-55 **9** *hd* **Eldorado**[19] 1470 6-8-8 **67**... FergusSweeney 4 60
(G L Moore) *chsd ldrs: hdwy to press ldrs and rdn over 3f out: wknd over 2f out* **14/1**
6-00 **10** *1 ½* **Tender Falcon**[13] 1621 7-9-2 **75**...................................... GeorgeBaker 14 67
(R J Hodges) *hld up in rr: n.d* **40/1**

526- **11** *shd* **Dubai Ace (USA)**[286] 3256 6-8-6 **65** ow3..................(p) NeilChalmers(3) 9 60
(Miss Sheena West) *towards rr: rdn ands struggling over 4f out: plugged on past btn horses fnl f* **50/1**

0-20 **12** *2 1/2* **Mister Right (IRE)**[33] 1148 6-9-3 **76**....................................(t) TQuinn 13 65
(D J S Ffrench Davis) *led tl rdn and hdd over 2f out: sn dropped out* **16/1**

-501 **13** *6* **Kayf Aramis**[7] 1793 5-9-0 **76** 6ex.............................. MarcHalford(3) 6 57
(J L Spearing) *chsd ldrs: ev ch and rdn 4f out: wknd 3f out* **11/2**[2]

66-0 **14** *8* **Stoop To Conquer**[33] 1148 7-9-6 **79**........................... DarryllHolland 11 51
(A W Carroll) *chsd ldrs: rdn and wknd 4f out* **9/1**[3]

012 **15** *15* **Newnham (IRE)**[29] 1253 6-8-11 **77**.................................. JackMitchell(7) 2 31
(J R Boyle) *w.w in midfield: stmbld bnd 10f out and dropped to rr: sme hdwy 6f out: wl bhd last 3f: eased: t.o* **10/1**

3m 27.23s (-3.56) **Going Correction** 0.0s/f (Good)
WFA 4 from 5yo+ 2lb **15** Ran SP% **120.9**
Speed ratings (Par 105):108,106,105,104,104 102,102,101,101,100 100,99,96,92,84
CSF £118.17 CT £3120.85 TOTE £18.70: £5.40, £2.50, £5.30; EX 161.90.
Owner The Chamberlain Addiscott Partnership **Bred** Schwindibode Ag **Trained** Mollington, Oxon
■ Stewards' Enquiry : Liam Jones one-day ban: careless riding (Jun 4)

FOCUS
They went a decent pace in this handicap and the form should prove solid, although there are slight doubts with the third out of the handicap. Full House ran to last year's Royal Ascot form. Both the second and fourth were hampered.
Mister Right(IRE) Official explanation: jockey said gelding ran too free
Stoop To Conquer Official explanation: jockey said gelding was unsuited by the good ground
Newnham(IRE) Official explanation: jockey said gelding slipped badly on first bend

1960 AVON INFLATABLES EBF MAIDEN FILLIES' STKS 6f
4:20 (4:21) (Class 5) 2-Y-O **£4,210** (£1,252; £625; £312) **Stalls** Low

Form RPR

6 **1** **Johar Jamal (IRE)**[13] 1636 2-9-0 0.................................... JHBowman 1 82
(M R Channon) *chsd ldrs: rdn to ld over 1f out: edgd rt fnl f: hld on wl* **6/1**[3]

2 *hd* **Regal Bird (USA)** 2-9-0 0.. EddieAhern 11 81
(M A Magnusson) *leggy: unf: led and sn crossed to stands rail: led for 2f: led again 3f out: hdd over 1f out: kpt on u.p: a jst hld* **13/2**

3 *2* **Lush (IRE)** 2-9-0 0.. JimmyFortune 3 78+
(R Hannon) *unf: leggy: v.s.a: wl bhd: hdwy on stands rail wl over 2f out: kpt on wl fnl f: nvr nrr* **6/1**[3]

5 **4** *3/4* **Perfect Flight**[24] 1354 2-9-0 0.. TedDurcan 5 73
(M Blanshard) *trckd ldrs: rdn over 1f out: kpt on same pce fnl f* **4/1**[2]

5 *1 3/4* **Bermacha** 2-9-0 0.. SteveDrowne 12 68
(W R Muir) *w'like: strong: chsd ldrs: rdn over 2f out: kpt on same pce* **20/1**

0 **6** *2 1/2* **Twilight Belle (IRE)**[26] 1285 2-9-0 0.. LDettori 6 60
(B J Meehan) *unf: hung rt: chsd ldr tl led after 2f tl 3f out: wknd qckly ins fnl f* **7/2**[1]

0 **7** *3/4* **Stand In Flames**[24] 1354 2-9-0 0.................................. DarryllHolland 10 58
(Pat Eddery) *prom on outer: rdn 2f out: wknd qckly 1f out* **12/1**

0 **8** *1 1/2* **Ostinata (IRE)**[5] 1832 2-9-0 0.. AdamKirby 9 54
(B W Duke) *sn rdn along: chsd ldrs to 1/2-way: sn wknd* **66/1**

0 **9** *hd* **In Decorum**[56] 814 2-9-0 0.. RichardThomas 4 53
(J A Geake) *swtg: chsd ldrs for 2f: sn rdn and struggling: no ch last 2f* **20/1**

10 *hd* **Limelight (USA)** 2-9-0 0.. SebSanders 13 52
(Sir Mark Prescott) *leggy: bit bkwd: in tch: rdn over 3f out: no ch last 2f* **8/1**

11 *2* **Jemiliah** 2-9-0 0.. BrettDoyle 8 46
(B J Meehan) *swtg: bit bkwd: slowly away: a bhd* **16/1**

12 *6* **Get Jealous (IRE)** 2-9-0 0.. RichardSmith 7 28
(R Hannon) *w'like: bit bkwd: v.s.a: a outpcd: wl bhd fr 1/2-way* **25/1**

13 *2 1/2* **Friction** 2-9-0 0.. JimCrowley 2 21
(J G Portman) *w'like: bit bkwd: slowly away: a outpcd: wl bhd fr 1/2-way* **50/1**

1m 13.54s (0.69) **Going Correction** -0.125s/f (Firm) **13** Ran SP% **125.6**
Speed ratings (Par 90):90,89,87,86,83 80,79,77,77,76 74,66,62
CSF £44.58 TOTE £7.90: £2.70, £2.80, £1.90; EX 59.80.
Owner Jaber Abdullah **Bred** Tally-Ho Stud **Trained** West Ilsley, Berks

FOCUS
Probably a decent race, with those with form stepping forward, although the level looks guessy at this stage.

NOTEBOOK
Johar Jamal(IRE) appreciated the extra furlong and improved for her debut outing at Nottingham. She was always going well towards the front of the pack and just held off the less-experienced Magnusson filly at the line. It is difficult to quantify the strength of the form. (op 15-2)
Regal Bird(USA), a $190,000 half-sister to Ghost Reply, a triple winner at around six to nine furlongs at three in the US, showed good speed from the gate to cross over and make the running next to the stands'-side rail. She rallied well after being headed by the more experienced Channon filly and was cutting her advantage back as they crossed the line. The worry for next time is that she was clearly buzzed up to do the job on her debut and may not have much improvement in her.
Official explanation: trainer said filly returned distressed (op 5-1 tchd 7-1)
Lush(IRE) ◆, a half-sister to Derivative, a dual winner at 7f and 1m1f at two and Listed placed over a mile at three, ran with plenty of promise, keeping on well in the closing stages after a bad start and shaping as though she will come on a good bit for the experience. (op 7-1)
Perfect Flight, unlucky in running at Windsor on her debut, looked likely to appreciate the extra furlong but she was a bit disappointing. She is likely to come up against better fillies now and might struggle before nurseries become an option. (op 6-1)
Bermacha, a half-sister to Megec Blis, a dual 7f winner at three, Nicowain, a multiple winner in Italy, and L'Enjoleuse, a dual 1m2f winner at three in France, was another who ran with a bit of promise. She hails from a stable who tend not to have juvenile winners first time out, and it is probably fair to assume that she will improve for the outing.
Twilight Belle(IRE), with the benefit of her debut run behind her, showed good pace but never looked comfortable, continually hanging right. (op 4-1)
Limelight(USA), who is closely related to Approach, a smart performer over 7f to 1m2f, and Intrigued, a useful performer over 1m at two, is also a half-sister to top-class miler Aussie Rules, out of a mare who won the Nassau Stakes here. While she would not be bred for the speed of some of her rivals here, the current form of her stable's juveniles meant that she was sent off a short enough price on her debut. She will do better over further in time. (op 6-1 tchd 17-2)

1961 WOODCOTE BUILDING SERVICES MAIDEN FILLIES' STKS 7f
4:55 (4:57) (Class 5) 3-Y-O
£3,739 (£1,119; £559; £280; £139; £70) **Stalls** High

Form RPR

22 **1** **Truly Enchanting (IRE)**[13] 1639 3-9-0 0.......................... SebSanders 1 75+
(J Noseda) *lw: hld up wl behnd: plld wd and hdwy 3f out: r.o wl to ld ins fnl f: rdn out* **10/11**[1]

02-4 **2** *1 1/4* **Cape Velvet (IRE)**[44] 996 3-9-0 72.. RHills 8 72
(J W Hills) *t.k.h: hld up in midfield: rdn 3f out: chsd ldr 2f out: ev ch tl nt pce of wnr ins fnl f* **14/1**

0 **3** *1* **Appleby**[20] 1447 3-9-0 0.. JimmyFortune 5 69
(J H M Gosden) *hld up towards rr: hdwy 3f out: pushed along over 1f out: kpt on steadily* **14/1**

4 *1/2* **Viva La Flag (USA)** 3-9-0 0.. TedDurcan 10 68+
(J L Dunlop) *leggy: s.i.s: sn racing in midfield: rdn 3f out: n.m.r 2f out: styd on fnl f: nrst fin* **9/1**

335- **5** *nk* **Millisecond**[210] 6187 3-9-0 74.. PhilipRobinson 4 67
(M A Jarvis) *led at gd pce: rdn 2f out: hdd ins fnl f: wknd last 50yds* **7/1**[3]

0-22 **6** *2* **Cassiara**[23] 1386 3-9-0 78.. KDarley 12 62
(J Pearce) *t.k.h: chsd ldr tl 2f out: sn wknd* **9/2**[2]

0-0 **7** *1 1/4* **Puissant Princess (IRE)**[20] 1447 3-9-0 0............................ TQuinn 11 58
(J W Hills) *hld up in midfield: shkn up and hung rt over 2f out: no hdwy after* **50/1**

4 **8** *1* **Pivotal Truth**[22] 1398 3-9-0 0.. MichaelHills 3 56
(B W Hills) *hld up bhd: rdn 3f out: sn btn* **8/1**

0- **9** *nk* **Day By Day**[223] 5950 3-9-0 0.. BrettDoyle 9 60+
(B J Meehan) *chsd ldng pair: rdn wl over 2f out: wknd over 1f out* **33/1**

U0 **10** *1 1/4* **Silver Surprise**[17] 1522 3-9-0 0.. AmirQuinn 2 51
(J J Bridger) *dropped in bhd sn after s: a bhd: rdn over 3f out: no prog* **100/1**

5-0 **11** *2 1/2* **Full Of Promise (USA)**[12] 1665 3-9-0 0.............................. JimCrowley 7 45
(Mrs A J Perrett) *chsd ldrs: rdn wl over 3f out: wknd 3f out: bhd last 2f* **33/1**

1m 27.9s (-0.14) **Going Correction** 0.0s/f (Good) **11** Ran SP% **126.3**
Speed ratings (Par 96):100,98,97,96,96 94,92,91,91,89 87
CSF £18.33 TOTE £1.90: £1.10, £3.20, £3.70; EX 16.30.
Owner Tom Ludt **Bred** Keatly Overseas Ltd **Trained** Newmarket, Suffolk

FOCUS
An ordinary fillies' maiden run at a fair gallop and the first four home all came from off the pace. The form makes sense.

1962 CHEVIOT ASSET MANAGEMENT STKS (H'CAP) 1m
5:30 (5:31) (Class 4) (0-85,85) 4-Y-O+ **£6,477** (£1,927; £963; £481) **Stalls** High

Form RPR

/5-0 **1** **Nawaqees**[26] 1287 4-8-6 **73**.. RHills 4 85
(J L Dunlop) *wl bhd: plld wd and hdwy 3f out: rdn to ld 2f out: hrd pressed and hung lft wl ins fnl f: r.o* **16/1**

423- **2** *3/4* **Ebert**[270] 4838 4-9-1 **82**... TQuinn 1 93
(P J Makin) *dropped in bhd sn after s: stl last over 3f out: plld wd and hdwy 3f out: chal 1f out: carried lft towards fin: no ex* **14/1**

02-0 **3** *2* **Bee Stinger**[22] 1395 5-9-1 **82**...................................(v1) KDarley 15 88
(I A Wood) *hld up: hdwy on rail 3f out: rdn and ev ch over 1f out: 3rd and hld whn edgd lft ins fnl f* **20/1**

0632 **4** *3/4* **Neardown Beauty (IRE)**[10] 1710 4-9-0 **81**.......................... LDettori 11 85+
(I A Wood) *hld up in midfield: nt clr run over 2f out: swtchd lft over 1f out: styd on wl ins fnl f: nt rch ldrs* **11/2**[3]

0-51 **5** *3/4* **Genari**[9] 1751 4-8-9 **76** 6ex.. TedDurcan 14 79+
(P F I Cole) *slowly away and stmbld s: hdwy on rail whn hmpd over 2f out: styng on same pce whn nt clr run ins fnl f* **5/2**[1]

63-4 **6** *1* **Master Pegasus**[42] 1013 4-9-4 **85**.................................. GeorgeBaker 9 86+
(C F Wall) *chsd ldrs: rdn and ev ch over 2f out: wknd 1f out* **11/2**[3]

004- **7** *nk* **Master Of The Race**[23] 6992 5-8-9 **76**....................(p) RichardThomas 7 76
(Tom Dascombe) *hld up bhd: effrt on rail whn nt clr run over 2f out: kpt on same pce fnl f* **25/1**

/5-2 **8** *2 1/2* **Mr Garston**[12] 1682 4-9-4 **85**.. DarryllHolland 8 79
(M P Tregoning) *chsd ldrs: effrt and hung rt over 2f out: wkng whn short of room 2f out* **9/2**[2]

0-00 **9** *shd* **Direct Debit (IRE)**[17] 1524 4-9-3 **84**................................ MichaelHills 5 78
(M L W Bell) *in tch: hdwy to chse ldrs 3f out: wknd 2f out* **16/1**

0-30 **10** *1* **Red Somerset (USA)**[13] 1619 4-9-2 **83**............................ JimmyQuinn 2 74
(R J Hodges) *hld up in midfield: short of room over 2f out: swtchd lft and rdn 2f out: wknd over 1f out* **33/1**

0000 **11** *3* **Hail The Chief**[38] 1060 10-8-6 **80**............................(p) HaddenFrost(7) 13 64
(R Hannon) *lw: led tl hdd 2f out: sn wknd* **25/1**

1110 **12** *6* **Lopinot (IRE)**[54] 842 4-9-2 **83**.................................... SebSanders 10 54
(P J Makin) *hld up in midfield: lost pl and nt clr run over 2f out: wknd 2f out* **16/1**

-000 **13** *3* **Nautical**[31] 1200 9-8-5 **72**.. SimonWhitworth 3 36
(A W Carroll) *plld hrd: racd wd in midfield: wknd over 3f out: no ch last 2f* **66/1**

0-00 **14** *17* **King's Majesty (IRE)**[22] 1395 5-8-10 **77**............................ AmirQuinn 6 2
(L A Dace) *lw: t.k.h: pressed ldrs: wknd qckly wl over 2f out: eased fnl f: t.o* **66/1**

0B-0 **15** *1 1/2* **Postgraduate (IRE)**[38] 1060 5-9-3 **84**..........................(v) PaulDoe 12 5
(W J Knight) *pressed ldr: rdn 3f out: wknd qckly over 2f out: eased fnl f: t.o* **16/1**

1m 38.83s (-1.44) **Going Correction** 0.0s/f (Good) **15** Ran SP% **126.1**
Speed ratings (Par 105):107,106,104,103,102 101,101,98,98,97 94,88,85,68,67
CSF £216.98 CT £4570.56 TOTE £22.30: £6.10, £3.90, £5.80; EX 304.20 Place 6 ££1816.74, Place 5 £191.06.
Owner Hamdan Al Maktoum **Bred** Shadwell Estate Company Limited **Trained** Arundel, W Sussex
■ Stewards' Enquiry : R Hills one-day ban: careless riding (Jun 4)

FOCUS
A competitive handicap run at a strong early pace with three helping force it from the off. However, they may have gone off too quick as the trio responsible were amongst the last five home. Solid form, the less exposed front pair a couple of lengths clear of the back-to-form third.
Genari Official explanation: jockey said gelding stumbled leaving stalls
Master Of The Race Official explanation: jockey said gelding was denied a clear run
Mr Garston Official explanation: jockey said gelding suffered interference in running
Direct Debit(IRE) Official explanation: jockey said gelding lost both hind shoes
Red Somerset(USA) Official explanation: jockey said gelding suffered interference in running
Postgraduate(IRE) Official explanation: vet said gelding returned lame
T/Jkpt: Not won. T/Plt: £2,284.20 to a £1 stake. Pool: £79,950.35. 25.55 winning tickets. T/Qpdt: £33.70 to a £1 stake. Pool: £5,328.80. 116.90 winning tickets. SP

[1743]NEWCASTLE (L-H)

Thursday, May 24

OFFICIAL GOING: Good (good to firm in places, 8.1)

Wind: fresh, half against

1963 EVERSHEDS MEDIAN AUCTION MAIDEN STKS 6f
2:20 (2:28) (Class 6) 2-Y-O **£2,266** (£674; £337; £168) **Stalls** Low

Form RPR

2 **1** **Pelican Prince**[17] 1528 2-9-3 0 PatCosgrave 11 81+
(K R Burke) *t.k.h: cl up centre: led over 2f out: drifted to stands rail 1f out: styd on strly* **2/1**[1]

0 **2** 3 ½ **Welcome Return (IRE)**[26] 1302 2-8-12 0 DavidAllan 5 66
(T D Easterby) *chsd centre ldrs: effrt over 2f out: kpt on fnl f: nt pce of wnr* **40/1**

3 ¾ **Borasco (USA)** 2-8-12 0 PhillipMakin 4 63
(T D Barron) *t.k.h: in tch centre: effrt over 1f out: kpt on same pce ins fnl f* **14/1**[3]

4 1 ¾ **Celtic Strand (IRE)** 2-9-3 0 MickyFenton 12 63
(T P Tate) *chsd stands' side ldrs: drvn and outpcd over 2f out: styd on wl fnl f: nrst fin* **16/1**

5 2 ½ **Madison Heights (IRE)** 2-9-3 0 TonyHamilton 14 56
(J Howard Johnson) *led stands' side to over 2f out: kpt on same pce* **16/1**

6 ½ **Firewalker** 2-8-12 0 J-PGuillambert 6 49
(B Smart) *led centre to over 2f out: kpt on same pce over 1f out* **28/1**

7 1 ¼ **Allahor** 2-8-12 0 PBradley[(5)] 7 50
(A Berry) *s.i.s: hld up centre: hdwy over 2f out: no imp over 1f out* **100/1**

0 **8** 2 ½ **Aquarian Dancer**[31] 1193 2-8-12 0 PaulMulrennan 8 38
(Jedd O'Keeffe) *chsd centre ldrs tl rdn and no ex fr over 2f out* **66/1**

60 **9** ¾ **Dhaka Dazzle**[26] 1291 2-9-3 0 EdwardCreighton 3 41
(M R Channon) *hld up centre: rdn 1/2-way: nvr rchd ldrs* **50/1**

0 **10** ½ **Moonlight Gambler (IRE)**[21] 1422 2-9-3 0 GrahamGibbons 13 39
(T D Easterby) *cl up stands' side: led that gp over 2f out to over 1f out: edgd lft and sn btn* **66/1**

53 **11** ½ **Natural Rhythm (IRE)**[13] 1622 2-9-3 0 RoystonFfrench 10 38
(Mrs A Duffield) *chsd ldrs: drvn 1/2-way: btn over 1f out* **13/2**[2]

0 **12** 3 ½ **Latin Dancer**[17] 1528 2-9-3 0 DO'Donohoe 2 27
(B S Rothwell) *hld up centre: drvn 1/2-way: nvr on terms* **80/1**

13 nk **Handsinthemist (IRE)** 2-8-7 0 RoryMoore[(5)] 16 21
(P T Midgley) *missed break: sn in tch stands' side: rdn and wknd over 2f out* **100/1**

0 **14** 3 ½ **Jolly Tipsy**[13] 1636 2-8-5 0 NSLawes[(7)] 17 —
(M W Easterby) *missed break: a wl bhd stands' side* **100/1**

1m 16.56s (1.47) **Going Correction** +0.10s/f (Good) **14** Ran SP% **80.1**

Speed ratings (Par 91):94,89,88,86,82 82,80,77,76,75 74,70,69,64

CSF £46.47 TOTE £2.30: £1.10, £5.40, £4.10; EX 43.10 TRIFECTA Not won..

Owner Market Avenue Racing Club Ltd **Bred** S H And Mrs A M Bayless **Trained** Middleham Moor, N Yorks

■ Drawnfromthepast (2/1) and Tuanku (10/1) were withdrawn after proving unruly at the s. R4 applies, deduct 35p in the £.

FOCUS

Probably just an average maiden, but the race should produce its share of winners. Pelican Prince stepped up on his debut form here.

NOTEBOOK

Pelican Prince, a promising second at this course on his debut, was expected to be suited by the extra furlong on this occasion and saw it out well despite racing keenly early on. He did most of his racing down the centre and, although drifting towards the stands' side, he had too much in hand, ultimately winning comfortably. This was just an average event, but he is clearly progressing. (op 9-4 tchd 5-2 and 11-4 in a place)

Welcome Return(IRE), too green to overcome a slow start on her debut, was another stepping up a furlong in distance and she looked a different horse, picking up having held a good position towards the far side and rallying for second. There is an ordinary maiden in her. (op 50-1)

Borasco(USA), a $60,000 purchase, got going late to fare best of the newcomers and, although losing out on second, she should have learned a good deal from the outing. There is an ordinary maiden at this distance in her. (op 9-1)

Celtic Strand(IRE), bred to appreciate further later on, comes from a stable who know how to ready a newcomer and he made a highly pleasing debut. There is probably a race in him at this distance, but he will not be at his best until tackling 7f-plus. (op 14-1)

Madison Heights(IRE), whose stable's juveniles are beginning to get going, was quite a costly purchase and he certainly knew his job, showing good early speed on the stands' side. He is entitled to improve for the experience and looks another likely winner. (op 12-1)

Firewalker, a cheap purchase, was responsible for the pace down the centre, but she got left behind when it mattered. She did at least demonstrate some ability though. (op 22-1)

1964 HALL & PARTNERS H'CAP 1m 3y(S)
2:55 (2:59) (Class 6) (0-65,65) 3-Y-O **£2,590** (£770; £385; £192) **Stalls** Low

Form RPR

355- **1** **The Grey Berry**[238] 5632 3-9-1 62 GrahamGibbons 4 73
(T D Walford) *missed break: hld up: hdwy over 2f out: qcknd to ld over 1f out: rdn clr* **25/1**

50-3 **2** 3 ½ **Grand Art (IRE)**[33] 1155 3-8-12 64 PatrickHills[(5)] 16 67
(M H Tompkins) *prom: effrt over 2f out: rallied over 1f out: hung lft and chsd wnr ins fnl f: r.o* **5/2**[1]

0-00 **3** nk **Grand Diamond (IRE)**[13] 1624 3-8-6 60 (p) GaryBartley[(7)] 2 62
(J S Goldie) *hld up: hdwy to chal wl over 1f out: kpt on same pce fnl f* **33/1**

-015 **4** 2 ½ **A Big Sky Brewing (USA)**[17] 1530 3-8-12 59 PaulFessey 11 55+
(T D Barron) *hld up: nt clr run and swtchd rt over 3f out: kpt on wl fnl f: nvr nrr* **3/1**[2]

6-30 **5** ¾ **Anne Bonney**[91] 522 3-8-11 58 (t) PatCosgrave 6 53+
(E J O'Neill) *sn midfield: effrt over 2f out: no imp appr fnl f* **14/1**

-010 **6** 2 **Alavana (IRE)**[22] 1410 3-8-11 58 RoystonFfrench 3 48
(D W Barker) *hld up: hdwy and prom over 2f out: rdn and no ex over 1f out* **22/1**

-300 **7** 3 **Foxxy**[17] 1531 3-8-6 60 NeilBrown[(7)] 8 43
(J R Norton) *hld up: effrt and hdwy over 2f out: nvr rchd ldrs* **50/1**

0-04 **8** 5 **Beaumont Boy**[18] 1489 3-8-8 55 DeanMcKeown 12 27
(G A Swinbank) *hld up: n.m.r and swtchd rt over 2f out: nvr rchd ldrs* **10/1**

10-6 **9** 1 **Smash N'Grab (IRE)**[23] 1383 3-8-11 58 DO'Donohoe 1 27
(K A Ryan) *led to over 1f out: sn rdn and btn* **28/1**

655- **10** 4 **Mineral Rights (USA)**[177] 6646 3-9-2 63 PhillipMakin 7 23
(I Semple) *chsd ldrs: effrt and ev ch 2f out: sn rdn and wknd* **16/1**

00-0 **11** nk **The Mighty Ogmore**[34] 1131 3-8-9 56 (p) PaulMulrennan 9 15
(R C Guest) *chsd ldrs: rdn over 3f out: wkng whn hmpd over 2f out* **20/1**

60-6 **12** ½ **Grethel (IRE)**[13] 1620 3-8-8 55 FrancisNorton 17 13
(A Berry) *bhd: rdn 1/2-way: nvr on terms* **25/1**

6-06 **13** ¾ **The Diamond Bond**[17] 1531 3-8-3 53 DuranFentiman[(3)] 15 9
(G R Oldroyd) *prom tl lost pl 3f out* **33/1**

60-6 **14** 5 **Grand Dream (IRE)**[26] 1303 3-9-4 65 TPQueally 13 10
(J G Given) *cl up: drvn over 3f out: wknd over 2f out* **11/1**

0-44 **15** 2 **Red Flare (IRE)**[10] 1712 3-8-6 53 TPO'Shea 5 —
(M R Channon) *midfield: drvn over 3f out: wknd over 2f out* **9/1**[3]

-600 **16** 1 ¼ **Seteem (USA)**[14] 1605 3-9-4 65 KimTinkler 10 2
(N Tinkler) *s.i.s: a bhd* **50/1**

1m 43.78s (1.88) **Going Correction** +0.10s/f (Good) **16** Ran SP% **123.6**

Speed ratings (Par 97):94,90,90,87,86 84,81,76,75,71 71,71,70,65,63 62

CSF £80.77 CT £2251.85 TOTE £28.10: £5.90, £1.40, £6.00, £1.40; EX 187.10 TRIFECTA Not won..

Owner N J Maher **Bred** G Deacon **Trained** Sheriff Hutton, N Yorks

■ Stewards' Enquiry : Dean McKeown three-day ban: careless riding (Jun 4-6)
Graham Gibbons three-day ban: careless riding (Jun 4-6)

FOCUS

A moderate yet competitive handicap. The Grey Berry put up an improved effort in causing a shock, but it was no fluke with the runner-up and third close to form.

Red Flare(IRE) Official explanation: jockey said gelding was never travelling

1965 NEWCASTLE INTERNATIONAL AIRPORT & NSPCC FULL STOP H'CAP 7f
3:30 (3:30) (Class 5) (0-75,73) 3-Y-O **£3,562** (£1,059; £529; £264) **Stalls** Low

Form RPR

100- **1** **Darfour**[227] 5866 3-8-9 71 GaryBartley[(7)] 11 77
(J S Goldie) *hld up: hdwy 2f out: str run fnl f to ld post* **16/1**

031 **2** shd **Royal Rock**[13] 1632 3-9-4 73 PaulMulrennan 2 79+
(C F Wall) *t.k.h: chsd ldrs: led gng wl over 1f out: shkn up to go clr fnl f: ct post* **7/4**[1]

60-0 **3** 3 **Bollin Fergus**[50] 931 3-8-4 59 oh1 DaleGibson 6 57
(T D Easterby) *bhd: rdn 1/2-way: hdwy wl over 1f out: kpt on fnl f: no ch w first two* **66/1**

3114 **4** ¾ **Pietersen (IRE)**[22] 1410 3-9-1 70 (b) PaulFessey 8 66
(T D Barron) *towards rr: hdwy and prom over 1f out: sn one pce* **10/1**

2-11 **5** 1 **Dressed To Dance (IRE)**[97] 478 3-8-11 66 (v[1]) RoystonFfrench 5 59
(N Tinkler) *t.k.h: in tch: nt clr run over 2f out to over 1f out: kpt on fnl f: no imp* **20/1**

44-5 **6** 2 **Celtic Change (IRE)**[22] 1403 3-9-1 70 PhillipMakin 4 58
(M Dods) *in tch: rdn whn n.m.r over 2f out: sn no imp* **8/1**[3]

0421 **7** 1 ½ **Pennyrock (IRE)**[16] 1558 3-8-7 62 GrahamGibbons 3 46
(J J Quinn) *cl up: ev ch 2f out: sn rdn and no ex* **8/1**[3]

-350 **8** nk **Bold Indian (IRE)**[17] 1531 3-8-13 68 (p) TonyHamilton 10 51
(I Semple) *chsd ldrs: ev ch over 2f out: wknd over 1f out* **9/1**

03-0 **9** 1 ½ **Charlie Tipple**[28] 1257 3-9-3 72 DavidAllan 13 51
(T D Easterby) *chsd ldrs: led over 2f out to over 1f out: sn wknd* **12/1**

-013 **10** ½ **Northern Dare (IRE)**[20] 1453 3-8-8 63 AdrianTNicholls 12 41
(D Nicholls) *t.k.h: hld up in tch: rdn over 2f out: sn wknd* **9/2**[2]

60-0 **11** 4 **Prince Rossi (IRE)**[35] 1108 3-9-4 73 PatCosgrave 1 40
(J D Bethell) *chsd ldrs tl rdn and wknd over 2f out* **80/1**

3-50 **12** 19 **Stepaside (IRE)**[13] 1625 3-8-7 65 (b[1]) GregFairley[(3)] 7 —
(M Johnston) *led to over 2f out: sn rdn and wknd* **28/1**

1m 28.76s (0.74) **Going Correction** +0.10s/f (Good) **12** Ran SP% **120.4**

Speed ratings (Par 99):99,98,95,94,93 91,89,89,87,86 82,60

CSF £43.93 CT £1938.19 TOTE £18.60: £4.10, £1.30, £10.00; EX 82.60 TRIFECTA Not won..

Owner J S Morrison **Bred** Hascombe And Valiant Studs **Trained** Uplawmoor, E Renfrews

FOCUS

A strange race with Royal Rock, who looked all over the winner when going clear, being claimed in a dramatic finish by Darfour. The winner, third and fourth were the last three at halfway. It has been rated through the third and fourth but the form looks less than cast-iron.

Dressed To Dance(IRE) Official explanation: jockey said filly was denied a clear run

Northern Dare(IRE) Official explanation: jockey said gelding ran too free

1966 NATS H'CAP 1m 4f 93y
4:05 (4:08) (Class 6) (0-60,60) 4-Y-O+ **£2,914** (£867; £433; £216) **Stalls** Centre

Form RPR

500- **1** **Fenners (USA)**[269] 4884 4-9-2 58 DaleGibson 14 69
(M W Easterby) *hld up: hdwy over 2f out: led 1f out: drvn and hld on wl* **6/1**[2]

00/0 **2** nk **Dance Sauvage**[12] 1671 4-8-6 48 DavidAllan 12 58
(C W Thornton) *hld up: hdwy over 2f out: chsd wnr ins fnl f: kpt on wl: jst hld* **40/1**

04-3 **3** 2 **Patavium (IRE)**[15] 1579 4-8-11 56 AndrewMullen[(3)] 3 63
(E W Tuer) *set decent gallop: hdd 1f out: kpt on same pce* **10/1**

0-00 **4** 1 **Fantastic Delight**[17] 1529 4-8-1 46 DuranFentiman[(3)] 11 51
(G M Moore) *hld up: hdwy to chse ldrs over 1f out: kpt on same pce fnl f* **28/1**

6615 **5** hd **Boppys Dancer**[10] 1717 4-8-8 50 (b) MickyFenton 4 55
(P T Midgley) *midfield: rdn 3f out: no imp fnl f* **28/1**

6/00 **6** 2 ½ **Silent Street**[15] 1579 4-8-4 46 oh1 PaulFessey 13 47
(K G Reveley) *bhd: rdn and hung rt over 4f out: swtchd rt and styd on wl fr over 1f out: nrst fin* **33/1**

60-0 **7** shd **Shekan Star**[28] 1258 5-8-4 53 DanielleMcCreery[(7)] 15 54
(K G Reveley) *missed break: bhd: hdwy ins 2f out: no imp fnl f* **18/1**

2301 **8** shd **Hugs Destiny (IRE)**[10] 1732 6-8-9 58 6ex (t) MCGeran[(7)] 8 59
(M A Barnes) *chsd ldrs: drvn over 2f out: sn no ex* **11/1**

4212 **9** hd **Diktatorship (IRE)**[10] 1732 4-8-8 50 TPO'Shea 5 50
(G A Swinbank) *trckd ldrs: effrt over 2f out: wknd over 1f out* **11/4**[1]

204/ **10** 1 ½ **Diamond Orchid (IRE)**[873] 6065 7-8-8 50 PaulMulrennan 7 48+
(G A Harker) *hld up in midfield: effrt whn nt clr run over 2f out to over 1f out: n.d* **28/1**

20-0 **11** ¾ **Knight Valliant**[22] 1406 4-8-11 53 PatCosgrave 9 50
(J Howard Johnson) *prom: drvn 3f out: wknd 2f out* **13/2**[3]

00-0 **12** 2 ½ **River Logic (IRE)**[15] 508 4-9-1 57 (p) SilvestreDeSousa 10 50
(A D Brown) *hld up: stdy hdwy over 4f out: rdn and wknd fr 3f out* **7/1**

04-0 **13** 2 **Peas 'n Beans (IRE)**[131] 121 4-8-6 48 FrancisNorton 16 38
(T Keddy) *midfield: effrt 3f out: wknd wl over 1f out* **10/1**

30-0 **14** hd **Just Waz (USA)**[25] 913 5-8-4 46 (v[1]) HayleyTurner 6 35
(R M Whitaker) *t.k.h: cl up tl rdn and wknd over 2f out* **12/1**

2m 42.67s (-0.88) **Going Correction** -0.025s/f (Good) **14** Ran SP% **122.0**

Speed ratings (Par 101):101,100,99,98,98 97,96,96,96,95 95,93,92,92

CSF £243.35 CT £2377.62 TOTE £9.40: £2.90, £10.30, £3.30; EX 283.40 TRIFECTA Not won..

Owner K Wreglesworth **Bred** Darley **Trained** Sheriff Hutton, N Yorks

FOCUS

This was just a moderate handicap, but the form has a solid feel to it overall despite the runner-up and fourth having shown nothing in maidens.

1967 MITIE H'CAP 1m 2f 32y
4:40 (4:42) (Class 6) (0-65,63) 4-Y-0+ £2,914 (£867; £433; £216) Stalls Centre

Form RPR
14-3 1 Royal Flynn[50] 928 5-9-2 61 PaulFessey 4 67+
(M Dods) hld up and bhd: gd hdwy 2f out: weaved through to ld ins fnl f: r.o 3/1[1]
326- 2 ½ Shiitake[262] 5063 4-9-1 60 DO'Donohoe 8 65
(Miss L A Perratt) hld up: gd hdwy to ld briefly ins fnl f: kpt on towards fin 16/1
2112 3 ¾ Jarvo[15] 1592 6-8-5 53 PatrickMathers(3) 5 57
(I W McInnes) hld up in tch: smooth hdwy and ev ch 2f out: kpt on same pce ins fnl f 7/1[2]
60-2 4 ½ Eijaaz (IRE)[16] 1554 6-8-8 53 RoystonFfrench 10 56
(G A Harker) midfield: hdwy to ld over 1f out: hdd and no ex ins fnl f 11/1
00-0 5 ½ Royal Citadel (IRE)[18] 1488 4-8-7 52 HayleyTurner 12 54
(Mrs L B Normile) hld up: effrt over 2f out: kpt on fnl f: no imp 50/1
160- 6 nk Rotuma (IRE)[223] 5954 8-8-8 53 (b) PhillipMakin 6 55
(M Dods) hld up in tch: effrt and ev ch ent fnl f: no ex 15/2[3]
465- 7 3½ Silver Sail[234] 5726 4-8-1 49 oh4 (p) DuranFentiman(3) 9 44
(J S Wainwright) hld up: hdwy and hung lft over 2f out: kpt on: no imp 66/1
00-4 8 shd Jordans Elect[18] 1488 7-9-1 63 MarkLawson(3) 13 58
(P Monteith) led to over 1f out: sn btn 10/1
5015 9 nk The Pen[17] 1532 5-9-0 59 PaulMulrennan 16 53
(C W Fairhurst) chsd ldrs tl rdn and no ex over 1f out 11/1
0460 10 1½ Wolds Way[17] 1532 5-9-2 61 (b) DavidAllan 14 52
(T D Easterby) hld up: effrt ins over 2f out: sn no imp 25/1
6-00 11 2 Soho Square[18] 1488 4-9-0 62 GregFairley(3) 11 49
(L Lungo) in tch tl drvn and wknd fr 3f out 25/1
0-00 12 nk Ruby Legend[22] 1416 9-8-11 56 (b) MickyFenton 2 43
(K G Reveley) hld up: drvn over 3f out: nvr rchd ldrs 12/1
0-00 13 13 Moonlight Fantasy (IRE)[21] 1435 4-8-4 49 oh1 KimTinkler 15 11
(N Tinkler) t.k.h: chsd ldrs tl wknd over 2f out 20/1
060- 14 1½ Motafarred (IRE)[290] 4203 5-9-4 63 PatCosgrave 17 22
(Micky Hammond) w ldr tl hung lft and wknd 2f out 33/1
66-4 15 2½ Musical Giant (USA)[20] 1455 4-8-7 52 TonyHamilton 7 7
(J Howard Johnson) hld up: drvn over 3f out: sn btn 16/1
36 16 ½ Rio (IRE)[23] 1385 5-9-0 62 AndrewElliott(3) 1 16
(J Balding) towards rr: drvn over 4f out: nvr on terms 9/1
17 43 My Causeway Dream (IRE)[260] 5121 4-8-10 55 GrahamGibbons 3 —
(J S Wainwright) plld hrd: in tch tl wknd 4f out: t.o 66/1

2m 11.02s (-0.78) **Going Correction** -0.025s/f (Good) 17 Ran SP% 124.8
Speed ratings (Par 101):102,101,101,100,100 99,97,97,96,95 94,93,83,82,80 79,45
CSF £52.53 CT £324.69 TOTE £4.20: £1.50, £4.60, £2.00, £3.00; EX 79.20 Trifecta £243.70 Part won. Pool: £343.29 - 0.34 winning units..
Owner J A Wynn-Williams **Bred** Highclere Stud Ltd **Trained** Denton, Co Durham

FOCUS
A competitive enough contest, run at a strong pace with the first two at the back of the field turning in. The winner did it quite nicely but the bare form is only modeest, rated through the third and fourth.

1968 CROFT TECHNOLOGY PLC MEDIAN AUCTION MAIDEN STKS 1m 4f 93y
5:15 (5:16) (Class 6) 3-4-Y-0 £2,266 (£674; £337; £168) Stalls Centre

Form RPR
04-4 1 Rock 'N' Roller (FR)[34] 1129 3-8-10 77 FrancisNorton 8 77+
(W R Muir) hld up: rdn 1/2-way: no imp tl hdwy over 2f out: led over 1f out: sn clr 8/13[1]
0-23 2 5 Spritza (IRE)[13] 1628 3-8-5 70 HayleyTurner 3 62
(M L W Bell) t.k.h: hld up: effrt over 2f out: styd on to chse wnr ins fnl f: no imp 3/1[2]
6 3 3 Flagstone (USA)[17] 1529 3-8-10 0 DaleGibson 4 62
(G A Swinbank) hld up in tch: rdn and outpcd 3f out: kpt on fnl f: no imp 12/1[3]
340- 4 ¾ Hunting Haze[51] 4884 4-9-13 57 MickyFenton 7 62
(Miss S E Hall) led to over 1f out: outpcd fnl f 20/1
46-6 5 3 Sendali (FR)[22] 1415 3-8-10 62 PatCosgrave 2 56
(J D Bethell) hld up in tch: effrt over 3f out: wknd over 2f out 12/1[3]
-05 6 3 Top Rocker[18] 1491 3-8-10 0 TonyHamilton 6 51
(E W Tuer) chsd ldrs tl rdn and wknd wl over 1f out 40/1
46-0 7 18 Miss Havisham (IRE)[52] 893 3-8-5 44 DO'Donohoe 10 18
(J R Weymes) chsd ldrs tl wknd fr 3f out 66/1
3-4 8 16 Lucky Find (IRE)[15] 1573 4-9-5 0 GregFairley(3) 5 —
(M Mullineaux) chsd ldrs to 1/2-way: sn rdn and btn 66/1

2m 43.72s (0.17) **Going Correction** -0.025s/f (Good)
WFA 3 from 4yo 17lb 8 Ran SP% 112.5
Speed ratings (Par 101):98,94,92,92,90 88,76,65
CSF £2.42 TOTE £1.70: £1.10, £1.30, £1.60; EX 3.00 Trifecta £10.20 Pool £880.52 - 60.95 winning units. Place 6 £31.80, Place 5 £19.82.
Owner D G Clarke & C L A Edginton **Bred** Eric Puerari, Oceanic Bloodstock Et Al **Trained** Lambourn, Berks
■ Stewards' Enquiry : Francis Norton caution: careless riding

FOCUS
A weak and uncompetitive maiden with six of the eight runners starting at 12-1 or longer. The market got it spot on and the winning time was about what you would expect, just over a second slower than the earlier handicap. The fourth looks the best guide.
T/Plt: £36.90 to a £1 stake. Pool: £60,592.05. 1,197.45 winning tickets. T/Qpdt: £38.80 to a £1 stake. Pool: £3,081.10. 58.70 winning tickets. RY

1781 SALISBURY (R-H)
Thursday, May 24

OFFICIAL GOING: Good to firm (good in places)
Wind: virtually nil

1969 BATHWICK TYRES LADY RIDERS' SERIES H'CAP 6f
6:10 (6:14) (Class 5) (0-70,70) 4-Y-0+ £3,123 (£968; £484; £242) Stalls High

Form RPR
-001 1 Stamford Blue[7] 1787 6-9-11 58 (b) MissFayeBramley 8 69
(R A Harris) chsd ldrs: chal 2f out: led appr fnl f: drvn out 13/2[2]
6050 2 1½ Ceredig[3] 1885 4-9-6 56 oh6 MrsMarieKing(3) 7 62
(P W Hiatt) pressed ldrs: chal fr 2f out and stl upsides over 1f out: kpt on same pce ins fnl f 25/1
00-0 3 ½ Roman Quintet (IRE)[18] 1507 7-9-10 62 MissABevan(5) 3 66
(R J Price) chsd ldrs: slt ld appr fnl 2f: hdd appr fnl f kpt on same pce 20/1
0-50 4 1½ Tamino (IRE)[12] 1669 4-9-7 59 MissVCartmel(5) 6 59
(H Morrison) chsd ldrs: pushed along fr 2f out: kpt on same pce ins fnl f 13/2[2]
3-02 5 ¾ Gracie's Gift (IRE)[18] 1507 5-10-1 62 (p) MissCHannaford 13 59
(A G Newcombe) s.i.s: sn mid-div: rdn 2f out: kpt on same pce fnl f 9/2[1]
6443 6 hd Digital[7] 1787 10-9-9 61 MissMichelleSaunders(5) 10 58+
(M R Channon) in rr tl str run appr fnl f: fin wl: nt rch ldrs 13/2[2]
0630 7 1¼ Arfinnit (IRE)[3] 1899 6-9-4 56 oh11 (p) MissHannahWatson(5) 11 49
(Mrs A L M King) chsd ldrs: pushed along and effrt over 1f out: sn one pce 50/1
6241 8 1 Imperium[16] 1564 6-9-11 65 MissJMHindle(7) 2 54
(Jean-Rene Auvray) wnt lft s: rr: hdwy over 1f out: kpt on but nt rch ldrs 12/1
0060 9 ½ Greenwood[2] 1931 9-10-3 64 MrsSMoore 17 52
(P G Murphy) in rr: hdwy 1/2-way: styd on fnl 2f but nvr gng pce to be competitive 10/1
-404 10 ¾ Chinalea (IRE)[19] 1465 5-10-2 68 (b[1]) MissJFerguson(5) 9 53
(C G Cox) rrd s: sn in tch: rdn over 2f out: wknd fnl f 9/1
4216 11 nk Over To You Bert[17] 8-9-4 56 oh3 MissZoeLilly(5) 12 40
(R J Hodges) towards rr: pushed along 1/2-way: nvr gng pce to be competitive 18/1
1011 12 1 Binnion Bay (IRE)[12] 1666 6-10-7 68 (b) MissLEllison 4 49
(J J Bridger) chsd ldrs over 4f 8/1[3]
-650 13 ¾ Montzando[3] 1899 4-9-2 56 oh6 MissDO'Brien(7) 15 35
(B R Millman) in rr: sme prog fnl 2f 16/1
60 14 ½ Spinetail Rufous (IRE)[76] 653 9-9-4 56 oh11 MissGDGracey-Davison(5) 16 33
(Miss Z C Davison) a towards rr 66/1
0000 15 ¾ Brandywell Boy (IRE)[3] 1885 4-10-2 70 MissJGeeson(7) 14 45
(D J S Ffrench Davis) outpcd 14/1
-600 16 4 Dancing Mystery[57] 810 13-9-13 67 (b) MissCNosworthy(7) 5 29
(E A Wheeler) led tl hdd & wknd qckly appr fnl f 33/1
040- 17 shd Summer Recluse (USA)[181] 6579 8-9-11 65 (t) MissHDavies(7) 1 27
(J M Bradley) wnt lft s: a outpcd 20/1

1m 15.17s (0.19) **Going Correction** +0.125s/f (Good) 17 Ran SP% 133.7
Speed ratings (Par 103):103,101,100,98,97 97,95,94,93,92 92,90,89,89,88 82,82
CSF £178.85 CT £3155.99 TOTE £7.60: £1.80, £6.50, £6.50, £2.30; EX 249.20.
Owner Brian Hicks **Bred** Mrs Wendy Miller **Trained** Earlswood, Monmouths
■ Stewards' Enquiry : Mrs S Moore two-day ban: careless riding (Jun 8-9)

FOCUS
A moderate lady riders' handicap. They headed towards the far side in the early stages, but the principals made their move more towards the centre of the track. The winning time was 1.39 seconds slower than the 71-85 handicap, but 0.25 seconds faster than the later fillies' maiden. The form looks solid despite the runner-up being 6lb wrong.

1970 "COME SHOPPING AT CASTLEPOINT" DOUGLAND SUPPORT SERVICES E B F MAIDEN STKS 5f
6:40 (6:40) (Class 4) 2-Y-0 £4,533 (£1,348; £674; £336) Stalls High

Form RPR
6 1 Stage Acclaim (IRE)[17] 1540 2-9-3 OscarUrbina 11 76+
(B R Millman) trcking ldrs whn nt clr run ins fnl 2f and sn swtchd sharply lft: rapid hdwy fnl f: led last stride 5/1[3]
2 shd Ramona Chase 2-9-3 DPMcDonogh 3 76
(S Kirk) front rnk tl led over 3f out: shkn up 2f and kpt on: rn wl fnl f: ct last stride 9/2[2]
3 ½ Hansinger (IRE) 2-9-0 RichardKingscote(3) 8 74
(B I Case) s.i.s: bhd: hdwy over 2f out: styd on wl fr over 1f out to chse ldr ins fnl f but a jst hld 66/1
0 4 1½ Ramblin Bob[17] 1540 2-9-3 JamesDoyle 10 68
(R M Beckett) pressed ldrs to 1/2-way: ridedn and swtchd lft over 1f out: one pce ins fnl f 16/1
5 1¼ Menadha (USA) 2-9-3 JHBowman 4 64
(M R Channon) slt ld tl over 3f out: styd pressing ldrs and rdn 2f out: outpcd ins fnl f 9/2[2]
6 nk Maybe I Will (IRE) 2-8-12 PatDobbs 2 58
(R Hannon) chsd ldrs: rdn over 2f out: outpcd fnl f 11/1
4 7 shd Straight And Level (CAN)[15] 1586 2-9-3 EddieAhern 6 63
(J W Hills) towards rr: drvn 1/2-way: kpt on fnl f but nvr gng pce to rch ldrs 17/2
8 ½ Stubbs Art (IRE) 2-9-0 MarcHalford(3) 1 61
(D R C Elsworth) in rr: pushed along 1/2-way: sme prog fnl f 20/1
6 9 ¾ What Katie Did (IRE)[7] 1781 2-9-3 IanMongan 9 58
(J A Osborne) trckd ldrs: n.m.r 2f out: sn rdn and effrt: nvr quite gng pce to rch ldrs: wknd ins fnl f 11/4[1]
10 shd Flying Applause 2-9-3 FergusSweeney 7 58
(A King) s.i.s and bmpd s: bhd: sme prog fr over 1f out 20/1
11 nk Maybe I Wont 2-9-3 PaulFitzsimons 5 57
(S Dow) s.i.s: outpcd most of way 66/1
12 nk Fervent Prince 2-9-3 SteveDrowne 12 55
(H Morrison) s.i.s: outpcd 16/1

62.55 secs (0.96) **Going Correction** +0.125s/f (Good) 12 Ran SP% 122.8
Speed ratings (Par 95):97,96,96,93,91 91,91,90,89,88 88,87
CSF £27.90 TOTE £9.50: £2.80, £2.70, £18.10; EX 67.20.
Owner You Boyz Is Lost **Bred** Oaks Stud **Trained** Kentisbeare, Devon
■ Stewards' Enquiry : Oscar Urbina caution: careless riding

FOCUS
The bare form of this juvenile maiden looks just ordinary, but a few interesting types lined up and the race should produce some winners. Quite a rough race, though, with these quite tightly bunched towards the far side, and several having to switch out for a run.

NOTEBOOK
Stage Acclaim(IRE) improved on the form he showed on his debut in just an ordinary maiden at Windsor with a narrow success. His effort is particularly creditable considering he lost a good early position after being short of room through the early stages and had to switch out widest of all with his challenge. He is seemingly held in quite high regard and could take in one of the juvenile races at Royal Ascot, as well as the Super Sprint. (op 6-1 tchd 13-2)
Ramona Chase ◆, a 90,000gns purchase, by High Chaparral, out of a very smart triple 1m-1m2f winner at three in France, made a most encouraging debut and looks a horse with a future. Quite clearly bred to be suited by middle-distances in time, he could have been expected to be run off his feet early, but he showed surprisingly good speed from the outset. He was also very green, though, not helping his chances by carrying his head at quite an ungainly angle, and continually looking around, taking in the new experience. Despite that, he kept responding to pressure when asked and ultimately just failed by the narrowest of margins. It will have to be hoped this experience does not have a negative effect, as he by no means had an easy race but, provided he goes the right way, he looks capable of developing into a very useful type. (op 11-4 tchd 5-1)

Hansinger(IRE), a 24,000gns Namid, is already a gelding, but this was a pleasing introduction. He stayed on well against the far rail and could have even more to offer when there is some cut in the ground.
Ramblin Bob could not reverse Windsor form with Stage Acclaim, but this was a respectable effort nonetheless. He showed plenty of dash and may be suited by a quicker track. Official explanation: jockey said colt hung let-handed in final 2f (tchd 18-1)
Menadha(USA), a $150,000 half-brother to useful Queen's Love, a dual 7f-1m winner at two and three, showed good speed but could not sustain his challenge late on. He should last a bit longer next time. (tchd 11-2)
Maybe I Will(IRE), the first foal of an unraced sister to high-class juvenile Chevalier, lacked the pace to pose a threat and is almost sure to benefit from a step up in trip. (op 9-1 tchd 12-1)
Straight And Level(CAN), fourth on his debut at Kempton, did not get the best of trips and never posed a threat. (op 12-1 tchd 15-2)
Stubbs Art(IRE), a 30,000gns first foal of a mare who was placed over 1m2f, struggled to stay in touch early on and was not given too hard a time once it was clear his chance was gone. He clearly wants further and should leave this form behind in time. (tchd 25-1)
What Katie Did(IRE) failed to build on the form he showed on his debut over course and distance the previous week, but this was a rough race and it would be unfair to be too harsh. (op 6-1 tchd 5-2)

1971 "COME SHOPPING AT CASTLEPOINT" K J PIKE & SONS LTD H'CAP 6f

7:10 (7:11) (Class 4) (0-85,85) 4-Y-0+ **£6,477** (£1,927; £963; £481) **Stalls** High

Form RPR
00-1 **1** **Orpsie Boy (IRE)**[34] [1121] 4-9-1 **82** JHBowman 9 95
(N P Littmoden) *in rr: hdwy fr 2f out: drvn to ld jst ins fnl f: r.o strly* **13/2**[1]
52-0 **2** 1 3/4 **Third Set (IRE)**[12] [1653] 4-9-4 **85** SteveDrowne 4 92
(R Charlton) *towards rr: hdwy on outside whn pushed lft ins fnl 2f: str run fr over 1f out: chsd wnr ins fnl f: no imp* **14/1**
-006 **3** 1/2 **Blue Tomato**[5] [1852] 6-8-13 **80** DarryllHolland 12 87+
(J M Bradley) *in rr: hdwy whn nt clr run 2f out tl hdwy over 1f out: kpt on wl fnl f but nt pce to chal* **15/2**[2]
4332 **4** shd **Adantino**[17] [1545] 8-8-11 **78** (b) JimCrowley 5 83
(B R Millman) *in rr: stl plenty to do 2f out: gd hdwy appr fnl f: fin wl* **12/1**
5-10 **5** 2 **Forest Dane**[12] [1653] 7-9-1 **82** JamesDoyle 6 81
(Mrs N Smith) *hdwy on outside whn pushed lft 2f out: styd on fnl f but nvr quite gng pce to chal* **14/1**
1620 **6** nk **Lucayos**[24] [1357] 4-8-6 **80** KylieManser(7) 15 78
(Mrs H Sweeting) *chsd ldrs: hdwy and veered rt ins fnl 2f: kpt on to chse ldrs 1f out: wknd last half f* **25/1**
00-0 **7** hd **Golden Dixie (USA)**[19] [1464] 8-8-13 **85** TolleyDean(5) 1 82
(R A Harris) *in rr: hdwy over 1f out: kpt on ins fnl f* **22/1**
20-0 **8** 1 **Blues In The Night (IRE)**[5] [1845] 4-8-13 **80** PatDobbs 8 74
(P J Makin) *in rr: drvn 2f out: hdwy fnl f: kpt on* **16/1**
-104 **9** nk **Border Music**[53] [867] 6-8-11 **83** (b) WilliamBuick(5) 3 76
(A M Balding) *trckd ldr tl led over 3f out: rdn and hdd jst ins fnl f: sn wknd* **15/2**[2]
0-14 **10** nk **Roman Maze**[12] [1682] 7-9-2 **83** TedDurcan 13 75+
(W M Brisbourne) *in tch: hdwy on rails whn bdly hmpd ins fnl 2f: nt rcvr but kpt on fnl f* **10/1**
612- **11** 1 **Don Pele (IRE)**[145] [6984] 5-9-1 **82** RobertHavlin 11 71
(P D Evans) *in tch effrt whn pushed lft 2f out: styd on same pce fr over 1f out* **16/1**
-030 **12** 1/2 **Phantom Whisper**[12] [1653] 4-9-4 **85** JimmyFortune 7 72+
(B R Millman) *in rr: hdwy on ins whn hmpd over 1f out: n.d after* **8/1**[3]
-403 **13** 1 **Peter Island (FR)**[14] [1607] 4-8-9 **79** JerryO'Dwyer(3) 17 63
(J Gallagher) *led tl hdd over 3f out: wknd appr fnl f* **20/1**
4-03 **14** 3/4 **Pic Up Sticks**[19] [1464] 8-9-0 **83** RichardKingscote(3) 16 66
(B G Powell) *chsd ldrs: rdn 2f out: wknd appr fnl f* **9/1**
00-0 **15** 2 1/2 **Russian Symphony (USA)**[17] [1545] 6-8-13 **80** (b) EddieAhern 18 54
(C R Egerton) *chsd ldrs: rdn and one pce whn hmpd on ins over 1f out: sn wknd* **22/1**
3-40 **16** hd **Briannsta (IRE)**[103] [419] 5-8-11 **78** AdamKirby 2 51
(C G Cox) *chsd ldrs: rdn and pushed lft 2f out: wknd sn after* **16/1**
053- **17** 2 1/2 **Scarlet Knight**[278] [4591] 4-8-4 **78** JackMitchell(7) 10 43
(P Mitchell) *chsd ldrs: wnt sharply lft 2f out: one pce whn hmpd and wknd over 1f out* **33/1**
600- **18** 7 **Jalamid (IRE)**[236] [5677] 5-9-4 **85** StephenCarson 14 28
(G C Bravery) *early spd: sn bhd* **25/1**

1m 13.78s (-1.20) **Going Correction** +0.125s/f (Good) **18** Ran SP% **129.8**
Speed ratings (Par 105):113,110,110,109,107 106,106,105,104,104 103,102,101,100,96 96,93,83
CSF £91.30 CT £743.34 TOTE £8.30: £2.50, £4.20, £2.10, £2.80; EX 158.90.
Owner Miss Vanessa Church **Bred** Minch Bloodstock **Trained** Newmarket, Suffolk
■ Stewards' Enquiry : Kylie Manser three-day ban: careless riding (Jun 4-6)

FOCUS
A good sprint handicap and strong form for the grade, with a career best from Orpsie Boy. Like the previous juvenile contest, a rough race with most of these trying to get a good position somewhere near the far rail. The leaders went off too quickly and set this up for the closers. The winning time was 1.39 seconds faster than the opening lady riders' handicap, and 1.64 seconds quicker than the later fillies' maiden.

1972 "COME SHOPPING AT CASTLEPOINT" ICE H'CAP 1m 4f

7:40 (7:41) (Class 6) (0-65,64) 3-Y-O **£3,238** (£963; £481; £240) **Stalls** High

Form RPR
000- **1** **Sumner (IRE)**[204] [6290] 3-9-4 **64** JimmyQuinn 6 73+
(M H Tompkins) *trckd ldrs: drvn to ld 2f out: hld on u.p ins fnl f* **8/1**[2]
004- **2** 1 **Calzaghe (IRE)**[194] [6447] 3-8-6 **57** (v[1]) WilliamBuick(5) 9 62
(A M Balding) *hld up in rr: plenty to do whn swtchd lft to outside over 2f out and hung rt: str run fr over 1f out: fin strly: nt rch wnr* **12/1**
50-0 **3** 2 1/2 **Proposal**[31] [1205] 3-8-9 **55** JamesDoyle 14 56
(A W Carroll) *in tch: hdwy 2f out: rdn and wnt sharply lft wl over 1f out: chsd ldrs but one pce fnl f* **33/1**
0-62 **4** hd **Linlithgow (IRE)**[30] [1224] 3-8-9 **55** EddieAhern 12 56
(J L Dunlop) *chsd ldrs: hrd drvn fr 2f out: styd on same pce ins fnl f* **9/2**[1]
0-32 **5** nk **Chiff Chaff**[17] [1536] 3-9-3 **63** DarryllHolland 8 64
(M L W Bell) *sn led: hdd 2f out: wknd ins fnl f* **9/2**[1]
04-0 **6** 1 **Last Flight (IRE)**[36] [1092] 3-9-1 **61** IanMongan 1 60
(J L Dunlop) *in rr and racd on outer: rdn 4f out: styd on fnl 2f but nvr gng pce to rch ldrs* **20/1**
65-0 **7** 3/4 **Disintegration (IRE)**[10] [1724] 3-9-4 **64** FergusSweeney 10 62
(A King) *rowards rr: sme hdwy whn hmpd wl over 1f out: styd on ins fnl f: but nvr in contention* **11/1**[3]
00-0 **8** 1 1/2 **Lightning Queen (USA)**[31] [1205] 3-8-10 **56** TedDurcan 13 51
(B W Hills) *towards rr tl hdwy 5f out: nvr gng pce to trble ldrs and one pce fnl 2f* **16/1**
000- **9** 2 1/2 **Pagan Rules (IRE)**[262] [5053] 3-9-4 **64** (b[1]) JimCrowley 4 55
(Mrs A J Perrett) *sn chsng ldr: chal fr over 4f out tl over 2f out: wknd appr fnl f* **25/1**
1033 **10** hd **It's No Problem (IRE)**[13] [1637] 3-8-9 **55** DavidKinsella 3 46
(M Salaman) *in rr tl hdwy 3f out: nvr quite gng pce to rch ldrs whn n.m.r wl over 1f out: sn btn* **8/1**[2]
00-0 **11** 3/4 **Down The Brick (IRE)**[64] [719] 3-9-3 **63** (b[1]) OscarUrbina 7 53
(B R Millman) *racd towards outside: hdwy to chse ldrs 6f out: wkng whn hmpd wl over 1f out: eased whn no ch ins fnl f* **16/1**
06-0 **12** 1 1/2 **Dr Light (IRE)**[31] [1204] 3-8-13 **59** LPKeniry 11 46
(S Kirk) *in tch early: towards rr fr 1/2-way* **40/1**
62-0 **13** 3/4 **Regal Ovation**[33] [1154] 3-8-12 **58** SteveDrowne 2 44
(W R Muir) *chsd ldrs: rdn and wkng whn bdly hmpd wl over 1f out* **20/1**
0033 **14** 14 **Marju's Gold**[17] [1536] 3-8-13 **59** JHBowman 5 23
(E J O'Neill) *t.k.h: hdwy to chse ldrs 4f out: wknd 2f out* **9/2**[1]

2m 38.95s (2.59) **Going Correction** +0.125s/f (Good) **14** Ran SP% **123.3**
Speed ratings (Par 97):96,95,93,93,93 92,92,91,89,89 88,87,87,78
CSF £95.69 CT £3020.55 TOTE £11.10: £3.10, £3.40, £14.30; EX 144.50.
Owner Mrs Beryl Lockey **Bred** Liam Ormsby **Trained** Newmarket, Suffolk
■ Stewards' Enquiry : James Doyle three-day ban: careless riding (Jun 7-9)
Eddie Ahern two-day ban: used whip with excessive frequency (Jun 5-6)

FOCUS
Just a modest middle-distance handicap, but the form looks solid with a pair of improvers coming clear of more exposed third, fourth and fifth.
Marju's Gold Official explanation: jockey said colt had run too freely

1973 "COME SHOPPING AT CASTLEPOINT" EMPRISE SERVICES PLC MAIDEN FILLIES' STKS 6f

8:10 (8:12) (Class 4) 3-Y-O+ **£4,857** (£1,445; £722; £360) **Stalls** High

Form RPR
2-00 **1** **Cartimandua**[18] [1496] 3-8-12 94 JimmyFortune 5 78+
(E S McMahon) *mde all: eased clr fnl 2f: v easily* **1/4**[1]
40-0 **2** 6 **Rogue**[88] [561] 5-9-7 57 LPKeniry 8 55
(Jane Southcombe) *in rr but in tch: hdwy fr 2f out: chsd wnr ins fnl f but nvr the remotest ch: hld on wl for 2nd* **16/1**
6/ **3** 1/2 **Exotic Venture**[535] [6502] 4-9-7 GeorgeBaker 2 53
(R M Beckett) *s.i.s: bhd: hdwy whn hmpd appr fnl f: swtchd lft and fin wl to take modest 3rd last strides* **25/1**
0 **4** nk **Rhapsilian**[61] [752] 3-8-12 RichardThomas 1 50
(J A Geake) *s.i.s and swtchd rt: hdwy 1/2-way: chsd ldrs 2f out but nvr nr easy wnr: one pce and lost 3rd last strides* **50/1**
4 **5** 1/2 **Glencal**[17] [1541] 3-8-12 SteveDrowne 7 49
(H Morrison) *t.k.h: chsd wnr to 1f out: sn wknd* **10/1**[2]
-005 **6** 1 1/2 **Night Falcon**[24] [1353] 3-8-12 45 JHBowman 4 44
(H Morrison) *chsd ldrs: rdn 2f out: wknd over 1f out* **25/1**
45-0 **7** 1 3/4 **To Party (IRE)**[13] [1620] 3-8-12 70 RobertHavlin 9 38
(P D Evans) *chsd ldrs: rdn 2f out: wknd appr fnl f* **14/1**[3]
0- **8** 11 **New Light**[239] [5622] 3-8-12 StephenCarson 3 3
(Eve Johnson Houghton) *chsd ldrs 4f* **22/1**

1m 15.42s (0.44) **Going Correction** +0.125s/f (Good)
WFA 3 from 4yo+ 9lb **8** Ran SP% **115.6**
Speed ratings (Par 102):102,94,93,92,92 90,87,73
CSF £5.38 TOTE £1.20: £1.02, £3.30, £4.30; EX 7.70.
Owner Mrs Fiona Williams **Bred** Mrs F S Williams **Trained** Lichfield, Staffs

FOCUS
Basically a one-horse race and the form is not worth dwelling on. The winning time was 1.64 seconds slower than the earlier 71-85 handicap, and 0.25 seconds slower than the opening lady riders' contest.
Exotic Venture Official explanation: jockey said filly had been unlucky in running
New Light Official explanation: jockey said filly hung right-handed

1974 "COME SHOPPING AT CASTLEPOINT" A3060 BOURNEMOUTH H'CAP 1m 1f 198y

8:40 (8:43) (Class 4) (0-80,80) 3-Y-O **£5,181** (£1,541; £770; £384) **Stalls** High

Form RPR
053- **1** **Camps Bay (USA)**[226] [5886] 3-8-11 **73** JimCrowley 11 80+
(Mrs A J Perrett) *hld up in tch: stdy hdwy fr 2f out: n.m.r over 1f out: qcknd to ld ins fnl f: kpt on strly* **16/1**
213 **2** nk **Warm Embraces (IRE)**[34] [1122] 3-8-10 **75** MarcHalford(3) 12 80
(D R C Elsworth) *in tch: hdwy over 2f out: drvn and str chal ins fnl f: no ex cl home* **7/2**[1]
3-1 **3** nk **Small Fortune**[22] [1409] 3-9-0 **76** SteveDrowne 13 80
(R Charlton) *chsd ldrs: chal u.p over 1f out tl led jst ins fnl f: sn hdd: kpt on same pce* **4/1**[2]
003- **4** 1/2 **Furmigadelagiusta**[265] [4992] 3-9-1 **77** NickyMackay 9 80
(L M Cumani) *led: hld slt advantage fr over 3f out: rdn 2f out: hdd jst ins fnl f: one pce* **14/1**
34-3 **5** 1/2 **Sunley Peace**[10] [1724] 3-8-9 **74** RichardKingscote(3) 3 76
(D R C Elsworth) *chsd ldrs and racd on outside: rdn over 2f out: kpt on fnl f but nt qckn nr fin* **4/1**[2]
00-3 **6** nk **Colonel Flay**[18] [1504] 3-8-6 **68** ow2 RobertHavlin 5 69
(Mrs P N Dutfield) *hld up in rr: hdwy and nt much fr fr 2f out: kpt on fnl f but nvr gng pce to rch ldrs* **20/1**
6-1 **7** 1 **Noojoom (IRE)**[124] [193] 3-9-0 **76** PatDobbs 4 75
(M P Tregoning) *chsd ldrs: rdn over 2f out: kpt on same pce appr fnl f* **6/1**[3]
61-0 **8** hd **Sam Lord**[31] [1202] 3-9-4 **80** JimmyFortune 2 79
(J H M Gosden) *trckd ldrs tl wnt upsides fr 5f out: rdn to chal fr 2f out: no ex and wknd ins fnl f* **6/1**[3]
41- **9** 3 **Zefooha (FR)**[301] [3868] 3-8-13 **75** JHBowman 8 68
(M R Channon) *in tch: rdn and effrt over 2f out: nvr quite gng pce to rch ldrs: wknd appr fnl f* **16/1**
640- **10** 3 1/2 **Altar (IRE)**[253] [5293] 3-9-1 **77** TedDurcan 7 63
(R Hannon) *in rr: sme hdwy on outside over 2f out: nvr rch ldrs and sn btn* **33/1**
0-4P **11** shd **Lights Of Vegas**[24] [1359] 3-8-13 **75** BrettDoyle 10 61
(B J Meehan) *towards rr most of way* **33/1**
34-0 **12** 1/2 **Aypeeyes (IRE)**[10] [1722] 3-8-9 **71** FrankieMcDonald 14 56
(S Kirk) *towards rr most of way* **40/1**

640- **13** 1 ¼ **Christalini**[219] 6023 3-9-0 **76** ... RichardSmith 1 58
(J C Fox) *towards rr most of way* **66/1**

2m 12.5s (4.04) **Going Correction** +0.125s/f (Good) 13 Ran SP% **123.8**
Speed ratings (Par 101):88,87,87,87,86 86,85,85,83,80 80,79,78
CSF £71.15 CT £281.32 TOTE £24.20: £5.30, £2.20, £2.10; EX 146.90 Place 6 £517.87, Place 5 £133.52.
Owner Mr & Mrs R Scott **Bred** Kidder,Cole,Marnakos,Graves & Beck **Trained** Pulborough, W Sussex

FOCUS
A messy contest, mainly due to there being no pace on at all early, and it developed into a four-furlong sprint. A large blanket would have covered the first six at the line and not surprisingly the winning time was very moderate for a race of its type. The form is hard to rate any more positively, but the first three are all improvers.
T/Plt: £985.00 to a £1 stake. Pool: £72,259.65. 53.55 winning tickets. T/Qpdt: £199.50 to a £1 stake. Pool: £4,664.40. 17.30 winning tickets. ST

1932 SOUTHWELL (L-H)
Thursday, May 24

OFFICIAL GOING: Standard
After the extended dry spell the surface was again reckoned to be riding on the slow side. The track was watered after each of the first three races.
Wind: Light 1/2 behind Weather: Fine, sunny and wam at first

1975 WELCOME TO THE PARTY IN THE PADDOCK MAIDEN AUCTION STKS 5f (F)
6:20 (6:20) (Class 5) 2-Y-O **£3,886** (£1,156; £577; £288) **Stalls** High

Form RPR
2 **1** **Diademas (USA)**[12] 1680 2-8-11 0 ... TPQueally 4 79+
(J A Osborne) *mde all: clr over 1f out: unchal* **11/8**[1]
3 **2** 5 **Carrickmacross (IRE)**[10] 1713 2-8-11 0 ... RichardMullen 6 61
(E S McMahon) *chsd ldrs: sn drvn along: styd on to take 2nd ins fnl f: no ch w wnr* **7/4**[2]
06 **3** nk **No Nines**[17] 1519 2-9-2 0 ... DaneO'Neill 5 65
(B W Hills) *sn chsng ldrs: rdn 2f out: kpt on same pce* **20/1**
4 15 **Kamal** 2-8-13 0 ... NCallan 2 8
(K A Ryan) *chsd ldrs: edgd lft and lost pl over 1f out: sn bhd* **4/1**[3]
5 2 **Seconds Out (IRE)** 2-8-13 0 ... JamieMackay 1 —
(Sir Mark Prescott) *dwlt: swvd lft s: sn detached in last* **16/1**
356 **6** 1 ¾ **Miss Willoughby**[29] 1235 2-8-4 0 ... ChrisCatlin 3 —
(J Ryan) *chsd ldrs: edgd lft and lost pl after 2f: sn bhd* **50/1**

59.40 secs (-0.90) **Going Correction** -0.35s/f (Stan) 6 Ran SP% **111.1**
Speed ratings (Par 93):93,85,84,60,57 54
CSF £3.93 TOTE £2.70: £1.40, £1.30; EX 3.60.
Owner Raymond Tooth **Bred** Carlos Perez **Trained** Upper Lambourn, Berks

FOCUS
The winner had clearly learnt plenty and was much too good for the weakish opposition. It is hard to gauge the merit of this, it being doubtful whether the third has improved as much as this suggests.

NOTEBOOK
Diademas(USA), a sharp type, really knew his job this time and came right away. The plan is to run him again soon under a penalty in a novices' event. (op 13-8 tchd 5-4)
Carrickmacross(IRE), who swished his tail in the paddock, is still learning the ropes and stayed on in encouraging fashion to claim second spot. A step up to six will be in his favour. (op 7-2)
No Nines, having his third outing, was left for dead by the winner and in the end even missed out on second spot. (op 14-1)
Kamal, a January foal, is a half-brother to five winners. A close-coupled individual, he moved very scratchily to post and, after showing good speed, edged markedly left and dropped right away. (op 11-4 tchd 9-2)
Seconds Out(IRE), a February foal, stands over plenty of ground. He showed a round action and was soon a long way behind. Even this trainer will have little difficulty getting this fellow into handicaps from a low mark. (op 8-1)

1976 3RD JUNE FAMILY FUN DAY MEDIAN AUCTION MAIDEN STKS 6f (F)
6:50 (6:50) (Class 5) 3-4-Y-O **£3,238** (£963; £481; £240) **Stalls** Low

Form RPR
0-4 **1** **Gold Flame**[15] 1587 4-9-9 0 ... DaneO'Neill 7 64
(H Candy) *trckd ldrs: led over 1f out: styd on strly* **5/4**[1]
0- **2** 3 ½ **Six Of Trumps (IRE)**[300] 3892 3-9-0 0 ... TPQueally 6 51
(J A Osborne) *trckd ldr: led over 2f out: hung lft and hdd over 1f out: kpt on same pce* **7/1**
26-0 **3** 1 **Mister Jingles**[14] 1594 4-9-4 44 ... MichaelJStainton(5) 4 50
(R M Whitaker) *chsd ldrs: kpt on same pce fnl 2f* **20/1**
4 nk **Morbick** 3-9-0 0 ... JoeFanning 3 47
(M Johnston) *dwlt: sn chsng ldrs: outpcd 3f out: hdwy on wd outside over 1f out: kpt on wl: improve* **7/2**[2]
40- **5** 1 ¼ **Gleaming Spirit (IRE)**[234] 5735 3-9-0 0 ... NCallan 1 43
(A P Jarvis) *led tl over 2f out: edgd lft over 1f out: sn fdd* **11/2**[3]
3560 **6** 11 **Splendidio**[103] 417 3-8-9 48 ... PaulQuinn 2 3
(Mrs Marjorie Fife) *chsd ldrs: lost pl over 2f out* **28/1**
36 **7** ½ **Singleb (IRE)**[27] 1278 3-9-0 0 ... ChrisCatlin 5 6
(T D Barron) *sn outpcd and in rr: swtchd wd over 4f out: sn detached: kpt on fnl 2f: nvr on terms* **9/1**
8 63 **Lord Of The Reins (IRE)** 3-8-11 0 ... SaleemGolam(3) 8 —
(D Shaw) *t.k.h to post: swvd rt s: sn trcking ldrs on outer: lost pl over 3f out: t.o 2f out: virtually p.u* **33/1**

1m 16.33s (-0.57) **Going Correction** -0.125s/f (Stan)
WFA 3 from 4yo 9lb 8 Ran SP% **115.7**
Speed ratings (Par 103):98,93,92,91,89 75,74,—
CSF £10.70 TOTE £2.20: £1.10, £2.30, £4.80; EX 16.70.
Owner Girsonfield Ltd **Bred** R W Huggins **Trained** Kingston Warren, Oxon

FOCUS
A weak spint maiden with the third rated just 44. An easy task for Gold Flame.
Gleaming Spirit(IRE) Official explanation: jockey said gelding ran green hanging both ways

1977 BARBARA & RICHARD YOUNG SILVER WEDDING ANNIVERSARY H'CAP 6f (F)
7:20 (7:20) (Class 4) (0-80,77) 3-Y-O+ **£6,477** (£1,927; £963; £481) **Stalls** Low

Form RPR
0111 **1** **Whitbarrow (IRE)**[10] 1718 8-9-2 **73** 6ex ... (b) JamesMillman(5) 5 88+
(B R Millman) *w ldr: led over 2f out: hld on towards fin* **6/4**[1]
44-0 **2** nk **Rosein**[57] 810 5-9-9 **75** ... JoeFanning 10 87
(Mrs G S Rees) *hld up in tch on outside: effrt 2f out: edgd lft and wnt 2nd ins fnl f: kpt on towards fin* **14/1**
6300 **3** 1 ½ **Figaro Flyer (IRE)**[14] 1607 4-9-11 **77** ... ChrisCatlin 9 84
(P Howling) *chsd ldrs: styd on same pce fnl f* **7/1**
0223 **4** 3 ½ **Effective**[29] 1252 7-9-10 **76** ... NCallan 4 72
(A P Jarvis) *chsd ldrs: effrt on outer over 2f out: n.m.r 1f out: kpt on same pce* **14/1**
5000 **5** ¾ **Pawan (IRE)**[9] 1754 7-9-5 **76** ... (b) AnnStokell(5) 8 70
(Miss A Stokell) *sn outpcd and bhd: hdwy 2f out: kpt on wl fnl f* **16/1**
2112 **6** 1 ¼ **Count Cougar (USA)**[16] 1565 7-9-8 **74** ... AdrianTNicholls 3 64
(S P Griffiths) *led tl over 2f out: wknd fnl f* **9/2**[2]
0214 **7** 1 **Owed**[2] 1935 5-9-7 **73** ... (p) StephenDonohoe 2 59
(R Bastiman) *chsd ldrs: outpcd and lost pl over 3f out: kpt on fnl f* **9/1**
5511 **8** 1 **Cool Sands (IRE)**[2] 1935 5-9-10 **76** 6ex ... (v) DaneO'Neill 7 59
(D Shaw) *in rr-div: drvn over 3f out: nvr nr ldrs* **5/1**[3]
2-00 **9** 8 **Tag Team (IRE)**[10] 1718 6-9-1 **67** ... (b) TPQueally 1 25
(John A Harris) *chsd ldrs on ins: lost pl over 1f out: sn bhd* **33/1**
21- **10** 3 ½ **Tilly's Dream**[274] 4691 4-9-3 **72** ... SaleemGolam(3) 6 18
(P S McEntee) *chsd ldrs: lost pl over 3f out: sn bhd* **25/1**

1m 15.51s (-1.39) **Going Correction** -0.125s/f (Stan) 10 Ran SP% **123.4**
Speed ratings (Par 105):104,103,101,96,95 94,92,91,80,76
CSF £28.25 CT £129.40 TOTE £2.20: £1.70, £3.10, £3.20; EX 29.70.
Owner Mrs H Brain **Bred** James Burns And A Moynan **Trained** Kentisbeare, Devon

FOCUS
The form looks rock solid and Whitbarrow, who confirmed his recent resurgence, may not be finished yet.
Pawan(IRE) Official explanation: jockey said gelding was slow into stride

1978 SOUTHWELL-RACECOURSE.CO.UK H'CAP 7f (F)
7:50 (7:50) (Class 4) (0-80,77) 3-Y-O **£6,477** (£1,927; £963; £481) **Stalls** Low

Form RPR
62-0 **1** **Radical Views**[38] 1062 3-8-13 **72** ... DaneO'Neill 9 89
(B W Hills) *trckd ldrs: led over 2f out: styd on wl fnl f: drvn rt out* **14/1**
441 **2** 1 ¾ **Gold Digger Miss (USA)**[32] 1175 3-8-8 **67** ... TPQueally 7 80
(J Noseda) *s.i.s: sn chsng ldrs: chal over 2f out: styd on same pce ins fnl f* **9/4**[1]
1561 **3** 5 **Divertimenti (IRE)**[42] 1008 3-8-13 **72** ... (p) EdwardCreighton 2 71
(C R Dore) *t.k.h: trckd ldrs: effrt over 2f out: kpt on to take 3rd ins fnl f* **14/1**
0-46 **4** 1 ½ **Chjimes (IRE)**[14] 1603 3-9-0 **73** ... NCallan 5 68
(K R Burke) *chsd ldrs: edgd lft 2f out: one pce* **10/1**
1322 **5** 1 ¼ **Sheriff's Silk**[32] 1176 3-8-13 **72** ... (b) PaulEddery 8 64
(B Smart) *drvn to ld after 1f: hdd over 2f out: wknd over 1f out* **4/1**[3]
2110 **6** 6 **Proper (IRE)**[14] 1603 3-8-8 **67** ... ChrisCatlin 3 42
(M R Channon) *chsd ldrs: drvn and lost pl over 3f out* **13/2**
3031 **7** 5 **Jord (IRE)**[21] 1437 3-8-7 **73** ... MCGeran(7) 1 35
(A J McCabe) *t.k.h in rr: effrt over 3f out: sn btn* **28/1**
01- **8** 6 **Ben Chorley**[239] 5614 3-9-4 **77** ... StephenDonohoe 6 23
(P W Chapple-Hyam) *led 1f: chsd ldrs: drvn over 3f out: sn outpcd: lost pl 2f out* **5/2**[2]

1m 28.18s (-2.62) **Going Correction** -0.125s/f (Stan) 8 Ran SP% **118.5**
Speed ratings (Par 101):109,107,101,99,98 91,85,78
CSF £47.59 CT £475.33 TOTE £20.70: £3.80, £1.80, £2.00; EX 74.50.
Owner Gainsborough **Bred** Gainsborough Stud Management Ltd **Trained** Lambourn, Berks

FOCUS
An interesting handicap and rock solid all-weather handicap form, the first two clear of two reliable yardsticks. The first two both looked well handicapped here.
Ben Chorley Official explanation: trainer's rep said gelding was possibly unsuited by the fibresand

1979 ARENA LEISURE PLC FILLIES' H'CAP 1m (F)
8:20 (8:20) (Class 4) (0-85,79) 3-Y-O+ **£6,477** (£1,927; £963; £481) **Stalls** Low

Form RPR
312 **1** **Lady Gloria**[12] 1672 3-8-12 **75** ... TPQueally 3 88+
(J G Given) *w ldr: led after 1f: edgd lft over 1f out: drew clr fnl f: readily* **2/1**[1]
1540 **2** 3 **Musical Beat**[12] 1649 3-8-9 **77** ... ColinHaddon(5) 7 81
(Miss V Haigh) *hld up in rr: n.m.r 3f out: hdwy and swtchd rt 2f out: styd on to take 2nd ins fnl f: no imp* **13/2**
-013 **3** 1 ½ **Indian's Feather (IRE)**[16] 1568 6-8-13 **69** ... MichaelJStainton(5) 2 73
(N Tinkler) *led 1f: w ldrs: styd on same pce appr fnl f* **12/1**
3-10 **4** 5 **Weekend Fling (USA)**[36] 1099 3-9-1 **78** ... JoeFanning 5 68
(M Johnston) *s.i.s: sn w ldrs: rdn and hung lft over 2f out: sn btn* **10/1**
2423 **5** 3 **Grand Symphony**[23] 1370 3-8-5 **68** ... RichardMullen 8 51
(W Jarvis) *t.k.h: effrt over 3f out: rdn and wknd 2f out* **14/1**
0550 **6** nk **Daring Affair**[12] 1649 6-9-13 **78** ... LeeEnstone 4 63
(K R Burke) *s.i.s: hdwy on outer over 3f out: rdn over 2f out: sn btn* **9/2**[3]
-560 **7** 2 ½ **Musical Mirage (USA)**[5] 1851 3-9-2 **79** ... TPO'Shea 1 55
(G A Swinbank) *trckd ldrs: drvn over 3f out: sn btn* **16/1**
01-5 **8** 4 **Sell Out**[22] 1407 3-9-1 **78** ... NCallan 6 45
(G Wragg) *chsd ldrs: rdn and lost pl over 2f out* **10/3**[2]

1m 42.45s (-2.15) **Going Correction** -0.125s/f (Stan)
WFA 3 from 6yo 12lb 8 Ran SP% **117.3**
Speed ratings (Par 102):105,102,100,95,92 92,89,85
CSF £16.18 CT £126.79 TOTE £3.00: £1.10, £2.30, £3.50; EX 20.60.
Owner M H Tourle **Bred** M H And Mrs G Tourle **Trained** Willoughton, Lincs

FOCUS
A slowly-run event. The winner is progressing nicely and took this with some authority. The placed horses ran to their pre-race marks.
Sell Out Official explanation: jockey said filly was unsuited by the fibresand

1980 JOURNEY SOUTH PLAY ON THE 30TH H'CAP 1m 4f (F)
8:50 (8:50) (Class 5) (0-70,70) 4-Y-O+ **£3,886** (£1,156; £577; £288) **Stalls** Low

Form RPR
/044 **1** **Newtonian (USA)**[10] 1717 8-8-8 **60** ... (p) JoeFanning 5 67+
(M Brittain) *trckd ldrs: led 3f out: hung rt over 1f out: styd on strly* **10/3**[1]
2501 **2** 2 ½ **Starcross Maid**[10] 1717 5-8-7 **59** 6ex ... ChrisCatlin 6 61
(J F Coupland) *trckd ldrs: wnt 2nd over 2f out: kpt on same pce fnl f* **7/2**[2]
/10- **3** 1 **Go Free**[194] 470 6-7-11 **56** oh6 ... MCGeran(7) 2 56
(J G M O'Shea) *dwlt: tk str hold in last: wl in tch: effoer over 3f out: one pce fnl 2f* **13/2**
1600 **4** 3 **Kylkenny**[28] 1263 12-8-13 **70** ... (t) TravisBlock(5) 1 65
(H Morrison) *t.k.h wl in tch: pushed along over 4f out: wknd over 1f out* **4/1**[3]
30-1 **5** 2 **Jeu D'Esprit (IRE)**[16] 1567 4-9-4 **70** ... TPQueally 3 62
(J G Given) *led: qcknd over 4f out: hrd rdn and hdd 3f out: wknd over 1f out* **4/1**[3]

0-02 **6** *39* **Surdoue**[10] 1717 7-8-4 **56** oh7 .... RichardMullen 4 —
(D Morris) *trckd ldr: drvn over 3f out: sn lost pl and bhd: eased fnl f: t.o*
6/1

2m 39.8s (-2.29) **Going Correction** -0.125s/f (Stan) **6** Ran SP% **112.9**
Speed ratings (Par 103):102,100,99,97,96 70
CSF £15.41 TOTE £3.60: £2.00, £2.30; EX 14.30 Place 6 £16.10, Place 5 £13.90.
Owner Ray Flegg **Bred** Jonabell Farm Inc, J Bell Iii & B Williams **Trained** Warthill, N Yorks

FOCUS

They ambled round for the first mile or so. In the end Newtonian, kept right up to his work, ran out a decisive winner. The form is only modest but makes sense with the placed horses running to their pre-race marks.

Surdoue Official explanation: jockey said gelding ran too free early stages

T/Plt: £11.90 to a £1 stake. Pool: £52,367.50. 3,187.30 winning tickets. T/Qpdt: £9.50 to a £1 stake. Pool: £4,234.40. 329.10 winning tickets. WG

1981 - 1983a (Foreign Racing) - See Raceform Interactive

1956 GOODWOOD (R-H)

Friday, May 25

OFFICIAL GOING: Good (good to firm in places on round course)

Wind: Virtually nil Weather: Sunny

1984 VINI'S GUCCI AND PUCCI H'CAP 7f

2:00 (2:02) (Class 4) (0-80,80) 4-Y-O+ **£5,181** (£1,541; £770; £384) **Stalls** High

Form RPR

-000 **1** **Scarlet Flyer (USA)**[13] 1666 4-8-7 **69** .... (b) FergusSweeney 12 79
(G L Moore) *s.i.s: bhd: weaved way through field fr over 1f out: swtchd lft jst ins fnl f: led fnl 100yds: r.o strly* **7/1**[3]

005- **2** *1 1/4* **Blue Java**[209] 6221 6-8-5 **72** .... TravisBlock(5) 3 79
(H Morrison) *prom: led 2f out: sn rdn: no ex whn hdd fnl 100yds* **4/1**[1]

05-6 **3** *1/2* **Angel Sprints**[27] 1292 5-8-13 **75** .... AlanDaly 10 81
(C J Down) *t.k.h trcking ldrs: rdn 2f out: sn swtchd rt: kpt on same pce* **33/1**

-520 **4** *nk* **Capricho (IRE)**[21] 1446 10-8-4 **66** oh6 .... (b) PaulDoe 2 71
(J Akehurst) *t.k.h in rr: hdwy on outer over 2f out: sn rdn: kpt on ins fnl f* **16/1**

06-6 **5** *shd* **Daniel Thomas (IRE)**[111] 340 5-9-4 **80** .... (e[1]) JimCrowley 6 85
(Mrs A J Perrett) *hld up towards rr: nt clr run over 2f out: swtchd lft over 1f out: r.o wl ins fnl f: nrst fin* **12/1**

11-2 **6** *3/4* **The Cayterers**[15] 1607 5-8-9 **76** .... LukeMorris(5) 1 79
(J M Bradley) *t.k.h in tch: hdwy 3f out: rdn to chal 2f out: hung rt and one pce fnl f* **9/2**[2]

00-0 **7** *1* **Marshman (IRE)**[10] 1747 8-8-13 **75** .... RHills 8 75
(M H Tompkins) *hld up towards rr: pushed along over 3f out: sme late prog: nvr trbld ldrs* **10/1**

460- **8** *1* **Landucci**[170] 6733 6-8-10 **77** .... PatrickHills(5) 9 75
(J W Hills) *virtually fell leaving stalls: bhd: shortlived effrt 2f out: sn one pce* **12/1**

0326 **9** *shd* **Sun Catcher (IRE)**[13] 1682 4-9-2 **78** .... (b) JimmyFortune 5 75
(R Hannon) *t.k.h: led for 1f: trckd ldr: rdn and ch over 2f out: wknd over 1f out* **8/1**

36-0 **10** *1 1/2* **First Show**[23] 1395 5-8-10 **72** .... (p) LDettori 4 65
(R A Harris) *in tch: effrt 3f out: wknd 2f out* **10/1**

0162 **11** *shd* **Raza Cab (IRE)**[23] 1401 5-8-9 **74** .... JerryO'Dwyer(3) 11 67
(Karen George) *chsd ldrs: rdn 3f out: wknd 2f out* **10/1**

400- **12** *6* **Material Witness (IRE)**[208] 6239 10-9-4 **80** .... RichardMullen 7 58
(W R Muir) *led after 1f: rdn 3f out: hdd 2f out: sn wknd* **16/1**

1m 28.03s (-0.01) **Going Correction** +0.10s/f (Good) **12** Ran SP% **119.2**
Speed ratings (Par 105):104,102,102,101,101 100,99,98,98,96 96,89
CSF £35.25 CT £893.08 TOTE £9.70: £3.00, £2.00, £8.60; EX 46.90.
Owner The Optima Partnership **Bred** Gary And Mrs Middlebrook **Trained** Woodingdean, E Sussex

FOCUS

An ordinary handicap for the grade and the pace was just steady through the early stages.

Landucci Official explanation: jockey said gelding stumbled badly leaving stalls

Sun Catcher(IRE) Official explanation: jockey said gelding ran too free

Material Witness(IRE) Official explanation: jockey said gelding slipped leaving stalls

1985 LETHEBY & CHRISTOPHER FESTIVAL STKS (LISTED RACE) 1m 1f 192y

2:35 (2:35) (Class 1) 4-Y-O+

£14,762 (£5,595; £2,800; £1,396; £699; £351) **Stalls** High

Form RPR

1342 **1** **Illustrious Blue**[23] 1392 4-8-12 107 .... PaulDoe 5 113
(W J Knight) *hld up in last trio: hdwy 3f out: sn rdn: led jst ins fnl f: drvn out* **11/4**[1]

0045 **2** *3/4* **Road To Love (IRE)**[23] 1392 4-8-12 105 .... RHills 1 111
(M Johnston) *led: rdn and hrd pressed fr 3f out: hdd jst ins fnl f: kpt on gamely but no ex nr fin* **11/2**

5-10 **3** *hd* **Imperial Star (IRE)**[36] 1104 4-9-1 110 .... JimmyFortune 2 114
(J H M Gosden) *hld up in last: hdwy over 2f out: sn rdn: wnt 3rd jst over 1f out: kpt on but a jst hld ins fnl f* **10/1**

1430 **4** *6* **Charlie Cool**[19] 1494 4-8-12 106 .... JoeFanning 3 99
(W J Haggas) *hld up in 4th: clsd on ldrs over 3f out: nt clr run briefly wl over 2f out: sn rdn: one pce fr over 1f out* **20/1**

521- **5** *1/2* **Into The Dark**[210] 6203 6-9-1 110 .... (t) LDettori 7 101
(Saeed Bin Suroor) *s.i.s: hld up in 5th: rdn wl over 2f out: no imp* **3/1**[2]

54-2 **6** *2 1/2* **Hard Top (IRE)**[13] 1664 5-8-12 112 .... SebSanders 4 93
(Sir Michael Stoute) *trckd ldrs: jnd ldrs and travelling wl over 2f out: sn rdn: grad fdd* **11/2**

6023 **7** *4* **Championship Point (IRE)**[18] 1550 4-8-12 105 .... DarryllHolland 6 85
(M R Channon) *trckd ldr: rdn to chal 3f out: wknd wl over 1f out* **5/1**[3]

2m 5.66s (-2.09) **Going Correction** +0.10s/f (Good) **7** Ran SP% **113.0**
Speed ratings (Par 111):112,111,111,106,106 104,100
CSF £17.73 TOTE £3.90: £1.90, £2.90; EX 21.50.
Owner Mr & Mrs I H Bendelow **Bred** B J & Mrs Crangle **Trained** Patching, W Sussex

FOCUS

A competitive Listed race run at a good pace throughout. The form looks solid for the grade.

NOTEBOOK

Illustrious Blue was not at his best when second to easy winner Cesare in this grade over 1m at Ascot on his previous start, but the step up in trip suited and he also benefited from the return to Goodwood, with his form figures at the course now reading 3131111. He was made to work very hard both to reel in long-time leader Road To Love and hold off Imperial Star's challenge, but he displayed the right attitude and ultimately just proved the strongest. His trainer has given him an entry in the Hardwicke Stakes at Royal Ascot and, looking at the way he races, there is every reason to believe he will stay 1m4f. (op 10-3 tchd 7-2 and 5-2)

Road To Love(IRE) finished miles behind Illustrious Blue when last of five in a 1m Listed race at Ascot on his previous start, but the step back up in trip suited and this was much more like it. He made this a proper test from the front, as he often does, and stuck to his task in willing fashion, confirming he is back to something like his best. (tchd 5-1)

Imperial Star(IRE) had a recurrence of his back problems when failing to run a race in the Earl Of Sefton on his previous start and, although this was obviously much better, he still gave the impression something is bothering him. Having been held up well out the back early, he was nursed into contention by Fortune, but began to wilt when asked for absolutely everything late on and flashed his tail under pressure. Strictly on the book, this was still a fine effort under his 3lb penalty, and he obviously possesses loads of ability, but one just suspects his physical problems are holding him back. (tchd 11-1)

Charlie Cool failed to beat a rival in a 1m1f handicap at Newmarket on his previous start, but this was better. His improvement seems to have levelled out for the time being, but he is clearly still capable of running well at this sort of level. (op 16-1)

Into The Dark had not been seen since bolting up in a similar race at Newmarket last backend and this must rate as a disappointing reappearance. Having been mounted on the course, he never posed a threat in the race itself and was below his best. It may be that softer ground would have suited better, but he could still have been expected to finish closer. (op 5-2)

Hard Top(IRE), second to Blue Ksar in a conditions race on his reappearance at Lingfield, looked one of the more likely winners when looming large travelling well two furlongs out, but he offered nothing under pressure and is becoming disappointing. (op 6-1)

Championship Point(IRE) shaped as though on the way back when third to Septimus at the Curragh on his previous start, but he was bitterly disappointing this time and has plenty to prove now. (op 13-2)

1986 BAKER TILLY TROPHY STKS (H'CAP) 5f

3:10 (3:10) (Class 2) (0-100,99) 4-Y-O+ **£10,363** (£3,083; £1,540; £769) **Stalls** Low

Form RPR

1261 **1** **Rowe Park**[14] 1630 4-8-6 **87** .... LPKeniry 2 95+
(Mrs L C Jewell) *chsd ldrs: edgd rt fr 2f out: rdn to ld over 1f out: r.o and a in command fnl f* **9/1**

135- **2** *1/2* **Loch Verdi**[275] 4717 4-7-13 **85** .... WilliamBuick(5) 7 91
(A M Balding) *prom: rdn 2f out: ev ch ent fnl f: kpt on but nt pce of wnr* **11/2**[2]

3130 **3** *1/2* **Lethal**[20] 1474 4-8-8 **89** ow4 .... DarryllHolland 10 93
(D K Ivory) *wnt rt s: prom: rdn and ev ch over 1f out: kpt on but nt pce of wnr* **6/1**[3]

0031 **4** *nk* **Magic Glade**[6] 1853 8-8-11 **92** 6ex .... JimCrowley 5 95
(Tom Dascombe) *hld up: rdn over 2f out: no imp tl r.o ins fnl f: nrst fin* **7/1**

-662 **5** *nk* **Talbot Avenue**[57] 818 9-8-7 **88** .... JoeFanning 6 90
(M Blanshard) *racd keenly: hld up: hdwy 2f out: sn rdn: kpt on ins fnl f* **11/1**

0061 **6** *1/2* **Classic Encounter (IRE)**[20] 1464 4-8-12 **93** .... FergusSweeney 3 93
(D M Simcock) *led: edgd rt fr 2f out: rdn and hdd over 1f out: no ex ins fnl f* **8/1**

-452 **7** *1 1/2* **Bluebok**[20] 1464 6-8-0 **86** ow1 .... (t) KevinGhunowa(5) 4 81
(J M Bradley) *chsd ldrs: rdn over 2f out: one pce ins fnl f* **5/1**[1]

1-00 **8** *hd* **Woodcote (IRE)**[20] 1474 5-9-0 **95** .... (p) DaneO'Neill 1 89
(C G Cox) *hung rt thrght: towards rr: rdn and sme hdwy over 2f out: no further imp fr over 1f out* **11/2**[2]

100- **9** *5* **Texas Gold**[195] 6445 9-9-4 **99** .... RichardMullen 8 75
(W R Muir) *in tch: effrt over 2f out: wknd over 1f out* **25/1**

5004 **10** *6* **The Lord**[6] 1853 7-8-11 **92** .... MatthewHenry 9 46
(W G M Turner) *chsd ldrs early: wknd over 2f out* **8/1**

57.68 secs (-1.37) **Going Correction** -0.075s/f (Good) **10** Ran SP% **118.6**
Speed ratings (Par 109):107,106,105,104,104 103,101,100,92,83
CSF £58.92 CT £333.93 TOTE £8.20: £2.50, £1.70, £2.80; EX 38.70 Trifecta £552.80 Part won. Pool: £778.72 - 0.70 winning tickets..
Owner Mrs Sue Ashdown And Mrs Lesley Hammond **Bred** J Baker **Trained** Sutton Valence, Kent

FOCUS

A good sprint handicap and typically competitive. The winning time was 0.75 seconds quicker than the later 51-65. They raced middle to stands' side, but there appeared no great bias.

NOTEBOOK

Rowe Park ◆ continued his improvement with a narrow success off a 6lb higher mark than when winning on the turf at Lingfield on his previous start. This was his sixth success from just 13 starts and he clearly remains a sprinter to follow. (op 8-1 tchd 10-1 in places)

Loch Verdi ◆, having her first run since last August, had little weight on her back with Buick taking off 5lb and this must rate as a pleasing return. She is bred to improve with age and looks worth keeping on the right side of. (tchd 6-1)

Lethal, an improved performer on Polytrack over the winter, showed himself every bit as effective on turf with a fine effort in defeat, and those who backed him could even feel a bit hard done by as his rider put up 4lb overweight. A strong-galloping type, he is fully effective between 5f-7f and remains worth keeping on the right side, even though the Handicapper is likely to take a dim view of this. (op 8-1)

Magic Glade was 2lb wrong under his 6lb penalty, but he is as good as ever and ran very well in defeat. (op 9-1)

Talbot Avenue has not won since July 2003, but incredibly he is still 3lb higher than when gaining that last success. He ran well, but is clearly very hard to win with. (op 16-1)

Classic Encounter(IRE), 8lb higher than when winning over course and distance on his previous start, showed his usual early speed but blew his chance by hanging to his right when asked for an effort. Official explanation: jockey said gelding hung right (op 13-2)

Bluebok, 3lb higher (including his jockey's overweight) than when second over course and distance on his previous start, failed to reverse form with Classic Encounter and was not quite at his best. (tchd 11-2)

Woodcote(IRE) was noted hanging right pretty much from the start and never posed a threat. Official explanation: jockey said gelding hung right (op 7-1 tchd 5-1)

1987 M-REAL STKS (H'CAP) 1m 3f

3:45 (3:48) (Class 4) (0-85,85) 3-Y-O **£7,124** (£2,119; £1,059; £529) **Stalls** Low

Form RPR

4-1 **1** **Record Breaker (IRE)**[46] 968 3-8-11 **78** .... JoeFanning 1 84+
(M Johnston) *mde all: hrd pressed fr 3f out: styd on gamely: all out* **13/8**[1]

01 **2** *hd* **Noticeable (IRE)**[22] 1433 3-9-2 **83** .... DarryllHolland 10 89
(M R Channon) *trckd wnr: rdn to chal over 2f out: kpt on strly fnl 30yds: jst failed* **33/1**

16 **3** *1 1/2* **Aajel (USA)**[79] 638 3-9-2 **83** .... RHills 9 86
(M P Tregoning) *trckd ldrs: hung lft ent st: sn rdn: styd on to go 3rd ins fnl f* **10/1**

01-3 **4** *1/2* **Sanbuch**[31] 1230 3-9-3 **84** .... DaneO'Neill 8 86+
(L M Cumani) *bmpd s: towards rr: hmpd after 3f: making hdwy whn carried wd by loose horse over 6f out: rdn and swtchd to centre 3f out: styd on fr over 1f out* **10/1**

13-2 **5** *1 3/4* **Mafeking (UAE)**[35] 1122 3-8-11 **78** .... FergusSweeney 6 77
(M R Hoad) *hld up towards rr: hdwy over 2f out to chse ldrs: sn rdn: kpt on same pce* **11/1**

6214 **6** *1* **Spiderback (IRE)**[6] 1843 3-8-13 **80**.................................(b) SebSanders 7 77
(R Hannon) *s.i.s: towards rr: smooth run on inner fr 6f out to trck ldrs ent st: sn rdn: one pce fnl f* **7/1**[3]

2-35 **7** *nk* **Bajan Pride**[19] 1505 3-8-6 **73**.. RichardSmith 4 70
(R Hannon) *hld up towards rr: smooth hdwy on inner fr 6f out: rdn over 2f out: kpt on same pce* **66/1**

-313 **8** *11* **Surrey Spinner**[28] 1277 3-9-3 **84**.. JimCrowley 2 62
(Mrs A J Perrett) *s.i.s: towards rr: stdy prog fr 6f out: trckd ldrs ent st: sn rdn: wknd 2f out* **8/1**

0-1 **9** *1/2* **Venerable**[17] 1560 3-9-3 **84**.. JimmyFortune 5 61
(J H M Gosden) *trckd ldrs: rdn 3f out: sn btn* **12/1**

0-15 **10** *5* **Sir Liam (USA)**[35] 1122 3-8-8 **75**.................................... RichardMullen 3 44
(P Mitchell) *mid-div tl hung lft ent st: wknd over 2f out* **25/1**

3-1 **U** **Fort Amhurst (IRE)**[39] 1062 3-9-4 **85**.. LDettori 11 —
(E A L Dunlop) *plld hrd in mid-div whn stmbld and uns rdr after 3f* **11/2**[2]

2m 26.22s (-0.99) **Going Correction** +0.10s/f (Good) **11** Ran SP% **119.6**
Speed ratings (Par 101):107,106,105,105,104 103,103,95,94,91 —
CSF £74.36 CT £438.74 TOTE £2.50: £1.30, £4.00, £3.00; EX 63.00.
Owner Leung Kai Fai & Vincent Leung **Bred** Sir E J Loder **Trained** Middleham Moor, N Yorks

FOCUS
A good three-year-old handicap, although slightly messy with Fort Amhurst unseating his rider early on and causing some interference. This race should produce its share of winners.
Spiderback(IRE) Official explanation: jockey said gelding hung right
Sir Liam(USA) Official explanation: jockey said colt lost a shoe

1988 SWORDFISH INVESTMENTS AND CAPITAL MANAGEMENT MAIDEN FILLIES' STKS 1m 1f
4:20 (4:22) (Class 5) 3-Y-O **£3,238** (£963; £481; £240) **Stalls** High

Form RPR

3 **1** **Jamboretta (IRE)**[23] 1409 3-9-0 0.. LDettori 10 81+
(Sir Michael Stoute) *prom: led after 3f: qcknd clr over 1f out: kpt up to work ins fnl f: comf* **5/6**[1]

25 **2** *3/4* **Zifaaf (USA)**[18] 1523 3-9-0 0... RHills 7 75+
(B W Hills) *mid-div: swtchd lft and stdy hdwy 2f out: r.o strly ins fnl f but a hld by wnr* **5/2**[2]

0- **3** *2* **Montjeu's Melody (IRE)**[285] 4400 3-9-0 0.............................. TQuinn 2 70
(J W Hills) *trckd ldrs: rdn to chal wnr 3f out: outpcd by wnr over 1f out: lost 2nd ins fnl f* **50/1**

4 *3* **Kokkokila** 3-9-0 0.. SebSanders 1 64+
(Lady Herries) *rn green: s.i.s: bhd: pushed along and stdy hdwy fr 3f out: wnt 4th nr fin* **33/1**

0-0 **5** *shd* **Cat Six (USA)**[14] 1639 3-9-0 0.. DaneO'Neill 3 63
(B J Meehan) *led for 3f: w wnr: rdn 3f out: one pce fr over 1f out* **66/1**

6 *2 1/2* **Catherine Palace** 3-9-0 0.. JimmyFortune 9 58
(E A L Dunlop) *trckd ldrs: rdn 3f out: grad fdd fnl 2f* **10/1**

00 **7** *2* **Luna Danza**[15] 1606 3-9-0 0... JoeFanning 8 53
(B J Meehan) *mid-div: rdn 3f out: wknd 2f out* **66/1**

5-3 **8** *1 1/2* **Run For Ede'S**[15] 1606 3-9-0 0.. IanMongan 6 49
(P M Phelan) *mid-div: hdwy 4f out: rdn 3f out: wknd 2f out* **7/1**[3]

4025 **9** *4* **Wassendale**[31] 1220 3-9-0 61.. DarryllHolland 5 40
(J W Hills) *racd keenly: hld up: sme hdwy over 3f out: sn rdn: wknd 2f out* **25/1**

1m 57.99s (1.13) **Going Correction** +0.10s/f (Good) **9** Ran SP% **116.5**
Speed ratings (Par 96):98,97,95,92,92 90,88,87,83
CSF £2.93 TOTE £1.90: £1.10, £1.30, £6.60; EX 4.00.
Owner Cheveley Park Stud **Bred** Castleton Group **Trained** Newmarket, Suffolk

FOCUS
An uncompetitive maiden and the early pace was just steady. It is hard to be confident about the form as those behind the front pair had previously shown little. The winner was value for extra.

1989 EBF TURFTV BETTING SHOP SERVICE MEDIAN AUCTION MAIDEN STKS (DIV I) 6f
4:55 (4:56) (Class 5) 2-Y-O **£2,914** (£867; £433; £216) **Stalls** Low

Form RPR

65 **1** **Outside Edge (IRE)**[20] 1469 2-9-3 0............................ DarryllHolland 9 68
(W R Swinburn) *sn pushed along towards rr: hdwy over 1f out: r.o through gap and struck on hd twice by rival's whip jst ins fnl f: led line: game* **5/1**[3]

63 **2** *shd* **Swindon Town Flyer (IRE)**[26] 1315 2-9-3 0.................. DaneO'Neill 11 68
(A B Haynes) *prom: rdn 2f out: led wl ins fnl f: ct line* **3/1**[1]

3 *nk* **Berbice (IRE)** 2-9-3 0.. JimmyFortune 2 67
(R Hannon) *s.i.s: towards rr: hdwy and nt clr run 2f out: swtchd lft and qcknd up wl to ld but hung rt 1f out: no ex whn hdd wl ins fnl f* **10/3**[2]

4 *shd* **Sofia's Star** 2-9-3 0... MatthewHenry 7 67
(P Winkworth) *chsd ldrs: rdn 2f out: ev ch ins fnl f: no ex nr fin* **16/1**

5 *1/2* **King's Wonder** 2-9-3 0.. RichardMullen 6 65
(W R Muir) *t.k.h: hld up: hdwy over 2f out: rdn and ch 1f out: kpt on* **16/1**

3 **6** *1 1/4* **Sheik'N'Knotsterd**[22] 1428 2-9-3 0..................................... JoeFanning 5 62+
(J Akehurst) *prom: led 3f out: rdn and hdd 1f out: hld whn n.m.r nr fin* **7/1**

7 *2 1/2* **Suite Francaise** 2-8-12 0.. SebSanders 3 49
(Sir Mark Prescott) *prom: rdn over 2f out: one pce ent fnl f* **16/1**

0 **8** *1 1/2* **Virtual Paddy**[24] 1367 2-9-3 0... LPKeniry 4 50
(M Blanshard) *chsd ldrs: hung rt over 2f out: sn rdn: wknd ins fnl f* **50/1**

9 *1 3/4* **Kristal Glory (IRE)** 2-9-3 0.. IanMongan 10 44+
(J L Dunlop) *s.i.s: bhd: sme late prog but nvr on terms* **14/1**

10 *1 3/4* **Latin Scholar (IRE)** 2-9-3 0.. FergusSweeney 1 39
(A King) *led for 3f: grad fdd* **7/1**

11 *11* **Kryptonite (IRE)** 2-9-3 0.. TQuinn 8 6
(J W Hills) *s.i.s: a wl bhd* **14/1**

1m 13.63s (0.78) **Going Correction** -0.075s/f (Good) **11** Ran SP% **122.7**
Speed ratings (Par 93):91,90,90,90,89 88,84,82,80,78 63
CSF £21.33 TOTE £6.40: £2.40, £1.50, £1.40; EX 26.30.
Owner Cricketers Club Racing Group **Bred** Tally-Ho Stud **Trained** Aldbury, Herts

FOCUS
The first five finished in a heap and, with the winning time 1.04 seconds slower than the second division, the bare form looks just modest and pretty weak for the track. The race has been rated through the runner-up.

NOTEBOOK
Outside Edge(IRE) had shown just moderate form on his two previous starts, including when only fifth in a 5f maiden here on his previous start, but the step up in trip brought about a much-improved performance. He would have been an unlucky loser had he not got up, for he was struck over the head by another rider's whip when looking for an opening, and had to force his way through a tight gap inside the final furlong. This represents pretty ordinary form, but he is clearly very tough. (op 8-1)
Swindon Town Flyer(IRE) improved as one might have expected for the step up to 6f and was just denied. He is only fair at best, but an ordinary race should come his way at some stage. (op 4-1)
Berbice(IRE), a 43,000gns Acclamation half-brother to Bibury Lodge, who was placed over 7f at two, out of a very lightly-raced 7f juvenile winner, looked to throw away a winning opportunity on his racecourse debut, perhaps through his inexperience. Having been forced to wait for a gap, he looked all over the winner when picking up against the near-side rail, but he carried his head at an awkward angle and did very little once in front. It will have to be hoped he was just running green, but he will have something to prove next time and does not appeal as one to take a short price about just yet. (op 7-2 tchd 4-1)
Sofia's Star, a 20,000gns half-sister to among others Chantilly Myth, a dual 6f-7f winner at two to three, shaped nicely on his racecourse bow, keeping on well widest of all.
King's Wonder, a half-brother to 5f juvenile winner Wonderful Mind, out of a 1m2f winner, shaped very nicely on his racecourse debut and looks the type to keep progressing. (op 20-1)
Sheik'N'Knotsterd gave the impression he may benefit from a return to 5f. (op 11-2 tchd 9-2)

1990 EBF TURFTV BETTING SHOP SERVICE MEDIAN AUCTION MAIDEN STKS (DIV II) 6f
5:25 (5:26) (Class 5) 2-Y-O **£2,914** (£867; £433; £216) **Stalls** Low

Form RPR

1 **Lindoro** 2-9-3 0.. DarryllHolland 7 81
(W R Swinburn) *s.i.s: sn niggled along towards rr: hdwy 3f out: rdn to ld and edgd lft jst ins fnl f: r.o wl* **5/1**

2 *1 1/4* **King's Icon (IRE)** 2-9-3 0.. SebSanders 8 77
(M P Tregoning) *prom: led 2f out: sn rdn: hdd jst ins fnl f: no ex* **10/3**[1]

3 *1 1/4* **Dream Eater (IRE)** 2-9-3 0.. LPKeniry 6 74
(A M Balding) *prom: sltly outpcd 2f out: kpt on again ins fnl f: wnt 3rd nr fin* **14/1**

06 **4** *shd* **Higgy's Boy (IRE)**[39] 1058 2-9-3 0.................................. DaneO'Neill 2 73
(R Hannon) *led: rdn and hdd 2f out: kpt on same pce* **8/1**

5 *3/4* **Scintillo** 2-9-3 0... RichardSmith 4 71
(R Hannon) *prom tl sltly outpcd over 2f out: kpt on again ins fnl f* **16/1**

6 *1 1/4* **Maximus Aurelius (IRE)** 2-8-10 0............................ GihanArnolda(7) 9 67
(J Jay) *t.k.h: trckd ldrs: effrt over 1f out: one pce ins fnl f* **4/1**[2]

7 *3 1/2* **Blandys Wood** 2-8-12 0.. EdwardCreighton 10 52
(M R Channon) *s.i.s: sn pushed along: a towards rr* **33/1**

8 *3/4* **Fortuity (IRE)** 2-9-3 0... JimmyFortune 3 54+
(J H M Gosden) *a mid-div* **9/2**[3]

9 *1* **Albaqaa** 2-9-3 0.. RHills 1 51
(E A L Dunlop) *s.i.s: bhd: hdwy 2f out: sn rdn: wknd 1f out* **7/1**

10 *3 1/2* **Fathsta (IRE)** 2-9-3 0.. JDSmith 5 41
(S Kirk) *prom for 4f* **33/1**

1m 12.59s (-0.26) **Going Correction** -0.075s/f (Good) **10** Ran SP% **120.0**
Speed ratings (Par 93):98,96,94,94,93 91,87,86,84,80
CSF £22.75 TOTE £6.70: £2.50, £1.50, £3.40; EX 28.70.
Owner Mrs P W Harris **Bred** Pigeon House Stud **Trained** Aldbury, Herts

FOCUS
A reasonable juvenile maiden and certainly much better than the first division although the level is less than solid; the winning time was 1.04 seconds quicker than division one.

NOTEBOOK
Lindoro, a 72,000gns half-brother to six winners at up to 1m, notably high-class 5f-6f winner Ringmoor Down, out of a 1m winner at three in France, did this quite convincingly on his racecourse debut, picking up nicely from just off the pace to reel in the favourite. There should be more to come and he deserves his chance in better company. (op 11-2)
King's Icon(IRE) ◆, a 62,000gns half-brother to among others quite useful 6f two-year-old winner Russian Rosie, out of a middle-distance winner in France, showed good speed throughout and kept on to the line. He finished nicely clear of the remainder and looks well up to winning a similar event. (op 7-2 tchd 4-1)
Dream Eater(IRE), a 40,000gns half-brother to 1m three-year-old winner Tremelo Pointe, out of a useful dual 1m2f winner, made a pleasing racecourse debut. He can be expected to improve and looks capable of finding a maiden in the coming weeks.
Higgy's Boy(IRE) had the benefit of previous experience and ran a respectable race. He helps give the form a solid look.
Scintillo ◆, a 30,000gns half-brother to four winners, including 1m winner Durer, out of a top-class miler, winner of the French 1,000 Guineas, showed up well for much of the way and this must rate as a pleasing debut. He is bred to improve with time and distance and looks worth keeping on the right side of. (op 25-1)
Maximus Aurelius(IRE), a 68,000gns brother to smart Dawnus, a triple 1m-1m2f winner at three, and 5f winner Maigue Violet, out of a dual 1m winner at three in France, was clearly well fancied. Although ultimately well held, he showed ability, producing a short-lived effort towards the outside, and is open to improvement.
Fortuity(IRE), a £90,000 purchase, out of a multiple winner over 1m1f-1m2f, showed signs of greenness and never posed a threat, but he is open to loads of improvement. (op 5-1)

1991 TURFTV.CO.UK APPRENTICE STKS (H'CAP) 5f
5:55 (5:57) (Class 6) (0-65,65) 4-Y-O+ **£3,238** (£963; £481; £240) **Stalls** Low

Form RPR

6-02 **1** **Matterofact (IRE)**[9] 1766 4-8-8 **57**................................. HaddenFrost(3) 3 66
(M S Saunders) *a.p: rdn 2f out: kpt on ins fnl f: led line* **7/1**[3]

3223 **2** *shd* **What Do You Know**[13] 1666 4-9-2 **65**.............................. NicolPolli(3) 15 74
(A M Hales) *a.p: drifted rt 2f out: rdn to ld 1f out: sn drifted lft: ct line* **8/1**

2461 **3** *hd* **Harrison's Flyer (IRE)**[4] 1885 6-8-11 **62** 6ex...............(p) AlanRutter(5) 4 70
(J M Bradley) *hld up in mid-div: rdn and hdwy 2f out: r.o ins fnl f* **11/2**[1]

3640 **4** *1* **Cosmic Destiny (IRE)**[13] 1669 5-8-6 **52**.......................... WilliamBuick 16 64+
(E F Vaughan) *rrd stalls: bhd: making gd hdwy on far side whn bdly hmpd and snatched up 2f out: sn swtchd lft: running on whn nt clr run ent fnl f: fin strly: unlucky* **11/1**

2-05 **5** *hd* **Musical Script (USA)**[13] 1681 4-9-0 **60**.............................. TravisBlock 12 64
(Mouse Hamilton-Fairley) *mid-div: rdn and hdwy over 1f out: styd on* **14/1**

-220 **6** *hd* **Quality Street**[109] 361 5-8-13 **64**.................................(p) JosephWalsh(5) 6 67
(P Butler) *led tl 3f out: sn rdn and remained cl up: kpt on again ins fnl f* **16/1**

2013 **7** *nk* **Monte Major (IRE)**[13] 1669 6-8-6 **55**..............................(v) PatrickHills(3) 1 57
(D Shaw) *hld up in rr: swtchd rt and hdwy over 2f out: sn rdn: styd on* **11/1**

00-5 **8** *1/2* **Multahab**[26] 1321 8-8-9 **60**...(t) BradleyRoper(5) 11 60
(Miss D A McHale) *rrd s: sn rcvrd to chse ldrs: led 3f out: drifted rt 2f out: hdd 1f out: no ex* **16/1**

1205 **9** *3/4* **Pride Of Joy**[11] 1729 4-9-2 **62**.. JamesMillman 2 60
(D K Ivory) *nvr bttr than mid-div* **20/1**

2105 **10** *nk* **Egyptian Lord**[10] 1754 4-8-10 **59**.....................(b) RussellKennemore(3) 19 56
(Peter Grayson) *chsd ldrs: rdn whn carried rt 2f out: kpt on same pce* **13/2**[2]

40- **11** *1 1/4* **King Egbert (FR)**[247] 5480 6-8-7 **53**................................ TolleyDean 18 45
(R A Harris) *chsd ldrs: carried rt 2f out: sn rdn: fdd ins fnl f* **13/2**[2]

-000 **12** *1/2* **Viewforth**[107] 383 9-8-5 **51** oh3.....................................(b) RoryMoore 7 41
(M A Buckley) *bhd: sme late prog: nvr a danger* **50/1**

0-00 **13** *hd* **Meikle Barfil**[23] 1405 5-8-2 **53**..................................(p) PietroRomeo(5) 20 43
(J M Bradley) *in tch: rdn whn carried rt 2f out: one pce after* **16/1**

000- **14** 3/4 **Parkside Pursuit**[248] 5453 9-8-0 **53** .... JakePayne(7) 14 — 40
(J M Bradley) *mid-div: rdn and hdwy whn rdr lost irons 2f out: wknd ins fnl f* **33/1**

5600 **15** 3/4 **Trinculo (IRE)**[13] 1669 10-8-11 **60** .... LukeMorris(3) 13 — 44
(R A Harris) *chsd ldrs: rdn over 2f out: sn wknd* **14/1**

6-00 **16** 3/4 **Hang Loose**[28] 1280 4-8-3 **52** .... (b) AmyBaker(3) 17 — 34
(S W Hall) *mid-div tl wknd over 1f out* **50/1**

0-00 **17** 2 1/2 **Silver Prelude**[13] 1669 6-9-0 **60** .... MarkFlynn 8 — 33
(D K Ivory) *s.i.s: sn mid-div: wknd over 1f out* **50/1**

6505 **18** 2 **Taboor (IRE)**[13] 1669 9-8-6 **55** .... JackMitchell(3) 5 — 20
(R M H Cowell) *rrd stalls: a bhd* **12/1**

58.43 secs (-0.62) **Going Correction** -0.075s/f (Good) **18** Ran SP% **134.6**
Speed ratings (Par 101):101,100,100,98,98 98,97,97,95,95 93,92,92,91,89 88,84,81
CSF £65.31 CT £354.04 TOTE £7.20: £2.10, £2.90, £1.20, £3.80; EX 87.60 Place 6 £33.83, Place 5 £13.52.
Owner Prempro Racing **Bred** Tony Gleeson **Trained** Green Ore, Somerset
■ Stewards' Enquiry : Bradley Roper three-day ban: careless riding (Jun 5-7)
Russell Kennemore five-day ban: careless riding (Jun 5-9)

FOCUS
A modest but competitive sprint handicap restricted to apprentices who had not ridden more than 50 winners. They were spread out across the track at the line, but there appeared no great bias. The winning time was 0.75 seconds slower than the earlier 86-100. The bare form is solid.
T/Plt: £56.70 to a £1 stake. Pool: £84,013.25. 1,081.40 winning tickets. T/Qpdt: £5.60 to a £1 stake. Pool: £4,145.30. 547.30 winning tickets. TM

1655 HAYDOCK (L-H)
Friday, May 25

OFFICIAL GOING: Good to firm
There were 12 non-runners due to the drying ground.
Wind: Moderate against Weather: Fine

1992 ARNOLD CLARK RENAULT MAIDEN AUCTION STKS (DIV I) — 5f
2:10 (2:10) (Class 5) 2-Y-O — £2,817 (£838; £418; £209) Stalls Centre

Form — RPR

1 **Little Big Boy (IRE)** 2-8-11 0 .... EddieAhern 7 — 77
(R Hannon) *hld up: hdwy over 2f out: rdn to ld jst over 1f out: edgd lft ins fnl f: r.o* **4/1**[2]

0 **2** hd **Supermassive Muse (IRE)**[13] 1680 2-8-9 0 .... GrahamGibbons 8 — 74
(E S McMahon) *a.p: rdn wl over 1f out: ev ch ins fnl f: r.o* **9/2**[3]

3 shd **Liberty Ship** 2-8-11 0 .... PatCosgrave 6 — 76
(J D Bethell) *s.i.s and wnt lft: hung lft over 3f out: rdn over 2f out: sn edgd rt: hdwy over 1f out: ev ch whn edgd rt wl ins fnl f: r.o* **12/1**

P **4** 1/2 **Look Busy (IRE)**[27] 1302 2-8-2 0 ow1 .... PatrickMathers(3) 5 — 68
(A Berry) *chsd ldrs: hung bdly lft over 3f out: sn lost pl: rallied over 1f out: kpt on ins fnl f* **50/1**

5 2 1/2 **El Tato** 2-8-11 0 .... DavidAllan 4 — 65
(T D Easterby) *dwlt: sn outpcd: late hdwy: nrst fin* **14/1**

6 hd **Alabama Spirit (USA)** 2-8-4 0 .... DeanMcKeown 10 — 57
(K R Burke) *chsd ldrs tl rdn and wknd jst over 1f out* **17/2**

7 1/2 **Richardthesecond (IRE)** 2-8-10 0 ow1 .... StephenDonohoe 2 — 62
(W M Brisbourne) *outpcd: nvr nrr* **25/1**

45 **8** 1/2 **Structura (USA)**[7] 1807 2-8-4 0 .... ChrisCatlin 3 — 54
(J S Moore) *led: rdn and hdd jst over 1f out: wknd ins fnl f* **3/1**[1]

5 **9** 12 **She's Our Dream**[34] 1150 2-8-7 0 ow1 .... MickyFenton 1 — 14+
(R C Guest) *t.k.h: prom: eased whn btn jst over 1f out* **4/1**[2]

62.59 secs (0.52) **Going Correction** -0.15s/f (Firm) **9** Ran SP% **113.9**
Speed ratings (Par 93):89,88,88,87,83 83,82,81,62
CSF £22.03 TOTE £3.50: £1.80, £1.90, £4.10; EX 25.00.
Owner Kemal Kurt **Bred** Tally-Ho Stud **Trained** East Everleigh, Wilts

FOCUS
This was probably the weaker of the two divisions, despite some promising performances. The runner-up helps set the level.

NOTEBOOK
Little Big Boy(IRE), who attracted money in the market before the off, was not rushed in the first couple of furlongs and gradually got into the race. He hit the front quite early and edged left a touch under pressure, so could be value for a bit more than the bare result suggests. (op 6-1)
Supermassive Muse(IRE) kept on really well throughout the final furlong and should easily get another furlong in time. He appears to be progressing the right away and should find an opening soon at the right level. (op 5-1 tchd 4-1)
Liberty Ship may well have won had he kept straight under pressure in the final furlong. Related to winners, he looks sure to pick up an ordinary maiden soon. (op 14-1)
Look Busy(IRE) was really green throughout but made tremendous late strides to finish strongly. This was obviously a massive improvement on her opening effort but it could also make the form look moderate.
El Tato missed the break badly and did amazingly well to finish as close as he did. If learning from this experience, he can go a great deal closer next time. Official explanation: jockey said colt suffered interference after start
Alabama Spirit(USA) does not look to have a great deal of substance yet and will need to improve a great deal to have any chance next time. (op 9-1 tchd 8-1)
Structura(USA) took the field along early but found disappointingly little when asked to win her race. She has got a bit to prove now after a promising start to her career. (op 9-4)
She's Our Dream raced prominently until fading quickly when appearing to go wrong just over a furlong from home. Official explanation: jockey said filly lost its action (op 9-2)

1993 ARNOLD CLARK RENAULT MAIDEN AUCTION STKS (DIV II) — 5f
2:45 (2:48) (Class 5) 2-Y-O — £2,817 (£838; £418; £209) Stalls Centre

Form — RPR

0 **1** **Captain Dunne (IRE)**[8] 1792 2-8-13 0 .... DavidAllan 10 — 75+
(T D Easterby) *mde all: clr over 1f out: rdn out fnl f: eased nr fin* **7/2**[1]

2 1 3/4 **I Dont Do Walkin (USA)** 2-8-7 0 ow1 .... SteveDrowne 3 — 63+
(B J Meehan) *mid-div: swtchd rt over 3f out: rdn over 2f out: hdwy fnl f: tk 2nd nr fin: nt trble wnr* **7/2**[1]

3 hd **Miss Firefly** 2-8-6 0 .... ChrisCatlin 9 — 61
(M R Channon) *chsd wnr: rdn 2f out: one pce fnl f* **8/1**

4 1 1/4 **Whiskey Creek** 2-8-9 0 .... TonyHamilton 8 — 59
(R A Fahey) *a.p: rdn over 2f out: one pce fnl f* **14/1**

6 **5** 3 **Fabuleux Cherie**[18] 1533 2-8-4 0 .... NickyMackay 1 — 44
(W R Muir) *chsd ldrs: rdn over 2f out: wknd over 1f out* **11/2**[2]

6 1/2 **Tenth Night (IRE)** 2-8-11 0 .... EddieAhern 6 — 49
(J A Osborne) *nvr trbld ldrs* **7/1**[3]

7 2 1/2 **Betty Burke** 2-8-4 0 .... RoystonFfrench 5 — 33
(W M Brisbourne) *dwlt: hung lft over 3f out: a bhd* **20/1**

8 3 1/2 **Charlie Green (IRE)** 2-8-11 0 .... DeanMcKeown 4 — 27
(Paul Green) *s.s: rdn over 2f out: a in rr* **16/1**

P **Everything** 2-8-7 0 ow3 .... MickyFenton 2 — —
(P T Midgley) *unruly stalls: s.s: sn p.u* **33/1**

62.21 secs (0.14) **Going Correction** -0.15s/f (Firm) **9** Ran SP% **103.7**
Speed ratings (Par 93):92,89,88,86,82 81,77,71,—
CSF £11.87 TOTE £3.50: £1.70, £1.30, £2.20; EX 13.60.
Owner Middleham Park Racing Xv **Bred** Ballybrennan Stud Ltd **Trained** Great Habton, N Yorks
■ Maracana Boy was withdrawn (9/2, unruly in stalls.) R4 applies, deduct 15p in the £.
■ Stewards' Enquiry : Steve Drowne one-day ban: careless riding (Jun 6)

FOCUS
Apart from the winner, who improved on his debut form, this looked a modest race, but the level is hard to gauge. The second, third and fourth all should be better for the run, while Tenth Night needs further.

NOTEBOOK
Captain Dunne(IRE), who made his debut in a good York maiden recently, never looked in any danger and came home a very easy winner. His experience certainly helped him and he will need to progress for the effort again to hold his own against stronger company. (op 9-4)
I Dont Do Walkin(USA) was well supported in the market before the off but failed to get on terms with the easy winner, like many in the field, and can be expected to benefit for the experience. She does not look overly big and ought to make it as a two-year-old. (op 11-1)
Miss Firefly, an unfurnished sort, showed good early dash but weakened slightly in the final furlong. She looks to have growing to do and should be better with time.
Whiskey Creek showed a good attitude from the off and should have little trouble finding an ordinary maiden somewhere in the north. (op 16-1)
Fabuleux Cherie was always in roughly the same spot during the race and failed to build on her opening effort. She looks like she will improve with time. (op 6-1 tchd 9-2)
Tenth Night(IRE) never really got into the race and came home in his own time. He is bred to stay further in time and certainly shaped like 5f is not his trip at all. (op 8-1)
Everything got very upset in the stalls and was pulled up quickly after a slow start.

1994 LOOKERS GROUP H'CAP — 6f
3:20 (3:24) (Class 4) (0-80,80) 3-Y-O — £5,505 (£1,637; £818; £408) Stalls Centre

Form — RPR

2-31 **1** **Kyle (IRE)**[19] 1501 3-8-13 **75** .... EddieAhern 5 — 86+
(R Hannon) *hld up in tch: rdn to ld wl ins fnl f: r.o* **5/1**[3]

1-3 **2** nk **Special Day**[13] 1658 3-9-2 **78** .... MichaelHills 9 — 88
(B W Hills) *hld up: hdwy over 1f out: rdn to ld and edgd lft ins fnl f: sn hdd: kpt on* **2/1**[1]

2013 **3** 3 1/2 **Mandurah (IRE)**[7] 1820 3-8-5 **67** .... AdrianTNicholls 7 — 67
(D Nicholls) *t.k.h: led: rdn 2f out: hdd and n.m.r briefly ins fnl f: no ex* **9/2**[2]

1-00 **4** 1/2 **Prospect Place**[16] 1577 3-9-3 **79** .... PhillipMakin 10 — 77
(M Dods) *hld up and bhd: rdn over 2f out: hdwy over 1f out: one pce fnl f* **16/1**

61-5 **5** nk **Sunnyside Tom (IRE)**[16] 1577 3-8-11 **78** .... JamieMoriarty(5) 11 — 75
(R A Fahey) *prom: hung lft fr 3f out: one pce fnl f* **11/2**

3116 **6** 2 1/2 **Arch Of Titus (IRE)**[29] 1257 3-9-4 **80** .... (t) MickyFenton 8 — 70
(M L W Bell) *hld up towards rr: rdn over 2f out: hdwy over 1f out: no further prog fnl f* **12/1**

31-0 **7** 3 1/2 **Crow's Nest Lad**[25] 1351 3-8-10 **72** .... DavidAllan 1 — 51
(T D Easterby) *prom: rdn over 2f out: wknd over 1f out* **50/1**

-612 **8** 14 **Polish World (USA)**[22] 1432 3-8-10 **72** .... DO'Donohoe 3 — 9
(E A L Dunlop) *t.k.h: prom: rdn over 2f out: sn wknd* **7/1**

562- **9** 9 **Pavlovia**[298] 3994 3-8-6 **68** .... PaulFessey 4 — —
(M Dods) *s.i.s: a bhd* **33/1**

540- **10** 3 **Mr Klick (IRE)**[231] 5788 3-9-1 **77** .... TonyHamilton 6 — —
(N Wilson) *a bhd* **33/1**

1m 14.68s (-0.22) **Going Correction** -0.15s/f (Firm) **10** Ran SP% **117.5**
Speed ratings (Par 101):95,94,89,89,88 85,80,62,50,46
CSF £15.33 CT £48.79 TOTE £6.00: £1.50, £1.40, £2.00; EX 15.90.
Owner Noodles Racing **Bred** John Cullinan **Trained** East Everleigh, Wilts
■ Stewards' Enquiry : Michael Hills caution: careless riding

FOCUS
A fair-looking sprint run at a solid tempo. The first two finished clear and a fairly positive view has been taken of the form with Kyle on the up and the second coming from a strong race here.
Mr Klick(IRE) Official explanation: jockey said gelding had no more to give

1995 RENAULT MANCHESTER MAIDEN STKS — 1m 30y
3:55 (3:57) (Class 5) 3-Y-O+ — £3,238 (£963; £481; £240) Stalls Low

Form — RPR

2- **1** **Fifty Cents**[252] 5339 3-8-13 0 .... SteveDrowne 16 — 66+
(R Charlton) *hld up in mid-div: hdwy over 2f out: led over 1f out: rdn and edgd lft ins fnl f: r.o* **4/11**[1]

0 **2** 1/2 **African Pursuits (USA)**[18] 1523 3-8-13 0 .... DavidKinsella 5 — 65
(H Morrison) *w ldr: rdn 4f out: ev ch over 1f out: r.o ins fnl f* **33/1**

3 3/4 **Sofie Tucker** 3-8-8 0 .... DavidAllan 4 — 58
(T D Easterby) *s.i.s: bhd: rdn and hdwy over 2f out: r.o ins fnl f* **33/1**

6 **4** 1/2 **Sweet Clover**[23] 1408 3-8-8 0 .... PatCosgrave 12 — 57
(K R Burke) *hld up in tch: rdn and ev ch over 1f out: nt clr run briefly ins fnl f: nt qckn* **14/1**

0 **5** 1/2 **Caluba**[14] 1620 3-8-8 0 .... PhillipMakin 11 — 56
(K R Burke) *hld up in mid-div: rdn and hdwy 2f out: kpt on ins fnl f* **33/1**

6 **6** 1 3/4 **Haasem (USA)**[46] 977 4-9-11 0 .... DO'Donohoe 10 — 66+
(E A L Dunlop) *hld up and bhd: rdn whn swtchd lft and hdwy on ins over 2f out: nt clr run ins fnl f: nt rch ldrs* **7/1**[2]

34 **7** hd **Gunfighter (IRE)**[11] 1714 4-9-11 0 .... TonyHamilton 2 — 59
(J S Wainwright) *led: rdn over 2f out: hdd over 1f out: wknd ins fnl f* **12/1**[3]

0/ **8** nk **Pivotal Era**[635] 4790 4-9-11 0 .... MichaelHills 14 — 59
(C F Wall) *hld up and bhd: hdwy on outside wl over 2f out: sn rdn: nvr trbld ldrs* **33/1**

00- **9** 2 1/2 **Gary's Indian (IRE)**[252] 5353 4-9-6 0 .... DeanMcKeown 6 — 48?
(B P J Baugh) *bhd: no ch whn bmpd over 1f out* **100/1**

10 nk **Screaming Reel** 4-9-11 0 .... MickyFenton 7 — 52?
(M Wellings) *s.v.s: no ch whn edgd lft over 1f out* **100/1**

0 **11** 4 **Cecina Marina**[41] 1045 4-9-6 0 .... LeeEnstone 17 — 38
(C W Thornton) *mid-div: wknd over 1f out* **80/1**

3 **12** nk **Steeley Fox**[18] 1541 4-9-4 0 .... BarrySavage(7) 13 — 42
(J M Bradley) *dwlt: plld hrd in mid-div: bhd fnl 2f* **25/1**

05- **13** 1 3/4 **Risk Challenge (USA)**[6] 6923 5-9-11 0 .... VinceSlattery 1 — 38
(C J Price) *s.i.s: plld hrd towards rr: rdn over 3f out: no ch whn hmpd over 1f out* **50/1**

66/- **14** 1/2 **Zamalik (USA)**[595] 5709 4-9-11 0 .... KDarley 15 — 47+
(E J Alston) *prom: rdn and wknd 2f out: sn eased* **20/1**

00- **15** 12 **Sheriff Star**[235] 5726 4-9-6 0 .... PaulMulrennan 3 — 5
(G P Kelly) *s.i.s: sn hld up in tch: rdn over 3f out: wknd over 2f out* **100/1**

16 *6* **Well Defined**[63] 4-9-6 0 AdrianTNicholls 9 —
(T H Caldwell) *s.s: a bhd* **100/1**

1m 45.21s (-0.30) **Going Correction** -0.15s/f (Firm)
WFA 3 from 4yo+ 12lb 16 Ran SP% **127.7**
Speed ratings (Par 103):95,94,93,93,92 91,90,90,88,87 83,83,81,81,69 63
CSF £29.29 TOTE £1.40: £1.02, £9.60, £7.60; EX 31.30.
Owner Mountgrange Stud **Bred** Belgrave Bloodstock **Trained** Beckhampton, Wilts
■ Stewards' Enquiry : Steve Drowne three-day ban: careless riding (Jun 7-9)
Micky Fenton one-day ban: careless riding (Jun 5)

FOCUS
A modest maiden, won unimpressively by the heavily-backed favourite who was some way below his debut form. It has been rated around the fourth and seventh. A number caught the eye in behind and will make their marks in handicap company.
Caluba Official explanation: jockey said filly hung left-handed in the straight
Haasem(USA) Official explanation: jockey said colt was denied a clear run
Pivotal Era Official explanation: jockey said gelding hung left-handed
Steeley Fox Official explanation: jockey said gelding ran too free early

1996 RENAULT VANS STKS (H'CAP) 1m 30y

4:30 (4:30) (Class 3) (0-90,93) 4-Y-0+ **£9,715** (£2,890; £1,444; £721) **Stalls** Low

Form RPR

0315 **1** **Daaweitza**[3] 1915 4-8-5 **77** RoystonFfrench 12 87
(B Ellison) *chsd ldr: led over 2f out: rdn over 1f out: drvn out* **3/1**[2]

0060 **2** *1 ¼* **Zato (IRE)**[6] 1842 4-9-0 **86** ChrisCatlin 2 93
(M R Channon) *a.p: rdn over 2f out: nt qckn ins fnl f* **5/1**[3]

1210 **3** *nk* **Harare**[4] 1905 6-8-5 **77** ow1 (v) JamesDoyle 1 83
(R J Price) *hld up in mid-div: hdwy over 2f out: rdn wl over 1f out: nt qckn ins fnl f* **16/1**

2014 **4** *4* **Councellor (FR)**[33] 1180 5-8-11 **83** (t) MickyFenton 5 80
(Stef Liddiard) *hld up in tch: rdn over 2f out: hung lft and wknd over 1f out* **12/1**

100- **5** *nk* **Vicious Warrior**[156] 6888 8-9-0 **86** DeanMcKeown 10 82
(R M Whitaker) *led: hdd over 2f out: wknd over 1f out* **18/1**

-600 **6** *2 ½* **Coeur Courageux (FR)**[13] 1651 5-8-8 **80** (t) TonyHamilton 11 70
(D Nicholls) *hld up and bhd: pushed along and sme hdwy over 2f out: nvr trbld ldrs* **9/1**

55-4 **7** *2 ½* **Macedon**[34] 1145 4-8-10 **82** EddieAhern 9 67
(J S Moore) *hld up in mid-div: rdn 4f out: no rspnse* **13/8**[1]

/5-0 **8** *3 ½* **Akram (IRE)**[45] 993 5-8-13 **90** JamieMoriarty(5) 13 67
(Jonjo O'Neill) *hld up and bhd: rdn over 4f out: no rspnse* **22/1**

001- **9** *2* **Ludovico**[172] 6694 4-8-9 **81** SteveDrowne 3 53
(J M Bradley) *a bhd* **25/1**

1m 43.02s (-2.49) **Going Correction** -0.15s/f (Firm) 9 Ran SP% **116.8**
Speed ratings (Par 107):106,104,104,100,100 97,95,91,89
CSF £18.76 CT £207.63 TOTE £4.90: £1.50, £2.30, £2.60; EX 23.60.
Owner Mrs Andrea M Mallinson **Bred** C Mallinson **Trained** Norton, N Yorks
■ Stewards' Enquiry : Royston Ffrench three-day ban: used whip with excessive force (Jun 5-7)

FOCUS
A strongly-run affair, with two horses that disappointed last time fighting out the finish. The favourite never featured at any stage and this form is pretty ordinary, although it does make sense.

NOTEBOOK
Daaweitza, who disappointed only three days earlier on a track not thought to suit, bounced right back to his best with a gritty display. He has been in fine form during the last few months, but will find things getting tougher for him after the Handicapper has his say again. (op 7-2 tchd 4-1 in places)
Zato(IRE), who ran badly at Newmarket the previous weekend, kept on well under really strong pressure to give the winner a scare late on. He is fairly handicapped and should remain competitive for a while in decent handicaps. (op 6-1)
Harare moved with ominous ease throughout the race, which he often does, but found little off the bridle and failed to give the winner any worries. He is quite high in the handicap and will probably struggle in this grade unless improving significantly. (tchd 14-1)
Councellor(FR) had every chance at the two-furlong pole but quickly emptied out under pressure. He is still 4lb higher in the handicap than his last winning mark and has not won on turf since the autumn of 2005. (tchd 14-1)
Vicious Warrior, making his seasonal debut, set a strong gallop in front and failed to get home. (op 16-1)
Coeur Courageux(FR) never got involved and looked one-paced in the final stages. (op 7-1)
Macedon was extremely disappointing and failed by a long way to reproduce his effort at Newbury last time. The stable do seem to be a bit quiet at the moment, so the run can probably be ignored. Official explanation: jockey said gelding lost a near-fore shoe (tchd 15-8)

1997 STONEACRE H'CAP 1m 2f 120y

5:05 (5:05) (Class 5) (0-75,75) 4-Y-0+ **£3,886** (£1,156; £577; £288) **Stalls** High

Form RPR

-001 **1** **Just Lille (IRE)**[19] 1488 4-8-13 **70** (p) RoystonFfrench 6 87
(Mrs A Duffield) *a.p: rdn to ld wl over 1f out: drvn clr fnl f: r.o wl* **13/2**

3012 **2** *6* **Cinematic (IRE)**[77] 652 4-9-4 **75** AmirQuinn 8 82
(J R Boyle) *hld up in tch: rdn over 2f out: edgd lft and wnt 2nd ins fnl f: no ch w wnr* **7/2**[2]

1210 **3** *½* **Shape Up (IRE)**[41] 1042 7-9-3 **74** (v) PaulFessey 10 80
(R Craggs) *chsd ldr: led 3f out: rdn and hdd wl over 1f out: one pce fnl f* **6/1**

5523 **4** *2 ½* **Pab Special (IRE)**[13] 1655 4-9-1 **72** LeeEnstone 3 74
(K R Burke) *hld up in tch: rdn over 2f out: one pce* **3/1**[1]

0024 **5** *¾* **Sforzando**[24] 1371 6-8-4 **68** KristinStubbs(7) 7 68+
(Mrs L Stubbs) *bhd: rdn 4f out: styd on fnl f: nvr nrr* **11/2**[3]

00-4 **6** *1* **Gallego**[14] 1638 5-7-12 **62** MCGeran(7) 12 61
(R J Price) *s.s: hld up and bhd: rdn and hdwy on outside over 2f out: no further prog* **9/1**

4205 **7** *3* **Top Jaro (FR)**[11] 1720 4-9-1 **72** ChrisCatlin 1 66
(Jennie Candlish) *led: hdd 3f out: sn rdn: wknd wl over 1f out* **12/1**

260- **8** *5* **Latif (USA)**[331] 2974 6-9-0 **71** DeanMcKeown 5 56
(Ms Deborah J Evans) *hld up towards rr: stdy hdwy 5f out: wknd over 2f out* **12/1**

20- **9** *nk* **Exit To Luck (GER)**[156] 6878 6-8-10 **67** SteveDrowne 4 52
(S Gollings) *a towards rr* **16/1**

00/0 **10** *10* **Another Choice (IRE)**[22] 1438 6-9-1 **72** (t) JamesDoyle 2 40
(N P Littmoden) *hld up towards rr: rdn 4f out: sn struggling* **33/1**

2m 13.42s (-4.31) **Going Correction** -0.15s/f (Firm) 10 Ran SP% **124.4**
Speed ratings (Par 103):109,104,104,102,101 101,99,95,95,87
CSF £31.67 CT £150.58 TOTE £4.50: £2.00, £1.90, £2.30; EX 24.60.
Owner Granville J Harper **Bred** Sweetmans Bloodstock **Trained** Constable Burton, N Yorks

FOCUS
An ordinary handicap containing few progressive types. An exception is Just Lille, who was much improved at this trip in a race rated through the third to his recent level.
Gallego Official explanation: jockey said gelding hung right-handed
Latif(USA) Official explanation: jockey said gelding had no more to give
Another Choice(IRE) Official explanation: jockey said gelding hung right-handed

1998 RENAULT LIVERPOOL MAIDEN STKS 1m 3f 200y

5:40 (5:41) (Class 5) 3-Y-0+ **£2,817** (£838; £418; £209) **Stalls** High

Form RPR

34- **1** **Lion Sands**[253] 5321 3-8-9 0 NickyMackay 10 98+
(L M Cumani) *chsd ldrs: led 3f out: sn rdn: r.o wl* **4/1**[3]

0-3 **2** *3 ½* **Samuel**[35] 1129 3-8-9 0 EddieAhern 13 90
(J L Dunlop) *hld up in mid-div: hdwy over 3f out: rdn and edgd lft 2f out: swtchd rt jst over 1f out: one pce* **9/2**

62 **3** *1 ¾* **Heron Bay**[15] 1605 3-8-9 0 SteveDrowne 12 87
(G Wragg) *s.i.s: sn hld up in mid-div: hdwy over 3f out: rdn over 2f out: one pce fnl f* **15/8**[1]

4-63 **4** *6* **Rhaam**[27] 1290 3-8-9 **81** MichaelHills 4 77
(B W Hills) *prom: wnt 2nd over 5f out: ev ch 3f out: sn rdn: wknd over 1f out* **9/4**[2]

P0 **5** *1 ¼* **Feeling (IRE)**[13] 1659 3-8-2 0 MCGeran(7) 5 75
(P W Chapple-Hyam) *chsd ldr tl over 5f out: rdn 3f out: wknd wl over 1f out* **40/1**

000- **6** *11* **Gigi Glamor**[233] 5768 5-9-7 **41** StephenDonohoe 17 53?
(W M Brisbourne) *nvr nr ldrs* **100/1**

3 **7** *5* **Master Halling**[25] 1358 3-8-9 0 ChrisCatlin 9 50
(R Charlton) *nvr bttr than mid-div* **8/1**

3 **8** *2 ½* **Modarab**[18] 1529 5-9-7 0 PJMcDonald(5) 1 46
(Mrs L B Normile) *broke wl: stdd into mid-div after 1f: nvr nrr* **80/1**

9 *3* **Zen Garden**[12] 6-9-7 0 DavidAllan 14 36
(W M Brisbourne) *s.i.s: nvr nr ldrs* **100/1**

00/ **10** *4* **Ashmolian (IRE)**[581] 6013 4-9-12 0 VinceSlattery 2 35
(Miss Z C Davison) *nvr bttr than mid-div* **125/1**

0/ **11** *2 ½* **Code (IRE)**[9] 2260 6-9-12 0 DeanMcKeown 6 31
(Miss Z C Davison) *s.i.s: a bhd* **100/1**

6 **12** *3* **Tri Chara (IRE)**[15] 1605 3-8-9 0 GrahamGibbons 15 26
(R Hollinshead) *plld hrd in mid-div: bhd fnl 3f* **50/1**

0/ **13** *1 ¾* **Black Wadi**[636] 4754 5-9-7 0 (t) AmirQuinn 7 18
(T Keddy) *led: clr 7f out: hdd 3f out: wknd qckly* **100/1**

-0 **14** *3 ½* **Roll Em Over**[7] 1804 4-9-7 0 LeeEnstone 3 12
(C W Thornton) *a bhd* **100/1**

15 *13* **Lilymay**[973] 7-9-4 0 AndrewElliott(3) 11 —
(B P J Baugh) *s.i.s: a bhd* **100/1**

2m 30.14s (-4.85) **Going Correction** -0.15s/f (Firm)
WFA 3 from 4yo+ 17lb 15 Ran SP% **127.2**
Speed ratings (Par 103):110,107,106,102,101 94,91,89,87,84 83,81,79,77,68
CSF £23.69 TOTE £5.60: £2.10, £2.20, £1.10; EX 35.20.
Owner Stronach Stables **Bred** Fittocks Stud **Trained** Newmarket, Suffolk

FOCUS
A well above-average maiden, run at a good tempo and won by a promising sort in Lion Sands. The fourth sets the standard, and the first three should all make classy handicappers at least.
Black Wadi Official explanation: jockey said mare had no more to give
Roll Em Over Official explanation: jockey said filly stumbled leaving stalls
Lilymay Official explanation: jockey said mare never travelled

1999 GEORGE DUFFIELD APPRENTICE H'CAP 5f

6:10 (6:10) (Class 5) (0-75,80) 3-Y-0+ **£3,238** (£722; £722; £240) **Stalls** Centre

Form RPR

-006 **1** **Peopleton Brook**[6] 1854 5-9-8 **75** BarrySavage(5) 16 87+
(J M Bradley) *chsd ldrs: rdn to ld ins fnl f: r.o wl* **7/1**

6223 **2** *2 ½* **No Time (IRE)**[3] 1914 7-8-10 **63** PatrickDonaghy(5) 5 66
(A J McCabe) *mid-div: rdn and hdwy over 1f out: kpt on ins fnl f* **4/1**[1]

3006 **2** *dht* **Desperate Dan**[22] 1431 6-9-3 **70** (b) SophieDoyle(5) 2 73
(J A Osborne) *a.p: led over 1f out: rdn and hdd ins fnl f: nt qckn* **10/1**

6-60 **4** *1 ¼* **Jilly Why (IRE)**[17] 1557 6-8-9 **62** (b[1]) JohnCavanagh(5) 14 61
(Paul Green) *s.i.s: sn mid-div: rdn and hdwy over 1f out: kpt on ins fnl f* **16/1**

50-2 **5** *1 ½* **Jakeini (IRE)**[20] 1483 4-9-10 **75** MCGeran(3) 10 68
(E S McMahon) *hld up and bhd: nt clr run and swtchd rt 2f out: rdn and hdwy over 1f out: nvr able to chal* **11/2**[3]

30-0 **6** *nk* **Our Little Secret (IRE)**[46] 964 5-9-1 **63** KellyHarrison 13 55+
(A Berry) *s.i.s: hdwy fr jst over 1f out: nvr nrr* **16/1**

0-66 **7** *2* **Malapropism**[31] 1214 7-9-2 **71** MatthewDavies(7) 17 56
(M R Channon) *led: rdn over 2f out: hdd over 1f out: wknd fnl f* **10/1**

000- **8** *1* **Johnston's Diamond (IRE)**[174] 6681 9-9-7 **72** GaryBartley(3) 12 53
(E J Alston) *mid-div: rdn and no hdwy fnl 2f* **25/1**

0-50 **9** *1 ¾* **Our Fugitive (IRE)**[13] 1669 5-8-12 **65** MarkCoumbe(5) 8 40
(A W Carroll) *chsd ldrs tl wknd over 1f out* **8/1**

00-0 **10** *nk* **Danjet (IRE)**[6] 1854 4-9-7 **72** WJCafferty(3) 15 46
(J M Bradley) *mid-div: rdn 2f out: no rspnse* **33/1**

03-0 **11** *¾* **The History Man (IRE)**[31] 1226 4-9-1 **63** SCreighton 9 34
(M Mullineaux) *rrd and s.s: a bhd* **33/1**

35-1 **12** *½* **Steel City Boy (IRE)**[17] 1565 4-9-1 **70** DavidHunt(7) 4 39
(D Carroll) *mid-div tl wknd wl over 1f out* **5/1**[2]

0-16 **13** *3* **Macademy Royal (USA)**[66] 717 4-9-6 **68** (t) ThomasO'Brien 1 27
(H Morrison) *a bhd* **9/1**

60.56 secs (-1.51) **Going Correction** -0.15s/f (Firm) 13 Ran SP% **125.3**
Speed ratings (Par 103):106,102,102,100,97 97,93,92,89,89 87,87,82
WIN: Peopleton Brook £7.10. PL: £2.70, Desperate Dan £2.60, No Time £2.00. EX: PB/DD £25.00, PB/NT £11.10. CSF: PB/DD £38.90, PB/NT £18.13. TRIC: PB/DD/NT £167.10, PB/NT/DD £149.04. Place 6 £32.39, Place 5 £11.89.
Owner G S Thompson & P Banfield **Bred** Lower Hill Farm Stud **Trained** Sedbury, Gloucs
■ Green Lagonda was withdrawn (7/1, no suitable jockey available.) R4 applies, deduct 10p in the £. New market formed.

FOCUS
A competitive sprint run at a solid pace. The form should work out, the runner-up rated to his recent level, and there should be more to come from Peopleton Brook.
T/Plt: £71.60 to a £1 stake. Pool: £49,868.90. 507.85 winning tickets. T/Qpdt: £18.80 to a £1 stake. Pool: £3,888.90. 152.70 winning tickets. KH

1840 NEWMARKET (ROWLEY) (R-H)

Friday, May 25

OFFICIAL GOING: Good to firm (good in places, 8.4)

Wind: Fresh, behind Weather: Overcast

2000 EUROPEAN BREEDERS' FUND MAIDEN FILLIES' STKS — 6f

2:20 (2:21) (Class 4) 2-Y-O — **£4,533** (£1,348; £674; £336) **Stalls** High

Form — RPR

5 **1** **Liberty Belle (IRE)**[7] 1821 2-8-11 0 ... StephaneBreux(3) 8 — 80+
(J R Best) *led 1f: chsd ldrs: rdn over 1f out: r.o to ld nr fin* **5/2**[1]

02 **2** *shd* **Pixie's Blue (IRE)**[7] 1814 2-9-0 0 ... RobertHavlin 7 — 80
(J H M Gosden) *lw: led 5f out: rdn over 1f out: hdd nr fin* **9/2**[2]

3 *1 1/2* **Dea Caelestis (FR)** 2-9-0 0 ... TedDurcan 2 — 75
(H R A Cecil) *neat: sn chsng ldr: rdn and edgd lft over 1f out: styd on same pce ins fnl f* **9/2**[2]

4 *1 1/4* **Relinquished** 2-9-0 0 ... TPQueally 3 — 71
(J Noseda) *wl grwn: s.i.s: hld up: hdwy over 2f out: swtchd lft over 1f out: hung rt ins fnl f: styd on* **5/1**[3]

5 *hd* **Geestring (IRE)** 2-9-0 0 ... PatDobbs 6 — 71
(R Hannon) *neat: chsd ldrs: rdn over 1f out: styd on same pce* **15/2**

6 *shd* **Sakhacity** 2-9-0 0 ... StephenCarson 4 — 71
(J R Jenkins) *w'like: hld up: hdwy 1/2-way: rdn over 1f out: styd on* **80/1**

7 *1 1/2* **Dresden Doll (USA)** 2-9-0 0 ... HayleyTurner 9 — 66
(M L W Bell) *gd sort: neat: chsd ldrs over 4f* **16/1**

8 *1 1/4* **Danamight (IRE)** 2-9-0 0 ... NeilPollard 5 — 62
(G G Margarson) *leggy: unf: b: s.s: outpcd* **33/1**

9 *nk* **Night Skier (IRE)** 2-9-0 0 ... KerrinMcEvoy 10 — 61
(J L Dunlop) *w'like: chsd ldrs: lost pl over 4f out: outpcd over 2f out: styd on ins fnl f* **12/1**

10 *4* **Aberavon** 2-9-0 0 ... MartinDwyer 1 — 49
(D R C Elsworth) *w'like: scope: bit bkwd: s.s: outpcd* **16/1**

1m 13.74s (0.64) **Going Correction** +0.125s/f (Good) **10 Ran SP% 117.0**
Speed ratings (Par 92):100,99,97,96,95 95,93,92,91,86
CSF £13.61 TOTE £3.70: £1.40, £1.80, £1.90; EX 11.00.
Owner Heading For The Rocks Partnership **Bred** Dr Dean Harron **Trained** Hucking, Kent

FOCUS
They did not go mad up front and it paid to race handily in this decent fillies' maiden. Experience came to the fore and the form seems sound enough, with Liberty Belle running to a similar level as on her debut.

NOTEBOOK
Liberty Belle(IRE) was a 100-1 shot when shaping with plenty of promise in Listed company on her debut at York a week earlier, but was a solid favourite on this drop in class and step up in trip. Just edging the result at the line, she was a workmanlike winner, but the ground might have been on the quick side for her and she is probably better than the bare form suggests. She could go to Royal Ascot next, where the Albany Stakes would look a suitable target. (op 3-1)
Pixie's Blue(IRE), runner-up over the course and distance a week earlier, is steadily improving with racing and was only narrowly denied having made most of the running. It has to be said that she did enjoy the run of the race, though. (op 4-1)
Dea Caelestis(FR) ◆, who is closely related to Enrique, who won the Greenham before finishing second in the 2000 Guineas, is the first juvenile to run from the yard this season. She ran a race full of promise behind two more experienced fillies, might prefer slightly easier ground and will soon be winning on this evidence. (op 4-1 tchd 5-1)
Relinquished, a half-sister to a number of winners, including 6f juvenile scorers Medley, Marching Song & Flower Market, looked to find the ground a bit too quick and can improve on this when she gets her toe in a bit. (op 9-2)
Geestring(IRE), whose dam placed over 7f at two and is a half-sister to one-time very useful sprinter Fast Heart, came in for a bit of support in the market and can do better with this run under her belt. (op 11-1 tchd 12-1)
Sakhacity, who is a half-sister to Chara, a 1m4f winner at three, is herself by Sakhee and bound to need further in time. This was a highly satisfactory debut effort in the circumstances. (op 66-1)

2001 HOME OF RACING CONDITIONS STKS — 1m

2:55 (2:55) (Class 4) 3-Y-O — **£6,477** (£1,927; £963; £481) **Stalls** High

Form — RPR

14 **1** **Chantilly Tiffany**[20] 1466 3-8-7 88 ... KerrinMcEvoy 1 — 91
(E A L Dunlop) *lw: chsd ldr: led over 2f out: rdn clr fr over 1f out* **12/1**

1-00 **2** *1 1/4* **Go On Be A Tiger (USA)**[13] 1662 3-8-12 85 ... TPO'Shea 5 — 93
(M R Channon) *a.p: rdn to chse wnr and hung lft over 1f out: hung rt ins fnl f: styd on* **25/1**

1 **3** *1 3/4* **One Hour**[116] 293 3-8-12 0 ... PatDobbs 4 — 89
(M P Tregoning) *hld up in tch: rdn and hung lft fnl 2f: styd on same pce fnl f* **11/10**[1]

11-5 **4** *hd* **Yazamaan**[14] 1617 3-8-12 100 ... MartinDwyer 2 — 89
(J H M Gosden) *b.hind: hld up: racd keenly: rdn and hung lft over 1f out: nt trble ldrs* **11/8**[2]

6- **5** *7* **Vorteeva (USA)**[272] 4825 3-8-12 98 ... (p) NCallan 3 — 72
(K R Burke) *led: rdn and hdd over 2f out: wknd over 1f out* **9/1**[3]

1m 39.45s (0.08) **Going Correction** +0.125s/f (Good) **5 Ran SP% 111.3**
Speed ratings (Par 101):104,102,101,100,93
CSF £172.56 TOTE £9.00: £2.60, £4.40; EX 45.70.
Owner Ballygallon Stud Ltd **Bred** Ballygallon Stud **Trained** Newmarket, Suffolk

FOCUS
A steadily-run race to halfway and it is questionable what the form is worth. Chantilly Tiffany stepped up a fair bit on her previous effort in Listed company.

2002 NEWMARKETRACECOURSES.CO.UK H'CAP — 1m 4f

3:30 (3:30) (Class 3) (0-90,89) 4-Y-0+ — **£7,772** (£2,312; £1,155; £577) **Stalls** High

Form — RPR

150- **1** **Rayhani (USA)**[267] 4951 4-9-4 89 ... MartinDwyer 9 — 105+
(M P Tregoning) *hld up: hdwy over 3f out: led over 1f out: hung rt ins fnl f: rdn out* **9/2**[1]

504- **2** *4* **Castle Howard (IRE)**[202] 6336 5-9-3 88 ... TPQueally 5 — 96+
(W J Musson) *lw: hld up: nt clr run fr over 2f out tl r.o ins fnl f: no ch w wnr* **9/2**[1]

1062 **3** *1/2* **Active Asset (IRE)**[18] 1542 5-9-2 87 ... FrancisNorton 6 — 91
(M Quinn) *hld up: rdn over 2f out: r.o ins fnl f: nt trble ldrs* **8/1**[3]

0236 **4** *hd* **Mustajed**[18] 1542 6-8-13 84 ... OscarUrbina 3 — 88
(B R Millman) *hld up: rdn and hung rt over 2f out: r.o ins fnl f: nvr trbld ldrs* **6/1**[2]

210- **5** *nk* **Topjeu (IRE)**[225] 5920 4-9-4 89 ... TedDurcan 2 — 92
(L M Cumani) *led: rdn and hdd over 1f out: no ex ins fnl f* **8/1**[3]

21-5 **6** *1 1/2* **Very Agreeable**[18] 1543 4-9-0 85 ... AdamKirby 4 — 86
(W R Swinburn) *chsd ldrs: rdn and ev ch 2f out: wknd fnl f* **9/2**[1]

00- **7** *1 1/2* **Magicalmysterytour (IRE)**[229] 5854 4-9-1 86 ... BrettDoyle 1 — 84
(W J Musson) *lw: hld up: rdn over 3f out: n.d* **17/2**

1140 **8** *1 3/4* **Art Modern (IRE)**[30] 1245 5-8-11 82 ... PatDobbs 8 — 78
(G L Moore) *chsd ldr: rdn and ev ch 2f out: wknd fnl f* **12/1**

35-0 **9** *5* **Spell Casting (USA)**[9] 1767 4-9-0 85 ... JimmyQuinn 7 — 73
(M H Tompkins) *chsd ldrs: ev ch over 2f out: sn rdn and wknd* **10/1**

2m 35.02s (1.52) **Going Correction** +0.125s/f (Good) **9 Ran SP% 118.4**
Speed ratings (Par 107):99,96,96,95,95 94,93,92,89
CSF £25.03 CT £159.55 TOTE £4.90: £2.30, £2.20, £2.50; EX 30.70.
Owner Sheikh Ahmed Al Maktoum **Bred** Darley **Trained** Lambourn, Berks

■ Stewards' Enquiry : Oscar Urbina two-day ban: used whip with excessive frequency without giving gelding time to respond (Jun 5-6)

FOCUS
A decent handicap. They did not go a strong gallop and it turned into something of a sprint, but the winner has clearly improved from three to four. The first two pulled clear and are both better than the bare form.

NOTEBOOK
Rayhani(USA) looks to have improved for a gelding operation last autumn and showed a smart turn of foot to put this race to bed inside the final furlong and a half. He is obviously going to take a hit from the Handicapper for this, but there could still be better to come, and the obvious race for him would appear to be the Duke of Edinburgh Stakes at Royal Ascot. (op 7-2 tchd 5-1)
Castle Howard(IRE), who like the winner was making his seasonal reappearance, did not enjoy the clearest of runs but he was keeping on well at the finish. There was a worry that this ground would be too quick for him but he handled it well enough and looks set for a good season. (op 11-2)
Active Asset(IRE), keen in the early stages off the ordinary gallop, looks to have been suited by the return to 1m4f, although he remains high enough in the handicap. (op 15-2)
Mustajed, who is always held up in his races, would have preferred a stronger gallop. He was staying on at the finish but was not seen to best effect. (op 8-1)
Topjeu(IRE), who looks the type on paper who should do better this year than last, was a market drifter and presumably it was thought that he needed this reappearance outing. He made most of the running at a fairly sedate gallop before dropping away inside the final two furlongs, and should come on for the run. (op 6-1)
Very Agreeable, who ran as though needing the race at Windsor on her reappearance, again travelled well but found little off the bridle. The ground may have been too quick for her, though. (op 13-2)

2003 NGK SPARK PLUGS H'CAP — 1m 2f

4:05 (4:07) (Class 4) (0-85,85) 4-Y-0+ — **£5,181** (£1,541; £770; £384) **Stalls** High

Form — RPR

02-4 **1** **Del Mar Sunset**[25] 1356 8-8-7 77 ... LiamJones(3) 15 — 86
(W J Haggas) *b: hld up: hdwy and nt clr run over 1f out: swtchd lft ins fnl f: r.o to ld post* **12/1**

-340 **2** *hd* **Pagan Sword**[30] 1245 5-9-1 82 ... KerrinMcEvoy 6 — 92+
(Mrs A J Perrett) *lw: hld up: hdwy over 2f out: n.m.r and hit over hd by rival's whip over 1f out: hmpd and led wl ins fnl f: hdd post* **9/2**[2]

111- **3** *1 1/2* **Khun John (IRE)**[195] 6432 4-9-0 81 ... BrettDoyle 2 — 87
(B J Meehan) *chsd ldr over 7f out: led over 3f out: rdn and hung lft over 1f out: hung rt and hdd wl ins fnl f* **15/2**[3]

4200 **4** *hd* **Quince (IRE)**[20] 1477 4-9-4 85 ... (v) TPQueally 14 — 90
(J Pearce) *hld up: hdwy 3f out: ev ch whn hmpd ins fnl f: styd on same pce* **12/1**

0-05 **5** *1 3/4* **Optimus (USA)**[18] 1542 5-8-4 74 ... RichardKingscote(3) 7 — 78+
(B G Powell) *b: hld up: hdwy 3f out: nt clr run and outpcd over 1f out: styd on ins fnl f* **8/1**

-156 **6** *1 1/4* **Robustian**[18] 1543 4-9-4 85 ... StephenCarson 8 — 85
(Eve Johnson Houghton) *chsd ldrs: rdn and ev ch over 1f out: wknd ins fnl f* **12/1**

1-60 **7** *hd* **Brief Goodbye**[18] 1543 7-8-13 80 ... TedDurcan 4 — 79
(John Berry) *lw: hld up: hdwy over 2f out: rdn and hung rt over 1f out: wknd ins fnl f* **14/1**

6550 **8** *3* **Prince Charlemagne (IRE)**[16] 1591 4-8-3 77 ow3 ... ESemaan(7) 10 — 71
(N P Littmoden) *hld up: hdwy over 2f out: sn rdn: wknd fnl f* **20/1**

-405 **9** *1 1/4* **James Caird (IRE)**[39] 1060 7-8-12 79 ... (b) JimmyQuinn 12 — 70
(M H Tompkins) *hld up: hdwy over 3f out: swtchd lft over 2f out: wknd fnl f* **8/1**

005- **10** *5* **Postage Stampe**[188] 6515 4-9-4 85 ... MartinDwyer 5 — 67
(D M Simcock) *lw: hld up: rdn over 3f out: n.d* **20/1**

5606 **11** *8* **Prime Contender**[22] 1434 5-8-7 74 ... PatDobbs 13 — 41
(G L Moore) *led 1f: chsd ldrs tl rdn over 3f out: sn wknd* **50/1**

-432 **12** *1/2* **The Aldbury Flyer**[7] 1819 4-8-8 75 ... AdamKirby 9 — 41+
(W R Swinburn) *trckd ldrs: racd keenly: ev ch over 2f out: wknd over 1f out: eased* **11/4**[1]

13 *1 1/4* **Kervriou (FR)**[203] 4-9-0 81 ... FrancisNorton 1 — 44
(A M Balding) *led 9f out: hdd over 3f out: wknd 2f out* **33/1**

2m 5.18s (-0.53) **Going Correction** +0.125s/f (Good) **13 Ran SP% 123.0**
Speed ratings (Par 105):107,106,105,105,104 103,102,100,99,95 89,88,87
CSF £64.60 CT £449.04 TOTE £15.20: £3.10, £2.00, £2.30; EX 89.40.
Owner R A Dawson **Bred** Woodsway Stud And Chao Racing And Bloodstock Ltd **Trained** Newmarket, Suffolk

FOCUS
A competitive handicap run at a good gallop that suited the held-up horses. The winner is rated to last year;s best, but may have been a shade fortunate as the runner-up was hampered. The form looks solid and should prove reliable.
Optimus(USA) Official explanation: jockey said gelding was denied a clear run
Prime Contender Official explanation: jockey said gelding lost a front shoe
The Aldbury Flyer Official explanation: jockey said gelding lost its action
Kervriou(FR) Official explanation: jockey said gelding ran too free early

2004 NEWMARKETEXPERIENCE.CO.UK H'CAP — 1m

4:40 (4:42) (Class 5) (0-75,75) 4-Y-0+ — **£3,886** (£1,156; £577; £288) **Stalls** High

Form — RPR

-600 **1** **Aggravation**[19] 1507 5-8-2 62 ... MarcHalford(3) 14 — 77
(D R C Elsworth) *b.hind: hld up: hdwy over 2f out: led and hung lft over 1f out: rdn out* **14/1**

50-0 **2** *2* **Night Cru**[32] 1198 4-9-1 72 ow1 ... GeorgeBaker 13 — 84+
(C F Wall) *hld up in tch: rdn and nt clr run over 1f out: styd on same pce ins fnl f* **12/1**

0-00 **3** *1 1/2* **San Antonio**[11] 765 7-9-3 74 ... (b) JimmyQuinn 7 — 81
(Mrs P Sly) *sn led: rdn and hdd over 1f out: styd on same pce* **16/1**

1-00 **4** *2* **Reeling N' Rocking (IRE)**[24] 1382 4-8-10 67 ... TPQueally 12 — 69
(B W Hills) *chsd ldr: rdn over 1f out: wknd ins fnl f* **12/1**

5044 **5** *1* **Treasure House (IRE)**[14] 1629 6-8-8 65 ... FrancisNorton 16 — 65
(M Blanshard) *hld up: hdwy u.p over 1f out: nt trble ldrs* **15/2**

343- **6** *3/4* **Colinca's Lad (IRE)**[249] 5422 5-8-6 63 ow1 ... SamHitchcott 6 — 61
(T T Clement) *chsd ldrs: rdn 1/2-way: wknd over 1f out* **22/1**

5300 **7** 2 1/2 **Marbaa (IRE)**[71] [685] 4-8-5 **62** .... PaulFitzsimons 10 55
(S Dow) *lw: hld up: rdn and hung rt over 1f out: n.d* **20/1**
0500 **8** 2 1/2 **Scroll**[26] [1318] 4-8-4 **61** oh12 .... (v) AdrianMcCarthy 2 48
(P Howling) *b: hld up: rdn over 2f out: n.d* **66/1**
350 **9** nk **Paraguay (USA)**[18] [1543] 4-8-11 **73** .... ColinHaddon(5) 8 59
(Miss V Haigh) *hld up in tch: rdn over 2f out: wknd over 1f out* **13/2**[3]
-460 **10** 1/2 **Snark (IRE)**[7] [1811] 4-8-13 **70** .... (t) NCallan 5 55
(P J Makin) *lw: chsd ldrs over 6f* **9/2**[1]
000- **11** nk **Aberlady Bay (IRE)**[164] [6794] 4-8-4 **61** oh16 .... JamieMackay 15 45
(T T Clement) *chsd ldrs over 5f* **100/1**
6-30 **12** 1/2 **Carmenero (GER)**[9] [1765] 4-9-4 **75** .... MartinDwyer 17 58
(W R Muir) *mid-div: rdn and wknd over 2f out* **12/1**
041- **13** 1 **Salonga (IRE)**[195] [6450] 4-8-10 **67** .... TedDurcan 4 48
(C F Wall) *s.i.s: hld up: rdn over 2f out: a in rr* **20/1**
2125 **14** 6 **Top Mark**[18] [1524] 5-9-3 **74** .... RobertHavlin 3 41
(J R Boyle) *chsd ldrs: rdn and wknd over 1f out: eased* **7/1**
231- **15** 3 1/2 **Esteem**[284] [4426] 4-9-3 **74** .... KerrinMcEvoy 9 33
(W Jarvis) *h.d.w: hld up: wknd 2f out* **11/2**[2]
0-54 **16** 7 **Soul Blazer (USA)**[109] [365] 4-8-8 **65** .... BrettDoyle 1 8
(Miss Gay Kelleway) *b: hld up: wknd over 2f out: eased* **28/1**

1m 37.91s (-1.46) **Going Correction** +0.125s/f (Good) **16 Ran SP% 126.6**
Speed ratings (Par 103):112,110,108,106,105 104,102,99,99,98 98,98,97,91,87 80
CSF £166.16 CT £2743.60 TOTE £20.80: £4.80, £3.50, £3.70, £3.00; EX 218.60.
Owner Perry, Vivian & Elsworth **Bred** John Khan **Trained** Newmarket, Suffolk
■ Stewards' Enquiry : Marc Halford two-day ban: careless riding (Jun 5-6)

FOCUS
Just a modest handicap for the track, but the form looks solid. Aggravation is rated back to his best, with the progressive runner-up rated as having finished a length closer than the winner.
Top Mark Official explanation: jockey said gelding lost its action
Esteem Official explanation: jockey said gelding did not handle the good to firm (good in places) ground

2005 DEVIL'S DYKE MAIDEN STKS 1m 2f
5:15 (5:17) (Class 4) 3-Y-O **£5,181** (£1,541; £770; £384) **Stalls High**

Form RPR
6-2 **1** **Tranquil Tiger**[32] [1204] 3-9-3 0 .... TedDurcan 11 87+
(H R A Cecil) *trckd ldrs: led over 3f out: rdn over 1f out: styd on* **1/1**[1]
2 2 **Purple Emperor (USA)** 3-9-3 0 .... KerrinMcEvoy 10 83
(Saeed Bin Suroor) *leggy: scope: bit bkwd: dwlt: racd keenly & sn prom: edgd lft & ev ch fr over 2f out: rdn over 1f out: styd on one pce ins fnl f* **10/3**[2]
3 3 **Louviere** 3-8-12 0 .... PatDobbs 1 72+
(Pat Eddery) *rangy: wnt lft s: hld up: hdwy over 3f out: outpcd over 2f out: styd on ins fnl f* **50/1**
5 **4** hd **Flavius (IRE)**[13] [1659] 3-9-3 0 .... J-PGuillambert 14 76
(Sir Michael Stoute) *lw: trckd ldrs: racd keenly: rdn over 2f out: sn edgd lft and outpcd: styd on ins fnl f* **12/1**
5 1 1/4 **Pathos (GER)** 3-9-3 0 .... AntonyProcter 13 74
(D R C Elsworth) *wl grwn: bkwd: s.s: hld up: hdwy over 3f out: hung lft over 1f out: no ex fnl f* **16/1**
6 1 **Horseford Hill** 3-9-0 0 .... MarcHalford(3) 4 72+
(D R C Elsworth) *leggy: scope: s.s: hld up: swtchd rt over 1f out: r.o ins fnl f: nvr nrr* **50/1**
2-2 **7** nk **Waymark (IRE)**[18] [1523] 3-9-3 0 .... PhilipRobinson 3 71
(M A Jarvis) *lw: led over 6f: rdn: edgd lft and wknd over 1f out* **4/1**[3]
8 3/4 **Spanish Diva** 3-8-12 0 .... RobertHavlin 6 65
(S C Williams) *neat: b.hind: mid-div: hdwy over 3f out: sn rdn: edgd lft and wknd over 1f out* **100/1**
50 **9** 6 **Day Of Days (IRE)**[11] [1725] 3-9-3 0 .... JimmyQuinn 5 58
(M H Tompkins) *chsd ldrs over 7f* **66/1**
10 2 1/2 **Southside Star** 3-8-12 0 .... OscarUrbina 7 48
(H J L Dunlop) *lt-f: unf: mid-div: hdwy over 3f out: rdn and wknd wl over 1f out* **66/1**
0 **11** 3/4 **Splinter Group**[37] [1093] 3-9-3 0 .... SimonWhitworth 2 51
(N A Callaghan) *hld up: a in rr: wknd over 2f out* **100/1**
0-0 **12** shd **Super Nebula**[6] [1840] 3-9-0 0 .... DominicFox(3) 9 51
(P L Gilligan) *chsd ldrs over 7f* **100/1**
13 40 **Man Of Gwent (UAE)** 3-9-3 0 .... BrettDoyle 8 —
(G A Huffer) *str: cmpt: bkwd: b: s.i.s: sn chsng ldrs: wknd over 3f out: eased* **50/1**

2m 7.65s (1.94) **Going Correction** +0.125s/f (Good) **13 Ran SP% 118.5**
Speed ratings (Par 101):97,95,93,92,91 91,90,90,85,83 82,82,50
CSF £4.20 TOTE £1.90: £1.10, £1.40, £6.20; EX 5.90.
Owner K Abdulla **Bred** Juddmonte Farms Ltd **Trained** Newmarket, Suffolk

FOCUS
They went a steady pace in this maiden and it turned into something of a sprint. The bare form is probably nothing out of the ordinary but this looks the sort of race that should throw up winners. Tranquil Tiger was 5lb off his Windsor form.

2006 BOLLINGER CHAMPAGNE CHALLENGE SERIES H'CAP (FOR GENTLEMAN AMATEUR RIDERS) 1m 2f
5:50 (5:52) (Class 5) (0-70,70) 4-Y-O+ **£3,747** (£1,162; £580; £290) **Stalls High**

Form RPR
0-00 **1** **Le Corvee (IRE)**[24] [501] 5-11-5 **70** .... MrMJJSmith(5) 13 81
(A W Carroll) *lw: chsd ldrs: led over 3f out: rdn and hdd over 1f out: styd on to ld nr fin* **12/1**
2205 **2** nk **Bavarica**[17] [1567] 5-10-13 **66** .... MrRBirkett(7) 1 76
(Miss J Feilden) *hld up: plld hrd: hdwy 1/2-way: led over 1f out: hung lft and hdd nr fin* **14/1**
213- **3** 3 **Sol Rojo**[179] [6621] 5-11-4 **67** .... (v) MrSPearce(3) 9 71
(J Pearce) *hld up: hdwy over 3f out: nt clr run over 1f out: swtchd lft and r.o ins fnl f* **9/1**
4-55 **4** 1/2 **Qualitair Wings**[7] [1819] 8-10-8 **59** .... MrBMcHugh(5) 4 62
(J Hetherton) *lw: dwlt: hld up: hdwy over 3f out: rdn over 1f out: styd on same pce* **11/2**[2]
3050 **5** 1 1/4 **Golden Alchemist**[22] [888] 4-10-10 **56** oh1 .... MrLeeNewnes 8 57
(M D I Usher) *hld up: hdwy over 3f out: rdn: hung rt and outpcd 2f out: styd on ins fnl f* **3/1**[1]
1260 **6** nk **Norwegian**[18] [1539] 6-10-3 **56** oh1 .... (p) MrJRavenall(7) 2 56
(Ian Williams) *chsd ldrs: ev ch 3f out: rdn and hung lft over 1f out: wknd fnl f* **11/2**[2]
230- **7** 6 **Prince Of Medina**[226] [5910] 4-10-3 **56** .... MrRHill(7) 12 44
(J R Best) *chsd ldr: led over 5f out: hdd over 3f out: rdn and wknd wl over 1f out* **12/1**
000- **8** 3/4 **Prince Zafonic**[167] [6321] 4-11-5 **65** .... (t) MrMatthewSmith 11 52
(Miss Gay Kelleway) *b: b.hind: chsd ldrs over 6f* **8/1**

0555 **9** 1 1/2 **Undeterred**[13] [1664] 11-10-7 **60** .... MrECookson(7) 5 44
(K J Burke) *hld up: hdwy over 2f out: rdn and wknd over 2f out* **16/1**
40-0 **10** hd **Thorny Mandate**[27] [1314] 5-10-8 **59** .... MrBenBrisbourne(5) 6 42
(W M Brisbourne) *hld up and bhd: hung rt over 2f out: n.d* **6/1**[3]
5400 **11** 12 **Royal Sailor (IRE)**[4] [1888] 5-10-3 **56** oh11 .... (b) MrDavidMcMinn(7) 10 15
(J Ryan) *lw: mid-div: wknd over 3f out* **33/1**
00P- **12** 3 **Bond Cruz**[318] [3378] 4-11-2 **69** oh11 ow13 .... MrGDavies(7) 14 22
(D Burchell) *led over 4f: wknd 4f out* **66/1**
000/ **13** 24 **Chisel**[60] [2936] 6-10-3 **56** oh11 .... MrJPearce(7) 3 —
(M Wigham) *b: dwlt: sn outpcd and bhd* **33/1**

2m 10.31s (4.60) **Going Correction** +0.125s/f (Good) **13 Ran SP% 126.5**
Speed ratings (Par 103):86,85,83,82,81 81,76,76,75,74 65,62,43
CSF £177.15 CT £1610.13 TOTE £20.00: £5.60, £5.00, £2.10; EX 211.10 Place 6 £992.06, Place 5 £727.02.
Owner J G Boyce **Bred** Forenaghts Stud And David O'Reilly **Trained** Cropthorne, Worcs

FOCUS
A modest handicap made up of exposed performers. The winner had slipped to a good mark on his old form. The second and third are better on the sand.
T/Jkpt: Not won. T/Plt: £425.90 to a £1 stake. Pool: £69,759.35. 119.55 winning tickets. T/Qpdt: £41.40 to a £1 stake. Pool: £4,551.30. 81.20 winning tickets. CR

1411 PONTEFRACT (L-H)
Friday, May 25

OFFICIAL GOING: Good (good to firm in places, 7.3)
There was a running rail in place from the 6f marker extending out and 7m wide at the line. The ground was described as 'generally firm'.
Wind: Light, half-behind Weather: Fine

2007 MAUREEN AND ERIC ARTIS GOLDEN WEDDING H'CAP 1m 4y
6:30 (6:30) (Class 6) (0-65,65) 4-Y-O+ **£3,238** (£963; £481; £240) **Stalls Low**

Form RPR
40-5 **1** **Society Music (IRE)**[32] [1198] 5-9-4 **65** .... (p) PaulMulrennan 1 74+
(M Dods) *trckd ldrs: edgd lft over 1f out: led 1f out: hld on wl* **11/2**[1]
6500 **2** 3/4 **Boy Dancer (IRE)**[19] [1488] 4-8-8 **55** .... (p) PaulQuinn 9 62
(D W Barker) *swtchd lft s: sn chsng ldrs: wnt 2nd 1f out: kpt on wl towards fin* **14/1**
500- **3** 1 **Dinner Date**[154] [6918] 5-8-5 **52** .... DaleGibson 10 57
(T Keddy) *in rr: hdwy on outside over 2f out: styd on fnl f: nt rch first 2* **11/1**
05-0 **4** 1 1/2 **Apsara**[23] [1413] 6-9-2 **63** .... PatCosgrave 5 65
(G M Moore) *chsd ldrs: one pce fnl 2f* **12/1**
6554 **5** 2 **Hoh Wotanite**[31] [1226] 4-9-1 **62** .... JHBowman 14 59
(R Hollinshead) *hld up in rr: hdwy over 2f out: kpt on same pce appr fnl f* **9/1**
300- **6** 1/2 **Tidy (IRE)**[164] [6008] 7-9-0 **64** .... (v[1]) GregFairley(3) 8 60
(Micky Hammond) *mid-div: kpt on fnl 2f: nvr nr ldrs* **20/1**
004- **7** nk **Gifted Flame**[240] [5617] 8-9-3 **64** .... PhillipMakin 17 59+
(T D Barron) *swtchd lft s: hld up in rr: styd on fnl 2f: nt rch ldrs* **7/1**[3]
1300 **8** 2 1/2 **Time To Regret**[91] [538] 7-8-11 **61** .... (p) PatrickMathers(3) 12 50
(I W McInnes) *mid-div: kpt on fnl 2f: nvr nr ldrs* **18/1**
122- **9** 1 1/2 **Bowl Of Cherries**[158] [6854] 4-8-4 **54** oh2 ow3 .... (b) SaleemGolam(3) 3 40
(I A Wood) *chsd ldrs: wkng whn n.m.r 2f out* **13/2**[2]
0-61 **10** nk **Bond Diamond**[37] [1086] 10-8-6 **58** ow1 .... MichaelJStainton(5) 2 43
(P T Midgley) *t.k.h: led: clr over 2f out: edgd rt and hdd 1f out: wknd* **7/1**[3]
55-6 **11** 2 1/2 **Bolton Hall (IRE)**[21] [1455] 5-8-10 **64** .... JamesRogers(7) 7 43
(R A Fahey) *mid-div: lost pl over 3f out: sn bhd* **10/1**
00-0 **12** 3/4 **Jaassey**[13] [1675] 4-8-5 **55** .... (p) DuranFentiman(3) 6 33
(A Crook) *prom: effrt over 2f out: sn wknd* **66/1**
5644 **13** nk **Garibaldi (GER)**[16] [1579] 5-8-8 **62** ow7 .... (b) JamesO'Reilly(7) 16 39
(J O'Reilly) *chsd ldrs: reminders 3f out: wkng whn n.m.r over 1f out* **11/1**
0-00 **14** 14 **Newcorp Lad**[120] [242] 7-8-4 **51** oh3 .... HayleyTurner 15 —
(Mrs G S Rees) *mid-div: lost pl over 2f out: bhd whn eased ins fnl f* **40/1**
00-4 **15** 3 1/2 **Seesawmilu (IRE)**[25] [1360] 4-8-4 **51** oh4 .... AdrianTNicholls 13 —
(E J Alston) *t.k.h: trckd ldrs: wknd over 2f out: sn bhd: eased ins fnl f* **14/1**

1m 44.95s (-0.75) **Going Correction** -0.075s/f (Good) **15 Ran SP% 124.5**
Speed ratings (Par 101):100,99,98,96,94 94,93,91,89,89 87,86,86,72,68
CSF £83.93 CT £856.39 TOTE £7.10: £2.40, £5.40, £5.40; EX 77.30.
Owner Henry Hewitson **Bred** John Weld **Trained** Denton, Co Durham

FOCUS
A low-grade handicap run at a strong pace. The form is sound, the front three having slipped to good marks. The runner-up is rated to this year's form and the winner will still be well in on her old form after this.
Seesawmilu(IRE) Official explanation: jockey said gelding ran too free and had no more to give

2008 MSK FILLIES' H'CAP 1m 2f 6y
7:00 (7:00) (Class 5) (0-70,67) 3-Y-O+ **£3,886** (£1,156; £577; £288) **Stalls Low**

Form RPR
05-0 **1** **Polyquest (IRE)**[141] [37] 3-8-2 **54** .... HayleyTurner 10 57
(G A Butler) *swtchd lft after s: stdy hdwy on outside 3f out: styd on wl appr fnl f: led ins fnl f: styd on wl* **16/1**
6-00 **2** 1 1/4 **Sweet Request**[15] [1606] 3-8-4 **59** ow1 .... AndrewMullen(3) 5 59
(R M Beckett) *trckd ldrs: swtchd rt over 1f out: styd on to take 2nd wl ins fnl f* **8/1**
420 **3** 2 **Anne Bronte**[41] [1044] 3-9-1 **67** .... KDarley 8 64
(M Johnston) *led: shkn up and qcknd over 3f out: hdd ins fnl f: wknd* **10/1**
4660 **4** nk **Giddywell**[11] [1731] 3-8-8 **60** .... PaulQuinn 4 56
(R Hollinshead) *mid-div: hdwy 3f out: styd on same pce fnl f* **33/1**
0411 **5** shd **Malinsa Blue (IRE)**[16] [1578] 5-9-9 **66** .... JamieMoriarty(5) 14 63
(B Ellison) *chsd ldrs: effrt 2f out: kpt on same pce fnl f* **15/8**[1]
02-2 **6** 1 1/2 **Charlotte Vale**[30] [914] 6-9-13 **65** .... PaulMulrennan 13 59
(Micky Hammond) *sn chsng ldrs: one pce whn sltly hmpd 1f out* **13/2**[3]
-030 **7** 3/4 **Susiedil (IRE)**[31] [1227] 6-9-0 **52** oh7 .... (v) AdrianTNicholls 1 45
(S T Mason) *chsd ldrs: one pce fnl 2f* **40/1**
0-31 **8** 1 1/4 **Princess Lavinia**[18] [1521] 4-9-13 **65** .... MickyFenton 12 55
(G Wragg) *in rr-div: effrt over 4f out: kpt on fnl f* **11/2**[2]
053- **9** hd **Etoile D'Or (IRE)**[227] [5898] 3-8-12 **67** .... SaleemGolam(3) 3 56
(M H Tompkins) *chsd ldrs: effrt over 3f out: one pce whn sltly hmpd 1f out* **9/1**
0554 **10** 2 1/2 **Jenny Soba**[13] [1671] 4-8-11 **54** .... MichaelJStainton(5) 9 39
(R M Whitaker) *in rr: kpt on fnl 2f: nvr on terms* **14/1**
06-0 **11** 4 **World At My Feet**[22] [1423] 5-8-7 **52** oh7 .... SuzzanneFrance(7) 7 29
(N Bycroft) *a in rr* **100/1**

-660 **12** *7* **Perfect Practice**[51] 924 3-8-4 **56** .... DaleGibson 6 19
(J A R Toller) *sn chsng ldrs: drvn 3f out: sn wknd* **20/1**
0106 **13** *11* **Raven Rascal**[19] 1489 3-7-11 **52** oh7 .... DuranFentiman(3) 2 —
(J F Coupland) *hld up in last: pushed along over 4f out: bhd and eased ins fnl f* **100/1**

2m 13.03s (-1.05) **Going Correction** -0.075s/f (Good)
WFA 3 from 4yo+ 14lb **13** Ran SP% **118.4**
Speed ratings (Par 100):101,100,98,98,98 96,96,95,95,93 89,84,75
CSF £132.77 CT £1358.75 TOTE £25.10: £5.10, £2.90, £2.80; EX 212.40.
Owner The Fairy Story Partnership **Bred** Deepwood Farm Stud **Trained** Blewbury, Oxon

FOCUS
A modest handicap and something of a tactical affair. It was an improved effort from each of the first four but none of them look on obviously good marks.

2009 GRIMETHORPE COLLIERY BAND SUPPORTED BY TOTESPORT YOUNGSTERS CONDITIONS STKS 6f
7:30 (7:30) (Class 2) 2-Y-O **£9,348** (£2,799; £1,399; £700; £349) **Stalls** Low

Form RPR
1 **1** **Burnwynd Boy**[10] 1743 2-9-0 0 .... PhillipMakin 3 87
(I Semple) *trckd ldrs: effrt 2f out: r.o to ld last 75yds: hld on wl* **7/2**[3]
41 **2** *hd* **Aaim To Storm (USA)**[11] 1706 2-8-11 0 .... JHBowman 4 83
(M R Channon) *led 2f: w ldr: shkn up to ld 1f out: hdd and no ex wl ins fnl f* **9/4**[2]
1 **3** *5* **Grand Fleet**[38] 1073 2-9-0 0 .... KDarley 1 71
(M Johnston) *w ldr: led after 2f: edgd rt and hdd 1f out: sn btn* **10/11**[1]
4 *20* **Bunty Malenoir** 2-8-3 0 .... DO'Donohoe 5 —
(I A Wood) *s.i.s: lost pl over 2f out: sn wl bhd* **33/1**
5 *3 1/2* **Our Joan** 2-8-7 0 ow4 .... MickyFenton 2 —
(P T Midgley) *s.i.s: lost pl over 2f out: sn wl bhd* **33/1**

1m 17.11s (-0.29) **Going Correction** -0.075s/f (Good) **5** Ran SP% **111.3**
Speed ratings (Par 99):98,97,91,64,59
CSF £11.88 TOTE £4.80: £2.10, £1.50; EX 12.80.
Owner Robert Reid **Bred** Mrs A F Tullie **Trained** Carluke, S Lanarks

FOCUS
Subsequent Royal Ascot winner Hellvelyn took this a year ago, but this race was not as strong. The third was disappointing after creating a good impression when winning on his debut at Nottingham, but take nothing away from the winner.

NOTEBOOK
Burnwynd Boy, who cost just 3,000gns as a yearling, has still not come in his coat. He was happy to track the two leaders and in the end did just enough. (op 5-2)
Aaim To Storm(USA), a grand, athletic type, had the leader covered. He looked to be travelling best when going on but in the end just missed out. A strongerrun race would suit him a lot better.
Grand Fleet, drawn one, made the running. He came away from the rail and in the end dropped away in disappointing fashion. He is surely better than he showed here. (op 6-4)
Bunty Malenoir, a half-sister to Im Spartacus bred for stamina rather than speed, is on the leg and narrow. She was thrown in at the deep end and had drowned at halfway. She still earned £700. (op 25-1)
Our Joan, a late foal, was a cheap buy. She looks as though she needs a lot more time yet and was left well behind going into the final turn. (op 40-1)

2010 CONSTANT SECURITY SERVICES H'CAP 1m 4y
8:00 (8:01) (Class 4) (0-85,84) 3-Y-O **£6,477** (£1,927; £963; £481) **Stalls** Low

Form RPR
2-13 **1** **Colorado Rapid (IRE)**[6] 1851 3-9-4 **84** .... KDarley 2 103+
(M Johnston) *hld up: effrt on inner and n.m.r over 2f out: chsng ldrs on inner whn nt clr run over 1f out: swtchd rt and qcknd to ld ins fnl f: r.o strly* **11/10**[1]
6-32 **2** *2 1/2* **Dream Lodge (IRE)**[22] 1439 3-8-11 **77** .... TPQueally 6 81
(J G Given) *trckd ldrs: chal 3f out: led 1f out: hdd and no ex ins fnl f: lft 2nd nr line* **8/1**[3]
0-02 **3** *1 3/4* **Lap Of Honour (IRE)**[17] 1563 3-7-12 **71** oh3 ow1... KirstyMilczarek(7) 1 71
(N A Callaghan) *led: qcknd over 3f out: hdd 1f out: kpt on same pce* **25/1**
5402 **4** *1/2* **Musical Beat**[1] 1979 3-8-11 **77** .... MickyFenton 5 78+
(Miss V Haigh) *hld up: effrt on outer over 3f out: kpt on same pce: bdly hmpd nr fin* **25/1**
3-24 **5** *10* **Leon Knights**[30] 1246 3-8-9 **75** .... RoystonFfrench 4 51
(G A Butler) *trckd ldrs: drvn over 3f out: wkng whn n.m.r 2f out: sn bhd and eased* **12/1**
324- **6** *3* **Flying Encore (IRE)**[221] 6018 3-8-11 **77** .... AdamKirby 3 46
(W R Swinburn) *trckd ldrs: wkng whn sltly hmpd 2f out: sn lost pl and eased* **20/1**
11 **F** **Sky More**[13] 1672 3-9-4 **84** .... PhilipRobinson 8 89
(M A Jarvis) *chsd ldrs: effrt over 2f out: 2nd and styng on whn broke fore leg and fell last 50yds: dead* **15/8**[2]

1m 43.81s (-1.89) **Going Correction** -0.075s/f (Good) **7** Ran SP% **113.7**
Speed ratings (Par 101):106,103,101,101,91 88,—
CSF £10.56 CT £134.31 TOTE £2.20: £1.30, £2.70; EX 11.10.
Owner Luke Lillingston **Bred** Mount Coote Stud And M Johnston **Trained** Middleham Moor, N Yorks
■ Stewards' Enquiry : Kirsty Milczarek one-day ban: careless riding (Jun 5)

FOCUS
A tactical affair but a most impressive winner in Colorado Rapid who was value for a lot more than the bare form and can go on from here. The form looks sound. The race was marred by the fatal injury to the hitherto unbeaten Sky More.

2011 CONSTANT SECURITY SERVING YORKSHIRE RACECOURSES H'CAP 1m 4f 8y
8:30 (8:33) (Class 4) (0-85,83) 4-Y-O+ **£6,477** (£1,927; £963; £481) **Stalls** Low

Form RPR
-554 **1** **La Estrella (USA)**[9] 1771 4-9-0 **79** .... TPQueally 7 92
(J G Given) *led: qcknd over 5f out: rdn clr over 1f out: styd on strly* **3/1**[1]
450- **2** *5* **Mceldowney**[230] 5811 5-9-4 **83** .... KDarley 9 88
(M Johnston) *chsd ldrs: drvn over 5f out: wnt 2nd 2f out: kpt on: no ch w wnr* **6/1**[3]
-313 **3** *nk* **Heathyards Pride**[14] 1621 7-8-9 **74** .... MickyFenton 10 79
(R Hollinshead) *hld up in rr: hdwy on outer over 1f out: styd on to take 3rd nr fin* **9/2**[2]
0-00 **4** *1* **Great View (IRE)**[20] 1470 8-8-5 **73** .... (p) GregFairley(3) 11 76
(Mrs A L M King) *trckd ldrs: t.k.h: drvn over 4f out: one pce fnl 2f* **28/1**
-000 **5** *1 1/4* **Dium Mac**[9] 1767 6-8-7 **79** .... SuzzanneFrance(7) 4 80+
(N Bycroft) *tk fierce hold towards rr: hdwy over 3f out: one pce fnl 2f* **8/1**
1044 **6** *1/2* **Cripsey Brook**[13] 1668 9-8-6 **78** .... (t) DanielleMcCreery(7) 1 78
(K G Reveley) *s.i.s: hld up in rr: effrt on ins and n.m.r over 2f out: kpt on fnl f* **8/1**
-456 **7** *1/2* **Mighty Moon**[8] 1794 4-8-10 **82** .... (bt) JamesO'Reilly(7) 6 81
(J O'Reilly) *s.i.s: sn chsng ldrs: hrd rdn 3f out: one pce* **14/1**

21-0 **8** *5* **Mulaazem**[22] 1438 4-9-2 **81** .... DaleGibson 2 72
(J Mackie) *chsd ldrs: effrt over 4f out: lost pl over 1f out* **25/1**
050- **9** *1 1/4* **Astrobella**[235] 5732 4-8-7 **75** .... SaleemGolam(3) 8 64
(M H Tompkins) *in rr: drvn over 5f out: kpt on fnl 2f: nvr nr ldrs* **20/1**
3204 **10** *1 1/4* **Wulimaster (USA)**[14] 1621 4-8-5 **70** .... DO'Donohoe 3 57
(D W Barker) *hld up in rr: effrt over 2f out: nvr on terms* **8/1**
4-06 **11** *11* **Nelsons Column (IRE)**[16] 1575 4-9-3 **82** .... RoystonFfrench 12 52
(G M Moore) *chsd ldr: drvn over 4f out: lost pl over 2f out: sn bhd* **10/1**

2m 37.83s (-2.47) **Going Correction** -0.075s/f (Good) **11** Ran SP% **118.6**
Speed ratings (Par 105):105,101,101,100,99 99,99,95,95,94 86
CSF £20.45 CT £81.27 TOTE £3.60: £1.60, £2.70, £2.20; EX 23.00.
Owner The G-Guck Group **Bred** Five Horses Ltd And Theatrical Syndicate **Trained** Willoughton, Lincs

FOCUS
The winner had his own way in front and in the end came right away to improve by 4lb on his York mark. This was not that strong a race though, with doubts over those at the head of the weights.

2012 ROCHDALE FOOTBALL CLUB CENTENARY MAIDEN STKS 6f
9:00 (9:03) (Class 5) 3-Y-O **£3,886** (£1,156; £577; £288) **Stalls** Low

Form RPR
022- **1** **Zonta Zitkala**[293] 4148 3-8-12 76 .... JamesDoyle 8 65
(R M Beckett) *trckd ldrs: styd on wl to ld last 75yds* **6/4**[1]
02- **2** *1* **Farefield Lodge (IRE)**[346] 2530 3-9-3 0 .... AdamKirby 1 66
(C G Cox) *mde most: hdd and no ex last 75yds* **11/4**[2]
20- **3** *nk* **Extravagance (IRE)**[217] 6073 3-8-12 0 .... NickyMackay 6 60
(L M Cumani) *chsd ldrs: styd on wl ins fnl f to take 3rd nr line* **5/1**[3]
0- **4** *3/4* **Tumbelini**[241] 5592 3-8-12 0 .... KDarley 3 58
(C F Wall) *trckd ldrs: chal over 1f out: no ex ins fnl f* **14/1**
66-0 **5** *1 1/4* **Nufoudh (IRE)**[18] 1530 3-9-3 57 .... PatCosgrave 9 59
(Miss Tracy Waggott) *w wnr: sltly outpcd over 1f out: kpt on wl ins fnl f* **100/1**
6 *1 3/4* **Julian Joachim (USA)** 3-9-3 0 .... DeanMcKeown 7 53
(G A Swinbank) *s.i.s: hdwy over 2f out: sn outpcd: styd on fnl f* **14/1**
0 **7** *1* **Piperman**[27] 1303 3-9-3 0 .... PhillipMakin 11 50
(M Dods) *mid-div: kpt on fnl 2f: nvr rchd ldrs* **100/1**
0- **8** *shd* **River Club**[212] 6175 3-9-3 0 .... JHBowman 12 50
(G A Swinbank) *in tch: outpcd over 2f out: kpt on wl fnl f* **7/1**
6 **9** *nk* **Musical Parkes**[13] 1679 3-8-9 0 .... AndrewMullen(3) 4 44
(W J H Ratcliffe) *chsd ldrs: one pce fnl 2f* **40/1**
00 **10** *1* **Hello Nod**[28] 1282 3-9-3 0 .... PaulMulrennan 14 46
(Miss J A Camacho) *swtchd lft after s: mid-div: kpt on fnl 2f: nvr a factor* **100/1**
11 *5* **Recovery Mission** 3-9-3 0 .... RoystonFfrench 5 30
(G M Moore) *s.i.s: a in rr: detached 2f out* **33/1**
0- **12** *3/4* **Buds Dilemma**[294] 4109 3-8-9 0 .... PatrickMathers(3) 10 22
(I W McInnes) *chsd ldrs on outer: lost pl over 2f out* **100/1**
13 *3* **Art Gamble (IRE)** 3-9-3 0 .... PaulEddery 13 18
(N A Callaghan) *s.s: a detached in rr* **20/1**
6 **14** *31* **Harts In Mo Shun (IRE)**[14] 1625 3-8-12 0 .... PBradley(5) 15 —
(A Berry) *s.i.s: detached in rr: lost tch over 2f out: t.o* **40/1**

1m 17.0s (-0.40) **Going Correction** -0.075s/f (Good) **14** Ran SP% **125.7**
Speed ratings (Par 99):99,97,97,96,94 92,90,90,90,89 82,81,77,36
CSF £5.52 TOTE £2.70: £1.40, £1.60, £2.10; EX 7.80 Place 6 £122.35, Place 5 £36.15.
Owner Lady Green **Bred** Lady Jennifer Green **Trained** Whitsbury, Hants

FOCUS
The first four have potential but the exposed fifth is rated just 57 and severely limits the form. The first three were all 8lb+ better than this on their pre-race marks.
River Club Official explanation: jockey said, regarding running and riding, his orders were to bounce gelding out of stalls, give it a chance and get its confidence in running, adding that it became unbalanced on the undulations final 2f
T/Plt: £156.40 to a £1 stake. Pool: £66,142.50. 308.65 winning tickets. T/Qpdt: £4.60 to a £1 stake. Pool: £4,371.50. 700.90 winning tickets. WG

2013 - 2017a (Foreign Racing) - See Raceform Interactive

1644 WEXFORD (R-H)
Friday, May 25

OFFICIAL GOING: Hurdle course - good to firm; flat course - good (good to firm in places)

2018a JOHN HARNEY BOOKMAKER RACE 1m 5f
7:40 (7:40) 4-Y-O+ **£5,135** (£1,196; £527; £304)

RPR
1 **Souvenance**[10] 1760 4-9-6 .... PJSmullen 5 93+
(Sir Mark Prescott) *trckd ldr in 2nd: pushed along fr under 6f out: led over 4f out: sn clr: pressed bef st where lft clr again: styd on wl* **1/3**[1]
2 *13* **Beliar (GER)**[6] 1326 4-9-11 62 .... (p) CO'Donoghue 7 76
(Eoin Doyle, Ire) *towards rr: rdn to go mod 4th under 3f out: mod 3rd bef st where lft 2nd: kpt on u.p* **66/1**
3 *6* **Misskinta (IRE)**[14] 1642 4-9-6 72 .... (b) FMBerry 1 63
(M J Grassick, Ire) *sn led: clr early: jnd 5f out: hdd over 4f out: 3rd and no ex fr over 3f out: kpt on same pce* **9/2**[2]
4 *1 1/4* **Fitzroy (IRE)**[21] 1462 6-9-2 76 .... CPGeoghegan(5) 3 62
(R Donohoe, Ire) *racd in mod 5th: 4th over 6f out: no imp u.p fr over 4f out: kpt on same pce* **20/1**
5 *11* **Balance Of Power**[247] 5479 5-9-0 .... (t) SJGray(7) 4 46
(D Broad, Ire) *v s.i.s: mod 6th over 4f out: sn no imp u.p* **14/1**[3]
6 *48* **Oporto (UAE)**[26] 1325 4-9-6 58 .... (p) MCHussey 2 —
(D M Fogarty, Ire) *chsd ldrs: mod 4th 1/2-way: wknd and trailing fr over 4f out: completely t.o* **50/1**
P **Artistic Lad**[30] 3128 7-9-2 84 .... ADLeigh(5) 8 —
(Mrs John Harrington, Ire) *chsd ldrs in mod 3rd: pushed along over 6f out: mod 2nd over 3f out: clsd bef st where broke down whn chalng: sn p.u* **16/1**

2m 41.1s (-6.20) **8** Ran SP% **114.0**
CSF £43.38 TOTE £1.40: £1.10, £40.60; DF 65.60.
Owner Miss K Rausing **Bred** Miss K Rausing **Trained** Newmarket, Suffolk

NOTEBOOK
Souvenance picked up another race for her astute trainer but this was by no means as easy as the result suggests, because Artistic Lad was making her work hard when he unfortunately broke down, leaving her clear. (op 2/7)
Artistic Lad Official explanation: jockey said gelding broke down turning for home

2019 - 2020a (Foreign Racing) - See Raceform Interactive

1912 BEVERLEY (R-H)

Saturday, May 26

OFFICIAL GOING: Good to firm (9.3)

After 4mm rain and 7mm water over the previous three days the ground was described as 'near perfect, just on the quick side of good'.
Wind: almost nil Weather: overcast, drizzle race 5 onwards

2021 TURF TV MEDIAN AUCTION MAIDEN STKS 5f
2:00 (2:01) (Class 4) 2-Y-O **£3,886** (£1,156; £577; £288) **Stalls High**

Form RPR

1 **Prime Performer (IRE)** 2-8-12 0 PaulEddery 10 73
(B Smart) *swvd rt s: sn trcking ldrs: hmpd and swtchd lft over 1f out: led jst ins fnl f: r.o* **6/1**[3]

22 2 1 1/2 **Irving Place**[24] 1411 2-8-12 0 LukeMorris(5) 5 73
(M L W Bell) *trckd ldrs: effrt 2f out: edgd lft and styd on fnl f* **5/2**[1]

6 3 shd **Rievaulx Valentino**[36] 1130 2-9-3 0 NCallan 7 73
(K A Ryan) *chsd ldrs: led over 1f out: hdd jst ins fnl f: no ex* **15/2**

5 4 2 1/2 **Angle Of Attack (IRE)**[10] 1772 2-9-3 0 TonyHamilton 1 64
(R A Fahey) *hung lft thrght: racd wd: chsd ldrs: rdn over 2f out: kpt on fnl f* **3/1**[2]

5 nk **Revue Princess (IRE)** 2-8-9 0 DuranFentiman(3) 6 58
(T D Easterby) *sn outpcd and in rr: hdwy over 1f out: styd on ins fnl f* **20/1**

6 1 3/4 **Daring Dream (GER)** 2-9-3 0 PaulQuinn 4 56
(T D Easterby) *sn outpcd and in rr: hdwy over 1f out: nvr nr ldrs* **12/1**

6 7 3 1/2 **Fyodorovich (USA)**[24] 1411 2-9-0 0 PatrickMathers(3) 9 44
(J S Wainwright) *sn prom: n.m.r and hung rt 2f out: wknd over 1f out* **9/1**

0 8 1 **Note Perfect**[28] 1285 2-8-12 0 PaulMulrennan 12 35
(M W Easterby) *chsd ldrs: hung rt and led over 2f out: wknd appr fnl f* **8/1**

00 9 7 **Blazing Bullet (IRE)**[38] 1087 2-8-10 0 LanceBetts(7) 11 15
(N Wilson) *led tl over 2f out: sn lost pl* **66/1**

10 3/4 **Frizzini** 2-9-3 0 PaulFessey 8 12
(N Tinkler) *dwlt: hdwy 3f out: wknd over 1f out* **33/1**

11 1 3/4 **Lay Down Darling** 2-8-12 0 KimTinkler 3 —
(N Tinkler) *swvd lft s: a outpcd and in rr* **50/1**

65.57 secs (1.57) **Going Correction** 0.0s/f (Good) **11 Ran SP% 119.6**
Speed ratings (Par 95):87,84,84,80,79 77,71,69,58,57 54
CSF £21.16 TOTE £7.60: £2.10, £1.40, £2.20; EX 25.40.
Owner Prime Equestrian **Bred** D & K Burnett **Trained** Hambleton, N Yorks

FOCUS
A modest median auction maiden race but the winner is a newcomer of some potential. The race has been rated through the runner-up for the time being.

NOTEBOOK
Prime Performer(IRE), a February foal, is lightly-made and still a bit on the leg. Forced to switch, she surged to the front inside the last and scored in decisive fashion. She will have learnt plenty from this and looks a fair prospect.
Irving Place, runner-up on his two previous starts, was draw wide. He stuck on to claim second spot but the winner was a cut above. (op 11-4 tchd 3-1)
Rievaulx Valentino, who ran way below expectations first time, shaped a lot better and can find a similar event. (op 6-1)
Angle Of Attack(IRE), drawn one, hung outwards and found himself with work to do at the halfway mark. He stuck on in the final furlong and will be much happier with a rail on his left side. Official explanation: jockey said colt hung left-handed (op 10-3 tchd 7-2)
Revue Princess(IRE), an April foal, is bred for speed. Carrying plenty of condition, she finished in pleasing style and will be much sharper next time. (op 16-1)
Daring Dream(GER), a January foal, has a fair bit of size and scope. He picked up late in the day and will improve a fair bit on this. (op 16-1)
Note Perfect, who showed a very scratchy action, hung badly towards the running rail and tired noticeably in the final furlong. Official explanation: jockey said filly hung left-handed throughout (tchd 15-2)

2022 BEVERLEY ELECTRIC 25 YEAR CELEBRATION CONDITIONS STKS 5f
2:30 (2:30) (Class 2) 3-Y-O+ **£11,217** (£3,358; £1,679; £840; £419; £210) **Stalls High**

Form RPR

33-1 1 **Pivotal's Princess (IRE)**[38] 1088 5-8-7 100 NCallan 3 103+
(E S McMahon) *trckd ldrs: smooth hdwy to ld 1f out: smoothly* **4/6**[1]

0/50 2 1 1/4 **Baron's Pit**[14] 1657 7-8-12 102 PaulMulrennan 4 104
(E F Vaughan) *led: hdd 1f out: kpt on same pce* **8/1**[3]

00-0 3 1 1/4 **Gift Horse**[10] 1770 7-8-12 104 DaneO'Neill 5 99
(D Nicholls) *pushed along in last: hdwy over 1f out: styd on to take 3rd nr line* **7/2**[2]

0-00 4 nk **Masta Plasta (IRE)**[9] 1788 4-8-12 92 PaulQuinn 6 98
(D Nicholls) *w ldr: wknd last 150yds* **16/1**

0-53 5 4 **Avertuoso**[8] 1825 3-8-4 88 PaulFessey 2 81
(B Smart) *dwlt: sn w ldrs: rdn 2f out: wknd fnl f* **16/1**

060- 6 11 **Chookie Heiton (IRE)**[336] 2847 9-8-12 99 TonyHamilton 1 44
(I Semple) *t.k.h: sn trcking ldrs: drvn over 2f out: lost pl appr fnl f: bhd whn eased ins fnl f* **12/1**

63.30 secs (-0.70) **Going Correction** 0.0s/f (Good)
WFA 3 from 4yo+ 8lb **6 Ran SP% 112.8**
Speed ratings (Par 109):105,103,101,100,94 76
CSF £7.01 TOTE £1.60: £1.10, £3.70; EX 7.40.
Owner R L Bedding **Bred** George Delahunt **Trained** Lichfield, Staffs

FOCUS
A decent sprint. Pivotals's Princess looks better than ever and made this golden opportunity look very simple. The race has been rated around the winner and second.

NOTEBOOK
Pivotal's Princess(IRE) really does look the finished article now. Best in on official figures, she made this look very plain sailing and should continue to give a very good account of herself. (op 8-11 tchd 4-5)
Baron's Pit, having his third outing after a long spell on the sidelines, made the running but was a sitting duck for the winner. Connections' patience deserves to bring some reward. (tchd 9-1)
Gift Horse, carrying a fair amount of condition, shaped a lot better and hopefully his 2005 Stewards' Cup victory will not prove his only highlight. (op 4-1 tchd 10-3)
Masta Plasta(IRE), who had plenty to find, showed a lot more dash but this 2005 Norfolk winner might go up in the handicap as a result of this. (op 12-1)
Avertuoso, who had his trainer with him at the start, had plenty to find but was by no means disgraced. (op 18-1 tchd 20-1)
Chookie Heiton(IRE), absent since June, looked very backward in his coat but at least showed he retains much of his old speed. Hopefully he will bounce back in due course. (op 14-1 tchd 11-1)

2023 GEORGE KILBURN MEMORIAL H'CAP 1m 100y
3:00 (3:02) (Class 5) (0-70,69) 4-Y-0+ **£3,562** (£1,059; £529; £264) **Stalls High**

Form RPR

5211 1 **Very Well Red**[14] 1673 4-8-2 60 WilliamCarson(7) 8 74+
(P W Hiatt) *led tl 7f out: trckd ldrs: led 2f out: drvn clr 1f out* **9/4**[1]

60-1 2 4 **Harvest Warrior**[14] 1655 5-9-1 69 DuranFentiman(3) 1 74
(T D Easterby) *s.i.s: swtchd rt after s: sn bhd and drvn along: hdwy over 1f out: swtchd rt and styd on strly ins fnl f* **11/2**[3]

-460 3 shd **Xpres Maite**[15] 1638 4-8-9 60 PaulEddery 5 65
(S R Bowring) *hld up in mid-div: effrt 3f out: wnt 2nd over 1f out: styd on same pce* **25/1**

2343 4 3/4 **Paparaazi (IRE)**[82] 612 5-8-13 67 (p) PatrickMathers(3) 6 70
(I W McInnes) *in rr: drvn over 4f out: hdwy on outside over 2f out: kpt on same pce* **9/1**

005- 5 3 1/2 **Kudbeme**[249] 5444 5-7-13 57 SuzzanneFrance(7) 3 52
(N Bycroft) *sn trcking ldrs: hmpd 7f out: effrt on outside over 3f out: sn chsng ldrs: wknd appr fnl f* **28/1**

50-6 6 nk **Trevian**[18] 1562 6-8-1 57 oh1 ow2 KevinGhunowa(5) 10 51
(J M Bradley) *t.k.h in rr: hdwy 3f out: sn chsng ldrs: wknd over 1f out* **8/1**

5463 7 1/2 **Skyelady**[17] 1576 4-9-2 67 (b[1]) PaulMulrennan 4 60
(Miss J A Camacho) *chsd ldr 7f out: led and hung rt over 2f out: sn hdd: wknd over 1f out* **10/1**

4205 8 7 **Volaticus (IRE)**[82] 612 6-8-9 59 TonyHamilton 9 36
(A D Brown) *hld up in mid-div: effrt 3f out: wknd over 1f out* **9/1**

-635 9 5 **Northern Boy (USA)**[24] 1413 4-9-4 69 PaulFessey 2 34
(T D Barron) *problems in stalls: dwlt: hdwy to ld 7f out: hdd over 2f out: lost pl over 1f out: eases ins fnl f* **11/4**[2]

-040 10 3 **Mister Minty (IRE)**[17] 1579 5-8-4 55 oh10 PaulQuinn 7 13
(Mrs S Lamyman) *trckd ldrs: t.k.h: effrt 3f out: sn lost pl* **50/1**

1m 46.68s (-0.72) **Going Correction** +0.025s/f (Good) **10 Ran SP% 122.3**
Speed ratings (Par 103):104,100,99,99,95 95,94,87,82,79
CSF £15.76 CT £260.11 TOTE £2.70: £1.70, £2.30, £6.40; EX 12.10.
Owner P W Hiatt **Bred** Butts Enterprises Limited **Trained** Hook Norton, Oxon
■ Stewards' Enquiry : Paul Fessey two-day ban: careless riding (Jun 6-7)

FOCUS
A modest handicap and solid form with the progressive Very Well Red taking another step up. She did much the best of those to chase the pace, the other principals coming from the rear, and could easily be another 7lb+ better. The placed form does not look strong.

2024 BRIAN YEARDLEY CONTINENTAL TWO YEAR OLD TROPHY (CONDITIONS STKS) (C&G) 5f
3:30 (3:30) (Class 2) 2-Y-O **£12,464** (£3,732; £1,866; £934; £466; £234) **Stalls High**

Form RPR

13 1 **Fred's Lad**[10] 1772 2-9-2 0 PaulMulrennan 6 83
(M W Easterby) *w ldrs: edgd lft after 1f: led over 1f out: hld on nr fin* **3/1**[2]

6 2 hd **Captain Gerrard (IRE)**[9] 1792 2-8-12 0 PaulFessey 3 78
(B Smart) *w ldrs: t.k.h: led over 2f out tl over 1f out: kpt on wl ins fnl f* **9/2**[3]

414 3 hd **Bahama Baileys**[10] 1772 2-8-12 0 DaneO'Neill 5 78
(M Johnston) *w ldrs: bmpd after 1f: outpcd 3f out: hdwy over 1f out: styd on wl towards fin* **6/1**

51 4 hd **Taurian**[20] 1487 2-9-0 0 FergusSweeney 2 79
(Mrs L Stubbs) *chsd ldrs: outpcd over 3f out: hdwy and edgd rt over 1f out: styd on strly* **10/1**

00 5 3 **Thomas Malory (IRE)**[7] 1832 2-8-12 0 ColinHaddon 4 66?
(Miss V Haigh) *sn outpcd: hdwy 2f out: nvr nr ldrs* **100/1**

6 3 **Do As I Say** 2-8-9 0 DuranFentiman 1 52
(T D Easterby) *dwlt: bhd: edgd rt 2f out: kpt on: nvr on terms* **40/1**

322 7 5 **Fast Feet**[17] 1580 2-8-12 0 NCallan 8 37
(K A Ryan) *t.k.h: led tl over 2f out: lost pl over 1f* **11/8**[1]

8 9 **Premier Class (IRE)** 2-8-9 0 TonyHamilton 7 2
(J S Wainwright) *s.i.s: a detached in last* **100/1**

63.70 secs (-0.30) **Going Correction** 0.0s/f (Good) **8 Ran SP% 113.1**
Speed ratings (Par 99):102,101,101,101,96 91,83,69
CSF £16.44 TOTE £4.90: £1.50, £1.70, £1.80; EX 21.70.
Owner Derek Pearson **Bred** A C M Spalding **Trained** Sheriff Hutton, N Yorks

FOCUS
Hand-timed. Quite a valuable two-year-old prize but a large blanket would have covered the first four at the line. The race took less winning than expected with the favourite below par but the form looks strong enough.

NOTEBOOK
Fred's Lad still does not look at his very best yet. He collided with the third early on but showed a good spirit. At the line there was nothing at all to spare.
Captain Gerrard(IRE), tending to race wide, was very keen to get on with it. He fought back when headed and in the end was only just denied. He will be better with some cover and is surely a winner waiting to happen. (op 6-1)
Bahama Baileys, bumped after a furlong, came back strongly after being tapped for toe and finished best of all. He is crying out for a sixth furlong.
Taurian, who did not impress at all going to post, struggled to keep up before the halfway mark. Edging towards the far rail, he finished with quite a flourish. (op 11-1 tchd 9-1)
Thomas Malory(IRE), unplaced in his first two starts, was picking up ground from halfway, perhaps suggesting the two leaders were stopping.
Do As I Say, a robust March foal, was carrying tons of condition and looked very inexperienced going to post. He kept on in his own time in the rear and this tough introduction will have taught him plenty. (op 33-1)
Fast Feet, having his fourth outing, wouldn't settle in front and ran himself to a standstill. It will be back to the drawing board with him now. Official explanation: trainer had no explanation for the poor form shown (op 5-4 tchd 6-4)

2025 COTTINGHAM PARK GOLF AND COUNTRY CLUB SPRINT (HANDICAP STKS) 5f
4:00 (4:00) (Class 4) (0-85,85) 4-Y-0+ **£6,477** (£1,927; £963; £481) **Stalls High**

Form RPR

-516 1 **Namir (IRE)**[4] 1914 5-8-1 71 oh2 (vt) DuranFentiman(3) 11 81
(D Shaw) *hld up on ins: hdwy 2f out: led 75yds out: drvn out* **5/1**[3]

1604 2 1/2 **Spanish Ace**[7] 1854 6-8-13 85 KevinGhunowa(5) 8 93
(J M Bradley) *sn chsng ldrs: kpt on wl fnl f: jst hld* **6/1**

52-0 3 1/2 **Bahamian Ballet**[17] 1574 5-8-2 72 PatrickMathers(3) 4 78
(E S McMahon) *led after 1f: edgd elft 1f out: hdd and no ex last 75yds* **16/1**

0024 4 nk **Bo McGinty (IRE)**[11] 1754 6-8-10 77 (b) TonyHamilton 2 82
(R A Fahey) *sn w ldr: hung rt over 1f out: no ex ins fnl f* **6/1**

6166 **5** *hd* **Efistorm**[11] [1754] 6-8-11 **78**.. PaulMulrennan 9 82+
(C R Dore) *led 1f: trckd ldrs tl nt clr run fr over 1f out: swtchd ins fnl 75yds: r.o* **12/1**

4040 **6** *1 1/2* **High Reach**[7] [1854] 7-8-3 **77**.. DeanHeslop(7) 3 76
(T D Barron) *chsd ldrs on outer: rdn and edgd rt 1f out: one pce* **20/1**

02-5 **7** *1 3/4* **Matsunosuke**[21] [1464] 5-8-5 **77**.. LukeMorris(5) 10 70
(A B Coogan) *hld up: effrt 2f out: kpt on: nvr rchd ldrs* **9/2[2]**

0/06 **8** *1/2* **Playful Dane (IRE)**[17] [1574] 10-8-12 **79**.. NCallan 6 70
(K A Ryan) *hmpd s: hdwy and c outside over 1f out: nvr nr ldrs* **7/2[1]**

0160 **9** *3/4* **Danzig River (IRE)**[7] [1852] 6-8-9 **76**.. PaulQuinn 1 64
(D Nicholls) *in rr on outer: effrt over 2f out: nvr a threat* **16/1**

-660 **10** *1/2* **Malapropism**[1] [1999] 7-8-4 **71**.. EdwardCreighton 5 57
(M R Channon) *trckd ldrs: wkng whn nt much oom 1f out* **11/1**

6-00 **11** *4* **The Bear**[11] [1754] 4-8-8 **75**..(v[1]) SamHitchcott 7 47
(J S Wainwright) *in rr: lost pl over 3f out: sn bhd* **33/1**

62.89 secs (-1.11) **Going Correction** 0.0s/f (Good) **11** Ran SP% **121.1**
Speed ratings (Par 105):108,107,106,105,105 103,100,99,98,97 91
CSF £36.33 CT £465.22 TOTE £6.70: £2.20, £1.80, £4.10; EX 55.50.
Owner ownaracehorse.co.uk (Shakespeare) **Bred** B Kennedy **Trained** Danethorpe, Notts

FOCUS
The high numbers as usual held sway in what was quite a rough sprint handicap. Solid form, the second and third good guides and the winner running his best race since early 2005. The fifth was arguably unlucky.
Efistorm Official explanation: jockey said gelding was denied a clear run
Playful Dane(IRE) Official explanation: jockey said gelding was hampered at the start
The Bear Official explanation: jockey said gelding was unsuited by the good to firm ground

2026 BRANTINGHAM STAYERS H'CAP 2m 35y
4:35 (4:36) (Class 5) (0-75,72) 4-Y-O+ **£3,562** (£1,059; £529; £264) **Stalls** High

Form RPR

0-01 **1** **Vice Admiral**[18] [1556] 4-8-5 **56**.. PaulMulrennan 2 64
(M W Easterby) *trckd ldr: styd on fnl 2f: edgd rt ins fnl f: led post* **9/2[3]**

30-6 **2** *shd* **Karlani (IRE)**[16] [1598] 4-8-12 **63**.. NCallan 4 71
(G A Swinbank) *hld up: hdwy over 5f out: hrd rdn over 3f out: hung rt: led over 1f out: jst ct* **6/1**

0-42 **3** *3/4* **Boxhall (IRE)**[14] [1677] 5-9-3 **66**.. TonyHamilton 7 73
(N Wilson) *led: qcknd over 3f out: hdd over 1f out: styng on same pce whn n.m.r nr fin* **6/1**

-144 **4** *6* **Mister Arjay (USA)**[9] [1794] 7-9-4 **72**.. PJMcDonald(5) 3 72
(B Ellison) *chsd ldrs: pushed along after 5f: outpcd over 3f out: styd on: nvr rchd ldrs* **7/2[2]**

0-00 **5** *6* **Compton Commander**[18] [1556] 9-7-11 **53** oh3.... DanielleMcCreery(7) 5 46
(E W Tuer) *hld up: effrt over 5f out: hung rt over 2f out: one pce* **40/1**

1542 **6** *2 1/2* **Rule For Ever**[18] [1556] 5-9-0 **66**.. PatrickMathers(3) 1 56
(I W McInnes) *chsd ldrs: rdn over 3f out: lost pl over 1f out* **13/2**

4-05 **7** *1/2* **Barton Belle**[18] [1566] 5-8-6 **58** ow1.. NeilChalmers(3) 8 47
(C N Kellett) *trckd ldrs: drvn over 5f out: lost pl over 1f out* **28/1**

3423 **8** *3* **Noddies Way**[2] [1959] 4-8-6 **57** ow1.. SamHitchcott 6 42
(J F Panvert) *rn in snatches: in rr: hdwy to chse ldrs 9f out: effrt on outside over 3f out: lost pl over 1f out* **9/4[1]**

3m 38.47s (-1.03) **Going Correction** +0.025s/f (Good)
WFA 4 from 5yo+ 2lb **8** Ran SP% **119.0**
Speed ratings (Par 103):103,102,102,99,96 95,95,93
CSF £32.90 CT £165.90 TOTE £5.10: £1.60, £2.30, £2.10; EX 34.20.
Owner A C R Stubbs **Bred** Barry Minty **Trained** Sheriff Hutton, N Yorks
■ Stewards' Enquiry : Paul Mulrennan caution: careless riding

FOCUS
Hand-timed. A steady gallop and a tight three-way finish to this modest stayers' handicap. Solid form, the first three clear and the front pair both improving on recent form.
Noddies Way Official explanation: jockey said gelding never travelled

2027 BEVERLEY LADY AMATEUR RIDERS' H'CAP 1m 1f 207y
5:10 (5:10) (Class 5) (0-70,76) 4-Y-O+ **£3,435** (£1,065; £532; £266) **Stalls** High

Form RPR

0011 **1** **Just Lille (IRE)**[1] [1997] 4-10-11 **76** 6ex..............................(p) MissJAKidd(5) 4 84
(Mrs A Duffield) *chsd ldrs: effrt over 2f out: carried lft and r.o to ld last 75yds* **3/1[2]**

3453 **2** *nk* **Augustine**[33] [1199] 6-10-4 **67**.. MrsMarieKing(3) 3 74
(P W Hiatt) *trckd ldrs: wnt 2nd over 3f out: led over 1f out: edgd lft: hdd and no ex ins fnl f* **4/1[3]**

0000 **3** *1 1/2* **Everest (IRE)**[11] [1744] 10-10-0 **67**.. MissJRRichards(7) 6 71
(B Ellison) *hld up towards rr: hdwy on outer over 2f out: styd on fnl f: nt rch 1st 2* **20/1**

0-00 **4** *1 1/2* **King's Account (USA)**[52] [928] 5-9-10 **56**..............................(p) MrsCBartley 11 57
(S Gollings) *led tl over 1f out: kpt on same pce* **20/1**

3-30 **5** *1* **Champagne Shadow (IRE)**[131] [142] 6-10-0 **65**........... MissARyan(5) 8 64
(K A Ryan) *hld up: hdwy 3f out: kpt on: nvr rchd ldrs* **8/1**

330- **6** *nk* **Parchment (IRE)**[235] [5750] 5-9-13 **59**.. MissADeniel 1 58
(A J Lockwood) *hld up in rr: hdwy over 2f out: kpt on: nvr rchd ldrs* **20/1**

2154 **7** *3* **The Grey One (IRE)**[11] [1755] 4-9-7 **60**..............................(p) MissHDavies(7) 2 53
(J M Bradley) *stdd s: t.k.h in rr: hdwy 3f out: hung rt: nvr rchd ldrs* **10/1**

60-4 **8** *1/2* **Chapter (IRE)**[18] [1562] 5-9-5 **56** oh1........... MissGDGracey-Davison(5) 10 48
(Mrs A L M King) *prom: effrt 3f out: one pce* **10/1**

1123 **9** *2* **Jarvo**[2] [1967] 6-9-10 **56** oh3.. MissLEllison 9 44
(I W McInnes) *in rr: effrt 3f out: nvr a factor* **5/2[1]**

1055 **10** *3* **Fuel Cell (IRE)**[5] [1906] 6-9-3 **56** oh11.. MissEHickey(7) 5 38
(J O'Reilly) *t.k.h towards rr: hdwy 4f out: nvr on terms* **33/1**

004/ **11** *1/2* **High Window (IRE)**[328] [2] 7-9-3 **56** oh11....... MissJoannaMason(7) 7 37
(G P Kelly) *chsd ldr: lost pl over 1f out* **100/1**

04-6 **12** *15* **Splodger Mac (IRE)**[17] [1578] 8-9-5 **56** oh8.. MrsLHannity(5) 12 7
(N Bycroft) *s.s: a in rr: lost tch 3f out* **25/1**

2m 8.50s (1.20) **Going Correction** +0.025s/f (Good) **12** Ran SP% **124.9**
Speed ratings (Par 103):96,95,94,93,92 92,89,89,87,85 85,73
CSF £14.89 CT £214.77 TOTE £4.40: £1.90, £1.70, £4.70; EX 17.10 Place 6 £ 63.55, Place 5 £40.61.
Owner Granville J Harper **Bred** Sweetmans Bloodstock **Trained** Constable Burton, N Yorks
■ Stewards' Enquiry : Mrs Marie King caution: careless riding

FOCUS
A modest lady amateur riders' handicap run at just a steady pace. Just ordinary form, with Just Lille 3lb off her Haydock form from the previous day.
T/Plt: £78.10 to a £1 stake. Pool: £50,168.80. 468.35 winning tickets. T/Qpdt: £38.40 to a £1 stake. Pool: £2,340.50. 45.00 winning tickets. WG

[1553] CATTERICK (L-H)
Saturday, May 26
OFFICIAL GOING: Good to firm (firm in places, 8.3)
Wind: almost nil

2028 TOTEPLACEPOT (S) STKS 5f 212y
2:40 (2:40) (Class 6) 2-Y-O **£2,730** (£806; £403) **Stalls** Low

Form RPR

060 **1** **Little Finch (IRE)**[23] [1422] 2-8-6 0..............................(b[1]) GrahamGibbons 1 55
(R C Guest) *mde all: rdn 2f out: kpt on wl fnl f* **10/1**

5 **2** *1 3/4* **Caught In Paradise (IRE)**[6] [1857] 2-8-11 0............ SilvestreDeSousa 6 55
(D Nicholls) *cl up: effrt and chsd wnr 2f out: kpt on fnl f: no imp* **7/2[2]**

3 *5* **Pearo (IRE)** 2-8-6 0.. LPKeniry 4 35
(J S Moore) *cl up: effrt over 2f out: wknd over 1f out* **4/1[3]**

4 *2 1/2* **Tanley** 2-8-8 0.. MarkLawson(3) 5 32
(James Moffatt) *chsd ldrs: outpcd 1/2-way: n.d after* **20/1**

5 *10* **Lavemill (IRE)** 2-8-6 0.. RoystonFfrench 2 —
(R F Fisher) *missed break: nvr on terms* **14/1**

4431 **U** **Amazing Day**[6] [1857] 2-8-10 0.. JackDean(7) 3 —
(W G M Turner) *chsd ldrs: outpcd over 3f out: sddle sn slipped: rn wd and uns rdr ent st* **1/1[1]**

1m 15.33s (1.33) **Going Correction** -0.025s/f (Good) **6** Ran SP% **112.7**
Speed ratings (Par 91):90,87,81,77,64 —
CSF £44.65 TOTE £12.70: £3.30, £2.40; EX 67.10.There was no bid for the winner. Amazing Day was claimed by S Parr for £6,000. Caught In Paradise was the subject of a friendly claim.
Owner S Harris **Bred** L Mulryan **Trained** Brancepeth, Co Durham

FOCUS
A weak event, further diluted when the market leader, and the only one with solid pre-race form, failed to complete. The pace was sound.

NOTEBOOK
Little Finch(IRE), down in grade and fitted with blinkers for the first time, did enough to win a poor event. She had the rub of things, though, and would not be an obvious one to follow up. (op 11-1)
Caught In Paradise(IRE) attracted support and bettered the form of his Ripon debut. He should stay 7f and is capable of winning a similar event. (op 15-2)
Pearo(IRE), a half-sister to a 5f winner, was not totally disgraced in a weak race on this racecourse debut. She may be capable of a bit better in due course. (op 7-2)
Tanley was easy to back and well beaten on this racecourse debut. He will have to improve a fair bit before he is a betting proposition. (op 16-1)
Lavemill(IRE), a half-sister to a fair winner up to middle distances in Ireland, showed nothing after missing the break on this racecourse debut. Official explanation: jockey said filly missed the break and hung right-handed throughout (op 10-1)
Amazing Day looked the one to beat after an improved effort at Ripon on his previous start but was already starting to struggle when his saddle slipped. He was claimed by Stephen Parr and is worth another chance in this grade. (op 10-11 tchd 5-6)

2029 TOTECOURSE TO COURSE MEDIAN AUCTION MAIDEN STKS 5f
3:15 (3:15) (Class 6) 3-Y-O **£2,730** (£806; £403) **Stalls** Low

Form RPR

300- **1** **Hawaii Prince**[296] [4088] 3-9-3 65.. SilvestreDeSousa 1 63
(S T Mason) *mde all: hld on wl fnl f* **8/1[3]**

-534 **2** *1/2* **Nomoreblondes**[22] [1453] 3-8-7 60..............................(p) RoryMoore(5) 5 56
(P T Midgley) *pressed wnr: ev ch 2f out: kpt on fnl f* **5/1[2]**

-023 **3** *nk* **Foxy Music**[15] [1616] 3-9-3 82.. FrancisNorton 4 60
(E J Alston) *chsd ldrs: rdn and outpcd wl over 1f out: styd on fnl f* **1/2[1]**

0020 **4** *4* **Mangano**[3] [1943] 3-9-3 47.. RoystonFfrench 3 45
(A Berry) *sn drvn along and outpcd: kpt on fnl f: no imp* **14/1**

00-0 **5** *1 1/2* **Croeso Bach**[15] [1635] 3-8-12 45.. VinceSlattery 6 34
(J L Spearing) *bhd: drvn 1/2-way: nt pce to chal* **50/1**

00 **6** *3/4* **Aslan**[21] [1482] 3-9-3 0..............................(e[1]) GrahamGibbons 7 36
(T D Easterby) *in tch to 1/2-way: sn rdn and btn* **20/1**

4U-3 **7** *4* **Fly Time**[10] [1763] 3-8-9 50.. LiamJones(3) 2 16
(Mrs L Williamson) *bhd and outpcd after 2f: nvr on terms* **16/1**

59.69 secs (-0.91) **Going Correction** -0.25s/f (Firm) **7** Ran SP% **113.7**
Speed ratings (Par 97):97,96,95,89,86 85,79
CSF £46.49 TOTE £9.80: £4.50, £3.80; EX 103.00.
Owner Dream On **Bred** Ms R A Myatt **Trained** Lanchester, Co. Durham

FOCUS
An uncompetitive event in which the pace was sound. Dubious maiden form, and in all likelihood a weak race.

2030 TOTESPORT.COM H'CAP 7f
3:45 (3:45) (Class 2) (0-100,100) 4-Y-O+ **£11,334** (£3,372; £1,685; £841) **Stalls** Low

Form RPR

0-31 **1** **Phluke**[14] [1682] 6-8-7 **89**.. StephenCarson 8 95
(Eve Johnson Houghton) *set stdy pce: rdn 2f out: hld on gamely fnl f* **13/2**

6502 **2** *hd* **Zomerlust**[8] [1826] 5-8-11 **93**.. GrahamGibbons 3 98
(J J Quinn) *prom: rdn and outpcd over 2f out: rallied over 1f out: kpt on wl fnl f: jst hld* **9/2[3]**

0623 **3** *nk* **Beckermet (IRE)**[8] [1826] 5-9-4 **100**.. RoystonFfrench 5 104
(R F Fisher) *trckd ldrs: effrt 2f out: kpt on fnl f: hld nr fin* **11/2**

2001 **4** *nk* **Dhaular Dhar (IRE)**[15] [1619] 5-8-9 **98**.. GaryBartley(7) 2 101+
(J S Goldie) *hld up in tch: effrt over 1f out: kpt on fnl f: nrst fin* **7/2[2]**

-310 **5** *1/2* **Malcheek (IRE)**[14] [1651] 5-8-7 **89**.. DaleGibson 4 91
(T D Easterby) *w wnr: ev ch tl no ex wl ins fnl f* **11/4[1]**

1-13 **6** *1 3/4* **Hiccups**[14] [1682] 7-8-4 **86** oh2.. FrancisNorton 6 83
(M Dods) *t.k.h: hld up in tch: rdn over 2f out: kpt on fnl f: no imp* **6/1**

0010 **7** *2* **King Marju (IRE)**[4] [1931] 5-8-1 **86** oh12..............................(v) AndrewElliott(3) 1 78?
(K R Burke) *hld up: drvn over 2f out: sn btn* **18/1**

1m 26.83s (-0.53) **Going Correction** -0.025s/f (Good) **7** Ran SP% **115.3**
Speed ratings (Par 109):102,101,101,101,100 98,96
CSF £36.09 CT £172.23 TOTE £6.30: £2.40, £4.00; EX 31.40.
Owner Mrs R F Johnson Houghton **Bred** Mrs R F Johnson Houghton **Trained** Blewbury, Oxon

FOCUS
A fair handicap but a very steady pace means the bare form of this race is best treated with caution. Phluke is improved this year and the runner-up is rated to his latest.

NOTEBOOK
Phluke showed a good attitude to notch his tenth race but the win owes plenty to the finely judged waiting in front ride by Stephen Carson. He will not be going up too much for this and will be of interest in similar company, especially if allowed the same rope in front. (op 11-2)
Zomerlust has yet to win over this trip but ran right up to his best and deserves plenty of credit given he would have preferred a much stronger gallop and possibly easier ground. He is capable of winning a similar event but his record suggests he would not be one to take too short a price about next time. (tchd 11-2)

Beckermet(IRE) is a consistent sort who was ideally placed in a messy race and ran right up to his best. However he is unlikely to be getting any respite after this very respectable run and is going to remain vulnerable to the more progressive and better handicapped types. (op 4-1)
Dhaular Dhar(IRE) ◆, 4lb higher than at Chester, did really well to finish as close as he did in a race that was not run to suit. An end-to-end gallop will see him in a much better light and he looks the sort to win a decent handicap this term when things drop right. (op 3-1)
Malcheek(IRE), below his best on easy ground at Ascot on his previous start, had the run of the race and ran creditably. All his turf wins have been over 7f on fast ground at Thirsk. (op 5-1)
Hiccups finished further behind today's winner than at Warwick but this race was not run to suit and he is well worth another chance in similar company when a better gallop looks assured. (op 7-1 tchd 15-2)

2031 TOTESPORT 0800 221 221 H'CAP — 1m 5f 175y
4:20 (4:20) (Class 4) (0-80,78) 4-Y-0+ — **£6,477** (£1,927; £963; £481) **Stalls** Low

Form — RPR
06-0 **1** **Doctor Scott**[15] 1621 4-9-6 **77** .... RoystonFfrench 5 — 86+
(M Johnston) *chsd ldr: rdn over 4f out: chal 3f out: styd on wl u.p to ld towards fin* **9/2**
-413 **2** *hd* **Osolomio (IRE)**[20] 1490 4-9-2 **73** .... DaleGibson 4 — 81+
(G A Swinbank) *led: rdn 3f out: styd on fnl f: hdd towards fin* **7/4**[1]
0-00 **3** *2 1/2* **Our Teddy (IRE)**[32] 1208 7-9-7 **78** .... FrankieMcDonald 1 — 83
(P A Blockley) *chsd ldrs: rdn over 3f out: outpcd 2f out: kpt on fnl f: nt rch first 2* **11/1**
0-52 **4** *1 1/4* **Balyan (IRE)**[20] 1490 6-8-13 **77** .... NeilBrown(7) 2 — 80
(J Howard Johnson) *stmbld s: hld up in tch: effrt over 3f out: no imp fr 2f out* **11/4**[2]
-022 **5** *7* **Danzatrice**[16] 1598 5-8-6 **63** .... FrancisNorton 3 — 56
(C W Thornton) *s.s: bhd: rdn 4f out: nvr on terms* **4/1**[3]
3m 2.50s (-2.00) **Going Correction** -0.025s/f (Good) — **5** Ran SP% **109.5**
Speed ratings (Par 105):104,103,102,101,97
CSF £12.71 TOTE £5.30: £2.70, £1.20; EX 13.30.
Owner Irene White And Helen Bogie **Bred** The Kingwood Partnership **Trained** Middleham Moor, N Yorks
■ Stewards' Enquiry : Royston Ffrench one-day ban: careless riding (Jun 8)

FOCUS
Not a strong handicap for the money and a race in which the pace was on the steady side. The winner was rated a bit higher last year, but a career best from the runner-up.
Balyan(IRE) Official explanation: jockey said gelding stumbled leaving stalls
Danzatrice Official explanation: jockey said mare missed the break

2032 TOTEEXACTA MEDIAN AUCTION MAIDEN FILLIES' STKS — 5f 212y
4:50 (4:54) (Class 6) 3-4-Y-0 — **£2,730** (£806; £403) **Stalls** Low

Form — RPR
30 **1** **Maia**[15] 1620 3-8-10 0 .... SilvestreDeSousa 11 — 61+
(D Nicholls) *hld up in midfield: effrt and swtchd lft over 1f out: qcknd to ld ins fnl f: comf* **7/2**[2]
220- **2** *1 1/4* **Onatopp (IRE)**[205] 6309 3-8-10 68 .... RoystonFfrench 4 — 57
(T D Easterby) *chsd ldrs: effrt over 1f out: chsd wnr ins fnl f: kpt on* **11/8**[1]
0-3 **3** *1 1/2* **Swift Princess (IRE)**[14] 1679 3-8-7 0 ....(v) AndrewElliott(3) 7 — 52
(K R Burke) *t.k.h: chsd ldrs: led over 1f out: hung rt and hdd ins fnl f: no ex* **9/2**[3]
0-32 **4** *3/4* **Miss Taboo (IRE)**[14] 1679 3-8-5 45 .... RoryMoore(5) 2 — 50
(P T Midgley) *led to over 1f out: nt qckn fnl f* **5/1**
6000 **5** *nk* **Smart Pick**[20] 1491 4-9-2 36 .... LiamJones(3) 8 — 51
(Mrs L Williamson) *bhd tl styd on fr 2f out: nrst fin* **66/1**
00-0 **6** *4* **Rose Of Inchinor**[14] 1679 4-9-2 52 .... MarkLawson(3) 10 — 38
(R E Barr) *w ldr tl rdn and wknd over 1f out* **20/1**
0 **7** *1* **Mary From Maryhill (IRE)**[15] 1625 3-8-10 0 .... DaleGibson 3 — 33
(Miss L A Perratt) *prom tl rdn and wknd fr 2f out* **40/1**
00- **8** *3* **Scene Three**[228] 5899 3-8-10 0 .... GrahamGibbons 6 — 23
(J J Quinn) *bhd: pushed along 1/2-way: nvr rchd ldrs* **14/1**
0 **9** *1 1/2* **Ducal Regancy Red**[73] 678 3-8-10 0 .... FrankieMcDonald 12 — 19
(C J Teague) *prom: lost pl over 3f out: sn btn* **100/1**
10 *3 1/2* **Maysridge Ofkuwait** 3-8-10 0 .... DavidKinsella 9 — 7
(A Berry) *s.i.s: nvr on terms* **40/1**
11 *18* **Flying Princess (IRE)** 3-8-10 0 .... FrancisNorton 1 — —
(A Berry) *s.i.s: sn wl bhd* **20/1**
1m 13.52s (-0.48) **Going Correction** -0.025s/f (Good)
WFA 3 from 4yo 9lb — **11** Ran SP% **122.7**
Speed ratings (Par 98):102,100,98,97,96 91,90,86,84,79 55
CSF £8.64 TOTE £6.00: £1.70, £1.40, £1.50; EX 14.10.
Owner Racegoers Club Owners Group **Bred** L C And Mrs A E Sigsworth **Trained** Sessay, N Yorks

FOCUS
A modest event in which the pace was sound throughout. It is doubtful if the winner had to improve. The form is dubious, rated through the third and fourth.

2033 TOTESPORTCASINO.COM H'CAP — 7f
5:20 (5:22) (Class 6) (0-65,64) 4-Y-0+ — **£2,730** (£806; £403) **Stalls** Low

Form — RPR
1620 **1** **Million Percent**[20] 1507 8-9-0 **63** .... LiamJones(3) 1 — 71
(C R Dore) *prom: rdn to ld 1f out: kpt on wl* **8/1**
35-0 **2** *1/2* **Turn Me On (IRE)**[15] 1640 4-7-13 **52** .... KellyHarrison(7) 2 — 59
(T D Walford) *trckd ldrs: effrt whn nt clr run over 1f out: squeezed through to chse wnr ent fnl f: r.o* **33/1**
100- **3** *3/4* **Desert Hunter (IRE)**[292] 4199 4-8-4 **50** .... DavidKinsella 14 — 55+
(Micky Hammond) *s.i.s: hld up: hdwy 2f out: r.o fnl f* **25/1**
3010 **4** *3/4* **Inca Soldier (FR)**[4] 1933 4-8-5 **51** ow1 .... GrahamGibbons 5 — 54
(R C Guest) *hld up: hdwy and prom whn swtchd rt over 1f out: kpt on fnl f* **10/1**
-021 **5** *2* **Sedge (USA)**[14] 1675 7-8-11 **62** ....(p) RoryMoore(5) 7 — 60+
(P T Midgley) *hld up in midfield: effrt over 1f out: kpt on fnl f: nrst fin* **9/2**[1]
0-13 **6** *1/2* **Maison Dieu**[32] 1226 4-9-2 **62** .... FrancisNorton 6 — 58
(E J Alston) *hld up: rdn over 2f out: kpt on fnl f: nrst fin* **7/1**[3]
044- **7** *1/2* **Dark Champion**[207] 6274 7-8-6 **55** ....(v) MarkLawson(3) 4 — 50
(R E Barr) *led to 1f out: sn btn* **40/1**
544- **8** *1/2* **No Grouse**[169] 6747 7-8-6 **57** ow1 .... TravisBlock(5) 10 — 51+
(E J Alston) *hld up: shkn up and hdwy over 1f out: nvr nr ldrs* **10/1**
6-36 **9** *1 1/2* **Joshua's Gold (IRE)**[11] 1755 6-9-2 **62** ....(v) StephenCarson 12 — 51
(D Carroll) *w ldr tl wknd appr fnl f* **8/1**
-013 **10** *nk* **Bessemer (JPN)**[112] 346 6-9-4 **64** ....(p) RoystonFfrench 15 — 53
(I W McInnes) *s.i.s: bhd tl sme late hdwy: nvr on terms* **20/1**
0062 **11** *1 1/2* **Jellytot (USA)**[15] 1640 4-8-7 **60** ow5 ....(b) JamesO'Reilly(7) 9 — 45
(J O'Reilly) *trckd ldrs tl wknd over 1f out* **6/1**[2]
26-3 **12** *hd* **Divine White**[25] 1379 4-8-7 **53** ....(p) LPKeniry 8 — 37
(P Bowen) *prom: drvn 3f out: wknd 2f out* **11/1**
001- **13** *2 1/2* **Pay Time**[268] 4961 8-8-10 **61** .... MichaelJStainton(5) 3 — 38
(R E Barr) *midfield: drvn over 2f out: sn wknd* **14/1**
300- **14** *1 1/4* **Dispol Katie**[220] 6060 6-8-7 **60** .... NeilBrown(7) 11 — 34
(T D Barron) *t.k.h: in tch tl rdn and wknd fr 2f out* **7/1**[3]
-043 **15** *hd* **Compton Plume**[14] 1675 7-8-13 **59** .... DaleGibson 13 — 32
(M W Easterby) *bhd: rdn 1/2-way: nvr on terms* **12/1**
1m 26.0s (-1.36) **Going Correction** -0.025s/f (Good) — **15** Ran SP% **134.6**
Speed ratings (Par 101):106,105,104,103,101 100,100,99,98,97 95,95,92,91,91
CSF £275.27 CT £6436.64 TOTE £11.20: £3.10, £6.90, £13.10; EX 179.00 Place 6 £1259.19, Place 5 £372.12.
Owner Ship Tottenham **Bred** D J And Mrs Deer **Trained** West Pinchbeck, Lincs
■ Stewards' Enquiry : Kelly Harrison two-day ban: careless riding (Jun 6-7)

FOCUS
An ordinary handicap but one in which the pace was sound throughout. Regulation form for the grade, rated through the winner and third.
Million Percent Official explanation: trainer's rep said, regarding apparent improvement in form, that the gelding was unable to get any cover early stages of its previous race.
Compton Plume Official explanation: jockey said gelding never travelled
T/Plt: £5,056.00 to a £1 stake. Pool: £43,634.55. 6.30 winning tickets. T/Qpdt: £40.30 to a £1 stake. Pool: £2,549.50. 46.70 winning tickets. RY

1992 HAYDOCK (L-H)
Saturday, May 26

OFFICIAL GOING: Good to firm (firm in places)
There were 17 non-runners after the ground had quickened further overnight and the hoped-for rain failed to materialise.
Wind: Light against Weather: Fine

2034 RECTANGLE GROUP H'CAP — 5f
2:05 (2:05) (Class 2) (0-105,105) 3-Y-0+ **£19,431** (£5,781; £2,889; £1,443) **Stalls** Centre

Form — RPR
-201 **1** **Sierra Vista**[14] 1657 7-9-7 **102** .... PatCosgrave 5 — 114
(D W Barker) *mde all: rdn wl over 1f out: r.o wl* **7/2**[2]
0-22 **2** *2 1/2* **River Falcon**[22] 1456 7-9-4 **99** .... J-PGuillambert 1 — 102
(J S Goldie) *broke wl: hld up: lost pl over 3f out: rdn and hdwy 2f out: chsd wnr over 1f out: no imp* **4/1**[3]
266- **3** *2* **Portmeirion**[216] 6121 6-8-7 **91** oh9 .... SaleemGolam(3) 4 — 87
(S C Williams) *hld up in tch: rdn over 1f out: one pce* **16/1**
-022 **4** *1 1/2* **Corridor Creeper (FR)**[9] 1788 10-8-11 **99** ....(p) BarrySavage(7) 7 — 90
(J M Bradley) *prom tl rdn and wknd over 1f out* **9/2**
020- **5** *nk* **Orientor**[252] 5358 9-9-10 **105** .... JHBowman 9 — 95
(J S Goldie) *hld up and bhd: rdn wl over 1f out: no rspnse* **16/1**
16-4 **6** *1 1/2* **Buachaill Dona (IRE)**[8] 1826 4-9-3 **98** .... AdrianTNicholls 2 — 82
(D Nicholls) *t.k.h: prom tl rdn and wknd jst over 1f out* **13/8**[1]
59.81 secs (-2.26) **Going Correction** -0.20s/f (Firm) — **6** Ran SP% **110.3**
Speed ratings (Par 109):110,106,102,100,99 97
CSF £16.99 CT £179.74 TOTE £4.20: £2.20, £2.00; EX 17.20.
Owner David T J Metcalfe **Bred** Mrs M Beddis **Trained** Scorton, N Yorks

FOCUS
A very good sprint handicap. The winner did not set a breakneck pace and she has not necessarily improved, although she does appear to have done so.

NOTEBOOK
Sierra Vista, who holds the course record, followed up her defeat of last year's Stewards' Cup winner Borderlescott over six here last time. Successful on each of her last four visits to Haydock, the plan is to bring her back for the Sprint Cup in September.
River Falcon remains in good form having gone up to a career-high mark after a couple of narrow defeats. (op 7-2)
Portmeirion ◆, 9lb out of a handicap, was the last off the bridle and this was a promising reappearance for one who is much better suited to 6f. (op 20-1 tchd 25-1)
Corridor Creeper(FR), 4lb lower than when landing this race two years ago, had beaten today's winner by half a length on 10lb better terms on much softer ground at Beverley last May.
Orientor was having his first race since breaking a pedal bone when a very respectable ninth in the Ayr Gold Cup last September. (tchd 20-1)
Buachaill Dona(IRE), dropping back to the minimum trip, raced keenly and, although he has won on fast ground, his best form has come with some cut. Official explanation: trainer had no explanation for the poor form shown (op 7-4 tchd 2-1)

2035 WATSON / MCCROHAN 50TH TRIBUTE SANDY LANE STKS (LISTED RACE) — 6f
2:35 (2:35) (Class 1) 3-Y-O
£14,762 (£5,595; £2,800; £1,396; £699; £351) **Stalls** Centre

Form — RPR
-210 **1** **Prime Defender**[21] 1473 3-9-3 109 .... MichaelHills 6 — 115+
(B W Hills) *hld up in tch: led over 1f out: rdn and r.o wl ins fnl f* **11/8**[1]
62-1 **2** *1 1/2* **Hoh Mike (IRE)**[24] 1394 3-9-3 110 .... MartinDwyer 5 — 110
(M L W Bell) *s.i.s: hdwy 2f out: sn rdn: kpt on ins fnl f* **5/2**[2]
45-1 **3** *1 1/2* **City Of Tribes (IRE)**[15] 1616 3-9-0 0 .... PhilipRobinson 7 — 102
(G M Lyons, Ire) *hld up and bhd: rdn and hdwy fnl f: r.o* **17/2**
4 **4** *hd* **Speed Dream (IRE)**[22] 1461 3-9-0 0 .... EddieAhern 2 — 101
(David Wachman, Ire) *hld up in mid-div: hdwy over 2f out: rdn over 1f out: no ex ins fnl f* **20/1**
2511 **5** *2* **Aahayson**[8] 1802 3-9-0 96 .... PatCosgrave 9 — 95
(K R Burke) *led: rdn and hdd over 1f out: wknd ins fnl f* **9/2**[3]
3012 **6** *3 1/2* **Northern Fling**[15] 1623 3-9-0 92 .... AdrianTNicholls 3 — 84
(D Nicholls) *s.i.s: rdn whn swtchd lft and hdwy 2f out: wknd 1f out* **16/1**
0-00 **7** *4* **Bazroy (IRE)**[38] 1099 3-9-0 92 .... StephenDonohoe 1 — 71
(P D Evans) *prom: rdn over 2f out: wknd wl over 1f out* **66/1**
20-0 **8** *4* **Invincible Force (IRE)**[14] 1656 3-9-0 103 .... JHBowman 4 — 58
(Paul Green) *prom: rdn over 2f out: wknd wl over 1f out* **20/1**
1m 12.19s (-2.71) **Going Correction** -0.20s/f (Firm) — **8** Ran SP% **116.3**
Speed ratings (Par 107):110,108,106,105,103 98,93,87
CSF £4.90 TOTE £2.60: £1.20, £1.50, £2.20; EX 5.80.
Owner S Falle, M Franklin, J Sumsion **Bred** Christopher J Mason **Trained** Lambourn, Berks

FOCUS
The form of this race looks strong with the first two having already been successful at this level. They are both improving and Prime Defender will be competitive in Group sprints before long. The third is rated for his latest Chester level.

NOTEBOOK
Prime Defender made a triumphant return to sprinting having finished down the field in the 2,000 Guineas after he had scraped home in the Free Handicap. His jockey thinks he has the speed to be equally effective over five although the July Cup seems on the agenda. (op 2-1)
Hoh Mike(IRE) stuck to his task against a sprinter who could well be going places. (op 15-8)

City Of Tribes(IRE), stepping up in class on this return to 6f, did his best work in the closing stages. He has won on firm ground but his trainer gave the impression he prefers it good in a pre-race interview. (op 8-1 tchd 15-2)

Speed Dream(IRE) was running in a hotter Listed event than at Cork but ran a sound race back against his own age group.

Aahayson adopted his usual tactics but this was a much tougher assignment than his back-to-back wins at Hamilton. (op 13-2)

Northern Fling had finished precisely the same distance behind Aahayson also at level weights at Hamilton. (op 22-1)

2036 E B F JOAN WESTBROOK PINNACLE STKS (LISTED RACE) (F&M) 1m 3f 200y

3:05 (3:05) (Class 1) 4-Y-0+

£19,873 (£7,532; £3,769; £1,879; £941; £472) **Stalls** High

Form	Pos	Dist	Horse	RPR
226-	1		**Trick Or Treat**[212] 6191 4-8-12 95 ... JamieMackay 1 (J G Given) *mde all: rdn over 1f out: r.o* **7/2**[2]	106
22-1	2	¾	**Wannabe Posh (IRE)**[21] 1477 4-8-12 92 ... EddieAhern 5 (J L Dunlop) *hld up in tch: rdn over 2f out: chsd wnr wl over 1f out: styd on towards fin* **13/8**[1]	105
11-0	3	3 ½	**Green Room (FR)**[35] 1144 4-9-1 101 ... MartinDwyer 7 (J L Dunlop) *hld up and bhd: rdn over 3f out: hdwy on ins 2f out: edgd rt over 1f out: edgd lft ins fnl f: one pce* **15/2**	102
14-4	4	3 ½	**Maroussies Wings (IRE)**[9] 1789 4-9-3 105 ... DeanMcKeown 2 (P C Haslam) *s.i.s: sn prom: rdn and carried hd high over 2f out: wknd over 1f out* **4/1**[3]	98
24-5	5	1 ¾	**Mango Mischief (IRE)**[14] 1650 6-8-12 101 ... JHBowman 3 (M R Channon) *s.i.s: hld up in rr: rdn over 3f out: no rspnse* **13/2**	91
34-0	6	3 ½	**Cresta Gold**[7] 1844 4-8-12 100 ... DavidAllan 6 (A Bailey) *chsd wnr: rdn over 2f out: wknd over 1f out* **10/1**	85

2m 30.77s (-4.22) **Going Correction** -0.20s/f (Firm) **6** Ran SP% **114.5**

Speed ratings (Par 111):106,105,103,100,99 97

CSF £9.94 TOTE £5.80: £2.50, £1.50; EX 12.30.

Owner Peter Onslow **Bred** P Onslow **Trained** Willoughton, Lincs

FOCUS

The finish of this distaff Listed contest was fought out by a couple of very progressive types. The overall form is not that strong.

NOTEBOOK

Trick Or Treat did not stop improving in the second half of last season and carried on where she left off. Dictating matters from the front, she was the last to come off the bit and always looked like holding on. She will now be aimed at a Group 3 at Cork in the middle of next month. (op 6-1)

Wannabe Posh(IRE) proved well up to this step up in grade but came up against another most progressive type. (op 2-1 tchd 5-2 in a place and 9-4 in places)

Green Room(FR) was inclined to drift away from the whip but that may well have been down to the fact that the ground was really too lively for her. This was a decent effort under the circumstances. (op 13-2 tchd 6-1)

Maroussies Wings(IRE), whose two wins have come on soft ground, had also looked very ungainly on a fast surface when second at Pontefract just over a year ago. (op 3-1)

Mango Mischief(IRE) settled much better this time with the help of a stronger gallop on this considerably faster ground. (op 11-2)

Cresta Gold has yet to come to hand this year. (tchd 9-1 and 11-1)

2037 TOTESPORT.COM SILVER BOWL (HERITAGE H'CAP) 1m 30y

3:40 (3:41) (Class 2) 3-Y-0

£62,320 (£18,660; £9,330; £4,670; £2,330; £1,170) **Stalls** Low

Form	Pos	Dist	Horse	RPR
6-20	1		**Tobosa**[21] 1473 3-9-7 104 ... MichaelHills 4 (W Jarvis) *hld up: nt clr run and lost pl after 1f: hdwy on outside over 1f out: rdn to ld ent fnl f: sn rdn and edgd lft: r.o wl* **10/3**[1]	115+
1131	2	2 ½	**Annemasse**[16] 1603 3-8-6 89 ... J-PGuillambert 11 (M Johnston) *t.k.h: led early: prom: rdn to ld wl over 1f out: hdd ent fnl f: nt qckn* **9/1**	93
04-5	3	hd	**Billy Dane (IRE)**[10] 1768 3-8-4 87 ... JimmyQuinn 9 (R A Fahey) *plld hrd: a.p: rdn over 2f out: hung lft fnl f: kpt on* **33/1**	91
0-15	4	1 ¼	**Voodoo Moon**[21] 1471 3-8-3 89 ... GregFairley(3) 14 (M Johnston) *a.p: rdn over 2f out: edgd lft over 1f out: sn swtchd rt: kpt on ins fnl f* **33/1**	90
13-4	5	hd	**Smart Instinct (USA)**[10] 1768 3-8-10 98 ... JamieMoriarty(5) 15 (R A Fahey) *hld up towards rr: rdn 3f out: hdwy fnl f: nrst fin* **8/1**	98
-166	6	nk	**Majuro (IRE)**[20] 1516 3-8-13 96 ... JHBowman 8 (M R Channon) *prom: led 6f out: rdn and hdd wl over 1f out: one pce* **40/1**	96
111	7	¾	**Regal Parade**[20] 1500 3-8-10 93 ... JoeFanning 16 (M Johnston) *sn led: hdd 6f out: chsd ldr tl rdn 2f out: btn whn nt clr run ins fnl f* **13/2**[3]	94+
1-26	8	½	**Tybalt (USA)**[29] 1275 3-8-9 92 ... RobertHavlin 5 (J H M Gosden) *hld up and bhd: nt clr run after 1f: bmpd over 5f out: hdwy on ins over 2f out: sn rdn: wknd ins fnl f* **7/1**	89
2-00	9	shd	**Valdan (IRE)**[56] 839 3-8-7 90 ow1 ... StephenDonohoe 10 (P D Evans) *nvr trbld ldrs* **66/1**	86
1-63	10	shd	**Thunder Storm Cat (USA)**[21] 1471 3-8-9 92 ... EddieAhern 13 (P F I Cole) *hld up in mid-div: rdn over 2f out: btn whn hung lft over 1f out* **8/1**	88
5-62	11	¾	**Ponty Rossa (IRE)**[10] 1768 3-8-10 93 ... DavidAllan 6 (T D Easterby) *hld up in mid-div: hdwy over 3f out: rdn over 2f out: wknd ins fnl f* **8/1**	87
1-11	12	2	**Kay Gee Be (IRE)**[23] 1439 3-8-7 90 ... PatCosgrave 7 (M J Wallace) *hld up in mid-div: nt clr run after 1f: bmpd over 5f out: nt clr run ent st: rdn over 2f out: sn bhd* **6/1**[2]	80
2-41	13	14	**Aqmaar**[21] 1471 3-8-10 93 ... MartinDwyer 12 (J L Dunlop) *t.k.h in rr: rdn over 3f out: sn struggling* **12/1**	51

1m 42.15s (-3.36) **Going Correction** -0.20s/f (Firm) **13** Ran SP% **124.0**

Speed ratings (Par 105):108,105,105,104,103 103,102,102,102,102 101,99,85

CSF £34.81 CT £899.30 TOTE £4.40: £1.90, £2.80, £4.90; EX 46.40 Trifecta £2043.30 Pool £23,599.36 - 8.20 winning units..

Owner Collins, Randall, Rich & Turnbull **Bred** G S Shropshire **Trained** Newmarket, Suffolk

■ Stewards' Enquiry : J-P Guillambert three-day ban: careless riding (Jun 6-8)

FOCUS

A good handicap but the form might not be as strong as recent renewals, with the fourth and sixth limiting it. Tobosa is yet another to underline the form of the 2,000 Guineas and is well up to a crack at Group races again. Leading ante-post fancies We'll Come and Gulf Express missed the cut.

NOTEBOOK

Tobosa produced a first-class performance to defy top weight with the form of his narrow defeat by Prime Defender in the Free Handicap having been enhanced earlier in the afternoon. He was disappointing after having plenty of use made of him in the 2,000 Guineas, but his trainer considered him to be a Group horse in a handicap here and it is hard to argue with that view given the way he won. (op 5-1 tchd 11-2)

Annemasse ran a cracking race over this slightly longer trip off a 3lb higher mark. His rider picked up a three-day ban for careless riding a furlong out. (op 8-1)

Billy Dane(IRE) ◆, described as big and lazy by his trainer, was all the better for his run at York. He proved that he stays a mile despite running freely and hanging left on this fast ground in the later stages. He should now be approaching his peak.

Voodoo Moon had disappointed her trainer despite not being beaten far at Newmarket last time. Confirming that she stays this trip, this was a fair performance for one who really likes to front-run.

Smart Instinct(USA) ◆ confirmed his trainer's belief that he would appreciate a longer trip and gave the impression that he might stay event further. He is one to keep in mind. (op 6-1)

Majuro(IRE) deserves credit for not caving in once headed. Official explanation: jockey said colt ran too freely early on (op 33-1)

Regal Parade did not look that harshly treated despite having again gone up 7lb. He would have finished a little closer but for running into trouble late on but this was a bit of a setback on the way to the Britannia at Royal Ascot. (op 11-2)

Tybalt(USA), with ground conditions in his favour, is probably a bit better than the bare form suggests given his troublesome passage. (op 11-1)

Kay Gee Be(IRE) was another who did not exactly get the run of the race. (op 8-1)

Aqmaar Official explanation: jockey said colt lost its action

2038 OPTION HYGIENE H'CAP 1m 30y

4:10 (4:10) (Class 4) (0-80,79) 4-Y-0+ **£6,477** (£1,927; £963; £481) **Stalls** Low

Form	Pos	Dist	Horse	RPR
5-45	1		**Bold Marc (IRE)**[21] 1481 5-9-4 79 ... LeeEnstone 7 (K R Burke) *led early: chsd ldr: led jst over 3f out: rdn wl over 1f out: hld on wl ins fnl f* **5/1**	86
36-2	2	hd	**Barons Spy (IRE)**[10] 1765 6-8-12 73 ... JamesDoyle 1 (R J Price) *hld up in tch: chsd wnr over 2f out: sn rdn: ev ch fnl f: r.o* **10/3**[2]	79
6-02	3	¾	**Mount Usher**[22] 1455 5-8-11 72 ... TPO'Shea 10 (G A Swinbank) *hld up: hdwy over 2f out: rdn and edgd lft over 1f out: nt qckn ins fnl f* **7/2**[3]	77
0-02	4	1 ¼	**Moody Tunes**[28] 1287 4-9-2 77 ... PatCosgrave 5 (K R Burke) *hld up in tch: rdn over 1f out: nt qckn* **3/1**[1]	79
6-61	5	nk	**Flighty Fellow (IRE)**[33] 1198 7-8-10 71 ... (b) DavidAllan 4 (T D Easterby) *hld up: swtchd rt over 2f out: rdn and edgd lft 1f out: nvr able to chal* **7/2**[3]	72
0-00	6	dist	**Nesno (USA)**[15] 1638 4-8-12 73 ... (v) JHBowman 11 (J D Bethell) *sn led: hdd jst over 3f out: eased over 2f out: virtually p.u over 1f out* **20/1**	—

1m 43.55s (-1.96) **Going Correction** -0.20s/f (Firm) **6** Ran SP% **114.0**

Speed ratings (Par 105):101,100,100,98,98 —

CSF £22.31 CT £65.04 TOTE £6.90: £2.80, £2.10; EX 23.90.

Owner Market Avenue Racing Club Ltd **Bred** Eamon D Delany **Trained** Middleham Moor, N Yorks

FOCUS

An open little handicap despite the field being decimated by five non-runners. The winner and second are rated to form.

2039 E B F NOBBY EDWARDS 65TH BIRTHDAY MAIDEN FILLIES' STKS 6f

4:40 (4:43) (Class 5) 2-Y-0 **£3,238** (£963; £481; £240) **Stalls** Centre

Form	Pos	Dist	Horse	RPR
	1		**Monaazalah (IRE)** 2-9-0 0 ... MartinDwyer 13 (B W Hills) *hld up and bhd: hdwy and bmpd over 3f out: led over 1f out: r.o wl* **7/4**[1]	77+
	2	1 ½	**Feisty Royale** 2-9-0 0 ... J-PGuillambert 11 (M Johnston) *w ldr: rdn and ev ch over 1f out: nt qckn ins fnl f* **10/1**	73
	3	¾	**Threestoneburn (USA)** 2-9-0 0 ... LeeEnstone 10 (P C Haslam) *hld up in mid-div: hung rt over 3f out: rdn over 2f out: r.o ins fnl f* **8/1**	70+
	4	¾	**Cat Whistle** 2-8-9 0 ... JamieMoriarty(5) 12 (R A Fahey) *a.p: rdn over 1f out: nt qckn fnl f* **14/1**	68
	5	½	**Starlight Girl** 2-9-0 0 ... DavidAllan 2 (T D Easterby) *led: rdn and hdd over 1f out: no ex ins fnl f* **25/1**	67
	6	shd	**Festivale (IRE)** 2-9-0 0 ... EddieAhern 4 (J L Dunlop) *mid-div: rn green and hung lft over 2f out: kpt on towards fin* **9/2**[3]	66+
	7	5	**Chica Guapa (IRE)** 2-9-0 0 ... JHBowman 9 (Paul Green) *chsd ldrs: rdn over 2f out: sn wknd* **25/1**	51
	8	hd	**Lavender Moon (IRE)** 2-8-11 0 ... AndrewMullen(3) 3 (K A Ryan) *rrd and uns rdr bef s: dwlt: outpcd: nvr nr ldrs* **10/1**	51+
	9	1	**Elegant Step** 2-9-0 0 ... PatCosgrave 8 (A P Jarvis) *a bhd* **20/1**	48
	10	2	**Miss Bouggy Wouggy** 2-9-0 0 ... JimmyQuinn 1 (M Blanshard) *a bhd* **18/1**	42
	11	2 ½	**Spoilt Madame** 2-9-0 0 ... StephenDonohoe 5 (P D Evans) *a bhd* **25/1**	34
3	12	¾	**Elusive Deal (USA)**[17] 1585 2-9-0 0 ... JoeFanning 6 (R A Fahey) *chsd ldrs: pushed along over 3f out: sn lost pl* **7/2**[2]	32

1m 15.68s (0.78) **Going Correction** -0.20s/f (Firm) **12** Ran SP% **134.3**

Speed ratings (Par 90):86,84,83,82,81 81,74,74,72,70 66,65

CSF £23.72 TOTE £2.90: £1.60, £3.90, £3.30; EX 30.30.

Owner Hamdan Al Maktoum **Bred** Shadwell Estate Company Limited **Trained** Lambourn, Berks

FOCUS

The first six finished clear in a race when the only one with previous racecourse experience trailed in last. A nice start from the winner, whose yard has strength in depth with its early juveniles, but the level is guessy at this stage.

NOTEBOOK

Monaazalah(IRE) ◆, a half-sister to recent Newmarket 1m4f winner Latanazul, has plenty of speed in her pedigree. Creating a favourable impression on her debut, only time will show the value of this form but she does look the sort who can go on from here. (op 13-8 tchd 9-4)

Feisty Royale ◆ is a half-sister to several winners at between 6f and 1m4f. Normal improvement should see her find a suitable opening. (op 12-1)

Threestoneburn(USA) ◆, a 68,000gns breeze-up purchase, showed signs of inexperience before the penny eventually dropped. She should not be hard to place. (op 7-1)

Cat Whistle is a sister to successful All-Weather staying handicapper Lady Pilot. Nibbled at on her debut, she had presumably been showing something at home and shaped well for one who should eventually need further. (op 20-1)

Starlight Girl was not beaten far after cutting out the running and should come on for the outing. (tchd 33-1)

Festivale(IRE) ◆ looked very inexperienced and only seemed to pick up after her rider had accepted the situation. She should have learnt a lot from this. Official explanation: jockey said, regarding running and riding, his orders were to jump out, get a position, get the filly balanced and finish as close as he could, adding that filly misbehaved in stalls, ran green and wandered throughout, adding further that in the closing stages when it began to run on, he felt he was running on to the heels of horses coming to the end of their run and was unable to ride out to the line (op 8-1)
Elusive Deal(USA), upped in trip after a promising debut at Chester, failed to give her running. Official explanation: jockey said filly never travelled (op 5-1)

2040 HAYDOCK PARK ANNUAL BADGEHOLDERS' CLUB H'CAP — 7f 30y

5:15 (5:17) (Class 3) (0-95,95) 3-Y-O — **£9,715** (£2,890; £1,444; £721) **Stalls** Low

Form			Horse	Jockey	RPR
1-53	**1**		**Lovelace**[8] [1817] 3-8-4 **81** (M Johnston) *chsd ldr: led 3f out: rdn over 1f out: r.o* **9/2**[3]	JoeFanning 6	86
31-2	**2**	*nk*	**Miss Lucifer (FR)**[20] [1500] 3-8-10 **87** (B W Hills) *stdd s: hld up in rr: hdwy 2f out: rdn and edgd lft ins fnl f: nt qckn* **9/4**[2]	MichaelHills 9	92
6-20	**3**	*nk*	**Love On Sight**[37] [1105] 3-7-13 **81** oh1 (A P Jarvis) *hld up in rr: hdwy 2f out: rdn and edgd lft over 1f out and ins fnl f: nt qckn* **20/1**	WilliamBuick(5) 2	85
00-5	**4**	*1 ¾*	**Soviet Palace (IRE)**[36] [1124] 3-8-5 **85** (K A Ryan) *a.p: rdn 2f out: one pce fnl f* **20/1**	AndrewMullen(3) 5	84
10-2	**5**	*nk*	**Jaasoos (IRE)**[36] [1124] 3-8-7 **84** (M A Jarvis) *a.p: rdn and ev ch 2f out: no ex ins fnl f* **7/4**[1]	PhilipRobinson 11	82
316-	**6**	*9*	**Manchurian**[231] [5805] 3-9-4 **95** (M J Wallace) *hld up: hdwy on ins over 3f out: wknd 2f out* **13/2**	PatCosgrave 4	69
4-06	**7**	*shd*	**Osteopathic Remedy (IRE)**[10] [1768] 3-8-3 **83** (M Dods) *led: hdd 3f out: sn wknd* **12/1**	SaleemGolam(3) 7	57
0263	**8**	*7*	**Copper King**[16] [1603] 3-7-11 **81** oh1 (P D Evans) *hld up towards rr: rdn over 2f out: sn struggling* **14/1**	MCGeran(7) 10	36

1m 29.85s (-2.21) **Going Correction** -0.20s/f (Firm) **8** Ran SP% **122.5**
Speed ratings (Par 103):104,103,103,101,100 90,90,82
CSF £16.30 CT £186.85 TOTE £7.60: £1.90, £1.50, £3.00; EX 20.80 Place 6 £70.37, Place 5 £22.24.
Owner Hamad Suhail **Bred** Mrs Mary Taylor **Trained** Middleham Moor, N Yorks

FOCUS
There were several unexposed sorts in this handicap, in which there were five non-runners. Reasonable form with the front pair improvers and the fourth and fifth coming from a strong Newbury race.

NOTEBOOK
Lovelace was well supported on the exchanges in the morning having not handled a drop back to six when struck into at Newmarket last time. There could well be more to come. (op 5-1 tchd 6-1)
Miss Lucifer(FR) confirmed that she handles fast ground but could not peg back the winner having gone up 2lb. (op 3-1 tchd 2-1)
Love On Sight came with a dangerous-looking run on the outside but her young rider would probably have been better off pulling his whip through to his left hand. (op 14-1)
Soviet Palace(IRE) again appeared to be unfancied despite a promising reappearance when 66/1 at Newbury. (op 16-1)
Jaasoos(IRE) had no excuses having been raised 2lb for his second at Newbury. (op 9-4 tchd 5-2)
Copper King Official explanation: trainer said gelding was unsuited by the good to firm (firm in places) ground
T/Plt: £96.70 to a £1 stake. Pool: £126,078.85. 951.20 winning tickets. T/Qpdt: £56.30 to a £1 stake. Pool: £4,049.90. 53.20 winning tickets. KH

2000 NEWMARKET (ROWLEY) (R-H)

Saturday, May 26

OFFICIAL GOING: Good to firm (9.0)
Wind: Light, behind Weather: Overcast

2041 EUROPEAN BREEDERS' FUND MAIDEN STKS — 6f

1:45 (1:46) (Class 4) 2-Y-O — **£4,533** (£1,348; £674; £336) **Stalls** Low

Form			Horse	Jockey	RPR
	1		**Luck Money (IRE)** 2-9-3 0 (P F I Cole) *leggy: scope: mde all: edgd lft and rdn clr fr over 1f out* **5/1**[1]	TQuinn 16	92
	2	*2 ½*	**Orientalist Art** 2-9-3 0 (P W Chapple-Hyam) *gd sort: chsd ldrs: rdn and edgd rt over 1f out: r.o* **5/1**[1]	SebSanders 3	85
	3	*½*	**Red Alert Day** 2-9-3 0 (N A Callaghan) *str: w'like: a.p: rdn and hung rt over 1f out: styd on* **50/1**	PatDobbs 15	83
	4	*nk*	**Seeking Star (IRE)** 2-9-3 0 (M R Channon) *w'like: scope: lw: prom: chsd wnr over 2f out: sn rdn and hung rt: no ex ins fnl f* **12/1**	DarryllHolland 10	82
	5	*1 ¾*	**Generous Thought** 2-9-3 0 (P Howling) *w'like: leggy: hld up: hdwy over 1f out: sn rdn: no ex ins fnl f* **66/1**	IanMongan 19	77
	6	*1 ½*	**Alwaabel** 2-9-3 0 (J L Dunlop) *gd sort: leggy: s.i.s: hld up: hung rt over 1f out: r.o ins fnl f: nrst fin* **13/2**[2]	RHills 7	73
	7	*1*	**Classical Rhythm (IRE)** 2-9-3 0 (J R Boyle) *w'like: scope: chsd wnr over 3f: rdn and wknd over 1f out* **100/1**	AmirQuinn 12	70
	8	*shd*	**Unnefer (FR)** 2-9-3 0 (H R A Cecil) *leggy: scope: s.i.s: hld up: hung rt over 1f out: r.o ins fnl f: nvr nrr* **7/1**[3]	TedDurcan 14	69
	9	*½*	**Pride Of India (USA)** 2-9-3 0 (J Noseda) *w'like: scope: lw: chsd ldrs over 4f* **5/1**[1]	(t) TPQueally 5	68
	10	*1 ¾*	**Seeking The Star (CAN)** 2-9-3 0 (D M Simcock) *w'like: unf: prom 4f* **50/1**	RichardMullen 17	63
	11	*nk*	**Bourse (IRE)** 2-9-3 0 (J H M Gosden) *gd sort: cmpt: chsd ldrs: rdn and hung rt over 2f out: sn wknd* **14/1**	JimmyFortune 1	62
0	**12**	*1 ¼*	**Rimrock (IRE)**[7] [1846] 2-9-3 0 (J Noseda) *dwlt: outpcd* **16/1**	SteveDrowne 9	58
	13	*nk*	**Mister Beano (IRE)** 2-9-0 0 (V Smith) *w'like: scope: s.i.s: hld up: wknd over 2f out* **100/1**	JerryO'Dwyer(3) 2	57
	14	*1*	**The Gatekeeper** 2-8-12 0 (M H Tompkins) *cmpt: scope: prom 4f* **80/1**	PatrickHills(5) 4	54
	15	*2 ½*	**Flash Of Fire (USA)** 2-9-3 0 (J M P Eustace) *cmpt: scope: prom to 1/2-way* **10/1**	KerrinMcEvoy 11	47
	16	*nk*	**Space Pirate** 2-9-3 0 (M L W Bell) *neat: mid-div: sn drvn along: wknd over 2f out* **66/1**	HayleyTurner 8	46
	17	*3 ½*	**Headache** 2-9-3 0 (B W Duke) *cmpt: bkwd: s.s: outpcd* **33/1**	MickyFenton 13	35
0	**18**	*13*	**Last Angel (IRE)**[12] [1727] 2-8-12 0 (M Wigham) *mid-div: wknd over 2f out* **100/1**	DO'Donohoe 6	—
	19	*7*	**Biased Opinion (IRE)** 2-9-3 0 (H J L Dunlop) *cmpt: bkwd: s.i.s: hld up: wknd over 2f out* **33/1**	KDarley 18	—

1m 13.74s (0.64) **Going Correction** +0.05s/f (Good) **19** Ran SP% **122.2**
Speed ratings (Par 95):97,93,93,92,90 88,86,86,86,83 83,81,81,80,76 76,71,54,44
CSF £26.95 TOTE £7.30: £2.50, £2.60, £17.80; EX 46.20.
Owner Mrs Stephanie Smith **Bred** Mrs Chris Harrington **Trained** Whatcombe, Oxon
■ Richard Quinn's first winner since coming out of retirement this week. Paul Cole also trained Quinn's first ever winner in 1981.

FOCUS
Only one of the 19 runners had run before, so very little previous form to go on, but some top stables were represented and this looked quite a good race beforehand. They raced middle to stands' side, but nobody wanted to know the near rail and those drawn high appeared to be at an advantage. The winning time was 1.19 seconds slower than the later 0-105 three-year-old handicap but the form looks likely to prove strong and should produce winners.

NOTEBOOK
Luck Money(IRE), a 160,000euros half-brother to among others useful 6f-7f winner Charlotte O Fraise, out of a 7f three-year-old scorer, showed good speed from the outset and sustained his effort to the line to make a winning debut in convincing fashion. It is hard to know exactly what he achieved, but there were some promising types in behind and he looks a very useful prospect. He may now be aimed at the Coventry Stakes at Royal Ascot. (op 11-2 tchd 6-1 and 9-2)
Orientalist Art ◆, a 50,000gns half-brother to Always First, who was a 7f winner at two and later high-class over 1m4f in the US, out of a useful dual 7f-1m winner at three, was always close to the pace and, although unable to seriously threaten the winner, kept on to the line to post a good effort from his unfavourable draw. His stable has been in fine form with their juveniles so far this season and this one should make his mark in good company. (op 9-2 tchd 11-2 in place)
Red Alert Day, a 40,000gns purchase, out of a smart triple 6f winner at two to three, belied his big odds with a promising debut. He was always close to the pace and kept on to the line.
Seeking Star(IRE), a 65,000gns purchase, out of a mare who was placed over 1m2f, showed up well for much of the way and this was a promising introduction. (op 16-1)
Generous Thought, a 28,000gns purchase, out of a 6f winner on her juvenile debut, made her move wide of the main pack towards the centre of the track and showed plenty of ability. (op 50-1)
Alwaabel ◆, a half-brother to smart triple 5f-7f winner Munaddam, out of a useful dual 7f-1m winner, was noted doing some good late work towards the near side and fared second best of those in a single-figure stall. He seemed to carry his head at a slight angle late on, but that may have been through greenness and he should improve. (tchd 7-1)
Classical Rhythm(IRE), a £24,000 half-brother to a juvenile winner in Belgium, out of a 1m2f winner at two in France, shaped nicely on his racecourse debut.
Unnefer(FR) ◆, the first foal of a mare who was placed over 1m2f in a light career, was another who was staying on quite nicely when the race was all over. He should improve plenty of the experience and looks a nice prospect. (op 15-2 tchd 8-1)
Pride Of India(USA), a $210,000 half-brother to I Want You, a sprint winner in US, out of a quite useful multiple winner at around 6f-1m1f at three in the US, was clearly well fancied but he never posed a serious threat. This could bring him on plenty and it would be no surprise to see a much-improved performance next time. (op 4-1)
Seeking The Star(CAN), out of a US juvenile winner on turf, showed up well in the early stages and has ability. (op 40-1)
Bourse(IRE), a half-brother to 1m2f winner Demi Voix, out of a smart triple 7f-1m winner, can be expected to improve a fair bit for this outing.
Rimrock(IRE) was the only runner in the line-up with the benefit of previous experience, but he had shown just a moderate level of form when beating only one rival in a novice event over course and distance the previous week and was well held.
Mister Beano(IRE) Official explanation: jockey said colt hung left under pressure
Biased Opinion(IRE) Official explanation: jockey said colt lost its action

2042 ONERAILWAY.COM FAIRWAY STKS (LISTED RACE) — 1m 2f

2:20 (2:23) (Class 1) 3-Y-O
£15,330 (£5,810; £2,907; £1,449; £726; £364) **Stalls** Low

Form			Horse	Jockey	RPR
21	**1**		**Lucarno (USA)**[19] [1522] 3-9-0 92 (J H M Gosden) *mde all: rdn clr fr over 1f out: eased nr fin* **11/4**[2]	JimmyFortune 5	116+
1-	**2**	*3 ½*	**Supersonic Dave (USA)**[239] [5659] 3-9-0 94 (B J Meehan) *hld up: hdwy over 2f out: rdn to chse wnr over 1f out: styd on same pce ins fnl f* **8/1**	RHills 3	109
-512	**3**	*1 ¼*	**Hearthstead Maison (IRE)**[14] [1662] 3-9-0 104 (M Johnston) *chsd ldrs: rdn over 2f out: styd on same pce appr fnl f* **13/8**[1]	KDarley 4	106
12-5	**4**	*6*	**Mythical Kid (USA)**[14] [1662] 3-9-0 106 (Saeed Bin Suroor) *prom: chsd wnr 4f out tl rdn and wknd over 1f out* **6/1**[3]	KerrinMcEvoy 6	94
6-14	**5**	*2*	**Many Volumes (USA)**[14] [1662] 3-9-0 99 (H R A Cecil) *lw: stmbld s: hld up: hdwy over 2f out: rdn and wknd over 1f out* **11/1**	TedDurcan 2	90
2-34	**6**	*3 ½*	**Monzante (USA)**[15] [1617] 3-9-0 102 (R Charlton) *chsd wnr 6f: wknd over 2f out* **7/1**	SteveDrowne 1	83

2m 4.79s (-0.92) **Going Correction** +0.05s/f (Good) **6** Ran SP% **111.0**
Speed ratings (Par 107):105,102,101,96,94 92
CSF £23.28 TOTE £3.80: £2.00, £2.50; EX 26.80.
Owner George Strawbridge **Bred** Augustin Stable **Trained** Newmarket, Suffolk

FOCUS
A Listed contest than can produce a decent type and this looked like a good, certainly interesting renewal. They raced up the middle of the track. Lucarno was allowed to dictate on his own terms, and he set just an ordinary gallop for much of the way, but still had them very well strung out at the line. The runner-up was also a big improver on his maiden win, and with the next three all having contested the Lingfield Derby Trial the form is worth taking at face value.

NOTEBOOK
Lucarno(USA) ◆, second to Diamond Tycoon on his debut at Newbury before running away with a Polytrack maiden at Kempton, benefited from the step up in trip and ran out a comfortable winner. Admittedly he was allowed to dictate on his own terms, setting no more than an ordinary pace for much of the way, but one could not fail to be impressed by the way he extended when asked for his effort and he soon had his five rivals well strung out, no mean effort considering the early gallop. His trainer is now considering a tilt at the Derby, and this hugely progressive colt will be fully deserving of his place in the line-up if taking his chance, although his stamina for 1m4f is far from guaranteed. Whether he goes to Epsom or not, he looks capable of reaching a high level at some stage this season. (op 5-2 tchd 3-1)
Supersonic Dave(USA) ◆, the winner of a 7f maiden here on his only start as a juvenile, was representing a trainer who had won this race with a subsequent Group 1 winner for the last two years, David Junior and Red Rocks. This was a very pleasing return to action and he looks a smart prospect.
Hearthstead Maison(IRE), runner-up in the Lingfield Derby Trial on his previous start, would have been unsuited by the steady pace and may not have been at his best. (op 2-1 tchd 9-4)
Mythical Kid(USA), well beaten behind Hearthstead Maison in the Lingfield Derby Trial on his previous start, again proved disappointing. He has not built on the promise he showed for Sir Michael Stoute last year and, even though a further drop in trip may suit, he looks best watched for the time being. (op 4-1)

Many Volumes(USA) could not confirm Lingfield Derby Trial form with Mythical Kid and was below his best. He stumbled slightly coming out of the stalls and that might have affected his performance. (op 9-1 tchd 8-1)
Monzante(USA) did not help his chance by racing keenly and he offered nothing when asked for his effort. (op 10-1)

2043 DARIAN HOMES KING CHARLES II STKS (LISTED RACE) 7f
2:50 (2:52) (Class 1) 3-Y-O

£15,330 (£5,810; £2,907; £1,449; £726; £364) **Stalls** Low

Form				RPR
3-50	1		**Tariq**[13] 1703 3-9-0 101 JimmyFortune 5 (P W Chapple-Hyam) *s.i.s: sn trcking ldrs: led over 1f out: hung lft ins fnl f: rdn out* **7/2**[2]	109
-222	2	1 ½	**Mr Napper Tandy**[19] 1547 3-9-0 106 DarryllHolland 4 (M R Channon) *lw: chsd ldr: rdn over 2f out: ev ch over 1f out: styd on same pce ins fnl f* **10/11**[1]	106
10-	3	hd	**Prince Forever (IRE)**[259] 5183 3-9-0 93 RHills 6 (M A Jarvis) *plld hrd: led: edgd lft and hdd over 1f out: styd on same pce* **8/1**	105
110-	4	4	**St Philip (USA)**[239] 5653 3-9-0 100 SebSanders 2 (R M Beckett) *lw: hld up: rdn: hung lft and wknd over 1f out* **4/1**[3]	96
210-	5	½	**Mimisel**[211] 6201 3-8-9 79 KerrinMcEvoy 1 (Rae Guest) *chsd ldrs: hung lft and wknd over 1f out* **33/1**	90?
2164	6	shd	**Knapton Hill**[5] 1903 3-8-9 63 TedDurcan 3 (R Hollinshead) *sn outpcd* **100/1**	90?

1m 25.66s (-0.84) **Going Correction** +0.05s/f (Good) 6 Ran SP% **109.6**
Speed ratings (Par 107):106,104,104,99,98 98
CSF £6.74 TOTE £4.70: £2.20, £1.10; EX 7.50.
Owner Saleh Al Homeizi & Imad Al Sagar **Bred** D R Botterill **Trained** Newmarket, Suffolk

FOCUS
The pace seemed reasonable enough, with Prince Forever soon in a clear lead, but the proximity of the 79-rated fifth and 63-rated sixth casts serious doubts over the worth of the form of this Listed contest. A race to treat with caution. Again, they raced up the middle of the track.

NOTEBOOK
Tariq missed the rest of his juvenile campaign after running third in the Coventry Stakes, and he had not shown a great deal in two runs since returning this year, beating only one rival in both the Greenham and the French Guineas. However, he showed he retains all of his ability with a decisive success, picking up well from just off the pace and settling this without too much fuss. The proximity of both the fifth and sixth horses suggest the bare form is not worth a great deal, but he is clearly back on track and deserves to take his chance in the Jersey Stakes, where he will bid to emulate Jeremy, who won this race last year before following up at Royal Ascot. (tchd 10-3)
Mr Napper Tandy had an outstanding chance judged on his recent second to Creachadoir at the Curragh but, although running with credit, he failed to really confirm the ability he showed in Ireland and may have been a touch flattered. (op 6-5 tchd 5-4)
Prince Forever(IRE), off the track since finishing last in the Champagne Stakes 259 days previously, raced a little freely in front and could not sustain his challenge. This was still a decent effort on his return though, and there could be better to come with this run taking the freshness out of him. (op 5-1)
St Philip(USA), a progressive juvenile but down the field in the Somerville Tattersall Stakes over course and distance when last seen 239 days previously, was not at his best and may have needed the outing. (tchd 9-2 in a place)
Mimisel, returning from a 211-day break, came into this with an official rating of just 79 and looks flattered to finish so close to a few of these, especially considering she only had half a length to spare over the 63-rated Knapton Hill. (tchd 25-1)
Knapton Hill had never achieved an RPR higher than 64 prior to this, so her proximity badly devalues the form and she is surely flattered. (op 66-1)

2044 CORAL SPRINT (HERITAGE H'CAP) 6f
3:20 (3:22) (Class 2) (0-105,95) 3-Y-O

£24,928 (£7,464; £3,732; £1,868; £932; £468) **Stalls** Low

Form				RPR
2-12	1		**Genki (IRE)**[14] 1658 3-8-6 80 SteveDrowne 9 (R Charlton) *hld up in tch: rdn over 1f out: r.o to ld nr fin* **13/2**[2]	89
60-1	2	shd	**Lipocco**[20] 1502 3-9-7 95 SebSanders 7 (R M Beckett) *lw: chsd ldrs: led 1/2-way: rdn over 1f out: hdd nr fin* **8/1**[3]	104
00-4	3	1 ¾	**Celtic Sultan (IRE)**[28] 1298 3-9-7 95 MickyFenton 16 (T P Tate) *led to 1/2-way: rdn and ev ch over 1f out: styd on same pce ins fnl f* **8/1**[3]	98
-005	4	shd	**Everymanforhimself (IRE)**[14] 1667 3-8-8 87 (b[1]) PatrickHills[(5)] 6 (J G Given) *hld up: hdwy and hung lft over 1f out: styd on* **33/1**	90
1-42	5	hd	**Luscivious**[8] 1817 3-9-4 92 (b) AdamKirby 2 (A J McCabe) *hld up: swtchd lft and hdwy over 1f out: rdn and hung rt ins fnl f: styd on* **25/1**	94
1-00	6	½	**College Scholar (GER)**[20] 1502 3-9-2 90 (v[1]) DarryllHolland 15 (M R Channon) *chsd ldrs: rdn over 1f out: styd on same pce ins fnl f* **33/1**	91
3-30	7	¾	**Steelcut**[15] 1616 3-9-0 88 PatDobbs 12 (R A Fahey) *hld up: hdwy over 1f out: nt trble ldrs* **40/1**	87
-241	8	3 ½	**Dickie Le Davoir**[14] 1667 3-9-5 93 RichardMullen 13 (K R Burke) *lw: s.i.s: hld up: nvr trbld ldrs* **16/1**	81
2-01	9	1 ¾	**Mason Ette**[9] 1786 3-8-7 81 KerrinMcEvoy 4 (C G Cox) *mid-div: rdn over 2f out: wknd over 1f out* **10/1**	64
3-05	10	nk	**Lady Lily (IRE)**[25] 1372 3-8-12 86 TedDurcan 11 (H R A Cecil) *lw: hld up in tch: rdn and wknd over 1f out* **12/1**	68
10-1	11	4	**Mambo Spirit (IRE)**[30] 1270 3-8-13 87 TPQueally 14 (J G Given) *trckd ldrs: racd keenly: rdn and wknd over 1f out* **14/1**	57
20-0	12	1 ¾	**All You Need (IRE)**[8] 1825 3-7-12 72 NickyMackay 5 (R Hollinshead) *mid-div: rdn and wknd over 2f out* **20/1**	37
1-00	13	7	**Fantasy Parkes**[20] 1496 3-9-2 90 DO'Donohoe 1 (K A Ryan) *sn pushed along in rr: wknd over 2f out* **20/1**	34
01-1	14	9	**Sandrey (IRE)**[14] 1660 3-9-0 88 JimmyFortune 10 (P W Chapple-Hyam) *chsd ldrs: wknd and eased wl over 1f out: lame* **7/4**[1]	5

1m 12.55s (-0.55) **Going Correction** +0.05s/f (Good) 14 Ran SP% **122.9**
Speed ratings (Par 105):105,104,102,102,102 101,100,95,93,93 87,85,76,64
CSF £53.71 CT £447.15 TOTE £7.60: £2.30, £2.70, £3.00; EX 54.30 Trifecta £609.50 Pool £1,287.82 - 1.50 winning unit..
Owner Ms Gillian Khosla **Bred** Rathbarry Stud **Trained** Beckhampton, Wilts

FOCUS
A very good three-year-old sprint handicap and typically competitive. They tended to race up the middle of the track but, unlike in the opening maiden, there did not appear to be a draw bias. The winning time was 1.19 seconds quicker than the opening juvenile maiden. Genki is rated to the level of his previous run, with a personal best from the progressive Lipocco.

NOTEBOOK
Genki(IRE) ◆ improved on the form he showed when second at Haydock on his previous start to narrowly defy a 3lb rise in the weights. There was plenty to like about the way he picked up from off the pace to reel in Lipocco, who had raced handy from the start, and he is clearly improving. He appeals as one to very much keep on the right side of and looks the type to go well in the William Hill Trophy at York. (op 7-1)
Lipocco ◆ ran a terrific race off a 4lb higher mark than when winning at Salisbury on his previous start and was just denied. He looks worth keeping on the right side of, especially while his yard is in such good form. (op 17-2 tchd 9-1)
Celtic Sultan(IRE) ◆ confirmed the promise he showed on his reappearance at Ripon with a good performance in third. He shapes as though he might be worth another try over 7f and remains one to have on-side. (op 17-2 tchd 9-1)
Everymanforhimself(IRE) improved on his recent efforts in first-time blinkers, keeping on well late on when switched out with his effort. (tchd 40-1)
Luscivious ◆ was noted travelling well for much of the way, but he was forced to wait for a gap and got going too late once switched left with his challenge. This ground would have been plenty fast enough for him and he could do better again when there is some give underfoot. Official explanation: jockey said gelding suffered interference 2f out
College Scholar(GER) is another who might have found this ground a touch on the quick side, but he still ran with credit in a first-time visor.
Dickie Le Davoir Official explanation: jockey said gelding was unsuited by the good to firm ground
All You Need(IRE) Official explanation: jockey said gelding did not feel right
Sandrey(IRE) was beaten a fair way out and never looked like following up his reappearance success at Lingfield off a 9lb higher mark on this much faster ground. He was later reported to have finished lame and can obviously be forgiven this. Official explanation: trainer said colt returned lame (op 9-4 tchd 5-2 in a place)

2045 NEWMARKETEXPERIENCE.CO.UK H'CAP 1m
3:55 (3:58) (Class 3) (0-90,87) 3-Y-O **£7,772** (£2,312; £1,155; £577) **Stalls** Low

Form				RPR
12-4	1		**Artimino**[30] 1257 3-9-1 84 (t) OscarUrbina 7 (J R Fanshawe) *hld up: hdwy and nt clr run over 1f out: rdn to ld ins fnl f: edgd lft: r.o* **9/2**[1]	97+
234-	2	1	**Bid For Glory**[222] 6010 3-9-3 86 DarryllHolland 14 (H J Collingridge) *chsd ldrs: led over 1f out: sn rdn: hdd ins fnl f: styd on same pce* **14/1**	93
-221	3	2	**Docofthebay (IRE)**[7] 1851 3-9-0 83 (p) TPQueally 5 (J A Osborne) *hld up: hdwy over 2f out: rdn adn hung lft over 1f out: styd on same pce* **7/1**[3]	86
21-4	4	nk	**Farleigh House (USA)**[21] 1471 3-9-4 87 TedDurcan 9 (M H Tompkins) *hld up: hdwy over 2f out: rdn and ev ch over 1f out: no ex ins fnl f* **10/1**	89
40-3	5	1	**Okikoki**[19] 1535 3-8-10 79 JimCrowley 17 (W R Muir) *hld up: hdwy over 2f out: rdn and ev ch over 1f out: no ex ins fnl f* **40/1**	79
111-	6	nk	**Sharpazmax (IRE)**[158] 6866 3-9-0 83 SebSanders 8 (P J Makin) *hld up: hdwy over 2f out: rdn over 1f out: one pce* **20/1**	82
4401	7	½	**Lazy Darren**[18] 1563 3-9-1 84 KerrinMcEvoy 12 (R Hannon) *chsd ldrs: rdn and hung lft over 1f out: n.m.r ins fnl f: styd on same pce* **9/1**	84+
0-1	8	2 ½	**Snaafy (USA)**[38] 1098 3-8-13 82 RHills 4 (B W Hills) *hld up: hdwy over 2f out: rdn and wknd over 1f out* **8/1**	74
0-51	9	hd	**Premio Loco (USA)**[26] 1343 3-9-2 85 IanMongan 13 (C F Wall) *lw: hld up: hdwy over 3f out: rdn over 1f out: wknd fnl f* **12/1**	77
1002	10	1	**Highland Harvest**[19] 1544 3-8-6 78 MarcHalford[(3)] 16 (D R C Elsworth) *lw: led: rdn and hdd over 1f out: wknd ins fnl f* **12/1**	67
1-50	11	1 ½	**Tredegar**[10] 1768 3-9-4 87 JimmyFortune 11 (P F I Cole) *lw: chsd ldrs: rdn: hung lft and wknd over 1f out* **12/1**	73
00-1	12	½	**Rudry Dragon (IRE)**[26] 1359 3-8-11 80 SimonWhitworth 10 (P A Blockley) *chsd ldrs: rdn over 2f out: wknd over 1f out* **20/1**	65
-323	13	¾	**New World Order (IRE)**[99] 483 3-9-2 85 RichardMullen 1 (K R Burke) *hld up: rdn over 2f out: n.d* **66/1**	68
-41	14	nk	**Yaroslav (USA)**[22] 1447 3-9-3 86 SteveDrowne 3 (R Charlton) *hld up: rdn over 2f out: n.d* **11/2**[2]	68
1-10	15	hd	**Hostage**[24] 1407 3-8-8 77 HayleyTurner 18 (M L W Bell) *lw: hld up: effrt over 2f out: sn wknd* **50/1**	59
013-	16	20	**Book Of Facts (FR)**[179] 6634 3-8-10 79 TQuinn 15 (J McAuley) *prom over 5f* **66/1**	15
2-10	17	46	**Autograph Hunter**[39] 1076 3-8-12 81 KDarley 2 (M Johnston) *s.i.s: hld up: bhd fr 1/2-way: eased* **33/1**	—

1m 38.24s (-1.13) **Going Correction** +0.05s/f (Good) **17** Ran SP% **125.9**
Speed ratings (Par 103):107,106,104,103,102 102,101,99,99,98 96,96,95,95,94 74,28
CSF £66.03 CT £464.27 TOTE £5.00: £2.00, £4.20, £2.00, £2.30; EX 89.50.
Owner Cheveley Park Stud **Bred** Cheveley Park Stud Ltd **Trained** Newmarket, Suffolk

FOCUS
A good three-year-old handicap run at a fair pace and the form looks strong for the grade. They all raced up the middle in the early stages, but a few of these drifted towards the stands' rail late on. The winning time was 2.06 seconds quicker than the following maiden.

NOTEBOOK
Artimino ◆ was a beaten favourite in a half-decent race at Beverley on his reappearance, but he has clearly come on for that outing and produced an improved performance. He was ultimately made to work quite hard to see off Bid For Glory, but he had travelled like a very useful horse for much of the way and one suspects he can go on again from this. He shapes as though he will stay further in time, but this trip seems fine for the time being and he will be well worth his place in the Britannia Stakes at Royal Ascot. (tchd 4-1 and 5-1)
Bid For Glory, tried in Listed company on his last start as a juvenile, showed himself on a good mark switched to handicaps off the back of a 222-day break, finding only a potentially decent sort too good late on. (tchd 16-1 in a place)
Docofthebay(IRE), 5lb higher than when winning at Thirsk on his previous start, is not straightforward and threw away any chance he might have had by wandering badly to his left under pressure. He has plenty of ability, and the Handicapper is by no means in charge just yet, but he is a hard ride. Interestingly, his only two wins have come on the only two occasions he has been partnered by Stephen Donohoe. Official explanation: jockey said colt hung left (op 8-1)
Farleigh House(USA) ran a respectable race without really building on the form he showed when fourth in a smaller field over course and distance on his reappearance. (tchd 9-1)
Okikoki, trying 1m for the first time, was produced with every chance and ran well. (op 33-1)
Sharpazmax(IRE) had not been seen since completing a hat-trick on the Polytrack towards the end of last year, but this was a pleasing performance on his return to action. (tchd 25-1 in places)
Lazy Darren had no easy task off a mark 7lb higher than when winning a lesser race at Chepstow on his previous start and he did not help his chance by drifting left in the closing stages. He might have been intimidated somewhat by the wondering Docofthebay, but he also edged left on his previous start and will need to run straighter to compete at this level in future. This was a creditable effort in the circumstances and he could be seen to even better effect when he has a rail to race against. Official explanation: jockey said gelding ran too keen and hung left (op 10-1 tchd 11-1 in a place)
Rudry Dragon(IRE) Official explanation: jockey said colt would not let itself down on the good to firm ground

Yaroslav(USA) never looked like winning and was well below his best. He has already shown he is better than this and there will be other days for him. Official explanation: jockey said colt never travelled (op 13-2)
Book Of Facts(FR) Official explanation: jockey said gelding got tired

2046 ROWLEY MILE MAIDEN STKS 1m
4:25 (4:30) (Class 4) 3-Y-O £5,181 (£1,541; £770; £384) **Stalls** Low

Form				RPR
3	1		**Jaleela (USA)**[24] 1391 3-8-12 0 RHills 2 (W J Haggas) *racd stands' side: chsd ldrs: rdn to ld over 1f out: r.o* **8/11**[1]	77+
26-6	2	2 1/2	**Saviour Sand (IRE)**[129] 160 3-9-3 73 TQuinn 1 (D R C Elsworth) *led stands' side: rdn and hdd over 1f out: styd on same pce* **16/1**	76
05	3	1 3/4	**Novikov**[7] 1840 3-9-3 0 JimmyFortune 3 (J H M Gosden) *lw: racd stands' side: hld up: nt clr run over 2f out: r.o ins fnl f: nvr nr to chal* **10/1**[3]	77+
	4	2	**Al Badeya (IRE)** 3-8-5 0 JamieHamblett(7) 7 (Sir Michael Stoute) *w'like: scope: racd centre tl jnd stands' side over 5f out: chsd ldrs: rdn over 1f out: wknd ins fnl f* **20/1**	62
	5	hd	**Tahdeed** 3-9-3 0 KerrinMcEvoy 10 (Sir Michael Stoute) *w'like: leggy: s.i.s and hamperd s: racd centre: hld up: jnd stands' side over 5f out: nt clr run over 1f out: nvr nr to chal* **11/4**[2]	73+
0	6	3/4	**Beau Michael**[19] 1522 3-9-3 0 AdamKirby 9 (W R Swinburn) *racd centre: sn chsng ldrs: jnd stands' side over 5f out: wknd over 1f out* **50/1**	65
	7	nk	**Scripted (USA)** 3-9-3 0 NickyMackay 5 (L M Cumani) *wl grwn: bkwd: led centre tl jnd stands' side over 5f out: chsd ldrs: wknd fnl f* **14/1**	65
	8	2	**Know The Law** 3-9-3 0 SebSanders 11 (D R C Elsworth) *w'like: wnt rt start: racd centre: hld up: jnd stands' side over 5f out: nt clr run over 2f out: n.d* **20/1**	60
4	9	nk	**Oh Mary (IRE)**[63] 758 3-8-12 0 TPQueally 6 (W J Haggas) *racd centre chsd ldrs: jnd stands' side over 5f out: wknd over 2f out* **14/1**	54
0-0	10	9	**Three Half Crowns (IRE)**[35] 1166 3-9-3 0 TedDurcan 4 (P Howling) *racd stands' side: chsd ldrs over 5f* **100/1**	39

1m 40.3s (0.93) **Going Correction** +0.05s/f (Good) **10** Ran SP% **125.4**
Speed ratings (Par 101):97,94,92,90,90 89,89,87,87,78
CSF £17.34 TOTE £1.70: £1.10, £3.10, £2.10; EX 13.30.
Owner Hamdan Al Maktoum **Bred** Shadwell Farm LLC **Trained** Newmarket, Suffolk

FOCUS
Plenty of late-maturing types, so the bare form is nothing special, but this looked like a maiden that should produce some winners in time. The runner-up set the standard and the winner was 9lb off the bare form of her debut win. They all congregated towards the stands'-side rail after a furlong or so and a low draw was no disadvantage. The pace was just ordinary and the winning time was 2.06 seconds slower than the previous 76-90 handicap.
Novikov Official explanation: jockey said colt hung left closing stages

2047 HOME OF HORSE RACING H'CAP 1m 6f
5:00 (5:05) (Class 4) (0-85,85) 4-Y-O+ £5,181 (£1,541; £770; £384) **Stalls** High

Form				RPR
6-12	1		**Right To Play (USA)**[23] 1438 4-9-7 **85** JimmyFortune 4 (J H M Gosden) *chsd ldrs: led 3f out: rdn over 1f out: hung rt ins fnl f: styd on u.p* **2/1**[1]	98+
314-	2	3/4	**Indonesia**[271] 4883 5-8-9 **73** JimCrowley 7 (T D Walford) *hld up: hdwy over 2f out: rdn to chse wnr over 1f out: hung lft: styd on* **11/2**	80
00-0	3	1 1/2	**Corum (IRE)**[17] 1582 4-9-5 **83** (p) TQuinn 5 (Mrs K Waldron) *hld up: hdwy over 3f out: rdn over 1f out: styd on same pce* **20/1**	88
03-4	4	3 1/2	**Annambo**[30] 1272 7-8-10 **74** RichardMullen 6 (D Morris) *chsd ldrs: rdn over 2f out: wknd ins fnl f* **12/1**	74
	5	8	**Mabel (IRE)**[281] 4583 4-8-6 **70** KerrinMcEvoy 1 (S C Williams) *hld up: rdn and wknd over 2f out* **16/1**	59
30-4	6	4	**Peppertree**[20] 1506 4-9-6 **84** OscarUrbina 3 (J R Fanshawe) *lw: unruly bef s: chsd ldr tl led over 3f out: sn hdd: wknd 2f out* **7/2**[2]	67
1-10	7	1/2	**Power Of Future (GER)**[9] 1794 4-9-6 **84** TedDurcan 2 (H R A Cecil) *hld up: rdn over 4f out: sn hung rt: wknd over 2f out* **4/1**[3]	67
1330	8	shd	**Mahmjra**[8] 1819 5-8-2 **66** oh1 NickyMackay 9 (C N Allen) *led over 10f: wknd over 2f out* **20/1**	48

3m 0.04s (-0.09) **Going Correction** +0.05s/f (Good) **8** Ran SP% **114.0**
Speed ratings (Par 105):102,101,100,98,94 91,91,91
CSF £13.37 CT £162.44 TOTE £2.30: £1.10, £1.80, £4.70; EX 15.40 Place 6 £58.79, Place 5 £27.06.
Owner H R H Princess Haya Of Jordan **Bred** And Mrs Robert A Witt **Trained** Newmarket, Suffolk

FOCUS
Not a strong race, particularly with the sixth and seventh not giving their running, but Right To Play did it well and there should be more to come. The runner-up is rated to form.
Peppertree Official explanation: jockey said filly was distressed
Power Of Future(GER) Official explanation: trainer's rep said race may have come too soon for filly
T/Jkpt: £10,277.30 to a £1 stake. Pool: £231,602.00. 16.00 winning tickets. T/Plt: £59.50 to a £1 stake. Pool: £113,688.60. 1,394.70 winning tickets. T/Qpdt: £7.70 to a £1 stake. Pool: £5,171.70. 495.85 winning tickets. CR

2048 - (Foreign Racing) - See Raceform Interactive

1546 CURRAGH (R-H)
Saturday, May 26

OFFICIAL GOING: Good to firm

2049a ISABEL MORRIS EUROPEAN BREEDERS FUND STKS (LISTED RACE) 5f
2:40 (2:41) 2-Y-O £25,512 (£7,485; £3,566; £1,214)

			RPR
1		**Pencil Hill (IRE)**[10] 1776 2-9-1 PShanahan 5 (Tracey Collins, Ire) *hld up in 5th: 3rd and hdwy under 1 1/2f out: led under 1f out: qcknd clr: eased nr fin* **12/1**[3]	105+
2	1 3/4	**You'resothrilling (USA)** 2-8-12 CO'Donoghue 6 (A P O'Brien, Ire) *bhd: last and outpcd bef 1/2-way: r.o strly fr over 1f out: nvr nrr* **16/1**	96+
3	1	**Tuscan Evening (IRE)**[10] 1774 2-8-12 DMGrant 3 (John Joseph Murphy, Ire) *prom: 2nd and chal after 1/2-way: 3rd and kpt on ins fnl f* **50/1**	92
4	1 1/2	**Achilles Of Troy (IRE)**[20] 1498 2-9-1 JAHeffernan 1 (A P O'Brien, Ire) *sn led: rdn under 2f out: hdd under 1f out: no ex* **2/5**[1]	91
5	shd	**Another Express (IRE)**[41] 1046 2-9-1 WMLordan 2 (T Stack, Ire) *chsd ldrs in 4th: 3rd and rdn 2f out: no ex fr over 1f out* **9/2**[2]	90
6	4	**Inzone (IRE)**[19] 1546 2-8-12 DPMcDonogh 4 (K J Condon, Ire) *towards rr: 6th 1/2-way: no imp fr 1 1/2f out* **33/1**	73
7	3 1/2	**Barraland**[15] 1631 2-9-1 MJKinane 7 (M R Channon) *cl 2nd to 1/2-way: sn wknd* **12/1**[3]	63

58.80 secs (-2.50) **Going Correction** -0.40s/f (Firm) **7** Ran SP% **115.8**
Speed ratings: 104,101,99,97,97 91,85
CSF £174.48 TOTE £9.00: £4.70, £6.30; DF 259.90.
Owner Mrs C Collins **Bred** Millsec Limited **Trained** The Curragh, Co Kildare

FOCUS
An interesting renewal of this good prize that attracted some promising previous winners.

NOTEBOOK
Pencil Hill(IRE) had created a very good impression when capturing a 6f winners' event at Naas on his debut and here ran out a commanding winner. A very promising sort, he will now be aimed at the Group 2 Railway Stakes and a bold showing there can be expected. The step back up to 6f will certainly be in his favour and he can be rated a very promising juvenile. (op 10/1)
You'resothrilling(USA), a sister to Giant's Causeway, made a highly encouraging start to her career. She raced at the rear of the field and looked to be struggling some way from home but she stayed on strongly from over a furlong out. This experience will bring her on considerably and she looks a fine prospect, particularly when she steps up in trip. (op 14/1)
Tuscan Evening(IRE) ran respectably in what looked a useful maiden at Naas last week and improved on that form. She was in the front rank from the outset and stuck to her task well over the final furlong. She should prove just as effective over further.
Achilles Of Troy(IRE) came away smartly to set a strong early pace and he had plenty of his rivals hard at work with over a furlong to run. However, his early exertions took their toll and he had no more to give over the final furlong. (op 2/5 tchd 4/11)
Another Express(IRE) was looking to build on an encouraging debut victory over this course and distance last month. He held a prominent position from the outset but could do no more heading towards the final furlong. (op 5/1)
Inzone(IRE) Official explanation: trainer said filly hung badly in running
Barralandclear winner of a Lingfield maiden last time, found this assignment beyond him. (op 16/1)

2050a WEATHERBYS IRELAND GREENLANDS STKS (GROUP 3) 6f
3:10 (3:10) 3-Y-O+ £35,135 (£10,270; £4,864; £1,621)

			RPR
1		**Benbaun (IRE)**[167] 6783 6-9-12 (b) PJSmullen 1 (M J Wallace) *trckd ldrs: 5th 1/2-way: smooth hdwy into 2nd under 2f out: led over 1f out: r.o wl: easily* **4/1**[2]	119
2	2 1/2	**Moss Vale (IRE)**[10] 1770 6-10-0 KJManning 6 (D Nicholls) *broke wl: led bef 1/2-way: rdn and strly pressed under 2f out: hdd over 1f out: kpt on same u.p* **7/2**[1]	113
3	1 1/2	**Theann**[20] 1496 3-8-11 104 JAHeffernan 11 (A P O'Brien, Ire) *chsd ldrs on outer: 5th and rdn 2f out: mod 3rd and kpt on ins fnl f* **13/2**	99
4	1/2	**Flash McGahon (IRE)**[22] 1461 3-9-0 100 MJKinane 10 (John M Oxx, Ire) *prom in centre: 3rd 2f out: kpt on same pce u.p* **16/1**	100
5	1 1/2	**Ashdown Express (IRE)**[14] 1657 8-9-9 GeorgeBaker 7 (C F Wall) *chsd ldrs: 6th 1/2-way: no imp fr 1 1/2f out* **9/1**	98
6	1 1/2	**Leitra (IRE)**[272] 4855 4-9-6 102 RPCleary 5 (M Halford, Ire) *hld up towards rr: prog under 2f out: mod 6th and kpt on fnl f* **20/1**	90
7	1 1/2	**Facchetti (USA)**[22] 1461 3-9-0 100 CO'Donoghue 3 (A P O'Brien, Ire) *led early: rdn 1/2-way: 6th under 2f out: sn no ex* **33/1**	89
8	1/2	**Silver Touch (IRE)**[224] 5962 4-9-6 OPeslier 4 (M R Channon) *towards rr: no imp fr 2f out* **9/2**[3]	84
9	hd	**Absolutelyfabulous (IRE)**[22] 1461 4-9-6 101 WMLordan 9 (David Wachman, Ire) *chsd ldrs to 1/2-way: sn no ex* **14/1**	83
10	3/4	**Majestic Times (IRE)**[328] 3124 7-9-9 105 NGMcCullagh 8 (Liam McAteer, Ire) *towards rr thrght* **33/1**	84
11	hd	**An Tadh (IRE)**[41] 1049 4-9-12 109 JMurtagh 2 (G M Lyons, Ire) *4th early: 2nd after 1/2-way: wknd fr 2f out: eased fnl f* **8/1**	87

1m 10.1s (-4.40) **Going Correction** -0.40s/f (Firm)
WFA 3 from 4yo+ 9lb **11** Ran SP% **118.0**
Speed ratings: 113,109,107,107,105 103,101,100,100,99 98
CSF £18.06 TOTE £5.20: £1.70, £1.50, £2.60; DF 13.40.
Owner Ransley, Birks, Hillen **Bred** Dr T A Ryan **Trained** Newmarket, Suffolk

FOCUS
The race has been rated through the third and fourth, with Benbaun in line with his winter form over this trip.

NOTEBOOK
Benbaun(IRE), on his first outing since taking third behind Absolute Champion and Silent Witness in Hong Kong last December, scored in decisive fashion on a course he likes. He seems to be improving with age, and the most significant aspect to this thoroughly convincing success is that it widens his sprinting options to include the major 6f events. All three of his previous course wins had been gained over the minimum distance, and this was only his second victory at the trip. He could go for the Prix du Gros Chene at Chantilly before a trip to Royal Ascot. (op 3/1)
Moss Vale(IRE), last year's winner and seeking a third success over course and distance, was up with the pace from the start and took a definite advantage from over 3f out but was picked off fairly effortlessly. This represented an improvement from his seasonal debut at York, and he should again be competitive at a high level this season. (op 3/1 tchd 4/1)
Theann, dropping in trip following her run in the 1000 Guineas, ran a sound race without sending out definite signals that she is truly a sprinting type. She ran well behind the John Oxx-trained pair Arch Swing and Four Sins over 7f at Leopardstown on her seasonal debut, and that is probably closer to her optimum trip. (op 7/1)
Flash McGahon(IRE), whose form ties in with the leading Irish sprinter Dandy Man, was able to hold a good position throughout. This was a perfectly respectable effort by the three-year-old against some seasoned campaigners, and he looks capable of picking up a decent prize this season. (op 14/1)
Ashdown Express(IRE), who was in action in Dubai during the winter, failed to show any improvement from a recent Haydock outing. He has lost the winning habit, and is not going to be particularly easy to place. (op 8/1 tchd 10/1)
Silver Touch(IRE) failed to make any impression on her first outing of the season. (op 5/1)

2051a BOYLESPORTS IRISH 2,000 GUINEAS (GROUP 1) (C&F) 1m
3:45 (3:46) 3-Y-O
£151,689 (£51,689; £24,662; £8,445; £5,743; £3,040)

			RPR
1		**Cockney Rebel (IRE)**[21] 1473 3-9-0 OPeslier 7 (G A Huffer) *settled 3rd: led under 2f out: rdn and strly pressed 1f out: r.o wl: comf* **6/4**[1]	121+

The Form Book, Raceform Ltd, Compton, RG20 6NL

2 1 **Creachadoir (IRE)**[13] 1703 3-9-0 114 KJManning 8 118
(J S Bolger, Ire) *trckd ldrs: 6th 1/2-way: 4th 2 1/2f out: 2nd and chal 1f out: kpt on wl* **7/1**[3]

3 1 **He's A Decoy (IRE)**[37] 1103 3-9-0 115 MJKinane 3 116+
(David Wachman, Ire) *hld up in rr: 7th and hdwy 2f out: 5th over 1f out: styd on* **40/1**

4 hd **Duke Of Marmalade (IRE)**[21] 1473 3-9-0 114 JAHeffernan 12 116
(A P O'Brien, Ire) *chsd ldrs: 4th and rdn over 2 1/2f out: 3rd and chal on far rail 2f out: kpt on same pce u.p* **9/4**[2]

5 ¾ **Followmyfootsteps (USA)**[13] 1703 3-9-0 108 WMLordan 5 114
(David Wachman, Ire) *towards rr: prog over 2f out: 5th over 1f out: kpt on* **33/1**

6 hd **Vital Equine (IRE)**[21] 1473 3-9-0 ChrisCatlin 1 113
(E J O'Neill) *disp ld: led 2 1/2f out: hdd under 2f out: 4th over 1f out: kpt on same pce* **8/1**

7 5 ½ **Confuchias (IRE)**[19] 1547 3-9-0 102 DPMcDonogh 4 101
(Francis Ennis, Ire) *hld up in tch: 6th and rdn 2 1/2f out: no ex fr under 2f out* **50/1**

8 ½ **Kingsdale Orion (IRE)**[19] 1549 3-9-0 78 PShanahan 2 100?
(Ms Florence Mills, Ire) *towards rr: 11th 1/2-way: kpt on fr under 2f out* **500/1**

9 1 ¼ **Traffic Guard (USA)**[56] 859 3-9-0 JohnEgan 13 97
(J S Moore) *mid-div: no imp fr over 2f out* **50/1**

10 3 **Fleeting Shadow (IRE)**[41] 1047 3-9-0 112 PJSmullen 11 90
(D K Weld, Ire) *towards rr: no imp fr over 2f out* **33/1**

11 ¾ **Ferneley (IRE)**[34] 1185 3-9-0 109 WSupple 9 88
(Francis Ennis, Ire) *s.i.s: settled in mid-div: rdn after 1/2-way: no ex fr over 2f out* **12/1**

12 ½ **Trinity College (USA)**[41] 1047 3-9-0 103 DavidMcCabe 1 87
(A P O'Brien, Ire) *disp ld: rdn and hdd 2 1/2f out: sn wknd: eased fnl f* **100/1**

1m 36.1s (-6.00) **Going Correction** -0.325s/f (Firm) **13** Ran SP% **115.5**
Speed ratings: 117,116,115,114,114 113,108,107,106,103 102,102
CSF £12.08 TOTE £2.50: £1.10, £1.60, £4.90; DF 13.30.
Owner Phil Cunningham **Bred** Oak Lodge Bloodstock **Trained** Newmarket, Suffolk

FOCUS
A good renewal with the Newmarket form upheld and tied in with the French equivalent by the runner-up. The proximity of the exposed eighth is a worry, but otherwise the form looks sound enough, with the seventh setting the standard.

NOTEBOOK
Cockney Rebel(IRE) completed the English/Irish Guineas double and, if there were any doubts about the merits of his Newmarket triumph, they were put to bed here in a race that binds together the form of the English, Irish and sub-standard French three-year-old milers. He was ridden closer to the pace in this much smaller field, and he showed the right attributes in shrugging off the attentions of a tough and rugged performer in Creachadoir, ultimately scoring with more comfort than is implied by the margin. He is going to take all the beating in the St James's Palace Stakes, with the main threat likely to come from one of several possible contenders from the Aidan O'Brien stable. Official explanation: jockey said colt shied from the winning post and the photographers (op 7/4)
Creachadoir(IRE) put up a performance which will only serve to fuel the "might have been" debate in relation to his sidelined stablemate Teofilo. However, he has emerged as a very substantial talent in his own right, and he confimed that he is a hearty competitor who takes his racing well, as this was his third outing inside less than three weeks. However, he will give Royal Ascot a miss and have a break now, with the Prix du Moulin named as a possible target. (op 8/1)
He's A Decoy(IRE) showed that he has progressed well since making his seasonal debut in the Craven. He had smart form as a two-year-old, including when third to Holy Roman Emperor at Longchamp, and the manner in which he stayed on suggests he will stay 1m2f.
Duke Of Marmalade(IRE), fourth at Newmarket, could do no better than replicate that finishing position. He had to be scrubbed along to keep close contact with the leaders under 3f out, and while there was no lack of response he failed to build his challenge further after getting into third place on the far side. He missed the latter part of last season, and at this stage it looks as if he still has a bit of catching up to do in order to attain Group 1 honours. (op 11/4 tchd 7/4)
Followmyfootsteps(USA), a stablemate of the third and sixth in the Poulains, also enhanced his reputation and should be able to supplement his Tipperary maiden win if his sights are lowered a little.
Vital Equine(IRE), the Newmarket runner-up, was prominent from the early stages and had a spell in the lead until the winner arrived travelling much better. He is capable of better than this.
Kingsdale Orion(IRE) looked thoroughly exposed and had no business finishing so close. It will be interesting to see if he can reproduce his apparent level of improvement.
Traffic Guard(USA), having his first run on turf this season after racing on dirt at the Dubai Carnival, never really got into contention and is another who may need his sights lowering in the short-term. (op 66/1)

2053a RIDGEWOOD PEARL STKS (GROUP 3) 1m
4:50 (4:51) 4-Y-0+ **£43,918** (£12,837; £6,081; £2,027)

RPR

1 **Cheyenne Star (IRE)**[20] 1510 4-8-12 108 PJSmullen 10 110
(Ms F M Crowley, Ire) *trckd ldrs in 6th: impr into 2nd under 2f out: chal on far rail fr over 1f out: led 50yds out: kpt on wl* **7/1**

2 ¾ **Heaven Sent**[14] 1649 4-8-12 MJKinane 4 109
(Sir Michael Stoute) *in tch: 5th and rdn 2 1/2f out: 3rd over 1f out: sn chal: kpt on wl cl home* **11/4**[1]

3 shd **Modeeroch (IRE)**[19] 1548 4-8-12 106 KJManning 1 109
(J S Bolger, Ire) *hld up early: smooth hdwy 3f out: led under 2f out: strly pressed fnl f: hdd 50yds out: kpt on* **5/1**[3]

4 3 **Anna Karenina (IRE)**[20] 1511 4-8-12 103 WMLordan 11 102
(David Wachman, Ire) *hld up in tch: 5th and hdwy 2f out: 4th and no imp fnl f* **7/1**

5 2 **Dani's Girl (IRE)**[19] 1548 4-8-12 90 (b[1]) FMBerry 2 97
(P A Fahy, Ire) *sn led: rdn and strly pressed whn wandered abt 2f out: sn hdd: kpt on same pce* **40/1**

6 hd **Bon Nuit (IRE)**[19] 1550 5-8-12 100 NGMcCullagh 7 97
(Mrs John Harrington, Ire) *prom: 2nd 1/2-way: 3rd 3f out: sn rdn and one pce* **16/1**

7 nk **Eastern Appeal (IRE)**[19] 1548 4-9-1 102 RPCleary 9 99
(M Halford, Ire) *chsd ldrs: 5th early: rdn and no imp fr over 2f out* **12/1**

8 2 **Dancing Sky (IRE)**[20] 1511 4-8-12 100 PShanahan 3 91
(D K Weld, Ire) *a towards rr* **33/1**

9 1 **Blessyourpinksox (IRE)**[10] 1777 6-8-12 99 DPMcDonogh 5 89
(Peter Casey, Ire) *4th early: lost pl 1/2-way: no ex fr 2 1/2f out* **14/1**

10 ½ **Ardbrae Lady**[19] 1548 4-9-1 103 JAHeffernan 6 91
(Joseph G Murphy, Ire) *sn prom: 2nd 3f out: rdn and wknd fr over 2f out* **12/1**

11 3 ½ **Deauville Vision (IRE)**[19] 1548 4-8-12 104 JMurtagh 8 80
(M Halford, Ire) *prom to 1/2-way: rdn and wknd over 2f out: eased fnl f* **10/3**[2]

1m 38.7s (-3.40) **Going Correction** -0.325s/f (Firm) **11** Ran SP% **124.7**
Speed ratings: 104,103,103,100,98 97,97,95,94,94 90
CSF £28.24 TOTE £8.60: £3.30, £1.30, £1.70; DF 34.00.
Owner Mrs Jacqueline Alder **Bred** Roland H Alder **Trained** Curragh, Co Kildare

FOCUS
Quite a decent Group 3 that attracted six previous Stakes winners. However, the fifth limits the overall level of the form.

NOTEBOOK
Cheyenne Star(IRE) posted a career-best effort to prevail, but she had run some sound races in defeat at Listed level last year. She should continue to pay her way at this level for the rest of the season and further stakes race success looks entirely possible. (op 6/1)
Heaven Sent was taking a step up in class after winning an Ascot handicap off 87 two weeks previously. She was under pressure over two furlongs from home but stayed on well and could be worth trying over further. She is well worth her place at this level. (op 3/1 tchd 7/2)
Modeeroch(IRE) made stylish headway to lead just inside the final quarter of a mile and it was only very late on that she gave best. A talented filly, she has now posted two good efforts in defeat this term and looks more than capable of adding to her stakes race haul. This trip may just have stretched her stamina. (op 4/1)
Anna Karenina(IRE) could never land a telling blow but was not at all disgraced in a stronger race than the Listed event she won at Gowran last time. (op 6/1)

2054 - (Foreign Racing) - See Raceform Interactive

2041
NEWMARKET (ROWLEY) (R-H)
Sunday, May 27

OFFICIAL GOING: Good to soft (good in places) changing to good to soft after race 2 (2.45) and to soft after race 5 (4.25)
Wind: Light, behind Weather: Raining

2055 BIDWELLS LADIES H'CAP (LADY AMATEUR RIDERS) (IN MEMORY OF LUCINDA STOPFORD-SACKVILLE) 1m 4f
2:10 (2:11) (Class 5) (0-70,72) 4-Y-0+ **£3,747** (£1,162; £580; £290) **Stalls** High

Form RPR

2213 **1** **They All Laughed**[15] 1683 4-9-6 **58** MrsMarieKing(3) 11 70+
(P W Hiatt) *hld up: hdwy over 3f out: led over 1f out: sn clr* **7/2**[1]

5402 **2** 4 **Flying Spirit (IRE)**[12] 1741 8-10-4 **72** (b) MissHayleyMoore(5) 5 76
(G L Moore) *chsd ldr: rdn over 2f out: styd on same pce appr fnl f* **10/1**

-124 **3** 1 ½ **Dark Parade (ARG)**[20] 1526 6-9-12 **64** MissEFolkes(3) 7 66
(P D Evans) *lw: chsd ldrs tl led 5f out: rdn and hdd over 1f out: no ex fnl f* **5/1**[2]

0550 **4** 5 **Blue Hedges**[13] 1730 5-9-4 **58** oh4 ow2 MissALHutchinson(5) 13 52
(H J Collingridge) *b. hld up: hdwy over 1f out: nt trble ldrs* **10/1**

0560 **5** ¾ **Lady's Law**[15] 1666 4-9-0 **56** oh11 MissEmma-JaneJenkins(7) 3 48
(Rae Guest) *lw: swtg: chsd ldrs: rdn over 3f out: wknd over 1f out* **50/1**

1-50 **6** 1 **Alexian**[6] 1886 4-9-12 **68** BrydieKilloran(7) 8 59
(D W P Arbuthnot) *hld up: effrt over 2f out: wknd over 1f out* **16/1**

030- **7** shd **Escobar (POL)**[7] 2636 6-9-3 **57** oh9 ow1 MrsCThompson(5) 6 48
(Mrs P Townsley) *hld up: n.d* **20/1**

6024 **8** 1 ½ **Come What July (IRE)**[18] 1592 6-9-7 **56** oh8 MrsMMorris 10 44
(D Shaw) *b. hld up: hdwy over 4f out: wknd over 1f out* **14/1**

32-0 **9** 1 **Cormorant Wharf (IRE)**[17] 1609 7-10-4 **72** ow4 MissJPowell(5) 14 59
(T E Powell) *hld up: hdwy over 4f out: wknd over 1f out* **7/2**[1]

60 **10** 10 **Red Wine**[15] 1668 8-9-13 **67** (be) MissJCDuncan(5) 15 38
(A J McCabe) *dwlt: hld up: a in rr* **8/1**[3]

4-00 **11** 4 **Cool Isle**[18] 1592 4-9-0 **56** oh8 (b) MissFGuillambert(7) 2 20
(P Howling) *hld up: hdwy over 3f out: wknd over 1f out* **33/1**

0065 **12** 9 **Love You Always (USA)**[12] 1742 7-9-2 **58** oh6 ow2(t) MissCCasey(7) 12 8
(Miss J Feilden) *b. hld up: a in rr* **50/1**

3014 **13** 39 **Bienheureux**[12] 1741 6-9-0 **56** oh3 (t) MissOMaylam(7) 4 —
(Miss Gay Kelleway) *b. led: clr 10f out: hdd 5f out: sn rdn and wknd: t.o* **16/1**

006- **14** 22 **Love And Affection**[176] 6668 4-9-1 **57** oh4 ow1.(t) MissGThorogood(7) 1 —
(P S McEntee) *lw: s.s: a in rr: t.o fr 1/2-way* **50/1**

2m 41.11s (7.61) **Going Correction** +0.40s/f (Good) **14** Ran SP% **122.4**
Speed ratings (Par 103):90,87,86,83,82 81,81,80,80,73 70,64,38,24
CSF £38.82 CT £177.43 TOTE £3.50: £1.70, £2.50, £2.70; EX 24.10.
Owner Clive Roberts **Bred** T G And B B Mills **Trained** Hook Norton, Oxon

FOCUS
A moderate lady amateur riders' contest and, with over half the field racing from out of the handicap, the form is dubious. The leaders went off very quickly considering the conditions. They raced towards the far side, but most of these wanted to avoid the rail.

2056 KNIGHTFRANK.CO.UK MAIDEN STKS 5f
2:45 (2:46) (Class 4) 2-Y-0 **£4,533** (£1,348; £674; £336) **Stalls** Low

Form RPR

3 **1** **Swiss Franc**[15] 1652 2-9-3 0 TedDurcan 8 87
(D R C Elsworth) *b. lw: trckd ldr: rdn to ld ins fnl f: r.o* **4/7**[1]

2 1 ¾ **Wolgan Valley (USA)** 2-9-3 0 KerrinMcEvoy 6 81
(Saeed Bin Suroor) *w'like: scope: bit bkwd: led: shkn up and hung rt over 1f out: hdd and unable qck ins fnl f* **9/2**[2]

3 1 ¾ **Let Us Prey** 2-9-3 0 JimmyFortune 2 74
(N A Callaghan) *leggy: scope: lw: stdd s: hld up: swtchd rt over 1f out: r.o ins fnl f: nrst fin* **14/1**

4 2 ½ **Creative (IRE)** 2-9-3 0 JimmyQuinn 7 65
(M H Tompkins) *chsd ldrs: rdn over 1f out: wknd ins fnl f* **22/1**

5 ½ **Notepad** 2-8-12 0 LPKeniry 4 59
(W Jarvis) *neat: unf: prom: pushed along 1/2-way: wknd over 1f out* **20/1**

0 **6** nk **Mister Fips (IRE)**[15] 1652 2-9-3 0 JHBowman 3 63
(Jane Chapple-Hyam) *chsd ldrs: rdn over 1f out: wknd ins fnl f* **6/1**[3]

7 3 **Race The Moon (IRE)** 2-9-0 0 JerryO'Dwyer(3) 5 52
(V Smith) *w'like: s.i.s: hdwy over 3f out: wknd over 1f out* **16/1**

8 shd **Bettys Touch** 2-8-12 0 RichardMullen 1 46
(P J McBride) *neat: hld up: wknd 2f out* **66/1**

62.20 secs (1.73) **Going Correction** +0.40s/f (Good) **8** Ran SP% **119.3**
Speed ratings (Par 95):102,99,96,92,91 91,86,86
CSF £3.66 TOTE £1.60: £1.10, £1.50, £2.30; EX 4.70.
Owner Lordship Stud **Bred** Lordship Stud **Trained** Newmarket, Suffolk

FOCUS
Hard to be confident about the value of the form, and the winner stood out, as his odds suggested he would. However, some nice types lined up and this maiden should produce some winners. They raced towards the stands' side.

NOTEBOOK

Swiss Franc ◆ shaped well when third in a decent-looking maiden on his debut at Ascot and confirmed that promise with a straightforward success, despite not looking totally happy on the ground. He gives the impression though a faster surface will suit better and he is potentially decent. (op 4-6)

Wolgan Valley(USA), a $1,450,000 half-brother to three winners on dirt in the US over 7f plus, including useful Indian War Dance, out of triple sprint winner in the US, was the stable's first juvenile runner of the year. He proved easy to back, but made a satisfactory debut behind the potentially decent winner. (op 3-1)

Let Us Prey ◆, a 42,000gns half-brother to 1m2f winner Grandretour, and 6f winner Entailment, out of a triple 7f-1m scorer, picked up nicely once switched to the outside and shaped with plenty of promise for the future. (op 12-1)

Creative(IRE), a 17,000euros half-brother to 2m winner Pendle Forest, later successful over hurdles, out of a 15-time winner over 6f-1m1f, showed some ability on his racecourse debut and should improve. (op 20-1 tchd 25-1)

Notepad, a 72,000gns half-sister to, among others, high-class 5f-7f juvenile winner Rag Top, out a 5f juvenile scorer, should be better for the experience.

Mister Fips(IRE) was well backed but he never looked like reversing Ascot form with Swiss Franc. (op 10-1)

2057 MATERIAL CHANGE AND GLOBAL RECYCLING SOLUTIONS H'CAP 1m 2f

3:15 (3:17) (Class 2) (0-100,96) 3-Y-O **£11,658** (£3,468; £1,733; £865) **Stalls** Low

Form RPR

00-0 **1** **Smokey Oakey (IRE)**[11] 1768 3-8-4 **82** .... JimmyQuinn 1 88
(M H Tompkins) *lw: hmpd s: hld up: hdwy 2f out: rdn to ld ins fnl f: r.o* **4/1**[3]

-231 **2** *shd* **Eradicate (IRE)**[26] 1369 3-8-13 **91** .... KDarley 4 97+
(M Johnston) *lw: led: rdn and edgd lft over 1f out: hdd ins fnl f: r.o* **6/4**[1]

011- **3** *3* **Ladies Best**[227] 5916 3-9-0 **92** .... KerrinMcEvoy 3 92
(Sir Michael Stoute) *h.d.w: chsd ldr: rdn over 2f out: edgd rt and styd on same pce fnl f* **2/1**[2]

22-1 **4** *5* **Coeur De Lionne (IRE)**[32] 1250 3-8-7 **85** .... ChrisCatlin 5 75
(R Charlton) *trckd ldrs: rdn over 2f out: wknd fnl f* **7/1**

10-0 **5** *37* **To The Max (IRE)**[39] 1097 3-9-4 **96** .... JimmyFortune 2 12
(R Hannon) *wnt lft s: sn chsng ldrs: rdn over 2f out: sn hung lft and wknd* **16/1**

2m 9.39s (3.68) **Going Correction** +0.40s/f (Good) **5** Ran SP% **111.7**

Speed ratings (Par 105):101,100,98,94,64

CSF £10.67 TOTE £4.30: £1.70, £1.70; EX 14.40.

Owner Judi Dench and Bryan Agar **Bred** Hyde Park Stud **Trained** Newmarket, Suffolk

FOCUS

Just the five runners, but a good three-year-old handicap and strong form. They raced up the middle of the track.

NOTEBOOK

Smokey Oakey(IRE) had never previously raced beyond 1m, but the step up in trip brought about an improved performance. Having travelled nicely for much of the way, he looked likely to win well when taking it up inside the final furlong, but the Johnston horse battled back and he may have been beaten in another stride or two. He is unexposed over this sort of trip, though, and could have more to offer. (op 7-1)

Eradicate(IRE) ◆ won his maiden on very firm ground at Bath last time, but that was a weak race and the return to an easier surface would have suited. He battled on well when headed by the winner and this must rate as a very useful performance. He gives the impression he might stay 1m4f and could go well in something like the King George V Handicap at Royal Ascot. (op 13-8 tchd 11-8)

Ladies Best ◆, stepped up two furlongs in trip off the back of a 227-day break, did not help his chance by racing a little keenly early on and this run should have taken the freshness out of him. A further step up in trip is almost sure to suit and he is another to consider for the King George V Handicap at Royal Ascot. (op 13-8 tchd 6-4 in places)

Coeur De Lionne(IRE) found this tougher than the Polytrack maiden he won on his previous start and was well beaten. (op 6-1)

To The Max(IRE) was beaten a long way and may have been unsuited by the ground. (op 14-1)

2058 CONNAUGHT SQUARE SQUIRREL HUNT H'CAP 6f

3:50 (3:50) (Class 2) (0-100,98) 4-Y-O+ **£11,658** (£3,468; £1,733; £865) **Stalls** Low

Form RPR

0006 **1** **Commando Scott (IRE)**[9] 1826 6-8-4 **84** oh2 .... RoystonFfrench 10 96
(I W McInnes) *trckd ldrs: racd keenly: rdn to ld ins fnl f: r.o* **17/2**

50-5 **2** *1* **Trafalgar Bay (IRE)**[15] 1653 4-8-9 **89** .... PatCosgrave 14 98
(K R Burke) *b. hld up: hung rt: hdwy over 2f out: rdn and ev ch ins fnl f: styd on same pce* **6/1**[2]

00-5 **3** *hd* **Ingleby Arch (USA)**[9] 1826 4-8-8 **88** .... PaulFessey 6 96
(T D Barron) *lw: chsd ldrs: rdn over 2f out: styd on* **6/1**[2]

-500 **4** *1 1/2* **Charles Darwin (IRE)**[15] 1653 4-8-7 **87** .... FrancisNorton 13 91
(M Blanshard) *chsd ldrs: rdn over 1f out: styd on same pce* **22/1**

046- **5** *nk* **Pearly Wey**[259] 5202 4-8-9 **89** .... PhilipRobinson 7 92
(C G Cox) *lw: hld up: rdn over 1f out: styd on ins fnl f: nt trble ldrs* **14/1**

0301 **6** *shd* **Ripples Maid**[8] 1836 4-9-3 **97** .... JHBowman 4 99+
(J A Geake) *lw: led: hdd and no ex ins fnl f* **3/1**[1]

005 **7** *1 1/4* **Romany Nights (IRE)**[5] 1931 7-8-4 **84** oh1 .... (bt) JimmyQuinn 8 82
(Miss Gay Kelleway) *b. s.i.s: hld up: styd on ins fnl f: nvr trbld ldrs* **25/1**

3616 **8** *3* **Mujood**[15] 1653 4-8-10 **90** .... (v) StephenCarson 1 79
(Eve Johnson Houghton) *hld up: rdn over 2f out: n.d* **12/1**

3300 **9** *shd* **One More Round (USA)**[15] 1651 9-9-1 **95** .... (b) JamesDoyle 12 83
(N P Littmoden) *hld up: rdn over 2f out: n.d* **20/1**

0000 **10** *1* **The Kiddykid (IRE)**[16] 1619 7-9-4 **98** .... StephenDonohoe 2 83
(P D Evans) *broke wl: chsd ldrs: rdn over 2f out: wknd over 1f out* **8/1**[3]

-000 **11** *5* **Coleorton Dancer**[15] 1651 5-8-5 **88** .... (p) AndrewMullen(3) 5 57
(K A Ryan) *chsd ldrs over 4f* **8/1**[3]

60-0 **12** *12* **Andronikos**[8] 1836 5-9-3 **97** .... (t) JimmyFortune 3 28
(P F I Cole) *lw: s.i.s: hld up: wknd 2f out: eased* **14/1**

1m 13.26s (0.16) **Going Correction** +0.40s/f (Good) **12** Ran SP% **120.3**

Speed ratings (Par 109):114,112,112,110,110 109,108,104,104,102 96,80

CSF £58.08 CT £340.97 TOTE £12.40: £2.10, £2.70, £2.40; EX 58.00 Trifecta £534.70 Part won. Pool £753.16 - 0.60 winning units..

Owner Mrs Ann Morris **Bred** Noel Finegan **Trained** Catwick, E Yorks

FOCUS

A decent sprint handicap and the form looks very strong for the grade. The winning time was 2.52 seconds quicker than the later fillies' 71-85. They raced up the middle of the track.

NOTEBOOK

Commando Scott(IRE) was 2lb lower than when gaining his last success a year previously, despite racing from out of the handicap, and ran out a decisive winner under his favoured conditions. (op 8-1 tchd 9-1)

Trafalgar Bay(IRE) ◆ built on the promise he showed on his reappearance/debut for this yard when fifth at Ascot with a good effort in second. He looks capable of winning a decent sprint handicap this season. (op 11-2)

Ingleby Arch(USA) ◆, 9lb lower than when last winning, ran a fine race on ground that was probably softer than is ideal He is another who should pick up a nice prize or two this term. (op 11-2 tchd 5-1)

Charles Darwin(IRE), only 1lb higher than when last winning, ran well on ground that may just have been on the soft side for him. (op 33-1)

Pearly Wey ◆ lost his way a touch last season, but there is no denying his talent when he is on song and this was a pleasing return from a 259-day break.

Ripples Maid could not defy a 5lb rise in the weights for her recent Newbury success, but she only gave way late on. She showed bags of early speed and could be worth another try over 5f. (op 11-4 tchd 100-30)

Andronikos Official explanation: jockey said horse was never travelling

2059 CAPITAL SPREADS MAIDEN STKS 7f

4:25 (4:25) (Class 4) 3-Y-O **£5,181** (£1,541; £770; £384) **Stalls** Low

Form RPR

4-23 **1** **Transcend**[8] 1841 3-9-3 85 .... JimmyFortune 6 84+
(J H M Gosden) *a.p: chsd ldr over 2f out: rdn to ld and hung lft ins fnl f: r.o* **10/11**[1]

3425 **2** *2* **Esteem Machine (USA)**[17] 1606 3-9-0 74 .... MarcHalford(3) 3 78
(D R C Elsworth) *lw: led: rdn and hung lft fr over 1f out: hdd and no ex ins fnl f* **15/2**[3]

3 *3* **Shadow The Wind (IRE)** 3-9-3 0 .... KerrinMcEvoy 9 70
(E F Vaughan) *gd sort: chsd ldrs: rdn and hung lft over 1f out: no ex* **10/1**

4 *1 1/2* **Cape Cobra** 3-9-3 0 .... RobertHavlin 7 66+
(J H M Gosden) *w'like: s.i.s: hld up: plld hrd: hdwy 1/2-way: wknd over 1f out* **20/1**

4 **5** *1/2* **Destour (IRE)**[22] 1468 3-9-3 0 .... SebSanders 11 65+
(J Noseda) *lw: s.i.s: hld up: hung rt and styd on fr over 1f out: nvr nrr* **8/1**

0-52 **6** *5* **Cavalry Guard (USA)**[16] 1634 3-9-3 74 .... (p) TedDurcan 4 52
(H R A Cecil) *mid-div: hdwy 1/2-way: rdn over 2f out: hung rt and wknd over 1f out* **9/2**[2]

7 *1* **Hot Property (IRE)** 3-9-3 0 .... RichardMullen 1 49
(W R Muir) *neat: hld up: rdn 1/2-way: n.d* **66/1**

8 *2* **Park Valley Prince** 3-9-3 0 .... FrancisNorton 8 44
(W R Muir) *neat: mid-div: lost pl 4f out: sn bhd* **66/1**

9 *7* **Upstairs** 3-9-3 0 .... TQuinn 5 26
(D R C Elsworth) *leggy: scope: s.s: outpcd* **33/1**

10 *1* **Word Of Warning** 3-9-3 0 .... EddieAhern 12 23
(G Wragg) *leggy: scope: hld up: wknd over 2f out* **33/1**

11 *8* **Apolina** 3-8-12 0 .... ChrisCatlin 2 —
(P S McEntee) *unf: s.i.s: outpcd* **66/1**

0- **12** *5* **Stravinsky's Art (USA)**[365] 2029 3-9-3 0 .... BrettDoyle 10 —
(D R C Elsworth) *lw: w ldr 3f: hung lft and wknd over 2f out* **33/1**

1m 29.14s (2.64) **Going Correction** +0.40s/f (Good) **12** Ran SP% **120.6**

Speed ratings (Par 101):100,97,94,92,92 86,85,82,74,73 64,58

CSF £8.03 TOTE £1.80: £1.20, £2.50, £2.40; EX 9.50.

Owner H R H Princess Haya Of Jordan **Bred** Keith Freeman **Trained** Newmarket, Suffolk

FOCUS

An ordinary maiden. The winning time was 0.34 seconds quicker than the later 56-70 handicap. They raced up the middle of the track.

2060 EUROPEAN BREEDERS' FUND FILLIES' H'CAP 6f

4:55 (4:57) (Class 4) (0-85,85) 3-Y-O **£5,829** (£1,734; £866; £432) **Stalls** Low

Form RPR

5-10 **1** **Goodbye Cash (IRE)**[17] 1604 3-8-12 **79** .... StephenDonohoe 9 80
(P D Evans) *lw: chsd ldrs: rdn over 1f out: led ins fnl f: hung lft: styd on u.p* **7/2**[1]

26-1 **2** *hd* **Ken's Girl**[33] 1207 3-8-8 **75** .... TQuinn 10 76
(W S Kittow) *led to 1/2-way: rdn and ev ch whn edgd rt ins fnl f: r.o* **4/1**[2]

10- **3** *1/2* **Pinkabout (IRE)**[302] 3925 3-9-4 **85** .... JimmyFortune 6 84
(J H M Gosden) *lw: trckd ldrs: rdn and ev ch ins fnl f: styd on* **4/1**[2]

01-0 **4** *3/4* **Miss Ippolita**[17] 1610 3-8-11 **78** .... KerrinMcEvoy 3 75
(J R Jenkins) *hld up: rdn over 2f out: outpcd over 1f out: r.o ins fnl f* **14/1**

2034 **5** *1 3/4* **Penny Post (IRE)**[13] 1710 3-9-2 **83** .... JoeFanning 11 78+
(M Johnston) *w ldr tl led 1/2-way: rdn over 1f out: hdd whn hmpd ins fnl f: no ex* **4/1**[2]

55-0 **6** *hd* **Bridge It Jo**[26] 1372 3-9-1 **85** .... JerryO'Dwyer(3) 2 75
(Miss J Feilden) *hld up: swtchd rt and hdwy over 1f out: sn rdn: no ex* **9/1**[3]

51-0 **7** *1/2* **Sacre Coeur**[15] 1670 3-9-1 **82** .... EddieAhern 7 71+
(J L Dunlop) *hld up in tch: nt clr run over 1f out: no ex fnl f* **4/1**[2]

1m 15.78s (2.68) **Going Correction** +0.40s/f (Good) **7** Ran SP% **118.9**

Speed ratings (Par 98):98,97,97,96,93 93,92

CSF £18.81 CT £58.98 TOTE £4.80: £2.00, £2.50; EX 23.80.

Owner D Healy **Bred** Mrs A C Peters **Trained** Pandy, Monmouths

■ Stewards' Enquiry : Stephen Donohoe one-day ban: careless riding (Jun 7)

FOCUS

A competitive fillies' handicap, but the pace was by no means frantic for a sprint and they finished in a bunch. The winning time was 2.52 seconds slower than the earlier 86-100. They tended to race up the middle of the track.

2061 COUNTRYSIDE RACEDAY H'CAP 7f

5:30 (5:33) (Class 5) (0-70,70) 3-Y-O **£3,886** (£1,156; £577; £288) **Stalls** Low

Form RPR

00-3 **1** **Oscarshall (IRE)**[16] 1634 3-8-8 **63** .... SaleemGolam(3) 15 75+
(M H Tompkins) *hmpd s: hld up: hdwy over 2f out: led 1f out: styd on wl* **10/1**

01-0 **2** *2 1/2* **Summer Dancer (IRE)**[9] 1815 3-8-13 **68** .... MarcHalford(3) 18 73
(D R C Elsworth) *lw: chsd ldrs: led 1/2-way: rdn and hdd 1f out: styd on same pce* **7/2**[1]

5325 **3** *2* **Kelamon**[35] 1176 3-8-12 **64** .... RobertHavlin 9 64
(M D I Usher) *b. chsd ldrs: rdn over 1f out: styd on same pce* **25/1**

0-54 **4** *hd* **Baby Dordan (IRE)**[20] 1534 3-8-10 **62** .... SebSanders 7 61
(H J L Dunlop) *chsd ldrs: rdn over 1f out: styd on same pce* **9/1**

6-15 **5** *hd* **Tifernati**[15] 1684 3-9-4 **70** .... KerrinMcEvoy 3 69+
(W J Haggas) *hld up: swtchd rt and hdwy over 1f out: nvr trbld ldrs* **7/1**[3]

-503 **6** *1* **Bold Saxon (IRE)**[31] 1261 3-8-8 **65** .... PatrickHills(5) 1 61
(M D I Usher) *hld up: hdwy over 2f out: no ex fnl f* **20/1**

-043 **7** *2* **Early Promise (IRE)**[6] 1903 3-8-5 **62** .... LukeMorris(5) 16 53
(P L Gilligan) *chsd ldrs: lost pl over 4f out: n.d after* **20/1**

30-5 **8** *1* **Bluebelle Dancer (IRE)**[9] 1815 3-9-2 **68** .... RichardMullen 2 56
(W R Muir) *hld up: swtchd lft and hdwy over 1f out: sn rdn: eased whn btn ins fnl f* **22/1**

04-3 **9** *1/2* **The Jay Factor (IRE)**[19] 1561 3-8-11 **63** .... ChrisCatlin 12 50
(Pat Eddery) *lw: prom: rdn over 2f out: wkng whn nt clr run over 1f out* **17/2**

The Form Book, Raceform Ltd, Compton, RG20 6NL

30-3 **10** *1* **Rumbled**[27] 1345 3-9-4 **70** ..... RichardThomas 14 54
(J A Geake) *wnt rt s: sn chsng ldrs: rdn over 2f out: wknd over 1f out* **25/1**

4-04 **11** *1 1/2* **Event Music (IRE)**[15] 1684 3-9-1 **67** ..... JHBowman 4 48
(M R Channon) *hld up: rdn over 2f out: n.d* **12/1**

0-24 **12** *2 1/2* **Tracer**[26] 1383 3-9-4 **70** ..... PatDobbs 11 44
(R Hannon) *lw: led to 1/2-way: wknd 2f out* **16/1**

01-0 **13** *2 1/2* **Ravinia (USA)**[8] 1837 3-9-0 **66** ..... BrettDoyle 17 34
(B J Meehan) *prom: rdn 1/2-way: wknd 2f out* **6/1**[2]

4340 **14** *1 1/4* **Realy Naughty (IRE)**[16] 1634 3-8-12 **64** ..... TQuinn 8 28
(B G Powell) *mid-div: rdn and wknd over 2f out* **16/1**

4155 **15** *2 1/2* **Slipasearcher (IRE)**[11] 1766 3-8-10 **62** ..... (b) StephenDonohoe 13 20
(P D Evans) *mid-div: rdn and wknd 2f out* **20/1**

0-43 **16** *3* **Red Current**[29] 1297 3-8-12 **64** ..... JimmyFortune 5 14
(J R Fanshawe) *prom over 4f* **10/1**

1m 29.48s (2.98) **Going Correction** +0.40s/f (Good) **16** Ran SP% **133.5**
Speed ratings (Par 99):98,95,92,92,92 91,88,87,87,86 84,81,78,77,74 70
CSF £44.16 CT £935.20 TOTE £13.70: £4.20, £2.10, £5.90, £3.10; EX 70.60 Place 6 £21.62, Place 5 £10.95.
Owner Roalco Limited **Bred** Shadwell Estate Company Limited **Trained** Newmarket, Suffolk

FOCUS
A modest but competitive handicap and the form looks sound for the level. The winning time was 0.34 seconds slower than the earlier maiden. They raced up the middle of the track.
Event Music(IRE) Official explanation: jockey said filly was unsuited by the soft ground
Ravinia(USA) Official explanation: vet said filly was in season
Realy Naughty(IRE) Official explanation: jockey said colt was unsuited by the soft ground
Slipasearcher(IRE) Official explanation: jockey said filly was unsuited by the soft ground
Red Current Official explanation: jockey said filly was unsuited by the soft ground
T/Jkpt: £7,100.00 to a £1 stake. Pool: £10,000.00. 0.50 winning tickets. T/Plt: £28.60 to a £1 stake. Pool: £80,401.35. 2,046.25 winning tickets. T/Qpdt: £15.50 to a £1 stake. Pool: £3,084.70. 147.00 winning tickets. CR

2048 CURRAGH (R-H)
Sunday, May 27

OFFICIAL GOING: Straight course - good; round course - good to firm

2064a TATTERSALLS GOLD CUP (GROUP 1) 1m 2f 110y
3:00 (3:02) 4-Y-0+ **£125,675** (£38,513; £18,243; £6,081; £2,027)

RPR

1 **Notnowcato**[30] 1274 5-9-0 ..... JMurtagh 9 127
(Sir Michael Stoute) *broke wl: settled 2nd: chal st: led over 2f out: sn rdn and strly pressed: kpt on wl u.p fr over 1f out: all out* **7/1**[2]

2 *hd* **Dylan Thomas (IRE)**[28] 1340 4-9-0 126 ..... JAHeffernan 3 127
(A P O'Brien, Ire) *settled 3rd: 4th 1/2-way: impr into cl 2nd and chal 2f out: ev ch fr over 1f out: kpt on wl u.p: jst failed* **1/2**[1]

3 *4* **Youmzain (IRE)**[57] 861 4-9-0 ..... RichardHughes 8 119
(M R Channon) *trckd ldrs in 5th: impr into 3rd after 1/2-way: 4th early st: mod 3rd and kpt on fr over 1f out* **7/1**[2]

4 *1 1/4* **Danak (IRE)**[14] 1696 4-9-0 113 ..... MJKinane 7 117
(John M Oxx, Ire) *hld up in tch: 5th into st: 4th under 2f out: rdn and no imp* **10/1**[3]

5 *3/4* **Fracas (IRE)**[20] 1550 5-9-0 109 ..... WMLordan 2 115
(David Wachman, Ire) *sn led: rdn and hdd over 2f out: 5th and no ex fr over 1f out* **20/1**

6 *2* **Mustameet (USA)**[20] 1550 6-9-0 117 ..... DPMcDonogh 6 111
(Kevin Prendergast, Ire) *hld up towards rr: 7th and prog ent st: 6th and no imp fr 2f out* **16/1**

7 *3* **Arch Rebel (USA)**[209] 6267 6-9-0 111 ..... FMBerry 5 105
(Noel Meade, Ire) *hld up in rr: kpt on same pce st* **66/1**

8 *hd* **Nightime (IRE)**[338] 2802 4-8-11 114 ..... PJSmullen 1 102
(D K Weld, Ire) *trckd ldrs on outer: 6th 4f out: no ex appr st* **25/1**

9 *5 1/2* **Heliostatic (IRE)**[35] 1184 4-9-0 112 ..... KJManning 4 94
(J S Bolger, Ire) *hld up towards rr: no imp st: wknd fr 2f out* **40/1**

2m 16.2s (0.50) **Going Correction** +0.20s/f (Good) **9** Ran SP% **119.2**
Speed ratings: 106,105,102,102,101 100,97,97,93
CSF £10.99 TOTE £8.30: £1.80, £1.10, £1.30; DF 21.30.
Owner Anthony & David de Rothschild **Bred** Southcourt Stud **Trained** Newmarket, Suffolk
■ Stewards' Enquiry : J Murtagh caution: used whip with excessive frequency

FOCUS
A top-class renewal with the first two clear.

NOTEBOOK
Notnowcato, all the better for last month's seasonal debut at Sandown, caused a minor upset in gaining his second Group 1 success, although he did beat the runner-up when taking the Juddmonte International last August. He took up a prominent position early on and raised the tempo from over 2f out as the pace-setter began to falter. He kept finding just enough to hold off the odds-on favourite and this consolidates his status as a fully-fledged Group 1 performer. The Prince Of Wales's Stakes at Royal Ascot and the Eclipse are the short term targets. (op 7/1 tchd 15/2)
Dylan Thomas(IRE) came here with a lot in his favour in his bid to reverse last August's York form with the winner following a convincing win in the Prix Ganay. He covered the winner's move 2f out but failed to find another gear to get past him and, although the overnight rain may have had some effect on his chance, the first two were clear and to say he was below par is to denigrate the winner. (op 1/2 tchd 4/7)
Youmzain(IRE), who might have been expected to benefit a little more from the rain, struggled to make any inroads in the final quarter-mile and probably needs a return to further. (op 11/2)
Danak(IRE) lost an unbeaten record that had comprised five wins, but there was no lack of merit as he was reported to have picked up a muscle injury in running. Connections are left no wiser as to whether he gets this trip, which he was attempting for the first time. On balance, it would seem to make sense to let him have another shot at the distance when he recovers fitness.
Fracas(IRE) has shown smart form this season, chasing home both Dylan Thomas and Septimus in previous races. He made the running here, and showed enough dash to suggest he should be able to pick up a race when his sights are lowered. (op 25/1)

2065a BOYLESPORTS IRISH 1,000 GUINEAS (GROUP 1) (FILLIES) 1m
3:35 (3:35) 3-Y-0
£151,689 (£51,689; £24,662; £8,445; £5,743; £3,040)

RPR

1 **Finsceal Beo (IRE)**[14] 1702 3-9-0 120 ..... KJManning 8 112
(J S Bolger, Ire) *trckd ldrs in 6th: hdwy over 2f out: rdn to ld over 1f out: strly pressed wl ins fnl f: kpt on wl u.p* **9/10**[1]

2 *nk* **Dimenticata (IRE)**[21] 1511 3-9-0 100 ..... CDHayes 11 111
(Kevin Prendergast, Ire) *trckd ldrs on far rail: 6th and switched lft 2f out: hdwy 1 1/2f out: 2nd and styd on strly ins fnl f: jst failed* **66/1**

3 *2* **Peeping Fawn (USA)**[11] 1780 3-9-0 94 ..... JAHeffernan 5 106
(A P O'Brien, Ire) *led: rdn 3f out: strly pressed 2f out: hdd over 1f out: kpt on same pce u.p* **12/1**

4 *shd* **Alexander Tango (IRE)**[14] 1694 3-9-0 104 ..... WMLordan 7 106
(T Stack, Ire) *prom: 3rd 1/2-way: 4th and rdn 2f out: kpt on u.p ins fnl f* **10/1**

5 *2 1/2* **Truly Mine (IRE)**[48] 987 3-9-0 98 ..... PShanahan 6 100
(D K Weld, Ire) *sn 2nd: chal under 3f out: no ex fr 1 1/2f out* **20/1**

6 *1/2* **Treat**[21] 1496 3-9-0 ..... JMurtagh 9 99
(M R Channon) *2nd early: 4th and rdn 2 1/2f out: 6th 1 1/2f out: kpt on same pce* **9/1**[3]

7 *1 1/4* **Diamond Necklace (USA)**[11] 1777 3-9-0 100 ..... CO'Donoghue 3 96
(A P O'Brien, Ire) *hld up in rr: kpt on same pce fr over 2f out* **66/1**

8 *2 1/2* **Gaudeamus (USA)**[14] 1694 3-9-0 103 ..... DJMoran 1 90
(J S Bolger, Ire) *hld up: 8th 1/2-way: no imp fr over 2f out* **100/1**

9 *4 1/2* **Silk Dress (IRE)**[21] 1499 3-9-0 102 ..... DMGrant 10 80
(John Joseph Murphy, Ire) *hld up towards rr: no ex fr 2f out* **150/1**

10 *1/2* **Offbeat Fashion (IRE)**[20] 1548 3-9-0 ..... PJSmullen 4 79
(D K Weld, Ire) *hld up towards rr: 10th 1/2-way: 8th 2f out: sn no ex* **25/1**

11 *7* **Arch Swing (USA)**[21] 1496 3-9-0 114 ..... MJKinane 2 63
(John M Oxx, Ire) *trckd ldrs on outer: 7th 1/2-way: wknd over 2f out: sn eased* **10/3**[2]

1m 39.3s (-2.80) **Going Correction** 0.0s/f (Good) **11** Ran SP% **115.7**
Speed ratings: 114,113,111,111,109 108,107,104,100,99 92
CSF £110.01 TOTE £2.10: £1.10, £11.40, £3.90; DF 102.80.
Owner M A Ryan **Bred** Rathberry Stud **Trained** Coolcullen, Co Carlow

FOCUS
Finsceal Beo completed the English/Irish Guineas double, and although the she confirmed Newmarket form with Treat, the pair are rated as having run 10lb below Newmarket form and were separated by several whose previous form limits confidence.

NOTEBOOK
Finsceal Beo(IRE) completed the British/Irish Guineas double but only just got home. However, the effect of three runs at Classic level in such a short time should not be underestimated, even for a filly such as this, blessed with both talent and toughness. The temptation to head for Royal Ascot will be hard for connections to resist, but it would be asking a lot after what she has done during May, and perhaps a break will be in order prior to an autumn campaign. (op 1/1)
Dimenticata(IRE), whose only win from nine previous starts came in a maiden at Leopardstown last season, was the surprise of the race on her fourth outing of the year, reversing form with a few who had previously finished in front of her previously. Having been switched out, she was closing throughout the final furlong and only just failed to collect for her apprentice rider. (op 50/1)
Peeping Fawn(USA), a recent Naas maiden winner, faced a huge task but there was no shortage of market confidence and she made the running and maintained her effort in a manner that augurs well for her future over longer distances. Having been unraced at two, she is making progress with every run. (op 10/1)
Alexander Tango(IRE), a Group 3 winner over the trip at Leopardstown, justified her place in the line-up with an honest display. She was always in the first in the first four and ended up only just touched off for third. (op 10/1 tchd 11/1)
Truly Mine(IRE), a lightly raced maiden, ran well and looks a sure-fire future winner at a lower level. (op 16/1)
Treat failed to match her fourth in the British equivalent, but finished virtually the same distance behind the winner. (op 8/1)
Arch Swing(USA) was the major disappointment of the race, having chased home Finsceal Beo at Newmarket. She may have had an excuse as the suggestion was that she picked up a knock on leaving the stalls. Official explanation: vet said filly was found to be blowing hard post race (op 3/1 tchd 7/2)

2066a AIRLIE STUD GALLINULE STKS (GROUP 3) 1m 2f
4:10 (4:10) 3-Y-0 **£35,189** (£10,324; £4,918; £1,675)

RPR

1 **Alexander Of Hales (USA)**[11] 1778 3-9-1 90 ..... JAHeffernan 5 109+
(A P O'Brien, Ire) *trckd ldrs in 3rd: 4th into st: 3rd whn nt clr run over 1f out: eadged lft to chal 1f out: sn led: styd on wl* **7/1**

2 *1/2* **Spanish Harlem (IRE)**[20] 1547 3-9-1 96 ..... CO'Donoghue 7 107
(A P O'Brien, Ire) *led: rdn over 2f out: hdd under 1f out: kpt on u.p* **10/1**

3 *1 3/4* **Eyshal (IRE)**[20] 1547 3-9-1 104 ..... MJKinane 8 104
(John M Oxx, Ire) *hld up in tch: cl 7th ent st: 4th 2f out: chal over 1f out: kpt on* **7/2**[1]

4 *1/2* **Big Robert**[38] 1103 3-9-1 ..... JMurtagh 3 103+
(W R Muir) *chsd ldrs in 5th: rdn 2f out: kpt on ins fnl f* **7/2**[1]

5 *nk* **Yeaman's Hall**[30] 1276 3-9-1 ..... MartinDwyer 2 102
(A M Balding) *settled 2nd: rdn to chal 2f out: sltly hmpd 1f out: no ex* **4/1**[2]

6 *2* **Dal Cais (IRE)**[7] 1868 3-9-1 96 ..... RPCleary 4 98
(Francis Ennis, Ire) *hld up towards rr: last into st: rdn and kpt on same pce fr 2f out* **20/1**

7 *3 1/2* **Capital Exposure (USA)**[231] 5851 3-9-1 ..... (b[1]) PJSmullen 6 91
(D K Weld, Ire) *hld up towards rr: 6th into st: no imp fr over 2f out: eased ins fnl f* **13/2**[3]

8 *1/2* **Ezima (IRE)**[21] 1512 3-8-12 93 ..... KJManning 1 87
(J S Bolger, Ire) *trckd ldrs on outer: 4th 1/2-way: 3rd appr st: sn rdn and no imp: eased ins fnl f* **10/1**

2m 9.60s (0.30) **Going Correction** +0.20s/f (Good) **8** Ran SP% **113.2**
Speed ratings: 106,105,104,103,103 101,99,98
CSF £71.70 TOTE £8.30: £2.10, £3.40, £1.30; DF 54.30.
Owner Mrs John Magnier **Bred** Barnett Enterprises **Trained** Ballydoyle, Co Tipperary

FOCUS
This was not the strongest of renewals of this Group 3 and is best rated around the third, fourth and sixth to recent form.

NOTEBOOK
Alexander Of Hales(USA), who showed a useful level form in reaching the frame in two maidens last year, had returned to action with victory in a 1m 2f maiden at Naas 11 days ago. This represented a much tougher assignment, but he rose to the challenge in fine style and could be in line for a quick reappearance in Sunday's French Derby. The French Derby will represent a major rise in class for the winner but he is a smart colt going the right way. He also looked here as though he could be worth trying over further. (op 11/2)
Spanish Harlem(IRE) could make no impression on his reappearance in the Tetrarch Stakes but shaped with much more promise and this was more like the form he showed to defeat Archipenko in a 7f maiden last October. (op 14/1)
Eyshal(IRE) was stepping up in trip following his third in the Tetrarch Stakes and seemed to see out this trip to post another sound effort. He looks capable of winning a Listed race. (op 4/1)
Big Robert ran respectably without ever being able to land a telling blow. He was stepping up in trip following his sixth in the Craven Stakes, where he did not enjoy a clear run and ran below his mark this time. (op 7/2 tchd 4/1)
Yeaman's Hall raced in second and held every chance from early in the straight but could do no more heading towards the final furlong. He looked a smart prospect when defeating Sunshine Kid in a Sandown conditions event last month and it is possible he is capable of better. (op 7/2 tchd 4/1)

2067a BOYLESPORTS 115 NATIONWIDE H'CAP (PREMIER) 1m 4f
4:40 (4:44) 3-Y-O+ £32,989 (£9,679; £4,611; £1,570)

RPR

1 **King Rama (USA)**[16] [1645] 6-8-11 88 MJKinane 9 94+
(John E Kiely, Ire) *mid-div on outer: 6th and hdwy appr st: 2nd under 2f out: led under 1f out: jnd cl home: regained ld on line* 6/1[1]

2 *shd* **Kempes (IRE)**[337] [2886] 4-9-9 100 NGMcCullagh 13 106+
(Ms F M Crowley, Ire) *prom: 4th and drvn along after 1/2-way: hdwy on inner under 2f out: chal ins fnl f: disp ld cl home: hdd on line* 9/1[3]

3 *hd* **Princess Nala (IRE)**[56] [875] 5-9-1 92 JMurtagh 1 98
(M Halford, Ire) *towards rr: hdwy on outer ent st: 6th and rdn 2f out: 3rd and chal ins fnl f: ev ch: jst failed* 14/1

4 *1* **Cool Touch (IRE)**[28] [1330] 4-9-9 105 OCasey(5) 6 109
(Peter Casey, Ire) *towards rr: hdwy early st: 6th 1 1/2f out: styd on ins fnl f* 12/1

5 *nk* **Galistic (IRE)**[14] [1692] 4-9-3 94 DMGrant 3 98
(Patrick J Flynn, Ire) *sn 3rd: led appr st: rdn clr over 2f out: hdd under 1f out: no ex* 10/1

6 *2 1/2* **Dolphin Bay (IRE)**[14] [1188] 7-8-4 77 RPCleary 7 81
(J G Burns, Ire) *hld up: prog early st: 8th under 1 1/2f out: styd on* 9/1[3]

7 *1 3/4* **Kapera (FR)**[35] [1187] 4-8-11 88 FMBerry 10 85
(Noel Lawlor, Ire) *hld up in rr: hdwy ent st: 7th 1 1/2f out: kpt on same pce* 11/1

8 *1* **Varsity**[14] [1692] 4-8-7 84 CO'Donoghue 12 80
(C F Swan, Ire) *trckd ldrs: 5th 1/2-way: prog into 2nd ent st: sn rdn and no imp: wknd fr over 1f out* 20/1

9 *3* **Fantoche (BRZ)**[24] [1438] 5-8-8 85 (t) DPMcDonogh 14 76
(M J Wallace) *settled 6th: dropped to mid-div after 1/2-way: no imp st* 10/1

10 *shd* **Rhythm 'N' Blues (IRE)**[14] [1692] 4-8-1 79 CDHayes(3) 8 72
(John M Oxx, Ire) *trckd ldrs: 6th 1/2-way: impr into 2nd 3f out: 3rd into st: sn no ex* 10/1

11 *1 1/2* **Salute Him (IRE)**[69] [5530] 4-9-3 94 RichardHughes 4 82
(A J Martin, Ire) *towards rr: no imp st* 12/1

12 *1/2* **Callow Lake (IRE)**[14] [4122] 7-8-4 81 (b) WMLordan 11 68
(Mrs John Harrington, Ire) *in rr of mid-div thrght* 12/1

13 *2 1/2* **Midnight Traveller**[17] [1615] 4-8-4 77 WSupple 5 64
(Thomas Cooper, Ire) *disp ld: rdn and hdd appr st: sn no ex* 20/1

14 *5* **Flare Star**[18] [1582] 4-8-3 85 DJMoran(5) 17 60
(T Hogan, Ire) *in rr of mid-div: pushed along 1/2-way: no ex st* 33/1

15 *10* **Moon Mix (FR)**[42] [1053] 4-9-2 93 PJSmullen 16 52
(D K Weld, Ire) *mid-div: rdn appr st: no ex fr over 2f out: eased* 8/1[2]

16 *5 1/2* **Marbeuf (USA)**[14] 6-8-13 90 (b) KJManning 15 41
(Noel Meade, Ire) *in rr of mid-div: wknd st* 25/1

17 *2 1/2* **Galilean (IRE)**[273] [4852] 4-8-11 88 (t) JAHeffernan 2 35
(Eoin Griffin, Ire) *disp ld: rdn and hdd 3f out: sn wknd* 16/1

2m 36.6s (-2.30) **Going Correction** +0.20s/f (Good) 17 Ran SP% 132.9
Speed ratings: 115,114,114,114,113 112,111,110,108,108 107,107,105,102,95 91,90
CSF £59.76 CT £762.98 TOTE £3.70: £1.20, £2.80, £3.60, £3.00; DF 48.50.
Owner Brainwave Syndicate **Bred** Ingalls Farm **Trained** Dungarvan, Co Waterford

NOTEBOOK
Fantoche(BRZ), who broke the track record when beating subsequent winner Right To Play at Wolverhampton, failed to make much impression on ground he has handled in the past. He may be worth another chance back on a left-handed track. (op 10/1)

2068 - 2069a (Foreign Racing) - See Raceform Interactive

1518
SAN SIRO (R-H)
Sunday, May 27

OFFICIAL GOING: Soft

2070a PREMIO MARIA INCISA (GROUP 3) (FILLIES) 1m 2f
4:00 (4:18) 3-Y-O £27,365 (£12,041; £6,568; £3,284)

RPR

1 **Shot Bless (IRE)**[26] 3-8-11 MEsposito 1 102
(M Guarnieri, Italy) *5th st: hdwy in middle fr 2f out: drvn to ld wl ins fnl f: r.o* 28/10[2]

2 *hd* **Moi Non Plus** 3-8-11 SMulas 3 101
(B Grizzetti, Italy) *hld up: 10th st: c to outside: str run fr over 1f out: ev ch ins fnl f: r.o* 74/10

3 *3/4* **Turfrose (GER)**[14] [1701] 3-8-11 SLandi 11 100
(P Giannotti, Italy) *led to wl ins fnl f: kpt on one pce* 19/10[1]

4 *3* **Vinea Federspiel (IRE)** 3-8-11 MTellini 4 95
(Werner Glanz, Germany) *hld up towards rr: hdwy over 2f out: kpt on one pce to take 4th last strides* 19/2

5 *shd* **La Spezia (IRE)**[21] [1499] 3-8-11 HayleyTurner 7 94
(M L W Bell) *a.p: wnt 2nd after 2f: rdn wl over 1f out: one pce* 41/10[3]

6 *2 1/2* **Miss Sultin (IRE)**[28] 3-8-11 GArena 10 90
(B Grizzetti, Italy) *6th st: one pce fnl 2f* 84/1

7 *3 1/2* **Sopran Slam (IRE)**[14] [1701] 3-8-11 PSirigu 8 84
(B Grizzetti, Italy) *hld up: last st: nvr a factor* 64/1

8 *1/2* **Red And Black (IRE)**[28] 3-8-11 DPorcu 2 83
(G Angellotti, Italy) *in rr to st: hdwy on far side to dispute 3rd 2f out: btn whn carried rt appr fnl f* 26/1

9 *nk* **Passionate Girl (IRE)**[35] 3-8-11 EBotti 5 82
(A & G Botti, Italy) *prom to 1/2-way: btn 2f out* 17/4

10 *4* **Gambara (IRE)**[26] 3-8-11 DVargiu 9 75
(B Grizzetti, Italy) *3rd st: rdn over 2f out: eased whn btn fnl f* 128/10

11 *4* **Discover Roma (IRE)**[26] 3-8-11 PConvertino 6 68
(F Magliari, Italy) *4th st: wknd 3f out* 22/1

2m 7.70s (1.00) 11 Ran SP% 138.9
(including one euro stakes): WIN 3.80; PL 1.51, 1.88, 1.36; DF 14.67.
Owner Scuderia Blu Fir **Bred** Patrick Doyle **Trained** Italy

NOTEBOOK
La Spezia(IRE), third in the Pretty Polly Stakes on her most recent start, probably ran to a similar level of form on this step up in grade. She is entered in the Ribblesdale Stakes but the step up in trip is not sure to suit.

CARLISLE (R-H)
Monday, May 28

OFFICIAL GOING: Good to firm (meeting abandoned after race 2 (2.50) due to unsafe ground) (10.6)
Wind: Fresh, half behind Weather: Overcast

2071 EUROPEAN BREEDERS' FUND MAIDEN STKS 5f
2:15 (2:17) (Class 5) 2-Y-O £3,465 (£1,030; £515; £257) Stalls High

Form RPR

2 1 **Art Advisor (IRE)**[12] [1772] 2-9-3 0 SebSanders 4 85+
(J Howard Johnson) *mde all: rdn 2f out: drew clr fnl f* 4/11[1]

05 2 *4* **Grudge**[14] [1706] 2-9-3 0 TonyHamilton 7 71
(D W Barker) *pressed wnr: drvn over 2f out: edgd lft and kpt on u.p fnl f* 80/1

3 *nk* **Cute Ass (IRE)** 2-8-12 0 PatCosgrave 2 65
(K R Burke) *prom: effrt over 1f out: kpt on same pce fnl f* 11/2[2]

6 4 *1/2* **Dalarossie**[39] [1107] 2-9-3 0 DaleGibson 6 68
(E J Alston) *in tch: drvn 1/2-way: kpt on fnl f: nrst fin* 25/1

5 *4* **Chatham Islands (USA)** 2-8-12 0 KDarley 3 48
(M Johnston) *cl up tl rdn and wknd over 1f out* 7/1[3]

6 *1 3/4* **Mr Lu** 2-9-3 0 TPO'Shea 8 47+
(G A Swinbank) *s.i.s: hung lft thrght: sn outpcd: nvr rchd ldrs* 12/1

3 7 *9* **Seein'Red (IRE)**[16] [1674] 2-9-3 0 LeeEnstone 1 15
(P T Midgley) *wnt bdly lft s: a wl bhd* 50/1

60.18 secs (-1.32) **Going Correction** -0.325s/f (Firm) 7 Ran SP% 115.9
Speed ratings (Par 93):97,90,90,89,82 80,65
CSF £58.07 TOTE £1.30: £1.10, £20.90; EX 31.90.
Owner Matthew Green and J H Johnson **Bred** Drumhass Stud **Trained** Billy Row, Co Durham

FOCUS
There didn't appear to be much strength in depth in this juvenile maiden. Comfortable winner Art Advisor was 9lb below his York form.

NOTEBOOK
Art Advisor(IRE), a fine second in much better grade at York, stood out in the paddock and needed only to run up to his debut form to take this. Making all, he drew away in the last furlong to score decisively. He'll probably head to Royal Ascot now but would not want the ground to be too firm. (op 4-9)

Grudge had run to RPRs of 42 and 56 on his two previous starts, and though he improved again on that, he puts the form into perspective.

Cute Ass(IRE), a half-sister to the very useful sprinter Peruvian Chief, amongst others, was a bit edgy in the paddock but came out best of the newcomers. (op 5-1 tchd 6-1 in places)

Dalarossie improved on his debut run to be fourth, without being able to get into the action. He slipped and came down when pulling up on the bend after the winning line. (op 33-1)

Chatham Islands(USA), a sprint-bred debutante, chased up the leaders but faded in the final furlong. She ought to improve with this experience under her belt. (tchd 15-2)

Seein'Red(IRE) Official explanation: jockey said gelding never travelled

2072 DOBIES CHEVROLET H'CAP 5f 193y
2:50 (3:16) (Class 5) (0-70,70) 4-Y-O+ £2,817 (£838; £418; £209) Stalls High

Form RPR

2-00 1 **Walnut Grove**[16] [1675] 4-8-4 **56** oh2 DaleGibson 4 65
(T D Barron) *mde all: rdn 2f out: styd on strly fnl f* 14/1

4330 2 *1 1/4* **Cross Of Lorraine (IRE)**[18] [1597] 4-9-1 **67** (b) TomEaves 17 72
(I Semple) *chsd wnr: effrt 2f out: kpt on fnl f* 11/1

-000 3 *3/4* **Stellite**[13] [1747] 7-8-11 **70** GaryBartley(7) 15 73
(J S Goldie) *cl up: effrt 2f out: edgd rt and kpt on u.p fnl f* 8/1

1440 4 *1* **Brigadore**[6] [1914] 8-9-1 **67** SebSanders 10 66
(J G Given) *midfield: drvn 2f out: kpt on fnl f: no imp* 5/1[2]

062 5 *nk* **Welcome Approach**[6] [1914] 4-8-8 **63** AndrewMullen(3) 11 61
(J R Weymes) *in tch: drvn over 2f out: kpt on same pce fnl f* 7/1

4-06 6 *1 1/2* **Petite Mac**[13] [1748] 7-8-1 **60** SuzzanneFrance(7) 14 54
(N Bycroft) *midfield: lost pl after 2f: effrt on outside 2f out: hung rt: kpt on fnl f: no imp* 12/1

0311 7 *1/2* **Violent Velocity (IRE)**[24] [1459] 4-8-9 **68** NeilBrown(7) 8 60
(J J Quinn) *t.k.h: hld up: effrt over 2f out: kpt on fnl f: n.d* 5/2[1]

4341 8 *2 1/2* **Dorn Dancer (IRE)**[5] [1940] 5-8-11 **63** 6ex PatCosgrave 7 47
(D W Barker) *midfield: drvn over 2f out: no imp over 1f out* 6/1[3]

000- 9 *3* **Orphan (IRE)**[222] [6048] 5-9-2 **68** KDarley 12 42
(E J Alston) *plld hrd: hld up: drvn over 2f out: n.d* 11/1

-000 10 *10* **Choreography**[20] [1555] 4-9-3 **69** AdrianTNicholls 3 11
(D Nicholls) *chsd ldrs tl wknd over 1f out: eased whn no ch fnl f* 28/1

00-0 11 *2 1/2* **Playtotheaudience**[35] [1198] 4-8-13 **65** (b[1]) TonyHamilton 5 —
(R A Fahey) *s.i.s: drvn 1/2-way: nvr on terms* 20/1

-050 12 *1 1/4* **Charles Parnell (IRE)**[16] [1678] 4-8-10 **65** (v) DuranFentiman(3) 2 —
(M Dods) *t.k.h: hld up on outside: rdn over 2f out: btn over 1f out* 20/1

1m 11.78s (-1.83) **Going Correction** -0.325s/f (Firm) 12 Ran SP% 127.1
Speed ratings (Par 103):99,97,96,95,94 92,91,88,84,71 67,66
CSF £166.07 CT £1368.41 TOTE £19.10: £3.90, £3.30, £3.10; EX 210.20 Place 6 £8.31, Place 5 £6.16.
Owner Mrs M West **Bred** Mrs M West **Trained** Maunby, N Yorks

FOCUS
After a horse had slipped up after the line in the opener, two of the bends were sanded prior to this race, leading to a delay. The order hardly changed throughout and nothing got into it from off the pace. Ordinary form.

Choreography Official explanation: jockey said gelding had no more to give

2073 CARLISLE BELL TRIAL H'CAP 7f 200y
() (Class 4) (0-80,) 4-Y-O+ £

2074 LLOYD LIMITED NEW HOLLAND CONSTRUCTION H'CAP 1m 1f 61y
() (Class 6) (0-65,) 4-Y-O+ £

2075 CUMBERLAND PLATE TRIAL H'CAP 1m 3f 107y
() (Class 4) (0-80,) 4-Y-O+ £

2076 FELIX THE FAST TRACTOR H'CAP 5f
() (Class 6) (0-60,) 4-Y-O+ £

T/Jkpt: £373.60 to a £1 stake. Pool: £10,000.00. 19.00 winning tickets. T/Plt: £6.10 to a £1 stake. Pool: £61,082.95. 7,273.00 winning tickets. RY

The Form Book, Raceform Ltd, Compton, RG20 6NL

1559 CHEPSTOW (L-H)

Monday, May 28

OFFICIAL GOING: Good to soft (5.9)

The ground had softened considerably after a lot of rain the previous day and the best ground seemed to be in the centre on the straight course.

Wind: Moderate behind Weather: Fine

2077 UNISON CONVENOR MAIDEN STKS — 1m 14y

2:20 (2:21) (Class 5) 3-Y-0+ **£2,849** (£847; £423; £211) **Stalls** High

Form / RPR

34- **1** **Atraas (IRE)**[230] 5892 3-9-1 0 MartinDwyer 3 — 79+
(M P Tregoning) *a.p: led over 2f out: rdn over 1f out: jinked rt to paddock exit ins fnl f: r.o wl* **1/1**[1]

0652 **2** 2 1/2 **First Princess (IRE)**[14] 1731 3-8-10 62 (p) RichardHughes 2 — 64
(J S Moore) *hld up and bhd: hdwy over 4f out: chsd wnr over 1f out: no imp* **9/2**[2]

0- **3** 4 **Halkerston**[230] 5891 3-9-1 0 GeorgeBaker 1 — 60
(C G Cox) *a.p: rdn over 3f out: one pce fnl 2f* **9/1**

0 **4** 1 1/4 **Arabiyah**[20] 1560 3-8-3 0 HeatherMcGee(7) 7 — 52+
(L M Cumani) *hld up and bhd: hdwy over 2f out: nvr nr to chal* **33/1**

05-0 **5** 2 **Three Counties (IRE)**[29] 1319 6-9-6 57 KylieManser(7) 4 — 55
(N I M Rossiter) *prom: led over 4f out tl over 2f out: sn hung lft: wknd fnl f* **50/1**

-40 **6** 6 **Spinal Tap (IRE)**[24] 1447 3-9-1 0 JohnEgan 10 — 39+
(C R Egerton) *hld up in mid-div: pushed along over 5f out: no hdwy fnl 3f* **10/1**

0-0 **7** nk **Kastan**[14] 1725 3-9-1 0 JamieMackay 8 — 38
(B Palling) *led: hdd over 4f out: rdn over 2f out: wknd over 1f out* **66/1**

00 **8** hd **Red Brick Road (IRE)**[9] 1838 3-9-1 0 EddieAhern 11 — 37
(A J Lidderdale) *nvr nr ldrs* **50/1**

06 **9** 3/4 **Officer Material (IRE)**[9] 1838 3-9-1 0 SamHitchcott 14 — 45+
(C G Cox) *prom tl rdn and wknd over 3f out* **16/1**

00- **10** 1 1/2 **Thornbill**[201] 6406 4-9-13 0 FergusSweeney 5 — 35
(H Candy) *t.k.h towards rr: rdn and short-lived effrt over 3f out* **33/1**

6066 **11** 1 1/4 **Fly By Jove (IRE)**[20] 1559 4-9-10 46 NeilChalmers(3) 16 — 32
(Jane Southcombe) *prom tl rdn and wknd over 3f out* **50/1**

-060 **12** 6 **Childish Thoughts**[128] 194 3-8-10 45 JamesDoyle 6 — 11
(Mrs Norma Pook) *t.k.h: prom: rdn over 3f out: sn wknd* **100/1**

0 **13** 20 **Terandeil**[35] 1197 3-8-3 0 MCGeran(7) 17 — —
(J G M O'Shea) *dwlt: hdwy over 5f out: hung lft over 4f out: rdn and wknd over 3f out: t.o* **66/1**

20 **14** 6 **Golden Platitude (IRE)**[18] 1606 4-9-13 0 TedDurcan 12 — —
(W R Swinburn) *dwlt: a bhd: t.o* **6/1**[3]

1m 37.64s (1.64) **Going Correction** +0.025s/f (Good)
WFA 3 from 4yo+ 12lb **14** Ran SP% **123.2**
Speed ratings (Par 103):92,89,85,84,82 76,75,75,75,73 72,66,46,40
CSF £5.32 TOTE £2.00: £1.20, £1.20, £3.00; EX 5.20 Trifecta £36.40 Pool: £176.17 - 3.43 winning tickets..
Owner Hamdan Al Maktoum **Bred** Shadwell Estate Co Ltd **Trained** Lambourn, Berks

■

FOCUS
Not much of a maiden, the fifth helping to hold down the form. The exposed runner-up looks the best guide. A moderate winning time, 1.82 seconds slower than the later handicap.
Arabiyah Official explanation: jockey said her orders were to jump filly out, sit nice and handy and ride filly to best of her ability, adding that filly became tired 4f out and then had run on in the closing stages

2078 UNISON ONE IN A MILLION (S) STKS — 6f 16y

2:55 (2:56) (Class 6) 2-Y-0 **£2,047** (£604; £302) **Stalls** High

Form / RPR

000 **1** **Ocean Transit (IRE)**[40] 1087 2-8-1 0 TolleyDean(5) 5 — 61+
(W G M Turner) *t.k.h: mde all: edgd lft fnl f: r.o wl* **15/8**[1]

2 1 1/2 **Giggling Monkey** 2-7-13 0 MCGeran(7) 2 — 54
(P D Evans) *sn w ldrs: rdn over 2f out: kpt on same pce fnl f* **10/1**

655 **3** 2 **Miss Antropist (IRE)**[14] 1728 2-8-3 0 LiamJones(3) 9 — 48
(R A Harris) *bhd: hdwy over 2f out: rdn and one pce fnl f* **9/1**

4 1 **Yes Meg** 2-8-6 0 EddieAhern 6 — 45
(P F I Cole) *hld up and bhd: hung lft over 3f out: swtchd rt wl over 2f out: rdn over 1f out: hdwy fnl f: nrst fin* **5/1**[3]

0 **5** 2 **Sailing By**[21] 1540 2-8-11 0 TedDurcan 7 — 44
(B R Millman) *prom: rdn over 2f out: wknd over 1f out* **9/2**[2]

036 **6** 1 1/4 **O'Casey (IRE)**[8] 1857 2-8-11 0 FergusSweeney 11 — 40
(J G M O'Shea) *prom tl wknd over 1f out* **12/1**

4 **7** 4 **Scrap N'Dust**[47] 1000 2-8-6 0 MatthewHenry 4 — 23
(W G M Turner) *w ldr tl wknd over 2f out* **25/1**

63 **8** 21 **Riskie Blue (IRE)**[47] 1000 2-8-6 0 (p) JohnEgan 8 — —
(J S Moore) *prom: rdn over 3f out: sn wknd: t.o* **10/1**

0 **9** 22 **Sonsue**[37] 1150 2-8-6 0 JamieMackay 10 — —
(B Palling) *rrd s: wnt bdly lft: a t.o* **10/1**

1m 14.11s (1.71) **Going Correction** +0.025s/f (Good) **9** Ran SP% **118.4**
Speed ratings (Par 91):89,87,84,83,80 78,73,45,16
CSF £23.02 TOTE £3.10: £1.60, £2.50, £2.80; EX 47.40 Trifecta £179.90 Part won. Pool: £253.47 - 0.44 winning tickets..The winner was bought in for 10,000 guineas. Giggling Monkey was subject to a friendly claim.
Owner Pride of the West Racing Club **Bred** Mike Channon Bloodstock Ltd **Trained** Sigwells, Somerset

FOCUS
A modest heat for the grade, but Ocean Transit ran out a ready winner and was value for further.

NOTEBOOK
Ocean Transit(IRE), who had shown more than enough in 5f maidens to suggest a race such as this was within her grasp, was upped a furlong in trip and saw it out well to run out a ready winner. Seemingly effective in the ground, she remains capable of further success at this level and may even be up to winning a small nursery later in the season. (op 7-4 tchd 9-4)
Giggling Monkey, a 5,000gns daughter of Fraam, certainly knew her job and was always up there, but could not go on with the winner. This was a promising enough debut and she did enough to suggest there is a race of this nature in her. (op 12-1)
Miss Antropist(IRE) is already exposed at this sort of level and she is likely to remain vulnerable to more progressive sorts. Official explanation: jockey said filly hung left-handed (op 12-1)
Yes Meg, related to a bunch of moderate performers, is clearly not up to much to be making her debut in this grade, but she came home in a fashion to suggest there is a race in her at this sort of level. (op 9-2 tchd 11-2)
Sailing By, never involved in a decent maiden on his debut at Windsor, was up in trip/down in grade, but he failed to run a race and proved most disappointing. (op 7-1 tchd 7-2)
Riskie Blue(IRE) Official explanation: jockey said filly moved poorly
Sonsue Official explanation: jockey said filly reared as the stalls opened

2079 UNISON PUBLIC SERVICES H'CAP — 1m 14y

3:30 (3:33) (Class 5) (0-70,70) 3-Y-0 **£3,044** (£905; £452; £226) **Stalls** High

Form / RPR

03-0 **1** **Princess Zada**[37] 1155 3-8-8 60 FergusSweeney 9 — 72
(B R Millman) *hld up in mid-div: hdwy over 4f out: led 3f out: clr whn edgd lft 1f out: r.o wl* **14/1**

02-0 **2** 3 1/2 **Venir Rouge**[14] 1722 3-9-3 69 GeorgeBaker 3 — 73
(M Salaman) *hld up in mid-div: hdwy over 4f out: rdn over 2f out: chsd wnr over 1f out: no imp* **11/1**

0012 **3** 2 1/2 **Private Peachey (IRE)**[21] 1538 3-8-7 59 TedDurcan 14 — 57+
(B R Millman) *prom: lost pl over 4f out: hdwy 3f out: sn rdn: one pce fnl f* **4/1**[2]

00-5 **4** 1 1/2 **Alloro**[29] 1316 3-8-4 56 oh1 JamesDoyle 10 — 51
(D J S Ffrench Davis) *chsd ldr: rdn over 3f out: lost 2nd over 1f out: no ex* **40/1**

4-03 **5** 1/2 **Bidable**[26] 1410 3-8-10 62 JamieMackay 8 — 56
(B Palling) *t.k.h in rr: swtchd lft over 5f out: rdn and hdwy 3f out: nvr able to chal* **11/1**

63-0 **6** hd **Penny From Heaven (IRE)**[35] 1203 3-9-3 69 RichardHughes 7 — 62+
(E A L Dunlop) *s.i.s: hld up and bhd: hdwy over 4f out: rdn over 3f out: wknd over 1f out* **13/2**[3]

-002 **7** nk **Goose Green (IRE)**[16] 1684 3-8-13 65 JohnEgan 12 — 58+
(R J Hodges) *chsd ldrs: rdn over 2f out: wknd over 1f out* **7/2**[1]

325- **8** 1 1/2 **Mo (USA)**[157] 6921 3-9-4 70 (t) EddieAhern 5 — 59
(R A Kvisla) *led: hdd 3f out: sn rdn: wknd over 1f out* **18/1**

400- **9** 1/2 **Everyman**[287] 4436 3-8-4 56 oh1 RichardThomas 1 — 44
(A W Carroll) *prom: rdn and lost pl over 4f out: n.d after* **33/1**

2130 **10** 6 **Mark Of Love (IRE)**[16] 1672 3-9-1 67 EdwardCreighton 4 — 41
(M R Channon) *t.k.h: sn chsng ldrs: rdn over 3f out: wknd over 2f out* **7/1**

2360 **11** 11 **L'Oiseau De Feu (USA)**[41] 1084 3-9-3 69 SamHitchcott 2 — 18
(Mrs K Waldron) *hld up towards rr: hdwy over 4f out: rdn over 3f out: wknd over 2f out* **25/1**

3-35 **12** 1 **Ravenna**[82] 635 3-8-11 63 (b[1]) MartinDwyer 11 — 10
(M P Tregoning) *s.i.s: rdn over 4f out: a bhd* **12/1**

00-6 **13** nk **Krikket**[24] 1452 3-8-11 66 LiamJones(3) 13 — 12
(W J Haggas) *rel to r and wnt rt s: a wl bhd* **11/1**

000- **14** 9 **Safari Sundowner (IRE)**[255] 5349 3-9-1 67 MatthewHenry 15 — —
(P Winkworth) *wl bhd fnl 4f* **28/1**

1m 35.82s (-0.18) **Going Correction** +0.025s/f (Good) **14** Ran SP% **125.4**
Speed ratings (Par 99):101,97,95,93,93 92,92,91,90,84 73,72,72,63
CSF £160.90 CT £765.19 TOTE £24.20: £5.50, £3.90, £2.30; EX 430.70 TRIFECTA Not won..
Owner Pimperne Syndicate **Bred** W V Poole And L And A Loake **Trained** Kentisbeare, Devon

FOCUS
A modest handicap, but the time compared favourably with that of the opening maiden. A personal best from the winner, with the second rated to his 2yo sand form and the third bringing solid form to the table.
Krikket Official explanation: jockey said filly missed the break and was reluctant to race

2080 UNISON CYMRU/WALES FILLIES' STKS (H'CAP) — 6f 16y

4:05 (4:05) (Class 5) (0-70,70) 3-Y-0 **£3,044** (£905; £452; £226) **Stalls** High

Form / RPR

6-23 **1** **Nobilissima (IRE)**[26] 1404 3-9-0 69 MarcHalford(3) 12 — 80
(J L Spearing) *chsd ldr: led over 3f out: edgd rt ins fnl f: comf* **11/2**[3]

0310 **2** 4 **Ensign's Trick**[12] 1766 3-8-9 64 LiamJones(3) 1 — 63
(W M Brisbourne) *a.p: chsd wnr wl over 1f out: sn rdn: no imp* **10/1**

4-31 **3** 1 1/2 **Twitch Hill**[25] 1430 3-9-0 66 FergusSweeney 7 — 60
(H Candy) *t.k.h in tch: rdn over 2f out: one pce fnl f* **7/4**[1]

22-0 **4** 3 **Izabela Hannah**[37] 1151 3-9-0 66 JamesDoyle 2 — 51
(R M Beckett) *hld up: rdn 3f out: edgd rt 2f out: no real prog* **10/3**[2]

660- **5** 1/2 **Montemayorprincess (IRE)**[210] 6257 3-8-8 60 TedDurcan 5 — 44
(D Haydn Jones) *led: hdd over 3f out: rdn over 2f out: wknd over 1f out* **14/1**

0-44 **6** 1 1/4 **Bonnet O'Bonnie**[27] 1386 3-8-4 56 oh1 EdwardCreighton 3 — 36
(J Mackie) *hld up in rr: rdn over 2f out: no rspnse* **11/1**

20-6 **7** 3/4 **Swiftly Addicted (IRE)**[20] 1561 3-8-8 60 EddieAhern 9 — 38
(A King) *hld up in tch: rdn over 2f out: wknd wl over 1f out* **8/1**

06-0 **8** 13 **Silver Flame**[37] 1151 3-8-4 56 oh1 RichardThomas 13 — —
(A W Carroll) *hld up: rdn 3f out: sn bhd* **25/1**

1m 12.54s (0.14) **Going Correction** +0.025s/f (Good) **8** Ran SP% **113.9**
Speed ratings (Par 96):100,94,92,88,88 86,85,68
CSF £57.55 CT £134.87 TOTE £5.20: £1.80, £1.80, £1.10; EX 30.10 Trifecta £51.40 Pool: £635.00 - 8.77 winning tickets..
Owner Nine Traders Syndicate **Bred** Sea Syndicate **Trained** Kinnersley, Worcs

FOCUS
Just a moderate sprint handicap. Improvement from the winner, but it is doubtful if either placed horse was at their best.

2081 UNISON RECRUITMENT MAIDEN STKS — 1m 4f 23y

4:40 (4:42) (Class 5) 3-Y-0 **£2,849** (£847; £423; £211) **Stalls** Low

Form / RPR

5-22 **1** **Brisk Breeze (GER)**[16] 1663 3-8-12 94 TedDurcan 8 — 64+
(H R A Cecil) *hld up: hdwy 4f out: led on bit over 1f out: v easily* **1/12**[1]

0500 **2** 7 **Whodunit (UAE)**[26] 1399 3-9-3 53 GeorgeBaker 6 — 47
(P W Hiatt) *led: clr over 5f out: rdn and hdd over 1f out: wknd ins fnl f* **50/1**

00- **3** shd **Apache Chant (USA)**[242] 5640 3-9-3 0 JamesDoyle 7 — 47
(A W Carroll) *hld up towards rr: rdn and hdwy over 3f out: edgd lft 2f out and ins fnl f: one pce* **66/1**

00 **4** hd **Best Of Gold (IRE)**[10] 1812 3-9-3 0 (b[1]) EddieAhern 2 — 47
(B J Meehan) *a.p: rdn over 2f out: one pce* **16/1**[3]

0 **5** 11 **Martinet (IRE)**[18] 1605 3-9-3 0 (t) JohnEgan 5 — 29
(P D Evans) *t.k.h in rr: rdn over 2f out: no rspnse* **14/1**[2]

00-0 **6** 2 1/2 **Acosta**[17] 1633 3-9-3 50 (e[1]) RichardThomas 1 — 25
(Dr J R J Naylor) *prom: rdn over 4f out: wknd 3f out* **66/1**

00-0 **7** 3/4 **Mazoran (FR)**[10] 1812 3-8-10 25 (p) MarkCoumbe(7) 4 — 24
(D G Bridgwater) *s.s: rdn 4f out: a bhd* **66/1**

00 8 3 ½ **Stafford Will (IRE)**[20] 1560 3-9-3 0 FergusSweeney 3 18
(J G M O'Shea) *hld up: rdn over 3f out: sn struggling* **16/1**[3]
2m 47.72s (9.00) **Going Correction** +0.45s/f (Yiel) **8** Ran SP% **117.2**
Speed ratings (Par 99):88,83,83,83,75 74,73,71
CSF £19.06 TOTE £1.10: £1.02, £3.30, £6.90; EX 6.20 Trifecta £40.40 Pool: £1,279.45 - 22.46 winning tickets..
Owner Ennismore Racing I **Bred** Dr R Wilhelms **Trained** Newmarket, Suffolk
■ Stewards' Enquiry : Eddie Ahern one-day ban: used whip with excessive frequency (Jun 8)
FOCUS
As uncompetitive as maidens come and 1/12 shot Brisk Breeze won as expected. The placed form looks poor. A very slow winning time, 4.12 seconds slower than the following fillies' handicap.

2082 EUROPEAN BREEDERS' FUND FILLIES' H'CAP 1m 4f 23y
5:15 (5:15) (Class 4) (0-80,80) 4-Y-0+ **£4,857** (£1,445; £722; £360) **Stalls** Low

Form RPR
00-4 1 **Vale De Lobo**[20] 1567 5-8-9 **71** TedDurcan 2 81
(B R Millman) *trckd ldr: led 4f out: rdn over 1f out: drvn out* **7/2**[3]
16-1 2 ¾ **Hanella (IRE)**[27] 1371 4-9-4 **80** GeorgeBaker 4 89
(R M Beckett) *hld up in rr: hdwy to chse wnr 3f out: rdn over 1f out: nt qckn ins fnl f* **5/2**[2]
5601 3 14 **Spring Dream (IRE)**[7] 1884 4-8-7 **69** 6ex SamHitchcott 3 55
(M R Channon) *t.k.h: hdwy 5f out: rdn and wnt 2nd briefly over 1f out: wknd over 2f out* **9/2**
6313 4 1 **Caucasienne (FR)**[7] 1884 4-8-10 **72** EddieAhern 1 57
(J W Hills) *led: hdd 4f out: sn wknd* **6/4**[1]
2m 43.6s (4.88) **Going Correction** +0.45s/f (Yiel) **4** Ran SP% **109.0**
Speed ratings (Par 102):101,100,91,90
CSF £12.17 TOTE £6.40; EX 14.00 Place 6 £60.72, Place 5 £47.46.
Owner Seasons Holidays **Bred** J B Haggas **Trained** Kentisbeare, Devon
FOCUS
This looked a tricky heat on paper, but the front pair came some 14 lengths clear. A weak race, the winner rated to last year's form from the progressive runner-up.
T/Plt: £93.90 to a £1 stake. Pool: £59,787.80. 464.50 winning tickets. T/Qpdt: £34.60 to a £1 stake. Pool: £2,436.80. 52.10 winning tickets. KH

1919 LEICESTER (R-H)
Monday, May 28

OFFICIAL GOING: Soft (heavy in places, 5.5)
There were 17 non-runners on account of the ground.
Wind: Light across Weather: Cloud, turning to rain after race 5

2083 KIBWORTH HARCOURT MEDIAN AUCTION MAIDEN STKS 7f 9y
2:00 (2:01) (Class 5) 3-Y-0 **£3,238** (£963; £481; £240) **Stalls** Centre

Form RPR
02 1 **Russian Epic**[9] 1840 3-9-3 0 PhilipRobinson 14 79
(M A Jarvis) *trckd ldrs: rdn to ld ins fnl f: edgd lft: styd on wl* **10/11**[1]
2 4 **Taghreed (IRE)** 3-8-12 0 DarryllHolland 3 64
(W Jarvis) *hld up: hdwy 1/2-way: led over 2f out: rdn over 1f out: hdd and no ex ins fnl f* **14/1**
4-46 3 ¾ **Ask Yer Dad**[14] 1726 3-9-3 60 (p) SteveDrowne 13 67
(Mrs P Sly) *hld up: hdwy 1/2-way: rdn over 1f out: styd on same pce* **14/1**
04-2 4 nk **Doyles Lodge**[19] 1587 3-9-3 72 DaneO'Neill 6 66
(H Candy) *chsd ldrs: rdn and hung rt over 1f out: no ex* **11/2**[2]
0 5 15 **Brackenridge**[17] 1635 3-9-3 0 PatDobbs 9 27
(Miss E C Lavelle) *chsd ldrs over 4f* **100/1**
550- 6 shd **Having A Ball**[264] 5113 3-9-3 53 ChrisCatlin 5 27
(P D Cundell) *prom over 4f* **33/1**
7 ¾ **King Of Legend (IRE)** 3-9-0 0 JerryO'Dwyer(3) 12 25
(Miss Gay Kelleway) *s.s: sme hdwy over 2f out: sn wknd* **66/1**
000- 8 3 **Danjoe**[157] 6905 3-8-12 47 KevinGhunowa(5) 1 17
(R Brotherton) *hld up: hdwy 1/2-way: rdn and wknd 2f out* **100/1**
450 9 6 **Toms Laughter**[82] 633 3-9-3 60 IanMongan 2 2
(B Palling) *hld up: bhd fr 1/2-way* **40/1**
03 10 ½ **Mabaahej (USA)**[21] 1522 3-8-12 0 MichaelHills 11 —
(B W Hills) *led over 4f: sn wknd* **7/1**
0 11 1 ¾ **Pixie Princess (IRE)**[17] 1620 3-8-7 0 ColinHaddon(5) 10 —
(Miss V Haigh) *chsd ldrs over 4f* **100/1**
12 10 **Golden Peacock** 3-9-3 0 AdamKirby 4 —
(M Appleby) *s.i.s: sn outpcd* **150/1**
622 13 30 **Sky Masterson**[14] 1716 3-9-3 73 RobertHavlin 8 —
(J H M Gosden) *chsd ldrs to 1/2-way* **6/1**[3]
1m 32.54s (6.44) **Going Correction** +0.775s/f (Yiel) **13** Ran SP% **118.4**
Speed ratings (Par 99):94,89,88,88,71 70,70,66,59,59 57,45,11
CSF £16.19 TOTE £1.80: £1.30, £2.50, £4.00; EX 17.90.
Owner Magno-Pulse Ltd **Bred** Derek R Price **Trained** Newmarket, Suffolk
FOCUS
A weak, uncompetitive maiden. The winning time was 1.37 seconds slower than the later fillies' 66-80. They raced up the middle of the track. It was a fair effort from the winner, but the overall level depends on how much improvement the 60-rated third finds.
Danjoe Official explanation: jockey said gelding hung right and lost a front shoe
Mabaahej(USA) Official explanation: trainer's rep said filly was unsuited by the soft (heavy patches) ground
Sky Masterson Official explanation: jockey said gelding stopped very quickly

2084 GILMORTON (S) STKS 1m 1f 218y
2:35 (2:36) (Class 6) 3-5-Y-0 **£2,590** (£770; £385; £192) **Stalls** High

Form RPR
0-66 1 **Press Express (IRE)**[26] 1413 5-9-7 61 SteveDrowne 4 63
(R A Fahey) *hld up: hdwy 1/2-way: rdn over 1f out: styd on to ld wl ins fnl f* **4/1**[2]
02 2 shd **Prince Des Neiges (FR)**[27] 1368 4-9-7 63 (p) ChrisCatlin 8 63
(Ian Williams) *led to 1/2-way: chsd ldr: wnt centre 4f out: rdn to ld and hung rt over 1f out: hdd wl ins fnl f: styd on u.p* **7/1**
6500 3 nk **Snake Hips**[28] 1361 3-8-4 54 (b[1]) RichardKingscote(3) 6 61
(B Palling) *chsd ldrs: rdn over 2f out: nt clr run over 1f out: ev ch ins fnl f: styd on* **33/1**
0-35 4 3 **Rowan Lodge (IRE)**[20] 1568 5-9-7 70 (b) MichaelHills 1 57
(M H Tompkins) *hld up: hdwy over 3f out: rdn over 1f out: no ex ins fnl f* **9/2**[3]
000- 5 nk **Shaika**[166] 6804 4-8-11 55 KevinGhunowa(5) 9 51
(G Prodromou) *hld up: hdwy over 3f out: sn rdn: hung rt over 1f out: no ex ins fnl f* **11/2**

0-40 6 nk **Viable**[33] 1249 5-9-0 57 JosephWalsh(7) 11 56
(Mrs P Sly) *chsd ldr tl led 1/2-way: rdn and hdd over 1f out: no ex ins fnl f* **7/1**
0025 7 ¾ **Faversham**[18] 1609 4-9-7 61 NickyMackay 10 54
(M Wigham) *prom: racd keenly: rdn and n.m.r over 1f out: no ex ins fnl f* **3/1**[1]
4/00 8 22 **Fixateur**[13] 1745 5-9-7 65 (v[1]) TPQueally 2 12
(J G Given) *s.i.s: hdwy over 8f out: rdn and wknd 4f out* **14/1**
-000 9 ½ **Digger Boy**[14] 603 4-9-4 60 JerryO'Dwyer(3) 12 11
(J Gallagher) *chsd ldrs 6f* **33/1**
0 10 23 **Long Gone**[30] 1296 4-9-2 0 StephenDonohoe 3 —
(John A Harris) *s.s: outpcd* **66/1**
00 11 1 ½ **Emma Gee**[59] 825 5-9-2 0 LPKeniry 5 —
(J Gallagher) *hld up: rdn and wknd over 4f out* **100/1**
0 12 39 **Worldwind**[80] 649 4-9-2 0 IanMongan 7 —
(Mrs L J Mongan) *hld up: bhd fr 1/2-way* **66/1**
2m 16.17s (7.87) **Going Correction** +0.775s/f (Yiel)
WFA 3 from 4yo+ 14lb **12** Ran SP% **120.1**
Speed ratings (Par 101):99,98,98,96,96 95,95,77,77,58 57,26
CSF £31.89 TOTE £6.10: £2.20, £2.10, £4.50; EX 45.40.There was no bid for the winner.
Owner Mark A Leatham **Bred** Tareq Al Mazeedi **Trained** Musley Bank, N Yorks
FOCUS
An ordinary seller in which they finished in a heap. Most of these are on the downgrade.
Worldwind Official explanation: trainer said filly was unsuited by the soft (heavy patches) ground

2085 LEICESTER MERCURY FAMILY FUN DAY FILLIES' H'CAP 7f 9y
3:10 (3:11) (Class 4) (0-80,79) 4-Y-0+
£6,232 (£1,866; £933; £467; £233; £117) **Stalls** Centre

Form RPR
011- 1 **Bakhoor (IRE)**[324] 3299 4-8-7 **68** ow1 DarryllHolland 3 81+
(W Jarvis) *hld up: hdwy over 2f out: led over 1f out: rdn out* **11/2**[3]
310- 2 2 ½ **Yandina (IRE)**[241] 5649 4-9-0 **75** MichaelHills 8 82
(B W Hills) *chsd ldr tl led 1/2-way: rdn: edgd lft and hdd over 1f out: styd on same pce* **11/2**[3]
5-05 3 1 **Misphire**[5] 1940 4-8-12 **73** (p) SteveDrowne 2 77
(M Dods) *hld up: hdwy over 1f out: styd on same pce ins fnl f* **14/1**
-341 4 ½ **Tender The Great (IRE)**[21] 1534 4-8-4 **68** RichardKingscote(3) 5 71
(B G Powell) *chsd ldrs: rdn and hung lft over 1f out: edgd rt and no ex fnl f* **5/1**[2]
0-04 5 7 **Tara Too (IRE)**[21] 1525 4-9-1 **79** EmmettStack(3) 1 64
(J G Portman) *chsd ldrs: rdn 1/2-way: wknd 2f out* **20/1**
00-2 6 1 ¼ **Rydal Mount (IRE)**[19] 1588 4-8-12 **73** ChrisCatlin 6 55
(W S Kittow) *led to 1/2-way: rdn and wknd wl over 1f out* **15/2**
-036 7 3 **Passion Fruit**[9] 1845 6-9-3 **78** DaneO'Neill 10 52
(C W Fairhurst) *s.i.s: sn pushed along in rr: hdwy 2f out: sn rdn and wknd* **11/4**[1]
4-20 8 8 **Inaminute (IRE)**[37] 1157 4-8-13 **77** AndrewElliott(3) 11 30
(K R Burke) *chsd ldrs: rdn 1/2-way: wknd 2f out* **7/1**
1m 31.17s (5.07) **Going Correction** +0.775s/f (Yiel) **8** Ran SP% **109.8**
Speed ratings (Par 102):102,99,98,97,89 88,84,75
CSF £32.70 CT £372.10 TOTE £6.60: £1.90, £2.30, £4.20; EX 44.00.
Owner Ziad A Galadari **Bred** Galadari Sons Stud Company Limited **Trained** Newmarket, Suffolk
FOCUS
This fillies' handicap was not a strong race, particularly with the favourite running poorly, but Bakhoor was quite impressive. The winning time was 1.37 seconds quicker than the earlier three-year-old maiden. They came up the middle of the track.
Tender The Great(IRE) Official explanation: trainer's rep said filly was unsuited by the soft (heavy patches) ground
Passion Fruit Official explanation: jockey said mare never travelled

2086 ENDERBY MEDIAN AUCTION MAIDEN STKS 5f 2y
3:45 (3:48) (Class 5) 2-Y-0 **£3,238** (£963; £481; £240) **Stalls** Low

Form RPR
1 **Mahusay (IRE)** 2-9-3 0 NickyMackay 6 81+
(L M Cumani) *chsd ldrs: shkn up to ld ins fnl f: r.o wl* **15/2**
3 2 1 ¾ **Advertisement**[23] 1469 2-9-3 0 DaneO'Neill 5 75
(C G Cox) *led over 3f: styd on same pce ins fnl f* **11/8**[1]
0 3 nk **Brixworth Scribe**[21] 1540 2-9-3 0 PaulEddery 10 74
(B Smart) *s.i.s: sn chsng ldrs: rdn to ld over 1f out: hdd and unable qck ins fnl f* **14/1**
4 7 **Galley Slave (IRE)** 2-9-3 0 SteveDrowne 9 48
(Mrs P Sly) *s.i.s: outpcd: r.o ins fnl f: nrst fin* **18/1**
0 5 3 **Theebah**[7] 1896 2-8-12 0 DarryllHolland 3 33
(M R Channon) *s.i.s: sn outpcd: effrt and edgd rt over 1f out: sn wknd* **11/1**
6 3 **Greystoke Prince** 2-9-3 0 AdamKirby 14 27
(W R Swinburn) *chsd ldr: rdn: hung rt and wknd over 1f out* **9/2**[3]
7 ¾ **Magnol** 2-8-12 0 PhilipRobinson 2 19
(M A Jarvis) *s.s: hung rt and outpcd* **4/1**[2]
0 8 shd **Validity**[17] 1636 2-8-7 0 (t) WilliamBuick(5) 7 19
(A J McCabe) *mid-div: sn drvn along: edgd rt fnl 3f: wknd 2f out* **28/1**
9 1 ½ **Jay Gee Wigmo** 2-9-3 0 RobertHavlin 15 18
(A W Carroll) *s.s: outpcd* **33/1**
64.58 secs (3.68) **Going Correction** +0.775s/f (Yiel) **9** Ran SP% **118.7**
Speed ratings (Par 93):101,98,97,86,81 76,75,75,73
CSF £18.75 TOTE £9.00: £2.40, £1.10, £3.10; EX 21.20.
Owner Sheikh Mohammed Obaid Al Maktoum **Bred** Darley **Trained** Newmarket, Suffolk
FOCUS
Just an ordinary juvenile maiden, but a nice performance from Mahusay and improvement from the runner-up. Sound form. They all raced towards the stands'-side rail.
NOTEBOOK
Mahusay(IRE) ◆, by Noverre and the first foal of a mare who was placed over 1m, picked up nicely from just off the pace to run out a comfortable winner on his racecourse debut. This represents just ordinary form, but he looks a nice type and should hold his own at a higher level. (op 7-1 tchd 13-2)
Advertisement, third in a reasonable maiden on his debut at Goodwood, was given every chance against the stands'-side rail and can have few excuses. (op 7-4 tchd 2-1 and 9-4 in places)
Brixworth Scribe, down the field in an ordinary maiden on his debut at Windsor, ran a respectable race in third and looks to be going the right way. (op 16-1 tchd 12-1)
Galley Slave(IRE), a 30,000gns half-brother to multiple 6f-1m winner Summer Magic, never posed a threat and should know more next time. (op 16-1 tchd 14-1 and 20-1)
Theebah, last on her debut at Windsor, hardly fared much better this time and may want better ground. (op 8-1 tchd 12-1)

Greystoke Prince ♦, a 24,000gns half-brother to 5f juvenile winner Howards Prince, and Howards Princess, a dual winner over 5-6f at three, out of a prolific 5f-6f two-year-old scorer, showed up well in the early stages before weakening out of contention. He finished up well beaten, but should be capable of better on a decent surface and should make his mark when the emphasis is on speed. (op 7-2 tchd 5-1)
Magnol, a half-sister to 1m winner One Upmanship, did not look happy on the ground and was well beaten on her racecourse debut. (op 11-2)

2087 SKEFFINGTON CLAIMING STKS — 5f 218y
4:20 (4:20) (Class 5) 2-Y-O — **£3,886** (£1,156; £577; £288) **Stalls** Centre

Form — RPR

1 **Star Of Rosanna** 2-8-5 0 ... RussellKennemore(5) 5 — 66
(R Hollinshead) *trckd ldrs: led over 1f out: rdn out* **14/1**

3522 **2** 1 1/4 **Rio Taffeta**[8] 1857 2-8-9 0 ... LPKeniry 9 — 61
(Peter Grayson) *hld up in tch: rdn to chse wnr and hung lft ins fnl f: styd on same pce* **5/2**[2]

004 **3** 3 **Lord Deevert**[29] 1315 2-8-4 0 ... JackDean(7) 6 — 54
(W G M Turner) *trckd ldr: plld hrd: sddle slipped sn after s: led over 2f out: rdn and hdd over 1f out: no ex ins fnl f* **7/2**[3]

314 **4** 1 3/4 **Echostar**[16] 1674 2-8-2 0 ... ChrisCatlin 3 — 40
(W R Muir) *awkward leaving stalls: chsd ldrs: rdn 1/2-way: wknd over 1f out* **5/1**

01 **5** 3 **Alexander Monarchy (IRE)**[14] 1728 2-8-10 0 ... MichaelHills 7 — 45+
(K A Ryan) *chsd ldrs: rdn and ev ch over 1f out: wknd ins fnl f* **7/4**[1]

05 **6** 12 **Danny Boy Blue**[25] 1428 2-8-11 0 ... IanMongan 1 — 4
(Mrs L J Mongan) *led over 3f: wknd over 1f out* **25/1**

1m 19.4s (6.20) **Going Correction** +0.775s/f (Yiel) **6** Ran SP% **114.3**
Speed ratings (Par 93):89,87,83,81,77 61
CSF £50.16 TOTE £15.20: £3.70, £1.70; EX 69.80.The winner was claimed by Kevin Ryan for £12,000.
Owner Mrs Debbie Hodson **Bred** R Hollinshead **Trained** Upper Longdon, Staffs
■ Stewards' Enquiry : L P Keniry one-day ban: used whip with excessive frequency (Jun 8)

FOCUS
The winning time was 2.95 seconds slower than the following 61-75 older-horse handicap. They raced up the middle of the track. Star Of Rosanna won well and it is doubtful if she was flattered, but this was a weak event.

NOTEBOOK
Star Of Rosanna, a half-sister to triple 7f-1m1f winner Pauline's Prince, proved good enough to make a winning debut. This represents just moderate form, but she is open to some improvement. (op 16-1 tchd 12-1)
Rio Taffeta, having his first start since being claimed out of Mick Channon's yard, looked to have every chance. He is not progressing. (op 11-4 tchd 9-4)
Lord Deevert is better than he was able to show as his saddle slipped early on. Official explanation: jockey said saddle slipped (tchd 4-1)
Echostar seemed unsuited by the soft ground and was below her best. (op 7-2)
Alexander Monarchy(IRE) could not follow up her recent Wolverhampton success and looked to get bogged down in the soft ground. Official explanation: trainer said filly was unsuited by the soft (heavy patches) ground (op 5-2)

2088 LEICESTERSHIRE AND RUTLAND LIFE H'CAP — 5f 218y
4:55 (4:56) (Class 5) (0-75,75) 4-Y-0+ — **£3,886** (£1,156; £577; £288) **Stalls** Centre

Form — RPR

53-0 **1** **Balakiref**[19] 1574 8-9-1 72 ... DarryllHolland 2 — 81+
(M Dods) *hld up: r.o u.p and hung rt ins fnl f: r.o to ld post* **3/1**[1]

5053 **2** hd **Cornus**[9] 1847 5-8-13 70 ... (be) AdamKirby 14 — 78
(A J McCabe) *chsd ldrs: nt clr run over 1f out: rdn to ld wl ins fnl f: hdd post* **10/1**

46-1 **3** nk **Guilded Warrior**[19] 1589 4-8-13 70 ... ChrisCatlin 17 — 77
(W S Kittow) *chsd ldrs: rdn and ev ch ins fnl f: styd on* **11/1**

5-63 **4** 3/4 **Angel Sprints**[3] 1984 5-9-4 75 ... AlanDaly 7 — 80
(C J Down) *hld up: hdwy and edgd rt over 2f out: rdn and ev ch ins fnl f: styng on same pce whn n.m.r nr fin* **10/1**

63-5 **5** 1 **Outer Hebrides**[16] 1666 6-8-9 73 ... (vt) BarrySavage(7) 12 — 75
(J M Bradley) *chsd ldrs: rdn and ev ch over 1f out: styd on same pce ins fnl f* **16/1**

2-55 **6** shd **Westport**[9] 1847 4-9-2 73 ... MichaelHills 9 — 75
(K A Ryan) *hld up in tch: rdn to ld over 1f out: hdd and no ex wl ins fnl f* **6/1**[3]

3-00 **7** nk **Kingscross**[35] 1200 9-9-3 74 ... LPKeniry 5 — 75
(M Blanshard) *s.i.s: hld up: hdwy over 1f out: n.m.r ins fnl f: nt trble ldrs* **14/1**

030- **8** 1 3/4 **Imperial Gain (USA)**[230] 5896 4-9-4 75 ... StephenDonohoe 15 — 70
(J M Bradley) *s.i.s: hld up: styd on ins fnl f: nvr trbld ldrs* **50/1**

24-2 **9** 1 1/4 **Prince Of Delphi**[22] 1501 4-9-1 72 ... DaneO'Neill 8 — 64
(H Candy) *hld up: hdwy and n.m.r over 2f out: wknd fnl f* **7/2**[2]

1264 **10** nk **George The Second**[62] 803 4-8-5 65 ... RichardKingscote(3) 4 — 56
(Mrs H Sweeting) *led: hdd over 4f out: led again over 2f out: rdn and hdd over 1f out: wknd ins fnl f* **16/1**

0-00 **11** 4 **Foreign Edition (IRE)**[9] 1847 5-9-1 72 ... (p) PhilipRobinson 13 — 51
(Miss J A Camacho) *led over 4f out: hdd over 2f out: wknd over 1f out* **16/1**

4-00 **12** 2 1/2 **Vanadium**[10] 1819 5-9-1 72 ... (p) TPQueally 16 — 43
(J G Given) *hld up: wknd over 1f out* **11/1**

1m 16.45s (3.25) **Going Correction** +0.775s/f (Yiel) **12** Ran SP% **122.6**
Speed ratings (Par 103):109,108,108,107,106 105,105,103,101,101 95,92
CSF £35.28 CT £307.49 TOTE £4.10: £2.30, £3.30, £3.60; EX 45.80.
Owner Septimus Racing Group **Bred** S R Hope And D Erwin **Trained** Denton, Co Durham

FOCUS
A fair sprint handicap. Sound form, the first four within a pound of their pre-race marks. The winning time was 2.95 seconds quicker than the juvenile claimer. They tended to race towards the far side and a high draw seemed to be at an advantage.

2089 TIGERS APPRENTICE H'CAP — 1m 3f 183y
5:25 (5:25) (Class 6) (0-60,63) 4-Y-0+ — **£2,590** (£770; £385; £192) **Stalls** High

Form — RPR

-000 **1** **Red River Rebel**[34] 1222 9-8-2 48 ow1 ... JamesRogers(5) 11 — 54
(J R Norton) *chsd ldrs: led 2 out: rdn over 1f out: styd on* **25/1**

5-43 **2** 1/2 **My Legal Eagle (IRE)**[26] 1406 13-8-5 46 oh1 ... JamieHamblett 12 — 51
(E G Bevan) *hld up: rdn over 3f out: hdwy over 1f out: styd on* **10/1**

-25 **3** hd **Near Germany (IRE)**[30] 1295 7-9-4 59 ... ThomasO'Brien 13 — 64+
(R Curtis) *s.i.s: hld up: hdwy over 4f out: ev ch fr over 1f out: nt qckn nr fin* **14/1**

1334 **4** 3 **Apache Fort**[10] 1819 4-9-3 58 ... PatrickHills 9 — 58
(T Keddy) *prom: rdn over 2f out: hung rt and no ex ins fnl f* **6/1**[3]

4604 **5** 5 **General Flumpa**[6] 1924 6-8-10 56 ... SophieDoyle(5) 2 — 48
(Miss Tor Sturgis) *hld up: hdwy 1/2-way: rdn and hung rt over 2f out: sn wknd* **14/1**

3050 **6** 3/4 **Synonymy**[16] 1683 4-8-10 56 ... (b) LauraReynolds(5) 6 — 47
(M Blanshard) *hld up: rdn over 3f out: styd on ins fnl f: nvr nrr* **8/1**

4221 **7** 1 1/2 **Recalcitrant**[12] 1764 4-9-5 60 ... HaddenFrost 3 — 48
(S Dow) *chsd ldr: led over 4f out: hdd & wknd 2f out* **11/2**[2]

000- **8** 3 **Bold Finch (FR)**[137] 4048 5-8-4 50 ... BarrySavage(5) 1 — 34
(J M Bradley) *chsd ldrs: rdn over 3f out: sn wknd* **14/1**

0-06 **9** nk **Phone In**[16] 1671 4-8-4 50 ... (p) JosephWalsh(5) 10 — 33
(R Brotherton) *led: clr 6f out: hdd over 4f out: wknd over 2f out* **25/1**

3/65 **10** 2 1/2 **Prelude**[6] 1926 6-8-13 54 ... LukeMorris 4 — 33
(W M Brisbourne) *hld up: rdn and wknd over 3f out* **14/1**

00-2 **11** 1 1/4 **Moonshine Creek**[16] 1671 5-8-8 52 ... WilliamCarson(3) 8 — 29
(P W Hiatt) *chsd ldrs: rdn over 2f out: hung rt and wknd wl over 1f out: eased* **13/2**

3-30 **12** 12 **Coffin Dodger**[20] 1570 4-8-5 46 oh1 ... KirstyMilczarek 5 — 4
(C N Allen) *s.s: a bhd* **33/1**

5551 **13** 4 **Medieval Maiden**[7] 1907 4-9-5 63 6ex ... AlanRutter(3) 7 — 15
(W J Musson) *hld up: rdn and wknd over 3f out* **3/1**[1]

2m 43.31s (8.81) **Going Correction** +0.775s/f (Yiel) **13** Ran SP% **125.5**
Speed ratings (Par 101):101,100,100,98,95 94,93,91,91,89 89,81,78
CSF £265.17 CT £3657.63 TOTE £28.20: £5.20, £2.20, £4.20; EX 164.70 Place 6 £173.09, Place 5 £105.20..
Owner Jeff Slaney **Bred** J Slaney **Trained** High Hoyland, S Yorks

FOCUS
A moderate handicap restricted to apprentices who had not ridden more than 25 winners. The pace was strong considering the conditions. The form has been rated through the first two.
Phone In Official explanation: jockey said gelding had no more to give
Moonshine Creek Official explanation: trainer's rep said gelding was unsuited by the soft (heavy patches) ground
Medieval Maiden Official explanation: trainer said filly was unsuited by the tactics
T/Plt: £117.70 to a £1 stake. Pool: £70,282.10. 435.55 winning tickets. T/Qpdt: £32.30 to a £1 stake. Pool: £3,379.40. 77.35 winning tickets. CR

REDCAR (L-H)
Monday, May 28

OFFICIAL GOING: Good to firm (firm in places, 9.1)
Wind: Moderate, half-against

2090 SAVILLS IN YORKSHIRE NOVICE AUCTION STKS — 5f
2:05 (2:05) (Class 5) 2-Y-O — **£2,817** (£838; £418; £209) **Stalls** Centre

Form — RPR

1 **Wigram's Turn (USA)** 2-8-9 ... FrancisNorton 2 — 81+
(A M Balding) *dwlt: sn rdn along: rn green and outpcd in rr: swtchd rt and hdwy wl over 1f out: styd on to ld ent fnl f: sn clr* **7/1**

3 **2** 4 **Select Committee**[25] 1422 2-8-9 ... GrahamGibbons 3 — 67
(J J Quinn) *trckd ldrs: effrt 2f out: rdn to ld over 1f out: hdd ent fnl f and nt pce of wnr* **5/2**[2]

210 **3** 1 3/4 **Artdeal**[19] 1580 2-9-4 ... (p) KerrinMcEvoy 1 — 69
(M J Wallace) *cl up: rdn and ev ch 2f out: sn drvn and edgd lft over 1f out: one pce* **3/1**[3]

6 **4** shd **Atephobia**[7] 1889 2-8-12 ... PaulMulrennan 5 — 63
(K R Burke) *cl up: rdn and ev ch 2f out: sn one pce* **33/1**

21 **5** 3 1/2 **Diademas (USA)**[4] 1975 2-9-4 ... JimCrowley 4 — 56
(J A Osborne) *led: rdn along 2f out: sn drvn and hdd over 1f out: wknd* **5/4**[1]

59.95 secs (1.25) **Going Correction** +0.225s/f (Good) **5** Ran SP% **113.5**
Speed ratings (Par 93):99,92,89,89,84
CSF £25.25 TOTE £10.90: £2.90, £2.00; EX 28.70.
Owner David Brownlow **Bred** Lone Cedar Thoroughbred Holdings, Llc **Trained** Kingsclere, Hants

FOCUS
This did not look a great race beforehand despite the presence of a couple of previous winners, but the winning time was decent for a contest of its type.

NOTEBOOK
Wigram's Turn(USA) ♦, a $25,000 half-brother to a winner in the US out of a juvenile winner in the same country, was the only debutant in the field and looked like it in the early stages as he was completely taken off his feet and looked more likely to finish a well-beaten last. However, he eventually got the hang of things and swept past his four rivals to win going away. This was a decent effort with two of his four rivals previous winners and with a longer trip likely to suit he looks capable of finding something rather better. (tchd 8-1)
Select Committee stepped up from his Catterick debut, did very little wrong, and was unfortunate to run into an unexposed and decent prospect in a race like this. There is a maiden waiting for him somewhere. (tchd 11-4)
Artdeal had every chance on the far side of the quintet, but was exposed for a lack of pace where it mattered. He was later reported to have bled, but even so he may need a stiffer test now and also faced a difficult task under his big penalty. Official explanation: trainer said gelding bled from the nose (op 7-2)
Atephobia faced a stiff task and was not disgraced under the circumstances, but this speedily-bred colt may be one for sprint nurseries late on. (op 25-1)
Diademas(USA), who bolted up in a Fibresand maiden four days earlier, found these conditions very different and although he showed up at the front for a while, he was ultimately the first beaten. Official explanation: trainer said colt was unsuited by the good to firm (firm in places) ground (op 11-8 tchd 6-4)

2091 MARKET CROSS JEWELLERS (S) STKS — 7f
2:40 (2:42) (Class 6) 3-5-Y-O — **£2,047** (£604; £302) **Stalls** Centre

Form — RPR

00-1 **1** **Sam's Secret**[7] 1893 5-9-8 62 ... DeanMcKeown 13 — 68
(G A Swinbank) *hld up in tch: swtchd rt and gd hdwy 2f out: led 1f out: sn rdn and styd on wl* **5/2**[1]

430- **2** 1 **Yo Pedro (IRE)**[14] 1733 5-9-7 ... (vt[1]) JimCrowley 12 — 64
(Barry Potts, Ire) *hld up: smooth hdwy over 2f out: rdn to chsd wnr ent fnl f: kpt on* **11/4**[2]

05-0 **3** 4 **Drum Dance (IRE)**[18] 1596 5-9-7 46 ... JoeFanning 6 — 53
(N Tinkler) *trckd ldrs: hdwy to ld wl over 1f out: rdn and hdd 1f out: sn drvn and one pce* **11/1**

00-4 **4** 3/4 **Andorran (GER)**[25] 1423 4-9-7 47 ... (tp) PaulMulrennan 2 — 51
(A Dickman) *trckd ldrs: effrt and ev ch over 2f out tl rdn and grad wknd fr over 1f out* **12/1**

616- **5** 1 **Chateau (IRE)**[15] 2240 5-9-4 58 ... (t) MarkLawson(3) 15 — 48
(M E Sowersby) *towards rr: hdwy on outer 3f out: kpt on fnl 2f: nrst fin* **12/1**

0350 **6** ¾ **Mister Maq**[48] 997 4-9-7 52 ....(b) DO'Donohoe 14 46
(A Crook) *sn rdn along and bhd tl styd on wl fnl 2f: nrst fin* **25/1**
2053 **7** 1¾ **Denton Hawk**[22] 1489 3-8-10 53 ....(b[1]) PaulFessey 9 42
(M Dods) *in rr and pushed along 1/2-way: kpt on u.p fnl 2f* **9/1**[3]
-000 **8** *shd* **Filey Buoy**[14] 1715 5-9-0 43 ....(v) PaulPickard(7) 7 41
(R M Whitaker) *cl up: rdn to ld briefly wl over 2f out: sn hdd and grad wknd* **40/1**
40-0 **9** ½ **Woodwee**[54] 912 4-9-7 47 .... FrancisNorton 11 40
(R E Barr) *led 2f: prom tl rdn along over 2f out and grad wknd* **28/1**
0400 **10** 2 **Following Flow (USA)**[7] 1893 5-9-2 52 .... PJMcDonald(5) 8 35
(R Allan) *chsd ldrs: rdn along wl over 2f out: wknd over 1f out* **20/1**
00-0 **11** *nk* **Lewis Lloyd (IRE)**[13] 1744 4-9-4 45 ....(t) StephaneBreux(3) 3 34
(R E Barr) *cl up: led after 2f: rdn along and hdd over 2f out: sn wknd* **33/1**
0 **12** 3½ **Shoot Out**[10] 1804 4-9-7 .... DavidAllan 10 24
(C W Thornton) *chsd ldrs: rdn along 1/2-way: sn wknd* **40/1**
05-0 **13** 9 **The Dandy Fox**[32] 1259 3-8-0 48 .... NataliaGemelova(5) 1 —
(R Bastiman) *cl up: rdn along 3f out: sn wknd* **28/1**

1m 27.7s (2.80) **Going Correction** +0.225s/f (Good)
WFA 3 from 4yo+ 11lb **13** Ran SP% **112.3**
Speed ratings (Par 101):93,91,87,86,85 84,82,82,81,79 79,75,64
CSF £7.18 TOTE £3.00: £1.20, £1.70, £3.30; EX 9.80.There was no bid for the winner. Yo Pedro was claimed by Mrs B. Ramsden for £6,000.
Owner Copskam Partnership **Bred** Dandy's Farm **Trained** Melsonby, N Yorks
■ Wiltshire (8/1, unruly in stalls) and Cadogen Square (50/1, vet's advice) were withdrawn. R4 applies, deduct 10p in the £.

FOCUS
A poor seller, lacking strength in depth and totally dominated by the two market leaders, who pulled a long way clear of the others. The race has been rated through the runner-up. The winning time was modest, even for a race like this.

2092 TOTESPORT 0800 221 221 H'CAP 1m 2f
3:15 (3:15) (Class 3) (0-90,87) 3-Y-O **£8,096** (£2,408; £1,203; £601) **Stalls** Low

Form RPR
1-01 **1** **Lacework**[18] 1610 3-9-3 83 .... KerrinMcEvoy 8 89+
(Sir Michael Stoute) *hld up in rr: hdwy over 3f out: pushed along over 2f out: swtchd outside and rdn wl over 1f out: styd on to ld wl ins fnl f* **5/4**[1]
11-4 **2** *1* **King Charles**[23] 1467 3-9-7 87 .... DO'Donohoe 5 91
(E A L Dunlop) *trckd ldrs: hdwy 3f out: rdn to chal over 1f out: drvn ins fnl f: tk 2nd nr fin* **9/1**
10-4 **3** *nk* **Plane Painter (IRE)**[28] 1365 3-8-11 77 .... JoeFanning 9 80
(M Johnston) *trckd ldr: hdwy to ld and edgd lft 2f out: sn rdn: drvn and hdd wl ins fnl f: lost 2nd nr line* **10/1**
4432 **4** 2½ **Arena's Dream (USA)**[16] 1676 3-8-5 71 .... JimmyQuinn 7 69
(R A Fahey) *chsd ldng pair: rdn along over 2f out: drvn and wknd ent fnl f* **8/1**
2-10 **5** *shd* **Salaasa (USA)**[31] 1277 3-9-7 87 .... RHills 10 85
(M Johnston) *led: rdn along 3f out: hdd and n.m.r 2f out: grad wknd* **11/2**[3]
3320 **6** 3½ **Deadline (UAE)**[9] 1851 3-8-4 70 .... PaulFessey 3 61
(P T Midgley) *a towards rr* **14/1**
20-1 **7** *15* **Packers Hill (IRE)**[21] 1531 3-8-9 75 .... DeanMcKeown 6 36
(G A Swinbank) *in tch: rdn along over 3f out: sn wknd* **5/1**[2]
342- **8** ¾ **Akiyama (IRE)**[230] 5900 3-8-3 69 .... FrancisNorton 2 28
(J Howard Johnson) *chsd ldrs on inner: rdn along over 3f out: sn wknd* **14/1**

2m 7.08s (0.28) **Going Correction** +0.225s/f (Good) **8** Ran SP% **120.0**
Speed ratings (Par 103):107,106,105,103,103 101,89,88
CSF £14.74 CT £85.14 TOTE £2.10: £1.10, £2.20, £3.10; EX 14.90.
Owner Cheveley Park Stud **Bred** Cheveley Park Stud Ltd **Trained** Newmarket, Suffolk
■ Stewards' Enquiry : Joe Fanning caution: careless riding

FOCUS
A decent pace for this three-year-old handicap and with the field finishing well spread out, the form looks rock solid. The first three were all improved by 5-6lb.

NOTEBOOK
Lacework, raised 6lb for her Windsor victory, was ridden with plenty of confidence on this first attempt at the trip. She came off the bridle a fair way out, but maintained her effort down the centre of the track to eventually win with a degree of comfort. She remains on an upwards curve and there should be a lot more to come from her. (op 11-8 tchd 13-8)
King Charles, stepped up from his Goodwood reappearance and had every chance, but could not cope with the progressive filly at the business end. He seems to get the trip well enough and should remain competitive off this sort of mark. (op 8-1)
Plane Painter(IRE), taking another step up in trip despite not appearing to see out the extended 1m at Wolverhampton last time, was not ridden as though lack of stamina was a problem and that did not seem to be the case. He was just not quite good enough on the day. (op 9-1)
Arena's Dream(USA), back in a handicap after running into a Stoute hotpot in a Thirsk maiden last time, did not appear to see out the longer trip and is proving a complete nightmare to place. (tchd 17-2)
Salaasa(USA) was given a positive ride, but was rather easily picked off in the home straight and it now looks as though he was put in on too stiff a mark following his Pontefract maiden victory. (op 13-2 tchd 7-1 and 9-2)
Deadline(UAE), who has become an exposed maiden, found this company too hot and needs more help from the Handicapper. (op 16-1)
Packers Hill(IRE), walloped 8lb for his Newcastle victory, was beaten even before stamina for this longer trip became an issue. Official explanation: vet said colt finished lame (op 11-2 tchd 6-1)
Akiyama(IRE) Official explanation: trainer's rep said gelding was unsuited by the good to firm (firm in places) ground

2093 TOTESPORT.COM ZETLAND GOLD CUP (HERITAGE H'CAP) 1m 2f
3:50 (3:51) (Class 2) (0-105,103) 3-Y-O+**£32,385** (£9,635; £4,815; £2,405) **Stalls** Lower

Form RPR
6041 **1** **Flipando (IRE)**[6] 1915 6-9-3 96 6ex .... PaulFessey 4 104
(T D Barron) *t.k.h early: trckd ldrs: hdwy over 2f out: rdn to ld ent fnl f: sn drvn and styd on wl* **14/1**
3-30 **2** *nk* **Wind Star**[23] 1480 4-8-8 87 .... DeanMcKeown 2 94+
(G A Swinbank) *hld up in tch on inner: effrt and nt clr run over 2f out: swtchd rt and rdn over 1f out: drvn and ev ch ins fnl f: kpt on* **28/1**
3523 **3** *hd* **Bailieborough (IRE)**[12] 1767 8-8-6 85 .... SilvestreDeSousa 7 92
(B Ellison) *trckd ldrs: effrt and n.m.r over 2f out: swtchd rt and rdn over 1f out: styd on wl fnl f* **12/1**
-000 **4** *nk* **Blue Spinnaker (IRE)**[12] 1767 8-8-5 84 .... PaulMulrennan 14 90
(M W Easterby) *hld up in rr: hdwy on wd outside over 2f out: rdn over 1f out: styd on strly ins fnl f: nrst fin* **18/1**
0050 **5** ½ **Collateral Damage (IRE)**[12] 1767 4-8-8 87 ....(t) DavidAllan 11 93+
(T D Easterby) *hld up in rr: hdwy whn nt clr run 2f out: swtchd ins 2f out and sn rdn: styd on strly ins fnl f: nt clear run towards fin* **20/1**
21-1 **6** ¾ **Hassaad**[26] 1395 4-8-7 86 .... RHills 6 90+
(W J Haggas) *hld up towards rr: hdwy 3f out: swtchd ins 2f out and sn nt clr run: styng on whn nt clr run ins fnl f: kpt on* **11/4**[1]
35-1 **7** *hd* **Dan Dare (USA)**[21] 1529 4-8-8 87 .... KerrinMcEvoy 3 91
(Sir Michael Stoute) *trckd ldng pair: pushed along 3f out: swtchd rt and rdn over 2f out: sn drvn and kpt on same pce appr fnl f* **9/2**[2]
0-00 **8** *hd* **Prince Of Light (IRE)**[22] 1494 4-9-10 103 ....(b[1]) JoeFanning 13 106
(M Johnston) *cl up: rdn to ld 2f out: drvn: hdd & wknd ent fnl f* **11/1**
0512 **9** 2 **Goodbye Mr Bond**[9] 1842 7-9-0 93 .... GrahamGibbons 8 92
(E J Alston) *hld up towards rr: effrt and sme hdwy 3f out: sn rdn along and no imp fr over 1f out* **12/1**
30-5 **10** *hd* **Motive (FR)**[10] 1822 6-8-12 91 .... MickyFenton 9 90
(J Howard Johnson) *hld up: effrt and sme hdwy on outer over 3f out: sn rdn and btn* **28/1**
0-23 **11** 2½ **Benandonner (USA)**[33] 1245 4-8-6 85 .... JimmyQuinn 5 79
(R A Fahey) *led: rdn along 3f out: hdd 2f out and sn wknd* **5/1**[3]
00-4 **12** 4 **Chantaco (USA)**[39] 1109 5-9-1 94 .... FrancisNorton 12 80
(A M Balding) *in tch: hdwy to chse ldrs over 3f out: sn rdn along and btn 2f out* **8/1**

2m 5.82s (-0.98) **Going Correction** +0.225s/f (Good) **12** Ran SP% **119.9**
Speed ratings (Par 109):112,111,111,111,110 110,110,110,108,108 106,103
CSF £362.07 CT £4754.20 TOTE £15.30: £4.00, £8.70, £3.20; EX 374.20.
Owner Mrs J Hazell **Bred** Denis McDonnell **Trained** Maunby, N Yorks
■ Stewards' Enquiry : Silvestre De Sousa one-day ban: used whip with excessive frequency (Jun 8)

FOCUS
A typically competitive Zetland Gold Cup run at a solid, if far from breakneck, pace. As is usually the case in this contest, a few did not enjoy the smoothest of passages. It is difficult to rate the bare form that positively, but the winner produced a personal best and the third ran to form.

NOTEBOOK
Flipando(IRE), 8lb higher than when winning at Beverley including his 6lb penalty, was always in a perfect position just behind the pace-setters and always had enough daylight to make his effort when he wanted to. His move, when he made it, proved decisive and this was a fine performance to win such a competitive event off a career-high mark. He also won this because he was given the best ride. (op 16-1)
Wind Star, trying this trip for the first time, was buried away in the pack and never had a great deal of room to play with, though he was not alone there. In truth he managed to get himself into a position where he had every chance had he been good enough, but found the winner too determined. He certainly stayed and this opens up a few more opportunities for him. (op 33-1)
Bailieborough(IRE), who finished just ahead of Flipando at York last time and was 6lb better off, was brought out towards the centre of the track for his effort and finished well but was never quite able to get there in time. He is wonderfully consistent and has never been better at the age of eight, but he is 8lb above his highest winning mark and is yet to win over this far.
Blue Spinnaker(IRE), a stone lower than when winning this race three years ago, has been rather disappointing since winning at York over a year ago and was well behind Bailieborough and Flipando at the same track last time. Given his usual patient ride, he negated any chance of getting caught in traffic by being pulled widest of all and flew home to such an extent that he would have been in front with a little further to go, but to be fair had he not been brought so wide he probably would not have got a run. He is extremely well handicapped if this is a sign of a general renaissance. (op 20-1)
Collateral Damage(IRE), who finished behind Bailieborough, Flipando and Blue Spinnaker when walking out of the stalls at York last time, was held up right out the back as usual but it was always asking a lot for him to weave his way through the entire field. Under the circumstances he did well, and was a bit fortunate, to finish right on the heels of the leaders. Softer ground would suit him even better and even though he looks weighted right up to his best, he looks capable of defying this sort of mark when getting the breaks. Official explanation: jockey said colt was denied a clear run
Hassaad, trying this trip for the first time and bidding for a hat-trick off a 6lb higher mark, was locked away on the inside for most of the way and it was always going to be a big ask to pick his way though his rivals in the straight. He managed to get past several, but when he tried to get up the inside of Prince Of Light well inside the last furlong his luck ran out. Official explanation: jockey said gelding was denied a clear run (tchd 3-1, 10-3 in places)
Dan Dare(USA), making his handicap debut after easily winning a Newcastle maiden, was close enough if good enough entering the last couple of furlongs and was by no means knocked about when it became obvious that he was making little impression. This was a tough race to make his handicap bow in and there will be other days. Official explanation: jockey said gelding was denied a clear run (op 4-1)
Prince Of Light(IRE) was ridden up with the pace in the first-time blinkers, but had to work hard to get to the front and after he did his stamina appeared to give out. He is beginning to look a 'twilight' horse at the moment. (op 12-1)
Benandonner(USA) tried to make every yard, but was never allowed an easy lead thanks to the attentions of Prince Of Light and folded fairly tamely once headed. He is 11lb higher than for his only victory and the form of his third in the City And Suburban may not amount to a great deal. (op 11-2)

2094 JOURNEY SOUTH & ETON ROAD MEDIAN AUCTION MAIDEN STKS 6f
4:25 (4:25) (Class 5) 3-Y-O **£2,817** (£838; £418; £209) **Stalls** Centre

Form RPR
30-3 **1** **Bid For Gold**[35] 1197 3-9-3 70 .... PaulMulrennan 5 56
(Jedd O'Keeffe) *trckd ldrs: effrt over 2f out and sn rdn: swtchd rt and drvn to ld ins fnl f: kpt on u.p* **4/6**[1]
00 **2** 1¼ **Sharpattack**[19] 1587 3-9-3 ....(t) KerrinMcEvoy 6 52
(M Botti) *hld up in rr: swtchd lft and hdwy wl over 1f out: swtchd rt and rdn to chse wnr ins fnl f: kpt on* **14/1**
0-60 **3** *1* **Baybshambles (IRE)**[25] 1425 3-9-0 45 .... MarkLawson(3) 3 49
(R E Barr) *dwlt: hdwy 1/2-way: rdn to chal over 1f out and ev ch tl drvn and one pce ent fnl f* **40/1**
5606 **4** 1½ **Splendidio**[4] 1976 3-8-12 48 .... DO'Donohoe 4 39
(Mrs Marjorie Fife) *led: rdn along 2f out: drvn over 1f out: hdd & wknd ins fnl f* **33/1**
0004 **5** 1¾ **Seaton Snooks**[16] 1679 3-9-3 50 ....(b) DavidAllan 7 39
(T D Easterby) *chsd ldrs on outer: rdn along 2f out and sn one pce* **13/2**[3]
6 2½ **New Year (IRE)** 3-9-3 .... MickyFenton 2 31
(T P Tate) *chsd ldrs: rdn along over 2f out: sn wknd* **4/1**[2]
0203 **7** 5 **Rue Soleil**[14] 1709 3-8-12 58 .... JoeFanning 1 10
(J R Weymes) *prom: rdn along over 2f out and sn wknd* **10/1**

1m 14.43s (2.73) **Going Correction** +0.225s/f (Good) **7** Ran SP% **114.5**
Speed ratings (Par 99):90,88,87,85,82 79,72
CSF £12.35 TOTE £1.50: £1.50, £5.40; EX 9.70.
Owner Paul Chapman And Ba'Tat Investments **Bred** B Minty **Trained** Middleham Moor, N Yorks

FOCUS
A poor and uncompetitive maiden with three of the seven runners officially rated 50 or lower and the winning time was moderate, even for a contest like this. The winner was 20lb off his 2yo best but only 5lb below the form of his reappearance.

2095 TOTECOURSE TO COURSE H'CAP — 1m 6f 19y
5:00 (5:00) (Class 5) (0-75,72) 4-Y-0+ — £2,817 (£838; £418; £209) Stalls Low

Form — RPR

1444 **1** **Mister Arjay (USA)**[2] [2026] 7-9-2 **72** .... PJMcDonald(5) 4 — 80
(B Ellison) *mde all: sn clr: rdn along wl over 2f out: drvn over 1f out: kpt on strly ins fnl f* **9/2**

0-62 **2** *nk* **Karlani (IRE)**[2] [2026] 4-8-12 **63** .... KerrinMcEvoy 2 — 71
(G A Swinbank) *hld up in rr: niggled along over 5f out: rdn and hdwy 3f out: drvn to chse wnr and hung lft ent fnl f: styd on* **7/4**[1]

-246 **3** *4* **Let It Be**[13] [1745] 6-8-8 **59** .... DavidAllan 3 — 61
(K G Reveley) *chsd wnr: rdn along and sltly outpcd 3f out: drvn and kpt on fnl 2f* **11/4**[3]

0004 **4** *½* **Ahlawy (IRE)**[8] [1862] 4-9-7 **72** .... PaulMulrennan 5 — 74
(M W Easterby) *hld up in rr: hdwy 5f out: effrt 3f out: rdn to chse wnr 2f out: drvn and edgd lft over 1f out: sn btn* **5/2**[2]

60-0 **5** *17* **Loch Awe**[21] [1529] 4-8-2 **53** oh7 ....(p) PaulFessey 1 — 31
(R E Barr) *chsd ldng pair: rdn along 5f out: outpcd and bhd fnl 3f* **33/1**

3m 6.77s (1.75) **Going Correction** +0.225s/f (Good) — **5** Ran SP% **112.7**
Speed ratings (Par 103):104,103,101,101,91
CSF £13.18 TOTE £5.60: £2.90, £1.10; EX 14.80.
Owner Keith Middleton **Bred** Barbara Hunter **Trained** Norton, N Yorks

FOCUS
Only five runners for this staying handicap, but the pace was solid thanks to the winner. The form seems sound enough.

2096 "COME RACING AT REDCAR TOMORROW!" MAIDEN H'CAP — 1m 6f 19y
5:30 (5:31) (Class 6) (0-65,60) 3-Y-0 — £2,047 (£604; £302) Stalls Low

Form — RPR

0532 **1** **Color Man**[26] [1397] 3-8-11 **50** ....(p) JoeFanning 7 — 55
(Mrs A J Perrett) *mde all: qcknd 3f out: rdn 2f out: drvn ent fnl f and styd on strly* **4/1**[2]

0-05 **2** *1* **Monet's Lady (IRE)**[28] [1361] 3-8-6 **45** .... JimmyQuinn 3 — 49
(R A Fahey) *in tch: hdwy on inner 4f out: rdn along to chse ldrs 2f out: drvn and kpt on ins fnl f* **11/2**[3]

64-3 **3** *½* **Hatton Flight**[34] [1220] 3-9-7 **60** ....(p) FrancisNorton 1 — 63
(A M Balding) *hld up in midfield: hdwy 3f out: rdn along 2f out: sn drvn and kpt on same pce ins fnl f* **5/2**[1]

0064 **4** *shd* **Park's Prodigy**[34] [1224] 3-8-11 **50** ....(t) DeanMcKeown 10 — 53
(P C Haslam) *hld up in tch: hdwy on outer 3f out: rdn and ch 2f out: sn drvn and one pce ent fnl f* **7/1**

0-40 **5** *2½* **Kingsmead (USA)**[34] [1224] 3-9-2 **55** .... MickyFenton 14 — 55
(Miss J Feilden) *hld up in rr: hdwy over 3f out: rdn along and styd on appr fnl f: nrst fin* **16/1**

6-00 **6** *½* **Decent Proposal**[44] [1045] 3-8-11 **50** .... DavidAllan 13 — 49
(T D Easterby) *in tch: hdwy to chse ldrs over 4f out: rdn along wl over 2f out: drvn and wknd over 1f out* **11/1**

0-20 **7** *1* **Ingleby Hill (IRE)**[19] [1579] 3-8-13 **52** .... PaulFessey 12 — 50
(T D Barron) *hld up in rr: stdy hdwy on wd outside 3f out: rdn to chse ldrs 2f out: sn drvn and btn* **9/1**

00-0 **8** *½* **Abbotts Account (USA)**[21] [1536] 3-9-2 **55** .... JimCrowley 15 — 52
(Mrs A J Perrett) *prom: hdwy 3f out and ev ch tl rdn and wknd wl over 1f out* **10/1**

-043 **9** *1¾* **Devilfishpoker Com**[19] [1573] 3-9-2 **55** ....(p) DO'Donohoe 11 — 49
(R C Guest) *chsd ldrs: pushed along 1/2-way: sn lost pl and bhd fnl 3f* **20/1**

0-00 **10** *4* **Wingsinmotion (IRE)**[34] [1220] 3-8-6 **45** ....(p) SilvestreDeSousa 2 — 34
(Miss Tracy Waggott) *prom: rdn along over 4f out and sn wknd* **40/1**

006 **11** *hd* **Malguru**[26] [1412] 3-9-5 **58** .... KerrinMcEvoy 8 — 47
(G A Swinbank) *trckd wnr: hdwy to chal over 3f out and ev ch tl rdn 2f out and sn wknd* **13/2**

0-06 **12** *36* **Dee Valley Boy (IRE)**[34] [1224] 3-8-8 **47** ....(v) DavidKinsella 5 — —
(J D Bethell) *s.i.s: a in rr* **33/1**

3m 10.36s (5.34) **Going Correction** +0.225s/f (Good) — **12** Ran SP% **133.2**
Speed ratings (Par 97):93,92,92,92,90 90,89,89,88,86 86,65
CSF £29.62 CT £70.98 TOTE £5.40: £2.40, £2.70, £1.30; EX 32.80 Place 6 £211.78, Place 5 £48.91.
Owner Mrs S L Whitehead **Bred** Milton Park Stud Partnership **Trained** Pulborough, W Sussex
■ Stewards' Enquiry : Dean McKeown caution: careless riding

FOCUS
A poor race and a moderate winning time for the class, but as in the previous contest over the same trip another brave all-the-way winner. The fourth looks the best guide to the form.
Decent Proposal Official explanation: jockey said filly hung right-handed in home straight
T/Plt: £103.80 to a £1 stake. Pool: £59,637.55. 419.20 winning tickets. T/Qpdt: £38.20 to a £1 stake. Pool: £3,130.20. 60.60 winning tickets. JR

2097 - 2099a (Foreign Racing) - See Raceform Interactive

1878 LONGCHAMP (R-H)
Monday, May 28

OFFICIAL GOING: Heavy

2100a PRIX DU PALAIS-ROYAL (GROUP 3) — 7f
1:20 (1:26) 3-Y-0+ — £27,027 (£10,811; £8,108; £5,405; £2,703)

RPR

1 **Garnica (FR)**[220] [6093] 4-9-6 .... C-PLemaire 3 — 112
(J-C Rouget, France) *racd in 4th: rdn to ld 100yds out: r.o wl* **53/10**[3]

2 *1* **Ridaar (FR)**[25] 7-9-4 .... RonanThomas 4 — 107
(J-P Gallorini, France) *led: rdn wl over 1f out: hdd 100yds out: one pce* **42/10**[2]

3 *¾* **Donatello (GER)**[11] [1800] 6-9-4 .... DBoeuf 5 — 105
(W Baltromei, Germany) *hld up in 8th on ins: swtchd outside 2f out: 9th over 1 1/2f out: fin strly to take 3rd on line* **77/10**

4 *nse* **Sabasha (FR)**[29] [1337] 4-9-1 .... RMarchelli 9 — 102
(F Rohaut, France) *racd in 5th: rdn and hdwy over 1f out: tk 3rd cl home: lost 3rd on line* **36/1**

5 *1* **Bertranicus (FR)**[31] 4-9-4 .... TThulliez 10 — 102
(L Urbano-Grajales, France) *wnt 2nd after 1f: rdn 1 1/2f out: lost 2nd 1f out: wknd* **16/1**

6 *1½* **Princess Jones**[26] [1421] 7-9-1 .... FVeron 7 — 95
(J-L Guillochon, France) *hld up in last: rdn over 1 1/2f out: styd on at same pce* **45/1**

7 *snk* **Law Lord**[26] [1420] 3-8-7 .... JVictoire 1 — 98
(A Fabre, France) *racd keenly early in midfield on ins: 6th st: one pce fr over 1f out: lost 6th cl home* **12/1**

8 *1* **Prior Warning**[26] [1420] 3-8-7 .... SPasquier 8 — 95
(D Smaga, France) *hld up in 7th: hdwy over 2f out: wnt 4th 1 1/2f out: lost 4th 1f out: wknd* **36/10**[1]

9 *2* **Sabana Perdida (IRE)**[25] 4-9-1 .... CSoumillon 11 — 87
(A De Royer-Dupre, France) *hld up in 9th: effrt on outside over 2f out: btn over 1f out* **54/10**

10 *2½* **Makaan (USA)**[43] [1056] 3-8-9 .... DBonilla 2 — 85
(F Head, France) *racd in 3rd on ins: wknd 2f out* **58/10**

1m 25.6s (3.20)
WFA 3 from 4yo+ 11lb — **10** Ran SP% **117.1**
PARI-MUTUEL: WIN 6.30; PL 2.60, 1.70, 2.30; DF 16.20.
Owner E A Gann **Bred** Jean-Pierre Dubois **Trained** Pau, France

NOTEBOOK
Garnica(FR) put up an excellent performance considering that this was his seasonal debut and he was carrying top weight. Asked for his effort a furlong and a half out, he took command inside the final furlong and drew away from the others at the end. He will be back over this course and distance next month for the Prix de la Porte Maillot, before taking in the Prix Maurice de Gheest at Deauville.
Ridaar(FR), as usual tried to make all the running, and he was very brave until the bitter end. Shaken up two out, he put his head down and stuck to his guns but could not hold the winner inside the last 100 yards.
Donatello(GER) was given a lot to do. He was well behind entering the straight and then finished well up the centre of the track, but he was a bit late making his final challenge.
Sabasha(FR) made some late progress from the furlong pole but never really threatened the winner and runner-up. She failed by inches to hold third place.

2101 - (Foreign Racing) - See Raceform Interactive

MUNICH (L-H)
Monday, May 28

OFFICIAL GOING: Good

2102a GERMAN TOTE - BAVARIAN CLASSIC (GROUP 3) — 1m 2f
3:55 (4:05) 3-Y-0 — £21,622 (£6,757; £3,378; £2,027)

RPR

1 **Persian Storm (GER)**[11] 3-9-2 .... THellier 6 — 111
(J Hirschberger, Germany) *mde all: rdn and fnd ex whn pressed appr fnl f: rdn out* **11/2**

2 *3* **Davidoff (GER)**[22] [1516] 3-9-2 .... AStarke 4 — 106
(P Schiergen, Germany) *racd in 4th: hdwy on ins to go 2nd 2f out: no ex fnl f: wkng cl home* **22/10**[1]

3 *1½* **First Stream (GER)**[27] 3-9-2 .... ASuborics 1 — 103
(Mario Hofer, Germany) *s.s: hld up in 7th: rdn 2f out: wnt 3rd 100yds out: fin wl* **29/10**[3]

4 *4* **Sassoaloro (GER)** 3-9-2 .... JMurtagh 7 — 96
(A Wohler, Germany) *racd in 2nd: rdn wl over 2f out: sn outpcd* **24/10**[2]

5 *½* **Lord Hill (GER)**[27] [1387] 3-9-2 .... J-PCarvalho 3 — 95
(C Zeitz) *broke out of stalls wout rdr bef s: sn ct: hld up: 5th st: rdn and one pce fnl 2f* **92/10**

6 *¾* **Welttraumer (GER)**[27] 3-9-2 .... ADeVries 2 — 94
(A Trybuhl, Germany) *racd in 6th: one pce fr over 2f out* **11/1**

7 *9* **Wellinas (GER)** 3-9-2 ....(b) AdrianMcCarthy 8 — 78
(W Hefter, Germany) *cl up: 3rd st: sn rdn and wknd* **50/1**

8 *22* **Allanit (GER)**[27] [1387] 3-9-2 .... KJManning 5 — 38
(J Hirschberger, Germany) *last thrght: t.o fnl f* **66/10**

2m 13.6s (4.63) — **8** Ran SP% **134.9**
(including ten euro stakes): WIN 65; PL 21, 12, 14; SF 250.
Owner Baron G Von Ullmann **Bred** Dr Christoph Berglar **Trained** Germany

2077 CHEPSTOW (L-H)
Tuesday, May 29

OFFICIAL GOING: Good (6.9)
The ground had dried out overnight but the centre again appeared to be the place to be on the straight course.
Wind: Light across Weather: Sunny

2103 BETDIRECT.COM MAIDEN STKS — 5f 16y
2:30 (2:33) (Class 5) 2-Y-0 — £2,849 (£847; £423; £211) Stalls High

Form — RPR

1 **Gaspar Van Wittel (USA)** 2-9-3 0 .... DaneO'Neill 10 — 84+
(N A Callaghan) *s.i.s: outpcd: edgd lft over 2f out: hdwy whn swtchd rt wl over 1f out: str run to ld ins fnl f: edgd lft: r.o wl* **8/1**

3 **2** *2½* **Elna Bright**[13] [1762] 2-9-3 0 .... PatDobbs 8 — 70
(R Hannon) *a.p: hung lft over 2f out: rdn over 1f out: nt qckn ins fnl f* **11/4**[2]

3 *1¼* **Sandy Par** 2-9-3 0 .... MatthewHenry 7 — 66
(P Winkworth) *chsd ldrs: hmpd over 2f out: kpt on same pce fnl f* **25/1**

4 *1* **Casla Beag (IRE)** 2-8-12 0 .... FergusSweeney 14 — 57
(B Palling) *led: hung lft fr 2f out: hdd and no ex ins fnl f* **7/1**[3]

04 **5** *nk* **Lord Of The Wing**[18] [1631] 2-9-3 0 .... GeorgeBaker 3 — 61
(R M Beckett) *a.p: rdn and no hdwy fnl 2f* **16/1**

0 **6** *nk* **Gillans Inn**[8] [1882] 2-8-12 0 .... KevinGhunowa(5) 4 — 60
(J M Bradley) *bhd: swtchd rt and hdwy over 2f out: rdn over 1f out: one pce* **100/1**

0 **7** *2½* **Lady Vibeeka**[17] [1652] 2-8-12 0 .... SteveDrowne 9 — 46
(Mrs H Sweeting) *hld up in mid-div: hdwy 3f out: wknd ins fnl f* **40/1**

6 **8** *nk* **Happy Hacker (IRE)**[28] [1367] 2-8-12 0 .... StephenDonohoe 5 — 45
(P D Evans) *hung lft sn after s: swtchd rt over 3f out: rdn and sme hdwy over 2f out: wknd over 1f out* **16/1**

9 *2½* **Berties Goodenough** 2-9-3 0 .... HayleyTurner 6 — 41
(Andrew Turnell) *s.i.s: a bhd* **50/1**

0 **10** *1¼* **The Name Is Frank**[12] [1781] 2-9-3 0 .... RichardThomas 13 — 36
(J W Mullins) *chsd ldrs: rdn 3f out: sn wknd* **8/1**

2 **11** *shd* **Latin Class (USA)**[11] [1801] 2-8-12 0 .... J-PGuillambert 12 — 31
(M Johnston) *half-rrd s: sn prom: hung lft fr over 3f out: rdn and wknd over 1f out* **9/4**[1]

12 *5* **Bid Art (IRE)** 2-9-3 0 .... LPKeniry 2 — 18
(A M Balding) *s.s: outpcd* **14/1**

13 *5* **Aries Magic** 2-8-12 0 .... FrankieMcDonald 11 —
(S C Burrough) *s.s: outpcd* **100/1**

61.19 secs (1.59) **Going Correction** +0.175s/f (Good) **13** Ran SP% **120.8**
Speed ratings (Par 93):94,90,88,86,85 85,81,80,76,74 74,66,58
CSF £29.95 TOTE £8.80: £2.50, £1.70, £6.70; EX 25.60 Trifecta £282.40 Part won. Pool: £397.80 - 0.74 winning units..
Owner Matthew Green **Bred** Barronstown Stud **Trained** Newmarket, Suffolk

FOCUS

Nearly half the field were newcomers in this interesting if low-grade maiden. There should be better to come from Gaspar Van Wittel, who is rated a 4l winner.

NOTEBOOK

Gaspar Van Wittel(USA) ◆, a 120,000gns colt, had been working well at home and created a good impression on his debut despite showing plenty of signs of inexperience. He should have learnt a lot from this and is likely to go to Royal Ascot. (op 13-2 tchd 6-1)

Elna Bright, who did the third no favours at halfway, probably came up against an above-average sort for this type of race. (op 9-2 tchd 5-2)

Sandy Par ◆, a half-brother to a couple of debut juvenile winners, found the runner-up hanging into him at halfway. Normal improvement should see him take a similar event. (op 16-1 tchd 28-1)

Casla Beag(IRE), a springer in the market, showed plenty of speed but drifted over from the centre to the far rail. She would probably have finished second or third had she kept straight but would not have beaten the winner. Official explanation: jockey said filly hung left-handed (op 12-1)

Lord Of The Wing seems to be progressing along the right lines for one whose breeding suggests he wants further. (op 11-1)

Gillans Inn ran better than he had done on his debut at Bath last week. (op 66-1)

The Name Is Frank Official explanation: jockey said colt was unsuited by the track

Latin Class(USA) played up leaving the stalls and then let her supporters down by persistently hanging. (op 2-1 tchd 5-2)

2104 BETDIRECT.COM GET INVOLVED CLAIMING STKS 5f 16y

3:00 (3:02) (Class 6) 3-Y-0+ **£1,943** (£578; £288; £144) **Stalls** High

Form RPR

-600 **1** **Seven No Trumps**[15] 1729 10-8-13 45 .... SteveDrowne 1 53
(J M Bradley) *a.p: rdn wl over 1f out: led wl ins fnl f: r.o* **9/1**

6000 **2** *¾* **Trinculo (IRE)**[4] 1991 10-9-8 60 .... (b) LukeMorris(5) 5 64
(R A Harris) *a.p: rdn over 1f out: kpt on ins fnl f* **17/2**

0-40 **3** *nk* **Luloah**[124] 239 4-8-6 42 .... FergusSweeney 2 42
(J G M O'Shea) *led: rdn over 1f out: hdd wl ins fnl f: kpt on* **20/1**

040 **4** *nk* **Savile's Delight (IRE)**[21] 1569 8-8-11 48 .... (v) J-PGuillambert 8 46
(Miss Joanne Priest) *towards rr: rdn and hdwy over 1f out: r.o ins fnl f* **5/1**[2]

4000 **5** *hd* **Saintly Place**[22] 6-9-3 40 .... FrancisNorton 6 51
(A W Carroll) *a.p: rdn over 1f out: nt qckn ins fnl f* **33/1**

2250 **6** *½* **Pat Will (IRE)**[8] 1899 3-8-2 55 .... CatherineGannon 11 42
(P D Evans) *chsd ldrs: rdn over 2f out: one pce fnl f* **16/1**

4003 **7** *½* **Ruby's Dream**[15] 1729 5-8-7 48 .... (p) KevinGhunowa(5) 9 43
(J M Bradley) *chsd ldrs: rdn over 1f out: one pce* **6/1**[3]

05-0 **8** *¾* **Mynd**[43] 1065 7-8-13 55 .... JamieMackay 3 41
(B Palling) *chsd ldrs: rdn and no hdwy fnl f* **7/1**

00-0 **9** *hd* **Zimbali**[40] 1112 5-8-0 45 ow1 .... KirstyMilczarek(7) 17 34
(J M Bradley) *towards rr: sme hdwy over 1f out: no further prog fnl f* **25/1**

30-2 **10** *¾* **Princely Vale (IRE)**[8] 1899 5-8-10 48 .... (p) JackDean(7) 7 41
(W G M Turner) *outpcd: nvr nr ldrs* **9/2**[1]

54-0 **11** *1* **Campeon (IRE)**[121] 287 5-8-11 45 .... StephenDonohoe 12 32
(J M Bradley) *mid-div: rdn 3f out: no hdwy fnl 2f* **10/1**

0000 **12** *nk* **Globe**[66] 751 4-8-8 41 .... HayleyTurner 15 28
(Mrs H Sweeting) *bmpd s: nvr nr ldrs* **66/1**

4005 **13** *hd* **Princess Kai (IRE)**[50] 978 6-8-6 40 .... RichardThomas 4 25
(R Ingram) *a towards rr* **33/1**

0-06 **14** *1¾* **Georges Pride**[28] 1373 3-8-7 50 .... (b[1]) LPKeniry 14 28
(J M Bradley) *hmpd s: a bhd* **50/1**

650- **15** *hd* **First Among Equals**[189] 6548 4-8-2 39 ow1 .... RoryMoore(5) 13 19
(D G Bridgwater) *wnt rt s: a bhd* **50/1**

0005 **16** *6* **Mind That Fox**[38] 1163 5-8-4 41 .... JosephWalsh(7) 10 1
(T Wall) *s.i.s: hld up: sme hdwy over 3f out: rdn and wknd over 1f out* **80/1**

2600 **17** *7* **Hornpipe**[67] 746 5-9-7 54 .... (v) AdrianMcCarthy 16 —
(M S Saunders) *hmpd s: a bhd* **14/1**

61.02 secs (1.42) **Going Correction** +0.175s/f (Good)
WFA 3 from 4yo+ 8lb **17** Ran SP% **124.9**
Speed ratings (Par 101):95,93,93,92,92 91,90,89,89,88 86,86,85,83,82 73,61
CSF £79.43 TOTE £14.50: £4.60, £3.90, £5.70; EX 191.70 TRIFECTA Not won..
Owner J M Bradley **Bred** Yeomanstown Stud **Trained** Sedbury, Gloucs

FOCUS

A poor claimer full of infrequent winners. It has been rated at face value and the form does not look that sound.

Princely Vale(IRE) Official explanation: jockey said gelding was slowly into stride

Hornpipe Official explanation: jockey said gelding stumbled leaving stalls

2105 BETDIRECTPOKER.COM H'CAP 1m 4f 23y

3:35 (3:35) (Class 6) (0-60,60) 3-Y-0 **£2,266** (£674; £337; £168) **Stalls** Low

Form RPR

0-51 **1** **Jafaru**[18] 1624 3-9-1 56 .... (b) FrancisNorton 15 70+
(G A Butler) *t.k.h: sn mid-div: hdwy over 6f out: led on bit over 3f out: pushed out ins fnl f* **7/2**[2]

00-1 **2** *¾* **Credit Slip**[29] 1361 3-9-2 57 .... IanMongan 11 65
(J L Dunlop) *hld up in mid-div: hdwy 4f out: rdn whn hung lft wl over 1f out: hung lft ins fnl f: nt qckn* **3/1**[1]

4036 **3** *1½* **Raquel White**[31] 1310 3-8-9 55 .... KevinGhunowa(5) 7 61
(J L Flint) *plld hrd in mid-div: hdwy 4f out: rdn over 2f out: one pce fnl f* **33/1**

6-00 **4** *7* **Anthea**[15] 1731 3-9-4 59 .... AdrianMcCarthy 2 54
(B R Millman) *prom: rdn over 4f out: wknd 3f out* **16/1**

0-00 **5** *nk* **Kanonkop**[45] 1039 3-8-10 51 .... FrankieMcDonald 6 45
(Miss J R Gibney) *hld up and bhd: rdn and hdwy over on ins over 2f out: nvr nr ldrs* **28/1**

60-0 **6** *½* **Lady Traill**[29] 1364 3-8-11 52 .... SamHitchcott 13 46
(B W Hills) *hld up and bhd: rdn and hdwy over 3f out: wknd 2f out* **14/1**

1542 **7** *shd* **King Of The Beers (USA)**[29] 1353 3-9-0 60 .... (p) TolleyDean(5) 10 53
(R A Harris) *hld up towards rr: rdn and hdwy over 3f out: no further prog fnl 2f* **8/1**

2330 **8** *1½* **Citrus Chief (USA)**[29] 1361 3-8-8 54 .... (b) LukeMorris(5) 4 45
(R A Harris) *nvr nr ldrs* **14/1**

5603 **9** *4* **Intensifier (IRE)**[29] 1353 3-8-13 54 .... (b) SimonWhitworth 17 39
(P A Blockley) *led over 1f: chsd ldr: led 4f out: sn hdd: rdn and wknd over 2f out* **25/1**

0-00 **10** *6* **Muffett's Dream**[12] 1785 3-8-13 54 .... PatDobbs 1 29
(J A Geake) *t.k.h: sn mid-div: lost pl over 3f out* **50/1**

0-00 **11** *2½* **Queens Quay**[12] 1784 3-9-4 59 .... DaneO'Neill 16 30
(R Hannon) *prom: rdn over 4f out: wknd over 3f out:* **10/1**

000 **12** *4* **Quite A Splash (USA)**[21] 1560 3-8-10 58 .... WilliamCarson(7) 5 23
(S Curran) *prom: rdn 3f out: sn wknd* **16/1**

50-0 **13** *3½* **Kings Art (IRE)**[27] 1410 3-9-5 60 .... (t) StephenDonohoe 8 19
(W M Brisbourne) *plld hrd: a in rr* **33/1**

05-5 **14** *6* **Francesco**[35] 1224 3-9-1 56 .... SteveDrowne 12 5
(M L W Bell) *a bhd* **11/2**[3]

560- **15** *76* **Hocinail (FR)**[270] 4980 3-9-0 55 .... MatthewHenry 9 —
(P Winkworth) *t.k.h: led over 11f out tl over 4f out: wknd qckly over 3f out: t.o* **50/1**

2m 43.39s (4.67) **Going Correction** +0.425s/f (Yiel) **15** Ran SP% **125.0**
Speed ratings (Par 97):101,100,99,94,94 94,94,93,90,86 84,82,79,75,25
CSF £13.93 CT £308.67 TOTE £4.40: £2.10, £1.80, £10.40; EX 15.00 Trifecta £170.10 Pool: £354.58 - 1.48 winning units..
Owner C McFadden **Bred** Nawara Stud Co Ltd **Trained** Blewbury, Oxon

FOCUS

A modest handicap. The first two were a couple who have improved since being stepped up in distance, albeit at a low level. The form looks sound enough.

Francesco Official explanation: jockey said gelding never travelled

Hocinail(FR) Official explanation: jockey said gelding ran too free

2106 LETHEBY & CHRISTOPHER H'CAP 1m 2f 36y

4:10 (4:11) (Class 5) (0-75,74) 4-Y-0+ **£3,886** (£1,156; £577; £288) **Stalls** Low

Form RPR

0-62 **1** **Uig**[6] 1951 6-8-5 61 ow1 .... SimonWhitworth 2 68
(H S Howe) *plld hrd: chsd ldr: rdn over 2f out: sustained chal to ld fnl strides* **12/1**

50-1 **2** *shd* **Nightspot**[11] 1811 6-9-3 73 .... SteveDrowne 8 80
(Eve Johnson Houghton) *led: rdn wl over 1f out: hdd fnl strides* **5/1**[2]

3332 **3** *3½* **Generous Lad (IRE)**[31] 1295 4-8-13 69 .... (p) DaneO'Neill 3 69
(A B Haynes) *hld up in tch: rdn and one pce fnl 2f* **8/1**

5211 **4** *2½* **Penang Cinta**[7] 1924 4-9-1 71 6ex .... StephenDonohoe 6 66
(P D Evans) *hld up in mid-div: rdn over 2f out: hdwy over 1f out: one pce fnl f* **7/4**[1]

-024 **5** *1* **Mae Cigan (FR)**[13] 1761 4-8-11 67 .... FrancisNorton 5 60
(M Blanshard) *hld up towards rr: hdwy on ins 4f out: no imp fnl 2f* **5/1**[2]

0230 **6** *1½* **First Friend (IRE)**[13] 1761 6-8-6 62 .... AdrianMcCarthy 9 52
(M Hill) *plld hrd: prom: rdn over 1f out: fdd fnl f* **25/1**

7 *1½* **Oldrik (GER)**[24] 4-8-8 64 .... JamieMackay 7 51
(P J Hobbs) *s.s: hld up: hdwy on outside 3f out: sn rdn: wknd over 1f out* **7/1**[3]

5310 **8** *½* **Jackie Kiely**[7] 1922 6-8-13 74 .... (t) TolleyDean(5) 4 60
(R Brotherton) *hld up in mid-div: hrd rdn over 3f out: wknd over 2f out* **25/1**

2214 **9** *1* **Can Can Star**[7] 1922 4-8-9 72 .... MarkCoumbe(7) 10 56+
(A W Carroll) *hld up and bhd: sddle slipped after 3f: n.d* **12/1**

06-0 **10** *shd* **Merchant Bankes**[8] 1886 4-8-6 62 .... MatthewHenry 1 46
(W G M Turner) *a bhd* **66/1**

2m 14.61s (4.71) **Going Correction** +0.425s/f (Yiel) **10** Ran SP% **117.9**
Speed ratings (Par 103):98,97,95,93,92 91,89,89,88,88
CSF £70.65 CT £519.48 TOTE £14.20: £3.50, £2.00, £2.70; EX 77.20 Trifecta £483.80 Part won. Pool: £681.46 - 0.68 winning units..
Owner B P Jones **Bred** Mrs Gillian A R Jones And John Balding **Trained** Oakford, Devon

FOCUS

A modest handicap in which the favourite was not at his best. The winner and second are returning to something like their best form of two seasons ago.

First Friend(IRE) Official explanation: vet said horse had a breathing problem

Can Can Star Official explanation: jockey said saddle slipped

2107 LETHEBY & CHRISTOPHER AT CHEPSTOW RACECOURSE H'CAP 1m 14y

4:40 (4:42) (Class 5) (0-70,70) 4-Y-0+ **£2,914** (£867; £433; £216) **Stalls** High

Form RPR

-500 **1** **The Gaikwar (IRE)**[30] 1318 8-8-5 62 .... (b) LukeMorris(5) 14 73
(R A Harris) *hld up and bhd: rdn and hdwy over 1f out: led ins fnl f: rdn out* **20/1**

-434 **2** *2½* **Merrymadcap (IRE)**[13] 1765 5-9-4 70 .... FrancisNorton 13 76
(M Blanshard) *hld up and bhd: hdwy over 1f out: rdn and kpt on ins fnl f* **8/1**[3]

-003 **3** *2* **Full Victory (IRE)**[13] 1765 5-9-4 70 .... DaneO'Neill 4 71
(R A Farrant) *hld up in mid-div: hdwy 3f out: rdn to ld over 1f out: hdd ins fnl f: no ex* **2/1**[1]

-516 **4** *hd* **Indian Edge**[13] 1765 6-9-2 68 .... FergusSweeney 9 69
(B Palling) *led: rdn over 2f out: hdd over 1f out: no ex ins fnl f* **7/1**[2]

-504 **5** *¾* **Bold Cross (IRE)**[8] 1886 4-8-8 60 .... PaulFitzsimons 8 59
(E G Bevan) *t.k.h: a.p: rdn and ev ch over 1f out: no ex ins fnl f* **20/1**

0210 **6** *½* **Seneschal**[8] 1886 6-9-0 66 .... SamHitchcott 16 64
(A B Haynes) *hld up: hdwy over 3f out: rdn 2f out: wknd ins fnl f* **14/1**

0000 **7** *shd* **Lockstock (IRE)**[21] 1562 9-8-4 56 oh4 .... (p) AdrianMcCarthy 3 53
(M S Saunders) *s.i.s: hdwy 5f out: wknd ins fnl f* **33/1**

500/ **8** *nk* **Kenwyn**[13] 3912 5-8-6 58 .... SimonWhitworth 5 55
(K Bishop) *nvr nrr* **50/1**

0600 **9** *hd* **Lizarazu (GER)**[8] 1886 8-8-5 62 .... (p) TolleyDean(5) 11 58
(R A Harris) *t.k.h: prom: rdn over 1f out: wknd ins fnl f* **25/1**

150- **10** *nk* **Red Rudy**[187] 6568 5-9-1 67 .... SteveDrowne 10 63
(A W Carroll) *hld up and bhd: hdwy 3f out: rdn 2f out: wknd ins fnl f* **14/1**

6351 **11** *1¼* **Convince (USA)**[7] 1921 6-8-7 64 6ex .... (p) KevinGhunowa(5) 15 57
(J M Bradley) *stdd s: rdn and hdwy over 2f out: wknd ins fnl f* **10/1**

-020 **12** *½* **Azreme**[13] 1761 7-8-11 63 .... J-PGuillambert 12 55
(P Howling) *hld up in mid-div: rdn 2f out: wknd fnl f* **8/1**[3]

0-00 **13** *5* **Gracechurch (IRE)**[13] 1765 4-9-1 67 .... GeorgeBaker 1 47
(R J Hodges) *a bhd* **12/1**

40-6 **14** *4* **High Class Problem (IRE)**[18] 1629 4-9-0 66 .... EdwardCreighton 2 37
(P F I Cole) *prom: rdn 3f out: wknd over 2f out* **14/1**

1m 37.04s (1.04) **Going Correction** +0.175s/f (Good) **14** Ran SP% **123.1**
Speed ratings (Par 103):101,98,96,96,95 95,94,94,94,94 92,92,87,83
CSF £167.48 CT £485.01 TOTE £26.30: £5.30, £2.40, £1.60; EX 266.70 TRIFECTA Not won..
Owner Leeway Group Limited **Bred** Burton Agnes Stud Co Ltd **Trained** Earlswood, Monmouths

FOCUS

A moderate handicap but the form looks sound. The winner is rated to the form of his course-and-distance win last July.

2108 BETFAIR APPRENTICE TRAINING SERIES H'CAP 6f 16y
5:10 (5:12) (Class 6) (0-65,68) 3-Y-0+ £2,072 (£616; £308; £153) Stalls High

Form RPR

0011 1 **Stamford Blue**[5] 1969 6-10-1 68 6ex..............................(b) JackDean(5) 17 81+
(R A Harris) *hld up and bhd: smooth hdwy over 3f out: led on bit wl over 1f out: rdn out* **4/1**[2]

-043 2 1 ¾ **Moon Forest (IRE)**[21] 1564 5-9-2 55..........................(p) BarrySavage(5) 6 60+
(J M Bradley) *hld up in mid-div: hdwy over 3f out: rdn over 1f out: chsd wnr fnl f: kpt on same pce* **5/1**[3]

20-0 3 2 ½ **Double Valentine**[139] 86 4-9-2 50.................................. JackMitchell 3 47
(R Ingram) *hld up in mid-div: rdn and swtchd rt wl over 2f out: hdwy 1f out: kpt on ins fnl f* **22/1**

4010 4 1 **Rainbow Bay**[6] 1946 4-9-10 58..............................(v) SCreighton 10 52
(P D Evans) *wnt lft s: led: rdn over 2f out: hdd wl over 1f out: wknd wl ins fnl f* **8/1**

000/ 5 1 ¼ **Sydneyroughdiamond**[533] 6555 5-9-0 48 oh3............ KirstyMilczarek 7 38
(M Mullineaux) *chsd ldrs: rdn over 2f out: no hdwy* **66/1**

0-00 6 hd **Enjoy The Buzz**[27] 1405 8-8-12 49... KMay(3) 5 38
(J M Bradley) *towards rr: swtchd lft and hdwy over 1f out: one pce fnl f* **33/1**

5206 7 1 **Prettilini**[8] 1902 4-8-9 48... MarkCoumbe(5) 14 34
(A W Carroll) *prom: rdn 3f out: wknd fnl f* **16/1**

-000 8 1 ¼ **Goodwood Spirit**[23] 1507 5-9-8 59.................................. AlanRutter(3) 12 41
(J M Bradley) *hld up and bhd: rdn and hdwy 2f out: no further prog fnl f* **8/1**

0-00 9 2 ½ **Mannello**[27] 1404 4-9-1 52.. WilliamCarson(3) 1 26
(B Palling) *prom: rdn 3f out: wknd over 1f out* **14/1**

5623 10 2 ½ **Mister Incredible**[14] 1753 4-8-9 48 oh1.......................(v) PietroRomeo(5) 4 14
(J M Bradley) *t.k.h: w ldr tl rdn and wknd over 2f out* **7/1**

0-00 11 2 **King Of Tricks**[7] 1932 3-8-7 55.................................. LauraReynolds(5) 2 15
(M D I Usher) *a towards rr* **33/1**

0-00 12 nk **Wee Ziggy**[28] 1381 4-8-9 48 oh3..............................(be[1]) SoniaEaton(5) 13 7
(M Mullineaux) *outpcd* **100/1**

0-00 13 5 **Pachello (IRE)**[25] 1459 5-9-9 57................................. JamieHamblett 11 —
(J M Bradley) *s.i.s: sn chsng ldrs: rdn over 2f out: eased whn btn over 1f out* **25/1**

-033 14 ¾ **Memphis Man**[19] 1597 4-9-2 55.................................. PatrickDonaghy(5) 8 —
(W M Brisbourne) *s.i.s: rdn over 3f out: a bhd* **7/2**[1]

1m 12.9s (0.50) **Going Correction** +0.175s/f (Good)
WFA 3 from 4yo+ 9lb **14 Ran SP% 122.7**
Speed ratings (Par 101):103,100,97,96,94 94,92,91,87,84 81,81,74,73
CSF £23.38 CT £415.91 TOTE £4.40: £1.90, £2.30, £5.50; EX 21.40 Trifecta £234.10 Part won. Pool: £329.74 - 0.69 winning units. Place 6 £ 265.53, Place 5 £ 106.40.
Owner Brian Hicks **Bred** Mrs Wendy Miller **Trained** Earlswood, Monmouths

FOCUS
A moderate handicap, but a career best from Stamford Blue who was effetively 6lb wrong and who could win again off his proper mark. The race has been rated through the second and fifth.
Memphis Man Official explanation: jockey said gelding ran flat
T/Jkpt: Not won. T/Plt: £400.30 to a £1 stake. Pool: £64,003.00. 116.70 winning tickets. T/Qpdt: £23.20 to a £1 stake. Pool: £3,878.60. 123.30 winning tickets. KH

2083 LEICESTER (R-H)
Tuesday, May 29

OFFICIAL GOING: Soft (heavy in places, 5.6)
Wind: Light across Weather: Cloudy with sunny spells

2109 EBF LADBROKES.COM MAIDEN FILLIES' STKS 5f 2y
2:20 (2:20) (Class 4) 2-Y-0 £5,047 (£1,510; £755; £377; £188) Stalls Low

Form RPR

2 1 **Just A Dancer (IRE)**[48] 999 2-9-0 0................................ MichaelHills 6 76+
(B W Hills) *trckd ldrs: racd keenly: rdn to ld and hung lft over 1f out: r.o* **8/13**[1]

2 3 **Drastic Measure** 2-9-0 0.. SebSanders 1 65+
(Sir Mark Prescott) *s.i.s: hld up: hdwy 2f out: rdn and ev ch over 1f out: hung rt and no ex ins fnl f* **5/2**[2]

3 1 ¼ **Romantic Destiny** 2-9-0 0... RichardHughes 9 61
(K A Ryan) *s.i.s: sn chsng ldrs: rdn 1/2-way: no ex fnl f* **10/1**[3]

0 4 2 ½ **Ponder Anew (IRE)**[29] 1354 2-9-0 0.................................. EddieAhern 3 52
(K R Burke) *chsd ldrs: rdn 1/2-way: wknd fnl f* **28/1**

0 5 nk **Rubytwosox (IRE)**[25] 1445 2-9-0 0.............................. RichardMullen 5 51
(W R Muir) *sn pushed along in rr: hdwy 1/2-way: wknd over 1f out* **50/1**

F 6 3 **Emma's Secrets**[22] 1528 2-8-11 0................................... NeilChalmers(3) 8 40
(Miss M E Rowland) *led: rdn and hdd over 1f out: sn wknd* **20/1**

63.39 secs (2.49) **Going Correction** +0.475s/f (Yiel) **6 Ran SP% 109.8**
Speed ratings (Par 92):99,94,92,88,87 82
CSF £2.16 TOTE £1.50: £1.10, £1.80; EX 2.30.
Owner John C Grant **Bred** Shefford Valley Stud **Trained** Lambourn, Berks

FOCUS
A fair fillies' juvenile maiden. The winner looks capable of rating higher.

NOTEBOOK
Just A Dancer(IRE) had no trouble with this different surface and showed a good attitude to put the race to bed nearing the final furlong. Indeed, she looked better the further she went, will no doubt come on again for the experience, and ought to get another furlong before the season's end. A step up in class now looks in order for this daughter of Choisir, although according to her connections it is unlikely to be in the Queen Mary next month as they already house a live chance for that with the unbeaten Janina. (op 4-6 tchd 4-7)
Drastic Measure, related to winners over further, was popular in the betting ahead of this racecourse bow. She momentarily looked like causing the winner trouble when making her challenge against the stands' rail passing the 2f pole, but ran green when the gun was put to her head and ultimately lacked the turn of foot to match that rival. She is entitled to come on for the experience and was a clear second best. A quicker surface may also prove more to her liking. (op 7-2)
Romantic Destiny, a half-sister to Queen Mary winners Romantic Myth and Romantic Liason, proved very easy to back for this first visit to the racecourse and ultimately ran too green to do herself full justice. She was not given a hard time when her chance became apparent and can be expected to be a lot sharper with this run under her belt. (op 13-2)
Ponder Anew(IRE) showed the benefit of her Windsor debut a month ago and displayed much more early dash this time. She was put in her place when the race became serious, but this was still a definite step in the right direction. (tchd 25-1)
Rubytwosox(IRE), as on her Lingfield debut earlier this month, was being ridden from an early stage and never really figured. She has scope, however, and looks the type to find her feet as she gains further experience. (op 40-1)

2110 LADBROKES.COM CLAIMING STKS 7f 9y
2:50 (2:50) (Class 5) 3-Y-0 £3,238 (£963; £481; £240) Stalls Centre

Form RPR

1226 1 **Mick Is Back**[8] 1903 3-8-10 64...(p) EddieAhern 10 62
(J R Boyle) *chsd ldrs: rdn to ld over 1f out: hung lft ins fnl f: styd on* **5/2**[1]

5-50 2 nk **Rebel Pearl (IRE)**[38] 1155 3-8-2 55................................ DominicFox(3) 1 56
(M G Quinlan) *chsd ldrs: led over 2f out: rdn and hdd over 1f out: hung rt ins fnl f: kpt on* **10/1**

5035 3 2 ½ **Tenterhooks (IRE)**[7] 1912 3-8-1 43 ow3..............(be) PatrickMathers(3) 2 48
(A J McCabe) *led over 4f: rdn over 1f out: styng on same pce whn n.m.r ins fnl f* **28/1**

5653 4 2 **Birdie Birdie**[14] 1750 3-7-13 49....................................(v) NickyMackay 13 38
(R A Fahey) *hld up: hdwy over 1f out: sn hung lft: nt trble ldrs* **9/2**[2]

4056 5 6 **Storm Mission (USA)**[22] 1538 3-8-11 48.................... ColinHaddon(5) 7 38
(Miss V Haigh) *hld up: nt clr run over 2f out: hdwy and n.m.r over 1f out: sn hung rt: n.d* **28/1**

5-05 6 5 **Road To Recovery**[22] 1541 3-9-4 59.........................(v) RichardHughes 9 27
(A M Balding) *prom: rdn over 2f out: sn wknd* **11/2**

3006 7 1 ¾ **Cherri Fosfate**[17] 1672 3-9-4 70..............................(b) DarryllHolland 3 22
(D Carroll) *s.i.s: hdwy 5f out: sn rdn swtchd rt over 2f out: sn wknd* **5/1**[3]

6266 8 3 **Homecroft Boy**[27] 1397 3-8-10 42.........................(v[1]) GrahamGibbons 14 6
(P D Evans) *hld up: rdn 1/2-way: a in rr* **14/1**

00-0 9 shd **Katie Kingfisher**[22] 1538 3-8-9 47................................ JamesDoyle 5 5
(R M Beckett) *mid-div: rdn 1/2-way: sn wknd* **25/1**

2600 10 hd **Flushed**[33] 1266 3-8-1 47..(be) AndrewElliott(3) 11 —
(A J McCabe) *rrd s: hdwy over 5f out: wknd 2f out* **25/1**

04-0 11 2 **Grand Officer (IRE)**[27] 1397 3-7-13 40............................ BillyCray(7) 6 —
(D J S Ffrench Davis) *sn outpcd* **66/1**

0-00 12 1 ¾ **Espejo (IRE)**[17] 1684 3-9-4 66....................................... RichardMullen 16 3
(K R Burke) *hld up: rdn over 4f out: a in rr* **16/1**

020- 13 1 **Our Toy Soldier**[323] 3351 3-9-0 64.................................. PaulEddery 8 —
(B Smart) *hld up: rdn 1/2-way: sn wknd* **25/1**

1m 29.64s (3.54) **Going Correction** +0.475s/f (Yiel) **13 Ran SP% 120.4**
Speed ratings (Par 99):98,97,94,92,85 79,77,74,74,74 71,69,68
CSF £26.77 TOTE £3.40: £1.80, £2.20, £9.30; EX 43.90.
Owner M Khan X2 **Bred** J E Abbey **Trained** Epsom, Surrey

FOCUS
A moderate three-year-old claimer. The first pair came clear and the third seem to limit the form.
Flushed Official explanation: jockey said gelding reared in stalls

2111 LADBROKES.COM ABBEY PARK CONDITIONS STKS 7f 9y
3:20 (3:20) (Class 4) 3-Y-0+ £6,232 (£1,866; £933) Stalls Centre

Form RPR

-130 1 **Eisteddfod**[17] 1651 6-9-9 104... EddieAhern 3 105
(P F I Cole) *trckd ldr: rdn over 2f out: styd on to ld wl ins fnl f* **7/2**[2]

-153 2 nk **Levera**[15] 1723 4-9-7 107.. RichardHughes 2 102
(A King) *led: shkn up over 1f out: edgd rt and hdd wl ins fnl f* **2/5**[1]

5502 3 ¾ **Fajr (IRE)**[11] 1818 5-9-4 90.. DarryllHolland 1 99+
(Miss Gay Kelleway) *trckd ldrs: pushed along over 2f out: nt clr run fr over 1f out: hmpd ins fnl f: swtchd rt: nvr able to chal* **7/1**[3]

1m 27.97s (1.87) **Going Correction** +0.475s/f (Yiel) **3 Ran SP% 106.2**
Speed ratings (Par 105):108,107,106
CSF £5.52 TOTE £3.80; EX 5.00.
Owner Elite Racing Club **Bred** Elite Racing Club **Trained** Whatcombe, Oxon

FOCUS
An interesting little conditions event, run at a solid pace. The form should be treated with a little caution, with the first two 7lb+ off their best.

2112 LADBROKESCASINO.COM H'CAP 1m 3f 183y
3:55 (3:55) (Class 5) (0-75,75) 3-Y-0 £3,886 (£1,156; £577; £288) Stalls High

Form RPR

60-1 1 **Intiquilla (IRE)**[23] 1505 3-9-3 74.................................... JimCrowley 2 79+
(Mrs A J Perrett) *chsd ldrs: outpcd over 3f out: rallied over 2f out: rdn to ld and edgd lft over 1f out: styd on wl* **14/1**

-056 2 2 ½ **Delta Shuttle (IRE)**[15] 1708 3-8-1 61 oh3.................. AndrewElliott(3) 1 62
(K R Burke) *hld up in tch: outpcd over 4f out: rallied over 1f out: styd on* **33/1**

50 3 nk **Kasban**[21] 1560 3-9-2 73... DO'Donohoe 5 74
(E A L Dunlop) *sn pushed along in rr: hdwy u.p over 3f out: chsd wnr and edgd lft over 1f out: styd on same pce ins fnl f* **16/1**

4-1 4 3 ½ **Market Forces**[20] 1573 3-9-4 75............................. RichardHughes 10 70
(H R A Cecil) *led: rdn over 2f out: hdd over 1f out: hung lft and wknd ins fnl f* **10/11**[1]

4-35 5 1 ½ **Irish Dancer**[22] 1536 3-8-10 67.. EddieAhern 7 60
(J L Dunlop) *chsd ldr: rdn and ev ch over 2f out: wknd over 1f out* **8/1**[3]

5-41 6 28 **Arctic Wings (IRE)**[15] 1724 3-9-2 73............................. RichardMullen 6 21
(W R Muir) *prom: rdn over 3f out: wknd over 2f out: t.o* **9/4**[2]

44-0 7 31 **Astral Charmer**[15] 1724 3-8-8 65.................................(b[1]) MichaelHills 3 —
(M H Tompkins) *dwlt: outpcd: t.o* **40/1**

2m 41.32s (6.82) **Going Correction** +0.475s/f (Yiel) **7 Ran SP% 112.2**
Speed ratings (Par 99):96,94,94,91,90 72,51
CSF £313.90 CT £7196.97 TOTE £9.00: £2.90, £20.60; EX 288.20.
Owner Lady Clague **Bred** Newberry Stud Farm Ltd **Trained** Pulborough, W Sussex

FOCUS
A fair three-year-old handicap, run at a sound enough pace. The field came stands' side in the home straight and the first three all came from the rear. The race has been rated through the runner-up.
Arctic Wings(IRE) Official explanation: trainer said colt was unsuited by the soft (heavy in places) ground

2113 LADBROKES.COM FOREST H'CAP 1m 1f 218y
4:30 (4:30) (Class 5) (0-70,69) 4-Y-0+ £3,886 (£1,156; £577; £288) Stalls High

Form RPR

5031 1 **Street Life (IRE)**[11] 1819 9-9-2 67................................. DavidKinsella 3 76
(W J Musson) *hld up in tch: rdn over 2f out: led ins fnl f: styd on* **11/4**[2]

4532 2 1 ¼ **Augustine**[3] 2027 6-8-13 67..................................... SaleemGolam(3) 1 74
(P W Hiatt) *trckd ldr: racd keenly: rdn over 2f out: styd on* **11/8**[1]

1142 3 ¾ **Sawwaah (IRE)**[21] 1559 10-8-9 65.............................(v) TravisBlock(5) 6 70
(Tom Dascombe) *s.i.s: hld up: hdwy over 2f out: led over 1f out: edgd lft: hdd and no ex ins fnl f* **13/2**

52-0 4 shd **Dan Buoy (FR)**[25] 1446 4-9-4 69................................ RobertHavlin 5 74
(A King) *led: rdn and hdd over 1f out: n.m.r sn after: styd on same pce* **9/2**[3]

00-0 5 27 **Zirkel (IRE)**[20] 1591 4-9-3 68..................................... DO'Donohoe 10 19
(Mrs A L M King) *chsd ldrs over 7f: t.o* **14/1**

022- 6 20 **Vehari**[365] [2066] 4-9-0 **68**.............................. PatrickMathers(3) 2 —
(G F Bridgwater) *hld up: plld hrd: bhd fr 1/2-way: t.o* **22/1**

2m 15.49s (7.19) **Going Correction** +0.475s/f (Yiel) **6** Ran SP% **111.3**
Speed ratings (Par 103):90,89,88,88,66 50
CSF £6.81 CT £19.05 TOTE £3.80: £2.20, £1.10; EX 8.50.
Owner W J Musson **Bred** Derek Veitch **Trained** Newmarket, Suffolk

FOCUS
A modest handicap. It produced a moderate winning time, due to the lack of early pace. The winner will still be on a fair mark based on his old forn, and the runner-up ran to his latest mark.

2114 LADBROKES.COM H'CAP 5f 218y
5:00 (5:00) (Class 4) (0-80,79) 3-Y-O **£5,047** (£1,510; £755; £377; £188) **Stalls** Low

Form RPR
16-6 **1** **Yerevan**[19] [1604] 3-8-13 **74**.............................. RobertHavlin 2 81
(R T Phillips) *mde all: qcknd over 2f out: r.o wl* **12/1**
1222 **2** 1 1/4 **Sohraab**[8] [1900] 3-8-9 **75**.............................. TravisBlock(5) 8 78
(H Morrison) *a.p: rdn over 2f out: chsd wnr fnl f: no imp* **1/1**[1]
4-00 **3** 3 **Rainbow Fox**[22] [1535] 3-8-9 **70**..............................(p) RichardMullen 6 64
(R A Fahey) *hld up: outpcd over 2f out: sn hung rt: r.o ins fnl f: nvr trbld ldrs* **12/1**
0115 **4** 3/4 **Nordic Light (USA)**[17] [1658] 3-8-10 **78**.............................. MCGeran(7) 3 70
(P W Chapple-Hyam) *trckd wnr: racd keenly: rdn over 1f out: edgd rt and wknd fnl f* **9/2**[3]
3434 **5** 3/4 **Go On Green (IRE)**[17] [1660] 3-8-13 **79**.............................. MarkFlynn(5) 5 69
(E A L Dunlop) *trckd ldrs: rdn over 2f out: wknd over 1f out* **5/2**[2]

1m 16.06s (2.86) **Going Correction** +0.475s/f (Yiel) **5** Ran SP% **112.1**
Speed ratings (Par 101):99,97,93,92,91
CSF £25.49 TOTE £14.60: £4.10, £1.10; EX 29.20 Place 6 £ 707.97, Place 5 £ 662.14.
Owner Bellflower Racing Limited **Bred** Jenny Hall Bloodstock Ltd **Trained** Adlestrop, Gloucs

FOCUS
A fair little sprint, but it was run at an uneven pace and the winner is somewhat flattered. The winner is up 9lb, with the runner-up rated to the bare form of his latest effort.
T/Plt: £214.00 to a £1 stake. Pool: £44,886.45. 153.05 winning tickets. T/Qpdt: £53.70 to a £1 stake. Pool: £1,988.70. 27.40 winning tickets. CR

2090 REDCAR (L-H)
Tuesday, May 29

OFFICIAL GOING: Good (good to soft in places)
After 1/2" rain overnight and before racing the ground was described as 'on the soft side, very dead'.
Wind: fresh 1/2 against Weather: dry but blustery and on the cold side

2115 EUROPEAN BREEDERS' FUND MEDIAN AUCTION MAIDEN FILLIES' STKS 6f
2:10 (2:11) (Class 5) 2-Y-O **£3,238** (£963; £481; £240) **Stalls** Centre

Form RPR
1 **Yasinisi (IRE)** 2-9-0 0.............................. ChrisCatlin 1 70
(E J O'Neill) *trckd ldrs on outer: effrt over 2f out: led over 1f out: edgd rt: hld on towards fin* **5/1**[2]
2233 **2** hd **Sinead Of Aglish (IRE)**[20] [1580] 2-8-11 0.............................. DuranFentiman(3) 6 70
(A B Haynes) *trckd ldrs: effrt 2f out: wnt 2nd ins fnl f: styd on towards fin* **7/4**[1]
2 **3** 2 1/2 **Montiboli (IRE)**[9] [1859] 2-9-0 0.............................. NCallan 2 62
(K A Ryan) *w ldrs: led over 2f out tl over 1f out: kpt on same pce* **7/4**[1]
4 2 **Lady Of Kintyre (IRE)** 2-9-0 0.............................. JimmyQuinn 3 56+
(E J Alston) *s.s: hld up: styd on fnl 2f: nvr trbld ldrs* **33/1**
5 2 1/2 **Planet Queen** 2-9-0 0.............................. PatCosgrave 4 49
(K R Burke) *s.i.s: hld up: hdwy over 2f out: nvr rchd ldrs* **14/1**
F62 **6** 1 **Miss Tilen**[34] [1235] 2-8-11 0.............................. LiamJones(3) 5 46
(V Smith) *t.k.h: w ldrs: led after 2f tl over 2f out: wknd over 1f out* **20/1**
7 5 **Mill Creek** 2-9-0 0.............................. TomEaves 10 31
(B Smart) *trckd ldrs: lost pl over 1f out* **10/1**[3]
0 **8** 1 3/4 **Welcome Inn**[9] [1857] 2-8-11 0..............................(t) MarkLawson(3) 8 25
(M E Sowersby) *s.s: hdwy to join ldrs 3f out: sn wknd* **200/1**
9 2 1/2 **Dawn Whisper** 2-9-0 0.............................. PaulMulrennan 9 18
(M E Sowersby) *s.i.s: in rr: bhd fnl 2f* **66/1**
0 **10** 3 1/2 **Foxies Bychance**[10] [1848] 2-9-0 0.............................. TonyHamilton 7 7
(R D E Woodhouse) *led 2f: lost pl over 1f out* **100/1**

1m 14.95s (3.25) **Going Correction** +0.375s/f (Good) **10** Ran SP% **115.8**
Speed ratings (Par 90):93,92,89,86,83 82,75,73,69,65
CSF £13.79 TOTE £5.90: £1.90, £1.30, £1.10; EX 16.40.
Owner Miss A H Marshall **Bred** Frank Dunne **Trained** Averham Park, Notts

FOCUS
A fair fillies' maiden in which Sinead Of Aglish looks the best guide to the strength of the form.

NOTEBOOK
Yasinisi(IRE), a half-sister to smart multiple sprint winner Ibiscus, out of a 6f winner at two, just proved good enough to make a winning debut. She beat a fair type in Sinead Of Aglish and should have more to offer. (op 7-1)
Sinead Of Aglish(IRE), third in the Lily Agnes on her previous start, had every chance and looked to run her race. She gives the impression she will benefit from a switch to easier ground. (op 13-8 tchd 15-8)
Montiboli(IRE), whose debut second at Ripon represented just modest form, was well held in third. (op 15-8)
Lady Of Kintyre(IRE), a 5,500euros half-sister to 1m juvenile winner Scotty Guest, and 1m2f scorer Lady For Life, who was also a multiple winner over hurdles, out of a dual 7f-1m1f winner, showed some ability on her racecourse debut and should benefit from a step up in trip. (op 25-1)
Planet Queen, a 19,000gns purchase, out of a quite useful dual 5f-6f juvenile winner, never posed a threat on her racecourse debut but is obviously open to improvement. (op 12-1)

2116 REDCARRACING.CO.UK CLAIMING STKS 1m 2f
2:40 (2:41) (Class 6) 3-Y-O **£2,047** (£604; £302) **Stalls** Low

Form RPR
2215 **1** **Skye But N Ben**[15] [1708] 3-8-10 58..............................(b) NeilBrown(7) 9 64
(T D Barron) *trckd ldrs: t.k.h: led over 2f out: styd on wl fnl f* **5/2**[2]
3430 **2** 1 1/4 **Winged Farasi**[11] [1815] 3-8-13 64.............................. NCallan 12 58
(Miss J Feilden) *chsd ldrs: chal over 2f out: edgd rt and one pce fnl f* **2/1**[1]
066- **3** 1 3/4 **Ellies Faith**[227] [5959] 3-8-2 45.............................. JimmyQuinn 4 43
(N Bycroft) *chsd ldrs: drvn over 4f out: kpt on one pce fnl 2f* **40/1**
6430 **4** nk **Irish Relative (IRE)**[15] [1712] 3-8-7 55.............................. PaulFessey 2 47
(T D Barron) *s.i.s: sn drvn along and in tch: one pce fnl 3f* **8/1**
0000 **5** 5 **Roca Redonda (IRE)**[20] [1579] 3-7-12 53 ow3..........(p) LiamJones(3) 10 31
(V Smith) *led tl over 2f out: sn wknd* **9/2**[3]
0- **6** 5 **Attila's Peintre**[234] [5814] 3-9-1 0.............................. WJCafferty(7) 1 42
(P C Haslam) *s.s: in rr: hdwy 2f out: nvr a factor* **11/1**
1060 **7** 1 1/2 **Raven Rascal**[4] [2008] 3-7-11 40.............................. DuranFentiman(3) 7 17
(J F Coupland) *hld up in rr: effrt over 3f out: nvr a factor* **40/1**
0000 **8** 5 **Play Straight**[8] [1894] 3-7-10 57 ow3.............................. NataliaGemelova(5) 8 8
(I W McInnes) *mid-div: drvn over 4f out: nvr a factor* **28/1**
9 1 **King Verti** 3-9-4 0.............................. LeeEnstone 13 23
(P C Haslam) *mid-div: rdn 4f out: nvr on terms* **25/1**
00-0 **10** 13 **Hesaguru (IRE)**[28] [1381] 3-8-2 42..............................(b[1]) AndrewMullen(3) 6 —
(J O'Reilly) *chsd ldrs: wknd over 2f out* **66/1**
00-0 **11** 77 **Redcliff (GER)**[17] [1672] 3-8-11 62..............................(b[1]) DaleGibson 5 —
(M W Easterby) *swvd rt and s.s: reluctant: sn wl t.o* **12/1**

2m 10.96s (4.16) **Going Correction** +0.375s/f (Good) **11** Ran SP% **120.9**
Speed ratings (Par 97):98,97,95,95,91 87,86,82,81,70 9
CSF £7.81 TOTE £3.30: £1.40, £1.90, £4.80; EX 10.10.Winged Farasi was claimed by R. A. Harris for £10,000
Owner Carequick Ltd-(air Conditioning) **Bred** Charles And David Hodge **Trained** Maunby, N Yorks
■ Stewards' Enquiry : W J Cafferty four-day ban: used whip with excessive force (Jun 9-12)

FOCUS
A weak-looking claimer which took little winning with the runner-up a disappointing sort. Skye But N Ben was up 4lb, with the third and fourth rated to their marks.
Redcliff(GER) Official explanation: trainer's rep said gelding failed to race with first time blinkers

2117 TURF TV BETTING SERVICE H'CAP 1m 1f
3:10 (3:10) (Class 5) (0-70,67) 4-Y-O+ **£2,817** (£838; £418; £209) **Stalls** Low

Form RPR
-004 **1** **King Of The Moors (USA)**[17] [1655] 4-8-11 **67**.............................. NeilBrown(7) 6 78
(T D Barron) *trckd ldrs: t.k.h: chal 3f out: edgd lft and led over 1f out: rdn clr* **3/1**[1]
-000 **2** 3 1/2 **Dark Charm (FR)**[17] [1655] 8-9-2 **65**.............................. TonyHamilton 2 69
(R A Fahey) *chsd ldrs: reminders after 2f: wnt 2nd over 1f out: no imp* **6/1**[3]
0-00 **3** 1 **Bright Sun (IRE)**[18] [1621] 6-9-4 **67**..............................(t) KimTinkler 1 69
(N Tinkler) *trckd ldrs: t.k.h: led over 2f out: hdd over 1f out: kpt on same pce* **11/2**[2]
-000 **4** 1 1/2 **Esoterica (IRE)**[8] [1892] 4-8-6 **62**.............................. GaryBartley(7) 9 60
(J S Goldie) *chsd ldrs: one pce fnl 2f* **12/1**
-000 **5** shd **Efidium**[14] [1747] 9-9-3 **66**.............................. ChrisCatlin 8 64
(N Bycroft) *hld up towards rr: hdwy over 3f out: styd on fnl 2f* **10/1**
360- **6** 1 1/2 **Royal Indulgence**[246] [5579] 7-8-3 **55**.............................. LiamJones(3) 11 50
(W M Brisbourne) *hld up in rr: hdwy over 3f out: kpt on: nvr trbld ldrs* **6/1**[3]
6020 **7** 3/4 **Green Pirate**[14] [1740] 5-8-1 **53**.............................. DuranFentiman(3) 5 46
(W M Brisbourne) *dwlt: hdwy over 3f out: hung rt: nvr nr ldrs* **12/1**
/210 **8** nk **Mr Mischief**[12] [1793] 7-8-13 **67**.............................. RussellKennemore(5) 7 60
(M C Chapman) *led tl hdd & wknd over 2f out* **15/2**
120- **9** 18 **Pianoforte (USA)**[312] [3716] 5-8-13 **62**.............................. JimmyQuinn 10 17
(E J Alston) *hld up in mid-div: effrt over 3f out: lost pl 2f out: eased ins fnl f* **8/1**

1m 56.59s (3.19) **Going Correction** +0.375s/f (Good) **9** Ran SP% **116.3**
Speed ratings (Par 103):100,96,96,94,94 93,92,92,76
CSF £21.10 CT £94.59 TOTE £3.30: £1.30, £1.40, £3.80; EX 16.10.
Owner G Fawcett **Bred** F Brown, Hedberg Hall & Keith Hernandez **Trained** Maunby, N Yorks

FOCUS
More moderate stuff, but King Of The Moors ran out a ready winner, up 3lb on his latest effort. The second and third have not been at their best so far this year.

2118 MATT SEYMOUR "FRIEND OF RACING IN THE NORTH" MAIDEN STKS 1m 2f
3:45 (3:46) (Class 5) 3-Y-O+ **£2,817** (£838; £418; £209) **Stalls** Low

Form RPR
34- **1** **Tartan Tie**[281] [4650] 3-8-7 0.............................. GregFairley(3) 4 83+
(M Johnston) *mde all: rdn over 2f out: styd on strly appr fnl f* **14/1**[3]
4-02 **2** 5 **Murbek (IRE)**[19] [1606] 3-8-10 84.............................. NCallan 10 73
(M A Jarvis) *trckd ldrs: smooth hdwy 4f out: chal gng wl over 2f out: rdn over 1f out: fnd nthing* **4/9**[1]
5 **3** 2 1/2 **Music Review**[45] [1045] 3-8-5 0.............................. DaleGibson 5 62
(R A Fahey) *sn chsng ldrs: drvn over 3f out: keeping on same pce whn bmpd and hit rail jst ins fnl f* **16/1**
5 **4** shd **Golden Wave (IRE)**[38] [1166] 3-8-5 0.............................. JimmyQuinn 11 62
(J Noseda) *chsd ldrs: drvn over 5f out: kpt on same pce fnl 2f: edgd lft jst ins fnl f* **5/1**[2]
240 **5** 3 1/2 **Ninetyninetreble (IRE)**[15] [1716] 4-9-10 0.............................. AdrianTNicholls 13 61
(D Nicholls) *swvd rt s: in rr: drvn 5f out: kpt on fnl 2f: nvr nr ldrs* **33/1**
6 3 **Adare (GER)**[20] 4-9-10 0.............................. ChrisCatlin 7 55
(T P Tate) *bhd: kpt on fnl 3f: nvr nr ldrs* **20/1**
7 nk **Still Dreaming** 3-8-5 0.............................. PaulFessey 8 48
(M Dods) *s.i.s: in rr: pushed along 4f out: nvr nr ldrs* **66/1**
0-00 **8** 4 **Finnegans Rainbow**[33] [1271] 5-9-5 42.............................. RussellKennemore(5) 6 46
(M C Chapman) *chsd ldrs: rdn 4f out: lost pl over 2f out* **150/1**
0000 **9** 1 1/4 **Alisdanza**[8] [1893] 5-9-5 43.............................. TonyHamilton 12 39
(N Wilson) *hld up in midfield: effrt over 3f out: sn wknd* **200/1**
10 15 **Fortuitous (IRE)** 3-8-10 0.............................. TomEaves 2 13
(I W McInnes) *s.i.s: drvn along in rr: bhd fnl 3f* **66/1**
00 **11** 7 **Feeling Peckish (USA)**[7] [1937] 3-8-5 0.............................. NicolPolli(5) 3 11
(M C Chapman) *chsd ldrs: rdn 4f out: sn lost pl* **200/1**

2m 9.34s (2.54) **Going Correction** +0.375s/f (Good)
WFA 3 from 4yo+ 14lb **11** Ran SP% **110.8**
Speed ratings (Par 103):104,100,98,97,95 92,92,89,88,76 75
CSF £19.43 TOTE £14.70: £2.60, £1.02, £2.80; EX 30.30.
Owner Mrs I Bird **Bred** D G Hardisty Bloodstock & Marston Stud **Trained** Middleham Moor, N Yorks

FOCUS
A weak maiden, the poor eighth limiting the form. Not form to trust with the favourite failing to stay, but there was no faulting the winner's effort. Connections will have to hope the Handicapper does not take this form too literally, though.

2119 REDCAR RACECOURSE CONFERENCE CENTRE H'CAP 5f
4:20 (4:20) (Class 4) (0-85,84) 3-Y-O **£4,728** (£1,406; £702; £351) **Stalls** Centre

Form RPR
3-64 **1** **The Nifty Fox**[11] [1825] 3-8-9 **75**.............................. TomEaves 3 79
(T D Easterby) *w ldrs: led over 1f out: kpt on wl* **15/8**[1]
20-0 **2** 1 1/4 **Ice Mountain**[38] [1160] 3-9-1 **84**.............................. MarkLawson(3) 4 84
(B Smart) *sn chsng ldrs: no ex ins fnl f* **6/1**
0034 **3** 1 **Feelin Foxy**[11] [1820] 3-8-1 **70** oh5..............................(v) LiamJones(3) 1 66+
(D Shaw) *dwlt: t.k.h in rr: hdwy over 2f out: n.m.r on inner over 1f out: swtchd lft jst ins fnl f: kpt on same pce* **8/1**

01-0 **4** *1* **Flying Valentino**[40] [1108] 3-8-12 **78** TPO'Shea 2 70
(G A Swinbank) *sn drvn along: hdwy 2f out: edgd lft and kpt on fnl f* **12/1**

15-5 **5** *1/2* **Tobermory (IRE)**[22] [1520] 3-9-3 **83** NCallan 6 74
(M A Jarvis) *led: edgd rt and hdd over 1f out: edgd lft ins fnl f: wknd fnl 75yds* **9/2**[3]

16-0 **6** *6* **Now Look Out**[20] [1577] 3-8-4 **73** GregFairley(3) 5 42
(E S McMahon) *sn trcking ldrs: lost pl over 1f out: sn bhd* **11/4**[2]

60.30 secs (1.60) **Going Correction** +0.375s/f (Good) **6** Ran SP% **112.7**
Speed ratings (Par 101):102,100,98,96,96 86
CSF £13.69 TOTE £2.50: £1.40, £2.90; EX 17.10.

Owner Roy Peebles **Bred** Mrs Norma Peebles **Trained** Great Habton, N Yorks

FOCUS
Just an ordinary sprint handicap. The winner was up a length on his latest effort but it is not hard to have doubts over the form.

2120 PARTY NIGHT HERE IN AUGUST H'CAP 6f
4:50 (4:50) (Class 5) (0-70,70) 3-Y-O £2,817 (£838; £418; £209) **Stalls** Centre

Form RPR

-544 **1** **Strathmore (IRE)**[22] [1530] 3-8-10 **62** TonyHamilton 10 73
(R A Fahey) *s.i.s: t.k.h: hdwy 2f out: led jst ins fnl f: sn clr* **5/1**[3]

3010 **2** *4* **Almora Guru**[21] [1561] 3-8-7 **62** LiamJones(3) 2 60
(W M Brisbourne) *hld up: effrt and edgd lft over 1f out: kpt on to take 2nd ins fnl f* **20/1**

100- **3** *3/4* **Triple Shadow**[241] [5681] 3-9-2 **68** JimmyQuinn 7 64
(T D Barron) *hld up: effrt over 2f out: kpt on fnl f* **7/1**

3116 **4** *3/4* **Jojesse**[34] [1240] 3-8-8 **60** TPO'Shea 1 53
(G A Swinbank) *chsd ldrs: effrt over 2f out: kpt on same pce fnl f* **7/1**

4-64 **5** *1* **Tenancy (IRE)**[18] [1634] 3-9-2 **68** NCallan 9 58
(J A Osborne) *led: hung bdly lft thrght: ended up far side: hdd jst ins fnl f: wknd towards fin* **15/8**[1]

4-61 **6** *3 1/2* **Multitude (IRE)**[22] [1530] 3-9-0 **69** DuranFentiman(3) 3 48
(T D Easterby) *chsd ldrs: rdn over 2f out: wknd over 1f out* **4/1**[2]

0-50 **7** *6* **Mambomoon**[17] [1679] 3-8-4 **56** oh11 (b) PaulQuinn 6 16
(T D Easterby) *sn chsng ldrs: lost pl over 1f out* **40/1**

235- **8** *14* **Riotous (IRE)**[285] [4519] 3-8-13 **70** MichaelJStainton(5) 4 —
(A Dickman) *s.i.s: lost pl over 2f out: bhd whn hmpd and swervd rt over 1f out* **12/1**

0-30 **F** **Uace Mac**[17] [1679] 3-8-1 **60** SuzzanneFrance(7) 8 —
(N Bycroft) *w ldrs: wkng whn sltly hmpd and fell heavily over 1f out* **28/1**

1m 13.46s (1.76) **Going Correction** +0.375s/f (Good) **9** Ran SP% **114.8**
Speed ratings (Par 99):103,97,96,95,94 89,81,63,—
CSF £97.04 CT £701.45 TOTE £6.20: £1.90, £4.30, £2.90; EX 138.60.

Owner Jonathan Gill **Bred** M Sharkey **Trained** Musley Bank, N Yorks

■ Stewards' Enquiry : Liam Jones nine-day ban: careless riding (Jun 9-17)

FOCUS
A fair race for the grade, the clear pick on times of the three 6f races, but the level is hard to pin down.

2121 BEVERLEY RACES TOMORROW EVENING AMATEUR RIDERS' MAIDEN H'CAP 6f
5:20 (5:27) (Class 6) (0-60,60) 4-Y-0+ £1,977 (£608; £304) **Stalls** Centre

Form RPR

0-03 **1** **Whozart (IRE)**[19] [1594] 4-10-7 **46** oh1 MrSDobson 8 52
(A Dickman) *stdd s: t.k.h: edgd lft and hdwy to ld on far side 2f out: hrd rdn: jst hld on* **9/2**[2]

00-0 **2** *hd* **Royal Composer (IRE)**[17] [1675] 4-11-0 **58** MissJCoward(5) 9 63
(T D Easterby) *chsd ldrs: edgd lft and styd on fnl f: kpt on towards fin* **8/1**

2040 **3** *nk* **Alucica**[19] [1594] 4-10-7 **46** oh1 (v) MrsMMorris 11 50
(D Shaw) *mid-div: hdwy over 2f out: sn chsng ldrs: edgd lft and styd on ins fnl f: n.m.r towards fin* **10/1**

30-3 **4** *1 1/2* **Butterfly Bud (IRE)**[18] [1640] 4-10-8 **54** MissEHickey(7) 14 53
(J O'Reilly) *led after 1f: hdd 2f out: kpt on same pce fnl f* **5/1**[3]

360- **5** *hd* **Lambency (IRE)**[232] [5864] 4-11-1 **54** MrsCBartley 1 53
(J S Goldie) *towards rr: hdwy 2f out: wandered: styd on wl ins fnl f* **12/1**

/0-0 **6** *3/4* **Crux**[70] [715] 5-10-7 **46** oh1 MissFayeBramley 5 42
(R E Barr) *chsd ldrs: sn drvn along: kpt on same pce fnl 2f* **33/1**

4544 **7** *3/4* **Cabourg (IRE)**[17] [1675] 4-11-0 **58** (b) MissRBastiman(5) 10 52
(R Bastiman) *s.i.s: hld up: hdwy over 2f out: kpt on same pce fnl f* **7/2**[1]

00-0 **8** *1 1/4* **Boreana**[27] [1413] 4-11-7 **60** MissLEllison 2 50
(Jedd O'Keeffe) *chsd ldrs: wknd fnl f* **8/1**

0400 **9** *3/4* **Boppys Dream**[14] [1748] 5-10-0 **46** oh1 (b[1]) MissWGibson(7) 13 33
(P T Midgley) *chsd ldrs: one pce fnl 2f* **40/1**

00-0 **10** *3/4* **Alone It Stands (IRE)**[18] [1625] 4-10-13 **52** MissADeniel 3 37
(D Nicholls) *chsd ldrs: lost pl over 1f out* **16/1**

0/0- **11** *1 3/4* **Maxolini**[399] [1218] 4-10-2 **46** oh1 MrBMcHugh(5) 6 25
(J J Quinn) *unruly s: sn in rr* **25/1**

00-0 **12** *11* **Height Of Esteem**[8] [1906] 4-10-4 **48** (t) MrBenBrisbourne(5) 12 —
(W M Brisbourne) *wnt lft s: led for 1f: lost pl over 2f out: sn bhd* **33/1**

44-0 **13** *1 1/2* **Electron Pulse**[7] [1918] 4-11-2 **58** (b[1]) MrOWilliams(3) 4 —
(M Dods) *mid-div: sn drvn along: lost pl over 2f out: sn bhd* **20/1**

0-06 **14** *3 1/2* **Rose Of Inchinor**[3] [2032] 4-10-8 **52** MissARyan(5) 15 —
(R E Barr) *prom: lost pl 3f out: sn bhd* **11/1**

1m 16.09s (4.39) **Going Correction** +0.375s/f (Good) **14** Ran SP% **127.2**
Speed ratings (Par 101):85,84,84,82,82 81,80,78,77,76 74,59,57,52
CSF £40.52 CT £358.66 TOTE £5.30: £2.40, £3.40, £3.30; EX 46.10 Place 6 £ 14.09, Place 5 £ 12.58.

Owner The Marooned Crew **Bred** Mrs E Mulhern, Sonarc Bloodstock And Tower Bloods **Trained** Sandhutton, N Yorks

■ Stewards' Enquiry : Miss J Coward caution: careless riding

Mr Ben Brisbourne one-day ban: failed to ride to draw (Jun 13)

FOCUS
A poor maiden handicap restricted to amateur riders. The winner was less exposed than most.

T/Plt: £38.00 to a £1 stake. Pool: £41,529.85. 796.70 winning tickets. T/Qpdt: £24.10 to a £1 stake. Pool: £1,683.80. 51.70 winning tickets. WG

1305 SANDOWN (R-H)
Tuesday, May 29

OFFICIAL GOING: Sprint course - soft (good to soft in places); round course - good to soft (soft in places)
Wind: Moderate against Weather: Sunshine and showers

2122 WBX.COM WORLD BET EXCHANGE EBF MAIDEN FILLIES' STKS 5f 6y
6:10 (6:11) (Class 5) 2-Y-O £3,886 (£1,156; £577; £288) **Stalls** High

Form RPR

20 **1** **Presto Levanter**[11] [1821] 2-9-0 0 RichardHughes 9 75+
(R Hannon) *mde all: cruising over 1f out: shkn up and sn asserted fnl f* **3/1**[1]

2 *1 1/2* **High Days (IRE)** 2-9-0 0 LDettori 13 70
(Sir Michael Stoute) *athletic: racd on inner in midfield: rdn 1/2-way: styd on fr over 1f out to take 2nd nr fin* **9/2**[3]

3 **3** *1/2* **Iamagrey (IRE)**[52] [942] 2-9-0 0 LPKeniry 1 68
(J S Moore) *t.k.h early: prom: chsd wnr wl over 1f out: no imp fnl f: lost 2nd nr fin* **25/1**

4 *1/2* **Tatbeeq (IRE)** 2-9-0 0 RHills 4 66+
(M A Jarvis) *w'like: str: s.s: hld up in rr: prog 2f out: effrt to dispute 2nd 1f out: kpt on same pce* **7/1**

5 *1/2* **Mizooka** 2-9-0 0 SebSanders 12 64+
(R M Beckett) *s.v.s: in tch in rr: pushed along and prog 2f out: nt clr run 1f out: nudged along and kpt on steadily* **12/1**

6 *nk* **Polite Society (IRE)** 2-9-0 0 JoeFanning 11 63+
(M Johnston) *leggy: rn green in midfield: lost pl and last of main gp 2f out: swtchd outside over 1f out: pushed along and r.o fnl 150yds* **13/2**

7 *1/2* **Eye Catching** 2-9-0 0 DarryllHolland 7 61
(J R Jenkins) *w'like: trckd ldrs for 2f: lost pl: struggling over 1f out: kpt on again ins fnl f* **20/1**

8 *nk* **Our Kally** 2-9-0 0 HayleyTurner 5 60
(M D I Usher) *w'like: dwlt: t.k.h early: sn in tch: cl up over 1f out: wknd fnl f* **50/1**

9 *1 3/4* **Pretty Bonnie** 2-9-0 0 EddieAhern 3 54+
(J G Portman) *leggy: s.s: racd on outer: in tch tl fdd fnl f* **50/1**

10 *nk* **Chelsea Girl** 2-9-0 0 PhilipRobinson 8 53
(C G Cox) *unf: trckd ldr to wl over 1f out: wknd* **4/1**[2]

11 *6* **Compton Abbess** 2-9-0 0 TedDurcan 14 31
(B R Millman) *leggy: s.s: rn v green and sn wl bhd* **12/1**

64.72 secs (2.51) **Going Correction** +0.425s/f (Yiel) **11** Ran SP% **116.9**
Speed ratings (Par 90):96,93,92,92,91 90,89,89,86,86 76
CSF £15.61 TOTE £4.20: £1.60, £2.30, £5.70; EX 20.90.

Owner B Bull **Bred** B Bull **Trained** East Everleigh, Wilts

FOCUS
The pace was not strong, which allowed the slow starters to recover. The winner obviously sets the standard but it would be a mistake to take the form too literally, despite some promising performances.

NOTEBOOK
Presto Levanter had experience on her side and pulled right away from her rivals in the final furlong. Taking a drop in class after running in Listed company last time on ground the trainer described as loose, there are no firm plans for her but she should continue to pay her way during the season if kept to a realistic level. (op 10-3 tchd 7-2)
High Days(IRE), out of a smart sister to Fantastic Light, was Stoute's first 2yo runner of the season. She was outpaced in the middle of the race before staying on in good style up the incline. One of the nicest sorts in the paddock before the race, she will improve for the run and should make progression. (op 4-1)
Iamagrey(IRE), who showed plenty of knee action, ran really well despite a very moderate draw. A less demanding track will probably suit her better, as she did not seem to get home.
Tatbeeq(IRE), who is closely related to the smart Crosspeace, showed plenty of pace when recovering her position after a slow start, but found less than looked likely off the bridle when asked to quicken. It was a promising effort and she ought to be good enough to land an ordinary maiden at least. (op 11-2)
Mizooka, a half-sister to a couple of middle-distance winners out of a mare who won at 15f, shaped with plenty of promise after starting very slowly. Her jockey did not give her a really hard time in the final furlong and she certainly shaped like a winner waiting to happen. As she is related to horses who stayed well, at least another furlong will suit her. (op 14-1)
Polite Society(IRE), whose dam won over a mile at two, kept on in pleasing style and will no doubt be suited by further in time. (op 5-1)
Our Kally ran really well for a long way and will be suited by an easy 5f in the coming weeks. (op 40-1)
Chelsea Girl showed some early speed but weakened badly throughout the final furlong. She will need to improve a lot to have any chance next time. (op 13-2)
Compton Abbess was very green leaving the stalls and could not be ridden properly as a result. (tchd 11-1)

2123 JOIN WBX.COM FOR £150 IN FREE BETS H'CAP 1m 14y
6:40 (6:40) (Class 3) (0-95,95) 4-Y-0+
£9,348 (£2,799; £1,399; £700; £349; £175) **Stalls** High

Form RPR

06-4 **1** **Killena Boy (IRE)**[22] [1524] 5-8-8 **85** PaulDoe 4 98+
(W Jarvis) *lw: hld up in 5th: prog over 2f out: rdn to chal jst over 1f out: led fnl 150yds: sn drew clr* **5/2**[2]

10-3 **2** *3* **Queen's Best**[25] [1449] 4-8-11 **88** LDettori 3 94
(Sir Michael Stoute) *hld up in 4th: prog 3f out: led 2f out: sn pressed and drvn: hdd and outpcd fnl 150yds* **9/4**[1]

2-61 **3** *1 1/2* **Presumptive (IRE)**[25] [1448] 7-8-12 **92** RichardKingscote(3) 7 94
(R Charlton) *hld up in last pair: prog over 2f out: chal over 1f out: nrly upsides ent fnl f: wknd* **7/1**

0-40 **4** *shd* **Invention (USA)**[52] [940] 4-8-9 **86** MartinDwyer 2 88
(Miss E C Lavelle) *led to 2f out: outpcd over 1f out: plugged on* **20/1**

00-0 **5** *1 1/4* **Moonlight Man**[59] [840] 6-8-6 **90** HaddenFrost(7) 6 89
(R Hannon) *t.k.h: trckd ldng pair to wl over 2f out: stl cl up over 1f out: fdd* **25/1**

0-05 **6** *1* **Ace Of Hearts**[23] [1494] 8-9-3 **94** EddieAhern 9 91
(C F Wall) *trckd ldr to wl over 2f out: sn u.p and struggling* **4/1**[3]

-053 **7** *1* **Adventuress**[17] [1649] 4-8-8 **85** KDarley 5 80
(B J Meehan) *t.k.h: hld up in last: rdn wl over 2f out: no prog* **13/2**

1m 45.25s (1.30) **Going Correction** +0.425s/f (Yiel) **7** Ran SP% **113.8**
Speed ratings (Par 107):110,107,105,105,104 103,102
CSF £8.48 CT £32.61 TOTE £3.30: £2.40, £1.40; EX 9.10.

Owner Capel (CS) Ltd **Bred** John Malone **Trained** Newmarket, Suffolk

■ Stewards' Enquiry : Paul Doe caution: used whip down the shoulder in the forehand position

FOCUS

All the runners came to the stands' side. The gallop was only ordinary in this fair handicap, which produced an easy winner in the generally progressive Killena Boy. The second and third ran to their turf form but the fourth lends a note of caution.

NOTEBOOK

Killena Boy(IRE), who was well supported in the market before the off, travelled easily throughout the race and came right away from his rivals when asked to quicken, despite getting hit across the face with a whip just over a furlong from home. It was an impressive performance but he would seem suited by turning tracks, so is unlikely to line up for a race such as the Hunt Cup at Royal Ascot. (op 7-2)

Queen's Best, who handles ease in the ground, did not help her cause by being a bit keen in the early stages and was left behind when the winner flew past her. An easy mile or even a drop to 7f will suit her, considering the way she travels during a race. (op 15-8 tchd 5-2 and 11-4 in places)

Presumptive(IRE) ran well but simply had no turn of foot when required. The Handicapper seems to have his measure for now, but he may have found the trip stretching his stamina at a course like Sandown.

Invention(USA), making his debut for the stable, was a winner over 1m2f last season and made most of the running until joined up the home straight. His handicap mark is starting to drop and his shrewd stable will find him the right opportunity.

Moonlight Man has come down to a winning mark again, but all of his best form has been shown on much quicker ground. (op 28-1 tchd 33-1)

Ace Of Hearts has taken a long time to come down to a winning mark but only shaped with a bit of promise. Quicker ground will be more to his advantage but he has something to prove now. Official explanation: jockey said gelding was unsuited by the good to soft (soft in places) ground (op 7-2)

Adventuress did not look the most willing of characters under pressure and never threatened to get involved. (op 8-1)

2124 BET NOW AT WBX.COM HERON STKS (LISTED RACE) 1m 14y

7:15 (7:16) (Class 1) 3-Y-O **£14,762** (£5,595; £2,800; £1,396) **Stalls** High

Form				RPR
20-6	1		**Massive (IRE)**[41] [1097] 3-8-12 102 ... DarryllHolland 1 (M R Channon) *mde all: rousted along and hrd pressed wl over 1f out: styd on fnl f and holding on nr fin* **12/1**	103
012-	2	nk	**Charlie Farnsbarns (IRE)**[220] [6104] 3-8-12 113 ... LDettori 4 (B J Meehan) *bit bkwd: trckd wnr: rdn to chal wl over 1f out: upsides ent fnl f: styd on but hld fnl 75yds* **2/5**[1]	102
03-0	3	1 1/4	**Jo'Burg (USA)**[24] [1473] 3-8-12 97 ... KDarley 5 (Mrs A J Perrett) *lw: unruly preliminaries: trckd ldng pair: effrt to chal over 1f out: ev ch tl no ex fnl 100yds* **5/1**[2]	99
-030	4	1 3/4	**Fishforcompliments**[24] [1473] 3-8-12 100 ... MartinDwyer 3 (R A Fahey) *hld up in last: outpcd over 1f out: shkn up and one pce after* **7/1**[3]	95

1m 46.7s (2.75) **Going Correction** +0.425s/f (Yiel) **4 Ran SP% 108.3**

Speed ratings (Par 107):103,102,101,99

CSF £18.24 TOTE £7.70; EX 15.80.

Owner Sheikh Ahmed Al Maktoum **Bred** Mrs S Lloyd And Dr M Klay **Trained** West Ilsley, Berks

FOCUS

A modest winning time for a Listed race, 1.45 seconds slower than the preceding handicap. The form is weak for the grade with the favourite disappointing, and the third looks the best guide.

NOTEBOOK

Massive(IRE), edgy in the paddock, was given a positive ride and repelled the opposition as they stacked up to challenge him. Disappointing in the Feilden Stakes last time, he is clearly much more at home on ground with ease in it and will probably be stepped up in class again if a suitable race can be found. Considering his size - presumably why he was given his name - it would not be unfair to presume he could still be improving. (op 10-1)

Charlie Farnsbarns(IRE), who was rated 11lb higher than the winner on official figures, gave him a fight in the final furlong but could not thrust his head in front. It has to be considered a disappointing effort on his Racing Post Trophy form last season, but he is entitled to improve for the run - he had a setback during the winter that delayed his return - and could make his next appearance in the Hampton Court Stakes at Royal Ascot as long as the ground has some ease in it. (tchd 4-9 and 1-2 in places)

Jo'Burg(USA), taking a drop in class after contesting the 2000 Guineas last time, does not look the most straightforward of characters but shows plenty of ability when racing, although his ears were flat back under pressure in the final furlong. A race such as the Jersey Stakes at Royal Ascot might be a fair target for him, especially if the ground came up quicker. (op 13-2 tchd 9-2)

Fishforcompliments, who finished well in front of today's winner when they met in the Feilden Stakes but just behind Jo'Burg in the 2000 Guineas, was not disgraced but rarely looked like taking a hand in the finish. He should provide his owners with plenty of fun this season but may not be very easy to place to have an obvious winning chance. (tchd 13-2)

2125 WBX.COM HENRY II STKS (GROUP 2) 2m 78y

7:50 (7:50) (Class 1) 4-Y-O+

£48,263 (£18,292; £9,154; £4,564; £2,286; £1,147) **Stalls** High

Form				RPR
33-5	1		**Allegretto (IRE)**[11] [1823] 4-9-0 108 ... (v[1]) SebSanders 3 (Sir Michael Stoute) *swtg: t.k.h early: trckd ldng pair 9f out: drvn to chal 2f out: narrow ld jst ins fnl f: styd on gamely* **12/1**	114
03-3	2	3/4	**Balkan Knight**[17] [1650] 7-9-2 106 ... JohnEgan 6 (D R C Elsworth) *b.hind: lw: hld up in last trio: prog 3f out: drvn and narrow ld 2f out: hdd jst ins fnl f: hld nr fin* **7/2**[3]	113
2-03	3	1 1/2	**Bulwark (IRE)**[11] [1823] 5-9-2 104 ... (be) JimCrowley 1 (Mrs A J Perrett) *hld up in last trio: prog to trck ldng pair wl over 1f out: sn rdn: carried hd to one side and fnd nil* **8/1**	111
10-1	4	6	**Mount Kilimanjaro (IRE)**[55] [929] 4-9-0 103 ... LDettori 8 (J L Dunlop) *chsd ldr: rdn 5f out: lost pl over 2f out: wknd over 1f out* **3/1**[2]	104
00-1	5	1	**Tungsten Strike (USA)**[27] [1393] 6-9-2 110 ... DarryllHolland 2 (Mrs A J Perrett) *mde most: hrd rdn and hdd 2f out: wknd* **5/2**[1]	103
6-34	6	27	**Under The Rainbow**[20] [1582] 4-8-11 100 ... KDarley 7 (B W Hills) *chsd ldng pair to 9f out: rdn whn hmpd 3f out: sn btn: eased and t.o* **6/1**	67
0-00	7	12	**Land 'n Stars**[82] [648] 7-9-2 0 ... PaulDoe 5 (R A Fahey) *a in last trio: lost tch 1/2-way: t.o fnl 4f* **16/1**	56

3m 39.47s (1.24) **Going Correction** +0.425s/f (Yiel)

WFA 4 from 5yo+ 2lb **7 Ran SP% 114.8**

Speed ratings (Par 115):113,112,111,108,108 94,88

CSF £53.87 TOTE £15.30: £4.10, £2.60; EX 88.80.

Owner Cheveley Park Stud **Bred** Miss K Rausing And Airlie Stud **Trained** Newmarket, Suffolk

FOCUS

The pace was sound and they came over to the stands' side in the home straight. This is solid form, rated through the third. An improved effort from Allegretto, and a slight career best from Balkan Knight.

NOTEBOOK

Allegretto(IRE), who made a reasonable reappearance in the Yorkshire Cup, built on that promise on this first try over 2m. Rather keen early on in the first-time visor, she threw down a challenge to the runner-up at the two pole and eventually got on top inside the last. The Doncaster Cup, a race her dam won a few seasons ago, could be an interesting target later in the season. (op 11-1)

Balkan Knight had his ground and ran a big race. Improving to show ahead on the stands' rail with two to run, he kept battling but the filly proved the stronger in the last half-furlong. He seemed to stay the 2m well enough this time. (op 13-2)

Bulwark(IRE) had finished two places and just over 6l in front of today's winner in the Yorkshire Cup recently but could not confirm the form on 2lb worse terms. He ran his usual sort of race, coming through from the back of the field, before shirking the issue when asked to battle. One day things will drop for him but he is obviously not one to place too much faith in. (op 11-1)

Mount Kilimanjaro(IRE), upped in class after winning a Listed event at Nottingham, was on his toes in the paddock. He tracked the leader into the straight but soon began to wander around under pressure and faded inside the last quarter mile. He has yet to really prove he stays this far. (op 9-4)

Tungsten Strike(USA) landed a weak renewal of this event last year in soft ground but really prefers a faster surface. Adopting the front-running tactics which landed him the Sagaro at Ascot, he brought the field over to the stands' side in the straight but was collared with two to run and soon on the retreat. Official explanation: jockey said gelding was unsuited by the good to soft (soft in places) ground (op 2-1)

Under The Rainbow ran a big race in the Chester Cup but was a long way off that form here. She did get hampered as the field tacked over to the near side in the home straight, but it was still disappointing the way she dropped away. (op 8-1)

Land 'n Stars, back from a World tour and having his first run since leaving Julian Poulton, was always trailing. Official explanation: jockey said gelding was unsuited by the good to soft (soft in places) ground (op 14-1)

2126 WBX.COM WE WILL MATCH YOUR COMMISSION RATE H'CAP 1m 2f 7y

8:20 (8:20) (Class 3) (0-90,87) 3-Y-O **£7,772** (£2,312; £1,155; £577) **Stalls** High

Form				RPR
6434	1		**Sahrati**[31] [1293] 3-8-10 79 ... EddieAhern 11 (C E Brittain) *trckd ldng pair: led over 2f out: rdn clr over 1f out: in n.d after* **9/2**[3]	89
1-50	2	3 1/2	**Mutadarrej (IRE)**[13] [1773] 3-9-3 86 ... RHills 2 (J L Dunlop) *hld up in last pair: prog over 2f out: styd on to take 2nd ins fnl f: no ch w wnr* **8/1**	89
4316	3	3/4	**Urban Warrior**[15] [1724] 3-8-4 73 ... JamesDoyle 1 (Mrs Norma Pook) *hld up towards rr: prog over 2f out: chsd wnr over 1f out: no imp: kpt on but lost 2nd ins fnl f* **10/1**	75
1-55	4	1 3/4	**Magic Mountain (IRE)**[19] [1603] 3-9-2 85 ... RichardHughes 4 (R Hannon) *lw: hld up in midfield: drvn over 2f out: kpt on same pce u.p: no ch w ldrs* **14/1**	83
1-01	5	3/4	**Happy Go Lily**[27] [1407] 3-9-1 84 ... AdamKirby 10 (W R Swinburn) *lw: trckd ldng pair: lost pl then hmpd over 2f out: nt rcvr: plugged on fnl f* **8/1**	84+
4-61	6	1 1/4	**Wester Ross (IRE)**[15] [1725] 3-8-9 78 ... MickyFenton 7 (J M P Eustace) *disp ld: led 1/2-way to over 2f out: wknd over 1f out* **6/1**	72
12-0	7	5	**Strikeen (IRE)**[52] [939] 3-9-4 87 ... DaneO'Neill 5 (T G Mills) *bit bwkd: s.i.s: hld up in last: rdn over 2f out: swtchd rt over 1f out: no prog* **25/1**	71
51-	8	1 3/4	**Ajaan**[239] [5730] 3-8-13 82 ... TedDurcan 8 (H R A Cecil) *lw: settled in rr: pushed along 1/2-way: rdn over 3f out: sme prog u.p wl over 1f out: no ch: wknd and eased ins fnl f* **10/3**[1]	71+
116-	9	17	**Old Romney**[280] [4680] 3-9-2 85 ... KDarley 9 (M Johnston) *disp ld to 1/2-way: wknd 3f out: t.o* **4/1**[2]	32

2m 13.67s (3.43) **Going Correction** +0.425s/f (Yiel) **9 Ran SP% 117.4**

Speed ratings (Par 103):103,100,99,98,97 96,92,91,77

CSF £40.93 CT £344.84 TOTE £5.10: £2.10, £2.80, £3.30; EX 44.30.

Owner Saeed Manana **Bred** Darley **Trained** Newmarket, Suffolk

FOCUS

Once more they came over to the stands' side. This was a fair handicap and solid enough form, the second and third running to their marks.

NOTEBOOK

Sahrati, on his toes in the paddock, was faced with easy ground for the first time since landing a Nottingham maiden last October. After easing his way to the front in the straight, he came soon clear and, keeping up the gallop, was never seriously threatened. He did it well but will be hit by the handicapper for this. (op 11-2)

Mutadarrej(IRE) left his York form behind and stayed on from the rear to chase home the winner, if never looking like catching him. (op 9-1)

Urban Warrior is the most exposed in the field and a decent guide to the worth of this form. After claiming the pitch against the stands' rail, he chased the winner in vain before being run out of second late on. This was a sound effort but he does look held off this mark . (op 12-1)

Magic Mountain(IRE), dropped 2lb since Chester, was ridden differently over this longer trip and could never get in a blow. He did seem to stay.

Happy Go Lily, 5lb higher than at Nottingham and on easier ground, was found wanting but would have finished a bit closer had she not met with trouble. She looks ready for a try over 12f. (tchd 9-1)

Wester Ross(IRE), on his handicap bow, was taken on for the lead and had little left in the tank when challenged in the straight. Official explanation: jockey said colt lost a shoe and hung right (op 9-2)

Ajaan, who won his maiden at two in soft ground, was a big disappointment on this seasonal and handicap debut. Running in snatches and coming off the bridle by halfway, he made a brief forward move under pressure once in line for home but soon appeared to hang and his rider called it a day. He looks less than straightforward. (op 11-4 tchd 7-2 in places)

Old Romney, off the track since the Ebor meeting last August, was unable to escape the attentions of Wester Ross at the head of affairs and dropped away tamely once into the home straight. He probably needs faster ground. (op 11-2)

2127 WBX.COM KEEPING COMMISSION RATES LOW MAIDEN STKS 1m 2f 7y

8:50 (8:56) (Class 5) 3-Y-O+ **£4,533** (£1,348; £674; £336) **Stalls** High

Form				RPR
1		**Winter Sunrise** 3-8-7 0 ow1 ... SebSanders 5 (Sir Michael Stoute) *w'like: scope: bit bkwd: chsd ldrs: shkn up over 4f out: prog over 2f out: drvn to ld over 1f out: hld on wl fnl f* **9/1**	82
2	3/4	**Spring City (GER)** 3-8-11 0 ... LDettori 13 (Saeed Bin Suroor) *w'like: lw: str: w ldr: led 3f out: drvn and hdd over 1f out: styd on fnl f: a hld* **4/1**[2]	84
42-3	3	1 1/2	**Black Rock (IRE)**[38] [1143] 3-8-11 87 ... PhilipRobinson 2 (M A Jarvis) *lw: trckd ldrs: nt qckn and lost pl over 2f out: sn hrd rdn: wnt 3rd fnl f: no real imp on ldng pair* **5/4**[1]	83+
05-	4	3	**Niqaab**[230] [5906] 3-8-6 0 ... RHills 8 (B W Hills) *mde most to 3f out: sn shkn up and outpcd: kpt on steadily again fnl f* **20/1**	70
32	5	1/2	**Haarth Sovereign (IRE)**[28] [1369] 3-8-11 0 ... AdamKirby 12 (W R Swinburn) *trckd ldrs: rdn to press ldng pair 2f out: nt qckn over 1f out: wknd fnl f* **12/1**	74

The Form Book, Raceform Ltd, Compton, RG20 6NL

00 **6** 1 **Fraternal**[11] [1812] 3-8-11 0........ DaneO'Neill 9 72+
(R Charlton) *in tch in midfield: lost pl sltly 3f out: kpt on fr over 1f out: n.d* **20/1**

7 shd **Stalking Tiger (IRE)** 3-8-8 0........ RichardKingscote(3) 4 72+
(R Charlton) *leggy: scope: settled wl in rr: stl in last trio 3f out: prog on outer fr over 2f out: chsd ldrs over 1f out: fdd fnl f* **33/1**

0 **8** 1 1/2 **Muraco**[17] [1665] 3-8-11 0........ JamesDoyle 16 69
(R M Beckett) *wl in tch: pushed along fr over 2f out: steadily fdd* **66/1**

9 2 **Sadler's Leap (IRE)** 4-9-6 0........ PaulEddery 1 61+
(Pat Eddery) *str: bit bkwd: s.v.s: wl in rr: plugged on fnl 2f: no ch* **13/2**[3]

4 **10** 3 1/2 **Marieschi (USA)**[17] [1665] 3-8-11 0........ TedDurcan 15 58
(H R A Cecil) *trckd ldrs: rdn over 2f out: sn wknd* **8/1**

0-0 **11** 1 1/4 **Time Upon Time**[15] [1725] 3-8-6 0........ PaulDoe 7 50
(W J Knight) *stdd s: a wl in rr: last 1/2-way: nvr on terms* **100/1**

0 **12** 1 **Almahaza (IRE)**[15] [1725] 3-8-11 0........ JimCrowley 11 53
(Mrs A J Perrett) *w'like: dwlt: sn in tch in midfield: lost pl and struggling 3f out: no ch after* **20/1**

13 1 1/2 **Irish Quest (IRE)** 3-8-11 0........ MatthewHenry 6 50
(M A Jarvis) *w'like: bit bkwd: in tch: rdn and green 3f out: steadily wknd* **33/1**

2m 14.82s (4.58) **Going Correction** +0.425s/f (Yiel)
WFA 3 from 4yo 14lb **13** Ran SP% **129.2**
Speed ratings (Par 103):98,97,96,93,93 92,92,91,89,86 85,85,83
CSF £45.65 TOTE £12.10: £3.40, £1.90, £1.40; EX 71.30 Place 6 £ 725.86, Place 5 £ 364.66.
Owner K Abdulla **Bred** Juddmonte Farms Ltd **Trained** Newmarket, Suffolk

FOCUS
The form might not be that solid down the field but the third set a good standard and the front pair have improvement in them.
T/Plt: £958.30 to a £1 stake. Pool: £80,537.75. 61.35 winning tickets. T/Qpdt: £368.00 to a £1 stake. Pool: £4,028.50. 8.10 winning tickets. JN

TABY (R-H)
Tuesday, May 29
OFFICIAL GOING: Good to firm

2131a STOCKHOLMS STORA PRIS (GROUP 3) 1m 1f 153y
8:09 (8:16) 4-Y-0+ **£30,246** (£15,123; £7,259; £4,839; £3,025)

RPR

1 **Funny Legend (NOR)**[226] 6-8-12........ FJohansson 5 98
(Wido Neuroth, Norway) *mid-div: hdwy to ld 1f out: r.o wl* **27/20**[1]

2 1 **Angel De Madrid (CHI)**[31] 6-9-2........ ESki 3 100
(Rune Haugen, Norway) *mid-div: prog 3f out: tk 2nd fnl 100yds* **33/2**

3 1/2 **Calistoga (DEN)**[31] 8-9-2........ MSantos 2 99
(L Reuterskiold, Sweden) *a cl up: wnt 2nd 2f out: no ex fnl 100yds* **22/1**

4 shd **Icaros (SWE)**[18] [1648] 4-9-2........ YvonneDurant 6 99
(Wido Neuroth, Norway) *mid-div: hdwy 3f out: chal 2f out: one pce fnl f* **61/10**[3]

5 hd **Ecology (IRE)**[345] 9-9-2........ GSolis 7 98
(M Robertz, Norway) *mid-div: hdwy to ld 3f out: hdd 1f out: one pce* **51/1**

6 nk **Crimson And Gold**[31] 5-9-2........ FDiaz 12 98
(L Reuterskiold, Sweden) *cl up to 1/2-way: no ex fr 2f out* **26/1**

7 1/2 **Art Attack (GER)**[262] 4-9-2........ MLarsen 4 97
(A Wohler, Germany) *towards rr to 1/2-way: nvr a factor* **48/10**[2]

8 1/2 **Maybach**[18] [1648] 6-9-2........ P-AGraberg 8 96
(B Bo, Sweden) *a in mid-div* **88/10**

9 1/2 **Alnitak (USA)**[12] 6-9-2........(b) AStarke 9 95
(B Olsen, Norway) *a towards rr: nvr a factor* **44/1**

10 shd **Fly Society (DEN)**[31] 6-9-2........ KAndersen 14 95
(S Jensen, Denmark) *last to 3f out: a towards rr* **16/1**

11 4 **Moltas (SWE)**[226] 5-9-2........ RebeccaColldin 11 88
() *prom to 4f out* **33/2**

12 2 **Mad Dog Slew (USA)**[289] [4420] 4-9-2........ DinaDanekilde 13 84
(F Reuterskiold, Sweden) *mid-div to 1/2-way* **45/2**

13 5 **Highway (IRE)**[18] [1648] 4-9-2........(b) LTorres 1 75
(F Castro, Sweden) *led to 3f out: wknd qckly* **12/1**

1m 59.0s (119.00) **13** Ran SP% **125.5**
(including one SKr stakes): WIN 2.35; PL 1.46, 3.14, 4.31; DF 46.08.
Owner Stall E & F **Bred** Stall E & F **Trained** Norway

2021 BEVERLEY (R-H)
Wednesday, May 30
OFFICIAL GOING: Good (good to firm in places, 8.6)
There was a golden highway against the stands' rail and several winners made use of it. The form of this meeting should therefore be treated with caution.
Wind: Slight, half across Weather: Overcast and showers

2132 SUPABED QUALITY PAPER BEDDING H'CAP 1m 4f 16y
6:20 (6:20) (Class 5) (0-70,70) 3-Y-0 **£3,562** (£1,059; £529; £264) **Stalls** High

Form RPR

2114 **1** **Dee Cee Elle**[19] [1637] 3-9-1 **67**........ JoeFanning 1 73
(M Johnston) *trckd ldr: hdwy to ld wl over 2f out: jnd and rdn wl over 1f out: drvn and styd on gamely fnl f* **2/1**[1]

-314 **2** 2 **Sonara (IRE)**[19] [1624] 3-9-0 **66**........ JimmyQuinn 5 68
(M H Tompkins) *hld up in rr: hdwy over 3f out: chal wl over 1f out and sn rdn: ev ch tl drvn and one pce ins fnl f* **2/1**[1]

4-22 **3** 4 **Bachnagairn**[29] [1370] 3-9-4 **70**........ NCallan 4 66
(R Charlton) *trckd ldrs: effrt over 3f out and sn pushed along: rdn 2f out: sn drvn and btn* **4/1**[2]

0420 **4** 1 3/4 **Chip N Pin**[11] [1850] 3-8-2 **57**........ DuranFentiman(3) 7 50
(T D Easterby) *t.k.h: chsd ldrs: rdn along over 3f out: kpt on same pce fnl 2f* **7/1**[3]

50-0 **5** 2 1/2 **Traditionalist (IRE)**[27] [1440] 3-9-1 **67**........(t) NickyMackay 6 56
(G A Butler) *hld up in tch: hdwy to chse ldrs over 3f out: sn rdn along and no imp fnl 2f* **12/1**

5-04 **6** 25 **Galingale (IRE)**[21] [1576] 3-8-8 **60**........ MickyFenton 3 9
(Mrs P Sly) *led: rdn along over 3f out: hdd wl over 2f out and sn wknd* **20/1**

2m 40.82s (0.61) **Going Correction** +0.15s/f (Good) **6** Ran SP% **111.6**
Speed ratings (Par 99):103,101,99,97,96 79
CSF £5.98 TOTE £2.80: £1.40, £1.60; EX 6.90.
Owner Douglas Livingston **Bred** Pollards Stables **Trained** Middleham Moor, N Yorks

FOCUS
A steadily-run handicap that turned into something of a sprint. The form has a solid look to it.
Traditionalist(IRE) Official explanation: jockey said colt hung badly right-handed throughout

2133 GUEST AND PHILIPS H'CAP 1m 100y
6:50 (6:51) (Class 5) (0-70,70) 3-Y-0 **£3,562** (£1,059; £529; £264) **Stalls** High

Form RPR

4340 **1** **Snow Dancer (IRE)**[10] [1863] 3-8-11 **63**........ FrancisNorton 9 71
(A Berry) *hld up in midfield: swtchd lft and hdwy wl over 2f out: rdn to ld appr fnl f: styd on strly* **33/1**

4-05 **2** 1 1/2 **Kindlelight Blue (IRE)**[23] [1531] 3-9-0 **66**........(e[1]) MickyFenton 11 71
(N P Littmoden) *s.i.s and bhd: swtchd wd to stands' rails st: sn rdn and styd on strly ins fnl f* **14/1**

0-50 **3** 2 1/2 **Cheshire Prince**[23] [1536] 3-8-8 **60**........ TPQueally 4 59
(W M Brisbourne) *led: rdn clr wl over 2f out: drvn and hdd appr fnl f: kpt on u.p* **16/1**

34-3 **4** nk **Chasing Memories (IRE)**[11] [1850] 3-8-6 **61**........ MarkLawson(3) 14 60
(B Smart) *midfield: rdn along 3f out: swtchd rt and drvn over 1f out: styd on wl u.p ins fnl f* **11/2**[2]

0-00 **5** nk **Smugglers Bay (IRE)**[12] [1827] 3-8-10 **62**........ DavidAllan 10 60
(T D Easterby) *dwlt: sn chsng ldrs on inner: rdn along over 2f out: drvn over 1f out: kpt on u.p ins fnl f* **18/1**

1144 **6** nk **Pietersen (IRE)**[6] [1965] 3-9-4 **70**........(b) PaulFessey 15 67
(T D Barron) *chsd ldr: effrt 3f out: rdn 2f out: drvn over 1f out and wknd ins fnl f* **5/1**[1]

3466 **7** 1 1/4 **Gold Response**[30] [1361] 3-8-1 **56** oh2........(v) DuranFentiman(3) 17 50
(D Shaw) *towards rr tl gd hdwy on inner over 1f out: styd on strly ins fnl f: nrst fin* **18/1**

0-42 **8** hd **Astroangel**[42] [1091] 3-8-8 **65**........ PatrickHills(5) 16 64+
(M H Tompkins) *in tch: effrt whn nt clr run 2f out: sn rdn and kpt on same pce fnl f* **11/2**[2]

040- **9** 1 **Bollin Freddie**[287] [4466] 3-8-2 **57** ow1........ AndrewMullen(3) 7 49
(A J Lockwood) *bhd tl styd on fnl 2f* **80/1**

4-00 **10** 1 1/4 **Pagan Starprincess**[32] [1303] 3-8-8 **60**........ PatCosgrave 2 49
(G M Moore) *chsd ldrs: rdn along wl over 2f out: sn drvn and grad wknd* **20/1**

0-34 **11** 3/4 **Leprechaun's Gold (IRE)**[11] [1850] 3-8-8 **60**........ JoeFanning 3 47
(M Johnston) *a in midfield* **9/1**

63-5 **12** 1 1/2 **Naughty Thoughts (IRE)**[28] [1408] 3-9-4 **70**........ NCallan 1 53
(K A Ryan) *chsd ldrs: hdwy 3f out: rdn over 2f out and sn wknd* **14/1**

31-0 **13** 1 1/4 **Putra Laju (IRE)**[35] [1247] 3-9-3 **69**........ MichaelHills 12 50
(J W Hills) *a towards rr* **16/1**

60-5 **14** 1 **Bobansheil (IRE)**[14] [1769] 3-8-10 **62**........ KDarley 13 40
(J S Wainwright) *bhd fr 1/2-way* **18/1**

030- **15** 3/4 **Miss Percy**[250] [5507] 3-8-12 **64**........ TonyHamilton 5 41
(R A Fahey) *t.k.h: in tch: rdn along 1/2-way and sn wknd* **20/1**

50-6 **16** 4 **Loch Tay**[30] [1359] 3-9-4 **70**........ HayleyTurner 8 37
(M L W Bell) *t.k.h: chsd ldrs: rdn wl over 2f out and sn wknd* **8/1**[3]

056- **17** 16 **Cornell Precedent**[232] [5900] 3-8-4 **56** oh2........ TPO'Shea 6 —
(J J Quinn) *towards rr whn bmpd after 1f: bhd after* **20/1**

1m 48.95s (1.55) **Going Correction** +0.15s/f (Good) **17** Ran SP% **127.9**
Speed ratings (Par 99):98,96,94,93,93 93,91,91,90,89 88,87,85,84,84 80,64
CSF £438.90 CT £7723.53 TOTE £42.90: £5.80, £3.10, £5.20, £2.00; EX 470.50.
Owner Anthony Hanlon **Bred** Liam Queally **Trained** Cockerham, Lancs

FOCUS
A competitive race in which the performance of the runner-up was the most informative, with regard to the rest of the card. The form is not rock solid with the winner surprisingly back to his All-Weather best.
Snow Dancer(IRE) Official explanation: trainer had no explanation for the apparent improvement in form

2134 HILARY NEEDLER TROPHY (FILLIES) (LISTED RACE) 5f
7:20 (7:22) (Class 1) 2-Y-O
£14,195 (£5,380; £2,692; £1,342; £672; £337) **Stalls** High

Form RPR

16 **1** **Loch Jipp (USA)**[12] [1821] 2-8-12 0........ KDarley 1 97
(J S Wainwright) *cl up stands' rail: hdwy to ld and overall ldr 2f out: sn rdn and styd on wl* **20/1**

14 **2** 2 1/2 **Primo Heights**[21] [1580] 2-8-12 0........ NickyMackay 2 88
(J S Goldie) *led stands' side gp: rdn along over 2f out: sn hdd: kpt on wl under u.p fnl f* **20/1**

6 **3** 2 **Eastern Romance**[32] [1285] 2-8-12 0........ FrancisNorton 5 81
(K A Ryan) *midfield: hdwy 2f out: sn rdn and styd on ins fnl f: nrst fin* **50/1**

13 **4** 1/2 **Cristal Clear (IRE)**[12] [1821] 2-8-12 0........(p) DavidAllan 6 79
(T D Easterby) *prom: hdwy to dispute ld centre over 2f out: rdn and edgd lft over 1f out: kpt on same pce* **7/4**[1]

1 **5** 1 3/4 **Rose Siog**[9] [1889] 2-8-12 0........ TonyHamilton 12 73
(R A Fahey) *cl up centre: rdn along 2f out: sn one pce* **8/1**

2 **6** 1 1/2 **Charlotti Carlotti (IRE)**[11] [1848] 2-8-12 0........ PaulFessey 3 67
(T D Barron) *chsd ldrs: pushed along and outpcd 1/2-way: styd on ins fnl f* **8/1**

3 **7** 1/2 **Sudden Impact (IRE)**[11] [1848] 2-8-12 0........ TPQueally 9 66
(Paul Green) *swtchd to far rail after 1f and in tch: hdwy on inner and ev ch 2f out: sn rdn and wknd over 1f out* **13/2**[3]

10 **8** 2 **Feeling Proud (USA)**[12] [1821] 2-8-12 0........ JimmyQuinn 8 58
(Jane Chapple-Hyam) *in tch: rdn along over 2f out and sn no imp* **40/1**

32 **9** 1/2 **Hucking Harmony (IRE)**[46] [1033] 2-8-12 0........ MickyFenton 11 57
(J R Best) *overall ldr centre: rdn along 1/2-way: hdd 2f out and grad wknd* **12/1**

31 **10** 1/2 **Tan Bonita (USA)**[22] [1553] 2-8-12 0........ PatCosgrave 10 55
(M J Wallace) *chsd ldrs centre: rdn along over 2f out: grad wknd* **14/1**

4 **11** 8 **Deal Flipper**[26] [1445] 2-8-12 0........ MichaelHills 7 26
(P Winkworth) *dwlt: a towards rr* **66/1**

043 **12** 8 **Zahwah**[16] [1727] 2-8-12 0........ JoeFanning 4 —
(J G Portman) *sn outpcd in rr* **50/1**

13 2 **Coachhouse Lady (USA)** 2-8-9 0........ NCallan 13 —
(K A Ryan) *prom: rdn along 1/2-way: wknd qckly wl over 1f out and eased* **5/1**[2]

64.75 secs (0.75) **Going Correction** +0.15s/f (Good) **13** Ran SP% **120.3**
Speed ratings (Par 98):100,96,92,92,89 86,86,82,82,81 68,55,52
CSF £350.02 TOTE £25.90: £5.90, £6.30, £7.70; EX 374.50.

Owner I Barran & P Rhodes **Bred** R L Quinichet And Lorraine R Quinichett **Trained** Kennythorpe, N Yorks

FOCUS

A fair renewal on paper but the result was heavily influenced by the bias towards the two runners who came stands' side in the straight, where the ground was clearly better there. Any assessment of the form ought to take that into account.

NOTEBOOK

Loch Jipp(USA), who ran a creditable race in similar company at York last time, came stands' side with Primo Heights, and they both proved to be at a big advantage racing on quicker ground. She mastered her only rival with two furlongs to run and came clear to win well. Whether she can be rated any higher than the 'winner' from the main pack is open to question, though. Obviously, the Queen Mary Stakes or the Albany Stakes are now the likely options. (tchd 25-1)

Primo Heights was the only other filly to race next to the stands'-side rail, where there was clearly a quicker strip of ground. Headed two furlongs out, she kept on well enough to maintain her advantage over the far-side group, but she was surely flattered by her final placing.

Eastern Romance ran with promise behind Janina at Haydock on her debut and has clearly improved since. Although a big price, there was no fluke about this effort and she stayed on well to win the race from the group that ran up the centre of the track. She will have no problem winning a maiden on this evidence. (op 80-1)

Cristal Clear(IRE), wearing cheekpieces for the first time, finished almost three lengths in front of Loch Jipp at York last time, and the main reason for the form being reversed on this occasion was the track bias, which played into her old rival's favour. (op 2-1 tchd 13-8 and 85-40 in places)

Rose Siog, a winner at Musselburgh on her debut, unseated her rider before the start and got upset in the stalls. She ran a fair race in the circumstances, especially as the easier ground would probably not have been in her favour. (op 7-1)

Charlotti Carlotti(IRE) is another who should have little trouble finding a maiden, but she is by Celtic Swing and will appreciate another furlong. (op 7-1)

Sudden Impact(IRE) ran very close to her Thirsk debut form with Charlotti Carlotti, who finished one place in front of her on both occasions. She will find things easier back in maiden company. Official explanation: jockey said filly struck into itself and pulled a shoe off (op 7-1 tchd 15-2)

Coachhouse Lady(USA), a $275,000 sister to Rahy's Secret, a smart multiple winner at around 6f to 1m1f in the US, was the only filly in the race making her racecourse debut, but her trainer sent out a debutante to win this race last year and, given her starting price, it seems that there were plenty of people willing to believe he could repeat the trick. Eased when beaten, it will be a surprise if this form is a true reflection of her ability. (op 4-1)

2135 ROLLITS SOLICITORS CONDITIONS STKS — 5f

7:50 (7:51) (Class 3) 3-Y-O — **£7,478** (£2,239; £1,119; £560; £279) **Stalls** High

Form				RPR
1221	1		**Morinqua (IRE)**[12] 1825 3-8-7 89 ... TPQueally 4 (J G Given) *mde all: rdn along wl over 1f out: kpt on* **5/4**[1]	98+
444-	2	1	**Siren's Gift**[264] 5154 3-8-10 101 ... FrancisNorton 6 (A M Balding) *chsd wnr: rdn along wl over 1f out: drvn ins fnl f and kpt on* **7/4**[2]	97
4-11	3	4	**Jack Rackham**[21] 1577 3-9-1 86 ... KDarley 3 (B Smart) *sn outpcd and bhd: hdwy 2f out: sn rdn and kpt on fnl f* **4/1**[3]	88
-000	4	11	**Deserted Dane (USA)**[39] 1160 3-9-1 87 ... TPO'Shea 1 (G A Swinbank) *chsd ldng pair: rdn along over 2f out: sn wknd* **17/2**	48
6	5	6	**Bovered (IRE)**[19] 1623 3-8-7 0 ... PaulQuinn 5 (A Berry) *a outpcd and bhd* **100/1**	19

63.43 secs (-0.57) **Going Correction** +0.15s/f (Good) **5** Ran SP% **112.3**

Speed ratings (Par 103):110,108,102,84,74

CSF £3.84 TOTE £2.30: £1.20, £1.70; EX 4.60.

Owner The Living Legend Racing Partnership **Bred** Corrin Stud **Trained** Willoughton, Lincs

FOCUS

An uncompetitive race, dominated by the pair best in at the weights, and the quintet all gradually made their way across to the favoured stands' rail. The order hardly changed throughout the contest, but the time was decent for a race of its type and the winner looks most progressive. Morinqua was up another 6lb, with the second and third to form.

NOTEBOOK

Morinqua(IRE) ◆ utilised her dazzling early pace once again to gain the early lead and she never looked like getting caught. She looks a most progressive filly, who seems to go on just about any ground, and it will be a surprise if she cannot land a Listed sprint at least this season. (op 7-4)

Siren's Gift was always in the same place and though she never looked like catching the favourite, she did at least keep trying and finished right on her heels. On the face of it she ran below form as she would have been 9lb better off with her rival in a handicap, but on the other hand she was returning from eight months off and was up against a very progressive performer. (op 11-8 tchd 15-8)

Jack Rackham, spectacular winner of a course-and-distance handicap last time, faced an impossible task again the two fillies with whom he would have been 11lb and 20lb better off respectively in a handicap. He could never get near them, but also finished a long way clear of a rival with whom he was only 1lb badly in so connections will be hoping he has not totally blown his mark. (op 7-2 tchd 10-3)

Deserted Dane(USA), even though he faced an impossible task against the front pair, should have performed better than this strictly on official ratings and it seems he has not trained on. (op 11-1)

Bovered(IRE), as on her debut, had no chance at this level and was suitably outclassed.

2136 WEATHERBYS BLOODSTOCK INSURANCE H'CAP — 1m 1f 207y

8:20 (8:20) (Class 4) (0-85,84) 4-Y-O+ — **£4,857** (£1,445; £722; £360) **Stalls** High

Form				RPR
3002	1		**Fortunate Isle (USA)**[10] 1862 5-9-2 82 ... (p) TonyHamilton 2 (R A Fahey) *trckd ldr: hdwy to ld and c wd to stands' rails wl over 2f out: sn rdn: drvn over 1f out and kpt on gamely fnl f* **7/2**[2]	91
6-03	2	1 1/4	**Sir Arthur (IRE)**[9] 1890 4-8-6 72 ... JoeFanning 4 (M Johnston) *led: rdn along 3f out and sn hdd: drvn: rallied and ev ch over 1f out tl no ex wl ins fnl f* **11/2**	79
105-	3	nk	**Sunisa (IRE)**[68] 5769 6-8-10 76 ... NickyMackay 3 (J Mackie) *hld up in tch: hdwy wl over 2f out: rdn over 1f out: kpt on wl u.p fnl f* **12/1**	82
-023	4	3/4	**Mount Usher**[4] 2038 5-8-6 72 ... TPO'Shea 1 (G A Swinbank) *hld up in rr: hdwy 3f out: rdn along to chse ldrs wl over 1f out: kpt onsame pce ent fnl f* **11/4**[1]	77
2020	5	2 1/2	**Blacktoft (USA)**[24] 1494 4-8-12 78 ... (e) KDarley 6 (S C Williams) *chsd ldng pair: rdn along 3f out: drvn and wknd wl over 1f out* **10/1**	78
200-	6	1 3/4	**Dash To The Front**[249] 5525 4-9-4 84 ... MichaelHills 9 (J R Fanshawe) *hld up in rr: hdwy 3f out: rdn along over 2f out and no imp fr over 1f out* **4/1**[3]	80
-020	7	1/2	**Along The Nile**[39] 1149 5-9-4 84 ... (t) DavidAllan 5 (K G Reveley) *a towards rr* **10/1**	79
362-	8	20	**Magic Sting**[255] 5403 6-9-0 80 ... HayleyTurner 8 (B S Rothwell) *chsd ldrs: rdn along 3f out: sn wknd* **16/1**	35

2m 8.09s (0.79) **Going Correction** +0.15s/f (Good) **8** Ran SP% **116.0**

Speed ratings (Par 105):102,101,100,100,98 96,96,80

CSF £23.46 CT £207.63 TOTE £4.20: £1.20, £1.60, £4.20; EX 21.10.

Owner The First Team **Bred** Gainsborough Stud Management Ltd **Trained** Musley Bank, N Yorks

FOCUS

A reasonable handicap run at just a fair gallop and once again the whole field came towards the stands' side in the home straight. Those that raced up with the pace were at an advantage as the front two were at the sharp end throughout. Just ordinary form, rated through the third.

2137 RACING AGAIN ON 13 JUNE MAIDEN FILLIES' STKS — 7f 100y

8:50 (8:52) (Class 5) 3-Y-O+ — **£3,238** (£963; £481; £240) **Stalls** High

Form				RPR
342	1		**Medici Pearl**[8] 1913 3-8-10 0 ... DavidAllan 8 (T D Easterby) *trckd ldrs on inner: hdwy and wd st to stands' rail and led wl over 2f out: sn rdn and styd on wl fnl f* **7/1**[3]	77
63-	2	1 1/4	**Furbeseta**[200] 6433 3-8-10 0 ... NickyMackay 1 (L M Cumani) *hld un in rr: gd hdwy over 3f out: rdn to chse wnr wl over 1f out: sn drvn and kpt on ins fnl f* **7/2**[1]	74+
0-4	3	6	**Goodbye**[11] 1841 3-8-10 0 ... TPO'Shea 12 (G A Swinbank) *hld up in tch gng wl: hdwy 3f out: swtchd towards stands' rail and hmpd 2f out: sn rdn and styd on ins fnl f: nrst fin* **7/2**[1]	64+
	4	3	**Haedi** 3-8-10 0 ... (t) KDarley 4 (Saeed Bin Suroor) *in tch: hdwy over 3f out: rdn to chse wnr over 2f out: drvn wl over 1f out and sn wknd* **7/2**[1]	52
6223	5	2 1/2	**Diksie Dancer**[8] 1923 3-8-10 72 ... NCallan 11 (K A Ryan) *chsd ldrs: rdn along 3f out: sn one pce* **9/2**[2]	45
00	6	nk	**Entre Chat**[19] 1639 3-8-10 0 ... (t) TPQueally 6 (M Botti) *bhd: rdn along 3f out: kpt on fnl 2f* **66/1**	45
30	7	1/2	**Verone (USA)**[44] 1068 3-8-5 0 ... (t) NicolPolli[(5)] 5 (M Botti) *a towards rr* **50/1**	43
00-4	8	2 1/2	**Cadi May**[23] 1537 3-8-10 51 ... PatCosgrave 9 (W M Brisbourne) *led: rdn along over 3f out: hdd wl over 2f out and sn wknd* **100/1**	37
	9	1 1/4	**Beresford Lady** 3-8-10 0 ... SilvestreDeSousa 3 (A D Brown) *a in rr* **100/1**	34
0-60	10	4	**Slip Star**[123] 270 4-9-4 32 ... GregFairley[(3)] 10 (T J Etherington) *chsd ldrs: rdn along over 3f out and sn wknd* **100/1**	24
00-5	11	nk	**Musical Chimes**[23] 1537 4-9-4 41 ... DuranFentiman[(3)] 7 (W M Brisbourne) *chsd ldrs: rdn along 3f out: sn wknd* **100/1**	23

1m 35.14s (0.83) **Going Correction** +0.15s/f (Good)

WFA 3 from 4yo 11lb **11** Ran SP% **104.8**

Speed ratings (Par 100):101,99,92,89,86 86,85,82,81,76 76

CSF £26.34 TOTE £10.10: £2.20, £1.70, £1.70; EX 33.60 Place 6 £699.38, Place 5 £564.58.

Owner Ryedale Partners No 3 **Bred** Larkwood Stud **Trained** Great Habton, N Yorks

■ Stewards' Enquiry : T P O'Shea three-day ban: careless riding (Jun 10-12)

FOCUS

Not as competitive a maiden as the numbers would suggest, with five of these plus the withdrawn Dragon Flower going off at 7-1 or less, whilst the other six started at 50-1 or longer. The quintet at the top of the market duly dominated, but this was another race determined by the huge track bias as the front two raced closest to the stands' rail in the straight. The winner was up 12lb on her recent course form.

T/Plt: £1,477.30 to a £1 stake. Pool: £75,185.30. 37.15 winning tickets. T/Qpdt: £207.20 to a £1 stake. Pool: £3,949.70. 14.10 winning tickets. JR

1737 BRIGHTON (L-H)

Wednesday, May 30

OFFICIAL GOING: Soft

The going was changed from good (good to soft in places) after the first race, but attempts by jockeys to take the wide "soft ground" route ended in failure.

Wind: Fresh, half against Weather: Rain before racing, mainly cloudy later

2138 E B F TONY BOWLES LIFETIME IN RACING MAIDEN STKS — 5f 213y

2:00 (2:01) (Class 5) 2-Y-O — **£3,562** (£1,059; £529; £264) **Stalls** Low

Form				RPR
005	1		**Sirjoshua Reynolds**[11] 1846 2-8-12 0 ... WilliamBuick[(5)] 1 (N A Callaghan) *sn towards rr: styd alone far side st: hdwy over 2f out: led over 1f out: rdn clr* **9/2**	84+
03	2	3	**Romany Princess (IRE)**[20] 1608 2-8-12 0 ... PatDobbs 7 (R Hannon) *prom: c stands' side st: chsd wnr fnl f: no imp* **4/1**[3]	70+
332	3	2	**Shatter Resistant (IRE)**[14] 1762 2-9-3 0 ... JHBowman 8 (M R Channon) *led after 1f: brought to centre st: grad c wdr: hdd over 1f out: no ex fnl f* **10/3**[1]	69
0	4	nk	**Golden Penny**[11] 1832 2-9-3 0 ... SteveDrowne 3 (H Morrison) *dwlt: sn in tch: c stands' side st: outpcd over 2f out: styd on fnl f* **15/2**	68
3	5	1 1/2	**Prunes**[10] 1858 2-8-12 0 ... SebSanders 4 (Sir Mark Prescott) *led 1f: c stands' side st: outpcd fnl 2f* **7/2**[2]	59
0	6	2 1/2	**Nathan Dee**[23] 1540 2-9-3 0 ... DaneO'Neill 2 (R Hannon) *in rr: c stands' side st: rdn 3f out: nvr nr ldrs* **33/1**	56
	7	5	**Spinning Ridge (IRE)** 2-9-3 0 ... JimCrowley 5 (R A Harris) *s.s: sn drvn along: c stands' side st: a bhd* **20/1**	41
0	8	6	**New Colossus**[19] 1622 2-9-3 0 ... RichardMullen 6 (E J O'Neill) *plld hrd early: stdd to chse ldrs: c stands' side st: wknd 3f out* **9/1**	23

1m 12.08s (1.98) **Going Correction** +0.175s/f (Good) **8** Ran SP% **113.0**

Speed ratings (Par 93):93,89,86,85,83 80,73,65

CSF £22.24 TOTE £7.30: £2.30, £1.60, £1.20; EX 36.50.

Owner Matthew Green **Bred** Hedsor Stud **Trained** Newmarket, Suffolk

FOCUS

A routine maiden, but a fair one for the track. The winner raced alone and was advantaged to some extent. The form has been rated at face value through the third.

NOTEBOOK

Sirjoshua Reynolds's jockey had walked the track beforehand, concluding that the far side was the place to be - in contrast to all the other riders, who took the traditional "soft ground" wide route. Though that undoubtedly helped the winner confirm his superiority, he had shown plenty of promise in previous races and, with the stable now hitting form, his victory cannot be regarded as a complete fluke. (op 13-2)

Romany Princess(IRE) did best of those who came wide, only to be trumped by the lone runner on the far side - which appeared to give the winner an advantage. A market drifter, she continues to look capable of finding a race, and her options will be significantly increased now she is qualified for handicaps. (op 11-4)

Shatter Resistant(IRE) is bred to get this extra furlong, but he had looked more effective over 5f in his previous three races. He has plenty of early speed, and the uphill finish found him out at this stage of his career, but he should stay up to a mile in due course if his pedigree is any guide. (op 4-1)
Golden Penny, whose dam was a high-class miler in South Africa, has run as if 7f would suit in both his races to date. When he is qualified for nurseries, this son of the champion juvenile Xaar should really come into his own. (op 10-1 tchd 7-1)
Prunes is falling just a bit short, even in routine maiden company like this. However, she is showing enough to have possibilities, with nurseries beckoning after one more run. (op 11-4)
Nathan Dee has lacked early pace in his two races to date, and this 28,000gns colt from a good family looks likely to be better suited by longer trips, particularly when qualified for handicaps.

2139 WEATHERBYS BLOODSTOCK INSURANCE H'CAP 5f 213y
2:35 (2:35) (Class 4) (0-80,80) 4-Y-0+ **£4,605** (£1,378; £689; £344; £171) **Stalls** Low

Form RPR
6206 **1** **Lucayos**[6] [1971] 4-8-11 **80** KylieManser(7) 2 90
(Mrs H Sweeting) *mde all: styd far side st: drvn along and hld on wl fnl f* **12/1**
0005 **2** 3/4 **Pawan (IRE)**[6] [1977] 7-8-9 **76** ow1 (b) AnnStokell(5) 8 84
(Miss A Stokell) *hld up in rr: c stands' side st: hdwy and edgd lft over 1f out: chsd wnr ins fnl f: kpt on* **16/1**
3111 **3** 1 1/4 **Misaro (GER)**[12] [1806] 6-8-12 **79** (b) TolleyDean(5) 4 83
(R A Harris) *trckd ldng pair: styd far side st: wnt 2nd over 2f out: hrd rdn over 1f out: one pce* **7/2**[1]
60-4 **4** 2 **Seamus Shindig**[28] [1401] 5-9-1 **77** DaneO'Neill 7 75
(H Candy) *in tch: c stands' side st: rdn and hung lft fnl 2f: one pce* **4/1**[2]
5114 **5** shd **Who's Winning (IRE)**[11] [1847] 6-9-1 **80** RichardKingscote(3) 10 78
(B G Powell) *in tch: c stands' side st: styd on same pce fnl 2f* **11/2**[3]
0230 **6** 1 1/4 **Marko Jadeo (IRE)**[20] [1607] 9-8-9 **71** JimCrowley 6 65
(R A Harris) *dwlt: in rr: styd far side st: hdwy over 2f out: no ex over 1f out* **9/1**
3412 **7** 5 **Dvinsky (USA)**[27] [1431] 6-8-11 **73** IanMongan 3 52
(P Howling) *w wnr early: c stands' side st: hung lft and wknd over 1f out* **4/1**[2]
-000 **8** 8 **Jayanjay**[7] [1946] 8-8-10 **72** (p) SebSanders 9 27
(P Mitchell) *in tch: c stands' side st: wknd over 2f out: eased whn no ch fnl f* **10/1**

1m 11.82s (1.72) **Going Correction** +0.425s/f (Yiel) 8 Ran SP% **110.3**
Speed ratings (Par 105):105,104,102,99,99 97,91,80
CSF £167.15 CT £778.61 TOTE £17.30: £4.20, £1.50, £1.60; EX 168.30.
Owner Alex Sweeting **Bred** P Sweeting **Trained** Lockeridge, Wilts

FOCUS
A fair race of its type, and a competitive one, but a weak early pace for the trip and a slow time. With the first race having gone to the lone runner on the far side, it was strange that five still elected to come wide, with the winner being one of the three sticking to the inside. The form is not solid, with the runner-up hard to pin down.
Misaro(GER) Official explanation: jockey said gelding was unsuited by the soft ground
Dvinsky(USA) Official explanation: jockey said gelding hung left
Jayanjay Official explanation: jockey said gelding moved poorly throughout

2140 ARGUS (S) STKS 1m 1f 209y
3:10 (3:11) (Class 6) 3-5-Y-0 **£1,943** (£578; £288; £144) **Stalls** High

Form RPR
5335 **1** **Birkside**[14] [1765] 4-9-8 61 PaulDoe 8 69
(S Dow) *hld up towards rr: smooth hdwy 4f out: rdn to ld over 1f out: styd on wl* **4/1**[3]
022 **2** 2 **Prince Des Neiges (FR)**[2] [2084] 4-9-8 63 (p) SebSanders 3 65
(Ian Williams) *chsd ldr: drvn to chal 2f out: styd on same pce* **5/2**[1]
2566 **3** 5 **Missie Baileys**[7] [1951] 5-9-3 49 (p) IanMongan 5 50
(Mrs L J Mongan) *mid-div: sme hdwy and rdn over 3f out: kpt on to take 3rd fnl f* **7/1**
36-5 **4** 5 **The Jailer**[36] [1210] 4-9-3 42 DaneO'Neill 6 40
(J G M O'Shea) *led: 3 l clr 1/2-way: hdd over 1f out: sn wknd* **16/1**
56-0 **5** 1/2 **Elmasong**[13] [1784] 3-8-3 50 FrankieMcDonald 12 39
(J J Bridger) *prom: rdn over 3f out: wknd 2f out* **33/1**
00 **6** 2 **Ceol Eile (IRE)**[36] [1206] 4-9-3 47 SteveDrowne 9 35
(D Haydn Jones) *bhd: rdn and sme hdwy 3f out: no imp whn edgd lft 2f out* **11/1**
00-0 **7** 2 1/2 **Flashing Feet (IRE)**[142] [68] 3-8-8 40 (p) LPKeniry 4 35
(Mrs L C Jewell) *mid-div: rdn and btn 4f out: n.d whn hung lft 2f out* **50/1**
0600 **8** 3/4 **Bluecrop Boy**[36] [1224] 3-8-8 43 JimCrowley 11 34
(D J S Ffrench Davis) *in tch: rdn 1/2-way: sn lost pl* **66/1**
6400 **9** 19 **Show Business (IRE)**[15] [1739] 3-8-8 45 (vt[1]) RichardThomas 2 —
(P Butler) *chsd ldrs: drvn along 4f out: sn wknd* **66/1**
5250 **10** 2 1/2 **Santaverti**[20] [1609] 4-9-8 53 (b[1]) FergusSweeney 1 —
(G L Moore) *t.k.h early: in tch: wknd over 4f out: no ch fnl 3f* **20/1**
5431 **P** **Liberty Run (IRE)**[15] [1742] 5-9-1 56 JamieHamblett(7) 7 —
(Mouse Hamilton-Fairley) *s.s: hld up and bhd: rdn over 3f out: p.u lame over 2f out* **11/4**[2]

2m 6.44s (3.84) **Going Correction** +0.425s/f (Yiel)
WFA 3 from 4yo+ 14lb 11 Ran SP% **114.6**
Speed ratings (Par 101):101,99,95,91,91 89,87,86,71,69 —
CSF £13.43 TOTE £4.80: £2.00, £1.40, £2.40; EX 18.70.The winner was bought in for 10,000gns. Prince Des Neiges was claimed by Gary Martin for £6,000.
Owner I Hedgecock **Bred** Pendley Farm **Trained** Epsom, Surrey

FOCUS
The rain was getting into the ground by this stage but the time was not bad. A routine seller, but containing some fair sorts at this level as well as the usual slowcoaches. Birkside is better than the average plater.
Ceol Eile(IRE) Official explanation: jockey said filly hung right

2141 WEATHERBYS PRINTING H'CAP 1m 1f 209y
3:45 (3:46) (Class 6) (0-60,59) 4-Y-0+ **£2,137** (£635; £317; £158) **Stalls** High

Form RPR
20-0 **1** **Alqaayid**[16] 6-8-7 **51** StephaneBreux(3) 6 59
(P W Hiatt) *hld up in rr: n.m.r over 4f out: rdn and hdwy over 2f out: styd on to ld ins fnl f* **16/1**
205- **2** 3/4 **Justcallmehandsome**[191] [6544] 5-7-13 **47** LauraReynolds(7) 9 53
(D J S Ffrench Davis) *chsd ldrs: effrt and swtchd rt over 2f out: rdn to chal 1f out: kpt on* **11/1**
2604 **3** 3/4 **Shaheer (IRE)**[31] [1319] 5-8-10 **51** JimCrowley 3 56
(J Gallagher) *led 4f: rdn and lost pl over 3f out: rallied to ld wl over 1f out: hdd and nt qckn ins fnl f* **9/2**[1]
60-2 **4** hd **Piano Man**[14] [1761] 5-9-0 **58** RichardKingscote(3) 13 62
(B G Powell) *hld up in midfield: hdwy to ld over 2f out: hdd wl over 1f out: one pce fnl f* **6/1**
0035 **5** 8 **Twilight Avenger (IRE)**[22] [1570] 4-8-0 **46** ow1 (b) KevinGhunowa(5) 10 34
(W M Brisbourne) *towards rr: rdn and sme hdwy fnl 3f: nvr nr to chal* **25/1**
-060 **6** 5 **Prince Valentine**[15] [1740] 6-8-9 **50** (p) FergusSweeney 4 28
(G L Moore) *hld up towards rr: rdn and sme hdwy 2f out: no ex over 1f out* **15/2**
365- **7** 5 **Fortune Point (IRE)**[228] [4240] 9-8-13 **54** JHBowman 11 22
(A W Carroll) *w ldrs tl wknd 2f out* **10/1**
00-6 **8** 6 **Zinging**[15] [1742] 8-8-2 **46** ow1 (b) MarcHalford(3) 5 2
(J J Bridger) *towards rr: rdn and bmpd over 4f out: sn bhd* **16/1**
0300 **9** 3 **Competitor**[29] [1368] 6-8-6 **47** (b) PaulDoe 8 —
(J Akehurst) *s.s: sn in tch: led 3f out tl wknd qckly over 2f out* **14/1**
6000 **10** 1 1/2 **Mustard Benn**[70] [723] 4-8-4 **45** FrankieMcDonald 2 —
(Mouse Hamilton-Fairley) *a bhd: rdn and no ch fnl 4f* **40/1**
4003 **11** 1 **Makai**[15] [1741] 4-8-9 **50** (b) MatthewHenry 7 —
(J J Bridger) *w ldrs: led 6f out tl 3f out: wknd 2f out* **5/1**[2]
036- **12** 3 **The Iron Giant (IRE)**[138] [6769] 5-8-11 **52** SebSanders 12 —
(B G Powell) *trckd ldrs tl wknd 3f out* **11/2**[3]

2m 7.69s (5.09) **Going Correction** +0.50s/f (Yiel) 12 Ran SP% **118.4**
Speed ratings (Par 101):99,98,97,97,91 87,83,78,76,74 74,71
CSF £181.12 CT £934.50 TOTE £20.60: £4.60, £3.00, £2.20; EX 303.50.
Owner S F Holder **Bred** Meon Valley Stud **Trained** Hook Norton, Oxon

FOCUS
A poor race, no better than a seller, and a slow time. The first four pulled clear and the race has been rated through the second and third to their marks.
The Iron Giant(IRE) Official explanation: jockey said gelding was unbalanced

2142 SDS GROUP FILLIES' H'CAP 1m 3f 196y
4:20 (4:20) (Class 6) (0-65,61) 4-Y-0+ **£2,137** (£635; £317; £158) **Stalls** High

Form RPR
0-03 **1** **Snake Skin**[21] [1592] 4-8-9 **52** JimCrowley 3 64
(J Gallagher) *chsd ldrs: led 2f out: drvn clr over 1f out: styd on wl* **10/3**[2]
-051 **2** 5 **Adage**[16] [1730] 4-8-12 **55** (t) FergusSweeney 4 61+
(David Pinder) *hld up towards rr: hdwy 3f out: chsd wnr over 1f out: edgd lft: no imp* **7/2**[3]
0-63 **3** 6 **Lady Diktat**[14] [1764] 5-9-4 **61** JHBowman 1 55
(Mouse Hamilton-Fairley) *hld up in tch: rdn over 2f out: one pce* **6/1**
-554 **4** 2 **Squirtle (IRE)**[9] [1884] 4-9-4 **61** DaneO'Neill 8 52
(W M Brisbourne) *dwlt: sn chsng ldr: led 3f out tl 2f out: wknd over 1f out* **11/4**[1]
0-00 **5** 6 **Katie Lawson (IRE)**[9] [1886] 4-8-13 **56** (p) SteveDrowne 5 38
(D Haydn Jones) *bhd: pushed along and outpcd over 4f out: n.d after* **20/1**
0500 **6** 5 **Flashing Floozie**[9] [1888] 4-8-4 **47** oh2 RichardThomas 2 21
(A W Carroll) *led 4f: wknd over 2f out* **12/1**
-006 **7** 10 **Be Wise Girl**[8] [1934] 6-7-13 **47** oh2 WilliamBuick(5) 6 —
(A W Carroll) *in tch: led after 4f tl 3f out: sn wknd* **17/2**

2m 37.17s (4.97) **Going Correction** +0.50s/f (Yiel) 7 Ran SP% **109.2**
Speed ratings (Par 98):103,99,95,94,90 87,80
CSF £13.94 CT £58.45 TOTE £3.80: £1.40, £2.50; EX 17.80.
Owner Adweb Ltd **Bred** The C H F Partnership **Trained** Moreton-in-Marsh, Gloucs

FOCUS
A pretty weak race for fillies and mares, not strongly run. The winner was the best suited by the conditions and is rated up 5lb.

2143 SDS GROUP H'CAP 6f 209y
4:55 (4:55) (Class 6) (0-60,60) 4-Y-0+ **£1,943** (£578; £288; £144) **Stalls** Low

Form RPR
32 **1** **Vegas Boys**[21] [1589] 4-9-4 **60** SebSanders 5 69+
(M Wigham) *trckd ldrs: effrt on bit ins fnl 2f: led jst ins fnl f: drvn out* **7/2**[1]
2644 **2** nk **Lady Duxyana**[18] [1673] 4-8-4 **46** oh1 (v) RichardSmith 11 54
(M D I Usher) *s.s: bhd: gd hdwy and edgd lft over 1f out: r.o to chse wnr fnl 75yds* **12/1**
2020 **3** 1 **Machinate (USA)**[30] [1366] 5-8-11 **53** DaneO'Neill 1 58
(W M Brisbourne) *mid-div: hdwy and hrd rdn over 1f out: kpt on fnl f* **11/1**
00-2 **4** 1 1/2 **Drawback (IRE)**[8] [1921] 4-8-8 **55** (p) TolleyDean(5) 8 57
(R A Harris) *chsd ldrs: rdn and lost pl over 2f out: styd on fnl f* **9/1**
0406 **5** shd **Bollywood (IRE)**[15] [1739] 4-8-4 **46** oh1 FrankieMcDonald 6 47
(J J Bridger) *towards rr: rdn and hdwy over 1f out: kpt on fnl f* **28/1**
60-0 **6** nk **Limonia (GER)**[23] [1534] 5-8-1 **48** KevinGhunowa(5) 3 48
(Mike Murphy) *led tl 2f out: one pce* **16/1**
5-03 **7** nk **Mamichor**[15] [1742] 4-8-4 **46** oh1 RichardThomas 14 46
(B R Johnson) *in tch on outside: drvn along and no prog 3f out: hung lft 2f out: kpt on fnl f* **16/1**
0502 **8** nk **Ceredig**[6] [1969] 4-8-8 **50** JimCrowley 9 49
(P W Hiatt) *prom: hrd rdn 2f out: sn btn* **13/2**[2]
400- **9** shd **Willofcourse**[323] [3389] 6-8-3 **52** AmyScott(7) 4 51
(H Candy) *prom: led 2f out tl jst ins fnl f: no ex* **33/1**
0000 **10** 1 3/4 **Drury Lane (IRE)**[9] [1893] 7-8-10 **57** oh1 ow11 (b) AnnStokell(5) 7 51?
(Miss A Stokell) *bhd: rdn along 1/2-way: nvr rchd ldrs* **66/1**
1-00 **11** hd **Megalala (IRE)**[20] [1612] 6-8-5 **50** MarcHalford(3) 15 44
(J J Bridger) *towards rr on outside: drvn along and n.d fnl 3f* **14/1**
0-00 **12** 3/4 **Spoilsport**[128] [210] 4-7-13 **46** oh1 WilliamBuick(5) 10 38
(G A Butler) *hld up in rr: c wd 3f out: rdn and nvr nr ldrs* **9/1**
2-46 **13** nk **Cree**[142] [66] 5-9-2 **58** JHBowman 2 49
(W R Muir) *hld up in tch: effrt 2f out: wknd 1f out: eased whn btn* **15/2**[3]
00-0 **14** 3/4 **Colonel Cotton (IRE)**[18] [1681] 8-9-0 **56** PaulDoe 13 45
(W J Knight) *prom 5f* **16/1**
4106 **15** 5 **King Of Charm (IRE)**[28] [1400] 4-8-6 **48** (b) FergusSweeney 12 24
(G L Moore) *mid-div tl rdn and wknd 2f out* **16/1**

1m 25.24s (2.54) **Going Correction** +0.50s/f (Yiel) 15 Ran SP% **121.4**
Speed ratings (Par 101):105,104,103,101,101 101,101,100,100,98 98,97,97,96,90
CSF £45.73 CT £440.22 TOTE £3.80: £2.00, £3.20, £2.10; EX 54.40.
Owner P R Iron **Bred** Brimpton Bloodstock **Trained** Newmarket, Suffolk

FOCUS
A low-grade, but very competitive, handicap. The level of form is sound amongst the principals and the winner was well in on sand form.
Mamichor Official explanation: jockey said gelding hung left
Cree Official explanation: jockey said gelding ran too free

2144 BRIGHTON'S JUICE 107.2 H'CAP — 5f 59y

5:25 (5:25) (Class 5) (0-75,74) 3-Y-O — **£2,849** (£847; £423; £211) **Stalls** Low

Form	Pos	Dist	Horse	RPR
215	**1**		**Telltime (IRE)**[26] 1450 3-8-11 **72** ... WilliamBuick(5) 7 (A M Balding) *cl up: rdn over 2f out: r.o to ld ins fnl f* **7/2**[3]	74
52	**2**	1	**Spiffing (IRE)**[15] 1737 3-8-12 **68** ... SebSanders 2 (R M Beckett) *led: hrd rdn over 1f out: hdd and nt qckn ins fnl f* **11/10**[1]	66
1664	**3**	½	**My Drop (IRE)**[15] 1738 3-8-7 **70** ... MCGeran(7) 1 (E J O'Neill) *plld hrd: cl up: effrt and n.m.r on rail fr over 1f out: kpt on* **3/1**[2]	66+
5100	**4**	nk	**Mr Loire**[26] 1450 3-9-4 **74** ... (v[1]) DaneO'Neill 4 (H J L Dunlop) *sn trcking ldr: drvn to chal over 1f out: no ex fnl f* **6/1**	69

65.41 secs (3.11) **Going Correction** +0.50s/f (Yiel) — **4** Ran SP% **109.1**
Speed ratings (Par 99):95,93,92,92
CSF £7.92 TOTE £3.90; EX 7.80 Place 6 £72.95, Place 5 £44.77.
Owner Mrs P McEnery **Bred** John McEnery **Trained** Kingsclere, Hants

FOCUS
With three intended runners pulled out, the race lacked numbers but the quality was fair. Modest form for the grade, rated through the runner-up, with Telltime up 5lb.
T/Jkpt: Not won. T/Plt: £126.20 to a £1 stake. Pool: £67,412.00. 389.75 winning tickets. T/Qpdt: £35.90 to a £1 stake. Pool: £3,440.30. 70.90 winning tickets. LM

1975 SOUTHWELL (L-H)

Wednesday, May 30

OFFICIAL GOING: Standard
Wind: Light, across Weather: Cloudy with the odd shower

2145 SOUTHWELL-RACECOURSE.CO.UK APPRENTICE H'CAP — 1m (F)

6:35 (6:37) (Class 6) (0-60,59) 4-Y-0+ — **£2,388** (£705; £352) **Stalls** Low

Form	Pos	Dist	Horse	RPR
3000	**1**		**Tabulate**[18] 1671 4-9-0 **54** ... MarkCoumbe 8 (P L Gilligan) *hld up: hdwy over 2f out: rdn to chse wnr and hung lft over 1f out: led ins fnl f: styd on wl* **20/1**	66
4210	**2**	3	**Government (IRE)**[8] 1933 6-8-4 **49** ... MJMurphy(5) 10 (M C Chapman) *led 7f out: hdd over 5f out: chsd ldr: outpcd over 2f out: styd on ins fnl f* **9/1**	54
010	**3**	1	**Feelin Irie (IRE)**[47] 1027 4-8-10 **55** ... (p) MatthewDavies(5) 2 (J R Boyle) *sn led: hdd 7f out: led again over 5f out: clr 1/2-way: rdn over 1f out: hdd and no ex ins fnl f* **5/1**[1]	58
0360	**4**	2	**Kumakawa**[21] 1592 9-8-9 **49** ... (b) PatrickDonaghy 5 (N P Littmoden) *mid-div: styd on fnl 2f: nvr trbld ldrs* **16/1**	47
-401	**5**	¾	**Middle Eastern**[29] 1379 5-9-4 **58** ... (p) SophieDoyle 3 (P A Blockley) *hld up: hdwy over 1f out: nt trble ldrs* **5/1**[1]	54
0342	**6**	½	**Don Pasquale**[15] 1750 5-8-5 **45** ... SoniaEaton 1 (J T Stimpson) *hld up: styd on appr fnl f: n.d* **12/1**	40
0003	**7**	3	**Key Partners (IRE)**[16] 1720 6-9-5 **59** ... DeanHeslop 12 (J T Stimpson) *hld up: hdwy over 2f out: wknd over 1f out* **6/1**[2]	47
5503	**8**	shd	**Spy Gun (USA)**[16] 1715 7-8-5 **45** ... JosephWalsh 9 (T Wall) *chsd ldrs: sn drvn along: wknd over 2f out* **12/1**	33
5026	**9**	2	**Kirkhammerton (IRE)**[16] 1717 5-8-7 **52** ... (b) AdamCarter(5) 14 (A J McCabe) *chsd ldrs: rdn 1/2-way: wknd 3f out* **15/2**[3]	35
0044	**10**	1¾	**Piccleyes**[16] 1719 6-8-0 **45** ... (be) PNolan(5) 6 (A J McCabe) *chsd ldrs over 5f* **25/1**	24
00-1	**11**	2	**Sonic Anthem (USA)**[21] 666 5-9-5 **59** ... ChrisHough 4 (P C Haslam) *hld up: rdn 1/2-way: a in rr* **5/1**[1]	34
000-	**12**	2	**Inchloss (IRE)**[327] 3263 6-8-4 **49** ow4 ... GaryEdwards(5) 11 (S Parr) *prom: lost pl 5f out: bhd fnl 3f* **66/1**	19
0505	**13**	11	**Barzak (IRE)**[15] 1750 7-8-0 **45** ... LeeTopliss(5) 7 (S R Bowring) *hld up: a in rr: bhd fnl 3f* **33/1**	—

1m 43.16s (-1.44) **Going Correction** -0.225s/f (Stan) — **13** Ran SP% **120.4**
Speed ratings (Par 101):98,95,94,92,91 90,87,87,85,83 81,79,68
CSF £186.08 CT £1085.06 TOTE £20.50: £5.80, £4.10, £3.10; EX 507.20.
Owner Harvey Bell **Bred** Millsec Limited **Trained** Newmarket, Suffolk
■ Stewards' Enquiry : Gary Edwards caution: used whip when out of contention

FOCUS
A moderate heat, run at strong early pace which rather set things up for the winner. The second and third were close to form.
Barzak(IRE) Official explanation: trainer said gelding finished lame

2146 3RD JUNE IS FAMILY FUN DAY CLAIMING STKS — 6f (F)

7:05 (7:05) (Class 6) 3-Y-O — **£2,184** (£644; £322) **Stalls** Low

Form	Pos	Dist	Horse	RPR
3160	**1**		**Totally Free**[14] 1763 3-8-10 58 ... (v) TravisBlock(5) 4 (M D I Usher) *sn outpcd: hdwy over 1f out: rdn to ld ins fnl f: comf* **9/1**	66
2535	**2**	1½	**Fractured Foxy**[16] 1710 3-9-2 70 ... GrahamGibbons 5 (J J Quinn) *s.i.s: hdwy over 4f out: rdn over 2f out: styd on* **11/10**[1]	63
-362	**3**	1	**Josr's Magic (IRE)**[8] 1912 3-8-6 63 ... (b) HaddenFrost(7) 3 (R M Stronge) *chsd ldr over 4f out: rdn to ld over 1f out: hdd and no ex ins fnl f* **5/2**[2]	57
-000	**4**	5	**Retaliate**[12] 1820 3-9-2 65 ... ChrisCatlin 1 (M Quinn) *chsd ldrs: rdn over 2f out: hung rt and wknd fnl f* **10/1**	45
0-06	**5**	4	**Maeve (IRE)**[14] 1763 3-8-6 45 ... EdwardCreighton 8 (E J Creighton) *hld up: rdr dropped whip over 2f out: wknd over 1f out* **28/1**	23
060-	**6**	1½	**Nepos**[240] 5738 3-8-11 58 ... AdamKirby 7 (A J McCabe) *sn rdn to ld: hdd over 1f out: wknd fnl f* **6/1**[3]	23

1m 16.9s **Going Correction** -0.225s/f (Stan) — **6** Ran SP% **113.0**
Speed ratings (Par 97):91,89,87,81,75 73
CSF £19.86 TOTE £8.80: £3.20, £1.70; EX 26.80.Josr's Magic was claimed by Mr K. Tyre for £8,000. Totally Free was the subject of a friendly claim.
Owner I Sheward **Bred** B Mills **Trained** Upper Lambourn, Berks

FOCUS
Just an ordinary claimer and the winning time was modest. It is doubtful whether the winner had to improve anywhere near as much as the figures would suggest.

2147 JOIN NODDY AND BIG-EARS ON SUNDAY MAIDEN AUCTION STKS — 6f (F)

7:35 (7:36) (Class 6) 2-Y-O — **£2,184** (£644; £322) **Stalls** Low

Form	Pos	Dist	Horse	RPR
	1		**Ellmau** 2-8-13 0 ... ChrisCatlin 7 (E J O'Neill) *w ldr tl led 1/2-way: drvn out* **7/1**[3]	78
50	**2**	hd	**Dubai Dynamo**[11] 1832 2-8-11 0 ... JohnEgan 5 (J S Moore) *chsd ldrs: rdn and hung lft over 2f out: r.o u.p* **3/1**[2]	75
02	**3**	¾	**Rub Of The Relic (IRE)**[16] 1713 2-9-1 0 ... SimonWhitworth 1 (P A Blockley) *led to 1/2-way: rdn over 1f out: styd on same pce ins fnl f* **7/1**[3]	77
22	**4**	1½	**Fol Hollow (IRE)**[16] 1706 2-8-9 0 ... AdrianTNicholls 8 (D Nicholls) *chsd ldrs: rdn over 1f out: edgd rt and no ex ins fnl f* **11/8**[1]	66+
54	**5**	10	**Countrywide Comet (IRE)**[9] 1889 2-9-1 0 ... DO'Donohoe 4 (K A Ryan) *s.i.s: hdwy over 4f out: rdn and wknd 2f out* **28/1**	42
60	**6**	hd	**Myriola**[22] 1553 2-8-10 0 ... DeanMcKeown 3 (J G Given) *chsd ldrs over 3f* **18/1**	37
	7	5	**Bonny's Babe** 2-8-6 0 ... PaulEddery 2 (B Smart) *s.i.s: outpcd* **22/1**	18
	8	¾	**Smith Esquire (USA)** 2-8-13 0 ... AdamKirby 9 (W R Swinburn) *mid-div: rdn over 3f out: sn wknd* **10/1**	22
	9	½	**Moss Way** 2-8-9 0 ... DavidKinsella 10 (W J Musson) *sn outpcd* **33/1**	17
0	**10**	5	**Lady Grantley**[10] 1859 2-8-2 0 ow3 ... NSLawes(7) 6 (M W Easterby) *sn outpcd* **66/1**	—
0	**11**	8	**Eighty Twenty**[32] 1285 2-8-6 0 ... DaleGibson 11 (M W Easterby) *mid-div: rdn and wknd over 3f out* **33/1**	—

1m 16.47s (-0.43) **Going Correction** -0.225s/f (Stan) — **11** Ran SP% **121.6**
Speed ratings (Par 91):93,92,91,89,76 76,69,68,67,61 50
CSF £28.02 TOTE £8.90: £2.20, £1.20, £1.60; EX 42.90.
Owner Premspace Ltd **Bred** Lady Hardy **Trained** Averham Park, Notts
■ Stewards' Enquiry : John Egan one-day ban: used whip with excessive frequency and without giving colt time to respond (Jun 10)

FOCUS
Just a modest maiden but a reasonable race for the track, the first four finishing clear. The runner-up stepped forward from his last run with the third rated to his mark.

NOTEBOOK
Ellmau, an 8,000gns half-brother to quite useful Laureldean Express, who was placed over 6f-1m at two, out of a 1m2f winner who was later successful over hurdles, ran out a narrow winner on his racecourse debut. This looked a modest race, but there could be more to come. (op 5-1 tchd 9-2)
Dubai Dynamo would have found this easier than the Newbury maiden he contested on his previous start and only just failed. (op 4-1)
Rub Of The Relic(IRE) improved for the step up in trip and is going the right way. (op 9-1 tchd 11-2)
Fol Hollow(IRE) was well below the form he had shown on his two previous starts and appeared unsuited by both the step up in trip and switch to sand. Official explanation: jockey said colt hung on bend (op 6-4 tchd 2-1 and 5-4)
Countrywide Comet(IRE) offered very little and could be more of a nursery type. (op 33-1)
Eighty Twenty Official explanation: jockey said filly hung left

2148 PETER AND LOUISE LANE WEDDING DAY H'CAP — 1m 6f (F)

8:05 (8:05) (Class 5) (0-75,72) 4-Y-0+ — **£3,071** (£906; £453) **Stalls** Low

Form	Pos	Dist	Horse	RPR
166	**1**		**Global Strategy**[13] 1793 4-9-3 **68** ... ChrisCatlin 1 (Rae Guest) *hld up: hdwy over 4f out: sn rdn: chsd ldr over 2f out: led and edgd lft over 1f out: styd on u.p* **6/4**[1]	82+
1202	**2**	2	**Arsad (IRE)**[15] 1752 4-9-6 **71** ... (b[1]) SebSanders 5 (C E Brittain) *sn drvn to chse clr ldr: led over 3f out: rdn and hdd over 1f out: edgd lft and no ex* **9/2**[3]	80
120	**3**	2	**Al Moulatham**[50] 994 8-8-6 **57** ... (bt) DO'Donohoe 4 (R Ford) *led and sn clr: rdn over 4f out: hdd over 3f out: styd on same pce fnl 2f* **12/1**	63
55-4	**4**	2	**Cotton Eyed Joe (IRE)**[15] 1752 6-9-1 **66** ... DeanMcKeown 2 (G A Swinbank) *hld up: hdwy over 4f out: sn rdn: wknd over 1f out* **3/1**[2]	69
-230	**5**	1¼	**Ha'Penny Beacon**[13] 1794 4-9-0 **65** ... GrahamGibbons 6 (D Carroll) *prom: rdn over 5f out: sn lost pl: n.d after* **18/1**	67
4351	**6**	1¼	**Eforetta (GER)**[15] 1752 5-9-1 **66** ... SamHitchcott 7 (D J Wintle) *hld up: rdn 10f out: hdwy over 6f out: over 1f out* **5/1**	66

3m 9.14s (-0.46) **Going Correction** -0.225s/f (Stan) — **6** Ran SP% **112.8**
Speed ratings (Par 103):92,90,89,88,87 87
CSF £8.77 TOTE £1.90: £1.80, £2.90; EX 7.40.
Owner E P Duggan **Bred** Keith Freeman **Trained** Newmarket, Suffolk

FOCUS
A very moderate winning time for the class, but the form looks sound enough rated through the second. Global Strategy, who is unbeaten round here, was value for a bit extra.

2149 JOURNEY SOUTH PLAY AFTER RACING H'CAP — 7f (F)

8:35 (8:35) (Class 6) (0-65,65) 4-Y-0+ — **£2,388** (£705; £352) **Stalls** Low

Form	Pos	Dist	Horse	RPR
1041	**1**		**Doctor's Cave**[15] 1755 5-9-3 **64** ... (b) SebSanders 11 (K O Cunningham-Brown) *led over 5f out: rdn and edgd rt fr over 1f out: styd on* **4/1**[2]	80
0060	**2**	1¾	**Lii Najma**[15] 1747 4-9-4 **65** ... JohnEgan 9 (C E Brittain) *chsd wnr 5f out: rdn over 2f out: styd on same pce ins fnl f* **12/1**	76
-400	**3**	1	**Scuba (IRE)**[19] 1640 5-8-5 **57** ... (b) TravisBlock(5) 6 (H Morrison) *chsd ldrs: rdn 1/2-way: styd on same pce fnl f* **15/2**	66
2632	**4**	1¼	**Cleveland**[15] 1755 5-8-11 **63** ... RussellKennemore(5) 3 (R Hollinshead) *hld up in tch: plld hrd: effrt over 2f out: no ex ins fnl f* **11/4**[1]	69+
4634	**5**	2½	**Modern Verse (USA)**[24] 1491 4-8-12 **59** ... DeanMcKeown 7 (G A Swinbank) *prom: rdn over 2f out: styd on same pce* **9/1**	58
5024	**6**	2	**Wainwright (IRE)**[15] 1753 7-8-5 **52** ... (t) AlanDaly 1 (P A Blockley) *hld up: hdwy u.p over 1f out: no imp fnl f* **11/1**	46
0010	**7**	½	**Alsadaa (USA)**[15] 1755 4-9-1 **62** ... DaleGibson 4 (M W Easterby) *s.i.s: hdwy 1/2-way: rdn and wknd 2f out* **7/1**[3]	55
5332	**8**	½	**Penel (IRE)**[15] 1744 6-8-1 **53** ow2 ... (p) RoryMoore(5) 10 (P T Midgley) *chsd ldrs over 4f* **8/1**	44
00-0	**9**	nk	**Top Dirham**[18] 1673 9-8-2 **56** ... NSLawes(7) 2 (M W Easterby) *hld up: rdn 1/2-way: wknd over 2f out* **22/1**	47
021	**10**	1	**Shaftesbury Avenue (USA)**[69] 728 4-8-6 **60** ... (bt) JamesO'Reilly(7) 5 (J O'Reilly) *s.i.s: outpcd* **8/1**	48
030-	**11**	8	**Sea Frolic (IRE)**[169] 6799 6-8-4 **51** oh6 ... AdrianTNicholls 8 (Jennie Candlish) *led: hdd over 5f out: rdn 1/2-way: wknd 2f out* **40/1**	18
44/0	**12**	11	**Lytham (IRE)**[15] 1755 6-8-10 **57** ... VinceSlattery 12 (D J Wintle) *mid-div: rdn and wknd over 2f out* **50/1**	—

1m 28.12s (-2.68) **Going Correction** -0.225s/f (Stan) — **12** Ran SP% **127.9**
Speed ratings (Par 101):106,104,102,101,98 96,95,95,94,93 84,71
CSF £55.30 CT £368.76 TOTE £7.60: £2.50, £3.80, £2.80; EX 65.70.

The Form Book, Raceform Ltd, Compton, RG20 6NL

Owner A J Richards & Michael A Richards **Bred** Tweenhills Stud And Genesis Green Stud **Trained** Nether Wallop, Hants

FOCUS
A decent winning time for the grade and the form looks fair for the class. Sound form too, with the first four all solid performers at around this trip.

2150 LET'S PARTY IN PADDOCK H'CAP 1m (F)
9:05 (9:05) (Class 5) (0-75,76) 3-Y-O **£3,071** (£906; £453) **Stalls** Low

Form RPR
-101 **1** **Tilapia (IRE)**[8] [1936] 3-9-7 **76** 6ex........ SebSanders 2 88+
(Sir Mark Prescott) *dwlt: sn led: rdn over 2f out: hung lft ins fnl f: drvn out* **5/6**[1]
01-0 **2** 3 1/2 **Sularno**[16] [1724] 3-8-10 **70**........ TravisBlock(5) 3 74
(H Morrison) *chsd ldrs: rdn over 3f out: styd on same pce ins fnl f* **5/1**[2]
415 **3** *hd* **Krakatau (FR)**[18] [1672] 3-8-7 **62**........ SamHitchcott 1 66
(D J Wintle) *w wnr tl rdn over 2f out: hung rt and no ex ins fnl f* **8/1**
2100 **4** 5 **Paymaster General (IRE)**[11] [1835] 3-9-4 **73**........ ChrisCatlin 6 65
(M D I Usher) *chsd ldrs: rdn over 3f out: wknd 2f out* **7/1**
6522 **5** 2 1/2 **First Princess (IRE)**[2] [2077] 3-8-7 **62**........(p) JohnEgan 4 48
(J S Moore) *chsd ldrs over 5f* **6/1**[3]
-001 **6** 6 **Cavort (IRE)**[16] [1731] 3-9-3 **72**........ PaulEddery 5 44
(Pat Eddery) *chsd ldrs: rdn over 3f out: wknd over 2f out* **10/1**

1m 41.76s (-2.84) **Going Correction** -0.225s/f (Stan) **6** Ran SP% **118.2**
Speed ratings (Par 99):105,101,101,96,93 87
CSF £6.00 TOTE £1.80: £1.90, £3.80; EX 7.30 Place 6 £56.22, Place 5 £18.16.
Owner G D Waters **Bred** G D Waters **Trained** Newmarket, Suffolk

FOCUS
A smart winning time for a race of its type and the form looks solid for the grade. The progressive Tilapia was up another 7lb.
Krakatau(FR) Official explanation: jockey said colt hung right in final furlong
T/Plt: £121.10 to a £1 stake. Pool: £58,399.10. 352.00 winning tickets. T/Qpdt: £14.70 to a £1 stake. Pool: £4,597.50. 230.60 winning tickets. CR

1267 YARMOUTH (L-H)
Wednesday, May 30
OFFICIAL GOING: Good (good to soft in places, 6.3)
Wind: strong across Weather: overcast

2151 EUROPEAN BREEDERS' FUND NOVICE STKS 6f 3y
2:10 (2:11) (Class 5) 2-Y-O **£3,469** (£1,038; £519; £259; £129) **Stalls** High

Form RPR
1 **1** **Spitfire**[18] [1680] 2-9-2 0........ KerrinMcEvoy 6 89+
(J R Jenkins) *hld up bhd ldrs: plld out and hdwy over 2f out: led 1f out: pushed clr: readily* **85/40**[1]
5 **2** 2 1/2 **Jebel Tara**[42] [1094] 2-8-12 0........ EddieAhern 7 76
(C E Brittain) *led tl 1/2-way: rdn 2f out: kpt on u.p to go 2nd ins fnl f: no ch w wnr* **4/1**[3]
1 **3** 1 **Rubirosa (IRE)**[10] [1859] 2-9-5 0........ DarryllHolland 5 80
(M Dods) *t.k.h: chsd ldr tl led 1/2-way: rdn and hdd 1f out: sn outpcd by wnr: lost 2nd ins fnl f* **9/4**[2]
4 2 1/2 **Mr Fantozzi (IRE)** 2-8-12 0........ BrettDoyle 2 65
(Miss J Feilden) *trckd ldrs on outer: rdn over 2f out: wknd over 1f out* **6/1**
0 **5** 4 **Insomnitas**[11] [1846] 2-8-12 0........ TedDurcan 3 53
(M G Quinlan) *hld up in tch: rdn over 2f out: sn wknd* **22/1**
6 4 **Wooden King (IRE)** 2-8-12 0........ StephenDonohoe 1 41
(P D Evans) *wnt lft sn after s: dropped in bhd: a last: rdn 1/2-way: sn lost tch* **11/1**

1m 18.89s (5.19) **Going Correction** +0.60s/f (Yiel) **6** Ran SP% **109.7**
Speed ratings (Par 93):89,85,84,81,75 70
CSF £10.44 TOTE £3.40: £2.00, £1.40; EX 9.40.
Owner The Spitfire Partnership **Bred** R B Hill **Trained** Royston, Herts

FOCUS
Spitfire impressed in what was probably a fair maiden for the time of year, although it is not too easy to set the level.

NOTEBOOK
Spitfire, a strong gelding with scope, powered clear of his rivals when asked to quicken and came home an impressive winner. Clearly heading in the right direction, he will need to up his game again when meeting classier types. (op 9-4 tchd 5-2 and 2-1)
Jebel Tara did not get the best of runs up the stands'-side rail, but kept on in pleasing style to suggest he will be winning races. A seventh furlong seems sure to be within his scope. (tchd 10-3)
Rubirosa(IRE), who was carrying top weight, was always close to the pace but did not get home in the face of a headwind. He does, however, remain a promising sort and should be capable of winning again. (tchd 11-4)
Mr Fantozzi(IRE), whose stable houses the exciting Spirit Of Sharjah, showed enough promise, despite getting little cover during the race, to suggest he will be winning races. He was not given a hard race by his jockey and looks to have plenty of scope for improvement physically. (op 5-1 tchd 9-2)
Insomnitas probably ran to much the same level as he did on his debut, and will be of more interest in nurseries later in the season. (op 25-1 tchd 28-1)
Wooden King(IRE) was far too green on his debut to do himself justice. (op 12-1 tchd 10-1)

2152 GREAT YARMOUTH MERCURY (S) STKS 6f 3y
2:45 (2:45) (Class 6) 2-Y-O **£1,943** (£578; £288; £144) **Stalls** High

Form RPR
3 **1** **Pearo (IRE)**[4] [2028] 2-8-1 0........ ColinHaddon(5) 2 57
(J S Moore) *wnt bdly lft s: sn chsng ldrs: rdn and edgd lft 2 fout: led wl over 1f out: styd on wl* **11/2**
0 **2** 1 3/4 **Bettys Touch**[3] [2056] 2-8-3 0........ SaleemGolam(3) 4 52
(P J McBride) *t.k.h: chsd ldr: ev ch 2f out: sn rdn and hung lft: nt qckn fnl f* **15/8**[1]
00 **3** 1/2 **Redbackcappuchino (IRE)**[11] [1848] 2-8-6 0........ EddieAhern 5 51
(J L Spearing) *t.k.h: trckd ldrs: rdn and outpcd wl over 1f out: kpt on again ins fnl f* **9/2**[3]
440 **4** 2 1/2 **Mama Leo**[32] [1285] 2-8-7 0 ow1........ StephenDonohoe 3 44
(P D Evans) *led: rdn 2f out: sn hdd: hung lft over 1f: wknd 1f out* **2/1**[2]
5 26 **Fahed** 2-8-11 0........ RobertHavlin 1 —
(J R Jenkins) *carried bdly lft s: sn wl outpcd: tailled off last 2f* **11/1**

1m 20.68s (6.98) **Going Correction** +0.60s/f (Yiel) **5** Ran SP% **110.0**
Speed ratings (Par 91):77,74,74,70,36
CSF £16.22 TOTE £5.20: £1.90, £1.80; EX 12.80.The winner was bought in for 7,600gns. Bettys Touch was claimed by W Musson for £5,000.
Owner Willie McKay **Bred** Johnny Kent **Trained** Upper Lambourn, Berks
■ Colin Haddon's first winner in Britain since 2005, following a spell in the United States.

FOCUS
A very slow winning time, even for a juvenile seller. An improved effort from the winner, but this was not a strong race for the grade.

NOTEBOOK
Pearo(IRE), third in this grade on her debut at Catterick, shot left coming out of the stalls but still managed to obtain a good early position and she then picked up strongly under pressure to win with a bit to spare. She can score again in a similar grade of contest and may go on to show herself a bit better than this in time. (tchd 15-2)
Bettys Touch, outclassed in a Newmarket maiden on her debut, appreciated the drop in grade and ran a solid race in second, appearing to appreciate the extra furlong. (op 5-2)
Redbackcappuchino(IRE) was kept under a strong hold early, but she took time to pick up when asked and could only keep on steadily under pressure. (op 6-1 tchd 7-2)
Mama Leo proved to be the disappointment of the race. Her form in maidens entitled her to go well here, but she hung under pressure and looks to have a bit to prove now. (op 11-8)
Fahed, making his debut at a lowly level, ran as though something was amiss and can probably be given another chance. (op 14-1)

2153 EXPRESS CAFES MAIDEN STKS 1m 3y
3:20 (3:21) (Class 5) 3-Y-O+ **£2,914** (£867; £433; £216) **Stalls** High

Form RPR
02-2 **1** **We'll Come**[25] [1471] 3-9-0 **84**........ PhilipRobinson 12 94+
(M A Jarvis) *s.i.s: t.k.h: sn chsng ldr in centre: led 2f out: rdn and hung rt fnl f: jst hld on* **4/6**[1]
2 *shd* **Gongidas** 3-9-0 0........ KerrinMcEvoy 7 94+
(Saeed Bin Suroor) *v.s.a: sn in midfield: hdwy 3f out: hung lft fr over 1f out: chsd wnr ins fnl f: jst failed* **6/1**[3]
4 **3** 3 1/2 **Fondled**[19] [1639] 3-8-9 0........ EddieAhern 14 81+
(J R Fanshawe) *s.i.s: t.k.h: sn chsng ldrs in centre: hdwy over 2f out: chsd wnr wl over 1f out: kpt on same pce fnl f* **7/2**[2]
2- **4** 1 3/4 **Sign Of The Cross**[203] [6393] 3-9-0 0........ GeorgeBaker 8 82+
(J R Fanshawe) *s.i.s: hld up in centre: hdwy 3f out: chsd ldrs and rdn wl over 1f out: no hdwy fnl f* **11/1**
4-30 **5** 7 **Alpes Maritimes**[32] [1290] 3-9-0 **75**........ DarryllHolland 6 66
(G Wragg) *led centre gp tl overall ldr over 2f out: sn hdd & wknd* **14/1**
6 10 **Littlemissdynamite** 4-9-7 0........ StephenDonohoe 5 41
(J McAuley) *s.i.s: bmpd sn after s: bhd in centre: sme hdwy 4f out: kpt on past btn horses last 2f: n.d* **250/1**
-223 **7** *shd* **Norman The Great**[43] [1075] 3-8-9 **75**........ MichaelJStainton(5) 15 43
(Jane Chapple-Hyam) *chsd ldr on stands' side: rdn 1/2-way: no ch last 2f* **28/1**
0 **8** 1/2 **Cosmic Apollo**[16] [1716] 5-9-12 0........ BrettDoyle 4 44
(Rae Guest) *chsd ldrs in centre: rdn wl over 2f out: sn wknd* **200/1**
9 6 **Reigning Monarch (USA)**[394] [1367] 4-9-12 0........ AdrianMcCarthy 11 31
(Miss Z C Davison) *led and overall ldr on stands' side tl wl over 2f out: sn wknd: t.o* **200/1**
0 **10** 17 **Formidable Guest**[11] [1840] 3-8-9 0........ J-PGuillambert 1 —
(J Pearce) *chsd ldrs in centre: rdn 3f out: sn wknd: t.o* **200/1**
0-50 **11** *shd* **Anatolian Prince**[30] [1359] 3-9-0 **59**........ TedDurcan 9 —
(J M P Eustace) *chsd ldrs: rdn 4f out: sn bhd: t.o* **80/1**
0 **12** 1 1/4 **Nothingtodeclaire**[51] [977] 3-8-11 0........ EmmettStack(3) 10 —
(G A Huffer) *in tch: rdn 1/2-way: sn wl bhd: t.o* **100/1**
13 12 **Adore Moi** 5-9-4 0........ AlanCreighton(3) 2 —
(R W Price) *s.i.s: veered rt sn after s: chsd ldrs after 1f tl rdn and dropped out qckly 1/2-way: t.o last 2f* **250/1**

1m 43.2s (3.30) **Going Correction** +0.60s/f (Yiel)
WFA 3 from 4yo+ 12lb **13** Ran SP% **119.5**
Speed ratings (Par 103):107,106,103,101,94 84,84,84,78,61 60,59,47
CSF £5.47 TOTE £1.80: £1.10, £2.10, £1.20; EX 7.00 TRIFECTA Pool £668.70 - 19.14 winning unit..
Owner Richie Baines & Stephen Dartnell **Bred** J A And P Duffy **Trained** Newmarket, Suffolk
■ Stewards' Enquiry : Ted Durcan caution: improper riding - struck colt in stalls

FOCUS
A good maiden in which the front four pulled clear in a decent time. The form should work out among the first four with Gongidas perhaps the brightest long-term prospect.
Anatolian Prince Official explanation: trainer said gelding had a breathing problem

2154 LETHEBY & CHRISTOPHER H'CAP 1m 3y
3:55 (4:05) (Class 6) (0-65,65) 4-Y-O+ **£2,137** (£635; £317; £158) **Stalls** High

Form RPR
0041 **1** **Networker**[8] [1918] 4-8-12 **59** 6ex........ BrettDoyle 5 77+
(P J McBride) *stdd s: hld up wl bhd: hdwy over 2f out: swtchd lft over 1f out: sn led and pushed clr: v easily* **15/8**[1]
00-6 **2** 7 **Convallaria (FR)**[26] [1447] 4-9-1 **62**........ EddieAhern 6 64+
(G Wragg) *led tl 6f out: pressed ldr tl led again over 2f out: hdd over 1f out: kpt on but no ch w wnr* **10/1**
0-00 **3** 3/4 **Major League (USA)**[32] [1295] 5-9-4 **65**........ GeorgeBaker 2 65
(D Morris) *hld up in bhd: hdwy wl over 2f out: ev ch and rdn over 1f out: sn outpcd by wnr: plugged on* **16/1**
055- **4** 1 3/4 **Desert Island Miss**[210] [6294] 4-9-0 **61**........(v[1]) TedDurcan 10 57
(W R Swinburn) *t.k.h: chsd ldrs: rdn over 2f out: wknd over 1f out* **14/1**
0-10 **5** 3/4 **The Bonus King**[23] [1539] 7-8-7 **54**........ PhilipRobinson 3 48
(J Jay) *chsd ldrs: rdn whn bmpd over 2f out: sn wknd* **8/1**
0244 **6** 3 **Postmaster**[20] [1612] 5-8-5 **52** ow1........ RobertHavlin 4 39
(R Ingram) *hld up bhd: rdn over 2f out: no imp* **4/1**[2]
2036 **7** 1 **Wodhill Schnaps**[16] [1715] 6-8-4 **51** oh6........ AdrianMcCarthy 7 36+
(D Morris) *t.k.h: w ldr tl led 6f out: hdd over 2f out: sn wknd* **25/1**
00-0 **8** 1 1/4 **Dream Master (IRE)**[18] [1671] 4-7-13 **51** oh3........ LukeMorris(5) 13 33
(J Ryan) *chsd ldng pair tl 1/2-way: sn rdn and wknd* **66/1**
22-0 **9** 5 **Bowl Of Cherries**[5] [2007] 4-8-7 **54** oh2 ow3........(b) StephenDonohoe 12 25
(I A Wood) *chsd ldrs: rdn and lost pl 1/2-way: no ch last 3f: t.o* **15/2**[3]
54-0 **10** 3 1/2 **Al Rayanah**[51] [979] 4-8-12 **62**........ SaleemGolam(3) 9 25
(G Prodromou) *stdd s: hld up bhd: hdwy 4f out: rdn and wknd over 2f out: t.o* **9/1**
64-0 **11** 10 **Haneen (USA)**[51] [980] 4-8-13 **60**........ JamieMackay 8 —
(R W Price) *bhd: rdn and lost tch 1/2-way: t.o last 2f* **33/1**
/60- **12** 2 **Grand Rebecca (IRE)**[239] [5761] 4-8-1 **51** oh6........ EmmettStack(3) 1 —
(G A Huffer) *chsd ldrs tl rdn and lost pl qckly 1/2-way: t.o last 2f* **50/1**
5500 **13** *nk* **Lough Neagh (USA)**[82] [650] 4-8-6 **56**........(b[1]) LiamJones(3) 14 —
(Miss D Mountain) *t.k.h: chsd ldrs tl 1/2-way: sn wl bhd: t.o last 2f* **16/1**

1m 44.18s (4.28) **Going Correction** +0.60s/f (Yiel) **13** Ran SP% **125.4**
Speed ratings (Par 101):102,95,94,92,91 88,87,86,81,78 68,66,65
CSF £22.95 CT £252.38 TOTE £2.90: £1.10, £3.40, £4.70; EX 31.00 Trifecta £258.60 Pool £488.23 - 1.34 winning units..
Owner P J McBride **Bred** T S And Mrs M E Child **Trained** Newmarket, Suffolk
■ Stewards' Enquiry : Brett Doyle one-day ban: careless riding (Jun 10)

FOCUS
The race had to be delayed due to a shambolic incident where the highest-numbered three stalls failed to open. Only Major League covered more than a couple of furlongs following the false start and he ran mighty well considering. This was a pretty weak race, but Networker did it well and was full value for his winning margin.
Major League(USA) Official explanation: jockey said gelding hung right

2155 BOS MAGAZINE H'CAP — 6f 3y
4:30 (4:31) (Class 5) (0-75,75) 4-Y-O+ **£2,839** (£849; £424; £212) **Stalls** High

Form RPR
-211 **1** **Brunelleschi**[11] [1847] 4-8-10 **72**..........(b) LukeMorris(5) 2 87
(P L Gilligan) *trckd ldrs: swtchd to centre over 3f out: rdn over 2f out: led last 100yds: r.o strly* **11/10**[1]
1450 **2** *3* **Methaaly (IRE)**[21] [1589] 4-8-9 **66**.......... KerrinMcEvoy 1 72
(Jane Chapple-Hyam) *led in centre: rdn over 1f out: hdd last 100yds: nt pce of wnr* **3/1**[2]
-220 **3** *½* **Mr Cellophane**[23] [1545] 4-9-4 **75**.......... EddieAhern 5 80
(J R Jenkins) *rrd as stalls opened: trckd ldrs: swtchd to centre over 3f out: rdn over 1f out: swtchd rt 1f out: nt qckn fnl f* **10/3**[3]
41-6 **4** *4* **Siraj**[16] [1718] 8-8-6 **63**.......... RobertHavlin 4 56
(J Ryan) *racd on stands' rail: chsd ldr: rdn 2f out: wknd over 1f out* **8/1**
1m 16.57s (2.87) **Going Correction** +0.60s/f (Yiel) **4** Ran SP% **106.8**
Speed ratings (Par 103):104,100,99,94
CSF £4.51 TOTE £2.00; EX 5.30.
Owner Dr Susan Barnes **Bred** Dr Susan Barnes **Trained** Newmarket, Suffolk
■ Stewards' Enquiry : Eddie Ahern caution (reduced from two-day ban on appeal): careless riding
FOCUS
The pace was reasonable for such a small field. The winner looks to be improving and won with quite a bit in hand, in a race rated through the runner-up.

2156 BANHAM POULTRY H'CAP — 1m 3f 101y
5:05 (5:07) (Class 6) (0-65,65) 4-Y-O+ **£2,137** (£635; £317; £158) **Stalls** Low

Form RPR
-533 **1** **Broughtons Revival**[23] [1521] 5-9-4 **65**.......... BrettDoyle 5 75
(W J Musson) *chsd ldrs: hdwy to chse ldr 2f out: styd on wl u.p to ld last stride* **9/4**[1]
4-04 **2** *shd* **Bronze Star**[14] [1764] 4-9-0 **61**.......... KerrinMcEvoy 7 71
(J R Fanshawe) *chsd ldr tl led over 2f out: rdn over 1f out: kpt on u.p: hdd last stride* **9/2**[2]
1205 **3** *6* **Turner's Touch**[15] [1741] 5-9-2 **63**..........(b) GeorgeBaker 4 63
(G L Moore) *stdd s: hld up bhd: hdwy 3f out: chsd ldng pair over 1f out: rdn and btn 1f out* **9/2**[2]
4546 **4** *1 ¼* **Amwell Brave**[12] [1822] 6-9-2 **63**.......... EddieAhern 6 61
(J R Jenkins) *chsd ldrs: hdwy over 3f out: rdn wl over 2f out: wknd wl over 1f out* **11/2**[3]
00-5 **5** *shd* **Shaika**[2] [2084] 4-8-5 **55**.......... SaleemGolam(3) 3 53
(G Prodromou) *s.i.s: hld up bhd: rdn over 2f out: kpt on u.p fnl f: n.d* **11/2**[3]
005- **6** *hd* **English Archer**[272] [4959] 4-8-1 **51** oh6.......... LiamJones(3) 8 48
(W M Brisbourne) *plld hrd: hld up towards rr: hdwy 3f out: chsd ldrs and rdn over 2f out: wknd over 1f out* **50/1**
04-6 **7** *6* **Pochard**[57] [903] 4-9-0 **61**.......... TedDurcan 9 48
(J M P Eustace) *chsd ldrs: rdn 5f out: wknd over 2f out* **20/1**
4-00 **8** *7* **Peas 'n Beans (IRE)**[6] [1966] 4-8-1 **53** oh3 ow2.......... ColinHaddon(5) 2 28
(T Keddy) *led: rdn 3f out: hdd & wknd qckly over 2f out* **12/1**
-300 **9** *7* **Coffin Dodger**[2] [2089] 4-7-13 **53** oh6 ow2.......... KirstyMilczarek(7) 1 16
(C N Allen) *stdd s: t.k.h: hld up in rr: hdwy over 4f out: rdn and lost pl over 3f out: sn no ch* **25/1**
2m 32.13s (4.63) **Going Correction** +0.45s/f (Yiel) **9** Ran SP% **116.2**
Speed ratings (Par 101):101,100,96,95,95 95,91,85,80
CSF £12.20 CT £41.81 TOTE £3.40: £1.30, £2.10, £1.80; EX 15.20 Trifecta £37.00 Pool £552.36 - 10.59 winning units..
Owner Broughton Thermal Insulation **Bred** Broughton Bloodstock And M Billings **Trained** Newmarket, Suffolk
FOCUS
A very moderate event, but the first two came clear and the winner has scope to improve.

2157 RACECOURSE VIDEO SERVICES H'CAP — 1m 2f 21y
5:35 (5:37) (Class 6) (0-65,62) 4-Y-O+ **£2,137** (£635; £317; £158) **Stalls** Low

Form RPR
/650 **1** **Kingscape (IRE)**[12] [1819] 4-9-4 **62**.......... KerrinMcEvoy 4 73+
(J R Fanshawe) *in tch: trckd ldrs over 2f out: swtchd lft and led ins fnl f: pushed out* **7/2**[2]
0040 **2** *1* **Art Investor**[12] [1811] 4-9-0 **58**..........(b) TedDurcan 6 64
(D R C Elsworth) *w.w in tch: hdwy 3f out: chal and rdn over 1f out: hld hd awkwardly: ev ch tl nt qckn fnl f* **10/1**
0000 **3** *1 ½* **Danzare**[8] [1918] 5-8-10 **54**.......... StephenDonohoe 7 57
(J L Spearing) *t.k.h: wl in tch: hdwy 4f out: led over 1f out: sn rdn: hdd and outpcd last 100yds* **12/1**
0015 **4** *nk* **Elopement (IRE)**[7] [1944] 5-8-8 **55**.......... LiamJones(3) 2 57
(W M Brisbourne) *trckd ldrs on rail: rdn over 2f out: keeping on same pce whn swtchd rt 1f out: kpt on* **6/1**
2000 **5** *2 ½* **Magic Amigo**[51] [982] 6-9-1 **59**.......... EddieAhern 10 56
(J R Jenkins) *w ldr: led over 2f out: rdn and hdd over 1f out: wknd fnl f* **9/2**[3]
1324 **6** *nk* **Gigs Magic (USA)**[8] [1918] 4-8-9 **53**.......... J-PGuillambert 3 50
(M Johnston) *t.k.h: hld up in midfield on rail: rdn over 3f out: swtchd rt 2f out: no imp* **7/4**[1]
000- **7** *1 ¾* **Debord (FR)**[215] [6206] 4-9-3 **61**..........(b[1]) RobertHavlin 9 54
(Jamie Poulton) *slowly away and reminders sn after s: rdn over 3f out: nvr trbld ldrs* **20/1**
4-00 **8** *¾* **Grand Court (IRE)**[22] [1562] 4-8-4 **48** oh1.......... JamieMackay 1 40
(M J Wallace) *s.i.s: hld up bhd: hdwy over 3f out: rdn over 2f out: wknd over 1f out* **25/1**
6500 **9** *1 ½* **Always A Story**[15] [1750] 5-8-3 **50** oh3 ow2.......... SaleemGolam(3) 5 39
(Miss D Mountain) *led tl rdn and hdd over 2f out: wknd qckly fnl f* **50/1**
-004 **10** *6* **Gala Jackpot (USA)**[15] [1742] 4-7-13 **48** oh3.......... LukeMorris(5) 8 25
(W M Brisbourne) *hld up in tch: effrt and rdn over 3f out: wknd over 2f out* **28/1**
2m 17.21s (9.11) **Going Correction** +0.45s/f (Yiel) **10** Ran SP% **121.9**
Speed ratings (Par 101):81,80,79,78,76 76,75,74,73,68
CSF £38.10 CT £390.31 TOTE £5.20: £2.00, £3.20, £4.20; EX 49.60 TRIFECTA Not won. Place 6 £10.58, Place 5 £ 5.85..
Owner Mrs V Shelton **Bred** E Tynan **Trained** Newmarket, Suffolk
FOCUS
A pedestrian winning time for the grade. The form looks very moderate indeed and may not prove reliable. Kingscape was value for a length or so more than the bare form.

T/Plt: £13.30 to a £1 stake. Pool: £48,985.80. 2,686.15 winning tickets. T/Qpdt: £5.20 to a £1 stake. Pool: £2,720.70. 385.50 winning tickets. SP

2158 - 2160a (Foreign Racing) - See Raceform Interactive

1690 LEOPARDSTOWN (L-H)
Wednesday, May 30

OFFICIAL GOING: Good to firm

2161a SEAMUS & ROSEMARY MCGRATH MEMORIAL SAVAL BEG STKS (LISTED RACE) — 1m 6f
7:30 (7:32) 4-Y-O+ **£28,591** (£8,388; £3,996; £1,361)

RPR
1 **Yeats (IRE)**[31] [1330] 6-9-8 121.......... JAHeffernan 4 122+
(A P O'Brien, Ire) *settled 2nd: led ent st: sn rdn clr: easily* **1/7**[1]
2 *6* **Mutakarrim**[17] [1692] 10-9-1 108..........(b) PJSmullen 3 106
(D K Weld, Ire) *settled 3rd: 4th 4f out: impr into 2nd and chsd wnr fr early st: no imp: kpt on* **9/1**[2]
3 *4 ½* **King In Waiting (IRE)**[23] [1550] 4-9-1 100..........(b[1]) MJKinane 2 100
(John M Oxx, Ire) *trckd ldrs in 4th: impr into 3rd 4f out: 4th and rdn st: kpt on same pce* **16/1**
4 *shd* **Clara Allen (IRE)**[31] [1330] 9-8-12 100.......... KJManning 6 97
(John E Kiely, Ire) *sn led: rdn and hdd ent st: 3rd and outpcd 2f out: no ex ins fnl f* **14/1**[3]
5 *1 ¾* **Sacrosanct (IRE)**[14] [1777] 4-8-12 87.......... CO'Donoghue 5 94
(Joseph Crowley, Ire) *hld up in rr: rdn st: kpt on same pce fr 2f out* **50/1**
2m 58.8s (-7.10) **Going Correction** -0.30s/f (Firm) **8** Ran SP% **112.0**
Speed ratings: 108,104,102,101,100
CSF £2.41 TOTE £1.10: £1.10, £1.40; DF 2.40.
Owner Mrs John Magnier **Bred** Barronstown Stud & Orpendale **Trained** Ballydoyle, Co Tipperary

NOTEBOOK
Yeats(IRE) warmed up for his bid to win the Ascot Gold Cup for a second time with a commanding display that underlined his wellbeing and the task that will face the pretenders to his crown next month. A stayer of the highest quality, he started off his season with a similarly impressive display at Navan last month and, although the Ascot Gold Cup will present him with a much tougher challenge than he has faced thus far this season, he goes there in fine form and will take all the beating. He was settled in second as Clara Allen went to the front early on and, entering the straight, he swept to the front with the minimum of effort. He soon stretched clear and his rider only needed to push him out for him to record another easy victory. (op 1/6)
Mutakarrim ran a creditable race in second, 17 days after winning a 1m4f handicap here off a mark of 104. Although no match for the winner, he stuck to his task from the turn in to finish a clear second. A thorough credit to his connections, he remains as good as ever and lost nothing in defeat against a rival of Yeats's quality. (op 8/1)
King In Waiting(IRE) was struggling to make an impression heading towards the final quarter of a mile and kept on under pressure to secure third. This was only his third run since he made a winning debut in a Curragh maiden in March 2006 and he will have to do better if he is to make an impact at this level.
Clara Allen(IRE) could do no more once the winner eased past and performed to a similar level with Yeats as when fourth to him at Navan. She showed towards the end of last season that she was more than capable of competing in premier handicaps off her current mark. (op 12/1)
Sacrosanct(IRE) had it all to do on ratings and was unable to land a telling blow. She will have to do better if she is to pick up black type.

2162 - 2164a (Foreign Racing) - See Raceform Interactive

1736 SAINT-CLOUD (L-H)
Wednesday, May 30

OFFICIAL GOING: Very soft

2165a PRIX CORRIDA (GROUP 2) (F&M) — 1m 2f 110y
1:50 (1:51) 4-Y-O+ **£50,068** (£19,324; £9,223; £6,149; £3,075)

RPR
1 **Mandesha (FR)**[241] [5713] 4-9-2.......... CSoumillon 1 115
(A De Royer-Dupre, France) *missed break: last early: impr to 2nd 1/2-way: pushed along to chal 2f out: led over 1f out: drvn out* **2/5**[1]
2 *¾* **Macleya (GER)**[28] [1421] 5-8-11.......... OPeslier 3 109
(A Fabre, France) *racd in 3rd: pushed along on ins st: rdn and disputing ld 1 1/2f out: no ex on fnl f: nt pce of wnr* **41/10**[2]
3 *½* **Musical Way (FR)**[171] [6785] 5-8-11.......... RonanThomas 2 108
(P Van De Poele, France) *first to show: racd in 2nd: dropped to last but wl in tch 1/2-way: 4th st: styd on wl fr 1f out: jst missed 2nd* **88/10**
4 *½* **La Dancia (IRE)**[38] [1190] 4-8-11.......... TMundry 4 107
(P Rau, Germany) *sn led: jnd 2f out: hdd over 1f out: no ex* **12/1**
5 *½* **Nickelle (FR)**[28] [1421] 4-8-9.......... C-PLemaire 5 104
(J-P Gallorini, France) *racd in 4th: last st: hld fr over 1f out* **79/10**[3]
2m 25.3s (5.70) **5** Ran SP% **120.2**
PARI-MUTUEL: WIN 1.40; PL 1.10, 1.20; SF 2.10.
Owner Princess Zahra Aga Khan **Bred** Princess Zahra Aga Khan **Trained** Chantilly, France

NOTEBOOK
Mandesha(FR), making her seasonal reappearance, probably produced a better performance than the bare form suggests as she would not have been suited by the steady pace and this ground was more testing than she really wants. Very much on her toes in the paddock, she sat back in the stalls when they opened and was slowly into her stride. That did not really matter, though, as the field were going along at just a hack canter and she was soon in second place. Taken to the lead up the centre of the track running into the last two furlongs, she stayed on well, albeit needing a few reminders to do so. She may now be aimed at the Prince of Wales's Stakes, but the Grand Prix de Saint-Cloud remains an alternative.
Macleya(GER), keen in the early stages, began her run from two out and stayed on nicely throughout the final furlong. She was another greatly disadvantaged by the way the race was run as she has won over 1m7f.
Musical Way(FR) was another who pulled hard early on, but she made late progress to take third place close home. This was a decent effort as she was making her seasonal debut.
La Dancia(IRE) was a reluctant leader, just cantering along at the head of affairs until the straight, and could not quicken as well as some of these.

[1938]AYR (L-H)

Thursday, May 31

OFFICIAL GOING: Good to firm (good in places)

Wind: Fresh, half behind

2166 PARADIGM EUROPEAN BREEDERS' FUND MAIDEN STKS 6f

2:20 (2:22) (Class 4) 2-Y-O **£5,181** (£1,541; £770; £384) **Stalls** High

Form RPR

1 **Bigfanofthat (IRE)** 2-9-3 0 .... PatCosgrave 7 79+
(K R Burke) *trckd ldrs: effrt over 1f out: led ins fnl f: kpt on strly* **12/1**[3]

4 2 ½ **Atabaas Pride**[29] [1411] 2-9-3 0 .... KDarley 6 77
(M Johnston) *led: rdn and hung lft 1f out: hdd ins fnl f: edgd rt: kpt on towards fin* **4/1**[2]

3 3 1 ¼ **Montaquila**[14] [1792] 2-9-3 0 .... TomEaves 5 73
(J Howard Johnson) *chsd ldrs: rdn 2f out: no ex ins fnl f* **2/5**[1]

6 4 nk **Dream Express (IRE)**[16] [1743] 2-9-3 0 .... PaulFessey 4 72
(M Dods) *s.i.s: bhd: rdn over 2f out: styd on wl fnl f: nrst fin* **25/1**

044 5 1 ¼ **Alpen Adventure (IRE)**[8] [1938] 2-9-3 0 ....(p) DavidAllan 3 68
(Mrs L Stubbs) *w ldr: rdn 2f out: no ex fnl f* **25/1**

6 nk **Transmission (IRE)** 2-9-3 0 .... RoystonFfrench 1 67
(B Smart) *in tch: rdn after 2f: no imp over 1f out* **22/1**

7 20 **Livvy Inn (USA)** 2-9-3 0 .... JoeFanning 2 3
(Miss Lucinda V Russell) *missed break: nvr on terms* **100/1**

1m 11.22s (-2.45) **Going Correction** -0.475s/f (Firm) 7 Ran SP% **112.2**

Speed ratings (Par 95):97,96,94,94,92 92,65

CSF £54.31 TOTE £11.90: £3.50, £1.40; EX 45.40.

Owner Mrs Maura Gittins **Bred** Paddocks Holdings **Trained** Middleham Moor, N Yorks

FOCUS

Little strength in depth and the market leader disappointed but plenty to like about the manner in which the winner went about his business.

NOTEBOOK

Bigfanofthat(IRE) ◆, who cost 70,000euros and is the first foal of an unraced half-sister to smart Mutakddim, a multiple six-furlong to a mile winner, created a favourable impression on this racecourse debut. He will stay seven furlongs and appeals as the type to win more races. (op 14-1 tchd 16-1 in places)

Atabaas Pride, who shaped with promise when just behind a subsequent winner on his debut, bettered that effort and, although wandering under pressure, kept trying and will be suited by seven furlongs. He is sure to win a similar event. (op 10-3)

Montaquila, who shaped with plenty of promise on his debut at York, was on his toes in the paddock and failed to build on that effort on this quicker ground. There is a chance that this may have come too quickly and he is worth another chance in this type of event. (op 1-2 tchd 8-15 in places)

Dream Express(IRE) more than confirmed the bit of promise shown on his debut and, while he may continue to look vulnerable to the better sorts in this grade, he will be of more interest over seven furlongs in ordinary nursery company in due course. (op 33-1)

Alpen Adventure(IRE), tried in the first-time cheekpieces, had the run of the race and ran creditably with no excuses. He is a good guide to the worth of this form but is likely to continue to look vulnerable in this type of event. (op 20-1)

Transmission(IRE), who cost 25,000gns and is out of a seven-furlong winner, was easy to back but was not totally disgraced on this racecourse debut. He shaped as though a stiffer test of stamina would be in his favour. (op 20-1 tchd 25-1)

2167 GILES INSURANCE CONSTRUCTION SPECIALISTS RATING RELATED MAIDEN STKS 6f

2:50 (2:51) (Class 5) 3-Y-O+ **£2,914** (£867; £433; £216) **Stalls** High

Form RPR

2040 1 **Distant Sun (USA)**[10] [1903] 3-9-1 62 .... TomEaves 4 60
(I Semple) *trckd ldrs: shkn up to ld ins fnl f: rdn and kpt on* **5/4**[1]

42-0 2 hd **Hansomis (IRE)**[20] [1625] 3-8-12 64 .... RoystonFfrench 2 57
(B Mactaggart) *led to ins fnl f: kpt on towards fin* **2/1**[2]

5 3 3 ½ **Vadinka**[19] [1679] 3-9-1 63 .... KimTinkler 1 48
(N Tinkler) *pressed ldr tl edgd lft and no ex appr fnl f* **3/1**[3]

000- 4 2 **Churchtown**[174] [6749] 3-9-1 45 .... PatCosgrave 3 42
(K R Burke) *prom: outpcd 2f out: n.d after* **14/1**

1m 11.63s (-2.04) **Going Correction** -0.475s/f (Firm) 4 Ran SP% **109.4**

Speed ratings (Par 103):94,93,89,86

CSF £4.10 TOTE £2.00; EX 4.00.

Owner Gordon McDowall **Bred** Forging Oaks Llc **Trained** Carluke, S Lanarks

FOCUS

An uncompetitive maiden in which the pace was just fair and doubtful if they ran to their marks.

2168 GRIFFIN WEBSTER H'CAP 1m 1f 20y

3:20 (3:21) (Class 6) (0-60,59) 4-Y-O+ **£2,590** (£770; £385; £192) **Stalls** Low

Form RPR

-561 1 **Bijou Dan**[8] [1944] 6-9-3 58 6ex ....(p) TonyHamilton 10 68+
(D W Thompson) *hld up: hdwy to ld appr fnl f: r.o strly* **7/2**[2]

60-0 2 2 ½ **Mandarin Rocket (IRE)**[21] [1595] 4-8-6 50 .... AndrewMullen(3) 9 55
(Miss L A Perratt) *chsd ldrs: effrt and ev ch over 1f out: kpt on fnl f: nt rch wnr* **66/1**

-620 3 nk **Mystical Ayr (IRE)**[8] [1944] 5-9-4 59 .... RoystonFfrench 5 63
(Miss L A Perratt) *t.k.h early: hld up: hdwy centre and ev ch over 1f out: kpt on ins fnl f* **7/1**[3]

-000 4 shd **Neil's Legacy (IRE)**[8] [1944] 5-8-9 55 .... JamieMoriarty(5) 8 59
(Miss L A Perratt) *bhd: hdwy over 2f out: chsng ldrs over 1f out: kpt on ins fnl f* **25/1**

450- 5 1 **Desert Lightning (IRE)**[187] [6606] 5-8-11 52 .... LeeEnstone 7 54
(K R Burke) *t.k.h: hld up in tch: hdwy to chal over 1f out: r.o same pce* **8/1**

0-00 6 1 ¼ **Apache Point (IRE)**[9] [1918] 10-9-0 55 .... KimTinkler 6 54
(N Tinkler) *prom: effrt and ev ch over 1f out: sn no ex* **14/1**

-223 7 3 **Queen's Echo**[8] [1944] 6-8-7 51 .... MarkLawson(3) 4 44
(P Monteith) *prom: effrt over 2f out: sn one pce* **11/4**[1]

0550 8 hd **Counterfactual (IRE)**[9] [1918] 4-8-13 54 .... PatCosgrave 11 46
(B Smart) *rrd s: bhd tl sme late hdwy: nvr on terms* **10/1**

-004 9 nk **Komreyev Star**[8] [1944] 5-8-9 50 ....(p) JoeFanning 2 42
(R E Peacock) *led to appr fnl f: sn btn* **8/1**

0-00 10 1 ¼ **Jordans Spark**[8] [1944] 6-8-12 53 ....(p) TomEaves 1 42
(P Monteith) *hld up: effrt over 2f out: btn over 1f out* **22/1**

00-0 11 7 **Orpen's Astaire (IRE)**[57] [928] 4-8-10 54 .... DuranFentiman(3) 3 28
(Jedd O'Keeffe) *w ldr tl rdn and wknd fr 2f out* **40/1**

66-0 12 1 **Ignition**[24] [1534] 5-8-4 48 ....(p) LiamJones(3) 12 20
(W M Brisbourne) *prom tl rdn and wknd over 2f out* **14/1**

1m 54.34s (-5.66) **Going Correction** -0.475s/f (Firm) 12 Ran SP% **118.2**

Speed ratings (Par 101):106,103,103,103,102 101,98,98,98,97 90,90

CSF £234.38 CT £1555.36 TOTE £4.30: £1.80, £12.40, £2.10; EX 204.60.

Owner Bert Markey **Bred** James Thom And Sons **Trained** Bolam, Co Durham

FOCUS

Just an ordinary handicap but one in which the pace was fair and the placed form looks sound.

Queen's Echo Official explanation: jockey said mare was unsuited by the good to firm, good in places ground

Counterfactual(IRE) Official explanation: jockey said gelding reared as stalls opened

Komreyev Star Official explanation: jockey said gelding changed its legs and lost its action, and was unsuited by the good to firm, good in places ground

2169 MACTAGGART AND MICKEL H'CAP 1m 1f 20y

3:50 (3:51) (Class 5) (0-75,73) 4-Y-O+ **£4,533** (£1,348; £674; £336) **Stalls** Low

Form RPR

0551 1 **Stolen Glance**[17] [1720] 4-8-10 63 .... DaleGibson 7 72
(M W Easterby) *chsd ldrs: drvn over 2f out: led ins fnl f: hld on wl* **5/1**[2]

0016 2 hd **Sedgwick**[9] [1924] 5-8-13 66 .... RoystonFfrench 5 75
(J G Given) *chsd ldrs: rdn over 2f out: disp ld ins fnl f: hld cl home* **5/1**[2]

0-40 3 2 ½ **Jordans Elect**[7] [1967] 7-8-7 63 ....(v) MarkLawson(3) 10 67
(P Monteith) *t.k.h: led: clr over 2f out: hdd and no ex ins fnl f* **6/1**[3]

1-53 4 1 ¾ **Spinning**[27] [1455] 4-9-0 67 .... PaulFessey 1 67
(T D Barron) *hld up: rdn 3f out: kpt on fnl f: edgd rt cl home: nrst fin* **9/2**[1]

00-6 5 ¾ **Tidy (IRE)**[6] [2007] 7-8-8 64 ....(v) GregFairley(3) 6 62
(Micky Hammond) *hld up: drvn and outpcd over 2f out: kpt on fnl f: no imp* **13/2**

4641 6 shd **Primo Way**[8] [1939] 6-9-3 73 6ex ....(b) DuranFentiman(3) 4 71
(I Semple) *t.k.h: in tch: effrt over 2f out: no imp over 1f out* **6/1**[3]

-350 7 2 **Anduril**[124] [263] 6-8-13 66 ....(b) PatCosgrave 2 60
(Miss M E Rowland) *hld up on ins: effrt over 2f out: sn btn* **20/1**

-401 8 shd **Flylowflylong (IRE)**[20] [1626] 4-8-8 64 .... AndrewMullen(3) 8 58
(I Semple) *hld up: rdn 3f out: n.d* **7/1**

00/4 9 13 **Verification**[26] [1479] 4-8-8 61 ow1 .... TomEaves 9 28
(J Howard Johnson) *chsd ldr to 3f out: sn rdn and lost pl* **33/1**

1m 54.12s (-5.88) **Going Correction** -0.475s/f (Firm) 9 Ran SP% **113.6**

Speed ratings (Par 103):107,106,104,103,102 102,100,100,88

CSF £29.66 CT £151.87 TOTE £6.00: £2.00, £1.90, £2.60; EX 32.50.

Owner R S Cockerill (Farms) Ltd **Bred** R S Cockerill (farms) Ltd **Trained** Sheriff Hutton, N Yorks

■ Stewards' Enquiry : Paul Fessey caution: careless riding

FOCUS

Another ordinary handicap but one in which the gallop was sound after a furlong or so. This form should stand up at a similar level.

Flylowflylong(IRE) Official explanation: jockey said filly hung right-handed throughout

2170 MACDONALD SOLICITORS H'CAP 1m 7f

4:20 (4:21) (Class 4) (0-85,85) 4-Y-O+ **£5,829** (£1,734; £866; £432) **Stalls** Low

Form RPR

4043 1 **Trance (IRE)**[14] [1793] 7-9-1 79 ....(p) PaulFessey 4 87
(T D Barron) *hld up: hdwy and prom after 6f: rdn to ld over 1f out: hld on gamely fnl f* **9/2**[3]

326- 2 hd **Falpiase (IRE)**[58] [5768] 5-9-2 80 .... TomEaves 8 88
(J Howard Johnson) *in tch: drvn 3f out: rallied over 1f out: kpt on fnl f: jst hld* **11/1**

50-2 3 nk **Mceldowney**[6] [2011] 5-9-5 83 .... JoeFanning 6 91
(M Johnston) *trckd ldrs: rdn to chal over 1f out: kpt on fnl f: hld cl home* **9/4**[1]

00-1 4 3 ½ **Monolith**[25] [1490] 9-9-4 85 .... GregFairley(3) 5 88
(L Lungo) *cl up: led 3f out to over 1f out: sn no ex* **7/2**[2]

400/ 5 nk **Turbo (IRE)**[8] [4639] 8-8-8 72 ....(t) DaleGibson 3 75
(M W Easterby) *hld up in tch: effrt over 2f out: no ex over 1f out* **14/1**

1-00 6 24 **Dr Sharp (IRE)**[22] [1582] 7-9-7 85 .... MickyFenton 1 56
(T P Tate) *led to 3f out: sn rdn and wknd* **7/2**[2]

3m 15.13s (-7.34) **Going Correction** -0.475s/f (Firm) 6 Ran SP% **108.4**

Speed ratings (Par 105):100,99,99,97,97 84

CSF £44.87 CT £122.21 TOTE £5.40: £2.40, £3.70; EX 30.00.

Owner Nigel Shields **Bred** Forenaghts Stud Co Ltd **Trained** Maunby, N Yorks

■ Stewards' Enquiry : Paul Fessey one-day ban: used whip with excessive frequency (Jun 11)
Tom Eaves caution: used whip with excessive frequency

FOCUS

A fair handicap but one in which the pace was only modest to the home straight. The form is rated around the winner and third.

Dr Sharp(IRE) Official explanation: jockey said gelding was unsuited by the good to firm, good in places ground

2171 KEPPIE DESIGN H'CAP 6f

4:50 (4:50) (Class 4) (0-85,84) 3-Y-O **£6,477** (£1,927; £963; £481) **Stalls** High

Form RPR

0-03 1 **Fish Called Johnny**[14] [1782] 3-8-4 70 ....(b1) DaleGibson 1 76
(Peter Grayson) *prom: rdn to ld ins fnl f: edgd lft: pushed clr* **10/1**

5-23 2 2 ½ **Mundo's Magic**[13] [1802] 3-8-7 73 .... RoystonFfrench 3 72
(G M Moore) *cl up: led over 1f out to ins fnl f: kpt on: nt pce of wnr* **13/8**[1]

-004 3 nk **Prospect Place**[6] [1994] 3-8-13 79 .... TomEaves 5 77
(M Dods) *prom: effrt and swtchd lft appr fnl f: no imp ins fnl f* **4/1**[2]

306- 4 4 **Opal Noir**[237] [5788] 3-8-13 84 .... JamieMoriarty(5) 6 70
(J Howard Johnson) *led to over 1f out: sn btn* **9/2**[3]

00-1 5 1 **Darfour**[7] [1965] 3-8-4 77 6ex .... GaryBartley(7) 2 60+
(J S Goldie) *racd alone in centre: outpcd after 2f: rallied over 1f out: no imp* **5/1**

-550 6 4 **Dolly Coughdrop (IRE)**[69] [737] 3-8-1 70 oh2 .... AndrewElliott(3) 4 41
(K R Burke) *cl up tl rdn and wknd over 1f out* **9/1**

1m 11.82s (-1.85) **Going Correction** -0.475s/f (Firm) 6 Ran SP% **112.0**

Speed ratings (Par 101):93,89,89,83,82 77

CSF £26.75 TOTE £7.50: £3.10, £1.20; EX 27.60.

Owner Richard Teatum **Bred** Mrs D O Joly **Trained** Formby, Lancs

FOCUS

An ordinary event in which the time was the slowest of the three over the trip. The form is rated around the placed horses.

Opal Noir Official explanation: jockey said gelding hung left throughout

2172 CARSWELL SECURITIES H'CAP 5f

5:20 (5:20) (Class 5) (0-70,70) 3-Y-O **£3,238** (£963; £481; £240) **Stalls** High

Form RPR

2632 1 **Baileys Outshine**[9] [1932] 3-9-4 70 .... JoeFanning 3 76
(J G Given) *mde all: rdn and r.o strly fnl f* **7/4**[1]

1456 **2** 1 3/4 **Ronnie Howe**[33] 1286 3-9-1 **67** TomEaves 6 67
(M Dods) *w wnr: rdn over 1f out: kpt on fnl f* **5/1**[3]
30-5 **3** 3/4 **Princess Ileana (IRE)**[16] 1748 3-8-10 **62** LeeEnstone 5 59
(K R Burke) *chsd ldrs: effrt 2f out: kpt on same pce fnl f* **10/3**[2]
6005 **4** 1/2 **Stoneacre Gareth (IRE)**[8] 1948 3-9-0 **66** (b) MickyFenton 1 62+
(Peter Grayson) *s.i.s: bhd tl hdwy over 1f out: kpt on fnl f* **10/1**
0102 **5** 2 1/2 **Almora Guru**[2] 2120 3-8-10 **62** DavidAllan 2 49
(W M Brisbourne) *prom tl edgd lft and no ex over 1f out* **11/2**
1040 **6** 1 3/4 **Pirner's Brig**[9] 1932 3-9-0 **66** DaleGibson 4 46
(M W Easterby) *prom tl rdn and wknd 2f out* **8/1**
58.68 secs (-1.76) **Going Correction** -0.475s/f (Firm) **6** Ran SP% **111.7**
Speed ratings (Par 99):95,92,91,90,86 83
CSF £10.73 TOTE £2.00: £1.30, £2.70; EX 12.90 Place 6 £546.37, Place 5 £147.70.
Owner G R Bailey Ltd (Baileys Horse Feeds) **Bred** P And Mrs A G Venner **Trained** Willoughton, Lincs

FOCUS
An ordinary handicap in which the pace was sound and the runner-up sets the standard.
Stoneacre Gareth(IRE) Official explanation: jockey said gelding reared as stalls opened
T/Plt: £934.60 to a £1 stake. Pool: £38,538.40. 30.10 winning tickets. T/Qpdt: £38.70 to a £1 stake. Pool: £3,752.30. 71.70 winning tickets. RY

1945 LINGFIELD (L-H)
Thursday, May 31

OFFICIAL GOING: Standard
Wind: Strong, behind Weather: overcast

2173 S G HAMBROS MAIDEN STKS (DIV I) 6f (P)
2:00 (2:02) (Class 5) 3-Y-O+ **£3,238** (£963; £481; £240) **Stalls** Low

Form RPR
5 **1** **Lochstar**[37] 1207 3-9-0 0 FrancisNorton 10 81+
(A M Balding) *chsd ldr: led jst ins fnl f: pushed out: readily* **4/1**[2]
20-3 **2** 1 1/2 **Obstructive**[41] 1117 3-9-0 73 JimCrowley 4 76
(D K Ivory) *led at gd pce: rdn over 2f out: hdd jst ins fnl f: kpt on but no ch w wnr* **10/3**[1]
3 1 3/4 **Vainglory (USA)** 3-9-0 0 MartinDwyer 8 71+
(D M Simcock) *racd in midfield: off the pce: rdn 1/2-way: c wd over 1f out: r.o strly fnl f: nvr nrr* **20/1**
0 **4** 3/4 **Conbextra**[29] 1398 3-9-0 0 JohnEgan 1 69
(J S Moore) *racd in midfield: rdn over 3f out: hdwy over 2f out: kpt on to chse ldng pair ins fnl f tl wknd towards fin* **8/1**
5 1 **Compulsion** 4-9-4 0 PaulEddery 5 63+
(Pat Eddery) *s.i.s: bhd: hdwy on inner over 2f out: kpt on wl fnl f: nvr nrr* **33/1**
3 **6** 1/2 **He's My Best (USA)**[35] 1267 3-9-0 0 EddieAhern 7 64
(J Noseda) *chsd ldrs: rdn to chse ldng pair over 2f out: no imp: wknd ins fnl f* **10/3**[1]
05-5 **7** 3 1/2 **Danehill Kikin (IRE)**[20] 1620 3-8-9 59 MichaelHills 2 49
(B W Hills) *chsd ldrs: rdn over 2f out: wknd over 1f out* **9/2**[3]
00 **8** 3 **Mix N Match**[9] 1913 3-9-0 0 SebSanders 3 45
(W J Haggas) *a outpcd: nvr on terms* **12/1**
60 **9** 3 **Simpleton**[9] 1928 4-9-9 0 DaneO'Neill 9 38
(J R Best) *dwlt: a outpcd in rr* **66/1**
0-0 **10** 4 **Fluters House**[20] 1633 3-9-0 0 JamesDoyle 6 24
(S Woodman) *a bhd: no ch last 2f* **66/1**
1m 11.48s (-1.33) **Going Correction** -0.125s/f (Stan)
WFA 3 from 4yo 9lb **10** Ran SP% **113.8**
Speed ratings (Par 103):103,101,98,97,96 95,91,87,83,77
CSF £16.77 TOTE £5.50: £1.90, £1.10, £7.40; EX 23.40.
Owner J C Smith **Bred** Littleton Stud **Trained** Kingsclere, Hants

FOCUS
A fair maiden and the form looks straightforward enough rated through the consistent runner-up.

2174 HEATWAVE LIVE AT LINGFIELDPARK.CO.UK CLASSIFIED STKS 5f (P)
2:30 (2:32) (Class 7) 4-Y-O+ **£2,388** (£705; £352) **Stalls** High

Form RPR
6300 **1** **Arfinnit (IRE)**[7] 1969 6-9-0 45 (v) EddieAhern 8 54
(Mrs A L M King) *in tch: hdwy to chse ldrs over 2f out: styd on u.p to ld nr fin* **8/1**[3]
30-1 **2** hd **Maromito (IRE)**[17] 1707 10-9-0 45 SebSanders 3 53
(R Bastiman) *taken down early: chsd ldr: rdn to ld wl over 1f out: edgd lft u.p fnl f: hdd nr fin* **5/4**[1]
6603 **3** 3/4 **Nawayea**[10] 1883 4-8-7 45 KirstyMilczarek(7) 6 51
(C N Allen) *bhd: hdwy on inner over 2f out: r.o wl ins fnl f: nrst fin* **12/1**
5555 **4** nk **Lady Hopeful (IRE)**[30] 1384 5-9-0 45 (b) LPKeniry 5 50
(Peter Grayson) *s.i.s: hdwy 3f out: chsd ldrs over 2f out: kpt on same pce u.p fnl f* **6/1**[2]
0000 **5** 1 **Auentraum (GER)**[65] 797 7-9-0 45 (e) JamesDoyle 7 46
(Ms J S Doyle) *bhd: hdwy over 2f out: plld out and rdn wl over 1f out: kpt on: nt trble ldrs* **20/1**
0002 **6** 3/4 **Orchestration (IRE)**[17] 1719 6-8-11 45 (v) DominicFox(3) 1 43
(S Parr) *s.i.s: sn chsng ldrs on inner: rdn and effrt over 2f out: kpt on same pce fnl f* **8/1**[3]
2040 **7** 2 1/2 **Katie Killane**[92] 581 5-9-0 45 (t) AdamKirby 2 34
(M Wellings) *sn led: rdn and hdd wl over 1f out: wknd ins fnl f* **14/1**
000- **8** 1 1/2 **Montillia (IRE)**[174] 6753 5-8-9 45 PatrickHills(5) 4 29
(J W Unett) *chsd ldrs: rdn and wknd over 2f out* **25/1**
0000 **9** 2 1/2 **The London Gang**[45] 1066 4-9-0 45 (vt) FergusSweeney 9 20
(Miss D A McHale) *a bhd: rdn 1/2-way: no ch last 2f* **14/1**
050- **10** 5 **Dhurwah (IRE)**[241] 5729 4-9-0 45 PaulDoe 10 —
(T Keddy) *a bhd: rdn and lost tch over 2f out* **16/1**
59.43 secs (-0.35) **Going Correction** -0.125s/f (Stan) **10** Ran SP% **116.5**
Speed ratings (Par 97):97,96,95,95,93 92,88,85,81,73
CSF £18.30 TOTE £10.70: £3.00, £1.30, £4.20; EX 25.90.
Owner All The Kings Horses **Bred** Robert De Vere Hunt **Trained** Wilmcote, Warwicks

FOCUS
A very weak event, run at a sound pace. The first four were closely covered at the finish with the third the best guide to the level.
Nawayea Official explanation: jockey said filly suffered interference soon after start
Katie Killane Official explanation: jockey said mare hung right

2175 S G HAMBROS MAIDEN STKS (DIV II) 6f (P)
3:00 (3:01) (Class 5) 3-Y-O+ **£3,238** (£963; £481; £240) **Stalls** Low

Form RPR
2 **1** **Arabian Gleam**[27] 1452 3-9-0 0 SebSanders 9 89+
(J Noseda) *chsd ldrs: led over 1f out: sn clr: v easily* **4/7**[1]
0 **2** 5 **Spinneret**[41] 1128 3-8-9 0 PhilipRobinson 6 63
(M A Jarvis) *sn chsng ldr: ev ch over 2f out: sn no ch w wnr: hld on to 2nd nr fin* **4/1**[2]
0 **3** nk **Hartmann (USA)**[24] 1522 3-9-0 0 RichardHughes 7 67
(B J Meehan) *chsd ldrs: rdn and effrt over 2f out: chsd ldrs 2f out: kpt on but no ch w wnr* **10/1**
0/0 **4** 1 1/4 **Pivotal Era**[6] 1995 4-9-9 0 IanMongan 4 65+
(C F Wall) *wnt rt s: hdwy into midfield 1/2-way: kpt on u.p last 2f: no ch w wnr* **20/1**
00-4 **5** 1/2 **Kind Of Fizzy**[9] 1923 3-8-9 0 SteveDrowne 3 57
(Rae Guest) *chsd ldrs: rdn over 2f out: kpt on same pce* **8/1**[3]
6 1/2 **Dirty Dancing** 3-9-0 0 MichaelHills 5 60+
(B W Hills) *hmpd s: t.k.h: hld up wl bhd: hdwy over 2f: swtchd rt over 1f out: r.o: n.d* **12/1**
0 **7** 2 **Capping (IRE)**[10] 1904 3-9-0 0 AdamKirby 1 54
(W R Swinburn) *chsd ldrs: rdn wl over 2f out: wknd 2f out* **33/1**
50 **8** 1 **Western Point (IRE)**[9] 1923 3-9-0 0 JamieMackay 10 51
(Sir Mark Prescott) *a bhd* **40/1**
040- **9** 1 1/2 **Batchworth Fleur**[333] 3118 4-9-4 42 StephenCarson 2 44
(E A Wheeler) *led tl hdd 2f out: wknd qckly over 1f out* **66/1**
00- **10** 1/2 **Chart Express**[244] 5659 3-8-11 0 StephaneBreux(3) 8 45
(J R Best) *a bhd: rdn 3f out: no ch last 2f* **50/1**
1m 12.12s (-0.69) **Going Correction** -0.125s/f (Stan)
WFA 3 from 4yo 9lb **10** Ran SP% **125.1**
Speed ratings (Par 103):99,92,91,90,89 88,86,84,82,82
CSF £3.34 TOTE £1.80: £1.10, £1.30, £2.60; EX 4.40.
Owner Saeed Suhail **Bred** P And Mrs A G Venner **Trained** Newmarket, Suffolk

FOCUS
This maiden was the stronger of the two divisions and the form makes sense rated through the fourth.
Dirty Dancing Official explanation: jockey said colt suffered interference in running

2176 KNIGHT FRANK H'CAP 1m 4f (P)
3:30 (3:30) (Class 6) (0-50,54) 4-Y-O+ **£3,238** (£963; £481; £240) **Stalls** Low

Form RPR
0500 **1** **Ganymede**[17] 1732 6-8-10 **48** IanMongan 15 62
(Mrs L J Mongan) *racd wd in midfield: hdwy 6f out: chsd ldr over 4f out: led over 2f out: rdn clr wl over 1f out: readily* **10/1**
54/0 **2** 4 **Selkirk Grace**[30] 1376 7-8-12 **50** EddieAhern 8 57
(K A Morgan) *in tch: hdwy 4f out: chsd wnr and rdn over 2f out: kpt on but no ch w wnr* **9/1**
2600 **3** 2 **War Feather**[9] 1925 5-8-10 **48** RobertHavlin 10 52
(T D McCarthy) *hld up towards rr: hdwy 6f out: rdn to chse ldng pair over 2f out: hung lft u.p: kpt on same pce* **20/1**
0662 **4** 3 **Khyberie**[8] 1950 4-8-10 **48** SteveDrowne 5 47
(G Wragg) *led for 1f: chsd ldrs: rdn over 2f out: wknd over 1f out* **6/4**[1]
4160 **5** 1/2 **Icannshift (IRE)**[22] 1590 7-8-5 **46** oh1 NeilChalmers(3) 9 44
(T M Jones) *bhd: rdn and hdwy over 2f out: kpt on fnl f: nvr able to chal* **14/1**
0001 **6** 1/2 **El Capitan (FR)**[10] 1906 4-8-9 **54** 6ex GihanArnolda(7) 6 52
(Miss Gay Kelleway) *chsd ldrs tl short of room and lost pl 4f out: rallied to chse ldrs over 2f out: wknd over 1f out* **11/2**[2]
0000 **7** nk **Atticus Trophies (IRE)**[59] 888 4-8-8 **46** oh1 (p) JamesDoyle 4 43
(Ms J S Doyle) *hld up in midfield: hdwy over 3f out: rdn over 2f out: sn wknd* **33/1**
6040 **8** 3 1/2 **Scuzme (IRE)**[22] 1590 4-8-2 **47** (p) JemmaMarshall(7) 1 39
(Miss Sheena West) *v.s.a: a bhd: sme hdwy past btn horses fnl f* **12/1**
30-0 **9** 2 **Royal Axminster**[29] 1402 12-8-4 **49** ow2 NBazeley(7) 13 37
(Mrs P N Dutfield) *led after 1f: rdn and hdd over 2f out: wknd qckly over 1f out* **33/1**
/0-0 **10** 7 **Muqarrar (IRE)**[9] 1934 8-8-8 **46** oh1 (vt) JohnEgan 16 23
(T J Fitzgerald) *t.k.h: hld up towards rr: hdwy u.p 3f out: sn no imp* **33/1**
000/ **11** 1 1/4 **Reason (IRE)**[689] 3400 9-8-8 **46** oh1 HayleyTurner 12 21
(D W Chapman) *chsd ldr after 2f tl over 4f out: sn rdn and wknd* **50/1**
0-03 **12** nk **Blue Quiver (IRE)**[99] 514 7-8-8 **46** PaulEddery 3 21
(C A Horgan) *v.s.a: a bhd* **8/1**[3]
02/0 **13** nk **Keynes (JPN)**[9] 887 5-8-1 **46** oh1 (t) SCreighton(7) 14 20
(E J Creighton) *hld up towards rr: rdn over 4f out: sn wl bhd* **66/1**
0000 **14** nk **Lady Lucas (IRE)**[10] 1884 4-8-6 **47** oh1 ow1 (t) AlanCreighton(3) 2 21
(E J Creighton) *hld up in midfield: rdn and lost pl wl over 3f out: no ch after* **100/1**
2m 31.97s (-2.42) **Going Correction** -0.125s/f (Stan) **14** Ran SP% **118.0**
Speed ratings (Par 101):103,100,99,97,96 96,96,93,92,87 86,86,86,86
CSF £89.93 CT £1772.09 TOTE £11.30: £3.10, £4.00, £3.10; EX 97.30.
Owner Condover Racing **Bred** Mrs A M Jenkins **Trained** Epsom, Surrey

FOCUS
A very poor handicap. The winner is value for a bit further than the winning margin and the third is the best guide to the level.

2177 BENTLEY, KENT H'CAP 1m 2f (P)
4:00 (4:01) (Class 5) (0-75,74) 3-Y-O **£5,181** (£1,541; £770; £384) **Stalls** Low

Form RPR
0-55 **1** **Mutual Friend (USA)**[31] 1343 3-8-13 **69** SebSanders 3 78+
(E A L Dunlop) *hld up in midfield: hdwy wl over 2f out: chsd ldr over 1f out: led ins fnl f: pushed out: readily* **7/2**[1]
4-10 **2** 1 1/2 **Jaady (USA)**[41] 1122 3-9-3 **73** MartinDwyer 11 77
(J H M Gosden) *chsd ldr after 2f: led wl over 2f out: rdn over 2f out: hdd ins fnl f: nt pce of wnr* **8/1**
1130 **3** 2 1/2 **Dan Tucker**[17] 1724 3-9-4 **74** (b[1]) RichardHughes 12 73
(B J Meehan) *stdd s: hld up towards rr: hdwy over 2f out: drvn 2f out: r.o fnl f: nrst fin* **11/2**[2]
006- **4** nk **Gib (IRE)**[248] 5563 3-8-6 **62** SamHitchcott 7 61
(B W Hills) *t.k.h: hld up in midfield: hdwy on outer over 3f out: chsd ldrs and rdn over 2f out: kpt on same pce* **33/1**
6-40 **5** nk **Forced Upon Us**[40] 1155 3-8-4 **60** oh2 HayleyTurner 5 58
(P J McBride) *t.k.h: chsd ldrs on inner: rdn over 2f out: kpt on same pce* **20/1**
2-00 **6** shd **Shouldntbethere (IRE)**[31] 1359 3-8-10 **66** RobertHavlin 8 64
(Mrs P N Dutfield) *taken down early: hld up towards rr: hdwy on outer wl over 2f out: kpt on u.p fnl f: nvr trbld ldrs* **20/1**

7 1 **Hill Queen (IRE)**[185] 3-9-1 **71**.. NickyMackay 9 67
(L M Cumani) *chsd ldrs: rdn to chse ldr over 2f out tl over 1f out: sn outpcd* **9/1**

0-02 **8** 1 3/4 **Up In Arms (IRE)**[10] 1887 3-8-11 **67**............................ StephenCarson 1 59
(P Winkworth) *hld up in rr: hdwy and swtchd rt over 2f out: kpt on u.p: nt rch ldrs* **8/1**

00-0 **9** 1 3/4 **Chunky's Choice (IRE)**[12] 1840 3-8-13 **69**........................ JohnEgan 14 58
(J Noseda) *hld up towards rr: hdwy 3f out: c wd bnd over 2f out: no real imp* **14/1**

1-40 **10** nk **Benny The Bat**[36] 1247 3-9-2 **72**...................................... SteveDrowne 4 60
(H Morrison) *t.k.h: chsd ldr for 2f: styd prom: rdn 3f out: wknd 2f out* **7/1**[3]

-230 **11** shd **Postsprofit (IRE)**[13] 1815 3-8-12 **68**................................ DaneO'Neill 10 56
(N A Callaghan) *t.k.h: dropped in bhd sn after s: rdn and effrt whn hmpd bnd over 2f out: no ch after* **10/1**

46-3 **12** 8 **Geordie's Pool**[22] 1587 3-8-11 **67**...................................... EddieAhern 2 39
(J W Hills) *in tch on inner: lost pl and nt clr run wl over 2f out: no ch last 2f: eased ins fnl f* **12/1**

050- **13** 19 **Crystal Plum (IRE)**[268] 5095 3-8-7 **63** ow1...................... MichaelHills 6 —
(B W Hills) *led tl hdd wl over 2f out: wknd rapidly: t.o* **20/1**

2m 6.33s (-1.46) **Going Correction** -0.125s/f (Stan) **13** Ran SP% **123.0**
Speed ratings (Par 99):100,98,96,96,96 96,95,94,92,92 92,85,70
CSF £30.42 CT £157.15 TOTE £4.10: £2.00, £2.20, £1.90; EX 23.20.
Owner Gainsborough **Bred** Gainsborough Farm Llc **Trained** Newmarket, Suffolk

FOCUS
A modest three-year-old handicap, but the form looks sound for the class, although limited by the fifth.
Crystal Plum(IRE) Official explanation: jockey said filly ran too free to post

2178 JASON DONOVAN LIVE AT LINGFIELDPARK.CO.UK H'CAP 1m (P)
4:30 (4:31) (Class 6) (0-60,60) 3-Y-O **£3,238** (£963; £481; £240) **Stalls** High

Form RPR

0060 **1** **Cavallo Di Ferro (IRE)**[36] 1238 3-9-2 **58**...................... AntonyProcter 6 63
(M J Gingell) *t.k.h: in tch: hdwy over 2f out: led jst ins fnl f: r.o strly* **33/1**

0-65 **2** 1 3/4 **Affiliation (IRE)**[17] 1726 3-9-3 **59**................................ RichardHughes 12 60
(R Hannon) *bhd: rdn over 4f out: hdwy on outer over 2f out: kpt on u.p to go 2nd wl ins fnl f: nt rch wnr* **4/1**[2]

0-66 **3** nk **Chant De Guerre (USA)**[17] 1731 3-9-3 **59**...................... DaneO'Neill 7 59
(H J L Dunlop) *racd in midfield: c wd over 2f out: rdn and hdwy jst over 2f out: kpt on steadily u.p: nt pce to trble wnr* **12/1**

0030 **4** nk **Inquisitress**[20] 1634 3-8-8 **57**.. RyanBird(7) 9 56
(J J Bridger) *chsd ldrs: rdn to ld 2f out: hdd jst ins fnl f: kpt on same pce* **16/1**

006- **5** 1/2 **Whaxaar (IRE)**[183] 6651 3-9-2 **58**............................ FrankieMcDonald 11 60+
(S Kirk) *v.s.a: hld up and bhd: swtchd rt over 2f out: hdwy over 1f out: styng on whn nt clr run and swtchd rt nr fin: nvr nrr* **20/1**

0-05 **6** 3 1/2 **Ireland Dancer (IRE)**[57] 924 3-9-2 **58**............................... IanMongan 8 48
(P M Phelan) *chsd ldr: rdn and ev ch over 2f out: wknd qckly fnl f* **15/2**[3]

2120 **7** 3/4 **Time For Change (IRE)**[10] 1903 3-9-4 **60**...................... MichaelHills 10 48
(B W Hills) *hld up and bhd: effrt whn nt clr run over 2f out: rdn and carried hd awkwardly over 1f out: no imp* **7/2**[1]

0-55 **8** 1 1/2 **Metropolitan Chief**[28] 1432 3-9-3 **59**........................... FergusSweeney 2 44+
(D M Simcock) *chsd ldrs on inner: lost pl and nt clr run 3f out tl wl over 1f out: no ch after* **4/1**[2]

0061 **9** 3/4 **Hayley's Flower (IRE)**[37] 1232 3-9-1 **57**.....................(b) PatDobbs 3 40
(J C Fox) *hld up and bhd: nt clr run 3f out tl 2f out: rdn and no prog after* **8/1**

5100 **10** 1 1/2 **Zaafira (SPA)**[115] 357 3-9-1 **60**................................. AlanCreighton(3) 4 40
(E J Creighton) *chsd ldrs: rdn wl over 2f out: wknd wl over 1f out* **20/1**

40-5 **11** nk **Blue Mistral (IRE)**[28] 1430 3-9-4 **60**....................................(t) PaulDoe 1 39
(W J Knight) *rrd s: sn led: rdn 3f out: hdd 2f out: sn wknd* **20/1**

1m 39.44s (0.01) **Going Correction** -0.125s/f (Stan) **11** Ran SP% **115.9**
Speed ratings (Par 97):94,92,91,91,91 87,86,85,84,83 82
CSF £152.34 CT £1741.39 TOTE £54.80: £9.30, £1.90, £2.70; EX 302.70.
Owner P Chakko & M J Gingell **Bred** Michael Dalton **Trained** North Runcton, Norfolk

FOCUS
A moderate handicap and, although the third and fifth ran to their marks, the form looks worth treating with a little caution.
Whaxaar(IRE) Official explanation: jockey said gelding missed the break
Metropolitan Chief Official explanation: jockey said gelding was denied a clear run

2179 TONY HADLEY LIVE AT LINGFIELDPARK.CO.UK H'CAP 1m (P)
5:00 (5:04) (Class 6) (0-50,50) 4-Y-O+ **£3,238** (£963; £481; £240) **Stalls** High

Form RPR

00-2 **1** **Nan Jan**[9] 1933 5-8-11 **49**...(t) RobertHavlin 6 61+
(R Ingram) *racd in midfield: rdn 4f out: hdwy on inner and nt clr run jst over 2f out: swtchd rt over 1f out: str run to ld last strides* **7/2**[1]

-453 **2** 3/4 **Labelled With Love**[113] 383 7-8-12 **50**..............................(t) AmirQuinn 9 55
(J R Boyle) *stdd s: t.k.h: hld up and bhd: hdwy over 2f out: rdn to ld wl ins fnl f: hdd last strides* **7/1**

0004 **3** 1 **Rafferty (IRE)**[9] 1933 8-8-12 **50**..(p) SebSanders 7 53
(S Dow) *hld up in midfield: hdwy and rdn jst over 2f out: chsd ldrs over 1f out: kpt on ins fnl f* **7/1**

5020 **4** 1/2 **Ceredig**[1] 2143 4-8-5 **50**.. WilliamCarson(7) 4 52
(P W Hiatt) *sn led: clr 5f out tl 3f out: rdn over 2f out: kpt on wl tl hdd and no ex wl ins fnl f* **13/2**[3]

6540 **5** 1 3/4 **Just Fly**[50] 1002 7-8-11 **49**...(v) DaneO'Neill 10 47
(Dr J R J Naylor) *racd in midfield on outer: rdn 4f out: hdwy to chse ldrs wl over 2f out: ev ch over 1f out: fdd last 100yds* **6/1**[2]

0014 **6** 1 1/4 **Jools**[16] 1740 9-8-11 **49**... SteveDrowne 12 44
(D K Ivory) *hld up and bhd: hdwy over 3f out: rdn 2f out: chsd ldrs whn nt clr run and snatched up jst over 1f out: nt rcvr* **10/1**

3505 **7** 3/4 **Ellen's Girl (IRE)**[16] 1740 4-8-8 **49**.................(v[1]) RichardKingscote(3) 11 42
(B G Powell) *prom: chsd ldr over 2f out: hung bdly lft over 1f out: sn wknd* **14/1**

5206 **8** 2 1/2 **Mid Valley**[31] 1350 4-8-12 **50**.......................................(v) RichardHughes 2 37
(J R Jenkins) *stdd s: hld up in tch on inner: lost pl over 3f out: c wd bnd over 2f out: no imp* **10/1**

300- **9** 3/4 **Trouble Maker**[373] 1913 6-8-11 **49**.. FrancisNorton 8 35
(A M Balding) *chsd ldr 5f out tl over 2f out: sn wknd* **13/2**[3]

-500 **10** 8 **Shinko (IRE)**[16] 1740 4-8-12 **50**..(p) PaulDoe 5 17
(Miss J Feilden) *chsd ldr for 3f: sn rdn: bhd last 3f* **28/1**

1m 38.82s (-0.61) **Going Correction** -0.125s/f (Stan) **10** Ran SP% **116.5**
Speed ratings (Par 101):98,97,96,95,94 92,92,89,88,80
CSF £27.90 CT £163.48 TOTE £4.70: £1.70, £2.20, £2.60; EX 32.50 Place 6 £126.49, Place 5 £63.10.
Owner The Waltons **Bred** Mrs S Ingram **Trained** Epsom, Surrey

FOCUS
A typically open handicap for the class and rated through the third to his recent best.
Jools ◆ Official explanation: jockey said gelding was denied a clear run
T/Jkpt: Not won. T/Plt: £1,403.10 to a £1 stake. Pool: £58,145.65. 30.25 winning tickets. T/Qpdt: £181.10 to a £1 stake. Pool: £3,549.00. 14.50 winning tickets. SP

2122 SANDOWN (R-H)
Thursday, May 31

OFFICIAL GOING: Good to soft (soft in places on sprint course)
A new fixture for Sandown, effectively replacing the traditional Whit Monday card.
Wind: Light, behind Weather: Fine

2180 BETFAIR GAMES H'CAP 1m 14y
6:10 (6:11) (Class 4) (0-80,80) 4-Y-O+ **£6,477** (£1,927; £963; £481) **Stalls** High

Form RPR

0033 **1** **Full Victory (IRE)**[2] 2107 5-8-8 **70**.............................. FergusSweeney 9 86
(R A Farrant) *lw: hld up towards rr: prog over 2f out: led over 1f out: hanging lft but sn rdn clr* **11/4**[1]

0-00 **2** 7 **Crocodile Bay (IRE)**[15] 1765 4-8-8 **70**................................ BrettDoyle 7 72
(B J Meehan) *t.k.h: prom: chsd ldr over 2f out: upsides over 1f out: sn nt qckn u.p* **25/1**

5344 **3** 1 1/4 **Shot To Fame (USA)**[8] 1939 8-9-3 **79**....................(t) AdrianTNicholls 10 78
(D Nicholls) *lw: led at decent pce: hdd over 1f out: sn outpcd: plugged on* **13/2**[3]

-050 **4** nk **Finsbury**[12] 1845 4-8-5 **74**.. AmyBaker(7) 5 72+
(Miss J Feilden) *dwlt: t.k.h: hld up in last: styd on in centre st but eventually c to nr side: bmpd along and kpt on same pce fnl 2f* **25/1**

0402 **5** 1 **Desert Dreamer (IRE)**[9] 1935 6-8-8 **70**.......................... MartinDwyer 8 66
(P R Chamings) *plld hrd early: hld up in rr: sme prog 2f out: shkn up over 1f out: nvr nr ldrs* **6/1**[2]

10-0 **6** nk **Fabrian**[9] 1922 9-9-1 **77**.. JamesDoyle 4 72+
(R J Price) *trckd ldr: styd alone towards far side in st: sn rdn: nt on terms over 1f out: no ch w wnr after* **10/1**

1061 **7** 6 **Bold Diktator**[33] 1308 5-9-3 **79**... JimCrowley 3 61
(Tom Dascombe) *t.k.h: prom: rdn over 2f out: wknd over 1f out* **6/1**[2]

0-10 **8** 2 **Cactus King**[36] 1245 4-9-4 **80**.. IanMongan 6 57
(P M Phelan) *t.k.h: trckd ldrs: rdn wl over 2f out: wknd wl over 1f out* **10/1**

022- **9** 5 **Calming Waters**[199] 6459 4-8-12 **74**..................................... JohnEgan 2 39
(D W P Arbuthnot) *t.k.h: hld up in midfield: rdn and wknd over 2f out* **8/1**

10-5 **10** 3 1/2 **Sotik Star (IRE)**[16] 1751 4-9-0 **76**..................................... TedDurcan 1 33
(P J Makin) *hld up in tch: rdn and lost pl whn hmpd over 2f out: floundering after* **8/1**

1m 43.92s (-0.03) **Going Correction** +0.15s/f (Good) **10** Ran SP% **116.7**
Speed ratings (Par 105):106,99,97,97,96 96,90,88,83,79
CSF £81.80 CT £347.67 TOTE £4.20: £1.60, £7.30, £2.30; EX 76.30.
Owner Friends of Saunton Sands **Bred** Larry Ryan **Trained** Upper Lambourn, Berks

FOCUS
Plenty raced keenly in this competitive-looking handicap which was eventually won in authoritative manner by Full Victory.
Desert Dreamer(IRE) Official explanation: jockey said gelding ran too free
Sotik Star(IRE) Official explanation: jockey said colt had no more to give

2181 BETFAIR POKER FILLIES' H'CAP 1m 1f
6:40 (6:40) (Class 5) (0-75,81) 3-Y-O+ **£3,886** (£1,156; £577; £288) **Stalls** High

Form RPR

3121 **1** **Lady Gloria**[7] 1979 3-9-7 **81** 6ex.. TPQueally 4 88+
(J G Given) *lw: trckd ldr after 2f: led wl over 2f out: drvn wl over 1f out: styd on wl fnl f* **5/2**[1]

5603 **2** 1 1/2 **Fangorn Forest (IRE)**[15] 1761 4-8-11 **63**....................(p) LukeMorris(5) 1 69
(R A Harris) *settled in last pair: rdn and prog fr over 2f out: wnt 2nd ins fnl f: no imp on wnr* **25/1**

303- **3** 1/2 **Boogie Dancer**[209] 6322 3-8-5 **65**.. MartinDwyer 12 68
(H S Howe) *led to wl over 2f out: chsd wnr after: hld over 1f out: lost 2nd ins fnl f* **33/1**

3-03 **4** 1 1/4 **House Maiden (IRE)**[30] 1386 3-7-9 **60**........................ WilliamBuick(5) 11 60
(D M Simcock) *t.k.h: hld up and sn in midfield: rdn over 2f out: prog over 1f out: kpt on same pce* **16/1**

1-52 **5** 1/2 **Colchium (IRE)**[21] 1610 3-8-13 **73**...................................... SteveDrowne 5 72
(H Morrison) *trckd ldrs: cl up and rdn 2f out: one pce u.p after* **6/1**

32-4 **6** 3/4 **Sister Maria (USA)**[13] 1815 3-9-1 **75**.............................. KerrinMcEvoy 3 73+
(E A L Dunlop) *lw: hld up wl in rr: prog 2f out: kpt on same pce fr over 1f out and no hdwy* **10/3**[2]

-130 **7** 4 **Going To Work (IRE)**[19] 1649 3-9-1 **75**................................ TedDurcan 6 64
(D R C Elsworth) *stdd s: hld up towards rr: effrt 2f out: no imp on ldrs over 1f out: wknd ins fnl f* **8/1**

43-5 **8** 2 **Lavenham (IRE)**[29] 1401 4-9-13 **74**............................... RichardHughes 8 61
(R Hannon) *trckd ldrs: effrt and cl up 2f out: drvn and wknd over 1f out* **5/1**[3]

0330 **9** 8 **It's No Problem (IRE)**[7] 1972 3-8-0 **60** oh5................. FrancisNorton 10 28
(M Salaman) *t.k.h: trckd ldr for 2f: wknd over 2f out: t.o* **33/1**

5-34 **10** 2 **Dansil In Distress**[17] 1731 3-8-4 **64**...................................... JohnEgan 7 28
(S Kirk) *hld up in rr: rdn and struggling over 3f out: t.o* **20/1**

3-00 **11** 3 **Greek Easter (IRE)**[13] 1813 4-9-8 **69**.................................. BrettDoyle 2 29
(B J Meehan) *hld up in tch: struggling over 3f out: sn btn and eased: t.o* **25/1**

1m 56.32s (0.21) **Going Correction** +0.15s/f (Good)
WFA 3 from 4yo 13lb **11** Ran SP% **117.9**
Speed ratings (Par 100):105,103,103,102,101 101,97,95,88,86 84
CSF £75.83 CT £1686.47 TOTE £3.20: £1.40, £4.20, £5.90; EX 79.50.
Owner M H Tourle **Bred** M H And Mrs G Tourle **Trained** Willoughton, Lincs

FOCUS
A fair fillies' handicap, but run at an ordinary early gallop. The whole field came stands' side in the straight this time.

2182 BETFAIR BRIGADIER GERARD STKS (GROUP 3) 1m 2f 7y
7:15 (7:15) (Class 1) 4-Y-O+
£28,390 (£10,760; £5,385; £2,685; £1,345; £675) **Stalls** High

Form RPR

4-32 **1** **Take A Bow**[17] 1723 6-9-0 **108**... JimCrowley 5 115
(P R Chamings) *lw: trckd ldr after 2f to 6f out: effrt over 2f out: narrow ld over 1f out: drvn fnl f: battled on and a jst holding on* **11/1**

3423 **2** *shd* **Mighty**^{25} [1495] 4-9-0 112 .... JohnEgan 4 115
(Jane Chapple-Hyam) *trckd ldr 6f out: led wl over 2f out to over 1f out: rallied u.p fnl f: jst hld* **8/1**

34-2 **3** *shd* **Mashaahed**^{34} [1274] 4-9-0 110 .... MartinDwyer 3 115
(B W Hills) *hld up in last pair: prog wl over 2f out: drvn to chal over 1f out: upsides fnl f: jst hld* **5/2**^{1}

0-12 **4** *8* **Pinpoint (IRE)**^{25} [1494] 5-9-0 111 .... AdamKirby 1 99
(W R Swinburn) *hld up in last pair: rdn 3f out: no prog and btn 2f out* **7/2**^{2}

05-4 **5** *½* **Papal Bull**^{25} [1495] 4-9-5 115 .... JMurtagh 6 103
(Sir Michael Stoute) *lw: dwlt and rousted along to go prom: rdn over 4f out: reluctant u.p over 2f out: sn wl btn* **15/2**^{3}

112- **6** *9* **Tam Lin**^{258} [5342] 4-9-3 115 .... LDettori 2 83
(Saeed Bin Suroor) *free to post: led to wl over 2f out: shkn up and capitulated tamely wl over 1f out* **5/2**^{1}

600- **7** *15* **Fire And Rain (FR)**^{244} [5657] 4-9-0 0 .... RichardHughes 7 50
(Miss E C Lavelle) *w ldr for 2f: last by 1/2-way: t.o* **33/1**

2m 8.75s (-1.49) **Going Correction** +0.15s/f (Good) **7** Ran SP% **113.5**
Speed ratings (Par 113):111,110,110,104,104 96,84
CSF £90.94 TOTE £12.70: £3.10, £3.50; EX 86.60.
Owner Mrs J E L Wright **Bred** Mrs A M Jenkins **Trained** Baughurst, Hants

FOCUS
A weak renewal. They finished well strung out behind the winner, who put up a career best effort, and the two placed horses, who were very close to their marks.

NOTEBOOK
Take A Bow was third in the Betfred Mile here last month and is suited by the stiff finish at this track, but this was still something of a shock result. One cannot crab his consistency, though, and he deserved to win a Pattern race for his performances over the past two years. (op 12-1)
Mighty is becoming a consistent performer at this sort of level himself, and he put up another fine effort to follow on from his second in the John Porter and third in the Jockey Club Stakes. Another two furlongs probably suits him ideally nowadays, and the way he rallied in the closing stages reinforces that impression. He is tough and one could easily see him pick up Group honours on the continent.
Mashaahed, runner-up to Red Rocks over this course and distance on his seasonal reappearance, looked to hold strong claims on that piece of form. He loomed up looking the likeliest winner a furlong out, but he was outbattled in the closing stages. While it seems a bit harsh, he does seem to disappoint a little too often for a horse of his ability. (op 9-4 tchd 11-4)
Pinpoint(IRE), a very smart and progressive handicapper, was stepping up into Group company for the first time but disappointed. He simply did not pick up when the leaders quickened and the ground cannot really be used as an excuse as he likes a bit of give. It remains to be seen whether he can cut it in this type of event rather than the hurly-burly of big-field handicaps with which he is familiar. (op 10-3 tchd 4-1 in places)
Papal Bull, lazy out of the stalls, never looked to be helping his rider much and in the straight he put his head up in the air and did not want to know, looking thoroughly unco-operative under pressure. He confirmed the impression left at Newmarket that he has gone the wrong way. (op 7-1 tchd 6-1)
Tam Lin, who joined Godolphin at the end of last season having looked a progressive three-year-old under the care of Sir Michael Stoute, looked fit and was backed into joint-favouritism on his seasonal reappearance. He disappointed, though, racing freely and dropping out very quickly after getting squeezed up and hampered two furlongs out. He is entitled to improve for the run, but will have to come on quite a bit if his Group 1 entries at Royal Ascot are to be taken seriously. Official explanation: jockey said colt ran too free (op 7-2)
Fire And Rain(FR), running his first race for this stable having been bought out of Ballydoyle for 40,000gns, has been gelded since his last run and will no doubt be going jumping in due course. (tchd 25-1)

2183 BETFAIR MOBILE NATIONAL STKS (LISTED RACE) 5f 6y
7:50 (7:51) (Class 1) 2-Y-O

£12,207 (£4,626; £2,315; £1,154; £578; £290) **Stalls** High

Form RPR

1 **1** **Sweepstake (IRE)**^{14} [1781] 2-8-9 0 .... RichardHughes 8 98
(R Hannon) *cl up: lost pl 1/2-way: trapped bhd rivals 2f out tl swtchd rt jst over 1f out: squeezed through and r.o to ld last 75yds* **11/4**^{2}

1 **2** *½* **Lady Avenger (IRE)**^{10} [1896] 2-8-9 0 .... KerrinMcEvoy 3 96
(J M P Eustace) *w'like: s.i.s: t.k.h and hld up: prog on outer over 1f out: hanging rt but rdn to ld ins fnl f: hdd last 75yds* **6/1**

3 **3** *1 ½* **Al Muheer (IRE)**^{44} [1073] 2-9-0 0 .... TedDurcan 6 96
(C E Brittain) *w'like: sn pushed along to stay in tch: last and struggling 2f out: styd on wl fnl f to take 3rd nr fin* **33/1**

421 **4** *½* **New Jersey (IRE)**^{15} [1772] 2-9-0 0 .... DO'Donohoe 7 94
(K A Ryan) *trckd ldr: pushed along 1/2-way: rdn to ld narrowly wl over 1f out: hdd and outpcd ins fnl f* **2/1**^{1}

34 **5** *1 ½* **Major Eazy (IRE)**^{29} [1390] 2-9-0 0 .... LDettori 4 89
(B J Meehan) *lw: hld up: smooth prog to chal 2f out: shkn up over 1f out: hanging rt and fdd* **9/2**^{3}

1362 **6** *2* **Baytown Blaze**^{21} [1608] 2-8-9 0 .... HayleyTurner 2 76
(P S McEntee) *led to wl over 1f out: hld whn hmpd 150yds out: fdd* **33/1**

1 **7** *1 ¼* **Carleton**^{17} [1721] 2-9-0 0 .... DarryllHolland 5 77
(M R Channon) *w'like: lw: chsd ldrs: prog to chal 2f out: wknd ins fnl f* **11/2**

62.72 secs (0.51) **Going Correction** +0.15s/f (Good) **7** Ran SP% **113.7**
Speed ratings (Par 101):101,100,97,97,94 91,89
CSF £19.27 TOTE £4.00: £2.40, £2.90; EX 11.90.
Owner B Bull **Bred** Calley House Uk **Trained** East Everleigh, Wilts

FOCUS
A good-looking renewal, featuring four last-time out winners. They went a good gallop and the principals came from off the pace.

NOTEBOOK
Sweepstake(IRE), an athletic and relaxed type whose debut form was hard to quantify, left no-one in any doubt that she is a smart filly after this performance. Racing on the rail for much of the way, she was angled out for her run but then got stuck behind horses and had to be switched back to the rail to challenge. Things got a bit tight there, though, and she had to show courage to take a narrow gap. The way she quickened up and really put her head down was impressive and there looks to be plenty more to come from her. The Queen Mary looks the obvious race for her now, although the Albany will come into the equation too. (op 3-1 tchd 7-2 and 4-1 in places)
Lady Avenger(IRE), who impressed when winning on her debut at Windsor, was always likely to appreciate the cut in the ground, being a daughter of Namid, and despite being on her toes beforehand she ran well, especially considering that she raced down the outer in the second half of the race, while the winner raced mainly close to the favoured far rail. (op 9-2)
Al Muheer(IRE) ran with promise on his debut at Nottingham but looked to be up against it in this company on only his second start. He ran well, though, is going to be very much suited by another furlong, and should have little difficulty winning a maiden before going on to better things.
New Jersey(IRE) won a novice race at York last time in similar conditions and was rightly sent off favourite to build on that in this higher grade. He did not get home on this stiffer track, though, having raced handily throughout in a race run at a good clip. (op 9-4)
Major Eazy(IRE) had shown useful form on his previous two starts without getting off the mark and again ran well in defeat in what was a decent race. He will appreciate a drop in grade and can win his maiden. (tchd 5-1)
Baytown Blaze, who finished runner-up to Spirit Of Sharjah in this grade at Goodwood last time, showed good early speed to cross over from stall two and make the running on the far-side rail. She had too much use made of her, though, and simply failed to get home after setting a fast pace.
Carleton, who was a bit of a shock winner on his debut at Windsor, could not build on that in this hotter company. (op 8-1)

2184 BETFAIR TEMPLE STKS (GROUP 2) 5f 6y
8:20 (8:23) (Class 1) 3-Y-O+

£48,263 (£18,292; £9,154; £4,564; £2,286; £1,147) **Stalls** High

Form RPR

2011 **1** **Sierra Vista**^{5} [2034] 7-9-1 100 .... PaulHanagan 7 114
(D W Barker) *mde all: shkn up over 1f out: styd on strly fnl f* **5/1**

5-02 **2** *1 ¼* **Moss Vale (IRE)**^{5} [2050] 6-9-8 116 .... AdrianTNicholls 8 117
(D Nicholls) *lw: prom: chsd wnr 1/2-way: hrd rdn over 1f out: no imp* **4/1**^{3}

01-1 **3** *hd* **Firenze**^{19} [1670] 6-9-1 99 .... LDettori 5 109+
(J R Fanshawe) *stdd s: settled in 6th: pushed along and prog fr 2f out: styd on fnl f and nrly snatched 2nd* **5/2**^{1}

445- **4** *3 ½* **The Trader (IRE)**^{268} [5087] 9-9-4 107 .... (b) TedDurcan 9 99
(M Blanshard) *lw: chsd clr ldrs: effrt to go 3rd briefly over 1f out: one pce and no imp after* **14/1**

212- **5** *nk* **Wi Dud**^{244} [5656] 3-9-0 116 .... DO'Donohoe 1 99
(K A Ryan) *awkward s: sn pushed along in 7th: styd on fnl f: gng on at fin* **10/1**

0001 **6** *4* **Angus Newz**^{11} [1861] 4-9-1 90 .... (v) FrancisNorton 6 81
(M Quinn) *chsd wnr to 1/2-way: sn btn* **33/1**

0022 **7** *4* **Excusez Moi (USA)**^{19} [1656] 5-9-4 102 .... KerrinMcEvoy 3 69
(C E Brittain) *chsd clr ldrs: struggling over 2f out: wknd over 1f out* **12/1**

10-2 **8** *5* **Red Clubs (IRE)**^{15} [1770] 4-9-8 113 .... MichaelHills 2 55
(B W Hills) *dwlt: outpcd and a last* **3/1**^{2}

61.02 secs (-1.19) **Going Correction** +0.15s/f (Good)
WFA 3 from 4yo+ 8lb **8** Ran SP% **116.6**
Speed ratings (Par 115):115,113,112,107,106 100,93,85
CSF £25.86 TOTE £6.10: £1.90, £1.70, £1.50; EX 26.90.
Owner David T J Metcalfe **Bred** Mrs M Beddis **Trained** Scorton, N Yorks

FOCUS
A weak race by the standard of the contest but Sierra Vista is improving at the age of seven and took another step up the ladder. Firenze also improved on her bare form and there should be more to come.

NOTEBOOK
Sierra Vista, who is in the form of her life at present, pinged the traps, grabbed the favoured far-side rail and set a strong gallop that the others struggled to match. Although strongly challenged by Moss Vale from two furlongs out, she kept finding more, as befits a mare who stays 6f. Her form in fields of nine runners or fewer over the minimum trip now reads 1141911, a clear sign that she enjoys dominating in a small field. A credit to her trainer, she will apparently skip Royal Ascot, and perhaps not have another race until her main target of her season, the Haydock Sprint Cup. (tchd 6-1)
Moss Vale(IRE), runner-up to Benbaun in Ireland five days earlier, was happy to take a lead from Sierra Vista next to the rail, but when it came to trying to get past the mare he proved incapable. Because he was carrying a 3lb penalty, though, he comes out the best horse in the race on the ratings. (tchd 9-2)
Firenze found it all happening a bit too quickly back at the minimum trip and, although she stayed on well from off the pace to almost take second place on the line, the conclusion has to be that she will be very much suited by a return to six. She is clearly still on the upgrade, though. (op 11-4 tchd 7-2)
The Trader(IRE), who finished runner-up in this race last year and has gone well fresh in the past, had the best of the draw. Switched off the rail for his challenge, he could muster only the one pace, and one would imagine that he will continue to struggle in this sort of company this year as he surely cannot be improving at the age of nine. (op 10-1)
Wi Dud was a smart juvenile last year, rounding off his season with a fine second to Dutch Art in the Middle Park Stakes, but he had a stiff task here on his return, taking on older horses under a 4lb penalty, and struggled to go the pace from an early stage. He looked fit enough, but he should still come on for the run, and he can also improve for quicker ground and another furlong. (tchd 15-2)
Angus Newz, who won a handicap off 88 last time out, had the lowest official rating in the race and faced a stiff task.
Excusez Moi(USA), whose stable is in form, was dropping back from 7f and was never a threat. (op 16-1)
Red Clubs(IRE) was poorly drawn and is ideally suited by further, but this performance was so far removed from what we know he can do that one must assume that he was just not at his best. Official explanation: vet said colt was found to be lame (tchd 11-4, 10-3 and 7-2 in places)

2185 BETFAIR SUPPORTS THE THOROUGHBRED REHABILITATION CENTRE H'CAP 1m 6f
8:50 (8:52) (Class 4) (0-85,83) 3-Y-O **£6,477** (£1,927; £963; £481) **Stalls** Centre

Form RPR

-314 **1** **Madaarek (USA)**^{13} [1810] 3-9-4 **80** .... MartinDwyer 9 86+
(E A L Dunlop) *lw: trckd ldng pair to over 6f out: styd cl up: effrt over 2f out: rdn to ld wl over 1f out: in command fnl f* **3/1**^{1}

35-5 **2** *1* **Squadron**^{17} [1724] 3-8-5 **67** .... JamesDoyle 8 69
(Mrs A J Perrett) *trckd ldng trio: lost pl 5f out: effrt again over 2f out: styd on u.p to take 2nd last strides* **8/1**

2-13 **3** *shd* **Actodos (IRE)**^{22} [1584] 3-9-7 **83** .... JimCrowley 4 85
(B R Millman) *led after 1f and set stdy pce: kicked on over 3f out: hdd wl over 1f out: one pce after: lost 2nd last strides* **3/1**^{1}

3-20 **4** *1 ¼* **Tempelstern (GER)**^{12} [1849] 3-9-4 **80** .... TedDurcan 1 80
(H R A Cecil) *hld up in 8th tl prog 6f out: disp 2nd fr 5f out: drvn 3f out: one pce fnl 2f* **7/2**^{2}

1053 **5** *¾* **Sweetheart**^{13} [1810] 3-8-12 **74** .... JohnEgan 10 73
(Jamie Poulton) *settled in 5th: lost pl over 5f out: drvn and effrt on outer over 2f out: kpt on same pce and unable to chal* **7/1**^{3}

2-55 **6** *2 ½* **Troialini**^{13} [1810] 3-9-4 **80** .... AdamKirby 3 76
(S W Hall) *hld up in 7th: lost pl and last 5f out: outpcd 3f out: drvn and sme prog 2f out: wandering and no hdwy over 1f out* **16/1**

323 **7** *1* **Guardian Of Truth (IRE)**^{25} [1505] 3-8-13 **75** .... PaulDoe 11 69
(W J Knight) *led for 1f: chsd ldr after: drvn 3f out: one pce and btn 2f out: wknd fnl f* **14/1**

-010 **8** *14* **Cry Presto (USA)**^{13} [1810] 3-8-13 **75** .... (bt) RichardHughes 5 50
(R Hannon) *s.s: hld up in last tl rapid prog to trck ldrs 6f out: rdn 3f out: sn btn: eased over 1f out* **25/1**

2-00 **9** *6* **Cavalry Twill (IRE)**^{13} [1810] 3-8-8 **70** .... SteveDrowne 6 36
(P F I Cole) *settled in 6th: rdn and wknd over 3f out: t.o* **20/1**

3m 14.66s (10.15) **Going Correction** +0.15s/f (Good) **9** Ran SP% **117.0**
Speed ratings (Par 101):77,76,76,75,75 73,73,65,61
CSF £28.20 CT £78.26 TOTE £3.80: £1.70, £1.80, £1.70; EX 30.40 Place 6 £593.15, Place 5 £253.45.

The Form Book, Raceform Ltd, Compton, RG20 6NL

Owner Hamdan Al Maktoum **Bred** Shadwell Farm LLC **Trained** Newmarket, Suffolk

FOCUS

They did not go a great gallop in this staying handicap and the form is not that sound. It was also far from a test of stamina. A much improved effort from the winner nevertheless.

T/Plt: £317.30 to a £1 stake. Pool: £101,144.85. 232.70 winning tickets. T/Qpdt: £42.80 to a £1 stake. Pool: £6,287.80. 108.60 winning tickets. JN

[2151]YARMOUTH (L-H)

Thursday, May 31

OFFICIAL GOING: Good

Wind: Light, against Weather: Fine

2186 WATERAID MEDIAN AUCTION MAIDEN STKS 6f 3y

2:10 (2:11) (Class 6) 3-5-Y-O **£1,943** (£578; £288; £144) **Stalls** High

Form				RPR
	1		**Big Noise** 3-9-3 0 ... DarryllHolland 1 (Dr J D Scargill) *trckd ldrs: shkn up to ld over 1f out: styd on wl* **4/1**[3]	71
500-	**2**	*5*	**Dragon Flame (IRE)**[230] 5949 4-9-12 55 ... (v[1]) ChrisCatlin 3 (M Quinn) *chsd ldr: led wl over 1f out: sn rdn and hdd: no ex ins fnl f* **20/1**	57
0-0	**3**	*3*	**Siesta (IRE)**[20] 1635 3-8-12 0 ... (e) OscarUrbina 4 (J R Fanshawe) *chsd ldrs: lost pl over 3f out: n.d after* **9/1**	40
0-06	**4**	*hd*	**Extractor**[20] 1634 3-9-3 54 ... (b[1]) JimmyQuinn 5 (J L Dunlop) *sn led: rdn and hdd wl over 1f out: wknd fnl f* **7/2**[2]	44
0	**5**	*nk*	**Apolina**[4] 2059 3-8-12 0 ... StephenDonohoe 6 (P S McEntee) *chsd ldrs: rdn and hung lft over 3f out: sn wknd* **33/1**	38
0-0	**6**	*1/2*	**She's A Softie (IRE)**[9] 1923 3-8-12 0 ... RichardMullen 7 (C F Wall) *chsd ldrs over 4f* **11/1**	37
4-	**7**	*1/2*	**Tawnybrack (IRE)**[295] 4251 3-9-3 0 ... GeorgeBaker 2 (Jane Chapple-Hyam) *s.i.s: hld up: nvr trbld ldrs* **13/8**[1]	40
0	**8**	*3/4*	**Art Gamble (IRE)**[6] 2012 3-8-10 0 ... BradleyRoper(7) 8 (N A Callaghan) *hld up: hdwy 1/2-way: rdn and wknd 2f out* **14/1**	38

1m 15.73s (2.03) **Going Correction** +0.35s/f (Good)

WFA 3 from 4yo 9lb **8** Ran SP% **113.0**

Speed ratings (Par 101):100,93,89,89,88 88,87,86

CSF £74.41 TOTE £4.40: £1.30, £3.30, £3.60; EX 70.20 Trifecta £203.10 Pool: £412.02 - 1.44 winning tickets..

Owner Mrs Susan Scargill **Bred** F B B White **Trained** Newmarket, Suffolk

FOCUS

A shocking contest and although the winner was impressive enough he beat little.

2187 AQUAZONE CLAIMING STKS 6f 3y

2:40 (2:40) (Class 6) 3-Y-0+ **£1,943** (£578; £288; £144) **Stalls** High

Form				RPR
0122	**1**		**Charlie Delta**[8] 1946 4-9-11 64 ... (b) JHBowman 9 (J R Boyle) *chsd ldrs: led over 1f out: sn rdn: r.o* **15/8**[2]	69
00-0	**2**	*hd*	**Currency**[19] 1681 10-9-0 56 ... BarrySavage(7) 6 (J M Bradley) *mid-div: rdn 1/2-way: hdwy over 1f out: r.o* **16/1**	64
0000	**3**	*1 1/2*	**Viewforth**[6] 1991 9-9-5 48 ... (b) DarryllHolland 11 (M A Buckley) *led over 4f out: sn clr: hdd over 1f out: styd on same pce ins fnl f* **18/1**	57
6150	**4**	*1 1/4*	**Doctor Ned**[23] 1561 3-8-6 50 ... WilliamBuick(5) 3 (N A Callaghan) *dwlt: hld up: hdwy over 1f out: nt trble ldrs* **11/1**	52
04-0	**5**	*1/2*	**Full Spate**[20] 1640 12-9-0 48 ... KevinGhunowa(5) 10 (J M Bradley) *s.s: bhd: hdwy over 1f out: rdn and edgd lft ins fnl f: nvr trbld ldrs* **33/1**	52
12-0	**6**	*1 1/2*	**Don Pele (IRE)**[7] 1971 5-9-11 82 ... StephenDonohoe 2 (P D Evans) *hld up: rdn over 1f out: nvr trbld ldrs* **13/8**[1]	53
0406	**7**	*shd*	**Blythe Spirit**[16] 1753 8-9-2 50 ... (v) PaulHanagan 5 (R A Fahey) *chsd ldrs: rdn over 1f out: wknd ins fnl f* **9/1**[3]	44
0413	**8**	*2*	**Blue Knight (IRE)**[31] 1360 8-9-7 41 ... (p) JimmyQuinn 4 (P Howling) *chsd ldrs over 4f* **14/1**	42
000-	**9**	*10*	**Bertie Bear**[241] 5733 4-8-9 36 ... JosephineBruning(7) 1 (G G Margarson) *chsd ldrs: lost pl 4f out: sn bhd* **150/1**	5
450-	**10**	*1/2*	**Swallow Senora (IRE)**[16] 6962 5-8-9 38 ... RussellKennemore(5) 8 (M C Chapman) *led: hdd over 4f out: losing pl whn sddle slipped over 2f out* **150/1**	—

1m 15.86s (2.16) **Going Correction** +0.35s/f (Good)

WFA 3 from 4yo+ 9lb **10** Ran SP% **113.3**

Speed ratings (Par 101):99,98,96,95,94 92,92,89,76,75

CSF £30.92 TOTE £3.00: £1.10, £4.60, £3.70; EX 37.80 Trifecta £322.30 Part won. Pool: £454.06 - 0.60 winning tickets..The winner was subject to a friendly claim. Blythe Spirit was claimed Mrs Lisa Williamson for £3,000. Don Pele was claimed by Robert Bailey for £12,000.

Owner M Khan X2 **Bred** P K Gardner **Trained** Epsom, Surrey

FOCUS

A competitive heat on paper, and sound enough, although the poor showing of Don Pele detracts from the form.

Viewforth Official explanation: jockey said gelding ran too free early and hung left

Swallow Senora(IRE) Official explanation: jockey said saddle slipped

2188 BLP WATERAID (S) STKS 5f 43y

3:10 (3:10) (Class 6) 2-Y-0 **£1,943** (£578; £288; £144) **Stalls** High

Form				RPR
00	**1**		**Longoria (IRE)**[12] 1848 2-8-6 0 ow2 ... JerryO'Dwyer(3) 4 (M G Quinlan) *dwlt: sn rcvrd to ld: clr 1/2-way: eased ins fnl f* **10/11**[1]	65
4	**2**	*4*	**Secret Meaning**[28] 1428 2-8-0 0 ... JackDean(7) 6 (W G M Turner) *prom: chsd wnr 1/2-way: sn rdn and hung lft: styd on same pce fnl f* **6/1**[3]	49
0	**3**	*1 3/4*	**Little Angel (IRE)**[8] 1945 2-8-2 0 ... ColinHaddon(5) 2 (Miss V Haigh) *chsd ldrs: rdn 1/2-way: wknd ins fnl f* **6/1**[3]	42
3566	**4**	*3 1/2*	**Miss Willoughby**[7] 1975 2-8-4 0 ... MarcHalford(3) 3 (J Ryan) *s.i.s: hld up: rdn 1/2-way: sn wknd* **16/1**	30
	5	*1/2*	**Sharps Gold** 2-8-7 0 ... EdwardCreighton 1 (P J McBride) *sn outpcd* **11/2**[2]	28
0240	**6**	*3 1/2*	**Portway Lane**[17] 1728 2-8-2 0 ... TolleyDean(5) 5 (W G M Turner) *chsd wnr tl rdn 1/2-way: sn wknd* **10/1**	15

66.16 secs (3.36) **Going Correction** +0.35s/f (Good) **6** Ran SP% **111.3**

Speed ratings (Par 91):87,80,77,72,71 65

CSF £6.72 TOTE £2.00: £1.80, £2.70; EX 7.80.The winner was bought in for 10,600gns.

Owner John Hanly **Bred** Cathal Ryan **Trained** Newmarket, Suffolk

FOCUS

A poor race won readily by favourite Longoria, although the time was modest.

NOTEBOOK

Longoria(IRE) had shown enough in two previous attempts in maidens to suggest a race of this nature was within her capabilities and she rarely had a moment's worry, coming right away before being eased down. She is probably capable of winning races at a higher level. (op 11-10 tchd 5-4)

Secret Meaning stepped up on her debut effort and kept on best of the rest, but the winner proved in a different league. There is probably a race at this level in her. (op 13-2 tchd 7-1 and 11-2)

Little Angel(IRE), beaten a long way on her debut at Lingfield, faced a much simpler assignment here and ran well, but will need to progress again before she can be considered a likely winner. (op 11-2 tchd 5-1)

Miss Willoughby is already exposed as moderate and she is likely to continue to fall short, even at the lowest level. (op 11-1)

Sharps Gold proved too inexperienced on this racecourse debut, but is taken to improve on this initial experience. (op 9-1 tchd 5-1)

2189 HOLLERAN H'CAP 1m 3y

3:40 (3:40) (Class 4) (0-80,80) 4-Y-0+ **£4,731** (£1,416; £708; £354; £176) **Stalls** High

Form				RPR
-024	**1**		**Moody Tunes**[5] 2038 4-9-1 77 ... JHBowman 10 (K R Burke) *hld up: hdwy 3f out: n.m.r over 2f out: led over 1f out: rdn out* **10/3**[1]	88+
0650	**2**	*2 1/2*	**Surwaki (USA)**[26] 1481 5-8-5 74 ... MCGeran(7) 1 (R M H Cowell) *chsd ldrs: led and edgd rt over 2f out: hdd over 1f out: styd on same pce ins fnl f* **12/1**	79
0202	**3**	*2 1/2*	**Orpen Wide (IRE)**[19] 1568 5-8-11 78 ... (b) RussellKennemore(5) 7 (M C Chapman) *chsd ldrs: rdn 5f out: sn lost pl: rallied and edgd lft over 1f out: styd on same pce fnl f* **8/1**	77
2112	**4**	*hd*	**Luckylover**[16] 1751 4-9-1 80 ... (t) JerryO'Dwyer(3) 6 (M G Quinlan) *led: rdn over 3f out: hdd over 2f out: hmpd sn after: wknd ins fnl f* **10/3**[1]	79
3-46	**5**	*1 1/2*	**Stargazer Jim (FR)**[13] 1819 5-8-6 68 ... PaulHanagan 8 (W J Haggas) *chsd ldrs: rdn whn hmpd 2f out: wknd over 1f out* **5/1**[2]	66+
0520	**6**	*11*	**Guildenstern (IRE)**[19] 1653 5-9-1 77 ... DarryllHolland 3 (P L Gilligan) *chsd ldrs: rdn and hung lft over 2f out: wknd over 1f out* **6/1**[3]	47
0-00	**7**	*2 1/2*	**Fast Bowler**[31] 1357 4-9-1 77 ... StephenDonohoe 4 (J M P Eustace) *hld up: wknd over 2f out* **16/1**	41
5340	**8**	*1 1/2*	**Sonny Parkin**[35] 1268 5-8-6 75 ... (v) StevenCorrigan(7) 5 (G A Huffer) *s.s: hld up: wknd over 2f out* **33/1**	36
-003	**9**	*2 1/2*	**Major League (USA)**[1] 2154 5-8-4 66 oh1 ... RichardMullen 9 (D Morris) *hld up: rdn over 4f out: wknd over 2f out* **16/1**	21
14-0	**10**	*12*	**Lincolneurocruiser**[23] 1568 5-8-12 74 ... JimmyQuinn 2 (Mrs N Macauley) *s.i.s: hdwy over 5f out: wknd over 2f out* **33/1**	1

1m 41.11s (1.21) **Going Correction** +0.35s/f (Good) **10** Ran SP% **113.6**

Speed ratings (Par 105):107,104,102,101,100 89,86,85,82,70

CSF £44.27 CT £298.78 TOTE £4.10: £2.10, £3.20, £2.90; EX 58.90 Trifecta £241.80 Part won. Pool: £340.64 - 0.78 winning tickets..

Owner Geoffrey Hamilton **Bred** Llety Stud **Trained** Middleham Moor, N Yorks

■ Stewards' Enquiry : J H Bowman three-day ban: careless riding (Jun 11-13)

FOCUS

An ordinary handicap in which the front five pulled 11 lengths clear, but hard to rate any higher with the fourth to previous turf form.

Stargazer Jim(FR) Official explanation: jockey said gelding hung right and suffered interference in running

Fast Bowler Official explanation: trainer's rep said gelding bled from the nose

Major League(USA) Official explanation: jockey said gelding ran flat

Lincolneurocruiser Official explanation: jockey said gelding lost its action

2190 ESSEX & SUFFOLK WATER H'CAP 7f 3y

4:10 (4:12) (Class 5) (0-70,67) 4-Y-0+ **£2,914** (£867; £433; £216) **Stalls** High

Form				RPR
2010	**1**		**High Ambition**[41] 1118 4-9-2 65 ... (v) DarryllHolland 9 (P W D'Arcy) *hld up: hdwy over 2f out: led ins fnl f: r.o wl* **9/2**[3]	84+
6163	**2**	*3 1/2*	**Flying Bantam (IRE)**[10] 1892 6-9-1 64 ... PaulHanagan 8 (R A Fahey) *chsd ldrs: rdn over 1f out: styd on same pce* **5/1**	72
0-00	**3**	*2 1/2*	**Joy And Pain**[16] 1755 6-8-8 57 ... (v) OscarUrbina 4 (M J Attwater) *chsd ldrs: led 2f out: sn rdn and hung rt: hdd & wknd ins fnl f* **10/1**	58
0432	**4**	*2*	**Moon Forest (IRE)**[2] 2108 5-7-13 55 ... (p) BarrySavage(7) 3 (J M Bradley) *trckd ldr: plld hrd: rdn over 1f out: wknd fnl f* **10/3**[1]	51
4003	**5**	*1*	**Plateau**[12] 1845 8-9-4 67 ... JHBowman 5 (C R Dore) *hld up: hdwy over 2f out: rdn over 1f out: wknd fnl f* **4/1**[2]	60
5-34	**6**	*shd*	**Mugeba**[30] 1377 6-8-6 55 ... (t) JimmyQuinn 7 (Miss Gay Kelleway) *hld up: effrt over 2f out: wknd over 1f out* **9/2**[3]	48
-604	**7**	*5*	**Out For A Stroll**[94] 571 8-8-6 62 ... FLenclud(7) 6 (S C Williams) *hld up: hdwy over 2f out: wknd over 1f out* **16/1**	41
200/	**8**	*5*	**Dorchester**[671] 3904 10-9-2 65 ... GeorgeBaker 10 (W J Musson) *led 5f: wknd over 1f out* **33/1**	31

1m 27.31s (0.71) **Going Correction** +0.35s/f (Good) **8** Ran SP% **114.0**

Speed ratings (Par 103):109,105,102,99,98 98,92,87

CSF £27.02 CT £213.07 TOTE £6.00: £2.10, £1.60, £2.40; EX 26.20 Trifecta £464.30 Part won. Pool: £654.07 - 0.34 winning tickets..

Owner Skeltools Ltd **Bred** A B Phipps **Trained** Newmarket, Suffolk

FOCUS

Not much of a contest and High Ambition won easily. The form looks sound rated around the runner-up, fourth and fifth.

2191 FAULKNERBROWNS H'CAP 5f 43y

4:40 (4:40) (Class 5) (0-75,75) 3-Y-0+ **£2,914** (£867; £433; £216) **Stalls** High

Form				RPR
0002	**1**		**Bold Minstrel (IRE)**[20] 1630 5-9-8 73 ... ChrisCatlin 1 (M Quinn) *mde all: rdn and edgd rt ins fnl f: r.o* **4/1**[2]	84
0400	**2**	*2*	**Kings College Boy**[13] 1806 7-9-0 65 ... (b) PaulHanagan 2 (R A Fahey) *a.p: rdn to chse wnr over 1f out: no imp* **7/1**	69
0061	**3**	*1 1/4*	**Peopleton Brook**[6] 1999 5-9-3 75 ... BarrySavage(7) 7 (J M Bradley) *hld up: hdwy over 1f out: sn rdn: nt rch ldrs* **5/4**[1]	74
3130	**4**	*1 1/2*	**Desert Master**[45] 1061 4-9-7 72 ... GeorgeBaker 9 (C F Wall) *chsd ldrs: rdn and edgd lft over 1f out: wknd ins fnl f* **5/1**[3]	66
1-0	**5**	*3/4*	**Tilly's Dream**[7] 1977 4-9-4 72 ... SaleemGolam(3) 6 (P S McEntee) *prom: rdn 1/2-way: wknd fnl f* **25/1**	63
4-26	**6**	*4*	**Overwing (IRE)**[24] 1525 4-9-3 75 ... MCGeran(7) 4 (R M H Cowell) *rrd s: sddle sn slipped: outpcd* **16/1**	52
0-00	**7**	*1*	**Danjet (IRE)**[6] 1999 4-9-3 68 ... StephenDonohoe 8 (J M Bradley) *chsd ldrs: rdn 1/2-way: wknd over 1f out* **20/1**	41
600	**8**	*nk*	**Spinetail Rufous (IRE)**[7] 1969 9-8-10 61 oh16 ... (b) AdrianMcCarthy 5 (Miss Z C Davison) *chsd ldrs over 3f* **150/1**	33

200 9 *hd* **Straight Face (IRE)**[56] 935 3-8-6 **65**.......... MatthewHenry 3 36
(M Wigham) *s.i.s: outpcd* **18/1**

64.26 secs (1.46) **Going Correction** +0.35s/f (Good)
WFA 3 from 4yo+ 8lb **9** Ran SP% **114.0**
Speed ratings (Par 103):102,98,96,94,93 86,85,84,84
CSF £30.87 CT £53.22 TOTE £4.50: £1.50, £1.80, £1.30; EX 29.20 Trifecta £112.00 Pool: £697.64 - 4.42 winning tickets..
Owner The Boys From The Shed Partnership **Bred** John & Denis Dunne **Trained** Newmarket, Suffolk

FOCUS
A decent race for the grade, Bold Minstrel dominated from the off and sets the standard.
Overwing(IRE) Official explanation: jockey said saddle slipped

2192 CARILLION H'CAP 1m 2f 21y
5:10 (5:12) (Class 6) (0-55,55) 3-Y-O **£2,137** (£635; £317; £158) **Stalls** Low

Form RPR

005- **1** **Raise The Goblet (IRE)**[187] 6603 3-8-10 **51**.......... DarryllHolland 14 57
(W J Haggas) *chsd ldrs: led 2f out: drvn out* **7/1**[3]

2160 **2** *nk* **A Mothers Love**[22] 1579 3-8-12 **53**.......... EdwardCreighton 6 58+
(P J McBride) *hld up: hdwy and nt clr run over 1f out: r.o* **7/1**[3]

50-0 **3** *1 1/4* **Blockley (USA)**[125] 257 3-9-0 **55**..........(t) GeorgeBaker 8 58
(Ian Williams) *chsd ldrs: rdn over 3f out: styd on same pce ins fnl f* **7/1**[3]

000- **4** *1/2* **Cushat Law (IRE)**[225] 6049 3-8-13 **54**.......... JHBowman 2 56+
(W Jarvis) *s.i.s: hld up: nt clr run over 2f out: hdwy over 1f out: styd on same pce ins fnl f* **6/1**[2]

600 **5** *1/2* **Pretty Demanding (IRE)**[24] 1537 3-8-10 **54**.......... JerryO'Dwyer(3) 4 58+
(M G Quinlan) *hld up: hmpd and nt clr run over 2f out: swtchd rt: nt clr run over 1f out: r.o: nvr able to chal* **14/1**

50-0 **6** *1* **Black Mogul**[24] 1522 3-9-0 **55**.......... RichardMullen 16 54
(W R Muir) *prom: rdn over 3f out: edgd lft over 2f out: no ex fnl f* **18/1**

000- **7** *nk* **Bold Adventure**[274] 4920 3-8-9 **50**.......... DavidKinsella 7 48
(W J Musson) *hld up: hdwy over 1f out: no imp fnl f* **11/2**[1]

-000 **8** *3* **Dancewiththestars (USA)**[9] 1917 3-9-0 **55**.......... OscarUrbina 1 47
(J R Fanshawe) *chsd ldrs: rdn and n.m.r over 2f out: wknd ins fnl f* **8/1**

00-5 **9** *2* **Sky Beam (USA)**[31] 1364 3-8-11 **52**.......... JimmyQuinn 13 40
(J L Dunlop) *hld up in tch: rdn over 2f out: wknd fnl f* **10/1**

060- **10** *3/4* **High Lite**[211] 6295 3-8-11 **55**.......... SaleemGolam(3) 5 42
(M L W Bell) *s.i.s: hld up: hdwy over 3f out: wknd over 1f out* **14/1**

000- **11** *1 1/4* **Slavonic Lake**[227] 6007 3-8-9 **50**..........(t) PaulHanagan 11 34
(I A Wood) *chsd ldrs: led over 3f out: rdn and hdd 2f out: wknd fnl f* **33/1**

00-0 **12** *1 1/4* **Best Warning**[23] 1566 3-8-6 **50**.......... MarcHalford(3) 10 32
(J Ryan) *hld up: rdn over 3f out: a in rr* **100/1**

000- **13** *2* **Better Off Red (USA)**[293] 4323 3-8-2 **50**.......... MCGeran(7) 12 28
(D M Simcock) *hld up: hdwy over 3f out: rdn and hung lft over 2f out: wknd over 1f out* **33/1**

000- **14** *1 1/4* **Rotation (IRE)**[234] 5871 3-8-7 **48**.......... MatthewHenry 9 23
(J W Hills) *hld up: rdn over 3f out: a in rr* **12/1**

-006 **15** *5* **Present**[20] 1637 3-8-11 **52**.......... ChrisCatlin 15 17
(D Morris) *sn led: rdn and hdd 3f out: wknd 2f out* **33/1**

2m 11.89s (3.79) **Going Correction** +0.35s/f (Good) **15** Ran SP% **123.5**
Speed ratings (Par 97):98,97,96,96,95 95,94,92,90,90 89,88,86,85,81
CSF £55.21 CT £366.42 TOTE £8.80: £3.20, £2.70, £2.90; EX 72.60 TRIFECTA Not won. Place 6 £102.31, Place 5 £30.66.
Owner J Hanson **Bred** Miss Eileen Grealish **Trained** Newmarket, Suffolk

FOCUS
Just a moderate handicap, but it was a relatively interesting one with so many unexposed sorts on show, 11 of which were making their handicap debut. The bare form is probably ordinary though.
T/Plt: £163.20 to a £1 stake. Pool: £45,844.20. 205.05 winning tickets. T/Qpdt: £7.30 to a £1 stake. Pool: £3,523.00. 352.60 winning tickets. CR

1882 BATH (L-H)
Friday, June 1

OFFICIAL GOING: Good (good to soft in places, 7.4)
Wind: almost nil Weather: Fine

2193 EUROPEAN BREEDERS' FUND AND BLACKTHORN MAIDEN STKS 5f 161y
6:30 (6:32) (Class 5) 2-Y-O **£3,562** (£1,059; £529; £264) **Stalls** Low

Form RPR

0 **1** **Spanish Bounty**[15] 1781 2-9-3 0.......... GeorgeBaker 11 83+
(J G Portman) *mde virtually all: rdn over 1f out: clr ins fnl f: r.o wl* **8/1**[3]

2 *3* **Aaim For Applause** 2-9-3 0.......... EdwardCreighton 1 73+
(M R Channon) *dwlt: outpcd and wl bhd: swtchd rt and hdwy 2f out: wnt 2nd wl ins fnl f: nt trble wnr* **10/1**

4 **3** *1/2* **Lady Sandicliffe (IRE)**[21] 1636 2-8-12 0.......... DaneO'Neill 8 66
(B W Hills) *a.p: rdn over 2f out: chsd wnr over 1f out: one pce* **4/5**[1]

4 **4** *2* **Midnite Blews (IRE)**[49] 1021 2-9-3 0.......... FrancisNorton 5 65
(A B Haynes) *mid-div: rdn over 2f out: hdwy over 1f out: no ex ins fnl f* **13/2**[2]

00 **5** *4* **Ostinata (IRE)**[8] 1960 2-8-12 0.......... MickyFenton 3 47
(B W Duke) *mid-div: rdn and outpcd over 3f out: styd on fnl f: n.d* **33/1**

6 *2 1/2* **Splash The Cash** 2-9-3 0.......... MatthewHenry 2 43
(P Winkworth) *w wnr: rdn over 2f out: wknd over 1f out* **12/1**

7 *shd* **Bilboa** 2-8-12 0.......... JamesMillman(5) 6 43
(B R Millman) *hung rt thrght: sn chsng ldrs: rn wd to stands' rail over 2f out: nt rcvr* **14/1**

0 **8** *2 1/2* **Mairead's Boy (IRE)**[16] 1762 2-9-3 0.......... LPKeniry 10 35
(J S Moore) *prom: rdn over 2f out: wknd 1f out* **40/1**

05 **9** *1* **Theebah**[4] 2086 2-8-12 0.......... SamHitchcott 4 27
(M R Channon) *s.i.s: rdn and hdwy on ins over 3f out: wknd 2f out* **25/1**

10 *3* **Penrice Castle** 2-8-12 0.......... RichardSmith 7 17
(R Hannon) *s.i.s: rdn and sme hdwy 3f out: wknd wl over 1f out* **20/1**

11 *2* **Fraamington** 2-8-10 0.......... ThomasO'Brien(7) 9 15
(M R Channon) *s.i.s: sn wl outpcd* **33/1**

1m 12.5s (1.30) **Going Correction** +0.10s/f (Good) **11** Ran SP% **120.4**
Speed ratings (Par 93):95,91,90,87,82 79,78,75,74,70 67
CSF £80.69 TOTE £10.50: £2.10, £2.90, £1.30; EX 137.90.
Owner The Farleigh Court Racing Partnership **Bred** Farleigh Court Racing Partnership **Trained** Compton, Berks

FOCUS
There was not much previous form to go on in this low-grade maiden, although the time was fair and the third is rated to her debut form.

NOTEBOOK
Spanish Bounty was all the better for his Salisbury debut where he had to recover from interference at the start. The last to come off the bridle, he soon had the race sewn up. (op 7-1 tchd 9-1)
Aaim For Applause ◆ is bred to be a juvenile sprinter despite being a half-brother to mile and ten furlong three-year-old winner Colton. Coming from a long way back to finish second, he will know a lot more next time. (op 8-1 tchd 11-1)
Lady Sandicliffe(IRE) had no problems at the start this time over this slightly longer trip but she is going to need even further by the look of it. (op 11-8)
Midnite Blews(IRE) could not sustain his effort over this extended five furlongs. (op 8-1 tchd 6-1)
Ostinata(IRE) was dropped in class after a couple of quick outings over six.
Splash The Cash seemed to pay the penalty for trying to go with the winner. (op 8-1)
Bilboa, a speedily-bred gelding, threw his chance away by hanging right. Official explanation: jockey said gelding hung right-handed (op 12-1)

2194 TAKE PRIDE - FULLERS.CO.UK H'CAP 1m 2f 46y
7:00 (7:03) (Class 5) (0-70,70) 4-Y-O+ **£2,914** (£867; £433; £216) **Stalls** High

Form RPR

4435 **1** **Our Kes (IRE)**[57] 933 5-8-8 **57** ow1.......... AmirQuinn 9 65
(P Howling) *hld up in mid-div: rdn and hdwy over 2f out: led ins fnl f: r.o* **4/1**[1]

3323 **2** *3/4* **Generous Lad (IRE)**[3] 2106 4-9-1 **69**.......... KevinGhunowa(5) 7 76
(A B Haynes) *chsd ldr: rdn to ld 2f out: hdd ins fnl f: nt qckn* **4/1**[1]

00-0 **3** *2 1/2* **Golden Applause (FR)**[16] 1765 5-9-5 **68**.......... SamHitchcott 5 70
(Mrs A L M King) *hld up in mid-div: rdn 3f out: hdwy on ins over 1f out: swtchd rt ins fnl f: tk 3rd last strides* **16/1**

440 **4** *nk* **Sopran Gath (ITY)**[14] 1811 4-9-5 **68**.......... TQuinn 3 70
(J W Hills) *led: rdn and hdd 2f out: no ex ins fnl f* **13/2**[3]

0-46 **5** *shd* **Gallego**[7] 1997 5-8-13 **62**.......... MatthewHenry 11 63
(R J Price) *s.i.s: hld up in rr: hdwy on outside over 2f out: rdn over 1f out: kpt on ins fnl f* **8/1**

5-20 **6** *2 1/2* **Piper's Song (IRE)**[21] 1638 4-9-7 **70**.......... DaneO'Neill 13 67
(H Candy) *hld up in tch: rdn over 2f out: fdd ins fnl f* **6/1**[2]

3600 **7** *2* **Mouseen (IRE)**[15] 1562 4-8-0 **54** ow1..........(t) TolleyDean(5) 8 47
(R J Price) *s.s: hld up in rr: rdn 3f out: sme hdwy on outside over 1f out: n.d* **20/1**

050- **8** *nk* **Ermine Grey**[198] 6497 6-8-6 **55**.......... FrancisNorton 10 50+
(A W Carroll) *hld up and bhd: rdn and sme hdwy over 2f out: eased whn btn ins fnl f* **12/1**

53-5 **9** *1* **Over Ice**[16] 1761 4-9-0 **63**.......... VinceSlattery 12 53
(Karen George) *hld up towards rr: rdn over 2f out: no rspnse* **20/1**

006/ **10** *3 1/2* **Pole Dancer**[585] 6068 4-8-2 **51** oh1.......... FrankieMcDonald 6 35
(W S Kittow) *prom: rdn over 3f out: wknd over 2f out* **14/1**

000- **11** *9* **Yenaled**[207] 6382 10-8-2 **51** oh1.......... AdrianMcCarthy 1 18
(J M Bradley) *hld up in mid-div: rdn and bhd fnl 3f* **33/1**

363- **12** *10* **Greenmeadow**[230] 5974 5-8-7 **56**.......... LPKeniry 2 4
(S Kirk) *hld up in mid-div: rdn over 3f out: wknd over 2f out* **12/1**

2m 10.47s (-0.53) **Going Correction** +0.025s/f (Good) **12** Ran SP% **119.1**
Speed ratings (Par 103):103,102,100,100,100 98,96,96,95,92 85,77
CSF £18.26 CT £234.70 TOTE £5.10: £2.10, £1.90, £4.10; EX 26.90.
Owner Mark Entwistle **Bred** Yeomanstown Stud **Trained** Newmarket, Suffolk

FOCUS
An open-looking moderate handicap but sound enough rated around the runner-up and fourth to recent form.
Mouseen(IRE) Official explanation: jockey said gelding threw its head up as stalls opened

2195 BLB SOLICITORS CLAIMING STKS 5f 11y
7:30 (7:32) (Class 6) 3-Y-O **£2,072** (£616; £308; £153) **Stalls** Low

Form RPR

2516 **1** **Scarlett Heart (IRE)**[9] 1948 3-8-7 66 ow1.......... TQuinn 7 68
(P J Makin) *hld up and bhd: hdwy over 2f out: rdn to ld ins fnl f: r.o wl* **11/8**[1]

-306 **2** *2 1/2* **Eastern Princess**[37] 1248 3-8-0 47..........(v) FrancisNorton 9 52
(J A Geake) *hld up in mid-div: rdn and hdwy over 1f out: kpt on to take 2nd nr fin: nt trble wnr* **8/1**

0-20 **3** *nk* **Tibinta**[9] 1943 3-8-3 54 ow1.......... MatthewHenry 11 54
(P D Evans) *hld up in mid-div: hdwy over 2f out: led wl over 1f out: hdd ins fnl f: one pce* **8/1**

4520 **4** *hd* **Temtation (IRE)**[9] 1943 3-8-1 59 ow1.......... FrankieMcDonald 2 51
(Peter Grayson) *t.k.h in tch: rdn over 1f out: kpt on same pce ins fnl f* **7/1**[3]

0164 **5** *2 1/2* **Mind The Style**[16] 1763 3-9-1 63.......... VinceSlattery 10 56
(W G M Turner) *w ldr: rdn and ev ch wl over 1f out: wknd wl ins fnl f* **7/1**[3]

3400 **6** *1/2* **Royal Dagger (IRE)**[49] 1031 3-8-4 48.......... SaleemGolam(3) 1 46
(Rae Guest) *hld up in mid-div: nt clr run and lost pl over 2f out: rdn and sme hdwy fnl f: n.d* **12/1**

0-00 **7** *hd* **Skiddaw Fox**[30] 1403 3-8-0 40.......... TolleyDean(5) 8 44
(Mrs L Williamson) *bhd: rdn and hdwy on outside over 2f out: wknd over 1f out* **50/1**

0000 **8** *shd* **Meadfoot**[15] 1782 3-8-8 47..........(t) AdrianMcCarthy 4 46
(B R Millman) *s.i.s: rdn and effrt on ins over 1f out: n.d* **40/1**

-052 **9** *4* **Shreddy Shrimpster**[38] 1213 3-8-2 45.......... DavidKinsella 3 26
(A B Haynes) *hld up in tch: nt clr run and lost pl over 1f out: n.d after* **11/2**[2]

040 **10** *shd* **Juce Of Hearts**[25] 1541 3-8-11 52.......... RichardThomas 6 35
(J L Spearing) *led: rdn and hdd wl over 1f out: sn wknd* **20/1**

0000 **11** *5* **Redflo**[37] 1248 3-7-8 44 ow1.......... SophieDoyle(7) 5 7
(Ms J S Doyle) *plld hrd: prom tl rdn and wknd over 1f out* **66/1**

63.27 secs (0.77) **Going Correction** +0.10s/f (Good) **11** Ran SP% **123.1**
Speed ratings (Par 97):97,93,92,92,88 87,87,86,80,80 72
CSF £13.69 TOTE £2.60: £1.20, £2.40, £3.00; EX 19.90.The winner was claimed by J Gallagher £8,000.
Owner Ten Horsepower **Bred** Mrs P J Makin **Trained** Ogbourne Maisey, Wilts

FOCUS
A poor claimer but the form makes sense with the winner to his mark backed up by the third and fourth.

2196 CHARTWELL GROUP MEDIAN AUCTION MAIDEN STKS 1m 5y
8:00 (8:03) (Class 6) 3-Y-O **£2,072** (£616; £308; £153) **Stalls** High

Form RPR

0-5 **1** **First To Call**[28] 1447 3-9-3 0.......... AmirQuinn 5 83
(P J Makin) *hld up in rr: hdwy on ins over 3f out: swtchd rt over 2f out: rdn to ld over 1f out: clr fnl f: r.o wl* **8/1**

3-32 **2** *5* **Spriggan**[27] 1468 3-9-3 77.......... GeorgeBaker 6 74+
(C G Cox) *a.p: nt clr run 2f out: rdn over 1f out: wnt 2nd ins fnl f: no ch w wnr* **5/4**[1]

3-33 **3** *nk* **Aussie Cricket (FR)**[18] 1731 3-8-12 66.......... EdwardCreighton 2 66
(D J Coakley) *hld up towards rr: rdn and hdwy over 3f out: one pce fnl f* **7/2**[2]

4 *nk* **Fleuret** 3-8-12 0 .... StephenCarson 12 66
(Eve Johnson Houghton) *s.i.s: t.k.h: sn in tch: rdn over 2f out: one pce fnl f* **7/1**[3]

5 *5* **Strut The Stage (IRE)**[14] [1830] 3-9-3 0 .... MickyFenton 10 59
(B W Duke) *prom: ev ch 2f out: rdn and wknd over 1f out* **12/1**

6 *1* **Glenisland** 3-8-7 0 .... RussellKennemore[(5)] 9 52
(Mrs L Williamson) *bhd: rdn over 3f out: hdwy over 1f out: nvr nr ldrs* **66/1**

-040 7 *2* **Murdoch**[29] [1440] 3-9-3 62 .... GrahamGibbons 11 52
(E S McMahon) *chsd ldr: led 4f out: rdn and hdd over 1f out: sn wknd* **14/1**

2005 8 *½* **Cantique (IRE)**[15] [1782] 3-8-12 52 .... DaneO'Neill 14 46
(Ms J S Doyle) *led: hdd 4f out: rdn and wknd 2f out* **25/1**

0- 9 *hd* **Pure Velvet (IRE)**[269] [5091] 3-8-12 0 .... LPKeniry 4 46
(S Kirk) *hld up in tch: rdn and wknd 2f out* **25/1**

10 *1* **Break Out** 3-9-3 0 .... StephenDonohoe 13 48
(J M Bradley) *s.s: a bhd* **80/1**

0-0 11 *1 ¾* **My Silver Monarch (IRE)**[26] [1501] 3-8-12 0 .... SimonWhitworth 7 39
(H S Howe) *s.s: a bhd* **50/1**

06 12 *¾* **Dark Druid (IRE)**[25] [1523] 3-9-0 0 .... LiamJones[(3)] 15 42
(I A Wood) *t.k.h in mid-div: rdn over 3f out: wknd over 2f out* **20/1**

0-00 13 *4* **Grazie Mille**[41] [1154] 3-8-7 49 .... (v[1]) TolleyDean[(5)] 16 28
(R Brotherton) *hld up in mid-div: rdn 4f out: wknd over 2f out* **66/1**

60-0 14 *3* **Spirit Rising**[24] [1561] 3-8-12 49 .... KevinGhunowa[(5)] 3 26
(J M Bradley) *hld up in mid-div: rdn 4f out: sn bhd* **50/1**

0000 15 *10* **Merlins Quest**[24] [1561] 3-8-10 52 .... BarrySavage[(7)] 8 3
(J M Bradley) *rdn 4f out: a bhd* **66/1**

1m 42.03s (0.93) **Going Correction** +0.025s/f (Good) **15** Ran SP% **126.7**
Speed ratings (Par 97):96,91,90,90,85 84,82,81,81,80 78,78,74,71,61
CSF £18.05 TOTE £10.30: £2.80, £1.30, £1.50; EX 26.10.
Owner Dr John Wilson and Partners **Bred** P J Makin **Trained** Ogbourne Maisey, Wilts

FOCUS
There was plenty of dead wood in this uncompetitive maiden and the form, rated through the reliable third, is not rock solid.
Grazie Mille Official explanation: jockey said filly lost its action 3f out

2197 BET NOW AT WBX.COM H'CAP 5f 161y
8:30 (8:33) (Class 4) (0-85,85) 3-Y-0+ **£4,857** (£1,445; £722; £360) **Stalls** Low

Form RPR

-530 1 **Matuza (IRE)**[20] [1653] 4-9-6 **77** .... DaneO'Neill 11 86
(W R Muir) *hld up in rr: hdwy on outside 2f out: hrd rdn to ld cl home* **7/1**

5226 2 *hd* **Chatshow (USA)**[11] [1885] 6-8-13 **70** .... FrancisNorton 9 78
(A W Carroll) *hld up in mid-div: hdwy over 2f out: rdn to ld jst over 1f out: hdd cl home* **13/2**

362 3 *4* **Carcinetto (IRE)**[24] [1564] 5-8-12 **69** .... StephenDonohoe 4 64
(P D Evans) *a.p: rdn over 2f out: one pce* **9/1**

6042 4 *1* **Spanish Ace**[6] [2025] 6-9-9 **85** .... KevinGhunowa[(5)] 5 77
(J M Bradley) *a.p: rdn over 2f out: wknd over 1f out* **11/2**[3]

-460 5 *nk* **Hoh Hoh Hoh**[14] [1826] 5-9-9 **83** .... LiamJones[(3)] 2 74
(R J Price) *t.k.h: prom: led 3f out: rdn and hdd jst over 1f out: wknd fnl f* **3/1**[2]

-030 6 *¾* **Pic Up Sticks**[8] [1971] 8-9-13 **84** .... MickyFenton 6 72
(B G Powell) *hld up and bhd: pushed along over 2f out: n.d* **14/1**

1-26 7 *½* **The Cayterers**[7] [1984] 5-9-0 **76** .... LukeMorris[(5)] 7 62
(J M Bradley) *hld up and bhd: rdn over 2f out: nvr trbld ldrs* **11/4**[1]

635- 8 *3* **Equuleus Pictor**[263] [5245] 3-8-2 **67** .... RichardThomas 3 43
(J L Spearing) *s.i.s: hld up in mid-div: rdn and wknd over 1f out* **40/1**

0030 9 *3* **Smokin Beau**[27] [1465] 10-9-6 **77** .... GeorgeBaker 1 44
(N P Littmoden) *led: hdd 3f out: wknd 2f out* **14/1**

1m 11.17s (-0.03) **Going Correction** +0.10s/f (Good)
WFA 3 from 4yo+ 8lb **9** Ran SP% **118.7**
Speed ratings (Par 105):104,103,98,97,96 95,95,91,87
CSF £53.29 CT £421.09 TOTE £9.40: £2.70, £2.60, £2.80; EX 82.40.
Owner The Eastwood Partnership **Bred** Round Hill Stud **Trained** Lambourn, Berks

FOCUS
The first two pulled clear in this sprint handicap and the form is solid backed up by a decent time.
Hoh Hoh Hoh Official explanation: jockey said gelding ran too free
The Cayterers Official explanation: jockey said gelding suffered interference shortly after start
Equuleus Pictor Official explanation: jockey said gelding stumbled on leaving stalls and ran too freely

2198 ATI STELLRAM FILLIES' H'CAP 5f 11y
9:05 (9:06) (Class 5) (0-70,71) 3-Y-O **£2,914** (£867; £433; £216) **Stalls** Low

Form RPR

3-03 1 **Ocean Blaze**[31] [1373] 3-8-13 **62** .... AdrianMcCarthy 1 66
(B R Millman) *mde all: rdn over 1f out: edgd rt ins fnl f: r.o wl* **15/2**

454- 2 *1 ¼* **Russian Gift (IRE)**[280] [4754] 3-9-6 **69** .... TQuinn 7 68
(C G Cox) *hld up and bhd: hdwy over 1f out: r.o ins fnl f: nt rch wnr* **12/1**

5-50 3 *½* **Wadnagin (IRE)**[21] [1634] 3-8-3 **55** .... LiamJones[(3)] 3 52
(I A Wood) *hld up in tch: rdn and nt qckn ins fnl f* **16/1**

1-24 4 *nk* **Aquilegia (IRE)**[16] [1766] 3-9-7 **70** .... GrahamGibbons 6 66
(E S McMahon) *hld up: rdn and hdwy on outside over 1f out: nt qckn ins fnl f* **6/4**[1]

54-2 5 *1* **Metal Guru**[38] [1207] 3-8-11 **65** .... RussellKennemore[(5)] 9 58
(R Hollinshead) *a.p: rdn and no ex ins fnl f* **7/1**

63-2 6 *7* **My Tiger Lilly**[29] [1430] 3-8-6 **55** .... PaulDoe 5 22
(W J Knight) *prom tl wknd over 2f out* **5/1**[3]

5-11 7 *3* **No Worries Yet (IRE)**[10] [1912] 3-9-8 **71** 6ex .... FrancisNorton 2 28
(J L Spearing) *chsd wnr: rdn and wknd 1f out: eased whn btn ins fnl f* **7/2**[2]

63.35 secs (0.85) **Going Correction** +0.10s/f (Good) **7** Ran SP% **116.7**
Speed ratings (Par 96):97,95,94,93,92 80,76
CSF £90.65 CT £1398.61 TOTE £9.50: £3.20, £4.00; EX 159.50.
Owner Ocean View Properties International Ltd **Bred** Longdon Stud And Robin Lawson **Trained** Kentisbeare, Devon

FOCUS
A modest fillies' handicap and ordinary form rated through the winner.
Aquilegia(IRE) Official explanation: jockey said filly was lame behind
T/Plt: £155.80 to a £1 stake. Pool: £64,799.10. 303.55 winning tickets. T/Qpdt: £110.70 to a £1 stake. Pool: £3,501.55. 23.40 winning tickets. KH

[2028]CATTERICK (L-H)
Friday, June 1

OFFICIAL GOING: Good to firm (8.8)
Wind: Virtually nil Weather: Fine and sunny

2199 E B F PEGGY'S 80TH BIRTHDAY NOVICE STKS 5f
1:50 (1:50) (Class 5) 2-Y-O **£3,562** (£1,059; £529; £264) **Stalls** Low

Form RPR

1 1 **Starlit Sands**[13] [1848] 2-9-0 0 .... JamieMackay 4 96+
(Sir Mark Prescott) *qckly away: mde all: shkn up and edgd rt over 1f out: comf* **5/4**[1]

42 2 *2* **Littlemisssunshine (IRE)**[30] [1390] 2-8-7 0 .... JohnEgan 5 82
(J S Moore) *chsd wnr: effrt and hdwy 2f out: sn rdn and edgd lft: sltly hmpdover 1f out: sn drvn and kpt on same pce* **11/8**[2]

5 3 *2 ½* **Kinout (IRE)**[26] [1498] 2-8-12 0 .... DO'Donohoe 3 78
(K A Ryan) *trckd ldrs: hdwy 2f out: sn rdn and kpt on same pce appr last* **15/2**[3]

2215 4 *2* **Ten Down**[22] [1608] 2-9-5 0 .... PaulHanagan 1 78
(J A Osborne) *chsd ldng pair: rdn along over 2f out and sn one pce* **9/1**

5 *½* **Curio** 2-8-5 0 ow3 .... MichaelJStainton[(5)] 6 67
(R M Whitaker) *in tch on outer: effrt and hdwy over 2f out: sn rdn and no imp* **66/1**

6 6 *1 ½* **Royal Sovereign (IRE)**[21] [1622] 2-8-7 0 .... JamieMoriarty[(5)] 2 64
(J Howard Johnson) *a in rr* **40/1**

59.59 secs (-1.01) **Going Correction** -0.125s/f (Firm) **6** Ran SP% **112.2**
Speed ratings (Par 93):103,99,95,92,91 89
CSF £3.24 TOTE £1.90: £1.30, £1.10; EX 2.60.
Owner Miss K Rausing **Bred** Miss K Rausing **Trained** Newmarket, Suffolk
■ Stewards' Enquiry : John Egan two-day ban: careless riding (Jun 12-13)

FOCUS
A good novice event and decent form rated through the runner-up.

NOTEBOOK
Starlit Sands ◆ improved on the bare form of her debut success at Thirsk with a straightforward victory. This represents very useful form and she will be worth her place in Pattern company. The Queen Mary at Royal Ascot could be a worthwhile target. (op 6-5 tchd 11-8)
Littlemisssunshine(IRE) seemed to run her race but the winner was too good. She should have little trouble in winning an ordinary maiden. (op 13-8 tchd 7-4 and 15-8 in a place)
Kinout(IRE), fifth on his debut at Newmarket, improved on that form with a creditable third. He is going the right way. (op 9-1 tchd 13-2)
Ten Down might be best when granted an uncontested lead, but he is basically not progressing. (op 8-1)
Curio, a half-sister to smart dual 5f juvenile winner Tabaret, out of a 6f winner, showed plenty of ability on her racecourse debut. (op 50-1)

2200 SCORTON CLAIMING STKS 7f
2:25 (2:26) (Class 6) 3-Y-O **£2,730** (£806; £403) **Stalls** Low

Form RPR

3500 1 **Bold Indian (IRE)**[8] [1965] 3-8-10 68 .... JamieMoriarty[(5)] 9 59
(I Semple) *trckd ldrs: hdwy 2f out: rdn to ld ent fnl f: edgd lft and styd on wl* **4/1**[2]

3-05 2 *1 ¾* **Riverside Dancer (USA)**[10] [1920] 3-9-0 72 .... DO'Donohoe 11 53
(K A Ryan) *rrd s and slowly away: bhd tl gd hdwy into midfield 1/2-way: effrt on outer 2f out: sn rdn and styd on wl fnl f* **4/1**[2]

56-0 3 *1 ¼* **Amazing King (IRE)**[30] [1399] 3-8-8 61 .... JackDean[(7)] 13 51
(W G M Turner) *midfield on inner: swtchd rt and effrt 2f out: sn rdn and styd on ins fnl f: nrst fin* **16/1**

6-00 4 *shd* **La Vecchia Scuola (IRE)**[9] [1943] 3-8-6 60 .... PaulQuinn 1 42
(D Nicholls) *t.k.h: chsd ldrs on inner: rdn along 2f out: drvn and kpt on same pce ent fnl f* **16/1**

5000 5 *nk* **Meathop (IRE)**[31] [1381] 3-8-11 41 .... PaulHanagan 8 46
(R F Fisher) *led: rdn over 2f out: drvn over 1f out: hdd & wknd ent fnl f* **50/1**

5352 6 *¾* **Fractured Foxy**[2] [2146] 3-8-7 70 .... NeilBrown[(7)] 4 47
(J J Quinn) *trckd ldrs: effrt over 2f out: sn rdn and no imp fr wl over 1f out* **11/8**[1]

-000 7 *1* **Espejo (IRE)**[3] [2110] 3-9-5 66 .... (p) PaulMulrennan 10 49
(K R Burke) *cl up: rdn 2f out: drvn and wknd over 1f out* **25/1**

R1-3 8 *2 ½* **Sad Times (IRE)**[10] [1921] 3-8-3 60 .... (p) LiamJones[(3)] 7 30
(W G M Turner) *in rr on inner: swtchd rt to outer and rdn wl over 1f out: sme late hdwy* **8/1**[3]

00-0 9 *1 ¼* **Newport Lass (IRE)**[108] [454] 3-8-6 49 .... PaulFessey 12 26
(K R Burke) *t.k.h: cl up: rdn along 2f out and grad wknd* **25/1**

0-00 10 *1* **Hesaguru (IRE)**[3] [2116] 3-8-7 42 .... (b) DavidAllan 2 24
(J O'Reilly) *dwlt: a in rr* **50/1**

0U00 11 *11* **Spinning Game**[9] [1943] 3-7-13 42 .... DuranFentiman[(3)] 6 —
(D W Chapman) *a in rr* **66/1**

40-5 12 *22* **Perfect Reflection**[18] [1709] 3-7-9 25 .... (b[1]) CharlotteKerton[(7)] 3 —
(A Berry) *a towards rr* **150/1**

1m 27.14s (-0.22) **Going Correction** -0.125s/f (Firm) **12** Ran SP% **118.7**
Speed ratings (Par 97):96,94,92,92,92 91,90,87,85,84 72,46
CSF £19.56 TOTE £4.40: £2.00, £1.90, £5.00; EX 27.00.There were no claims in this race.
Owner R Hyndman **Bred** Dunderry Stud **Trained** Carluke, S Lanarks

FOCUS
A modest claimer with the form limited by the proximity of the fifth.
Newport Lass(IRE) Official explanation: jockey said filly hung left throughout

2201 LIONWELD KENNEDY H'CAP 1m 3f 214y
3:00 (3:00) (Class 5) (0-70,70) 4-Y-0+ **£3,238** (£963; £481; £240) **Stalls** Low

Form RPR

3246 1 **Gigs Magic (USA)**[2] [2157] 4-8-4 **53** .... KDarley 8 69
(M Johnston) *hld up: hdwy to trck ldrs over 4f out: rapid hdwy on outer to ld wl over 2f out and sn clr: rdn out* **9/2**[2]

0-24 2 *5* **Eijaaz (IRE)**[8] [1967] 6-8-4 **53** .... PaulFessey 6 61
(G A Harker) *hld up in rr: hdwy over 4f out: effrt to chse wnr wl over 1f out: sn drvn and no imp ins fnl f* **13/2**[3]

03-0 3 *nk* **Sporting Gesture**[48] [1042] 10-8-11 **67** .... NSLawes[(7)] 4 75+
(M W Easterby) *trckd ldrs on inner: hdwy 3f out: n.m.r and swtchd rt wl over 1f out: sn rdn and kpt on ins fnl f* **14/1**

2-26 4 *hd* **Charlotte Vale**[7] [2008] 6-9-2 **65** .... PaulMulrennan 2 72
(Micky Hammond) *trckd ldrs: effrt and hdwy 3f out: rdn over 2f out and kpt on same pce* **7/1**

43- **5** *1* **Hilltime (IRE)**[14] 4256 7-8-3 **52** .... JimmyQuinn 9 58
(J S Wainwright) *prom: rdn along wl over 2f out: sn drvn and one pce* **9/2**[2]

0-40 **6** *5* **Richtee (IRE)**[11] 1907 6-8-6 **55** .... PaulHanagan 1 53
(R A Fahey) *hld up in rr: effrt and hdwy on outer over 2f out: sn rdn and btn* **10/1**

6325 **7** *3* **Bernix**[13] 1849 5-9-7 **70** .... (t) DavidAllan 5 63
(T D Easterby) *led: rdn along over 3f out: hdd over 2f out and sn wknd* **16/1**

50-6 **8** *2* **Gifted Musician**[17] 1752 5-8-13 **67** .... TravisBlock(5) 7 57
(H Morrison) *t.k.h: cl up tl rdn along 3f over 3f out and sn wknd* **12/1**

11-3 **9** *1 1/2* **Scutch Mill (IRE)**[6] 976 5-8-10 **62** .... (t) JerryO'Dwyer(3) 3 49
(P C Haslam) *dwlt: a in rr* **7/2**[1]

2m 35.05s (-3.95) **Going Correction** -0.125s/f (Firm) **9** Ran SP% **113.8**
Speed ratings (Par 103):108,104,104,104,103 100,98,97,96
CSF £33.23 CT £375.29 TOTE £3.30: £1.60, £1.90, £3.60; EX 42.30.
Owner J Barson **Bred** R McDonald **Trained** Middleham Moor, N Yorks

FOCUS
A weak handicap rated through the runner-up and may not prove that solid.
Gifted Musician Official explanation: jockey said gelding was unsuited by the good to firm ground
Scutch Mill(IRE) Official explanation: jockey said gelding ran flat

2202 LESLIE PETCH H'CAP 5f 212y
3:35 (3:35) (Class 4) (0-80,78) 4-Y-0+ **£5,181** (£1,541; £770; £384) **Stalls** Low

Form RPR

0104 **1** **Rainbow Bay**[3] 2108 4-7-9 **59** oh1 .... (v) MCGeran(7) 4 70
(P D Evans) *trckd ldrs: hdwy 2f out: rdn to ld and edgd rt ins fnl f: styd on* **3/1**[1]

00-5 **2** *1 1/2* **Mulligan's Gold (IRE)**[10] 1914 4-8-8 **65** .... DavidAllan 9 71
(T D Easterby) *chsd ldng pair: hdwy 2f out: sn rdn and led briefly over 1f out: hdd and hmpd ins fnl f: kpt on same pce* **4/1**[2]

0050 **3** *nk* **Bel Cantor**[13] 1847 4-8-11 **71** .... AndrewMullen(3) 11 76
(W J H Ratcliffe) *chsd ldrs: hdwy on outer 2f out: rdn over 1f out and ev ch tl sltly hmpd and no ex ins fnl f* **15/2**[3]

0-00 **4** *3 1/2* **Guest Connections**[13] 1852 4-9-7 **78** .... (v) PaulQuinn 5 72
(D Nicholls) *hld up in tch: hdwy over 2f out: sn rdn and kpt on same pce fr over 1f out* **16/1**

25-6 **5** *hd* **Riquewihr**[66] 796 7-8-10 **67** .... TonyHamilton 6 60
(J S Wainwright) *chsd clr ldr: rdn along over 2f out: drvn and ev ch over 1f out: wknd ent fnl f* **12/1**

2232 **6** *shd* **No Time (IRE)**[7] 1999 7-8-6 **63** .... JimmyQuinn 7 56
(A J McCabe) *hld up in tch: effrt over 2f out: swtchd lft and rdn wl over 1f out: sn no imp* **3/1**[1]

0500 **7** *shd* **Charles Parnell (IRE)**[4] 2072 4-8-8 **65** .... (b1) PaulMulrennan 10 58
(M Dods) *v.s.a and bhd tl styd on wl fnl 2f* **14/1**

3-00 **8** *1/2* **The History Man (IRE)**[7] 1999 4-8-2 **66** ow3 .... (b) SCreighton(7) 2 57
(M Mullineaux) *led and sn clr: rdn along over 2f out: drvn and hdd over 1f out: sn wknd* **22/1**

2-00 **9** *3/4* **Stonecrabstomorrow (IRE)**[13] 1852 4-9-1 **77** .... JamieMoriarty(5) 3 66
(R A Fahey) *s.i.s: a in rr* **8/1**

1m 12.7s (-1.30) **Going Correction** -0.125s/f (Firm) **9** Ran SP% **117.5**
Speed ratings (Par 105):103,101,100,95,95 95,95,94,93
CSF £15.31 CT £82.99 TOTE £4.40: £1.70, £1.80, £2.20; EX 21.80.
Owner Dusktilldawn Racing I **Bred** Ms R A Myatt **Trained** Pandy, Monmouths
■ Stewards' Enquiry : M C Geran caution: careless riding

FOCUS
A modest sprint handicap for the grade rated around the placed horses.
No Time(IRE) Official explanation: jockey said horse slipped at start
Charles Parnell(IRE) Official explanation: jockey said gelding was slowly away

2203 ELLERY HILL RATING RELATED MAIDEN STKS (DIV I) 7f
4:15 (4:16) (Class 6) 3-Y-0+ **£2,047** (£604; £302) **Stalls** Low

Form RPR

20-0 **1** **Barataria**[9] 1944 5-9-3 50 .... JamieMoriarty(5) 1 62
(R Bastiman) *dwlt: hld up and bhd: swtchd outside and hdwy 2f out: sn rdn and str run to ld wl ins fnl f* **16/1**

0-60 **2** *1 1/2* **Cheery Cat (USA)**[18] 1712 3-8-12 50 .... (p) TonyHamilton 4 54
(D W Barker) *cl up: led wl over 2f out and sn rdn: drvn over 1f out: hdd and nt qckn wl ins fnl f* **10/1**

60-0 **3** *3/4* **Palmetto Point**[36] 1266 3-8-7 52 .... TravisBlock(5) 7 52
(H Morrison) *hld up: swtchd outside and hdwy wl over 1f out: sn rdn and styd on ins fnl f: nrst fin* **20/1**

050- **4** *hd* **Froissee**[190] 6569 3-8-9 60 .... J-PGuillambert 5 48
(N A Callaghan) *hld up towards rr: hdwy 2f out: swtchd lft and rdn wl over 1f out: styd on u.p ins fnl f* **11/4**[1]

042 **5** *1* **Prince Noel**[18] 1712 3-8-12 52 .... (p) KDarley 2 52+
(N Wilson) *led: rdn along and hdd wl over 2f out: sn drvn and one pce ent fnl f* **3/1**[2]

06-0 **6** *3/4* **Pitbull**[38] 1226 4-9-8 59 .... JimmyQuinn 13 51
(Mrs G S Rees) *in tch: hdwy over 2f out: rdn to chse ldrs wl over 1f out: sn drvn and kpt on same pce* **15/2**

400- **7** *1/2* **Underthemistletoe (IRE)**[272] 5023 5-8-12 38 .... NeilBrown(7) 6 46
(R E Barr) *chsd ldrs: rdn along over 2f out: sn drvn and wknd ent fnl f* **100/1**

0-56 **8** *1* **Stormburst (IRE)**[25] 1530 3-8-9 58 .... PaulFessey 3 40
(M Dods) *midfield on inner: rdn along over 2f out: n.d* **9/2**[3]

-200 **9** *2 1/2* **Bathwick Fancy (IRE)**[29] 1432 3-8-9 52 .... (t) PaulHanagan 10 33
(J G Portman) *hld up: a in rr* **16/1**

0660 **10** *nk* **Cottam Eclipse**[10] 1918 6-9-3 54 .... PJMcDonald(5) 8 39
(I W McInnes) *chsd ldrs: rdn along wl over 2f out and sn wknd* **12/1**

3606 **11** *11* **O'Dwyer (IRE)**[18] 1711 3-8-12 48 .... (p) PaulMulrennan 11 5
(A D Brown) *chsd ldrs: rdn along 1/2-way: sn wknd* **33/1**

1m 27.05s (-0.31) **Going Correction** -0.125s/f (Firm)
WFA 3 from 4yo+ 10lb **11** Ran SP% **118.9**
Speed ratings (Par 101):96,94,93,93,92 91,90,89,86,86 73
CSF £165.49 TOTE £24.20: £6.20, £2.50, £5.20; EX 178.70.
Owner Coal Trade Partnership **Bred** Hesmonds Stud Ltd **Trained** Cowthorpe, N Yorks

FOCUS
A maiden restricted to horses rated 60 or lower, so very weak form rated around the first two. The winning time was 0.09 seconds quicker than the previous division.
Bathwick Fancy(IRE) Official explanation: jockey said filly had a breathing problem

2204 GO RACING AT THIRSK ON MONDAY H'CAP 1m 7f 177y
4:45 (4:45) (Class 5) (0-70,67) 4-Y-0+ **£3,238** (£963; £481; £240) **Stalls** Low

Form RPR

5361 **1** **Silver Mont (IRE)**[10] 1934 4-8-5 **51** 6ex .... (b) DO'Donohoe 7 57
(S R Bowring) *t.k.h: trckd ldng pair: hdwy over 3f out: rdn to ld 2f out: sn clr: comf* **9/1**

-002 **2** *2* **Toparudi**[17] 1745 6-9-6 **65** .... JimmyQuinn 5 69
(M H Tompkins) *hld up in rr: hdwy over 3f out: rdn to chse wnr over 1f out: sn drvn and no imp ins fnl f* **5/1**[3]

-553 **3** *3 1/2* **True (IRE)**[24] 1556 6-8-3 **48** oh2 .... PaulFessey 3 47
(Mrs S Lamyman) *prom: hdwy to ld 3f out: sn rdn and hdd 2f out: drvn and one pce fr over 1f out* **7/1**

2012 **4** *3/4* **Ronsard (IRE)**[10] 1925 5-8-2 **54** 6ex .... MCGeran(7) 4 53
(P D Evans) *t.k.h: trckd ldrs: hdwy over 3f out: rdn wl over 2f out and sn btn* **11/4**[1]

46-0 **5** *1 1/2* **Riodan (IRE)**[15] 1793 5-9-3 **67** .... JamieMoriarty(5) 2 64
(J J Quinn) *set stdy pce: qcknd 5f out: rdn along and hdd 3f out: grad wknd* **9/2**[2]

2365 **6** *3 1/2* **Toni Alcala**[17] 1745 8-8-3 **48** oh2 .... (p) PaulHanagan 6 41
(R F Fisher) *trckd ldrs: rdn along 4f out: sn wknd* **5/1**[3]

6-00 **P** **Kristoffersen**[27] 1152 7-8-5 **50** .... KDarley 1 —
(Ian Williams) *hld up in tch: effrt and rdn along 4f out: sn wknd and bhd whn p.u over 1f out* **7/1**

3m 43.38s (11.98) **Going Correction** -0.125s/f (Firm)
WFA 4 from 5yo+ 1lb **7** Ran SP% **113.2**
Speed ratings (Par 103):65,64,62,61,61 59,—
CSF £51.64 CT £334.08 TOTE £11.70: £4.30, £2.90; EX 63.90.
Owner Clark Industrial Services Partnership **Bred** Clark Industrial Services Partnership **Trained** Edwinstowe, Notts

FOCUS
A moderate staying handicap and, with the pace very steady for much of the way, the form does not look very reliable.
Kristoffersen Official explanation: jockey said gelding pulled up lame, but returned sound

2205 RACING AGAIN HERE NEXT FRIDAY APPRENTICE H'CAP 5f
5:15 (5:16) (Class 6) (0-65,69) 3-Y-O **£2,730** (£806; £403) **Stalls** Low

Form RPR

50-1 **1** **Ishetoo**[9] 1943 3-9-10 **64** 6ex .... MichaelJStainton 8 81
(A Dickman) *trckd ldng pair: hdwy 2f out: rdn to ld ent fnl f: sn clr* **4/1**[1]

5342 **2** *4* **Nomoreblondes**[6] 2029 3-9-6 **60** .... (p) RoryMoore 7 63
(P T Midgley) *led: rdn along 2f out: drvn over 1f out: hdd ent fnl f: kpt on same pce* **9/2**[2]

0204 **3** *1 3/4* **Mangano**[6] 2029 3-8-2 **47** .... KellyHarrison(5) 2 44
(A Berry) *in tch: hdwy 2f out: sn rdn and kpt on ins fnl f: nrst fin* **17/2**

2500 **4** *nk* **La Marmotte (IRE)**[13] 1850 3-8-12 **57** .... MCGeran(5) 4 53
(R E Barr) *sn outpcd and bhd: hdwy 2f out: swtchd outside and rdn wl over 1f out: edgd lft and styd on ins fnl f: nrst fin* **15/2**

0303 **5** *hd* **Nou Camp**[38] 1213 3-8-9 **54** .... BradleyRoper(5) 11 49
(N A Callaghan) *in tch: hdwy over 2f out: sn rdn and kpt on same pce fr wl over 1f out* **13/2**[3]

60-0 **6** *1* **Miss Capricorn**[30] 1403 3-8-0 **47** ow2 .... (t) PNolan(7) 5 38
(K A Ryan) *chsd ldrs: rdn 2f out: sn wknd:* **20/1**

5041 **7** *2* **New York Oscar (IRE)**[9] 1948 3-9-10 **69** 6ex .... (b) PatrickDonaghy(5) 10 53
(A J McCabe) *chsd ldrs on outer: rdn along over 2f out: sn btn* **9/2**[2]

0300 **8** *nk* **Minimum Fuss (IRE)**[37] 1240 3-8-12 **52** .... (b) PJMcDonald 6 35
(M C Chapman) *cl up: rdn along over 2f out: sn drvn and wknd* **16/1**

600- **9** *6* **Only A Splash**[195] 6518 3-8-10 **50** .... JamieMoriarty 1 11
(D W Chapman) *spd to 1/2-way: sn wknd* **18/1**

60-6 **10** *25* **Shantina's Dream (USA)**[17] 1738 3-9-4 **58** .... TravisBlock 9 —
(H Morrison) *rrd bdly s: sddle slipped: a bhd* **10/1**

59.49 secs (-1.11) **Going Correction** -0.125s/f (Firm) **10** Ran SP% **117.0**
Speed ratings (Par 97):103,96,93,93,93 91,88,87,78,38
CSF £21.93 CT £149.13 TOTE £5.60: £1.90, £1.50, £2.60; EX 21.20.
Owner John H Sissons **Bred** Longdon Stud Ltd **Trained** Sandhutton, N Yorks

FOCUS
A modest sprint handicap restricted to apprentices who had not ridden more than 50 winners. The form looks worth treating positively.
New York Oscar(IRE) Official explanation: jockey said gelding was unsuited by the track
Shantina's Dream(USA) Official explanation: jockey said saddle slipped

2206 ELLERY HILL RATING RELATED MAIDEN STKS (DIV II) 7f
5:45 (5:45) (Class 6) 3-Y-0+ **£2,047** (£604; £302) **Stalls** Low

Form RPR

4-40 **1** **Strabinios King**[43] 1111 3-8-12 60 .... KDarley 12 57
(P C Haslam) *cl up: led wl over 2f out: rdn clr over 1f out: comf* **7/2**[2]

03-0 **2** *4* **Storm Path (IRE)**[42] 1129 3-8-9 54 .... JerryO'Dwyer(3) 5 46
(Eve Johnson Houghton) *towards rr: hdwy on outer wl over 1f out: sn rdn and styd on wl fnl f: nrst fin* **15/2**

0-00 **3** *nk* **Musette (IRE)**[20] 1679 4-8-12 35 .... NeilBrown(7) 4 46
(R E Barr) *chsd ldrs: rdn along 2f out: kpt on u.p ins fnl f* **50/1**

0-34 **4** *3/4* **Butterfly Bud (IRE)**[3] 2121 4-9-1 54 .... JamesO'Reilly(7) 8 47
(J O'Reilly) *s.i.s and bhd: hdwy 1/2-way: rdn to chse wnr 2f out: sn drvn and wknd ent fnl f* **5/2**[1]

-000 **5** *2* **Rambling Socks**[88] 620 4-9-2 36 .... DuranFentiman(3) 3 39
(S R Bowring) *towards rr: hdwy over 2f out: sn rdn and kpt on same pce* **66/1**

00-6 **6** *4* **Aussie Blue (IRE)**[39] 1197 3-8-7 52 .... MichaelJStainton(5) 2 27
(R M Whitaker) *chsd ldrs: rdn along wl over 2f out: grad wknd* **9/2**

0-00 **7** *3* **Immaculate Red**[18] 1719 4-9-3 41 .... (b) JamieMoriarty(5) 9 23
(R Bastiman) *led: rdn along and hdd over 2f out: grad wknd* **20/1**

6400 **8** *6* **Imperial Beach (USA)**[9] 1943 3-8-12 57 .... PaulFessey 1 2
(T D Barron) *chsd ldrs on inner: rdn along 1/2-way and sn wknd* **4/1**[3]

0-60 **9** *3/4* **Grethel (IRE)**[8] 1964 3-8-9 55 .... TonyHamilton 7 —
(A Berry) *chsd ldrs to 1/2-way: sn wknd* **20/1**

00-4 **10** *10* **Cranworth Blaze**[18] 1709 3-8-9 50 .... PaulHanagan 6 —
(T J Etherington) *a bhd* **33/1**

1m 27.14s (-0.22) **Going Correction** -0.125s/f (Firm)
WFA 3 from 4yo 10lb **10** Ran SP% **116.7**
Speed ratings (Par 101):96,91,91,90,87 83,79,73,72,60
CSF £27.67 TOTE £5.40: £1.70, £2.60, £11.60; EX 27.10 Place 6 £744.92, Place 5 £670.20.
Owner Mrs R J Jacobs **Bred** Newsells Park Stud Limited **Trained** Middleham Moor, N Yorks

FOCUS
Another very moderate maiden and the winning time was 0.09 seconds slower than the first division. The form is poor limited by the third and fifth.
Grethel(IRE) Official explanation: jockey said filly failed to handle the bend

T/Plt: £4,699.40 to a £1 stake. Pool: £42,809.90. 6.65 winning tickets. T/Qpdt: Part won. £1,704.30 to a £1 stake. Pool: £2,303.20. 0.20 winning tickets. JR

[1242] EPSOM (L-H)

Friday, June 1

OFFICIAL GOING: Good to soft (soft in places, 6.3)

Wind: light across Weather: overcast, becoming sunny

2207 PRINCESS ELIZABETH STKS (SPONSORED BY VODAFONE) (GROUP 3) (F&M) 1m 114y

1:40 (1:43) (Class 1) 3-Y-O+

£28,390 (£10,760; £5,385; £2,685; £1,345; £675) **Stalls** Low

Form RPR

25-1 **1** **Echelon**[27] 1472 5-9-9 109 KerrinMcEvoy 6 104+
(Sir Michael Stoute) *hld up towards rr: hdwy jst over 2f out: edgd lft but r.o to ld ins fnl f: pushed out* **7/4**[1]

33-2 **2** ¾ **Bahia Breeze**[34] 1305 5-9-6 106 PJSmullen 4 99
(Rae Guest) *lw: taken down early: chsd ldng pair tl rdn and outpcd over 3f out: rallied u.p over 1f out: ev ch ins fnl f: no ex nr fin* **7/2**[2]

345- **3** 1 ¼ **Nannina**[243] 5713 4-9-6 115 RobertHavlin 5 96+
(J H M Gosden) *lw: t.k.h: w.w in midfield: hdwy 3f out: rdn and hung lft fr over 2f out: styd on steadily fnl f* **5/1**[3]

3441 **4** nk **Nans Joy (IRE)**[14] 1804 3-8-8 78 ChrisCatlin 9 93
(E J O'Neill) *sn led: rdn over 3f out: hdd 2f out: kpt on same pce u.p* **66/1**

45-1 **5** 1 **Harvest Queen (IRE)**[27] 1466 4-9-6 105 SebSanders 10 93
(P J Makin) *t.k.h: sn chsng ldr: rdn to ld 2f out: hdd ins fnl f: fdd last 100yds* **7/1**

41-0 **6** 1 ¾ **Edaara (IRE)**[20] 1651 4-9-6 82 RHills 2 89
(W J Haggas) *lw: t.k.h: hld up in rr: rdn and effrt on inner 3f out: kpt on u.p: nvr able to chal* **14/1**

3-00 **7** ¾ **Puggy (IRE)**[26] 1496 3-8-9 102 ow1 (t) CSoumillon 8 86
(R A Kvisla) *stdd s: hld up bhd: rdn and effrt wl over 2f out: no imp fr over 1f out* **8/1**

-206 **8** 1 ¾ **Fann (USA)**[20] 1649 4-9-6 77 RichardHughes 3 83
(C E Brittain) *t.k.h: rdn over 3f out: sn outpcd: bhd whn hung rt 2f out* **66/1**

2-12 **9** nk **Apply Dapply**[20] 1649 4-9-6 75 SteveDrowne 7 83
(H Morrison) *t.k.h: hld up towards rr on outer: rdn over 3f out: sn outpcd: bhd last 2f* **28/1**

213- **10** 3 **Sabah**[285] 4628 4-9-6 90 NeilChalmers 1 76
(A M Balding) *chsd ldr tl rdn and wknd over 2f out* **25/1**

1m 47.67s (1.93) **Going Correction** +0.45s/f (Yiel)
WFA 3 from 4yo+ 12lb **10** Ran SP% **115.8**
Speed ratings (Par 113):109,108,107,106,106 104,103,102,102,99
CSF £7.46 TOTE £2.70: £1.40, £1.60, £2.10; EX 9.30 Trifecta £18.50 Pool £1,153.98 - 44.26 winning units..
Owner Cheveley Park Stud **Bred** Cheveley Park Stud Ltd **Trained** Newmarket, Suffolk

FOCUS
This race was spoiled to a degree by a very moderate early pace, though things quickened up in the second half of the contest and the final time was respectable for a race of its type. Despite there being some ease in the ground, the jockeys decided to stay on the inside on reaching the home straight.

NOTEBOOK
Echelon won this race last year, but her chances of landing the double looked pretty remote early on as she did not travel at all well down the hill in the first half of the contest. However, once into the home straight she found her stride and produced a strong run down the outside to finally score with a degree of comfort. She is likely to have another crack at higher Group company now, but as consistent as she is, she still looks a little way below the very best fillies and mares. (op 2-1)
Bahia Breeze, a couple of lengths behind Echelon when fifth in this last year and a fine second to Jeremy in the Betfred Mile last time out, was always in touch with the leaders, but looked likely to finish out of the frame when coming under pressure and apparently going nowhere soon after turning in. To her credit, she found her stride on reaching the rising ground but the favourite was finishing even more strongly on her outside. She continues to just miss out at Group level, but it is not for the want of trying. (tchd 3-1)
Nannina, having her first start since finishing fifth behind Mandesha in the Prix de l'Opera last October, was keen enough early but was putting in some good late work down the inside rail without ever quite looking like getting there. This was a long way off last year's best, but her trainer had made it plain beforehand that he had concerns over the ground and that this was a stepping-stone to future targets, so he must have been delighted. She is in a couple of races at Royal Ascot, with the Windsor Forest, where she could meet the winner again, looking the most viable option. (op 4-1 tchd 11-2 in a place)
Nans Joy(IRE), who had only broken her maiden at the eighth attempt at Hamilton last time and had been beaten a few times off a mark in the low 70s in handicaps prior to that, had no chance at these weights, but she was able to gain an uncontested lead in a race run at a modest early pace and it was that which enabled her to keep going for much longer than would have been expected. As creditable as this effort was, her future now lies in the hands of the Handicapper, and if he decided to take this effort at anything like face value, she could be a very hard filly to place.
Harvest Queen(IRE), whose three victories have all been gained on fast ground, raced prominently, which was an advantage in a race run this way, and having taken up the running she was still in front well inside the last furlong. However, these conditions appeared to expose a lack of stamina and she stopped very quickly, losing four places in the last half-furlong. (tchd 15-2)
Edaara(IRE), for whom the ground would not have been a problem but who had a mountain to climb at these weights, was switched off out the back early, but that was not the ideal position in a moderately run contest and she never threatened to play a part. (op 16-1 tchd 18-1)
Puggy(IRE) did not do much for the 1,000 Guineas form, but was probably at a disadvantage in being held up in a steadily run race. (op 9-1 tchd 15-2)

2208 VODAFONE MILE (H'CAP) 1m 114y

2:10 (2:12) (Class 2) (0-105,102) 4-Y-O+

£21,812 (£6,531; £3,265; £1,634; £815; £409) **Stalls** Low

Form RPR

60-2 **1** **Unshakable (IRE)**[25] 1524 8-8-8 **86** PaulEddery 4 97
(Bob Jones) *chsd ldrs: hdwy to chse ldr 2f out: led over 1f out: rdn and r.o wl fnl f* **10/1**

-001 **2** 1 ¼ **Montpellier (IRE)**[25] 1524 4-8-9 **87** KerrinMcEvoy 9 95
(E A L Dunlop) *lw: dropped in bhd after s: hmpd 5f out: gd hdwy 3f out: chsd wnr 1f out: rdn and unable qck ins fnl f* **6/1**[2]

1-03 **3** 1 **Ordnance Row**[14] 1818 4-9-0 **92** RichardHughes 14 99+
(R Hannon) *chsd ldrs: rdn to chse ldng pair 3f out: nt clr run 2f out tl over 1f out: kpt on u.p last 100yds* **9/2**[1]

220- **4** hd **Tucker**[237] 5808 5-9-10 **102** AdamKirby 8 107
(W R Swinburn) *chsd ldng pair: wnt 2nd wl over 3f out: led over 2f out: sn rdn: hdd over 1f out: hung lft and one pce fnl f* **20/1**

0100 **5** 3 **Wavertree Warrior (IRE)**[20] 1651 5-8-13 **91** JamesDoyle 5 89
(N P Littmoden) *hld up in rr: rdn over 3f out: kpt on u.p last 2f: nvr able to chal* **20/1**

0000 **6** ¾ **Uhoomagoo**[69] 759 9-9-3 **95** (b) NCallan 11 91
(K A Ryan) *racd in midfield: rdn over 4f out: plugged on same pce u.p last 2f* **25/1**

-030 **7** 1 **Prince Of Thebes (IRE)**[20] 1651 6-9-2 **94** PaulDoe 1 88
(J Akehurst) *swtg: w.w in midfield: hdwy over 3f out: chsd ldrs and drvn 2f out: wknd over 1f out* **16/1**

6100 **8** 1 ¾ **Waterside (IRE)**[15] 1791 8-8-13 **91** SebSanders 7 81
(G L Moore) *w.w in tch: rdn wl over 2f out: wknd over 1f out* **14/1**

00-6 **9** 2 ½ **Spanish Don**[13] 1842 9-8-7 **85** NeilPollard 2 69
(D R C Elsworth) *b: a bhd: rdn and lost tch wl over 3f out: sme late hdwy* **33/1**

-110 **10** 1 ½ **Future's Dream**[20] 1651 4-8-7 **85** PatCosgrave 3 66
(K R Burke) *lw: led tl rdn and hdd over 2f out: sn wknd* **15/2**[3]

0602 **11** 1 **Zato (IRE)**[7] 1996 4-8-6 **84** ChrisCatlin 6 63
(M R Channon) *hld up bhd: rdn and effrt 3f out: wknd over 2f out: eased ins fnl f* **12/1**

2-25 **12** 16 **Rio Riva**[12] 1860 5-9-7 **99** TomEaves 12 41
(Miss J A Camacho) *hld up in rr: rdn wl over 3f out: lost tch over 2f out: eased ins fnl f: t.o* **9/2**[1]

0560 **13** 1 ½ **Rain Stops Play (IRE)**[13] 1842 5-8-5 **83** oh1 FrancisNorton 13 21
(M Quinn) *sn chsng ldr tl wl over 3f out: sn rdn and dropped out: eased ins fnl f: t.o* **12/1**

-501 **14** 2 **Plum Pudding (IRE)**[13] 1842 4-8-13 **98** HaddenFrost(7) 10 32
(R Hannon) *lw: hld up towards rr: rdn over 3f out: sn bhd: eased ins fnl f: t.o* **11/1**

1m 46.45s (0.71) **Going Correction** +0.45s/f (Yiel) **14** Ran SP% **124.1**
Speed ratings (Par 109):114,112,112,111,109 108,107,106,103,102 101,87,86,84
CSF £67.62 CT £325.86 TOTE £12.30: £3.70, £2.20, £2.30; EX 45.40 Trifecta £203.30 Pool: £1,489.30 - 5.20 winning units..
Owner Unshakable Partnership **Bred** Timothy Coughlan **Trained** Wickhambrook, Suffolk
■ Stewards' Enquiry : Hadden Frost two-day ban: careless riding (Jun 12-13)

FOCUS
With Future's Dream going off at a rate of knots, this race was run at a much stronger pace than the fillies in the opener and the time was 1.22 seconds quicker. This time the riders decided to take the more traditional route on easy ground here and came over to the stands' side in the home straight. Solid form.

NOTEBOOK
Unshakable(IRE), a most encouraging second to Montpellier on his return from seven months off on the Kempton Polytrack last time, was 3lb better off with that rival for just over a length and managed to turn the form around after having held a decent position just behind the leaders throughout. He perhaps does not win as often as his talent suggests he should, but when he does hit the target there is usually a decent prize involved and this was another example. He may go for the Royal Hunt Cup under a 5lb penalty, but may be of more interest if turning out for the Totesport Mile at Glorious Goodwood, a race he won two years ago off a 1lb higher mark. (op 9-1 tchd 11-1)
Montpellier(IRE) ◆, raised 5lb for his Kempton victory, was given a much more patient ride than the winner and may not have been helped by making his effort further from the stands' rail than his rival. He could not confirm the Kempton form with Unshakable on 3lb worse terms, but this was still a decent effort and he remains a progressive handicapper. (op 13-2 tchd 11-2)
Ordnance Row, who came from a mile back when third at Newmarket last time, had no excuses in relation to his position this time as he raced much more prominently over this longer trip and was close enough if good enough. The problem was that the took far too long to respond when put under pressure and when he finally did on reaching the rising ground, it was far too late. He has the ability to win off this mark, but it is going to require a finely-judged ride in order for him to do it. (op 4-1)
Tucker, gelded since he was last seen, ran a blinder on his first start in seven months, racing close to the pace throughout and holding every chance. It was always going to be tough to give weight away to some tough and talented handicappers and his new yard are still learning about him, but he remains on an awkward mark and has not won for over two years.
Wavertree Warrior(IRE) ◆, busy on the Polytrack since his last start on turf last October, got the strong pace he needs but was another who may not have been helped by having to make his effort furthest from the stands' rail. He is 8lb above his last winning mark on turf, but looks capable of winning off it when things go his way.
Uhoomagoo, ridden closer to the pace than he normally is, was always in about the same place and this ground did not really help him produce his famed power-packed finish. He is more likely to get his ground if aimed at the Buckingham Palace Handicap at Royal Ascot, which he landed last year off a 5lb lower mark.
Prince Of Thebes(IRE) had every chance, but failed to see out the trip in the ground.
Waterside(IRE) has winning form on this track, but this is not his ground and it found him out over this trip.
Spanish Don Official explanation: vet said gelding had been struck into
Future's Dream, given his usual attacking ride, is not finding that it works so well in competitive handicaps back on grass as it did on Fibresand. As soon as he lost the advantage, he fell in a hole. (op 9-1 tchd 7-1)
Rio Riva Official explanation: trainer said gelding did not handle the track
Plum Pudding(IRE) would not have found this track to his liking. Official explanation: trainer said gelding was unsuited by the track and the good to soft (soft in places) ground (op 12-1 tchd 14-1 and 10-1 in places)

2209 VODAFONE ROSE BOWL (HERITAGE H'CAP) 1m 2f 18y

2:45 (2:48) (Class 2) 4-Y-O+

£46,740 (£13,995; £6,997; £3,502; £1,747; £877) **Stalls** Low

Form RPR

-661 **1** **Lake Poet (IRE)**[37] 1244 4-9-5 **95** SebSanders 1 104
(C E Brittain) *chsd ldrs: wnt 2nd 6f out: rdn and upsides ldr over 2f out: led narrowly wl over 1f out: forged clr last 100yds* **6/1**[3]

6-00 **2** 1 ¼ **Wovoka (IRE)**[12] 1862 4-8-6 **82** MartinDwyer 4 88
(M R Channon) *led: hrd pressed and rdn wl over 2f out: hdd wl over 1f out: battled on gamely tl no ex last 100yds* **33/1**

623- **3** 1 ½ **Resonate (IRE)**[181] 6673 9-8-9 **85** KerrinMcEvoy 11 88+
(A G Newcombe) *t.k.h: hld up whn hdwy 4f out: rdn and edgd lft over 1f out: kpt on steadily: wnt 3rd last 100yds: nrst fin* **14/1**

1541 **4** ¾ **Tabadul (IRE)**[28] 1449 6-9-9 **99** RHills 8 101
(E A L Dunlop) *chasd ldr tl 6f out: styd handy: rdn and chsd ldng pair wl over 2f out: no imp ins fnl f* **13/2**

30-3 **5** 2 **John Terry (IRE)**[25] 1543 4-8-11 **87** MJKinane 13 85
(Mrs A J Perrett) *s.i.s: hld up in rr: hdwy on stands rail 3f out: hanging lft fr over 2f out: styd on ins fnl f: n.d* **15/2**

-005 **6** ¾ **Red Lancer**[10] 1922 6-8-3 **79** SilvestreDeSousa 2 75
(D Nicholls) *hld up: hdwy and rdn over 3f out: no imp over 2f 11th* **8/1**

6-10 **7** nk **Forroger (CAN)**[16] 1771 4-8-8 **84** PhilipRobinson 10 79+
(M A Jarvis) *t.k.h: hld up in midfield: effrt and rdn 3f out: wknd over 2f out* **11/4**[1]

4004 **8** *¾* **Prince Samos (IRE)**[12] [1860] 5-8-8 **84**....................(v) AdrianTNicholls 12 78
(D Nicholls) *t.k.h: hld up in rr: rdn wl over 3f out: sme hdwy fnl f: nvr on terms* **16/1**

24-0 **9** *hd* **Press The Button (GER)**[30] [1395] 4-8-6 **82**.................. NickyMackay 7 76
(J R Boyle) *chsd ldrs: rdn and hdwy over 3f out: wknd over 2f out* **20/1**

0-20 **10** *1 ¾* **Kings Quay**[48] [940] 5-9-2 **92**......................................(t) GrahamGibbons 5 82
(J J Quinn) *lw: t.k.h: rdn and effrt 3f out: wknd over 2f out* **14/1**

10-2 **11** *7* **Stotsfold**[23] [1583] 4-9-10 **100**.. AdamKirby 9 76
(W R Swinburn) *lw: stdd sn after s: hld up in rr: rdn and effrt 3f out: no prog* **11/2**[2]

0 **12** *4* **Bazart**[23] [1583] 5-9-6 **96**... PatCosgrave 3 64
(K R Burke) *hld up in midfield: hmpd 4f out: rdn and outpcd 3f out: eased ins fnl f* **25/1**

2m 11.61s (2.57) **Going Correction** +0.45s/f (Yiel) **12** Ran SP% **123.3**
Speed ratings (Par 109):107,106,104,104,102 102,101,101,101,99 94,90
CSF £200.07 CT £2679.29 TOTE £5.90: £1.90, £11.20, £4.10; EX 386.70 TRIFECTA Not won..
Owner Mohammed Rashid **Bred** Philip And Mrs Jane Myerscough And Charles O'Brien **Trained** Newmarket, Suffolk

FOCUS
Considering this was a decent prize, the early pace was very disappointing and it suited those that raced handily, with the winner, second and fourth all up with the pace throughout. As in the previous contest, the whole field came over to the stands' side in the home straight, but this was a messy contest and the form is probably not totally reliable.

NOTEBOOK
Lake Poet(IRE), boasted a record of just two wins from 24 starts coming into this, but he did run well when a close third behind Stage Gift in the big three-year-old handicap over course and distance at this meeting a year ago and came into this off the back of a victory in the Great Metropolitan Handicap here back in April. Raised 8lb for that, the key to this victory was racing close to the pace in a moderately run race, which helped negate the shorter trip, and once he hit the front he was never going to stop. (op 8-1)
Wovoka(IRE), who ran too badly to be true at Ripon last time, showed that effort to be all wrong. He was able to dictate at just an ordinary pace, which enabled him to keep something in reserve, and only the winner was able to get past him. Although undeniably flattered, he is on a much more feasible mark now and may be suited by dropping back slightly in trip. (op 50-1)
Resonate(IRE) was suited by these conditions, having won over course and distance on similar ground last August. Now 11lb higher, he deserves plenty of credit as he did much the best of those held up and was also reappearing from six months off. He was by far the oldest in the field and will need to be better than ever in order to defy this sort of mark, but this performance suggests it is not impossible. (op 16-1)
Tabadul(IRE) ran with a lot of credit, but was another of those suited by racing close to the pace. Raised 4lb for his Lingfield Polytrack victory last month, his successes on sand and his win on grass in Dubai mean that he is now 19lb above his last winning mark in a domestic turf handicap, and that makes him look very vulnerable. (op 7-1 tchd 15-2)
John Terry(IRE) was not at all helped by the way the race was run, over what still looks an indequate trip, and he never looked like getting there in time. (op 8-1 tchd 9-1)
Red Lancer ♦, without a win since landing the Chester Vase more than three years ago, was another that tried to come from off the pace but at least as big a problem was that he was trying to do so furthest from the stands' rail and that probably was not ideal. He does look very well handicapped now and as he was only having his third outing for the yard, he remains one to be interested in. (op 6-1)
Forroger(CAN) had conditions in his favour, but he basically destroyed his chance by pulling like a train early so it was no surprise that he found nothing off the bridle. He is better than this and a race like the John Smiths' Cup would probably bring out the best in him. (op 4-1 tchd 9-2 in places)
Stotsfold was very disappointing, even though the easy ground and the way the race was run would not have been in his favour. This was too bad to be true and he is worth another chance to confirm the favourable impression he gave in the second-half of last season. (op 9-2)

2210 VODAFONE CORONATION CUP (GROUP 1) 1m 4f 10y
3:25 (3:26) (Class 1) 4-Y-0+

£141,950 (£53,800; £26,925; £13,425; £6,725; £3,375) **Stalls** Centre

Form RPR

50-2 **1** **Scorpion (IRE)**[21] [1618] 5-9-0 0... MJKinane 2 123
(A P O'Brien, Ire) *swtg: chsd ldrs tl wnt 2nd 6f out: rdn to ld over 2f out: styd on wl u.p fnl f* **8/1**

10-1 **2** *1 ¼* **Septimus (IRE)**[25] [1550] 4-9-0 0.. JMurtagh 3 121
(A P O'Brien, Ire) *led: after 2f: rdn wl over 3f out: hdd over 2f out: kpt on same pce u.p* **3/1**[2]

5-11 **3** *½* **Maraahel (IRE)**[22] [1600] 6-9-0 120...(b) RHills 7 120
(Sir Michael Stoute) *lw: led for 2f: chsd ldr tl 6f out: 3rd and rdn 3f out: kpt on u.p fnl f* **7/1**

55-0 **4** *3 ½* **Rising Cross**[14] [1823] 4-8-11 110.. TedDurcan 6 112
(J R Best) *hld up in rr: hdwy and plld out wl over 2f out: kpt on steadily: nt pce to rch ldrs* **33/1**

3014 **5** *½* **Hattan (IRE)**[22] [1600] 5-9-0 107... SebSanders 5 114
(C E Brittain) *lw: hld up in last pair: hdwy and rdn over 3f out: kpt on same pce last 2f* **66/1**

10-4 **6** *hd* **Sir Percy**[62] [861] 4-9-0 121.. MartinDwyer 1 114
(M P Tregoning) *swtg: chsd ldng pair tl 1/2-way: rdn and outpcd 3f out: hdwy on rail 2f out: no imp fnl f* **7/2**[3]

10-1 **7** *3 ½* **Sixties Icon**[26] [1495] 4-9-0 122.. LDettori 4 108
(J Noseda) *hld up in tch: hdwy 3f out: sn rdn: wknd over 1f out: eased ins fnl f* **11/8**[1]

2m 40.82s (2.09) **Going Correction** +0.45s/f (Yiel) **7** Ran SP% **117.4**
Speed ratings (Par 117):111,110,109,107,107 107,104
CSF £33.51 TOTE £8.10: £3.00, £3.20; EX 47.40.
Owner Mrs John Magnier & M Tabor **Bred** Grangemore Stud **Trained** Ballydoyle, Co Tipperary

FOCUS
A fascinating race on paper and well up to scratch standard-wise, with a Derby winner and two St Leger winners in opposition. Hwever, it was run at a rather uneven gallop which probably did not suit a few of these and resulted in a time 0.44 seconds slower than the Oaks. With the fourth and fifth a bit close for comfort and a couple of the big names disappointing, it is not form one could be confident about. On this occasion the sextet all decided to stay on the inside of the track in the home straight.

NOTEBOOK
Scorpion(IRE) has had his problems over the last 18 months or so and was a beaten favourite in the Ormonde Stakes at Chester on his return last month, but he may well have needed that run more than was obvious at the time. It was a different story here though, as despite getting edgy beforehand he travelled very well just off the pace on ground that was ideal for him whilst his stable-companion messed up Maraahel, and then when asked to go and win his race he fairly bounded clear. The strict form is perhaps questionable given how the race was run, but this did at least suggest that his problems may be behind him and his overall record shows that he is perfectly capable of winning again at this level. (op 12-1 tchd 14-1 and 16-1 in places)
Septimus(IRE), disappointing in last year's Derby, but fit and well having won his first start since at Leopardstown last month, had conditions in his favour here but was given a much more positive ride than might have been expected and apart from giving his stable companion a nice lead, it also did not help Maraahel's chances. He was unable to match Scorpion's turn of foot in the home straight, but never stopped trying and managed to keep on for a brave second. (op 7-2 tchd 11-4 and 5-2 in places)
Maraahel(IRE) has been in great form this season, with two victories since blinkers replaced the visor, but he could have done without Septimus taking him on for the early lead here and his rider eventually decided not to try get involved in a battle and settle him just behind. When asked for his effort in the home straight, he merely stayed on at one pace and fell just short at Group 1 winning level for the 11th time. (op 9-1 tchd 10-1)
Rising Cross, runner-up in last year's Oaks, probably needs further than this these days whilst this was a tough race in general for those held up. Under the circumstances she probably achieved as much as could be expected. The Gold Cup is next on the agenda, and she could improve for the extreme distance. (op 66-1)
Hattan(IRE) ran fairly close to form with Maraahel on their Chester running, but had no real chance and only finished ahead of two of the market principals because they underperformed.
Sir Percy, back to the scene of his greatest triumph, was awkward when being saddled and was disappointingly left behind down the home straight. Things have not gone his way since last year's Derby and he may have had excuses here with the ground and the way the race was run, but you can only make so many. It is always disappointing when a Derby winner cannot confirm his status. (op 11-4 tchd 9-4)
Sixties Icon, very well backed for this following his impressive win in a slowly run Jockey Club Stakes at Newmarket, was close enough turning in but found nothing at all off the bridle and was allowed to coast home. This was obviously not his running. Official explanation: trainer had no explanation for the poor form shown (tchd 15-8 and 2-1 in places)

2211 VODAFONE OAKS (GROUP 1) (FILLIES) 1m 4f 10y
4:05 (4:08) (Class 1) 3-Y-O

£222,350 (£84,272; £42,175; £21,028; £10,534; £5,286) **Stalls** Centre

Form RPR

1-11 **1** **Light Shift (USA)**[23] [1581] 3-9-0 106.................................. TedDurcan 11 121
(H R A Cecil) *lw: hld up in midfield: hdwy 4f out: 4th st: led over 2f out: sn rdn and clr over 1f out: hrd pressed ins fnl f: fnd ex and r.o wl* **13/2**[3]

3 **2** *½* **Peeping Fawn (USA)**[5] [2065] 3-9-0 0.................................. MartinDwyer 9 120
(A P O'Brien, Ire) *leggy: scope: plld hrd: chsd ldrs for 1f: stmbld after 2f: bhd: 12th st: gd hdwy on outer wl over 2f out: edgd lft 2f out: ev ch ins fnl f: no ex and hld last 50yds* **20/1**

2 **3** *4* **All My Loving (IRE)**[23] [1581] 3-9-0 0.................................. CSoumillon 6 113
(A P O'Brien, Ire) *lw: hld up in midfield: hdwy to trck ldrs 7f out: 2nd st: rdn to ld 3f out: hdd over 2f out: kpt on same pce* **5/1**[2]

0-21 **4** *5* **Four Sins (GER)**[16] [1777] 3-9-0 0.. MJKinane 13 105
(John M Oxx, Ire) *w'like: lengthy: chsd ldrs: 3rd st: sn rdn: struggling whn bmpd 2f out: kpt on same pce after* **5/1**[2]

2 **5** *1 ½* **Cherry Hinton**[16] [1777] 3-9-0 0... JAHeffernan 7 103
(A P O'Brien, Ire) *w'like: hld up in rr: 13th st: gd hdwy and edgd lft over 2f out: no imp last 2f* **66/1**

11-3 **6** *8* **Simply Perfect**[26] [1496] 3-9-0 112.. JMurtagh 5 90
(J Noseda) *hmpd sn after s: plld hrd: hld up bhd: hmpd 7f out: 11th st: swtchd rt and hdwy 3f out: sn no imp* **8/1**

5-1 **7** *2* **Dance Of Light (USA)**[15] [1784] 3-9-0 0....................... KerrinMcEvoy 10 87
(Sir Michael Stoute) *lw: hld up bhd on outer: hmpd 5f out: hdwy on outer and 9th st: sn rdn and outpcd: no ch last 2f* **33/1**

11-1 **8** *nk* **Passage Of Time**[16] [1769] 3-9-0 110............................. RichardHughes 8 87
(H R A Cecil) *lw: chsd ldrs: 5th and rdn st: wknd 3f out* **9/4**[1]

1-1 **9** *½* **Kayah**[20] [1663] 3-9-0 0.. SebSanders 12 86
(R M Beckett) *lw: led tl rdn and hdd 3f out: wknd qckly* **16/1**

-000 **10** *2* **Darrfonah (IRE)**[26] [1496] 3-9-0 103..................................(t) EddieAhern 3 83
(C E Brittain) *hld up in midfield: hdwy over 4f out: 7th st: sn rdn and wknd* **66/1**

1-1 **11** *shd* **Dalvina**[26] [1499] 3-9-0 109.. OPeslier 4 82
(E A L Dunlop) *hmpd sn after s: sn chsng ldrs: 6th and rdn st: sn wknd* **11/1**

0-02 **12** *1 ¾* **Nell Gwyn (IRE)**[19] [1694] 3-9-0 0.. NCallan 2 80
(A P O'Brien, Ire) *str: s.i.s: hld up in rr: last st: sn lost tch and no ch last 3f:* **66/1**

1-1 **13** *nk* **Measured Tempo**[14] [1809] 3-9-0 98.. LDettori 14 79
(Saeed Bin Suroor) *lw: t.k.h: hdwy to trck ldrs 8f out: 8th and wkng st: sn wl bhd* **9/1**

42-3 **14** *48* **Sues Surprise (IRE)**[16] [1769] 3-9-0 0.................................. MichaelHills 1 2
(B W Hills) *pressed ldr tl wl over 3f out: 10th and wkng rapidly st: virtually p.u last 2f* **66/1**

2m 40.38s (1.65) **Going Correction** +0.45s/f (Yiel) **14** Ran SP% **126.4**
Speed ratings (Par 110):112,111,109,105,104 99,98,97,97,96 96,94,94,62
CSF £140.53 TOTE £9.10: £2.70, £6.30, £2.70; EX 201.10 Trifecta £1680.20 Pool: £8,283.04 - 3.50 winning units..
Owner Niarchos Family **Bred** Flaxman Holdings Ltd **Trained** Newmarket, Suffolk
■ Henry Cecil's 24th domestic Classic, and his eighth Oaks, equalling Alec Taylor's record. Ted Durcan's first Classic winner.
■ Stewards' Enquiry : Martin Dwyer one-day ban: careless riding (Jun 12)

FOCUS
A competitive Oaks in terms of numbers, though only a couple had previously triumphed at Group 1 level. The pace was solid enough and the time was 0.44 seconds quicker than the Coronation Cup. Once again the whole field decided to stay on the inside in the home straight. The Cheshire Oaks, which has not been a great pointer to this race, proved the key trial this time as the first two there finished first and third here. Light Shift has been raised 14lb since then and her Oaks win has been rated a shade above the average for the last 10 years.

NOTEBOOK
Light Shift(USA) may have been stepping up a good deal in class having never tackled anything above Listed company before, but she is extremely tough and knows how to win. She did not exactly enjoy the smoothest of passages here, racing out wide for most of the way, but she travelled into the race supremely well and when she swept to the front passing the two-furlong pole, she looked like winning by a decent margin. She then faced a big challenge from the runner-up and it seemed as though she might be caught, but the toughness that has marked her previous victories this term came to her rescue and she found plenty more when she needed it. She would need supplementing for the Irish Oaks, which may in any case come too soon for her, and connections are inclined to wait for the Nassau and the Yorkshire Oaks (op 6-1 tchd 15-2)
Peeping Fawn(USA), stepping up half a mile in trip after finishing third in the Irish 1,000 Guineas the previous weekend, did not enjoy a smooth passage at all and had plenty to do starting up the home straight. Pulled out wide for her effort, she produced an amazing turn of speed to haul back the leaders but, due to the camber, for every two strides forward she took one to her left, smashing into Four Sins as she did so, and finished up right alongside the winner. Even so, it looked as though her impetus would still take her to the front, but she was up against a rival with guts in abundance and having got there, she could not find any more in the final run to the line. She stayed the trip perfectly well and, given a less dramatic journey at the Curragh, she will prove a formidable rival. (op 33-1)

The Form Book, Raceform Ltd, Compton, RG20 6NL

All My Loving(IRE) ◆, beaten less than a length by Light Shift in the Cheshire Oaks, made her bid for glory turning for home but could never get away from her old rival and ended up being beaten further this time. Although one place further back in this race than her sisters Quarter Moon and Yesterday, this was still a fine effort and as she is even less experienced than the front pair - this was only her third career start - she ought to pick up a Group race in due course. (op 7-1 tchd 9-2)
Four Sins(GER) ◆ would probably have preferred the rains not to have come, but she had every chance and had run her race by the time she received a left hook from Peeping Fawn passing the two-furlong pole. With the ground likely to be more suitable, it would be no surprise to her get a lot closer at the Curragh. (op 7-1 tchd 15-2)
Cherry Hinton ◆ was given plenty to do, but stayed on quite nicely up the home straight and finished a length closer to Four Sins than at Naas last month. Still a maiden after just three outings, the best of her is probably still to be seen.
Simply Perfect, third in the 1,000 Guineas last time, is proven at Group 1 level but the trip was always going to be an issue and she was ridden accordingly. She also did not help herself by being a bit too keen early, having been edgy and warm beforehand, and although she stayed on past beaten rivals to finish a respectable sixth, she was never within shouting distance of the principals. (op 10-1 tchd 7-1)
Dance Of Light(USA) came into this off the back of a victory in a very slowly run Salisbury maiden. She made a brief effort turning in, but it amounted to very little and she needs her sights lowering a bit. (op 25-1)
Passage Of Time, the stable's first string on the face of it, seemed to be in the ideal position throughout so it was very disappointing to see her fade so tamely. The ground should not have been a problem and given the way she won the Musidora it is hard to blame lack of stamina, even though connections were inclined to so so. The well-documented problem with the throat abscess might have contributed, but either way it would be no surprise if we did not see her for some considerable time. Official explanation: jockey said filly stopped quickly (op 2-1 tchd 5-2)
Kayah, supplemented for this following her Lingfield Oaks Trial victory, had conditions in her favour and was given a positive ride in order to make her stamina count, but as soon as she was taken on for the lead turning in she folded very quickly. This was probably too stiff a task for her at this stage of her career, but she is still relatively inexperienced.
Darrfonah(IRE), a relatively exposed filly trying further than a mile for the first time, is bred to stay and this was probably more a case of her not being good enough rather than lack of stamina.
Dalvina ◆, whose connections expressed fears over the easy ground, seemed to have those fears realised as she never really got involved and ended up well beaten. She should not be written off yet and is well worth another chance back on faster ground. (op 10-1 tchd 12-1)
Nell Gwyn(IRE) is not up to this class and never made any impression from off the pace over this longer trip.
Measured Tempo, whose participation had been briefly in doubt due to a foot abscess appearing five days earlier, was in a fair enough position in the first half of the contest, but she could not handle the downhill sectiion and there was no way back. Perhaps the foot was still troubling her, but whatever the cause, this was well below the form of her Newbury victory. (op 10-1 tchd 11-1)
Sues Surprise(IRE), who ran with some credit against Passage Of Time in the Musidora when able to enjoy an uncontested lead, did not have that luxury here and having taken part in a battle for the lead for over a mile, she capitulated completely once in line for home. Official explanation: trainer said filly finished distressed

2212 VODAFONE SURREY STKS (LISTED RACE) 7f

4:50 (4:51) (Class 1) 3-Y-O

£19,873 (£7,532; £3,769; £1,879; £941; £472) **Stalls** Low

Form				RPR
5-33	**1**		**Howya Now Kid (IRE)**[14] 1808 3-8-13 0 .... JMurtagh 2 (G M Lyons, Ire) *hld up in tch: hdwy 3f out: rdn to chse ldr over 1f out: led ins fnl f: drvn out* **17/2**	101
1-54	**2**	*3/4*	**Solid Rock (IRE)**[30] 1394 3-8-13 95 .... MJKinane 3 (T G Mills) *wnt rt s: sn led: rdn 3f out: hrd pressed wl over 1f out: hdd ins fnl f: kpt on same pce* **12/1**	99
1-02	**3**	*3/4*	**Whazzis**[13] 1837 3-8-8 85 .... KerrinMcEvoy 10 (W J Haggas) *hld up in midfield: c to stands' rail and racd alone over 3f out: styd on wl ins fnl f: nt rch ldrs* **13/2**[3]	92+
1440	**4**	*1 1/4*	**Mastership (IRE)**[19] 1703 3-8-13 100 ....(b) EddieAhern 8 (C E Brittain) *hld up: hdwy 3f out: chsd ldrs and rdn wl over 1f out: kpt on same pce* **9/1**	94
1312	**5**	*4*	**Annemasse**[6] 2037 3-8-13 89 .... JoeFanning 1 (M Johnston) *lw: chsd ldr: rdn 3f out: wknd jst over 1f out* **7/2**[1]	83
2-14	**6**	*2 1/2*	**Mofarij**[25] 1544 3-8-13 98 .... LDettori 6 (Saeed Bin Suroor) *hmpd s: t.k.h: hld up in last pair: rdn 3f out: no prog* **11/2**[2]	76
15-0	**7**	*shd*	**Heroes**[16] 1768 3-8-13 90 .... EmmettStack 7 (G A Huffer) *t.k.h: hld up in last: rdn 3f out: no hdwy: hung lft fnl f* **20/1**	76+
031	**8**	*1 1/4*	**Heywood**[22] 1604 3-8-13 92 .... DarryllHolland 4 (M R Channon) *hmpd s: hld up in tch: hmpd over 4f out: rdn and outpcd 3f out: n.d after* **9/1**	72
14-4	**9**	*1*	**Opera Music**[35] 1276 3-8-13 95 .... RichardHughes 9 (S Kirk) *chsd ldrs: rdn over 3f out: wknd over 2f out* **20/1**	70

1m 25.55s (1.60) **Going Correction** +0.45s/f (Yiel) **9** Ran SP% **98.7**
Speed ratings (Par 107):108,107,106,104,100 97,97,95,94
CSF £67.92 TOTE £7.10: £1.90, £2.30, £2.20; EX 69.10 Trifecta £176.40 Pool: £571.56 - 2.30 winning units..

Owner Glenview House Stud **Bred** Miss Jill Finegan **Trained** Dunsany, Co. Meath

FOCUS
Not a strong Listed event, and it was weakened by the late withdrawal of the favourite Escape Route after he got out from under the front of the stalls (3/1, deduct 25p in the £ under Rule 4.). The pace was decent and the time reasonable, even though it was 0.46 seconds slower than the following handicap over the same trip. There was a difference of opinion as to where the best ground was in this contest, with the bulk of the field staying on the inside in the straight, whilst the eventual third came stands' side.

NOTEBOOK
Howya Now Kid(IRE) proved well suited by this step back up to 7f. Never far away, he took a while to get on top of the leader, but gradually wore him down and was well on top at the line. There looks to be more to come from him over this sort of trip and he would not be out of place in the Jersey Stakes. (op 8-1 tchd 10-1)
Solid Rock(IRE), back over a more suitable trip, was given a positive ride and seemed to be holding the Irish raider for much of the home straight, but his rival's persistence finally got the better of him. This performance shows that he is not just a Polytrack performer, especially when there is some cut in the ground. (op 11-1)
Whazzis ◆, stepping up in class, had plenty to do against the boys on official ratings. Her rider decided that he was going to come over to the stands' rail turning in, even though the others all stayed on the inside, and without any company to race against it is impossible to be sure if it was to her advantage or not. Given the task she faced at the weights, it is probably best to give both her and her rider the benefit of the doubt. (op 9-1)
Mastership(IRE) was totally out of his depth in the French 2,000 Guineas and is more exposed than most, but even though he could never get on terms with the principals, he finished clear of the others and emerges with some credit. He is not without hope at this level, especially back on faster ground or, if an opportunity can be found, back on sand, but his best effort was at 6f. (tchd 11-1 and 12-1 in places)
Annemasse, given a prominent ride from the inside stall, had every chance but was rather easily brushed aside over the last couple of furlongs. Strictly at the weights he had a bit to find, but he still might have been expected to last a bit longer and perhaps this came too soon after his hard race at Haydock, or he needs quicker ground. (op 4-1 tchd 10-3)
Mofarij never looked like taking a hand. Although the yard have had a few winners over the last month or so, many of their representatives are still underperforming. (op 13-2 tchd 7-1 in a place)

2213 VODAFONE GROUP SERVICES (H'CAP) 7f

5:25 (5:25) (Class 2) (0-100,95) 3-Y-O

£18,696 (£5,598; £2,799; £1,401; £699; £351) **Stalls** Low

Form				RPR
1-22	**1**		**Vitznau (IRE)**[64] 815 3-8-3 **77** .... MartinDwyer 1 (R Hannon) *hld up: swtchd rt and hdwy over 2f out: led ins fnl f: hung lft: rdn out* **5/2**[1]	90+
3-	**2**	*1*	**Little White Lie (IRE)**[68] 784 3-9-7 **95** .... JMurtagh 9 (G M Lyons, Ire) *w'like: lw: chsd ldr: rdn to ld over 2f out: hdd ins fnl f: short of room and swtchd wl ins fnl f: kpt on* **7/1**[3]	103
4-03	**3**	*3*	**Salient**[39] 1202 3-8-5 **79** .... PaulDoe 4 (J Akehurst) *hld up: swtchd rt after 2f: rdn 3f out: chsd ldng pair over 1f out: hung lft and no imp fnl f* **10/1**	79
4-06	**4**	*2 1/2*	**Lunces Lad (IRE)**[26] 1500 3-8-8 **82** .... DarryllHolland 10 (M R Channon) *lw: in tch: c stands' side and racd alone over 3f out: chsd ldrs 1f out: wknd fnl f* **7/1**[3]	75+
2-44	**5**	*1 1/4*	**Dubai Magic (USA)**[110] 433 3-8-8 **82** .... TedDurcan 3 (C E Brittain) *chsd ldrs: hdwy on inner 3f out: no hdwy u.p over 1f out* **20/1**	72
0-00	**6**	*2 1/2*	**Don't Panic (IRE)**[26] 1500 3-8-11 **85** .... RichardHughes 2 (P W Chapple-Hyam) *led tl over 2f out: sn wknd* **12/1**	68
1-05	**7**	*1 3/4*	**Cheap Street**[14] 1817 3-8-13 **87** .... NickyMackay 7 (J G Portman) *hld up: rdn and hmpd over 3f out: no imp* **16/1**	65
1222	**8**	*4*	**Captain Jacksparra (IRE)**[13] 1851 3-8-11 **85** .... NCallan 11 (K A Ryan) *lw: hld up in tch: rdn 3f out: sltly hmpd over 2f out: sn wknd* **9/2**[2]	53
0-30	**9**	*6*	**Mystery Ocean**[16] 1768 3-8-10 **84** .... SebSanders 8 (R M Beckett) *swtg: hld up: rdn 3f out: hung lft and no hdwy: eased ins fnl f: t.o* **7/1**[3]	35
-020	**10**	*9*	**Cesc**[42] 1124 3-9-2 **90** .... EddieAhern 5 (P J Makin) *in tch: rdn and hmpd over 3f out: wknd qckly 2f out: eased ins fnl f: t.o:* **12/1**	17+
2410	**11**	*1/2*	**Dickie Le Davoir**[6] 2044 3-9-5 **93** .... PhilipRobinson 6 (K R Burke) *sn outpcd in last: no ch fr 1/2-way: t.o:* **9/1**	19+

1m 25.09s (1.14) **Going Correction** +0.45s/f (Yiel) **11** Ran SP% **129.4**
Speed ratings (Par 105):111,109,106,103,102 99,97,92,85,75 75
CSF £22.82 CT £165.75 TOTE £3.90: £1.70, £2.60, £3.70; EX 21.80 Trifecta £95.90 Pool £ 1,175.20 - 8.70 winning units. Place 6 £388.99, Place 5 £314.85.

Owner Louis Stalder **Bred** John McLoughlin **Trained** East Everleigh, Wilts

■ Stewards' Enquiry : Darryll Holland three-day ban (reduced from four days on appeal): careless riding (Jun 12-14)

FOCUS
A fair handicap of its type. They went a decent pace which resulted in the field finishing spread out all over Surrey and a time 0.46 seconds quicker than the preceding Listed event. As in the previous race, all bar one of the field stayed on the inside of the track after turning in.

NOTEBOOK
Vitznau(IRE) ◆, twice narrowly beaten on Polytrack this year, was racing off a 6lb higher mark. He was still 4lb better off with Captain Jacksparra for a beating of just under a length at Lingfield last time, and compehensively turned that form around having been given a patient ride off the strong pace. Once produced with his effort, he was always doing enough despite hanging left down the camber to the inside rail. There may be more to come. (op 7-2)

Little White Lie(IRE), bidding for a quick double for the yard, might have preferred the ground to have been more testing that this, but still ran a cracker having been up with the pace throughout. His jockey did have to stop riding for a couple of strides when the winner went across him inside the last furlong, but the favourite had his measure by then and it made no difference to the result. (op 13-2 tchd 11-2)

Salient, given plenty to do, stayed on well down the centre of the track and showed that his decent effort at a huge price at Windsor last time was no fluke. He is still to win on turf, but it is only a matter of time and he shaped here as though he will appreciate a return to a mile. (op 8-1 tchd 11-1)

Lunces Lad(IRE), whose eight career outings have all been over this trip, was the only one to come stands' side in the home straight and he seemed to have every chance until getting tired and hanging back down the camber near the line. As was the case with Whazzis in the previous race, it is impossible to be sure whether the tactics were a help or a hindrance. (op 8-1 tchd 6-1)

Dubai Magic(USA), busy on the sand in the winter but reappearing from four months off, had every chance on the inside and there seemed no real excuses. (op 28-1 tchd 33-1)

Don't Panic(IRE), a headstrong sort, was allowed to stride on, which were the tactics used for his only previous victory, but they did not work this time as he faded very tamely once headed. (op 16-1)

Captain Jacksparra(IRE), who finished in front of the winner on Polytrack back in March, was 4lb worse off but still did not run his race and was not helped by running into the back of Cesc passing the two-furlong pole. (tchd 11-2)

Cesc, a much-improved performer on Polytrack during the winter, finds himself on a very stiff mark back on grass as a result. This did not tell us much more about his true ability on turf though, as after he seemed to get caught from behind by Captain Jacksparra two furlongs out, it was not long before his rider eased him right off. Official explanation: jockey said colt lost its action (op 16-1 tchd 20-1)

Dickie Le Davoir failed to handle the downhill run at all over the first couple of furlongs and was not hard pressed from then on. It may be best to ignore this effort. Official explanation: jockey said gelding was unsuited by the track (op 7-1)

T/Jkpt: Not won. T/Plt: £810.60 to a £1 stake. Pool: £209,258.16. 188.45 winning tickets. T/Qpdt: £572.90 to a £1 stake. Pool: £13,317.30. 17.20 winning tickets. SP

[1984]GOODWOOD (R-H)

Friday, June 1

OFFICIAL GOING: Good

Wind: slight across

2214 HAMBURGER UNION H'CAP (FOR AMATEUR RIDERS) 1m 1f
6:20 (6:22) (Class 6) (0-65,68) 4-Y-0+ £3,123 (£968; £484; £242) Stalls High

Form RPR

0-00 1 **Monashee River (IRE)**[65] 812 4-10-2 **45**............... MissFayeBramley 5 54
(Miss V Haigh) *led after 2f: rdn whn rdr lost whip over 1f out: kpt on wl* **50/1**

1540 2 1 1/4 **The Grey One (IRE)**[6] 2027 4-10-10 **60**..................(p) MissHDavies(7) 10 66
(J M Bradley) *t.k.h: a.p: chsd wnr fr over 2f out* **12/1**

-643 3 1 **Foolish Groom**[20] 1673 6-10-5 **53**...................... MrStephenHarrison(5) 2 57
(R Hollinshead) *prom on outside: styd on ins fnl 2f* **6/1**[2]

-535 4 nk **Agilete**[70] 741 5-10-11 **57**.. MrSPearce(3) 7 60
(J Pearce) *bhd tl styd on fr over 2f out: fin wl: nvr nrr* **9/1**

-422 5 2 1/2 **Murrumbidgee (IRE)**[22] 1612 4-11-5 **62**...................... MissEJJones 16 60
(J W Hills) *mid-div: rdn over 2f out: kpt on one pce* **6/1**[2]

0-00 6 shd **Mythical Charm**[138] 130 8-10-11 **54**..........................(t) MissLEllison 14 52
(J J Bridger) *nvr bttr than mid-div* **16/1**

00-0 7 1 **Bold Finch (FR)**[4] 2089 5-10-2 **50**............................ MissSBradley(5) 11 46
(J M Bradley) *led for 2f: styd prom tl wknd fnl f* **33/1**

3000 8 nk **Marbaa (IRE)**[7] 2004 4-11-2 **62**................................. MrDHutchison(3) 18 57
(S Dow) *slowly away: hdwy over 2f out: nvr nr to chal* **7/1**[3]

5001 9 1/2 **The Gaikwar (IRE)**[3] 2107 8-11-4 **68** 6ex.......................(b) MrRPFlint(7) 6 62
(R A Harris) *a.p: rdn over 2f out: one pce after* **11/2**[1]

0650 10 shd **Love You Always (USA)**[5] 2055 7-10-0 **50**..................(t) MrRBirkett(7) 3 44
(Miss J Feilden) *slowly away: in rr tl hdwy and nt clr run over 2f out: swtchd lft over 1f out: no hdwy* **33/1**

00-5 11 1 1/2 **Adobe**[25] 1539 12-10-2 **50**.................................... MrBenBrisbourne(5) 17 41
(W M Brisbourne) *slowly away: in rr: mde sme late hdwy* **12/1**

-000 12 1 **Wizby**[24] 1564 4-10-2 **50**.. MrRichardEvans(5) 13 39
(P D Evans) *a towards rr* **25/1**

60-0 13 1/2 **Mixing**[22] 1612 5-10-3 **46**..(b[1]) MrMatthewSmith 8 34
(W Jarvis) *nvr bttr than mid-div* **16/1**

50-4 14 1 3/4 **Dispol Veleta**[21] 1627 6-11-5 **62**... MrSDobson 1 46
(Miss T Spearing) *v.s.a: a bhd* **14/1**

000- 15 3/4 **Dancing Melody**[10] 5897 4-9-10 **46**..........................(p) MrDHannig(7) 15 28
(J A Geake) *mid-div tl wknd 2f out* **40/1**

4520 16 3/4 **Charlie Bear**[26] 1507 6-10-8 **56**.................. MissGDGracey-Davison(5) 9 37
(Miss Z C Davison) *in tch tl rdn and wknd over 2f out* **9/1**

3640 17 3 **Reaching Out (IRE)**[31] 928 5-11-0 **64**.................(b) MissHollyHall(7) 12 38
(N P Littmoden) *slowly away: sn mid-div: wkng whn hmpd over 2f out* **16/1**

-004 18 14 **Secam (POL)**[32] 1347 8-9-11 **45**............................ MrsCThompson(5) 4 —
(Mrs P Townsley) *chsd ldrs tl wknd over 3f out* **50/1**

2m 1.77s (4.91) **Going Correction** +0.30s/f (Good) **18** Ran SP% **132.2**
Speed ratings (Par 101):90,88,88,87,85 85,84,84,83,83 82,81,81,79,78 78,75,63
CSF £590.88 CT £4246.26 TOTE £104.80: £18.60, £3.20, £1.70, £2.80; EX 1505.80.
Owner R J Budge **Bred** Christopher John Strain **Trained** Wiseton, Notts

FOCUS

A modest but competitive race for amateur riders, run at a disappointingly weak early pace. The runner-up is rated as having run to form and is the best guide to the level.

Bold Finch(FR) Official explanation: vet said gelding was lame

Dispol Veleta Official explanation: jockey said mare hung right

2215 SOIL ASSOCIATION EUROPEAN BREEDERS' FUND MAIDEN STKS 6f
6:50 (6:50) (Class 5) 2-Y-0 £3,562 (£1,059; £529; £264) Stalls Low

Form RPR

1 **Bobs Surprise** 2-9-3 .... MichaelHills 11 87+
(B W Hills) *hld up: hdwy to ld over 1f out: qcknd clr: promising* **9/1**[3]

2 4 **Atheer Dubai (IRE)** 2-9-3 .... EddieAhern 7 75+
(C E Brittain) *hld up in tch: styd on wl fnl f to go 2nd post* **16/1**

2 3 shd **Nawaaff**[15] 1792 2-9-3 .... JHBowman 9 75
(M R Channon) *led tl hdd over 1f out: rdn and lost 2nd post* **4/6**[1]

4 1/2 **Captain Esteem** 2-9-3 .... ChrisCatlin 10 73
(B W Hills) *plld hrd: trckd ldrs: ev ch over 1f out: kpt on one pce* **66/1**

5 1 1/2 **Barbarossa** 2-9-3 .... RichardHughes 8 69+
(R Hannon) *hld up: nt clr run over 2f out: swtchd rt: nvr nr to chal* **12/1**

0 6 3/4 **Merchant Navy**[12] 1858 2-9-3 .... MartinDwyer 2 66+
(E A L Dunlop) *slowly away: sn in tch: rdn over 2f out: wknd ins fnl f* **40/1**

0 7 1 **Vigano (IRE)**[13] 1832 2-9-3 .... JohnEgan 1 63
(S Kirk) *prom tl wknd wl over 1f out* **25/1**

8 1 3/4 **Mymumsaysimthebest** 2-9-3 .... PatDobbs 4 58
(R Hannon) *slowly away: nvr on terms* **16/1**

9 1/2 **Sparton Duke (IRE)** 2-9-3 .... RichardMullen 5 57
(E J O'Neill) *trckd ldrs: rdn and wknd over 1f out* **4/1**[2]

10 3 **Palm Court** 2-9-3 .... SteveDrowne 12 48+
(R Charlton) *swvd bdly rt s: a bhd* **25/1**

11 hd **Benhavis** 2-9-3 .... IanMongan 6 47
(J L Dunlop) *t.k.h: prom tl rdn and wknd over 1f out* **50/1**

12 3/4 **Lisselan Prospect (USA)** 2-9-3 .... JimCrowley 3 45
(Mrs A J Perrett) *prom: rdn 1/2-way: sn btn* **66/1**

1m 13.93s (1.08) **Going Correction** +0.075s/f (Good) **12** Ran SP% **124.5**
Speed ratings (Par 93):95,89,89,88,86 85,84,82,81,77 77,76
CSF £137.75 TOTE £9.00: £2.20, £4.90, £1.10; EX 205.70.
Owner A L R Morton **Bred** Wyck Hall Stud Ltd **Trained** Lambourn, Berks

FOCUS

An above-average maiden, run at a decent pace and producing a smart-looking winner.

NOTEBOOK

Bobs Surprise ◆ completed an eye-catching debut, swiftly picking up from behind and leaving his rivals standing a furlong from home. By the speedy Bertonlini, and half-brother to several decent sprinters, this 60,000gns yearling looks set for a trip to Royal Ascot, and on this evidence thoroughly deserves to take his chance. (tchd 8-1)

Atheer Dubai(IRE), a son of the high-class Dubai Destination, is bred to come into his own at around a mile. The way he ran seemed to confirm that slightly longer trips will suit him as the season progresses, but there was plenty to like about this first effort. (op 12-1)

Nawaaff failed to live up to his market position, but he showed plenty of speed and still looks capable of finding a race before long. In being taken on for the lead by so many others, he may have gone a shade too fast, setting the race up for the come-from-behind winner. (op 5-6)

Captain Esteem, a 60,000gns Mark Of Esteem colt, is out of a 6f/7f mare, so should be best at trips up to a mile. Too impetuous on this debut, he nonetheless showed plenty of ability at a surprisingly big price for the stable, suggesting that he produced much more here than he had at home beforehand. (tchd 50-1)

Barbarossa, a 57,000gns yearling, is by the top-class middle-distance performer Beat All, and out of the speedy mare Gagajulu - who has already produced three smart offspring up to a mile. Thanks to the influence of his sire, he may stay a bit farther than his half-siblings, and this was an encouraging first effort. (op 14-1)

Merchant Navy again missed the kick, but ran better than he had on his debut. This son of Green Desert seems to be benefiting from experience, and will do even better when he learns to break on terms. (op 50-1)

Vigano(IRE), a 115,000euro son of Noverre, and from a good family, stepped up a on his debut effort. He showed much more early speed this time, and will be well at home in handicaps after one more run. (tchd 22-1)

Mymumsaysimthebest, 24,000gns son of Sussex Stakes winner Reel Buddy, hails from a speedy family, so is bred to be useful up to a mile. This was a satisfactory if unspectacular debut, but improvement is likely. (op 14-1)

Sparton Duke(IRE), a 42,000gns son of Xaar, looks on breeding as if he will settle down around seven furlongs or a mile. He lacks nothing in pace, and should be able to last longer with experience. (tchd 6-1)

Palm Court, a Green Desert colt whose dam stayed a mile, should come into his own over slightly longer trips. He needed this experience, and should benefit for the run. (op 28-1)

Benhavis Official explanation: jockey said gelding was struck into

2216 HILDON STKS (REGISTERED AS THE TAPSTER STAKES) (LISTED RACE) 1m 4f
7:20 (7:21) (Class 1) 4-Y-0+ £16,595 (£6,274; £3,136; £1,568) Stalls High

Form RPR

6-63 1 **Ivy Creek (USA)**[22] 1600 4-9-0 108................................... SteveDrowne 7 114+
(G Wragg) *hld up in rr: hdwy over 2f out: nt clr run tl over 1f out: strly rdn to ld wl ins fnl f* **8/1**

1/6- 2 1/2 **Shahin (USA)**[264] 5204 4-9-0 93... MartinDwyer 3 111
(M P Tregoning) *hld up and soon wl bhd: rapid hdwy on outside over 1f out: ev ch ins fnl f: hld cl home* **25/1**

40-3 3 1 1/2 **Foxhaven**[20] 1664 5-9-3 105... JimCrowley 8 112
(P R Chamings) *led tl rdn and drifted rt and hdd wl ins fnl f* **14/1**

21-5 4 1 3/4 **Into The Dark**[7] 1985 6-9-3 110..........................(t) KerrinMcEvoy 4 109
(Saeed Bin Suroor) *in tch: rdn over 1f out: edgd rt and nt qckn ins fnl f* **15/2**

01-0 5 1/2 **Alfie Flits**[69] 761 5-9-3 114.. TPO'Shea 9 108+
(G A Swinbank) *in tch on ins: n.m.r 3f out: rdn and one pce fnl f* **4/1**[2]

24-2 6 2 1/2 **Day Flight**[13] 1833 6-9-0 113.. RichardHughes 5 101
(J H M Gosden) *trckd ldr: wkng whn n.m.r and squeezed out ent fnl f* **6/4**[1]

6024 7 1/2 **Akarem**[14] 1805 6-9-0 105.. PatCosgrave 2 101
(K R Burke) *mid-div: rdn over 3f out: one pce fnl 2f* **33/1**

44/6 8 6 **Kong (IRE)**[20] 1650 5-9-0 100.. JHBowman 10 91
(J L Dunlop) *hld up: short-lived effrt over 2f out: n.d* **25/1**

-033 9 2 1/2 **Group Captain**[13] 1833 5-9-0 104.. JohnEgan 6 87
(R Charlton) *mid-div: hdwy over 2f out: sn edgd rt and btn* **14/1**

4-13 10 6 **Steppe Dancer (IRE)**[21] 1618 4-9-3 105........................... EddieAhern 1 80
(D J Coakley) *t.k.h: trckd ldrs: rdn and wknd 2f out* **7/1**[3]

2m 38.38s (-0.54) **Going Correction** +0.30s/f (Good) **10** Ran SP% **119.3**
Speed ratings (Par 111):113,112,111,110,110 108,108,104,102,98
CSF £191.87 TOTE £8.70: £2.60, £6.60, £3.40; EX 187.20.
Owner Mollers Racing **Bred** Eleanor Drake Rose Trust Et Al **Trained** Newmarket, Suffolk

FOCUS

A hot Listed race, run at an even gallop which stepped up inside the final half-mile. The winner is rated back to his best but the form is limited by the proximity of the placed horses.

NOTEBOOK

Ivy Creek(USA) was having his first crack at the trip, and came through with flying colours, making impressive late headway despite meeting trouble in running. Likely to improve again, he can make his mark back in Group company. (op 15-2 tchd 7-1)

Shahin(USA) ◆ ran an extraordinary race, looking likely to be tailed off early in the straight, but in the end only just being held by the Pattern-class winner. Still relatively unexposed, he can find a nice race over this distance. (op 20-1)

Foxhaven battled gamely after setting the pace and, with only two talented types finishing in front of him, emerged with plenty of credit. (op 16-1)

Into The Dark has not been quite at his best this season, but should step up a bit when the stable hits top form. (op 8-1 tchd 7-1)

Alfie Flits's stamina only began to kick in too late, but by then the superior class of the first two home had taken the race by storm. However, he showed distinct signs of a revival here, leaving his poor performance on the All-Weather in the Winter Derby behind him. (op 11-2)

Day Flight was a strong favourite, but has not reached his peak in two races this season, and the way he faded was disappointing. Official explanation: jockey said horse lost its action and was wrong behind (tchd 7-4)

Group Captain made a promising effort early in the straight, but he again found this level beyond him when it came to the crunch. That said, he had run better than this in Listed company on his previous outing.

Steppe Dancer(IRE) Official explanation: jockey said colt was unsuited by the track and the good ground

2217 ORGANIC RESEARCH CENTRE STKS (H'CAP) 6f
7:50 (7:50) (Class 5) (0-70,66) 4-Y-0+ £3,238 (£963; £481; £240) Stalls Low

Form RPR

0-01 1 **Osiris Way**[9] 1946 5-9-6 **64** 6ex.. JimCrowley 1 83+
(P R Chamings) *mde all: pushed clr fnl f* **7/2**[2]

21 2 3 **Vegas Boys**[2] 2143 4-9-8 **66** 6ex...................................... SteveDrowne 7 76
(M Wigham) *wnt lft s: hdwy over 2f out: r.o to chse wnr fnl f* **2/1**[1]

2640 3 2 **George The Second**[4] 2088 4-9-4 **65**................. RichardKingscote(3) 2 69
(Mrs H Sweeting) *chsd wnr tl one pce fnl f* **10/1**

/000 4 2 1/2 **Charming Ballet (IRE)**[13] 1847 4-9-1 **59**........................(p) JHBowman 9 56
(N P Littmoden) *racd wd in tch: wknd ins fnl f* **12/1**

20-0 5 shd **Inka Dancer (IRE)**[42] 1118 5-9-1 **59**......................... CatherineGannon 4 55
(B Palling) *chsd ldrs 4f* **25/1**

3-40 6 1 1/4 **Supreme Kiss**[38] 1212 4-8-10 **54**..................................(b) EddieAhern 3 46
(Mrs N Smith) *in tch: rdn over 2f out: wknd 1f out* **16/1**

2206 7 shd **Quality Street**[7] 1991 5-8-13 **64**...........................(v[1]) JosephWalsh(7) 6 56
(P Butler) *squeezed out s: prom after 2f: rdn 1/2-way: wknd over 1f out* **10/1**

500- 8 10 **Marker**[188] 6595 7-8-6 **57**... HaddenFrost(7) 5 19
(J D Frost) *wnt rt s: a bhd: eased ins fnl f* **4/1**[3]

1m 13.08s (0.23) **Going Correction** +0.075s/f (Good) **8** Ran SP% **111.2**
Speed ratings (Par 103):101,97,94,91,90 89,89,75
CSF £10.25 CT £58.50 TOTE £4.00: £1.70, £1.30, £3.40; EX 7.80.

Owner Mrs Alexandra J Chandris **Bred** Whitsbury Manor Stud **Trained** Baughurst, Hants

FOCUS

A modest sprint, but with an improving winner who was relatively unexposed at the trip. The form looks solid rated through the runner-up.

2218 ECOLOGIST STKS (H'CAP) 1m 1f 192y

8:20 (8:21) (Class 4) (0-80,80) 4-Y-0+ £5,181 (£1,541; £770; £384) Stalls High

Form RPR

0560 **1** **Fort Churchill (IRE)**[14] 1822 6-9-7 **80**.........................(bt) PatCosgrave 1 94
(B Ellison) *mid-div: hdwy over 2f out: led wl over 1f out: rdn clr fnl f* **7/2**[1]

1135 **2** 5 **Lisathedaddy**[15] 1783 5-9-4 **80**............................ RichardKingscote(3) 2 84
(B G Powell) *hld up in rr: hdwy over 2f out: chsd wnr fnl f* **9/2**[2]

0-00 **3** 2 ½ **Kavachi (IRE)**[20] 1655 4-8-3 **62** oh1 ow1.................. RichardMullen 3 61
(G L Moore) *hld up: hdwy whn n.m.r 2f out: r.o fnl f: nvr nrr* **11/1**

00 **4** ½ **Paraguay (USA)**[7] 2004 4-8-9 **73**.............................. ColinHaddon(5) 8 71
(Miss V Haigh) *hld up in rr: rdn over 2f out: styd on fnl f: nvr nr to chal* **12/1**

5060 **5** 2 **Cape Greko**[10] 1922 5-9-3 **76**.. JHBowman 9 70
(B G Powell) *chsd ldrs: led briefly 2f out: wknd fnl f* **8/1**

5-02 **6** 1 **Shout (IRE)**[10] 1922 4-9-3 **76**.. EddieAhern 11 68
(J W Hills) *chsd ldrs: rdn over 3f out: wknd ins fnl f* **11/2**[3]

6-00 **7** ¾ **Punta Galera (IRE)**[25] 1524 4-9-5 **78**.......................(b) RichardHughes 5 69
(R Hannon) *bhd: rdn over 2f out: styd on past btn horses* **12/1**

06-6 **8** 3 **Jamaahir (USA)**[14] 1811 4-8-4 **63**................................ ChrisCatlin 6 48
(S Lycett) *led tl rdn and hdd 2f out: steadily wknd* **12/1**

3-40 **9** 3 **Duelling Banjos**[25] 1521 8-8-5 **64**.................................. JohnEgan 12 43
(J Akehurst) *mid-div: rdn over 3f out: wknd over 1f out* **12/1**

0640 **10** 5 **Prime Powered (IRE)**[14] 1813 6-8-13 **72**....................... JamesDoyle 4 41
(R M Beckett) *mid-div: effrt 3f out: sn btn* **12/1**

0-50 **11** 6 **Barathea Dreams (IRE)**[14] 1819 6-8-11 **70**.................... MartinDwyer 7 27
(J S Moore) *trckd ldrs tl wknd over 2f out* **9/1**

2m 9.34s (1.59) **Going Correction** +0.30s/f (Good) **11** Ran SP% **123.7**

Speed ratings (Par 105):105,101,99,98,97 96,95,93,90,86 82

CSF £19.88 CT £163.96 TOTE £5.50: £2.10, £1.90, £3.80; EX 24.80.

Owner L D Gamble and Mr & Mrs J H Mathias **Bred** P H Betts **Trained** Norton, N Yorks

■ Stewards' Enquiry : Richard Mullen two-day ban: careless riding (Jun 12-13)

FOCUS

A moderate handicap that could be a little better than rated. The pace did not look anything special, with the front-runners fading though lack of stamina rather than because they went too fast.

Barathea Dreams(IRE) Official explanation: jockey said gelding moved badly and hung

2219 GOODWOOD FARM SHOP MAIDEN FILLIES' STKS 1m

8:55 (8:58) (Class 5) 3-Y-0+ £3,238 (£963; £481; £240) Stalls High

Form RPR

5-3 **1** **Passing Hour (USA)**[21] 1620 3-8-9 .... JHBowman 16 70+
(G A Butler) *hld up: rdn to ld over 1f out: drvn out* **5/2**[2]

5 **2** nk **Royal Secrets (IRE)**[20] 1685 3-8-9 .... ChrisCatlin 15 66
(E A L Dunlop) *s.i.s: hdwy over 3f out: pressed wnr ins fnl f* **16/1**

0 **3** 1 ¼ **Roxie Princess (IRE)**[13] 1841 3-8-9 .... TPO'Shea 2 63
(J A R Toller) *chsd ldrs: kpt on ins fnl f* **66/1**

30 **4** ¾ **Etain (IRE)**[21] 1639 3-8-9 .... AdamKirby 3 61
(W R Swinburn) *chsd ldrs: styd on one pce ins fnl 2f* **12/1**

5 ¾ **Safwa (IRE)** 3-8-9 .... MartinDwyer 8 60+
(Sir Michael Stoute) *slowly away: twrds rr when hmpd on ins 4f out: sn rdn: kpt on but nvr nr to chal* **7/4**[1]

06 **6** ½ **Jawaaneb (USA)**[21] 1632 3-8-9 .... EddieAhern 11 58
(J L Dunlop) *trckd ldrs: effrt 3f out: one pce after* **20/1**

7 hd **Bundle Up** 4-9-6 .... IanMongan 6 58+
(Mrs L J Mongan) *slowly away: in rr: hdwy whn nt clr run over 3f out: kpt on but nvr nr to chal* **66/1**

43 **8** nk **Crown Office (USA)**[29] 1433 3-8-9 .... JimCrowley 10 57
(H Morrison) *led tl rdn and hdd wl over 1f out: sn wknd* **14/1**

9 2 ½ **Atayeb (USA)** 3-8-10 ow1................................ RichardHughes 4 52
(M P Tregoning) *slowly away: nvr bttr than mid-div* **6/1**[3]

U00 **10** hd **Silver Surprise**[8] 1961 3-8-6 .... MarcHalford(3) 12 51
(J J Bridger) *chsd ldrs: rdn over 3f out: wknd over 1f out* **100/1**

4- **11** 1 ½ **Dramatic Touch**[169] 6821 3-8-9 .... SteveDrowne 9 48+
(G Wragg) *in tch tl wknd wl over 1f out* **16/1**

00 **12** 1 ½ **Condi (IRE)**[11] 1901 3-8-9 .... JohnEgan 7 44
(A J Lidderdale) *a in rr* **33/1**

13 1 ¼ **Rustenberg** 3-8-9 .... RichardMullen 13 41
(E F Vaughan) *chsd ldrs tl wknd 3f out* **33/1**

14 13 **Krasivaya (IRE)** 3-8-9 .... PatCosgrave 5 11
(J R Boyle) *slowly away: a wl in rr* **16/1**

00 **F** **Fraamtastic Too**[22] 1606 3-8-6 .... RichardKingscote(3) 14 —
(Jamie Poulton) *in rr whn stmbld and fell 4f out* **100/1**

1m 45.02s (4.75) **Going Correction** +0.30s/f (Good)

WFA 3 from 4yo 11lb **15** Ran SP% **126.8**

Speed ratings (Par 100):88,87,86,85,84 84,84,83,81,81 79,78,77,64,—

CSF £43.27 TOTE £3.50: £1.70, £2.90, £8.60; EX 60.70.

Owner Sangster Family **Bred** Swettenham Stud **Trained** Blewbury, Oxon

■ Stewards' Enquiry : Martin Dwyer one-day ban: careless riding (Jun 13)

FOCUS

A fair maiden, but there was a modest pace and the well-backed favourite met trouble in running. The form makes some sense but is far from solid.

T/Plt: £210.50 to a £1 stake. Pool: £69,461.45. 240.80 winning tickets. T/Qpdt: £26.80 to a £1 stake. Pool: £3,978.20. 109.70 winning tickets. JS

1902 WOLVERHAMPTON (A.W) (L-H)

Friday, June 1

OFFICIAL GOING: Standard

Wind: Almost nil Weather: Overcast

2220 STAY AT THE WOLVERHAMPTON HOLIDAY INN CLAIMING STKS 5f 216y(P)

2:00 (2:00) (Class 6) 3-Y-0+ £2,730 (£806; £403) Stalls Low

Form RPR

2204 **1** **Mistral Sky**[11] 1899 8-9-5 63...(v) MickyFenton 8 60
(Stef Liddiard) *sn led: hdd over 4f out: led over 2f out: drvn out* **3/1**[1]

2214 **2** 1 ¼ **Blackheath (IRE)**[11] 1891 11-9-1 56.................................... SimonWhitworth 6 54+
(D Nicholls) *chsd ldrs: nt clr run and hmpd over 1f out: r.o wl towards fin* **9/2**[2]

0036 **3** nk **Boisdale (IRE)**[32] 1344 9-9-3 41.................................... RichardThomas 9 53
(P S Felgate) *chsd ldrs: rdn: edgd lft and ev ch over 1f out: styd on same pce ins fnl f* **40/1**

4514 **4** ¾ **Phinerine**[88] 622 4-9-0 54...(b) TolleyDean(5) 1 53
(Miss J E Foster) *hld up: hdwy 1/2-way: rdn over 1f out: edgd lft and styd on same pce ins fnl f* **8/1**

0510 **5** hd **Le Chiffre (IRE)**[18] 1729 5-9-0 57.................................(b) LukeMorris(5) 11 52
(R A Harris) *mid-div: rdn 1/2-way: hdwy over 1f out: styd on* **13/2**

-006 **6** 2 ½ **Superjain**[10] 1912 3-8-2 54.................................... DavidKinsella 10 36
(J M Jefferson) *mid-div: rdn and lost pl 1/2-way: hung lft and styd on ins fnl f* **40/1**

0000 **7** nk **Dark Moon**[58] 912 4-8-8 48.................................(v[1]) DeanMcKeown 3 33
(D Shaw) *s.s: a in rr* **10/1**

-000 **8** shd **Tag Team (IRE)**[8] 1977 6-9-5 65.................................(v) StephenDonohoe 7 44
(John A Harris) *led over 4f out: rdn and hdd over 2f out: wknd fnl f* **11/2**[3]

-050 **9** nk **Dancing Deano (IRE)**[10] 1921 5-8-10 49.........(v) RussellKennemore(5) 5 39
(R Hollinshead) *sn pushed along in rr: hmpd over 4f out: hung lft ins fnl f: n.d* **10/1**

3430 **10** 1 ½ **Laith (IRE)**[22] 1596 4-9-2 48...(p) ColinHaddon(5) 2 40
(Miss V Haigh) *s.i.s: hdwy over 2f out: wknd over 1f out* **10/1**

-500 **11** 5 **Brynris**[35] 1282 3-8-5 36.................................... EdwardCreighton 4 15
(Mrs G S Rees) *chsd ldrs: rdn over 2f out: sn wknd: in rr whn hmpd ins fnl f* **100/1**

1m 15.15s (-0.66) **Going Correction** -0.075s/f (Stan)

WFA 3 from 4yo+ 8lb **11** Ran SP% **116.2**

Speed ratings (Par 101):101,99,98,97,97 94,93,93,93,91 84

CSF £15.73 TOTE £4.00: £1.60, £2.00, £5.40; EX 17.80 TRIFECTA Not won..There were no claims in this race.

Owner Shefford Valley Stud **Bred** Peter Nelson **Trained** Great Shefford, Berks

■ Stewards' Enquiry : Colin Haddon three-day ban: careless riding (Jun 12-14)

FOCUS

A run-of-the mill claimer but the form appears sound enough, despite the proximity of the third.

Le Chiffre(IRE) Official explanation: jockey said gelding hung right-handed

Superjain Official explanation: jockey said filly hung left-handed

2221 SPONSOR A RACE BY CALLING 0870 220 2442 H'CAP 5f 20y(P)

2:35 (2:35) (Class 6) (0-55,53) 3-Y-0+ £2,388 (£705; £352) Stalls Low

Form RPR

0000 **1** **Sir Loin**[21] 1640 6-8-8 **50**.................................(b[1]) DanielleMcCreery(7) 9 63
(N Tinkler) *chsd ldr: r.o to ld wl ins fnl f* **25/1**

4-30 **2** 1 ½ **One Way Ticket**[24] 1557 7-9-3 **52**.................................(p) MickyFenton 11 60
(J M Bradley) *sn led: rdn over 1f out: edgd rt and hdd wl ins fnl f* **5/1**[1]

-005 **3** ½ **Davids Mark**[30] 1405 7-9-0 **52**.................................... PatrickMathers(3) 3 58
(J R Jenkins) *hld up: hdwy u.p over 1f out: r.o: nt rch ldrs* **6/1**[3]

0205 **4** nk **Dysonic (USA)**[11] 1902 5-8-12 **50**.................................(v) AndrewElliott(3) 10 55
(J Balding) *a.p: rdn over 1f out: edgd lft and styd on same pce ins fnl f* **11/2**[2]

6404 **5** 1 ¾ **Cosmic Destiny (IRE)**[7] 1991 5-9-3 **52**.................................... LPKeniry 6 51
(E F Vaughan) *trckd ldrs: rdn over 1f out: no ex fnl f* **5/1**[1]

2330 **6** nk **Thoughtsofstardom**[60] 892 4-9-3 **52**.........................(be) HayleyTurner 5 50
(P S McEntee) *s.i.s: hld up: styd on appr fnl f: nvr nrr* **6/1**[3]

0002 **7** 1 ½ **City For Conquest (IRE)**[18] 1729 4-9-1 **50**.........(b) StephenDonohoe 12 42
(John A Harris) *s.i.s: hld up: nvr nrr* **7/1**

6-00 **8** ¾ **Dukestreet**[9] 1946 6-9-4 **53**.................................... DeanMcKeown 8 42
(D Shaw) *hld up: rdn and hung lft fr over 1f out: n.d* **50/1**

0-00 **9** ¾ **Alone It Stands (IRE)**[3] 2121 4-9-3 **52**.................(v[1]) SimonWhitworth 7 39
(D Nicholls) *hld up: n.d* **25/1**

-300 **10** 2 **Glenargo (USA)**[112] 403 4-8-10 **50**.................... RussellKennemore(5) 1 30
(S T Lewis) *chsd ldrs: rdn 1/2-way: wknd over 1f out* **22/1**

2106 **11** hd **Kitchen Sink (IRE)**[70] 743 5-9-3 **52**.........................(e) FergusSweeney 13 31
(Jean-Rene Auvray) *mid-div: rdn over 2f out: sn wknd* **14/1**

006- **12** shd **Knead The Dough**[221] 6142 6-8-12 **52**.................... NataliaGemelova(5) 2 30
(A E Price) *chsd ldrs over 3f* **16/1**

62.18 secs (-0.64) **Going Correction** -0.075s/f (Stan) **12** Ran SP% **116.3**

Speed ratings (Par 101):102,99,98,98,95 95,92,91,90,87 86,86

CSF £138.97 CT £876.83 TOTE £23.00: £3.70, £2.00, £2.90; EX 161.60 TRIFECTA Not won..

Owner W F Burton **Bred** Britton House Stud And C Gregson **Trained** Langton, N Yorks

FOCUS

An open-looking sprint handicap but only two got seriously involved. The form appears sound with the placed horses to form.

2222 COMBINE BUSINESS WITH PLEASURE (S) STKS 1m 5f 194y(P)

3:10 (3:10) (Class 6) 4-Y-0+ £2,047 (£604; £302) Stalls Low

Form RPR

1303 **1** **Mister Completely (IRE)**[41] 1152 6-9-4 55............. EdwardCreighton 7 68
(Ms J S Doyle) *chsd ldrs: led over 5f out: rdn over 1f out: edgd lft: all out* **4/1**[3]

0040 **2** nk **Birthday Star (IRE)**[34] 1314 5-8-13 57.................................... BrettDoyle 2 63
(W J Musson) *chsd ldrs: rdn over 2f out: r.o wl towards fin* **5/2**[2]

2443 **3** 1 ¼ **Tresor Secret (FR)**[11] 1907 7-8-13 57.................................... LPKeniry 1 61
(J Gallagher) *led 1f: chsd ldr: rdn over 1f out: styng on same pce whn hit over hd by rival's whip ins fnl f* **5/4**[1]

3000 **4** 7 **Reminiscent (IRE)**[18] 1730 8-8-11 52.........................(b) JackMitchell(7) 6 56
(B P J Baugh) *hld up: hdwy over 5f out: rdn: hung lft and wknd over 1f out* **10/1**

0/ **5** 156 **Nibbles (IRE)**[1012] 4997 5-8-13 0.................................... DeanMcKeown 3 —
(D W Chapman) *dwlt: hld up: plld hrd: bhd fnl 8f* **25/1**

/00- **6** 45 **Royalties**[242] 5741 5-8-4 38 ow1.................................... ColinHaddon(5) 4 —
(M A Allen) *led after 1f: hdd & wknd over 5f out* **33/1**

3m 9.81s (2.44) **Going Correction** -0.075s/f (Stan) **6** Ran SP% **108.9**

Speed ratings (Par 101):90,89,89,85,— —

CSF £13.49 TOTE £4.00: £1.90, £1.70; EX 14.40.Birthday Star was claimed by A Juckes for £6,000.

Owner Ms J S Doyle **Bred** Eamonn Griffin **Trained** Upper Lambourn, Berks

FOCUS

A long-distance seller that was run at a very slow early pace. The form is rated through the winner but probably does not amount to much.

Royalties Official explanation: vet said mare finished distressed

2223 HOTEL & CONFERENCING AT WOLVERHAMPTON H'CAP 1m 4f 50y(P)

3:45 (3:45) (Class 5) (0-70,68) 3-Y-0 £3,238 (£963; £481; £240) Stalls Low

Form RPR

305- **1** **Abounding**[248] 5597 3-8-8 **55**.................................... FergusSweeney 6 69+
(R M Beckett) *hld up: hdwy over 5f out: chsd ldr over 2f out: led over 1f out: drvn out* **14/1**

04-2 **2** hd **Calzaghe (IRE)**[8] 1972 3-8-5 **57**.................................(v) WilliamBuick(5) 2 71
(A M Balding) *hld up: hdwy over 3f out: chsd wnr over 1f out: sn rdn and hung lft: styd on* **15/8**[1]

4203 **3** *14* **Anne Bronte**[7] [2008] 3-9-3 **67** .... GregFairley(3) 10 58
(M Johnston) *chsd ldr: led over 8f out: hdd & wknd over 1f out* **5/1**[3]

6-24 **4** *½* **Distant Sunset (IRE)**[10] [1917] 3-8-12 **59** .... DeanMcKeown 4 49
(B W Hills) *sn pushed along and prom: hmpd and stmbld after 1f: chsd ldr over 6f out: rdn over 2f out: sn hung lft and wknd* **2/1**[2]

00-0 **5** *1 ½* **Sew In Character**[41] [1166] 3-8-3 **50** .... RichardThomas 5 38
(M Blanshard) *led: hdd over 8f out: rdn over 5f out: wknd over 2f out* **50/1**

0464 **6** *hd* **Danalova**[32] [1353] 3-8-2 **49** oh4 .... HayleyTurner 3 37
(R A Fahey) *plld hrd and prom: rdn and wknd over 2f out* **16/1**

0-50 **7** *5* **Shady Green (IRE)**[37] [1238] 3-8-3 **53** .... DaleGibson 9 30
(M W Easterby) *prom 9f* **22/1**

004 **8** *34* **Camp Counsellor**[97] [553] 3-9-4 **65** .... BrettDoyle 8 —
(J A Osborne) *prom 8f* **8/1**

2m 39.05s (-3.37) **Going Correction** -0.075s/f (Stan) **8** Ran SP% **114.8**
Speed ratings (Par 99):108,107,98,98,97 97,93,71
CSF £40.91 CT £155.62 TOTE £20.60: £3.90, £1.10, £1.60; EX 51.00 TRIFECTA Not won..

Owner A D G Oldrey **Bred** A D G Oldrey **Trained** Whitsbury, Hants

■ Stewards' Enquiry : William Buick two-day ban: used whip with excessive frequency and without giving gelding time to respond (Jun 12-13)

FOCUS
A modest but interesting handicap, featuring several unexposed sorts, and two of those fought out the finish. The sixth is probably the best guide to the level.

Danalova Official explanation: jockey said filly hung right-handed

2224 DINE IN HORIZONS RESTAURANT H'CAP 1m 141y(P)
4:25 (4:26) (Class 6) (0-65,63) 3-Y-O **£2,388** (£705; £352) **Stalls** Low

Form RPR

00-5 **1** **Mountain Cat (IRE)**[83] [661] 3-9-0 **59** .... DavidKinsella 5 65+
(W J Musson) *chsd ldr: rdn to ld 1f out: r.o* **12/1**

0-20 **2** *1 ¼* **Susanna's Prospect (IRE)**[18] [1731] 3-9-4 **63** ....(b[1]) BrettDoyle 1 66
(B J Meehan) *led: rdn and hdd 1f out: no ex towards fin* **7/1**

-403 **3** *1 ¼* **Ice Box (IRE)**[29] [1432] 3-8-7 **55** .... GregFairley(3) 3 55
(M Johnston) *chsd ldrs: rdn over 3f out: edgd lft ins fnl f: styd on* **9/2**[1]

5654 **4** *¾* **Here's Blue Chip (IRE)**[20] [1672] 3-9-0 **59** ....(v) StephenDonohoe 9 57
(P W D'Arcy) *hld up: hdwy over 2f out: sn rdn: styd on same pce fnl f* **5/1**[2]

0-05 **5** *1* **Lindhoven (USA)**[31] [1375] 3-9-3 **62** ....(b[1]) HayleyTurner 8 58
(C E Brittain) *hld up in tch: rdn over 2f out: hung lft over 1f out: styd on same pce* **14/1**

06-5 **6** *1* **Exit Strategy (IRE)**[13] [1850] 3-8-7 **57** .... PatrickHills(5) 2 51
(W J Haggas) *chsd ldrs: rdn over 2f out: wknd ins fnl f* **11/2**[3]

0063 **7** *nk* **Sixfields Flyer (IRE)**[25] [1538] 3-8-8 **60** .... KMay(7) 4 53
(Pat Eddery) *mid-div: outpcd over 2f out: styd on ins fnl f* **11/2**[3]

660- **8** *2 ½* **Namarian (IRE)**[258] [5366] 3-8-7 **52** .... SimonWhitworth 12 39
(T D Easterby) *dwlt: hld up: rdn and wknd over 2f out* **33/1**

-500 **9** *½* **Hard As Iron**[30] [1399] 3-8-7 **52** .... DaleGibson 10 38
(M Blanshard) *hld up: hdwy u.p over 2f out: hung lft and wknd over 1f out* **9/1**

0-04 **10** *9* **Wisdom's Kiss**[27] [1482] 3-8-11 **59** .... AndrewElliott(3) 11 25
(J D Bethell) *sn outpcd* **11/1**

1m 51.72s (-0.04) **Going Correction** -0.075s/f (Stan) **10** Ran SP% **113.8**
Speed ratings (Par 97):97,95,94,94,93 92,92,89,89,81
CSF £91.08 CT £437.92 TOTE £15.20: £2.80, £2.60, £1.40; EX 94.50 Trifecta £42.90 Part won. Pool £60.56 - 0.20 winning units..

Owner S Rudolf **Bred** Mrs Mary Gallagher **Trained** Newmarket, Suffolk

FOCUS
A modest contest that was steadily run and close to the pace was the place to be. The race could be rated a little higher.

2225 BOOK ONLINE AT WOLVERHAMPTON-RACECOURSE.CO.UK H'CAP 7f 32y(P)
5:00 (5:00) (Class 6) (0-60,60) 4-Y-O+ **£2,388** (£705; £352) **Stalls** High

Form RPR

3060 **1** **Royal Orissa**[11] [1885] 5-8-11 **53** .... BrettDoyle 7 59
(D Haydn Jones) *plld hrd: trckd ldr tl led over 5f out: rdn over 1f out: jst hld on* **11/2**[2]

6200 **2** *hd* **Lucius Verrus (USA)**[9] [1947] 7-9-2 **58** ....(v) DeanMcKeown 1 63
(D Shaw) *chsd ldrs: rdn over 1f out: r.o* **13/2**[3]

0-64 **3** *¾* **Champain Sands (IRE)**[30] [1413] 8-9-2 **58** .... StephenDonohoe 8 61
(E J Alston) *s.i.s: hld up: hdwy over 1f out: r.o* **7/2**[1]

2000 **4** *shd* **Benny The Bus**[20] [1673] 5-8-13 **55** .... DaleGibson 5 58
(Mrs G S Rees) *led: hdd over 5f out: chsd wnr: rdn and ev ch ins fnl f: no ex towards fin* **10/1**

2020 **5** *nk* **Dasheena**[9] [1946] 4-8-10 **55** ....(be) GregFairley(3) 2 60+
(A J McCabe) *hld up in tch: lost pl 4f out: nt clr run over 2f out: r.o ins fnl f: nt rch ldrs* **11/2**[2]

21-0 **6** *shd* **Ours (IRE)**[35] [1280] 4-8-13 **58** ....(p) AndrewElliott(3) 4 60
(J D Bethell) *mid-div: hdwy over 2f out: rdn over 1f out: styd on* **7/1**

3403 **7** *1 ¼* **Golden Spectrum (IRE)**[11] [1886] 8-8-11 **58** ....(b) LukeMorris(5) 3 57
(R A Harris) *mid-div: hdwy u.p over 1f out: styd on same pce ins fnl f* **7/1**

60-0 **8** *5* **Regal Dream (IRE)**[46] [1064] 5-8-11 **58** .... PatrickHills(5) 11 43
(J W Unett) *s.s: hmpd 4f out: sme hdwy over 1f out: n.d* **10/1**

06-0 **9** *¾* **Psycho Cat**[23] [142] 4-8-12 **59** .... RussellKennemore(5) 9 42
(S T Lewis) *hld up: rdn over 3f out: hung lft fnl f: n.d* **50/1**

1005 **10** *nk* **Mister Benji**[66] [806] 8-8-6 **55** ....(p) SoniaEaton(7) 10 37
(B P J Baugh) *chsd ldrs 5f* **16/1**

1m 30.09s (-0.31) **Going Correction** -0.075s/f (Stan) **10** Ran SP% **117.3**
Speed ratings (Par 101):98,97,96,96,96 96,94,89,88,88
CSF £41.44 CT £147.16 TOTE £6.20: £2.50, £2.60, £1.50; EX 70.10 Trifecta £44.40 Part won. Pool £62.58 - 0.20 winning units. Place 6 £61.91, Place 5 £36.18.

Owner Llewelyn, Runeckles **Bred** Hellwood Stud Farm **Trained** Efail Isaf, Rhondda C Taff

FOCUS
A moderate but competitive handicap with the winner rated to this year's best and the runner-up back to form.

T/Plt: £34.80 to a £1 stake. Pool: £40,613.50. 850.30 winning tickets. T/Qpdt: £10.80 to a £1 stake. Pool: £2,418.80. 165.00 winning tickets. CR

2226 - 2230a (Foreign Racing) - See Raceform Interactive

[2207]EPSOM (L-H)
Saturday, June 2

OFFICIAL GOING: Good
Wind: Almost nil Weather: Sunny, warm

2231 VODAFONE MAKE THE MOST OF NOW STKS (HERITAGE H'CAP) 1m 2f 18y
2:00 (2:01) (Class 2) (0-105,98) 3-Y-O
£46,740 (£13,995; £6,997; £3,502; £1,747; £877) **Stalls** Low

Form RPR

1131 **1** **Zaham (USA)**[14] [1835] 3-9-2 **93** .... RHills 10 103+
(M Johnston) *pressed ldr: rdn to ld over 2f out: hdd ins fnl f: sn led again: styd on wl* **7/2**[2]

-311 **2** *nk* **Fever**[19] [1722] 3-8-3 **80** .... JimmyQuinn 1 89+
(R Hannon) *prom: 3rd and rdn st: chsd ldr over 1f out: led ins fnl f but hung lft and sn hdd: nt rcvr* **14/1**

6-00 **3** *3* **Golden Dagger (IRE)**[14] [1835] 3-8-8 **85** .... NCallan 2 89
(K A Ryan) *lw: trckd ldrs: 5th st: effrt over 2f out: chsd ldng pair fnl f: hanging lft and no imp* **33/1**

2-45 **4** *2* **Buccellati**[14] [1835] 3-8-9 **86** .... FrancisNorton 12 86+
(A M Balding) *hld up in last trio: 12th st: prog sn after: styd on wl fr 2f out to take 4th nr fin: hopeless task* **11/2**[3]

611- **5** *½* **Ekhtiaar**[230] [5989] 3-9-0 **91** .... MartinDwyer 4 93+
(J H M Gosden) *lw: hld up wl in rr: stmbld bdly over 4f out: 13th st: styd on wl fnl 2f: nt rch ldrs* **20/1**

1221 **6** *½* **Bergonzi (IRE)**[12] [1898] 3-8-8 **85** .... SteveDrowne 8 83
(J H M Gosden) *chsd ldrs: 6th st: no imp on ldrs 2f out: kpt on* **16/1**

-432 **7** *nk* **Duke Of Tuscany**[14] [1835] 3-9-7 **98** .... RichardHughes 5 95
(R Hannon) *b: led at str pce: rdn and hdd over 2f out: hanging lft after: wknd fnl f* **10/1**

1-26 **8** *nk* **Regal Flush**[14] [1835] 3-9-1 **92** .... KerrinMcEvoy 14 89
(Sir Michael Stoute) *lw: hld up: prog and 7th st: rdn over 2f out: one pce and no imp on ldrs* **11/4**[1]

-430 **9** *1 ¾* **Bed Fellow (IRE)**[17] [1773] 3-8-5 **82** .... JohnEgan 3 79+
(A P Jarvis) *swtg: hld up in midfield: 8th and gng wl enough st: rdn and no prog 2f out* **25/1**

4-53 **10** *14* **Billy Dane (IRE)**[7] [2037] 3-8-13 **90** .... PaulHanagan 7 57
(R A Fahey) *t.k.h early: hld up on inner: 10th st: effrt 3f out: no prog 2f out: wknd: t.o* **20/1**

02-1 **11** *5* **Toccata (IRE)**[21] [1685] 3-8-1 **78** .... NickyMackay 13 35
(D M Simcock) *prom: 4th st: sn wknd: t.o* **28/1**

2-12 **12** *1 ¼* **Jeer (IRE)**[17] [1773] 3-8-9 **86** .... DO'Donohoe 9 41
(E A L Dunlop) *a wl in rr: last and rdn st: no prog: t.o* **7/1**

6204 **13** *1 ½* **Putra Square**[23] [1605] 3-9-1 **92** .... TQuinn 11 44
(P F I Cole) *lw: hld up in last trio: 11th st: brief effrt 3f out: sn btn: eased fnl 2f: t.o* **33/1**

20-6 **14** *nk* **Frosty Night (IRE)**[44] [1110] 3-8-8 **85** .... JoeFanning 6 37
(M Johnston) *settled in midfield: 9th and wkng st: bhd and eased 2f out: t.o* **28/1**

2m 7.94s (-1.10) **Going Correction** +0.025s/f (Good) **14** Ran SP% **124.6**
Speed ratings (Par 105):105,104,102,100,100 99,99,99,98,86 82,81,80,80
CSF £48.41 CT £1421.01 TOTE £4.80: £2.10, £3.20, £6.50; EX 64.00 Trifecta £1398.40 Part won. Pool: £1,969.70 - 0.30 winning units..

Owner Hamdan Al Maktoum **Bred** London Thoroughbred Services Ltd **Trained** Middleham Moor, N Yorks

■ Stewards' Enquiry : Jimmy Quinn one-day ban: careless riding (Jun 13)

FOCUS
A decent, competitive handicap in which Newbury's London Gold Cup provided the key. The pace was not that strong and the form might be quite as hot as ususal, but it nevertheless looks a race that should provide more than its share of future winners.

NOTEBOOK
Zaham(USA) ◆ is a progressive individual and, ridden up with the pace as usual, confirmed form with those that had finished behind him in the London Gold Cup at Newbury in the gamest fashion. After cruising into the lead at the quarter-mile pole, he looked sure to be beaten as the runner-up drew alongside and went a neck up inside the final furlong. However, as that rival drifted down the camber and faltered, he took his chance to snatch back the lead and was increasing it at the finish. He has several options at Royal Ascot, but the Hampton Court Stakes over this trip looks the most suitable, and he will take some beating there. (op 9-2 tchd 5-1 in places)
Fever, another progressive colt, was taking a big step up in class having dead-heated in a 0-75 Class 5 handicap at Windsor last time. He delivered his challenge at what looked like the perfect time and went a neck ahead, but he drifted down the camber and faltered, and the game winner needed no second bidding. Considering his owners it is likely he will go to Royal Ascot, and if they wish to avoid the winner the choice appears to be between the Britannia and King George V Handicaps. (op 16-1 tchd 20-1 in places)
Golden Dagger(IRE), who had been unlucky in running behind today's winner at Newbury, got a clear passage this time and finished closer on 8lb better terms. She is a likeable sort and looks capable of picking up a good handicap this season, although there are a number of fillies' Listed races at around this trip which could give her the chance to earn black type.
Buccellati, whose style of racing tends to mean he meets trouble in running, found the gaps this time, but he had been given an awful lot to do and was never going to get there in time. He remains capable of better. (op 5-1)
Ekhtiaar ◆, who has been gelded since winning twice on Lingfield's Polytrack at the end of last season, was the unlucky horse of the race, getting squeezed against the rail and stumbling at the halfway mark before running on really well in the straight. He looks capable of winning a good race with this seasonal debut under his belt and he is another who will be interesting if connections opt for one of the handicaps at Royal Ascot.
Bergonzi(IRE), another stepping up in grade, was also dropping in trip and, having been close enough if good enough turning in, could not find the extra gear requirred at this level. However, he is a consistent sort and helps set the level of the form. (op 14-1)
Duke Of Tuscany, who had been runner-up to today's winner at Newbury, was better off with that rival but had been raised 3lb himself. He adopted similar tactics to that race, but this time could not respond when taken on by his old rival. He has had some pretty stiff tasks this season and does not give himself an easy time in his races, so might be ready for a break. (op 12-1)
Regal Flush was well backed to put a slightly disappointing effort at Newbury behind him, but was forced to race wide from his draw and never got competitive, finishing behind all of those who re-opposed here. (op 10-3 tchd 7-2 in places)
Bed Fellow(IRE), coltish beforehand, was a stone better off with the winner for a three and a half-length beating at Kempton earlier in the season. He stuck to the rail throughout, but was not good enough to land a serious blow. He seems best around a mile on soft ground.
Billy Dane(IRE) Official explanation: trainer said gelding did not handle the track
Toccata(IRE) Official explanation: trainer said filly was unsuited by the track
Frosty Night(IRE) got warm and misbehaved beforehand. (op 33-1)

2232 VODAFONE WOODCOTE STKS (LISTED RACE) 6f
2:30 (2:31) (Class 1) 2-Y-O

£17,034 (£6,456; £3,231; £1,611; £807; £405) Stalls High

Form RPR

1 **1** **Declaration Of War (IRE)**[14] 1846 2-9-0 0.................. RobertHavlin 11 100+
(P W Chapple-Hyam) *lw: racd wd: in tch: 9th st: rdn and prog over 2f out: chsd ldr 1f out: styd on wl to ld last 75yds* **9/2**[3]

1 **2** *1* **Bespoke Boy**[13] 1858 2-9-0 0.. LDettori 9 97
(P C Haslam) *lw: trckd ldr: carried wd and lft in ld ent st: kicked 2l clr wl over 1f out: collared last 75yds* **6/1**

11 **3** *nk* **Mount Pleasure (USA)**[31] 1390 2-9-3 0......................... MartinDwyer 1 99
(J A Osborne) *prom: lft chsng ldr ent st: rdn 2f out: clsd grad but lost 2nd 1f out: hanging lft but kpt on* **8/1**

3 **4** *1 1/2* **Berbice (IRE)**[8] 1989 2-9-0 0.. EddieAhern 8 92
(R Hannon) *hld up in tch: 8th st: prog over 2f out: chsd ldrs 1f out: one pce and no imp after* **20/1**

011 **5** *2* **Cracking (IRE)**[24] 1580 2-9-5 0............................ RichardHughes 6 91
(R Hannon) *lw: chsd ldrs: 7th and wl in tch st: outpcd 2f out: no real imp after* **11/1**

13 **6** *1/2* **Kersaint (IRE)**[31] 1390 2-9-0 0.. NCallan 10 84
(K A Ryan) *trckd ldrs: 5th st: cl enough over 2f out: sn outpcd: one pce after* **25/1**

1 **7** *nk* **Meeriss (IRE)**[22] 1622 2-9-0 0... JHBowman 4 83
(M R Channon) *prom: chsd ldng pair ent st: sn rdn: lost pl and struggling 2f out: one pce after* **14/1**

3 **8** *1* **Irish Jig (IRE)**[20] 1690 2-9-0 0... JMurtagh 13 80
(G M Lyons, Ire) *w'like: str: lw: restless stalls: racd wd in tch: 10th st: effrt over 2f out: sn outpcd and btn* **7/2**[1]

521 **9** *1/2* **Cee Bargara**[31] 1411 2-9-0 0... MJKinane 7 79
(J A Osborne) *hld up: sn outpcd: 12th and wl off the pce st: kpt on fnl 2f: no ch* **33/1**

1 **10** *7* **Lieutenant Pigeon**[15] 1801 2-9-0 0.................................... TedDurcan 2 58
(B Smart) *str: sn outpcd: 11th and wl off the pce st: no prog* **16/1**

11 **11** *2* **Mister Hardy**[49] 1043 2-9-0 0.. PaulHanagan 5 52
(R A Fahey) *w'like: t.k.h: trckd ldrs: 6th st: wknd over 2f out* **4/1**[2]

3626 **12** *6* **Baytown Blaze**[2] 2183 2-8-9 0.. JohnEgan 3 29
(P S McEntee) *led: rn v wd ent st and hdd: wknd 2f out* **66/1**

13 *5* **Jermajesty (IRE)** 2-9-0 0.. AmirQuinn 12 19
(J R Boyle) *str: bit bkwd: s.i.s: bdly outpcd and a t.o* **100/1**

1m 10.45s (-0.18) **Going Correction** +0.025s/f (Good) **13** Ran SP% **120.7**

Speed ratings (Par 101):102,100,100,98,95 94,94,93,92,83 80,72,65

CSF £30.58 TOTE £5.20: £2.00, £2.00, £2.60; EX 40.40 Trifecta £180.40 Pool: £1,880.40 - 7.40 winning units..

Owner Mrs Violet Mercer **Bred** St Simon Foundation **Trained** Newmarket, Suffolk

FOCUS

An above-average renewal of this traditional Listed contest for juveniles, with 11 of the 13 being previous winners. It was strongly run and the form as some solidity down the field, with the sixth, seventh of ninth all close to their previous marks.

NOTEBOOK

Declaration Of War(IRE) ◆, who had scored at Newmarket despite looking in need of the experience, had clearly learned from that and, despite not handling the turn into the straight that well, stayed on strongly to get to the front near the finish. He will get further in time and, although his trainer would prefer to wait for a 7f event at Newmarket, the owners are reportedly keen to go to Royal Ascot for the Coventry Stakes, and this improving colt should go well in that event. (op 10-3)

Bespoke Boy, an athletic type who made all to win on his debut at Ripon, again showed plenty of speed and raced prominently, but he was carried slightly wide by the errant Baytown Blaze off the bend into the straight before being left in front. He looked sure to score halfway up the straight, but was caught late on. It would be no surprise if he renewed rivalry with today's winner at Royal Ascot, although he looks to have the speed for 5f. (op 15-2 tchd 8-1)

Mount Pleasure(USA), who won what looked a decent conditions stakes at Ascot on his previous outing, handled the extra furlong and easier ground well enough and made the most of his draw on the inside. He was keeping on well in the last furlong and is a fair guide to the level of the form. (tchd 15-2)

Berbice(IRE) ◆, who ran green when beaten in a maiden auction at Goodwood, showed the benefit of that outing by keeping on to finish on the heels of the principals. He looks sure to be winning his maiden soon and is bred to appreciate another furlong in time. (op 25-1)

Cracking(IRE), a speedy colt who won the Lily Agnes last time, was not sure to appreciate the extra furlong and easier ground, although the track should not have been a problem. He had his chance but did not pick up halfway up the straight and had to switch before running past tiring rivals. This exposed his limitations and a return to 5f for something like the Windsor Castle seems a likely option. (op 10-1 tchd 9-1)

Kersaint(IRE) finished further behind the today's third than he had done in the Garter Stakes. He did not appear totally comfortable on the track and faded in the last furlong and a half.

Meeriss(IRE), an athletic type stepping up following his maiden win at Hamilton, showed plenty of pace before tiring and may have more to offer, with his pedigree suggesting he will stay a fair bit further.

Irish Jig(IRE) came into this with some decent Irish maiden form and was well backed. Drawn on the outside, he was another who looked uncomfortable on the track and he failed to pick up when asked. Official explanation: jockey said colt was upset in the stalls (op 11-2)

Mister Hardy, the winner of his two previous races including the Brocklesby, showed plenty of early pace but his rider would have preferred him to settle better and it was no surprise that he faded out of contention in the straight. (op 7-2)

Baytown Blaze Official explanation: jockey said filly hung right

2233 VODAFONE DIOMED STKS (GROUP 3) 1m 114y
3:00 (3:00) (Class 1) 3-Y-O+ £42,585 (£16,140; £8,077; £4,027; £2,017) Stalls Low

Form RPR

2031 **1** **Blythe Knight (IRE)**[16] 1791 7-9-4 102...................... GrahamGibbons 2 113
(J J Quinn) *lw: hld up in 3rd: squeezed through to ld jst ins fnl 2f: rdn and styd on wl* **4/1**[2]

11-1 **2** *1* **Blue Ksar (FR)**[21] 1664 4-9-4 115...................................(t) LDettori 3 111
(Saeed Bin Suroor) *slowly away: hld up in last: smooth prog to chal 2f out: hung lft and nt qckn after* **4/5**[1]

20-0 **3** *3* **Welsh Emperor (IRE)**[17] 1770 8-9-4 113........................ MickyFenton 4 104
(T P Tate) *mde most to jst ins fnl 2f: one pce after: wkng nr fin* **8/1**

0543 **4** *3/4* **King Jock (USA)**[20] 1699 6-9-4 0.. PShanahan 5 102
(R J Osborne, Ire) *hld up in 4th: prog to chal 2f out: btn over 1f out: wknd fnl f* **13/2**[3]

-033 **5** *5* **Ordnance Row**[1] 2208 4-9-4 92.................................... RichardHughes 1 91
(R Hannon) *w ldr: nrly upsides 2f out: wknd wl over 1f out* **9/1**

1m 43.36s (-2.38) **Going Correction** +0.025s/f (Good) **5** Ran SP% **110.0**

Speed ratings (Par 113):111,110,107,106,102

CSF £7.70 TOTE £4.30: £1.90, £1.10; EX 8.20.

Owner Maxilead Limited **Bred** Gainsborough Stud Management Ltd **Trained** Settrington, N Yorks

FOCUS

A below-par renewal of this Group 3, but a worthy winner.

NOTEBOOK

Blythe Knight(IRE), whose attitude has been transformed since joining his current trainer and going hurdling, followed up his good win at York by taking his first Group 3. He had a tough task judged on official ratings, but always travelled well and, once squeezed through between the two leaders, he picked up well for pressure to hold off the favourite. His trainer had planned to give him a break after this, and will do so if the ground dries up. But he will bring him back in the autumn with the Prix Dollar at the Arc meeting in mind, and possibly then a return to hurdles, with the Champion Hurdle the long-term aim. (op 7-2)

Blue Ksar(FR), who missed the break and whose rider got Welsh Emperor's blindfold tangled around his arm, was settled at the back and came to have every chance, but edged down the camber when challenging and was always being kept at bay. He was top on official ratings but has not won above Listed class yet, which tends to confirm this was not the strongest of races for the grade. Connections feel he wants softer ground. (tchd 10-11 and Evens in a place)

Welsh Emperor(IRE) is a high-class performer at 6-7f, having been touched off in the Prix de la Foret last season. He was trying a new trip and did not get an uncontested lead, but battled back after being headed without totally convincing that he will be seen to best effect at this distance. Seven furlongs, a flat track and soft ground seem to be his ideal conditions. (op 7-1)

King Jock(USA), a fair performer at a similar level with form in Ireland and Dubai, is arguably best on a fast surface and, although he appeared to have every chance, he was left behind when the principals joined issue. (op 7-1)

Ordnance Row, who finished third in the handicap here the previous day, had a stiff task judged on official ratings. He kept the third company in front until fading in the closing stages. (op 16-1)

2234 VODAFONE "DASH" STKS (HERITAGE H'CAP) 5f
3:30 (3:31) (Class 2) 3-Y-O+

£46,740 (£13,995; £6,997; £3,502; £1,747; £877) Stalls High

Form RPR

00-3 **1** **Hogmaneigh (IRE)**[16] 1788 4-9-1 99........................ SaleemGolam(3) 15 109
(S C Williams) *settled wl in rr: prog and threaded through fr 2f out: drvn and r.o to ld last 75yds* **7/1**[2]

1032 **2** *nk* **Moorhouse Lad**[14] 1853 4-8-9 90.................................. TedDurcan 16 99
(B Smart) *b.hind: mostly chsd ldr: rdn to ld over 1f out: hdd and one pce last 75yds* **15/2**[3]

0-01 **3** *shd* **Caribbean Coral**[23] 1601 8-8-9 90 4ex..................... GrahamGibbons 17 99
(J J Quinn) *s.i.s: towards rr against nr side rail: prog over 1f out: got through ins fnl f: jst outpcd last 75yds* **10/1**

5-40 **4** *3/4* **Holbeck Ghyll (IRE)**[14] 1854 5-7-7 79 oh2.............(p) WilliamBuick(5) 12 85+
(A M Balding) *dwlt: wl in rr: nt clr run 3f out: swtchd to outer and rapid prog over 1f out: fin strly* **20/1**

00-1 **5** *hd* **Green Manalishi**[43] 1125 6-9-10 105...................................... NCallan 19 110
(K A Ryan) *pressed ldrs: rdn 1/2-way: clsd to chal 1f out: kpt on same pce last 100yds* **6/1**[1]

-601 **6** *shd* **Wyatt Earp (IRE)**[15] 1826 6-8-11 92 4ex......................... PaulHanagan 9 97+
(R A Fahey) *wl in rr: struggling u.p 2f out: str run fnl f: fin wl* **12/1**

2230 **7** *1/2* **Bond City (IRE)**[17] 1770 5-9-6 101... LDettori 13 104
(G R Oldroyd) *racd towards outer in midfield: prog fr 2f out: chsd ldrs ins fnl f: one pce last 100yds* **6/1**[1]

-165 **8** *3/4* **Merlin's Dancer**[29] 1456 7-9-0 95.. JohnEgan 5 95
(S Dow) *fast away: led and crossed to nr side rail: hdd over 1f out: wknd ins fnl f* **33/1**

0224 **9** *shd* **Corridor Creeper (FR)**[7] 2034 10-8-7 95...............(p) BarrySavage(7) 11 95
(J M Bradley) *w ldrs: lost pl u.p jst over 1f out: hanging lft and no ex ins fnl f* **16/1**

4530 **10** *1 1/4* **Machinist (IRE)**[21] 1651 7-8-9 90.................................. KerrinMcEvoy 14 86
(D Nicholls) *lw: outpcd: last 1/2-way: styd on against nr side rail fnl f: nrst fin* **16/1**

-242 **11** *1 1/4* **Handsome Cross (IRE)**[10] 1941 6-8-7 88.............. SilvestreDeSousa 8 79+
(D Nicholls) *chsd ldng gp: one pce and no prog over 1f out: fdd* **14/1**

35-2 **12** *1/2* **Loch Verdi**[8] 1986 4-8-4 85.. MartinDwyer 4 74
(A M Balding) *racd on outer in midfield: effrt 2f out: no prog fnl f* **8/1**

1040 **13** *nk* **Fire Up The Band**[16] 1788 8-9-2 97........................... AdrianTNicholls 18 85
(D Nicholls) *racd against nr side rail: pressed ldrs to 1/2-way: lost pl and struggling over 1f out* **12/1**

/4-0 **14** *3/4* **Overstayed (IRE)**[23] 1601 4-8-8 89...............................(p) DaneO'Neill 10 74
(I Semple) *b.off hind: wl in rr and nt handling trck: nvr a factor* **50/1**

30-6 **15** *hd* **Fantasy Explorer**[40] 1195 4-8-7 88.................................. JimmyQuinn 7 73
(J J Quinn) *w ldrs for over 3f: wknd* **14/1**

1005 **16** *1 3/4* **Cape Royal**[14] 1853 7-8-7 93.................................(bt) KevinGhunowa(5) 2 71
(J M Bradley) *w ldrs for 3f: wknd over 1f out* **33/1**

5660 **17** *1* **Bigalos Bandit**[16] 1788 5-8-8 89................................... FrancisNorton 6 81+
(D Nicholls) *lw: a in rr: hanging bdly over 1f out* **40/1**

-300 **18** *hd* **Steelcut**[7] 2044 3-8-1 89.. DO'Donohoe 1 63
(R A Fahey) *a towards rr: struggling fr 1/2-way* **66/1**

55.16 secs (-0.52) **Going Correction** +0.125s/f (Good)

WFA 3 from 4yo+ 7lb **18** Ran SP% **130.1**

Speed ratings (Par 109):109,108,108,107,106 106,105,104,104,102 100,99,99,98,97 94,93,93

CSF £58.55 CT £393.59 TOTE £7.90: £2.10, £2.60, £2.80, £6.40; EX 79.90 Trifecta £509.00 Pool: £4,229.78 - 5.90 winning units..

Owner Mrs Lucille Bone **Bred** John Malone **Trained** Newmarket, Suffolk

FOCUS

A typically competitive renewal of this high-class sprint handicap, producing a close finish. The winner got the splits when he needed them and showed improved form, but we may have still to see the best of him.

NOTEBOOK

Hogmaneigh(IRE) ◆, a lightly-raced and generally progressive sprinter, built on his recent run at York and, coming from well off the pace, was able to get a relatively untroubled passage through the middle of the pack to hit the front late on. This was a fine performance and, with the ability to quicken off a strong pace, he has the makings of a Group-class performer. He has been made favourite for the Wokingham, but he will have a penalty and he will not want the ground too fast. It will be no surprise therefore if he is campaigned sparingly in the summer, with end-of-season targets such as the Portland, Ayr Gold Cup and possibly the Prix de L'Abbaye in mind. (op 13-2)

Moorhouse Lad ◆, another progressive performer, had run well here at the April meeting from stall one and looked to have a major chance drawn near the rail. He made a bold bid, being in the front rank all the way, but was probably forced to do a little too much at an early stage to hold his place after being crossed by Merlin's Dancer and, although bravely holding several challenges, could not resist the winner's late surge. He deserves to pick up a good handicap before long, and the Gosforth Park Cup appeals as a race that might suit him. (op 9-1 tchd 10-1 in places)

Caribbean Coral, who won this race in 2004, ran well under his 4lb penalty and got a gap against the rail when needed. He is in good form and could be a contender for the Gosforth Park Cup at the end of the month, although he also likes Chester and would be of interest if found a race there. (op 9-1 tchd 8-1)

Holbeck Ghyll(IRE) ◆ has been running pretty well this season but has slipped a little in the handicap so that he was racing from 2lb out of the handicap on this occasion. In first-time cheekpieces and having his first experience of the track, he did not get the clearest of passages from the rear but finished really strongly and would have been in the photo in another few strides. He looks sure to pick up a race on this evidence and faster ground will be in his favour. (op 25-1)

Green Manalishi, who made a good start for new connections when scoring at Newbury, had a stiff task off his revised mark despite having the plum rail draw. He ran with plenty of credit, being close to the leaders throughout and keeping on right to the line. A return to Listed races beckons, but he can be expected to hold his own in the big 5f handicaps, especially if there is a little ease in the ground. (op 11-2 tchd 13-2 in places and 7-1 in a place)

Wyatt Earp(IRE) ◆, whose winning form has been over 6f and 7f, not surprisingly could not lay up in the early stages, but he ran on really well in the closing stages and was going on at the finish. He is in the Wokingham and looks likely to be a major contender for that race, especially as all ground comes alike to him.

Bond City(IRE) likes this track, having been runner-up in this last year before scoring at the August Bank Holiday meeting, and he ran well again before being run out of the placings by the fast finishers. He is in good heart and the Scottish Sprint Cup may be on the agenda next. (op 7-1)

Merlin's Dancer, on his toes on this first outing for new connections, flew out of the stalls from his low draw and got across to near the stands' rail. However, the early exertions took their toll on the climb to the line. He seems to like Goodwood and could give a good account of himself in the Stewards' Cup later in the season. (op 50-1)

Corridor Creeper(FR) is a regular in this race, having been in the first seven in his three previous tries, with third being his best placing. He again ran his race but appeared to get buffeted around in the closing stages and faded, although only beaten about two and a half lengths.

Machinist(IRE) struggled to go the gallop before running on in the closing stages. (tchd 18-1 in a place)

Handsome Cross(IRE), on his toes beforehand, ran well from a less than favourable draw and will be suited by the return to a flatter track, with his next target likely to be a repeat success in the Scottish Sprint Cup, although he will have 10lb more to carry this year. (op 16-1)

Loch Verdi, a relatively lightly-raced daughter of Lochsong, ran with credit from her low draw and will be of interest on similarly sharp tracks when the ground is faster. (op 10-1)

Overstayed(IRE) Official explanation: jockey said gelding was hanging

Fantasy Explorer Official explanation: jockey said gelding was unsuited by the track

2235 VODAFONE DERBY STKS (GROUP 1) (ENTIRE COLTS & FILLIES) 1m 4f 10y

4:20 (4:21) (Class 1) 3-Y-O

£709,750 (£269,000; £134,625; £67,125; £33,625; £16,875) **Stalls** Centre

Form				RPR
31-1	**1**		**Authorized (IRE)**[16] 1790 3-9-0 116 .... LDettori 14 (P W Chapple-Hyam) *swtg: dwlt: rchd midfield after 5f: 9th st: stdy prog on outer fr 3f out: led over 1f out: shkn up and stormed clr impressively* **5/4**[1]	130+
14-5	**2**	*5*	**Eagle Mountain**[28] 1473 3-9-0 0 .... JMurtagh 8 (A P O'Brien, Ire) *wl in rr: 15th st: rdn and prog on outer fr 3f out: styd on wl to take 2nd ins fnl f: no ch w wnr* **6/1**[2]	121
32-1	**3**	*2 1/2*	**Aqaleem**[21] 1662 3-9-0 112 .... RHills 2 (M P Tregoning) *swtg: wl plcd: 6th st: effrt 3f out: rdn to dispute cl 2nd 2f out: outpcd over 1f out* **9/1**	117
211	**4**	*hd*	**Lucarno (USA)**[7] 2042 3-9-0 92 .... SteveDrowne 17 (J H M Gosden) *lw: wl plcd: 4th st: chsd ldr over 3f out to 2f out: one pce after* **16/1**	117+
2-11	**5**	*1/2*	**Soldier Of Fortune (IRE)**[23] 1602 3-9-0 0 .... WMLordan 9 (A P O'Brien, Ire) *swtg: prom: 5th st: effrt to dispute 2nd 2f out: one pce after* **14/1**	116
-121	**6**	*3/4*	**Salford Mill (IRE)**[28] 1475 3-9-0 105 .... TedDurcan 11 (D R C Elsworth) *lw: wl in rr: 14th st: prog over 2f out: kpt on fnl f: n.d* **20/1**	115
2-23	**7**	*1 3/4*	**Kid Mambo (USA)**[21] 1662 3-9-0 104 .... JoeFanning 19 (T G Mills) *led at str pce: kicked 3l clr 3f out: hdd & wknd over 1f out* **50/1**	112
-502	**8**	*nk*	**Yellowstone (IRE)**[20] 1693 3-9-0 0 .... CO'Donoghue 16 (A P O'Brien, Ire) *wl in rr: 13th st: kpt on u.p fr over 2f out: no ch* **28/1**	112
2	**9**	*3 1/2*	**Acapulco (IRE)**[28] 1475 3-9-0 0 .... FMBerry 5 (A P O'Brien, Ire) *pushed up to go prom: 3rd and drvn st: wknd fr over 2f out* **66/1**	106
1-01	**10**	*shd*	**Admiralofthefleet (USA)**[22] 1617 3-9-0 0 .... JAHeffernan 15 (A P O'Brien, Ire) *trckd ldrs: 7th st: sn rdn: wknd wl over 2f out* **14/1**	106
	11	*6*	**Mahler**[27] 1512 3-9-0 0 .... PJSmullen 6 (A P O'Brien, Ire) *w'like: str: nvr bttr than midfield: 10th and rdn st: no prog* **20/1**	96
1-51	**12**	*2*	**Anton Chekhov**[25] 1572 3-9-0 0 .... DPMcDonogh 4 (A P O'Brien, Ire) *w'like: str: chsd ldr to over 3f out: sn wknd* **50/1**	93
20-1	**13**	*8*	**Regime (IRE)**[35] 1306 3-9-0 110 .... MartinDwyer 7 (M L W Bell) *wl in rr: 12th and brief effrt st: sn no prog and btn* **20/1**	80
42	**14**	*2 1/2*	**Leander**[27] 1505 3-9-0 0 .... MarkGallagher 3 (B R Johnson) *dwlt: a in rr: last and tailing off st: passed 3 toiling rivals fnl f* **100/1**	76
0-10	**15**	*1*	**Petara Bay (IRE)**[35] 1306 3-9-0 105 .... DaneO'Neill 12 (T G Mills) *lw: nvr gng wl in midfield: 11th and u.p st: sn wknd* **100/1**	75
13-0	**16**	*13*	**Strategic Prince**[28] 1473 3-9-0 117 .... EddieAhern 18 (P F I Cole) *lw: chsd ldrs: 8th st: sn wknd: t.o* **20/1**	54
1	**17**	*4*	**Archipenko (USA)**[20] 1693 3-9-0 0 .... MJKinane 10 (A P O'Brien, Ire) *w'like: scope: swtg: a wl in rr: 16th and struggling st: no prog: t.o* **13/2**[3]	48

2m 34.77s (-3.96) **Going Correction** +0.025s/f (Good) **591** Ran SP% **131.2**

Speed ratings (Par 113):114,110,109,108,108 108,106,106,104,104 100,98,93,91,91 82,79

CSF £8.08 CT £56.92 TOTE £2.30: £1.10, £2.70, £2.60; EX 13.60 Trifecta £120.00 Pool: £37,212.72 - 220.16 winning units..

Owner Saleh Al Homeizi & Imad Al Sagar **Bred** Marengo Investments And Knighton House Ltd And M **Trained** Newmarket, Suffolk

■ Frankie Dettori's first Derby winner, and Peter Chapple-Hyam's second. Aidan O'Brien saddled eight runners, a race record.

FOCUS

A strong Derby, won impressively by a top-class colt who was full value for the winning margin. It ought to take an exceptional performance to beat him. The runner-up represented 2000 Guineas form, and with trial winners filling the next four places the form should stand up. The time was the fastest of the day and well up to standard for the grade

NOTEBOOK

Authorized(IRE), who had been all the rage for this race since spread-eagling his field in the Dante Stakes, repeated the dose in impressive style. Settled off the pace travelling well, he moved into contention with little apparent effort, and when asked he put daylight between himself and his rivals without hesitation. He looks the best Derby winner since High Chaparral on this evidence and, although the Irish Derby would appear a formality, he is likely to go for the Eclipse before a tilt at the King George. He is clearly the best of the middle-distance three-year-old colts we have seen - although Teofilo has yet to reappear - and if he can beat older rivals in the two all-aged Group 1 races he will be well on the way to the Horse of the Year title. (op 11-10 tchd 11-8 in places and 6-4 in a place)

Eagle Mountain, on his toes beforehand, had finished closer to the winner in the Racing Post Trophy but had to come from some way back this time and deserves plenty of credit for his effort. He would have been a decisive winner without Authorized in the race and, if the winner declines what looks an easy opportunity in the Irish Derby, this colt can take full advantage. His three-length fifth in the 2000 Guineas gives a line to the comparative merits of the winner and Cockney Rebel, and if that pair clash at Sandown at the intermediate trip that race could be one of the season's highlights. (op 9-1)

Aqaleem, who won the Lingfield Derby Trial last time, was given a positive ride and put up a fine staying performance. He is in the King Edward VII at Royal Ascot and would be a short-priced favourite if taking his chance. Whether he goes there or not, the St Leger is definitely on the agenda, and he shapes like a stayer even though the dam's side of his pedigree suggests he is not guaranteed to get the trip. (op 11-1)

Lucarno(USA), one of the least experienced runners in the line-up, having only made his racecourse debut six weeks previously, put up a performance worthy of plenty of credit. Always close up, he appeared to have every chance in the straight but could find no extra in the last quarter mile, with a faint suspicion that he did not quite stay the trip. He is in the King Edward VII at Royal Ascot, but it may be worth connections giving him time to recover from a hard race and his second in seven days, and target the Grand Prix De Paris instead. (tchd 20-1 in a place)

Soldier Of Fortune(IRE), winner of the Chester Vase, ran a decent race but was keeping on at just the one pace in the closing stages. He could well take his chance in the King Edward VII and/or Irish Derby, but has a bit to find with those that finished in front of him and he is another who may make up into a St Leger horse. (op 16-1 tchd 20-1)

Salford Mill(IRE) ◆ was noted staying on really well from the rear in the wake of the runner-up. He looks a progressive sort and, possessing a pedigree packed with stamina, could well have progressed past a couple of those that finished ahead of him here come St Leger time.

Kid Mambo(USA), third behind Aqaleem in the Lingfield Derby Trial, put up a brave performance from the front and finished a length closer to that rival on this occasion. He is a decent colt and deserves to win a good race, but it may be at Listed or Group 3 level, and it may be at a slightly shorter distance. (op 66-1 tchd 80-1)

Yellowstone(IRE), runner-up to Archipenko in the Derrinstown Derby Trial, never got involved but gives a fair indication of where his stable companion and Leopardstown conqueror would have finished had he run his race. (op 33-1 tchd 40-1)

Acapulco(IRE), runner-up to Salford Mill in the Newmarket Stakes, was on his toes beforehand and finished further behind that rival this time over a trip that should have suited him. He is still relatively inexperienced and may have more to offer on softer ground.

Admiralofthefleet(USA), winner of the Dee Stakes, got warm beforehand and ran as if he did not get the trip. Presumably he will be campaigned at shorter from now on. (op 16-1)

Mahler, a progressive type at a lower level, was in trouble rounding Tattenham Corner. (tchd 25-1 in a place)

Anton Chekhov chased the leader until into the straight but dropped right out. He never looked to be travelling with any fluency and the ground may have been quick enough for him.

Regime(IRE) was always at the back and failed to run his race, but his jockey felt he might have tweaked a muscle early on as he was never really going. (op 25-1)

Strategic Prince showed up well before dropping out in the straight. Connections felt the ground was not as quick as he would have liked, but he ran as though lack of stamina was the problem, despite being out of a Lingfield Oaks Trial winner who was a half-sister to an Oaks winner. (tchd 25-1)

Archipenko(USA), the Derrinstown Derby Trial winner, was beaten a long way from home and his jockey reported he had lost his action coming down the hill. Official explanation: trainer's rep said colt lost its action coming down the hill (op 8-1)

2236 VODAFONE LIVE! MUSIC STKS (H'CAP) 1m 4f 10y

5:05 (5:07) (Class 2) (0-100,97) 4-Y-O+

£24,928 (£7,464; £3,732; £1,868; £932; £468) **Stalls** Centre

Form				RPR
31-1	**1**		**Nosferatu (IRE)**[26] 1542 4-8-12 **88** .... JimCrowley 16 (Mrs A J Perrett) *prom: cl 3rd st: rdn over 2f out: led over 1f out: styd on* **9/2**[2]	97
14/4	**2**	*1 1/4*	**Misty Dancer**[26] 1542 8-8-4 **80** .... FrancisNorton 1 (Miss Venetia Williams) *hld up towards rr: 10th st: prog over 2f out: n.m.r over 1f out: styd on to take 2nd nr fin* **33/1**	87
64/5	**3**	*shd*	**Night Hour (IRE)**[38] 1244 5-8-12 **88** .... SteveDrowne 9 (J H M Gosden) *trckd ldrs: cl 6th st: tried to chal fr 2f out: hanging lft and nt qckn over 1f out: kpt on* **25/1**	94
0430	**4**	*hd*	**Dzesmin (POL)**[24] 1582 5-7-13 **80** ....(p) RoryMoore(5) 15 (R C Guest) *lw: dwlt: t.k.h and hld up in rr: 12th but wl in tch st: nt clr run over 2f out and over 1f out: r.o ins fnl f: nrst fin* **20/1**	89+
55-1	**5**	*shd*	**Hernando Royal**[24] 1591 4-8-5 **86** .... TravisBlock(5) 8 (H Morrison) *led for 3f: trckd ldr after: rdn to ld briefly wl over 1f out: one pce fnl f* **14/1**	92
5541	**6**	*1/2*	**La Estrella (USA)**[8] 2011 4-8-11 **87** .... JoeFanning 13 (J G Given) *lw: led after 3f: rdn over 2f out: hdd wl over 1f out: fdd ins fnl f* **10/1**	92
010-	**7**	*nk*	**Oh Glory Be (USA)**[304] 4039 4-8-11 **87** .... RichardHughes 18 (R Hannon) *lw: hld up in rr: 14th st: prog on outer over 2f out: styd on fr over 1f out: nt rch ldrs* **25/1**	92
013-	**8**	*1/2*	**Leslingtaylor (IRE)**[21] 5952 5-8-2 **78** .... JimmyQuinn 11 (J J Quinn) *hld up in midfield: 8th st: sn pushed along: one pce and no real imp on ldrs fnl 2f* **4/1**[1]	82
-001	**9**	*hd*	**My Arch**[13] 1862 5-8-11 **87** .... NCallan 4 (K A Ryan) *lw: cl up: 4th st: effrt on inner over 2f out: pressed ldrs over 1f out: fdd fnl f* **25/1**	91
10-1	**10**	*4*	**Cape Secret (IRE)**[27] 1506 4-8-11 **87** .... TedDurcan 3 (R M Beckett) *hld up in midfield: 9th st: hmpd wl over 2f out: nvr on terms after* **20/1**	84
60-5	**11**	*1 1/4*	**Gavroche (IRE)**[35] 1304 6-9-5 **95** .... MartinDwyer 10 (J R Boyle) *trbld passage in midfield: 11th and losing pl st: struggling over 2f out* **12/1**	90
6-43	**12**	*3*	**Tilt**[24] 1575 5-8-10 **86** .... DaneO'Neill 12 (B Ellison) *racd wd in rr: 13th st: sn struggling and bhd* **13/2**[3]	76
0324	**13**	*1/2*	**Nakheel**[15] 1822 4-9-7 **97** .... RHills 7 (M Johnston) *s.s: last tl sme prog on outer wl over 2f out: hanging lft and sn btn: eased* **9/1**	87
0/0-	**14**	*1/2*	**Adopted Hero (IRE)**[21] 5010 7-8-4 **87** .... JackMitchell(7) 14 (G L Moore) *trbld passage in first half of r and dropped to rr: 15th st: sn bhd* **25/1**	76
-122	**15**	*11*	**Flying Clarets (IRE)**[17] 1767 4-8-12 **88** .... PaulHanagan 5 (R A Fahey) *trckd ldrs: 7th st: sn lost pl: eased whn wl btn* **14/1**	59
551-	**16**	*1*	**Great Hawk (USA)**[269] 5110 4-9-6 **96** .... KerrinMcEvoy 17 (Sir Michael Stoute) *lw: trckd ldrs: cl 5th st: wknd over 2f out: eased* **8/1**	66

2m 39.16s (0.43) **Going Correction** +0.025s/f (Good) **16** Ran SP% **130.6**

Speed ratings (Par 109):99,98,98,97,97 97,97,97,96,94 93,91,91,90,83 82

CSF £161.17 CT £3444.34 TOTE £6.70: £2.00, £4.30, £6.40, £5.50; EX 238.80 TRIFECTA Not won..

Owner Lady Clague **Bred** Newberry Stud Company **Trained** Pulborough, W Sussex

■ Vacation was withdrawn (lame at start): Rule 4 does not apply.

■ Stewards' Enquiry : Francis Norton two-day ban: used whip with excessive frequency and without giving gelding time to respond (Jun 13-14)
N Callan two-day ban: careless riding (Jun 13-14)

FOCUS

A good competitive handicap, but it was run at a slow early pace and the time was 4.39sec slower than the Derby. The form is messy, and the fourth was particularly unfortunate.

NOTEBOOK

Nosferatu(IRE) has been lightly raced but progressive and took this step up in grade off a higher mark in his stride. Always close to the pace, he went on halfway up the straight and battled to resist several challenges. He may well go to Royal Ascot for the Duke Of Edinburgh Handicap now, although he would not want the ground too fast. The Ebor is a feasible target later in the season. (tchd 5-1, 11-2 in places)

Misty Dancer, a course and distance winner just under two years ago, had won three times over fences since. On 4lb better terms, he finished closer to the winner than he had at Windsor last time, and connections may be hopeful of getting even closer if taking him on again at Royal Ascot, as he did not get the best of runs.

Night Hour(IRE) ◆, who finished fifth in the Great Metropolitan over course and distance at the April meeting on his return from the best part of two years off, had been given time to recover and ran a fine race to reverse placings with two that finished in front of him there. He is not especially well handicapped but looks to have more to offer and is one to keep in mind for a similar contest. (tchd 33-1)

Dzesmin(POL) ◆, who finished ahead of the third at the April meeting, looked the unlucky horse of the race as he missed the break and had to switch on more than one occasion in the straight before running on well near the finish. Strictly on a line through the third he would just about have won with a clear passage and he could be the sort for the Northumberland Plate if connections opt to go there, although he still has to prove his stamina for 2m. (op 16-1)

Hernando Royal, whose two previous wins were on the All-Weather, ran a fine race but could not find an extra gear once the winner went on. He has not had much racing and looks to have the potential to do better, possibly over a longer trip. (tchd 16-1)

La Estrella(USA), a clear-cut winner last time, was 8lb higher and up in grade but performed with credit, having been prominent throughout. (op 12-1)

Oh Glory Be(USA), having her first outing since August, was noted making good headway late on, having been held up from her wide draw. She looks capable of improvement with this under her belt, and will be of especial interest if returning to Salisbury, where she has gained both her previous successes. (op 16-1)

Leslingtaylor(IRE), a progressive performer both on the Flat and over hurdles in the last year, included the valuable and competitive Swinton Hurdle among his victories. He was well supported beforehand and appeared to have every chance in the race but could not pick up. He seems best on flat tracks and may not have been happy on this course. (tchd 7-2, 9-2 in places)

My Arch, stepping back up in trip, was ridden close to the pace but weakened in the closing stages as if he does not quite stay this far. (tchd 28-1)

Tilt, had a sound chance on his running in the Great Metropolitan, but failed to run up to that form. He should have been involved in the finished judged on the efforts of today's third and fourth, who finished either side of him there. (op 11-1)

Nakheel Official explanation: jockey said colt lost its action

Great Hawk(USA), stepping up in distance and with the visor left off this time, travelled well enough but dropped out quickly and was eased as if something was amiss. (op 10-1)

2237 VODAFONE SPRINT STKS (H'CAP) 6f

5:40 (5:41) (Class 2) (0-100,100) 4-Y-0+

£24,928 (£7,464; £3,732; £1,868; £932; £468) **Stalls High**

Form				RPR
4-53	**1**		**Song Of Passion (IRE)**[22] 1619 4-9-0 **90** ... RichardHughes 9 (R Hannon) *trckd ldr: led wl over 1f out: rdn clr and in n.d fnl f* **10/1**	105+
0-04	**2**	*2 ½*	**Prince Namid**[16] 1788 5-8-9 **85** ... WSupple 1 (Mrs A Duffield) *trckd ldrs: 7th st: nt clr run 2f out and swtchd rt twice: r.o to take 2nd ins fnl f: no ch w wnr* **11/2**[2]	92+
5022	**3**	*1 ¾*	**Bahamian Pirate (USA)**[14] 1852 12-9-3 **93** ... AdrianTNicholls 11 (D Nicholls) *sn outpcd: 14th st: prog 2f out: styd on strly fnl f to snatch 3rd last strides* **10/1**	95
-000	**4**	*½*	**Fantasy Believer**[21] 1651 9-9-10 **100** ... JimmyQuinn 7 (J J Quinn) *hld up in midfield: 8th st: prog and hanging lft 2f out: wnt 2nd briefly 1f out: one pce after* **25/1**	101
-000	**5**	*1*	**Turnkey**[15] 1826 5-9-0 **90** ... SilvestreDeSousa 14 (D Nicholls) *dwlt: outpcd: last st: r.o wl fr over 1f out: nrst fin* **50/1**	88
5-15	**6**	*nk*	**Beaver Patrol (IRE)**[21] 1651 5-9-6 **96** ... KerrinMcEvoy 5 (Eve Johnson Houghton) *towards rr: 10th st: nt on terms over 2f out: styd on wl fnl f: nrst fin* **5/2**[1]	93+
-000	**7**	*nk*	**Idle Power (IRE)**[21] 1653 9-8-11 **87** ... AmirQuinn 10 (J R Boyle) *t.k.h: prom: 3rd st: nt clr run over 1f out: lost pl and n.d after* **33/1**	83
0061	**8**	*½*	**Commando Scott (IRE)**[6] 2058 6-8-12 **88** 6ex ... PaulHanagan 13 (I W McInnes) *trckd ldrs: 5th st: rdn over 2f out: no prog: wknd fnl f* **15/2**[3]	82
0040	**9**	*nk*	**Tournedos (IRE)**[16] 1788 5-9-7 **97** ... MartinDwyer 16 (D Nicholls) *swtg: led to wl over 1f out: wknd fnl f* **25/1**	90
60-0	**10**	*hd*	**Pacific Pride**[16] 1788 4-9-3 **93** ... GrahamGibbons 6 (J J Quinn) *trckd ldrs: 4th st: rdn and effrt whn n.m.r over 1f out: no ch after* **9/1**	86
0306	**11**	*1*	**Pic Up Sticks**[1] 2197 8-8-8 **84** ... TQuinn 12 (B G Powell) *hld up in midfield towards outer: 9th st: outpcd over 2f out: no ch after* **33/1**	74
2061	**12**	*½*	**Lucayos**[3] 2139 4-8-6 **85** 6ex ... RichardKingscote(3) 15 (Mrs H Sweeting) *lw: wl in rr and wd: 13th st: hanging bdly lft and struggling over 2f out* **20/1**	73
-000	**13**	*shd*	**Indian Trail**[15] 1826 7-9-2 **92** ...(v[1]) FrancisNorton 2 (D Nicholls) *hmpd and snatched up on inner over 4f out: 11th st: smooth prog on inner over 2f out: nowhere to go after and no ch* **14/1**	80+
0014	**14**	*1 ½*	**Dhaular Dhar (IRE)**[7] 2030 5-9-8 **98** ... TedDurcan 17 (J S Goldie) *a in rr and nt handling trck: 15th st: struggling after* **12/1**	81
1303	**15**	*1 ¾*	**Lethal**[8] 1986 4-8-13 **89** ... JimCrowley 8 (D K Ivory) *swtg: dwlt: plld hrd and hld up: 12th st and racing on outer: no prog fnl 2f* **10/1**	67
6-00	**16**	*3*	**Guto**[16] 1788 4-8-13 **89** ...(p) NCallan 4 (K A Ryan) *swtg: trckd ldrs: 6th st: cl up whn bdly hmpd over 1f out: nt rcvr and heavily eased* **33/1**	82+

69.38 secs (-1.25) **Going Correction** +0.025s/f (Good) **16 Ran SP% 130.6**

Speed ratings (Par 109):109,105,103,102,101 100,100,99,99,99 97,97,97,95,92 88

CSF £64.04 CT £614.54 TOTE £9.10: £2.00, £2.10, £2.20, £4.20; EX 98.10 Trifecta £380.60 Pool: £2,144.28 - 4.00 winning units. Place 6 £213.37, Place 5 £63.43..

Owner Thurloe Thoroughbreds XVI **Bred** Mrs Stephanie Hanly **Trained** East Everleigh, Wilts

■ Stewards' Enquiry : Amir Quinn three-day ban: careless riding (Jun 13-15)

FOCUS

A good sprint handicap run at a decent pace and the time was 1.08 sec faster than the earlier Listed juvenile contest. The winner showed much improved form and on the face of it looks close to Listed level.

NOTEBOOK

Song Of Passion(IRE) ◆, one of the few unexposed runners at this trip, having done all of her winning over 7f, had however won on the track and handled it particularly well. She was close to the pace throughout and, committing for home halfway up the straight, her stamina came into play and she won decisively. She looks to have more to offer and it will be no surprise if connections have another try at earning black type with this half-sister to Hurricane Alan. (op 11-1)

Prince Namid, runner-up in this race last season when drawn on the wide outside, had the best draw this time but, as a hold-up horse, it did not particularly help him. He also did not have much luck in running and, although he came through well in the last furlong after being switched wid, the winner was already home and hosed. He has not scored for over a year now, but is close to his previous winning mark and deserves to pick up a decent handicap. (op 5-1 tchd 9-2)

Bahamian Pirate(USA), a tough and consistent veteran, repeated last year's performance of finishing third in this race, and ran close to that form with the runner-up.

Fantasy Believer ◆, who finished sixth in this last season, improved on that effort despite being 15lb higher in the ratings thanks to five subsequent victories. He tends to find his form in mid-summer and is one to bear in mind for similar races from now on. (op 20-1)

Turnkey has not shown much since returning from a ten-month absence, but has dropped 10lb in that time and this effort indicated he was on the way back. (op 66-1)

Beaver Patrol(IRE), last year's winner, was racing off a 7lb higher mark following his win at Newmarket last month. He never really got involved this time, although he was keeping on well in the closing stages. He may need to drop a few pounds before he can win again. (op 7-2)

Idle Power(IRE), fourth in this race last year, has been running reasonably lately but without making the frame, and was consequently 3lb lower. This showed that the spark was still there and he is one to watch out for back here or at Goodwood, a track where he has four successes to his name.

Commando Scott(IRE), under a 6lb penalty, was slightly hampered early but soon recovered to track the leaders. He faded in the closing stages and seems happier on a more conventional track. (tchd 8-1)

Tournedos(IRE) made a fast start from his wide stall and was soon at the head of affairs. However, he used up a fair amount of energy getting to the front and was a sitting target for the strong finishers in the straight.

Pacific Pride, having just his second outing for new connections, showed the ability is still there and will be happier returned to a flat track, particularly York, where he has a good record. (op 7-1)

Indian Trail ◆ was a real eyecatcher and appeared very unlucky. Having finished fifth in this race last year, he was 2lb lower in the handicap and had the visor on for the first time. He was hampered on the descent to the straight but got a clear run up the rail once in line for home that took him onto the heels of the leader. However, from that point his path was blocked and the gap never opened and he was boxed in, so his rider had to sit and suffer. Last year's form entitled him to finish much closer than he did and, providing the headgear has the same effect, he looks capable of gaining compensation. Official explanation: jockey said gelding was denied a clear run

Guto would have been a lot closer but for being badly hampered. However, he was beaten at the time. Official explanation: jockey said gelding suffered interference in running

T/Jkpt: £13,033.70 to a £1 stake. Pool: £64,251.00. 3.50 winning tickets. T/Plt: £139.00 to a £1 stake. Pool: £299,914.25. 1,574.90 winning tickets. T/Qpdt: £23.90 to a £1 stake. Pool: £16,954.35. 523.70 winning tickets. JN

1428 FOLKESTONE (R-H)

Saturday, June 2

OFFICIAL GOING: Good (good to firm in places)

Wind: Virtually nil

2238 INTERCASINO.CO.UK FOLKESTONE DERBY DAY H'CAP 1m 4f

2:05 (2:05) (Class 4) (0-85,84) 4-Y-0+ **£6,477** (£1,927; £963; £481) **Stalls Low**

Form				RPR
-002	**1**		**Pocketwood**[15] 1813 5-8-8 **71** ... StephenCarson 1 (Jean-Rene Auvray) *mde all: rdn 2f out: r.o gamely fnl f* **8/1**	78
-310	**2**	*nk*	**Fregate Island (IRE)**[14] 1844 4-9-5 **82** ... BrettDoyle 7 (B J Meehan) *w.w in tch: rdn 2f out: chsd wnr ins fnl f: r.o* **9/2**[2]	89
10-2	**3**	*1*	**Swan Queen**[16] 1783 4-9-7 **84** ... PhilipRobinson 5 (J L Dunlop) *chsd ldng pair tl wnt 2nd 6f out: rdn 2f out: kpt on same pce* **15/8**[1]	89
0-05	**4**	*2*	**Rawdon (IRE)**[22] 1638 6-8-9 **72** ...(v) HayleyTurner 8 (M L W Bell) *t.k.h: chsd wnr tl 6f out: rdn 2f out: kpt on same pce* **17/2**	74
5-00	**5**	*½*	**Transvestite (IRE)**[17] 1771 5-9-3 **80** ... MichaelHills 3 (J W Hills) *t.k.h: hld up in tch: hdwy on outer over 2f out: rdn 2f out: kpt on same pce* **11/2**[3]	81
-266	**6**	*4*	**Nero's Return (IRE)**[10] 1949 6-8-13 **76** ... FergusSweeney 4 (G L Moore) *s.i.s: hld up in last pair: hdwy on outer over 2f out: rdn 2f out: wknd over 1f out* **10/1**	71
1061	**7**	*shd*	**Wild Pitch**[10] 1949 6-8-12 **82** ...(b) JackMitchell(7) 6 (P Mitchell) *s.i.s: hld up in last pair: outpcd 3f out: rdn 2f out: no imp* **13/2**	76

2m 44.8s (4.30) **Going Correction** 0.0s/f (Good) **7 Ran SP% 112.4**

Speed ratings (Par 105):85,84,84,82,82 79,79

CSF £41.90 CT £94.80 TOTE £10.20: £3.40, £3.00; EX 59.20 Trifecta £172.60 Pool: £272.38 - 1.12 winning units..

Owner Lambourn Racing **Bred** M J Lewin **Trained** Upper Lambourn, Berks

FOCUS

The winner made every yard, but he recorded a very slow winning time for the class and the form is not rock solid.

2239 PLAY BLACKJACK AT INTERCASINO.CO.UK H'CAP 7f (S)

2:35 (2:36) (Class 3) (0-90,91) 4-Y-0+ **£9,067** (£2,697; £1,348; £673) **Stalls Low**

Form				RPR
0-00	**1**		**South Cape**[21] 1651 4-8-13 **82** ... TPO'Shea 13 (M R Channon) *trckd ldrs far side: hdwy 3f out: chsd ldr and rdn over 2f out: led narrowly 1f out: styd on: all out* **14/1**	92
000-	**2**	*shd*	**Cape Of Luck (IRE)**[154] 6986 4-8-12 **88** ... JackMitchell(7) 10 (P Mitchell) *hld up in midfield far side: hdwy 3f out: rdn over 2f out: ev ch 1f out: a jst hld* **50/1**	98
0-14	**3**	*2 ½*	**Mcnairobi**[21] 1649 4-9-0 **83** ... DarryllHolland 6 (P D Cundell) *hld up and bhd on far side: hdwy 3f out: styd on u.p fr 2f out: nt rch ldrs* **5/1**[2]	86
0-32	**4**	*1 ¼*	**Neon Blue**[14] 1845 6-8-3 **72** ... HayleyTurner 2 (R M Whitaker) *racd stands' side: sn rdn and wl outpcd: hdwy over 1f out: styd on fnl f: nrst fin* **10/1**	72+
2000	**5**	*¾*	**Yarqus**[27] 1494 4-9-5 **88** ... RichardMullen 8 (C E Brittain) *chsd ldrs on far side: rdn over 2f out: kpt on same pce u.p* **16/1**	86
52-4	**6**	*¾*	**Irony (IRE)**[15] 1818 8-9-2 **88** ...(p) NeilChalmers(3) 3 (A M Balding) *led and clr of rival stands' side: prom overall: rdn over 2f out: wknd fnl f* **14/1**	84+
11-0	**7**	*hd*	**Trimlestown (IRE)**[21] 1651 4-8-13 **82** ... FergusSweeney 9 (H Candy) *chsd ldr on far side: overall ldr after 2f: rdn 2f out: hdd 1f out: wknd* **7/2**[1]	77

23-4 **8** *½* **Gloved Hand**[14] [1836] 5-9-7 **90** .... JamesDoyle 4 84
(R M Beckett) *swtchd to r far side: hdwy to chse ldrs 3f out: hung lft u.p over 1f out: sn wknd* **8/1**
4000 **9** *nk* **Gallantry**[15] [1818] 5-9-0 **83** .... OscarUrbina 12 76
(D Shaw) *s.i.s: hld up in rr on far side: hdwy 2f out: rdn and no hdwy fnl f* **16/1**
0500 **10** *1* **Compton's Eleven**[14] [1836] 6-9-3 **86** .... ChrisCatlin 1 76
(M R Channon) *swtchd to r far side: sn pushed along: nvr on terms* **14/1**
-311 **11** *hd* **Phluke**[7] [2030] 6-9-8 **91** .... StephenCarson 11 81
(Eve Johnson Houghton) *racd far side: overall ldr for 2f: chsd ldr tl over 2f out: wknd over 1f out* **7/1**[3]
00-0 **12** *3 ½* **Our Putra**[14] [1845] 4-8-7 **76** ow3 .... PhilipRobinson 5 56
(M A Jarvis) *swtchd to r far side: chsd ldrs tl 3f out: sn wknd* **20/1**
-610 **13** *2 ½* **Bonnie Prince Blue**[15] [1818] 4-8-11 **80** .... MichaelHills 7 54
(B W Hills) *s.i.s: racd far side: a bhd* **7/1**[3]

1m 26.68s (-1.22) **Going Correction** 0.0s/f (Good) **13** Ran SP% **122.6**
Speed ratings (Par 107):106,105,103,101,100 99,99,99,98,97 97,93,90
CSF £573.41 CT £4088.00 TOTE £19.30: £4.40, £11.80, £3.00; EX 184.70 TRIFECTA Not won..
Owner Heart Of The South Racing **Bred** John And Mrs Caroline Penny **Trained** West Ilsley, Berks

FOCUS
Two horses stayed stands' side while the rest went far side, but there appeared little bias. A decent handicap for the track but not the most straightforward form to assess, with the winner having shown little previously this season and the second not obviously well treated.

NOTEBOOK
South Cape, running off a career-low mark, was suited by the good pace and came clear with the runner-up in the closing stages. There was not a lot between the pair at the line. He has a number of entries in the coming week, has run well in two races close together in the past and will not mind a return to a mile. (op 16-1)
Cape Of Luck(IRE), having his first outing since December, was not at all fancied according to the market, but he picked up well with the eventual winner to go clear inside the last. He was only just denied and, if building on this, should soon be returning to winning ways. (op 66-1)
Mcnairobi, who ran well in a decent contest at Ascot last time, needs a mile really and was staying on all too late. She has yet to win on turf but, in a strongly-run race over a mile on decent ground, she will put that right at some point. (op 7-1)
Neon Blue, who has been running well this spring, was one of only two to stay stands' side and he beat his only companion Irony by a length and a half.
Yarqus, who has done his winning over further, was suited by the good gallop and his stamina came into play late on.
Irony(IRE), with the cheekpieces back on, set a good pace on the stands' side and ended up setting it up for his only rival on that side of the course. (op 16-1)
Trimlestown(IRE), who ran a fair race in the Victoria Cup on his seasonal reappearance, once again had too much use made of him early on and merely help set it up for the closers. (op 10-3 tchd 4-1 in places)
Gloved Hand Official explanation: jockey said mare had been hanging left
Phluke Official explanation: jockey said gelding had run flat

2240 INTERCASINO.CO.UK FILLIES' H'CAP 6f
3:05 (3:06) (Class 4) (0-85,80) 4-Y-0+ **£6,477** (£1,927; £963; £481) **Stalls** Low

Form RPR
3312 **1** **Keyaki (IRE)**[14] [1847] 6-9-2 **80** .... PatrickHills(5) 2 92+
(C F Wall) *led stands' side: overall ldr thrght: clr over 2f out: pushed out fnl f* **3/1**[2]
11-1 **2** *2* **Bakhoor (IRE)**[5] [2085] 4-9-0 **73** 6ex .... DarryllHolland 9 79
(W Jarvis) *racd far side: in tch: rdn to chse far side ldr wl over 1f out: styd on to chse wnr ins fnl f* **11/8**[1]
0242 **3** *½* **Shes Minnie**[10] [1940] 4-9-0 **73** .... FergusSweeney 6 78
(J G M O'Shea) *chsd ldr on far side: rdn to ld far side over 2f out: hung rt wl over 1f out: kpt on same pce fnl f: lost overall 2nd nr fin* **14/1**
5233 **4** *nk* **Sweet Pickle**[11] [1935] 6-8-11 **70** ....(e) MichaelHills 1 74
(J R Boyle) *chsd wnr stands' side: rdn and effrt over 1f out: kpt on same pce fnl f* **8/1**[3]
-000 **5** *2 ½* **Golden Asha**[13] [1861] 5-9-7 **80** .... OscarUrbina 5 77
(G G Margarson) *racd stands' side: nvr gng pce of other pair on stands' side: no hdwy last 2f* **16/1**
-031 **6** *2 ½* **Linda Green**[17] [1766] 6-9-2 **75** .... ChrisCatlin 7 64
(M R Channon) *bhd on far side: rdn 3f out: sn outpcd* **8/1**[3]
-005 **7** *nk* **Kaveri (USA)**[93] [590] 4-8-11 **70** .... RichardMullen 4 58
(C E Brittain) *t.k.h: chsd ldrs on far side tl 1/2-way: sn wknd: no ch last 2f* **16/1**
00-6 **8** *1* **Bowness**[21] [1670] 5-9-6 **79** .... JamieMackay 3 64
(J G Given) *swtchd to r far side: led far side tl over 2f out: sn wknd* **14/1**
25-0 **9** *17* **Musical Romance (IRE)**[32] [1372] 4-9-0 **73** ....(b) BrettDoyle 8 7
(B J Meehan) *stdd s: hld up on far side: rdn and wknd qckly 2f out: eased over 1f out: t.o* **33/1**

1m 12.74s (-0.86) **Going Correction** 0.0s/f (Good) **9** Ran SP% **117.4**
Speed ratings (Par 102):105,102,101,101,97 94,94,92,70
CSF £7.62 CT £48.16 TOTE £4.60: £1.50, £1.10, £2.90; EX 9.40 Trifecta £56.60 Pool: £322.51 - 4.04 winning units..
Owner S Oldroyd **Bred** Rathbarry Stud **Trained** Newmarket, Suffolk

FOCUS
A faitr handicap and once again the field split and there was no discernible advantage in racing on either side. The form is rated around the third and fourth.

2241 INTERCASINO.CO.UK MAIDEN AUCTION STKS 6f
3:35 (3:38) (Class 5) 2-Y-0 **£3,886** (£1,156; £577; £288) **Stalls** Low

Form RPR
4 **1** **Ruff Diamond (USA)**[21] [1652] 2-9-1 0 .... GeorgeBaker 1 86
(J R Best) *mde all on stands' side: edgd rt briefly jst ins fnl f: sn rcvrd: pushed out and r.o wl last 100yds* **7/2**[2]
2 *1 ¾* **Archived (IRE)** 2-8-9 0 .... BrettDoyle 14 75
(M G Quinlan) *led far side: hung bdly lft fr 2f out: ev ch 1f out: outpcd last 100yds* **16/1**
2 **3** *3* **Nijoom Dubai**[15] [1807] 2-8-4 0 .... ChrisCatlin 11 61
(M R Channon) *chsd ldrs far side: rdn 1/2-way: hung lft fr 2f out: styd on to go 3rd nr fin: nt pce to rch ldrs* **11/10**[1]
3 **4** *shd* **Bosun Breese**[51] [1007] 2-8-9 0 .... DarryllHolland 8 65
(P W D'Arcy) *t.k.h: chsd far side ldr: rdn and hung lft fr 2f out: wknd jst ins fnl f* **4/1**[3]
5 *1* **Karky Schultz (GER)** 2-8-12 0 .... HayleyTurner 2 65
(J M P Eustace) *chsd ldrs on stands' side: kpt on fnl f: nvr able to chal* **33/1**
6 *2* **Mudhish (IRE)** 2-8-9 0 .... RichardMullen 12 56
(C E Brittain) *sn pushed along: chsd ldrs on far side: rdn and hung lft fr 2f out: kpt on same pce* **33/1**
35 **7** *nk* **Fox's Den**[12] [1882] 2-8-9 0 ....(b[1]) JamesDoyle 4 56
(R M Beckett) *pressed wnr on stands' side: rdn wl over 2f out: wknd over 1f out* **16/1**
8 *nk* **Lady Nova (IRE)** 2-8-7 0 .... SimonWhitworth 3 53
(J S Moore) *outpcd in rr on stands' side: rdn over 3f out: n.d* **33/1**
9 *shd* **Isander (USA)** 2-8-12 0 .... OscarUrbina 5 57
(Mrs A J Perrett) *chsd ldrs on stands' side: rdn wl over 2f out: wknd over 1f out* **18/1**
10 *1* **Ruby Delta** 2-8-9 0 .... FergusSweeney 7 51
(P D Cundell) *s.i.s: a bhd on stands' side: n.d* **40/1**
11 *nk* **Howdigo** 2-8-12 0 .... StephaneBreux(3) 6 56
(J R Best) *slowly away: a outpcd on stands' side* **33/1**
12 *hd* **Jelly Mo** 2-8-8 0 ow1 .... MichaelHills 9 49
(J W Hills) *racd far side: a outpcd: rdn 3f out: hung lft last 2f: n.d* **33/1**
6 **13** *1* **Tenth Night (IRE)**[8] [1993] 2-8-12 0 .... PhilipRobinson 10 50
(J A Osborne) *racd far side: a outpcd* **20/1**

1m 14.06s (0.46) **Going Correction** 0.0s/f (Good) **13** Ran SP% **128.8**
Speed ratings (Par 93):96,93,89,89,88 85,85,84,84,83 82,82,81
CSF £58.09 TOTE £5.00: £2.10, £7.40, £1.10; EX 129.90 Trifecta £61.40 Part won. Pool: £86.57 - 0.34 winning units..
Owner John Griffin Owen Mullen **Bred** W B Harrigan **Trained** Hucking, Kent
■ Seconds Out (40/1) was withdrawn (unruly in stalls); Rule 4 does not apply.

FOCUS
A fair maiden and not easy to rate with confidence as arguably the third and fourth were not at their best.

NOTEBOOK
Ruff Diamond(USA), who ran well in a better maiden on his debut at Ascot, showed good pace to make every yard on the stands' side and saw the extra furlong out strongly. He looks the type who will progress with racing, and should be able to hold his own in better company. (op 9-2)
Archived(IRE), a half-brother to Time For You, a 6f winner at two, made the running on the far side before drifting over to the stands' side in the closing stages. He clearly has the ability to pick up an ordinary race, especially if he improves for this outing. (op 20-1)
Nijoom Dubai was getting weight from all her rivals and, having made a promising debut in a conditions race at Newbury, it was easy to see why she was sent off a short price on this drop in grade, especially as the step up in trip was also likely to suit her. This has to go down as a disappointing effort in the circumstances. (tchd Evens and 5-4 and 11-8 in places)
Bosun Breese was not obviously suited by the step up to 6f, but he did race keenly in the early stages and that probably contributed to his downfall. Official explanation: jockey said gelding hung left (op 6-1)
Karky Schultz(GER), who is out of a mare who won the German 1000 Guineas, is a half-brother to Kaleo, a winner over a mile at two in Germany, Musical Gift, a dual 1m to 1m1f winner, and Kantorka, a sprint winner at three in Italy. He ran a promising race, should improve for the experience and will get further in time.
Mudhish(IRE), whose dam did not run but is a half-sister to Taxman, a multiple 1m4f to 2m winner, and 1m winner Silver Bracelet, has a fair amount of speed in his pedigree and did not shape badly on his debut.

2242 INTERCASINO.CO.UK MAIDEN STKS 5f
4:05 (4:08) (Class 5) 3-Y-0+ **£3,886** (£1,156; £577; £288) **Stalls** Low

Form RPR
4324 **1** **Everygrainofsand (IRE)**[11] [1931] 4-9-7 72 .... GeorgeBaker 3 73
(J R Best) *mde all: rdn over 2f out: hanging rt fr 2f out: hld on wl last 100yds* **9/4**[1]
34-2 **2** *nk* **Excessive**[22] [1635] 3-8-9 65 .... DarryllHolland 6 64
(W Jarvis) *trckd ldrs: hdwy over 1f out: styd on u.p to press wnr ins fnl f: hld towards fin* **7/2**[3]
54 **3** *1* **Golden Brown (IRE)**[22] [1633] 3-9-0 0 .... FergusSweeney 1 65
(David Pinder) *chsd ldrs on rail: rdn and outpcd over 2f out: rallied over 1f out: kpt on ins fnl f* **20/1**
020- **4** *¾* **Even Bolder**[236] [5872] 4-9-7 65 .... SimonWhitworth 7 66
(R Simpson) *t.k.h: hld up: hdwy over 2f out: chsd ldrs and rdn over 1f out: kpt on same pce last 100yds* **14/1**
0-02 **5** *hd* **Lady Lafitte (USA)**[30] [1429] 3-8-9 67 .... MichaelHills 5 57
(B W Hills) *chsd wnr: ev ch and rdn 2f out: wknd ins fnl f* **11/4**[2]
6-5 **6** *1 ½* **Millsini**[12] [1883] 3-8-9 0 .... ChrisCatlin 2 52
(Rae Guest) *hld up and bhd: outpcd 2f out: kpt on fnl f* **33/1**
20- **7** *2* **Awwal Malika (USA)**[231] [5966] 3-8-9 0 .... RichardMullen 9 44
(C E Brittain) *s.i.s: a bhd: rdn over 2f out: sn btn* **6/1**
204- **8** *nk* **Kindallachan**[180] [6704] 4-9-2 42 .... PatDobbs 8 46
(G C Bravery) *chsd ldrs: rdn over 2f out: wknd over 1f out* **50/1**
26-0 **9** *1 ½* **Isobel Rose (IRE)**[33] [1345] 3-8-9 65 ....(b[1]) PhilipRobinson 10 38
(E A L Dunlop) *s.i.s: effrt and rdn over 2f out: wknd wl over 1f out* **12/1**

60.75 secs (-0.05) **Going Correction** 0.0s/f (Good)
WFA 3 from 4yo 7lb **9** Ran SP% **118.0**
Speed ratings (Par 103):100,99,97,96,96 94,90,90,87
CSF £10.46 TOTE £3.10: £1.20, £1.70, £4.10; EX 14.30 Trifecta £66.80 Pool: £191.94 - 2.04 winning units..
Owner John Mayne **Bred** Mrs C Hartery **Trained** Hucking, Kent

FOCUS
Mainly pretty exposed types in this modest maiden, and the whole field raced stands' side. It looks easy to rate based on the performances of the runner-up and fourth.

2243 £600 FREE AT INTERCASINO.CO.UK H'CAP 7f (S)
4:50 (4:51) (Class 4) (0-85,85) 3-Y-0 **£5,505** (£1,637; £818; £408) **Stalls** Low

Form RPR
0-21 **1** **Slate (IRE)**[21] [1684] 3-9-7 **85** .... PhilipRobinson 1 97+
(J A Osborne) *hld up on stands' side: hdwy over 2f out: led wl over 1f out: hrd pressed ins fnl f: hld on wl towards fin* **10/3**[2]
341- **2** *nk* **Danehillsundance (IRE)**[164] [6887] 3-8-12 **76** .... PatDobbs 3 87
(R Hannon) *chsd ldr on stands' side: rdn wl over 2f out: rallied over 1f out: ev ch ins fnl f: hld towards fin* **16/1**
0-60 **3** *4* **La Roca (IRE)**[23] [1610] 3-9-2 **80** .... GeorgeBaker 10 80
(R M Beckett) *hld up on far side: rdn and hdwy jst over 2f out: swtchd rt over 1f out: styd on: wnt 3rd last 100yds* **25/1**
23-1 **4** *¾* **Bold Abbott (USA)**[28] [1468] 3-9-5 **83** .... OscarUrbina 12 81+
(Mrs A J Perrett) *trckd ldrs on far side: hdwy to ld far side over 1f out: hung bdly lft to stands' rail ins fnl f: nt rcvr* **10/1**
-025 **5** *1 ¼* **King's Bastion (IRE)**[15] [1820] 3-9-3 **81** .... HayleyTurner 2 76
(M L W Bell) *taken down early: hld up on stands' side: hdwy and rdn over 2f out: no hdwy fnl f* **12/1**
14-0 **6** *1* **Steam Cuisine**[46] [1076] 3-9-0 **81** .... JerryO'Dwyer(3) 5 73
(M G Quinlan) *hld up on stands' side: rdn and hdwy over 2f out: no imp over 1f out* **25/1**
0-36 **7** *1* **Karoo Blue (IRE)**[21] [1662] 3-9-7 **85** .... RichardMullen 9 74
(C E Brittain) *w.w on far side: rdn and effrt over 2f out: btn wl over 1f out* **11/1**

020- **8** ½ **Oi Vay Joe (IRE)**[251] [5546] 3-9-7 **85**................................ DarryllHolland 7 73
(W Jarvis) *chsd ldrs on far side: rdn over 2f out: wknd 1f out* **8/1**
61 **9** ½ **Azeema (IRE)**[22] [1620] 3-8-13 **77**.. MichaelHills 11 64
(B W Hills) *led far side tl over 1f out: wknd and edgd lft over 1f out* **5/2**[1]
00-6 **10** *1* **Hythe Bay**[29] [1450] 3-8-7 **74**.. StephaneBreux(3) 6 58
(J R Best) *mounted on crse and taken down early: racd stands' side: led: clr tl wl over 2f out: hdd wl over 1f out: sn wknd* **25/1**
1106 **11** 2½ **Proper (IRE)**[9] [1978] 3-9-1 **79**.. ChrisCatlin 4 56
(M R Channon) *chsd ldrs on stands' side: rdn wl over 2f out: sn btn* **25/1**
1-44 **12** 2½ **Roodolph**[26] [1535] 3-8-13 **77**.. StephenCarson 8 47
(Eve Johnson Houghton) *chsd ldr on far side tl 1/2-way: sn rdn and lost pl: no ch last 2f* **11/2**[3]

1m 26.58s (-1.32) **Going Correction** 0.0s/f (Good) **12** Ran SP% **124.5**
Speed ratings (Par 101):107,106,102,101,99 98,97,96,96,95 92,89
CSF £55.78 CT £1141.57 TOTE £4.10: £1.80, £3.40, £7.10; EX 50.90 TRIFECTA Not won. Place 6 £168.45, Place 5 £46.85..
Owner Mountgrange Stud **Bred** Swordlestown Stud **Trained** Upper Lambourn, Berks

FOCUS
A fair little handicap in which the field split equally and the stands'-side group won the day.
Bold Abbott(USA) Official explanation: jockey said colt hung left
Azeema(IRE) Official explanation: trainer's rep had no explanation for the poor form shown
T/Plt: £420.90 to a £1 stake. Pool: £55,100.55. 95.55 winning tickets. T/Qpdt: £13.40 to a £1 stake. Pool: £2,572.50. 141.80 winning tickets. SP

1889 MUSSELBURGH (R-H)
Saturday, June 2

OFFICIAL GOING: Good (good to firm in places, 8.6)
Wind: virtually nil Weather: Fine

2244 TOTESCOOP6 H'CAP 5f
2:20 (2:20) (Class 4) (0-85,84) 3-Y-O+ **£6,477** (£1,927; £963; £481) **Stalls** Low

Form RPR
1105 **1** **Raccoon (IRE)**[15] [1806] 7-8-11 **72**.................................. PJMcDonald(5) 9 86
(D W Chapman) *cl up: led after 1f: rdn wl over 1f out: styd on strly* **11/2**[2]
21-1 **2** 1¼ **How's She Cuttin' (IRE)**[54] [964] 4-9-0 **70**...................... PaulFessey 10 80+
(T D Barron) *trckd ldrs: hdwy 2f out: rdn and ev ch ent fnl f: sn drvn: hung rt and one pce towards fin* **11/4**[1]
0244 **3** *1* **Bo McGinty (IRE)**[7] [2025] 6-9-2 **77**..........................(b) JamieMoriarty(5) 7 83
(R A Fahey) *hld up in tch: n.m.r and swtchd rt 2f out: sn rdn and ev ch ent fnl f: nt qckn* **7/1**
4355 **4** *nk* **Nusoor (IRE)**[10] [1941] 4-8-10 **69**..............................(b) PatrickMathers(3) 4 74
(Peter Grayson) *towards rr and nt clr run on inner over 2f out: swtchd rt and rdn wl over 1f out: styd on strly ins fnl f: nrst fin* **16/1**
-550 **5** *1* **Ptarmigan Ridge**[10] [1941] 11-9-2 **72**............................ RoystonFfrench 8 73
(Miss L A Perratt) *hld up: hdwy whn hmpd 2f out: sn rdn and kpt on ins fnl f* **20/1**
0005 **6** ½ **Glenviews Youngone (IRE)**[25] [1565] 4-8-8 **69**(b) RussellKennemore(5) 12 69
(Peter Grayson) *prom: rdn along 2f out: sn drvn and kpt on same pce* **20/1**
0101 **7** *nk* **Colorus (IRE)**[14] [1854] 4-9-8 **78**... DaleGibson 2 77
(M W Easterby) *chsd ldrs: rdn along 2f out: grad wknd* **8/1**
2-50 **8** *hd* **Matsunosuke**[7] [2025] 5-9-5 **75**.. DeanMcKeown 5 73
(A B Coogan) *towards rr: hdwy 2f out: sn rdn and kpt on same pce ins fnl f* **9/1**
1-63 **9** 2½ **Blazing Heights**[10] [1941] 4-9-2 **79**................................. GaryBartley(7) 11 68
(J S Goldie) *hld up in rr: hdwy on outer 1/2-way: effrt whn sltly hmpd 2f out: sn rdn and wknd ent fnl f* **6/1**[3]
0400 **10** *5* **First Order**[14] [1854] 6-10-0 **84**..(v) TomEaves 1 55
(I Semple) *chsd ldrs: rdn along over 2f out: grad wknd* **9/1**
-000 **11** *6* **Sokoke**[15] [1806] 6-8-9 **65** oh20.................................... PaulMulrennan 13 14
(D A Nolan) *led 1f: sn rdn along and wknd 1/2-way* **200/1**
00-0 **12** 1½ **Mister Marmaduke**[27] [1492] 6-8-9 **68** oh20 ow3.......... MarkLawson(3) 6 12
(D A Nolan) *dwlt: hdwy towards outer whn hmpd 2f out: sn wknd* **200/1**

60.19 secs (-0.31) **Going Correction** 0.0s/f (Good) **12** Ran SP% **116.3**
Speed ratings (Par 105):102,100,98,97,96 95,95,94,90,82 73,70
CSF £19.95 CT £107.69 TOTE £6.30: £2.40, £1.20, £2.60; EX 22.20.
Owner P D Savill **Bred** P D Savill **Trained** Stillington, N Yorks
■ Stewards' Enquiry : Patrick Mathers two-day ban: used whip with excessive force (Jun 13-14)

FOCUS
This looked a decent sprint on paper, but the winning time was nearly a second slower than the 41-rated Dematraf took to win the claimer later on the card. However, the form appears solid.

2245 TOTESPORT 0800 221 221 H'CAP 1m 6f
2:50 (2:50) (Class 3) (0-95,95) 4-Y-O+ **£11,217** (£3,358; £1,679; £840; £419; £210) **Stalls** High

Form RPR
1-60 **1** **All The Good (IRE)**[15] [1822] 4-9-7 **95**............................... PatCosgrave 1 103+
(G A Butler) *hld up in rr: smooth hdwy on inner 3f out: rdn to ld wl over 1f out: hit rail ins fnl f: styd on wl* **11/4**[1]
55-2 **2** *1* **Sin City**[31] [1416] 4-8-3 **77**.. DaleGibson 2 82
(R A Fahey) *hld up in tch: hdwy 3f out: rdn wl over 1f out: styd on to chse wnr ins fnl f* **3/1**[2]
4-26 **3** *1* **Lets Roll**[15] [1805] 6-8-13 **92**.. PJMcDonald(5) 5 96
(C W Thornton) *a.p: effrt 3f out and ev ch tl drvn over 1f out and kpt on same pce* **14/1**
6-01 **4** 2½ **Doctor Scott**[7] [2031] 4-8-4 **78**.. KDarley 6 78
(M Johnston) *trckd ldr: hdwy 3f out and sn ev ch: rdn 2f out and kpt on same pce* **3/1**[2]
1025 **5** 2½ **Kames Park (IRE)**[15] [1805] 5-9-0 **88**.................................. TomEaves 7 85
(I Semple) *hld up in rr: hdwy over 2f out: swtchd wd and rdn wl over 1f out: sn btn* **8/1**
30/ **6** 1¼ **Astronomic**[77] [3716] 7-8-6 **85**.. JamieMoriarty(5) 3 80
(J Howard Johnson) *hld up: a towards rr* **33/1**
-362 **7** 1¼ **Baizically (IRE)**[39] [1208] 4-9-1 **89**................................ DeanMcKeown 8 82
(J A Osborne) *led: rdn along over 3f out: drvn and edgd lft 2f out: sn hdd & wknd* **11/2**[3]

3m 2.49s (-3.21) **Going Correction** 0.0s/f (Good) **7** Ran SP% **112.8**
Speed ratings (Par 107):109,108,107,106,105 104,103
CSF £10.97 CT £93.06 TOTE £3.40: £2.10, £2.40; EX 5.90.
Owner Future In Mind Partnership **Bred** Mount Coote Partnership **Trained** Blewbury, Oxon

FOCUS
Just a fair gallop to this staying handicap which is best rated through the third.

NOTEBOOK
All The Good(IRE) came from last to first to win with a tad to spare. Getting a peach of a run up the inner, he did not do an awful lot after striking the front and faltered for a stride or two after losing concentration and touching the rail, but he was never going to be beaten. There could be more to come from him. (op 3-1 tchd 5-2)
Sin City, stepping back up in trip, took time to really find his stride after the race developed in earnest in the last 3f, but kept on to the line. He gives the impression that he may save a little for himself, but he probably came across a progressive winner here. (op 4-1 tchd 11-4, 9-2 in places)
Lets Roll ran a decent race on ground that would have been lively enough for him.
Doctor Scott was found wanting in the last couple of furlongs. (op 11-4 tchd 7-2)
Kames Park(IRE), not for the first time, gave the impression that things have to fall just right for him. (op 7-1 tchd 9-1)

2246 TOTESPORT.COM TRADESMAN'S DERBY H'CAP 1m 4f
3:20 (3:29) (Class 4) (0-85,83) 3-Y-O **£12,464** (£3,732; £1,866; £934; £466; £234) **Stalls** High

Form RPR
21 **1** **Secret Tune**[18] [1746] 3-9-7 **83**.. PaulEddery 1 92+
(Pat Eddery) *a.p: hdwy to chse ldr over 3f out: rdn to chal 2f out: sn drvn: styd on wl u.p ins fnl f to ld last 50yds* **4/1**[2]
1-26 **2** ½ **Gull Wing (IRE)**[21] [1663] 3-9-0 **79**.............................. AndrewElliott(3) 3 87
(M L W Bell) *hld up towards rr: gd hdwy wl over 2f out: rdn wl over 1f out: styd on strly ins fnl f* **5/1**[3]
331- **3** *shd* **Aureate**[190] [6581] 3-9-2 **78**... KDarley 2 86
(M Johnston) *prom: led over 8f out: qcknd 3f out: pushed along 2f out: rdn over 1f out: drvn ins fnl f: hdd and nt qckn last 50yds* **9/4**[1]
0061 **4** 2½ **Sadler's Kingdom (IRE)**[11] [1917] 3-7-12 **60** oh2............... DaleGibson 6 64
(R A Fahey) *trckd ldrs: hdwy over 3f out: rdn along over 2f out: drvn wl over 1f out and kpt on same pce* **8/1**
4220 **5** *5* **My Secrets**[12] [1898] 3-9-3 **79**.. J-PGuillambert 4 75
(M Johnston) *led over 3f: cl up: rdn along 3f out: drvn 2f out: grad wknd appr fnl f* **14/1**
1100 **6** ½ **Chookie Hamilton**[14] [1851] 3-8-10 **72**............................ TonyHamilton 10 67
(I Semple) *hld up: a towards rr* **33/1**
5-01 **7** ¾ **Polyquest (IRE)**[8] [2008] 3-8-1 **63** ow2.......................... RoystonFfrench 7 57
(G A Butler) *hld up in rr: effrt and hdwy on outer over 2f out: sn rdn and no imp* **7/1**
5-61 **8** ½ **Patavian (IRE)**[27] [1491] 3-8-7 **69** ow1.................................(p) TomEaves 8 62
(I Semple) *in tch: rdn along over 3f out: sn no hdwy* **25/1**
10 **9** 3½ **Rumpus (GER)**[22] [1637] 3-8-4 **69**................................ DuranFentiman(3) 9 57
(T P Tate) *hld up: a towards rr* **25/1**

2m 40.14s (3.24) **Going Correction** 0.0s/f (Good) **9** Ran SP% **108.3**
Speed ratings (Par 101):89,88,88,86,83 83,82,82,80
CSF £21.08 CT £46.72 TOTE £2.50: £1.40, £1.50, £1.20; EX 14.10.
Owner K Abdulla **Bred** Juddmonte Farms Ltd **Trained** Nether Winchendon, Bucks
■ Fushe Jo was withdrawn (14/1, injured in stalls.) Rule 4 applies, deduct 5p in the pound.

FOCUS
A decent prize for this staying handicap and a thrilling finish to a messy event. A race run a pedestrian gallop early on, and only a modest one afterwards, did not begin in earnest until the final half-mile. A very slow winning time for a race of its type but still rated relatively positively.

2247 VORWERK THERMOMIX GERMANY (S) STKS 5f
3:55 (3:57) (Class 4) 2-Y-O **£6,477** (£1,927; £963; £481) **Stalls** High

Form RPR
66 **1** **Glenluji**[10] [1938] 2-8-5 **0**... GaryBartley(7) 8 64
(J S Goldie) *sn outpcd and bhd: hdwy 2f out: swtchd outside and rdn wl over 1f out: styd on ins fnl f to ld nr fin* **8/1**
5 **2** *nk* **Prignsov Dancer (IRE)**[21] [1674] 2-8-12 **0**......................... LeeEnstone 5 63
(P C Haslam) *trckd ldrs: smooth hdwy 2f out: rdn to ld and hung lft over 1f out: sn drvn: hdd and no ex nr fin* **3/1**[2]
500 **3** *5* **Areweplayingout (IRE)**[12] [1889] 2-8-4 **0** ow2.... RussellKennemore(5) 3 42
(Peter Grayson) *chsd ldrs: rdn wl over 1f out: bmpd ent fnl f: kpt on u.p* **16/1**
35 **4** *nk* **La Guancha**[12] [1889] 2-8-7 **0**.. PaulFessey 7 39
(T D Barron) *s.i.s: hdwy on outer to chse ldrs 2f out: sn rdn and hung lft ent fnl f: one pce* **5/2**[1]
5 *4* **Ten On Line (IRE)** 2-8-12 **0**.. DeanMcKeown 1 30
(J A Osborne) *cl up: rdn along over 2f out: grad wknd* **6/1**
000 **6** *1* **Blazing Bullet (IRE)**[7] [2021] 2-8-12 **0**..........................(b[1]) TonyHamilton 10 26+
(N Wilson) *led: rdn along 2f out: hdd and wkng whn n.m.r ent fnl f* **40/1**
0601 **7** ¾ **Little Finch (IRE)**[7] [2028] 2-8-7 **0** ow2............................(b) NeilBrown(7) 2 25
(R C Guest) *chsd ldrs: rdn along and wkng whn n.m.r ent fnl f* **13/2**
5 **8** ½ **Quarrymaster (IRE)**[29] [1454] 2-8-12 **0**................................ TomEaves 6 21+
(J Howard Johnson) *cl up: rdn along 2f out: grad wknd and in rr whn n.m.r ent fnl f* **5/1**[3]

61.69 secs (1.19) **Going Correction** 0.0s/f (Good) **8** Ran SP% **117.3**
Speed ratings (Par 95):90,89,81,81,74 73,71,71
CSF £33.17 TOTE £11.60: £2.20, £1.50, £4.50; EX 39.00.There was no bid for the winner.
Owner Jim Goldie Racing Club **Bred** J S Goldie **Trained** Uplawmoor, E Renfrews
■ Stewards' Enquiry : Paul Fessey three-day ban: careless riding (Jun 13-15)

FOCUS
A valuable prize for this juvenile seller and above-average form for the grade, with the placed horses and sixth to form.

NOTEBOOK
Glenluji, dropped in class on his third outing and not unbacked, was outpaced early on but came home strongly down the outside to get on top inside the last. He will be better over 6f and may prove a nursery type. Official explanation: trainer said, regarding apparent improvement in form, that the colt benefited from a drop in class. (op 14-1)
Prigsnov Dancer(IRE) did not appear to help himself. He hung to his left and carried his head a little high after striking the front, but, given every assistance, was worried out of it near the finish. (op 10-3 tchd 11-4, 7-2 in places)
Areweplayingout(IRE), dropped in class after showing a small amount of ability in three maidens, had no chance with the front pair but was not disgraced and she may appreciate an extra furlong. (op 20-1 tchd 22-1)
La Guancha, who missed a beat at the start, looks a modest performer. (op 9-4 tchd 11-4, 3-1 in a place)
Ten On Line(IRE), a 31,000euros full-brother to Bogaz, showed little promise on this debut and may appreciate a bit further in time. (op 15-2)

2248 TOTEEXACTA H'CAP 1m 1f
4:40 (4:40) (Class 6) (0-65,69) 3-Y-O **£3,238** (£963; £481; £240) **Stalls** High

Form RPR
6211 **1** **Jewelled Dagger (IRE)**[12] [1894] 3-9-11 **69**........................(b) TomEaves 3 75
(I Semple) *trckd ldrs: pushed along and hdwy 2f out: swtchd rt and rdn to ld ins fnl f: drvn out* **9/4**[2]

4400 **2** ½ **Cap St Jean (IRE)**[61] 894 3-8-10 **54** .... LeeEnstone 4 58
(P C Haslam) *dwlt: hld up in tch: hdwy over 2f out: rdn over 1f out: ev ch whn drvn and edgd rt ins fnl f: kpt on* **25/1**

330 **3** 1 **Marju's Gold**[9] 1972 3-8-13 **57** .... DeanMcKeown 5 59
(E J O'Neill) *s.i.s and bhd: hdwy 2f out: sn rdn and styd on ins fnl f: nrst fin* **8/1**

00-0 **4** nk **Fistral**[19] 1712 3-8-1 **48** .... PatrickMathers(3) 2 49
(J Hetherton) *t.k.h: trckd ldrs: hdwy over 2f out and sn ev ch: rdn wl over 1f out and no ex ins fnl f* **40/1**

0-32 **5** nk **Grand Art (IRE)**[9] 1964 3-9-1 **66** .... HaddenFrost(7) 1 67
(M H Tompkins) *t.k.h: cl up: rn wd home turn and sn pushed along: rdn wl over 2f out: styd on same pce appr fnl f* **2/1**[1]

425 **6** nk **Prince Noel**[1] 2203 3-8-8 **52** .... (p) TonyHamilton 7 52
(N Wilson) *led: rdn along and hdd over 2f out: cl up and drvn tl wknd ins fnl f* **15/2**

-002 **7** hd **Desert Soul**[12] 1894 3-9-4 **62** .... J-PGuillambert 6 61
(M Johnston) *cl up: led over 2f out and sn rdn: drvn over 1f out: hdd & wknd ins fnl f* **4/1**[3]

1m 54.77s (0.91) **Going Correction** 0.0s/f (Good) **7** Ran SP% **113.3**
Speed ratings (Par 97):95,94,93,93,93 92,92
CSF £50.29 TOTE £2.50: £1.50, £7.30; EX 24.30.

Owner A R M Galbraith **Bred** Ballyhane Stud **Trained** Carluke, S Lanarks

■ Stewards' Enquiry : Hadden Frost five-day ban: used whip with excessive frequency (Jun 14-18)

Dean McKeown two-day ban: careless riding (Jun 13-14)

Lee Enstone one-day ban: careless riding (Jun 13); caution: used whip down shoulder in forehand position

FOCUS
Another messy race, run at dawdling gallop through the early exchanges. All in all, this is not a race to rely on as an accurate guide for the future, given the lack of early pace.

2249 TOTE TEXT BETTING 60021 CLAIMING STKS 5f
5:15 (5:15) (Class 6) 3-Y-O+ **£3,238** (£963; £481; £240) **Stalls** Low

Form RPR

26-2 **1** **Dematraf (IRE)**[12] 1891 5-8-2 41 .... PatrickMathers(3) 7 55
(Peter Grayson) *towards rr: gd hdwy 2f out: swtchd lft and chal over 1f out: rdn to ld ins fnl f: styd on wl* **10/1**

4300 **2** 1 ¼ **Sharp Hat**[25] 1557 13-8-10 52 .... DeanMcKeown 4 55
(D W Chapman) *led: rdn over 1f out: hdd and nt qckn ins fnl f* **12/1**

4612 **3** 1 ½ **Spirit Of Coniston**[12] 1902 4-9-7 50 .... (b) DuranFentiman(3) 10 64
(C J Teague) *outpcd and bhd: hdwy 2f out: sn rdn and kpt on ins fnl f* **15/2**[2]

0406 **4** hd **High Reach**[7] 2025 7-8-13 75 .... NeilBrown(7) 6 59
(T D Barron) *trckd ldrs: hdwy 2f out: sn rdn and one pce* **4/6**[1]

0402 **5** ¾ **She's Our Beauty (IRE)**[23] 1594 4-8-0 45 .... (p) PatrickDonaghy(7) 5 44
(S T Mason) *chsd ldrs: rdn along 2f out: sn one pce* **8/1**[3]

4033 **6** 7 **Rothesay Dancer**[12] 1891 4-9-2 52 .... (b[1]) GaryBartley(7) 2 34
(J S Goldie) *cl up: rdn along over 2f out: sn wknd* **8/1**[3]

00-0 **7** 1 **Tombalina**[23] 1594 4-8-4 43 .... KellyHarrison(7) 1 19
(C J Teague) *chsd ldrs: rdn along 1/2-way: sn wknd* **33/1**

0-00 **8** 2 ½ **Alfie Lee (IRE)**[12] 1891 10-8-9 33 ow2 .... MarkLawson(3) 9 11
(D A Nolan) *a towards rr* **100/1**

0060 **U** **Howards Princess**[23] 1594 5-8-7 41 ow2 .... (b) TonyHamilton 8 —
(J Hetherton) *rrd and uns rdr s* **28/1**

59.86 secs (-0.64) **Going Correction** 0.0s/f (Good) **9** Ran SP% **118.1**
Speed ratings (Par 101):105,103,100,100,99 87,86,82,—
CSF £121.15 TOTE £11.40: £2.60, £3.10, £2.20; EX 139.70.Dematraf was claimed by P. D. Evans for £5,000.

Owner Alan Williams **Bred** Edward Ryan **Trained** Formby, Lancs

FOCUS
A poor claimer with the odds-on High Reach failing to produce the goods, but the winning time was almost a second quicker than the earlier handicap. The third rated to last year's form sets the level.

2250 TOTESPORTCASINO.COM H'CAP 1m 6f
5:50 (5:50) (Class 5) (0-70,69) 4-Y-O+ **£4,533** (£1,348; £674; £336) **Stalls** High

Form RPR

0022 **1** **Toparudi**[1] 2204 6-8-10 **65** .... HaddenFrost(7) 4 73
(M H Tompkins) *dwlt: hld up in rr: hdwy on inner over 2f out: rdn to chal wl over 1f out: styd on to ld nr fin* **3/1**[2]

3010 **2** hd **Hugs Destiny (IRE)**[9] 1966 6-8-6 **54** .... (t) DeanMcKeown 7 62
(M A Barnes) *trckd ldrs: hdwy 3f out: led 2f out: sn jnd and rdn: drvn ins fnl f: hdd and no ex nr fin* **8/1**

-423 **3** 3 ½ **Boxhall (IRE)**[7] 2026 5-9-7 **69** .... TonyHamilton 5 72
(N Wilson) *led: rdn along 3f out: hdd 2f out and kpt on same pce* **4/1**[3]

136 **4** 6 **Kyber**[12] 1895 6-8-1 **52** .... DuranFentiman(3) 6 47
(J S Goldie) *chsd ldr: rdn along 3f out: wknd over 2f out* **8/1**

/520 **5** 2 ½ **Alrida (IRE)**[16] 1793 8-9-2 **69** .... JamieMoriarty(5) 2 60
(R A Fahey) *hld up: a in rr* **11/4**[1]

4550 **6** 1 ½ **Grey Outlook**[16] 1793 4-8-7 **60** .... RussellKennemore(5) 1 49
(Miss L A Perratt) *chsd ldrs: rdn along over 3f out and sn wknd* **12/1**

6-01 **7** hd **Toshi (USA)**[12] 1890 5-9-1 **66** .... MarkLawson(3) 3 55
(P Monteith) *plld hrd: chsd ldrs: cl up 1/2-way: rdn along 3f out and sn wknd* **4/1**[3]

3m 2.96s (-2.74) **Going Correction** 0.0s/f (Good) **7** Ran SP% **121.6**
Speed ratings (Par 103):107,106,104,101,100 99,99
CSF £29.01 TOTE £4.10: £2.30, £4.20; EX 41.40 Place 6 £143.77, Place 5 £83.33..

Owner M P Bowring **Bred** M P Bowring **Trained** Newmarket, Suffolk

■ Stewards' Enquiry : Hadden Frost two-day ban: used whip with excessive frequency (Jun 24-25)

FOCUS
A fair time for a race like this, just around half a second slower than the earlier Class 3 handicap over the same trip, and solid form with the winner back to something like his best.

T/Plt: £502.70 to a £1 stake. Pool: £58,269.30. 84.60 winning tickets. T/Qpdt: £139.30 to a £1 stake. Pool: £2,127.60. 11.30 winning tickets. JR

[1963]NEWCASTLE (L-H)
Saturday, June 2

OFFICIAL GOING: Good (good to soft in places)
The ground had dried out rapidly and was described as 'mainly good, faster than that in places'. The stands' side rail was a big advantage.
Wind: Light, half-behind Weather: Fine and mild

2251 SENDRIG MAIDEN AUCTION STKS 6f
6:30 (6:32) (Class 5) 2-Y-O **£3,368** (£1,002; £500; £250) **Stalls** High

Form RPR

1 **Maze (IRE)** 2-9-1 0 .... RoystonFfrench 11 87+
(B Smart) *dwlt: sn chsng ldrs: n.m.r after 1f: drvn 3f out: chal 1f out: styd on to ld last 75yds* **5/1**[2]

0 **2** ½ **La Chicaluna**[35] 1285 2-8-5 0 .... PaulQuinn 5 75
(J G Given) *swtchd rt after s: led: hdd and no ex wl ins fnl f* **33/1**

533 **3** 3 **Runswick Bay**[18] 1743 2-8-11 0 .... AndrewElliott(3) 6 75
(G M Moore) *chsd ldrs: effrt 2f out: kpt on same pce* **13/2**[3]

2 **4** ¾ **Abolition (USA)**[18] 1743 2-9-0 0 .... KDarley 10 73
(M Johnston) *trckd ldrs: hmpd after 1f: rdn over 1f out: sn btn* **1/2**[1]

44 **5** ¾ **Berrymead**[19] 1713 2-8-4 0 .... DaleGibson 3 61
(M W Easterby) *swvd lft s: mid-div: effrt and rn green 2f out: kpt on wl ins fnl f* **20/1**

0 **6** 1 ½ **Discanti (IRE)**[19] 1713 2-8-13 0 .... (t) DavidAllan 8 65
(T D Easterby) *n.m.r after 1f: mid-div: hdwy over 1f out: styd on ins fnl f* **20/1**

005 **7** 6 **Thomas Malory (IRE)**[7] 2024 2-8-9 0 .... ColinHaddon(5) 4 48
(Miss V Haigh) *w ldrs: hung lft and lost pl over 1f out* **16/1**

8 9 **Utrillo's Art (IRE)** 2-8-3 0 ow2 .... NSLawes(7) 7 17
(M W Easterby) *s.i.s: in rr: bhd fnl 2f* **100/1**

5 **9** nk **Lavemill (IRE)**[7] 2028 2-8-1 0 .... AndrewMullen(3) 1 10
(R F Fisher) *swvd lft s: sn chsng ldrs: lost pl over 1f out: sn eased* **100/1**

10 8 **Woodford** 2-8-10 0 .... PaulMulrennan 2 —
(M W Easterby) *s. s: a detached in rr* **66/1**

1m 13.33s (-1.76) **Going Correction** -0.225s/f (Firm) **10** Ran SP% **118.5**
Speed ratings (Par 93):102,101,97,96,95 93,85,73,72,62
CSF £152.45 TOTE £6.60: £2.00, £10.00, £2.00; EX 147.40.

Owner Pinnacle Dr Fong Partnership **Bred** Millsec Limited **Trained** Hambleton, N Yorks

■ Stewards' Enquiry : Paul Quinn one-day ban: careless riding (Jun 13)

FOCUS
A fair contest and sound enough rated around the third and fifth. The runner-up sqeezed them up early on. She had the favoured stands'-side rail to race against and the winner deserves credit.

NOTEBOOK
Maze(IRE), a March foal, is on the leg. After missing a beat at the start and then tightened up when the winner made a bee-line for the stands'-side rail, he deserves credit for the way he put his head down and really battled. Well thought of, seven furlongs will suit him even better. (op 9-2 tchd 6-1)
La Chicaluna, drawn on the outer, made a bee-line for the stands'-side rail. Only edged out near the line, she had the best of the ground but will surely find a race.
Runswick Bay, having his fourth outing, was forced to race rather wide. (op 7-1 tchd 8-1)
Abolition(USA), a big type, had finished ahead of Runswick Bay on his debut here on his debut here. He was knocked out of his stride at the end of the first furlong and was in big trouble coming to the final furlong and may need more time yet. (op 4-6 tchd 4-5 and 8-11 i8n places)
Berrymead, happy to be back on turf, still looks very inexperienced. Picking up in good style late on, she looks more of a nursery type.
Discanti(IRE), wearing a tongue-tie this time, picked up in encouraging fashion late on and will be even better suited by a step up to seven. (tchd 25-1)

2252 SENDRIG CONSTRUCTION H'CAP 2m 19y
7:00 (7:00) (Class 6) (0-65,63) 4-Y-O+ **£2,914** (£867; £433; £216) **Stalls** Low

Form RPR

625- **1** **Gallileo Figaro (USA)**[175] 6766 4-9-8 **63** .... KDarley 4 71+
(N B King) *chsd ldrs: led over 3f out: clr over 1f out: jst hld on* **10/1**

06-2 **2** nk **Kristiansand**[10] 1942 7-8-10 **50** .... PatCosgrave 14 58+
(P Monteith) *hld up in rr: hdwy 5f out: nt clr run 2f out: styd on strly ins fnl f: jst failed* **5/1**[1]

/362 **3** 1 ½ **Theflyingscottie**[24] 1590 5-8-5 **45** .... (v) DaleGibson 2 51
(D Shaw) *hld up: hdwy 7f out: sn chsng ldrs: kpt on same pce appr fnl f* **11/2**[2]

-441 **4** 2 **York Cliff**[10] 1942 9-9-6 **60** .... DavidAllan 3 64
(W M Brisbourne) *chsd ldrs: styd on same pce fnl 2f* **5/1**[1]

30/5 **5** 4 **Brave Vision**[10] 1942 11-8-2 **45** .... AndrewMullen(3) 12 44+
(A C Whillans) *mid-div: drvn 6f out: hdwy to chse ldrs 3f out: wknd over 1f out* **14/1**

-000 **6** 3 **Time Marches On**[12] 1895 9-7-12 **45** .... DanielleMcCreery(7) 15 40
(K G Reveley) *hld up in rr: hdwy 6f out: kpt on fnl 3f: nvr rchd ldrs* **20/1**

06-1 **7** shd **Singhalongtasveer**[12] 1895 5-8-9 **52** .... (vt) AndrewElliott(3) 5 47
(W Storey) *in rr: drvn along 9f out: kpt on fnl 3f: nvr rchd ldrs* **9/1**

/66- **8** 3 **Woodford Consult**[126] 6178 5-8-11 **51** .... PaulMulrennan 6 42
(M W Easterby) *chsd ldrs: drvn over 5f out: wknd over 2f out* **16/1**

/006 **9** 1 **Silent Street**[9] 1966 4-8-4 **45** .... PaulQuinn 9 35
(K G Reveley) *t.k.h in rr: kpt on fnl 3f: nvr nr ldrs* **12/1**

-422 **10** ¾ **Bulberry Hill**[114] 389 6-8-9 **56** .... KirstyMilczarek(7) 7 45
(R W Price) *trckd ldrs: led after 3f tl over 3f out: lost pl over 1f out* **13/2**[3]

66-0 **11** 2 ½ **The Dunion**[10] 1942 4-7-13 **47** ow2 .... JamesRogers(7) 8 33
(Miss L A Perratt) *dwlt: in rr: bhd fnl 6f* **80/1**

00-5 **12** 3 ½ **Borsch (IRE)**[12] 1895 5-8-0 **45** .... TolleyDean(5) 1 27
(Miss L A Perratt) *led 3f: chsd ldrs: drvn over 3f out: sn wknd* **33/1**

02-0 **13** 5 **Good Investment**[32] 240 5-8-8 **48** .... (b) DeanMernagh 10 24
(Miss Tracy Waggott) *hld up in mid-div: hdwy 5f out: rdn and one pce fnl 3f* **50/1**

00/3 **14** 1 **Roman Army (IRE)**[27] 1491 5-9-3 **57** .... (p) RoystonFfrench 16 32
(James Moffatt) *prom: effrt over 3f out: sn lost pl* **12/1**

02/0 **15** 6 **Alghaazy (IRE)**[59] 913 6-8-5 **45** .... PaulFessey 13 13
(Micky Hammond) *mid-div: drvn 5f out: lost pl over 2f out* **33/1**

-304 **F** **Arcangela**[54] 965 4-8-1 **47** ow2 .... ColinHaddon(5) 11 —
(Miss Tracy Waggott) *in rr-div: fell bnd after 6f* **33/1**

3m 36.65s (1.45) **Going Correction** -0.125s/f (Firm)
WFA 4 from 5yo+ 1lb **16** Ran SP% **125.9**
Speed ratings (Par 101):91,90,90,89,87 85,85,84,83,83 81,80,77,77,74 —
CSF £57.92 CT £316.13 TOTE £12.30: £3.10, £1.40, £2.20, £1.60; EX 56.00.

Owner The Not Over Big Partnership **Bred** Finger Rock Farm **Trained** Newmarket, Suffolk

FOCUS
A very steady pace for this modest stayers' handicap. The form looks sound though rated through the runner-up and the fourth.

The Form Book, Raceform Ltd, Compton, RG20 6NL

2253 **SENDRIG CONSTRUCTION MAIDEN STKS** **1m 2f 32y**
7:30 (7:34) (Class 5) 3-Y-0+ **£3,303** (£982; £491; £245) **Stalls** Centre

Form RPR
1 **Bogside Theatre (IRE)** 3-8-4 0 AndrewElliott(3) 5 73
(G M Moore) *chsd ldrs: qcknd to ld over 1f out: drew clr* **100/1**
53 **2** 6 **Honorable Love**^{21} [1659] 3-8-7 0 TomEaves 8 61
(M Dods) *hld up in tch: effrt 2f out: styd on to take 2nd ins fnl f* **11/2**^{3}
4 **3** 2 **Candy Mountain**^{25} [1560] 3-8-7 0 KDarley 4 57
(L M Cumani) *trckd ldrs: chal over 2f out: kpt on same pce appr fnl f* **4/1**^{2}
0/2 **4** 1/2 **Grizebeck (IRE)**^{39} [1231] 5-9-11 0 PhillipMakin 2 61
(R F Fisher) *led 3f: chsd ldrs: kpt on same pce fnl 2f* **40/1**
2040 **5** 1 1/4 **Wulimaster (USA)**^{8} [2011] 4-9-11 69 (p) PatCosgrave 3 58
(D W Barker) *sn drvn along: chsng ldrs: one pce fnl 2f* **13/2**
3 **6** 2 **Crispian (IRE)**^{63} [849] 3-8-12 0 PaulMulrennan 9 54
(W J Haggas) *hld up in mid-div: effrt over 2f out: nvr trbld ldrs* **11/8**^{1}
03 **7** hd **White Moss (IRE)**^{15} [1816] 3-8-7 0 DaleGibson 7 49
(M H Tompkins) *t.k.h: trckd ldr: led after 3f tl over 1f out: wknd* **11/1**
00-0 **8** nk **Bottomless Wallet**^{18} [1744] 6-9-6 35 PaulFessey 15 48
(F Watson) *in rr: kpt on fnl 2f: nvr nr ldrs* **100/1**
9 nk **Solid Silver**^{15} 6-9-11 0 DavidAllan 12 52
(K G Reveley) *s.i.s: hld up in rr: kpt on fnl 2f: nvr nr ldrs* **33/1**
30 **10** 3 **Modarab**^{6} [1998] 5-9-6 0 PJMcDonald(5) 14 46
(Mrs L B Normile) *in rr: nvr a factor* **66/1**
2400 **11** 1 1/4 **Jiminor Mack**^{101} [514] 4-9-6 40 RoystonFfrench 13 39
(W J H Ratcliffe) *in rr: kpt on fnl 2f: nvr on terms* **33/1**
23 **12** 1 1/4 **Campli (IRE)**^{14} [1849] 5-9-6 0 MichaelJStainton(5) 11 41
(Micky Hammond) *in rr-div: drvn over 3f out: nvr on terms* **10/1**
06 **13** 1 1/4 **Little Nipper**^{19} [1716] 3-8-9 0 AndrewMullen(3) 6 39
(W J H Ratcliffe) *prom: drvn 6f out: lost pl 4f out* **100/1**
14 3 1/2 **Ringo (IRE)**^{24} 7-9-8 0 DougieCostello(3) 10 32
(R Johnson) *s.i.s: hld up in mid-div: effrt over 3f out: lost pl over 2f out* **66/1**

2m 11.11s (-0.69) **Going Correction** -0.125s/f (Firm)
WFA 3 from 4yo+ 13lb **14 Ran SP% 122.5**
Speed ratings (Par 103):97,92,90,90,89 87,87,87,86,84 83,82,81,78
CSF £599.98 TOTE £124.30: £39.60, £2.00, £2.00; EX 1380.70.
Owner B Lappin **Bred** Crone Stud Farms Ltd **Trained** Middleham Moor, N Yorks

FOCUS
A modest maiden won by a 100/1 newcomer and not that solid with the 35-rated eighth tying down the form.
White Moss(IRE) Official explanation: jockey said filly ran too free

2254 **SENDRIG SUPPORTS CHILDREN'S HOPE H'CAP** **1m 2f 32y**
8:00 (8:04) (Class 6) (0-65,67) 4-Y-0+ **£2,914** (£867; £433; £216) **Stalls** Centre

Form RPR
0-00 **1** **Best Of The Lot (USA)**^{10} [1942] 5-8-13 **57** PatCosgrave 8 69
(R A Fahey) *hld up in tch: smooth hdwy on ins 3f out: led over 1f out: sn clr: drvn out* **12/1**
03-0 **2** 1 3/4 **Hawkit (USA)**^{22} [1627] 6-9-6 **64** DaleGibson 7 73
(P Monteith) *hld up in midfield: hdwy over 3f out: wnt 2nd 1f out: kpt on wl* **20/1**
-000 **3** 2 **Ruby Legend**^{9} [1967] 9-8-8 **52** (b) KDarley 5 57
(K G Reveley) *hld up in rr: hdwy 3f out: styd on same pce fnl f* **18/1**
0400 **4** shd **Dechiper (IRE)**^{19} [1715] 5-8-3 **50** AndrewElliott(3) 1 55+
(R Johnson) *chsd ldrs: outpcd and nt clr run over 1f out: styd on wl ins fnl f* **20/1**
0154 **5** 1 3/4 **Elopement (IRE)**^{3} [2157] 5-8-11 **55** DavidAllan 15 56
(W M Brisbourne) *chsd ldrs: styd on same pce fnl 2f* **13/2**^{2}
0004 **6** nk **Neil's Legacy (IRE)**^{2} [2168] 5-8-1 **50** TolleyDean(5) 16 50
(Miss L A Perratt) *s.i.s: hdwy over 3f out: kpt on fnl 2f: nt rch ldrs* **7/1**^{3}
4-31 **7** 1/2 **Royal Flynn**^{9} [1967] 5-9-9 **67** PaulFessey 13 66+
(M Dods) *stdd s: hld up detached in rr: hdwy and nt clr run over 2f out: styd on: nt rch ldrs* **11/4**^{1}
60-6 **8** 1 **Rotuma (IRE)**^{9} [1967] 8-8-9 **53** (b) PhillipMakin 10 50
(M Dods) *hld up in rr: hdwy over 2f out: kpt on: nvr nr ldrs* **7/1**^{3}
6424 **9** hd **Tour D'Amour (IRE)**^{22} [1626] 4-8-10 **61** NeilBrown(7) 6 58
(R Craggs) *sn chsng ldrs: kpt on same pce fnl 2f* **12/1**
104- **10** 8 **Thornaby Green**^{163} [6899] 6-8-0 **51** DeanHeslop(7) 4 32
(T D Barron) *mde most: hdd & wknd over 1f out* **16/1**
0 **11** 3 **My Causeway Dream (IRE)**^{9} [1967] 4-8-8 **52** (v^{1}) PaulQuinn 3 27
(J S Wainwright) *bhd: hdwy over 3f out: sn chsng ldrs: wknd 2f out* **100/1**
320- **12** 2 1/2 **Turn Of Phrase (IRE)**^{202} [5904] 8-9-2 **60** TomEaves 12 30
(B Ellison) *in rr-div: effrt 3f out: nvr a factor* **11/1**
60-0 **13** 1 1/2 **Fadansil**^{25} [1569] 4-8-1 **48** oh1 ow2 AndrewMullen(3) 14 15
(J Wade) *mid-div: lost pl over 3f out* **50/1**
641- **14** 6 **Roman History (IRE)**^{264} [5240] 4-8-11 **55** J-PGuillambert 9 10
(Miss Tracy Waggott) *chsd ldrs: lost pl 3f out* **33/1**
0 **15** 22 **Besi**^{22} [1627] 5-8-13 **57** RoystonFfrench 2 —
(P Monteith) *prom: drvn 4f out: sn lost pl: eased whn bhd* **40/1**
3-06 **16** 49 **Tranos (USA)**^{10} [1532] 4-8-12 **56** PaulMulrennan 11 —
(Micky Hammond) *w ldrs: lost pl over 4f out: bhd and virtually p.u over 2f out: t.o* **14/1**

2m 10.19s (-1.61) **Going Correction** -0.125s/f (Firm) **16 Ran SP% 124.4**
Speed ratings (Par 101):101,99,98,97,96 96,95,95,94,88 86,84,82,78,60 22
CSF £245.26 CT £4279.05 TOTE £14.10: £3.00, £4.00, £3.60, £6.10; EX 253.50.
Owner Mike Browne **Bred** Team Half Moon Farm **Trained** Musley Bank, N Yorks

FOCUS
A low-grade handicap with plenty of traffic problems. The fifth is the key to the overall value of the form.
Besi Official explanation: jockey said gelding was unsuited by the good ground

2255 **SENDRIG H'CAP** **5f**
8:30 (8:30) (Class 5) (0-75,68) 3-Y-0 **£3,562** (£1,059; £529; £264) **Stalls** High

Form RPR
1440 **1** **Darcy's Pride (IRE)**^{26} [1530] 3-8-9 **56** TomEaves 7 66
(D W Barker) *mde all: styd on wl fnl f: drvn rt out* **7/2**^{1}
65-0 **2** 1 1/2 **Bollin Franny**^{35} [1286] 3-9-3 **64** DavidAllan 6 68
(T D Easterby) *chsd wnr: styd on same pce ins fnl f* **7/2**^{1}
0343 **3** shd **Feelin Foxy**^{4} [2119] 3-9-4 **65** (v) KDarley 3 69
(D Shaw) *t.k.h in rr: effrt 2f out: sn chsng ldrs: no ex ins fnl f* **7/2**^{1}
26-4 **4** 1 1/2 **Morristown Music (IRE)**^{43} [1135] 3-9-4 **65** TonyHamilton 5 64
(J S Wainwright) *hld up: effrt over 2f out: kpt on same pce appr fnl f* **12/1**
240- **5** nk **Gap Princess (IRE)**^{242} [5748] 3-8-13 **65** JamieMoriarty(5) 8 63+
(R A Fahey) *hld up: effrt 2f out: styd on ins fnl f* **4/1**^{2}
4116 **6** 3 **Bentley**^{103} [502] 3-9-7 **68** (v) DeanMcKeown 4 55
(D Shaw) *chsd ldrs: wknd over 1f out* **10/1**
4-00 **7** 6 **Only A Grand**^{18} [1748] 3-8-3 **55** NataliaGemelova(5) 1 20
(R Bastiman) *sn outpcd in rr: sme hdwy on outer over 2f out: lost pl over 1f out* **16/1**
5-43 **8** 3 **Mickleberry (IRE)**^{11} [1932] 3-9-1 **62** PatCosgrave 2 16
(J D Bethell) *w ldrs on outer: rdn over 2f out: lost pl over 1f out* **8/1**^{3}

60.74 secs (-0.76) **Going Correction** -0.225s/f (Firm) **8 Ran SP% 120.4**
Speed ratings (Par 99):97,94,94,92,91 86,77,72
CSF £16.92 CT £47.09 TOTE £6.50: £2.00, £2.10, £1.10; EX 23.40.
Owner Ms Jenny Hanson **Bred** Leo Cox **Trained** Scorton, N Yorks

FOCUS
The winner had the advantage of racing hard against the stands'-side rail. This modest handicap has been rated through the runner-up.

2256 **JAMES BURRELL BUILDERS MERCHANTS H'CAP** **7f**
9:00 (9:00) (Class 5) (0-70,70) 4-Y-0+ **£3,562** (£1,059; £529; £264) **Stalls** High

Form RPR
-064 **1** **Viva Volta**^{18} [1747] 4-9-5 **68** (b) DavidAllan 17 81+
(T D Easterby) *mde all against stands' side rail: drvn clr over 1f out: rdn rt out* **7/2**^{1}
5200 **2** 1 1/4 **Parkview Love (USA)**^{14} [1847] 6-9-0 **63** (v) DeanMcKeown 16 70
(D Shaw) *hld up: hdwy stands' side 2f out: styd on wl to take 2nd ins fnl f* **20/1**
105- **3** 3 **Rigat**^{231} [5961] 4-9-0 **70** NeilBrown(7) 12 69+
(T D Barron) *hld up: hdwy over 2f out: edgd lft and wnt 2nd 1f out: kpt on same pce* **14/1**
0-00 **4** 1/2 **Top Dirham**^{3} [2149] 9-8-7 **56** DaleGibson 10 54
(M W Easterby) *hld up in rr: hdwy stands' side 2f out: styd on wl ins fnl f* **16/1**
1-00 **5** 1 3/4 **Prospect Court**^{23} [1597] 5-8-3 **55** AndrewMullen(3) 5 48
(A C Whillans) *w ldrs: one pce fnl 2f* **20/1**
306 **6** 1 **The Osteopath (IRE)**^{18} [1747] 4-9-6 **69** (b) TomEaves 14 59
(M Dods) *trckd ldrs: t.k.h: effrt over 2f out: kpt on same pce* **7/2**^{1}
25-0 **7** 3/4 **Dazzler Mac**^{61} [892] 6-8-7 **56** ow1 TonyHamilton 8 44
(N Bycroft) *chsd ldrs: kpt on same pce fnl 2f* **10/1**^{3}
05-2 **8** 1/2 **Zhitomir**^{59} [912] 9-8-9 **58** PhillipMakin 7 45
(M Dods) *trckd ldrs: one pce fnl 2f* **12/1**
122- **9** nk **Scotland The Brave**^{217} [6211] 7-9-7 **70** (v) PatCosgrave 6 56
(J D Bethell) *w ldrs: wknd appr fnl f* **11/1**
3410 **10** shd **Dorn Dancer (IRE)**^{5} [2072] 5-8-13 **62** RoystonFfrench 13 48
(D W Barker) *mid-div: hung lft over 2f out: kpt on fnl f* **8/1**^{2}
00-0 **11** hd **Dispol Katie**^{7} [2033] 6-8-9 **58** PaulFessey 3 43
(T D Barron) *chsd ldrs: one pce fnl 2f* **14/1**
450- **12** nk **Miss Sure Bond (IRE)**^{227} [6061] 4-8-5 **57** DuranFentiman(3) 9 41
(G R Oldroyd) *hld up in rr: kpt on fnl 2f: nvr nr ldrs* **50/1**
220- **13** 1 1/4 **Penzo (IRE)**^{261} [5312] 4-8-13 **67** JamieMoriarty(5) 2 48
(J Howard Johnson) *in rr: nvr on terms* **25/1**
/5-0 **14** 7 **Brace Of Doves**^{40} [1198] 5-8-11 **65** PJMcDonald(5) 1 27
(D W Whillans) *chsd ldrs: lost pl over 2f out* **50/1**
0100 **15** 8 **Alsadaa (USA)**^{3} [2149] 4-9-2 **65** PaulMulrennan 11 5
(M W Easterby) *chsd ldrs: wknd 2f out: bhd whn eased ins fnl f* **10/1**^{3}
50-0 **16** 7 **Titinius (IRE)**^{25} [1555] 7-8-13 **62** KDarley 15 —
(Micky Hammond) *chsd ldrs: hung lft and lost pl over 1f out: heavily eased and sn bhd* **16/1**

1m 25.77s (-2.25) **Going Correction** -0.225s/f (Firm) **16 Ran SP% 132.2**
Speed ratings (Par 103):103,101,98,97,95 94,93,93,92,92 92,91,90,82,73 65
CSF £88.51 CT £678.39 TOTE £5.30: £1.40, £4.90, £6.40, £4.70; EX 59.00 Place 6 £323.13, Place 5 £92.54.
Owner Mrs Jennifer E Pallister **Bred** T W H And Mrs Dancer **Trained** Great Habton, N Yorks

FOCUS
The stands'-side rail was the place to be and the winner, runner-up and strong-finishing fourth raced there. The race has been rated through the runner-up.
Titinius(IRE) Official explanation: jockey said gelding hung left-handed final 2f
T/Plt: £1,615.50 to a £1 stake. Pool: £72,591.15. 32.80 winning tickets. T/Qpdt: £226.40 to a £1 stake. Pool: £4,895.50. 16.00 winning tickets. WG

2220 WOLVERHAMPTON (A.W) (L-H)
Saturday, June 2

OFFICIAL GOING: Standard
Wind: Light behind Weather: Warm and sunny

2257 **X K R SPRINT FILLIES' H'CAP** **7f 32y(P)**
6:40 (6:46) (Class 6) (0-65,64) 4-Y-0+ **£2,388** (£705; £352) **Stalls** High

Form RPR
2-30 **1** **Fairdonna**^{98} [548] 4-8-11 **54** AdamKirby 2 62
(D J Coakley) *mid-div: hdwy over 2f out: rdn over 1f out: r.o to ld post* **11/2**^{3}
04-0 **2** shd **Antigoni (IRE)**^{27} [1507] 4-9-5 **62** LPKeniry 5 69
(A M Balding) *chsd ldrs: rdn 1/2-way: led over 1f out: hdd post* **13/2**
0-34 **3** 1 1/2 **Bens Georgie (IRE)**^{10} [1946] 5-8-12 **55** RobertHavlin 8 58
(D K Ivory) *prom: lost pl 4f out: hdwy over 1f out: styd on u.p* **6/1**
6442 **4** 1 1/4 **Lady Duxyana**^{3} [2143] 4-8-2 **45** (v) RichardSmith 7 45
(M D I Usher) *s.i.s: sn pushed along in rr: hdwy over 1f out: nt rch ldrs* **7/2**^{2}
-301 **5** 1 1/2 **Pappas Ruby (USA)**^{11} [1933] 4-8-13 **56** (b) SebSanders 4 52
(R M Beckett) *led 1f: chsd ldrs: led again 1/2-way: rdn and hdd over 1f out: wknd ins fnl f* **5/2**^{1}
2040 **6** 1 1/2 **My Michelle**^{17} [1765] 6-9-7 **64** CatherineGannon 6 56
(B Palling) *chsd ldrs: rdn over 2f out: wknd over 1f out* **8/1**
0/00 **7** 11 **Miss Lovat**^{23} [1596] 4-7-13 **45** LiamJones(3) 11 7
(W M Brisbourne) *sn pushed along in rr: bhd fr 1/2-way* **50/1**
100- **8** 2 1/2 **Penny Glitters**^{178} [6725] 4-8-1 **47** DominicFox(3) 10 2
(S Parr) *chsd ldrs over 4f* **28/1**
0-06 **9** 1 1/2 **Limonia (GER)**^{3} [2143] 5-8-3 **51** ow3 KevinGhunowa(5) 9 2
(Mike Murphy) *led 6f out: hdd 1/2-way: wknd over 2f out* **13/2**
0 **10** 1 3/4 **Minstrel Flyer (IRE)**^{21} [1673] 5-8-2 **45** FrankieMcDonald 1 —
(E J Creighton) *unruly in stalls: sn pushed along in rr: bhd fr 1/2-way* **50/1**

1m 29.35s (-1.05) **Going Correction** -0.10s/f (Stan) **10 Ran SP% 125.6**
Speed ratings (Par 98):102,101,100,98,97 95,82,79,78,76
CSF £44.06 CT £234.42 TOTE £8.00: £1.70, £2.90, £2.50; EX 61.60.

Owner James Kerr Max Moccia **Bred** Sir Gordon Brunton **Trained** West Ilsley, Berks

FOCUS

A very ordinary fillies' handicap with the winner getting off the mark at the 11th attempt, but with three vying for the lead from the start at least the pace was decent. The form is limited, but reliable enough.

Limonia(GER) Official explanation: jockey said mare ran flat

2258 STRATSTONE THOROUGHBRED (S) STKS — 1m 141y(P)
7:10 (7:13) (Class 6) 4-Y-0+ — **£2,047** (£604; £302) **Stalls** Low

Form — RPR

6-04 **1** **Dante's Diamond (IRE)**^{11} [1921] 5-8-12 55.................. MickyFenton 11 — 63
(D Burchell) *outpcd: hdwy over 2f out: rdn over 1f out: hung lft ins fnl f: styd on to ld nr fin* **7/1**^{3}

2 *hd* **Lady Aspen (IRE)**^{31} [1418] 4-8-4 0.................................... CDHayes(3) 4 — 58
(Enda Kelly, Ire) *led: hdd over 6f out: led again 4f out: rdn over 1f out: hdd nr fin* **8/1**

1420 **3** *nk* **Samuel Charles**^{22} [1638] 9-9-1 73..............................(p) LiamJones(3) 1 — 68+
(C R Dore) *chsd ldrs: rdn and hung lft fr over 2f out: nt clr run ins fnl f: r.o nr fin* **6/4**^{1}

66 **4** *4* **Itcanbedone Again (IRE)**^{21} [1673] 8-8-12 52.................. SebSanders 9 — 53
(Ian Williams) *in rr: hdwy over 1/2-way: rdn over 1f out: wknd ins fnl f* **7/2**^{2}

0260 **5** *1* **Kirkhammerton (IRE)**^{3} [2145] 5-8-12 52..................(b) AdamKirby 8 — 51
(A J McCabe) *sn pushed along in rr: styd on ins fnl f: nvr nrr* **22/1**

3060 **6** *5* **Fulvio (USA)**^{12} [1906] 7-8-12 46..(p) LPKeniry 3 — 39
(P Howling) *prom 6f* **22/1**

-030 **7** *shd* **Baby Barry**^{32} [1368] 10-8-9 45.................................. DominicFox(3) 10 — 39
(S Parr) *prom: rdn over 3f out: wknd 2f out* **33/1**

0605 **8** *1* **Mine The Balance (IRE)**^{12} [1899] 4-8-5 50............ ThomasO'Brien(7) 6 — 37
(H J Manners) *hld up: rdn over 3f out: sn wknd* **25/1**

4600 **9** *½* **Bathwick Emma (IRE)**^{70} [768] 4-8-6 45.......................(p) MCGeran(7) 7 — 37
(M A Doyle) *outpcd* **50/1**

60-0 **10** *2½* **Tamworth (IRE)**^{145} [72] 5-8-5 47..............................(vt^{1}) SCreighton(7) 2 — 30
(E J Creighton) *chsd ldrs 6f* **50/1**

6026 **11** *1¼* **Shannon Arms (USA)**^{12} [1906] 6-8-7 48...............(b) KevinGhunowa(5) 5 — 27
(R Brotherton) *hld up: plld hrd: rdn over 3f out: sn wknd* **14/1**

0500 **12** *2½* **Danettie**^{10} [1951] 6-8-2 47... LukeMorris(5) 13 — 16
(W M Brisbourne) *mid-div: hdwy to ld over 6f out: hdd 4f out: rdn over 2f out: sn wknd* **25/1**

00-1 **13** *16* **Hilversum**^{35} [1311] 5-8-10 48....................................(p) EmmettStack(3) 12 — —
(Miss J A Camacho) *chsd ldrs 6f* **11/1**

1m 50.76s (-1.00) **Going Correction** -0.10s/f (Stan) — **13 Ran** SP% **124.1**

Speed ratings (Par 101):100,99,99,96,95 90,90,89,89,87 85,83,69

CSF £59.38 TOTE £8.40: £2.00, £2.40, £1.40; EX 84.10.There was no bid for the winner. Lady Aspen was claimed by Ian Williams for £6,000.

Owner The Goodfellas **Bred** William Granville **Trained** Briery Hill, Blaenau Gwent

FOCUS

A wide range of abilities in this ordinary seller in which the pace was not that strong. The finish was dominated by the market leaders, with the pair best in at the weights and an Irish challenger pulling clear of the rest.

Shannon Arms(USA) Official explanation: trainer said gelding ran too free early stages

Hilversum Official explanation: jockey said mare ran flat

2259 JAGUAR HERITAGE CARS H'CAP — 1m 4f 50y(P)
7:40 (7:40) (Class 6) (0-65,62) 3-Y-0 — **£2,388** (£705; £352) **Stalls** Low

Form — RPR

5420 **1** **King Of The Beers (USA)**^{4} [2105] 3-9-2 62...............(p) LukeMorris(5) 7 — 71
(R A Harris) *bmpd s: sn pushed along in rr: rdn over 7f out: hdwy over 2f out: led over 1f out: drvn clr* **7/2**^{1}

5560 **2** *3½* **Conny Nobel (IRE)**^{42} [1164] 3-8-4 50...................(p) KevinGhunowa(5) 1 — 53
(J L Flint) *mid-div: hdwy 5f out: led wl over 1f out: sn rdn and hdd: no ex ins fnl f* **10/1**

000- **3** *1¼* **Kentucky Boy (IRE)**^{214} [6270] 3-8-6 47......................... NickyMackay 2 — 48
(Jedd O'Keeffe) *mid-div: hdwy over 2f out: rdn and hung lft over 1f out: styd on u.p* **25/1**

4 *2½* **Tarellia**^{21} [1686] 3-8-10 54... CDHayes(3) 5 — 51
(Enda Kelly, Ire) *led: hdd 9f out: chsd ldrs: n.m.r: lost pl and stmbld 3f out: rallied 2f out: nt clr run and swtchd rt sn after: hung lft and no ex appr fnl f* **22/1**

00-0 **5** *2* **Salto Chico**^{39} [1224] 3-8-5 49.. LiamJones(3) 11 — 43
(W M Brisbourne) *sn pushed along in rr: effrt over 3f out: edgd lft and wknd over 1f out* **20/1**

6 *½* **Patwish**^{62} [874] 3-8-6 47.. DO'Donohoe 4 — 40
(Enda Kelly, Ire) *s.i.s: hld up: nt clr run over 2f out: rdn and hung lft over 1f out: n.d* **10/1**

0-00 **7** *1½* **Piano Key**^{26} [1541] 3-8-4 45... RichardSmith 9 — 36
(M D I Usher) *hld up: hdwy over 2f out: edgd lft and wknd over 1f out* **28/1**

002 **8** *¾* **Laughing Game**^{31} [1396] 3-9-6 61.................................. MickyFenton 12 — 50
(M L W Bell) *hld up: rdn to ld 9f out: rn in snatches afterwards: hdd wl over 1f out: sn wknd* **11/2**^{2}

-400 **9** *10* **Mud Monkey**^{11} [1927] 3-9-2 57... AdamKirby 6 — 30
(B G Powell) *chsd ldrs: rdn over 3f out: wknd over 2f out* **8/1**

1505 **10** *1¾* **Always Best**^{11} [1916] 3-9-4 62..............................(v^{1}) GregFairley(3) 10 — 33
(M Johnston) *chsd ldrs: rdn and wknd 2f out* **7/2**^{1}

-520 **11** *1¾* **Royal Tender (IRE)**^{26} [1536] 3-9-4 59............................ RobertHavlin 3 — 27
(B G Powell) *chsd ldrs: rdn over 2f out: sn wknd* **20/1**

6604 **12** *1¼* **Giddywell**^{8} [2008] 3-9-5 60.. SebSanders 8 — 26
(R Hollinshead) *bmpd s: hld up: hdwy over 2f out: edgd lft and wknd wl over 1f out* **13/2**^{3}

2m 40.91s (-1.51) **Going Correction** -0.10s/f (Stan) — **12 Ran** SP% **123.6**

Speed ratings (Par 97):101,98,97,96,94 94,93,93,86,85 84,83

CSF £38.52 CT £785.52 TOTE £5.90: £1.60, £3.60, £12.20; EX 71.00.

Owner Dr Simon Clarke **Bred** Liberation Farm, Oratis Thoroughbreds Et Al **Trained** Earlswood, Monmouths

FOCUS

A very modest three-year-old handicap and a strange race in some ways, as the eventual winner and third were receiving hefy reminders with a circuit still to race, even though the early pace did not look that strong. Not much solid form, but the winner still seems to be getting better.

Always Best Official explanation: trainer had no explanation for the poor form shown

2260 ROSIE WARD DASH H'CAP — 5f 216y(P)
8:10 (8:14) (Class 5) (0-70,70) 3-Y-0 — **£3,238** (£963; £481; £240) **Stalls** Low

Form — RPR

646 **1** **Dramatic**^{102} [505] 3-8-0 52.. CDHayes(3) 9 — 78+
(Sir Mark Prescott) *hdwy to chse ldr 4f out: led over 2f out: rdn clr fnl f* **3/1**^{1}

4212 **2** *5* **Drifting Gold**^{10} [1948] 3-9-7 70..(b) AdamKirby 4 — 77
(C G Cox) *hld up: hdwy to chse wnr over 1f out: sn rdn: hung lft and no ex* **9/2**^{2}

400- **3** *3* **Call Me Rosy (IRE)**^{199} [6488] 3-9-0 63.............................. SebSanders 1 — 60
(C F Wall) *hld up: hdwy over 1f out: sn rdn and wknd* **5/1**^{3}

0016 **4** *shd* **Charlotte Grey**^{15} [1820] 3-9-2 65......................... EdwardCreighton 5 — 62
(C N Allen) *sn led: hdd over 2f out: sn rdn: wknd fnl f* **11/1**

2224 **5** *1¾* **Welsh Auction**^{22} [1635] 3-9-1 67.................................. EmmettStack(3) 2 — 58
(G A Huffer) *chsd ldrs: rdn and wknd over 1f out* **9/2**^{2}

-065 **6** *6* **Maeve (IRE)**^{3} [2146] 3-8-2 51 oh6.............................. FrankieMcDonald 3 — 23
(E J Creighton) *sn pushed along in rr: wknd over 2f out* **66/1**

0530 **7** *8* **Bahamian Love**^{11} [1932] 3-8-9 58...................................... NickyMackay 6 — 5
(B W Hills) *led early: chsd ldrs: rdn over 2f out: sn wknd* **10/1**

0-60 **8** *9* **Smash N'Grab (IRE)**^{9} [1964] 3-8-6 55............................ DO'Donohoe 8 — —
(K A Ryan) *chsd ldrs over 3f* **22/1**

1m 14.41s (-1.40) **Going Correction** -0.10s/f (Stan) — **8 Ran** SP% **101.3**

Speed ratings (Par 99):105,98,94,94,91 83,73,61

CSF £12.12 CT £34.52 TOTE £3.80: £1.90, £1.70, £1.70; EX 11.60.

Owner Cheveley Park Stud **Bred** Cheveley Park Stud **Trained** Newmarket, Suffolk

FOCUS

A fair little sprint handicap and a most impressive winner. This form looks absolutely rock solid, for the runner-up was on a good mark and the third and fourth have solid Wolverhampton form.

2261 JAGUAR LE MANS EVENT MAIDEN STKS — 1m 141y(P)
8:40 (8:41) (Class 5) 3-Y-0 — **£2,968** (£876; £438) **Stalls** Low

Form — RPR

0 **1** **Grand Vizier (IRE)**^{15} [1812] 3-9-0 0.............................. LiamJones(3) 13 — 67+
(C F Wall) *s.i.s: hdwy 1/2-way: rdn to ld ins fnl f: styd on* **33/1**

04- **2** *½* **Pivotalia (IRE)**^{203} [6433] 3-8-12 0.................................... AdamKirby 7 — 61
(W R Swinburn) *led: rdn over 1f out: hdd ins fnl f: styd on* **11/1**

5 **3** *1¼* **Gone Gold (USA)**^{33} [1358] 3-9-3 0.................................. SteveDrowne 5 — 63+
(J Noseda) *hld up in tch: outpcd over 2f out: rallied over 1f out: edgd lft ins fnl f: r.o* **10/11**^{1}

00 **4** *shd* **Mr Grand Lodge (FR)**^{13} [1863] 3-9-3 0............................ NickyMackay 1 — 63+
(L M Cumani) *chsd ldrs: rdn over 1f out: edgd lft: styd on same pce* **16/1**

0-0 **5** *¾* **Soldier Field**^{26} [1522] 3-9-0 0..................................... NeilChalmers(3) 6 — 61+
(A M Balding) *trckd ldrs: rdn over 1f out: hmpd ins fnl f: styd on* **50/1**

0-5 **6** *½* **Expedience (USA)**^{22} [1639] 3-8-12 0............................. SebSanders 4 — 55+
(Sir Michael Stoute) *hld up: plld hrd: hdwy over 2f out: rdn over 1f out: edgd lft and no ex fnl f* **9/4**^{2}

7 *1¾* **Victory Mile (USA)** 3-9-3 0... BrettDoyle 3 — 56+
(B J Meehan) *mid-div: rdn over 5f out: hdwy over 1f out: nt trble ldrs* **10/1**^{3}

8 *nk* **Mega Dame (IRE)** 3-8-12 0... RobertHavlin 12 — 50
(D Haydn Jones) *chsd ldrs: rdn over 3f out: wknd over 1f out* **66/1**

00 **9** *hd* **Movie Mogul**^{22} [1639] 3-8-12 0....................................... MickyFenton 8 — 50+
(M L W Bell) *hld up: plld hrd: shkn up over 1f out: hung lft ins fnl f: nvr trbld ldrs* **40/1**

0- **10** *hd* **Tykie Two**^{264} [5231] 3-8-12 0... TPO'Shea 11 — 49
(E J O'Neill) *hld up: rdn over 2f out: n.d* **20/1**

0 **11** *1½* **New Star (UAE)**^{23} [1605] 3-8-12 0................................. LukeMorris(5) 2 — 51
(W M Brisbourne) *prom: rdn over 2f out: sn wknd* **33/1**

0 **12** *7* **River Hunter (IRE)**^{11} [1928] 3-8-12 0................................ LPKeniry 9 — 30
(S Kirk) *chsd ldrs: rdn and wknd over 1f out* **66/1**

13 *½* **Cardington Queen** 3-8-9 0.. EmmettStack(3) 10 — 29
(M Mullineaux) *dwlt: a in rr* **100/1**

1m 54.37s (2.61) **Going Correction** -0.10s/f (Stan) — **13 Ran** SP% **125.5**

Speed ratings (Par 99):84,83,82,82,81 81,79,79,79,79 77,71,71

CSF £358.80 TOTE £47.10: £8.40, £2.50, £1.10; EX 1735.10.

Owner Hintlesham SP Partners **Bred** Yeomanstown Stud **Trained** Newmarket, Suffolk

■ Stewards' Enquiry : Nicky Mackay two-day ban: careless riding (Jun 13-14)

FOCUS

Despite the size of the field, this was run at an early crawl and the winning time was 3.61 seconds slower than the seller. That has to put a big question mark over the true value of the form, which is hard to rate positively.

Movie Mogul Official explanation: jockey said filly hung left-handed

2262 SPONSOR A RACE BY CALLING 0870 220 2442 H'CAP — 7f 32y(P)
9:10 (9:14) (Class 6) (0-60,64) 3-Y-0 — **£2,388** (£705; £352) **Stalls** High

Form — RPR

3-00 **1** **Nashharry (IRE)**^{19} [1726] 3-9-4 60........................... FrankieMcDonald 5 — 64
(S Kirk) *led 1f: chsd ldrs: rdn over 2f out: led and hung lft ins fnl f: r.o* **25/1**

4500 **2** *½* **Toms Laughter**^{5} [2083] 3-9-4 60............................... CatherineGannon 1 — 62
(B Palling) *led 6f out: sn hdd: chsd ldrs: rdn and ev ch ins fnl f: styd on* **16/1**

3442 **3** *nk* **Strike Force**^{17} [1763] 3-8-10 57..............................(p) LukeMorris(5) 3 — 59
(R A Harris) *chsd ldrs: rdn over 2f out: nt clr run ins fnl f: styd on* **3/1**^{2}

0346 **4** *hd* **Comptonspirit**^{30} [1437] 3-9-2 58............................ EdwardCreighton 9 — 59
(B P J Baugh) *chsd ldrs: rdn over 3f out: sn outpcd: r.o ins fnl f* **16/1**

30-3 **5** *nk* **Oh So Saucy**^{33} [1346] 3-9-1 57.. SebSanders 8 — 60+
(C F Wall) *hld up: hdwy and nt clr run over 1f out: running on whn n.m.r and eased nr fin* **5/2**^{1}

1601 **6** *1* **Totally Free**^{3} [2146] 3-9-3 64 6ex.........................(v) TravisBlock(5) 11 — 61
(M D I Usher) *led over 5f out: clr 3f out: hdd and no ex ins fnl f* **13/2**^{3}

000- **7** *nk* **Little Iris**^{249} [5592] 3-8-13 55.. NickyMackay 10 — 52+
(L M Cumani) *hld up: rdn over 3f out: hdwy and nt clr run ins fnl f: nvr trbld ldrs* **8/1**

4544 **8** *¾* **Head To Head (IRE)**^{35} [1313] 3-8-13 55............................ LPKeniry 2 — 50
(Peter Grayson) *trckd ldrs: rdn over 2f out: wknd over 1f out* **12/1**

64-0 **9** *1¼* **Doonigan (IRE)**^{31} [1399] 3-8-13 55............................(v^{1}) MickyFenton 6 — 46
(A M Balding) *swvd lft s: a in rr* **20/1**

-002 **10** *7* **Dancing Duo**^{12} [1903] 3-9-5 61..............................(v) SteveDrowne 12 — 33
(D Shaw) *s.i.s: sn chsng ldrs: wknd over 2f out* **7/1**

1m 30.97s (0.57) **Going Correction** -0.10s/f (Stan) — **10 Ran** SP% **118.6**

Speed ratings (Par 97):92,91,91,90,90 89,89,88,86,78

CSF £376.77 CT £1205.22 TOTE £26.90: £5.70, £5.10, £1.40; EX 159.30 Place 6 £94.63, Place 5 £24.16.

Owner Club ISM **Bred** Forenaght Partnership No 2 **Trained** Upper Lambourn, Berks

FOCUS

This was a poor contest with the bulk of the field finishing in a heap, so the form probably does not amount to much.

Doonigan(IRE) Official explanation: jockey said gelding jumped awkwardly leaving stalls

T/Plt: £184.20 to a £1 stake. Pool: £66,463.80. 263.40 winning tickets T/Qpdt: £39.80 to a £1 stake. Pool: £3,419.90. 63.50 winning tickets. CR

2263 - 2269a (Foreign Racing) - See Raceform Interactive

1856 CHANTILLY (R-H)

Saturday, June 2

OFFICIAL GOING: Soft

2270a PRIX DE ROYAUMONT (GROUP 3) (FILLIES) 1m 4f

2:50 (3:01) 3-Y-O **£27,027** (£10,811; £8,108; £5,405; £2,703)

RPR

1 **Legerete (USA)**[48] [1055] 3-9-0 OPeslier 5 105
(A Fabre, France) *disp 3rd: hdwy to press ldr over 1f out: styd on u.p to ld cl home* **26/10**[3]

2 *shd* **La Hernanda (IRE)**[20] [1705] 3-9-0 JVictoire 2 105
(H-A Pantall, France) *racd in 2nd tl led over 2f out: r.o gamely u.p whn strly pressed fr over 1f out: hdd and no ex cl home* **10/1**

3 *5* **Artistica (IRE)**[29] 3-9-0 CSoumillon 4 97
(A Fabre, France) *hld up in 5th: wnt 3rd over 1 1/2f out: outpcd by first two* **5/2**[2]

4 *6* **Chill (FR)**[32] [1388] 3-9-0 C-PLemaire 3 88
(J-C Rouget, France) *disp 3rd: wknd 2f out* **9/4**[1]

5 *15* **Dancing Lady (FR)**[20] [1705] 3-9-0 SPasquier 1 66
(J-M Beguigne, France) *uns rdr and lost shoe bhd stalls: rn loose for 5 minutes: reshod: led to over 2f out: wknd qckly* **43/10**

6 *10* **Taffetas (FR)**[14] 3-9-0 WMongil 6 51
(T Doumen, France) *a in rr: reminders and lost tch over 4f out* **27/1**

2m 30.4s (-3.00) **6** Ran SP% **118.6**
PARI-MUTUEL: WIN 3.60; PL 2.30, 3.80; SF 26.90.
Owner Wertheimer Et Frere **Bred** Wertheimer Et Frere **Trained** Chantilly, France
■ Stewards' Enquiry : J Victoire 100 euros fine: whip abuse

NOTEBOOK
Legerete(USA) tackling this trip for the first time, showed her class and paid a compliment to dual 1000 Guineas winner Finsceal Beo who was ahead of her in the Prix Marcel Boussac last October. She relaxed in fourth position in the early stages before starting her challenge a furlong and a half out. Joining the battle for the lead running into the last furlong, she battled on gamely to win by a narrow margin. Certainly still on the upgrade, she is likely to go for the Prix de Malleret and looks a possible candidate for the Prix Vermeille later in the year.
La Hernanda(IRE) lost nothing in defeat and stuck to her guns right to the line. She was tucked in behind the leaders early on before taking up the running at the two-furlong post. Digging deep, she just failed to hold the winner in the final few strides.
Artistica(IRE), dropped out in the early stages, never really settled in the early parts. By the time she started to run on in the straight, the race was over, and she is probably better than this effort shows.
Chill(FR) was given every chance, but failed to kick when things warmed up and this distance looks beyond her limitations.

2138 BRIGHTON (L-H)

Sunday, June 3

OFFICIAL GOING: Good to firm
Wind: Moderate, against

2271 E B F SPORTING BOOKMAKERS IN ST JAMES'S STREET NOVICE MEDIAN AUCTION STKS 5f 213y

2:20 (2:20) (Class 6) 2-Y-O **£2,849** (£847; £423; £211) **Stalls** Low

Form RPR

6 **1** **Drawnfromthepast (IRE)**[22] [1652] 2-8-12 JimCrowley 3 89+
(J A Osborne) *trckd ldrs: led over 2f out: drew clr fnl f: easily* **5/2**[2]

1 **2** *6* **Alizadora**[23] [1636] 2-8-13 SebSanders 1 80+
(Sir Mark Prescott) *s.i.s: led after 1f: rdn and hdd whn hmpd on ins over 2f out: swtchd rt over 1f out: styd on to go 2nd ins fnl f* **8/15**[1]

0 **3** *¾* **Evenstorm (USA)**[13] [1896] 2-8-7 JimmyQuinn 4 64
(B Gubby) *in tch whn hung lft over 2f out: chsd wnr tl rdn and wknd ins fnl f* **20/1**

4 *3½* **Victorian Bounty** 2-8-12 FrancisNorton 2 58
(E J O'Neill) *led for 1f: hung rt over 3f out: wknd over 1f out* **9/1**[3]

F626 **5** *2* **Miss Tilen**[5] [2115] 2-8-2 WilliamBuick(5) 5 47
(V Smith) *outpcd and a bhd* **66/1**

1m 10.22s (0.12) **Going Correction** -0.025s/f (Good) **5** Ran SP% **110.1**
Speed ratings (Par 91):98,90,89,84,81
CSF £4.20 TOTE £3.30: £1.60, £1.10; EX 4.80.
Owner Elaine and Martyn Booth **Bred** D And Mrs D Veitch **Trained** Upper Lambourn, Berks

FOCUS
Hard to weigh up, but probably a little above average for this level for Brighton.

NOTEBOOK
Drawnfromthepast(IRE) is stoutly bred on his dam's side, and this extra furlong was just what he needed, though he was flattered a little by the fact that the favourite did not act on the track and was hampered. A trip to Royal Ascot for the Coventry Stakes is a possibility, where the opposition will obviously be much stronger. (op 11-4 tchd 10-3 and 9-4 in places)
Alizadora, like the winner, looked sure to be suited by the sixth furlong, but she did not look happy on the downhill run into the straight and being hampered was the final straw. She will come into her own on a more conventional track, and should stay even farther as the season progresses. (op 4-7 tchd 4-9)
Evenstorm(USA) was trying an extra furlong, and on breeding should stay even farther in due course, but this 70,000$ yearling with a decent American pedigree needs a bit more time to fully develop her stamina. In any case, she looks like a nursery type after one more run. (tchd 25-1)
Victorian Bounty, a 10,000gns Bahamian Bounty colt from a speedy family mainly up to 7f, is bred to be quick. He would be more at home on a flatter track, and a drop to 5f should not be a problem. (op 8-1)
Miss Tilen could not go the pace down the hill, and is now ready for the switch to nurseries. Another option would be to have another crack at selling company, in which she ran her best race to date. (op 50-1)

2272 BERNS BRETT 40TH ANNIVERSARY H'CAP 6f 209y

2:50 (2:51) (Class 5) (0-75,72) 4-Y-O+ **£2,775** (£830; £415; £207; £103) **Stalls** Low

Form RPR

5135 **1** **Takitwo**[60] [923] 4-8-12 **63** SebSanders 6 69+
(P D Cundell) *hld up in tch: rdn wl over 1f out: tk hold of bit in fnl f: r.o strly to ld post* **2/1**[1]

0216 **2** *shd* **Quantum Leap**[12] [1931] 10-9-1 **66** (p) JimmyQuinn 5 72
(S Dow) *a.p: rdn to ld wl ins fnl f: ct post* **7/1**

5504 **3** *½* **Ivory Lace**[31] [1431] 6-9-7 **72** JimCrowley 8 77
(S Woodman) *hld up: rdn 2f out: r.o wl fnl f: nvr nrr* **7/2**[2]

-022 **4** *½* **Danawi (IRE)**[19] [1740] 4-7-11 **53** oh2 WilliamBuick(5) 1 56
(M R Hoad) *t.k.h: led tl hdd wl ins fnl f: no ex* **9/2**[3]

4110 **5** *nk* **Franksalot (IRE)**[24] [1597] 7-9-1 **66** RoystonFfrench 4 68
(I W McInnes) *trckd ldr: rdn and ev ch over 1f out: fdd ins fnl f* **15/2**

4436 **6** *¾* **Digital**[10] [1969] 10-8-9 **60** EdwardCreighton 7 60
(M R Channon) *slowly away: rdn over 2f out: kpt on fnl f but nvr nr to chal* **8/1**

1-64 **7** *1¾* **Siraj**[4] [2155] 8-8-12 **63** (p) RobertHavlin 2 59
(J Ryan) *trckd ldrs: rdn to chal over 2f out: wknd ins fnl f* **16/1**

1m 23.82s (1.12) **Going Correction** -0.025s/f (Good) **7** Ran SP% **115.0**
Speed ratings (Par 103):92,91,91,90,90 89,87
CSF £16.93 CT £46.12 TOTE £2.90: £1.70, £3.00; EX 24.10 Trifecta £35.10 Pool: £297.28 - 6.00 winning units.
Owner Miss M C Fraser **Bred** Roden House Stud **Trained** Compton, Berks

FOCUS
A typical Brighton handicap, moderate in quality and run in a slow time, but containing some decent sorts at this level, and producing a close finish.

2273 MICHAEL & CLAIRE SILVER WEDDING (S) STKS 6f 209y

3:20 (3:20) (Class 6) 3-Y-O+ **£1,943** (£578; £288; £144) **Stalls** Low

Form RPR

0001 **1** **Magroom**[19] [1739] 3-9-3 53 (v) RichardSmith 7 58
(B R Johnson) *a in tch: hdwy over 2f out: rdn to ld wl ins fnl f* **7/2**[2]

2160 **2** *nk* **Over To You Bert**[10] [1969] 8-9-6 53 HaddenFrost(7) 3 61
(R J Hodges) *led: edgd lft over 4f out: rdn over 1f out: hdd wl ins fnl f* **11/2**[3]

0505 **3** *1* **Napoletano (GER)**[12] [1921] 6-9-7 50 (p) SebSanders 4 52
(S Dow) *stdd s: hmpd over 4f out: hdwy over 2f out: styd on fnl f: nvr nrr* **5/2**[1]

4065 **4** *2½* **Bollywood (IRE)**[4] [2143] 4-9-0 45 RyanBird(7) 11 46
(J J Bridger) *in rr: hdwy 1/2-way: styd on one pce fnl f* **10/1**

0-20 **5** *3½* **Tipsy Lad**[12] [1933] 5-9-7 46 (bt) SimonWhitworth 5 37
(D J S Ffrench Davis) *w ldr tl rdn and wknd ent fnl f* **11/1**

500- **6** *nk* **Bogaz (IRE)**[179] [6726] 5-9-0 40 KylieManser(7) 9 46+
(Mrs H Sweeting) *wnt rt s: making hdwy but hld whn n.m.r ins fnl f* **40/1**

0/0- **7** *1¼* **Good Wee Girl (IRE)**[179] [6726] 5-8-11 40 (p) KevinGhunowa(5) 8 28
(S Woodman) *hld up: hdwy over 2f out: sn hung lft and no hdwy appr fnl f* **50/1**

-040 **8** *2½* **Dawson Creek (IRE)**[48] [1059] 3-8-11 49 (p) RoystonFfrench 1 22
(B Gubby) *chsd ldrs: hmpd over 4f out: rdn 2f out: sn wknd* **8/1**

0000 **9** *7* **Campbeltown (IRE)**[13] [1899] 4-9-7 50 JimmyQuinn 6 8
(M R Hoad) *in rr: rdn and hdwy 1/2-way: wknd 2f out* **14/1**

0-00 **10** *6* **All Talk**[27] [1537] 3-7-13 40 LauraReynolds(7) 2 —
(M J Gingell) *chsd ldrs tl wknd 1/2-way* **50/1**

00-0 **11** *10* **Meru Camp (IRE)**[12] [1921] 3-8-11 50 (b) JimCrowley 10 —
(P Winkworth) *hmpd s: towards rr whn rdn 1/2-way: wl btn whn eased ins fnl f* **14/1**

1m 22.67s (-0.03) **Going Correction** -0.025s/f (Good)
WFA 3 from 4yo+ 10lb **11** Ran SP% **114.4**
Speed ratings (Par 101):99,98,97,94,90 90,88,86,78,71 59
CSF £22.23 TOTE £4.60: £1.80, £2.30, £1.20; EX 19.00 Trifecta £42.00 Pool: £338.09 - 5.71 winning units..The winner was sold to Bob Andrews for 8,200gns.
Owner Tann Racing **Bred** Mrs M Chaworth-Musters **Trained** Ashtead, Surrey
■ Stewards' Enquiry : Hadden Frost five-day ban: careless riding (Jun 19-23)

FOCUS
A routine non-handicap seller, with the runners reasonably well-matched on official figures, and run at a good gallop. Difficult to rate it positively.
Good Wee Girl(IRE) Official explanation: jockey said mare hung right

2274 CONNAUGHT 5C'S MAIDEN STKS 1m 3f 196y

3:50 (3:53) (Class 5) 3-Y-O+ **£2,849** (£847; £423; £211) **Stalls** High

Form RPR

5-62 **1** **Set The Scene (IRE)**[22] [1685] 3-8-7 74 RobertHavlin 5 72+
(J H M Gosden) *trckd ldr: led over 2f out: drew clr fnl f: easily* **5/2**[1]

06 **2** *3½* **Driving Miss Suzie**[22] [1659] 3-8-2 WilliamBuick(5) 8 62
(A M Balding) *hld up on ins: hdwy 2f out: hung lft fr over 1f out: r.o to go 2nd ins fnl f* **33/1**

3252 **3** *1½* **Sowdrey**[24] [1611] 3-8-12 73 TPO'Shea 1 65
(M R Channon) *in rr: rdn over 3f out: styd on one pce fr over 1f out* **11/2**[3]

32 **4** *shd* **Artless (USA)**[12] [1937] 4-9-8 SebSanders 4 60
(Sir Mark Prescott) *led tl rdn and hdd over 2f out: wknd ins fnl f* **5/2**[1]

5 *1½* **Lion Ridge (IRE)** 3-8-12 NickyMackay 7 62
(L M Cumani) *chsd ldrs tl rdn and wknd 1f out* **15/2**

0/0 **6** *11* **Code (IRE)**[9] [1998] 6-9-13 JimCrowley 2 45?
(Miss Z C Davison) *a wl in rr* **100/1**

2 **7** *3* **Mercury Blue**[17] [1785] 3-8-7 JohnEgan 3 35+
(S Kirk) *in tch: rdn over 3f out: wknd over 2f out: eased whn wl btn ins fnl f* **3/1**[2]

2m 30.72s (-1.48) **Going Correction** -0.025s/f (Good)
WFA 3 from 4yo+ 15lb **7** Ran SP% **113.2**
Speed ratings (Par 103):103,100,99,99,98 91,89
CSF £73.63 TOTE £3.80: £2.00, £5.90; EX 107.10 Trifecta £169.10 Pool: £405.02 - 1.70 winning units..
Owner Carwell Equities Ltd **Bred** Carwell Equities Ltd **Trained** Newmarket, Suffolk

FOCUS
A maiden contested by some good stables, and not bad for the track. Improved form from the winner, who could make her mark in handcaps, assuming connections sidestep the Ribblesdale.

2275 MANTA FINANCE SUPPORTS THE ROCKINGHORSE H'CAP 1m 1f 209y

4:20 (4:21) (Class 6) (0-65,65) 4-Y-O+ **£2,072** (£616; £308; £153) **Stalls** High

Form RPR

1423 **1** **Sawwaah (IRE)**[5] [2113] 10-9-7 **65** (v) JimCrowley 6 78+
(Tom Dascombe) *hld up in rr: hdwy and hung lft fr over 1f out: r.o strly to ld ins fnl f: won gng away* **9/2**[2]

0030 **2** *3½* **Makai**[4] [2141] 4-8-1 **50** (b) TolleyDean(5) 4 54
(J J Bridger) *mid-div: hdwy to chse ldrs over 2f out: styd on to go 2nd ins fnl f* **14/1**

024- **3** *½* **Factual Lad**[269] [5127] 9-9-4 **62** GeorgeBaker 7 65
(B R Millman) *led: rdn 2f out: hdd & wknd ins fnl f* **17/2**

0-24 **4** *1* **Piano Man**[4] [2141] 5-9-0 **58** TQuinn 9 59
(B G Powell) *mid-div: chsd ldrs over 3f out: wknd appr fnl f* **10/3**[1]

0306 **5** *½* **Christmas Truce (IRE)**[19] [1740] 8-8-6 **50** (b) JimmyQuinn 12 50
(M R Hoad) *mid-div: hdwy over 2f out: hung lft over 1f out: sn btn* **20/1**

1230 **6** *1¼* **Jarvo**[8] [2027] 6-8-11 **55** RoystonFfrench 2 53
(I W McInnes) *in rr: mde mod late hdwy* **7/1**[3]

45-0 **7** *4* **Border Edge**[13] 1886 9-9-1 **64**.................................... JamesMillman(5) 5 54
(J J Bridger) *trckd ldrs: rdn over 2f out: wknd fnl f* **14/1**

5-03 **8** *nk* **Hansomelle (IRE)**[19] 1740 5-8-6 **53** ow3.................... NeilChalmers(3) 11 42
(Miss Sheena West) *slowly away: racd wd: nvr on terms* **15/2**

5-0 **9** *nk* **Something Simple (IRE)**[8] 332 4-8-6 **55**..........(b[1]) KevinGhunowa(5) 8 43
(R Ford) *a towards rr* **33/1**

6640 **10** *2 1/2* **Moving Target (IRE)**[80] 685 8-8-11 **58**.................... JerryO'Dwyer(3) 10 41
(Luke Comer, Ire) *trckd ldr tl rdn and wknd qckly 2f out* **33/1**

05-2 **11** *9* **Justcallmehandsome**[4] 2141 5-7-10 **47**.................. LauraReynolds(7) 3 12
(D J S Ffrench Davis) *a bhd* **9/2**[2]

365- **12** *nk* **Shamwari Fire (IRE)**[186] 4266 7-7-11 **46** oh1............. WilliamBuick(5) 1 11
(I W McInnes) *mid-div: rdn over 3f out: sn bhd* **25/1**

2m 2.08s (-0.52) **Going Correction** -0.025s/f (Good) **12** Ran SP% **122.1**
Speed ratings (Par 101):101,98,97,97,96 95,92,92,91,89 82,82
CSF £64.64 CT £524.42 TOTE £6.10: £2.00, £5.80, £2.40; EX 89.90 Trifecta £273.60 Part won. Pool: £385.38 - 0.10 winning units..
Owner Alan Solomon **Bred** Shadwell Estate Company Limited **Trained** Lambourn, Berks

FOCUS
A modest handicap, with the winner having recently switched back from selling and claiming company. It has been rated through the second and third to the level of last year's course and distance wins.
Jarvo Official explanation: jockey said gelding was unsuited by the track
Something Simple(IRE) Official explanation: jockey said gelding ran too free
Justcallmehandsome Official explanation: vet said gelding had been struck into on right hind

2276 CONNAUGHT COMMUNITY CHALLENGE H'CAP 5f 59y
4:50 (4:50) (Class 5) (0-75,74) 3-Y-0 **£2,775** (£830; £415; £207; £103) **Stalls** Low

Form RPR

00-6 **1** **Divalini**[17] 1786 3-8-2 **55** oh6.. NickyMackay 3 55
(J Akehurst) *trckd ldr: rdn to ld ins fnl f: hld on wl* **14/1**

1004 **2** *nk* **Mr Loire**[4] 2144 3-9-7 **74**..(b[1]) SebSanders 1 73
(H J L Dunlop) *trckd ldrs: r.o wl to go 2nd ins fnl f* **7/2**[3]

0214 **3** *3* **Hereford Boy**[11] 1948 3-9-6 **73**... RobertHavlin 2 61
(D K Ivory) *led tl rdn and hdd ins fnl f: fdd* **13/8**[1]

060 **4** *3/4* **Sherjawy (IRE)**[18] 1763 3-8-2 **55** oh7...........................(b) JimmyQuinn 7 41
(Miss Z C Davison) *wnt rt s: hld up: rdn 1/2-way: kpt on fnl f but nvr on terms* **25/1**

4331 **5** *nk* **Diminuto**[12] 1932 3-8-8 **66**.. PatrickHills(5) 6 50
(M D I Usher) *in tch: effrt over 2f out: wknd over 1f out* **7/4**[2]

-000 **6** *11* **Princely Royal**[17] 1782 3-8-2 **55** oh10...................(b) FrankieMcDonald 5 —
(J J Bridger) *t.k.h: bhd fr 1/2-way* **50/1**

61.99 secs (-0.31) **Going Correction** -0.025s/f (Good) **6** Ran SP% **109.2**
Speed ratings (Par 99):101,100,95,94,94 76
CSF £58.25 TOTE £16.60: £4.90, £2.30; EX 38.40 Place 6 £134.84, Place 5 £125.96.
Owner R P Tullett and Friends **Bred** T E Pocock **Trained** Epsom, Surrey

FOCUS
A mixed bag, with the runners having previously shown a wide range of ability. Some of the form horses may have been below their best.
T/Plt: £220.20 to a £1 stake. Pool: £67,254.45. 222.95 winning tickets. T/Qpdt: £57.10 to a £1 stake. Pool: £3,512.20. 45.50 winning tickets. JS

2277 - 2289a (Foreign Racing) - See Raceform Interactive

2270 CHANTILLY (R-H)
Sunday, June 3

OFFICIAL GOING: Good to soft

2290a PRIX DE SANDRINGHAM MITSUBISHI MOTORS (GROUP 2) (FILLIES) 1m
2:10 (2:14) 3-Y-O **£50,068** (£19,324; £9,223; £6,149; £3,074)

RPR

1 **All Is Vanity (FR)**[30] 3-8-11 .... FBlondel 2 108
(W J S Cargeeg, France) *mde all: jnd 1 1/2f out: rdn and fnd more: r.o strly fnl f* **16/1**

2 *2 1/2* **Majestic Roi (USA)**[43] 1146 3-8-11 .... DarryllHolland 3 103
(M R Channon) *hld up in 6th: drvn and r.o in centre 1 1/2f out: styd on and tk 2nd on line* **3/1**[3]

3 *snk* **Just Little (FR)**[35] 1339 3-8-11 .... C-PLemaire 8 103
(J-C Rouget, France) *racd in 2nd: chal 2f out: disp ld 1 1/2f out: rdn and kpt on tl no ex fnl 50yds* **9/4**[1]

4 *snk* **Elva (IRE)**[35] 1339 3-8-11 .... CSoumillon 4 102
(J-C Rouget, France) *disp 3rd: 3rd st: pushed along 2f out: rdn 1 1/2f out: styd on at one pce* **11/4**[2]

5 *2* **Viola Carlita (FR)**[24] 3-8-11 .... JVictoire 5 98
(J-P Gallorini, France) *hld up in last: rdn over 1 1/2f out: n.d* **33/1**

6 *1/2* **Terra Incognita**[33] 1388 3-8-11 .... JMurtagh 1 97
(Y De Nicolay, France) *disp 3rd: 4th st: sn pushed along: hdwy on ins 2f out: drvn and wnt 3rd 1 1/2f out: no ex fr over 1f out* **6/1**

7 *6* **Party Girl (FR)**[35] 1339 3-8-11 .... OPeslier 6 85
(R Pritchard-Gordon, France) *racd in 5th: pushed along over 2f out: unable qck* **14/1**

1m 37.8s (-2.50) **Going Correction** -0.125s/f (Firm) **7** Ran SP% **112.2**
Speed ratings: 107,104,104,104,102 101,95
PARI-MUTUEL: WIN 11.70; PL 4.50, 2.70; DF 26.70.
Owner Mme I Corbani **Bred** Jedburgh Stud **Trained** France
■ The first Group winner for English trainer Stuart Cargeeg, a former jump jockey.

NOTEBOOK
All Is Vanity(FR) completely routed her opponents on her first run in a Group event. Making all and brought up the middle of the track in the straight, she quickened again and never looked in danger of defeat. She was landing a four-timer and appears to have further scope for improvement. Considerable offers have been made for her and her English trainer is now having a look at the Falmouth and Nassau Stakes as the Coronation Stakes comes a little too soon.
Majestic Roi(USA), upped in trip after landing the Fred Darling, only got into top gear when the race was virtually over. Sixth rounding the final turn in a race run at a decent pace, she was a bit caught for speed when the winner quickened things up in the straight and was putting in her best work at the finish, pinching second place in the last few strides.
Just Little(FR) was given every possible chance but was always in the winner's wake. She tried bravely to make a challenge halfway up the straight but could never get on terms and lost second place in the final few strides. A return to a slightly longer trip might be an advantage.
Elva(IRE) appeared to have no excuses and was given every possible chance. Third rounding the final turn, she challenged away from the rail up the straight and battled on gamely to the line.

2291a PRIX DU GROS-CHENE MITSUBISHI MOTORS (GROUP 2) 5f
2:45 (2:44) 3-Y-O+ **£50,068** (£19,324; £9,223; £6,149; £3,074)

RPR

1 **Beauty Is Truth (IRE)**[21] 1704 3-8-6 ....(b) TThulliez 9 117+
(Robert Collet, France) *trckd Moss Vale towards outside: disputing 4th 1/2-way: pushed along 2f out: drvn to chal 1 1/2f out: led appr fnl f: r.o strly* **13/2**

2 *2 1/2* **Peace Offering (IRE)**[21] 1704 7-9-2 .... TedDurcan 10 113
(D Nicholls) *prom on outside: 2nd 1/2-way: ev ch 2f out: rdn over 1f out: styd on fnl f: tk 2nd 100yds out* **9/2**[2]

3 *1 1/2* **Moss Vale (IRE)**[3] 2184 6-9-2 .... AdrianTNicholls 11 108
(D Nicholls) *cl up towards outside: led after 2f: rdn and r.o over 2f out: hdd appr fnl f: kpt on: lost 2nd 100yds out* **5/2**[1]

4 *nk* **New Girlfriend (IRE)**[21] 1704 4-8-13 .... OPeslier 1 104
(Robert Collet, France) *in tch on rail: 8th 1/2-way: pushed along 2 1/2f out: styd on steadily* **9/1**

5 *nk* **Conquest (IRE)**[18] 1770 3-9-0 ....(b) JHBowman 7 107
(W J Haggas) *towards rr: disputing 9th and pushed along 1/2-way: styd on down outside fr over 1f out* **20/1**

6 *1/2* **Manzila (FR)**[21] 1704 4-8-9 .... DBonilla 8 97
(F Head, France) *prom: disputing 4th 1/2-way: rdn and r.o fr 2f out tl no ex fnl f* **16/1**

7 *1* **Patavellian (IRE)**[22] 1657 9-8-13 ....(b) JimmyFortune 5 97
(R Charlton) *in rr: last 1/2-way: r.o fnl 1 1/2f but n.d* **10/1**

8 *3/4* **Val Jaro (FR)**[40] 1234 4-8-13 .... THuet 4 94
(S Morineau, France) *led 2f: cl 3rd 1/2-way: wknd 1 1/2f out* **40/1**

9 *2* **Place Vendome (FR)**[12] 3-8-3 .... TJarnet 3 81
(Mlle S-V Tarrou, France) *mid-div: 6th 1/2-way: n.d* **33/1**

10 *1 1/2* **Presto Shinko (IRE)**[28] 1497 6-9-2 .... RichardHughes 6 85
(R Hannon) *towards rr: disputing 9th 1/2-way: nvr a factor* **5/1**[3]

11 **Blue Echo**[22] 1670 3-8-3 .... SPasquier 2 76
(M A Jarvis) *in tch on rail: pushed along in 7th 1/2-way: one pce fr 2f out* **14/1**

57.30 secs (-3.00) **Going Correction** -0.225s/f (Firm)
WFA 3 from 4yo+ 7lb **11** Ran SP% **118.5**
Speed ratings: 115,111,108,108,107 106,105,104,100,98 98
PARI-MUTUEL: WIN 7.20 (coupled with New Girlfriend); PL 2.30, 1.70,1.40; DF 14.90.
Owner R C Strauss **Bred** Kilfrush Stud **Trained** Chantilly, France

NOTEBOOK
Beauty Is Truth(IRE) relaxed behind the leaders after being smartly into her stride before coming through at the furlong marker to win with something in hand. Although she wears blinkers, she is a thoroughly game individual. Her trainer has no specific plans but Ascot, the July Cup and the Nunthorpe are possibilities.
Peace Offering(IRE) beat Beauty Is Truth in a Group 3 at Longchamp but the filly reversed the order in spectacular fashion. Given every possible chance, he was one of the leaders at the two pole but could do nothing when the winner came charging past a little later. It was another genuine effort from this seven-year-old who is now likely to be seen out at Ascot later in the month.
Moss Vale(IRE), last year's winner, was making a quick reappearance. Quickly out of the stalls from his outside draw and soon at the head of affairs, he led two out but was collared approaching the last and was eventually comfortably beaten by his stablemate for second place. He is another likely to be seen out at Royal Ascot.
New Girlfriend(IRE), always thereabouts, fought bravely to the line, but was a little one-paced and an extra furlong would certainly be an advantage to her.
Conquest(IRE), given a waiting ride, did run on but not fast enough. A return to 6f may be an advantage for this Gimcrack winner.
Patavellian(IRE) still had plenty to do at the halfway stage and was badly interfered with at the two-furlong marker. Once balanced, he ran on again inside the final furlong. It was a decent effort from this dear old campaigner.
Presto Shinko(IRE) ran below his best and was never really seen with a chance. He was hampered a little over a furlong out and was unable to quicken as the race came to an end.
Blue Echo was smartly into her stride, but was a spent force by the two marker and certainly ran well below her best for some reason.

2292a GRAND PRIX DE CHANTILLY MITSUBISHI MOTORS (GROUP 2) 1m 4f
3:50 (3:49) 4-Y-O+ **£50,068** (£19,324; £9,223; £6,149; £3,074)

RPR

1 **Saddex**[42] 1190 4-9-2 .... TMundry 2 121
(P Rau, Germany) *disputing 6th: 5th on ins st: hdwy 1 1/2f out: chal appr fnl f: rdn to ld 100yds out: drvn out* **12/1**

2 *1 1/2* **Vison Celebre (IRE)**[41] 4-8-12 .... OPeslier 5 114
(A Fabre, France) *hld up disputing 6th: 7th st: fin wl on outside fnl f: tk 2nd on line* **5/1**

3 *nse* **Mountain High (IRE)**[22] 1650 5-8-12 .... KerrinMcEvoy 3 114
(Sir Michael Stoute) *racd in 3rd: wnt 2nd 4f out: led over 2f out: rdn 1 1/2f out: hdd 100yds out: lost 2nd on line* **9/2**[3]

4 *1 1/2* **Irish Wells (FR)**[35] 1340 4-9-2 .... DBoeuf 8 116
(F Rohaut, France) *racd in 2nd: 3rd st: hrd rdn and disp 2nd 1 1/2f out: no ex u.p fnl f* **3/1**[1]

5 *2* **Champs Elysees**[26] 1571 4-8-12 .... SPasquier 7 108
(A Fabre, France) *disp 4th: 6th st: sn pushed along: rdn 1 1/2f out: no imp* **4/1**[2]

6 *snk* **Daramsar (FR)**[14] 1881 4-9-2 .... CSoumillon 1 112
(A De Royer-Dupre, France) *in tch disputing 4th: 4th and pushed along st: rdn and disputing 2nd 1 1/2f out: wknd fnl 100yds* **4/1**[2]

7 *snk* **Walk In The Park (IRE)**[391] 1558 5-8-12 .... TGillet 4 108
(J E Hammond, France) *hld up in last: pushed along st: hdwy on ins 2f out to over 1f out: one pce after* **12/1**

8 *15* **Sign Of The Wolf**[35] 1340 7-8-12 .... F-XBertras 6 84
(F Rohaut, France) *drvn to ld: hdd over 2f out: eased* **100/1**

2m 28.7s (-4.70) **Going Correction** -0.125s/f (Firm) **8** Ran SP% **116.2**
Speed ratings: 110,109,108,107,106 106,106,96
PARI-MUTUEL: WIN 10.60; PL 3.10, 3.00, 3.50; DF 46.10.
Owner Stall Avena **Bred** The Niarchos Family **Trained** Germany

NOTEBOOK
Saddex, a rapidly improving German challenger, won with something in hand. Coming from the rear on the far rail, he took control halfway through the final furlong. This bargain colt, who has been given plenty of time by his connections, now goes for the Deutschland Preis at Dusseldorf at the end of July and then the Grosser Preis Von Baden at the beginning of September, before hopefully a tilt at the Arc.
Vison Celebre(IRE) was dropped out in the early stages. Brought with a run up the centre of the track, he finished best of all and was slightly hampered by the third inside the final furlong before taking second place in the final few strides. This distance looks perfect for this promising colt, who was running for just the third time. It would be no surprise to see him run in the Grand Prix de Saint-Cloud later in the month.

Mountain High(IRE), given a fine ride, acquitted himself well. After tracking the leaders, he took a decent advantage with a quarter of a mile to run but was run out of it late on. He hung left a little when under pressure and this might have cost him second place. He may next be seen out in the Hardwicke Stakes at Royal Ascot.
Irish Wells(FR) was slightly disappointing. Always handy, his pacemaker doing an excellent job, he was asked for an effort halfway up the straight but he didn't have his normal kick at the business end and just stayed on at the same pace. He will now have a rest and could go for back-to-back wins in the Grand Prix de Deauville later in the season.
Daramsar(FR), down in trip, should have appreciated the ground and was a little disappointing.

2293a PRIX DU JOCKEY CLUB MITSUBISHI MOTORS (GROUP 1) 1m 2f 110y

4:35 (4:48) 3-Y-O **£579,122** (£231,689; £115,845; £57,872; £28,986)

RPR

1 **Lawman (FR)**[25] 1593 3-9-2 .... LDettori 5 119
(J-M Beguigne, France) *mde all: drvn and r.o 1 1/2f out: rdn out* **4/1**[1]
2 1 1/2 **Literato (FR)**[49] 1057 3-9-2 .... C-PLemaire 9 116
(J-C Rouget, France) *hld up in mid-div: hdwy in centre fr 1 1/2f out: rdn and r.o wl fnl f: tk 2nd 100yds out: nrest at fin* **9/1**[3]
3 snk **Shamdinan (FR)**[35] 3-9-2 .... CSoumillon 1 116
(A De Royer-Dupre, France) *hld up on ins: pushed along and r.o fr 2f out: rdn and disputing 2nd 100yds out: styd on* **16/1**
4 snk **Zambezi Sun**[35] 3-9-2 .... SPasquier 14 115
(P Bary, France) *towards rr: pushed along on outside st: rdn and styd on fr 1 1/2f out: fin strly fnl f* **6/1**[2]
5 2 1/2 **Castlereagh (UAE)**[12] 3-9-2 .... KerrinMcEvoy 7 110
(A Fabre, France) *mid-div: pushed along appr st: drvn 2f out: styd on at one pce fr 1 1/2f out* **25/1**
6 1/2 **No Dream (USA)**[40] 1233 3-9-2 .... OPeslier 8 109
(C Laffon-Parias, France) *prom: 2nd 1/2-way: pushed along 2f out: rdn to keep pl 1 1/2f out: sn one pce* **25/1**
7 nse **Sagara (USA)**[20] 1736 3-9-2 ....(p) TGillet 20 109
(J E Pease, France) *towards rr: last st: rdn and hdwy down outside 1 1/2f out: nrest at fin* **12/1**
8 snk **Loup Breton (IRE)**[25] 3-9-2 .... TThulliez 4 109
(E Lellouche, France) *prom: 4th st: rdn 2f out: wnt 2nd 1 1/2f out: no ex fnl 150yds* **40/1**
9 1 1/2 **Brooklyn Boy (USA)**[66] 3-9-2 .... IMendizabal 2 106
(J-C Rouget, France) *prom on rail: 4th 1/2-way: 3rd st: hdwy 1 1/2f out: disputing 2nd 150yds out: wknd* **50/1**
10 1/2 **Indian Spring (IRE)**[19] 3-9-2 .... GBenoist 17 105
(D Smaga, France) *mid-div: effrt to chse ldrs ent st: sn no ex* **100/1**
11 shd **Raincoat**[17] 1790 3-9-2 .... RichardHughes 6 105
(J H M Gosden) *mid-div: rdn 2f out: nvr in chalng position* **4/1**[1]
12 nk **Sunshine Kid (USA)**[20] 1736 3-9-2 .... JimmyFortune 15 104
(J H M Gosden) *nvr bttr than mid-div* **33/1**
13 5 **Quest For Honor**[20] 1736 3-9-2 .... JVictoire 3 94
(A Fabre, France) *prom on ins: 6th and pushed along st: rdn and u.p 2f out: wknd fnl f* **16/1**
14 1/2 **Spirit One (FR)**[21] 1703 3-9-2 .... DBoeuf 11 93
(P Demercastel, France) *mid-div: shkn up 4f out: effrt on outside st: rdn and one pce fr 1 1/2f out* **14/1**
15 hd **Halicarnassus (IRE)**[10] 1957 3-9-2 .... DarryllHolland 16 93
(M R Channon) *in rr: last 1/2-way: drvn over 2f out and styd on on rail tl one pce fr over 1f out* **20/1**
16 3/4 **Alexander Of Hales (USA)**[7] 2066 3-9-2 .... JAHeffernan 12 91
(A P O'Brien, Ire) *prom on outside to 1/2-way: towards rr whn drvn ent st: sn no ex* **14/1**
17 nk **Beltanus (GER)**[14] 3-9-2 .... TMundry 19 91
(Frau Ira Ferentschak, Germany) *towards rr: n.d* **100/1**
18 shd **Visionario (IRE)**[21] 1703 3-9-2 .... MSautjeau 10 91
(A Fabre, France) *prom: 5th st: drvn 2f out: one pce fr appr fnl f* **16/1**
19 nk **Chinese Whisper (IRE)**[25] 1593 3-9-2 .... JMurtagh 13 90
(A P O'Brien, Ire) *hld up: drvn 2 1/2f out: sltly hmpd by Spirit One 2f out but nvr looked dangerous* **12/1**
20 1 1/2 **Medicine Path**[44] 1126 3-9-2 .... RichardMullen 18 87
(E J O'Neill) *broke wl on outside: racd in mid-div: 19th st: sn rdn and btn* **25/1**

2m 5.90s (-4.60) **Going Correction** -0.125s/f (Firm) **20 Ran SP% 136.3**
Speed ratings: 111,109,109,109,107 107,107,107,106,105 105,105,101,101,101 100,100,100,100,99
PARI-MUTUEL: WIN 4.50; PL 2.20, 2.70, 3.90; DF 13.50.
Owner C Marzocco **Bred** Petra Bloodstock Agency **Trained** France
■ Dettori completed a memorable Derby double most recently achieved by Lester Piggott, Willie Carson and Pat Eddery.
■ Stewards' Enquiry : C Soumillon two-day ban: careless riding (jun 12-13) and four-day ban: whip abuse (Jun 14-17)

FOCUS
As is usual these days, this was a weaker race than its Epsom counterpart and Lawman has been rated a long way behind Authorized, and also a couple of pounds below Eagle Mountain. A false start was followed by a messy race, but Dettori avoided any traffic problems on the winner, whom he gave a fine front-running ride.

NOTEBOOK
Lawman(FR) was fractious during the preliminaries when he unshipped his jockey, so Dettori broke the parade to take him to post early. He was also a little difficult after a false start, but did absolutely nothing wrong in the race and won in fine style under a terrific front-running ride, Dettori setting a sensible pace before giving him a little breather round the final turn and then quickening things up at the two-furlong marker and soon having the race in the bag. The colt has been beautifully prepared and further progress can be expected. He will now be rested and his trainer is thinking about his international reputation, which could be further enhanced in races like the Irish Champion Stakes and the Arc.
Literato(FR), given plenty to do, was brought with his run up the centre of the track. He quickened well one and a half out but never threatened the winner. This thoroughly genuine colt will probably be given a holiday now and has an entry in the Arc.
Shamdinan(FR) was well behind coming into the straight but really began to motor from one and a half out up the rail and was still making ground at the finish. He rather barged his way through in the straight and his jockey was suspended for an unusual manoeuvre on the rail in the straight. He may go for the Grand Prix de Paris in July.
Zambezi Sun, who had finished well ahead of the third when they last met at Longchamp, was well behind at the entrance to the straight and did not have much luck when making his challenge. He finished well and this was a decent effort from an individual who was only racing for the third time, and in a Group race for the first occasion. With a better draw he would undoubtedly have been closer, and he may well be seen out next in the Grand Prix de Paris.
Raincoat, slowly into his stride, was never really seen with a chance of taking a hand in the finish. Ninth turning in, he was asked to make an effort near the rail in the straight and was hampered a little at the furlong marker. He finished quite well and his trainer feels he needs a longer trip, so he could be in the line-up for the King Edward VII Stakes at Royal Ascot.
Sunshine Kid(USA), not well drawn on the outside, was never really seen with a chance.
Halicarnassus(IRE), held up, was unable to quicken in the straight and was always towards the back of the field.
Medicine Path should have liked the ground but was never beyond mid-division.

1338 DUSSELDORF (R-H)

Sunday, June 3

OFFICIAL GOING: Good

2294a HENKEL PREIS DER DIANA - GERMAN OAKS (GROUP 1) (FILLIES) 1m 3f

4:05 (4:17) 3-Y-O **£135,135** (£54,054; £27,027; £13,514; £6,757)

RPR

1 **Mystic Lips (GER)**[35] 1338 3-9-2 .... AHelfenbein 9 115
(Andreas Lowe, Germany) *mde all: clr fnl f: r.o wl* **5/1**[2]
2 5 **Dominante (GER)**[6] 3-9-2 .... MickyFenton 12 107
(A Wohler, Germany) *hld up towards rr to st: gd hdwy on outside fr 2f out: r.o to take 2nd fnl 100yds: no ch w wnr* **8/1**
3 1/2 **Avanti Polonia (GER)** 3-9-2 .... AStarke 4 106
(P Schiergen, Germany) *6th st: hdwy to go 3rd 1 1/2f out: 2nd 1f out: one pce* **61/10**[3]
4 4 **Scoubidou (GER)**[28] 1515 3-9-2 .... FJohansson 6 100
(H Blume, Germany) *a.p: 2nd st: wknd appr fnl f* **21/10**[1]
5 hd **Naomia (GER)**[15] 1855 3-9-2 .... WMongil 8 100
(P Rau, Germany) *a.p: 3rd st: wknd appr fnl f* **109/10**
6 1 1/2 **Meridia (GER)**[28] 1515 3-9-2 .... KJManning 7 97
(J Hirschberger, Germany) *a in tch: 5th st: one pce fnl 2f* **13/2**
7 shd **Nouvelle Europe (GER)** 3-9-2 .... ABest 3 97
(P Rau, Germany) *a mid-div* **30/1**
8 3/4 **Zuckerpuppe (GER)**[28] 1515 3-9-2 .... VSchulepov 13 96
(Frau E Mader, Germany) *played up in stalls and lost 10 l at s: bhd to st: nvr a factor* **123/10**
9 8 **Highness (GER)** 3-9-2 .... J-PCarvalho 2 83
(W Baltromei, Germany) *hld up in rr: nvr a factor* **125/10**
10 3 1/2 **Chantra (GER)**[35] 1338 3-9-2 .... DaneO'Neill 11 78
(P Rau, Germany) *in tch: 7th st: sn btn* **155/10**
11 3 **Loa Loa (GER)**[55] 3-9-2 .... EPedroza 10 73
(A Wohler, Germany) *prom 7f* **109/10**
12 11 **Palace Princess (GER)** 3-9-2 ....(b) NRichter 5 55
(U Ostmann, Germany) *a towards rr* **31/1**

2m 16.31s (35.15) **12 Ran SP% 131.6**
(Including 10 Euros stake): WIN 60; PL 22, 35, 23; SF 571.
Owner Stall Lintec **Bred** Gestut Erlenhof **Trained** Germany

FOCUS
Pre-race favourite Miramare was withdrawn after proving unruly in the stalls.

2070 SAN SIRO (R-H)

Sunday, June 3

OFFICIAL GOING: Heavy

2295a PREMIO EMILIO TURATI (GROUP 2) 1m

3:30 (3:35) 3-Y-O+ **£38,767** (£17,057; £9,304; £4,652)

RPR

1 **Apollo Star (GER)**[42] 5-9-6 .... ASuborics 6 106
(Mario Hofer, Germany) *led after 1 1/2f: 2 l clr fr 2f out: pushed out: comf (1.63/1)* **8/5**[1]
2 2 **Icelandic**[14] 5-9-6 .... MSanna 7 102
(Frank Sheridan, Italy) *5th st: hrd rdn and chsd wnr fr over 1f out: no imp* **77/10**
3 1 1/2 **Miles Gloriosus (USA)**[22] 4-9-6 .... GMarcelli 9 99
(R Menichetti, Italy) *mid-div: 6th st: styd on one pce fnl 2f to take 3rd in clsng stages* **11/1**
4 3/4 **Rattle And Hum (ITY)**[22] 4-9-6 .... SLandi 1 98
(F & L Camici, Italy) *led 1 1/2f: 2nd st: one pce fr wl over 1f out* **37/10**[3]
5 2 **Scartozz**[49] 5-9-6 ....(b) EBotti 3 94
(A & G Botti, Italy) *4th st: one pce fnl 2f* **13/1**
6 5 1/2 **Moriwood (ITY)**[14] 1873 3-8-9 .... URispoli 8 83
(A & G Botti, Italy) *last st: nvr a factor* **11/1**
7 1/2 **Amante Latino**[35] 1336 3-8-9 .... SMulas 2 82
(V Caruso, Italy) *prom: 3rd st: btn over 2f out* **19/10**[2]
8 7 1/2 **Momix**[49] 4-9-3 .... PConvertino 5 64
(B Grizzetti, Italy) *7th st: a bhd* **21/1**

1m 41.7s (-0.40)
WFA 3 from 4yo+ 11lb **8 Ran SP% 134.1**
(including one euro stakes): WIN 2.63; PL 1.68, 2.22, 2.69; DF 10.49.
Owner J Spranke **Bred** H Gerwin **Trained** Germany

2296a PREMIO PAOLO MEZZANOTTE (GROUP 3) (F&M) 1m 2f

4:40 (4:45) 3-Y-O+ **£24,628** (£10,836; £5,911; £2,955)

RPR

1 **Wickwing**[217] 6251 4-8-9 .... EBotti 8 102
(A & G Botti, Italy) *a in tch: 4th st: hdwy fr over 1f out: r.o to ld last strides (22.29/1)* **223/10**
2 1/2 **Fair Breeze (GER)**[32] 1421 4-8-9 .... ASuborics 2 101
(Mario Hofer, Germany) *sn racing in 2nd bhd clr ldr: drvn to ld jst ins fnl f: hrd rdn and ct last strides* **6/5**[1]
3 snk **Irene Watts**[579] 6222 4-8-9 .... PConvertino 5 101
(F Folco, Italy) *hld up: hdwy 2f out: styd on: nrest at fin* **112/10**
4 hd **Mara Spectrum (IRE)**[350] 2694 4-8-9 .... GBietolini 10 101
(B Grizzetti, Italy) *hld up: 6th st: hdwy 3f out: kpt on one pce fr over 1f out: nrest at fin* **10/1**
5 2 **Veronica Franco (ITY)**[350] 2694 4-8-9 .... GArena 4 97
(E Borromeo, Italy) *clr ldr to over 1f out: hdd jst ins fnl f: kpt on one pce* **10/1**
6 shd **Opatja**[49] 5-8-9 .... SMulas 7 97
(L Camici, Italy) *mid-div: styd on fnl 2f: nvr in chalng position* **25/1**
7 1/2 **Snow Gretel (IRE)**[28] 1517 4-8-9 .... MEsposito 1 96
(M Botti) *racd in 3rd to st: one pce fnl 2f* **82/10**

8 1 **Sexy Lady (GER)**[319] 3661 4-8-9 .... MDemuro 6 94
(P Rau, Germany) *hld up: last st: nvr a factor* **26/10[2]**
9 3 ½ **Cockayne (IRE)**[210] 6362 4-8-9 .... NPinna 11 88
(V Valiani, Italy) *a in rr* **103/10**
10 4 ½ **Twardowska (ITY)**[350] 2694 4-8-9 .... GMarcelli 3 80
(G Dolfi, Italy) *5th st: btn over 2f out* **15/2[3]**
11 11 **Desert Quiet (IRE)**[49] 5-8-9 .... SLandi 9 60
(P Giannotti, Italy) *mid-div to 1/2-way: bhd fnl 2f* **119/10**

2m 6.70s 11 Ran SP% **147.0**
WIN 23.29; PL 4.07, 1.36, 2.63; DF 34.67.
Owner Scuderia Francesca **Bred** G S Shropshire **Trained** Italy

NOTEBOOK
Snow Gretel(IRE) ran quite well in the circumstances, given the combination of a longer trip, first try in Pattern company and much softer ground than she had previously encountered. Prominent in the chasing pack behind clear leader Veronica Franco, she still had a chance of a place approaching the final furlong.

2071 CARLISLE (R-H)

Monday, June 4

OFFICIAL GOING: Good (good to firm in places in home straight; 8.5)
Following the early abandonment of a meeting at this course due to unsafe conditions last week, the runners in all races came centre to stands side.
Wind: Fresh, half against Weather: Fine

2297 JOIN WBX.COM FOR £150 FREE BETS MEDIAN AUCTION MAIDEN STKS 5f
2:20 (2:22) (Class 6) 2-Y-O **£1,943** (£578; £288; £144) **Stalls** High

Form RPR
1 **Philario (IRE)** 2-9-3 0 .... PhillipMakin 3 81
(K R Burke) *prom: effrt over 1f out: styd on to ld nr fin* **11/1**
4 2 nk **Mazzanti**[13] 1919 2-9-3 0 .... DO'Donohoe 6 80
(K A Ryan) *chsd ldrs: led over 2f out: r.o wl fnl f: hdd cl home* **3/1[2]**
6 3 2 ½ **Firewalker**[11] 1963 2-8-12 0 .... RoystonFfrench 8 66
(B Smart) *chsd ldrs: ev ch over 2f out: one pce fnl f* **25/1**
4 nk **Chain Of Gold** 2-9-3 0 .... RichardMullen 7 70
(E S McMahon) *s.i.s: bhd: hdwy on outside and prom over 2f out: edgd rt u.p and one pce fnl f* **5/4[1]**
0 5 1 ½ **Bazguy**[58] 942 2-9-3 0 .... DAllen 4 65
(P D Evans) *led to over 2f out: no ex over 1f out* **33/1**
4 6 1 ¼ **Gain Share**[28] 1528 2-9-3 0 .... PaulFessey 2 60
(T D Barron) *unruly bef s: plld hrd: disp ld tl wknd over 1f out* **10/1[3]**
7 ¾ **Blue Cross Boy (USA)** 2-8-12 0 .... JamieMoriarty(5) 9 57
(J Howard Johnson) *bhd and outpcd tl hdwy fnl f: nvr on terms* **14/1**
8 ½ **Terry's Tip (IRE)** 2-9-3 0 .... TomEaves 11 56
(Mrs L Stubbs) *s.i.s: bhd: effrt on outside 1/2-way: btn over 1f out* **14/1**
9 1 **Stormy Journey** 2-8-12 0 .... PJMcDonald(5) 1 52
(Mrs K Walton) *bhd and outpcd: nvr on terms* **150/1**
4 10 1 **Whiskey Creek**[10] 1993 2-9-3 0 .... PaulHanagan 10 48
(R A Fahey) *prom tl rdn and wknd over 2f out* **12/1**
11 4 **Smilodon** 2-8-9 0 .... PatrickMathers(3) 5 29
(A Berry) *s.i.s: nvr on terms* **200/1**

61.94 secs (0.44) **Going Correction** -0.125s/f (Firm) 11 Ran SP% **115.8**
Speed ratings (Par 91):91,90,86,86,83 81,80,79,78,76 70
CSF £42.93 TOTE £16.00: £4.10, £1.10, £5.60; EX 71.20.
Owner Philip Richards **Bred** David Barry **Trained** Middleham Moor, N Yorks

FOCUS
Probably ordinary form behind the front two but the runner-up set a good standard and the form should prov reliable. The early pace was not strong.

NOTEBOOK
Philario(IRE), who cost 27,000gns and is a half brother to multiple 7f winner Saxon Lil, was easy to back but showed a good attitude to make a winning debut. He will have no problems with 6f and appeals as the type to win more races. (op 9-1 tchd 12-1)
Mazzanti, who shaped well on his debut, confirmed that promise and, although caught in the closing stages, finished clear of the remainder and appeals as the type to win a similar event. (tchd 11-4)
Firewalker had shown only a modest level of form on her debut but she fared a good deal better with that experience behind her. While vulnerable to the better types in this grade, she will stay 6f and looks the sort to pick up a minor event. (op 16-1)
Chain Of Gold ◆, who attracted plenty of support, showed his inexperience on this racecourse debut and is almost certainly a fair bit better than the bare form suggests. He is well worth another chance with this experience behind him. (op 9-4)
Bazguy showed only a modest level of form on his racecourse debut at Kempton but fared better on this first start on turf. He is going to need a step into nursery company or his sights lowering before he gets off the mark, though. (tchd 50-1)
Gain Share, keen when showing ability on his debut at Newcastle, looked a real handful both before and during the race this time. There is little doubting he has plenty of ability but it remains to be seen whether his temperament gets the better of him and he is one to tread carefully with at present. (op 11-2)

2298 CARLISLE CONFERENCE GROUP & WAVERLEY TBS CLAIMING STKS 7f 200y
2:50 (2:55) (Class 6) 3-Y-O+ **£2,047** (£604; £302) **Stalls** High

Form RPR
2050 1 **Top Jaro (FR)**[10] 1997 4-9-6 70 .... LiamTreadwell(3) 6 62
(Jennie Candlish) *in tch: effrt over 2f out: led ins fnl f: styd on wl* **7/2[2]**
/00- 2 1 ½ **Slavonic (USA)**[248] 3139 6-9-2 55 .... TomEaves 14 52
(B Storey) *led: rdn over 2f out: edgd rt over 1f out: hdd ins fnl f: kpt on* **50/1**
0652 3 ¾ **Nevinstown (IRE)**[14] 1893 7-9-7 52 .... TonyHamilton 9 55
(C Grant) *in tch: effrt over 2f out: edgd rt over 1f out: kpt on fnl f* **12/1**
00-0 4 shd **Noble Edge**[20] 1744 4-9-9 41 ....(p) FTahir 4 57
(Karen McLintock) *midfield: hdwy over 1f out: kpt on fnl f: nrst fin* **100/1**
16-5 5 1 **Chateau (IRE)**[7] 2091 5-9-1 58 ....(t) MarkLawson(3) 3 49
(M E Sowersby) *hld up: hdwy on outside over 2f out: hung rt over 1f out: kpt on same pce ins fnl f* **16/1**
1111 6 shd **Blue Sky Thinking (IRE)**[20] 1744 8-9-6 71 .... AndrewElliott(3) 11 54
(K R Burke) *t.k.h: cl up: effrt over 2f out: edgd rt and no ex over 1f out* **10/11[1]**
-060 7 5 **Khetaab (IRE)**[28] 1539 5-9-5 50 .... DavidAllan 7 39
(E J Alston) *prom tl rdn and wknd over 1f out* **8/1[3]**
-000 8 3 ½ **Distant Vision (IRE)**[73] 743 4-8-11 35 .... PaulFessey 2 23
(A Berry) *bhd: rdn 3f out: n.d* **200/1**
-000 9 ½ **Ho Pang Yau**[14] 1893 9-8-11 44 .... GaryBartley(7) 1 28
(J S Goldie) *towards rr: drvn 1/2-way: n.d* **25/1**
30-0 10 1 ½ **Briery Blaze**[42] 1197 4-8-11 48 .... PJMcDonald(5) 15 23
(Mrs K Walton) *stdd s: n.d* **50/1**
2660 11 5 **Homecroft Boy**[6] 2110 3-8-6 42 .... RoystonFfrench 12 12
(P D Evans) *hld up: rdn 3f out: sn btn* **20/1**
204- 12 2 ½ **Quaker Boy**[340] 3023 4-9-1 56 .... AndrewMullen(3) 10 8
(A C Whillans) *t.k.h: hld up: rdn 3f out: sn btn* **33/1**
000- 13 23 **Auburndale**[71] 4635 5-9-2 30 .... PaulHanagan 5 —
(A Crook) *prom tl wknd over 3f out* **200/1**
14 1 ¾ **Walker (CZE)**[211] 3-8-9 30 ....(b[1]) PatrickMathers(3) 13 —
(A Berry) *chsd ldrs tl wknd over 3f out* **80/1**
-060 15 25 **Ross Is Boss**[23] 1676 5-9-5 25 .... PaddyAspell 8 —
(C J Teague) *bhd: t.o fr 1/2-way* **150/1**

1m 40.47s (0.38) **Going Correction** +0.075s/f (Good)
WFA 3 from 4yo+ 11lb 15 Ran SP% **118.6**
Speed ratings (Par 101):101,99,98,98,97 97,92,89,88,87 82,79,56,54,29
CSF £177.41 TOTE £4.90: £1.70, £9.70, £2.30; EX 299.60.There was no bid for the winner.
Owner Alan Baxter **Bred** Jean Biraben And Robert Labeyrie **Trained** Basford Green, Staffs

FOCUS
A run-of-the-mill event in which the pace was sound throughout. The winner and sixth stood out beforehand and the form is tricky to rate.

2299 BET NOW AT WBX.COM WORLD BET EXCHANGE FILLIES' H'CAP 1m 1f 61y
3:20 (3:21) (Class 5) (0-70,68) 3-Y-O **£2,817** (£838; £418; £209) **Stalls** High

Form RPR
00-0 1 **Amanda Carter**[57] 954 3-8-2 49 oh1 .... PaulHanagan 4 63+
(R A Fahey) *in tch: green and outpcd 4f out: gd hdwy and squeezed through on stands' side rail to ld over 1f out: sn clr: eased nr fin* **7/2[3]**
-043 2 4 **Falimar**[39] 1256 3-9-1 62 ....(p) TomEaves 7 64
(Miss J A Camacho) *t.k.h: cl up: led over 2f out to over 1f out: no ch w wnr* **2/1[1]**
0-00 3 5 **The Mighty Ogmore**[11] 1964 3-8-1 51 ow1 ....(p) AndrewMullen(3) 3 43
(R C Guest) *s.i.s: bhd: plenty to do 4f out: gd hdwy over 1f out: kpt on fnl f* **12/1**
400- 4 3 ½ **Reflective Glory (IRE)**[192] 6582 3-8-5 52 .... RoystonFfrench 6 36
(J S Wainwright) *in tch: effrt over 2f out: sn no imp* **16/1**
00-0 5 1 ½ **Fairy Slipper**[33] 1412 3-7-13 49 oh4 .... DuranFentiman(5) 8 30
(Jedd O'Keeffe) *hld up: rdn and wandered over 2f out: nvr rchd ldrs* **33/1**
0040 6 1 ¾ **Noravana (IRE)**[74] 731 3-8-2 52 .... PatrickMathers(3) 9 29
(Miss V Haigh) *chsd ldrs: rdn 3f out: sn wknd* **22/1**
634- 7 4 **Golden Topaz (IRE)**[281] 4830 3-9-2 68 .... JamieMoriarty(5) 10 37
(J Howard Johnson) *led to over 2f out: sn rdn and btn* **5/2[2]**
62-0 8 69 **Pavlovia**[10] 1994 3-9-4 65 .... PaulFessey 5 —
(M Dods) *sn bhd and struggling: t.o fr 1/2-way* **10/1**

1m 59.33s (1.77) **Going Correction** +0.075s/f (Good) 8 Ran SP% **114.1**
Speed ratings (Par 96):95,91,87,83,82 81,77,16
CSF £10.86 CT £72.48 TOTE £4.50: £1.50, £1.10, £3.50; EX 11.10.
Owner Mrs Janis Macpherson **Bred** James G Thom **Trained** Musley Bank, N Yorks
■ Princess Palatine was withdrawn (6/1, vet's advice.) R4 applies, deduct 10p in the £.

FOCUS
A modest handicap but a sound pace throughout. The form is rated through the runner-up and the winner is value for extra.
Pavlovia Official explanation: jockey said filly lost its action

2300 WBX.COM WORLD BET EXCHANGE H'CAP 5f 193y
3:50 (3:50) (Class 6) (0-65,62) 3-Y-O **£2,047** (£604; £302) **Stalls** High

Form RPR
-500 1 **Mambomoon**[6] 2120 3-8-6 47 ow2 ....(b) DavidAllan 8 54
(T D Easterby) *mde all: rdn and styd on wl fnl f* **20/1**
0363 2 2 **Missus Molly Brown**[12] 1943 3-8-5 46 ....(b[1]) PaulHanagan 4 47
(R A Fahey) *blkd s: sn prom: rdn over 2f out: styd on wl fnl f to take 2nd cl home: nt rch wnr* **7/2[1]**
66-4 3 nk **Ishibee (IRE)**[32] 1426 3-8-9 50 ....(p) RoystonFfrench 11 50
(Mrs A Duffield) *cl up: effrt over 2f out: kpt on fnl f: lost 2nd cl home* **7/1[3]**
1550 4 2 **Slipasearcher (IRE)**[8] 2061 3-9-0 62 ....(b) MCGeran(7) 6 56+
(P D Evans) *hld up: nt clr run briefly over 2f out: hdwy over 1f out: nrst fin* **8/1**
5-05 5 2 **Soviet Sound (IRE)**[12] 1943 3-8-7 53 ow1 .... JamieMoriarty(5) 13 41
(Jedd O'Keeffe) *prom: effrt over 2f out: one pce over 1f out* **17/2**
02-0 6 1 ¼ **Ocean Of Champagne**[43] 1175 3-8-9 55 ....(v) MichaelJStainton(5) 9 39
(A Dickman) *hld up: rdn and effrt over 2f out: kpt on fnl f: nvr rchd ldrs* **14/1**
6-03 7 shd **Karmest**[20] 1749 3-9-0 55 .... PaulMulrennan 2 39
(E S McMahon) *cl up tl rdn and wknd over 1f out* **7/1[3]**
-606 8 3 **Avoncreek**[24] 1635 3-8-11 52 .... PaulFessey 7 27
(B P J Baugh) *midfield: effrt over 2f out: wknd over 1f out* **16/1**
0640 9 2 **Tomorrow's Dancer**[21] 1712 3-8-12 53 .... DO'Donohoe 14 22
(K A Ryan) *hld up: shortlived effrt over 2f out: sn btn* **11/2[2]**
000- 10 3 **Anybody's Guess (IRE)**[250] 5614 3-8-9 50 .... TonyHamilton 3 10
(J S Wainwright) *cl up to 1/2-way: sn rdn and wknd* **50/1**
5-40 11 2 **Livalex**[13] 1913 3-9-2 57 .... PhillipMakin 1 11
(M Dods) *hld up: rdn over 2f out: sn btn* **12/1**
00-5 12 1 ¾ **Mystic**[27] 1558 3-8-9 50 .... PaulQuinn 5 —
(D W Barker) *bmpd s: sn prom: rdn and wknd fr 1/2-way* **20/1**
606- 13 18 **Waiheke Island**[249] 5632 3-9-5 60 .... TomEaves 15 —
(B Mactaggart) *in tch tl wknd qckly 1/2-way: t.o* **25/1**

1m 14.26s (0.65) **Going Correction** -0.125s/f (Firm) 13 Ran SP% **119.8**
Speed ratings (Par 97):90,87,86,84,81 79,79,75,73,69 66,64,40
CSF £85.99 CT £578.00 TOTE £27.30: £5.40, £1.70, £2.30; EX 148.10.
Owner Miss Betty Duxbury **Bred** Hyperion Bloodstock **Trained** Great Habton, N Yorks

FOCUS
A weak handicap, rated through the second, with a big step up from Mambomoon. In all probability this took little winning. Although the pace seemed sound throughout, it was a modest winning time for a race of its type.
Karmest Official explanation: jockey said filly was unsuited by the good (good to firm in places) ground

2301 BORDER CONSTRUCTION H'CAP 5f
4:20 (4:20) (Class 6) (0-60,62) 3-Y-O **£2,047** (£604; £302) **Stalls** High

Form RPR
4401 1 **Darcy's Pride (IRE)**[2] 2255 3-9-3 62 6ex .... AndrewMullen(3) 6 74
(D W Barker) *mde all: rdn 2f out: kpt on strly fnl f* **7/2[2]**
5250 2 3 **Moonlight Applause**[12] 1943 3-8-8 50 .... DavidAllan 4 51
(T D Easterby) *towards rr: hdwy u.p over 1f out: chsd wnr ins fnl f: no imp* **5/1[3]**

5-26 **3** *1 1/4* **Smirfys Gold (IRE)**[13] 1932 3-9-0 **56**........................(v) PaulMulrennan 3 53
(E S McMahon) *trckd ldrs: effrt over 1f out: nt qckn fnl f* **8/1**

6-05 **4** *hd* **Nufoudh (IRE)**[10] 2012 3-8-13 **60**.......................... JamieMoriarty(5) 2 56
(Miss Tracy Waggott) *chsd ldrs: outpcd over 1f out: kpt on fnl f: no imp* **16/1**

0-50 **5** *shd* **Dotty's Daughter**[21] 1707 3-8-8 **50**..........................(p) RoystonFfrench 1 45+
(Mrs A Duffield) *in tch: rdn whn n.m.r and swtchd rt appr fnl f: no imp* **16/1**

2043 **6** *hd* **Mangano**[3] 2205 3-8-10 **52**................................. PaulHanagan 5 47
(A Berry) *bhd: drvn 1/2-way: kpt on fnl f: nrst fin* **11/1**

2414 **7** *nk* **Princess Ellis**[12] 1943 3-8-8 **57**........................ GaryBartley(7) 8 51
(E J Alston) *cl up tl rdn and wknd appr fnl f* **5/2**[1]

6425 **8** *3 1/2* **Kilvickeon (IRE)**[40] 1248 3-8-4 **51** ow2.............. RussellKennemore(5) 7 32
(Peter Grayson) *prom: effrt over 2f out: wknd over 1f out* **6/1**

60.78 secs (-0.72) **Going Correction** -0.125s/f (Firm) **8** Ran SP% **113.0**
Speed ratings (Par 97):100,95,93,92,92 92,91,86
CSF £20.79 CT £127.94 TOTE £4.20: £1.60, £2.40, £2.30; EX 23.40.
Owner Ms Jenny Hanson **Bred** Leo Cox **Trained** Scorton, N Yorks

FOCUS
An ordinary event but another improved performance from the winner, who is thriving at present. The form seems sound enough.
Dotty's Daughter Official explanation: jockey said filly was denied a clear run

2302 JOIN WBX.COM FOR £150 FREE BETS APPRENTICE H'CAP 7f 200y
4:50 (4:50) (Class 6) (0-65,65) 4-Y-0+ **£2,047** (£604; £302) **Stalls** High

Form RPR

0120 **1** **Holiday Cocktail**[33] 1413 5-9-2 **57**........................ RoryMoore 10 69
(J J Quinn) *hld up: hdwy over 2f out: led ins fnl f: styd on strly* **12/1**

0-06 **2** *1 1/4* **Dakota Rain (IRE)**[23] 1655 5-9-10 **65**.................. LiamTreadwell 6 74
(Jennie Candlish) *led: rdn over 2f out: hdd ins fnl f: kpt on wl* **11/1**

230- **3** *3* **Spring Time Girl**[156] 6281 5-8-1 **47** oh1 ow1............... LanceBetts(5) 15 49
(B Ellison) *bhd: rdn over 3f out: kpt on fr 2f out: nrst fin* **20/1**

00-0 **4** *1/2* **Catherines Cafe (IRE)**[34] 1378 4-8-0 **46**.................. MCGeran(5) 7 47
(A C Whillans) *prom: effrt over 2f out: one pce over 1f out* **50/1**

30-3 **5** *hd* **William John**[26] 1578 4-8-13 **59**..........................(t) PatrickDonaghy(5) 8 59
(P C Haslam) *chsd ldrs: effrt 2f out: sn one pce* **8/1**

4-00 **6** *2 1/2* **First Rhapsody (IRE)**[13] 1918 5-8-9 **50**.............. RussellKennemore 17 45
(T J Etherington) *midfield: drvn over 2f out: no imp over 1f out* **33/1**

0104 **7** *1* **Inca Soldier (FR)**[9] 2033 4-8-4 **50**........................ GaryBartley(5) 14 42
(R C Guest) *plld hrd in midfield: effrt over 2f out: n.d* **9/1**

0000 **8** *3/4* **Apache Nation (IRE)**[12] 1944 4-8-13 **54**................... PJMcDonald 1 45
(M Dods) *midfield: pushed along over 2f out: nvr rchd ldrs* **14/1**

04-0 **9** *1/2* **Gifted Flame**[10] 2007 8-9-5 **63**........................... NeilBrown(3) 11 53
(T D Barron) *hld up: rdn whn hung rt over 2f out: nvr rchd ldrs* **4/1**[1]

5002 **10** *1* **Boy Dancer (IRE)**[10] 2007 4-9-3 **58**........................(p) AndrewMullen 12 45
(D W Barker) *s.i.s: a bhd* **6/1**[2]

0-03 **11** *hd* **Terenzium (IRE)**[13] 1918 5-8-11 **52**.......................... JamieMoriarty 9 39
(Micky Hammond) *hld up: pushed along 3f out: nvr on terms* **7/1**[3]

5-00 **12** *3/4* **Entranced**[14] 1892 4-9-1 **56**.................................. GregFairley 16 41
(L Lungo) *in tch: drvn over 3f out: btn over 1f out* **14/1**

5-60 **13** *1 1/4* **Bolton Hall (IRE)**[10] 2007 5-9-1 **61**........................ JamesRogers(5) 5 43
(R A Fahey) *s.i.s: nvr on terms* **12/1**

30-0 **14** *3/4* **Sea Frolic (IRE)**[5] 2149 6-8-5 **46** oh1........................ PatrickMathers 4 26
(Jennie Candlish) *prom tl hung rt and wknd fr 3f out* **66/1**

0054 **15** *1 1/2* **Red Lantern**[28] 1527 6-8-3 **49** oh1 ow3............................ NSLawes(5) 2 26
(M W Easterby) *hld up: pushed along over 2f out: sn btn* **33/1**

346- **16** *1* **Tequila Sheila (IRE)**[219] 6211 5-8-10 **51**...................... AndrewElliott 3 26
(K R Burke) *cl up tl rdn and wknd over 2f out* **14/1**

340- **17** *12* **Lady Lochinver (IRE)**[194] 5581 4-8-7 **48**.............. MichaelJStainton 13 —
(Micky Hammond) *towards rr: drvn and wknd fr 1/2-way* **66/1**

1m 39.32s (-0.77) **Going Correction** +0.075s/f (Good) **17** Ran SP% **127.2**
Speed ratings (Par 101):106,104,101,101,101 98,97,96,96,95 95,94,93,92,90 89,77
CSF £136.13 CT £2738.55 TOTE £15.30: £3.30, £2.80, £4.80, £9.90; EX 237.90 Place 6 £3338.50, Place 5 £123.45.
Owner Team Suffolk **Bred** Mrs W H Gibson Fleming **Trained** Settrington, N Yorks

FOCUS
Astrongly-run race and a fair winning time for the grade. The form looks modest but pretty reliable for the grade, rated through the runner-up.
Holiday Cocktail Official explanation: trainer said, regarding apparent improvement in form, that the gelding was better suited by not wearing a visor.
Boy Dancer(IRE) Official explanation: jockey said gelding was struck into
T/Jkpt: Not won. T/Plt: £333.30 to a £1 stake. Pool: £54,565.00. 119.50 winning tickets. T/Qpdt: £31.30 to a £1 stake. Pool: £4,105.40. 96.90 winning tickets. RY

2109 LEICESTER (R-H)
Monday, June 4

OFFICIAL GOING: Soft (5.2)
Wind: Light, across Weather: Cloudy

2303 PYTCHLEY MAIDEN STKS 5f 218y
2:00 (2:01) (Class 4) 2-Y-0 **£4,533** (£1,348; £674; £336) **Stalls** Low

Form RPR

1 **Golan Knight (IRE)** 2-9-3 0.......................... CatherineGannon 12 79+
(K A Ryan) *led over 4f out: pushed clr fnl f* **14/1**

02 **2** *3 1/2* **Ink Spot**[12] 1938 2-9-3 0.................................. HayleyTurner 4 65
(M L W Bell) *chsd ldrs: rdn over 1f out: styd on same pce* **7/2**[2]

0 **3** *1/2* **Always Ready**[20] 1743 2-9-3 0................................ TedDurcan 2 64
(C E Brittain) *mid-div: hdwy 1/2-way: rdn over 1f out: styng on same pce whn hung rt fr over 1f out* **14/1**

0 **4** *1 1/2* **An Scaribh**[13] 1919 2-9-3 0.......................... SimonWhitworth 8 59
(P D Evans) *mid-div: hdwy over 2f out: edgd rt ins fnl f: nt trble ldrs* **100/1**

6 **5** *hd* **King Bathwick (IRE)**[24] 1631 2-9-3 0........................ DaneO'Neill 6 58
(B R Millman) *chsd ldrs: rdn and hung rt over 1f out: wknd ins fnl f* **20/1**

6 *1 1/4* **Berrynarbor** 2-8-12 0.................................... FergusSweeney 10 50
(A G Newcombe) *sn outpcd: hdwy and nt clr run over 1f out: nt trble ldrs* **66/1**

4 **7** *1/2* **Galley Slave (IRE)**[7] 2086 2-9-3 0........................ MickyFenton 3 53
(Mrs P Sly) *sn outpcd: nvr nrr* **25/1**

8 *1* **Tapas Lad (IRE)** 2-9-0 0................................ JerryO'Dwyer(3) 9 50
(V Smith) *s.i.s: outpcd* **100/1**

64 **9** *3/4* **American Art (IRE)**[16] 1832 2-9-3 0........................ MichaelHills 7 48
(B W Hills) *led: hdd over 4f out: rdn over 2f out: wknd over 1f out* **5/4**[1]

10 *1 3/4* **Enactment** 2-9-3 0.. KerrinMcEvoy 11 43
(Sir Michael Stoute) *prom: rdn 1/2-way: wknd over 1f out* **9/2**[3]

11 *nk* **Penchesco (IRE)** 2-9-3 0................................ RichardHughes 5 42
(Pat Eddery) *s.i.s: hdwy over 2f out: wknd over 1f out* **12/1**

1m 16.35s (3.15) **Going Correction** +0.45s/f (Yiel) **11** Ran SP% **118.0**
Speed ratings (Par 95):97,92,91,89,89 87,87,85,84,82 82
CSF £61.13 TOTE £25.10: £5.00, £1.40, £4.50; EX 117.40 Trifecta £168.90 Part won. Pool £237.99 - 0.34 winning units..
Owner S Carr **Bred** M J Halligan **Trained** Hambleton, N Yorks

FOCUS
With the favourite running poorly, the race took less winning than might otherwise have been the case, but the winner could hardly have been more impressive and the time was solid, 1.25 seconds quicker than the following older-horse seller.

NOTEBOOK
Golan Knight(IRE) ◆, a 26,000euros colt out of a winner over a mile, did not go unsupported on this debut and, up with the pace from the start, ended up running his rivals into the ground. He may not have beaten much, but could hardly have done much more and his pedigree suggests that he will improve further as he goes up in trip. (op 20-1)
Ink Spot was always in about the same place but could never get on terms with the winner. He was one of the most experienced in the field and could find a modest maiden somewhere, but the nurseries start next month and that will provide him with other opportunities. (tchd 4-1 in places)
Always Ready stepped up from his debut in a Newcastle maiden that is starting to work out well. The way he stayed on here, and his pedigree, suggests that another furlong will suit. (op 11-1)
An Scaribh was doing his best work late and stepped up on his debut effort at this track on this easier ground. He looks a likely type for nurseries later on.
King Bathwick(IRE) looked more gathered this time and showed a bit more. He should continue to improve with racing. (op 14-1)
American Art(IRE) was up there early, but gradually lost his place as the race progressed and ended up running a stinker. This was miles below his Newbury effort. Official explanation: jockey said colt became upset in stalls (op 6-4 tchd 13-8 in places)

2304 HICKLING (S) STKS 5f 218y
2:30 (2:32) (Class 6) 3-5-Y-O **£2,590** (£770; £385; £192) **Stalls** Low

Form RPR

5-03 **1** **Drum Dance (IRE)**[7] 2091 5-8-13 46.............................. KDarley 8 53
(N Tinkler) *racd stands' side: mid-div: pushed along 1/2-way: hdwy and nt clr run over 1f out: rdn to ld wl ins fnl f* **2/1**[1]

50-6 **2** *shd* **Having A Ball**[7] 2083 3-8-5 53.............................. NickyMackay 9 51
(P D Cundell) *racd stands' side: chsd ldrs: rdn to ld 1f out: hdd wl ins fnl f: 2nd of 10 in gp* **4/1**[2]

0-03 **3** *1 1/4* **Valeesha**[13] 1912 3-7-13 45.............................. LukeMorris(5) 10 46
(W G M Turner) *racd stands' side: chsd ldrs: led wl over 1f out: rdn and hdd 1f out: styd on same pce: 3rd of 10 in gp* **14/1**

-000 **4** *1 3/4* **Tantien**[37] 1311 5-8-4 30 ow1..........................(p) ColinHaddon(5) 7 40
(T Keddy) *racd stands' side: mid-div: rdn 1/2-way: hdwy and hung rt fr over 1f out: styd on: 4th of 10 in gp* **40/1**

020- **5** *shd* **Bold Haze**[215] 6300 5-9-7 54..........................(v) MickyFenton 6 51
(Miss S E Hall) *racd stands' side: mid-div: rdn over 3f out: styd on ins fnl f: nt trble ldrs: 5th of 10 in gp* **11/2**[3]

0000 **6** *hd* **Dark Moon**[3] 2220 4-9-7 48..........................(v) DaneO'Neill 5 51
(D Shaw) *racd stands' side: hld up: r.o u.p ins fnl f: nrst fin: 6th of 10 in gp* **10/1**

2506 **7** *3* **Pat Will (IRE)**[6] 2104 3-8-5 54.......................... BernadetteQuinn(7) 1 39
(P D Evans) *racd stands' side: chsd ldr: rdn and edgd rt over 1f out: wknd ins fnl f: 7th of 10 in gp* **14/1**

5000 **8** *1* **Silly Gilly (IRE)**[13] 1912 3-7-11 49 ow4..................(p) KellyHarrison(7) 15 28
(K R Burke) *racd centre: wnt rt s: sn chsng ldrs: led that trio over 2f out: rdn and wknd over 1f out: 1st of 3 in gp* **7/1**

0-00 **9** *1 1/4* **Demi Sec**[76] 714 4-8-8 36.............................. DaleGibson 2 22
(Dr J D Scargill) *racd stands' side: sn outpcd: no ch whn hung rt ins fnl f: 8th of 10 in gp* **25/1**

0-0 **10** *6* **Tora Warning**[20] 1749 3-9-3 0.......................... SimonWhitworth 3 19
(John A Harris) *racd stands' side: s.i.s: a in rr: 9th of 10 in gp* **50/1**

200- **11** *7* **Baytown Valentina**[295] 4389 4-9-1 38..................(p) KevinGhunowa(5) 11 —
(R Brotherton) *racd centre: led that trio over 3f: wknd wl over 1f out: 2nd of 3 in gp* **66/1**

5000 **12** *5* **Brynris**[3] 2220 3-8-13 36.................................. JimmyQuinn 13 —
(Mrs G S Rees) *racd centre: chsd ldr over 3f: wknd wl over 1f out: last of 3 in gp* **66/1**

0600 **13** *19* **Bee Magic**[45] 1136 4-9-11 41..........................(b[1]) AdamKirby 4 —
(C N Kellett) *racd stands' side: overall ldr tl hdd & wknd wl over 1f out: last of 10 in gp* **33/1**

1m 17.6s (4.40) **Going Correction** +0.45s/f (Yiel)
WFA 3 from 4yo+ 8lb **13** Ran SP% **117.8**
Speed ratings (Par 101):88,87,86,83,83 83,79,78,75,67 58,51,26
CSF £8.80 TOTE £2.50: £1.70, £1.40, £3.40; EX 12.20 Trifecta £72.90 Part won. Pool £102.76 - 0.44 winning units..The winner was sold to Martin Hill for 4,500gns.
Owner Peter Alderson **Bred** J P And Miss M Mangan **Trained** Langton, N Yorks

FOCUS
A moderate time even for a seller, 1.25 seconds slower than the preceding two-year-old maiden. The three drawn highest raced on their own for the first part of the race, but had joined up with the main group before the two-furlong pole. This was a poor seler, rated at face value through the winner.

2305 BELVOIR CASTLE H'CAP 1m 1f 218y
3:00 (3:01) (Class 4) (0-85,85) 3-Y-O **£5,181** (£1,541; £770; £384) **Stalls** High

Form RPR

150- **1** **Greek Envoy**[235] 5916 3-9-6 **84**.............................. MickyFenton 6 95
(T P Tate) *hld up in tch: lost pl 1/2-way: hdwy over 3f out: led over 1f out: drvn out* **16/1**

31 **2** *1/2* **Mad Rush (USA)**[23] 1659 3-9-2 **80**........................ NickyMackay 2 90+
(L M Cumani) *sn pushed along in rr: hdwy over 2f out: rdn over 1f out: hung rt ins fnl f: r.o* **10/3**[3]

3-41 **3** *6* **Fretwork**[18] 1785 3-9-6 **84**.............................. RichardHughes 7 82
(R Hannon) *chsd ldrs: rdn over 2f out: no ex fnl f* **2/1**[1]

1-22 **4** *shd* **Giant Slalom**[13] 1936 3-8-10 **74**........................ KerrinMcEvoy 5 72
(W J Haggas) *sn led: rdn over 2f out: hdd over 1f out: no ex fnl f* **11/4**[2]

-043 **5** *3* **Dee Jay Wells**[21] 1708 3-8-2 **66** oh1..........................(b) DaleGibson 4 58
(R A Fahey) *prom: chsd ldr 7f out: rdn over 2f out: wknd fnl f* **33/1**

3-61 **6** *4* **Aegis (IRE)**[21] 1716 3-8-13 **77**.............................. MichaelHills 3 61
(B W Hills) *hld up: hdwy over 4f out: rdn over 2f out: hung rt and wknd over 1f out* **12/1**

12- **7** *dist* **Five A Side**[293] 4458 3-9-7 **85**.............................. KDarley 8 —
(M Johnston) *chsd ldr 3f: remained handy tl rdn and wknd 3f out: eased fnl 2f* **8/1**

06 **8** *dist* **Without Excuse (USA)**[30] [1467] 3-9-5 **83** .... TedDurcan 1 —
(M Botti) *sn outpcd: rdn and wknd over 3f out: eased fnl 2f* **33/1**

2m 11.41s (3.11) **Going Correction** +0.45s/f (Yiel) **8** Ran SP% **113.6**

Speed ratings (Par 101):105,104,99,99,97 94,—,—

CSF £68.02 CT £155.19 TOTE £24.00: £5.00, £1.40, £1.30; EX 63.30 Trifecta £214.90 Part won. Pool £302.80 - 0.64 winning units..

Owner T P Tate **Bred** Worksop Manor Stud **Trained** Tadcaster, N Yorks

FOCUS

A fair handicap. It was run at a decent pace and, with the front pair pulling well clear, the form looks sound. The winner improved by 9lb.

2306 CHARNWOOD FOREST FILLIES' CONDITIONS STKS 7f 9y

3:30 (3:30) (Class 2) 3-Y-O **£9,971** (£2,985; £1,492; £747) **Stalls** Low

Form RPR

514- **1** **Lady Grace (IRE)**[219] [6217] 3-8-5 90 .... KerrinMcEvoy 3 101+
(W J Haggas) *chsd ldr tl led over 2f out: rdn clr over 1f out: eased towards fin* **9/4**[2]

41-3 **2** *5* **Medley**[33] [1394] 3-8-9 95 .... RichardHughes 2 89
(R Hannon) *trckd ldrs: rdn to chse wnr over 1f out: styd on same pce* **5/4**[1]

-500 **3** *8* **Princess Valerina**[29] [1496] 3-8-9 84 .... MichaelHills 1 68
(B W Hills) *sn led: rdn and hdd over 2f out: wknd over 1f out* **3/1**[3]

-101 **4** *5* **Goodbye Cash (IRE)**[8] [2060] 3-8-5 79 .... SimonWhitworth 4 51
(P D Evans) *s.i.s: sn chsng ldrs: rdn and wknd over 2f out* **10/1**

1m 28.12s (2.02) **Going Correction** +0.45s/f (Yiel) **4** Ran SP% **109.3**

Speed ratings (Par 102):106,100,91,85

CSF £5.54 TOTE £3.50; EX 6.50.

Owner F C T Wilson **Bred** Frank Barry **Trained** Newmarket, Suffolk

FOCUS

Despite only the four runners, this was run at a solid pace hence the big margins separating the quartet at the line and the creditable winning time. Not easy to assess, but the winner has been rated as having improved.

NOTEBOOK

Lady Grace(IRE), fourth behind Passage Of Time when last seen seven months earlier, travelled strongly up with the pace, and as soon as she got the better of Princess Valerina, she was away and clear. She obviously likes to get her toe in and looks well worth another crack at a fillies-only Listed event under those conditions, with the Sandringham Handicap at Royal Ascot a potential target. (op 2-1)

Medley, on soft ground for the first time, seemed to be ridden with the extra furlong in mind, but although she plugged on when pulled out for her effort the winner was already long gone. (op 11-8 tchd 6-4)

Princess Valerina, beaten a long way in the 1,000 Guineas, was ridden aggressively and tried to make all but she was made to look very ordinary once the winner swept past. The ground should not have been an issue and it is beginning to look as though she has not trained on. (op 4-1)

Goodbye Cash(IRE) was much more exposed than the other three - this was her 14th start - and she had a bit to find on official ratings too. She eventually found the demands too great and needs a drop in trip and to return to handicaps. (op 8-1)

2307 RACECOURSE VIDEO SERVICES CLAIMING STKS 1m 1f 218y

4:00 (4:01) (Class 5) 4-Y-O+ **£3,238** (£963; £481; £240) **Stalls** High

Form RPR

3002 **1** **Bay Boy**[12] [1939] 5-9-1 72 ....(b) KDarley 11 70
(M Johnston) *chsd ldr tl led over 3f out: rdn and hung lft over 1f out: styd on* **6/4**[1]

00/4 **2** *3/4* **Tizzy May (FR)**[14] [1893] 7-9-5 70 .... DaneO'Neill 5 72
(B Ellison) *plld hrd and prom: chsd wnr over 3f out: rdn and ev ch ins fnl f: nt qckn* **5/1**[2]

0006 **3** *3* **King's Ransom**[19] [1764] 4-9-5 61 .... RichardHughes 4 66+
(W R Muir) *s.i.s: hld up: swtchd rt and hdwy over 3f out: rdn over 1f out: styd on same pce* **13/2**[3]

0610 **4** *4* **Experimental (IRE)**[21] [1730] 13-8-11 48 .... SimonWhitworth 6 50
(John A Harris) *hld up: hdwy over 3f out: rdn and hung rt over 1f out: sn wknd* **20/1**

6044 **5** *3 1/2* **Ming Vase**[20] [1750] 5-8-7 45 .... MickyFenton 12 39
(P T Midgley) *chsd ldrs: rdn over 2f out: wknd over 1f out* **25/1**

60-0 **6** *nk* **Kuster**[28] [1542] 11-8-8 80 .... MJMurphy(7) 10 46
(L M Cumani) *hld up: shkn up over 3f out: nvr trbld ldrs* **5/1**[2]

-000 **7** *3* **Sheriff's Deputy**[27] [1570] 7-8-3 39 ow1 .... KevinGhunowa(5) 1 33
(C N Kellett) *hld up: hdwy over 3f out: rdn and wknd over 2f out* **66/1**

0/ **8** *3* **Princess Zaha**[745] [1847] 5-9-0 0 .... FergusSweeney 7 33
(A G Newcombe) *hld up: sme hdwy 2f out: sn wknd* **40/1**

0-00 **9** *10* **Evolution Ex (USA)**[47] [1086] 5-8-2 52 .... NataliaGemelova(5) 2 6
(I W McInnes) *hld up: a in rr* **16/1**

5453 **10** *20* **Rose Muwasim**[14] [1906] 4-7-13 47 ....(v) DominicFox(3) 3 —
(S Parr) *led over 6f: wknd over 2f out: eased* **14/1**

0/ **11** *8* **Steak N Kidney (USA)**[121] [5711] 4-9-1 0 .... NickyMackay 8 —
(M Wigham) *hld up: in rr whn nt clr run wl over 3f out: sn wknd* **50/1**

00 **12** *3/4* **Arthur Parker**[23] [1665] 6-8-11 0 ow2 ....(t) VinceSlattery 9 —
(J A B Old) *plld hrd and prom: lost pl over 5f out: sn bhd* **100/1**

2m 12.15s (3.85) **Going Correction** +0.45s/f (Yiel) **12** Ran SP% **114.7**

Speed ratings (Par 103):102,101,99,95,93 92,90,87,79,63 57,56

CSF £7.83 TOTE £1.90: £1.10, £2.40, £2.40; EX 10.90 Trifecta £9.30 Pool £471.77 - 35.88 winning units..The winner was claimed by I W McInnes for £10,000.

Owner Mrs Louise H Boggs **Bred** Mark Johnston Racing Ltd **Trained** Middleham Moor, N Yorks

FOCUS

A wide variety of abilities in this claimer and they finished well spread out. They went a decent gallop and it paid to race up with the pace, with four having gone clear by halfway, which included the eventual first two home. Ordinary form for the grade, the level not rock solid.

2308 COPLOW MAIDEN STKS 1m 3f 183y

4:30 (4:34) (Class 5) 3-Y-O **£3,238** (£963; £481; £240) **Stalls** High

Form RPR

4 **1** **Wing Express (IRE)**[37] [1296] 3-9-3 0 .... NickyMackay 7 87+
(L M Cumani) *chsd ldrs: n.m.r 5f out: led over 1f out: shkn up and r.o wl* **4/1**[3]

2- **2** *2* **Dawn Sky**[215] [6298] 3-9-3 0 .... PhilipRobinson 8 81+
(M A Jarvis) *led 10f out: hdd 9f out: chsd ldrs: led over 2f out: rdn and hdd over 1f out: styd on same pce ins fnl f* **5/2**[2]

0-6 **3** *9* **Mirthful (USA)**[45] [1127] 3-8-12 0 .... RichardHughes 12 61
(B W Hills) *led 2f: chsd ldrs: led over 4f out: rdn and hdd over 2f out: wknd over 1f out* **7/1**

-2 **4** *nk* **Hazarayna**[23] [1665] 3-8-12 0 .... TedDurcan 9 61
(H R A Cecil) *chsd ldrs: ev ch over 2f out: rdn and wknd over 1f out* **11/1**

06 **5** *4* **Rainbow Flame**[12] [1950] 3-9-3 0 ....(b) AdamKirby 2 60
(W R Swinburn) *hld up in tch: rdn over 3f out: wknd over 2f out* **50/1**

64 **6** *2* **Ancient Culture**[17] [1812] 3-9-3 0 .... KerrinMcEvoy 6 56
(Sir Michael Stoute) *s.i.s: sn pushed along in rr: nvr nrr* **15/8**[1]

0 **7** *hd* **Sister Agnes (IRE)**[21] [1725] 3-8-12 0 .... OscarUrbina 4 54+
(J R Fanshawe) *hld up: hdwy over 3f out: rdn and hung rt over 2f out: wknd wl over 1f out: eased ins fnl f* **66/1**

0-4 **8** *20* **Wild Gardenia**[17] [1816] 3-8-12 0 .... JimmyFortune 10 19
(J H M Gosden) *hld up: rdn over 3f out: sn wknd: t.o* **16/1**

00 **9** *3 1/2* **Holiday Rock**[13] [1937] 3-9-3 0 .... NeilPollard 1 18
(A J McCabe) *chsd ldrs: led 9f out: hdd over 4f out: sn rdn and wknd: t.o* **300/1**

10 *16* **Precious Mettle** 3-8-12 0 .... JimmyQuinn 3 —
(H R A Cecil) *s.i.s: outpcd: wknd over 4f out: t.o* **40/1**

00 **11** *1/2* **Highbourne Lady**[17] [1816] 3-8-12 0 .... VinceSlattery 5 —
(B N Pollock) *prom 8f: t.o* **300/1**

000- **12** *hd* **Diverse Forecast (IRE)**[288] [4630] 3-9-3 40 .... MickyFenton 11 —
(Mrs P Sly) *s.i.s: a in rr: wknd 4f out: t.o* **100/1**

2m 39.29s (4.79) **Going Correction** +0.45s/f (Yiel) **12** Ran SP% **117.6**

Speed ratings (Par 99):102,100,94,94,91 90,90,77,74,64 63,63

CSF £14.31 TOTE £5.50: £2.00, £1.50, £2.10; EX 15.80 Trifecta £279.10 Part won. Pool: £393.10 - 0.84 wiining units..

Owner JMC Breed & Race Limited **Bred** Stonethorn Stud Farms Ltd **Trained** Newmarket, Suffolk

FOCUS

Not as competitive a maiden as the numbers might suggest, but the front pair pulled miles clear of the others and may be above-average types. The third and sixth were not at their best and the race has been rated through the fifth.

2309 SIS FILLIES' H'CAP 7f 9y

5:00 (5:00) (Class 5) (0-70,69) 3-Y-O+ **£3,886** (£1,156; £577; £288) **Stalls** Low

Form RPR

460- **1** **What A Treasure (IRE)**[250] [5606] 3-9-5 **66** .... NickyMackay 5 74
(L M Cumani) *trckd ldrs: rdn to ld 1f out: styd on* **9/2**[3]

4-61 **2** *3/4* **Fealeview Lady (USA)**[14] [1903] 3-9-3 **69** .... TravisBlock(5) 8 75
(H Morrison) *hld up in tch: rdn to ld over 1f out: sn edgd lft and hdd: styd on same pce ins fnl f* **15/8**[1]

43-5 **3** *5* **Angel Voices (IRE)**[43] [1177] 4-10-0 **65** .... LeeEnstone 2 62
(K R Burke) *w ldr tl led over 2f out: rdn and hdd over 1f out: wknd ins fnl f* **7/2**[2]

5000 **4** *8* **Kineta (USA)**[39] [1260] 4-8-12 **49** .... AdamKirby 4 25
(W R Muir) *chsd ldrs: rdn over 2f out: wknd over 1f out* **6/1**

0-56 **5** *3/4* **Safranine (IRE)**[21] [1710] 10-8-10 **52** .... AnnStokell(5) 7 26
(Miss A Stokell) *sn pushed along in rr: effrt over 2f out: wknd over 1f out* **8/1**

6600 **6** *2 1/2* **Dictatrix**[19] [1766] 4-9-11 **65** ....(b) JerryO'Dwyer(3) 3 33
(J M P Eustace) *led over 4f: wknd wl over 1f out* **9/1**

1m 30.27s (4.17) **Going Correction** +0.45s/f (Yiel)

WFA 3 from 4yo+ 10lb **6** Ran SP% **110.6**

Speed ratings (Par 100):94,93,87,78,77 74

CSF £12.98 CT £29.82 TOTE £4.90: £2.90, £1.10; EX 11.00 Trifecta £37.20 Pool: £346.10 - 6.60 winning units. Place 6 £58.05, Place 5 £18.36.

Owner Scuderia Archi Romani **Bred** Serpentine Bloodstock Et Al **Trained** Newmarket, Suffolk

FOCUS

They went a very modest pace in this, but the first two still pulled right away. The form is pretty weak behind the front pair. The winning time was understandably modest, 2.15 seconds slower than the earlier fillies' conditions event.

T/Plt: £58.80 to a £1 stake. Pool: £59,386.35. 736.05 winning tickets. T/Qpdt: £12.30 to a £1 stake. Pool: £3,854.90. 230.20 winning tickets. CR

1848 THIRSK (L-H)

Monday, June 4

OFFICIAL GOING: Good to firm (firm in places; 10.7)

The ground was described as 'firm but no jar and a good cover of grass'.

Wind: moderate 1/2 against Weather: fine

2310 BUCK INN THORNTON WATLASS FILLIES' (S) STKS 6f

6:15 (6:16) (Class 5) 2-Y-O **£3,886** (£1,156; £577; £288) **Stalls** High

Form RPR

4 **1** **Yes Meg**[7] [2078] 2-8-12 0 .... TomEaves 2 59+
(P F I Cole) *mde all: clr over 1f out: v readily* **5/2**[1]

42 **2** *3* **Secret Meaning**[4] [2188] 2-8-5 0 .... JackDean(7) 3 50
(W G M Turner) *dwlt: sn chsng ldrs: kpt on to take 2nd towards fin: no ch w wnr* **10/3**[2]

6553 **3** *3/4* **Miss Antropist (IRE)**[7] [2078] 2-8-12 0 .... JoeFanning 6 48
(R A Harris) *hld up: effrt and swtchd lft over 3f out: sn outpcd: hdwy to chse wnr 2f out: wknd ins fnl f* **5/2**[1]

6010 **4** *5* **Little Finch (IRE)**[2] [2247] 2-9-3 0 ....(b) PhillipMakin 4 38
(R C Guest) *chsd ldrs: wknd over 1f out* **4/1**[3]

6 **5** *3 1/2* **Next Best**[29] [1487] 2-8-12 0 .... TonyHamilton 8 23
(A Berry) *dwlt: sn chsng ldrs and hanging lft: rdn over 2f out: lost pl over 1f out* **10/1**

00 **6** *2* **Welcome Inn**[6] [2115] 2-8-9 0 ....(t) MarkLawson(3) 1 17
(M E Sowersby) *swvd lft s: sn rdn and chsng ldrs: lost pl over 2f out* **28/1**

1m 14.76s (2.26) **Going Correction** -0.075s/f (Good) **6** Ran SP% **112.8**

Speed ratings (Par 90):81,77,76,69,64 62

CSF £11.26 TOTE £2.90: £1.90, £2.50; EX 10.10.The winner was bought in for 8,600gns.

Owner R A Instone **Bred** R A Instone **Trained** Whatcombe, Oxon

FOCUS

A weak seller, rated through the runner-up, run in a very slow winning time even for a race like this.

NOTEBOOK

Yes Meg, who showed promise in this grade on her debut in easy ground, knew much more this time and was far too good for some poor opposition. A half-sister to Being There, a recent 2m4f hurdles winner, she will get further than this and might be up to winning in slightly better company. (op 2-1 tchd 11-4)

Secret Meaning , making a quick reappearance after finishing second in this grade at Yarmouth, kept on in a manner which suggested she was suited by this step up in trip. (op 9-2 tchd 3-1)

Miss Antropist(IRE), who finished in front of today's winner at Chepstow, is thoroughly exposed in this grade. A drop back to 5f might help. (op 7-2)

Little Finch(IRE) was back up in trip following her run at Musselburgh two days earlier. Her Catterick win came in a poor event. (op 11-4)

Next Best, down in grade, again started slowly and is showing no promise. (op 14-1)

2311 WHITE HORSE MUSEUM CONSULTANCY H'CAP 1m
6:45 (6:45) (Class 5) (0-75,75) 4-Y-O+ **£3,886** (£1,156; £577; £288) **Stalls Low**

Form RPR
-503 **1** **Hula Ballew**[13] 1915 7-9-7 **75**........ PhillipMakin 2 86
(M Dods) *chsd ldrs: styd on wl to ld ins fnl f: r.o* **11/2**[2]
P0-0 **2** 1 1/2 **Heureux (USA)**[27] 1555 4-9-1 **69**........(b) TomEaves 4 77
(J Howard Johnson) *mid-div: hdwy over 2f out: styd on to take 2nd ins fnl f* **20/1**
5-32 **3** 3/4 **Il Castagno (IRE)**[27] 1555 4-9-4 **75**........ MarkLawson(3) 8 81
(B Smart) *w ldr: led over 5f out: hung lft and hdd ins fnl f: no ex* **5/1**[1]
6-33 **4** 2 **Tough Love**[27] 1555 8-8-13 **67**........(p) DavidAllan 7 68+
(T D Easterby) *in rr-div: hdwy over 2f out: kpt on fnl f* **6/1**[3]
3000 **5** nk **Time To Regret**[10] 2007 7-8-6 **60**........(p) RoystonFfrench 1 61
(I W McInnes) *led tl over 5f out: w ldr: wknd ins fnl f* **28/1**
0005 **6** 1 **Efidium**[6] 2117 9-8-12 **66**........ PaulFessey 3 64
(N Bycroft) *s.i.s: hdwy on wd outside over 2f out: styd on fnl f: nt rch ldrs* **12/1**
5234 **7** nk **Pab Special (IRE)**[10] 1997 4-9-3 **71**........(p) PaulMulrennan 6 69
(K R Burke) *chsd ldrs: one pce fnl 2f* **7/1**
-643 **8** 1/2 **Champain Sands (IRE)**[3] 2225 8-8-11 **65**........ KDarley 11 61
(E J Alston) *mid-div: hdwy but n.m.r over 2f out: hung lft: nvr trbld ldrs* **6/1**[3]
5-30 **9** 1 3/4 **Coup D'Etat**[19] 1765 5-9-4 **72**........(p) PaulHanagan 12 64
(R A Harris) *hld up: effrt over 2f out: nvr nr ldrs* **7/1**
55-0 **10** 4 **Sake (IRE)**[16] 1845 5-9-3 **71**........ KimTinkler 10 54
(N Tinkler) *prom: rdn over 2f out: lost pl over 1f out* **20/1**
20-0 **11** 7 **Pianoforte (USA)**[6] 2117 5-8-8 **62**........ DaleGibson 9 29
(E J Alston) *chsd ldrs: drvn over 3f out: lost pl 2f out: eased* **33/1**
2020 **12** 2 1/2 **Sir Bond (IRE)**[13] 1918 6-7-13 **56**........ DuranFentiman(3) 5 17
(G R Oldroyd) *mid-div: effrt over 2f out: sn lost pl: eased* **11/1**

1m 37.66s (-2.04) **Going Correction** -0.075s/f (Good) **12** Ran SP% **117.6**
Speed ratings (Par 103):107,105,104,102,102 101,101,100,98,94 87,85
CSF £114.64 CT £597.74 TOTE £5.20: £1.90, £5.10, £2.50; EX 111.30.
Owner Mrs J W Hutchinson & Mrs P A Knox **Bred** T K & Mrs P A Knox **Trained** Denton, Co Durham

FOCUS
Solid-looking form rated through the winner and third. The runner-up was back to something like last summer's best.
Sir Bond(IRE) Official explanation: jockey said gelding lost its action closing stages

2312 OSWALDS RESTAURANT WITH ROOMS MAIDEN STKS 7f
7:15 (7:17) (Class 5) 3-Y-O+ **£3,886** (£1,156; £577; £288) **Stalls Low**

Form RPR
3-32 **1** **Shevchenko (IRE)**[31] 1447 3-9-2 79........ KDarley 10 79
(J Noseda) *w ldrs: led over 2f out: drvn out* **5/6**[1]
20-2 **2** 2 **Onatopp (IRE)**[9] 2032 3-8-11 64........ DavidAllan 13 69
(T D Easterby) *s.i.s: hdwy over 2f out: styd on wl to take 2nd ins fnl f* **20/1**
2- **3** 2 **Flying Goose (IRE)**[213] 6324 3-9-2 0........ DO'Donohoe 3 69
(L M Cumani) *s.i.s: hdwy 5f out: sn chsng ldrs: hung lft and wnt 2nd over 1f out: kpt on same pce* **9/4**[2]
23-5 **4** 4 **Apache Dawn**[17] 1804 3-9-2 75........ NCallan 9 58
(K A Ryan) *mde most tl over 2f out: wknd fnl f* **8/1**[3]
4 **5** 1 **Morbick**[11] 1976 3-9-2 0........ JoeFanning 6 55
(M Johnston) *mid-div: outpcd over 3f out: kpt on fnl 2f* **12/1**
0-6 **6** 1/2 **Lilac Moon (GER)**[13] 1913 3-8-11 0........ RoystonFfrench 2 49
(Mrs A Duffield) *settled in rr: kpt on fnl 2f: nvr on terms* **50/1**
0-06 **7** shd **Crux**[6] 2121 5-9-9 45........ MarkLawson(3) 12 57?
(R E Barr) *in rr: kpt on fnl 2f: nvr on terms* **100/1**
0- **8** 1/2 **Forrest Flyer (IRE)**[213] 6318 3-9-2 0........ PaulMulrennan 5 52
(Miss L A Perratt) *chsd ldrs: outpcd over 3f out: kpt on fnl 2f* **100/1**
03- **9** 1/2 **Four Tel**[216] 6284 3-9-2 0........ PaulFessey 8 51
(N J Vaughan) *stdd s: t.k.h in rr: sme hdwy 2f out: nvr on terms* **28/1**
50/ **10** 8 **Don Jose (USA)**[591] 6009 4-9-12 0........ PaulHanagan 11 33
(N J Vaughan) *plld hrd in midfield: bhd fnl 3f* **33/1**
05 **11** 2 1/2 **Dendor**[32] 1425 3-9-2 0........ TonyHamilton 4 22
(D W Barker) *w ldrs: wknd over 2f out* **50/1**
0 **12** 2 **Recovery Mission**[10] 2012 3-9-2 0........ PhillipMakin 7 17
(G M Moore) *in rr: bhd fnl 3f* **100/1**

1m 25.43s (-1.67) **Going Correction** -0.075s/f (Good)
WFA 3 from 4yo+ 10lb **12** Ran SP% **122.2**
Speed ratings (Par 103):106,103,101,96,95 95,95,94,93,84 81,79
CSF £26.66 TOTE £1.80: £1.10, £3.20, £1.30; EX 24.80.
Owner M Tabor, Mrs J Magnier & D Smith **Bred** Jim Fleming **Trained** Newmarket, Suffolk

FOCUS
A straightforward opportunity for the winner in this ordinary maiden in which few were seen with a chance. The poor seventh limits the form.
Lilac Moon(GER) Official explanation: jockey said, regarding running and riding, his orders were to get a position and do his best, adding that the filly lost its action turning into the straight; trainer confirmed, adding that the filly is a poor mover
Crux Official explanation: jockey said gelding lost its action
Four Tel Official explanation: jockey said gelding failed to handle the bend

2313 OTTERINGTON SHORTHORN H'CAP 7f
7:45 (7:45) (Class 4) (0-85,84) 3-Y-O **£5,181** (£1,541; £770; £384) **Stalls Low**

Form RPR
3-36 **1** **White Deer (USA)**[19] 1773 3-9-7 **84**........ JoeFanning 7 94
(M Johnston) *led after 1f: pushed along over 2f out: styd on strly fnl f* **5/2**[2]
3-14 **2** 1 **Hazzard County (USA)**[29] 1500 3-9-3 **80**........ PaulHanagan 5 87
(D M Simcock) *trckd ldrs: wnt 2nd over 1f out: sn rdn: no ex ins fnl f* **2/1**[1]
4-14 **3** 3 **Baltimore Jack (IRE)**[23] 1667 3-9-4 **81**........ DaleGibson 4 80
(M W Easterby) *led 1f: chsd ldrs: kpt on same pce appr fnl f* **6/1**
431- **4** nk **Tarraburn (USA)**[245] 5721 3-8-6 **74**........ JamieMoriarty(5) 6 72
(J Howard Johnson) *t.k.h: rapid hdwy to join wnr over 4f out: one pce fnl 2f* **10/1**
2-10 **5** 3/4 **Shake On It**[42] 1202 3-8-12 **75**........(t) StephenCarson 3 71
(Eve Johnson Houghton) *t.k.h: trckd ldrs: nt clr run over 2f out: kpt on same pce: nvr a threat* **9/2**[3]
0-45 **6** 3 **Pegasus Dancer (FR)**[17] 1802 3-8-11 **74**........ NCallan 1 62
(K A Ryan) *hld up in rr: effrt over 2f out: nvr nr ldrs* **14/1**
35-0 **7** 1/2 **Karma Llama (IRE)**[23] 1684 3-8-4 **67**........ RoystonFfrench 2 54
(B Smart) *hld up in rr: effrt on outer over 3f out: lost pl over 1f out* **14/1**

1m 26.29s (-0.81) **Going Correction** -0.075s/f (Good) **7** Ran SP% **116.8**
Speed ratings (Par 101):101,99,96,96,95 91,91
CSF £8.27 TOTE £3.70: £1.90, £2.00; EX 8.50.
Owner Jaber Abdullah **Bred** Fleetwood Bloodstock Et Al **Trained** Middleham Moor, N Yorks

FOCUS
White Deer set a modest pace under a good front-running ride. The race has been rated around the placed horses.

2314 CARLETON FURNITURE H'CAP 1m 4f
8:15 (8:16) (Class 3) (0-90,87) 4-Y-O+ **£7,772** (£2,312; £1,155; £577) **Stalls Low**

Form RPR
0-50 **1** **Luna Landing**[19] 1771 4-8-10 **76**........ PaulMulrennan 4 84
(Jedd O'Keeffe) *mde all: rdn and styd on wl fnl 2f* **14/1**
512/ **2** 1 1/4 **Clueless**[12] 5608 5-8-13 **84**........(b) JamieMoriarty(5) 1 90
(N G Richards) *trckd ldr: rdn and outpcd 3f out: styd on fnl 2f: wnt 2nd ins fnl f* **5/1**
0-21 **3** 1 1/4 **Tcherina (IRE)**[19] 1771 5-8-10 **79**........ DuranFentiman(3) 7 83
(T D Easterby) *trckd ldrs: wnt 2nd over 3f out: rdn 2f out: styd on same pce* **7/2**[2]
0623 **4** 2 **Active Asset (IRE)**[10] 2002 5-9-7 **87**........ NCallan 5 88
(M Quinn) *t.k.h: hdwy 4f out: sn rdn: one pce fnl 2f* **4/1**[3]
2103 **5** 1/2 **Shape Up (IRE)**[10] 1997 7-8-8 **74**........(v) PaulFessey 2 74
(R Craggs) *in tch: effrt over 3f out: kpt on same pce* **7/1**
-231 **6** 2 **Just Observing**[33] 1416 4-8-10 **76**........(p) MickyFenton 6 73
(P T Midgley) *hld up: effrt on outside over 3f out: nvr trbld ldrs* **17/2**
0-50 **7** 8 **Florimund**[16] 1844 4-9-3 **83**........ PaulHanagan 3 67
(Sir Michael Stoute) *sn chsng ldr: hrd drvn over 4f out: lost pl 3f out: sn bhd* **3/1**[1]

2m 34.45s (-0.75) **Going Correction** -0.075s/f (Good) **7** Ran SP% **113.6**
Speed ratings (Par 107):99,98,97,96,95 94,89
CSF £80.02 TOTE £20.20: £5.50, £2.50; EX 162.00.
Owner W R B Racing 47 (wrbracing.com) **Bred** Chippenham Lodge Stud Ltd **Trained** Middleham Moor, N Yorks

FOCUS
A very moderate winning time for a race of its class. All-the-way winner Luna Landing is rated back to the sort of form which he showed when winning at Catterick last season.

NOTEBOOK
Luna Landing had finished behind Tcherina at York but enjoyed a 12lb pull here. Allowed a soft lead, he set only a fair pace and saw off his pursuers in determined fashion. (op 16-1 tchd 20-1)
Clueless, progressive on the Flat in 2005 when in the care of William Haggas, came here fit from hurdling. This was a pleasing run and the blinkers have obviously helped him return to some sort of form. (op 11-2 tchd 6-1)
Tcherina(IRE), raised 7lb for her York win, where she had Luna Landing back in eleventh, looked menacing when moving into second but could only keep on at the same pace. She seems to reserve her best for the Knavesmire and is probably more effective on easier ground. (op 10-3)
Active Asset(IRE) is performing consistently this season but is currently 4lb above his highest winning mark, which could continue to prove a stumbling block. (op 9-2)
Shape Up(IRE) could never get into the action in a race run at just a modest gallop. (op 6-1)
Just Observing, back up in trip, was found wanting under a 6lb rise for his Pontefract win. (op 8-1 tchd 7-1 and 9-1)
Florimund was the first to come under pressure and capitulated tamely in the straight. He has run well below form on his last two starts and now has questions to answer. Official explanation: trainer's rep had no explanation for the poor form shown (op 10-3 tchd 11-4 and 7-2 in a place)

2315 WHITE HORSE 150TH ANNIVERSARY FILLIES' H'CAP 5f
8:45 (8:45) (Class 5) (0-75,75) 3-Y-O+ **£3,886** (£1,156; £577; £288) **Stalls High**

Form RPR
-235 **1** **Mimi Mouse**[16] 1854 5-10-0 **75**........ DavidAllan 11 89
(T D Easterby) *racd stands' side: w ldr: led ins fnl f: r.o* **7/2**[2]
0002 **2** 3/4 **Coconut Moon**[32] 1427 5-9-9 **70**........ KDarley 1 81+
(E J Alston) *swvd lft s: racd alone in centre: overall ldr: hdd and no ex ins fnl f* **8/1**
-021 **3** 2 **Matterofact (IRE)**[10] 1991 4-8-13 **60**........ NCallan 12 64
(M S Saunders) *chsd ldrs: styd on same pce fnl 2f* **9/4**[1]
0-06 **4** 1 **Our Little Secret (IRE)**[10] 1999 5-8-9 **61**........ KevinGhunowa(5) 3 61
(A Berry) *racd wd: chsd ldrs: kpt on same pce appr fnl f* **11/1**
5001 **5** 1 1/4 **Champagne Cracker**[20] 1748 6-8-12 **59**........ PhillipMakin 9 55
(M Dods) *mid-div: outpcd over 2f out: styd on fnl f* **5/1**[3]
0-00 **6** nk **Hello Roberto**[19] 1766 6-8-10 **62**........(p) MichaelJStainton(5) 8 57
(R A Harris) *in tch: outpcd over 2f out: kpt on fnl f* **16/1**
-066 **7** 1/2 **Petite Mac**[7] 2072 7-8-8 **60**........ JamieMoriarty(5) 5 53
(N Bycroft) *mid-div: outpcd over 2f out: kpt on fnl f* **12/1**
6300 **8** 1/2 **Town House**[81] 680 5-8-2 **56** oh11........ SoniaEaton(7) 4 47
(B P J Baugh) *racd wd: chsd ldrs: one pce fnl 2f* **66/1**
4540 **9** 3 1/2 **Muara**[20] 1748 5-8-11 **58**........ PaulHanagan 7 37
(D W Barker) *mid-div: outpcd and lost pl over 2f out:* **7/1**
036- **10** 2 1/2 **Bella Marie**[245] 5727 4-8-9 **56** oh1........ TonyHamilton 6 26
(L R James) *swvd rt s a outpcd and in rr* **50/1**
-000 **11** nk **Toy Top (USA)**[16] 1854 4-9-6 **67**........(b) TomEaves 10 36
(M Dods) *outpcd and lost pl after 1f: sn bhd* **20/1**

58.85 secs (-1.05) **Going Correction** -0.075s/f (Good) **11** Ran SP% **123.4**
Speed ratings (Par 100):105,103,100,99,97 96,95,94,89,85 84
CSF £33.15 CT £79.85 TOTE £4.90: £1.90, £2.70, £1.80; EX 28.70 Place 6 £59.05, Place 5 £31.29.
Owner Mrs Jean P Connew **Bred** Mrs P A Clark **Trained** Great Habton, N Yorks

FOCUS
An ordinary handicap which nothing got into from the rear. The winner and third raced on the rail, the runner-up on her own down the centre. Mimi Mouse is rated to last year's form.
T/Plt: £105.30 to a £1 stake. Pool: £60,542.50. 419.60 winning tickets. T/Qpdt: £29.60 to a £1 stake. Pool: £3,615.00. 90.30 winning tickets. WG

1896 WINDSOR (R-H)
Monday, June 4

OFFICIAL GOING: Good to firm (good in places; 8.8)
Wind: virtually nil Weather: fair

2316 BERNARD SUNLEY CHARITABLE FOUNDATION E B F NOVICE STKS 5f 10y
6:30 (6:31) (Class 5) 2-Y-O **£4,533** (£1,348; £674; £336) **Stalls High**

Form RPR
5 **1** **Hatta Fort**[13] 1919 2-8-12 0........ JHBowman 8 95+
(M R Channon) *led 1f: styd chsng ldr tl ld again over 1f out: styd on strly ins fnl f* **4/1**[3]
31 **2** 1 **Swiss Franc**[8] 2056 2-9-5 0........ TedDurcan 6 98+
(D R C Elsworth) *t.k.h: chsd ldrs: swtchd rt over 1f out: styd on to chse wnr ins fnl f but a hld* **9/4**[1]

1 **3** *1 ¼* **In Uniform**[34] 1367 2-9-0 0 ..... RichardMullen 5 89
(E S McMahon) *chsd ldrs: wnt 2nd u.p over 1f out: styd on same pce ins fnl f* **11/4**[2]
5 **4** *2* **Paveroc**[23] 1652 2-8-12 0 ..... JohnEgan 4 79
(J S Moore) *wnt lft s: sn rdn and outpcd: styd on fnl f but nvr gng pce to rch ldrs* **16/1**
52 **5** *1 ½* **Alexander Nepotism (IRE)**[34] 1367 2-8-7 0 ..... BrettDoyle 9 69
(B J Meehan) *chsd ldrs: outpcd 1/2-way: hdwy 2f out: swtchd lft over 1f out: sn no imp* **10/1**
61 **6** *1* **Stage Acclaim (IRE)**[11] 1970 2-9-0 0 ..... JamesMillman(5) 7 77
(B R Millman) *t.k.h: chsd ldrs: rdn 2f out: sn btn* **8/1**
0 **7** *3 ½* **Hold That Call (USA)**[23] 1652 2-8-12 0 ..... RichardHughes 2 58
(R Hannon) *bmpd s: rcvrd to ld after 1f: hdd over 1f out and wknd qckly* **11/1**
8 *26* **Queen's Treasure (IRE)** 2-8-7 0 ..... DarryllHolland 1 —
(M P Tregoning) *rrd stalls and v.s.a: a wl bhd* **25/1**

60.08 secs (-1.02) **Going Correction** -0.025s/f (Good) **8** Ran SP% **115.7**
Speed ratings (Par 93):107,105,103,100,97 96,90,49
CSF £13.63 TOTE £5.40: £1.80, £1.30, £1.40; EX 15.80.
Owner Sheikh Ahmed Al Maktoum **Bred** Wellsummers Farm **Trained** West Ilsley, Berks

FOCUS
This is often a very good novice event and this is decent form, rated fairly positively, with the front pair sizeable improvers. The winning time was outstanding for a race like this.

NOTEBOOK
Hatta Fort ◆ attracted strong support in the market throughout the day and duly improved significantly on the form he showed when an eye-catching fifth on his debut at Leicester. He looks Royal Ascot material and the Windsor Castle is apparently now the plan, but it is interesting to note that his stable see Yem Kinn as their Coventry horse. They both look very useful and must head to Ascot with every chance. (op 7-2 tchd 5-1)
Swiss Franc ◆ may have failed to justify favouritism, but this must rate as a very useful effort indeed conceding 7lb to such a promising sort. He does not look very far off pattern class and will also be worth his place at Royal Ascot. (tchd 11-4)
In Uniform looked to improve on the form he showed when winning on his debut at Bath, but just found a couple too good. (op 7-2)
Paveroc was never a danger, but this probably still represented a slight improvement on the form he showed behind Hatta Fort's stablemate, Yem Kinn, at Ascot. He should pick up an ordinary maiden. (op 14-1)
Alexander Nepotism(IRE) ran a respectable race but she just does not seem to be progressing. (op 9-1)
Stage Acclaim(IRE) struggled under the penalty he picked up for winning at Salisbury on his previous start. (op 9-1)
Queen's Treasure(IRE) Official explanation: jockey said filly reared on leaving stalls and was slowly away

2317 COLLYER BRISTOW SOLICITORS H'CAP — 1m 67y
7:00 (7:00) (Class 5) (0-70,70) 3-Y-O **£3,238** (£963; £481; £240) **Stalls High**

Form RPR
5345 **1** **Baltic Belle (IRE)**[21] 1731 3-9-7 **70** ..... PatDobbs 4 76
(R Hannon) *chsd ldr: led 2f out: sn rdn: hdd ins fnl f: rallied gamely to ld again last strides* **9/1**
4-04 **2** *hd* **Voice**[37] 1312 3-9-5 **68** ..... RichardHughes 13 74
(H R A Cecil) *chsd ldrs: wnt 2nd 3f out: rdn over 2f out: led ins fnl f: hdd and no ex last strides* **11/2**[3]
4235 **3** *2 ½* **Grand Symphony**[11] 1979 3-9-3 **66** ..... DarryllHolland 12 66+
(W Jarvis) *in tch: rdn 2f out: swtchd rt and hdwy appr fnl f: styd on ins fnl f but nvr gng pce to rch ldrs* **16/1**
314- **4** *1 ¼* **Nicada (IRE)**[167] 6872 3-9-4 **67** ..... (p) JohnEgan 14 64+
(J S Moore) *in rr: rdn 3f out: styd on u.p fnl 2f but nt rch ldrs* **20/1**
23-4 **5** *½* **Cleide Da Silva (USA)**[44] 1153 3-9-7 **70** ..... SebSanders 1 66
(J Noseda) *chsd ldrs: rdn and effrt over 2f out: wknd ins fnl f* **12/1**
223- **6** *nk* **Risque Heights**[157] 6976 3-9-6 **69** ..... JHBowman 9 64
(G A Butler) *t.k.h: chsd ldrs: rdn 3f out: stl wl there 2f out: wknd fnl f* **4/1**[1]
3-01 **7** *nk* **Princess Zada**[7] 2079 3-9-3 **66** 6ex ..... FergusSweeney 3 60
(B R Millman) *chsd ldrs: rdn and effrt over 2f out: wknd ins fnl f* **9/2**[2]
00-4 **8** *¾* **The Wily Woodcock**[28] 1522 3-9-5 **68** ..... RobertHavlin 6 65+
(G Wragg) *in rr: pushed along over 2f out: sme prog fnl f but nvr in contention* **8/1**
350- **9** *shd* **Law Of The Land (IRE)**[208] 6394 3-8-13 **62** ..... RichardMullen 5 55
(W R Muir) *t.k.h: stdd rr after 2f: rdn over 2f out: sme prog fnl f* **40/1**
-240 **10** *½* **Tracer**[8] 2061 3-9-7 **70** ..... TedDurcan 8 61+
(R Hannon) *stmbld stalls and bhd: sme hdwy fnl 2f but nvr in contention* **14/1**
5036 **11** *shd* **Bold Saxon (IRE)**[8] 2061 3-9-2 **65** ..... RichardSmith 7 56
(M D I Usher) *chsd ldrs: rdn 3f out: wknd fr 2f out* **14/1**
25-5 **12** *2* **Little Miss Tara (IRE)**[64] 864 3-9-7 **70** ..... DaneO'Neill 11 57
(A B Haynes) *led tl hdd 2f out: sn wknd: no ch whn n.m.r over 1f out* **28/1**
2330 **13** *1* **Henry The Seventh**[35] 1359 3-9-1 **64** ..... TQuinn 2 48
(J W Hills) *in tch: rdn 3f out: nvr gng pce to trble ldrs and sn btn* **33/1**
54-6 **14** *¾* **Joyful Tears (IRE)**[26] 1588 3-9-5 **68** ..... KerrinMcEvoy 10 51
(E A L Dunlop) *in rr: hdwy 3f out: one pce whn hmpd over 1f out* **20/1**

1m 45.51s (0.81) **Going Correction** -0.025s/f (Good) **14** Ran SP% **119.9**
Speed ratings (Par 99):94,93,91,90,89 89,88,88,88,87 87,85,84,83
CSF £53.77 CT £817.75 TOTE £11.50: £3.60, £2.50, £5.50; EX 96.00.
Owner Thurloe Thoroughbreds Viii **Bred** Ocal Bloodstock **Trained** East Everleigh, Wilts

FOCUS
A modest handicap and, with the gallop steady, it paid to be close to the pace. The winner is rated to her handicap form, with the second up 4lb.
Grand Symphony Official explanation: jockey said filly hung right-handed
Risque Heights Official explanation: jockey said gelding ran very freely
Tracer Official explanation: jockey said colt slipped on leaving stalls

2318 CANNON KIRK H'CAP — 6f
7:30 (7:30) (Class 4) (0-80,83) 4-Y-O+ **£6,477** (£1,927; £963; £481) **Stalls High**

Form RPR
3324 **1** **Adantino**[11] 1971 8-9-0 **78** ..... (b) JamesMillman(5) 12 87
(B R Millman) *hld up towards rr: hdwy 2f out: qcknd to ld ins fnl f: sn in command* **11/2**[1]
-400 **2** *1 ½* **Briannsta (IRE)**[11] 1971 5-9-2 **75** ..... PhilipRobinson 10 80
(C G Cox) *chsd ldrs: rdn 2f out: styd on to chse wnr ins fnl f but no imp* **14/1**
2234 **3** *hd* **Effective**[11] 1977 7-9-0 **73** ..... JHBowman 9 77
(A P Jarvis) *led: rdn over 2f out: styd on tl hdd and no ex ins fnl f* **17/2**[3]
3003 **4** *½* **Figaro Flyer (IRE)**[11] 1977 4-9-4 **77** ..... IanMongan 15 79+
(P Howling) *chsd ldrs: rdn and kpt on fr over 1f oyt but nvr quite gng pce to trble ldrs* **11/2**[1]
0020 **5** *1 ¼* **Fromsong (IRE)**[30] 1464 9-9-7 **80** ..... RobertHavlin 4 79
(D K Ivory) *chsd ldrs: travelling wl gng to fnl f: sn rdn: one pce ins fnl f* **20/1**
000- **6** *1* **Crimson Silk**[231] 6009 7-9-4 **77** ..... (p) PaulEddery 13 73
(B Smart) *broke wl: sn rdn and outpcd: styd on fnl f but nvr in contention* **7/1**[2]
0-01 **7** *hd* **Abwaab**[28] 1545 4-9-7 **80** ..... (b) LDettori 1 77+
(Eve Johnson Houghton) *pressed ldrs on outside: rdn 2f out: wknd fnl f: eased whn no ch* **7/1**[2]
53-0 **8** *hd* **Scarlet Knight**[11] 1971 4-8-9 **75** ..... JackMitchell(7) 8 69+
(P Mitchell) *in rr: hdwy 1/2-way: chsng ldrs whn rdr dropped reins and edgd lft over 1f out: wknd ins fnl f* **40/1**
600- **9** *hd* **Alfie Tupper (IRE)**[251] 5590 4-9-4 **77** ..... GeorgeBaker 6 71+
(S Kirk) *rrd stall and slowly away: pushed along and hdwy finasl f: nvr gng pce to be competitive* **16/1**
5301 **10** *1 ¼* **Matuza (IRE)**[3] 2197 4-9-10 **83** 6ex ..... RichardMullen 5 73
(W R Muir) *chsd ldrs: rdn over 1f out: wknd ins fnl f* **11/2**[1]
4025 **11** *½* **Desert Dreamer (IRE)**[4] 2180 6-9-0 **73** ..... PaulDoe 2 62
(P R Chamings) *in rr: hdwy over 2f out: sn rdn: wknd fnl f* **10/1**
-000 **12** *1 ½* **Kingscross**[7] 2088 9-9-1 **74** ..... TedDurcan 16 58
(M Blanshard) *a outpcd* **14/1**
000- **13** *1 ¼* **Fisberry**[250] 5627 5-9-4 **77** ..... FrancisNorton 11 57
(M S Saunders) *s.i.s: sn rcvrd to chse ldrs: wknd over 1f out* **16/1**

1m 12.81s (-0.86) **Going Correction** -0.025s/f (Good) **13** Ran SP% **123.1**
Speed ratings (Par 105):104,102,101,101,99 98,97,97,97,95 94,92,91
CSF £86.99 CT £663.25 TOTE £6.70: £2.10, £4.30, £2.70; EX 153.40.
Owner Tarka Two Racing **Bred** S D Bevan **Trained** Kentisbeare, Devon

FOCUS
A fair sprint handicap. The winning time was 1.15 seconds slower than the following Listed contest. Sound form, the reliable Adantino rated back to his best.
Alfie Tupper(IRE) Official explanation: jockey said gelding reared in stalls and was slowly away
Fisberry Official explanation: jockey said horse ran too freely early stages

2319 SEI INVESTMENTS STKS (REGISTERED AS THE LEISURE STAKES) (LISTED RACE) — 6f
8:00 (8:00) (Class 1) 3-Y-O+
£14,762 (£5,595; £2,800; £1,396; £699; £351) **Stalls High**

Form RPR
4-25 **1** **Assertive**[19] 1770 4-9-0 **106** ..... RichardHughes 8 113
(R Hannon) *trckd ldr: led ins fnl 2f: drvn and styd on strly fnl f* **11/4**[2]
62-2 **2** *½* **Borderlescott**[23] 1657 5-9-0 **109** ..... SebSanders 6 111+
(R Bastiman) *trckd ldrs: rdn 2f out: styng on whn n.m.r jst ins fnl f: kpt on cl home but a jst hld* **7/4**[1]
160- **3** *shd* **Something (IRE)**[394] 1487 5-9-0 **102** ..... DaneO'Neill 4 111
(T G Mills) *chsd ldrs: drvn to chal ins fnl f: nvr quite gng pce of wnr: no ex nr fin* **14/1**
211- **4** *nk* **Bygone Days**[234] 5942 6-9-7 **110** ..... LDettori 9 117+
(Saeed Bin Suroor) *trckd ldrs: n.m.r over 1f out and sn swtchd lft: styd on to chse ldrs ins fnl f but a jst hld* **6/1**[3]
0-40 **5** *¾* **Balthazaar's Gift (IRE)**[23] 1656 4-9-0 **109** ..... NickyMackay 5 108
(L M Cumani) *s.i.s: towards rr but in tch: rdn and qcknd to chse ldrs ins fnl f but nvr quite gng pce to chal* **9/1**
5-30 **6** *5* **Fayr Jag (IRE)**[19] 1770 8-9-0 **107** ..... TQuinn 2 93
(T D Easterby) *chsd ldrs: rdn 2f out: wknd fnl f* **16/1**
-010 **7** *½* **Kostar**[23] 1657 6-9-0 **102** ..... PhilipRobinson 7 91
(C G Cox) *led: hdd ins fnl 2f: wknd fnl f* **16/1**
20-4 **8** *1 ¼* **Baltic King**[46] 1102 7-9-0 **110** ..... (t) JimmyFortune 3 88
(H Morrison) *in rr: rdn and sme prog fr over 2f out: nvr gng pce to trble ldrs: wknd over 1f out* **7/1**
1/6 **9** *shd* **Prince Woodman (USA)**[23] 1657 4-9-0 **100** ..... BrettDoyle 1 87
(B J Meehan) *t.k.h in rr: sme hdwy over 2f out: nvr in contention: wknd appr fnl f* **33/1**

1m 11.66s (-2.01) **Going Correction** -0.025s/f (Good) **9** Ran SP% **121.2**
Speed ratings (Par 111):112,111,111,110,109 103,102,100,100
CSF £8.44 TOTE £4.00: £1.70, £1.40, £3.90; EX 11.10.
Owner A J Ilsley, K T Ivory & Lady Whent **Bred** Raffin Bloodstock **Trained** East Everleigh, Wilts

FOCUS
A good, competitive Listed race, but the early pace could have been stronger. The winning time was 1.15 seconds quicker than the previous 61-80 handicap. The form makes some sense around the winner and fourth but might not prove that reliable form for better races.

NOTEBOOK
Assertive found this slightly easier than the Duke of York Stakes and just proved good enough, improving significantly on last year's ninth of ten in this race. This and perhaps Group 3 company looks to be his level for the time being. (op 7-2)
Borderlescott was staying on well at the finish and gave the impression he would have benefited from a more positive ride. This was still a smart effort in defeat and he should make his mark in pattern company this season. (op 2-1 tchd 9-4 and 5-2 in a place)
Something(IRE), gelded since he was last seen over a year ago, produced a huge effort on his return to action and looks better than ever. He could pick up a nice prize this season provided he goes the right way from this. (tchd 16-1)
Bygone Days had a stiff task conceding 7lb all round, but this was a pleasing reappearance and he should go on from this. (tchd 13-2)
Balthazaar's Gift(IRE) would have preferred a stronger end-to-end gallop, but this was still an improvement on his recent efforts. (op 12-1)
Baltic King could not build on the form he showed when fourth on his reappearance at Newmarket. (op 11-2)

2320 SCOTT WILSON MAIDEN STKS — 1m 2f 7y
8:30 (8:31) (Class 5) 3-Y-O **£3,238** (£963; £481; £240) **Stalls Low**

Form RPR
1 **Moon Quest (IRE)** 3-9-3 0 ..... LDettori 6 89+
(Saeed Bin Suroor) *trckd ldrs: led ins fnl 2f: c readily clr ins fnl f: easily* **1/1**[1]
2 *1 ¾* **Fourteenth** 3-9-3 0 ..... SebSanders 10 80
(Sir Michael Stoute) *chsd ldrs: drvn and one pce over 2f out: kpt on fr over 1f out to chse wnr ins fnl f but nvr any ch* **14/1**
0- **3** *1 ¾* **Baba Ganouge (IRE)**[241] 5784 3-8-12 0 ..... BrettDoyle 14 72
(B J Meehan) *led after 1f: rdn 3f out: hdd ins fnl 2f: one pce fnl f* **66/1**
0 **4** *1 ¾* **Eastern Emperor**[42] 1204 3-9-3 0 ..... AdamKirby 9 73
(W R Swinburn) *chsd ldrs: pushed along and one pce over 2f oyt: swtchd lft and sme prog fnl f but nvr a danger* **50/1**
5 *1 ½* **Dar Es Salaam** 3-9-3 0 ..... JimmyFortune 12 70+
(E A L Dunlop) *bmpd s: in rr: pushed along over 2f out: kpt on fr over 1f out but nvr in contention* **12/1**

6-3 **6** 1 **Mia's Boy**^{31} [1452] 3-9-3 0 .... TedDurcan 2 68
(P W Chapple-Hyam) *led 1f: styd chsd ldrs: rdn over 2f out: styd on same pce fr over 1f out* **7/2**^{2}

0 **7** 1 3/4 **Garden Party**^{28} [1523] 3-9-3 0 .... KerrinMcEvoy 7 65
(Sir Michael Stoute) *s.i.s: towards rr: rdn and sme prog over 2f out: nvr in contention and sn outpcd* **20/1**

0-4 **8** 3/4 **Hope Road**^{15} [1863] 3-9-3 0 .... OscarUrbina 11 63+
(J R Fanshawe) *bmpd s: towards rr: sme prog fr 3f out: nvr quite gng pce to rch ldrs: wknd over 1f out* **11/2**^{3}

30 **9** 1 1/4 **Master Halling**^{10} [1998] 3-9-3 0 .... DaneO'Neill 13 61+
(R Charlton) *in rr: sme prog 3f out: nvr in contention* **14/1**

00 **10** 2 1/2 **Almahaza (IRE)**^{6} [2127] 3-9-3 0 .... JimCrowley 5 56
(Mrs A J Perrett) *a towards rr and nvr in contention* **50/1**

6 **11** 1/2 **Hot Diamond**^{16} [1840] 3-9-3 0 .... JohnEgan 3 55
(D R C Elsworth) *t.k.h: stdd into mid-div: hdwy 3f out: wknd fr 2f out* **20/1**

0 **12** 3/4 **Surprise Act**^{21} [1725] 3-9-3 0 .... GeorgeBaker 8 53
(P R Chamings) *a towards rr* **100/1**

2m 8.40s (0.10) **Going Correction** -0.025s/f (Good) **12** Ran SP% **124.6**
Speed ratings (Par 99):98,96,95,93,92 91,90,89,88,86 86,85
CSF £18.47 TOTE £2.00: £1.10, £3.50, £10.70; EX 21.90.
Owner Godolphin **Bred** Darley **Trained** Newmarket, Suffolk

FOCUS
This looked like quite a good maiden for the time of year, but the pace was just ordinary. Not easy to assess what the comfortable winner achieved but he was value for extra and has better to come. Like the second and third, he was well placed through the race.
Mia's Boy Official explanation: jockey said colt lost a front shoe
Hope Road Official explanation: vet said gelding was struck into
Master Halling Official explanation: jockey said colt was hampered on bend into straight

2321 ARENA LEISURE H'CAP 1m 3f 135y
9:00 (9:02) (Class 5) (0-75,77) 4-Y-0+ **£3,238** (£963; £481; £240) **Stalls** Low

Form RPR

0-30 **1** **Ocean Avenue (IRE)**^{28} [1542] 8-9-4 **71** .... DarryllHolland 4 77
(C A Horgan) *mde all: hrd drvn fnl 2f: r.o gamely whn strly chal thrght fnl f: jst hld on* **11/2**^{2}

06-0 **2** shd **Olimpo (FR)**^{17} [1813] 6-8-12 **70** .... JamesMillman(5) 8 76
(B R Millman) *hld up in tch: hdwy over 2f out: qcknd to mount str chal thrght fnl f: upsides fnl 50yds: jst failed* **8/1**

0/15 **3** 1/2 **Charmatic (IRE)**^{14} [1884] 6-9-0 **67** .... FrancisNorton 13 72
(Andrew Turnell) *inrr: hdwy fr 3f out: drvn to chal thrght fnl f: no ex cl home* **25/1**

0-00 **4** 2 1/2 **Rawaabet (IRE)**^{21} [1592] 5-8-2 **55** oh8 .... AdrianMcCarthy 15 56
(P W Hiatt) *in rr tl hdwy fr 3f out: chsd ldrs fnl f: kpt on same pce* **66/1**

0-00 **5** 1 **Pactolos Way**^{17} [1811] 4-8-13 **66** .... JimCrowley 9 65
(P R Chamings) *sn chsng wnr: rdn over 2f out: wknd ins fnl f* **14/1**

-040 **6** nk **Broughtons Folly**^{34} [1378] 4-8-13 **66** .... BrettDoyle 10 65
(W J Musson) *in rr: hdwy over 2f out: nvr quite gng pce to rch ldrs* **20/1**

0043 **7** shd **Hatch A Plan (IRE)**^{17} [1811] 6-8-9 **67** .... TravisBlock(5) 12 65
(Mouse Hamilton-Fairley) *in rr: hdwy fr 2f out but nvr quite gng pce to rch ldrs* **7/1**

060/ **8** hd **Fourth Dimension (IRE)**^{635} [3835] 8-8-12 **65** .... AdamKirby 3 63
(Miss T Spearing) *in rr: hdwy 3f out: chsd ldrs 2f out: wknd fnl f* **66/1**

2624 **9** 1 1/4 **Ross Moor**^{12} [1949] 5-9-3 **70** .... (b) TQuinn 16 66
(Mike Murphy) *s.i.s: bhd: sme hdwy 2f out but nvr in contention* **14/1**

30-3 **10** 1/2 **True Companion**^{17} [1813] 8-9-6 **73** .... SamHitchcott 5 68
(Miss E C Lavelle) *in rr: rdn and sme hdwy fr 3f out: nvr trbld leaaders* **12/1**

-611 **11** 1 1/4 **Royal Premier (IRE)**^{25} [1609] 4-9-1 **68** .... (v) SebSanders 2 61
(H J Collingridge) *chsd ldrs: rdn and wkng whn not much room ins fnl 2f* **7/2**^{1}

5545 **12** 3 **Smart Cat (IRE)**^{12} [1951] 4-8-5 **58** .... JohnEgan 7 46
(A P Jarvis) *in tch: wkng whn n.m.r 2f out* **16/1**

1-56 **13** nk **And Again (USA)**^{18} [1783] 4-9-3 **70** .... TedDurcan 14 57
(R A Teal) *a towards rr* **25/1**

-120 **14** shd **Love Always**^{18} [1783] 5-9-7 **74** .... DaneO'Neill 1 61
(S Dow) *chsd ldrs tl wknd over 2f out* **20/1**

2153 **15** 25 **Musango**^{31} [1451] 4-9-1 **68** .... RichardSmith 11 13
(B R Johnson) *chsd ldrs tl wknd and eased over 2f out* **6/1**^{3}

2m 28.38s (-1.72) **Going Correction** -0.025s/f (Good) **15** Ran SP% **122.6**
Speed ratings (Par 103):104,103,103,101,101 101,101,100,100,99 98,96,96,96,79
CSF £45.60 CT £1032.48 TOTE £6.40: £2.10, £3.40, £7.30; EX 49.60 Place 6 £112.95, Place 5 £93.74.
Owner Mr & Mrs D Tapper & C Horgan **Bred** Steve Starkey **Trained** Uffcott, Wilts

FOCUS
A fair and competitive handicap in which the winner got a good ride from the front. The form does not look that strong, rated through the third to his Flat best.
Ross Moor Official explanation: jockey said gelding was slow into stride
T/Plt: £127.10 to a £1 stake. Pool: £113,722.60. 653.05 winning tickets. T/Qpdt: £24.40 to a £1 stake. Pool: £5,578.10. 168.60 winning tickets. ST

2322 - 2323a (Foreign Racing) - See Raceform Interactive

1774 NAAS (L-H)
Monday, June 4

OFFICIAL GOING: Good to yielding

2324a NAAS SPRINT STKS (LISTED RACE) 5f
3:40 (3:40) 3-Y-0+ **£21,993** (£6,452; £3,074; £1,047)

RPR

1 **Tax Free (IRE)**^{29} [1497] 5-9-12 .... AdrianTNicholls 8 118
(D Nicholls) *trckd ldrs: 6th early: impr into 3rd 1/2-way: led over 1f out: drvn out and r.o wl: comf* **7/2**^{2}

2 1 **Dandy Man (IRE)**^{44} [1171] 4-9-10 115 .... PShanahan 6 112+
(Tracey Collins, Ire) *a.p: 2nd 1/2-way: chal fr under 2f out: kpt on ins fnl f* **9/10**^{1}

3 1 3/4 **Desert Lord**^{176} [6783] 7-10-0 112 .... (b) NCallan 5 110
(K A Ryan) *led: rdn and strly pressed fr 2f out: hdd over 1f out: 3rd and kpt on ins fnl f* **13/2**^{3}

4 3/4 **Snaefell (IRE)**^{19} [1775] 3-9-0 96 .... JMurtagh 11 97
(M Halford, Ire) *hld up: mod 7th 2f out: styd on ins fnl f* **33/1**

5 2 **Flash McGahon (IRE)**^{9} [2050] 3-9-3 100 .... MJKinane 2 93
(John M Oxx, Ire) *chsd ldrs on far side: 4th and rdn 1/2-way: no ex ins fnl f* **12/1**

6 3 **Osterhase (IRE)**^{44} [1171] 8-9-10 112 .... (b) FMBerry 7 85
(J E Mulhern, Ire) *prom: 2nd early: 5th and rdn 2f out: sn no ex* **12/1**

7 1 3/4 **King Of Swords (IRE)**^{19} [1775] 3-9-0 93 .... WSupple 10 73
(Tracey Collins, Ire) *hld up in rr: kpt on same pce fr over 2f out* **50/1**

8 1 1/4 **Extraterrestrial**^{15} [1867] 3-9-0 99 .... CDHayes 1 69
(Kevin Prendergast, Ire) *sn outpcd: kpt on same pce fr over 2f out* **33/1**

9 3/4 **Facchetti (USA)**^{9} [2050] 3-9-0 98 .... JAHeffernan 9 66
(A P O'Brien, Ire) *nvr a factor: rdn and no imp fr 1/2-way* **16/1**

10 2 **Spirit Of Pearl (IRE)**^{196} [6546] 3-8-11 .... KJManning 4 56
(Nicholas Cox, Ire) *3rd early: no ex fr over 2f out* **33/1**

11 1 3/4 **Miswadah (IRE)**^{12} [1946] 4-9-4 59 .... WMLordan 3 52
(Kevin F O'Donnell, Ire) *a bhd* **100/1**

57.80 secs (-4.20)
WFA 3 from 4yo+ 7lb **11** Ran SP% **121.2**
CSF £7.00 TOTE £6.30: £1.10, £1.20, £2.00; DF 8.60.
Owner Ian Hewitson **Bred** Denis & Mrs Teresa Bergin **Trained** Sessay, N Yorks

FOCUS
A quality Listed race featuring classy performers in the potentially top drawer Dandy Man, last year's Prix de l'Abbaye winner Desert Lord, the Palace House Stakes hero Tax Free and the seven-time Stakes winner Osterhase. The fourth limits the form a little.

NOTEBOOK
Tax Free(IRE) emerged victorious to follow up his Group 3 victory at Newmarket last month. The five-year-old held a good position from the outset and improved to challenge for the lead inside the final two furlongs. He led just over a furlong out and stayed on well in the closing stages to keep Dandy Man at bay. Dandy Nicholls intends to\n\x\x aim him at the King's Stand Stakes at Royal Ascot and on this evidence it is not hard to envisage him playing a leading role there. The winning trainer added that the recent rain would not have been a help to his charge, who can hold his own in top sprints over the remainder of the season. (op 4/1)
Dandy Man(IRE), who made a most impressive start to his season over this course and distance in April, faced a much tougher assignment on ground that was slower than ideal, and turned in a sound effort in defeat. He travelled well for much of the race and looked a likely winner with two furlongs to run but just could not match Tax Free. He too heads to Ascot for the King's Stand and remains a leading contender for that race. The faster ground there should show him off to better effect and an improved performance is expected. (op 9/10 tchd 8/11)
Desert Lord, another who would have appreciated quicker ground, was having his first run since finishing unplaced in a top-class sprint in Hong Kong in December. He was in the front rank from the outset, but was unable to match the front pair inside the final furlong. This run can be expected to bring him on considerably and connections were understandably pleased with this effort. He too is destined to take his chance in the King's Stand. (op 5/1 tchd 7/1)
Snaefell(IRE) could never land a telling blow, but was keeping on at the finish and posted a sound effort. He was probably helped by not racing up with the searing early pace but this should not detract from his best effort of the season. He showed signs here of returning to the form that carried him into fourth in last year's Windsor Castle Stakes. (op 25/1)
Flash McGahon(IRE) raced virtually on his own over on the far side of the track and did not run at all badly. This trip probably suits him best and he should be able to hold his own in good company over the coming months – it is worth remembering that this was an exceptionally strong Listed race. (op 14/1)
Osterhase(IRE) helped to force the pace but was starting to struggle with two furlongs to run. He is another that is at his best on quicker ground and it would be unwise to start drawing any conclusions from this. (op 8/1)
King Of Swords(IRE), who holds a rating of 93, ran as well as could be expected.
Extraterrestrial, whose rating of 99 looks harsh for what he has achieved, was predictably outclassed. He will not be easy to place.

2325a SWORDLESTOWN STUD SPRINT STKS (GROUP 3) (FILLIES) 6f
4:10 (4:11) 2-Y-0 **£43,986** (£12,905; £6,148; £2,094)

RPR

1 **You'resothrilling (USA)**^{9} [2049] 2-8-12 .... JAHeffernan 5 100+
(A P O'Brien, Ire) *trckd ldrs in 4th: hdwy 2f out: led under 1f out: r.o wl: comf* **13/8**^{1}

2 1 **Saoirse Abu (USA)**^{8} [2063] 2-8-12 .... KJManning 9 94
(J S Bolger, Ire) *cl up and disp ld: rdn and hdd 2f out: chal 1f out: kpt on u.p* **7/2**^{2}

3 1 1/4 **May Day Queen (IRE)**^{14} [1896] 2-8-12 .... JMurtagh 2 91
(R Hannon) *led and disp: def advantage 2f out: hdd under 1f out: kpt on: no ex nr fin* **10/1**

4 1 **Pretty Ballerina (USA)**^{19} [1774] 2-8-12 .... CO'Donoghue 1 88
(John Joseph Murphy, Ire) *chsd ldrs on far rail: 5th and rdn 2f out: edgd rt over 1f out: kpt on* **33/1**

5 1/2 **The Loan Express (IRE)**^{28} [1546] 2-8-12 .... WMLordan 4 86
(T Stack, Ire) *hld up: 7th 2f out: kpt on fr over 1f out* **9/1**

6 3 1/2 **Raja (IRE)**^{19} [1774] 2-8-12 .... DPMcDonogh 7 76
(Kevin Prendergast, Ire) *cl up and disp ld: rdn 2f out: bmpd over 1f out: no ex* **9/2**^{3}

7 3 **Porto Marmay (IRE)**^{56} [983] 2-8-12 .... PJSmullen 6 67
(K J Condon, Ire) *chsd ldrs: 5th 1/2-way: no ex fr 2f out* **16/1**

8 1/2 **Aspen Shadow (USA)** 2-8-12 .... FMBerry 3 65
(David Wachman, Ire) *a towards rr* **33/1**

9 14 **Reine De Coeur (IRE)**^{10} [2013] 2-8-12 .... MJKinane 8 23
(David Marnane, Ire) *a bhd: eased over 1f out* **8/1**

1m 10.4s (-2.80) **9** Ran SP% **120.5**
CSF £7.68 TOTE £2.20: £1.50, £1.50, £2.60; DF 8.20.
Owner Michael Tabor **Bred** Pacelco **Trained** Ballydoyle, Co Tipperary

FOCUS
An intriguing renewal of this Group 3 that brought together a number of promising and lightly-raced fillies.

NOTEBOOK
You'resothrilling(USA), a sister to Giant's Causeway, had created a good impression when coming home strongly to finish second to Pencil Hill in the Marble Hill Stakes at the Curragh recently, and that effort marked her down as a juvenile of some potential. She duly delivered on the promise of that run. Always well placed, she improved into the front rank with two furlongs to run. Without her rider having to get all that vigorous, she started to edge ahead inside the final furlong and kept on well under pressure in the closing stages to see off Saoirse Abu. She looked as though that first run had brought her on considerably and she won this with something to spare. She can be rated a very bright prospect and is undoubtedly Royal Ascot material. The Queen Mary or the Albany Stakes are firmly on her agenda and she goes there with every chance of victory. (op 6/4 tchd 11/8)
Saoirse Abu(USA) was an emphatic maiden winner over this trip at the Curragh last month and made good progress from that outing to turn in a fine effort in defeat. She was close up from the outset and kept on well once coming under pressure. Her trainer has already indicated that she wants further than this distance and she can continue to progress as the season goes on. A stakes race victory should not be long in coming her way. (op 3/1 tchd 4/1)
May Day Queen(IRE), the sole English raider, was looking to improve on her debut third to Lady Avenger in a Windsor maiden last month and fully vindicated connections' decision to pitch her in at this level. She made most of the running and only gave best inside the final furlong. She will have no trouble opening her account and can continue to hold her own in good company.
Pretty Ballerina(USA) made a most encouraging debut here last month when finishing second to Raja and confirmed the promise of that run. She will have no trouble winning a maiden. (op 25/1)

The Loan Express(IRE), already a 5f winner and stakes placed, met some interference early on that saw her drop to the rear. She started to get back into the reckoning inside the final two furlongs, but had no more to give in the closing stages. She would certainly have finished closer with a clear run and may prove most effective over 5f. (op 7/1)
Raja(IRE) looked to have a leading chance on the form of her maiden victory where she had both today's second and fourth behind her. However, she had no more to give from over a furlong out after racing prominently, although she did receive a bump heading into the final furlong. She is probably capable of better. (op 13/2)
Reine De Coeur(IRE), a promising maiden winner at Tipperary recently, could never get involved and something must have been amiss with her. (op 10/1)

2326 - 2330a (Foreign Racing) - See Raceform Interactive

2173 LINGFIELD (L-H)

Tuesday, June 5

OFFICIAL GOING: Turf course - good to firm (8.5); all-weather - standard

2331 CHESNEY HAWKES LIVE AT LINGFIELDPARK.CO.UK CLAIMING STKS 7f (P)

2:15 (2:16) (Class 6) 3-Y-O+ £2,047 (£604; £302) Stalls Low

Form RPR
0300 **1** **Leonard Charles**[15] [1887] 3-9-4 72 ....(b[1]) SebSanders 6 68
(Sir Mark Prescott) *s.i.s: rousted along and jnd ldr after 1f: rdn 1/2-way: led over 2f out: hld on u.p fnl f* **5/1**[3]
4532 **2** *nk* **Labelled With Love**[5] [2179] 7-9-2 50 ....(t) AmirQuinn 7 55
(J R Boyle) *s.i.s: hld up off the pce: prog on inner gng easily over 2f out: plld out and effrt 1f out: clsng fin: too much to do* **4/1**[2]
6201 **3** *shd* **Million Percent**[10] [2033] 8-9-9 71 .... LiamJones(3) 11 65
(C R Dore) *chsd ldrs: prog 3f out: drvn to go 2nd wl over 1f out: chal and upsides ins fnl f: nt qckn* **5/2**[1]
0001 **4** *1/2* **Crafty Fox**[22] [1719] 4-9-10 52 ....(v) RichardMullen 8 61
(A P Jarvis) *chsd ldng pair: u.p fr 1/2-way: kpt on fr over 1f out: nvr able to chal* **16/1**
0043 **5** *1 1/4* **Rafferty (IRE)**[5] [2179] 8-9-2 49 ....(p) JimmyQuinn 14 50
(S Dow) *chsd ldrs: rdn over 3f out: one pce and nvr quite on terms* **16/1**
0-40 **6** *hd* **Millfield (IRE)**[13] [1947] 4-9-5 54 .... TravisBlock(5) 4 57
(P R Chamings) *dwlt: hld up wl in rr: sn outpcd: prog over 2f out: styd on fnl f: no ch* **8/1**
6000 **7** *3 1/2* **Alwariah**[21] [1740] 4-8-4 47 .... SophieDoyle(7) 9 35
(Ms J S Doyle) *chsd ldrs: urged along fr 3f out: no imp 2f out: fdd* **66/1**
0004 **8** *shd* **Fire At Will**[35] [1380] 5-8-9 42 .... MarkCoumbe(7) 12 40
(A W Carroll) *dwlt: settled wl in rr: outpcd and rdn after 2f: kpt on fr over 1f out: n.d* **50/1**
6650 **9** *1 1/4* **Calloff The Search**[19] [1782] 3-8-5 53 ....(p) TolleyDean(5) 5 40
(W G M Turner) *mde most: set str pce after 1f: hdd over 2f out: wknd over 1f out* **33/1**
1465 **10** *2 1/2* **Mountain Pass (USA)**[28] [1564] 5-9-3 57 ....(p) HaddenFrost(7) 1 38
(B J Llewellyn) *trckd ldrs: rdn over 3f out: wknd 2f out* **8/1**
4020 **11** *nk* **Savoy Chapel**[29] 5-9-2 45 .... DarryllHolland 13 29
(A W Carroll) *outpcd and rdn over 5f out: detached in last trio over 2f out: pushed along and kpt on: nvr nr ldrs* **20/1**
0-00 **12** *3/4* **African Concerto (IRE)**[15] [1899] 4-9-0 42 .... FrankieMcDonald 3 25
(S Kirk) *nvr beyond midfield: wknd 2f out* **66/1**
506- **13** *3/4* **Pink Bay**[56] [5474] 5-8-6 48 ....(b) KevinGhunowa(5) 10 20
(K F Clutterbuck) *struggling u.p after 2f: a wl bhd* **33/1**
0600 **14** *3/4* **Childish Thoughts**[8] [2077] 3-8-5 45 .... JohnEgan 2 22
(Mrs Norma Pook) *nvr beyond midfield: wknd over 2f out* **100/1**

1m 24.88s (-1.01) **Going Correction** -0.05s/f (Stan)
WFA 3 from 4yo+ 10lb 14 Ran SP% 115.8
Speed ratings (Par 101):103,102,102,101,100 100,96,96,94,91 91,90,89,89
CSF £23.02 TOTE £5.50: £2.20, £1.80, £1.40; EX 24.70 Trifecta £61.50 Pool: £378.90 - 4.37 winning units..The winner was claimed by C. R. Dore for £12,000. Labelled With Love was claimed by J R Auvray for £6,000.
Owner John Brown & Megan Dennis **Bred** John Brown & Megan Dennis **Trained** Newmarket, Suffolk

FOCUS
An ordinary claimer in which the firtst three were not at their best.
Savoy Chapel Official explanation: jockey said gelding was never travelling

2332 JASON DONOVAN LIVE AT LINGFIELDPARK.CO.UK H'CAP 1m 4f (P)

2:45 (2:45) (Class 6) (0-60,60) 4-Y-O+ £2,047 (£604; £302) Stalls Low

Form RPR
0000 **1** **Blackmail (USA)**[32] [1451] 9-8-12 **54** ....(b) TQuinn 5 62
(P Mitchell) *trckd ldrs: wnt 2nd over 3f out: drvn 2f out: kpt on to ld ins fnl f* **16/1**
0-03 **2** *1 1/4* **Bob's Your Uncle**[26] [1609] 4-8-13 **55** .... SebSanders 12 61
(J G Portman) *hld up in rr: prog on outer fr 3f out: rdn to go 3rd 2f out: styd on to take 2nd last strides* **5/1**[2]
3012 **3** *hd* **Mighty Kitchener (USA)**[15] [1907] 4-9-3 **59** .... IanMongan 6 65
(P Howling) *hld up tl pressed ldr after 3f: led 4f out: kicked over 2 l clr wl over 1f out: hdd and folded ins fnl f* **11/2**[3]
2400 **4** *1 1/4* **Hallings Overture (USA)**[32] [1451] 8-9-2 **58** .... PaulEddery 3 62
(C A Horgan) *usual slow s: hld up in last pair: gng wl whn nt clr run over 2f out: gd prog over 1f out: effrt petered out last 100yds* **9/1**
0-06 **5** *4* **Lady Ambitious**[15] [1907] 4-8-6 **48** oh1 ow2 .... RobertHavlin 10 45
(D K Ivory) *hld up wl in rr: rdn over 2f out: styd on one pce: nvr rchd ldrs* **50/1**
2204 **6** *1/2* **Veba (USA)**[15] [1906] 4-8-4 **46** .... HayleyTurner 7 42
(M D I Usher) *t.k.h: hld up in midfield: nt clr run over 2f out: sn outpcd: rdn over 1f out: plugged on* **10/1**
3000 **7** *1/2* **Competitor**[6] [2141] 6-9-1 **57** ....(v) DaneO'Neill 8 53
(J Akehurst) *hld up: prog fr 3f out: rdn to dispute 3rd 2f out: wknd fnl f* **8/1**
000- **8** *1 1/2* **St Fris**[208] [6410] 4-8-10 **52** ....(v[1]) TPO'Shea 13 45
(J A R Toller) *trckd ldrs: rdn and lost pl over 3f out: sn toiling: kpt on ins fnl f* **50/1**
6264 **9** *1/2* **Carlton Scroop (FR)**[22] [1730] 4-8-11 **60** ....(b) GihanArnolda(7) 1 52
(J Jay) *led at slow pce for 3f: sn pushed along: rdn and steadily lost pl fnl 3f* **9/2**[1]
0000 **10** *1/2* **Atticus Trophies (IRE)**[5] [2176] 4-8-4 **46** oh1 ....(p) EdwardCreighton 2 38
(Ms J S Doyle) *hld up towards rr on inner: stl there over 2f out: no ch whn rdn fnl f* **40/1**
324/ **11** *hd* **Captain Marryat**[936] [6624] 6-9-0 **56** .... PaulDoe 9 47
(J Akehurst) *stdd s: racd wd: hld up in rr: effrt over 4f out: wknd wl over 2f out* **12/1**
000- **12** *2 1/2* **Book Of Days (IRE)**[176] [6792] 4-8-4 **46** oh1 .... JimmyQuinn 11 33
(Evan Williams) *s.i.s: plld hrd: led after 3f to 4f out: wknd 3f out* **10/1**
0-53 **13** *1* **Star Berry**[14] [1926] 4-8-10 **52** .... BrettDoyle 4 38
(B J Meehan) *trckd ldr for 3f: styd cl up tl wknd fr 3f out* **8/1**

2m 34.16s (-0.23) **Going Correction** -0.05s/f (Stan) 13 Ran SP% 120.6
Speed ratings (Par 101):98,97,97,96,93 93,92,91,91,91 91,89,88
CSF £94.41 CT £509.28 TOTE £14.20: £4.20, £2.20, £1.80; EX 110.00 Trifecta £164.30 Part won. Pool: £231.42 - 0.10 winning units..
Owner Peter Crate **Bred** Skymarc Farm Inc **Trained** Epsom, Surrey

FOCUS
A moderate handicap and, with the pace steady for much of the way, the form does not look worth a great deal. It has been rated through the second and third.

2333 TONY HADLEY LIVE AT LINGFIELDPARK.CO.UK MEDIAN AUCTION MAIDEN STKS 5f

3:15 (3:17) (Class 6) 2-Y-O £2,730 (£806; £403) Stalls High

Form RPR
1 **Swallow Star** 2-8-12 0 .... SebSanders 12 76
(R M Beckett) *racd against nr side rail: led over 3f out: mde rest: drvn 2f out: kpt on wl fnl f* **11/1**
06 **2** *1 1/4* **Mister Fips (IRE)**[9] [2056] 2-9-3 0 .... JohnEgan 1 77
(Jane Chapple-Hyam) *chsd ldng gp on outer: rdn and green over 2f out: styd on wl u.p to take 2nd wl ins fnl f* **7/1**[3]
4423 **3** *3/4* **Ben**[24] [1680] 2-9-3 0 .... RobertHavlin 3 74
(P G Murphy) *chsd ldrs on outer: rdn to chal 2f out: nt qckn over 1f out: one pce after* **9/4**[1]
4 *shd* **Dalkey Girl (IRE)** 2-8-9 0 .... JerryO'Dwyer(3) 2 69
(V Smith) *racd in centre: outpcd: drvn 1/2-way: r.o fnl f: gaining at fin* **66/1**
6 **5** *nk* **Really Really Wish**[15] [1897] 2-9-3 0 .... GeorgeBaker 5 73
(J R Best) *w ldrs: upsides 2f out: fdd ins fnl f* **8/1**
6 *nk* **Cosmic Art** 2-9-3 0 .... DaneO'Neill 8 71
(E A L Dunlop) *cl up: rdn to chal 2f out: nt qckn over 1f out: one pce after* **5/2**[2]
0 **7** *1* **A Wish For You**[32] [1445] 2-8-12 0 .... DavidKinsella 13 63
(D K Ivory) *dwlt: racd towards nr side rail and sn cl up: urged along and one pce over 1f out* **25/1**
8 *2 1/2* **Ellemujie** 2-9-3 0 .... TQuinn 4 59
(D K Ivory) *dwlt: rn green and outpcd: wl bhd tl modest late prog* **50/1**
0 **9** *hd* **Victory Shout (USA)**[24] [1652] 2-9-0 0 .... StephaneBreux(3) 6 58
(J R Best) *sn outpcd and rn green: a struggling in rr* **25/1**
35 **10** *2* **Bookiebasher Dude**[27] [1585] 2-9-3 0 .... DarryllHolland 9 51
(M Quinn) *chsd ldrs to 1/2-way: sn wknd u.p* **8/1**
11 *3 1/2* **Treacle Noir (IRE)** 2-8-12 0 .... JimCrowley 7 33
(Tom Dascombe) *dwlt: outpcd and a bhd* **14/1**
0 **12** *3* **Patsymartin**[30] [1498] 2-9-3 0 .... BrettDoyle 11 28
(J Ryan) *in touh to 1/2-way: sn struggling* **100/1**
0 **13** *14* **Ruby's Smile**[38] [1285] 2-8-7 0 .... TolleyDean(5) 10 —
(R Brotherton) *led to over 3f out: wknd rapidly 1/2-way: t.o* **66/1**

59.41 secs (0.47) **Going Correction** -0.10s/f (Good) 13 Ran SP% 122.7
Speed ratings (Par 91):92,90,88,88,88 87,86,82,81,78 72,68,45
CSF £84.90 TOTE £10.40: £2.90, £2.30, £1.40; EX 86.30 TRIFECTA Not won..
Owner G C Myddelton **Bred** Mrs A M Upsdell **Trained** Whitsbury, Hants

FOCUS
Just an ordinary juvenile maiden, rated through the third. They raced middle to near side, and the near rail looked advantageous.

NOTEBOOK
Swallow Star, a 12,000gns purchase, is by Observatory, out of a close relation to a smart juvenile in the US. Drawn against the favoured rail, she showed good speed throughout to take full advantage and sustained her challenge to the line. It is worth keeping in mind when assessing the form that she raced on the best part of the track and it remains to be seen how much improvement there is to come. (tchd 12-1)
Mister Fips(IRE) had his sights lowered after contesting hot races at Ascot and Newmarket and ran well. His effort is all the more creditable considering he made his move wide, more towards the middle of the track. (op 11-2)
Ben has shown a modest to fair level of form on all of his starts so far, but he is just not progressing. (tchd 11-4)
Dalkey Girl(IRE), a half-sister to dual 1m4f-1m6f winner Tilla, shaped quite nicely on her racecourse debut and should improve.
Really Really Wish showed good early speed and could find his level in the nursery season. (tchd 10-1)
Cosmic Art, a 17,000gns first foal of a triple 1m1f-1m2f winner, ran below market expectations on his racecourse debut. (op 3-1 tchd 9-4)
Ellemujie Official explanation: jockey said gelding missed the break

2334 HEATWAVE LIVE AT LINGFIELDPARK.CO.UK H'CAP 6f

3:45 (3:51) (Class 6) (0-60,66) 3-Y-O+ £2,047 (£604; £302) Stalls High

Form RPR
212 **1** **Vegas Boys**[4] [2217] 4-10-0 **66** 6ex .... DO'Donohoe 6 73+
(M Wigham) *dwlt: grad worked way over fr low draw to nr side rail: wl in rr: prog and drvn 2f out: r.o to ld wl ins fnl f* **10/3**[1]
-005 **2** *1/2* **Smile For Us**[33] [1436] 4-9-8 **60** ....(b) RobertHavlin 18 66
(C Drew) *cl up on nr side: effrt over 2f out: hanging bdly lft after: chal 1f out: nt qckn* **12/1**
50-6 **3** *nk* **Tilsworth Charlie**[34] [1404] 4-8-10 **51** ....(v) PatrickMathers(3) 3 56
(J R Jenkins) *racd in centre: outpcd and sn rdn: overall last over 2f out: styd on strly on wd outside fnl f* **50/1**
0-02 **4** *hd* **Rogue**[12] [1973] 5-9-5 **57** .... LPKeniry 8 61
(Jane Southcombe) *w ldrs in centre but nt on terms w nr side gp early: clsd over 2f out: overall ldr 1f out: hdd and nt qckn wl ins fnl f* **20/1**
-165 **5** *1* **Piddies Pride (IRE)**[34] [1400] 5-9-5 **57** ....(v) JohnEgan 12 63+
(Miss Gay Kelleway) *trckd nr side ldrs: rdn 1/2-way: nt clr run over 1f out: styd on ins fnl f* **12/1**
40-0 **6** *hd* **King Egbert (FR)**[11] [1991] 6-8-9 **52** .... TolleyDean(5) 4 53
(R A Harris) *hld up in centre: prog over 2f out: tried to chal 1f out: fdd* **20/1**
-343 **7** *shd* **Bens Georgie (IRE)**[3] [2257] 5-9-3 **55** .... TQuinn 2 56
(D K Ivory) *racd on wd outside: nt on terms: prog fr 2f out: one pce and no imp fnl f* **6/1**[2]
0000 **8** *2* **Goodwood Spirit**[7] [2108] 5-9-2 **59** ....(p) KevinGhunowa(5) 10 54
(J M Bradley) *nt on terms in centre gp: chsd ldrs: kpt on fnl 2f: nvr able to chal* **20/1**
2041 **9** *1/2* **Mistral Sky**[4] [2220] 8-10-0 **66** 6ex ....(v) AmirQuinn 7 59
(Stef Liddiard) *w ldrs in centre but nt on terms early: carried hd high and nt qckn 2f out* **12/1**

The Form Book, Raceform Ltd, Compton, RG20 6NL

0003 **10** 3/4 **Going Skint**[15] 1899 4-9-4 **56**..........(v) AdamKirby 17 47
(M Wellings) *rousted along early: w overall ldr nr side to 1f out: hanging and wknd: eased* **12/1**

3006 **11** 1 **Whistleupthewind**[101] 555 4-9-0 **52**..........(b) HayleyTurner 5 40
(J M P Eustace) *trckd ldrs in centre but nt on terms: nt clr run 1/2-way: n.d after* **33/1**

0-03 **12** shd **Double Valentine**[7] 2108 4-8-12 **50**.......... SebSanders 15 37
(R Ingram) *racd nr side: mde most to 1f out: wknd rapidly* **7/1**

-003 **13** hd **Joy And Pain**[5] 2190 6-9-5 **57**..........(v) DaneO'Neill 11 44
(M J Attwater) *dwlt: racd nr side: wl in rr of gp: sme prog u.p 2f out: nt clr run briefly over 1f out: hanging lft after* **13/2**[3]

60-0 **14** 2 1/2 **Hard To Catch (IRE)**[15] 1885 9-9-2 **54**.......... JimCrowley 1 33
(Mike Murphy) *racd on outer: chsd ldrs in gp but nvr on terms: wknd over 1f out* **66/1**

1060 **15** 1 **Kitchen Sink (IRE)**[4] 2221 5-9-0 **52**.......... StephenCarson 9 28
(Jean-Rene Auvray) *mde most in centre to 1/2-way but nt on terms w nr side gp: sn wknd* **33/1**

0-00 **16** 2 1/2 **Jodrell Bank (IRE)**[21] 1753 4-8-11 **49**.......... BrettDoyle 16 18
(J Ryan) *racd nr side: wl in rr fr 1/2-way* **66/1**

45-0 **17** 3 **Royal Senga**[65] 866 4-9-0 **52**.......... FergusSweeney 14 12
(C A Horgan) *w nr side ldrs to 1/2-way: wknd rapidly* **14/1**

1m 11.21s (-0.46) **Going Correction** -0.10s/f (Good) **17** Ran SP% **125.7**
Speed ratings (Par 101):99,98,97,97,96 96,95,93,92,91 90,90,89,86,85 81,77
CSF £41.53 CT £1800.23 TOTE £3.90: £1.50, £3.20, £7.70, £4.10; EX 50.20 TRIFECTA Not won..
Owner P R Iron **Bred** Brimpton Bloodstock **Trained** Newmarket, Suffolk

FOCUS
A moderate but competitive sprint handicap. They raced middle to near side, with the near rail again looking like the place to be. Not many came here in form and the winner did not need to be at his best.
Mistral Sky Official explanation: jockey said gelding hit his head on the stalls

2335 W B SIMPSON & SONS TILING H'CAP 7f
4:15 (4:20) (Class 5) (0-75,75) 3-Y-O **£2,914** (£867; £433; £216) **Stalls** High

Form RPR
031 **1** **Sweet Gale (IRE)**[21] 1749 3-9-6 **74**..........(t) SebSanders 11 81+
(J Noseda) *trckd ldrs: swtchd to r against nr side rail and drvn over 1f out: r.o to ld wl ins fnl f* **3/1**[1]

40-0 **2** 1/2 **The Fifth Member (IRE)**[14] 1927 3-8-9 **63**.......... DarryllHolland 15 69
(R M Flower) *w ldrs: upsides ins fnl f: jst outpcd nr fin* **25/1**

3250 **3** 1/2 **Satyricon**[18] 1815 3-8-11 **70**..........(b) NicolPolli(5) 14 75
(M Botti) *t.k.h: cl up nr side: led over 2f out: hdd and one pce wl ins fnl f* **9/1**

-110 **4** 1/2 **Ambrosiano**[49] 1076 3-9-6 **74**.......... AdamKirby 1 77+
(C G Cox) *sn crossed towards nr side: pressed ldr: upsides 1f out: fdd last 100yds* **11/1**

-456 **5** 1 3/4 **Tipsy Prince**[14] 1920 3-9-3 **71**.......... FergusSweeney 17 70+
(David Pinder) *hld up wl in rr nr side: prog wl over 1f out: styd on: nt rch ldrs* **8/1**[3]

1-06 **6** hd **Buckie Massa**[15] 1900 3-9-4 **72**.......... FrankieMcDonald 9 70
(S Kirk) *hld up in rr: prog 2f out: hanging lft over 1f out: drvn and styd on fnl f: nt rch ldrs* **16/1**

0-60 **7** 1 3/4 **Hythe Bay**[3] 2243 3-9-6 **74**.......... GeorgeBaker 3 67
(J R Best) *sn crossed to r towards nr side: mde most to over 2f out: wknd over 1f out* **33/1**

1640 **8** 1 1/2 **Hucking Heat (IRE)**[25] 1634 3-8-13 **67**.......... DaneO'Neill 12 56
(J R Best) *hld up nr side: effrt over 2f out: no prog wl over 1f out* **20/1**

00-3 **9** 1 1/2 **Pango's Legacy**[19] 1786 3-9-0 **73**.......... TravisBlock(5) 10 58
(H Morrison) *racd towards centre: pressed ldrs for 4f: sn struggling* **11/1**

3150 **10** 1 1/4 **Convivial Spirit**[24] 1658 3-8-13 **67**..........(t) LPKeniry 8 49
(E F Vaughan) *racd towards centre: u.p and struggling 3f out* **16/1**

0-65 **11** 1/2 **Optical Illusion (USA)**[32] 1452 3-9-3 **71**.......... DO'Donohoe 16 51
(E A L Dunlop) *stdd s: hld up and swtchd fr high draw towards centre: nvr a factor* **8/1**[3]

-061 **12** 3/4 **Jack Oliver**[25] 1634 3-9-7 **75**.......... BrettDoyle 6 53
(B J Meehan) *t.k.h: hld up towards centre: n.m.r over 5f out: effrt over 2f out: wknd over 1f out* **9/2**[2]

046- **13** 3/4 **Give Evidence**[183] 6699 3-8-11 **65**.......... RichardMullen 7 41
(A P Jarvis) *nvr beyond midfield: u.p and struggling 3f out* **25/1**

10-0 **14** 6 **Victory Spirit**[29] 1535 3-9-2 **70**.......... JimmyQuinn 18 30
(H J L Dunlop) *t.k.h: w ldrs and racd nr side: losing pl whn hmpd 3f out* **20/1**

10-0 **15** shd **Loves Bidding**[18] 1820 3-9-4 **72**..........(v1) RobertHavlin 5 32
(R Ingram) *prom on outer over 4f: wknd rapidly and eased* **33/1**

050- **16** 2 **Only Hope**[190] 6625 3-8-10 **64**..........(v) TQuinn 4 19
(P S McEntee) *racd on outer: already struggling whn given slt nudge 2f out: hung lft and wknd rapidly* **50/1**

1m 23.2s (-1.01) **Going Correction** -0.10s/f (Good) **16** Ran SP% **128.9**
Speed ratings (Par 99):101,100,99,99,97 97,95,93,91,90 89,88,87,81,80 78
CSF £93.53 CT £648.78 TOTE £4.00: £1.70, £4.30, £3.00, £3.50; EX 82.10 TRIFECTA Not won..
Owner Vimal Khosla **Bred** Rozelle Bloodstock **Trained** Newmarket, Suffolk

FOCUS
An ordinary handicap for the grade. They were once more spread out across the track, but again those close to the near-rail rail looked to be at an advantage. The winning time was 0.50 seconds faster than the following older-horse 46-55. The winner should do better still and the second confirmed his 2yo form.
Tipsy Prince Official explanation: jockey said gelding was denied a clear run
Pango's Legacy Official explanation: vet said colt was struck into
Only Hope Official explanation: jockey said filly was hampered 2f out

2336 GO WEST LIVE AT LINGFIELDPARK.CO.UK H'CAP 7f
4:45 (4:47) (Class 6) (0-55,55) 4-Y-O+ **£2,047** (£604; £302) **Stalls** High

Form RPR
0-24 **1** **Drawback (IRE)**[6] 2143 4-8-9 **55**..........(p) LukeMorris(5) 16 63
(R A Harris) *racd nr side: w ldrs: rdn to ld over 2f out: hdd jst ins fnl f: rallied to ld fnl 50yds* **11/2**[2]

0644 **2** nk **Beneking**[13] 1947 7-8-4 **52**..........(p) HaddenFrost(7) 5 59
(D Burchell) *chsd ldrs in centre: rdn 1/2-way: prog to chal 2f out: led jst ins fnl f: wknd and hdd fnl 50yds* **9/1**

5053 **3** 1/2 **Napoletano (GER)**[2] 2273 6-8-9 **50**..........(p) JohnEgan 14 56+
(S Dow) *w ldrs to wl over 1f out: nt qckn and lost pl: rallied fnl 100yds and clsng at fin* **5/1**[1]

0505 **4** 1/2 **Blue Empire (IRE)**[14] 1918 6-8-11 **55**.......... LiamJones(3) 10 59
(C R Dore) *w ldrs to over 2f out: nt qckn wl over 1f out: styd on again fnl f: a hld* **11/1**

0-66 **5** nk **Trevian**[10] 2023 6-8-8 **54**.......... KevinGhunowa(5) 9 57+
(J M Bradley) *settled wl in rr nr side: rdn over 2f out: styd on fr over 1f out: gaining at fin* **14/1**

5236 **6** nk **Marmooq**[14] 1921 4-9-0 **55**.......... DaneO'Neill 2 58
(M J Attwater) *hld up in centre: rdn wl over 2f out: styd on fr over 1f out: unable to chal* **6/1**[3]

5000 **7** nk **Scroll**[11] 2004 4-8-8 **49**..........(v) JimCrowley 8 51
(P Howling) *dwlt: hld up wl in rr: effrt over 1f out: r.o ins fnl f: nvr nrr* **20/1**

-016 **8** shd **Firework**[76] 723 9-8-7 **48**.......... StephenCarson 15 50
(E A Wheeler) *dwlt: sn trckd nr side ldrs: rdn and lost pl over 2f out: swtchd to r against rail over 1f out: styd on* **14/1**

002- **9** shd **Milton's Keen**[246] 5729 4-9-0 **55**.......... BrettDoyle 1 56
(John Berry) *wl in rr in centre: prog on wd outside over 2f out: one pce and no imp fnl f* **14/1**

5/02 **10** 1/2 **Burford Lass (IRE)**[13] 1947 4-9-0 **55**.......... RobertHavlin 17 55
(D K Ivory) *racd against nr side rail: narrow ld tl edgd lft and hdd over 2f out: fdd* **7/1**

-346 **11** nk **Mugeba**[5] 2190 6-8-11 **55**..........(t) JerryO'Dwyer(3) 4 54
(Miss Gay Kelleway) *hld up in rr in centre: effrt 2f out: plugged on: nt rch ldrs* **12/1**

5036 **12** 1 3/4 **Piccostar**[13] 1947 4-8-13 **54**.......... FergusSweeney 6 48
(A B Haynes) *towards rr in centre: drvn and struggling 3f out* **16/1**

40-0 **13** 1 1/2 **Cove Mountain (IRE)**[41] 1251 5-9-0 **55**.......... LPKeniry 7 45
(S Kirk) *a wl in rr: struggling u.p 3f out* **33/1**

000- **14** hd **Hey Presto**[235] 5937 7-8-9 **50**.......... PaulDoe 11 40
(R Rowe) *racd nr side: chsd ldrs to 1/2-way: sn btn* **33/1**

54-0 **15** 1/2 **Simplify**[53] 1025 5-8-6 **47**..........(b) FrankieMcDonald 13 36
(T M Jones) *t.k.h: w ldrs to 2f out: wknd* **50/1**

/000 **16** 3/4 **Fancy (IRE)**[14] 1918 4-8-4 **50**.......... WilliamBuick(5) 3 36
(R A Farrant) *struggling on wd outside bef 1/2-way: no ch after* **20/1**

1m 23.7s (-0.51) **Going Correction** -0.10s/f (Good) **16** Ran SP% **128.1**
Speed ratings (Par 101):98,97,97,96,96 95,95,95,95,94 94,92,90,90,89 88
CSF £53.89 CT £284.52 TOTE £7.10: £1.60, £2.30, £2.00, £2.60; EX 72.50 Trifecta £246.10 Pool: £346.71 - 0.60 winning units. Place 6 £ 61.03, Place 5 £ 47.01.
Owner B & T Hicks Transport Limited **Bred** Mrs H B Raw **Trained** Earlswood, Monmouths

FOCUS
A moderate handicap, the winner and third running similar races to the Leicester seller in which they ran last month. The winning time was 0.50 seconds slower than the previous 56-75 for three-year-olds.
T/Jkpt: Not won. T/Plt: £23.10 to a £1 stake. Pool: £78,524.15. 2,477.00 winning tickets. T/Qpdt: £8.00 to a £1 stake. Pool: £3,960.70. 362.40 winning tickets. JN

1857 RIPON (R-H)
Tuesday, June 5

OFFICIAL GOING: Good to firm
13mm water had been put on the track over the previous four nights but the riders still reported the going to be 'very quick, mostly firm'.
Wind: light 1/2 against Weather: fine and sunny

2337 E B F MAN ERF MAIDEN STKS 5f
2:30 (2:31) (Class 5) 2-Y-O **£4,210** (£1,252; £625; £312) **Stalls** Low

Form RPR
1 **Roker Park (IRE)** 2-9-3 0.......... PatCosgrave 2 89+
(K R Burke) *chsd ldrs: swtchd rt over 1f out: led jst ins finasl f: r.o strly* **9/1**

2 2 **Befortyfour** 2-9-3 0.......... PhilipRobinson 9 82
(M A Jarvis) *w ldr: led over 1f out: hdd jst ins fnl f: no ex* **11/4**[1]

0 **3** 1 3/4 **Hadaf (IRE)**[19] 1781 2-9-3 0.......... RHills 3 76
(M P Tregoning) *chsd ldrs: effrt 2f out: upsides 1f out: kpt on same pce* **3/1**[2]

4 3/4 **Rocking** 2-8-12 0.......... MichaelHills 5 68+
(W J Haggas) *in rr-div: hdwy 2f out: kpt on wl ins fnl f* **5/1**

5 **5** 1 3/4 **Starlight Girl**[10] 2039 2-8-12 0.......... DavidAllan 6 62
(T D Easterby) *led tl 2f out: wknd fnl f* **4/1**[3]

6 2 **Our Sunnie** 2-9-3 0.......... AdrianTNicholls 8 59
(D Nicholls) *gave problems s: swvd rt s: mid-div: wandered over 1f out: nvr nr ldrs* **33/1**

7 6 **Jafra (IRE)** 2-8-12 0.......... MichaelJStainton(5) 1 38
(R M Whitaker) *s.s: a bhd* **16/1**

0 **8** 3/4 **Banus Flyer (IRE)**[19] 1792 2-9-3 0.......... KimTinkler 10 35
(N Tinkler) *chsd ldrs: swtchd lft after 1f: lost pl over 1f out* **66/1**

9 nk **Glenshee (IRE)** 2-9-3 0.......... NCallan 7 34
(J J Quinn) *hmpd s: a in rr* **18/1**

10 2 **Red River Boy** 2-9-3 0.......... PaulMulrennan 4 27
(C W Fairhurst) *s.i.s: a bhd* **50/1**

60.51 secs (0.31) **Going Correction** +0.05s/f (Good) **10** Ran SP% **115.9**
Speed ratings (Par 93):99,95,93,91,89 85,76,75,74,71
CSF £33.56 TOTE £9.60: £2.60, £1.10, £1.50; EX 40.40.
Owner T Alderson **Bred** Dr Dean Harron **Trained** Middleham Moor, N Yorks

FOCUS
A fair juvenile maiden with the first two possessing a fair amount of potential. Not much form to go on, with the fifth the best guide.

NOTEBOOK
Roker Park(IRE), a good-bodied May foal, was very noisy beforehand. Pulled off the fence to get a run, he swept to the front and scored in most decisive fashion, maintaining his stable's good recent run with their juveniles. (tchd 8-1 and 10-1)
Befortyfour, a February foal, is bred exclusively for speed. A well-made newcomer, he too was inclined to be noisy in the paddock. He had the leader covered, but after striking the front was gunned down by the winner. He will have no difficulty going one better. (op 9-4)
Hadaf(IRE), a sharp type, had made his debut on totally different ground. He worked hard to get almost upsides entering the last but then had his limitations exposed. (op 5-2 tchd 10-3)
Rocking, her dam's sixteenth foal, is a half-sister to six winners including the stable's smart sprinter Superstar Leo. A May foal, she is only small and was all at sea on the undulating track until picking up in good style late in the day. Even one win will make her a valuable asset at stud. (tchd 4-1)
Starlight Girl still looks very much on the weak side and is bred to need further in due course. (op 5-1 tchd 11-2)
Our Sunnie, a narrow March foal, gave problems going into the stalls. She ducked and dived and looked very inexperienced. (op 40-1)

2338 ROCK AT THE RACES TOMORROW NIGHT H'CAP — 1m 1f 170y
3:00 (3:00) (Class 5) (0-70,73) 4-Y-0+ **£3,238** (£722; £722; £240) **Stalls High**

Form RPR

2-55 **1** **Wasalat (USA)**[34] [1416] 5-9-5 **67** .... PaulHanagan 10 — 76
(D W Barker) *s.i.s: hdwy 4f out: led 2f out: jst hld on* **12/1**

0-12 **2** *shd* **Harvest Warrior**[10] [2023] 5-9-7 **69** .... DavidAllan 11 — 78
(T D Easterby) *s.i.s: hdwy on ins over 2f out: squeezed through to chal ins fnl f: jst failed* **5/1**[3]

2461 **2** *dht* **Gigs Magic (USA)**[4] [2201] 4-8-10 **58** 6ex .... JoeFanning 5 — 67
(M Johnston) *hld up: hdwy over 3f out: chalng whn edgd rt over 1f out: kpt on wl* **5/2**[1]

-003 **4** *3* **Bright Sun (IRE)**[7] [2117] 6-9-5 **67** .... KimTinkler 8 — 70
(N Tinkler) *chsd ldrs: one pce fnl 2f* **10/1**

3-30 **5** *1/2* **Inside Story (IRE)**[127] [297] 5-9-6 **68** ....(b) PaulMulrennan 7 — 70
(M W Easterby) *in rr: hdwy over 2f out: kpt on same pce* **20/1**

60-0 **6** *5* **Latif (USA)**[11] [1997] 6-9-0 **69** .... JohnCavanagh(7) 3 — 61
(Ms Deborah J Evans) *hld up in rr: hdwy over 2f out: wknd over 1f out* **40/1**

031- **7** *shd* **Moonstreaker**[166] [6897] 4-8-6 **59** .... MichaelJStainton(5) 6 — 51
(R M Whitaker) *w ldrs: led over 3f out: hdd 2f out: sn wknd* **33/1**

0041 **8** *1 1/4* **King Of The Moors (USA)**[7] [2117] 4-9-4 **73** 6ex .... NeilBrown(7) 9 — 62
(T D Barron) *chsd ldrs: wknd over 2f out* **7/2**[2]

60-0 **9** *1/2* **Motafarred (IRE)**[12] [1967] 5-8-11 **59** .... PatCosgrave 1 — 47
(Micky Hammond) *trckd ldrs on outer: slipped bdly bnd over 5f out: lost pl over 2f out* **50/1**

0-U0 **10** *1 1/2* **Billy One Punch**[49] [1078] 5-9-3 **65** .... JHBowman 2 — 50
(G G Margarson) *hld up in tch: smooth hdwy to chal over 2f out: sn wknd* **12/1**

5-04 **11** *1* **Apsara**[11] [2007] 6-9-0 **62** .... TomEaves 4 — 45
(G M Moore) *mid-div: lost pl over 3f out* **8/1**

4240 **12** *nk* **Tour D'Amour (IRE)**[3] [2254] 4-8-13 **61** .... NCallan 12 — 44
(R Craggs) *led tl over 3f out: sn lost pl* **28/1**

2m 3.85s (-1.15) **Going Correction** +0.05s/f (Good) **12 Ran SP% 118.6**
Speed ratings (Par 103):106,105,105,103,103 99,99,98,97,96 95,95
TOTE £16.00: £4.20 TRIFECTA Pl HW 2.40, GM 1.50; Ex W-HW-54.90, W-GM 29.10; CSF W-HW 33.76, W-GM 20.10; T/C W-HW-GM 101.36; W-GM-HW 88.56.
Owner Miss Daphne Downes **Bred** Darley **Trained** Scorton, N Yorks

FOCUS
The first three came from off the pace. The winner is back to her best, Harvest Warrior ran to his Haydock winning mark.

2339 NICK WILMOT-SMITH MEMORIAL H'CAP — 6f
3:30 (3:30) (Class 3) (0-95,87) 3-Y-0+
£9,348 (£2,799; £1,399; £700; £349; £175) **Stalls Low**

Form RPR

0-00 **1** **Desert Commander (IRE)**[18] [1826] 5-9-11 **85** ....(b1) NCallan 3 — 94+
(K A Ryan) *chsd ldrs: led 1f out: hld on wl* **5/1**[2]

41-0 **2** *3/4* **Yorkshire Blue**[24] [1653] 8-8-13 **80** .... GaryBartley(7) 6 — 87
(J S Goldie) *sn outpcd and detached in rr: hdwy on wd outside over 1f out: kpt on wl ins fnl f: no ex cl home* **16/1**

0-02 **3** *nk* **Gallery Girl (IRE)**[16] [1861] 4-9-8 **82** .... DavidAllan 8 — 88
(T D Easterby) *s.i.s: hdwy and swtchd outside over 2f out: no ex ins fnl f* **10/1**

60-1 **4** *1 1/4* **Trojan Flight**[24] [1678] 6-9-5 **79** .... PaulHanagan 7 — 81
(R A Fahey) *hld up in rr: shkn up 4f out: nt clr run over 2f out tl over 1f out: styd on: nt rch ldrs* **7/1**

4-03 **5** *3* **Lake Chini (IRE)**[17] [1852] 5-9-2 **76** ....(b) PaulMulrennan 9 — 69
(M W Easterby) *w ldrs: wknd fnl f* **20/1**

3-35 **6** *hd* **Countdown**[18] [1818] 5-9-4 **78** .... KDarley 1 — 71+
(T D Easterby) *in rr-div on inner: nt clr run over 2f and over 1f out: no ch* **6/1**[3]

5004 **7** *nk* **Charles Darwin (IRE)**[9] [2058] 4-9-13 **87** .... FrancisNorton 4 — 79
(M Blanshard) *w ldrs: led over 1f out: sn hdd & wknd* **5/1**[2]

53-1 **8** *1 1/2* **My Gacho (IRE)**[17] [1852] 5-9-10 **84** ....(b) PhillipMakin 5 — 71
(T D Barron) *trckd ldrs: t.k.h: wknd fnl f* **7/2**[1]

4-04 **9** *1* **Steel Blue**[17] [1852] 7-8-13 **78** .... MichaelJStainton(5) 2 — 62
(R M Whitaker) *led tl hdd & wknd over 1f out* **13/2**

1m 13.09s (0.09) **Going Correction** +0.05s/f (Good) **9 Ran SP% 115.4**
Speed ratings (Par 107):101,100,99,97,93 93,93,91,89
CSF £80.04 CT £775.06 TOTE £5.20: £2.10, £4.20, £2.50; EX 55.00.
Owner R J H Limited **Bred** Gainsborough Stud Management Ltd **Trained** Hambleton, N Yorks

FOCUS
A tight-knit sprint handicap with Trojan Flight and to a lesser extent Countdown robbed of their chance of victory. Desert Commander won a stronger running of this last year when 4lb higher. The race has been rated through the third.

NOTEBOOK
Desert Commander(IRE), in first-time blinkers, repeated his win in this last year when racing off a 4lb higher mark. Official explanation: trainer said, regarding the improved form shown, gelding was suited by wearing blinkers for the first time (op 7-1)
Yorkshire Blue as usual loitered in the rear. Making ground on the wide outside, in the end he was just found lacking. (op 20-1)
Gallery Girl(IRE), 2lb higher, is still potentially very well treated. Following a tardy start and after being forced to pull wide for a run, in the end she was just found wanting. It remains a fact though that her one win was in a maiden at two. (op 8-1)
Trojan Flight, 6lb higher, had no luck at all in running. When he did get racing room it was far too late. Frustrating in the past, he is just the type this trainer does so well with.
Lake Chini(IRE), drawn on the wide outside, has recorded his two career wins on the All-Weather. (op 14-1)
Countdown, dropping back in distance, was twice badly stopped in his run but it is debatable if he possesses the raw speed for a sharp 6f. Official explanation: jockey said gelding was denied a clear run (op 8-1)
My Gacho(IRE), just 1lb higher, saw a lot of daylight on the outer and was simply too keen for his own good. (tchd 4-1)

2340 WEATHERBYS BANK H'CAP — 1m 1f 170y
4:00 (4:00) (Class 4) (0-80,80) 3-Y-0 **£5,047** (£1,510; £755; £377; £188) **Stalls High**

Form RPR

2-01 **1** **Calabash Cove (USA)**[24] [1665] 3-9-7 **80** .... LDettori 7 — 85+
(Saeed Bin Suroor) *led 2f: trckd ldrs: qcknd to ld 4f out: hld on towards fin* **5/2**[2]

2612 **2** *nk* **Tetouan**[14] [1929] 3-9-6 **79** .... RichardHughes 4 — 84+
(R Charlton) *trckd ldrs: chal 4f out: no ex wl ins fnl f* **2/1**[1]

5130 **3** *nk* **New Beginning (IRE)**[20] [1773] 3-9-6 **79** .... PaulHanagan 5 — 83
(Mrs S Lamyman) *hld up: hdwy over 1f out: styd on strly ins fnl f* **11/1**

1-00 **4** *1 1/2* **Sam Lord**[12] [1974] 3-9-6 **79** .... JimmyFortune 2 — 80
(J H M Gosden) *hld up: hdwy to trck ldrs over 5f out: drvn over 3f out: kpt on same pce appr fnl f* **10/1**

0023 **5** *5* **Nota Liberata**[14] [1936] 3-8-7 **66** .... PatCosgrave 8 — 57
(G M Moore) *t.k.h: w ldrs: led after 2f tl 4f out: lost pl over 1f out* **22/1**

0-43 **6** *3/4* **Plane Painter (IRE)**[8] [2092] 3-9-4 **77** .... JoeFanning 3 — 67
(M Johnston) *trckd ldrs: chal over 3f out: wknd appr fnl f* **5/1**[3]

5204 **7** *1 1/2* **Colditz (IRE)**[22] [1708] 3-8-4 **63** .... PaulQuinn 6 — 50
(D W Barker) *s.i.s: t.k.h: sn trcking ldrs: outpcd over 3f out: sn lost pl* **50/1**

44-2 **8** *7* **Ideally (IRE)**[57] [973] 3-8-13 **72** .... MichaelHills 1 — 55+
(B W Hills) *hld up: hdwy on outer over 5f out: chsng ldrs over 3f out: lost pl over 1f out: eased* **13/2**

2m 5.28s (0.28) **Going Correction** +0.05s/f (Good) **8 Ran SP% 115.6**
Speed ratings (Par 101):100,99,99,98,94 93,92,86
CSF £8.03 CT £44.08 TOTE £3.10: £1.40, £1.30, £2.70; EX 8.20.
Owner Godolphin **Bred** Gainsborough Farm Llc **Trained** Newmarket, Suffolk

FOCUS
Just a steady gallop. Fair form, limited by the third and fourth, but with better to come from the first two.

2341 DAVENHAM PROPERTY FINANCE MAIDEN STKS — 1m
4:30 (4:31) (Class 5) 3-Y-O **£3,562** (£1,059; £529; £264) **Stalls High**

Form RPR

3-34 **1** **Costume**[23] [1702] 3-8-12 108 .... RichardHughes 7 — 49+
(J H M Gosden) *mde all: nudged along 1f out: v easily* **1/16**[1]

3 **2** *1 1/4* **Sofie Tucker**[11] [1995] 3-8-12 0 .... DavidAllan 2 — 46+
(T D Easterby) *trckd wnr: upsides 3f out: kpt on: no ch* **12/1**[2]

00-0 **3** *3* **Iced Tango**[38] [1297] 3-9-3 48 .... TomEaves 6 — 44
(F Jordan) *trckd ldrs: one pce fnl 2f* **100/1**

4 *3/4* **Derricks Dotty** 3-9-3 0 .... PaulHanagan 3 — 42
(N J Vaughan) *hld up: kpt on same pce fnl 2f: nvr a threat* **33/1**[3]

00- **5** *nk* **Forsters Plantin**[234] [5959] 3-8-12 0 .... PatCosgrave 4 — 37
(J J Quinn) *trckd ldrs: drvn over 2f out: one pce* **80/1**

U **Sky Chart (IRE)** 3-9-3 0 .... PhillipMakin 1 — —
(N J Vaughan) *s.s: hdwy and prom over 3f out: rdn, swvd bdly lft and uns rdr over 1f out* **33/1**[3]

1m 45.67s (4.57) **Going Correction** +0.05s/f (Good) **6 Ran SP% 109.9**
Speed ratings (Par 99):79,77,74,74,73 —
CSF £1.38 TOTE £1.10: £1.02, £2.30; EX 1.70.
Owner K Abdulla **Bred** Juddmonte Farms Ltd **Trained** Newmarket, Suffolk

FOCUS
A non-event resulting in a pedestrian winning time. Costume had nothing to beat and the form looks unreliable.

2342 HORWATH CLARK WHITEHILL H'CAP — 1m 4f 10y
5:00 (5:00) (Class 5) (0-75,74) 4-Y-0+ **£3,238** (£963; £481; £240) **Stalls High**

Form RPR

4132 **1** **Osolomio (IRE)**[10] [2031] 4-9-6 **73** .... JHBowman 6 — 81+
(G A Swinbank) *led: qcknd over 5f out: edgd lft over 1f out: styd on: readily* **5/4**[1]

63-0 **2** *1 3/4* **Fossgate**[20] [1771] 6-9-7 **74** .... NCallan 5 — 79
(J D Bethell) *trckd wnr: rdn over 2f out: kpt on same pce* **9/1**

00-1 **3** *shd* **Fenners (USA)**[12] [1966] 4-8-10 **63** .... DaleGibson 4 — 68
(M W Easterby) *chsd ldrs: drvn over 6f out: outpcd over 3f out: styd on fnl 2f* **4/1**[2]

-111 **4** *3 1/2* **Court Of Appeal**[28] [1554] 10-8-13 **71** ....(tp) JamieMoriarty(5) 7 — 70
(B Ellison) *s.s: drvn along in rr: kpt on fnl 2f: nvr on terms* **10/1**

44-6 **5** *1* **Platinum Charmer (IRE)**[15] [1890] 7-8-0 **56** oh5 ow1(p) AndrewElliott(3) 3 — 54
(K R Burke) *trckd ldrs: outpcd 3f out: kpt on appr fnl f: nvr a threat* **20/1**

0310 **6** *3* **Sudden Impulse**[20] [1771] 6-9-0 **67** .... TomEaves 1 — 60
(A D Brown) *hld up: pushed along over 5f out: hdwy 3f out: lost pl over 1f out* **5/1**[3]

5052 **7** *2* **Maneki Neko (IRE)**[15] [1890] 5-8-10 **68** .... PJMcDonald(5) 2 — 58
(E W Tuer) *hld up: hdwy to join wnr after 3f: lost pl over 2f out* **8/1**

2m 35.65s (-1.35) **Going Correction** +0.05s/f (Good) **7 Ran SP% 116.1**
Speed ratings (Par 103):106,104,104,102,101 99,98
CSF £14.28 TOTE £2.20: £1.40, £3.60; EX 15.50 Place 6 £ 16.88, Place 5 £ 10.70.
Owner Hokey Cokey Partnership (2) **Bred** Dr T A Ryan **Trained** Melsonby, N Yorks

FOCUS
A fine tactical ride from the front by Hugh Bowman, enjoying his first success at this track. The form looks sound rated through the runner-up.
T/Plt: £44.70 to a £1 stake. Pool: £67,237.65. 1,097.65 winning tickets. T/Qpdt: £18.80 to a £1 stake. Pool: £3,595.70. 141.10 winning tickets. WG

2145 SOUTHWELL (L-H)
Tuesday, June 5

OFFICIAL GOING: Standard
Wind: Cloudy Weather: Fresh across

2343 SOUTHWELL-RACECOURSE.CO.UK CLASSIFIED STKS — 7f (F)
6:40 (6:42) (Class 7) 4-Y-0+ **£1,876** (£554; £277) **Stalls Low**

Form RPR

0360 **1** **Wodhill Schnaps**[6] [2154] 6-9-0 45 ....(b) HayleyTurner 7 — 57+
(D Morris) *sn pushed along in rr: hdwy u.p over 1f out: led ins fnl f: hung rt: styd on* **7/2**[1]

2040 **2** *1 1/2* **Shadow Jumper (IRE)**[50] [1066] 6-8-9 45 ....(v) RoryMoore(5) 5 — 53
(J T Stimpson) *chsd ldr tl led over 2f out: rdn over 1f out: hdd and unable qck ins fnl f* **11/1**

6-03 **3** *3 1/2* **Mister Jingles**[12] [1976] 4-8-9 44 .... MichaelJStainton(5) 8 — 44
(R M Whitaker) *chsd ldrs: rdn over 2f out: styd on same pce appr fnl f* **8/1**

0-00 **4** *3* **Preskani**[28] [1569] 5-9-0 43 ....(p) AlanDaly 13 — 36
(Mrs N Macauley) *mid-div: outpcd 1/2-way: styd on appr fnl f* **20/1**

5030 **5** *shd* **Spy Gun (USA)**[6] [2145] 7-8-7 44 .... JosephWalsh(7) 4 — 36
(T Wall) *chsd ldrs: rdn 1/2-way: no imp fnl 2f* **12/1**

2060 **6** *2 1/2* **Prettilini**[7] [2108] 4-9-0 45 .... SebSanders 6 — 29
(A W Carroll) *mid-div: rdn 1/2-way: wknd over 1f out* **9/2**[2]

0050 **7** *1* **Gem Bien (USA)**[15] [1906] 9-9-0 45 ....(p) PaulMulrennan 9 — 27
(D W Chapman) *sn outpcd: sme hdwy over 1f out: wknd ins fnl f* **12/1**

000 **8** *nk* **Winds Of Kildare (IRE)**[28] [1566] 4-9-0 45 ....(t) PFredericks 1 — 26
(C N Allen) *sn outpcd* **50/1**

-565 **9** *4* **Safranine (IRE)**[1] [2309] 10-8-9 45 .... AnnStokell(5) 10 — 16
(Miss A Stokell) *mid-div: rdn over 3f out: wknd 2f out* **20/1**

0003 **10** *3 1/2* **Titian Saga (IRE)**[22] [1719] 4-8-7 45 AdeleRothery(7) 14 7
(D Nicholls) *led over 4f: wknd over 1f out* **7/1**[3]

0440 **11** *nk* **Piccleyes**[6] [2145] 6-9-0 43 (be) NeilPollard 11 6
(A J McCabe) *s.s: hdwy 1/2-way: wknd over 2f out* **10/1**

340- **12** *1* **Suhezy (IRE)**[278] [4943] 4-9-0 44 TonyHamilton 12 3
(J S Wainwright) *chsd ldrs 5f* **22/1**

000- **13** *7* **Bahhmirage (IRE)**[301] [4223] 4-9-0 45 (bt) SamHitchcott 3 —
(C N Kellett) *s.s: outpcd* **50/1**

2654 **14** *10* **A Teen**[57] [978] 9-9-0 45 JoeFanning 2 —
(P Howling) *sn outpcd* **9/1**

1m 29.26s (-1.54) **Going Correction** -0.225s/f (Stan) **14** Ran SP% **124.6**
Speed ratings (Par 97):99,97,93,89,89 86,85,85,80,76 76,75,67,55
CSF £41.70 TOTE £3.80: £1.50, £4.30, £2.80; EX 73.30.
Owner Miss S Graham **Bred** Wodhill Stud **Trained** Newmarket, Suffolk

FOCUS
A poor race, but at least the pace was solid throughout and they finished well spread out. Wodhill Schnaps finally delivered, while it has been a long time since the runner-up rated this high.
Suhezy(IRE) Official explanation: jockey said filly had no more to give
Bahhmirage(IRE) Official explanation: jockey said filly would not face the blinkers

2344 RACING AGAIN ON 21ST MAIDEN FILLIES' STKS 6f (F)
7:10 (7:11) (Class 5) 2-Y-O **£3,238** (£963; £481; £240) **Stalls** Low

Form RPR

2 **1** **Bastakiya (IRE)**[13] [1945] 2-9-0 0 JimmyFortune 11 90+
(J H M Gosden) *trckd ldr: led on bit over 1f out: shkn up and sn clr* **1/2**[1]

06 **2** *11* **Twilight Belle (IRE)**[12] [1960] 2-9-0 0 (b1) PaulEddery 5 57
(B J Meehan) *sn led: rdn and hdd over 1f out: wknd ins fnl f* **4/1**[2]

0 **3** *2* **Suite Francaise**[11] [1989] 2-9-0 0 SebSanders 2 51
(Sir Mark Prescott) *hld up: shkn up over 1f out: nvr nr to chal* **9/1**[3]

4 *hd* **Bohobe (IRE)** 2-9-0 0 HayleyTurner 9 50
(J G Given) *chsd ldrs: rdn over 2f out: wknd over 1f out* **20/1**

0 **5** *nk* **Marmite (IRE)**[29] [1533] 2-8-11 0 SaleemGolam(3) 7 50
(E F Vaughan) *chsd ldrs: lost pl over 4f out: n.d after* **40/1**

0 **6** *3/4* **Magnol**[8] [2086] 2-9-0 0 MatthewHenry 4 47+
(M A Jarvis) *s.s: outpcd: styd on ins fnl f* **14/1**

7 *1 1/4* **Bookiebasher Babe (IRE)** 2-9-0 0 SamHitchcott 10 44
(M Quinn) *prom: rdn over 3f out: wknd over 1f out: hung lft ins fnl f* **33/1**

8 *1 1/4* **Nice Dream** 2-9-0 0 JoeFanning 6 40
(C E Brittain) *chsd ldrs: rdn over 2f out: wknd over 1f out* **12/1**

00 **9** *7* **Jolly Tipsy**[12] [1963] 2-9-0 0 PaulMulrennan 1 19
(M W Easterby) *chsd ldrs: rdn over 3f out: wknd over 1f out* **100/1**

00 **10** *hd* **Lady Grantley**[6] [2147] 2-8-7 0 NSLawes(7) 3 18
(M W Easterby) *s.i.s: outpcd* **100/1**

1m 16.0s (-0.90) **Going Correction** -0.225s/f (Stan) **10** Ran SP% **123.1**
Speed ratings (Par 90):97,82,79,79,79 78,76,74,65,65
CSF £2.92 TOTE £1.40: £1.02, £1.20, £3.50; EX 2.90.
Owner H R H Princess Haya Of Jordan **Bred** Old Carhue Stud **Trained** Newmarket, Suffolk
■ Stewards' Enquiry : Sam Hitchcott one-day ban: used whip with excessive force (Jun 16)

FOCUS
As uncompetitive a maiden as you can get, but the favourite could hardly have done much more and the time was solid. She could have been rated as high as the mid 90s but a conservative view has been taken. The beaten horses will need to improve a huge amount if they are to win races.

NOTEBOOK
Bastakiya(IRE), beaten a nostril on her Lingfield debut, hacked her way around before tearing these rivals apart over the last furlong or so and probably worked harder going down to the start. The quality of the opposition almost certainly made this look better than it was, but to be fair the time was fair enough and best of her is still to be seen. (op 8-15 tchd 8-13)
Twilight Belle(IRE), who attracted market support on this switch to sand after finishing unplaced in two turf maidens, was given a positive ride in the first-time blinkers but it was obvious from a long way out that the favourite was several classes above her. Although she was still good enough to hang on for second, she may not have achieved that much and she may not be easy to place unless connections decide to drop her in grade. (op 13-2 tchd 7-1 and 7-2)
Suite Francaise plugged on to make the frame, but probably did not step up much from her turf debut. Her pedigree is all stamina though, so the best of her will not be seen until she is handicapped and stepped right up in trip. (op 10-1 tchd 11-1)
Bohobe(IRE), a half-sister to three winners, did best of the newcomers though that is not saying a great deal in this contest. Her breeding suggests that she would not get much further than this. (op 12-1)
Marmite(IRE), last on her debut, did not achieve that much more here. (op 33-1)
Magnol seemed to hate the soft ground on her turf debut and appeared to be hating this surface too, including the kickback. In a race where it is hard to find too much encouragement amongst the also-rans, she could be an exception and may be capable of a bit more when tried on a sound surface back on grass. Official explanation: jockey said filly was slowly into stride (op 10-1)
Bookiebasher Babe(IRE) Official explanation: jockey said filly hung left in final stages

2345 CORRUGATED CASE CO. 10TH ANNIVERSARY H'CAP 1m 6f (F)
7:40 (7:41) (Class 6) (0-50,54) 4-Y-O+ **£2,388** (£705; £352) **Stalls** Low

Form RPR

53-3 **1** **Orchard House (FR)**[35] [1376] 4-8-5 50 (b) GihanArnolda(7) 11 61
(J Jay) *s.i.s: hld up: hdwy over 3f out: led over 1f out: rdn and hung lft ins fnl f: styd on* **9/1**

3611 **2** *1* **Silver Mont (IRE)**[4] [2204] 4-9-2 54 6ex (b) PaulEddery 7 63
(S R Bowring) *s.i.s: hld up: hmpd over 4f out: hdwy u.p over 1f out: chsng wnr ins fnl f: styd on* **15/8**[1]

12/5 **3** *3 1/2* **Toledo Sun**[14] [1934] 7-8-8 46 oh1 AlanDaly 8 50
(S Curran) *a.p: chsd ldr over 4f out: rdn to ld over 3f out: hdd over 1f out: no ex ins fnl f* **28/1**

0664 **4** *5* **Piccolomini**[15] [1895] 5-8-8 46 oh1 (b) TonyHamilton 3 43
(E W Tuer) *led: rdn and hdd over 3f out: wknd over 1f out* **16/1**

0306 **5** *hd* **Lady Suffragette (IRE)**[14] [615] 4-8-5 46 oh1 SaleemGolam(3) 12 43
(John Berry) *hld up: hdwy 6f out: rdn over 2f out: wknd fnl f* **16/1**

00-0 **6** *1* **Squiffy**[20] [1764] 4-8-12 50 SebSanders 10 46
(P D Cundell) *hld up: hdwy over 3f out: sn rdn: wknd over 1f out* **7/2**[2]

0303 **7** *3/4* **Cragganmore Creek**[14] [1934] 4-8-8 46 oh1 (b) HayleyTurner 2 41
(D Morris) *prom: racd keenly: rdn over 3f out: wknd over 1f out* **6/1**[3]

0365 **8** *8* **Montecristo**[36] [1362] 14-8-8 46 oh1 NeilPollard 1 29
(Rae Guest) *s.i.s: hld up: wknd over 3f out* **33/1**

0466 **9** *3* **Red River Rock (IRE)**[34] [1402] 5-8-8 46 oh1 (be) TomEaves 5 25
(T J Fitzgerald) *prom: racd keenly: n.m.r and lost pl over 4f out: wknd over 3f out* **7/1**

/0-0 **10** *nk* **Wavertree One Off**[15] [1888] 5-8-12 50 DaleGibson 6 29
(J Ryan) *hld up in tch: racd keenly: wknd over 3f out* **25/1**

000- **11** *19* **Thou Shalt Not**[223] [6177] 4-8-8 46 oh1 MatthewHenry 9 —
(P S Felgate) *chsd ldrs: rdn over 3f out: sn wknd: eased fnl 2f* **80/1**

00/0 **12** *30* **Reason (IRE)**[5] [2176] 9-8-8 46 oh1 PaulMulrennan 4 —
(D W Chapman) *chsd ldr tl rdn over 4f out: sn wknd: eased fnl 3f* **50/1**

3m 9.22s (-0.38) **Going Correction** -0.225s/f (Stan) **12** Ran SP% **119.0**
Speed ratings (Par 101):92,91,89,86,86 85,85,80,79,79 68,51
CSF £25.34 CT £475.45 TOTE £9.20: £2.00, £2.00, £7.10; EX 54.20.
Owner The Snell Brothers **Bred** J Jay **Trained** Newmarket, Suffolk
■ Stewards' Enquiry : Alan Daly caution: used whip without allowing time for response
Gihan Arnolda two-day ban: used whip in the incorrect place without giving gelding time to respond (Jun 16-17)

FOCUS
They went no pace at all for much of this staying contest which resulted in a very moderate winning time. Despite that, the front pair came from off the pace and were in fact last and last-but-one with a circuit to race. With all bar four out of the weights even at this low level, this was a weak race.

2346 SOUTHWELL-RACECOURSE.CO.UK H'CAP 1m (F)
8:10 (8:10) (Class 4) (0-85,84) 4-Y-O+ **£4,857** (£1,445; £722; £360) **Stalls** Low

Form RPR

20-4 **1** **Yakimov (USA)**[21] [1751] 8-9-3 80 VinceSlattery 6 93+
(D J Wintle) *trckd ldrs: led 2f out: sn rdn and edgd rt: r.o: eased towards fin* **12/1**

5511 **2** *2* **Stolen Glance**[5] [2169] 4-8-3 66 6ex DaleGibson 2 74
(M W Easterby) *prom: drvn along thrght: styd on ins fnl f: nt trble wnr* **5/2**[1]

-004 **3** *1 1/4* **Nevada Desert (IRE)**[14] [1915] 7-9-0 82 MichaelJStainton(5) 1 87
(R M Whitaker) *chsd ldrs: rdn over 1f out: no ex ins fnl f* **7/2**[3]

2023 **4** *1/2* **Orpen Wide (IRE)**[5] [2189] 5-8-12 78 (b) GregFairley(3) 4 82
(M C Chapman) *chsd ldrs: hrd rdn fr over 3f out: ev ch 2f out: no ex fnl f* **7/2**[3]

110- **5** *3 1/2* **Secret Liaison**[274] [5070] 4-9-7 84 SebSanders 3 80
(Sir Mark Prescott) *led 6f: wknd fnl f* **3/1**[2]

0 **6** *10* **Kaballero (GER)**[14] [1915] 6-9-3 80 TomEaves 5 53
(S Gollings) *dwlt: hdwy over 3f out: wknd over 2f out* **20/1**

1m 41.48s (-3.12) **Going Correction** -0.225s/f (Stan) **6** Ran SP% **110.5**
Speed ratings (Par 105):106,104,102,102,98 88
CSF £40.73 TOTE £12.30: £3.80, £1.90; EX 37.80.
Owner B E T Partnership **Bred** Jane & Jeff Wooder **Trained** Naunton, Gloucs

FOCUS
A decent little handicap run a good pace and all six runners made for the stands'-side half of the track after turning in. It is a long time since the winner rated this high.
Kaballero(GER) Official explanation: jockey said gelding hung right throughout

2347 LADIES DAY IS 19TH AUGUST H'CAP 7f (F)
8:40 (8:40) (Class 4) (0-80,78) 4-Y-O+ **£4,857** (£1,445; £722; £360) **Stalls** Low

Form RPR

0133 **1** **Indian's Feather (IRE)**[12] [1979] 6-8-11 68 TomEaves 6 77
(N Tinkler) *chsd ldrs: led 1f out: r.o wl* **4/1**

4-02 **2** *5* **Rosein**[12] [1977] 5-9-7 78 SebSanders 3 76+
(Mrs G S Rees) *chsd ldrs: led over 5f out: hdd over 3f out: led again 2f out: hdd 1f out: styd on same pce ins fnl f* **9/4**[1]

0052 **3** *3 1/2* **Pawan (IRE)**[6] [2139] 7-8-12 74 (b) AnnStokell(5) 2 61
(Miss A Stokell) *s.i.s: sn chsng ldrs: led over 3f out: rdn and hdd 2f out: wknd fnl f* **7/2**[3]

1215 **4** *1/2* **Union Jack Jackson (IRE)**[13] [1947] 5-8-2 62 (b) AndrewElliott(3) 1 48
(John A Harris) *led: hdd over 5f out: rdn over 2f out: wknd fnl f* **10/3**[2]

5/1- **5** *6* **Amorist (IRE)**[159] [223] 5-9-3 74 TonyHamilton 4 44
(J Howard Johnson) *chsd ldrs: hung rt: lost pl over 4f out: wknd over 3f out* **8/1**

1m 28.95s (-1.85) **Going Correction** -0.225s/f (Stan) **5** Ran SP% **107.2**
Speed ratings (Par 105):101,95,91,90,83
CSF £12.61 TOTE £6.00: £2.70, £1.60; EX 14.40.
Owner James Marshall & Mrs Susan Marshall **Bred** The Duke Of Roxburghe's Stud, Beckhampton House St **Trained** Langton, N Yorks

FOCUS
Just the five runners and the pace was ordinary. The way the contest unfolded rather confirmed the impression of the previous race, that it was an advantage to come over towards the stands' side in the home straight. A race that probably did not take much winning.
Amorist(IRE) Official explanation: vet said gelding was lame

2348 BOOK TICKETS ON-LINE H'CAP 1m 3f (F)
9:10 (9:10) (Class 5) (0-70,68) 4-Y-O+ **£3,238** (£963; £481; £240) **Stalls** Low

Form RPR

3300 **1** **Mahmjra**[10] [2047] 5-9-7 68 EdwardCreighton 4 82
(C N Allen) *chsd ldr tl led over 4f out: rdn clr fr over 1f out: eased towards fin* **5/2**[1]

20-0 **2** *7* **Exit To Luck (GER)**[11] [1997] 6-9-3 64 TomEaves 3 66
(S Gollings) *sn pushed along in rr: hdwy over 7f out: outpcd over 4f out: styd on appr fnl f: no ch w wnr* **16/1**

5012 **3** *7* **Starcross Maid**[12] [1980] 5-8-12 59 SebSanders 5 49
(J F Coupland) *hld up: hdwy 6f out: chsd wnr over 3f out: sn rdn: wknd over 1f out* **11/4**[2]

-026 **4** *3* **Surdoue**[12] [1980] 7-8-4 51 (p) HayleyTurner 1 36
(D Morris) *led: hdd over 4f out: sn rdn: wknd over 2f out: hung rt ins fnl f* **10/1**

3604 **5** *2 1/2* **Kumakawa**[6] [2145] 9-7-13 49 (b) DuranFentiman(3) 2 30
(N P Littmoden) *hld up: bhd fr 1/2-way* **8/1**[3]

6-40 **6** *1 1/4* **Musical Giant (USA)**[12] [1967] 4-8-3 50 (b1) DaleGibson 7 29
(J Howard Johnson) *chsd ldrs over 7f* **20/1**

0441 **7** *10* **Newtonian (USA)**[12] [1980] 8-9-6 67 (p) JoeFanning 6 29
(M Brittain) *chsd ldrs: rdn and lost pl over 4f out: wknd over 3f out* **5/2**[1]

2m 25.26s (-3.64) **Going Correction** -0.225s/f (Stan) **7** Ran SP% **114.7**
Speed ratings (Par 103):104,98,93,91,89 88,81
CSF £41.44 TOTE £6.10: £2.40, £8.50; EX 58.90 Place 6 £ 34.24, Place 5 £ 14.36.
Owner Travel Spot Ltd **Bred** Darley **Trained** Newmarket, Suffolk

FOCUS
Thanks to a contested lead between Mahmjra and Surdoue, this race was run at a decent pace and they finished very well spread out. An improved effort from Mahmjra, who has a good record here.
Newtonian(USA) Official explanation: vet said gelding was lame
T/Plt: £30.60 to a £1 stake. Pool: £63,902.40. 1,523.45 winning tickets. T/Qpdt: £21.50 to a £1 stake. Pool: £3,941.00. 135.50 winning tickets. CR

[1586]KEMPTON (A.W) (R-H)

Wednesday, June 6

OFFICIAL GOING: Standard

It proved hard to make up significant amounts of ground, with the track appearing to favour those who raced prominently.

Wind: Moderate, across Weather: Fine becoming overcast

2349 CAMEL AND PIG RACING MEDIAN AUCTION MAIDEN STKS 5f (P)

6:10 (6:12) (Class 6) 2-Y-O £2,047 (£604; £302) Stalls High

Form				RPR
232	1		**Concertmaster**[38] [1315] 2-9-3 0 .... SebSanders 11 (R M Beckett) *mde all: drvn over 1f out: hung lft but kpt on wl fnl f* **5/2**[1]	81
3	2	1 1/4	**Rio Princess (IRE)**[19] [1807] 2-8-12 0 .... DaneO'Neill 7 (T G Mills) *chsd wnr: drvn over 1f out: nt qckn and hld fnl f* **13/2**	72
0	3	3/4	**Fortuity (IRE)**[12] [1990] 2-9-3 0 .... JimmyFortune 6 (J H M Gosden) *sn chsd ldng pair: rdn and outpcd wl over 1f out: kpt on fnl f* **13/2**	74
625	4	1	**Avertitop**[36] [1367] 2-9-3 0 .... RichardHughes 4 (R Hannon) *pushed along to chse ldrs and nt on terms: styd on fr over 1f out: nrst fin* **9/2**[3]	70
0	5	1/2	**Choisky (IRE)**[21] [1762] 2-9-3 0 .... JimmyQuinn 1 (J Akehurst) *off the pce in midfield: pushed along and styd on steadily fr over 1f out: nrst fin* **40/1**	68+
	6	1 1/2	**Little Knickers** 2-8-9 0 .... SaleemGolam(3) 10 (D K Ivory) *dwlt: off the pce in rr and racd wd: sme prog whn sltly impeded and rn green 1f out: kpt on* **33/1**	58+
6	7	hd	**Dome Rock (IRE)**[15] [1919] 2-9-3 0 .... NickyMackay 8 (L M Cumani) *off the pce in midfield: sme prog over 1f out: shkn up and no imp fnl f* **10/3**[2]	62+
33	8	1/2	**Iamagrey (IRE)**[8] [2122] 2-8-12 0 .... LPKeniry 3 (J S Moore) *sn in 4th: outpcd 2f out: wknd jst over 1f out* **9/1**	55
	9	1 1/2	**Gross Prophet** 2-9-3 0 .... EdwardCreighton 5 (Tom Dascombe) *s.s: outpcd in last pair: nvr a factor* **50/1**	55
	10	6	**Connor's Choice** 2-9-3 0 .... SamHitchcott 12 (Andrew Turnell) *awkward s: outpcd and a in last trio* **33/1**	33
0	11	1	**Planet Paradise (IRE)**[23] [1727] 2-8-12 0 .... SimonWhitworth 2 (D Shaw) *s.i.s: chsd clr ldrs for 3f: wknd rapidly* **66/1**	25

61.84 secs (1.44) **Going Correction** +0.05s/f (Slow) 11 Ran SP% **118.3**
Speed ratings (Par 91):90,88,86,85,84 82,81,80,78,68 67
CSF £18.84 TOTE £3.40: £1.20, £2.60, £2.30; EX 17.90.

Owner The Millennium Madness Partnership **Bred** B Whitehouse **Trained** Whitsbury, Hants

FOCUS
A funny race, with a few of these seemingly failing to up to form, and it looked just a fair maiden at best. Slight improvement from the winner.

NOTEBOOK
Concertmaster had the best of draw and took full advantage, appearing to improve slightly on his previous efforts. (op 4-1 tchd 9-4)
Rio Princess(IRE) was third at Newbury on her debut in what looked a hot race at the time, but she failed to build on that in this lesser contest and did not look at home on this tight track. (op 7-2 tchd 7-1)
Fortuity(IRE) improved on the form he showed on his debut at Goodwood and seems to be going the right way. (op 11-1)
Avertitop again failed to run up to the form he showed when a close second at Windsor on his second career start and is not progressing. (op 5-1)
Choisky(IRE) had the worst of the draw but he still managed to improve markedly on the form he showed on his debut at Bath. He gave the impression he can progress again. (op 33-1)
Little Knickers, the first foal of a 7f winner, showed some ability on her racecourse debut, despite meeting trouble over a furlong out, and should improve.
Dome Rock(IRE) failed to build on his debut effort at Leicester and has to be considered disappointing. (op 11-4)
Iamagrey(IRE) was well below the form she had shown when filling third on both her previous starts and was disappointing. (op 8-1)

2350 BUGLER DEVELOPMENTS H'CAP 5f (P)

6:40 (6:42) (Class 5) (0-70,69) 3-Y-O+ £2,914 (£867; £433; £216) Stalls High

Form				RPR
2232	1		**What Do You Know**[12] [1991] 4-9-11 **67** .... RichardHughes 1 (A M Hales) *wl away fr wd draw: pressed ldr: led 1f out: rdn and sn in command* **7/2**[1]	79
2442	2	1 1/2	**Willhewiz**[16] [1885] 7-9-8 **64** .... JimmyFortune 3 (M S Saunders) *fast away fr wd draw: led: rdn and hdd 1f out: one pce* **7/1**	71
-055	3	nk	**Musical Script (USA)**[12] [1991] 4-9-4 **60** .... JimmyQuinn 12 (Mouse Hamilton-Fairley) *chsd ldrs: effrt to go 3rd jst over 1f out: styd on same pce u.p* **6/1**	66
4-60	4	1/2	**Heavens Walk**[26] [1630] 6-9-13 **69** .... (t) SebSanders 11 (P J Makin) *stdd s: settled in rr: effrt and prog to chse ldrs 1f out: one pce fina 150yds* **11/2**[3]	73
0-50	5	3/4	**Duke Of Milan (IRE)**[44] [1200] 4-9-6 **62** .... PatDobbs 5 (G C Bravery) *hld up in detached last: effrt 1f out: pushed along and styd on: hopeless task* **14/1**	63
0130	6	shd	**Monte Major (IRE)**[12] [1991] 6-9-3 **59** .... (v) DaneO'Neill 6 (D Shaw) *towards rr: drvn on outer 2f out: kpt on fnl f but no ch* **10/1**	60
603	7	1/2	**Mambazo**[14] [1946] 5-9-2 **58** .... (e) AdamKirby 8 (S C Williams) *chsd ldrs: drvn 2f out: one pce over 1f out* **4/1**[2]	57
2050	8	hd	**Pride Of Joy**[12] [1991] 4-9-4 **60** .... JimCrowley 10 (D K Ivory) *in tch in rr: rdn over 1f out: no prog* **14/1**	58
06-0	9	1/2	**Clipper Hoy**[100] [566] 5-9-3 **62** .... RichardKingscote(3) 9 (Mrs H Sweeting) *chsd ldng pair to jst over 1f out: fdd* **33/1**	58

60.70 secs (0.30) **Going Correction** +0.05s/f (Slow) 9 Ran SP% **109.8**
Speed ratings (Par 103):99,96,96,95,94 93,93,92,92
CSF £25.55 CT £121.67 TOTE £4.70: £1.20, £2.50, £2.30; EX 18.00.

Owner Brick Farm Racing **Bred** C G Reid **Trained** Preston Capes, Northants

FOCUS
A modest sprint handicap and, as was the general theme for the evening, it proved hard to make up significant amounts of ground. Fair form for the grade, and solid enough, with a personal best from the winner.

2351 SPILLERS REDFERN H'CAP 1m 2f (P)

7:10 (7:10) (Class 3) (0-95,95) 4-Y-O+

£6,855 (£2,052; £1,026; £513; £256; £128) Stalls High

Form				RPR
/43-	1		**Familiar Territory**[284] [4805] 4-9-7 **95** .... KerrinMcEvoy 7 (Saeed Bin Suroor) *t.k.h: trckd ldng pair: wnt 2nd 2f out: rdn to ld over 1f out: grad asserted fnl f* **9/4**[1]	105+
65-4	2	1/2	**Bandama (IRE)**[32] [1477] 4-9-7 **95** .... JimCrowley 12 (Mrs A J Perrett) *trckd ldr: led jst over 2f out: rdn and hdd over 1f out: pressed wnr but hld last 100yds* **9/2**[3]	104
21	3	1/2	**Cedar Mountain (IRE)**[29] [1566] 4-9-0 **88** .... JimmyFortune 10 (J H M Gosden) *chsd ldrs: drvn and effrt on inner wl over 1f out: styd on but nvr quite able to chal* **7/2**[2]	96+
10-0	4	hd	**Ogee**[32] [1477] 4-8-8 **89** .... JamieHamblett(7) 4 (Sir Michael Stoute) *hld up towards rr: effrt on inner whn hmpd and lost pl 2f out: r.o fnl f: nt rcvr* **9/1**	99+
-140	5	2	**I Have Dreamed (IRE)**[42] [1244] 5-8-11 **85** .... (p) DaneO'Neill 5 (T G Mills) *settled towards rr: prog on outer and rdn over 2f out: chsd ldrs over 1f out: one pce after* **12/1**	89
-000	6	hd	**Counsel's Opinion (IRE)**[42] [1245] 10-9-2 **90** .... GeorgeBaker 1 (C F Wall) *hld up in midfield: prog on outer to chse ldrs 4f out: rdn 3f out: one pce fnl 2f* **25/1**	93
2-11	7	2 1/2	**William's Way**[36] [1385] 5-8-12 **86** .... SebSanders 8 (I A Wood) *stdd s: hld up in last pair: gng wl enough 2f out: pushed along and sme prog over 1f out: nvr nr ldrs* **14/1**	84
0136	8	nk	**Weightless**[35] [1393] 7-9-4 **92** .... TedDurcan 6 (N P Littmoden) *settled midfield: pushed along 1/2-way: hanging u.p bnd 3f out: no prog over 1f out* **16/1**	90
4550	9	1	**Atlantic Quest (USA)**[96] [608] 8-8-8 **82** .... AmirQuinn 3 (Miss Venetia Williams) *racd on outer in rr: rdn 3f out: struggling wl over 1f out* **33/1**	78
43-5	10	2	**Bobby Charles**[140] [164] 6-8-4 **78** .... RichardMullen 9 (Dr J D Scargill) *awkward s: racd in last pair: drvn over 2f out: no prog* **11/1**	70
000-	11	13	**Chancellor (IRE)**[159] [6336] 9-9-2 **90** .... (t) DarryllHolland 11 (D K Ivory) *in tch tl dropped to last wl over 3f out: sn t.o* **50/1**	56
0244	12	shd	**Tufton**[33] [1449] 4-9-1 **89** .... (t) PaulDoe 13 (M Botti) *racd v freely in ld: hdd & wknd rapidly jst over 2f out: t.o* **16/1**	54

2m 6.99s (-2.01) **Going Correction** +0.05s/f (Slow) 12 Ran SP% **124.4**
Speed ratings (Par 107):110,109,109,109,107 107,105,105,104,102 92,92
CSF £12.69 CT £36.71 TOTE £3.60: £1.60, £2.10, £1.60; EX 17.30.

Owner Godolphin **Bred** P And Mrs Venner **Trained** Newmarket, Suffolk

FOCUS
A good handicap and the form looks strong, even allowing for the track favouring those who raced handily. There should be more to come from the winner.

NOTEBOOK
Familiar Territory is very lightly raced, but it was interesting such a powerful stable were prepared to persevere with him, and he justified that decision with a very useful effort on his seasonal return/Polytrack debut. He was made to work quite hard, but he gave the impression this run will bring him on plenty and he is likely to go on from this. (op 3-1 tchd 10-3)
Bandama(IRE) looked to produce a career-best effort in defeat. He will go back up in the weights for this, but his connections have clearly not got to the bottom of his just yet. (op 11-2 tchd 6-1)
Cedar Mountain(IRE) ◆ was a real unknown quantity coming into this off the back of an easy success in a weak Southwell maiden, but he showed himself very useful at the very least with a solid effort in defeat. This was only his third career start and there really should be more to come. (op 10-3)
Ogee ◆ fared best of those held up and would have been even closer had he not been hampered by the weakening Tufton on the turn for home. This was a big improvement on the form he showed first time up this season and he appears to be on the way back. Official explanation: jockey said gelding suffered interference in running (op 8-1)
I Have Dreamed(IRE) ran a respectable race in first-time cheekpieces and helps give the form a solid look. (op 11-1)
Counsel's Opinion(IRE) has dropped to a reasonable mark and hinted that he might be able to find a similar race at some point this year.
William's Way had no easy task bidding for the hat-trick off an 8lb higher mark than when winning at Wolverhampton on his previous start, but things did not fall his way in any case and he is better than he showed. Having been held up on a track suiting those who raced prominently, he was short of room both on the home bend and around a furlong out. (op 12-1)
Tufton Official explanation: jockey said colt ran too free

2352 DIGIBET ACHILLES STKS (LISTED RACE) 5f (P)

7:40 (7:43) (Class 1) 3-Y-O+

£14,762 (£5,595; £2,800; £1,396; £699; £351) Stalls High

Form				RPR
-354	1		**Dazed And Amazed**[31] [1502] 3-8-10 94 .... RichardHughes 5 (R Hannon) *chsd ldng pair: wnt 2nd 2f out: led over 1f out: drvn out* **12/1**	102
25-2	2	1	**Intrepid Jack**[18] [1836] 5-9-3 100 .... JimmyFortune 6 (H Morrison) *hmpd after 100yds and sn last: taken wd and rapid prog jst over 1f out: r.o wl to snatch 2nd on post* **9/4**[1]	102+
2611	3	hd	**Rowe Park**[12] [1986] 4-9-3 91 .... LPKeniry 3 (Mrs L C Jewell) *chsd ldrs: drvn and nt qckn wl over 1f out: styd on to chse wnr ins fnl f: no imp: lost 2nd last stride* **8/1**	101
1040	4	1/2	**Border Music**[13] [1971] 6-9-7 103 .... (b) FrancisNorton 10 (A M Balding) *n.m.r after 100yds: sn in tch: prog wl over 1f out: disp 2nd ins fnl f: kpt on same pce* **15/2**[3]	103
0616	5	1	**Classic Encounter (IRE)**[12] [1986] 4-9-3 92 .... FergusSweeney 4 (D M Simcock) *racd wd: chsd ldrs: effrt over 1f out: one pce fnl f* **25/1**	96
/502	6	1/2	**Baron's Pit**[11] [2022] 7-9-3 102 .... (b) TedDurcan 9 (E F Vaughan) *n.m.r after 100yds: sn in midfield: sltly outpcd 1/2-way: drvn and prog over 1f out: kpt on same pce after* **9/2**[2]	94
00-3	7	1/2	**Empress Jain**[36] [1372] 4-8-12 92 .... PhilipRobinson 12 (M A Jarvis) *led at str pce to over 1f out: wknd fnl f* **8/1**	87
55-6	8	1	**Elhamri**[35] [1394] 3-8-10 103 .... MartinDwyer 1 (S Kirk) *settled wl in rr: wd and off the pce 2f out: shuffled along and kpt on steadily* **15/2**[3]	85
4-00	9	6	**Biniou (IRE)**[24] [1704] 4-9-3 105 .... RichardMullen 2 (R M H Cowell) *sltly hmpd after 100yds: wl in rr: prog on inner wl over 1f out: drvn and wknd 1f out* **25/1**	67
0-46	10	2 1/2	**Cav Okay (IRE)**[31] [1502] 3-8-10 92 .... DaneO'Neill 11 (R Hannon) *pressed ldr tl hung lft and wd bnd 2f out: sn wknd* **20/1**	55

416/ **11** *3* **Playful**[628] 5261 4-8-12 92 SebSanders 7 42
(R M Beckett) *v awkward after 1f and dropped to rr: bhd fnl 2f* **28/1**

59.85 secs (-0.55) **Going Correction** +0.05s/f (Slow)
WFA 3 from 4yo+ 7lb **11** Ran SP% **118.3**
Speed ratings (Par 111):106,104,104,103,101 100,100,98,88,84 80
CSF £37.68 TOTE £15.80: £3.10, £1.60, £2.70; EX 54.10.
Owner Mrs R Ablett **Bred** Whitsbury Manor Stud And Pigeon House Stud **Trained** East Everleigh, Wilts
■ Intoxicating was withdrawn (66/1, refused to enter stalls.)
■ Stewards' Enquiry : Richard Hughes three-day ban: careless riding (Jun 17,18,24)

FOCUS
Once more it paid to race up with the pace. A controversial race with Dazed And Amazed keeping the race after hampering the unlucky Intrepid Jack early on. A clear personal best from the winner, but this is pretty ordinary Listed form.

NOTEBOOK
Dazed And Amazed, who showed he acted on this surface when third here in April, recorded his second Listed success. The drop back to 5f did not trouble him and he won with a bit to spare, although he had to survive an enquiry after an early incident involving the runner-up. This was a good performance by a three-year-old taking on his elders. (op 16-1)
Intrepid Jack ◆, back down to the minimum trip, was an unlucky loser. Finding himself in last place after the eventual winner edged across him in the first half-furlong, he had an awful lot to do on straightening up but ran on very strongly down the outside for second. One consolation for this defeat is that he escapes a penalty for the Wokingham, for which he should be on the shortlist. (tchd 2-1 and 5-2 in a place)
Rowe Park has made rapid improvement in recent months, both on Polytrack and turf, and he acquitted himself with credit on this Listed debut, only deprived of second on the line. He should continue to progress. (op 15-2)
Border Music, who was involved in a bumping match with Baron's Pit early on, is most effective over an extra furlong and this was a creditable effort. (tchd 9-1)
Classic Encounter(IRE), unable to get to the front this time, tried to close down the leaders in the straight but the effort flattened out in the final furlong.
Baron's Pit had the blinkers back on for the first time this year. Caught up in jostling for room with Border Music early on, he did make headway in the straight but in truth was never close enough to mount a challenge. (op 8-1)
Empress Jain showed bags of pace on this Polytrack debut but could not hold on in the straight. (op 6-1 tchd 11-2)
Elhamri was never a factor on this Polytrack debut but was keeping on at the end. It is a bit early to be writing him off at this stage. (op 8-1)

2353 DIGIBET SPORTS BETTING E B F NOVICE STKS 6f (P)
8:10 (8:14) (Class 4) 2-Y-O **£5,181** (£1,541; £770; £384) **Stalls** High

Form RPR
5210 **1** **Cee Bargara**[4] 2232 2-9-5 0 JimCrowley 4 92
(J A Osborne) *mde virtually all: rdn and hung across crse to end up on nr side rail 1f out: r.o wl* **8/1**
3 **2** *2* **Dream Eater (IRE)**[12] 1990 2-8-12 0 LPKeniry 9 79
(A M Balding) *chsd ldng pair: wnt 2nd 2f out: followed wnr by hanging bdly lft across trck after: kpt on but no imp* **13/2**
53 **3** *1 1/2* **Master Chef (IRE)**[18] 1846 2-8-12 0 JimmyFortune 5 75
(J H M Gosden) *settled in tch: shkn up and nt qckn 2f out: kpt on fnl f to take 3rd nr fin* **15/8**[1]
064 **4** *nk* **Higgy's Boy (IRE)**[12] 1990 2-8-12 0 RichardHughes 8 74
(R Hannon) *in tch: rdn to chse ldng pair fnl f: no imp: lost 3rd nr fin* **20/1**
0 **5** *1 1/2* **Seeking The Star (CAN)**[11] 2041 2-8-12 0 MartinDwyer 10 69
(D M Simcock) *hld up in rr: prog over 1f out: one pce fnl f* **33/1**
6 *2 1/2* **Captain Royale (IRE)** 2-8-12 0 SebSanders 6 62
(J Noseda) *green and awkward towards rr over 4f out: effrt on outer over 2f out: outpcd over 1f out* **9/2**[3]
315 **7** *2* **Dan Tucket**[22] 1743 2-9-2 0 DarryllHolland 7 60
(M R Channon) *hld up in last in modly run event: pushed along fnl 2f: nvr on terms* **10/1**
53 **8** *3* **Mansii**[31] 1498 2-8-12 0 KerrinMcEvoy 3 47
(C E Brittain) *chsd wnr to 2f out: wknd* **4/1**[2]

1m 13.61s (-0.09) **Going Correction** +0.05s/f (Slow) **8** Ran SP% **114.2**
Speed ratings (Par 95):102,99,97,96,94 91,88,84
CSF £58.39 TOTE £9.20: £2.40, £1.80, £1.20; EX 68.20.
Owner A Taylor **Bred** Mrs R Pease **Trained** Upper Lambourn, Berks

FOCUS
An ordinary novice event, but a useful performance from Cee Bargara and it is doubtful if he is flattered despite him being another all-the-way winner on the card. These two-year-olds were spread all over the track at the line, with a few of them possibly following the hanging winner.

NOTEBOOK
Cee Bargara failed to land a blow in the Woodcote Stakes at Epsom four days earlier, but he produced an improved effort in this lower grade, readily conceding weight all round despite hanging right the way over to the stands'-side rail late on. While his hanging was not ideal, he did not slow down, and looks worth another try in better company. (tchd 17-2)
Dream Eater(IRE) confirmed the promise he showed when third on his debut at Goodwood, but found the winner too strong. He hung towards the stands' rail, but basically just looked to be following Cee Bargara. (op 9-2)
Master Chef(IRE) failed to build on his recent third to subsequent Woodcote winner Declaration Of War at Newmarket and was a little disappointing. (op 11-4 tchd 3-1 in places)
Higgy's Boy(IRE) seemed to run his race and looks one of the better guides to the level of the form. (tchd 25-1)
Seeking The Star(CAN) showed some ability on his debut at Newmarket and this was another promising effort. (tchd 28-1)
Captain Royale(IRE), a 56,000gns half-brother to among others the quite useful Peacefally, a dual winner at around 7f in France and the US, out of a quite useful 1m winner, should improve plenty of this experience. Official explanation: jockey said colt ran green (op 7-2 tchd 10-3 and 5-1)
Mansii was well below form stepped up in trip on his Polytrack debut. (tchd 9-2)

2354 DIGITOTE LONDON MILE H'CAP (LONDON MILE QUALIFIER) 1m (P)
8:40 (8:46) (Class 4) (0-80,82) 3-Y-O **£4,728** (£1,406; £702; £351) **Stalls** High

Form RPR
6-22 **1** **Cape Hawk (IRE)**[18] 1839 3-9-2 75 JimCrowley 9 86
(R Hannon) *trckd ldrs: rdn over 2f out: r.o to ld over 1f out: drvn clr* **10/1**
633- **2** *2* **Malt Or Mash (USA)**[239] 5893 3-9-5 78 PatDobbs 6 85
(R Hannon) *chsd ldr for 3f: styd cl up on inner: drvn 2f out: styd on same pce* **25/1**
1011 **3** *nk* **Tilapia (IRE)**[7] 2150 3-9-9 82 6ex SebSanders 3 88
(Sir Mark Prescott) *led after 1f: drvn and hdd over 1f out: one pce fnl f* **6/1**[2]
2516 **4** *1* **Shot Gun**[13] 1956 3-9-4 77 DarryllHolland 5 81
(M R Channon) *dwlt: pushed up to go prom: chsd ldr 5f out: drvn to chal 2f out: upsides over 1f out: fdd* **8/1**
-312 **5** *1 3/4* **Last Sovereign**[35] 1399 3-9-3 76 ChrisCatlin 4 76
(R Charlton) *led for 1f: lost pl on inner after 3f: effrt over 2f out: one pce after* **7/1**[3]
1100 **6** *shd* **Alfresco**[29] 1563 3-9-7 80 (b) JimmyFortune 8 79+
(Pat Eddery) *slowly away: hld up in rr: gng wl enough but off the pce over 2f out: shkn up over 1f out: one pce and nvr on terms* **16/1**
1-50 **7** *2* **Sell Out**[13] 1979 3-9-5 78 RobertHavlin 14 73+
(G Wragg) *lost pl on inner over 6f out and sn in last pair: effrt 2f out: one pce and no prog fnl f* **40/1**
2-1 **8** *5* **Sea Land (FR)**[123] 342 3-9-3 76 DaneO'Neill 10 59
(M P Tregoning) *nvr bttr than midfield: rdn and no prog 3f out: struggling after* **9/2**[1]
14-0 **9** *3 1/2* **History Boy**[43] 1230 3-9-5 78 TedDurcan 11 53
(D J Coakley) *s.i.s and rousted along 1st f: a in rr: rdn and no prog over 2f out* **33/1**
5-10 **10** *1/2* **Hannicean**[31] 1504 3-9-5 78 PhilipRobinson 1 52
(M A Jarvis) *racd on outer: chsd ldrs: v wd bnd 3f out and sn wl in rr* **11/1**
-233 **11** *1 1/4* **Maslak (IRE)**[19] 1804 3-9-5 78 MartinDwyer 12 49
(E A L Dunlop) *prom 1f: sn lost pl and wl in rr: rdn over 2f out: no prog* **16/1**
1-6 **12** *nk* **Flower Of Kent (USA)**[35] 1407 3-9-2 75 RichardHughes 2 46
(J H M Gosden) *stdd s: hld up in last: nvr a factor* **12/1**

1m 38.73s (-2.07) **Going Correction** +0.05s/f (Slow) **12** Ran SP% **102.2**
Speed ratings (Par 101):112,110,109,108,106 106,104,99,96,95 94,94
CSF £177.49 CT £1033.36 TOTE £8.60: £2.50, £4.10, £1.70; EX 152.00.
Owner Thurloe Thoroughbreds XVII **Bred** John And Leslie Young **Trained** East Everleigh, Wilts
■ Dream Lodge was withdrawn (9/2, rdr K. McEvoy injured.) R4 applies, deduct 15p in the £.

FOCUS
A decent handicap, run at a sound gallop, and again it was important to race up with the pace as nothing got into it from the rear. The winner is progressive and this lookd solid form which should work out.
Hannicean Official explanation: jockey said colt hung left

2355 WEATHERBYS PRINTING APPRENTICE H'CAP (ROUND 1) 1m 4f (P)
9:10 (9:10) (Class 6) (0-65,71) 4-Y-0+ **£2,388** (£705; £352) **Stalls** Centre

Form RPR
440- **1** **Stolen Hours (USA)**[252] 5628 7-9-7 62 LukeMorris 2 70
(J Akehurst) *t.k.h: mde all: set slow pce for 3f: kicked on 3f out: kpt on fr over 1f out: unchal* **7/4**[1]
2200 **2** *3* **Raise The Heights (IRE)**[39] 1314 4-9-7 62 ThomasO'Brien 5 65
(C Tinkler) *s.s: sn cl up: rdn to chse wnr over 2f out: nt qckn and no imp over 1f out* **10/3**[3]
300 **3** *1 3/4* **Longhill Tiger**[15] 1924 4-9-7 62 JamieHamblett 7 62
(G G Margarson) *plld hrd early and hld up in 4th: rdn and nt qckn over 2f out: styd on same pce fr over 1f out* **5/1**
61-0 **4** *nk* **Montosari**[14] 1949 8-9-10 65 JackMitchell 1 65
(P Mitchell) *mostly trckd wnr to over 2f out: rdn and one pce after* **5/2**[2]
000- **5** *22* **Wanna Shout**[170] 6854 9-8-0 46 oh1 JosephWalsh(5) 6 11
(R Dickin) *dwlt: a last: wknd over 2f out: t.o* **20/1**

2m 39.12s (2.22) **Going Correction** +0.05s/f (Slow) **5** Ran SP% **109.4**
Speed ratings (Par 101):94,92,90,90,75
CSF £7.78 TOTE £2.70: £1.40, £2.20; EX 7.50 Place 6 £42.78, Place 5 £21.50.
Owner A D Spence **Bred** Allen E Paulson **Trained** Epsom, Surrey

FOCUS
The winner dictated a slow pace in this uncompetitive handicap. He need not need to improve to score.
T/Jkpt: Not won. T/Plt: £26.70 to a £1 stake. Pool: £65,510.00. 1,790.40 winning tickets. T/Qpdt: £10.20 to a £1 stake. Pool: £3,748.60. 271.90 winning tickets. JN

2331 LINGFIELD (L-H)
Wednesday, June 6

OFFICIAL GOING: Turf course - good to firm (8.8); all-weather - standard
Wind: Virtually nil

2356 MICHAEL VARAH MEMORIAL (S) STKS 5f (P)
1:50 (1:50) (Class 6) 2-Y-O **£2,047** (£604; £302) **Stalls** High

Form RPR
0043 **1** **Lord Deevert**[9] 2087 2-8-4 0 JackDean(7) 3 61+
(W G M Turner) *trckd ldr: led 1f out: sn clr: easily* **11/8**[1]
00 **2** *2* **Never Sold Out (IRE)**[25] 1680 2-8-11 0 DarryllHolland 4 52
(Pat Eddery) *chsd ldrs in 3rd: rdn 2f out: styd on to chse wnr ins fnl f but nvr any ch* **6/1**
31 **3** *4* **Pearo (IRE)**[7] 2152 2-8-11 0 LPKeniry 2 38
(J S Moore) *led: rdn 2f out: hdd 1f out: wknd rapidly ins fnl f* **9/4**[2]
5 **4** *nk* **Ten On Line (IRE)**[4] 2247 2-8-11 0 JimCrowley 1 37
(J A Osborne) *racd in 4th: outpcd 1/2-way and hrd drvn: mod prog fnl f* **7/2**[3]

60.99 secs (1.21) **Going Correction** +0.025s/f (Slow) **4** Ran SP% **109.4**
Speed ratings (Par 91):91,87,81,80
CSF £9.34 TOTE £2.30; EX 8.90.The winner was bought in for 7,200gns. Never Sold Out was claimed by W Baddiley for £6,000.
Owner Mrs M S Teversham **Bred** Mrs M S Teversham **Trained** Sigwells, Somerset

FOCUS
A weak juvenile seller, with the third not running her race.

NOTEBOOK
Lord Deevert was well held in a soft-ground claimer at Leicester on his previous start, but he was the clear form pick judged on his earlier fourth behind Cracking at Brighton, and found this an easy opportunity to gain his first success. He did not beat a great deal, but won with plenty in hand and may just be slightly better than this level. (op 6-4 tchd 13-8)
Never Sold Out(IRE) had beaten only one rival in two starts in maiden company, so he would have benefited from the drop in grade. However, he was no match for the winner and appeared to run to a very moderate level of form. (op 13-2)
Pearo(IRE) could not repeat the form of her recent Yarmouth success and appeared unsuited by both the drop in trip and switch to Polytrack. (op 7-4)
Ten On Line(IRE) is seemingly very moderate indeed. (op 9-2)

2357 REAL THING LIVE AT LINGFIELDPARK.CO.UK CLAIMING STKS 6f (P)
2:20 (2:20) (Class 6) 3-Y-O+ **£2,047** (£604; £302) **Stalls** High

Form RPR
-066 **1** **Calypso King**[15] 1935 4-10-0 67 SebSanders 10 68
(R M Beckett) *hld up towards rr: stdy hdwy over 2f out: str run to ld 1f out: sn clr* **7/4**[1]
-400 **2** *2* **New Proposal (IRE)**[14] 1947 5-9-10 50 JimCrowley 5 58
(A P Jarvis) *chsd ldrs: rdn and styd on same pce fnl 2f* **6/1**[3]

0000 3 1 ¼ **Detonate**[89] 653 5-9-0 44 .... JimmyQuinn 9 44
(Ms J S Doyle) *s.i.s: in rr: hdwy fr 3f out: rdn and kpt on fnl 2f but nvr gng pce to be competitive* **10/1**

3040 4 2 ½ **Time Share (IRE)**[21] 1763 3-8-1 52 .... FrankieMcDonald 1 30
(J A Osborne) *disp ld tl ins fnl 3f: sn hrd rdn and outpcd: mod prog u.p fnl f* **8/1**

5455 5 nk **Legal Set (IRE)**[16] 1891 11-8-13 44 ....(b) AnnStokell(5) 11 40
(Miss A Stokell) *mde most tl hdd 1f out: wknd rapidly* **20/1**

0005 6 3 **Auentraum (GER)**[6] 2174 7-9-6 45 .... DarryllHolland 8 33
(Ms J S Doyle) *chsd ldrs over 3f* **12/1**

0004 7 1 **Beverley Beau**[23] 1707 5-8-9 44 .... KristinStubbs(7) 3 26
(Mrs L Stubbs) *s.i.s: sn chsng ldrs: wknd over 2f out* **15/2**

2500 8 3 **Santaverti**[7] 2140 4-9-0 56 ....(b) FergusSweeney 4 15
(G L Moore) *s.i.s: outpcd most of way* **11/2**[2]

050- 9 nk **Safari**[40] 2187 4-8-6 41 .... EmmettStack(3) 6 9
(A J Chamberlain) *early spd: sn bhd* **50/1**

1m 13.07s (0.26) **Going Correction** +0.025s/f (Slow)
WFA 3 from 4yo+ 8lb **9** Ran SP% **112.4**
Speed ratings (Par 101):99,96,94,91,90 86,85,81,81
CSF £11.82 TOTE £3.00: £1.10, £3.40, £3.00; EX 14.60 Trifecta £169.70 Part won. Pool: £239.06 - 0.40 winning units..The winner was claimed by R Teatum for £12,000.
Owner Norman Brunskill **Bred** A Parker **Trained** Whitsbury, Hants

FOCUS
An ordinary claimer run at a good pace. The winner was 8lb off his best form of the last year or so but was still a class above, in a race rated through the second.
Time Share(IRE) Official explanation: jockey said filly hung badly right on the bend

2358 BESPOKE H'CAP 1m (P)
2:50 (2:50) (Class 5) (0-75,75) 4-Y-0+ **£2,914** (£867; £433; £216) **Stalls High**

Form RPR

-300 1 **Carmenero (GER)**[12] 2004 4-9-3 71 .... MartinDwyer 6 81
(W R Muir) *hld up in rr: hdwy fr 3f out: styd on to ld 1f out: drvn out* **11/2**[2]

-002 2 1 ¼ **Crocodile Bay (IRE)**[6] 2180 4-9-2 70 .... BrettDoyle 2 80+
(B J Meehan) *chsd ldrs: nt clr run ins fnl 2f and over 1f out: swtchd rt: styd on again ins fnl f but a hld by wnr* **8/1**

4603 3 ¾ **Western Roots**[12] 1366 6-8-7 61 ....(p) JimCrowley 4 66
(M Appleby) *in rr: rdn and hdwy over 2f out: styd on fnl f but nvr quite gng pce to get to ldrs* **16/1**

0001 4 shd **Tabulate**[7] 2145 4-7-11 56 oh2 .... LukeMorris(5) 9 61+
(P L Gilligan) *chsd ldrs: wnt 2nd 3f out: led ins fnl 2f: hdd 1f out and sn one pce* **11/2**[2]

0110 5 nk **Binnion Bay (IRE)**[13] 1969 6-9-7 75 ....(b) AmirQuinn 8 79
(J J Bridger) *t.k.h: chsd ldrs tl led 4f out: rdn and hdd ins fnl 2f: sn outpcd* **9/2**[1]

5001 6 3 **Glencalvie (IRE)**[15] 1931 6-9-5 73 ....(v) JimmyQuinn 5 70
(J Akehurst) *chsd ldr 3f: outpcd over 3f out: mod prog again fnl f* **9/2**[1]

20-0 7 ½ **James Street (IRE)**[26] 1629 4-8-11 68 ....(b) StephaneBreux(3) 1 64
(J R Best) *in tch: rdn over 2f out: sn btn* **16/1**

30-2 8 2 **Yo Pedro (IRE)**[9] 2091 5-8-11 65 ....(vt) TedDurcan 3 57
(D Carroll) *s.i.s: bhd most of way* **8/1**

0560 9 hd **Seldemosa**[23] 1715 6-8-2 56 oh11 .... FrancisNorton 7 47
(M S Saunders) *a in rr* **50/1**

2-03 10 ¾ **Titus Lumpus (IRE)**[26] 1629 4-8-7 61 .... DarryllHolland 10 51
(R M Flower) *led to 1/2-way: sn wknd* **6/1**[3]

1m 38.68s (-0.75) **Going Correction** +0.025s/f (Slow) **10** Ran SP% **117.4**
Speed ratings (Par 103):104,102,102,101,101 98,98,96,95,95
CSF £49.36 CT £667.16 TOTE £5.50: £1.70, £2.60, £3.50; EX 57.50 Trifecta £229.90 Part won. Pool: £323.84 - 0.84 winning units..
Owner Middleham Park Racing XXXVIII **Bred** Graf And Grafin Von Stauffenberg **Trained** Lambourn, Berks

FOCUS
A competitive-looking handicap run at just a steady pace. Carmenero took advantage of a good mark and was back to his sand best, but Crocodile Bay was unlucky.
Glencalvie(IRE) Official explanation: vet said gelding lost a front shoe

2359 TONY HADLEY LIVE AT LINGFIELDPARK.CO.UK MAIDEN FILLIES' STKS (DIV I) 1m 2f
3:20 (3:21) (Class 5) 3-Y-0+ **£2,266** (£674; £337; £168) **Stalls Low**

Form RPR

2 1 **Wise Little Girl**[51] 1068 3-8-9 0 .... PhilipRobinson 8 73+
(M A Jarvis) *sn led: drvn 3 l clr approachiung fnl f: hld on wl u.p* **6/4**[1]

0 2 nk **Demisemiquaver**[25] 1659 3-8-9 0 .... SebSanders 11 69
(J Noseda) *sn chsng wnr: rdn and outpcd 2f out: 3 l down appr fnl f: rallied u.p ins fnl f: nt quite get up* **9/1**[3]

33 3 ½ **Orama's Ghost**[25] 1685 3-8-9 0 .... KerrinMcEvoy 5 68+
(Sir Michael Stoute) *s.i.s: bhd: stl plenty to do over 2f out: rdn and hdwy sn after: edgd lft u.p ins fnl f: kpt on cl home* **13/8**[2]

4 2 ½ **Woolfall Rose** 3-8-9 0 .... NeilPollard 7 63
(G G Margarson) *in rr: hdwy on outside 4f out: chsd ldrs and rdn 2f out: kpt on same pce ins fnl f* **50/1**

5 1 ¼ **Berry Hill Lass (IRE)** 3-8-9 0 .... FergusSweeney 4 61
(J G M O'Shea) *chsd ldrs: rdn 3f out: wknd fnl f* **66/1**

-00 6 ¾ **Shine Like A Star**[25] 1665 3-8-9 0 .... TedDurcan 10 59
(J L Dunlop) *wnt wd bnd over 3f out: a towards rr* **50/1**

7 1 ¾ **Dot's Delight** 3-8-6 0 .... SaleemGolam(3) 3 56
(M H Tompkins) *a towards rr* **33/1**

0- 8 1 **Galloise (IRE)**[231] 6050 3-8-9 0 .... AdamKirby 2 54
(C G Cox) *chsd ldrs: rdn over 2f out: wknd over 1f out* **25/1**

6 9 nk **Catherine Palace**[12] 1988 3-8-9 0 .... DO'Donohoe 1 53
(E A L Dunlop) *t.k.h: in tch tl wknd over 2f out* **14/1**

0 10 17 **Moonfinder (IRE)**[20] 1784 3-8-9 0 .... IanMongan 9 19
(J L Dunlop) *wnt wd into st: a towards rr* **12/1**

2m 11.54s (1.82) **Going Correction** +0.225s/f (Good) **10** Ran SP% **114.7**
Speed ratings (Par 100):101,100,100,98,97 96,95,94,94,80
CSF £14.82 TOTE £2.60: £1.20, £2.30, £1.30; EX 19.90 Trifecta £21.40 Pool £299.92 - 9.95 winning units..
Owner Sheikh Mohammed **Bred** Darley **Trained** Newmarket, Suffolk

FOCUS
No more than a modest maiden, but it was the quicker of the two divisions by 2.26sec. The winner is a bit better than the bare form, and the third is the best guide, but this is not form to be confident about.

2360 TONY HADLEY LIVE AT LINGFIELDPARK.CO.UK MAIDEN FILLIES' STKS (DIV II) 1m 2f
3:50 (3:50) (Class 5) 3-Y-0+ **£2,266** (£674; £337; £168) **Stalls Low**

Form RPR

6 1 **Marzelline (IRE)**[44] 1203 3-8-9 0 .... AdamKirby 6 72+
(W R Swinburn) *trckd ldr: chal over 2f out: led ins fnl quarter m: rdn out* **15/8**[1]

0-32 2 ½ **Ravarino (USA)**[17] 1863 3-8-9 74 .... JDSmith 9 71
(Sir Michael Stoute) *chsd ldrs: wd into st: styd on to chse wnr fnl f: kpt on cl home but a hld* **2/1**[2]

66 3 3 **Central Force**[20] 1785 3-8-9 0 .... KerrinMcEvoy 7 65
(E A L Dunlop) *led: rdn 3f out: hdd ins fnl 2f: wknd ins fnl f* **10/1**

3 4 shd **Djalalabad (FR)**[20] 1784 3-8-9 0 .... PhilipRobinson 2 65
(M A Jarvis) *trckd ldrs: shkn up and no imp on ldrs fnl f* **10/3**[3]

5 1 ½ **Looktheotherway (IRE)** 3-8-9 0 .... FergusSweeney 11 62
(J G M O'Shea) *in rr: drvn over 2f out: styd on fnl f but nvr in contention* **66/1**

00 6 hd **Hermanita**[20] 1784 3-8-9 0 .... TedDurcan 5 61+
(G Wragg) *in rr: pushed along over 2f out: sme prog fnl f: nvr in contention* **33/1**

7 ¾ **Rhondda Valley** 3-8-9 0 .... JimCrowley 3 60
(Mrs A J Perrett) *chsd ldrs: rdn and hung lft over 2f out: sn btn* **20/1**

06 8 9 **Miss Invincible**[66] 864 3-8-9 0 .... SebSanders 1 42
(A P Jarvis) *a bhd* **25/1**

2m 13.8s (4.08) **Going Correction** +0.225s/f (Good) **8** Ran SP% **113.3**
Speed ratings (Par 100):92,91,89,89,87 87,87,79
CSF £5.60 TOTE £2.80: £1.40, £1.10, £1.80; EX 5.70 Trifecta £24.30 Pool £401.53 - 11.73 winning units..
Owner Mrs P W Harris **Bred** Pendley Farm **Trained** Aldbury, Herts

FOCUS
A steady pace and the slower of the two divisions by 2.26sec. The principals were never far off the pace. The form looks fair at best but makes more sense than that of division one, rated around the placed horses. The winner should get a nice mark to wor from in handicaps.

2361 STANLEY POWELL MEMORIAL FILLIES' H'CAP 1m 2f
4:20 (4:20) (Class 5) (0-75,77) 4-Y-0+ **£2,914** (£867; £433; £216) **Stalls Low**

Form RPR

0052 1 **Wassfa**[22] 1742 4-8-6 59 .... KerrinMcEvoy 6 67
(C E Brittain) *in tch: drvn: hdwy and hung lft over 1f out: styd on to ld last strides* **6/1**[3]

-031 2 nk **Snake Skin**[7] 2142 4-8-5 58 6ex .... JimCrowley 3 65
(J Gallagher) *chsd ldrs: slt ld 2f out: sn hrd drvn: styd on: ct last strides* **7/2**[1]

2052 3 1 ½ **Bavarica**[12] 2006 5-8-9 69 .... AmyBaker(7) 8 73
(Miss J Feilden) *s.i.s: in rr: hdwy on rails fr 3f out to press ldr 1f out: no ex ins fnl f* **10/1**

0-41 4 ½ **Vale De Lobo**[9] 2082 5-9-10 77 6ex .... TedDurcan 2 80
(B R Millman) *chsd ldrs: rdn and effrt over 1f out: styd on same pce ins fnl f* **4/1**[2]

-621 5 1 ½ **Uig**[8] 2106 6-9-2 69 6ex .... SimonWhitworth 1 69
(H S Howe) *led: rdn 3f out: hdd 2f out: wknd fnl f* **7/1**

0-05 6 2 **Cortesia (IRE)**[19] 1813 4-9-7 74 .... JimmyFortune 4 70
(P W Chapple-Hyam) *in tch: rdn 3f out: sn btn* **7/2**[1]

5050 7 2 ½ **Compton Express**[15] 1926 4-8-2 55 oh10 .... FrancisNorton 7 46
(Jamie Poulton) *a towards rr* **40/1**

0-15 8 7 **Jeu D'Esprit (IRE)**[13] 1980 4-9-2 69 .... SebSanders 5 46
(J G Given) *a towards rr* **10/1**

2m 10.52s (0.80) **Going Correction** +0.225s/f (Good) **8** Ran SP% **111.9**
Speed ratings (Par 100):105,104,103,103,101 100,98,92
CSF £26.05 CT £202.65 TOTE £6.70: £2.00, £1.10, £3.10; EX 37.00 Trifecta £204.70 Pool £397.88 - 91.38 winning units..
Owner Saeed Manana **Bred** Darley **Trained** Newmarket, Suffolk

FOCUS
A modest fillies' handicap. The winner was still around 10lb below her figures from this time last year. The fourth and fifth were both badly in under penalties.

2362 HEATWAVE LIVE AT LINGFIELDPARK.CO.UK H'CAP 1m 3f 106y
4:50 (4:51) (Class 6) (0-60,60) 3-Y-0 **£2,047** (£604; £302) **Stalls High**

Form RPR

6005 1 **Pretty Demanding (IRE)**[6] 2192 3-8-12 54 .... TedDurcan 9 69+
(M G Quinlan) *hld up towards rr: stdy hdwy fr 4f out: led 2f out: sn in command: easily* **5/1**[3]

5-55 2 3 ½ **Silver Mitzva (IRE)**[46] 1153 3-9-0 56 ....(v[1]) DarryllHolland 12 65
(M Botti) *led 9f out: hdd and rdn 2f out kpt on wl for clr 2nd but no ch w wnr* **25/1**

0-00 3 6 **Down The Brick (IRE)**[13] 1972 3-8-13 60 ....(b) JamesMillman(5) 6 59
(B R Millman) *in rr: hdwy on outside fr 3f out: styd on to take 3rd fnl f but no ch w ldng pair* **8/1**

0-03 4 ¾ **Proposal**[13] 1972 3-8-13 55 .... FrancisNorton 7 53
(A W Carroll) *towards rr: rdn and hdwy on ins fnl over 2f out: kpt on but nvr gng pce to be competitive* **10/1**

0363 5 ½ **Raquel White**[8] 2105 3-8-8 55 .... KevinGhunowa(5) 4 52+
(J L Flint) *in rr: rdn and hdwy on outside over 2f out: hung lft and nt rch ldrs* **9/1**

50-0 6 1 ¼ **Ski For Luck (IRE)**[46] 1154 3-8-12 54 .... IanMongan 8 49
(J L Dunlop) *chsd ldrs: rdn over 3f out: wknd fr 2f out* **50/1**

000- 7 nk **Strobe**[250] 5645 3-9-4 60 .... KerrinMcEvoy 16 54
(J A Osborne) *in rr: pushed along and kpt on fnl 2f: nvr nr ldrs* **14/1**

606- 8 1 ½ **Alleviate (IRE)**[211] 6386 3-9-2 58 .... SebSanders 10 50
(Sir Mark Prescott) *in tch: chsd ldrs 5f out: sn rdn: wknd 2f out* **3/1**[1]

3563 9 1 ¼ **Picky**[73] 776 3-9-3 59 .... FergusSweeney 11 49
(C Tinkler) *in tch: rdn into mid-div over 3f out: sn hrd drvn and wknd* **33/1**

60-0 10 1 **Hocinail (FR)**[8] 2105 3-8-13 55 .... AdamKirby 1 43
(P Winkworth) *slowly in to stride: bhd: rdn and styd on on fnl 2f: nvr in contention* **100/1**

0240 11 2 **Tenement (IRE)**[26] 1634 3-8-11 53 .... RobertHavlin 5 37
(Jamie Poulton) *a towards rr* **33/1**

0-00 12 6 **Revisionist (IRE)**[23] 1724 3-9-2 58 .... PatDobbs 13 32
(R Hannon) *led after 2f to 9f out: wknd 4f out* **14/1**

6535 13 14 **Razzano (IRE)**[15] 1928 3-9-4 60 .... JimmyQuinn 3 10
(A M Hales) *chsd ldrs: wknd 4f out* **16/1**

0050 14 1 ¾ **Cantique (IRE)**[5] 2196 3-8-7 52 .... SaleemGolam(3) 2 —
(Ms J S Doyle) *led 2f: wknd over 4f out* **33/1**

0-01 **15** *2* **Kyloe Belle (USA)**[38] 1320 3-9-3 **59**................................ JimCrowley 15 3
(Mrs A J Perrett) *chsd ldrs: wknd 4f out* **10/3**[2]

2m 30.27s (0.35) **Going Correction** +0.225s/f (Good) **15** Ran SP% **129.8**
Speed ratings (Par 97):107,104,100,99,99 98,98,96,96,95 93,89,79,78,76
CSF £140.37 CT £1025.10 TOTE £7.80: £3.60, £6.30, £3.30; EX 211.50 TRIFECTA Not won. Place 6 £32.78, Place 5 £14.40..
Owner L Mulryan & M C Fahy **Bred** Moyglare Stud Farm Ltd **Trained** Newmarket, Suffolk

FOCUS

Plenty of no-hopers, but the pace was strong, and Pretty Demanding had them well strung out. A group of five, including the winner and second, were clear turning into the straight. The first two are both on the upgrade.

Down The Brick(IRE) Official explanation: jockey said gelding missed the break
Raquel White Official explanation: jockey said filly hung left
Picky Official explanation: jockey said gelding lost its action

T/Plt: £100.00 to a £1 stake. Pool: £46,728.80. 341.10 winning tickets. T/Qpdt: £14.30 to a £1 stake. Pool: £3,371.80. 174.20 winning tickets. ST

1667 NOTTINGHAM (L-H)

Wednesday, June 6

OFFICIAL GOING: Good (good to firm in back straight; 8.8)
Wind: Light, behind Weather: Overcast

2363 BEST UK RACECOURSES ON TURF TV H'CAP 6f 15y

1:40 (1:41) (Class 5) (0-75,75) 3-Y-O **£3,238** (£963; £481; £240) **Stalls** Centre

Form RPR

5-51 **1** **Pusey Street Lady**[30] 1541 3-9-2 **70**.................................. JoeFanning 2 82+
(J Gallagher) *trckd ldrs: racd keenly: led and hung lft over 1f out: rdn out* **11/2**[3]

1-4 **2** *3/4* **My Love Thomas (IRE)**[20] 1786 3-9-4 **72**......................... JHBowman 8 82
(E A L Dunlop) *hld up: hdwy over 2f out: hung lft and chsd wnr fnl f: r.o* **9/2**[2]

0-14 **3** *2 1/2* **Fuschia**[18] 1837 3-9-7 **75**.. NCallan 4 78
(R Charlton) *chsd ldrs: rdn over 2f out: edgd lft over 1f out: styd on same pce* **11/4**[1]

1020 **4** *3/4* **Comrade Cotton**[14] 1948 3-8-11 **65**..................................... JohnEgan 3 65
(N A Callaghan) *mid-div: rdn 1/2-way: hdwy over 2f out: styd on same pce appr fnl f* **20/1**

5441 **5** *1/2* **Strathmore (IRE)**[8] 2120 3-9-0 **68** 6ex............................ PaulHanagan 5 67
(R A Fahey) *broke wl: stdd and lost pl sn after: rdn 1/2-way: edgd lft over 1f out: nt trble ldrs* **11/4**[1]

0001 **6** *nk* **Mr Forthright**[16] 1883 3-8-2 **56**.............................. AdrianMcCarthy 9 54
(J M Bradley) *chsd ldrs: rdn over 2f out: wknd fnl f* **18/1**

310 **7** *1 3/4* **Jord (IRE)**[13] 1978 3-8-6 **65**.. WilliamBuick(5) 6 58
(A J McCabe) *s.i.s: sn led: rdn and hdd over 1f out: sn edgd lft: wknd fnl f* **12/1**

3-35 **8** *3 1/2* **Billy Ruffian**[32] 1484 3-8-11 **65**...(b[1]) DavidAllan 1 47
(T D Easterby) *chsd ldrs over 4f* **20/1**

154- **9** *3/4* **Hill Of Lujain**[373] 2076 3-9-5 **73**.................................. ChrisCatlin 12 53
(Ian Williams) *hld up: rdn over 2f out: sn wknd* **22/1**

20-0 **10** *3 1/2* **Our Toy Soldier**[8] 2110 3-8-10 **64**................................(b[1]) PaulEddery 10 33
(B Smart) *s.i.s: a in rr: rdn and wknd over 2f out* **66/1**

1m 13.44s (-1.56) **Going Correction** -0.425s/f (Firm) **10** Ran SP% **115.2**
Speed ratings (Par 99):93,92,88,87,87 86,84,79,78,73
CSF £28.51 CT £84.50 TOTE £7.40: £2.40, £1.70, £1.30; EX 41.10.
Owner C R Marks (Banbury) **Bred** S R Hope **Trained** Moreton-in-Marsh, Gloucs

FOCUS

A fair sprint handicap in which the improving first two pulled clear. The form seems solid.

2364 EUROPEAN BREEDERS' FUND MAIDEN FILLIES' STKS (DIV I) 5f 13y

2:10 (2:10) (Class 5) 2-Y-O **£2,914** (£867; £433; £216) **Stalls** Centre

Form RPR

1 **Regal Step** 2-9-0 0.. RichardMullen 9 86
(R M H Cowell) *mde all: rdn out* **25/1**

2 *2* **Unilateral (IRE)** 2-9-0 0.. PaulEddery 1 79
(B Smart) *a.p: chsd wnr 2f out: sn rdn: styd on same pce fnl f* **10/1**

3 *3/4* **Speed Song** 2-9-0 0.. MichaelHills 3 76
(W J Haggas) *chsd ldrs: rdn over 1f out: styd on same pce* **13/2**

4 *shd* **Sophie's Girl** 2-9-0 0.. NCallan 6 76
(P W Chapple-Hyam) *chsd ldrs: rdn 1/2-way: styd on same pce fnl f* **5/1**[3]

5 *3 1/2* **Kashoof** 2-9-0 0.. RHills 8 63+
(J L Dunlop) *s.i.s: hdwy 1/2-way: wknd fnl f* **7/2**[2]

0 **6** *1/2* **Eye Catching**[8] 2122 2-9-0 0.................................... StephenCarson 2 61
(J R Jenkins) *chsd wnr 3f: wknd fnl f* **10/1**

7 *1* **Marie Camargo** 2-9-0 0.. PaulHanagan 11 58+
(R A Fahey) *mid-div: lost pl over 3f out: sn bhd* **33/1**

8 *1/2* **Eva's Request (IRE)** 2-9-0 0.. JHBowman 7 56
(M R Channon) *s.i.s: a in rr* **10/1**

9 *1 1/4* **Francesca D'Gorgio (USA)** 2-9-0 0.................................... LDettori 10 51
(J Noseda) *chsd ldrs: hung lft thrght: rdn and lost pl 1/2-way: sn bhd* **3/1**[1]

10 *3 1/2* **Missabeat (IRE)** 2-9-0 0.. DavidAllan 4 39
(T D Easterby) *s.i.s: outpcd* **66/1**

60.53 secs (-1.27) **Going Correction** -0.425s/f (Firm) **10** Ran SP% **112.8**
Speed ratings (Par 90):93,89,88,88,82 82,80,79,77,72
CSF £244.19 TOTE £38.10: £6.70, £3.10, £2.80; EX 920.90.
Owner Bottisham Heath Stud **Bred** Bottisham Heath Stud **Trained** Six Mile Bottom, Cambs

FOCUS

A decent maiden on paper and the faster of the two divisions, just 0.14sec slower than the later older-horse maiden, and a decisive winner.

NOTEBOOK

Regal Step ◆, a half-sister to among others the speedy juvenile Smooch, showed all her sister's speed on this debut. Racing close to the pace, she asserted in the final furlong to score in emphatic style and the time was quicker than the second division. Her trainer thinks she is very good as she works with some of his useful older sprinters at home and she will now head for the Queen Mary (op 33-1)

Unilateral(IRE) ◆, an 85,000gns yearling who is a half-sister to top-class juvenile and successful sire Danehill Dancer, was soon close up and moved into contention over a furlong out, but she made no impression on the winner inside the last. She should win races and could develop into a fair sort with time. (op 14-1)

Speed Song, a speedily-bred half-sister to the useful Enticing, looked as if she needed the experience and just stayed on in the closing stages. She will be sharper next time. (op 11-2 tchd 9-2)

Sophie's Girl, another speedily-bred filly, being a sister to Paradise Isle and Murfreesboro, was another to run a decent race and only faded out of it in the closing stages. (op 7-1)

Kashoof, the first foal of a 6-7f winner who was a half-sister to the high-class Mehthaaf and Elnadim, ran a little green and missed the break. She was staying on steadily without ever getting near the leaders but can do better with this behind her. (op 3-1)

Eye Catching, a half-sister to Goodbye Mr Bond and Anfield Dream, had finished closer to the winner on her debut on soft going, but this is potentially a better contest on faster ground. (op 12-1 tchd 17-2)

Francesca D'Gorgio(USA), a $250,000 American-bred yearling who cost $530,000 when resold earlier this year, was sent off favourite but tended to hang and was in trouble before the halfway mark. She can be given another chance but needs to improve a fair amount on this to live up to her price tag. (op 5-2 tchd 10-3 and 7-2 in places)

2365 EUROPEAN BREEDERS' FUND MAIDEN FILLIES' STKS (DIV II) 5f 13y

2:40 (2:40) (Class 5) 2-Y-O **£2,914** (£867; £433; £216) **Stalls** Centre

Form RPR

1 **Fleeting Spirit (IRE)** 2-9-0 0.. LDettori 3 85+
(J Noseda) *mde all: shkn up and hung lft fr over 1f out: r.o* **4/1**[3]

4 **2** *2* **Miss Emma May (IRE)**[19] 1814 2-9-0 0.................................... JohnEgan 7 78
(D R C Elsworth) *a.p: rdn to chse wnr and hung lft over 1f out: styd on same pce* **3/1**[2]

3 *1 3/4* **Cute** 2-9-0 0.. JoeFanning 10 72+
(C E Brittain) *s.i.s: outpcd: r.o ins fnl f: nrst fin* **14/1**

4 *1 1/4* **Narmeen** 2-9-0 0.. JHBowman 1 67
(M R Channon) *chsd ldrs: rdn 1/2-way: sn outpcd* **5/1**

4 **5** *2* **Pantherii (USA)**[19] 1807 2-9-0 0.................................... TQuinn 8 60
(P F I Cole) *chsd ldrs: rdn 1/2-way: wknd fnl f* **9/4**[1]

0 **6** *nk* **Linnet Park**[23] 1727 2-9-0 0.................................... KDarley 4 59
(J G Given) *chsd wnr over 3f: sn wknd* **14/1**

7 *3 1/2* **Clifton Dancer** 2-9-0 0.. RichardThomas 2 46
(Tom Dascombe) *s.i.s: outpcd* **14/1**

0 **8** *3 1/2* **Beyabi**[16] 1896 2-9-0 0.................................... StephenCarson 5 34
(J R Jenkins) *s.s: outpcd* **100/1**

60.67 secs (-1.13) **Going Correction** -0.425s/f (Firm) **8** Ran SP% **113.4**
Speed ratings (Par 90):92,88,86,84,80 80,74,69
CSF £16.15 TOTE £5.10: £1.50, £1.50, £3.30; EX 13.80.
Owner The Searchers **Bred** Mrs Bernadette Hayden **Trained** Newmarket, Suffolk

FOCUS

The slower of the two divisions of this maiden, but a taking performance from the winner. However this looked the weaker division on paper.

NOTEBOOK

Fleeting Spirit(IRE) ◆, who cost 35,000euros as a yearling and was resold for 90,000gns this year, is speedily-bred and knew her job on this debut, making all for an emphatic victory. It seems that she will go to Royal Ascot next, with a choice between the Queen Mary and the Windsor Castle Stakes. She should come on for the outing and is likely to make her presence felt whatever her preferred target. (op 3-1)

Miss Emma May(IRE), from the family of Zilzal and Polish Precedent, is bred to be more effective at longer trips. She had made her debut over 6f and this drop in trip did not appear to be in her favour, but she stayed on to chase home the winner without ever looking likely to trouble that rival. She looks capable of winning her maiden back over further. (op 11-4 tchd 5-2)

Cute ◆, another who on her dam's side is bred to stay further in time, is nevertheless by a sprinter. She looked in need of the experience having missed the break and been behind, but finished to good effect and should come on a lot for the race. (op 20-1)

Narmeen, the first foal of the useful Protectorate, was backed beforehand but ran as if the experience was needed. She should be a fair bit sharper next time. (op 15-2)

Pantherii(USA) set the standard on her debut in a Newbury maiden that normally produces a decent performer but is not working out that well this season. After having every chance she was well held and looks as if she will be better off in nurseries over further in time. (op 2-1 tchd 5-2)

Linnet Park, a half-sister to Mimi Mouse, showed plenty of pace as her breeding entitled her to do and had clearly improved for her debut. However, she could not sustain the effort and is another more likely to make her mark once handicapped. (op 25-1)

2366 WBX.COM WORLD BET EXCHANGE MEDIAN AUCTION MAIDEN STKS 5f 13y

3:10 (3:12) (Class 5) 3-5-Y-O **£2,914** (£867; £433; £216) **Stalls** Centre

Form RPR

02-2 **1** **Farefield Lodge (IRE)**[12] 2012 3-9-0 **78**.................................. KDarley 2 69
(C G Cox) *chsd ldrs: rdn 1/2-way: r.o to ld post* **4/6**[1]

20-5 **2** *shd* **Castano**[71] 798 3-9-0 **70**.. JHBowman 8 69
(B R Millman) *hld up: hdwy over 1f out: rdn to ld ins fnl f: hdd post* **11/4**[2]

60 **3** *2 1/2* **Musical Parkes**[12] 2012 3-8-6 0.................................. AndrewMullen(3) 6 55
(W J H Ratcliffe) *w ldr: rdn to ld over 1f out: hdd and no ex ins fnl f* **20/1**

-060 **4** *3/4* **Mujart**[30] 1538 3-8-10 **50** ow1.. NCallan 7 53
(J A Pickering) *chsd ldrs: rdn and ev ch over 1f out: styd on same pce ins fnl f* **18/1**[3]

005- **5** *2* **Dora's Green**[198] 6533 4-9-2 **45**..(p) ChrisCatlin 3 48
(S W Hall) *led over 3f: wknd fnl f* **33/1**

00 **6** *4* **Art Gamble (IRE)**[6] 2186 3-9-0 0.................................... PaulEddery 5 36
(N A Callaghan) *outpcd* **40/1**

0-0 **7** *4* **Stravinsky's Art (USA)**[10] 2059 3-9-0 0.......................... GeorgeBaker 9 21
(D R C Elsworth) *chsd ldrs over 3f* **18/1**[3]

8 *2* **Verbal Kint** 3-9-0 0.. RichardMullen 4 14
(E S McMahon) *s.s: hung lft: outpcd* **20/1**

0 **9** *1 1/4* **Lord Of The Reins (IRE)**[13] 1976 3-9-0 0.......................... PatCosgrave 1 10
(D Shaw) *bhd fr 1/2-way* **66/1**

60.49 secs (-1.31) **Going Correction** -0.425s/f (Firm)
WFA 3 from 4yo 7lb **9** Ran SP% **113.6**
Speed ratings (Par 103):93,92,88,87,84 78,71,68,66
CSF £2.23 TOTE £1.50: £1.02, £1.10, £6.80; EX 2.80.
Owner The Beechdown Braves **Bred** Millsec Limited **Trained** Lambourn, Berks

FOCUS

An uncompetitive maiden where they bet 18/1 bar two and that pair drew clear of the rest to produce a close finish. The first two did not produce their best here.

2367 TURFTV.CO.UK H'CAP 1m 6f 15y

3:40 (3:40) (Class 5) (0-75,75) 4-Y-O+ **£2,914** (£867; £433; £216) **Stalls** Low

Form RPR

5- **1** **Megaton**[14] 1213 6-9-0 **68**.. LDettori 1 78+
(P Bowen) *chsd ldrs: lost pl 8f out: hdwy 5f out: led 2f out: rdn clr: eased nr fin* **2/1**[1]

0-0 **2** *2* **Debord (FR)**[7] 2157 4-8-7 **61**.. JohnEgan 6 64
(Jamie Poulton) *hld up: hdwy over 3f out: rdn over 1f out: styd on same pce* **20/1**

0500 **3** *nk* **Blue Hills**[16] 1888 6-8-2 **56** oh2...(b) ChrisCatlin 3 59
(P W Hiatt) *led: hdd 12f out: chsd ldr tl led over 2f out: sn rdn and hdd: no ex fnl f* **15/2**

/064 **4** 1 3/4 **Naughty Nod (IRE)**[14] 1942 4-8-0 **57** oh6 ow1........... AndrewElliott(3) 7 57
(K R Burke) *wnt rt s: sn chsng ldrs: rdn over 5f out: outpcd over 3f out: styd on ins fnl f* **6/1**

21-6 **5** 1/2 **Height Of Fury (IRE)**[25] 1668 4-9-7 **75**............................. JHBowman 5 74
(J L Dunlop) *chsd ldrs: led 12f out: rdn and hdd over 2f out: wknd fnl f* **10/3**[2]

21-5 **6** 6 **Sa Nau**[64] 747 4-7-13 **58**.. WilliamBuick(5) 4 49
(T Keddy) *chsd ldrs: rdn over 3f out: wknd wl over 1f out* **7/2**[3]

3m 5.66s (-1.44) **Going Correction** -0.275s/f (Firm) **6** Ran SP% **109.4**
Speed ratings (Par 103):93,91,91,90,90 86
CSF £37.48 TOTE £2.90: £1.30, £4.30; EX 26.00.
Owner Swansea Bay Syndicate **Bred** Juddmonte Farms **Trained** Little Newcastle, Pembrokes

FOCUS
Just a fair staying handicap which did not take much winning. Megaton, well treated on his jumps form, is value for around double his winning margin.
Height Of Fury(IRE) Official explanation: jockey said colt ran too free early stages

2368 WBX.COM WE'LL MATCH YOUR COMMISSION RATE CONDITIONS STKS 1m 54y
4:10 (4:10) (Class 2) 3-Y-0+
£11,217 (£3,358; £1,679; £840; £419; £210) **Stalls** Centre

Form RPR
4304 **1** **Charlie Cool**[12] 1985 4-9-1 104...(v1) NCallan 2 111
(W J Haggas) *trckd ldrs: rdn over 1f out: styd on u.p to ld ins fnl f* **7/1**

215- **2** 2 **Shumookh (IRE)**[217] 6299 4-9-1 102.. RHills 3 106
(M A Jarvis) *led: rdn over 1f out: edgd rt: hdd and unable qck ins fnl f* **5/2**[2]

50-0 **3** 1 3/4 **Hinterland (IRE)**[125] 331 5-9-1 102.. LDettori 5 102
(Saeed Bin Suroor) *trckd ldr: rdn over 2f out: wknd wl ins fnl f* **11/8**[1]

3-03 **4** 2 **Jo'Burg (USA)**[8] 2124 3-8-7 97.. JoeFanning 6 98
(Mrs A J Perrett) *hld up: racd keenly: shkn up over 1f out: nvr trbld ldrs* **11/2**[3]

5425 **5** 6 **Chicken Soup**[60] 941 5-9-1 103.. JohnEgan 1 84
(T J Pitt) *hld up: rdn over 3f out: wknd 2f out* **12/1**

-100 **6** 15 **Kew Green (USA)**[20] 1791 9-9-7 96.. TQuinn 4 55
(P R Webber) *hld up in tch: wknd over 3f out: eased* **33/1**

1m 41.94s (-4.46) **Going Correction** -0.275s/f (Firm)
WFA 3 from 4yo+ 11lb **6** Ran SP% **109.2**
Speed ratings (Par 109):111,109,107,105,99 84
CSF £23.43 TOTE £7.40: £2.50, £1.90; EX 19.90.
Owner W J Gredley **Bred** Middle Park Stud Ltd **Trained** Newmarket, Suffolk

FOCUS
A decent conditions event, run at a strong early pace, and the form is almost Listed-class. It has been rated through the winner and fourth.

NOTEBOOK
Charlie Cool, equipped with the first-time visor, appreciated the decent pace over this shorter trip and bounced back to something like his best with a fairly decisive success. He has proved disappointing since returning from Dubai and evidently the headgear worked the oracle, but he has always looked at his best in a strongly-run race. Future hopes rely on the visor having the same effect in the future and he is far from easy to place from this sort of official rating. (op 13-2 tchd 6-1)
Shumookh(IRE), making his seasonal return, put up a solid effort in defeat from the front and enjoyed the sound surface. He should come on for the run and can be found further success this term, but is another who is not simple to place. (op 9-4 tchd 15-8 and 11-4 in places)
Hinterland(IRE), having his first run since disappointing in Dubai 125 days previously, was always handy and had his chance. He tired in the final furlong and should improve for this outing, but like so many in this type of event he is not at all easy to place from this sort of mark. (op 15-8 tchd 2-1)
Jo'Burg(USA) again advertised his quirks and did not help his cause by refusing to settle early on. The decent early pace eventually saw him keep on for a respectable fourth on this first outing against his elders, but he is proving very hard to catch right at present and looks well worth a try over 7f now. (op 6-1 tchd 5-1)
Chicken Soup, whose stable have been under a cloud for the past two months or so, was having his first outing on the turf since August last year and shaped as though he would come on for this first run for two months. He does look weighted to the hilt at present, however. (op 9-1)
Kew Green(USA) Official explanation: trainer said gelding ran too free to start

2369 E.B.F./ BET NOW AT WBX.COM FILLIES' H'CAP 1m 54y
4:40 (4:40) (Class 4) (0-85,88) 3-Y-0 **£5,181** (£1,541; £770; £384) **Stalls** Centre

Form RPR
221 **1** **Truly Enchanting (IRE)**[13] 1961 3-9-2 **80**............................. LDettori 9 90
(J Noseda) *hld up: swtchd rt over 3f out: hdwy over 2f out: rdn to chse ldr and hung lft over 1f out: r.o to ld wl ins fnl f: comf* **9/2**[3]

1211 **2** nk **Lady Gloria**[6] 2181 3-9-10 **88** 6ex.. JHBowman 4 97
(J G Given) *plld hrd: sn trcking ldr: led over 2f out: rdn over 1f out: hdd wl ins fnl f* **3/1**[1]

-226 **3** 5 **Cassiara**[13] 1961 3-8-12 **76**.. JohnEgan 13 74
(J Pearce) *hld up: hdwy u.p over 2f out: edgd lft: styd on same pce fnl f* **33/1**

4-61 **4** 1 **Arabian Treasure (USA)**[35] 1408 3-8-13 **77**....................... NCallan 10 73
(Sir Michael Stoute) *led: rdn and hdd over 2f out: no ex fnl f* **9/2**[3]

24-6 **5** nk **Flying Encore (IRE)**[12] 2010 3-8-11 **75**...................... StephenCarson 3 70
(W R Swinburn) *hld up: hdwy over 3f out: rdn and n.m.r over 1f out: styd on same pce* **33/1**

31 **6** nk **Jaleela (USA)**[11] 2046 3-9-7 **85**.. RHills 7 79
(W J Haggas) *s.i.s: hld up: hdwy over 3f out: sn rdn: edgd lft over 1f out: no ex* **4/1**[2]

106- **7** 5 **Miss Jenny (IRE)**[228] 6100 3-8-10 **81**.............................. KMay(7) 12 64
(B J Meehan) *hld up: nvr trbld ldrs* **100/1**

246- **8** 2 1/2 **Guacamole**[221] 6216 3-9-6 **84**.. MichaelHills 8 61
(B W Hills) *s.i.s: sn in midfield: rdn over 2f out: wknd wl over 1f out* **18/1**

01-0 **9** 2 1/2 **Milliegait**[18] 1851 3-8-13 **77**.. DavidAllan 2 48
(T D Easterby) *chsd ldrs over 5f* **25/1**

1-16 **10** 2 **Malyana**[27] 1610 3-9-1 **79**.. MatthewHenry 6 46
(M A Jarvis) *plld hrd and prom: wknd 2f out* **15/2**

000- **11** 1 3/4 **Samdaniya**[250] 5648 3-8-10 **74**.. JoeFanning 5 37
(C E Brittain) *trckd ldrs: plld hrd: wknd over 2f out* **25/1**

005- **12** 7 **Split Briefs (IRE)**[298] 4373 3-8-8 **72**.............................. PaulEddery 11 18
(D J Daly) *hld up: a in rr* **28/1**

1m 43.14s (-3.26) **Going Correction** -0.275s/f (Firm) **12** Ran SP% **116.4**
Speed ratings (Par 98):105,104,99,98,98 98,93,90,88,86 84,77
CSF £16.71 CT £403.05 TOTE £5.20: £1.60, £1.60, £8.00; EX 20.50.
Owner Tom Ludt **Bred** Keatly Overseas Ltd **Trained** Newmarket, Suffolk

FOCUS
A decent fillies' handicap and the form looks strong with the first two finishing clear. The time was good too. The front pair both produced improvement in the region of 11lb.

Jaleela(USA) Official explanation: jockey said filly became fractious in stalls
Guacamole Official explanation: jockey said filly had no more to give

2370 PERTEMPS PEOPLE DEVELOPMENT "HANDS AND HEELS" APPRENTICE SERIES H'CAP 1m 1f 213y
5:10 (5:12) (Class 6) (0-60,58) 4-Y-0+ **£2,388** (£705; £352) **Stalls** Low

Form RPR
051- **1** **Saluscraggie**[235] 5960 5-8-13 **51**............................. DanielleMcCreery 2 61+
(K G Reveley) *s.i.s: hld up: swtchd rt and hdwy over 2f out: edgd lft ins fnl f: r.o to ld post* **8/1**

6-45 **2** hd **Gizmondo**[37] 1347 4-9-3 **58**.. ChrisHough(3) 12 65
(M L W Bell) *chsd ldrs: effrt and hung lft over 1f out: led ins fnl f: hdd post* **13/2**[3]

0-20 **3** 1 **Moonshine Creek**[9] 2089 5-8-13 **51**............................. WilliamCarson 8 56
(P W Hiatt) *chsd ldr: led 1/2-way: pushed along 2f out: hdd and unable qck ins fnl f* **4/1**[1]

3426 **4** nk **Don Pasquale**[7] 2145 5-8-7 **45**.. SoniaEaton 7 49
(J T Stimpson) *hld up: hdwy over 3f out: styd on same pce ins fnl f* **12/1**

0300 **5** nk **Desert Hawk**[39] 1314 6-8-4 **50**...........................(b) Julie-AnneCumine(8) 3 55+
(W M Brisbourne) *hld up: plld hrd: hdwy over 3f out: n.m.r over 1f out: no ex towards fin* **25/1**

-004 **6** shd **King's Account (USA)**[11] 2027 5-9-1 **53**.........................(p) MCGeran 11 57
(S Gollings) *sn led: hdd 1/2-way: pushed along over 2f out: styd on same pce ins fnl f* **9/2**[2]

0300 **7** 2 **Baby Barry**[4] 2258 10-8-6 **52**.. GaryEdwards(8) 13 52
(S Parr) *plld hrd and prom: effrt over 2f out: no ex ins fnl f* **33/1**

00-0 **8** 1 **Inchloss (IRE)**[7] 2145 6-8-7 **45**.. MarkCoumbe 5 43
(S Parr) *chsd ldrs: effrt over 2f out: styd on same pce* **50/1**

0-00 **9** 3/4 **Grandad Bill (IRE)**[62] 932 4-9-1 **56**.............................. AlanRutter(3) 10 52
(W J Musson) *s.i.s: hld up: nvr trbld ldrs* **25/1**

65-0 **10** 13 **Silver Sail**[13] 1967 4-8-7 **45**.......................................(p) PatrickDonaghy 4 15
(J S Wainwright) *hld up: wknd over 3f out* **16/1**

305 **11** nk **Voice Mail**[16] 1886 8-8-9 **55**.......................................(v) DavidProbert(8) 6 25
(A M Balding) *chsd ldrs over 7f* **9/1**

-000 **12** 1 1/2 **Right Ted (IRE)**[34] 1435 4-8-7 **45**.. DeanHeslop 16 12
(T Wall) *hld up: wknd over 3f out* **40/1**

5000 **13** 2 **Orpen Quest (IRE)**[23] 1715 5-8-7 **45**.............................. JosephWalsh 1 8
(M J Attwater) *hld up: a bhd* **25/1**

00-0 **14** 1 1/2 **By Storm**[54] 1025 4-8-9 **47**.. HeatherMcGee 14 7
(John Berry) *chsd ldrs over 7f* **16/1**

0000 **15** 1 1/2 **Didnt Tell My Wife**[132] 243 8-8-7 **45**.......................(be) SophieDoyle 9 2
(P S McEntee) *hld up: wknd over 3f out* **80/1**

2102 **16** dist **Government (IRE)**[7] 2145 6-8-6 **49**.............................. MJMurphy(5) 15 —
(M C Chapman) *chsd ldrs: lost pl over 4f out: sn bhd: t.o* **14/1**

2m 9.44s (-0.26) **Going Correction** -0.275s/f (Firm) **16** Ran SP% **118.9**
Speed ratings (Par 101):90,89,89,88,88 88,86,86,85,75 74,73,72,70,69 —
CSF £53.86 CT £242.81 TOTE £10.50: £3.50, £1.90, £1.70, £3.60; EX 75.60.
Owner H B E Van Cutsem **Bred** Hilborough Stud Farm Ltd **Trained** Lingdale, Redcar & Cleveland

FOCUS
A typically weak handicap of its type, run at an ordinary pace. The form is fairly sound rated around the second, third and sixth.
Silver Sail Official explanation: trainer said filly got struck into on a hind leg
Orpen Quest(IRE) Official explanation: trainer said gelding was found to have bled after the race
Government(IRE) Official explanation: jockey said gelding had bled from the nose
T/Plt: £113.90 to a £1 stake. Pool: £44,812.90. 287.20 winning tickets. T/Qpdt: £8.40 to a £1 stake. Pool: £2,680.20. 235.10 winning tickets. CR

2337 RIPON (R-H)
Wednesday, June 6

OFFICIAL GOING: Good to firm
2 1/2mm water had been put on the track since the previous day. The ground was much the same, 'quick but no jar whatsoever'.
Wind: Moderate, half against Weather: Overcast and very cool

2371 EURA AUDIT UK YORKSHIRE'S SMALL BUSINESS ACCOUNTANTS MAIDEN STKS 6f
6:50 (6:51) (Class 5) 2-Y-0 **£3,238** (£963; £481; £240) **Stalls** Low

Form RPR
3 **1** **Russian Reel**[14] 1938 2-9-3 0.. NCallan 4 75+
(K A Ryan) *trckd ldr: led over 3f out: edgd rt and styd on strly ins fnl f* **7/2**[3]

2 **2** 1 1/2 **Nickel Silver**[17] 1858 2-9-3 0.. TomEaves 8 70
(B Smart) *w ldrs: upsides over 1f out: no ex ins fnl f* **15/8**[1]

24 **3** nk **Mission Impossible**[20] 1792 2-9-3 0.............................. LeeEnstone 2 69
(P C Haslam) *trckd ldrs: effrt 2f out: kpt on wl ins fnl f* **11/4**[2]

4 1 1/2 **Hurstpierpoint (IRE)** 2-8-7 0.............................. JamieMoriarty(5) 6 60+
(R A Fahey) *swvd rt s: sn bhd: hdwy 2f out: styd on wl ins fnl f: improve* **50/1**

54 **5** 1/2 **Timewatch**[33] 1454 2-9-3 0.. KDarley 9 63
(M Johnston) *mid-div: outpcd over 3f out: kpt on fnl 2f* **12/1**

5 **6** 1/2 **The Last Bottle (IRE)**[20] 1792 2-9-3 0.............................. MickyFenton 7 62
(T P Tate) *restless in stalls: chsd ldrs: sn drvn along: outpcd over 3f out: swtchd rt over 2f out: kpt on: nvr a threat* **9/2**

6 **7** nk **Rich James (IRE)**[17] 1859 2-9-3 0.............................. PatCosgrave 10 61
(J D Bethell) *mid-div: kpt on fnl 2f: nvr nr ldrs* **50/1**

0 **8** 9 **Handsinthemist (IRE)**[13] 1963 2-8-12 0....................... PaulMulrennan 1 29
(P T Midgley) *led tl over 3f out: lost pl over 1f out* **100/1**

9 5 **Astrol** 2-8-12 0.. TonyHamilton 3 14
(T D Easterby) *s.i.s: in rr: bhd fnl 2f* **66/1**

0 **10** 10 **Limelight (USA)**[13] 1960 2-8-12 0.............................. PaulHanagan 5 —
(Sir Mark Prescott) *dwlt: sn outpcd in rr: bhd fnl 2f* **40/1**

1m 14.98s (1.98) **Going Correction** +0.15s/f (Good) **10** Ran SP% **118.4**
Speed ratings (Par 93):92,90,89,87,86 86,85,73,67,53
CSF £10.57 TOTE £5.40: £2.00, £1.70, £1.10; EX 9.30.
Owner John Browne **Bred** Bearstone Stud **Trained** Hambleton, N Yorks

FOCUS
The placed horses are fair yardsticks and this looked an above-average juvenile maiden. Solid form, the winner improving from Ayr.

NOTEBOOK
Russian Reel, a good-bodied individual, has a fair amount of size about him. Happy to accept a lead, he seemed to appreciate the much quicker ground and was firmly in command at the line. A drop back to five will not be a problem and he should improve again. (op 4-1)
Nickel Silver is not very big but is very solidly made. He looked likely to give the winner a real fight entering the last but at the line was very much second best. He can surely go one better. (op 13-8 tchd 9-4 and 5-2 in places)

Mission Impossible, on the leg and narrow, did nothing wrong but did not see out the sixth furlong quite as well as the first two. (op 10-3 tchd 7-2 and 4-1 in a place)
Hurstpierpoint(IRE), a March foal, is out of a mare that won over a mile and a half. Only small, after going sideways at the start she put in some sterling late work. She will know a lot more next time. (tchd 66-1)
Timewatch, still carrying plenty of condition, shaped as though he still needs time and a step up to seven. (op 14-1 tchd 16-1)
The Last Bottle(IRE), very agitated in the stalls, was never galloping on an even keel. Seven furlongs and a much more galloping track will see him in a much more favourable light when he returns to action after being gelded. (tchd 7-2 and 5-1)
Rich James(IRE), though never a threat, showed a good deal more than he had done on his debut two weeks earlier.
Limelight(USA) (op 33-1)

2372 BOROUGHBRIDGE (S) H'CAP 1m 4f 10y
7:20 (7:20) (Class 6) (0-60,52) 4-5-Y-O **£2,590** (£770; £385; £192) **Stalls** High

Form RPR
000- **1** **Revolving World (IRE)**[159] 6972 4-8-13 47 ....(t) KDarley 3 56
(L R James) *t.k.h in rr: hdwy over 3f out: styd on to ld towards fin* **14/1**
-000 **2** 3/4 **Hits Only Life (USA)**[16] 1906 4-9-0 48 ....(b[1]) NCallan 1 56
(J Pearce) *hld up in rr: hdwy over 3f out: wnt 2nd 1f out: styd on to ld last 75yds: hdd nr fin* **12/1**
0000 **3** 1 1/2 **Danceinthevalley (IRE)**[37] 1362 5-8-11 45 .... TonyHamilton 10 51
(I W McInnes) *led: t.k.h: clr after 3f: rn wd bnd over 5f out: hung lft: wknd and hdd ins fnl f* **12/1**
064- **4** 4 **Tiltili (IRE)**[15] 5365 4-9-0 48 .... LeeEnstone 7 47
(P C Haslam) *s.i.s: hdwy on ins 3f out: nvr rchd ldrs* **20/1**
0-00 **5** 1 1/4 **Just Waz (USA)**[13] 1966 5-8-6 45 ....(v) MichaelJStainton[(5)] 5 42
(R M Whitaker) *t.k.h in mid-div: effrt and hmpd over 2f out: kpt on fnl f* **5/1**[3]
50-5 **6** 1/2 **Desert Lightning (IRE)**[6] 2168 5-9-4 52 .... JHBowman 9 48
(K R Burke) *chsd ldrs: wnt 2nd 2f out: wknd 1f out* **2/1**[1]
0-05 **7** nk **Loch Awe**[9] 2095 4-8-9 46 .... MarkLawson[(3)] 6 42
(R E Barr) *chsd ldrs: rdn 4f out: edgd lft and wknd 2f out* **22/1**
0040 **8** 1 1/2 **Gala Jackpot (USA)**[7] 2157 4-8-11 45 .... PaulMulrennan 2 39
(W M Brisbourne) *in rr: effrt 4f out: edgd lft and lost pl 2f out* **28/1**
500- **9** nk **Sweet Lavinia**[216] 6305 4-8-11 45 .... PatCosgrave 8 38
(J D Bethell) *chsd ldrs: drvn over 3f out: lost pl over 1f out* **15/2**
53-3 **10** 1 3/4 **Inchdhuaig (IRE)**[11] 1671 4-8-11 52 ....(p) NeilBrown[(7)] 4 42
(P C Haslam) *hld up in mid-div: hdwy over 4f out: wknd 2f out* **4/1**[2]

2m 38.63s (1.63) **Going Correction** +0.15s/f (Good) **10** Ran SP% **116.4**
Speed ratings: 100,99,98,95,95 94,94,93,93,92
CSF £163.84 CT £2074.42 TOTE £17.90: £4.90, £2.60, £4.70; EX 133.20.There was no bid for the winner.
Owner L R James Limited **Bred** Kilboy Stud **Trained** Norton, N Yorks

FOCUS
A rock-bottom selling handicap with the clear leader only being overhauled late on. The race has been rated through the runner-up for the time being.

2373 SKY TELEVISION H'CAP 6f
7:50 (7:50) (Class 4) (0-85,84) 3-Y-O **£5,047** (£1,510; £755; £377; £188) **Stalls** Low

Form RPR
-120 **1** **King's Apostle (IRE)**[18] 1851 3-9-2 79 .... PaulMulrennan 7 84
(W J Haggas) *w ldrs: led 2f out: hung fire and edgd lft over 1f out: hld on wl towards fin* **8/1**
6-22 **2** 3/4 **Valley Of The Moon (IRE)**[19] 1802 3-8-12 75 .... PaulHanagan 1 78+
(R A Fahey) *trckd ldrs: effrt and nt clr run appr fnl f: squeezed through: styd on towards fin* **6/1**[3]
1-00 **3** shd **Handsome Falcon**[25] 1658 3-8-11 74 .... TonyHamilton 8 77+
(R A Fahey) *swtchd lft after s: hdwy 2f out: styd on same pce ins fnl f* **16/1**
-016 **4** 2 **Lord Theo**[15] 1930 3-9-3 80 .... JHBowman 5 77
(N P Littmoden) *chsd ldrs: carried lft over 1f out: kpt on same pce* **9/1**
-232 **5** 2 1/2 **Mundo's Magic**[6] 2171 3-8-10 73 .... TomEaves 3 66+
(G M Moore) *led tl 2f out: keeping on same pce whn hmpd appr fnl f* **6/1**[3]
21-3 **6** nk **Musca (IRE)**[21] 1768 3-9-2 84 .... JamieMoriarty[(5)] 2 72
(J Howard Johnson) *chsd ldrs: t.k.h: nt clr run over 2f out: wknd fnl f* **5/2**[1]
01- **7** 6 **Fabuleux Millie (IRE)**[252] 5606 3-9-1 78 .... NCallan 4 48
(R M Beckett) *t.k.h in midfield: rdn and hung rt 2f out: sn wknd* **11/4**[2]
0-00 **8** 2 1/2 **Prince Rossi (IRE)**[13] 1965 3-8-0 66 ow1 ....(p) AndrewElliott[(3)] 6 29
(J D Bethell) *chsd ldrs: rdn and lost pl over 2f out* **25/1**

1m 13.67s (0.67) **Going Correction** +0.15s/f (Good) **8** Ran SP% **114.6**
Speed ratings (Par 101):101,100,99,97,93 93,85,82
CSF £55.07 CT £757.38 TOTE £9.50: £2.60, £1.90, £3.10; EX 36.80.
Owner Wentworth Racing (pty) Ltd **Bred** Wentworth Racing **Trained** Newmarket, Suffolk

FOCUS
A tight-knit sprint but a fair amount of traffic problems with the consistent runner-up out of luck. Sound form.

2374 DIRECTORS CUP (HANDICAP STKS) 1m
8:20 (8:20) (Class 3) (0-95,95) 4-Y-O+
£9,348 (£2,799; £1,399; £700; £349; £175) **Stalls** High

Form RPR
2630 **1** **Royal Dignitary (USA)**[25] 1651 7-8-11 85 .... AdrianTNicholls 11 96
(D Nicholls) *mde all: styd on wl fnl 2f: drvn out* **20/1**
0312 **2** 1 1/4 **Exit Smiling**[41] 1264 5-8-2 76 oh2 .... HayleyTurner 1 84+
(P T Midgley) *in rr: hdwy over 2f out: swtchd lft over 1f out: styd on wl to take 2nd ins fnl f: no real imp* **20/1**
-120 **3** 1 1/4 **Bustan (IRE)**[19] 1818 8-9-5 93 .... NCallan 6 98
(G C Bravery) *chsd ldrs: kpt on same pce fnl 2f* **8/1**[3]
1566 **4** 1 **Robustian**[12] 2003 4-8-10 84 .... StephenCarson 12 87
(Eve Johnson Houghton) *chsd ldrs: chal 3f out: kpt on same pce* **8/1**[3]
60-0 **5** 1 1/4 **Bajan Parkes**[18] 1852 4-8-6 80 .... KDarley 3 80
(E J Alston) *s.s: bhd tl styd on wl fnl 2f* **50/1**
10-2 **6** 1/2 **Stonehaugh (IRE)**[33] 1458 4-8-6 80 ow1 ....(t) JohnEgan 8 79
(J Howard Johnson) *mid-div: effrt over 3f out: sn chsng ldrs: hung rt and wknd appr fnl f* **9/1**
00-5 **7** shd **Vicious Warrior**[12] 1996 8-8-6 85 .... MichaelJStainton[(5)] 5 84
(R M Whitaker) *chsd ldrs: edgd lft over 2f out: one pce* **25/1**
0-3 **8** 8 **Desert Chief**[125] 325 5-9-7 95 .... LDettori 9 75
(Saeed Bin Suroor) *hld up in rr: hdwy 4f out: n.m.r over 2f out: hung rt and wknd over 1f out* **13/8**[1]
-451 **9** 1/2 **Bold Marc (IRE)**[11] 2038 5-8-7 81 .... PatCosgrave 7 60
(K R Burke) *chsd ldrs: chal 3f out: lost pl over 1f out* **11/1**
-062 **10** 1 **Little Jimbob**[19] 1040 6-8-6 80 .... PaulHanagan 10 57
(R A Fahey) *trckd ldrs: wknd 2f out* **16/1**
00-5 **11** 1 3/4 **Black Charmer (IRE)**[20] 1791 4-9-4 92 .... JoeFanning 2 65
(M Johnston) *chsd ldrs: sn drvn along: wandered and lost pl over 1f out* **11/2**[2]
62-0 **12** 6 **Magic Sting**[7] 2136 6-8-6 80 .... SilvestreDeSousa 4 39
(B S Rothwell) *dwlt: a in rr: bhd fnl 3f* **66/1**

1m 39.82s (-1.28) **Going Correction** +0.15s/f (Good) **12** Ran SP% **116.7**
Speed ratings (Par 107):112,110,109,108,107 106,106,98,98,97 95,89
CSF £343.04 CT £3482.93 TOTE £20.60: £5.60, £5.10, £3.10; EX 574.80.
Owner Middleham Park Racing XXXVI **Bred** Bentley Smith, J Michael O'Farrell Jr , Joan Thor **Trained** Sessay, N Yorks

FOCUS
The winner had his own way out in front from an ideal draw. A fair handicap, and the form has a reasonably solid look about it.

NOTEBOOK
Royal Dignitary(USA), ideally drawn, is a natural front-runner and, given his own way here, he kept up the gallop all the way to the line. A turning mile is his cup of tea.
Exit Smiling, 2lb out of the handicap, had to switch wide for a run. He stayed on in determined fashion to follow the winner home but in truth was never going to seriously trouble him. (op 18-1)
Bustan(IRE) put a poor effort at Newmarket last time behind him and looked rejuvenated this year. (tchd 15-2)
Robustian, dropping back in trip, had the sound pace he needs but he is still 2lb higher than his Pontefract win. (op 17-2 tchd 9-1)
Bajan Parkes, having just his second outing for this stable, blew his chance at the start. He made considerable late ground and seemed well suited by the step up to a mile.
Stonehaugh(IRE), 2lb higher, made his effort hard against the running rail but in the end the extra furlong found him out. (op 8-1)
Desert Chief, third behind Sir Gerard at Nad Al Sheba in February, looked in good nick, but after being left short of room he hung in towards the fence and dropped right out of it. (op 9-4)
Black Charmer(IRE), who moved poorly to post, was never happy and never seemed to be racing on an even keel. He may have a problem. (op 7-2 tchd 6-1)

2375 RIPON FARM SERVICES H'CAP 2m
8:50 (8:50) (Class 5) (0-75,67) 4-Y-O+ **£3,562** (£1,059; £529; £264) **Stalls** Low

Form RPR
120- **1** **Industrial Star (IRE)**[13] 3955 6-9-7 67 ....(p) KDarley 5 74
(Micky Hammond) *chsd ldr: led 3f out: edgd rt over 1f out: styd on* **11/1**
026- **2** nk **Thewhirlingdervish (IRE)**[215] 6321 9-9-3 63 .... DavidAllan 7 70
(T D Easterby) *chsd ldrs: effrt on inner over 4f out: upsides 1f out: no ex towards fin* **6/1**
/326 **3** 3 1/2 **Garnett (IRE)**[11] 691 6-9-5 65 ....(v) PatCosgrave 6 68
(D E Cantillon) *hld up: effrt over 3f out: kpt on to take 3rd ins fnl f* **3/1**[2]
6013 **4** nk **Spring Dream (IRE)**[9] 2082 4-9-5 66 .... JHBowman 3 68
(M R Channon) *hld up: hdwy over 3f out: sn edgd rt: rdn 2f out: kpt on one pce* **9/2**[3]
-504 **5** 2 1/2 **Rose Bien**[20] 1793 5-8-13 62 ....(p) DuranFentiman[(3)] 1 61
(P J McBride) *hld up: hdwy to chse ldrs 5f out: sltly hmpd 3f out: wknd over 1f out* **15/8**[1]
00-0 **6** 3/4 **Our Monogram**[42] 1253 11-9-7 67 .... JosedeSouza 2 66
(R M Beckett) *led: hung lft 10f out: sn pushed along: hdd 3f out: lost pl over 1f out* **7/1**

3m 36.07s (3.07) **Going Correction** +0.15s/f (Good)
WFA 4 from 5yo+ 1lb **6** Ran SP% **113.1**
Speed ratings (Par 103):98,97,96,95,94 94
CSF £72.81 TOTE £9.80: £3.40, £1.90; EX 29.50.
Owner Racing Management & Training Ltd **Bred** Emanuele Patruno **Trained** Middleham Moor, N Yorks

FOCUS
Just a steady gallop and a bit of a sprint finish to this ordinary stayers' handicap, rated through the runner-up and the fourth.

2376 EURA AUDIT UK MAIDEN STKS 1m 1f 170y
9:20 (9:21) (Class 5) 3-Y-O+ **£3,238** (£963; £481; £240) **Stalls** High

Form RPR
6-2 **1** **Jalil (USA)**[19] 1812 3-8-11 0 .... LDettori 6 78
(Saeed Bin Suroor) *mde all: drvn over 2f out: hld on towards fin* **2/9**[1]
4 **2** 1/2 **Fantastic Morning**[75] 745 3-8-11 0 .... JoeFanning 2 77
(M Johnston) *hld up: hdwy 4f out: edgd rt over 1f out: styd on ins fnl f* **10/1**[3]
-533 **3** 1 3/4 **King Joshua (IRE)**[16] 1898 3-8-11 74 .... JohnEgan 4 73
(D R C Elsworth) *t.k.h: trckd ldrs: rdn and edgd lft over 2f out: kpt on same pce* **4/1**[2]
4 14 **Go But Go** 3-8-11 0 .... NCallan 3 45
(E J O'Neill) *dwlt: sn chsng wnr: drvn over 4f out: lost pl 3f out* **25/1**
00 **5** 14 **Miss Lightning**[23] 1716 4-9-5 0 .... TomEaves 5 12
(R Bastiman) *hld up in last: drvn 4f out: sn lost tch* **100/1**

2m 5.35s (0.35) **Going Correction** +0.15s/f (Good)
WFA 3 from 4yo 13lb **5** Ran SP% **115.8**
Speed ratings (Par 103):104,103,102,91,79
CSF £4.20 TOTE £1.40: £1.10, £4.80; EX 3.70 Place 6 £3,285.81, Place 5 £2,757.56.
Owner Godolphin **Bred** And Mrs Martin J Wygod **Trained** Newmarket, Suffolk

FOCUS
The winner had his own way in front but in the end he had to be kept right up to his work. The 74-rated third sets the standard, with Jalil not needing to match his Newbury form.
T/Plt: £1,143.50 to a £1 stake. Pool: £67,751.80. 43.25 winning tickets. T/Qpdt: £55.30 to a £1 stake. Pool: £4,656.40. 62.25 winning tickets. WG

2377 - 2378a (Foreign Racing) - See Raceform Interactive

2158 LEOPARDSTOWN (L-H)
Wednesday, June 6

OFFICIAL GOING: Good

2379a BALLYOGAN STKS (GROUP 3) (F&M) 6f
7:00 (7:00) 3-Y-O+ **£30,743** (£8,986; £4,256; £1,418)

RPR
1 **Liscanna (IRE)**[24] 1694 3-8-12 100 .... WMLordan 4 103
(David Wachman, Ire) *towards rr: hdwy early st: 3rd 1f out: sn chal: led cl home* **7/1**
2 nk **That's Hot (IRE)**[33] 1461 4-9-6 100 .... DPMcDonogh 5 104
(G M Lyons, Ire) *trckd ldrs: mod 3rd 1/2-way: 4th and rdn early st: led wl ins fnl f: hdd cl home* **11/2**[2]
3 3/4 **Absolutelyfabulous (IRE)**[11] 2050 4-9-6 101 .... MJKinane 8 102+
(David Wachman, Ire) *chsd ldrs early: 8th 1/2-way: prog early st: 4th under 1f out: kpt on wl cl home* **12/1**

4 *nk* **Grecian Dancer**[19] 1829 4-9-6 95 .... FMBerry 2 101
(Charles O'Brien, Ire) *chsd ldrs: mod 2nd 1/2-way: hdwy ent st: led and edgd lft 1 1/2f out: hdd wl ins fnl f: no ex cl home* **10/1**

5 *2 1/2* **Theann**[11] 2050 3-8-12 102 .... JAHeffernan 1 92
(A P O'Brien, Ire) *trckd ldrs: mod 4th 1/2-way: 3rd and hdwy early st: hmpd 1 1/2f out: no ex* **11/8**[1]

6 *1 3/4* **Million Spirits (IRE)**[10] 2068 3-8-12 88 .... KJManning 6 86
(Kevin Prendergast, Ire) *in rr: rdn and kpt on st* **50/1**

7 *2* **Folga**[25] 1670 5-9-6 .... PJSmullen 7 82
(J G Given) *chsd ldrs: 6th 1/2-way: no ex st* **8/1**

8 *7* **Divert (IRE)**[5] 2227 3-8-12 88 .... CDHayes 9 59
(Edward Lynam, Ire) *led and sn wl clr: reduced advantage early st: hdd whn hmpd 1 1/2f out: no ex and wknd* **20/1**

9 *1/2* **Leitra (IRE)**[11] 2050 4-9-6 102 .... JMurtagh 3 60
(M Halford, Ire) *chsd ldrs: mod 5th 1/2-way: no imp st: eased fnl f* **6/1**[3]

1m 12.8s (-0.70) **Going Correction** +0.15s/f (Good)
WFA 3 from 4yo+ 8lb **9** Ran SP% **118.9**
Speed ratings: 110,109,108,108,104 102,99,90,89
CSF £46.62 TOTE £8.90: £2.40, £2.10, £3.20; DF 114.90.
Owner Mrs E M Stockwell **Bred** Western Bloodstock **Trained** Goolds Cross, Co Tipperary
■ Stewards' Enquiry : F M Berry four -day ban: careless riding (Jun 15-18)

FOCUS
A competitive Group 3 that attracted just one previous Stakes winner. The fourth and sixth set the level.

NOTEBOOK
Liscanna(IRE) produced a career-best effort to score. She showed she had made good progress over the winter with a close fourth to Arch Swing here in April and a respectable fifth to Alexander Tango last month. In a race run at a strong pace, she was given a patient ride as she dropped back to this trip for the first time since winning the Birdcatcher. She still had plenty to do turning in but stayed on strongly under pressure from over a furlong out and got to the front close home. He trainer reported that she likes an ease in the ground and that this surface was as quick as she would like. The Brownstown Stakes over 7f here next month could be next for her. (op 7/1 tchd 8/1)
That's Hot(IRE), who was an unlucky second in a Cork Listed race last time, ran a fine race in defeat. She stuck to her task well to take charge inside the final furlong but was just unable to fend off the winner. A reliable sort, she deserves to get her turn at Stakes level. (op 11/2 tchd 6/1)
Absolutelyfabulous(IRE) stayed on quite well over the final two furlongs and returned to the form she showed when winning a Listed race at Cork last month. She provides a good guide to the value of the form and once again looked as though she could be worth trying over 7f. (op 8/1)
Grecian Dancer has been in most progressive form in handicaps and turned in a solid effort stepped up to Stakes level. On this evidence she will prove capable of picking up black-type. (op 8/1)
Theann, previously a fine third to Benbaun and Moss Vale in the Greenlands Stakes, along with Divert was tightened up by Grecian Dancer inside the final quarter of a mile, and was not at her best. She was in contention two furlongs from home but was soon unable to raise her effort. (op 7/4 tchd 5/4)
Folga, who was placed in a Listed race at Bath last month, would have preferred a faster surface and she was found out in this slightly better grade. (op 7/1 tchd 10/1)

2380 - 2383a (Foreign Racing) - See Raceform Interactive

FONTAINEBLEAU
Wednesday, June 6

OFFICIAL GOING: Soft

2384a PRIX MELISANDE (GRAND PRIX DE FONTAINEBLEAU) (LISTED RACE) (FILLIES) 1m 2f
2:35 (2:36) 3-Y-O **£17,568** (£7,027; £5,270; £3,514; £1,757)

RPR

1 **Kaloura (IRE)**[24] 1705 3-8-12 .... CSoumillon 5 99
(A Fabre, France)

2 *1* **Party (IRE)**[228] 6105 3-8-12 .... SPasquier 7 97
(R Hannon) *prom: 3rd st: pushed along to chal 1 1/2f out: disp ld 150yds out: r.o* **76/10**[1]

3 *3/4* **Claire Et Bleu (FR)**[24] 1705 3-8-12 .... TThulliez 1 96
(Mme M Bollack-Badel, France)

4 *hd* **Sismix (IRE)**[36] 1388 3-9-2 .... OPeslier 2 100
(C Laffon-Parias, France)

5 *3/4* **Singapore Creek (FR)**[7] 3-8-12 .... SMaillot 6 94
(Robert Collet, France)

6 *snk* **Noble Ginger (FR)**[17] 3-8-12 .... THuet 3 94
(J E Pease, France)

7 *1* **Carolines Secret**[241] 5858 3-8-12 .... ASuborics 4 92
(Mario Hofer, Germany)

2m 0.90s (120.90) **7** Ran SP% **11.6**
PARI-MUTUEL (including 1 Euro stake): WIN 1.70; PL 1.30, 2.40; DF 5.80.
Owner H H Aga Khan **Bred** His Highness The Aga Khan's Studs S C **Trained** Chantilly, France

NOTEBOOK
Party(IRE) put up an excellent performance considering she was making her seasonal debut against six fillies who had already appeared this season. Always well placed, she took over the lead for a short time a furlong out and was then run out of it in the final half furlong. This outing will have certainly brought her on, and she could well run in the Ribbesdale Stakes at Royal Ascot next. The longer trip may well suit.

1801 HAMILTON (R-H)
Thursday, June 7

OFFICIAL GOING: Good to firm (good in places) changing to good to firm after race 5 (4.05)
Wind: Almost nil

2385 TARTAN TURF TOURS MAIDEN AUCTION STKS 6f 5y
2:00 (2:01) (Class 6) 2-Y-O **£2,590** (£770; £385; £192) **Stalls** Centre

Form RPR

24 1 **Lady Benjamin**[24] 1727 2-8-8 0 .... LeeEnstone 3 67
(P C Haslam) *mde all: rdn 2f out: hld on wl fnl f* **7/4**[1]

4 2 *shd* **Creative (IRE)**[11] 2056 2-8-11 0 .... JimmyQuinn 6 70
(M H Tompkins) *trckd ldrs: effrt over 1f out: chal ins fnl f: jst failed* **7/4**[1]

3 *1* **Rahere (IRE)** 2-9-0 0 .... JoeFanning 1 70
(M Johnston) *t.k.h: cl up: shkn up over 1f out: kpt on fnl f* **9/2**[2]

00 4 *7* **Zaplamation (IRE)**[21] 1792 2-9-2 0 .... TonyHamilton 4 51
(D W Barker) *prom tl hung rt and outpcd fr 2f out* **6/1**[3]

5 *4* **Premium Port** 2-8-5 0 .... PatrickMathers[(3)] 2 31
(A Berry) *bhd and sn outpcd: nvr on terms* **50/1**

6 *36* **Robslastcall** 2-8-3 0 .... PaulQuinn 5 —
(A Berry) *s.i.s: sn t.o* **25/1**

1m 13.19s (0.09) **Going Correction** -0.35s/f (Firm) **6** Ran SP% **111.0**
Speed ratings (Par 91):85,84,83,74,68 20
CSF £4.73 TOTE £2.90: £1.70, £1.20; EX 5.40.
Owner S A B Dinsmore & Geoffrey Lampard **Bred** Llety Stud **Trained** Middleham Moor, N Yorks
■ Stewards' Enquiry : Jimmy Quinn two-day ban: used whip with excessive frequency (Jun 18, 24)

FOCUS
Just an ordinary maiden but one in which the pace seemed fair throughout. Probably a moderate race.

NOTEBOOK
Lady Benjamin, returned to turf, appreciated the step up to 6f and showed a good attitude to get off the mark. She should stay 7f and may be capable of a bit better when the nursery season gets under way. (op 15-8)
Creative(IRE), who shaped with credit on his debut at Newmarket, bettered that effort over this longer trip and on this quicker ground. He has scope for improvement and looks capable of landing a similar event. (op 15-8)
Rahere(IRE) ◆, from a stable whose juveniles have generally struggled this term, was green but shaped with promise against two more experienced rivals on this racecourse debut. He should be better for this run and is the type to win a similar event. (op 10-3 tchd 3-1 in a place early)
Zaplamation(IRE), who had shown only modest form in two starts, looked ill at ease on this course and again had his limitations exposed in this type of event. He may do better in ordinary handicaps in due course. (op 9-1)
Premium Port, out of a modest winner over 7f and 1m, offered little immediate promise on this racecourse debut. (op 66-1)
Robslastcall, a cheap purchase, was soundly beaten after a tardy start. Official explanation: trainer said filly was in season

2386 HEALTH MATTERS FOR MEN H'CAP 5f 4y
2:30 (2:32) (Class 6) (0-65,64) 3-Y-O+ **£2,388** (£705; £352) **Stalls** Centre

Form RPR

6523 1 **Katie Boo (IRE)**[15] 1940 5-9-3 54 .... JoeFanning 12 62
(A Berry) *chsd ldrs: led over 1f out: overall ldr ins fnl f: r.o* **7/1**[3]

0610 2 *1/2* **Brut**[30] 1557 5-9-7 58 .... (p) TonyHamilton 13 64+
(D W Barker) *racd alone far side: overall ldr: rdn over 2f out: edgd lft and hdd wl ins fnl f: r.o* **15/2**

6001 3 *shd* **Seven No Trumps**[9] 2104 10-9-0 51 6ex .... NCallan 6 57
(J M Bradley) *in tch: effrt over 1f out: kpt on fnl f: nrst fin* **12/1**

0002 4 *1* **Trinculo (IRE)**[9] 2104 10-9-6 57 .... (b) PhillipMakin 10 59
(R A Harris) *prom: drvn over 2f out: kpt on ins fnl f* **8/1**

4000 5 *hd* **Sandwith**[20] 1806 4-9-8 64 .... (p) PJMcDonald[(5)] 8 66
(J S Wainwright) *led to over 1f out: kpt on same pce* **11/1**

00-0 6 *3/4* **Parkside Pursuit**[13] 1991 9-9-1 52 .... PaulMulrennan 9 51+
(J M Bradley) *towards rr: rdn 1/2-way: effrt over 1f out: nvr nrr* **18/1**

0-06 7 *nk* **Hotham**[30] 1557 4-9-8 59 .... JimmyQuinn 5 57
(N Wilson) *cl up tl rdn and no ex over 1f out* **6/1**[2]

6362 8 *nk* **Divine Spirit**[26] 1681 6-9-7 58 .... (b) TomEaves 3 55
(M Dods) *prom: effrt 2f out: sn no ex* **10/3**[1]

00-0 9 *1 1/2* **Strawberry Patch (IRE)**[20] 1806 8-8-10 54 .... (p) GaryBartley[(7)] 1 45
(J S Goldie) *bhd and rdn along: nvr rchd ldrs* **16/1**

0-60 10 *2* **Flying Tackle**[115] 441 9-8-8 48 .... (v) AndrewElliott[(3)] 14 32
(I W McInnes) *bhd: shortlived effrt over 2f out: n.d* **28/1**

14-0 11 *nk* **The Old Soldier**[43] 1241 9-8-12 52 .... DuranFentiman[(3)] 11 35
(A Dickman) *dwlt: n.d* **14/1**

261- 12 *1 1/4* **Rosie's Result**[294] 4523 7-8-5 45 .... AndrewMullen[(3)] 2 24
(M Todhunter) *in tch to 1/2-way: sn btn* **16/1**

0-00 13 *3 1/2* **Howards Prince**[17] 1891 4-8-7 47 ow2 .... (p) MarkLawson[(3)] 4 13
(D A Nolan) *in tch 2f: sn rdn and btn* **200/1**

59.41 secs (-1.79) **Going Correction** -0.35s/f (Firm) **13** Ran SP% **116.4**
Speed ratings (Par 101):100,99,99,97,97 95,95,94,92,89 88,86,81
CSF £57.13 CT £642.15 TOTE £6.50: £2.30, £3.20, £2.90; EX 55.60.
Owner The Early Doors Partnership **Bred** Michael McGlynn **Trained** Cockerham, Lancs

FOCUS
A modest handicap in which all except runner-up Brut raced centre to stands' side. The pace was sound. Ordinary form, rated through the third and fourth.

2387 BETRESCUE ANTEPOSTMAG.COM CLAIMING STKS 6f 5y
3:00 (3:00) (Class 6) 3-4-Y-O **£2,388** (£705; £352) **Stalls** Centre

Form RPR

-052 1 **Riverside Dancer (USA)**[6] 2200 3-8-9 70 .... NCallan 2 68
(K A Ryan) *chsd stands' side ldrs: led 1/2-way: edgd rt ins fnl f: hld on wl* **7/4**[1]

-430 2 *1* **Howards Tipple**[31] 1530 3-8-6 64 .... (v) TomEaves 3 64
(I Semple) *prom stands' side: stdy hdwy to press wnr over 2f out: effrt over 1f out: one pce fnl f* **10/3**[2]

5506 3 *8* **Dolly Coughdrop (IRE)**[7] 2171 3-8-0 68 ow5 .... AndrewElliott[(3)] 5 35
(K R Burke) *prom far side: rdn to ld that gp ins fnl f: no ch w stands' side* **7/1**

0-00 4 *2* **Lucky Bee (IRE)**[31] 1530 3-8-11 67 .... DeanMcKeown 7 37
(G A Swinbank) *in tch far side: effrt and edgd rt over 2f out: no imp fnl f* **12/1**

5144 5 *3/4* **Phinerine**[6] 2220 4-9-0 54 .... (b) SebSanders 6 30
(Miss J E Foster) *led far side to ins fnl f: sn btn* **8/1**

00-0 6 *3 1/2* **Signor Whippee**[32] 1493 4-9-1 49 .... (b) TonyHamilton 9 20
(A Berry) *chsd far side ldrs to over 2f out: sn btn* **40/1**

4423 7 *2 1/2* **Strike Force**[5] 2262 3-8-8 57 .... (b[1]) JoeFanning 4 14
(R A Harris) *cl up stands' side to over 2f out: sn btn* **9/2**[3]

00- 8 *1* **Northern Candy**[242] 5835 3-8-3 0 .... (p) DuranFentiman[(3)] 8 9
(A Dickman) *cl up far side tl rdn and wknd over 2f out* **100/1**

0 9 *1/2* **Maysridge Ofkuwait**[12] 2032 3-8-3 0 .... PaulQuinn 1 4
(A Berry) *led stands' side to 1/2-way: sn btn* **125/1**

1m 11.03s (-2.07) **Going Correction** -0.35s/f (Firm)
WFA 3 from 4yo 8lb **9** Ran SP% **113.2**
Speed ratings (Par 101):99,97,87,84,83 78,75,74,73
CSF £7.38 TOTE £2.10: £1.20, £1.30, £2.30; EX 10.80.The winner was claimed by T. J. Pitt for £16,000.
Owner J K Shannon **Bred** Dr Walter W And Mrs Zent **Trained** Hambleton, N Yorks
■ Stewards' Enquiry : N Callan caution: careless riding

FOCUS
A modest event in which the field split evenly but the two market leaders, who raced in the stands'-side group, pulled clear in the last quarter mile. The first two were slightly up on this year's form.

2388 DM HALL H'CAP (QUALIFIER FOR THE HAMILTON PARK HANDICAP SERIES FINAL) 1m 65y
3:35 (3:36) (Class 5) (0-70,70) 4-Y-0+ **£3,886** (£1,156; £577; £288) **Stalls High**

Form RPR
0411 **1** **Networker**[8] 2154 4-9-1 **64** 6ex.. NCallan 1 70+
(P J McBride) *hld up: effrt whn nt clr run over 2f out: swtchd lft and hdwy wl over 1f out: styd on wl to ld towards fin* **11/8**[1]
-650 **2** *nk* **Defi (IRE)**[85] 674 5-9-3 **66**..(b) TomEaves 7 71
(I Semple) *cl up: led over 1f out: kpt on: hdd towards fin* **20/1**
1-50 **3** *hd* **Anthemion (IRE)**[27] 1627 10-8-4 **56**.......................... AndrewMullen(3) 5 61
(Mrs J C McGregor) *led: rdn and hdd over 1f out: kpt on ins fnl f* **66/1**
0063 **4** *nk* **Mayadeen (IRE)**[17] 1893 5-8-0 **52**........................(b) DuranFentiman(3) 10 56
(I Semple) *hld up on ins: hdwy over 2f out: styd on wl towards fin* **9/1**
2111 **5** *3/4* **Very Well Red**[12] 2023 4-8-13 **69**.......................... WilliamCarson(7) 4 71
(P W Hiatt) *cl up: effrt and ev ch over 2f out: kpt on same pce fnl f* **4/1**[2]
0-02 **6** *shd* **Mandarin Rocket (IRE)**[7] 2168 4-8-2 **51** oh1................. JimmyQuinn 8 53
(Miss L A Perratt) *trckd ldrs: effrt over 2f out: one pce fnl f* **33/1**
6350 **7** *nk* **Northern Boy (USA)**[12] 2023 4-9-4 **67**............................ PhillipMakin 3 68
(T D Barron) *hld up: hdwy over 2f out: no imp fnl f* **12/1**
-000 **8** *1/2* **Regent's Secret (USA)**[28] 1599 7-9-0 **70**...................... GaryBartley(7) 9 70+
(J S Goldie) *hld up and wl bhd: stdy hdwy over 1f out: nvr nr ldrs* **13/2**[3]
2230 **9** *2* **Queen's Echo**[7] 2168 6-8-4 **53**.. JoeFanning 6 48
(P Monteith) *hld up: outpcd over 3f out: nvr on terms* **14/1**
0-51 **10** *hd* **Society Music (IRE)**[13] 2007 5-9-7 **70**....................(p) PaulMulrennan 2 65
(M Dods) *prom: rdn over 2f out: wknd over 1f out* **16/1**

1m 44.71s (-4.59) **Going Correction** -0.475s/f (Firm) **10** Ran SP% **114.9**
Speed ratings (Par 103):103,102,102,102,101 101,101,100,98,98
CSF £35.40 CT £1272.93 TOTE £2.20: £1.20, £5.20, £15.10; EX 43.10.
Owner P J McBride **Bred** T S And Mrs M E Child **Trained** Newmarket, Suffolk
■ Stewards' Enquiry : Duran Fentiman one-day ban: careless riding (Jun 18)

FOCUS
An ordinary event but one in which the pace was only fair and the winner did well to come from behind after meeting trouble. There was a bunch finish, but the form seems sound.

2389 RECTANGLE GROUP H'CAP 1m 3f 16y
4:05 (4:06) (Class 6) (0-65,65) 3-Y-0 **£2,388** (£705; £352) **Stalls High**

Form RPR
060- **1** **Copernican**[253] 5607 3-9-0 **58**.. SebSanders 11 66+
(Sir Mark Prescott) *hld up: hdwy 3f out: edgd rt and led appr fnl f: drvn out* **13/8**[1]
1322 **2** *3/4* **News Of The Day (IRE)**[42] 1256 3-9-2 **63**.................. MarkLawson(3) 4 70
(P Monteith) *cl up: led over 3f out to appr fnl f: kpt on ins fnl f* **16/1**
1 **3** *1 3/4* **Silent Lucidity (IRE)**[32] 1489 3-8-11 **60**..................... JamieMoriarty(5) 9 64
(P D Niven) *chsd ldrs: drvn and outpcd 2f out: kpt on fnl f* **5/1**[3]
33-2 **4** *1/2* **Four Miracles**[23] 1746 3-9-7 **65**.. JimmyQuinn 6 68
(M H Tompkins) *chsd ldrs: effrt over 2f out: kpt on same pce fnl f* **5/1**[3]
0562 **5** *5* **Delta Shuttle (IRE)**[9] 2112 3-9-0 **58**...................................... NCallan 10 53
(K R Burke) *prom: outpcd 3f out: kpt on fnl f: no imp* **9/1**
0154 **6** *nk* **A Big Sky Brewing (USA)**[14] 1964 3-9-1 **59**..................... PhillipMakin 5 53
(T D Barron) *midfield: outpcd 3f out: rallied over 1f out: no imp* **7/2**[2]
50-6 **7** *1 1/2* **Zain (IRE)**[24] 1712 3-8-0 **47** ow1..................................(t) AndrewElliott(3) 2 39
(J G Given) *prom tl outpcd over 3f out: n.d after* **25/1**
4-03 **8** *1 1/4* **Strathaird (IRE)**[132] 253 3-8-3 **47**...................................... JoeFanning 3 36
(P C Haslam) *hld up: struggling over 3f out: sn btn* **50/1**
-056 **9** *1 1/2* **Top Rocker**[14] 1968 3-8-9 **53**.. PaulMulrennan 7 40
(E W Tuer) *led to over 3f out: wknd over 2f out* **100/1**
0-00 **10** *8* **Danni Di Guerra (IRE)**[24] 1711 3-7-13 **46** oh1......... DuranFentiman(3) 1 19
(J Barclay) *hld up: rdn over 3f out: sn btn* **150/1**

2m 21.17s (-5.09) **Going Correction** -0.475s/f (Firm) **10** Ran SP% **117.0**
Speed ratings (Par 97):99,98,97,96,93 92,91,90,89,84
CSF £31.63 CT £112.65 TOTE £2.60: £1.90, £2.20, £2.10; EX 19.30.
Owner Lady Katharine Watts **Bred** Gestut Gorlsdorf **Trained** Newmarket, Suffolk

FOCUS
Not a strong race and just an ordinary gallop but likely there is plenty more to come from the workmanlike winner as he gains in experience. The form has been rated fairly positively.

2390 SAM COLLINGWOOD-CAMERON H'CAP 6f 5y
4:35 (4:37) (Class 5) (0-70,69) 3-Y-0+ **£3,562** (£1,059; £529; £264) **Stalls Centre**

Form RPR
340 **1** **Gunfighter (IRE)**[13] 1995 4-9-7 **67**.......................... JamieMoriarty(5) 12 78+
(J S Wainwright) *bhd: gd hdwy over 1f out: led ins fnl f: r.o wl* **12/1**
0-02 **2** *1* **Currency**[7] 2187 10-9-1 **56**... JoeFanning 1 64
(J M Bradley) *prom: led over 1f out to ins fnl f: kpt on* **5/1**[2]
0605 **3** *1/2* **Borodinsky**[35] 1423 6-8-6 **50** oh5............................ DuranFentiman(3) 7 56
(R E Barr) *prom: outpcd 1/2-way: rallied fnl f: kpt on* **66/1**
0224 **4** *1* **Throw The Dice**[20] 1806 5-9-0 **55**.............................(v) TonyHamilton 10 58
(D W Barker) *led and clr: hdd over 1f out: no ex* **9/2**[1]
0-10 **5** *1* **Exponential (IRE)**[36] 1405 5-9-9 **64**.. NCallan 6 64
(J M Bradley) *chsd clr ldr: effrt and ev ch over 1f out: no ex ins fnl f* **11/2**[3]
4233 **6** *hd* **Oeuf A La Neige**[20] 1806 7-8-6 **50**.......................... AndrewMullen(3) 5 49
(Miss L A Perratt) *bhd tl hdwy over 1f out: n.d* **7/1**
-001 **7** *1/2* **Walnut Grove**[10] 2072 4-8-12 **60** 6ex............................... NeilBrown(7) 13 58
(T D Barron) *prom: drvn over 2f out: no ex over 1f out* **11/2**[3]
3-00 **8** *nk* **Regal Raider (IRE)**[23] 1747 4-10-0 **69**.................................. TomEaves 11 66
(I Semple) *midfield: effrt over 2f out: btn fnl f* **16/1**
60-5 **9** *1/2* **Lambency (IRE)**[9] 2121 4-8-6 **54**.............................. GaryBartley(7) 9 50
(J S Goldie) *dwlt: bhd tl sme late hdwy: nvr on terms* **25/1**
0205 **10** *3/4* **Local Poet**[28] 1597 6-8-12 **53**......................................(b) PhillipMakin 8 46
(I Semple) *midfield: drvn over 2f out: sn no imp* **13/2**
0-00 **11** *2 1/2* **Obe One**[24] 1711 7-8-6 **50** oh3.............................. PatrickMathers(3) 3 36
(A Berry) *dwlt: bhd and sn rdn along: nvr on terms* **50/1**
00-0 **12** *5* **Orphan (IRE)**[10] 2072 5-9-13 **68**.. JimmyQuinn 14 39
(E J Alston) *in tch to 1/2-way: sn wknd* **16/1**
00-3 **13** *2* **Frimley's Mattery**[31] 1527 7-8-9 **50** oh3........................ PaulMulrennan 4 15
(R E Barr) *bhd: drvn 1/2-way: nvr on terms* **40/1**
00-0 **14** *1 3/4* **Pays D'Amour (IRE)**[28] 1596 10-8-8 **52** oh5 ow2......(t) MarkLawson(3) 2 12
(D A Nolan) *dwlt: bhd and rdn 1/2-way: sn btn* **200/1**

1m 11.48s (-1.62) **Going Correction** -0.35s/f (Firm) **14** Ran SP% **121.1**
Speed ratings (Par 103):96,94,94,92,91 91,90,90,89,88 85,78,75,73
CSF £70.05 CT £3935.09 TOTE £16.90: £4.90, £2.20, £16.90; EX 101.40.
Owner M Sawers **Bred** Round Hill Stud **Trained** Kennythorpe, N Yorks

FOCUS
A modest event in which the field converged centre to stands'-side. The pace was sound. The winner did best of the hold-up horses and is up 6lb on his maiden form. The race has been rated through he second and third.

2391 TURF TV BETTING SHOP SERVICE H'CAP 1m 5f 9y
5:05 (5:06) (Class 5) (0-70,70) 4-Y-0+ **£3,562** (£1,059; £529; £264) **Stalls High**

Form RPR
-230 **1** **Bronze Dancer (IRE)**[21] 1794 5-9-5 **68**...................................... NCallan 5 76
(G A Swinbank) *hld up in tch: hdwy to ld over 1f out: rdn out* **3/1**[2]
2131 **2** *1 1/2* **They All Laughed**[11] 2055 4-9-1 **64** 6ex............................ SebSanders 7 70
(P W Hiatt) *hld up: rdn over 3f out: hdwy to chse wnr ins fnl f: kpt on: no imp* **5/2**[1]
4-33 **3** *1 3/4* **Patavium (IRE)**[14] 1966 4-8-8 **57**.. PaulMulrennan 2 60
(E W Tuer) *led to over 1f out: lost 2nd and no ex ins fnl f* **9/1**
4 *nk* **Nero West (FR)**[72] 6-8-10 **59**..(p) TomEaves 8 62
(I Semple) *prom: rdn 3f out: kpt on same pce fnl f* **33/1**
-010 **5** *4* **Toshi (USA)**[5] 2250 5-8-12 **66**.. PJMcDonald(5) 1 63
(P Monteith) *hld up: hdwy on outside over 3f out: no ex over 1f out* **10/1**
000/ **6** *1 1/4* **Named At Dinner**[26] 5431 6-8-1 **53** oh6 ow2............. AndrewMullen(3) 4 48?
(Miss Lucinda V Russell) *bhd: outpcd over 4f out: kpt on fnl f: nvr on terms* **80/1**
-430 **7** *1/2* **Magic Moth**[28] 1598 4-9-7 **70**...(b[1]) JoeFanning 11 64
(M Johnston) *cl up tl rdn and wknd fnl f 2f out* **11/2**
00-0 **8** *4* **Zabeel Tower**[17] 1890 4-8-3 **52**.. JimmyQuinn 10 40
(R Allan) *hld up in tch: effrt over 3f out: btn over 1f out* **66/1**
0-00 **9** *shd* **Shekan Star**[14] 1966 5-7-9 **51**...................................... DanielleMcCreery(7) 6 39
(K G Reveley) *missed break: stdy hdwy 4f out: sn rdn and n.d* **5/1**[3]
-403 **10** *3* **Jordans Elect**[7] 2169 7-8-10 **62**.. MarkLawson(3) 9 45
(P Monteith) *trckd ldrs: pushed along 1/2-way: drvn and wknd over 2f out* **14/1**

2m 47.77s (-5.63) **Going Correction** -0.475s/f (Firm) **10** Ran SP% **117.0**
Speed ratings (Par 103):98,97,96,95,93 92,92,89,89,87
CSF £10.92 CT £59.70 TOTE £4.20: £1.60, £1.60, £2.20; EX 15.10 Place 6 £74.29, Place 5 £57.63.
Owner Mrs I Gibson **Bred** Lisieux Stud **Trained** Melsonby, N Yorks

FOCUS
An ordinary handicap in which the pace was only fair. The winner is rated as running to form, but the proximity of the sixth holds down the level.
Bronze Dancer(IRE) Official explanation: trainer said, regarding apparent improvement in form, that the gelding's last run may have come too soon after its previous run on May 12
Magic Moth Official explanation: jockey said colt hung left throughout
Shekan Star Official explanation: jockey said mare missed the break
T/Plt: £64.70 to a £1 stake. Pool: £48,256.20. 544.35 winning tickets. T/Qpdt: £12.50 to a £1 stake. Pool: £2,703.00. 159.20 winning tickets. RY

2034 HAYDOCK (L-H)
Thursday, June 7

OFFICIAL GOING: Good to firm (7.6)
Wind: Very light, behind Weather: overcast

2392 ENTERPRISE MAIDEN CLAIMING STKS 5f
2:20 (2:21) (Class 5) 2-Y-0 **£2,817** (£838; £418; £209) **Stalls Centre**

Form RPR
52 **1** **Caught In Paradise (IRE)**[12] 2028 2-8-10 0.......... AdrianTNicholls 4 60
(D Nicholls) *led: hdd 3f out: remained prom: regained ld ins fnl f: r.o* **13/2**[3]
52 **2** *nk* **Prigsnov Dancer (IRE)**[5] 2247 2-9-1 0.................................... KDarley 5 64
(P C Haslam) *racd keenly: w ldr: led 3f out: hdd ins fnl f: nt qckn fnl strides* **11/4**[1]
3 *1/2* **Carry On Cleo** 2-8-7 0.. CatherineGannon 2 54
(P D Evans) *dwlt: rn green: bhd: hdwy over 1f out: chsd ldrs ins fnl f: nt qckn fnl strides* **20/1**
4 *nk* **Baby Jack** 2-8-12 0... SilvestreDeSousa 8 58
(D Nicholls) *s.i.s: bhd: rdn and hung lft fr 1/2-way: hdwy over 1f out: styd on ins fnl f: nt pce of ldrs* **7/1**
4 **5** *1/2* **Tanley**[12] 2028 2-8-7 0.. DO'Donohoe 7 51
(James Moffatt) *s.i.s: in tch: pushed along and outpcd 2f out: styd on ins fnl f: eased towards fin* **50/1**
6 *1* **Rio Rocket (IRE)** 2-8-10 0... TPO'Shea 3 51
(G A Swinbank) *dwlt: sn in tch: rdn 1/2-way: btn whn n.m.r ent fnl f* **12/1**
5222 **7** *shd* **Rio Taffeta**[10] 2087 2-8-10 0..(b[1]) LPKeniry 6 50
(Peter Grayson) *prom: rdn over 1f out: sn wknd* **11/4**[1]
0 **8** *1 3/4* **Drumalee Lass (IRE)**[22] 1774 2-8-10 0.................................. JHBowman 1 44
(Patrick Mooney, Ire) *wnt lft s: prom: rdn 2f out: wknd ent fnl f* **4/1**[2]

61.94 secs (1.82) **Going Correction** -0.15s/f (Firm) **8** Ran SP% **113.6**
Speed ratings (Par 93):95,94,93,93,92 90,90,87
CSF £24.40 TOTE £7.40: £2.30, £1.50, £3.30; EX 20.10.The winner was claimed by R. E. R. Williams for £10,000.
Owner Middleham Park Racing Iii **Bred** G Swift **Trained** Sessay, N Yorks

FOCUS
Ordinary form and fairly easy to rate.

NOTEBOOK
Caught In Paradise(IRE), beaten in sellers on his first two starts, battled on gamely having been strongly challenged by Prigsnov Dancer, who raced in the same colours, from three furlongs out. The form may not amount to much, but he has the right attitude, and a return to 6f ought to help him. (op 7-1)
Prigsnov Dancer(IRE), who had plenty in common with the winner, being also owned by the Middleham Park Racing Syndicate, having the same form figures and entering the race with an identical RPR of 76 having finished runner-up in a seller last time, hit the front with three furlongs to run but did not put distance between himself and the rest, and in the end he was outbattled. (tchd 3-1)
Carry On Cleo, whose dam was a prolific winning sprinter, is a half-sister to Mick Is Back, dual 7f winner at three, and Princess Cleo, a 6f winner at two. Beginning her racing career at a modest level, she ran green but showed ability, and she should improve for the outing. (op 16-1)
Baby Jack, a half-brother to eight winners, including Gurrun, a multiple 1m to 1m4f winner at three, dual 5f juvenile winner Moon At Midnight, and Bright Moon, a 7f winner at two, ran with some promise on his debut, but he is likely to need a stiffer test in time. (op 8-1)
Tanley ran a better race than on his debut in a seller at Catterick when seven and a half lengths behind Caught In Paradise.
Rio Taffeta, the most experienced runner in the line-up, was blinkered for the first time and the headgear cannot be said to have had a positive effect, although the fast ground may have been the main reason for his below-par effort. Official explanation: trainer's rep said gelding was unsuited by the good to firm ground (op 4-1)
Drumalee Lass(IRE), an Irish raider who had not shown much in three previous starts, was taking on much weaker opposition this time, but she was disappointing. (op 3-1 tchd 9-2 in places)

2393 ENTERPRISE.PLC.UK MAIDEN STKS 6f
2:50 (2:51) (Class 5) 3-Y-0+ **£2,817** (£838; £418; £209) **Stalls** Centre

Form RPR
1 **Bee Eater (IRE)** 3-8-11 0 PaulHanagan 9 76+
(Sir Mark Prescott) *s.i.s and wnt lft s: rn green towards rr: hdwy into midfield over 3f out: rdn to cl over 1f out: edgd lft and r.o to ld fnl stride* **4/1**[3]
2 *hd* **Jimmy Styles** 3-9-2 0 KDarley 4 80
(C G Cox) *chsd ldrs: pushed along and outpcd bef 1/2-way: rallied fr 2f out: r.o to ld wl ins fnl f: hdd fnl stride* **4/1**[3]
5-5 3 *1 1/4* **Galipette**[27] 1632 3-8-11 0 RichardHughes 1 72
(H R A Cecil) *led: rdn and edgd rt over 1f out: hdd wl ins fnl f: no ex cl home* **3/1**[2]
45 4 *1* **Destour (IRE)**[11] 2059 3-9-2 0 LDettori 6 73
(J Noseda) *chsd ldrs: wnt 2nd 1/2-way: rdn 2f out: lost 2nd over 1f out: no ex wl ins fnl f* **5/2**[1]
04- 5 *hd* **Gwyllion (USA)**[229] 6098 3-8-11 0 TedDurcan 10 67+
(J H M Gosden) *stdd s: hld up: hdwy and edgd lft over 2f out: styd on ins fnl f: nrst fin* **7/1**
30 6 *6* **Steeley Fox**[13] 1995 4-9-5 0 KevinGhunowa(5) 7 56
(J M Bradley) *in tch: rdn over 2f out: wknd over 1f out* **33/1**
63-0 7 *1/2* **Forzarzi (IRE)**[27] 1625 3-8-11 53 PBradley(5) 5 53
(A Berry) *bhd after 1f: n.d after* **100/1**
6 8 *7* **New Year (IRE)**[10] 2094 3-9-2 0 MickyFenton 3 32
(T P Tate) *chsd ldr to 1/2-way: sn pushed along and wknd* **66/1**
9 *3 1/2* **Invincible Lad (IRE)** 3-9-2 0 DavidAllan 2 21
(E J Alston) *s.i.s: rn green and a bhd* **25/1**

1m 13.89s **Going Correction** -0.15s/f (Firm)
WFA 3 from 4yo 8lb 9 Ran SP% **115.3**
Speed ratings (Par 103):100,99,98,96,96 88,87,78,73
CSF £19.89 TOTE £5.60: £1.50, £1.80, £1.50; EX 26.40.
Owner Sir Edmund Loder **Bred** Sir E J Loder **Trained** Newmarket, Suffolk

FOCUS
An interesting maiden, with the winner looking likely to do better and one or two in behind looking likely handicap winners over further. Solid maiden form, with fair efforts from the front pair.

2394 ENTERPRISE SUPPORTS CORPUS CHRISTI COLLEGE H'CAP 6f
3:25 (3:25) (Class 5) (0-75,78) 4-Y-0+ **£2,817** (£838; £418; £209) **Stalls** Centre

Form RPR
0-03 1 **Roman Quintet (IRE)**[14] 1969 7-8-8 62 TQuinn 6 75
(R J Price) *mde all: shkn up ins fnl f: pushed out towards fin* **14/1**
6-00 2 *1 1/4* **John Keats**[28] 1597 4-8-5 59 AdrianTNicholls 12 68+
(J S Goldie) *towards rr: hdwy over 2f out: r.o ins fnl f: gaining at fin* **33/1**
2343 3 *shd* **Effective**[3] 2318 7-9-5 73 JHBowman 2 82
(A P Jarvis) *a.p: rdn over 1f out: kpt on ins fnl f* **7/1**[3]
4040 4 *shd* **Chinalea (IRE)**[14] 1969 5-8-12 66 (b) KDarley 1 74+
(C G Cox) *a.p: rdn over 1f out: nt qckn towards fin* **8/1**
-046 5 *1 1/2* **Ocean Gift**[26] 1678 5-9-0 68 CatherineGannon 16 72
(P D Evans) *in tch: rdn over 1f out: styd on same pce fnl f* **14/1**
0532 6 *1 3/4* **Cornus**[10] 2088 5-9-2 70 (be) LDettori 5 69
(A J McCabe) *hmpd s: hld up: hdwy over 1f out: one pce ins fnl f* **9/2**[2]
1600 7 *1 1/2* **Danzig River (IRE)**[12] 2025 6-8-13 74 AdeleRothery(7) 9 68
(D Nicholls) *racd keenly: midfield: rdn over 2f out: nt pce to chal* **16/1**
3-55 8 *1/2* **Outer Hebrides**[10] 2088 6-9-5 73 (vt) TedDurcan 14 66
(J M Bradley) *hld up: rdn over 1f out: no imp on ldrs* **16/1**
5041 9 *1* **Makabul**[17] 1899 4-8-10 69 ow1 JamesMillman(5) 15 59
(B R Millman) *hld up: hdwy 1/2-way: sn rdn: btn fnl f* **10/1**
0-50 10 *nk* **Glasshoughton**[19] 1854 4-9-7 75 DarryllHolland 4 64
(M Dods) *wnt rt s: midfield: rdn over 1f out: no hdwy* **11/1**
2111 11 *5* **Brunelleschi**[8] 2155 4-9-5 78 6ex (b) LukeMorris(5) 11 52
(P L Gilligan) *hld up: rdn 2f out: nvr on terms* **3/1**[1]
3-5 12 *1 1/4* **High Ridge**[31] 1545 8-8-12 71 (p) KevinGhunowa(5) 13 41
(J M Bradley) *midfield: rdn over 2f out: wknd fnl f* **11/1**
00/5 13 *1* **Sydneyroughdiamond**[9] 2108 5-7-9 56 oh11 SoniaEaton(7) 10 23
(M Mullineaux) *chsd ldrs tl rdn and wknd over 2f out* **100/1**

1m 13.46s (-0.43) **Going Correction** -0.15s/f (Firm) 13 Ran SP% **121.6**
Speed ratings (Par 103):103,101,101,101,99 96,94,94,92,92 85,84,82
CSF £411.21 CT £3603.01 TOTE £18.50: £4.80, £5.60, £2.90; EX 435.00.
Owner Ms S A Gray, Mrs S J Howell, P A Kelly **Bred** Colin Kennedy **Trained** Ullingswick, H'fords

FOCUS
A competitive sprint in which it paid to race up with the pace. Sound form, the third the best guide.
Makabul Official explanation: jockey said gelding went too freely to post
Brunelleschi Official explanation: trainer had no explanation for the poor form shown
High Ridge Official explanation: jockey said gelding lost its action

2395 E B F ENTERPRISE SUPPORT SERVICES H'CAP 6f
3:55 (3:57) (Class 3) (0-95,91) 3-Y-0 **£9,715** (£2,890; £1,444; £721) **Stalls** Centre

Form RPR
0-21 1 **Express Wish**[23] 1737 3-9-0 84 LDettori 4 95+
(J Noseda) *mde all: rdn and edgd rt over 1f out: hrd pressed ins fnl f: fnd ex towards fin* **10/11**[1]
-253 2 *nk* **Mac Gille Eoin**[15] 1948 3-8-2 72 FrancisNorton 7 82
(J Gallagher) *in tch: rdn and hdwy whn hung lft over 1f out: ev ch ins fnl f: nt qckn fnl strides* **11/1**
2031 3 *shd* **El Bosque (IRE)**[16] 1930 3-9-2 91 JamesMillman(5) 3 101
(B R Millman) *midfield: rdn and hdwy over 1f out: r.o ins fnl f* **8/1**[3]
26-5 4 *3* **Thunderousapplause**[49] 1105 3-8-7 77 DO'Donohoe 9 78
(K A Ryan) *towards rr: pushed along and hdwy over 3f out: rdn whn chsd ldrs over 1f out: no ex ins fnl f* **6/1**[2]
-603 5 *nk* **Averticus**[26] 1667 3-8-7 77 (p) TedDurcan 8 77
(B W Hills) *dwlt: hld up: rdn over 1f out: kpt on: nt pce to chal* **11/1**
1-55 6 *nk* **Sunnyside Tom (IRE)**[13] 1994 3-8-6 76 (v1) PaulHanagan 10 78+
(R A Fahey) *in rr: hdwy 1/2-way: sn rdn: nt clr run over 1f out: styd on ins fnl f: nt rch ldrs* **16/1**
-641 7 *2* **The Nifty Fox**[9] 2119 3-8-11 81 6ex DavidAllan 2 74
(T D Easterby) *chsd ldrs: rdn over 1f out: wknd ins fnl f* **20/1**
320- 8 *1/2* **Rainbow Mirage (IRE)**[243] 5809 3-9-7 91 GrahamGibbons 6 83
(E S McMahon) *racd keenly: chsd ldrs: hmpd over 1f out: sn wknd* **16/1**
5-14 9 *1/2* **Our Blessing (IRE)**[120] 385 3-8-13 83 JHBowman 5 73
(A P Jarvis) *prom: rdn over 2f out: wkng whn n.m.r over 1f out* **40/1**
-000 10 *nk* **Bazroy (IRE)**[12] 2035 3-9-4 88 CatherineGannon 1 77
(P D Evans) *prom: rdn over 2f out: edgd lft over 1f out: sn wknd* **66/1**
-031 11 *2 1/2* **Fish Called Johnny**[7] 2171 3-8-6 76 6ex (b) DaleGibson 11 58
(Peter Grayson) *a bhd* **12/1**

1m 13.07s (-0.82) **Going Correction** -0.15s/f (Firm) 11 Ran SP% **122.6**
Speed ratings (Par 103):106,105,105,101,101 100,98,97,96,96 92
CSF £12.97 CT £59.60 TOTE £1.90: £1.30, £2.60, £2.60; EX 16.10.
Owner Peter Mitchell **Bred** Cranford Stud **Trained** Newmarket, Suffolk

FOCUS
The first three came clear in this three-year-olds' handicap, and the form looks solid rated around the placed horses.

NOTEBOOK
Express Wish, an easy maiden winner at Brighton last time out, was well backed into odds-on and justified the support, albeit only narrowly. His rider was not too hard on him and there is every chance that he will improve again on this. The valuable William Hill Trophy at York on June 16th looks a suitable target now, but his trainer is a little worried that the three-year-old may not have the experience for that competitive race at this stage of his career. (op 5-4 tchd 11-8)
Mac Gille Eoin found 5f on the short side last time out and appreciated the return to 6f. Only narrowly beaten by a well-handicapped rival, he should remain dangerous in similar company off this sort of mark. (op 10-1 tchd 12-1)
El Bosque(IRE) just got home over 7f last time and coped perfectly well with the return to 6f. He stayed on well in the closing stages and is always going to appreciate a good gallop at this trip. (op 10-1)
Thunderousapplause, who had not been getting home in maiden company over 7f, kept on well and won the separate race behind the first three. Together with the winner, she was the least experienced in the line-up, and is open to improvement for this handicap debut. (op 4-1)
Averticus, wearing cheekpieces for the first time, wandered about under pressure but kept on well enough. He does not look to have as much in hand of the Handicapper as some. (op 12-1)
Sunnyside Tom(IRE), visored for the first time, was putting in all his best work at the finish and might be suited to a stiffer 6f. (tchd 18-1)

2396 BANK OF SCOTLAND CORPORATE STKS (REGISTERED AS THE JOHN OF GAUNT STAKES) (LISTED RACE) 7f 30y
4:25 (4:27) (Class 1) 4-Y-0+
£15,898 (£6,025; £3,015; £1,503; £753; £378) **Stalls** Low

Form RPR
20-0 1 **Mine (IRE)**[21] 1791 9-9-0 107 (v) TQuinn 3 109
(J D Bethell) *bhd: hdwy 2f out: r.o to ld ins fnl f: rdn out* **16/1**
6233 2 *1/2* **Beckermet (IRE)**[12] 2030 5-9-0 100 PaulHanagan 9 108
(R F Fisher) *in tch: led over 2f out: sn rdn: hdd ins fnl f: kpt on* **25/1**
14/3 3 *1 1/2* **Soldier's Tale (USA)**[22] 1770 6-9-0 112 LDettori 7 104
(J Noseda) *midfield: shkn up 4f out: hdwy over 2f out: rdn whn chsd ldrs over 1f out: no imp on front pair cl home* **4/6**[1]
-060 4 *hd* **Quito (IRE)**[22] 1770 10-9-5 105 (b) KDarley 1 108
(D W Chapman) *bhd: rdn and hdwy over 2f out: styd on u.p: one pce cl home* **16/1**
0-50 5 *4* **Suggestive**[26] 1651 9-9-0 106 (b) DarryllHolland 4 93
(W J Haggas) *chsd ldrs: rdn over 2f out: hung lft over 1f out: wknd fnl f* **20/1**
/30- 6 *1 1/2* **Early March**[346] 2941 5-9-0 108 RichardHughes 6 89
(J H M Gosden) *in tch: rn wd on bnd wl over 5f out: rdn 2f out: wknd ins fnl f* **8/1**[3]
00-0 7 *3 1/2* **Jedburgh**[40] 1305 6-9-0 103 (b) TedDurcan 10 79
(J L Dunlop) *a towards rr: rdn over 2f out: nvr on terms* **20/1**
63-5 8 *1 1/2* **Sunderland Echo (IRE)**[26] 1670 4-8-9 90 (t) SamHitchcott 5 70
(B Ellison) *midfield: pushed along 4f out: bhd fnl 2f* **100/1**
1-30 9 *1* **King's Caprice**[75] 759 6-9-0 104 (t) LPKeniry 2 72
(J A Geake) *led at str gallop: rdn and hdd over 2f out: wknd over 1f out* **33/1**
0-15 10 *34* **New Seeker**[24] 1723 7-9-5 109 (b) JHBowman 8 —
(P F I Cole) *racd w ldr at str gallop: ev ch 3f out: rdn over 2f out: wknd and eased over 1f out: t.o* **9/2**[2]

1m 28.88s (-3.18) **Going Correction** -0.15s/f (Firm) 10 Ran SP% **118.3**
Speed ratings (Par 111):112,111,109,109,104 103,99,97,96,57
CSF £350.01 TOTE £14.00: £3.10, £3.40, £1.10; EX 260.70 Trifecta £426.80 Pool: £721.38 - 1.20 winning tickets..
Owner M J Dawson **Bred** David John Brown **Trained** Middleham Moor, N Yorks
■ Stewards' Enquiry : J H Bowman one-day ban: allowed gelding to be loaded in wrong stall (Jun 18)
Richard Hughes one-day ban: allowed horse to be loaded in wrong stall (Jul 4)

FOCUS
A very strongly-run Listed race that suited those that were held up in rear early. The pace-setters finished last and second-last. Mine did not have to be at his best, in a race rated through the runner-up.

NOTEBOOK
Mine(IRE), all the better for his reappearance outing at York and with conditions as he would like them, got the strong pace he needs and came from well back to record his first win at Listed level. The Criterion Stakes at Newmarket is his next objective, but once again his performance is likely to be dictated by the pace set for him by others. (op 14-1)
Beckermet(IRE), who has been running consistently this season, did by far the best of those who raced close to the strong early gallop. Taking up the running with two furlongs to run, he was headed inside the last by the staying-on Mine, but he kept on well to hold on to second place. Just one win from his last 40 starts is not a great return, but he has run a number of good races in defeat and it would not be a surprise to see him go one better soon.
Soldier's Tale(USA) was a well-backed favourite on the back of his promising return to action in the Group 2 Duke of York Stakes. The extra furlong was of no concern, but the quicker ground was, and it seemed to find him out, as he otherwise had everything go his way in being held up off a strong early pace. He can leave this form behind back on easy ground. (op 4-5 tchd 8-13 and 10-11 in a place)
Quito(IRE), who won this race last year, has not been in the best of form so far this term and he had a 5lb penalty to carry on this occasion. On the plus side, he had the race very much run to suit, and he stayed on in his usual way to finish clear of the rest.
Suggestive, another previous winner of this race (2004) struggling for form this season, chased the two clear leaders in the early stages and he paid the price in the latter part of the race. (tchd 25-1)
Early March, formerly trained in France where he reached the frame in Group company on more than one occasion, was entitled to need his first outing for 346 days, and he was another who raced too close to the fast pace set by King's Caprice and New Seeker. He might do a lot better next time. (op 9-1 tchd 10-1)
Jedburgh had conditions to suit and was held up in a strongly-run race, so he can have few excuses. (op 16-1)
New Seeker Official explanation: jockey said gelding hung left-handed

2397 ENTERPRISE H'CAP 1m 2f 120y
4:55 (4:56) (Class 4) (0-85,85) 4-Y-0+ £5,505 (£1,637; £818; £408) Stalls High

Form RPR
-000 1 **Peruvian Prince (USA)**[22] [1771] 5-8-13 77 PaulHanagan 6 88
(R A Fahey) *chsd ldrs: led 1f out: sn qcknd clr and edgd lft: wl in command at fin* 25/1
0-12 2 3 1/2 **Nightspot**[9] [2106] 6-8-9 73 KDarley 3 77
(Eve Johnson Houghton) *led: rdn over 2f out: hdd 1f out: nt pce of wnr ins fnl f* 9/2[3]
11-3 3 hd **Khun John (IRE)**[13] [2003] 4-9-3 81 LDettori 9 85
(B J Meehan) *midfield: hdwy 3f out: rdn to chal wl over 1f out: styd on u.p* 13/8[1]
60-2 4 hd **United Nations**[17] [1905] 6-8-12 76 TQuinn 4 80
(N Wilson) *chsd ldr: rdn and ev ch over 1f out: styd on same pce ins fnl f* 10/1
00-0 5 3/4 **Kingdom Of Dreams (IRE)**[18] [1862] 5-8-9 73 AdrianTNicholls 10 75
(J Mackie) *hld up: rdn over 2f out: hdwy over 1f out: styd on ins fnl f* 66/1
2004 6 1/2 **Quince (IRE)**[13] [2003] 4-9-7 85 (v) DarryllHolland 2 86
(J Pearce) *chsd ldrs: rdn over 1f out: one pce ins fnl f* 11/1
540- 7 1 1/4 **Diktatorial**[123] [6097] 5-9-5 83 DavidAllan 1 82
(J Howard Johnson) *s.i.s: hld up: pushed along and outpcd 2f out: nvr on terms* 16/1
1-00 8 hd **Mulaazem**[13] [2011] 4-8-13 77 DaleGibson 5 75
(J Mackie) *midfield: rdn over 1f out: no real imp* 20/1
3402 9 1 **Pagan Sword**[13] [2003] 5-9-6 84 JHBowman 8 81+
(Mrs A J Perrett) *s.v.s losing 10 l: in rr of main gp after 2f: rdn and hdwy 2f out: hung rt over 1f out: wknd ins fnl f* 3/1[2]
2015 10 6 **Frank Crow**[15] [1939] 4-8-11 75 TedDurcan 7 60
(J S Goldie) *hld up: rdn over 2f out: sn btn* 33/1

2m 16.27s (0.13) **Going Correction** -0.15s/f (Firm) 10 Ran SP% **117.6**
Speed ratings (Par 105):99,96,96,96,95 95,94,94,93,89
CSF £131.63 CT £294.85 TOTE £25.60: £4.40, £1.90, £1.20; EX 140.10 Place 6 £62.11, Place 5 £27.14.
Owner R G Leatham **Bred** Alexander-Groves Thoroughbreds **Trained** Musley Bank, N Yorks

FOCUS
A fair handicap run at quite a steady pace. The winner sprang a surprise, rated on a par with his improved sand form.
Pagan Sword Official explanation: jockey said gelding missed the break
T/Jkpt: Not won. T/Plt: £84.30 to a £1 stake. Pool: £71,038.70. 615.15 winning tickets. T/Qpdt: £20.00 to a £1 stake. Pool: £4,004.25. 147.60 winning tickets. DO

2180 SANDOWN (R-H)
Thursday, June 7
OFFICIAL GOING: Good (good to firm in places in back straight)
Wind: Moderate, across Weather: Overcast

2398 REUTERS, FIRST FOR NEWS MAIDEN AUCTION STKS 5f 6y
6:20 (6:29) (Class 5) 2-Y-0 £3,886 (£1,156; £577; £288) Stalls High

Form RPR
0 1 **Grylls (USA)**[19] [1832] 2-8-11 0 PatDobbs 14 84+
(R Hannon) *pressed ldr: led wl over 1f out and clr of rest: pushed out and wl in command fnl f* 4/1[3]
25 2 1 3/4 **Hobson**[22] [1762] 2-8-9 0 StephenCarson 11 76
(Eve Johnson Houghton) *leggy: unf: led: clr of rest whn hdd by wnr wl over 1f out: kpt on same pce* 3/1[1]
3 2 1/2 **Ten Meropa (USA)** 2-8-13 0 (t) JamieSpencer 7 71+
(J A Osborne) *wlike: str: dwlt: sn wl off the pce in last trio: gd prog fr 1/2-way: wnt 3rd 1f out: no ch w ldng pair but kpt on wl* 7/1
0 4 1 1/2 **Ruby Delta**[5] [2241] 2-8-9 0 FergusSweeney 4 62
(P D Cundell) *w'like: outpcd and rdn over 3f out: styd on fr 2f out: nrst fin* 33/1
32 5 nk **Shamrock Lady (IRE)**[17] [1896] 2-8-5 0 ow1 JohnEgan 3 57
(Pat Eddery) *w'like: leggy: racd on outer: chsd ldrs: outpcd 1/2-way: carried lft after: styd on again and edgd rt fnl f* 7/2[2]
0 6 1 1/2 **Fathsta (IRE)**[13] [1990] 2-8-9 0 FrankieMcDonald 5 55
(S Kirk) *chsd ldrs: outpcd fr 1/2-way: no imp after* 33/1
6 7 hd **Wooden King (IRE)**[8] [2151] 2-8-13 0 SimonWhitworth 13 58
(P D Evans) *leggy: pushed along to chse ldrs: effrt to go 3rd fr 1/2-way to 1f out: wknd* 28/1
6 8 1 1/2 **Diamond Soles (IRE)**[33] [1469] 2-8-8 0 KerrinMcEvoy 9 48
(B J Meehan) *chsd ldng pair to 1/2-way: hanging lft after: wknd over 1f out* 12/1
9 hd **Lunar Limelight** 2-9-2 0 EddieAhern 6 55
(P J Makin) *b/like: bit bwkd: pushed along in midfield: prog to dispute 3rd over 1f out: wknd rapidly fnl f* 20/1
10 3 **Lord's Bidding** 2-8-9 0 RobertHavlin 12 37
(R Ingram) *w'like: bit bkwd: nvr on terms: struggling in last trio fr 1/2-way* 33/1
11 nk **City Wizzard** 2-8-13 0 HayleyTurner 16 40
(M L W Bell) *w'like: s.i.s: rchd midfield after 2f but sn rdn: wknd over 1f out* 11/1
12 2 **Two Imposters (USA)** 2-8-10 0 StephaneBreux(3) 10 33
(J R Best) *w'ile bit bkwd: outpcd in last trio: nvr a factor* 20/1
13 17 **Peter's Joy (USA)** 2-8-9 0 DaneO'Neill 8 —
(Jean-Rene Auvray) *unf: bit bwkd: dwlt: a struggling in last trio: t.o: lame* 33/1

61.54 secs (-0.67) **Going Correction** -0.175s/f (Firm) 13 Ran SP% **120.5**
Speed ratings (Par 93):98,95,91,88,88 85,85,83,82,78 77,74,47
CSF £15.01 TOTE £4.40: £1.70, £1.80, £2.50; EX 16.50.
Owner Mrs J K Powell **Bred** Margaux Farm Llc & Margaux Farm Inc **Trained** East Everleigh, Wilts

FOCUS
A maiden lacking strength in depth and the draw played its part. The front pair were both berthed high and they were also at the sharp end throughout. Sound form from the front two.

NOTEBOOK
Grylls(USA) ◆, who did show some ability despite only beating two home on his Newbury debut, was backed off the boards and his supporters got it right. He and the favourite had the race to themselves from the off and he saw it out much the better. The stiff finish compensated for the drop in trip and there should be more to come from him. (op 12-1)
Hobson put his modest Bath performance behind him with a solid effort from the front. He could not cope with the winner, but was never in any danger from the others and he should find an opportunity in similar company before too long. (op 10-3 tchd 11-4)
Ten Meropa(USA), out of a half-sister to Pride, looked clueless early but eventually realised what the game was about and made up a lot of ground from off the pace to fare much the best of the newcomers. The performance was all the more meritorious given that the front pair were in those positions throughout and it should not be long before he hits the target. (op 13-2)
Ruby Delta, who showed nothing on his Folkestone debut just five days earlier, fared much better this time and was staying on nicely at the end having started from a moderate draw. A half-brother to the winning juvenile Pommes Frites, he should find a race himself and may be suited by a return to further.
Shamrock Lady(IRE), placed in both of her starts, did not improve on those efforts though to be fair she was always marooned out in the centre of the track from her low draw. She may be worth another chance. (op 5-2 tchd 4-1)
Fathsta(IRE) showed up for a while and improved from his Goodwood debut. All three of his siblings are winners and there is a mix of speed and stamina in his pedigree, so he may improve for a return to further. (op 40-1)
Diamond Soles(IRE) Official explanation: jockey said filly hung left
Peter's Joy(USA) Official explanation: vet said colt returned lame

2399 STERLING SOLUTIONS H'CAP 5f 6y
6:50 (6:59) (Class 4) (0-85,85) 3-Y-0+ £5,181 (£1,541; £770; £384) Stalls High

Form RPR
2-61 1 **Bertoliver**[17] [1900] 3-9-5 83 KerrinMcEvoy 1 89+
(D K Ivory) *fast away: mde all and sn crossed to far rail fr wd draw: drew 2 l clr over 1f out: jst hld on* 16/1
0300 2 shd **Phantom Whisper**[14] [1971] 4-9-12 83 JimCrowley 7 92
(B R Millman) *prom: rdn to chse wnr over 1f out: clsd fnl f: jst failed* 17/2
1665 3 1 **Efistorm**[12] [2025] 6-9-7 78 JamieSpencer 6 83
(C R Dore) *settled wl in rr: gd prog on outer fr wl over 1f out: r.o fnl f: nrst fin* 7/1[2]
00-0 4 3/4 **Zowington**[19] [1836] 5-10-0 85 GeorgeBaker 14 88
(C F Wall) *cl up on inner: rdn and effrt over 1f out: styd on same pce fnl f* 15/2[3]
40-0 5 nk **Roman Quest**[52] [1063] 4-8-10 72 TravisBlock(5) 5 74
(H Morrison) *towards rr: prog fr 2f out: kpt on fnl f: no ch w ldrs* 16/1
5161 6 hd **Namir (IRE)**[12] [2025] 5-8-13 75 (vt) PatrickHills(5) 11 76+
(D Shaw) *wl in rr: nt clr run wl over 2f out: prog wl over 1f out: styd on: nvr nrr* 9/1
-000 7 3/4 **Royal Challenge**[20] [1826] 6-9-8 82 SaleemGolam(3) 13 80+
(M H Tompkins) *racd on inner in midfield: shkn up wl over 1f out: one pce and nvr able to rch ldrs* 12/1
-266 8 nk **Overwing (IRE)**[7] [2191] 4-9-4 75 EddieAhern 2 72
(R M H Cowell) *lw: racd on outer and wl in rr: prog 1/2-way: no imp over 1f out: kpt on last 150yds* 50/1
-404 9 nk **Holbeck Ghyll (IRE)**[5] [2234] 5-9-1 77 (p) WilliamBuick(5) 10 73+
(A M Balding) *slowest away: wl in rr: effrt and nt clr run wl over 2f out: sme prog over 1f out: styd on: no ch* 6/4[1]
0024 10 2 1/2 **Azygous**[27] [1630] 4-9-5 76 MartinDwyer 4 63
(J Akehurst) *prom tl wknd over 1f out* 20/1
00-0 11 1 1/2 **Art Market (CAN)**[19] [1836] 4-9-11 82 RyanMoore 8 64
(G L Moore) *a wl in rr: lost tch over 2f out* 50/1
/04- 12 nk **Nigella**[392] [1604] 4-10-0 85 JimmyFortune 3 66
(E S McMahon) *chsd wnr to over 1f out: wknd rapidly* 50/1
0021 13 nk **Bold Minstrel (IRE)**[7] [2191] 5-9-8 79 6ex ChrisCatlin 9 58
(M Quinn) *chsd ldrs for 3f: sn wknd* 12/1
/00- 14 1/2 **Saxon Saint**[351] [2756] 4-9-0 71 HayleyTurner 12 49
(M D I Usher) *hld up wl in rr: nt clr run wl over 2f out: no ch after* 66/1

60.79 secs (-1.42) **Going Correction** -0.175s/f (Firm)
WFA 3 from 4yo+ 7lb 14 Ran SP% **124.1**
Speed ratings (Par 105):104,103,102,101,100 100,99,98,98,94 91,91,90,89
CSF £145.87 CT £1088.36 TOTE £15.00: £3.20, £2.50, £2.60; EX 305.20.
Owner Mrs A Shone **Bred** Pillar To Post Racing **Trained** Radlett, Herts
■ Stewards' Enquiry : William Buick two-day ban: careless riding (Jun 18, 24)

FOCUS
A more competitive sprint handicap than the market would have suggested and again the inside rail was the place to be as, despite starting from the outside stall, the winner was soon racing against it. The winner is generally progressive and the race has been rated through the runner-up.
Holbeck Ghyll(IRE) Official explanation: jockey said gelding missed the break

2400 ROY WRIGHT CELEBRATION H'CAP 7f 16y
7:25 (7:28) (Class 4) (0-85,85) 3-Y-0 £6,477 (£1,927; £963; £481) Stalls High

Form RPR
0-1 1 **Zaahid (IRE)**[19] [1838] 3-8-8 72 MartinDwyer 4 85
(B W Hills) *swtg: mde all: drew clr over 1f out: edgd lft but wl in command fnl f* 10/1
-431 2 3 1/2 **Masai Moon**[16] [1920] 3-9-4 82 JHBowman 1 86
(B R Millman) *chsd wnr: rdn 2f out: outpcd fr over 1f out: hld on for 2nd* 10/1
13 3 hd **Lone Wolfe**[41] [1276] 3-9-1 79 JohnEgan 9 82+
(Jane Chapple-Hyam) *lw: hld up in midfield: prog on outer fr 2f out: styd on fnl f: nrly snatched 2nd* 9/1
-311 4 1 **Kyle (IRE)**[13] [1994] 3-9-4 82 RichardHughes 5 83+
(R Hannon) *hld up towards rr: pushed along and sme prog 2f out: shkn up and kpt on fnl f: nvr able to chal* 10/1
1 5 3/4 **Laa Rayb (USA)**[24] [1714] 3-9-1 82 GregFairley(3) 6 81+
(M Johnston) *scope: swtg: t.k.h: chsd ldng pair to 1f out: fdd* 9/1
01 6 nk **Ragheed (USA)**[33] [1482] 3-8-13 77 RHills 7 75+
(W J Haggas) *t.k.h: hld up bhd ldrs: rdn over 2f out: one pce and no imp* 8/1[3]
1-42 7 1 1/2 **Curzon Prince (IRE)**[16] [1920] 3-9-3 81 KerrinMcEvoy 15 75+
(C F Wall) *hld up in midfield: rdn over 2f out: kpt on but nt pce to trble ldrs* 4/1[1]
2201 8 shd **Eau Good**[45] [1202] 3-9-7 85 GeorgeBaker 8 79
(B G Powell) *sn in last trio: shkn up and sme prog 2f out: kpt on same pce fnl f: nvr nr ldrs* 14/1
003 9 shd **Samsons Son**[27] [1632] 3-8-3 67 RichardThomas 10 60
(J R Best) *t.k.h: hld up in midfield: effrt on outer 2f out: fdd fnl f* 33/1
01- 10 hd **Russki (IRE)**[208] [6434] 3-9-4 82 JimCrowley 12 75
(Mrs A J Perrett) *h.d.w: wl in rr: pushed along on inner whn nt clr run 2f out to 1f out: no prog fnl f* 11/2[2]
11-6 11 2 **Sharpazmax (IRE)**[12] [2045] 3-9-5 83 EddieAhern 2 70
(P J Makin) *hld up wl in rr: rdn 2f out: one pce and no real prog* 9/1
15-0 12 shd **Apollo Five**[32] [1500] 3-9-0 78 (v[1]) AdamKirby 11 65
(D J Coakley) *a wl in rr: rdn and struggling over 2f out* 50/1
0040 13 hd **Dora Explora**[16] [1920] 3-8-11 75 DaneO'Neill 14 62
(P D Evans) *in tch in midfield: losing pl whn n.m.r over 1f out* 33/1
100- 14 1/2 **Suki Bear**[258] [5503] 3-8-12 76 JamieSpencer 3 61
(W R Muir) *dwlt: hld up and a in last trio: no ch fnl 2f* 25/1

0-21 15 7 **Buxton**[17] 1904 3-9-2 80 ... RobertHavlin 13 46
(R Ingram) *t.k.h: prom to 2f out: wknd v rapidly: t.o* **20/1**

1m 28.96s (-0.38) **Going Correction** -0.175s/f (Firm) 15 Ran SP% **126.9**
Speed ratings (Par 101):105,101,100,99,98 98,96,96,96,96 93,93,93,93,85
CSF £105.53 CT £976.76 TOTE £11.40: £3.50, £3.40, £3.10; EX 147.70.
Owner Hamdan Al Maktoum **Bred** Shadwell Estate Company Limited **Trained** Lambourn, Berks

FOCUS
A decent little handicap, but one probably influenced to a degree by a pace bias as the first two home held those positions throughout. Hold-up horses had little chance and this is dubious form, rated through the runner-up.

2401 IG INDEX MILE H'CAP — 1m 14y
7:55 (7:57) (Class 3) (0-90,91) 4-Y-O+ **£7,772** (£2,312; £1,155; £577) **Stalls** High

Form RPR
000- 1 **Pintle**[224] 6190 7-9-3 85 ... KerrinMcEvoy 12 97
(J L Spearing) *mde all: kicked 3 l clr 2f out: rdn over 1f out: styd on wl: unchal* **50/1**
3-46 2 2 1/2 **Master Pegasus**[14] 1962 4-9-1 83 ... GeorgeBaker 13 89
(C F Wall) *prom: chsd wnr over 2f out: rdn and kpt on fr over 1f out but no imp* **14/1**
6-41 3 3/4 **Killena Boy (IRE)**[9] 2123 5-9-9 91 6ex ... PaulDoe 10 96
(W Jarvis) *lw: hld up in midfield: prog on outer to chse ldng pair 2f out: styd on same pce: no ch w wnr* **9/2**[2]
64-0 4 1 **Tumbleweed Glory (IRE)**[19] 1842 4-8-10 78 ... BrettDoyle 5 80
(B J Meehan) *hld up wl in rr: prog over 2f out: styd on fnl f: no ch* **33/1**
0331 5 1/2 **Full Victory (IRE)**[7] 2180 5-8-8 76 6ex ... FergusSweeney 2 77+
(R A Farrant) *hld up wl in rr: rdn and styd on fr over 2f out: nvr pce to rch ldrs* **7/1**[3]
1-16 6 hd **Hassaad**[10] 2093 4-9-4 86 ... RHills 8 87+
(W J Haggas) *lw: settled in last pair: rdn and struggling over 3f out: styd on u.p fnl 2f: n.d* **11/8**[1]
0-55 7 1/2 **It's A Dream (FR)**[19] 1842 4-8-7 78 ... MarcHalford(3) 9 77
(D R C Elsworth) *lw: hld up in rr: nt clr run over 2f out: sme prog over 1f out: kpt on same pce fnl f* **12/1**
4550 8 2 1/2 **Marajaa (IRE)**[31] 1524 5-9-4 86 ... DavidKinsella 14 80
(W J Musson) *hld up towards rr on inner: effrt over 2f out: one pce and no imp over 1f out* **16/1**
0-06 9 1 1/2 **Fabrian**[7] 2180 9-8-5 76 ... LiamJones(3) 4 71+
(R J Price) *prom: rdn 3f out: losing pl whn hmpd over 2f out: sn in rr: styng on again last 100yds* **25/1**
0062 10 shd **Langford**[16] 1915 7-8-11 82 ... SaleemGolam(3) 3 72
(M H Tompkins) *hld up towards rr: nt clr run over 2f out: sme prog wl over 1f out: fdd fnl f* **12/1**
-056 11 3/4 **The Snatcher (IRE)**[19] 1836 4-9-7 89 ... RichardHughes 7 77
(R Hannon) *prom: hrd rdn over 2f out: wknd wl over 1f out* **12/1**
0144 12 nk **Councellor (FR)**[13] 1996 5-8-12 80 ...(t) MickyFenton 6 68
(Stef Liddiard) *a in rr: drvn and hanging lft over 2f out: no prog* **33/1**
13 1 1/2 **Voliere**[244] 5799 4-9-0 82 ... AdamKirby 15 66
(S C Williams) *hld up bhd ldrs on inner: effrt 2f out and in tch: pushed along and lost pl over 1f out: wknd* **66/1**
4342 14 hd **Merrymadcap (IRE)**[9] 2107 5-7-9 70 ... LauraReynolds(7) 1 54
(M Blanshard) *slowest away: hld up in last: nvr a factor* **33/1**
0210 15 12 **General Knowledge (USA)**[19] 1842 4-9-0 82 ...(t) OscarUrbina 11 38
(B G Powell) *chsd wnr to over 2f out: wknd rapidly: t.o* **50/1**

1m 41.3s (-2.65) **Going Correction** -0.175s/f (Firm) 15 Ran SP% **126.5**
Speed ratings (Par 107):106,103,102,101,101 101,100,98,96,96 95,95,93,93,81
CSF £647.02 CT £3786.91 TOTE £44.50: £8.20, £5.70, £2.60; EX 1021.10.
Owner Robert Heathcote **Bred** R And Mrs Heathcote **Trained** Kinnersley, Worcs

FOCUS
This had looked a decent handicap on paper beforehand, despite the very short-priced favourite, but this was another contest where it paid to race up with the pace and the winner made every yard against the inside rail. Nothing got into it from the rear. The winenr is rated to the best view of her previous form.

NOTEBOOK
Pintle, who has gained four of her previous wins under McEvoy, had shown very little in her last few starts but as a result was back down to a mark off which she was only just denied at Warwick last July. Crucially, she was able to gain an uncontested lead against the inside rail and, with the track appearing to be suiting front-runners, never really looked in much danger of getting caught.
Master Pegasus was never far away from his decent draw and kept on battling right to the line, if never able to get to the winner. He is gradually running into form as he edges down the weights and would be especially interesting back on easier ground. (op 20-1)
Killena Boy(IRE), carrying a 6lb penalty for his course-and-distance victory the previous week, was well backed and moved smoothly into contention approaching the last quarter-mile, but once off the bridle he could not find much more. He does like this track, but will have to find improvement from somewhere to defy this sort of mark. (op 13-2)
Tumbleweed Glory(IRE) made up a lot of ground from well off the pace in the home straight. He is yet to win on turf, but looks capable and may appreciate a return to further. (op 25-1)
Full Victory(IRE) did not perform badly under a 6lb penalty for his course-and-distanec win, making up quite a bit of ground from well off the pace in the home straight, but this was a race dominated by the pace-setters. (op 6-1)
Hassaad was never travelling well at any stage and all he could do was plod on down the outside to reach his final position. He could have done with the penalty for winning this to improve his chances of getting into the Royal Hunt Cup, but on this showing he would have no chance there anyway. Perhaps he had a harder race in the Zetland Gold Cup than it appeared. Official explanation: jockey said gelding ran flat (op 6-4)
It's A Dream(FR) ◆, not for the first time this season, ran better than his finishing position might suggest. He is yet to make the frame in six outings on turf after making a successful racecourse debut on Polytrack, but looks more than capable of better, especially back over further.
General Knowledge(USA) Official explanation: jockey said gelding lost a shoe

2402 IGINDEX.COM MAIDEN STKS — 1m 2f 7y
8:30 (8:31) (Class 5) 3-Y-O **£3,886** (£1,156; £577; £288) **Stalls** High

Form RPR
2-0 1 **Walking Talking**[47] 1143 3-9-3 0 ... RichardHughes 1 88+
(H R A Cecil) *lw: cl up: rdn over 2f out: sn pressed ldr: led jst over 1f out: styd on wl* **11/4**[2]
2 2 2 **Purple Emperor (USA)**[13] 2005 3-9-3 0 ... LDettori 3 85+
(Saeed Bin Suroor) *lw: sn trckd ldr: led over 2f out: rdn and hdd jst over 1f out: nt qckn: hld whn n.m.r nr fin* **8/11**[1]
0- 3 3 **Harry Tricker**[222] 6220 3-9-3 0 ... JimCrowley 11 78
(Mrs A J Perrett) *prom: rdn over 2f out: styd on to take 3rd 1f out: no ch w ldng pair* **33/1**
4-2 4 2 **Coastal Command**[26] 1659 3-9-3 0 ... DaneO'Neill 10 74+
(R Charlton) *t.k.h: hld up in midfield: pushed along over 2f out: sme prog whn nt clr run over 1f out: styd on steadily fnl f* **16/1**
0 5 1 1/4 **Silver Suitor (IRE)**[19] 1841 3-9-3 0 ... JohnEgan 13 72+
(D R C Elsworth) *dwlt: hld up in last trio: pushed along over 2f out: stl only 10th jst over 1f out: swtchd to inner and styd on wl last 100yds* **66/1**
02 6 3/4 **Shavansky**[30] 1560 3-9-3 0 ... JimmyFortune 9 70
(J H M Gosden) *hld up in midfield: shkn up over 2f out: outpcd fr over 1f out* **11/1**
02 7 shd **Officer**[36] 1412 3-9-3 0 ... KerrinMcEvoy 7 70
(Sir Michael Stoute) *led to over 2f out: wknd fnl f* **16/1**
0 8 hd **Irish Quest (IRE)**[9] 2127 3-9-3 0 ... RHills 4 69
(M A Jarvis) *hld up in midfield: effrt on outer over 2f out: pushed along and outpcd over 1f out: fdd* **40/1**
524- 9 2 **Minnis Bay (CAN)**[233] 6031 3-9-3 79 ... MartinDwyer 12 65
(E F Vaughan) *trckd ldrs: shkn up over 2f out: steadily wknd* **50/1**
45 10 shd **Gold Prospect**[45] 1204 3-9-3 0 ... JamieSpencer 5 65+
(M L W Bell) *hld up in last trio: sme prog but repeatedly rn into trble fr over 2f out: shuffled along and nvr nr ldrs* **10/1**[3]
0 11 1 **Kings Story (IRE)**[20] 1812 3-9-3 0 ... AdamKirby 2 63+
(W R Swinburn) *sn detached in last: shkn up and no real prog over 2f out* **33/1**
00 12 3 1/2 **April The Second**[16] 1937 3-8-12 0 ... TolleyDean(5) 8 56
(R J Price) *nvr bttr than midfield: rdn and racing awkwardly in rr 3f out: no ch after* **100/1**
13 1 **Magic Show** 3-9-3 0 ... RobertHavlin 6 54
(J H M Gosden) *w'like: bit bkwd: s.s: a wl in rr: rdn and struggling 3f out* **50/1**

2m 9.90s (-0.34) **Going Correction** -0.175s/f (Firm) 13 Ran SP% **128.5**
Speed ratings (Par 99):94,92,90,88,87 86,86,86,84,84 84,81,80
CSF £5.31 TOTE £4.10: £1.40, £1.10, £7.90; EX 7.10.
Owner K Abdulla **Bred** Juddmonte Farms Ltd **Trained** Newmarket, Suffolk

FOCUS
Not as competitive a maiden as the numbers would suggest and it developed into a two-horse race as the betting said it would be. The pace was also ordinary, but six of these were qualifying for a handicap mark in this, so are likely to eventually do better in that sphere. The form makes sense at face value.
Gold Prospect ◆ Official explanation: jockey said colt was denied a clear run

2403 IG INDEX H'CAP — 1m 2f 7y
9:00 (9:00) (Class 4) (0-80,80) 4-Y-O+ **£5,181** (£1,541; £770; £384) **Stalls** High

Form RPR
4-26 1 **Greek Well (IRE)**[22] 1771 4-9-3 76 ... KerrinMcEvoy 11 92+
(Sir Michael Stoute) *lw: trckd clr ldrs: clsd to ld 2f out: idled briefly over 1f out: sn rdn clr* **9/4**[1]
00-1 2 3 **Le Soleil (GER)**[54] 1042 6-8-8 67 ... JamieSpencer 9 77
(B J Curley) *settled towards rr: rdn over 2f out: prog u.str.p to go 2nd 1f out: styd on but no ch w wnr* **3/1**[2]
50-4 3 1 1/2 **Parnassian**[20] 1811 7-8-9 68 ...(v[1]) RichardThomas 7 75
(J A Geake) *settled wl in rr: rdn wl over 3f out: gd prog on outer fr 2f out: styd on wl: nrst fin* **33/1**
0402 4 nk **Prince Nureyev (IRE)**[31] 1543 7-9-7 80 ... OscarUrbina 8 86
(B R Millman) *lw: wl in rr: u.p 3f out: styd on fr 2f out: nrst fin* **14/1**
-032 5 1 1/4 **Sir Arthur (IRE)**[8] 2136 4-8-10 72 ... GregFairley(3) 13 76
(M Johnston) *chsd clr ldng pair: drvn to cl over 2f out: fdd fnl f* **8/1**[3]
6-02 6 3/4 **Trans Sonic**[20] 1811 4-8-9 68 ow1 ...(v) JHBowman 6 70
(A P Jarvis) *lw: plld hrd: trckd ldr to over 2f out: grad wknd* **14/1**
60-0 7 hd **Zamboozle (IRE)**[40] 1308 5-9-0 73 ... JohnEgan 14 75
(D R C Elsworth) *dwlt: hld up in rr: sme prog on inner 2f out: no imp over 1f out* **25/1**
0104 8 1/2 **Double Spectre (IRE)**[28] 1609 5-8-8 67 ... DaneO'Neill 2 68
(Jean-Rene Auvray) *chsd clr ldrs: rdn and struggling over 2f out: one pce after* **20/1**
2-41 9 1/2 **Del Mar Sunset**[13] 2003 8-9-4 80 ... LiamJones(3) 3 80+
(W J Haggas) *hld up wl in rr: rdn and effrt on inner over 2f out: no prog over 1f out* **9/1**
-055 10 1 **Optimus (USA)**[13] 2003 5-9-0 73 ... GeorgeBaker 5 71
(B G Powell) *hld up wl in rr: gng wl enough 3f out: rdn and no prog over 2f out* **14/1**
04-0 11 1/2 **Master Of The Race**[14] 1962 5-9-2 75 ...(p) JimCrowley 12 72
(Tom Dascombe) *settled towards rr: drvn and prog 2f out: nvr rchd ldrs: wknd fnl f* **14/1**
-033 12 1 1/2 **Wee Charlie Castle (IRE)**[24] 1717 4-8-4 63 ... ChrisCatlin 10 57
(G C H Chung) *chsd clr ldrs: wknd 2f out* **50/1**
-002 13 shd **Wovoka (IRE)**[6] 2209 4-9-5 78 ... MartinDwyer 4 71+
(M R Channon) *racd freely: led at str pce: hdd 2f out: sn btn: heavily eased fnl f* **8/1**[3]
44-0 14 12 **Colton**[36] 1416 4-8-13 72 ... RichardHughes 1 41
(J M P Eustace) *hld up in last: no prog 3f out: wknd: t.o* **33/1**
111- 15 11 **Mostarsil (USA)**[336] 3209 9-8-6 72 ... JemmaMarshall(7) 15 19
(G L Moore) *nvr beyond midfield: wknd rapidly 2f out: t.o* **20/1**

2m 8.77s (-1.47) **Going Correction** -0.175s/f (Firm) 15 Ran SP% **135.9**
Speed ratings (Par 105):98,95,94,94,93 92,92,92,91,90 90,89,89,79,70
CSF £9.06 CT £201.41 TOTE £3.50: £1.60, £2.00, £7.90; EX 28.60 Place 6 £260.97, Place 5 £165.58.
Owner Ballymacoll Stud **Bred** Ballymacoll Stud Farm Ltd **Trained** Newmarket, Suffolk

FOCUS
A decent handicap, even though the time was nothing special, and both the front pair were very well backed which suggests the form is reliable enough, rated through the third and fourth. Greek Well is getting his act together now.
Wovoka(IRE) Official explanation: jockey said gelding ran too free
T/Plt: £357.20 to a £1 stake. Pool: £93,830.50. 191.75 winning tickets. T/Qpdt: £108.00 to a £1 stake. Pool: £5,035.60. 34.50 winning tickets. JN

2404 - 2408a (Foreign Racing) - See Raceform Interactive

2102 MUNICH (L-H)
Thursday, June 7

OFFICIAL GOING: Good

2409a GROSSER CANON-PREIS (LISTED RACE) — 1m 6f
3:25 (4:04) 4-Y-O+ **£8,108** (£2,973; £1,622; £811)

RPR
1 **Dragon Fly (GER)**[26] 1689 5-8-11 ... WMongil 5 102
(Frau Jutta Mayer, Germany) **2/1**[1]
2 7 **Brisant (GER)**[26] 1689 5-8-11 ... DPorcu 8 93
(M Trybuhl, Germany) **15/1**

3 4 **Rhapsody In Blue (GER)**[218] 4-8-4 DMoffatt 2 81
(D K Richardson, Germany) **94/10**
4 1 1/4 **Caudillo (GER)**[45] 4-9-4 ASchikora 1 93
(Dr A Bolte, Germany) **27/10**[3]
5 13 **Carus (GER)**[26] 1689 8-9-4 GHind 6 76
(D K Richardson, Germany) **23/1**
6 7 **Evinado (GER)**[284] 8-9-4 CCzachary 9 67
(Werner Glanz, Germany) **18/1**
7 35 **Foreign Affairs**[19] 1833 9-9-4 PatCosgrave 3 21
(Sir Mark Prescott) *led: pushed along most of the way: reminders 1/2-way: hdd 5f out: 3rd st: sn wknd: eased* **26/10**[2]
8 2 **Brigentia (GER)**[355] 4-8-7 TBitala 7 —
(Frau Ira Ferentschak, Germany) **31/2**
9 30 **Jump For You (FR)**[46] 5-9-4 YLerner 4 —
(W Baltromei, Germany) **63/10**

3m 5.48s (185.48) 9 Ran SP% **133.2**
(including ten euro stakes): WIN 30; PL 15, 31, 21; SF 405.
Owner Gestut Park Wiedingen **Bred** Gestut Park Wiedingen **Trained** Germany

NOTEBOOK
Foreign Affairs again put the pace to the race, but he was struggling from some way out and eventually dropped out to be well beaten. His trainer suggested that the nine-year-old, a winner of 12 races in his career, including nine in Listed company, may now be retired.

2271 BRIGHTON (L-H)
Friday, June 8

OFFICIAL GOING: Firm
Wind: Moderate, half behind Weather: Hazy sunshine; muggy

2410 TOTEPLACEPOT MEDIAN AUCTION MAIDEN STKS 5f 213y
2:20 (2:21) (Class 5) 2-Y-O **£2,914** (£867; £433; £216) **Stalls** Low

Form RPR
32 1 **Elna Bright**[10] 2103 2-9-3 0 RyanMoore 8 76
(R Hannon) *hld up in tch: plld wd over 1f out: strly rdn to ld fnl 50yds* **2/1**[2]
2332 2 1/2 **Sinead Of Aglish (IRE)**[10] 2115 2-8-12 0 SebSanders 4 70
(A B Haynes) *led: rdn and hdd ent fnl 50yds* **1/1**[1]
3323 3 1 1/2 **Shatter Resistant (IRE)**[9] 2138 2-9-3 0 TPO'Shea 2 70
(M R Channon) *t.k.h: in tch tl hung lft appr fnl f: one pce* **13/2**[3]
05 4 3/4 **Rubytwosox (IRE)**[10] 2109 2-8-12 0 SamHitchcott 7 63
(W R Muir) *trckd ldr tl over 1f out: wknd ins fnl f* **33/1**
40 5 1 1/4 **Straight And Level (CAN)**[15] 1970 2-8-12 0 PatrickHills(5) 6 64
(J W Hills) *prom on outside: rdn and hung lft over 1f out: wknd* **14/1**
0 6 4 **Fraamington**[7] 2193 2-9-3 0 EdwardCreighton 1 52
(M R Channon) *prom tl rdn over 1f out: wknd* **50/1**
7 shd **Poppy Perfect** 2-8-9 0 JerryO'Dwyer(3) 5 47
(J M P Eustace) *slowly away: a outpcd* **18/1**
0 8 18 **Adam Eterno (IRE)**[20] 1832 2-9-3 0 BrettDoyle 3 —
(B J Meehan) *a bhd: t.o* **25/1**

1m 11.13s (1.03) **Going Correction** +0.075s/f (Good) 8 Ran SP% **117.3**
Speed ratings (Par 93):96,95,93,92,90 85,85,61
CSF £4.39 TOTE £3.10: £1.40, £1.10, £1.10; EX 5.10 Trifecta £10.50 Pool: £471.53 - 31.78 winning tickets..
Owner David Mort **Bred** D R Tucker **Trained** East Everleigh, Wilts
■ Ryan Moore's first winner on just his second ride back since breaking his arm in March.

FOCUS
Just an ordinary juvenile maiden. The third and fifth set the level, with the winner showing improved form but the second 9lb off her best.

NOTEBOOK
Elna Bright proved suited by the step up in trip and improved on his recent second to Gaspar Van Wittel at Chepstow to get off the mark at the third attempt. He can probably be rated a little better than the bare form as he did not look comfortable on this undulating track and hung right near the finish. (op 9-4 tchd 15-8)
Sinead Of Aglish(IRE) made a bold bid to gain that elusive first success, but she again just found one too good. She did little wrong but, being by Captain Rio, she will probably appreciate some cut in the ground. (op 5-4)
Shatter Resistant(IRE) could not confirm earlier Bath form with Elna Bright and seemed to find this ground a bit on the quick side. (op 9-2 tchd 7-1)
Rubytwosox(IRE) ran a respectable race without posing a serious threat and could find her level in the nursery season. (op 40-1)
Straight And Level(CAN) did not improve as one might have expected for the step up in trip and was a little bit disappointing. (op 12-1)

2411 TOTESPORT.COM H'CAP 5f 59y
2:55 (2:55) (Class 4) (0-80,75) 3-Y-O+ **£4,605** (£1,378; £689; £344; £171) **Stalls** Low

Form RPR
16-3 1 **Safari Mischief**[18] 1885 4-9-5 **70** SaleemGolam(3) 5 81
(P Winkworth) *trckd ldr: led over 1f out: rdn: jst hld on* **15/2**
2262 2 hd **Chatshow (USA)**[7] 2197 6-9-7 **69** SebSanders 2 79
(A W Carroll) *chsd ldrs: rdn to go 2nd wl ins fnl f: r.o: jst failed* **2/1**[1]
-302 3 1 **One Way Ticket**[7] 2221 7-9-5 **67** (p) HayleyTurner 1 74
(J M Bradley) *led tl hdd over 1f out: rdn and lost 2nd wl ins fnl f* **7/1**[3]
005- 4 nk **Perfect Treasure (IRE)**[171] 6865 4-9-2 **64** TPO'Shea 4 69
(J A R Toller) *in tch: outpcd over 2f out: styng on whn hung lft appr fnl f* **20/1**
2321 5 hd **What Do You Know**[2] 2350 4-9-8 **73** 6ex JerryO'Dwyer(3) 3 78
(A M Hales) *in tch tl outpcd over 2f out: styd on fnl f* **5/1**[2]
4613 6 1 3/4 **Harrison's Flyer (IRE)**[14] 1991 6-8-11 **64** (p) KevinGhunowa(5) 6 63
(J M Bradley) *a bhd* **5/1**[2]
6600 7 nk **Malapropism**[13] 2025 7-9-6 **68** SamHitchcott 7 66
(M R Channon) *a bhd* **12/1**
3000 8 4 **Night Prospector**[36] 1431 7-9-5 **72** (p) LukeMorris(5) 9 56
(R A Harris) *slowly away and stmbld whn hood removed s: a bhd* **12/1**
000- 9 14 **Rare Cross (IRE)**[180] 6776 5-9-13 **75** JimmyQuinn 8 10
(R A Teal) *racd wd: a bhd* **20/1**

61.57 secs (-0.73) **Going Correction** +0.075s/f (Good) 9 Ran SP% **115.8**
Speed ratings (Par 105):108,107,106,105,105 102,102,95,73
CSF £22.96 CT £109.61 TOTE £9.40: £2.20, £1.30, £2.30; EX 25.80 Trifecta £502.10 Pool: £735.49 - 1.04 winning tickets..
Owner P Winkworth **Bred** Bearstone Stud **Trained** Chiddingfold, Surrey

FOCUS
The top weight was rated just 75 and this was an ordinary sprint handicap for the grade, albeit very competitive.

2412 TOTEEXACTA CLAIMING STKS 7f 214y
3:30 (3:30) (Class 6) 4-Y-O+ **£1,943** (£578; £288; £144) **Stalls** Low

Form RPR
-030 1 **Mamichor**[9] 2143 4-8-13 45 (p) RichardSmith 7 52
(B R Johnson) *mde all: rdn out fnl f* **3/1**[2]
0-00 2 2 **Colonel Cotton (IRE)**[9] 2143 8-8-5 56 JimmyQuinn 4 40
(W J Knight) *chsd wnr to over 2f out: rdn to regain 2nd ins fnl f: no imp on wnr* **9/2**[3]
0040 3 nk **Fire At Will**[3] 2331 5-8-11 42 SebSanders 3 45
(A W Carroll) *chsd ldrs: wnt 2nd over 2f out tl hung lft and lost 2nd ins fnl f* **7/4**[1]
0600 4 3 **Lady Edge (IRE)**[60] 975 5-8-10 55 (b[1]) ChrisCatlin 2 37
(A W Carroll) *t.k.h: trckd ldrs: rdn 1/2-way: no hdwy fr wl over 1f out* **9/2**[3]
505 5 2 1/2 **Rowan Pursuit**[39] 1344 6-7-7 39 (b) DavidProbert(7) 1 21
(E A Wheeler) *a bhd* **12/1**
0000 6 7 **Homebred Star**[38] 1368 6-8-8 36 JerryO'Dwyer(3) 5 16
(G P Enright) *hld up in rr: lost tch 2f out* **16/1**
00-0 7 3/4 **Aberlady Bay (IRE)**[14] 2004 4-8-6 41 SamHitchcott 6 10
(T T Clement) *a towards rr* **11/1**

1m 35.97s (0.93) **Going Correction** +0.075s/f (Good) 7 Ran SP% **119.6**
Speed ratings (Par 101):98,96,95,92,90 83,82
CSF £18.05 TOTE £4.70: £2.80, £2.20; EX 23.20.
Owner Cwmbach Racing **Bred** Nant Loyw Stud **Trained** Ashtead, Surrey

FOCUS
A very moderate claimer and not a race to dwell on. The winner is rated as having improved slightly on his 3yo best.
Homebred Star Official explanation: jockey said gelding lost its action
Aberlady Bay(IRE) Official explanation: trainer said filly was unsuited by the track

2413 TOTESPORT 0800 221 221 H'CAP 1m 1f 209y
4:05 (4:11) (Class 5) (0-70,75) 3-Y-O **£2,849** (£847; £423; £211) **Stalls** High

Form RPR
0-65 1 **Seeking The Buck (USA)**[17] 1913 3-9-7 **69** (t) ChrisCatlin 2 74
(M A Magnusson) *a in tch: rdn 3f out: wnt 2nd 3f out: led over 1f out: drvn out* **8/1**[3]
-551 2 1/2 **Mutual Friend (USA)**[8] 2177 3-9-13 **75** 6ex RyanMoore 4 79
(E A L Dunlop) *trckd ldrs: chal over 1f out: hung lft: kpt on but no imp cl home* **13/8**[1]
0-01 3 3/4 **Lapina (IRE)**[38] 1370 3-8-11 **59** (b) JimmyQuinn 1 61
(Pat Eddery) *hld up: r.o ins fnl f on outside: nvr nrr* **11/1**
-663 4 hd **Summer Of Love (IRE)**[17] 1927 3-9-3 **65** JosedeSouza 5 67
(P F I Cole) *led for 1f: styd prom: rdn 2f out: no hdwy ins fnl f* **6/1**[2]
0-05 5 2 **Cat Six (USA)**[14] 1988 3-9-4 **66** BrettDoyle 6 64
(B J Meehan) *led after 1f: hdd over 1f out: wknd ins fnl f* **20/1**
-340 6 1/2 **Zelos (IRE)**[95] 611 3-9-0 **65** RichardKingscote(3) 8 62
(J A Osborne) *w.w: rdn 3f out: no hdwy fr over 2f out* **16/1**

2m 5.16s (2.56) **Going Correction** +0.075s/f (Good) 6 Ran SP% **82.5**
Speed ratings (Par 99):92,91,91,90,89 88
CSF £11.41 CT £38.20 TOTE £7.60: £2.70, £1.20; EX 11.20 Trifecta £98.00 Pool: £278.97 - 2.02 winning tickets..
Owner Eastwind Racing Ltd and Martha Trussell **Bred** Flaxman Holdings Ltd **Trained** Upper Lambourn, Berks
■ Crossing the Line (7/4, unruly in stalls) & Krikket (40/1, ref to enter stalls) were withdrawn. R4 applies, deduct 35p in the £.

FOCUS
This race lost much of its interest with two horses withdrawn at the start, particularly Crossing The Line, who was disputing favouritism at the time. Surprisingly enough, though, it still looked a reasonable contest for the level, even if the early gallop was pretty ordinary. The bare form does not look that solid, however.
Zelos(IRE) Official explanation: jockey said gelding did not come down the hill

2414 TOTESPORTCASINO.COM H'CAP 6f 209y
4:40 (4:40) (Class 5) (0-70,71) 4-Y-O+ **£2,775** (£830; £415; £207; £103) **Stalls** Low

Form RPR
0503 1 **Purus (IRE)**[17] 1931 5-9-5 **67** ChrisCatlin 6 77
(R A Teal) *trckd ldrs: chal 3f out: sn led: rdn out fnl f* **16/1**
0101 2 1 1/4 **High Ambition**[8] 2190 4-9-9 **71** 6ex (v) SebSanders 3 78+
(P W D'Arcy) *hld up: hdwy on ins over 2f out: hung lft but wnt 2nd 1f out: kpt on but no imp* **7/4**[1]
2162 3 2 1/2 **Quantum Leap**[5] 2272 10-9-4 **66** (p) JimmyQuinn 1 66+
(S Dow) *bhd tl hdwy over 1f out: styd on fnl f: nvr nrr* **7/1**[3]
0360 4 1 1/2 **Piccostar**[3] 2336 4-8-6 **54** (b[1]) SamHitchcott 5 50
(A B Haynes) *trckd ldr: led over 4f out: hdd wl over 2f out: sn btn* **14/1**
0000 5 shd **Nautical**[15] 1962 9-9-7 **69** TPO'Shea 4 65
(A W Carroll) *t.k.h: hld up: rdn over 1f out: no ex* **20/1**
0111 6 2 **Stamford Blue**[10] 2108 6-8-9 **62** (b) LukeMorris(5) 7 52+
(R A Harris) *slowly away: rdn whn hung lft over 1f out: no hdwy after* **7/4**[1]
4101 7 4 **Night Wolf (IRE)**[40] 1318 7-8-8 **59** (t) RichardKingscote(3) 2 38
(Jamie Poulton) *led for over 2f: wknd over 2f out* **13/2**[2]

1m 23.07s (0.37) **Going Correction** +0.075s/f (Good) 7 Ran SP% **115.9**
Speed ratings (Par 103):100,98,95,94,93 91,87
CSF £45.77 TOTE £16.20: £5.30, £1.40; EX 55.20.
Owner J Morton **Bred** K Nercessian **Trained** Headley, Surrey
■ A first winner as a trainer for Roger Teal, a former assistant to Philip Mitchell.

FOCUS
A modest handicap and, with the early gallop steady, it paid to be close to the pace. It is doubtful if the form can be taken at face value, although the winner was operating at a highet level than this last summer.
Stamford Blue Official explanation: trainer had no explanation for the poor form shown

2415 TOTE TEXT BETTING 60021 H'CAP 5f 213y
5:15 (5:15) (Class 5) (0-75,73) 3-Y-O **£2,775** (£830; £415; £207; £103) **Stalls** Low

Form RPR
4412 1 **Gold Digger Miss (USA)**[15] 1978 3-9-6 **72** SebSanders 4 79+
(J Noseda) *chsd ldrs: rdn and str burst to ld ins fnl f: won gng away* **4/5**[1]
-066 2 1 **Buckie Massa**[3] 2335 3-9-6 **72** JDSmith 6 76
(S Kirk) *hld up: hdwy over 2f out: led over 1f out: hdd and nt pce of wnr ins fnl f* **11/2**[2]
0-30 3 2 1/2 **Rosie Cross (IRE)**[39] 1345 3-8-4 **56** HayleyTurner 2 52
(Eve Johnson Houghton) *mde most tl hdd over 1f out: one pce fnl f* **12/1**
-605 4 3/4 **Dowlleh**[27] 1660 3-9-7 **73** SamHitchcott 7 67
(T T Clement) *bhd: making hdwy whn hung lft over 1f out: nvr nr to chal* **8/1**
0204 5 3/4 **Comrade Cotton**[2] 2363 3-8-6 **65** BradleyRoper(7) 1 57
(N A Callaghan) *bhd on ins: rdn 1/2-way: sn btn* **7/1**[3]

035- **6** *1* **Path To Glory**[168] 6912 3-8-2 **54** oh1 ChrisCatlin 5 43
(Mrs L J Mongan) *a bhd* **25/1**
055 **7** *1 ¾* **Zahour Al Yasmeen**[22] 1786 3-9-7 **73** TPO'Shea 3 56
(M R Channon) *s.i.s: sn in tch: led briefly 2f out: wknd over 1f out* **7/1**[3]
1m 10.18s (0.08) **Going Correction** +0.075s/f (Good) 7 Ran SP% **118.6**
Speed ratings (Par 99):102,100,97,96,95 94,91
CSF £6.17 TOTE £1.60: £1.10, £4.20; EX 7.90 Place 6 £13.23, Place 5 £12.30.
Owner Tom Ludt **Bred** Grapestock Llc & Westwood Thoroughbreds Llc **Trained** Newmarket, Suffolk
FOCUS
A modest sprint handicap in which there was not a lot of turf form to go on. The winner is progressive and the second is rated back to form.
Dowlleh Official explanation: jockey said gelding hung left
T/Plt: £27.60 to a £1 stake. Pool: £63,166.10. 1,666.65 winning tickets. T/Qpdt: £15.10 to a £1 stake. Pool: £2,435.70. 118.60 winning tickets. JS

2199 CATTERICK (L-H)
Friday, June 8

OFFICIAL GOING: Good to firm (9.0)
Wind: Almost nil Weather: fine and sunny

2416 STAPLETON MAIDEN AUCTION FILLIES' STKS 5f
2:00 (2:00) (Class 6) 2-Y-O **£2,730** (£806; £403) **Stalls** Low

Form RPR
3 **1** **Style Award**[31] 1553 2-8-1 0 AndrewMullen(3) 6 67
(W J H Ratcliffe) *chsd ldrs: wnt 2nd over 1f out: led last 75yds: jst hld on* **17/2**
22 **2** *shd* **Speedy Senorita (IRE)**[25] 1727 2-8-4 0 FrancisNorton 7 67
(K R Burke) *led tl ins fnl f: hrd rdn and styd on towards fin: jst hld* **1/1**[1]
0 **3** *3* **Pretty Bonnie**[10] 2122 2-8-4 0 PaulHanagan 3 56+
(J G Portman) *w ldrs: fdd fnl f* **10/3**[2]
4 *6* **Sawpit Sunshine (IRE)** 2-8-10 0 DeanMcKeown 1 41
(J L Spearing) *sn drvn along and chsng ldrs: outpcd 2f out: sn lost pl* **8/1**[3]
5 *2* **Day Shift (IRE)** 2-8-7 0 DavidAllan 2 30
(Rae Guest) *chsd ldrs: outpcd over 2f out: sn lost pl* **12/1**
6 *4* **On Instinct (IRE)** 2-8-10 0 TomEaves 4 19
(B Smart) *dwlt: sn w ldrs: wknd qckly over 1f out* **8/1**[3]
60.93 secs (0.33) **Going Correction** -0.125s/f (Firm) 6 Ran SP% **113.5**
Speed ratings (Par 88):92,91,87,77,74 67
CSF £18.01 TOTE £9.80: £3.80, £1.30; EX 17.60.
Owner Bolton Hall Partnership 1 **Bred** Mrs S F Dibben **Trained** Wensley, N Yorks
■ Stewards' Enquiry : Francis Norton two-day ban: used whip with excessive frequency and in the incorrect position (Jun 24-25)
FOCUS
A modest maiden auction fillies' race with the luckless runner-up the best guide.
NOTEBOOK
Style Award knew a lot more this time and never looked like deviating from a straight line. In the end the line came just in time. (tchd 9-1)
Speedy Senorita(IRE), the pick of the paddock, was bidding to make it third time lucky. With everything thrown at her, she was coming back for more at the line and needed just one more stride. (op 5-6 tchd 8-11 and 11-10, 5-1 in places)
Pretty Bonnie, racing on totally different ground and a much sharper track, matched strides but didn't see it out anywhere near as well as the first two. (op 9-2)
Sawpit Sunshine(IRE), a neat, narrow newcomer, was very keen to post. Driven along to keep up, she dropped right away in the final two furlongs. (tchd 9-1)
Day Shift(IRE), a May foal, lacks size and scope and was in trouble at the halfway mark. (op 28-1)
On Instinct(IRE), a close-coupled newcomer, was keen to post. She stopped to nothing coming to the final furlong. (op 9-1 tchd 10-1)

2417 NOEL & GEORGINA VERNON 11TH WEDDING ANNIVERSARY (S) STKS 1m 5f 175y
2:30 (2:30) (Class 6) 4-Y-0+ **£2,730** (£806; £403) **Stalls** Low

Form RPR
004/ **1** **Cadeaux Rouge (IRE)**[144] 4026 6-8-7 0 (tp) TonyHamilton 1 47
(D W Thompson) *mde all: qcknd pce 4f out: hrd rdn fnl 2f: jst hld on* **5/1**[3]
64-4 **2** *shd* **Tiltili (IRE)**[2] 2372 4-8-7 **48** KDarley 4 47
(P C Haslam) *trckd ldrs: wnt clr 2nd over 3f out: rdn over 2f out: kpt on: jst denied* **6/4**[1]
40-0 **3** *8* **High Frequency (IRE)**[16] 1556 6-8-12 **42** (p) TomEaves 6 41
(A Crook) *chsd ldrs: drvn over 6f out: outpcd over 4f out: kpt on one pce* **5/1**[3]
0/0- **4** *3 ½* **Court One**[16] 3135 9-8-12 **39** PaddyAspell 2 36
(R E Barr) *hld up: pushed along 5f out: outpcd over 3f out: kpt on ins fnl f to take 4th nr line* **9/1**
6600 **5** *½* **Kristalchen**[16] 1942 5-8-7 **42** (v[1]) PaulFessey 7 30
(D W Thompson) *s.s: hld up in last: hdwy 7f out: sn chsng ldrs: outpcd over 3f out: lost 4th nr line* **7/2**[2]
000- **6** *17* **Phoenix Nights (IRE)**[294] 4568 7-8-12 **38** FrancisNorton 3 11
(A Berry) *chsd ldrs: outpcd 4f out: lost pl over 2f out: sn bhd* **14/1**
3m 7.37s (2.87) **Going Correction** +0.125s/f (Good) 6 Ran SP% **112.2**
Speed ratings (Par 101):96,95,91,89,89 79
CSF £13.00 TOTE £6.10: £2.90, £1.10; EX 11.30.There was no bid for the winner.
Owner D Morland **Bred** Stein Enqvist **Trained** Bolam, Co Durham
FOCUS
A dire seller, shortlisted for worst race of the year. The first two finished clear.

2418 GO RACING AT PONTEFRACT ON MONDAY H'CAP 5f
3:05 (3:06) (Class 5) (0-70,69) 3-Y-0+ **£3,238** (£963; £481; £240) **Stalls** Low

Form RPR
-064 **1** **Our Little Secret (IRE)**[4] 2315 5-9-6 **61** FrancisNorton 7 78
(A Berry) *mde all: styd on strly to draw clr fnl f* **7/1**[3]
30-0 **2** *3 ½* **Strensall**[31] 1557 10-9-8 **63** PaulHanagan 2 67
(R E Barr) *chsd wnr: styd on same pce fnl f* **9/1**
004 **3** *hd* **Henry Hall (IRE)**[17] 1914 11-9-9 **64** KimTinkler 6 67
(N Tinkler) *chsd ldrs: kpt on same pce fnl f* **7/1**[3]
3002 **4** *1* **Sharp Hat**[6] 2249 13-8-11 **52** DaleGibson 3 51
(D W Chapman) *chsd ldrs: one pce fnl 2f* **20/1**
6-00 **5** *nk* **Conjecture**[41] 1309 5-8-12 **58** JamieMoriarty(5) 9 56+
(R Bastiman) *s.i.s: in rr: styd on fnl 2f: nt rch ldrs* **11/2**[2]
3000 **6** *¾* **Minimum Fuss (IRE)**[7] 2205 3-7-11 **52** MCGeran(7) 4 44
(M C Chapman) *in tch: kpt on wl fnl 2f* **40/1**
2054 **7** *1 ½* **Dysonic (USA)**[7] 2221 5-8-9 **50** oh1 (v) DavidAllan 11 39
(J Balding) *chsd ldrs on outer: kpt on same pce fnl 2f* **9/1**
0431 **8** *hd* **Whinhill House**[18] 1891 7-9-5 **60** (v) PatCosgrave 5 49
(D W Barker) *chsd ldrs: one pce fnl 2f* **11/2**[2]
600 **9** *½* **Littledodayno (IRE)**[18] 1885 4-9-5 **60** DO'Donohoe 8 47+
(M Wigham) *s.i.s: kpt on fnl 2f: stmbld 1f out: nvr on terms: lame* **16/1**
0000 **10** *shd* **Toy Top (USA)**[4] 2315 4-9-12 **67** (b) PhillipMakin 1 53
(M Dods) *sn drvn along and in tch: no imp fnl 2f* **18/1**
03 **11** *1* **Silver Hotspur**[127] 322 3-9-0 **62** AdrianTNicholls 15 42
(M Wigham) *s.i.s: hdwy on inner 2f out: nvr on terms* **25/1**
61-0 **12** *½* **Rosie's Result**[1] 2386 7-8-6 **50** oh5 AndrewMullen(3) 13 31
(M Todhunter) *s.i.s: a in rr* **25/1**
000- **13** *¾* **Bond Becks (IRE)**[248] 5752 7-8-7 **55** ow1 NeilBrown(7) 12 33
(G R Oldroyd) *prom on outer: lost pl 2f out* **40/1**
14 *5* **Green Lagonda (AUS)**[188] 5-10-0 **69** KDarley 10 28
(J G Given) *prom on outer: lost pl 2f out: eased ins fnl f* **9/2**[1]
60-6 **15** *2* **Violet's Pride**[48] 1151 3-8-3 **58** ow3 MarkCoumbe(7) 14 6
(S Parr) *in tch on wd outside: lost pl over 2f out* **33/1**
59.69 secs (-0.91) **Going Correction** -0.125s/f (Firm)
WFA 3 from 4yo+ 7lb 15 Ran SP% **125.4**
Speed ratings (Par 103):102,96,96,94,94 92,90,90,89,89 87,86,85,77,74
CSF £65.57 CT £468.73 TOTE £8.70: £2.20, £2.60, £4.30; EX 64.60.
Owner J Berry **Bred** Camogue Stud Ltd **Trained** Cockerham, Lancs
FOCUS
A modest handicap but the form looks sound at this level with the speedy winner turning in a personal best. The three veterans who chased her home are all probably regressive these days.
Littledodayno(IRE) Official explanation: jockey said, regarding running and riding, his orders were to jump out, keep mid-div and finish as well as he could, adding that the filly missed the break and was outpaced early stages, approaching the furlong marker it stumbled, appeared to go wrong, and so he did not ride vigorously closing stages; trainer confirmed adding that the filly lost both front shoes in running and appeared lame; vet confirmed filly lame

2419 BOOK ON-LINE AT CATTERICKBRIDGE.CO.UK H'CAP 5f 212y
3:40 (3:40) (Class 4) (0-85,78) 4-Y-0+ **£5,181** (£1,541; £770; £384) **Stalls** Low

Form RPR
1041 **1** **Rainbow Bay**[7] 2202 4-8-0 **64** 6ex (v) MCGeran(7) 1 74
(P D Evans) *hld up: effrt over 2f out: r.o to ld ins fnl f* **3/1**[1]
0-52 **2** *¾* **Mulligan's Gold (IRE)**[7] 2202 4-8-6 **63** DavidAllan 5 70
(T D Easterby) *trckd ldrs: led 2f out: hdd and no ex ins fnl f* **3/1**[1]
0241 **3** *nk* **H Harrison (IRE)**[31] 1555 7-8-10 **70** AndrewElliott(3) 2 76+
(I W McInnes) *chsd ldrs: edgd lft 1f out: kpt on same pce* **5/1**[3]
3110 **4** *¾* **Violent Velocity (IRE)**[11] 2072 4-8-11 **68** GrahamGibbons 5 72
(J J Quinn) *chsd ldrs: outpcd over 3f out: kpt on same pce fnl 2f* **9/2**[2]
0100 **5** *¾* **King Marju (IRE)**[13] 2030 5-8-13 **70** (v) PhillipMakin 3 72
(K R Burke) *s.i.s: hdwy over 2f out: edgd rt over 1f out: kpt on same pce* **7/1**
/060 **6** *½* **Playful Dane (IRE)**[13] 2025 10-9-7 **78** PatCosgrave 7 78
(K A Ryan) *chsd ldrs: kpt on same pce appr fnl f* **8/1**
110- **7** *10* **Alugat (IRE)**[217] 6315 4-8-10 **67** (p) DO'Donohoe 4 35
(Mrs A Duffield) *led tl 2f out: sn wknd and eased* **16/1**
1m 13.96s (-0.04) **Going Correction** +0.125s/f (Good) 7 Ran SP% **114.3**
Speed ratings (Par 105):105,104,103,102,101 100,87
CSF £11.99 TOTE £3.80: £1.90, £1.70; EX 10.90.
Owner Dusktilldawn Racing I **Bred** Ms R A Myatt **Trained** Pandy, Monmouths
■ Stewards' Enquiry : Pat Cosgrave one-day ban: used whip above shoulder height (Jun 24)
FOCUS
A modest event and little between the first six at the line. The runner-up is the best guide and the form is probably not that solid.
Alugat(IRE) Official explanation: jockey said gelding lost its action

2420 BARTON MAIDEN STKS 1m 3f 214y
4:15 (4:15) (Class 5) 3-Y-0+ **£3,238** (£963; £481; £240) **Stalls** Low

Form RPR
1 **Turbo Linn**[56] 4-9-7 0 DeanMcKeown 1 87+
(G A Swinbank) *w ldr: led after 3f: clr over 1f out: v easily* **1/12**[1]
6-00 **2** *10* **Toboggan Lady**[30] 1579 3-8-6 **45** DO'Donohoe 4 55
(Mrs A Duffield) *chsd ldrs: drvn 6f out: kpt on to take modest 2nd over 1f out* **16/1**[3]
0 **3** *3 ½* **Still Dreaming**[10] 2118 3-8-6 0 PaulFessey 3 49
(M Dods) *hld up in tch: outpcd and lost pl over 4f out: kpt on fnl 2f: tk modest 3rd ins fnl f* **14/1**[2]
0- **4** *4* **Santera (IRE)**[202] 6523 3-8-6 0 PaulHanagan 6 43
(Mrs A Duffield) *hld up in tch: effrt and wnt 2nd over 3f out: wknd over 1f out* **80/1**
6 **5** *8* **Square Dealer**[20] 1849 6-9-12 0 (b) PaddyAspell 5 35
(J R Norton) *led 3f: chsd ldrs: lost pl 3f out* **14/1**[2]
000 **6** *12* **Feeling Peckish (USA)**[10] 2118 3-8-4 0 CharlotteKerton(7) 7 16
(M C Chapman) *trckd ldrs: drvn over 5f out: sn lost pl: bhd fnl 3f* **100/1**
7 *dist* **After Nine** 3-8-7 0 ow1 TonyHamilton 2 —
(F Watson) *s.s: v green: sn detached in rr: t.o 5f out: rn wd bnd 3f out: virtually p.u* **50/1**
2m 37.23s (-1.77) **Going Correction** +0.125s/f (Good)
WFA 3 from 4yo+ 15lb 7 Ran SP% **115.7**
Speed ratings (Par 103):110,103,101,98,93 85,—
CSF £3.51 TOTE £1.10: £1.02, £5.40; EX 4.10.
Owner J Nelson **Bred** James Nelson **Trained** Melsonby, N Yorks
FOCUS
Smart bumper filly Turbo Linn had nothing more than a good workout in this weak maiden.

2421 PEN HILL H'CAP 5f 212y
4:50 (4:50) (Class 6) (0-65,63) 3-Y-0+ **£2,730** (£806; £403) **Stalls** Low

Form RPR
1540 **1** **Winthorpe (IRE)**[17] 1914 7-9-5 **60** JamieMoriarty(5) 4 71
(J J Quinn) *trckd ldrs: shkn up to ld jst ins fnl f: jst hld on* **6/1**[3]
631- **2** *shd* **Observatory Star (IRE)**[227] 6159 4-9-13 **63** (b) GrahamGibbons 11 73
(T D Easterby) *hld up: hdwy over 2f out: str chal ins fnl f: jst hld* **10/1**
44-0 **3** *3 ½* **Dark Champion**[13] 2033 7-9-1 **54** (v) MarkLawson(3) 5 53
(R E Barr) *led: hung rt over 1f out: hdd jst ins fnl f: one pce* **14/1**
00-3 **4** *1* **Desert Hunter (IRE)**[13] 2033 4-9-1 **51** PaulHanagan 12 47
(Micky Hammond) *trckd ldrs: drvn and outpcd over 3f out: hdwy on ins over 2f out: sn chsng ldrs: fdd ins fnl f* **7/2**[2]
0430 **5** *nk* **Compton Plume**[13] 2033 7-9-9 **59** DaleGibson 7 54
(M W Easterby) *chsd ldrs: sn drvn along: kpt on same pce appr fnl f* **9/1**
5504 **6** *¾* **Slipasearcher (IRE)**[4] 2300 3-8-11 **62** (b) MCGeran(7) 2 53
(P D Evans) *s.i.s: hdwy to chse ldrs 3f out: hung lft over 1f out: one pce* **6/1**[3]
0010 **7** *nk* **Walnut Grove**[1] 2390 4-9-3 **60** 6ex NeilBrown(7) 1 52
(T D Barron) *sn w ldr: edgd rt over 1f out: fdd jst ins fnl f* **7/4**[1]

0-35 **8** *7* **Chairman Bobby**[25] 1711 9-9-0 **50**....................(p) TomEaves 6 19
(D W Barker) *chsd ldrs: hung lft and lost pl over 1f out* **10/1**

1m 14.23s (0.23) **Going Correction** +0.125s/f (Good)
WFA 3 from 4yo+ 8lb **8** Ran SP% **122.0**
Speed ratings (Par 101):103,102,98,96,96 95,95,85
CSF £67.45 CT £824.56 TOTE £9.80: £2.50, £2.40, £3.80; EX 58.60.
Owner Green Roberts Savage Whittall Williams **Bred** M Conaghan **Trained** Settrington, N Yorks

FOCUS
A low-grade sprint handicap, the first two clear in the end and the only ones to show their form.

2422 TURF TV BETTING SHOP SERVICE FILLIES' H'CAP 7f
5:25 (5:25) (Class 5) (0-75,70) 3-Y-0+ **£3,238** (£963; £481; £240) **Stalls** Low

Form RPR
05-5 **1** **Kudbeme**[13] 2023 5-8-13 **55**....................PaulFessey 1 63
(N Bycroft) *broke ahd of rest and led early: lost pl over 4f out: gd hdwy 2f out: styd on wl fnl f: led last strides* **10/3**[2]
50-0 **2** *shd* **Damelza (IRE)**[18] 1905 4-9-6 **65**....................DuranFentiman(3) 5 73
(T D Easterby) *w ldrs: led over 1f out: hdd nr fin* **13/2**
01-0 **3** *5* **Pay Time**[13] 2033 8-8-12 **61**....................NeilBrown(7) 3 55
(R E Barr) *w ldrs: chal 2f out: one pce fnl f* **7/1**
-100 **4** *¾* **Grand Lucre**[39] 1345 3-8-13 **65**....................FrancisNorton 7 53
(J W Hills) *sn led: hdd over 5f out: kpt on same pce appr fnl f* **13/2**
0005 **5** *nk* **Smart Pick**[13] 2032 4-8-6 **51** oh6....................GregFairley(3) 4 42
(Mrs L Williamson) *s.i.s: hdwy and hmpd 3f out: kpt on fnl f* **12/1**
0106 **6** *1 ½* **Alavana (IRE)**[15] 1964 3-8-4 **56**....................PaulHanagan 6 39
(D W Barker) *in rr: sn pushed along: kpt on fnl 2f: nvr a threat* **3/1**[1]
2334 **7** *1* **Sweet Pickle**[6] 2240 6-10-0 **70**....................(e) PatCosgrave 9 55
(J R Boyle) *s.i.s: kpt on fnl 2f: nvr nr ldrs* **5/1**[3]
50-0 **8** *shd* **The Keep**[27] 1679 5-8-4 **51** oh6....................(v) NataliaGemelova(5) 2 35
(R E Barr) *w ldrs: led over 5f out tl over 1f out: sn wknd* **66/1**
00-0 **9** *6* **Underthemistletoe (IRE)**[7] 2203 5-8-9 **51** oh6....................TomEaves 8 19
(R E Barr) *chsd ldrs on outer: lost pl over 1f out* **50/1**

1m 28.1s (0.74) **Going Correction** +0.125s/f (Good)
WFA 3 from 4yo+ 10lb **9** Ran SP% **115.1**
Speed ratings (Par 100):100,99,94,93,92 91,90,90,83
CSF £25.25 CT £142.99 TOTE £4.30: £1.40, £3.20, £2.50; EX 28.10 Place 6 £76.03, Place 5 £45.08.
Owner Cavalier Racing **Bred** Mrs R W Gore-Andrews **Trained** Brandsby, N Yorks
■ Stewards' Enquiry : Duran Fentiman one-day ban: careless riding (Jun 24)

FOCUS
A pretty weak fillies' handicap, the first two clear in the end. They were the only ones to really show their form.
T/Plt: £31.00 to a £1 stake. Pool: £40,398.55. 951.20 winning tickets. T/Qpdt: £13.10 to a £1 stake. Pool: £2,226.30. 125.30 winning tickets. WG

2214 GOODWOOD (R-H)
Friday, June 8

OFFICIAL GOING: Straight course - good; round course - good to firm
Wind: Almost nil Weather: Fine, warm

2423 GOODWOOD AVIATION STKS (H'CAP) 1m 1f
2:10 (2:14) (Class 5) (0-70,70) 4-Y-0+ **£3,562** (£1,059; £529; £264) **Stalls** High

Form RPR
0-01 **1** **Logsdail**[29] 1612 7-9-5 **68**....................(p) GeorgeBaker 7 81+
(G L Moore) *hld up in midfield: stdy prog on outer fr over 2f out: chsd ldr over 1f out: shkn up to ld jst ins fnl f: sn clr* **7/2**[2]
0162 **2** *2* **Sedgwick**[8] 2169 5-9-2 **65**....................KerrinMcEvoy 6 73+
(J G Given) *led: kicked 2 l clr over 2f out: drvn and hdd jst ins fnl f: one pce* **5/2**[1]
000- **3** *½* **Darghan (IRE)**[227] 6158 7-8-7 **56**....................TedDurcan 1 63
(W J Musson) *dropped in fr wd draw and hld up in last: prog fr 3f out: drvn and styd on to take 3rd fnl f* **16/1**
00-3 **4** *2* **Dinner Date**[14] 2007 5-8-4 **53**....................PaulDoe 12 56
(T Keddy) *prom: chsd ldr wl over 2f out to over 1f out: wknd fnl f* **9/2**[3]
2606 **5** *shd* **Norwegian**[14] 2006 6-8-5 **54**....................(p) MartinDwyer 13 56+
(Ian Williams) *towards rr: rdn 4f out: prog u.p 2f out: nt clr run briefly 1f out: styd on* **8/1**
00-6 **6** *nk* **Ile Michel**[18] 1886 10-8-9 **58**....................PatDobbs 4 60
(Lady Herries) *settled towards rr: pushed along 4f out: no prog tl styd on fnl 2f: nrst fin* **20/1**
-006 **7** *5* **Mythical Charm**[7] 2214 8-8-2 **54**....................(t) MarcHalford(3) 5 45
(J J Bridger) *racd wd: trckd ldrs: cl up over 2f out: wknd wl over 1f out* **25/1**
060- **8** *1 ¼* **Maud's Cat (IRE)**[171] 6870 4-8-6 **55**....................RichardMullen 10 43
(A P Jarvis) *t.k.h: trckd ldng pair to 1/2-way: wknd u.p 2f out* **28/1**
0-60 **9** *1* **Zinging**[9] 2141 8-8-2 **51** oh6....................(b) FrankieMcDonald 11 37
(J J Bridger) *t.k.h: hld up in last trio: rdn and struggling 3f out* **66/1**
04 **10** *¾* **Paraguay (USA)**[7] 2218 4-9-2 **70**....................ColinHaddon(5) 8 54
(Miss V Haigh) *t.k.h: hld up in last trio: gng wl enough over 3f out: bmpd along and no prog over 2f out* **5/1**
6040 **11** *2 ½* **Todlea (IRE)**[45] 1209 7-9-4 **67**....................(t) DaneO'Neill 3 46
(Jean-Rene Auvray) *pressed ldr to 3f out: wknd sn after* **9/1**

1m 54.95s (-1.91) **Going Correction** -0.075s/f (Good) **11** Ran SP% **126.2**
Speed ratings (Par 103):105,103,102,101,100 100,96,95,94,93 91
CSF £13.24 CT £134.83 TOTE £5.20: £2.00, £1.30, £6.80; EX 14.50.
Owner D T L Limited **Bred** Stetchworth Park Stud Ltd **Trained** Woodingdean, E Sussex
■ Near Germany was withdrawn (8/1, bolted before start.) R4 applies, deduct 10p in the £.

FOCUS
A modest handicap. It is a couple of years since Logsdail rated this high but the overall level of the form seems sound enough.

2424 CASCO EBF MAIDEN STKS 6f
2:45 (2:45) (Class 4) 2-Y-0 **£5,019** (£1,493; £746; £372) **Stalls** Low

Form RPR
2 **1** **King's Icon (IRE)**[14] 1990 2-9-3 0....................MartinDwyer 9 82+
(M P Tregoning) *mde all: hrd pressed and drvn over 1f out: drew clr fnl f* **11/8**[1]
2 *2* **Alsadeek (IRE)** 2-9-3 0....................RHills 1 82+
(J L Dunlop) *w'like: swtg: sn settled wl in rr: pushed along and prog against nr side rail jst over 1f out: r.o to take 2nd last stride: promising* **10/1**
5 **3** *shd* **Barbarossa**[7] 2215 2-9-3 0....................RichardHughes 12 76
(R Hannon) *pressed wnr: drvn and nrly upsides 1f out and clr of rest: wknd last 100yds* **4/1**[2]
4 *hd* **Bailey (IRE)** 2-9-3 0....................TedDurcan 6 75
(B J Meehan) *unf: scope: rn green in rr: shkn up 1/2-way: prog 2f out: styd on wl fnl f: fair debut* **33/1**
5 *1* **Gasmanfightsback** 2-9-3 0....................DaneO'Neill 7 72
(Evan Williams) *w'like: str: towards rr: prog on outer fr 1/2-way: shkn up and kpt on steadily fr over 1f out: nt pce to chal* **33/1**
6 *shd* **Art Sale** 2-9-3 0....................GeorgeBaker 2 72+
(G L Moore) *w'like: athletic: s.s: rn green in rr: taken to outer and prog wl over 1f out: kpt on steadily fnl f* **25/1**
7 *½* **Little Wing (IRE)** 2-9-3 0....................JamieSpencer 4 70
(J A Osborne) *athletic: settled midfield tl prog to trck ldng pair 1/2-way: wknd jst over 1f out* **17/2**
0 **8** *1 ¾* **Lisselan Prospect (USA)**[7] 2215 2-9-3 0....................JimCrowley 11 65
(Mrs A J Perrett) *chsd ldng pair to 1/2-way: sn rdn and lost pl* **50/1**
9 *shd* **Prince Desire (IRE)** 2-9-3 0....................MichaelHills 8 65
(B W Hills) *athletic: s.s: rcvrd on wd outside and in tch 1/2-way: wknd over 1f out* **9/1**
0 **10** *½* **Tiger's Rocket (IRE)**[22] 1781 2-9-3 0....................PatDobbs 3 63
(R Hannon) *w'like: chsd ldrs: pushed along and lost pl steadily fr over 2f out* **66/1**
0 **11** *1 ¼* **Bourse (IRE)**[13] 2041 2-9-3 0....................JimmyFortune 5 60
(J H M Gosden) *a in rr: struggling fr 1/2-way* **13/2**[3]
12 *shd* **Mighty Alfred (IRE)** 2-9-3 0....................JHBowman 10 59
(M R Channon) *w'like: neat: bit bkwd: chsd ldrs to 1/2-way: wknd* **14/1**

1m 14.15s (1.30) **Going Correction** -0.075s/f (Good) **12** Ran SP% **124.9**
Speed ratings (Par 95):88,85,85,84,83 83,82,80,80,79 78,77
CSF £17.37 TOTE £2.20: £1.20, £3.00, £1.70; EX 21.00.
Owner Lady Tennant **Bred** C J Foy **Trained** Lambourn, Berks

FOCUS
A fair maiden, dominated for the most part by the market principals, who both had previous racecourse experience. There is better to come from the first two but the form is hard to rate any higher than they have been.

NOTEBOOK
King's Icon(IRE) had shaped with plenty of promise over this course and distance on his debut, and he was able to build on that experience to get off the mark at the second time of asking. He did enjoy the run of the race, but impressed in beating off his chief market rival inside the last and deserves a crack at a bigger prize now. (op 7-4 tchd 15-8 in a place)
Alsadeek(IRE) ◆, who was coltish beforehand and on his toes, is a half-brother to Miswadah, a 7f winner at four, out of a mare who finished runner-up in the Lowther. Held up out the back on his debut, his rider did not find the clearest of runs but, once switched to the inside rail, his mount absolutely flew home. This son of Fasliyev looks sure to benefit a great deal from this experience and will be one to look out for on his next start. (op 7-1 tchd 11-1)
Barbarossa, who ran with promise behind the impressive Bobs Surprise here on his debut, gave the eventual winner a real race but was seen off inside the last and collared for second on the line. This was a fair race and he can win an ordinary maiden. (op 10-3 tchd 9-2 in places)
Bailey(IRE) ◆, whose dam won over 7f at two, will have appreciated the watering of the ground, being by Captain Rio, and there was promise in this debut effort for a yard whose juveniles always come on for a run. Edgy in the prelims, he showed signs of inexperience in the race itself as well and should be more professional next time.
Gasmanfightsback, retained for just 1,800gns at the sales, is a half-brother to Petit Lulu, a triple 6f to 1m winner at three in Italy, and he hails from a stable better known for its jumpers. He ran with promise, though, and is certainly bred to be fairly speedy. (tchd 40-1)
Art Sale, whose dam was a useful sprinter, is bred to go a bit, but his stable do not tend to strike first time out with its juveniles and the market reflected that. He was another who ran green and looked as though the experience would bring him on a bit, and he should know more next time.
Prince Desire(IRE), a half-brother to Macaw, a multiple 1m to 1m2f winner at home and in the US, to Nakos, a dual 1m to 1m2f winner in France, and Rutters Rebel, a dual 1m to 1m3f winner, showed more ability than his finishing position suggests and he will improve for a step up in distance in time. (op 7-1 tchd 10-1)
Bourse(IRE), who ran in a decent maiden at Newmarket on his debut, was the subject of a gamble from 20-1, but he was always out the back and never threatened to get involved. (op 20-1)

2425 INTERNATIONAL BUREAU OF AVIATION STKS (H'CAP) 1m
3:20 (3:21) (Class 5) (0-75,75) 3-Y-0 **£3,562** (£1,059; £529; £264) **Stalls** High

Form RPR
4-46 **1** **Murrin (IRE)**[44] 1247 3-9-6 **74**....................DaneO'Neill 10 83
(T G Mills) *hld up in last trio: prog and swtchd to wd outside 2f out: str run to ld ins fnl f: edgd rt but sn clr* **9/1**[3]
3-43 **2** *1 ¾* **Common Purpose (USA)**[32] 1523 3-9-4 **72**....................RichardHughes 14 77
(J H M Gosden) *lw: hld up in midfield: prog on inner over 2f out: rdn to chal and upsides ins fnl f: sn outpcd by wnr* **7/2**[2]
5-1 **3** *hd* **Cherie's Dream**[30] 1587 3-8-10 **69**....................WilliamBuick(5) 6 73
(A M Balding) *t.k.h: trckd ldr: led over 2f out: hdd and outpcd ins fnl f* **16/1**
-306 **4** *hd* **Kalasam**[17] 1929 3-9-2 **70**....................RichardMullen 12 74
(W R Muir) *settled towards rr: prog fr over 2f out: drvn and styd on fnl f: unable to chal* **12/1**
3-00 **5** *1 ¼* **Monkey Glas (IRE)**[20] 1851 3-9-4 **72**....................JHBowman 5 73
(K R Burke) *t.k.h: trckd ldrs: rdn to try to chal over 1f out: wknd ins fnl f* **10/1**
10-5 **6** *1 ½* **Swift Cut (IRE)**[131] 275 3-9-4 **72**....................JohnEgan 8 70
(A P Jarvis) *hld up in midfield: rdn to chse ldrs wl over 1f out: wknd fnl f* **20/1**
0-60 **7** *nk* **Anthill**[20] 1838 3-8-7 **61**....................JoeFanning 11 58+
(I A Wood) *swtg: t.k.h: trckd ldng pair: lost pl and nt clr run over 2f out: tried to rally over 1f out: wknd fnl f* **50/1**
0-40 **8** *4* **Rustic Gold**[17] 1927 3-8-6 **60**....................MartinDwyer 9 48
(J R Best) *dwlt: settled towards rr: effrt on inner fr 3f out: no imp on ldrs fnl 2f* **20/1**
50-6 **9** *5* **Art Gallery**[37] 1399 3-8-2 **56** oh2....................DavidKinsella 13 32
(G L Moore) *hld up in midfield: tried to cl on ldrs over 2f out: wknd over 1f out* **33/1**
04-1 **10** *hd* **Leptis Magna**[25] 1726 3-9-7 **75**....................TQuinn 3 51
(D R C Elsworth) *swtg: free to post and edgy bef s: hld up in last: effrt 3f out: sn struggling* **7/2**[2]
100- **11** *5* **Sunley Gift**[263] 5434 3-9-6 **74**....................GeorgeBaker 7 38
(B G Powell) *led at str pce to over 2f out: wknd rapidly* **40/1**
0-54 **12** *5* **Alloro**[11] 2079 3-8-2 **56** oh1....................FrankieMcDonald 2 9
(D J S Ffrench Davis) *a towards rr: u.p on outer and struggling 3f out* **33/1**
-552 **13** *6* **Super Cross (IRE)**[25] 1708 3-9-5 **73**....................JamieSpencer 4 12
(E A L Dunlop) *lw: t.k.h: hld up in midfield: taken to outer 3f out: hanging and nt moving wl 2f out: sn eased* **11/4**[1]
0-00 **14** *2 ½* **Itsawindup**[28] 1634 3-8-2 **56** oh1....................(v[1]) MatthewHenry 1 —
(W J Knight) *swtg: t.k.h: prom over 4f: wknd rapidly: t.o* **66/1**

1m 38.78s (-1.49) **Going Correction** -0.075s/f (Good) **14** Ran SP% **125.1**
Speed ratings (Par 99):104,102,102,101,100 99,98,94,89,89 84,79,73,71
CSF £39.58 CT £532.10 TOTE £11.50: £3.10, £1.60, £3.20; EX 42.40.

Owner Craig Faulkner **Bred** E Campion **Trained** Headley, Surrey

FOCUS

There was a decent pace to this handicap and the leaders paid the price for going off too quick. A couple of the fancied runners failed to run their races. The winner is rated up 7lb.

Art Gallery Official explanation: jockey said colt hung left-handed

Leptis Magna Official explanation: jockey said gelding boiled over in preliminaries

Super Cross(IRE) Official explanation: jockey said bit slipped through colt's mouth so he eased it final 2f

2426 THOMAS EGGAR STKS (H'CAP) 1m 1f 192y

3:55 (3:56) (Class 4) (0-85,83) 3-Y-O **£7,124** (£2,119; £1,059; £529) **Stalls** High

Form RPR

0-02 **1** **Rock Anthem (IRE)**[25] [1726] 3-8-10 **72** KerrinMcEvoy 5 79+
(J L Dunlop) *hld up in last trio: stdy prog towards inner fr 3f out: got through to chal 1f out: rdn to ld ins fnl f* **8/1**

1-01 **2** ¾ **Mr Aviator (USA)**[15] [1956] 3-9-6 **82** RichardHughes 3 88
(R Hannon) *trckd clr ldr: clsd gng easily over 2f out: led over 1f out: rdn and hdd ins fnl f: nt qckn* **4/1**[2]

511- **3** nk **Zoom One**[255] [5585] 3-9-4 **80** MartinDwyer 9 85
(M P Tregoning) *swtg: t.k.h: hld up off the pce: stdy prog on inner fr 3f out: rdn to chal 1f out: styd on* **13/2**

-011 **4** 1 **Guiseppe Verdi (USA)**[17] [1916] 3-9-5 **81** JimmyFortune 7 84
(J H M Gosden) *hld up wl off the pce: urged along to cl fr 3f out: drvn 2f out: plugged on same pce* **6/1**[3]

11 **5** 1 **Padlocked (IRE)**[17] [1929] 3-9-7 **83** JohnEgan 4 84
(J Noseda) *swtg: hld up in chsng gp: effrt to chse ldng pair 3f out: sn rdn: cl enough 2f out: fdd fnl f* **11/4**[1]

31-3 **6** 1¾ **Aureate**[6] [2246] 3-9-2 **78** JoeFanning 2 76
(M Johnston) *lw: pushed into ld: sn racing freely and 4 l clr: hdd over 1f out: wknd* **11/4**[1]

0-50 **7** 9 **Monachello (USA)**[21] [1810] 3-8-12 **74** JimCrowley 8 54
(Mrs A J Perrett) *prom in chsng gp tl wknd over 3f out* **66/1**

2-40 **8** 6 **Nordic Affair**[50] [1106] 3-9-5 **81** TQuinn 1 49
(D R C Elsworth) *a in fnl pair: t.o last fr 1/2-way* **40/1**

10- **9** 1¼ **One To Follow**[223] [6216] 3-9-7 **83** AdamKirby 6 48
(C G Cox) *prom in chsng gp: rdn 4f out: sn wknd: t.o* **14/1**

2m 6.73s (-1.02) **Going Correction** -0.075s/f (Good) **9** Ran SP% **122.7**

Speed ratings (Par 101):101,100,100,99,98 97,89,85,84

CSF £42.66 CT £228.88 TOTE £9.10: £2.30, £1.70, £2.70; EX 49.60.

Owner Mrs M E Slade **Bred** Mervyn Stewkesbury **Trained** Arundel, W Sussex

FOCUS

Probably a fairly useful handicap and it would be a surprise if it did not throw up a winner or two. The form has been rated positively with the first four all improving.

Nordic Affair Official explanation: jockey said gelding never travelled

One To Follow Official explanation: jockey said gelding hung right-handed

2427 GOODWOOD AERO CLUB STKS (H'CAP) 7f

4:30 (4:32) (Class 4) (0-85,85) 4-Y-O+ **£6,800** (£2,023; £1,011; £505) **Stalls** Low

Form RPR

2255 **1** **Barney McGrew (IRE)**[18] [1905] 4-8-8 **72** OscarUrbina 10 84+
(J A R Toller) *t.k.h: trckd ldr for 1f: 3rd after: effrt 2f out: rdn to ld 1f out: pushed along and r.o wl* **8/1**

00-6 **2** ¾ **Binanti**[37] [1395] 7-9-7 **85** GeorgeBaker 5 94
(P R Chamings) *hld up in 7th: smooth prog on outer over 2f out: produced to chal 1f out: fnd nil* **8/1**

1-05 **3** 2 **Rubenstar (IRE)**[20] [1845] 4-9-0 **78** TedDurcan 8 82
(M H Tompkins) *settled in 6th: rdn 2f out: nt qckn whn n.m.r over 1f out: styd on ins fnl f* **13/2**[3]

00-1 **4** nk **Grizedale (IRE)**[20] [1845] 8-8-13 **77** (t) PaulDoe 2 80
(J Akehurst) *trckd ldr after 1f: led wl over 1f out: hdd 1f out: wknd tamely* **10/1**

3600 **5** 3 **Small Stakes (IRE)**[17] [1931] 5-7-11 **66** (vt) WilliamBuick(5) 3 61
(P J Makin) *swtg: t.k.h: hld up in 8th: rdn wl over 2f out: no prog tl styd on ins fnl f* **16/1**

00-0 **6** hd **Material Witness (IRE)**[14] [1984] 10-8-11 **75** MartinDwyer 9 70
(W R Muir) *led to wl over 1f out: wknd fnl f* **16/1**

05-0 **7** ¾ **Loyal Royal (IRE)**[27] [1653] 4-9-7 **85** JohnEgan 6 78
(A M Balding) *t.k.h: trckd ldng trio: rdn and hanging rt fr 2f out: wknd fnl f* **14/1**

-605 **8** ¾ **China Cherub**[32] [1525] 4-8-8 **72** ow1 RichardHughes 11 63
(R Hannon) *settled in 5th: rdn over 2f out: wknd over 1f out* **17/2**

6-65 **9** ½ **Daniel Thomas (IRE)**[14] [1984] 5-9-2 **80** (e) JimCrowley 1 69
(Mrs A J Perrett) *swtg: hld up in 10th: rdn and effrt over 2f out: wknd wl over 1f out* **9/1**

6312 **10** 8 **Spring Goddess (IRE)**[65] [930] 6-8-12 **76** JamieSpencer 7 44
(A P Jarvis) *hld up in 9th: effrt on inner over 2f out: no prog* **7/2**[1]

2-03 **11** 4 **Bee Stinger**[15] [1962] 5-9-4 **82** (v) JoeFanning 4 39
(I A Wood) *b.hind: t.k.h: hld up in last: struggling fnl 3f* **5/1**[2]

1m 26.65s (-1.39) **Going Correction** -0.075s/f (Good) **11** Ran SP% **122.5**

Speed ratings (Par 105):104,103,100,100,97 96,96,95,94,85 80

CSF £73.64 CT £459.41 TOTE £8.10: £2.80, £3.10, £2.80; EX 99.30.

Owner M A Whelton **Bred** Mrs H B Raw **Trained** Newmarket, Suffolk

FOCUS

There was not a great pace on here and it turned into something of a sprint. Ordinary form, rated through the runner-up.

Spring Goddess(IRE) Official explanation: trainer had no explanation for the poor form shown

2428 GOODWOOD FLYING SCHOOL MAIDEN FILLIES' STKS (DIV I) 1m

5:05 (5:10) (Class 5) 3-Y-O **£2,914** (£867; £433; £216) **Stalls** High

Form RPR

3-2 **1** **Ballroom Dancer (IRE)**[37] [1398] 3-9-0 0 JohnEgan 4 74
(J Noseda) *cl up: trckd ldng pair 3f out: hrd rdn to ld narrowly last 150yds: jst hld on* **11/4**[2]

02 **2** hd **Medicea Sidera**[28] [1620] 3-9-0 0 MartinDwyer 10 74
(E F Vaughan) *neat: swtg: led: drvn 2f out: narrowly hdd ins fnl f: kpt on wl: jst hld* **7/1**

3 1¼ **Rolexa** 3-9-0 0 JHBowman 8 71+
(C G Cox) *athletic: bit bkwd: hld up towards rr: shkn up and effrt over 2f out: styd on and got through ins fnl f: nrst fin* **20/1**

52 **4** ½ **Angel Kate (IRE)**[37] [1409] 3-9-0 0 TedDurcan 9 70
(H R A Cecil) *trckd ldng pair to 3f out: sn rdn: styd on again fnl f: nt pce to chal* **4/1**[3]

43 **5** ¾ **Jacaranda Ridge**[28] [1639] 3-9-0 0 JamieSpencer 7 68
(M A Jarvis) *trckd ldr: rdn to chal 2f out: nt qckn over 1f out: wknd ins fnl f* **15/8**[1]

26 **6** ¾ **Pendulum Star**[18] [1901] 3-9-0 0 AdamKirby 6 67
(W R Swinburn) *neat: hld up towards rr: effrt over 2f out: rdn and kpt on fr over 1f out* **6/1**

7 1 **Blue Space** 3-9-0 0 AmirQuinn 11 64+
(P J Makin) *leggy: green to post: s.s: racd awkwardly in last trio: plugged on fr over 1f out: nvr nrr* **50/1**

06- **8** 12 **Barbs Pink Diamond (USA)**[246] [5773] 3-9-0 0 JimCrowley 1 37
(Mrs A J Perrett) *a in rr: struggling u.p over 3f out: t.o* **33/1**

9 1 **Pragmatist** 3-9-0 0 StephenCarson 3 34
(P Winkworth) *w'like: leggy: in tch tl wknd 3f out: t.o* **66/1**

1m 39.86s (-0.41) **Going Correction** -0.075s/f (Good) **9** Ran SP% **119.4**

Speed ratings (Par 96):99,98,97,97,96 95,94,82,81

CSF £22.31 TOTE £3.60: £1.40, £2.30, £3.50; EX 21.30.

Owner Mrs P G M Jamison **Bred** David Jamison Bloodstock **Trained** Newmarket, Suffolk

FOCUS

A fair maiden and the quicker of the two divisions by 0.92sec. The winner did not need to step up on her All-Weather form.

Jacaranda Ridge Official explanation: jockey said filly ran flat

2429 GOODWOOD FLYING SCHOOL MAIDEN FILLIES' STKS (DIV II) 1m

5:40 (5:40) (Class 5) 3-Y-O **£2,914** (£867; £433; £216) **Stalls** High

Form RPR

42- **1** **Contentious (USA)**[241] [5891] 3-9-0 0 IanMongan 6 81+
(J L Dunlop) *lw: t.k.h early: trckd ldrs: prog on outer 2f out: led jst over 1f out: rdn clr* **9/4**[1]

0-20 **2** 1¾ **Apple Blossom (IRE)**[28] [1620] 3-9-0 **83** JoeFanning 9 77
(G Wragg) *trckd ldrs: rdn to ld 2f out: hdd jst over 1f out: hld after: wkng nr fin* **9/2**[3]

3 nk **Areyaam (USA)** 3-9-0 0 StephenCarson 3 77+
(L M Cumani) *w'like: scope: bit bkwd: plld hrd & rn green: hld up last: wl off the pce 3f out: gd prog over 1f out: r.o wl last 150yds: improve* **25/1**

6- **4** 1¾ **Saaratt**[209] [6433] 3-9-0 0 PatDobbs 10 73
(M P Tregoning) *cl up: wnt 2nd briefly 3f out: rdn and one pce fnl 2f* **10/1**

4 **5** ¾ **Al Badeya (IRE)**[13] [2046] 3-9-0 0 KerrinMcEvoy 4 71
(Sir Michael Stoute) *lw: led to 2f out: shkn up over 1f out: grad fdd* **7/1**

3 **6** 3 **Blackberry Pie (USA)**[37] [1408] 3-9-0 0 RichardHughes 11 64
(R Charlton) *hld up in midfield: shkn up and no rspnse over 2f out: btn after* **3/1**[2]

7 1½ **Madam Vouvray** 3-9-0 0 JimmyFortune 7 61
(B J Meehan) *leggy: hld up in last pair: outpcd fr 3f out: plugged on* **40/1**

8 3 **Pulsate** 3-9-0 0 JimCrowley 5 54
(Mrs A J Perrett) *w'like: leggy: a towards rr: rdn and struggling wl over 2f out* **28/1**

9 2½ **Instantly (IRE)** 3-9-0 0 JHBowman 2 48
(W Jarvis) *w'like: s.s: a in rr: rdn and no prog over 2f out* **14/1**

005- **10** hd **Wickedish**[269] [5271] 3-9-0 **50** (t) RichardMullen 1 48
(C F Wall) *w'like: bit bkwd: trckd ldr to 3f out: wknd* **66/1**

5- **11** ½ **Rangali Belle**[266] [5340] 3-9-0 0 FergusSweeney 8 46
(C A Horgan) *bit bkwd: t.k.h: hld up towards rr: wknd over 2f out* **20/1**

1m 40.78s (0.51) **Going Correction** -0.075s/f (Good) **47** Ran SP% **118.2**

Speed ratings (Par 96):94,92,91,90,89 86,84,81,79,79 78

CSF £11.84 TOTE £3.00: £1.60, £1.80, £6.50; EX 14.90.

Owner Phipps Stable **Bred** O M Phipps **Trained** Arundel, W Sussex

FOCUS

A fair race featuring one or two interesting types, but it was the slower of the two divisions by 0.92sec. Not an easy race to rate with not much solid form to go on.

Rangali Belle Official explanation: jockey said filly ran too free

2430 GOODWOOD AIRCRAFT ENGINEERING STKS (H'CAP) 2m

6:10 (6:10) (Class 5) (0-70,67) 4-Y-O+ **£4,210** (£1,252; £625; £312) **Stalls** Low

Form RPR

600/ **1** **Commemoration Day (IRE)**[6] 6-9-3 **62** (t) TQuinn 8 70
(M F Harris) *hld up in midfield: effrt whn nt clr run 3f out: sn rdn: prog over 2f out: styd on to ld last 50yds* **9/2**[2]

5001 **2** ½ **Ganymede**[8] [2176] 6-8-9 **54** 6ex IanMongan 14 61
(Mrs L J Mongan) *in tch: prog to ld 3f out and sn drvn clr: tired and hdd last 50yds* **8/1**

63-0 **3** 1¼ **Cockatoo (USA)**[35] [618] 4-9-0 **60** (b) FergusSweeney 3 66
(G L Moore) *trckd clr ldrs: wnt 2nd 3f out: tried to cl 2f out: kpt on but lost 2nd fnl f* **8/1**

323/ **4** 3½ **Croix De Guerre (IRE)**[13] [5654] 7-8-8 **53** (b) DaneO'Neill 9 54
(P J Hobbs) *hld up in midfield: rdn and prog fr 3f out: tried to cl over 1f out: nt qckn* **3/1**[1]

32-0 **5** 2½ **Coda Agency**[18] [1888] 4-8-9 **55** KerrinMcEvoy 6 53
(D W P Arbuthnot) *chsd clr ldrs: effrt to go 3rd over 2f out: fdd over 1f out* **14/1**

-064 **6** 6 **Bobsleigh**[17] [1925] 8-8-3 **48** oh1 (b) DavidKinsella 10 39
(H S Howe) *led after 1f and sn clr: hdd 3f out: sn wknd* **16/1**

4/0- **7** nk **Screenplay**[423] [420] 6-9-8 **67** GeorgeBaker 1 58
(G L Moore) *settled wl in rr: rdn 4f out: no prog: plugged on u.p* **16/1**

3330 **8** ½ **Follow On**[22] [1793] 5-9-5 **64** JohnEgan 11 54
(A P Jarvis) *hld up in last trio: rdn and struggling over 3f out: no ch after: plugged on* **11/2**[3]

04-6 **9** 1¼ **Phoenix Hill (IRE)**[75] [775] 5-8-10 **55** TedDurcan 2 44
(D R Gandolfo) *settled in rr: u.p and struggling 4f out: no ch after* **10/1**

0-54 **10** 3½ **Gatecrasher**[37] [1396] 4-9-1 **61** PaulEddery 7 45
(Pat Eddery) *trckd ldrs: lost pl bef 1/2-way: struggling in rr 4f out* **16/1**

/0-0 **11** 7 **Don'Tcallmeginger (IRE)**[43] [1263] 4-8-11 **60** SaleemGolam(3) 5 36
(M H Tompkins) *chsd clr ldrs: rdn 6f out: wknd 3f out* **50/1**

-462 **12** 9 **Theatre Royal**[18] [1884] 4-9-1 **61** JHBowman 13 26
(Mouse Hamilton-Fairley) *fast away: led 1f: stdd bhd ldr: wknd 3f out* **12/1**

-000 **13** nk **Peas 'n Beans (IRE)**[9] [2156] 4-8-0 **51** oh3 ow3 ColinHaddon(5) 4 16
(T Keddy) *hld up in last: nvr a factor* **50/1**

3m 28.33s (-2.46) **Going Correction** -0.075s/f (Good)

WFA 4 from 5yo+ 1lb **13** Ran SP% **125.8**

Speed ratings (Par 103):103,102,102,100,99 96,95,95,95,93 89,85,85

CSF £42.99 CT £289.84 TOTE £6.50: £2.50, £3.20, £3.70; EX 41.60 Place 6 £143.42, Place 5 £80.49.

Owner Alan Bosley **Bred** Reg Griffin & Jim McGrath **Trained** Edgcote, Northants

FOCUS

A modest staying handicap in which the leader, Bobsleigh, went off at unrealistic pace. The winner was on a fair mark based on his progressive hurdles form.

Phoenix Hill(IRE) Official explanation: jockey said gelding lost its action

T/Jkpt: Not won. T/Plt: £171.20 to a £1 stake. Pool: £91,348.40. 389.30 winning tickets. T/Qpdt: £64.00 to a £1 stake. Pool: £3,590.70. 41.50 winning tickets. JN

[2392] HAYDOCK (L-H)

Friday, June 8

OFFICIAL GOING: Good to firm (8.0)

Wind: Almost nil Weather: warm and sunny

2431 LAMBRINI H'CAP STKS (FOR LADY AMATEUR RIDERS) 1m 2f 120y

6:50 (6:51) (Class 6) (0-65,65) 4-Y-O+ **£2,867** (£882; £441) **Stalls** High

Form RPR

/05- **1** **Coronado's Gold (USA)**[469] [498] 6-9-12 **53**.................. MissLEllison 4 60
(B Ellison) *a promienent: led 4f out: rdn over 2f out: rdr dropped hands briefly cl home: kpt on* **11/1**

-242 **2** ½ **Eijaaz (IRE)**[7] [2201] 6-9-13 **54**.. MrsCBartley 12 60
(G A Harker) *midfield: hdwy over 2f out: chsd wnr over 1f out: rdr dropped whip ins fnl f: r.o: gaining cl home* **4/1**[1]

1000 **3** 1 ¼ **Alsadaa (USA)**[6] [2256] 4-10-5 **65**................................ MissJCoward(5) 9 69
(M W Easterby) *midfield: hdwy over 2f out: r.o ins fnl f: nt rch ldrs* **18/1**

0-00 **4** 3 ½ **Thorny Mandate**[14] [2006] 5-10-2 **57**.............................. MissEJJones 11 54
(W M Brisbourne) *midfield: hdwy over 3f out: sn hung lft: one pce ins fnl f* **14/1**

600- **5** *shd* **Colinette**[233] [6052] 4-10-1 **61**.................................... MissJAKidd(5) 7 58
(R T Phillips) *hld up: hdwy over 3f out: hung lft u.p over 2f out: kpt on ins fnl f: nt rch ldrs* **14/1**

/25- **6** 4 **Front Rank (IRE)**[43] [4451] 7-9-13 **61** ow1..................... MissNSayer(7) 17 51
(Mrs Dianne Sayer) *sn in rr: rdn over 2f out: styd on fr over 1f out: nvr trbld ldrs* **16/1**

-030 **7** ¾ **Terenzium (IRE)**[4] [2302] 5-9-4 **52**.................................... MrsGHogg(7) 8 40
(Micky Hammond) *bhd: styd on fr over 1f out: nvr on terms* **14/1**

0102 **8** ½ **Hugs Destiny (IRE)**[6] [2250] 6-9-8 **54**..................(t) MissAngelaBarnes(5) 13 41
(M A Barnes) *in tch: rdn over 2f out: wknd fnl f* **4/1**[1]

0-05 **9** 1 **Royal Citadel (IRE)**[15] [1967] 4-9-6 **52**......................... MrsLHannity(5) 1 37
(Mrs L B Normile) *prom: led over 5f out: hdd 4f out: rdn over 2f out: hung lft and wknd over 1f out* **14/1**

0-00 **10** 1 ¾ **Jaassey**[14] [2007] 4-9-2 **50**.. MrsJEPugh(7) 15 32
(A Crook) *midfield: rdn over 2f out: no hdwy* **50/1**

-305 **11** 1 **Champagne Shadow (IRE)**[13] [2027] 6-10-4 **64**.......(p) MissARyan(5) 10 44
(K A Ryan) *towards rr: sn pushed along: sme hdwy over 2f out: nvr on terms w ldrs* **8/1**[2]

060- **12** 12 **Emperor's Well**[214] [6380] 8-9-5 **53**.................(b) MissJoannaMason(7) 5 10
(M W Easterby) *trckd ldrs tl wknd over 3f out* **25/1**

-001 **13** 1 **Monashee River (IRE)**[7] [2214] 4-9-10 **51** 6ex........ MissFayeBramley 14 6
(Miss V Haigh) *prom tl rdn and wknd over 2f out* **10/1**[3]

-256 **14** *hd* **Thunderwing (IRE)**[18] [1893] 5-10-5 **65**......................(p) MissKellyBurke(5) 3 20
(K R Burke) *led: hdd over 5f out: wknd over 2f out* **14/1**

6000 **15** 2 ½ **Bathwick Emma (IRE)**[6] [2258] 4-9-6 **52**.....................(p) MissABevan(5) 2 2
(M A Doyle) *towards rr: nvr on terms* **28/1**

00/6 **16** 7 **Perfect Picture**[31] [1554] 8-9-2 **50**..............................(p) MissWGibson(7) 6 —
(P T Midgley) *prom tl rdn and wknd over 3f out* **66/1**

034- **17** 10 **Penmara**[13] [4263] 4-9-4 **50**.. MissJFoster(5) 16 —
(Miss J E Foster) *cl up tl wknd over 4f out* **33/1**

2m 18.96s (2.82) **Going Correction** +0.175s/f (Good) **17** Ran SP% **126.7**

Speed ratings (Par 101):102,101,100,98,98 95,94,94,93,92 91,82,82,81,80 75,67

CSF £53.99 CT £823.69 TOTE £16.00: £3.80, £1.80, £4.40, £2.40; EX 98.60.

Owner S Hawe Brian Ellison **Bred** H J Hendrick Et Al **Trained** Norton, N Yorks

■ Stewards' Enquiry : Miss E J Jones four-day ban: used whip with excessive frequency (Jun 25,28,29 Jul 2)

Miss J A Kidd four-day ban: used whip with excessive frequency and without giving filly time to respond (Jun 25,28-29, Jul 2)

FOCUS

A weak lady riders' handicap, in which the result looks more down to the jockeys than the horses. It has been rated through the third.

2432 EBF KIRSTY DOYLE & THE MAGAZINE MAIDEN STKS 6f

7:20 (7:24) (Class 5) 2-Y-O **£3,238** (£963; £481; £240) **Stalls** Centre

Form RPR

1 **Bere Davis (FR)** 2-9-3 0.. DeanMcKeown 9 77
(P D Evans) *chsd ldrs: led narrowly 2f out: sn hung lft: r.o whn continually pressed ins fnl f: a holding on* **25/1**

3 **2** *hd* **Romantic Destiny**[10] [2109] 2-8-12 0.. NCallan 8 71
(K A Ryan) *prom: led after 2f: hdd narrowly 2f out: continued to press wnr: hld towards fin* **13/2**[3]

3 1 ½ **Muhajaar (IRE)** 2-9-3 0.. NickyMackay 5 71+
(L M Cumani) *squeezed out s: sn trckd ldrs racing keenly: rdn over 1f out: styd on towards fin: nt pce of front pair* **5/2**[2]

4 ½ **Siberian Tiger (IRE)** 2-9-3 0.. DavidAllan 12 70
(M R Channon) *in tch: clsd 1/2-way: ev ch 2f out: hung lft over 1f out: nt qckn over 1f out: styd on towards fin* **14/1**

4 **5** *nk* **Rockfield Tiger (IRE)**[20] [1846] 2-9-3 0.......................... PhilipRobinson 10 69
(J A Osborne) *in tch: clsd 1/2-way: ev ch 2f out: rdn over 1f out: no ex ins fnl f* **5/4**[1]

6 2 **Cairnbrae** 2-9-3 0.. PaulMulrennan 7 63
(Miss J A Camacho) *midfield: pushed along over 2f out: nt pce to chal* **66/1**

7 ½ **Feeling Fresh (IRE)** 2-9-3 0.. AdrianTNicholls 6 62
(Paul Green) *hld up: rdn over 2f out: nt pce to chal* **66/1**

8 3 **Laterly (IRE)** 2-9-3 0.. MickyFenton 1 53
(T P Tate) *s.s: a bhd* **40/1**

9 *hd* **Saturday Boy** 2-9-0 0.. PatrickMathers(3) 11 52
(Paul Green) *s.i.s: bhd: rdn over 2f out: nvr on terms* **66/1**

10 1 **Cross Fell (USA)** 2-9-3 0.. KDarley 4 49
(M Johnston) *led: hdd after 2f: remained cl up tl rdn and wknd over 1f out* **8/1**

0 **11** *hd* **Noplace For A Lady**[19] [1858] 2-8-12 0.................................. KimTinkler 3 43
(N Tinkler) *in tch: wknd 2f out* **100/1**

1m 16.76s (2.87) **Going Correction** -0.075s/f (Good) **11** Ran SP% **115.9**

Speed ratings (Par 93):84,83,81,81,80 78,77,73,73,71 71

CSF £163.06 TOTE £38.30: £5.60, £1.90, £1.30; EX 264.40.

Owner H J Sweeney **Bred** C Quellier & Mme Svetlana Timon **Trained** Pandy, Monmouths

■ Balata was withdrawn (14/1, refused to enter stalls.) R4 applies, deduct 5p in the £.

■ Stewards' Enquiry : Dean McKeown three-day ban: used whip with excessive frequency (Jun 24-26)

FOCUS

A fair maiden that ought to produce some winners. The runner-up found improvement from her debut effort, with the favourite just off his Newmarket form.

NOTEBOOK

Bere Davis(FR), a 90,000euros half-brother to among others 1m-1m2f winner Vettorio, out of a multiple 6f-1m winner, was very easy to back, but he defied that market weakness with a useful effort on his racecourse debut. He went for home plenty soon enough, but kept responding to pressure and was always going to hold on. He may now be aimed at the Coventry Stakes, but that would require a significant step up. (tchd 22-1)

Romantic Destiny improved significantly on the form she showed when third over 5f on her debut at Leicester and was just held. She looks up to finding a maiden, especially if switched to fillies-only company. (tchd 6-1)

Muhajaar(IRE) ◆, out of a very smart 6f-7f winner at two, made a respectable debut back in third. He just lacked the pace to go with the front two late on, but should sharpen up plenty and ought to go close in similar company next time. (tchd 3-1)

Siberian Tiger(IRE), a 60,000euros half-brother to dual 5f-6f juvenile winner Fabuleux Millie, out of a triple 6f winner at two to three, shaped nicely on his debut. He is another who can be expected to improve for the experience and can find a maiden in the coming weeks. (op 12-1 tchd 11-1)

Rockfield Tiger(IRE) failed to build on the form he showed when fourth in a good race on his debut at Newmarket and was a little disappointing. (op 6-4 tchd 7-4 and 6-5)

2433 OCS GROUP MAIDEN STKS 1m 30y

7:50 (7:52) (Class 5) 3-Y-O+ **£2,817** (£838; £418; £209) **Stalls** Low

Form RPR

1 **Samira Gold (FR)** 3-8-9 0.. NickyMackay 9 71+
(L M Cumani) *in rr: nudged along early: hdwy 3f out: led 1f out: r.o wl and won gng away* **11/2**[3]

0 **2** 4 **Wells Of Badr (IRE)**[50] [1105] 3-8-9 0.......................... AdrianMcCarthy 1 62
(P W Chapple-Hyam) *a.p: led 4f out: rdn over 2f out: hdd 1f out: one pce ins fnl f* **16/1**

66 **3** 1 ¼ **Haasem (USA)**[14] [1995] 4-9-11 0.. MartinDwyer 4 67
(E A L Dunlop) *prom: rdn and ev ch 2f out: kpt on same pce ins fnl f* **5/2**[2]

4 ½ **Honest Prospector (USA)** 3-9-0 0.................................. JamieSpencer 5 63+
(Sir Michael Stoute) *s.i.s: hld up: hdwy over 2f out: rn green: one pce fnl f* **10/11**[1]

5 1 ½ **King Of Connacht** 4-9-11 0.. RichardThomas 7 62
(B P J Baugh) *bhd: sn struggling: rdn 3f out: plld out and sme hdwy over 2f out: one pce over 1f out* **40/1**

0 **6** 9 **Screaming Reel**[14] [1995] 4-9-11 0.. MickyFenton 3 42
(M Wellings) *s.s: sn in midfield: rdn and wknd over 2f out* **33/1**

7 *shd* **Shahadah (IRE)**[726] [2527] 5-9-6 0.. NCallan 2 36
(R J Price) *racd keenly: trckd ldrs: rdn and wknd over 2f out* **14/1**

00-0 **8** 6 **Gary's Indian (IRE)**[14] [1995] 4-9-6 0.............................. PaulMulrennan 6 23
(B P J Baugh) *led: hdd 4f out: rdn and wknd over 2f out* **33/1**

1m 46.4s (0.89) **Going Correction** +0.175s/f (Good)

WFA 3 from 4yo+ 11lb **8** Ran SP% **117.2**

Speed ratings (Par 103):102,98,96,96,94 85,85,79

CSF £83.20 TOTE £7.10: £1.70, £3.10, £1.10; EX 68.90.

Owner Jaber Abdullah **Bred** L L C Woodside Farms **Trained** Newmarket, Suffolk

■ Stewards' Enquiry : Adrian McCarthy three-day ban: used whip with excessive frequency without giving filly time to respond (Jun 24-26)

Jamie Spencer caution: used whip above shoulder height

FOCUS

An ordinary maiden, run at just a steady pace, but a clear-cut winner in the form of Samira Gold. The race has been rated through the third.

2434 TONY AND KIERAN MEMORIAL H'CAP 1m 6f

8:20 (8:21) (Class 5) (0-70,68) 4-Y-O+ **£2,817** (£838; £418; £209) **Stalls** Low

Form RPR

101/ **1** **Mickmacmagoole (IRE)**[13] [2048] 5-9-2 **63**.................... JamieSpencer 2 73+
(Seamus G O'Donnell, Ire) *in tch: hdwy 3f out: led and hung lft 2f out: styd on wl to draw clr fnl f* **15/8**[1]

10 **2** 3 **Pentasilea**[21] [1811] 4-9-3 **64**.. PhilipRobinson 3 70
(H J L Dunlop) *a.p: rdn over 2f out: wnt 2nd over 1f out: kpt on ins fnl f: nt trble wnr* **13/2**[3]

5-14 **3** 1 ½ **Trafalgar Day**[27] [1683] 4-8-13 **60**...................................... MartinDwyer 10 64
(W M Brisbourne) *hld up: hdwy 7f out: led 3f out: sn rdn: hdd 2f out: no ex ins fnl f* **5/1**[2]

02 **4** 3 **Great Quest (IRE)**[55] [1042] 5-9-7 **68**.. KDarley 8 68
(James Moffatt) *trckd ldrs: lost pl over 6f out: rallied over 2f out: edgd lft over 1f out: one pce* **9/1**

2463 **5** 1 **Let It Be**[11] [2095] 6-8-12 **59**.. PaulHanagan 5 57
(K G Reveley) *led: hdd 3f out: one pce fnl 2f* **13/2**[3]

0124 **6** 2 ½ **Ronsard (IRE)**[7] [2204] 5-8-6 **56**.................................. PatrickMathers(3) 6 51
(P D Evans) *racd keenly: midfield: hdwy 6f out: rdn 3f out: wknd over 1f out* **10/1**

3514 **7** 2 **Treason Trial**[37] [1406] 6-8-7 **54**.. MickyFenton 7 46
(Stef Liddiard) *hld up: bmpd on bnd after 2f: rdn over 2f out: no imp* **7/1**

0/02 **8** 2 ½ **Dance Sauvage**[15] [1966] 4-8-5 **52**.. DavidAllan 4 41
(C W Thornton) *hld up: rdn over 2f out: nvr on terms* **12/1**

300 **9** 2 **Mustakhlas (USA)**[20] [792] 6-7-13 **51** oh4 ow2.................. TolleyDean(5) 9 37
(B P J Baugh) *prom: rdn 5f out: sn wknd* **66/1**

-006 **10** 1 ¾ **Nesno (USA)**[13] [2038] 4-9-7 **68**.. DarryllHolland 1 51
(J D Bethell) *a bhd* **33/1**

3m 6.91s (0.62) **Going Correction** +0.175s/f (Good) **10** Ran SP% **121.8**

Speed ratings (Par 103):105,103,102,100,100 98,97,96,95,94

CSF £15.27 CT £55.92 TOTE £3.00: £1.50, £2.60, £2.20; EX 16.30.

Owner Mrs Edel O'Donnell **Bred** Tower Bloodstock **Trained** Ballinalard, Co Tipperary

FOCUS

A modest staying handicap and there was not a great deal of early pace. The form may not prove reliable, but Mickmacmagoole did it well. The race has been rated through the placed horses.

2435 ELECTROLUX H'CAP 5f

8:50 (8:51) (Class 4) (0-80,80) 3-Y-O **£6,477** (£1,927; £963; £481) **Stalls** Centre

Form RPR

0-11 **1** **Ishetoo**[7] [2205] 3-8-4 **63**.. PaulHanagan 9 74+
(A Dickman) *hld up: hdwy over 2f out: led ins fnl f: r.o* **4/5**[1]

3110 **2** 1 ½ **Windjammer**[21] [1820] 3-8-11 **70**.. DavidAllan 2 75
(T D Easterby) *led: rdn over 1f out: hdd ins fnl f: nt qckn* **13/2**[3]

4140 **3** ¾ **Princess Ellis**[4] [2301] 3-8-2 **61** oh4.............................. RichardThomas 6 63
(E J Alston) *outpcd and bhd: hdwy and edgd lft over 1f out: chsd ldng pair ins fnl f: gaining at fin* **14/1**

0133 **4** 3 ½ **Mandurah (IRE)**[14] [1994] 3-8-8 **67**.............................. AdrianTNicholls 8 56
(D Nicholls) *chsd ldrs: rdn over 2f out: fdd ins fnl f* **9/2**[2]

6-61 **5** 4 **Yerevan**[10] [2114] 3-9-7 **80** 6ex.. FrancisNorton 7 54
(R T Phillips) *hld up: rdn and edgd lft over 1f out: no imp* **8/1**

65-0 **6** *shd* **Give Her A Whirl**[17] [1923] 3-8-5 **64**.............................. DeanMcKeown 5 37
(G A Swinbank) *priminent tl shkn up and wknd over 1f out* **14/1**

30-0 **7** *1 3/4* **Russian Silk**[30] [1577] 3-8-11 **70**........................ PaulMulrennan 4 36
(Jedd O'Keeffe) *in tch: rdn and wknd over 1f out* **25/1**

0054 **8** *3 1/2* **Stoneacre Gareth (IRE)**[8] [2172] 3-8-3 **65**..............(b) PatrickMathers(3) 3 18
(Peter Grayson) *chsd ldrs: rdn over 2f out: wknd over 1f out* **25/1**

61.00 secs (0.88) **Going Correction** -0.075s/f (Good) **8** Ran SP% **119.2**
Speed ratings (Par 101):105,102,101,95,89 89,86,80
CSF £7.15 CT £42.64 TOTE £1.80: £1.10, £1.40, £4.00; EX 8.40.
Owner John H Sissons **Bred** Longdon Stud Ltd **Trained** Sandhutton, N Yorks

FOCUS
A fair three-year-old sprint handicap. Solid form, but the winner was 12lb well in and didn't need to improve. The runner-up is mostly progressive but the third limits the form a little from out of the handicap.
Mandurah(IRE) Official explanation: jockey said gelding hung right-handed
Yerevan Official explanation: trainer's rep said filly was unsuited by the good to firm ground

2436 BLYTHEWOOD MAIDEN STKS 1m 3f 200y
9:20 (9:20) (Class 5) 3-Y-0+ **£2,817** (£838; £418; £209) **Stalls** High

Form RPR

03 **1** **Galianna (IRE)**[21] [1812] 3-8-6 0........................ JamieSpencer 3 79+
(Pat Eddery) *in tch: effrt over 2f out: sn chalng strly: hung lft fnl f: r.o to ld post* **15/8**[1]

34- **2** *shd* **Starry Messenger**[261] [5475] 3-8-6 0........................ MartinDwyer 9 79+
(M P Tregoning) *hld up: hdwy 3f out: rdn to ld 2f out: a hrd pressed: r.o u.p: hdd post* **3/1**[2]

P05 **3** *6* **Feeling (IRE)**[14] [1998] 3-8-11 0........................ AdrianMcCarthy 8 74
(P W Chapple-Hyam) *prom: rdn and ev ch 2f out: hung lft after: one pce and no ch w front pair fnl f* **10/1**

00-2 **4** *shd* **Crystal Prince**[48] [1153] 3-8-11 74........................ MickyFenton 5 74
(T P Tate) *led: rdn and hdd 2f out: one pce after* **8/1**

2 **5** *nk* **Pugnacious Lady**[22] [1784] 3-8-6 0........................ KDarley 7 68
(J W Hills) *hld up: rdn over 2f out: hdwy over 1f out: styd on ins fnl f: nvr able to chal* **5/1**[3]

0-0 **6** *6* **Pelleas**[46] [1204] 3-8-11 0........................ NCallan 1 64
(R Charlton) *midfield: rdn over 2f out: no imp* **14/1**

3 **7** *shd* **Compton Falcon**[38] [1369] 3-8-11 0........................ NickyMackay 4 64+
(G A Butler) *midfield: hdwy over 3f out: rdn whn hung lft and wknd over 1f out* **13/2**

0 **8** *3* **Zen Garden**[14] [1998] 6-9-7 0........................ DavidAllan 2 54?
(W M Brisbourne) *hld up: rdn over 2f out: nvr on terms* **100/1**

0 **9** *39* **Lilymay**[14] [1998] 7-9-7 0........................ DeanMcKeown 6 —
(B P J Baugh) *prom: wknd qckly over 3f out: t.o* **100/1**

2m 36.24s (1.25) **Going Correction** +0.175s/f (Good)
WFA 3 from 6yo+ 15lb **9** Ran SP% **118.6**
Speed ratings (Par 103):102,101,97,97,97 93,93,91,65
CSF £7.79 TOTE £3.10: £1.30, £1.60, £2.60; EX 9.00 Place 6 £37.74, Place 5 £13.62..
Owner Pat Eddery Racing (Polygamy) **Bred** Frank Dunne **Trained** Nether Winchendon, Bucks

FOCUS
An ordinary maiden. Quite a tight race on figues with a lot of these closely matched. It has been rated through the third and fourth.
Compton Falcon Official explanation: jockey said colt hung left-handed
T/Plt: £144.70 to a £1 stake. Pool: £70,910.50. 357.55 winning tickets. T/Qpdt: £26.40 to a £1 stake. Pool: £4,604.00. 128.90 winning tickets. DO

2437 - 2439a (Foreign Racing) - See Raceform Interactive

2423 GOODWOOD (R-H)
Saturday, June 9

OFFICIAL GOING: Straight course - good; round course - good to firm
Wind: Almost nil Weather: Fine, becoming hazy, warm

2440 EMPIRE PROPERTY GROUP H'CAP 6f
2:20 (2:22) (Class 2) (0-100,100) 3-Y-0+
£16,514 (£4,944; £2,472; £1,237; £617; £310) **Stalls** Low

Form RPR

50-0 **1** **Dingaan (IRE)**[21] [1836] 4-8-7 **84**........................ WilliamBuick(5) 6 93
(A M Balding) *s.s: racd on wd outside: last tl prog over 2f out: rdn and r.o wl to ld last strides* **20/1**

00-0 **2** *hd* **Bentong (IRE)**[35] [1474] 4-10-0 **100**..............(t) EddieAhern 5 108
(P F I Cole) *hld up in midfield: rdn and prog over 2f out: r.o to chal last 75yds: jst outpcd* **8/1**

-105 **3** *hd* **Forest Dane**[16] [1971] 7-8-2 **81**........................ MCGeran(7) 15 88
(Mrs N Smith) *chsd ldrs: prog to ld jst over 1f out: collared last strides* **12/1**

6160 **4** *1/2* **Mujood**[13] [2058] 4-9-3 **89**..............(p) StephenCarson 2 95
(Eve Johnson Houghton) *racd against nr side rail: w ldrs: drvn 2f out: kpt on same pce* **14/1**

00-0 **5** *1/2* **Greenslades**[21] [1836] 8-9-9 **95**........................ PatDobbs 8 99
(P J Makin) *w ldrs: rdn over 2f out: nt qckn wl over 1f out: kpt on ins fnl f* **12/1**

111- **6** *nk* **Cape**[254] [5643] 4-9-0 **86**........................ OscarUrbina 7 90+
(J R Fanshawe) *t.k.h: hld up in rr: shkn up 2f out: prog whn nt clr run over 1f out: styd on ins fnl f* **5/1**[2]

-030 **7** *nk* **Diane's Choice**[28] [1653] 4-8-12 **84**........................ SimonWhitworth 9 87
(J Akehurst) *mde most to jst over 1f out: fdd* **16/1**

11- **8** *shd* **Utmost Respect**[267] [5334] 3-8-10 **90**........................ DO'Donohoe 11 90+
(R A Fahey) *hld up in rr: nt clr run 2f out tl ins fnl f: styng on nr fin: no ch* **9/1**

46-5 **9** *1/2* **Pearly Wey**[13] [2058] 4-9-2 **88**........................ DaneO'Neill 14 89
(C G Cox) *taken down early: w ldrs: upsides over 1f out: wknd fnl f* **8/1**

22-4 **10** *1/2* **Viking Spirit**[47] [1195] 5-9-8 **94**........................ JHBowman 1 93+
(W R Swinburn) *hld up in midfield: prog and cl up 2f out: gng wl but trapped bhd rivals after: no ch to rcvr* **4/1**[1]

00-0 **11** *1* **Texas Gold**[15] [1986] 9-9-10 **96**........................ PaulDoe 13 92
(W R Muir) *racd on outer in midfield: rdn and effrt to chse ldrs over 1f out: fdd fnl f* **22/1**

6000 **12** *shd* **Connect**[23] [1788] 10-8-2 **81** oh1..............(b) AshleyMorgan(7) 12 77
(M H Tompkins) *chsd ldrs tl wknd over 1f out* **50/1**

0-00 **13** *1/2* **Captain Hurricane**[21] [1836] 5-9-1 **87**........................ RyanMoore 3 89+
(B J Meehan) *t.k.h: hld up in rr: effrt 2f out: nt clr run fr over 1f out: no ch to rcvr* **14/1**

3053 **14** *1/2* **Green Park (IRE)**[21] [1853] 4-8-11 **88**........................ JamieMoriarty(5) 4 86+
(R A Fahey) *rrd s: hld up in last trio: rdn 2f out: effrt whn hmpd 1f out: no room and no ch after* **15/2**[3]

000- **15** *2 1/2* **Royal Storm (IRE)**[350] [2846] 8-9-9 **95**........................ JimCrowley 10 81
(Mrs A J Perrett) *w ldrs over 3f: sn lost pl and struggling* **25/1**

1m 11.42s (-1.43) **Going Correction** -0.175s/f (Firm)
WFA 3 from 4yo+ 8lb **15** Ran SP% **130.2**
Speed ratings (Par 109):102,101,101,100,100 99,99,99,98,97 96,96,95,95,91
CSF £178.39 CT £2094.55 TOTE £32.80: £8.00, £3.20, £4.50; EX 385.20 TRIFECTA Not won..
Owner Lady C S Cadbury **Bred** Mrs Gill Wilson **Trained** Kingsclere, Hants
■ Stewards' Enquiry : Oscar Urbina three-day ban: careless riding (Jun 24-26)

FOCUS
A very good sprint handicap and, as one would expect, hugely competitive. Although they raced towards the stands' side, most of these shunned the rail, and the winner made his move widest of all, more towards the centre of the track. There were some hard-luck stories, several of them concerning sprinters with valuable targets in the coming weeks. The form is sound among the principals.

NOTEBOOK
Dingaan(IRE)'s three previous wins came on the Polytrack and he did not show a great deal on his reappearance at Newbury, but that run clearly brought him on and he returned to something like his best, taking advantage of a handicap mark 4lb lower than when last successful. His attitude has looked questionable in the past, but he did little wrong this time and may have turned the corner. (tchd 22-1)
Bentong(IRE) ◆ improved on the form he showed on his reappearance at Newmarket and was just held. He seemed to lose his way a touch last season, but he is clearly back to his very best now and looks one to have on side. He is entered in the Wokingham at Royal Ascot and could run a big race if allowed to take his chance. (op 10-1)
Forest Dane, supported in the market, confirmed he is very much still improving with a storming effort. He probably just took up the running a little too soon and was reeled in late on. (op 20-1)
Mujood was the only horse to race right against the near-side rail throughout and he kept on to the line to post a respectable effort. (op 16-1)
Greenslades was only 1lb higher than when last winning and seemed to have every chance.
Cape ◆, most progressive in ordinary company last year, was unlucky not to finish closer on her seasonal reappearance. Asked to come from an unpromising position, she was denied a clear run and failed to land a serious blow. This outing should bring her on and, with better luck, she should go close off this mark next time. She is in the Wokingham. Official explanation: jockey said filly was denied a clear run (op 4-1 tchd 11-2)
Utmost Respect ◆, the winner of both his starts as a juvenile, including a nursery off a mark of 81 when last seen 267 days previously, caught the eye on his seasonal return. He would have been in the shake up with a clear run and looks one to keep on the right side of this summer. The William Hill Trophy could be a suitable target. Official explanation: jockey said gelding became unbalanced and hung left (op 8-1)
Pearly Wey not for the first time appeared to have too much use made of him. He has loads of speed, but seems to have only a short finishing burst and wants riding with more patience. He is another who holds a Wokingham entry. (op 17-2 tchd 9-1)
Viking Spirit ◆ had nowhere to go throughout the closing stages and hardly came off the bridle at any stage. He would have gone mighty close with a clear run and has to be considered very unlucky. He is clearly up to winning off this sort of mark and looks one of the likelier types for the Wokingham if allowed his chance. Official explanation: jockey said gelding was denied a clear run (op 11-2)
Captain Hurricane, with Ryan Moore taking over from a 7lb claimer, would have been closer with a clear run but was not as unlucky as some. Official explanation: jockey said gelding was denied a clear run
Green Park(IRE) is another who would have been closer with a clearer run. (op 8-1 tchd 17-2)

2441 EMPIRE PROPERTY GROUP CONDITIONS STKS 1m 4f
2:50 (2:51) (Class 3) 4-Y-0+ **£9,815** (£2,938; £1,469; £735) **Stalls** Low

Form RPR

5-36 **1** **Munsef**[22] [1823] 5-8-9 110..............(b[1]) RHills 1 111+
(J L Dunlop) *mde all: shkn up and drew clr fr over 2f out: eased nr fin: comf* **5/6**[1]

41-0 **2** *3 1/2* **High Heel Sneakers**[28] [1650] 4-9-0 105........................ RyanMoore 2 106
(P F I Cole) *hld up in last: prog 3f out: sn rdn: def 2nd over 1f out but no ch w wnr* **9/2**[3]

0240 **3** *1 1/2* **Akarem**[8] [2216] 6-8-9 105........................ JHBowman 4 99
(K R Burke) *chsd wnr: rdn wl over 2f out: sn outpcd* **4/1**[2]

63-5 **4** *1 1/2* **Summer's Eve**[23] [1789] 4-8-4 99........................ FrankieMcDonald 3 91
(H Candy) *t.k.h: hld up in 3rd: effrt 3f out: sn rdn: fdd over 1f out* **11/2**

2m 38.92s **Going Correction** -0.05s/f (Good) **4** Ran SP% **108.1**
Speed ratings (Par 107):98,95,94,93
CSF £4.83 TOTE £1.50; EX 3.30.
Owner Hamdan Al Maktoum **Bred** Shadwell Estate Company Limited **Trained** Arundel, W Sussex

FOCUS
Quality rather than quantity for this conditions contest. Comfortable winner Munsef set a muddling gallop and the bare form should not be taken too literally.

NOTEBOOK
Munsef was on a losing run stretching back to his Listed-race success in 2005, but he had been pitched in at Group level in every start since then, and this drop in class was just what was required. Fitted with blinkers for the first time, he was allowed to dictate on his own terms and came home an easy winner. This should have boosted his confidence and he ought to run well when returned to Listed or Group company. (tchd 10-11)
High Heel Sneakers had no easy task conceding weight all round, but she ran a respectable race considering the stop-start gallop would not have been ideal and managed to reverse recent Ascot form with Akarem. (op 11-2)
Akarem was unsuited by the way the race was run and this ground would also have been quick enough. (op 7-2)
Summer's Eve compromised her chance by racing keenly and would have appreciated a stronger pace. (op 5-1 tchd 6-1)

2442 EMPIRE PROPERTY GROUP ON THE HOUSE STKS (LISTED RACE) 1m
3:25 (3:27) (Class 1) 3-Y-0+ **£17,034** (£6,456; £3,231; £1,611; £807) **Stalls** High

Form RPR

0-03 **1** **Dunelight (IRE)**[38] [1392] 4-9-5 105..............(v) DaneO'Neill 2 113+
(C G Cox) *mde all and sn clr: breather 1/2-way: drew rt away again fr 2f out: styd on strly* **7/2**[2]

2-61 **2** *4* **Army Of Angels (IRE)**[26] [1723] 5-9-8 110........................ LDettori 3 105
(Saeed Bin Suroor) *3rd tl chsd wnr 1/2-way: rdn 3f out: hanging rt after: no ch wl over 1f out* **5/4**[1]

0-60 **3** *hd* **Babodana**[23] [1791] 7-9-5 100........................ EddieAhern 7 102+
(M H Tompkins) *chsd wnr to 1/2-way: outpcd whn hmpd 2f out: styd on again fnl f* **16/1**

1-2 **4** *1* **Supersonic Dave (USA)**[14] [2042] 3-8-8 106........................ RHills 1 99
(B J Meehan) *hld up in 4th: rdn 3f out: no prog and sn btn* **4/1**[3]

01-0 **5** *5* **Nayyir**[93] [646] 9-9-8 0..............(t) JHBowman 6 91
(G A Butler) *hld up last: rdn 3f out: no prog: eased ins fnl f* **4/1**[3]

1m 37.56s (-2.71) **Going Correction** -0.05s/f (Good)
WFA 3 from 4yo+ 11lb **5** Ran SP% **112.5**
Speed ratings (Par 111):111,107,106,105,100
CSF £8.58 TOTE £4.70: £2.10, £1.40; EX 10.40.

Owner Mr And Mrs P Hargreaves **Bred** D And B Egan **Trained** Lambourn, Berks
■ Stewards' Enquiry : L Dettori one-day ban: careless riding (Jun 24)

FOCUS
This looked like a good Listed race beforehand, but Dunelight was allowed his own way up front and, with at least a couple of his rivals underperforming, he came home unchallenged in the straight. The winning time was 0.23 seconds faster than the later 81-100 handicap.

NOTEBOOK
Dunelight(IRE) was soon in a good rhythm out on his own up front and, able to get a breather in before the straight, he never looked in any danger. He deserved this first Listed-race success, and there is no doubting this was a smart effort, but it would probably be unwise to get too carried away as at least a couple of his main rivals appeared to run below form. (op 4-1 tchd 9-2 and 5-1 in a place)
Army Of Angels(IRE), a Listed winner on his return to the UK on easy ground at Windsor, hung badly when asked to challenge the long-time leader Dunelight and appeared to hate these much faster conditions. He was not at his best and will surely appreciate a return to softer ground next time. (op 7-4 tchd 15-8)
Babodana has not been at his best so far this season, but this was a creditable effort in defeat, especially considering he was short of room about two furlongs out. (op 20-1)
Supersonic Dave(USA) could not build on his recent second to subsequent Derby fourth Lucarno. He appeared unsuited by the drop in trip, but it's worth bearing in mind that his stable is hardly in the best of form at present. (op 11-4 tchd 5-2)
Nayyir, having his first run since returning from Dubai, was fitted with a tongue-tie for the first time, but had the headgear left off. He was held up in a race in which the winner made all, which would not have been ideal, but he was basically just well below his best.

2443 EMPIRE PROPERTY GROUP MAIDEN AUCTION STKS (DIV I) 6f
3:55 (3:58) (Class 5) 2-Y-O **£2,752** (£818; £409; £204) **Stalls** Low

Form RPR
4 **1** **Sofia's Star**[15] [1989] 2-8-13 0 JimCrowley 7 86
(P Winkworth) *w ldrs: rdn over 2f out: led jst over 1f out: forged clr* **10/3**[1]
53 **2** *2 ½* **Primed And Poised (USA)**[17] [1945] 2-8-8 0 EddieAhern 10 74
(J W Hills) *hld up bhd ldrs gng wl: rdn and nt qckn 2f out: styd on fnl f to take 2nd nr fnish* **6/1**
3 *nk* **Meydan Dubai (IRE)** 2-9-1 0 DaneO'Neill 8 80+
(J R Best) *squeezed s: sn w ldrs: upsides and rdn 2f out: chsd wnr 1f out: no imp: lost 2nd nr fin* **9/2**[2]
0 **4** *2* **Blandys Wood**[15] [1990] 2-8-4 0 EdwardCreighton 6 63+
(M R Channon) *cl up: rdn and outpcd fr 2f out: kpt on ins fnl f* **25/1**
4233 **5** *hd* **Ben**[4] [2333] 2-8-9 0 DO'Donohoe 4 67
(P G Murphy) *mde most to jst over 1f out: wknd ins fnl f* **11/2**[3]
0 **6** *nk* **Blue Zenith (IRE)**[59] [999] 2-8-0 0 ow1 TolleyDean(5) 9 62
(J S Moore) *dwlt and bmpd s: sn w ldrs on outer: wknd 1f out* **25/1**
7 *2 ½* **Wave Hill (IRE)** 2-8-13 0 LDettori 2 63+
(B J Meehan) *hanging rt thrght: cl up: jnd ldrs 1/2-way: wknd over 1f out* **9/1**
8 *1 ¾* **Synge Street** 2-8-11 0 RyanMoore 3 55
(R Hannon) *dwlt: in tch to 2f out: sn btn* **9/2**[2]
00 **9** *10* **Virtual Paddy**[15] [1989] 2-8-11 0 LPKeniry 5 25
(M Blanshard) *prom to 1/2-way: wknd rapidly* **40/1**
10 *dist* **Powys Lad** 2-9-2 0 JHBowman 1 —
(K R Burke) *s.s: sddle slipped and sn t.o* **9/1**
0 **11** *7* **Ba Speedbird (IRE)**[61] [972] 2-8-8 0 SamHitchcott 11 —
(M R Channon) *t.k.h for 2f: rdn and wknd rapidly 1/2-way: virtually p.u 2f out* **16/1**

1m 12.79s (-0.06) **Going Correction** -0.175s/f (Firm) 11 Ran SP% **125.1**
Speed ratings (Par 93):93,89,89,86,86 85,82,80,66,— —
CSF £24.81 TOTE £4.50: £1.60, £2.10, £2.10; EX 27.10.
Owner David Holden **Bred** Bearstone Stud **Trained** Chiddingfold, Surrey

FOCUS
A decent maiden for the grade, rated through the runner-up. Just as in the earlier sprint handicap, they raced stands' side, but not many of these wanted to know the rail. The winning time was 0.43 seconds slower than the second division.

NOTEBOOK
Sofia's Star improved on the form he showed when a close fourth in a modest course-and-distance maiden on his debut, running out a most decisive winner. The bare form does not look anything special, but he won well and looks a useful prospect. (op 5-1)
Primed And Poised(USA), third behind a couple of nice types on the Polytrack at Lingfield on her previous start, again ran well, but she basically just got going too late, having hit a bit of a flat spot when initially asked for her challenge. She is still learning. (op 11-2)
Meydan Dubai(IRE), a 40,000euros purchase, out of a mare who was placed over 6f on her juvenile debut, was extremely well backed on his racecourse debut. He failed to land the gamble, but showed good speed after recovering from being short of room at the start and clearly has plenty of ability. This should sharpen him up and, with normal improvement, he ought to pick up a similar event. (op 14-1)
Blandys Wood improved on the form she showed over course and distance on her debut and looks to be going the right way. (op 22-1)
Ben, upped in trip, tried his luck against the stands' rail and seemed to have every chance. He is not progressing and may need dropping into claiming company. (op 9-2 tchd 4-1)
Blue Zenith(IRE) received a bump at the start and did not fare too badly in the circumstances.
Synge Street, a 12,000gns half-brother to four winners, including 5f juvenile scorer Pivotal Guest, never got in a blow but should improve significantly with the benefit of this experience. (op 5-1)
Powys Lad Official explanation: jockey said saddle slipped
Ba Speedbird(IRE) Official explanation: jockey said filly lost its action

2444 EMPIRE PROPERTY GROUP SPRINT STKS (H'CAP) 5f
4:30 (4:30) (Class 5) (0-70,70) 3-Y-O **£3,562** (£1,059; £529; £264) **Stalls** Low

Form RPR
2122 **1** **Drifting Gold**[7] [2260] 3-9-0 **63** (b) LDettori 8 71
(C G Cox) *racd on outer: wl on terms: rdn over 1f out: led jst ins fnl f: drvn out* **6/4**[1]
40-5 **2** *½* **Gleaming Spirit (IRE)**[16] [1976] 3-8-13 **62** EddieAhern 3 68
(A P Jarvis) *cl up: rdn to chal over 1f out: styd on ins fnl f: a hld* **14/1**
0-10 **3** *1 ¼* **Pretty Miss**[19] [1900] 3-9-7 **70** DaneO'Neill 2 71
(H Candy) *racd against nr side rail: mde most: edgd rt and hdd jst ins fnl f: fdd* **5/1**[2]
225 **4** *1* **Ioweyou**[25] [1738] 3-8-6 **55** (b) LPKeniry 9 53
(J S Moore) *racd on wd outside: chsd ldrs: rdn 2f out: kpt on same pce* **12/1**
-510 **5** *½* **Game Lady**[24] [1766] 3-9-1 **69** JamieMoriarty(5) 4 65
(I A Wood) *chsd ldrs: rdn and nt qckn 2f out: one pce after* **14/1**
3035 **6** *2* **Nou Camp**[8] [2205] 3-7-12 **52** WilliamBuick(5) 6 41
(N A Callaghan) *w ldrs to 1/2-way: sn rdn and lost pl: nt qckn* **7/1**[3]
2000 **7** *nk* **Suhayl Star (IRE)**[33] [1538] 3-8-8 **57** DO'Donohoe 1 45
(S W Hall) *s.i.s: outpcd in last: nvr a factor* **25/1**
04-4 **8** *hd* **Damhsoir (IRE)**[19] [1883] 3-7-11 **51** oh1 LukeMorris(5) 5 38
(H S Howe) *restless stalls: awkward s: rdn in rr 1/2-way: nt keen after* **20/1**
3604 **9** *1* **Majestic Cheer**[35] [1484] 3-9-7 **70** JHBowman 7 53
(M R Channon) *prom 3f: wknd* **5/1**[2]

58.41 secs (-0.64) **Going Correction** -0.175s/f (Firm) 9 Ran SP% **115.5**
Speed ratings (Par 99):98,97,95,93,92 89,89,88,87
CSF £25.53 CT £87.99 TOTE £2.00: £1.10, £3.60, £2.10; EX 20.90.
Owner Martin C Oliver **Bred** Witney And Warren Enterprises Ltd **Trained** Lambourn, Berks
■ Stewards' Enquiry : L Dettori one-day ban: used whip with excessive frequency without giving filly time to respond (Jun 25)

FOCUS
A modest but competitive sprint handicap. The majority opted to race towards the middle of the track. The winner was 6lb off her AW form, but on the other hand the runner-up improved by a similar amount on his best form in maidens.
Suhayl Star(IRE) Official explanation: jockey said gelding had a breathing problem
Damhsoir(IRE) Official explanation: trainer said filly was found to be in season

2445 EMPIRE INVESTMENTS STKS (H'CAP) 1m 3f
5:05 (5:06) (Class 5) (0-70,68) 3-Y-O **£3,724** (£1,108; £553; £276) **Stalls** Low

Form RPR
600- **1** **Raffaas**[253] [5647] 3-9-2 **68** WilliamBuick(5) 7 78+
(M P Tregoning) *settled in midfield: pushed along over 4f out: effrt over 2f out: clsd and squeezed through 1f out: led last 150yds: pushed out* **8/1**
-511 **2** *1* **Jafaru**[11] [2105] 3-9-1 **62** (b) LDettori 1 66+
(G A Butler) *prom: trckd ldr 7f out: poised to chal over 2f out: rdn and nt qckn wl over 1f out: kpt on* **5/4**[1]
-420 **3** *nk* **Best Selection**[42] [1289] 3-9-6 **67** JHBowman 4 70
(A P Jarvis) *led: set stdy pce for 7f: rdn over 2f out: hdd and one pce last 150yds* **12/1**
-355 **4** *1 ¼* **Irish Dancer**[11] [2112] 3-9-4 **65** EddieAhern 11 66
(J L Dunlop) *prom: effrt on inner 2f out: chal 1f out: wknd fnl 150yds* **9/2**[2]
-232 **5** *1 ¼* **Spritza (IRE)**[16] [1968] 3-8-13 **65** LukeMorris(5) 8 64
(M L W Bell) *trckd ldrs: rdn and cl up 2f out: nt qckn over 1f out: fdd* **6/1**[3]
630- **6** *1 ½* **Tivers Song (USA)**[198] [6569] 3-9-7 **68** JimCrowley 6 64+
(Mrs A J Perrett) *hld up in rr: rdn over 2f out: no prog tl kpt on fnl f: n.d* **20/1**
000- **7** *shd* **Roxy Singer**[302] [4334] 3-8-2 **49** oh4 DavidKinsella 9 45?
(W J Musson) *unruly preliminaries: hld up in last pair: sme prog over 2f out: sn no hdwy and btn* **66/1**
344- **8** *1* **Bantry Bere (IRE)**[187] [6699] 3-9-5 **66** DaneO'Neill 3 60
(J R Best) *hld up in midfield: rdn over 2f out: no prog* **22/1**
0035 **9** *1* **Tumble Jill (IRE)**[38] [1397] 3-7-9 **49** oh4 KMay(7) 5 42
(J J Bridger) *trckd ldr for 4f: lost pl 1/2-way: effrt on inner and chsng ldrs wl over 1f out: wknd fnl f* **50/1**
25-0 **10** *1 ½* **Heights Of Golan**[26] [1722] 3-8-13 **65** JamieMoriarty(5) 2 55
(I A Wood) *hld up in rr: rdn and no prog wl over 2f out* **15/2**
6-05 **11** *4* **Elmasong**[10] [2140] 3-8-2 **49** oh4 FrankieMcDonald 10 32
(J J Bridger) *t.k.h: hld up in rr: last and struggling 4f out* **100/1**

2m 29.99s (2.78) **Going Correction** -0.05s/f (Good) 11 Ran SP% **121.0**
Speed ratings (Par 99):87,86,86,85,84 83,83,82,81,80 77
CSF £18.35 CT £129.29 TOTE £9.60: £2.90, £1.10, £4.00; EX 23.60.
Owner Sheikh Ahmed Al Maktoum **Bred** Darley **Trained** Lambourn, Berks

FOCUS
Just a modest handicap and, with the pace very steady, those who raced close to the lead were at an advantage, suggesting this was a better effort than it might look from the held-up Raffaas. The third and fourth are the best guides and there are doubts about the overall reliability of the form.

2446 EMPIRE PROPERTY GROUP FINALE STKS (H'CAP) 1m
5:40 (5:40) (Class 2) (0-100,99) 4-Y-O+
£13,087 (£3,918; £1,959; £980; £489; £245) **Stalls** High

Form RPR
-310 **1** **King Of Argos**[28] [1651] 4-9-3 **95** LDettori 7 105+
(E A L Dunlop) *hld up in last: clsd over 2f out: plld out and effrt over 1f out: pressed ldr fnl f: forced ahd last strides* **5/2**[1]
-604 **2** *shd* **Audience**[21] [1842] 7-8-7 **85** PaulDoe 2 95
(J Akehurst) *dwlt: hld up in last trio: rdn and prog on outer over 2f out: led wl over 1f out: hrd pressed fnl f: hdd last strides* **6/1**[3]
0335 **3** *¾* **Ordnance Row**[7] [2233] 4-9-0 **92** PatDobbs 5 100
(R Hannon) *trckd clr ldng pair: clsd over 2f out: drvn to chal on inner and upsides over 1f out: styd on same pce fnl f* **6/1**[3]
23-2 **4** *½* **Ebert**[16] [1962] 4-8-8 **86** EddieAhern 6 95+
(P J Makin) *hld up in last trio: prog on inner whn nt clr run briefly over 1f out: pressed ldrs ins fnl f: hld whn n.m.r nr fin* **4/1**[2]
4-60 **5** *3 ½* **Dansili Dancer**[34] [1494] 5-9-7 **99** JHBowman 4 98
(C G Cox) *hld up in 5th: prog to chal and upsides 2f out: wknd jst over 1f out* **6/1**[3]
1000 **6** *2* **Waterside (IRE)**[8] [2208] 8-8-11 **89** RyanMoore 1 83
(G L Moore) *w ldr at str pce to 1/2-way: lost pl and btn over 2f out* **15/2**
0241 **7** *¾* **Moody Tunes**[9] [2189] 4-8-1 **84** LukeMorris(5) 3 77
(K R Burke) *settled in 4th: clsd to chal 2f out: n.m.r over 1f out: wknd* **12/1**
30-6 **8** *1* **St Andrews (IRE)**[20] [1860] 7-8-12 **97** MartinGuest(7) 8 87
(M A Jarvis) *led at str pce: hdd & wknd wl over 1f out* **33/1**

1m 37.79s (-2.48) **Going Correction** -0.05s/f (Good) 8 Ran SP% **113.8**
Speed ratings (Par 109):110,109,109,108,105 103,102,101
CSF £17.70 CT £80.67 TOTE £3.30: £1.40, £2.40, £2.20; EX 23.40.
Owner P G Goulandris **Bred** Chippenham Lodge Stud Ltd **Trained** Newmarket, Suffolk

FOCUS
A good handicap and, with St Andrews and Waterside taking each other on up front, the pace was strong. The winning time was 0.23 seconds slower than the earlier Listed race. Solid form, and there is more to come from King Of Argos.

NOTEBOOK
King Of Argos bounced right back to form having flopped when favourite for the Victoria Cup on his previous start. Held up last for much of the way, the strong pace would have suited, and he stayed on best when switched to the outside in the straight, although he had to work hard to see off Audience, with that one displaying a particularly willing attitude. He is entered in the Royal Hunt Cup, but has picked up a 3lb penalty for that race and does not really appeal. (op 11-4)
Audience had been dropped 4lb since the start of the season, despite running some decent races in good company, and he very nearly took advantage, keeping on strongly for pressure right the way to the line. He could pick up a nice prize this season. (tchd 8-1)
Ordnance Row would have found this more realistic than the Group 3 he contested at Epsom the previous weekend and ran well on ground that might have been a little quicker than he really wants. (op 11-2)
Ebert could not defy a 4lb rise in the weights for his recent course-and-distance second, but he may well have been third had his jockey not had to stop riding when short of room near the finish. Official explanation: jockey said gelding was denied a clear run (op 9-2 tchd 7-2)

Dansili Dancer was well held off a mark 12lb higher than when winning this race last year. (tchd 5-1)
Waterside(IRE) was taken on for the lead by St Andrews and ended up doing too much. (op 8-1)

2447 EMPIRE PROPERTY GROUP MAIDEN AUCTION STKS (DIV II) 6f
6:10 (6:11) (Class 5) 2-Y-O **£2,752** (£818; £409; £204) **Stalls** Low

Form				RPR
502	1		**Dubai Dynamo**[10] [2147] 2-8-9 0 .... SimonWhitworth 10 (J S Moore) *trckd ldr: led wl over 1f out: edgd lft but styd on wl* **3/1**[1]	77
3	2	2	**Miss Firefly**[15] [1993] 2-8-10 0 .... JHBowman 2 (M R Channon) *led to wl over 1f out: clr of rest after but readily hld by wnr* **4/1**[3]	72
36	3	3	**Sheik'N'Knotsterd**[15] [1989] 2-8-9 0 .... DaneO'Neill 4 (J Akehurst) *in tch: chsd ldng pair 1/2-way: sn outpcd: kpt on* **8/1**	62+
	4	1 ¾	**Feasible** 2-8-13 0 .... FrankieMcDonald 8 (J G Portman) *racd on outer: chsd ldrs: rdn 1/2-way: outpcd 2f out: one pce after* **25/1**	61+
	5	½	**Farthermost (IRE)** 2-8-9 0 .... PatDobbs 6 (R Hannon) *in tch: outpcd over 2f out: one pce fnl 2f* **12/1**	55+
5	6	3	**Xtravaganza (IRE)**[19] [1896] 2-8-6 0 .... EddieAhern 9 (J W Hills) *dwlt: in tch in rr: outpcd over 2f out* **7/2**[2]	43
	7	5	**Sun In Splendour (USA)** 2-9-2 0 .... LDettori 3 (A P Jarvis) *chsd ldng pair to 1/2-way: hanging rt and wknd: eased* **4/1**[3]	38+
0	8	10	**Maddie's Pearl (IRE)**[22] [1807] 2-8-0 0 ow1 .... ThomasO'Brien(7) 5 (M R Channon) *dwlt: in tch over 3f: wknd and sn bhd* **33/1**	—
	9	10	**Spanish Heroine** 2-8-10 0 .... StephenCarson 1 (P Winkworth) *a last and rn green: t.o fnl 2f* **16/1**	—

1m 12.36s (-0.49) **Going Correction** -0.175s/f (Firm) **9** Ran SP% **118.7**
Speed ratings (Par 93):96,93,89,87,86 82,75,62,49
CSF £15.71 TOTE £3.40: £1.10, £1.90, £2.90; EX 12.40 Place 6 £42.24, Place 5 £ 4.77..
Owner Mrs Fitri Hay **Bred** T K And Mrs P A Knox **Trained** Upper Lambourn, Berks

FOCUS
Another fair juvenile maiden, run in a time 0.43 seconds faster than the first division. The race has been rated through the third, with steps up from both the front two. They all raced towards the stands' side, not shunning the rail this time.

NOTEBOOK
Dubai Dynamo had shown ability on all three of his three previous starts and found this a straightforward opportunity to gain his first-career success. He looks a nice type for the nursery season later in the year. (op 11-4 tchd 5-2)
Miss Firefly confirmed the promise she showed on her debut at Goodwood, but she proved no match for the winner. She looks the type to keep improving. (op 3-1)
Sheik'N'Knotsterd is only modest but this was a respectable effort. (op 7-1)
Feasible, a 14,500gns brother to 1m juvenile winner Petross, out of a dual 5f-6f winner, showed some ability on his racecourse debut and is entitled to improve for the experience. (op 20-1)
Farthermost(IRE), a half-brother to among others quite useful 7f-1m winner Easaar, out of a 6f juvenile scorer, never got in a blow on his racecourse debut, but he should improve plenty. (op 10-1)
Xtravaganza(IRE) attracted support in the market, but she failed to build on the promise she showed on her debut at Windsor. (op 13-2 tchd 3-1)
Sun In Splendour(USA), a 30,000gns purchase, out of a triple winner at around 6f-1m1f in the US, was beaten some way out and failed to justify strong market support on his racecourse debut. (op 7-1)
T/Plt: £118.90 to a £1 stake. Pool: £102,361.60. 628.25 winning tickets. T/Qpdt: £5.30 to a £1 stake. Pool: £5,328.30. 739.90 winning tickets. JN

2431 HAYDOCK (L-H)
Saturday, June 9

OFFICIAL GOING: Good to firm
Wind: Almost nil Weather: Hot and sunny

2448 J.W.LEES H'CAP 1m 3f 200y
2:05 (2:06) (Class 2) (0-100,93) 3-Y-O
£14,022 (£4,198; £2,099; £1,050; £524; £263) **Stalls** High

Form				RPR
2312	1		**Eradicate (IRE)**[13] [2057] 3-9-7 93 .... KDarley 3 (M Johnston) *a.p: led 3f out: rdn over 1f out: r.o wl and a in command fnl f* **7/2**[2]	101+
631	2	2	**Philatelist (USA)**[17] [1950] 3-9-4 90 .... PhilipRobinson 7 (M A Jarvis) *t.k.h: a.p: rdn 2f out: wnt 2nd wl over 1f out: kpt on: nt trble wnr* **6/1**[3]	94
12	3	¾	**Dansant**[22] [1803] 3-9-4 90 .... FrancisNorton 8 (G A Butler) *hld up: rdn 2f out: hdwy over 1f out: styd on ins fnl f* **9/1**	93
1-34	4	nk	**Sanbuch**[15] [1987] 3-9-1 87 .... NickyMackay 2 (L M Cumani) *hld up: rdn and outpcd over 3f out: hdwy 2f out: kpt on ins fnl f* **5/2**[1]	91+
16-0	5	1 ¾	**Old Romney**[11] [2126] 3-8-6 81 .... AndrewMullen(3) 4 (M Johnston) *led: hdd 3f out: sn rdn: wknd ins fnl f: eased whn btn towards fin* **25/1**	81
21-4	6	5	**Cabinet (IRE)**[16] [1956] 3-8-10 82 .... JimmyQuinn 5 (Sir Michael Stoute) *midfield: rdn and hdwy 3f out: hung lft 2f out: wknd over 1f out* **7/2**[2]	74
-556	7	9	**Troialini**[9] [2185] 3-8-7 79 .... ChrisCatlin 6 (S W Hall) *hld up: hdwy 5f out: rdn and wknd over 2f out* **40/1**	56
3-13	8	3	**Small Fortune**[16] [1974] 3-8-6 78 .... DarryllHolland 9 (R Charlton) *cl up: n.m.r whn hmpd and lost pl after 2f: sn wnt prom: wknd qckly 3f out* **16/1**	51
61-4	9	53	**Wait For The Light**[19] [1898] 3-8-9 81 .... JamieSpencer 1 (E A L Dunlop) *s.i.s: t.k.h: hld up in tch: lost pl 6f out: struggling 3f out: sn eased whn btn: t.o* **8/1**	—

2m 31.98s (-3.01) **Going Correction** -0.125s/f (Firm) **9** Ran SP% **120.6**
Speed ratings (Par 105):105,103,103,102,101 98,92,90,55
CSF £26.16 CT £179.03 TOTE £3.50: £1.60, £2.20, £3.00; EX 20.10 Trifecta £76.10 Pool: £418.30 - 3.90 winning units..
Owner A D Spence **Bred** Sir Eric Parker **Trained** Middleham Moor, N Yorks

FOCUS
A decent handicap, but run at only a modest pace. The front four are all progressive, and Eradicate could emulate his stable's 2006 winner Soapy Danger and prove himself a Group horse in due course.

NOTEBOOK
Eradicate(IRE), whose four previous runs were all over 1m2f, proved well suited by the step up in trip and stayed on strongly despite not doing a great deal in front. The King George V Handicap remains an option for this progressive colt, but connections regard him as a Group horse in the making and are reportedly considering the King Edward VII Stakes too. (op 11-4)
Philatelist(USA), who got off the mark in a weak race on Polytrack, acquitted himself well on this handicap debut but never promised to haul in the progressive winner. (op 7-1)
Dansant, runner-up in a weakly contested Listed event last time, kept on from the rear of the field but lacked the pace to mount a challenge. He probably needs a true test at this trip. (op 8-1)
Sanbuch was raised 3lb following his defeat at Goodwood. Caught out when the pace lifted early in the home straight, he was staying on at the end and, after being short of room briefly inside the last, might have been third had his rider not eased him off slightly near the line. (op 10-3)
Old Romney ran poorly on his recent return to action on easy ground but this was a better effort. After setting a moderate pace, he was headed by his stablemate early in the home straight but remained in contention for a place until fading inside the final furlong.
Cabinet(IRE) improved with three to run but soon began to hang under pressure. The trip looked to stretch him and the ground may well have been faster than he cares for. (op 4-1 tchd 9-2)
Wait For The Light Official explanation: trainer had no explanation for the poor form shown

2449 JOHN WILLIES STKS (H'CAP) 2m 45y
2:35 (2:36) (Class 2) (0-100,100) 4-Y-O+
£14,022 (£4,198; £2,099; £1,050; £524; £263) **Stalls** Low

Form				RPR
60-0	1		**Colloquial**[21] [1844] 6-8-8 86 ....(v) FergusSweeney 6 (H Candy) *a.p: led over 3f out: rdn 2f out: styd on wl* **9/1**	98
50-0	2	2	**River Alhaarth (IRE)**[21] [1844] 5-8-12 90 .... RobertHavlin 2 (P W Chapple-Hyam) *trckd ldrs: rdn to chse wnr over 2f out: kpt on fnl f: a hld* **6/4**[1]	100
-106	3	5	**Melpomene**[126] [345] 4-8-8 87 .... KDarley 9 (M Johnston) *midfield: rdn and hdwy over 3f out: chsd front pair 2f out: no imp fnl f* **12/1**	91
11-0	4	4	**Desert Sea (IRE)**[28] [1654] 4-8-3 82 .... FrancisNorton 8 (D W P Arbuthnot) *midfield: effrt 3f out: sn one pce* **6/1**[2]	81
202-	5	½	**The Nawab (IRE)**[14] [2054] 5-8-5 83 ....(t) PaulFessey 4 (Barry Potts, Ire) *midfield: hdwy over 5f out: rdn over 3f out: wknd over 1f out* **9/1**	81
40-0	6	nk	**Kasthari (IRE)**[22] [1823] 8-9-8 100 .... DarryllHolland 3 (J D Bethell) *prom: led after 3f: hdd over 3f out: sn rdn: wknd over 1f out* **28/1**	98
000-	7	¾	**Mr Ed (IRE)**[23] [5963] 9-8-3 81 oh5 ....(p) JimmyQuinn 7 (P Bowen) *hld up: rdn over 4f out: no imp* **10/1**	78
03-0	8	7	**Winged D'Argent (IRE)**[31] [1582] 6-8-12 90 .... MickyFenton 1 (B J Llewellyn) *led for 3f: remained prom: rdn 6f out: wknd 2f out* **25/1**	79
4-20	9	3 ½	**Billich**[91] [662] 4-8-2 81 .... ChrisCatlin 5 (E J O'Neill) *hld up: struggling 4f out: nvr on terms* **12/1**	65
1-40	P		**Escayola (IRE)**[28] [1654] 7-8-7 85 ....(b) JamieSpencer 10 (Grant Tuer) *hld up: broke leg and p.u over 3f out: dead* **13/2**[3]	—

3m 32.51s (-5.39) **Going Correction** -0.125s/f (Firm)
WFA 4 from 5yo+ 1lb **10** Ran SP% **119.4**
Speed ratings (Par 109):108,107,104,102,102 102,101,98,96,—
CSF £23.42 CT £172.98 TOTE £12.00: £3.00, £1.10, £3.70; EX 24.20 Trifecta £239.70 Part won. Pool: £337.70 - 0.30 winning units..
Owner Mrs David Blackburn & M Blackburn **Bred** Mrs M J Blackburn **Trained** Kingston Warren, Oxon

FOCUS
This was run at just a steady pace and developed into something of a sprint up the straight. Colloquial was back to form with the visor and ran to a similar level to last year, when it was a stronger race.

NOTEBOOK
Colloquial, runner-up to Bulwark in this event twelve months previously when visored for the first time, was 2lb lower here and had the headgear back in place. Tracking the leader into the straight, he kicked with a quarter of a mile to run and, maintaining the gallop, was never in much danger of being caught. (op 17-2 tchd 8-1)
River Alhaarth(IRE), who cracked a cannonbone last season, was sharper for his recent return to the fray at Newmarket but was beaten fair and square by the winner. He is pretty consistent but not proving easy to win with. (op 7-4 tchd 15-8 and 11-8 in places)
Melpomene, lightly raced on turf and tackling fast ground for the first time, had been off the track since a substandard effort on Polytrack in February. He plugged on without making much impression on the pair in front of him.
Desert Sea(IRE), who pulled for his head in the early stages, stuck on to reach the frame but was beaten a fair way. (op 7-1)
The Nawab(IRE), trained last season by John Dunlop, had been well beaten over inadequate trips in two runs for this yard in Ireland this spring. Always in a similar position, he could not quicken up when the sprint to the line began. (op 8-1)
Kasthari(IRE), well beaten in the Yorkshire Cup last time following a couple of non-completions over fences, has since left Howard Johnson. In front after three furlongs, but setting just a steady pace, he could not counter when headed by the eventual winner. He still has plenty to prove. (op 25-1 tchd 33-1)

2450 TIMEFORM SILVER SALVER (REGISTERED AS THE CECIL FRAIL STKS) (LISTED RACE) (F&M) 6f
3:10 (3:11) (Class 1) 3-Y-O+
£14,762 (£5,595; £2,800; £1,396; £699; £351) **Stalls** Centre

Form				RPR
-001	1		**Cartimandua**[16] [1973] 3-8-8 94 .... GrahamGibbons 4 (E S McMahon) *mde all: rdn clr ins fnl f: r.o wl* **11/1**	111
3016	2	4	**Ripples Maid**[13] [2058] 4-9-6 97 .... RobertHavlin 5 (J A Geake) *a.p: rdn over 1f out: nt pce of wnr ins fnl f* **8/1**[3]	104
/1-0	3	1 ¾	**Riotous Applause**[28] [1670] 4-9-2 92 .... JamieSpencer 7 (J R Fanshawe) *bmpd and lost pl sn after s: bhd: hdwy 2f out: styd on ins fnl f: nt rch front pair* **9/2**[2]	94+
50-5	4	½	**Alderney (USA)**[34] [1502] 3-8-8 95 .... PhilipRobinson 8 (M A Jarvis) *bhd after 1f: rdn and hdwy over 1f out: gng on at fin* **12/1**	91+
5-62	5	¾	**Leopoldine**[28] [1661] 4-9-2 89 .... FrancisNorton 9 (H Morrison) *prom: rdn over 1f out: kpt on same pce ins fnl f* **12/1**	90
2530	6	1	**Paradise Isle**[34] [1497] 6-9-2 104 .... KDarley 14 (C F Wall) *in tch on nr-side: rdn 2f out: one pce fnl f* **13/8**[1]	87
-222	7	3	**Perfect Story (IRE)**[28] [1670] 5-9-2 90 .... FergusSweeney 3 (J A R Toller) *midfield: rdn over 2f out: nt pce to chal* **10/1**	78
2064	8	1 ½	**Woodnook**[39] [1372] 4-9-2 90 .... GeorgeBaker 1 (J A R Toller) *towards rr: hdwy over 2f out: rdn to chse ldrs over 1f out: faltered ent fnl f: sn eased* **33/1**	73+
-104	9	2	**Lady Livius (IRE)**[28] [1670] 4-9-2 93 .... RichardMullen 2 (R Hannon) *chsd ldrs: rdn 2f out: wknd fnl f* **33/1**	66
2-43	10	nk	**Creative Mind (IRE)**[28] [1661] 4-9-2 87 ....(p) ChrisCatlin 10 (E J O'Neill) *prom: rdn over 2f out: wknd over 1f out* **20/1**	65
66-3	11	1 ¼	**Portmeirion**[14] [2034] 6-9-2 84 .... PaulFessey 15 (S C Williams) *hld up nr-side: rdn over 1f out: no imp* **20/1**	61
2125	12	5	**Sparkling Eyes**[22] [1808] 3-8-8 81 .... JimmyQuinn 12 (C E Brittain) *midfield: rdn over 2f out: wknd over 1f out* **33/1**	43

00- **13** *nk* **She's My Outsider**[240] 5919 5-9-2 76 PaulMulrennan 11 44
(I A Wood) *midfield: rdn 1/2-way: wknd over 2f out* **100/1**

0-40 **14** *18* **Sweet Afton (IRE)**[39] 1372 4-9-2 91 DarryllHolland 6 —
(M S Saunders) *edgy in stalls: s.i.s: a bhd* **33/1**

350- **P** **Daniella**[240] 5919 5-9-2 82 (p) MickyFenton 13 —
(Rae Guest) *in tch: lost pl 1/2-way: hung lft fr 2f out: t.o whn p.u and dismntd ins fnl f* **50/1**

1m 12.16s (-1.73) **Going Correction** -0.25s/f (Firm)
WFA 3 from 4yo+ 8lb **15** Ran SP% **124.4**
Speed ratings (Par 111):108,102,100,99,98 97,93,91,88,88 86,79,79,55,—
CSF £90.92 TOTE £13.50: £4.20, £3.20, £2.20; EX 201.30 TRIFECTA Not won..
Owner Mrs Fiona Williams **Bred** Mrs F S Williams **Trained** Lichfield, Staffs

FOCUS
A well contested Listed event and an impressive winner in Cartimandua, who had finished in midfield in the 1,000 Guineas. The favourite disappointed, but this looks solid form nevertheless.

NOTEBOOK
Cartimandua, who enjoyed a confidence booster in a maiden last time, made all the running down the centre of the track and, kicking approaching the final furlong, came clear to spreadeagle her field. A smart sprinter in the making, she will be well worth her place back in Group company. (op 10-1 tchd 12-1)
Ripples Maid was no match for the winner, but this was still a commendable effort under her penalty, particularly as she would probably have preferred easier ground. (tchd 17-2)
Riotous Applause, back on a more suitable surface, found herself towards the rear after taking a bump soon after the start. She improved travelling strongly, but by the time she was let down the winner had gone for home and she could not get to the runner-up either. She is capable of winning in this grade when things go her way. (op 5-1 tchd 4-1, 11-2 in places)
Alderney(USA), back up in grade, passed several rivals in the final furlong and looks well worth another try over further.
Leopoldine, no match for Wake Up Maggie in a Lingfield Group 3 last time, showed plenty of pace back over this shorter trip. (op 10-1)
Paradise Isle, last year's winner, came here via the same route, having taken in the Abernant and Palace House Stakes at Newmarket. She seemed unsuited by racing towards the stands' side when the main action was taking place down the centre and could never launch an effective challenge. (op 7-4 tchd 15-8)
Woodnook, back up in trip, was in the process of running a reasonable race when she began to edge to her left and was eased with a furlong or so to run. Official explanation: jockey said filly lost its action
Sweet Afton(IRE) Official explanation: jockey said filly missed the break
Daniella Official explanation: jockey said mare lost a front shoe and hung left

2451 E B F MARTIN BURGESS 65TH BIRTHDAY MAIDEN STKS 5f
3:40 (3:45) (Class 5) 2-Y-O **£3,238** (£963; £481; £240) **Stalls** Centre

Form RPR

03 **1** **Secret Asset (IRE)**[19] 1889 2-9-3 0 RichardMullen 2 86
(W M Brisbourne) *mde all: rdn and edgd rt over 1f out: r.o* **16/1**

2 **2** *1 1/4* **Wolgan Valley (USA)**[13] 2056 2-9-3 0 JamieSpencer 8 81
(Saeed Bin Suroor) *midfield: hdwy 1/2-way: rdn to chse wnr over 1f out: kpt on* **5/4**[1]

62 **3** *3/4* **Captain Gerrard (IRE)**[14] 2024 2-9-3 0 PhilipRobinson 11 79
(B Smart) *racd keenly in tch: rdn over 1f out: kpt on ins fnl f* **13/8**[2]

5 **4** *2* **Menadha (USA)**[16] 1970 2-9-3 0 DarryllHolland 10 71
(M R Channon) *prom: rdn over 1f out: kpt on same pce ins fnl f* **7/1**[3]

0 **5** *1/2* **Ridge Wood Dani (IRE)**[49] 1150 2-9-3 0 KDarley 3 69
(E J Alston) *in tch: rdn and outpcd over 1f out: kpt on towards fin* **40/1**

426 **6** *1* **Cayman Fox**[21] 1848 2-8-12 0 PaulMulrennan 7 61
(James Moffatt) *plld hrd: wnt lft s: prom: rdn and hung lft over 1f out: wknd ins fnl f* **14/1**

0 **7** *1/2* **Allahor**[16] 1963 2-8-12 0 PBradley(5) 6 64
(A Berry) *s.i.s and hmpd s: bhd: kpt on fnl f: nvr rchd chalng position* **80/1**

8 *3 1/2* **Waterloo Dock** 2-9-3 0 FrancisNorton 9 51
(M Quinn) *s.s: a bhd* **25/1**

9 *nk* **Skhilling Pride** 2-8-12 0 PaulFessey 1 45
(T D Barron) *in tch: rdn 2f out: sn wknd* **28/1**

10 *nk* **Rio Sabotini** 2-9-3 0 GrahamGibbons 5 49
(G A Swinbank) *s.i.s: midfield: rdn over 1f out: sn wknd* **33/1**

11 *shd* **Keep Shining** 2-8-12 0 MickyFenton 4 43
(E J Alston) *dwlt: a bhd* **66/1**

61.27 secs (1.15) **Going Correction** -0.25s/f (Firm) **11** Ran SP% **123.0**
Speed ratings (Par 93):96,94,92,89,88 87,86,80,80,79 79
CSF £37.16 TOTE £17.20: £2.70, £1.40, £1.30; EX 55.20.
Owner Kinsale Racing **Bred** Mrs C Hartery **Trained** Great Ness, Shropshire

FOCUS
Not much strength in depth to this maiden. Not easy to assess, with several stepping forward, including the runner-up, but the seventh sounds a note of caution.

NOTEBOOK
Secret Asset(IRE), who built on his debut form when a close third at Musselburgh, made every yard to land a bit of a gamble. He hung over to the stands' rail from his low draw, but kept going too strongly for the big guns. (op 25-1 tchd 14-1)
Wolgan Valley(USA) went in pursuit with over a furlong to run but was unable to reel in the winner, who cost a mere fraction of his purchase price. His turn should come, perhaps over 7f. (tchd 6-4, 7-4 in a place and 13-8 in places)
Captain Gerrard(IRE), the form pick on his close second at Beverley, was slightly disappointing. Having raced keenly, he could not find a change of gear when asked for his effort. (op 2-1 tchd 9-4 and 6-4 in places)
Menadha(USA) ran to a similar level as on his Goodwood debut last month and looks one for nurseries after one more run. (op 15-2 tchd 13-2)
Ridge Wood Dani(IRE), well beaten on his Nottingham debut in April, was keeping on determinedly at the end. His dam was a decent performer at 6f and he looks a likely type for nurseries over that trip later in the season. (op 50-1)
Cayman Fox, having her fourth run, looked a difficult ride as she failed to settle then hung under pressure. She might not have liked the ground. (op 16-1)
Rio Sabotini Official explanation: trainer's rep said the colt was unsuited by the good to firm ground

2452 TOMBOY CAVANAGH H'CAP 1m 30y
4:10 (4:13) (Class 3) (0-90,84) 3-Y-O+ **£9,715** (£2,890; £1,444; £721) **Stalls** Low

Form RPR

-425 **1** **Will He Wish**[133] 261 11-9-8 78 ChrisCatlin 8 87
(S Gollings) *a.p: led over 2f out: drvn out* **22/1**

2103 **2** *1* **Harare**[15] 1996 6-9-6 76 (v) PhilipRobinson 10 83
(R J Price) *midfield: hdwy over 2f out: chsd wnr over 1f out: sn rdn: styd on towards fin* **11/1**

4010 **3** *1 1/4* **Lazy Darren**[14] 2045 3-9-3 84 DarryllHolland 2 85+
(R Hannon) *s.i.s: hld up: rdn and hdwy over 1f out: styd on towards fin* **7/2**[2]

-130 **4** *3/4* **Just Bond (IRE)**[110] 501 5-9-6 76 GrahamGibbons 7 78
(G R Oldroyd) *in rr: hung rt on bnd over 5f out: hdwy 2f out: n.m.r and hmpd over 1f out: edgd rt and kpt on ins fnl f* **14/1**

131- **5** *1/2* **Prince Evelith (GER)**[263] 5446 4-9-7 77 JamieSpencer 5 78+
(G A Swinbank) *midfield: hdwy over 2f out: rdn and swtchd lft over 1f out whn chsd ldrs: fdd towards fin* **9/2**[3]

5-00 **6** *2 1/2* **Akram (IRE)**[15] 1996 5-9-13 83 GeorgeBaker 1 79
(Jonjo O'Neill) *in tch: lost pl 5f out: sn rdn and outpcd: kpt on fnl f: nt rch ldrs* **33/1**

4510 **7** *1/2* **Bold Marc (IRE)**[3] 2374 5-9-11 81 LeeEnstone 6 75
(K R Burke) *led for 1f: remained prom: regained ld 3f out: sn rdn and hdd: wknd fnl f* **15/2**

-515 **8** *2* **Genari**[16] 1962 4-9-9 79 KDarley 4 69
(P F I Cole) *trckd ldrs: rdn 3f out: wknd 2f out: btn whn n.m.r and hmpd over 1f out* **9/4**[1]

1316 **9** *3 1/2* **Wahoo Sam (USA)**[124] 364 7-9-2 72 FrancisNorton 3 54
(K A Ryan) *led after 1f: hdd 3f out: wknd over 1f out* **11/1**

46-0 **10** *1 3/4* **Zabeel House**[18] 1931 4-8-13 72 MarcHalford(3) 9 50
(J A R Toller) *bhd: rdn over 4f out: nvr on terms* **20/1**

1m 43.84s (-1.67) **Going Correction** -0.125s/f (Firm)
WFA 3 from 4yo+ 11lb **10** Ran SP% **118.3**
Speed ratings (Par 107):103,102,100,100,99 97,96,94,91,89
CSF £241.81 CT £1089.27 TOTE £30.00: £5.50, £3.10, £2.00; EX 177.20.
Owner Mrs D Dukes **Bred** Mrs C Buckland **Trained** Scamblesby, Lincs
■ Stewards' Enquiry : Jamie Spencer two-day ban: careless riding (Jun 24-25)

FOCUS
An ordinary handicap, but run at a sound pace and straightforward form.

NOTEBOOK
Will He Wish, off the track since January, was well suited by the strong gallop and he stuck his neck out willingly to hold off his challengers. He will still be fairly handicapped despite the rise for this and will not mind a drop back to 7f. (op 20-1)
Harare, eased a pound in the weights, ran his race and had no excuses. He should continue to give a good account, but he does keep a little back for himself. (op 9-1)
Lazy Darren was slowly away and still last turning into the home straight. Sticking to the inside rail, he was slightly short of room with over a furlong to run but was staying on well at the line. Official explanation: jockey said gelding missed the break (op 4-1)
Just Bond(IRE), off the track since February and returning to turf, was improving from the rear when becoming caught up in scrimmaging approaching the final furlong. While this was a decent effort, his head carriage did give cause for concern. (op 25-1)
Prince Evelith(GER), progressive last season, was 6lb higher than when last seen in September. Short of room over a furlong out, and causing trouble when extricated, his effort just flattened out in the final furlong. (op 4-1 tchd 5-1 in places)
Akram(IRE), already 12lb lower than at the start of the season, was keeping on at the end without ever threatening the principals. (op 25-1)
Bold Marc(IRE), making a quick reappearance, was taken on for the lead and eventually faded in the final furlong. (op 9-1)
Genari had excuses at Goodwood but there seemed none here, as he was already beaten when hampered with over a furlong to run. (op 5-2)
Wahoo Sam(USA) Official explanation: jockey said gelding stumbled shortly after start

2453 SPORTING INDEX H'CAP 1m 30y
4:45 (4:46) (Class 5) (0-75,74) 3-Y-O **£3,238** (£963; £481; £240) **Stalls** Low

Form RPR

3333 **1** **Eager Igor (USA)**[16] 1956 3-9-5 72 KDarley 12 79
(Eve Johnson Houghton) *hld up: hdwy over 2f out: led over 1f out: r.o wl in command ins fnl f* **11/4**[1]

3-30 **2** *3* **Laish Ya Hajar (IRE)**[22] 1815 3-9-5 72 DarryllHolland 7 72
(M R Channon) *racd keenly: a.p: led over 2f out: hdd over 1f out: styd on same pce ins fnl f* **9/1**

3401 **3** *1* **Snow Dancer (IRE)**[10] 2133 3-9-2 69 FrancisNorton 2 67+
(A Berry) *bhd: rdn and hdwy 2f out: hung rt over 1f out: styd on ins fnl f* **13/2**[3]

6-06 **4** *nk* **Caviar Heights (IRE)**[34] 1491 3-8-2 55 oh2 (b[1]) PaulFessey 4 52
(Miss L A Perratt) *bhd: rdn and hdwy over 1f out: styd on ins fnl f: one pce towards fin* **40/1**

5-20 **5** *1/2* **Perfect Courtesy (IRE)**[26] 1726 3-9-3 70 PhilipRobinson 6 66
(G A Swinbank) *midfield: rdn and hdwy over 2f out: kpt on same pce ins fnl f* **7/2**[2]

2-50 **6** *nk* **Jawaab (IRE)**[26] 1722 3-9-3 70 RobertHavlin 5 65
(M A Buckley) *midfield: hdwy 3f out: rdn and ev ch 2f out: no ex ins fnl f* **8/1**

00-3 **7** *1 1/2* **Tullythered (IRE)**[37] 1425 3-8-0 56 oh1 ow1 AndrewElliott(3) 1 48
(K R Burke) *in tch: pushed along and outpcd 4f out: no imp after* **14/1**

4-62 **8** *nk* **Run Free**[21] 1850 3-9-2 69 GrahamGibbons 9 60
(N Wilson) *prom tl rdn and wknd over 2f out* **7/1**

21-0 **9** *1 3/4* **Stanley George (IRE)**[22] 1815 3-9-7 74 MatthewHenry 11 66
(M A Jarvis) *hld up: rdn and hdwy 3f out: wknd 1f out: eased whn btn ins fnl f* **10/1**

1-60 **10** *9* **Milson's Point (IRE)**[28] 1658 3-9-0 67 PaulMulrennan 8 33
(I Semple) *sn led: rdn and hdd over 2f out: sn wknd* **18/1**

000 **11** *1 1/2* **Danehill Warrior (IRE)**[73] 807 3-8-2 58 oh10 ow3.. AndrewMullen(3) 3 21
(R C Guest) *midfield: hdwy 3f out: rdn and ev ch over 2f out: wknd over 1f out: sn eased whn btn* **66/1**

53-4 **12** *3 1/2* **Sangreal**[28] 1676 3-8-11 64 RichardMullen 13 19
(K R Burke) *racd keenly: prom tl rdn and wknd over 2f out* **18/1**

1m 44.8s (-0.71) **Going Correction** -0.125s/f (Firm) **12** Ran SP% **126.0**
Speed ratings (Par 99):98,95,94,93,93 92,91,91,89,80 78,75
CSF £30.67 CT £159.33 TOTE £3.90: £1.30, £4.10, £2.40; EX 36.80 Place 6 £83.92, Place 5 £31.99..
Owner G C Stevens **Bred** Crown Bloodstock & Chelsea Bloodstock **Trained** Blewbury, Oxon

FOCUS
This was run at a reasonable pace, but there didn't appear ro be anything particularly progressive in the field and it certainly wasn't a strong three-year-old handicap.

T/Jkpt: Not won. T/Plt: £91.50 to a £1 stake. Pool: £117,085.65. 933.95 winning tickets. T/Qpdt: £18.60 to a £1 stake. Pool: £4,472.10. 177.70 winning tickets. DO

2356 LINGFIELD (L-H)

Saturday, June 9

OFFICIAL GOING: Turf course - good to firm (good in places; 8.2); all weather - standard

Wind: virtually nil Weather: warm and muggy

2454 CHESNEY HAWKES LIVE AT LINGFIELDPARK.CO.UK (S) STKS 1m 4f (P)
5:50 (5:51) (Class 6) 3-Y-O £2,047 (£604; £302) Stalls Low

Form RPR

-263 1 **Right Option (IRE)**[38] 1397 3-8-12 55 SebSanders 11 57+
(S Dow) *hld up: stdy hdwy 7f out: chsd ldrs and rdn over 2f out: led over 1f out: drvn out* **5/2**[1]

00-0 2 ¾ **Converti**[56] 1039 3-8-12 52 JosedeSouza 4 54
(P F I Cole) *t.k.h: prom: rdn over 3f out: styd on u.p to chse wnr ins fnl f: kpt on* **7/1**

-040 3 2 ½ **Barney's Dancer**[106] 534 3-8-7 42 NeilPollard 2 45
(C L Popham) *t.k.h: chsd ldr after 2f: rdn to ld over 2f out: hdd over 1f out: no ex* **28/1**

4602 4 ½ **Best Woman**[74] 794 3-8-13 48 DaleGibson 6 50
(P Howling) *hld up: hdwy and rdn over 4f out: kpt on u.p fnl f: nvr trbld ldrs* **5/1**[2]

6655 5 1 ¼ **Gertie (IRE)**[76] 776 3-8-0 44 SCreighton(7) 8 42
(E J Creighton) *hld up in midfield: hdwy 5f out: rdn 3f out: kpt on same pce* **14/1**

0040 6 4 **Camp Counsellor**[8] 2223 3-8-12 62 (b[1]) VinceSlattery 3 41
(J A Osborne) *dwlt: sn led: rdn over 3f out: hdd over 2f out: wknd over 1f out* **6/1**

0000 7 1 ¾ **Tranquility**[47] 1204 3-8-7 44 (t) AdrianMcCarthy 13 33
(J Pearce) *t.k.h: hld up in rr: rdn and effrt over 3f out: sn no hdwy* **11/2**[3]

40 8 1 ¼ **Murdol (IRE)**[123] 373 3-8-12 43 AlanDaly 9 36
(C R Dore) *hld up in rr: rdn wl over 4f out: sn lost tch* **20/1**

0 9 1 ¼ **Augustus Caeser (IRE)**[68] 884 3-8-9 0 AlanCreighton(3) 5 34
(E J Creighton) *t.k.h: hld up in midfield: rdn and lost pl over 4f out: no ch after* **14/1**

0-00 10 9 **Flashing Feet (IRE)**[10] 2140 3-8-12 40 (v[1]) SamHitchcott 1 20
(Mrs L C Jewell) *t.k.h: chsd ldr for 2f: styd prom tl rdn and wknd wl over 3f out: t.o:* **25/1**

0-00 11 5 **Just A Flash (IRE)**[40] 1343 3-8-12 40 RichardSmith 12 12
(B R Johnson) *hld up in rr on outer: rdn 5f out: sn wl bhd: eased fnl f: t.o* **12/1**

R0 12 79 **Supercraft (IRE)**[26] 1725 3-8-7 0 (b[1]) TravisBlock(5) 10 —
(M Quinn) *chsd ldrs: rdn 6f out: dropped out rapidly over 4f out: wl t.o last 2f* **33/1**

2m 34.49s (0.10) **Going Correction** -0.10s/f (Stan) 12 Ran SP% **123.4**
Speed ratings (Par 97):95,94,92,92,91 89,87,87,86,80 76,24
CSF £20.14 TOTE £3.10: £1.40, £3.60, £5.10; EX 31.30.There was no bid for the winner. Converti was the subject of a friendly claim.
Owner P Wheatley **Bred** Paul Monaghan, R Berns And P Sexton **Trained** Epsom, Surrey

FOCUS
A weak seller, but the placed horses were relatively unexposed at this level. The winner did not need to improve on his winter form.

2455 MOTT MACDONALD MAIDEN STKS 1m 2f (P)
6:20 (6:25) (Class 5) 3-Y-O £2,914 (£867; £433; £216) Stalls Low

Form RPR

1 **Come April** 3-8-12 0 SebSanders 7 79+
(Sir Mark Prescott) *s.i.s: sn in tch in rr: hdwy over 3f out: nt clr run on inner over 2f out: swtchd rt 2f out: str run fnl f: led post* **5/1**[2]

2 shd **Cybersnow (USA)** 3-9-3 0 RichardHughes 11 77
(Mrs A J Perrett) *pressed ldr: led over 2f out: sn rdn: styd on wl tl ct on line* **12/1**

0- 3 2 ½ **Abyla**[282] 4964 3-8-12 0 DaleGibson 8 68
(M P Tregoning) *t.k.h: led for 2f: stdd to trck ldrs after: rdn to chse ldr over 2f out: kpt on same pce fnl f* **5/1**[2]

2230 4 ½ **Norman The Great**[10] 2153 3-9-3 75 AdrianMcCarthy 3 72+
(Jane Chapple-Hyam) *hld up in midfield: hdwy on inner over 3f out: chsd ldrs 2f out: kpt on same pce fnl furlong* **15/2**[3]

5 ¾ **Meynell** 3-8-12 0 CatherineGannon 10 65+
(M A Jarvis) *v s.i.s: reminders early: hld up in rr: hdwy on inner over 2f out: styd on fnl f: nt rch ldrs* **16/1**

6 3 ½ **Eastwell Smiles** 3-8-12 0 (t) TravisBlock(5) 13 64
(R T Phillips) *s.i.s: hld up in rr on outer: rdn 3f out: outpcd over 2f out: kpt on steadily ins fnl f* **50/1**

6- 7 nk **Valrhona (IRE)**[224] 6215 3-8-12 0 VinceSlattery 2 58+
(J Noseda) *hld up in midfield: rdn and effrt wl over 2f out: short of room briefly wl over 1f out: kpt on fnl f: nt pce to trble ldrs* **2/1**[1]

8 3 ½ **Chelsea Ballad (USA)** 3-8-12 0 JimmyFortune 14 51
(J H M Gosden) *rrd and s.i.s: sn in midfield: hdwy to chse ldrs 3f out: rdn 2f out: wknd 1f out* **8/1**

0 9 shd **Shirley A Star (USA)**[30] 1606 3-8-12 0 BrettDoyle 6 51
(B J Meehan) *rdn to ld after 2f: hdd over 2f out: sn wknd* **16/1**

10 ¾ **Who's This (IRE)** 3-9-3 0 AdamKirby 5 55
(W R Swinburn) *chsd ldrs: rdn over 2f out: wknd qckly over 1f out* **16/1**

11 13 **Arabian Sun** 3-9-3 0 RichardSmith 1 30
(M J Attwater) *s.i.s: hld up bhd: rdn over 3f out: sn lost tch: t.o* **66/1**

06 12 nk **Belinda Rose (IRE)**[26] 1725 3-8-12 0 DO'Donohoe 12 24
(B J Meehan) *w.w in midfield: rdn over 3f out: wknd over 2f out: t.o* **33/1**

00 13 25 **Ridgeway Place**[29] 1633 3-8-12 0 SamHitchcott 4 —
(A B Haynes) *in tch on outer: rdn wl over 3f out: sn bhd: wl t.o last 2f* **80/1**

2m 5.71s (-2.08) **Going Correction** -0.10s/f (Stan) 13 Ran SP% **122.5**
Speed ratings (Par 99):104,103,101,101,100 98,97,95,95,94 84,83,63
CSF £64.65 TOTE £6.90: £2.10, £3.60, £2.10; EX 72.50.
Owner Faisal Salman **Bred** M Lightbody **Trained** Newmarket, Suffolk

FOCUS
Many unraced and unexposed types from leading stables, and probably a reasonable maiden which should produce its share of winners. The fourth looks the best guide.

2456 HS WALSH & SONS 60TH ANNIVERSARY H'CAP 1m 2f (P)
6:50 (6:53) (Class 6) (0-60,60) 3-Y-O £2,047 (£604; £302) Stalls Low

Form RPR

-000 1 **Revisionist (IRE)**[3] 2362 3-9-2 58 RichardHughes 4 62
(R Hannon) *chsd ldr: upsides wl over 3f out: rdn over 2f out: led 1f out: forged ahd last 100yds* **7/1**

000 2 1 ¼ **My Mentor (IRE)**[19] 1904 3-9-3 59 SebSanders 1 61
(Sir Mark Prescott) *led: rdn and hrd pressed wl over 3f out: hdd 1f out: no ex last 100yds* **15/2**

056- 3 shd **Papradon**[199] 6562 3-8-8 53 StephaneBreux(3) 6 54
(J R Best) *racd in midfield: rdn 4f out: styd on to chse ldrs over 1f out: hung rt ins fnl f: kpt on: nt rch ldrs* **14/1**

5031 4 ½ **Featherlight**[38] 1397 3-8-13 55 AdrianMcCarthy 7 55
(Jamie Poulton) *hld up towards rr: hdwy 5f out: rdn and no hdwy 3f out: c wd wl over 1f out: r.o fnl f: nt rch ldrs* **4/1**[1]

340 5 nk **Encores**[37] 1440 3-9-4 60 JimmyFortune 8 60
(N A Callaghan) *w.w in bhd ldrs: rdn to chse ldng pair over 2f out: no hdwy and edgd rt ins fnl f* **8/1**

6063 6 shd **Brean Dot Com (IRE)**[44] 1266 3-8-5 54 NBazeley(7) 3 54
(Mrs P N Dutfield) *hld up bhd on inner: hdwy but nt clr run over 2f out: swtchd rt wl over 1f out: styd on fnl f: nt rch ldrs* **14/1**

00-0 7 ¾ **Neon**[38] 1403 3-9-4 60 DO'Donohoe 2 58
(J W Hills) *w.w in tch on inner: rdn 3f out: kpt on same pce last 2f* **16/1**

5066 8 shd **Silca Key**[22] 1815 3-9-2 58 SamHitchcott 11 56
(M R Channon) *t.k.h: hld up bhd: rdn 3f out: no hdwy tl kpt on wl ins fnl f: n.d* **7/1**

0-06 9 ½ **Black Mogul**[9] 2192 3-8-13 55 JamieSpencer 10 52
(W R Muir) *in tch: hdwy and rdn over 3f out: no hdwy wl over 1f out: eased last 100yds* **9/2**[2]

5200 10 nk **Royal Tender (IRE)**[7] 2259 3-9-1 57 (b[1]) AdamKirby 12 53
(B G Powell) *stdd and dropped in bhd after s: sme hdwy 3f out: hrd rdn over 2f out: nvr nr ldrs* **33/1**

6-50 11 hd **The Graig**[32] 1566 3-8-7 54 TravisBlock(5) 14 50
(C Drew) *stdd s: dropped in bhd: hdwy on inner wl over 1f out: nvr on terms* **50/1**

000 12 ¾ **Luna Danza**[15] 1988 3-9-1 57 (b[1]) BrettDoyle 5 51
(B J Meehan) *t.k.h: chsd ldrs: rdn wl over 2f out: wknd over 1f out* **50/1**

000- 13 5 **Like To Golf (USA)**[263] 5460 3-9-3 59 JimCrowley 9 43
(Mrs A J Perrett) *hld up in midfield: rdn over 3f out: sn wknd: wl bhd last 2f* **13/2**[3]

00 14 7 **King Canute (IRE)**[38] 1399 3-9-1 57 VinceSlattery 13 27
(M J Wallace) *hld up on outer: rdn over 3f out: sn lost tch: no ch last 2f* **50/1**

2m 7.89s (0.10) **Going Correction** -0.10s/f (Stan) 14 Ran SP% **127.4**
Speed ratings (Par 97):95,94,93,93,93 93,92,92,92,91 91,91,87,81
CSF £61.40 CT £734.15 TOTE £11.80: £3.40, £2.30, £5.80; EX 94.30.
Owner Wood Street Syndicate III **Bred** Forenaghts Stud **Trained** East Everleigh, Wilts

FOCUS
An interesting handicap containing a number of horses with little or no experience in this company. The first two dominated throughout, but the pack were closing at the finish and they finished in a bunch. Not particularly solid form.

2457 EUROPEAN BREEDERS' FUND MAIDEN FILLIES' STKS 6f
7:20 (7:25) (Class 5) 2-Y-O £3,238 (£963; £481; £240) Stalls High

Form RPR

6 1 **Festivale (IRE)**[14] 2039 2-9-0 0 EddieAhern 4 82+
(J L Dunlop) *trckd ldrs: chal over 1f out: led jst over 1f out: rdn clr: r.o strly* **11/4**[2]

2 3 **Change Tack (USA)** 2-9-0 0 RichardHughes 9 73
(Mrs A J Perrett) *in tch: hdwy over 2f out: nt clr run 2f out: swtchd rt over 1f out: styd on ins fnl f: wnt 2nd nr fin: no ch w wnr* **6/1**

2 3 nk **Carolina Belle (USA)**[36] 1445 2-9-0 0 JamieSpencer 7 72
(M J Wallace) *hld up: hdwy and edgd lft over 2f out: chsd ldrs and rdn wl over 1f out: kpt on same pce ins fnl f* **5/1**[3]

4 4 ½ **Petit Parc**[17] 1945 2-9-0 0 DaneO'Neill 8 70
(R A Teal) *led: rdn and hdd jst over 1f out: hung lft ins fnl f: lost 2 pls nr fin* **9/1**

0 5 ¾ **Night Skier (IRE)**[15] 2000 2-9-0 0 DO'Donohoe 5 68+
(J L Dunlop) *racd wd: sn pushed along: outpcd after 2f: hdwy over 1f out: r.o ins fnl f: nvr nrr* **33/1**

6 shd **Celtic Slipper (IRE)** 2-9-0 0 HayleyTurner 13 68+
(R M Beckett) *t.k.h: chsd ldr tl 3f out: lost pl 2f out: kpt on same pce fnl f* **20/1**

7 nk **Moonlight Angel** 2-9-0 0 AdamKirby 10 67+
(W R Swinburn) *hld up towards rr: hdwy over 2f out: rdn wl over 1f out: keeping on same pce whn short of room briefly ins fnl f* **11/1**

4 8 shd **Relinquished**[15] 2000 2-9-0 0 SebSanders 3 71+
(J Noseda) *prom: chsd ldr 3f out: ev ch and rdn wl over 1f out: wkng whn snatched up ins fnl f* **2/1**[1]

9 shd **Tenjack Queen (IRE)** 2-9-0 0 JimCrowley 11 66+
(J A Osborne) *s.i.s: bhd: hdwy 2f out: kpt on ins fnl f: nvr able to chal* **33/1**

6 10 1 **Tamara Moon (IRE)**[34] 1503 2-9-0 0 TPO'Shea 12 72+
(M R Channon) *chsd ldrs for 2f: sn lost pl: hdwy over 1f out: keeping on but no ch whn nt clr run ins fnl f* **20/1**

5 11 6 **Notepad**[13] 2056 2-9-0 0 PaulDoe 2 45
(W Jarvis) *racd wd: slowly away and wnt lft s: wl bhd last 3f* **33/1**

12 11 **Lady Charlemagne** 2-9-0 0 VinceSlattery 6 12
(N P Littmoden) *slowly away: a outpcd: t.o fr 1/2-way* **66/1**

1m 11.25s (-0.42) **Going Correction** -0.25s/f (Firm) 12 Ran SP% **129.1**
Speed ratings (Par 90):92,88,87,86,85 85,85,85,85,83 75,61
CSF £20.14 TOTE £4.20: £1.80, £2.30, £2.30; EX 31.10.
Owner Prince A A Faisal **Bred** Nawara Stud Co Ltd **Trained** Arundel, W Sussex

FOCUS
Mainly debutants, but a couple of unexposed sorts who had already shown plenty of promise, and probably a decent maiden. It featured a number of likely improvers. Pretty solid form.

NOTEBOOK
Festivale(IRE) showed the benefit of her eyecatching first run with a decisive victory which bodes well for her future. She should go on to better things from here. (tchd 9-4 and 3-1 in places)
Change Tack(USA) ◆ is by Mizzen Mast, a high-class performer in France and on dirt in the USA; while her dam, Jibe, is a half-sister to Warning, Commander In Chief and Dushyantor. That gives her a lot to live up to, but this was a fine debut behind a useful-looking juvenile, and trips up to 1m2f should suit her as she matures. (op 16-1)
Carolina Belle(USA) has run well in her two races to date. The two who finished in front of her here looked better than average, so she is good enough to win a typical maiden (op 7-2)
Petit Parc ran a more positive race that on her only previous start, but there was considerable merit in both performances and she is one to keep in mind. (op 16-1)
Night Skier(IRE)'s dam, Ski For Me, won over 1m as a juvenile, so looks sure to improve over longer trips. This daughter of Night Shift is going the right way and should be kept on the right side. (op 25-1)
Celtic Slipper(IRE) is a 40,000gns daughter of the top-class sprinter Anabaa, whose progeny often stay farther than he did. Her dam needed at least 1m, so improvement can be expected over longer trips, and this debut offered plenty of encouragement.

Moonlight Angel, a 36,000gns daughter of top-class sprinter Kyllachy, and out of a mare who needed 1m, made a promising debut and should improve with experience. (op 10-1 tchd 12-1)
Relinquished was held when hampered in the final furlong, but she had run well for a long way and the weight of money suggested she can do better. (op 11-4)
Tenjack Queen(IRE)'s dam Kooyong won over 6f as a juvenile, and this 44,000euros daughter of top-class miler Intikhab has produced some speedy youngsters. Though never in a challenging position, she made an encouraging debut and was not beaten far, so is one to keep tabs on.
Tamara Moon(IRE) has shown some ability in her two races to date, and looks to be one for nursery company after one more run. Official explanation: jockey said filly was denied a clear run (tchd 28-1)

2458 10TH YEAR OF THE DAVID WOODHOUSE BIRTHDAY H'CAP 7f
7:50 (7:53) (Class 5) (0-75,73) 4-Y-O+ £2,914 (£867; £433; £216) Stalls High

Form				RPR
5043	1		**Ivory Lace**[6] 2272 6-9-6 72 JimCrowley 8 (S Woodman) *w.w in midfield: pushed along over 2f out: hdwy 1f out: swtchd rt ins fnl f: qcknd to ld wl ins fnl f: r.o wl* **7/1**	87+
-440	2	1 1/4	**Fiefdom (IRE)**[36] 1458 5-9-7 73 SebSanders 1 (I W McInnes) *chsd ldrs: wnt 2nd 2f out: rdn to ld over 1f out: hdd wl ins fnl f: nt pce of wnr nr fin* **11/4**[1]	82
0-30	3	1 1/2	**Torquemada (IRE)**[18] 1931 6-8-12 64 PaulDoe 2 (W Jarvis) *stdd s: t.k.h: hld up: hdwy over 2f out: rdn to chal 1f out: no ex last 100yds* **9/2**[3]	69
3241	4	1 1/4	**Everygrainofsand (IRE)**[7] 2242 4-9-6 72 DaneO'Neill 7 (J R Best) *led: rdn over 2f out: hdd over 1f out: btn whn bmpd ins fnl f* **10/3**[2]	74
4-00	5	nk	**Lincolneurocruiser**[9] 2189 5-9-1 72 ColinHaddon(5) 4 (Mrs N Macauley) *hld up in rr: swtchd lft and hdwy over 1f out: no imp last 100yds* **33/1**	73
4520	6	1 1/4	**Border Artist**[21] 1847 8-8-10 62 RichardHughes 9 (J Pearce) *trckd ldrs on rail: rdn wl over 1f out: wknd jst ins fnl f* **12/1**	59
0035	7	1/2	**Plateau**[9] 2190 8-9-0 66 JamieSpencer 6 (C R Dore) *s.i.s: hld up bhd: rdn and effrt 2f out: sn no imp* **8/1**	62
00-0	8	2	**Goodenough Mover**[21] 1847 11-9-1 67 HayleyTurner 5 (Andrew Turnell) *chsd ldr tl 2f out: sn rdn and wknd* **16/1**	58
1360	9	1	**Special Place**[21] 1845 4-8-12 64 EddieAhern 3 (J A R Toller) *racd in midfield: rdn 3f out: wknd over 1f out* **8/1**	52

1m 22.55s (-1.66) **Going Correction** -0.25s/f (Firm) 9 Ran SP% **119.2**
Speed ratings (Par 103):99,97,95,94,94 92,92,89,88
CSF £27.51 CT £99.40 TOTE £5.50: £1.90, £1.70, £2.10; EX 23.00.
Owner Sally Woodman J Lenaghan D Mortimer **Bred** D R Tucker **Trained** East Lavant, W Sussex

FOCUS
A routine handicap, but containing a couple of nicely handicapped runners who are returning to their best. Sound enough form.

2459 WORKFORCE WINDOW FILLIES' H'CAP 5f
8:25 (8:26) (Class 5) (0-70,62) 3-Y-O+ £2,817 (£838; £418; £209) Stalls High

Form				RPR
0213	1		**Matterofact (IRE)**[5] 2315 4-9-12 60 SebSanders 10 (M S Saunders) *mde all: hung lft thrght: rdn wl over 1f out: styd on wl* **5/4**[1]	73+
1340	2	1 1/2	**Ashes (IRE)**[22] 1806 5-10-0 62 HayleyTurner 9 (K R Burke) *taken down early: trckd ldrs: hdwy to chse wnr over 2f out: sn rdn: kpt on same pce fnl f* **6/1**[3]	69
4045	3	nk	**Cosmic Destiny (IRE)**[8] 2221 5-9-2 50 JimCrowley 1 (E F Vaughan) *hld up in tch: hdwy over 2f out: rdn to chal over 1f out: kpt on same pce fnl f* **9/2**[2]	56
5554	4	1/2	**Lady Hopeful (IRE)**[9] 2174 5-8-8 45 (b) PatrickMathers(3) 5 (Peter Grayson) *sn outpcd and bhd: hdwy over 1f out: r.o fnl f: nrst fin* **16/1**	49
00-0	5	3	**Jucebabe**[24] 1766 4-9-8 56 AdamKirby 3 (J L Spearing) *sn bhd: rdn 2f out: sme late hdwy: nvr on terms* **12/1**	49
5204	6	1 1/4	**Temtation (IRE)**[8] 2195 3-8-12 53 (b[1]) FrankieMcDonald 6 (Peter Grayson) *chsd ldrs: rdn and hung lft over 1f out: sn btn* **25/1**	38
0-61	7	1 3/4	**Divalini**[6] 2276 3-9-0 55 6ex RichardHughes 4 (J Akehurst) *prom: rdn over 2f out: wknd wl over 1f out* **7/1**	33
-406	8	1	**Supreme Kiss**[8] 2217 4-8-9 50 (b) MCGeran(7) 7 (Mrs N Smith) *v.s.a: nvr on terms* **11/1**	28
06-6	9	1 3/4	**Autumn Storm**[46] 1213 3-8-13 54 EddieAhern 8 (R Ingram) *chsd ldr tl 1/2-way: sn rdn and wknd* **25/1**	22
060-	10	1 3/4	**Birbalini**[295] 4556 4-8-8 45 StephaneBreux(3) 2 (J R Best) *sn struggling in rr: no ch fr 1/2-way* **33/1**	9

57.59 secs (-1.35) **Going Correction** -0.25s/f (Firm)
WFA 3 from 4yo+ 7lb 10 Ran SP% **122.0**
Speed ratings (Par 100):100,97,97,96,91 89,86,85,82,79
CSF £9.44 CT £29.03 TOTE £2.60: £1.10, £2.10, £1.90; EX 7.30 Place 6 £103.20, Place 5 £47.71..
Owner Prempro Racing **Bred** Tony Gleeson **Trained** Green Ore, Somerset

FOCUS
A modest fillies-only sprint, but containing some experienced performers of their type. Improved form from the winner, with the runner-up to this year's turf form and the third to the level she showed over the course and distance last year.
Divalini Official explanation: jockey said filly ran flat
T/Plt: £140.70 to a £1 stake. Pool: £55,394.35. 287.40 winning tickets. T/Qpdt: £33.30 to a £1 stake. Pool: £4,210.50. 93.45 winning tickets. SP

2244 MUSSELBURGH (R-H)
Saturday, June 9

OFFICIAL GOING: Good (good to firm in places on round course; 9.0)
Wind: Virtually nil Weather: Fine

2460 E B F / BALFOUR KILPATRICK SUPPLY CHAIN MEDIAN AUCTION MAIDEN STKS 5f
2:15 (2:15) (Class 5) 2-Y-O £3,886 (£1,156; £577; £288) Stalls Low

Form				RPR
4	1		**Victorian Bounty**[6] 2271 2-9-3 0 JoeFanning 4 (E J O'Neill) *hld up: swtchd to outside and gd hdwy 2f out: rdn to ld over 1f out: styd on wl* **9/1**	75
23	2	1 3/4	**Rebel Aclaim (IRE)**[29] 1636 2-8-9 0 JerryO'Dwyer(3) 2 (M G Quinlan) *led: rdn along 2f out: hdd appr fnl f: sn drvn and kpt on same pce* **2/1**[2]	64
6	3	hd	**Do As I Say**[14] 2024 2-9-3 0 DavidAllan 5 (T D Easterby) *cl up: effrt 2f out: sn pushed along and and ev ch tl kpt on same pce fnl f* **5/1**[3]	68
54	4	1 1/2	**Angle Of Attack (IRE)**[14] 2021 2-9-3 0 PaulHanagan 1 (R A Fahey) *trckd ldrs: rdn along 2f out: sn no imp* **15/8**[1]	63+
	5	3/4	**The Game** 2-9-3 0 PatCosgrave 3 (J R Boyle) *cl up: rdn along and edgd rt 2f out: sn wknd* **13/2**	60

61.56 secs (1.06) **Going Correction** -0.10s/f (Good) 5 Ran SP% **108.1**
Speed ratings (Par 93):87,84,83,81,80
CSF £26.32 TOTE £11.80: £4.60, £1.40; EX 31.20.
Owner Victory Racing **Bred** Mrs P D Gray And Mr H Farr **Trained** Averham Park, Notts

FOCUS
A moderate juvenile maiden, run at a solid early pace. Guessy form, rated through the runner-up and fourth.

NOTEBOOK
Victorian Bounty got off the mark at the second attempt with a ready display. He enjoyed the switch to a more conventional track, looked better the further he went this time, and should improve a deal again for this experience. (op 7-1)
Rebel Aclaim(IRE) again set off at a decent pace and paid for her early exertions at the business end of the race. She is now looking rather exposed, but has done little wrong in her career to date and looks worth a try over another furlong now. (op 7-4)
Do As I Say, sixth in a much better race at Beverley on his debut a fortnight previously, had every chance but again left the impression this experience would be to his benefit. (op 15-2)
Angle Of Attack(IRE), well backed, had the benefit of a rail to race against this time yet failed to raise his game and was below his recent level. He has a bit to prove now. (op 9-4)
The Game, whose sales price nearly doubled at the breeze-ups, has a pedigree that suggests a mix of speed and stamina. He showed early pace before tiring and should last a little longer next time. (op 6-1)

2461 SMIRNOFF SPRINT TROPHY H'CAP 5f
2:45 (2:45) (Class 3) 3-Y-O+ £9,348 (£2,799; £1,399; £700; £349; £175) Stalls Low

Form				RPR
1-12	1		**How's She Cuttin' (IRE)**[7] 2244 4-9-3 73 (b[1]) PhillipMakin 12 (T D Barron) *trckd ldrs: gd hdwy to ld over 1f out: rdn and hung bdly rt ins fnl f: jst hld on* **3/1**[2]	86+
-630	2	nk	**Blazing Heights**[7] 2244 4-9-1 78 GaryBartley(7) 10 (J S Goldie) *hld up in tch: gd hdwy over 2f out: rdn to chse wnr ins fnl f: kpt on wl: jst failed* **11/1**	90
0-60	3	1 3/4	**Puskas (IRE)**[25] 1754 4-9-3 78 KevinGhunowa(5) 13 (J M Bradley) *chsd ldrs on outer: rdn wl over 1f out: kpt on same pce ins fnl f* **16/1**	84
1051	4	1 1/4	**Raccoon (IRE)**[7] 2244 7-9-4 79 PJMcDonald(5) 2 (D W Chapman) *led: rdn along and hdd wl over 1f out: sn drvn and one pce* **11/4**[1]	81
-020	5	shd	**Compton Classic**[19] 1891 5-7-12 54 oh4 (p) SilvestreDeSousa 3 (J S Goldie) *cl up: rdn along 2f out: sn drvn and grad wknd* **25/1**	55
5505	6	nk	**Ptarmigan Ridge**[7] 2244 11-8-11 70 GregFairley(3) 4 (Miss L A Perratt) *trckd ldrs: effrt and n.m.r over 1f out: sn rdn and kpt on same pce* **16/1**	70
0-00	7	nk	**Strawberry Patch (IRE)**[2] 2386 8-7-9 54 (p) DuranFentiman(3) 8 (J S Goldie) *sn outpcd in rr: swtchd rt and hdwy 2f out: kpt on appr fnl f: nrst fin* **14/1**	53
4002	8	shd	**Kings College Boy**[9] 2191 7-8-9 65 (b) PaulHanagan 6 (R A Fahey) *hdwy to chse ldrs over 2f out: sn rdn and no imp appr fnl f* **8/1**	64
0004	9	1 3/4	**Deserted Dane (USA)**[10] 2135 3-9-5 82 DeanMcKeown 11 (G A Swinbank) *prom: rdn along wl over 1f out: sn wknd* **20/1**	74
4310	10	3/4	**Whinhill House**[1] 2418 7-8-7 63 ow3 (v) PatCosgrave 1 (D W Barker) *dwlt: sn cl up: rdn along 2f out and sn wknd* **7/1**[3]	53
0336	11	nk	**Rothesay Dancer**[7] 2249 4-7-12 54 oh2 PaulQuinn 9 (J S Goldie) *a towards rr* **40/1**	43
-010	12	1 1/2	**Oranmore Castle (IRE)**[21] 1853 5-9-10 80 AdrianTNicholls 7 (D Nicholls) *dwlt: a towards rr* **14/1**	63
0-00	13	5	**Mister Marmaduke**[7] 2244 6-8-1 57 oh9 ow3 RoystonFfrench 5 (D A Nolan) *s.i.s: a in rr* **200/1**	22

59.72 secs (-0.78) **Going Correction** -0.10s/f (Good)
WFA 3 from 4yo+ 7lb 13 Ran SP% **120.3**
Speed ratings (Par 107):102,101,98,96,96 96,95,95,92,91 90,88,80
CSF £35.32 CT £373.27 TOTE £4.20: £1.90, £2.70, £4.30; EX 50.80.
Owner Chris McHale **Bred** A M Burke **Trained** Maunby, N Yorks

FOCUS
A consolation race for horses which failed to make the cut in the Scottish Sprint Cup, and a competitive sprint for the grade. The first two finished nicely clear. Solid form which should prove reliable. The progressive winner is up 5lb.

NOTEBOOK
How's She Cuttin'(IRE), equipped with first-time blinkers, got back to winning ways with another improved effort despite again hanging to her right when under maximum pressure late on. It is hard to know just how much more progression she has left in her, but she is at the top of her game at present and is developing into a very likeable sprinter. (op 4-1)
Blazing Heights showed his true colours and was just denied by the progressive winner. He was nicely clear of the remainder in second, and is still evidently capable of defying this sort of mark when in the mood, but his inconsistency at present dictates he is not really one for win-only purposes. (op 12-1)
Puskas(IRE) posted by far his best effort to date for current connections. He had lost his way after a decent juvenile campaign, but has fallen in the handicap as a result and surely his trainer will find a winning opportunity for him during the summer months.
Raccoon(IRE), up another 7lb for scoring over course and distance a week previously, showed his customary early dash and did little wrong in defeat. He remains in good heart. (tchd 3-1)
Strawberry Patch(IRE) struggled to go the early pace, but he picked up strongly nearing the final furlong and this was a much more encouraging effort in defeat. He seems to save his best for this track and looks well worth another try over a sixth furlong now. (op 25-1)

2462 BENTLEY EDINBURGH GRAND CUP STKS (LISTED RACE) 1m 6f
3:15 (3:15) (Class 1) 4-Y-O+ £15,898 (£6,025; £3,015; £1,503; £753) Stalls High

Form				RPR
3-32	1		**Balkan Knight**[11] 2125 7-9-0 105 JohnEgan 2 (D R C Elsworth) *hld up: hdwy over 3f out and sn pushed along: effrt to chse wnr wl over 1fout: drvn ins fnl f: styd on to ld nr line* **6/4**[2]	112
1-05	2	hd	**Alfie Flits**[8] 2216 5-9-3 114 NCallan 5 (G A Swinbank) *trckd wnr: hdwy 3f out: led 2f out and sn clr: rdn ins fnl f: drvn: hdd and nt qckn nr fin* **1/1**[1]	115
/06-	3	8	**Golden Quest**[291] 4677 6-9-0 106 JoeFanning 1 (M Johnston) *trckd ldng pair: hdwy and cl up 4f out: led 3f out: rdn and hdd 2f out: sn drvn and one pce* **7/1**[3]	101

0-53 **4** *4* **Acropolis (IRE)**[22] 1805 6-9-0 94.. TomEaves 3 95
(I Semple) *trckd ldrs: effrt 3f out: sn rdn along and no hdwy* **20/1**

-464 **5** *33* **Hovering (IRE)**[34] 1518 4-8-9 91.................................... JerryO'Dwyer 4 44
(M G Quinlan) *led and sn clr: rdn along over 4f out: hdd 3f out and sn wknd* **40/1**

3m 1.62s (-4.08) **Going Correction** -0.10s/f (Good) **5** Ran SP% **109.7**
Speed ratings (Par 111):107,106,102,100,81
CSF £3.30 TOTE £2.10: £1.50, £1.10; EX 3.90.
Owner Raymond Tooth **Bred** Sheikh Mohammed Bin Rashid Al Maktoum **Trained** Newmarket, Suffolk

FOCUS
A good little staying Listed contest, run at a sound pace, and good form for the grade. The two market leaders came well clear.

NOTEBOOK
Balkan Knight, who recorded a career-best effort when runner-up in the Group 2 Henry II Stakes at Sandown 11 days previously, was given a peach of a ride from Egan and just did enough to regain winning ways on this drop back in trip. He needs producing as late as possible in his races and, while opportunities are not easy to find for him, he deserved this success and remains right at the top of his game. (op 13-8 tchd 7-4)

Alfie Flits was produced to have every chance and did little wrong in defeat, but simply found the concession of weight to the winner beyond him. He got the trip without fuss and was well clear of the remainder at the finish. (op 5-6)

Golden Quest, making his seasonal return, was given a positive ride and shaped as though the run was needed. He has yet to really prove that he is the force of old, but he can build on this encouraging reappearance. (op 10-1)

Acropolis(IRE) failed to really raise his game for the step up to this longer trip. He faced a stiff task at the weights, however. (op 18-1 tchd 16-1)

2463 GNER SCOTTISH SPRINT CUP (HERITAGE H'CAP) 5f
3:45 (3:46) (Class 2) (0-105,105) 3-Y-0+
£31,160 (£9,330; £4,665; £2,335; £1,165; £585) **Stalls** Low

Form RPR

-130 **1** **Aegean Dancer**[21] 1854 5-8-1 82................................ RoystonFfrench 8 94+
(B Smart) *a.p: led over 1f out: sn rdn and hung lft ins fnl f: styd on* **10/1**[3]

6045 **2** *1* **Celtic Mill**[34] 1497 9-9-7 102..(p) PatCosgrave 11 110
(D W Barker) *cl up: ev ch over 1f out: sn rdn and kpt on wl fnl f* **14/1**

2300 **3** *nk* **Bond City (IRE)**[7] 2234 5-9-0 102.............................. NeilBrown(7) 12 109
(G R Oldroyd) *hld up in midfield: gd hdwy 2f out: rdn ent fnl f and kpt on wl* **11/1**

-503 **4** *½* **Fullandby (IRE)**[28] 1651 5-8-9 93.................................. GregFairley(3) 3 98+
(T J Etherington) *sn pushed along in rr: hdwy 2f out: rdn and styd on strly ins fnl f* **17/2**[2]

0-31 **5** *¾* **The Tatling (IRE)**[36] 1456 10-9-0 100..................... KevinGhunowa(5) 13 103
(J M Bradley) *chsd ldrs: hdwy on wd outside 2f out: rdn and ev ch over 1f out: drvn and one pce ins fnl f* **4/1**[1]

0400 **6** *nk* **Tournedos (IRE)**[7] 2237 5-9-0 95............................... AdrianTNicholls 14 96
(D Nicholls) *towards rr: hdwy 2f out: rdn over 1f out: styd on ins fnl f: nrst fin* **10/1**[3]

0004 **7** *nk* **Fantasy Believer**[7] 2237 9-9-4 99................................ TonyHamilton 6 99+
(J J Quinn) *outpcd and rdn along in rr: hdwy over 1f out: styd on wl fnl f* **10/1**[3]

4106 **8** *shd* **Harry Up**[21] 1853 6-8-8 89 ow1... NCallan 9 89
(K A Ryan) *led: rdn along and hdd over 1f out: sn wknd* **33/1**

0314 **9** *shd* **Magic Glade**[15] 1986 8-8-11 92.. JoeFanning 15 92
(Tom Dascombe) *chsd ldrs: rdn along 2f out: grad wknd appr fnl f* **16/1**

2420 **10** *1 ½* **Handsome Cross (IRE)**[7] 2234 6-8-7 88................. SilvestreDeSousa 2 82
(D Nicholls) *chsd ldrs: rdn along 2f out: sn wknd* **10/1**[3]

20-5 **11** *shd* **Orientor**[14] 2034 9-8-12 100.. GaryBartley(7) 16 94
(J S Goldie) *bhd tl sme late hdwy* **25/1**

5-30 **12** *shd* **Fonthill Road (IRE)**[24] 1770 7-9-10 105....................... PaulHanagan 17 99
(R A Fahey) *a towards rr* **12/1**

-100 **13** *hd* **Geojimali**[28] 1653 5-8-3 87 ow2................................... SaleemGolam(3) 5 80
(J S Goldie) *s.i.s: a towards rr* **14/1**

-222 **14** *1* **River Falcon**[14] 2034 7-9-3 98... PhillipMakin 1 87
(J S Goldie) *a towards rr* **11/1**

0424 **15** *hd* **Spanish Ace**[8] 2197 6-8-7 88 ow1...................................... TomEaves 10 76
(J M Bradley) *a towards rr* **40/1**

/00- **16** *hd* **Nota Bene**[399] 1485 5-9-10 105.. AntonyProcter 7 93
(D R C Elsworth) *cl up: rdn along over 2f out and sn wknd* **28/1**

4520 **17** *2* **Bluebok**[15] 1986 6-8-1 85..(t) DuranFentiman(3) 4 66
(J M Bradley) *bmpd s: sn prom: rdn along 1/2-way: sn wknd* **20/1**

58.93 secs (-1.57) **Going Correction** -0.10s/f (Good) **17** Ran SP% **127.9**
Speed ratings (Par 109):108,106,105,105,103 103,102,102,102,100 100,99,99,98,97 97,94
CSF £140.20 CT £1599.28 TOTE £12.50: £2.50, £3.30, £4.80, £2.70; EX 227.80 Trifecta £4976.00 Pool: £23,829.07 - 3.40 winning units..
Owner Pinnacle Piccolo Partnership **Bred** Theobalds Stud **Trained** Hambleton, N Yorks

FOCUS
A very competitive sprint for the class. The form looks solid rated through the placed horses. The progressive Aegean Dancer is up another 7lb.

NOTEBOOK
Aegean Dancer ran out a comfortable winner under bottom weight on this step up in class. He has been in good form since resuming this season, but this was by far his best effort to date and there is no doubt he is a progressive five-year-old. The Handicapper will have his say after this, but the way he travelled here suggests we have yet to see the best of him. (tchd 11-1)

Celtic Mill, with his usual cheekpieces back on for this return to handicap company, showed his customary early pace and ran with credit in defeat. This was certainly no disgrace in conceding the progressive winner so much weight and he is still very much in love with his racing. (op 16-1)

Bond City(IRE) fared the best of those who came from off the pace and posted a solid effort in defeat. He simply looks held by the Handicapper and rates a decent benchmark for this form. (op 12-1)

Fullandby(IRE) ◆ was doing his best work towards the finish and really needs another furlong to be seen at his best. This was a fine effort in the circumstances and his turn is not too far off again. (op 9-1)

The Tatling(IRE), back to winning ways over course and distance 36 days previously, had his chance and did nothing wrong in defeat. He is another who gives this form a solid look. (op 11-2 tchd 6-1 in places)

Tournedos(IRE) is better when ridden with patience, which was not the case at Epsom a week previously over 6f, and he was doing his best work towards the finish on this drop to the minimum trip. Similar tactics back over another furlong should see him get closer again. (tchd 9-1)

Fantasy Believer not surprisingly got himself outpaced over this inadequate test, but he finished his race with some promise and looks to be coming back to himself again now. One to keep an eye on.

2464 STEPHEN HAY AND ASSOCIATES LTD MAIDEN STKS 1m 1f
4:20 (4:20) (Class 5) 3-Y-0+ **£3,886** (£1,156; £577; £288) **Stalls** High

Form RPR

5 **1** **Pathos (GER)**[15] 2005 3-9-0 0... AntonyProcter 5 80+
(D R C Elsworth) *hld up in rr: hdwy 3f out: effrt and nt clr run wl over 1f out: swtchd lft and n.m.r over 1f out: sn rdn and styd on to ld nr fin* **3/1**[2]

4324 **2** *hd* **Arena's Dream (USA)**[12] 2092 3-9-0 71............................ PaulHanagan 1 73
(R A Fahey) *led: rdn along over 2f out: drvn and edgd lft ins fnl f: hdd and no ex nr fin* **9/2**[3]

0-2 **3** *2 ½* **Freya Tricks**[22] 1804 3-8-9 0... TomEaves 8 63
(I Semple) *hld up in tch: hdwy 3f out: rdn to chal wl over 1f out and ev ch tl drvn and hung lft ins fnl f: sn wknd* **3/1**[2]

5-6 **4** *3* **The Quantum Kid**[49] 1153 3-9-0 0.................................. RoystonFfrench 6 61
(T J Etherington) *chsd ldrs on inner: rdn along over 3f out and sn wknd* **25/1**

045- **5** *5* **Private Reason (USA)**[235] 6023 3-9-0 73.............................. NCallan 2 50
(K A Ryan) *chsd ldrs: effrt 3f out and ev ch tl rdn 2f out and sn wknd* **11/1**

05 **6** *2 ½* **Caluba**[15] 1995 3-8-9 0.. PatCosgrave 3 40
(K R Burke) *t.k.h: chsd ldr: effrt to chal 3f out and ev ch tl rdn 2f out and sn wknd* **20/1**

4-22 **7** *1 ½* **Stark Contrast (USA)**[44] 1259 3-9-0 76...........................(t) JohnEgan 4 41
(G A Butler) *chsd ldrs: effrt 3f out: sn rdn and wknd wl over 1f out* **9/4**[1]

1m 54.91s (1.05) **Going Correction** -0.10s/f (Good) **7** Ran SP% **115.9**
Speed ratings (Par 103):91,90,88,85,81 79,77
CSF £17.38 TOTE £4.50: £2.30, £2.50; EX 16.20.
Owner D R C Elsworth **Bred** K Nercessian **Trained** Newmarket, Suffolk

FOCUS
A modest maiden, run at an average pace. The first pair came clear and the winner is value for a little further. The third and the favourite were not at their best and the runner-up is the best guide.

2465 CHAMPAGNE POMMERY H'CAP 1m 6f
4:55 (4:55) (Class 4) (0-85,83) 4-Y-0+ **£6,232** (£1,866; £933; £467) **Stalls** High

Form RPR

-636 **1** **Oddsmaker (IRE)**[52] 1090 6-8-8 70..............................(t) DeanMcKeown 3 77
(M A Barnes) *set stdy pce: qckng 5f out: qcknd again over 3f out: rdn along 2f out and styd on wl* **2/1**[1]

4441 **2** *4* **Mister Arjay (USA)**[12] 2095 7-8-10 77........................... PJMcDonald(5) 1 78
(B Ellison) *chsd wnr: rdn along 4f out: drvn over 2f out: kpt on u.p fnl f* **5/2**[2]

50-1 **3** *5* **Stretton (IRE)**[29] 1621 9-9-7 83.. NCallan 2 77
(J D Bethell) *hld up: effrt and hdwy 3f out: sn rdn and no imp fnl 2f* **9/2**[3]

0-01 **4** *hd* **Alfonso**[10] 1598 6-8-7 69... PatCosgrave 4 63
(P Monteith) *trckd ldng pair: hdwy 3f out: rdn over 2f out: sn drvn and btn* **5/2**[2]

3m 4.39s (-1.31) **Going Correction** -0.10s/f (Good) **4** Ran SP% **108.7**
Speed ratings (Par 105):99,96,93,93
CSF £7.19 TOTE £2.70; EX 6.40.
Owner D Maloney **Bred** Margaret Conlon **Trained** Farlam, Cumbria

FOCUS
This staying handicap proved a tactical affair and the winner made all under a shrewd ride. It is doubtful if he had to improve, with the runner-up 3lb off his latest form and the other pair disappointing.

2466 NABCAPITAL H'CAP 7f 30y
5:25 (5:25) (Class 4) (0-85,91) 4-Y-0+ **£5,505** (£1,637; £818; £408) **Stalls** High

Form RPR

2413 **1** **H Harrison (IRE)**[1] 2419 7-8-3 70.................................... GregFairley(3) 6 89
(I W McInnes) *cl up: effrt 3f out: rdn to ld 2f out: carried hd high and drvn clr ent fnl f: styd on* **7/1**

0641 **2** *6* **Viva Volta**[7] 2256 4-8-10 74..(b) DavidAllan 10 77
(T D Easterby) *led: pushed along 3f out: rdn and hdd 2f out: kpt on same pce appr fnl f* **15/2**

6301 **3** *2* **Royal Dignitary (USA)**[3] 2374 7-9-13 91 6ex............ AdrianTNicholls 9 88
(D Nicholls) *chsd ldng pair: rdn along wl over 2f out: sn drvn and kpt on same pce* **4/1**[1]

1033 **4** *1 ¾* **Emerald Bay (IRE)**[17] 1939 5-9-7 85.................................. TomEaves 7 78
(I Semple) *dwlt: sn chsng ldrs: rdn along over 2f out and sn one pce* **10/1**

0003 **5** *shd* **Stellite**[12] 2072 7-8-6 70.. PaulHanagan 3 62
(J S Goldie) *hld up towards rr: stdy hdwy on inner over 2f out: rdn and one pce appr fnl f* **16/1**

4-22 **6** *1 ¼* **Angaric (IRE)**[35] 1481 4-8-11 75..................................... RoystonFfrench 1 64
(B Smart) *wnt lft s: sn in tch: hdwy over 3f out: sn rdn and no imp* **9/2**[2]

0063 **7** *nk* **Blue Tomato**[16] 1971 6-8-11 80................................ KevinGhunowa(5) 2 68
(J M Bradley) *sn rdn along and a towards rr* **11/2**[3]

61-1 **8** *1 ½* **La Matanza**[26] 1710 4-8-11 75.. PhillipMakin 5 59
(T D Barron) *hld up: a towards rr* **17/2**

-250 **9** *5* **Electric Warrior (IRE)**[28] 1682 4-9-2 80........................ PatCosgrave 8 51
(K R Burke) *hld up: a towards rr* **10/1**

0-02 **10** *2 ½* **King Harson**[25] 1747 8-8-13 77.. JoeFanning 4 41
(J D Bethell) *chsd ldrs: rdn along 3f out: sn wknd and eased* **12/1**

1m 27.62s (-2.32) **Going Correction** -0.10s/f (Good) **10** Ran SP% **120.1**
Speed ratings (Par 105):109,102,99,97,97 96,95,94,88,85
CSF £60.45 CT £242.86 TOTE £9.20: £2.20, £3.20, £2.30; EX 84.50 Place 6 £161.43, Place 5 £67.46. .
Owner David Lees **Bred** Margaret Conlon **Trained** Catwick, E Yorks

FOCUS
A fair handicap. The winner is full value for his winning margin, running to his best form of the past three years.

T/Plt: £329.20 to a £1 stake. Pool: £81,413.20. 180.50 winning tickets. T/Qpdt: £37.80 to a £1 stake. Pool: £3,500.00. 68.40 winning tickets. JR

1832 NEWBURY (L-H)
Saturday, June 9

OFFICIAL GOING: Good to firm (7.8)
Wind: virtually nil

2467 BATHWICK TYRES LADY RIDERS' H'CAP 1m 2f 6y
6:30 (6:31) (Class 5) (0-70,71) 4-Y-0+ **£3,747** (£1,162; £580; £290) **Stalls** High

Form RPR

231 **1** **Sawwaah (IRE)**[6] 2275 10-10-5 71 6ex.................(v) MissMSowerby(5) 10 86+
(Tom Dascombe) *b: hld up in rr: stdy hdwy fr 3f out to chal on bit 1f out: shkn up and led fnl half f: readily* **4/1**[2]

The Form Book, Raceform Ltd, Compton, RG20 6NL

0/42 **2** *2* **Tizzy May (FR)**[5] [2307] 7-10-9 **70**.................................... MissLEllison 13 78
(B Ellison) *b: trckd ldrs: chal 4f out: led over 3f out: sn hrd drvn: hdd and one pce last half f* **3/1**[1]

2-00 **3** *1 1/2* **Cormorant Wharf (IRE)**[13] [2055] 7-10-3 **69** ow3.......... MissJPowell(5) 4 74
(T E Powell) *lw: in rr: c wd and hdwy over 2f out: kpt on fnl f but nvr gng pce to chal* **9/1**

4225 **4** *nk* **Murrumbidgee (IRE)**[8] [2214] 4-10-1 **62**.......................... MissEJJones 7 66
(J W Hills) *hld up in rr: stdy hdwy fr 3f out: pressed ldrs over 1f out: kpt on same pce ins fnl f* **9/1**

-310 **5** *shd* **Royal Flynn**[7] [2254] 5-10-6 **67**... MrsCBartley 2 71
(M Dods) *in rr: hdwy on ins 4f out: kpt on fnl 2f but nvr quite gng pce to chal* **8/1**[3]

-465 **6** *hd* **Gallego**[8] [2194] 5-9-8 **60**.. MissABevan(5) 11 64
(R J Price) *lw: in rr: c wd and hdwy over 2f out: kpt on fnl f but nvr gng pce to chal* **11/1**

2153 **7** *3* **Majehar**[73] [809] 5-9-8 **55**... MissCHannaford 1 53
(A G Newcombe) *chsd ldrs: rdn and outpcd 3f out: kpt on again ins fnl f* **17/2**

1125 **8** *3* **Scottish River (USA)**[22] [1811] 8-10-2 **66**................. MissEFolkes(3) 5 58
(M D I Usher) *lw: in rr: hdwy over 2f out: sn chsng ldrs but nvr quite gng pce to be competitive* **12/1**

5605 **9** *3 1/2* **Lady's Law**[13] [2055] 4-8-11 **51** oh6......................... MissFGuillambert(7) 3 36
(Rae Guest) *chsd ldrs: rdn 3f out: wknd fr 2f out* **33/1**

2-60 **10** *nk* **Mucho Loco (IRE)**[19] [1906] 4-9-4 **51** oh4..................(b) MissSBeddoes 6 35
(R Curtis) *in rr: c wd home st and mod hdwy fnl 2f* **50/1**

-500 **11** *5* **Barathea Dreams (IRE)**[8] [2218] 6-10-5 **66**..................(p) MrsSBosley 9 40
(J S Moore) *chsd ldrs: rdn 3f out: sn wknd* **20/1**

0010 **12** *3/4* **Monashee River (IRE)**[1] [2431] 4-9-4 **51**................. MissFayeBramley 12 24
(Miss V Haigh) *sn led: hdd over 3f out: wknd 2f out* **25/1**

0404 **13** *2 1/2* **Valart**[18] [1926] 4-9-4 **56**...(tp) MissZoeLilly(5) 8 24
(A J Lidderdale) *chsd ldr: led over 6f out: hdd over 3f out: sn btn* **14/1**

506 **14** *4* **Alexian**[13] [2055] 4-9-11 **65**.. BrydieKilloran(7) 15 25
(D W P Arbuthnot) *bhd fr 1/2-way* **16/1**

366- **15** *11* **Divine River**[254] [5644] 4-10-4 **70**............................... MissKellyBurke(5) 14 8
(A P Jarvis) *s.i.s: sn in tch: chsd ldrs 5f out: c wd and wknd fr 3f out* **16/1**

2m 6.47s (-2.24) **Going Correction** -0.175s/f (Firm) **15** Ran SP% **134.6**
Speed ratings (Par 103):101,99,98,97,97 97,95,92,90,89 85,85,83,80,71
CSF £17.73 CT £113.30 TOTE £5.00: £1.70, £2.10, £3.30; EX 19.40.
Owner Alan Solomon **Bred** Shadwell Estate Company Limited **Trained** Lambourn, Berks

FOCUS
The leaders went off much too fast in this handicap and five of the first six home came from well off the pace. Sound form, more reliable than most races of this type, with the third the best guide.

2468 BETFAIR MAIDEN AUCTION FILLIES' STKS 6f 8y
7:00 (7:02) (Class 4) 2-Y-O **£6,477** (£1,927; £963; £481) **Stalls** Centre

Form RPR

1 **Fanatical** 2-8-3 0.. RichardKingscote(3) 7 84+
(E F Vaughan) *athletic: b.off hind: mde all: drvn and styd on strly fr over 1f out* **25/1**

2 *1 1/2* **Gypsy Baby (IRE)** 2-8-11 0... TedDurcan 10 80+
(R Hannon) *w'like: lw: s.i.s: pushed along in mid-div 1/2-way: qcknd over 1f out to chse wnr ins fnl f: gng on cl home but a hld* **11/2**

2 **3** *1 1/4* **Miss Versatile (IRE)**[40] [1354] 2-8-4 0.......................... NickyMackay 13 69
(J S Moore) *in tch: hdwy and drvn 2f out: styd on ins fnl f* **9/2**[3]

2 **4** *1 1/2* **I Dont Do Walkin (USA)**[15] [1993] 2-8-8 0................................ RHills 14 68
(B J Meehan) *w'like: scope: chsd ldrs: rdn over 2f out: styd on same pce fnl f* **3/1**[2]

5 *3 1/2* **Talamahana** 2-8-8 0... LPKeniry 9 58
(S Kirk) *str: bit bkwd: in tch: rdn over 2f out: kpt on fnl f but nvr gng pce to be competitive* **25/1**

4 **6** *nk* **Lowry's Art**[23] [1781] 2-8-6 0... WilliamBuick(5) 6 60
(R M Beckett) *lw: sn chsng wnr: rdn over 2f out: wknd fnl f* **2/1**[1]

7 *1/2* **Bahamarama (IRE)** 2-8-6 0.. FergusSweeney 8 53
(J R Boyle) *leggy: chsd ldrs: rdn 2f out: wknd appr fnl f* **25/1**

8 *1 1/4* **Agon Eyes (USA)** 2-8-6 0...................................... EdwardCreighton 11 50
(D J Coakley) *tall: w'like: bit bkwd: in rr: sme prog fnl f* **20/1**

9 *1/2* **Softly Killing Me** 2-8-4 0.. RichardThomas 12 46
(J Gallagher) *w'like: bit bkwd: s.i.s: bhd: kpt on ins fnl f but nvr in contention* **50/1**

10 *1/2* **Ronsai (USA)** 2-8-4 0... MartinDwyer 4 45
(R Hannon) *w'like: in tch: drvn to chse ldrs over 2f out: wknd over 1f out* **14/1**

11 *1* **Meridian Line (IRE)** 2-8-5 0... EmmettStack(3) 2 46
(J G Portman) *w'like: bit bkwd: t.k.h: chsd ldrs: rdn 2f out: sn wknd* **40/1**

4 **12** *hd* **Bunty Malenoir**[15] [2009] 2-7-13 0................................... TolleyDean(5) 5 41
(I A Wood) *leggy: lt-f: a outpcd* **66/1**

13 *nk* **Spectrana** 2-8-6 0.. PaulEddery 16 42
(Mrs A J Perrett) *w'like: bit bkwd: s.i.s: outpcd* **28/1**

14 *1* **Ever Hopeful** 2-8-6 0... JimmyQuinn 3 39
(H J L Dunlop) *mid-div: rdn and sme prog over 2f out: sn wknd* **20/1**

0 **15** *1* **Elegant Step**[14] [2039] 2-7-13 0...................................... JosephWalsh(7) 15 36
(A P Jarvis) *w'like: a wl bhd* **33/1**

1m 13.1s (-1.22) **Going Correction** -0.175s/f (Firm) **15** Ran SP% **131.9**
Speed ratings (Par 92):101,99,97,95,90 90,89,87,87,86 85,85,84,83,81
CSF £157.32 TOTE £50.20: £11.00, £2.20, £2.40; EX 280.60.
Owner C J Murfitt **Bred** Bearstone Stud **Trained** Newmarket, Suffolk

FOCUS
Probably a fair fillies' maiden and a taking performance from the winner, who made every yard and was value for at least 3l. The form looks sound enough.

NOTEBOOK
Fanatical ◆, whose dam was unraced but is a half-sister to Sadima, a 1m2f winner at three and later dam of top-class 1m4f colt Youmzain, and miler Creachadoir, showed bags of toe and was in control throughout. Her rider eased her down in the end but she was value for more like four lengths, and she looks a sprinting juvenile to follow, capable of paying her way at Pattern level. The Empress Stakes at Newmarket was mentioned. (op 20-1)
Gypsy Baby(IRE), a half-sister to Embossed, a 7f winner at two and later a three-time winner between 9f and 1m4f in the US, ran a promising race on her debut and, although she is flattered by her proximity to the eased-down winner, there should be a maiden in her as she beat two horses into third and fourth that brought fair form to the race. (op 5-1 tchd 4-1 and 6-1)
Miss Versatile(IRE), runner-up on her debut at Windsor, got the extra furlong well enough and her performance gives the form a fairly solid look. She might be more of a nursery type in time. Official explanation: jockey said filly hung left-handed (op 10-3 tchd 6-1)
I Dont Do Walkin(USA), who had shaped as though she would appreciate this step up in trip on her debut at Haydock, also ran a second race, having been given every chance. (op 4-1 tchd 11-4)
Talamahana, a half-sister to Captain Saif, a triple 7f winner at two, and Futures Dream, a triple winner over 1m at three and four, looked as though she would come on for the run beforehand. This was a promising debut and she should improve. (tchd 22-1)
Lowry's Art failed to progress from her debut effort and did not seem to get home over the extra furlong, despite her breeding suggesting she would improve for it. (op 10-3 tchd 7-2)

2469 WEDGEWOOD ESTATES H'CAP 1m (S)
7:30 (7:32) (Class 4) (0-85,83) 4-Y-O+ **£5,505** (£1,637; £818; £408) **Stalls** Centre

Form RPR

00-0 **1** **Habshan (USA)**[38] [1395] 7-9-5 **81**... GeorgeBaker 5 92
(C F Wall) *in tch: hdwy 3f out: chal 2f out: sn rdn to ld: drvn out fnl f* **14/1**

5-01 **2** *1 1/4* **Nawaqees**[16] [1962] 4-9-3 **79**.. RHills 11 87+
(J L Dunlop) *in rr: hdwy whn nt clr run ins fnl 2f: squeezed through and r.o wl fnl f to take 2nd but no ch w wnr* **9/2**[2]

33-5 **3** *1/2* **Gaelic Princess**[28] [1649] 7-9-4 **80**.............................. FergusSweeney 10 87
(A G Newcombe) *in tch: rdn and hdwy over 1f out: kpt on ins fnl f: gng on cl home* **16/1**

6252 **4** *1 1/4* **Cross The Line (IRE)**[38] [1395] 5-9-6 **82**......................... JHBowman 4 86
(A P Jarvis) *s.i.s: hdwy fr 3f out: kpt on u.p fnl f but nvr gng pce to rch ldrs* **4/1**[1]

0-31 **5** *1* **Ashes Regained**[19] [1905] 4-9-7 **83**.............................. KerrinMcEvoy 15 85
(B W Hills) *in tch: hdwy fr 2f out: styd on same pce ins fnl f* **7/1**[3]

0610 **6** *shd* **Bold Diktator**[9] [2180] 5-9-3 **79**................................... RichardThomas 1 80
(Tom Dascombe) *chsd ldrs: rdn to chal 2f out: wknd fnl f* **16/1**

1100 **7** *1 3/4* **Lopinot (IRE)**[16] [1962] 4-9-4 **80**.. TedDurcan 2 77
(P J Makin) *stdd s: towards rr: rdn and sme hdwy fr 2f out: nvr gng pce to be competitive* **20/1**

00-4 **8** *2* **Tempsford Flyer (IRE)**[19] [1905] 4-9-2 **78**.................................. TQuinn 13 71
(J W Hills) *in rr: rdn and styd on u.p fr 2f out: nvr gng pce to be competitive* **9/1**

60-0 **9** *1 3/4* **Glenmuir (IRE)**[54] [1060] 4-8-12 **77**.................(b[1]) RichardKingscote(3) 12 66
(B R Millman) *led after 2f: rdn ins fnl 3f: hdd jst ins fnl 2f: sn btn* **28/1**

6-22 **10** *shd* **Barons Spy (IRE)**[14] [2038] 6-7-7 **74**................................ TolleyDean(5) 8 63
(R J Price) *chsd ldrs: rdn over 2f out: sn wknd* **12/1**

225- **11** *1 1/4* **Don Pietro**[212] [6418] 4-9-2 **78**.. MartinDwyer 14 64
(D J Coakley) *t.k.h in rr: sme hdwy over 2f out: sn wknd* **7/1**[3]

0-56 **12** *1* **Cool Ebony**[15] [1481] 4-8-12 **74**.. NickyMackay 3 57
(M Dods) *chsd ldrs: rdn 3f out: wknd over 2f out* **14/1**

-003 **13** *2 1/2* **San Antonio**[15] [2004] 7-8-12 **74**..(p) MickyFenton 7 52
(Mrs P Sly) *led 2f: rdn 3f out: wknd 2f out* **16/1**

5-40 **14** *1* **Macedon**[15] [1996] 4-9-6 **82**.. LPKeniry 9 57
(J S Moore) *lw: mid-div: rdn 3f out: sn bhd* **12/1**

4000 **15** *3* **Chief Commander (FR)**[29] [1619] 4-9-4 **80**....................(p) JimmyQuinn 6 48
(Jane Chapple-Hyam) *t.k.h in mid-div: wknd over 2f out* **33/1**

1m 38.07s (-2.55) **Going Correction** -0.175s/f (Firm) **15** Ran SP% **130.7**
Speed ratings (Par 105):105,103,103,102,101 100,99,97,95,95 94,93,90,89,86
CSF £80.19 CT £1090.67 TOTE £21.60: £6.20, £2.60, £3.20; EX 136.10.
Owner Alan & Jill Smith **Bred** Darley Stud Management, L L C **Trained** Newmarket, Suffolk

FOCUS
A fair handicap and solid form, with the winner and third running to their marks.
Nawaqees Official explanation: jockey said colt had been denied a clear run
Tempsford Flyer(IRE) Official explanation: jockey said gelding hung left
Glenmuir(IRE) Official explanation: jockey said gelding had run too freely
Cool Ebony Official explanation: jockey said gelding had no more to give
Macedon Official explanation: vet said gelding finished lame on the left-fore

2470 R W ARMSTRONG & SONS 50TH ANNIVERSARY MAIDEN STKS 6f 8y
8:00 (8:03) (Class 5) 3-Y-O **£4,857** (£1,445; £722; £360) **Stalls** Centre

Form RPR

3 **1** **Shadow The Wind (IRE)**[13] [2059] 3-9-3 0...................... KerrinMcEvoy 7 70+
(E F Vaughan) *lw: trckd ldrs: chal ins fnl f: styd on strly to ld last strides* **11/8**[1]

65 **2** *hd* **Silca Elegance**[21] [1838] 3-9-3 0... JHBowman 12 69+
(M R Channon) *lw: in rr: gd hdwy fr 2f out: to ld jst ins fnl f: hung lft u.p: kpt on but hdd last strides* **7/1**[3]

3 *1 1/2* **Gimme Some Lovin (IRE)** 3-8-12 0......................... FergusSweeney 9 64+
(D W P Arbuthnot) *unf: scope: bit bkwd: s.i.s: bhd: hdwy and nt clr run over 1f out: swtchd lft and r.o strly fnl f: gng on cl home* **16/1**

0 **4** *1 1/2* **Tamarack (IRE)**[18] [1923] 3-9-3 0...................................... GeorgeBaker 11 60
(W R Muir) *cmpt: in rr: rdn over 2f out: styd on wl: fnl f but nvr gng pce to rch ldrs* **16/1**

00-0 **5** *1/2* **Land Ahoy**[17] [1948] 3-9-3 74.. MartinDwyer 5 59
(D W P Arbuthnot) *led tl hdd jst ins fnl f: sn wknd* **7/1**[3]

0 **6** *1* **Navene (IRE)**[21] [1840] 3-8-12 0..................................... StephenCarson 14 51+
(C F Wall) *lw: s.i.s: t.k.h in rr: sme hdwy whn hmpd jst ins fnl f: rn green after and nvr in contention* **28/1**

7 *1/2* **Le Riche** 3-8-9 0.. RichardKingscote(3) 6 49
(Miss J R Gibney) *leggy: in rr: hdwy over 2f out: kpt on fnl f but nvr gng pce to be competitive* **33/1**

04 **8** *nk* **Rhapsilian**[16] [1973] 3-8-12 0... RichardThomas 4 48
(J A Geake) *pressed ldrs: rdn over 2f out: wknd 1f out* **16/1**

9 *3 1/2* **Confucius Classic (IRE)** 3-9-3 0.. TQuinn 13 43
(J R Boyle) *w'like: lengthy: bit bkwd: chsd ldrs: rdn over 2f out: wknd fnl f* **9/1**

6 **10** *hd* **Hello Nemo**[37] [1429] 3-9-3 0... JimmyQuinn 10 42
(T E Powell) *bit bkwd: s.i.s: sn rcvrd to chse ldrs: wknd over 1f out* **40/1**

04 **11** *nk* **Conbextra**[9] [2173] 3-9-3 0.. LPKeniry 3 41
(J S Moore) *b: chsd ldrs: rdn over 2f out: wknd sn after* **9/2**[2]

05 **12** *6* **Brackenridge**[12] [2083] 3-9-3 0.. MickyFenton 1 23
(Miss E C Lavelle) *chsd ldrs 4f* **33/1**

1m 13.06s (-1.26) **Going Correction** -0.175s/f (Firm) **12** Ran SP% **124.7**
Speed ratings (Par 99):101,100,98,96,96 94,94,93,89,88 88,80
CSF £11.76 TOTE £2.50: £1.40, £2.20, £2.70; EX 9.60.
Owner M J C Hawkes and E J C Hawkes **Bred** Hirschmann Nolan And Sullivan Partnership **Trained** Newmarket, Suffolk

FOCUS
A modest maiden for Newbury and solid enough form. The winner improved slightly on his debut effort.
Gimme Some Lovin(IRE) ◆ Official explanation: jockey said filly was denied a clear run
Confucius Classic(IRE) Official explanation: jockey said gelding hung right-handed to rail

2471 BETFAIR MOBILE H'CAP 1m 5f 61y
8:35 (8:35) (Class 5) (0-75,73) 4-Y-O+ **£3,238** (£963; £481; £240) **Stalls** High

Form RPR

3-44 **1** **Annambo**[14] [2047] 7-9-6 **72**... TedDurcan 1 82
(D Morris) *lw: hld up in rr: stdy hdwy whn hmpd over 2f out: swtchd rt and drvn to chal ins fnl f: asserted last half f* **5/1**[3]

3344 **2** ¾ **Apache Fort**[12] 2089 4-8-5 **57**.......... NickyMackay 2 66
(T Keddy) *swtg: mid-div: hdwy 3f out: swtchd sharply rt over 2f out: narrow ld sn after: hrd rdn: hdd last half f* **9/2**[2]
5304 **3** 7 **Tranquilizer**[23] 1783 5-9-7 **73**..........(t) JimmyQuinn 6 71
(D J Coakley) *lw: chsd ldrs: drvn to chal appr fnl 2f: wknd fnl f* **4/1**[1]
0060 **4** ½ **Darusso**[19] 1888 4-8-4 **56** ow1..........(p) SimonWhitworth 3 54
(J S Moore) *b: mid-div: hdwy and rdn to chse ldrs over 2f out: wknd over 1f out* **16/1**
-206 **5** 2½ **Star Of Canterbury (IRE)**[31] 1591 4-9-6 **72**.......... JHBowman 10 66
(A P Jarvis) *chsd ldr: rdn and effrt 3f out: wknd ins fnl 2f* **8/1**
0355 **6** 2 **Most Definitely (IRE)**[16] 1959 7-9-5 **71**..........(b) GeorgeBaker 5 62
(R M Stronge) *in rr until hdwy 3f out: trckd ldrs over 2f out: shkn up and wknd over 1f out* **5/1**[3]
2210 **7** 1¾ **Recalcitrant**[12] 2089 4-8-3 **60**.......... WilliamBuick(5) 8 48
(S Dow) *led: rdn and hdd 2f out: wknd qckly* **11/2**
0-00 **8** 3½ **Freddy (ARG)**[22] 1813 8-9-4 **70**..........(bt) MartinDwyer 11 53
(D K Ivory) *in rr: hrd drvn 3f out: nt run on* **25/1**
-000 **9** 1¼ **Sterling Moll**[18] 1925 4-7-9 **54** oh9.......... CharlotteKerton(7) 7 35
(W De Best-Turner) *slowly away: sn mid-div: chsd ldrs 5f out: wknd fr 3f out* **66/1**
5300 **P** **Theatre Groom (USA)**[22] 1813 8-8-12 **64**..........(p) FergusSweeney 12 —
(M R Bosley) *p.u over 7f out: lame* **10/1**

2m 50.74s (-0.25) **Going Correction** -0.175s/f (Firm) **10** Ran SP% **118.3**
Speed ratings (Par 103):93,92,88,87,86 85,84,81,81,—
CSF £28.26 CT £99.98 TOTE £6.30: £2.10, £1.70, £1.90; EX 22.30.
Owner Bloomsbury Stud **Bred** Sheikh Mohammed Bin Rashid Al Maktoum **Trained** Newmarket, Suffolk
■ Stewards' Enquiry : Nicky Mackay three-day ban: careless riding (Jun 24-26)
Charlotte Kerton five-day ban: used whip with excessive frequency and when out of contention (Jun 20-24)

FOCUS
A modest handicap but it was run at a good clip and stamina came to the fore. The first two came clear and the form has been rated through the runner-up.
Theatre Groom(USA) Official explanation: jockey said gelding had been lame

2472 RELYON CLEANING NEWBURY FILLIES' H'CAP 7f (S)
9:05 (9:09) (Class 5) (0-75,75) 3-Y-0+ **£3,238** (£963; £481; £240) **Stalls** Centre

Form RPR
3-50 **1** **Lavenham (IRE)**[9] 2181 4-9-10 **71**.......... RyanMoore 2 86
(R Hannon) *lw: hld up in rr: gd hdwy over 2f out: str run u.p fnl f to ld fnl 100yds* **9/2**[2]
-634 **2** 3½ **Angel Sprints**[12] 2088 5-9-9 **75**.......... WilliamBuick(5) 3 84+
(C J Down) *trckd ldrs: led over 2f out: rdn and kpt on tl sddle slipped and hdd fnl 100yds: stl managed to hold on for 2nd* **8/1**
3623 **3** ½ **Carcinetto (IRE)**[8] 2197 5-9-2 **68**.......... TolleyDean(5) 10 72
(P D Evans) *b.hind: chsd ldrs: rdn to go 2nd 2f out: hung lft u.p and no imp fnl f* **5/1**[3]
-004 **4** ½ **Reeling N' Rocking (IRE)**[15] 2004 4-9-5 **66**.......... KerrinMcEvoy 5 69
(B W Hills) *lw: chsd ldrs: rdn 2f out: one pce fnl f* **9/2**[2]
30-0 **5** hd **Veenwouden**[30] 1610 3-9-4 **75**.......... JHBowman 4 73
(J R Fanshawe) *chsd ldrs: rdn over 2f out: styd on same pce* **8/1**
0316 **6** 1 **Linda Green**[7] 2240 6-9-7 **75**.......... ThomasO'Brien(7) 6 75
(M R Channon) *lw: in rr: rdn and styd on fr over 1f out: nvr gng pce to be competitive* **12/1**
0-00 **7** 5 **Puissant Princess (IRE)**[16] 1961 3-8-9 **66**.......... TQuinn 9 48
(J W Hills) *t.k.h in rr: sme prog and rdn 2f out: nvr in contention* **33/1**
4-60 **8** 1¼ **Becharm**[40] 1358 3-8-8 **65**.......... FergusSweeney 12 44
(A G Newcombe) *t.k.h: sn in tch: rdn over 2f out: sn btn* **50/1**
20-3 **9** 2½ **Extravagance (IRE)**[15] 2012 3-9-1 **72**.......... NickyMackay 13 44
(L M Cumani) *hld up in tch: rdn over 2f out: sn btn* **7/2**[1]
12-0 **10** 1¾ **Welsh Cake**[33] 1534 4-9-5 **66**..........(bt) TedDurcan 1 37
(Mrs A J Perrett) *wnt lft s: sn rcvrd to chse ldrs: wknd qckly 2f out* **9/1**
036- **11** 4 **Rosie's Glory (USA)**[244] 5828 3-9-4 **75**.......... PaulEddery 11 32
(B J Meehan) *chsd ldrs tl wknd over 2f out* **25/1**
0-P0 **12** nk **Reflecting (IRE)**[19] 1886 4-8-9 **56** oh1..........(v¹) JimmyQuinn 7 16+
(A W Carroll) *led after 1f: hdd over 2f out: eased fnl f* **50/1**
0000 **13** 10 **Princess Arwen**[74] 801 5-8-9 **56** oh11..........(b) LPKeniry 14 —
(Mrs Barbara Waring) *led 1f: wknd fr 3f out* **100/1**
20-0 **14** 17 **And I**[30] 1609 4-9-8 **69**.......... MartinDwyer 8 —
(C A Horgan) *lost tch fr 1/2-way* **40/1**

1m 25.21s (-1.79) **Going Correction** -0.175s/f (Firm)
WFA 3 from 4yo+ 10lb **14** Ran SP% **129.3**
Speed ratings (Par 100):103,99,98,97,97 96,90,89,86,84 79,79,68,48
CSF £42.03 CT £201.02 TOTE £7.50: £2.60, £3.70, £2.60; EX 77.70 Place 6 £136.32, Place 5 £77.20..
Owner Mrs J Wood **Bred** M Ervine **Trained** East Everleigh, Wilts

FOCUS
A modest fillies' handicap. Improvement from the winner, with the placed form sound.
Rosie's Glory(USA) Official explanation: jockey said filly suffered interference in running
Reflecting(IRE) Official explanation: jockey said filly lost her action
T/Plt: £194.90 to a £1 stake. Pool: £82,108.50. 307.45 winning tickets. T/Qpdt: £34.30 to a £1 stake. Pool: £4,112.35. 88.50 winning tickets. ST

2316 WINDSOR (R-H)
Saturday, June 9
OFFICIAL GOING: Good (good to firm in places; 8.0)
Wind: Nil Weather: Overcast

2473 EUROPEAN BREEDERS' FUND MAIDEN STKS (DIV I) 6f
2:30 (2:31) (Class 5) 2-Y-0 **£2,914** (£867; £433; £216) **Stalls** High

Form RPR
6 **1** **Nacho Libre**[50] 1123 2-9-3 0.......... MichaelHills 7 78
(B W Hills) *chsd ldrs: rdn and hung rt over 1f out: led ins fnl f: r.o wl* **3/1**[2]
2 1½ **Crystal Reign (IRE)** 2-9-3 0.......... JimmyFortune 12 74
(P W Chapple-Hyam) *chsd ldrs: led over 1f out: hdd and unable qck ins fnl f* **6/4**[1]
0 **3** 1 **Maybe I Wont**[16] 1970 2-9-3 0.......... PaulFitzsimons 11 71+
(S Dow) *a.p: rdn and nt clr run over 1f out: swtchd lft ins fnl f: styd on* **25/1**
0 **4** 1½ **Palm Court**[8] 2215 2-9-0 0.......... RichardKingscote(3) 1 66+
(R Charlton) *s.i.s: hld up: r.o ins fnl f: nvr nrr* **33/1**
5 hd **Compton Ridge** 2-9-3 0.......... MartinDwyer 4 65
(Mrs A J Perrett) *s.i.s: sn pushed along in rr: r.o ins fnl f: nrst fin* **20/1**
6 ½ **Natmana** 2-9-3 0.......... TPO'Shea 10 64
(M R Channon) *led: rdn and hdd over 1f out: wknd ins fnl f* **12/1**
00 **7** ¾ **Rimrock (IRE)**[14] 2041 2-9-3 0.......... TedDurcan 9 62
(J Noseda) *hld up: hdwy over 2f out: sn rdn: wknd fnl f* **14/1**
8 1 **Determind Stand (USA)** 2-9-3 0.......... KerrinMcEvoy 6 59
(Sir Michael Stoute) *chsd ldrs over 4f* **5/1**[3]
0 **9** shd **Aberavon**[15] 2000 2-8-12 0.......... TQuinn 2 53
(D R C Elsworth) *s.i.s: hld up: rdn over 2f out: wknd over 1f out* **20/1**
0 **10** nk **Bid Art (IRE)**[11] 2103 2-9-3 0.......... SebSanders 3 57
(A M Balding) *s.i.s: sn chsng ldrs: rdn and hung lft over 2f out: wknd fnl f* **40/1**
0 **11** hd **Flash Of Fire (USA)**[14] 2041 2-9-3 0.......... HayleyTurner 5 57
(J M P Eustace) *mid-div: rdn 1/2-way: wkng whn hmpd over 1f out* **33/1**

1m 13.83s (0.16) **Going Correction** -0.125s/f (Firm) **11** Ran SP% **117.7**
Speed ratings (Par 93):93,91,89,87,87 86,85,84,84,83 83
CSF £7.09 TOTE £3.90: £1.60, £1.40, £4.50; EX 8.40 Trifecta £165.80 Part won. Pool: £233.63 - 0.40 winning units..
Owner R J Arculli & John C Grant **Bred** Lostford Manor Stud **Trained** Lambourn, Berks

FOCUS
A fair maiden, but marginally the slower of the two divisions. Nacho Libre did it well but it is hard to rate the bare form too highly.

NOTEBOOK
Nacho Libre, who looked in need of the run, despite being sent off second-favourite on his debut at Newbury, appreciated the extra furlong and stayed on well to beat the gambled-on favourite. He could well go for the Coventry now, although connections are keen to avoid very quick ground as he came back from Newbury with sore shins. (op 4-1 tchd 9-2)
Crystal Reign(IRE), a half-brother to Sotik Star, a dual 1m winner at three, was all the rage in the market beforehand, and had been handed the best of the draw on his debut. He ran well, but the more experienced winner had his measure in the closing stages. (op 2-1)
Maybe I Wont, half-brother to Factual Lad, a prolific winner between 6f and 1m2f, had a good draw too and stepped up significantly on his debut effort at Salisbury. He looks more of a nursery type in time. (op 40-1)
Palm Court again shaped as though this was an insufficient test, but he finished well from the worst draw of all and looks another who will come into his own once nurseries become an option.
Compton Ridge, a brother to Cesc, a multiple winner over 7f and 1m at two, struggled to go the early pace but was putting in some good work at the finish. He is from a stable whose juveniles usually come on quite a bit for their debut outings and, as he is bred to appreciate 7f plus, should do better as he is stepped up in distance. (op 18-1)
Natmana, a half-brother to High Style, a 6f winner at two, Godsend, a 5f winner at two, and Instinct, a 6f winner at three, showed plenty of early speed from his decent draw and, given that his stable's juveniles have been improving for a run this term, he could hang on out there a bit longer next time.
Determind Stand(USA), who cost 200,000gns, is out of a mare who won three times at three, including over 1m2f in Listed company. (op 4-1 tchd 11-2)

2474 BISHOP METAL RECYCLING H'CAP 1m 3f 135y
3:00 (3:01) (Class 4) (0-85,85) 4-Y-0+ **£6,477** (£1,927; £963; £481) **Stalls** Low

Form RPR
20-6 **1** **Kerriemuir Lass (IRE)**[29] 1621 4-9-5 **83**.......... SebSanders 2 95
(M A Jarvis) *mde all: rdn over 1f out: styd on wl* **13/2**[2]
3113 **2** 1¾ **Kilimandscharo (USA)**[22] 1822 5-9-5 **83**.......... RichardHughes 1 92
(P J McBride) *hld up: hdwy over 2f out: rdn to chse wnr fnl f: no imp* **3/1**[1]
00-0 **3** 1 **Magicalmysterytour (IRE)**[15] 2002 4-9-6 **84**.......... BrettDoyle 10 91
(W J Musson) *hld up in tch: rdn over 1f out: styd on same pce ins fnl f* **7/1**[3]
1-56 **4** 1¼ **Very Agreeable**[15] 2002 4-9-6 **84**.......... AdamKirby 3 89
(W R Swinburn) *hld up: hdwy over 2f out: sn rdn: styd on same pce fnl f* **10/1**
0-02 **5** 2 **Cavallini (USA)**[31] 1591 5-8-8 **72**.......... TedDurcan 12 74
(G L Moore) *chsd ldrs: rdn over 2f out: wknd fnl f* **7/1**[3]
110- **6** 1 **Rationale (IRE)**[245] 5804 4-9-7 **85**.......... J-PGuillambert 8 85
(S C Williams) *prom: racd keenly: rdn over 2f out: wknd fnl f* **15/2**
2222 **7** ½ **Lemonette (USA)**[17] 1949 4-9-2 **80**.......... MichaelHills 4 79
(J W Hills) *mid-div: effrt over 2f out: nvr trbld ldrs* **9/1**
0311 **8** ½ **Street Life (IRE)**[11] 2113 9-8-6 **70**.......... DavidKinsella 7 68
(W J Musson) *hld up: sme hdwy over 1f out: n.d* **12/1**
1630 **9** 5 **Polish Power (GER)**[24] 1771 7-9-0 **83**.......... JamesMillman(5) 9 73
(J S Moore) *hld up: effrt over 2f out: a in rr* **33/1**
666- **10** 3½ **Pinch Of Salt (IRE)**[162] 5284 4-8-12 **76**.......... MartinDwyer 11 60
(A M Balding) *trckd ldrs: racd keenly: rdn and wknd 2f out* **33/1**
0210 **11** 5 **Fantoche (BRZ)**[13] 2067 5-9-7 **85**..........(t) JimmyFortune 5 70
(M J Wallace) *chsd ldrs: rdn over 3f out: wknd 2f out: eased* **10/1**
/00- **12** 6 **Sharmy (IRE)**[300] 4393 11-8-2 **66** oh1.......... TPO'Shea 6 31
(Ian Williams) *s.i.s: hld up: rdn over 3f out: sn wknd* **66/1**

2m 26.32s (-3.78) **Going Correction** -0.125s/f (Firm) **12** Ran SP% **118.3**
Speed ratings (Par 105):107,105,105,104,103 102,102,101,98,96 92,88
CSF £25.89 CT £143.91 TOTE £8.90: £2.20, £1.70, £3.40; EX 29.40 TRIFECTA Not won..
Owner Thurloe Thoroughbreds XV **Bred** P D Savill **Trained** Newmarket, Suffolk

FOCUS
This was dominated from flag-fall by Kerriemuir Lass, but it looks a strong handicap for the grade and should work out. The first four all look quite progressive.
Lemonette(USA) Official explanation: jockey said filly pulled front shoe off
Fantoche(BRZ) Official explanation: jockey said horse was hanging throughout

2475 KATE HARPHAM PRIME FILLIES' H'CAP 1m 2f 7y
3:35 (3:35) (Class 4) (0-80,75) 3-Y-0 **£6,477** (£1,927; £963; £481) **Stalls** Low

Form RPR
31-0 **1** **Encircled**[26] 1722 3-9-3 **71**.......... MichaelHills 5 81+
(D Haydn Jones) *hld up: hdwy over 4f out: led 2f out: sn rdn: edgd lft fnl f: styd on* **10/1**[3]
21- **2** 2½ **Algarade**[171] 6879 3-9-7 **75**.......... SebSanders 6 79+
(Sir Mark Prescott) *chsd ldrs: rdn and nt clr run over 1f out: swtchd lft: styd on same pce ins fnl f* **8/13**[1]
1300 **3** nk **Going To Work (IRE)**[9] 2181 3-9-6 **74**.......... TQuinn 7 77
(D R C Elsworth) *hld up: hdwy and hung lft over 1f out: styd on same pce ins fnl f* **7/1**[2]
40-6 **4** 1 **Vallemeldee (IRE)**[29] 1639 3-8-13 **67**.......... KerrinMcEvoy 4 68
(P W D'Arcy) *chsd ldr: rdn and ev ch 2f out: no ex ins fnl f* **16/1**
5230 **5** 2 **Miss Saafend Plaza (IRE)**[40] 1355 3-8-13 **67**..........(b) RichardHughes 2 64
(R Hannon) *led: rdn and hdd 2f out: wknd fnl f* **16/1**
-100 **6** 1¼ **Hostage**[14] 2045 3-9-5 **73**.......... TedDurcan 3 68
(M L W Bell) *hld up: effrt and nt clr run over 2f out: n.d* **12/1**
6-30 **7** nk **Paradise Walk**[26] 1726 3-8-8 **65**.......... RichardKingscote(3) 8 59
(R Charlton) *s.i.s: hld up: effrt and hung lft over 3f out: wknd over 1f out* **28/1**

-034 **8** *1* **House Maiden (IRE)**[9] [2181] 3-8-5 **59**.............................. MartinDwyer 1 51
(D M Simcock) *plld hrd and prom: rdn over 2f out: wkng whn hmpd sn after* **11/1**

2m 8.28s (-0.02) **Going Correction** -0.125s/f (Firm) **8** Ran SP% **114.7**
Speed ratings (Par 98):95,93,92,91,90 89,89,88
CSF £16.70 CT £49.89 TOTE £14.10: £3.10, £1.02, £2.20; EX 21.30 TRIFECTA Not won..
Owner Mrs M L Parry & P Steele-Mortimer **Bred** M H Ings **Trained** Efail Isaf, Rhondda C Taff

FOCUS
The bare form may not be all that strong, but it was still a much improved effort from Encircled to beat the well-treated odds-on chance Algarade, who remains capable of better.
Paradise Walk Official explanation: jockey said filly ran too free
House Maiden(IRE) Official explanation: jockey said filly ran too free

2476 GOLDRINGSECURITY.COM H'CAP 1m 67y
4:05 (4:05) (Class 3) (0-95,95) 3-Y-0+
£7,478 (£2,239; £1,119; £560; £279; £140) **Stalls** High

Form RPR
002 **1** **Humungous (IRE)**[42] [1307] 4-10-0 **95**.......................... RichardHughes 7 105+
(C R Egerton) *led over 7f out: rdn and hung lft fr over 1f out: r.o wl* **10/3**[2]
0205 **2** *2* **Blacktoft (USA)**[10] [2136] 4-8-10 **77**.....................(e) J-PGuillambert 8 81
(S C Williams) *led: hdd over 7f out: rdn over 3f out: styd on same pce fnl f* **22/1**
02-0 **3** *3/4* **Woodcote Place**[22] [1818] 4-9-7 **88**.......................... TedDurcan 2 90+
(P R Chamings) *s.i.s: hld up: hdwy over 2f out: sn rdn: styd on same pce fnl f* **12/1**
0-05 **4** *hd* **Moonlight Man**[11] [2123] 6-8-13 **87**.......................... HaddenFrost(7) 3 89
(R Hannon) *chsd ldrs: rdn over 1f out: no ex fnl f* **25/1**
-660 **5** *1/2* **Acheekyone (IRE)**[21] [1842] 4-9-6 **87**.......................... JimmyFortune 6 88
(B J Meehan) *chsd ldrs: rdn over 2f out: no ex fnl f* **10/1**
6-12 **6** *1 1/2* **Gulf Express (USA)**[30] [1603] 3-8-8 **86**.......................... KerrinMcEvoy 5 80
(Sir Michael Stoute) *hld up: hdwy over 2f out: rdn over 1f out: wknd ins fnl f* **11/10**[1]
1005 **7** *2* **Wavertree Warrior (IRE)**[8] [2208] 5-9-9 **90**.......................... IanMongan 4 83
(N P Littmoden) *hld up in tch: lost pl over 2f out: rdn and wknd over 1f out* **14/1**
-002 **8** *4* **Cool Box (USA)**[18] [1930] 3-8-5 **83**.......................... MartinDwyer 1 63
(Mrs A J Perrett) *hld up: hdwy over 4f out: rdn and wknd over 1f out: eased ins fnl f* **11/2**[3]

1m 42.41s (-2.29) **Going Correction** -0.125s/f (Firm)
WFA 3 from 4yo+ 11lb **8** Ran SP% **117.7**
Speed ratings (Par 107):106,104,103,103,102 101,99,95
CSF £71.79 CT £806.07 TOTE £4.90: £1.60, £5.40, £2.70; EX 173.40 TRIFECTA Not won..
Owner Exors of the Late Mrs E A Hankinson **Bred** Quay Bloodstock **Trained** Chaddleworth, Berks

FOCUS
This looked a fairly decent little contest beforehand, but the poor performances of the favourite and third-favourite put a question mark on the value of the form. The front two dominated.

NOTEBOOK
Humungous(IRE), who was well backed, usually contests better races than this, like at Sandown last time, and as he has made the running in the past it made perfect sense to take up the pace-setting duties early on in this easier company. He hung badly left in the closing stages but it made no difference as he had plenty in hand, and the Hunt Cup is now on the agenda, a race for which he is a best priced 28-1 with Paddy Power. (op 7-1)
Blacktoft(USA), who is not the easiest of rides, ran well to chase the class-dropping winner home, but the Handicapper seems to have his measure at present. (op 25-1 tchd 20-1)
Woodcote Place, who is arguably happier over 7f, ran a better race than on his reappearance at Newmarket, but he too looks on a stiff enough mark right now. (op 14-1)
Moonlight Man has only won one of his last 25 starts, albeit that success came off a higher mark than he was running off here, and he is another arguably better over shorter. (op 18-1)
Acheekyone(IRE) put in another below-par effort but his stable is not in the best of form at the moment. (tchd 14-1)
Gulf Express(USA), who did not have things go his way at Chester, was made a short price to get back on the winning trail, but he never really got involved and proved disappointing. He is better than this. Official explanation: trainer's rep had no explanation for the poor form shown (op 5-6 tchd 4-5)
Cool Box(USA) was another to fail to run up to the form of his recent efforts, although the step up in trip could have been an excuse for him. (op 7-1)

2477 GOLDRING SUPPORT SERVICES MEDIAN AUCTION MAIDEN STKS 1m 67y
4:40 (4:41) (Class 5) 3-Y-0 **£3,238** (£963; £481; £240) **Stalls** High

Form RPR
2 **1** **Gongidas**[10] [2153] 3-9-3 0.......................... KerrinMcEvoy 11 77+
(Saeed Bin Suroor) *hld up in tch: led over 2f out: rdn and hung lft fr over 1f out: jst hld on* **1/5**[1]
0 **2** *shd* **Cactus Rose**[21] [1839] 3-9-0 0.......................... RichardKingscote(3) 14 77
(R Charlton) *a.p: chsd wnr over 1f out: sn rdn and ev ch: r.o* **40/1**
0 **3** *6* **Nelly's Glen**[33] [1523] 3-8-12 0.......................... MartinDwyer 10 58+
(R Hannon) *s.i.s: hld up: styd on fr over 1f out: nvr trbld ldrs* **33/1**
0- **4** *hd* **El Dottore**[263] [5460] 3-9-3 0.......................... HayleyTurner 4 63
(M L W Bell) *mid-div: effrt over 2f out: n.d* **33/1**
02 **5** *nk* **Velocity's Gift**[21] [1838] 3-9-3 0.......................... PaulEddery 7 62
(Pat Eddery) *chsd ldrs: rdn over 1f out: sn outpcd* **9/1**[2]
0 **6** *1 3/4* **Arithmatix (USA)**[38] [1403] 3-8-10 0.......................... HaddenFrost(7) 13 58+
(G A Butler) *chsd ldrs 6f* **25/1**
0- **7** *shd* **Sunburn (IRE)**[240] [5918] 3-9-3 0.......................... TedDurcan 3 58
(Mrs A J Perrett) *hld up: hdwy and hung lft over 2f out: wknd over 1f out* **40/1**
0 **8** *1 3/4* **Victory Mile (USA)**[7] [2261] 3-9-3 0.......................... BrettDoyle 2 54
(B J Meehan) *mid-div: hdwy over 3f out: rdn and hung lft over 2f out: sn wknd* **33/1**
0 **9** *2 1/2* **Willie Ever**[21] [1841] 3-9-3 0.......................... RichardHughes 12 48
(W J Musson) *led over 5f: wknd over 1f out* **66/1**
0-3 **10** *1* **Halkerston**[12] [2077] 3-9-3 0..........................(t) AdamKirby 9 46
(C G Cox) *chsd ldrs: rdn over 3f out: wknd over 1f out* **16/1**[3]
11 *1 1/4* **My Spring Rose** 3-8-9 0.......................... PatrickMathers(3) 1 38
(J R Jenkins) *s.i.s: hld up: in rr whn hmpd over 2f out* **100/1**
12 *1 1/4* **Slip Silver** 3-8-12 0.......................... AmirQuinn 6 35
(P J Makin) *hld up: hdwy over 3f out: wkng whn hmpd 2f out* **40/1**
13 *5* **Panda Power** 3-8-12 0.......................... J-PGuillambert 5 23
(S C Williams) *s.i.s: rdn over 3f out: in rr whn hmpd 2f out* **66/1**
0 **14** *5* **Rosemary And Thyme**[36] [1452] 3-8-12 0.......................... MichaelHills 8 12
(J W Hills) *hld up: hung lft over 2f out: a in rr* **100/1**

1m 44.42s (-0.28) **Going Correction** -0.125s/f (Firm) **14** Ran SP% **124.2**
Speed ratings (Par 99):96,95,89,89,89 87,87,85,83,82 81,79,74,69
CSF £24.06 TOTE £1.20: £1.02, £8.40, £7.80; EX 21.00 TRIFECTA Not won..
Owner Godolphin **Bred** Karl-Dieter Ellerbracke **Trained** Newmarket, Suffolk
■ Stewards' Enquiry : Hayley Turner two-day ban: careless riding (Jun 24-25)

FOCUS
Not much strength in depth to this maiden. Quite messy form, and far from solid, but there were some likely improvers down the field.

2478 EUROPEAN BREEDERS' FUND MAIDEN STKS (DIV II) 6f
5:15 (5:15) (Class 5) 2-Y-0 **£2,914** (£867; £433; £216) **Stalls** High

Form RPR
4 **1** **Seeking Star (IRE)**[14] [2041] 2-9-3 0.......................... TPO'Shea 11 82
(M R Channon) *chsd ldrs: rdn and ev ch fr over 2f out: styd on to ld post* **11/10**[1]
0 **2** *shd* **Dresden Doll (USA)**[15] [2000] 2-8-12 0.......................... HayleyTurner 7 77
(M L W Bell) *led: rdn over 1f out: sn edgd lft: hdd post* **16/1**
3 *3/4* **Shifting Star (IRE)** 2-9-3 0.......................... AdamKirby 3 79
(W R Swinburn) *chsd ldrs: rdn over 1f out: styd on* **4/1**[2]
4 *2* **Azeer (USA)** 2-9-3 0.......................... MichaelHills 10 73+
(P W Chapple-Hyam) *s.i.s: hld up: hdwy over 1f out: styd on same pce ins fnl f* **6/1**[3]
0 **5** *2 1/2* **Stubbs Art (IRE)**[16] [1970] 2-9-3 0.......................... TQuinn 6 66
(D R C Elsworth) *trckd ldrs: racd keenly: rdn over 1f out: edgd rt and wknd fnl f* **11/1**
6 *nk* **Wannarock (IRE)** 2-9-3 0.......................... KerrinMcEvoy 12 65
(E A L Dunlop) *s.i.s: hld up: hdwy over 1f out: wknd fnl f* **7/1**
7 *6* **Royal Intruder** 2-9-3 0.......................... MartinDwyer 9 47+
(R Hannon) *chsd ldrs: hung lft over 2f out: sn wknd: eased fnl f* **14/1**
8 *3* **Asian Power (IRE)** 2-9-3 0.......................... J-PGuillambert 4 38
(P J O'Gorman) *s.i.s: hdwy over 3f out: wknd 2f out* **40/1**
9 *3* **Valentino Sky (USA)** 2-9-0 0.......................... RichardKingscote(3) 2 29
(N P Littmoden) *dwlt: outpcd* **50/1**
05 **10** *2* **Abfabfong (IRE)**[33] [1519] 2-9-3 0.......................... TedDurcan 5 23
(P F I Cole) *hld up: wknd over 2f out* **66/1**

1m 13.55s (-0.12) **Going Correction** -0.125s/f (Firm) **10** Ran SP% **121.2**
Speed ratings (Par 93):95,94,93,91,87 87,79,75,71,68
CSF £24.00 TOTE £2.10: £1.20, £3.00, £2.20; EX 20.50 Trifecta £288.90 Part won. Pool: £406.92 - 0.50 winning units..
Owner Jaber Abdullah **Bred** Pier House Stud **Trained** West Ilsley, Berks

FOCUS
Probably a fair maiden and marginally the quicker of the two divisions.

NOTEBOOK
Seeking Star(IRE), fourth in a much stronger maiden at Newmarket on his debut, was well drawn and looked to have plenty going for him. He only got home narrowly, though, and will have to improve on this bare form if he is to compete at a higher level – his connections have plans to run him in the Coventry Stakes at Royal Ascot. (op 6-4 tchd 13-8)
Dresden Doll(USA), the only filly in the race, stepped up on the form she showed on her debut in a race restricted to her own sex. She is bred to relish quick ground and, as a half-sister to that top-class filly Crimplene, she looks the type to improve again. (op 14-1)
Shifting Star(IRE), for whom there was market support during the day, is out of a half-sister to top-class 11-time winner Siberian Express, who won at up to 1m2f. From a stable not known for having first-time-up juvenile winners, he ran really well against rivals who had the benefit of a previous outing, and he should come on quite a bit for the run. (op 11-4 tchd 5-2 and 9-2)
Azeer(USA) is a half-brother to five winners, including Alyzig, who placed at Grade 1 level over 7f in the US. There was not a tremendous amount of support for him beforehand and it is likely that he will be all the better for this debut outing. Another furlong will suit him in time. (op 7-1 tchd 8-1 in places)
Stubbs Art(IRE), who is another that will get 7f later in the year, stepped up on his debut outing over 5f and looks to be going the right way. Official explanation: jockey said colt suffered interference shortly after start (op 10-1 tchd 12-1)
Wannarock(IRE), whose sales price rose from 20,000gns as a foal to 72,000gns as a yearling, is closely related to Tanami, a dual sprint winner at two and dam of high-class 7f winner Cairns. He will do better with this debut experience under his belt. (op 12-1)
Royal Intruder Official explanation: jockey said colt lost its action

2479 COME RACING 11TH JUNE CIRQUE NIGHT H'CAP 5f 10y
5:45 (5:46) (Class 5) (0-75,74) 3-Y-0+ **£3,238** (£963; £481; £240) **Stalls** High

Form RPR
2-03 **1** **Bahamian Ballet**[14] [2025] 5-9-13 **73**.......................... J-PGuillambert 4 83
(E S McMahon) *w ldrs: racd keenly: rdn to ld ins fnl f: edgd lft: r.o* **3/1**[1]
03-1 **2** *1/2* **Gwilym (GER)**[47] [1200] 4-9-5 **70**.......................... PatrickHills(5) 9 78
(D Haydn Jones) *chsd ldrs: led over 1f out: rdn and hdd ins fnl f: styd on* **7/2**[2]
001- **3** *shd* **Gold Express**[295] [4573] 4-9-7 **67**.......................... KerrinMcEvoy 5 75+
(P J O'Gorman) *s.i.s: hdwy over 3f out: rdn and ev ch over 1f out: edgd lft and unable qck nr fin* **4/1**[3]
4-0P **4** *2* **Xaluna Bay (IRE)**[40] [1357] 4-9-12 **72**.......................... MichaelHills 8 72+
(W R Muir) *hld up: swtchd lft over 1f out: r.o ins fnl f: nt rch ldrs* **16/1**
0-60 **5** *hd* **Calabaza**[21] [1847] 5-8-11 **60**.......................... RichardKingscote(3) 3 60
(W Jarvis) *s.i.s: hld up: hdwy over 1f out: nt trble ldrs* **11/2**
00-0 **6** *1 1/4* **Blue Aura (IRE)**[40] [1357] 4-10-0 **74**..........................(p) TedDurcan 6 69
(R M Beckett) *trckd ldrs: rdn whn nt clr run over 1f out: styd on same pce* **8/1**
0062 **7** *shd* **Desperate Dan**[15] [1999] 6-9-3 **70**..........................(b) SophieDoyle(7) 1 65
(J A Osborne) *chsd ldrs: styd on same pce fnl f* **6/1**
6000 **8** *3/4* **Dancing Mystery**[16] [1969] 13-8-12 **65**..........................(b) JackMitchell(7) 2 57
(E A Wheeler) *led: edgd lft 1/2-way: hung rt and hdd over 1f out: wknd ins fnl f* **33/1**
0-00 **9** *3 1/2* **Blessed Place**[136] [236] 7-9-4 **64**.......................... TQuinn 7 44
(D J S Ffrench Davis) *w ldrs over 3f: wknd fnl f* **20/1**

60.10 secs (-1.00) **Going Correction** -0.125s/f (Firm) **9** Ran SP% **121.6**
Speed ratings (Par 103):103,102,102,98,98 96,96,95,89
CSF £14.49 CT £44.05 TOTE £4.20: £1.70, £1.80, £1.90; EX 15.50 Trifecta £46.10 Pool: £396.38 - 6.10 winning units. Place 6 £10.18, Place 5 £7.17..
Owner B N Toye **Bred** B N And Mrs Toye **Trained** Lichfield, Staffs

FOCUS
A competitive little sprint and there was not too much between the first three home at the line. Solid form.
Xaluna Bay(IRE) Official explanation: jockey said filly was denied a clear run

T/Plt: £45.90 to a £1 stake. Pool: £62,125.75. 987.35 winning tickets. T/Qpdt: £23.90 to a £1 stake. Pool: £3,257.70. 100.50 winning tickets. CR

2480 - 2482a (Foreign Racing) - See Raceform Interactive

2062 CURRAGH (R-H)

Saturday, June 9

OFFICIAL GOING: Straight course - good; round course - good to firm

2483a GALLO FAMILY VINEYARDS SILVER STKS (LISTED RACE) 1m 2f

7:00 (7:02) 3-Y-0+ **£24,192** (£7,097; £3,381; £1,152)

RPR

1 **Fracas (IRE)**[13] 2064 5-9-9 111 WMLordan 3 113
(David Wachman, Ire) *mde all: rdn and styd on wl fr 2f out: comf* **9/10**[1]

2 2 **Trinity College (USA)**[14] 2051 3-8-10 100 KFallon 5 108+
(A P O'Brien, Ire) *hld up in rr: rdn 2f out: prog on outer over 1f out: mod 2nd ins fnl f: kpt on wl* **9/2**[3]

3 1 1/4 **Arch Rebel (USA)**[13] 2064 6-9-12 111 JMurtagh 2 109
(Noel Meade, Ire) *settled 2nd: rdn to chal early st: 3rd over 1f out: kpt on same pce u.p* **11/2**

4 hd **Cool Touch (IRE)**[13] 2067 4-9-9 107 PJSmullen 1 106
(Peter Casey, Ire) *dwlt: sn 4th: 3rd and hdwy 2f out: 2nd briefly 1f out: one pce* **4/1**[2]

5 2 **Diamond Necklace (USA)**[13] 2065 3-8-7 100 JAHeffernan 4 98
(A P O'Brien, Ire) *settled 3rd: drvn along ent st: 4th 2f out: no ex ins fnl f* **10/1**

2m 6.60s (-2.70) **Going Correction** -0.175s/f (Firm)
WFA 3 from 4yo+ 13lb 5 Ran SP% **115.3**
Speed ratings: 103,101,100,100,98
CSF £5.79 TOTE £1.70: £1.10, £2.70; DF 9.20.
Owner Joseph Joyce **Bred** Mrs Eileen Purcell **Trained** Goolds Cross, Co Tipperary

FOCUS
The race has been rated through the runner-up and the fifth.

NOTEBOOK
Fracas(IRE), well backed to record his first success since he completed an early season hat-trick as a three-year-old, appreciated this drop in class and made virtually every yard. Sent on when the gate opened, last month's Tattersalls Gold Cup fifth behind Notnowcato set a steady clip until quickening the tempo approaching the straight. Having recorded a couple of creditable placed efforts in top company behind the likes of Dylan Thomas and Septimus, it came as no surprise when he soon had his chasing rivals in trouble passing the two-furlong pole. He will be kept to this grade or Group 3 company over the coming months according to his trainer. (op 5/4)
Trinity College(USA), the better fancied of the Ballydoyle pair, did not enjoy the clearest of passages. Boxed in travelling well in last place with nowhere to go passing the two pole, he had to be switched left to mount his challenge. By the time he got going, the race was as good as over but he stayed on best of the rest. On this evidence he has a similar race or better within his compass. (op 4/1)
Arch Rebel(USA) had finished several lengths behind Fracas in the Tattersalls Gold Cup and, considering he was 3lb worse off under these race conditions, he appeared to have a tough task on his hands, even though that was his first race of the current campaign. When the pace quickened he was soon struggling to get on terms and was eventually collared for the runner-up berth. This three-time winner at Listed level should not be written off, though, as he may still have needed the run. (op 4/1)
Cool Touch(IRE), successful in four handicaps last season, had finished behind Arch Rebel when they clashed in a Group 3 contest at Leopardstown in September. He had been performing well recently, though, reaching the frame in a couple of starts, and held every chance if good enough this time. (op 9/2)
Diamond Necklace(USA), the only filly in the field, had previously run seventh in the Irish 1000 Guineas. In third entering the final quarter, she began to feel the pace and eventually dropped out.

2484 - 2486a (Foreign Racing) - See Raceform Interactive

BELMONT PARK (L-H)

Saturday, June 9

OFFICIAL GOING: Dirt course - fast; turf course - firm

2487a BELMONT STKS (GRADE 1) (DIRT) 1m 4f (D)

11:25 (11:29) 3-Y-0 **£306,122** (£102,040; £56,122; £30,612; £15,306)

RPR

1 **Rags To Riches (USA)**[36] 3-8-9 JRVelazquez 7 119
(T Pletcher, U.S.A) **43/10**[2]

2 hd **Curlin (USA)**[21] 1882 3-9-0 RAlbarado 3 124
(S Asmussen, U.S.A) **11/10**[1]

3 5 1/2 **Tiago (USA)**[35] 1486 3-9-0 MESmith 2 115
(J Shirreffs, U.S.A) **68/10**

4 5 1/2 **Hard Spun (USA)**[21] 1882 3-9-0 GKGomez 6 106
(J Larry Jones, U.S.A) **49/10**[3]

5 4 1/4 **C P West (USA)**[21] 1882 3-9-0 EPrado 4 99
(N Zito, U.S.A) **124/10**

6 1 3/4 **Imawildandcrazyguy (USA)**[35] 1486 3-9-0 (b) MGuidry 1 97
(W Kaplan, U.S.A) **93/10**

7 17 **Slew's Tizzy (USA)**[28] 3-9-0 RBejarano 5 69
(Gregory Fox, U.S.A) **183/10**

2m 28.74s (-0.22) 7 Ran SP% **118.6**
PARI-MUTUEL: WIN 10.60; PL (1-2) 4.40, 3.00; SHOW (1-2-3) 3.20, 2.30, 3.70; SF 25.20.
Owner Smith & Tabor **Bred** Skara Glen Stables **Trained** USA
■ Rags To Riches became the first filly to win the Belmont Stakes since Tanya in 1905.

NOTEBOOK
Rags To Riches(USA), bred to be a star, being a half-sister to Jazil, the winner of this race in 2006, had won her previous four races, the last three in Grade 1 company, and in beating the Preakness Stakes winner Curlin in a driving finish, she confirmed herself as a top-class filly and finally provided her trainer with his first win in a Triple Crown race. Given a smart ride, wide of the rail where the surface is generally deeper, she was travelling well turning into the straight. Sent on, she was immediately challenged by Curlin, and the pair went on to fight it out, with her stamina just seeing her through in the end. The Alabama at Saratoga in August and the Breeders' Cup Classic are now her main targets for the rest of the season, and she looks sure to be a major player in both races.
Curlin(USA), third in the Kentucky Derby and winner of the Preakness, was sent off a short-priced favourite to follow up in the final leg of the Triple Crown. Stuck on the inside in the straight, which was probably not ideal, he went down with all guns blazing, battling back to be beaten by only a narrow margin by a filly bred to stay a bit better than him. He is very tough and that will always make him a formidable adversary, and he looks sure to win plenty more races, with the Breeders' Cup Classic looking the natural long-term target.
Tiago(USA), seventh in the Kentucky Derby, skipped the Preakness as the longer distance here was expected to suit him. He finished on his own in third, but was well held by the front pair.
Hard Spun(USA), second at Churchill Downs and third at Pimlico, has plenty of pace and that was the worry over this longer trip. There was not a mad gallop on early but he was still beaten for stamina, and he will be far more effective when dropped back in distance.

2193 BATH (L-H)

Sunday, June 10

OFFICIAL GOING: Firm (11.4)
Not surprisingly the ground was fast as the course has no watering system.
Wind: Moderate, behind Weather: Sunny and humid

2488 TOTEPLACEPOT MEDIAN AUCTION MAIDEN FILLIES' STKS 5f 161y

2:10 (2:16) (Class 6) 2-Y-O **£2,266** (£674; £337; £168) **Stalls** Low

Form RPR

46 1 **Aide Memoir (IRE)**[25] 1762 2-8-9 0 WilliamBuick(5) 5 73+
(S Kirk) *in rr tl hdwy on outside over 1f out: r.o to ld ins fnl f: won gng away* **4/1**[2]

2 1 1/2 **Nothing Likea Dame** 2-9-0 0 EdwardCreighton 3 68
(D J Coakley) *mid-div: rdn hdwy on ins over 1f out: r.o to chse wnr ins fnl f* **25/1**

3 3 1/2 **Midnight Fling**[20] 1882 2-9-0 0 SteveDrowne 14 66
(R Charlton) *mid-div: rdn to chse ldr 2f out tl ins fnl f: styd on* **2/1**[1]

503 4 3/4 **Carolina Blini**[34] 1519 2-9-0 0 (b[1]) RyanMoore 4 64
(B J Meehan) *trckd ldr to 2f out: one pce fnl f* **12/1**

6 5 1/2 **Star In The East**[23] 1807 2-9-0 0 HayleyTurner 2 62
(A M Balding) *trckd ldrs: rdn over 1f out: one pce after* **6/1**

6 6 nk **Cocabana**[20] 1896 2-9-0 0 AdamKirby 13 61
(J G Portman) *led: rdn over 1f out: hdd & wknd ins fnl f* **9/2**[3]

60 7 2 1/2 **Happy Hacker (IRE)**[12] 2103 2-9-0 0 CatherineGannon 9 53
(P D Evans) *trckd ldrs: rdn and wknd over 1f out* **28/1**

0 8 6 **Orbital Orchid**[27] 1727 2-9-0 0 JHBowman 6 33+
(W S Kittow) *mid-div: rdn 1/2-way: nvr on terms* **33/1**

9 nk **Chemise (IRE)** 2-8-7 0 HaddenFrost(7) 15 32
(R J Hodges) *hung rt and rn wd into st: nvr on terms* **33/1**

00 10 1 1/4 **Bold Diva**[34] 1533 2-9-0 0 DavidKinsella 7 28
(A W Carroll) *mid-div: rdn 1/2-way: wknd over 1f out* **100/1**

00 11 5 **Bantham Bay**[27] 1727 2-9-0 0 TQuinn 8 12
(B J Meehan) *in tch tl wknd over 1f out* **50/1**

12 2 **Kintyre Lass (IRE)** 2-9-0 0 JimCrowley 11 5
(B R Millman) *a bhd* **20/1**

13 2 1/2 **Princess Namid (IRE)** 2-8-9 0 LukeMorris(5) 1 —
(R A Harris) *slowly away: a bhd* **50/1**

0430 14 11 **Zahwah**[11] 2134 2-8-11 0 EmmettStack(3) 10 —
(J G Portman) *a bhd* **15/2**

15 16 **Kay One (IRE)** 2-8-9 0 TolleyDean(5) 12 —
(R J Price) *slowly away: a bhd* **66/1**

69.96 secs (-1.24) **Going Correction** -0.125s/f (Firm) **15** Ran SP% **129.6**
Speed ratings (Par 88):103,101,100,99,98 98,94,86,86,84 78,75,72,57,36
CSF £112.29 TOTE £6.10: £2.20, £6.10, £1.30; EX 312.90 Trifecta £86.00 Part won. Pool £121.16. - 0.44 winning units..
Owner J C Smith **Bred** Secret Justice Syndicate **Trained** Upper Lambourn, Berks
■ Stewards' Enquiry : Hadden Frost 8-day ban (reduced from 14 days and breach of Rule 157 on appeal); in breach of Rule 158 (Jun 29-Jul 6)

FOCUS
This juvenile maiden fillies' contest looked ordinary but it was run at a furious pace and the time was very smart for a race like this. A good effort from the winner, building on her debut promise here.

NOTEBOOK
Aide Memoir(IRE) had run well on her debut but had disappointed here last time. However, she did little wrong on this occasion and seemed well suited by the tow into the race she got. On this evidence she will have no problems with a bit further. (op 6-1 tchd 7-1)
Nothing Likea Dame stayed on well on her debut and gave the impression she is up to taking one of these in due course, but she is going to be suited by a little further as well. (op 50-1)
Midnight Fling had gone into some notebooks when finishing with some purpose on her debut over 5f. She effectively had every chance here but could not pick up when things got busy. She maybe better over another furlong and after another run which will see her qualified for nurseries. (op 6-4 tchd 9-4)
Carolina Blini has had four chances already now so she looks ordinary. Official explanation: trainer said filly was unsuited by the firm ground (op 8-1)
Star In The East showed some promise on her debut but failed to build on that as she had her chance up the inside rail. She is another who is likely to take the nursery route. (op 9-2)
Chemise(IRE) bolted on the way to the start and had to be resaddled. In the race she darted out of the stalls and was never in real contention. However, the performance attracted the attention of the Stewards. (op 50-1)

Bold Diva Official explanation: trainer said filly was unsuited by the firm ground
Kay One(IRE) Official explanation: jockey said filly ran very green

2489 TOTECOURSE TO COURSE H'CAP 1m 5y

2:40 (2:44) (Class 6) (0-60,59) 3-Y-O **£2,072** (£616; £308; £153) **Stalls** High

Form RPR

0123 1 **Private Peachey (IRE)**[13] 2079 3-8-13 **59** JamesMillman(5) 2 72+
(B R Millman) *mde all: pushed clr over 2f out: comf* **6/4**[1]

0400 2 3 **Just Oscar (GER)**[20] 1903 3-9-4 **59** GeorgeBaker 16 65
(W M Brisbourne) *v.s.a: bhd tl stdy hdwy fr 3f out: chsd easy wnr fr wl over 1f out* **10/1**

4440 3 6 **Brave Jack (IRE)**[50] 1154 3-8-12 **53** SteveDrowne 8 51+
(J R Best) *s.i.s: sn in tch: lost pl 1/2-way: rdn and styd on ins fnl 2f* **15/2**[3]

00-6 4 nk **La Cuvee**[24] 1782 3-8-9 **50** TQuinn 10 42
(B G Powell) *bhd: hdwy over 1f out: n.m.r inside final f: kept on* **16/1**

05-0 5 nk **Inimical**[27] 1731 3-9-0 **55** (v[1]) JHBowman 13 46
(W S Kittow) *in rr: effrt 3f out: styng on whn edgd lft ins fnl f* **33/1**

2600 6 1 **The Tinker Man**[34] 1538 3-8-6 **47** HayleyTurner 9 36
(M D I Usher) *in rr: hdwy over 1f out: swtchd rt and short of room ins fnl f* **14/1**

0056 7 3 **Night Falcon**[17] 1973 3-8-4 **45** EdwardCreighton 1 27
(H Morrison) *chsd ldrs: rdn over 3f out: wknd fnl f* **18/1**

60-0 8 nk **The Skerret**[34] 1538 3-9-2 **57** JimCrowley 11 38
(P Winkworth) *trckd ldrs: wknd appr fnl f* **14/1**

004 9 3/4 **Kyburg**[26] 1749 3-8-6 **47** JosedeSouza 3 26
(P F I Cole) *mid-div: rdn 3f out: wknd 2f out* **14/1**

0044 10 shd **Pajada**[40] 1381 3-8-4 **45** RichardSmith 7 24
(M D I Usher) *trckd ldrs tl wknd over 3f out* **14/1**

 The Form Book, Raceform Ltd, Compton, RG20 6NL

0-00 **11** *4* **Spirit Rising**[9] 2196 3-8-0 **46** ow1..........................(p) KevinGhunowa(5) 4 16
(J M Bradley) *slowly away: sn in tch: rdn over 2f out: wknd over 1f out* **50/1**

6-41 **12** *1 1/4* **Shandelight (IRE)**[26] 1750 3-8-6 **47**.......................(p) RoystonFfrench 15 14
(Mrs A Duffield) *broke wl: bhd bef 1/2-way* **11/2**[2]

600- **13** *3/4* **Porjenski**[214] 6401 3-7-11 **45**...................................... JosephWalsh(7) 12 10
(A B Haynes) *a bhd* **66/1**

0-50 **14** *4* **Zameliana**[24] 1782 3-8-4 **45**.. RichardThomas 6 —
(Dr J R J Naylor) *trckd ldrs tl rdn and wknd over 2f out* **100/1**

0406 **15** *1/2* **Noravana (IRE)**[6] 2299 3-8-6 **52**................................ ColinHaddon(5) 14 7
(Miss V Haigh) *mid-div: rdn over 2f out: sn wknd* **66/1**

00-0 **16** *16* **Lordship (IRE)**[29] 1684 3-9-3 **58**.............................. FrancisNorton 5 —
(A W Carroll) *t.k.h: pressed wnr to over 3f out: wknd rapidly* **40/1**

1m 39.88s (-1.22) **Going Correction** -0.125s/f (Firm) **16** Ran SP% **125.4**
Speed ratings (Par 97):101,98,92,91,91 90,87,87,86,86 82,81,80,76,75 59
CSF £17.33 CT £100.50 TOTE £2.50: £1.10, £2.10, £2.60, £2.60; EX 17.80 Trifecta £101.30 Part won. Pool £142.78. - 0.30 winning units..
Owner The Peachey Syndicate **Bred** Paradime Ltd **Trained** Kentisbeare, Devon
■ Stewards' Enquiry : J H Bowman caution: careless riding

FOCUS
A low-grade handicap, but the winner came away from the runner-up who was, in turn, well clear of the third home so the form is probably as solid as it can be for the grade.
The Tinker Man Official explanation: jockey said colt was denied a clear run
Lordship(IRE) Official explanation: jockey said gelding ran too free

2490 TOTESPORT.COM H'CAP 1m 2f 46y
3:10 (3:10) (Class 6) (0-65,65) 3-Y-0+ **£2,202** (£655; £327; £163) **Stalls** High

Form RPR
010 **1** **Siena Star (IRE)**[46] 1249 9-10-0 **63**................................... JHBowman 11 72
(Stef Liddiard) *mid-div: rdn and hdwy 3f out: kpt on to ld wl ins fnl f* **12/1**

6043 **2** *1 1/4* **Shaheer (IRE)**[11] 2141 5-9-2 **51**.. JimCrowley 6 58
(J Gallagher) *mid-div: hdwy 3f out: rdn to ld over 1f out: hdd wl ins fnl f* **13/2**[2]

00-0 **3** *1/2* **She's So Pretty (IRE)**[19] 1927 3-9-1 **63**......................(p) AdamKirby 13 68
(W R Swinburn) *trckd ldr: led over 2f out: hdd over 1f out: no ex fnl f* **14/1**

64-6 **4** *3* **Spice Bar**[22] 1850 3-9-0 **62**...(p) FrancisNorton 9 61
(A M Balding) *s.i.s: rdn and hdwy over 2f out: kpt on one pce fnl f* **4/1**[1]

5602 **5** *5* **Conny Nobel (IRE)**[8] 2259 3-7-13 **52**............................ LukeMorris(5) 2 42
(J L Flint) *mid-div: rdn 3f out: one pce fnl 2f* **12/1**

4351 **6** *shd* **Our Kes (IRE)**[9] 2194 5-9-12 **61**....................................... AmirQuinn 3 52
(P Howling) *led tl rdn and hdd over 2f out: wknd over 1f out* **4/1**[1]

0156 **7** *2 1/2* **Monmouthshire**[25] 1761 4-8-9 **49**...............................(v) TolleyDean(5) 10 35
(R J Price) *mid-div: rdn over 3f out: wknd over 1f out* **8/1**

65-6 **8** *1 1/2* **Mystical Moon**[20] 1887 3-9-3 **65**.. PatDobbs 1 47
(Lady Herries) *in tch: rdn 3f out: wknd 2f out* **15/2**[3]

00-0 **9** *hd* **Yenaled**[9] 2194 10-8-8 **48**... KevinGhunowa(5) 7 31
(J M Bradley) *towards rr: effrt 3f out and sme hdwy: wknd over 1f out* **50/1**

0005 **10** *1 3/4* **Lawyer To World**[42] 1320 3-7-12 **46** oh1.................. FrankieMcDonald 4 24
(N A Callaghan) *s.i.s: a bhd* **33/1**

0-50 **11** *3* **Adobe**[9] 2214 12-8-8 **48**.. WilliamBuick(5) 8 22
(W M Brisbourne) *mid-div: wknd over 2f out* **14/1**

65-0 **12** *1 3/4* **Fortune Point (IRE)**[11] 2141 9-9-4 **53**.............................. SteveDrowne 5 23
(A W Carroll) *chsd ldrs to over 2f out: wknd qckly over 1f out* **25/1**

6005 **13** *7* **My Mirasol**[19] 1927 3-9-0 **62**... TQuinn 12 18
(D E Cantillon) *trckd ldrs tl wknd over 3f out* **20/1**

000- **P** **Grand Place**[372] 2223 5-9-3 **52**.....................................(b[1]) GeorgeBaker 14 —
(J G Portman) *t.k.h in mid-div: bhd whn p.u and dismntd over 2f out* **66/1**

2m 9.11s (-1.89) **Going Correction** -0.125s/f (Firm)
WFA 3 from 4yo+ 13lb **14** Ran SP% **119.9**
Speed ratings (Par 101):102,101,100,98,94 94,92,90,90,89 86,85,79,—
CSF £83.57 CT £1122.89 TOTE £13.60: £3.40, £2.40, £2.70; EX 95.00 TRIFECTA Not won..
Owner ownaracehorse.co.uk (Shefford) **Bred** Mrs A J Brudenell **Trained** Great Shefford, Berks

FOCUS
Another moderate handicap and there was a host of horses in with a chance up the straight, but in the end the front three came away. The level looks pretty sound.
Our Kes(IRE) Official explanation: jockey said mare ran too free
Lawyer To World Official explanation: jockey said colt suffered interference in running
My Mirasol Official explanation: jockey said filly hung left
Grand Place Official explanation: jockey said gelding lost its action on the bend

2491 TOTEEXACTA FILLIES' H'CAP 1m 3f 144y
3:40 (3:41) (Class 6) (0-65,65) 4-Y-0+ **£2,202** (£655; £327; £163) **Stalls** High

Form RPR
60 **1** **Tibouchina (IRE)**[30] 1628 4-9-0 **58**.................................... JamesDoyle 6 67+
(R M Beckett) *hld up: hdwy over 2f out: led 1f out: rdn out* **5/2**[2]

0-00 **2** *2 1/2* **Joy In The Guild (IRE)**[62] 976 4-8-7 **51**...................... FrancisNorton 3 55
(W S Kittow) *trckd ldrs: rdn and chsd wnr ins fnl f* **6/1**

2162 **3** *3/4* **Chia (IRE)**[66] 933 4-9-1 **59**.. HayleyTurner 4 62
(D Haydn Jones) *slowly away: sn in tch: t.k.h: hung lft fr over 1f out but r.o ins fnl f* **7/2**[3]

00-6 **4** *hd* **Gigi Glamor**[16] 1998 5-8-1 **50**.. WilliamBuick(5) 2 52
(W M Brisbourne) *led for 2f: led 2f out to 1f out: no ex ins fnl f* **5/1**

001- **5** *11* **Helen Wood**[20] 5733 4-9-0 **58**.. RyanMoore 5 48
(D E Pipe) *led after 2f: rdn and hdd 2f out: wknd appr fnl f* **15/8**[1]

2m 29.75s (-0.55) **Going Correction** -0.125s/f (Firm) **5** Ran SP% **116.5**
Speed ratings (Par 98):96,94,93,93,86
CSF £17.83 TOTE £3.60: £1.60, £2.10; EX 27.80.
Owner James M Egan **Bred** Benedikt Fassbender **Trained** Whitsbury, Hants

FOCUS
A weak fillies' handicap. There was no real pace on until things quickened up dramatically a quarter of a mile out, so the form might have a little question mark over it. The winner is rated in line with last year's Irish form.

2492 TOTESPORT 0800 221 221 H'CAP 1m 5y
4:10 (4:11) (Class 5) (0-70,69) 4-Y-0+ **£2,914** (£867; £433; £216) **Stalls** High

Form RPR
3414 **1** **Tender The Great (IRE)**[13] 2085 4-9-3 **68**........... RichardKingscote(3) 3 79+
(B G Powell) *trckd ldrs: rdn to ld over 1f out: edgd lft but r.o and in command fnl f* **4/1**[1]

0-02 **2** *2* **Wrighty Almighty (IRE)**[20] 1886 5-8-7 **55**.............................. PaulDoe 2 60
(P R Chamings) *trckd ldrs: rdn to ld briefly 2f out: no imp on wnr fnl f* **4/1**[1]

665 **3** *hd* **Trevian**[5] 2336 6-8-6 **54**... LPKeniry 6 59
(J M Bradley) *hld up in mid-div: hdwy over 2f out: rdn over 1f out: wnt 3rd ins fnl f* **8/1**[3]

0200 **4** *1* **Green Pirate**[12] 2117 5-7-11 **50** oh1.............................. WilliamBuick(5) 9 52+
(W M Brisbourne) *s.i.s: hld up in rr: hdwy over 2f out: styd on fnl f: nvr nrr* **12/1**

2306 **5** *nk* **First Friend (IRE)**[12] 2106 6-8-5 **60**............................ HaddenFrost(7) 1 62
(M Hill) *led after 1f: hdd 2f out: one pce fnl f* **8/1**[3]

2410 **6** *1 3/4* **Imperium**[17] 1969 6-9-2 **64**.. PatDobbs 8 62
(Jean-Rene Auvray) *stdd s: rdn and hdwy on ins over 2f out: one pce ins fnl 2f* **10/1**

0010 **7** *1/2* **The Gaikwar (IRE)**[9] 2214 8-9-2 **69**..........................(b) LukeMorris(5) 12 65
(R A Harris) *a in rr* **9/1**

61-3 **8** *1* **Wind Chime (IRE)**[33] 1562 10-8-7 **55**......................... RichardThomas 4 49
(A G Newcombe) *hld up: effrt 2f out: wknd fnl f* **6/1**[2]

/050 **9** *3* **Lockerley Man**[33] 1560 4-8-6 **54**................................ RoystonFfrench 5 41
(W S Kittow) *led for 1f: trckd ldr tl rdn and wknd over 2f out* **14/1**

0000 **10** *14* **Lockstock (IRE)**[12] 2107 9-8-4 **52**.................................(p) HayleyTurner 10 7
(M S Saunders) *mid-div: rdn over 2f out: sn wknd* **14/1**

2000 **11** *13* **Golden Square**[29] 1673 5-8-2 **50**................................... FrancisNorton 11 —
(A W Carroll) *chsd ldrs: rdn 1/2-way: sn wknd* **33/1**

1m 39.67s (-1.43) **Going Correction** -0.125s/f (Firm) **11** Ran SP% **119.6**
Speed ratings (Par 103):102,100,99,98,98 96,96,95,92,78 65
CSF £19.24 CT £124.63 TOTE £4.50: £1.50, £2.50, £4.20; EX 20.20 Trifecta £57.10 Pool £283.50. - 3.52 winning units..
Owner Miss Kwok-Mei Ada Yip **Bred** Y Wai Kwan **Trained** Lambourn, Berks

FOCUS
One of the better-class races on an uninspiring card. Not much got into it from the rear. Pretty sound form.
Golden Square Official explanation: jockey said gelding lost its action

2493 TOTESPORTCASINO.COM H'CAP 2m 1f 34y
4:40 (4:40) (Class 6) (0-60,63) 4-Y-0+ **£2,072** (£616; £308; £153) **Stalls** Low

Form RPR
60-0 **1** **Jayer Gilles**[29] 1683 7-8-5 **52**.................................(v[1]) KevinGhunowa(5) 4 61
(Dr J R J Naylor) *trckd ldrs: led over 3f out: pushed out fnl f* **12/1**[3]

015- **2** *1 1/2* **Sharaab (USA)**[21] 6132 6-8-6 **48**.......................................(t) LPKeniry 12 55
(D E Cantillon) *trckd ldrs: rdn to chse wnr 3f out: no imp fnl f* **9/2**[1]

0640 **3** *5* **Lord Nellsson**[20] 1888 11-8-7 **49**..................................... HayleyTurner 10 50
(Andrew Turnell) *mid-div: hdwy to chse ldrs 3f out: one pce fnl 2f* **9/2**[1]

000/ **4** *2* **Montgomery**[914] 6838 6-8-4 **46** oh1............................ RichardThomas 8 45
(A G Newcombe) *bhd: rdn over 3f out: styd on one pce past btn horses* **25/1**

60/6 **5** *1/2* **Honour High**[32] 1590 5-8-4 **46** oh1.............................. RoystonFfrench 2 44
(Lady Herries) *trckd ldr to over 3f out: wknd 2f out* **5/1**[2]

5544 **6** *nk* **Squirtle (IRE)**[11] 2142 4-8-11 **59**................................ WilliamBuick(5) 1 57
(W M Brisbourne) *hld up in rr: rdn 4f out: hdwy on outside over 2f out: wknd appr fnl f* **5/1**[2]

65-6 **7** *5* **Top Trees**[20] 1888 9-8-4 **46** oh1..................................... FrancisNorton 13 38
(W S Kittow) *t.k.h: mid-div: hdwy to chse ldrs 4f out: wknd over 1f out* **9/2**[1]

00-0 **8** *1* **Noble Calling (FR)**[7] 10-8-4 **46** oh1............................... DavidKinsella 11 36
(R J Hodges) *s.i.s: a bhd* **16/1**

033/ **9** *7* **Reflex Blue**[32] 6606 10-8-0 **47** oh1 ow1............................ TolleyDean(5) 6 29
(R J Price) *hld up in mid-div: rdn 4f out: wknd over 1f out* **14/1**

0000 **10** *17* **Digger Boy**[13] 2084 4-8-7 **50**... JimCrowley 3 12
(J Gallagher) *led: wkng whn hdd over 3f out* **14/1**

3m 47.52s (-2.08) **Going Correction** -0.125s/f (Firm)
WFA 4 from 5yo+ 1lb **10** Ran SP% **118.6**
Speed ratings (Par 101):99,98,95,95,94 94,92,91,88,80
CSF £66.50 CT £287.24 TOTE £14.70: £2.90, £2.10, £2.00; EX 92.10 TRIFECTA Not won..
Owner Mrs Susan Brimble **Bred** D E Hazzard **Trained** Shrewton, Wilts

FOCUS
The outcome to this modest staying handicap, which was no better than a seller, appeared to be an improved performance from the winner. Weak form.

2494 TOTE TEXT BETTING 60021 H'CAP 5f 161y
5:10 (5:11) (Class 4) (0-85,83) 3-Y-0+ **£4,857** (£1,445; £722; £360) **Stalls** Low

Form RPR
-140 **1** **Roman Maze**[17] 1971 7-9-13 **83**... RyanMoore 9 91
(W M Brisbourne) *hld up in rr: swtchd lft and hdwy over 1f out: squeezed through ins fnl f to ld cl home* **8/1**[3]

1145 **2** *nk* **Who's Winning (IRE)**[11] 2139 6-9-6 **79**............... RichardKingscote(3) 2 86
(B G Powell) *trckd ldrs and swtchd lft over 1f out: ev ch ins fnl f* **9/1**

0-00 **3** *shd* **Golden Dixie (USA)**[17] 1971 8-9-8 **83**............................ LukeMorris(5) 4 90
(R A Harris) *in tch: rdn 2f out: rdn 2f out: led ins fnl f: hdd and lost 2nd cl home* **8/1**[3]

3-50 **4** *1 1/2* **High Ridge**[3] 2394 8-8-10 **71**....................................(p) KevinGhunowa(5) 3 73
(J M Bradley) *towards rr: hdwy 2f out: rdn and ev ch ins fnl f: nt qckn cl home* **9/1**

0411 **5** *1/2* **Rainbow Bay**[7] 2419 4-8-7 **70** 6ex.................................(v) MCGeran(7) 12 70
(P D Evans) *in tch: rdn to chse ldrs 2f out: one pce fnl f* **9/2**[2]

3060 **6** *1/2* **Pic Up Sticks**[8] 2237 8-9-11 **81**.. TQuinn 7 79
(B G Powell) *trckd ldr: rdn to ld 2f out: hdd & wknd ins fnl f* **10/1**

40-0 **7** *3/4* **Summer Recluse (USA)**[17] 1969 8-8-8 **64** oh1....................(t) LPKeniry 8 60
(J M Bradley) *mid-div on ins: rdn 2f out: no hdwy after* **33/1**

2512 **8** *hd* **Saviours Spirit**[36] 1465 6-9-7 **77**...................................... SteveDrowne 10 72
(T G Mills) *towards rr: rdn over 2f out: nvr on terms* **9/4**[1]

2-30 **9** *2 1/2* **Fairfield Princess**[20] 1900 3-9-3 **81**................................... JHBowman 5 67
(M S Saunders) *led tl hdd & wknd 2f out* **25/1**

0-00 **10** *shd* **Mine Behind**[30] 1619 7-9-10 **80**...................................... GeorgeBaker 11 66
(J R Best) *a bhd* **12/1**

625 **11** *nk* **Welcome Approach**[13] 2072 4-8-8 **69**........................ WilliamBuick(5) 13 54
(J R Weymes) *trckd ldrs: rdn and wknd over 1f out* **16/1**

01-0 **F** **Ludovico**[16] 1996 4-8-12 **75**.......................................(bt) BarrySavage(7) 6 —
(J M Bradley) *rrd up and fell leaving stalls: dead* **50/1**

69.95 secs (-1.25) **Going Correction** -0.125s/f (Firm)
WFA 3 from 4yo+ 8lb **12** Ran SP% **122.6**
Speed ratings (Par 105):103,102,102,100,99 98,97,94,94 94,—
CSF £79.64 CT £614.44 TOTE £8.70: £2.20, £2.90, £3.50; EX 75.50 TRIFECTA Not won. Place 6 £89.51, Place 5 £52.84..
Owner The Jenko and Thomo Partnership **Bred** Juddmonte Farms **Trained** Great Ness, Shropshire

FOCUS
A tight finish to this sprint handicap where a lot of the usual suspects were taking each other on again. Sound enough form. Roman Maze was back to last year's best, with the second posting his best figure since 2005.
Saviours Spirit Official explanation: jockey said gelding was short of room
Fairfield Princess Official explanation: jockey said filly ran too free

T/Jkpt: Part won. £184,416.41 to a £1 stake. Pool: £259,741.50. 0.50 winning tickets. T/Plt: £101.40 to a £1 stake. Pool: £79,151.15. 569.30 winning tickets. T/Qpdt: £51.70 to a £1 stake. Pool: £3,660.70. 52.30 winning tickets. JS

2495 - 2498a (Foreign Racing) - See Raceform Interactive

2290 CHANTILLY (R-H)
Sunday, June 10

OFFICIAL GOING: Good

2499a PRIX PAUL DE MOUSSAC (GROUP 3) (C&G) 1m
2:15 (2:21) 3-Y-O **£27,027** (£10,811; £8,108; £5,405; £2,703)

RPR

1 **Asperity (USA)**[43] [1306] 3-8-10 ..... LDettori 1 108
(J H M Gosden) *led: rdn over 1f out: hdd 100yds out: drvn to ld again on line* **5/2**[2]

2 *nse* **Stoneside (IRE)**[21] [1878] 3-8-10 ..... TGillet 6 107
(Rod Collet, France) *trckd wnr: chal 2f out: drvn to take narrow ld 100yds out: r.o: ct on line* **13/2**[3]

3 *1 ½* **Grand Vista**[21] [1878] 3-8-10 ..... SPasquier 2 104
(A Fabre, France) *racd in 3rd to st: trcking wnr on rails fr over 2f out: swtchd out 1f out: r.o ins last 100yds* **10/1**

4 *2 ½* **Battle Paint (USA)**[28] [1703] 3-8-10 ..... C-PLemaire 3 98
(J-C Rouget, France) *hld up: last st: nvr able to chal* **13/8**[1]

5 *nk* **Lost Ark (IRE)**[27] 3-8-10 ..... OPeslier 4 98
(E Lellouche, France) *hld up in 5th to st: kpt on one pce* **13/2**[3]

6 *3* **Knowledge (FR)**[56] [1056] 3-8-10 ..... CSoumillon 7 91
(Y De Nicolay, France) *racd in 4th to st: btn over 1f out* **14/1**

7 *snk* **Bernando (FR)**[17] 3-8-10 ..... TThulliez 5 90
(P Bary, France) *6th st: hdwy on ins to go 4th: rdn over 2f out: btn over 1f out* **14/1**

1m 35.6s (-4.70) **Going Correction** -0.375s/f (Firm) 7 Ran SP% **115.8**
Speed ratings: 108,107,106,103,103 100,100
PARI-MUTUEL: WIN 5.00; PL 2.70, 3.70; SF 31.70.
Owner George Strawbridge **Bred** Equine Stable Ltd **Trained** Newmarket, Suffolk

NOTEBOOK
Asperity(USA) gave a thoroughly genuine effort and seemed suited by the drop back in distance. He fought really well in the final stages to regain a lead which he just lost half a furlong out. The colt was asked to make all the running and was still going well halfway up the straight when tackled by the runner-up. He was then put under strong pressure and just won this Group 3 event on the nod. Connections will now probably have a good look at the Group 1 Prix Jean Prat back over course and distance next month.
Stoneside(IRE), an ex-Spanish-trained colt, ran his heart out and looked the likely winner running into the last 50 yards. He pulled out all the stops and only lost by inches. Equipped with cheekpieces here, he is another who could line up for the Jean Prat.
Grand Vista, well placed from the start, was given every possible chance but could not quicken when things warmed up from the two-furlong marker. He just stayed on one-paced and is not quite up to this level.
Battle Paint(USA) was a most disappointing favourite and never really looked likely to take a hand in the finish. He was last early on and asked to make his run from the two-furlong marker, but there was nothing in the tank. He had good two-year-old form but has yet to reproduce it this season.

2500a PRIX DU CHEMIN DE FER DU NORD (GROUP 3) 1m
2:50 (2:49) 4-Y-O+ **£27,027** (£10,811; £8,108; £5,405; £2,703)

RPR

1 **Spirito Del Vento (FR)**[45] [1273] 4-8-12 ..... KFallon 2 113
(J-M Beguigne, France) *hld up in 4th: hdwy over 1f out: drvn to ld 150yds out: r.o wl* **7/1**

2 *2* **Multiplex**[45] [1273] 4-8-12 ..... SPasquier 5 109
(A Fabre, France) *disp 2nd to st: rdn & clsd up over 1f out: ev ch 150 yds out: one pce* **10/3**[3]

3 *1* **Passager (FR)**[22] [1834] 4-9-0 ..... C-PLemaire 6 109
(Mme C Head-Maarek, France) *set gd pce: led to 150yds out: one pce* **5/4**[1]

4 *2 ½* **Kentucky Dynamite (USA)**[40] [1389] 4-8-12 ..... CSoumillon 3 102
(A De Royer-Dupre, France) *disp 2nd to st: trcking ldr til rdn & btn over 1f out* **5/2**[2]

5 *2 ½* **Luisant**[38] 4-8-12 ..... JMurtagh 4 97
(F Doumen, France) *last thrght: rdn & btn 2f out* **20/1**

1m 34.6s (-5.70) **Going Correction** -0.375s/f (Firm) 5 Ran SP% **113.4**
Speed ratings: 113,111,110,107,105
PARI-MUTUEL: WIN 4.90; PL 2.00, 2.10; SF 9.40.
Owner L Ciampi **Bred** Haras Des Sablonnets **Trained** France
■ Kieren Fallon's first ride in France since returning from a six-month suspension.

NOTEBOOK
Spirito Del Vento(FR) broke the record time for the race and is certainly a top-class gelding when on form. Slightly detached during the early part of the race, he quickened impressively to strike the front inside the last and drew away to win with plenty in hand. Connections will now be looking at races like the Sussex Stakes and the Jacques Le Marois.
Multiplex looked the likely winner but was one-paced when tackled inside the final furlong. Always well up, he had done away with the favourite by the furlong post but could not match the finishing speed of the winner.
Passager(FR), who recorded a personal best to finish third in the Lockinge last time, proved a huge disappointment and was made to look paceless. He set out to make all the running but did not kick sufficiently when the race warmed up. He just stayed on in third place and is possibly better with more cut in the ground.
Kentucky Dynamite(USA) was well placed and given every possible chance but was going nowhere at the furlong marker. He will strip much fitter next time.

2501a PRIX DE DIANE HERMES (GROUP 1) (FILLIES) 1m 2f 110y
3:35 (3:36) 3-Y-O **£308,865** (£123,568; £61,784; £30,865; £15,459)

RPR

1 **West Wind**[32] 3-9-0 ..... LDettori 9 116
(H-A Pantall, France) *mid-div: 8th st: hdwy on outside whn sltly hmpd & carried rt wl over 1f out: led 1 1/f out: drvn out & r.o wl* **9/2**[2]

2 *1 ½* **Mrs Lindsay (USA)**[62] [989] 3-9-0 ..... JMurtagh 1 113
(F Rohaut, France) *led to 1 1/2f out: r.o same pce* **14/1**

3 *nk* **Diyakalanie (FR)**[42] [1339] 3-9-0 ..... TThulliez 6 113
(J Boisnard, France) *7th st on ins: hdwy 2f out: kpt on to take 3rd ins fnl f* **40/1**

4 *½* **Anabaa's Creation (IRE)**[21] [1880] 3-9-0 ..... GMosse 3 112
(A De Royer-Dupre, France) *trckd ldr: 2nd st: rdn & ev ch 1 1/2f out: one pce* **20/1**

5 *¾* **Beatrix Kiddo (FR)**[42] 3-9-0 ..... ODoleuze 4 111
(Robert Collet, France) *a cl up: 4th st: nvr able to chal but kpt on steadily fnl 2f* **33/1**

6 *1 ½* **Believe Me (IRE)**[21] [1880] 3-9-0 ..... OPeslier 2 108
(J-M Beguigne, France) *trckd ldrs: 3rd st: rdn wl over 1f out: one pce* **15/2**

7 *nk* **Marie Rossa**[17] 3-9-0 ..... ACrastus 5 107
(P Demercastel, France) *hld up: 12th st: hdwy over 2f out: kpt on one pce: nrest at fin* **33/1**

8 *2* **Vadapolina (FR)**[40] [1388] 3-9-0 ..... CSoumillon 10 104
(A Fabre, France) *in tch: 6th st: hdwy on outside: ev ch whn edgd rt wl over 1f out: rdn & hung lft 1 1/2f out: wknd fr dist* **11/4**[1]

9 *2* **Fontcia (FR)**[40] [1388] 3-9-0 ..... DBoeuf 14 100
(D Sepulchre, France) *hld up: 13th st: sme late prog: nvr a factor* **40/1**

10 *2 ½* **Cinnamon Bay**[22] [1856] 3-9-0 ..... SPasquier 12 96
(A Fabre, France) *prom: 5th st: btn wl over 1f out* **13/2**[3]

11 *shd* **Sequoia (SLO)**[28] 3-9-0 ..... WMongil 8 96
(J P Lopez, Slovakia) *hld up: last to st: nvr a factor* **100/1**

12 *½* **Sweet Lilly**[25] [1769] 3-9-0 ..... DarryllHolland 7 95
(M R Channon) *11th st: a in rr* **14/1**

13 *1 ½* **Topka (FR)**[21] [1880] 3-9-0 ..... TJarnet 13 92
(F Doumen, France) *mid-div on outside: 9th st: sn btn* **66/1**

14 *10* **Coquerelle (IRE)**[21] [1880] 3-9-0 ..... C-PLemaire 11 74
(J-C Rouget, France) *bandaged front: mid-div: 10th st: sn wknd & eased* **11/4**[1]

2m 6.30s (-4.20) **Going Correction** -0.125s/f (Firm) 14 Ran SP% **128.0**
Speed ratings: 110,108,108,108,107 106,106,105,103,101 101,101,100,92
PARI-MUTUEL: WIN 8.10; PL 3.60,5.00,9.70; DF 55.30.
Owner Sheikh Mohammed **Bred** Darley **Trained** France
■ A Prix du Jockey Club/Prix de Diane Classic double for Frankie Dettori.

NOTEBOOK
West Wind, a supplementary entry, had reportedly done a remarkable piece of work the Tuesday before this race. A little free early on, she was then put in a pocket before following the favourite in the early part of the straight. She burst into the lead at the furlong marker and won going away, dominating the final stages of this Classic. She looks to have plenty of scope for further improvement as this was only her fourth race, and she will now have a short rest. There is a likelihood that she will be supplemented into the Irish Oaks and she looks capable of getting 1m4f.
Mrs Lindsay(USA), given a two-month break, looked in great shape in the paddock and was taken into the lead soon after the start as there were no other takers for this role. She was passed in the straight and looked likely to drop back before rallying again inside the final furlong, losing nothing in defeat. Her trainer is now looking at the Prix de la Nonette at Deauville in August.
Diyakalanie(FR), virtually ignored in the betting, had reasonable previous form and ran well up to expectations. She began her career in the Provinces and this was just her second run at a major French track. Mid-division early on, she began her forward move from the two-furlong marker up the far rail but could not quite catch the runner-up. There are no plans for this filly at the moment and connections will probably have a look for a Listed or Group 3 event.
Anabaa's Creation(IRE), who has always been well thought of, was given an excellent ride and ran a blinder. She was well up there from the start and still there halfway up the straight. She battled on well to the line and more cut in the ground would have been an advantage. There are no plans for this filly at the moment.
Vadapolina(FR), impressive winner of a Group 3 at Saint-Cloud on her most recent outing, moved strongly into contention and held every chance, but she soon began to tire from well over a furlong out and proved most disappointing.
Sweet Lilly, narrowly denied by the overrated Passage Of Time in the Musidora, could not quicken in the straight and was simply not good enough.
Coquerelle(IRE) came here unbeaten in four races, including a defeat of West Wind when conceding 3lb at Longchamp in April and a win in the Group 1 Prix Saint-Alary last time. Bitterly disappointing, she is now set to continue her career in the USA where she can race on medication.

1515 COLOGNE (R-H)
Sunday, June 10

OFFICIAL GOING: Good

2502a OPPENHEIM-UNION-RENNEN (GROUP 2) 1m 3f
4:15 (4:34) 3-Y-O **£40,541** (£15,541; £8,108; £3,378)

RPR

1 **Axxos (GER)**[40] [1387] 3-9-2 ..... AStarke 1 105
(P Schiergen, Germany) *mde all: qcknd two l clr over 1f out: drvn out* **43/10**

2 *¾* **Appel Au Maitre (FR)**[40] [1387] 3-9-2 ..... FJohansson 4 104
(Wido Neuroth, Norway) *racd in 2nd: rdn over 1 1/2f out: kpt on gamely u.p whn chal for 2nd clsng stages* **191/10**

3 *nse* **Conillon (GER)**[24] 3-9-2 ..... EPedroza 6 104
(A Wohler, Germany) *racd in 4th: rdn 2f out: disp 2nd ins fnl f: lost 2nd and no ex cl home* **2/1**[1]

4 *½* **Sommersturm (GER)** 3-9-2 ..... THellier 2 103
(J Hirschberger, Germany) *racd in 3rd: kpt on steadily on ins fnl 1 1/2f* **33/10**[3]

5 *¾* **Antek (GER)**[24] 3-9-2 ..... ADeVries 3 102
(H Blume, Germany) *5th thrght: kpt on at same pce fnl 2f* **3/1**[2]

6 *3* **Global Dream (GER)**[35] [1516] 3-9-2 ..... AHelfenbein 5 97
(U Ostmann, Germany) *6th thrght: a in rr* **46/10**

7 *1 ½* **Kaleo**[56] [1054] 3-9-2 ..... ASuborics 7 95
(A Wohler, Germany) *last thrght: a bhd* **123/10**

2m 21.9s (1.10) 7 Ran SP% **130.8**
(including ten euro stakes): WIN 53; PL 19, 21, 14: SF 789.
Owner Gestut Ittlingen **Bred** Gestut Hof Ittlingen **Trained** Germany

NOTEBOOK
Axxos(GER) made all under a canny ride, but this was an inconclusive German Derby trial with only two lengths covering the first five home.

FRAUENFELD (R-H)

Sunday, June 10

OFFICIAL GOING: Good

2503a DAVIDOFF SWISS DERBY — 1m 4f

2:30 (2:38) 3-Y-O **£20,084** (£8,033; £6,025; £4,017; £2,008)

RPR

1 **Meshugah (IRE)**[22] 3-9-2 .... FSpanu 10 97
(R Gibson, France)

2 *5* **Cesar Le Peintre (FR)**[27] 3-9-2 .... GToupel 6 89
(H-A Pantall, France)

3 *nk* **Ganderas (GER)** 3-9-2 .... RobertHavlin 13 89
(M Weiss, Switzerland)

4 *2* **Best Of Thurgau (GER)** 3-9-2 .... GBocskai 12 86
(Carmen Bocskai, Switzerland)

5 *1 3/4* **Pont Des Arts (FR)**[360] [2596] 3-9-2 .... OPlacais 7 83
(K Schafflutzel, Switzerland)

6 *nk* **Mascarpone (GER)** 3-9-2 .... RKaderli 4 83
(M Weiss, Switzerland)

7 *1* **Swiss Act**[32] [1584] 3-9-2 .... JoeFanning 9 81
(M Johnston) *unruly in stall: removed & put in last: wnt lft s: midfield early: wnt 2nd on outside after 4f: hrd rdn 3f out: wknd over 1 1/2f out*

8 *1 1/2* **Auenritter (GER)**[40] 3-9-2 .... TCastanheira 3 79
(Karin Suter, Switzerland)

9 *1 3/4* **Big Honor (IRE)**[17] 3-9-2 .... SLadjadj 11 76
(U Suter, France)

10 *8* **Song Of Victory (GER)** 3-9-2 .... FergusSweeney 8 64
(M Weiss, Switzerland)

11 *8* **Ansermo (GER)** 3-9-2 .... ASanglard 2 52
(Christina Bucher, Germany)

12 *5* **Mamborock (FR)**[32] 3-9-2 .... AGavilan 1 45
(J-L Pelletan, France)

13 *dist* **Mission Apollo (FR)**[41] 3-9-2 .... F-XBertras 5 —
(J-L Pelletan, France)

2m 33.95s (153.95) **13** Ran
(including SwFr1 stake): WIN 7.80; PL 2.70, 3.20, 14.50; DF 13.90.
Owner E Mordukhovitch **Bred** Barronstown Stud & Orpendale **Trained** Lamorlaye, France

NOTEBOOK
Meshugah(IRE), one of five challengers from France, ran out an impressive winner.
Pont Des Arts(FR) had won his last five races, including the Swiss 2000 Guineas.
Swiss Act reacted badly to the hot weather and got upset in the stalls. The tight track was also against him and this run is probably best forgotten.

[2007]PONTEFRACT (L-H)

Monday, June 11

OFFICIAL GOING: Good to firm (good in places)
Wind: Nil Weather: Fine and dry

2504 RENAULT VANS MAIDEN AUCTION FILLIES' STKS — 6f

6:45 (6:46) (Class 5) 2-Y-O **£3,886** (£1,156; £577; £288) **Stalls** Low

Form RPR

02 1 **La Chicaluna**[9] [2251] 2-8-4 0 .... PaulHanagan 7 74
(J G Given) *mde all: rdn along wl over 1f out: kpt on u.p ins fnl f* **4/5**[1]

36 2 *1 3/4* **Lake Sabina**[28] [1727] 2-8-6 0 .... EdwardCreighton 2 71
(E S McMahon) *trckd ldrs: hdwy to chse wionner 2f out: rdn and ch ent fnl f: sn drvn and kpt on* **15/2**[2]

3 *1 1/2* **Suzi Spends (IRE)** 2-8-6 0 .... JoeFanning 1 66
(M Johnston) *in tch: hdwy over 2f out: rdn to chse ldng pair over 1f out: edgd lft ins fnl f: kpt on* **12/1**

5 4 *1 1/4* **Carnival Dream**[19] [1938] 2-8-4 0 ....(b) RoystonFfrench 9 61
(A Berry) *chsd wnr: rdn along over 2f out: sn drvn and kpt on same pce* **50/1**

5 *hd* **Serena's Storm (IRE)** 2-8-8 0 .... GrahamGibbons 12 64
(J J Quinn) *slowly in to stride and bhd: gd hdwy on inner 2f out: styng on whn n.m.r and eased ins fnl f* **33/1**

02 6 *2 1/2* **Welcome Return (IRE)**[18] [1963] 2-8-5 0 ow1 .... DavidAllan 13 53
(T D Easterby) *dwlt: sn in tch on wd outside: pushed along over 2f out: sn rdn and noimp appr fnl f* **15/2**[2]

50 7 *3/4* **Majigal**[31] [1636] 2-8-1 0 .... AndrewMullen(3) 6 50
(M W Easterby) *chsd ldrs: rdn along 2f out: kpt on same pce* **100/1**

8 *1 3/4* **Cryptonite Diamond (USA)** 2-8-13 0 .... AdamKirby 10 54+
(W R Swinburn) *towards rr: effrt and rn green 2f out: kpt on appr fnl f* **10/1**[3]

9 *1 1/2* **Calza Di Seta** 2-8-1 0 .... AndrewElliott(3) 8 40
(G M Moore) *a in rr* **66/1**

10 *hd* **Nisbah** 2-8-6 0 .... KDarley 4 42
(C E Brittain) *s.i.s: a in rr* **12/1**

0 11 *5* **Chica Guapa (IRE)**[16] [2039] 2-8-4 0 .... AdrianTNicholls 11 25
(Paul Green) *a in rr* **50/1**

0 12 *1/2* **Got Green (FR)**[30] [1680] 2-8-8 0 .... SebSanders 5 27
(R Hannon) *chsd ldrs: rdn along 1/2-way: sn wknd* **12/1**

00 13 *8* **Aquarian Dancer**[18] [1963] 2-8-1 0 .... DuranFentiman(3) 3 —
(Jedd O'Keeffe) *in tch: rdn along 1/2-way: sn wknd* **50/1**

1m 17.41s (0.01) **Going Correction** -0.125s/f (Firm) **13** Ran **SP% 122.6**
Speed ratings (Par 90):94,91,89,88,87 84,83,81,79,78 72,71,60
CSF £7.27 TOTE £1.90: £1.10, £2.80, £2.90; EX 8.70.
Owner The Living Legend Racing Partnership **Bred** Gainsborough Stud Ltd **Trained** Willoughton, Lincs

FOCUS
A fair fillies' maiden. The winner did not need to match her debut effort, but slight improvement from the second and fourth.

NOTEBOOK
La Chicaluna, who improved significantly on her debut running to finish second at Newcastle last time, put her previous experience to good use and was soon out in front. Responding gamely to pressure, she was always doing enough and could be of interest in nurseries. (op 6-5 tchd 5-4 in places)
Lake Sabina has shown ability on each start and improved again for the step up in distance. She is bred to get further still and is now qualified for nurseries. (op 8-1)
Suzi Spends(IRE), whose dam stayed middle distances, comes from a stable whose juveniles have been struggling and as a result this was a promising debut. She will benefit from an extra furlong in time and has a maiden in her. (op 11-1)
Carnival Dream started out in blinkers and again had them on here. She is not without ability and is more of a nursery type. (op 40-1)
Serena's Storm(IRE), a 30,000euros daughter of Statue Of Liberty, caught the eye back in fifth and is definitely one to be interested in next time. Slowly away, she was doing her best work late and was value for finishing a bit closer.
Welcome Return(IRE) improved on her initial effort when second at Newcastle last time, but she failed to progress again and was slightly disappointing. She is now qualified for nurseries. (op 7-1 tchd 8-1)
Cryptonite Diamond(USA), whose stable have made a bright start with their juveniles, did not get the clearest of runs and showed distinct signs of greenness. She is one to be interested in next time. (op 13-2)
Nisbah Official explanation: jockey said filly had missed the break

2505 TONY BETHELL MEMORIAL H'CAP — 2m 1f 22y

7:15 (7:15) (Class 4) (0-80,79) 4-Y-0+ **£5,181** (£1,541; £770; £384) **Stalls** Low

Form RPR

2212 1 **Great As Gold (IRE)**[25] [1793] 8-8-13 **70** .... TomEaves 1 80
(B Ellison) *hld up in tch: gd hdwy over 4f out: rdn along to chse ldng pair 3f out: sn drvn and outpcd: styd on wl u.p ent fnl f to ld least 75yds* **3/1**[3]

313- 2 *1 1/2* **Alambic**[280] [5069] 4-9-7 **79** .... SebSanders 7 87+
(Sir Mark Prescott) *hld up in rr: stdy hdwy 6f out: chal 3f out: rdn to ld ent fnl f: sn edgd lft: hdd and no ex last 75yds* **11/8**[1]

14-2 3 *3* **Indonesia**[16] [2047] 5-9-4 **75** .... GrahamGibbons 4 79+
(T D Walford) *trckd ldrs: smooth hdwy to ld 3f out: sn jnd and rdn over 2f out: drvn and hdd ent fnl f: one pce* **5/2**[2]

1513 4 *1 3/4* **Rocknest Island (IRE)**[21] [1895] 4-8-0 **61** ow1 ....(p) AndrewMullen(3) 3 63
(P D Niven) *chsd ldrs: rdn along 4f out: drvn 3f out and plugged on same pce* **16/1**

660/ 5 *10* **Hello It's Me**[18] [4394] 6-9-8 **79** ....(b) PaddyAspell 5 69
(D McCain Jnr) *prom: pushed along 5f out: rdn over 3f out and sn wknd* **18/1**

-000 6 *10* **Jamaican Flight (USA)**[49] [1196] 14-8-3 **60** oh15 .... PaulHanagan 6 38
(Mrs S Lamyman) *led 7f: prom tl rdn along and wknd over 3f out* **100/1**

-020 7 *46* **Imperial Harry**[24] [1813] 4-8-12 **70** .... KDarley 2 —
(V Smith) *t.k.h: chsd ldrs: hdwy to ld after 7f: pushed along and hdd 3f out: sn rdn and wknd* **14/1**

3m 45.67s (-4.83) **Going Correction** -0.125s/f (Firm)
WFA 4 from 5yo+ 1lb **7** Ran **SP% 114.5**
Speed ratings (Par 105):106,105,103,103,98 93,72
CSF £7.55 TOTE £4.10: £2.20, £1.30; EX 6.80.
Owner Keith Middleton **Bred** Rathasker Stud **Trained** Norton, N Yorks

FOCUS
The front four drew clear of the remainder in what was a decent staying handicap. It has been rated through the runner-up, with the winner better than ever.

2506 DIXONS BARNSLEY RENAULT H'CAP — 1m 2f 6y

7:45 (7:46) (Class 4) (0-85,85) 3-Y-O **£6,477** (£1,927; £963; £481) **Stalls** Low

Form RPR

61 1 **Pipedreamer**[32] [1606] 3-9-7 **85** .... JimmyFortune 2 98+
(J H M Gosden) *trckd ldrs: swtchd rt and hdwy 3f out: rdn to ld over 1f out: edgd lft and clr ins fnl f: kpt on* **11/4**[1]

2-10 2 *1* **Prince Sabaah (IRE)**[23] [1835] 3-9-1 **79** .... SebSanders 8 87
(R Hannon) *hld up in tch: effrt and pushed along 3f out: rdn 2f out: chsd wnr and hung lft ent fnl f: kpt on u.p* **6/1**[3]

-313 3 *3 1/2* **El Dececy (USA)**[23] [1843] 3-9-3 **81** .... RHills 4 82
(J L Dunlop) *led: rdn along over 2f out: drvn and hdd over 1f out: kpt on same pce* **11/4**[1]

1303 4 *1/2* **New Beginning (IRE)**[6] [2340] 3-9-1 **79** .... PaulHanagan 7 79
(Mrs S Lamyman) *hld up in rr: hdwy 3f out: swtchd ins and rdn over 1f out: kpt on same pce* **7/1**

1115 5 *2 1/2* **Fongs Gazelle**[24] [1827] 3-9-2 **83** .... GregFairley(3) 3 78
(M Johnston) *prom: rdn along to chal 3f out: drvn over 2f out and wknd wl over 1f out* **5/1**[2]

1 6 *1 1/2* **Bogside Theatre (IRE)**[9] [2253] 3-9-1 **82** .... AndrewElliott(3) 5 74
(G M Moore) *chsd ldrs: rdn along over 3f out: sn drvn and wknd over 2f out* **20/1**

21-4 7 *7* **Persian Peril**[24] [1827] 3-8-13 **77** .... DeanMcKeown 6 55
(G A Swinbank) *chsd ldrs: rdn along and nt much room 3f out: sn btn* **8/1**

05-4 8 *4* **Monsieur Dumas (IRE)**[40] [1415] 3-8-2 **66** oh1 .... RoystonFfrench 1 36
(T P Tate) *a in rr* **40/1**

2m 10.38s (-3.70) **Going Correction** -0.125s/f (Firm) **8** Ran **SP% 115.1**
Speed ratings (Par 101):109,108,105,105,103 101,96,93
CSF £20.04 CT £48.72 TOTE £4.40: £1.40, £2.30, £1.40.
Owner Cheveley Park Stud **Bred** Cheveley Park Stud Ltd **Trained** Newmarket, Suffolk

FOCUS
A good handicap, with the winner progressive and the next two to form. A decent winning time for a race like this.

2507 WEATHERBYS BANK PIPALONG STKS (LISTED RACE) (F&M) — 1m 4y

8:15 (8:15) (Class 1) 4-Y-0+
£19,631 (£7,472; £3,741; £1,869; £934; £469) **Stalls** Low

Form RPR

6612 1 **Expensive**[37] [1466] 4-9-1 100 .... EddieAhern 6 90
(C F Wall) *mde all: qcknd 2f out and sn rdn: drvn ins fnl f and kpt on wl* **6/4**[1]

140- 2 *shd* **Mont Etoile (IRE)**[275] [5185] 4-8-12 107 .... MichaelHills 3 86
(W J Haggas) *tracked ldrs: swtchd rt ancd hdwy 2f out: rdn to chal over 1f out and ev ch tl drvn and nt qckn nr line* **7/4**[2]

0360 3 *1/2* **Passion Fruit**[14] [2085] 6-8-12 76 .... DeanMcKeown 2 85
(C W Fairhurst) *hld up in rr: gd hdwy on outer wl over 1f out: rdn and hung lft ins fnl f: styd on strly towards fin* **40/1**

2060 4 *1* **Fann (USA)**[10] [2207] 4-8-12 77 .... SebSanders 1 84+
(C E Brittain) *trckd ldrs: hdwy 2f out: rdn and ch whn nt clr run ins fnl f and eased* **12/1**

040- 5 *1 1/2* **Home Sweet Home (IRE)**[228] [6190] 4-8-12 92 .... NickyMackay 4 80
(L M Cumani) *chsd wnr: rdn along over 2f out: wknd over 1f out* **9/2**[3]

6324 6 *shd* **Neardown Beauty (IRE)**[18] [1962] 4-8-12 82 .... KDarley 5 79
(I A Wood) *dwlt: sn chsng ldrs: rdn along over 2f out: wknd over 1f out* **12/1**

1m 44.81s (-0.89) **Going Correction** -0.125s/f (Firm) **6** Ran **SP% 112.4**
Speed ratings (Par 111):99,98,98,97,95 95
CSF £4.41 TOTE £2.50: £1.70, £1.30; EX 3.90.

Owner M Tilbrook **Bred** Genesis Green Stud **Trained** Newmarket, Suffolk

FOCUS

A moderate winning time for a race of its status and the close proximity of 76-rated Passion Fruit is worrying. Misleading Listed form all told, with the front pair not at their best.

NOTEBOOK

Expensive has developed into a decent filly at this level and she made it two wins in her last three with a hard-fought victory over the classy Mont Etoile. Ridden positively, she kept finding and has probably earned herself another crack at Group level. (op 13-8 tchd 2-1)

Mont Etoile(IRE), a narrow winner of last season's Ribblesdale, ran most respectably in the Irish Oaks and the St Leger on her last two starts at three and this was a fine reappearance effort considering it was over 1m. She looked likely to win a furlong out, but Expensive kept finding and she was narrowly denied. This was a highly pleasing return and she can soon get back to winning ways once stepped back up in trip. (op 15-8 tchd 2-1)

Passion Fruit stood no chance at the weights and her prominent showing does little for the form. She is little better than a fair handicapper and this is likely to be a career highlight. (tchd 33-1)

Fann(USA) found this easier than her recent Epsom assignment and was probably a little unlucky not to finish closer up. She is capable of gaining some black type. (op 10-1)

Home Sweet Home(IRE), making her debut for connections, did not offer a great deal on this seasonal reappearance and needs to step up if she is to make an impact at this level. (op 5-1)

Neardown Beauty(IRE) was another with plenty to find at the weights and it was no surprise to see her struggle. (tchd 11-1)

2508 HARRATTS WAKEFIELD RENAULT H'CAP — 6f

8:45 (8:45) (Class 5) (0-70,70) 3-Y-O+ **£3,886** (£1,156; £577; £288) **Stalls** Low

Form — RPR

1105 **1** **Franksalot (IRE)**^{8} [2272] 7-9-10 **66** .... RoystonFrench 3 — 76
(I W McInnes) *in tch: swtchd rt and hdwy over 2f out: sn rdn and chal ins fnl f: drvn and stdy on to ld nr line* **9/1**

5-02 **2** *shd* **Turn Me On (IRE)**^{16} [2033] 4-8-13 **55** .... GrahamGibbons 4 — 65
(T D Walford) *chsd ldrs on inner: hdwy over 2f out: rdn to ld jst ins fnl f: sn jnd and drvn: hdd and no ex nr line* **9/2**^{2}

4404 **3** *3* **Brigadore**^{14} [2072] 8-9-10 **66** .... SebSanders 9 — 66
(J G Given) *midfield: hdwy on outer 2f out: rdn and edgd lft over 1f out: kpt on u.pfnl f* **4/1**^{1}

5000 **4** *1* **Charles Parnell (IRE)**^{10} [2202] 4-9-6 **62** .... PaulMulrennan 12 — 59+
(M Dods) *s.i.s and bhd: hdwy on outer wl over 1f out: sn rdn and edgd lft: styd on: nrst fin* **25/1**

-136 **5** *nk* **Maison Dieu**^{16} [2033] 4-9-5 **61** .... KDarley 14 — 57
(E J Alston) *in tch: hdwy to chse ldrs over 2f out: drvn over 1f out and kpt on same pce ins fnl f* **8/1**

-150 **6** *shd* **Sir Orpen (IRE)**^{27} [1747] 4-9-13 **69** .... PhillipMakin 1 — 65
(T D Barron) *midfield: hdwy over 2f out: rdn wl over 1f out: kpt on same pce u.p ins fnl f* **7/1**^{3}

6-00 **7** *shd* **Paris Bell**^{30} [1678] 5-10-0 **70** .... PaulQuinn 10 — 65
(T D Easterby) *s.i.s and bhd: gd hdwy on inner wl over 1f out: kpt on ins fnl f* **16/1**

-045 **8** *1 1/4* **Snow Bunting**^{21} [1892] 9-8-10 **55** .... AndrewElliott$^{(3)}$ 15 — 48+
(Jedd O'Keeffe) *t.k.h: hld up in rr: hdwy 2f out: nt clr run and swtchd rt ins fnl f: styd on wl towards fin* **12/1**

-000 **9** *1* **Breaking Shadow (IRE)**^{28} [1718] 5-9-9 **65** .... JimmyQuinn 5 — 53
(M A Peill) *midfield: effrt over 2f out: sn rdn and no imp appr fnl f* **14/1**

0-00 **10** *hd* **It's Unbelievable (USA)**^{63} [967] 4-9-4 **60** .... (p) LeeEnstone 7 — 47
(P T Midgley) *led: rdn clr 2f out: drvn over 1f out: hdd & wknd ins fnl f* **40/1**

411- **11** *4* **Minnow**^{167} [6939] 3-9-1 **65** .... J-PGuillambert 2 — 40
(S C Williams) *in tch: rdn along 1/2-way: sn wknd* **11/1**

-000 **12** *1* **Foreign Edition (IRE)**^{14} [2088] 5-9-12 **68** .... (b^{1}) TomEaves 11 — 39
(Miss J A Camacho) *chsd ldrs: rdn along 1/2-way: sn wknd* **16/1**

5-65 **13** *1 1/2* **Riquewihr**^{10} [2202] 7-9-9 **65** .... TonyHamilton 8 — 32
(J S Wainwright) *prom: rdn along over 2f out: sn wknd* **11/1**

0-64 **14** *7* **Picture Frame**^{44} [1286] 3-8-11 **66** .... RoryMoore$^{(5)}$ 17 — 8
(J T Stimpson) *prom: rdn along over 2f out: sn wknd* **25/1**

1m 16.39s (-1.01) **Going Correction** -0.125s/f (Firm)
WFA 3 from 4yo+ 8lb **14 Ran SP% 124.7**
Speed ratings (Par 103):101,100,96,95,95 95,94,93,91,91 86,84,82,73
CSF £50.06 CT £195.64 TOTE £12.70: £3.60, £2.40, £2.00; EX 62.40.

Owner Stephen Hackney And Martin Higgins **Bred** J P Hardiman **Trained** Catwick, E Yorks

FOCUS

The front two came away in what was a modest handicap. Sound enough form, the winner rated to his best effort in the last couple of years.

Charles Parnell(IRE) Official explanation: jockey said gelding missed the break

Breaking Shadow(IRE) Official explanation: jockey said gelding was denied a clear run

2509 DIXON HULL RENAULT H'CAP — 5f

9:15 (9:17) (Class 6) (0-65,64) 4-Y-O+ **£3,238** (£963; £481; £240) **Stalls** Low

Form — RPR

-060 **1** **Hotham**^{4} [2386] 4-9-2 **59** .... JimmyQuinn 16 — 69
(N Wilson) *hld up in rr: gd hdwy on outer wl over 1f out: rdn to ld ins fnl f: drvn out* **14/1**

0100 **2** *1 1/4* **Paddywack (IRE)**^{20} [1914] 10-8-12 **62** .... (b) DanielleMcCreery$^{(7)}$ 15 — 67+
(D W Chapman) *dwlt and bhd: gd hdwy on outer wl over 1f out: sn rdn and styd on wl fnl f* **16/1**

3620 **3** *nk* **Divine Spirit**^{4} [2386] 6-9-1 **58** .... RoystonFrench 13 — 62
(M Dods) *hld up towards rr: hdwy on outer wl over 1f out: sn rdn and styd on wl u.p ins fnl f* **8/1**

0003 **4** *3/4* **Viewforth**^{11} [2187] 9-8-7 **50** .... (b) KDarley 3 — 51+
(M A Buckley) *led: rdn wl over 1f out: drvn and hdd ins fnl f: kpt on u.p* **8/1**

-002 **5** *1 1/4* **John Keats**^{4} [2394] 4-9-2 **59** .... PaulHanagan 11 — 55+
(J S Goldie) *hld up towards rr: hdwy over 2f out: swtchd ins and n.m.r briefly wl over 1f out: sn rdn and styd on wl fnl f* **9/2**^{1}

043 **6** *1/2* **Henry Hall (IRE)**^{3} [2418] 11-9-7 **64** .... KimTinkler 9 — 58
(N Tinkler) *chsd ldrs: rdn wl over 1f out: kpt on same pce ins fnl f* **11/2**^{2}

2400 **7** *nk* **Navigation (IRE)**^{32} [1596] 5-7-13 **45** .... (b) DuranFentiman$^{(3)}$ 12 — 38
(T J Etherington) *midfield: hdwy on outer top chse ldrs 2f out: sn rdn and kpt on same pce ins fnl f* **25/1**

-056 **8** *1 3/4* **Jun Fan (USA)**^{36} [1493] 5-8-8 **51** ow1 .... TomEaves 6 — 38
(B Ellison) *prom: effrt and ev ch over 1f out: sn rdn and one pce* **9/1**

0020 **9** *1/2* **City For Conquest (IRE)**^{10} [2221] 4-7-12 **48** .... (b) MCGeran$^{(7)}$ 5 — 33
(John A Harris) *dwlt and towards rr: n.m.r 2f out: swtchd wd and rdn over 1f out: styd on ins fnl f* **20/1**

0001 **10** *nk* **Majestical (IRE)**^{21} [1902] 5-8-8 **51** ow1 .... (p) SebSanders 8 — 35
(V Smith) *a in midfield* **6/1**^{3}

5050 **11** *nk* **Taboor (IRE)**^{17} [1991] 9-8-9 **52** .... GrahamGibbons 1 — 34
(R M H Cowell) *prominent: rdn along 2f out: drvn and wknd over 1f out* **14/1**

0-40 **12** *2* **Newcastles Owen (IRE)**^{28} [1719] 4-8-0 **46** ow1 .... AndrewElliott$^{(3)}$ 7 — 21
(R Johnson) *chsd ldrs: rdn along over 2f out: sn wknd* **100/1**

500 **13** *1* **Whithorn**^{20} [1921] 4-8-4 **47** .... EdwardCreighton 4 — 18
(J Balding) *towards rr on inner: effrt and rdn along whn hmpd 2f out: sn bhd* **66/1**

-350 **14** *1/2* **Chairman Bobby**^{3} [2421] 9-8-7 **50** .... PatCosgrave 2 — 19
(D W Barker) *chsd ldrs: rdn along 2f out: edgd lft and drvn wl over 1f out: sn wknd* **8/1**

0000 **15** *1/2* **Polish Emperor (USA)**^{68} [915] 7-9-3 **60** .... (v) TonyHamilton 10 — 27
(D W Barker) *s.i.s: a in rr* **28/1**

63.31 secs (-0.49) **Going Correction** -0.125s/f (Firm) **15 Ran SP% 124.9**
Speed ratings (Par 101):98,96,95,94,92 91,91,88,87,86 86,83,81,80,80
CSF £217.17 CT £1231.94 TOTE £13.90: £4.30, £4.70, £3.40; EX 459.40 Place 6 £27.80, Place 5 £20.50..

Owner Paul & Linda Dixon **Bred** Capt J H Wilson **Trained** Flaxton, N Yorks

FOCUS

A modest sprint handicap where the front three (drawn high) all came from off the gallop round the outside of the field as the leaders probably went off too quick. Straightforward form.

T/Plt: £36.20 to a £1 stake. Pool: £71,913.35. 1,447.25 winning tickets. T/Qpdt: £16.70 to a £1 stake. Pool: £3,683.10. 163.20 winning tickets. JR

2473 WINDSOR (R-H)

Monday, June 11

OFFICIAL GOING: Good to firm (8.8)

Wind: Light behind Weather: Fine but cloudy, warm

2510 TOTESPORT.COM SUPPORTING THE MATT HAMPSON TRUST E B F MEDIAN AUCTION MAIDEN STKS — 6f

6:35 (6:36) (Class 5) 2-Y-O **£4,210** (£1,252; £625; £312) **Stalls** High

Form — RPR

1 **Eternal Luck (IRE)** 2-9-3 0 .... PhilipRobinson 10 — 73
(M A Jarvis) *chsd ldrs: effrt over 1f out: swtchd lft ent fnl f: drvn to ld last 75yds: hld on* **15/2**

2 *hd* **Baronovici (IRE)** 2-9-3 0 .... RichardHughes 12 — 72
(R Hannon) *trckd ldrs: effrt against nr side rail over 1f out: str run fnl f but hung bdly lft: jst hld* **11/1**

05 **3** *nk* **Bazguy**^{7} [2297] 2-9-3 0 .... JamesDoyle 11 — 71
(P D Evans) *pressed ldr: rdn to chal over 1f out: narrow ld ins fnl f: hdd last 75yds: kpt on* **16/1**

4 *3/4* **Artsu** 2-9-3 0 .... RichardSmith 6 — 69
(M L W Bell) *pressed ldr: narrow ld over 1f out to ins fnl f: no ex last 75yds* **20/1**

3 **5** *1/2* **Hansinger (IRE)**^{18} [1970] 2-9-0 0 .... RichardKingscote$^{(3)}$ 13 — 67
(B I Case) *trckd ldrs: rdn 2f out: swtchd lft 1f out and then trapped bhd rivals: nt rcvr* **9/2**^{2}

32 **6** *1/2* **Advertisement**^{14} [2086] 2-9-3 0 .... TQuinn 14 — 66
(C G Cox) *led: hanging badly lft fr over 2f out: hdd over 1f out: stl veering lft and btn fnl f* **11/8**^{1}

7 *2* **Relative Order** 2-9-3 0 .... GeorgeBaker 16 — 60
(J R Best) *s.s: rn green and wl outpcd in rr: styd on fr over 1f out: gng on at fin* **16/1**

8 *3/4* **Follow The Band** 2-9-3 0 .... RyanMoore 9 — 58
(R Hannon) *bmpd s: off the pce towards rr: kpt on fnl f: n.d* **6/1**^{3}

9 *1/2* **Distant Noble** 2-8-12 0 .... KevinGhunowa$^{(5)}$ 4 — 56
(M J Wallace) *chsd ldrs: outpcd fr 2f out: no imp after* **66/1**

10 *1/2* **Marning Star** 2-9-3 0 .... IanMongan 8 — 55+
(M R Channon) *bmpd s: rn green and outpcd: styd on fnl f: no ch* **16/1**

0 **11** *11* **Jay Gee Wigmo**^{14} [2086] 2-9-3 0 .... SteveDrowne 3 — 22
(A W Carroll) *rn v green and outpcd: a bhd* **100/1**

12 *1 1/4* **Little Bones** 2-8-12 0 .... MartinDwyer 7 — 13
(Rae Guest) *s.s: outpcd and a wl bhd* **33/1**

13 *14* **Captain Jack Black** 2-9-3 0 .... JimCrowley 2 — —
(M R Bosley) *sn rdn and struggling in rr: t.o* **50/1**

1m 13.52s (-0.15) **Going Correction** -0.15s/f (Firm) **13 Ran SP% 124.5**
Speed ratings (Par 93):95,94,94,93,92 92,89,88,87,87 72,70,52
CSF £87.73 TOTE £8.30: £2.30, £2.40, £6.20; EX 50.40.

Owner H R H Sultan Ahmad Shah **Bred** Kevin B Lynch **Trained** Newmarket, Suffolk

FOCUS

A bunch finish and just a fair maiden, but it should produce some winners. The principals ended up racing down the centre of the track in the straight, with some of these inexperienced horses following a couple who edged to their left under pressure. Sound enough form.

NOTEBOOK

Eternal Luck(IRE), a 42,000gns brother to multiple 6f-1m winner Golden Tagula, and multiple sprint scorer Beaver Patrol, out of a winner over 1m5f, created a good impression on his racecourse debut. He proved relatively easy to back beforehand, but was always in touch just in behind the leaders and ultimately stayed on best. This represents just fair form, but he is obviously open to improvement and deserves his chance in better company. (op 5-1)

Baronovici(IRE), a 20,000euros first foal of a 7f winner, lacked the sharpness of some of these through the early stages, but he got the hang of things late on and just failed. (op 17-2 tchd 8-1)

Bazguy seemed a little free through the early stages, but he kept on to the line and this represented his best effort yet. He looks capable of winning an ordinary maiden and is the type to do well during the nursery season. (op 25-1)

Artsu, a 42,000gns half-brother to among others triple 7f-1m winner All Quiet, showed up well for a long way and this was a pleasing introduction. He could last a bit longer next time and may be up to finding a similar race.

Hansinger(IRE), a promising third on his debut in a 5f Salisbury maiden, was denied a clear run well inside the final furlong and looked unlucky not to be in the shake-up. He clearly possesses enough ability to pick up an ordinary contest and is another who looks capable of making his mark in nurseries later in the season. Official explanation: jockey said gelding was denied a clear run (op 7-1 tchd 8-1)

Advertisement, up a furlong in trip and switched to better ground, showed good speed through the early stages, but he compromised his chance by hanging left for much of the way up the straight and veering when hit with the whip on the right-hand side. This was disappointing considering he had shaped well on his two previous starts, but perhaps a return to easier ground will help. Official explanation: jockey said colt hung (op 2-1 tchd 5-4)

Follow The Band, a brother to dual 6f winner Sussex Lad, out of a triple 5f juvenile scorer, never posed a threat after receiving a bump at the start, but he should know a lot more next time. (tchd 5-1)

2511 CHG MERIDIAN CLAIMING STKS — 1m 3f 135y
7:05 (7:06) (Class 5) 3-Y-0+ £3,238 (£963; £481; £240) Stalls Low

Form — RPR

5663 **1** **Missie Baileys**[12] 2140 5-9-0 48........................(p) IanMongan 7 — 55
(Mrs L J Mongan) *wl plcd in chsng gp: rdn over 3f out: clsd u.p to ld over 1f out: hld on gamely* — **10/1**

0055 **2** *nk* **Treetops Hotel (IRE)**[20] 1925 8-9-6 48.................. RichardSmith 10 — 60
(B R Johnson) *hld up in last and wl off the pce: stdy prog over 3f out: clsd to chal 1f out: styd on: jst hld* — **16/1**

0063 **3** *½* **King's Ransom**[7] 2307 4-9-10 61.................. RichardHughes 3 — 63
(W R Muir) *stdd s: hld up in last trio: stdy prog fr 3f out: plld out to chal fnl f: fnd nil* — **5/1**[3]

0222 **4** *shd* **Prince Des Neiges (FR)**[12] 2140 4-9-5 60..............(p) JerryO'Dwyer(3) 9 — 61
(A M Hales) *wl plcd in chsng gp: clsd over 3f out: rdn to chal and upsides over 1f out: carried hd high and gave up* — **6/1**

-220 **5** *9* **Black Falcon (IRE)**[64] 955 7-9-7 70......................(p) WilliamBuick(5) 6 — 52
(M A Peill) *hld up in last trio: stdy prog fr 4f out to press ldrs over 2f out: wknd over 1f out* — **3/1**[2]

06-1 **6** *5* **Nuit Sombre (IRE)**[34] 1559 7-9-8 75......................(p) DarryllHolland 11 — 37
(J G M O'Shea) *led at str pce: hdd & wknd rapidly over 1f out* — **5/1**[3]

2000 **7** *5* **Bathwick Fancy (IRE)**[10] 2203 3-8-1 50 ow1..............(t) FrancisNorton 4 — 23
(J G Portman) *wl in rr: modest prog over 2f out but nvr on terms: wknd over 1f out* — **50/1**

5235 **8** *5* **Countback (FR)**[19] 1229 8-9-4 45.........................(v[1]) SteveDrowne 5 — 16
(A W Carroll) *chsd clr ldng pair to over 5f out: wknd 4f out* — **33/1**

2666 **9** *5* **Nero's Return (IRE)**[9] 2238 6-9-8 72......................(b) RyanMoore 2 — 12
(G L Moore) *dwlt: pushed up to chse ldr and sn clr of rest: rdn 4f out: wknd over 2f out: eased* — **5/2**[1]

0000 **10** *nk* **Atticus Trophies (IRE)**[6] 2332 4-9-5 49......................(p) JamesDoyle 1 — 8
(Ms J S Doyle) *chsd clr ldrs: wknd 3f out: eased whn no ch* — **100/1**

2m 28.27s (-1.83) **Going Correction** -0.15s/f (Firm)
WFA 3 from 4yo+ 15lb — 10 Ran SP% **122.1**
Speed ratings (Par 103):100,99,99,99,93 90,86,83,80,79
CSF £160.70 TOTE £14.70: £3.00, £3.20, £2.00; EX 87.00.There was no bid for the winner. Nuit Sombre was claimed by G Harker for £10,000.
Owner Mrs P J Sheen **Bred** Mrs J Wotherspoon **Trained** Epsom, Surrey

FOCUS
Some of the likelier types failed to run their races and this was a very moderate claimer. The pace was strong throughout, with both Nuit Sombre and Nero's Return looking to go off too quickly, yet the principals still finished in a bit of a heap. The race has been rated through the first two.

2512 MAXIMS AND COLONY CLUB CASINOS H'CAP — 1m 2f 7y
7:35 (7:37) (Class 4) (0-80,80) 4-Y-0+ £6,477 (£1,927; £963; £481) Stalls Low

Form — RPR

0-02 **1** **Night Cru**[17] 2004 4-9-1 74.................................. GeorgeBaker 6 — 86+
(C F Wall) *prom: led over 3f out: in command fnl 2f: pushed out* — **13/2**

-416 **2** *2* **Oscar Snowman**[102] 587 4-9-2 75.............................. MartinDwyer 10 — 82
(M P Tregoning) *t.k.h: hld up in midfield: rdn and prog on outer over 2f out: chsd wnr and hung across three rivals over 1f out: a hld* — **5/1**[3]

003 **3** *3* **Kavachi (IRE)**[10] 2218 4-7-11 61 oh1.......................... WilliamBuick(5) 7 — 65+
(G L Moore) *hld up in last: stdy prog fr 3f out: trying to cl whn bdly hmpd over 1f out: kpt on* — **9/2**[2]

0122 **4** *3½* **Cinematic (IRE)**[17] 1997 4-9-2 75.............................. AmirQuinn 4 — 70+
(J R Boyle) *t.k.h: hld up bhd ldrs: effrt 3f out: disputing 2nd but wl hld whn hmpd over 1f out* — **10/1**

610- **5** *4* **Crossbow Creek**[60] 5430 9-9-7 80.............................. JimCrowley 2 — 67+
(M G Rimell) *prom: w wnr briefly over 3f out: chsng after: sing to weaken whn hmpd over 1f out* — **20/1**

-100 **6** *shd* **Cactus King**[11] 2180 4-9-4 77.............................. IanMongan 12 — 64
(P M Phelan) *t.k.h: hld up in rr: plenty to do whn effrt 3f out: plugged on one pce* — **16/1**

0504 **7** *4* **Finsbury**[11] 2180 4-8-6 72.............................. AmyBaker(7) 1 — 51
(Miss J Feilden) *hld up in rr: sme prog into midfield 1/2-way: taken wd in st and sn no hdwy* — **33/1**

0 **8** *3* **Kervriou (FR)**[17] 2003 4-9-3 76.............................. FrancisNorton 11 — 50
(A M Balding) *hld up last tl plld way through rnd bnd to ld 1/2-way: hdd & wknd over 3f out* — **33/1**

000- **9** *1¼* **Foodbroker Founder**[219] 2989 7-8-12 74.................. MarcHalford(3) 9 — 45
(D R C Elsworth) *a towards rr: u.p and struggling 4f out* — **33/1**

6032 **10** *½* **Fangorn Forest (IRE)**[11] 2181 4-8-6 65..................(p) JamesDoyle 5 — 35
(R A Harris) *a in rr: wd in st and struggling fr 3f out* — **14/1**

-006 **11** *1½* **Faith And Reason (USA)**[31] 1638 4-8-12 71.............. JamieSpencer 8 — 38
(B J Curley) *trckd ldrs: rdn 4f out: wknd fr 3f out: eased* — **15/8**[1]

-000 **12** *6* **Punta Galera (IRE)**[10] 2218 4-9-5 78..................(v[1]) RichardHughes 3 — 34
(R Hannon) *drvn to ld: hdd 1/2-way: wknd over 3f out* — **14/1**

2m 5.98s (-2.32) **Going Correction** -0.15s/f (Firm) — 12 Ran SP% **124.9**
Speed ratings (Par 105):103,101,99,96,93 92,89,87,86,85 84,79
CSF £39.71 CT £164.25 TOTE £6.40: £2.10, £2.20, £2.30; EX 32.40.
Owner Archangels 2 **Bred** Jeremy Green And Sons **Trained** Newmarket, Suffolk

FOCUS
A fair handicap and the pace was reasonable enough, although it predictably steadied rounding the bottom bend. The winner is progressive. The third and fourth were hampered by the runner-up.
Oscar Snowman Official explanation: jockey said gelding ducked sharply right-handed
Kervriou(FR) Official explanation: jockey said gelding ran too free
Faith And Reason(USA) Official explanation: jockey said gelding had to snatch up on bend 3f out

2513 MAN GLOBAL STRATEGIES H'CAP — 5f 10y
8:05 (8:08) (Class 4) (0-80,80) 3-Y-0 £6,477 (£1,927; £963; £481) Stalls High

Form — RPR

0-32 **1** **Obstructive**[11] 2173 3-9-0 73.............................. JimCrowley 10 — 82
(D K Ivory) *reluctant to enter stalls: mde virtually all: hrd drvn wl over 1f out: edgd lft but hld on wl* — **7/1**

-031 **2** *1¼* **Ocean Blaze**[10] 2198 3-8-8 67.............................. AdrianMcCarthy 5 — 71
(B R Millman) *pressed wnr: upsides 1f out: nt qckn ins fnl f* — **10/1**

663- **3** *nk* **Star Strider**[246] 5829 3-8-11 70.............................. FrancisNorton 8 — 73+
(A M Balding) *dwlt: hld up in rr: prog on nr side over 1f out: hanging bdly lft fnl f: styd on* — **14/1**

-330 **4** *1¼* **Black Moma (IRE)**[54] 1099 3-9-2 75.............................. RichardHughes 2 — 73
(R Hannon) *dwlt: rcvrd to press ldrs on outer: hrd rdn over 1f out: kpt on same pce* — **8/1**

-215 **5** *shd* **Rocker**[79] 755 3-9-3 76.............................. JohnEgan 11 — 74
(B R Johnson) *pushed along to chse ldrs: effrt over 1f out: edgd lft and fnd little fnl f* — **9/1**

3433 **6** *nk* **Feelin Foxy**[9] 2255 3-8-7 69.............................. (v) SaleemGolam(3) 1 — 66
(D Shaw) *dwlt: wl in rr on outer: hrd rdn and sme prog over 1f out: no imp fnl f* — **20/1**

-310 **7** *nk* **Cuppacocoa**[33] 1577 3-9-1 74.............................. PhilipRobinson 9 — 71+
(C G Cox) *chsd ldrs: rdn 2f out: one pce and no imp fnl f* — **6/1**[3]

1654 **8** *½* **Gower**[21] 1900 3-9-7 80.............................. (v[1]) SteveDrowne 4 — 75+
(R Charlton) *awkward s: sn in midfield: drvn to chse ldrs over 1f out: fdd fnl f* — **5/1**[2]

3060 **9** *2* **Grange Lili (IRE)**[24] 1825 3-8-10 69.............................. (b) LPKeniry 12 — 56
(Peter Grayson) *s.s: outpcd and detached in last: kpt on fnl f* — **33/1**

6321 **10** *½* **Baileys Outshine**[11] 2172 3-9-3 76.............................. JamieSpencer 3 — 68+
(J G Given) *pressed ldrs: stl nrly upsides over 1f out: wknd and eased fnl f* — **7/1**

0-50 **11** *shd* **Camissa**[19] 1948 3-8-11 70.............................. MartinDwyer 6 — 55
(D K Ivory) *uns rdr in stalls: a in rr: rdn and no prog over 1f out* — **33/1**

-322 **12** *2½* **Bookiesindex Boy**[24] 1820 3-9-0 73.............................. (b) RobertHavlin 7 — 49+
(J R Jenkins) *hld up in midfield: gng wl enough wl over 1f out: nt clr run sn after: rdn and floundering after* — **7/2**[1]

59.91 secs (-1.19) **Going Correction** -0.15s/f (Firm) — 12 Ran SP% **125.7**
Speed ratings (Par 101):103,101,100,98,98 97,97,96,93,92 92,88
CSF £78.28 CT £984.83 TOTE £10.30: £3.20, £4.00, £4.90; EX 102.50.
Owner A S Reid **Bred** A S Reid **Trained** Radlett, Herts

FOCUS
An ordinary sprint handicap. Things got a bit messy late on but the form seems pretty sound among the second-fifth, with the winner up 9lb on his AW form.
Star Strider Official explanation: jockey said gelding hung left closing stages
Cuppacocoa Official explanation: jockey said filly ducked right leaving stalls

2514 WBX.COM PROUD TO SUPPORT SPINAL RESEARCH H'CAP — 1m 67y
8:35 (8:35) (Class 5) (0-75,69) 4-Y-0+ £3,238 (£963; £481; £240) Stalls High

Form — RPR

6001 **1** **Aggravation**[17] 2004 5-9-4 69.............................. MarcHalford(3) 1 — 77+
(D R C Elsworth) *dwlt and stdd s: hld up in last: prog and weaved through fr 2f out: led 1f out: idled whn in command: jst hld on* — **9/4**[1]

4-22 **2** *hd* **Veiled Applause**[43] 1318 4-9-7 69.............................. GeorgeBaker 5 — 76
(R M Beckett) *prom: led 2f out: hdd 1f out: styd on wl and gaining on wnr at fin* — **7/2**[2]

20-1 **3** *hd* **Jill Dawson (IRE)**[35] 1539 4-8-6 61.............................. KirstyMilczarek(7) 4 — 67+
(John Berry) *chsd ldrs: effrt over 2f out: intimidated and veered rt over 1f out: rdn and styd on fnl f* — **7/1**

534- **4** *1* **Mitanni (USA)**[231] 6144 4-9-5 67.............................. JimCrowley 6 — 71
(Mrs A J Perrett) *chsd ldrs: rdn 3f out: swtchd lft over 1f out: cl up after: one pce fnl f* — **14/1**

0146 **5** *¾* **Jools**[11] 2179 9-8-5 53.............................. HayleyTurner 11 — 55
(D K Ivory) *hld up towards rr: nt clr run on inner over 2f out: prog over 1f out: one pce fnl f* — **6/1**[3]

4600 **6** *1¾* **Snark (IRE)**[17] 2004 4-9-5 67.............................. (tp) TQuinn 10 — 65
(P J Makin) *hld up in midfield: rdn over 2f out: one pce and no imp whn carried lft over 1f out* — **8/1**

6040 **7** *1¼* **Out For A Stroll**[11] 2190 8-8-9 60.............................. SaleemGolam(3) 8 — 55
(S C Williams) *rrd s: hld up wl in rr: prog on outer over: hrd rdn over 1f out: wknd* — **20/1**

0-60 **8** *1¾* **High Class Problem (IRE)**[13] 2107 4-9-1 63..............(b) RyanMoore 9 — 54
(P F I Cole) *towards rr: rdn and no imp fr over 2f out* — **10/1**

6-00 **9** *2* **First Show**[17] 1984 5-9-7 69..............................(p) JamieSpencer 3 — 56
(R A Harris) *led for 1f: trckd ldr: chal 3f out: upsides 2f out: wandering and wknd over 1f out* — **16/1**

0400 **10** *4* **Todlea (IRE)**[3] 2423 7-9-0 67..............................(bt[1]) WilliamBuick(5) 2 — 45
(Jean-Rene Auvray) *t.k.h: led after 1f and set gd pce: hdd 2f out: wkng whn hmpd over 1f out* — **40/1**

000- **11** *nk* **Deeper In Debt**[177] 6841 9-9-0 62.............................. RobertMiles 7 — 39
(J Akehurst) *hld up in rr: brought wd in st: no prog 2f out: wknd* — **25/1**

1m 43.17s (-1.53) **Going Correction** -0.15s/f (Firm) — 11 Ran SP% **123.6**
Speed ratings (Par 103):101,100,100,99,98 97,95,94,92,88 87
CSF £10.19 CT £50.18 TOTE £3.20: £1.70, £1.80, £2.40; EX 9.30.
Owner Perry, Vivian & Elsworth **Bred** John Khan **Trained** Newmarket, Suffolk

FOCUS
A modest but competitive handicap run at a strong pace throughout. Aggravation is rated to his course-and-distance mark last year, with a slight personal best from the runner-up.
Out For A Stroll Official explanation: jockey said gelding fly-jumped out of stalls

2515 MASSERIA SAN DOMENICO HOTEL FILLIES' H'CAP — 6f
9:05 (9:06) (Class 5) (0-70,70) 3-Y-0 £3,238 (£963; £481; £240) Stalls High

Form — RPR

1-00 **1** **Kondakova (IRE)**[23] 1837 3-9-7 70.............................. JamieSpencer 15 — 75+
(M L W Bell) *hld up in rr: prog whn nt clr run briefly wl over 1f out: got through and r.o to ld last 100yds: hung lft and hld on* — **4/1**[1]

-503 **2** *½* **Wadnagin (IRE)**[10] 2198 3-8-1 55.............................. WilliamBuick(5) 16 — 58+
(I A Wood) *hld up in rr: prog whn nt clr run 2f out to 1f out: squeezed through and r.o fnl f: nt quite rch wnr* — **11/1**

-203 **3** *nk* **Tibinta**[10] 2195 3-8-3 52.............................. CatherineGannon 13 — 54
(P D Evans) *trckd ldrs against nr side rail: effrt over 1f out: hung lft but r.o fnl f: nrst fin* — **16/1**

-115 **4** *nk* **Dressed To Dance (IRE)**[18] 1965 3-9-2 65..................(v) JohnEgan 4 — 66
(N Tinkler) *settled in rr: prog fr 2f out: rdn to chal 1f out: carried lft and hld nr fin* — **12/1**

5161 **5** *½* **Scarlett Heart (IRE)**[10] 2195 3-9-2 65.............................. JimCrowley 7 — 64
(J Gallagher) *hld up in midfield: prog to chal over 1f out: upsides ins fnl f: hld whn n.m.r last 100yds* — **8/1**

610 **6** *¾* **Poppy's Rose**[31] 1634 3-8-12 61.............................. HayleyTurner 5 — 58+
(I W McInnes) *chsd ldrs: wnt v wd at intersection of crse 1/2-way: prog on outer and cl up 1f out: no ex* — **9/1**

52-0 **7** *1¼* **Aaron's Way**[40] 1408 3-9-2 65.............................. FrancisNorton 11 — 60+
(A W Carroll) *plld hrd: hld up in midfield: cl enough but hanging over 1f out: eased whn no ch last 100yds* — **33/1**

6012 **8** *½* **Scarlet Oak**[89] 679 3-9-0 63.............................. TQuinn 12 — 54
(D J S Ffrench Davis) *pressed ldrs: upsides over 1f out: fdd ins fnl f* — **5/1**[3]

3102 **9** *nk* **Ensign's Trick**[14] 2080 3-9-1 64.............................. JamesDoyle 2 — 54
(W M Brisbourne) *t.k.h: w ldrs to jst over 1f out: fdd* — **14/1**

044- **10** *1¾* **Lawyers Choice**[192] 6663 3-9-7 70.............................. RyanMoore 6 — 55
(Pat Eddery) *a in rr: rdn and struggling fr 1/2-way* — **16/1**

0-53 **11** *½* **Princess Ileana (IRE)**[11] 2172 3-8-11 60.............................. FergusSweeney 10 — 43
(K R Burke) *cl up tl wknd over 1f out* — **17/2**

54-2 **12** *1* **Russian Gift (IRE)**[10] 2198 3-9-6 69.............................. PhilipRobinson 9 — 49
(C G Cox) *restless stalls: led to over 1f out: wknd rapidly* — **9/2**[2]

0020 **13** *14* **Dancing Duo**[9] [2262] 3-8-9 **61**....................................(v) SaleemGolam(3) 3 —
(D Shaw) *restless stalls: s.v.s: a wl bhd* **33/1**

1m 13.24s (-0.43) **Going Correction** -0.15s/f (Firm) **13** Ran SP% **126.8**

Speed ratings (Par 96):96,95,94,94,93 92,91,90,90,87 87,85,67

CSF £52.09 CT £494.95 TOTE £5.90: £2.30, £4.40, £3.50; EX 85.80 Place 6 £1436.35, Place 5 £238.64..

Owner Luke Lillingston **Bred** Mount Coote Stud And Partners **Trained** Newmarket, Suffolk

■ Stewards' Enquiry : Jim Crowley caution: careless riding

FOCUS

Just a modest fillies' handicap, although quite competitive. Sound, with the first seven all close to form, but most of the field are pretty exposed and this is not a race to get carried away with.

Poppy's Rose Official explanation: jockey said filly hung left

Russian Gift(IRE) Official explanation: jockey said filly became upset in stalls

Dancing Duo Official explanation: jockey said filly became upset in stalls

T/Jkpt: Not won. T/Plt: £3,371.90 to a £1 stake. Pool: £105,317.10. 22.80 winning tickets. T/Qpdt: £57.60 to a £1 stake. Pool: £7,607.90. 97.70 winning tickets. JN

2257 WOLVERHAMPTON (A.W) (L-H)

Monday, June 11

OFFICIAL GOING: Standard

Wind: Light across Weather: Overcast

2516 WILLIAM HILL 0800 44 40 40 H'CAP — 5f 20y(P)

2:15 (2:15) (Class 6) (0-60,60) 3-Y-O+ **£2,388** (£705; £352) **Stalls** Low

Form RPR

1306 **1** **Monte Major (IRE)**[5] [2350] 6-9-3 **59**..............................(v) PatrickHills(5) 4 75
(D Shaw) *chsd ldrs: led over 1f out: rdn out* **5/1**[2]

-000 **2** *2 1/2* **Silver Prelude**[17] [1991] 6-9-4 **55**.. NCallan 3 62
(D K Ivory) *led over 3f: sn rdn: no ex ins fnl f* **9/1**[3]

030 **3** *1/2* **Mambazo**[5] [2350] 5-9-2 **58**..(e) WilliamBuick(5) 5 63+
(S C Williams) *hld up: swtchd rt over 1f out: r.o wl ins fnl f: nt rch ldrs* **9/2**[1]

-045 **4** *1/2* **Ryedane (IRE)**[34] [1557] 5-9-9 **60**.. DavidAllan 12 63
(T D Easterby) *mid-div: hdwy 1/2-way: rdn and hung lft over 1f out: styd on same pce* **9/2**[1]

0046 **5** *1/2* **Sands Crooner (IRE)**[19] [1946] 4-9-7 **58**...................(v) FrancisNorton 13 59
(D Shaw) *s.i.s: outpcd: hdwy over 1f out: nt rch ldrs* **20/1**

6540 **6** *shd* **Formidable Will (FR)**[28] [1718] 5-9-5 **56**..............(vt) CatherineGannon 10 57
(D Shaw) *hld up: hdwy over 1f out: nt trble ldrs* **25/1**

1-00 **7** *hd* **Decider (USA)**[21] [1885] 4-9-7 **58**.. LPKeniry 11 58
(J M Bradley) *trckd ldrs: plld hrd: rdn and hung lft over 1f out: styd on same pce* **10/1**

0205 **8** *2 1/2* **Dasheena**[10] [2225] 4-9-3 **54**...(be) AdamKirby 9 45
(A J McCabe) *s.i.s: outpcd: nvr nrr* **14/1**

450- **9** *1* **Talcen Gwyn (IRE)**[259] [5575] 5-9-9 **60**........................... DavidKinsella 7 47
(M F Harris) *hld up: nt clr run over 1f out: hmpd ins fnl f: n.d* **16/1**

0-00 **10** *1 1/4* **Alexia Rose (IRE)**[28] [1707] 5-8-12 **52**........................ PatrickMathers(3) 2 34
(A Berry) *chsd ldrs: rdn and hung rt 1/2-way: wkng whn hung lft fr over 1f out* **33/1**

-000 **11** *1/2* **The History Man (IRE)**[10] [2202] 4-9-8 **59**...................(b) JamieSpencer 1 39
(M Mullineaux) *mid-div: hdwy 1/2-way: rdn and wknd over 1f out* **9/1**[3]

0001 **12** *shd* **Sir Loin**[10] [2221] 6-8-12 **56**...................................(b) DanielleMcCreery(7) 8 36
(N Tinkler) *chsd ldrs: rdn 1/2-way: wknd over 1f out* **12/1**

0430 **13** *1 1/2* **Royal Envoy (IRE)**[23] [1847] 4-9-9 **60**............................ DeanMcKeown 6 34
(D Shaw) *mid-div: lost pl 1/2-way: sn bhd* **9/1**[3]

62.05 secs (-0.77) **Going Correction** -0.025s/f (Stan) **13** Ran SP% **123.9**

Speed ratings (Par 101):105,101,100,99,98 98,98,94,92,90 89,89,87

CSF £50.47 CT £191.37 TOTE £6.00: £1.60, £3.30, £2.10; EX 56.30 Trifecta £120.10 Pool £223.30 - 1.32 winning units..

Owner Danethorpe Racing Ltd **Bred** B Kennedy **Trained** Danethorpe, Notts

FOCUS

A typical Wolverhampton sprint handicap run at a decent pace. The draw played its part with the first three drawn five or lower and the first two home were always at the sharp end. A career best from the winner who has a good record here, but the form may not be entirely solid.

Talcen Gwyn(IRE) Official explanation: jockey said gelding was denied a clear run

Alexia Rose(IRE) Official explanation: jockey said mare hung right

The History Man(IRE) Official explanation: jockey said gelding had no more to give

Sir Loin Official explanation: jockey said gelding hung right

2517 BET ONLINE @ WILLIAMHILL.CO.UK (S) STKS — 5f 20y(P)

2:45 (2:48) (Class 6) 2-Y-O **£2,047** (£604; £302) **Stalls** Low

Form RPR

5003 **1** **Areweplayingout (IRE)**[9] [2247] 2-8-9 0..............................(b[1]) LPKeniry 7 54
(Peter Grayson) *s.i.s: sn chsng ldrs: rdn and hung lft fr over 1f out: led ins fnl f: r.o* **5/1**[2]

65 **2** *1/2* **Next Best**[7] [2310] 2-8-9 0...(p) FrancisNorton 8 52
(A Berry) *chsd ldrs: rdn whn nt clr run and hung lft over 1f out: r.o* **25/1**

5664 **3** *1/2* **Miss Willoughby**[11] [2188] 2-8-9 0.. ChrisCatlin 6 50
(J Ryan) *chsd ldrs: outpcd 1/2-way: rallied over 1f out: r.o* **12/1**

06 **4** *3/4* **Nathan Dee**[12] [2138] 2-9-0 0...(bt[1]) HayleyTurner 5 53
(P S McEntee) *s.i.s: outpcd: hdwy u.p over 1f out: nrst fin* **6/1**[3]

40 **5** *3/4* **Scrap N'Dust**[14] [2078] 2-8-2 0.. JackDean(7) 3 45
(W G M Turner) *prom: outpcd over 3f out: rallied over 1f out: r.o* **16/1**

0 **6** *1/2* **Hi High**[28] [1728] 2-8-9 0.. AdrianMcCarthy 10 43
(D K Ivory) *chsd ldr: led over 1f out: sn rdn: hdd whn hmpd ins fnl f: no ex* **14/1**

7 *1 3/4* **Amber Ridge** 2-9-0 0... RobertHavlin 9 42
(D K Ivory) *s.s: outpcd: hdwy over 1f out: nvr nrr* **9/1**

8 *2 1/2* **Madam Zorro** 2-8-6 0.. DominicFox(3) 4 28+
(S Parr) *dwlt: hung lft: outpcd* **11/1**

0006 **9** *2* **Blazing Bullet (IRE)**[9] [2247] 2-9-0 0..............................(b) JimmyQuinn 2 26
(N Wilson) *led over 3f: wknd fnl f* **7/1**

5533 **10** *21* **Miss Antropist (IRE)**[7] [2310] 2-8-4 0.............................(b[1]) TolleyDean(5) 1 —
(R A Harris) *s.s: outpcd* **4/1**[2]

65.61 secs (2.79) **Going Correction** -0.025s/f (Stan) **10** Ran SP% **117.8**

Speed ratings (Par 91):76,75,74,73,72 71,68,64,61,27

CSF £72.21 TOTE £3.60: £1.60, £5.00, £2.20; EX 61.60 Trifecta £192.80 Part won. Pool £271.68 - 0.34 winning units..There was no bid for the winner. Amber Ridge was claimed by B Baugh for £6,000. Nathan Dee was claimed by H Sweeting for £6,000.

Owner Men Behaving Badly Two **Bred** Mount Coote Stud **Trained** Formby, Lancs

■ Stewards' Enquiry : L P Keniry one-day ban: careless riding (Jun 24)

FOCUS

A dreadful seller, run in a time 3.56 seconds slower than the opener, which is pedestrian even for a race like this.

NOTEBOOK

Areweplayingout(IRE), a fair third, though well beaten, in a valuable seller at Musselburgh earlier this month, had blinkers on for the first time. After moving through smoothly to deliver her effort, she hung away to her left and eventually made very hard work of it. She did not attract any interest at the auction and will do well to find another race as weak as this. (op 3-1)

Next Best, well beaten in two outings on turf including one at this level, was staying on towards the finish but she has already been beaten out of sight over 6f and her proximity does nothing for the form. (op 22-1)

Miss Willoughby, who has only beaten a total of six horses in five previous outings including a few times at this level, seemed to put up a much better performance but this race was so bad that it means little. (tchd 14-1)

Nathan Dee, wearing an eyeshield, blinkers and a tongue-tie for the first time, did not get going until it was too late. The form adds up to little, but one ray of hope is that he is bred to need much further than this. He was subsequently claimed by Heidi Sweeting for £6,000. (op 8-1)

Scrap N'Dust seemed to find this an inadequate test even though she failed to stay when tried over an extra furlong on turf last time. (tchd 20-1)

Hi High, last of nine in a course-and-distance claimer on her only previous start, showed a little more in this poor contest, but was already fighting a losing battle when the winner squeezed her out against the inside rail a furlong out. (op 8-1)

Blazing Bullet(IRE) ran his usual sort of race, making most but not lasting home, and finished further behind today's winner than he had at Musselburgh last time. He looks a short runner. (op 16-1)

Miss Antropist(IRE) had the form to win this, especially from such a good draw, but she was weak in the market and whether it was the first-time blinkers, for some reason she ran no race at all. Official explanation: jockey said filly failed to face first time blinkers (op 11-4 tchd 9-2)

2518 CHIPS @ WILLIAMHILLCASINO.COM H'CAP — 5f 216y(P)

3:15 (3:15) (Class 4) (0-85,85) 3-Y-O **£4,857** (£1,445; £722; £360) **Stalls** Low

Form RPR

1-35 **1** **Diamond Diva**[23] [1837] 3-9-5 **83**.. EddieAhern 3 97+
(J W Hills) *trckd ldrs: led on bit over 1f out: shkn up and sn clr* **5/2**[2]

1166 **2** *5* **Bentley**[9] [2255] 3-8-0 **67**...(v) DuranFentiman(3) 5 61
(D Shaw) *s.i.s: outpcd: hdwy over 1f out: no ch w wnr* **20/1**

4-11 **3** *1* **Rasaman (IRE)**[38] [1450] 3-9-7 **85**..................................... PhilipRobinson 7 76
(M A Jarvis) *trckd ldrs: rdn and hung lft over 1f out: sn outpcd* **8/11**[1]

1500 **4** *1/2* **Convivial Spirit**[6] [2335] 3-8-8 **72**..(t) ChrisCatlin 8 62
(E F Vaughan) *sn outpcd: styd on ins fnl f: nvr nrr* **8/1**[3]

0310 **5** *1/2* **Fish Called Johnny**[4] [2395] 3-8-13 **77**...................................(b) LPKeniry 6 65
(Peter Grayson) *s.i.s: outpcd: styd on ins fnl f: nvr nrr* **8/1**[3]

0410 **6** *shd* **New York Oscar (IRE)**[10] [2205] 3-8-8 **72**...............................(b) AdamKirby 2 60
(A J McCabe) *led: rdn: edgd rt and hdd over 1f out: hung lft and wknd ins fnl f* **14/1**

0- **7** *nk* **Mulligans Pursuit (IRE)**[22] [1866] 3-8-2 **66**...................... HayleyTurner 4 53
(M D I Usher) *chsd ldrs: rdn over 3f out: wknd over 1f out* **22/1**

1m 14.69s (-1.12) **Going Correction** -0.025s/f (Stan) **7** Ran SP% **124.5**

Speed ratings (Par 101):106,99,98,97,96 96,96

CSF £52.46 CT £71.61 TOTE £3.20: £1.80, £7.20; EX 56.70 Trifecta £72.80 Pool £511.70 - 4.99 winning units..

Owner Mrs L Meagher and Donald M Kerr **Bred** Glebe Stud And Mrs F Woodd **Trained** Upper Lambourn, Berks

FOCUS

This had looked quite a competitive handicap, but was turned into a one-horse race by the winner whilst the other six all finished in a heap. He is value for a bit extra, but things fell for him here with the favourite not running his race. The winning time was smart for a race like this.

2519 HEADS-UP @ WILLIAMHILLPOKER.COM H'CAP — 1m 4f 50y(P)

3:45 (3:46) (Class 6) (0-60,59) 4-Y-O+ **£2,388** (£705; £352) **Stalls** Low

Form RPR

-004 **1** **Thorny Mandate**[3] [2431] 5-9-2 **57**.................................... JamieSpencer 9 66
(W M Brisbourne) *hld up: hdwy over 2f out: chsd ldr over 1f out: shkn up to ld ins fnl f: hung lft: r.o* **11/4**[2]

0123 **2** *1 1/2* **Mighty Kitchener (USA)**[6] [2332] 4-9-4 **59**........................... TedDurcan 5 66
(P Howling) *a.p: chsd ldr over 7f out: led over 3f out: rdn clr over 1f out: hdd and unable qck ins fnl f* **5/2**[1]

2046 **3** *2* **Veba (USA)**[6] [2332] 4-8-5 **46**... HayleyTurner 1 50
(M D I Usher) *s.i.s: hld up: racd keenly: hdwy over 1f out: nt rch ldrs* **5/1**[3]

4/00 **4** *3* **Lytham (IRE)**[12] [2149] 6-8-9 **50**.. VinceSlattery 10 49
(D J Wintle) *hld up: hdwy 3f out: rdn and hung lft over 1f out: styd on same pce* **25/1**

0030 **5** *1/2* **Key Partners (IRE)**[12] [2145] 6-8-12 **58**................ RussellKennemore(5) 4 56
(J T Stimpson) *chsd ldrs: nt clr run and lost pl over 2f out: styd on ins fnl f* **8/1**

2605 **6** *hd* **Kirkhammerton (IRE)**[9] [2258] 5-8-9 **50**.................................(be) LPKeniry 3 48
(A J McCabe) *hld up in tch: racd keenly: rdn over 3f out: edgd lft over 1f out: styd on same pce* **9/1**

40-0 **7** *3 1/2* **Never Say Deya**[32] [1596] 4-8-4 **45**.. ChrisCatlin 7 37
(M J Wallace) *hld up: rdn over 2f out: n.d* **16/1**

0/0- **8** *3* **Norman Norman**[402] [1467] 5-8-4 **45**..................................... JimmyQuinn 2 32
(W S Kittow) *hld up: plld hrd: rdn over 2f out: n.d* **25/1**

05-2 **9** *3 1/2* **Rock Haven (IRE)**[21] [1906] 5-8-9 **53**........................ DuranFentiman(3) 6 35
(G F Bridgwater) *chsd ldrs: led over 9f out: rdn and hdd over 3f out: wknd over 1f out* **8/1**

00-0 **10** *shd* **Thou Shalt Not**[6] [2345] 4-8-4 **45**................................... RichardThomas 11 27
(P S Felgate) *prom: rdn over 3f out: wknd over 2f out* **66/1**

0060 **11** *6* **Be Wise Girl**[12] [2142] 6-8-4 **45**....................................... FrancisNorton 8 17
(A W Carroll) *sn led: hdd over 9f out: rdn and wknd over 2f out* **20/1**

2m 41.79s (-0.63) **Going Correction** -0.025s/f (Stan) **11** Ran SP% **124.0**

Speed ratings (Par 101):101,100,98,96,96 96,93,91,89,89 85

CSF £10.26 CT £34.26 TOTE £4.00: £2.10, £1.10, £3.00; EX 12.80 Trifecta £27.10 Pool £357.12 - 9.35 winning units..

Owner R C Naylor **Bred** Major W R Hern And W H Carson **Trained** Great Ness, Shropshire

FOCUS

An ordinary and uncompetitive middle-distance handicap run at a modest early pace, and things did not quicken up until inside the last half-mile. The contest was dominated by the two market leaders. The winner was 3lb off his best in a race rated through the runner-up.

Key Partners(IRE) Official explanation: trainer's rep said gelding was denied a clear run on home bend

Norman Norman Official explanation: jockey said gelding ran too free

Rock Haven(IRE) Official explanation: jockey said gelding ran too free

The Form Book, Raceform Ltd, Compton, RG20 6NL

2520 PLAY BACKGAMMON @ WILLHILL.COM MEDIAN AUCTION MAIDEN STKS 1m 1f 103y(P)
4:15 (4:15) (Class 6) 3-4-Y-0 £2,388 (£705; £352) Stalls Low

Form RPR

1 **Hazy Days** 3-8-9 0 .... JimmyQuinn 4 59+
(Sir Mark Prescott) *hld up: hdwy and nt clr run over 1f out: rdn and hung rt wl ins fnl f: led nr fin* **7/1**[3]

22-0 2 *nk* **Calming Waters**[11] [2180] 4-9-12 72 .... EddieAhern 2 65
(D W P Arbuthnot) *trckd ldrs: rdn to ld ins fnl f: sn hung rt: hdd nr fin* **5/1**[2]

2 3 *1* **Commandment (IRE)**[28] [1725] 3-9-0 0 .... JamieSpencer 9 61
(E A L Dunlop) *hld up: rdn over 3f out: hung lft over 1f out: styd on ins fnl f* **2/5**[1]

0- 4 *½* **Fluffy**[380] [2028] 4-9-7 0 .... NCallan 8 57
(K A Ryan) *chsd ldrs: led and hung lft over 1f out: hdd and no ex ins fnl f: nt clr run towards fin* **12/1**

-340 5 *nk* **Cavendish**[20] [1917] 3-9-0 52 .... (b) DaleGibson 3 59
(J M P Eustace) *sn drvn to ld: rdn and hdd 2f out: no ex ins fnl f* **25/1**

0 6 *3 ½* **Mega Dame (IRE)**[9] [2261] 3-8-9 0 .... RobertHavlin 5 47
(D Haydn Jones) *hld up: rdn over 5f out: hdwy over 2f out: wknd ins fnl f* **33/1**

043- 7 *3* **Oedipuss (IRE)**[244] [5884] 3-9-0 46 .... (t) CatherineGannon 6 45?
(K J Burke) *chsd ldr: rdn to ld 2f out: sn hdd: wknd ins fnl f* **66/1**

0 8 *4* **Altos Reales**[21] [1904] 3-8-9 0 .... FrancisNorton 7 31
(D Shaw) *s.i.s: hld up: plld hrd: a in rr* **66/1**

4003 9 *11* **Chart Oak**[59] [1030] 4-9-12 47 .... TedDurcan 1 12
(P Howling) *chsd ldrs: rdn over 2f out: wknd over 1f out* **20/1**

2m 3.50s (0.88) **Going Correction** -0.025s/f (Stan)
WFA 3 from 4yo 12lb **9** Ran SP% **122.8**
Speed ratings (Par 101):95,94,93,93,93 90,87,83,74
CSF £41.71 TOTE £9.40: £2.10, £1.50, £1.02; EX 51.90 Trifecta £61.60 Pool £373.40 - 4.30 winning units..
Owner Lordship Stud **Bred** Lordship Stud Limited **Trained** Newmarket, Suffolk
■ Stewards' Enquiry : Eddie Ahern two-day ban: careless riding (Jun 24-25)
Jimmy Quinn caution: careless riding

FOCUS
This looked a moderate maiden and the pace was ordinary. With the long odds-on favourite disappointing it may not have taken much winning, and the fifth and seventh limit the form, but Hazy Days is entitled to progress.

2521 CALL HOUSE @ WILLIAMHILLBINGO.COM H'CAP 1m 1f 103y(P)
4:45 (4:45) (Class 5) (0-70,68) 4-Y-0+ £2,914 (£867; £433; £216) Stalls Low

Form RPR

6033 1 **Western Roots**[5] [2358] 6-9-0 61 .... (p) JimmyQuinn 5 70
(M Appleby) *hld up: swtchd rt and hdwy over 1f out: r.o u.p to ld post* **7/1**

1215 2 *shd* **Scamperdale**[30] [1655] 5-9-7 68 .... (p) DeanMcKeown 6 77
(B P J Baugh) *chsd ldrs: rdn to ld over 1f out: edgd lft ins fnl f: hdd post* **8/1**

41-0 3 *1 ½* **Salonga (IRE)**[17] [2004] 4-9-6 67 .... TedDurcan 2 73
(C F Wall) *led: hdd 7f out: rdn over 3f out: ev ch over 1f out: styd on same pce ins fnl f* **10/1**

0-34 4 *1* **Lord Of Dreams (IRE)**[56] [1069] 5-9-0 61 .... EddieAhern 1 65
(D W P Arbuthnot) *hld up in tch: nt clr run over 2f out: rdn over 1f out: no ex ins fnl f* **7/2**[1]

0-21 5 *hd* **Nan Jan**[11] [2179] 5-8-7 54 .... (t) RobertHavlin 9 57
(R Ingram) *hld up: rdn over 3f out: hdwy over 1f out: hung lft ins fnl f: nt rch ldrs* **9/2**[3]

054- 6 *1 ½* **Tafiya**[226] [6225] 4-9-5 66 .... ChrisCatlin 4 66
(J W Hills) *hld up: styd on appr fnl f* **33/1**

0406 7 *nk* **My Michelle**[9] [2257] 6-9-1 62 .... CatherineGannon 8 61
(B Palling) *chsd ldr: led 7f out: rdn and hdd over 1f out: wknd ins fnl f* **20/1**

30-0 8 *3 ½* **Bordello**[44] [1287] 4-9-7 68 .... NCallan 10 60
(K A Ryan) *chsd ldrs: rdn over 2f out: wknd fnl f* **14/1**

4030 9 *nk* **Golden Spectrum (IRE)**[10] [2225] 8-8-5 57 .... (b) LukeMorris(5) 7 48
(R A Harris) *hld up: racd keenly: hdwy over 2f out: rdn and wknd over 1f out* **16/1**

6065 10 *16* **Norwegian**[3] [2423] 6-9-1 62 .... (p) JamieSpencer 11 20
(Ian Williams) *hld up: hdwy u.p over 2f out: wknd over 1f out: eased* **4/1**[2]

360 11 *¾* **Rio (IRE)**[18] [1967] 5-8-13 60 .... DaleGibson 3 16
(J Balding) *prom: n.m.r and lost pl 7f out: wknd over 2f out* **16/1**

2m 1.41s (-1.21) **Going Correction** -0.025s/f (Stan) **11** Ran SP% **119.2**
Speed ratings (Par 103):104,103,102,101,101 100,99,96,96,82 81
CSF £62.93 CT £567.19 TOTE £9.60: £3.00, £2.10, £4.20; EX 76.40 Trifecta £255.20 Part won. Pool £359.44 - 0.34 winning units..
Owner Sarnian Racing **Bred** Stratford Place Stud **Trained** Shrewley, Warwicks

FOCUS
An ordinary handicap, but at least the pace was solid and the winning time was 2.09 seconds faster than the preceding maiden. The winner is back to his early-season form, with another step forward from the runner-up.
Norwegian Official explanation: jockey said gelding never travelled and had no more to give
Rio(IRE) Official explanation: jockey said gelding was hampered on first bend
T/Plt: £123.10 to a £1 stake. Pool: £56,479.20. 334.80 winning tickets. T/Qpdt: £20.50 to a £1 stake. Pool: £4,161.20. 150.20 winning tickets. CR

2522 - 2525a (Foreign Racing) - See Raceform Interactive

1616 CHESTER (L-H)
Tuesday, June 12

OFFICIAL GOING: Good (good to firm in places)
After 18mm water had been put down over the previous eight days and 3mm rain overnight the ground was described as 'near perfect, a deep pile carpet'.
Wind: light 1/2 against Weather: fine

2526 KEMIRA GROWHOW EBF MAIDEN STKS 5f 16y
6:45 (6:46) (Class 4) 2-Y-0 £5,181 (£1,541; £770; £384) Stalls Low

Form RPR

433 1 **Brassini**[21] [1919] 2-9-3 0 .... JamieSpencer 2 79+
(B R Millman) *trckd ldrs: led jst ins fnl f: drvn out* **11/10**[1]

P4 2 *1 ½* **Look Busy (IRE)**[18] [1992] 2-8-9 0 .... PatrickMathers(3) 4 69
(A Berry) *unruly s: chsd ldrs: kpt on to take 2nd ins fnl f: no real imp* **16/1**

64 3 *1 ½* **Dalarossie**[15] [2071] 2-9-3 0 .... KDarley 1 68
(E J Alston) *led tl jst ins fnl f: wknd towards fin* **5/1**[3]

53 4 *½* **Kinout (IRE)**[11] [2199] 2-9-3 0 .... MichaelHills 9 66
(K A Ryan) *chsd ldrs: styd on same pce fnl 2f* **8/1**

0 5 *2 ½* **Altercation**[32] [1636] 2-8-12 0 .... J-PGuillambert 8 52+
(W Jarvis) *swvd rt s: hld up in rr: hdwy over 1f out: nvr nr ldrs* **40/1**

6 *2 ½* **Maryolini** 2-8-9 0 .... AndrewElliott(3) 5 43
(N J Vaughan) *s.s: sme hdwy over 2f out: nvr nr ldrs* **33/1**

4 7 *nk* **Harlech Castle**[53] [1123] 2-9-3 0 .... EddieAhern 10 47
(P F I Cole) *reminders after 1f: sn detached in last: kpt on appr fnl f: nvr on terms* **10/3**[2]

5 8 *1 ¼* **Curio**[11] [2199] 2-8-12 0 .... MickyFenton 6 38
(R M Whitaker) *chsd ldrs: wknd over 1f out* **16/1**

0 9 *1 ½* **Charlie Green (IRE)**[18] [1993] 2-9-3 0 .... (v[1]) FrancisNorton 7 37
(Paul Green) *in rr: sn drvn along: sme hdwy 2f out: sn wknd* **50/1**

60.84 secs (-1.21) **Going Correction** -0.325s/f (Firm) **9** Ran SP% **117.6**
Speed ratings (Par 95):96,93,91,90,86 82,81,79,77
CSF £22.92 TOTE £2.10: £1.10, £2.20, £1.80; EX 22.90.
Owner The Links Partnership **Bred** B N And Mrs Toye **Trained** Kentisbeare, Devon

FOCUS
Just an average maiden with the winner running to form in seeing off the improved runner-up and the well-drawn third.

NOTEBOOK
Brassini, on the leg and narrow, in the end did more than enough. He didn't look entirely happy on the track and may be better going right-handed. (op 6-5 tchd 5-4)
Look Busy(IRE), a handful behind the stalls, stuck on to claim second spot and will be suited by a slightly stiffer test.
Dalarossie, very keen to post, took them along but in the end did not quite last home. This at least opens up the nursery route for him. (op 7-1 tchd 9-2)
Kinout(IRE), a close-coupled type, had an outside draw and to his credit kept going all the way to the line. A 6f nursery should come his way. (op 15-2)
Altercation went sideways leaving the stalls. She picked up in her own time late on and should improve again. Official explanation: jockey said filly missed the break
Maryolini, carrying tons of condition, was very green to post. After a slow start she was getting the grasp of things once in line for home and a fair bit better can be expected.
Harlech Castle, a lazy walker, moved very short to post. Soon detached in last and given some sharp reminders, he picked up in his own time late on. Perhaps this very sharp track was against him. Official explanation: trainer's rep had no explanation for the poor form shown (tchd 7-2)

2527 ERNST & YOUNG H'CAP 1m 2f 75y
7:15 (7:17) (Class 4) (0-85,81) 4-Y-0+ £5,505 (£1,637; £818; £408) Stalls High

Form RPR

3126 1 **Torrens (IRE)**[21] [1922] 5-9-0 74 .... PaulHanagan 6 83
(R A Fahey) *hld up in midfield: effrt over 2f out: hdwy on ins to ld over 1f out: all out* **11/4**[1]

0056 2 *shd* **Red Lancer**[11] [2209] 6-9-3 77 .... SilvestreDeSousa 1 86
(D Nicholls) *trckd ldrs: chal over 1f out: jst hld* **3/1**[2]

-305 3 *2* **Inside Story (IRE)**[7] [2338] 5-8-8 68 .... (b) DavidAllan 7 73
(M W Easterby) *s.s: hld up in rr: hdwy over 2f out: kpt on to take 3rd ins fnl f* **8/1**

22-3 4 *1 ½* **Whatizzit**[36] [1542] 4-9-7 81 .... JamieSpencer 8 83
(E A L Dunlop) *led: hdd over 1f out: wknd ins fnl f* **11/4**[1]

300- 5 *5* **Pirouetting**[215] [6411] 4-9-0 74 .... MichaelHills 5 67
(B W Hills) *trckd ldrs: effrt over 2f out: wknd over 1f out* **13/2**[3]

0-06 6 *2 ½* **Latif (USA)**[7] [2338] 6-8-9 69 .... J-PGuillambert 4 57
(Ms Deborah J Evans) *s.v.s: hdwy 3f out: sn hrd rdn: nvr nr ldrs* **16/1**

56-0 7 *nk* **Top Seed (IRE)**[153] [89] 6-8-6 66 ow4 .... DeanMcKeown 2 54
(A J Chamberlain) *in rr: pushed along over 4f out: nvr nr ldrs* **20/1**

00-0 8 *14* **Canina**[155] [66] 4-7-9 62 oh7 .... MCGeran(7) 3 23
(Paul Green) *unruly and led to s rdrless: plld v hrd: trckd ldrs: lost pl over 2f out: sn bhd* **66/1**

2m 10.3s (-2.84) **Going Correction** -0.325s/f (Firm) **8** Ran SP% **114.9**
Speed ratings (Par 105):98,97,96,95,91 89,88,77
CSF £11.35 CT £57.05 TOTE £3.60: £1.40, £1.50, £2.40; EX 11.60.
Owner Mrs Catherine Reynard **Bred** Dermot Cantillon And Forenaghts Stud **Trained** Musley Bank, N Yorks

FOCUS
A modest winning time for the grade. Sound, with the front three to form.
Whatizzit Official explanation: vet said filly finished distressed
Latif(USA) Official explanation: jockey said gelding missed the break

2528 HIGHSTREETVOUCHERS.COM H'CAP 7f 2y
7:45 (7:46) (Class 3) (0-95,92) 4-Y-0-£8,832 (£2,643; £1,321; £660; £329) Stalls Low

Form RPR

4131 1 **H Harrison (IRE)**[3] [2466] 7-8-2 76 6ex .... AndrewElliott(3) 3 86
(I W McInnes) *chsd ldrs: led ins fnl f: hld on towards fin* **7/2**[2]

0000 2 *hd* **Gallantry**[10] [2239] 5-8-11 82 .... DeanMcKeown 5 92
(D Shaw) *hld up towards rr: hdwy 3f out: styd on to take 2nd wl ins fnl f: no ex nr fin* **14/1**

0-14 3 *nk* **Giganticus (USA)**[32] [1619] 4-9-7 92 .... MichaelHills 2 101
(B W Hills) *sn chsng ldrs: effrt over 1f out: no ex fnl 75yds* **11/4**[1]

3443 4 *½* **Shot To Fame (USA)**[12] [2180] 8-8-6 77 .... (t) AdrianTNicholls 10 85
(D Nicholls) *led tl ins fnl f: fdd towards fin* **16/1**

1401 5 *1 ½* **Roman Maze**[2] [2494] 7-9-4 89 6ex .... EddieAhern 7 93
(W M Brisbourne) *hld up in midfield: hdwy over 2f out: styd on same pce appr fnl f* **9/1**

3110 6 *2* **Phluke**[10] [2239] 6-9-6 91 .... StephenCarson 4 90
(Eve Johnson Houghton) *chsd ldrs: rdn 2f out: fdd appr fnl f* **15/2**[3]

-613 7 *shd* **Presumptive (IRE)**[14] [2123] 7-9-7 92 .... ChrisCatlin 8 91
(R Charlton) *in rr: sn pushed along: hdwy over 1f out: kpt on: nvr trbld ldrs* **9/1**

-000 8 *shd* **Stonecrabstomorrow (IRE)**[11] [2202] 4-8-3 74 .... PaulHanagan 6 72
(R A Fahey) *chsd ldrs: one pce fnl 2f* **9/1**

3105 9 *2* **Malcheek (IRE)**[17] [2030] 5-9-4 89 .... DavidAllan 13 82
(T D Easterby) *hld up in rr: n.m.r over 2f out: hdwy on wd outside over 1f out: nvr nr ldrs* **12/1**

-136 10 *shd* **Hiccups**[17] [2030] 7-8-12 83 .... NCallan 12 76
(M Dods) *hld up in rr: effrt on ins 2f out: nvr on terms* **10/1**

050 11 *1* **Romany Nights (IRE)**[16] [2058] 7-8-11 82 .... (bt) FrancisNorton 11 72
(Miss Gay Kelleway) *chsd ldrs: lost pl over 1f out* **33/1**

0-00 12 *¾* **Obezyana (USA)**[33] [1599] 5-8-11 82 .... (bt) MickyFenton 9 70
(A Bailey) *hld up in midfield: effrt 2f out: sn btn* **50/1**

0-00 13 *4* **Campo Bueno (FR)**[32] [1619] 5-8-7 78 .... (b) DavidKinsella 1 56
(A Berry) *hld up in rr: effrt over 2f out: lost pl over 1f out* **33/1**

1m 24.22s (-4.25) **Going Correction** -0.325s/f (Firm) course record **13** Ran SP% **127.8**
Speed ratings (Par 107):111,110,110,109,108 105,105,105,103,103 102,101,96
CSF £55.76 CT £154.86 TOTE £3.70: £1.80, £5.00, £1.80; EX 79.90.
Owner David Lees **Bred** Margaret Conlon **Trained** Catwick, E Yorks

FOCUS
Fast and furious resulting in a fair time for the class of contest. The winner is right at the top of his game and the form looks rock solid.

NOTEBOOK

H Harrison(IRE), in the form of his life, again carried his head rather high but in the end did just enough. He is a great credit to his trainer. (op 11-4 tchd 4-1 in a place)

Gallantry, back on the same mark as his last two wins, likes a turning track. He weaved his way through and in the end was just denied. (op 16-1)

Giganticus(USA), 4lb higher than Newcastle, stuck to his guns and in the end was just found wanting. (op 9-2)

Shot To Fame(USA), running from a career low-mark, did amazingly well to take them along at a strong pace from his double-figure draw. It was hardly a surprise that he had no more to give near the line and, turned out in fine fettle here, he is surely about to end his three-year drought.

Roman Maze, making a quick return to action under his penalty, travelled strongly in midfield. He stuck on in the home straight without ever threatening to land a blow. (tchd 10-1)

Phluke, a winner here in the past, was unable to dominate this time. (op 8-1)

Malcheek(IRE) Official explanation: jockey said gelding suffered interference in running

2529 INTERACTIVE WORLD H'CAP — 5f 16y

8:15 (8:18) (Class 4) (0-85,83) 3-Y-O+ **£5,505** (£1,637; £818; £408) **Stalls** Low

Form — RPR

4605 **1** **Hoh Hoh Hoh**[11] 2197 5-9-13 **82** ... JamieSpencer 8 — 93
(R J Price) *hld up in rr: effrt and swtchd outside over 1f out: str run: edgd lft and led nr fin* **5/1**[3]

-604 **2** *nk* **Jilly Why (IRE)**[18] 1999 6-8-9 **64** oh4 ... (b) FrancisNorton 3 — 74
(Paul Green) *w ldr: led over 1f out: hdd and no ex towards fin* **6/1**

0022 **3** *½* **Coconut Moon**[8] 2315 5-9-1 **70** ... KDarley 6 — 78
(E J Alston) *chsd ldrs: kpt on same pce ins fnl f: n.m.r nr fin* **4/1**[2]

0020 **4** *nk* **Kings College Boy**[3] 2461 7-8-10 **65** ... (b) PaulHanagan 1 — 72
(R A Fahey) *chsd ldrs: edgd lft ins fnl f: no ex* **9/4**[1]

4026 **5** *¾* **Canadian Danehill (IRE)**[20] 1941 5-9-9 **78** ... (p) NCallan 5 — 82
(R M H Cowell) *mid-div: hdwy over 1f out: kpt on same pce: nvr rchd ldrs* **8/1**

3300 **6** *hd* **Garstang**[41] 1401 4-8-8 **66** ... (b) PatrickMathers(3) 4 — 71+
(Peter Grayson) *prom: effrt on inner over 1f out: keeping on same pce whn n.m.r towards fin* **14/1**

-002 **7** *nk* **Continent**[24] 1854 10-10-0 **83** ... AdrianTNicholls 7 — 86
(D Nicholls) *in rr: effrt on outer over 1f out: kpt on: nvr rchd ldrs* **10/1**

0233 **8** *2* **Foxy Music**[17] 2029 3-9-6 **82** ... DavidAllan 2 — 77
(E J Alston) *led tl over 1f out: kpt on same pce* **9/1**

0-25 **9** *2* **Jakeini (IRE)**[18] 1999 4-9-5 **74** ... J-PGuillambert 11 — 62
(E S McMahon) *chsd ldrs: lost pl over 1f out* **16/1**

3000 **10** *1 ½* **Town House**[8] 2315 5-8-2 **64** oh19 ... SoniaEaton(7) 9 — 47
(B P J Baugh) *prom: outpcd 2f out: sn lost pl* **100/1**

59.89 secs (-2.16) **Going Correction** -0.325s/f (Firm)
WFA 3 from 4yo+ 7lb — **10** Ran SP% **125.5**
Speed ratings (Par 105):104,103,102,102,101 100,100,97,93,91
CSF £38.10 CT £140.15 TOTE £6.90: £2.20, £2.60, £1.50; EX 52.40.
Owner Multi Lines 2 **Bred** D R Botterill **Trained** Ullingswick, H'fords
■ Stewards' Enquiry : Paul Hanagan one-day ban: careless riding (Jun 24)
Francis Norton two-day ban: used whip with excessive frequency (Jun 26-27)

FOCUS
A large blanket would have covered the first seven home. The winner came from last to first and deserves full marks. The form looks very reliable with the winner back to something like his best and the race could work out.
Garstang Official explanation: jockey said gelding was denied a clear run

2530 TRADEONLY.CO.UK H'CAP — 1m 2f 75y

8:45 (8:47) (Class 5) (0-70,70) 3-Y-O **£3,562** (£1,059; £529; £264) **Stalls** High

Form — RPR

0052 **1** **Yes One (IRE)**[21] 1927 3-9-6 **69** ... EddieAhern 2 — 75+
(J W Hills) *trckd ldrs: nt clr run on inner over 1f out: styd on to ld nr fin: all out* **9/2**[1]

-503 **2** *shd* **Cheshire Prince**[13] 2133 3-8-10 **59** ... DavidAllan 3 — 63
(W M Brisbourne) *trckd ldrs: t.k.h: narrow advantage 1f out: hdd and kpt on wl towards fin* **9/1**

6-50 **3** *shd* **Mujma**[25] 1810 3-9-1 **64** ... (v[1]) RHills 8 — 68
(Sir Michael Stoute) *hld up in rr: hdwy on outer over 2f out: styd on wl fnl f: jst hld* **7/1**[3]

4013 **4** *1 ¾* **Snow Dancer (IRE)**[3] 2453 3-9-6 **69** ... FrancisNorton 13 — 69
(A Berry) *swtchd lft after s: hld up in rr: hdwy over 2f out: kpt on same pce fnl f* **9/1**

-340 **5** *1 ½* **Mystery River (USA)**[25] 1815 3-9-6 **69** ... NCallan 4 — 67
(B J Meehan) *chsd ldrs: chal over 1f out: fdd ins fnl f* **16/1**

040- **6** *½* **Danehill Silver**[223] 6297 3-9-1 **64** ... MickyFenton 1 — 61
(R Hollinshead) *led tl hdd 1f out: wknd towards fin* **33/1**

6-44 **7** *1 ¼* **Riguez Dancer**[73] 849 3-9-7 **70** ... LeeEnstone 11 — 64
(P C Haslam) *hld up in rr: hdwy on ins 2f out: kpt on: nvr nr ldrs* **10/1**

-445 **8** *nk* **Valley Observer (FR)**[21] 1929 3-9-6 **69** ... KDarley 6 — 63
(W R Swinburn) *hld up in mid-div: effrt over 2f out: kpt on same pce: nvr rchd ldrs* **8/1**

2151 **9** *nk* **Skye But N Ben**[14] 2116 3-8-7 **63** ... (b) NeilBrown(7) 10 — 56
(T D Barron) *chsd ldrs: one pce fnl 2f* **10/1**

-164 **10** *¾* **Pigeon Flight**[21] 1916 3-9-3 **66** ... JamieSpencer 5 — 58
(M L W Bell) *mid-div: effrt on outer over 1f out: kpt on one pce: nvr a threat* **6/1**[2]

-023 **11** *3 ½* **Lap Of Honour (IRE)**[18] 2010 3-8-11 **67** ... KirstyMilczarek(7) 12 — 52
(N A Callaghan) *in rr: effrt 3f out: nvr a factor* **8/1**

3560 **12** *10* **Hubble Bubble (USA)**[21] 1916 3-9-0 **63** ... J-PGuillambert 14 — 29
(M Johnston) *chsd ldrs: lost pl over 2f out: sn bhd* **20/1**

50-5 **13** *3* **Alberts Story (USA)**[22] 1894 3-8-2 **51** ... PaulHanagan 9 — 11
(R A Fahey) *trckd ldrs: t.k.h: lost pl 2f out: sn bhd* **16/1**

0-00 **14** *17* **Kings Art (IRE)**[14] 2105 3-8-8 **57** ... (t) ChrisCatlin 7 — —
(W M Brisbourne) *s.i.s: a bhd: t.o 3f out* **50/1**

2m 11.66s (-1.48) **Going Correction** -0.325s/f (Firm) — **14** Ran SP% **126.8**
Speed ratings (Par 99):92,91,91,90,89 88,87,87,87,86 83,75,73,59
CSF £46.55 CT £292.77 TOTE £4.10: £1.90, £2.60, £3.20; EX 44.70.
Owner Yes-One **Bred** C E Holt **Trained** Upper Lambourn, Berks

FOCUS
Just a steady gallop, resulting in a moderate winning time for a race of its type, 1.36 seconds slower than the earlier all-aged handicap. Solid form, the second and fourth to their marks and the less-exposed winner and third improving.
Snow Dancer(IRE) Official explanation: jockey said filly was denied a clear run
Pigeon Flight Official explanation: jockey said gelding hung right-handed

2531 DOUBLE TAKE STUDIOS H'CAP (FOR LADY AMATEUR RIDERS) — 1m 4f 66y

9:15 (9:15) (Class 5) (0-70,70) 4-Y-O+ **£3,435** (£1,065; £532; £266) **Stalls** Low

Form — RPR

/650 **1** **Prelude**[15] 2089 6-9-4 **52** ... MrsSBosley 16 — 59
(W M Brisbourne) *t.k.h in mid-div: hdwy over 4f out: styd on fnl 2f: led towards fin* **33/1**

033- **2** *¾* **Acuzio**[52] 5725 6-9-9 **57** ... MissNCarberry 14 — 63+
(W M Brisbourne) *trckd ldrs: led 2f out: hung lft: hdd wl ins fnl f* **3/1**[2]

06-0 **3** *nk* **Compton Dragon (USA)**[22] 1895 8-9-5 **53** ... MissEJJones 11 — 59
(W M Brisbourne) *s.i.s: in rr: hdwy 4f out: styd on wl: no ex wl ins fnl f* **40/1**

00/5 **4** *1 ½* **Turbo (IRE)**[12] 2170 8-10-3 **70** ... (t) MissJCoward(5) 6 — 73
(M W Easterby) *hld up in rr: effrt over 2f out: hrd rdn and styd on strly fnl f* **12/1**

/422 **5** *1 ¼* **Tizzy May (FR)**[3] 2467 7-10-8 **70** ... MissLEllison 4 — 71
(B Ellison) *chsd ldrs: effrt over 2f out: one pce* **2/1**[1]

-011 **6** *1 ½* **Vice Admiral**[17] 2026 4-9-5 **60** ... MissJoannaMason(7) 2 — 59
(M W Easterby) *set str pce: hdd 2f out: wknd ins fnl f* **13/2**

-406 **7** *½* **Richtee (IRE)**[11] 2201 6-9-4 **52** ... (p) MissSBrotherton 12 — 50
(R A Fahey) *in tch: effrt over 2f out: one pce* **8/1**

1250 **8** *3 ½* **Credential**[112] 507 5-9-12 **60** ... MrsMMorris 8 — 52
(John A Harris) *hld up in rr: sme hdwy 3f out: swtchd rt over 1f out: nvr on terms* **25/1**

-200 **9** *1 ¼* **Ariodante**[45] 1295 5-9-9 **64** ... MissCAMadgin(7) 13 — 54
(J M P Eustace) *s.i.s: kpt on fnl 3f: nvr on terms* **20/1**

36/- **10** *nk* **Moment Of Clarity**[482] 4994 5-9-3 **51** oh2 ... MissFayeBramley 5 — 41
(R C Guest) *chsd ldrs: lost pl over 1f out* **66/1**

/60- **11** *1* **Last Pioneer (IRE)**[2] 4914 5-9-5 **60** ... MissPHermansson(7) 1 — 48
(R Ford) *hmpd after s: kpt on fnl 2f: nvr a factor* **11/2**[3]

00-0 **12** *1 ¼* **Sunny Parkes**[16] 1229 4-8-12 **51** oh6 ... MissMMullineaux(5) 9 — 37
(M Mullineaux) *s.i.s: bhd: sme hdwy over 3f out: nvr on terms* **40/1**

00-0 **13** *¾* **Prince Zafonic**[18] 2006 4-9-8 **63** ... (t) MissOMaylam(7) 7 — 48
(Miss Gay Kelleway) *chsd ldrs: chal over 2f out: hmpd and lost pl over 1f out* **33/1**

0-00 **14** *2 ½* **Makfly**[21] 1918 4-9-0 **55** ... (p) MissRKneller(7) 3 — 36
(R Hollinshead) *mid-div: outpcd 6f out: no ch after* **40/1**

-000 **15** *23* **Dream Of Paradise (USA)**[22] 1906 4-9-4 **52** ... (p) MissPaulineRyan 10 — —
(Mrs L Williamson) *w ldr: wknd over 3f out: sn bhd: t.o* **40/1**

2m 39.47s (-1.18) **Going Correction** -0.325s/f (Firm) — **15** Ran SP% **131.6**
Speed ratings (Par 103):90,89,89,88,87 86,86,83,82,82 82,81,80,79,63
CSF £133.28 CT £4202.57 TOTE £69.40: £12.10, £1.70, £11.30; EX 146.70 Place 6 £55.92, Place 5 £42.31..
Owner A P Burgoyne **Bred** Cheveley Park Stud Ltd **Trained** Great Ness, Shropshire
■ A one-two-three for trainer Mark Brisbourne.
■ Stewards' Enquiry : Mrs M Morris one-day ban: careless riding (Jun 25)

FOCUS
The two leaders went off very fast, which suited the keen-going winner in this modest lady amateur riders' handicap. Not strong form at face value, with none of the first three obviously well treated.
T/Jkpt: £108,807.00 to a £1 stake. Pool: £536,372.75. 3.50 winning tickets. T/Plt: £49.40 to a £1 stake. Pool: £126,381.70. 1,864.80 winning tickets. T/Qpdt: £25.80 to a £1 stake. Pool: £4,586.80. 131.10 winning tickets. WG

2115 REDCAR (L-H)

Tuesday, June 12

OFFICIAL GOING: Good to firm (firm in places, 9.9)
Wind: Nil Weather: Overcast

2532 REDCAR RACECOURSE CONFERENCE CENTRE MEDIAN AUCTION MAIDEN STKS — 6f

2:30 (2:31) (Class 5) 2-Y-O **£2,817** (£838; £418; £209) **Stalls** Centre

Form — RPR

1 **Mutabayen (USA)** 2-9-3 0 ... TedDurcan 15 — 69+
(B Smart) *s.i.s: in rr and hanging lft 1/2-way: hdwy wl over 1f out: str run ins fnl f to ld nr fin* **12/1**

2 *½* **Boomtown** 2-9-3 0 ... JoeFanning 9 — 68+
(M Johnston) *a.p: rdn wl over 1f out: led ins fnl f: hung lft: hdd and nt qckn nr fin* **7/1**

3 *hd* **Wotashirtfull (IRE)** 2-9-3 0 ... NCallan 14 — 67+
(K A Ryan) *towards rr: hdwy over 2f out: rdn over 1f out and styd on wl fnl f* **3/1**[2]

3 **4** *½* **Rocheport**[25] 1801 2-9-3 0 ... TomEaves 3 — 66
(J Howard Johnson) *sn led: rdn along 2f out: hdd over 1f out: rallied u.p ins fnl f: kpt on* **25/1**

5 *shd* **Zabougg** 2-9-3 0 ... DeanMcKeown 10 — 65
(G A Swinbank) *in tch: hdwy to chse ldrs and edgd lft 2f out: sn rdn and kpt on ins fnl f* **16/1**

3 **6** *¾* **Borasco (USA)**[19] 1963 2-8-12 0 ... PhillipMakin 11 — 58
(T D Barron) *trckd ldrs: hdwy over 2f out: ev ch over 1f out: sn rdn: edgd lft and one pce ins fnl f* **5/1**[3]

0 **7** *1 ½* **Tharaya**[28] 1743 2-8-12 0 ... DavidAllan 12 — 54
(T D Easterby) *t.k.h: hld up towards rr: hdwy 2f out: sn pushed along and styd on ins fnl f: nrst fin* **50/1**

8 *¾* **Kiwi Princess** 2-8-12 0 ... DeanMernagh 8 — 51
(M Brittain) *towards rr tl styd on fnl 2f* **50/1**

4 **9** *nk* **Kingstyle (IRE)**[25] 1801 2-8-10 0 ... PatrickDonaghy(7) 5 — 55
(M Brittain) *prom: rdn along 1/2-way: drvn: edgd lft and grad wknd fnl 2f* **100/1**

10 *1 ¼* **Somarini** 2-8-12 0 ... PaulHanagan 7 — 47
(J G Given) *in tch on outer: rdn along over 2f out: sn no imp* **20/1**

0 **11** *1* **Sparton Duke (IRE)**[11] 2215 2-9-3 0 ... ChrisCatlin 6 — 49
(E J O'Neill) *hld up: effrt over 2f out: sn rdn along and nvr a factor* **2/1**[1]

12 *8* **Reel Buddy Blaze** 2-9-3 0 ... MickyFenton 4 — 25
(T P Tate) *s.i.s: a in rr* **20/1**

0 **13** *hd* **Premier Class (IRE)**[17] 2024 2-9-3 0 ... TonyHamilton 1 — 24
(J S Wainwright) *in tch on outer whn hung bdly lft after 1f: bhd fr 1/2-way* **66/1**

14 *1 ¾* **Brilliantsensation (IRE)** 2-9-3 0 ... PatCosgrave 13 — 19
(J G Given) *racd wd: in midfield: rdn along over 2f out and sn wknd* **33/1**

1m 13.49s (1.79) **Going Correction** +0.125s/f (Good) — **14** Ran SP% **123.8**
Speed ratings (Par 93):93,92,92,91,91 90,88,87,86,85 83,73,72,70
CSF £89.35 TOTE £15.30: £4.10, £2.10, £1.50; EX 62.70.

Owner A M A Al Shorafa **Bred** B Walker & Steve Schwartz **Trained** Hambleton, N Yorks

FOCUS

A modest maiden, run at a sound enough pace. The first six were closely covered at the finish, limiting enthusiasm for the form which has been rated as just below average for the grade and track.

NOTEBOOK

Mutabayen(USA), a 30,000gns purchase whose dam was a 1m winner in France, got his career off to a perfect start and maintained the recent good form of his stable in the process. He did especially well to overcome a slow start, left the definite impression he would improve for the experience, and clearly has a future. (op 9-1)

Boomtown ♦, closely related to some smart juvenile winners, proved very easy to back ahead of this debut most probably due to the fact that his leading stable has been surprisingly struggling to hit the mark with its juvenile runners of late. However, he ran a very pleasing race in defeat and only got picked off by the winner late in the day. He should come on for this experience and could just be the one to signal a rise in fortune for his trainer's two-year-old runners now. (op 9-2)

Wotashirtfull(IRE), a 55,000euros purchse bred for speed, was popular in the betting ring and posted an encouraging start to his career. He got the hang of things too late here, so can be expected to prove plenty sharper next time and should not remain a maiden for too long. (op 11-4 tchd 10-3, tchd 7-2 in a place)

Rocheport, third on his debut over 5f at Hamilton, showed the benefit of that experience and put up a bold effort from the front over this extra furlong. He rates a fair benchmark for this form and is going the right way.

Zabougg, who cost 20,000euros and is bred to be effective at around this trip at two, ultimately proved too green to do himself full justice on this racecourse bow. He was still not beaten far, however, and is another who should get closer with this experience under his belt. (op 25-1)

Borasco(USA), despite being a little free early on, ran her race and was just found wanting inside the final furlong. (op 13-2)

Tharaya took an age to settle through the early parts and still looked distinctly inexperienced. The manner in which she finished her race suggests she has ability, however, and she looks the type to do better over another furlong in due course.

Sparton Duke(IRE), as was the case on his Goodwood debut, was well backed and has clearly been showing the right signs on the gallops. However, he again dropped out of it nearing the final furlong and proved most disappointing. He is bred to appreciate a little further in due course, but looks well worth dropping back to the minimum trip for the short term in an attempt to restore his reputation. Official explanation: trainer had no explanation for the poor form shown (op 3-1 tchd 10-3)

2533 TURFTV BETTING SERVICE (S) STKS 6f

3:00 (3:00) (Class 6) 2-Y-O **£2,047** (£604; £302) **Stalls** Centre

Form RPR

0 **1** **Bonny's Babe**[13] 2147 2-8-6 0 PaulEddery 1 61+
(B Smart) *trckd ldrs: hdwy 2f out: rdn to ld 1 1/2f out: hung bdly lft ent fnl f: sn clr* **10/3**[3]

50 **2** *3* **Shipboard Romance (IRE)**[42] 1367 2-8-6 0 PaulHanagan 3 49
(P D Evans) *cl up: rdn to ld 2f out: sn drvn and hdd 1 1/2f out: kpt on same pce* **5/2**[2]

354 **3** *2* **La Guancha**[10] 2247 2-8-6 0 PaulFessey 6 43
(T D Barron) *trckd ldrs: hdwy 2f out: rdn and ev ch wl over 1f out: sn one pce* **11/8**[1]

50 **4** *1½* **Lavemill (IRE)**[10] 2251 2-8-6 0 ChrisCatlin 2 39
(R F Fisher) *a in rr* **12/1**

0104 **5** *6* **Little Finch (IRE)**[8] 2310 2-8-11 0 (b) GrahamGibbons 4 26
(R C Guest) *led: rdn along and hdd 2f out: sn wknd* **7/1**

1m 13.86s (2.16) **Going Correction** +0.125s/f (Good) **5** Ran SP% **113.9**

Speed ratings (Par 91):90,86,83,81,73

CSF £12.46 TOTE £5.10: £2.40, £1.50; EX 14.90.The winner was bought in for 13,000gns

Owner Mason Gill Racing **Bred** Mason Gill Racing **Trained** Hambleton, N Yorks

■ Misk Hills was withdrawn on vet's advice (11/1, deduct 5p in the £ under Rule 4.) New market formed.

FOCUS

A weak juvenile event, rated through the third. The winner is value for double her winning margin and is a fair sort for the grade.

NOTEBOOK

Bonny's Babe, seventh on her debut at Southwell, relished the drop in grade and got off the mark in decisive fashion. She did hang badly left shortly after hitting the front, but had the race in the bag at that stage and it was probably due to her lack of experience. This should do her confidence good for an impending return to a higher level. (old market op 9-2 tchd 5-1, new market op 7-2)

Shipboard Romance(IRE) had her chance on this drop in class and finished nicely clear of the remainder. However, she has now clearly found her level. (old market op 3-1, new market op 9-4)

La Guancha, up in trip and down in class, again hung when put under maximum pressure and has to rate very disappointing. One to avoid. (old market op 6-4 tchd 7-4, new market op 13-8)

Lavemill(IRE), back down in grade, was never in the hunt from off the pace and is going to prove very hard to place successfully. (old market op 16-1 tchd 14-1)

Little Finch(IRE) dropped out tamely once headed at the 2f pole and has gone badly the wrong way since winning at Catterick in May. (old market tchd 10-1, new market op 8-1)

2534 ANDERSON BARROWCLIFF H'CAP 7f

3:30 (3:32) (Class 5) (0-75,75) 3-Y-O **£2,817** (£838; £418; £209) **Stalls** Centre

Form RPR

2503 **1** **Satyricon**[7] 2335 3-8-11 **70** (v[1]) NicolPolli(5) 8 81
(M Botti) *trckd ldrs: smooth hdwy to ld wl over 2f out: sn clr: edgd rt ins fnl f: kpt on* **7/2**[1]

4-56 **2** *½* **Celtic Change (IRE)**[19] 1965 3-9-0 **68** TomEaves 1 78
(M Dods) *prom on outer: hdwy to chse wnr over 2f out: sn rdn: styd on u.p ins fnl f* **7/1**[3]

-446 **3** *5* **Coconut Queen (IRE)**[21] 1916 3-9-2 **70** DO'Donohoe 6 66
(Mrs A Duffield) *dwlt and bhd: hdwy 2f out: sn rdn and styd on wl fnl f* **20/1**

225- **4** *½* **Cassie's Choice (IRE)**[252] 5748 3-9-0 **71** MarkLawson(3) 3 66
(B Smart) *prom: rdn along over 2f out: sn drvn and one pce* **16/1**

125 **5** *hd* **Sea Rover (IRE)**[25] 1825 3-9-1 **69** DeanMernagh 4 63
(M Brittain) *led: pushed along 1/2-way: hdd wl over 2f out: sn rdn and wknd over 1f out* **7/2**[1]

-003 **6** *1¼* **Rainbow Fox**[14] 2114 3-9-0 **68** (p) PaulHanagan 9 59
(R A Fahey) *stmbld s: in tch: effrt over 2f out: sn rdn and no imp* **12/1**

0-22 **7** *½* **Onatopp (IRE)**[8] 2312 3-8-10 **64** DavidAllan 12 53
(T D Easterby) *chsd ldrs: rdn along over 2f out: sn drvn and grad wknd* **4/1**[2]

2-46 **8** *3½* **Teasing**[36] 1535 3-9-7 **75** JimmyQuinn 10 55
(J Pearce) *nvr bttr than midfield* **16/1**

0-00 **9** *2* **Mandy's Maestro (USA)**[33] 1595 3-8-6 **60** ow3 DeanMcKeown 5 35
(R M Whitaker) *a in rr* **50/1**

3-50 **10** *½* **Naughty Thoughts (IRE)**[13] 2133 3-9-0 **68** NCallan 7 41
(K A Ryan) *chsd ldrs to 1/2-way: sn wknd* **12/1**

6544 **11** *hd* **Here's Blue Chip (IRE)**[11] 2224 3-8-4 **58** (v) ChrisCatlin 11 31
(P W D'Arcy) *a in rr* **11/1**

1m 24.92s (0.02) **Going Correction** +0.125s/f (Good) **11** Ran SP% **119.1**

Speed ratings (Par 99):104,103,97,97,96 95,94,90,88,88 87

CSF £28.77 CT £442.64 TOTE £5.00: £1.50, £2.60, £6.50; EX 28.30.

Owner Effevi Snc Di Villa Felice & C **Bred** Sir Eric Parker **Trained** Newmarket, Suffolk

FOCUS

A modest handicap, but the form still looks solid for the class with the first pair coming clear. The first two have both improved, but maybe not as much as they might seem to have at face value as the third is not progressing and the fourth seems on a stiffish mark.

Sea Rover(IRE) Official explanation: jockey said colt ran too free; vet said colt finished lame left-fore

2535 JOURNEY SOUTH HERE IN AUGUST MEDIAN AUCTION MAIDEN STKS 1m

4:00 (4:02) (Class 6) 3-5-Y-O **£2,047** (£604; £302) **Stalls** Centre

Form RPR

60 **1** **Distant Pleasure**[21] 1913 3-8-8 0 TomEaves 5 56
(M Dods) *dwlt and bhd: hdwy over 2f out: rdn and styd on wl fnl f to ld nr line* **25/1**

32 **2** *½* **Sofie Tucker**[7] 2341 3-8-8 0 DavidAllan 1 55
(T D Easterby) *cl up: led over 2f out: sn rdn: hdd ins fnl f: rallied to ld last 50yds: hdd and no ex nr line* **3/1**[2]

0-06 **3** *nk* **Henry Bernstein (USA)**[24] 1841 3-8-13 75 TedDurcan 6 59
(H R A Cecil) *sn led: pushed along and hdd over 2f out: rdn and wandered over 1f out: rallied to ld ins fnl f: sn drvn: hdd and no ex last 50yds* **4/5**[1]

0-0 **4** *1* **Tykie Two**[10] 2261 3-8-8 0 ChrisCatlin 9 52
(E J O'Neill) *chsd ldrs: rdn along 2f out: drvn over 1f out: kpt on u.p ins fnl f: gng on towards fin* **12/1**

-003 **5** *2½* **Musette (IRE)**[11] 2206 4-9-0 47 MichaelJStainton(5) 8 49
(R E Barr) *prom: rdn along over 2f out: sn drvn and kpt on same pce* **25/1**

6 *nk* **Spring Creek** 3-8-8 0 PaulMulrennan 10 45
(M W Easterby) *hld up: hdwy 3f out: swtchd lft and rdn over 2f out: sn drvn and kpt on same pce* **33/1**

00- **7** *2½* **Averti Star**[355] 2783 3-8-13 0 PaulHanagan 13 44
(Mrs A Duffield) *in tch: hdwy on outer to chse ldrs 3f out: rdn over 2f out and sn one pce* **20/1**

0-00 **8** *5* **The Keep**[4] 2422 5-9-0 38 (v) NataliaGemelova(5) 12 31
(R E Barr) *chsd ldrs: rdn along over 2f out: drvn wl over 1f out: wknd ent fnl f* **40/1**

000/ **9** *3* **Eastfields Lad**[555] 6498 5-9-10 0 (b[1]) PaulEddery 2 29
(S R Bowring) *a in rr* **100/1**

0005 **10** *2½* **Rambling Socks**[11] 2206 4-9-2 41 DuranFentiman(3) 7 18
(S R Bowring) *a towards rr* **40/1**

000/ **11** *3* **Running On Empty**[619] 5627 4-9-7 31 (v) SaleemGolam(3) 3 17
(P D Evans) *a in rr* **100/1**

00 **12** *½* **Piperman**[18] 2012 3-8-13 0 PhillipMakin 11 12
(M Dods) *a in rr* **10/1**[3]

1m 39.39s (1.59) **Going Correction** +0.125s/f (Good)

WFA 3 from 4yo+ 11lb **12** Ran SP% **119.6**

Speed ratings (Par 101):97,96,96,95,92 92,89,84,81,79 76,75

CSF £95.58 TOTE £53.10: £5.40, £1.10, £1.20; EX 183.80.

Owner M J K Dods **Bred** Mrs M T Dawson **Trained** Denton, Co Durham

■ Stewards' Enquiry : Paul Eddery caution: used whip down shoulder in forehand position

FOCUS

A modest three-year-old maiden in which the first four came clear. It is doubtful if the form will prove solid, with a surprise winner and some very moderate horses not beaten far. The second and third were a fair way off their best after taking each other on.

Distant Pleasure Official explanation: trainer said, regarding apparent improvement in form, the filly was better suited by the straight mile.

2536 JOHN SMITH'S REDCAR STRAIGHT-MILE CHAMPIONSHIP (H'CAP) (QUALIFIER) 1m

4:30 (4:31) (Class 3) (0-95,87) 3-Y-O+

£7,790 (£2,332; £1,166; £583; £291; £146) **Stalls** Centre

Form RPR

-323 **1** **Il Castagno (IRE)**[8] 2311 4-9-2 **75** TomEaves 3 89
(B Smart) *mde all: qcknd wl over 2f out: rdn over 1f out: drvn and edgd lft ins fnl f: hld on wl* **7/1**[3]

305- **2** *¾* **Webbow (IRE)**[387] 1864 5-8-10 **69** DavidAllan 7 81
(T D Easterby) *hld up in rr: gd hdwy wl over 2f out: chsd wnr over 1f out: rdn and ev ch ins fnl f: hld whn hit on nose by rival's whip last 50yds* **40/1**

221 **3** *hd* **Soccerjackpot (USA)**[21] 1913 3-8-7 **77** DeanMcKeown 12 86
(G A Swinbank) *hld up towards rr: gd hdwy over 2f out: rdn to chse ldng pair ent fnl f: drvn and kpt on wl u.p* **13/8**[1]

-003 **4** *4* **Nanton (USA)**[23] 1862 5-9-11 **87** JamieMoriarty(3) 9 89
(N Wilson) *hld up towards rr: swtchd lft and hdwy 1/2-way: effrt to chal over 2f out and sn rdn: ev ch tl drvn and one pce over 1f out* **11/2**[2]

1-15 **5** *hd* **Shy Glance (USA)**[46] 1283 5-9-1 **74** DaleGibson 11 76
(P Monteith) *hld up: hdwy 3f out: rdn to chse ldrs wl over 1f out: sn drvn and kpt on ins fnl f* **12/1**

4251 **6** *¾* **Will He Wish**[3] 2452 11-9-11 **84** 6ex ChrisCatlin 8 84
(S Gollings) *in tch: effrt and hdwy over 2f out: sn rdn and no imp appr fnl f* **12/1**

66 **7** *1* **Waterline Twenty (IRE)**[87] 702 4-9-1 **77** SaleemGolam(3) 6 75
(P D Evans) *chsd ldrs: rdn along 2f out: sn drvn and one pce appr fnl f* **40/1**

0005 **8** *shd* **Dium Mac**[18] 2011 6-9-4 **77** JimmyQuinn 2 75
(N Bycroft) *in midfield: hdwy 3f out: sn rdn along and no imp fnl 2f* **12/1**

-324 **9** *5* **Neon Blue**[10] 2239 6-8-7 **71** MichaelJStainton(5) 13 57
(R M Whitaker) *hld up: hdwy on outer to chse ldrs over 2f out: sn rdn along and no imp* **12/1**

210- **10** *nk* **Just Dust**[242] 5940 3-9-0 **84** PaulMulrennan 1 66
(M W Easterby) *prom: rdn along wl over 2f out and grad wknd* **40/1**

104- **11** *6* **Wigwam Willie (IRE)**[227] 6210 5-9-9 **82** (p) NCallan 10 54
(K A Ryan) *in midfield: effrt 3f out: sn rdn along and no hdwy* **12/1**

1000 **12** *2½* **Stoic Leader (IRE)**[39] 1458 7-9-5 **78** PaulHanagan 4 44
(R F Fisher) *t.k.h: prom: rdn along 2f out: sn drvn and wknd over 1f out* **20/1**

240- **13** *24* **Riley Boys (IRE)**^{299} [4508] 6-9-12 **85**.................................. JoeFanning 5 —
(J G Given) *rdr had trble removing blindfold and stmbld s: v.s.a and a t.o* **18/1**

1m 36.98s (-0.82) **Going Correction** +0.125s/f (Good)
WFA 3 from 4yo+ 11lb **13** Ran SP% **121.8**
Speed ratings (Par 107):109,108,108,104,103 103,102,102,97,96 90,88,64
CSF £274.18 CT £687.22 TOTE £9.10: £2.80, £13.10, £1.20; EX 422.40 Trifecta £249.60 Part won. Pool £351.60 - 0.20 winning units..
Owner Pinnacle Night Shift Partnership **Bred** Millsec Limited **Trained** Hambleton, N Yorks

FOCUS
A fair handicap. Solid form, the progressive winner up 5lb and the second probably running his best race too.

NOTEBOOK
Il Castagno(IRE) has been running consistently well and fully deserved this win, leading throughout and battling on doggedly when challenged throughout the final quarter mile. He continues to progress and there is no reason why he should not continue to pay his way. (op 8-1 tchd 9-1)
Webbow(IRE), an unexposed sort making his seasonal reappearance, took a keen grip early on, but made good headway two furlongs out to hold every chance, only for lack of a recent outing to tell in the end. He was held when getting hit over the head by a rival jockey's whip, but can gain compensation before long if going the right way from this.
Soccerjackpot(USA), easily the least exposed in the line-up, readily broke his maiden at Beverley last time, but this was obviously going to be tougher and it was surprising to see him ridden with such restraint. He was putting in some good late work and remains capable of better. (op 7-4, tchd 15-8 in a place)
Nanton(USA), although sure to be there or thereabouts, was always likely to be vulnerable to an improver or two and this was as good a run as connections could have hoped for. (tchd 6-1)
Shy Glance(USA) was another who was doing his best work towards the finish and he remains in fine form.
Will He Wish, shouldering a 6lb penalty for his recent Haydock win, had every chance if good enough and might have benefited from more positive tactics. (op 8-1)
Riley Boys(IRE) Official explanation: jockey said gelding missed the break and stumbled on leaving stalls after blindfold got stuck on bridle

2537 REDCARRACING.CO.UK CLAIMING STKS 1m 6f 19y
5:00 (5:00) (Class 6) 4-Y-0+ **£2,047** (£604; £302) **Stalls** Low

Form RPR
-005 **1** **Just Waz (USA)**^{6} [2372] 5-8-8 43.............................. MichaelJStainton(5) 3 57
(R M Whitaker) *hld up towards rr: stdy hdwy 4f out: effrt to chal over 1f out: rdn to ld and edgd lft ins fnl f: styd on* **12/1**
5533 **2** *3/4* **True (IRE)**^{11} [2204] 6-8-8 47.. PaulFessey 6 51
(Mrs S Lamyman) *hld up in rr: hdwy 1/2-way: effrt 3f out: rdn to ld over 2f out: jnd and drvn over 1f out: hdd ins fnl f: kpt on* **11/4**^{1}
0006 **3** *1 1/4* **Time Marches On**^{10} [2252] 9-7-12 43.................... DanielleMcCreery(7) 9 46
(K G Reveley) *hld up in rr: stdy hdwy 4f out: rdn to chse ldrs 2f out: drvn and ch over 1f out: kpt on same pce* **14/1**
4-65 **4** *shd* **Platinum Charmer (IRE)**^{7} [2342] 7-8-11 50..............(p) PaulMulrennan 7 52
(K R Burke) *trckd ldrs: smooth hdwy 4f out: cl up whn n.m.r over 2f out: swtchd rt and sn rdn: kpt on same pce* **9/2**^{2}
0-42 **5** *6* **Mystified (IRE)**^{22} [1895] 4-8-10 47..............................(b) MarkLawson(3) 8 46
(R F Fisher) *led and sn clr: rdn along wl over 3f out: hdd over 2f out and sn wknd* **6/1**
6 *43* **Drumossie (AUS)**^{38} 7-8-4 0 ow1.....................................(t) JoeFanning 2 —
(R C Guest) *a in rr* **6/1**
214- **7** *1* **Mister Fizzbomb (IRE)**^{12} [3145] 4-8-13 57.................(v) TonyHamilton 1 —
(J S Wainwright) *chsd clr ldr: rdn along 5f out: sn wknd* **5/1**^{3}
420/ **8** *2 1/2* **Colourful Life (IRE)**^{168} [5949] 11-8-13 0............................. TomEaves 4 —
(K G Reveley) *prom: rdn along 6f out: sn wknd* **12/1**
0005 **9** *12* **Orphir (IRE)**^{60} [1030] 4-9-3 32.. VHalliday 10 —
(Mrs N Macauley) *in tch: rdn along over 6f out: sn wknd* **100/1**

3m 7.22s (2.20) **Going Correction** +0.125s/f (Good) **9** Ran SP% **113.1**
Speed ratings (Par 101):98,97,96,96,93 —,—,—,—
CSF £44.22 TOTE £16.60: £4.60, £1.60, £3.20; EX 49.80.Platinum Charmer was claimed by Ferdy Murphy for £9,000.
Owner Waz Developments Ltd **Bred** Lochlow Farm **Trained** Scarcroft, W Yorks

FOCUS
A poor claimer, not a race that took much winning. The form makes sense at face value but could be dubious as the time was slow.
Colourful Life(IRE) Official explanation: jockey said gelding hung left

2538 GO RACING AT BEVERLEY TOMORROW H'CAP 1m 2f
5:30 (5:35) (Class 6) (0-55,55) 3-Y-0 **£2,047** (£604; £302) **Stalls** Low

Form RPR
0-00 **1** **Sir Duke (IRE)**^{61} [1011] 3-8-12 **53**...................................... TedDurcan 12 64
(P W D'Arcy) *hld up in rr: hdwy on outer 3f out: swtchd lft and rdn to chse ldrs wl over 1f out: styd on ent fnl f: led last 100yds* **12/1**
0-01 **2** *1 1/4* **Amanda Carter**^{8} [2299] 3-8-10 **54** 6ex...................... JamieMoriarty(3) 14 63
(R A Fahey) *hld up in rr: hdwy on outer 3f out: rdn to chse ldrs 2f out: drvn to ld ent fnl f: hdd and no ex last 100yds* **5/4**^{1}
300 **3** *3 1/2* **Bivouac (UAE)**^{51} [1177] 3-8-11 **52**................................ PatCosgrave 13 54
(G A Swinbank) *hld up towards rr: stdy hdwy on outer over 3f out: chsd ldrs 2f out: rdn and edgd lft over 1f out: sn drvn and one pce* **4/1**^{2}
300- **4** *1 3/4* **Jardines Bazaar**^{258} [5615] 3-9-0 **55**................................ JimmyQuinn 15 54
(T D Easterby) *a.p: rdn to ld 2f out: drvn and hdd ent fnl f: wknd* **33/1**
-060 **5** *1* **High Five Society**^{24} [1850] 3-8-13 **54**..........................(p) PaulEddery 8 51
(S R Bowring) *chsd ldrs: rdn along over 3f out: drvn 2f out and kpt on same pce* **20/1**
30-0 **6** *3 1/2* **Xaar Too Busy**^{24} [1850] 3-9-0 **55**....................................(p) DO'Donohoe 6 45
(Mrs A Duffield) *chsd ldrs: rdn along over 3f out: drvn 2f out and grad wknd* **40/1**
3000 **7** *3/4* **Foxxy**^{19} [1964] 3-9-0 **55**.. PaddyAspell 4 44
(J R Norton) *in tch: effrt over 3f out: sn rdn along and no hdwy* **20/1**
6-03 **8** *nk* **Pegasus Prince (USA)**^{29} [1712] 3-8-9 **50**............................ TomEaves 7 38
(Miss J A Camacho) *a in midfield* **13/2**^{3}
-200 **9** *7* **Ingleby Hill (IRE)**^{15} [2096] 3-8-11 **52**.............................. PaulFessey 9 27
(T D Barron) *led and sn clr: rdn along 3f out: hdd 2f out and sn wknd* **8/1**
56-0 **10** *5* **Cornell Precedent**^{13} [2133] 3-8-10 **51**........................ GrahamGibbons 2 17
(J J Quinn) *prom: rdn along 4f out: sn wknd* **20/1**
-003 **11** *9* **The Mighty Ogmore**^{8} [2299] 3-8-9 **50**.......................(p) JoeFanning 11 —
(R C Guest) *a in rr* **25/1**
000- **12** *25* **Mr Wall Street**^{210} [6480] 3-8-11 **52**.................................. PaulMulrennan 5 —
(M W Easterby) *in midfield: rdn along and wknd over 4f out: virtually p.u fnl 2f* **66/1**

2m 8.71s (1.91) **Going Correction** +0.125s/f (Good) **12** Ran SP% **121.6**
Speed ratings (Par 97):97,96,93,91,91 88,87,87,81,77 70,50
CSF £26.05 CT £78.24 TOTE £16.00: £3.10, £1.20, £2.10; EX 49.80 Place 6 £64.62, Place 5 £19.65..

Owner Mrs Jan Harris **Bred** Southern Bloodstock **Trained** Newmarket, Suffolk

FOCUS
Not the worst race for the grade, containing some likely improvers, but the time was modest and the form has not been rated too positively. The first three all came from off the pace and those drawn high dominated.
T/Plt: £84.60 to a £1 stake. Pool: £56,220.75. 484.70 winning tickets. T/Qpdt: £10.40 to a £1 stake. Pool: £5,529.20. 393.30 winning tickets. JR

1969 SALISBURY (R-H)
Tuesday, June 12

OFFICIAL GOING: Good to firm (8.4)
Wind: Nil

2539 GEORGE SMITH HORSEBOXES MAIDEN AUCTION STKS 6f
2:15 (2:25) (Class 5) 2-Y-0 **£3,238** (£963; £481; £240) **Stalls** High

Form RPR
04 **1** **Ramblin Bob**^{19} [1970] 2-8-12 0... SebSanders 2 70
(R M Beckett) *chsd ldrs: chal fr 2f out tl led over 1f out: drvn and hld on wl fnl f* **3/1**^{1}
03 **2** *nk* **Ballinskelligs Boy**^{32} [1631] 2-8-9 0.................................. RyanMoore 10 66
(R Hannon) *hld up in rr: swtchd to outside and gd hdwy fr over 2f out: str run to press wnr ins fnl f but a jst hld* **3/1**^{1}
00 **3** *shd* **The Name Is Frank**^{14} [2103] 2-8-9 0.............................. SteveDrowne 8 66
(J W Mullins) *sn led: rdn 2f out: hdd over 1f out: styd on u.p tl no ex last strides* **14/1**
4 *2* **Afram Blue** 2-8-12 0.. TQuinn 11 63
(W J Knight) *chsd ldrs: pushed along 2f out: outpcd fnl f* **20/1**
5 *shd* **Distant Charm (IRE)** 2-8-12 0................................... RichardHughes 4 63+
(R Hannon) *chsd ldrs: rdn 2f out: kpt on same pce ins fnl f* **9/1**^{2}
6 *1 1/4* **Solent Ridge (IRE)** 2-8-12 0... LPKeniry 13 59
(J S Moore) *in tch: rdn: edgd lft and green over 1f out: kpt on ins fnl f* **25/1**
7 *2 1/2* **El Fuser** 2-8-12 0... JimmyFortune 16 51
(P J Makin) *chsd ldrs: pushed along over 2f out: fdd fnl f* **14/1**
0 **8** *1 1/2* **Hyper Viper (IRE)**^{22} [1882] 2-8-11 0............................... TolleyDean(5) 9 51
(J S Moore) *in rr: swtchd lft to outside 2f out and kpt on u.p fnl f but nvr in contention* **20/1**
9 *hd* **Illusionary** 2-8-10 0 ow1.. AdamKirby 17 44
(J G Portman) *mid-div: pushed along 1/2-way: nvr gng pce to be competitive* **66/1**
00 **10** *shd* **In Decorum**^{19} [1960] 2-8-4 0.. RichardThomas 5 38
(J A Geake) *in rr tl drvn and mod late hdwy* **50/1**
60 **11** *1* **Charlie Be (IRE)**^{26} [1781] 2-8-9 0............................ FergusSweeney 3 40
(Mrs P N Dutfield) *in tch: chsd ldrs 1/2-way: sn wknd* **33/1**
04 **12** *nk* **An Scaribh**^{8} [2303] 2-8-9 0...................................... CatherineGannon 14 45+
(P D Evans) *chsd ldrs tl rdn and wknd 2f out* **10/1**^{3}
13 *1 1/2* **I Certainly May** 2-9-2 0.. PaulFitzsimons 7 50+
(S Dow) *s.i.s: bhd: hdwy whn n.m.r and rn green ins fnl 2f: n.d after* **25/1**
0 **14** *nk* **Goldhill Fair**^{73} [845] 2-8-2 0... JackDean(7) 1 34
(W G M Turner) *a towards rr* **11/1**
15 *1 1/4* **Rosy Dawn** 2-8-7 0.. PaulDoe 15 28
(H J L Dunlop) *early pce: sn bhd* **20/1**
16 *1 3/4* **Morforwyn** 2-8-4 0.. RichardKingscote(3) 18 23
(J A Osborne) *in tch whn hmpd on rails over 3f out: sn bhd* **16/1**
17 *5* **Alannah (IRE)** 2-8-6 0 ow2... RobertHavlin 12 7
(Mrs P N Dutfield) *s.i.s: a in rr* **66/1**

1m 16.35s (1.37) **Going Correction** -0.025s/f (Good) **17** Ran SP% **126.5**
Speed ratings (Par 93):89,88,88,85,85 84,80,78,78,78 76,76,74,74,72 70,63
CSF £9.03 TOTE £4.00: £1.60, £1.90, £4.50; EX 12.40.
Owner Alan & Christine Briars **Bred** D R Tucker **Trained** Whitsbury, Hants

FOCUS
A moderate maiden, not a race to be positive about. The first three finished in a heap with the winner and third both posting slight improvement.

NOTEBOOK
Ramblin Bob, who did not seem to have an ideal draw, enjoyed the step up in trip and just held on under pressure. He seems sure to get a bit further. (op 7-2 tchd 4-1)
Ballinskelligs Boy, stepping up a furlong in trip, is still progressing with racing and came very close to landing his first race. He ought to get his head in front soon. (op 9-2)
The Name Is Frank does not look devoid of talent and will be one to consider in a low-grade nursery when they start. (op 20-1 tchd 25-1)
Afram Blue did the best of the newcomers, but this did not look a strong event and he will need to progress to go close next time.
Distant Charm(IRE) made a fair start to his career and is certainly bred to win races. His trainer is a master at placing his juveniles and he is sure to find the right races for him. (op 7-1)
Solent Ridge(IRE) stayed on well after running green in the early stages. Normal progression should see him go much closer next time. Official explanation: jockey said colt ran very green (op 33-1)

2540 PETER WEST "LIFETIME IN RACING" CLAIMING STKS 6f 212y
2:45 (2:53) (Class 5) 3-Y-0+ **£3,238** (£963; £481; £240) **Stalls** High

Form RPR
1221 **1** **Charlie Delta**^{12} [2187] 4-9-10 64....................................(b) KerrinMcEvoy 2 73
(J R Boyle) *hld up in rr: stdy hdwy on outside to ld appr fnl f: sn clr: easily* **5/2**^{1}
-000 **2** *3 1/2* **Mannello**^{14} [2108] 4-8-13 49... CatherineGannon 3 52
(B Palling) *in rr tl drvn and hdwy fr 3f out to take slt ld appr fnl 2f: hdd appr fnl f: kpt on but no ch w easy wnr* **33/1**
4030 **3** *1 1/2* **Chalentina**^{31} [1655] 4-8-12 60.. IanMongan 13 47
(P Howling) *in rr: hdwy over 3f out to chse ldrs over 2f out: sn ev ch: one pce fnl f* **15/2**
60 **4** *1 1/4* **Stagnite**^{37} [1507] 7-8-13 49....................................... JerryO'Dwyer(3) 6 47
(Karen George) *chsd ldrs: rdn and ev ch 2f out: wknd ins fnl f* **14/1**
000- **5** *1 1/4* **Wild Lass**^{172} [6904] 6-8-12 37...(p) PatDobbs 11 40
(J C Fox) *towards rr tl hdwy 3f out: styd on to chse ldrs 2f out: kpt on same pce* **25/1**
0003 **6** *2 1/2* **Detonate**^{6} [2357] 5-9-2 44.. SebSanders 7 37
(Ms J S Doyle) *chsd ldrs: rdn to chal fr over 2f out: wknd fnl f* **14/1**
510 **7** *2* **Convince (USA)**^{14} [2107] 6-9-5 58..................................(p) RyanMoore 15 35
(J M Bradley) *chsd ldrs: drvn and ev ch 2f out: wknd appr fnl f* **3/1**^{2}
0/00 **8** *2* **Bahrall**^{43} [1350] 4-9-7 34.......................................(v^{1}) RichardHughes 1 31
(A P Jarvis) *in rr: mod prog fnl f* **66/1**
6-00 **9** *shd* **Useful**^{97} [637] 4-8-11 40..(p) SamHitchcott 12 21
(A B Haynes) *in tch: rdn 3f out: wknd 2f out* **66/1**

-205 **10** *1* **Tipsy Lad**[9] [2273] 5-9-3 46........(vt) AdamKirby 8 24
(D J S Ffrench Davis) *chsd ldrs: rdn over 2f out: wknd sn after* **20/1**

00-6 **11** *hd* **Lady Shirley Hunt**[36] [1537] 3-8-2 40........ RichardThomas 14 19
(A D Smith) *chsd ldrs: rdn and n.m.r over 2f out: sn wknd* **33/1**

-600 **12** *nk* **Zinging**[4] [2423] 8-8-10 39........ RyanBird(7) 9 23
(J J Bridger) *pressed ldrs to 3f out: sn wknd* **40/1**

50-0 **13** *1* **Safari**[6] [2357] 4-8-8 41........(b[1]) EmmettStack(3) 16 14
(A J Chamberlain) *a in rr* **100/1**

5322 **14** *5* **Labelled With Love**[7] [2331] 7-9-5 51........(t) FergusSweeney 5 9
(Jean-Rene Auvray) *a in rr* **5/1[3]**

0000 **15** *3* **Alwariah**[7] [2331] 4-8-12 47........ JamesDoyle 18 —
(Ms J S Doyle) *sn slt lded hdd over 3f out: wknd qckly* **33/1**

6-00 **16** *3* **Zantero**[83] [723] 5-9-2 44........ SteveDrowne 4 —
(M A Doyle) *chsd ldrs: led over 3f out: hdd & wknd rapidly over 2f out* **80/1**

0056 **17** *3 1/2* **Auentraum (GER)**[6] [2357] 7-9-5 44........ GeorgeBaker 17 —
(Ms J S Doyle) *chsd ldrs over 3f* **33/1**

1m 28.25s (-0.81) **Going Correction** -0.025s/f (Good)
WFA 3 from 4yo+ 10lb **17** Ran SP% **123.4**
Speed ratings (Par 103):103,99,97,95,94 91,89,87,86,85 85,85,84,78,74 71,67
CSF £100.60 TOTE £3.50: £1.50, £8.90, £2.60; EX 127.50.Charlie Delta was claimed by J. M. Bradley for £13,000.
Owner M Khan X2 **Bred** P K Gardner **Trained** Epsom, Surrey

FOCUS
A very moderate race, rated through the fifth. The winner apart, all of the runners are going to struggle to get involved in any sort of race in the short-term.
Labelled With Love Official explanation: jockey said gelding was lame behind

2541 WISE CATERING MAIDEN STKS (DIV I) 6f 212y
3:15 (3:20) (Class 4) 3-Y-0 **£4,210** (£1,252; £625; £312) **Stalls** High

Form RPR

0 **1** **Pagan Belief**[24] [1840] 3-9-3 0........ GeorgeBaker 10 74+
(J A R Toller) *t.k.h: chsd ldrs: drvn and qcknd to ld appr fnl f: c readily clr* **14/1**

4 **2** *2 1/2* **Cape Cobra**[16] [2059] 3-9-3 0........ JimmyFortune 1 67
(J H M Gosden) *in tch: rdn to chse ldrs and edgd lft 2f out: kpt on fnl f to take 2nd but no imp on wnr* **11/8[1]**

25 **3** *3/4* **Six Of Hearts**[29] [1714] 3-9-0 0........ RichardKingscote(3) 5 65
(J A Osborne) *led: rdn over 2f out: hdd appr fnl f: kpt on same pce and lost 2nd ins fnl f* **14/1**

5-4 **4** *hd* **Nice To Know (FR)**[24] [1838] 3-8-12 0........ RichardHughes 7 59
(E A L Dunlop) *bmpd and slowly away s: hld up towards rr: hdwy fr 2f out: kpt on fnl f but nvr gng pce to trble ldrs* **13/2[3]**

-0 **5** *nk* **Woodins Way**[24] [1839] 3-9-3 0........ SebSanders 11 65+
(P J Makin) *in rr: rdn and hdwy over 2f out: chsd ldrs over 1f out: sn one pce* **8/1**

5 **6** *3/4* **Up The Chimney**[41] [1398] 3-9-3 0........ BrettDoyle 9 62
(A P Jarvis) *chsd ldrs: rdn over 2f out: wknd ins fnl f* **11/1**

2-42 **7** *1 3/4* **Cape Velvet (IRE)**[19] [1961] 3-8-12 77........ RyanMoore 3 52
(J W Hills) *t.k.h: chsd ldrs: rdn 2f out: wknd over 1f out* **11/4[2]**

8 *3* **Come On Nellie (IRE)** 3-8-12 0........ FergusSweeney 4 44
(J G M O'Shea) *a outpcd in rr* **66/1**

0 **9** *6* **Qatar Way (GR)**[34] [1587] 3-8-12 0........ RobertHavlin 8 28
(P R Chamings) *bmpd s: outpcd most of the way* **66/1**

00- **10** *8* **Our Archie**[334] [3457] 3-8-12 0........ KevinGhunowa(5) 6 11
(M J Attwater) *wnt rt s: early spd: sn bhd* **100/1**

1m 28.98s (-0.08) **Going Correction** -0.025s/f (Good) **10** Ran SP% **118.9**
Speed ratings (Par 101):99,96,95,95,94 93,91,88,81,72
CSF £34.46 TOTE £18.70: £3.30, £1.20, £3.40; EX 52.20.
Owner The Gap Partnership **Bred** Redmyre Bloodstock & Helen Wadsworth Bloodstock **Trained** Newmarket, Suffolk

FOCUS
The slower of the two divisions - and slower than the claimer on the card - but some fairly promising displays, especially with handicaps in mind. It has been rated through the fourth, with improvement from the three in front of her.
Our Archie Official explanation: jockey said gelding jumped right on leaving stalls and ran too keen

2542 WISE CATERING MAIDEN STKS (DIV II) 6f 212y
3:45 (3:50) (Class 4) 3-Y-0 **£4,210** (£1,252; £625; £312) **Stalls** High

Form RPR

0-3 **1** **Parisian Dream**[24] [1839] 3-9-3 0........ RyanMoore 3 82
(B W Hills) *towards rr: hdwy 3f out: kpt on u.p to chse wnr fnl f: styd on to ld last strides* **6/1[3]**

4252 **2** *hd* **Esteem Machine (USA)**[16] [2059] 3-9-0 74........ MarcHalford(3) 6 81
(D R C Elsworth) *led 1f: styd w ldr tl led again over 3f out: 3 l clr 2f out and sn rdn: hdd and no ex last strides* **6/4[1]**

0 **3** *6* **Emperor Court (IRE)**[38] [1468] 3-9-3 0........ SebSanders 1 65
(P J Makin) *in tch: rdn along 3f out: styd on to take modest 3rd appr fnl f* **12/1**

0 **4** *4* **Hot Property (IRE)**[16] [2059] 3-9-3 0........ KerrinMcEvoy 5 54
(W R Muir) *in rr: pushed along 3f out: modest prog to take 4th ins fnl f* **12/1**

03 **5** *2* **Appleby**[19] [1961] 3-8-12 0........ JimmyFortune 11 44
(J H M Gosden) *sn racing in 3rd but nvr nr ldng pair: hrd drvn over 2f out: wknd over 1f out* **5/2[2]**

04- **6** *1/2* **Storm Petrel**[210] [6480] 3-8-12 0........ IanMongan 8 42
(N P Littmoden) *in rr tl modest hdwy fnl 2f* **14/1**

00 **7** *shd* **Capping (IRE)**[12] [2175] 3-9-3 0........(t) AdamKirby 2 47+
(W R Swinburn) *in rr: pushed along and mod prog fnl 2f: nvr in contention* **66/1**

8 *4* **Ravenhill Ralph (IRE)** 3-9-3 0........ FergusSweeney 10 36
(J G M O'Shea) *slowly away: in rr: nvr in contention* **100/1**

5 **9** *8* **Now You See Me**[88] [689] 3-8-12 0........ RichardHughes 9 10+
(K McAuliffe) *w ldr slt advantage after 1f: hdd over 3f out: wknd 2f out* **20/1**

10 *3* **Miss Gibraltar** 3-8-12 0........ NickyMackay 4 —
(L M Cumani) *rdn along after 2f: sn bhd* **12/1**

0-0 **11** *2* **Astarte**[25] [1816] 3-8-12 0........ PaulDoe 7 —
(P R Chamings) *a in rr* **100/1**

1m 27.77s (-1.29) **Going Correction** -0.025s/f (Good) **37** Ran SP% **120.8**
Speed ratings (Par 101):106,105,98,94,92 91,91,86,77,74 71
CSF £15.63 TOTE £5.90: £1.70, £1.30, £3.50; EX 15.40.
Owner J Hanson **Bred** Mrs A D Bourne **Trained** Lambourn, Berks

FOCUS
A good tempo set and quicker than the first division. The firt two finished clear. A slightly postive view has been taken of the form in light of the way the Newmarket race in which the second and fourth ran has been working out.
Appleby Official explanation: vet said filly returned lame behind
Ravenhill Ralph(IRE) Official explanation: jockey said gelding hung left
Now You See Me Official explanation: jockey said filly lost its action

2543 EBF MARGADALE FILLIES' H'CAP 1m 1f 198y
4:15 (4:16) (Class 4) (0-85,82) 3-Y-0+ **£6,800** (£2,023; £1,011; £505) **Stalls** High

Form RPR

52-1 **1** **Gold Hush (USA)**[31] [1676] 3-9-2 **82**........ KerrinMcEvoy 5 94+
(Sir Michael Stoute) *hld up in rr but in tch: gd hdwy fr over 3f out to ld appr fnl 2f: pushed clr fnl f: readily* **7/2[2]**

21-0 **2** *3/4* **Pentatonic**[21] [1922] 4-9-10 **77**........ NickyMackay 8 82
(L M Cumani) *hld up in rr: rdn over 2f out: styd on u.p fr over 1f out: kpt on to take 2nd nr fin but no ch w wnr* **11/4[1]**

1352 **3** *1/2* **Lisathedaddy**[11] [2218] 5-9-13 **80**........ GeorgeBaker 2 84
(B G Powell) *towards rr tl gd hdwy on outside to trck ldrs 3f out: chal 2f out: sn outpcd by wnr: lost 2nd cl home* **4/1[3]**

200- **4** *shd* **Noora (IRE)**[245] [5895] 6-9-10 **77**........(v) AdamKirby 4 81
(C G Cox) *hld up in rr: rdn and hdwy over 2f out: styd on u.p ins fnl f but nvr gng pce to rch ldrs* **16/1**

05-0 **5** *2 1/2* **Postage Stampe**[18] [2003] 4-9-11 **81**........ RichardKingscote(3) 3 80
(D M Simcock) *chsd ldr tl led ins fnl 4f: hdd over 3f out: wknd over 1f out* **20/1**

6215 **6** *1 1/2* **Uig**[6] [2361] 6-9-0 **67**........ SimonWhitworth 1 63
(H S Howe) *chsd ldrs: led over 3f out: hdd appr fnl 2f: sn btn* **12/1**

05-3 **7** *2* **Sunisa (IRE)**[13] [2136] 6-9-10 **77**........ SteveDrowne 7 69
(J Mackie) *chsd ldrs: rdn 3f out: wknd qckly 2f out* **11/1**

1-02 **8** *dist* **Ronaldsay**[41] [1407] 3-9-0 **80**........ RichardHughes 6 —
(R Hannon) *slt ld tl hdd ins fnl 4f: sn wknd: virtually p.u fnl 2f* **7/2[2]**

2m 10.89s (2.43) **Going Correction** +0.20s/f (Good)
WFA 3 from 4yo+ 13lb **8** Ran SP% **117.8**
Speed ratings (Par 102):98,97,97,96,94 93,92,—
CSF £14.07 CT £40.04 TOTE £4.20: £1.70, £1.60, £1.70; EX 11.60.
Owner Gainsborough **Bred** Gainsborough Farm Llc **Trained** Newmarket, Suffolk

FOCUS
A competitive event but the form, for this trip, may not be that reliable due to the lack of any early pace. However, the first two look capable of a bit better and it was a good performance by the winner, as she is only three.
Ronaldsay Official explanation: vet said filly was found to have an irregular heart beat

2544 DUTTON GREGORY H'CAP 1m 4f
4:45 (4:45) (Class 5) (0-75,73) 4-Y-0+ **£3,238** (£963; £481; £240) **Stalls** High

Form RPR

-032 **1** **Wild Fell Hall (IRE)**[21] [1924] 4-9-7 **73**........ AdamKirby 4 81
(W R Swinburn) *mde virtually all: hrd drvn ins fnl 2f out: kpt on strly fnl f* **9/4[2]**

-550 **2** *1 3/4* **Eldorado**[19] [1959] 6-8-13 **65**........ RyanMoore 3 70
(G L Moore) *in tch: hdwy 3f out: hrd drvn and styd on to chse wnr fnl f but a hld* **2/1[1]**

0430 **3** *1 1/2* **Hatch A Plan (IRE)**[8] [2321] 6-9-1 **67**........ TQuinn 7 70
(Mouse Hamilton-Fairley) *towards rr tl hdwy 4f out: drvn to chse ldrs 2f out: kpt on same pce* **8/1**

-310 **4** *2* **Princess Lavinia**[18] [2008] 4-8-13 **65**........ SteveDrowne 6 65
(G Wragg) *sn trcking wnr: rdn over 2f out and no imp: wknd fnl f* **6/1**

003/ **5** *9* **Almavara (USA)**[62] [4788] 5-8-12 **64**........ LPKeniry 5 49
(C P Morlock) *reminders to chse ldrs after 2f: lost pl u.p 3f out: n.d after* **33/1**

2503 **6** *hd* **Three Thieves (UAE)**[28] [1752] 4-9-4 **70**........ SebSanders 1 55
(M S Saunders) *a in rr* **4/1[3]**

00-0 **7** *1* **Bouzouki (USA)**[27] [1765] 4-8-8 **60**........ FergusSweeney 2 43
(Karen George) *t.k.h: in rr tl rapid hdwy to chse ldrs over 7f out: wknd over 2f out* **50/1**

2m 37.65s (1.29) **Going Correction** +0.20s/f (Good) **7** Ran SP% **114.4**
Speed ratings (Par 103):103,101,100,99,93 93,92
CSF £7.19 TOTE £3.10: £1.70, £1.90; EX 8.00.
Owner Mrs P W Harris **Bred** M H Dixon **Trained** Aldbury, Herts

FOCUS
An even pace to this handicap, even though the winner was given an easy time in front, and the front four pulled miles clear of the other three. The winning time, and that of the preceding contest, suggested the ground was less quick on the loop than on the straight course. The winner is rated to his latest form.
Three Thieves(UAE) Official explanation: vet said gelding returned lame in front and behind

2545 MILFORD HALL HOTEL H'CAP 6f 212y
5:15 (5:19) (Class 6) (0-65,65) 3-Y-0 **£3,238** (£963; £481; £240) **Stalls** High

Form RPR

3300 **1** **Prince Of Charm (USA)**[32] [1634] 3-9-2 **60**........(p) GeorgeBaker 9 73
(R A Teal) *s.i.s: in rr tl stdy hdwy over 2f out: qcknd to ld appr fnl f: pushed out* **25/1**

3400 **2** *3 1/2* **Realy Naughty (IRE)**[16] [2061] 3-9-4 **62**........ TQuinn 2 66
(B G Powell) *in rr: drvn along over 2f out: styd on u.p fr over 1f out to chse wnr ins fnl f but a wl hld* **16/1**

6-56 **3** *2* **Exit Strategy (IRE)**[11] [2224] 3-8-8 **57**........(b[1]) PatrickHills(5) 4 55
(W J Haggas) *chsd ldrs tl led ins fnl 4f: 4 l clr and hung rt to far rail over 2f out: hdd and no ex appr fnl f* **8/1**

-060 **4** *1/2* **Beckenham's Secret**[29] [1726] 3-8-13 **62**........ JamesMillman(5) 11 59
(B R Millman) *led tl hdd ins fnl 4f: styd chsng ldrs tl wknd fnl f* **13/2[2]**

-550 **5** *3* **Metropolitan Chief**[17] [2178] 3-9-0 **58**........ FergusSweeney 5 47
(D M Simcock) *sn chsng ldrs: rdn and styd on same pce fnl 2f* **11/1**

5500 **6** *3* **Follow The Flag (IRE)**[45] [1297] 3-9-7 **65**........(b) SebSanders 1 46
(N P Littmoden) *towards rr tl drvn and hdwy to chse ldrs over 2f out: wknd appr fnl f* **14/1**

5002 **7** *1/2* **Toms Laughter**[10] [2262] 3-8-11 **55**........ CatherineGannon 7 34
(B Palling) *chsd ldrs: rdn 3f out: wknd 2f out* **14/1**

0-02 **8** *2* **Fun In The Sun**[26] [1782] 3-8-6 **55**........ TolleyDean(5) 10 29+
(P D Evans) *chsd ldrs: rdn 3f out: wknd fr 2f out* **9/2[1]**

6-20 **9** *1/2* **Emma Jean Lad (IRE)**[64] [974] 3-9-2 **60**........ LPKeniry 17 33
(J S Moore) *in tch: rdn 3f out: wknd 2f out* **12/1**

-040 **10** *1* **Event Music (IRE)**[16] [2061] 3-9-6 **64**........ JimmyFortune 3 34
(M R Channon) *in tch: hrd drvn and hdwy to chse ldrs over 2f out: sn wknd* **9/1**

0-20 **11** *1 3/4* **Whipchord (IRE)**[32] [1634] 3-9-4 **62**........ RyanMoore 8 27
(R Hannon) *a towards rr* **11/1**

-350 **12** *3* **Ravenna**[15] [2079] 3-9-0 **58**........(p) AdamKirby 15 15
(M P Tregoning) *rdn 1/2-way: a towards rr* **12/1**

-056 **13** *3* **Ireland Dancer (IRE)**[12] [2178] 3-9-2 **60**........ IanMongan 6 9
(P M Phelan) *chsd ldrs over 3f* **33/1**

3000 **14** *5* **Lordswood (IRE)**[81] 737 3-8-8 **59** ow1 RyanBird(7) 16 —
(J J Bridger) *s.i.s: sn in tch: wknd 1/2-way* **40/1**
0020 **15** *4* **Goose Green (IRE)**[15] 2079 3-9-7 **65** SteveDrowne 14 —
(R J Hodges) *stmbld s: sn rcvrd: wknd fr 1/2-way* **7/1**[3]
3-00 **16** *hd* **Situla (IRE)**[22] 1887 3-9-6 **64** PaulDoe 12 —
(H J L Dunlop) *pressed ldrs to 1/2-way* **33/1**
00-0 **17** *4* **Dumas (IRE)**[69] 931 3-9-5 **63** NickyMackay 18 —
(A P Jarvis) *pressed ldrs to 1/2-way* **20/1**

1m 28.61s (-0.45) **Going Correction** -0.025s/f (Good) **17** Ran SP% **133.3**
Speed ratings (Par 97):101,97,94,94,90 87,86,84,83,82 80,77,73,68,63 63,58
CSF £395.05 CT £3626.46 TOTE £34.30: £6.50, £5.20, £2.70, £2.40; EX 659.30.
Owner J R Stephens **Bred** Juddmonte Farms Inc **Trained** Headley, Surrey

FOCUS
An ordinary handicap, but the big field made it very competitive. Sound enough, the winner reproducing his AW form on sand for the first time. The pace looked no more than fair and although they finished very well spread out and the front pair came from a long way back, the next three home were up there throughout so there seemed no great bias either way. The centre of the track looked the place to be though.
Prince Of Charm(USA) Official explanation: trainer said, regarding apparent improvement in form, that in its previous race the gelding missed the break, was rushed into the race and emptied in the final furlong.
Whipchord(IRE) Official explanation: jockey said saddle slipped
Goose Green(IRE) Official explanation: jockey said gelding never travelled
Dumas(IRE) Official explanation: jockey said saddle slipped

2546 AXMINSTER CARPETS APPRENTICE H'CAP (WHIPS SHALL BE CARRIED BUT NOT USED) 6f
5:45 (5:48) (Class 5) (0-75,75) 4-Y-0+ **£3,238** (£963; £481; £240) **Stalls** High

Form RPR
-022 **1** **Currency**[5] 2390 10-8-1 **57** BarrySavage(5) 10 68
(J M Bradley) *trckd ldrs: wnt 2nd 2f out: str chal ins fnl f: led last strides* **5/1**[2]
0-44 **2** *nk* **Seamus Shindig**[13] 2139 5-9-3 **75** AmyScott(7) 1 85
(H Candy) *trckd ldrs: chal over 3f out tl led appr fnl 2f: edgd rt ins fnl f: ct last strides* **8/1**
444- **3** *2* **Unlimited**[215] 6193 5-8-2 **58** (p) SophieDoyle(5) 9 62
(R Simpson) *stdd s: plld hrd and sn in tch: drvn and styd on fnl f but nvr gng pce to rch ldrs* **10/1**
0-04 **4** *2* **Bold Argument (IRE)**[26] 1787 4-8-7 **63** NBazeley(5) 5 61
(Mrs P N Dutfield) *in rr: drvn along 1/2-way: sme late hdwy* **8/1**
1623 **5** *shd* **Quantum Leap**[4] 2414 10-8-10 **66** (p) ThomasBubb(5) 7 64
(S Dow) *in rr tl pushed along and hdwy fr 2f out: nvr rchd ldrs* **8/1**
5206 **6** *shd* **Guildenstern (IRE)**[12] 2189 5-9-5 **75** (t) MarkCoumbe(5) 2 72
(P L Gilligan) *in rr: drvn and mod hdwy fr over 1f out* **6/1**[3]
30-0 **7** *shd* **Imperial Gain (USA)**[15] 2088 4-9-6 **74** AlanRutter(3) 6 71
(J M Bradley) *in rr: drvn along 1/2-way: kpt on fnl f but nvr in contention* **14/1**
4120 **8** *1 1/2* **Dvinsky (USA)**[13] 2139 6-9-8 **73** WilliamCarson 4 66
(P Howling) *bolted bef s: led tl hdd appr fnl 2f: wknd over 1f out* **9/1**
0553 **9** *nk* **Musical Script (USA)**[6] 2350 4-8-9 **60** JamieHamblett 3 52
(Mouse Hamilton-Fairley) *chsd ldrs: rdn 3f out: wknd over 1f out* **13/2**
4002 **10** *1/2* **Briannsta (IRE)**[8] 2318 5-9-5 **75** JosephWalsh(5) 8 65
(C G Cox) *chsd ldrs 4f* **4/1**[1]

1m 14.63s (-0.35) **Going Correction** -0.025s/f (Good) **10** Ran SP% **123.4**
Speed ratings (Par 103):101,100,97,95,95 95,94,92,92,91
CSF £47.58 CT £404.70 TOTE £4.80: £1.70, £3.00, £3.70; EX 45.00 Place 6 £13.58, Place 5 £7.06..
Owner Robert Bailey **Bred** Limestone Stud **Trained** Sedbury, Gloucs

FOCUS
An ordinary sprint handicap in which the apprentices were not allowed to use their whips, and given the narrow winning margin, the result might have been different had they done so. That is only significant in terms of the reliability of the form, however, as this type of contest does serve its purpose. The winner is still below last year's peak but is at the veteran stage now.
T/Plt: £22.70 to a £1 stake. Pool: £63,753.30. 2,042.80 winning tickets. T/Qpdt: £9.60 to a £1 stake. Pool: £3,134.10. 240.90 winning tickets. ST

LE LION-D'ANGERS (R-H)
Tuesday, June 12

OFFICIAL GOING: Good to soft

2547a PRIX URBAN SEA (LISTED RACE) (FILLIES) 1m 3f 110y
3:05 (3:06) 3-Y-0 **£17,568** (£7,027; £5,270; £3,514; £1,757)

RPR
1 **Orion Girl (GER)**[21] 3-8-11 JVictoire 3 97
(H-A Pantall, France)
2 *1* **Shawhill**[29] 1724 3-8-11 DBonilla 4 96
(Tom Dascombe) *racd in 2nd: pushed along and disputing ld 2 1/2f out: led ent st to 100yds out: kpt on* **38/10**[1]
3 *3* **Une Pivoine (FR)**[44] 1339 3-8-11 C-PLemaire 8 91
(J E Pease, France)
4 *hd* **Furusato (USA)**[44] 1339 3-8-11 TJarnet 7 91
(M Delzangles, France)
5 *5* **Nabati (USA)**[52] 3-8-11 GToupel 2 83
(H-A Pantall, France)
6 *5* **Sahara Lady (IRE)**[46] 3-8-11 FVeron 1 75
(H-A Pantall, France)
7 *2* **Takaniya (IRE)**[24] 3-8-11 MSautjeau 9 71
(A Fabre, France)
8 *6* **Bocabelle (FR)**[87] 705 3-8-11 IMendizabal 5 62
(J-C Rouget, France)
9 *dist* **Graceful Steps (IRE)**[21] 1927 3-8-11 TThulliez 6 —
(E J O'Neill) *mid-div: 4th and reminders 1/2-way: sn u.p: last and btn st: t.o* **14/1**[2]

2m 20.2s (140.20) **9** Ran SP% **27.5**
PARI-MUTUEL (Including 1 Euro stake): WIN 5.10; PL 1.90, 4.80, 2.20;DF 51.60.
Owner H Rapp **Bred** H Rapp **Trained** France

NOTEBOOK
Shawhill ran a cracking race and battled right the way to the line. Beautifully placed throughout, she took up the running a furlong and a half out and looked likely to end up in the winner's enclosure, but she was passed by Orion Girl inside the final furlong.
Graceful Steps(IRE), in mid-division for much of this event, was under pressure before the straight and eventually dropped out to finish a distant last.

2131 TABY (R-H)
Tuesday, June 12

OFFICIAL GOING: Firm

2548a JOCKEYKLUBBENS JUBILEUMSLOPNING (C&G) 1m
7:53 (7:53) 3-Y-0
£19,679 (£9,052; £3,946; £2,755; £1,968; £1,181)

RPR
1 **Champollion (SWE)** 3-9-4 FDiaz 12 —
(L Reuterskiold, Sweden) **136/10**
2 *3 1/2* **Royal Miswaki (IRE)** 3-9-4 JohnFortune 5 —
(Wido Neuroth, Norway) **54/10**[3]
3 *1 1/2* **Alaska State (SWE)** 3-9-4 (b) ILopez 7 —
(J Malmborg) **24/1**
4 *1* **Spinning Fun (IRE)** 3-9-4 JJohansen 8 —
(F Reuterskiold, Sweden) **15/1**
5 *1 1/2* **Supergill (IRE)**[59] 3-9-4 KAndersen 3 —
(Are Hyldmo, Norway) **24/10**[2]
6 *1/2* **Premier Cru (DEN)** 3-9-4 NCordrey 11 —
(P Wahl, Sweden) **19/10**[1]
7 *hd* **Mo (USA)**[15] 2079 3-9-4 YvonneDurant 2 —
(R A Kvisla) *led to 1 1/2f out: wknd qckly* **76/10**
8 *1* **El Rey (IRE)** 3-9-4 (b) P-AGraberg 10 —
(F Castro, Sweden) **26/1**
9 *dist* **Zimon** 3-9-4 MLarsen 9 —
(Ms C Erichsen, Norway) **83/10**
P **Sambalando (SWE)** 3-9-4 MSantos 4 —
(Annike Bye Nunez) **27/1**

1m 38.4s (98.40) **10** Ran SP% **126.3**
(including one krona stakes); WIN 14.58; PL 4.60, 2.54, 7.51; DF195.25.
Owner Stall Gransater **Bred** B Helander **Trained** Sweden

NOTEBOOK
Mo(USA), just a modest maiden in Britain, showed good speed but did not get home. He has yet to prove his stamina for this trip.

2132 BEVERLEY (R-H)
Wednesday, June 13

OFFICIAL GOING: Good to firm (8.9)
After 25mm water over the previous five days and 6mm rain the previous day the ground was described as 'easy side of good'.
Wind: blustery 1/2 behind Weather: overcast

2549 NEW EVENING FIXTURE HERE NEXT THURSDAY CLAIMING STKS 5f
2:20 (2:20) (Class 6) 2-Y-0 **£2,914** (£867; £433; £216) **Stalls** High

Form RPR
2103 **1** **Artdeal**[16] 2090 2-9-5 0 (p) PaulHanagan 3 70
(M J Wallace) *mde all: drvn out* **8/13**[1]
015 **2** *2* **Alexander Monarchy (IRE)**[16] 2087 2-9-0 0 PatCosgrave 2 58
(K A Ryan) *chsd ldrs: wnt 2nd over 2f out: sn rdn: styd on: no real imp* **7/2**[2]
00 **3** *4* **Handsinthemist (IRE)**[7] 2371 2-9-0 0 MickyFenton 4 43
(P T Midgley) *sn chsng ldrs: sltly hmpd after 100yds: lost pl over 3f out: wandered and kpt on appr fnl f: tk 3rd ins fnl f* **33/1**
0 **4** *1 1/2* **Amy Lionheart**[56] 1087 2-8-2 0 KimTinkler 5 26
(N Tinkler) *s.i.s: hdwy to go 3rd over 2f out: fdd ins fnl f* **25/1**
1U **5** *7* **My Sheilas Dream (IRE)**[32] 1674 2-8-3 0 JackDean(7) 1 9
(W G M Turner) *swvd lft s: sn chsng wnr: edgd lft over 2f out: sn lost pl* **9/2**[3]

64.39 secs (0.39) **Going Correction** -0.05s/f (Good) **5** Ran SP% **109.1**
Speed ratings (Par 91):94,90,84,82,70
CSF £3.01 TOTE £1.60: £1.10, £1.30; EX 2.70.The winner was subject to a friendly claim.
Owner Matthew Green **Bred** Miss A Shaykhutdinova **Trained** Newmarket, Suffolk
■ Stewards' Enquiry : Paul Hanagan 16-day ban (takes into account previous offences): careless riding (Jul 3-14; 4 days deferred)

FOCUS
An uncompetitive seller with the winner not having to be at his best to account for the runner-up, who ran very much to her pre-race mark.

NOTEBOOK
Artdeal, who bled from the nose at Redcar, was excitable in the paddock and thought twice about going to post. In the end he had to be kept right up to his work and was retained in the face of three hostile claims. Whether he is going the right way remains to be seen. (tchd 4-7 and 4-6)
Alexander Monarchy(IRE), happier on this quicker surface, went in pursuit of the winner. She never gave up the fight but was always definitely second best. She deserves another success at this low level. (op 4-1)
Handsinthemist(IRE), in selling company for the first time, still looks very inexperienced. (tchd 40-1)
Amy Lionheart, twice as far behind today's winner on her debut here two months ago, still looks weak and inexperienced. (op 33-1)
My Sheilas Dream(IRE), who refused to race and lost her rider at the start last time, swerved leaving the gates then edged out towards the centre before dropping right out. She is one to have severe doubts about now. Official explanation: vet said filly was heard to cough after (op 4-1 tchd 5-1)

2550 LINDA BRADBURY 60TH BIRTHDAY H'CAP 7f 100y
2:50 (2:51) (Class 5) (0-70,72) 4-Y-0+ **£3,886** (£1,156; £577; £288) **Stalls** High

Form RPR
1632 **1** **Flying Bantam (IRE)**[13] 2190 6-9-2 **65** PaulHanagan 14 75
(R A Fahey) *prom: drvn over 2f out: styd on to ld last 100yds* **9/2**[2]
0-00 **2** *3/4* **Motafarred (IRE)**[8] 2338 5-8-10 **59** PaulMulrennan 13 67
(Micky Hammond) *led: hdd and no ex ins fnl f* **25/1**
4603 **3** *1* **Xpres Maite**[18] 2023 4-8-8 **60** MarcHalford(3) 11 66
(S R Bowring) *t.k.h: trckd ldrs: upsides 1f out: no ex* **15/2**
0-11 **4** *1 1/4* **Sam's Secret**[16] 2091 5-8-11 **60** J-PGuillambert 10 63
(G A Swinbank) *hld up in tch: effrt on inner over 2f out: kpt on same pce appr fnl f* **5/1**[3]
1051 **5** *3* **Franksalot (IRE)**[2] 2508 7-9-9 **72** 6ex RoystonFfrench 6 67
(I W McInnes) *mid-div: hdwy over 2f out: kpt on: nvr rchd ldrs* **7/2**[1]

0203 **6** *nk* **Machinate (USA)**^{14} [2143] 5-8-2 **54**............................ AndrewMullen$^{(3)}$ 1 48+
(W M Brisbourne) *swtchd rt after s: bhd: hdwa on inner over 2f out: hmpd over 1f out: nvr nr ldrs* **16/1**

5-45 **7** *1 ½* **Ryedale Ovation (IRE)**^{50} [1223] 4-9-0 **68**.............. NataliaGemelova$^{(5)}$ 2 59
(T D Easterby) *sn chsng ldrs: wnt rt over 1f out: sn wknd* **11/1**

3320 **8** *½* **Penel (IRE)**^{14} [2149] 6-8-2 **56** ow5.......................(p) RoryMoore$^{(5)}$ 7 45
(P T Midgley) *chsd ldrs: outpcd 3f out: kpt on fnl 2f* **22/1**

0215 **9** *1 ½* **Sedge (USA)**^{18} [2033] 7-8-13 **62**.....................................(p) MickyFenton 9 48
(P T Midgley) *in rr-div: drvn over 4f out: nvr on terms* **11/1**

20-0 **10** *1* **Advancement**^{29} [1751] 4-9-4 **70**................................ JamieMoriarty$^{(3)}$ 8 53
(R A Fahey) *s.i.s: a in rr* **20/1**

-260 **11** *3* **Musicmaestroplease (IRE)**^{23} [1892] 4-8-8 **60**............. DominicFox$^{(3)}$ 4 36+
(S Parr) *t.k.h in rr: hdwy on ins over 2f out: styng on whn bdly hmpd over 1f out: nt rcvr and eased* **40/1**

1m 33.04s (-1.27) **Going Correction** -0.05s/f (Good) **11** Ran SP% **106.8**
Speed ratings (Par 103):105,104,103,101,98 97,96,95,93,92 89
CSF £103.02 CT £532.92 TOTE £5.70: £1.60, £5.00, £2.50; EX 83.60.
Owner The Matthewman Partnership **Bred** Robinski Bloodstock Limited **Trained** Musley Bank, N Yorks
■ Stewards' Enquiry : Rory Moore two-day ban: used whip when out of contention (Jun 24-25)
Natalia Gemelova four-day ban: careless riding (Jun 24-27)

FOCUS
Those drawn high dominated and in the end avoided the trouble caused by Ryedale Ovation. The form looks sound among the principals, the winner rated to last year's best.
Musicmaestroplease(IRE) Official explanation: jockey said colt suffered interference in running

2551 DEAN MORSE CAFE SOCIETY H'CAP 1m 1f 207y
3:20 (3:20) (Class 4) (0-80,80) 4-Y-0+ **£5,181** (£1,541; £770; £384) **Stalls** High

Form RPR

0-00 **1** **Zaif (IRE)**^{37} [1542] 4-9-7 **80**.................................... AntonyProcter 4 87
(D R C Elsworth) *hld up in last: effrt and swtchd outside over 2f out: r.o to ld ins fnl f* **3/1**^{2}

0325 **2** *½* **Sir Arthur (IRE)**^{6} [2403] 4-9-0 **73**... KDarley 1 79
(M Johnston) *led: qcknd over 3f out: rdn and edgd lft 1f out: hdd and no ex ins fnl f* **11/8**^{1}

0130 **3** *3* **Bessemer (JPN)**^{18} [2033] 6-8-3 **62**............................(p) RoystonFfrench 3 62
(I W McInnes) *hld up: effrt over 3f out: sn chsng ldrs: hung rt over 1f out: kpt on same pce* **9/1**

2316 **4** *2* **Just Observing**^{9} [2314] 4-9-3 **76**....................................(p) MickyFenton 6 72
(P T Midgley) *trckd ldrs: drvn over 3f out: one pce* **6/1**

0002 **5** *3 ½* **Dark Charm (FR)**^{15} [2117] 8-8-7 **66**...........................(p) PaulHanagan 2 55
(R A Fahey) *chsd ldrs: drvn 3f out: wknd appr fnl f* **4/1**^{3}

2m 7.14s (-0.16) **Going Correction** -0.05s/f (Good) **5** Ran SP% **111.4**
Speed ratings (Par 105):98,97,95,93,90
CSF £7.69 TOTE £4.10: £2.20, £1.20; EX 10.60.
Owner Miss R Wakeford **Bred** Bobby Donworth And Miss Honora Corridan **Trained** Newmarket, Suffolk
■ Stewards' Enquiry : K Darley caution: careless riding

FOCUS
Just a steady gallop and the winner did well to come from off the pace. Sound enough form, rated through the second and third.

2552 DRABBLE AND CO SOLICITORS OF SCARBOROUGH H'CAP 1m 4f 16y
3:50 (3:50) (Class 6) (0-55,55) 3-Y-O **£2,914** (£867; £433; £216) **Stalls** High

Form RPR

-606 **1** **Mr Crystal (FR)**^{22} [1917] 3-8-7 **53**.................. MichaelJStainton$^{(5)}$ 1 60
(Micky Hammond) *trckd ldrs: styd on to ld fnl 75yds* **13/2**^{3}

00-4 **2** *¾* **Cushat Law (IRE)**^{13} [2192] 3-9-0 **55**.. KDarley 4 61
(W Jarvis) *t.k.h: hdwy on outside to trck ldrs after 4f: led over 1f out: hdd and no ex wl ins fnl f* **5/2**^{1}

0644 **3** *2* **Park's Prodigy**^{16} [2096] 3-8-6 **50**.............................(t) AndrewElliott$^{(3)}$ 10 53
(P C Haslam) *prom: drvn over 4f out: wandered over 1f out: styd on* **4/1**^{2}

0-50 **4** *¾* **Sky Beam (USA)**^{13} [2192] 3-8-9 **50**........................... RoystonFfrench 9 51
(J L Dunlop) *hld up towards rr: effrt 3f out: kpt on: nt rch ldrs* **13/2**^{3}

400- **5** *nk* **Admiral Savannah (IRE)**^{284} [5025] 3-8-9 **50**.................. MickyFenton 8 51
(T D Easterby) *drvn to sn chse ldrs: hung rt and n.m.r over 1f out: kpt on* **12/1**

065 **6** *¾* **Celtic Memories (IRE)**^{22} [1917] 3-8-12 **53**.................. PaulMulrennan 3 53
(M W Easterby) *led: rdn and hung lft 3f out: hdd over 1f out: one pce* **8/1**

40-0 **7** *6* **Bollin Freddie**^{14} [2133] 3-8-10 **54**............................ AndrewMullen$^{(3)}$ 12 44
(A J Lockwood) *chsd ldrs: drvn and outpcd 4f out: lost pl over 2f out* **10/1**

0500 **8** *2* **Woodygo**^{44} [1355] 3-8-11 **52**..................................(v^{1}) RichardThomas 11 39
(J R Best) *plld hrd in rr: drvn and lost pl 4f out: no ch after* **14/1**

0-00 **9** *2* **Firestorm (IRE)**^{22} [1917] 3-8-3 **51**................................ KellyHarrison$^{(7)}$ 2 35
(C W Fairhurst) *prom: drvn over 4f out: lost pl 3f out* **33/1**

00-4 **10** *5* **Reflective Glory (IRE)**^{9} [2299] 3-8-11 **52**........................ TonyHamilton 6 28
(J S Wainwright) *chsd ldrs: lost pl over 2f out* **25/1**

0-50 **11** *17* **Bobansheil (IRE)**^{14} [2133] 3-8-11 **55**.......................... JamieMoriarty$^{(3)}$ 5 —
(J S Wainwright) *bhd and drvn along: t.o 3f out* **16/1**

2m 40.58s (0.37) **Going Correction** -0.05s/f (Good) **11** Ran SP% **122.5**
Speed ratings (Par 97):96,95,94,93,93 92,88,87,86,82 71
CSF £24.07 CT £76.92 TOTE £8.70: £3.00, £1.30, £1.50; EX 24.30.
Owner S Henderson **Bred** Gerard Schence **Trained** Middleham Moor, N Yorks

FOCUS
A very steady gallop to this low-grade handicap. The form looks sound for the grade, the front pair up 4lb and the race rated through the third.
Bollin Freddie Official explanation: trainer said gelding finished lame

2553 VK VODKA KICK FILLIES' H'CAP 5f
4:20 (4:21) (Class 6) (0-65,65) 3-Y-0+ **£2,914** (£867; £433; £216) **Stalls** High

Form RPR

45-0 **1** **Sahara Silk (IRE)**^{144} [190] 6-9-3 **61**.........................(v) KellyHarrison$^{(7)}$ 1 71
(D Shaw) *led one other stands' side: led overall 2f out: styd on wl* **18/1**

-504 **2** *1 ¾* **Princess Cleo**^{21} [1940] 4-9-9 **60**..................................... MickyFenton 14 64
(T D Easterby) *chsd ldrs towards far side: hung lft and racd stands' side over 2f out: styd on to take 2nd ins fnl f* **5/1**^{1}

6-00 **3** *nk* **Pick A Nice Name**^{25} [1847] 5-9-9 **65**.................. MichaelJStainton$^{(5)}$ 5 68
(R M Whitaker) *chsd ldrs on outer: kpt on same pce fnl f* **12/1**

0010 **4** *hd* **Mystery Pips**^{23} [1902] 7-8-13 **50**...(v) KimTinkler 3 52
(N Tinkler) *w wnr stands' side: kpt on same pce ins fnl f* **28/1**

40-5 **5** *nk* **Gap Princess (IRE)**^{11} [2255] 3-9-5 **63**............................ PaulHanagan 13 61+
(R A Fahey) *in rr far side: hdwy to ld that side 1f out: kpt on wl* **15/2**

5400 **6** *3 ½* **Muara**^{9} [2315] 5-9-4 **58**..(p) AndrewMullen$^{(3)}$ 15 46
(D W Barker) *chsd ldrs far side: wknd fnl f* **13/2**^{3}

2-00 **7** *2 ½* **Flower Of Cork (IRE)**^{37} [1538] 3-8-6 **55**..........(b^{1}) NataliaGemelova$^{(5)}$ 12 31
(T D Easterby) *sn outpcd and in rr: sme hdwy 2f out: nvr on terms* **40/1**

0-45 **8** *1 ¼* **Cut Ridge (IRE)**^{65} [967] 8-8-11 **48**.............................. PaulMulrennan 11 23+
(J S Wainwright) *stall only half opened: s.s: bhd tl kpt on fnl 2f* **11/1**

0-00 **9** *hd* **Smart Cassie**^{33} [1640] 4-8-12 **49**..................................(p) VinceSlattery 2 23
(H J Evans) *chsd ldrs towards stands' side: outpcd fnl 2f* **80/1**

0-63 **10** *shd* **Tilsworth Charlie**^{8} [2334] 4-9-0 **51**......................................(v) KDarley 10 25
(J R Jenkins) *s.i.s: in rr tl kpt on fnl 2f: nvr on terms* **5/1**^{1}

0-60 **11** *¾* **Violet's Pride**^{5} [2418] 3-8-8 **55**.. DominicFox$^{(3)}$ 16 23+
(S Parr) *led overall towards far side: sddle slipped and hdd 2f out: heavily eased fnl f* **14/1**

0006 **12** *1 ¼* **Minimum Fuss (IRE)**^{5} [2418] 3-7-13 **50**................. CharlotteKerton$^{(7)}$ 17 13
(M C Chapman) *chsd ldrs far side: wknd over 1f out* **22/1**

-200 **13** *1 ½* **Miss Mujahid Times**^{23} [1902] 4-8-11 **48**.................(v^{1}) RichardThomas 9 9
(A D Brown) *sn outpcd and in rr* **28/1**

6-44 **14** *nk* **Morristown Music (IRE)**^{11} [2255] 3-9-5 **63**.................... TonyHamilton 8 20
(J S Wainwright) *in tch: lost pl over 3f out* **16/1**

0015 **15** *¾* **Champagne Cracker**^{9} [2315] 6-9-8 **59**........................ RoystonFfrench 7 16
(M Dods) *charged gate: chsd ldrs: wknd 2f out* **6/1**^{2}

63.54 secs (-0.46) **Going Correction** -0.05s/f (Good)
WFA 3 from 4yo+ 7lb **15** Ran SP% **121.5**
Speed ratings (Par 98):101,98,97,97,96 91,87,85,85,84 83,81,79,78,77
CSF £101.31 CT £1178.84 TOTE £26.90: £5.40, £2.20, £5.10; EX 193.00.
Owner Danethorpe Racing Ltd **Bred** John Cullinan **Trained** Danethorpe, Notts

FOCUS
As at the previous meeting the stands' side held sway, the first four ending up on that side. The form is best treated with caution but the winner is worth this figure on her All-Weather form.
Cut Ridge(IRE) Official explanation: jockey said mare had missed the break
Violet's Pride Official explanation: jockey said saddle slipped
Champagne Cracker Official explanation: jockey said mare had missed the break

2554 RACING HERE ON MIDSUMMER'S NIGHT 21 JUNE MAIDEN STKS 7f 100y
4:50 (4:53) (Class 5) 3-Y-0+ **£3,886** (£1,156; £577; £288) **Stalls** High

Form RPR

03 **1** **Trivia (IRE)**^{25} [1840] 3-8-8 0.. MickyFenton 9 75
(N A Callaghan) *trckd ldrs: swtchd stands' side 2f out: led over 1f out: jst hld on* **15/8**^{2}

0 **2** *shd* **Know The Law**^{18} [2046] 3-8-10 0.................................. MarcHalford$^{(3)}$ 6 79
(D R C Elsworth) *swvd lft s: hdwy over 2f out: carried stands' side fnl f: kpt on wl: jst failed* **12/1**

3 *1 ¼* **Red Blossom** 3-8-8 0.. PaulHanagan 10 71
(Sir Mark Prescott) *chsd ldrs: hung bdly lft appr fnl f and ended up stands' side: no ex fnl 75yds* **6/4**^{1}

02P **4** *7* **Ammeyrr**^{30} [1714] 3-8-10 0...................................... AndrewMullen$^{(3)}$ 4 58
(A Crook) *in rr and sn pushed along: swtchd stands' side over 2f out: kpt on: nvr nr ldrs* **33/1**

4 **5** *1 ¾* **Jibajaba (USA)**^{22} [1913] 3-8-13 0..................................... TonyHamilton 3 53
(R A Fahey) *chsd ldrs: swtchd stands' side over 2f out: kpt on one pce* **13/2**^{3}

-060 **6** *½* **Crux**^{9} [2312] 5-9-4 44... MichaelJStainton$^{(5)}$ 13 55?
(R E Barr) *prminent: hmpd over 5f out: hdwy to chse ldrs far side 2f out: one pce* **33/1**

45 **7** *1* **Morbick**^{9} [2312] 3-8-13 0... KDarley 11 50+
(M Johnston) *s.i.s: sn bhd: t.o 3f out: styd on steadily* **8/1**

600- **8** *nk* **Ivana Illyich (IRE)**^{291} [4506] 5-9-1 31.......................... JamieMoriarty$^{(3)}$ 5 47?
(J S Wainwright) *t.k.h: in tch: swtchd stands' side over 2f out: no imp* **66/1**

0-0 **9** *2 ½* **River Club**^{19} [2012] 3-8-13 0.. PaulMulrennan 8 42+
(G A Swinbank) *t.k.h in midfield: swtchd stands' side over 2f out: nvr a threat* **28/1**

000- **10** *½* **Chilsdown**^{211} [6473] 4-9-6 42....................................... AndrewElliott$^{(3)}$ 12 44
(J G Given) *t.k.h: w ldr: led 4f out tl over 2f out: lost pl over 1f out* **100/1**

0/- **11** *1 ¾* **Princess Charlmane (IRE)**^{658} [4677] 4-9-4 0................. PaddyAspell 1 34
(C J Teague) *unruly s: a in rr* **100/1**

00- **12** *½* **Bishop Auckland (IRE)**^{222} [6318] 3-8-13 0................ RoystonFfrench 7 35
(Mrs A Duffield) *dwlt: hld up in rr: nvr a factor* **50/1**

13 *2* **Summer Gift**^{334} 4-8-11 0.. JamesO'Reilly$^{(7)}$ 2 28
(J O'Reilly) *t.k.h: led tl 4f out: led over 2f out: hdd & wknd qckly over 1f out* **100/1**

1m 33.93s (-0.38) **Going Correction** -0.05s/f (Good)
WFA 3 from 4yo+ 10lb **13** Ran SP% **122.7**
Speed ratings (Par 103):100,99,98,90,88 87,86,86,83,82 80,80,78
CSF £24.48 TOTE £3.30: £1.20, £2.40, £1.20; EX 32.10 Place 6 £15.30, Place 5 £13.77..
Owner Michael Tabor **Bred** Mrs Jean O'Brien **Trained** Newmarket, Suffolk

FOCUS
In the end the first five raced on the stands' side. The sixth, first home on the far side, is rated just 44 and the form is far from solid. Steps forward from the first two, especially the runner-up.
T/Plt: £26.90 to a £1 stake. Pool: £42,243.55. 1,143.60 winning tickets. T/Qpdt: £5.80 to a £1 stake. Pool: £2,230.50. 282.90 winning tickets. WG

2410 BRIGHTON (L-H)
Wednesday, June 13

OFFICIAL GOING: Firm
Wind: Moderate, across Weather: Fine, occasional sea frets

2555 SOUTHERN FM H'CAP 5f 59y
2:00 (2:00) (Class 6) (0-60,60) 3-Y-0+ **£2,072** (£616; £308; £153) **Stalls** Low

Form RPR

0453 **1** **Cosmic Destiny (IRE)**^{4} [2459] 5-8-13 **50**.......................... JimCrowley 12 61
(E F Vaughan) *mid-div: hdwy to ld wl over 1f out: drvn clr* **4/1**^{2}

3306 **2** *2* **Thoughtsofstardom**^{12} [2221] 4-8-13 **50**.....................(be) HayleyTurner 10 54
(P S McEntee) *mid-div: hdwy 2f out: drvn to chse wnr ins fnl f: nt qckn* **16/1**

0-00 **3** *nk* **Zimbali**^{15} [2104] 5-8-2 **46** oh1................................ KirstyMilczarek$^{(7)}$ 14 49
(J M Bradley) *outpcd towards rr: gd hdwy over 1f out: kpt on same pce* **40/1**

0-50 **4** *nk* **Multahab**^{19} [1991] 8-9-8 **59**..(t) DaneO'Neill 3 61+
(Miss D A McHale) *disp ld: led and edgd towards stands' rail fr over 2f out: hdd wl over 1f out: one pce* **5/1**^{3}

060- **5** *¾* **Peruvian Style (IRE)**^{217} [6399] 6-9-2 **53**......................... SteveDrowne 1 52
(J M Bradley) *chsd ldng pair: hrd rdn over 1f out: one pce* **9/1**

-006 **6** *hd* **Enjoy The Buzz**^{15} [2108] 8-8-3 **47**................................ BarrySavage$^{(7)}$ 4 46
(J M Bradley) *dwlt: bhd: hdwy over 1f out: nrst fin* **12/1**

4555 **7** *½* **Legal Set (IRE)**^{7} [2357] 11-8-4 **46** oh1........................(b) AnnStokell$^{(5)}$ 7 43
(Miss A Stokell) *mid-div on rail: hrd rdn and hdwy 2f out: one pce appr fnl f* **33/1**

-000 **8** *nk* **Jodrell Bank (IRE)**[8] 2334 4-8-12 **49**....................(b[1]) TQuinn 15 45
(J Ryan) *sltly hmpd early: sn wl bhd: pushed along and styd on fnl 2f* **80/1**

4-00 **9** *3/4* **Campeon (IRE)**[15] 2104 5-8-5 **47** oh1 ow1.............. KevinGhunowa(5) 13 40+
(J M Bradley) *stmbld s and sddle slipped: sn wl bhd: r.o fr over 1f out: nvr nrr* **25/1**

3001 **10** *nk* **Arfinnit (IRE)**[13] 2174 6-8-11 **48**....................(v) SebSanders 16 40
(Mrs A L M King) *mid-div on outside: rdn and no imp fnl 2f* **8/1**

1060 **11** *nk* **King Of Charm (IRE)**[14] 2143 4-8-10 **47**..............(b) StephenCarson 8 38
(G L Moore) *chsd ldrs 3f: hrd rdn: grad lost pl* **14/1**

0005 **12** *1 1/4* **Saintly Place**[15] 2104 6-8-9 **46** oh1.................. CatherineGannon 11 32
(A W Carroll) *in tch tl rdn and wknd 2f out* **25/1**

0002 **13** *2* **Silver Prelude**[2] 2516 6-8-13 **55**.................... JamesMillman(5) 6 34+
(D K Ivory) *disp ld: carried towards stands' rail over 2f out: sn wknd* **7/2**[1]

06- **14** *1 1/4* **Ballybunion (IRE)**[279] 5131 8-8-13 **55**.................... LukeMorris(5) 9 30
(R A Harris) *chsd ldrs: drvn along 1/2-way: sn wknd* **18/1**

62.56 secs (0.26) **Going Correction** +0.05s/f (Good) **14** Ran SP% **119.8**
Speed ratings (Par 101):99,95,95,94,93 93,92,92,90,90 89,87,84,82
CSF £62.72 CT £2252.62 TOTE £5.50: £1.90, £7.60, £12.30; EX 85.10 TRIFECTA Not won..
Owner A M Pickering **Bred** The Cruelle People **Trained** Newmarket, Suffolk

FOCUS
A low-grade but competitive sprint, run at a strong gallop. Ordinary form but sound enough for the grade
Multahab Official explanation: jockey said gelding hung right
Campeon(IRE) Official explanation: jockey said saddle slipped
King Of Charm(IRE) Official explanation: jockey said gelding hung right

2556 DJMT MAGNOTHERAPY HORSE RUG H'CAP 6f 209y
2:30 (2:31) (Class 6) (0-65,59) 4-Y-0+ **£2,266** (£674; £337; £168) **Stalls** Low

Form RPR

00- **1** **Bucharest**[168] 6949 4-9-7 **59**.................... SteveDrowne 8 69
(M Wigham) *mde all: rdn and in control fnl 2f: styd on wl* **3/1**[1]

6004 **2** *1 3/4* **Lady Edge (IRE)**[5] 2412 5-8-12 **55**.................... KevinGhunowa(5) 13 60
(A W Carroll) *mid-div: hdwy 2f out: drvn to chse wnr over 1f out: kpt on same pce* **50/1**

4346 **3** *1 3/4* **Fantasy Defender (IRE)**[124] 402 5-8-4 **47**.............. LukeMorris(5) 6 47
(R M H Cowell) *towards rr: hrd rdn and hdwy over 1f out: edgd lft: nrst fin* **16/1**

0533 **4** *nk* **Napoletano (GER)**[8] 2336 6-8-12 **50**....................(p) TQuinn 2 50
(S Dow) *chsd ldrs: hrd rdn and one pce fnl 2f* **6/1**[3]

0-00 **5** *nk* **Sands Of Barra (IRE)**[32] 1675 4-9-4 **56**..............(p) SebSanders 14 55
(I W McInnes) *towards rr: rdn and r.o fnl 2f: nvr nrr* **6/1**[3]

-406 **6** *1 3/4* **Millfield (IRE)**[8] 2331 4-8-11 **54**.................... TravisBlock(5) 5 48+
(P R Chamings) *s.s: hld up and bhd: hdwy into midfield whn involved in scrimmaging ins fnl 2f: unable to chal* **4/1**[2]

4424 **7** *1* **Lady Duxyana**[11] 2257 4-8-11 **49**....................(v) RichardSmith 1 49+
(M D I Usher) *dwlt: sn chsng ldrs: one pce fnl 2f: 4th and btn wn hmpd and eased wl ins fnl f* **14/1**

0224 **8** *1/2* **Danawi (IRE)**[10] 2272 4-8-13 **51**.................... DaneO'Neill 7 41
(M R Hoad) *chsd wnr tl wknd over 1f out: b.b.v* **13/2**

0303 **9** *1/2* **Sham Ruby**[45] 1317 5-8-7 **45**....................(t) HayleyTurner 16 34
(M R Bosley) *in tch: drvn along 3f out: btn whn edgd lft ins fnl 2f* **33/1**

5-05 **10** *nk* **Three Counties (IRE)**[16] 2077 6-8-12 **57**.............. KylieManser(7) 3 45
(N I M Rossiter) *hld up towards rr: sme hdwy on rail whn hmpd ins fnl 2f: n.d after* **66/1**

000- **11** *2* **Dado Mush**[186] 6762 4-9-1 **53**.................... JimCrowley 9 36
(T T Clement) *sn wl bhd: nvr trbld ldrs* **40/1**

-460 **12** *16* **Cree**[14] 2143 5-9-2 **54**.................... PaulDoe 12 —
(W R Muir) *stdd s: hld up towards rr: effrt and n.m.r 3f out: sn rdn and n.d: b.b.v* **16/1**

000- **13** *11* **Halfwaytoparadise**[177] 6855 4-9-5 **57**..............(p) MatthewHenry 11 —
(W G M Turner) *chsd ldrs: rdn whn pushed wd 3f out: sn bhd* **50/1**

0000 **14** *dist* **Drury Lane (IRE)**[14] 2143 7-8-3 **46**..............(b) AnnStokell(5) 10 —
(Miss A Stokell) *chsd ldrs: wknd 3f out: bhd whn lost action and virtually p.u 1f out* **50/1**

1m 22.56s (-0.14) **Going Correction** +0.05s/f (Good) **14** Ran SP% **118.1**
Speed ratings (Par 101):102,100,98,97,97 95,94,93,93,92 90,72,59,—
CSF £181.22 CT £2148.92 TOTE £3.60: £1.90, £12.00, £6.50; EX 146.10 TRIFECTA Not won..
Owner D T L Limited **Bred** Juddmonte Farms Ltd **Trained** Newmarket, Suffolk
■ Stewards' Enquiry : Luke Morris two-day ban: careless riding (Jun 24-25)
Richard Smith three-day ban: careless riding (Jun 24-26)

FOCUS
A modest race, with the well-backed favourite landing the money. A bit of a messy race, but the form seems sound enough with the winner back to last year's form.
Fantasy Defender(IRE) Official explanation: jockey said gelding hung left
Napoletano(GER) Official explanation: jockey said horse hung both ways
Danawi(IRE) Official explanation: trainer said gelding bled from the nose
Cree Official explanation: trainer said gelding bled from the nose
Drury Lane(IRE) Official explanation: jockey said gelding lost its action

2557 BRIGHTON INTERNATIONAL ARENA (S) STKS 1m 1f 209y
3:00 (3:01) (Class 6) 3-5-Y-0 **£1,943** (£578; £288; £144) **Stalls** High

Form RPR

0003 **1** **Danceinthevalley (IRE)**[7] 2372 5-9-4 40.................... SebSanders 3 59+
(I W McInnes) *mde all: sn 15 l clr: rdn 2f out: eased fnl 75yds: unchal* **7/4**[2]

0200 **2** *13* **Savoy Chapel**[8] 2331 5-9-4 40.................... SteveDrowne 6 30
(A W Carroll) *3rd tl wnt 15 l 2nd 1/2-way: rdn and no imp fnl 3f* **8/1**

3000 **3** *1* **Coffin Dodger**[14] 2156 4-8-6 42.................... KirstyMilczarek(7) 4 23
(C N Allen) *lost 10 l s: wnt mod 3rd 3f out: no imp: no ch whn hung lft and hit rail over 1f out* **6/1**[3]

0000 **4** *9* **Play Straight**[15] 2116 3-8-0 45.................... HayleyTurner 2 5
(I W McInnes) *mod 2nd tl 1/2-way: wknd over 3f out* **14/1**

/000 **5** *2* **Ghail Force**[8] 1344 5-9-1 41....................(p) AlanCreighton(3) 5 6
(P Butler) *reluctant to s: a bhd: rdn and no ch fnl 3f* **28/1**

0-04 **L** **Hester Brook (IRE)**[27] 1782 3-7-8 53 ow1.................... MCGeran(7) 1 —
(J G M O'Shea) *tk 2 steps forwards then reversed through the starting stall: uns rdr and tk no part* **6/4**[1]

2m 4.53s (1.93) **Going Correction** +0.05s/f (Good)
WFA 3 from 4yo+ 13lb **6** Ran SP% **111.9**
Speed ratings (Par 101):94,83,82,75,74 —
CSF £15.65 TOTE £2.30: £1.50, £2.80; EX 8.20.The winner was sold to D. Ivory for 9,000gns.
Owner Horses 4 Courses **Bred** Peter Mooney **Trained** Catwick, E Yorks

FOCUS
A non-contest, with the favourite backing out of the stalls as they opened and her market rival subsequently never seeing another horse. A very weak race, and hard to put accurate figures on.

2558 JOHN BLOOR MEMORIAL H'CAP (FOR THE OPERATIC SOCIETY CHALLENGE CUP) 1m 3f 196y
3:30 (3:31) (Class 5) (0-70,70) 3-Y-0 **£2,849** (£847; £423; £211) **Stalls** High

Form RPR

60-1 **1** **Copernican**[6] 2389 3-9-1 **64** 6ex.................... SebSanders 4 76+
(Sir Mark Prescott) *hdwy 7f out: reminder 4f out: led 3f out: drvn along and hung rt: styd on* **4/9**[1]

00-0 **2** *4* **Pagan Rules (IRE)**[20] 1972 3-8-12 **61**....................(b) JimCrowley 6 64
(Mrs A J Perrett) *prom: chsd wnr fnl 3f: hrd rdn: nt qckn* **16/1**

0-00 **3** *1 1/4* **Lightning Queen (USA)**[20] 1972 3-8-4 **53**.................... PaulDoe 5 54
(B W Hills) *chsd ldr: led 4f out to 3f out: hrd rdn: one pce* **16/1**

4201 **4** *7* **King Of The Beers (USA)**[11] 2259 3-8-8 **62**..............(p) LukeMorris(5) 7 52
(R A Harris) *towards rr: rdn 5f out: wnt mod 4th fnl 2f: lacked pce to chal* **6/1**[2]

00-3 **5** *1* **Apache Chant (USA)**[16] 2081 3-8-6 **55**.................... CatherineGannon 3 43
(A W Carroll) *rdn and n.d fnl 4f* **33/1**

0-60 **6** *1 3/4* **Opera Crown (IRE)**[23] 1887 3-9-7 **70**.................... TQuinn 1 55
(P F I Cole) *a bhd: rdn 5f out: no ch fnl 3f: eased fnl f* **17/2**[3]

-400 **7** *nk* **Benny The Bat**[13] 2177 3-9-7 **70**....................(b[1]) SteveDrowne 8 55
(H Morrison) *led tl 4f out: sn wknd: bhd whn eased over 1f out* **16/1**

2m 31.39s (-0.81) **Going Correction** +0.05s/f (Good) **7** Ran SP% **114.7**
Speed ratings (Par 99):104,101,100,95,95 94,93
CSF £9.93 CT £56.99 TOTE £1.20: £1.30, £7.00; EX 8.40 Trifecta £123.80 Pool £603.76 - 3.46 winning units..
Owner Lady Katharine Watts **Bred** Gestut Gorlsdorf **Trained** Newmarket, Suffolk

FOCUS
A moderate race and an ordinary gallop. The progressive winner probably had little to beat but should improve with racing.

2559 BRIGHTON INTERNATIONAL ARENA APPRENTICE CLAIMING STKS 7f 214y
4:00 (4:01) (Class 6) 3-Y-0+ **£1,943** (£578; £288; £144) **Stalls** Low

Form RPR

311 **1** **Sawwaah (IRE)**[4] 2467 10-9-12 65....................(v) TravisBlock 1 61+
(Tom Dascombe) *s.s and rdn early: settled in rr: eased out and hdwy 2f out: r.o to ld fnl 30yds: cleverly* **8/13**[1]

6-54 **2** *1/2* **The Jailer**[14] 2140 4-8-12 42....................(p) MCGeran(5) 3 51
(J G M O'Shea) *led: drvn 3 l ahd over 1f out: hdd and no ex fnl 30yds* **12/1**

00-0 **3** *nk* **Jalamid (IRE)**[20] 1971 5-10-0 80....................(t) JamesMillman 8 61
(G C Bravery) *hld up in tch: rdn to chse ldr 2f out: kpt on fnl f* **3/1**[2]

3065 **4** *2 1/2* **Christmas Truce (IRE)**[10] 2275 8-9-5 50..............(b) JackMitchell(3) 4 50
(M R Hoad) *towards rr: hrd rdn and outpcd 3f out: hdwy over 1f out: styd on same pce* **11/1**[3]

00-6 **5** *3 1/2* **Bogaz (IRE)**[10] 2273 5-9-2 40.................... KylieManser(5) 2 41
(Mrs H Sweeting) *chsd ldr tl 2f out: wknd over 1f out* **20/1**

5055 **6** *7* **Rowan Pursuit**[5] 2412 6-8-9 39....................(b) DavidProbert(7) 9 19
(E A Wheeler) *prom tl hrd rdn and wknd 2f out* **50/1**

/0-0 **7** *18* **Good Wee Girl (IRE)**[10] 2273 5-8-12 40..............(p) JosephWalsh(5) 10 —
(S Woodman) *dwlt: n.d: rdn and no ch fnl 3f* **100/1**

0000 **P** **Winds Of Kildare (IRE)**[8] 2343 4-9-5 45.................. KirstyMilczarek(3) 6 —
(C N Allen) *plld hrd: chsd ldrs: hrd rdn and wknd over 2f out: hung lft: no ch whn p.u over 1f out: lame* **66/1**

1m 35.73s (0.69) **Going Correction** +0.05s/f (Good) **8** Ran SP% **112.2**
Speed ratings (Par 101):98,97,97,94,91 84,66,—
CSF £9.05 TOTE £1.60: £1.02, £2.10, £1.20; EX 6.10 Trifecta £22.00 Pool £662.56 - 21.36 winning units..There was no bid for the winner.
Owner Alan Solomon **Bred** Shadwell Estate Company Limited **Trained** Lambourn, Berks

FOCUS
A modest claimer, but the decent gallop suited the in-form veteran winner. Not form to be taken at face value, and it is probable that Sawwaah did not have to be at his best.

2560 JOHN SMITH'S H'CAP 5f 213y
4:30 (4:30) (Class 6) (0-65,62) 3-Y-0 **£2,266** (£674; £337; £168) **Stalls** Low

Form RPR

6-43 **1** **Ishibee (IRE)**[9] 2300 3-8-9 **50**....................(p) SebSanders 1 55
(Mrs A Duffield) *chsd ldrs: effrt on rail 2f out: led over 1f out: drvn out* **3/1**[2]

4002 **2** *1* **Realy Naughty (IRE)**[1] 2545 3-9-7 **62**.................... TQuinn 5 64
(B G Powell) *hdwy 2f out: rdn to chse ldrs over 1f out: r.o to take 2nd fnl 75yds* **9/4**[1]

4-02 **3** *1 1/4* **Lost All Alone**[128] 360 3-8-5 **49**.................... RichardKingscote(3) 3 48
(D M Simcock) *prom: hrd rdn 2f out: one pce appr fnl f* **5/1**[3]

-324 **4** *1/2* **Marist Madame**[29] 1739 3-8-4 **45**.................... MatthewHenry 6 42
(D K Ivory) *in tch: outpcd and hrd rdn 2f out: styd on fnl f* **5/1**[3]

-505 **5** *1/2* **Dotty's Daughter**[9] 2301 3-8-6 **50**..............(p) SaleemGolam(3) 4 46
(Mrs A Duffield) *pressed ldr tl ins fnl 2f: one pce* **15/2**

0-00 **6** *nk* **She Wont Wait**[28] 1763 3-8-6 **50** ow5..............(b) NeilChalmers(3) 2 45
(T M Jones) *led tl over 1f out: sn wknd* **40/1**

3-26 **7** *1/2* **My Tiger Lilly**[12] 2198 3-8-13 **54**.................... DaneO'Neill 8 47
(W J Knight) *towards rr: rdn 3f out: n.d* **10/1**

0-00 **8** *6* **Fluters House**[13] 2173 3-8-4 **45**....................(b[1]) HayleyTurner 7 20
(S Woodman) *dwlt: rdn 3f out: a bhd* **33/1**

1m 10.62s (0.52) **Going Correction** +0.05s/f (Good) **8** Ran SP% **115.3**
Speed ratings (Par 97):98,96,95,94,93 93,92,84
CSF £10.30 CT £31.87 TOTE £3.90: £1.50, £1.10, £1.80; EX 12.30 Trifecta £124.90 Pool £1,056.15 - 6.00 winning units. Place 6 £47.64, Place 5 £8.52..
Owner D K Barker & Lee Bolingbroke **Bred** Ambersham Stud **Trained** Constable Burton, N Yorks

FOCUS
A weak sprint for three-year-olds. The form makes some sense, with the winner rated to her latter juvenile level.

T/Plt: £92.40 to a £1 stake. Pool: £56,355.50. 445.00 winning tickets. T/Qpdt: £5.60 to a £1 stake. Pool: £4,009.90. 529.10 winning tickets. LM

2385 **HAMILTON** (R-H)
Wednesday, June 13
OFFICIAL GOING: Good (good to firm in places, 8.7)
Wind: Breezy, half against Weather: Overcast

2561 **F&C INVESTMENTS AMATEUR RIDERS' H'CAP** **6f 5y**
6:40 (6:42) (Class 6) (0-60,60) 4-Y-O+ **£2,637** (£811; £405) **Stalls** Low

Form				RPR
6102	1		**Brut**[6] 2386 5-11-0 **58**........(p) MissARyan(5) 9 (D W Barker) *mde all: rdn 2f out: hld on wl* **5/1**[2]	70
-031	2	1	**Whozart (IRE)**[15] 2121 4-10-10 **49**........MrSDobson 6 (A Dickman) *missed break: bhd tl hdwy over 2f out: kpt on wl fnl f: nt rch wnr* **7/1**	58+
44-0	3	1 1/4	**No Grouse**[18] 2033 7-10-9 **55**........MissWGibson(7) 8 (E J Alston) *towards rr: rdn 1/2-way: kpt on fnl f: nrst fin* **16/1**	60
2050	4	shd	**Local Poet**[6] 2390 6-10-7 **53**........(b) MrCMcGaffin(7) 1 (I Semple) *bhd tl hdwy over 1f out: r.o fnl f* **12/1**	58
2154	5	1/2	**Union Jack Jackson (IRE)**[8] 2347 5-11-0 **60**........(b) MrCAHarris(7) 4 (John A Harris) *cl up tl edgd rt and no ex over 1f out* **11/1**	63
2336	6	1/2	**Oeuf A La Neige**[6] 2390 7-10-11 **50**........MissSBrotherton 7 (Miss L A Perratt) *midfield: rdn over 2f out: no imp over 1f out* **6/1**[3]	52
0353	7	1 1/2	**Tuscan Flyer**[65] 978 9-10-2 **46** oh1........(b) MissRBastiman(5) 2 (R Bastiman) *prom tl rdn and one pce over 1f out* **16/1**	43
00-1	8	1 3/4	**Hit's Only Money (IRE)**[34] 1597 7-11-4 **57**........MrsCBartley 13 (J S Goldie) *hmpd s: sn wl bhd: styd on fnl f: nrst fin* **7/2**[1]	49+
0204	9	shd	**Ceredig**[13] 2179 4-10-13 **55**........MrsMarieKing(3) 3 (P W Hiatt) *s.i.s: sn in midfield: effrt and prom 1/2-way: edgd rt and wknd over 1f out* **12/1**	47
0-01	10	1/2	**Coalite (IRE)**[34] 1596 4-10-13 **52**........(p) MissLEllison 5 (A D Brown) *sn outpcd and rdn along: nvr rchd ldrs* **12/1**	42
-000	11	nk	**Obe One**[6] 2390 7-10-1 **47**........MrKJames(7) 12 (A Berry) *sn outpcd: no ch fr 1/2-way* **33/1**	37
2142	12	8	**Blackheath (IRE)**[12] 2220 11-10-7 **53**........MissERamstrom(7) 11 (D Nicholls) *hung rt thrght: prom tl wknd over 2f out* **9/1**	19
/00-	13	6	**Hebenus**[247] 5865 8-10-2 **46** oh1........MissHCuthbert(5) 10 (T A K Cuthbert) *prom tl rdn and wknd over 2f out* **150/1**	—
-000	14	6	**Howards Prince**[6] 2386 4-10-4 **46** oh1........(p) MrOWilliams(3) 14 (D A Nolan) *wnt lft and blkd s: in tch to 1/2-way: sn btn* **150/1**	—

1m 13.8s (0.70) **Going Correction** -0.025s/f (Good) **14** Ran SP% **123.1**
Speed ratings (Par 101):94,92,91,90,90 89,87,85,85,84 84,73,65,57
CSF £40.94 CT £535.77 TOTE £6.50: £2.50, £2.40, £3.70; EX 42.20.
Owner D W Barker **Bred** Mrs Deborah O'Brien **Trained** Scorton, N Yorks
■ Stewards' Enquiry : Mr C McGaffin ten-day ban: failed to ride out for third place (Jun 25,29, Jul 8,27-28, Aug 2,16-17,22,26)

FOCUS
A modest handicap but one in which the pace was sound throughout and this form should prove reliable.

2562 **PERSIMMON PARTNERSHIPS CHAMPAGNE MAIDEN STKS** **6f 5y**
7:10 (7:10) (Class 4) 2-Y-O **£4,533** (£1,348; £674; £336) **Stalls** Low

Form				RPR
	1		**Double Attack (FR)** 2-8-9 0........GregFairley(3) 1 (M Johnston) *t.k.h early: mde all: rdn and styd on strly to draw clr fnl f* **9/1**	79+
	2	5	**Papillio (IRE)** 2-9-3 0........PatCosgrave 6 (K R Burke) *prom: effrt and chsd wnr 2f out: kpt on same pce fnl f* **5/6**[1]	69
	3	3/4	**Binario Uno** 2-9-3 0........SilvestreDeSousa 4 (D Nicholls) *chsd ldrs: effrt over 2f out: one pce over 1f out* **28/1**	67
	4	1	**Casino Night** 2-8-12 0........AdrianTNicholls 3 (M Johnston) *cl up: edgd lft and outpcd 2f out: kpt on fnl f: no imp* **11/1**	62+
	5	shd	**Flying Sommelier (USA)** 2-9-3 0........PhillipMakin 5 (T D Barron) *missed break: bhd: hdwy over 2f out: no imp fnl f* **13/2**[3]	63
	6	8	**Moon Spray (USA)** 2-9-3 0........TomEaves 2 (K A Ryan) *in tch: drvn and outpcd 1/2-way: edgd rt and sn btn* **10/3**[2]	39

1m 13.91s (0.81) **Going Correction** -0.025s/f (Good) **6** Ran SP% **112.7**
Speed ratings (Par 95):93,86,85,84,83 73
CSF £17.35 TOTE £11.30: £4.40, £1.30; EX 21.30.
Owner R W Huggins **Bred** Newsells Park Stud Ltd **Trained** Middleham Moor, N Yorks
■ Stewards' Enquiry : Pat Cosgrave one-day ban: careless riding (Jun 25)

FOCUS
This was confined to juveniles which had never run. Not a strong race, but a reasonable gallop and a pleasing first run from Double Attack, who looks the type to win more races. The runner-up was disappointing.

NOTEBOOK
Double Attack(FR) ◆, the first foal of a winning half-sister to the stable's former very smart stayer Double Honour, was easy to back but created a favourable impression on this racecourse debut. She will be equally at home over 7f and is sure to win more races. (op 6-1)
Papillio(IRE), a 100,000 euros half-brother to triple juvenile winner Ponty Rossa, was the subject of favourable reports from a stable whose juveniles have been winning first time but this one failed to land the odds on this racecourse debut. However he is open to plenty of improvement and is sure to win a similar event. (op 4-5 tchd 8-11 and Evens, 11-10 in places)
Binario Uno looked in good shape in the paddock for this racecourse debut and showed ability. He should stay 7f and is likely to be placed to best advantage when his stable really hit top gear. (tchd 33-1)
Casino Night, a 26,000gns yearling, who is a half-sister to a couple of fair sorts, looked as though the race would do her good but showed ability on this debut. She will stay 7f, is in good hands and may do better. (op 8-1 tchd 12-1)
Flying Sommelier(USA), the first foal of an unraced half-sister to a champion turf horse in Canada, shaped better than the bare form on this racecourse debut after missing the break. He should improve for this experience and is the type to fare better in due course. (op 7-1 tchd 6-1)
Moon Spray(USA), a £35,000 half-brother to a fairly useful juvenile winner, attracted support but proved a disappointment on this racecourse debut. He had obviously been showing a fair bit at home and would not be one to write off yet. (op 7-1)

2563 **PATERSONS OF GREENOAKHILL (S) STKS** **1m 65y**
7:40 (7:43) (Class 6) 3-Y-O+ **£2,590** (£770; £385; £192) **Stalls** High

Form				RPR
352-	1		**Ballyhurry (USA)**[27] 6241 10-10-1 66........PhillipMakin 10 (J S Goldie) *hld up: hdwy over 2f out: styd on wl to ld nr fin* **6/1**[3]	67
0046	2	nk	**Neil's Legacy (IRE)**[11] 2254 5-9-7 54........AndrewMullen(3) 8 (Miss L A Perratt) *chsd ldrs: outpcd over 3f out: rallied to ld over 1f out: kpt on: hdd towards fin* **8/1**	61
0000	3	7	**Ho Pang Yau**[9] 2298 9-9-8 44........(p) GaryBartley(7) 13 (J S Goldie) *midfield: outpcd 3f out: styng on u.p whn edgd rt ins fnl f: no imp* **66/1**	50
0600	4	3/4	**Khetaab (IRE)**[9] 2298 5-9-9 50........DavidAllan 14 (E J Alston) *hld up: drvn over 3f out: kpt on fnl f: nrst fin* **8/1**	42
-000	5	1/2	**Jordans Spark**[13] 2168 6-10-1 46........TonyHamilton 9 (P Monteith) *midfield: outpcd and drvn over 3f out: r.o fnl f* **40/1**	47
6	6	hd	**Knight Of Kintyre (IRE)**[34] 1594 4-9-4 0........PatCosgrave 11 (Barry Potts, Ire) *led to over 3f out: wknd fr 2f out* **20/1**	36
0-44	7	3/4	**Andorran (GER)**[16] 2091 4-9-9 47........(tp) PaulHanagan 1 (A Dickman) *hld up: rdn over 3f out: styng on but no imp whn hmpd ins fnl f* **20/1**	39
52-3	8	2	**Quicks The Word**[34] 1596 7-9-12 46........GregFairley(3) 15 (T A K Cuthbert) *prom: led over 3f tl over 1f out: sn btn* **12/1**	41
6502	9	1	**Defi (IRE)**[6] 2388 5-10-1 66........(b) TomEaves 2 (I Semple) *w ldr: ev ch tl wknd fr 2f out* **13/8**[1]	38
00-2	10	3/4	**Slavonic (USA)**[9] 2298 6-9-10 55........PJMcDonald(5) 12 (B Storey) *prom: outpcd and hung rt over 3f out: sn n.d* **22/1**	37
-000	11	4	**City Miss**[30] 1711 4-9-1 36........DuranFentiman(3) 4 (Miss L A Perratt) *bhd: drvn over 4f out: nvr on terms* **100/1**	16
0	12	3	**King Verti**[15] 2116 3-8-12 0........RoystonFfrench 5 (P C Haslam) *prom to 1/2-way: sn rdn and btn* **50/1**	14
0-00	13	7	**Merlins Dreams**[34] 338 4-9-2 35........WJCafferty(7) 7 (P C Haslam) *unruly bef s: s.i.s: hdwy on outside and prom over 3f out: hung rt and wknd 2f out* **125/1**	—
4000	14	11	**Following Flow (USA)**[16] 2091 5-10-1 45........(v[1]) PaulMulrennan 3 (R Allan) *hld up: rdn 4f out: btn over 2f out* **100/1**	—
1210	15	8	**Just James**[30] 1711 8-10-1 64........AdrianTNicholls 6 (D Nicholls) *in tch: lost pl qckly over 4f out: eased whn no ch* **5/1**[2]	—

1m 48.86s (-0.44) **Going Correction** -0.025s/f (Good)
WFA 3 from 4yo+ 11lb **15** Ran SP% **121.5**
Speed ratings (Par 101):101,100,93,92,92 92,91,89,88,87 83,80,73,62,54
CSF £49.23 TOTE £8.60: £2.40, £2.90, £9.70; EX 74.50.The winner was bought in for £4,800.
Owner John Breslin **Bred** J Hettinger **Trained** Uplawmoor, E Renfrews

FOCUS
A run-of-the-mill seller in which the market leader disappointed. It has been rated through the second and third. The pace was sound.
Andorran(GER) Official explanation: jockey said gelding was denied a clear run

2564 **WALTER SCOTT SAINTS & SINNERS CHALLENGE CUP H'CAP** **1m 65y**
8:10 (8:13) (Class 4) (0-80,73) 4-Y-O+ **£6,477** (£1,927; £963; £481) **Stalls** High

Form				RPR
-465	1		**Stargazer Jim (FR)**[13] 2189 5-9-0 **66**........(v[1]) PaulMulrennan 1 (W J Haggas) *mde all: rdn over 2f out: kpt on wl fnl f* **9/2**[3]	83
4010	2	5	**Flylowflylong (IRE)**[13] 2169 4-8-12 **64**........TonyHamilton 4 (I Semple) *chsd ldrs: effrt over 2f out: edgd rt over 1f out: one pce* **16/1**	69
0000	3	1 1/4	**Regent's Secret (USA)**[6] 2388 7-9-4 **70**........(p) PaulHanagan 9 (J S Goldie) *bhd: plenty to do and rdn 1/2-way: kpt on fr 2f out: nrst fin* **7/2**[1]	72
6203	4	nk	**Mystical Ayr (IRE)**[13] 2168 5-8-7 **59**........RoystonFfrench 6 (Miss L A Perratt) *prom: drvn over 3f out: one pce fr 2f out* **8/1**	60
0220	5	shd	**Fortress**[21] 1944 4-8-7 **59**........AdrianTNicholls 10 (E J Alston) *hld up: rdn over 3f out: kpt on fnl f: nrst fin* **14/1**	60
-005	6	2	**Middlemarch (IRE)**[29] 1747 7-9-7 **73**........PhillipMakin 7 (J S Goldie) *hld up: rdn over 3f out: kpt on fnl f: n.d* **4/1**[2]	70
0634	7	3/4	**Mayadeen (IRE)**[6] 2388 5-7-13 **54** oh2........(b) DuranFentiman(3) 2 (I Semple) *prom: effrt over 2f out: wknd over 1f out* **5/1**	49
6416	8	2 1/2	**Primo Way**[13] 2169 6-9-7 **73**........(b) TomEaves 3 (I Semple) *hld up: drvn over 3f out: nvr on terms* **16/1**	62
3160	9	2 1/2	**Wahoo Sam (USA)**[4] 2452 7-9-6 **72**........PatCosgrave 5 (K A Ryan) *cl up: effrt and ev ch over 3f out: wknd 2f out* **8/1**	55

1m 46.24s (-3.06) **Going Correction** -0.025s/f (Good) **9** Ran SP% **117.7**
Speed ratings (Par 105):114,109,107,107,107 105,104,102,99
CSF £74.01 CT £283.92 TOTE £5.70: £1.90, £3.00, £1.90; EX 59.80.
Owner Nicholas J Hughes **Bred** Sarl Le Lieu Calice And Peter Kavanagh **Trained** Newmarket, Suffolk

FOCUS
A decent gallop resulted in an improved effort by the winner and a very smart winning time for a race like this.

2565 **HUDSON WINNING WAYS CLAIMING STKS** **1m 3f 16y**
8:40 (8:41) (Class 6) 3-Y-O **£2,590** (£770; £385; £192) **Stalls** High

Form				RPR
315	1		**Stringsofmyheart**[25] 1843 3-9-0 72........(p) PaulMulrennan 4 (W J Haggas) *led to over 4f out: hd high and outpcd over 3f out: no imp tl rallied u.p appr fnl f: led nr fin* **8/11**[1]	63
0-6	2	shd	**Attila's Peintre**[15] 2116 3-9-0 0........PhillipMakin 10 (P C Haslam) *bhd: drvn and outpcd over 4f out: rallied 2f out: led briefly wl ins fnl f: jst hld* **28/1**	63
2040	3	1 1/4	**Colditz (IRE)**[8] 2340 3-8-9 63........TonyHamilton 5 (D W Barker) *cl up: led over 4f out: rdn over 2f out: hdd wl ins fnl f: no ex* **8/1**	56
-610	4	shd	**Patavian (IRE)**[11] 2246 3-9-3 65........TomEaves 3 (I Semple) *cl up: effrt and ev ch over 3f out: one pce ins fnl f* **11/2**[3]	64
6650	5	hd	**Firebird Annie (IRE)**[21] 1943 3-8-2 50 ow3........AndrewMullen(3) 7 (A Bailey) *in tch: effrt over 2f out: nt qckn fnl f* **20/1**	51?
66-0	6	6	**Terry Molloy (IRE)**[46] 1289 3-9-5 65........PatCosgrave 1 (K R Burke) *midfield: effrt and prom over 3f out: sn rdn: wknd over 1f out* **4/1**[2]	55
0-0	7	28	**Hillside Smoki (IRE)**[22] 1913 3-8-9 0........DavidAllan 9 (A Berry) *bhd: struggling 1/2-way: nvr on terms* **100/1**	—
	8	3	**Bluto** 3-9-0 0........AdrianTNicholls 8 (P C Haslam) *plld hrd: cl up tl wknd fr 5f out* **20/1**	—
-000	9	5	**Danni Di Guerra (IRE)**[6] 2389 3-8-3 35........RoystonFfrench 6 (J Barclay) *towards rr: drvn 1/2-way: nvr on terms* **100/1**	—
-060	10	27	**Dee Valley Boy (IRE)**[16] 2096 3-8-7 43........(b[1]) PaulHanagan 2 (J D Bethell) *a wl bhd* **40/1**	—

2m 27.28s (1.02) **Going Correction** -0.025s/f (Good) **10** Ran SP% **121.8**
Speed ratings (Par 97):95,94,94,93,93 89,69,66,63,43
CSF £36.89 TOTE £1.80: £1.10, £7.30, £1.90; EX 30.70.
Owner Mrs Denis Haynes **Bred** Wretham Stud **Trained** Newmarket, Suffolk

FOCUS
A modest event and one in which the pace was just fair. They finished in a heap and the form is dubious.

2566 COFFEE EXPRESS H'CAP 6f 5y
9:10 (9:11) (Class 3) (0-90,90) 4-Y-0+ £10,363 (£3,083; £1,540; £769) Stalls Low

Form RPR
5300 1 Machinist (IRE)[11] 2234 7-9-5 88 SilvestreDeSousa 8 101
(D Nicholls) *chsd ldrs: led over 1f out: rdn and r.o strly* 8/1
0-14 2 1 1/2 Trojan Flight[8] 2339 6-8-10 79 PaulHanagan 11 87
(R A Fahey) *hld up bhd ldrs: effrt over 2f out: chsd wnr ins fnl f: r.o* 12/1
0-53 3 3/4 Ingleby Arch (USA)[17] 2058 4-9-7 90 PhillipMakin 7 96
(T D Barron) *slt ld to over 1f out: kpt on same pce fnl f* 7/2[1]
0-01 4 shd Sunrise Safari (IRE)[21] 1941 4-9-0 83 (v) TonyHamilton 14 88
(I Semple) *t.k.h: hld up bhd ldrs: effrt over 2f out: kpt on ins fnl f* 16/1
-356 5 1/2 Countdown[8] 2339 5-8-9 78 DavidAllan 9 82+
(T D Easterby) *bhd tl hdwy over 1f out: nrst fin* 11/1
6-00 6 nk Ice Planet[32] 1653 6-9-5 88 AdrianTNicholls 13 91
(D Nicholls) *cl up centre tl rdn and nt qckn over 1f out* 12/1
-500 7 shd Curtail (IRE)[25] 1852 4-9-2 85 TomEaves 12 88
(I Semple) *wl plcd centre: rdn over 2f out: no ex over 1f out* 25/1
1-02 8 shd Yorkshire Blue[8] 2339 8-8-4 80 GaryBartley(7) 4 82
(J S Goldie) *bhd: rdn over 2f out: kpt on fnl f: nvr rchd ldrs* 6/1[3]
-405 9 1/2 High Curragh[25] 1852 4-9-3 89 AndrewMullen(3) 6 90
(K A Ryan) *w ldrs tl no ex over 1f out* 9/1
042 10 3/4 Prince Namid[11] 2237 5-9-4 87 RoystonFfrench 5 86
(Mrs A Duffield) *prom: drvn over 2f out: btn fnl f* 11/2[2]
0-04 11 nk Kenmore[21] 1941 5-9-0 83 PatCosgrave 1 81
(D Nicholls) *hld up: rdn over 2f out: sn btn* 20/1
2010 12 3/4 Dig Deep (IRE)[25] 1853 5-9-2 85 PaulMulrennan 3 81
(W J Haggas) *plld hrd: hld up bhd ldrs: rdn over 2f out: btn over 1f out* 6/1[3]
0035 13 shd Stellite[4] 2466 7-7-13 71 oh1 DuranFentiman(3) 2 66
(J S Goldie) *w ldrs to 2f out: sn wknd* 50/1

1m 11.54s (-1.56) **Going Correction** -0.025s/f (Good) 13 Ran SP% 127.5
Speed ratings (Par 107):109,107,106,105,105 104,104,104,103,102 102,101,101
CSF £105.20 CT £408.98 TOTE £11.20: £3.80, £3.90, £1.80; EX 165.40.
Owner Berry & Gould Partnership **Bred** Ballymacoll Stud Farm Ltd **Trained** Sessay, N Yorks

FOCUS
A competitive race run at a sound pace throughout. The winner produced his best ever figure and the runner-up his best run since 2005. Good form which should prove reliable.

NOTEBOOK
Machinist(IRE), taken off his feet over five at Epsom on his previous start, proved well suited by the step up to this distance and step down in grade and ran as well as he ever has done. Life will be tougher from a mark in the low to mid-90s but he is an honest sort who should continue to give a good account. (op 9-1 tchd 10-1)
Trojan Flight, who has been in good form for his current stable, had the race run to suit and ran right up to his recent best. He has always been the type that needs things to drop right but should continue to go well in this type of event. (op 11-1)
Ingleby Arch(USA) has not won for over a year and has little margin for error from his current mark but ran right up to the pick of his form from this year. This effort means he will get little respite from the handicapper though, and he is likely to remain vulnerable to the more progressive or better handicapped horses in this type of event. (op 9-2 tchd 10-3, 5-1 in places)
Sunrise Safari(IRE), 5lb higher than when successful at Ayr on his previous start, ran to a similar level in this better contest. He is with a stable that does well with this type and he may be capable of even better when he learns to settle better. (op 14-1)
Countdown is a consistent sort who ran a typical race and he should be suited by the return to 7f in a truly-run race. Effective in softer ground, he may be able to win again for his current stable this term. (op 9-1 tchd 12-1)
Ice Planet, a consistent sort, ran respectably after racing in the centre of the track. The gelding, who has not won for nearly two years, is unlikely to get much respite from the handicapper, though, and is likely to remain vulnerable to the more progressive sorts in this type of race. (op 11-1)
Yorkshire Blue, whose style of running means he needs things to drop right, was not disgraced and looks worth another try over 7f when there looks likely to be a decent gallop on. (op 7-1 tchd 8-1 in places)

2567 BELSTANE RACING STABLES H'CAP 1m 5f 9y
9:40 (9:40) (Class 5) (0-70,74) 4-Y-0+ £3,886 (£1,156; £577; £288) Stalls High

Form RPR
4612 1 Gigs Magic (USA)[8] 2338 4-8-12 62 GregFairley(3) 6 70
(M Johnston) *cl up: rdn and led over 2f out: hld on wl fnl f* 2/1[1]
4 2 1/2 Nero West (FR)[6] 2391 6-8-12 59 (p) TomEaves 1 66
(I Semple) *cl up: led over 4f out to over 2f out: rdn and styd upsides: kpt on: hld nr fin* 10/1
453- 3 2 Crathorne (IRE)[11] 4954 7-9-1 62 PatCosgrave 8 66
(M Todhunter) *chsd ldrs: rdn and outpcd over 2f out: r.o fnl f: nt rch first two* 5/1[3]
5506 4 2 1/2 Grey Outlook[11] 2250 4-8-10 57 RoystonFfrench 7 58
(Miss L A Perratt) *hld up: effrt over 3f out: sn outpcd: kpt on fnl f: nrst fin* 8/1
2301 5 1 3/4 Bronze Dancer (IRE)[6] 2391 5-9-8 74 6ex PJMcDonald(5) 5 72
(G A Swinbank) *in tch: effrt 3f out: outpcd fr 2f out* 5/2[2]
364 6 9 Kyber[11] 2250 6-8-3 50 PaulHanagan 4 34
(J S Goldie) *led to over 4f out: wknd over 2f out* 9/1
6-00 7 3 The Dunion[11] 2252 4-7-13 49 oh4 DuranFentiman(3) 10 29
(Miss L A Perratt) *bhd: drvn 4f out: nvr on terms* 100/1
00-4 8 7 Brabazon (IRE)[34] 1598 4-9-3 64 PaulMulrennan 2 33
(Barry Potts, Ire) *hld up: drvn 4f out: nvr on terms* 16/1
0-50 9 1 Borsch (IRE)[11] 2252 5-8-2 52 oh4 ow3 AndrewMullen(3) 9 20
(Miss L A Perratt) *bhd: drvn over 4f out: sn btn* 80/1
000- 10 29 Farne Isle[26] 3215 8-8-8 55 (tp) TonyHamilton 3 —
(G A Harker) *prom tl wknd over 4f out: t.o* 33/1

2m 51.17s (-2.23) **Going Correction** -0.025s/f (Good) 10 Ran SP% 119.8
Speed ratings (Par 103):105,104,103,101,100 95,93,89,88,70
CSF £24.25 CT £92.29 TOTE £2.70: £1.40, £2.80, £2.00; EX 29.60 Place 6 £146.80, Place 5 £33.30.
Owner J Barson **Bred** R McDonald **Trained** Middleham Moor, N Yorks

FOCUS
A run-of-the-mill event in which the gallop was just fair. Probably weak form, with the fifth not running his race and the winner not needing to improve on his recent level.
T/Plt: £187.00 to a £1 stake. Pool: £68,553.00. 267.50 winning tickets. T/Qpdt: £34.10 to a £1 stake. Pool: £4,235.00. 91.90 winning tickets. RY

2349 KEMPTON (A.W) (R-H)
Wednesday, June 13

OFFICIAL GOING: Standard
Wind: Light, half behind Weather: Overcast, warm

2568 WEATHERBYS PRINTING APPRENTICE H'CAP (ROUND 2) 1m (P)
6:20 (6:21) (Class 5) (0-75,74) 4-Y-0+ £2,914 (£867; £433; £216) Stalls High

Form RPR
0400 1 Out For A Stroll[2] 2514 8-8-3 56 FLenclud(7) 6 62
(S C Williams) *cl up: trckd ldr 1/2-way: led jst over 2f out: kpt on wl and gng away nr fin* 7/1
1331 2 1 1/2 Indian's Feather (IRE)[8] 2347 6-10-0 74 6ex DanielleMcCreery 2 77
(N Tinkler) *hld up in 4th: prog to chal over 2f out: pressed wnr after: nt qckn fnl f* 11/4[2]
0014 3 nk Tabulate[7] 2358 4-8-9 60 MarkCoumbe(5) 1 62
(P L Gilligan) *hld up in last: prog to press ldng pair 2f out: nt qckn over 1f out: kpt on same pce* 9/2[3]
5-00 4 2 Border Edge[10] 2275 9-8-13 64 RyanBird(5) 3 62
(J J Bridger) *chsd ldr to 1/2-way: sn rdn: struggling over 2f out* 10/1
2236 5 nk Magic Warrior[34] 1612 7-9-3 68 JosephWalsh(5) 4 65
(J C Fox) *t.k.h: hld up in 5th: rdn and no prog whn hmpd on inner over 1f out: no hdwy after* 5/2[1]
023- 6 2 1/2 October Ben[276] 5211 4-9-6 66 ThomasO'Brien 5 57
(M D I Usher) *sn led and racd freely: hdd jst over 2f out: immediately btn* 5/1

1m 42.82s (2.02) **Going Correction** +0.125s/f (Slow) 6 Ran SP% 111.7
Speed ratings (Par 103):94,92,92,90,89 87
CSF £26.16 TOTE £9.70: £3.30, £1.90; EX 44.10.
Owner The Nomads **Bred** Exors Of The Late Mrs F G Allen **Trained** Newmarket, Suffolk
■ The first winner for French apprentice Freddie Lenclud.
■ Stewards' Enquiry : Ryan Bird two-day ban: careless riding (Jun 24-25)

FOCUS
A moderate apprentice handicap, made even more so by the withdrawal of the probable favourite Parkview Love. The early pace was modest and the winning time was moderate for the grade.

2569 SPILLERS MAIDEN AUCTION STKS 6f (P)
6:50 (6:52) (Class 5) 2-Y-O £2,914 (£867; £433; £216) Stalls High

Form RPR
0 1 Ellemujie[8] 2333 2-8-10 0 PatDobbs 12 74
(D K Ivory) *sn in midfield: rdn and prog 2f out: edgd lft but r.o wl to ld last 100yds: sn clr* 18/1
6 2 1 1/4 Cosmic Art[8] 2333 2-8-11 0 DaneO'Neill 9 71
(E A L Dunlop) *chsd ldrs: rdn over 2f out: styd on to ld 1f out: hdd and outpcd fnl 100yds* 9/4[1]
405 3 2 Straight And Level (CAN)[5] 2410 2-8-10 0 RHills 4 64
(J W Hills) *trckd ldr: clsd to chal over 1f out: hld whn checked jst ins fnl f* 7/1[3]
0 4 hd Penrice Castle[12] 2193 2-8-5 0 RichardSmith 6 58
(R Hannon) *led: hung bdly lft fr 2f out and ended on nr side rail: hdd 1f out: one pce* 20/1
5 5 Sarah Park (IRE) 2-8-6 0 SteveDrowne 2 44
(B J Meehan) *dwlt: hld up wl in rr and off the pce: sme prog on inner 2f out: plugged on: n.d* 16/1
0 6 nk Classical Rhythm (IRE)[18] 2041 2-8-12 0 EddieAhern 3 50
(J R Boyle) *pushed along in midfield after 2f: nvr gng pce to trble ldes: no hdwy u.p 2f out* 9/4[1]
7 1 Eastbourne 2-8-10 0 StephenCarson 5 45
(Eve Johnson Houghton) *dwlt: hld up at rr of main gp: outpcd and shkn up fr 2f out: n.d after* 12/1
0 8 nk Insured[51] 1201 2-8-11 0 VHalliday 11 45
(A J McCabe) *chsd ldng pair to over 2f out: wknd over 1f out* 40/1
0 9 4 Moss Way[14] 2147 2-8-9 0 DavidKinsella 7 31
(W J Musson) *outpcd over 3f out: struggling after* 50/1
10 3 It's My Day (IRE) 2-8-10 0 TQuinn 10 23
(Jane Chapple-Hyam) *chsd ldrs: pushed along over 3f out: wknd 2f out* 13/2[2]
11 4 Honest Yankee (USA) 2-8-10 0 AdamKirby 8 11
(Mrs L C Jewell) *s.s: a bhd: detached in last pair 1/2-way* 25/1
12 21 Shybutwilling (IRE) 2-8-6 0 ow2 RobertHavlin 1 —
(Mrs P N Dutfield) *s.s: sn t.o* 33/1

1m 15.31s (1.61) **Going Correction** +0.125s/f (Slow) 12 Ran SP% 122.2
Speed ratings (Par 93):94,92,89,89,82 82,81,80,75,71 65,37
CSF £57.75 TOTE £31.60: £5.40, £1.20, £2.80; EX 107.80.
Owner Mrs J A Cornwell & John G Smith **Bred** Mrs J A Cornwell **Trained** Radlett, Herts

FOCUS
A modest juvenile maiden. The form is rated through the third.

NOTEBOOK
Ellemujie, well behind Cosmic Art when proving distinctly green on his debut on Lingfield's turf eight days previously, showed the clear benefit of that experience and readily reversed form with that rival to score. He relished the extra furlong and should have more to offer now he has got his head in front, but his future lies with the Handicapper all the same. (op 14-1 tchd 20-1)
Cosmic Art was always handy and looked like doing the business when hitting the front, but simply failed to see out the extra furlong as well as the winner, who had been behind him at Lingfield. He got the trip and finished nicely clear in second, but may just be better off reverting to 5f in an attempt to lose his maiden tag. (tchd 5-2)
Straight And Level(CAN) ran his race and peformed close to his recent level. He helps to set the level of this form. (op 11-2)
Penrice Castle showed decent early speed, but hung her chance away in the home straight and is clearly not all that straightforward. A drop back to 5f now looks in order.
Classical Rhythm(IRE), seventh on his debut in what looked a decent maiden at Newmarket 18 days previously, was very well backed for this lesser contest but he never really got into at any stage. He did not have the best of draws and still looked green, however, so should not be totally written off on the back of this display. (op 3-1 tchd 2-1)

2570 DIGIBET H'CAP 6f (P)
7:20 (7:23) (Class 4) (0-80,80) 3-Y-O £4,728 (£1,406; £702; £351) Stalls High

Form RPR
0312 1 Royal Rock[20] 1965 3-9-4 77 GeorgeBaker 6 89+
(C F Wall) *hld up in 6th: prog on outer to ld jst over 1f out: sn wl in command* 5/4[1]
1 2 1 1/2 Big Noise[13] 2186 3-8-12 71 RobertHavlin 7 75
(Dr J D Scargill) *hld up in last trio: effrt wl over 1f out: r.o fnl f to take 2nd last strides: no ch w wnr* 8/1[3]

31- 3 1/2 **Sunoverregun**[221] 6330 3-9-7 **80** JimmyFortune 1 83
(J R Boyle) *crossed fr wd draw and trckd ldr: led briefly over 1f out: styd on but readily outpcd by wnr: lost 2nd last strides* **8/1**[3]

0-1 4 1 **Double Bill (USA)**[22] 1923 3-9-6 **79** TQuinn 8 79
(P F I Cole) *cl up on inner: rdn to chal over 1f out: one pce fnl f* **7/2**[2]

5-00 5 1 1/4 **Hart Of Gold**[20] 1956 3-9-4 **77** EddieAhern 5 73
(M J Wallace) *uns rdr and bolted a m bef s: trckd ldrs: gng wl enough over 1f out: one pce after* **16/1**

1-04 6 3 **Miss Ippolita**[17] 2060 3-9-4 **77** StephenCarson 2 64
(J R Jenkins) *led and crossed fr outside draw: hdd & wknd over 1f out* **25/1**

1-0 7 1 1/4 **Galaxy Stars**[40] 1450 3-8-13 **72** (t) PatDobbs 3 55
(P J Makin) *hld up in last: rdn and struggling over 2f out* **33/1**

1-40 8 nk **Roshanak (IRE)**[25] 1837 3-9-5 **78** RichardHughes 4 60
(B J Meehan) *trckd ldrs tl wknd tamely over 1f out* **9/1**

5-00 9 hd **Disco Dan**[22] 1930 3-9-4 **77** SebSanders 9 59
(D M Simcock) *hld up in last trio but wl in tch: rdn on inner over 2f out: wknd over 1f out* **12/1**

1m 13.5s (-0.20) **Going Correction** +0.125s/f (Slow) 9 Ran SP% **119.3**
Speed ratings (Par 101):106,104,103,102,100 96,94,94,94
CSF £12.87 CT £61.56 TOTE £2.30: £1.10, £1.80, £3.10; EX 12.60.
Owner S Fustok **Bred** Deerfield Farm **Trained** Newmarket, Suffolk

FOCUS
The early pace did not appear that strong, but things eventually quickened up appreciably and the winning time was decent for a race of its type, so the form should work out. Decent form for the type of race, with the winner rated a length better than the bare form.

2571 DIGIBET SPORTS BETTING FILLIES' H'CAP 7f (P)
7:50 (7:52) (Class 5) (0-70,72) 3-Y-0 **£2,914** (£867; £433; £216) **Stalls** High

Form RPR

6-00 1 **On The Map**[42] 1399 3-8-9 **58** (v[1]) PatDobbs 2 62
(A P Jarvis) *mde virtually all: hrd pressed and rdn over 2f out: kpt on u.p fnl f* **33/1**

-001 2 nk **Nashharry (IRE)**[11] 2262 3-8-13 **62** RichardHughes 1 65
(S Kirk) *trckd ldr: chal over 2f out: hrd drvn fr over 1f out: nt qckn* **6/1**[3]

5-64 3 hd **Kashmir Lady (FR)**[30] 1726 3-9-3 **66** DaneO'Neill 4 68
(H Candy) *t.k.h: hld up bhd ldrs: effrt to chal jst over 2f out: w wnr to over 1f out: kpt on same pce u.p* **7/4**[1]

0304 4 3/4 **Inquisitress**[13] 2178 3-8-2 **56** TolleyDean(5) 3 56
(J J Bridger) *hld up: prog on outer 1/2-way: chal over 2f out: nt qckn wl over 1f out: kpt on* **14/1**

4-10 5 3/4 **Blue Bamboo**[25] 1837 3-9-6 **69** JimCrowley 8 67
(Mrs A J Perrett) *trckd ldng pair: lost pl over 2f out but stl cl up: drvn and one pce over 1f out* **7/2**[2]

2-44 6 hd **Kassuta**[41] 1437 3-8-12 **64** SaleemGolam(3) 6 62
(S C Williams) *trckd ldrs: rdn over 2f out: nt qckn u.p fr over 1f out* **9/1**

0430 7 5 **Early Promise (IRE)**[17] 2061 3-8-7 **61** LukeMorris(5) 5 45
(P L Gilligan) *a in last pair: pushed along 1/2-way: struggling over 2f out* **8/1**

20-0 8 1 1/4 **Awwal Malika (USA)**[11] 2242 3-9-7 **70** SebSanders 7 51
(C E Brittain) *hld up in last pair: rdn over 2f out: no prog and sn btn* **6/1**[3]

1m 28.78s (1.98) **Going Correction** +0.125s/f (Slow) 8 Ran SP% **117.9**
Speed ratings (Par 96):93,92,92,91,90 90,84,83
CSF £223.71 CT £543.95 TOTE £41.60: £7.40, £1.50, £1.40; EX 220.40.
Owner Eurostrait Ltd **Bred** P Balding **Trained** Twyford, Bucks

FOCUS
A moderate fillies' handicap in which the pace was ordinary and that suited those that raced handily. The order did not really change that much during the contest and the form looks weak, with the favourite not at her best.

2572 DIGITOTE H'CAP 1m 3f (P)
8:20 (8:21) (Class 6) (0-65,65) 3-Y-0+ **£2,047** (£604; £302) **Stalls** High

Form RPR

0-25 1 **Pothos Way (GR)**[37] 1521 4-9-11 **62** PaulDoe 9 68
(P R Chamings) *trckd ldr: led 1/2-way: kicked 2 l clr 3f out: drvn 2f out: jst hld on* **12/1**

-406 2 hd **Spinal Tap (IRE)**[16] 2077 3-8-9 **60** RobertHavlin 6 66
(C R Egerton) *drvn after tardy s to go prom: wnt 2nd 1/2-way: nt qckn 3f out: grad clsd fnl 2f: nt quite rch wnr* **7/1**[3]

5510 3 hd **Medieval Maiden**[16] 2089 4-10-0 **65** BrettDoyle 7 70+
(W J Musson) *settled midfield: stdy prog over 2f out: urged along wl over 1f out: styd on fnl f: nt quite get up* **8/1**

0312 4 1/2 **Snake Skin**[7] 2361 4-9-9 **60** JimCrowley 14 64
(J Gallagher) *cl up: rdn on inner over 2f out: grad clsd fr over 1f out: tried to chal fnl f: no ex last 75yds* **9/2**[1]

0304 5 2 **Rowan Warning**[37] 1521 5-9-4 **55** (b) SteveDrowne 12 56
(J R Boyle) *trckd ldrs: rdn to dispute 2nd 2f out: clsd on wnr briefly: fdd fnl f* **16/1**

4004 6 1 **Hallings Overture (USA)**[8] 2332 8-9-7 **58** PaulEddery 2 58+
(C A Horgan) *s.s: hld up in last: sme prog fr 3f out: shkn up and no imp over 1f out* **7/1**[3]

0005 7 1 1/2 **Magic Amigo**[14] 2157 6-9-4 **55** (p) EddieAhern 4 52
(J R Jenkins) *settled in rr: rdn 3f out: kpt on same pce fr over 2f out: nvr rchd ldrs* **20/1**

00 8 1/2 **Red Wine**[17] 2055 8-9-13 **64** (be) AdamKirby 8 60
(A J McCabe) *hmpd on inner over 9f out and wl in rr: effrt 3f out: kpt on one pce fnl 2f and nvr rchd ldrs* **20/1**

06-0 9 1 1/4 **The Composer**[26] 1811 5-9-13 **64** SebSanders 11 58
(M Blanshard) *nvr bttr than midfield: rdn over 4f out: brief effrt over 2f out: sn fdd* **12/1**

-030 10 1 1/4 **Hansomelle (IRE)**[10] 2275 5-8-10 **50** NeilChalmers(3) 1 42
(Miss Sheena West) *wl in rr: rdn over 4f out: plugged on one pce u.p: n.d* **33/1**

0001 11 16 **Revisionist (IRE)**[4] 2456 3-8-13 **64** 6ex (v[1]) RichardHughes 5 29
(R Hannon) *led to 1/2-way: wknd rapidly 3f out: t.o* **15/2**

0-00 12 5 **A Peaceful Man**[33] 1634 3-8-1 **52** ow2 FrankieMcDonald 13 8
(Mrs L C Jewell) *dropped to last u.p over 4f out: sn t.o* **66/1**

0302 13 1 1/4 **Makai**[10] 2275 4-8-10 **52** (b) TolleyDean(5) 3 6
(J J Bridger) *a in rr: drvn over 4f out: sn btn: t.o* **18/1**

5023 14 25 **Revolve**[34] 1612 7-9-9 **60** (b) IanMongan 10 —
(Mrs L J Mongan) *trckd ldrs tl wknd 3f out: virtually p.u over 1f out* **5/1**[2]

2m 23.83s (1.15) **Going Correction** +0.125s/f (Slow) 14 Ran SP% **123.2**
WFA 3 from 4yo+ 14lb
Speed ratings (Par 101):100,99,99,99,97 97,96,95,94,93 82,78,77,59
CSF £92.22 CT £731.28 TOTE £18.30: £5.30, £3.80, £3.60; EX 175.90.
Owner Mrs Alexandra J Chandris **Bred** Ippotour Stud **Trained** Baughurst, Hants
■ Stewards' Enquiry : Frankie McDonald four-day ban: careless riding (Jun 24-27)
Robert Havlin five-day ban: used whip with excessive frequency and down shoulder in forehand position (Jun 24-28)

FOCUS
A modest handicap, run at an uneven pace. Little got into it from the rear. The winner was less exposed than some but did not need to improve much on his previous form. Improvement from the runner-up on his handicap debut.
Revisionist(IRE) Official explanation: jockey said gelding hung badly right
Revolve Official explanation: vet said gelding bled from the nose

2573 TFM NETWORKS H'CAP 7f (P)
8:50 (8:50) (Class 4) (0-85,84) 4-Y-0+ **£4,728** (£1,406; £702; £351) **Stalls** High

Form RPR

0120 1 **Sailor King (IRE)**[25] 1845 5-8-12 **75** JimCrowley 9 86
(D K Ivory) *trckd ldrs: gap appeared towards inner 2f out and got through to chal: led 1f out: drvn out* **8/1**

2000 2 3/4 **Resplendent Nova**[25] 1845 5-9-7 **84** TQuinn 7 93
(P Howling) *trckd ldr: led over 2f out: drvn and hdd 1f out: kpt on same pce* **10/1**

6100 3 3/4 **Bonnie Prince Blue**[11] 2239 4-9-2 **79** RHills 4 86+
(B W Hills) *t.k.h: hld up in last trio: nt clr run over 2f out tl over 1f out: r.o fnl f: gaining at fin* **8/1**

6403 4 1/2 **Katiypour (IRE)**[40] 1446 10-8-11 **74** SebSanders 11 80
(P Mitchell) *trckd ldrs: effrt on inner and cl up 2f out: nt qckn over 1f out: one pce after* **7/1**[3]

3260 5 nk **Sun Catcher (IRE)**[19] 1984 4-8-13 **76** RichardHughes 3 81
(R Hannon) *s.i.s and swtchd to inner: hld up in last trio: prog 2f out to chse ldrs 1f out: nt qckn after* **4/1**[2]

0-00 6 1/2 **Blues In The Night (IRE)**[20] 1971 4-9-1 **78** JimmyFortune 5 81+
(P J Makin) *hld up in last trio: nt clr run briefly 2f out: sn rdn: no prog tl styd on fnl f* **16/1**

1620 7 3/4 **Raza Cab (IRE)**[19] 1984 5-8-9 **75** JerryO'Dwyer(3) 1 76
(Karen George) *in tch towards rr: rdn 3f out: struggling after but plugged on* **16/1**

60-0 8 nk **Landucci**[19] 1984 6-8-9 **77** PatrickHills(5) 8 78
(J W Hills) *trckd ldrs: effrt wl over 1f out and sn cl up: nt qckn and btn ent fnl f: fdd* **14/1**

5534 9 1 **Josh**[126] 384 5-9-0 **77** DO'Donohoe 2 75
(K A Ryan) *cl up in midfield: rdn over 2f out: fdd over 1f out* **7/1**[3]

122 10 1 **His Master's Voice (IRE)**[22] 1931 4-8-13 **76** EddieAhern 6 71
(D W P Arbuthnot) *prom: chal and upsides over 2f out: btn over 1f out: wkng whn n.m.r ins fnl f* **11/4**[1]

0-00 11 6 **Arrivee (FR)**[32] 1661 4-8-12 **75** (p) SteveDrowne 10 54
(Mrs P Sly) *led to over 2f out: wknd* **25/1**

1m 26.84s (0.04) **Going Correction** +0.125s/f (Slow) 11 Ran SP% **125.3**
Speed ratings (Par 105):104,103,102,101,101 100,99,99,98,97 90
CSF £91.14 CT £690.86 TOTE £11.50: £2.70, £5.00, £4.10; EX 174.80.
Owner John Stocker **Bred** Janus Bloodstock **Trained** Radlett, Herts
■ Stewards' Enquiry : Patrick Hills one-day ban: careless riding (Jun 24)

FOCUS
A fair handicap. The first eight were fairly closely covered at the finish and the form has not been rated too positively.

2574 BARRETTSTOWN STUD H'CAP 1m 4f (P)
9:20 (9:20) (Class 4) (0-85,85) 3-Y-0 **£4,728** (£1,406; £702; £351) **Stalls** Centre

Form RPR

-621 1 **Audit (IRE)**[22] 1937 3-9-2 **80** (b) J-PGuillambert 4 84
(Sir Michael Stoute) *hld up in 4th or 5th: prog over 2f out: drvn and styd on to ld wl ins fnl f* **7/2**[2]

-015 2 nk **Happy Go Lily**[15] 2126 3-9-6 **84** AdamKirby 1 87
(W R Swinburn) *led: 2l clr and had rest in trble over 2f out: hung bdly lft wl over 1f out: hdd wl ins fnl f: nt rcvr* **9/1**

1303 3 shd **Dan Tucker**[13] 2177 3-8-8 **72** RichardHughes 3 75
(B J Meehan) *hld up in last plenty to do 3f out: rdn over 2f out: prog to press ldrs ins fnl f: kpt on* **4/1**[3]

1141 4 shd **Dee Cee Elle**[14] 2132 3-8-6 **70** EddieAhern 5 73
(M Johnston) *hld up tl prog to chse ldr 4f out: rdn 3f out: clsd to chal fnl f: nt qckn last 100yds* **9/4**[1]

-102 5 5 **Jaady (USA)**[13] 2177 3-8-12 **76** RHills 2 71
(J H M Gosden) *t.k.h: trckd ldng pair to 1/2-way: shkn up over 2f out: sn btn* **5/1**

212- 6 14 **Sagredo (USA)**[219] 6379 3-9-7 **85** SebSanders 6 58
(Sir Mark Prescott) *t.k.h: trckd ldr to 4f out: wknd over 2f out* **9/2**

2m 35.85s (-1.05) **Going Correction** +0.125s/f (Slow) 6 Ran SP% **117.8**
Speed ratings (Par 101):108,107,107,107,104 95
CSF £34.60 TOTE £4.40: £2.10, £5.10; EX 43.60 Place 6 £310.05, Place 5 £113.38.
Owner Highclere Thoroughbred Racing XXXVIII **Bred** Barronstown Stud And Pacelco S A **Trained** Newmarket, Suffolk
■ Stewards' Enquiry : J-P Guillambert one-day ban: used whip in incorrect place (Jun 24)

FOCUS
Despite a small field and the front four being separated by less than half a length at the line, this was a truly-run contest and the time was very decent. The form looks sound with the fourth the best guide.
T/Plt: £498.30 to a £1 stake. Pool: £56,220.20. 82.35 winning tickets. T/Qpdt: £65.50 to a £1 stake. Pool: £3,957.55. 44.70 winning tickets. JN

2363 NOTTINGHAM (L-H)
Wednesday, June 13

OFFICIAL GOING: Good to firm (good in places, 8.5)
Wind: Virtually nil Weather: Fine and sunny

2575 EUROPEAN BREEDERS' FUND MAIDEN STKS 6f 15y
1:40 (1:41) (Class 5) 2-Y-0 **£3,562** (£1,059; £529; £264) **Stalls** High

Form RPR

1 **Easy Target (FR)** 2-9-3 0 PaulEddery 10 73+
(B Smart) *dwlt: sn trcking ldrs: hdwy 2f out: rdn and edgd lft ins fnl f: styd on wl to ld last 100yds* **10/1**

2 1/2 **Quick Release (IRE)** 2-9-3 0 RichardHughes 1 72+
(D M Simcock) *hld up in rr: hdwy 2f out: rdn and styd on wl fnl f* **22/1**

6 3 nk **Polite Society (IRE)**[15] 2122 2-8-12 0 JoeFanning 9 66
(M Johnston) *cl up: effrt over 2f out: rdn to ld wl over 1f out: edgd lft ins fnl f: hdd and no ex last 100yds* **5/2**[1]

06 4 2 **Merchant Navy**[12] 2215 2-9-3 0 JimmyFortune 2 65
(E A L Dunlop) *trckd ldrs: hdwy to chal wl over 1f out and ev ch tl rdn and wknd ins fnl f* **12/1**

0 **5** *nk* **Shannersburg (IRE)**[32] 1652 2-9-3 0 ChrisCatlin 3 64+
(E J O'Neill) *midfield: pushed along and outpcd 1/2-way: kpt on appr fnl f: nrst fin* **11/2**[3]

6 *hd* **Merchant Of Dubai** 2-9-3 0 TPO'Shea 6 64+
(G A Swinbank) *midfield: green and sn pushed along: styd on appr fnl f* **11/2**[3]

7 *1/2* **Highland Homestead** 2-9-3 0 RobertHavlin 4 62+
(B R Millman) *s.i.s: sn bhd and pushed along: hdwy 2f out: styd on wl fnl f: nrst fin* **50/1**

8 *3 1/2* **Indian Days** 2-9-3 0 EddieAhern 5 52
(J G Given) *prom on outer: rdn along over 2f out and sn wknd* **14/1**

02 **9** *1 1/4* **Smileforawhile (IRE)**[33] 1622 2-9-3 0 DO'Donohoe 8 48
(K A Ryan) *prom: rdn along 1/2-way: sn wknd* **4/1**[2]

0 **10** *nk* **Biased Opinion (IRE)**[18] 2041 2-9-3 0 PhilipRobinson 11 47
(H J L Dunlop) *led: rdn along over 2f out: hdd wl over 1f out and sn wknd* **50/1**

60 **11** *32* **Orpen's Art (IRE)**[22] 1919 2-9-3 0 JamieSpencer 7 —
(N A Callaghan) *stdd s: t.k.h and hld up: hdwy to chse ldrs 1/2-way: sn rdn and wknd: eased* **25/1**

1m 15.45s (0.45) **Going Correction** -0.025s/f (Good) **11** Ran SP% **114.9**
Speed ratings (Par 93):96,95,94,92,91 91,90,86,84,84 41
CSF £208.06 TOTE £10.80: £2.80, £5.60, £1.30; EX 228.20.
Owner Prime Equestrian **Bred** David Brown **Trained** Hambleton, N Yorks

FOCUS

A modest maiden, run at a sound pace. The runners came down the middle of the track and the form looks solid enough.

NOTEBOOK

Easy Target(FR), a 60,000gns purchase whose pedigree suggests a mix of speed and stamina, proved easy to back ahead of his racecourse debut largely as he proved very keen to post. However, once overcoming a sluggish start he settled well in behind the leaders and showed a good attitude to get on top where it mattered. His stable is in flying form at present and he should have a deal more to offer yet. (op 13-2)

Quick Release(IRE) ◆, who cost 53,000euros and whose dam is an unraced half-sister to Oaks heroine Casual Look, was doing all of his best work towards the finish and may well have gone one better had his rider asked for an effort earlier than he did. However, he was undoubtedly green on this debut and looks a winner waiting to happen in the coming weeks.

Polite Society(IRE), very well backed to step up on her recent Sandown debut, did just that yet failed to see out the extra furlong as well as the front pair. She did little wrong in defeat and will no doubt be found an opening before too long. (op 11-4 tchd 10-3)

Merchant Navy broke on terms this time and emerged to have every chance. He is going the right way, indeed this was his best effort to date, and rated a sound benchmark for the form. However, he is unlikely to be seen at best until tackling nurseries in due course, for which he is now qualified.

Shannersburg(IRE) showed improved form from his Ascot debut a month ago, but failed to really raise his game as could have been expected for the extra furlong and indeed shaped as though he now wants 7f. One to keep an eye on. (op 6-1 tchd 9-2)

Merchant Of Dubai, out of a half-sister to top-class sprinter Owington, met support in the betting ring for this racecourse bow yet ultimately proved too green to do himself full justice. He was far from disgraced, however, and like so many juveniles from his stable he ought to come on a deal for the experience. (op 7-1)

Highland Homestead, out of a half-sister to his stable's former useful sprinter Lord Kintyre, fell out of the stalls and his chance was apparent before halfway. He was still noted as finishing his race with some promise, however, and should learn a great deal for this debut experience. (op 40-1)

Smileforawhile(IRE), up in trip, dropped out disappointingly before the 2f pole and this effort leaves him with a good deal to prove now. (tchd 3-1)

Orpen's Art(IRE) Official explanation: jockey said colt hung left throughout

2576 TOTEEXACTA H'CAP — 6f 15y

2:10 (2:10) (Class 6) (0-65,65) 3-Y-O+ **£2,388** (£705; £352) **Stalls** High

Form RPR

-062 **1** **Dakota Rain (IRE)**[9] 2302 5-9-11 **65** LiamTreadwell(3) 5 77
(Jennie Candlish) *cl up: rdn 2f out: drvn and styd on to ld ins fnl f* **8/1**[2]

-000 **2** *1 1/4* **Falmassim**[34] 1597 4-9-6 **57** (p) KerrinMcEvoy 6 65
(Miss J A Camacho) *overall ldr centre: rdn along 2f out: drvn and hdd ins fnl f: kpt on* **9/1**[3]

130- **3** *1* **Markestino**[282] 5062 4-8-13 **50** GrahamGibbons 7 55
(T D Easterby) *in tch: hdwy over 2f out: sn rdn and styd on wl appr fnl f: nrst fin* **33/1**

0410 **4** *nk* **Mistral Sky**[8] 2334 8-9-9 **60** (p) JamieSpencer 14 64
(Stef Liddiard) *chsd ldr stands' side: rdn along 2f out: kpt on u.p appr fnl f: nrst fin* **8/1**[2]

3015 **5** *hd* **Pappas Ruby (USA)**[11] 2257 4-9-5 **56** (b) JamesDoyle 16 59
(R M Beckett) *led stands' side gp: rdn along and hdd over 2f out: sn drvn and kpt on: 2nd in gp* **12/1**

0030 **6** *2 1/2* **Joy And Pain**[8] 2334 6-9-6 **57** (v) EddieAhern 13 52
(M J Attwater) *in tch: hdwy to chse ldrs 1/2-way: rdn over 2f out and sn one pce* **9/1**[3]

-005 **7** *1* **Cayman Breeze**[131] 339 7-8-13 **50** JoeFanning 8 42
(J M Bradley) *hmpd s and bhd tl styd on fnl 2f: nrst fin* **16/1**

4366 **8** *nk* **Digital**[10] 2272 10-9-2 **60** MatthewDavies(7) 15 51
(M R Channon) *dwlt and towards rr tl styd on fnl 2f* **11/1**

4-44 **9** *2 1/2* **Briery Lane (IRE)**[33] 1640 6-9-4 **55** (p) RyanMoore 3 38
(J M Bradley) *chsd ldrs: rdn along wl over 2f out and sn wknd* **6/1**[1]

25-0 **10** *1* **Make My Dream**[154] 86 4-9-1 **52** (v[1]) ChrisCatlin 11 32
(J Gallagher) *wnt lft s: chsd ldrs: rdn along over 2f out and sn wknd* **14/1**

5545 **11** *1 3/4* **Hoh Wotanite**[19] 2007 4-9-10 **61** (p) TedDurcan 17 35
(R Hollinshead) *chsd ldng pair stands' side: rdn along over 2f out and no hdwy: 3rd in that gp* **8/1**[2]

0-00 **12** *2* **Dispol Katie**[11] 2256 6-8-11 **55** NeilBrown(7) 10 23
(T D Barron) *s.i.s: a in rr* **20/1**

0052 **13** *2* **Smile For Us**[8] 2334 4-9-9 **60** (b) RobertHavlin 1 22
(C Drew) *racd wd: in tch: rdn along 1/2-way: sn wknd* **8/1**[2]

1445 **14** *1/2* **Phinerine**[6] 2387 4-9-3 **54** (b) AdrianMcCarthy 9 14
(Miss J E Foster) *hmpd s: a in rr* **50/1**

6-00 **15** *1 1/4* **Kansas Gold**[25] 1847 4-9-13 **64** DaleGibson 4 20
(J Mackie) *chsd ldrs: rdn along 1/2-way: sn wknd* **25/1**

1m 13.97s (-1.03) **Going Correction** -0.025s/f (Good)
WFA 3 from 4yo+ 8lb **15** Ran SP% **120.8**
Speed ratings (Par 101):105,103,102,101,101 98,96,96,92,91 89,86,83,83,81
CSF £74.83 CT £2267.89 TOTE £8.60: £3.00, £4.00, £5.90; EX 99.20.
Owner P and Mrs G A Clarke **Bred** Islanmore Stud **Trained** Basford Green, Staffs

FOCUS

A moderate sprint, where the main bulk of the field again elected to race down the middle, and the first pair came clear. Solid form, the winner running to something like last year's best.

2577 TOTESPORT.COM H'CAP — 1m 54y

2:40 (2:40) (Class 4) (0-85,85) 3-Y-O **£4,857** (£1,445; £722; £360) **Stalls** Centre

Form RPR

41-2 **1** **Danehillsundance (IRE)**[11] 2243 3-9-4 **82** RichardHughes 3 87
(R Hannon) *cl up: effrt over 2f out: rdn to ld wl over 1f out: drvn and kpt on wl fnl f* **9/2**[2]

2213 **2** *nk* **Docofthebay (IRE)**[18] 2045 3-9-5 **83** RyanMoore 8 87+
(J A Osborne) *hld up in rr: hdwy wl over 2f out: rdn and styd on to chal ins fnl f: drvn and no ex towards fin* **7/2**[1]

13-5 **3** *1/2* **Practicallyperfect (IRE)**[25] 1851 3-8-11 **75** TedDurcan 7 78
(H R A Cecil) *trckd ldng pair: hdwy to chal 2f out: sn rdn and ev ch tl no ex wl ins fnl f* **8/1**

2-01 **4** *1 1/2* **Radical Views**[20] 1978 3-8-13 **77** MichaelHills 2 76
(B W Hills) *led: qcknd wl over 2f out: rdn and hdd wl over 1f out: kpt on same pce* **5/1**[3]

322 **5** *1/2* **Dream Lodge (IRE)**[19] 2010 3-8-13 **77** EddieAhern 4 75
(J G Given) *trckd ldrs on inner: rdn along over 2f out: sn one pce* **7/2**[1]

1-04 **6** *nk* **Flying Valentino**[15] 2119 3-8-12 **76** TPO'Shea 10 74
(G A Swinbank) *in tch: hdwy on outer 3f out: rdn along to chse ldrs 2f out: sn drvn and kpt on same pce* **50/1**

-014 **7** *1 1/2* **Flores Sea (USA)**[26] 1802 3-8-13 **77** JamieSpencer 6 71
(T D Barron) *stdd s: hld up in rr: swtchd violently rt over 1f out: nvr a factor* **11/2**

60-4 **8** *shd* **Adaptation**[33] 1623 3-9-7 **85** JoeFanning 1 79
(M Johnston) *dwlt: sn chsng ldrs: rdn along over 2f out: sn drvn and wknd wl over 1f out* **20/1**

1m 46.42s (0.02) **Going Correction** -0.025s/f (Good) **8** Ran SP% **112.5**
Speed ratings (Par 101):98,97,97,95,95 94,93,93
CSF £19.93 CT £120.80 TOTE £4.60: £1.60, £1.70, £2.40; EX 18.20.
Owner J P Hardiman **Bred** J P Hardiman **Trained** East Everleigh, Wilts

FOCUS

A fair three-year-old handicap, run at a modest early pace. The first three fought out a tight finish, but the overall form should be treated with a little caution.

Flores Sea(USA) Official explanation: jockey said colt was denied a clear run

2578 UNITED PALLET NETWORK H'CAP — 1m 54y

3:10 (3:10) (Class 3) (0-95,90) 3-Y-O **£7,124** (£2,119; £1,059; £529) **Stalls** Centre

Form RPR

34-2 **1** **Bid For Glory**[18] 2045 3-9-7 **90** RichardHughes 3 98
(H J Collingridge) *trckd ldrs on inner: effrt and n.m.r over 2f out: swtchd rt and rdn to chse ldr over 1f out: drvn and styd on strly to ld nr line* **11/4**[2]

2112 **2** *hd* **Lady Gloria**[7] 2369 3-9-4 **87** EddieAhern 2 94
(J G Given) *prom: hdwy to ld over 2f out: rdn clr over 1f out: drvn ins fnl f: hdd and no ex nr line* **2/1**[1]

1-44 **3** *1 1/4* **Farleigh House (USA)**[18] 2045 3-9-4 **87** KerrinMcEvoy 4 92+
(M H Tompkins) *hld up in tch: pushed along over 3f out: effrt and nt clr run 2f out: sn swtchd lft and rdn: styd on wl fnl f* **4/1**[3]

4024 **4** *2* **Musical Beat**[19] 2010 3-8-8 **77** PhilipRobinson 5 77
(Miss V Haigh) *hld up in tch: hdwy on outer over 2f out: rdn to chse ldrs wl over 1f out: poon drvn and kpt on same pce* **28/1**

-110 **5** *1/2* **Kay Gee Be (IRE)**[18] 2037 3-9-7 **90** JamieSpencer 7 89
(M J Wallace) *stdd s: sn niggled along in rr: hdwy on outer over 2f out: sn rdn and one pce* **5/1**

10-6 **6** *nk* **The Illies (IRE)**[39] 1471 3-8-13 **82** MichaelHills 8 80
(B W Hills) *sn led: rdn along 3f out: hdd over 2f out: sn drvn and grad wknd* **12/1**

150- **7** *3* **Millestan (IRE)**[228] 6217 3-9-6 **89** TedDurcan 6 80
(H R A Cecil) *trckd ldrs: hdwy 3f out: rdn along over 2f out and grad wknd over 1f out* **28/1**

10-0 **8** *21* **Atlantic Light**[46] 1298 3-9-4 **87** JoeFanning 1 30
(M Johnston) *prom: rdn along wl over 2f out: sn wknd and eased* **33/1**

1m 44.19s (-2.21) **Going Correction** -0.025s/f (Good) **8** Ran SP% **114.2**
Speed ratings (Par 103):110,109,108,106,106 105,102,81
CSF £8.49 CT £20.46 TOTE £3.90: £1.30, £1.30, £1.60; EX 8.80.
Owner Harraton Court One **Bred** Llety Stud **Trained** Exning, Suffolk

FOCUS

A decent three-year-old handicap, run at a solid pace. The first pair came clear and the form looks solid.

NOTEBOOK

Bid For Glory, who found only the progressive Artimino too good at Newmarket on his seasonal bow 18 days previously, deservedly got back to winning ways under a neat ride from Hughes. He is clearly still improving, the strong pace over this trip played right into his hands, and he looks ready to tackle a little further now. (op 3-1)

Lady Gloria again just got pegged back near the finish and posted another rock-solid display in defeat. This most consistent filly sets a decent standard for this form and richly deserves to regain the winning thread, but will most likely go up another pound or two for this. (op 15-8 tchd 9-4)

Farleigh House(USA), behind today's winner at Newmarket last time, failed to reverse form with that rival despite a 4lb pull in the weights. However, he must be rated better than the bare form as he was forced to wait for his challenge at a crucial stage and found the front two getting first run on him entering the final furlong. He should not be too long in finding another race. Official explanation: jockey said colt was denied a clear run (op 5-1)

Musical Beat ran with credit, enjoying the decent pace, and again left the impression she now wants a longer trip. No doubt she will go up in the weights for this effort, however. (tchd 33-1)

Kay Gee Be(IRE), luckless in a hot handicap at Haydock last time, was given a patient ride and proved disappointingly one-paced when asked for his effort on the outside of the pack. He is capable of better on his day. (tchd 9-2)

The Illies(IRE) paid nearing the 2f pole for his exertions at the head of affairs and was not totally disgraced. He is not going to prove that simple to place from his current rating on this evidence. (op 10-1)

Millestan(IRE), who had some decent form at two, shaped as though this seasonal return was much needed and can do better. (op 22-1)

2579 TOTESPORT 0800 221 221 FILLIES' H'CAP — 1m 1f 213y

3:40 (3:40) (Class 5) (0-75,73) 3-Y-O+ **£3,238** (£963; £481; £240) **Stalls** Low

Form RPR

6-33 **1** **Magic Echo**[22] 1916 3-9-4 **71** JamieSpencer 11 82+
(M Dods) *led and sn clr at stdy pce: qcknd 3f out: rdn wl over 1f out: styd on* **11/2**[3]

-120 **2** *1 3/4* **Its Moon (IRE)**[26] 1827 3-9-0 **67** GrahamGibbons 2 73
(T D Walford) *chsd ldrs and rdn along 1/2-way: drvn 3f out: styd on u.p from over 1f out: tk 2nd towards fin* **10/1**

2-46 **3** *3/4* **Sister Maria (USA)**[13] 2181 3-9-6 **73** JimmyFortune 12 78
(E A L Dunlop) *chased wnr: rdn along to cl over 2f out: sn drvn and one pce: lost 2nd last 50yds* **7/1**

51-1 **4** *7* **Saluscraggie**[7] 2370 5-8-11 **51** JoeFanning 4 42
(K G Reveley) *hld up in rr: hdwy on inner over 3f out: rdn along 2f out: sn no imp* **7/2**[2]

-002 **5** *1 ¾* **Sweet Request**[19] 2008 3-8-9 **62** JamesDoyle 3 49
(R M Beckett) *chsd ldrs: rdn along over 3f out: sn drvn and no imp* **15/2**

63-2 **6** *¾* **Furbeseta**[14] 2137 3-9-5 **72** RyanMoore 5 60+
(L M Cumani) *hld up and bhd: hdwy on outer over 3f out: poor 4th wl over 1f out: eased ins fnl f* **3/1**[1]

2114 **7** *4* **Nicomedia (IRE)**[23] 1887 3-9-5 **72** RichardHughes 7 50
(R Hannon) *towards rr: rdn along and sme hdwy over 3f out: nvr a factor* **12/1**

0-03 **8** *6* **Golden Applause (FR)**[12] 2194 5-9-13 **67** SamHitchcott 9 33
(Mrs A L M King) *midfield: rdn alonng and hdwy over 4f out: drvn along over 3f out: sn btn* **16/1**

6040 **9** *1 ½* **Giddywell**[11] 2259 3-8-5 **58** KerrinMcEvoy 8 21
(R Hollinshead) *a in rr* **33/1**

0041 **10** *82* **Lunar River (FR)**[21] 1951 4-9-13 **67** FergusSweeney 10 —
(David Pinder) *chsd ldrs: rdn along over 3f out: sn wknd and eased* **22/1**

2m 8.01s (-1.69) **Going Correction** -0.025s/f (Good)
WFA 3 from 4yo+ 13lb **10** Ran SP% **116.8**
Speed ratings (Par 100):105,103,103,97,96 95,92,87,86,20
CSF £59.42 CT £392.00 TOTE £7.10: £2.70, £3.40, £3.00; EX 95.80.
Owner D C Batey **Bred** D C Batey **Trained** Denton, Co Durham

FOCUS
Magic Echo appeared to set a reasonable pace - the winning time was 2.98 seconds quicker than the later 46-60 - but she was allowed too much rope and won almost unchallenged, with those held up unable to make any impression. As a result, the bare form of this fillies' handicap could be a little misleading. None of the front three are fully exposed, though.
Furbeseta Official explanation: jockey said filly was never travelling and hung left in the straight
Lunar River(FR) Official explanation: trainer said filly had a breathing problem

2580 TOTEPOOL MAIDEN STKS (DIV I) 1m 54y
4:10 (4:11) (Class 5) 3-Y-0+ **£2,266** (£674; £337; £168) **Stalls** Centre

Form RPR

2-4 **1** **Sign Of The Cross**[14] 2153 3-9-0 0 JamieSpencer 2 84+
(J R Fanshawe) *mde all: clr wl over 2f out: styd on strly* **6/5**[2]

4- **2** *3 ½* **Thinking Positive**[267] 5456 3-8-9 0 JimmyFortune 6 70+
(J H M Gosden) *trckd ldrs: hdsway to chse wnr 2f out: sn rdn and no imp* **11/10**[1]

04 **3** *5* **Arabiyah**[16] 2077 3-8-9 0 TedDurcan 4 53
(L M Cumani) *trckd ldrs: hdwy to chse wnr after 3f: rdn along over 3f out: sn drvn and wknd over 2f out* **12/1**[3]

0 **4** *1 ½* **Montrachet**[54] 1127 3-8-9 0 EddieAhern 5 50
(M L W Bell) *chsd ldrs: rdn along over 3f out: sn drvn and plugged on one pce* **20/1**

00-0 **5** *6* **Vampyrus**[23] 1886 4-9-11 50 (v[1]) FergusSweeney 10 44
(H Candy) *chsd wnr 3f: rdn along over 3f out: sn drvn and wknd* **40/1**

U **6** *1 ½* **Sky Chart (IRE)**[8] 2341 3-9-0 0 DO'Donohoe 7 38
(N J Vaughan) *midfield: rdn along over 3f out: no hdwy* **100/1**

00- **7** *6* **Presque Perdre**[242] 5959 3-9-0 0 JoeFanning 9 24
(K G Reveley) *a towards rr* **80/1**

0 **8** *1 ½* **Cardington Queen**[11] 2261 3-8-9 0 ChrisCatlin 8 15
(M Mullineaux) *a in rr* **100/1**

9 *¾* **Tavares (IRE)** 4-9-11 0 BrettDoyle 11 22
(P S McEntee) *v.s.a: a bhd* **40/1**

10 *9* **Watt A Will** 4-9-6 0 LPKeniry 1 —
(J M Bradley) *s.i.s: a bhd* **100/1**

11 *1 ¼* **Own Gift** 3-8-9 0 PaulEddery 3 —
(S Parr) *a bhd* **150/1**

1m 46.9s (0.50) **Going Correction** -0.025s/f (Good)
WFA 3 from 4yo 11lb **11** Ran SP% **115.3**
Speed ratings (Par 103):96,92,87,86,80 78,72,71,70,61 60
CSF £2.61 TOTE £2.10: £1.10, £1.10, £2.00; EX 3.00.
Owner T R G Vestey **Bred** T R G Vestey **Trained** Newmarket, Suffolk

FOCUS
An uncompetitive maiden and they finished well strung out. The winning time was 1.24 seconds slower than the second division and the slowest of the four races over course and distance. The first two were both eased and are better than the bare form.
Montrachet Official explanation: jockey said filly was unsuited by the good to firm, good in places ground

2581 TOTEPOOL MAIDEN STKS (DIV II) 1m 54y
4:40 (4:41) (Class 5) 3-Y-0+ **£2,266** (£674; £337; £168) **Stalls** Centre

Form RPR

022- **1** **First Buddy**[196] 6651 3-9-0 74 KerrinMcEvoy 9 82+
(W J Haggas) *mde all: rdn along over 2f out: styd on strly appr fnl f* **9/1**[2]

6-56 **2** *4* **Handset (USA)**[32] 1685 3-8-9 68 RichardHughes 6 68
(H R A Cecil) *a chsng wnr: rdn 2f out and sn no imp* **16/1**

3 *3 ½* **Pivotal Answer (IRE)** 3-8-9 0 EddieAhern 8 60+
(J Noseda) *midfield: pushed along and outpcd over 3f out: swtchd rigjht and sn rdn: styd on wl appr fnl f* **12/1**[3]

63 **4** *3 ½* **Flagstone (USA)**[20] 1968 3-9-0 0 DaleGibson 2 57
(G A Swinbank) *chsd ldrs: rdn along over 3f out: sn drvn and plugged on same pce* **50/1**

0 **5** *7* **Break Out**[12] 2196 3-9-0 0 LPKeniry 10 41
(J M Bradley) *chsd ldrs: rdn along over 3f out: grad wknd* **300/1**

3 **6** *4* **Ionian**[23] 1904 4-9-11 0 PaulEddery 3 35+
(Pat Eddery) *hld up: hdwy and in tch 1/2-way: sn rdn along and wkng whn sltly hmpd 2f out* **25/1**

0004 **7** *2 ½* **Kineta (USA)**[9] 2309 4-9-6 49 (b[1]) JoeFanning 7 24
(W R Muir) *a towards rr* **250/1**

0- **8** *4* **Gizmo**[177] 6861 4-9-8 0 MarkLawson(3) 11 20
(B Smart) *chsd ldrs on outer: rdn along over 3f out: grad wknd* **125/1**

2 **9** *8* **Sister Act**[54] 1128 3-8-9 0 JamieSpencer 5 —
(J R Fanshawe) *stdd s: keen and hld up in rr: hdwy 4f out: shkn up to chse ldrs 3f out: eased 2f out whn lost action: virtually p.u* **2/7**[1]

00- **10** *5* **Soylent Green**[240] 6012 3-8-9 0 ChrisCatlin 4 —
(S Parr) *a bhd* **400/1**

1m 45.66s (-0.74) **Going Correction** -0.025s/f (Good)
WFA 3 from 4yo 11lb **10** Ran SP% **108.9**
Speed ratings (Par 103):102,98,94,91,84 80,77,73,65,60
CSF £111.57 TOTE £7.50: £1.40, £3.40, £2.40; EX 103.40.
Owner W J Gredley **Bred** Tarworth Bloodstock Investments Ltd **Trained** Newmarket, Suffolk

FOCUS
This maiden lost much of its interest with the red-hot favourite Sister Act failing to run her race, but First Buddy still managed to record a time 1.24 seconds quicker than the first division and is up 9lb on his 2yo form.
Sister Act Official explanation: jockey said filly lost its action

2582 TOTESPORTCASINO.COM H'CAP 1m 1f 213y
5:10 (5:10) (Class 6) (0-60,60) 4-Y-0+ **£2,388** (£705; £352) **Stalls** Low

Form RPR

4264 **1** **Don Pasquale**[7] 2370 5-8-4 **46** oh1 ChrisCatlin 8 55
(J T Stimpson) *towards rr: gd hdwy on outer 3f out: rdn to ld wl over 1f out: drvn entlast and hld on gamely* **8/1**

04-0 **2** *nk* **Thornaby Green**[11] 2254 6-8-0 **49** DeanHeslop(7) 14 57
(T D Barron) *led: rdn along 3f out: hdd 2f out: rallied gamely fnl f* **25/1**

0003 **3** *1 ½* **Ruby Legend**[11] 2254 9-8-11 **53** (b) JoeFanning 6 58+
(K G Reveley) *in tch on inner: hdwy 3f out: rdn over 2f out: kpt on u.p ins fnl f* **8/1**

60-6 **4** *nk* **Royal Indulgence**[15] 2117 7-8-11 **53** RyanMoore 13 57+
(W M Brisbourne) *s.i.s and bhd: hdwy on outer over 3f out: rdn along over 2f out: styd on wl fnl f* **7/1**[3]

000- **5** *2 ½* **Moving Story**[352] 2940 4-8-7 **49** FrankieMcDonald 12 48
(P T Midgley) *chsd ldrs: rdn and n.m.r 2f out: sn drvn and kpt on same pce* **66/1**

0250 **6** *1 ½* **Faversham**[16] 2084 4-9-4 **60** JamieSpencer 4 56
(M Wigham) *trckd ldrs: effrt and n.m.r over 2f out: sn rdden: drvn over 1f out: wknd ins fnl f* **11/4**[1]

0-40 **7** *4* **Chapter (IRE)**[18] 2027 5-8-11 **53** (p) SamHitchcott 10 41
(Mrs A L M King) *midfield: hdwy and in tch over 3f out: rdn over 2f out and sn no iompression* **14/1**

0000 **8** *1 ½* **Takes Tutu (USA)**[41] 808 8-8-13 **55** PhilipRobinson 9 40
(C R Dore) *bhd tl sme late hdwy* **20/1**

00-0 **9** *8* **Monsignor Fred**[22] 1924 5-9-2 **58** FergusSweeney 2 27
(H Candy) *a towards rr* **25/1**

5500 **10** *3* **Counterfactual (IRE)**[13] 2168 4-8-7 **52** MarkLawson(3) 15 15
(B Smart) *prom: rdn along 3f out: drvn over 2f out and sn wknd* **12/1**

4600 **11** *3 ½* **Wolds Way**[11] 1967 5-9-3 **59** (b) GrahamGibbons 3 15
(T D Easterby) *dwlt: sn chsng ldrs: pushed along 1/2-way and sn wknd* **33/1**

0016 **12** *1* **El Capitan (FR)**[13] 2176 4-8-13 **55** BrettDoyle 7 9
(Miss Gay Kelleway) *chsd ldrs: rdn along over 3f out: sn wknd* **12/1**

4530 **13** *2* **Rose Muwasim**[9] 2307 4-8-5 **47** (p) DaleGibson 16 —
(S Parr) *chsd ldrs: rdn along over 3f out: sn wknd* **50/1**

-222 **14** *¾* **Don't Mind Me**[71] 903 4-9-1 **57** KerrinMcEvoy 5 6
(T Keddy) *midfield: effrt and pushed along whn n.m.r 3f out: sn wknd* **7/2**[2]

2m 10.99s (1.29) **Going Correction** -0.025s/f (Good) **14** Ran SP% **124.5**
Speed ratings (Par 101):93,92,91,91,89 88,84,83,77,74 72,71,69,69
CSF £206.19 CT £1673.75 TOTE £9.60: £2.90, £9.50, £2.90; EX 223.00 Place 6 £ 74.76, Place 5 £32.36..
Owner J T Stimpson **Bred** Chippenham Lodge Stud Ltd **Trained** Newcastle-Under-Lyme, Staffs

FOCUS
A very moderate handicap, as a winning time 2.98 seconds slower than the earlier 58-75 fillies' handicap suggests. The form has not been rated too positively.
Don't Mind Me Official explanation: trainer said filly was unsuited by the good to firm, good in places ground
T/Jkpt: Not won. T/Plt: £84.10 to a £1 stake. Pool: £46,474.20. 403.15 winning tickets. T/Qpdt: £9.00 to a £1 stake. Pool: £3,299.50. 270.30 winning tickets. JR

2583 - 2585a (Foreign Racing) - See Raceform Interactive

2377 LEOPARDSTOWN (L-H)
Wednesday, June 13

OFFICIAL GOING: Good

2586a BALLYCORUS STKS (GROUP 3) 7f
7:30 (7:31) 3-Y-0+ **£30,743** (£8,986; £4,256; £1,418)

RPR

1 **Lord Admiral (USA)**[24] 1867 6-9-9 109 (b) MJKinane 6 112
(Charles O'Brien, Ire) *trckd ldr in 2nd: chal ent st: led 1 1/2f out: strly pressed ins fnl f: kpt on wl u.p: all out* **12/1**

2 *hd* **Modeeroch (IRE)**[18] 2053 4-9-6 106 DPMcDonogh 3 108
(J S Bolger, Ire) *trckd ldrs: 5th 1/2-way: 3rd and hdwy early st: 2nd and chal ins fnl f: ev ch: jst failed* **7/4**[1]

3 *1 ½* **Eastern Appeal (IRE)**[18] 2053 4-9-9 102 JMurtagh 9 107+
(M Halford, Ire) *hld up: 7th 1/2-way: 5th and rdn ent st: 3rd and kpt on wl fnl f* **16/1**

4 *nk* **Duff (IRE)**[24] 1867 4-9-9 102 FMBerry 7 106
(Edward Lynam, Ire) *led: rdn and strly pressed st: hdd 1 1/2f out: no ex ins fnl f* **7/1**[3]

5 *1 ¾* **King Jock (USA)**[11] 2233 6-9-12 107 PShanahan 4 104
(R J Osborne, Ire) *trckd ldrs on outer: 4th 1/2-way: 3rd into st: no imp fr over 1f out* **11/1**

6 *1* **Hard Rock City (USA)**[7] 2381 7-9-9 104 JAHeffernan 2 99
(M J Grassick, Ire) *chsd ldrs: 6th 1/2-way: 5th briefly under 2f out: kpt on same pce* **14/1**

7 *1 ¼* **Absolutelyfabulous (IRE)**[7] 2379 4-9-6 100 KFallon 8 92
(David Wachman, Ire) *hld up: 8th and rdn ent st: no imp* **11/2**[2]

8 *2* **Fleeting Shadow (IRE)**[18] 2051 3-8-13 108 (b[1]) PJSmullen 1 90
(D K Weld, Ire) *prom: 3rd 1/2-way: 5th early st: sn wknd* **8/1**

9 *¾* **Vanderlin**[32] 1656 8-9-9 CDHayes 5 88
(A M Balding) *hld up towards rr: last 3f out: effrt ent st: sn no ex* **7/1**[3]

10 *1* **Summit Surge (IRE)**[52] 1185 3-8-13 101 (t) NGMcCullagh 10 85
(G M Lyons, Ire) *a towards rr* **16/1**

1m 26.3s (-5.90) **Going Correction** -0.50s/f (Hard)
WFA 3 from 4yo+ 10lb **10** Ran SP% **122.3**
Speed ratings: 113,112,111,110,108 107,106,103,103,101
CSF £35.02 TOTE £12.30: £2.90, £1.30, £3.90; DF 53.10.
Owner Dr M V O'Brien **Bred** London Thrghbrd Services/Derry **Trained** Straffan, Co Kildare

FOCUS
A decent Group 3 and by far the fastest of the four 7f races on the card, very much as it should have been. The form looks sound.

NOTEBOOK
Lord Admiral(USA) ended a long losing sequence - he had been in the first three 13 times since achieving his previous win in a 1m Listed race at this track two years ago - by holding on under strong pressure over a trip which is a bit short of his best. Always prominent, he hit the front a furlong and a half out and won all out. (op 10/1)
Modeeroch(IRE), a four-time winner whose three Listed successes include two over this course and trip, had been placed on her two previous starts this season. She was dropping back from 1m here and having tracked the leaders from four furlongs out, she arrived with a strong challenge inside the final furlong and ran on under pressure. (op 5/2)

Eastern Appeal(IRE) successful at this level over this trip at the Curragh last month, had finished behind Modeeroch on her previous start. She made headway over the last two furlongs and was doing her best work in the closing stages. (op 12/1)
Duff(IRE), runner-up to Hard Rock City at Gowran Park last month when his jockey had to ride without irons for most of the journey, made the running and kept on when headed by the winner. (op 7/1 tchd 13/2)
King Jock(USA), whose seven wins include a Group 3 event over 1m here and two Listed events in the UAE, had finished fourth behind Blythe Knight at Epsom on his previous start. Fourth into the straight, he could make little impression in the closing stages. (op 10/1 tchd 12/1)
Hard Rock City(USA) had run moderately for the first time in his career in a 1m Listed event here a week previously. He made a forward move turning for home, but never really threatened to get seriously involved. (op 10/1)
Vanderlin, who was held up in rear, made a forward move turning for home but his effort proved short-lived. (op 6/1)

2587 - 2589a (Foreign Racing) - See Raceform Interactive

[2454] LINGFIELD (L-H)

Thursday, June 14

OFFICIAL GOING: Standard

Wind: Light, behind Weather: Fine but cloudy

2590 HEATWAVE LIVE AT LINGFIELDPARK.CO.UK MAIDEN STKS 6f (P)

2:30 (2:32) (Class 5) 2-Y-O £2,817 (£838; £418; £209) **Stalls** Low

Form RPR

1 **Strike The Deal (USA)** 2-9-3 0 SebSanders 8 78+
(J Noseda) *mde all: jnd 1/2-way: drvn into def advantage again over 1f out: styd on wl* **11/4**[1]

05 2 2 **Flying Indian**[39] [1503] 2-8-12 0 LPKeniry 9 67
(A M Balding) *trckd wnr: upsides 1/2-way to wl over 1f out: tired and jst hld on to 2nd nr fin* **9/2**[3]

4 3 ½ **L'Art Du Silence (IRE)**[29] [1762] 2-9-3 0 FergusSweeney 6 71
(J R Boyle) *chsd ldrs: rdn over 2f out: hanging lft over 1f out: r.o fnl f to take 3rd nr fin* **4/1**[2]

6 4 shd **Maybe I Will (IRE)**[21] [1970] 2-8-12 0 PatDobbs 5 65
(R Hannon) *chsd ldrs: outpcd over 2f out: styd on fr over 1f out on inner: nrst fin* **6/1**

5 nk **Cracking Nick (IRE)** 2-9-3 0 OscarUrbina 2 69
(W R Swinburn) *trckd ldrs: wnt 3rd over 2f out but outpcd by ldng pair: kpt on but lost 2 pls nr fin* **15/2**

6 6 **Bencorr (USA)** 2-9-3 0 TPO'Shea 7 51
(M J Wallace) *s.s: wl in rr: rdn and effrt over 3f out but already wl outpcd: plugged on fr over 1f out* **12/1**

0 7 shd **Jemiliah**[21] [1960] 2-8-12 0 BrettDoyle 4 46
(B J Meehan) *chsd clr ldrs: lft bhd fr 1/2-way: rdn and no ch after* **25/1**

8 1 **Listed Art** 2-9-3 0 DavidKinsella 12 48
(B J Meehan) *outpcd and wl in rr after 2f: no ch after: plugged on* **20/1**

0 9 ½ **Ballyhealy Lady**[41] [1445] 2-8-12 0 AdrianMcCarthy 10 42
(D K Ivory) *t.k.h: chsd ldng pair to over 2f out: wknd rapidly over 1f out* **25/1**

00 10 ¾ **Victory Shout (USA)**[9] [2333] 2-9-3 0 GeorgeBaker 1 44
(J R Best) *settled in rr: wl outpcd bef 1/2-way: bhd after* **25/1**

0 11 12 **Jermajesty (IRE)**[12] [2232] 2-9-3 0 MatthewHenry 11 8
(J R Boyle) *led to post: pushed along in midfield: outpcd bef 1/2-way: wknd 2f out: t.o* **33/1**

12 dist **Frammenti** 2-8-12 0 DO'Donohoe 3 —
(A J McCabe) *s.v.s: v green and a wl t.o* **33/1**

1m 13.71s (0.90) **Going Correction** +0.075s/f (Slow) 12 Ran SP% **120.8**
Speed ratings (Par 93):97,94,93,93,93 85,85,83,83,82 66,—
CSF £13.74 TOTE £3.60: £1.70, £2.10, £1.80; EX 21.90.
Owner The Searchers **Bred** Five-D Thoroughbreds, Llc **Trained** Newmarket, Suffolk

FOCUS
An average juvenile maiden, rated through the runner-up and the time. The winner could rate higher.

NOTEBOOK
Strike The Deal(USA), who cost 140,000gns and is out of a choicely-bred dam, was well backed to make a winning start to his career and duly rewarded his supporters by making all in resolute fashion. He was well on top at the finish and has the physical scope to rate higher, so it will be fascinating to see how he handles the transition to turf in due course. (op 10-3 tchd 7-2)
Flying Indian tried to go with the winner from the off, but it was clear nearing the final furlong that she was losing that battle, and she was a tired horse at the finish. She can find an opportunity in which to go one better and should be happier over this trip when ridden with slightly more patience. (tchd 5-1)
L'Art Du Silence(IRE) hung fire when the gun was really put to his head nearing the final furlong, but he ran on again when his rider straightened him up and ultimately ran an improved race. The extra furlong proved much to his liking. (op 9-2 tchd 7-2)
Maybe I Will(IRE) adopted a decent early position just behind the leaders, but hit a flat spot at a crucial stage before keeping on again all too late. This looks her trip at present and she is worth trying on a more galloping track again. (op 9-2)
Cracking Nick(IRE) ◆, whose dam was a smart 6-7f winner at two and has already produced two 7f juvenile winners, showed ability on this racecourse debut and left the clear impression that he would be emulating his half-brothers when upped to another furlong in due course. (op 7-1 tchd 8-1)
Bencorr(USA), half-brother to six winners in the US, never figured after a slow start and looked much in need of this debut experience. He should get closer next time. (op 10-1)
Frammenti Official explanation: jockey said filly missed the break

2591 GO WEST LIVE AT LINGFIELDPARK.CO.UK (S) STKS 7f (P)

3:00 (3:00) (Class 6) 3-Y-0+ £2,047 (£604; £302) **Stalls** Low

Form RPR

-030 1 **Blue Quiver (IRE)**[14] [2176] 7-9-7 46 SimonWhitworth 11 61
(C A Horgan) *taken down early: hld up in last pair: gng best fr 1/2-way and stdy prog fr 3f out: gap appeared and led over 1f out: drvn out* **14/1**

0000 2 2 **Scroll**[9] [2336] 4-9-7 54 (v) AdrianMcCarthy 5 56
(P Howling) *pushed along in rr after 2f: urged along fr 1/2-way: prog fr 2f out to chse wnr jst ins fnl f: limited rspnse and no imp* **7/2**[2]

0435 3 1½ **Rafferty (IRE)**[9] [2331] 8-9-7 49 (p) SebSanders 12 52
(S Dow) *racd on outer in midfield: prog 3f out: cl up 2f out: nt qckn u.p over 1f out: kpt on* **9/4**[1]

0606 4 1 **Fulvio (USA)**[12] [2258] 7-9-0 45 (v) JackMitchell[(7)] 4 49
(P Howling) *pushed along early to go prom: effrt to chse ldr over 2f out to wl over 1f out: wknd ins fnl f* **10/1**

0253 5 ½ **Dexileos (IRE)**[44] [1381] 8-9-0 47 ChrisCavanagh[(7)] 13 48
(David Pinder) *mostly trckd ldr to over 2f out: styd cl up on inner: fdd fnl f* **8/1**

0000 6 nk **Alwariah**[2] [2540] 4-8-9 47 SophieDoyle[(7)] 2 42
(Ms J S Doyle) *nvr beyond midfield: bmpd along on inner over 2f out: swtchd wd and kpt on one pce over 1f out* **40/1**

0353 7 nk **Tenterhooks (IRE)**[16] [2110] 3-8-6 49 (be) LPKeniry 6 37
(A J McCabe) *pressed ldng pair: drvn 1/2-way: sn lost pl: plugged on* **9/1**

0006 8 3½ **Dark Moon**[10] [2304] 4-9-8 45 (v) DO'Donohoe 9 37
(D Shaw) *s.s: sn in tch in last pair: rdn 3f out: no prog and wl btn fnl 2f* **16/1**

6060 9 hd **O'Dwyer (IRE)**[13] [2203] 3-8-11 48 (b[1]) SilvestreDeSousa 7 32
(A D Brown) *led to over 1f out: wknd rapidly* **33/1**

3244 10 11 **Marist Madame**[1] [2560] 3-8-6 52 DavidKinsella 8 —
(D K Ivory) *chsd ldrs: u.p 1/2-way: wknd 2f out: eased over 1f out* **5/1**[3]

1m 26.82s (0.93) **Going Correction** +0.075s/f (Slow)
WFA 3 from 4yo+ 10lb 10 Ran SP% **117.8**
Speed ratings (Par 101):97,94,93,91,91 90,90,86,86,73
CSF £63.33 TOTE £22.90: £6.70, £1.40, £1.50; EX 112.50.There was no bid for the winner.
Owner C A Horgan **Bred** Mrs B Sumner **Trained** Uffcott, Wilts

FOCUS
A solid-looking seller, run at a strong early pace. The winner bounced back to form and the third is probably the best guide.
Marist Madame Official explanation: jockey said filly lost its action

2592 HENRY STREETER FILLIES' H'CAP 7f (P)

3:35 (3:35) (Class 6) (0-65,63) 3-Y-0+ £2,047 (£604; £302) **Stalls** Low

Form RPR

0403 1 **Alucica**[16] [2121] 4-8-7 47 (v) PatrickHills[(5)] 8 51
(D Shaw) *chsd ldr after 1f: rdn 2f out: edgd rt u.p and looked hld: kpt on to ld last strides* **12/1**

-000 2 hd **Nightstrike (IRE)**[101] [614] 4-9-6 55 GeorgeBaker 7 58
(Luke Comer, Ire) *mde most: drvn over 1f out: looked like holding on tl wknd and hdd last strides* **10/1**

0-35 3 ½ **Oh So Saucy**[12] [2262] 3-8-12 57 SebSanders 2 55
(C F Wall) *s.i.s: n.m.r after 2f: prog fr 4f out to chse ldng pair over 1f out: hrd rdn and nt qckn* **5/2**[1]

0-00 4 1¼ **Parthenope**[39] [1507] 4-8-10 45 RichardThomas 10 44
(J A Geake) *chsd ldng pair after 1f: rdn 1/2-way: lost 3rd over 1f out: one pce* **50/1**

5-40 5 shd **Boogie Board**[34] [1639] 3-8-8 53 DO'Donohoe 9 47
(S Parr) *towards outer in midfield: rdn and nt qckn over 2f out: kpt on ins fnl f* **50/1**

/020 6 shd **Burford Lass (IRE)**[9] [2336] 4-9-1 55 JamesMillman[(5)] 5 53
(D K Ivory) *hld up: nt clr run 1/2-way and nt wl plcd after: effrt on inner and n.m.r over 1f out: plugged on* **8/1**

-030 7 ½ **Double Valentine**[9] [2334] 4-8-7 49 JackMitchell[(7)] 6 46
(R Ingram) *s.i.s: racd wd in tch: rdn whn v wd bnd 2f out: no ch after: plugged on* **16/1**

2013 8 ½ **Pearl Farm**[22] [1947] 6-9-7 56 FergusSweeney 3 52
(C A Horgan) *hld up: lost pl and last after 2f: effrt 3f out: rdn and one pce fnl 2f: no prog* **10/3**[3]

4-02 9 1½ **Antigoni (IRE)**[12] [2257] 4-10-0 63 LPKeniry 1 55
(A M Balding) *chsd ldrs on inner: rdn over 2f out: no imp wl over 1f out: wknd ins fnl f* **3/1**[2]

00-0 10 22 **Liskaveen Beauty**[85] [721] 4-8-10 45 (b) TPO'Shea 4 —
(T J Fitzgerald) *t.k.h early: chsd ldr 1f: lost pl: last and tailing off 3f out* **25/1**

1m 27.0s (1.11) **Going Correction** +0.075s/f (Slow)
WFA 3 from 4yo+ 10lb 10 Ran SP% **118.2**
Speed ratings (Par 98):96,95,95,93,93 93,92,92,90,65
CSF £125.09 CT £408.00 TOTE £15.90: £3.50, £3.50, £1.10; EX 139.60.
Owner D R Tucker **Bred** D R Tucker **Trained** Danethorpe, Notts

FOCUS
A weak fillies' handicap. The from looks dubious with the fourth 3lb out of the weights.
Nightstrike(IRE) Official explanation: jockey said filly hung right final bend
Pearl Farm Official explanation: jockey said mare lost off-fore shoe

2593 THE GREAT PRETENDER LIVE AT LINGFIELDPARK.CO.UK MEDIAN AUCTION MAIDEN STKS 7f (P)

4:10 (4:10) (Class 6) 3-4-Y-0 £2,730 (£806; £403) **Stalls** Low

Form RPR

-522 1 **Napoleon Dynamite (IRE)**[42] [1437] 3-9-0 70 SebSanders 3 69+
(J W Hills) *trckd ldr over 4f out: led over 2f out: drew clr wl over 1f out: rdn out* **8/13**[1]

2 3 **Neboisha** 3-8-9 0 AdrianMcCarthy 4 53
(P Howling) *chsd ldrs: rdn 1/2-way: prog u.p over 1f out: wnt 2nd ins fnl f: no ch w wnr* **16/1**

3 nk **Affrettando (IRE)** 3-9-0 0 TPO'Shea 5 57+
(J A R Toller) *s.s: in tch in rr: rdn 1/2-way: stl only 7th and hanging over 1f out: styd on fnl f to press for 2nd nr fin* **11/2**[3]

00-0 4 1¾ **Ma Ridge**[23] [1928] 3-9-0 50 RichardThomas 7 52?
(T D McCarthy) *racd on outer in tch: rdn and prog over 2f out: disp modest 2nd ent fnl f: wknd* **33/1**

5 1½ **Black Meyeden (FR)** 3-8-9 0 DO'Donohoe 1 43
(S W Hall) *racd freely: led after 1f to over 2f out: chsd wnr tl wknd ins fnl f* **20/1**

0360 6 ¾ **Bold Saxon (IRE)**[10] [2317] 3-9-0 64 (v[1]) PatDobbs 2 46
(M D I Usher) *chsd ldrs: rdn 1/2-way: no prog u.p 2f out* **7/2**[2]

00-0 7 nk **Thornbill**[17] [2077] 4-9-10 47 FergusSweeney 8 49
(H Candy) *led 1f: restrained: tried to chal 3f out: btn 2f out: wknd over 1f out* **25/1**

00 8 5 **Stoneacre Donny (IRE)**[123] [429] 3-9-0 0 LPKeniry 6 32
(Peter Grayson) *last and struggling over 4f out: bhd over 2f out* **33/1**

1m 26.98s (1.09) **Going Correction** +0.075s/f (Slow)
WFA 3 from 4yo 10lb 8 Ran SP% **119.9**
Speed ratings (Par 101):96,92,92,90,88 87,87,81
CSF £13.22 TOTE £1.70: £1.02, £4.20, £1.80; EX 11.30.
Owner Richard Tufft and Partners **Bred** Humphrey Okeke **Trained** Upper Lambourn, Berks

FOCUS
No strength in depth here and the 70-rated winner scored as he was entitled to, value for a bit more than the bare form. The form is put into perspective by the 50-rated fourth.

2594 JACKSON LIFTS GROUP H'CAP 6f (P)

4:45 (4:45) (Class 5) (0-70,69) 3-Y-O £2,817 (£838; £418; £209) **Stalls** Low

Form RPR

6461 1 **Dramatic**[12] [2260] 3-9-2 64 SebSanders 3 82+
(Sir Mark Prescott) *pressed ldr: led over 3f out: sn jnd: drvn and drew clr wl over 1f out* **2/5**[1]

4-30 **2** 2 ½ **The Jay Factor (IRE)**[18] 2061 3-9-0 **62** .... PatDobbs 6 65
(Pat Eddery) *hld up bhd ldng gp: rdn and outpcd 2f out: r.o over 1f out to take 2nd last 100yds: no real ch w wnr* **17/2**[3]

-600 **3** 2 **Hythe Bay**[9] 2335 3-9-7 **69** .... GeorgeBaker 2 66
(J R Best) *prom: w wnr over 3f out to 2f out: wknd rapidly ins fnl f and lost 2nd last 100yds* **14/1**

1662 **4** ½ **Bentley**[3] 2518 3-9-0 **67** ....(v) PatrickHills(5) 5 63
(D Shaw) *chsd ldrs: rdn 3f out: outpcd fr 2f out: no ch after* **15/2**[2]

0540 **5** nk **Stoneacre Gareth (IRE)**[6] 2435 3-9-2 **64** ....(b) LPKeniry 4 59
(Peter Grayson) *t.k.h: cl up: rdn to chse ldng pair over 2f out: sn outpcd and btn: fdd* **22/1**

-654 **6** 1 **Billy Red**[23] 1932 3-8-12 **60** ....(b[1]) FergusSweeney 9 52
(J R Jenkins) *t.k.h: racd wd and hld up in tch: jnd ldrs 3f out: outpcd 2f out: no ch after* **16/1**

-234 **7** nk **Rann Na Cille (IRE)**[108] 567 3-9-0 **62** .... DO'Donohoe 8 53
(K A Ryan) *rdn in last pair early: effrt 2f out: nt clr run after and eased* **11/1**

4250 **8** 8 **Kilvickeon (IRE)**[10] 2301 3-8-2 **50** oh1 .... TPO'Shea 1 17
(Peter Grayson) *led to over 3f out: sn wknd: t.o* **25/1**

016- **9** 5 **Lay The Cash (USA)**[208] 6525 3-8-12 **65** ....(b) TolleyDean(5) 7 17
(J S Moore) *sn outpcd and rdn: t.o bef 1/2-way* **16/1**

1m 12.74s (-0.07) **Going Correction** +0.075s/f (Slow) 9 Ran SP% **128.7**
Speed ratings (Par 99):103,99,97,96,95 94,94,83,76
CSF £6.11 CT £32.40 TOTE £1.50: £1.02, £2.80, £4.00; EX 7.50.
Owner Cheveley Park Stud **Bred** Cheveley Park Stud **Trained** Newmarket, Suffolk

FOCUS
A modest sprint handicap and the progressive winner is value for further. Sound form, although the winner has effectively been ignored for rating this.
Rann Na Cille(IRE) Official explanation: jockey said filly was denied a clear run

2595 JASON DONOVAN LIVE AT LINGFIELDPARK.CO.UK H'CAP 1m 4f (P)
5:15 (5:17) (Class 6) (0-55,60) 4-Y-0+ **£2,047** (£604; £302) **Stalls** Low

Form RPR

-032 **1** **Bob's Your Uncle**[9] 2332 4-9-0 **55** .... SebSanders 2 65
(J G Portman) *hld up towards rr: prog over 3f out: rdn to chse ldrs 2f out: led 1f out: drvn and hld on wl* **11/4**[1]

4 **2** 1 **Super Sensation (GER)**[6] 496 6-8-10 **51** .... PatDobbs 14 59
(G L Moore) *hld up in midfield: smooth prog over 3f out: rdn to press ldrs 2f out: upsides 1f out: nt qckn* **10/3**[2]

0140 **3** hd **Bienheureux**[18] 2055 6-8-12 **53** ....(t) SimonWhitworth 8 61
(Miss Gay Kelleway) *dwlt: hld up wl in rr: prog whn snatched up over 3f out: hdwy again over 2f out: rdn to chal 1f out: nt qckn* **12/1**

3000 **4** 2 **Chimes At Midnight (USA)**[91] 683 10-8-2 **46** oh1(b) EmmettStack(3) 3 50
(Luke Comer, Ire) *in tch in midfield: bdly outpcd over 3f out: r.o strly again fnl f* **33/1**

4/02 **5** ½ **Selkirk Grace**[14] 2176 7-8-2 **50** .... WilliamCarson(7) 1 54
(K A Morgan) *hld up in last: wl outpcd fr 3f out: bhd over 2f out: r.o wl over 1f out: nrst fin* **10/1**

0240 **6** ½ **Come What July (IRE)**[18] 2055 6-8-2 **48** .... PatrickHills(5) 4 51
(D Shaw) *dwlt: hld up wl in rr: outpcd by ldng gp 3f out: styd on over 1f out: no ch* **8/1**[3]

06-6 **7** 1 ½ **Mr Belvedere**[45] 1366 6-8-6 **47** oh1 ow1 ....(p) LPKeniry 13 47
(A J Lidderdale) *trckd ldr: rdn to ld 2f out: hdd & wknd 1f out* **50/1**

430- **8** 2 ½ **Amnesty**[395] 1724 8-8-6 **47** oh1 ow2 .... FergusSweeney 10 43
(G L Moore) *hld up in rr: outpcd and racing wd 3f out: no ch after: kpt on* **25/1**

1605 **9** shd **Icannshift (IRE)**[14] 2176 7-8-5 **49** oh1 ow3 .... NeilChalmers(3) 6 45
(T M Jones) *led to 2f out: wknd rapidly* **25/1**

0036 **10** 1 ¼ **Royal Auditon**[23] 1926 6-8-9 **50** ....(p) DO'Donohoe 16 44
(T T Clement) *prom: trckd ldng pair over 4f out: drvn on inner over 2f out: wknd over 1f out* **16/1**

0001 **11** hd **Blackmail (USA)**[9] 2332 9-8-12 **60** 6ex ....(b) JackMitchell(7) 9 54
(P Mitchell) *settled midfield: lost pl and rdn 5f out: struggling in rr after: kpt on fnl f* **8/1**[3]

-432 **12** shd **My Legal Eagle (IRE)**[11] 2089 13-7-12 **46** oh1 .... MCGeran(7) 15 40
(E G Bevan) *racd on outer in midfield: outpcd over 3f out: no ch after* **10/1**

-530 **13** 8 **Star Berry**[9] 2332 4-8-11 **52** ....(b[1]) BrettDoyle 7 33
(B J Meehan) *prom: drvn and wknd rapidly wl over 2f out* **16/1**

0-00 **14** dist **Muqarrar (IRE)**[14] 2176 8-8-5 **46** oh1 ....(vt) TPO'Shea 12 —
(T J Fitzgerald) *dwlt: sn in tch in midfield: wknd rapidly 3f out: t.o* **66/1**

6/3- **P** **Iftikhar (USA)**[521] 72 8-8-12 **53** .... GrahamGibbons 5 —
(S Wynne) *chsd ldng pair to over 4f out: wknd rapidly: t.o whn p.u 1f out: dismntd* **16/1**

2m 34.04s (-0.35) **Going Correction** +0.075s/f (Slow) 15 Ran SP% **129.6**
Speed ratings (Par 101):104,103,103,101,101 101,100,98,98,97 97,97,92,—,—
CSF £11.82 CT £103.33 TOTE £3.60: £1.40, £1.80, £3.90; EX 13.10 Place 6 £ 6.49, Place 5 £5.08..
Owner A S B Portman **Bred** Wheelersland Stud **Trained** Compton, Berks

FOCUS
A modest handicap, run at a solid early pace. The form looks solid, the winner up 4lb on his recent course form.
Royal Auditon Official explanation: trainer said filly was found to have pulled muscles in her back after the race
Blackmail(USA) Official explanation: jockey said gelding hung right throughout
Iftikhar(USA) Official explanation: vet said gelding pulled up lame
T/Plt: £6.20 to a £1 stake. Pool: £47,910.30. 5,606.75 winning tickets. T/Qpdt: £2.70 to a £1 stake. Pool: £2,428.30. 645.80 winning tickets. JN

2467 NEWBURY (L-H)
Thursday, June 14

OFFICIAL GOING: Good to firm changing to good to firm (good in places) after race 5 (4.25)
Race 9: charity race not under Rules, won by John Reid on Bonchester Bridge.
Wind: virtually nil

2596 BETDAQ FIRST FOR MULTIPLES MAIDEN STKS (DIV I) 6f 8y
2:10 (2:11) (Class 3) 2-Y-0 **£5,829** (£1,734; £866; £432) **Stalls** High

Form RPR

1 **Midships (USA)** 2-9-0 0 .... RichardHughes 1 87+
(Mrs A J Perrett) *mde all: shkn up and r.o strly fr over 1f out: unchal* **16/1**

6 **2** 1 ¾ **Alwaabel**[19] 2041 2-9-0 0 .... RHills 2 82+
(J L Dunlop) *chsd wnr thrght: pushed along and effrt over 1f out but nvr quite gng pce to chal: kpt on wl for 2nd* **13/8**[1]

3 1 ½ **Legal Eagle (IRE)** 2-9-0 0 .... JimmyFortune 4 78+
(J H M Gosden) *racd in 3rd thrght: rdn and effrt to dispute 2nd over 1f out: one pce ins fnl f* **9/2**[2]

4 nk **Ghetto** 2-9-0 0 .... RyanMoore 5 77
(R Hannon) *chsd ldrs: drvn along over 2f out: styd on same pce fnl f* **11/1**

5 1 ¼ **Landikhaya (IRE)** 2-9-0 0 .... RichardSmith 6 73
(R Hannon) *chsd ldrs 1/2-way: sn pushed along and outpcd over 1f out: kpt on again ins fnl f* **33/1**

4 **6** 2 **Captain Esteem**[13] 2215 2-9-0 0 .... MichaelHills 3 67
(B W Hills) *t.k.h: chsd ldrs: pushed along 2f out: wknd fnl f* **9/2**[2]

7 hd **Tango Jack (USA)** 2-9-0 0 .... StephenCarson 10 66
(Eve Johnson Houghton) *s.i.s: bhd: drvn along 2f out: kpt on ins fnl f but nvr in contention* **25/1**

8 3 **Zabeel Tiger** 2-9-0 0 .... JamieSpencer 8 57
(M R Channon) *in tch 1/2-way: drvn over 2f out: wknd over 1f out* **13/2**[3]

9 ¾ **Ezthegezza** 2-9-0 0 .... EddieAhern 11 55
(J S Moore) *slowly away: sn prom: rdn 1/2-way: wknd fr 2f out* **50/1**

10 ½ **Dinarius** 2-9-0 0 .... MickyFenton 9 54
(T P Tate) *chsd ldrs tl wknd 2f out* **25/1**

11 3 **We Have A Dream** 2-9-0 0 .... MartinDwyer 7 45
(W R Muir) *a outpcd* **50/1**

1m 13.11s (-1.21) **Going Correction** -0.20s/f (Firm) 11 Ran SP% **116.6**
Speed ratings (Par 97):100,97,95,95,93 90,90,86,85,85 81
CSF £40.49 TOTE £19.00: £3.40, £1.30, £2.10; EX 60.30.
Owner K Abdulla **Bred** Juddmonte Farms Inc **Trained** Pulborough, W Sussex

FOCUS
This looked like a good juvenile maiden, although the early pace was just ordinary and those who raced handy appeared to be at an advantage. The winning time was 0.30 seconds slower than the first division. The majority of these tended to race down the middle of the track. The level of the form is guessy, but this was certainly a nice start from Midships.

NOTEBOOK
Midships(USA) ◆, a half-brother to several three-year-old winners over 1m1f plus, out of a smart 1m2f performer, made a very pleasing introduction. Allowed his own way up front, he set just an ordinary gallop for much of the way and had saved plenty for the closing stages, responding well when asked to readily hold off the favourite. He looks a very useful prospect. (tchd 20-1 in a place)
Alwaabel confirmed the promise he showed when an eye-catcher in a good maiden on his debut at Newmarket, but just found one too good. This was a useful effort in defeat and he really should find a similar race. (op 6-4 tchd 7-4)
Legal Eagle(IRE) ◆, a 300,000euros half-brother to among others multiple 6f-1m winner Lupo's Boy, out of a quite useful dual winner at three in Germany, made a pleasing debut back in third. His trainer's horses tend to improve plenty for a run and he should go close in similar company next time. (tchd 11-2)
Ghetto, a 66,000gns brother to 6f juvenile winner Hythe Bay, out of a 1m winner, showed plenty of ability on his racecourse debut and is another open to improvement. (op 12-1 tchd 10-1)
Landikhaya(IRE), a 20,000gns half-brother to 6f juvenile scorer Nebraska Lady, out of a 7f three-year-old winner, would have found this trip plenty short enough, but he ran well. He should improve on this form when stepped up in trip.
Captain Esteem failed to build on the form he showed when fourth at big odds on his debut at Goodwood and was disappointing. (tchd 4-1)

2597 DOYLE CLAYTON MAIDEN FILLIES' STKS 1m 2f 6y
2:40 (2:43) (Class 5) 3-Y-0 **£4,210** (£1,252; £625; £312) **Stalls** High

Form RPR

00 **1** **Shirley A Star (USA)**[5] 2455 3-9-0 0 ....(b[1]) RichardHughes 12 80
(B J Meehan) *sn 6l clr: reminders 3f out: hrd drvn fr over 1f out and styd on gamely u.p thrght fnl f* **66/1**

33- **2** 1 ½ **Circle Of Love**[268] 5456 3-9-0 0 .... RyanMoore 2 77
(J L Dunlop) *racd in 3rd tl chsd wnr 5f out: rdn over 2f out: effrt over 1f out but nvr quite gng pce to chal and sn one pce* **5/4**[1]

0 **3** 1 **Soul Mountain (IRE)**[56] 1105 3-9-0 0 .... MichaelHills 13 75
(B W Hills) *in rr: rdn along and hdwy fr 2f out: styd on to go 3rd ins fnl f: gng on cl home but nvr gng pce of ldrs* **12/1**

252 **4** 1 **Zifaaf (USA)**[20] 1988 3-9-0 **76** .... RHills 3 73
(B W Hills) *chsd ldrs: rdn over 2f out: styd on same pce fnl f* **13/2**[3]

0- **5** nk **Unreachable Star**[287] 4964 3-9-0 0 .... JimCrowley 9 72
(Mrs A J Perrett) *hld up in mid-div: drvn and outpcd 3f out: kpt on again fnl f* **20/1**

2-40 **6** 1 ½ **Fidelia (IRE)**[36] 1581 3-9-0 **89** .... EddieAhern 4 69
(G Wragg) *chsd ldrs: rdn over 2f out: no imp: wknd fnl f* **3/1**[2]

7 ½ **Sugarbush** 3-9-0 0 .... JamieSpencer 7 68
(J R Fanshawe) *in rr: stl plenty to do over 2f out: kpt on fnl f but nvr in contention* **14/1**

8 5 **Dabawiyah (IRE)** 3-9-0 0 .... JimmyFortune 10 58
(L M Cumani) *s.i.s: sn rcvrd to mid-div: chsd ldrs 4f out: wknd over 2f out* **16/1**

0-4 **9** 5 **Dangerous Dancer (IRE)**[28] 1784 3-9-0 0 .... SteveDrowne 14 48
(R Charlton) *in rr: rdn 4f out: nvr in contention and sn wknd* **25/1**

10 2 ½ **Gemstone Lass (FR)** 3-9-0 0 .... PaulEddery 6 43
(Pat Eddery) *slowly away: a towards rr* **50/1**

6 **11** ¾ **Hayward's Heath**[28] 1784 3-9-0 0 .... MickyFenton 11 42
(B W Duke) *chsd wnr to 5f out: wknd 3f out* **66/1**

4 **12** dist **Anna Towkaska**[23] 1928 3-9-0 0 .... AdamKirby 5 —
(W R Swinburn) *in rr: rdn and lost tch fnl 4f: virtually p.u fnl f* **20/1**

2m 6.40s (-2.31) **Going Correction** -0.20s/f (Firm) 12 Ran SP% **121.3**
Speed ratings (Par 96):101,99,99,98,97 96,96,92,88,86 85,—
CSF £147.02 TOTE £66.60: £11.60, £1.20, £3.30; EX 319.60.
Owner Star Crown Stables **Bred** Carl Rosen Associates **Trained** Manton, Wilts

FOCUS
A fair fillies' maiden, but a surprise result. Shirley A Star set a strong pace, but she was given plenty of rope in front and did not come back to the field as some of her rivals might have expected. The race has been rated around the fourth but the form looks a little dubious. The winning time was 0.63 seconds quicker than the later three-year-old fillies' Listed contest.
Anna Towkaska Official explanation: jockey said filly shortened its stride

2598 BATHWICK TYRES H'CAP 1m (S)
3:15 (3:18) (Class 5) (0-75,75) 3-Y-0 **£3,886** (£1,156; £577; £288) **Stalls** High

Form RPR

40-0 **1** **Altar (IRE)**[21] 1974 3-9-5 **73** .... RyanMoore 8 77
(R Hannon) *disp ld over 2f: styd chsng ldrs: rdn over 2f out: kpt on u.p fnl f to ld last strides* **16/1**

3-10 **2** shd **Rule Of Life**[23] 1920 3-9-7 **75** .... RichardHughes 16 79
(B W Hills) *stdd s: sn in tch: reminders 3f out: hrd drvn over 1f out and strong run u.p ins fnl f: fin wl: nt quite get up* **7/1**

10-1 **3** *shd* **Oceana Gold**[27] 1815 3-9-0 **73** WilliamBuick(5) 1 77
(A M Balding) *sn slt ld: pushed along over 2f out: kpt on wl fnl f tl ct last strides* **9/4**[1]

-105 **4** *1 1/4* **Shake On It**[10] 2313 3-9-7 **75** (t) StephenCarson 9 76
(Eve Johnson Houghton) *chsd ldrs: rdn to chal ins fnl 2f: styd pressing ldr tl wknd cl home* **14/1**

-155 **5** *1/2* **Tifernati**[18] 2061 3-9-2 **70** (p) J-PGuillambert 14 70
(W J Haggas) *chsd ldrs: rdn over 2f out: kpt on under presure fnl f but no ex* **10/1**

351 **6** *3* **Ridgewell (USA)**[96] 661 3-9-5 **73** JimmyFortune 6 66
(B J Meehan) *chsd ldrs: rdn over 2f out: wknd fnl f* **25/1**

-150 **7** *1 1/4* **Sir Liam (USA)**[20] 1987 3-9-7 **75** JamieSpencer 10 65
(P Mitchell) *in rr: rdn and sme hdwy 2f out: nvr gng pce to be competitive* **20/1**

0-11 **8** *shd* **Golden Prospect**[26] 1850 3-9-3 **71** EddieAhern 2 61
(J W Hills) *trckd ldrs: stl travelling wl over 2f out: rdn over 1f out: sn wknd* **5/1**[2]

35-3 **9** *5* **Fairly Honest**[31] 1722 3-9-3 **71** TQuinn 3 49
(D R C Elsworth) *mid-div: rdn and sme prog 3f out: nvr rchd ldrs: wknd 2f out* **11/1**

614- **10** *1* **Tom Paris**[213] 6458 3-9-7 **75** MartinDwyer 13 51
(W R Muir) *s.i.s: a towards rr* **33/1**

34-1 **11** *12* **Atraas (IRE)**[17] 2077 3-9-7 **75** RHills 15 23
(M P Tregoning) *chsd ldrs: rdn 3f out: sn wknd* **6/1**[3]

41-0 **12** *3* **Zefooha (FR)**[21] 1974 3-9-5 **73** SamHitchcott 5 15
(M R Channon) *rdn into mid-div 1/2-way: nvr in contention and sn wknd* **20/1**

40-0 **13** *3* **Christalini**[21] 1974 3-9-3 **71** RichardSmith 12 6
(J C Fox) *s.i.s: a in rr* **66/1**

-4P0 **14** *4* **Lights Of Vegas**[21] 1974 3-9-3 **71** PJSmullen 7 —
(B J Meehan) *bhd fr 1/2-way* **40/1**

1m 38.55s (-2.07) **Going Correction** -0.20s/f (Firm) **14** Ran SP% **124.4**
Speed ratings (Par 99):102,101,101,100,100 97,95,95,90,89 77,74,71,67
CSF £118.94 CT £366.02 TOTE £21.70: £5.90, £2.40, £1.70; EX 165.50.
Owner Highclere Thoroughbred Racing XLII **Bred** James Nally **Trained** East Everleigh, Wilts
■ Stewards' Enquiry : Ryan Moore one-day ban: used whip with excessive frequency (Jun 25)
Richard Hughes one-day ban: used whip with excessive frequency (Jun 25)

FOCUS
A modest handicap, but just 5lb separated the entire field and it was very competitive. The form is probably sound, rated though the second and third, but hard to rate too positively. They raced up the middle of the track.
Fairly Honest Official explanation: jockey said gelding hung left
Atraas(IRE) Official explanation: trainer said gelding had a breathing problem

2599 LORD WEINSTOCK MEMORIAL STKS (REGISTERED AS THE BALLYMACOLL STUD STAKES) (LISTED RACE) (FILLIES) 1m 2f 6y
3:50 (3:51) (Class 1) 3-Y-O

£14,762 (£5,595; £2,800; £1,396; £699; £351) **Stalls High**

Form RPR

0000 **1** **Darrfonah (IRE)**[13] 2211 3-8-12 **96** (t) RyanMoore 2 97
(C E Brittain) *hld up in rr: drvn and hdwy over 2f out: led 1f out: drvn out* **11/1**[3]

0-04 **2** *3/4* **Russian Rosie (IRE)**[27] 1824 3-8-12 **89** EddieAhern 1 95
(J G Portman) *in tch: trckd ldrs over 2f out: drvn to chal over 1f out: kpt on ins fnl f but a jst hld by wnr* **33/1**

6-53 **3** *shd* **Majounes Song**[26] 1855 3-8-12 **88** J-PGuillambert 3 97+
(M Johnston) *chsd ldrs: rdn and n.m.r 2f out: swtchd rt to outside and r.o fnl f but nvr gng pce to chal* **25/1**

2-46 **4** *2 1/2* **Treat**[18] 2065 3-8-12 **108** JamieSpencer 4 90
(M R Channon) *hld up in rr: pushed along over 3f out: styd on u.p to press ldrs fr 2f out: wknd ins fnl furlonh* **8/13**[1]

31- **5** *1/2* **Basaata (USA)**[176] 6886 3-8-12 **84** RHills 8 89
(M P Tregoning) *chsd ldrs: led appr fnl 2f: sn rdn: hdd 1f out: sn wknd* **6/1**[2]

4-03 **6** *1/2* **Ransom Captive (USA)**[27] 1809 3-8-12 **91** SteveDrowne 5 88
(M A Magnusson) *led tl hdd over 2f out: styd on same pce u.p* **16/1**

0 **7** *2 1/2* **Thiella (USA)**[11] 2289 3-8-12 **0** PJSmullen 6 83
(D K Weld, Ire) *in tch: rdn and sme prog fr 4f out: nvr quite gng pce to rch ldrs: wknd fr 2f out* **6/1**[2]

-621 **8** *7* **Set The Scene (IRE)**[11] 2274 3-8-12 **74** JimmyFortune 7 69
(J H M Gosden) *chsd ldr to 3f out: chal u.p over 2f out: sn wknd* **16/1**

2m 7.03s (-1.68) **Going Correction** -0.20s/f (Firm) **8** Ran SP% **117.4**
Speed ratings (Par 104):98,97,97,95,94 94,92,86
CSF £290.23 TOTE £11.30: £2.30, £5.70, £5.90; EX 279.60.
Owner Saeed Manana **Bred** Darley **Trained** Newmarket, Suffolk

FOCUS
Just an ordinary fillies' Listed contest, as is to be expected considering it falls bang in between the Oaks and Royal Ascot. The favourite was clearly not at her best and Darrfonah probably did not run up to the pick of her 2yo form. The third was a little unlucky. The early pace was nothing special and the winning time was 0.63 seconds slower than the earlier fillies' maiden.

NOTEBOOK
Darrfonah(IRE) would have appreciated this drop in grade having finished well beaten in both the 1000 Guineas and the Oaks and she was able to gain her first success since landing a conditions event here as a juvenile. She was held up last of all in a race run at no more than an ordinary gallop, but impressed with the ease in which she moved into contention and picked up well when asked. She is now likely to be aimed at the Coronation Stakes, but that will be a big ask dropping back to 1m in Group 1 company, and something like the Nassau Stakes later in the season could be more suitable if her connections continue to pitch her in at the highest level. (op 12-1)
Russian Rosie(IRE) was not beaten that far in a 1m Listed race at York on her previous start and this was an even better performance. She is clearly still improving and could well pick up some more black type.
Majounes Song, third in a Listed race in Germany on her previous start, was denied a clear run when trying to stay on and looked unlucky not to finish second, finishing strongly once switched into the clear. She might even have given the winner something to think about with more luck, although that one did look to be idling in front. (op 20-1)
Treat was well below the smart level of form she had shown when running creditably in both the English and Irish 1000 Guineas and was very disappointing. She looked to be in trouble before stamina became an issue and basically just looked to have an off day. Her connections felt she failed to stay and she is likely to be dropped back in trip next time. Official explanation: trainer said filly did not suit the trip (op 4-5 tchd 5-6 in places)
Basaata(USA), off the track since winning a 7f maiden on the Polytrack 176 days previously, ran with credit stepped up significantly in class and could build on this. (op 13-2 tchd 7-1)
Ransom Captive(USA) managed to pick up some black type in a weak race over course and distance on her previous start, but she was well held this time.
Thiella(USA) had a bit to find judged on the form she had shown in three runs in Ireland and she finished up well beaten. (op 11-2 tchd 5-1)
Set The Scene(IRE) Official explanation: jockey said filly hung left

2600 BETDAQ FIRST FOR MULTIPLES MAIDEN STKS (DIV II) 6f 8y
4:25 (4:27) (Class 3) 2-Y-O **£5,829** (£1,734; £866; £432) **Stalls High**

Form RPR

1 **River Proud (USA)** 2-9-0 **0** TQuinn 2 90+
(P F I Cole) *trckd ldrs: led appr fnl 2f: drvn and forged clr fnl f: impressive* **17/2**

2 *5* **Billion Dollar Kid** 2-9-0 **0** RichardHughes 4 75+
(R Hannon) *chsd ldrs: rdn over 2f out: styd on to go 2nd ins fnl f and styd on but nvr any ch w wnr* **7/1**

3 *3/4* **Carniolan** 2-9-0 **0** AdamKirby 9 73+
(W R Swinburn) *towards rr but in tch whn nt clr run ins fnl 2f: swtchd lft and hdwy fr over 1f out: kpt on wl fnl f but nvr in contention* **7/1**

4 *1 1/2* **Kyrie Eleison (IRE)** 2-9-0 **0** RyanMoore 10 68+
(R Hannon) *in rr: drvn along over 2f out: styd on thrght fnl f but nvr gng pce to rch ldrs* **25/1**

5 *1 1/4* **Good Gorsoon (USA)** 2-9-0 **0** MichaelHills 5 65
(B W Hills) *s.i.s: sn in tch: qcknd to chse wnr 2f out: sn rdn and one pce: wknd ins fnl f* **5/2**[1]

6 *1* **Jasmines Hero (USA)** 2-9-0 **0** EddieAhern 8 62+
(J S Moore) *s.i.s: rr: hdwy and nt clr run ins fnl 2f: swtchd lft and kpt on but nvr nr ldrs* **50/1**

45 **7** *3* **Rockfield Tiger (IRE)**[6] 2432 2-9-0 **0** JimCrowley 7 53+
(J A Osborne) *sn led: rdn 3f out: hdd over 2f out: wkng whn hmpd on rail over 1f out* **11/2**[3]

6 **8** *shd* **Liberty Island (IRE)**[26] 1846 2-9-0 **0** SteveDrowne 6 52
(B J Meehan) *chsd ldrs: rdn 3f out: wknd ins fnl 2f* **10/1**

9 *5* **Excape (IRE)** 2-9-0 **0** JamieSpencer 1 37
(D R C Elsworth) *slowly away: a struggling* **5/1**[2]

1m 12.81s (-1.51) **Going Correction** -0.20s/f (Firm) **9** Ran SP% **111.0**
Speed ratings (Par 97):102,95,94,92,90 89,85,85,78
CSF £60.84 TOTE £11.10: £2.80, £2.40, £2.10; EX 79.40.
Owner Mrs Michael Spencer **Bred** Brereton C Jones And B Ned Jones **Trained** Whatcombe, Oxon
■ Raven's Pass was withdrawn (10/1, broke out of stalls.) R4 applies, deduct 5p in the £.

FOCUS
This looked like quite a good maiden, but River Proud took them apart and looks potentially smart. The winning time was 0.30 seconds quicker than the first division. They raced towards the stands' side.

NOTEBOOK
River Proud(USA) ◆, a $75,000 half-brother to Lexi's Hoss, who was placed over 6f-1m at two, was always travelling well towards the outside of the leading group and blew his eight rivals away when asked to extend. He took around half a furlong or so to hit full stride, but he was really motoring close home and drew well clear without having to be given too hard a time. He may well join his stablemate Luck Money in the Coventry Stakes at Royal Ascot and could go close if the race does not come too soon. (op 8-1 tchd 15-2 and 9-1)
Billion Dollar Kid, a 75,000gns half-brother to 7f juvenile scorer Dora Explora, out of a multiple 7f-1m2f winner, proved no match for the impressive winner, but still quite shaped nicely back in second. He is open to improvement and should win a similar race in the coming weeks. (op 9-2)
Carniolan, an 80,000gns brother to quite useful juvenile Feathers Flying, out of a 1m winner, was denied a clear run and may have been slightly unlucky not to take second. This was an encouraging debut and he is another who should pick up a similar race. (op 5-1 tchd 8-1)
Kyrie Eleison(IRE), a 48,000gns first foal of a mare who was placed over 5f-6f, proved easy to back but this was a pleasing introduction. There should be plenty of improvement to come. (op 20-1)
Good Gorsoon(USA), $35,000 purchase, out of a winner over 1m plus in the US, failed to justify strong market support on his racecourse debut, weakening out of the places rather disappointingly late on. Official explanation: trainer said colt had a breathing problem (op 9-2)
Jasmines Hero(USA), 38,000gns half-brother to six winners, including very smart Sensation, a triple winner over 6f-7f at two in the US, out of a triple sprint scorer in the States, showed ability and might have finished closer with a clearer run. (op 40-1)
Rockfield Tiger(IRE) was well below the form he had shown on his two previous starts and this was a disappointing run. (op 9-2 tchd 4-1)
Excape(IRE), a 65,000gns purchase, out of a useful 1m-1m2f filly, attracted good market support, but he blew his chance with a very slow start. (op 7-1 tchd 8-1)

2601 BARRETTSTOWN STUD H'CAP 7f (S)
4:55 (4:57) (Class 5) (0-75,73) 3-Y-O **£3,562** (£1,059; £529; £264) **Stalls High**

Form RPR

1-02 **1** **Summer Dancer (IRE)**[18] 2061 3-9-5 **71** TQuinn 12 73+
(D R C Elsworth) *stdd s: plld hrd and settled in rr: hdwy over 2f out: hrd drvn and r.o strly fnl f to ld last strides* **2/1**[1]

4-24 **2** *nk* **Doyles Lodge**[17] 2083 3-9-6 **72** DaneO'Neill 13 74
(H Candy) *chsd ldrs: drvn to chal thrght fnl f tl no ex last strides* **9/1**

0662 **3** *hd* **Buckie Massa**[6] 2415 3-9-1 **72** WilliamBuick(5) 2 73
(S Kirk) *chsd ldrs: slt advantage appr fnl 2f: rdn and kpt on thrght fnl f tl hdd last strides* **4/1**[2]

0200 **4** *1 1/2* **Goose Green (IRE)**[2] 2545 3-8-13 **65** JimCrowley 1 62
(R J Hodges) *chsd ldrs: drvn to chal 2f out: outpcd ins fnl f* **11/1**

23-6 **5** *1/2* **Risque Heights**[10] 2317 3-9-3 **69** SteveDrowne 4 65
(G A Butler) *towards rr but in tch: rdn and hdwy over 2f out: nvr quite gng pce to rch ldrs and one pce ins fnl f* **7/1**

4565 **6** *nk* **Tipsy Prince**[9] 2335 3-9-5 **71** AdamKirby 5 66
(David Pinder) *t.k.h: chsd ldrs: chal over 2f out tl over 1f out: wknd ins fnl f* **5/1**[3]

306- **7** *nk* **Queen Noverre (IRE)**[246] 5906 3-9-7 **73** EddieAhern 6 67
(J W Hills) *in tch: drvn to chse ldrs fr 2f out: wknd fnl f* **14/1**

46-0 **8** *5* **Give Evidence**[9] 2335 3-8-13 **65** (v[1]) PaulHanagan 10 45
(A P Jarvis) *t.k.h: chsd ldrs: wknd qckly 2f out* **40/1**

0-00 **9** *1/2* **Loves Bidding**[9] 2335 3-9-6 **72** SamHitchcott 11 51
(R Ingram) *t.k.h: ld tl hdd over 2f out: wknd qckly* **66/1**

-052 **10** *2* **Kindlelight Blue (IRE)**[15] 2133 3-9-3 **69** (e) MickyFenton 8 43
(N P Littmoden) *in rr: rdn and sme prog fr 3f out: nvr rchd ldrs: wknd fr 2f out* **11/1**

1m 26.71s (-0.29) **Going Correction** -0.20s/f (Firm) **10** Ran SP% **119.8**
Speed ratings (Par 99):93,92,92,90,90 89,89,83,83,80
CSF £22.17 CT £70.36 TOTE £3.10: £1.10, £2.80, £1.80; EX 22.70.
Owner The Sunday Lunch Partnership **Bred** Eddie O'Leary **Trained** Newmarket, Suffolk

FOCUS
Just an ordinary handicap and the early pace was noticeably steady. They raced middle to stands' side. The form has been rated through the third, with the winner capabale of better.
Risque Heights Official explanation: jockey said gelding hung right
Tipsy Prince Official explanation: jockey said gelding ran too free

The Form Book, Raceform Ltd, Compton, RG20 6NL

2602 BATHWICK TYRES SWINDON H'CAP 1m 4f 5y
5:25 (5:27) (Class 5) (0-75,75) 3-Y-O £3,562 (£1,059; £529; £264) Stalls High

Form RPR

10-5 **1** **Hi Calypso (IRE)**[24] 1898 3-9-5 **73** RyanMoore 12 85
(Sir Michael Stoute) *hld up in rr: stdy hdwy over 3f out to ld appr fnl 2f: drvn and styd on wl fnl f* **15/2**

3-33 **2** *2* **Coyote Creek**[24] 1887 3-9-5 **73** JimmyFortune 6 82
(E F Vaughan) *chsd ldrs: drvn to chal appr fnl 2f: styd chsng wnr but a hld fr over 1f out* **4/1**[1]

4-35 **3** *1* **Sunley Peace**[21] 1974 3-9-6 **74** MichaelHills 3 81
(D R C Elsworth) *in tch: hdwy over 3f out: chsd ldrs fr 2f out and kpt on same pce u.p* **15/2**

1420 **4** *3/4* **Serpentaria**[27] 1827 3-9-7 **75** PaulHanagan 11 81
(Sir Mark Prescott) *led: rdn 3f out: hdd appr fnl 2f: one pce fr over 1f out* **10/1**

-006 **5** *hd* **Shine And Rise (IRE)**[23] 1927 3-8-8 **62** JimCrowley 10 67
(C G Cox) *in rr tl hdwy over 3f out: drvn to chse ldrs 2f out: sn one pce* **20/1**

4-22 **6** *1/2* **Calzaghe (IRE)**[13] 2223 3-8-6 **65** (v) WilliamBuick(5) 15 70
(A M Balding) *hld up in rr: swtchd to outside and styd on fr over 3f out: nvr quite gng pce to rch ldrs and one pce fr over 1f out* **5/1**[2]

3541 **7** *3 1/2* **Pret A Porter (UAE)**[38] 1536 3-9-3 **71** CatherineGannon 1 70
(P D Evans) *slowly away: bhd tl rdn and kpt on fr 3f out but nvr gng pce to rch ldrs* **33/1**

02-0 **8** *6* **Silmi**[47] 1290 3-9-4 **72** MartinDwyer 13 61
(E A L Dunlop) *in rr: pushed along 4f out: styd on one pce and nvr in contention* **16/1**

65-6 **9** *3 1/2* **Polish Red**[52] 1205 3-9-6 **74** EddieAhern 7 58
(G G Margarson) *in rr: rdn and sme prog into mid-div 3f out: nvr in contention after* **25/1**

63-1 **10** *3 1/2* **Mujahaz (IRE)**[27] 1810 3-9-4 **72** RHills 4 50
(J L Dunlop) *chsd ldr: rdn over 3f out: wknd over 2f out* **7/1**[3]

1 **11** *10* **Moraine**[51] 1217 3-9-7 **75** RichardHughes 16 37
(R Charlton) *rdn 5f out: a towards rr* **10/1**

-000 **12** *3* **Cavalry Twill (IRE)**[14] 2185 3-9-0 **68** TQuinn 14 25
(P F I Cole) *in tch to 1/2-way: sn rdn and wknd* **25/1**

3-05 **13** *4* **Composing (IRE)**[37] 1560 3-9-0 **68** SteveDrowne 5 19
(H Morrison) *chsd ldrs: rdn 3f out: wknd qckly sn after* **40/1**

2205 **14** *1 1/4* **My Secrets**[12] 2246 3-9-7 **75** J-PGuillambert 9 24
(M Johnston) *chsd ldrs: rdn 5f out: wknd over 3f out* **14/1**

-416 **15** *13* **Arctic Wings (IRE)**[16] 2112 3-9-5 **73** JamieSpencer 8 —
(W R Muir) *chsd ldrs tl wknd qckly 3f out: eased fnl 2f* **14/1**

2m 33.16s (-2.83) **Going Correction** -0.20s/f (Firm) **15** Ran SP% **127.9**
Speed ratings (Par 99):101,99,99,98,98 98,95,91,89,87 80,78,75,74,66
CSF £37.28 CT £246.32 TOTE £8.20: £3.90, £1.90, £2.80; EX 53.20.

Owner Philip Newton **Bred** Philip Newton **Trained** Newmarket, Suffolk

■ Stewards' Enquiry : Jimmy Fortune two-day ban: used whip with excessive force (Jun 25-26)

FOCUS
A modest but very competitive handicap. The pace seemed fair throughout and the time was decent, and the form has been rated positively with the unexposed winner up 8lb.

2603 BOLLINGER CHAMPAGNE CHALLENGE SERIES H'CAP (FOR GENTLEMAN AMATEUR RIDERS) 1m 2f 6y
5:55 (5:55) (Class 5) (0-70,69) 4-Y-0+ £3,435 (£1,065; £532; £266) Stalls High

Form RPR

0523 **1** **Bavarica**[8] 2361 5-11-3 **69** MrRBirkett(7) 1 79
(Miss J Feilden) *trckd ldrs: led over 2f out: shkn up and kpt on wl fnl f* **15/2**

1201 **2** *2* **Holiday Cocktail**[10] 2302 5-10-10 **58** ow1 MrMWalford(3) 9 64+
(J J Quinn) *hld up in rr: swtchd rt to outside and stdy hdwy fr 3f out to chse wnr appr fnl f: no imp ins fnl f* **5/2**[1]

1250 **3** *1 3/4* **Scottish River (USA)**[5] 2467 8-11-7 **66** MrLeeNewnes 3 69
(M D I Usher) *hld up in rr: hdwy fr 3f out: chsd ldrs and one pce fr over 1f out* **6/1**[3]

50-0 **4** *2* **Ermine Grey**[13] 2194 6-10-6 **54** MrMJJSmith(3) 6 53
(A W Carroll) *s.i.s: in rr: hrd rdn and sme hdwy to chse ldrs 2f out: sn one pce* **10/1**

3005 **5** *nk* **Desert Hawk**[8] 2370 6-10-0 **50** (b) MrBenBrisbourne(5) 8 48
(W M Brisbourne) *mid-div: rdn over 3f out: kpt on fr over 1f out but nvr in contention* **9/1**

-004 **6** *3/4* **Rawaabet (IRE)**[10] 2321 5-10-5 **55** oh3 MrSWalker 7 46
(P W Hiatt) *in rr: sme hdwy fr 3 out: nvr rchd ldrs and one pce fnl 2f* **6/1**[3]

5040 **7** *1/2* **Casablanca Minx (IRE)**[37] 1562 4-10-0 **50** oh2.. MrRichardEvans(5) 11 45
(P D Evans) *in tch: slt ld 3f out tl hdd over 2f out: wknd fr 2f out* **20/1**

13-3 **8** *1 1/2* **Sol Rojo**[20] 2006 5-11-5 **67** (v) MrSPearce(3) 5 59
(J Pearce) *plld hrd: chsd ldrs: rdn 3f out: sn btn* **9/2**[2]

0-00 **9** *6* **James Street (IRE)**[8] 2358 4-11-2 **68** (b) MrRHill(7) 4 48
(J R Best) *chsd ldrs to 3f out* **25/1**

4000 **10** *8* **Royal Sailor (IRE)**[20] 2006 5-9-12 **50** oh5 MrDavidMcMinn(7) 10 14
(J Ryan) *pressed ldr tl led over 4f out: hdd 3f out: sn btn* **100/1**

/00- **11** *7* **A One (IRE)**[344] 3194 8-9-12 **50** MrDBass(7) 2 —
(H J Manners) *led tl hdd over 4f out: sn btn* **66/1**

2m 11.85s (3.14) **Going Correction** -0.20s/f (Firm) **11** Ran SP% **117.3**
Speed ratings (Par 103):79,77,76,74,74 73,73,71,67,60 55
CSF £25.78 CT £122.87 TOTE £9.20: £2.10, £1.50, £2.30; EX 41.40 Place 6 £498.93, Place 5 £323.38..

Owner Hoofbeats Racing Club **Bred** Juddmonte Farms **Trained** Exning, Suffolk
■ The first winner for Ross Birkett, son of winning trainer Julia Feilden.

FOCUS
A moderate amateur riders' handicap and, with the pace very steady through the first few furlongs, before increasing significantly rounding the home bend, the form probably wants treating with some caution. It is hard to rate positively with the winner having been beaten off this mark or lower on her last six runs. The principals tended to race down the centre of the track in the straight.

T/Jkpt: Not won. T/Plt: £750.80 to a £1 stake. Pool: £73,898.25. 71.85 winning tickets. T/Qpdt: £389.80 to a £1 stake. Pool: £3,371.70. 6.40 winning tickets. ST

2186 YARMOUTH (L-H)
Thursday, June 14

OFFICIAL GOING: Soft
Wind: Fresh, half-behind Weather: Overcast

2604 NELSON'S COUNTY MAIDEN AUCTION STKS 6f 3y
2:20 (2:22) (Class 6) 2-Y-0 £2,047 (£604; £302) Stalls High

Form RPR

52 **1** **Jebel Tara**[15] 2151 2-8-13 0 JoeFanning 5 80
(C E Brittain) *mde virtually all: rdn out* **9/4**[2]

2 *1 3/4* **Sir George (IRE)** 2-8-12 0 TedDurcan 4 74
(P W Chapple-Hyam) *chsd wnr: rdn over 1f out: styd on same pce ins fnl f* **6/4**[1]

5 **3** *1 1/2* **Karky Schultz (GER)**[12] 2241 2-9-0 0 HayleyTurner 12 71
(J M P Eustace) *sn pushed along and prom: rdn over 1f out: r.o* **10/1**

00 **4** *3* **Una Auroraborealis**[56] 1101 2-8-4 0 AdrianTNicholls 8 52
(J Ryan) *chsd ldrs: rdn over 2f out: wknd ins fnl f* **100/1**

5 *3* **Metal Madness (IRE)** 2-8-11 0 JerryO'Dwyer(3) 13 53
(M G Quinlan) *hld up in tch: rdn over 2f out: wknd over 1f out* **33/1**

6 *4* **Rapidity** 2-8-13 0 ChrisCatlin 3 40
(E J O'Neill) *s.i.s: sn pushed along into mid-div: rdn 1/2-way: wknd wl over 1f out* **11/2**[3]

0 **7** *3/4* **Tapas Lad (IRE)**[10] 2303 2-8-9 0 SaleemGolam(3) 16 37
(V Smith) *sn outpcd* **50/1**

0 **8** *nk* **Utrillo's Art (IRE)**[12] 2251 2-8-8 0 DaleGibson 14 32
(M W Easterby) *s.i.s: outpcd* **150/1**

9 *hd* **No Guilt (IRE)** 2-8-3 0 MarcHalford(3) 9 30
(J L Spearing) *s.s: outpcd* **50/1**

6 **10** *2* **Purple Ransom (IRE)**[61] 1033 2-8-13 0 EdwardCreighton 10 31
(I A Wood) *chsd ldrs over 3f* **100/1**

0 **11** *2 1/2* **Woodford**[12] 2251 2-8-10 0 PaulMulrennan 1 20
(M W Easterby) *chsd ldrs: hmpd and wknd over 2f out* **100/1**

12 *3* **Milne Bay (IRE)** 2-8-12 0 RichardMullen 2 13
(D M Simcock) *chsd ldrs: rdn: hung lft and wknd over 2f out* **33/1**

1m 16.48s (2.78) **Going Correction** +0.325s/f (Good) **12** Ran SP% **108.7**
Speed ratings (Par 91):94,91,89,85,81 76,75,74,74,72 68,64
CSF £4.84 TOTE £2.80: £1.30, £1.10, £2.40; EX 5.60 Trifecta £32.10 Pool £280.79 - 6.21 winning units..

Owner Saeed Manana **Bred** Mrs G P Booth & J Porteous **Trained** Newmarket, Suffolk
■ Slugger O'Toole was withdrawn (8/1, unruly in stalls.) R4 applies, deduct 10p in the £.

FOCUS
A modest event. The action took place down the centre and the pace was only steady. The winner had the run of things and won well enough, while the next two should also win races.

NOTEBOOK
Jebel Tara, runner-up in a novice event here last month, was soon in front and ran on strongly to get off the mark at the third time of asking. He handled the underfoot conditions well and is set to go the nursery route in time. (op 5-2 tchd 11-4 and 2-1)
Sir George(IRE), who cost 22,000 euros as a yearling, is a out of a mare who has produced several winners in Italy. He was never far from the action, but lacked the pace of the more experienced winner in the latter stages. He does lack a bit of scope but can win in ordinary company. (op 11-8 tchd 5-4 and 7-4)
Karky Schultz(GER) ◆, by the same sire as the winner, built on his debut experience and ran a promising race, running on in taking style through the final furlong. He should get 7f and a modest race can be found for him. (op 14-1 tchd 20-1)
Una Auroraborealis, tackling 6f for the first time, showed pace but could not stick with the principals in the latter stages. She is now qualified for nurseries.
Metal Madness(IRE) is a half-brother to Beautiful Madness, placed over 6f for the same connections last year, out of a half-sister to top-class miler Air Express. He faded in the closing stages after showing up well. (op 25-1)
Rapidity has a mixture of speed and stamina in his pedigree, as his sire was a sprinter and his dam comes from the family of middle-distance stayers Moon Madness and Sheriff's Star. A scopey sort, he was distinctly green on this debut and is going to require time, but still showed signs of ability and is one to keep an eye on. (op 10-1 tchd 5-1)

2605 GREAT YARMOUTH FRIDAY GATEWAY CLUB (S) STKS 7f 3y
2:50 (2:51) (Class 6) 2-Y-0 £1,943 (£578; £288; £144) Stalls Low

Form RPR

6643 **1** **Miss Willoughby**[3] 2517 2-8-6 0 ChrisCatlin 1 50
(J Ryan) *led: hdd over 4f out: led over 1f out: edgd rt ins fnl f: drvn out* **14/1**

0 **2** *1 1/4* **Distant Noble**[3] 2510 2-8-6 0 KevinGhunowa(5) 2 52
(M J Wallace) *s.i.s: sn chsng ldrs: rdn over 1f out: styd on same pce ins fnl f* **7/4**[1]

003 **3** *1 1/2* **Redbackcappuchino (IRE)**[15] 2152 2-8-6 0 AdrianTNicholls 4 43
(J L Spearing) *trckd wnr: racd keenly: led over 4f out: hdd over 1f out: sn rdn: styd on same pce fnl f* **7/2**[3]

422 **4** *1* **Secret Meaning**[10] 2310 2-8-3 0 (p) SaleemGolam(3) 3 41
(W G M Turner) *plld hrd and prom: rdn over 2f out: no ex fnl f* **9/4**[2]

06 **5** *9* **Fraamington**[6] 2410 2-8-11 0 EdwardCreighton 5 23
(M R Channon) *chsd ldrs: rdn and hung lft over 2f out: wknd over 1f out* **8/1**

6 *15* **Culzean Bay** 2-8-6 0 RichardMullen 6 —
(A Bailey) *dwlt: sn pushed along in rr: wknd 1/2-way* **16/1**

1m 32.08s (5.48) **Going Correction** +0.325s/f (Good) **6** Ran SP% **113.0**
Speed ratings (Par 91):81,79,77,76,66 49
CSF £39.63 TOTE £10.00: £4.20, £1.50; EX 40.60.There was no bid for the winner. Distant Noble was claimed by Roy Brotherton for £5,000.

Owner B Liversage **Bred** Mrs J M Langmead **Trained** Newmarket, Suffolk

FOCUS
A modest seller, typical form for the grade, with an improved showing from the winner. They raced down the centre and the pace was only steady.

NOTEBOOK
Miss Willoughby, the most experienced in the line-up, had put up an improved showing when third on the Polytrack just three days earlier. Always up with the pace, she was back in front over a furlong out and answered her rider's calls willingly. This longer trip suited her. (op 10-1)
Distant Noble, down the field in a 6f maiden at Windsor on his debut, could not capitalise on this drop in grade. He stuck to his task and could win a similarly weak event. (op 2-1 tchd 5-2)
Redbackcappuchino(IRE), an unimaginatively named filly, has already been beaten in this grade. Collared by the winner approaching the final furlong, she stuck on and seemed to stay this longer trip. (tchd 3-1)
Secret Meaning, upped another furlong in trip, was equipped with cheekpieces for the first time and raced too keenly to get home. (op 11-4 tchd 3-1)

2606 HKB WILTSHIRES SOLICITORS MAIDEN STKS 6f 3y
3:25 (3:25) (Class 5) 3-Y-0+ £2,849 (£847; £423; £211) Stalls High

Form RPR
3 1 Vainglory (USA)[14] 2173 3-9-0 0 ... RichardMullen 16 84
(D M Simcock) *hld up: hdwy 2f out: led 1f out: r.o wl* 13/2
2 2 3 Taghreed (IRE)[17] 2083 3-8-9 0 ... TedDurcan 1 69
(W Jarvis) *s.i.s: sn chsng ldrs: led and hung rt over 1f out: hdd 1f out: styd on same pce* 11/4[2]
652 3 1 Silca Elegance[5] 2470 3-9-0 0 ... JHBowman 14 71
(M R Channon) *hld up: hdwy over 1f out: sn rdn: styd on same pce* 5/2[1]
00-2 4 5 Dragon Flame (IRE)[14] 2186 4-9-8 55 ... (v) ChrisCatlin 2 57
(M Quinn) *chsd ldrs: led over 4f out: rdn, hdd and hmpd over 1f out: sn wknd* 20/1
5 shd Bold Bobby 3-8-9 0 ... DaleGibson 5 50
(J M P Eustace) *chsd ldrs: rdn whn hmpd over 1f out: sn wknd* 16/1
6 3/4 Red Barnet 3-8-7 0 ... NSLawes[(7)] 6 52
(M W Easterby) *prom 4f* 100/1
02 7 1 1/4 Spinneret[14] 2175 3-8-9 0 ... PhilipRobinson 4 43
(M A Jarvis) *led: hdd over 4f out: wknd over 1f out* 11/2[3]
0- 8 1 1/4 Water Margin (IRE)[260] 5607 3-9-0 0 ... RobertHavlin 10 44
(T G Mills) *prom: rdn over 2f out: wknd over 1f out* 20/1
00-0 9 2 Samdaniya[8] 2369 3-8-9 74 ... NashRawiller 7 33
(C E Brittain) *chsd ldrs: wkng whn hmpd over 1f out* 14/1
10 1/2 Buffy Boo 4-9-3 0 ... JoeFanning 13 33
(C R Egerton) *hld up: swtchd lft over 3f out: hdwy over 2f out: wknd fnl f* 50/1
0 11 1 1/4 Bidding Time[55] 1128 3-8-9 0 ... HayleyTurner 12 27
(M L W Bell) *hld up: rdn over 3f out: a in rr* 40/1
40 12 1 1/4 Oh Mary (IRE)[19] 2046 3-8-9 0 ... PaulMulrennan 3 23
(W J Haggas) *mid-div: lost pl 1/2-way: sn bhd* 22/1
05 13 6 Apolina[14] 2186 3-8-6 0 ... SaleemGolam[(3)] 8 4
(P S McEntee) *prom: lost pl 5f out: sn bhd* 100/1
14 1/2 Sea Willow (IRE) 3-8-11 0 ... MarcHalford[(3)] 9 7
(D R C Elsworth) *s.s: outpcd* 33/1
15 3 With Ease (IRE) 3-9-0 0 ... IanMongan 15 —
(P W D'Arcy) *s.s: outpcd* 28/1

1m 15.03s (1.33) **Going Correction** +0.325s/f (Good)
WFA 3 from 4yo 8lb 15 Ran SP% **123.1**
Speed ratings (Par 103):104,100,98,92,91 90,89,87,84,84 82,80,72,72,68
CSF £22.65 TOTE £8.60: £2.70, £1.50, £1.20; EX 27.00 Trifecta £69.60 Pool £258.95 - 2.64 winning units..
Owner DXB Bloodstock Ltd **Bred** Darley **Trained** Newmarket, Suffolk

FOCUS
A modest maiden in which the first three finished clear. The form seems fairly solid. Vainglory did it well but may pay for it with the Handicapper.

2607 JUNE'S SPECIAL BIRTHDAY FILLIES' H'CAP 1m 3y
4:00 (4:02) (Class 6) (0-65,65) 3-Y-0 £1,943 (£578; £288; £144) Stalls Low

Form RPR
-202 1 Susanna's Prospect (IRE)[13] 2224 3-9-0 65 ... KMay[(7)] 7 79
(B J Meehan) *chsd ldrs: led over 2f out: rdn over 1f out: jst hld on* 7/1
50-4 2 shd Froissee[13] 2203 3-8-4 55 ... KirstyMilczarek[(7)] 9 69
(N A Callaghan) *a.p: chsd wnr over 1f out: sn rdn: styd on* 13/2[3]
-502 3 4 Rebel Pearl (IRE)[16] 2110 3-8-8 55 ... DominicFox[(3)] 4 59
(M G Quinlan) *led: hdd 6f out: led again over 4f out: rdn and hdd over 2f out: wknd ins fnl f* 4/1[2]
-544 4 1 Baby Dordan (IRE)[18] 2061 3-9-4 62 ... PhilipRobinson 6 64
(H J L Dunlop) *chsd ldrs: rdn over 2f out: wknd ins fnl f* 9/4[1]
-420 5 3 1/2 Astroangel[15] 2133 3-9-6 64 ... JimmyQuinn 3 58
(M H Tompkins) *hld up: hdwy 1/2-way: rdn over 2f out: wknd over 1f out* 11/1
6-00 6 7 Isobel Rose (IRE)[12] 2242 3-9-2 60 ... JHBowman 2 38
(E A L Dunlop) *s.i.s: hld up: hdwy over 2f out: rdn adn wknd wl over 1f out* 20/1
000- 7 1 1/2 Kimono My House[205] 6558 3-9-0 58 ... JoeFanning 8 32
(J G Given) *chsd ldrs over 5f* 16/1
65-5 8 nk Meeting Of Minds[157] 73 3-8-10 54 ... TedDurcan 16 28
(W Jarvis) *s.s: swtchd lft sn after s: a in rr* 14/1
0-06 9 9 She's A Softie (IRE)[14] 2186 3-8-6 50 ... RichardMullen 12 —
(C F Wall) *trckd ldrs: racd keenly: rdn and wknd over 2f out* 25/1
60-0 10 2 High Lite[14] 2192 3-8-9 53 ... (v[1]) ChrisCatlin 17 —
(M L W Bell) *s.i.s: a in rr* 33/1
4-00 11 2 Millyjean[107] 577 3-8-8 52 ... AdrianTNicholls 10 —
(John Berry) *hld up: rdn 1/2-way: sn wknd* 50/1
-430 12 6 Red Current[18] 2061 3-9-4 62 ... TomEaves 1 —
(J R Fanshawe) *hld up in tch: rdn over 3f out: wknd over 2f out* 12/1
4-40 13 8 Above And Below (IRE)[51] 1232 3-8-6 50 ... NeilPollard 13 —
(M Quinn) *led 6f out: hdd over 4f out: wknd over 3f out* 25/1
300 14 8 Verone (USA)[15] 2137 3-9-1 64 ... (t) NicolPolli[(5)] 14 —
(M Botti) *prom: rdn and lost pl over 4f out: sn bhd* 40/1

1m 42.42s (2.52) **Going Correction** +0.325s/f (Good) 14 Ran SP% **125.0**
Speed ratings (Par 94):100,99,95,94,91 84,82,82,73,71 69,63,55,47
CSF £50.10 CT £214.00 TOTE £9.20: £2.80, £2.90, £2.20; EX 67.40 Trifecta £210.70 Part won. Pool £296.79 - 0.10 winning units..
Owner Mrs Susanna O'Reilly Hyland **Bred** Rathbarry Stud **Trained** Manton, Wilts

FOCUS
A moderate fillies' handicap, run at a fair pace. The first pair came clear and the winner was up 7lb, but the form has not been rated as positively as it could have been.
Meeting Of Minds Official explanation: jockey said filly had no more to give
Millyjean Official explanation: jockey said filly had no more to give

2608 BARLEY CHALU H'CAP 6f 3y
4:35 (4:35) (Class 5) (0-75,72) 3-Y-0+ £2,914 (£867; £433; £216) Stalls High

Form RPR
0500 1 Soto[23] 1914 4-9-7 63 ... PaulMulrennan 4 72
(M W Easterby) *mde all: rdn over 1f out: r.o* 9/4[1]
3460 2 hd Mugeba[9] 2336 6-8-11 53 ... (t) JimmyQuinn 2 61+
(Miss Gay Kelleway) *hld up: hdwy over 1f out: rdn and ev ch ins fnl f: r.o* 10/3[3]
1-05 3 3 Tilly's Dream[14] 2191 4-9-11 70 ... SaleemGolam[(3)] 5 69
(P S McEntee) *trckd ldrs: plld hrd: rdn over 1f out: no ex ins fnl f* 6/1
1304 4 4 Desert Master[14] 2191 4-10-0 70 ... TedDurcan 6 57
(C F Wall) *trckd ldrs: racd keenly: rdn over 1f out: sn wknd* 3/1[2]
0006 5 2 Dunn Deal (IRE)[39] 1492 7-8-9 51 oh1 ... RichardMullen 1 32
(J Balding) *plld hrd: sn trcking wnr: rdn over 2f out: wknd over 1f out* 5/1

1m 15.73s (2.03) **Going Correction** +0.325s/f (Good)
WFA 3 from 4yo+ 8lb 5 Ran SP% **109.8**
Speed ratings (Par 103):99,98,94,89,86
CSF £9.88 TOTE £3.90: £1.50, £2.10; EX 11.90.
Owner D Sugars & J Crickmore **Bred** D Sugars And B Parker **Trained** Sheriff Hutton, N Yorks

FOCUS
A modest sprint handicap, run at an uneven pace. The winner had more the run of the race than the second. Pretty ordinary form.
Desert Master Official explanation: jockey said gelding hung right
Dunn Deal(IRE) Official explanation: jockey said gelding hung right

2609 BBC RADIO NORFOLK H'CAP 1m 3f 101y
5:05 (5:08) (Class 6) (0-65,65) 3-Y-0 £1,943 (£578; £288; £144) Stalls Low

Form RPR
0051 1 Pretty Demanding (IRE)[8] 2362 3-9-4 62 6ex ... TedDurcan 2 77+
(M G Quinlan) *hld up: hdwy over 4f out: rdn to ld over 1f out: sn hung lft: styd on* 2/1[1]
05-1 2 3/4 Raise The Goblet (IRE)[14] 2192 3-8-13 57 ... PaulMulrennan 4 68
(W J Haggas) *a.p: chsd ldr over 4f out: rdn over 2f out: nt clr run ent fnl f: styd on* 7/2[2]
-552 3 1 1/4 Silver Mitzva (IRE)[8] 2362 3-8-7 56 ... (b[1]) NicolPolli[(5)] 9 65
(M Botti) *led over 10f out: clr 1/2-way: rdn and hdd over 1f out: styd on same pce ins fnl f* 13/2
200- 4 18 Watch Out[247] 5901 3-8-1 48 ow1 ... AndrewMullen[(3)] 7 28
(M W Easterby) *hld up: rdn over 7f out: nvr nrr* 66/1
0-00 5 3/4 Super Nebula[20] 2005 3-8-12 59 ... DominicFox[(3)] 6 38
(P L Gilligan) *led 1f: chsd ldr tl rdn over 4f out: wknd over 3f out* 22/1
0640 6 4 President Dan[52] 1194 3-9-2 60 ... IanMongan 8 33
(M R Channon) *prom: lost pl 1/2-way: rdn and wknd over 4f out* 40/1
0-03 7 3/4 Blockley (USA)[14] 2192 3-8-13 57 ... (t) TomEaves 14 28
(Ian Williams) *chsd ldrs: rdn over 6f out: wknd over 4f out* 11/2[3]
-055 8 shd Lindhoven (USA)[13] 2224 3-9-2 60 ... (b) RichardMullen 3 31
(C E Brittain) *hld up: hdwy 1/2-way: rdn over 4f out: sn wknd* 14/1
-440 9 26 Astrolibra[23] 1917 3-8-13 57 ... JimmyQuinn 1 —
(M H Tompkins) *mid-div: hdwy 1/2-way: rdn and wknd over 3f out* 15/2
050- 10 23 Glorious View[266] 5495 3-8-4 48 ... DaleGibson 13 —
(M W Easterby) *hld up: reminders 8f out: wknd 1/2-way: eased fnl 4f* 40/1
225- P Go Dude[167] 6976 3-9-7 65 ... (p) RobertHavlin 5 —
(J Ryan) *s.i.s: a in rr: lost tch fnl 4f: t.o whn p.u over 1f out* 28/1

2m 34.33s (6.83) **Going Correction** +0.55s/f (Yiel) 11 Ran SP% **116.9**
Speed ratings (Par 97):97,96,95,82,81 79,78,78,59,42 —
CSF £8.25 CT £37.97 TOTE £2.80: £1.10, £1.80, £2.20; EX 10.20 Trifecta £24.90 Pool £364.01 - 10.35 winning units..
Owner L Mulryan & M C Fahy **Bred** Moyglare Stud Farm Ltd **Trained** Newmarket, Suffolk

FOCUS
Three progressive horses pulled some 18 lengths clear in what was a modest handicap with not much strength in depth. The form could be underrated, but the soft ground strikes a cautious note.
Go Dude Official explanation: jockey said gelding never travelled

2610 GREAT YARMOUTH MERCURY H'CAP 1m 6f 17y
5:35 (5:36) (Class 5) (0-70,70) 3-Y-0 £2,914 (£867; £433; £216) Stalls Low

Form RPR
0-12 1 Credit Slip[16] 2105 3-8-11 60 ... IanMongan 14 72+
(J L Dunlop) *s.i.s: hld up: hdwy 8f out: lost pl 6f out: hdwy over 4f out: led and hung rt over 2f out: rdn and hung lft over 1f out: jst hld on* 9/4[1]
4-06 2 nk Last Flight (IRE)[21] 1972 3-8-11 60 ... PhilipRobinson 12 70
(J L Dunlop) *hld up: hdwy 8f out: rdn over 2f out: styd on u.p* 14/1
3452 3 9 Dana Music (USA)[23] 1916 3-9-7 70 ... JHBowman 1 67
(M R Channon) *chsd ldrs: led 4f out: hdd over 2f out: wknd fnl f* 13/2[2]
0-25 4 1 1/2 Super Sifted (GER)[22] 1950 3-9-0 63 ... TedDurcan 5 58
(H R A Cecil) *hld up in tch: rdn over 2f out: sn wknd* 8/1
-000 5 2 1/2 Tobougg Welcome (IRE)[118] 484 3-8-3 52 oh6 ow1 AdrianTNicholls 10 43
(S C Williams) *hld up: rdn over 4f out: nvr nrr* 20/1
5321 6 3 1/2 Color Man[17] 2096 3-8-5 54 ... (p) DaleGibson 11 41
(Mrs A J Perrett) *sn pushed along and prom: led 7f out: rdn and hdd 4f out: hung lft and wknd over 2f out* 7/1[3]
4044 7 nk Personal Column[31] 1724 3-9-6 69 ... RobertHavlin 7 55
(T G Mills) *led: hdd over 11f out: chsd ldrs tl rdn and wknd over 2f out* 10/1
0000 8 14 Dancewiththestars (USA)[14] 2192 3-8-3 52 ... RichardMullen 6 18
(J R Fanshawe) *s.i.s: hld up: rdn over 4f out: n.d* 25/1
-405 9 3 Kingsmead (USA)[17] 2096 3-8-3 55 ow2 ... (p) SaleemGolam[(3)] 4 17
(Miss J Feilden) *chsd ldrs 10f* 16/1
0-00 10 27 Best Warning[14] 2192 3-7-13 51 oh6 ... DominicFox[(3)] 13 —
(J Ryan) *chsd ldrs over 10f* 100/1
535 11 18 Force Celebre (IRE)[23] 1937 3-9-7 70 ... JimmyQuinn 3 —
(M H Tompkins) *hld up: rdn over 6f out: bhd fnl 4f* 7/1[3]
0020 12 10 Laughing Game[12] 2259 3-8-9 58 ... HayleyTurner 2 —
(M L W Bell) *hld up: plld hrd: rdn oevr 5f out: sn wknd* 20/1
2033 13 36 Anne Bronte[13] 2223 3-9-2 65 ... JoeFanning 9 —
(M Johnston) *w ldr tl led over 11f out: hdd 7f out: lost pl 6f out: sn wknd* 12/1

3m 14.96s (9.66) **Going Correction** +0.55s/f (Yiel) 13 Ran SP% **123.9**
Speed ratings (Par 99):94,93,88,87,86 84,84,76,74,59 48,43,22
CSF £37.31 CT £191.66 TOTE £2.80: £1.40, £5.40, £3.20; EX 35.40 TRIFECTA Not won. Place 6 £11.43, Place 5 £9.44..
Owner Hesmonds Stud **Bred** Hesmonds Stud Ltd **Trained** Arundel, W Sussex

FOCUS
Just a modest handicap, but the two Dunlop runners put distance between themselves and the remainder. The winner is not straightforward but is better than this bare form, with the second up 9lb.
Force Celebre(IRE) Official explanation: jockey said gelding never travelled
Laughing Game Official explanation: trainer's rep said filly was in season
Anne Bronte Official explanation: jockey said filly never travelled
T/Plt: £12.10 to a £1 stake. Pool: £52,696.25. 3,162.95 winning tickets. T/Qpdt: £4.00 to a £1 stake. Pool: £2,398.00. 437.30 winning tickets. CR

2611 - 2616a (Foreign Racing) - See Raceform Interactive

2100 LONGCHAMP (R-H)

Thursday, June 14

OFFICIAL GOING: Good

2617a LA COUPE (GROUP 3) 1m 2f

2:50 (2:53) 4-Y-O+ **£27,027** (£10,811; £8,108; £5,405; £2,703)

RPR

1 **Stage Gift (IRE)**105 600 4-9-2 .... KerrinMcEvoy 4 115
(Saeed Bin Suroor) *mde all: rdn over 1f out: drvn out* **18/10**2

2 ¾ **Willywell (FR)**25 1879 5-8-12 .... IMendizabal 1 109
(J-P Gauvin, France) *trckd wnr: chal and ev ch over 1f out: rdn 1f out: one pce* **89/10**

3 2 **Atlantic Air (FR)**98 642 5-8-12 .... OPeslier 2 105
(Y De Nicolay, France) *disp 3rd: 4th st: nvr able to chal* **21/1**

4 8 **Numide (FR)**14 4-8-12 .... C-PLemaire 8 89
(J-C Rouget, France) *disp 3rd on outside: 3rd st: btn wl over 1f out* **6/5**1

5 dist **Blushing King (FR)**14 5-8-12 .... YGourraud 6 —
(J-L Guillochon, France) *last whn bdly hmpd by fallers wl over 2f out: completed crse* **41/1**

B **Musical Way (FR)**15 2165 5-8-13 .... RonanThomas 3 —
(P Van De Poele, France) *6th whn b.d wl over 2f out* **73/10**3

S **Formal Decree (GER)**75 862 4-9-2 .... LDettori 7 —
(Saeed Bin Suroor) *5th whn slipped up on turn wl over 2f out* **18/10**2

P **Kilometre Neuf (FR)**19 4-8-12 .... DBoeuf 5 —
(F Doumen, France) *7th whn bdly hmpd by fallers wl over 2f out: p.u* **12/1**

2m 6.60s (-1.40) **8** Ran SP% **153.7**

PARI-MUTUEL: WIN 2.80 (coupled with Formal Decree); PL 5.10, 3.10,5.50; DF 83.20.

Owner Godolphin **Bred** Ballymacoll Stud Farm Ltd **Trained** Newmarket, Suffolk

NOTEBOOK

Stage Gift(IRE) was the stable second-string on jockey bookings, but Dettori's mount, Formal Decree, slipped up early on. He proved an able deputy, responding well to pressure in the straight having led at a sensible pace, and he ultimately looked to win with a little bit in hand.

Willywell(FR), immediately settled behind the leader, was given every possible chance but was always being held.

Atlantic Air(FR), in mid-division in the early part of the race, missed the multiple fall and was still fourth coming into the straight. He ran on for pressure but never looked like catching the front two.

Numide(FR) was nervous before the start, something that has happened in the past, and was a very disappointing favourite. He came back with a shoe missing and that may go some way to explaining this below-par showing.

Formal Decree(GER), who did not settle well in the early part of the race, did not handle the bend that well and slipped up. Happily, neither jockey nor horse were worse for wear.

2103 CHEPSTOW (L-H)

Friday, June 15

OFFICIAL GOING: Good to soft changing to soft after race 1 (6:30)

Wind: Nil Weather: Heavy showers

2618 WATERAID IN WALES /E.B.F. NOVICE STKS 6f 16y

6:30 (6:30) (Class 4) 2-Y-O **£4,533** (£1,348; £674; £336) **Stalls High**

Form RPR

1 1 **Gaspar Van Wittel (USA)**17 2103 2-9-5 0 .... DaneO'Neill 3 95+
(N A Callaghan) *s.i.s: hld up: hdwy to chse ldr 3f out: rdn to ld 1f out: sn clr* **2/7**1

1 2 8 **Star Of Rosanna**18 2087 2-8-7 0 .... KDarley 4 59
(K A Ryan) *led: rdn and hdd 1f out: sn btn* **7/2**2

10 3 3 **Nestor Protector (IRE)**25 1882 2-8-12 0 .... SteveDrowne 2 55
(A B Haynes) *hld up in tch: hung lft fr over 4f out: wknd wl over 1f out* **25/1**3

05 4 nk **Insomnitas**16 2151 2-8-10 0 ow1 .... JerryO'Dwyer(3) 5 55
(M G Quinlan) *hld up: outpcd 3f out: n.d after* **25/1**3

5 3½ **Whatalotofbuts** 2-8-12 0 .... LPKeniry 1 44
(B De Haan) *chsd ldr 3f: sn rdn and wknd* **50/1**

1m 16.12s (3.72) **Going Correction** +0.65s/f (Yiel) **5** Ran SP% **109.6**

Speed ratings (Par 95):101,90,86,85,81

CSF £1.50 TOTE £1.30: £1.02, £1.60; EX 1.50.

Owner Matthew Green **Bred** Barronstown Stud **Trained** Newmarket, Suffolk

FOCUS

Gaspar Van Wittel impressed again and looks a decent prospect. He could have been rated up to 5lb higher, in a race best assessed through the fourth.

NOTEBOOK

Gaspar Van Wittel(USA) followed up his win in a 5f maiden here on his debut, form that has been boosted by the subsequent victory of runner-up Elna Bright. He had to work a bit to get to the leader, but streaked away in the final furlong to win in impressive style. Scoring despite the ground, he will miss Ascot and may go for the July Stakes at Newmarket next. (tchd 1-4 and 3-10)

Star Of Rosanna, winner of a claimer for Reg Hollinshead on her debut, was loaded with the help of a Monty Roberts rug. Making the running against the stands' rail, she briefly went clear before being left for dead by the smart winner in the final furlong. (tchd 4-1)

Nestor Protector(IRE), beaten in this company last time after winning a seller on his debut, was hanging from an early stage and did not see out this longer trip. Official explanation: jockey said colt hung left-handed (tchd 22-1)

Insomnitas, who beat just a single rival in his first two starts in similar company, could not go with the leaders from halfway but was not given a hard time when held and has now qualified for nurseries. (op 33-1)

Whatalotofbuts, the first foal of a mare who won at 1m7f on the Flat before going on to make quite a useful hurdler/chaser for the same owners, was not surprisingly outpaced in the second half of the contest. (op 40-1)

2619 WHITLAND ENGINEERING CLAIMING STKS 7f 16y

7:00 (7:01) (Class 6) 3-Y-O+ **£1,943** (£578; £288; £144) **Stalls High**

Form RPR

-000 1D **Zantero**3 2540 5-8-8 44 .... KevinGhunowa(5) 3 53
(M A Doyle) *hld up: hdwy 2f out: rdn to ld ins fnl f: drvn out; fin1st, 1l; disq* **50/1**

2261 1 **Mick Is Back**17 2110 3-8-12 61 ....(p) FergusSweeney 5 55
(J R Boyle) *hld up in mid-div: hdwy over 3f out: sn rdn and edgd lft: led over 1f out tl ins fnl f: nt qckn: fin 2nd, 1l: subs awrdd r* **2/1**1

0002 2 2 **Mannello**3 2540 4-8-12 49 ....(p) CatherineGannon 12 47
(B Palling) *a.p: rdn over 1f out: ev ch ins fnl f: nt qckn: fin 3rd, 1l & 1l: plcd 2nd* **13/2**3

2535 3 2½ **Dexileos (IRE)**1 2591 8-8-10 42 ow2 .... ChrisCavanagh(7) 11 45
(David Pinder) *a.p: led 3f out: rdn and hdd over 1f out: no ex fnl f: fin4th, plcd 3rd* **16/1**

0000 4 1½ **Filey Buoy**18 2091 5-8-8 43 ....(v) NataliaGemelova(5) 15 37
(R M Whitaker) *w ldrs: rdn over 3f out: ev ch 2f out: sn edgd lft: wknd 1f out: fin 5th, plcd 4th* **33/1**

6-00 5 ½ **She Whispers (IRE)**24 1933 4-8-10 41 .... LPKeniry 6 33
(R Hollinshead) *hld up in tch: nt clr run wl over 1f out: sn swtchd rt and rdn: wknd ins fnl f: fin 6th, plcd 5th* **66/1**

4-05 6 nk **Full Spate**15 2187 12-9-3 48 .... SteveDrowne 13 39
(J M Bradley) *hld up: sn mid-div: rdn over 2f out: no hdwy fnl f: fin 7th, plcd 6th* **10/1**

6050 7 nk **Mine The Balance (IRE)**13 2258 4-8-8 48 .... ThomasO'Brien(7) 14 37
(H J Manners) *led over 2f: rdn over 3f out: wknd wl over 1f out: fin 8th, plcd 7th* **25/1**

000- 8 2 **What-A-Dancer (IRE)**212 6493 10-8-12 59 ....(b) JamesMillman(5) 7 33
(R A Harris) *t.k.h in mid-div: bhd fnl 4f: fin 9th, plcd 8th* **11/1**

404 9 1¾ **Savile's Delight (IRE)**17 2104 8-8-13 48 ....(v) KDarley 16 25
(Miss Joanne Priest) *chsd ldrs: rdn 2f out: wknd over 1f out: fin 10th, plcd 9th* **11/1**

6000 10 hd **Lizarazu (GER)**17 2107 8-9-4 58 ....(p) LukeMorris(5) 4 34
(R A Harris) *t.k.h: prom: led over 4f out to 3f out: sn rdn: wknd over 1f out: fin 11th, plcd 10th* **4/1**2

200- 11 12 **Emperor Cat (IRE)**206 6552 6-9-3 47 .... RobertHavlin 2 —
(Mrs N S Evans) *hld up in mid-div: rdn over 3f out: sn bhd; fin 12th, plcd 11th* **50/1**

0000 12 4 **Goodwood Spirit**10 2334 5-8-10 55 ....(p) BarrySavage(7) 10 —
(J M Bradley) *s.i.s: a bhd: fin 13th, plcd 12th* **15/2**

1m 27.43s (4.13) **Going Correction** +0.65s/f (Yiel)

WFA 3 from 4yo+ 10lb **13** Ran SP% **122.3**

Speed ratings (Par 101):102,100,99,96,95 94,94,93,91,89 89,75,71

CSF £150.24 TOTE £94.00: £17.10, £1.30, £2.40; EX 157.40.Mannello was claimed by Diane Cooper for £7,000

Owner The Duncow Racing Partnership **Bred** Stanley Estate And Stud Co **Trained** Leominster, H'fords

■ Trainer Mark Doyle's first and only winner, and he lost it when Zantero was later disqualified.

FOCUS

A poor claimer but Zantero was subs. disq (methylprednisolone in sample) M. Doyle fined £750

Zantero Official explanation: trainer said, regarding apparent improvement in form, that the gelding was better suited by being held up.

2620 DANIEL CONTRACTORS SUPPORTING WATERAID IN WALES MAIDEN FILLIES' STKS 1m 4f 23y

7:35 (7:35) (Class 5) 3-Y-O+ **£2,914** (£867; £433; £216) **Stalls Low**

Form RPR

0-3 1 **Baba Ganouge (IRE)**11 2320 3-8-12 0 .... KDarley 7 81+
(B J Meehan) *mde all: clr over 1f out: r.o wl* **7/1**

0 2 11 **Sadler's Leap (IRE)**17 2127 4-9-13 0 .... PaulEddery 1 63
(Pat Eddery) *a.p: rdn 3f out: sn outpcd: tk 2nd ins fnl f: no ch w wnr* **5/1**3

0-03 3 ¾ **Ashmal (USA)**29 1785 3-8-12 75 .... DaneO'Neill 2 62+
(J L Dunlop) *chsd ldrs: wnt 2nd over 3f out: rdn over 2f out: wknd over 1f out* **3/1**2

5 4 nk **Berry Hill Lass (IRE)**9 2359 3-8-12 0 .... RobertHavlin 9 61
(J G M O'Shea) *hld up towards rr: hdwy 5f out: hung lft over 2f out: one pce* **20/1**

20-0 5 5 **Nimra (USA)**29 1793 4-9-13 75 .... FrancisNorton 4 53
(G A Butler) *hld up in mid-div: rdn over 3f out: sn btn* **2/1**1

0 6 15 **Esclarmonde (IRE)**29 1785 3-8-12 0 .... NickyMackay 11 29
(L M Cumani) *a bhd* **15/2**

5 7 1¾ **Looktheotherway (IRE)**9 2360 3-8-12 0 .... FergusSweeney 6 27
(J G M O'Shea) *chsd wnr tl wknd over 3f out* **33/1**

0-0 8 22 **Pure Velvet (IRE)**14 2196 3-8-12 0 .... LPKeniry 10 —
(S Kirk) *a bhd: lost tch fnl 4f: t.o* **66/1**

50- 9 nk **Corviglia**254 5770 4-9-13 0 .... SamHitchcott 5 —
(C E Longsdon) *hld up in mid-div: shortlived effrt on outside over 4f out: t.o* **66/1**

10 shd **Boekenhoutskloof (IRE)** 3-8-12 0 .... SteveDrowne 3 —
(E F Vaughan) *a bhd: t.o* **16/1**

0-0 11 12 **Fancy Woman**28 1816 3-8-12 0 .... ChrisCatlin 8 —
(J L Dunlop) *a bhd: t.o fnl 5f* **40/1**

2m 45.47s (6.75) **Going Correction** +0.65s/f (Yiel)

WFA 3 from 4yo 15lb **11** Ran SP% **118.3**

Speed ratings (Par 100):103,95,95,94,91 81,80,65,65,65 57

CSF £40.46 TOTE £6.00: £2.00, £2.10, £1.60; EX 26.50.

Owner Miss C A Green **Bred** T W Bloodstock Ltd **Trained** Manton, Wilts

FOCUS

Baba Ganouge ran out a wide-margin winner of this maiden, but it is hard to know what she achieved as several rivals failed to run their race.

2621 YOUNG BROS CIVIL ENGINEERING H'CAP 1m 2f 36y

8:10 (8:11) (Class 5) (0-75,73) 4-Y-O+ **£2,914** (£867; £433; £216) **Stalls Low**

Form RPR

6-02 1 **Olimpo (FR)**11 2321 6-8-13 70 .... JamesMillman(5) 8 79
(B R Millman) *n.m.r s: hld up and bhd: hdwy 3f out: rdn to ld ins fnl f: r.o* **11/4**1

5322 2 ¾ **Augustine**17 2113 6-9-2 68 .... ChrisCatlin 6 76
(P W Hiatt) *t.k.h: chsd ldrs: rdn and ev ch 2f out: r.o ins fnl f* **9/2**3

0 3 1¼ **Oldrik (GER)**17 2106 4-8-10 62 .... KDarley 9 67
(P J Hobbs) *hld up in tch: rdn to ld over 1f out: hdd ins fnl f: no ex* **7/1**

04-0 4 2½ **Dove Cottage (IRE)**35 1638 5-9-4 70 .... LPKeniry 10 70
(W S Kittow) *w ldr: led over 2f out: rdn and hdd over 1f out: sn btn* **8/1**

0550 5 4 **Optimus (USA)**8 2403 5-9-7 73 ....(b1) FergusSweeney 4 65
(B G Powell) *hld up in rr: hung lft fr over 3f out: nvr trbld ldrs* **9/1**

-300 6 2 **Coup D'Etat**11 2311 5-9-1 72 ....(p) LukeMorris(5) 2 60
(R A Harris) *wnt rt s: t.k.h: led: hdd over 2f out: wknd wl over 1f out* **8/1**

-310 7 18 **Montchara (IRE)**28 1813 4-9-0 66 .... SteveDrowne 5 18
(G Wragg) *n.m.r s: hld up: rdn over 3f out: sn struggling* **10/3**2

2m 16.47s (6.57) **Going Correction** +0.65s/f (Yiel) **7** Ran SP% **112.6**

Speed ratings (Par 103):99,98,97,95,92 90,76

CSF £14.87 CT £75.78 TOTE £3.30: £2.40, £1.90; EX 9.90.

Owner Christine And Aubrey Loze **Bred** Ewar Stud Farm **Trained** Kentisbeare, Devon

FOCUS

A fair handicap and straightforward to rate, with Olimpo back to last year's course form.

Montchara(IRE) Official explanation: jockey said gelding had no more to give

2622 BURDENS WATERAID CHALLENGE MAIDEN H'CAP 6f 16y

8:45 (8:47) (Class 5) (0-70,65) 3-Y-O+ **£2,914** (£867; £433; £216) **Stalls High**

Form RPR

0020 1 **Toms Laughter**3 2545 3-9-1 55 .... CatherineGannon 4 63
(B Palling) *s.i.s: rdn and hdwy over 2f out: r.o to ld nr fin* **8/1**

53 2 nk **Kelamon**19 2061 3-9-10 64 .... RobertHavlin 2 71
(M D I Usher) *hld up in mid-div: hdwy over 2f out: rdn to ld over 1f out: hdd nr fin* **5/2**1

600- **3** *4* **Beat The Bully**[202] 6592 3-9-3 **57** KDarley 15 52
(I A Wood) *outpcd: sn swtchd lft: rdn and hdwy over 1f out: r.o ins fnl f: tk 3rd post* **20/1**
00-0 **4** *shd* **Willofcourse**[16] 2143 6-8-13 **52** AmyScott(7) 8 49
(H Candy) *w ldr: led wl over 1f out: sn hdd: wknd wl ins fnl f* **13/2**[3]
30-0 **5** *2* **Turkish Sultan (IRE)**[38] 1564 4-10-0 **60** LPKeniry 3 51
(J M Bradley) *a.p: rdn over 1f out: wknd wl ins fnl f* **13/2**[3]
-600 **6** *hd* **Kyllachy Storm**[30] 1763 3-9-0 **54** (b) SteveDrowne 10 42
(R J Hodges) *a.p: rdn over 2f out: wknd fnl f* **16/1**
2040 **7** *½* **Ceredig**[2] 2561 4-9-2 **55** WilliamCarson(7) 12 44
(P W Hiatt) *led: rdn over 2f out: hdd wl over 1f out: wknd ins fnl f* **5/1**[2]
0/50 **8** *3* **Sydneyroughdiamond**[8] 2394 5-8-13 **45** FergusSweeney 7 25
(M Mullineaux) *mid-div: rdn over 2f out: wkng whn hung lft over 2f out* **16/1**
0000 **9** *¾* **Fancy You (IRE)**[126] 403 4-8-13 **45** FrancisNorton 1 22
(A W Carroll) *prom tl wknd over 1f out* **33/1**
0-45 **10** *¾* **Kind Of Fizzy**[15] 2175 3-9-11 **65** ChrisCatlin 11 38
(Rae Guest) *mid-div: rdn 3f out: no rspnse* **10/1**
560 **11** *¾* **Fervent**[24] 1923 3-9-1 **60** KevinGhunowa(5) 6 31
(J M Bradley) *a bhd* **14/1**
06-0 **12** *5* **Knead The Dough**[14] 2221 6-8-13 **50** NataliaGemelova(5) 13 8
(A E Price) *chsd ldrs: rdn over 3f out: sn wknd* **20/1**
-060 **13** *9* **Georges Pride**[17] 2104 3-8-1 **48** ow3 (b) BarrySavage(7) 14 —
(J M Bradley) *chsd ldrs: rdn 3f out: sn wknd* **33/1**

1m 15.6s (3.20) **Going Correction** +0.65s/f (Yiel)
WFA 3 from 4yo+ 8lb 13 Ran SP% **125.9**
Speed ratings (Par 103):104,103,98,98,95 95,94,90,89,88 87,80,68
CSF £28.50 CT £418.82 TOTE £8.00: £2.90, £1.90, £3.80; EX 38.80.
Owner Five To Follow **Bred** Mrs D J Hughes **Trained** Tredodridge, Vale Of Glamorgan

FOCUS
A weak event and obviously limited form, with the winner producing much his best turf run.
Sydneyroughdiamond Official explanation: jockey said gelding hung left-handed
Fancy You(IRE) Official explanation: jockey said filly had no more to give

2623 WATERAID H'CAP 7f 16y
9:15 (9:18) (Class 5) (0-75,71) 3-Y-O+ **£3,238** (£963; £481; £240) **Stalls** High

Form RPR
6-13 **1** **Guilded Warrior**[18] 2088 4-10-0 **71** FergusSweeney 2 83
(W S Kittow) *t.k.h: set stdy pce: shkn up over 1f out: pushed clr ins fnl f: comf* **11/2**[3]
1350 **2** *3 ½* **Call My Bluff (FR)**[26] 1862 4-9-9 **66** ChrisCatlin 7 69
(Rae Guest) *plld hrd: a.p: edgd lft fr over 1f out: kpt on to take 2nd ins fnl f: no ch w wnr* **9/1**
2306 **3** *1 ¾* **Marko Jadeo (IRE)**[16] 2139 9-9-7 **69** LukeMorris(5) 4 67
(R A Harris) *t.k.h in tch: rdn and wnt 2nd over 1f out: no ex ins fnl f* **9/1**
-612 **4** *hd* **Fealeview Lady (USA)**[11] 2309 3-9-2 **69** SteveDrowne 1 67
(H Morrison) *a.p: rdn over 2f out: one pce fnl f* **11/4**[1]
50-0 **5** *4* **Red Rudy**[17] 2107 5-9-8 **65** FrancisNorton 3 53
(A W Carroll) *plld hrd: sn in rr: rdn and shortlived effrt 2f out* **10/3**[2]
4324 **6** *2* **Moon Forest (IRE)**[15] 2190 5-8-7 **55** (p) KevinGhunowa(5) 5 37
(J M Bradley) *plld hrd: prom: rdn and wknd over 1f out* **11/4**[1]

1m 28.57s (5.27) **Going Correction** +0.65s/f (Yiel)
WFA 3 from 4yo+ 10lb 6 Ran SP% **111.8**
Speed ratings (Par 103):95,91,89,88,84 81
CSF £49.56 TOTE £7.20: £2.70, £3.10; EX 49.30 Place 6 £ 107.87, Place 5 £ 106.84.
Owner The Racing Guild **Bred** Manor Farm Packers Ltd **Trained** Blackborough, Devon
■ Stewards' Enquiry : Luke Morris one-day ban: arrived at start after appointed start time (Jun 26)

FOCUS
A modest handicap in which the runners made for the centre of the track leaving the stalls. They went no pace at all until halfway with the whole field pulling, and the form is dubious.
Moon Forest(IRE) Official explanation: jockey said gelding ran too free
T/Plt: £13.20. Pool £75,490.30. 4,153.35 winning tickets T/Qpdt: £8.90. Pool £4,196.20. 346.10 winning tickets KH

2440 GOODWOOD (R-H)
Friday, June 15

OFFICIAL GOING: Straight course - good; round course - good to firm (8.0)
Wind: fresh across Weather: cloudy with bright spells

2624 EBF SOUTHERN DAILY ECHO MEDIAN AUCTION MAIDEN STKS 6f
6:20 (6:20) (Class 4) 2-Y-O **£5,019** (£1,493; £746; £372) **Stalls** Low

Form RPR
34 **1** **Berbice (IRE)**[13] 2232 2-9-3 0 RyanMoore 2 85+
(R Hannon) *mde all: rdn 1f out: edgd rt fnl f: a holding runner-up* **2/5**[1]
2 **2** *nk* **Aaim For Applause**[14] 2193 2-9-3 0 JHBowman 5 84+
(M R Channon) *pressed wnr thrght: rdn and ev ch fnl f: a hld* **7/2**[2]
0 **3** *8* **Kristal Glory (IRE)**[21] 1989 2-9-3 0 IanMongan 6 60
(J L Dunlop) *t.k.h: hld up in tch: rdn to chse ldng pair over 2f out: sn outpcd* **33/1**
0 **4** *½* **Poppy Dean (IRE)**[25] 1896 2-8-12 0 (t) EddieAhern 4 54
(J G Portman) *t.k.h: hld up in last pair: hdwy and rdn over 2f out: sn outpcd* **20/1**
00 **5** *1 ¼* **Lisselan Prospect (USA)**[7] 2424 2-9-3 0 DarryllHolland 1 55
(Mrs A J Perrett) *trckd ldrs: rdn over 2f out: sn struggling* **66/1**
6 *1* **Irish Artist (FR)** 2-9-3 0 RichardHughes 3 52+
(R Hannon) *hld up in last: rdn over 2f out: sn outpcd* **14/1**[3]

1m 13.37s (0.52) **Going Correction** +0.10s/f (Good) 6 Ran SP% **109.5**
Speed ratings (Par 95):100,99,88,88,86 85
CSF £1.87 TOTE £1.30: £1.10, £1.90; EX 2.00.
Owner Jim McCarthy **Bred** W Flynn **Trained** East Everleigh, Wilts

FOCUS
A weak pace for the trip, which favoured the front-running market leaders. The first two finished clear, both improving, and the form could have been rated a bit higher.

NOTEBOOK
Berbice(IRE) had a simple task on previous form, and the fact that the others allowed him to dictate the pace at a dawdle made it even simpler. He had to fight harder than expected, but this scopey grey can do even better when fully tested. (op 4-9 tchd 4-11)
Aaim For Applause was favoured, like the winner, by being prominent in a slowly-run affair, but he gave the odds-on favourite a good race and finished well clear of the others. He should win his share of races. (tchd 10-3)
Kristal Glory(IRE) is from a family that needs at least a mile, with his dam having won over 2m, so he will come into his own when handicapped over longer trips. (op 28-1)
Poppy Dean(IRE) is out of a dam who won over trips as far as 2m, so 7f and a mile should suit her as the season progresses. Though well beaten here, she showed some promise - as she had on her debut - and will be more in her element in nurseries. (op 16-1)
Lisselan Prospect(USA) has struggled in three maidens at this track, and looks the type for nurseries in time. His sire and dam were useful performers in the USA, and he has shown early speed himself, so there is potential for some improvement. (op 40-1)
Irish Artist(FR), a 60,000euro son of top-class miler Orpen, will need at least that distance in the long term, as his family stayed up to 1m4f. Though showing little here behind his odds-on stablemate, being held up in a race run at a funereal pace was not ideal and there is probably better to come. Official explanation: jockey said colt hung left (op 12-1)

2625 GABEM MAIDEN STKS 1m
6:50 (6:51) (Class 5) 3-Y-O **£3,562** (£1,059; £529; £264) **Stalls** High

Form RPR
52 **1** **Royal Secrets (IRE)**[14] 2219 3-8-12 0 RyanMoore 7 74+
(E A L Dunlop) *hld up in tch: nt clr run wl over 2f out tl over 1f out: swtchd lft and str run jst over 1f out: led fnl 100yds: r.o strly* **9/2**[2]
52-4 **2** *1 ¼* **Castara Bay**[46] 1358 3-9-3 78 RichardHughes 8 76
(R Hannon) *led: rdn and hrd pressed over 1f out: hdd fnl 100yds: nt pce of wnr* **11/4**[1]
4 **3** *shd* **Viva La Flag (USA)**[22] 1961 3-8-12 0 TedDurcan 5 71
(J L Dunlop) *hld up in midfield: hdwy 3f out: rdn to chal and edgd rt jst over 1f out: kpt on same pce fnl f* **11/4**[1]
0 **4** *2 ½* **Atayeb (USA)**[14] 2219 3-8-12 0 RHills 1 65
(M P Tregoning) *s.i.s: sn chsng ldrs: pressed ldr over 2f out: sn rdn: ev ch tl wknd fnl 100yds* **7/1**[3]
0- **5** *½* **Orchestrator (IRE)**[182] 6826 3-9-3 0 JimmyFortune 2 69+
(T G Mills) *s.i.s: t.k.h and dropped in bhd: nt clr run over 2f out tl over 1f out: swtchd lft 1f out: styd on fnl f: nt trble ldrs* **10/1**
00- **6** *½* **Bring It On Home**[268] 5475 3-9-3 0 PatDobbs 4 68
(G L Moore) *hld up in midfield: rdn wl over 2f out: outpcd 2f out: kpt on ins fnl f: nvr trbld ldrs* **33/1**
0- **7** *¾* **Inchinata (IRE)**[230] 6215 3-8-12 0 MartinDwyer 6 61
(B W Hills) *s.i.s: bhd: rdn 3f out: styd on past btn horses fnl f: n.d* **25/1**
03 **8** *nk* **Roxie Princess (IRE)**[14] 2219 3-8-12 0 TPO'Shea 12 60
(J A R Toller) *t.k.h: trckd ldrs on rail: rdn over 2f out: wknd over 1f out* **14/1**
0 **9** *1 ½* **Practical Joke (IRE)**[44] 1398 3-9-3 0 PaulDoe 9 62
(W J Knight) *chsd ldr tl over 2f out: wknd wl over 1f out* **33/1**
10 *1* **Quaglino Way (GR)** 3-9-3 0 JimCrowley 3 60
(P R Chamings) *s.i.s: hdwy on outer 5f out: rdn 3f out: wknd wl over 2f out* **12/1**
11 *1* **Sibo Baggins (IRE)** 3-9-3 0 SimonWhitworth 10 57
(J S Moore) *s.i.s: t.k.h: hld up towards rr: rdn over 2f out: sn wknd* **40/1**

1m 42.02s (1.75) **Going Correction** +0.10s/f (Good) 11 Ran SP% **119.6**
Speed ratings (Par 99):95,93,93,91,90 90,89,89,87,86 85
CSF £17.02 TOTE £5.50: £1.80, £1.40, £1.40; EX 19.00.
Owner Mohammed Jaber **Bred** Barronstown Stud And Orpendale **Trained** Newmarket, Suffolk

FOCUS
A modest maiden for the track, with the winning jockey talking it down afterwards, and run at a moderate pace. The form is rated through the runner-up.
Orchestrator(IRE) Official explanation: jockey said gelding ran too free

2626 PETERS OPAL STKS (H'CAP) 7f
7:25 (7:25) (Class 4) (0-80,78) 4-Y-O+ **£7,124** (£2,119; £1,059; £529) **Stalls** High

Form RPR
0431 **1** **Ivory Lace**[6] 2458 6-9-8 **78** 6ex JimCrowley 1 89
(S Woodman) *dropped in sn after s: hld up bhd: plld out wl over 2f out: hdwy to chal over 1f out: rdn to ld ins fnl f: r.o strly* **14/1**
05-2 **2** *1 ¼* **Blue Java**[21] 1984 6-8-12 **73** TravisBlock(5) 7 81
(H Morrison) *chsd ldr: ev ch fr 3f out: kpt on wl u.p tl no ex fnl 50yds* **11/4**[1]
0-06 **3** *¾* **Material Witness (IRE)**[7] 2427 10-9-5 **75** MartinDwyer 9 81
(W R Muir) *led: hrd pressed fr 3f out: rdn over 1f out: hdd ins fnl f: no ex fnl 100yds* **14/1**
0001 **4** *shd* **Scarlet Flyer (USA)**[21] 1984 4-9-3 **73** (b) RyanMoore 8 78
(G L Moore) *hld up in midfield: hdwy 2f out: chsd ldrs over 1f out: kpt on same pce u.p fnl f* **7/2**[2]
5204 **5** *½* **Capricho (IRE)**[21] 1984 10-8-9 **65** (b) PaulDoe 4 69
(J Akehurst) *t.k.h: hld up bhd: hdwy on rail over 3f out: swtchd lft 2f out: effrt to chse ldrs over 1f out: keeping on same pce whn nt clr run ins fnl f* **11/1**
1105 **6** *¾* **Binnion Bay (IRE)**[9] 2358 6-8-12 **68** (b) J-PGuillambert 10 70
(J J Bridger) *trckd ldrs on rail: rdn over 2f out: kpt on same pce fnl f* **10/1**[3]
-045 **7** *6* **Tara Too (IRE)**[18] 2085 4-9-7 **77** EddieAhern 5 63
(J G Portman) *stdd s: t.k.h: sn in tch: lost pl and rdn wl over 2f out: bhd last 2f* **28/1**
0556 **8** *½* **Gavarnie Beau (IRE)**[27] 1847 4-9-0 **70** (b) TedDurcan 3 54
(M Blanshard) *hld up bhd: rdn wl over 2f out: sn struggling: no ch last 2f* **20/1**
11-1 **9** *½* **California Laws**[143] 227 5-9-0 **70** SebSanders 2 59+
(R M Beckett) *chsd ldrs: rdn wl over 2f out: sn btn: eased ins fnl f* **7/2**[2]
4200 **10** *3* **Grey Boy (GER)**[34] 1682 6-9-2 **72** DarryllHolland 6 47
(A W Carroll) *in tch in midfield: rdn 3f out: btn over 2f out* **12/1**

1m 27.37s (-0.67) **Going Correction** +0.10s/f (Good) 10 Ran SP% **117.8**
Speed ratings (Par 105):107,105,104,104,104 103,96,95,95,91
CSF £53.08 CT £579.69 TOTE £10.50: £2.50, £1.70, £4.40; EX 63.40.
Owner Sally Woodman J Lenaghan D Mortimer **Bred** D R Tucker **Trained** East Lavant, W Sussex
■ Stewards' Enquiry : Darryll Holland one-day ban: used whip when out of contention (Jun 26)

FOCUS
A fair handicap, with the runners soon stepping it up to a medium gallop for the trip. Sound form, the second, fourth and fifth closely matched on their course-and-distance meeting, with a career best from the winner.

2627 CRIMBOURNE STUD STKS (H'CAP) 1m 1f 192y
8:00 (8:02) (Class 4) (0-80,80) 3-Y-O **£7,124** (£2,119; £1,059; £529) **Stalls** High

Form RPR
33-2 **1** **Malt Or Mash (USA)**[9] 2354 3-9-5 **78** PatDobbs 2 85
(R Hannon) *led for 1f: chsd ldr tl led again over 2f out: styd on wl u.p* **6/1**[3]
2214 **2** *1 ¼* **Emerald Wilderness (IRE)**[27] 1835 3-9-5 **78** JHBowman 4 82
(M R Channon) *t.k.h: chsd ldrs: hdwy to chse wnr over 2f out: ev ch and rdn wl over 1f out: no ex fnl 100yds* **8/1**
53-1 **3** *hd* **Camps Bay (USA)**[22] 1974 3-9-4 **77** JimCrowley 5 81
(Mrs A J Perrett) *hld up in midfield: rdn over 3f out: hdwy to chse ldng pair 2f out: kpt on u.p: nrst fin* **9/1**
3441 **4** *nk* **Six Of Diamonds (IRE)**[25] 1887 3-9-3 **76** JamieSpencer 11 79+
(J A Osborne) *t.k.h: hld up in midfield: lost pl over 4f out: hdwy over 2f out: styd on u.p: nt rch ldrs* **15/2**

-224 **5** 1 1/4 **Vanquisher (IRE)**[24] 1937 3-9-2 **75**.....................(v[1]) TedDurcan 8 79+
(W J Haggas) *s.i.s: hld up: hdwy on rail over 3f out: bmpd over 2f out: swtchd lft and bmpd again 2f out: kpt on: nt able to chal* **16/1**

14 **6** *nk* **Woodcraft**[30] 1773 3-9-7 **80**.......................... RichardHughes 12 80
(B W Hills) *chsd ldrs: rdn over 3f out: kpt on same pce last 2f* **9/2**[1]

3331 **7** 1 1/2 **Eager Igor (USA)**[6] 2453 3-9-5 **78** 6ex.................. StephenCarson 13 75+
(Eve Johnson Houghton) *hld up towards rr: hdwy and edgd rt over 2f out: sn rdn to chse ldrs: nt clr run tl over 1f out: nt rcvr* **13/2**

-350 **8** *shd* **Bajan Pride**[21] 1987 3-8-12 **71**.......................... RyanMoore 9 68+
(R Hannon) *hld up in rr: hdwy and nt clr run over 2f out: no ch after* **12/1**

2-00 **9** 3/4 **Strikeen (IRE)**[17] 2126 3-8-13 **79**.......................... JackMitchell[(7)] 10 75
(T G Mills) *unruly in stalls: v.s.a: t.k.h: hdwy into midfield 8f out: rdn over 2f out: sn wknd* **33/1**

-144 **10** 3 1/2 **Nassmaan (IRE)**[58] 1089 3-9-4 **77**.......................... JimmyFortune 6 66
(P W Chapple-Hyam) *chsd ldrs: rdn over 3f out: wkng whn bmpd over 1f out* **18/1**

0-00 **11** *2* **Chunky's Choice (IRE)**[15] 2177 3-8-7 **66** ow1.............. SebSanders 1 51
(J Noseda) *hld up bhd: rdn 4f out: no ch last 2f* **25/1**

1-0 **12** 1/2 **Samorra (IRE)**[22] 1956 3-9-3 **76**.......................... MartinDwyer 7 60
(M P Tregoning) *hld up in midfield: rdn whn short of room and snatched up over 2f out: no ch after* **11/2**[2]

3-25 **13** *3* **Mafeking (UAE)**[21] 1987 3-9-5 **78**.......................... DarryllHolland 3 56
(M R Hoad) *pushed up to ld after 1f: rdn over 3f out: hdd over 2f out: sn wknd: eased whn wl btn ins fnl f* **11/1**

2m 9.52s (1.77) **Going Correction** +0.10s/f (Good) **13** Ran SP% **128.0**
Speed ratings (Par 101):96,95,94,94,93 93,92,92,91,88 87,86,84
CSF £57.64 CT £447.73 TOTE £7.10: £2.50, £2.80, £2.70; EX 65.10.
Owner A P Patey **Bred** Delahanty Stock Farm **Trained** East Everleigh, Wilts
■ Stewards' Enquiry : Stephen Carson two-day ban: careless riding (Jun 26-27)

FOCUS
Several relatively unexposed sorts here who should improve with experience. There was plenty of interference in the home straight but the front pair kept out of trouble, the winner not needing to improve on his solid Kempton form.
Six Of Diamonds(IRE) Official explanation: jockey said colt stumbled very badly

2628 TAURUS WASTE RECYCLING MAIDEN H'CAP 1m 6f
8:35 (8:36) (Class 5) (0-75,75) 3-Y-O **£3,562** (£1,059; £529; £264) **Stalls** High

Form RPR

5-52 **1** **Squadron**[15] 2185 3-9-1 **69**.......................... RyanMoore 11 73
(Mrs A J Perrett) *hld up: stdy hdwy 10f out: chsd ldng pair 6f out: rdn 5f out: led 2f out: kpt on u.p: all out: fin lame* **2/1**[1]

3230 **2** *nk* **Guardian Of Truth (IRE)**[15] 2185 3-9-7 **75**.................. PaulDoe 3 78
(W J Knight) *chsd ldr tl led after 2f: sn clr: rdn and hdd 2f out: kpt on wl u.p tl unable qck nr fin* **16/1**

6-26 **3** 1/2 **Adversane**[28] 1810 3-9-1 **69**.......................... SebSanders 10 71
(J L Dunlop) *hld up in midfield: pushed along 5f out: hdwy over 3f out: chsd ldng pair last 2f: unable qck wl ins fnl f* **5/1**[2]

503 **4** 3/4 **Kasban**[17] 2112 3-9-5 **73**.......................... RHills 7 74
(E A L Dunlop) *hld up: hdwy 7f out: rdn and outpcd 5f out: hdwy and n.m.r over 1f out: styng on whn nt clr run wl ins fnl f* **5/1**[2]

0-53 **5** *1* **I Predict A Riot (IRE)**[36] 1611 3-9-0 **68**.................. EddieAhern 12 68+
(J W Hills) *hld up in midfield: hdwy and nt clr run over 2f out: styd on u.p to chse ldrs 1f out: keeping on whn nt clr run wl ins fnl f* **12/1**

2523 **6** *1* **Sowdrey**[12] 2274 3-9-5 **73**.......................... JHBowman 1 71
(M R Channon) *hld up bhd: rdn wl over 3f out: kpt on steadily u.p last 2f: nt rch ldrs* **9/1**

-340 **7** *nk* **Crimson Monarch (USA)**[35] 1637 3-9-0 **68**..............(b) JimCrowley 9 66
(Mrs A J Perrett) *hld up in rr: rdn over 3f out: little rspnse tl styd on ins fnl f: nt rch ldrs* **10/1**

-624 **8** *2* **Linlithgow (IRE)**[22] 1972 3-8-2 **56** oh1.................. TPO'Shea 5 51
(J L Dunlop) *towards rr: lost pl 7f and rdn 6f out: sme hdwy undr press 5f out: kpt on same pce after* **15/2**[3]

-000 **9** *3* **Muffett's Dream**[17] 2105 3-8-2 **56** oh6.................. DavidKinsella 13 47
(J A Geake) *chsd ldrs: rdn 4f out: sn struggling: no ch last 2f* **66/1**

2243 **10** *7* **Reciprocation (IRE)**[23] 1950 3-9-7 **75**..............(v[1]) RichardHughes 14 56
(K McAuliffe) *led for 2f: chsd ldr tl over 2f out: sn rdn: btn 1f out: eased fnl f* **16/1**

-200 **11** *5* **Into Action**[53] 1205 3-8-13 **67**.......................... PatDobbs 4 41
(R Hannon) *racd in midfield: lost pl and rdn 5f out: sn no ch: eased fnl f* **25/1**

3m 7.37s (3.40) **Going Correction** +0.10s/f (Good) **11** Ran SP% **122.3**
Speed ratings (Par 99):94,93,93,93,92 91,91,90,88,84 82
CSF £41.42 CT £151.16 TOTE £3.10: £1.30, £4.60, £1.90; EX 33.10.
Owner Highclere Thoroughbred Racing XXXVI **Bred** B Root **Trained** Pulborough, W Sussex

FOCUS
A fair staying race for three-year-olds, with several runners trying a longer trip after proving one-paced around 1m4f. The runner-up soon went clear, and set a decent gallop, though the pace steadied at halfway until 4f out. The form is sound enough, but the principals finished in aheap and it is hard to rate the race positively.
Reciprocation(IRE) Official explanation: jockey said colt hung right

2629 ABIMARA STKS (H'CAP) 6f
9:05 (9:06) (Class 4) (0-85,84) 3-Y-O **£7,124** (£2,119; £1,059; £529) **Stalls** Low

Form RPR

2532 **1** **Mac Gille Eoin**[8] 2395 3-8-9 **72**.......................... JimCrowley 3 85+
(J Gallagher) *s.i.s: pushed along early: hdwy on outer 3f out: led over 1f out: sn hung lft: drvn clr: r.o strly* **2/1**[1]

151 **2** *4* **Telltime (IRE)**[16] 2144 3-8-13 **76**.......................... MartinDwyer 4 77+
(A M Balding) *hld up in tch: hdwy whn nt clr run over 2f out: sn rdn and outpcd: styd on ins fnl f: wnt 2nd last 100yds: no ch w wnr* **12/1**

-010 **3** *1* **Mason Ette**[20] 2044 3-9-3 **80**.......................... PhilipRobinson 5 78
(C G Cox) *pressed ldr: rdn and edgd rt over 1f out: kpt on same pce fnl f* **9/2**[3]

12-1 **4** 1/2 **Shustraya**[146] 199 3-9-7 **84**.......................... SebSanders 9 81
(P J Makin) *chsd ldrs on outer: rdn and ev ch wl over 1f out: kpt on same pce fnl f* **4/1**[2]

2155 **5** *nk* **Rocker**[4] 2513 3-8-13 **76**..............(v[1]) RichardSmith 6 72
(B R Johnson) *sn led: edgd rt wl over 1f out: hdd over 1f out: kpt on same pce* **16/1**

011- **6** 1/2 **Bateleur**[269] 5461 3-9-6 **83**.......................... EdwardCreighton 2 77
(M R Channon) *hld up in tch: hdwy over 2f out: ev ch and rdn over 1f out: one pce fnl f* **14/1**

0-65 **7** *13* **Ede's Dot Com (IRE)**[78] 815 3-8-11 **74**.................. IanMongan 8 29
(P M Phelan) *chsd ldrs tl wl over 2f out: sn rdn and wknd: t.o* **33/1**

-231 **8** 1 1/4 **Nobilissima (IRE)**[18] 2080 3-8-11 **77**.................. MarcHalford[(3)] 7 28
(J L Spearing) *chsd ldrs: rdn and lost pl 1/2-way: no ch last 2f: t.o* **11/2**

1-00 **9** *11* **Sacre Coeur**[19] 2060 3-9-2 **79**.......................... EddieAhern 1 —
(J L Dunlop) *unruly in stalls: chsd ldrs on rail tl rdn and wknd qckly wl over 2f out: wl t.o fnl f* **7/1**

1m 12.22s (-0.63) **Going Correction** +0.10s/f (Good) **9** Ran SP% **122.6**
Speed ratings (Par 101):108,102,101,100,100 99,82,80,65
CSF £30.96 CT £103.87 TOTE £3.10: £1.30, £2.20, £2.00; EX 26.60 Place 6 £ 22.93, Place 5 £ 20.97.
Owner M C S D Racing Partnership **Bred** M C S D Racing Ltd **Trained** Moreton-in-Marsh, Gloucs

FOCUS
A race of reasonable quality, and run at a good sprint tempo. The first two came from the rear and the winner ran to the same mark as he had in a good race at Haydock.
T/Plt: £19.50. Pool £76,577.75. 2,858.35 winning tickets T/Qpdt: £14.40. Pool £3,615.60. 185.15 winning tickets SP

2398 SANDOWN (R-H)
Friday, June 15

OFFICIAL GOING: Sprint course - good to soft (good in places, 7.2); round course - good (good to soft in places, 8.0)
Wind: Virtually nil

2630 BANK OF IRELAND REAL ESTATE FINANCE E B F MAIDEN STKS 5f 6y
2:10 (2:18) (Class 5) 2-Y-O **£3,886** (£1,156; £577; £288) **Stalls** High

Form RPR

34 **1** **Bosun Breese**[13] 2241 2-9-3 0.......................... DarryllHolland 10 77
(P W D'Arcy) *unf: mde all: pushed along over 1f out: r.o strly ins fnl f* **3/1**[1]

00 **2** 1 1/2 **Vigano (IRE)**[14] 2215 2-9-3 0.......................... JohnEgan 5 72
(S Kirk) *leggy: towards rr tl drvn and qcknd to chse wnr ins fnl 2f: kpt on ins fnl f but a hld* **9/1**

00 **3** 3/4 **Hold That Call (USA)**[11] 2316 2-9-3 0.................. RyanMoore 2 69
(R Hannon) *towards rr: pushed along 2f out: hdwy over 1f out: kpt on wl fnl f but nvr gng pce to rch ldrs* **9/2**[3]

4 *hd* **Blues Minor (IRE)** 2-9-3 0.......................... RichardHughes 4 68
(R Hannon) *lengthy: lw: towards rr tl pushed along and hdwy fr 2f out: swtchd lft 1f out: hung lft ins fnl f: kpt on cl home but nvr gng pce to rch ldrs* **4/1**[2]

03 **5** *hd* **Evenstorm (USA)**[12] 2271 2-8-12 0.................. JimCrowley 6 62
(B Gubby) *chsd ldrs: rdn fr 2f out: styd on same pce ins fnl f* **16/1**

0 **6** 1 1/2 **Our Kally**[17] 2122 2-8-12 0.......................... HayleyTurner 8 57
(M D I Usher) *chsd wnr tl ins fnl 2f: wknd ins fnl f* **10/1**

7 3 1/2 **Mistress Cooper** 2-8-12 0.......................... BrettDoyle 1 44
(W J Musson) *strong: bit bkwd: towards rr tl pushed along and sme prog fr 1/2-way: wknd fnl f* **40/1**

8 1 1/2 **Saoodah (IRE)** 2-8-12 0.......................... PhilipRobinson 11 39
(M A Jarvis) *neat: bit bkwd: s.i.s: nvr in contention* **6/1**

05 **9** *1* **Choisky (IRE)**[9] 2349 2-9-3 0.......................... TQuinn 7 40
(J Akehurst) *chsd ldrs: rdn 1/2-way: wknd qckly fnl f* **9/1**

10 *2* **Kaystar Ridge** 2-9-3 0.......................... RobertHavlin 9 33
(D K Ivory) *s.i.s: sn mid-div: rdn 1/2-way and sn in rr* **66/1**

63.49 secs (1.28) **Going Correction** 0.0s/f (Good) **10** Ran SP% **116.4**
Speed ratings (Par 93):89,86,85,85,84 82,76,74,72,69
CSF £30.99 TOTE £3.90: £1.50, £2.80, £2.10; EX 41.90.
Owner Lodge Hyson Delnevo And Breese Racing **Bred** Lady Lonsdale **Trained** Newmarket, Suffolk

FOCUS
A modest event dominated by those who had run before. The drop back in trip by a furlong did not go against Bosun Breese, who won nicely. The form has been rated around him. The runner-up and third both look likely nursery types, while the fourth might be the best horse to emerge from the race.

NOTEBOOK
Bosun Breese, who was dropping down by a furlong in trip, grabbed the rail from a decent draw and kept on in good style under pressure. His previous form entitled him to go close, but he will no doubt find things more difficult against other winners next time, although as a gelding he is likely to be kept to nurseries or conditions events in the short-term. The big sales race at Newmarket in October is reportedly his long-term objective. (op 11-4 tchd 5-2 and 10-3 and 7-2 in places)
Vigano(IRE) had shown some reasonable form in decent maidens and kept on nicely in the final stages. An ordinary contest is within his grasp before some of the better later-season maidens are run. (op 10-1)
Hold That Call(USA) did not have the best of the draw and could not get involved until the latter stages. He is one to bear in mind for nurseries when they start. (op 15-2)
Blues Minor(IRE) ◆ came down the middle of the course and was certainly not given a hard time while slightly drifting to his left under pressure. He should learn plenty for the run and go even closer next time. (op 9-2 tchd 5-1)
Evenstorm(USA) did not run too badly again and might be capable of going close in a low-grade nursery later in the season. The stiff finish appeared to find her out (tchd 20-1)
Our Kally helped to share the early gallop but weakened inside the final furlong. A less demanding course will suit her. (tchd 14-1)
Mistress Cooper did not shape quite as badly as her finishing position suggests. (op 50-1)
Saoodah(IRE) was very weak in the market and ruined any chance she had with a slow start. Official explanation: jockey said filly reared as stalls opened (op 9-2 tchd 4-1)

2631 FLEMING RUSSELL STENT H'CAP 5f 6y
2:40 (2:46) (Class 5) (0-75,75) 3-Y-O **£4,533** (£1,348; £674; £336) **Stalls** High

Form RPR

6-21 **1** **Sundae**[35] 1635 3-9-2 **70**.......................... TedDurcan 7 87+
(C F Wall) *lw: hld up in tch: nt clr run and swtchd lft over 1f out: qcknd to ld ins fnl f: sn clr: easily* **5/1**[2]

521- **2** 1 1/2 **Gentle Guru**[245] 5950 3-9-4 **72**.......................... SebSanders 2 83
(R T Phillips) *fit: in tch: drvn and hdwy to ld over 1f out: hdd ins fnl f and hung lft: kpt on but no ch w wnr* **7/1**

3304 **3** *4* **Black Moma (IRE)**[4] 2513 3-9-2 **75**.................. TravisBlock[(5)] 4 72
(R Hannon) *chsd ldrs: rdn fr 2f out: chsd ldrs fnl f but a wl hld* **9/1**

0-52 **4** 1/2 **Gleaming Spirit (IRE)**[6] 2444 3-8-8 **62**.................. JimCrowley 8 57
(A P Jarvis) *slt ld: rdn over 2f out: hdd over 1f out: sn wknd* **5/1**[2]

0-52 **5** *shd* **Castano**[9] 2366 3-9-2 **70**.......................... JHBowman 3 65+
(B R Millman) *slowly away: in rr tl sme prog fr over 1f out: kpt on ins fnl f but nvr in contention* **12/1**

4011 **6** 2 1/2 **Darcy's Pride (IRE)**[11] 2301 3-9-1 **69** 6ex.................. JamieSpencer 1 55
(D W Barker) *chsd ldrs: rdn over 2f out: wknd over 1f out* **7/2**[1]

040 **7** 1/2 **Punching**[24] 1923 3-8-10 **64**..............(t) StephenCarson 9 48
(Eve Johnson Houghton) *in rr: rdn and mod prog fr over 1f out: nvr in contention* **25/1**

3100 **8** 1 1/2 **Cuppacocoa**[4] 2513 3-9-6 **74**.......................... PhilipRobinson 6 53
(C G Cox) *w ldr to 1/2-way: sn rdn: wknd over 1f out* **10/1**

0-05 **9** 1 1/4 **Land Ahoy**[6] 2470 3-9-6 **74**.......................... KerrinMcEvoy 5 48
(D W P Arbuthnot) *a outpcd* **20/1**

114 **10** *1* **Halsion Chancer**[100] [639] 3-9-2 **70** LDettori 10 41
(J R Best) *chsd ldrs tl wknd qckly 2f out* **11/2**[3]
61.65 secs (-0.56) **Going Correction** 0.0s/f (Good) **10** Ran SP% **118.8**
Speed ratings (Par 99):104,101,95,94,94 90,89,87,85,83
CSF £40.79 CT £316.78 TOTE £5.60: £2.50, £2.30, £3.00; EX 53.90.
Owner Peter Gregory **Bred** Jeremy Green And Sons **Trained** Newmarket, Suffolk
FOCUS
An interesting handcap run at a solid pace. The first two were both potentially well treated and came clear, with the improving winner travelling strongly and winning with something to spare.
Castano Official explanation: jockey said gelding missed the break
Darcy's Pride(IRE) Official explanation: trainer had no explanation for the poor form shown
Cuppacocoa Official explanation: jockey said filly was unsuited by the ground

2632 BANK OF IRELAND BUSINESS & CORPORATE BANKING MAIDEN STKS 7f 16y
3:15 (3:22) (Class 4) 2-Y-O **£5,181** (£1,541; £770; £384) **Stalls** High

Form RPR
1 **Firestreak** 2-9-3 0 RyanMoore 1 79+
(R Hannon) *w'like: in tch: sltly hmpd over 3f out: drvn and qcknd to ld jst ins fnl 2f and edgd rt: sn in command and kpt on strly* **6/1**
2 *2 1/2* **Donegal (USA)** 2-9-3 0 FrancisNorton 8 73
(A M Balding) *neat: lw: in tch: pushed along 3f out: styd on fnl 2f and tk 2nd ins fnl f but nvr any ch w wnr* **25/1**
3 *1 1/4* **Strategic Mission (IRE)** 2-9-3 0 TQuinn 10 69
(P F I Cole) *w'like: scope: lw: led: pushed along 3f out: hrd drvn and hdd ins fnl 2f: no ex and lost 2nd ins fnl f* **11/4**[2]
4 *1/2* **By Command** 2-9-3 0 KerrinMcEvoy 3 68+
(J L Dunlop) *w'like: bit bkwd: s.i.s: bhd: hdwy 3 out: shkn up and styd on to go 4th ins fnl f but nvr gng pce to rch ldrs* **15/2**
5 *3/4* **La Voile Rouge** 2-9-3 0 LDettori 12 66
(B J Meehan) *unf: scope: chsd ldrs: edgd lft u.p over 3f out: drvn to chse ldr over 2f out: wknd ins fnl f* **10/1**
6 *2* **Hampstead Heath (IRE)** 2-9-3 0 JoeFanning 9 61+
(M Johnston) *w'like: scope: bit bkwd: pressed ldr: rdn 3f out: lost 2nd over 2f out: wknd appr fnl f* **5/2**[1]
0 **7** *2 1/2* **Howdigo**[13] [2241] 2-9-0 0 StephaneBreux(3) 7 55+
(J R Best) *w'like: in rr: pushed along 3f out: sme prog fnl f* **22/1**
00 **8** *3 1/2* **Adam Eterno (IRE)**[7] [2410] 2-9-3 0 BrettDoyle 4 46
(B J Meehan) *chsd ldrs: rdn and sltly hmpd over 3f out: wknd fr 2f out* **66/1**
9 *3/4* **Native Talent** 2-9-3 0 RichardHughes 2 44
(B W Hills) *w'like: slowly away: towards rr: rdn and sme prog whn hung lft fr 2f out: nvr in contention and veered bdly lft ins fnl f* **11/2**[3]
0 **10** *29* **Two Imposters (USA)**[8] [2398] 2-9-3 0 TedDurcan 11 —
(J R Best) *lengthy: a in rr* **33/1**
1m 31.36s (2.02) **Going Correction** 0.0s/f (Good) **10** Ran SP% **118.4**
Speed ratings (Par 95):98,95,93,93,92 90,87,83,82,49
CSF £147.07 TOTE £7.30: £2.50, £4.20, £1.20; EX 154.50.
Owner The Queen **Bred** The Queen **Trained** East Everleigh, Wilts
■ Stewards' Enquiry : L Dettori four-day ban: careless riding (Jun 26-29); two-day ban: used whip with excessive frequency down shoulder in forehand position (Jun 30-Jul 1)
FOCUS
A fair-looking maiden, and an early 7f event for 2yos in England. The winner impressed and should do better, but the overall level of the form is guessy at this stage.
NOTEBOOK
Firestreak, a Green Desert colt from a useful middle-distance family, was a bit edgy in the paddock, but showed good acceleration when asked to quicken and came right away from his rivals in smooth style. If going the right way, which some of his relations have not done, he should make up into a nice sort. (op 8-1 tchd 9-1)
Donegal(USA), an American-bred colt; stayed on really nicely up the incline and shaped like a future winner. The stable seem to be doing well with their 2yos this season. (op 28-1)
Strategic Mission(IRE), whose stable have already produced a couple of smart 2yos, was really well supported before the off and helped to set the pace early. He kept on when joined, but was firmly put in his place by the winner and may have been a bit too keen early. (op 11-2)
By Command ◆, who is related to many decent horses, was kept quite wide and ran green early in the straight. The jockey was not too hard on him in the last furlong, but he finished strongly when hitting the rising ground and should come on a lot for the race. (op 5-1 tchd 9-2)
La Voile Rouge went left when beginning his effort but improved to have his chance 2f from home before failing to see out the trip as well as some others. It was a satisfactory debut and he can win a race. (op 15-2)
Hampstead Heath(IRE) helped to share the pace, where he was possibly a bit keen, before weakening in the final stages. His stable has yet to really hit top gear with their 2yos and he can be given another chance. (op 2-1)
Howdigo stayed on well from the back and, although well beaten, looks to have enough ability to be competitive in lower-grade contests. (op 20-1)
Native Talent started slowly and almost ran off the track up the home straight. He clearly needs to improve his attitude. (op 5-1 tchd 6-1)

2633 MOUSETRAP CHALLENGE CUP H'CAP 1m 14y
3:50 (3:56) (Class 4) (0-85,84) 3-Y-O **£6,477** (£1,927; £963; £481) **Stalls** High

Form RPR
15 **1** **Laa Rayb (USA)**[8] [2400] 3-9-5 **82** JoeFanning 10 102+
(M Johnston) *trckd ldr tl led appr fnl 3f: pushed along and c readily clr fnl 2f: easily* **15/2**
3-13 **2** *5* **Gyroscope**[27] [1837] 3-9-3 **80** KerrinMcEvoy 9 88
(Sir Michael Stoute) *prom: chsd wnr ins fnl 3f but nvr any ch: kpt on wl for clr 2nd* **11/4**[2]
3-13 **3** *3* **Monte Alto (IRE)**[24] [1920] 3-9-0 **77** NickyMackay 7 78
(L M Cumani) *lw: towards rr: rdn 3f out: styd on u.p fnl 2f but nvr gng pce to rch ldrs* **9/4**[1]
1104 **4** *1* **Ambrosiano**[10] [2335] 3-8-11 **74** PhilipRobinson 8 73
(C G Cox) *in tch: rdn fr 3f out: styd on same pce and nvr in contention* **7/1**
6-00 **5** *2 1/2* **Our Herbie**[28] [1815] 3-8-7 **70** (t) TQuinn 2 63
(J W Hills) *bmpd s: bhd: drvn along over 3f out: mod prog fr over 1f out* **33/1**
01-0 **6** *1/2* **Russki (IRE)**[8] [2400] 3-9-5 **82** JimCrowley 1 74
(Mrs A J Perrett) *lw: in rr tl pushed along and mod prog fnl 2f* **10/1**
-554 **7** *7* **Magic Mountain (IRE)**[17] [2126] 3-9-7 **84** (b[1]) RichardHughes 6 60
(R Hannon) *lw: led tl rdn and hdd appr fnl 3f: sn btn* **16/1**
51-6 **8** *8* **Cat De Mille (USA)**[27] [1851] 3-9-1 **78** AdrianMcCarthy 5 36
(P W Chapple-Hyam) *in tch tl rdn and wknd 3f out* **13/2**[3]
01 **9** *6* **Grand Vizier (IRE)**[13] [2261] 3-8-13 **76** TedDurcan 3 20
(C F Wall) *wnt lft s: chsd ldrs tl wknd fr 3f out* **25/1**
1m 42.92s (-1.03) **Going Correction** 0.0s/f (Good) **9** Ran SP% **116.8**
Speed ratings (Par 101):105,100,97,96,93 93,86,78,72
CSF £28.79 CT £62.50 TOTE £8.70: £2.20, £1.70, £1.50; EX 30.20.
Owner Sheikh Ahmed Al Maktoum **Bred** Darley **Trained** Middleham Moor, N Yorks
FOCUS
A good three-year-old handicap won impressively by the smart-looking Laa Rayb. The race should produce its share of winners.
Our Herbie Official explanation: jockey said gelding was hampered leaving stalls

2634 BRISTOL & WEST PROPERTY FINANCE H'CAP 1m 2f 7y
4:25 (4:30) (Class 4) (0-85,84) 4-Y-O+ **£7,772** (£2,312; £1,155; £577) **Stalls** High

Form RPR
-261 **1** **Greek Well (IRE)**[8] [2403] 4-9-5 **82** 6ex KerrinMcEvoy 3 91
(Sir Michael Stoute) *lw: trckd ldr: led appr fnl 3f: drvn fr over 1f out and styd on wl thrght fnl f* **1/1**[1]
-600 **2** *nk* **Brief Goodbye**[21] [2003] 7-9-1 **78** TedDurcan 5 86
(John Berry) *stdd in rr: rdn and outpcd 3f out: r.o strly fr over 1f out to chse wnr ins fnl f: gng on cl home but a jst hld* **20/1**
-443 **3** *1 1/2* **Cleaver**[23] [1949] 6-8-13 **76** SebSanders 2 81
(Lady Herries) *led tl hdd appr fnl 3f: no ch w wnr fr over 1f out and lost 2nd fnl f* **4/1**[3]
4024 **4** *1 1/4* **Prince Nureyev (IRE)**[8] [2403] 7-9-3 **80** JHBowman 4 83
(B R Millman) *chsd ldrs: rdn fr 3f out: one pce fnl 2f* **8/1**
31- **5** *15* **Clear Sailing**[254] [5770] 4-9-7 **84** RichardHughes 1 57
(Mrs A J Perrett) *stdd in rr: hdwy 4f out: rdn over 2f out: fnd little and sn btn: eased whn no ch ins fnl f* **7/2**[2]
2m 11.81s (1.57) **Going Correction** 0.0s/f (Good) **5** Ran SP% **108.1**
Speed ratings (Par 105):93,92,91,90,78
CSF £19.62 TOTE £1.80: £1.30, £3.50; EX 17.60.
Owner Ballymacoll Stud **Bred** Ballymacoll Stud Farm Ltd **Trained** Newmarket, Suffolk
FOCUS
This was not a particularly strong event and recent scorer Greek Well did not achieve much in beating some well exposed handicappers, with the only other interesting runner Clear Sailing running as though something was amiss.

2635 BANK OF IRELAND SPECIALIST DEPOSIT BUSINESS H'CAP 1m 2f 7y
4:55 (5:02) (Class 5) (0-75,74) 3-Y-O **£4,533** (£1,348; £674; £336) **Stalls** High

Form RPR
043- **1** **Starparty (USA)**[198] [6651] 3-9-1 **68** JimCrowley 6 75
(Mrs A J Perrett) *chsd ldr: rdn and styd on fr 2f out to ld 1f out: hld on all out* **20/1**
-003 **2** *1/2* **Trump Call (IRE)**[28] [1815] 3-9-0 **67** SebSanders 7 73+
(R M Beckett) *towards rr: rdn over 3f out: styd on fr 2f out to chse wnr wl ins fnl f: kpt on cl home but a jst hld* **2/1**[1]
0-44 **3** *1 3/4* **Rowan River**[24] [1927] 3-9-0 **67** PaulDoe 9 69
(M H Tompkins) *led: 4 l clr 3f out: rdn 2f out: hdd 1f out but kpt on tl wknd and lost 2nd wl ins fnl f* **10/1**
0-40 **4** *2 1/2* **The Wily Woodcock**[11] [2317] 3-9-1 **68** JimmyFortune 10 65
(G Wragg) *lw: chsd ldrs: rdn 3f out: one pce fnl 2f* **8/1**
0100 **5** *2 1/2* **Cry Presto (USA)**[15] [2185] 3-9-6 **73** PatDobbs 4 65
(R Hannon) *in rr: rdn over 3f out: kpt on fr over 1f out but nvr in contention* **25/1**
3163 **6** *shd* **Urban Warrior**[17] [2126] 3-9-6 **73** JamesDoyle 1 65
(Mrs Norma Pook) *chsd ldrs: rdn fr over 3f out: no imp: wknd fr 2f out* **6/1**[3]
0444 **7** *3/4* **Mango Masher (IRE)**[24] [1936] 3-9-3 **70** JohnEgan 2 60
(C R Egerton) *b. in tch: reminders 5f out: nvr in contention after* **14/1**
0630 **8** *1/2* **Sixfields Flyer (IRE)**[14] [2224] 3-8-7 **60** RichardMullen 8 49
(Pat Eddery) *bhd most of way* **33/1**
531- **9** *hd* **Mardi**[188] [6757] 3-9-6 **73** KerrinMcEvoy 5 62
(W J Haggas) *chsd ldr: rdn 3f out: wknd 2f out: eased whn no ch fnl f* **9/2**[2]
2130 **10** *14* **Resplendent Ace (IRE)**[22] [1956] 3-9-7 **74** TQuinn 3 35
(P Howling) *racd wd: a towards rr* **7/1**
2m 11.24s (1.00) **Going Correction** 0.0s/f (Good) **10** Ran SP% **116.7**
Speed ratings (Par 99):96,95,94,92,90 90,89,89,88,77
CSF £59.14 CT £447.07 TOTE £21.80: £5.10, £1.30, £1.90; EX 93.20 Place 6 £62.25, Place 5 £34.77.
Owner Mr & Mrs R Scott **Bred** Bruce Hundley **Trained** Pulborough, W Sussex
FOCUS
Just a modest handicap, but it was run in a quicker time than that recorded by Greek Well in the previous contest, and the race should produce the odd winner at a similar level. Solid form.
Resplendent Ace(IRE) Official explanation: jockey said colt never travelled
T/Plt: £74.80 to a £1 stake. Pool: £88,333.80. 861.40 winning tickets. T/Qpdt: £8.80 to a £1 stake. Pool: £5,212.30. 437.40 winning tickets. ST

1821 YORK (L-H)
Friday, June 15
2636 Meeting Abandoned - Waterlogged

2642 - 2649a (Foreign Racing) - See Raceform Interactive

2488 BATH (L-H)
Saturday, June 16
OFFICIAL GOING: Good to soft
The going was changed from good after a mini downpour just before racing.
Wind: Light against Weather: Heavy shower just before first race

2650 BATHWICK TYRES BRIDGEND AND EUROPEAN BREEDERS' FUND NOVICE STKS 5f 11y
2:15 (2:16) (Class 4) 2-Y-O **£4,533** (£1,348; £674; £336) **Stalls** Centre

Form RPR
10 **1** **Carleton**[16] [2183] 2-9-5 0 DarryllHolland 1 92+
(M R Channon) *hld up: hdwy over 2f out: led over 1f out: edgd lft ins fnl f: pushed out* **7/2**[3]
01 **2** *1 1/2* **Spanish Bounty**[15] [2193] 2-9-5 0 SebSanders 3 87
(J G Portman) *chsd ldr: rdn and ev ch over 1f out: nt qckn ins fnl f* **13/8**[1]
21 **3** *3* **Just A Dancer (IRE)**[18] [2109] 2-8-7 0 ChrisGlenister(7) 2 71+
(B W Hills) *chsd ldrs: rdn and ev ch over 1f out: no ex ins fnl f* **7/4**[2]
201 **4** *7* **Only In Jest**[25] [1919] 2-8-9 0 TolleyDean(5) 5 46
(W G M Turner) *led: rdn and hdd over 1f out: wknd fnl f* **9/1**
65.81 secs (3.31) **Going Correction** +0.35s/f (Good) **4** Ran SP% **106.7**
Speed ratings (Par 95):87,84,79,68
CSF £9.33 TOTE £4.60; EX 7.50.

Owner Capital **Bred** Peter Taplin **Trained** West Ilsley, Berks

FOCUS

A typically small field for this novice contest won in a time a second and a half slower than the following maiden auction race. Not easy to assess, but the winner was quite impressive and could be a fair bit better than he has been rated.

NOTEBOOK

Carleton, highly tried last time, does seem to relish some give in the ground and regained the winning thread with something in hand. (tchd 9-4)

Spanish Bounty had more on his plate than when successful over slightly further here last time and could not cope with the winner. (op 2-1 tchd 6-4)

Just A Dancer(IRE) had no excuses and had nothing more to offer in the closing stages. Official explanation: jockey said saddle slipped (op 6-4 tchd 9-4)

Only In Jest failed to get home in the rain-softened ground. Official explanation: trainer said filly was unsuited by the good to soft ground (op 8-1 tchd 10-1)

2651 BATHWICK TYRES CARDIFF MAIDEN AUCTION STKS 5f 11y

2:50 (2:51) (Class 6) 2-Y-O £2,072 (£616; £308; £153) Stalls Centre

Form RPR

02 **1** **Supermassive Muse (IRE)**^{22} [1992] 2-8-9 0 SebSanders 5 75+
(E S McMahon) *bhd: rdn over 2f out: hdwy over 1f out: led ins fnl f: drvn out* **2/1**^{1}

5 **2** ¾ **Gasmanfightsback**^{8} [2424] 2-8-9 0 ChrisCatlin 8 72
(Evan Williams) *w ldr: led over 2f out: rdn and hdd ins fnl f: kpt on* **13/2**

3 2½ **Katrina Bee (IRE)** 2-8-9 0 ow1 PatDobbs 9 63
(R Hannon) *s.i.s: hdwy over 1f out: rdn and edgd lft wl ins fnl f: one pce* **13/2**

4 ¾ **Lambrini Lace (IRE)** 2-8-3 0 TolleyDean$^{(5)}$ 10 60
(Mrs L Williamson) *chsd ldrs: rdn over 2f out: edgd lft ins fnl f: one pce* **50/1**

54 **5** ½ **Perfect Flight**^{23} [1960] 2-8-8 0 AdamKirby 3 58
(M Blanshard) *chsd ldrs: rdn over 1f out: one pce fnl f* **8/1**

00 **6** 3 **Lady Vibeeka**^{18} [2103] 2-8-4 0 HayleyTurner 2 43
(Mrs H Sweeting) *mid-div: rdn over 2f out: sn lost pl: n.d after* **50/1**

24 **7** 1½ **I Dont Do Walkin (USA)**^{7} [2468] 2-8-8 0 DarryllHolland 1 42+
(B J Meehan) *prom tl rdn and wknd 2f out* **3/1**^{2}

8 2 **Little By Luck (IRE)** 2-7-13 0 LukeMorris$^{(5)}$ 4 30
(W G M Turner) *outpcd* **50/1**

65 **9** 1¾ **Fabuleux Cherie**^{22} [1993] 2-8-6 0 RichardMullen 6 26+
(W R Muir) *prom tl rdn and wknd 2f out* **33/1**

4 **10** nk **Casla Beag (IRE)**^{18} [2103] 2-8-4 0 CatherineGannon 7 23+
(B Palling) *led: rdn and hdd over 2f out: wknd over 1f out* **5/1**^{3}

64.26 secs (1.76) **Going Correction** +0.35s/f (Good) **10** Ran SP% **121.6**

Speed ratings (Par 91):99,97,93,92,91 87,84,81,78,78

CSF £16.41 TOTE £3.00: £1.10, £2.50, £2.50; EX 17.30 Trifecta £147.60 Pool: £405.47 - 1.95 winning units..

Owner Nick Hughes **Bred** Richard O' Hara **Trained** Lichfield, Staffs

FOCUS

This low-grade affair was a second and a half quicker than the opening novice event. The winner came on for his debut and the first two finished 9lb clear of the third, but a few of these raced on slower ground.

NOTEBOOK

Supermassive Muse(IRE) again gave the impression that he will be suited by further and came from off the pace to score. He is going the right way. (op 5-2)

Gasmanfightsback ◆ probably found the rain-softened ground helping him on this drop back from six. A reproduction of this performance should see him take a similar event. (op 8-1)

Katrina Bee(IRE) ◆ showed why she was a springer on her debut after not getting the best of breaks. Improvement can be expected. (op 11-1)

Lambrini Lace(IRE) is a half-sister to an Irish 1m4f winner who went on to score over hurdles. She may do better over further.

Perfect Flight could not raise her game sufficiently on this return to five. (op 7-1)

Fabuleux Cherie Official explanation: trainer said filly was unsuited by the good to soft ground

2652 BATHWICK TYRES NEWBURY (S) STKS 5f 161y

3:25 (3:25) (Class 6) 3-Y-O+ £1,943 (£578; £288; £144) Stalls Low

Form RPR

0060 **1** **Mafaheem**^{28} [1852] 5-9-4 78 SebSanders 1 59
(S Dow) *hld up in mid-div: hdwy over 2f out: rdn to ld over 1f out: edgd rt ins fnl f: r.o* **3/1**^{1}

356- **2** 1¼ **Danehill Stroller (IRE)**^{176} [6906] 7-9-1 48 JerryO'Dwyer$^{(3)}$ 11 55
(A M Hales) *chsd ldrs: rdn to ld wl over 1f out: sn hdd: nt qckn ins fnl f* **15/2**^{3}

0036 **3** 2½ **Detonate**^{4} [2540] 5-9-4 44 (b) DarryllHolland 3 46
(Ms J S Doyle) *bhd: hdwy over 2f out: rdn over 1f out: kpt on same pce fnl f* **14/1**

0050 **4** hd **Saintly Place**^{3} [2555] 6-9-3 45 MarkCoumbe$^{(7)}$ 10 51
(A W Carroll) *s.i.s: sn mid-div: rdn and hdwy 2f out: kpt on same pce fnl f* **40/1**

-050 **5** 2½ **Full Spate**^{1} [2619] 12-9-4 48 ChrisCatlin 5 37
(J M Bradley) *s.s: rdn and hdwy over 2f out: kpt on ins fnl f: nvr trbld ldrs* **14/1**

0030 **6** ¾ **Ruby's Dream**^{18} [2104] 5-8-6 45 (p) BarrySavage$^{(7)}$ 9 29
(J M Bradley) *prom: rdn over 2f out: wknd ins fnl f* **14/1**

6500 **7** 1 **Montzando**^{23} [1969] 4-8-13 48 (v) JamesMillman$^{(5)}$ 4 31
(B R Millman) *bhd: nt clr run over 1f out: late hdwy: nrst fin* **9/1**

-335 **8** ½ **Tang**^{103} [619] 3-8-1 55 TolleyDean$^{(5)}$ 7 22
(W G M Turner) *mid-div: rdn over 2f out: no hdwy fnl f* **12/1**

0030 **9** shd **Going Skint**^{11} [2334] 4-9-10 53 (b^{1}) AdamKirby 12 35
(M Wellings) *led: rdn over 2f out: hdd wl over 1f out: wknd fnl f* **9/1**

5060 **10** nk **Pat Will (IRE)**^{12} [2304] 3-8-6 48 RichardMullen 6 21
(P D Evans) *s.i.s: rdn and hdwy 3f out: wknd over 1f out* **20/1**

-000 **11** 2 **Campeon (IRE)**^{3} [2555] 5-8-13 44 KevinGhunowa$^{(5)}$ 15 21
(J M Bradley) *s.i.s: rdn and hdwy over 2f out: wknd over 1f out* **5/1**^{2}

6-0 **12** 2 **Ballybunion (IRE)**^{3} [2555] 8-8-13 55 LukeMorris$^{(5)}$ 2 14
(R A Harris) *prom: rdn over 2f out: edgd rt over 1f out: sn wknd* **14/1**

3000 **13** 4 **Glenargo (USA)**^{15} [2221] 4-8-13 47 RussellKennemore$^{(5)}$ 8 1
(S T Lewis) *prom: rdn over 2f out: n.m.r over 1f out: sn wknd* **66/1**

2100 **14** 1½ **Borzoi Maestro**^{33} [1729] 6-9-7 52 (p) RichardKingscote$^{(3)}$ 17 2
(G F Bridgwater) *prom: rdn 3f out: sn wknd* **33/1**

0400 **15** 1¼ **Juce Of Hearts**^{15} [2195] 3-8-8 50 (p) MarcHalford$^{(3)}$ 14 —
(J L Spearing) *s.i.s: rdn whn hmpd over 2f out: a bhd* **40/1**

6000 **16** 1¼ **Hornpipe**^{18} [2104] 5-9-4 50 VinceSlattery 16 —
(M S Saunders) *mid-div: rdn 3f out: sn bhd* **20/1**

0-00 **17** 3½ **Auction Oasis**^{39} [1561] 3-8-6 54 CatherineGannon 13 —
(B Palling) *outpcd* **12/1**

1m 13.35s (2.15) **Going Correction** +0.35s/f (Good)

WFA 3 from 4yo+ 7lb **17** Ran SP% **134.3**

Speed ratings (Par 101):99,97,94,93,90 89,88,87,87,86 84,81,76,74,72 70,66

CSF £25.68 TOTE £4.20: £1.80, £4.00, £4.50; EX 36.60 Trifecta £227.60 Part won. Pool: £320.70 - 0.60 winning units..The winner was sold to David Evans for 5,000gns.

Owner T G Parker **Bred** J H And J M Wall **Trained** Epsom, Surrey

FOCUS

The winner was the clear pick on ratings in this big field of platers but did not run anywhere near to his mark. A poorish seller overall.

Montzando Official explanation: jockey said gelding hung right

Glenargo(USA) Official explanation: jockey said gelding suffered interference in running

2653 BATHWICK TYRES TETBURY H'CAP 1m 3f 144y

4:00 (4:00) (Class 5) (0-70,70) 3-Y-O £2,979 (£886; £442; £221) Stalls Low

Form RPR

0040 **1** **Bathwick Breeze**^{25} [1917] 3-8-7 56 DavidKinsella 2 63
(A B Haynes) *set stdy pce: qcknd 4f out: rdn 2f out: r.o wl* **11/1**

0-12 **2** 4 **Potentiale (IRE)**^{25} [1917] 3-8-11 60 DarryllHolland 12 66+
(J W Hills) *hld up: nt clr run and lost pl over 7f out: rdn over 2f out: hdwy over 1f out: wnt 2nd ins fnl f: nt trble wnr* **5/4**^{1}

6634 **3** 2½ **Summer Of Love (IRE)**^{8} [2413] 3-8-11 65 TolleyDean$^{(5)}$ 4 61
(P F I Cole) *sn chsng wnr: rdn over 2f out: wknd ins fnl f* **7/1**

5140 **4** 2 **Beau Sancy**^{33} [1722] 3-9-2 70 LukeMorris$^{(5)}$ 7 62
(R A Harris) *hld up: hdwy over 6f out: rdn 3f out: edgd rt 1f out: sn wknd* **12/1**

-003 **5** nk **Down The Brick (IRE)**^{10} [2362] 3-8-11 60 (b) RichardMullen 5 52
(B R Millman) *s.i.s: hld up: hdwy over 4f out: rdn over 2f out: no imp whn hmpd 1f out* **5/1**^{2}

3406 **6** 3½ **Zelos (IRE)**^{8} [2413] 3-8-11 63 RichardKingscote$^{(3)}$ 11 49
(J A Osborne) *t.k.h in mid-div: rdn 4f out: hdwy over 2f out: wknd over 1f out* **16/1**

303 **7** 1½ **Marju's Gold**^{14} [2248] 3-8-9 58 ChrisCatlin 3 41
(E J O'Neill) *stdd s: a in rr* **6/1**^{3}

050- **8** ½ **Vietnam**^{263} [5597] 3-8-9 58 FrankieMcDonald 9 40
(S Kirk) *prom: rdn over 3f out: wknd over 1f out* **25/1**

00-0 **P** **Everyman**^{19} [2079] 3-8-0 54 ow3 KevinGhunowa$^{(5)}$ 6 —
(A W Carroll) *plld hrd in mid-div: sddle slipped: lost pl over 5f out: t.o whn p.u over 1f out* **16/1**

2m 34.97s (4.67) **Going Correction** +0.35s/f (Good) **9** Ran SP% **119.5**

Speed ratings (Par 99):98,95,93,92,92 89,88,88,—

CSF £26.12 CT £112.19 TOTE £12.90: £2.80, £1.10, £2.20; EX 28.10 Trifecta £311.00 Pool: £762.38 - 1.74 winning units..

Owner W Clifford **Bred** Miss C Tagart **Trained** Limpley Stoke, Bath

FOCUS

The winner took advantage of a soft lead in this field of hold-up horses, although the time was not bad and he was not totally flattered. The runer-up would have gone close had he not had trouble rounding the bend.

Potentiale(IRE) Official explanation: jockey said gelding lost its action

Everyman Official explanation: jockey said saddle slipped

2654 BATHWICK TYRES BRISTOL FILLIES' H'CAP 1m 5y

4:35 (4:38) (Class 5) (0-70,70) 3-Y-O+ £2,914 (£867; £433; £216) Stalls Low

Form RPR

21-3 **1** **World Spirit**^{33} [1726] 3-9-7 70 RichardMullen 7 77+
(Rae Guest) *chsd ldr: rdn to ld over 1f out: r.o wl* **6/4**^{1}

0602 **2** 3 **Lii Najma**^{17} [2149] 4-10-0 67 DarryllHolland 8 69
(C E Brittain) *sn led: rdn and hdd over 1f out: one pce fnl f* **9/2**^{3}

-000 **3** 1½ **Corrib (IRE)**^{30} [1787] 4-9-10 63 CatherineGannon 4 62
(B Palling) *hld up in mid-div: hdwy over 2f out: sn rdn: one pce fnl f* **12/1**

-413 **4** nk **Blue Line**^{24} [1951] 5-8-12 54 MarcHalford$^{(3)}$ 2 52
(M Madgwick) *hld up towards rr: hdwy over 2f out: rdn wl over 1f out: one pce fnl f* **10/3**^{2}

0320 **5** ¾ **Fangorn Forest (IRE)**^{5} [2512] 4-9-7 65 (p) LukeMorris$^{(5)}$ 6 61
(R A Harris) *hld up and bhd: nt clr run and swtchd rt 2f out: sn rdn: styd on fnl f: n.d* **5/1**

-000 **6** 1½ **Spoilsport**^{17} [2143] 4-8-9 48 oh3 HayleyTurner 1 41
(G A Butler) *hld up and bhd: rdn and hdwy over 2f out: wknd fnl f* **14/1**

000- **7** ¾ **Beshairt**^{217} [6441] 3-8-0 49 oh3 ow1 FrankieMcDonald 9 40?
(D Burchell) *prom: rdn over 3f out: wknd over 2f out* **50/1**

000- **8** 1¼ **Ishismart**^{210} [6520] 3-8-1 50 oh3 ow2 ChrisCatlin 3 36?
(R Hollinshead) *hld up in tch: rdn and wknd over 1f out* **25/1**

1m 44.73s (3.63) **Going Correction** +0.35s/f (Good)

WFA 3 from 4yo+ 10lb **8** Ran SP% **118.1**

Speed ratings (Par 100):95,92,90,90,89 87,87,85

CSF £9.01 CT £59.96 TOTE £2.30: £1.20, £1.60, £2.40; EX 8.90 Trifecta £31.40 Pool: £977.93 - 22.06 winning units..

Owner R J Searle **Bred** Chippenham Lodge Stud Ltd **Trained** Newmarket, Suffolk

FOCUS

A modest handicap run at an ordinary pace. Pretty weak form overall, rated through the run ner-up, but an improved run from World Spirit.

2655 BATHWICK TYRES SWINDON H'CAP 5f 161y

5:05 (5:06) (Class 4) (0-80,79) 3-Y-O+ £4,792 (£1,425; £712; £355) Stalls Low

Form RPR

23 **1** **Gilded Cove**^{56} [1165] 7-8-8 64 RussellKennemore$^{(5)}$ 6 73
(R Hollinshead) *s.i.s: in rr whn rdn over 3f out: hdwy 1f out: r.o to ld cl home* **12/1**

6136 **2** nk **Harrison's Flyer (IRE)**^{8} [2411] 6-8-5 63 (p) BarrySavage$^{(7)}$ 7 71
(J M Bradley) *hld up and bhd: rdn and hdwy over 1f out: ev ch whn edgd lft towards fin: r.o* **7/1**

-550 **3** hd **Outer Hebrides**^{9} [2394] 6-9-0 70 (t) KevinGhunowa$^{(5)}$ 3 77
(J M Bradley) *s.i.s: hdwy 3f out: rdn 2f out: led ins fnl f: hdd cl home* **12/1**

1452 **4** ¾ **Who's Winning (IRE)**^{6} [2494] 6-9-11 79 RichardKingscote$^{(3)}$ 11 83
(B G Powell) *chsd ldrs: rdn 2f out: ev ch 1f out: nt qckn towards fin* **11/2**^{3}

2622 **5** 1¾ **Chatshow (USA)**^{8} [2411] 6-9-0 72 MarkCoumbe$^{(7)}$ 2 71
(A W Carroll) *hld up: hdwy 3f out: rdn and ev ch 1f out: wknd wl ins fnl f* **9/2**^{1}

2131 **6** nk **Matterofact (IRE)**^{7} [2459] 4-9-1 66 FergusSweeney 12 63
(M S Saunders) *w ldr: led over 2f out: rdn over 1f out: hdd ins fnl f: wknd* **7/1**

113 **7** ¾ **Misaro (GER)**^{17} [2139] 6-9-9 79 (b) LukeMorris$^{(5)}$ 14 74
(R A Harris) *chsd ldrs: rdn over 1f out: wknd fnl f* **5/1**^{2}

3215 **8** 1 **What Do You Know**^{8} [2411] 4-9-4 72 JerryO'Dwyer$^{(3)}$ 4 64
(A M Hales) *hld up in mid-div: rdn over 2f out: no hdwy* **7/1**

-000 **9** *nk* **Blessed Place**[7] 2479 7-8-11 **62** ChrisCatlin 9 53
(D J S Ffrench Davis) *led: hdd over 2f out: rdn and wknd ins fnl f* **33/1**

0000 **10** *1 3/4* **Night Prospector**[8] 2411 7-9-7 **72** (p) RichardThomas 10 57
(R A Harris) *chsd ldrs: rdn over 2f out: wknd over 1f out* **20/1**

6233 **11** *1 3/4* **Carcinetto (IRE)**[7] 2472 5-9-2 **67** RichardMullen 13 46
(P D Evans) *prom tl rdn and wknd over 2f out* **15/2**

1m 12.4s (1.20) **Going Correction** +0.35s/f (Good) **11** Ran SP% **122.6**
Speed ratings (Par 105):106,105,105,104,102 101,100,99,98,96 94
CSF £97.55 CT £1053.16 TOTE £17.50: £4.20, £1.70, £4.00; EX 68.80 Trifecta £347.30 Part won. Pool: £489.24 - 0.20 winning units..
Owner M Johnson **Bred** R Hollinshead And M Johnson **Trained** Upper Longdon, Staffs

FOCUS
Several came into this open sprint handicap in decent form. Sound form, rated through the third.

2656 BATHWICK TYRES CHIPPENHAM H'CAP 1m 2f 46y
5:40 (5:42) (Class 6) (0-55,59) 4-Y-0+ **£2,184** (£644; £322) **Stalls** Low

Form RPR

-241 **1** **Drawback (IRE)**[11] 2336 4-8-13 **59** (p) LukeMorris(5) 5 69
(R A Harris) *t.k.h: a.p: rdn and wnt 2nd over 2f out: led wl over 1f out: r.o wl* **7/1**[3]

456- **2** *1 1/2* **Soviet Sceptre (IRE)**[283] 1548 6-8-10 **51** (t) FergusSweeney 15 58
(Evan Williams) *hld up and bhd: hdwy on outside over 2f out: sn rdn: chsd wnr fnl f: nt qckn* **12/1**

4000 **3** *1* **Stravara**[29] 1811 4-8-6 **52** RussellKennemore(5) 7 57
(R Hollinshead) *s.i.s: hld up and bhd: rdn and hdwy on ins over 2f out: nt clr run over 1f out: kpt on ins fnl f* **12/1**

5-20 **4** *nk* **Rock Haven (IRE)**[5] 2519 5-8-9 **53** RichardKingscote(3) 3 57
(G F Bridgwater) *t.k.h: prom: led over 6f out: rdn and hdd wl over 1f out: no ex ins fnl f* **9/1**

0-00 **5** *2 1/2* **Cove Mountain (IRE)**[11] 2336 5-8-11 **52** JDSmith 8 51
(S Kirk) *a.p: rdn over 2f out: wknd ins fnl f* **14/1**

0003 **6** *1/2* **Danzare**[17] 2157 5-8-10 **54** MarcHalford(3) 12 52
(J L Spearing) *hld up in mid-div: hdwy on ins 3f out: sn rdn: wknd ins fnl f* **6/1**[2]

0000 **7** *hd* **Atticus Trophies (IRE)**[5] 2511 4-7-13 **47** SophieDoyle(7) 16 45
(Ms J S Doyle) *hld up in tch: rdn over 2f out: wknd over 1f out* **40/1**

6442 **8** *1 1/4* **Beneking**[11] 2336 7-8-13 **54** ChrisCatlin 13 50
(D Burchell) *hld up and bhd: rdn and hdwy on outside over 2f out: wknd ins fnl f* **9/2**[1]

6035 **9** *3* **Kilmeena Magic**[46] 1380 5-8-5 **46** oh1 PaulFitzsimons 17 36
(J C Fox) *prom early: sn mid-div: rdn over 2f out: no hdwy* **25/1**

0-00 **10** *shd* **Yenaled**[6] 2490 10-8-2 **48** KevinGhunowa(5) 14 37
(J M Bradley) *hld up towards rr: sme hdwy 3f out: sn rdn: wknd over 1f out* **25/1**

664 **11** *1 1/2* **Itcanbedone Again (IRE)**[14] 2258 8-7-12 **46** oh1 KMay(7) 10 32
(Ian Williams) *mid-div: lost pl 3f out: n.d after* **8/1**

1560 **12** *12* **Monmouthshire**[6] 2490 4-8-3 **49** (v) TolleyDean(5) 6 11
(R J Price) *hld up in mid-div: rdn over 2f out: sn wknd* **8/1**

050 **13** *6* **Voice Mail**[10] 2370 8-8-4 **52** (v) DavidProbert(7) 1 —
(A M Balding) *hld up in mid-div: rdn over 2f out: sn bhd* **6/1**[2]

6-00 **14** *13* **Psycho Cat**[15] 2225 4-8-9 **53** JerryO'Dwyer(3) 2 —
(S T Lewis) *s.i.s: hdwy to ld after 1f: hdd over 6f out: rdn and wknd over 2f out: sn eased* **25/1**

4506 **15** *18* **Myrtle Bay (IRE)**[47] 1342 4-8-5 **46** (p) HayleyTurner 9 —
(J C Tuck) *led 1f: rdn over 4f out: wknd qckly over 3f out: sn eased* **10/1**

0- **16** *1/2* **World Supremacy (IRE)**[204] 6584 4-8-6 **47** AlanDaly 11 —
(G A Ham) *prom: lost pl 7f out: lost tch over 3f out: eased fnl 2f* **50/1**

2m 14.01s (3.01) **Going Correction** +0.35s/f (Good) **16** Ran SP% **138.6**
Speed ratings (Par 101):101,99,99,98,96 96,96,95,92,92 91,81,77,66,52 51
CSF £96.35 CT £1044.70 TOTE £10.10: £3.20, £4.10, £4.10, £2.80; EX 152.70 TRIFECTA Not won. Place 6 £349.82, Place 5 £47.95.
Owner B & T Hicks Transport Limited **Bred** Mrs H B Raw **Trained** Earlswood, Monmouths

FOCUS
A distinctly modest handicap in which the winner is rated up 5lb on his Lingfield win over shorter.
Rock Haven(IRE) Official explanation: jockey said gelding ran too free
Psycho Cat Official explanation: jockey said gelding hung left
T/Plt: £428.30 to a £1 stake. Pool: £90,136.85. 153.60 winning tickets. T/Qpdt: £26.70 to a £1 stake. Pool: £5,180.40. 143.10 winning tickets. KH

2303 LEICESTER (R-H)
Saturday, June 16

OFFICIAL GOING: Soft (heavy in places)
There were no fewer than 26 non-runners on account of the worsening ground conditions.
Wind: Light behind Weather: Showers

2657 CITY LIFE AND COUNTY LIVING MAGAZINE FILLIES' H'CAP 5f 218y
6:45 (6:45) (Class 5) (0-70,67) 3-Y-0+ **£4,533** (£1,348; £674; £336) **Stalls** Low

Form RPR

-060 **1** **Limonia (GER)**[14] 2257 5-8-2 **48** oh2 ThomasO'Brien(7) 10 57
(Mike Murphy) *chsd ldrs: led over 4f out: edgd rt ins fnl f: rdn out* **6/1**[3]

-650 **2** *1 1/2* **Riquewihr**[5] 2508 7-9-9 **65** JamieMoriarty(3) 3 70
(J S Wainwright) *s.i.s: hld up: hdwy over 1f out: sn rdn: r.o* **13/2**

1655 **3** *1/2* **Piddies Pride (IRE)**[11] 2334 5-9-4 **57** (b[1]) JohnEgan 15 60
(Miss Gay Kelleway) *s.i.s: outpcd: hdwy over 2f out: styd on u.p* **11/2**[2]

2 **4** *1 1/4* **Lady Aspen (IRE)**[14] 2258 4-10-0 **67** TPO'Shea 11 66
(Ian Williams) *a.p: rdn over 1f out: no ex ins fnl f* **17/2**

0155 **5** *2 1/2* **Pappas Ruby (USA)**[3] 2576 4-9-3 **56** (v[1]) GeorgeBaker 1 48
(R M Beckett) *chsd ldrs: drvn along thrght: hung rt over 1f out: no ex* **3/1**[1]

0606 **6** *1* **Prettilini**[11] 2343 4-8-9 **48** oh3 J-PGuillambert 2 37
(A W Carroll) *led: hdd over 4f out: hung rt over 1f out: wknd fnl f* **12/1**

4060 **7** *1 1/4* **Noravana (IRE)**[6] 2489 3-7-9 **48** DanielleMcCreery(7) 14 33
(Miss V Haigh) *hld up: rdn over 3f out: bhd whn hmpd 2f out: nvr nrr* **66/1**

40-0 **8** *shd* **Suhezy (IRE)**[11] 2343 4-8-6 **48** oh2 AndrewElliott(3) 12 33
(J S Wainwright) *prom: rdn 1/2-way: wknd over 1f out* **18/1**

000- **9** *3/4* **Sapphire Dream**[407] 1465 5-8-2 **48** oh3 AmyBaker(7) 6 30
(A Bailey) *hld up: hdwy 1/2-way: wknd over 1f out* **25/1**

5-01 **10** *1/2* **Sahara Silk (IRE)**[3] 2553 6-9-7 **67** 6ex (v) KellyHarrison(7) 4 48
(D Shaw) *chsd ldrs: lost pl over 3f out: wknd wl over 1f out* **13/2**

0 **11** *17* **Shahadah (IRE)**[8] 2433 5-8-13 **55** SaleemGolam(3) 8 —
(R J Price) *s.i.s: outpcd* **22/1**

1m 15.94s (2.74) **Going Correction** +0.40s/f (Good)
WFA 3 from 4yo+ 7lb **11** Ran SP% **114.5**
Speed ratings (Par 100):97,95,94,92,89 88,86,86,85,84 61
CSF £42.63 CT £230.02 TOTE £8.60: £2.10, £1.60, £1.80; EX 46.10.
Owner M Murphy **Bred** D Furstin Zu Oettingen-Wallerstein **Trained** Westoning, Beds
■ The first winner for trainer Mike Murphy.

FOCUS
A very moderate fillies' handicap. The form is sound enough, rated though the fourth, but none of these are likely improvers.
Prettilini Official explanation: jockey said filly hung right-handed closing stages

2658 EAST MIDLANDS PREMIER LIFESTYLE MAGAZINE MAIDEN FILLIES' STKS 5f 218y
7:15 (7:16) (Class 4) 2-Y-O **£5,047** (£1,510; £755; £377; £188) **Stalls** Low

Form RPR

1 **Highland Daughter (IRE)** 2-9-0 0 PhilipRobinson 4 86+
(C G Cox) *hld up: swtchd rt and hdwy to ld over 1f out: shkn up and sn clr: edgd lft ins fnl f: eased nr fin* **12/1**

2 *3 1/2* **Red And White (IRE)** 2-9-0 0 JoeFanning 9 76
(M Johnston) *chsd ldrs: ev ch 2f out: sn hung lft and outpcd: hung rt and styd on ins fnl f* **16/1**

4 **3** *1 3/4* **Tatbeeq (IRE)**[18] 2122 2-9-0 0 RHills 12 70
(M A Jarvis) *trckd ldrs: racd keenly: led over 4f out: rdn and hdd over 1f out: edgd lft and no ex ins fnl f* **9/2**[3]

4 *1* **Patio** 2-9-0 0 RichardHughes 5 67
(Mrs A J Perrett) *stdd s: hld up in tch: rdn and ev ch 2f out: wkng whn hmpd ins fnl f* **12/1**

5 **5** *3/4* **Mizooka**[18] 2122 2-9-0 0 GeorgeBaker 2 65
(R M Beckett) *led: racd keenly: hdd over 4f out: ev ch 2f out: sn rdn and wknd* **3/1**[2]

2 **6** *3 1/2* **High Days (IRE)**[18] 2122 2-9-0 0 LDettori 1 55+
(Sir Michael Stoute) *chsd ldrs: rdn over 2f out: hung rt and wknd over 1f out* **7/4**[1]

7 *5* **Princess India (IRE)** 2-9-0 0 JohnEgan 3 40
(P Winkworth) *chsd ldrs: rdn over 2f out: wknd over 1f out* **33/1**

43 **8** *8* **Lady Sandicliffe (IRE)**[15] 2193 2-9-0 0 MichaelHills 13 16
(B W Hills) *chsd ldrs over 3f: eased over 1f out* **8/1**

1m 16.28s (3.08) **Going Correction** +0.40s/f (Good) **8** Ran SP% **114.9**
Speed ratings (Par 92):95,90,88,86,85 81,74,63
CSF £179.66 TOTE £12.90: £2.80, £4.80, £1.80; EX 250.30.
Owner Highland Thoroughbred Ltd **Bred** Dr Francesco Magliari **Trained** Lambourn, Berks

FOCUS
This looked a fair juvenile fillies' maiden. The debutante winner is value for around double her winning margin. The third, fifth and sixth all came from the same Sandown maiden.

NOTEBOOK
Highland Daughter(IRE) ◆, whose stable took this event last year with the very useful Hope'n'charity, got her career off to a perfect start with a most decisive debut success. She showed a neat turn of foot to settle the issue entering the final furlong and should be rated value for at least double her winning margin. Not surprisingly being by Kyllachy she had no trouble with this easy ground, in fact she looked most suited by it, and a step up in class now surely beckons. (tchd 9-1)
Red And White(IRE), a 40,000gns purchase whose dam scored over 1m at two, showed up well until wandering about under pressure at the 1f marker and ultimately proved too green to do herself full justice. This must rate an encouraging start to her career and she will no doubt relish a stiffer test before the season is out. (op 14-1)
Tatbeeq(IRE), fourth at Sandown over 5f on her debut, broke on terms this time and was given a positive ride. However, she paid late on for refusing to settle early and still looks in need of further experience. She helps to set the level of this form. (tchd 4-1 and 5-1)
Patio, a half-sister to three winners from 6f to 1m 6f, came through to hold every chance at the 2f pole but she tired thereafter and was treading water prior to being hampered late in the day. She should build on this next time and may be suited by faster ground. (op 9-1 tchd 14-1)
Mizooka failed to really build on the promise of her Sandown debut over this extra distance and simply proved too keen through the early parts. She can do better. (op 5-1 tchd 11-2 and 11-4)
High Days(IRE), in front of today's third and fifth when second on her debut at Sandown 18 days previously, obviously ran below that level here and shaped as though she needs a sounder surface. She should not be written off. Official explanation: trainer's rep said filly may have been unsuited by the soft ground (op 5-4 tchd 11-10 and 2-1)

2659 CITY LIFE AND COUNTY LIVING MAGAZINE SPRINT H'CAP 5f 2y
7:45 (7:49) (Class 3) (0-95,93) 3-Y-O **£9,348** (£2,799; £1,399; £700) **Stalls** Low

Form RPR

0-01 **1** **Fathom Five (IRE)**[29] 1820 3-8-13 **85** LDettori 6 96
(B Smart) *racd centre: led over 3f out: clr fnl f: comf* **11/8**[1]

-104 **2** *5* **Ebn Reem**[29] 1817 3-9-4 **90** (p) PhilipRobinson 2 83
(M A Jarvis) *led stands' side: hdd over 3f out: outpcd fr over 1f out* **9/4**[2]

-222 **3** *4* **Valley Of The Moon (IRE)**[10] 2373 3-8-4 **76** PaulHanagan 9 55+
(R A Fahey) *s.i.s: racd centre: outpcd* **7/2**[3]

0-10 **4** *13* **Mambo Spirit (IRE)**[21] 2044 3-9-1 **87** J-PGuillambert 4 19
(J G Given) *chsd ldr stands' side to 1/2-way* **7/1**

62.52 secs (1.62) **Going Correction** +0.40s/f (Good) **4** Ran SP% **107.6**
Speed ratings (Par 103):103,95,88,67
CSF £4.67 TOTE £2.00; EX 4.80.
Owner Hintlesham Racing **Bred** Eamonn Connolly **Trained** Hambleton, N Yorks

FOCUS
This was decimated by the non-runners and the form should be treated with some caution. The winner still did the job very well, however.

NOTEBOOK
Fathom Five(IRE) ◆ followed up his Newmarket success a month ago with a career-best effort from an 8lb higher mark. He is thriving at present, went through the softer ground without any fuss, and has relished the drop back to this trip the last twice. It could prove that he is a bit flattered by his winning margin, but while his stable remains in such good form he should be capable of handling another rise back up the class ladder. (op 13-8 tchd 5-4)
Ebn Reem, equipped with first-time cheekpices, was given a positive ride on the stands' rail yet was made to look one-paced entering the final furlong. He ideally needs another furlong, but has been disappointing to date this term and is one to have reservations about at present. (op 10-3)
Valley Of The Moon(IRE) was never in the hunt after missing the break and did not prove suited by the drop back to this trip. She also prefers a sounder surface. Official explanation: jockey said filly missed the break (op 9-4 tchd 4-1)
Mambo Spirit(IRE) dropped out tamely after the halfway stage and, while this was very disappointing, he simply must have a faster surface. (op 11-2 tchd 15-2)

2660 CITYLIFEMEDIA.COM H'CAP 1m 1f 218y
8:15 (8:15) (Class 5) (0-75,74) 4-Y-0+ £4,533 (£1,348; £674; £336) Stalls High

Form				RPR
/000	1		Prize Fighter (IRE)[27] 1862 5-9-7 74.....(b[1]) TedDurcan 4 (H R A Cecil) mde all: rdn clr fnl f 14/1	86
0-40	2	4	Dispol Veleta[15] 2214 6-8-8 61..... DeanMcKeown 8 (Miss T Spearing) a.p: rdn over 3f out: chsd wnr over 1f out: styd on same pce 20/1	65
00-0	3	1	Sharmy (IRE)[7] 2474 11-8-5 58..... TPO'Shea 2 (Ian Williams) sn chsng ldrs: rdn over 3f out: styd on same pce appr fnl f 50/1	60
-060	4	3/4	Fabrian[9] 2401 9-9-7 74..... GeorgeBaker 7 (R J Price) trckd wnr: shkn up over 2f out: styd on same pce appr fnl f 13/2	75
6501	5	3 1/2	Kingscape (IRE)[17] 2157 4-9-1 68..... LDettori 11 (J R Fanshawe) hld up: rdn over 2f out: nvr trbld ldrs 10/3[2]	66+
0245	6	3	Mae Cigan (FR)[18] 2106 4-8-12 65..... NCallan 6 (M Blanshard) hld up: rdn over 3f out: n.d 11/4[1]	53+
0-05	7	4	Kingdom Of Dreams (IRE)[9] 2397 5-9-5 72..... AdrianTNicholls 9 (J Mackie) chsd ldrs: rdn over 3f out: wknd wl over 1f out 15/2	52
-600	8	3	Bolton Hall (IRE)[12] 2302 5-8-5 58..... PaulHanagan 3 (R A Fahey) s.i.s: hld up: rdn over 3f out: a in rr 14/1	32
-253	9	3/4	Near Germany (IRE)[19] 2089 7-8-0 60..... ThomasO'Brien(7) 1 (R Curtis) dwlt: hld up: swtchd rt and hdwy over 2f out: sn rdn and wknd 9/2[3]	32

2m 16.83s (8.53) **Going Correction** +0.95s/f (Soft) 9 Ran SP% **113.1**
Speed ratings (Par 103):103,99,99,98,95 93,90,87,87
CSF £249.36 CT £12727.79 TOTE £10.60: £4.60, £6.40, £8.40; EX 203.00.

Owner Diamond Racing Ltd **Bred** G Dunne **Trained** Newmarket, Suffolk

FOCUS
A moderate handicap in which those racing handily proved at an advantage. The winner returned to some form in the blinkers but there are big doubts over what he beat.

2661 ENQUIRIES@SALESCITYLIFEMEDIA.COM H'CAP 5f 218y
8:45 (8:45) (Class 6) (0-60,59) 3-Y-0 £3,238 (£963; £481; £240) Stalls Low

Form				RPR
0604	1		Mujart[10] 2366 3-8-9 50..... DeanMcKeown 13 (J A Pickering) chsd ldrs: rdn to ld over 1f out: edgd lft ins fnl f: jst hld on 7/1	48
0-00	2	hd	The Skerret[6] 2489 3-9-2 57..... PaulEddery 2 (P Winkworth) s.i.s: outpcd: hdwy u.p over 1f out: r.o 11/2[3]	54
-055	3	nk	Soviet Sound (IRE)[12] 2300 3-8-9 50..... PaulMulrennan 18 (Jedd O'Keeffe) chsd ldrs: led 1/2-way: rdn and hdd over 1f out: styd on 4/1[1]	46
000	4	1/2	Cornerstone[109] 573 3-8-4 45.....(b[1]) AdrianTNicholls 7 (S C Williams) s.i.s: outpcd: r.o ins fnl f: nrst fin 14/1	40
0040	5	5	Kyburg[6] 2489 3-8-7 48 ow1..... TQuinn 8 (P F I Cole) sn outpcd 4/1[1]	28
0000	6	shd	Flamestone[32] 1750 3-7-13 45..... NataliaGemelova(5) 4 (A E Price) chsd ldrs: rdn 1/2-way: wknd over 1f out 25/1	24
0006	7	1	Abadia[24] 1943 3-8-1 45..... AndrewElliott(3) 12 (J G Given) s.i.s: outpcd 13/2	21
3-30	8	1 1/4	Come What May[24] 1943 3-9-0 55..... LDettori 1 (Rae Guest) led to 1/2-way: wknd over 1f out 9/2[2]	27
-400	9	2	Meridian Grey (USA)[28] 1850 3-9-2 57.....(b[1]) NCallan 6 (K A Ryan) chsd ldrs 4f 10/1	23

1m 17.44s (4.24) **Going Correction** +0.65s/f (Yiel) 9 Ran SP% **119.0**
Speed ratings (Par 97):97,96,96,95,89 88,87,85,83
CSF £46.66 CT £178.94 TOTE £8.20: £2.10, £2.10, £1.70; EX 66.80.

Owner J A Pickering **Bred** S Kitching And Mr J A Pickering **Trained** Sharnford, Leics

■ Stewards' Enquiry : Paul Eddery five-day ban: used whip with excessive frequency (Jun 27-Jul 1)

FOCUS
A poor three-year-old sprint handicap. The first four came clear in a bunch finish.

2662 CITY LIFE AND COUNTY LIVING MAGAZINE H'CAP 7f 9y
9:15 (9:16) (Class 4) (0-80,77) 3-Y-0 £6,309 (£1,888; £944; £472; £235) Stalls Low

Form				RPR
01	1		Look So[28] 1839 3-9-1 71..... GeorgeBaker 7 (R M Beckett) chsd ldr: led 2f out: rdn out 2/1[2]	81+
0610	2	2 1/2	Jack Oliver[11] 2335 3-9-4 74..... LDettori 2 (B J Meehan) led 5f: sn rdn: styd on same pce fnl f 9/2[3]	77
0-31	3	1	Bid For Gold[19] 2094 3-9-0 70..... PaulMulrennan 9 (Jedd O'Keeffe) plld hrd and prom: rdn over 2f out: no ex fnl f 9/1	70
0-31	4	2	Oscarshall (IRE)[20] 2061 3-8-12 71..... SaleemGolam(3) 1 (M H Tompkins) trckd ldrs: rdn over 2f out: hung rt over 1f out: sn wknd 13/8[1]	66
-460	5	3 1/2	Dr Dream (IRE)[26] 1904 3-8-2 63..... WilliamBuick(5) 6 (D M Simcock) hld up in tch: racd keenly: rdn over 2f out: sn wknd 9/1	48
13-0	6	6	Book Of Facts (FR)[21] 2045 3-9-7 77..... PaulEddery 8 (J McAuley) hld up: rdn over 2f out: sn wknd 33/1	46

1m 33.27s (7.17) **Going Correction** +1.05s/f (Soft) 6 Ran SP% **112.6**
Speed ratings (Par 101):101,98,97,94,90 83
CSF £11.45 CT £62.97 TOTE £2.90: £1.50, £2.30; EX 14.70 Place 6 £1,952.42, Place 5 £930.45.

Owner J H Richmond-Watson **Bred** Lawn Stud **Trained** Whitsbury, Hants

FOCUS
A modest three-year-old handicap, run at an average pace. The lightly-raced winner looks capable of rating higher but the form is not entirely solid.

T/Plt: £2,808.20 to a £1 stake. Pool: £97,902.60. 25.45 winning tickets. T/Qpdt: £106.90 to a £1 stake. Pool: £4,582.40. 31.70 winning tickets. CR

2590 LINGFIELD (L-H)
Saturday, June 16

OFFICIAL GOING: Turf course - good; all-weather - standard
Wind: Fresh, behind Weather: cloudy bright

2663 PLATINUM ABBA LIVE AT LINGFIELDPARK.CO.UK MEDIAN AUCTION MAIDEN FILLIES' STKS 5f
5:55 (5:56) (Class 5) 2-Y-O £2,817 (£838; £418; £209) Stalls High

Form				RPR
	1		Raymi Coya (CAN) 2-9-0 0..... OscarUrbina 2 (M Botti) s.i.s: hdwy on outer 1/2-way: chal over 1f out: led ins fnl f: pushed out 20/1	81+
4	2	1	Sophie's Girl[10] 2364 2-9-0 0..... SebSanders 8 (P W Chapple-Hyam) led: rdn 2f out: hdd ins fnl f: one pce 4/7[1]	77
00	3	2 1/2	A Wish For You[11] 2333 2-9-0 0..... RobertHavlin 1 (D K Ivory) prom: ev ch and rdn over 1f out: wknd last 100yds 18/1	68
	4	3	Lavande 2-9-0 0..... PatDobbs 4 (M J Wallace) chsd ldrs: rdn over 2f out: outpcd wl over 1f out: kpt on same pce fnl f 33/1	57
	5	1 1/4	Maddy 2-9-0 0..... JamesDoyle 7 (R M Beckett) sn outpcd and pushed along in rr: nvr on terms 10/1	53
	6	nk	Heavenly Saint 2-9-0 0..... JHBowman 3 (M R Channon) sn pushed along and outpcd: n.d 14/1	52
	7	nk	Memphis Kate 2-9-0 0..... JamieSpencer 5 (M L W Bell) chsd ldr: ev ch and rdn over 2f out: edgd rt wl over 1f out: sn wknd 7/1[3]	54+
2	8	3/4	Giggling Monkey[19] 2078 2-9-0 0..... StephenDonohoe 10 (P D Evans) s.i.s: sn rdn: a outpcd 6/1[2]	48
03	9	1 3/4	Little Angel (IRE)[16] 2188 2-8-9 0..... ColinHaddon(5) 9 (Miss V Haigh) sn outpcd: rdn after 2f: nvr on terms 50/1	42

58.06 secs (-0.88) **Going Correction** -0.225s/f (Firm) 9 Ran SP% **121.1**
Speed ratings (Par 90):98,96,92,87,85 85,84,83,80
CSF £33.21 TOTE £22.50: £5.60, £1.10, £5.10; EX 49.10.

Owner C Pizarro **Bred** Anderson Farms Ont Inc & Marrette Farrell **Trained** Newmarket, Suffolk

FOCUS
A modest-looking contest, with the runner-up the guide to the form. The winner could be rated a bit better than the bare result, while the second should be winning soon in similar company.

NOTEBOOK
Raymi Coya(CAN) did not get the best of starts but soon caught up and eventually won going away. She has some decent relations in her pedigree and it would be unwise to discount her in a slight better grade.
Sophie's Girl attempted to make most down the stands' side, despite slightly hanging away from the rail, but had no answer to the winner as she swept past. Another nicely-bred sort, she is capable of winning a similar event. (op 8-13 tchd 4-6, 8-11 in places)
A Wish For You travelled really well in the early stages but just did not have another gear when required. Although soundly beaten by the first two, she was clear of the fourth. (op 20-1)
Lavande showed plenty of early pace but seemed to be caught out by a lack of experience at the vital stage of the race. Keeping on well inside the final furlong, there are races to be won with her. (op 25-1)
Maddy could not go the early gallop but stayed on quite nicely in the final stages. (op 12-1)
Memphis Kate tracked Sophie's Girl in the early stages, but completely lost the plot about a furlong and a half from home and weakened very quickly. (op 11-2)
Giggling Monkey never went the pace and failed to improve on her debut effort. (op 10-1 tchd 11-1)

2664 RAY QUINN & BEN MILLS LIVE AT LINGFIELDPARK.CO.UK H'CAP 6f
6:25 (6:25) (Class 6) (0-65,60) 3-Y-0+ £2,047 (£604; £302) Stalls High

Form				RPR
0004	1		Charming Ballet (IRE)[15] 2217 4-9-7 55.....(b) JamesDoyle 10 (N P Littmoden) mde all: rdn 2f out: 2 l clr 1f out: jst hld on 16/1	68
0221	2	shd	Currency[4] 2546 10-9-9 57..... JamieSpencer 7 (J M Bradley) taken down early: chsd wnr for 2f: rdn 1/2-way: chsd wnr again 1f out: r.o u.p: jst failed 7/4[1]	70
60-0	3	2 1/2	Ruman (IRE)[36] 1640 5-8-11 52..... JosephWalsh(7) 13 (M J Attwater) chsd ldrs early: sddn and hld up: hdwy 1/2-way: outpcd 2f out: rallied and swtchd lft 1f out: kpt on: nt trble ldrs 16/1	58
0330	4	3/4	Inwaan (IRE)[24] 1946 4-9-10 58.....(t) PatDobbs 4 (P R Webber) s.i.s: bhd: rdn 1/2-way: kpt on u.p last 2f: nrst fin 8/1[3]	61
6230	5	nk	Mister Incredible[18] 2108 4-8-11 45.....(v) JHBowman 1 (J M Bradley) chsd wnr after 2f: rdn over 1f out: nt qckn: btn whn rdr dropped whip ins fnl f 12/1	47
4130	6	1/2	Blue Knight (IRE)[16] 2187 8-8-11 45.....(p) AmirQuinn 8 (P Howling) bhd: rdn wl over 2f out: r.o fnl f: nvr nrr 16/1	46
10-0	7	1 1/2	Endless Summer[35] 1681 10-9-12 60..... FrancisNorton 11 (A W Carroll) hld up and bhd: rdn 2f out: sme late hdwy: n.d 12/1	56
4-00	8	hd	Simplify[11] 2336 5-8-12 46 ow1.....(b) NashRawiller 5 (T M Jones) racd in midfield: hdwy to chse ldrs 1/2-way: rdn 2f out: sn wknd 50/1	42
-505	9	nk	Duke Of Milan (IRE)[10] 2350 4-9-12 60..... SebSanders 6 (G C Bravery) chsd ldrs: rdn 2f out: wknd 1f out 9/2[2]	55
2330	10	1 1/4	Mind Alert[32] 1753 6-8-11 45.....(v) AdrianMcCarthy 12 (D Shaw) stdd s: t.k.h: hld up in rr: rdn over 2f out: no hdwy 12/1	39+
2033	11	1 3/4	Tibinta[5] 2515 3-8-11 52..... StephenDonohoe 2 (P D Evans) in tch in midfield: rdn and hdwy 2f out: wknd over 1f out 10/1	36
-000	12	2 1/2	Batchworth Blaise[32] 1737 4-8-11 45.....(b) StephenCarson 3 (E A Wheeler) bhd: rdn 1/2-way: sn lost tch 66/1	23
5015	13	3 1/2	Mustammer[124] 441 4-9-4 55..... DuranFentiman(3) 9 (D Shaw) a bhd: rdn 3f out: no ch last 2f 33/1	23

1m 10.76s (-0.91) **Going Correction** -0.225s/f (Firm)
WFA 3 from 4yo+ 7lb 13 Ran SP% **121.9**
Speed ratings (Par 101):97,96,93,92,92 91,89,89,88,87 84,81,76
CSF £44.70 CT £513.37 TOTE £22.90: £5.80, £1.30, £5.80; EX 67.10.

Owner Jason Gibbons **Bred** Brian Donlon **Trained** Newmarket, Suffolk

FOCUS
A very moderate event which the winner probably nicked from the front. The form is questionable, but does seem to make sense.

2665 THE REAL THING LIVE AT LINGFIELDPARK.CO.UK H'CAP 7f
6:55 (6:55) (Class 6) (0-65,65) 3-Y-0+ £2,047 (£604; £302) Stalls High

Form				RPR
5334	1		Napoletano (GER)[3] 2556 6-9-0 51.....(p) SebSanders 13 (S Dow) taken down early: hld up towards rr on rail: hdwy 2f out: rdn over 1f out: r.o wl to ld last 50yds 7/2[1]	57+

00-3 **2** ½ **Beat The Bully**[1] 2622 3-8-11 **57** .... LPKeniry 16 58
(I A Wood) *led: rdn 2f out: hdd jst over 1f out: hung lft ins fnl f: unable qck nr fin* **25/1**

-504 **3** shd **Tamino (IRE)**[23] 1969 4-9-2 **58** .... (t) TravisBlock(5) 11 63+
(H Morrison) *trckd ldrs: hdwy over 2f out: rdn to ld narrowly jst over 1f out: hdd last 50yds: no ex* **6/1**[3]

-050 **4** 1 ¾ **Three Counties (IRE)**[3] 2556 6-8-13 **57** .... KylieManser(7) 6 57+
(N I M Rossiter) *s.i.s: dropped in bhd: nt clr run over 2f out tl ins fnl f: r.o wl: wnt 4th nr fin: nvr nrr* **50/1**

4002 **5** nk **New Proposal (IRE)**[10] 2357 5-9-1 **52** .... JimCrowley 10 51
(A P Jarvis) *chsd ldr: rdn and ev ch 2f out: kpt on same pce ins fnl f* **18/1**

-U00 **6** 1 ¾ **Billy One Punch**[11] 2338 5-9-12 **63** .... JHBowman 18 57
(G G Margarson) *in tch: rdn and effrt 2f out: kpt on same pce fnl f* **12/1**

-022 **7** ½ **Wrighty Almighty (IRE)**[6] 2492 5-9-4 **55** .... PaulDoe 4 48+
(P R Chamings) *hld up in midfield on outer: hdwy over 2f out: kpt on same pce u.p over 1f out* **5/1**[2]

0306 **8** shd **Joy And Pain**[3] 2576 6-8-11 **55** .... JosephWalsh(7) 9 48
(M J Attwater) *t.k.h: prom: rdn over 2f out: wknd 1f out* **20/1**

1404 **9** 1 ¾ **King After**[48] 1318 5-9-3 **54** .... (v) JamieSpencer 14 42
(J R Best) *t.k.h: trckd ldrs: rdn 2f out: sn btn: hung lft ins fnl f* **10/1**

0-00 **10** ½ **Salisbury Plain**[30] 1787 6-9-2 **53** .... StephenDonohoe 17 40
(N I M Rossiter) *s.i.s: a bhd: rdn 3f out: n.d* **50/1**

0002 **11** 1 ¼ **Scroll**[2] 2591 4-8-12 **49** .... (v) AdrianMcCarthy 2 32
(P Howling) *towards rr: rdn and bhd over 3f out: no ch after* **16/1**

0300 **12** 1 ½ **Double Valentine**[2] 2592 4-8-10 **47** .... RobertHavlin 3 26
(R Ingram) *chsd ldrs: rdn wl over 2f out: sn wknd* **16/1**

-056 **13** 3 **Royal Amnesty**[132] 351 4-10-0 **65** .... OscarUrbina 15 36
(G C H Chung) *hld up in midfield: rdn wl over 2f out: sn btn* **16/1**

0445 **14** ½ **Treasure House (IRE)**[22] 2004 6-9-12 **63** .... FrancisNorton 12 33
(M Blanshard) *a bhd: no ch last 2f* **8/1**

0160 **15** nk **Firework**[11] 2336 9-8-11 **48** .... StephenCarson 5 17
(E A Wheeler) *taken down early: a bhd* **33/1**

3516 **16** 5 **Our Kes (IRE)**[6] 2490 5-9-10 **61** .... AmirQuinn 1 17
(P Howling) *v.s.a: a wl bhd: no ch last 3f* **14/1**

2002 **17** hd **Lucius Verrus (USA)**[15] 2225 7-8-13 **53** .... (v) DuranFentiman(3) 7 8
(D Shaw) *a bhd: rdn after 2f: no ch last 3f* **25/1**

1m 23.23s (-0.98) **Going Correction** -0.225s/f (Firm)
WFA 3 from 4yo+ 9lb **17** Ran SP% **130.0**
Speed ratings (Par 101):96,95,95,93,92 90,90,90,88,87 86,84,81,80,80 74,74
CSF £107.91 CT £537.71 TOTE £5.30: £1.90, £9.10, £2.30, £7.80; EX 416.00.
Owner Miss Helen Chamberlain **Bred** Gestut Hof Ittlingen **Trained** Epsom, Surrey

FOCUS
A weak-looking handicap. The winner has been beaten in sellers recently and the form is unlikely to prove to be very strong.
King After Official explanation: jockey said gelding hung badly left
Our Kes(IRE) Official explanation: jockey said mare ran flat

2666 BRIEFCASE BLUES BROTHERS LIVE AT LINGFIELDPARK.CO.UK MEDIAN AUCTION MAIDEN STKS 1m 4f (P)
7:25 (7:26) (Class 6) 3-4-Y-O **£2,590** (£770; £385; £192) **Stalls** Low

Form RPR

1 **Double Harness (USA)** 3-8-11 0 .... RobertHavlin 1 78
(H Morrison) *hld up in tch: hdwy over 3f out: chsd ldr 3f out: rdn 2f out: led ins fnl f: forged ahd nr fin* **4/1**[3]

0-53 **2** nk **Kailasha (IRE)**[33] 1725 3-8-7 70 ow1 .... SebSanders 6 73
(C F Wall) *chsd ldr after 2f tl led over 4f out: rdn over 2f out: kpt on wl tl hdd and no ex wl ins fnl f* **13/8**[1]

5-22 **3** 10 **Snake's Head**[25] 1928 3-8-6 76 .... KerrinMcEvoy 4 56
(J L Dunlop) *led for 1f: stdd to chse ldrs: sltly hmpd wl over 3f out: sn rdn and outpcd: no ch after: wnt modest 3rd ins fnl f* **15/8**[2]

0 **4** 2 **Bundle Up**[15] 2219 4-9-6 0 .... IanMongan 5 53
(Mrs L J Mongan) *hld up in last pair: hdwy 5f out: chsd ldng pair and rdn wl over 2f out: sn outpcd* **12/1**

0 **5** 8 **Beauchamp Viking**[29] 1812 3-8-11 0 .... (t) StephenCarson 3 45
(G A Butler) *hld up in last: rdn over 3f out: sn outpcd and no ch* **12/1**

0-0 **6** dist **Agent Eleven (IRE)**[24] 1950 4-9-11 0 .... StephenDonohoe 7 —
(A J Lidderdale) *pushed up to ld after 1f: rdn and hdd over 4f out: sn dropped out: eased and no ch last 2f* **66/1**

2m 32.64s (-1.75) **Going Correction** -0.125s/f (Stan)
WFA 3 from 4yo 14lb **6** Ran SP% **109.8**
Speed ratings (Par 101):100,99,93,91,86 —
CSF £10.45 TOTE £5.00: £2.80, £1.30; EX 12.60.
Owner Mrs B Oppenheimer **Bred** B D Oppenheimer **Trained** East Ilsley, Berks

FOCUS
An ordinary maiden dominated by the first two, who came clear of the disappointing third in the home straight.
Snake's Head Official explanation: jockey said filly hung right

2667 GO WEST LIVE AT LINGFIELDPARK.CO.UK H'CAP 1m 2f (P)
7:55 (7:55) (Class 5) (0-70,70) 4-Y-O+ **£2,817** (£838; £418; £209) **Stalls** Low

Form RPR

351 **1** **Birkside**[17] 2140 4-9-1 **64** .... JamieSpencer 7 71+
(S Dow) *hld up in last pair: hdwy on outer 2f out: str run to ld last 100yds: pushed out* **7/2**[2]

26/- **2** hd **Wicked Daze (IRE)**[722] 2873 4-9-7 **70** .... SebSanders 2 77
(Sir Mark Prescott) *led: rdn over 2f out: 2 l clr 1f out: hdd last 100yds: rallied but a hld by wnr* **3/1**[1]

1530 **3** 3 **Musango**[12] 2321 4-9-5 **68** .... (t) RichardSmith 9 69
(B R Johnson) *hld up in tch: rdn 3f out: hdwy over 2f out: chsd ldr briefly 1f out: outpcd last 100yds* **7/1**

-005 **4** 1 **Pactolos Way**[12] 2321 4-9-5 **68** .... JimCrowley 4 67
(P R Chamings) *hld up in bhd ldrs: hdwy to chse ldng pair 3f out: sn rdn: no ex fnl f* **6/1**[3]

-521 **5** ¾ **Watchmaker**[122] 459 4-9-3 **66** .... PaulDoe 3 64
(W J Knight) *w.w in midfield: rdn and hdwy over 3f out: no imp u.p wl over 1f out* **3/1**[1]

200 **6** 1 **Golden Platitude (IRE)**[19] 2077 4-9-2 **65** .... (t) AdamKirby 5 61
(W R Swinburn) *hld up in last pair: rdn and effrt 2f out: no imp* **14/1**

-030 **7** shd **Titus Lumpus (IRE)**[10] 2358 4-8-9 **58** .... DarryllHolland 6 55+
(R M Flower) *chsd ldr: rdn 4f out: ev ch tl 2f out: wknd over 1f out: btn whn short of room ins fnl f* **12/1**

2-00 **8** 6 **Bowl Of Cherries**[17] 2154 4-8-8 **57** .... (b) StephenDonohoe 1 40
(I A Wood) *chsd ldrs: rdn and lost pl over 3f out: no ch last 2f* **16/1**

2m 6.77s (-1.02) **Going Correction** -0.125s/f (Stan) **8** Ran SP% **119.2**
Speed ratings (Par 103):99,98,96,95,95 94,94,89
CSF £15.20 CT £70.75 TOTE £4.70: £1.60, £1.60, £3.60; EX 28.90.
Owner I Hedgecock **Bred** Pendley Farm **Trained** Epsom, Surrey
■ Stewards' Enquiry : Richard Smith caution: careless riding

FOCUS
A pretty ordinary event with a few horses having a few question marks over them. It would be difficult to get too carried away with the form, although Birkside is capable of better based on his best form of last winter.

2668 CHESNEY HAWKES LIVE AT LINGFIELDPARK.CO.UK H'CAP 1m (P)
8:25 (8:25) (Class 6) (0-60,65) 3-Y-O **£2,047** (£604; £302) **Stalls** High

Form RPR

0002 **1** **My Mentor (IRE)**[7] 2456 3-9-5 **61** .... SebSanders 12 69
(Sir Mark Prescott) *sn prom: reminder over 3f out: sn chsng ldr: rdn to ld 2f out: hld on grimly fnl f* **9/2**[3]

3044 **2** ½ **Inquisitress**[3] 2571 3-8-9 **56** .... TolleyDean(5) 10 63
(J J Bridger) *hld up and bhd: hdwy and rdn wl over 2f out: chsd ldrs over 2f out: ev ch over 1f out: wnt 2nd last 100yds: no ex nr fin* **12/1**

-405 **3** 1 **Forced Upon Us**[16] 2177 3-9-1 **57** .... JamieSpencer 11 62
(P J McBride) *racd wd: hld up wl bhd: pushed along and hdwy over 2f out: rdn and hung lft fr wl over 1f out: kpt on: nt quite rch ldrs* **11/4**[2]

1231 **4** nk **Private Peachey (IRE)**[6] 2489 3-9-4 **65** 6ex .... JamesMillman(5) 4 69
(B R Millman) *sn chsng ldr: led over 4f out: rdn and narrowly hdd 2f out: ev ch tl fdd last 100yds* **5/2**[1]

0660 **5** 1 **Silca Key**[7] 2456 3-9-1 **57** .... JHBowman 6 59
(M R Channon) *hld up in tch on rail: hdwy on inner over 2f out: kpt on same pce fnl f* **8/1**

1000 **6** 5 **Zaafira (SPA)**[16] 2178 3-8-6 **55** .... SCreighton(7) 9 45
(E J Creighton) *chsd ldrs: hdwy to chse ldng pair and rdn 3f out: wknd wl over 1f out* **33/1**

-663 **7** 1 ½ **Chant De Guerre (USA)**[16] 2178 3-9-3 **59** .... IanMongan 5 46
(H J L Dunlop) *sn rdn along in midfield: lost pl 3f out: n.d after* **10/1**

0610 **8** hd **Hayley's Flower (IRE)**[16] 2178 3-9-0 **56** .... (b) PatDobbs 8 42
(J C Fox) *hld up wl bhd: nvr on terms* **16/1**

400 **9** 3 **Mandalay Prince**[56] 1166 3-9-1 **57** .... BrettDoyle 2 36
(W J Musson) *s.i.s: bhd: hdwy over 3f out: sn outpcd* **10/1**

5440 **10** 2 ½ **Head To Head (IRE)**[14] 2262 3-8-13 **55** .... LPKeniry 7 29
(Peter Grayson) *t.k.h: hld up in midfield: hdwy to chse ldrs 3f out: sn rdn and wknd: eased whn btn fnl f* **33/1**

50-0 **11** 24 **Crystal Plum (IRE)**[16] 2177 3-9-4 **60** .... OscarUrbina 1 —
(B W Hills) *taken down early: led tl over 4f out: wknd qckly 3f out: t.o and eased fnl f* **25/1**

1m 39.01s (-0.42) **Going Correction** -0.125s/f (Stan) **11** Ran SP% **126.0**
Speed ratings (Par 97):97,96,95,95,94 89,87,87,84,82 58
CSF £60.75 CT £167.98 TOTE £5.40: £1.30, £4.30, £2.20; EX 72.60 Place 6 £38.98, Place 5 £25.25.
Owner Mr And Mrs Arthur Finn **Bred** B D Burnett **Trained** Newmarket, Suffolk

FOCUS
Not a strong race but the form looks fairly sound for the grade with the winner improving by 6lb on his previous best.
Forced Upon Us Official explanation: jockey said, regarding running and riding, his orders were to drop the gelding in, as it had raced keenly before, adding that on settling in rear it resented the kickback, which caused him to ease his mount to the outside, adding that it then raced smoothly and he nursed it into contention turning for home being only 2 lengths behind 2nd horse entering straight, it made up ground one-paced on leaders and was never quite able to get on terms; trainer said gelding returned lame near-fore
T/Plt: £35.80 to a £1 stake. Pool: £67,678.65. 1,377.45 winning tickets. T/Qpdt: £17.40 to a £1 stake. Pool: £3,835.20. 162.50 winning tickets. SP

2630 SANDOWN (R-H)
Saturday, June 16

OFFICIAL GOING: Good to soft
The 5mm of rain the course had seen led to jockeys tacking across towards the stands' side in races.
Wind: Virtually nil

2669 CHERRIES RACING H'CAP 1m 1f
1:50 (2:05) (Class 3) (0-90,90) 3-Y-O **£7,772** (£2,312; £1,155; £577) **Stalls** High

Form RPR

13 **1** **One Hour**[22] 2001 3-9-6 **89** .... MartinDwyer 8 95
(M P Tregoning) *mde virtually all: hrd drvn fr 2f out: r.o gamely fnl f and in command whn edgd lft cl home* **8/1**

2-21 **2** ¾ **Royal Rationale (IRE)**[25] 1928 3-8-12 **81** .... JamieSpencer 1 86
(W J Haggas) *t.k.h: hld up in rr: hdwy on ins fr 3f out: n.m.r 2f out: r.o u.p to take 2nd wl ins fnl f: nt pce of wnr* **11/1**

021 **3** nk **Russian Epic**[19] 2083 3-8-9 **78** .... PhilipRobinson 10 82
(M A Jarvis) *chsd ldrs: rdn over 2f out: styd on u.p thrght fnl f but nt qckn nr fin* **11/4**[1]

15-0 **4** ½ **Gold Option**[28] 1835 3-9-6 **89** .... RichardHughes 4 92
(J H M Gosden) *lw: chsd ldr: chal fr 4f out: shkn up and stl ev ch 2f out: one pce ins fnl f and hld whn nt mcuh room cl home* **7/1**[3]

10- **5** hd **Divine Right**[339] 3415 3-9-7 **90** .... MJKinane 9 92
(B J Meehan) *towards rr but in tch: hdwy 3f out rdn to chse ldrs 2f out: kpt on same pce ins fnl f* **12/1**

1 **6** 3 **Idle No More (USA)**[46] 1375 3-9-7 **90** .... JimmyFortune 3 86
(J H M Gosden) *w'like: towards rr: rdn and flashed tail over 2f out: nvr in contention* **4/1**[2]

1-20 **7** 3 **Hunting Tower**[31] 1773 3-9-1 **84** .... RyanMoore 5 73
(R Hannon) *lw: prom early: dropped towards rr 5f out: rdn over 3f out and nvr in contention* **11/4**[1]

-050 **8** 5 **Cheap Street**[15] 2213 3-9-1 **84** .... JimCrowley 2 62
(J G Portman) *chsd ldrs: rdn 4f out: wknd over 2f out* **20/1**

1m 57.38s (1.27) **Going Correction** +0.175s/f (Good) **8** Ran SP% **117.7**
Speed ratings (Par 103):101,100,100,99,99 96,94,89
CSF £92.54 CT £308.59 TOTE £9.40: £2.50, £2.70, £1.20; EX 92.00 Trifecta £362.40 Pool: £510.55 - 1.00 winning units..
Owner Sheikh Ahmed Al Maktoum **Bred** Darley **Trained** Lambourn, Berks

FOCUS
A good three-year-old handicap, likely to work out well, in which they all came across towards the stands' rail. Improvement from the first five, although none of them looked obviously well treated going into this.

NOTEBOOK

One Hour, unraced at two, ran out a ready winner on his debut at Lingfield back in January, but could not go on from that when returning in a conditions event at Newmarket, looking rather paceless. With that run under his belt and up a furlong, he was able to make a successful switch to handicaps, being made plenty of use of and battling on doggedly under strong pressure to hold off numerous challengers. A further rise in distance is going to suit the son of Halling and he looks capable of further improvement. (op 6-1)

Royal Rationale(IRE), ready winner of an average maiden at Lingfield last month, took a keen grip early on for what was his handicap debut, but that did not prevent him seeing his race out strongly. It looked likely he would pass the winner when emerging against the stands' rail inside the final furlong, but he could not get past. He is clearly progressing and there are more races in him. (tchd 10-1)

Russian Epic, off the mark at the third attempt when dropped to 7f at Leicester last time, had appeared not to stay 1m2f on his debut, but he saw his race out well on this step back up in distance and, although unable to justify the market support, it still represented an improved showing. (op 10-3 tchd 7-2)

Gold Option ◆ is of more interest than most for the future. A disappointment when sent off favourite for the Royal Lodge at two, his effort that day could safely be put down to the soft ground and he was again faced with slow conditions for his seasonal debut when down the field at Newbury. He could really have done without the rain the course saw and as a result this has to go down as a fine effort, only just losing out on the placings. There is a decent prize in him this season. (op 8-1)

Divine Right, unable to handle the rise to Group 2 level when seventh behind Sander Camillo in the Cherry Hinton at two, had not been seen since, but her debut victory showed her to be a filly of definite ability and she made a pleasing reappearance for a yard who have been going through a rough spell. She is another who could have a decent race in her this season. (op 14-1)

Idle No More(USA), a stablemate of Gold Option, made a highly pleasing debut when winning by eight lengths at Southwell and the betting suggested he was the stable's first string on this handicap debut. On a stiffish mark of 90, he was ridden with restraint, but could never really get into it and it was disconcerting to see him flashing his tail. He may be better than this, but is one to tread carefully with. (op 10-3 tchd 9-2)

Hunting Tower proved rather disappointing on this drop back down in distance and has a fair bit to prove now. (op 4-1)

Cheap Street is not bred to stay and it was no surprise to see him fade out of it in the final quarter mile.

2670 RBS H'CAP 7f 16y

2:25 (2:34) (Class 2) (0-100,99) 3-Y-O+

£12,464 (£3,732; £1,866; £934; £466; £234) **Stalls** High

Form				RPR
0-50	**1**		**Black Charmer (IRE)**[10] 2374 4-9-5 **90** J-PGuillambert 12 (M Johnston) *lw: led after 1f: hrd drvn 2f out: c clr over 1f out: kpt on strly* **8/1**	107+
0-62	**2**	*3*	**Binanti**[8] 2427 7-9-2 **87** PaulDoe 11 (P R Chamings) *lw: towards rr: hdwy and rdn fr 2f out: styd on to chse wnr ins fnl f and hung lft: kpt on for clr 2nd but nvr any ch* **11/1**	94
2-46	**3**	*2*	**Irony (IRE)**[14] 2239 8-9-2 **87** FrancisNorton 9 (A M Balding) *led 1f: styd chsng wnr to 3f out: sn one pce: styd on again fnl f to retake 3rd* **16/1**	89
-054	**4**	*3/4*	**Moonlight Man**[7] 2476 6-9-1 **86** RyanMoore 5 (R Hannon) *prom: chsd wnr 3f out: sn rdn and no imp: wknd fnl f* **10/1**	86
-143	**5**	*3/4*	**Mcnairobi**[14] 2239 4-8-11 **82** DaneO'Neill 2 (P D Cundell) *in tch: rdn and styd on same pce fnl 2f* **13/2**[2]	80
0050	**6**	*hd*	**Wavertree Warrior (IRE)**[7] 2476 5-8-10 **88** JackMitchell(7) 7 (N P Littmoden) *chsd ldrs: rdn 3f out: wknd fnl f* **10/1**	85
050	**7**	*1*	**Bahiano (IRE)**[35] 1653 6-9-6 **91** JMurtagh 8 (C E Brittain) *chsd ldrs: pushed along 3f out: sn outpcd* **12/1**	85
1-44	**8**	*1/2*	**Partners In Jazz (USA)**[35] 1651 6-10-0 **99** JamieSpencer 4 (T D Barron) *lw: t.k.h: hld up towards rr: pushed along over 2f out: sn edgd rt: mod prog fnl f* **5/2**[1]	92
00-0	**9**	*4*	**Jamieson Gold (IRE)**[28] 1842 4-9-3 **88** MichaelHills 10 (B W Hills) *rdn 3f out: a towards rr* **7/1**[3]	70
0560	**10**	*2*	**The Snatcher (IRE)**[9] 2401 4-9-2 **87** RichardHughes 1 (R Hannon) *chsd ldrs: shkn up 3f out: wknd qckly over 2f out* **9/1**	64
066-	**11**	*2 1/2*	**Prime Number (IRE)**[168] 4112 5-8-12 **83** MartinDwyer 3 (J Akehurst) *a in rr* **20/1**	53

1m 30.38s (1.04) **Going Correction** +0.175s/f (Good) **11** Ran SP% **120.4**

Speed ratings (Par 109):111,107,105,104,103 103,102,101,97,94 91

CSF £94.96 CT £945.30 TOTE £9.80: £2.90, £3.40, £5.60; EX 121.80 Trifecta £1461.30 Pool: £25,727.63 - 12.50 winning units..

Owner A D Spence **Bred** Annalee Bloodstock & Rockhart Trading Ltd **Trained** Middleham Moor, N Yorks

FOCUS

Again runners came towards the stands' side and, as was the case in the opening event, it paid to race on the pace. The form of the first two seems sound but a number of the others were below their best.

NOTEBOOK

Black Charmer(IRE) looked a horse to follow this season following a highly pleasing comeback run at York, but he ran too bad to be true at Ripon last time and as a result came into this with a bit to prove. However, he showed that latest running to be all wrong and made full use of his draw, pressing on from an early stage and galloping on relentlessly in the straight. This was a taking performance from the one-time smart juvenile and he is now on course to take his chance in next week's Royal Hunt Cup, for which he is a general 25/1 shot. That though will prove much more difficult and all evidence so far points to him being better at short of 1m. Official explanation: trainer's rep had no explanation for the apparent improvement in form (op 7-1)

Binanti often goes well over this course and he came through to claim second, but was left for dead by the easy winner. He tends to run well without winning these days and that is likely to continue to be the case. (op 8-1)

Irony(IRE), running in this contest for the third time, was not helped by being headed early by the winner and as a result he ran quite well back in third. This was his best finish in this race to date and he should continue to pay his way without winning. (op 20-1)

Moonlight Man, back down in distance, held every chance in the straight, but did not see it out as well as those around him. He has apparently taken time to get fit this season and as a result could be worth watching out for in the coming weeks as he is back down to a reasonable mark. (op 11-1 tchd 9-1 and 12-1 in places)

Mcnairobi is a most consistent filly, but she could only make limited headway from the rear in a race where it was an advantage to race prominently. (op 15-2 tchd 6-1)

Partners In Jazz(USA) has been running well without suggesting he is up to defying this kind of mark and he proved rather disappointing, finding little for pressure. (op 3-1 tchd 10-3 in places)

Jamieson Gold(IRE) has yet to show much in two starts back, but he is not yet one to give up on. (op 13-2 tchd 8-1)

2671 PADDYPOWER.COM H'CAP 7f 16y

3:00 (3:04) (Class 3) (0-90,90) 3-Y-O **£7,772** (£2,312; £1,155; £577) **Stalls** High

Form				RPR
53-1	**1**		**Mutanaseb (USA)**[45] 1398 3-9-5 **88** RHills 6 (M A Jarvis) *trckd ldrs: wnt 2nd over 2f out: sn rdn: styd on u.p to ld fnl 100yds: kpt on wl* **3/1**[2]	100+
44-1	**2**	*1 1/4*	**Endiamo (IRE)**[122] 456 3-9-4 **87** MartinDwyer 10 (M P Tregoning) *lw: led: hrd drvn fr 2f out: hdd and one pce fnl 100yds* **7/2**[3]	96
3-14	**3**	*4*	**Bold Abbott (USA)**[14] 2243 3-9-0 **83** JimCrowley 9 (Mrs A J Perrett) *chsd ldr tl over 2f out: styd on u.p fr over 1f out* **11/1**	81
-360	**4**	*shd*	**Karoo Blue (IRE)**[14] 2243 3-9-1 **84** (b[1]) JMurtagh 2 (C E Brittain) *chsd ldrs: rdn over 2f out and kpt on one pce* **14/1**	82
-603	**5**	*shd*	**La Roca (IRE)**[14] 2243 3-8-11 **80** JamesDoyle 8 (R M Beckett) *in tch: rdn and kpt on fnl 2f but nvr gng pce to be competitive* **14/1**	77
-202	**6**	*2*	**Southandwest (IRE)**[35] 1667 3-9-5 **88** JohnEgan 7 (J S Moore) *stdd s: towards rr: rdn over 2f out: edgd lft u.p over 1f out and nvr in contention* **11/1**	80
-231	**7**	*9*	**Transcend**[20] 2059 3-9-0 **83** JimmyFortune 4 (J H M Gosden) *lw: chsd ldrs: rdn 3f out: wknd fr over 2f out: eased whn no ch ins fnl f* **2/1**[1]	51
0-05	**8**	*21*	**To The Max (IRE)**[20] 2057 3-9-6 **89** RichardHughes 1 (R Hannon) *lw: s.i.s: reminders sn after: drvn and mod prog over 3f out: sn bhd: eased whn no ch fnl f* **25/1**	—

1m 31.02s (1.68) **Going Correction** +0.175s/f (Good) **8** Ran SP% **114.4**

Speed ratings (Par 103):107,105,101,100,100 98,88,64

CSF £13.99 CT £99.92 TOTE £4.10: £1.50, £1.70, £3.50; EX 14.70 Trifecta £122.60 Pool: £881.36 - 5.10 winning units..

Owner Hamdan Al Maktoum **Bred** Spendthrift Farm Llc **Trained** Newmarket, Suffolk

FOCUS

Two unexposed sorts came nicely clear in what was a fair handicap. Both are progressive, and the overall form looks sound.

NOTEBOOK

Mutanaseb(USA) ◆ showed some useful form in a couple of starts at two and confirmed that promise when scoring in a 7f Kempton maiden on his return. Not overly burdened off a mark of 88 for this handicap debut, he was given a fine ride by Richard Hills who did not go for the colt too soon and he edged past Endiamo in the final half-furlong, winning with a bit to spare. He should get 1m, but looks happy enough at this distance for the time being and it would not surprise to see him tried at pattern level should he continue to progress. (op 11-4, tchd 10-3 in a place)

Endiamo(IRE), another to have shown useful form in all starts at two, readily shed his maiden status in a maiden at Lingfield back in February and looked a major player on this first start since. In a bid to repeat the all-the-way tactics of the first race, Dwyer soon had the gelding out in front and he looked the likely winner two out, but he could not shake off Mutanaseb and he was worn down in the final half-furlong. This was still a fine effort and he pulled nicely clear of the remainder. (op 4-1)

Bold Abbott(USA), readily held off this mark at Folkestone last time, is not as progressive as the front two, but he kept on well to just snatch third and will find easier opportunities. (tchd 12-1)

Karoo Blue(IRE), sporting first-time blinkers, showed a slight improvement in form, but still held every chance and was simply not good enough. He needs to progress further, but the headgear is not certain to have the same effect in future.

La Roca(IRE) was unable to confirm her Folkestone superiority over Bold Abbott or Karoo Blue, but still ran well and only lost out on the placings by short heads.

Transcend, off the mark when winning a moderate maiden by Newmarket standards latest, has proved himself to be most effective with cut in the ground in the past, so that cannot be put forward as an excuse for this dismal showing. The way he dropped out suggested something may have been amiss. (op 9-4 tchd 15-8 and 5-2 in a place)

To The Max(IRE) continues to race like a horse with a problem, whether it be mental or physical. (tchd 28-1 and 33-1 in a place)

2672 CHERRIESRACING.COM SCURRY STKS (LISTED RACE) 5f 6y

3:35 (3:36) (Class 1) 3-Y-O

£14,762 (£5,595; £2,800; £1,396; £699; £351) **Stalls** High

Form				RPR
2-12	**1**		**Hoh Mike (IRE)**[21] 2035 3-9-2 **110** JamieSpencer 4 (M L W Bell) *lw: hld up towards rr but in tch: hdwy: qcknd to chal and edgd rt 1f out: led sn after: sn clr: comf* **7/4**[2]	112+
5-13	**2**	*2 1/2*	**City Of Tribes (IRE)**[21] 2035 3-8-13 **0** JMurtagh 6 (G M Lyons, Ire) *led tl hdd jst insde fnl f: sn no ch w wnr but hld on wl for 2nd* **13/2**[3]	100
	3	*3/4*	**Contest (IRE)**[31] 1775 3-8-13 **0** MJKinane 3 (David Wachman, Ire) *lw: strong: athletic: wnt lft s: chsd ldrs: rdn to chal fr 2f out: styng on same pce whn pushed rt 1f out* **6/4**[1]	97
44-2	**4**	*1 1/4*	**Siren's Gift**[17] 2135 3-8-8 **98** FrancisNorton 2 (A M Balding) *awkward s and pushed lft: sn in tch: rdn over 2f out: kpt on but nvr gng pce to be competitive* **8/1**	88
5-60	**5**	*shd*	**Elhamri**[10] 2352 3-9-2 **103** DPMcDonogh 7 (S Kirk) *lw: chsd ldrs: rdn 1/2-way: wknd appr fnl f* **14/1**	95
01-3	**6**	*1 1/2*	**Ishi Adiva**[26] 1900 3-8-8 **85** JimCrowley 5 (Tom Dascombe) *pressed ldrs: chal 2f out tl hmpd and wknd 1f out* **20/1**	91+
0600	**7**	*2 1/2*	**Grange Lili (IRE)**[5] 2513 3-8-8 **69** LPKeniry 1 (Peter Grayson) *rrd s and bmpd: a outpcd* **200/1**	73?

63.19 secs (0.98) **Going Correction** +0.375s/f (Good) **7** Ran SP% **112.7**

Speed ratings (Par 107):107,103,101,99,99 97,93

CSF £13.22 TOTE £2.80: £1.60, £2.50; EX 9.20.

Owner M Lynch & the late D Allport **Bred** John Malone **Trained** Newmarket, Suffolk

FOCUS

Not a bad race for the grade and Hoh Mike put up a noteworthy performance. The race has been rated through the first two based on their Haydock meeting. The time though did not compare favourably to that set by the 79-rated Efistorm in the following contest.

NOTEBOOK

Hoh Mike(IRE) looked the outstanding sprinting juvenile in the early part of last season, but he struggled following his slightly unlucky defeat at the Royal meeting. There can be no doubting however that he has returned a better performer this season and the drop back down to 5f brought about an impressive performance, the strong-looking colt speeding clear having shown a fine turn of foot. He has done very well physically over the winter and connections expect him to get even better as a four-year-old, but he is likely to return here on Eclipse day for a Group 3 and, if all goes according to plan, will probably be allowed to take his chance in the Abbaye, where a bit of cut in the ground should suit. (tchd 15-8)

City Of Tribes(IRE) has quickly developed into a very useful sprinter, improving on his Chester win with two solid efforts in defeat at this level. He was unable to reverse Haydock form with the winner, but there is a race in him at this level and his blistering early speed is likely to continue to be an advantage. (op 15-2)

Contest(IRE), who has confirmed the promise of his debut effort with two subsequent wins dropped back to sprinting distances, latterly in a handicap off a mark of 90 at Naas, was understandably made favourite, but he was unable to cope with this distance against similarly smart sprinters and there was also the thought that this ground, the softest he has tackled to date, did not suit the son of Danehill Dancer. He is better than he showed here, but connections' pre-race aspirations of running him in the July Cup will surely have been dashed by this defeat. (tchd 13-8)
Siren's Gift, who reappeared with a sound effort in defeat behind the highly progressive Morinqua at Beverley, had slower ground to contend with here and she did not seem quite so effective in it, failing to pick up when asked for her effort. She deserves another chance.
Elhamri, last year's Windsor Castle winner, has yet to make much impression as a three-year-old, but there have been glimpses in his races to suggest he still has the ability and he could be of more interest once his stable begin to fire. Official explanation: jockey said colt stumbled on leaving stalls (tchd 16-1)
Ishi Adiva, a good third at Windsor on her recent handicap debut, would not have won, but would certainly have finished a good bit closer, had she not been hampered racing inside the final quarter mile. (op 25-1)

2673 DIAMOND SPORTS BETS H'CAP 5f 6y
4:10 (4:10) (Class 4) (0-80,79) 4-Y-O+ **£5,181** (£1,541; £770; £384) **Stalls** High

Form				RPR
6653	1		**Efistorm**[9] 2399 6-9-7 79 ... JamieSpencer 6 (C R Dore) *trckd ldrs: led 2f out: rdn out fnl f* **3/1**[2]	91
1616	2	1	**Namir (IRE)**[9] 2399 5-9-0 75 ...(vt) DuranFentiman(3) 2 (D Shaw) *hld up in rr: rdn and hdwy over 1f out: styd on to chse wnr ins fnl f but no imp* **7/1**	83
00-0	3	1 1/4	**Matty Tun**[28] 1854 8-9-0 72 ... RichardHughes 5 (J Balding) *hld up towards rr: pushed along 2f out: n.m.r over 1f out: kpt on wl fnl f but nvr gng pce to rch ldrs* **14/1**	77+
0205	4	hd	**Fromsong (IRE)**[12] 2318 9-9-6 78 ... RobertHavlin 7 (D K Ivory) *lw: chsd ldrs: rdn over 2f out: kpt on same pce fnl f* **12/1**	81
0404	5	1/2	**Chinalea (IRE)**[9] 2394 5-8-8 66 ...(b) PhilipRobinson 10 (C G Cox) *in tch: pushed along and n.m.r fr over 1f out: styd on ins fnl f but nvr gng pce to be competitive* **11/4**[1]	74+
-603	6	1/2	**Puskas (IRE)**[7] 2461 4-9-6 78 ... RyanMoore 11 (J M Bradley) *chsd ldrs: rdn over 2f out: wknd fnl 100yds* **6/1**	77
3554	7	1	**Nusoor (IRE)**[14] 2244 4-8-11 69 ...(b) LPKeniry 1 (Peter Grayson) *in tch: rdn 1/2-way: styd on same pce fr over 1f out* **16/1**	65
4422	8	2 1/2	**Willhewiz**[10] 2350 7-8-6 64 ... FrancisNorton 12 (M S Saunders) *led tl hdd 2f out: wknd fnl f* **11/2**[3]	51
20-4	9	4	**Even Bolder**[14] 2242 4-8-6 64 ...(p) SimonWhitworth 3 (R Simpson) *early spd: bhd fr 1/2-way* **20/1**	36

63.52 secs (1.31) **Going Correction** +0.375s/f (Good) **9 Ran SP% 118.8**
Speed ratings (Par 105): **104,102,100,100,99 98,96,92,86**
CSF £25.28 CT £259.17 TOTE £3.80: £1.40, £2.50, £2.80; EX 23.00.
Owner Sean J Murphy **Bred** E Duggan And D Churchman **Trained** West Pinchbeck, Lincs
Stewards' Enquiry : Jamie Spencer caution: used whip in an incorrect place

FOCUS
An average sprint handicap.
Fromsong(IRE) Official explanation: vet said gelding lost a hind shoe

2674 RBS MAIDEN STKS 1m 2f 7y
4:45 (4:45) (Class 5) 3-Y-O **£3,886** (£1,156; £577; £288) **Stalls** High

Form				RPR
2-33	1		**Black Rock (IRE)**[18] 2127 3-9-3 86 ... PhilipRobinson 2 (M A Jarvis) *lw: trckd ldr: rdn over 2f out: led appr fnl f and styd on dourly u.p* **6/4**[2]	96
2	2	3/4	**Spring City (GER)**[18] 2127 3-9-3 0 ... KerrinMcEvoy 4 (Saeed Bin Suroor) *sn led: rdn 2f out: hdd appr fnl f: styd pressing wnr tl no ex fnl 100yds* **4/6**[1]	95
64	3	29	**Mawaared**[119] 492 3-8-12 0 ... MartinDwyer 1 (M P Tregoning) *racd in 3rd thrght: lost tch over 3f out* **14/1**[3]	44+
	4	13	**Coloso** 3-9-3 0 ... JHBowman 3 (P D Cundell) *w'like: scope: strong: a last: lost tch 4f out* **33/1**	11

2m 12.19s (1.95) **Going Correction** +0.175s/f (Good) **4 Ran SP% 109.6**
Speed ratings (Par 99): **99,98,75,64**
CSF £2.90 TOTE £2.50; EX 2.90.
Owner A D Spence **Bred** Rockhart Trading Ltd **Trained** Newmarket, Suffolk

FOCUS
The expected match materialised and Black Rock managed to reverse recent course form with the favourite. Spring City still improved on that form but Black Rock was back to his strong Newbury form here.

2675 RBS PRIVATE BANKING H'CAP 1m 6f
5:15 (5:16) (Class 4) (0-85,85) 4-Y-O+ **£5,181** (£1,541; £770; £384) **Stalls** Centre

Form				RPR
0-23	1		**Swan Queen**[14] 2238 4-9-6 84 ... KerrinMcEvoy 6 (J L Dunlop) *trckd ldrs: led and veered lft 3f out: rdn and continued to hang lft fr over 1f out: jst hld on* **15/8**[1]	99+
-516	2	nk	**Takafu (USA)**[23] 1959 5-9-0 78 ... JimCrowley 3 (W S Kittow) *lw: trckd ldrs: rdn over 2f out: styd on u.p to chse wnr ins fnl f: kpt on wl cl home but nt quite get up* **4/1**[2]	86
	3	3	**Gabier**[20] 4-9-3 81 ... RyanMoore 7 (G L Moore) *in tch: rdn along 3f out: hdwy fr 2f out to chse wnr over 1f out: nvr gng pce to chal and lost 2nd ins fnl f* **9/2**[3]	85
13-0	4	3 1/2	**Velvet Heights (IRE)**[28] 1844 5-9-7 85 ... IanMongan 8 (J L Dunlop) *towards rr but in tch: rdn over 3f out: styd on fnl 2f but nvr gng pce to rch ldrs* **9/2**[3]	84
06-0	5	6	**Dance World**[27] 811 7-8-3 67 ... SimonWhitworth 2 (Miss J Feilden) *led tl hdd 3f out: sn btn* **33/1**	58
-560	6	1 3/4	**Flame Creek (IRE)**[56] 1148 11-8-9 76 ... AlanCreighton(3) 5 (E J Creighton) *chsd ldrs: rdn 3f out: sn wknd* **20/1**	64
5	7	2	**Mabel (IRE)**[21] 2047 4-8-4 68 ... MartinDwyer 4 (S C Williams) *chsd ldr to 4f out: sn rdn: wknd 3f out* **11/1**	53
02	8	shd	**Debord (FR)**[10] 2367 4-8-2 66 oh6 ... FrancisNorton 1 (Jamie Poulton) *a towards rr* **11/1**	51

3m 7.75s (3.24) **Going Correction** +0.175s/f (Good) **8 Ran SP% 115.5**
Speed ratings (Par 105): **97,96,95,93,89 88,87,87**
CSF £9.58 CT £29.05 TOTE £2.70: £1.40, £1.60, £1.70; EX 13.30 Place 6 £411.21, Place 5 £160.35.
Owner Sir Thomas Pilkington **Bred** Sir Thomas Pilkington **Trained** Arundel, W Sussex

FOCUS
Not the strongest of contests, but Swan Queen is rated value for a 4l victory. The form is sound enough with the second and third running to their marks.
T/Jkpt: £7,608.30 to a £1 stake. Pool: £21,431.89. 2.00 winning tickets. T/Plt: £300.60 to a £1 stake. Pool: £177,775.75. 431.65 winning tickets. T/Qpdt: £27.30 to a £1 stake. Pool: £7,744.20. 209.90 winning tickets. ST

[1821]YORK (L-H)
Saturday, June 16
2676 Meeting Abandoned - Waterlogged

[2295]SAN SIRO (R-H)
Saturday, June 16
OFFICIAL GOING: Good to soft

2684a PREMIO PRIMI PASSI (GROUP 3) 6f
4:30 (4:31) 2-Y-O **£24,628** (£10,836; £5,911; £2,955)

			RPR
1		**Magritte (ITY)**[14] 2-8-8 ... CFiocchi 1 (R Menichetti, Italy) *mde all: r.o wl fnl f (1.97-1)* **39/20**[2]	101
2	3 1/2	**Cima On Fly (IRE)** 2-8-11 ... DVargiu 3 (B Grizzetti, Italy) *hld up: fin wl fr 2f out: styd on to take 2nd ins fnl f* **22/1**	94
3	3/4	**Black Mambazo (IRE)**[14] 2-8-11 ... GMarcelli 4 (L Riccardi, Italy) *racd in 2nd: pushed along 2f out: stmbld 1 1/2f out: styd on tl no ex and lost 2nd ins fnl f* **18/10**[1]	92
4	1/2	**Sirjoshua Reynolds**[17] 2138 2-8-11 ... EBotti 11 (N A Callaghan) *broke wl on outside and in tch in mid-div: pushed along and u.p 2f out: rcvrd to stay on wl fnl f* **15/2**	90
5	3/4	**Ristant (IRE)** 2-8-11 ... MDemuro 9 (A & G Botti, Italy) *towards rr on outside: styd on fr over 1f out: nrest at fin* **8/1**	88
6	2	**Gladiatorus (USA)** 2-8-11 ... LManiezzi 10 (R Menichetti, Italy) *racd on outside in mid-div: pushed along 2f out: styd on at one pce* **39/20**[2]	82
7	snk	**Eldest (IRE)** 2-8-11 ... SMulas 8 (V Caruso, Italy) *towards rr: nvr a factor* **87/10**	81
8	1 1/2	**Golden Virginy (IRE)**[14] 2-8-8 ... PConvertino 6 (M & G Fratini, Italy) *a in rr* **90/1**	74
9	5	**Ashantee (GER)** 2-8-8 ... MSautjeau 2 (M Rulec, Germany) *racd in tch on ins: wknd 2f out* **6/1**[3]	59
10	1/2	**Robybat (IRE)**[14] 2-8-11 ... GArena 7 (B Grizzetti, Italy) *cl up tl wknd qckly fnl f* **20/1**	60
11	dist	**Rudebox (IRE)** 2-8-11 ... SLandi 5 (A Peraino, Italy) *in rr: outpcd* **50/1**	—

1m 12.5s (0.70) **11 Ran SP% 163.2**
(Including 1 Euro stake): WIN 2.97 (coupled with Gladiatorus); PL1.38, 3.32, 1.38; DF 46.80.
Owner Scuderia Razza Dell'Olmo **Bred** Azienda Agricola Le Ferriere **Trained** Italy

NOTEBOOK
Sirjoshua Reynolds showed useful form to win a Brighton maiden by three lengths last time out and ran well on this step up in grade. A bit of cut does seem to suit him.

[2238]FOLKESTONE (R-H)
Sunday, June 17
OFFICIAL GOING: Good (good to firm in places)
Wind: Brisk, across Weather: Fine, sunny

2686 LADBROKES CARD APPRENTICE H'CAP 1m 7f 92y
2:20 (2:20) (Class 5) (0-70,68) 4-Y-O+ **£3,238** (£963; £481; £240) **Stalls** Low

Form				RPR
3362	1		**Sand Repeal (IRE)**[54] 1222 5-8-13 62 ...(v) AmyBaker(5) 9 (Miss J Feilden) *mde all: kicked on over 2f out: hung lft u.p over 1f out: kpt on wl* **9/2**[3]	71
0424	2	1 1/2	**Madiba**[33] 1745 8-8-5 49 ... RichardKingscote 8 (P Howling) *cl up: trckd wnr 3f out: rdn to chal over 1f out: fnd nil and readily hld fnl f* **9/2**[3]	56
30-0	3	3	**Prince Of Medina**[23] 2006 4-8-10 54 ... StephaneBreux 7 (J R Best) *s.s: in tch in last pair: hit rail 3f out: prog to chse ldng pair over 1f out: one pce* **12/1**	57
5140	4	1/2	**Treason Trial**[9] 2434 6-8-9 53 ... JamieMoriarty 4 (Stef Liddiard) *t.k.h: hld up: last tl prog 1/2-way: disp 2nd on outer 3f out: nt qckn over 2f out: one pce after* **7/2**[2]	55
42-4	5	3 1/2	**Sendinpost**[156] 112 4-9-5 63 ... SaleemGolam 2 (S C Williams) *cl up: dropped to last pair 1/2-way: n.m.r 3f out: sn rdn and outpcd: no ch after* **7/2**[2]	61
0-10	6	7	**Himba**[36] 1683 4-8-12 56 ... JamesDoyle 5 (Mrs A J Perrett) *trckd wnr to 3f out: sn wknd* **11/4**[1]	45

3m 29.29s (2.09) **Going Correction** +0.175s/f (Good) **6 Ran SP% 115.2**
Speed ratings (Par 103): **101,100,98,98,96 92**
CSF £25.35 CT £226.42 TOTE £5.70: £3.10, £2.70; EX 35.30 TRIFECTA Not won..
Owner The Sultans of Speed **Bred** Don Commins **Trained** Exning, Suffolk
Squiffy was withdrawn on vet's advice (8/1.). Rule 4 applies, deduct 10p in the £.

FOCUS
A moderate apprentice handicap in which the winner set just an ordinary pace. He is rated in line with his winter sand form here.
Himba Official explanation: jockey said gelding stopped very quickly

2687 EUROPEAN BREEDERS' FUND MEDIAN AUCTION MAIDEN STKS 6f
2:50 (2:54) (Class 4) 2-Y-O **£5,505** (£1,637; £818; £408) **Stalls** Low

Form				RPR
2	1		**Archived (IRE)**[15] 2241 2-9-3 0 ... BrettDoyle 7 (M G Quinlan) *trckd ldr: led 2f out: strly pressed 1f out: styd on wl nr fin* **8/11**[1]	75
03	2	1	**Maybe I Wont**[8] 2473 2-9-3 0 ... DaneO'Neill 4 (S Dow) *dwlt: hld up bhd ldrs: prog to chse wnr over 1f out: str chal ent fnl f: no ex last 75yds* **8/1**	72
3	3	3 1/2	**Sandy Par**[19] 2103 2-9-3 0 ... MatthewHenry 3 (P Winkworth) *taken down early and sddle slipped on way to post: led: racd freely and sddle sn slipped: hdd 2f out: one pce* **11/1**	62+
	4	1 3/4	**Ordinance (USA)** 2-9-3 0 ... TQuinn 6 (T G Mills) *s.s: sn trckd ldrs on outer: cl up 2f out: shkn up and wknd over 1f out* **9/2**[2]	56

5 2 1/2 **All That Brass** 2-9-3 0 ... RichardMullen 2 49
(E J O'Neill) *cl up on inner: hanging and rn green fr 2f out: steadily wknd* **15/2[3]**

6 9 **Flash Of Colour** 2-9-3 0 ... JimCrowley 8 22
(Mrs A J Perrett) *s.s: rn green and sn t.o* **14/1**

1m 14.17s (0.57) **Going Correction** -0.025s/f (Good) **6** Ran SP% **114.0**
Speed ratings (Par 95):95,93,89,86,83 71
CSF £7.66 TOTE £1.80: £1.10, £3.10; EX 6.30 Trifecta £20.50 Pool £66.61. - 2.30 winning units..
Owner Swan Racing **Bred** Mrs J M Langmead **Trained** Newmarket, Suffolk

FOCUS
An ordinary juvenile maiden. A slight step forward from the winner and the second and the form should stand up.

NOTEBOOK
Archived(IRE) confirmed the promise he showed when runner-up over course and distance on his previous start, although he was made to work quite hard. (op 5-4)
Maybe I Wont was clear of the remainder in second and this looked like his best effort yet. He is progressing. (op 6-1)
Sandy Par did well to finish so close considering his saddle slipped quite early on. His rider was trying his best in the closing stages, but was obviously unable to given him absolutely everything. Official explanation: jockey said saddle slipped (op 10-1 tchd 12-1)
Ordinance(USA), a £42,000 half-sister to quite useful Cole Express, a sprint winner at two in the US, and to three other winners in the States, out of a 1m juvenile winner who was later useful in the US, raced widest of all but showed ability. He is open to improvement. (tchd 11-2)
All That Brass, a 36,000gns purchase, out of a fair 5f-6f winner at two, proved easy to back and looked in need of the experience. (op 7-1 tchd 6-1)

2688 EASTWELL MANOR H'CAP 6f
3:20 (3:20) (Class 2) (0-100,98) 3-Y-O+
£13,710 (£4,105; £2,052; £1,027; £512; £257) **Stalls** Low

Form RPR

6-50 **1** **Pearly Wey**[8] [2440] 4-9-0 **86** ... PhilipRobinson 6 96+
(C G Cox) *stdd s: hld up and swtchd to r against nr side rail: prog 1/2-way: gd run through to ld last 150yds: rdn clr* **13/2[3]**

1053 **2** 1 1/4 **Forest Dane**[8] [2440] 7-8-11 **83** ... JamesDoyle 5 89
(Mrs N Smith) *trckd ldrs gng wl: clsd over 1f out: rdn to chal and upsides ent fnl f: nt qckn* **12/1**

-000 **3** nk **Mine Behind**[7] [2494] 7-8-8 **80** ... TedDurcan 7 85
(J R Best) *sn last: outpcd wl over 2f out: clsd over 1f out: nt clr run sn after: styd on ins fnl f on inner: nrst fin* **33/1**

0000 **4** 3/4 **Idle Power (IRE)**[15] [2237] 9-8-13 **85** ... AmirQuinn 8 88
(J R Boyle) *trckd ldr: clr of rest 1/2-way: led over 1f out: hdd and fdd last 150yds* **16/1**

11-6 **5** 1/2 **Cape**[8] [2440] 4-9-0 **86** ... OscarUrbina 1 87+
(J R Fanshawe) *stdd s: barging match w rival in rr after 1f: rdn and effrt 2f out: trbld run after: kpt on u.p: no ch* **5/4[1]**

44-5 **6** 3/4 **Swinbrook (USA)**[29] [1836] 6-8-12 **84** ... (v) MartinDwyer 3 83
(J A R Toller) *dwlt: barging match in rr w rival after 1f: rdn over 2f out: effrt and taken to outer over 1f out: kpt on one pce u.p* **7/1**

0610 **7** shd **Lucayos**[15] [2237] 4-8-9 **84** ... RichardKingscote(3) 2 83
(Mrs H Sweeting) *chsd ldng pair: u.p and lost pl over 2f out: tried to rally jst over 1f out: one pce* **25/1**

3121 **8** 2 1/2 **Keyaki (IRE)**[15] [2240] 6-8-10 **87** ... PatrickHills(5) 9 78
(C F Wall) *trckd ldrs: rdn on outer over 2f out: wknd over 1f out* **9/2[2]**

0523 **9** 4 **Pawan (IRE)**[12] [2347] 7-8-2 **79** oh1 ... (b) AnnStokell(5) 10 58
(Miss A Stokell) *spd on wd outside: wknd 2f out* **33/1**

2410 **10** 1 **Maltese Falcon**[58] [1125] 7-9-12 **98** ... (t) TQuinn 4 74
(P F I Cole) *led at str pce: hdd & wknd over 1f out: eased fnl f* **12/1**

1m 11.99s (-1.61) **Going Correction** -0.025s/f (Good) **10** Ran SP% **119.5**
Speed ratings (Par 109):109,107,106,105,105 104,104,100,95,94
CSF £81.24 CT £2379.40 TOTE £9.60: £2.80, £3.10, £5.30; EX 95.10 Trifecta £321.40 Part won. Pool £452.73. - 0.10 winning units..
Owner Dennis Shaw **Bred** Leydens Farm Stud **Trained** Lambourn, Berks
■ Stewards' Enquiry : James Doyle two-day ban: careless riding (Jun 28-29)

FOCUS
A good sprint handicap, but it was a bit messy with favourite Cape one of the sufferers. Pearly Wey shaped a bit better than the bare form and seems back to his best, with the runner-up the most solid guide.

NOTEBOOK
Pearly Wey ◆ has often had too much use made of him, but he was finally ridden with some patience and produced a very useful effort. Having raced a little keenly, he was initially denied a clear run when trying to pick up, but he soon had this won once in the clear. He is now set to take his chance in the Wokingham and a 5lb penalty may not be enough to stop him making the frame. (op 15-2)
Forest Dane ran a terrific race off a career-high mark and continues to improve. (op 16-1)
Mine Behind had been badly out of form for quite a while coming into this, but he had dropped to a mark 4lb lower than when last winning as a result and this was more like it. He just got going too late having struggled to lay up early on and will be interesting if returned to 7f.
Idle Power(IRE) was 5lb lower than when last successful and ran a respectable race.
Cape would have gone very close indeed with a clearer run on her reappearance at Goodwood, but she failed to build on that this time. Admittedly she was again messed about a bit, and might have finished a little closer, but she was not an unlucky loser. Better can be expected when things fall right, but she is in quite a few notebooks at the moment and is unlikely to represent value in the coming weeks. Official explanation: jockey said filly was unsuited by the good ground (op 11-10 tchd 11-8 in places)
Keyaki(IRE) was not ideally drawn in stall nine and could not defy a 7lb rise in the weights for her recent course-and-distance success.
Pawan(IRE) Official explanation: jockey said gelding was unsuited by the good ground
Maltese Falcon Official explanation: jockey said gelding hung right from 3f out

2689 IRISH LOTTO, ANY 2 WILL DO H'CAP 7f (S)
3:50 (3:50) (Class 4) (0-85,84) 3-Y-O+ **£7,772** (£2,312; £1,155; £577) **Stalls** Low

Form RPR

10-2 **1** **Yandina (IRE)**[20] [2085] 4-9-5 **75** ... PhilipRobinson 6 83
(B W Hills) *pressed ldr: led after 3f: mde rest: hrd pressed and drvn fnl f: hld on wl* **9/4[2]**

5000 **2** 1/2 **Compton's Eleven**[15] [2239] 6-10-0 **84** ... TPO'Shea 1 91
(M R Channon) *hld up in touh: pushed along and sltly outpcd 1/2-way: effrt to chse wnr wl over 1f out: chal fnl f: nt qckn and hld nr fin* **11/2[3]**

1351 **3** 1/2 **Takitwo**[14] [2272] 4-8-9 **65** oh1 ... DaneO'Neill 7 71
(P D Cundell) *t.k.h: racd on outer: in tch: sltly outpcd 1/2-way: clsd 2f out: tried to chal fnl f: kpt on* **2/1[1]**

0-00 **4** 1 **Russian Symphony (USA)**[24] [1971] 6-9-7 **77** ... TedDurcan 3 80
(C R Egerton) *led against nr side rail for 3f: chsd wnr to wl over 1f out: one pce* **14/1**

0-35 **5** 2 1/2 **Dr Synn**[31] [1787] 6-8-9 **65** oh3 ... PaulDoe 2 61
(J Akehurst) *last and outpcd 1/2-way: plugged on fnl 2f: n.d* **9/1**

4-30 **6** 3 **Non Compliant**[30] [1817] 3-9-3 **82** ... MartinDwyer 5 70
(J W Hills) *t.k.h: cl up tl wknd 2f out* **7/1**

114- **7** 6 **Hucking Hill (IRE)**[179] [6881] 3-8-10 **75** ... (b) TQuinn 4 47
(J R Best) *t.k.h: hld up in tch: outpcd 3f out: sn wknd* **14/1**

1m 26.9s (-1.00) **Going Correction** -0.025s/f (Good)
WFA 3 from 4yo+ 9lb **7** Ran SP% **115.3**
Speed ratings (Par 105):104,103,102,101,98 95,88
CSF £15.37 TOTE £3.40: £2.20, £3.00; EX 16.80.
Owner M C & Mrs D A Throsby **Bred** Epona Bloodstock Ltd **Trained** Lambourn, Berks

FOCUS
Just an ordinary handicap for the grade, and it probably took little winning. The winner is less exposed than the others and could do better but she did not achieve a great deal here.
Hucking Hill(IRE) Official explanation: jockey said gelding had no more to give

2690 CHLOE ASLING MAIDEN STKS 1m 4f
4:20 (4:20) (Class 4) 3-Y-O+ **£5,181** (£1,541; £770; £384) **Stalls** Low

Form RPR

1 **Speed Gifted** 3-8-13 0 ... MartinDwyer 2 81+
(L M Cumani) *dwlt: rn green in last and wl off the pce: stl last 3f out: rapid prog over 2f out: storming run to ld ins fnl f: sn clr* **8/1[3]**

2-2 **2** 2 1/2 **Dawn Sky**[13] [2308] 3-8-13 0 ... PhilipRobinson 6 77+
(M A Jarvis) *trckd ldng pair: effrt to ld 5f out: drew clr 2f out: no answer whn hdd ins fnl f* **30/100[1]**

00 **3** 6 **Sister Agnes (IRE)**[13] [2308] 3-8-8 0 ... OscarUrbina 8 62
(J R Fanshawe) *mostly in 5th/6th and off the pce: outpcd 5f out: kpt on fr over 2f out take modest 3rd ins fnl f* **20/1**

4 1 1/2 **Arctiz (USA)** 3-8-13 0 ... TQuinn 1 65+
(P F I Cole) *t.k.h: trckd ldr to 1/2-way: clr of rest in 3rd 4f out: wknd 2f out* **11/1**

0 **5** 1/2 **Arabian Sun**[8] [2455] 3-8-13 0 ... PaulFitzsimons 3 64?
(M J Attwater) *chsd ldng trio: outpcd fr over 4f out and rdn: tried to cl 2f out: no hdwy after* **66/1**

042 **6** 1 1/2 **Mowadeh (IRE)**[29] [1849] 3-8-13 **75** ... TPO'Shea 5 62
(M R Channon) *mostly 7th and pushed along 7f out: wl off the pce after* **13/2[2]**

334 **7** 2 1/2 **Just Julie (USA)**[25] [1950] 3-8-8 **68** ... DaneO'Neill 4 53
(N A Callaghan) *led at str pce: hdd 5f out: stl 2nd over 1f out: wknd rapidly* **10/1**

0- **8** 11 **By The River**[275] [5348] 3-8-13 0 ... PaulDoe 7 40
(P Winkworth) *racd in 5th/6th and off the pce: rdn after 4f: wl outpcd over 4f out: t.o* **33/1**

2m 40.96s (0.46) **Going Correction** +0.175s/f (Good) **8** Ran SP% **128.0**
Speed ratings (Par 105):105,103,99,98,98 97,95,88
CSF £12.12 TOTE £11.40: £2.20, £1.02, £5.60; EX 17.10 Trifecta £266.60 Part won. Pool £375.51. - 0.10 winning units..
Owner JMC Breed & Race Limited **Bred** B W Hills & R A N Bonnycastle **Trained** Newmarket, Suffolk

FOCUS
A weakish maiden, but a nice winner in the form of Speed Gifted. Dawn Sky did not run to his Leicester level and could have paid for kicking off a moderate pace with half a mile to run. The first two finished clear.
By The River Official explanation: jockey said gelding had no more to give

2691 NEW MONDEO AT INVICTA MOTORS ASHFORD FILLIES' H'CAP 1m 1f 149y
4:50 (4:50) (Class 4) (0-85,85) 3-Y-O **£6,477** (£1,927; £963; £481) **Stalls** Low

Form RPR

4-04 **1** **Rose Of Petra (IRE)**[26] [1929] 3-8-10 **81** ... JamieHamblett(7) 8 86+
(Sir Michael Stoute) *hld up in 5th: hmpd over 3f out and detached in last: effrt on inner 2f out: styd on wl to ld last 50yds* **11/4[1]**

0016 **2** 1/2 **Cavort (IRE)**[18] [2150] 3-8-8 **72** ... DaneO'Neill 1 73
(Pat Eddery) *hld up in 4th: prog to trck ldr 1/2-way: chal 2f out: narrow ld 1f out: hdd fnl 50yds* **10/1**

0244 **3** 1 **Musical Beat**[4] [2578] 3-8-6 **75** ... ColinHaddon(5) 6 74
(Miss V Haigh) *t.k.h: hld up in last: prog on outer over 2f out: rdn to chal and upsides over 1f out: one pce last 100yds* **11/4[1]**

03-3 **4** hd **Boogie Dancer**[17] [2181] 3-8-3 **67** ow1 ... MartinDwyer 5 66
(H S Howe) *led at decent pce: rdn over 2f out: narrowly hdd 1f out: no ex last 100yds* **10/3[2]**

0-03 **5** 4 **Baldovina**[120] [491] 3-8-3 **67** ... RichardThomas 4 58
(Tom Dascombe) *cl up: lost pl over 4f out: no hdwy 2f out: wknd* **11/2[3]**

5-30 **6** 7 **Run For Ede'S**[23] [1988] 3-8-6 **70** ... PaulDoe 3 47
(P M Phelan) *s.i.s: hld up in 6th: prog to dispute 2nd over 4f out: wknd 2f out* **16/1**

0-00 **U** **Harvest Joy (IRE)**[39] [1581] 3-9-2 **85** ... (p) JamesMillman(5) 2 —
(B R Millman) *t.k.h: trckd ldr to 1/2-way: lost pl: pushed along whn stmbld and uns rdr over 3f out* **15/2**

2m 6.17s (0.94) **Going Correction** +0.175s/f (Good) **7** Ran SP% **118.5**
Speed ratings (Par 98):103,102,101,101,98 92,—
CSF £32.28 CT £83.70 TOTE £3.40: £2.30, £3.50; EX 25.20 Trifecta £102.10 Pool £217.23 - 1.51 winning units. Place 6 £214.10, Place 5 £48.91..
Owner Ballymacoll Stud **Bred** Ballymacoll Stud Farm Ltd **Trained** Newmarket, Suffolk
■ Stewards' Enquiry : Jamie Hamblett one-day ban: careless riding (Jun 28)

FOCUS
Ordinary handicap form for the grade, the runner-up setting the standard. The winner is a bit better than the bare form.
T/Plt: £266.30 to a £1 stake. Pool: £81,690.35. 223.90 winning tickets. T/Qpdt: £83.90 to a £1 stake. Pool: £4,517.10. 39.80 winning tickets. JN

2539 SALISBURY (R-H)
Sunday, June 17

OFFICIAL GOING: Good to firm (good in the last 3 furlongs, 8.7)
Wind: Nil Weather: Sunny, dry

2692 ALBERT SAMUEL "CITY BOWL" H'CAP 1m 4f
2:00 (2:02) (Class 4) (0-85,84) 4-Y-O+ **£5,181** (£1,541; £770; £384) **Stalls** High

Form RPR

2364 **1** **Mustajed**[23] [2002] 6-9-7 **84** ... JHBowman 9 92
(B R Millman) *trckd ldrs: led 2f out: kpt on wl: rdn out* **3/1[1]**

1200 **2** 3 **Love Always**[13] [2321] 5-8-9 **72** ... RyanMoore 3 75
(S Dow) *hld up: rdn and hdwy over 2f out: styd on to go 2nd nr fin* **4/1[2]**

221/ **3** *nk* **Bull Market (IRE)**[554] 6538 4-9-4 **81** .... JimmyFortune 7 84
(J A Osborne) *led: rdn and hdd 2f out: kpt on same pce fnl f: lost 2nd nr fin* **4/1**[2]
6300 **4** *1* **Polish Power (GER)**[8] 2474 7-9-3 **80** .... LPKeniry 6 81
(J S Moore) *s.i.s: sn in tch: rdn 3f out: kpt on same pce fnl 2f* **14/1**
440- **5** *1 1/4* **Graham Island**[401] 1631 6-9-3 **80** .... SteveDrowne 2 79
(G Wragg) *hld up in tch: tk clsr order 4f out: sn rdn: one pce fnl 2f* **14/1**
40-1 **6** *shd* **Stolen Hours (USA)**[11] 2355 7-8-4 **67** .... JimmyQuinn 4 66
(J Akehurst) *trckd ldrs: rdn over 3f out: wknd wl ins fnl f* **8/1**
6-01 **7** *1 1/4* **Inchmahome**[26] 1926 4-8-3 **66** .... ChrisCatlin 5 63
(E F Vaughan) *rdn over 3f out: a towards rr* **11/2**[3]
11-0 **8** *1 1/2* **Mostarsil (USA)**[10] 2403 9-8-9 **72** ....(p) FergusSweeney 1 66
(G L Moore) *pumped along over 5f out: a towards rr* **12/1**

2m 39.17s (2.81) **Going Correction** +0.375s/f (Good) **8** Ran SP% **112.5**
Speed ratings (Par 105):105,103,102,102,101 101,100,99
CSF £14.49 CT £46.67 TOTE £3.90: £1.20, £1.80, £1.80; EX 14.00.
Owner Double P Partnership **Bred** Shadwell Estate Company Limited **Trained** Kentisbeare, Devon

FOCUS
A moderate handicap and solid enough form for the grade, but the consistent winner did not need to improve to score.
Stolen Hours(USA) Official explanation: jockey said he eased prematurely for fear of clipping a rival's heels

2693 CHAS H. BAKER MAIDEN FILLIES' STKS 1m
2:30 (2:34) (Class 5) 3-Y-O £4,857 (£1,445; £722; £360) **Stalls** High

Form RPR
0-3 **1** **El Toreador (USA)**[29] 1838 3-9-0 0 .... JHBowman 10 80+
(G A Butler) *mid-div: rdn and hdwy over 2f out: led over 1f out: kpt on wl* **8/1**[3]
0- **2** *1* **Josephine Malines**[232] 6215 3-9-0 0 .... FergusSweeney 13 78
(C G Cox) *in tch: rdn and hdwy over 1f out: kpt on to chse wnr jst ins fnl f: a hld* **33/1**
2 **3** *3 1/2* **Duchess Royale (IRE)**[37] 1632 3-9-0 0 .... RyanMoore 12 70+
(Sir Michael Stoute) *hld up towards rr: swtchd lft and hdwy 2f out: styd on to go 3rd ins fnl f: nt rch ldrs* **11/10**[1]
6 **4** *2* **Rustic Flame (IRE)**[29] 1839 3-9-0 0 .... RobertHavlin 3 65
(C R Egerton) *in tch: tk clsr order 3f out: rdn 2f out: ev ch 1f out: no ex* **50/1**
4-0 **5** *1/2* **Dramatic Touch**[16] 2219 3-9-0 0 .... SteveDrowne 15 64+
(G Wragg) *mid-div: rdn 4f out: styd on fnl f* **40/1**
03 **6** *3/4* **Nelly's Glen**[8] 2477 3-9-0 0 .... PatDobbs 8 62
(R Hannon) *chsd ldrs: rdn over 2f out: kpt on same pce* **16/1**
4 **7** *shd* **Fleuret**[16] 2196 3-9-0 0 .... StephenCarson 1 62
(Eve Johnson Houghton) *chsd ldrs: rdn 3f out: sn one pce* **12/1**
5-4 **8** *nk* **Balliasta (IRE)**[64] 1045 3-9-0 0 .... MichaelHills 6 61
(B W Hills) *mid-div: swtchd lft and rdn 3f out: one pce fnal f* **8/1**[3]
00- **9** *nk* **Peppermint Green**[275] 5344 3-9-0 0 .... NickyMackay 14 60
(L M Cumani) *a mid-div* **9/2**[2]
00 **10** *hd* **Poppets Sweetlove**[26] 1913 3-9-0 0 .... DavidKinsella 7 60
(A B Haynes) *chsd ldrs: led over 2f out: rdn and hdd over 1f out: wknd* **66/1**
11 *3 1/2* **Idesia (IRE)** 3-9-0 0 .... AdamKirby 2 51+
(W R Swinburn) *s.i.s: a towards rr* **20/1**
30- **12** *4* **Serene Highness (IRE)**[303] 4553 3-9-0 0 .... JimmyQuinn 11 42+
(J L Dunlop) *s.i.s: mainly in rr* **16/1**
13 *8* **Cumae (USA)** 3-9-0 0 .... LPKeniry 4 22
(Miss Diana Weeden) *s.i.s: towards rr: wknd 2f out* **66/1**
14 *1* **Roymar** 3-9-0 0 .... ChrisCatlin 9 20
(M Appleby) *a bhd* **100/1**
4- **15** *8* **Swing On A Star (IRE)**[228] 6290 3-9-0 0 .... JimmyFortune 5 1
(W R Swinburn) *led: rdn and hdd over 2f out: sn wknd: eased ins fnl f* **10/1**

1m 42.45s (-0.64) **Going Correction** -0.025s/f (Good) **15** Ran SP% **132.6**
Speed ratings (Par 96):102,101,97,95,95 94,94,93,93,93 89,85,77,76,68
CSF £268.40 TOTE £10.20: £3.00, £13.40, £1.20; EX 529.10.
Owner Abdulla Al Khalifa **Bred** Windsworth Farms **Trained** Blewbury, Oxon

FOCUS
A fair fillies' maiden, more strongly-run than most. The winner is highly thought of and the form looks pretty solid.
Idesia(IRE) Official explanation: jockey said filly missed the break
Swing On A Star(IRE) Official explanation: jockey said filly ran too free

2694 FLAXMILLGALLERY.COM H'CAP 5f
3:00 (3:02) (Class 4) (0-85,85) 3-Y-O+ £5,181 (£1,541; £770; £384) **Stalls** High

Form RPR
-003 **1** **Golden Dixie (USA)**[7] 2494 8-9-6 **83** .... LukeMorris(5) 5 96+
(R A Harris) *hld up: pushed along over 3f out: hdwy 2f out: led wl ins fnl f: r.o wl* **5/1**[3]
0410 **2** *1 1/4* **Makabul**[10] 2394 4-8-6 **66** oh1 .... RobertHavlin 4 74
(B R Millman) *hld up: sltly outpcd over 2f out: hdwy over 1f out: r.o ins fnl f: wnt 2nd nr fin* **10/1**
4040 **3** *1/2* **Holbeck Ghyll (IRE)**[10] 2399 5-9-2 **79** ....(p) WilliamBuick(5) 1 85
(A M Balding) *s.i.s: sn prom: led 3f out: rdn 2f out: no ex whn hdd ins fnl f* **10/3**[1]
0-04 **4** *1* **Zowington**[10] 2399 5-9-13 **85** .... GeorgeBaker 2 88
(C F Wall) *sn prom: rdn and ev ch over 1f out: kpt on same pce* **10/3**[1]
0613 **5** *1 1/4* **Peopleton Brook**[17] 2191 5-9-10 **82** .... RyanMoore 7 80
(J M Bradley) *chsd ldrs: rdn over 2f out: one pce fnl f* **7/2**[2]
0606 **6** *nk* **Pic Up Sticks**[7] 2494 8-9-9 **81** .... IanMongan 9 78
(B G Powell) *chsd ldrs: rdn over 2f out: one pce fnl f* **11/1**
0240 **7** *shd* **Azygous**[10] 2399 4-9-2 **74** .... JimmyQuinn 6 71
(J Akehurst) *led for 2f: prom: rdn over 2f out: wknd ins fnl f* **14/1**
-003 **8** *1 1/2* **Cashel Mead**[29] 1854 7-9-9 **84** .... MarcHalford(3) 8 75+
(J L Spearing) *hld up: rdn and hdwy over 1f out: abt to chal on rails whn short of room and snatched up on rails ent fnl f: nt rcvr* **10/1**

61.05 secs (-0.54) **Going Correction** -0.025s/f (Good) **8** Ran SP% **118.2**
Speed ratings (Par 105):103,101,100,98,96 96,95,93
CSF £54.92 CT £192.03 TOTE £6.70: £1.80, £3.50, £1.80; EX 77.60.
Owner Mrs Vicki Davies **Bred** G Strawbridge Jr **Trained** Earlswood, Monmouths

FOCUS
A competitive little sprint. Sound form amongst the principals.
Cashel Mead Official explanation: jockey said mare was denied a clear run

2695 AXMINSTER CARPETS CATHEDRAL STKS (LISTED RACE) 6f
3:30 (3:31) (Class 1) 3-Y-O+
£17,034 (£6,456; £3,231; £1,611; £807; £405) **Stalls** High

Form RPR
4-11 **1** **Sakhee's Secret**[30] 1808 3-9-0 **108** .... SteveDrowne 8 124+
(H Morrison) *trckd ldrs: swtchd lft wl over 1f out: led jst ins fnl f: stormed clr: v impressive* **7/4**[2]
2101 **2** *4* **Prime Defender**[22] 2035 3-9-0 **111** .... MichaelHills 6 112
(B W Hills) *trckd ldr: rdn to chal 2f out: ev ch 1f out: nt pce of wnr* **11/10**[1]
2-40 **3** *1 1/4* **Presto Shinko (IRE)**[14] 2291 6-9-3 **107** ....(p) RyanMoore 2 106
(R Hannon) *cl up: swtchd lft over 2f out: sn rdn: kpt on ins fnl f* **8/1**[3]
103- **4** *hd* **Pivotal Point**[308] 4410 7-9-3 **111** .... PatDobbs 1 106
(P J Makin) *t.k.h: trckd ldr: led over 2f out: rdn and hdd jst ins fnl f: kpt on same pce* **14/1**
2645 **5** *nk* **Ashdown Express (IRE)**[22] 2050 8-9-3 **105** .... GeorgeBaker 7 105
(C F Wall) *hld up: rdn and hdwy over 1f out: kpt on ins fnl f* **14/1**
45-4 **6** *2 1/2* **The Trader (IRE)**[17] 2184 9-9-3 **104** ....(b) FergusSweeney 4 97
(M Blanshard) *hld up: rdn over 2f out: no imp* **28/1**
-350 **7** *shd* **Patavellian (IRE)**[14] 2291 9-9-3 **103** ....(b) JimmyFortune 5 97
(R Charlton) *led: rdn and hdd over 2f out: grad fdd* **28/1**

1m 12.59s (-2.39) **Going Correction** -0.025s/f (Good)
WFA 3 from 6yo+ 7lb **7** Ran SP% **115.3**
Speed ratings (Par 111):114,108,107,106,106 103,102
CSF £4.09 TOTE £2.70: £1.50, £1.60; EX 4.30.
Owner Miss B Swire **Bred** Miss B Swire **Trained** East Ilsley, Berks

FOCUS
A top-quality Listed event run in a good time which resulted in a one-two for the three-year-olds. The impressive Sakhee's Secret can probably be rated the leading domestic sprinter now although there is a little doubt about the form of the older horses he beat here.

NOTEBOOK
Sakhee's Secret, who bolted up in a weak Listed race last time, had tougher competition to deal with here but he was even more impressive, picking up in great style and clearing away to win in very impressive fashion. He is a very smart sprinter and will be worthy of his place in all the top races later this year, with the July Cup the obvious mid-season target. (op 5-2)
Prime Defender, who appreciated the return to sprinting at Haydock last time, was sent off a fairly short price to follow up. He had every chance, beat the older horses well enough, but had no answer to the impressive winner, who travelled well in behind and quickened up past him in striking fashion. He will not always run into such a smart rival at this or Group 3 level. (tchd 10-11)
Presto Shinko(IRE), back over his ideal distance and with the cheekpieces on again, came out best of the older horses. Best with some cut in the ground, it was probably to his advantage that times suggested that the ground was riding closer to good than to the official good to firm. (op 7-1)
Pivotal Point, who does not always settle in his races, was a bit keen on his seasonal reappearance and was tiring a bit towards the end. He should come on for the run. (op 12-1)
Ashdown Express(IRE) has not been easy to win with for some time now. (tchd 12-1)
The Trader(IRE), who is on a losing run of over two years, is at his best over the minimum trip. (op 25-1)
Patavellian(IRE) set a decent gallop up front but was easily brushed aside. (op 33-1)

2696 DANCO MARQUEES FILLIES' H'CAP 6f 212y
4:00 (4:04) (Class 5) (0-70,70) 3-Y-O+ £3,238 (£963; £481; £240) **Stalls** High

Form RPR
030- **1** **Our Faye**[234] 6189 4-10-0 **69** .... GeorgeBaker 7 78
(S Kirk) *hld up: steadily swtchd to centre fr over 2f out: rdn and r.o strly ins fnl f: led cl home* **10/1**
-024 **2** *1/2* **Rogue**[12] 2334 5-9-3 **58** .... LPKeniry 9 65
(Jane Southcombe) *chsd ldrs: rdn over 2f out: led jst ins fnl f: ct cl home* **7/1**
4240 **3** *2* **Lady Duxyana**[4] 2556 4-8-9 **50** oh1 ....(v) RichardSmith 1 52
(M D I Usher) *trckd ldrs: led over 3f out: rdn and hdd jst ins fnl f: no ex* **8/1**
3604 **4** *hd* **Piccostar**[9] 2414 4-8-11 **52** ....(b) SamHitchcott 5 53
(A B Haynes) *s.i.s: bhd: rdn over 2f out: hdwy over 1f out: kpt on* **11/1**
5450 **5** *1/2* **Smart Cat (IRE)**[13] 2321 4-9-0 **55** .... JHBowman 4 55
(A P Jarvis) *trckd ldrs: rdn over 2f out: kpt on same pce fnl f* **9/2**[3]
60-1 **6** *4* **What A Treasure (IRE)**[13] 2309 3-9-6 **70** .... NickyMackay 6 56
(L M Cumani) *mid-div: rdn over 2f out: wknd ins fnl f* **9/4**[1]
0060 **7** *nk* **Mythical Charm**[9] 2423 8-8-11 **52** ....(t) SteveDrowne 3 41
(J J Bridger) *in tch: hdwy 3f out: sn rdn: wknd 1f out* **14/1**
0-60 **8** *1 1/4* **Lady Shirley Hunt**[5] 2540 3-8-0 **50** oh5 .... JimmyQuinn 8 32
(A D Smith) *led: hdd over 3f out: sn rdn: wknd over 1f out* **66/1**
-200 **9** *3 1/2* **Whipchord (IRE)**[5] 2545 3-8-12 **62** .... RyanMoore 2 35
(R Hannon) *hld up: rdn over 2f out: wknd over 1f out* **4/1**[2]
000- **10** *4* **Kerswell**[275] 5349 3-8-9 **59** .... RobertHavlin 10 21
(B R Millman) *mid-div: rdn over 2f out: wknd over 1f out* **25/1**

1m 28.42s (-0.64) **Going Correction** -0.025s/f (Good)
WFA 3 from 4yo+ 9lb **10** Ran SP% **122.0**
Speed ratings (Par 100):102,101,99,98,98 93,93,92,88,83
CSF £81.87 CT £617.29 TOTE £13.70: £3.80, £2.20, £2.50; EX 83.50.
Owner J B J Richards **Bred** J B J Richards **Trained** Upper Lambourn, Berks

FOCUS
Moderate handicap form, but sound enough. The winner is less exposed than most of her rivals.
Whipchord(IRE) Official explanation: jockey said filly ran flat

2697 PERTEMPS PEOPLE DEVELOPMENT "HANDS AND HEELS" APPRENTICE SERIES H'CAP 1m
4:30 (4:35) (Class 6) (0-65,65) 3-Y-O £3,238 (£963; £481; £240) **Stalls** High

Form RPR
4302 **1** **Winged Farasi**[19] 2116 3-9-2 **57** .... AlanRutter 13 66
(R A Harris) *trckd ldr: led over 3f out: kpt on wl* **11/8**[1]
-440 **2** *2* **Red Flare (IRE)**[24] 1964 3-8-1 **50** .... MatthewDavies(8) 14 54
(M R Channon) *mid-div: rdn to chse ldrs over 2f out: wnt 2nd 1f out: kpt on* **11/2**[2]
6-60 **3** *hd* **The King And I (IRE)**[31] 1786 3-9-2 **65** .... JosephLoveridge(8) 10 69
(J S Moore) *hld up towards rr: hdwy over 2f out: steadily swtchd lft: styd on strly fnl f: nrst fin* **12/1**
-340 **4** *3 1/2* **Dansil In Distress**[17] 2181 3-9-5 **60** .... WilliamCarson 8 56
(S Kirk) *trckd ldrs: jnd wnr over 3f out: rdn and ev ch 2f out: kpt on same pce* **7/1**[3]
6006 **5** *hd* **The Tinker Man**[7] 2489 3-8-6 **47** .... BarrySavage 5 42
(M D I Usher) *s.i.s: towards rr: hdwy 2f out: styd on fnl f: nvr trbld ldrs* **8/1**
-000 **6** *2* **Piano Key**[15] 2259 3-8-5 **46** oh1 .... MCGeran 9 37
(M D I Usher) *towards rr: rdn and styd on fr 2f out: nrst fin* **25/1**
0440 **7** *1* **Pajada**[7] 2489 3-8-5 **46** oh1 .... LauraReynolds 7 35
(M D I Usher) *hld up bhd: styd on fr 2f out: nvr trbld ldrs* **16/1**

The Form Book, Raceform Ltd, Compton, RG20 6NL

-540 **8** *hd* **Alloro**[9] [2425] 3-8-3 **52**.......... BillyCray(8) 6 40
(D J S Ffrench Davis) *chsd ldrs over 5f* **16/1**

600 **9** *3 1/2* **Just An Angel (IRE)**[30] [1812] 3-8-6 **47**.......... JosephWalsh 3 27
(A P Jarvis) *chsd ldrs: rdn over 2f out: wknd over 1f out* **9/1**

0-03 **10** *2* **Iced Tango**[12] [2341] 3-8-11 **52**.......... ChrisHough 16 27
(F Jordan) *led tl over 3f out: fdd fr 2f out* **20/1**

00-0 **11** *3* **Kiss Chase (IRE)**[37] [1632] 3-8-11 **55**..........(p) JackMitchell(3) 15 24
(P Mitchell) *a towards rr* **25/1**

0000 **12** *7* **Lordswood (IRE)**[5] [2545] 3-9-3 **58**.......... KMay 11 10
(J J Bridger) *dwlt: a towards rr* **25/1**

4000 **13** *3/4* **Show Business (IRE)**[18] [2140] 3-8-7 **53** oh1 ow7.....(tp) LaurenShea(5) 1 4
(P Butler) *mid-div tl wknd 2f out* **50/1**

U000 **14** *5* **Silver Surprise**[16] [2219] 3-8-13 **57**.......... RyanBird(3) 2 —
(J J Bridger) *s.i.s: a towards rr* **25/1**

-000 **15** *4* **Acece**[41] 3-8-5 **46** oh1.......... SoniaEaton 12 —
(M Appleby) *prom early: bhd fnl 3f* **50/1**

4000 **P** **Jonny Behave**[47] [1381] 3-8-5 **46** oh1.......... SophieDoyle 4 —
(I A Wood) *in tch: rdn 3f out: btn whn p.u over 1f out: dead* **25/1**

1m 44.73s (1.64) **Going Correction** -0.025s/f (Good) **16** Ran SP% **138.5**
Speed ratings (Par 97):90,88,87,84,84 82,81,80,77,75 72,65,64,59,55 —
CSF £9.03 CT £80.32 TOTE £2.40: £1.20, £2.10, £3.00, £2.10; EX 14.60 Place 6 £22.63, Place 5 £16.80..
Owner Leeway Group Limited **Bred** The National Stud **Trained** Earlswood, Monmouths

FOCUS
Very moderate fare but a clear-cut win for Winged Farasi who has been given a big chance by the handicapper. The second and third ran to form..
T/Jkpt: Not won. T/Plt: £50.20 to a £1 stake. Pool: £81,514.00. 1,184.25 winning tickets. T/Qpdt: £21.40 to a £1 stake. Pool: £4,188.20. 144.20 winning tickets. TM

1828 CORK (R-H)

Sunday, June 17

OFFICIAL GOING: Sprint course - good; round course - good to firm

2702a KERRY GROUP NOBLESSE STKS (GROUP 3) (F&M) 1m 4f

4:25 (4:26) 3-Y-0+ **£43,918** (£12,837; £6,081; £2,027)

RPR

1 **Nick's Nikita (IRE)**[32] [1777] 4-9-9 **100**.......... RPCleary 10 107
(M Halford, Ire) *hld up early: 7th 1/2-way: 5th 4f out: 2nd and chal 2f out: led 1 1/2f out: styd on wl fr over 1f out: comf* **7/1**

2 *1* **Athenian Way (IRE)**[42] [1511] 3-8-9 **100**.......... MJKinane 11 105
(John M Oxx, Ire) *trckd ldrs: 4th 1/2-way: nt clr run early st: 3rd over 1f out: kpt on u.p* **8/1**

3 *shd* **Wannabe Posh (IRE)**[22] [2036] 4-9-9.......... EddieAhern 4 105
(J L Dunlop) *hld up early: 6th and prog 1/2-way: 3rd 4f out: led over 2f out: hdd 1 1/2f out: kpt on u.p ins fnl f* **9/2**[2]

4 *1* **Downtown (IRE)**[24] [1981] 3-8-9 **84**.......... KFallon 3 104
(David Wachman, Ire) *prom early: settled in mid-div: 7th early st: 4th and rdn under 2f out: kpt on same pce* **10/1**

5 *nk* **Reform Act (USA)**[32] [1777] 4-9-9 **104**.......... PJSmullen 7 103
(D K Weld, Ire) *hld up in rr: prog on outer early st: 5th over 1f out: kpt on wout threatening* **5/1**[3]

6 *4* **Mount Eliza (IRE)**[11] [2381] 5-9-9 **97**.......... PShanahan 8 97
(Charles O'Brien, Ire) *hld up towards rr: 8th and prog early st: 6th under 2f out: kpt on same pce* **33/1**

7 *5 1/2* **You're Beautiful (USA)**[32] [1777] 3-8-9 **94**.......... WMLordan 6 88
(David Wachman, Ire) *disp ld: hdd bef 1/2-way: 2nd 4f out: 3rd u.p early st: no ex fr under 2f out* **25/1**

8 *nk* **Green Room (FR)**[22] [2036] 4-9-9.......... DPMcDonogh 1 88
(J L Dunlop) *hld up towards rr: rdn and no imp st* **10/1**

9 *1 1/4* **Trick Or Treat**[22] [2036] 4-9-9.......... JAHeffernan 9 86
(J G Given) *disp ld: led bef 1/2-way: hdd over 2f out: sn wknd* **4/1**[1]

10 *1* **Whoneedswings (IRE)**[77] [875] 5-9-9 **87**.......... CO'Donoghue 5 84
(David Wachman, Ire) *towards rr: rdn and no imp st* **33/1**

11 *15* **High Heel Sneakers**[8] [2441] 4-9-9.......... KJManning 2 60
(P F I Cole) *6th early: impr into 3rd appr 1/2-way: wknd 4f out: bhd whn virtually p.u fr over 1f out* **6/1**

2m 29.6s (-18.30)
WFA 3 from 4yo+ 14lb **11** Ran SP% **120.7**
CSF £62.44 TOTE £7.80: £2.70, £2.10, £2.00; DF 122.40.
Owner Nicholas Hartery **Bred** Mount Coote Stud **Trained** the Curragh, Co Kildare

FOCUS
A competitive renewal of this Group 3 prize that attracted a four-strong British challenge and a total of five previous stakes winners. It has been rated through the third, with the first two open to improvement.

NOTEBOOK
Nick's Nikita(IRE) had yet to win outside handicap company, but had shown enough to suggest that she could score at stakes level. She had progressed well through handicaps last term, coming here off a fine third to Four Sins in a 1m2f Group 3 at Naas last month, and produced a career-best effort to score over this longer trip. In a race run at a strong pace, she turned for home in fifth and ran on well under pressure to lead over a furlong out. She found plenty in the closing stages and kept on well to the line. Her trainer felt that this trip made all the difference and that she might even be better suited by more ease in the ground. (op 6/1)
Athenian Way(IRE) ran a cracking race and appreciated the step up to this trip following her fourth to Anna Karenina in an extended 1m1f Listed event at Gowran last month. She had to be angled out from the rail to deliver her challenge early in the straight and ran on well late on. She should be able to win a stakes race over this trip. (op 8/1 tchd 9/1)
Wannabe Posh(IRE) fared best of the English raiding party. Rated 98, she reversed form emphatically with Trick Or Treat, who defeated her in a Listed event at Haydock last month. She took over in front early in the straight and ran on well once tackled by the winner, but could do no more in the closing stages. She should be able to record a black-type success. (op 5/1)
Downtown(IRE) was taking a major step up in class from the 1m2f Clonmel maiden that she won last month. After racing prominently early, she then lost her place and dropped towards the rear but was coming back strongly over the final quarter-mile. She can do better over a longer trip and has further room for improvement. (op 8/1)
Reform Act(USA), who chased home Yeats on her reappearance, ran to a similar level with the winner as when fifth in a Group 3 at Naas last month. She was keeping on in the straight here, but could never work her way into a challenging position. She might be worth trying over further.
Mount Eliza(IRE) was unable to match the form that carried her into fourth in a 1m Listed event won by Quinmaster at Leopardstown recently.
You're Beautiful(USA) held a good position for much of the race, but could do no more nearing the final furlong. She will do better back over 1m2f.
Trick Or Treat showed up for a long way, but was a spent force from early in the straight. (op 5/1 tchd 11/2)
High Heel Sneakers was in trouble a long way out and was way below her best. Something was surely amiss with her and she was reported never to have travelled. Official explanation: jockey said filly never travelled in the race (op 9/2)

2698 - 2701a, 2703 - 2704a (Foreign Racing) - See Raceform Interactive

DORTMUND (R-H)

Sunday, June 17

OFFICIAL GOING: Good

2705a GROSSER PREIS DER WIRTSCHAFT (GROUP 3) 1m 165y

4:15 (4:28) 3-Y-0+ **£21,622** (£6,757; £3,378; £2,027)

RPR

1 **Soldier Hollow**[35] [1700] 7-9-7.......... AStarke 4 113
(P Schiergen, Germany) *hld up in 4th to st: hdwy on outside fr 2f out: led 1f out: pushed out and r.o wl* **1/2**[1]

2 *1* **Banknote**[35] [1699] 5-9-5.......... FrancisNorton 2 109
(A M Balding) *cl 3rd to st: led over 2f out: rdn over 1f out: hdd 1f out: kpt on same pce* **22/10**[2]

3 *2 1/2* **Forthe Millionkiss (GER)**[19] 3-8-3.......... J-PCarvalho 5 99
(U Ostmann, Germany) *led to over 2f out: sn one pce* **7/1**

4 *3 1/2* **Willingly (GER)**[35] [1699] 8-9-0.......... ADeVries 1 93
(M Trybuhl, Germany) *hld up in rr to st: nvr a factor* **16/1**

5 *1/2* **Oriental Hero (GER)** 3-8-3.......... NRichter 3 92
(Frau K Haustein, Germany) *trckd ldr to st: rdn and btn 2f out* **9/2**[3]

1m 48.45s (108.45)
WFA 3 from 5yo+ 11lb **5** Ran SP% **134.5**
(including ten euro stakes) WIN 15; PL 11, 15; SF 18.
Owner Gestut Park Wiedingen **Bred** Car Colston Hall Stud **Trained** Germany

NOTEBOOK
Banknote, who won a Group 3 at Baden-Baden last time out, found Soldier Hollow too strong but probably still ran right up to his best in defeat. He should continue to be a force at this level on the continent.

2684 SAN SIRO (R-H)

Sunday, June 17

OFFICIAL GOING: Soft

2706a GRAN PREMIO DI MILANO (GROUP 1) 1m 4f

4:10 (4:16) 3-Y-0+ **£97,297** (£42,811; £23,351; £11,676)

RPR

1 **Sudan (IRE)**[40] [1571] 4-9-6.......... LDettori 3 116
(E Lellouche, France) *racd in 3rd to st: led 1 1/2f out: drvn out: jst hld on (1.88/1)* **19/10**[1]

2 *nse* **Hattan (IRE)**[16] [2210] 5-9-6.......... SebSanders 1 116
(C E Brittain) *hld up: 4th st: swtchd off rails wl over 1f out: one l bhd 1f out: r.o u.str driving: jst failed* **27/10**[3]

3 *3* **Exhibit One (USA)**[28] [1874] 5-9-3.......... EBotti 2 109
(V Valiani, Italy) *sn led: hdd 1 1/2f out: one pce* **24/10**[2]

4 *1 1/2* **Dickens (GER)**[245] [6004] 4-9-6.......... ASuborics 7 109
(H Blume, Germany) *hld up: 5th st: hdwy fnl 2f: nvr nr to chal* **12/1**

5 *hd* **Donaldson (GER)**[28] [1872] 5-9-6.......... TMundry 5 109
(P Rau, Germany) *hld up: racd wd in bk st: cl 6th st: nvr a factor* **11/1**

6 *4 1/2* **Vol De Nuit**[28] [1874] 6-9-6.......... MDemuro 6 102
(L Brogi, Italy) *first to show: racd wd in bk st: 2nd st: pressed ldr tl wkng qckly over 2f out* **33/10**

2m 32.1s (0.60)
WFA 3 from 4yo+ 14lb **6** Ran SP% **130.2**
(including one euro stake) WIN 2.88; PL 1.85, 2.01; DF 5.21.
Owner Gary A Tanaka **Bred** Dayton Investments Ltd **Trained** Lamorlaye, France

NOTEBOOK
Sudan(IRE) probably hit the front too soon as he idled in front and just held on at the line. He is now due to join Michael Jarvis and is likely to be campaigned in the US at some point down the line.
Hattan(IRE), who finished fourth in this race last year, came with a good late run and just failed to catch the idling winner. Regularly held in Group company in Britain, his best chance of success will come on the continent.

2707a OAKS D'ITALIA (GROUP 2) (FILLIES) 1m 3f

5:25 (5:35) 3-Y-0 **£121,622** (£53,514; £29,189; £14,595)

RPR

1 **Fashion Statement**[39] [1581] 3-8-11.......... NCallan 9 104
(M A Jarvis) *a.p: 3rd st: rdn to ld 1 1/2f out: r.o wl (2.01/1)* **2/1**[1]

2 *1 3/4* **Moi Non Plus**[21] [2070] 3-8-11.......... LDettori 8 101
(B Grizzetti, Italy) *hld up in rr to st: hdwy on ins 3f out: ev ch 1f out: one pce* **42/10**[3]

3 *nk* **Scatina (IRE)**[42] [1515] 3-8-11.......... ASuborics 4 101
(Mario Hofer, Germany) *a.p: 2nd st: outpcd 2f out: r.o again ins fnl f* **24/10**[2]

4 *1 1/4* **Turfrose (GER)**[21] [2070] 3-8-11.......... SLandi 13 99
(P Giannotti, Italy) *hdwy on rails fnl 1 1/2f to take 4th on line* **15/1**

5 *shd* **Biz Bar**[14] 3-8-11.......... EBotti 11 98
(M Guarnieri, Italy) *styd on steadily on outside fnl 1 1/2f: nrest at fin* **34/1**

6 *shd* **Lokaloka**[35] [1701] 3-8-11.......... DVargiu 2 98
(B Grizzetti, Italy) *hld up: hdwy fr wl over 1f out: 4th and hrd rdn ins fnl f: one pce* **71/10**

7 *nk* **Red Diva**[29] [1855] 3-8-11.......... TMundry 12 98
(Mario Hofer, Germany) *last st: hdwy and nt clr run fr 3f out to ins fnl 2f: styd on: nvr nr to chal* **24/10**[2]

8 *2 1/2* **Cosi** 3-8-11.......... URispoli 3 94
(L Brogi, Italy) *led to 1 1/2f out* **24/1**

9 *nk* **Miss Sultin (IRE)**[21] [2070] 3-8-11.......... SMulas 6 93
(B Grizzetti, Italy) *nvr a factor* **71/1**

10 *4* **Shot Bless (IRE)**[21] [2070] 3-8-11.......... MEsposito 7 87
(M Guarnieri, Italy) *nvr a factor* **66/10**

11 *hd* **Spectra (IRE)**[55] 3-8-11.......... MSautjeau 5 87
(M Rulec, Germany) *bhd fnl 3f* **38/1**

12 *8* **Connessa (IRE)**[47] 3-8-11.......... CColombi 10 74
(V Valiani, Italy) *mid-div tl wkng wl over 1f out* **20/1**

U **Miss Annaleo (IRE)**[35] 1701 3-8-11 .... MarcoMonteriso 1 —
(I Bugattella, Italy) *saddle slipped and uns rdr shortly after s* **8/1**

2m 21.1s (2.50) **13** Ran SP% **169.8**
WIN 3.01; PL 1.45, 1.78, 1.43.
Owner P D Savill **Bred** P D Savill **Trained** Newmarket, Suffolk
■ This race has been downgraded from Group 1 level.

NOTEBOOK
Fashion Statement, third to Light Shift in the Cheshire Oaks, gave another boost to that form with a clear-cut success in this Group 2 contest. She stays well, is suited by a galloping track and now has the Yorkshire Oaks as her next target.

LES LANDES

Friday, June 15

OFFICIAL GOING: Good (good to firm in places)

2708a COUTTS OFFSHORE EUROPE H'CAP 1m 4f
7:05 (7:05) 3-Y-0+ **£1,460** (£525; £315)

RPR

1 **Khuzdar (IRE)**[12] 8-10-2 .... AdamJones —
(Mrs A Malzard, Jersey) **7/4**[1]

2 *1* **Groomsman**[12] 5-9-10 ....(p) AntonyProcter —
(Ms V S Lucas, Jersey) **9/4**[2]

3 *4* **Flashing Floozie**[16] 2142 4-8-5 oh4.............................. MarkCoumbe —
(A W Carroll) **6/1**

4 *3* **Flaxby**[12] 5-8-13 .... EmmettStack —
(Mrs J L Le Brocq, Jersey) **10/1**

5 *7* **Robinzal**[12] 5-9-10 ....(e[1]) VinceSlattery —
(Mrs J L Le Brocq, Jersey) **11/2**[3]

2m 40.0s (-10.00) **5** Ran SP% **105.9**
DF £1.90.
Owner Mrs Y Burnett, Messrs D Le Poidevin and H Le Poide **Bred** P J B O'Callaghan **Trained** St Ouen, Jersey

NOTEBOOK
Flashing Floozie, who won on Guernsey last month, was racing from 4lb out of the handicap on this occasion and was well held in the end.

2297 CARLISLE (R-H)

Monday, June 18

OFFICIAL GOING: Good to soft (6.5)
Wind: Breezy, half behind Weather: Overcast

2709 ANDIDRAIN CLAIMING STKS 1m 1f 61y
2:15 (2:15) (Class 6) 3-Y-0+ **£2,047** (£604; £302) **Stalls** High

Form RPR

0620 **1** **Little Jimbob**[12] 2374 6-9-12 78........................ PaulHanagan 7 78
(R A Fahey) *mde all: rdn over 2f out: hld on wl fnl f* **3/1**[2]

0003 **2** *1* **Everest (IRE)**[23] 2027 10-9-9 67........................ TomEaves 10 73
(B Ellison) *in tch: drvn over 3f out: effrt over 1f out: styd on to chse wnr towards fin* **10/3**[3]

0501 **3** *½* **Top Jaro (FR)**[14] 2298 4-9-9 70........................ SaleemGolam(3) 3 75
(Jennie Candlish) *t.k.h early: chsd ldrs: effrt and ev ch over 1f out: no ex and lost 2nd towards fin* **13/8**[1]

6-00 **4** *5* **Miss Havisham (IRE)**[25] 1968 3-8-0 42........................ DaleGibson 4 49
(J R Weymes) *chsd ldrs tl rdn and no ex over 1f out* **16/1**

0000 **5** *9* **Distant Vision (IRE)**[14] 2298 4-8-11 35........................ TonyHamilton 6 31
(A Berry) *hld up in tch: rdn 3f out: btn over 1f out* **100/1**

00-6 **6** *1 ¾* **Phoenix Nights (IRE)**[10] 2417 7-8-13 36........................ PBradley(5) 5 34
(A Berry) *bhd: drvn 1/2-way: nvr on terms* **150/1**

0-03 **7** *¾* **Procrastinate (IRE)**[19] 1744 5-9-4 49........................ AdrianTNicholls 1 32
(R F Fisher) *s.i.s: sn prom: rdn over 3f out: btn 2f out* **15/2**

3506 **8** *5* **Mister Maq**[21] 2091 4-9-3 52........................(b) DO'Donohoe 9 21
(A Crook) *towards rr: drvn over 3f out: nvr on terms* **16/1**

2m 0.12s (2.56) **Going Correction** +0.20s/f (Good)
WFA 3 from 4yo+ 11lb **8** Ran SP% **111.4**
Speed ratings (Par 101):96,95,94,90,82 80,80,75
CSF £12.69 TOTE £4.00: £1.40, £1.30, £1.10; EX 10.20.There was no bid for the winner.
Owner Dale Scaffolding Co Ltd **Bred** D R Tucker **Trained** Musley Bank, N Yorks

FOCUS
A modest event in which the pace was fair. The field came stands' side in the straight. The first three are not bad for the grade, but the fourth limits the form.

2710 EDINBURGH WOOLLEN MILL MAIDEN AUCTION STKS 5f 193y
2:45 (2:48) (Class 5) 2-Y-0 **£2,968** (£876; £438) **Stalls** High

Form RPR

522 **1** **Guertino (IRE)**[28] 1889 2-8-11 0........................ PaulEddery 11 86
(B Smart) *chsd ldrs: rdn to ld 1f out: edgd rt: kpt on wl* **9/4**[1]

224 **2** *1 ½* **Fol Hollow (IRE)**[19] 2147 2-8-9 0........................ AdrianTNicholls 5 80
(D Nicholls) *j. path afer 1f: led to 1f out: edgd rt and kpt on fnl f* **5/2**[2]

4 **3** *2* **Cat Whistle**[23] 2039 2-8-11 0........................ PaulHanagan 3 76
(R A Fahey) *towards rr: hdwy over 2f out: rdn and kpt on same pce fnl f* **7/1**[3]

R **4** *4* **Toto Skyllachy**[29] 1859 2-8-12 0........................ RoystonFfrench 4 65
(T P Tate) *bhd: drvn and plenty to do 1/2-way: styd on wl fnl f: nrst fin* **11/1**

63 **5** *1 ¼* **Do As I Say**[9] 2460 2-9-2 0........................ DavidAllan 8 65
(T D Easterby) *cl up: j. path after 1f: rdn and outpcd wl over 1f out* **10/1**

206 **6** *5* **Mujada**[35] 1713 2-7-11 0........................ AndrewHeffernan(7) 10 38
(M Brittain) *in tch: drvn over 2f out: btn over 1f out* **50/1**

7 *hd* **Scruffy Skip (IRE)** 2-8-11 0........................ DaleGibson 1 44
(M Dods) *in tch tl rdn and wknd over 2f out* **20/1**

4 **8** *½* **Shabnaam**[28] 1896 2-8-11 0........................ DO'Donohoe 6 43+
(K A Ryan) *in tch: rdn over 2f out: sn btn* **7/1**[3]

00 **9** *17* **Lucky Stream**[29] 1859 2-8-4 0........................ DeanMernagh 7 —
(M Brittain) *bhd: shortlived effrt on outside over 2f out: sn btn* **100/1**

10 *28* **Northwest** 2-8-11 0........................ TonyHamilton 9 —
(A Berry) *s.i.s: bhd and sn struggling* **33/1**

1m 15.55s (1.94) **Going Correction** +0.20s/f (Good) **10** Ran SP% **112.4**
Speed ratings (Par 93):95,93,90,85,83 76,76,75,53,15
CSF £7.37 TOTE £3.20: £1.10, £1.30, £1.90; EX 6.70.
Owner Prime Equestrian **Bred** Mrs T Marnane **Trained** Hambleton, N Yorks

FOCUS
Not the strongest of maidens but a decent gallop and a race that went largely as expected from a form perspective. The field again raced centre to stands' side.

NOTEBOOK
Guertino(IRE) has improved with every outing and turned in his best effort yet over this longer trip and on this first start away from a sound surface. He should continue to give a good account. (tchd 11-4)
Fol Hollow(IRE), who looked in good shape, bettered the form of his recent Fibresand debut. He settled better than at Southwell, pulled a couple of lengths clear of the remainder and, although he has had a few chances, he looks sure to win an ordinary event. (op 9-4 tchd 2-1)
Cat Whistle, who shaped with credit on her debut on fast ground at Haydock in May, ran to a similar level on this first start on easy ground and fared the best of those coming from just off the pace. She will be suited by 7f and is likely to be placed to best advantage. (op 8-1 tchd 13-2)
Toto Skyllachy, who refused to race on his intended debut at Ripon, looked as though the race would do him good in the preliminaries but he showed he possesses ability on effectively his first run. The step up to 7f will suit, he has physical scope and he looks capable of better. (op 20-1)
Do As I Say had run creditably in a modest event on his previous start but failed to step up on that form over this longer trip and on this easier ground. On this evidence he is likely to continue to look vulnerable in this type of event. Official explanation: jockey said colt jumped the road and ran green (tchd 11-1)
Mujada, who has shown ability at a modest level on artificial surfaces, again had her limitations ruthlessly exposed returned to turf. She is going to struggle to win a race of this nature. (op 40-1)
Shabnaam, a leggy, unfurnished sort who caught the eye on her debut at Windsor, failed by a long chalk to reproduce that effort over this longer trip and on easier ground. Official explanation: jockey said filly hung right-handed final 2f (op 11-2)

2711 ARCHITECTS PLUS H'CAP 5f 193y
3:15 (3:16) (Class 6) (0-60,60) 3-Y-0+ **£2,047** (£604; £302) **Stalls** High

Form RPR

20-5 **1** **Bold Haze**[14] 2304 5-8-10 52........................(v) MichaelJStainton(5) 15 69
(Miss S E Hall) *bhd: hdwy centre over 2f out: led wl ins fnl f: r.o* **16/1**

-005 **2** *nk* **Prospect Court**[16] 2256 5-9-0 54........................ AndrewMullen(3) 9 70
(A C Whillans) *prom: led over 1f out: edgd rt: hdd wl ins fnl f: kpt on* **7/1**[1]

2-30 **3** *4* **Quicks The Word**[5] 2563 7-8-6 46........................ GregFairley(3) 8 49
(T A K Cuthbert) *in tch: effrt and chsd ldrs wl over 1f out: kpt on same pce fnl f* **14/1**

3366 **4** *1 ¼* **Oeuf A La Neige**[5] 2561 7-8-13 50........................ DO'Donohoe 17 49
(Miss L A Perratt) *bhd tl kpt on fr 2f out: nrst fin* **9/1**[3]

60-5 **5** *¾* **Takanewa (IRE)**[38] 1625 4-8-13 50........................ PaulMulrennan 10 47
(J Howard Johnson) *cl up: rdn and outpcd over 2f out: kpt on fnl f: no imp* **25/1**

-042 **6** *hd* **Eternal Legacy (IRE)**[38] 1625 5-9-1 52........................ KDarley 7 57+
(E J Alston) *bhd: effrt whn nt clr run over 2f out: swtchd lft over 1f out: kpt on fnl f: nrst fin* **7/1**[1]

14-0 **7** *2* **George The Best (IRE)**[51] 1299 6-9-9 60........................ PaulHanagan 4 50
(Micky Hammond) *bhd tl sme late hdwy: nvr rchd ldrs* **8/1**[2]

6505 **8** *hd* **Attacca**[41] 1569 6-8-9 46........................ PhillipMakin 16 35
(J R Weymes) *hld up: effrt over 2f out: sn no imp* **12/1**

0000 **9** *¾* **Funfair Wane**[69] 992 8-9-6 57........................ AdrianTNicholls 3 44
(D Nicholls) *led to over 1f out: sn btn* **12/1**

06-3 **10** *1* **Misaine (IRE)**[54] 1248 3-8-6 53........................ SaleemGolam(3) 14 35
(T J Etherington) *midfield: drvn 1/2-way: no imp fr over 1f out* **33/1**

0540 **11** *¾* **Dysonic (USA)**[10] 2418 5-8-9 49........................(v) AndrewElliott(3) 13 30
(J Balding) *chsd ldrs tl hung rt and wknd over 1f out* **22/1**

5-00 **12** *nk* **Dazzler Mac**[16] 2256 6-9-3 54........................ PaulFessey 1 34
(N Bycroft) *towards rr: nt clr run over 2f and wl over 1f out: n.d* **8/1**[2]

0660 **13** *nk* **Petite Mac**[14] 2315 7-9-3 57........................ JamieMoriarty(3) 6 36
(N Bycroft) *bhd and sn rdn along: nvr on terms* **8/1**[2]

5-00 **14** *1 ¾* **Making Music**[42] 1534 4-8-13 50........................ DavidAllan 12 24
(T D Easterby) *cl up tl rdn and wknd over 1f out* **10/1**

00-0 **15** *3* **Hebenus**[5] 2561 8-8-9 46 oh1........................ TonyHamilton 5 10
(T A K Cuthbert) *midfield: drvn along 1/2-way: sn outpcd* **100/1**

060- **16** *8* **Stanley Wolfe (IRE)**[232] 6234 4-8-12 49........................ RoystonFfrench 2 —
(Garry Moss) *midfield: outpcd 1/2-way: sn btn* **28/1**

55-0 **17** *1* **Bayberry King (USA)**[43] 1488 4-9-2 53........................ TomEaves 11 —
(J S Goldie) *s.i.s: nvr on terms* **25/1**

1m 14.88s (1.27) **Going Correction** +0.20s/f (Good)
WFA 3 from 4yo+ 7lb **17** Ran SP% **124.8**
Speed ratings (Par 101):99,98,93,91,90 90,87,87,86,85 84,83,83,80,76 66,64
CSF £117.41 CT £1697.27 TOTE £12.90: £3.10, £2.50, £4.80, £2.00; EX 196.80.
Owner Mrs Joan Hodgson **Bred** R F And S D Knipe **Trained** Middleham Moor, N Yorks

FOCUS
A modest event but one run at a sound pace throughout. The field raced centre to stands' side in the straight and the first pair finished clear.
Eternal Legacy(IRE) Official explanation: jockey said gelding was denied a clear run
Dazzler Mac Official explanation: jockey said gelding was denied a clear run
Making Music Official explanation: jockey said gelding had no more to give
Stanley Wolfe(IRE) Official explanation: jockey said gelding had no more to give

2712 LAKELAND WILLOW WATER H'CAP 5f
3:45 (3:46) (Class 5) (0-70,66) 3-Y-0+ **£3,238** (£963; £481; £240) **Stalls** High

Form RPR

0205 **1** **Compton Classic**[9] 2461 5-8-6 50........................(p) SaleemGolam(3) 12 59
(J S Goldie) *hld up in midfield: hdwy on outside to ld 1f out: hld on wl* **8/1**

6203 **2** *nk* **Divine Spirit**[7] 2509 6-9-2 57........................ RoystonFfrench 13 65
(M Dods) *bhd tl hdwy over 1f out: kpt on to take 2nd nr fin* **8/1**

3061 **3** *shd* **Monte Major (IRE)**[7] 2516 6-8-11 59 6ex........................(v) GaryBartley(7) 11 67
(D Shaw) *midfield on outside: hdwy to dispute ld appr fnl f: kpt on: lost 2nd nr fin* **11/1**

5231 **4** *hd* **Katie Boo (IRE)**[11] 2386 5-9-2 57........................ KDarley 1 65+
(A Berry) *chsd ldrs: drvn 1/2-way: rallied and edgd rt whn n.m.r over 1f out: kpt on fnl f* **9/1**

6123 **5** *½* **Spirit Of Coniston**[16] 2249 4-8-7 55........................(b) KellyHarrison(7) 14 60
(C J Teague) *cl up: effrt and ev ch over 1f out: edgd lft: kpt on ins fnl f* **25/1**

0601 **6** *nk* **Hotham**[7] 2509 4-9-5 63 6ex........................ JamieMoriarty(3) 8 67+
(N Wilson) *midfield: effrt whn n.m.r over 2f and ins fnl f: kpt on towards fin* **8/1**

0204 **7** *hd* **Kings College Boy**[6] 2529 7-9-9 64........................(b) PaulHanagan 7 68+
(R A Fahey) *prom: effrt and rdn whn nt clr run over 1f out: kpt on fnl f* **13/2**[2]

2244 **8** *1* **Throw The Dice**[11] 2390 5-8-13 54........................(v) TonyHamilton 5 54
(D W Barker) *led to 1f out: sn no ex* **5/1**[1]

1002 **9** *nk* **Paddywack (IRE)**[7] 2509 10-9-0 62........................(b) DanielleMcCreery(7) 6 61
(D W Chapman) *s.i.s: bhd tl kpt on over 1f out: nrst fin* **8/1**

-522 **10** *1* **Mulligan's Gold (IRE)**[10] 2419 4-9-11 **66** DavidAllan 10 61
(T D Easterby) *chsd ldrs tl rdn and wknd over 1f out* **7/1**[3]
0465 **11** *1/2* **Sands Crooner (IRE)**[7] 2516 4-9-3 **58** (v) DeanMcKeown 3 52
(D Shaw) *dwlt: bhd: rdn 1/2-way: nvr rchd ldrs* **20/1**
526- **12** *3 1/2* **Fern House (IRE)**[232] 6233 5-8-6 **47** oh2 PaulFessey 4 28
(Garry Moss) *dwlt: bhd and rdn 1/2-way: nvr on terms* **33/1**
1-00 **13** *shd* **Rosie's Result**[10] 2418 7-8-3 **47** oh2 AndrewMullen(3) 9 28
(M Todhunter) *in tch tl rdn and wknd fr 2f out* **66/1**
10-0 **14** *4* **Alugat (IRE)**[10] 2419 4-9-10 **65** (p) DO'Donohoe 2 31
(Mrs A Duffield) *cl up tl rdn and wknd 2f out: eased whn no ch ins fnl f* **28/1**

61.87 secs (0.37) **Going Correction** +0.20s/f (Good) **14** Ran SP% **121.8**
Speed ratings (Par 103):105,104,104,104,103 102,102,100,100,98 97,92,92,85
CSF £67.42 CT £512.05 TOTE £10.90: £3.30, £3.10, £3.90; EX 67.80.
Owner Jim Goldie Racing Club **Bred** James Thom And Sons And Peter Orr **Trained** Uplawmoor, E Renfrews
■ Stewards' Enquiry : Saleem Golam one-day ban: used whip with excessive frequency (Jun 29)
Kelly Harrison one-day ban: careless riding (Jun 29)

FOCUS
Just a modest event run at a decent gallop and the action again unfolded centre to stands' side in the straight. Sound form for the grade, the winner taking advantage of a good mark.

2713 CLARK DOOR LTD FILLIES' H'CAP 6f 192y
4:15 (4:20) (Class 5) (0-70,70) 3-Y-O **£2,817** (£838; £418; £209) **Stalls** High

Form RPR
4463 **1** **Coconut Queen (IRE)**[6] 2534 3-9-7 **70** (p) RoystonFfrench 8 74
(Mrs A Duffield) *in tch: effrt outside over 2f out: ev ch fnl f: led post* **4/1**[2]
-532 **2** *shd* **Five Wishes**[26] 1943 3-8-7 **56** PaulFessey 9 60
(M Dods) *t.k.h: led 3f: led again over 1f out: edgd rt ins fnl f: hdd post* **7/4**[1]
-600 **3** *3 1/2* **Smash N'Grab (IRE)**[16] 2260 3-8-3 **52** DO'Donohoe 4 46
(K A Ryan) *cl up: led after 3f to over 1f out: kpt on same pce fnl f* **33/1**
5-00 **4** *3/4* **Karma Llama (IRE)**[14] 2313 3-9-0 **63** PaulEddery 10 55
(B Smart) *chsd ldrs: effrt over 2f out: one pce fnl f* **15/2**
6-20 **5** *2 1/2* **Kyrenia Girl (IRE)**[57] 1175 3-8-7 **56** ow1 DavidAllan 5 42
(T D Easterby) *midfield: outpcd over 3f out: rallied fnl f: nrst fin* **22/1**
1066 **6** *shd* **Alavana (IRE)**[10] 2422 3-8-2 **54** AndrewMullen(3) 1 39
(D W Barker) *chsd ldrs tl hung rt and wknd over 1f out* **10/1**
-600 **7** *1/2* **Grethel (IRE)**[17] 2206 3-8-2 **51** oh2 PaulQuinn 6 35
(A Berry) *bhd: rdn over 2f out: edgd rt: nvr rchd ldrs* **80/1**
0-06 **8** *2 1/2* **Xaar Too Busy**[6] 2538 3-8-3 **55** (p) SaleemGolam(3) 3 32
(Mrs A Duffield) *prom: effrt and drvn over 2f out: btn over 1f out* **18/1**
2-02 **9** *shd* **Hansomis (IRE)**[18] 2167 3-8-12 **61** PaulHanagan 7 38
(B Mactaggart) *prom tl rdn and wknd over 2f out* **7/1**[3]
2-06 **10** *1 1/2* **Ocean Of Champagne**[14] 2300 3-8-3 **52** (v) AdrianTNicholls 11 25
(A Dickman) *s.i.s: a bhd* **10/1**
06-0 **11** *nk* **Waiheke Island**[14] 2300 3-8-8 **57** ow2 TomEaves 12 29
(B Mactaggart) *hld up: drvn 3f out: sn btn* **100/1**
5063 **12** *1* **Dolly Coughdrop (IRE)**[11] 2387 3-8-11 **60** PhillipMakin 2 29
(K R Burke) *hld up: rdn 3f out: sn btn* **14/1**

1m 29.12s (2.02) **Going Correction** +0.20s/f (Good) **12** Ran SP% **120.3**
Speed ratings (Par 96):96,95,91,91,88 88,87,84,84,82 82,81
CSF £11.27 CT £209.64 TOTE £6.10: £2.00, £1.30, £8.90; EX 16.20.
Owner Middleham Park Racing Xi **Bred** Bakewell Bloodstock **Trained** Constable Burton, N Yorks
■ Stewards' Enquiry : D O'Donohoe caution: used whip with excessive frequency

FOCUS
A weak handicap but one in which the pace seemed sound throughout. The field raced centre to stands side but the principals came down the centre. Few of these had shown much this term, the front pair exceptions.

2714 BAINES WILSON H'CAP 7f 200y
4:45 (4:48) (Class 5) (0-70,68) 4-Y-0+ **£2,817** (£838; £418; £209) **Stalls** High

Form RPR
0003 **1** **Regent's Secret (USA)**[5] 2564 7-9-7 **68** (p) PaulHanagan 3 82
(J S Goldie) *hld up: hdwy centre over 2f out: led ins fnl f: kpt on strly* **4/1**[1]
0-04 **2** *2* **Catherines Cafe (IRE)**[14] 2302 4-8-1 **51** oh4 ow2.. AndrewMullen(3) 15 60
(A C Whillans) *prom: ev ch fr 2f out: kpt on fnl f: nt rch wnr* **20/1**
60-0 **3** *hd* **Emperor's Well**[10] 2431 8-8-4 **51** (b) DaleGibson 4 60
(M W Easterby) *cl up: ev ch 2f out: kpt on same pce ins fnl f* **25/1**
40-4 **4** *1/2* **Riverhill (IRE)**[45] 1459 4-8-3 **50** PaulFessey 5 58
(J Howard Johnson) *led to ins fnl f: kpt on same pce* **4/1**[1]
0-50 **5** *3/4* **Kirkby's Treasure**[34] 1747 9-8-13 **60** DeanMcKeown 9 66
(G A Swinbank) *hld up: hdwy over 2f out: rdn over 1f out: kpt on ins fnl f* **11/1**
-006 **6** *1 3/4* **First Rhapsody (IRE)**[14] 2302 5-7-13 **49** oh1 DominicFox(3) 10 51
(T J Etherington) *midfield: effrt over 2f out: no imp over 1f out* **16/1**
3-40 **7** *3 1/2* **Haifa (IRE)**[38] 1627 4-8-13 **60** (p) RoystonFfrench 8 54
(Mrs A Duffield) *bhd: drvn 3f out: rdn fnl f: nrst fin* **7/1**[2]
345 **8** *shd* **Modern Verse (USA)**[19] 2149 4-8-11 **58** PaulQuinn 7 52
(G A Swinbank) *bhd: drvn 3f out: nvr rchd ldrs* **14/1**
0-01 **9** *2* **Barataria**[17] 2203 5-8-8 **58** JamieMoriarty(3) 16 47
(R Bastiman) *hld up: hdwy centre over 2f out: n.d* **16/1**
0-00 **10** *2* **Orpen's Astaire (IRE)**[18] 2168 4-7-9 **49** DanielleMcCreery(7) 14 34
(Jedd O'Keeffe) *chsd ldrs tl wknd over 2f out* **40/1**
-004 **11** *1 3/4* **Top Dirham**[16] 2256 9-8-8 **55** PaulMulrennan 12 36
(M W Easterby) *in tch: rdn and hung rt 2f out: sn btn* **8/1**[3]
405- **12** *2 1/2* **Red Chairman**[12] 5483 5-8-3 **50** PaulEddery 2 25
(R Johnson) *hld up in tch: rdn and wknd over 2f out* **20/1**
5-00 **13** *nk* **Brace Of Doves**[16] 2256 5-8-13 **60** TomEaves 1 34
(D W Whillans) *bhd: drvn over 3f out: sn btn* **28/1**
30-0 **14** *3 1/2* **Emotive**[20] 1488 4-8-10 **57** ow2 (b) PhillipMakin 6 23
(F P Murtagh) *midfield: drvn and wkng whn hung rt over 2f out: b.b.v* **66/1**
46-0 **15** *7* **Tequila Sheila (IRE)**[14] 2302 5-8-0 **50** ow1 AndrewElliott(3) 13 —
(K R Burke) *chsd ldrs tl wknd fr 3f out* **12/1**

1m 40.2s (0.11) **Going Correction** +0.20s/f (Good) **15** Ran SP% **118.8**
Speed ratings (Par 103):107,105,104,104,103 101,98,98,96,94 92,89,89,86,79
CSF £92.30 CT £1818.83 TOTE £4.70: £1.60, £4.50, £10.10; EX 80.20 TRIFECTA Not won..
Owner Mrs M Craig **Bred** Adena Springs **Trained** Uplawmoor, E Renfrews

FOCUS
An ordinary handicap but a decent gallop resulted in a fair winning time for a race like this. The principals raced in the centre. Despite the runner-up racing from out of the weights the form looks sound enough.
Emotive Official explanation: jockey said gelding bled from the nose

2715 ROSS LLOYD COMMERCIAL INSURANCE BROKERS H'CAP 1m 6f 32y
5:15 (5:15) (Class 5) (0-70,69) 4-Y-0+ **£2,817** (£838; £418; £209) **Stalls** High

Form RPR
5-44 **1** **Cotton Eyed Joe (IRE)**[19] 2148 6-8-13 **66** PJMcDonald(5) 3 73
(G A Swinbank) *hld up: hdwy over 3f out: styd on wl fnl f to ld nr fin* **8/1**
2224 **2** *nk* **Prince Des Neiges (FR)**[7] 2511 4-8-9 **60** AndrewElliott(3) 5 67
(A M Hales) *t.k.h: led: rdn over 2f out: kpt on fnl f: hdd nr fin* **15/2**[3]
0221 **3** *7* **Toparudi**[16] 2250 6-9-4 **69** SaleemGolam(3) 6 66
(M H Tompkins) *plld hrd: pressed ldr: rdn and hung rt 2f out: sn no ex* **5/2**[2]
0-35 **4** *14* **William John**[14] 2302 4-8-9 **57** (t) PaulMulrennan 8 35
(P C Haslam) *hld up: hdwy over 3f out: rdn and no imp fr 2f out* **14/1**
-425 **5** *3* **Mystified (IRE)**[6] 2537 4-8-3 **51** oh4 ow1 (b) AdrianTNicholls 1 24
(R F Fisher) *chsd clr ldrs: drvn 1/2-way: wknd fr 3f out* **16/1**
61 **6** *6* **Global Strategy**[19] 2148 4-9-4 **66** PaulHanagan 7 31
(Rae Guest) *hld up in tch: effrt over 3f out: rdn and btn 2f out* **13/8**[1]
0405 **7** *3 1/2* **Wulimaster (USA)**[16] 2253 4-9-7 **69** TonyHamilton 2 29
(D W Barker) *prom in chsng gp: rdn and wknd over 3f out* **10/1**
66-3 **8** *24* **King's Envoy (USA)**[32] 965 8-8-1 **52** oh5 ow2 AndrewMullen(3) 4 —
(Mrs J C McGregor) *hld up: drvn over 4f out: wknd over 3f out: t.o* **66/1**

3m 9.50s (2.20) **Going Correction** +0.20s/f (Good) **8** Ran SP% **112.7**
Speed ratings (Par 103):101,100,96,88,87 83,81,67
CSF £63.81 CT £192.23 TOTE £8.80: £2.10, £2.20, £1.40; EX 74.90 Place 6 £65.29, Place 5 £56.36..
Owner Mrs S Sanbrook **Bred** Tally-Ho Stud **Trained** Melsonby, N Yorks

FOCUS
A run-of-the-mill handicap featuring mainly exposed sorts. The pace was sound throughout. The winner is rated back to his best but the form is not strong.
Global Strategy Official explanation: jockey said gelding was unsuited by the good to soft ground
T/Jkpt: Not won. T/Plt: £81.90 to a £1 stake. Pool: £73,199.80. 651.85 winning tickets. T/Qpdt: £31.40 to a £1 stake. Pool: £3,155.70. 74.30 winning tickets. RY

1680 WARWICK (L-H)
Monday, June 18

OFFICIAL GOING: Soft (heavy in places)
Wind: Light behind Weather: Cloudy with sunny spells

2716 RACING UK AMATEUR RIDERS' H'CAP 1m 22y
6:45 (6:45) (Class 6) (0-60,59) 4-Y-0+ **£1,977** (£608; £304) **Stalls** Low

Form RPR
00-0 **1** **Bahhmirage (IRE)**[13] 2343 4-10-0 **45** MissSusannahWileman(7) 1 54
(C N Kellett) *s.i.s: sn chsng ldrs: led over 2f out: styd on wl* **80/1**
0-04 **2** *2 1/2* **Ermine Grey**[4] 2603 6-10-13 **54** MrMJJSmith(3) 14 58
(A W Carroll) *hld up: hmpd over 5f out: hdwy over 2f out: sn rdn: styd on* **7/1**[3]
30-3 **3** *3/4* **Spring Time Girl**[14] 2302 5-10-7 **45** MissLEllison 6 47
(B Ellison) *s.i.s: hld up: hdwy over 2f out: rdn over 1f out: styd on same pce ins fnl f* **11/2**[2]
0003 **4** *1 1/2* **Music Celebre (IRE)**[42] 1539 7-11-7 **59** (b) MrsSBosley 11 58
(S Curran) *plld hrd and prom: lost pl over 5f out: hdwy 3f out: rdn and ev ch over 1f out: no ex ins fnl f* **17/2**
0000 **5** *5* **Royal Sailor (IRE)**[4] 2603 5-10-0 **45** (b) MrDavidMcMinn(7) 4 32
(J Ryan) *s.i.s: hdwy over 5f out: rdn over 2f out: wknd fnl f* **80/1**
0100 **6** *hd* **Monashee River (IRE)**[9] 2467 4-10-7 **50** MissVHaigh(5) 2 37
(Miss V Haigh) *chsd ldrs: led over 3f out: hung rt and hdd over 2f out: wknd over 1f out* **20/1**
6433 **7** *shd* **Foolish Groom**[17] 2214 6-10-12 **55** (v) MrStephenHarrison(5) 3 41
(R Hollinshead) *chsd ldrs: rdn over 2f out: wknd fnl f* **5/1**[1]
104- **8** *1 3/4* **Band**[203] 6628 7-10-9 **54** MissEGeorge(7) 8 36
(E S McMahon) *chsd ldrs over 5f* **11/2**[2]
0-00 **9** *1/2* **Sea Frolic (IRE)**[14] 2302 6-10-7 **45** MrSWalker 5 26
(Jennie Candlish) *chsd ldrs: rdn over 2f out: sn wknd* **25/1**
5354 **10** *5* **Agilete**[17] 2214 5-11-3 **58** MrSPearce(3) 17 28
(J Pearce) *s.i.s: hld up: nvr trbld ldrs* **15/2**
6500 **11** *1/2* **Love You Always (USA)**[17] 2214 7-10-10 **48** (t) MrMatthewSmith 12 17
(Miss J Feilden) *mid-div: rdn over 3f out: wknd over 2f out* **18/1**
-500 **12** *nk* **Adobe**[8] 2490 12-10-5 **48** MrBenBrisbourne(5) 13 16
(W M Brisbourne) *chsd ldrs: lost pl over 5f out: sn bhd* **16/1**
6503 **13** *7* **Sun Bian**[46] 1435 5-10-5 **50** (b[1]) MrJHerbert(7) 9 2
(L P Grassick) *chsd ldrs: hung rt and wknd over 2f out* **14/1**
000- **14** *17* **Ten To The Dozen**[198] 6674 4-11-0 **55** MrsMarieKing(3) 15 —
(P W Hiatt) *chsd ldrs over 5f* **18/1**
140- **15** *2* **Hows That**[233] 6213 5-10-2 **45** (p) MissKellyBurke(5) 7 —
(K R Burke) *led over 4f: wknd over 2f out* **16/1**
5-00 **16** *6* **Fateful Attraction**[28] 1885 4-10-8 **53** (b) MrCMartin(7) 16 —
(I A Wood) *hld up: bhd fr 1/2-way* **25/1**

1m 44.59s (4.99) **Going Correction** +0.375s/f (Good) **16** Ran SP% **126.1**
Speed ratings (Par 101):90,87,86,85,80 80,79,78,77,72 72,71,64,47,45 39
CSF £583.81 CT £3792.17 TOTE £100.10: £13.10, £1.90, £1.80, £2.50; EX 367.10.
Owner Miss S Walley **Bred** Centaur Bloodstock Agency **Trained** Woodlane, Staffs
■ Susannah Wileman's first winner.
■ Stewards' Enquiry : Mr Matthew Smith three-day ban: used whip with excessive force and when gelding was out of contention (Jun 29, Jul 8, 27)

FOCUS
A very moderate amateur riders' handicap and not a race to dwell on. They were spread all over the track at the line. The winner had shown nothing for a year and the form is rated through the third.

2717 EUROPEAN BREEDERS' FUND MAIDEN FILLIES' STKS 5f
7:15 (7:16) (Class 5) 2-Y-O **£3,562** (£1,059; £529; £264) **Stalls** Centre

Form RPR
3322 **1** **Sinead Of Aglish (IRE)**[10] 2410 2-9-0 0 JamieSpencer 7 79
(A B Haynes) *chsd ldr: rdn over 1f out: styd on u.p to ld post* **11/8**[1]
3 **2** *hd* **Cute Ass (IRE)**[21] 2071 2-9-0 0 PatCosgrave 5 78
(K R Burke) *hld up: hdwy over 1f out: rdn to ld and edgd rt ins fnl f: hdd post* **9/2**[3]
4266 **3** *3/4* **Cayman Fox**[9] 2451 2-9-0 0 NCallan 8 76
(James Moffatt) *led: clr 3f out: rdn over 1f out: hdd and unable qck ins fnl f* **7/1**
22 **4** *1 1/2* **Far Gone**[38] 1636 2-9-0 0 HayleyTurner 6 70
(M L W Bell) *chsd ldrs: rdn over 1f out: edgd lft and no ex ins fnl f* **4/1**[2]
06 **5** *3* **Eye Catching**[12] 2364 2-9-0 0 KerrinMcEvoy 3 59
(J R Jenkins) *chsd ldrs: rdn over 1f out: wknd fnl f* **8/1**

4 **6** 1 1/4 **Lady Of Kintyre (IRE)**[20] 2115 2-8-7 0........................ RonanKeogh(7) 1 55
(E J Alston) *hld up: rdn over 1f out: n.d* **14/1**
7 2 1/2 **Jastaanhi** 2-8-9 0.. RussellKennemore(5) 4 46
(J A Pickering) *s.i.s: a in rr* **66/1**
8 3 1/2 **Naming Problems** 2-9-0 0.. J-PGuillambert 2 33
(K J Burke) *s.i.s: outpcd* **40/1**

61.74 secs (2.34) **Going Correction** -0.175s/f (Firm) **8** Ran SP% **114.5**
Speed ratings (Par 90):74,73,72,70,65 63,59,53
CSF £7.81 TOTE £2.00: £1.10, £1.30, £2.60; EX 8.00.
Owner Men At Work Racing **Bred** Oghill House Stud **Trained** Limpley Stoke, Bath

FOCUS
An ordinary fillies' maiden, but the winner was back to her best and the form looks solid.

NOTEBOOK
Sinead Of Aglish(IRE) would have appreciated the switch to soft ground and gained a deserved first success following a string of consistent efforts. She had to work very hard and probably deserves a bit of a break now. (op 9-4 tchd 7-4 in a place)
Cute Ass(IRE) confirmed the promise she showed when third over 5f on fast ground at Carlisle and was only just held. (op 9-4)
Cayman Fox showed terrific early speed and should be able to find an ordinary race on a slightly quicker surface (op 10-1)
Far Gone was below the form she had shown on her two previous starts and may have been unsuited by the soft ground. (op 7-2)
Eye Catching should find her level during the nursery season. (tchd 17-2)
Naming Problems Official explanation: jockey said filly missed the break

2718 GLOW-WORM COMBI FILLIES' H'CAP 6f
7:45 (7:46) (Class 6) (0-65,65) 3-Y-O **£2,730** (£806; £403) **Stalls** Centre

Form RPR
-030 **1** **Karmest**[14] 2300 3-8-8 **52**... GrahamGibbons 11 59
(E S McMahon) *chsd ldrs: led 1/2-way: rdn and hung rt ins fnl f: styd on wl* **8/1**
0-33 **2** 3/4 **Swift Princess (IRE)**[23] 2032 3-8-10 **54**.......................... PatCosgrave 1 59
(K R Burke) *chsd ldrs: rdn and ev ch 1f out: sn hung rt: styd on* **7/1**
3464 **3** 1 **Comptonspirit**[16] 2262 3-9-0 **58**................................(p) J-PGuillambert 14 60
(B P J Baugh) *chsd ldr: ev ch form 1/2-way tl no ex wl ins fnl f* **25/1**
5032 **4** nk **Wadnagin (IRE)**[7] 2515 3-8-11 **55**.................................. JamieSpencer 5 56+
(I A Wood) *chsd ldrs: lost pl 4f out: r.o ins fnl f* **7/2**[1]
2-00 **5** 1 1/4 **Aaron's Way**[7] 2515 3-9-7 **65**... SteveDrowne 6 62
(A W Carroll) *s.i.s: sn chsng ldrs: rdn 1/2-way: styd on same pce fnl f* **8/1**
1403 **6** hd **Princess Ellis**[10] 2435 3-9-3 **61**...................................... RichardThomas 8 57
(E J Alston) *s.i.s: hdwy over 3f out: rdn over 1f out: styd on same pce* **13/2**[3]
-560 **7** 1 **Stormburst (IRE)**[17] 2203 3-8-10 **54**.................................... NCallan 16 47
(M Dods) *mid-div: hdwy 1/2-way: rdn over 1f out: sn hung lft: styd on* **10/1**
6041 **8** 4 **Mujart**[2] 2661 3-8-7 **56** 6ex.. TolleyDean(5) 15 37
(J A Pickering) *chsd ldrs: rdn over 1f out: wknd ins fnl f* **10/1**
3530 **9** 1 3/4 **Tenterhooks (IRE)**[4] 2591 3-8-5 **49**........................(be) StephenCarson 3 25
(A J McCabe) *led to 1/2-way: sn rdn: wknd over 1f out* **12/1**
400- **10** 2 **Little Hotpotch**[249] 5923 3-8-6 **50**... TPO'Shea 4 20
(J R Jenkins) *sn outpcd* **66/1**
0000 **11** shd **Tizzydore (IRE)**[32] 1782 3-7-13 **46** oh1........................(p) LiamJones(3) 2 16
(A G Newcombe) *chsd ldrs to 1/2-way* **25/1**
40-0 **12** 7 **Afric Star**[27] 1912 3-8-2 **46** oh1.................................. FrankieMcDonald 7 —
(John A Harris) *chsd ldrs: n.m.r and lost pl over 3f out: n.d after* **66/1**
2-30 **13** 1 1/2 **Millachy**[27] 1923 3-9-6 **64**... KerrinMcEvoy 12 8
(B W Hills) *s.i.s: outpcd* **6/1**[2]

1m 14.11s (-0.17) **Going Correction** -0.175s/f (Firm) **13** Ran SP% **121.1**
Speed ratings (Par 94):94,93,91,91,89 89,88,82,80,77 77,68,66
CSF £62.31 CT £1396.16 TOTE £8.60: £2.40, £3.50, £5.10; EX 89.00.
Owner J A Porteous **Bred** Charles B B Booth **Trained** Lichfield, Staffs
■ The first race over the new straight 6f track at Warwick, starting in the extended chute.

FOCUS
A moderate fillies' handicap. The principals ended up middle to stands' side at the line. The third and fifth are the best guides to the form.
Millachy Official explanation: jockey said filly stumbled leaving stalls

2719 PRICEWATERHOUSECOOPERS H'CAP 7f 26y
8:15 (8:15) (Class 4) (0-80,78) 4-Y-O+ **£4,857** (£1,445; £722; £360) **Stalls** Low

Form RPR
066 **1** **The Osteopath (IRE)**[16] 2256 4-8-10 **67**....................(p) JamieSpencer 4 79
(M Dods) *hld up: c stands' side and hdwy over 2f out: rdn to ld ins fnl f: hung rt: r.o* **3/1**[2]
040- **2** 3 1/2 **Valentino Swing (IRE)**[215] 6489 4-8-13 **70**.................. KerrinMcEvoy 1 73
(Miss T Spearing) *a.p: c stands' side over 2f out: chsd ldr over 1f out: sn rdn and ev ch: no ex ins fnl f* **7/1**
1124 **3** 1/2 **Luckylover**[18] 2189 4-9-4 **78**......................................(t) JerryO'Dwyer(3) 7 80
(M G Quinlan) *chsd ldr: rdn and hung towards stands' side over 2f out: styd on same pce fnl f* **9/2**[3]
0411 **4** 3/4 **Doctor's Cave**[19] 2149 5-8-4 **61**...................................(b) StephenCarson 6 61
(K O Cunningham-Brown) *led: c stands' side over 2f out: hdd & wknd ins fnl f* **6/1**
22-0 **5** 3 1/2 **Scotland The Brave**[16] 2256 7-8-13 **70**...............................(v) LDettori 3 61
(J D Bethell) *s.i.s: sn chsng ldrs: lost pl 5f out: hdwy and c stands' side over 2f out: wknd fnl f* **11/4**[1]
41-0 **6** 7 **Ochre Bay**[158] 102 4-8-9 **71**.................................... RussellKennemore(5) 2 43
(R Hollinshead) *chsd ldrs to 1/2-way: in rr whn c stands' side over 2f out* **33/1**
1440 **7** 13 **Councellor (FR)**[11] 2401 5-9-6 **77**......................................(vt[1]) NCallan 5 16
(Stef Liddiard) *hld up: wknd 3f out: sn c stands' side* **8/1**
100- **8** 2 **Proud Killer**[334] 3644 4-9-2 **73**... J-PGuillambert 9 6
(J R Jenkins) *chsd ldrs 4f: in rr whn c stands' side sn after* **28/1**

1m 26.0s (1.80) **Going Correction** +0.375s/f (Good) **8** Ran SP% **114.1**
Speed ratings (Par 105):104,100,99,98,94 86,71,69
CSF £24.15 CT £93.10 TOTE £4.00: £1.80, £2.50, £1.50; EX 20.30.
Owner Kevin Kirkup **Bred** Joe Rogers **Trained** Denton, Co Durham

FOCUS
This looked like a very ordinary handicap for the grade, but the pace was strong. They all raced stands' side in the straight. Solid form, the winner back to his 3yo best.
Councellor(FR) Official explanation: jockey said gelding was unsuited by the soft (heavy in places) ground

2720 TWEENHILLS FARM AND STUD WARWICKSHIRE OAKS STKS (LISTED RACE) (F&M) 1m 2f 188y
8:45 (8:45) (Class 1) 4-Y-O+
£14,762 (£5,595; £2,800; £1,396; £699; £351) **Stalls** Low

Form RPR
00-6 **1** **Dash To The Front**[19] 2136 4-8-12 **81**............................ OscarUrbina 2 96
(J R Fanshawe) *a.p: c stands' side and chsd ldr over 2f out: rdn to ld over 1f out: styd on* **33/1**
0-32 **2** 1 3/4 **Queen's Best**[20] 2123 4-8-12 **89**...................................... KerrinMcEvoy 1 99+
(Sir Michael Stoute) *hld up in tch: lost pl and hmpd over 3f out: c stands' side over 2f out: hdwy and hung lft over 1f out: nt rch wnr* **6/1**[3]
40 **3** 1/2 **Glitter Baby (IRE)**[31] 1805 4-8-12 **88**.. NCallan 8 92
(M G Quinlan) *s.i.s: hld up: plld hrd: hdwy over 3f out: c stands' side over 2f out: sn rdn: styd on same pce ins fnl f* **25/1**
4-55 **4** shd **Mango Mischief (IRE)**[23] 2036 6-8-12 **94**........................... TPO'Shea 4 92
(M R Channon) *chsd ldr tl c stands' side and led over 2f out: rdn and hdd over 1f out: no ex ins fnl f* **8/1**
4-24 **5** 9 **Abhisheka (IRE)**[44] 1472 4-8-12 **100**..................................... LDettori 10 75
(Saeed Bin Suroor) *hld up in tch: c stands' side and rdn over 2f out: wknd over 1f out* **11/8**[1]
0521 **6** 2 **Wassfa**[12] 2361 4-8-12 **63**... NashRawiller 7 71
(C E Brittain) *s.i.s: hld up: rdn and c stands' side over 2f out: sn wknd* **66/1**
4645 **7** 13 **Hovering (IRE)**[9] 2462 4-8-12 **87**...................................... JerryO'Dwyer 9 46
(M G Quinlan) *led: rdn and hdd over 2f out: sn wknd* **50/1**
3043 **8** 2 **Tranquilizer**[9] 2471 5-8-12 **72**..(t) HayleyTurner 5 42
(D J Coakley) *chsd ldrs tl rdn and wknd 3f out* **33/1**
15-3 **P** **Portal**[32] 1789 4-8-12 **104**.. JamieSpencer 11 —
(J R Fanshawe) *hld up: p.u over 6f out* **15/8**[2]

2m 21.29s (1.89) **Going Correction** +0.375s/f (Good) **9** Ran SP% **115.5**
Speed ratings (Par 111):108,106,106,106,99 98,88,87,—
CSF £210.01 TOTE £30.20: £5.60, £2.00, £3.00; EX 114.70.
Owner Helena Springfield Ltd **Bred** Meon Valley Stud **Trained** Newmarket, Suffolk

FOCUS
They raced stands' side in the straight. The front two in the betting failed to give their running and this was a weak fillies' & mares' Listed contest, although the pace was good. Dash To The Front was up 10lb on her previous best, with the runner-up unlucky and the third the best guide to the form.

NOTEBOOK
Dash To The Front did not look an obvious winner beforehand, having been well held on her two previous attempts at this level and having finished down the field in a handicap off a mark of just 84 on her reappearance, but she was able to take advantage of a couple of the more fancied runners failing to perform, proving suited by both the step up in trip and soft ground. It would be unwise to get carried away with this performance, but she could pick up some more black type when conditions are suitable.
Queen's Best, pitched in at Listed level for the first time over the furthest trip she has tried to date, was in an unpromising position turning into the straight after being hampered and she never looked like doing enough. (op 11-2 tchd 9-2)
Glitter Baby(IRE) was held up well off the pace with her inferior stablemate setting a solid gallop and the tactics worked a treat as she was able to gain some valuable black type.
Mango Mischief(IRE) has yet to run up to her best this season, but this wasn't a bad effort. (op 12-1)
Abhisheka(IRE) had a big chance judged on the form of her fourth in the Dahlia Stakes at Newmarket on 2000 Guineas day, and the soft ground should have suited too, but she ran a stinker, weakening very tamely when asked for her challenge. (op 6-4 tchd 5-4 and 13-8 in places)
Portal, along with Abhisheka, was entitled to go very close if at her best, but she was pulled up early on and was reported by Jamie Spencer to be sore. (tchd 9-4)

2721 WARWICK FESTIVAL FROLICS H'CAP 1m 2f 188y
9:15 (9:15) (Class 6) (0-65,63) 4-Y-O+ **£2,388** (£705; £352) **Stalls** Low

Form RPR
1545 **1** **Elopement (IRE)**[16] 2254 5-8-13 **55**................................ JamieSpencer 5 60
(W M Brisbourne) *mde all: c stands' side and qcknd over 2f out: drvn out* **9/2**[2]
0-03 **2** 1 1/4 **Sharmy (IRE)**[2] 2660 11-9-2 **58**... TPO'Shea 7 61
(Ian Williams) *hld up in tch: c stands' side over 2f out: rdn to chse wnr over 1f out: styd on* **5/1**[3]
10-0 **3** 2 **Sovietta (IRE)**[76] 903 6-8-8 **55**....................................(t) TravisBlock(5) 3 54+
(A G Newcombe) *hld up: c stands' side over 2f out: hung rt and r.o ins fnl f: nrst fin* **9/1**
5-20 **4** 1 1/2 **Justcallmehandsome**[15] 2275 5-7-12 **47**.............. LauraReynolds(7) 13 43
(D J S Ffrench Davis) *chsd wnr: c stands' side over 2f out: sn rdn: styd on same pce fnl f* **12/1**
0003 **5** hd **Stravara**[2] 2656 4-8-5 **52**... RussellKennemore(5) 2 48
(R Hollinshead) *hld up: racd keenly: c stands' side over 2f out: hdwy over 1f out: styd on same pce ins fnl f* **15/8**[1]
05-6 **6** 2 1/2 **English Archer**[19] 2156 4-8-0 **45**..................................... LiamJones(3) 9 36
(W M Brisbourne) *plld hrd and prom: c stands' side over 2f out: sn rdn and hung lft: wknd fnl f* **17/2**
-600 **7** 3/4 **High Class Problem (IRE)**[7] 2514 4-9-7 **63**........................ NCallan 10 52
(P F I Cole) *hld up: c stands' side over 2f out: rdn over 1f out: wknd ins fnl f* **10/1**
5045 **8** 3 **Bold Cross (IRE)**[20] 2107 4-9-2 **58**.............................. PaulFitzsimons 8 42
(E G Bevan) *s.i.s: hld up: plld hrd: c stands' side over 2f out: rdn and wknd over 1f out* **14/1**
0 **9** 1 3/4 **Investment Pearl (IRE)**[11] 1378 4-9-4 **60**...................... SteveDrowne 11 40
(D R Gandolfo) *prom: racd keenly: c stands' side over 2f out: sn rdn: wknd over 1f out* **50/1**

2m 34.15s (14.75) **Going Correction** +0.375s/f (Good) **9** Ran SP% **115.6**
Speed ratings (Par 101):61,60,58,57,57 55,55,52,51
CSF £27.31 CT £194.10 TOTE £4.50: £1.50, £2.20, £2.60; EX 35.80 Place 6 £446.66, Place 5 £160.71..
Owner Stratford Bards Racing **Bred** Haras Du Mezeray **Trained** Great Ness, Shropshire

FOCUS
A moderate handicap and, with the winner allowed to dictate a steady pace pretty much until they turned into the straight, the bare form wants treating with caution. An incredibly slow winning time, 12.86 seconds (or about 65 lengths) slower than the preceding fillies' Listed event.
Bold Cross(IRE) Official explanation: trainer said gelding finished distressed
T/Plt: £690.00 to a £1 stake. Pool: £75,049.95. 79.40 winning tickets. T/Qpdt: £190.80 to a £1 stake. Pool: £4,048.90. 15.70 winning tickets. CR

2510 WINDSOR (R-H)
Monday, June 18

OFFICIAL GOING: Good to soft (good in places)
Wind: Moderate, behind Weather: Sunny

2722 TRAILFINDERS H'CAP — 1m 67y
6:35 (6:35) (Class 5) (0-75,75) 4-Y-O+ £3,238 (£963; £481; £240) Stalls High

Form RPR
-222 1 **Veiled Applause**[7] 2514 4-9-2 69 SebSanders 2 79
(R M Beckett) *trckd clr ldng pair: led gp of 5 to far side in st: overall ldr 2f out and sn clr: drvn out* 2/1[1]

5164 2 2 **Indian Edge**[20] 2107 6-9-1 68 CatherineGannon 5 73+
(B Palling) *chsd clr ldr and clr of rest: styd nr side in st: def 2nd bhd clr wnr on far side over 1f out: kpt on* 9/1

0-00 3 2 **Glenmuir (IRE)**[9] 2469 4-9-7 74 (b) RyanMoore 11 74
(B R Millman) *hld up in 4th and wl off the pce: rdn to chse wnr on far side over 1f out: kpt on but no imp* 5/1[3]

0011 4 1 **Aggravation**[7] 2514 5-9-5 75 6ex MarcHalford(3) 9 73
(D R C Elsworth) *hld up in last and wl off the pce: prog 2f out: chsd far side ldng pair fnl f: kpt on one pce* 3/1[2]

1465 5 7 **Jools**[7] 2514 9-8-4 57 oh2 ow2 MartinDwyer 6 39
(D K Ivory) *hld up in 5th and wl off the pce: shkn up on far side 2f out: no prog* 7/1

0030 6 2 **San Antonio**[9] 2469 7-9-6 73 (b) MickyFenton 3 50
(Mrs P Sly) *rdn to ld and set furious pce: at least 6 l clr 1/2-way: styd nr side tl wnt across 3f out: hdd & wknd 2f out* 9/1

5200 7 7 **Charlie Bear**[17] 2214 6-8-2 55 (p) AdrianMcCarthy 10 16
(Miss Z C Davison) *hld up in 6th and wl off the pce: no prog on far side 3f out: eased fnl f* 28/1

1m 44.36s (-0.34) **Going Correction** +0.05s/f (Good) 7 Ran SP% 110.9
Speed ratings (Par 103):103,101,99,98,91 89,82
CSF £19.47 CT £74.58 TOTE £2.90: £1.80, £3.00; EX 22.50.
Owner The Wright And Wrong Partnership **Bred** P J McCalmont **Trained** Whitsbury, Hants

FOCUS
A modest handicap, run at a strong early pace. All bar the runner-up went far side in the home straight. The winner was up a length on his latest form.
Charlie Bear Official explanation: trainer said a subsequent test showed horse's blood to be wrong

2723 SIMCORP DIMENSION SOFTWARE FOR ASSET MANAGERS (S) STKS — 6f
7:05 (7:05) (Class 5) 2-Y-O £3,238 (£963; £481; £240) Stalls High

Form RPR
2220 1 **Rio Taffeta**[11] 2392 2-8-11 0 LPKeniry 1 66+
(Peter Grayson) *trckd far side ldrs: overall ldr wl over 2f out: sn clr: rdn out* 3/1[1]

2 3 **Liani (IRE)** 2-8-6 0 ChrisCatlin 6 52
(W M Brisbourne) *trckd far side ldrs: drvn to chse wnr wl over 1f out: no real imp* 22/1

05 3 2 **Sailing By**[21] 2078 2-8-11 0 (b[1]) JimmyFortune 8 51
(B R Millman) *led nr side gp thrght: kpt on u.p but nvr on terms w far side ldrs* 10/1

000 4 nk **Bold Diva**[8] 2488 2-8-1 0 KevinGhunowa(5) 2 45
(A W Carroll) *rdn and outpcd in far side gp over 3f out: plugged on fr over 1f out: n.d* 33/1

60 5 nk **Tenth Night (IRE)**[16] 2241 2-8-11 0 MartinDwyer 9 49
(J A Osborne) *pushed along nr side and outpcd over 3f out: kpt on to go 2nd in gp fnl f: no ch* 10/3[2]

502 6 3/4 **Shipboard Romance (IRE)**[6] 2533 2-8-7 0 ow1 StephenDonohoe 4 43
(P D Evans) *overall ldr far side to wl over 2f out: wknd over 1f out* 9/2[3]

54 7 hd **Ten On Line (IRE)**[12] 2356 2-8-8 0 RichardKingscote(3) 11 46
(J A Osborne) *pushed along nr side and outpcd over 3f out: nvr on terms after* 16/1

0 8 3 1/2 **Friction**[25] 1960 2-8-6 0 NickyMackay 7 31
(J G Portman) *dwlt: sn chsd nr side ldr: wknd over 1f out* 16/1

405 9 1 1/4 **Scrap N'Dust**[7] 2517 2-8-1 0 LukeMorris(5) 5 27
(W G M Turner) *pressed overall ldr far side to 1/2-way: wknd* 33/1

0 10 10 **Poppy Perfect**[10] 2410 2-8-6 0 CatherineGannon 12 —
(J M P Eustace) *bdly outpcd in last nr side: taken to far side over 2f out: t.o after* 8/1

11 6 **Golden Dane (IRE)** 2-8-11 0 SebSanders 10 —
(I A Wood) *s.s: chsd nr side ldrs tl wnt across over 3f out and wl in rr of that gp: sn wknd: t.o* 10/1

1m 13.9s (0.23) **Going Correction** -0.125s/f (Firm) 11 Ran SP% 117.5
Speed ratings (Par 93):93,89,86,85,85 84,84,79,77,64 56
CSF £73.55 TOTE £4.20: £1.80, £4.20, £3.10; EX 92.60.The winner was bought in for £6,600. Tenth Night was claimed by P Midgley for £6,000.
Owner Richard Teatum **Bred** And Mrs P Trant & Mrs **Trained** Formby, Lancs

FOCUS
A fair juvenile seller with Rio Taffeta finally delivering on his earlier promise and producing a good effort for the grade.

NOTEBOOK
Rio Taffeta, placed on five of his nine previous outings, had the blinkers left off for this step back up to 6f and ran out a ready winner, finally breaking his maiden tag in the process. He is clearly also happier with some cut in the ground and, on this evidence, should get another furlong before the season is out. (op 7-2 tchd 4-1 in a place)
Liani(IRE), bred to make her mark at around this trip at two, showed ability and finished a clear second best. The fact that she was making her debut at the bottom level strongly suggests that she is only moderate, however. (op 20-1)
Sailing By was lit up by the first-time blinkers and posted an improved effort in defeat. He is not going to prove at all easy to place successfully, though. (op 11-1 tchd 12-1)
Bold Diva showed her most encouraging form to date on this drop in grade, but left the impression she will be better suited by a stiffer test. (op 25-1)
Tenth Night(IRE) failed to really raise his game for the drop into this class and again became outpaced. He probably already needs a seventh furlong. (op 4-1 tchd 9-2 in a place)

2724 VC CASINO.COM E B F MAIDEN STKS — 5f 10y
7:35 (7:36) (Class 4) 2-Y-O £5,505 (£1,637; £818; £408) Stalls High

Form RPR
4 1 **Rocking**[13] 2337 2-8-12 0 MichaelHills 1 80
(W J Haggas) *restless stalls: sn settled bhd ldng trio: swtchd to outer 1/2-way: prog to ld 1f out: rdn out* 2/1[1]

03 2 1 1/4 **Luscious Lips**[31] 1814 2-8-12 0 PatDobbs 14 76
(R Hannon) *w ldrs: led wl over 1f out to 1f out: one pce* 4/1[2]

3 1 1/2 **Zippi Jazzman (USA)** 2-9-3 0 SebSanders 6 75
(R M Beckett) *pressed ldr: led 1/2-way: hdd and rn green wl over 1f out: kpt on* 6/1

4 1 3/4 **Orton Park** 2-9-3 0 MickyFenton 7 69
(Mrs P Sly) *dwlt: rn green in tch: prog to chse ldng trio over 1f out: pushed along and styd on steadily* 33/1

06 5 5 **Gillans Inn**[20] 2103 2-8-12 0 KevinGhunowa(5) 3 51
(J M Bradley) *restless stalls: chsd ldrs: rdn and outpcd fr 2f out* 25/1

60 6 1/2 **What Katie Did (IRE)**[25] 1970 2-9-3 0 MartinDwyer 2 55+
(J A Osborne) *led: hanging bdly lft and hdd 1/2-way: wknd over 1f out* 9/2[3]

7 nk **Binfield (IRE)** 2-8-12 0 TQuinn 10 50+
(B G Powell) *free to post: dwlt: hld up in rr: edgd lft fr 2f out: no ch but gng wl enough whn rn into trble ent fnl f* 14/1

8 1/2 **Isinkso (IRE)** 2-9-3 0 JamesDoyle 5 46
(R M Beckett) *dwlt: sn in tch: shkn up and outpcd fr 2f out: no ch after* 16/1

9 1 3/4 **Far Song (IRE)** 2-8-12 0 FrancisNorton 13 35
(A M Balding) *chsd ldrs: rn green but stl in tch over 2f out: fdd* 14/1

10 1 **Charlevoix (IRE)** 2-8-12 0 TedDurcan 4 31
(C F Wall) *dwlt: outpcd and a struggling in rr* 10/1

11 1 1/2 **Pennyspider (IRE)** 2-8-12 0 FergusSweeney 8 26
(M S Saunders) *nvr on terms w ldrs: bhd over 1f out* 33/1

60.95 secs (-0.15) **Going Correction** -0.125s/f (Firm) 11 Ran SP% 123.8
Speed ratings (Par 95):96,94,91,88,80 80,79,78,75,74 71
CSF £10.15 TOTE £2.90: £1.40, £1.50, £2.20; EX 7.90.
Owner Hirschfeld/Piggott/Scott/Healey/Malone **Bred** L K Piggott & A Hirschfeld **Trained** Newmarket, Suffolk

FOCUS
A fair juvenile maiden which saw the first four come clear. The level is a little guessy but the race has been rated on the positive side.

NOTEBOOK
Rocking ◆, fourth on her debut at Ripon, got off the mark in workmanlike fashion but should be rated better than the bare form. She proved restless in the stalls and really shaped as though she will be more at home when returning to faster ground in due course, but still had the class to come home well on top of her rivals. It will be interesting to see where she is pitched in next and this well-related filly could well be a likely type for something such as the Molecomb at Goodwood next month. (op 5-2 tchd 3-1)
Luscious Lips defied market weakness with a sound effort in defeat on this return to the minimum trip. She already appeals as a likely sort for nurseries and, with better ground in the future likely to suit again, has a race or two within her compass this term when reverting to a slightly stiffer test. (op 5-2)
Zippi Jazzman(USA) ◆, a 23,000gns purchase whose dam was a sprint winner in the US, was nibbled at in the betting ahead of this racecourse bow and rewarded each-way support with a pleasing effort. He left the clear impression he would benefit for the experience and should be placed to advantage before too long. (tchd 5-1)
Orton Park, bred for speed, turned in a promising debut effort and shaped a little better than the bare form. He can be expected to prove a deal sharper next time.
What Katie Did(IRE), again well backed, showed early speed yet did not look happy on this soft ground as he was hanging under pressure. He has it to prove. Official explanation: jockey said colt hung left (op 7-1)
Binfield(IRE) Official explanation: jockey said filly was denied a clear run

2725 VC CASINO.COM H'CAP — 6f
8:05 (8:05) (Class 4) (0-80,80) 4-Y-O+ £6,477 (£1,927; £963; £481) Stalls High

Form RPR
6050 1 **China Cherub**[10] 2427 4-8-10 69 (b[1]) RyanMoore 1 84
(R Hannon) *pressed ldrs: led 2f out and grabbed far side rail: sn wl in command: clr fnl f* 5/1[2]

0-26 2 2 1/2 **Rydal Mount (IRE)**[21] 2085 4-8-13 72 FergusSweeney 3 79
(W S Kittow) *towards rr: prog towards far side rail over 2f out: chsd wnr over 1f out: styd on but no imp* 10/1

006 3 2 1/2 **Regal Royale**[42] 1545 4-8-11 70 (b[1]) LPKeniry 6 70
(Peter Grayson) *dwlt: in tch nr far side rail: rdn and styd on to take 3rd ins fnl f: no ch w ldng pair* 14/1

-010 4 1/2 **Abwaab**[14] 2318 4-9-7 80 (b) MickyFenton 12 78
(Eve Johnson Houghton) *led and racd towards far side: hdd 2f out: grad fdd* 7/1

5503 5 1 1/4 **Outer Hebrides**[2] 2655 6-8-11 70 (t) DarryllHolland 16 64
(J M Bradley) *racd on outer: chsd ldrs: outpcd fr 2f out: n.d after: kpt on* 9/2[1]

3-00 6 1/2 **Scarlet Knight**[14] 2318 4-8-6 72 JackMitchell(7) 10 65
(P Mitchell) *sltly hmpd s: wl in rr: sme prog over 2f out: bmpd over 1f out: plugged on* 14/1

0465 7 nk **Ocean Gift**[11] 2394 5-8-7 66 StephenDonohoe 9 58
(P D Evans) *rdn in rr bef 1/2-way: kpt on one pce fnl 2f: no ch* 11/2[3]

0-00 8 1/2 **Imperial Gain (USA)**[6] 2546 4-8-10 74 KevinGhunowa(5) 11 64
(J M Bradley) *squeezed out s: wl in rr: effrt on outer of gp 2f out: no real prog* 25/1

00-0 9 1 **Fisberry**[14] 2318 5-9-0 73 FrancisNorton 8 60
(M S Saunders) *taken down early: hld up in rr: effrt against far side rail 2f out: no prog fnl f* 16/1

0-41 10 6 **Gold Flame**[25] 1976 4-8-13 72 DaneO'Neill 15 41
(H Candy) *pressed ldrs on outer tl wknd rapidly wl over 1f out* 11/2[3]

-0P4 11 8 **Xaluna Bay (IRE)**[9] 2479 4-8-11 70 MartinDwyer 13 15
(W R Muir) *pressed ldrs over 3f: wkng whn hmpd over 1f out: eased: t.o* 12/1

00-0 12 1 1/4 **Saxon Saint**[11] 2399 4-8-6 65 RichardSmith 7 7
(M D I Usher) *pressed ldrs over 2f: sn wknd: t.o* 50/1

1m 12.07s (-1.60) **Going Correction** -0.125s/f (Firm) 12 Ran SP% 119.9
Speed ratings (Par 105):105,101,98,97,96 95,94,94,92,84 74,72
CSF £55.15 CT £494.38 TOTE £5.70: £2.10, £4.00, £5.60; EX 50.60.
Owner J Connolly R Goward J Jenkins W Thornton **Bred** Wayne And Hilary Thornton **Trained** East Everleigh, Wilts
■ Stewards' Enquiry : Stephen Donohoe £275 fine: changed boots after weighing out; three-day ban: weighed in 3lb more than weighing out (Jun 29-30, Jul 1)

FOCUS
A fair sprint for the grade. With stalls 2,4 and 5 all non-runners, effectively the bottom three stalls still filled the first three placings. The winner was up 6lb on her 3yo form.
Regal Royale Official explanation: jockey said gelding hung right
Xaluna Bay(IRE) Official explanation: jockey said filly lost a shoe

2726 PLAY AT VC CASINO.COM MAIDEN STKS — 1m 2f 7y
8:35 (8:37) (Class 5) 3-Y-O+ — **£3,238** (£963; £481; £240) **Stalls** Low

Form — RPR

2 **1** **Fourteenth**[14] [2320] 3-9-0 0 .... RyanMoore 11 — 81+
(Sir Michael Stoute) *trckd ldr: led over 3f out: sn 2 l clr: hrd pressed ins fnl f: drvn and hld on* **8/11**[1]

5 **2** *1/2* **Lady Friend**[63] [1068] 5-9-2 0 .... PatrickHills(5) 16 — 72
(J W Hills) *hld up in midfield: prog on outer over 3f out: hanging lft but hdwy to go 2nd 1f out: clsd on wnr fnl f: jst hld* **33/1**

00 **3** *3* **Muraco**[20] [2127] 3-9-0 0 .... JamesDoyle 5 — 71+
(R M Beckett) *hld up wl in rr: stdy prog fr over 2f out: nudged along and styd on steadily fr over 1f out: tk 3rd nr fin: do bttr* **50/1**

4 *hd* **Exclusionist** 3-9-0 0 .... SebSanders 15 — 71
(J Noseda) *reluctant to enter stalls: prom: chsd wnr over 3f out: rn green u.p 2f out: lost 2nd 1f out: one pce* **11/2**[2]

0 **5** *1/2* **Bee Sting**[30] [1841] 3-9-0 0 .... AdamKirby 3 — 70+
(W R Swinburn) *settled in rr: prog 3f out: pushed along and styd on steadily fnl 2f: nrst fin* **16/1**

6 *1/2* **Kwazulu (USA)** 3-9-0 0 .... JimmyFortune 8 — 69+
(J H M Gosden) *dwlt: wl in rr: prog 3f out: urged along and styd on fr over 1f out: nvr nrr* **15/2**[3]

7 *2* **Trans Siberian** 3-9-0 0 .... TQuinn 10 — 65
(P F I Cole) *dwlt: hld up in midfield: gng wl enough and cl up over 3f out: steadily fdd fnl 2f* **25/1**

8 *2 1/2* **Precept** 3-8-9 0 .... DaneO'Neill 4 — 55
(H Candy) *prom: shkn up 3f out: wkng whn carried lft over 1f out* **33/1**

00 **9** *5* **Irish Quest (IRE)**[11] [2402] 3-9-0 0 .... PhilipRobinson 9 — 50
(M A Jarvis) *hld up in midfield: cl enough 3f out: nudged along and wknd 2f out* **16/1**

4-5 **10** *hd* **Ommadawn (IRE)**[32] [1784] 3-8-9 0 .... MichaelHills 2 — 44
(J R Fanshawe) *settled in rr: sme prog over 2f out: sn wknd* **12/1**

11 *1 1/2* **Laurentian Lad** 3-9-0 0 .... ChrisCatlin 6 — 46
(Rae Guest) *s.s: a wl in rr: detached and struggling over 3f out* **100/1**

06 **12** *1/2* **Beau Michael**[23] [2046] 3-9-0 0 .... TedDurcan 1 — 45
(W R Swinburn) *prom to 3f out: wknd and flashed tail 2f out* **33/1**

05 **13** *11* **Martinet (IRE)**[21] [2081] 3-8-7 0 .... BernadetteQuinn(7) 7 — 23
(P D Evans) *led: rn v wd bnds 6f out and 5f out: hdd over 3f out: veering all over the crse and wknd* **100/1**

14 *8* **Damascus Gold** 3-9-0 0 ....(p) SamHitchcott 13 — 7
(Miss Z C Davison) *s.v.s: a last and wl bhd: t.o* **100/1**

2m 11.31s (3.01) **Going Correction** +0.30s/f (Good)
WFA 3 from 5yo 12lb — **14** Ran SP% **122.1**
Speed ratings (Par 103):99,98,96,96,95 95,93,91,87,87 86,85,77,70
CSF £43.85 TOTE £1.80: £1.10, £7.20, £14.50; EX 33.60.
Owner K Abdulla **Bred** Juddmonte Farms Ltd **Trained** Newmarket, Suffolk

FOCUS
This should prove to be a fair three-year-old maiden, but it was falsely-run. A slight improvement from Fourteenth on his debut effort here, but there was little solid form to go on. A number of these will do better when qualified for handicaps.
Muraco Official explanation: jockey said gelding hung left
Ommadawn(IRE) Official explanation: jockey said filly ran too free

2727 PLAY BLACKJACK AT VC CASINO.COM H'CAP — 1m 2f 7y
9:05 (9:09) (Class 5) (0-70,70) 3-Y-O — **£3,238** (£963; £481; £240) **Stalls** Low

Form — RPR

004- **1** **Ballet Boy (IRE)**[275] [5364] 3-9-0 **63** .... SebSanders 7 — 70+
(Sir Mark Prescott) *reluctant to enter stalls: led after 1f: reminder after 2f: mde rest: hrd pressed and u.str.p fnl 2f: hld on* **7/2**[2]

-400 **2** *1/2* **Rustic Gold**[10] [2425] 3-8-5 **57** .... StephaneBreux(3) 11 — 63
(J R Best) *dwlt: t.k.h: hld up towards rr: prog 4f out: wnt 2nd 2f out on outer: chal fnl f: jst hld* **20/1**

06-4 **3** *1 1/4* **Gib (IRE)**[18] [2177] 3-8-11 **60** .... MichaelHills 14 — 63
(B W Hills) *t.k.h: hld up in rr: prog on outer over 2f out: rdn and styd on over 1f out: nrst fin* **16/1**

60-4 **4** *nk* **Marlyn Ridge**[47] [1399] 3-8-13 **62** .... RobertHavlin 13 — 64
(D K Ivory) *trckd wnr after 2f to 5f out: styd prom: one pce fnl 2f* **50/1**

-001 **5** *1/2* **Sir Duke (IRE)**[6] [2538] 3-8-10 **59** 6ex .... TedDurcan 15 — 60+
(P W D'Arcy) *hld up in rr: rdn over 2f out: prog wl over 1f out: urged along and styd on ins fnl f* **4/1**[3]

043 **6** *1/2* **Natural Action**[27] [1928] 3-9-7 **70** .... DarryllHolland 5 — 70+
(W Jarvis) *dwlt: hld up wl in rr: stdy prog against far rail fr 3f out: urged along and styd on fr over 1f out: nrst fin* **14/1**

-550 **7** *shd* **Calculating (IRE)**[31] [1815] 3-9-7 **70** .... JimmyFortune 1 — 70+
(J H M Gosden) *dwlt: settled wl in rr: effrt on outer 3f out: hrd rdn and styd on fnl 2f: nrst fin* **12/1**

1-00 **8** *shd* **Doubly Guest**[35] [1722] 3-9-6 **69** .... TQuinn 16 — 69
(G G Margarson) *t.k.h: hld up towards rr: reminders and prog 2f out: edgd lft fr over 1f out: styd on* **20/1**

-013 **9** *1/2* **Lapina (IRE)**[10] [2413] 3-8-10 **59** ....(b) RichardMullen 3 — 58
(Pat Eddery) *wl in rr: drvn in last trio 4f out: no prog tl styd on wl fr over 1f out* **25/1**

3142 **10** *1 3/4* **Sonara (IRE)**[19] [2132] 3-8-12 **66** .... PatrickHills(5) 6 — 66+
(M H Tompkins) *in tch in midfield: u.p on outer 2f out: one pce* **3/1**[1]

-020 **11** *nk* **Up In Arms (IRE)**[18] [2177] 3-9-2 **70** .... LukeMorris(5) 8 — 65
(P Winkworth) *a towards rr: rdn over 2f out: one pce and no prog* **16/1**

1004 **12** *1* **Paymaster General (IRE)**[19] [2150] 3-9-2 **65** .... DaneO'Neill 4 — 58
(M D I Usher) *t.k.h: hld up in tch: rdn and no prog over 2f out: fdd* **25/1**

-006 **13** *9* **Shouldntbethere (IRE)**[18] [2177] 3-8-13 **62** .... JamesDoyle 2 — 37
(Mrs P N Dutfield) *dwlt: hld up in rr: prog into midfield 1/2-way: wknd over 2f out* **50/1**

000 **14** *1/2* **Bubbly Girl**[30] [1841] 3-8-6 **62** .... SCreighton(7) 10 — 36
(P J McBride) *a towards rr: wknd 2f out* **50/1**

4-00 **15** *19* **Sofia Royale**[28] [1901] 3-9-1 **64** .... PhilipRobinson 9 — —
(B Palling) *led for 1f: prom tl wknd over 3f out: eased: t.o* **25/1**

663 **16** *8* **Central Force**[12] [2360] 3-9-5 **68** .... RyanMoore 12 — —
(E A L Dunlop) *prom: trckd wnr 5f out: upsides 3f out: wknd rapidly and eased: t.o* **9/1**

2m 11.5s (3.20) **Going Correction** +0.30s/f (Good) — **16** Ran SP% **130.3**
Speed ratings (Par 99):99,98,97,97,96 96,96,96,96,94 94,93,86,85,70 64
CSF £82.23 CT £1036.23 TOTE £3.50: £1.90, £5.10, £2.80, £10.50; EX 135.20 TRIFECTA IPlace 6 £156.26, Place 5 £68.12..
Owner Syndicate 2005 **Bred** Knocklong House Stud **Trained** Newmarket, Suffolk
■ Stewards' Enquiry : Seb Sanders three-day ban: used whip with excessive frequency (Jun 29-30, Jul 1)
Stephane Breux three-day ban: used whip with excessive frequency (Jun 29-30, Jul 1)

FOCUS
An interesting three-year-old handicap, featuring some unexposed handicappers, but it was not strongly run. The winner can rate a deal higher but the lack of pace renders the form dubious.
Shouldntbethere(IRE) Official explanation: jockey said gelding missed the break and was carried wide on bend
Central Force Official explanation: jockey said filly lost its action
T/Plt: £377.80 to a £1 stake. Pool: £98,885.35. 191.05 winning tickets. T/Qpdt: £104.60 to a £1 stake. Pool: £6,037.40. 42.70 winning tickets. JN

2728 - 2731a (Foreign Racing) - See Raceform Interactive

1649 ASCOT (R-H)
Tuesday, June 19

OFFICIAL GOING: Straight course - good to firm; round course - good
Wind: Moderate, behind Weather: Sunny early, clouding over

2732 COVENTRY STKS (GROUP 2) — 6f
2:30 (2:35) (Class 1) 2-Y-O
£45,424 (£17,216; £8,616; £4,296; £2,152; £1,080) **Stalls** Centre

Form — RPR

1 **1** **Henrythenavigator (USA)**[44] [1508] 2-9-1 0 .... MJKinane 17 — 110
(A P O'Brien, Ire) *tall: str: scope: lw: t.k.h to post: chsd ldrs: led jst ins fnl f: drvn out* **11/4**[1]

312 **2** *3/4* **Swiss Franc**[15] [2316] 2-9-1 0 .... TedDurcan 11 — 108
(D R C Elsworth) *lw: b: mid-div: n.m.r 1/2-way: rdn and hdwy 2f out: r.o to take 2nd nr fin* **25/1**

1 **3** *shd* **Luck Money (IRE)**[24] [2041] 2-9-1 0 .... TQuinn 10 — 107
(P F I Cole) *cl up: rdn to press ldrs whn jinked lft 1f out: continued to edge lft: nt qckn fnl 100yds* **13/2**

1 **4** *3/4* **Pencil Hill (IRE)**[24] [2049] 2-9-1 0 .... PShanahan 19 — 105
(Tracey Collins, Ire) *gd sort: lw: prom towards centre: led 2f out tl jst ins fnl f: one pce* **6/1**[3]

113 **5** *1 1/2* **Mount Pleasure (USA)**[17] [2232] 2-9-1 0 .... MartinDwyer 5 — 101+
(J A Osborne) *s.s: sn in midfield: drvn along 1/2-way: styd on fnl 2f: nvr nrr* **25/1**

2101 **6** *hd* **Cee Bargara**[13] [2353] 2-9-1 0 .... RyanMoore 2 — 100+
(J A Osborne) *led tl 2f out: wknd 1f out* **66/1**

1 **7** *1 3/4* **Bobs Surprise**[18] [2215] 2-9-1 0 .... MichaelHills 12 — 95
(B W Hills) *hld up towards rr: hdwy over 2f out: sn rdn and no imp* **9/1**

11 **8** *1/2* **Declaration Of War (IRE)**[17] [2232] 2-9-1 0 .... RobertHavlin 9 — 93
(P W Chapple-Hyam) *mid-div: rdn 1/2-way: nt pce to chal* **9/2**[2]

9 *nk* **South Dakota (IRE)**[34] [1776] 2-9-1 0 .... JMurtagh 1 — 92+
(A P O'Brien, Ire) *tall: str: lw: prom: outpcd 1/2-way: kpt on again fnl f* **14/1**

11 **10** *nk* **Burnwynd Boy**[25] [2009] 2-9-1 0 .... TomEaves 8 — 92
(I Semple) *lw: sn bhd: drvn along 1/2-way: nvr rchd ldrs* **33/1**

2 **11** *1* **Atheer Dubai (IRE)**[18] [2215] 2-9-1 0 .... EddieAhern 3 — 89+
(C E Brittain) *prom over 3f* **66/1**

3 **12** *1/2* **Greek Mythology (USA)**[20] [2159] 2-9-1 0 .... JAHeffernan 13 — 87
(A P O'Brien, Ire) *in tch: rdn along 1/2-way: sn btn* **33/1**

412 **13** *1 1/2* **Aaim To Storm (USA)**[25] [2009] 2-9-1 0 .... DarryllHolland 4 — 83
(M R Channon) *chsd ldrs to 1/2-way* **50/1**

1 **14** *1/2* **Yem Kinn**[38] [1652] 2-9-1 0 .... JHBowman 7 — 81
(M R Channon) *in tch: rdn and btn over 2f out* **20/1**

31 **15** *nk* **Coasting**[31] [1832] 2-9-1 0 .... JimCrowley 14 — 80
(Mrs A J Perrett) *towards rr: sme hdwy over 2f out: sn btn* **33/1**

16 *3 1/2* **Ernie Owl (USA)** 2-9-1 0 .... JamieSpencer 15 — 73+
(B J Meehan) *cmpt: scope: lw: s.s: a towards rr* **66/1**

1 **17** *1 1/4* **Bere Davis (FR)**[11] [2432] 2-9-1 0 .... DeanMcKeown 16 — 66+
(P D Evans) *prom: tried to jump path and stmbld bdly after 2f: nt rcvr and sn bhd* **66/1**

5021 **18** *1 1/4* **Dubai Dynamo**[10] [2447] 2-9-1 0 .... JohnEgan 6 — 62
(J S Moore) *prom to 1/2-way* **100/1**

1 **19** *1 3/4* **Lindoro**[25] [1990] 2-9-1 0 .... AdamKirby 20 — 57
(W R Swinburn) *v keen to post: trckd ldrs in centre: rdn over 2f out: sn wknd* **33/1**

41 **20** *47* **Ruff Diamond (USA)**[17] [2241] 2-9-1 0 .... GeorgeBaker 18 — —
(J R Best) *mid-div: hmpd after 2f: sn wl bhd: virtually p.u over 1f out* **50/1**

1m 12.46s (-2.44) **Going Correction** -0.20s/f (Firm) 2y crse rec — **20** Ran SP% **124.2**
Speed ratings (Par 105):108,107,106,105,103 103,101,100,100,99 98,97,95,95,94 90,88,86,84,21
CSF £81.90 TOTE £3.70: £1.80, £7.60, £2.90; EX 89.10 Trifecta £2723.50 Pool: £5,753.97, 1.50 winning units.
Owner Mrs John Magnier **Bred** Westrn Bloodstock **Trained** Ballydoyle, Co Tipperary
■ A fifth Coventry winner in 11 years for Aidan O'Brien.

FOCUS
An up-to-scratch renewal of the Coventry Stakes and the proximity of the likes of Pencil Hill and Mount Pleasure, who both have smart Listed form to their name, helps give the race a very solid look. The winning time was both a juvenile and all-aged course record for the trip. The first four home raced up the middle of the track but, with both Mount Pleasure and Cee Bargara running as well as could have been expected towards the stands' side, it is hard to believe there was any track bias.

NOTEBOOK
Henrythenavigator(USA) ◆ looked a smart prospect when winning a 7f maiden at Gowran by seven lengths on his debut and he confirmed that impression on this step up in class. The drop in trip did not pose him any problems whatsoever and, having mastered one of his main dangers strictly on the book, Pencil Hill, quite readily, he was always doing enough. He will have to step up again to develop into a serious Guineas candidate next year, for which he is now available at 10/1, but that is highly likely considering this was just his second career start and he is bred to appreciate at least 1m in time. His trainer saddled subsequent French Guineas winner Landseer to win this race in 2001, with our own 2000 Guineas winner Rock Of Gibraltar back in sixth, so there should be no concerns about this race's history of producing Classic winners. Whatever the case, that's a long way off and he could try and take the next step up in the ladder in the Group 1 Phoenix Stakes at the Curragh in August. Races like the National Stakes and Dewhurst will also no doubt be considered later in the year. (op 5-2 tchd 3-1, 10-3 in places)
Swiss Franc ◆ produced a smart effort in defeat when conceding 7lb to Hatta Fort (third in the Windsor Castle on this card) over 5f at Windsor on his previous start and he improved again to take a fine second behind a potential top notcher. Having travelled as well as anything for much of the way, he just hit a bit of a flat spot, having had to make his way through a tight gap to get into the clear, and he got going too late. He gives the impression he will come on again for this and he could be very hard to beat if taking his chance in the July Stakes. Later in the season, he looks a proper Middle Park horse.
Luck Money(IRE) improved significantly on the form he showed when winning well on his debut at Newmarket, but he lugged left under pressure near the line, feeling the ground according to his trainer, and possibly still displaying signs of inexperience. He would not have been far away had he stayed straight and he looks a serious prospect. His connections are keen to give him time to mature and may wait for the Richmond Stakes at Goodwood. (tchd 7-1 in places)

Pencil Hill(IRE) was one of the best juveniles seen out so far this year coming into the race, having won a winners' event on his debut and followed up in a Listed contest, and his proximity helps set the standard. He was still battling it out with the eventual winner around a furlong out when his rider lost his whip and he was ultimately just outstayed by those who finished in front of him. A May foal, he was the youngest in the field, and should stay this trip better in time, but a drop back to 5f is unlikely to inconvenience him. (op 13-2 tchd 7-1 in places)

Mount Pleasure(USA) ran to the same sort of form he showed when third in the Woodcote Stakes on Derby day and is another who helps give the form a very solid look. He might just want dropping back into Listed company.

Cee Bargara hung badly left when winning at Kempton on his previous start, so the stands' rail would have been a big help, and he ran a fine race in defeat, showing his earlier Woodcote running to be all wrong. He is very tough and is the type who should give his connections a lot of fun in some nice races for most of the season.

Bobs Surprise produced a useful effort when winning on his debut at Goodwood and he confirmed he is a colt of some potential with a creditable run. This was only his second outing and there should be more to come. (tchd 10-1 in places)

Declaration Of War(IRE) was well below the form he showed when winning the Woodcote Stakes on his previous start and was disappointing. Official explanation: jockey said colt was unsuited by the good to firm ground (op 5-1)

South Dakota(IRE) was weighted to reverse Naas form with Pencil Hill, but that one has clearly progressed to another level. He has plenty of size, so the hurly-burly of a race like this may not have been ideal, and he can yet do better. (op 16-1)

Burnwynd Boy came into this having won the same conditions event at Pontefract that last year's Coventry winner, Hellvelyn, had picked up, but he never got in a blow. He has already shown enough to suggest he can develop into a very useful sort and it would be unwise to assume this is as good as he is. (tchd 40-1 in a place)

Atheer Dubai(IRE) finished closer to Bobs Surprise than he did at Goodwood on his debut and this was an improved performance. (tchd 125-1 in a place)

Greek Mythology(USA) looked the third string on jockey bookings and this may have come a little too soon in his career.

Aaim To Storm(USA) could not reverse Pontefract form with Burnwynd Boy. (op 66-1)

Yem Kinn looked an interesting type for this race when winning over 5f here on his debut, but he never featured.

Coasting could not build on his Newbury maiden success, failing to confirm form with Greek Mythology.

Ernie Owl(USA) ◆, a $425,000 purchase, out of a smart prolific winning sprinter in the US at two to six, made a highly respectable debut considering he was faced with such a tough task. It might be worth taking the hint that his connections felt he was worth his place in such a line-up. (op 50-1)

Bere Davis(FR) looked a nice type when winning on his debut at Haydock, but he lost his chance when seeming to lose his action after attempting to jump the path after a couple of furlongs. Official explanation: jockey said gelding stumbled

Dubai Dynamo was outclassed.

Lindoro looked useful when winning on his debut at Goodwood, but this was a lot tougher.

Ruff Diamond(USA), a recent Folkestone maiden winner, lost his chance when hampered by the stumbling Bere Davis not long after the start. Official explanation: jockey said colt suffered interference and lost its action (tchd 66-1 in places)

2733 KING'S STAND STKS (BRITISH LEG OF THE GLOBAL SPRINT CHALLENGE) (GROUP 2) 5f

3:05 (3:10) (Class 1) 3-Y-O+

£121,259 (£45,958; £23,000; £11,468; £5,744; £2,883) **Stalls** Centre

Form				RPR
	1		**Miss Andretti (AUS)**[101] 6-9-1 0 ... CNewitt 19 (Lee Freedman, Australia) *lw: in tch: clsd over 2f out: led jst over 1f out: r.o wl and in command towards fin* **3/1**[1]	125+
3-12	**2**	*1 3/4*	**Dandy Man (IRE)**[15] 2324 4-9-4 0 ... PShanahan 1 (Tracey Collins, Ire) *in tch towards nr side: rdn and hung rt fr 2f out: r.o to take 2nd wl ins fnl f: nt rch wnr* **15/2**[3]	122+
	3	*nk*	**Magnus (AUS)**[86] 5-9-4 0 ... (b) DMOliver 17 (P Moody, Australia) *w'like: chsd ldrs: rdn to ld over 1f out: sn hdd: styd on same pce towards fin* **14/1**	120
301-	**4**	*1/2*	**Takeover Target (AUS)**[24] 8-9-4 0 ... JayFord 14 (J Janiak, Australia) *lw: midfield: rdn and hdwy 2f out: r.o ins fnl f: gaining towards fin* **11/2**[2]	119
03-1	**5**	*1 1/2*	**Enticing (IRE)**[49] 1372 3-8-9 115 ... JamieSpencer 12 (W J Haggas) *hld up: hdwy 2f out: fin wl* **8/1**	109
10-3	**6**	*1 3/4*	**Desert Lord**[15] 2324 7-9-4 117 ... (b) NCallan 20 (K A Ryan) *sn w ldr: rdn to ld over 2f out: hdd over 1f out: no ex wl ins fnl f* **25/1**	107
-321	**7**	*hd*	**Beauty Is Truth (IRE)**[16] 2291 3-8-9 0 ... (b) TThulliez 10 (Robert Collet, France) *hld up: rdn and hdwy over 1f out: r.o ins fnl f: nt rch ldrs* **14/1**	102
-315	**8**	*1/2*	**The Tatling (IRE)**[10] 2463 10-9-4 100 ... DarryllHolland 15 (J M Bradley) *s.i.s: towards rr: rdn and hdwy over 1f out: styd on wl fnl f: nvr nrr* **66/1**	105
0-15	**9**	*1/2*	**Green Manalishi**[17] 2234 6-9-4 105 ... TedDurcan 21 (K A Ryan) *hld up: rdn and hdwy 2f out: styd on wl fnl f: nvr rchd ldrs* **66/1**	103
0322	**10**	*1 1/4*	**Moorhouse Lad**[17] 2234 4-9-4 93 ... TomEaves 18 (B Smart) *b.hind: led: rdn and hdd over 2f out: wknd ins fnl f* **100/1**	99
0111	**11**	*hd*	**Tax Free (IRE)**[15] 2324 5-9-4 110 ... AdrianTNicholls 7 (D Nicholls) *midfield in centre gp: pushed along over 2f out: no imp* **14/1**	98
53-1	**12**	*shd*	**Benbaun (IRE)**[24] 2050 6-9-4 115 ... (v) PJSmullen 5 (M J Wallace) *midfield in centre gp: rdn over 2f out: nvr able to chal* **10/1**	98
03-4	**13**	*1/2*	**Pivotal Point**[2] 2695 7-9-4 111 ... SebSanders 4 (P J Makin) *midfield in centre gp: rdn and edgd rt over 1f out: no imp* **40/1**	96
0223	**14**	*hd*	**Moss Vale (IRE)**[16] 2291 6-9-4 114 ... LDettori 11 (D Nicholls) *lw: rrd s: midfield: rdn over 2f out: one pce fnl f* **25/1**	95
6-05	**15**	*shd*	**Conquest (IRE)**[16] 2291 3-8-12 114 ... (b) JHBowman 9 (W J Haggas) *hld up: rdn and n.d whn n.m.r and hmpd over 1f out* **50/1**	93
66	**16**	*1*	**Manzila (FR)**[16] 2291 4-9-1 0 ... OPeslier 2 (F Head, France) *w'like: lw: racd towards nr side: a bhd* **150/1**	88
1-11	**17**	*1*	**King Orchisios (IRE)**[87] 762 4-9-4 108 ... (p) DO'Donohoe 6 (K A Ryan) *midfield in centre gp: rdn and wknd over 2f out* **66/1**	87
500	**18**	*nk*	**Matsunosuke**[17] 2244 5-9-4 75 ... JMurtagh 8 (A B Coogan) *lw: midfield in centre gp: lost pl 2f out: bhd after* **200/1**	86
3541	**19**	*5*	**Dazed And Amazed**[13] 2352 3-8-12 94 ... RichardHughes 16 (R Hannon) *chsd ldrs: rdn over 2f out: wknd over 1f out* **100/1**	66
	20	*1/2*	**Bentley Biscuit (AUS)**[38] 6-9-4 0 ... NashRawiller 3 (Mrs Gai Waterhouse, Australia) *str: lw: swtchd rt after s: in rr: edgd rt and sme hdwy wl over 1f out: eased whn n.d ins fnl f* **9/1**	67

57.44 secs (-3.96) **Going Correction** -0.20s/f (Firm) course record
WFA 3 from 4yo+ 6lb **20** Ran SP% **122.1**
Speed ratings (Par 115):123,120,119,118,116 113,113,112,111,109 109,109,108,108,108 106,104,104,96,95
CSF £22.65 TOTE £4.20: £2.20, £3.00, £5.30; EX 36.80 Trifecta £535.90 Pool: £10,899.86, 14.44 winning units.
Owner P S Buckley, D B Mueller, Ms G Guenzi **Bred** K & Mrs P Beauglehole **Trained** Australia
■ The first winner in Britain for top Australian trainer Lee Freedman and jockey Craig Newitt.

FOCUS

A decent renewal, featuring four raiders from Australia and, for the first time, Group 1 winners were not required to carry a penalty. It was run at a strong gallop and in a very smart winning time, even for a Group 2, which took 2.35sec off the existing course record. The form looks rock solid, confirming the superiority of the Aussie sprinters overall, with a probable career best from the progressive Miss Andretti.

NOTEBOOK

Miss Andretti(AUS), successful in 16 of her previous 24 career starts and unbeaten in four starts over the minimum trip, was widely considered to be the strongest candidate from down under, and she proved herself a top-notcher with a highly impressive success, quickening up well from her compatriot Magnus and comfortably holding off Dandy Man, who raced on the other side of the track. She broke a track record for the third time in her last four starts and it was understandable that bookmakers took evasive action with regard to her chance in the Golden Jubilee on Saturday, for which she is now a best-priced 2-1. Further down the line, the July Cup is likely to be on the agenda. (tchd 10-3 in places and 7-2 in a place)

Dandy Man(IRE) ◆ got beaten on an easier surface last time out but bounced right back to form on this quick ground. Forced to race on his own for most of the race while the main action took place towards the centre to far side of the track, he ran on strongly to finish second, the only horse from a single-figure box to make the first ten, and had he been drawn higher it is quite possible that he would have won. His trainer said it was unlikely that he would reoppose the winner in the Golden Jubilee, although 6f ought not to inconvenience him this year, and he will probably take the Aussies on again in the July Cup. Granted fast ground, though, the Nunthorpe at York in August should be the ideal race for him. (op 10-1 tchd 12-1 in places)

Magnus(AUS), who had finished behind Miss Andretti on a couple of occasions earlier this season, was once again unable to match the speedy mare. He still ran well, though, leading over a furlong out before being done for toe by the winner inside the last. The Golden Jubilee remains a possible for him, but it is difficult to see him reversing form with the winner. (op 12-1)

Takeover Target(AUS), who won this race last year, struggled a little to go the strong gallop but he stayed on well in the closing stages and one would have to believe that he will be suited by the furlong-longer trip in the Golden Jubilee on Saturday, which is the race his trainer claims has been his number one target all along. (tchd 6-1 in places)

Enticing(IRE) was impressive in winning a fillies' Listed race on her reappearance but had a lot more on her plate here. She bounces off fast ground, though, and ran a fine race against older, more experienced rivals. She remains open to further improvement as the season develops. (tchd 9-1 in places)

Desert Lord, last year's Abbaye winner, finished one place behind Dandy Man in Ireland last time, but he was 4lb better off at the weights here. He went too fast on this occasion, giving himself little chance of seeing out the trip, especially on a track with a stiff finish like this. (op 20-1)

Beauty Is Truth(IRE), a clear winner of a Group 2 at Chantilly last time out and supplemented for this, was another three-year-old filly by Pivotal to run with credit, especially as the ground would have been plenty quick enough for her. (tchd 16-1 in a place)

The Tatling(IRE), winner of this race back in 2004, was another staying on late, but he is in the veteran stage now and his best days are certainly behind him.

Green Manalishi was outclassed in this company but he has graduated through the handicapping ranks and could well win a Listed race this season.

Moorhouse Lad, a natural front-runner, set the strong pace which led to a very smart winning time.

Tax Free(IRE), on a roll this year, was poorly drawn in a single-figure stall, and he never really threatened. His form with Dandy Man was comprehensively turned around despite the fact that the Irish colt had to deal with an even lower draw.

Benbaun(IRE), runner-up in this race last year, was another who was poorly drawn and failed to get competitive.

Pivotal Point, third in this race last year, again finished one place behind Benbaun, but on this occasion their battle was for very minor positions only.

Bentley Biscuit(AUS) has shown his best form over 6f and 7f in Australia, and the Golden Jubilee was expected to be his best chance of success at the meeting, but it was still disappointing to see him run so badly. Apparently he got badly jarred up, finding the ground far too fast for his liking, and Saturday's race is now likely to be skipped in favour of the July Cup next month. (op 15-2)

2734 ST JAMES'S PALACE STKS (GROUP 1) (COLTS) 1m (R)

3:45 (3:50) (Class 1) 3-Y-O

£141,950 (£53,800; £26,925; £13,425; £6,725; £3,375) **Stalls** High

Form				RPR
31-4	**1**		**Excellent Art**[37] 1703 3-9-0 ... JamieSpencer 1 (A P O'Brien, Ire) *hld up in rr: shkn up and gd hdwy over 1f out: drvn to ld ins fnl f* **8/1**[3]	123
2-44	**2**	*nk*	**Duke Of Marmalade (IRE)**[24] 2051 3-9-0 ... MJKinane 7 (A P O'Brien, Ire) *lw: led at modest pce: qcknd 3f out: hrd rdn and hdd ins fnl f: kpt on wl* **11/1**	122
1-61	**3**	*1 1/4*	**Astronomer Royal (USA)**[37] 1703 3-9-0 ... CO'Donoghue 6 (A P O'Brien, Ire) *lw: t.k.h: trckd ldng pair: drvn to chal over 1f out: nt qckn ins fnl f* **14/1**	119
1-23	**4**	*hd*	**Dutch Art**[45] 1473 3-9-0 118 ... JimmyFortune 4 (P W Chapple-Hyam) *lw: hld up in tch: drvn to chal over 1f out: one pce fnl f* **10/3**[2]	118
3-11	**5**	*shd*	**Cockney Rebel (IRE)**[24] 2051 3-9-0 120 ... OPeslier 3 (G A Huffer) *hld up towards rr: eased outside and hdwy over 1f out: ch whn hung bdly lft fnl f: nt rcvr* **1/1**[1]	118+
4122	**6**	*1*	**Creachadoir (IRE)**[24] 2051 3-9-0 ... KJManning 8 (J S Bolger, Ire) *tall: str: lw: hld up in tch: effrt and nt clr run wl over 1f out: swtchd sharply lft: drvn along and nt pce to chal* **12/1**	116
46-2	**7**	*2 1/2*	**Jack Junior (USA)**[80] 859 3-9-0 ... LDettori 2 (B J Meehan) *trckd ldr: hrd rdn 2f out: wknd over 1f out* **33/1**	110
0-43	**8**	*3/4*	**He's A Decoy (IRE)**[24] 2051 3-9-0 ... KerrinMcEvoy 5 (David Wachman, Ire) *hld up on outside in 6th: hrd rdn over 2f out: sn btn* **12/1**	109

1m 39.33s (-2.77) **Going Correction** -0.05s/f (Good) **8** Ran SP% **117.5**
Speed ratings (Par 113):111,110,109,109,109 108,105,104
CSF £92.37 TOTE £7.30: £1.60, £2.80, £3.60; EX 89.50 Trifecta £395.80 Pool: £29,039.55, 52.09 winning units.
Owner Mrs John Magnier **Bred** Cheveley Park Stud Ltd **Trained** Ballydoyle, Co Tipperary
■ Not for the first time in a race at this level, Aidan O'Brien trained the first three home.

FOCUS
This renewal looked up to standard, with the English and Irish Guineas winner Cockney Rebel reopposed by the third and fourth from Newmarket and the placed horses from the Curragh. In addition, the French Guineas winner was joined by the runner-up and unlucky-in-running fourth at Longchamp. The form is best rated through the runner-up but the result does not conclusively establish the pecking order of the top 3yo milers, especially with Cockney Rebel picking up an injury.

NOTEBOOK
Excellent Art, unlucky in running at Longchamp when only fourth in the French Guineas, got the breaks this time and was produced with great timing to challenge between his stablemates inside the final furlong. He quickened up well through the gap and held on well at the finish. He deserved this Group 1 success, and should remain competitive at this level throughout the rest of the campaign as all ground seems to come alike to him. The one worry with him is that he clearly needs to be held up in his races, and that means he requires luck in running. The Sussex Stakes could be next on his agenda. (op 13-2)

Duke Of Marmalade(IRE), in a race lacking any natural front-runner, was sent to the front by Kinane and was able to dictate a gallop to suit himself. He made a bold bid to make all, only finding his stablemate Excellent Art in possession of a smart turn of foot in the closing stages, but the way he battled on well suggests that he should get 1m2f without much trouble, and it would not be a surprise to see him turn out for the Eclipse next month. (op 12-1 tchd 14-1 in places)

Astronomer Royal(USA), an outsider when successful in the French Guineas, was again rather dismissed in the betting. He ran well again, though, despite racing keenly off the steady early gallop, and might do better in a stronger-run race. (tchd 16-1 in places)

Dutch Art, third in the 2000 Guineas at Newmarket, when he won his race on the far side, managed to reverse the form with Cockney Rebel but he was still a shade disappointing. His trainer blamed himself for not giving the rider the right instructions, as the colt raced a touch freely without sufficient cover. It is too early to write him off and the Jacques le Marois and the Sussex Stakes are to be considered. (op 3-1 tchd 7-2)

Cockney Rebel(IRE), sent off a short price following his successes in the English and Irish 2000 Guineas, was held up as usual and brought to challenge inside the final two furlongs. Once asked to pick up, though, he hung badly left and failed to run on as we know he can. The ground was no excuse as he relished a fast surface at Newmarket, and the real reason was revealed later when it was discovered that he had sustained a stress fracture to his pelvis. The good news is that the injury is not expected to keep him off the track for long, however, and his trainer believes that his charge could still take his chance in the Prix Jacques le Marois at Deauville in August. (op 5-4)

Creachadoir(IRE), runner-up in both the French and Irish 2000 Guineas, did not get the best of runs and had to be switched for his challenge, but he did not really pick up even once in the clear and it might just be that a busy first half of the campaign is catching up with him. (tchd 14-1, 16-1 in places)

Jack Junior(USA) finished runner-up, albeit well beaten, to Asiatic Boy on his last start on the dirt in Dubai, but is still a maiden. This represented another tough assignment and he did not disgrace himself. He should be able to win any maiden going, but can make his mark at Pattern level in time. (op 50-1)

He's A Decoy(IRE) ran above himself to finish third in the Irish 2000 Guineas, but he has generally struggled against the best, and trailed in last here. (op 20-1)

2735 QUEEN ANNE STKS (GROUP 1) — 1m (S)
4:20 (4:26) (Class 1) 4-Y-O+

£152,170 (£57,673; £28,863; £14,391; £7,209; £3,618) **Stalls** Centre

Form				RPR
13-2	**1**		**Ramonti (FR)**[31] 1834 5-9-0 116 .....(t) LDettori 2 (Saeed Bin Suroor) *lw: led: rdn and hdd 2f out: gamely regained ld towards fin* **5/1[3]**	121
0-15	**2**	*shd*	**Jeremy (USA)**[31] 1834 4-9-0 112 ..... RyanMoore 6 (Sir Michael Stoute) *hld up: hdwy 3f out: led 2f out: sn rdn and drifted rt: hdd towards fin* **14/1**	121
-222	**3**	*shd*	**Turtle Bowl (IRE)**[30] 1879 5-9-0 .....(t) OPeslier 3 (F Rohaut, France) *a.p: rdn 2f out: r.o u.p towards fin* **33/1**	120
316-	**4**	*hd*	**George Washington (IRE)**[227] 6345 4-9-0 ..... MJKinane 8 (A P O'Brien, Ire) *lw: plld hrd: in tch: rdn and nt qckn wl over 1f out: r.o and gaining towards fin* **10/11[1]**	120
15-1	**5**	*¾*	**Cesare**[48] 1392 6-9-0 ..... JMurtagh 4 (J R Fanshawe) *lw: hld up: effrt 2f out: lugged rt ins fnl f: styd on: nt pce of ldrs* **9/2[2]**	118
2-11	**6**	*1 ¾*	**Racinger (FR)**[49] 1389 4-9-0 ..... CSoumillon 5 (F Head, France) *w'like: lw: midfield: rdn wl over 1f out: nvr able to chal* **16/1**	114
15-1	**7**	*½*	**Red Evie (IRE)**[31] 1834 4-8-11 115 ..... JamieSpencer 7 (M L W Bell) *lw: b.hind: hld up in rr: hdwy over 2f out: chsd ldrs over 1f out: wknd towards fin* **15/2**	110
2-06	**8**	*10*	**Notability (IRE)**[130] 413 5-9-0 110 ..... KerrinMcEvoy 1 (Saeed Bin Suroor) *prom: rdn 2f out: sn wknd: eased whn btn ins fnl f* **50/1**	90

1m 37.21s (-4.59) **Going Correction** -0.20s/f (Firm) course record **8** Ran SP% **116.4**
Speed ratings (Par 117):114,113,113,113,112 111,110,100
CSF £71.40 TOTE £5.20: £1.40, £3.90, £3.30; EX 58.30 Trifecta £807.20 Pool: £14,462.39 - 12.72 winning units..
Owner Godolphin **Bred** S P A Siba **Trained** Newmarket, Suffolk

■ Frankie Dettori's first Group 1 winner in Britain for Godolphin since Sulamani won the International Stakes in 2004.

■ Stewards' Enquiry : M J Kinane one-day ban: used whip with excessive force (Jun 30)

L Dettori 14-day ban: improper riding - used whip with excessive frequency and without giving horse time to respond (Jul 13-26)

Ryan Moore two-day ban: used whip with excessive frequency (Jul 1-2)

FOCUS
An unsatisfactory renewal of the Queen Anne Stakes with eventual winner Ramonti setting just a steady pace for much of the way, and the first seven covered by just over three lengths at the line. Ramonti and Jeremy were both up 3lb, with Turtle Bowl running his best race but George Washington 10lb below his top form. Surprisingly considering the slow early gallop, the course record was lowered by 0.65 seconds. The field raced down the middle of the track for much of the way, but ended up towards the far side at the line, with some of these following the drifting Jeremy.

NOTEBOOK
Ramonti(FR) confirmed the promise he showed when second in the Lockinge Stakes on his reappearance/debut for Godolphin, but he was made to work extremely hard, with his rider appearing to go for the whip around 25 times in the closing stages, for which he has been referred to the HRA. He was allowed his own way in front at just a steady pace, and in most cases that would be ideal, but if anything he would have been better served by setting a stronger gallop, as he was outpaced by Jeremy when that one went for home, only to rally and get back up near the line. On this evidence, he may be capable of even better back over a longer trip, and it is surprising he has been kept to 1m-1m1f since finishing second over 1m4f in the 2005 Italian Derby. He would have to be of interest if supplemented for the Eclipse. (tchd 11-2 in places and 6-1 in a place)

Jeremy(USA) is fully effective over 7f, as he showed when winning the Jersey Stakes at this meeting last season, so the steady pace would not have inconvenienced him as much as some of the others, and he looked the most likely winner when taking it up two furlongs from the finish. However, he drifted over to the far rail close home and that ultimately looked to cost him the race. (tchd 16-1 in places)

Turtle Bowl(IRE), a five-length second to Manduro in the Prix d'Ispahan on his previous run, would probably have been more accustomed to the steady early pace than some of these and ran a terrific race in defeat. He may now be aimed at the Prix Jacques le Marois.

George Washington(IRE) ◆ showed himself to be one of the best milers of recent times with impressive victories in both the 2000 Guineas and Queen Elizabeth II Stakes last year, but he suffered from fertility problems when packed off to stud after his sixth in the Breeders' Cup Classic, successfully covering just a few mares, and was returned to training. He looked fit enough beforehand, but was very keen for some of the way to the start, and also pulled hard in the race itself, proving inconvenienced by the steady pace. He was clearly very fresh and, having looked likely to finish well back when failing to respond after initially coming under pressure, he eventually ran on for a close fourth. This was a highly satisfactory return to action - not too dissimilar to his third in last year's Celebration Mile off the back of a break prior to winning the Queen Elizabeth II Stakes - and he should improve significantly on the bare form next time. He may well be given another try over 1m2f, with his only previous attempt at that distance having come on dirt, but one suspects he can still show his very best over 1m granted a strong pace. Whether he turns out to be an out-an-out miler, or stays further, he can win at least one more Group 1 before presumably being given another try at stud. (op 6-5 tchd 5-4, 11-8 in places)

Cesare, winner of the Hunt Cup at last year's Royal meeting off a mark of 94, showed improved form this year when bolting up in a course-and-distance Listed event. Supplemented into his first Group contest, he ran well in defeat, especially considering a stronger-run race might have suited better. It remains to be seen, though, whether he is quite up to this level. (tchd 5-1 in places)

Racinger(FR) had just denied Turtle Bowl on two starts at a slightly lower level this year, but he failed to confirm form upped to Group 1 company and probably found this ground plenty quick enough.

Red Evie(IRE), much improved since winning the Sandringham Stakes off a mark of 96 at this meeting last year, could not match the form she showed when landing the Lockinge on her reappearance, a race in which she had both Ramonti and Jeremy behind. She looked set to finish a little closer for much of the final furlong, but weakened worryingly quickly near the line. (op 13-2 tchd 8-1 in places)

Notability(IRE) would have found this ground far too fast.

2736 ASCOT STKS (H'CAP) — 2m 4f
4:55 (5:01) (Class 2) (0-95,95) 4-Y-O+

£34,276 (£10,263; £5,131; £2,568; £1,281; £643) **Stalls** High

Form				RPR
40-1	**1**		**Full House (IRE)**[26] 1959 8-9-1 **86** ..... JimmyFortune 4 (P R Webber) *lw: hld up in midfield: hdwy over 3f out: led 2f out: drvn to hold on fnl f* **20/1**	98
11-0	**2**	*½*	**Juniper Girl (IRE)**[31] 1844 4-9-1 **93** ..... LukeMorris(5) 7 (M L W Bell) *hld up in midfield: rdn and hdwy over 2f out: styd on wl to take 2nd on line* **16/1**	104
16-5	**3**	*shd*	**Som Tala**[41] 1582 4-8-12 **85** ..... JHBowman 2 (M R Channon) *hld up towards rr: hdwy 3f out: drvn to go 2nd 1f out: clsd on wnr but lost 2nd on line* **15/2[3]**	96
111/	**4**	*2*	**Leg Spinner (IRE)**[33] 2574 6-9-1 **86** ..... JMurtagh 3 (A J Martin, Ire) *mid-div: hdwy over 2f out: n.m.r and hrd rdn over 1f out: styd on same pce* **5/1[2]**	95
-150	**5**	*1 ¼*	**Odiham**[41] 1582 6-9-5 **90** ..... SteveDrowne 17 (H Morrison) *chsd ldrs: rdn and one pce fnl 2f* **33/1**	97
/0-0	**6**	*2*	**Afrad (FR)**[41] 1582 6-9-5 **90** ..... MichaelHills 9 (N J Henderson) *stdd s: wd and t.k.h towards rr: rdn and styd on fnl 3f: nvr nrr* **50/1**	95
31/1	**7**	*2 ½*	**Princelet (IRE)**[38] 1654 5-9-0 **85** ..... FMBerry 16 (N J Henderson) *lw: hld up towards rr: gd hdwy over 2f out: rdn and hung rt over 1f out: no ex* **8/1**	89+
411-	**8**	*1*	**Raslan**[25] 3269 4-8-13 **86** ..... RyanMoore 10 (D E Pipe) *in tch: rdn 6f out: led 3f out tl 2f out: disputing 4th and hld whn n.m.r over 1f out: eased* **10/1**	90+
1063	**9**	*6*	**Melpomene**[10] 2449 4-8-13 **86** ..... J-PGuillambert 12 (M Johnston) *prom: hrd rdn over 2f out: wknd over 1f out* **33/1**	81
100-	**10**	*5*	**Nobelix (IRE)**[38] 5678 5-9-0 **85** ..... JamieSpencer 8 (J R Fanshawe) *bhd: hdwy towards outside over 2f out: eased whn no imp ins fnl f* **33/1**	83+
3-00	**11**	*1*	**Winged D'Argent (IRE)**[10] 2449 6-9-0 **85** .....(b) NCallan 13 (B J Llewellyn) *mid-div: drvn along 7f out: outpcd fnl 3f* **50/1**	73
02-0	**12**	*2*	**Inchnadamph**[33] 1794 7-8-12 **83** .....(t) PhilipRobinson 15 (T J Fitzgerald) *lw: chsd ldrs tl n.m.r and wknd 3f out* **20/1**	69
1-16	**13**	*1*	**Raucous (GER)**[31] 1844 4-8-11 **84** ..... MickyFenton 19 (T P Tate) *disp ld: led 4f out tl 3f out: wknd 2f out* **10/1**	69
5-03	**14**	*11*	**Enjoy The Moment**[41] 1582 4-9-5 **92** ..... MartinDwyer 20 (J A Osborne) *hld up in tch on rail: effrt whn hmpd 3f out and again bdly ent st: nt rcvr* **9/2[1]**	65+
0-23	**15**	*12*	**Mceldowney**[19] 2170 5-8-13 **84** ..... JoeFanning 5 (M Johnston) *prom: pushed along 8f out: n.m.r and wknd 3f out* **12/1**	44
013-	**16**	*5*	**Scotland Yard (UAE)**[49] 3882 4-8-12 **85** .....(v) CSoumillon 18 (D E Pipe) *hld up in tch: n.m.r on bnd after 7f: rdn whn hmpd and wknd over 3f out: eased whn no ch fnl 2f* **25/1**	39
/0-0	**17**	*4*	**Adopted Hero (IRE)**[17] 2236 7-8-11 **82** .....(p) TedDurcan 14 (G L Moore) *towards rr: hmpd bnd after 7f: dropped to last 8f out: no ch fnl 4f* **50/1**	32
0-06	**18**	*2*	**Kasthari (IRE)**[10] 2449 8-9-10 **95** ..... DarryllHolland 6 (J D Bethell) *disp ld tl 4f out: wknd 3f out* **66/1**	42
4/0-	**19**	*1 ¼*	**Liss Ard (IRE)**[18] 1017 6-9-0 **85** .....(b[1]) JAHeffernan 11 (John Joseph Murphy, Ire) *w'like: lw: mid-div: rdn and wknd 5f out: sn bhd* **100/1**	31
	20	*20*	**Grafton Street (IRE)**[65] 1051 4-9-4 **91** ..... MJKinane 1 (A P O'Brien, Ire) *wl grwn: lw: a bhd: no ch fnl 4f* **8/1**	15

4m 18.29s (-6.31) **Going Correction** -0.05s/f (Good)
WFA 4 from 5yo+ 2lb **20** Ran SP% **131.2**
Speed ratings (Par 109):110,109,109,108,108 107,106,106,103,101 101,100,100,95,91 89,87,86,86,78
CSF £303.33 CT £2648.29 TOTE £23.40: £4.40, £3.20, £2.90, £1.80; EX 286.50 Trifecta £5030.40 Part won. Pool: £7,085.14 - 0.40 winning units..
Owner The Chamberlain Addiscott Partnership **Bred** Schwindibode Ag **Trained** Mollington, Oxon

FOCUS
A competitive handicap run at a decent gallop, and in a time that took 2.16sec off the course record. The form looks solid, with the runner-up and third progressive types and the fourth running close to the mark he achieved when successful in this race in 2005.

NOTEBOOK

Full House(IRE), who ran out a clear winner at Goodwood last time out, had been raised 8lb for that success which meant he was also racing off an 8lb higher mark than when only fourth in this race last year. He is in the form of his life at present, though, appreciates fast ground and travelled well before asserting two furlongs out. He might well run in the Queen Alexandra on Saturday, but he also has an alternative target in the Northumberland Plate at the end of the month.

Juniper Girl(IRE), a progressive stayer last autumn, probably needed her reappearance over an inadequate trip at Newmarket last month, and had clearly been prepared with this race in mind. She ran a blinder off a 9lb higher mark than when last successful, especially considering that the ground would have been on the fast side for her. She might run in the Queen Alexandra on Saturday, and connections will be hoping for rain.

Som Tala, who did not get the best of runs when fifth in the Chester Cup, just lost second close home to the staying-on Juniper Girl, but this was still a fine effort and confirms him to be a progressive stayer. He is another possible for the Queen Alexandra on Saturday.

Leg Spinner(IRE), last seen on the Flat winning this race when the meeting took place at York in 2005, was 3lb higher this time but has been in good form over hurdles of late and ran a good race in his attempt to repeat that success from two years ago. He probably ran to a similar level as it happens. (tchd 11-2, 6-1 in a place)

Odiham, who has not won on turf for over three years, ran well over a trip that probably stretches his stamina a bit. He was first home of those drawn high in a race that has in the past strongly favoured those drawn in the high numbers. The stats were overturned this year, largely due, no doubt, to the reduction of the safety limit to 20 runners.

Afrad(FR), 2lb above his last winning mark on the Flat, ran poorly in this race last year, but no doubt the smaller field helped him this time as his rider was able to keep him wide - he does not like to be crowded.

Princelet(IRE), 5lb higher than when winning on soft ground over 2m here last month, hung right in the closing stages and was probably feeling the ground a bit. He will be happier back on an easier surface. (op 7-1 tchd 9-1 in a place)

Raslan, last seen on the Flat racking up a couple of wins at Warwick last July, was 7lb higher than for the last of those successes, but he has had a good spell over hurdles since and there was every reason to believe that he would return to the Flat an improved performer. He ran well given that he was never far off the decent gallop, and there is better to come from him, perhaps at Glorious Goodwood. Official explanation: jockey said gelding ran out of room (tchd 11-1 in a place)

Melpomene was well placed throughout but, as it turned out, the pace he was chasing was too strong and he paid for racing close to it in the closing stages.

Raucous(GER) helped set the strong pace that played into the hands of the hold-up horses. (op 11-1 tchd 12-1 in places)

Enjoy The Moment, third in the Chester Cup on his previous start, loves fast ground and was a well-backed favourite. He was just trying to get involved when badly hampered, and could not recover. He deserves another chance, and Goodwood may provide a suitable opportunity. (op 7-1 tchd 15-2 in a place)

Scotland Yard(UAE) shaped like a non-stayer.

Grafton Street(IRE), stepping up from 1m4f, had his stamina to prove and was never really seen with a chance.

2737 WINDSOR CASTLE STKS (LISTED RACE) 5f

5:30 (5:37) (Class 1) 2-Y-O

£31,229 (£11,836; £5,923; £2,953; £1,479; £742) **Stalls** Centre

Form				RPR
61	**1**		**Drawnfromthepast (IRE)**[16] 2271 2-9-3 0 .... MartinDwyer 15 (J A Osborne) *w ldr: rdn to ld over 2f out: r.o gamely whn hrd pressed ins fnl f* **9/1**	99
	2	*hd*	**Kingsgate Native (IRE)** 2-9-3 0 .... GeorgeBaker 9 (J R Best) *midfield: hdwy 3f out: rdn over 1f out: ev ch whn edgd lft ins fnl f: r.o* **66/1**	98+
51	**3**	*½*	**Hatta Fort**[15] 2316 2-9-3 0 .... JHBowman 11 (M R Channon) *midfield: rdn and hdwy over 1f out: r.o towards fin* **3/1**[1]	96
32	**4**	*½*	**Dream Eater (IRE)**[13] 2353 2-9-3 0 .... LPKeniry 8 (A M Balding) *hld up: rdn over 1f out: r.o strly ins fnl f: nrst fin* **50/1**	95
54	**5**	*nk*	**Paveroc**[15] 2316 2-9-3 0 .... JohnEgan 17 (J S Moore) *outpcd: hdwy whn nt clr run over 1f out: r.o and gaining towards fin* **33/1**	94+
10	**6**	*nk*	**Fat Boy (IRE)**[48] 1390 2-9-3 0 .... RichardHughes 19 (R Hannon) *midfield: rdn and hdwy over 1f out: styd on ins fnl f* **20/1**	93
345	**7**	*½*	**Major Eazy (IRE)**[19] 2183 2-9-3 0 .... LDettori 12 (B J Meehan) *stdd s: bhd: rdn over 1f out: styd on ins fnl f: nvr nrr* **12/1**	91
1	**8**	*hd*	**Vhujon (IRE)**[69] 999 2-9-3 0 .... StephenDonohoe 1 (P D Evans) *gd spd: rdn and lost pl wl over 1f out: styd on towards fin* **15/2**	90
062	**9**	*nk*	**Mister Fips (IRE)**[14] 2333 2-9-3 0 .... JimmyFortune 21 (Jane Chapple-Hyam) *midfield: rdn over 2f out: styd on fr over 1f out: nt pce of ldrs* **66/1**	89
131	**10**	*¾*	**Fred's Lad**[24] 2024 2-9-7 0 .... PaulMulrennan 14 (M W Easterby) *led: hdd over 2f out: rdn over 1f out: wknd ins fnl f* **25/1**	90
21	**11**	*hd*	**Dark Angel (IRE)**[41] 1585 2-9-3 0 .... MichaelHills 5 (B W Hills) *in tch: rdn and lost pl 2f out: kpt on ins fnl f* **7/1**[3]	86
015	**12**	*shd*	**Enodoc**[29] 1897 2-9-3 0 .... RichardMullen 16 (W R Muir) *midfield: rdn and hdwy over 2f out: no ex ins fnl f* **100/1**	85
2	**13**	*nk*	**Befortyfour**[14] 2337 2-9-3 0 .... PhilipRobinson 4 (M A Jarvis) *in tch: rdn over 1f out: kpt on same pce ins fnl f* **25/1**	84
14	**14**	*nk*	**Achilles Of Troy (IRE)**[24] 2049 2-9-3 0 .... CSoumillon 7 (A P O'Brien, Ire) *prom: rdn over 1f out: wknd ins fnl f* **7/2**[2]	83
31	**15**	*½*	**Russian Reel**[13] 2371 2-9-3 0 .... NCallan 18 (K A Ryan) *prom: rdn over 2f out: wknd ins fnl f* **20/1**	81
22	**16**	*½*	**Magical Speedfit (IRE)**[36] 1721 2-9-3 0 .... TQuinn 20 (G G Margarson) *towards rr: kpt on ins fnl f: nt pce to trble ldrs* **50/1**	79
012	**17**	*1 ¾*	**Little Pete (IRE)**[29] 1882 2-9-3 0 .... FergusSweeney 6 (R A Farrant) *midfield: outpcd 2f out* **100/1**	73
30	**18**	*6*	**Sudden Impact (IRE)**[20] 2134 2-8-12 0 .... KerrinMcEvoy 10 (Paul Green) *wnt rt s: in tch: wknd over 2f out* **33/1**	46
52	**19**	*3*	**Gasmanfightsback**[3] 2651 2-9-3 0 .... JimCrowley 3 (Evan Williams) *sn outpcd and bhd* **100/1**	41
323	**20**	*hd*	**Party In The Park**[33] 1781 2-9-3 0 .... RyanMoore 2 (R Hannon) *a bhd* **33/1**	40

59.77 secs (-1.63) **Going Correction** -0.20s/f (Firm) **20** Ran SP% **125.1**

Speed ratings (Par 101):105,104,103,103,102 102,101,101,100,99 99,98,98,97,97 96,93,83,79,78

CSF £522.61 TOTE £13.20: £4.30, £25.00, £1.90; EX 1716.30 TRIFECTA Not won. Place 6 £ 626.92, Place 5 £ 291.32.

Owner Elaine and Martyn Booth **Bred** D And Mrs D Veitch **Trained** Upper Lambourn, Berks

■ Stewards' Enquiry : J H Bowman one-day ban: used whip without giving colt time to respond (Jun 30)

FOCUS

The Windsor Castle is often one of the weakest juvenile contests of the meeting and this year's renewal looked particularly ordinary. They finished in a heap and it would probably be unwise to get carried away with the bare form, but Drawnfromthpast stepped forward and debutant Kingsgate Native ran a cracker on his debut. The winning time took 1.05 seconds off the existing juvenile course record. The runners tended to race towards the middle of the track.

NOTEBOOK

Drawnfromthepast(IRE) looked a very useful prospect in the making when bolting up in a minor event at Brighton on his second start and he coped with the step up in class, putting his experience to good use to narrowly hold off the newcomer Kingsgate Native. He was reportedly unlikely to take up his engagement in the Norfolk later in the week, but would obviously be worthy of respect if his connections did allow him to take his chance. In the longer term, it would be no surprise to see him follow a similar path to the stable's 2001 winner of this race, Irony, and head for the Molecomb at Goodwood. (op 10-1 tchd 12-1 in a place)

Kingsgate Native(IRE), a 20,000gns half-brother 7f three-year-old winner Assumption, out of a 1m winner, ran a mighty race on his debut. He clearly knew his job, although he did edge left a touch late on, and only just failed to pull off what would have been one of the shocks of the meeting. Provided he takes this race okay, he could make a quick reappearance in the Norfolk, and he could not be ruled out by any means. He is obviously a colt of some potential, but it is hard to know how such a tough start to his career will affect him in the longer term.

Hatta Fort had subsequent Coventry runner-up Swiss Franc back in second, albeit conceding 7lb, when winning at Windsor on his previous start, so it could be argued this effort was a shade disappointing. He ran as though he needs 6f now. (op 10-3 tchd 7-2 in places)

Dream Eater(IRE), whose form also received a boost in the Coventry courtesy of his Kempton conqueror Cee Bargara, ran his best race yet in fourth. The way he stayed on suggests he will have even more to offer when stepped back up in trip.

Paveroc could not reverse Windsor form with Hatta Fort, but ran very well nonetheless and is another who looks as though he will benefit from a step up to 6f. (tchd 40-1 in places)

Fat Boy(IRE) had not been seen since disappointing over course and distance over a month previously, but he bounced back with by far his best performance yet. (op 25-1 tchd 40-1 in a place)

Major Eazy(IRE) had some useful form to his name in defeat coming into this and this was another decent effort. He could be hard to beat if returned to maiden company next time and gives the impression 6f may suit. (op 14-1)

Vhujon(IRE) had not been seen since blitzing his rivals on his debut at Bath over two months previously and he might just have lacked sharpness for such a tough assignment. (op 13-2)

Mister Fips(IRE) was not beaten far and stepped up on his previous efforts. He is clearly well suited by quick ground.

Fred's Lad had it all to do conceding weight all round and probably ran about as well as could have been expected. (op 33-1)

Dark Angel(IRE) looked one of the more likely winners beforehand, but he was rather disappointing. (tchd 8-1 in a place)

Enodoc would have found this company a bit hot, but he did not fare too badly.

Befortyfour could be a tough opponent if returned to maiden company next time.

Achilles Of Troy(IRE) looked a serious prospect when hacking up at Newmarket on his second run, but he did not progress in a good race on his next start and this was another disappointing effort. (tchd 4-1, 9-2 in places)

Russian Reel failed to build on his Ripon maiden success.

Magical Speedfit(IRE) was never going and that was confirmed by his rider. Official explanation: jockey said colt never travelled

T/Jkpt: Not won. T/Plt: £1,898.20 to a £1 stake. Pool: £489,119.81. 188.10 winning tickets. T/Qpdt: £170.80 to a £1 stake. Pool: £16,892.00. 73.15 winning tickets. LM

2310 THIRSK (L-H)

Tuesday, June 19

OFFICIAL GOING: Good to soft

Wind: Nil Weather: Warm and overcast

2738 "SQUEAK" HOLDEN (S) STKS 6f

2:15 (2:28) (Class 5) 2-Y-O **£3,886** (£1,156; £577; £288) **Stalls** High

Form				RPR
	1		**Little Firecracker** 2-8-6 0 .... AndrewElliott(3) 1 (G M Moore) *cl up: effrt 2f out: rdn to ld over 1f out: sn hung bdly lft: clr ins fnl f* **6/1**[3]	60
0	**2**	*3 ½*	**Lavender Moon (IRE)**[24] 2039 2-8-6 0 .... AndrewMullen(3) 7 (K A Ryan) *wnt rt s: sn pushed along to chse ldrs: rdn along over 2f out: styd on to chse wnr ent fnl f: sn no imp* **5/4**[1]	49
652	**3**	*3*	**Next Best**[8] 2517 2-8-9 0 .... (p) FrancisNorton 5 (A Berry) *cl up: led wl over 2f out: rdn and hdd over 1f out: sn wknd* **7/2**[2]	40
	4	*8*	**Arabian Fern** 2-8-9 0 .... RoystonFfrench 4 (M E Sowersby) *s.i.s: a bhd* **25/1**	16
04	**5**	*2*	**Amy Lionheart**[6] 2549 2-8-9 0 .... KimTinkler 6 (N Tinkler) *led: rdn along 1/2-way: sn hdd & wknd* **8/1**	10

1m 16.23s (3.73) **Going Correction** +0.425s/f (Yiel) **5** Ran SP% **95.9**

Speed ratings (Par 93):92,87,83,72,70

CSF £10.54 TOTE £7.20: £2.90, £1.10; EX 14.70.The winner was sold to G Robotti for 10,000gns

Owner J B Wallwin **Bred** Palm Tree Thoroughbreds **Trained** Middleham Moor, N Yorks

FOCUS

A relatively valuable seller, though this looked a weak event especially following the withdrawal of the 5/1 third-favourite Make Acquaintance, who managed to get loose beforehand and delayed the race for 13 minutes (deduct 15p in the £ under Rule 4.). The winner does have a bit of scope but the next two home were disappointing.

NOTEBOOK

Little Firecracker, a half-sister to two winners, did well to win this in such convincing fashion as she saw plenty of daylight on the outside and was inclined to hang away into the centre of the track once in front. Although she is by a top-class sprinter, her dam won over 1m4f so it would be no surprise if she got a bit further than this. She was sold for 10,000gns at the subsequent auction. (tchd 11-2)

Lavender Moon(IRE), who was a very naughty girl prior to her Haydock debut, was taking a drop in class but again fluffed the start and took an age to get into gear. Even so she was no match for the winner and it will not be easy for her to find many weaker races than this. Like the winner there is plenty of stamina on the dam's side of her pedigree and her only hope is that she improves for a longer trip. (tchd 6-4 and 13-8 in a place)

Next Best, the most experienced of the field, seemed to find 5f too sharp at Wolverhampton a week earlier, but not for the first time the extra furlong appeared to find her out here. It will be a poor race she wins. (op 9-2)

Arabian Fern, a cheap yearling, looked clueless on this debut. However, her dam is a half-sister to Javelin who scored several times on the Flat and over hurdles at up to 2m5f, so any ability she does possess is likely to be shown over a longer trip much further down the line. (op 20-1)

Amy Lionheart may have already been beaten twice in modest company, but she might have been expected to have performed rather better than this, so the extra furlong cannot have been the only problem.

2739 GEORGE WIMPEY MEDIAN AUCTION MAIDEN STKS 7f
2:50 (2:53) (Class 5) 2-Y-O £3,886 (£1,156; £577; £288) Stalls Low

Form RPR

4 **1** **Apollo Shark (IRE)**[30] 1859 2-9-3 0 PaulHanagan 7 74+
(J Howard Johnson) *a.p: hdwy 3f out: rdn to ld wl over 1f out: pushed out* **4/1**[3]

0 **2** 3/4 **Marning Star**[8] 2510 2-9-3 0 TPO'Shea 16 72
(M R Channon) *cl up: led after 2f: rdn along over 2f out: hdd wl over 1f out: sn drvn and kpt on* **7/2**[2]

3 1 3/4 **Red Cauldron** 2-9-3 0 ChrisCatlin 12 68
(E J O'Neill) *s.i.s and bhd: hdwy on inner over 2f out: swtchd rt and rdn over1f out: styd on wl fnl f* **8/1**

4 **4** 3/4 **Celtic Strand (IRE)**[26] 1963 2-9-3 0 RoystonFfrench 5 66
(T P Tate) *chsd ldrs: rdn along and outpcd 1/2-way: styd on fnl 2f* **5/2**[1]

5 2 **Flop (IRE)** 2-8-12 0 DeanMernagh 8 56
(M Brittain) *chsd ldrs: rdn along 3f out: drvn and kpt on same pce fnl 2f* **40/1**

6 3 1/2 **Parliamentary (JPN)** 2-9-0 0 GregFairley(3) 4 52
(M Johnston) *trckd ldrs: pushed along 3f out: rdn and one pce fnl 2f* **5/1**

0 **7** 5 **Motherwell**[30] 1858 2-8-5 0 PatrickDonaghy(7) 6 35
(M Brittain) *towards rr: hdwy 3f out: sn rdn and kpt on u.p fnl 2f: nt rch ldrs* **80/1**

0 **8** 1 1/2 **Astrol**[13] 2371 2-8-9 0 DuranFentiman(3) 1 31
(T D Easterby) *sn led: hdd after 2f: cl up tl rdn along 3f out and grad wknd* **50/1**

9 1 1/4 **Cobbold Point** 2-8-10 0 NSLawes(7) 2 33
(M W Easterby) *dwlt and bhd tl sme late hdwy* **50/1**

00 **10** 5 **Foxies Bychance**[21] 2115 2-8-12 0 TonyHamilton 13 15
(R D E Woodhouse) *a towards rr* **100/1**

11 nk **Uncle Harry** 2-9-3 0 GrahamGibbons 10 20
(J J Quinn) *s.i.s and a in rr* **18/1**

12 3 **Horologist** 2-9-3 0 DaleGibson 9 12
(M W Easterby) *a towards rr* **25/1**

00 **13** 1/2 **Eboracum Dream**[31] 1848 2-8-12 0 PaulQuinn 3 6
(T D Easterby) *dwlt: a towards rr* **12/1**

14 5 **Royal Musketeer (IRE)** 2-9-3 0 KDarley 14 —
(T D Easterby) *in tch: rdn along on outer 3f out: wknd over 2f out* **11/1**

15 10 **Filthygorgeous (IRE)** 2-8-9 0 JamieMoriarty(3) 11 —
(J R Weymes) *t.k.h in midfield tl rn wd on home turn and bhd after* **28/1**

1m 29.4s (2.30) **Going Correction** +0.25s/f (Good) **15** Ran SP% **135.7**
Speed ratings (Par 93):96,95,93,92,90 86,80,78,77,71 71,67,67,61,49
CSF £20.23 TOTE £4.30: £1.80, £2.60, £3.00; EX 21.40.
Owner Transcend Bloodstock LLP **Bred** Churchtown House Stud **Trained** Billy Row, Co Durham

FOCUS
Not the most competitive of maidens and few managed to get involved from off the pace. However, some of these gave the impression they would improve on this in time.

NOTEBOOK
Apollo Shark(IRE) showed the benefit of his Ripon debut and demonstrated a willing attitude after having been up with the pace throughout. He should continue to improve and could be the type for nurseries over this sort of trip from now on. (op 7-2)
Marning Star ◆, who had the worst of the draw, had given the impression on his recent Windsor debut that he would appreciate a longer trip and he duly did so. He kept on battling away even after the winner had gone past him and it should not take him long to go one better. (op 10-1)
Red Cauldron ◆, a half-brother to Casterossa and Avertuoso, not only did best of the newcomers but he also did much the best of those held up. It was a little surprising that he was staying on so well at the end over this trip considering his speedy pedigree, but in any case this was a debut full of promise. (op 6-1)
Celtic Strand(IRE), up a furlong from his debut, seemed to find even this trip inadequate and he stayed on again after getting outpaced. He will have to wait until August before he can tackle a mile and there should still be plenty of improvement in him. (op 4-1)
Flop(IRE), a half-sister to Confide, ran well for a long way at a big price and appears to possess some ability. (op 33-1)
Parliamentary(JPN), a brother to a winner in Greece and a half-brother to a winner in the US, was in a good position for most of the way but did not find a great deal off the bridle. His dam won three times over 1m4f so he may well improve for further in time. (op 4-1)
Eboracum Dream Official explanation: jockey said filly lost its action
Royal Musketeer(IRE) Official explanation: jockey said colt lost its action
Filthygorgeous(IRE) Official explanation: jockey said filly hung right-handed throughout

2740 FIRST TRANSPENNINE EXPRESS MAIDEN STKS 7f
3:30 (3:33) (Class 5) 3-Y-O £3,886 (£1,156; £577; £288) Stalls Low

Form RPR

6-36 **1** **Mia's Boy**[15] 2320 3-9-3 0 KDarley 3 74+
(P W Chapple-Hyam) *trckd ldrs: pushed along over 3f out: rdn 2f out: drvn to ld ins fnl f: kpt on* **1/2**[1]

2 1 1/2 **Trees Of Green (USA)** 3-9-3 0 ChrisCatlin 6 70+
(Saeed Bin Suroor) *a.p: effrt over 2f out: rdn and ev ch over 1f out tl drvn and one pce ins fnl f* **5/1**[2]

60-2 **3** 1/2 **Kunte Kinteh**[35] 1749 3-9-3 65 FrancisNorton 2 69
(D Nicholls) *a cl up: rdn 2f out: drvn to ld over 1f out: hdd ins fnl f: no ex* **8/1**[3]

42-0 **4** nk **Akiyama (IRE)**[22] 2092 3-9-3 67 TonyHamilton 8 68
(J Howard Johnson) *led: rdn along over 2f out: drvn and hdd appr fnl f: kpt on same pce* **10/1**

0-0 **5** 7 **Buds Dilemma**[25] 2012 3-8-12 0 LeeEnstone 1 44
(I W McInnes) *in tch: hdwy to chse ldrs 3f out: sn drvn and kpt on same pce fnl 2f* **100/1**

0-0 **6** nk **Day By Day**[26] 1961 3-8-12 0 PaulHanagan 13 43+
(B J Meehan) *hld up: hdwy 3f out: rdn 2f out: kpt on appr fnl f: nrst fin* **16/1**

7 1 1/2 **Treasure Isle** 3-8-9 0 JamieMoriarty(3) 7 39+
(R A Fahey) *a towards rr* **50/1**

8 shd **Lady Johanna (USA)** 3-8-12 0 PatCosgrave 12 39+
(K R Burke) *towards rr: hdwy on outer over 2f out: sn rdn along and nvr a factor* **33/1**

0-0 **9** 3 1/2 **Bunderos (IRE)**[57] 1197 3-8-12 0 RoystonFfrench 5 30
(Mrs A Duffield) *chsd ldrs: rdn along 1/2-way: sn wknd* **100/1**

0 **10** 3 1/2 **Archimage (USA)**[28] 1923 3-9-3 0 PhillipMakin 11 25+
(T D Barron) *a in rr* **33/1**

00 **11** 8 **Cardington Queen**[6] 2580 3-8-9 0 GregFairley(3) 4 —
(M Mullineaux) *a towards rr* **100/1**

12 16 **Scruffy (IRE)** 3-9-0 0 DuranFentiman(3) 10 —
(C J Teague) *s.i.s: a bhd* **80/1**

13 19 **Ronnies Girl** 3-8-12 0 PaulQuinn 9 —
(C J Teague) *s.i.s: a bhd* **100/1**

1m 27.65s (0.55) **Going Correction** +0.25s/f (Good) **13** Ran SP% **122.5**
Speed ratings (Par 99):106,104,103,103,95 95,93,93,89,85 76,57,36
CSF £3.32 TOTE £1.50: £1.02, £1.80, £2.40; EX 4.90.
Owner Iraj Parvizi **Bred** Sir Eric Parker **Trained** Newmarket, Suffolk

FOCUS
Once again those that raced handily were favoured and at first glance this may have looked a moderate maiden with the long odds-on favourite making very hard work of it and the fourth having run poorly last time, but the winning time was smart and the front four pulled miles clear, so there is plenty of hope for them.

2741 PERSONAL TOUCHES BEDALE H'CAP 7f
4:05 (4:05) (Class 5) (0-75,73) 3-Y-O+ £3,886 (£1,156; £577; £288) Stalls Low

Form RPR

-334 **1** **Tough Love**[15] 2311 8-9-9 67 (p) DuranFentiman(3) 1 76
(T D Easterby) *trckd ldrs on inner: swtchd outside and hdwy 2f out: rdn over 1f out: styd onto ld wl ins fnl f* **11/2**[2]

0-00 **2** 1/2 **Looks Could Kill (USA)**[28] 1921 5-9-10 65 KDarley 3 73
(E J Alston) *chsd ldr: led after 2f tl hdd wl over 2f out: rdn to ld again 1 1/2f out: drvn and hdd wl ins fnl f: edgd rt towards fin* **16/1**

6053 **3** 3/4 **Borodinsky**[12] 2390 6-8-9 50 PaulHanagan 2 56
(R E Barr) *chsd ldrs on inner: rdn along 2f out: drvn ent fnl f and kpt on* **16/1**

0000 **4** shd **Breaking Shadow (IRE)**[8] 2508 5-9-10 65 FrancisNorton 7 72+
(M A Peill) *chsd ldrs: hdwy 2f out: rdn and ev ch over 1f out: drvn and hld in 3rd whn n.m.r and snatched up nr fin* **10/1**

661 **5** hd **The Osteopath (IRE)**[1] 2719 4-10-4 73 6ex (p) PhillipMakin 5 78
(M Dods) *hld up in rr: hdwy over 2f out: rdn wl over 1f out: styd on ins fnl f: nrst fin* **11/8**[1]

6435 **6** 1/2 **General Feeling (IRE)**[49] 1382 6-8-12 53 PatCosgrave 4 57
(K R Burke) *stdd s and hld up in rr: hdwy over 2f out: rdn to chse ldrs wl over 1fout: sn drvn and one pce ins fnl f* **6/1**[3]

1506 **7** 1/2 **Sir Orpen (IRE)**[8] 2508 4-10-0 69 PaulFessey 8 71
(T D Barron) *led 2f: cl up tl rdn to ld again wl over 2f out: drvn and hdd 1 1/2f out: kpt on same pce* **17/2**

5-51 **8** 2 **Kudbeme**[11] 2422 5-9-6 61 RoystonFfrench 6 58
(N Bycroft) *hld up: hdwy on outer to chse ldrs 3f out: rdn along 2f out: sn drvn and wknd over 1f out* **8/1**

1m 28.42s (1.32) **Going Correction** +0.25s/f (Good) **8** Ran SP% **114.3**
Speed ratings (Par 103):102,101,100,100,100 99,99,96
CSF £85.42 CT £943.82 TOTE £5.10: £1.70, £5.20, £4.30; EX 71.70 Place 6 £ 66.86, Place 5 £ 49.28.
Owner D A West **Bred** Branston Stud Ltd **Trained** Great Habton, N Yorks

FOCUS
An ordinary handicap in which they finished in a heap and the winning time was 0.77 seconds slower than the preceding three-year-old maiden. The form is not the strongest, Tough Love 3lb off his winning form in this last year.

2742 SOLBERGE HALL HOTEL FILLIES' H'CAP 1m
4:40 (4:40) (Class 3) (0-90,81) 3-Y-O+ £7,772 (£2,312; £1,155; £577) Stalls Low

Form RPR

11-6 **1** **Amy Louise (IRE)**[30] 1861 4-9-11 78 KDarley 4 86+
(T D Barron) *chsd ldng pair: hdwy 3f out: rdn to ld 1 1/2f out: drvn and edgd lft ent fnl f: kpt on wl* **4/1**[3]

1031 **2** 1/2 **Dispol Isle (IRE)**[29] 1892 5-8-11 71 NeilBrown(7) 3 78
(T D Barron) *chsd ldrs: hdwy over 2f out: sn rdn and styd on u.p ins fnl f: nrst fin* **5/1**

3603 **3** 1/2 **Passion Fruit**[8] 2507 6-9-9 76 RoystonFfrench 5 82
(C W Fairhurst) *dwlt: hld up in rr: hdwy over 2f out: rdn to chse ldrs over 1f out: drvn and nt qckn ins fnl f* **5/2**[2]

5031 **4** 1 3/4 **Hula Ballew**[15] 2311 7-10-0 81 PhillipMakin 2 83
(M Dods) *led: rdn along over 2f out: drvn and hdd 1 1/2f out: kpt on same pce* **2/1**[1]

34-0 **5** 9 **Golden Topaz (IRE)**[15] 2299 3-8-5 68 PaulHanagan 1 47
(J Howard Johnson) *in tch: effrt 3f out: rdn along 2f out and sn btn* **25/1**

-104 **6** 7 **Weekend Fling (USA)**[26] 1979 3-8-10 76 GregFairley(3) 7 39
(M Johnston) *cl up: rdn along 3f out: wknd 2f out* **9/1**

1m 41.63s (1.93) **Going Correction** +0.25s/f (Good)
WFA 3 from 4yo+ 10lb **6** Ran SP% **112.4**
Speed ratings (Par 104):100,99,99,97,88 81
CSF £23.75 TOTE £5.10: £2.20, £2.30; EX 23.30.
Owner P D Savill **Bred** P D Savill **Trained** Maunby, N Yorks

FOCUS
A routine fillies' handicap run at an even pace and the finish became a war of attrition. The form looks pretty solid.

NOTEBOOK
Amy Louise(IRE), all the better for her return to action over an inadequate 6f at Ripon last month, was always in a good position and responded well to pressure to get to the front, but the way she hung over to the inside rail in the closing stages suggested there was not much left in the locker and she is probably best over 7f. (op 7-2)
Dispol Isle(IRE), raised 3lb for her Musselburgh win, was doing all her best work late but could never quite get there in time. Stamina was not an issue even though all five of her career wins have come over 7f, but she will need to find a bit of improvement to defy this mark. (op 11-2 tchd 6-1)
Passion Fruit was not raised by the Handicapper despite finishing close behind a couple of fillies rated 100 and 107 in a Pontefract Listed race last time, and that turned out to be correct. She tried to come from well off the pace, but was never quite doing it quickly enough. She has won six times in her career, but never over this far. (op 11-4 tchd 3-1)
Hula Ballew, whose last three wins have come over course and distance, including this race last year off a 12lb lower mark, tried to make every yard but although she never stopped trying, she was found wanting for pace in the latter stages. A 6lb rise for her most recent victory seems to have found her out. (op 9-4)
Golden Topaz(IRE), still a maiden, is yet to convince over this far and has not returned in great form this term. (op 20-1)
Weekend Fling(USA) dropped tamely away and is another yet to prove her stamina for the trip. She probably needs quicker ground in any case. (op 8-1 tchd 10-1)

2743 SILKS RESTAURANT H'CAP 1m 4f
5:15 (5:15) (Class 4) (0-80,80) 4-Y-O+ £5,181 (£1,541; £770; £384) Stalls Low

Form RPR

-264 **1** **Charlotte Vale**[18] 2201 6-8-3 65 GregFairley(3) 6 74
(Micky Hammond) *trckd ldng pair: hdwy to ld wl over 2f out and sn rdn: drvn over 1f out and kept on wl u.p ins fnl f* **9/4**[2]

-661 **2** 1 3/4 **Press Express (IRE)**[22] 2084 5-8-2 61 PaulHanagan 3 67
(R A Fahey) *hld up: stdy hdwy 4f out: chsd wnr 2f out: sn rdn and ev ch tl drvn and one pce ins fnl f* **2/1**[1]

3-03 **3** 1 **Sporting Gesture**[18] 2201 10-8-8 **67**.................. DaleGibson 2 71
(M W Easterby) *hld up: pushed along 1/2-way: hdwy over 3f out: rdn over 2f out and styd on fnl f* **6/1**

1035 **4** nk **Shape Up (IRE)**[15] 2314 7-9-0 **73**..................(b) PatCosgrave 1 77
(R Craggs) *cl up: led 4f out: rdn along and hdd wl over 2f out: sn drvn and kpt on same pce ent fnl f* **6/1**

5 28 **Gloucester**[322] 4-9-4 **77**.................. GrahamGibbons 7 36
(J J Quinn) *led: pushed along and hdd 4f out: rdn 3f out: sn wknd and eased* **11/2**[3]

2m 37.65s (2.45) **Going Correction** +0.25s/f (Good) 5 Ran SP% **108.1**
Speed ratings (Par 105):101,99,99,98,80
CSF £6.86 TOTE £2.80: £1.40, £1.60; EX 5.70.
Owner Peter J Davies **Bred** Snailwell Stud Co Ltd **Trained** Middleham Moor, N Yorks

FOCUS
A modest handicap and the pair that disputed the early lead ended up last and last but one. Ordinary form, the winner cashing in on a good mark.

2744 LADIES DAY ON 3RD JULY H'CAP 6f
5:45 (5:46) (Class 4) (0-85,84) 3-Y-0+ **£5,181** (£1,541; £770; £384) **Stalls** High

Form RPR

0020 **1** **Continent**[7] 2529 10-9-11 **83**.................. SilvestreDeSousa 17 91
(D Nicholls) *trckd ldrs stands' side: hdwy 2f out: rdn over 1f out: drvn inside last to ld fnl 100yds* **11/1**

4064 **2** ½ **High Reach**[17] 2249 7-8-7 **72**.................. DeanHeslop(7) 14 79
(T D Barron) *overall ldr stands' side: rdn along 2f out: jnd and drvn over 1f out: hdd and nt qckn fnl 100yds* **16/1**

5326 **3** nk **Cornus**[12] 2394 5-9-0 **72**..................(be) KDarley 19 78
(A J McCabe) *in tch stands' side: hdwy 2f out: swtchd rt and rdn ent fnl f: styd on wl towards fin* **12/1**

0-20 **4** shd **Imperial Echo (USA)**[46] 1458 6-9-11 **83**.................. PaulFessey 2 89
(T D Barron) *prom far side: hdwy to ld that gp over 1f out: sn rdn and ev ch tl nt qckn nr fin* **12/1**

3-01 **5** ½ **Balakiref**[22] 2088 8-9-3 **75**.................. PhillipMakin 10 79+
(M Dods) *dwlt and swtchd rt s: in rr stands' side tl gd hdwy over 1f out: rdn and styd on strly ins fnl f: nrst fin* **12/1**

-400 **6** shd **River Thames**[31] 1854 4-9-1 **73**.................. CatherineGannon 4 77
(K A Ryan) *chsd ldrs far side: hdwy 2f out: rdn and ev ch ent fnl f: no ex towards fin* **25/1**

-004 **7** hd **Guest Connections**[18] 2202 4-9-4 **76**..................(v) FrancisNorton 15 79
(D Nicholls) *chsd ldrs stands' side: rdn along and hdwy 2f out: drvn over 1f out and on same pce ins fnl f* **33/1**

0-04 **8** ½ **Give Me The Night (IRE)**[30] 1861 4-9-6 **78**.................. RoystonFfrench 9 80
(B Smart) *prom stands' side: effrt 2f out: sn rdn and ev ch tl drvn and one pce ins fnl f* **20/1**

-556 **9** nk **Westport**[22] 2088 4-9-0 **72**.................. PatCosgrave 16 73
(K A Ryan) *chsd ldrs stands' side: rdn along 2f out: drvn and kpt on same pce ent fnl f* **12/1**

0503 **10** nk **Bel Cantor**[18] 2202 4-8-10 **71**.................. AndrewMullen(3) 5 71
(W J H Ratcliffe) *led far side gp: rdn along 2f out: ev ch over 1f out: sn drvn and hdd: kpt on same pce* **13/2**[2]

-040 **11** ¾ **Kenmore**[6] 2566 5-9-11 **83**.................. ChrisCatlin 13 81
(D Nicholls) *chsd ldrs stands' side: rdn along over 2f out and grad wknd* **7/1**[3]

-040 **12** nk **Steel Blue**[14] 2339 7-9-0 **77**.................. MichaelJStainton(5) 3 74
(R M Whitaker) *prom far side: rdn along 2f out: grad wknd* **16/1**

50-1 **13** nk **Wanchai Lad**[41] 1574 6-9-12 **84**.................. TonyHamilton 20 80
(T D Easterby) *chsd ldrs stands' side: rdn along 2f out: sn btn* **7/2**[1]

-420 **14** 2 **River Kirov (IRE)**[40] 1607 4-9-1 **80**.................. MCGeran(7) 1 70
(P W Chapple-Hyam) *chsd ldrs far side: rdn along over 2f out and sn wknd* **9/1**

0020 **15** 3 **Monashee Brave (IRE)**[41] 1574 4-9-1 **73**.................. GrahamGibbons 8 54
(J J Quinn) *cl up stands' side: rdn along 2f out and grad wknd* **20/1**

06-4 **16** 2½ **Opal Noir**[19] 2171 3-9-1 **80**.................. PaulHanagan 6 53
(J Howard Johnson) *in tch stands' side: rdn along over 2f out and sn wknd* **40/1**

-053 **17** 1 **Misphire**[22] 2085 4-8-10 **71**..................(p) JamieMoriarty(3) 11 41
(M Dods) *in tch on outer stands' side: effrt over 2f out: sn rdn and wknd* **22/1**

1m 14.23s (1.73) **Going Correction** +0.425s/f (Yiel)
WFA 3 from 4yo+ 7lb 17 Ran SP% **132.0**
Speed ratings (Par 105):105,104,103,103,103 103,102,102,101,101 100,99,99,96,92 89,88
CSF £172.65 CT £1322.61 TOTE £15.90: £3.90, £5.00, £2.00, £5.40; EX 234.70.
Owner Lucayan Stud and G G N Bloodstock **Bred** Juddmonte Farms **Trained** Sessay, N Yorks

FOCUS
A competitive sprint handicap in which the field split into two, with the larger group of 11 staying on the stands' side whilst six went far side. Although the first three were all drawn high, those that raced far side finished close enough to suggest there was not a great deal between the two groups.
Opal Noir Official explanation: jockey said gelding hung right throughout
T/Plt: £99.80 to a £1 stake. Pool: £50,339.20. 368.15 winning tickets. T/Qpdt: £25.60 to a £1 stake. Pool: £2,639.80. 76.20 winning tickets. JR

2604 YARMOUTH (L-H)
Tuesday, June 19

OFFICIAL GOING: Good to soft (good in places, 6.5)
Wind: moderate across becoming fresh across Weather: bright and sunny becoming overcast

2745 4HEAD APPRENTICE H'CAP 1m 2f 21y
6:30 (6:33) (Class 6) (0-60,60) 4-Y-0+ **£1,943** (£578; £288; £144) **Stalls** Low

Form RPR

0055 **1** **Desert Hawk**[5] 2603 6-8-9 **50**.................. LiamJones 7 61
(W M Brisbourne) *hld up in midfield: pushed along and hdwy over 4f out: led over 2f out: clr over 1f out: rdn out* **5/1**[3]

00-0 **2** 5 **Lucefer (IRE)**[35] 1742 9-8-2 **46** oh1.................. WilliamBuick(3) 10 47
(G C H Chung) *hld up in last: hdwy over 4f out: chsd wnr 2f out: rdn over 1f out: fnd little and fin weakly* **40/1**

6045 **3** ¾ **General Flumpa**[22] 2089 6-8-7 **53**.................. KirstyMilczarek(5) 6 53
(Miss Tor Sturgis) *hld up in midfield: rdn and effrt 4f out: kpt on u.p last 2f: no ch w wnr* **3/1**[2]

0050 **4** ½ **Magic Amigo**[6] 2572 6-9-1 **56**..................(p) PatrickMathers 9 55
(J R Jenkins) *hld up in midfield on outer: rdn 4f out: plugged on u.p last 2f: no ch w wnr* **17/2**

0264 **5** 9 **Surdoue**[14] 2348 7-8-6 **50**..................(p) RussellKennemore(3) 5 32
(D Morris) *led tl 4f out: ev ch tl rdn and wknd qckly wl over 2f out* **33/1**

-000 **6** 2½ **Panshir (FR)**[41] 1592 6-8-5 **46**..................(t) MarcHalford 2 23
(Mrs C A Dunnett) *t.k.h: trckd ldrs: rdn 3f out: sn wknd* **8/1**

6045 **7** 3½ **Kumakawa**[14] 2348 9-8-5 **46** oh1.................. JamesDoyle 11 16
(N P Littmoden) *hld up in rr: c wd and rdn 4f out: sn wl bhd: no ch last 2f* **22/1**

-452 **8** hd **Gizmondo**[13] 2370 4-8-12 **60**.................. ChrisHough(7) 4 30
(M L W Bell) *hld up in tch: hdwy 4f out: chsd ldrs and rdn 3f out: sn btn* **9/4**[1]

0-55 **9** 7 **Shaika**[20] 2156 4-8-9 **50**.................. SaleemGolam 3 6
(G Prodromou) *s.i.s: reminders early: short of room bnd over 5f out: sn rdn: sme hdwy over 4f out: sn bhd: t.o* **7/1**

5000 **10** 13 **Always A Story**[20] 2157 5-8-2 **46** oh1.................. NicolPolli(3) 1 —
(Miss D Mountain) *prom: led 4f out: rdn and hdd over 2f out: sn dropped out: t.o* **80/1**

00-0 **11** 30 **King Of Chav's (IRE)**[52] 1311 4-8-0 **46** oh1....(b[1]) DanielleMcCreery(5) 8 —
(A Bailey) *t.k.h: chse ldr tl 5f out: wknd 4f out: sn t.o: eased last 2f* **66/1**

2m 13.27s (5.17) **Going Correction** +0.55s/f (Yiel) 11 Ran SP% **119.0**
Speed ratings (Par 101):101,97,96,96,88 86,84,83,78,67 43
CSF £196.03 CT £708.50 TOTE £8.10: £2.30, £5.50, £1.70; EX 141.00.
Owner J Jones Racing Ltd **Bred** C J Mills **Trained** Great Ness, Shropshire

FOCUS
A weak handicap, confined to apprentice riders, run at a sound early pace. The winner is rated to his old turf form, but the second had shown little for some time.
Kumakawa Official explanation: jockey said gelding never travelled

2746 AEROPAK MAIDEN AUCTION STKS 5f 43y
7:00 (7:00) (Class 6) 2-Y-0 **£1,943** (£578; £288; £144) **Stalls** High

Form RPR

4 **1** **Dalkey Girl (IRE)**[14] 2333 2-8-0 0.................. WilliamBuick(5) 7 71+
(V Smith) *sn outpcd and pushed along: swtchd lft 1/2-way: hdwy wl over 1f out: led fnl 100yds: r.o strly and sn clr* **6/4**[1]

320 **2** 3 **Hucking Harmony (IRE)**[20] 2134 2-8-6 0.................. StephaneBreux(3) 2 64
(J R Best) *led: rdn over 1f out: hung rt 1f out: hdd fnl 100yds: sn outpcd* **3/1**[2]

0 **3** ¾ **The Magic Blanket (IRE)**[80] 845 2-8-12 0.................. DaneO'Neill 6 64
(Mrs L Stubbs) *w ldrs: ev ch and rdn wl over 1f out tl outpcd by wnr fnl 100yds* **15/2**

03 **4** 1 **Pretty Bonnie**[11] 2416 2-8-8 0.................. NickyMackay 1 57
(J G Portman) *chsd ldrs: rdn over 2f out: kpt on same pce fnl f* **6/1**

5 1 **Mac Dalia** 2-8-5 0.................. JerryO'Dwyer(3) 4 53
(M G Quinlan) *pressed ldr: rdn 2f out: sltly hmpd 1f out: kpt on same pce after* **11/2**[3]

0 **6** 8 **Bookiebasher Babe (IRE)**[14] 2344 2-8-7 0 ow1.................. SamHitchcott 3 23
(M Quinn) *s.i.s: a outpcd: no ch last 2f* **33/1**

7 1 **Locum** 2-8-11 0.................. JimmyQuinn 5 24
(M H Tompkins) *s.i.s: a outpcd in last: no ch fr 1/2-way* **20/1**

64.33 secs (1.53) **Going Correction** +0.175s/f (Good) 7 Ran SP% **114.1**
Speed ratings (Par 91):94,89,88,86,84 72,70
CSF £6.11 TOTE £2.90: £1.50, £2.60; EX 8.90.
Owner V Smith **Bred** G Gaffney & Kerr & Co Ltd **Trained** Exning, Suffolk

FOCUS
A moderate juvenile maiden. The winner did the job well and the fourth is a guide to the form.

NOTEBOOK
Dalkey Girl(IRE) ◆ struggled to go the pace early on, but she kept responding to her rider's urgings and eventually came through to win this going away. She is clearly going the right way, looks sure to improve again for the experience, and went through the soft ground well. Another furlong should also see her in a better light. (op 9-4 tchd 5-2)
Hucking Harmony(IRE), unplaced in the Hilary Needler last time, had her chance from the front and could not match the winner for speed at the business end. She may not have been too happy on this softer ground. (op 2-1)
The Magic Blanket(IRE), very well backed, held every chance and showed improvement from his debut effort at Newcastle 80 days previously. He can do even better when faced with another furlong. (op 16-1 tchd 7-1)
Pretty Bonnie looked to run close to her recent level on this easier ground and helps to set the level of this form. (op 7-1 tchd 15-2)
Mac Dalia, whose dam scored over this trip at two, was done few favours when the runner-up hung across her nearing the final furlong and could not find a change of gear when put under pressure thereafter. She should come on a bundle for this debut experience. (op 3-1)

2747 DIOMED DEVELOPMENTS (S) STKS 1m 3y
7:30 (7:30) (Class 6) 3-Y-O **£1,943** (£578; £288; £144) **Stalls** High

Form RPR

00-0 **1** **Joint Expectations (IRE)**[52] 1311 3-8-12 40..................(b[1]) DMylonas 4 44
(Mrs C A Dunnett) *chsd ldrs: wnt 2nd over 3f out: rdn wl over 1f out: led fnl 75yds: sn clr* **40/1**

6505 **2** 4 **Firebird Annie (IRE)**[6] 2565 3-8-0 50..................(b[1]) AmyBaker(7) 1 30
(A Bailey) *led: clr and rdn wl over 1f out: hung bdly lft fnl f: hdd fnl 75yds:* **7/2**[3]

1-30 **3** ½ **Sad Times (IRE)**[18] 2200 3-8-9 54..................(p) LiamJones(3) 3 34
(W G M Turner) *s.i.s: bhd: rdn 5f out: lost tch 1/2-way: styd on u.p last 2f: nrly snatched 2nd: nvr nrr* **11/4**[2]

060- **4** 3½ **Dee Burgh**[279] 5296 3-8-7 54.................. JimmyQuinn 8 21
(J Pearce) *t.k.h: hld up in midfield: hdwy to chse ldng pair: over 3f out: rdn and wknd 2f out* **9/2**

650 **5** 16 **Musical Box**[35] 1749 3-8-7 50.................. AdrianMcCarthy 5 —
(G Prodromou) *taken down early: chsd ldrs on stands' rail: swtchd to join others after 3f: rdn over 3f out: sn wknd: t.o* **12/1**

-000 **6** 7 **All Talk**[16] 2273 3-8-0 34.................. LauraReynolds(7) 2 —
(M J Gingell) *t.k.h: chsd ldr tl over 3f: sn wknd: t.o* **66/1**

R00 **7** 16 **Supercraft (IRE)**[10] 2454 3-8-12 0..................(b) NeilPollard 9 —
(M Quinn) *s.i.s: sn rdn: hrd rdn and hung lft 5f out: sn wl bhd: t.o last 3f* **66/1**

0005 **8** 25 **Roca Redonda (IRE)**[9] 2116 3-8-2 48..................(p) WilliamBuick(5) 7 —
(V Smith) *sn rdn along in rr: lost tch 5f out: t.o and eased last 3f* **2/1**[1]

1m 44.32s (4.42) **Going Correction** +0.175s/f (Good) 8 Ran SP% **113.5**
Speed ratings (Par 97):84,80,79,76,60 53,37,12
CSF £173.08 TOTE £32.80: £6.20, £1.60, £1.10; EX 717.80.There was no bid for the winner
Owner Christine Dunnett Racing **Bred** Tally-Ho Stud **Trained** Hingham, Norfolk
■ The first winner in Britain for Cypriot jockey Dimitris Mylonas.
■ Stewards' Enquiry : Liam Jones four-day ban: used whip with excessive frequency (Jun 30, Jul 1-3)

FOCUS
A pedestrian time, even for a race like this, 4.25 seconds slower than the following handicap. Very weak form, unlikely to have any bearing outside the very lowliest races.

2748 FREEDERM H'CAP — 1m 3y
8:00 (8:00) (Class 5) (0-75,75) 3-Y-0+ **£2,914** (£867; £433; £216) **Stalls** High

Form				RPR
0-42	1		**Froissee**[5] [2607] 3-7-8 **56** oh1 ... WilliamBuick(5) 3	79
			(N A Callaghan) *hld up in tch: led gng wl over 3f out: rdn clr over 2f out: sn in total command: pushed out fnl f* **9/4**[1]	
2506	2	11	**Professor Twinkle**[36] [1722] 3-9-0 **71** ... (v[1]) DaneO'Neill 5	69
			(W J Knight) *hld up in midfield: rdn and effrt over 3f out: chsd wnr wl over 2f out: no imp* **12/1**	
-354	3	1	**Rowan Lodge (IRE)**[22] [2084] 5-8-10 **60** ... (v) SaleemGolam(3) 4	56
			(M H Tompkins) *hld up bhd: hdwy wl over 3f out: rdn wl over 2f out: plugged on but no ch w wnr* **9/2**[2]	
6322	4	4	**Hits Only Cash**[28] [1918] 5-8-13 **60** ... DeanMcKeown 2	47
			(J Pearce) *in tch: rdn over 3f out: plugged on but no ch w wnr* **15/2**	
34-0	5	hd	**Emily's Place (IRE)**[164] [48] 4-9-3 **64** ... JimmyQuinn 8	50
			(J Pearce) *hld up: swtchd lft after 3f: rdn and effrt wl over 2f out: sn outpcd: kpt on ins fnl f: no ch w wnr* **33/1**	
-124	6	1 1/2	**Josh You Are**[134] [369] 4-8-10 **57** ... MickyFenton 11	40
			(D E Cantillon) *unruly in stalls: bhd: rdn and outpcd after 4f out: styd on past btn horse fnl f: n.d* **14/1**	
6502	7	1 1/4	**Surwaki (USA)**[19] [2189] 5-10-0 **75** ... SebSanders 10	55
			(R M H Cowell) *led for 1f: prom: ev ch and rdn over 3f out: sn wknd* **9/2**[2]	
0022	8	1	**Crocodile Bay (IRE)**[13] [2358] 4-9-11 **72** ... BrettDoyle 9	49
			(B J Meehan) *hld up: hdwy wl over 3f out: chsd ldrs and rdn over 2f out: wknd fnl f* **6/1**[3]	
0030	9	5	**Major League (USA)**[19] [2189] 5-9-3 **64** ... HayleyTurner 7	30
			(D Morris) *hld up in midfield: rdn wl over 3f out: sn bhd* **25/1**	
0000	10	16	**She's Dunnett**[54] [1271] 4-8-9 **56** oh11 ... (t) DMylonas 6	—
			(Mrs C A Dunnett) *prom tl 1/2-way: sn bhd: t.o over 1f out* **33/1**	
00-0	11	8	**Patitiri (USA)**[156] [129] 4-8-6 **56** oh11 ... (t) MarcHalford(3) 1	—
			(Mrs C A Dunnett) *wnt lft s: t.k.h: led after 1f tl after 3f out: sn wknd: t.o and eased last 2f* **66/1**	

1m 40.07s (0.17) **Going Correction** +0.175s/f (Good)
WFA 3 from 4yo+ 10lb — 11 Ran SP% **118.8**
Speed ratings (Par 103):106,95,94,90,89 88,87,86,81,65 57
CSF £31.44 CT £116.37 TOTE £4.10: £1.60, £3.40, £2.20; EX 47.40.
Owner Mrs T A Foreman **Bred** Rosyground Stud **Trained** Newmarket, Suffolk
■ Stewards' Enquiry : Dean McKeown two-day ban (reduced from three days on appeal): careless riding (Jun 30, Jul 1)

FOCUS
A modest handicap which saw a very easy winner in Froissee, who is value for further than her already wide-winning margin. There was no fluke about this but the opposition was not strong.
She's Dunnett Official explanation: jockey said filly had a breathing problem
Patitiri(USA) Official explanation: jockey said filly ran too freely to post

2749 ADIOS RATING RELATED MAIDEN STKS — 7f 3y
8:30 (8:30) (Class 5) 3-Y-0 **£3,071** (£906; £453) **Stalls** High

Form				RPR
0030	1		**Samsons Son**[12] [2400] 3-9-3 65 ... DaneO'Neill 8	75
			(J R Best) *hld up bhd: hdwy over 2f out: rdn and edgd lft over 1f out: led 1f out: r.o wl* **7/1**	
225-	2	1 1/2	**Corlough Mountain**[182] [6867] 3-8-12 70 ... WilliamBuick(5) 9	74+
			(N A Callaghan) *hld up bhd: rdn and hdwy 2f out: styng on whn swtchd rt ins fnl f: wnt 2nd nr fin: nt rch wnr* **10/3**[1]	
-506	3	nk	**Jawaab (IRE)**[10] [2453] 3-9-3 68 ... DeanMcKeown 1	70
			(M A Buckley) *t.k.h: trckd ldrs: rdn to chse ldr over 2f out tl over 1f out: kpt on same pce: lost 2nd nr fin* **7/2**[2]	
320-	4	1 1/2	**Beautiful Madness (IRE)**[260] [5735] 3-8-11 66 ... JerryO'Dwyer(3) 2	63
			(M G Quinlan) *led: rdn 2f out: hdd 1f out: no ex last 100yds* **16/1**	
-463	5	6	**Ask Yer Dad**[22] [2083] 3-9-3 65 ... (p) MickyFenton 3	50
			(Mrs P Sly) *in tch: rdn and lost pl 5f out: rallied u.p over 2f out: no imp over 1f out* **4/1**[3]	
-323	6	nk	**Hessian (IRE)**[126] [449] 3-9-0 70 ... HayleyTurner 5	47
			(M L W Bell) *t.k.h: chsd ldr tl over 2f out: sn rdn and wknd* **11/2**	
0-00	7	5	**Hamilton House**[31] [1841] 3-9-3 68 ... JimmyQuinn 4	37
			(M H Tompkins) *stdd s: hld up in tch: rdn 3f out: sn wknd* **14/1**	
6220	8	22	**Sky Masterson**[22] [2083] 3-9-3 70 ... SebSanders 7	—
			(J H M Gosden) *chsd ldrs: rdn wl over 3f out: wknd wl over 2f out: eased fnl f: t.o* **17/2**	

1m 27.18s (0.58) **Going Correction** +0.175s/f (Good) — 8 Ran SP% **116.3**
Speed ratings (Par 99):103,101,100,99,92 92,86,61
CSF £31.15 TOTE £11.40: £2.30, £1.70, £1.80; EX 55.80.
Owner M Folan **Bred** J R Best **Trained** Hucking, Kent

FOCUS
A modest maiden for three-year-olds. The form is sound, rated through the third and fourth.

2750 BAZUKA H'CAP — 6f 3y
9:00 (9:02) (Class 6) (0-65,70) 3-Y-0 **£2,137** (£635; £317; £158) **Stalls** High

Form				RPR
4611	1		**Dramatic**[5] [2594] 3-9-13 **70** 6ex ... SebSanders 4	81+
			(Sir Mark Prescott) *sn led: mde rest: rdn 2f out: drvn and fnd ex 1f out: in command fnl f:* **4/9**[1]	
044-	2	1	**Hucking Hope (IRE)**[223] [6400] 3-9-7 **64** ... DaneO'Neill 5	68
			(J R Best) *bhd: rdn over 3f out: hdwy over 2f out: chsd wnr over 1f out: kpt on u.p fnl f* **16/1**	
0004	3	nk	**Cornerstone**[3] [2661] 3-8-2 **45** ... (b) JimmyQuinn 2	48
			(S C Williams) *s.i.s: bhd: hdwy 3f out: rdn over 2f out: kpt on steadily fnl f: nrst fin* **8/1**[2]	
0356	4	1 1/4	**Nou Camp**[10] [2444] 3-8-2 **50** ... WilliamBuick(5) 9	49
			(N A Callaghan) *plld hrd: prom: ev ch 2f out: rdn and hanging lft over 1f out: kpt on same pce ins fnl f* **12/1**[3]	
02-0	5	4	**Go Imperial (IRE)**[67] [1022] 3-9-3 **63** ... JerryO'Dwyer(3) 1	50
			(M G Quinlan) *prom on outer: rdn 2f out: wknd over 1f out* **28/1**	
1020	6	3 1/2	**Ensign's Trick**[8] [2515] 3-9-4 **64** ... LiamJones(3) 10	41
			(W M Brisbourne) *unruly in stalls: pressed ldrs: rdn 3f out: wknd over 2f out* **16/1**	
3240	7	3	**Thunderbolt Jaxon**[29] [1903] 3-9-3 **60** ... AdrianMcCarthy 6	28
			(P W Chapple-Hyam) *chsd ldrs: rdn and lost pl over 3f out: no ch after* **14/1**	
0004	8	2 1/2	**Retaliate**[20] [2146] 3-9-3 **60** ... NeilPollard 3	20
			(M Quinn) *prom for 2f: sn rdn and struggling: no ch last 2f* **25/1**	

1m 16.04s (2.34) **Going Correction** +0.175s/f (Good) — 8 Ran SP% **113.8**
Speed ratings (Par 97):91,89,89,87,82 77,73,70
CSF £9.47 CT £29.39 TOTE £1.40: £1.02, £3.30, £1.90; EX 7.90 Place 6 £ 17.76, Place 5 £ 5.41.
Owner Cheveley Park Stud **Bred** Cheveley Park Stud **Trained** Newmarket, Suffolk

FOCUS
A moderate handicap and the progressive winner is value for a bit further than the winning margin. There should be more to come from him. The form seems sound enough amongst the placed horses. It was a very moderate time for a race of its type.
T/Plt: £96.90 to a £1 stake. Pool: £64,909.10. 488.90 winning tickets. T/Qpdt: £18.00 to a £1 stake. Pool: £4,929.40. 202.40 winning tickets. SP

2616 LONGCHAMP (R-H)
Tuesday, June 19

OFFICIAL GOING: Soft

2751a PRIX DU LYS (GROUP 3) (C&G) — 1m 4f
2:55 (2:56) 3-Y-0 **£27,027** (£10,811; £8,108; £5,405; £2,703)

			RPR
1		**Airmail Special (IRE)**[26] 3-8-11 ... SPasquier 3	103
		(A Fabre, France) *disp 3rd: 3rd 1/2-way: led over 1f out: fin wl fnl 100yds: drvn out* **2/5**[1]	
2	snk	**Le Paradis (FR)**[75] 3-8-11 ... DBonilla 5	103
		(F Head, France) *racd in last pl: drvn on outside ent st: styd on fnl f: fin 3rd, 2l & snk: plcd 2nd* **14/1**	
3	nk	**Garda (USA)**[31] 3-8-11 ... TGillet 6	103
		(Mme C Head-Maarek, France) *led 2f: 2nd st: sltly short of room 2f out: drvn and outpcd 1 1/2f out: rdn and styd on again ins fnl f: fin 4th, 2l, snk & nk: plcd 3rd* **15/2**[3]	
4	2	**Cristobal (USA)**[72] 3-8-11 ... (b) C-PLemaire 1	103
		(J-C Rouget, France) *led after 2f: qcknd pce 5f out: hdd over 1f out: kpt on: fin 2nd, 2l: disq & plcd 4th* **69/10**[2]	
5	hd	**Incanto Dream**[20] 3-8-11 ... YLerner 4	99
		(C Lerner, France) *racd in 5th: 4th 5f out: rdn 1 1/2f out: no ex ins fnl f* **76/10**	
6	6	**Tastumaki**[96] 3-8-11 ... ACrastus 2	90
		(F Caenepeel, France) *disp 3rd: 4th 1/2-way: 5th and pushed along st: qckly btn* **37/1**	

2m 38.1s (3.10) — 6 Ran SP% **116.8**
PARI-MUTUEL: WIN 1.40; PL 1.10, 2.40; SF 7.80.
Owner Sheikh Mohammed **Bred** Shirley Blue Syndicate **Trained** Chantilly, France
■ Stewards' Enquiry : C-P Lemaire two-day ban: careless riding (Jun 28-29)

NOTEBOOK
Airmail Special(IRE) raced in fourth early on off the steady early pace before moving up to third rounding the home turn. He took the advantage a furlong and a half out and stayed on well to win by two lengths, just being kept up to his work with hands and heels by his jockey. A very good-looking three-year-old, he has enormous scope for future improvement, and will next be seen out in the Grand Prix de Paris.
Le Paradis(FR), held up out the back for much of the race, improved up the straight on the outside and finished third, but he was promoted to second when the runner-up was demoted to fourth position. He never looked like catching the winner but this was a step up in class for him, and he is likely to improve.
Garda(USA), who raced prominently for much of the race, made his move halfway up the straight but was interfered with by the second horse at the two-furlong pole which stopped his momentum. He finished fourth but after a Stewards' enquiry was promoted to third position. He holds an entry for the Grand Prix de Paris.
Cristobal(USA), who led the field along at a very steady pace, was overtaken by the winner three out, but stayed on well to take second position. He wavered off a true line, though, and after a Stewards' enquiry he was demoted to fourth.

2732 ASCOT (R-H)
Wednesday, June 20

OFFICIAL GOING: Round course - good; straight course - good to firm); (overall: 9.3, round 8.3, straight 10.7)
5mm of overnight rain did not make much difference, although some jockeys felt it was riding good ground.
Wind: Moderate, behind Weather: Sunny spells

2752 JERSEY STKS (GROUP 3) — 7f
2:30 (2:31) (Class 1) 3-Y-0
£36,907 (£13,988; £7,000; £3,490; £1,748; £877) **Stalls** Centre

Form				RPR
-501	1		**Tariq**[25] [2043] 3-9-1 107 ... JimmyFortune 8	116
			(P W Chapple-Hyam) *hld up: swtchd rt whn hdwy ent fnl 2f: r.o to ld and edgd lft ins fnl f: qcknd away towards fin* **15/2**[2]	
10	2	2 1/2	**US Ranger (USA)**[46] [1473] 3-9-1 0 ... C-PLemaire 16	109
			(J-C Rouget, France) *lw: in tch: impr to ld over 2f out: rdn over 1f out: hdd ins fnl f: nt pce of wnr towards fin* **6/5**[1]	
21	3	1 1/4	**Arabian Gleam**[20] [2175] 3-9-1 90 ... LDettori 4	106
			(J Noseda) *neat: lw: n.m.r leaving stalls: racd towards nr-side early: midfield: rdn over 2f out: hdwy over 1f out: edgd rt ins fnl f: r.o and gaining towards fin* **14/1**	
2260	4	hd	**Traffic Guard (USA)**[25] [2051] 3-9-1 105 ... (p) JohnEgan 5	105
			(J S Moore) *racd towards nr-side early: midfield: rdn and hdwy 2f out: edgd rt whn chsd ldrs ins fnl f: nt qckn towards fin* **66/1**	
0-60	5	nk	**Vital Statistics**[45] [1496] 3-8-12 103 ... TQuinn 9	101
			(D R C Elsworth) *hld up: swtchd rt and hdwy over 2f out: sn rdn: styd on ins fnl f: nt pce to chal ldrs* **33/1**	
4-20	6	3	**Sonny Red (IRE)**[46] [1473] 3-9-1 109 ... JamieSpencer 6	96
			(R Hannon) *lw: racd towards nr-side: prom: rdn and hung rt whn chalng over 1f out: wknd wl ins fnl f* **16/1**	
3035	7	3/4	**Theann**[14] [2379] 3-8-12 0 ... CSoumillon 11	91
			(A P O'Brien, Ire) *in tch: rdn 2f out: styd on same pce fnl f* **25/1**	
5-35	8	shd	**Thousand Words**[38] [1703] 3-9-4 112 ... RichardHughes 15	97
			(B W Hills) *led: rdn and hdd over 2f out: wknd over 1f out* **9/1**	
3-20	9	3/4	**Ferneley (IRE)**[25] [2051] 3-9-1 0 ... TedDurcan 13	92
			(Francis Ennis, Ire) *w'like: hld up: rdn and sme hdwy over 2f out: kpt on same pce fnl f* **25/1**	
2610	10	2	**Fares (IRE)**[52] [1336] 3-9-1 102 ... (b) SebSanders 12	86
			(C E Brittain) *trckd ldrs: rdn and hung rt fr 2f out: wknd 1f out* **50/1**	
-542	11	1/2	**Solid Rock (IRE)**[19] [2212] 3-9-1 95 ... JMurtagh 7	85
			(T G Mills) *racd towards nr-side: prom tl rdn and wknd over 2f out* **33/1**	

The Form Book, Raceform Ltd, Compton, RG20 6NL

46 **12** *shd* **Charriots Of Fire (IRE)**[16] 2323 3-9-1 0 (t) MJKinane 2 85
(David Wachman, Ire) *w'like: scope: racd towards nr-side: rdn over 2f out: a bhd* **12/1**
3-00 **13** *shd* **Strategic Prince**[18] 2235 3-9-6 111 EddieAhern 10 89
(P F I Cole) *midfield: rdn over 2f out: sn wknd* **8/1**[3]
2026 **14** *1 3/4* **Southandwest (IRE)**[4] 2671 3-9-1 88 LPKeniry 14 80
(J S Moore) *tracd keenly: a bhd* **100/1**
23-5 **15** *1/2* **Silca Chiave**[60] 1146 3-8-12 107 JHBowman 17 75
(M R Channon) *prom: rdn 3f out: wknd wl over 1f out* **20/1**
1m 26.76s (-1.34) **Going Correction** 0.0s/f (Good) **15** Ran SP% **121.4**
Speed ratings (Par 109):107,104,102,102,102 98,97,97,96,94 94,93,93,91,91
CSF £15.50 TOTE £10.20: £3.30, £1.20, £2.60; EX 20.30 Trifecta £154.30 Pool £7,943.31 - 36.54 winning units..
Owner Saleh Al Homeizi & Imad Al Sagar **Bred** D R Botterill **Trained** Newmarket, Suffolk
■ A first Royal Ascot winner outside of two-year-old company for Peter Chapple-Hyam.

FOCUS
A renewal well up to scratch and a really impressive display by Tariq, up 7lb on his Newmarket form. The runner-up was a similar amount off his Guineas form. The form is probably sound despite outsiders finishing fourth and fifth.

NOTEBOOK
Tariq ◆, injured during the race when third in last season's Coventry Stakes, disappointed on his seasonal debut when fifth in the Greenham, but he showed quite a bit more before being badly interfered with in the French 2000 Guineas and confirmed himself to be well on the way back to peak form when taking a Listed contest at Newmarket last time. Still appearing to have a bit to find with US Ranger, he was a solid second favourite, but appeared to be given an awful lot to do as he sat some way off the pace and did not make his move until going into the final quarter mile, at which point it became clear he was making rapid headway. He hit the front inside the final furlong and drew clear in the style of a very smart peformer, leaving the favourite trailing. Only now is he beginning to fulfil connections' initial expectations and his trainer was quick to nominate the Sussex Stakes for the colt, who had not been put in the Prix Jean Prat as it was initially felt this was his trip, but whose rider seemed in no doubt afterwards that 1m would be within his stamina range. He could be the type to rapidly progress now he has found his groove. (op 8-1 tchd 9-1 in places)
US Ranger(USA) created a stir in the 2000 Guineas market with a most impressive winning effort in the Prix Djebel back in April and, although only able to finish seventh at Newmarket, there was sufficient promise in that effort as he made his challenge more towards the centre of the track and committed a fair way from home. He did not completely convince with his head carriage, but he is a big horse and was perhaps reluctant to let himself down on the ground. Once going to the front he did not extend his lead, holding around a length's advantage over the others throughout the final furlong and a half, and the winner's late change of gear left him for dead. Connections are now planning on dropping him in trip for the July Cup followed by the Prix Maurice de Gheest if all goes well. (op 5-4 tchd 11-10 and 11-8 in places)
Arabian Gleam, thrown in deep following his ready Lingfield maiden success, comes from a stable with a fine record in this event and he showed himself to be a classy colt with a fine effort in third, sticking on well under pressure towards the stands' side. This was only his third outing and the son of Kyllachy looks capable of winning races at this level, with further progress likely. (tchd 12-1)
Traffic Guard(USA) has been asked some difficult questions of late, twice behind Asiatic Boy in Dubai and most recently in the Irish 2000 Guineas, and the drop back down in grade enabled him to show his true form. Sporting first-time cheekpieces, he moved into contention two out and stuck on well for pressure, but could not match the classier colts late on. There is a decent race in him this season.
Vital Statistics, down the field in the 1000 Guineas, made good late headway, staying on past beaten rivals, and fared best of the fillies. This was easily her best effort to date and this Listed winner looks capable of further success at that level.
Sonny Red(IRE), a good sprinting juvenile, reappeared with a fine effort in the Craven behind Adagio, but was unable to build on that when finishing down the field in the Guineas. The drop to 7f was always likely to suit and he showed up well for a long way, suggesting he can return to winning ways once having his sight lowered to Listed level. (op 14-1)
Theann has been kept busy of late and she seemed to benefit from the step back up in trip, keeping on at the one pace under pressure having held a good early position. She is probably no better than Listed level and is not going to be easy to place. (op 20-1)
Thousand Words brought solid form into this, having finished third in the Craven and fifth in the French Guineas, but having towed them along early he was always likely to be vulnerable and he dropped away disappointingly when things began to heat up. (op 10-1)
Ferneley(IRE), outclassed in the Irish Guineas latest, had previously run a cracker when second to Mores Wells in the Ballysax, but that came over 1m2f and there were obvious question marks as to how he would cope with this drop back down to 7f. He simply lacked the speed, being ridden quite early on and only plugging on at the one pace under pressure. (op 28-1)
Strategic Prince, one of last season's better juveniles, has not built on a pleasing Guineas effort, and this significant drop in trip, having contested the Derby latest, was not the answer. It is probable he has not trained on. (tchd 17-2)

2753 WINDSOR FOREST STKS (GROUP 2) (F&M) 1m (S)
3:05 (3:05) (Class 1) 4-Y-0+
£73,814 (£27,976; £14,001; £6,981; £3,497; £1,755) **Stalls** Centre

Form RPR
45-3 **1** **Nannina**[19] 2207 4-8-12 115 JimmyFortune 7 113
(J H M Gosden) *trckd ldrs: bmpd over 2f out: sn led: drvn clr and edgd rt fnl f: r.o strly* **3/1**[1]
56-2 **2** *3* **Satwa Queen (FR)**[49] 1421 5-8-12 LDettori 5 106
(J De Roualle, France) *leggy: wnt rt s: hld up in rr: rdn and hdwy 2f out: chsd wnr over 1f out: no imp* **3/1**[1]
43-0 **3** *3/4* **Sabana Perdida (IRE)**[23] 2100 4-8-12 C-PLemaire 2 104
(A De Royer-Dupre, France) *w'like: trckd ldr tl swtchd rt and bmpd over 2f out: sltly outpcd: kpt on fnl f* **50/1**
0604 **4** *3/4* **Fann (USA)**[9] 2507 4-8-12 77 RyanMoore 8 102
(C E Brittain) *dwlt: hld up in rr: swtchd outside and hung rt 2f out: drvn along and styd on: nt rch ldrs* **100/1**
5-11 **5** *1* **Echelon**[19] 2207 5-8-12 109 KerrinMcEvoy 9 100
(Sir Michael Stoute) *trckd ldrs: bmpd over 2f out: sn rdn and one pce* **3/1**[1]
23-6 **6** *2* **Flashy Wings**[81] 862 4-8-12 112 JamieSpencer 10 95
(M R Channon) *hld up in rr: effrt whn bmpd over 2f out: sn hrd rdn and btn* **13/2**[2]
13-4 **7** *shd* **Wasseema (USA)**[39] 1661 4-8-12 109 RHills 6 95
(Sir Michael Stoute) *led tl 2f out: sn outpcd* **7/1**[3]
2-54 **8** *4* **Gwenseb (FR)**[50] 1389 4-8-12 OPeslier 4 86
(C Laffon-Parias, France) *w'like: in tch: rdn along 1/2-way: wknd 3f out* **14/1**
6121 **9** *23* **Expensive**[9] 2507 4-8-12 100 EddieAhern 1 33
(C F Wall) *prom tl wknd over 2f out* **20/1**
1m 40.97s (-0.83) **Going Correction** 0.0s/f (Good) **9** Ran SP% **115.2**
Speed ratings (Par 115):104,101,100,99,98 96,96,92,69
CSF £11.49 TOTE £4.20: £1.70, £1.40, £7.90; EX 14.20 Trifecta £601.40 Pool £6,166.81 - 7.28 winning units..
Owner Cheveley Park Stud **Bred** Cheveley Park Stud Ltd **Trained** Newmarket, Suffolk
■ Stewards' Enquiry : C-P Lemaire three-day ban: careless riding (Jul 1-3)

FOCUS
A fair race for the grade, but slightly questionable form. The pace was not strong. The winner was by far the best horse in the race, but the performances of the third and fourth do cause plenty of concern as to the true value of the form; it seems unlikely that either Sabana Perdida or Fann will go this close in Group 2 company again.

NOTEBOOK
Nannina, winner of the Group 1 Coronation Stakes at last year's meeting, stamped her authority over the opposition with a terrific turn of foot just over a furlong from home. She readily outclassed her rivals and still maintained a healthy winning advantage despite drifting to the inside rail from the middle of the track under pressure. (op 5-2 tchd 10-3 in places)
Satwa Queen(FR), her trainer's first runner in Britain, and having her first run over a mile since early 2006, never had the toe to go with the winner but kept on in good style, as befits a horse who stays further. She will be much better suited to 10f and is likely to be campaigned in that way. (tchd 10-3)
Sabana Perdida(IRE) ran out of her skin to finish so close, considering her previous record. Her performance does appear to devalue the form in general, and it is not easy to see why she ran so well against such classy opposition. Her trainer suggested that she is a fast-ground lover, but all of her previous form does not back this up.
Fann(USA) only has an official mark of 78 and was another in the field that could give the race a modest look, although she was not beaten too far by the winner when they met at Epsom earlier in the month. She has already spurned a recent chance to at least get a win in Listed company, so it is impossible to know what to make of her. One suspects that she will need to come out fairly quickly again if she is to ever land a handicap again.
Echelon, who finished in front of Nannina at Epsom last time, ran most disappointingly and was beaten on merit despite receiving a hefty bump when the tempo lifted. She is better than this, as there seems little reason to believe the third and fourth horses are of a higher class, but is probably more at home in a slightly lesser grade. (tchd 10-3, 7-2 in places)
Flashy Wings, making her first appearance since a modest effort in Dubai, was a bit keen in the early stages and the jockey tried to find as much cover as he could. She was another in the race who got a bump at the crucial stage of the race, but it seemed to have little bearing on the final outcome and she weakened tamely under pressure. She might have been suited by a stronger pace but, even so, has a lot to prove now after having such a lofty reputation at one point of her career. (tchd 7-1 in places)
Wasseema(USA) had an easy lead but failed to make any impact when the pace increased. Arguably, she should have run better than she did. (op 10-1)
Gwenseb(FR) was never going the pace, which seemed a bit strange considering the modest tempo, and never landed a blow. Her best form has come on easier ground and she could be given another chance when encountering those conditions. (op 12-1)
Expensive was not given a hard time once her chance was gone and the distance she was beaten is not a true reflection of how she ran. (op 33-1)

2754 PRINCE OF WALES'S STKS (GROUP 1) 1m 2f
3:45 (3:45) (Class 1) 4-Y-0+
£211,207 (£80,049; £40,061; £19,975; £10,006; £5,021) **Stalls** High

Form RPR
2-11 **1** **Manduro (GER)**[31] 1879 5-9-0 0 SPasquier 4 131
(A Fabre, France) *swtg: trckd ldrs in 3rd pl: led 2f out: r.o wl and in command towards fin* **15/8**[1]
-112 **2** *1 1/4* **Dylan Thomas (IRE)**[24] 2064 4-9-0 0 CSoumillon 1 128
(A P O'Brien, Ire) *lw: hld up in 4th pl: hdwy to chse wnr 2f out: ev ch and hung rt ins fnl f: nt qckn towards fin* **2/1**[2]
0-41 **3** *4* **Notnowcato**[24] 2064 5-9-0 121 JMurtagh 7 120
(Sir Michael Stoute) *b: trckd ldr: rdn and outpcd 2f out: kpt on u.p and no ch w front pair fnl f* **13/2**
1-01 **4** *3/4* **Red Rocks (IRE)**[54] 1274 4-9-0 121 LDettori 5 119
(B J Meehan) *swtg: hld up: effrt 2f out: kpt on one pce fnl f: nt pce of ldrs* **4/1**[3]
3-12 **5** *1 1/2* **Pressing (IRE)**[38] 1700 4-9-0 0 OPeslier 2 116
(M A Jarvis) *w'like: hld up: rdn over 2f out: no imp* **25/1**
0-46 **6** *3/4* **Sir Percy**[19] 2210 4-9-0 121 MartinDwyer 3 114
(M P Tregoning) *led: rdn and hdd 2f out: wknd 1f out* **11/1**
2m 5.91s (-2.09) **Going Correction** +0.15s/f (Good) **6** Ran SP% **113.6**
Speed ratings (Par 117):114,113,109,109,108 107
CSF £6.10 TOTE £2.80: £1.60, £1.80; EX 6.60.
Owner Baron G Von Ullmann **Bred** Rolf Brunner **Trained** Chantilly, France

FOCUS
With so much top-class Group 1 form on show, this has to go down as the classiest race of the week, and the form looks sound. Manduro has finally shed his unlucky tag from last season and has really matured into a serious racehorse, the top middle-distance turf performer currently. Dylan Thomas came to have every chance rounding the home bend but found the winner in no mood to give up. They were nicely clear of Notnowcato and there seems little reason to not believe this race was not of the highest order.

NOTEBOOK
Manduro(GER), on his toes beforehand, has really come of age this season and sealed a fine first half of the campaign with a tremendous display of tenacity, staying on strongly under pressure. He beat some really good yardsticks and looks sure to be a very tough nut to crack wherever he turns up for the rest of the season. Connections are keen to try him over 1m4f later in the season - he does hold a King George entry - but he will have to prove that he can truly stay that sort of distance at the highest level, considering his form at a mile and 1m2f. The suggestion after the race was that he will head for the Prix Jaques le Marois in August over a mile next, a race he was only just beaten in last season, and then have a tilt at the Arc afterwards before a crack at the Americans in the Breeders' Cup Classic. (op 9-4 tchd 5-2 in places)
Dylan Thomas(IRE) moved with real menace turning into the home straight and pretty much started his effort at the same time as the eventual winner. However, he was completely outbattled by Manduro and could never get on terms when they drew clear. There was a slight hint of quirkiness when he was placed under pressure - his head carriage looked ungainly and he rolled around a touch - and it might be that easier ground is more to his liking. That all said, it was another top-class performance and he is sure to win at the highest level again. (op 9-4 tchd 5-2 in places and 15-8 in places)
Notnowcato could not confirm the form with Dylan Thomas from their recent Curragh meeting, and the trainer reported afterwards that his horse would have preferred more ease in the ground. However, an inspection of his form does not suggest that ease in the ground is essential - the official going was good - and it is more than likely that he was just beaten on merit. (op 6-1 tchd 7-1, 8-1 in a place)
Red Rocks(IRE), who was held up in last place, could never really make his presence felt and once again shaped as though a longer trip would suit him. Connections have nominated the Eclipse as his next race, but one would have thought a race such as the King George would have been a much more suitable target to aim for. (op 7-2)
Pressing(IRE) had shown some good form for Roberto Feligioni in Italy but not nearly enough to have suggested he was a threat to the best of his rivals. Supplemented for £25,000 and making his debut for the stable, he ran a decent race but will find much easier opportunities in the future.
Sir Percy has proved a disappointment since landing the Derby and, with ground conditions to suit, really should have run much better. It is very difficult to see where his next victory will come from and one wonders how long connections will keep him in training. (op 12-1)

2755 ROYAL HUNT CUP (HERITAGE H'CAP) 1m (S)

4:20 (4:22) (Class 2) 3-Y-0+

£62,320 (£18,660; £9,330; £4,670; £2,330; £1,170) **Stalls** Centre

Form				RPR
0-20	**1**		**Royal Oath (USA)**^{45} [1494] 4-9-0 **96**........................(b^{1}) JimmyFortune 14 (J H M Gosden) *lw: racd centre: hld up in midfield: hdwy over 2f out: led wl over 1f out: sn qcknd clr: rdn out* **9/1^{3}**	113
0411	**2**	*4*	**Flipando (IRE)**^{23} [2093] 6-9-2 **98** 5ex............................ JamieSpencer 19 (T D Barron) *racd centre: hld up in rr: hdwy over 2f out: rdn and r.o to take 2nd nr fin: nt rch wnr* **16/1**	106
0230	**3**	*½*	**Vortex**^{40} [1648] 8-9-10 **106**..(t) JMurtagh 4 (Miss Gay Kelleway) *lw: hld up towards rr stands' side: smooth hdwy 2f out: styd on: nt pce to trble wnr* **50/1**	113
50-1	**4**	*hd*	**Supaseus**^{45} [1494] 4-9-2 **98**.. JohnEgan 30 (H Morrison) *lw: racd alone on far rail: gd spd to match ldrs in centre and stands' side tl no ex fnl f* **17/2^{2}**	104+
0005	**5**	*nk*	**Yarqus**^{18} [2239] 4-8-6 **88**...(t) RichardMullen 6 (C E Brittain) *hld up in rr stands' side: rdn and hdwy 2f out: edgd rt 1f out: styd on: nt pce to chal* **66/1**	94
5012	**6**	*½*	**My Paris**^{31} [1860] 6-9-1 **97**... NCallan 3 (K A Ryan) *lw: chsd stands' side ldr: led gp and overall ldr over 2f out tl wl over 1f out: one pce* **20/1**	102
0406	**7**	*5*	**Lundy's Lane (IRE)**^{117} [544] 7-9-0 **96**........................... FrancisNorton 5 (A M Balding) *in tch stands' side: rdn and outpcd fnl 2f* **100/1**	89
-302	**8**	*2*	**Skhilling Spirit**^{39} [1651] 4-9-2 **98**.................................... PaulFessey 16 (T D Barron) *dwlt: towards rr in centre: effrt over 2f out: nt rch ldrs* **16/1**	86
254/	**9**	*hd*	**Fantastic View (USA)**^{1013} [5439] 6-9-1 **97**..................... SebSanders 25 (J Noseda) *towards rr in centre: hdwy over 2f out: hrd rdn over 1f out: no imp* **12/1**	85
00-1	**10**	*nk*	**Trafalgar Square**^{33} [1818] 5-8-7 **89**................................ DaneO'Neill 23 (J Akehurst) *mid-div in centre: effrt 3f out: no imp fnl 2f* **14/1**	76
-406	**11**	*1*	**Pentecost**^{39} [1651] 8-8-10 **97**.. WilliamBuick$^{(5)}$ 9 (A M Balding) *lw: hld up towards rr in centre: effrt and nt clr run 2f out: swtchd lft: nvr rchd ldrs* **20/1**	82
5010	**12**	*nk*	**Plum Pudding (IRE)**^{19} [2208] 4-9-2 **98**............................ RyanMoore 13 (R Hannon) *lw: in tch in centre tl rdn and btn 2f out* **33/1**	82
0012	**13**	*shd*	**Montpellier (IRE)**^{19} [2208] 4-8-5 **87**............................... KerrinMcEvoy 21 (E A L Dunlop) *lw: chsd ldrs in centre tl rdn and wknd 2f out* **6/1^{1}**	71
5120	**14**	*1*	**Goodbye Mr Bond**^{23} [2093] 7-8-11 **93**................................. KDarley 26 (E J Alston) *mid-div in centre: rdn 3f out: outpcd fnl 2f* **50/1**	75
-000	**15**	*nk*	**Prince Of Light (IRE)**^{23} [2093] 4-9-7 **103**.......................(b) JoeFanning 2 (M Johnston) *led stands' side gp tl over 2f out: wknd over 1f out* **25/1**	84
0010	**16**	*shd*	**Capable Guest (IRE)**^{39} [1651] 5-8-10 **92**......................(v) JHBowman 12 (M R Channon) *mid-div in centre: rdn over 2f out: no imp* **25/1**	73
0-06	**17**	*½*	**Crooked Throw (IRE)**^{25} [2052] 8-8-9 **94**............................. WJLee$^{(3)}$ 20 (C F Swan, Ire) *bhd in centre: rdn over 2f out: sme late hdwy* **33/1**	74
00-3	**18**	*shd*	**Minority Report**^{46} [1480] 7-8-11 **93**................................. NickyMackay 1 (L M Cumani) *wnt rt and bmpd s: sn chsng stands' side ldrs: wknd 2f out* **14/1**	72
2-03	**19**	*1 ¾*	**Woodcote Place**^{11} [2476] 4-8-6 **88**..................................... JimCrowley 7 (P R Chamings) *dwlt: sn chsng ldrs on stands' side of centre gp: btn whn hmpd over 2f out* **33/1**	63
533-	**20**	*½*	**Military Cross**^{312} [4356] 4-8-12 **94**.................................. CSoumillon 17 (L M Cumani) *prom in centre: rdn over 2f out: wknd wl over 1f out* **11/1**	68
-120	**21**	*1 ¼*	**Count Trevisio (IRE)**^{117} [544] 4-9-6 **102**............................. LDettori 10 (Saeed Bin Suroor) *prom in centre: led gp over 2f out tl wknd wl over 1f out* **18/1**	73
-056	**22**	*¾*	**Ace Of Hearts**^{22} [2123] 8-8-12 **94**...................................... EddieAhern 29 (C F Wall) *swtchd lft to join far side of centre gp after 1f: chsd ldrs: rdn over 2f out: sn wknd* **25/1**	64
0021	**23**	*1*	**Humungous (IRE)**^{11} [2476] 4-9-4 **100** 5ex............................ OPeslier 18 (C R Egerton) *led centre gp tl over 2f out: wknd wl over 1f out* **20/1**	67
50-4	**24**	*1*	**Eden Rock (IRE)**^{139} [331] 6-8-11 **93**................................. MJKinane 24 (Pat Eddery) *racd centre: a bhd* **10/1**	58
-302	**25**	*3*	**Wind Star**^{23} [2093] 4-8-5 **87**.. DeanMcKeown 8 (G A Swinbank) *chsd ldrs in centre over 5f* **25/1**	45
-000	**26**	*¾*	**Beringoer (FR)**^{131} [411] 4-8-13 **95**..................................... LPKeniry 28 (A M Balding) *hld up towards rr on far side of centre gp: rdn and btn over 2f out* **33/1**	51

1m 39.78s (-2.02) **Going Correction** 0.0s/f (Good) **26** Ran SP% **138.1**

Speed ratings (Par 109):110,106,105,105,105 104,99,97,97,97 96,95,95,94,94 94,93,93,91,91 90,89,88,87,84 83

CSF £128.96 CT £6883.88 TOTE £11.10: £3.00, £4.10, £14.10, £2.90; EX 165.00 Trifecta £6543.60 Part won. Pool £9,216.36 - 0.20 winning units.

Owner W S Farish & William S Farish Jnr **Bred** Farish And Farish Llc **Trained** Newmarket, Suffolk

■ A 339/1 treble for Jimmy Fortune.

FOCUS

Despite the late absence of fancied duo Sound Of Nature and Pride Of Nation, this was a hugely competitive handicap, as is to be expected for this race, but the first-time blinkered Royal Oath destroyed his rivals and turned it into something of a procession. It was a good even split with none of the centre, the stands' side or Supaseus, who raced alone on the far side, appearing to be at a disadvantage. Strong form.

NOTEBOOK

Royal Oath(USA), whose reappearance second in the Spring Cup at Newbury pointed to there being a big handicap in him, flopped badly behind Supaseus at Newmarket last time and as a result connections opted to fit blinkers for the first time. Solid enough in the market, he produced a spectacular winning effort, bursting clear of the main pack down the centre of the course and winning with any amount in hand, looking a Group performer in the making. The long-term plan is to pick up a Group 1 at Keeneland in the Autumn for his American-based owners, but it remains to be seen whether the headgear will continue to have the same effect. (op 8-1 tchd 10-1 in places)

Flipando(IRE), on a hat-trick following wins at Beverley and most recently in the Zetland Gold Cup at Redcar, was dropping back a quarter of a mile in distance, but he is fully effective at a mile and looked a player. However, nobody was counting on Royal Oath winning like he did and he was unfortunate to bump into one. Perhaps if his rider had the chance again he would have made a bit more use of him, but he remains on an upward curve and now heads for the John Smith's Cup at York.

Vortex ran an absolute blinder and recorded an RPR equal to that of the winner. The eight-year-old has not been at his best of late, but he travelled supremely well towards the stands' side and kept fighting right the way to the line, just being anchored by his weight. This has to go down as one of the best efforts of his career considering his age. (op 66-1)

Supaseus, who returned to action with a career-best at Newmarket, narrowly prevailing from Pinpoint, raced solo on the far rail. He has never been the most consistent, but he managed to put two good runs together with a highly creditable effort here off a new 6lb higher mark. It would have been interesting to see how he would have fared in company with other horses. (op 8-1 tchd 9-1)

Yarqus has dropped to a decent mark now and the reapplication of the tongue tie enabled him to run a storming race, just missing out on the placings. Towards the rear of the small stands'-side group, he came with a strong run and kept on right the way to the line, suggesting there is a decent prize in him off this sort of mark.

My Paris has been in good form and, although finding this a bit competitive, he gave his all. He found himself as the overall leader two out, but could do nothing about the winner, and is likely to continue to give a good account in top handicaps. He was clear of the remainder. (op 25-1 tchd 28-1 in a place)

Lundy's Lane(IRE), fresh from an unsuccessful spell in Dubai, was the rank outsider of the whole field but out-ran his odds and did enough to show connections they have something to work with.

Skhilling Spirit, who could have done with some rain, briefly threatened to make a run for the placings, but he could not quicken on the ground. (tchd 20-1 in places)

Fantastic View(USA), off since September 2004, was a smart two-year-old for Richard Hannon and the fact he had been kept in training suggested he was not one to dismiss too readily. He looked fit and ran well, but horses running well on returns from lengthy lay-offs do not always progress. (op 14-1 tchd 16-1 in places)

Trafalgar Square, up 5lb for his recent return to winning ways at Newmarket, ran well for a long way, but was not quite so effective on this step back up to 1m. (tchd 16-1 in places)

Pentecost was a little unlucky not to finish closer, not getting a run when he wanted it before keeping on at the one pace under pressure.

Montpellier(IRE), a progressive gelding since being dropped to this distance, winning comfortably at Kempton before a fine effort in defeat at Epsom recently, was a strongly supported favourite, but no sooner had he started to come with his run in the centre it became clear he was running on empty and he dropped right away. This was disappointing and perhaps he is best with more of a break between his races. (op 13-2 tchd 7-1 in a place)

Prince Of Light(IRE) took the small stands'-side group along for a long way and strikes as a horse who will one day become very backable in a big handicap such as this, assuming the Handicapper begins to relent.

Military Cross, making his debut for connections, dropped right out having shown up well early and this was a stiff ask on his first start of the season. (op 10-1)

Count Trevisio(IRE) Official explanation: jockey said colt lost its action.

Beringoer(FR) Official explanation: jockey said gelding banged its head in the stalls.

2756 QUEEN MARY STKS (GROUP 2) (FILLIES) 5f

4:55 (4:59) (Class 1) 2-Y-0

£39,746 (£15,064; £7,539; £3,759; £1,883; £945) **Stalls** Centre

Form				RPR
	1		**Elletelle (IRE)**^{14} [2378] 2-8-12 0.. JMurtagh 13 (G M Lyons, Ire) *w'like: s.i.s: hld up: hdwy over 1f out: nt clr run briefly over 1f out: r.o ins fnl f to ld towards fin* **20/1**	103
11	**2**	*½*	**Starlit Sands**^{19} [2199] 2-8-12 0... SebSanders 14 (Sir Mark Prescott) *w'like: lw: led: rdn 2f out: hdd towards fin* **4/1^{1}**	101
25	**3**	*shd*	**The Loan Express (IRE)**^{16} [2325] 2-8-12 0...................... WMLordan 18 (T Stack, Ire) *neat: racd keenly: hld up: hdwy and hung rt over 1f out: r.o and clsng towards fin* **66/1**	101
0	**4**	*½*	**Francesca D'Gorgio (USA)**^{14} [2364] 2-8-12 0........................ LDettori 7 (J Noseda) *str: lw: in tch: effrt 2f out: r.o towards fin* **20/1**	99+
113	**5**	*shd*	**Cake (IRE)**^{30} [1897] 2-8-12 0... RyanMoore 20 (R Hannon) *chsd ldrs: rdn 2f out: styd on same pce towards fin* **14/1**	99
422	**6**	*½*	**Littlemisssunshine (IRE)**^{19} [2199] 2-8-12 0...................... JohnEgan 12 (J S Moore) *chsd ldrs: rdn over 2f out: nt qckn towards fin* **66/1**	97
12	**7**	*1*	**Lady Avenger (IRE)**^{20} [2183] 2-8-12 0........................... KerrinMcEvoy 1 (J M P Eustace) *hld up: hdwy and hung rt fr 2f out: r.o ins fnl f: nt rch ldrs* **20/1**	93
1	**8**	*hd*	**Fanatical**^{11} [2468] 2-8-12 0.. DaneO'Neill 16 (E F Vaughan) *prom: rdn 2f out: one pce ins fnl f* **16/1**	93
3	**9**	*shd*	**Tuscan Evening (IRE)**^{25} [2049] 2-8-12 0............................... DMGrant 8 (John Joseph Murphy, Ire) *str: s.i.s: midfield: rdn over 2f out: kpt on ins fnl f: nt pce of ldrs* **50/1**	92
12	**10**	*hd*	**Tia Mia**^{33} [1821] 2-8-12 0.. JamieSpencer 17 (J G Given) *lw: prom: rdn over 1f out: no ex ins fnl f* **10/1**	91
1	**11**	*1 ¼*	**Polar Circle (USA)**^{33} [1807] 2-8-12 0................................... MJKinane 15 (P W Chapple-Hyam) *lw: midfield: rdn 2f out: eased whn no imp ins fnl f* **9/1**	89+
21	**12**	*1*	**Bastakiya (IRE)**^{15} [2344] 2-8-12 0................................. JimmyFortune 19 (J H M Gosden) *lw: hld up: effrt 2f out: no imp on ldrs* **8/1^{3}**	83+
4	**13**	*shd*	**Perfect Paula (USA)**^{30} [1897] 2-8-12 0.......................... SteveDrowne 21 (B J Meehan) *w'like: hld up: rdn over 2f out: nt pce to chal* **66/1**	83+
1	**14**	*1*	**Regal Step**^{14} [2364] 2-8-12 0.. EddieAhern 3 (R M H Cowell) *w'like: scope: in tch: rdn and outpcd 2f out* **8/1^{3}**	79
1	**15**	*¾*	**Monaazalah (IRE)**^{25} [2039] 2-8-12 0... RHills 10 (B W Hills) *hld up: rdn 2f out: nvr trbld ldrs* **11/1**	77
1	**16**	*2 ½*	**Kylayne**^{72} [972] 2-8-12 0... DarryllHolland 6 (P W D'Arcy) *str: racd keenly: midfield: hmpd over 2f out: edgd rt whn n.d over 1f out* **40/1**	68+
035	**17**	*1 ¾*	**Evenstorm (USA)**^{5} [2630] 2-8-12 0.................................. JimCrowley 11 (B Gubby) *midfield: rdn and outpcd over 2f out* **200/1**	61
13	**18**	*3 ½*	**Piece Of My Heart**^{37} [1721] 2-8-12 0.. TQuinn 4 (P F I Cole) *w'like: racd keenly: in tch: wknd over 2f out* **100/1**	49+
11	**19**	*½*	**Sweepstake (IRE)**^{20} [2183] 2-8-12 0............................. RichardHughes 9 (R Hannon) *chsd ldrs tl lost pl qckly over 2f out: n.d after* **9/2^{2}**	47+
	20	*¾*	**L'Orage** 2-8-12 0... BrettDoyle 2 (J Ryan) *unf: s.s: a bhd* **100/1**	44
134	**21**	*1 ¼*	**Cristal Clear (IRE)**^{21} [2134] 2-8-12 0..................................(b^{1}) KDarley 5 (T D Easterby) *racd keenly: midfield: bdly hmpd and lost pl over 3f out: bhd after* **33/1**	40+

60.64 secs (-0.76) **Going Correction** 0.0s/f (Good) **21** Ran SP% **129.0**

Speed ratings (Par 102):106,105,105,104,104 103,101,101,101,100 98,97,97,95,94 90,87,81,81,79 77

Part won. Pool £5,405.49 - 0.20 winning units. Pool £4,324.39 carried forward to Saturday. CSF £95.14 TOTE £25.30: £6.50, £2.50, £20.50; EX 157.40 Trifecta £3837.80 w/u.

Owner Jesse Club Syndicate **Bred** Timothy Gleeson & Ashley O'Lea **Trained** Dunsany, Co. Meath

FOCUS

A fair winning time for a race of its stature. Starlit Sands showed tremendous early speed to take the field along, but was just caught out by the fast finishing Elletelle in the final 100 yards. The first ten finished in a heap and this was probably only a very average renewal, but the form looks very solid indeed.

NOTEBOOK

Elletelle(IRE), who went off at a terrific price considering her debut effort, was very keen in the early stages but still found more than enough under pressure to grab Starlit Sands close to the line. This was her first time at 5f, so it was not surprising to see her doing all of her best work in the final stages, and one would suspect a step back up in trip is quite likely. Very much a 2yo in looks, she has plenty of options both in England and Ireland to aim for during the season and has created a good standard to aim at. (tchd 25-1 in places)

Starlit Sands, an athletic type, is a very quick filly and was basically just outstayed by the winner in the final stages. Her breeding does suggest that a sixth furlong is within her scope, but for now 5f looks ideal and a race like the Molecomb would seem a logical target for her. (op 5-1)

The Loan Express(IRE), another who came from Ireland with very solid form, was doing all of her best work late on and, much like the winner, will stay at least another furlong. Hanging a little under pressure, she might well have got past Starlit Sands had she stayed a bit straighter.
Francesca D'Gorgio(USA) left her disappointing debut effort well behind her with a promising display. She was staying on really well in the final stages and looks sure to be even better over at least another furlong, and the Cherry Hinton at Newmarket - a race connections won last season with Sander Camillo - would probably suit her in the coming weeks'.
Cake(IRE) was never far away and seemed to have every chance. The minimum trip looks to suit her well and she is probably the sort to head for the Molecomb at Goodwood or the Weatherbys Super Sprint at Newbury rather than try slightly further. (op 16-1)
Littlemisssunshine(IRE) pretty much ran up to the form she had with Starlit Sands and looks more than capable of landing a decent contest before the end of the season. She may well benefit from another furlong.
Lady Avenger(IRE) ran a remarkable race, as she had plenty to do from a moderate draw and still had lots of horses to pass inside the final furlong. She seemed to finish with something still to give and should leave this form well behind when given an even chance. Official explanation: jockey said filly hung right-handed.
Fanatical showed plenty of early pace but did not get home as well as a few others in the race, which is slightly surprising as she won over 6f on her debut. The conclusion must be that the step up in class caught her out and a return to a lesser grade will help her. (tchd 20-1 in places)
Tuscan Evening(IRE) did not look to be suited by the 5f trip at all and should be more effective over at least a furlong more.
Tia Mia helped to set the gallop but did not get home as a result. She looked very tired inside the final furlong. (op 14-1 tchd 16-1 in places)
Polar Circle(USA) did not look suited to the quick early pace and stayed on quite well in the final stages without suggesting that she was really unlucky. It seems highly likely that she will run over 6f next time. (op 8-1)
Bastakiya(IRE) appeared to have every chance but was not good enough on the day. (tchd 9-1 in places)
Regal Step appeared to run well below the form she showed on her debut - although she did start at 25/1 on that occasion - but it later transpired that she was heavily in season, so at least has an excuse for the effort. Official explanation: trainer said filly was found to be in season after the race (op 15-2 tchd 10-1 in a place and 9-1 in a place)
Monaazalah(IRE) looks an athletic type. Official explanation: jockey said filly was struck into behind (op 10-1 tchd 12-1 in places)
Kylayne was just starting to be ridden along when badly hampered over 2f from home. Official explanation: jockey said filly suffered interference in running. (op 33-1)
Piece Of My Heart Official explanation: jockey said filly suffered interference.
Sweepstake(IRE) was bang there with a couple of furlongs to go but dropped out tamely once put under serious pressure. The ground was initially blamed, but it transpired that she had pulled muscles in her back, probably when leaving the stalls. Official explanation: jockey sadi filly was unsuited by the good to firm ground. (op 4-1 tchd 5-1 in places)

2757 SANDRINGHAM H'CAP (LISTED RACE) (FILLIES) 1m (S)

5:30 (5:35) (Class 1) (0-110,108) 3-Y-O

£31,229 (£11,836; £5,923; £2,953; £1,479; £742) **Stalls** Centre

Form					RPR
-150	**1**		**Barshiba (IRE)**[45] [1496] 3-8-8 **95** (D R C Elsworth) *t.k.h in rr: hdwy and hmpd 3f out: nt clr run over 2f out: swtchd rt: r.o to ld fnl 100yds*	TQuinn 13 **16/1**	107+
11-0	**2**	*1 1/4*	**Selinka**[45] [1496] 3-8-11 **98** (R Hannon) *lw: sn pushed along and bhd: rapid hdwy 2f out: led over 1f out: hdd and nt qckn fnl 100yds*	RyanMoore 3 **33/1**	104
-341	**3**	*hd*	**Costume**[15] [2341] 3-9-7 **108** (J H M Gosden) *lw: hld up in midfield: stdy hdwy 2f out: drvn to join ldrs over 1f out: kpt on same pce*	RichardHughes 19 **5/1**[2]	114
54-1	**4**	*4*	**Italian Girl**[49] [1391] 3-9-2 **103** (A P Jarvis) *lw: hld up in rr: hdwy 2f out: rdn to join ldrs 1f out: no ex ins fnl f*	JamieSpencer 18 **10/3**[1]	100
4-12	**5**	*3/4*	**In Safe Hands (IRE)**[33] [1809] 3-8-7 **94** oh2 (C G Cox) *chsd ldrs: hrd rdn 2f out: one pce*	(p) MJKinane 8 **14/1**	89
2211	**6**	*3/4*	**Truly Enchanting (IRE)**[14] [2369] 3-8-7 **94** oh6 (J Noseda) *stdd and swtchd rt s: hld up towards rr: effrt and swtchd lft over 1f out: drvn along and styd on*	EddieAhern 2 **10/1**	91+
1122	**7**	*hd*	**Lady Gloria**[7] [2578] 3-8-8 **95** (J G Given) *chsd ldrs: rdn and n.m.r over 1f out: one pce*	LDettori 16 **8/1**[3]	88+
33-1	**8**	*1 3/4*	**Cliche (IRE)**[30] [1901] 3-8-12 **99** (Sir Michael Stoute) *prom tl wknd over 1f out*	KerrinMcEvoy 17 **5/1**[2]	88
14-1	**9**	*1/2*	**Lady Grace (IRE)**[16] [2306] 3-9-0 **101** (W J Haggas) *t.k.h: in tch: rdn and n.m.r over 2f out: sn btn*	MichaelHills 1 **12/1**	89
0010	**10**	*1 3/4*	**Precocious Star (IRE)**[63] [1096] 3-8-7 **94** oh4 (K R Burke) *chsd ldrs: rdn over 2f out: sn outpcd*	FergusSweeney 20 **100/1**	78
6-3	**11**	*nk*	**Divine Night (IRE)**[38] [1694] 3-8-12 **99** (David Wachman, Ire) *w'like: plld hrd in midfield: rdn 3f out: sn outpcd*	WMLordan 12 **25/1**	82
0-	**12**	*2 1/2*	**Miss Gorica (IRE)**[21] [2160] 3-8-7 **94** oh7 (Ms Joanna Morgan, Ire) *cmpt: disp ld: led after 3f: hrd rdn 2f out: hdd & wknd qckly over 1f out*	RPCleary 21 **25/1**	71
0-40	**13**	*2 1/2*	**So Sweet (IRE)**[27] [1958] 3-8-7 **94** (M R Channon) *chsd ldrs: hmpd and lost pl 3f out: rdn and n.d after*	DarryllHolland 15 **66/1**	66
12-6	**14**	*1/2*	**Hollow Ridge**[42] [1581] 3-8-7 **94** oh1 (B W Hills) *disp ld 3f: wknd over 2f out: wl btn whn bmpd wl over 1f out*	SPasquier 6 **40/1**	64
313	**15**	*3/4*	**Graduation**[33] [1824] 3-8-7 **94** oh2 (E A L Dunlop) *hld up in tch: rdn and btn whn n.m.r wl over 1f out*	NCallan 11 **12/1**	63
141	**16**	*5*	**Chantilly Tiffany**[26] [2001] 3-8-7 **94** oh3 (E A L Dunlop) *mid-div tl wknd 2f out*	C-PLemaire 10 **16/1**	51
-403	**17**	*5*	**Laurentina**[46] [1466] 3-8-7 **94** oh2 (B J Meehan) *chsd ldrs: hrd rdn over 2f out: sn wknd*	KDarley 4 **40/1**	40
2005	**18**	*16*	**Satulagi (USA)**[33] [1824] 3-8-13 **100** (J S Moore) *edgy in stalls: mid-div: rdn over 3f out: sn wknd: eased whn no ch over 1f out*	JohnEgan 14 **50/1**	9
0-54	**19**	*43*	**Alderney (USA)**[11] [2450] 3-8-7 **94** oh2 (M A Jarvis) *a towards rr: wl bhd fnl 3f*	PhilipRobinson 5 **25/1**	—

1m 40.22s (-1.58) **Going Correction** 0.0s/f (Good) **19** Ran SP% **134.2**
Speed ratings (Par 104):107,105,105,101,100 100,99,98,97,95 95,93,90,90,89 84,79,63,20
CSF £500.62 CT £3106.34 TOTE £23.30: £5.20, £8.00, £2.30, £1.30; EX 751.10 TRIFECTA Not won. Pool £5,718.39 Place 6 £81.75, Place 5 £58.49..
Owner J C Smith **Bred** Littleton Stud **Trained** Newmarket, Suffolk

FOCUS
A highly competitive Listed Handicap contested by some classy fillies and the decent gallop allowed three to draw four lengths clear. Half the field were out of the weights, but the form looks strong with Oh So Sharp Stakes winner Selinka and French Guineas fourth Costume claiming two of the three places behind the unexposed and visually impressive winner Barshiba.

NOTEBOOK
Barshiba(IRE) ◆, a useful-looking juvenile last season who broke her maiden with an impressive victory over the smart Zaham at Lingfield, reappeared with a highly creditable effort over an inadequate 7f in the Nell Gwyn and her latest effort in the Guineas could be safely ignored as she got badly hampered at an early stage. Off since and back down in grade, she has always been quite highly thought of, but she took a really strong grip early on and a lesser filly would have pulled her chance away. However, despite twice getting blocked when attempting to challenge inside the final three furlongs, she eventually got into the clear and quickened up in the style of a very smart filly, ultimately winning comfortably. This was a taking performance from the daughter of Barathea and, considering she still looked quite green under pressure, it would not surprise to see a good deal of further improvement in the coming months. She may not be able to replicate last year's winner Red Evie by going on to multiple Group 1 success, but fully deserves her place back at Group level and can prove a force when learning to settle better. (tchd 20-1 in places)
Selinka, winner of the Listed Oh So Sharp Stakes on her final start at two, showed a definite preference for a slow surface as a juvenile and, although she could be forgiven her 100/1 last on her reappearance in the Guineas, she looked one of the unlikelier ones here off a mark of 98. The rest has clearly enabled her to come to herself though and, having been switched, she produced a sustained run towards the stands' side to go into the lead over a furlong out, but Barshiba produced a fine change of pace and it proved too much for her. Had she been able to hold her position early she may well have been the victor, but this was a big step back in the right direction and she looks well worth her place back in Group races.
Costume brought the single best piece of form into this, her fourth placing in the French 1000 Guineas two starts back, and a recent confidence booster when winning her maiden easily at Ripon should have put her spot on for this. Conceding upwards of 5lb to all her rivals was never going to be easy, but she gave it a bold go and held every chance over a furlong out, only to lack the winner's change of pace. She is unlikely to find it too hard winning a race at this level and is in the right hands to keep progressing. (op 11-2 tchd 6-1 in places)
Italian Girl, who actually finished behind Selinka in the Oh So Sharp Stakes on her final outing in 2006, impressed many with her visually impressive display in a course-and-distance conditions event on her three-year-old debut, even though the runner-up - subsequent Listed scorer Silver Pivotal - was unlucky not to get a bit closer to her that day. Up 8lb for this handicap debut, she raced close to both Barshiba and Costume towards the rear early on, but made her move racing into the final quarter mile and briefly appeared to be going best, before it soon became clear there was little left in the tank and she was left trailing in the final half-furlong. This still represented an improved effort and there is a Listed contest in her this season. (op 6-1 tchd 13-2 in a place)
In Safe Hands(IRE) has gone from strength to strength since joining current connections from Ireland, winning her maiden at Nottingham before running the useful Measured Tempo close at Newbury last time over 1m2f. Back down in trip, she was sporting first-time cheekpieces and fared best of those to have raced near the pace, keeping on at the one pace under pressure. This represented another step forward.
Truly Enchanting(IRE), beaten by In Safe Hands at Nottingham, has since gone from strength to strength herself, winning at Goodwood and Nottingham, and she should probably have reversed form with her old rival, just getting going a bit too late under her 6lb penalty. (tchd 12-1, 33-1 in places)
Lady Gloria, who had yet to finish out the first three in seven starts, is enjoying a fine first season, but she has been going up for not winning and was racing here off a stone higher mark than when last successful. Beaten by Truly Enchanting two starts back, she was unable to reverse the form and may remain vulnerable off this mark in handicaps for the time being. (op 10-1)
Cliche(IRE), a workmanlike winner on her reappearance at Windsor, had shown useful placed form at two - most notably when third in a big Sales race at the Curragh - but she was starting out off a stiff enough mark and may have paid for sitting too close to the early pace, weakening right out of it in the final furlong. She is probably a bit better than this and can gain some black type this season, but was simply not as good as the principals on this occasion. (op 4-1 tchd 11-2 in places)
Lady Grace(IRE), an easy winner on her reappearance at Leicester, had been raised a harsh 11lb for that victory and the combination of the return to 1m on the fastest ground she has tackled to date was enough to find her out. (tchd 14-1 in places)
Precocious Star(IRE), who had to race from 4lb out of the handicap, is already a winner at this level, but she was always likely to struggle against so many unexposed sorts and this was probably as good a run as connections could have hoped for.
Divine Night(IRE) brought some decent form into this, but she raced keenly in the early stages before fading out in the final quarter mile.
Chantilly Tiffany, ready winner of a conditions event at Newmarket, saw the form boosted when third-placed One Hour scored at the weekend, but she was unable to make an impact in this more competitive contest. It may be worth giving her another chance though as she was done no favours by the rapidly weakening Hollow Ridge.
Satulagi(USA) Official explanation: jockey said filly was in season.
Alderney(USA) Official explanation: trainer said filly finished distressed.
T/Jkpt: Not won. T/Plt: £109.00 to a £1 stake. Pool: £482,171.09. 3,227.35 winning tickets. T/Qpdt: £40.60 to a £1 stake. Pool: £16,879.30. 307.60 winning tickets. DO

2561 HAMILTON (R-H)

Wednesday, June 20

OFFICIAL GOING: Good (good to soft in places, 7.7)
Wind: Light, half behind

2758 LANARKSHIRE CHAMBER OF COMMERCE MAIDEN AUCTION STKS 6f 5y

2:10 (2:10) (Class 6) 2-Y-O **£2,266** (£674; £337; £168) **Stalls** Low

Form					RPR
00	**1**		**Gin Genereux**[30] [1889] 2-8-13 0 (M Johnston) *mde all: rdn and drifted rt over 1f out: hld on wl*	GregFairley(3) 9 **16/1**	77+
03	**2**	*3/4*	**Brixworth Scribe**[23] [2086] 2-8-11 0 (B Smart) *dwlt: outpcd: plenty to do 1/2-way: gd hdwy to chse wnr ins fnl f: r.o*	RoystonFfrench 1 **9/4**[1]	70+
3	**3**	*1 1/4*	**Binario Uno**[7] [2562] 2-8-12 0 (D Nicholls) *cl up: rdn over 2f out: kpt on fnl f*	AdrianTNicholls 4 **8/1**[3]	67
655	**4**	*6*	**Turn And River (IRE)**[40] [1622] 2-7-13 0 (M Brittain) *t.k.h: chsd ldrs: drvn over 2f out: edgd rt and sn one pce*	PatrickDonaghy(7) 6 **22/1**	43
0	**5**	*1 3/4*	**Keep Shining**[11] [2451] 2-8-4 0 (E J Alston) *prom tl rdn and wknd fr 2f out*	PaulQuinn 5 **100/1**	36
5	**6**	*3/4*	**Planet Queen**[22] [2115] 2-8-11 0 (K R Burke) *sn bhd: hung rt thrght: rdn and outpcd fr 1/2-way*	PatCosgrave 3 **7/1**[2]	41
4	**7**	*1/2*	**Hurstpierpoint (IRE)**[14] [2371] 2-8-7 0 (R A Fahey) *sn bhd and outpcd: no ch fr 1/2-way*	PaulHanagan 2 **9/4**[1]	35
	8	*3*	**Victorian Princess (IRE)** 2-8-9 0 (E J O'Neill) *prom tl rdn and wknd over 2f out*	ChrisCatlin 7 **7/1**[2]	28

1m 13.46s (0.36) **Going Correction** 0.0s/f (Good) **8** Ran SP% **108.9**
Speed ratings (Par 91):97,96,94,86,84 83,82,78
CSF £47.40 TOTE £15.30: £3.60, £1.60, £2.00; EX 66.50.
Owner Mrs R J Jacobs **Bred** Newsells Park Stud Limited **Trained** Middleham Moor, N Yorks

FOCUS
An ordinary bunch on looks but the pace seemed sound throughout and this bare form should prove reliable. The first three finished clear, with step ups from the winner and third and the second running to form without improving.

NOTEBOOK

Gin Genereux, well beaten over 5f on a sound surface on his first two starts, turned in a much improved effort over this longer trip and on this easier ground, despite wandering off a true line. He may be the type to progress again for his current stable. Official explanation: trainer was unable to explain the improvement in form (op 12-1)

Brixworth Scribe, who turned in an improved effort on soft ground on his previous start, ran to a similar level in terms of form over this longer trip after being unable to hold an early position. He has little in the way of physical scope, though, and may remain vulnerable to the better sorts in this type of event.

Binario Uno, who shaped with credit on his recent debut over this course and distance, ran to a similar level and again left the impression that the step up to 7f would be to his liking. (op 10-1)

Turn And River(IRE), who had shown ability at a modest level in maidens, again had her limitations firmly exposed in this type of event. She may do better in run-of-the-mill nursery company. (op 25-1)

Keep Shining, soundly beaten on her debut at Haydock, was beaten a similar level in this ordinary event. She is likely to continue to look vulnerable in this type of race.

Planet Queen, who hinted at ability on her debut, failed to build on that effort but looked ill at ease on this course and she may do better in ordinary nursery company over further in due course. (op 9-2)

Hurstpierpoint(IRE), a sturdy individual, failed by a long chalk to reproduce her debut promise on this easier ground. However she is in good hands and will be worth another chance in similar company back on a sound surface. Official explanation: trainer had no explanation for the poor form shown (op 11-4 tchd 2-1 and 3-1 in a place)

2759 TURFTV BETTING SHOP SERVICE H'CAP — 1m 65y

2:45 (2:45) (Class 6) (0-60,60) 3-Y-O — **£2,266** (£674; £337; £168) **Stalls** High

Form — RPR

000- **1** **Surprise Pension (IRE)**^{253} [5901] 3-8-8 **50**............ GrahamGibbons 12 — 56
(J J Quinn) *hld up: smooth hdwy and ev ch over 2f out: rdn over 1f out: styd on wl to ld nr fin* **12/1**

-410 **2** *hd* **Shandelight (IRE)**^{10} [2489] 3-8-5 **47**........................(p) RoystonFfrench 1 — 53
(Mrs A Duffield) *chsd ldrs: effrt and led over 3f out: sn hrd pressed: kpt on fnl f: hdd nr fin* **12/1**

465 **3** *½* **John Dillon (IRE)**^{71} [991] 3-9-3 **59**.................................... LeeEnstone 8 — 64
(P C Haslam) *hld up: smooth hdwy and cl up over 2f out: disp ld ins fnl f: hld cl home* **12/1**

0-04 **4** *8* **Fistral**^{18} [2248] 3-8-7 **49** ow1.. TomEaves 10 — 35
(J Hetherton) *hld up: effrt over 3f out: rdn and no imp wl over 1f out* **16/1**

4002 **5** *nk* **Just Oscar (GER)**^{10} [2489] 3-9-3 **59**.............................. PaulMulrennan 3 — 45
(W M Brisbourne) *t.k.h: hld up: hdwy centre and in tch over 3f out: rdn and outpcd fr 2f out* **7/1**

-340 **6** *½* **Leprechaun's Gold (IRE)**^{21} [2133] 3-8-13 **58**.............. GregFairley$^{(3)}$ 5 — 43
(M Johnston) *dwlt: hld up: effrt centre over 3f out: outpcd fr 2f out* **5/1**^{2}

00-6 **7** *2½* **Lady Pickpocket**^{43} [1566] 3-9-4 **60**........................... JimmyQuinn 11 — 39
(M H Tompkins) *in tch tl rdn and wknd over 2f out* **25/1**

0403 **8** *3½* **Colditz (IRE)**^{7} [2565] 3-9-3 **59**....................................... TonyHamilton 9 — 30
(D W Barker) *chsd ldrs: effrt over 2f out: edgd rt and sn btn* **13/2**^{3}

000- **9** *5* **Eldon Endeavour**^{276} [5402] 3-8-2 **47** oh1 ow1........... AndrewMullen$^{(3)}$ 2 — 6
(B Storey) *led 2f: cl up tl rdn and wknd over 2f out* **150/1**

005 **10** *2½* **Pearl Valley**^{36} [1749] 3-8-4 **46** oh1.............................(v^{1}) DaleGibson 4 — —
(R A Fahey) *t.k.h: led after 2f to over 3f out: sn btn* **66/1**

500 **11** *11* **Western Point (IRE)**^{20} [2175] 3-9-0 **56**........................ PaulHanagan 7 — —
(Sir Mark Prescott) *prom: rdn over 3f out: sn wknd* **15/8**^{1}

050 **R** **Polish Star**^{32} [1850] 3-8-9 **54**... JamieMoriarty$^{(3)}$ 6 — —
(J S Wainwright) *ref to r* **14/1**

1m 49.1s (-0.20) **Going Correction** 0.0s/f (Good) — **12** Ran SP% **118.9**

Speed ratings (Par 97):101,100,100,92,92 91,89,85,80,78 67,—

CSF £147.12 CT £1805.64 TOTE £23.30: £5.40, £3.00, £3.90; EX 373.20.

Owner P J Carr **Bred** Gabriel Bell **Trained** Settrington, N Yorks

■ Stewards' Enquiry : Royston Ffrench caution: used whip down the shoulder in the forehand position

FOCUS

Hand-timed. The pace was just fair. A low-grade handicap and one weakened by the below-par showing of the market leader. The winner was up 7lb on his previous best.

Western Point(IRE) Official explanation: trainer had no explanation for the poor form shown

2760 TURFTV FILLIES' H'CAP — 1m 1f 36y

3:20 (3:20) (Class 5) (0-70,70) 3-Y-O+ — **£3,886** (£1,156; £577; £288) **Stalls** High

Form — RPR

6-00 **1** **Ignition**^{20} [2168] 5-8-9 **49** oh4... PaulHanagan 8 — 58
(W M Brisbourne) *led 1f: chsd ldrs: led again over 1f out: kpt on strly* **25/1**

2034 **2** *2½* **Mystical Ayr (IRE)**^{7} [2564] 5-9-2 **59**...................... JamieMoriarty$^{(3)}$ 11 — 63
(Miss L A Perratt) *hld up: drvn over 3f out: kpt on fnl 2f: chsd wnr towards fin* **7/2**^{1}

112 **3** *hd* **Stolen Glance**^{15} [2346] 4-10-0 **68**.............................. PaulMulrennan 6 — 72
(M W Easterby) *prom: smooth hdwy over 3f out: effrt 2f out: nt qckn fnl f* **5/1**^{3}

02-0 **4** *1½* **Peintre's Wonder (IRE)**^{40} [1639] 3-9-2 **67**...................... ChrisCatlin 9 — 66
(E J O'Neill) *midfield: rdn over 3f out: rallied 2f out: kpt on same pce fnl f* **9/1**

0-23 **5** *1¾* **Freya Tricks**^{11} [2464] 3-9-5 **70**.. TomEaves 10 — 66
(I Semple) *bhd: hdwy over 3f out: flashed tail u.p over 1f out: kpt on: no imp* **4/1**^{2}

4-34 **6** *3½* **Chasing Memories (IRE)**^{21} [2133] 3-8-9 **60**............. RoystonFfrench 3 — 48
(B Smart) *hld up: outpcd over 3f out: sme late hdwy: nvr on terms* **9/1**

4666 **7** *hd* **Reveur**^{44} [1539] 4-8-12 **52**... PatCosgrave 5 — 41
(K R Burke) *hld up: hdwy to ld over 2f out: hdd over 1f out: sn btn* **10/1**

0-30 **8** *4* **Spirit Of Ecstacy**^{36} [1746] 3-8-8 **62**..............................(t) GregFairley$^{(3)}$ 2 — 42
(G M Moore) *cl up tl rdn and wknd over 2f out* **33/1**

0462 **9** *2* **Neil's Legacy (IRE)**^{7} [2563] 5-8-11 **54**.................... AndrewMullen$^{(3)}$ 1 — 30
(Miss L A Perratt) *hld up in midfield: effrt over 3f out: wknd 2f out* **13/2**

/000 **10** *5* **Miss Lovat**^{18} [2257] 4-8-9 **49** oh4.. PaulQuinn 7 — 15
(W M Brisbourne) *hld up: rdn over 3f out: sn btn* **100/1**

5-02 **11** *18* **Zell (IRE)**^{28} [1944] 4-8-13 **53**.. JimmyQuinn 4 — —
(E J Alston) *s.i.s: plld hrd and led after 1f: hdd over 2f out: sn wknd: eased whn no ch* **9/1**

1m 58.99s (-0.67) **Going Correction** 0.0s/f (Good)

WFA 3 from 4yo+ 11lb — **11** Ran SP% **119.1**

Speed ratings (Par 100):102,99,99,98,96 93,93,89,88,83 67

CSF £111.42 CT £529.55 TOTE £25.10: £5.00, £2.00, £1.60; EX 196.20.

Owner M F Hyman **Bred** M F Hyman **Trained** Great Ness, Shropshire

FOCUS

Just a modest handicap in which the pace was fair. The winner had slipped to a good mark and the form seems sound enough.

Ignition Official explanation: trainer was unable to explain the improved form

Miss Lovat Official explanation: jockey said filly had no more to give

Zell(IRE) Official explanation: jockey said filly had no more to give

2761 LADIES NIGHT AT HAMILTON PARK CLAIMING STKS — 5f 4y

4:00 (4:00) (Class 6) 3-Y-O+ — **£2,266** (£674; £337; £168) **Stalls** Low

Form — RPR

3062 **1** **Thoughtsofstardom**^{7} [2555] 4-8-11 **50**......................(be) LukeMorris$^{(5)}$ 4 — 57
(P S McEntee) *midfield: rdn and effrt over 2f out: styd on fnl f to ld nr fin* **9/1**

-403 **2** *nk* **Luloah**^{22} [2104] 4-8-2 **42**.. JamieHamblett$^{(7)}$ 9 — 49
(J G M O'Shea) *led: rdn over 1f out: kpt on fnl f: hdd nr fin* **20/1**

4302 **3** *½* **Howards Tipple**^{13} [2387] 3-9-0 **64**.. TomEaves 8 — 56
(I Semple) *stdd in rr: hdwy over 1f out: kpt on fnl f: nrst fin* **5/2**^{1}

6643 **4** *1* **My Drop (IRE)**^{21} [2144] 3-8-12 **69**..................................... ChrisCatlin 2 — 51
(E J O'Neill) *in tch: rdn over 2f out: sn outpcd: kpt on fnl f* **11/4**^{2}

000 **5** *hd* **Alexia Rose (IRE)**^{9} [2516] 5-8-11 **44**....................(b^{1}) StephenDonohoe 6 — 45
(A Berry) *prom: rdn and hung rt over 2f out: kpt on ins fnl f* **50/1**

3360 **6** *¾* **Rothesay Dancer**^{11} [2461] 4-8-12 **50**........................ GaryBartley$^{(7)}$ 5 — 50
(J S Goldie) *prom: smooth hdwy 2f out: rdn and one pce fnl f* **14/1**

4240 **7** *1¼* **Beamsley Beacon**^{45} [1493] 6-9-2 **48**....................(tp) SilvestreDeSousa 1 — 43
(S T Mason) *sn towards rr: drvn 1/2-way: hdwy over 1f out: n.d* **9/1**

1420 **8** *½* **Blackheath (IRE)**^{7} [2561] 11-8-10 **53**.......................... AdrianTNicholls 7 — 35
(D Nicholls) *prom: effrt over 2f out: edgd rt and no ex over 1f out* **5/1**^{3}

0040 **9** *2* **Beverley Beau**^{14} [2357] 5-8-5 **43**.............................. KristinStubbs$^{(7)}$ 3 — 30
(Mrs L Stubbs) *prom tl rdn and wknd fr 2f out* **18/1**

3500 **10** *¾* **Chairman Bobby**^{9} [2509] 9-8-10 **48**............................(p) TonyHamilton 10 — 25
(D W Barker) *racd alone far side: rdn and outpcd fr 1/2-way* **14/1**

00 **11** *2½* **Maysridge Ofkuwait**^{13} [2387] 3-8-5 **0**.................................. PaulQuinn 13 — 15
(A Berry) *sn bhd and outpcd: nvr on terms* **100/1**

60.72 secs (-0.48) **Going Correction** 0.0s/f (Good)

WFA 3 from 4yo+ 6lb — **11** Ran SP% **118.2**

Speed ratings (Par 101):103,102,101,100,99 98,96,95,92,91 87

CSF £172.56 TOTE £13.20: £2.90, £4.50, £1.40; EX 100.00.

Owner Eventmaker Racehorses **Bred** B Bargh **Trained** Newmarket, Suffolk

FOCUS

Another modest event but one run at a decent gallop throughout. The winner is rated to his recent form.

2762 RAEBURN BRICK H'CAP — 6f 5y

4:35 (4:36) (Class 5) (0-75,75) 3-Y-O+ — **£3,886** (£1,156; £577; £288) **Stalls** Low

Form — RPR

1021 **1** **Brut**^{7} [2561] 5-9-4 **65** 6ex...(p) TonyHamilton 8 — 74
(D W Barker) *mde all: rdn and kpt on wl fnl f* **5/1**^{3}

0504 **2** *½* **Local Poet**^{7} [2561] 6-8-7 **57** oh6 ow1..........................(b) MarkLawson$^{(3)}$ 6 — 64
(I Semple) *hld up in tch: effrt over 2f out: kpt on fnl f: hld towards fin* **11/2**

1040 **3** *1¾* **Inca Soldier (FR)**^{16} [2302] 4-8-9 **56** oh7................................ PaulEddery 7 — 58
(R C Guest) *hld up: hdwy over 2f out: kpt on same pce ins fnl f* **16/1**

5401 **4** *hd* **Winthorpe (IRE)**^{12} [2421] 7-9-0 **64**.............................. JamieMoriarty$^{(3)}$ 5 — 65
(J J Quinn) *in tch: rdn whn checked over 1f out: kpt on fnl f: no imp* **7/1**

015 **5** *shd* **Balakiref**^{1} [2744] 8-10-0 **75**.. PhillipMakin 1 — 76
(M Dods) *s.i.s: hld up: hdwy over 1f out: no imp fnl f* **11/4**^{1}

6/00 **6** *2* **Royal Engineer**^{133} [384] 4-9-10 **74**............................... GregFairley$^{(3)}$ 2 — 69
(M Johnston) *chsd ldrs: drvn over 2f out: no ex over 1f out* **11/1**

0330 **7** *1¼* **Memphis Man**^{22} [2108] 4-8-9 **56** oh3.................................. JimmyQuinn 4 — 47
(W M Brisbourne) *s.i.s: hld up in tch: drvn and outpcd over 2f out: n.d after* **11/2**

-035 **8** *nk* **Lake Chini (IRE)**^{15} [2339] 5-10-0 **75**................................(b) DaleGibson 9 — 65
(M W Easterby) *chsd ldrs tl rdn and wknd over 1f out* **4/1**^{2}

1m 12.7s (-0.40) **Going Correction** 0.0s/f (Good) — **8** Ran SP% **120.8**

Speed ratings (Par 103):102,101,99,98,98 95,94,93

CSF £34.51 CT £419.19 TOTE £3.70: £1.20, £2.40, £4.50; EX 26.10.

Owner D W Barker **Bred** Mrs Deborah O'Brien **Trained** Scorton, N Yorks

FOCUS

Another ordinary handicap in which the early pace was not overly strong. Slightly questionable form, with both the second and third out of the handicap.

2763 SCOTTISH RACING MEDIAN AUCTION MAIDEN STKS — 1m 1f 36y

5:10 (5:14) (Class 5) 3-5-Y-O — **£3,071** (£906; £453) **Stalls** High

Form — RPR

4 **1** **Go But Go**^{14} [2376] 3-9-1 **0**... ChrisCatlin 4 — 70
(E J O'Neill) *prom: effrt and rdn over 2f out: led ins fnl f: styd on wl* **16/1**

3-24 **2** *1½* **Four Miracles**^{13} [2389] 3-8-10 **65**....................................... JimmyQuinn 6 — 62
(M H Tompkins) *hld up in tch: smooth hdwy to ld over 2f out: rdn over 1f out: hdd ins fnl f: no ex nr fin* **6/5**^{1}

3 **3** *nk* **Ducal Pip Squeak**^{36} [1746] 3-8-10 **0**................................ PhillipMakin 10 — 61
(M Dods) *prom: effrt and drvn over 2f out: kpt on wl fnl f: nrst fin* **4/1**^{3}

35-0 **4** *5* **Bret Maverick (IRE)**^{40} [1624] 3-8-12 **57**..................... JamieMoriarty$^{(3)}$ 3 — 55
(J R Weymes) *bhd: outpcd over 3f out: kpt on fnl f: no imp* **33/1**

00-0 **5** *3* **Dream On Dreamers (IRE)**^{53} [1303] 3-9-1 **33**..............(b^{1}) PaulEddery 1 — 49?
(R C Guest) *hld up in tch: drvn over 3f out: btn 2f out* **100/1**

6 **6** *2* **Glenisland**^{19} [2196] 3-8-5 **0**.. RussellKennemore$^{(5)}$ 9 — 39
(Mrs L Williamson) *towards rr: struggling over 3f out: sn btn* **25/1**

000- **7** *1* **View From The Top**^{179} [6933] 3-9-1 **68**.......................... PaulMulrennan 8 — 42
(Sir Mark Prescott) *led to over 2f out: sn wknd* **6/1**

8 *18* **Pay Or Pay**^{46} 5-9-7 **0**... MichaelJStainton$^{(5)}$ 2 — 3
(P S McEntee) *s.i.s: rdn and lost tch fr over 4f out* **66/1**

4 **9** *19* **Allaire**^{79} [884] 3-8-7 **0**... GregFairley$^{(3)}$ 7 — —
(M Johnston) *unruly bef s and in stalls: chsd ldrs tl wknd qckly over 3f out* **7/2**^{2}

2m 0.22s (0.56) **Going Correction** 0.0s/f (Good)

WFA 3 from 5yo 11lb — **9** Ran SP% **117.1**

Speed ratings (Par 103):97,95,95,90,88 86,85,69,52

CSF £36.08 TOTE £15.50: £2.60, £1.10, £1.60; EX 42.90.

Owner John E Rose **Bred** J E Rose **Trained** Averham Park, Notts

FOCUS

A weak maiden in which the pace was just fair, run in a slower time than the earlier fillies' handicap. Improvement from the winner, but the runner-up was below par.

Allaire Official explanation: jockey said filly became upset in the stalls

2764 BETFAIR APPRENTICE TRAINING SERIES H'CAP (ROUND 1) ("BETFAIR APPRENTICE TRAINING RACE" SERIES) — 1m 4f 17y

5:45 (5:46) (Class 6) (0-60,55) 4-Y-O+ — **£2,388** (£705; £352) **Stalls** High

Form — RPR

6-03 **1** **Compton Dragon (USA)**^{8} [2531] 8-9-3 **53**................ KirstyMilczarek 13 — 61
(W M Brisbourne) *hld up: hdwy over 2f out: led ins fnl f: hung lft: r.o wl* **8/1**

4024 **2** ½ **Qaasi (USA)**[124] 482 5-9-0 **55** .... PatrickDonaghy(5) 11 62
(M Brittain) *led: rdn over 3f out: hdd ins fnl f: rallied towards fin* **9/1**

4560 **3** 4 **Regency Red (IRE)**[30] 1907 9-8-7 **50** .... Julie-AnneCumine(7) 12 52+
(W M Brisbourne) *prom: ev ch over 3f out: no ex over 1f out: eased cl home* **20/1**

621- **4** 1 **Master Nimbus**[18] 4380 7-8-11 **47** .... LukeMorris 4 46
(J J Quinn) *t.k.h: trckd ldrs: effrt 3f out: edgd lft and no ex over 1f out* **9/4[1]**

5 4 **Camolin (IRE)**[40] 1641 4-8-6 **45** .... AmyKathleenParsons(3) 6 38
(Michael McElhone, Ire) *towards rr: hdwy 3f out: nvr rchd ldrs* **20/1**

10-3 **6** 1 ¾ **Go Free**[17] 1980 6-8-12 **48** .... JamieHamblett 9 38
(J G M O'Shea) *dwlt: bhd tl styd on fr 2f out: n.d* **4/1[2]**

/62- **7** ½ **Rossin Gold (IRE)**[66] 5061 5-8-11 **47** .... NeilBrown 1 36
(P Monteith) *prom tl rdn and no ex over 2f out* **11/2[3]**

60/0 **8** 6 **Kid'Z'Play (IRE)**[10] 1490 11-9-0 **53** .... GaryBartley(3) 8 32
(J S Goldie) *chsd ldrs tl rdn and wknd fr 3f out* **14/1**

0/0- **9** 3 **Little Task**[39] 2788 9-8-9 **45** .... DanielleMcCreery 5 20
(J S Wainwright) *bhd: rdn 4f out: nvr on terms* **33/1**

60-0 **10** 1 ½ **Kyle Of Lochalsh**[10] 1457 7-8-11 **52** .... DeanHeslop(5) 3 24
(Miss Lucinda V Russell) *towards rr: drvn 4f out: sn n.d* **14/1**

0355 **11** 8 **Twilight Avenger (IRE)**[21] 2141 4-8-9 **45** ....(b) WilliamCarson 10 4
(W M Brisbourne) *tk keen holf: cl up: ev ch over 3f out: wknd over 2f out* **12/1**

00-0 **12** *dist* **Howards Dream (IRE)**[10] 955 9-8-4 **47** ow2........(t) GaryEdwards(7) 2 —
(D A Nolan) *bhd: lost tch 4f out: t.o* **100/1**

2m 39.79s (0.61) **Going Correction** 0.0s/f (Good) **12** Ran SP% **121.7**
Speed ratings (Par 101):97,96,94,93,90 89,89,85,83,82 76,—
CSF £76.99 CT £1410.09 TOTE £9.20: £2.10, £3.10, £5.70; EX 60.30 Place 6 £274.23, Place 5 £124.54..
Owner John Connor **Bred** Orpendale & Partners **Trained** Great Ness, Shropshire

FOCUS
A low-grade apprentice handicap in which the pace was sound. Very ordinary form.
T/Plt: £1,022.80 to a £1 stake. Pool: £40,072.70. 28.60 winning tickets. T/Qpdt: £30.20 to a £1 stake. Pool: £3,306.50. 80.90 winning tickets. RY

2568 KEMPTON (A.W) (R-H)
Wednesday, June 20

OFFICIAL GOING: Standard
Wind: Fresh behind Weather: Bright & breezy

2765 WEATHERBYS FINANCE APPRENTICE H'CAP (ROUND 3) 1m 2f (P)
6:10 (6:10) (Class 4) (0-80,80) 4-Y-O+ **£4,728** (£1,406; £702; £351) **Stalls** High

Form RPR

1250 **1** **Top Mark**[26] 2004 5-9-7 **78** .... HarryPoulton(3) 6 87
(J R Boyle) *mde all: hrd pressed and rdn 2f out: hld on gamely* **5/1**

-021 **2** *shd* **Night Cru**[9] 2512 4-9-12 **80** 6ex........ ThomasO'Brien 5 89
(C F Wall) *lw: chsd wnr: upsides 2f out: pushed along wl over 1f out: jst hld* **9/4[1]**

331 **3** 2 ½ **Broughtons Revival**[21] 2156 5-8-13 **70** .... AlanRutter(3) 2 74
(W J Musson) *chsd ldng pair: swtchd lft and rdn wl over 1f out: kpt on same pce* **4/1[3]**

-500 **4** ¾ **Burgundy**[42] 1591 10-9-0 **68** ....(b) JackMitchell 4 71
(P Mitchell) *hld up in midfield: hdwy over 3f out: chsd ldrs and rdn over 2f out: kpt on same pce* **14/1**

-005 **5** *hd* **Transvestite (IRE)**[18] 2238 5-9-6 **77** .... MCGeran(3) 1 79
(J W Hills) *hld up bhd: hdwy on outer 3f out: rdn over 2f out: kpt on same pce* **11/4[2]**

000- **6** 5 **Ringsider (IRE)**[333] 3748 6-9-2 **75** .... MarkCoumbe(5) 7 67
(Declan Gillespie, Ire) *rrd in stalls and slowly away: hld up in last: clsd over 3f out: rdn wl over 2f out: sn outpcd* **16/1**

2/1- **7** 3 ½ **Sir Haydn**[532] 33 7-9-1 **74** .... JosephWalsh(5) 3 59
(J R Jenkins) *t.k.h: hld up in midfield: hdwy over 3f out: rdn over 2f out: sn outpcd* **12/1**

2m 9.95s (0.95) **Going Correction** -0.05s/f (Stan) **7** Ran SP% **114.3**
Speed ratings (Par 105):94,93,91,91,91 87,84
CSF £16.70 TOTE £6.30: £3.60, £1.80; EX 23.70.
Owner M Khan X2 **Bred** Ewar Stud Farms **Trained** Epsom, Surrey

FOCUS
This was run at a very sedate pace and the best place to be in races run like this is at the front. The first two home occupied those positions throughout and the winning time was 2.84 seconds slower than the following fillies' maiden. Modest form for the grade, unlikely to prove reliable.

2766 DAY TIME, NIGHT TIME, GREAT TIME, MAIDEN FILLIES' STKS 1m 2f (P)
6:40 (6:44) (Class 5) 3-Y-0+ **£2,914** (£867; £433; £216) **Stalls** High

Form RPR

1 **Rose Street (IRE)** 3-8-12 0........ PhilipRobinson 2 81+
(M A Jarvis) *tall: lengthy: scope: lw: chsd ldr 8f out: led jst over 2f out: rdn and styd on wl* **4/1[2]**

2 1 ½ **Salsa Verdi (USA)** 3-8-12 0........ TedDurcan 13 78+
(Saeed Bin Suroor) *lengthy: tall: lw: in tch: pushed along and hdwy 6f out: rdn to chse wnr 2f out: sn hung rt: no imp fnl f* **4/1[2]**

3 3 ½ **Alma Mater** 4-9-10 0........ SebSanders 11 74+
(Sir Mark Prescott) *w'like: str: bit bkwd: pushed along and dropped to rr after 1f: hdwy over 3f out: nt clr run wl over 1f out: swtchd rt and squeezed through over 1f out: chsd ldng pair 1f out: kpt on* **9/4[1]**

0 **4** 2 **Madam Vouvray**[12] 2429 3-8-12 0........ SteveDrowne 6 67
(B J Meehan) *chsd ldrs: rdn over 3f out: kpt on same pce u.p last 2f* **25/1**

0-3 **5** ½ **Montjeu's Melody (IRE)**[26] 1988 3-8-12 0........ EddieAhern 1 66
(J W Hills) *lw: chsd ldrs: rdn and lost pl 4f out: kpt on past btn horses u.p fnl f* **14/1**

5-0 **6** 1 ½ **Tebee**[61] 1127 3-8-12 0........ JimmyFortune 5 63+
(J H M Gosden) *lw: led tl over 8f out: chsd ldrs: rdn wl over 2f out: sn wknd wl over 1f out* **13/2**

00- **7** 3 ½ **Dubai Shadow (IRE)**[299] 4765 3-8-12 0........ HayleyTurner 12 56
(C E Brittain) *bit bkwd: hld up towards rr: pushed along 7f out: sme hdwy over 3f out: wknd 2f out* **50/1**

60 **8** *hd* **Catherine Palace**[14] 2359 3-8-12 0........ JHBowman 4 56
(E A L Dunlop) *s.i.s: racd in midfield: hdwy to chse ldrs 5f out: rdn over 3f out: wknd over 2f out* **50/1**

9 *shd* **Thermidora** 3-8-12 0........ OscarUrbina 8 55
(J R Fanshawe) *unruly in stalls: hld up in midfield: hdwy on inner 4f out: wkng whn bmpd over 1f out: no ch after* **25/1**

10 *shd* **Adorabella (IRE)**[103] 4-9-10 0........ DaneO'Neill 14 55
(A King) *hld up towards rr: rdn wl over 2f out: no prog* **33/1**

0-2 **11** 2 ½ **Hypoteneuse (IRE)**[33] 1816 3-8-12 0........ RyanMoore 3 50
(Sir Michael Stoute) *pushed along to ld over 8f out: rdn and hdd jst over 2f out: sn wknd* **9/2[3]**

6 **12** 9 **Littlemissdynamite**[21] 2153 4-9-10 0........ RobertHavlin 10 32
(J McAuley) *swtg: hld up in rr: rdn over 3f out: wknd over 2f out: eased whn no ch fnl f* **66/1**

0-00 **13** 34 **Astarte**[8] 2542 3-8-12 0........ JimCrowley 9 —
(P R Chamings) *v.s.a: bhd and rn wd bnd over 7f out: t.o and eased last 2f* **66/1**

2m 7.11s (-1.89) **Going Correction** -0.05s/f (Stan)
WFA 3 from 4yo 12lb **13** Ran SP% **126.5**
Speed ratings (Par 100):105,103,101,99,99 97,95,94,94,94 92,85,58
CSF £20.78 TOTE £6.60: £2.20, £1.90, £1.40; EX 34.00.
Owner Mr & Mrs Raymond Anderson Green **Bred** Margaret Conlon **Trained** Newmarket, Suffolk
■ Stewards' Enquiry : Seb Sanders two-day ban: careless riding (Jul 2-3)

FOCUS
Probably a decent maiden, with the first three all well-bred newcomers. The time was reasonable and the fifth, seventh and eighth give some substance to the bare form.
Hypoteneuse(IRE) Official explanation: trainers' representative said filly had a breathing problem

2767 AZURE HOSPITALITY H'CAP 1m 2f (P)
7:10 (7:12) (Class 4) (0-85,81) 3-Y-0 **£4,728** (£1,406; £702; £351) **Stalls** High

Form RPR

0114 **1** **Guiseppe Verdi (USA)**[12] 2426 3-9-7 **81** .... JimmyFortune 5 92
(J H M Gosden) *lw: s.i.s: led 8f out: mde rest: rdn and qcknd over 1f out: r.o wl* **7/4[1]**

450 **2** 1 ¼ **Gold Prospect**[13] 2402 3-9-3 **77** .... JamieSpencer 1 85+
(M L W Bell) *s.i.s: dropped in bhd: last and plld wd 2f out: sn rdn: r.o wl to chse wnr ins fnl f: nvr nrr* **4/1[3]**

1-00 **3** 1 ½ **Feeling Wonderful (IRE)**[44] 1531 3-8-5 **65** .... JoeFanning 8 70
(M Johnston) *t.k.h: led tl 8f out: chsd wnr after: rdn 2f out: sn hung rt and nt qckn: lost 2nd ins fnl f* **20/1**

5512 **4** 1 ¾ **Mutual Friend (USA)**[12] 2413 3-9-4 **78** .... SebSanders 7 81+
(E A L Dunlop) *plld hrd: trckd ldng pair: rdn over 1f out: n.m.r and no imp fnl f* **5/2[2]**

1500 **5** *nk* **Sir Liam (USA)**[6] 2598 3-9-1 **75** .... JimCrowley 6 76
(P Mitchell) *t.k.h: hld up in tch: rdn and effrt 2f out: kpt on same pce fnl f* **14/1**

10-0 **6** 1 **Emulate**[29] 1929 3-9-3 **77** .... RichardHughes 2 76
(B W Hills) *s.i.s: hld up in last pair: rdn jst over 1f out: no imp* **16/1**

1006 **7** ½ **Alfresco**[14] 2354 3-9-5 **79** ....(b) DaneO'Neill 3 77
(Pat Eddery) *s.i.s: rdn and effrt wl over 1f out: kpt on same pce* **7/1**

0-05 **8** 5 **Soldier Field**[18] 2261 3-8-8 **68** .... FrancisNorton 4 56
(A M Balding) *s.i.s: hdwy 3f out: rdn over 2f out: wknd over 1f out* **33/1**

2m 8.47s (-0.53) **Going Correction** -0.05s/f (Stan) **8** Ran SP% **117.7**
Speed ratings (Par 101):100,99,97,96,96 95,94,90
CSF £9.49 CT £103.94 TOTE £2.60: £1.30, £1.50, £3.40; EX 11.10.
Owner H R H Princess Haya Of Jordan **Bred** Runnymede Farm Inc And Catesby W Clay **Trained** Newmarket, Suffolk

FOCUS
The pace was modest until the favourite took the race by the scruff of the neck with a circuit left. The first two home received contrasting rides and it was the winner that was in the ideal place as things turned out. The winner is progressive and the form has been rated positively, around the fourth. The runner-up is better than the bare form.
Emulate Official explanation: jockey said filly was denied a clear run.

2768 EUROPEAN BREEDERS' FUND MAIDEN FILLIES' STKS 7f (P)
7:40 (7:41) (Class 5) 2-Y-0 **£3,562** (£1,059; £529; £264) **Stalls** High

Form RPR

1 **Dixey** 2-9-0 0........ PhilipRobinson 10 84+
(M A Jarvis) *w'like: scope: lengthy: lw: wnt lft s: t.k.h: chsd ldrs: hdwy over 3f out: rdn to ld over 1f out: edgd lft but r.o wl fnl f* **20/1**

2 **2** 1 ½ **Gypsy Baby (IRE)**[11] 2468 2-9-0 0........ RyanMoore 4 80
(R Hannon) *hld up in tch: hdwy 3f out: rdn to ld 2f out: hdd jst over 1f out: edgd lft and no ex fnl f* **1/1[1]**

6 **3** *shd* **Lady Aquitaine (USA)**[33] 1814 2-9-0 0........ SteveDrowne 1 80
(B J Meehan) *hld up in tch: hdwy over 3f out: rdn and ev ch wl over 2f out: edgd lft and one pce fnl f* **14/1**

4 2 **Kay Es Jay (FR)** 2-9-0 0........ MichaelHills 5 75+
(B W Hills) *w'like: scope: str: bhd: hdwy wl over 2f out: r.o wl fnl f: nt rch ldrs* **9/2[3]**

5 3 **Pampas (USA)** 2-9-0 0........ RichardHughes 2 67
(R Charlton) *hld up in midfield: hdwy 4f out: rdn 3f out: edgd rt and kpt on same pce after* **20/1**

022 **6** ¾ **Pixie's Blue (IRE)**[26] 2000 2-9-0 0........ JimmyFortune 6 65
(J H M Gosden) *lw: pressed ldr: rdn over 2f out: wknd qckly over 1f out* **11/4[2]**

7 2 ½ **Starfala** 2-9-0 0........ TQuinn 8 59
(P F I Cole) *neat: str: towrds rr: rdn over 3f out: outpcd 3f out: kpt on* **33/1**

8 5 **Dawn Wind** 2-9-0 0........ JimCrowley 7 46
(I A Wood) *unf: scope: bit bkwd: sn rdn and outpcd: nvr on terms* **66/1**

03 **9** *hd* **Suite Francaise**[15] 2344 2-9-0 0........ SebSanders 9 45
(Sir Mark Prescott) *hld up in midfield: rdn 3f out: sn wknd* **16/1**

00 **10** 1 **Fly Kiss**[39] 1680 2-9-0 0........ EddieAhern 11 42
(C E Brittain) *led tl rdn and hdd 2f out: sn wknd* **66/1**

11 6 **Safiyeh** 2-9-0 0........ PaulFitzsimons 12 27
(M J Attwater) *pushed along and bhd: hdwy on inner 4f out: rdn and wknd wl over 2f out* **66/1**

12 6 **Infinite Patience** 2-9-0 0........ JohnEgan 3 11+
(J S Moore) *unf: s.i.s: hung lft thrght: hdwy 5f out: chsd ldrs over 3f: wknd wl over 2f out: eased fnl f* **16/1**

1m 26.98s (0.18) **Going Correction** -0.05s/f (Stan) **12** Ran SP% **130.2**
Speed ratings (Par 90):96,94,94,91,88 87,84,79,78,77 70,63
CSF £42.91 TOTE £19.10: £3.90, £1.20, £3.00; EX 67.20.
Owner T G Warner **Bred** Red House Stud **Trained** Newmarket, Suffolk

FOCUS
This was run at a good pace and the time was good for the type of contest. They finished well spread out. The winner made a nice debut, but just how good this form is remains to be seen.

NOTEBOOK
Dixey ◆, a sister to the yard's multiple sand winner Dichoh, was always close to the pace and when it looked as though she might be overhauled, she pulled out a bit more and was well on top at the line. She should improve and there are likely to be plenty more races to be won with her. (op 16-1)
Gypsy Baby(IRE), up a furlong from her promising Newbury debut, had every chance but ran into a talented newcomer and there seemed to be no excuses. She will get further than this in time and should find her maiden before too much longer. (op 13-8)

Lady Aquitaine(USA), another tackling an extra furlong on her second start, was brought with a withering run down the wide outside in the home straight but her effort flattened out in the closing stages. There should be a similar race in her, especially when her yard is in generally better form. (tchd 12-1)

Kay Es Jay(FR) ◆, a 100,000euros sister to a winning juvenile in Scandinavia, was noted putting in some good late work on this racecourse debut and she can be expected to improve from this. (op 6-1 tchd 4-1)

Pampas(USA), a sister to the smart Exterior and half-sister to the useful Acrobatic and Verbose, showed enough on this debut to suggest she will not let the family down and she should improve with racing over a bit further. (op 16-1)

Pixie's Blue(IRE), the most experienced in the field, showed up for a long away but dropped away rather tamely and this was a step backwards. It does appear she is better on turf than on sand.
Official explanation: jockey said filly ran too free (op 5-2 tchd 7-2)

2769 DIGIBET H'CAP 6f (P)

8:10 (8:10) (Class 4) (0-80,82) 3-Y-O £4,728 (£1,406; £702; £351) Stalls High

Form RPR

5321 1 **Mac Gille Eoin**[5] 2629 3-9-9 82 6ex................................ JimCrowley 3 90
(J Gallagher) *mde all: rdn over 1f out: stormed clr fnl f* 7/4[1]

1-0 2 2 1/2 **Fabuleux Millie (IRE)**[14] 2373 3-9-4 77.......................... GeorgeBaker 8 78
(R M Beckett) *t.k.h: trckd ldrs: rdn over 2f out: styd on u.p fnl f: wnt 2nd wl ins fnl f: no ch w wnr* 10/1

-210 3 hd **Buxton**[13] 2400 3-9-7 80.. RobertHavlin 7 80
(R Ingram) *hld up in midfield: rdn and effrt 2f out: styd on u.p fnl f: wnt 3rd nr fin: no ch w wnr* 16/1

31-3 4 hd **Sunoverregun**[7] 2570 3-9-7 80....................................... JimmyFortune 1 79
(J R Boyle) *lw: sn chsng wnr: rdn over 2f out: kpt on same pce: lost 2 pls wl ins fnl f* 9/4[2]

0042 5 1 3/4 **Mr Loire**[17] 2276 3-9-4 77..(b) DaneO'Neill 6 71
(H J L Dunlop) *hld up in tch: rdn and effrt 2f out: no imp fnl f* 16/1

532 6 1/2 **Kelamon**[5] 2622 3-8-5 64.. HayleyTurner 5 57
(M D I Usher) *t.k.h: hld up in rr on outer: rdn over 3f out: n.d after* 8/1

6-12 7 shd **High Tribute**[140] 312 3-9-2 75.......................................(t) SebSanders 9 67
(Sir Mark Prescott) *t.k.h: chsd ldrs: rdn and chsd wnr briefly jst over 2f out: wknd over 1f out* 4/1[3]

50-0 8 3/4 **Pelican Key (IRE)**[60] 1160 3-9-5 78........................... RichardHughes 2 68
(D M Simcock) *s.i.s: effrt on rail 2f out: sn no imp: wknd fnl f* 33/1

1m 13.63s (-0.07) **Going Correction** -0.05s/f (Stan) 8 Ran SP% 122.0
Speed ratings (Par 101):98,94,94,94,91 91,91,90
CSF £22.51 CT £227.59 TOTE £2.70: £1.10, £2.80, £6.80; EX 24.90.
Owner M C S D Racing Partnership **Bred** M C S D Racing Ltd **Trained** Moreton-in-Marsh, Gloucs

FOCUS
A fair little sprint handicap in which the favourite had the run of the race out in front and made the most of it. He has improved again, but neither placed horse came into the race looking well treated.

2770 DIGIBET SPORTS BETTING H'CAP 2m (P)

8:40 (8:41) (Class 6) (0-65,65) 4-Y-O+ £2,047 (£604; £302) Stalls High

Form RPR

213 1 **Colwyn Bay (IRE)**[28] 1942 5-8-10 54.........................(p) JamieSpencer 7 65
(Jane Chapple-Hyam) *lw: hld up in midfield: c wd and hdwy 3f out: led over 1f out: veered lft ins fnl f: rdn out* 2/1[1]

3031 2 1 1/2 **Mister Completely (IRE)**[19] 2222 6-9-5 63.................. JamesDoyle 14 72
(Ms J S Doyle) *lw: chsd ldrs: rdn and hdwy 4f out: drvn to ld 2f out: hdd jst over 1f out: kpt on same pce* 20/1

-211 3 3 **Gaelic Roulette (IRE)**[29] 1925 7-8-8 52......................... JoeFanning 12 57
(J Jay) *hld up in midfield: rdn and hdwy over 3f out: ev ch wl over 1f out: outpcd fnl f* 7/2[2]

2-05 4 2 1/2 **Coda Agency**[12] 2430 4-8-11 55.. JimCrowley 5 57
(D W P Arbuthnot) *lw: hld up in rr: gd hdwy 4f out: chsd ldrs and rdn over 2f out: wknd fnl f* 12/1

31-5 5 4 **Grasp**[15] 302 5-9-2 60...(v) RyanMoore 8 58
(G L Moore) *lw: hld up wl in tch: rdn over 3f out: sn btn* 8/1

0/34 6 2 1/2 **Festive Chimes (IRE)**[25] 913 6-9-0 61..................... JerryO'Dwyer(3) 1 56
(N B King) *chsd ldr for 4f: wnt 2nd again 6f out: rdn over 3f out: wknd wl over 1f out* 16/1

0012 7 1 1/4 **Ganymede**[12] 2430 6-8-13 57... IanMongan 3 50
(Mrs L J Mongan) *squeezed s: dropped in bhd: rdn and effrt on outer 5f out: kpt on fnl f: nvr able to chal* 13/2[3]

610/ 8 1/2 **In Deep**[610] 5320 6-8-9 53.. RobertHavlin 10 46
(Mrs P N Dutfield) *hld up bhd: rdn 5f out: wknd 3f out* 50/1

0-00 9 nk **Don'Tcallmeginger (IRE)**[12] 2430 4-8-9 56............ SaleemGolam(3) 13 48
(M H Tompkins) *hld up in midfield: rdn over 3f out: sn struggling: no ch last 2f* 50/1

102 10 5 **Pentasilea**[12] 2434 4-9-7 65.. SebSanders 4 51
(H J L Dunlop) *lw: prom: chsd ldr after 4f: led 8f out: rdn 3f out: hdd 2f out: sn wknd* 17/2

-540 11 4 **Gatecrasher**[12] 2430 4-9-2 60......................................(v[1]) JimmyFortune 2 41
(Pat Eddery) *sn led: hdd 8f out: chsd ldr tl 6f out: rdn and wknd over 3f out* 16/1

600/ 12 2 **Cambo (FR)**[47] 1586 6-8-9 56.. NeilChalmers(3) 11 35
(Miss Sheena West) *a bhd: rdn and lost tch 3f out* 50/1

3m 29.03s (-2.37) **Going Correction** -0.05s/f (Stan) 12 Ran SP% 120.6
Speed ratings (Par 101):103,102,100,99,97 96,95,95,95,92 90,89
CSF £47.91 CT £121.37 TOTE £2.90: £1.10, £3.70, £1.70; EX 52.20.
Owner Philip M Hickey **Bred** Tower Bloodstock **Trained** Newmarket, Suffolk
■ Broughtons Folly was withdrawn (10/1, refused to enter stalls.) R4 applies, deduct 5p in the £.

FOCUS
A truly-run handicap. The winner was up 5lb, while the runner-up produced a personal best.

2771 DIGITOTE H'CAP 7f (P)

9:10 (9:10) (Class 4) (0-85,85) 3-Y-O+ £4,728 (£1,406; £702; £351) Stalls High

Form RPR

10-5 1 **Secret Liaison**[15] 2346 4-9-11 82...................................... SebSanders 11 93
(Sir Mark Prescott) *prom: led 5f out: mde rest: rdn over 2f out: hld on gamely u.p fnl f: edgd lft nr fin: all out* 7/1

2500 2 nk **Electric Warrior (IRE)**[11] 2466 4-9-6 77..................... FergusSweeney 1 87
(K R Burke) *hld up in tch on outer: rdn and effrt jst over 2f out: str run fnl f: wnt 2nd nr fin: nvr nrr* 20/1

0002 3 nk **Resplendent Nova**[7] 2573 5-9-13 84.............................. JamieSpencer 3 93
(P Howling) *hld up in tch: gd hdwy on inner over 2f out: sn ev ch: unable qck and edgd lft nr fin* 11/2[2]

1604 4 3/4 **Mujood**[11] 2440 4-9-9 80...(v) StephenCarson 4 87
(Eve Johnson Houghton) *lw: sn pressing ldrs: rdn 3f out: kpt on u.p fnl f* 10/1

-462 5 1 1/2 **Master Pegasus**[13] 2401 4-10-0 85................................ GeorgeBaker 10 88
(C F Wall) *lw: hld up in tch: hdwy on inner 4f out: chsd wnr over 3f out: ev ch 2f out: wknd ins fnl f* 4/1[1]

0000 6 1/2 **Hollow Jo**[29] 1931 7-8-12 69... EddieAhern 7 71
(J R Jenkins) *lw: t.k.h: trckd ldrs: rdn 3f out: kpt on same pce u.p* 33/1

1201 7 1/2 **Sailor King (IRE)**[7] 2573 5-9-10 81 6ex............................ JimCrowley 2 81
(D K Ivory) *s.i.s: hld up in rr: rdn and effrt over 2f out: kpt on: nt pce to rch ldrs* 8/1

2151 8 3 **Nikki Bea (IRE)**[28] 1947 4-8-9 66 oh1.................................. JohnEgan 9 58
(Jamie Poulton) *trckd ldrs: rdn wl over 2f out: wknd over 1f out* 10/1

1003 9 1 1/4 **Bonnie Prince Blue**[7] 2573 4-9-8 79................................ MichaelHills 5 68
(B W Hills) *hld up in rr: rdn wl over 2f out: no imp* 4/1[1]

-100 10 21 **Autograph Hunter**[25] 2045 3-9-1 81.................................. JoeFanning 6 13
(M Johnston) *stdd sn after s: racd in midfield: rdn over 4f out: btn 3f out: eased fnl f: t.o* 16/1

600- 11 3 1/2 **Namid Reprobate (IRE)**[250] 5943 4-9-12 83........................ TQuinn 8 6
(P F I Cole) *led for 2f: rdn 4f out: wknd 3f out: eased fnl f: t.o* 6/1[3]

1m 25.93s (-0.87) **Going Correction** -0.05s/f (Stan)
WFA 3 from 4yo+ 9lb 11 Ran SP% 125.0
Speed ratings (Par 105):102,101,101,100,98 98,97,94,92,68 64
CSF £145.64 CT £856.35 TOTE £8.80: £2.00, £7.60, £2.60; EX 172.00 Place 6 £15.03, Place 5 £7.10..
Owner W E Sturt - Osborne House **Bred** Cheveley Park Stud Ltd **Trained** Newmarket, Suffolk

FOCUS
A fair handicap and the form looks pretty solid, rated through the third and fourth.
Bonnie Prince Blue Official explanation: trainer had no explanation for the poor form shown
T/Plt: £19.50 to a £1 stake. Pool: £56,273.00. 2,096.75 winning tickets. T/Qpdt: £8.80 to a £1 stake. Pool: £6,176.50. 514.30 winning tickets. SP

2371 RIPON (R-H)

Wednesday, June 20

2772 Meeting Abandoned - Waterlogged

2778 - 2784a (Foreign Racing) - See Raceform Interactive

2752 ASCOT (R-H)

Thursday, June 21

OFFICIAL GOING: Good to firm (firm in places on straight course; good in places on round course) (overall: 10.0; straight 12.0; round 8.7)
Wind: Moderate, across Weather: Showers

2785 NORFOLK STKS (GROUP 2) 5f

2:30 (2:32) (Class 1) 2-Y-O

£39,746 (£15,064; £7,539; £3,759; £1,883; £945) Stalls Centre

Form RPR

1 1 **Winker Watson**[62] 1123 2-9-1 0.................................... JimmyFortune 16 107+
(P W Chapple-Hyam) *lw: dwlt: hld up: hdwy over 2f out: led 1f out: sn hung lft: r.o and in command towards fin* 2/1[1]

21 2 1 1/4 **Art Advisor (IRE)**[24] 2071 2-9-1 0.................................... SebSanders 3 101
(J Howard Johnson) *lw: a.p: rdn and edgd lft over 1f out: ev ch ins fnl f: nt qckn towards fin* 14/1

11 3 shd **Spirit Of Sharjah (IRE)**[42] 1608 2-9-1 0........................ KerrinMcEvoy 6 100
(Miss J Feilden) *racd keenly: hld up: rdn and hdwy over 2f out: r.o towards fin* 9/2[3]

2232 4 1 **Silver Guest**[33] 1846 2-9-1 0.. DarryllHolland 4 97
(M R Channon) *s.i.s: hld up: nt clr run over 1f out: r.o ins fnl f: pushed along and gaining towards fin* 33/1

1 5 hd **Strike The Deal (USA)**[7] 2590 2-9-1 0.............................. JMurtagh 10 96
(J Noseda) *racd keenly: a.p: led over 2f out: hdd 1f out: no ex towards fin* 25/1

101 6 1/2 **Carleton**[5] 2650 2-9-1 0... JHBowman 8 94
(M R Channon) *lw: hld up bhd ldrs: effrt whn nt clr run over 1f out: sn swtchd rt: styd on ins fnl f* 66/1

1 7 3/4 **Roker Park (IRE)**[16] 2337 2-9-1 0.................................... PatCosgrave 2 91
(K R Burke) *midfield: rdn 2f out: hung lft fr over 1f out: nt pce of ldrs* 16/1

12 8 1 3/4 **Bespoke Boy**[19] 2232 2-9-1 0.. LDettori 15 85
(P C Haslam) *led: hdd over 2f out: rdn over 1f out: wknd ins fnl f* 6/1

521 9 nk **Jebel Tara**[7] 2604 2-9-1 0.. RyanMoore 9 84
(C E Brittain) *w'like: prom: rdn 2f out: wknd over 1f out* 50/1

1 10 3/4 **Warsaw (IRE)**[45] 1546 2-9-1 0... MJKinane 11 81+
(A P O'Brien, Ire) *cmpt: in tch: rdn over 2f out: wknd over 1f out: eased whn btn wl ins fnl f* 3/1[2]

0115 11 5 **Cracking (IRE)**[19] 2232 2-9-1 0..................................... RichardHughes 1 63
(R Hannon) *wnt lft s: midfield: rdn over 2f out: sn lost pl and bhd* 25/1

60.83 secs (-0.57) **Going Correction** -0.05s/f (Good) 11 Ran SP% 117.4
Speed ratings (Par 105):102,100,99,98,97 97,95,93,92,91 83
CSF £30.82 TOTE £3.40: £1.70, £3.40, £1.90; EX 37.00 Trifecta £154.80 Pool: £12,155.38 - 55.75 winning tickets..
Owner The Comic Strip Heroes & Mrs J D Trotter **Bred** Mrs John Trotter **Trained** Newmarket, Suffolk
■ The fifth and final winner of the week for Jimmy Fortune, the meeting's top rider.

FOCUS
A step up from the impressive Winker Watson, although he is still 5lb off the figure recorded by his stablemate Dutch Art last year. The next three all improved too and the form is very solid.

NOTEBOOK

Winker Watson ◆ won the same Newbury maiden as Turtle Island, Chapple-Hyam's Norfolk winner in 1993. After a slow start, he made up the ground towards the far side before picking up well to lead with a furlong to run. He hung left in front and possibly idled a little, but was not unduly troubled and won with a bit to spare. A step up to 6f will suit him and races like the Prix Morny and the Middle Park Stakes look obvious targets for this bright prospect. (op 9-4 tchd 7-4)

Art Advisor(IRE), whose stable won this at York two years ago with Masta Plasta, was always in the front rank. He stuck on well, and there was no disgrace in this defeat by a smart opponent. Genuine good ground will suit him and the Gimcrack at York could be his next port of call. (op 16-1 tchd 20-1 in places)

Spirit Of Sharjah(IRE) ◆, already a winner at Listed level, ran well on this step up in grade. A keen individual, able to get some cover in a strongly-run race, he ran on well inside the last and would have been second in another stride. He will appreciate another furlong. (op 5-1 tchd 11-2 in places)

Silver Guest, who was a bit slow away from the stalls, briefly had to wait for a run but was keeping on nicely inside the last without his rider getting too tough with him. A return to 6f will suit and he is overdue his first success, although it could be that he is the type to run well in defeat. (op 50-1)

Strike The Deal(USA), who made a winning debut on the Lingfield Polytrack a week earlier, showed plenty of pace on this turf debut and only faded out of the frame inside the last.
Carleton, making a quick reappearance, came home strongly after having to be switched over a furlong out. A step up to 6f ought to suit him.
Roker Park(IRE), successful in an ordinary event at Ripon on his debut, ran creditably on this step up in class but hung across the track under pressure in the latter stages. (tchd 20-1 in places)
Bespoke Boy, who failed to handle the track at Epsom, showed bright early pace on this first try over the minimum trip. (tchd 13-2)
Warsaw(IRE), winner of both his previous starts including a Listed event in which he had today's fourth behind, was never really travelling and failed to run his race. Official explanation: trainer had no explanation for the poor form shown (op 9-4 tchd 7-2)
Cracking(IRE) Official explanation: jockey said colt never travelled

2786 RIBBLESDALE STKS (GROUP 2) (FILLIES) 1m 4f

3:05 (3:05) (Class 1) 3-Y-O

£79,446 (£30,110; £15,069; £7,513; £3,763; £1,888) **Stalls** High

Form RPR

121 **1** **Silkwood**[55] [1277] 3-8-12 92 PhilipRobinson 2 117
(M A Jarvis) *t.k.h: settled towards rr on outside: gd hdwy ent st: led wl over 1f out: hung left: rdn clr* **4/1**[2]

23 **2** *5* **All My Loving (IRE)**[20] [2211] 3-8-12 MJKinane 8 109
(A P O'Brien, Ire) *lw: dwlt: sn rdn up to chse ldrs: pshd along fr 1/2-wy: kpt on u.p to take 2nd ins fnl f: nt pce of wnr* **15/8**[1]

1-10 **3** *1 1/4* **Dalvina**[20] [2211] 3-8-12 109 JamieSpencer 5 107+
(E A L Dunlop) *hld up towards rr: gd hdwy on outside over 2f out: briefly wnt 2nd over 1f out: one pce* **8/1**

16- **4** *3/4* **Baroness Richter (IRE)**[55] 3-8-12 C-PLemaire 1 106
(J-C Rouget, France) *b: hld up in rr: styd on u.p fnl 2f: nvr nrr* **16/1**

61 **5** *nk* **Marzelline (IRE)**[15] [2360] 3-8-12 AdamKirby 11 105
(W R Swinburn) *hld up towards rr: sme hdwy and hrd rdn 2f out: nt pce to chal* **33/1**

-533 **6** *3 1/2* **Majounes Song**[7] [2599] 3-8-12 88 J-PGuillambert 3 100
(M Johnston) *lw: led tl wl over 1f out: sn wknd* **16/1**

11 **7** *3 1/2* **Cosmodrome (USA)**[28] [1958] 3-8-12 103 LDettori 4 94
(L M Cumani) *in tch: hrd rdn over 2f out: sn btn* **5/1**[3]

3-45 **8** *6* **Hanging On**[43] [1581] 3-8-12 92 TedDurcan 6 85
(W R Swinburn) *mid-div: rdn and lost pl 5f out: n.d after* **50/1**

14-4 **9** *1 1/2* **Shorthand**[36] [1769] 3-8-12 101 KerrinMcEvoy 12 82
(Sir Michael Stoute) *hld up in midfield: effrt on ins 3f out: sn wknd: btn whn n.m.r over 2f out* **9/1**

11-2 **10** *3* **Party (IRE)**[15] [2384] 3-8-12 94 RichardHughes 10 77
(R Hannon) *prom: shkn up 5f out: hrd rdn and wknd over 2f out* **16/1**

0-04 **11** *9* **Lost In Wonder (USA)**[28] [1958] 3-8-12 92 (v[1]) RyanMoore 9 63
(Sir Michael Stoute) *lw: sn chsng ldr: wknd qckly over 2f out* **25/1**

3-56 **12** *14* **Fascinatin Rhythm**[46] [1499] 3-8-12 82 SebSanders 7 41
(V Smith) *a bhd* **100/1**

2m 30.23s (-2.77) **Going Correction** +0.025s/f (Good) **12** Ran SP% **119.9**
Speed ratings (Par 108):110,106,105,105,105 102,100,96,95,93 87,78
CSF £11.72 TOTE £5.60: £2.00, £1.20, £2.90; EX 14.70 Trifecta £92.90 Pool: £10,042.04 - 76.68 winning tickets..
Owner Sheikh Mohammed **Bred** Darley **Trained** Newmarket, Suffolk

FOCUS

A typically intriguing renewal of this Group 2 prize, run at a searching early pace. Silkwood produced a most taking display and is an above-average winner of this race. She looks a Group 1 filly in the making and has been rated only 3lb behind Oaks winner Light Shift, even though the runner-up might not have been at her best here.

NOTEBOOK

Silkwood ◆, a handicap winner from a mark of 83 on her turf debut at Sandown in April, is clearly highly regarded and had been nibbled at in the ante-post betting for the Oaks, but her connections opted to miss that on account of the soft ground. That decision paid dividends here and she confirmed her reputation with a most taking success on this big step up in class. Despite the strong early pace she still took her time to settle under restraint, but when her rider asked her to improve she made up her ground easily and produced a potent turn of foot to settle the issue nearing the final furlong. On this evidence she is a Group 1 filly in the making and, taking the runner-up as a guide, she would have surely gone very close to winning at Epsom had the ground been in her favour there. Considering this was just her fourth career start and first attempt at the distance, there should be more to come and she still looks to be learning her trade. Her connections will surely be very tempted to step her up again and supplement her for what is now shaping up to be a cracking renewal of the Irish Oaks at the Curragh next month, where she could take on the Oaks heroine Light Shift. (op 5-1 tchd 11-2 in places)
All My Loving(IRE), the Oaks third, was never really travelling with any fluency after a sluggish start and was made to look pedestrian when the winner asserted at the top of the home straight. It is to her credit that she kept to her task and bagged second, leaving the impression that she would ideally prefer easier ground - which she got at Epsom. She still rates a decent benchmark for this form and remains open to a bit more improvement. Looking further ahead, she could be the type to enjoy an even stiffer test in the Park Hill at Doncaster in September. (op 6-4 tchd 2-1 and 85-40 in places)
Dalvina, who lost her unbeaten tag when failing to handle the track and soft ground in the Oaks last time, was given a fair bit to do from off the pace yet came through to run a much-improved race which went a long way to restoring her reputation on this return to a more galloping track. She got the trip without much fuss, and further improvement looks assured, but the suspicion is that she could prove at her very best over 10f. The faster the ground the better. (op 15-2)
Baroness Richter(IRE), having her first outing in Britain since leaving Richard Hannon at the start of the year, came into this on the back of a Listed win in France over 1m2f and was ridden to get this longer trip. She had to angle out for her effort in the home straight, but when in the clear she was motoring home inside the final furlong and should be rated a little better than the bare form. Another lightly-raced filly, she can make her mark at this level before the season's end. (op 25-1 tchd 28-1)
Marzelline(IRE) ◆, a maiden winner over 1m2f last time, ran a perfectablty respectable race on this big step up in grade and is clearly a most progressive filly. She may just be better off reverting to 1m2f for the short term and can regain the winning thread when dropping into Listed company. (tchd 66-1 in a place)
Majounes Song, third in Listed company the last twice, went off too fast for her own good on this further step up in trip and not surprisingly proved a sitting duck in the home straight. This was still another improved effort in defeat, however, and she deserves to get her head in front again. No doubt she will have to drop back down in grade in order to do so, however.
Cosmodrome(USA), a Goodwood Listed winner on just her second outing 28 days previously, lost her unbeaten tag and found this all too hot. She still has to prove she gets this far, but is still too soon to write off one so inexperienced. (tchd 11-2)
Shorthand, who flopped on her seasonal bow in the Musidora, moved well until finding just the same pace off the home turn and was well beaten before meeting a little trouble on the rail around 2f marker. On the level of her final outing at two in the Rockfel behind Finsceal Beo she really ought to have the engine to make her mark in Pattern company this year, and she probably found this ground fast enough on this first attempt over 12f. However, she still has it all to prove at present.

2787 GOLD CUP (GROUP 1) 2m 4f

3:45 (3:47) (Class 1) 4-Y-O+

£127,755 (£48,420; £24,232; £12,082; £6,052; £3,037) **Stalls** High

Form RPR

0-11 **1** **Yeats (IRE)**[22] [2161] 6-9-2 0 MJKinane 2 122+
(A P O'Brien, Ire) *midfield: hdwy over 5f out: led over 2f out: asserted over 1f out: jinked sltly lft and kpt up to work ins fnl f: r.o wl and in command towards fin* **8/13**[1]

-252 **2** *1 1/2* **Geordieland (FR)**[34] [1823] 6-9-2 109 JamieSpencer 5 119
(J A Osborne) *hld up and bhd: hdwy whn nt clr run over 2f out: chsd wnr over 1f out: styd on: hld towards fin* **12/1**[3]

3-25 **3** *3 1/2* **Le Miracle (GER)**[32] [1881] 6-9-2 0 DBoeuf 7 115
(W Baltromei, Germany) *leggy: in tch: hdwy over 2f out: chsd wnr wl over 1f out: sn lost 2nd: one pce ins fnl f* **50/1**

0-34 **4** *3 1/2* **Finalmente**[33] [1844] 5-9-2 101 JMurtagh 3 112
(N A Callaghan) *trckd ldrs: rdn over 3f out: hung rt and carried hd high over 2f out: sn hung lft: no ch w front trio fnl f* **66/1**

1-03 **5** *1 1/4* **Montare (IRE)**[32] [1881] 5-8-13 0 (p) OPeslier 14 107+
(J E Pease, France) *w'like: leggy: lw: in tch: nt clr run and hmpd over 2f out: sn swtchd rt: kpt on one pce after* **12/1**[3]

14-1 **6** *7* **Lord Du Sud (FR)**[32] [1881] 6-9-2 0 C-PLemaire 8 103
(J-C Rouget, France) *w'like: leggy: led: rdn and hdd over 2f out: wknd over 1f out* **25/1**

00-2 **7** *2 1/2* **Baddam**[50] [1393] 5-9-2 108 IanMongan 6 101
(M R Channon) *midfield: hdwy over 5f out: rdn 3f out: edgd rt over 2f out: sn no imp on ldrs: wknd fnl f* **20/1**

31-4 **8** *1 1/2* **Cherry Mix (FR)**[39] [1700] 6-9-2 118 (t) LDettori 9 99
(Saeed Bin Suroor) *midfield: hdwy over 5f out: rdn whn bmpd over 2f out: wknd over 1f out* **14/1**

3-51 **9** *nk* **Allegretto (IRE)**[23] [2125] 4-8-11 107 (v) SebSanders 13 96
(Sir Michael Stoute) *racd keenly: in tch: lost pl over 5f out: n.d after* **14/1**

-033 **10** *5* **Bulwark (IRE)**[23] [2125] 5-9-2 106 (be) JimCrowley 1 94
(Mrs A J Perrett) *lw: hld up: cajoled along on bnd after 7f: rdn over 3f out: hung lft and rt over 2f out: nvr on terms* **66/1**

-23P **11** *2 1/2* **The Last Drop (IRE)**[34] [1823] 4-9-0 110 KerrinMcEvoy 4 91
(B W Hills) *prom: rdn over 2f out: wknd over 1f out* **66/1**

5-04 **12** *5* **Rising Cross**[20] [2210] 4-8-11 109 TedDurcan 10 83
(J R Best) *hld up: rdn over 2f out: no imp: eased whn btn ins fnl f* **66/1**

0-15 **13** *1 1/2* **Tungsten Strike (USA)**[23] [2125] 6-9-2 110 RyanMoore 11 85
(Mrs A J Perrett) *trckd ldrs: wnt 2nd after 5f: rdn and ev ch 3f out: wknd 2f out: eased whn btn ins fnl f* **50/1**

3-41 **14** *25* **Sergeant Cecil**[34] [1823] 8-9-2 116 JimmyFortune 12 60
(B R Millman) *hld up: rdn over 2f out: no imp: eased whn btn fnl f: t.o* **13/2**[2]

4m 20.78s (-3.82) **Going Correction** +0.025s/f (Good)
WFA 4 from 5yo+ 2lb **14** Ran SP% **122.5**
Speed ratings (Par 117):108,107,106,104,104 101,100,99,99,97 96,94,93,83
CSF £8.77 TOTE £1.80: £1.10, £3.10, £6.60; EX 12.10 Trifecta £367.40 Pool: £33,422.66 - 64.58 winning tickets..
Owner Mrs John Magnier & Mrs David Nagle **Bred** Barrowsdale Stud & Orpendale **Trained** Ballydoyle, Co Tipperary
■ The bicentenary of the Gold Cup, which was first run in 1807.

FOCUS

A high-class renewal. Yeats looks as good as ever, while this was a career best from Geordieland. Le Miracle has been rated to the balance of his French form, with the fourth an improver over the longer trip. The pace dropped significantly on the run downhill to Swinley Botton and the time was 2.49 sec slower than Tuesday's Ascot Stakes.

NOTEBOOK

Yeats(IRE) ◆, an outstanding stayer, followed up his win of 12 months ago and ran to the sme RPR in doing so. Quickening up smartly to lead early in the straight, he jinked to his left inside the last as the runner-up threatened to close but was in no trouble once straightened up. His itinerary for the rest of the season is likely to be similar to last year, although he could give Goodwood a miss before going for the Irish St Leger and the Melbourne Cup. All being well he will return here next year and bid to emulate Sagaro, the only horse to have won the Gold Cup three times. (op 4-6 tchd 8-11 and 4-5 in places)
Geordieland(FR), held up travelling well, was still last turning for home with his rider anxious to play his hand late. After threading his way through, he went after the favourite over a furlong out and just for a moment it looked as if he might trouble him, but he was held in the last half-furlong. There was no disgrace in this and a major prize should come his way. He too is likely to be aimed for the Melbourne Cup again. (op 14-1 tchd 16-1 in places)
Le Miracle(GER) is trained in Germany but his last 13 races before today were in France. Suited by this ground, he was briefly in second place in the straight and stuck on for a highly creditable third.
Finalmente, the lowest rated in the field, was climbing markedly in grade after contesting a couple of Newmarket handicaps last month. Turning for home in third place and staying on despite hanging and carrying his head high, this was a career-best effort but on the downside he is going to be hard to place from now on with the Handicapper sure to hit him for this.
Montare(IRE) had the cheekpieces back in place and ground conditions to suit. She was well enough placed straightening up for home, but soon ran up the backs of rivals and, when switched, she could not produce a change of gear. (op 14-1)
Lord Du Sud(FR) made the running as usual but, once headed by Yeats early in the home straight, he was soon on the retreat. This fast ground was not ideal.
Baddam, a dual winner at last year's Royal meeting, ran respectably but is likely to continue to find it a struggle in this sort of company. He stays extra well.
Cherry Mix(FR), having his first run beyond 1m6f, was keen to go faster when the pace slackened on the approach to Swinley Bottom. He was under pressure once into the straight and did not get home, as connections had feared would be the case. (op 20-1)
Allegretto(IRE), upped in trip once again, was again keen in the visor and she could never make her presence felt.
Bulwark(IRE) continues to struggle in Pattern company.
The Last Drop(IRE), without the tongue tie, showed up prominently but the extended trip eventually took its toll. (op 100-1)
Rising Cross, always at the back of the field, probably doesn't stay this far.
Tungsten Strike(USA) failed to stay last year and that was again the case.
Sergeant Cecil looked the main danger to Yeats but failed to give his running and was beaten by five horses who had finished behind him in the Yorkshire Cup, notably today's runner-up. Held up towards the rear, he was keen running downhill towards Swinley Bottom and when asked for his effort early in the straight he failed to pick up and was allowed to coast home in the final furlong. Connections could find nothing physically wrong with him and were of the opinion that the gelding does not like being crowded. Hopefully he can bounce back from this, with the Lonsdale Cup at York looking the obvious race. Official explanation: trainer had no explanation for the poor form shown (op 11-2 tchd 7-1 in places)

2788 BRITANNIA STKS (HERITAGE H'CAP) (C&G) 1m (S)

4:20 (4:25) (Class 2) (0-105,104) 3-Y-O

£34,276 (£10,263; £5,131; £2,568; £1,281; £643) **Stalls** Centre

Form RPR

2-33 **1** **Eddie Jock (IRE)**45 [1544] 3-9-7 **104**.................................... JMurtagh 29 113
(M L W Bell) *hld up in midfield: hdwy 3f out: led 2f out: drvn to hold on fnl f* **33/1**

6-16 **2** ½ **Ea (USA)**41 [1617] 3-8-7 **90**.................................... RyanMoore 2 98+
(Sir Michael Stoute) *hld up in midfield: gd hdwy 2f out: edgd rt and pressed wnr fnl f: r.o* **16/1**

10-4 **3** *nk* **St Philip (USA)**26 [2043] 3-8-13 **96**.................................... SebSanders 15 103+
(R M Beckett) *hld up and bhd: gd hdwy 2f out: edgd lft ins fnl f: styd on wl* **33/1**

2-41 **4** 1 ¾ **Artimino**26 [2045] 3-8-8 **91**....................................(t) JamieSpencer 20 94
(J R Fanshawe) *lw: stdd s: hld up and bhd: hdwy on far rail 2f out: rdn and styd on* **4/1**[1]

11-5 **5** ½ **Ekhtiaar**19 [2231] 3-8-8 **91**.................................... MartinDwyer 27 93
(J H M Gosden) *hld up in midfield: hdwy to press ldrs 2f out: one pce fnl f* **9/1**[3]

3125 **6** *hd* **Annemasse**20 [2212] 3-8-9 **92**.................................... J-PGuillambert 11 93
(M Johnston) *lw: prom: led briefly over 2f out: one pce appr fnl f* **25/1**

1140 **7** *shd* **Players Please (USA)**33 [1835] 3-8-5 **88**.................................... JoeFanning 24 89+
(M Johnston) *in tch: swtchd lft and outpcd over 2f out: rallied and r.o fnl f* **33/1**

03-3 **8** 1 ¾ **Furnace (IRE)**46 [1500] 3-8-9 **92** ow1.................................... OPeslier 28 89
(M L W Bell) *stdd s: sn in tch: rdn to chse ldrs 2f out: no ex fnl f* **20/1**

9 1 **Canongate**24 3-8-9 **92**.................................... C-PLemaire 18 87
(R Gibson, France) *bhd: rdn and hdwy 2f out: nvr rchd ldrs* **50/1**

-443 **10** ¾ **Farleigh House (USA)**8 [2578] 3-8-4 **87**.................................... JimmyQuinn 5 80
(M H Tompkins) *mid-div: rdn to chse ldrs over 2f out: one pce appr fnl f* **33/1**

-131 **11** *nk* **Colorado Rapid (IRE)**27 [2010] 3-8-11 **94**.................................... KDarley 12 86+
(M Johnston) *lw: in tch: bmpd after 3f: rdn and btn 2f out* **9/2**[2]

5-00 **12** ½ **Heroes**20 [2212] 3-8-2 **88**.................................... EmmettStack(3) 23 79
(G A Huffer) *towards rr: rdn and sme hdwy 2f out: n.d* **100/1**

13 *shd* **De La Grandera (USA)**15 [2377] 3-8-3 **86**.................................... WMLordan 21 77
(David Wachman, Ire) *str: travelled wl in tch: drvn to press ldrs over 2f out: wknd over 1f out* **16/1**

1110 **14** 1 **Regal Parade**26 [2037] 3-8-10 **93**.................................... LDettori 22 89+
(M Johnston) *lw: hld up towards rr: hdwy over 2f out: chsng ldrs but hld whn squeezed for room 1f out* **12/1**

-126 **15** ½ **Gulf Express (USA)**12 [2476] 3-8-3 **86**.................................... KerrinMcEvoy 10 74+
(Sir Michael Stoute) *hld up and bhd: sme hdwy wn nt clr rn and swtchd rt 2f out: pushed along and styd on* **22/1**

-123 **16** ¾ **Dubai Twilight**33 [1835] 3-8-9 **92**.................................... MichaelHills 30 78
(B W Hills) *mid-div: shkn up and sme hdwy 2f out: no imp* **25/1**

4-40 **17** *hd* **Opera Music**20 [2212] 3-8-9 **92**.................................... LPKeniry 1 77
(S Kirk) *in tch: hrd rdn over 2f out: sn btn* **66/1**

0-6 **18** ½ **Dal Cais (IRE)**25 [2066] 3-8-13 **96**.................................... TedDurcan 19 80
(Francis Ennis, Ire) *w'like: lw: in tch tl hrd rdn and wknd 2f out* **66/1**

3500 **19** 2 **Danebury Hill**33 [1835] 3-8-12 **95**....................................(t) JimmyFortune 25 75
(B J Meehan) *towards rr most of wy: brief effrt 2f out: n.d* **50/1**

-034 **20** *nk* **Jo'Burg (USA)**15 [2368] 3-9-2 **99**.................................... MJKinane 16 78
(Mrs A J Perrett) *bhd: shkn up 2f out: nvr a factor* **33/1**

-454 **21** 2 **Buccellati**19 [2231] 3-8-3 **86**.................................... FrancisNorton 13 60
(A M Balding) *mid-div: rdn 3f out: sn outpcd* **12/1**

-530 **22** *nk* **Billy Dane (IRE)**19 [2231] 3-8-7 **90**.................................... PaulHanagan 7 64+
(R A Fahey) *dwlt: sn in mid-div: bdly squeezed and lost pl after 3f: nt rcvr* **100/1**

216- **23** 8 **Tudor Prince (IRE)**265 [5655] 3-8-5 **88**.................................... SteveDrowne 26 43
(B J Meehan) *mde most tl over 2f out: sn wknd* **80/1**

-000 **24** *shd* **Valdan (IRE)**26 [2037] 3-8-5 **88**.................................... DeanMcKeown 3 43
(P D Evans) *mid-div: outpcd 3f out: sn bhd* **100/1**

-630 **25** 1 ¾ **Thunder Storm Cat (USA)**26 [2037] 3-8-9 **92**.................................... TQuinn 4 43
(P F I Cole) *chsd ldrs: rdn 1/2-way: wknd over 2f out* **66/1**

-211 **26** 2 ½ **Slate (IRE)**19 [2243] 3-8-9 **92**.................................... EddieAhern 9 37
(J A Osborne) *chsd ldrs tl wknd over 2f out: eased whn wl btn over 1f out* **20/1**

1666 **27** *shd* **Majuro (IRE)**26 [2037] 3-8-13 **96**.................................... DarryllHolland 6 41
(M R Channon) *t.k.h: chsd ldrs: bmpd after 3f: rdn and btn whn n.m.r over 2f out* **100/1**

15-0 **28** ¾ **Kilburn**55 [1275] 3-8-6 **89** ow3....................................(p) PhilipRobinson 14 32
(C G Cox) *w ldr 5f: sn wknd* **33/1**

2-11 **29** 1 ¼ **Shmookh (USA)**36 [1768] 3-8-6 **89**.................................... RHills 17 29
(J L Dunlop) *lw: chsd ldrs: wnt lft and bmpd after 3f: wknd over 2f out* **9/1**[3]

430 **30** 8 **Norisan**54 [1306] 3-9-3 **100**.................................... RichardHughes 8 22
(R Hannon) *chsd ldrs 5f: btn whn n.m.r over 2f out* **100/1**

1m 39.93s (-1.87) **Going Correction** -0.05s/f (Good) **30** Ran SP% **139.1**

Speed ratings (Par 105):107,106,106,104,103 103,103,101,100,100 99,99,99,98,97 97,96,96,94,94 92,91,83,83,81 79,79,78

CSF £462.16 CT £16269.82 TOTE £35.60: £6.80, £6.00, £8.20, £2.10; EX 1081.30 TRIFECTA Not won. Pool £8,140.11.

Owner C A Gershinson **Bred** J Egan, J Corcoran And J Judd **Trained** Newmarket, Suffolk

FOCUS

A hugely competitive handicap, and the form looks typically solid for this race. High numbers were favoured, which makes the runner-up's performance all the more meritorious. The third is also rated better than the bare form. Eddie Jock was a surprise winner but there was no fluke about it.

NOTEBOOK

Eddie Jock(IRE), third in a warm renewal of the Free Handicap before failing to run his race in a muddling affair at Windsor, put up a fine weight carrying performance. Drawn high, and held up near the far rail, he showed ahead with two to run and held on bravely. He clearly likes this venue, having won the Shergar Cup Juvenile on a previous visit. (tchd 40-1 in a place)

Ea(USA) ◆, who failed to act on the track when last of six in the Group 3 Dee Stakes at Chester, was dropping back to a mile. Drawn on the opposite side of the track to the winner, he found himself in a small group which raced apart from the main bunch in the early stages. Edging across the track as he closed on the leaders, he ran on strongly inside the last but was just held. He would have won with a more favourable draw and is well up to winning a nice prize.

St Philip(USA) ◆, fourth to Jersey Stakes winner Tariq in a Newmarket Listed race on his seasonal debut, was running over a mile for the first time. Held up on the far side, he made rapid headway when pulled out but was just held near the line. This was a taking performance and he will be worth another crack at a Listed race.

Artimino was raised 7lb for his win at Newmarket, form which has been well advertised since. Held up some way off the pace, he improved up the far rail but, despite running on, was never quite pegging back the leaders. (op 5-1)

Ekhtiaar, down in trip after an unfortunate run at Epsom, had his chance but could not quicken up when push came to shove. (op 10-1)

Annemasse, who disappointed on soft ground in an Epsom Listed race last time, was always in the front wave and stuck on to do best of the four Johnston runners. (tchd 33-1 in places)

Players Please(USA), who raced freely from a wide draw at Newbury, was down at a mile for the first time in his career. After losing his pitch with over two furlongs to run, he found his stride late on and finished well.

Furnace(IRE), a stablemate of the winner, ran well for a long way but was held inside the last. He gave the impression that he will stay a bit further than this. (op 18-1)

Colorado Rapid(IRE), raised 10lb after his Pontefract win, was unable to get into the action after receiving an early bump, but he is highly regarded and is worth another chance. (op 5-1)

De La Grandera(USA), a useful maiden making his handicap debut, travelled strongly but faded once the pressure was on inside the final quarter mile. (op 20-1 tchd 25-1 in places)

Regal Parade, ridden differently on this occasion, would have finished closer had he not been hampered slightly entering the final furlong, after which his rider accepted the situation. (op 16-1)

Billy Dane(IRE) Official explanation: jockey said gelding suffered interference

Tudor Prince(IRE) showed good pace on his seasonal debut but failed to stay this first attempt at a mile. A drop back in trip on an easier surface will suit him.

Shmookh(USA), having his first run beyond 7f, took an early bump and was on the retreat in the last quarter mile. (op 11-1 tchd 12-1 in places)

2789 HAMPTON COURT STKS (LISTED RACE) 1m 2f

4:55 (5:01) (Class 1) 3-Y-O

£31,229 (£11,836; £5,923; £2,953; £1,479; £742) **Stalls** High

Form RPR

1311 **1** **Zaham (USA)**19 [2231] 3-9-2 100.................................... RHills 9 112
(M Johnston) *led for 1f: trckd ldr after: rdn over 2f out: led over 1f out: r.o gamely whn pressed ins fnl f: hld on wl* **7/2**[1]

-403 **2** *hd* **Al Shemali**35 [1790] 3-9-2 104.................................... RyanMoore 2 112
(Sir Michael Stoute) *lw: hld up in midfield: swtchd wd whn rdn and hdwy over 2f out: fin strly* **6/1**[3]

0-12 **3** *nk* **Desert Dew (IRE)**41 [1617] 3-9-2 103.................................... MichaelHills 6 111
(B W Hills) *lw: midfield: rdn and hdwy over 2f out: ev ch and str chal ins fnl f: r.o: hld fnl strides* **8/1**

-230 **4** *hd* **Kid Mambo (USA)**19 [2235] 3-9-2 108.................................... TQuinn 15 111
(T G Mills) *s.i.s: bustled along to ld after 1f: rdn and hdd over 1f out: r.o and continued str chal ins fnl f: hld fnl strides* **5/1**[2]

6-21 **5** 1 ¾ **Tranquil Tiger**27 [2005] 3-9-2 88.................................... RichardHughes 14 108
(H R A Cecil) *lw: in tch: rdn to chse ldrs over 2f out: edgd lft ins fnl f: nt qckn towards fin* **10/1**

-230 **6** 1 ¼ **Chinese Whisper (IRE)**18 [2293] 3-9-2 0.................................... JMurtagh 8 105
(A P O'Brien, Ire) *midfield: hdwy over 2f out: sn rdn: lugged rt over 1f out: styd on same pce ins fnl f* **10/1**

5-64 **7** 2 ½ **Big Robert**25 [2066] 3-9-2 104....................................(t) MartinDwyer 4 100
(W R Muir) *hld up: rdn over 2f out: styd on fnl f: nt rch ldrs* **16/1**

-231 **8** ½ **Champery (USA)**32 [1873] 3-9-7 107.................................... JoeFanning 16 104
(M Johnston) *trckd ldrs: rdn over 2f out: wknd over 1f out* **14/1**

5430 **9** 2 ½ **Habalwatan (IRE)**32 [1875] 3-9-2 95....................................(b) JimmyFortune 3 94
(C E Brittain) *hld up in midfield: effrt over 2f out: no imp over 1f out* **66/1**

51 **10** 3 **Ascalon**33 [1841] 3-9-2 87.................................... MJKinane 10 88
(Pat Eddery) *towards rr: rdn over 2f out: nvr on terms* **14/1**

1-24 **11** *shd* **Supersonic Dave (USA)**12 [2442] 3-9-2 106.................................... JamieSpencer 7 88
(B J Meehan) *hld up: rdn over 2f out: nvr trbld ldrs* **12/1**

0304 **12** 14 **Fishforcompliments**23 [2124] 3-9-2 98.................................... PaulHanagan 11 60
(R A Fahey) *midfield: rdn over 2f out: sn wknd* **50/1**

1-03 **13** 2 ½ **Glen Nevis (USA)**105 [641] 3-9-2 102.................................... LDettori 1 55
(Saeed Bin Suroor) *trckd ldrs: rdn over 2f out: sn wknd* **25/1**

-602 **14** ½ **Trinity College (USA)**12 [2483] 3-9-2 0.................................... CO'Donoghue 5 54
(A P O'Brien, Ire) *rdn 3f out: a bhd* **12/1**

2m 6.27s (-1.73) **Going Correction** +0.025s/f (Good) **30** Ran SP% **124.4**

Speed ratings (Par 107):107,106,106,106,105 104,102,101,99,97 97,85,83,83

CSF £24.19 TOTE £4.30: £2.00, £2.80, £3.40; EX 27.60 Trifecta £144.60 Pool: £5,882.95 - 28.87 winning tickets..

Owner Hamdan Al Maktoum **Bred** London Thoroughbred Services Ltd **Trained** Middleham Moor, N Yorks

FOCUS

A competitive renewal of this three-year-old Listed event. It was run at a fair pace and the first four came clear in a very tight finish. Rock solid form.

NOTEBOOK

Zaham(USA) ◆, unraced at two and a winner of four of his previous six outings, maintained his progression on this debut in Listed company and just did enough to gamely fend off his pursuers near the line. He had the run of the race just behind the leader for most of the way, but again showed a turn of foot when asked to win his race and really does possess a fantastic attitude. He is no doubt worth his place in Group company but could be due a well-deserved break first. (tchd 4-1 and 9-2 in places)

Al Shemali ◆, third in the Dante behind Authorized last time, has to rate an unlucky loser. He was forced to race wide throughout from his low draw and had plenty to do turning for home, but he displayed a potent turn of foot when put under maximum pressure and only just failed at the finish. Indeed he was in front shortly after passing the line and richly deserves to get his head back in front again now. He also shaped as though he is now ready to tackle a little further. (op 7-1 tchd 8-1 in a place)

Desert Dew(IRE), second in the Group 3 Dee Stakes at Chester 41 days previously, came through from off the pace to hold every chance on this drop in class and was another just held at the finish. He retains a progressive profile and can be placed to strike at this level before too long.

Kid Mambo(USA), seventh in the Derby last time, had to be rushed up to adopt his favoured position at the head of affairs after a sluggish start and then set a decent enough tempo. He could not match the winner for speed when that rival asserted for home, but he again showed battling qualities and proved most game thereafter. Not beaten at all far, his style of running dictates he will always have to do it the hard way, but no doubt he can strike in this sort of company, perhaps when reverting to a stiffer test. (op 9-2 tchd 11-2 and 6-1 in places)

Tranquil Tiger ◆ ran a perfectably respectable race on this step up from maiden company and is clearly still an improving colt. He was nicely clear in fifth and left the impression he will be winning again when stepping up to a stiffer test. (tchd 12-1 in places)

Chinese Whisper(IRE) had his chance and posted a more encouraging effort in defeat. He should be found a winning opportunity in his native Ireland at this level. (op 12-1)

Big Robert, equipped with a first-time tongue tie, ran a little freely out the back through the early parts and ultimately stayed on too late in the day. He needs to settle better, but certainly deserves to be ridden a little more positively and it may be that we have yet to see the best of him. (tchd 20-1 and 14-1 in places)

Supersonic Dave(USA) Official explanation: vet said colt returned lame behind

The Form Book, Raceform Ltd, Compton, RG20 6NL

2790 KING GEORGE V STKS (HERITAGE H'CAP) 1m 4f
5:30 (5:35) (Class 2) (0-105,100) 3-Y-O

£34,276 (£10,263; £5,131; £2,568; £1,281; £643) **Stalls** High

Form RPR

623 **1** **Heron Bay**[27] 1998 3-8-11 **90**.............................. SteveDrowne 5 103
(G Wragg) *lw: hld up in tch: effrt over 2f out: led over 1f out: narrowly hdd 100yds out: rallied gamely to ld nr fin* **20/1**

1-31 **2** *hd* **Filios (IRE)**[34] 1827 3-8-11 **90**.............................. LDettori 15 103
(L M Cumani) *hld up in midfield: rdn and gd hdwy fr 2f out: slt ld 100yds out: kpt on wl: hdd nr fin* **6/1**[2]

2-01 **3** *4* **Walking Talking**[14] 2402 3-8-11 **90**.............................. RichardHughes 6 97
(H R A Cecil) *lw: hld up towards rr: stdy hdwy 5f out: drvn along and edgd rt fnl 2f: styd on: nvr nrr* **12/1**

3121 **4** *2* **Eradicate (IRE)**[12] 2448 3-9-7 **100**.............................. KDarley 2 104
(M Johnston) *lw: prom: led over 2f out tl over 1f out: no ex fnl f* **9/2**[1]

2-13 **5** *nk* **Western Adventure (USA)**[34] 1803 3-8-9 **88**..........(b[1]) JimmyFortune 9 91+
(E A L Dunlop) *hld up towards rr: sltly outpcd 5f out: hdwy and swtchd lft over 1f out: drvn along: nrst fin* **25/1**

4-11 **6** *1 1/2* **Record Breaker (IRE)**[27] 1987 3-8-7 **86**.............................. JoeFanning 10 87
(M Johnston) *lw: prom: rdn to press ldrs over 2f out: wknd over 1f out* **15/2**[3]

6312 **7** *hd* **Philatelist (USA)**[12] 2448 3-8-13 **92**.............................. PhilipRobinson 16 92
(M A Jarvis) *chsd ldrs: rdn 5f out: no ex fnl 2f* **16/1**

11-3 **8** *hd* **Ladies Best**[25] 2057 3-8-13 **92**.............................. KerrinMcEvoy 18 92+
(Sir Michael Stoute) *hld up towards rr: effrt over 2f out: eased outside over 1f out: nt rch ldrs* **15/2**[3]

012 **9** *1 1/4* **Noticeable (IRE)**[27] 1987 3-8-10 **89**.............................. JHBowman 11 87
(M R Channon) *t.k.h: in tch tl rdn and btn 2f out* **25/1**

2211 **10** *hd* **Man Of Vision (USA)**[54] 1293 3-8-10 **89**.............................. DarryllHolland 7 87
(M R Channon) *led after 2f tl over 2f out: sn wknd* **8/1**

-163 **11** *nk* **Celestial Halo (IRE)**[42] 1602 3-9-5 **98**.............................. MichaelHills 12 95
(B W Hills) *led 2f: chsd ldrs tl wknd over 2f out* **66/1**

123 **12** *1* **Dansant**[12] 2448 3-8-11 **90**.............................. OPeslier 19 86
(G A Butler) *stdd s: t.k.h towards rr: rdn over 3f out: nvr nr ldrs* **22/1**

3112 **13** *2* **Fever**[19] 2231 3-8-6 **85**.............................. JimmyQuinn 17 77
(R Hannon) *mid-div: rdn along fr 6f out: hdwy on rail 4f out: drvn and in tch whn hmpd 2f out: sn wknd* **14/1**

305- **14** *hd* **Red Rock Canyon (IRE)**[18] 2289 3-9-1 **94**.............................. MJKinane 4 86
(A P O'Brien, Ire) *hld up in rr: rdn 3f out: nvr a factor* **14/1**

-502 **15** *1 1/4* **Mutadarrej (IRE)**[23] 2126 3-8-8 **87**.............................. RHills 14 77
(J L Dunlop) *hld up in rr: sme hdwy into midfield over 3f out: rdn and wknd 2f out* **40/1**

4341 **16** *shd* **Sahrati**[23] 2126 3-8-8 **87**.............................. RyanMoore 8 77
(C E Brittain) *hld up towards rr: sltly hmpd after 3f: bhd fnl 3f* **25/1**

5-13 **17** *nk* **Wandle**[63] 1106 3-9-3 **96**.............................. JMurtagh 3 85
(T G Mills) *stdd s: plld hrd and bhd: no ch whn edgd lft over 2f out* **20/1**

1-10 **18** *2* **Swiss Act**[11] 2503 3-8-10 **89**.............................. J-PGuillambert 1 75
(M Johnston) *mid-div on outside: rdn 4f out: wknd over 2f out* **28/1**

-003 **19** *1 3/4* **Golden Dagger (IRE)**[19] 2231 3-8-7 **86**.............................. DO'Donohoe 13 69
(K A Ryan) *towards rr: mod effrt 5f out: wknd 3f out* **66/1**

2m 30.11s (-2.89) **Going Correction** +0.025s/f (Good) **47 Ran SP% 128.3**
Speed ratings (Par 105):110,109,107,105,105 104,104,104,103,103 103,102,101,101,100 100,100,98,97
CSF £128.09 CT £1550.84 TOTE £26.80: £4.10, £1.90, £3.40, £1.90; EX 208.20 Trifecta £1921.10 Pool: £7,305.67 - 2.70 winning tickets. Place 6 £19.15, Place 5 £11.60.
Owner Mollers Racing **Bred** Car Colston Hall Stud **Trained** Newmarket, Suffolk

FOCUS
A typically open renewal full of unexposed and highly progressive three-year-olds, but it was run at no more than a fair gallop. The first pair came clear, with Heron Bay up a stone on his maiden form and Filios also a big improver. The form is typically solid for this race and there were plenty of future winners down the field.

NOTEBOOK
Heron Bay, making his handicap debut after three decent efforts in maiden company this term, broke his duck with a narrow success on this marked step up in class. He effortlessly made up his ground nearing the turn for home and displayed a neat turn of foot to take it up nearing the final furlong, but he looked in trouble when Filios loomed up to him. He would not be denied, however, and was probably idling as he showed real battling qualities at the business end. His trainer has always regarded him highly and plans to now up him further in class in the Gordon Stakes at Goodwood, in an attempt to test his credentials for a possible tilt at the St Leger. No doubt he will have to improve again to figure there, but that is entirely possible as this was just his fourth outing.

Filios(IRE), raised 11lb for winning at York 34 days previously, looked to have been laid out for this event and proved popular in the betting ring. Given a patient ride, he picked up strongly when asked to make his challenge and looked the most likely winner when looming up to Heron Bay inside the final furlong. He nosed ahead briefly but was just held again where it mattered. He has to rate unfortunate as he was clear of the remainder at the finish and is clearly still an improving colt. The Handicapper will hike him up again for this, however, and he may be better off making the move into Listed or Group company now as he is still relatively unexposed. (op 7-1 tchd 8-1 in a place)

Walking Talking, off the mark in a Sandown maiden a fortnight previously, put in another improved effort on this handicap bow and finished nicely clear in third. He too remains open to improvement and should have learnt a lot from this experience.

Eradicate(IRE) ◆, 7lb higher than when making all at Haydock 12 days previously, was far from disgraced under top weight considering he was unable to dictate from his low draw. It is still likely that we have yet to see the best of him and he is the type his trainer does so well with. (op 11-2 tchd 6-1 in places)

Western Adventure(USA), third in the Glasgow Stakes 34 days previously, responded positively to the first-time blinkers and was doing his best work towards the finish on this further step up in distance. He looks another improver, but whether the blinkers have the same effect in the future remains to be seen.

Record Breaker(IRE), up 8lb for his Goodwood success 27 days previously, was always handy and held every chance. He looks worth dropping back in trip for the short term, however. (op 13-2)

Philatelist(USA), just behind the winner at Chester on his second outing this term, proved one paced when it mattered and was never travelling with any real fluency.

Ladies Best should be rated a little better than the bare form as he had to wait for his challenge and by the time he hit full stride the race was effectively over. He is capable of rating higher still. (op 13-2)

T/Jkpt: £148,054.09 to a £1 stake. Pool: £208,527.00. 1.00 winning ticket. T/Plt: £19.80 to a £1 stake. Pool: £466,431.66. 17,162.85 winning tickets. T/Qpdt: £9.70 to a £1 stake. Pool: £15,932.75. 1,205.45 winning tickets. DO

2549 BEVERLEY (R-H)
Thursday, June 21

OFFICIAL GOING: Good to soft
Wind: Virtually nil Weather: Heavy thunder showers

2791 BOOK TICKETS ON-LINE AT BEVERLEY-RACECOURSE.CO.UK CLASSIFIED STKS 5f
6:30 (6:33) (Class 7) 3-Y-O+ **£2,266** (£674; £337; £168) **Stalls** High

Form RPR

2305 **1** **Mister Incredible**[5] 2664 4-8-11 45..........................(v) BarrySavage(7) 16 57
(J M Bradley) *led far side gp: rdn along and overall ldr wl over 1f out: clr ins fnl f* **9/2**[1]

6033 **2** *2 1/2* **Nawayea**[21] 2174 4-8-11 45.............................. KirstyMilczarek(7) 17 48
(C N Allen) *chsd wnr far side: rdn along 2f out: drvn ent fnl f: kpt on* **8/1**

4025 **3** *shd* **She's Our Beauty (IRE)**[19] 2249 4-9-1 45..........(p) DuranFentiman(3) 12 48
(S T Mason) *swtchd to stands' side and overall ldr after 2f: rdn and hdd wl over 1f out: kpt on u.p ins fnl f* **10/1**

3530 **4** *1 1/2* **Tuscan Flyer**[8] 2561 9-9-1 45..............................(b) JamieMoriarty(3) 14 42
(R Bastiman) *chsd ldng pair far side: rdn along 2f out: kpt on u.p fnl f* **12/1**

00-0 **5** *hd* **Orotund**[79] 910 3-8-12 45.............................. GrahamGibbons 15 40
(T D Easterby) *swtchd lft to r stands' side after 1f: a chsng ldrs: rdn along over 1f out: kpt on same pce* **33/1**

5544 **6** *2 1/2* **Lady Hopeful (IRE)**[12] 2459 5-8-13 45............(b) RussellKennemore(5) 9 33
(Peter Grayson) *towards rr stands' side: hdwy 2f out: sn rdn and kpt on fnl f* **7/1**

04-0 **7** *1/2* **Kindallachan**[19] 2242 4-9-4 45.............................. NCallan 11 31
(G C Bravery) *in tch on outer of stands' side gp: rdn along 2f out and kpt on same pce* **12/1**

3000 **8** *1 1/2* **Piccolo Prince**[38] 1719 6-9-4 45.............................. PaulQuinn 3 25
(Mrs Marjorie Fife) *chsd ldrs stands' side: rdn along 2f out: sn drvn and grad wknd* **25/1**

0363 **9** *1* **Boisdale (IRE)**[20] 2220 9-9-4 45.............................. RichardThomas 5 22
(P S Felgate) *towards rr stands' side: effrt and sme hdwy 2f out: sn rdn and no imp* **6/1**[2]

4000 **10** *3/4* **Navigation (IRE)**[10] 2509 5-9-4 45..........................(v[1]) RoystonFfrench 1 19
(T J Etherington) *overall ldr stands' side: hdd after 2f and sn pushed along: rdn 2f out and grad wknd* **14/1**

0306 **11** *1 3/4* **Ruby's Dream**[5] 2652 5-9-4 45..............................(p) ChrisCatlin 10 13
(J M Bradley) *chsd ldrs stands' side: rdn along over 2f out: grad wknd* **13/2**[3]

06-4 **12** *3 1/2* **Trombone Tom**[31] 1902 4-9-4 45.............................. PaulMulrennan 8 —
(J R Norton) *in tch stands' side: rdn along over 2f out: n.d* **11/1**

0000 **13** *7* **Jodrell Bank (IRE)**[8] 2555 4-9-4 45..............................(b) BrettDoyle 6 —
(J Ryan) *a in rr stands' side* **33/1**

0-00 **14** *3* **Bahamian Bay**[52] 1349 5-9-4 45.............................. DeanMernagh 2 —
(M Brittain) *chsd ldrs stands' side: rdn along 1/2-way: sn wknd* **11/1**

67.72 secs (3.72) **Going Correction** +0.675s/f (Yiel)
WFA 3 from 4yo+ 6lb **14 Ran SP% 126.9**
Speed ratings (Par 97):97,93,92,90,90 86,85,82,81,80 77,71,60,55
CSF £41.50 TOTE £7.50: £3.10, £2.80, £4.80; EX 34.00.
Owner racingshares.co.uk **Bred** R J H West **Trained** Sedbury, Gloucs

FOCUS
A poor affair dominated by those racing high. The form looks sound with to first three to recent form.

Lady Hopeful(IRE) Official explanation: jockey said mare ran flat
Trombone Tom Official explanation: trainer said gelding was unsuited by the good to soft ground
Bahamian Bay Official explanation: trainer said mare was found to be coughing after the race

2792 RACING AGAIN ON 26 JUNE MEDIAN AUCTION MAIDEN STKS 1m 100y
7:00 (7:00) (Class 5) 3-4-Y-O **£3,724** (£1,108; £553; £276) **Stalls** High

Form RPR

4- **1** **Rhuepunzel**[268] 5592 3-8-9 0.............................. HayleyTurner 5 66
(G A Butler) *hld up in rr: gd hdwy on outer over 2f out: rdn to ld jst ins fnl f: styd on wl* **11/4**[3]

45 **2** *1 1/4* **Jibajaba (USA)**[8] 2554 3-9-0 0.............................. TonyHamilton 9 68
(R A Fahey) *trckd ldrs: hdwy on inner 3f out: led 2f out and sn rdn: drvn and hdd jst ins fnl f: kpt on* **9/4**[2]

322 **3** *2 1/2* **Sofie Tucker**[9] 2535 3-8-6 0.............................. DuranFentiman(3) 2 58
(T D Easterby) *trckd ldng pair: effrt over 2f out: rdn and ev ch over 1f out: sn drvn and one pce* **11/8**[1]

0 **4** *5* **Beresford Lady**[22] 2137 3-8-9 0.............................. SilvestreDeSousa 3 47
(A D Brown) *cl up: led after 3f: rdn along and hdd 2f out: sn drvn and grad wknd* **25/1**

00 **5** *4* **Cecina Marina**[27] 1995 4-9-5 0.............................. LeeEnstone 6 40
(C W Thornton) *hld up: a in rr* **20/1**

0-05 **6** *4* **Village Storm (IRE)**[93] 714 4-9-3 32.............................. KellyHarrison(7) 1 36?
(C J Teague) *led 3f: cl up tl rdn over wl 2f out and sn wknd* **33/1**

1m 53.46s (6.06) **Going Correction** +0.775s/f (Yiel)
WFA 3 from 4yo 10lb **6 Ran SP% 111.1**
Speed ratings (Par 103):100,98,96,91,87 83
CSF £9.05 TOTE £3.20: £1.50, £1.90; EX 8.90.
Owner The Fairy Story Partnership **Bred** Deepwood Farm Stud **Trained** Blewbury, Oxon

FOCUS
Just an average maiden rated around the runner-up to his debut form.

2793 TURFTV FILLIES' H'CAP 1m 4f 16y
7:30 (7:30) (Class 6) (0-60,60) 3-Y-O **£2,590** (£770; £385; £192) **Stalls** High

Form RPR

3635 **1** **Raquel White**[15] 2362 3-8-8 **55**.............................. KevinGhunowa(5) 1 63
(J L Flint) *hld up towards rr: gd hdwy on outer 4f out: led wl over 2f out: rdn wl over 1fout: styd on gamely u.p fnl f* **12/1**

06-0 **2** *3* **Alleviate (IRE)**[15] 2362 3-9-0 **56**.............................. NCallan 9 59
(Sir Mark Prescott) *in tch: hdwy to trck ldrs 4f out: effrt to chse wnr over 1f out: drvn ins fnl f and no imp* **15/8**[1]

0-06 **3** *3/4* **Lady Traill**[23] 2105 3-8-8 **50**.............................. ChrisCatlin 3 52
(B W Hills) *midfield: rdn along: outpcd and hung lft 3f out: drvn 2f out: styd on wl u.p fnl f: nrst fin* **12/1**

1602 **4** *1/2* **A Mothers Love**[21] 2192 3-9-2 **58**.............................. EdwardCreighton 12 59
(P J McBride) *hld up: gd hdwy on outer wl over 2f out: rdn to chse ldrs over 1f out: sn drvn and no ex ins fnl f* **7/1**[3]

405 **5** *shd* **Windbeneathmywings (IRE)**[31] 1887 3-9-4 **60**............. JamesDoyle 8 61
(J W Hills) *towards rr: hdwy whn bmpd wl over 2f out: sn rdn and styng on whn hung rt ins fnl f: kpt on wl towards fin* **10/1**

-000 **6** *1/2* **Pagan Starprincess**[22] 2133 3-9-1 **57**.............................. TomEaves 10 57
(G M Moore) *in tch: pushed along 4f out: rdn and outpcd 3f out: styd on u.p ins fnl f* **8/1**

246 **7** *3* **Serhaaphim**[30] 1928 3-9-3 **59**.. HayleyTurner 6 54
(M L W Bell) *hld up: effrt and hdwy 3f out: sn rdn along and no imp fr wl over 1f out* **6/1**[2]

4204 **8** *4* **Chip N Pin**[22] 2132 3-8-10 **55**.................................... DuranFentiman(3) 7 44
(T D Easterby) *cl up: led 1/2-way: rdn along and hdd wl over 2f out: sn drvn and wknd wl over 1f out* **8/1**

-006 **9** *1 3/4* **Decent Proposal**[24] 2096 3-8-6 **48**............................ GrahamGibbons 2 34
(T D Easterby) *chsd ldrs: rdn along over 3f out: drvn wl over 2f out and sn wknd* **16/1**

0-45 **10** *6* **Snow Ballerina**[42] 1611 3-9-4 **60**.................................. PaulMulrennan 5 36
(E A L Dunlop) *in tch: effrt over 3f out: sn rdn along and wknd over 2f out* **25/1**

656 **11** *20* **Celtic Memories (IRE)**[8] 2552 3-8-11 **53**......................(b) DaleGibson 4 —
(M W Easterby) *led to 1/2-way: cl up tl rdn along 3f out and sn wknd: bhd and eased wl over 1f out* **22/1**

00-0 **12** *18* **Atlantic Dame (USA)**[35] 1785 3-8-13 **55**.......................... BrettDoyle 11 —
(Mrs A J Perrett) *chsd ldrs: rdn along 4f out: sn wknd and bhd: eased* **40/1**

2m 46.39s (6.18) **Going Correction** +0.775s/f (Yiel) **12** Ran SP% **124.8**
Speed ratings (Par 94):110,108,107,107,107 106,104,102,100,96 83,71
CSF £35.91 CT £300.39 TOTE £15.30: £4.30, £1.20, £3.70; EX 65.70.
Owner N Poacher **Bred** C And Mrs Wilson **Trained** Kenfig Hill, Bridgend
■ The first winner on the Flat for trainer John Flint.
■ Stewards' Enquiry : N Callan one-day ban: careless riding (Jul 2)

FOCUS
Just a moderate handicap but solid form rated around the fourth and fifth.

2794 MIDSUMMER'S NIGHT FILLIES' H'CAP 1m 1f 207y
8:00 (8:00) (Class 4) (0-85,80) 3-Y-O+ **£6,477** (£1,927; £963) **Stalls** High

Form RPR

-331 **1** **Magic Echo**[8] 2579 3-9-2 **77** 6ex....................................... PhillipMakin 4 82
(M Dods) *led: pushed along over 2f out: rdn and hdd over 1f out: drvn ins fnl f: rallied gamely to ld again nr fin* **8/11**[1]

5-30 **2** *hd* **Sunisa (IRE)**[9] 2543 6-10-0 **77**.. NCallan 6 82
(J Mackie) *trckd wnr: hdwy over 2f out: rdn to ld over 1f out: drvn ins fnl f: hdd and no ex nr fin* **10/3**[3]

212- **3** *8* **Princess Cocoa (IRE)**[323] 4040 4-9-7 **73**.................. JamieMoriarty(3) 3 62
(R A Fahey) *hld up in tch: effrt over 2f out: sn rdn along and no hdwy* **3/1**[2]

2m 13.42s (6.12) **Going Correction** +0.775s/f (Yiel)
WFA 3 from 4yo+ 12lb **3** Ran SP% **106.0**
Speed ratings (Par 102):106,105,99
CSF £3.23 TOTE £2.00; EX 2.90.
Owner D C Batey **Bred** D C Batey **Trained** Denton, Co Durham
■ Stewards' Enquiry : Phillip Makin four-day ban: used whip with excessive frequency down shoulder in forehand position (Jul 3-6)

FOCUS
A depleted field and the in-form Magic Echo narrowly justified favouritism but the form is not entirely solid.

2795 SHEILA AND COLIN STAMFORD 38TH WEDDING ANNIVERSARY H'CAP 1m 1f 207y
8:30 (8:30) (Class 6) (0-50,51) 4-Y-O+ **£2,590** (£770; £385; £192) **Stalls** High

Form RPR

2641 **1** **Don Pasquale**[8] 2582 5-8-13 **51** 6ex.................................. ChrisCatlin 16 59
(J T Stimpson) *hld up towards rr: gd hdwy on outer wl over 2f out: rdn to ld over 1f out: edgd rt and clr ins fnl f: styd on* **9/2**[3]

0/00 **2** *1 1/4* **Reason (IRE)**[16] 2345 9-8-8 **46** oh1............................(b) HayleyTurner 12 52
(D W Chapman) *sn bhd and rdn along: hdwy wl over 2f out: chsd ldrs over 1f out: swtchd rt ins fnl f and fin wl* **40/1**

4000 **3** *1 3/4* **Jiminor Mack**[19] 2253 4-8-5 **46** oh1.......................(b) AndrewMullen(3) 14 48
(W J H Ratcliffe) *dwlt and towards rr: hdwy 4f out: rdn over 2f out: drvn to chse wnr ent fnl f: kpt on same pce* **12/1**

4-02 **4** *3* **Thornaby Green**[8] 2582 6-8-4 **49**.................................. DeanHeslop(7) 5 45
(T D Barron) *sn led: rdn along over 2f out: drvn and hdd over 1f out: sn one pce* **10/3**[1]

0300 **5** *2* **Susiedil (IRE)**[27] 2008 6-8-10 **48**..............................(v) AdrianTNicholls 4 40
(S T Mason) *chsd ldrs: hdwy 3f out: rdn and ev ch 2f out: sn drvn and wknd appr fnl f* **9/1**

00-5 **6** *3/4* **Moving Story**[8] 2582 4-8-11 **49**.. MickyFenton 9 40
(P T Midgley) *trckd ldrs: effrt 3f out: rdn and ev ch 2f out: sn drvn and wknd* **7/2**[2]

0000 **7** *hd* **Didnt Tell My Wife**[15] 2370 8-8-3 **46** oh1............. NataliaGemelova(5) 10 36
(P S McEntee) *in tch: hdwy to chse ldrs 3f out: rdn 2f out: sn drvn and wknd over 1f out* **20/1**

5-00 **8** *nk* **Silver Sail**[15] 2370 4-8-5 **46** oh1........................(p) DuranFentiman(3) 13 36
(J S Wainwright) *bhd and swtchd to stands' rail 3f out: sn rdn and styd on fnl 2f: nt rch ldrs* **12/1**

-600 **9** *1 3/4* **No Inkling (IRE)**[11] 467 4-8-3 **46** oh1.................... KevinGhunowa(5) 11 32
(Miss M E Rowland) *towards rr: gd hdwy on inner 3f out: chsd ldrs 2f out: sn rdn and wknd over 1f out* **50/1**

5300 **10** *3 1/2* **Rose Muwasim**[8] 2582 4-8-9 **47**..(v) PaulEddery 3 26
(S Parr) *a towards rr* **33/1**

000- **11** *36* **Mccormack (IRE)**[29] 3484 5-8-8 **46** oh1............................... TomEaves 1 —
(Micky Hammond) *in tch: rdn along over 4f out: sn wknd* **20/1**

-000 **12** *7* **Evolution Ex (USA)**[17] 2307 5-8-12 **50**......................... RoystonFfrench 15 —
(I W McInnes) *a bhd* **10/1**

40-0 **13** *2* **Lady Lochinver (IRE)**[17] 2302 4-8-8 **46**.............................. DaleGibson 7 —
(Micky Hammond) *a in rr* **20/1**

000- **14** *nk* **Salisbury World (IRE)**[276] 5432 4-8-8 **46** oh1........... GrahamGibbons 6 —
(J F Coupland) *cl up: rdn along 3f out: sn wknd* **50/1**

-000 **15** *3/4* **Tamatave (IRE)**[126] 466 5-8-12 **50**.............................. PaulMulrennan 8 —
(M W Easterby) *trckd ldrs: rdn along wl over 2f out: sn wknd* **11/1**

2m 14.34s (7.04) **Going Correction** +0.775s/f (Yiel) **15** Ran SP% **129.9**
Speed ratings (Par 101):102,101,99,97,95 95,94,94,93,90 61,56,54,54,53
CSF £192.81 CT £2087.49 TOTE £6.10: £2.10, £11.70, £4.80; EX 268.30.
Owner J T Stimpson **Bred** Chippenham Lodge Stud Ltd **Trained** Newcastle-Under-Lyme, Staffs

FOCUS
A bad handicap won readily by the in-form Don Pasquale and rated through the third.
Thornaby Green Official explanation: jockey said gelding hung left throughout

2796 GO RACING AT REDCAR TOMORROW H'CAP 1m 100y
9:00 (9:00) (Class 6) (0-60,60) 3-Y-O **£2,590** (£770; £385; £192) **Stalls** High

Form RPR

-005 **1** **Smugglers Bay (IRE)**[22] 2133 3-9-4 **60**.................(b[1]) PaulMulrennan 14 70
(T D Easterby) *chsd ldrs: hdwy 3f out: led 2f out and sn rdn: drvn ent fnl f and kpt on wl* **13/2**[2]

-046 **2** *2 1/2* **Giovanni D'Oro (IRE)**[53] 1317 3-8-10 **52**................. RoystonFfrench 10 56
(Miss M E Rowland) *towards rr: stdy hdwy 3f out: rdn wl over 1f out: styd on to chse wnr ins fnl f: sn drvn and no imp* **14/1**

050- **3** *3/4* **Harry The Hawk**[257] 5814 3-9-4 **60**........................... GrahamGibbons 15 62
(T D Walford) *in tch on inner: hdwy to chse ldrs 3f out: rdn and ch wl over 1f out tl drvn and one pce ent fnl f* **10/1**

000 **4** *1/2* **Mix N Match**[21] 2173 3-8-12 **54**.. NCallan 8 55+
(W J Haggas) *in tch: hdwy to chse ldrs 3f out: rdn over 2f out: sn drvn and kpt on same pce appr fnl f* **3/1**[1]

4000 **5** *7* **Mandalay Prince**[5] 2668 3-8-12 **54**....................................... BrettDoyle 4 39+
(W J Musson) *in rr: hdwy 3f out: rdn and in tch 2f out: sn drvn and no imp* **8/1**

6-60 **6** *1/2* **Cape Dancer (IRE)**[30] 1916 3-9-1 **57**.......................... TonyHamilton 13 41
(J S Wainwright) *chsd ldr: led 3f out: rdn and hdd 2f out: sn drvn and wknd appr fnl f* **16/1**

4304 **7** *3/4* **Irish Relative (IRE)**[23] 2116 3-8-2 **51** ow1.................. DeanHeslop(7) 11 33
(T D Barron) *chsd ldrs: rdn along 3f out: drvn 2f out and sn wknd* **10/1**

0000 **8** *1* **Quite A Splash (USA)**[23] 2105 3-8-12 **54**..................... MickyFenton 12 34
(S Curran) *bhd tl swtchd wd and sme hdwy 2f out: nvr a factor* **25/1**

4002 **9** *2* **Cap St Jean (IRE)**[19] 2248 3-9-1 **57**.................................. LeeEnstone 3 32
(P C Haslam) *stdd and swtchd rt s: hld up towards rr: hdwy over 4f out: rdn to chse ldrs over 2f out: sn drvn: edgd rt and btn* **7/1**[3]

4660 **10** *1* **Gold Response**[22] 2133 3-8-9 **54**.........................(v) DuranFentiman(3) 6 27
(D Shaw) *a in rr* **12/1**

-040 **11** *1 1/4* **Wisdom's Kiss**[20] 2224 3-9-2 **58**... TomEaves 7 28
(J D Bethell) *a bhd* **16/1**

0440 **12** *9* **Mr Chocolate Drop (IRE)**[56] 1266 3-8-6 **53**.......... KevinGhunowa(5) 16 2
(Miss M E Rowland) *chsd ldrs: rdn along 1/2-way and sn wknd* **14/1**

0-00 **13** *5* **Three Half Crowns (IRE)**[26] 2046 3-8-11 **53**................ ChrisCatlin 5 —
(P Howling) *midfield: rdn along and lost pl over 3f out: sn bhd* **16/1**

400 **14** *3* **Jentris Girl (IRE)**[33] 1849 3-8-13 **55**..............................(b[1]) DaleGibson 2 —
(T D Easterby) *racd wd: led: rdn along 4f out: hdd 3f out and c wd to stands' rails: wknd qckly* **20/1**

1m 54.46s (7.06) **Going Correction** +0.775s/f (Yiel) **14** Ran SP% **127.4**
Speed ratings (Par 97):95,92,91,91,84 83,83,82,80,79 77,68,63,60
CSF £100.32 CT £929.79 TOTE £9.80: £3.50, £3.90, £4.30; EX 154.80 Place 6 £ 254.25, Place 5 £ 102.35.
Owner C H Stevens **Bred** P G Lyons **Trained** Great Habton, N Yorks

FOCUS
Another weak handicap in which the front four drew clear. The form is rated around the placed horses, although neither are solid.
Mr Chocolate Drop(IRE) Official explanation: jockey said gelding was unsuited by the good to soft ground
T/Plt: £296.60 to a £1 stake. Pool: £62,019.40. 152.60 winning tickets. T/Qpdt: £53.20 to a £1 stake. Pool: £3,705.20. 51.50 winning tickets. JR

2663 LINGFIELD (L-H)
Thursday, June 21

OFFICIAL GOING: Standard
Meeting transferred from Southwell, where parts of the site were flooded.
Wind: Fresh, behind Weather: Overcast

2797 CHESNEY HAWKES LIVE AT LINGFIELD PARK MAIDEN AUCTION FILLIES' STKS 5f (P)
2:20 (2:21) (Class 5) 2-Y-O **£2,968** (£876; £438) **Stalls** High

Form RPR

04 **1** **Penrice Castle**[8] 2569 2-8-9 0 ow1... PatDobbs 3 68
(R Hannon) *chsd ldrs: rdn to ld ins fnl f: r.o* **11/2**[2]

5034 **2** *1 1/4* **Carolina Blini**[11] 2488 2-8-5 0...(b) KMay(7) 1 66
(B J Meehan) *led: rdn over 1f out: hdd and unable qckn ins fnl f* **7/1**

0 **3** *1/2* **Bahamarama (IRE)**[12] 2468 2-8-10 0......................... FergusSweeney 6 62
(J R Boyle) *hld up: rdn over 1f out: r.o ins fnl f: nt rch ldrs* **10/1**

4 *1* **Erin Thomas (IRE)** 2-8-6 0.. JohnEgan 2 55
(M G Quinlan) *w ldr: rdn and ev ch 1f out: no ex ins fnl f* **14/1**

222 **5** *shd* **Speedy Senorita (IRE)**[13] 2416 2-8-6 0......................(p) FrancisNorton 4 54
(K R Burke) *trckd ldrs: plld hrd: rdn and hung lft over 1f out: styd on same pce* **5/6**[1]

6 *hd* **Rightcar Ellie (IRE)** 2-8-10 0.. LPKeniry 5 58
(Peter Grayson) *hld up in tch: rdn over 1f out: nt trble ldrs* **14/1**

65 **7** *nk* **Star In The East**[11] 2488 2-8-5 0............................... WilliamBuick(5) 7 56
(A M Balding) *sn outpcd* **6/1**[3]

3 **8** *nk* **Carry On Cleo**[14] 2392 2-8-4 0.................................. CatherineGannon 8 49
(P D Evans) *s.i.s: outpcd* **17/2**

60.21 secs (0.43) **Going Correction** 0.0s/f (Stan) **8** Ran SP% **129.7**
Speed ratings (Par 90):96,94,93,91,91 91,90,90
CSF £49.45 TOTE £8.00: £2.70, £3.40, £4.60; EX 57.30.
Owner D J Deer **Bred** D J And Mrs Deer **Trained** East Everleigh, Wilts

FOCUS
Modest maiden form, especially with the odds-on favourite failing to run her race, but worth a chance at this level.

NOTEBOOK
Penrice Castle had shaped as though she would be suited by a drop back to the minimum trip at Kempton last time, and it certainly did the trick, as she travelled well throughout before nipping through on the inside in the straight. She won comfortably in the end and should make her mark in nurseries in due course. (tchd 6-1)
Carolina Blini once again had every chance but found one too good. It was not a good sign to see her flash her tail under pressure in the closing stages. (op 15-2)
Bahamarama(IRE), a half-sister to three winners, including sprint juvenile winners Ivory's Promise and Coley, ran on late down the outside but was never a real threat to the winner. She shapes as though she needs to return to 6f.
Erin Thomas(IRE), a half-sister to Lyrical Girl, a dual 1m-1m2f winner at two to three, and to Catch Fire, a multiple winner at three to five in Holland, showed speed and, providing she improves for this debut, there could be a little race in her. (tchd 16-1)
Speedy Senorita(IRE) did not run to her best and was very disappointing, failing to settle in the first-time cheekpieces and hanging left in the straight. (op 5-4)

The Form Book, Raceform Ltd, Compton, RG20 6NL

2798 LINGFIELDPARK.CO.UK (S) H'CAP 7f (P)
2:55 (2:55) (Class 6) (0-60,55) 3-Y-O+ **£2,184** (£644; £322) **Stalls** Low

Form RPR
0400 **1** **Ceredig**[6] 2622 4-8-8 47 .... WilliamCarson(7) 9 54
(P W Hiatt) *hld up: hdwy over 2f out: rdn to ld ins fnl f: r.o* **8/1**
6500 **2** ¾ **Calloff The Search**[16] 2331 3-8-8 52 ....(v) SaleemGolam(3) 4 54
(W G M Turner) *prom: outpcd 2f out: r.o ins fnl f* **16/1**
4353 **3** *nk* **Rafferty (IRE)**[7] 2591 8-8-9 48 ....(p) ThomasBubb(7) 3 52
(S Dow) *chsd ldrs: shkn up over 1f out: styd on* **7/1**
5105 **4** *shd* **Le Chiffre (IRE)**[20] 2220 5-9-4 55 ....(b) LukeMorris(5) 5 59
(R A Harris) *chsd ldrs: rdn over 2f out: styd on* **7/1**
0020 **5** ½ **Scroll**[5] 2665 4-9-6 52 ....(v) AdrianMcCarthy 10 54
(P Howling) *hld up: r.o ins fnl f: nvr nrr* **12/1**
103 **6** *shd* **Feelin Irie (IRE)**[22] 2145 4-9-9 55 ....(p) FergusSweeney 7 57
(J R Boyle) *chsd ldr tl led 3f out: rdn over 1f out: hdd and no ex ins fnl f* **6/1**[2]
1602 **7** 1 **Over To You Bert**[18] 2273 8-9-7 53 .... RobertHavlin 12 52
(R J Hodges) *hld up: hdwy u.p over 1f out: styd on same pce fnl f* **13/2**[3]
5343 **8** *hd* **Primarily**[31] 1902 5-9-2 48 .... GeorgeBaker 14 47
(Peter Grayson) *hld up: hdwy over 1f out: one pce fnl f* **11/2**[1]
6635 **9** 1½ **Wodhill Be**[30] 1933 7-9-0 46 .... OscarUrbina 13 41
(D Morris) *hld up: hdwy u.p over 1f out: wknd ins fnl f* **11/1**
6064 **10** 1 **Fulvio (USA)**[7] 2591 7-8-11 46 ....(v) RichardKingscote(3) 6 38
(P Howling) *s.i.s: a in rr:* **14/1**
351- **11** 5 **Gifted Heir (IRE)**[218] 6487 3-9-0 55 .... CatherineGannon 1 31
(I A Wood) *mid-div: rdn 1/2-way: wknd over 2f out* **8/1**
05-5 **12** 2 **Dora's Green**[15] 2366 4-8-10 45 ....(p) JerryO'Dwyer(3) 8 18
(S W Hall) *mid-div: rdn over 2f out: sn wknd* **33/1**
0363 **13** 7 **Detonate**[5] 2652 5-8-8 45 ....(b) WilliamBuick(5) 2 —
(Ms J S Doyle) *sn led: racd keenly: hdd 3f out: wknd 2f out* **9/1**

1m 25.74s (-0.15) **Going Correction** 0.0s/f (Stan)
WFA 3 from 4yo+ 9lb **13** Ran SP% **131.7**
Speed ratings (Par 101):100,99,98,98,98 98,96,96,94,93 88,85,77
CSF £142.87 CT £997.66 TOTE £5.10: £3.90, £7.50, £4.10; EX 461.40.The winner was sold to Mrs L Mongan for 8,000gns.
Owner P W Hiatt **Bred** Usk Valley Stud **Trained** Hook Norton, Oxon

FOCUS
Moderate handicap form rated through the third and fifth to previous course and distance form.
Primarily Official explanation: vet said gelding returned lame post-race

2799 CELEBRATE YOUR BIRTHDAY AT LINGFIELD PARK H'CAP 6f (P)
3:30 (3:30) (Class 6) (0-60,60) 3-Y-O+ **£2,388** (£705; £352) **Stalls** Low

Form RPR
303 **1** **Mambazo**[10] 2516 5-9-3 57 ....(e) RichardKingscote(3) 9 67
(S C Williams) *chsd ldrs: rdn to ld over 1f out: edgd lft: r.o* **10/3**[1]
/0-0 **2** 1½ **Berti Bertolini**[38] 1718 4-9-3 54 .... FergusSweeney 10 59
(Rae Guest) *s.i.s: hdwy over 3f out: rdn over 1f out: styd on* **14/1**
104 **3** ½ **Mistral Sky**[8] 2576 8-9-8 59 ....(v) JohnEgan 12 63
(Stef Liddiard) *chsd ldrs: rdn over 1f out: styd on same pce ins fnl f* **5/1**[2]
5050 **4** 1½ **Duke Of Milan (IRE)**[5] 2664 4-9-7 58 .... GeorgeBaker 6 57
(G C Bravery) *hld up: rdn over 1f out: edgd lft and r.o ins fnl f: nt rch ldrs* **6/1**[3]
3430 **5** 1¼ **Bens Georgie (IRE)**[16] 2334 5-9-2 53 .... RobertHavlin 3 48
(D K Ivory) *hld up: hdwy over 1f out: r.o: nt rch ldrs* **5/1**[2]
3120 **6** *shd* **Grand Palace (IRE)**[116] 560 4-9-2 56 ....(v) SaleemGolam(3) 1 51
(D Shaw) *led over 4f: wknd ins fnl f* **15/2**
0125 **7** *nk* **Balerno**[73] 980 8-9-5 56 .... AmirQuinn 4 50
(Mrs L J Mongan) *mid-div: rdn over 2f out: nt clr run over 1f out: swtchd rt: nt trble ldrs* **5/1**[2]
-006 **8** 5 **Hello Roberto**[17] 2315 6-9-4 60 ....(p) LukeMorris(5) 7 39
(R A Harris) *chsd ldrs: rdn over 2f out: wknd fnl f* **20/1**
02/ **9** 1½ **Sabre's Edge (IRE)**[217] 955 6-8-13 55 .... TravisBlock(5) 5 30
(R J Hodges) *hld up: a in rr* **25/1**
0150 **10** *hd* **Mustammer**[5] 2664 4-9-2 53 .... CatherineGannon 2 27
(D Shaw) *s.i.s: a in rr* **25/1**
0400 **11** 5 **Punching**[6] 2631 3-9-2 60 ....(bt[1]) StephenCarson 8 19
(Eve Johnson Houghton) *chsd ldr: rdn over 2f out: wknd over 1f out* **16/1**

1m 12.47s (-0.34) **Going Correction** 0.0s/f (Stan)
WFA 3 from 4yo+ 7lb **11** Ran SP% **124.1**
Speed ratings (Par 101):102,100,99,97,95 95,95,88,86,86 79
CSF £55.19 CT £207.40 TOTE £3.90: £2.20, £5.20, £1.50; EX 72.00.
Owner D G Burge **Bred** Barry Taylor **Trained** Newmarket, Suffolk

FOCUS
Just an ordinary handicap, but it was truly run. the runner-up is rated to old juvenile form but the third and fourth are not solid guides.

2800 CONFERENCES AT LINGFIELD PARK CLAIMING STKS 1m 4f (P)
4:10 (4:10) (Class 5) 3-Y-O+ **£2,968** (£876; £438) **Stalls** Low

Form RPR
3050 **1** **Champagne Shadow (IRE)**[13] 2431 6-9-9 68 ....(p) JohnEgan 7 56
(K A Ryan) *chsd ldrs: led 1f out: rdn clr* **11/10**[1]
-065 **2** 3 **Lady Ambitious**[16] 2332 4-9-4 40 .... RobertHavlin 3 46
(D K Ivory) *s.i.s: hld up: hdwy over 5f out: rdn to ld over 1f out: sn hdd: styd on same pce* **10/1**
602- **3** ½ **North Walk (IRE)**[7] 6898 4-9-11 70 .... SaleemGolam(3) 1 55
(Jennie Candlish) *led 2f: chsd ldrs: rdn over 2f out: styd on same pce fnl f* **7/1**[3]
6631 **4** ½ **Missie Baileys**[10] 2511 5-8-9 48 ....(p) JackMitchell(7) 6 42
(Mrs L J Mongan) *hld up: rdn over 3f out: styd on ins fnl f: nt trble ldrs* **11/4**[2]
0500 **5** *hd* **Cantique (IRE)**[15] 2362 3-7-9 49 .... WilliamBuick(5) 8 40
(Ms J S Doyle) *plld hrd and prom: led over 3f out: rdn and hdd over 1f out: no ex ins fnl f* **12/1**
0- **6** 11 **Cocobean**[11] 6522 3-8-7 0 ....(b[1]) SimonWhitworth 5 29
(M Appleby) *hld up: led 10f out: rdn and hdd over 3f out: wknd 2f out* **66/1**
-110 **7** 5 **Vanishing Dancer (SWI)**[60] 618 10-10-0 62 ....(bt) VinceSlattery 9 28
(K J Burke) *s.i.s: sn pushed along in rr: rdn and wknd over 3f out* **7/1**[3]
00/0 **8** *dist* **Running On Empty**[9] 2535 4-9-4 31 .... CatherineGannon 2 —
(P D Evans) *lost tch 10f out: t.o fnl 8f* **33/1**

2m 37.47s (3.08) **Going Correction** 0.0s/f (Stan)
WFA 3 from 4yo+ 14lb **8** Ran SP% **120.5**
Speed ratings (Par 103):89,87,86,86,86 78,75,—
CSF £15.14 TOTE £2.30: £1.30, £2.90, £2.20; EX 14.40.The winner was claimed by Miss Tor Sturgis for £10,000.
Owner John Duddy **Bred** Mrs Kate Watson **Trained** Hambleton, N Yorks

FOCUS
They went a very steady pace in this claimer and it turned into something of a sprint. The bare form is poor, with the runner-up rated only 40.
Running On Empty Official explanation: jockey said gelding lost its action

2801 PERFECT WEDDING VENUE H'CAP 1m 4f (P)
4:45 (4:46) (Class 6) (0-65,69) 3-Y-O **£2,388** (£705; £352) **Stalls** Low

Form RPR
00-0 **1** **Strobe**[15] 2362 3-9-0 58 .... JohnEgan 13 67
(J A Osborne) *hld up: hdwy u.p over 2f out: led and edgd lft ins fnl f: styd on wl* **12/1**
00-4 **2** 1¾ **Alnwick**[87] 790 3-8-13 57 .... FergusSweeney 7 63
(P D Cundell) *hld up in tch: rdn over 4f out: styd on same pce ins fnl f* **6/1**[3]
04-1 **3** ½ **Ballet Boy (IRE)**[3] 2727 3-9-11 69 6ex .... GeorgeBaker 16 74+
(Sir Mark Prescott) *s.i.s: rcvrd to ld after 1f: hdd over 9f out: led again 1/2-way: rdn clr over 3f out: hdd and unable qckn ins fnl f* **6/4**[1]
54-5 **4** 2½ **Duty Free (IRE)**[104] 649 3-9-7 65 .... RobertHavlin 6 66
(H Morrison) *chsd ldrs: rdn over 2f out: no ex fnl f* **5/1**[2]
-325 **5** *nk* **Chiff Chaff**[28] 1972 3-9-5 63 .... OscarUrbina 14 64
(M L W Bell) *chsd ldrs: rdn over 2f out: no ex fnl f* **6/1**[3]
030 **6** 4 **Fizzy Bella**[31] 1904 3-9-4 65 .... JerryO'Dwyer(3) 10 59
(M G Quinlan) *hld up: hdwy u.p over 2f out: nt trble ldrs* **33/1**
6406 **7** 13 **President Dan**[7] 2609 3-8-11 55 ....(v[1]) SamHitchcott 11 28
(M R Channon) *hld up: n.d* **33/1**
00-0 **8** ¾ **Slavonic Lake**[21] 2192 3-8-4 48 ....(t) CatherineGannon 15 20
(I A Wood) *chsd ldrs: led over 9f out: hdd 1/2-way: wknd over 2f out* **40/1**
00-0 **9** 5 **Roxy Singer**[12] 2445 3-7-11 46 oh1 .... LukeMorris(5) 3 10
(W J Musson) *mid-div: lost pl whn hmpd over 8f out: n.d* **33/1**
-055 **10** *hd* **Cat Six (USA)**[13] 2413 3-8-11 62 .... KMay(7) 1 26
(B J Meehan) *chsd ldrs over 8f* **25/1**
0-02 **11** 3 **Converti**[12] 2454 3-8-3 52 .... WilliamBuick(5) 12 11
(P F I Cole) *s.i.s: hld up: hdwy 1/2-way: wknd 4f out* **7/1**
0000 **12** 24 **Acece**[4] 2697 3-7-11 46 oh1 .... NicolPolli(5) 2 —
(M Appleby) *mid-div: lost pl whn hmpd over 8f out: sn bhd* **66/1**
0-00 **13** 1¾ **Time Upon Time**[23] 2127 3-8-8 52 .... PatDobbs 4 —
(W J Knight) *led 1f: lost pl over 8f out* **33/1**
0-06 **14** 2 **Ski For Luck (IRE)**[15] 2362 3-8-6 50 .... TPO'Shea 9 —
(J L Dunlop) *mid-div: rdn over 4f out: sn wknd* **25/1**
5002 **15** ½ **Whodunit (UAE)**[24] 2081 3-8-11 58 .... SaleemGolam(3) 8 —
(P W Hiatt) *trckd ldrs: plld hrd: wknd over 3f out* **12/1**

2m 31.83s (-2.56) **Going Correction** 0.0s/f (Stan) **15** Ran SP% **136.5**
Speed ratings (Par 97):108,106,106,104,104 101,93,92,89,89 87,71,70,68,68
CSF £87.10 CT £180.00 TOTE £20.30: £5.80, £1.80, £1.10; EX 112.70.
Owner Kerr-Dineen Pallett Tullett **Bred** Old Mill Stud **Trained** Upper Lambourn, Berks

FOCUS
They went a strong gallop in this modest event and the form should work out.
Roxy Singer Official explanation: vet said filly lost a shoe

2802 LINGFIELD PARK GOLF COURSE H'CAP 1m (P)
5:20 (5:21) (Class 5) (0-70,66) 4-Y-O+ **£3,071** (£906; £453) **Stalls** High

Form RPR
-215 **1** **Nan Jan**[10] 2521 5-8-9 54 ....(t) RobertHavlin 1 68+
(R Ingram) *hld up in tch: swtchd rt over 2f out: rdn to ld ins fnl f: r.o wl* **11/4**[1]
4003 **2** 3 **Scuba (IRE)**[22] 2149 5-8-7 57 ....(b) TravisBlock(5) 10 64
(H Morrison) *chsd ldrs: led over 2f out: rdn over 1f out: hdd and unable qckn ins fnl f* **5/1**[3]
3600 **3** 1½ **Special Place**[12] 2458 4-9-4 63 .... OscarUrbina 6 67
(J A R Toller) *hld up: hdwy over 2f out: rdn over 1f out: styd on same pce* **10/3**[2]
1530 **4** *hd* **Majehar**[12] 2467 5-9-0 59 .... AmirQuinn 9 62
(A G Newcombe) *hld up: hdwy over 1f out: nt rch ldrs* **11/2**
00-0 **5** 2 **Hey Presto**[16] 2336 7-7-10 48 oh2 ow1 .... RichardRowe(7) 7 46
(R Rowe) *hld up: r.o ins fnl f: nvr nrr* **25/1**
540 **6** 1 **Ganache (IRE)**[38] 1714 5-9-6 65 .... JohnEgan 4 61
(P R Chamings) *trckd ldrs: racd keenly: lost pl and hmpd over 2f out: n.d after* **14/1**
0300 **7** *hd* **Titus Lumpus (IRE)**[5] 2667 4-8-12 57 .... FergusSweeney 11 53
(R M Flower) *led over 5f: wknd fnl f* **9/1**
0331 **8** 2½ **Western Roots**[10] 2521 6-9-7 66 ....(p) GeorgeBaker 3 56
(M Appleby) *s.i.s: hld up: rdn over 1f out: n.d* **6/1**
550 **9** 2½ **Undeterred**[27] 2006 11-8-10 55 ....(b) VinceSlattery 5 39
(K J Burke) *chsd ldrs over 5f* **25/1**
4404 **10** ¾ **Sopran Gath (ITY)**[20] 2194 4-9-2 66 .... PatrickHills(5) 2 49
(J W Hills) *trckd ldr: plld hrd: rdn and wknd over 1f out* **7/1**

1m 39.34s (-0.09) **Going Correction** 0.0s/f (Stan) **10** Ran SP% **132.9**
Speed ratings (Par 103):100,97,95,95,93 92,92,89,87,86
CSF £19.76 CT £52.32 TOTE £3.30: £1.90, £2.50, £2.10; EX 24.20 Place 6 £25.46, Place 5 £136.04.
Owner The Waltons **Bred** Mrs S Ingram **Trained** Epsom, Surrey

FOCUS
An ordinary handicap that is anchored by the fifth but otherwise seems sound.
T/Plt: £408.50 to a £1 stake. Pool: £41,835.85. 74.75 winning tickets. T/Qpdt: £5.60 to a £1 stake. Pool: £3,225.60. 424.05 winning tickets. CR

2371 RIPON (R-H)
Thursday, June 21

OFFICIAL GOING: Soft
After 6" of rain since the weekend the ground was reckoned 'very testing'. There were 25 non-runners owing to the conditions.
Wind: Moderate, half-behind Weather: fine, sunny and warm

2803 E B F INGHAM UNDERWRITING MAIDEN STKS (DIV I) 6f
1:40 (1:45) (Class 5) 2-Y-O **£3,562** (£1,059; £529; £264) **Stalls** High

Form RPR
6 **1** **Captain Royale (IRE)**[15] 2353 2-9-3 0 .... DaneO'Neill 7 86+
(J Noseda) *mde all: pushed clr over 1f out: edgd lft ins fnl f: v readily* **13/8**[1]
34 **2** 5 **Demure Princess**[32] 1858 2-8-5 0 .... JackDean(7) 2 60
(W G M Turner) *hld up: hdwy 3f out: styd on to take 2nd ins fnl f: no ch w wnr* **14/1**

06 **3** 1 3/4 **Discanti (IRE)**[19] 2251 2-9-3 0....................................(t) GrahamGibbons 6 60
(T D Easterby) *trckd ldrs: wnt 2nd over 1f out: kpt on same pce* **10/1**
4 2 **Cobo Bay** 2-9-3 0.. NCallan 4 54
(K A Ryan) *swvd lft s: hdwy to chse ldrs over 3f out: hung rt over 1f out: kpt on* **16/1**
4 **5** 2 1/2 **Choisette**[47] 1478 2-8-12 0.. RoystonFfrench 8 41
(B Smart) *w ldrs: n.m.r after 2f: lost pl over 1f out* **8/1**[3]
2 **6** 3/4 **Boomtown**[9] 2532 2-9-0 0... GregFairley[(3)] 1 44
(M Johnston) *w ldrs: edgd lft 2f out: sn lost pl* **7/4**[2]
7 3 **Duke Of Touraine (IRE)** 2-9-3 0................................... LeeEnstone 11 35+
(P C Haslam) *got loose and rn abt on trck bef being sddled: sn chsng ldrs: edgd lft and lost pl over 2f out* **25/1**
8 17 **Lady From Westow** 2-8-12 0.. MickyFenton 9 —
(P T Midgley) *s.i.s: sn outpcd and bhd fnl 2f* **100/1**
50 **9** 1 1/4 **Sandies Choice**[32] 1859 2-8-12 0................................... DeanMernagh 10 —
(M Brittain) *w ldrs: wknd rapidly over 1f out* **100/1**

1m 15.66s (2.66) **Going Correction** +0.275s/f (Good) **9 Ran SP% 113.0**
Speed ratings (Par 93):93,86,84,81,78 77,73,50,48
CSF £24.67 TOTE £2.70: £1.20, £2.60, £2.50; EX 31.90.
Owner D Margolis and A Michaels **Bred** Skymarc Farm Inc **Trained** Newmarket, Suffolk

FOCUS
Marginally the slower of the two divisions but a winner of some potential and the race could be rated 5lb higher.

NOTEBOOK
Captain Royale(IRE), a quality-looking colt, travelled strongly in the bad ground and in the end came right away. He looks a fair prospect. (op 15-8 tchd 9-4)
Demure Princess, a strongly-made filly, still does not look 100% fit. Improving with every outing having started life in claiming company, she can surely find an opening. (op 18-1)
Discanti(IRE), still carrying plenty of condition, again showed ability and looks a likely nursery type. (op 12-1)
Cobo Bay, a robust, good-bodied May foal, looked very inexperienced. The outing should have taught him plenty. (op 9-1)
Choisette, who is only small, came off worst in a bumping match at the end of the first two furlongs. (op 7-1)
Boomtown, making a quick return, really took the eye in the paddock. He was all at sea on the undulating track and soft ground and must be given another chance after his bold effort on his debut just nine days earlier. (op 15-8 tchd 6-4 and 9-4 in places)
Sandies Choice Official explanation: jockey said filly had no more to give

2804 E B F INGHAM UNDERWRITING MAIDEN STKS (DIV II) 6f
2:10 (2:10) (Class 5) 2-Y-0 **£3,562** (£1,059; £529; £264) **Stalls** High

Form RPR
1 **Upper Class (IRE)** 2-9-0 0... GregFairley[(3)] 2 73+
(M Johnston) *sn in rr and pushed along: hdwy over 2f out: hung rt and led appr fnl f: styd on wl* **9/2**[2]
6 **2** 2 1/2 **Our Sunnie**[16] 2337 2-9-3 0... AdrianTNicholls 9 66
(D Nicholls) *led tl hdd appr fnl f: kpt on same pce* **5/1**[3]
3 shd **Silk Drum (IRE)** 2-9-3 0... TomEaves 8 65+
(J Howard Johnson) *sn outpcd and in last: swtchd outside over 1f out: styd on wl ins fnl f* **10/1**
6 **4** 1/2 **Daring Dream (GER)**[26] 2021 2-9-3 0.................................... NCallan 6 64
(T D Easterby) *sn chsng ldrs: chal 3f out: kpt on same pce appr fnl f* **9/2**[2]
0 **5** 1 3/4 **Glenshee (IRE)**[16] 2337 2-9-3 0.................................. GrahamGibbons 4 58
(J J Quinn) *chsd ldrs: sn drvn along: one pce fnl 2f* **10/1**
6 1 1/2 **Calmdownmate (IRE)** 2-9-3 0... PhillipMakin 1 54
(K R Burke) *in rr: sme hdwy over 2f out: nvr nr ldrs* **7/2**[1]
00 **7** 3/4 **Tharaya**[9] 2532 2-8-12 0... TonyHamilton 3 47
(T D Easterby) *chsd ldrs: fdd appr fnl f* **7/1**
0 **8** 6 **Transcendent (IRE)**[54] 1291 2-9-3 0.................................. PaulMulrennan 7 34
(J D Bethell) *sn trcking ldrs: effrt 2f out: sn wknd* **12/1**
0 **9** dist **Big Slick (IRE)**[35] 1792 2-9-3 0..................................... DeanMernagh 5 —
(M Brittain) *chsd ldrs: lost pl and heavily eased over 2f out: virtually p.u: sddle slipped* **33/1**

1m 15.83s (2.83) **Going Correction** +0.275s/f (Good) **9 Ran SP% 116.6**
Speed ratings (Par 93):92,88,88,87,85 83,82,74,—
CSF £27.58 TOTE £4.30: £1.60, £1.90, £2.70; EX 26.40.
Owner Sheikh Mohammed **Bred** Darley **Trained** Middleham Moor, N Yorks

FOCUS
Slightly quicker then the first division. The winner looks a fair prospect but overall it was probably the weaker half and the form looks modest at best.

NOTEBOOK
Upper Class(IRE), a May foal, is on the leg and looked very inexperienced beforehand. He warmed to his task and despite showing definite signs of greenness, in the end ran out a most decisive winner. (op 4-1 tchd 11-2)
Our Sunnie improved on his debut effort behaing much better beforehand this time. He should improve again. (op 13-2)
Silk Drum(IRE), a March foal, is a robust, round-barrelled individual. He struggled to keep up but when pulled wide put in some pleasing late work. He needs seven already. (op 8-1)
Daring Dream(GER) im proved on his debut effort and there should be even better to come with a little more time. (op 4-1)
Glenshee(IRE), a neat individual, had to be driven along to keep up. He is still learning what it is all about. (op 12-1)
Calmdownmate(IRE), a March foal, is on the leg at present. He was never in the contest but will be a lot wiser when he next appears. He is almost certainly capable of a fair bit better than he showed on his debut here. (tchd 10-3)
Big Slick(IRE) Official explanation: jockey said saddle slipped

2805 LEGAL AND RECEIVABLES H'CAP 5f
2:45 (2:47) (Class 5) (0-75,74) 3-Y-0+ **£3,562** (£1,059; £529; £264) **Stalls** High

Form RPR
0-50 **1** **Highland Warrior**[47] 1483 8-9-12 **72**................................. MickyFenton 13 87
(P T Midgley) *sn chsng ldrs against far side rail: led 1f out: styd on wl* **14/1**
1362 **2** 1 1/2 **Harrison's Flyer (IRE)**[5] 2655 6-8-10 **63**..................(p) BarrySavage[(7)] 9 73
(J M Bradley) *trckd ldrs: kpt on same pce ins fnl f* **5/1**[2]
-053 **3** 1 **Tilly's Dream**[7] 2608 4-9-10 **70**... NCallan 7 76
(P S McEntee) *t.k.h: nt clr run over 2f out: swtchd outside over 1f out: styd on ins fnl f* **14/1**
0641 **4** nk **Our Little Secret (IRE)**[13] 2418 5-9-5 **70**........................ PBradley[(5)] 2 75
(A Berry) *led on outer: hdd 1f out: wknd towards fin* **6/1**[3]
-105 **5** 1/2 **Exponential (IRE)**[14] 2390 5-8-12 **63**......................... KevinGhunowa[(5)] 4 67
(J M Bradley) *trckd ldrs: kpt on same pce appr fnl f* **8/1**
5030 **6** 2 1/2 **Bel Cantor**[2] 2744 4-9-8 **71**...................................... AndrewMullen[(3)] 8 66
(W J H Ratcliffe) *in rr: hdwy on outside 2f out: nvr rchd ldrs* **7/2**[1]
5042 **7** 3/4 **Princess Cleo**[8] 2553 4-9-0 **60**.................................... PaulMulrennan 12 52
(T D Easterby) *chsd ldrs towards far side: wknd appr fnl f* **7/1**

4020 **8** nk **Never Without Me**[38] 1718 7-9-0 **60**................................. DaneO'Neill 10 51
(J F Coupland) *in rr: effrt over 2f out: nvr nr ldrs* **12/1**
0-00 **9** 1/2 **Westbrook Blue**[33] 1854 5-9-0 **67**..............................(tp) JackDean[(7)] 5 56
(W G M Turner) *chsd ldrs on outer: sn drvn along: lost pl over 1f out* **16/1**
-026 **10** 3 **Mr Rooney (IRE)**[53] 1321 4-9-7 **67**............................... AdrianTNicholls 1 45
(D Nicholls) *chsd ldrs on outer: wknd 2f out* **22/1**

61.02 secs (0.82) **Going Correction** +0.275s/f (Good) **10 Ran SP% 108.0**
Speed ratings (Par 103):104,101,100,99,98 94,93,93,92,87
CSF £66.07 CT £655.33 TOTE £17.80: £4.40, £2.00, £3.00; EX 101.80.
Owner Frank & Annette Brady **Bred** Rowcliffe Stud **Trained** Westow, N Yorks
■ Hotham was withdrawn (11/2, refused to enter stalls.) R4 applies, deduct 15p in the £.

FOCUS
A modest handicap in which the winner took full advantage of a favourable mark and should continue to run well for this yard. The runner-up ran to his mark, the third is back to something like her best.

2806 GO RACING IN YORKSHIRE CLAIMING STKS 6f
3:20 (3:20) (Class 5) 3-Y-0+ **£3,238** (£963; £481; £240) **Stalls** High

Form RPR
-002 **1** **Looks Could Kill (USA)**[2] 2741 5-9-2 65........................ DavidKinsella 8 73
(E J Alston) *hld up: smooth hdwy over 2f out: led over 1f out: sn qcknd clr: easily* **2/1**[2]
1545 **2** 6 **Union Jack Jackson (IRE)**[8] 2561 5-9-2 60........(b) StephenDonohoe 9 55
(John A Harris) *drvn and lost pl after 2f: hdwy on ins 2f out: styd on to take 2nd ins fnl f* **4/1**[3]
-300 **3** 3/4 **Spiritual Peace (IRE)**[29] 1941 4-9-6 77.............................(p) NCallan 12 57
(K A Ryan) *led: edgd lft 2f out: sn hdd: kpt on same pce* **15/8**[1]
3200 **4** nk **Penel (IRE)**[8] 2550 6-8-10 51....................................(p) MickyFenton 1 46
(P T Midgley) *swvd lft s and rdr briefly lost iron: in rr and drvn along: hdwy on wd outside 2f out: styd on ins fnl f* **9/1**
0-20 **5** 1 1/4 **Princely Vale (IRE)**[23] 2104 5-8-5 50................................(p) JackDean[(7)] 5 44
(W G M Turner) *chsd ldrs: one pce fnl 2f* **10/1**
000- **6** 1 3/4 **Zap Attack**[255] 5865 7-8-12 36... DeanMernagh 3 39
(M Brittain) *chsd ldrs: hung rt over 1f out: one pce* **50/1**
-000 **7** 1 3/4 **The Keep**[9] 2535 5-8-0 39......................................(v) NataliaGemelova[(5)] 7 27
(R E Barr) *drvn in rr: lost pl over 2f out* **40/1**
060- **8** 10 **Born For Diamonds (IRE)**[278] 5368 5-8-5 36.......... RoystonFfrench 10 —
(R E Barr) *prom: hung rt and lost pl 2f out: sn bhd* **33/1**

1m 14.2s (1.20) **Going Correction** +0.275s/f (Good) **8 Ran SP% 114.5**
Speed ratings (Par 103):103,95,94,93,91 89,87,73
CSF £10.41 TOTE £3.50: £1.30, £1.80, £1.30; EX 12.10.The winner was claimed by A. B. Haynes for £12,000.
Owner Mr & Mrs G Middlebrook **Bred** Maple Leaf Farm **Trained** Longton, Lancs

FOCUS
With Spiritual Peace again below his best this took little winning but Looks Could Kill could hardly have taken it in better style, revelling in the easy ground.
Penel(IRE) Official explanation: jockey said gelding stumbled leaving stalls
Born For Diamonds(IRE) Official explanation: jockey said mare had no more to give

2807 ROYAL BANK OF SCOTLAND H'CAP 1m 1f
4:00 (4:00) (Class 3) (0-90,88) 4-Y-0+
£9,348 (£2,799; £1,399; £700; £349; £175) **Stalls** High

Form RPR
0021 **1** **Fortunate Isle (USA)**[22] 2136 5-9-6 **87**........................(p) TonyHamilton 5 95
(R A Fahey) *mde all: hld on towards fin* **7/2**[2]
3315 **2** 1/2 **Full Victory (IRE)**[14] 2401 5-8-8 **80**........................... KevinGhunowa[(5)] 4 87
(R A Farrant) *hld up: hdwy on ins to chse wnr over 2f out: rdn and hung violently lft over 1f out: styd on towards fin* **5/1**[3]
0505 **3** 4 **Collateral Damage (IRE)**[24] 2093 4-9-3 **87**............. DuranFentiman[(3)] 6 86
(T D Easterby) *trckd ldrs: effrt over 3f out: outpcd whn nt clr run over 2f out: styd on to go modest 3rd 1f out* **7/4**[1]
006- **4** 2 1/2 **Kamanda Laugh**[175] 6678 6-9-7 **88**.. NCallan 8 81
(K A Ryan) *trckd ldrs: wkng whn n.m.r 2f out* **11/2**
350- **5** hd **Baan (USA)**[188] 6836 4-9-2 **86**.. GregFairley[(3)] 3 79
(M Johnston) *chsd wnr: drvn 4f out: lost pl over 2f out* **7/1**
-320 **6** 1/2 **Fremen (USA)**[48] 1458 7-9-0 **81**..................................... AdrianTNicholls 2 73
(D Nicholls) *t.k.h in rr: effrt on outer over 3f out: sn chsng ldrs: wknd fnl f* **10/1**

1m 55.24s (1.39) **Going Correction** +0.275s/f (Good) **6 Ran SP% 112.2**
Speed ratings (Par 107):104,103,100,97,97 97
CSF £20.84 CT £38.91 TOTE £4.30: £2.10, £3.00; EX 14.90.
Owner The First Team **Bred** Gainsborough Stud Management Ltd **Trained** Musley Bank, N Yorks
■ Stewards' Enquiry : Kevin Ghunowa caution: careless riding

FOCUS
A good handicap which saw the first pair come clear and the race could be rated a little better.

NOTEBOOK
Fortunate Isle(USA), 5lb higher for his Beverley success, followed up by making all for a game success. He is now coming good for connections and is reportedly being considered for a tilt at the John Smith's Cup at York next month - a race his yard won with Vintage Premium in 2004. (op 11-4)
Full Victory(IRE) again showed his liking for soft ground and came through from off the pace with every chance, before hanging his chance away entering the final furlong. He will most likely go up again in the weights for this. (tchd 6-1)
Collateral Damage(IRE), well backed, had just started to hit a flat spot before meeting trouble nearing the 2f marker. He could muster just the one pace when in the clear, however, and remains a very hard horse to catch right. (op 2-1 tchd 9-4)
Kamanda Laugh, last seen over hurdles in December last year, was beating a retreat prior to being hampered 2f out. He should strip a deal fitter with this run under his belt. (tchd 5-1)
Baan(USA), who lost his way last term, was another who left the impression he would be sharper for this seasonal bow. (op 10-1 tchd 13-2)

2808 TOTAL BUTLER H'CAP 1m 4f 10y
4:35 (4:36) (Class 4) (0-85,83) 3-Y-0 **£5,047** (£1,510; £755; £377; £188) **Stalls** High

Form RPR
0-11 **1** **Copernican**[8] 2558 3-8-9 71 6ex...................................... PaulMulrennan 6 84+
(Sir Mark Prescott) *mde all: qcknd over 4f out: shkn up and clr over 1f out: unchal* **7/4**[1]
532 **2** 5 **Honorable Love**[19] 2253 3-8-9 **71**.. PhillipMakin 2 76
(M Dods) *t.k.h early: hld up: hdwy to chse wnr over 3f out: hung rt over 1f out: no imp* **14/1**
-013 **3** 5 **Highland Legacy**[41] 1624 3-8-8 **73**................................. AndrewElliott[(3)] 9 70
(M L W Bell) *rn in snatches: hdwy over 5f out: outpcd over 3f out: kpt on to take modest 3rd nr fin* **4/1**[3]
51-2 **4** 1/2 **Bayonyx (IRE)**[41] 1624 3-8-13 **75**.. TomEaves 7 71
(J Howard Johnson) *chsd ldrs: rdn over 3f out: wknd fnl f* **7/2**[2]

6-65 **5** *8* **Sendali (FR)**[28] 1968 3-7-13 **64** oh4 .... DuranFentiman(3) 4 47
(J D Bethell) *in tch: effrt over 4f out: lost pl 3f out* **40/1**

32-0 **6** *20* **Sivota (IRE)**[34] 1827 3-8-5 **67** .... PaulEddery 8 18
(T P Tate) *dwlt: in rr: pushed along and outpcd over 6f out: lost pl over 4f out: bhd whn eased fnl 2f* **7/1**

1414 **7** *10* **Dee Cee Elle**[8] 2574 3-8-5 **70** .... GregFairley(3) 5 —
(M Johnston) *chsd ldrs: pushed along 7f out: rdn and lost pl over 4f out: bhd whn eased fnl f* **4/1**[3]

2m 38.79s (1.79) **Going Correction** +0.275s/f (Good) **7** Ran SP% **120.2**
Speed ratings (Par 101):105,101,98,98,92 79,72
CSF £30.76 CT £92.32 TOTE £2.10: £1.40, £4.00; EX 22.10.
Owner Lady Katharine Watts **Bred** Gestut Gorlsdorf **Trained** Newmarket, Suffolk

FOCUS
A fair handicap in which the progressive winner ran his rivals ragged from the front. The form is rated positively for now.
Sivota(IRE) Official explanation: jockey said gelding became upset in stalls
Dee Cee Elle Official explanation: trainer's rep had no explanation for the poor form shown

2809 RACING AT REDCAR TOMORROW AND SATURDAY H'CAP 1m
5:10 (5:10) (Class 6) (0-65,65) 4-Y-0+ **£2,590** (£770; £385; £192) **Stalls** High

Form RPR

0000 **1** **Apache Nation (IRE)**[17] 2302 4-8-8 **52** .... PhillipMakin 10 64+
(M Dods) *trckd ldrs on inner: nt clr run and swtchd lft over 2f out: led appr fnl f: edgd lft: styd on strly* **4/1**[1]

5402 **2** *2 1/2* **The Grey One (IRE)**[20] 2214 4-9-0 **63** ....(p) KevinGhunowa(5) 7 69
(J M Bradley) *tk fierce hold: sn trcking ldrs: led 2f out: hdd appr fnl f: no ex* **9/2**[2]

0200 **3** *1 3/4* **Azreme**[23] 2107 7-9-3 **61** .... DaneO'Neill 8 63
(P Howling) *in rr: hdwy over 3f out: chsng ldrs over 1f out: kpt on same pce* **9/2**[2]

6523 **4** *4* **Nevinstown (IRE)**[17] 2298 7-8-8 **52** .... TonyHamilton 16 45
(C Grant) *led: hdd 2f out: one pce* **5/1**[3]

0-65 **5** *3* **Tidy (IRE)**[21] 2169 7-9-1 **62** ....(p) GregFairley(3) 4 48
(Micky Hammond) *sn prom: drvn 4f out: wknd over 1f out* **7/1**

0-00 **6** *nk* **Pianoforte (USA)**[17] 2311 5-9-0 **58** .... DavidKinsella 12 43
(E J Alston) *hld up in mid-div: kpt on fnl 3f: nvr rchd ldrs* **12/1**

-000 **7** *1 3/4* **Orpen's Astaire (IRE)**[3] 2714 4-8-2 **49** .... AndrewElliott(3) 3 30
(Jedd O'Keeffe) *sn chsng ldrs: chal over 3f out: wknd over 1f out* **12/1**

40-0 **8** *1 3/4* **Hows That**[3] 2716 5-7-12 **49** oh1 ow3 ....(p) KellyHarrison(7) 6 26
(K R Burke) *chsd ldrs: chal over 3f out: wknd over 1f out* **16/1**

5000 **9** *hd* **Suffolk House**[45] 1527 5-8-3 **50** oh1 ow4 .... AndrewMullen(3) 15 27
(M Brittain) *hld up in mid-div: effrt 3f out: nvr a threat* **20/1**

3500 **10** *15* **Anduril**[21] 2169 6-9-7 **65** ....(b) MickyFenton 2 7
(Miss M E Rowland) *swvd lft s: sn bhd: lost tch fnl 2f* **18/1**

1m 42.86s (1.76) **Going Correction** +0.275s/f (Good) **10** Ran SP% **116.8**
Speed ratings (Par 101):102,99,97,93,90 90,88,86,86,71
CSF £21.92 CT £84.36 TOTE £3.50: £1.10, £1.80, £2.30; EX 23.80.
Owner Doug Graham **Bred** Crone Stud Farms Ltd **Trained** Denton, Co Durham
■ Stewards' Enquiry : Phillip Makin one-day ban: careless riding (Jul 2)

FOCUS
A moderate handicap and modest form, although the first three were suited by the ground.
Suffolk House Official explanation: trainer said gelding did not handle the soft ground

2810 BEAUMONT ROBINSON LADIES' DERBY H'CAP (LADY AMATEUR RIDERS) 1m 4f 10y
5:45 (5:46) (Class 6) (0-65,65) 4-Y-0+ **£3,123** (£968; £484; £242) **Stalls** High

Form RPR

60/6 **1** **Gardasee (GER)**[29] 1942 5-9-1 **48** .... MissJAKidd(5) 4 58
(T P Tate) *led tl 7f out: led 3f out: rdn ins fnl f: all out* **7/2**[1]

0-00 **2** *shd* **Prince Zafonic**[9] 2531 4-10-2 **63** ....(t) MissALHutchinson(5) 8 73
(Miss Gay Kelleway) *s.i.s: effrt on inner whn n.m.r 4f out: gd hdwy 2f out: chal wl ins fnl f: jst hld* **33/1**

000/ **3** *1 3/4* **Grey Samurai**[195] 4139 7-9-4 **46** oh1 .... MissLEllison 5 53
(B Ellison) *sn chsng ldrs: kpt on same pce appr fnl f* **9/2**[2]

1146 **4** *7* **Atlantic Gamble (IRE)**[90] 740 7-10-3 **64** ....(p) MissKellyBurke(5) 10 60
(K R Burke) *s.i.s: hdwy 3f out: kpt on: nvr nr ldrs* **14/1**

-333 **5** *3/4* **Patavium (IRE)**[14] 2391 4-10-1 **57** .... MissADeniel 1 52
(E W Tuer) *trckd ldr: led 7f out tl 3f out: wknd over 1f out* **17/2**

0-00 **6** *3* **Inchloss (IRE)**[15] 2370 6-9-4 **46** oh1 .... MissFayeBramley 11 36
(S Parr) *trckd ldrs: t.k.h: edgd lft over 2f out: sn wknd* **22/1**

6050 **7** *hd* **Lady's Law**[12] 2467 4-9-1 **46** oh1 .... MissARyan(3) 6 36
(Rae Guest) *hld up in mid-div: effrt on inner and n.m.r 4f out: wknd 2f out* **22/1**

6501 **8** *2* **Prelude**[9] 2531 6-10-2 **58** 6ex .... MissEJJones 7 44
(W M Brisbourne) *hld up in mid-div: effrt over 3f out: edgd lft: hung rt and lost pl over 1f out* **7/1**

0003 **9** *6* **Alsadaa (USA)**[13] 2431 4-10-4 **65** .... MissJCoward(5) 13 42
(M W Easterby) *prom: edgd lft over 3f out: rdn and hung rt over 2f out: sn lost pl* **12/1**

0046 **10** *35* **King's Account (USA)**[15] 2370 5-9-11 **53** ....(p) MrsCBartley 9 —
(S Gollings) *t.k.h in rr: edgd rt 4f out: sn lost pl: eased ins fnl f: t.o* **11/2**[3]

6-56 **11** *14* **Fiddlers Creek (IRE)**[21] 685 8-9-1 **46** ....(p) JenniferRiding(3) 12 —
(R Allan) *trckd ldrs: effrt and hung lft over 3f out: lost pl over 2f out: bhd and eased ins fnl f* **18/1**

2m 43.16s (6.16) **Going Correction** +0.275s/f (Good) **32** Ran SP% **110.1**
Speed ratings (Par 101):90,89,88,84,83 81,81,80,76,52 43
CSF £110.55 CT £397.27 TOTE £4.10: £1.90, £9.50, £1.90; EX 120.90 Place 6 £212.97, Place 5 £55.22.
Owner A S Helaissi **Bred** Gestut Romerhof **Trained** Tadcaster, N Yorks
■ Richtee was withdrawn (8/1, rein broke on way to start.) R4 applies, deduct 10p in the £.

FOCUS
Moderate handicap form, the winner running his best race since early last year.
Prelude Official explanation: trainer said mare spread a plate
King's Account(USA) Official explanation: trainer said gelding was unsuited by the soft ground
Fiddlers Creek(IRE) Official explanation: jockey said gelding lost its action
T/Plt: £83.00 to a £1 stake. Pool: £43,884.65. 385.75 winning tickets. T/Qpdt: £9.60 to a £1 stake. Pool: £2,739.75. 210.90 winning tickets. WG

2499 CHANTILLY (R-H)
Thursday, June 21
OFFICIAL GOING: Good to soft

2811a PRIX HAMPTON (LISTED RACE) 5f
1:20 (1:22) 3-Y-0+ **£17,568** (£7,027; £5,270; £3,514; £1,757)

RPR

1 **Arc De Triomphe (GER)**[35] 1800 5-9-5 .... JVictoire 1 106
(D Fechner, Germany)

2 *hd* **Sacho (GER)**[51] 9-9-5 .... AlxiBadel 5 105
(W Kujath, Germany)

3 *nk* **Rakiza (IRE)**[30] 3-8-7 .... DBonilla 7 98
(F Head, France)

4 *1 1/2* **Tycoon's Hill (IRE)**[39] 1704 8-9-5 .... CSoumillon 8 99
(Robert Collet, France)

5 *snk* **Salute The Sun (FR)**[19] 4-8-13 .... RonanThomas 2 92
(L Urbano-Grajales, France)

6 *1* **Fulminant (IRE)**[60] 1189 6-9-2 ....(b) WMongil 4 92
(W Kujath, Germany)

7 *5* **Biniou (IRE)**[15] 2352 4-9-5 .... SPasquier 6 77
(R M H Cowell) *led or disp ld to 1/2-way: rdn and sn btn 2f out: eased* **8/1**[1]

58.60 secs (-1.70)
WFA 3 from 4yo+ 6lb **7** Ran SP% **11.1**
PARI-MUTUEL: WIN 6.00; PL 3.10, 4.40; DF 21.20.
Owner Frau B Stenzel **Bred** Frau B Stenzel **Trained** Baden-Baden, Germany
■ Stewards' Enquiry : Alxi Badel 100 fine: whip abuse
Ronan Thomas 100 fine: whip abuse

NOTEBOOK
Biniou(IRE) was quickly into his stride and amongst the leaders but was beginning to struggle at halfway and faded away tamely to finish last of the seven runners. He did not look happy on the ground in the final stages and his trainer said he would take him home for a thorough health check.

2785 ASCOT (R-H)
Friday, June 22
OFFICIAL GOING: Good to soft (soft in places on round course)
Wind: Light to moderate, against Weather: Sunny spells and heavy showers

2812 ALBANY STKS (GROUP 3) (FILLIES) 6f
2:30 (2:33) (Class 1) 2-Y-0
£34,068 (£12,912; £6,462; £3,222; £1,614; £810) **Stalls** Centre

Form RPR

23 **1** **Nijoom Dubai**[20] 2241 2-8-12 0 .... JamieSpencer 11 103+
(M R Channon) *swtchd rt s: hld up: swtchd rt and hdwy over 2f out: edgd lft and led over 1f out: drvn out and r.o ins fnl f* **50/1**

21 **2** *1 1/4* **You'resothrilling (USA)**[18] 2325 2-8-12 0 .... MJKinane 15 102+
(A P O'Brien, Ire) *fly-jmpd leaving stalls: hld up: swtchd rt and hdwy over 2f out: hmpd by wnr over 1f out: sn swtchd rt: wnt 2nd ins fnl f: r.o: a hld* **7/4**[1]

1 **3** *2* **Baffled (USA)**[30] 1945 2-8-12 0 .... LDettori 17 96+
(J Noseda) *lw: midfield: hdwy 3f out: rdn over 2f out: hmpd over 1f out: lugged rt ins fnl f: styd on* **6/1**[3]

461 **4** *hd* **Aide Memoir (IRE)**[12] 2488 2-8-12 0 .... MartinDwyer 18 92
(S Kirk) *hld up: hdwy 3f out: led jst over 2f out: rdn and hdd over 1f out: styd on same pce ins fnl f* **33/1**

3 **5** *1* **Cute**[16] 2365 2-8-12 0 .... RyanMoore 20 89
(C E Brittain) *midfield: pushed along and hdwy over 2f out: styd on ins fnl f: nt pce of ldrs* **16/1**

11 **6** *1 3/4* **Janina**[35] 1821 2-8-12 0 .... RHills 1 84
(B W Hills) *hld up in tch: effrt 2f out: chsd ldrs over 1f out: one pce ins fnl f* **4/1**[2]

31 **7** *1/2* **Waveline (USA)**[32] 1882 2-8-12 0 .... JimmyFortune 19 83
(B J Meehan) *rdr briefly lost iron leaving stalls: s.i.s: bhd: hdwy 2f out: styd on over 1f out: one pce wl ins fnl f* **33/1**

42 **8** *3/4* **Miss Emma May (IRE)**[16] 2365 2-8-12 0 .... TedDurcan 4 80
(D R C Elsworth) *racd keenly: hld up: rdn over 2f out: hdwy over 1f out: kpt on ins fnl f: nt troube ldrs* **50/1**

161 **9** *1/2* **Loch Jipp (USA)**[23] 2134 2-8-12 0 .... KDarley 6 79
(J S Wainwright) *in tch: rdn and outpcd 3f out: kpt on fr over 1f out: nt pce of ldrs* **25/1**

23 **10** *1 1/2* **Miss Versatile (IRE)**[13] 2468 2-8-12 0 .... LPKeniry 9 74
(J S Moore) *prom: rdn over 2f out: wknd over 1f out* **100/1**

1 **11** *hd* **Festoso (IRE)**[35] 1814 2-8-12 0 .... PhilipRobinson 21 74
(H J L Dunlop) *lw: midfield: hdwy 3f out: ev ch over 2f out: wknd ins fnl f* **20/1**

21 **12** *2 1/2* **Eileen's Violet (IRE)**[32] 1897 2-8-12 0 .... StephenDonohoe 7 66
(P D Evans) *midfield: pushed along over 3f out: sn outpcd* **25/1**

51 **13** *shd* **Liberty Belle (IRE)**[28] 2000 2-8-12 0 .... KerrinMcEvoy 16 66
(J R Best) *lw: prom: ev ch over 2f out: edgd lft u.p over 1f out: wknd ins fnl f* **12/1**

12 **14** *3* **Alizadora**[19] 2271 2-8-12 0 ....(b[1]) SebSanders 3 57
(Sir Mark Prescott) *gd spd: ev ch over 2f out: wknd ent fnl 2f* **12/1**

42 **15** *6* **Sophie's Girl**[6] 2663 2-8-12 0 .... DarryllHolland 12 39
(P W Chapple-Hyam) *lw: prom tl rdn and wknd 2f out* **40/1**

33 **16** *3 1/2* **May Day Queen (IRE)**[18] 2325 2-8-12 0 .... DaneO'Neill 10 29
(R Hannon) *lw: midfield tl wknd over 2f out* **16/1**

6 **17** *4* **Bellalatino (IRE)**[49] 1445 2-8-12 0 .... JMurtagh 14 17
(Mrs Norma Pook) *s.i.s: sn bhd* **150/1**

18 *3/4* **Miss Deeds (IRE)** 2-8-12 0 .... JHBowman 8 14
(N P Littmoden) *neat: led: rdn and hdd jst over 2f out: sn wknd* **100/1**

014 **19** *7* **Affirmatively**[43] 1608 2-8-12 0 .... JohnEgan 5 —
(D R C Elsworth) *midfield: lost pl 3f out: n.d after* **66/1**

004 **20** *4* **Una Auroraborealis**[8] 2604 2-8-12 0 .... ChrisCatlin 13 —
(J Ryan) *midfield tl wknd over 2f out* **100/1**

1m 15.55s (0.65) **Going Correction** +0.125s/f (Good) **20** Ran SP% **127.6**
Speed ratings (Par 100):100,98,95,95,94 91,91,90,89,87 87,83,83,79,71 67,61,60,51,46
CSF £132.94 TOTE £74.20: £13.90, £1.50, £2.00; EX 339.10 Trifecta £1858.90 Pool: £5,760.17 - 2.20 winning units..

Owner Jaber Abdullah **Bred** Bloodhorse International Limited **Trained** West Ilsley, Berks
■ Petit Parc was withdrawn (100/1, refused to enter stalls.)

FOCUS

Sander Camillo won this last year, but it remains to be seen if there was anything of her calibre in a big field. The surprise winner was not flattered but the second was 6lb off her Irish form. With the weather turning nasty afterwards they had the best of the ground for this contest, but the bias towards those drawn on the far side was still evident, with the first five all berthed 11 or higher. Time comparisons with other races on the card are difficult with the ground subsequently deteriorating, but to the naked eye the pace looked solid without being breakneck.

NOTEBOOK

Nijoom Dubai hardly came into this with the strongest credentials having been a beaten into third when favourite for a Folkestone maiden auction last time, though to be fair the pair that finished either side of her have both subsequently won. She proved a revelarion here though, scything through her rivals over on the far side before winning going away and on this evidence she will be worth her place in the top two-year-old fillies' events from now on, though the evidence is that she may need some cut to show her best. Her owner and trainer have enjoyed a lot of luck with their two-year-old fillies at this meeting in recent years and hopefully this filly will carry her talent right through to next season. (op 40-1)

You'resothrilling(USA) was a little errant leaving the stalls which meant that she had a bit of running to do from an early stage, but no more so than the eventual winner. She tried to follow her through towards the latter stages, but never really looked like getting to her and had to be contest with clear second-best. She had her conditions here so can have few excuses though she does shape as though she would appreciate another furlong. (op 11-8 tchd 15-8 and 2-1 in places)

Baffled(USA) ◆, game winner of a Polytrack maiden on her debut, hit a flat spot just after halfway but was in the process of rallying when taking a broadside from the weakening Liberty Belle over a furlong out which briefly knocked her out of her stride. To her great credit, she stayed on again to snatch third place near the line and given her lack of experience, especially on turf, this was a cracking effort. There should be more to come from her as she steps up in trip. (op 15-2 tchd 8-1 in places)

Aide Memoir(IRE) ◆, who improved to win a strongly run Bath maiden last time, showed that performance to be no fluke in this much stronger company. She made a big move over on the far side to hit the front around a quarter of a mile out, but could not get away and was eventually overhauled. If she can be held on to a little longer, there should be a nice race to be won with her. (op 40-1 tchd 50-1)

Cute ◆, third in a Nottingham maiden on her debut, was doing all her best work late and reversed form with Miss Emma May, who finished ahead of her at Nottingham, though admittedly she was much the best drawn of the pair here. She should not be underestimated though and she will show her true worth over longer trips than this. Official explanation: jockey said filly hung left throughout (op 25-1)

Janina ◆ lost her unbeaten record, but faced an impossible task as it turned out. Not only was she worst drawn, she was also the only one to start from her bank of stalls and with the filly intended to come of stall 2 a late withdrawal, she found herself berthed three horse-widths away from her nearest rival. Given the way the straight track has been riding this week, that was hugely significant and she did wonders to get herself into any sort of contention at all. A big line can be drawn through this effort and she deserves to gain compensation at this level at the earliest opportunity. (tchd 9-2 in places, 7-2 in places)

Waveline(USA), up a furlong and on easier ground, like the runner-up was awkward leaving the stalls and gave herself plenty to do. She did stay on towards the far side in the latter stages without ever looking a threat, but still posted a creditable effort. Official explanation: jockey said filly jumped awkwardly from the stalls and lost an iron (tchd 50-1)

Miss Emma May(IRE) had little chance from her draw and failed to confirm Nottingham running with Cute, though she did reverse earlier Newmarket form with Festoso. She shapes as though she will relish a step up to 7f, though it may be best to give her a confidence-booster in a maiden before returning her to Pattern company.

Loch Jipp(USA), whose Hilary Needler victory posed more questions than it answered, found herself on the wrong side this time but she finished a bit closer to Janina than she had previously done at York, so probably performed as well as could be expected under the circumstances.

Miss Versatile(IRE) did not perform at all badly on this softer ground in this much tougher company and she should find a race before too long.

Festoso(IRE), having only her second start, looked like taking a hand at one stage but she did not get home and failed to confirm Newmarket running with Miss Emma May, even though she was drawn much the better of the pair here. Perhaps the easier ground exposed a lack of stamina in this better company, but whatever the reason, she still looks a nice filly. (op 25-1)

Eileen's Violet(IRE), surprise winner of a Windsor condtions event last time, was not totally disgraced from her ordinary draw.

Liberty Belle(IRE) showed good speed for a long way, but did not seem to see out the trip in this ground. (op 16-1)

Alizadora, beaten at odds-on by Tuesday's Windsor Castle Stakes-winner Drawnfromthepast at Brighton last time, was up there from the start in the first-time blinkers, but a combination of a poor draw and the easier ground appeared to find her out. (op 14-1 tchd 16-1 in places)

Miss Deeds(IRE), a 40,000gns two-year-old out of a half-sister to a high-class performer at up to 1m2f in France, faced a very stiff task on this racecourse debut, but showed good speed from her ordinary draw for much of the way before fading. She will find much easier opportunities than this.

2813 KING EDWARD VII STKS (GROUP 2) (C&G) 1m 4f

3:05 (3:08) (Class 1) 3-Y-O

£113,560 (£43,040; £21,540; £10,740; £5,380; £2,700) **Stalls** High

Form				RPR
1121	1		**Boscobel**[35] [1803] 3-8-12 100 ... JoeFanning 3 (M Johnston) *mde all: rdn and qcknd over 2f out: hld on wl fnl f* **7/1**	116
2114	2	1	**Lucarno (USA)**[20] [2235] 3-8-12 113 ... JimmyFortune 7 (J H M Gosden) *lw: settled 2nd gng wl: effrt and hrd rdn over 1f out: pressed wnr fnl f: a jst hld* **5/2**[1]	114
5020	3	1 ½	**Yellowstone (IRE)**[20] [2235] 3-8-12 0 ... JMurtagh 9 (A P O'Brien, Ire) *in tch: hrd rdn and outpcd over 2f out: rallied and r.o fnl f* **8/1**	112
34-1	4	1 ½	**Lion Sands**[28] [1998] 3-8-12 100 ... LDettori 6 (L M Cumani) *chsd ldrs: rdn 3f out: one pce fnl 2f* **4/1**[2]	110
011	5	½	**Spice Route**[37] [1773] 3-8-12 95 ... JamieSpencer 5 (M L W Bell) *lw: hld up in 6th: effrt and swtchd to outside 2f out: rdn and kpt on: nt pce to chal* **12/1**	109
	6	1 ¼	**Ashkazar (FR)**[25] [2101] 3-8-12 0 ... CSoumillon 4 (A De Royer-Dupre, France) *str: lw: dwlt: hld up and bhd: effrt over 2f out: nvr nr to chal* **14/1**	107
1216	7	3	**Salford Mill (IRE)**[20] [2235] 3-8-12 105 ... TedDurcan 2 (D R C Elsworth) *t.k.h in rr: hrd rdn over 2f out: edgd rt and no rspnse* **11/2**[3]	102
5-1	8	nk	**Harland**[83] [849] 3-8-12 92 ... PhilipRobinson 1 (M A Jarvis) *hld up in rr: hdwy into midfield on outside 5f out: hrd rdn and wknd 2f out* **10/1**	102
3-51	9	7	**Al Tharib (USA)**[43] [1605] 3-8-12 101 ... RHills 8 (Sir Michael Stoute) *prom tl wknd 2f out* **12/1**	90

2m 37.13s (4.13) **Going Correction** +0.475s/f (Yiel) 9 Ran SP% **118.7**

Speed ratings (Par 111): 105,104,103,102,102 101,99,98,94

CSF £25.61 TOTE £8.90: £2.30, £1.30, £3.00; EX 33.20 Trifecta £210.70 Pool: £11,070.32 - 37.29 winning units..

Owner Sheikh Mohammed **Bred** Darley **Trained** Middleham Moor, N Yorks

FOCUS

Judging by the way the runners were making a print in the turf running down to Swinley Bottom, the heavy rain which preceded this contest had made a difference to the ground. The pace was also modest however, which resulted in a modest time for a race of its stature even allowing for the going. The ideal place to be in circumstances like this is out in front and the first two home held those positions throughout, whilst several of those held up were thrown very wide rounding the home bend. Boscobel was up 11lb on his Hamilton form. It is doubtful if Lucarno was at his best and the third is the best guide.

NOTEBOOK

Boscobel, winner of four of his previous five races, may have been stepping up in class but one thing you can guarantee with a Johnston inmate is that if you allow them a soft lead, whatver the grade, they will prove very hard to pass and that is how it turned out. He looked to be a sitting duck for the favourite the whole way but, sticking tight to the inside rail throughout, he took a length or two out of his rivals turning for home and there was no way he was going to throw it away after that. He is a very nice type and the St Leger has been rightly mentioned, but the way this race was run almost certainly flatters him and he probably still has to truly prove himself at such a lofty level. A race like the Great Voltigeur may be the ideal sort of contest for him to show what he is truly capable of.

Lucarno(USA), representing the Derby form, had a question mark against him with regard to the softening ground, but he was in the perfect position throughout and travelled as if conditions were not bothering him at all. It seemed as though he could pick the leader off when he wanted, but his rival rather got away from him turning in and, try as he might, he could never make up the leeway in time. Whilst this effort may not have advertised the Derby form in glowing terms, he is worth another chance on better ground and still looks up to winning races at Group level. (op 9-4 tchd 11-4 in places)

Yellowstone(IRE) did not perform badly in a race domnated by the two pace-setters, and the way he kept on suggested he would have preferred a stronger all-round pace. He did finish a bit closer to Lucarno than he had done at Epsom, but is obviously not amongst the very best at Ballydoyle so may not be an easy horse to place. (op 11-1 tchd 12-1 in places)

Lion Sands, taking a huge step up in class following his Haydock maiden victory in which Thursday's King George V Handicap winner Heron Bay finished third, was in a good position just behind the front two throughout, but when asked to go and pick them up he did not find that much. He did face a stiff task here, but may be worth another chance in Pattern company on a sounder surface. (op 5-1 tchd 11-2 in places)

Spice Route, stepping up from handicap company, had it all to do on official ratings and, as was true of all those held up, failed to make much impression from off the pace, especially as he was forced very wide in order to see daylight. He still does not have that many miles on the clock though, and remains capable of making his mark in Listed company. (op 14-1)

Ashkazar(FR) was proven in the ground, but this was a much stiffer task than those he had been facing. Kept wide throughout, even on the run down to Swinley Bottom, he came very wide into the home straight and never looked like getting involved. (op 16-1)

Salford Mill(IRE) never picked up from off the pace and ran much the worst of the trio that contested the Derby, but he was not in the ideal position in a steadily run race and it did appear that the ground had gone against him. He is worth another chance to show this running to be all wrong back on better ground. (op 4-1 tchd 6-1 in places)

Harland, not seen since winning his maiden on the opening day of the turf season, would not have minded the softer ground but he had the lowest offcial rating in the field and was right up against it. A brief move on the run up from Swinley Bottom came to little and he will surely find much easier opportunities than this. (tchd 11-1 and 12-1 in places)

Al Tharib(USA), whose Chester maiden victory has worked out well, was very disappointing as he was handy enough for much of the way but dropped away very tamely. He is surely better than this, but while the ground may have been an issue, he has run well on it before.

2814 CORONATION STKS (GROUP 1) (FILLIES) 1m (R)

3:45 (3:48) (Class 1) 3-Y-O

£141,950 (£53,800; £26,925; £13,425; £6,725; £3,375) **Stalls** High

Form				RPR
1-25	1		**Indian Ink (IRE)**[47] [1496] 3-9-0 111 ... RichardHughes 2 (R Hannon) *lw: hld up: pushed along over 2f out: hdwy ent fnl 2f: led 1f out: sn qcknd clr: impressive* **8/1**[3]	121
1	2	6	**Mi Emma (GER)**[54] [1338] 3-9-0 0 ... EPedroza 1 (A Wohler, Germany) *lt-f: handy on outside: rdn 2f out: ev ch 1f out: sn nt pce of wnr* **10/3**[1]	108
11	3	hd	**Darjina (FR)**[40] [1702] 3-9-0 0 ... CSoumillon 7 (A De Royer-Dupre, France) *str: lw: trckd ldrs: rdn over 2f out: ev ch over 1f out: styd on same pce fnl f* **7/2**[2]	107
-120	4	1	**Arch Swing (USA)**[26] [2065] 3-9-0 0 ... MJKinane 11 (John M Oxx, Ire) *lw: trckd ldrs: 5th and in contention for plcs whn n.m.r and hmpd ins fnl f: gng on at fin* **10/1**	109+
51-2	5	½	**Missvinski (USA)**[68] [1055] 3-9-0 0 ... C-PLemaire 5 (J-C Rouget, France) *cmpt: lw: s.i.s: sn in midfield: pushed along over 2f out: sn nt clr run: styd on ins fnl f* **25/1**	104
0-10	6	nk	**Scarlet Runner**[47] [1496] 3-9-0 107 ... KerrinMcEvoy 6 (J L Dunlop) *swtg: led for 1f: remained prom: led jst over 2f out: hdd 1f out: fdd ins fnl f* **50/1**	103
1-12	7	shd	**Majestic Roi (USA)**[19] [2290] 3-9-0 108 ... JamieSpencer 8 (M R Channon) *lw: hld up: hung rt fr over 2f out: hdwy ent fnl 2f: styd on: one pce towards fin* **25/1**	103
-121	8	½	**Finsceal Beo (IRE)**[26] [2065] 3-9-0 0 ... KJManning 3 (J S Bolger, Ire) *midfield: hdwy gng wl over 2f out: rdn whn chalng over 1f out: no ex ins fnl f* **10/3**[1]	102
3-16	9	2	**Yaqeen**[47] [1496] 3-9-0 107 ... RHills 9 (M A Jarvis) *midfield: nt clr run ent fnl 2f: nvr trbld ldrs* **14/1**	97
12-3	10	1 ½	**Rahiyah (USA)**[40] [1702] 3-9-0 113 ... TedDurcan 4 (J Noseda) *lw: in tch: nt clr run 2f out: sn rdn and outpcd: n.d after* **10/1**	94
-000	11	5	**Puggy (IRE)**[21] [2207] 3-9-0 102 ... (t) LDettori 10 (R A Kvisla) *racd keenly: hld up: pushed along over 2f out: nvr on terms* **22/1**	82
25	12	1	**Cherry Hinton**[21] [2211] 3-9-0 0 ... JMurtagh 13 (A P O'Brien, Ire) *led after 1f: rdn and hdd jst over 2f out: wknd over 1f out* **33/1**	80
12-0	13	8	**Silk Blossom (IRE)**[62] [1146] 3-9-0 112 ... MichaelHills 12 (B W Hills) *s.i.s: towards rr: pushed along 3f out: bhd fnl 2f* **50/1**	61

1m 42.26s (0.16) **Going Correction** +0.475s/f (Yiel) 13 Ran SP% **123.2**

Speed ratings (Par 110): 118,112,111,110,110 110,109,109,107,105 100,99,91

CSF £33.60 TOTE £13.00: £3.80, £1.90, £1.30; EX 51.90 Trifecta £477.50 Pool: £18,962.33 - 28.19 winning units..

Owner Raymond Tooth **Bred** Killeen Castle Stud **Trained** East Everleigh, Wilts

■ Stewards' Enquiry : Kerrin McEvoy caution: used whip in forehand position down neck

FOCUS

This was a cracking renewal of the Coronation Stakes, featuring the winners of the English, Irish, French and German 1,000 Guineas, plus other fillies that had been successful at Group 1 level. Despite that, it was turned into a one-horse race and the time was hugely impressive when allowing for the deteriorating ground. Impossible form to assess with confidence, but Indian Ink, though ground dependant, has been rated ahead of Finsceal Beo.

NOTEBOOK

Indian Ink(IRE) ◆ put up a superb performance, though it was obvious that the ground had come just right for her as it was soft for two of her victories as a juvenile, including in the Cheveley Park. Given a patient ride, in truth she was not travelling quite as well as several in front of her rounding the home bend, but once she was brought with her effort down the wide outside the burst of speed she produced to settle the race was devastating. Obviously where she goes and how she fares from now on will depend much on the going and there are more opportunites for top-class fillies these days, but when there is some give she looks as though she would give the boys and the older horses a decent run for their money. (op 12-1 tchd 14-1 in places)

Mi Emma(GER) ◆ came into this off the back of a devastating nine-length victory in the German 1,000 Guineas, and even though the standard of that Group 2 race may have fallen short of the equivalent contests in England, Ireland and France, that did not stop punters backing her down to joint favourite. She ran with a lot of credit too, always holding a good position close to the pace, and she never stopped trying even after it became obvious the winner was in a different parish. There should be more decent races to be won with her around Europe. (op 7-2 tchd 4-1 in places)

Darjina(FR) ◆, never far away, battled on to confirm French 1,000 Guineas form with Finsceal Beo and Rahiyah but the devasting turn of foot she produced to win at Longchamp was missing on this holding ground. She is still relatively inexperienced and remains capable of winning again at the highest level under more suitable conditions. (op 3-1 tchd 4-1 and 9-2 in places)

Arch Swing(USA) ◆ had finished behind Finsceal Beo in her last two starts including in the Irish 1,000 Guineas, but did have an excuse there as she banged herself leaving the stalls. On this occasion she travelled extremely well just behind the leaders but, just as Indian Ink was flying down the outside to claim the race, she ran into trouble when trying for a gap between Darjina and Scarlet Runner and lost her momentum. She would never have got near the winner, but the way she kept on again suggests that with a clear run she might have finished second. (tchd 12-1 in places)

Missvinski(USA), closely matched with Darjina on Prix de la Grotte running, stayed on without looking a threat and on a line through her old rival she probably ran to form. She seems to stay this trip even though she has not yet won beyond an extended 6f, but is fairly well exposed now and is yet to win above Listed company.

Scarlet Runner ran another brave race from the front but again the mile looked beyond her, at this level at least. She may need a drop in trip and a return to lesser Group company. (op 66-1)

Majestic Roi(USA) attempted the same come-from-behind tactics that enabled her to floor Indian Ink on her return in the Fred Darling, but although she made up a lot of ground down the wide outside in the home straight, she was not making up any more ground in the final furlong. Both her wins have come on fast ground and she probably has a better chance of getting this trip under those conditions. Official explanation: jockey said filly was unsuited by the good to soft ground (op 33-1)

Finsceal Beo(IRE), bidding to add this prestigious prize to her victories in the English and Irish 1,000 Guineas, ran a rather strange race. She came there on the bridle passing the two-furlong pole and it looked a question of how far, but once asked to go and win her race she found absolutely nothing and, in the end, finished very tired. Connections' opinion that the ground had gone against her are probably valid despite her impressive victory on rain-softened ground in the Rockfel last October, but despite the impressions she might have given over her wellbeing coming into this, she has had a lot of very hard races at the highest level this spring and they may very well have left their mark. She deserves a nice break and owes no-one anything, and if she does come back it will hopefully be when conditions are more suitable. Official explanation: jockey said filly was unsuited by the good to soft ground (op 4-1 tchd 9-2 in places)

Yaqeen ◆, behind three of these including Indian Ink when sixth in the 1,000 Guineas, did not have a great deal of room to play with on the inside in the home straight, but she did not excactly fly home when there was daylight. She still has time on her side and the best of her is probably to be seen, whilst all three of her previous starts have been on fast ground which is probably what she needs. (tchd 12-1)

Rahiyah(USA) should have done better judged on her form behind Finsceal Beo in last year's Rockfel and the same filly and Darjina in the French 1,000 Guineas. Perhaps she is another that needs faster ground as she is much better than this. (op 7-1)

Puggy(IRE) is repeatedly being found out at this level and is yet to show that she has trained on. (op 66-1 tchd 100-1 in a place)

Cherry Hinton taking a big drop in trip after her fine fifth in the Oaks, was given a positive ride but was swamped soon after turning for home. This looked to be the wrong move, but she has too much ability to remain a maiden. (op 40-1 tchd 50-1)

Silk Blossom(IRE), who only beat one home in the Fred Darling on her return to action, had the ground to suit this time but ran another shocker. It is beginning to look as though she has not trained on. (tchd 100-1 in a place)

2815 WOLFERTON H'CAP (LISTED RACE) 1m 2f

4:20 (4:22) (Class 1) (0-110,110) 4-Y-O+

£31,229 (£11,836; £5,923; £2,953; £1,479; £742) **Stalls** High

Form				RPR
0230	**1**		**Championship Point (IRE)**[28] 1985 4-9-2 **105**............ DarryllHolland 3 (M R Channon) *bhd: drvn along and hdwy 2f out: styd on to ld fnl 100yds* **25/1**	114
-312	**2**	*1*	**Heaven Sent**[27] 2053 4-9-1 **104**.......................... KerrinMcEvoy 1 (Sir Michael Stoute) *hld up in midfield: hdwy 3f out: led 2f out: hdd and nt qckn fnl 100yds* **4/1**[2]	111
3041	**3**	*1 1/4*	**Charlie Cool**[16] 2368 4-9-3 **106**..............................(v) NCallan 10 (W J Haggas) *lw: hld up in tch: squeezed through and drvn to chse ldrs over 1f out: styd on same pce* **11/1**	110
034-	**4**	*shd*	**Purple Moon (IRE)**[138] 5804 4-8-8 **97**.................. JamieSpencer 5 (L M Cumani) *bhd: rdn and styd on fnl 3f: nvr nrr* **10/1**	101
23-1	**5**	*nk*	**Emirates Skyline (USA)**[37] 1767 4-9-0 **103**.................. LDettori 4 (Saeed Bin Suroor) *hld up in midfield: hdwy 2f out: hung rt: one pce appr fnl f* **3/1**[1]	106
00-4	**6**	*1 3/4*	**Star Of Light**[41] 1650 6-8-10 **99**.......................... RichardHughes 8 (B J Meehan) *stdd s: hld up towards rr: hrd rdn and hdwy 2f out: no further prog* **16/1**	99
	7	*1 1/2*	**Worldly Wise**[9] 2587 4-8-7 **96**.. KDarley 7 (Patrick J Flynn, Ire) *neat: lw: trckd ldrs: rdn to chal over 2f out: wknd wl over 1f out* **16/1**	93
6611	**8**	*1/2*	**Lake Poet (IRE)**[21] 2209 4-8-12 **101**........................ SebSanders 11 (C E Brittain) *chsd ldrs: rdn over 2f out: btn whn n.m.r ins fnl 2f* **13/2**[3]	97
0000	**9**	*22*	**Prince Of Light (IRE)**[2] 2755 4-8-13 **102**......................(b) JoeFanning 6 (M Johnston) *dwlt: towards rr: rdn over 2f out: no rspnse* **25/1**	54
0452	**10**	*5*	**Road To Love (IRE)**[28] 1985 4-9-4 **107**...................... RyanMoore 13 (M Johnston) *lw: chsd ldr: led 7f out to 6f out: led over 3f out tl wknd qckly 2f out* **7/1**	49
20-4	**11**	*3*	**Tucker**[21] 2208 5-8-13 **102**..(p) HayleyTurner 16 (W R Swinburn) *lw: racd freely in front: led 3f: led 6f out tl over 3f out: drvn along and wknd ent st* **9/1**	38
5414	**12**	*1 1/2*	**Tabadul (IRE)**[21] 2209 6-8-10 **99**.. RHills 15 (E A L Dunlop) *prom tl wknd qckly 3f out* **14/1**	32

2m 10.84s (2.84) **Going Correction** +0.475s/f (Yiel) **12** Ran SP% **124.4**

Speed ratings (Par 111):107,106,105,105,104 103,102,101,84,80 77,76

CSF £128.64 CT £1205.00 TOTE £38.00: £7.90, £1.90, £3.10; EX 192.30 TRIFECTA Not won. Pool £5,037.46.

Owner John Livock Bloodstock Limited **Bred** Mount Coote Stud **Trained** West Ilsley, Berks

■ Stewards' Enquiry : N Callan one-day ban: careless riding (Jul 3)

FOCUS

This decent handicap was run at a strong early pace and the runners elected to race wide under the trees coming back from Swinley Bottom. It suited those coming from off the pace. Championship Point recorded hs best ever figure, but the form does seem sound with the runner-up also an improver and the next two close to their marks.

NOTEBOOK

Championship Point(IRE) bounced right back to form on this return to handicap company and came from last to first in the home straight to score going away. He has been very hard to predict since running in the Derby last year, and this was his first success since landing the Predominate Stakes, but he has run some sound races in defeat all the same. The return to more patient tactics worked the oracle, plus he clearly enjoyed the soft ground, so it will be very interesting to see whether he can now build on this confidence-boosting success when tackling minor Group races again. (tchd 33-1 and 50-1 in places)

Heaven Sent ◆, third in a Group 3 at the Curragh last time, was given a patient ride before making her move turning for home. She looked all over the winner when hitting the front 2f out, but she was in front plenty soon enough on this first attempt at the longer trip and it was clear inside the final furlong that she was a sitting duck for the eventual winner. This must rate another improved effort, on ground she would have found plenty soft enough, and there is little doubt that she can go one better in this sort of company before the season's end. (op 9-2 tchd 5-1 in places)

Charlie Cool, back to winning ways in the first-time visor in a conditions event last time, had finished in front of the winner when fourth at Goodwood on his penultimate outing. He looked a threat when making up his ground in the home straight, but his effort petered out at the business end and he simply looks weighted to his best in handicaps. A sound benchmark for the form. (op 14-1)

Purple Moon(IRE) ◆, who failed to meet expectations as a hurdler during the winter, was having his first start for Luca Cumani and was nibbled at in the betting ring on this first outing for 138 days. He ran with real credit in defeat and left the impression he has a decent prize within his grasp when stepping back up to a suitably longer trip in due course, perhaps the Old Newton Cup at Haydock next month - a race his trainer has won in the past. (op 12-1 tchd 14-1 in a place)

Emirates Skyline(USA), 6lb higher than when scoring readily on his seasonal bow at York 37 days previously, came through to have his chance yet hung right under maximum pressure and probably found this ground a bit too soft for his liking. He remains lightly raced for his age and should have a little more to offer still. (op 11-4 tchd 10-3 and 7-2 in places)

Star Of Light was another who enjoyed being ridden with patience and was not disgraced, but he again left the impression he is held by the Handicapper. He is another who helps to set the level of this form. (tchd 20-1 in a place)

Worldly Wise, back up in trip, fared the best of those to race up with the pace and was not disgraced on ground that had gone against him. He has a big prize within his grasp when reverting to decent ground, but he may just be at his very best over 1m. (op 14-1)

Lake Poet(IRE), bidding for a hat-trick from a 6lb higher mark, was starting to tread water prior to being short of room nearing two out. He now has to prove he is up to this new rating, but should not be totally written off when returning to 12f. (op 7-1 tchd 15-2 in places)

Road To Love(IRE) failed to convince on this soft ground and, while he still looks high enough in the handicap at present, should be seen to better effect again when faced with faster ground in due course. (op 6-1 tchd 11-2)

Tucker proved too free for his own good at the head of affairs and not surprisingly folded when challenged for the lead. (op 14-1)

Tabadul(IRE) looked all at sea on this soft surface and should be given another chance. Official explanation: jockey said gelding was unsuited by the good to soft ground (op 11-1 tchd 16-1)

2816 QUEEN'S VASE (GROUP 3) 2m

4:55 (4:56) (Class 1) 3-Y-O

£34,068 (£12,912; £6,462; £3,222; £1,614; £810) **Stalls** High

Form				RPR
0	**1**		**Mahler**[20] 2235 3-9-1 0.. MJKinane 11 (A P O'Brien, Ire) *lw: trckd ldrs: led over 3f out: styd on wl and in command fnl f* **7/1**	103
-211	**2**	*3 1/2*	**Veracity**[34] 1843 3-9-1 87.................................. PhilipRobinson 8 (M A Jarvis) *trckd ldrs: ev ch 3f out: sn rdn: styd on same pce fnl f* **11/1**	99
211	**3**	*hd*	**Secret Tune**[20] 2246 3-9-1 86.............................. RichardHughes 17 (Pat Eddery) *midfield: reminder over 6f out: hdwy 5f out: rdn to chal over 2f out: kpt on same pce fnl f* **11/1**	99
-211	**4**	*8*	**Serengeti**[48] 1467 3-9-1 97...................................... SebSanders 14 (M Johnston) *hld up: hdwy 1/2-way: ev ch 3 fout: wknd over 1f out* **7/2**[1]	89
-353	**5**	*hd*	**Sunley Peace**[8] 2602 3-9-1 74.................................. MichaelHills 7 (D R C Elsworth) *hld up: hdwy over 5f out: rdn to chse ldrs over 3f out: one pce fnl f* **40/1**	89
1-14	**6**	*1/2*	**Metaphoric (IRE)**[43] 1602 3-9-1 94...................... JamieSpencer 15 (M L W Bell) *lw: s.s: hld up: effrt whn nt clr run 4f out: sn swtchd rt: styd on fr 2f out: nt trble ldrs and one pce wl ins fnl f* **12/1**	88
1-46	**7**	*6*	**Shimoni**[29] 1958 3-8-12 89...................................... RyanMoore 13 (W J Knight) *lw: hld up: hdwy over 5f out: no imp on ldrs* **40/1**	78
5410	**8**	*7*	**Pret A Porter (UAE)**[8] 2602 3-8-12 71...................... JimmyFortune 1 (P D Evans) *upset in stalls: bhd: sme hdwy 3f out: nvr rchd ldrs* **80/1**	70
	9	*1/2*	**Darestan (IRE)**[15] 3-9-1 0...................................... CSoumillon 12 (A De Royer-Dupre, France) *neat: lw: hld up: hdwy over 3f out: no imp on ldrs: wknd and eased over 1f out* **5/1**[2]	72
-221	**10**	*1 1/2*	**Brisk Breeze (GER)**[25] 2081 3-8-12 94...................... TedDurcan 2 (H R A Cecil) *lw: midfield: hdwy over 5f out: drvn to chse ldrs ent fnl 3f: wknd 2f out* **10/1**	67
	11	*6*	**Consulate (IRE)**[16] 2382 3-9-1 0.............................. WMLordan 5 (David Wachman, Ire) *str: lw: racd keenly: in tch: rdn and wknd over 5f out* **15/2**	63
042	**12**	*1*	**Ask The Butler**[34] 1843 3-9-1 81.......................... DarryllHolland 3 (A W Carroll) *prom tl rdn and wknd 4f out* **66/1**	62
-133	**13**	*27*	**Actodos (IRE)**[22] 2185 3-9-1 85.............................. JimCrowley 4 (B R Millman) *led: rdn and hdd over 3f out: sn wknd: dismntd after line: lame* **33/1**	30
420	**14**	*1 1/2*	**Leander**[20] 2235 3-9-1 78.......................................(t) NCallan 9 (K J Burke) *midfield tl wknd over 6f out: lame* **100/1**	28

5123 **15** *39* **Hearthstead Maison (IRE)**[27] 2042 3-9-1 104 JoeFanning 10 —
(M Johnston) *in tch: rdn and wknd over 4f out: eased over 2f out: t.o* **6/1**[3]

3m 32.65s (2.49) **Going Correction** +0.475s/f (Yiel) **15** Ran SP% **122.4**
Speed ratings (Par 109):112,110,110,106,106 105,102,99,99,98 95,94,81,80,61
CSF £80.26 TOTE £7.50: £2.40, £3.80, £3.80; EX 106.70 Trifecta £483.40 Pool: £7,693.66 - 11.30 winning units..
Owner Mrs John Magnier, M Tabor & D Smith **Bred** Pegasus Racing Ltd **Trained** Ballydoyle, Co Tipperary

FOCUS
Traditionally the first real stamina test at this level for three-year-olds. The field finished strung out behind the comfortable winner. He should be rated value for further, but with the placed horses rated in the mid 80s he probably did not need to improve on his Derby Trial form and it remains to be seen how the form works out.

NOTEBOOK
Mahler, who found little go his way when down the field in the Derby last time, has always shaped as though he would relish a real test of stamina and he delivered on that promise in some style here, running out a comfortable winner. He was always travelling with ease, despite not being certain to enjoy the soft ground, and should be rated value for further. It would be little surprise to see him develop into a Cup horse now, and he deserves to take in the St Leger later in the year, but in beating two rivals rated in the 80s here one should not go overboard about the current ante-post quotes of around 7-1, especially as past winners of this event have a very mixed record. (op 8-1 tchd 9-1 in a place)
Veracity maintained his progression and this lazy colt clearly stayed every yard of the longer trip. He is also suited by some give underfoot and, in very good hands, it is unlikely we have still to see the best of him. (op 9-1)
Secret Tune, who like the runner-up came into this after winning his last two races at a lower level, ran in snatches yet clearly got the longer trip and is still improving. He is now likely to head to the Bahrain Trophy at Newmarket next month. (tchd 12-1 in a place)
Serengeti, the winner of three of his four previous outings to date, was going nicely at halfway and looked a big player. However, he was in trouble turning for home and has to rate a non-stayer over the longer trip on this softer ground. It is a fair bet that he is up to making his mark at this level when dropping back in distance, but he looked to have a very hard race all the same and may need some time to recover. (op 9-2 tchd 5-1in places)
Sunley Peace, still a maiden, enjoyed the stiffer test of stamina yet was never a serious threat. His proximity at the finish helps to put this form into perspective. (op 100-1)
Metaphoric(IRE) was never really going after a sluggish start, but he was not totally done with prior to meeting a bit of trouble nearing the turn for home. He kept on without ever threatening, but where he goes from here is now up in the air and he is not going to prove easy to place.
Darestan(IRE), progressive opn this sort of ground over 1m4f in France, ran a tame race and never looked like getting invloved. (op 6-1 tchd 13-2 in a place)
Brisk Breeze(GER) showed up well until her stamina gave way at the top of the home straight. She needs to drop back in trip, but could find a Listed race on this sort of ground in the future. (op 8-1 tchd 12-1 in places)
Consulate(IRE), a winner over this trip in handicap company at Leopardstown 16 days previously, gave himself little chance of lasting home by refusing to settle early on. (op 8-1)
Ask The Butler Official explanation: jockey said gelding was unsuited the good to soft ground
Actodos(IRE) Official explanation: vet said gelding finished lame in front
Leander Official explanation: vet said colt finished lame
Hearthstead Maison(IRE), easy to back, was beaten too far out for this to have been his true running and shaped as though something was amiss. He can leave this form behind when reverting to faster ground. (op 4-1 tchd 13-2 in places)

2817 BUCKINGHAM PALACE STKS (HERITAGE H'CAP) 7f

5:30 (5:33) (Class 2) (0-105,104) 3-Y-O+

£34,276 (£10,263; £5,131; £2,568; £1,281; £643) **Stalls** Centre

Form				RPR
-622	**1**		**Binanti**[6] 2670 7-8-7 87 FrancisNorton 21	99
			(P R Chamings) *prom: rdn to ld 1f out: edgd left and leant on runner-up fnl f: all out* **33/1**	
5023	**2**	*1*	**Fajr (IRE)**[24] 2111 5-9-1 95 JohnEgan 10	104+
			(Miss Gay Kelleway) *trckd ldrs gng wl: effrt over 2f out: str chal whn carried lft by wnr fnl f: nt qckn nr fin* **25/1**	
53-0	**3**	*1*	**Dabbers Ridge (IRE)**[41] 1651 5-9-5 99 MichaelHills 11	106
			(B W Hills) *led and trvld wl in frnt: rdn and hdd 1f out: one pace* **12/1**[3]	
-112	**4**	*½*	**Wise Dennis**[36] 1791 5-9-10 104 JHBowman 6	109+
			(A P Jarvis) *lw: towards rr: nt clr run over 2f out: hdwy and edgd rt over 1f out: styd on* **4/1**[1]	
-001	**5**	*1*	**South Cape**[20] 2239 4-8-6 86 TPO'Shea 1	89
			(M R Channon) *towards rr: rdn and gd hdwy fnl 2f: edgd rt: nrst fin* **12/1**[3]	
03-3	**6**	*1 ½*	**Pride Of Nation (IRE)**[36] 1791 5-9-5 99 MartinDwyer 25	98
			(L M Cumani) *lw: trckd ldrs: chal and rdn 2f out: no ex 1f out* **4/1**[1]	
2042	**7**	*1 ¼*	**Ceremonial Jade (UAE)**[49] 1448 4-9-0 94 CSoumillon 19	89
			(M Botti) *hld up in rr: hdwy into midfield whn squeezed for room over 2f out: styd on fnl f* **25/1**	
06-3	**8**	*1 ¼*	**Racer Forever (USA)**[49] 1448 4-9-10 104 JimmyFortune 18	96
			(J H M Gosden) *hld up and bhd: hdwy 2f out: hrd rdn and no imp over 1f out* **20/1**	
0-52	**9**	*1 ¼*	**Trafalgar Bay (IRE)**[26] 2058 4-8-11 91 PatCosgrave 24	79
			(K R Burke) *hld up in rr: hdwy whn bmpd over 2f out: tried to rally and nt clr run over 1f out: nt rcvr* **14/1**	
16-6	**10**	*¾*	**Signor Peltro**[35] 1818 4-8-6 86 FergusSweeney 27	72
			(H Candy) *hld up in rr: hdwy 3f out: rdn to chal 2f out: wknd jst over 1f out* **25/1**	
0-01	**11**	*½*	**Dingaan (IRE)**[13] 2440 4-8-2 87 WilliamBuick(5) 9	72
			(A M Balding) *awkward leaving stalls: t.k.h in rr: hrd rdn over 2f out: sme late hdwy* **40/1**	
-533	**12**	*2*	**Ingleby Arch (USA)**[9] 2566 4-8-10 90 PaulFessey 7	70
			(T D Barron) *hld up towards rr: hdwy into midfield whn hmpd over 2f out: n.d after* **40/1**	
0000	**13**	*½*	**Indian Trail**[20] 2237 7-8-12 92 (v) JoeFanning 29	70
			(D Nicholls) *lw: plld hrd in midfield: smooth hdwy to press ldrs over 2f out: wknd over 1f out* **16/1**	
-501	**14**	*1*	**Black Charmer (IRE)**[6] 2670 4-9-1 95 5ex J-PGuillambert 4	71
			(M Johnston) *prom tl hrd rdn and wknd 2f out* **9/1**[2]	
0223	**15**	*hd*	**Bahamian Pirate (USA)**[20] 2237 12-8-13 93 AdrianTNicholls 13	68
			(D Nicholls) *dwlt: sn chsng ldrs: wknd 2f out* **33/1**	
1203	**16**	*1 ¾*	**Bustan (IRE)**[16] 2374 8-8-13 93 SebSanders 28	63
			(G C Bravery) *dwlt: sn chsng ldrs: hrd rdn 2f out: sn wknd* **66/1**	
00-0	**17**	*nk*	**Royal Storm (IRE)**[13] 2440 8-8-10 90 JimCrowley 14	59
			(Mrs A J Perrett) *prom tl wknd 2f out* **80/1**	
500	**18**	*1*	**Bahiano (IRE)**[6] 2670 6-8-11 91 JMurtagh 26	58
			(C E Brittain) *in tch: rdn whn bmpd over 2f out: sn wknd: eased whn no ch fnl f* **33/1**	
2-02	**19**	*¾*	**Third Set (IRE)**[29] 1971 4-8-6 86 ChrisCatlin 2	51
			(R Charlton) *prom tl wknd over 2f out* **20/1**	
-625	**20**	*1 ½*	**Leopoldine**[13] 2450 4-8-9 89 SteveDrowne 20	50
			(H Morrison) *in tch: rdn whn bdly squeezed over 2f out: n.d after* **33/1**	
1050	**21**	*1*	**Malcheek (IRE)**[10] 2528 5-8-9 89 MJKinane 23	47
			(T D Easterby) *w ldrs 5f: sn wknd: eased whn no ch fnl f* **66/1**	
2020	**22**	*4*	**Sendalam (FR)**[113] 597 5-9-1 100 TolleyDean(5) 8	47
			(J S Moore) *swtg: dwlt: a bhd: hrd rdn and no ch over 2f out* **100/1**	
6016	**23**	*5*	**Wyatt Earp (IRE)**[20] 2234 6-8-13 93 PaulHanagan 15	27
			(R A Fahey) *plld hrd in midfield: rdn and outpcd whn hmpd over 2f out: sn bhd* **16/1**	
0006	**24**	*1 ½*	**Uhoomagoo**[21] 2208 9-8-13 93 (b) NCallan 17	23
			(K A Ryan) *sn bhd and rdn along: no ch whn sltly hmpd and swvd rt over 2f out* **14/1**	
-531	**P**		**Song Of Passion (IRE)**[20] 2237 4-9-4 98 RichardHughes 22	—
			(R Hannon) *prssd ldrs: rdn and beginning to lose pl whn bdly hmpd and nrly f appr 2f out: sn p.u* **16/1**	

1m 29.28s (1.18) **Going Correction** +0.40s/f (Good) **25** Ran SP% **139.3**
Speed ratings (Par 109):109,107,106,106,105 103,101,100,99,98 97,95,94,93,93 91,91,89,89,87 86,81,75,74,—
CSF £726.92 CT £10112.99 TOTE £55.60: £7.90, £4.50, £4.50, £1.90; EX 611.60 Trifecta £4890.60 Part won. Pool: £6,888.28 - 0.50 winning units. Place 6 £ 266.44, Place 5 £ 156.96.
Owner Mrs J E L Wright **Bred** Wheelersland Stud **Trained** Baughurst, Hants
■ The first Royal Ascot winner for trainer Pat Chamings. Eisteddfod was withdrawn (25/1, broke out of stalls.)
■ Stewards' Enquiry : Francis Norton three-day ban: careless riding (Jul 3-5)

FOCUS
A decent and competitive handicap. The runners came up the middle of the track from halfway and there appeared to be no real draw bias. Sound form, with Binanti rated back to his best.

NOTEBOOK
Binanti, third in this race last season from a 3lb lower mark, came into this in decent form having finished second the last twice. His attitude in a finish has often come under scrutiny and he did the runner-up no favours at all when hanging into that rival in the final furlong, but he was on top at the finish and would have been unlucky to have lost the race in the subsequent Stewards' enquiry. Where he goes from here is not certain, but perhaps the Bunbury Cup at Newmarket in July. A hike in the weights is now assured, but his consistency should ensure he remains competitive all the same. (op 28-1)
Fajr(IRE), unlucky at Leicester last time, was racing from a 5lb higher mark here and ran a huge race in defeat. He was always travelling well near the head of affairs but was unfortunately carried left by the winner inside the final furlong. He is another whose attitude under maximum pressure has never totally convinced, but his connections were adamant the winner's antics cost him the race and he could bag a decent prize after this.
Dabbers Ridge(IRE) left his Victoria Cup run well behind with a solid effort in defeat from the front. This puts him right back on track and he should make a bold bid to defend his title if turning up again for the totesport International next month.
Wise Dennis, 8lb higher than when landing the Victoria Cup, found the easing ground in his favour and was very well backed. He was again ridden with great patience and did not get the best of passages from off the pace, but while he still came through to run another solid race, he was never quite going to get to the leaders. He remains in top form and was far from disgraced under top weight. (op 6-1)
South Cape, 4lb higher than when winning at Folkestone 20 days previously, shaped better than his finishing position suggests as he got no cover from his draw in 1. He was motoring home inside the final furlong and left the impression he will be better served by returning to a mile in such company. However, he will no doubt go up again in the weights for this. (op 16-1 tchd 20-1 in places)
Pride Of Nation(IRE), who missed the Royal Hunt Cup earlier in the week due to the quick surface, had the ground come right for him here and looked set to run a big race. He came there with every chance passing the 2f marker, but his effort was short-lived and he proved one paced when it really mattered. Official explanation: jockey said horse had no more to give (op 7-2 tchd 9-2)
Ceremonial Jade(UAE) did well to finish as he did after being hampered nearing 2f out and deserves to be rated better than the bare form. This was just about his best effort to date on the turf.
Racer Forever(USA), who looked to have been laid out for this, proved easy to back after the ground had eased and ran creditably in the circumstances. He can do better when returning to a quicker surface. (tchd 33-1 in a place)
Trafalgar Bay(IRE) was another who was unfortunate to have been hampered on more than one occasion and is better than the bare form. (op 16-1)
Indian Trail, who missed the cut in the Wokingham, eventually paid for refusing to settle early on and not surprisingly failed to last home over a trip that stretches his stamina. He again showed that the engine is still there, however, and it would not be a surprise to see him win again over 6f before too long when things go more his way.
Black Charmer(IRE), penalised for readily beating the winner at Sandown six days previously, dropped out tamely when put under pressure and it was clear nearing 2f out that he was not going to confirm that form. He may be better in smaller fields. Official explanation: jockey said gelding ran flat (op 10-1)
Uhoomagoo, winner of this race last year from a 3lb lower mark, was never in the hunt from off the pace and hated the ground. Official explanation: jockey said gelding was unsuited by the good to soft ground
Song Of Passion(IRE) was beating a retreat at the time, but almost came down when badly hampered nearing 2f out and her rider was quick to pull her up thereafter.
T/Jkpt: Not won. T/Plt: £193.70 to a £1 stake. Pool: £482,122.56. 1,816.10 winning tickets. T/Qpdt: £45.70 to a £1 stake. Pool: £16,996.60. 275.10 winning tickets. DO

2166 AYR (L-H)

Friday, June 22

OFFICIAL GOING: Good
Wind: Breezy, half against Weather: Fine

2818 PARK'S MAIDEN AUCTION STKS 5f

2:20 (2:21) (Class 5) 2-Y-O

£3,238 (£963; £481; £240) **Stalls** High

Form				RPR
26	**1**		**Charlotti Carlotti (IRE)**[23] 2134 2-8-10 0 TomEaves 6	78+
			(T D Barron) *mde all: pushed out fnl f* **4/11**[1]	
63	**2**	*2*	**Rievaulx Valentino**[27] 2021 2-9-2 0 PaulMulrennan 2	77
			(K A Ryan) *pressed wnr thrght: rdn 2f out: edgd lft: kpt on same pce fnl f* **5/1**[2]	
606	**3**	*¾*	**Myriola**[23] 2147 2-8-7 0 RoystonFfrench 7	65
			(J G Given) *prom: drvn over 2f out: kpt on u.p fnl f* **12/1**[3]	
	4	*1 ½*	**Personal Choice** 2-7-13 0 ow1 PatrickDonaghy(7) 5	59
			(M Brittain) *hld up in tch: effrt 2f out: sn no imp* **40/1**	
0	**5**	*2 ½*	**Invincible Rose (IRE)**[34] 1848 2-8-4 0 DeanMernagh 3	48
			(M Brittain) *cl up tl rdn and wknd wl over 1f out* **22/1**	
0	**6**	*¾*	**Frizzini**[27] 2021 2-9-0 0 TonyHamilton 4	55
			(N Tinkler) *dwlt: hld up: shkn up 2f out: n.d* **80/1**	

0 7 9 **Rio Sabotini**[13] 2451 2-8-13 0 DeanMcKeown 1 22
(G A Swinbank) *chsd ldrs tl hung lft and wknd 2f out* **16/1**
60.83 secs (0.39) **Going Correction** +0.05s/f (Good) 7 Ran SP% **111.6**
Speed ratings (Par 93):98,94,93,91,87 86,71
CSF £2.33 TOTE £1.30: £1.10, £1.70; EX 2.00.
Owner P D Savill **Bred** P D Savill **Trained** Maunby, N Yorks

FOCUS
An uncompetitive event in which the market leader did not have to improve to win with more in hand than the winning margin suggested. The winner was basically to form although not totally confident it will work out.

NOTEBOOK
Charlotti Carlotti(IRE), who was not disgraced in a Listed event at Beverley on her previous start, did not have to improve to win an uncompetitive event with more in hand than the winning margin suggested. She will stay six furlongs and looks the type to win more races. (op 4-9)
Rievaulx Valentino, who turned in a much-improved performance at Beverley on his previous start, had the run of the race and confirmed that promise against a potentially fair sort. He looks capable of winning an ordinary event. (op 9-2)
Myriola had been soundly beaten on her two previous starts but returned to something like the form she showed on her debut at Pontefract. She should appreciate the step up to seven furlongs and may do better in ordinary nursery company.
Personal Choice, the first foal of a five-furlong juvenile winner, showed ability on this racecourse debut. She left the impression that another furlong would be in her favour but she is likely to remain vulnerable in this type of event. (op 33-1)
Invincible Rose(IRE) bettered the form of her racecourse debut at Thirsk but she did not show anywhere near enough to suggest she will be winning in this grade in the near future. (tchd 25-1)
Frizzini, soundly beaten on her debut at Beverley, fared better this time. He will be suited by further and appeals as the sort to be suited by modest handicap company in due course. (op 50-1)

2819 ARNOLD CLARK MAIDEN AUCTION STKS 6f
2:55 (2:57) (Class 5) 2-Y-O **£3,562** (£1,059; £529; £264) **Stalls** High

Form RPR
1 **Bahamian Gift** 2-8-4 0 DeanMernagh 6 61
(M Brittain) *unruly bef s: prom: rdn to ld appr fnl f: kpt on wl* **16/1**
0445 2 1 1/4 **Alpen Adventure (IRE)**[22] 2166 2-8-9 0 (p) TomEaves 7 62
(Mrs L Stubbs) *chsd ldrs: n.m.r and outpcd over 2f out: styd wl fnl f: nt rch wnr* **9/4**[1]
0 3 1/2 **Richardthesecond (IRE)**[28] 1992 2-8-9 0 DeanMcKeown 8 61
(W M Brisbourne) *upset in stalls: led tl hung lft and hdd appr fnl f: no ex and lost 2nd cl home* **3/1**[2]
04 4 hd **Willyn (IRE)**[47] 1487 2-8-1 0 AndrewElliott(3) 4 55
(J R Weymes) *prom: drvn and outpcd over 2f out: kpt on fnl f: no imp* **9/2**[3]
64 5 nk **Atephobia**[25] 2090 2-9-1 0 PaulMulrennan 3 65
(K R Burke) *cl up: outpcd 2f out: rallied 1f out: no imp towards fin* **6/1**
4 6 1/2 **Bohobe (IRE)**[17] 2344 2-8-7 0 RoystonFfrench 1 56
(J G Given) *in tch: rdn and ev ch over 2f out: no ex fnl f* **5/1**
7 25 **Caribbean Cruiser** 2-8-12 0 TonyHamilton 5 —
(Garry Moss) *dwlt and wnt lft s: sn wl bhd* **20/1**
1m 15.93s (2.26) **Going Correction** +0.05s/f (Good) 7 Ran SP% **115.5**
Speed ratings (Par 93):86,84,83,83,83 82,49
CSF £53.35 TOTE £15.10: £4.00, £1.60; EX 60.00.
Owner Mel Brittain **Bred** Eurostrait Ltd **Trained** Warthill, N Yorks

FOCUS
Low grade stuff and, although the pace seemed fair, this was a moderate winning time for a race of this ilk and the form has been rated negatively.

NOTEBOOK
Bahamian Gift, a half-sister to five winners up to a mile, proved a handful at the start but showed ability to make a winning debut. This was not much of a race and, although open to improvement, she will find life tougher under a penalty. (op 20-1)
Alpen Adventure(IRE), with the cheekpieces again fitted, has had a few chances but looked unlucky not to finish closer after getting squeezed out at a crucial stage. He has the ability to win a similar event and is worth a try over 7f, but is vulnerable to the more progressive sorts in this grade. (tchd 11-4)
Richardthesecond(IRE), who showed ability at a modest level on his debut, attracted support and bettered that effort, despite getting stirred up in the stalls and showing a tendency to hang left under pressure. He may be capable of a bit better. (op 5-1)
Willyn(IRE), who had shown ability at an ordinary level on her two previous starts, was not disgraced but left the impression that a stiffer overall test of stamina would have been in her favour. She may do better in run-of-the-mill nursery company. (op 7-2)
Atephobia again had his limitations exposed in this type of event and, although not disgraced on this first run over six furlongs, may be the type to fare better in ordinary nursery company when his stable is back among the winners. (op 4-1)
Bohobe(IRE), who showed only a modicum of ability on her debut on Fibresand, was not disgraced having raced on the outside of the field for this turf bow. She is likely to continue to look vulnerable in this type of event, though. (op 7-1 tchd 9-2)

2820 JOIN THE RANGERS SUPPORTERS TRUST H'CAP 1m 1f 20y
3:30 (3:31) (Class 6) (0-55,58) 4-Y-0+ **£2,590** (£770; £385; £192) **Stalls** Low

Form RPR
0-00 1 **Zabeel Tower**[15] 2391 4-8-8 **49** TomEaves 8 57
(R Allan) *mde all: rdn 2f out: hrd pressed fnl f: hld on wl* **14/1**
-050 2 1/2 **Royal Citadel (IRE)**[14] 2431 4-8-3 **51** KellyHarrison(7) 9 58
(Mrs L B Normile) *prom on outside: effrt and edgd lft over 1f out: ev ch ins fnl f: hld towards fin* **14/1**
0-56 3 3/4 **Desert Lightning (IRE)**[16] 2372 5-8-6 **50** AndrewElliott(3) 2 55
(K R Burke) *t.k.h: prom: effrt over 1f out: kpt on fnl f: no ex fnl 50yds* **15/2**
2050 4 1 1/2 **Volaticus (IRE)**[27] 2023 6-9-0 **55** SilvestreDeSousa 10 57
(A D Brown) *prom: drvn over 2f out: one pce over 1f out* **9/2**[2]
0300 5 nk **Terenzium (IRE)**[14] 2431 5-8-8 **49** (p) DeanMcKeown 3 50
(Micky Hammond) *hld up: effrt over 2f out: edgd lft: nvr able to chal* **7/1**
0-64 6 1 1/2 **Royal Indulgence**[9] 2582 7-8-9 **53** LiamJones(3) 12 51
(W M Brisbourne) *missed break: hld up on outside: effrt over 2f out: no imp over 1f out* **11/4**[1]
0005 7 hd **Jordans Spark**[9] 2563 6-8-5 **46** DaleGibson 5 43
(P Monteith) *hld up outside: effrt and hung lft 2f out: sn no imp* **7/1**
-026 8 7 **Mandarin Rocket (IRE)**[15] 2388 4-8-10 **51** RoystonFfrench 7 33
(Miss L A Perratt) *midfield: outpcd 3f out: sn btn* **6/1**[3]
000- 9 3 **Admiral Compton**[249] 5621 6-9-0 **55** TonyHamilton 4 30
(B Storey) *hld up: rdn over 3f out: sn btn* **28/1**
-000 10 shd **Soho Square**[29] 1967 4-8-11 **55** (b) MarkLawson(3) 1 30
(L Lungo) *in tch: rdn and outpcd over 3f out: sn btn* **20/1**
504- 11 13 **Strife (IRE)**[191] 6812 4-8-2 **50** PatrickDonaghy(7) 6 —
(W M Brisbourne) *s.i.s: nvr on terms* **16/1**
1m 56.78s (-3.22) **Going Correction** -0.35s/f (Firm) 11 Ran SP% **123.3**
Speed ratings (Par 101):100,99,98,97,97 95,95,89,86,86 75
CSF £203.84 CT £1600.84 TOTE £22.00: £6.30, £4.50, £2.60; EX 274.10.
Owner David Doughty **Bred** Gainsborough Stud Management Ltd **Trained** Duns, Scottish Borders
■ Dick Allan's first winner from his new yard near Greenlaw.
■ Stewards' Enquiry : Tom Eaves caution: used whip with excessive frequency

FOCUS
A modest handicap and the ordinary gallop played to the strengths of those racing prominently. The form is moderate but sound, rated through the third.
Zabeel Tower Official explanation: trainer said, regarding apparent improvement in form, that the gelding appreciated the drop back in trip

2821 PARK'S H'CAP 6f
4:10 (4:10) (Class 4) (0-80,80) 3-Y-O **£5,829** (£1,734; £866; £432) **Stalls** High

Form RPR
-143 1 **Baltimore Jack (IRE)**[18] 2313 3-9-7 **80** DaleGibson 5 82
(M W Easterby) *w ldr: rdn 2f out: styd on wl to ld towards fin* **2/1**[1]
2 1/2 **Aye Aye Definitely (IRE)**[30] 1955 3-8-12 **71** TonyHamilton 3 71
(R A Fahey) *hld up in tch: effrt 2f out: edgd lft ins fnl f: kpt on fnl f: jst hld* **15/2**
-456 3 hd **Pegasus Dancer (FR)**[18] 2313 3-8-12 **71** RoystonFfrench 2 70
(K A Ryan) *led: rdn 2f out: kpt on fnl f: hdd towards fin* **8/1**
14-0 4 3/4 **Davaye**[49] 1453 3-8-3 **65** AndrewElliott(3) 7 62
(K R Burke) *chsd ldrs: drvn over 2f out: kpt on fnl f* **12/1**
0401 5 nk **Distant Sun (USA)**[22] 2167 3-8-7 **66** ow1 TomEaves 6 62
(I Semple) *hld up: hdwy over 1f out: kpt on fnl f: nrst fin* **9/2**[3]
0043 6 4 **Prospect Place**[22] 2171 3-9-4 **77** PaulMulrennan 4 61
(M Dods) *t.k.h: chsd ldrs tl wknd appr fnl f* **3/1**[2]
40-0 7 7 **Mr Klick (IRE)**[28] 1994 3-9-0 **73** PaddyAspell 1 36
(N Wilson) *prom on outside: rdn over 2f out: sn btn* **16/1**
1m 13.81s (0.14) **Going Correction** +0.05s/f (Good) 7 Ran SP% **113.0**
Speed ratings (Par 101):101,100,100,99,98 93,84
CSF £17.24 TOTE £2.70: £1.60, £3.60; EX 15.40.
Owner D Swales **Bred** P Monagnan And J Collins And G Dillon **Trained** Sheriff Hutton, N Yorks

FOCUS
An ordinary event in which the form makes sense but is limited by the proximity of the fifth.
Prospect Place Official explanation: jockey said gelding ran too free

2822 ARNOLD CLARK H'CAP 1m 1f 20y
4:45 (4:48) (Class 4) (0-85,83) 4-Y-0+ **£5,829** (£1,734; £866; £432) **Stalls** Low

Form RPR
32- 1 **Avoriaz (IRE)**[263] 5726 4-9-7 **83** TonyHamilton 6 92
(R A Fahey) *cl up: led over 2f out: styd on strly fnl f* **13/2**
-155 2 1 3/4 **Shy Glance (USA)**[10] 2536 5-8-12 **74** DaleGibson 1 79
(P Monteith) *trckd ldrs: effrt and chsd wnr over 1f out: kpt on fnl f: nt rch wnr* **5/1**[3]
31-5 3 2 1/2 **Prince Evelith (GER)**[13] 2452 4-9-1 **77** DeanMcKeown 8 77
(G A Swinbank) *in tch: effrt outer over 2f out: hung lft over 1f out: nt qckn* **10/3**[2]
-560 4 hd **Cool Ebony**[13] 2469 4-8-10 **72** TomEaves 7 71
(M Dods) *prom: drvn and outpcd over 2f out: rallied fnl f: kpt on* **8/1**
0150 5 1 **Frank Crow**[15] 2397 4-8-6 **75** GaryBartley(7) 5 72
(J S Goldie) *led after 2f to over 2f out: sn rdn and no ex* **14/1**
3053 6 nk **Inside Story (IRE)**[10] 2527 5-8-6 **68** (b) PaulMulrennan 3 64
(M W Easterby) *hld up in tch: hdwy over 2f out: outpcd wl over 1f out: no imp after* **7/1**
622 7 1/2 **Sedgwick**[14] 2423 5-8-8 **70** RoystonFfrench 4 65
(J G Given) *led 2f: cl up: ev ch over 2f out: btn fnl f* **11/4**[1]
264- 8 19 **Rodeo**[300] 4806 4-9-3 **82** MarkLawson(3) 2 35
(C W Thornton) *bhd: struggling fr 1/2-way: t.o* **33/1**
1m 57.09s (-2.91) **Going Correction** -0.35s/f (Firm) 8 Ran SP% **113.0**
Speed ratings (Par 105):98,96,94,94,93 92,92,75
CSF £37.84 CT £126.26 TOTE £7.00: £2.30, £1.70, £1.60; EX 49.40.
Owner R Thompson & M Charlton **Bred** Jean Charles Coude **Trained** Musley Bank, N Yorks
■ Stewards' Enquiry : Dean McKeown caution: careless riding

FOCUS
A fair handicap but one run at only an ordinary gallop. The form is rated through the runner-up and could be a little higher.
Rodeo Official explanation: jockey said gelding never travelled

2823 AYR RUGBY CLUB 110 YEARS H'CAP 1m 1f 20y
5:20 (5:21) (Class 6) (0-65,65) 4-Y-0+ **£2,590** (£770; £385; £192) **Stalls** Low

Form RPR
303- 1 **Whittinghamvillage**[257] 5839 6-8-0 **47** AndrewElliott(3) 10 56
(D W Whillans) *chsd ldrs: led over 2f out: hrd pressed 1f out: hld on wl* **20/1**
0342 2 nk **Mystical Ayr (IRE)**[2] 2760 5-9-1 **59** DeanMcKeown 8 67
(Miss L A Perratt) *chsd ldrs: effrt and ev ch fr over 1f out: carried hd high: kpt on fnl f: hld towards fin* **10/3**[2]
5611 3 4 **Bijou Dan**[22] 2168 6-9-7 **65** (p) TonyHamilton 4 64
(D W Thompson) *hld up: rdn over 2f out: hdwy over 1f out: nrst fin* **11/4**[1]
0004 4 1/2 **Esoterica (IRE)**[24] 2117 4-8-7 **58** (b) GaryBartley(7) 5 56
(J S Goldie) *t.k.h: hld up: rdn over 2f out: hdwy over 1f out: nvr rchd ldrs* **13/2**
-002 5 2 **Motafarred (IRE)**[9] 2550 5-8-13 **57** PaulMulrennan 11 51
(Micky Hammond) *led to over 2f out: sn no ex* **4/1**[3]
0/0- 6 hd **Tiger King (GER)**[376] 976 6-9-7 **65** DaleGibson 6 58
(P Monteith) *chsd ldrs: effrt over 2f out: no ex over 1f out* **25/1**
0000 7 6 **City Miss**[9] 2563 4-8-3 **47** oh1 ow1 DeanMernagh 7 27
(Miss L A Perratt) *hld up: drvn and outpcd 3f out: n.d after* **66/1**
1303 8 1 3/4 **Bessemer (JPN)**[9] 2551 6-9-4 **62** (p) RoystonFfrench 1 38
(I W McInnes) *midfield: drvn and outpcd 3f out: n.d after* **13/2**
/0-0 9 nk **Showtime Annie**[89] 462 6-7-13 **46** oh1 (p) LiamJones(3) 9 22
(A Bailey) *midfield: struggling over 2f out: sn btn* **14/1**
1m 56.68s (-3.32) **Going Correction** -0.35s/f (Firm) 9 Ran SP% **113.2**
Speed ratings (Par 101):100,99,96,95,93 93,88,86,86
CSF £82.93 CT £246.31 TOTE £29.50: £3.40, £1.50, £1.20; EX 103.40.
Owner Flex Racing **Bred** T And M A Bibby **Trained** Hawick, Borders

FOCUS
A low-grade handicap in which the ordinary pace again suited those racing prominently. The form looks weak though.

2824 AYR FAMILY DAY ON 8TH JULY APPRENTICE H'CAP 1m 5f 13y
5:55 (5:55) (Class 5) (0-75,67) 4-Y-0+ **£2,914** (£867; £433; £216) **Stalls** Low

Form RPR
646 1 **Kyber**[9] 2567 6-8-4 **50** GaryBartley(3) 4 58
(J S Goldie) *chsd ldrs: outpcd over 2f out: styd on wl fnl f: led nr fin* **13/2**

-143 **2** *hd* **Trafalgar Day**[14] [2434] 4-8-11 **59**.............................. PatrickDonaghy(5) 5 67
(W M Brisbourne) *cl up: rdn and led over 1f out: edgd lft ins fnl f: hdd cl home* **7/4**[1]
-014 **3** *3* **Alfonso**[13] [2465] 6-9-10 **67**.. WilliamCarson 3 70
(P Monteith) *led to over 1f out: nt qckn fnl f* **7/2**[2]
5064 **4** *3* **Grey Outlook**[9] [2567] 4-8-9 **57**.. NSLawes(5) 6 56
(Miss L A Perratt) *chsd ldrs: effrt over 2f out: no ex over 1f out* **9/2**
0225 **5** *3 1/2* **Danzatrice**[27] [2031] 5-9-4 **61**.. KellyHarrison 1 54
(C W Thornton) *s.s: sn rcvrd and hld up: rdn and hung lft 3f out: sn btn* **4/1**[3]
300 **6** *29* **Modarab**[20] [2253] 5-8-9 **57**.. JamesRogers(5) 2 7
(Mrs L B Normile) *chsd ldrs to 1/2-way: sn struggling: t.o* **16/1**
2m 53.15s (-3.46) **Going Correction** -0.35s/f (Firm) **6** Ran SP% **116.0**
Speed ratings (Par 103):96,95,94,92,90 72
CSF £19.18 TOTE £10.40: £4.20, £1.10; EX 49.10 Place 6 £ 156.72, Place 5 £ 146.08.
Owner Great Northern Partnership **Bred** P B Holmes **Trained** Uplawmoor, E Renfrews

FOCUS
Not a strong handicap and a steady pace to the straight resulted in a modest winning time and the form is unlikely to amount to much.
Kyber Official explanation: trainer's rep said, regarding apparent improvement in form, that the gelding was better suited by the galloping track
Danzatrice Official explanation: jockey said mare missed the break
Modarab Official explanation: jockey said gelding was unsuited by the good ground
T/Plt: £140.80 to a £1 stake. Pool: £41,969.35. 217.50 winning tickets. T/Qpdt: £48.30 to a £1 stake. Pool: £2,073.00. 31.70 winning tickets. RY

2460 MUSSELBURGH (R-H)
Friday, June 22
OFFICIAL GOING: Good (good to soft in places, 7.8)
Wind: Nil Weather: Overcast

2825 BOLLINGER CHAMPAGNE CHALLENGE SERIES H'CAP (FOR GENTLEMAN AMATEUR RIDERS) 2m
6:50 (6:51) (Class 6) (0-65,65) 4-Y-0+ £3,123 (£968; £484; £242) Stalls Low

Form RPR
16-0 **1** **Ostfanni (IRE)**[41] [913] 7-11-1 **61**.............................. MrCPHuxley(5) 10 69
(M Todhunter) *trckd ldrs: hdwy over 4f out: rdn along to chse ldr 3f out: led 2f out: drvn and styd on wl fnl f* **5/2**[1]
4414 **2** *3* **York Cliff**[20] [2252] 9-11-0 **60**.............................. MrBenBrisbourne(5) 1 64
(W M Brisbourne) *hld up towards rr: stdy hdwy over 4f out: rdn to chse ldrs 3f out: drvn and styd on fnl f* **4/1**[3]
6-22 **3** *hd* **Kristiansand**[12] [2252] 7-10-13 **54**.............................. MrSWalker 11 58
(P Monteith) *trckd ldrs: hdwy to ld 4f out: rdn clr 3f out: hdd and drvn 2f out: wknd ent fnl f* **10/3**[2]
5426 **4** *2 1/2* **Rule For Ever**[27] [2026] 5-11-10 **65**.............................. MrSDobson 7 66
(I W McInnes) *hld up: hdwy over 4f out: rdn along to chse ldng pair wl over 2f out: sn drvn and kpt on same pce* **11/2**
-300 **5** *10* **Mulligan's Pride (IRE)**[27] [1556] 6-10-2 **50**...............(b) MrMGarnett(7) 14 39
(James Moffatt) *prom: rdn along 4f out: outpcd fnl 3f* **8/1**
006/ **6** *3 1/2* **Rightful Ruler**[24] [5061] 5-10-11 **55**.............................. MrMJJSmith(3) 8 40
(N Wilson) *chsd ldrs: rdn along 4f out: plugged on same pce fnl 3f* **9/1**
-000 **7** *8* **The Dunion**[9] [2567] 4-10-2 **46** oh1.............................. MrSPearce(3) 6 21
(Miss L A Perratt) *a towards rr* **40/1**
00-0 **8** *5* **On Every Street**[31] [1934] 6-10-2 **46** oh1...............(v) MrPCallaghan(3) 13 15
(R Bastiman) *chsd ldrs: rdn along 4f out: drvn over 3f out and sn wknd* **40/1**
-500 **9** *hd* **Borsch (IRE)**[9] [2567] 5-9-12 **46** oh1.............................. MrGRSmith(7) 4 15
(Miss L A Perratt) *a in rr* **33/1**
6-30 **10** *14* **King's Envoy (USA)**[4] [2715] 8-9-12 **46** oh1.............................. MrBAdams(7) 2 —
(Mrs J C McGregor) *a in rr* **50/1**
00/0 **11** *13* **Chisel**[8] [2006] 6-9-12 **46** oh1.............................. MrJPearce(7) 3 —
(M Wigham) *sn outpcd and a bhd* **50/1**
/00- **12** *2 1/2* **Welcome Spirit**[257] [5837] 4-9-12 **46** oh1.............................. MrAdamNicol(7) 12 —
(J S Haldane) *led: rdn along 5f out: sn hdd & wknd* **100/1**
304F **13** *1/2* **Arcangela**[20] [2252] 4-9-12 **46** oh1.............................. MrJWaggott(7) 5 —
(Miss Tracy Waggott) *chsd ldrs: rdn along over 5f out: sn wknd* **40/1**
0060 **14** *4* **Bournonville**[31] [1934] 4-10-0 **46** oh1.............................. MrSRees(5) 9 —
(M Wigham) *cl up tl wknd qckly over 5f out* **33/1**
3m 38.69s (4.79) **Going Correction** +0.225s/f (Good) **14** Ran SP% **126.3**
Speed ratings (Par 101):97,95,95,94,89 87,83,80,80,73 67,66,65,63
CSF £12.60 CT £36.10 TOTE £4.10: £1.60, £1.60, £1.80; EX 19.80.
Owner Ian Hall Racing **Bred** Mrs Brigitte Schlueter **Trained** Orton, Cumbria

FOCUS
A moderate handicap, confined to amateur riders, but it was run at a fair pace and the form looks straightforward enough.

2826 TURFTV (S) STKS 5f
7:20 (7:37) (Class 6) 3-Y-0 £3,238 (£963; £481; £240) Stalls Low

Form RPR
-004 **1** **La Vecchia Scuola (IRE)**[21] [2200] 3-8-4 52..........(v1) AndrewMullen(3) 3 51
(D Nicholls) *wnt lft s: chsd ldrs and rdn along 1/2-way: hdwy over 1f out: styd on u.p to ld ins fnl f* **15/8**[1]
0000 **2** *2* **Silly Gilly (IRE)**[18] [2304] 3-8-7 48.............................. PaulMulrennan 7 44
(K R Burke) *led: rdn along wl over 1f out: sn drvn: hdd and no ex ins fnl f* **20/1**
2046 **3** *1 1/2* **Temtation (IRE)**[13] [2459] 3-8-4 50.............................. PatrickMathers(3) 11 38
(Peter Grayson) *in tch: hdwy on outer 2f out: sn rdn and styd on ins fnl f* **6/1**[3]
00-0 **4** *1 1/4* **Northern Candy**[15] [2387] 3-8-12 30...............(p) DaleGibson 8 39
(A Dickman) *prom: rdn along 2f out: drvn and wknd appr fnl f* **66/1**
2-05 **5** *shd* **Go Imperial (IRE)**[3] [2750] 3-8-9 63.............................. JerryO'Dwyer(3) 5 39
(M G Quinlan) *chsd ldrs: rdn along 1/2-way: drvn over 1f out and sn one pce* **11/4**[2]
4006 **6** *1 3/4* **Royal Dagger (IRE)**[21] [2195] 3-8-12 48.............................. RoystonFfrench 4 32
(Rae Guest) *cl up: rdn along 2f out: drvn and wknd ent fnl f* **10/1**
60-6 **7** *3 1/2* **Nepos**[23] [2146] 3-8-12 55.............................. DeanMcKeown 9 20
(A J McCabe) *a towards rr* **14/1**
0 **8** *1 1/2* **Irish Mickey**[60] [1197] 3-8-12 0.............................. TomEaves 2 14
(James Moffatt) *hmpd s: a bhd* **50/1**
60-0 **9** *3 1/2* **Senora Lenorah**[30] [1943] 3-8-3 35 ow3.............................. PaulPickard(7) 1 —
(D A Nolan) *bdly hmpd s: a bhd* **100/1**
61.77 secs (1.27) **Going Correction** +0.125s/f (Good) **9** Ran SP% **100.7**
Speed ratings (Par 97):94,90,88,86,86 83,77,75,69
CSF £30.32 TOTE £2.50: £1.10, £3.60, £1.40; EX 24.60.The winner was sold to R W Johnson for £6,200.
Owner The Three K's **Bred** Maurice Craig **Trained** Sessay, N Yorks
■ This race was delayed by 15 minutes to allow jockeys more time to complete their journey from the afternoon fixture at Ayr.

FOCUS
A dire event and not one to dwell on. Bungie was withdrawn (4/1, refused to enter stalls.) R4 applies, deduct 20p in the £.

2827 TPS H'CAP 7f 30y
7:50 (8:00) (Class 6) (0-65,65) 4-Y-0+ £3,238 (£963; £481; £240) Stalls High

Form RPR
4630 **1** **Skyelady**[27] [2023] 4-9-7 **65**.............................. TomEaves 6 77
(T D Barron) *hld up in rr: hdwy 3f out: swtchd lft and rdn wl over 1f out: styd on strly ins fnl f to ld nr line* **9/2**[2]
-005 **2** *shd* **Sands Of Barra (IRE)**[9] [2556] 4-8-12 **56**...............(p) RoystonFfrench 8 68
(I W McInnes) *prom: hdwy to ld wl over 1f out and sn rdn clr: drvn wl ins fnl f: hdd nr line* **7/1**[3]
5050 **3** *3* **Attacca**[4] [2711] 6-8-1 **48** ow2.............................. PatrickMathers(3) 12 52
(J R Weymes) *hld up towards rr: hdwy 3f out: rdn to chse ldrs wl over 1f out: kpt on same pce u.p ent fnl f* **10/1**
-503 **4** *shd* **Anthemion (IRE)**[15] [2388] 10-8-10 **57**.............................. AndrewMullen(3) 11 61
(Mrs J C McGregor) *cl up: led 3f out: rdn along: hdd and outpcd wl over 2f out: rallied u.p over 1f out: kpt on same pce ent fnl f* **7/1**[3]
0004 **5** *2 1/2* **Charles Parnell (IRE)**[11] [2508] 4-9-4 **62**.............................. PaulMulrennan 13 59
(M Dods) *hld up: hdwy 3f out: rdn and nt clr run 2f out: sn drvn and no imp* **10/1**
0-50 **6** *1* **Lambency (IRE)**[15] [2390] 4-8-7 **51**.............................. TonyHamilton 5 45
(J S Goldie) *in tch: rdn along 3f out: grad wknd* **20/1**
0450 **7** *1/2* **Snow Bunting**[11] [2508] 9-8-8 **55**.............................. AndrewElliott(3) 7 48
(Jedd O'Keeffe) *hld up in rr: effrt 3f out: sn pushed along and no hdwy* **8/1**
-113 **8** *hd* **Megalo Maniac**[38] [1755] 4-9-1 **62**.............................. JamieMoriarty(3) 10 54
(R A Fahey) *chsd ldrs: rdn along whn n.m.r over 2f out: grad wknd* **3/1**[1]
1004 **9** *2* **Mozakhraf (USA)**[43] [1597] 5-9-5 **63**.............................. DO'Donohoe 1 50
(K A Ryan) *led: cl up tl led again wl over 2f out: sn rdn and edgd lft: hdd wl over 1f out: sn drvn and wknd* **10/1**
00-0 **10** *3* **The Thrifty Bear**[33] [1862] 4-8-2 **46** oh1.............................. SilvestreDeSousa 3 25
(C W Fairhurst) *chsd ldrs: rdn along 3f out: wknd fnl 2f* **33/1**
10-0 **11** *15* **Red Contact (USA)**[129] [451] 6-8-12 **56**...............(p) DaleGibson 9 —
(A Dickman) *t.k.h: in tch: pushed along over 3f out and sn wknd* **18/1**
1m 30.93s (0.99) **Going Correction** +0.225s/f (Good) **11** Ran SP% **119.5**
Speed ratings (Par 101):103,102,99,99,96 95,94,94,92,88 71
CSF £36.82 CT £309.57 TOTE £6.90: £1.80, £2.60, £3.90; EX 53.30.
Owner David W Armstrong **Bred** Manor Farm Stud (rutland) **Trained** Maunby, N Yorks

FOCUS
A modest handicap, but it was run at a solid pace and the form looks sound for the class.
Megalo Maniac Official explanation: jockey said gelding had been unsuited by the good, good to soft in places ground

2828 NCB (STOCKBROKERS) CLAIMING STKS 1m 1f
8:20 (8:21) (Class 6) 4-Y-0+ £3,238 (£963; £481; £240) Stalls High

Form RPR
52-1 **1** **Ballyhurry (USA)**[9] [2563] 10-8-4 66.............................. GaryBartley(7) 4 70
(J S Goldie) *hld up in tch: hdwy wl over 2f out: rdn to chse ldng pair over 1f out: styd on u.p to ld last 100yds* **10/3**[2]
6201 **2** *1/2* **Little Jimbob**[4] [2709] 6-9-2 78.............................. JamieMoriarty(3) 7 77
(R A Fahey) *t.k.h: trckd ldng pair: hdwy 3f out: rdn to chal 2f out and sn ev ch: drvn ent fnl f and kpt on towards fin* **5/6**[1]
1600 **3** *3/4* **Wahoo Sam (USA)**[9] [2564] 7-9-5 70.............................. DO'Donohoe 5 75
(K A Ryan) *cl up: led wl over 3f out: jnd and rdn 2f out: drvn over 1f out: hdd and no ex last 100yds* **10/1**
4160 **4** *4* **Primo Way**[9] [2564] 6-9-3 73.............................. TomEaves 3 64
(I Semple) *hld up in rr: hdwy 3f out: rdn to chse ldrs wl over 1f out: sn drvn and one pce* **4/1**[3]
5 *12* **Raguany (IRE)**[24] 5-8-9 0.............................. RoystonFfrench 1 28
(B Mactaggart) *chsd ldrs: rdn along over 3f out: sn wknd* **50/1**
0040 **6** *14* **Second Reef**[7] [1554] 5-8-12 48...............(vt) PaulMulrennan 2 —
(J R Weymes) *hld up: effrt and sme hdwy 3f out: sn rdn and btn* **28/1**
00 **7** *2 1/2* **Shoot Out**[25] [2091] 4-8-9 0.............................. DeanMcKeown 6 —
(C W Thornton) *led: rdn along and hdd wl over 3f out: sn wknd* **80/1**
1m 56.13s (2.27) **Going Correction** +0.225s/f (Good) **7** Ran SP% **113.4**
Speed ratings (Par 101):98,97,96,93,82 70,68
CSF £6.39 TOTE £4.10: £2.80, £1.10; EX 8.60.
Owner Jim Goldie Racing Club **Bred** J Hettinger **Trained** Uplawmoor, E Renfrews

FOCUS
A typically modest event of its type. It was run at an uneven pace and the form should be treated with some caution.

2829 NAIRN'S OAT CAKES H'CAP 7f 30y
8:50 (8:50) (Class 6) (0-65,64) 3-Y-0 £3,238 (£963; £481; £240) Stalls High

Form RPR
5023 **1** **Rebel Pearl (IRE)**[8] [2607] 3-8-9 **55**.............................. JerryO'Dwyer(3) 2 68+
(M G Quinlan) *mde all: rdn clr over 1f out: styd on strly* **6/1**[2]
5322 **2** *4* **Five Wishes**[4] [2713] 3-8-13 **56**.............................. PaulMulrennan 7 58
(M Dods) *trckd ldrs: effrt 3f out: sn rdn along: styd on u.p to chse wnr ins fnl f: no imp* **5/2**[1]
-003 **3** *1 1/2* **Grand Diamond (IRE)**[29] [1964] 3-8-12 **62**...............(p) GaryBartley(7) 12 60
(J S Goldie) *hld up in tch: hdwy on inner 3f out: n.m.r and swtchd lft wl over 1f out: sn rdn and styd on ins fnl f: nrst fin* **10/1**
55-0 **4** *hd* **Mineral Rights (USA)**[29] [1964] 3-9-3 **60**.............................. TomEaves 14 57
(I Semple) *chsd ldrs: rdn along 3f out: drvn 2f out and kpt on same pce* **18/1**
0235 **5** *3/4* **Nota Liberata**[17] [2340] 3-9-4 **64**.............................. JamieMoriarty(3) 6 59
(G M Moore) *midfield: effrt and hdwy wl over 2f out: sn rdn and styd on appr fnl f: nrst fin* **7/1**[3]
0-03 **6** *2 1/2* **Bollin Fergus**[29] [1965] 3-9-1 **58**.............................. SilvestreDeSousa 11 47
(T D Easterby) *towards rr: effrt 3f out: sn rdn along and styd on appr fnl f: nrst fin* **7/1**[3]
-401 **7** *3/4* **Strabinios King**[21] [2206] 3-9-3 **60**.............................. DeanMcKeown 1 47
(P C Haslam) *chsd wnr: rdn along over 2f out: sn drvn and wknd appr fnl f* **8/1**
2340 **8** *4* **Rann Na Cille (IRE)**[8] [2594] 3-9-5 **62**.............................. DO'Donohoe 9 38
(K A Ryan) *towards rr: effrt and sme hdwy 3f out: sn rdn along and no imp fnl 2f* **40/1**
3-40 **9** *3* **Sangreal**[13] [2453] 3-9-2 **62**.............................. AndrewElliott(3) 4 30
(K R Burke) *a towards rr* **50/1**

The Form Book, Raceform Ltd, Compton, RG20 6NL

-210 **10** *1 1/2* **Falcon's Fire (IRE)**[46] [1538] 3-9-5 **62**.......................... RoystonFfrench 3 26
(Mrs A Duffield) *chsd ldrs on outer: pushed along 3f out: sn rdn and wknd fnl 2f* **12/1**

00-0 **11** *2* **Lovers Kiss**[59] [1219] 3-8-8 **51**.......................................(b) TonyHamilton 13 9
(N Wilson) *chsd ldrs: rdn along 3f out: wknd 2f out* **33/1**

00-0 **12** *12* **Anybody's Guess (IRE)**[18] [2300] 3-8-1 **47** ow2......... AndrewMullen[(3)] 8 —
(J S Wainwright) *a bhd* **80/1**

0-40 **13** *hd* **Didactic**[31] [1913] 3-8-3 **49**.......................................(be) PatrickMathers[(3)] 5 —
(A J McCabe) *t.k.h: chsd ldrs on outer: rdn along over 3f out and sn wknd* **22/1**

6534 **14** *5* **Birdie Birdie**[24] [2110] 3-8-2 **45**.......................................(v) DaleGibson 10 —
(R A Fahey) *hld up: a bhd* **14/1**

1m 31.02s (1.08) **Going Correction** +0.225s/f (Good) **14** Ran SP% **120.6**
Speed ratings (Par 97):102,97,95,95,94 91,90,86,82,81 78,65,64,59
CSF £20.47 CT £157.31 TOTE £9.60: £3.80, £1.70, £2.90; EX 16.30.
Owner L Cashman **Bred** Miss Niamh Cashman **Trained** Newmarket, Suffolk

FOCUS
A moderate handicap, but the winner was full value for her winning margin and improved again. The second is not living up to expectations though, and the third ran a little below his latest form.
Strabinios King Official explanation: jockey said gelding hung right

2830 TURFTV.CO.UK H'CAP 5f
9:20 (9:20) (Class 6) (0-65,63) 4-Y-0+ **£3,238** (£963; £481; £240) **Stalls** Low

Form RPR

2051 **1** **Compton Classic**[4] [2712] 5-8-7 **56** 6ex.......................(p) GaryBartley[(7)] 12 71
(J S Goldie) *trckd ldrs: hdwy on outer 2f out: rdn and qcknd to ld ent fnl f: kpt on* **7/2**[2]

2032 **2** *1 3/4* **Divine Spirit**[4] [2712] 6-9-1 **57**....................................... RoystonFfrench 10 66
(M Dods) *hmpd s and bhd: gd hdwy on outer 2f out: rdn over 1f out and ev ch tl drvn and nt qckn ins fnl f* **15/8**[1]

3606 **3** *1 1/2* **Rothesay Dancer**[2] [2761] 4-8-1 **50**................................ KellyHarrison[(7)] 7 53+
(J S Goldie) *in tch: hdwy and nt clr run wl over 1f out: sn swtchd lft and rdn: styd on fnl f* **12/1**

0024 **4** *1 1/4* **Sharp Hat**[14] [2418] 13-8-8 **50**.. DaleGibson 4 49
(D W Chapman) *hmpd s and bhd: hdwy 2f out: rdn and styd on wl fnl f: nrst fin* **12/1**

-000 **5** *hd* **Strawberry Patch (IRE)**[13] [2461] 8-8-10 **52**..............(p) PaulMulrennan 5 50+
(J S Goldie) *in tch: effrt and nt clr run wl over 1f out: sn rdn and styd on ins fnl f* **9/2**[3]

0005 **6** *shd* **Sandwith**[15] [2386] 4-9-4 **63**................................(p) JamieMoriarty[(3)] 6 61
(J S Wainwright) *cl up: led after 1 1/2f: rdn wl over 1f out: drvn and hdd ent fnl f: sn wknd* **9/1**

-000 **7** *2* **Rosie's Result**[1] [2712] 7-8-0 **45**................................ AndrewMullen[(3)] 11 36
(M Todhunter) *chsd ldrs: rdn along wl over 1f out: grad wknd* **16/1**

0-12 **8** *8* **Maromito (IRE)**[22] [2174] 10-8-10 **52**................................ TomEaves 3 14
(R Bastiman) *wnt rt s: a towards rr* **6/1**

000- **9** *7* **Mutayam**[323] [4091] 7-8-3 **45**..............................(t) SilvestreDeSousa 2 —
(D A Nolan) *led 1 1/2f: cl up tl rdn 2f out and sn wknd* **100/1**

100- **10** *6* **Orpenlina (IRE)**[267] [5631] 4-8-0 **45**........................... PatrickMathers[(3)] 9 —
(Peter Grayson) *wnt rt s: plld hrd and cl up: rdn along 2f out and sn wknd* **33/1**

60.73 secs (0.23) **Going Correction** +0.125s/f (Good) **10** Ran SP% **124.7**
Speed ratings (Par 101):103,100,97,95,95 95,92,79,68,58
CSF £11.30 CT £75.00 TOTE £5.20: £1.70, £1.40, £2.30; EX 11.80 Place 6 £11.65, Place 5 £9.21.
Owner Jim Goldie Racing Club **Bred** James Thom And Sons And Peter Orr **Trained** Uplawmoor, E Renfrews

FOCUS
A weak sprint handicap. There were a couple short of room in behind, but the first two avoided trouble from their high draws. The form of the principals looks sound enough and the winner has been raised significantly.
Maromito(IRE) Official explanation: jockey said gelding was denied a clear run
T/Plt: £25.80 to a £1 stake. Pool: £60,313.30. 1,702.70 winning tickets. T/Qpdt: £28.20 to a £1 stake. Pool: £3,159.40. 82.80 winning tickets. JR

2055
NEWMARKET (JULY) (R-H)
Friday, June 22

OFFICIAL GOING: Good
Wind: Virtually nil Weather: Overcast

2831 UNICORN APPRENTICE H'CAP 1m
6:00 (6:02) (Class 5) (0-70,72) 4-Y-0+ **£3,886** (£1,156; £577; £288) **Stalls** Low

Form RPR

43-6 **1** **Colinca's Lad (IRE)**[28] [2004] 5-9-3 **62**............................ PJMcDonald 14 71
(T T Clement) *stdd s: rdn and prog 3f out: led over 1f out: sn clr: kpt on wl* **12/1**

030- **2** *2 1/2* **Silent Applause**[273] [5504] 4-9-7 **69**.............................. JackMitchell[(3)] 10 72
(Dr J D Scargill) *bhd: hdwy on outside fnl 2f: passed 3 rivals ins fnl f: fin wl but nt rch wnr* **16/1**

-025 **3** *1/2* **Gracie's Gift (IRE)**[29] [1969] 5-9-3 **62**................................(p) LukeMorris 5 64
(A G Newcombe) *hld up: effrt 3f out: ev ch over 1f out: rdn and one pce* **6/1**[2]

3543 **4** *nk* **Rowan Lodge (IRE)**[3] [2748] 5-8-8 **60**......................(v) AshleyMorgan[(7)] 2 61
(M H Tompkins) *prom: led over 2f out tl over 1f out: nt qckn after* **8/1**[3]

3502 **5** *hd* **Call My Bluff (FR)**[7] [2623] 4-9-7 **66**................................ PatrickHills 1 67
(Rae Guest) *midfield: effrt 3f out: hung rt and racd v awkwardly whn styng on at one pce after* **9/1**

4-00 **6** *4* **Al Rayanah**[23] [2154] 4-8-12 **60**.............................. KirstyMilczarek[(3)] 6 52
(G Prodromou) *dwlt: bhd tl sme prog fnl 2f: nvr nr ldrs* **33/1**

-000 **7** *1 1/4* **Salisbury Plain**[6] [2665] 6-8-6 **56** ow3............................ KylieManser[(5)] 11 45
(N I M Rossiter) *bhd tl modest late prog fnl 2f* **33/1**

06-0 **8** *1 1/2* **Love And Affection**[26] [2055] 4-8-2 **52**............................(t) MCGeran[(5)] 8 37
(P S McEntee) *dwlt: nvr nr ldrs* **50/1**

0-00 **9** *3 1/2* **Oh Danny Boy**[27] [1717] 6-8-4 **56**.................................... MJMurphy[(7)] 9 33
(M C Chapman) *cl up tl 1/2-way: struggling over 2f out* **40/1**

4651 **10** *nk* **Stargazer Jim (FR)**[9] [2564] 5-9-10 **72** 6ex..........(v) JamieHamblett[(3)] 12 48
(W J Haggas) *prom: hrd drvn over 3f out: no rspnse and lost pl v tamely* **5/4**[1]

2600 **11** *nk* **Tancredi (SWE)**[34] [1847] 5-9-7 **66**.............................. RussellKennemore 4 42
(N B King) *struggling after 5f* **20/1**

150- **12** *nk* **Riolo (IRE)**[270] [5576] 5-8-7 **55**..................................(b) SCreighton[(3)] 13 30
(K F Clutterbuck) *prom: led over 3f out: sn rdn: hdd over 2f out: tied up bdly ins fnl f* **33/1**

3462 **13** *shd* **Favouring (IRE)**[38] [1753] 5-8-5 **50** oh2..................................(v) NicolPolli 15 25
(M C Chapman) *led on outside tl hdd over 3f out: sn lost pl* **16/1**

0143 **14** *3/4* **Tabulate**[9] [2568] 4-8-10 **60**.. MarkCoumbe[(5)] 3 33
(P L Gilligan) *a bhd* **20/1**

0300 **15** *6* **Magical Music**[46] [1524] 4-8-11 **63**......................... JosephineBruning[(7)] 16 22
(J Pearce) *a toiling in rr* **16/1**

1m 41.98s (1.55) **Going Correction** +0.175s/f (Good) **15** Ran SP% **127.9**
Speed ratings (Par 103):99,96,96,95,95 91,90,88,85,84 84,84,84,83,77
CSF £186.18 CT £1311.11 TOTE £17.40: £3.90, £4.90, £2.40; EX 193.20.
Owner Andreas Charalambous & Partners **Bred** Peter Charles **Trained** Newmarket, Suffolk

FOCUS
There had been 1.2mm of rain overnight and early in the day, but the going stick showed 7.9, indicating good ground. This apprentice handicap was run at only a steady pace and the form is modest, rated through the third.
Al Rayanah Official explanation: jockey said filly never travelled

2832 UNICORN ASSET MANAGEMENT JULY COURSE SERIES MAIDEN STKS (QUALIFIER) 6f
6:35 (6:36) (Class 3) 2-Y-O **£6,477** (£1,927; £963; £481) **Stalls** Low

Form RPR

3 **1** **Shifting Star (IRE)**[13] [2478] 2-9-3 0.. AdamKirby 5 79+
(W R Swinburn) *chsd ldrs: nt clr run over 1f out: rdn to ld ins fnl f: r.o* **2/1**[2]

03 **2** *1 1/4* **Fortuity (IRE)**[16] [2349] 2-9-3 0.. RobertHavlin 3 75
(J H M Gosden) *led: rdn over 1f out: hdd and unable qckn ins fnl f* **10/1**[3]

3 *1 3/4* **Rio De La Plata (USA)** 2-9-3 0...................................... LDettori 2 70+
(Saeed Bin Suroor) *mid-div: outpcd 1/2-way: r.o ins fnl f: nt trble ldrs* **11/10**[1]

4 *1/2* **Incomparable** 2-9-3 0.. StephenDonohoe 12 69
(A J McCabe) *hld up: hdwy over 2f out: rdn over 1f out: styd on* **50/1**

5 *2 1/2* **Astania** 2-8-12 0.. DarryllHolland 1 56+
(P W D'Arcy) *chsd ldrs: hmpd sn after s: shkn up over 1f out: styd on same pce* **50/1**

6 *nk* **Flawed Genius** 2-9-3 0.. JDSmith 6 60
(Sir Michael Stoute) *hld up: nt clr run over 1f out: r.o ins fnl f: nvr trbld ldrs* **16/1**

02 **7** *shd* **Bettys Touch**[23] [2152] 2-8-12 0.................................... DavidKinsella 8 55
(W J Musson) *chsd ldr: rdn and ev ch over 1f out: wknd fnl f* **33/1**

8 *1 1/4* **Redesdale** 2-9-3 0.. DaneO'Neill 4 59+
(P W D'Arcy) *s.i.s: hld up: rdn and nt clr run over 1f out: n.d* **50/1**

9 *nk* **Close To Paradise (IRE)** 2-8-12 0.............................. JamieSpencer 13 50
(E A L Dunlop) *s.i.s: hld up: effrt and n.m.r over 1f out: n.d* **16/1**

4 **10** *2* **Mr Fantozzi (IRE)**[23] [2151] 2-9-3 0................................ BrettDoyle 9 49
(Miss J Feilden) *chsd ldrs: rdn over 2f out: wknd over 1f out* **11/1**

0 **11** *hd* **Asian Power (IRE)**[13] [2478] 2-9-0 0.............................. SaleemGolam[(3)] 7 49
(P J O'Gorman) *hld up: n.d* **66/1**

0 **12** *shd* **Mister Beano (IRE)**[27] [2041] 2-9-3 0.............................. SimonWhitworth 10 48
(V Smith) *mid-div: racd keenly: rdn and wknd over 1f out* **66/1**

13 *1 3/4* **Tobogganist** 2-9-3 0.. TedDurcan 11 43
(W Jarvis) *s.i.s: hld up: rdn over 2f out: wknd over 1f out* **25/1**

14 *nk* **Bury Treasure (IRE)** 2-9-3 0...................................... JimmyQuinn 14 42
(Miss Gay Kelleway) *prom: rdn over 2f out: n.m.r and wknd over 1f out* **50/1**

15 *3* **Piscean (USA)** 2-9-3 0.. MickyFenton 16 33
(T Keddy) *racd keenly: sn prom: hung rt fr over 2f out: wknd over 1f out* **33/1**

16 *2 1/2* **Weight In Gold** 2-8-12 0.. EdwardCreighton 15 21
(P J McBride) *s.i.s: a in rr* **66/1**

1m 14.65s (1.30) **Going Correction** +0.175s/f (Good) **16** Ran SP% **132.2**
Speed ratings (Par 97):98,96,94,93,90 89,89,87,87,84 84,84,82,81,77 74
CSF £23.71 TOTE £3.40: £1.30, £3.00, £1.10; EX 22.70.
Owner Night Shadow Syndicate **Bred** Hardys Of Kilkeel Ltd **Trained** Aldbury, Herts

FOCUS
An uncompetitive race and not a strong maiden for the track, best rated through the winner to his debut form.

NOTEBOOK
Shifting Star(IRE), a nice prospect, was entitled to have come on for the experience of his debut and travelled well before going on to win his race inside the final furlong. He should get further but it remains to be seen how the Handicapper assesses him. (tchd 15-8)
Fortuity(IRE) is progressing, albeit it at a modest rate having been third in an unexceptional Kempton maiden auction last time. His future is likely to lie in nurseries. (op 9-1)
Rio De La Plata(USA) ◆, an 170,000gns purchase at the breeze-ups, showed signs of greenness but shaped encouragingly in the closing 2f and will certainly know a lot more next time. It would be no surprise if he made significant improvement over the coming months. (op 13-8 tchd 7-4 in places)
Incomparable produced a promising enough display, staying on nicely. A race can be found for him over the summer, allowing for natural progression.
Astania, a son of Shahrastani, ran a fair race and, on breeding, is likely to enjoy going further in time. (op 66-1)
Flawed Genius, who is related to juvenile winners, did not get the best of runs and should know better next time.
Bettys Touch, beaten in a seller last time, not surprisingly found this more difficult but did not fare too badly. (op 40-1)
Close To Paradise(IRE) Official explanation: jockey said filly missed the break
Piscean(USA) would have been assisted by some cover, as he raced a little eagerly on the outside. (op 40-1)

2833 UNICORNAM.COM H'CAP 1m 4f
7:05 (7:10) (Class 5) (0-75,74) 4-Y-0+ **£3,886** (£1,156; £577; £288) **Stalls** High

Form RPR

0-12 **1** **Le Soleil (GER)**[15] [2403] 6-9-3 **70**.................................... JamieSpencer 11 84+
(B J Curley) *settled in midfield: clsd 3f out: chal but rdn and hanging lft fnl 2f: led 1f out: drvn along w ears pricked and a jst holding rival* **13/8**[1]

6/-2 **2** *shd* **Wicked Daze (IRE)**[6] [2667] 4-9-3 **70**.................................... JimmyQuinn 6 84+
(Sir Mark Prescott) *pressed ldr in slowly run r: led over 2f out: hdd 1f out: hrd rdn and pressed idling wnr all way to line* **5/1**[2]

-042 **3** *5* **Bronze Star**[23] [2156] 4-8-12 **65**.................................... KerrinMcEvoy 3 71
(J R Fanshawe) *set v modest pce: rdn and hdd over 2f out: outpcd by ldng pair 1f out* **5/1**[2]

1-00 **4** *1/2* **Lady Romanov (IRE)**[36] [1794] 4-9-0 **70**.............................. SaleemGolam[(3)] 9 75
(M H Tompkins) *prom: drvn and outpcd over 2f out: kpt on again fnl f but n.d* **33/1**

-004 **5** *1 1/2* **Great View (IRE)**[28] [2011] 8-9-5 **72**.................................(p) TedDurcan 8 75
(Mrs A L M King) *prom: hrd drvn 3f out: btn wl over 1f out* **14/1**

3110 **6** *1/2* **Street Life (IRE)**[13] [2474] 9-8-10 **70**................................ AlanRutter[(7)] 1 72
(W J Musson) *trckd ldrs on outer: effrt 3f out: outpcd wl over 1f out* **12/1**

0402 **7** *shd* **Art Investor**[23] [2157] 4-8-7 **60**.......................................(b) DaneO'Neill 10 62
(D R C Elsworth) *t.k.h in midfield: effrt 3f out: sn rdn: outpcd wl over 1f out* **14/1**

5464 **8** *5* **Amwell Brave**[23] [2156] 6-8-6 **59**....................................... NickyMackay 2 53
(J R Jenkins) *midfield: wnt cl up 4f out: rdn and wknd 2f out* **14/1**

003 **9** *1 1/4* **Longhill Tiger**[16] [2355] 4-8-3 **63** ow2........................ JamieHamblett(7) 5 55
(G G Margarson) *dropped out last: nvr on terms* **40/1**

3400 **10** *3/4* **Sonny Parkin**[22] [2189] 5-9-6 **73**......................................(v) AdamKirby 7 64
(G A Huffer) *t.k.h in rr: hdwy 3f out: flattered briefly: sn drvn w no rspnse* **33/1**

0-00 **11** *hd* **Zamboozle (IRE)**[15] [2403] 5-9-0 **70**...................... MarcHalford(3) 12 60
(D R C Elsworth) *plld v hrd in rr: hdwy 4f out: rdn and btn over 2f out* **8/1**[3]

000- **12** *nk* **Regal Sunset (IRE)**[22] [5953] 4-8-9 **62**................................ LPKeniry 13 52
(D E Cantillon) *t.k.h: effrt 4f out: flattered over 2f out: sn lost pl* **33/1**

0000 **13** *shd* **Fantasy Ride**[35] [1819] 5-9-2 **69**......................................(b[1]) PatDobbs 4 59
(J Pearce) *s.s: sn in tch and t.k.h in rr: stuggling fnl 3f* **33/1**

0200 **14** *6* **Imperial Harry**[11] [2505] 4-9-3 **70**..................................... MickyFenton 14 50
(V Smith) *t.k.h towards rr: struggling fnl 3f* **25/1**

15 *17* **Roi De L'Odet (FR)**[820] 7-9-7 **74**................................ DarryllHolland 15 27
(N J Henderson) *stdd s: wl bhd: lost tch 4f out: eased and t.o* **14/1**

2m 33.99s (1.08) **Going Correction** +0.175s/f (Good) **15** Ran SP% **134.9**
Speed ratings (Par 103):103,102,99,99,98 97,97,94,93,93 93,92,92,88,77
CSF £9.92 CT £40.30 TOTE £2.90: £1.40, £2.20, £2.30; EX 13.50.
Owner Curley Leisure **Bred** Gestut Wittekindshof **Trained** Newmarket, Suffolk

FOCUS
This was only an ordinary handicap, in which they went a modest pace early on, and not the most reliable form despite the third being solid enough.
Zamboozle(IRE) Official explanation: jockey said gelding ran too free
Fantasy Ride Official explanation: jockey said gelding was slowly away
Roi De L'Odet(FR) Official explanation: jockey said gelding moved poorly throughout, frequently changing its leading leg

2834 CHELMSFORD CITY FC H'CAP 1m
7:40 (7:42) (Class 5) (0-75,74) 3-Y-O £3,886 (£1,156; £577; £288) Stalls Low

Form RPR

55-1 **1** **The Grey Berry**[29] [1964] 3-9-4 **71**........................... GrahamGibbons 8 85
(T D Walford) *hld up: hdwy and edgd lft over 1f out: rdn to ld wl ins fnl f: r.o* **17/2**

-562 **2** *1/2* **Celtic Change (IRE)**[10] [2534] 3-9-1 **68**......................... JamieSpencer 6 80
(M Dods) *chsd ldrs: led over 2f out: rdn over 1f out: edgd rt and hdd wl ins fnl f* **9/4**[1]

-305 **3** *1 1/2* **Alpes Maritimes**[23] [2153] 3-9-6 **73**............................ DarryllHolland 10 82
(G Wragg) *hld up: hdwy over 2f out: rdn and ev ch ins fnl f: edgd rt: styd on same pce* **14/1**

000- **4** *1/2* **Sun Of The Sea**[235] [6255] 3-8-11 **64**.......................... StephenDonohoe 2 72
(N P Littmoden) *hld up: hdwy over 1f out: r.o ins fnl f: nvr nrr* **22/1**

36-1 **5** *2 1/2* **Keidas (FR)**[51] [1410] 3-9-7 **74**... RHills 9 76
(C F Wall) *led: hdd over 6f out: ev ch over 2f out: no ex fnl f* **9/1**

5520 **6** *1 1/2* **Super Cross (IRE)**[14] [2425] 3-9-6 **73**................................. RyanMoore 13 72
(E A L Dunlop) *chsd ldrs: rdn and ev ch over 1f out: wknd ins fnl f* **10/1**

-600 **7** *nk* **Becharm**[13] [2472] 3-8-9 **62**... LPKeniry 7 60
(A G Newcombe) *hld up: hdwy 2f out: rdn whn hmpd over 1f out: no ex* **50/1**

0621 **8** *3/4* **Cnoc Moy (IRE)**[79] [924] 3-9-4 **71**.. GeorgeBaker 15 67
(C F Wall) *hld up: hdwy and edgd rt over 1f out: nt trble ldrs* **7/1**[3]

1555 **9** *shd* **Tifernati**[8] [2598] 3-9-3 **70**...(b[1]) RobertHavlin 14 66
(W J Haggas) *chsd ldrs: rdn over 2f out: wknd over 1f out* **14/1**

0-51 **10** *hd* **Mountain Cat (IRE)**[21] [2224] 3-8-11 **64**........................... BrettDoyle 16 60
(W J Musson) *hld up in tch: rdn over 1f out: wknd fnl f* **6/1**[2]

04-0 **11** *1 3/4* **Effigy**[43] [1606] 3-9-2 **69**.. DaneO'Neill 3 61
(H Candy) *hld up: effrt over 2f out: wknd over 1f out* **20/1**

2353 **12** *1/2* **Grand Symphony**[18] [2317] 3-8-13 **66**................................. TedDurcan 5 56
(W Jarvis) *chsd ldrs: rdn over 2f out: wknd over 1f out* **16/1**

53-0 **13** *shd* **Etoile D'Or (IRE)**[28] [2008] 3-8-12 **65**.............................. JimmyQuinn 11 55
(M H Tompkins) *hld up: racd keenly: rdn over 2f out: sn wknd* **33/1**

1-00 **14** *7* **Stanley George (IRE)**[13] [2453] 3-9-3 **70**........................ JimCrowley 12 44
(M A Jarvis) *chsd ldrs: rdn over 2f out: wknd wl over 1f out* **20/1**

0-60 **15** *10* **Loch Tay**[23] [2133] 3-9-1 **68**.. KerrinMcEvoy 1 19
(M L W Bell) *led over 6f out: racd keenly: hdd over 2f out: wkng whn hmpd wl over 1f out* **14/1**

000- **16** *1 1/4* **Addictive**[256] [5866] 3-8-9 **65**...................................... SaleemGolam(3) 4 13
(S C Williams) *hld up: rdn over 2f out: sn wknd* **20/1**

1m 40.24s (-0.19) **Going Correction** +0.175s/f (Good) **16** Ran SP% **136.6**
Speed ratings (Par 99):107,106,105,104,102 100,100,99,99,99 97,96,96,89,79 78
CSF £28.59 CT £297.81 TOTE £12.00: £2.10, £1.40, £3.70, £7.50; EX 22.00.
Owner N J Maher **Bred** G Deacon **Trained** Sheriff Hutton, N Yorks

FOCUS
An interesting contest, with plenty of lightly raced types open to plenty of improvement. The time was good and the form has been rated fairly positively, with the winner progressing again.
Super Cross(IRE) Official explanation: jockey said colt hung left
Loch Tay Official explanation: jockey said gelding ran too free to post and suffered interference in running

2835 NATIONAL STUD OWNER BREEDERS' CLUBS H'CAP 7f
8:10 (8:12) (Class 3) (0-95,94) 3-Y-O+ £7,772 (£2,312; £1,155; £577) Stalls Low

Form RPR

3-40 **1** **Gloved Hand**[20] [2239] 5-9-8 **88**.. GeorgeBaker 16 101
(R M Beckett) *dropped out last: stl plenty to do 3f out: gd hdwy to ld jst ins fnl f: kpt on stoutly* **12/1**

0234 **2** *nk* **Orpen Wide (IRE)**[17] [2346] 5-8-5 **76**...............(b) RussellKennemore(5) 7 88
(M C Chapman) *prom: rdn to ld briefly over 1f out: chsd wnr after: r.o gamely but a jst hld* **25/1**

-000 **3** *1 1/4* **Direct Debit (IRE)**[29] [1962] 4-9-2 **82**......................... JamieSpencer 14 91
(M L W Bell) *racd alone centre: tacked over to rest of gp after 2f and chsd ldrs: rdn and outpcd 2f out: kpt on again ins fnl f* **14/1**

0002 **4** *1 1/2* **Compton's Eleven**[5] [2689] 6-9-4 **84**................................. TPO'Shea 3 89
(M R Channon) *chsd ldrs: drvn wl over 1f out: no imp after* **15/2**

0-05 **5** *1 1/2* **Greenslades**[13] [2440] 8-10-0 **94**...................................... PatDobbs 4 95
(P J Makin) *t.k.h and sn led: hdd over 1f out: wknd fnl 100yds* **20/1**

1-12 **6** *3* **Bakhoor (IRE)**[20] [2240] 4-8-9 **75** oh1.......................... DarryllHolland 1 68
(W Jarvis) *prom: rdn and ev ch over 1f out: sn wknd* **7/2**[1]

-160 **7** *1/2* **Bobski (IRE)**[35] [1818] 5-9-5 **85**... AdamKirby 11 76
(G A Huffer) *hmpd s: nvr rchd ldrs* **40/1**

1-00 **8** *1/2* **Trimlestown (IRE)**[20] [2239] 4-9-0 **80**.............................. DaneO'Neill 8 70
(H Candy) *s.s: sme hdwy 2f out: faltered 1f out: sn wl btn* **4/1**[2]

-06 **9** *3/4* **Edaara (IRE)**[21] [2207] 4-9-2 **82**.. RHills 13 70
(W J Haggas) *cl up tl rdn and folded tamely 2f out* **5/1**[3]

-550 **10** *2* **It's A Dream (FR)**[15] [2401] 4-8-11 **77**................................. TedDurcan 12 59
(D R C Elsworth) *midfield: drvn over 2f out: sn btn* **17/2**

0 **11** *nk* **Voliere**[15] [2401] 4-8-10 **79**.. SaleemGolam(3) 10 61
(S C Williams) *wnt rt s: a bhd* **40/1**

200 **12** *1/2* **Secret Night**[48] [1474] 4-8-8 **77**.................................. MarcHalford(3) 15 57
(J A R Toller) *midfield: rdn over 2f out: sn wknd* **25/1**

0-00 **13** *hd* **Art Market (CAN)**[15] [2399] 4-8-12 **78**................................. RyanMoore 6 58
(G L Moore) *drvn 1/2-way: struggling after* **16/1**

2220 **14** *1 1/2* **Perfect Story (IRE)**[13] [2450] 5-9-8 **88**.......................... KerrinMcEvoy 9 64
(J A R Toller) *t.k.h in midfield: rdn 1/2-way: sn btn* **10/1**

-005 **15** *3* **Mubaashir (IRE)**[31] [1930] 3-8-12 **87**............................ StephenDonohoe 5 55
(E A L Dunlop) *a towards rr: no ch fnl 3f* **50/1**

1m 26.13s (-0.65) **Going Correction** +0.175s/f (Good)
WFA 3 from 4yo+ 9lb **15** Ran SP% **129.8**
Speed ratings (Par 107):110,109,108,106,104 101,100,100,99,97 96,96,95,94,90
CSF £301.84 CT £4322.40 TOTE £17.60: £5.40, £6.20, £4.00; EX 430.10.
Owner Mrs M V Chaworth-Musters **Bred** Mrs M Chaworth Musters **Trained** Whitsbury, Hants

FOCUS
A fair handicap containing some hardened campaigners and a couple of interesting types who were open to improvement, but a number were not at their best on the day. The first two both recorded career bests on turf.

NOTEBOOK
Gloved Hand ◆, who has been easing in the weights but was still 8lb above her highest winning mark, gained her first win for almost two years. Held up, it opened up for her approaching the final furlong and she quickened smartly to score. She is clearly in good order and if she can reproduce this sort of form over the coming weeks there is no reason why she should not continue to be competitive, despite the inevitable rise in the weights.
Orpen Wide(IRE) is a hardy individual and has not been far away from success on each of his last four starts. Suffering a narrow reverse here, he has to be of interest in similar contests although his present mark is a shade higher than he has ever won off.
Direct Debit(IRE), another 2lb lower, showed something of a return to form without threatening to win. A step back up to a mile should suit him.
Compton's Eleven ran a fair race and is well handicapped on the pick of his form, but it is hard to get away from the fact that he has not won since January 2006 and for three years in Britain. (op 9-1)
Greenslades, tackling 7f for the first time in two years, made a lot of the running but his stamina did not quite hold out.
Bakhoor(IRE) came here in fine form and there was an excuse for her rather disappointing showing. Official explanation: jockey said filly lost its action (op 4-1 tchd 3-1)
Edaara(IRE), beaten only around five lengths in an Epsom Group 3 on her previous outing, was the main disappointment. (op 4-1)

2836 UNICORN INVESTMENT MANAGERS MAIDEN STKS 1m 2f
8:40 (8:47) (Class 4) 3-Y-O £5,181 (£1,156; £1,156; £384) Stalls High

Form RPR

6 **1** **Horseford Hill**[28] [2005] 3-9-0 0..................................... MarcHalford(3) 15 71
(D R C Elsworth) *s.i.s: hld up: hdwy 1/2-way: rdn to ld over 1f out: styd on* **9/2**[2]

5 **2** *1/2* **Dar Es Salaam**[18] [2320] 3-9-3 0.. RyanMoore 12 70
(E A L Dunlop) *chsd ldrs: rdn over 4f out: r.o u.p ins fnl f* **9/4**[1]

2 *dht* **Take The Gold (IRE)** 3-8-12 0.. NCallan 6 65
(M A Jarvis) *chsd ldrs: rdn and ev ch over 1f out: styd on* **16/1**

04 **4** *1 1/4* **Eastern Emperor**[18] [2320] 3-9-3 0.. AdamKirby 1 67
(W R Swinburn) *hld up: hdwy over 2f out: rdn over 1f out: styd on* **7/1**[3]

5 *3 1/2* **Legend Erry (IRE)** 3-9-3 0... JimmyQuinn 7 60
(Jane Chapple-Hyam) *prom: rdn over 3f out: wknd over 1f out* **16/1**

6 *nk* **Hannahbecc** 3-8-12 0.. TedDurcan 16 54
(H R A Cecil) *hld up: rdn over 2f out: nvr trbld ldrs* **10/1**

7 *shd* **Sierra Rose** 3-8-12 0... EdwardCreighton 5 54
(P J McBride) *prom: led 3f out: rdn and hdd over 1f out: sn wknd* **66/1**

0 **8** *2 1/2* **Panda Power**[13] [2477] 3-8-12 0....................................... J-PGuillambert 10 49
(S C Williams) *led: hdd 7f out: rdn and wknd over 1f out* **50/1**

9 *nk* **Corkscrew Hill (IRE)** 3-8-12 0... DaneO'Neill 2 49
(N A Callaghan) *s.i.s: a in rr* **33/1**

0 **10** *shd* **Two Timer (IRE)**[65] [1093] 3-9-3 0....................................... AntonyProcter 8 53
(D R C Elsworth) *s.s: plld hrd: hdwy to ld 7f out: hdd 3f out: sn hung rt: wknd over 1f out* **14/1**

0 **11** *1/2* **Dot's Delight**[16] [2359] 3-8-9 0.. SaleemGolam(3) 13 47
(M H Tompkins) *hld up: rdn over 2f out: a in rr* **33/1**

0- **12** *1 3/4* **Iceman George**[237] [6220] 3-9-3 0.. BrettDoyle 14 49
(D Morris) *hld up: rdn over 4f out: sn wknd* **50/1**

2m 13.02s (6.58) **Going Correction** +0.175s/f (Good) **12** Ran SP% **100.3**
Speed ratings (Par 101):80,79,79,78,75 75,75,73,73,73 72,71
WIN: Horseford Hill £5.20. PL: £1.70, Dar Es Salaam £1.30, Take The Gold £2.20. EX: HH/DES £3.40, HH/TTG £39.10. CSF: HH/DES £4.66, HH/TTG £20.91..
Owner Raymond Tooth **Bred** Darley **Trained** Newmarket, Suffolk
■ Harry Tricker was withdrawn (9/4JF, unruly in stalls.) R4 applies, deduct 30p in the £.
■ Stewards' Enquiry : Ryan Moore two-day ban: used whip with excessive frequency (Jul 3-4)

FOCUS
A slowly-run race and a pedestrian winning time for a race of its type. Only fair form, but it makes sense based around the winner, second and fourth.
Corkscrew Hill(IRE) Official explanation: jockey said filly hung left
Two Timer(IRE) Official explanation: jockey said colt ran too free early
Dot's Delight Official explanation: jockey said filly ran too free to post

2837 UNICORN FINALE H'CAP 5f
9:10 (9:13) (Class 5) (0-75,73) 3-Y-O £3,886 (£1,156; £577; £288) Stalls Low

Form RPR

-300 **1** **Come What May**[6] [2661] 3-8-3 **55**...................................(bt[1]) ChrisCatlin 5 60
(Rae Guest) *chsd ldrs: sn pushed along: drvn up on outside to chal fnl f: str run to ld cl home* **12/1**

1102 **2** *1 1/4* **Windjammer**[14] [2435] 3-9-6 **72**.. PaulEddery 4 72
(T D Easterby) *set brisk pce: rdn over 1f out: ct nr fin* **11/4**[1]

4106 **3** *3/4* **New York Oscar (IRE)**[11] [2518] 3-9-6 **72**...............(b) StephenDonohoe 8 69
(A J McCabe) *prom but racing awkwardly w hd high: ev ch 1f out: no imp after* **12/1**

6624 **4** *3/4* **Bentley**[8] [2594] 3-9-1 **67**..(v) NCallan 9 62
(D Shaw) *dwlt: outpcd 3f out: kpt on ins fnl f but no threat* **13/2**[3]

30 **5** *nk* **Silver Hotspur**[14] [2418] 3-8-8 **60**....................................... BrettDoyle 6 54?
(M Wigham) *hld up towards rr: elbowed along 2f out: kpt on promisingly ins fnl f* **12/1**

6054 **6** *shd* **Dowlleh**[14] [2415] 3-9-5 **71**.. SamHitchcott 2 64
(T T Clement) *midfield: outpcd after 2f: sme hdwy ins fnl f* **13/2**[3]

3220 **7** 3/4 **Bookiesindex Boy**[11] 2513 3-9-7 **73**............................(v) RobertHavlin 7 63
(J R Jenkins) *prom: hrd drvn over 1f out: sn fnd little* **7/2**[2]
0-00 **8** 3/4 **Stravinsky's Art (USA)**[16] 2366 3-7-11 **54** oh9........... WilliamBuick(5) 3 42
(D R C Elsworth) *sed awkwardly and plld hrd: bhd: nvr able to chal* **25/1**
00-0 **9** 3/4 **Sunley Gift**[14] 2425 3-9-4 **70**... GeorgeBaker 1 55
(B G Powell) *chsd ldrs: rdn 1/2-way: btn over 1f out* **14/1**
000 **10** 1 1/4 **Straight Face (IRE)**[22] 2191 3-8-8 **60**........................... NickyMackay 10 41
(M Wigham) *fly j. s: rdn in last: nvr on terms* **8/1**
60.88 secs (1.32) **Going Correction** +0.175s/f (Good) **10** Ran SP% **120.3**
Speed ratings (Par 99):96,94,92,91,91 90,89,88,87,85
CSF £46.57 CT £423.02 TOTE £12.70: £2.50, £1.80, £4.50; EX 43.70 Place 6 £230.96, Place 5 £44.77.
Owner Storm Again Syndicate Sentinel Bloodstock **Bred** Matthews Breeding And Racing Ltd **Trained** Newmarket, Suffolk
■ Stewards' Enquiry : Brett Doyle 33-day ban: breach of Rule 157 - failed to ask for sufficient effort (Jul 21-Aug 22); M Wigham fined £7,500: in breach of Rule 155 (ii)

FOCUS
The runner-up probably went off too fast which set things up for the winner, and the form may not prove too solid. The race has been rated through the third.
Silver Hotspur ◆ Official explanation: jockey said, regarding running and riding, his orders were to relax the gelding and do his best, adding that it was restless in the stalls and moved poorly only staying on in later stages past tired horses and, although concerned about its welfare, he did employ his usual riding style at the finish; trainer confirmed, adding that the gelding returned lame; vet said following two examinations she found no sign of lameness other than conceding that the gelding had an unusual gait behind; 40-day ban (Jul 21-Aug 29)
T/Plt: £355.20 to a £1 stake. Pool: £57,785.90. 118.75 winning tickets. T/Qpdt: £70.30 to a £1 stake. Pool: £4,908.10. 51.60 winning tickets. CR

2532 REDCAR (L-H)
Friday, June 22

OFFICIAL GOING: Good to soft (good in places, 9.6)
After 4" rain over the previous eight days the track had dried out remarkably well and the going was reckoned 'just on the slow side of good'.
Wind: Light, half-behind Weather: Overcast

2838 TURFTV BETTING SHOP SERVICE (S) STKS 7f
2:10 (2:11) (Class 6) 2-Y-O **£1,943** (£578; £288; £144) **Stalls** Centre

Form RPR
003 **1** **Indecision**[33] 1857 2-8-11 0... PhillipMakin 4 58
(M W Easterby) *mde all: clr over 1f out: hld on towards fin* **5/2**[2]
06 **2** *nk* **Magnol**[17] 2344 2-8-6 0... CatherineGannon 2 52+
(M A Jarvis) *dwlt: hdwy over 2f out: styd on ins fnl f: jst hld* **5/2**[2]
6431 **3** 7 **Miss Willoughby**[8] 2605 2-8-12 0.................................. DO'Donohoe 8 41
(J Ryan) *w ldrs: chal over 2f out: wknd fnl f* **9/4**[1]
0 **4** 1 1/4 **Madam Zorro**[11] 2517 2-8-3 0.. DominicFox(3) 6 32
(S Parr) *hld up: effrt over 2f out: hung lft: kpt on fnl f* **16/1**[3]
4 **5** 3/4 **Arabian Fern**[3] 2738 2-8-5 0 ow2.................................... GregFairley(3) 9 32
(M E Sowersby) *chsd ldrs: outpcd over 1f out: kpt on towards fin* **20/1**
0 **6** 11 **Misk Hills**[33] 1858 2-8-11 0... LeeEnstone 3 7
(P T Midgley) *w ldrs: hung lft thrght: lost pl 2f out* **25/1**
006 **7** 5 **Welcome Inn**[18] 2310 2-8-6 0.. RichardThomas 7 —
(M E Sowersby) *w ldrs: wknd 3f out: sn bhd* **50/1**
0 **8** 2 **Lay Down Darling**[27] 2021 2-8-6 0.................................... KimTinkler 5 —
(N Tinkler) *w ldrs: rdn and hung bdly lft over 2f out: sn bhd* **16/1**[3]
1m 27.44s (2.54) **Going Correction** +0.125s/f (Good) **8** Ran SP% **110.2**
Speed ratings (Par 91):90,89,81,80,79 66,61,58
CSF £8.38 TOTE £3.20: £1.10, £1.40, £1.10; EX 9.00.The winner was bought in for 6,000gns. Magnol was claimed by Gary Roberts for £6,000. Arabian Fern was the subject of a friendly claim
Owner K Wreglesworth **Bred** K Wreglesworth **Trained** Sheriff Hutton, N Yorks

FOCUS
A poor seller and they came home well strung out with the third back to her previous level.

NOTEBOOK
Indecision, well backed, appreciated the step up to seven but in the end the post came just in time. (op 4-1 tchd 9-4)
Magnol, a leggy, narrow filly, continually swished her tail in the paddock. She was fast closing down the winner at the line and was claimed. Whether she is one to rely on remains to be seen. (op 9-4)
Miss Willoughby is only small and, having her eighth start already, is fully exposed. (op 7-4 tchd 5-2 in a place)
Madam Zorro improved on her debut effort but veered across the track before sticking on towards the finish.
Arabian Fern was making a quick return to action having only made her debut three days earlier. (op 18-1)

2839 JACKSONS-CPL SOLICITORS RUBY TUESDAY H'CAP 2m 4y
2:45 (2:45) (Class 6) (0-65,65) 4-Y-O+ **£1,943** (£578; £288; £144) **Stalls** Low

Form RPR
3263 **1** **Garnett (IRE)**[16] 2375 6-9-7 **65**...............................(b[1]) CatherineGannon 5 75
(D E Cantillon) *hld up wl in tch: hdwy to trck ldrs 9f out: led on bit over 2f out: drvn out* **3/1**[2]
5134 **2** 3 **Rocknest Island (IRE)**[11] 2505 4-8-12 **59**.............(p) AndrewMullen(3) 3 65
(P D Niven) *w ldr: led over 4f out: hdd over 2f out: kpt on: no imp* **3/1**[2]
-005 **3** 7 **Compton Commander**[27] 2026 9-7-10 **47**........(p) DanielleMcCreery(7) 4 45
(E W Tuer) *hld up in rr: effrt 4f out: kpt on to take modest 3rd 1f out* **8/1**
020- **4** 5 **Figaro's Quest (IRE)**[298] 4900 5-8-9 **58**.............. MichaelJStainton(5) 7 50
(C N Kellett) *t.k.h: w ldr: rdn 3f out: eased ins fnl f: jst retained 4th pl* **14/1**
5332 **5** *hd* **True (IRE)**[10] 2537 6-8-0 **47**.. DuranFentiman(3) 2 39
(Mrs S Lamyman) *hld up wl in tch: effrt over 3f out: lost pl over 1f out* **11/4**[1]
0-02 **6** 30 **Exit To Luck (GER)**[17] 2348 6-9-5 **63**................................ DO'Donohoe 1 19
(S Gollings) *trckd ldrs: drvn 5f out: lost pl over 2f out: bhd whn eased fnl f* **11/2**[3]
005 **7** 1 **Miss Lightning**[16] 2376 4-8-2 **46** oh1.......................... RichardThomas 6 1
(R Bastiman) *led tl over 4f out: sn lost pl: t.o 2f out* **66/1**
3m 37.92s (6.42) **Going Correction** +0.45s/f (Yiel) **7** Ran SP% **111.3**
Speed ratings (Par 101):101,99,96,93,93 78,77
CSF £11.74 TOTE £3.00: £2.50, £1.80; EX 11.20.
Owner Mrs Sue Catt **Bred** James Reardon **Trained** Newmarket, Suffolk

FOCUS
A low-grade stayers' handicap run at a very steady pace. In the end the versatile winner made it look plain sailing and the first two appear on the upgrade.

2840 SPORTING LODGE INNS MAIDEN STKS 1m 2f
3:20 (3:23) (Class 5) 3-Y-O+ **£2,817** (£838; £418; £209) **Stalls** Low

Form RPR
00- **1** **Step To The Stars (IRE)**[238] 6200 3-8-4 0..................... GregFairley(3) 2 82
(M Johnston) *trckd ldr: tk fierce hold: led over 4f out: styd on wl fnl 2f: unchal* **16/1**
23-3 **2** 2 1/2 **Font**[34] 1842 4-9-10 **89**.. OscarUrbina 4 82
(J R Fanshawe) *hld up wl in tch: drvn and wnt 2nd over 2f out: edgd lft: no real imp* **2/9**[1]
03 **3** 3 **Still Dreaming**[14] 2420 3-8-7 0...................................... PhillipMakin 9 71
(M Dods) *chsd ldrs: effrt over 3f out: kpt on same pce* **50/1**
53 **4** 7 **Music Review**[24] 2118 3-8-6 0 ow2.............................. JamieMoriarty(3) 3 59
(R A Fahey) *dwlt: sn chsng ldrs: effrt 3f out: hung lft: wknd appr fnl f* **14/1**
5 **5** 9 **Lion Ridge (IRE)**[19] 2274 3-8-12 0................................. DO'Donohoe 5 44
(L M Cumani) *t.k.h in rr: drvn 4f out: nvr on terms* **12/1**[3]
40- **6** 3 **Wishing On A Star**[282] 5287 3-8-7 0............................... RichardMullen 7 33
(E J O'Neill) *pushed along to ld: hdd over 4f out: lost pl over 2f out* **10/1**[2]
0-00 **7** 2 **Shotley Mac**[31] 1912 3-8-5 **48**...................................... GihanArnolda(7) 6 34
(N Bycroft) *hld up in rr: bhd fnl 3f* **100/1**
-000 **8** 3/4 **Firestorm (IRE)**[9] 2552 3-8-12 **51**..........................(b[1]) CatherineGannon 1 33
(C W Fairhurst) *hld up in rr: effrt over 4f out: sn btn* **100/1**
0-4 **9** 4 **Santera (IRE)**[14] 2420 3-8-4 0................................... AndrewMullen(3) 8 20
(Mrs A Duffield) *hld up in rr: rdn over 3f out: sn bhd* **100/1**
2m 8.73s (1.93) **Going Correction** +0.45s/f (Yiel)
WFA 3 from 4yo 12lb **9** Ran SP% **116.1**
Speed ratings (Par 103):110,108,105,100,92 90,88,88,85
CSF £20.59 TOTE £19.80: £3.90, £1.02, £11.00; EX 68.10.
Owner S R Counsell **Bred** Frank Towey **Trained** Middleham Moor, N Yorks

FOCUS
An uncompetitive contest but a very smart winning time for a race of its type. The winner had first run but there seemed no real excuse for the runner-up in a maiden lacking any strength in depth.

2841 JACKSONS-CPL SOLICITORS ELEANOR RIGBY H'CAP 6f
4:00 (4:00) (Class 3) (0-95,90) 3-Y-O+ **£9,715** (£2,890; £1,444; £721) **Stalls** Centre

Form RPR
-006 **1** **Ice Planet**[9] 2566 6-9-9 **88**... AndrewMullen(3) 5 98
(D Nicholls) *mid-div: effrt over 2f out: led and edgd rt over 1f out: hld on wl* **5/1**[1]
0005 **2** 3/4 **Turnkey**[20] 2237 5-9-5 **88**... AdeleRothery(7) 7 96
(D Nicholls) *hld up: hdwy on wd outside 2f out: no ex wl ins fnl f* **12/1**
0-40 **3** 1/2 **King's Gait**[35] 1826 5-9-12 **88**..............................(b) RichardMullen 14 94
(T D Easterby) *hld up: hdwy over 2f out: chsng ldrs over 1f out: no ex ins fnl f* **11/2**[2]
3565 **4** 3/4 **Countdown**[9] 2566 5-8-12 **77**..................................... DuranFentiman(3) 9 81
(T D Easterby) *chsd ldrs: outpcd over 2f out: styd on strly fnl f* **15/2**[3]
0201 **5** 1 **Continent**[3] 2744 10-9-6 **89** 6ex.................................... OliveGaule(7) 8 90
(D Nicholls) *w ldrs: styd on same pce appr fnl f* **12/1**
4050 **6** 1 1/2 **High Curragh**[9] 2566 4-9-13 **89**.. DO'Donohoe 3 86
(K A Ryan) *chsd ldrs: sn drvn along: kpt on same pce fnl 2f* **12/1**
0-20 **7** 1 **Mr Wolf**[43] 1601 6-10-0 **90**.. CatherineGannon 2 84
(D W Barker) *led: hdd and sltly hmpd over 1f out: sn wknd* **10/1**
-060 **8** 3/4 **Osteopathic Remedy (IRE)**[27] 2040 3-8-13 **82**............ PhillipMakin 15 71
(M Dods) *sn outpcd and bhd: hdwy over 2f out: kpt on wl fnl f* **9/1**
-300 **9** *shd* **Bond Boy**[38] 1754 10-8-8 **77**......................................(v) SladeO'Hara(7) 10 68
(G R Oldroyd) *w ldrs: wknd over 1f out* **25/1**
0506 **10** 1 1/4 **Danum Dancer**[35] 1825 3-8-9 **85**.............................(b) GihanArnolda(7) 4 70
(N Bycroft) *chsd ldrs: rdn over 2f out: wknd over 1f out* **12/1**
310- **11** *nk* **Damika (IRE)**[273] 5501 4-9-8 **89**................................ MichaelJStainton(5) 11 75
(R M Whitaker) *s.i.s: hdwy 3f out: upsides over 1f out: sn wknd* **16/1**
1000 **12** 7 **Geojimali**[13] 2463 5-9-9 **85**.. LeeEnstone 12 50
(J S Goldie) *mid-div: sn drvn along: lost pl 2f out* **12/1**
0400 **13** 1 1/4 **Kenmore**[3] 2744 5-9-2 **83**... HMuya(5) 13 45
(D Nicholls) *mid-div: effrt over 2f out: edgd rt and sn wknd* **10/1**
3-50 **14** *nk* **Sunderland Echo (IRE)**[15] 2396 4-9-11 **90**.............(t) JamieMoriarty(3) 6 51
(B Ellison) *s.s: a bhd* **33/1**
1m 11.06s (-0.64) **Going Correction** +0.125s/f (Good)
WFA 3 from 4yo+ 7lb **14** Ran SP% **123.1**
Speed ratings (Par 107):109,108,107,106,105 103,101,100,100,98 98,89,87,87
CSF £66.35 CT £359.57 TOTE £6.30: £2.40, £4.50, £2.70; EX 84.50.
Owner David Faulkner **Bred** L C And Mrs A E Sigsworth **Trained** Sessay, N Yorks

FOCUS
A competitive sprint handicap with the action down the middle of the track. The form has a rock-solid look about it.

NOTEBOOK
Ice Planet, without a win since the 2005 Great St Wilfrid at Ripon, is proven on easy ground and in the end he did enough to repel his stablemate's challenge. (op 7-1)
Turnkey, without a win for over two years ago, really took the eye beforehand and had the ease in the ground he relishes. He came from off the pace down the wide outside and in the end was just held. He deserves to break his drought soon. (op 10-1)
King's Gait, quite keen early, was in the end just found wanting and now may be the time to give him a try over seven. (op 7-1)
Countdown, tapped for toe soon after halfway, was putting in some sterling late work and is crying out for a return to seven. (op 7-1)
Continent, under his 6lb penalty and ridden by an inexperienced apprentice, ran out of his skin and the old boy is clearly in very good heart. (op 10-1)
High Curragh, without a win since his juvenile career, is surely overdue some leniency. (op 14-1 tchd 16-1)
Osteopathic Remedy(IRE), tackling his elders, stayed on from way off the pace and really needs 7f. (op 11-1)
Sunderland Echo(IRE) Official explanation: trainer said filly would not face the tongue strap

2842 JOHN SMITH'S REDCAR STRAIGHT-MILE CHAMPIONSHIP STKS (H'CAP) (QUALIFIER) 1m
4:35 (4:35) (Class 5) (0-75,73) 3-Y-O+ **£2,817** (£838; £418; £209) **Stalls** Centre

Form RPR
0056 **1** **Efidium**[18] 2311 9-8-10 **62**... GihanArnolda(7) 6 70
(N Bycroft) *in rr: swtchd to stands' side over 2f out: led over 1f out: styd on* **5/1**[3]
-534 **2** 1 3/4 **Spinning**[22] 2169 4-9-7 **66**.. PhillipMakin 4 70
(T D Barron) *sn in rr: hdwy on outer and hung lft over 3f out: upsides over 1f out: kpt on same pce* **10/3**[1]
5-00 **3** 2 1/2 **Sake (IRE)**[18] 2311 5-9-10 **69**.. KimTinkler 3 67
(N Tinkler) *led tl over 1f out: one pce* **5/1**[3]
1-03 **4** 3/4 **Pay Time**[14] 2422 8-8-12 **60**....................................... DuranFentiman(3) 2 57
(R E Barr) *trckd ldrs: effrt over 2f out: kpt on same pce* **14/1**

0056 **5** ½ **Middlemarch (IRE)**[9] [2564] 7-10-0 **73**............................(b) LeeEnstone 1 68
(J S Goldie) *chsd ldrs drvn 3f out: fdd over 1f out* **13/2**

0-05 **6** 1 **Dream On Dreamers (IRE)**[2] [2763] 3-7-13 **54** oh9(b[1])
CatherineGannon 5 45?
(R C Guest) *trckd ldr: rdn over 2f out: one pce* **33/1**

0200 **7** 6 **Sir Bond (IRE)**[18] [2311] 6-8-8 **56**...................................... GregFairley(3) 7 35
(G R Oldroyd) *mid-div: hdwy to chse ldrs 3f out: lost pl over 1f out* **17/2**

05-3 **8** 7 **Rigat**[20] [2256] 4-9-4 **70**.. NeilBrown(7) 9 33
(T D Barron) *t.k.h and sn in rr: hdwy on stands' side over 3f out: lost pl over 2f out: sn bhd* **7/2**[2]

1m 38.13s (0.33) **Going Correction** +0.125s/f (Good)
WFA 3 from 4yo+ 10lb **8** Ran SP% **112.1**
Speed ratings (Par 103):103,101,98,98,97 96,90,83
CSF £21.13 CT £85.70 TOTE £4.80: £1.80, £1.20, £1.70; EX 21.50.

Owner Hambleton Racing Partnership **Bred** T Umpleby **Trained** Brandsby, N Yorks

■ Moonstreaker (7/1) was withdrawn on vet's advice. R4 applies, deduct 10p in the £. New market formed.

FOCUS
A low-grade handicap run at a sound pace and overall the form looks fairly sound.

Rigat Official explanation: jockey said gelding ran too free early

2843 JACKSONS-CPL SOLICITORS PENNY LANE CLAIMING STKS 1m 2f
5:10 (5:11) (Class 6) 3-Y-0+ **£2,047** (£604; £302) **Stalls** Low

Form RPR

0-60 **1** **Rotuma (IRE)**[20] [2254] 8-9-8 52..(b) PhillipMakin 5 54
(M Dods) *trckd ldr: led 4f out: rallied to regain ld post* **2/1**[1]

-006 **2** *shd* **Apache Point (IRE)**[22] [2168] 10-9-6 52.................................... KimTinkler 2 52
(N Tinkler) *hld up: effrt on ins over 3f out: wnt 2nd 2f out: slt ld 75yds out: hdd post* **9/2**[3]

0002 **3** 2½ **Arabellas Homer**[44] [1573] 3-8-6 45........................... DuranFentiman(3) 6 48
(Mrs N Macauley) *hld up in rr: hdwy on outside over 3f out: kpt on to take modest 3rd over 1f out* **20/1**

6-55 **4** ¾ **Chateau (IRE)**[18] [2298] 5-9-4 50.................................(t) RichardThomas 8 44
(M E Sowersby) *sn trcking ldrs: one pce fnl 2f* **11/1**

0445 **5** 1 **Ming Vase**[18] [2307] 5-9-4 43.. LeeEnstone 3 42
(P T Midgley) *ld tl 4f out: one pce fnl 2f* **9/1**

00/0 **6** 1 **Pre Eminance (IRE)**[34] [1849] 6-8-11 60........................... NeilBrown(7) 9 40
(J S Wainwright) *sn trcking ldrs: one pce fnl 2f* **11/1**

0-66 **7** 1¼ **Phoenix Nights (IRE)**[4] [2709] 7-9-3 36............................. PBradley(5) 4 41
(A Berry) *trckd ldrs: wknd fnl 2f* **100/1**

0050 **8** 7 **Orphir (IRE)**[10] [2537] 4-9-7 32.....................................(b[1]) ColinHaddon(5) 7 31
(Mrs N Macauley) *s.i.s: a in rr* **80/1**

0033 **9** ¾ **Ruby Legend**[9] [2582] 9-9-3 53..(b) GregFairley(3) 1 24
(K G Reveley) *chsd ldrs: rdn 4f out: lost pl over 2f out* **5/2**[2]

2m 12.33s (5.53) **Going Correction** +0.45s/f (Yiel)
WFA 3 from 4yo+ 12lb **9** Ran SP% **113.7**
Speed ratings (Par 101):95,94,92,92,91 90,89,84,83
CSF £11.05 TOTE £3.40: £1.20, £1.80, £4.30; EX 12.00.

Owner Denton Hall Racing Ltd **Bred** Sean Twomey **Trained** Denton, Co Durham

■ Stewards' Enquiry : Lee Enstone one-day ban: used whip down shoulder in forehand position (Jul 3)

FOCUS
A poor claimer run at a very steady pace with the proximity of the third and the seventh holding down the value of the form..

Ruby Legend Official explanation: trainer had no explanation for the poor form shown

2844 REDCAR LADIES' DAY TOMORROW MAIDEN H'CAP 5f
5:45 (5:46) (Class 5) (0-70,69) 3-Y-0+ **£2,817** (£838; £418; £209) **Stalls** Centre

Form RPR

-004 **1** **Miacarla**[43] [1595] 4-8-9 **45**.. LeeEnstone 5 56
(A Berry) *hmpd s: sn trcking ldrs: t.k.h: led 1f out: styd on* **14/1**

0-05 **2** 1½ **Orotund**[1] [2791] 3-8-3 **45**.. PaulQuinn 1 49
(T D Easterby) *w ldrs: upsides 1f out: styd on same pce* **12/1**

0246 **3** 1½ **Wolfman**[43] [1595] 5-8-13 **49**......................................(p) CatherineGannon 8 50
(D W Barker) *chsd ldrs: kpt on fnl f* **9/2**[2]

62-4 **4** 1½ **Inspainagain (USA)**[51] [1403] 3-9-4 **60**.............................. PhillipMakin 6 53
(T D Barron) *chsd ldrs: sltly hmpd 2f out: kpt on same pce* **11/4**[1]

-600 **5** ½ **Violet's Pride**[9] [2553] 3-8-9 **54**.................................(v[1]) DominicFox(3) 7 45
(S Parr) *led: hung lft 2f out: hdd 1f out: sn wknd* **12/1**

-000 **6** 1 **Flower Of Cork (IRE)**[9] [2553] 3-8-10 **55**................(b) DuranFentiman(3) 9 43
(T D Easterby) *reminders sn after s: kpt on fnl 2f: nvr nr ldrs* **33/1**

3632 **7** *nk* **Missus Molly Brown**[18] [2300] 3-8-5 **47**...................(b) RichardThomas 14 34
(R A Fahey) *sn outpcd and in rr: kpt on fnl 2f* **5/1**[3]

0436 **8** *shd* **Mangano**[18] [2301] 3-8-3 **50**...................................... NataliaGemelova(5) 11 36
(A Berry) *swvd rt s: outpcd and in rr: kpt on fnl 2f* **12/1**

5505 **9** ½ **Danethorpe (IRE)**[43] [1594] 4-8-9 **45**...............................(v) OscarUrbina 12 32
(D Shaw) *hmpd s: sn outpcd: sme hdwy 2f out: nvr on terms* **7/1**

36-4 **10** ¾ **Dilwin (IRE)**[74] [968] 3-9-6 **69**....................................... OliveGaule(7) 4 51
(D Nicholls) *wnt rt s: chsd ldrs: outpcd over 2f out* **14/1**

5000 **11** 3 **Whithorn**[11] [2509] 4-8-8 **47**.. GregFairley(3) 2 20
(J Balding) *in tch: rdn over 2f out: sn lost pl* **22/1**

000- **12** 1 **My Maite Mickey**[234] [6278] 3-7-10 **45**..................... DanielleMcCreery(7) 10 12
(R C Guest) *chsd ldrs: rdn and lost pl over 2f out* **22/1**

430- **13** 6 **Fly So Free (IRE)**[325] [4017] 3-9-4 **67**......................... AdeleRothery(7) 13 13
(D Nicholls) *in rr: bhd fnl 2f* **20/1**

59.04 secs (0.34) **Going Correction** +0.125s/f (Good)
WFA 3 from 4yo+ 6lb **13** Ran SP% **126.8**
Speed ratings (Par 103):102,99,97,94,94 92,91,91,90,89 84,83,73
CSF £173.27 CT £924.16 TOTE £22.00: £5.70, £5.00, £2.30; EX 414.60 Place 6 £ 10.01, Place 5 £ 9.06.

Owner J D Riches **Bred** Primrose Cottage **Trained** Cockerham, Lancs

FOCUS
A low-grade maiden sprint handicap but in the end quite a ready winner. The form is limited but looks reliable at this level.

Missus Molly Brown Official explanation: jockey said filly never travelled

T/Plt: £16.80 to a £1 stake. Pool: £44,676.90. 1,938.45 winning tickets. T/Qpdt: £4.90 to a £1 stake. Pool: £2,489.30. 370.70 winning tickets. WG

2845 - 2850a (Foreign Racing) - See Raceform Interactive

2683 LIMERICK (R-H)
Friday, June 22

OFFICIAL GOING: Yielding changing to yielding to soft after race 1 (5.55)

2851a MCINERNEY HOMES MARTIN MOLONY STKS (LISTED RACE) 1m 3f 70y
7:25 (7:28) 3-Y-0+ **£24,192** (£7,097; £3,381; £1,152)

RPR

1 **Honolulu (IRE)**[9] [2589] 3-8-10 99... KFallon 3 110+
(A P O'Brien, Ire) *chsd ldr in 2nd: pushed along 1/2-way: chal appr st: led 2f out: edgd rt under 1 1/2f out: clr whn wandered abt and hit rail ins fnl f: styd on* **11/4**[1]

2 1½ **Athenian Way (IRE)**[5] [2702] 3-8-7 100.......................... NGMcCullagh 6 105
(John M Oxx, Ire) *led: strly pressed appr st: hdd 2f out: sltly hmpd under 1 1/2f out: kpt on u.p ins fnl f* **11/2**[3]

3 *hd* **Arch Rebel (USA)**[13] [2483] 6-9-12 109..................................(b) FMBerry 8 111
(Noel Meade, Ire) *slowly away and hld up in rr: hdwy 3f out: mod 5th under 2f out: 3rd and styd on wl ins fnl f: nvr nrr* **5/1**[2]

4 5 **Cool Touch (IRE)**[13] [2483] 4-9-9 107... WSupple 1 100
(Peter Casey, Ire) *trckd ldrs: 6th appr 1/2-way: hdwy into 3rd over 3f out: rdn and no imp st: 4th and no ex fnl f* **8/1**

5 3 **Jalmira (IRE)**[33] [1868] 6-9-6 88... WJLee 4 92
(C F Swan, Ire) *hld up: 7th 1/2-way: mod 6th early st: kpt on* **20/1**

6 ¾ **Uimhir A Haon (IRE)**[235] [6261] 3-8-7 90.......................... JAHeffernan 7 91
(A P O'Brien, Ire) *hld up: 6th over 4f out: prog into 4th appr st: sn rdn and no imp* **9/1**

7 16 **Attercliffe (IRE)**[240] [6185] 4-9-9 .... NPMadden 9 68
(Noel Meade, Ire) *trckd ldrs: 3rd 1/2-way: 4th over 3f out: sn no ex and wknd* **11/2**[3]

8 18 **Boca Dancer (IRE)**[243] [6113] 3-8-10 .... DPMcDonogh 5 39
(Kevin Prendergast, Ire) *3rd early: wknd after 1/2-way: trailing whn eased bef st* **5/1**[2]

2m 33.8s (153.80)
WFA 3 from 4yo+ 13lb **9** Ran SP% **116.6**
CSF £18.53 TOTE £3.00: £1.20, £2.80, £1.80; DF 39.50.

Owner Derrick Smith **Bred** Kilfrush Stud **Trained** Ballydoyle, Co Tipperary

FOCUS
This Listed race attracted quite a useful field that contained two previous stakes winners. The third is a good guide to the form.

NOTEBOOK
Honolulu(IRE), the previous week's Leopardstown maiden winner, coped very well with a sharp step up in class to confirm himself a colt with a bright future. The son of Montjeu was being pushed along some way out and showed distinct signs of greenness when wandering about inside the final furlong - he hit the far rail in the process - but was firmly in control at the finish. There could well be more to come from him. (op 7/2 tchd 4/1)
Athenian Way(IRE), on ground that was slower than she would like, made a bold bid from the front just five days after chasing home Nick's Nikita in a 1m4f Group 3 at Cork. She stuck to her task well when headed by the winner and was slightly hampered when that rival came across her at one stage, but that made no difference to the result. She is good enough to win at this level.
Arch Rebel(USA), a triple Listed winner who had conditions to suit, ran his best race of the season. He was towards the rear turning in, but came home well and was gaining on the front two. He can be win at this level. (op 4/1)
Cool Touch(IRE) ran respectably, but has not been at his best lately and would probably prefer quicker ground. A prolific handicap winner last season, he has previously shown enough to suggest that he can pick up a Listed race and may well do that when he returns to his best.

2852 - 2854a (Foreign Racing) - See Raceform Interactive

2812 ASCOT (R-H)
Saturday, June 23

OFFICIAL GOING: Straight course - good changing to good to soft after race 2 (3.05); round course - good to soft (soft in places) changing to soft after race 2 (3.05)

Wind: Light, across Weather: Showers

2855 CHESHAM STKS (LISTED RACE) 7f
2:30 (2:30) (Class 1) 2-Y-0
£31,229 (£11,836; £5,923; £2,953; £1,479; £742) **Stalls** Centre

Form RPR

1 **1** **Maze (IRE)**[21] [2251] 2-9-3 0.. RoystonFfrench 10 96
(B Smart) *athletic: scope: lw: chsd ldng pair: rdn to ld and edgd rt over 1f out: hld on wl u.p fnl f: edgd lft nr fin* **11/2**[2]

2 *nk* **Pegasus Again (USA)** 2-9-3 0.. LDettori 5 95+
(T G Mills) *w'like: str: s.i.s: hld up in last pair: rdn and gd hdwy jst over 2f out: ev ch fnl f: no ex nr fin* **14/1**

1 **3** *nk* **Feared In Flight (IRE)**[37] [1792] 2-9-3 0.................................. MJKinane 9 96+
(B W Hills) *w.w in midfield: hdwy over 2f out: ev ch whn short of room wl over 1f out: rallied u.p fnl f: nt quite rch ldrs* **15/8**[1]

2 **4** *hd* **Ramona Chase**[30] [1970] 2-9-3 0...................................... DPMcDonogh 1 96+
(S Kirk) *w'like: t.k.h: hld up in rr: stdy hdwy over 2f out: swtchd lft over 1f out: r.o fnl f: carried lft nr fin* **8/1**

5 ¾ **Jedediah** 2-9-3 0.. NashRawiller 11 92
(A M Balding) *leggy: s.i.s: hld up in midfield: hdwy over 2f out: ev ch and edgd lft wl over 1f out: kpt on same pce last 100yds* **40/1**

3 **6** *hd* **Meydan Dubai (IRE)**[14] [2443] 2-9-3 0............................... GeorgeBaker 4 91
(J R Best) *t.k.h: hld up in midfield: rdn and hdwy 2f out: ev ch over 1f out: keeping on same pce whn carried lft nr fin* **33/1**

5 **7** ¾ **Scintillo**[29] [1990] 2-9-3 0... RichardHughes 3 90
(R Hannon) *hld up in tch: rdn and lost pl 3f out: styd on u.p last 2f: nt rch ldrs* **25/1**

4 **8** ¾ **Azeer (USA)**[14] [2478] 2-9-3 0... JimmyFortune 12 88
(P W Chapple-Hyam) *leggy: stdd s: hld up in rr: hdwy wl over 2f out: swtchd rt over 2f out: no imp fnl f* **11/1**

9 3 **The Bogberry (USA)**[16] [2404] 2-9-5 0.. JMurtagh 2 82
(A P O'Brien, Ire) *w'like: scope: towards rr: rdn over 3f out: no imp* **7/1**[3]

1 **10** 3 **Golan Knight (IRE)**[19] [2303] 2-9-3 0... NCallan 7 72
(K A Ryan) *led: rdn and edgd rt wl over 1f out: hdd over 1f out: sn wknd* **12/1**

1 **11** 5 **Double Attack (FR)**[10] [2562] 2-8-12 0.................................. JoeFanning 8 54+
(M Johnston) *w'like: t.k.h: rdn over 2f out: wkng whn squeezed out wl over 1f out: no ch after* **8/1**

The Form Book, Raceform Ltd, Compton, RG20 6NL

12 1 3/4 **Resplendent Light** 2-9-3 0 .... KerrinMcEvoy 6 54
(W R Muir) *w'like: leggy: chsd ldrs: rdn 3f out: wknd over 2f out* **33/1**

1m 29.28s (1.18) **Going Correction** +0.25s/f (Good) **12** Ran SP% **119.7**
Speed ratings (Par 101):103,102,102,102,101 101,100,99,95,92 86,84
CSF £77.46 TOTE £7.50: £2.30, £2.70, £1.20; EX 123.60 Trifecta £295.90 Pool £8,611.24 - 20.66 winning units..
Owner Pinnacle Dr Fong Partnership **Bred** Millsec Limited **Trained** Hambleton, N Yorks
■ Royston Ffrench's first Royal Ascot winner.
■ Stewards' Enquiry : D P McDonogh three-day ban: used whip down neck in forehand position and without allowing time to respond (Jul 4-6)
Royston Ffrench five-day ban: careless riding (Jul 4-6, 8); used whip with excessive frequency (Jul 9)
George Baker

FOCUS
The Chesham has not produced many superstars in recent years though the 2005 winner Championship Point did win here earlier in the week. This year's renewal was most notable for being a rough race, with a couple of horses seriously impeded and withthe first eight covered by less than three lengths it seems unlikely that any of these will go right to the top. It should, however, produce its fair share of winners.

NOTEBOOK
Maze(IRE), stepping up a furlong from his winning debut in a maiden at Newcastle from which the second and third have subsequently won, travelled particularly well just behind the leading pair until taking it up a furlong out. He stayed on well despite facing some stern challenges on either side, but nearly threw it away by diving out to his left near the line, hampering the fourth and six horses in the process. That pair would not have beaten him even without the interference so he was allowed to keep the race, but his jockey received a ban totalling five days for careless riding and excessive use of the whip. He is likely to be aimed at the Racing Post Trophy in the autumn and soft ground there will not be a problem. Neither will the 1m trip, but he will still have to improve a lot from this in the meantime to be a serious candidate there. (tchd 6-1)
Pegasus Again(USA) ◆, a £75,000 two-year-old out of a multiple winning dam at up to 1m1f in the US, faced a very stiff task on this debut but ran a blinder. Given a patient ride, he ran on really strongly once switched over to the far rail over the last furlong or so but the winner, who was racing more towards the centre of the track, was always just holding him. Highly regarded at home, he is sure to be sharper for the experience and his connections are never shy of taking on the very best. (op 16-1)
Feared In Flight(IRE), up a furlong from his winning debut at the York Dante meeting in a contest that has only produced one subsequent winner, did not enjoy the run of the race. He was badly hampered when trying for a run between Golan Knight and Jedediah well over a furlong out which saw him receive a right old buffeting. To his great credit, he stayed on very well after that and there is a strong argument that he would have won with a clear passage. This looks to be his sort of ground, so he may be one to keep in mind for the autumn. (op 5-2 tchd 11-4)
Ramona Chase ◆ could hardly have faced more constrasting conditions to when runner-up on his Salisbury debut, this being two furlongs further and the ground much easier. He is bred to be more suited by these conditions, however, and duly posted a decent effort. Putting in a strong late run down the outside after not enjoying the smoothest of passages, he was carried right out to the left by the hanging winner near the line but it was too late to suggest that this particular incident affected the result. He should not remain a maiden for too much longer. (op 12-1 tchd 7-1)
Jedediah ◆, a 35,000gns yearling out of the three-time winner Penelewey, ran a fine debut in the face of a stiff task and was probably not helped by getting into a barging match with Feared In Flight over a furlong from home. Despite his dam's victories coming over 6f and 7f, there is still plenty of stamina on that side of his pedigree, plus the influence of his sire, so he is likely to improve as he goes up in trip. (op 50-1)
Meydan Dubai(IRE), third when well backed on his Goodwood debut, almost certainly improved significantly on that performance here. He had every chance down the outside and even though he found himself at the end of the chain reaction started by the antics of the winner near the line it did not affect his finishing position. An ordinary maiden should be his for the taking.
Scintillo ◆, despite the extra furlong and easier ground, ran a very similar sort of race to his Goodwood debut in that he stayed on again after seeming to lose his place. He will have to wait until August before he can tackle a mile, but on the evidence so far that is what he wants.
Azeer(USA) never managed to land a blow from off the pace and will be better off trying to break his maiden. (op 12-1)
The Bogberry(USA), who gave Kieren Fallon a winning return from his six-month suspension earlier this month, was obviously without his services here and this effort suggests the race he won at Tipperary was decidedly weak. (op 11-2 tchd 5-1 in places)
Golan Knight(IRE) was a winner on soft ground on his Leicester debut, but the form has not worked out at all and similar forcing tactics did not do the trick over the extra furlong at this level. Official explanation: jockey said colt hung right (op 10-1)
Double Attack(FR) was a bit disappointing in view of how impressive she was on her Hamilton debut, as she was already fighting a losing battle when hampered by the hanging Golan Knight entering the last quarter-mile. Official explanation: jockey said filly suffered interference in running (op 5-1)

2856 HARDWICKE STKS (GROUP 2) 1m 4f

3:05 (3:05) (Class 1) 4-Y-O+

£79,492 (£30,128; £15,078; £7,518; £3,766; £1,890) **Stalls** High

Form RPR

-113 **1** **Maraahel (IRE)**[22] [2210] 6-9-0 120 .... (b) RHills 4 119
(Sir Michael Stoute) *t.k.h: chsd ldrs: wnt 2nd 4f out: rdn to ld 2f out: hld on wl last 100yds* **10/3**[2]

0-21 **2** 1/2 **Scorpion (IRE)**[22] [2210] 5-9-5 0 .... MJKinane 5 123
(A P O'Brien, Ire) *swtg: chsd ldrs tl 4f out: rdn 3f out: hdwy to chse wnr over 1f out: edgd rt u.p: ev ch last 100yds: hld towards fin* **4/5**[1]

4232 **3** 2 1/2 **Mighty**[23] [2182] 4-9-0 112 .... JohnEgan 2 114
(Jane Chapple-Hyam) *hld up in tch: bmpd wl over 3f out: sn rdn: styd on u.p fnl f: wnt 3rd last 100yds: nt trble ldrs* **10/1**

3-52 **4** 1/2 **Admiral's Cruise (USA)**[48] [1495] 5-9-0 112 .... (b) JimmyFortune 8 113
(B J Meehan) *t.k.h: hld up in tch: rdn and effrt 2f out: kpt on same pce fnl f* **9/1**[3]

2512 **5** 1/2 **Blue Bajan (IRE)**[44] [1600] 5-9-0 110 .... MichaelHills 7 113
(Andrew Turnell) *t.k.h: hld up in tch in rr: hdwy on outer and bmpd over 3f out: chsd ldrs and rdn over 1f out: kpt on same pce* **11/1**

6142 **6** 3/4 **Diamond Quest (SAF)**[107] [645] 6-9-0 110 .... JHBowman 6 111
(A M Balding) *w'like: leggy: t.k.h: hld up in tch in rr: plld out and rdn over 2f out: kpt on but nt pce to rch ldrs: lame* **20/1**

2403 **7** 5 **Akarem**[14] [2441] 6-9-0 105 .... (v[1]) NCallan 3 103
(K R Burke) *swtg: t.k.h: led tl rdn and hdd 2f out: wknd over 1f out* **33/1**

2m 35.47s (2.47) **Going Correction** +0.55s/f (Yiel) **7** Ran SP% **113.8**
Speed ratings (Par 115):113,112,111,110,110 109,106
CSF £6.28 TOTE £4.00: £2.20, £1.30; EX 5.70 Trifecta £32.30 Pool £8,796.94 - 193.20 winning units..
Owner Hamdan Al Maktoum **Bred** Shadwell Estate Company Limited **Trained** Newmarket, Suffolk
■ Stewards' Enquiry : M J Kinane four-day ban: used whip several times on number cloth (Jul 4-6,8)

FOCUS
Not the classiest Hardwicke in terms of strength in depth, but the front pair are proven at this level and more, so the standard was probably maintained. The form seems sound. The pace was only fair for much of the race and did not pick up until around half a mile out.

NOTEBOOK
Maraahel(IRE), winner of this race last year, was 5lb better off with Scorpion compared to the Coronation Cup, but more significant was that this race was run to suit him more and he owes much of this victory to a well-judged ride. Keen enough just behind the pacemaker for much of the contest, the key moment came when he was sent into a clear second place starting the home bend which enabled him to take a length or so out of the favourite. Sent for home soon after straightening up, he then faced a stern challenge from his old rival, but the cup had come loose on the left-hand side of his blinkers and it seemed that as soon as he saw Scorpion range alongside, he pulled out a bit more. This was his seventh Group-race victory and although success at the top level continues to elude him, he does not owe anyone anything. (op 3-1 tchd 7-2)
Scorpion(IRE), bidding to confirm Coronation Cup form with Maraahel, had a 5lb penalty and was not so well suited by the way this race was run. He was always in a good position, but became outpaced for a time rounding the long home bend which enabled his old rival to just get away from him. He stayed on strongly once in line for home but, try as he might, he could not get past the determined winner. If he returns here for the King George next month, he should get the strong pace he needs. (op 10-11 tchd 8-11, evens in places and 11-10 in a place)
Mighty, just a neck behind Maraahel at Newbury in April, has done marvellously well for a horse that only broke his maiden on the Lingfield Polytrack in January. Given a patient ride, he got into all sorts of trouble with Blue Bajan when trying to pull out rounding the home bend and it is testament to his courage that he plugged on to snatch a very creditable third. He is wonderfully consistent and is well worth his place in this sort of company, so it would be a shame if he ended the season without a victory in Listed company at the very least. (op 11-1 tchd 12-1)
Admiral's Cruise(USA) was quite coltish in the paddock and got warm. Closely matched with Mighty on their running in the John Porter and Jockey Club Stakes, he ran close to form with that rival but his second place to Sixties Icon in the latter contest probably flatters him, as that race was run at a crawl. Held up for a late run here, he never looked like winning and needs to drop down a level. (op 8-1 tchd 10-1)
Blue Bajan(IRE) just a head behind Maraahel at Chester, was 5lb worse off with him here. He travelled really well off the pace, even after getting involved in some argy-bargy with Mighty rounding the home bend, and although he was still on the bridle starting up the home straight his effort soon petered out. He has winning form over this trip, but that was against much inferior rivals than these and he does look better over 1m2f. (op 12-1)
Diamond Quest(SAF), a winner in Dubai for Mike de Kock earlier in the year and successful over distances ranging from 1m to 2m in the past 12 months, was making his debut for his new yard after over three months off. Keen enough out the back for much of the way, he was brought out very wide for his effort in the home straight, but could never get involved. He was entitled to need this, but is still to show that he is up to this class and was reportedly lame afterwards.
Akarem was keen enough out in front in the first-time visor, but merely set the race up for the big guns. Still paying for his win in a Listed race here more than a year ago, he has become the archetypal twilight horse.

2857 GOLDEN JUBILEE STKS (BRITISH LEG OF THE GLOBAL SPRINT CHALLENGE) (GROUP 1) 6f

3:45 (3:46) (Class 1) 3-Y-O+

£198,730 (£75,320; £37,695; £18,795; £9,415; £4,725) **Stalls** Centre

Form RPR

4/33 **1** **Soldier's Tale (USA)**[16] [2396] 6-9-4 112 .... (v[1]) JMurtagh 11 124
(J Noseda) *chsd ldrs: rdn over 2f out: r.o ins fnl f to ld post* **9/1**

01-4 **2** hd **Takeover Target (AUS)**[4] [2733] 8-9-4 0 .... JayFord 10 123
(J Janiak, Australia) *lw: led: rdn over 1f out: hdd post* **8/1**

02-1 **3** 1/2 **Asset (IRE)**[65] [1102] 4-9-4 113 .... RichardHughes 12 121
(R Hannon) *lw: trckd ldrs: rdn over 1f out: r.o and gaining cl home* **14/1**

0-20 **4** 1/2 **Red Clubs (IRE)**[23] [2184] 4-9-4 114 .... MichaelHills 22 120
(B W Hills) *hld up: hdwy 1/2-way: rdn and pressed ldr ins fnl f: no ex fnl strides* **25/1**

5-40 **5** 2 **Drayton (IRE)**[49] [1473] 3-8-11 0 .... WMLordan 20 112
(M F De Kock, South Africa) *s.s: racd keenly: hld up: hdwy over 2f out: sn rdn: r.o ins fnl f: nt pce to rch ldrs* **100/1**

11-4 **6** 1 1/4 **Bygone Days**[19] [2319] 6-9-4 110 .... LDettori 8 110
(Saeed Bin Suroor) *hld up in midfield: rdn 2f out: hdwy over 1f out: styd on ins fnl f: gng on at fin* **18/1**

0-40 **7** nk **Baltic King**[19] [2319] 7-9-4 110 .... (t) JimmyFortune 13 109
(H Morrison) *bmpd s: hld up and bhd: hdwy over 1f out: r.o and gaining towards fin* **50/1**

2-22 **8** shd **Borderlescott**[19] [2319] 5-9-4 109 .... RoystonFfrench 17 109
(R Bastiman) *in tch: rdn over 1f out: kpt on same pce ins fnl f* **20/1**

1-13 **9** 3/4 **Firenze**[23] [2184] 6-9-1 103 .... JamieSpencer 4 104
(J R Fanshawe) *swtchd rt sn after s: hld up and bhd: nt clr run over 1f out: sn rdn: styd on ins fnl f: nvr rchd ldrs* **25/1**

11-6 **10** 1/2 **Al Qasi (IRE)**[38] [1770] 4-9-4 107 .... KerrinMcEvoy 15 105
(P W Chapple-Hyam) *lw: midfield: rdn over 1f out: one pce ins fnl f* **8/1**

35-1 **11** 2 **Amadeus Wolf**[38] [1770] 4-9-4 114 .... NCallan 7 99
(K A Ryan) *lw: in tch: rdn over 2f out: sn btn* **13/2**[2]

-403 **12** 1/2 **Presto Shinko (IRE)**[6] [2695] 6-9-4 107 .... (p) JHBowman 9 98
(R Hannon) *midfield: rdn over 2f out: nt pce to chal* **100/1**

12-5 **13** 3/4 **Wi Dud**[23] [2184] 3-8-11 116 .... MJKinane 19 93
(K A Ryan) *stmbld s: towards rr: nvr rchd chalng position* **40/1**

3 **14** 3/4 **Magnus (AUS)**[4] [2733] 5-9-4 0 .... (b) DMOliver 21 93
(P Moody, Australia) *gd spd w ldr: rdn and wknd over 1f out: eased whn btn ins fnl f* **15/2**[3]

1 **15** 1/2 **Miss Andretti (AUS)**[4] [2733] 6-9-1 0 .... CNewitt 16 89
(Lee Freedman, Australia) *racd keenly: chsd ldrs tl rdn and wknd over 2f out* **2/1**[1]

-251 **16** 2 **Assertive**[19] [2319] 4-9-4 106 .... RyanMoore 14 86
(R Hannon) *midfield: pushed along 3f out: no imp* **66/1**

0604 **17** 1 3/4 **Quito (IRE)**[16] [2396] 10-9-4 105 .... (b) KDarley 18 80
(D W Chapman) *a in rr-div: eased whn btn fnl f* **66/1**

1540 **18** 2 1/2 **Appalachian Trail (IRE)**[42] [1656] 6-9-4 108 .... (b) TomEaves 2 73
(I Semple) *towards rr: rdn over 2f out: nvr on terms* **100/1**

1-14 **19** 3/4 **Rising Shadow (IRE)**[38] [1770] 6-9-4 110 .... JimmyQuinn 1 71
(T D Barron) *s.i.s: a bhd* **25/1**

-306 **20** 1 **Fayr Jag (IRE)**[19] [2319] 8-9-4 107 .... JohnEgan 5 68
(T D Easterby) *midfield: rdn over 2f out: wknd over 1f out* **100/1**

10-0 **21** nk **Hamoody (USA)**[66] [1095] 3-8-11 105 .... OPeslier 6 65
(P W Chapple-Hyam) *swtchd rt after 1f: midfield: rdn over 2f out: sn wknd* **100/1**

1m 14.51s (-0.39) **Going Correction** +0.30s/f (Good)
WFA 3 from 4yo+ 7lb **21** Ran SP% **131.2**
Speed ratings (Par 117):114,113,113,112,109 108,107,107,106,105 103,102,101,100,99 97,94,91,90,89 88
CSF £76.82 TOTE £14.30: £4.70, £3.40, £4.00; EX 186.20 Trifecta £4456.50 Pool £16,947.62 - 2.70 winning units..
Owner Budget Stable **Bred** Budget Stables Inc **Trained** Newmarket, Suffolk
■ Stewards' Enquiry : J Murtagh six-day ban: used whip with excessive frequency (Jul 4-9)

FOCUS

A cracking sprint in terms of quality, featuring several of the top domestic speedballs, plus three of the Australian raiders that contested Tuesday's King's Stand Stakes, but that trio finished in reverse order this time and only one of them figured in the finish, which shows how much ground conditions had changed. The action all unfolded centre to far side of the track and the trio who raced alone more towards the stands' side never figured, though they were outsiders. The form makes plenty of sense amongst the first four and the only negative to this cracking contest was that the winning time was only 0.4 seconds quicker than the Wokingham, when it might have been expected to have been more.

NOTEBOOK

Soldier's Tale(USA), who looked a potentially high-class sprinter in 2005 before going missing for a season due to a whole string of physical problems, had shown that he retained all his ability with his fine third in the Duke Of York last month, and there is the possibility that he was the victim of the bounce when beaten at odds-on at Haydock last time. Visored for the first time, and with the ground very much in his favour, he was always close to the pace but looked to be in trouble passing the two-furlong pole. However, he found reserves from somewhere and put in a strong effort to snatch the race near the line. Fourth in the 2005 July Cup before his career went on hold, his chances there this time around will depend greatly on whether there is enough give in the ground, as there was here. (op 16-1 tchd 20-1 in places)

Takeover Target(AUS), fourth in Tuesday's King's Stand and third in this race last year after winning the King's Stand, was expected to do better in this race this time and comprehensively turned Tuesday's form around with his two compatriots. Always up at the sharp end, he looked in trouble when joined by Red Clubs inside the last furlong, but battled on bravely until the race was snatched from him on the line. He looks as good as ever at the age of eight and his presence has lit up this meeting for the past two years, but connections suggested he was unlikely to return in 2008. (op 15-2)

Asset(IRE) ◆, yet to win at above Listed level, confirmed the impression he created when an impressive winner of the Abernant in April and ran a cracking race in defeat. Always up with the pace, he never gave in for an instant and was still going forwards at the line. He must go to the July Cup with a great chance, especially as quicker ground there would be a big plus.

Red Clubs(IRE), who split Amadeus Wolf and Soldier's Tale in the Duke Of York on his return, showed his subsequent miserable effort when dropped to the minimum trip in the Temple Stakes to have been all wrong. Given a much more patient ride than the front three, he moved up strongly to challenge and may have hit the front for a few strides, but he could not maintain it and had to settle for a highly commendable fourth. He will no doubt continue to be campaigned in the classier sprints throughout the season, including the Diadem, which he won over this course and distance last year.

Drayton(IRE), beaten out of sight in the 2,000 Guineas on his British debut, found this drop in trip much more to his liking and, despite fluffing the start, ran a fine race at a huge price over on the far side of the track. He did much the best of the trio of three-year-olds and if he can build on this, he looks capable of picking up a decent sprint over here.

Bygone Days ◆, all the better for his Windsor return, can be given extra credit for this staying-on effort as he was racing away from the main action and did best of those drawn in single figures. He should be able to pick up another Group sprint somewhere this term. (op 25-1)

Baltic King, winner of the Wokingham at this meeting last year when Borderlescott and Firenze were just behind him, has been mainly struggling in Pattern sprints in the meantime, including behind several of today's rivals. He was not disgraced, even though he never looked like winning, and the proximity of the aforementioned duo suggests he ran his race. (tchd 40-1)

Borderlescott kept battling away and was far from disgraced, but although he has shown himself well up to lesser-Group and Listed company, this was something different.

Firenze ◆ had no chance from her draw, so her her rider tried to overcome that by switching to race with the main group soon after the start. She could ill-afford to give away that sort of ground at this level and did very well to finish so close under the circumstances. These are her conditions and she is worth another chance.

Al Qasi(IRE) was fancied by many to have progressed enough from his reappearance in the Duke Of York to reverse the form with the quintet who finished ahead of him there, especially as this ground should have suited him, but he had every chance and was plainly not good enough. (tchd 15-2 and 9-1 in places)

Amadeus Wolf held several of these, including the winner, on his victory in the Duke Of York. His draw was not ideal, but he never looked happy at any stage and was very disappointing. Official explanation: jockey said colt ran flat; trainer said colt was found to have an inflamed throat after the race (op 7-1)

Magnus(AUS), well backed to come out best of the Australians, helped force the early pace with his compatriot Takeover Target, but eventually dropped away very tamely. (op 10-1 tchd 7-1)

Miss Andretti(AUS), so devastating here on Tuesday, broke well enough but was one of the first beaten and the contrast with her King's Stand victory could hardly have been greater. She did drift significantly in the market beforehand, which seemed to suggest that many people expected the softer ground to find her out, but equally she may not be at her best when returned to the track quickly. (op 13-8 tchd 5-2)

2858 WOKINGHAM STKS (HERITAGE H'CAP) 6f

4:25 (4:26) (Class 2) (0-110,109) 3-Y-O+

£49,856 (£14,928; £7,464; £3,736; £1,864; £936) **Stalls** Centre

Form — RPR

00-4 **1** **Dark Missile**[49] 1474 4-8-6 **96**.................................... WilliamBuick(5) 27 — 109
(A M Balding) *lw: chsd ldr on far side: led 2f out: styd on wl u.p fnl f* **22/1**

5-22 **2** *nk* **Intrepid Jack**[17] 2352 5-9-1 **100**.................................... SteveDrowne 23 — 112
(H Morrison) *hld up in tch on far side: hdwy over 2f out: rdn to chse wnr over 1f out: unable qckn last 100yds* **10/1**[3]

-405 **3** *1 1/2* **Balthazaar's Gift (IRE)**[19] 2319 4-9-10 **109**.......................... LDettori 22 — 117
(L M Cumani) *hld up in rr on far side: rdn and hdwy 2f out: chsd ldrs over 1f out: no imp last 100yds* **12/1**

60-3 **4** *1/2* **Something (IRE)**[19] 2319 5-9-3 **102**.................................. JMurtagh 20 — 108
(T G Mills) *swtg: chsd ldrs on far side: rdn and ev ch 2f out: no ex ins fnl f* **14/1**

4143 **5** *1/2* **Grantley Adams**[49] 1474 4-9-5 **104**.................................... JHBowman 9 — 109
(M R Channon) *stmbld s: sn in midfield in centre gp: hdwy over 2f out: kpt on u.p fnl f* **25/1**

02-0 **6** *1/2* **Burning Incense (IRE)**[49] 1474 4-8-11 **96**................. RichardHughes 6 — 99
(R Charlton) *swtchd rt after s: hld up in rr of centre gp: hdwy wl over 1f out: edgd rt u.p but r.o wl fnl f: nvr able to chal* **20/1**

4-41 **7** *nk* **Zidane**[42] 1653 5-9-1 **100**.. JamieSpencer 4 — 102
(J R Fanshawe) *lw: swtchd rt after s: hld up in rr of centre gp: swtchd rt* and hdwy wl over 1f out: kpt on and edgd lft u.p fnl f: nvr able to chal **4/1**[1]

-100 **8** *2* **Protector (SAF)**[92] 6-8-10 **95**..(v[1]) DMOliver 24 — 91
(Miss Gay Kelleway) *taken down early: chsd ldrs on far side: rdn over 2f out: no hdwy over 1f out* **50/1**

5026 **9** *nk* **Baron's Pit**[17] 2352 7-9-3 **102**.......................................(v[1]) JimCrowley 16 — 97
(E F Vaughan) *led centre gp and overall ldr tl 2f out: wknd u.p 1f out* **50/1**

22-6 **10** *nk* **Knot In Wood (IRE)**[37] 1788 5-8-10 **95**....................(b[1]) PaulHanagan 11 — 89
(R A Fahey) *lw: rrd in stalls: chsd ldrs in centre gp: rdn over 2f out: fdd ins fnl f* **7/1**[2]

-156 **11** *2 1/2* **Beaver Patrol (IRE)**[21] 2237 5-8-11 **96**.............................. MJKinane 3 — 83
(Eve Johnson Houghton) *s.i.s: outpcd in stands' side trio: sme late hdwy u.p: n.d* **20/1**

0-31 **12** *1/2* **Hogmaneigh (IRE)**[21] 2234 4-9-2 **104** 5ex................. SaleemGolam(3) 7 — 89
(S C Williams) *hld up in rr in centre gp: rdn and effrt 2f out: nvr on terms* **10/1**[3]

6455 **13** *1/2* **Ashdown Express (IRE)**[6] 2695 8-9-6 **105**.................. GeorgeBaker 12 — 89
(C F Wall) *hld up towards rr of centre gp: drvn and sme hdwy 2f out: sn no imp* **33/1**

226- **14** *1 1/2* **One Putra (IRE)**[251] 6005 5-9-6 **105**.. RHills 8 — 84
(M A Jarvis) *chsd ldrs in centre gp: rdn and btn over 2f out* **66/1**

0-02 **15** *1/2* **Bentong (IRE)**[14] 2440 4-8-10 **100**..............................(t) TolleyDean(5) 1 — 78
(P F I Cole) *led stands' side trio: rdn over 2f out: n.d to ldrs after* **50/1**

0-00 **16** *hd* **Royal Storm (IRE)**[1] 2817 8-8-11 **96** ow1.............................. OPeslier 2 — 73
(Mrs A J Perrett) *chsd ldr in stands' side trio: rdn 1/2-way: n.d* **100/1**

3-03 **17** *1 1/4* **Out After Dark**[35] 1836 6-8-12 **97**...(p) KDarley 10 — 70
(C G Cox) *chsd ldrs in centre gp: rdn 2f out: sn struggling* **12/1**

00-0 **18** *2* **Nota Bene**[14] 2463 5-9-6 **105**... TQuinn 28 — 72
(D R C Elsworth) *a bhd in far side gp: no ch last 2f* **40/1**

2332 **19** *hd* **Beckermet (IRE)**[16] 2396 5-9-1 **100**............................ JimmyFortune 21 — 67
(R F Fisher) *s.i.s: racd far side: rdn 3f out: n.d after* **16/1**

0352 **20** *1 1/2* **Mutamared (USA)**[49] 1474 7-9-2 **101**...................................... NCallan 13 — 63
(K A Ryan) *racd in centre gp: n.d* **25/1**

-300 **21** *hd* **King's Caprice**[16] 2396 6-9-0 **104**..............................(t) TravisBlock(5) 18 — 66
(J A Geake) *taken down early: chsd ldrs in centre gp: rdn wl over 2f out: sn wknd* **25/1**

3020 **22** *nk* **Bonus (IRE)**[48] 1497 7-8-11 **96**..(t) EddieAhern 17 — 57
(G A Butler) *a in rr of centre gp: rdn and effrt 2f out: nvr trbld ldrs* **66/1**

1650 **23** *5* **Merlin's Dancer**[21] 2234 7-8-10 **95**...................................... JohnEgan 26 — 41
(S Dow) *led far side gp tl over 2f out: sn wknd* **100/1**

0-03 **24** *hd* **Gift Horse**[28] 2022 7-9-0 **99**... RyanMoore 15 — 44
(D Nicholls) *s.i.s: hld up in midfield of centre gp: rdn over 2f out: sn wknd* **12/1**

0162 **25** *5* **Ripples Maid**[14] 2450 4-8-12 **97**.................................... KerrinMcEvoy 19 — 27
(J A Geake) *lw: chsd ldrs on far side of centre gp: rdn over 2f out: sn dropped out* **16/1**

2240 **26** *1 3/4* **Corridor Creeper (FR)**[21] 2234 10-8-6 **98**................(p) BarrySavage(7) 5 — 23
(J M Bradley) *chsd ldrs in centre gp tl 1/2-way: sn rdn and wknd* **66/1**

1m 14.91s (0.01) **Going Correction** +0.30s/f (Good) **26** Ran SP% **135.3**

Speed ratings (Par 109):111,110,108,107,107 106,106,103,103,102 99,98,98,96,95 95,93,90,90,88 88,87,81,80,74 71

CSF £214.77 CT £1657.23 TOTE £28.90: £5.80, £2.50, £2.70, £5.00; EX 102.00 Trifecta £4646.60 Pool £100,786.41 - 15.40 winning units..

Owner J C Smith **Bred** Littleton Stud **Trained** Kingsclere, Hants

■ A first winner at the Royal meeting for both Andrew Balding and apprentice William Buick.

FOCUS

A typically strong Wokingham, but the draw played a key role, with the first four home all among a group of eight who raced down the far side. The majority came up the centre, with three drawn lowest isolated down the stands' rail. Solid form, at least amongst the high-drawn principals.

NOTEBOOK

Dark Missile, a winner over course and distance on Shergar Cup day last August, had been kept back for this since her promising reappearance at Newmarket. Taking full advantage of her high draw, she showed ahead with a quarter of a mile to run and held on determinedly. Connections will presumably try and win some black type with her now. (op 16-1)

Intrepid Jack, tenth to stablemate Baltic King last year, ran a cracker on ground that had gone against him. Another to race in the far-side octet, he was briefly outpaced with around two to run but was clawing back the winner's advantage late on. Runner-up in five of his last seven starts, he deserves a change of luck. (op 9-1)

Balthazaar's Gift(IRE), the topweight, put up his best performance since finishing second to Les Arcs in last year's Golden Jubilee Stakes when trained by Kevin Ryan. Favourably drawn on the far side, he came through to have his chance but was just held in the final half-furlong.

Something(IRE) had finished a length in front of Balthazaar's Gift in a Listed race at Windsor last time but could not confirm that form on 7lb better terms. Another blessed with a high draw, he was right there with two to run but faded inside the last on this rain-softened ground. (op 11-1)

Grantley Adams ◆ overcame a stumble leaving the stalls to finish on top in the large group which raced down the centre. He is well up to winning a big handicap - perhaps the Stewards' Cup - if the draw is kind to him.

Burning Incense(IRE), still without the blinkers, was switched leaving the stalls to join the large group which raced down the centre. He could not get to the leaders on the far side, but he came home in good style and this was a fine effort from his draw. (op 16-1)

Zidane, who was 11lb higher than when scoring over course and distance last month, was undone by his low draw. Switched leaving the stalls to tack on to the group racing down the centre, he made eyecatching progress with over a furlong to run but could not sustain the momentum inside the last. (op 9-2 tchd 5-1)

Protector(SAF), something of a Globe-trotter, was making his first appearance for the Kelleway yard. With a visor replacing the blinkers he had worn on his latest start in the UAE in March, he ran a decent race but was helped by his high draw. (op 40-1)

Baron's Pit, tried in a first-time visor, was 5lb lower than when he last ran in a handicap. He showed fine speed to lead the field down the centre of the course but was always fighting a losing battle against the far-side group.

Knot In Wood(IRE) ◆, fitted with blinkers in an attempt to sharpen him up, soon tracked the leaders down the centre but could produce no extra in the final furlong. He should not be written off, with races like the Portland and Ayr Gold Cup likely targets later in the season. (tchd 13-2, 6-1 in places and 8-1 in places)

Beaver Patrol(IRE) had no chance from his draw but did beat the pair who accompanied him on the stands' rail. (op 25-1)

Hogmaneigh(IRE), 5lb higher under his penalty and stepped back up to 6f, was never able to get into the race but it emerged that there was a valid excuse. Official explanation: jockey said gelding lost a front shoe (op 9-1)

Bentong(IRE) was disadvantaged both by his low draw and the rain-softened ground, so a line can be drawn through this performance. Official explanation: jockey said gelding was unsuited by the good to soft ground (op 40-1)

Royal Storm(IRE), fourth to Lafi in this event three years ago, was well beaten for the second time in two days but his low draw was a major hindrance here. (op 80-1)

Out After Dark has become well handicapped but was found out by this stiff 6f, although the Ascot track seems to be easier than it was. (op 16-1 tchd 20-1 in places)

Nota Bene, lightly raced in the last two years, was well beaten despite being drawn on the right side. (tchd 50-1)

Beckermet(IRE), runner-up to Iffraaj in this event at York two years ago, was well drawn but put in an uncharacteristic below-par performance. Official explanation: jockey said gelding was unsuited by the good to soft ground

Merlin's Dancer towed the far-side group along but his exertions took their toll in the last quarter-mile. He is happier over 5f. (op 66-1)

Gift Horse Official explanation: jockey said gelding ran flat

Ripples Maid ought to have enjoyed the underfoot conditions but was not herself. Official explanation: jockey said filly lost its action

2859 DUKE OF EDINBURGH STKS (HERITAGE H'CAP) 1m 4f

5:00 (5:00) (Class 2) (0-105,104) 3-Y-O+

£34,276 (£10,263; £5,131; £2,568; £1,281; £643) **Stalls** High

Form				RPR
65-0	**1**		**Pevensey (IRE)**[38] 1767 5-8-10 **90**.............................. GrahamGibbons 2 (J J Quinn) *racd wd early: hld up: hdwy 3f out: r.o ins rail over 2f out: swtchd off rail to chal over 1f out: nosed ahd ent fnl f: kpt on and hld on wl* **8/1**	101
5-26	**2**	*hd*	**Solent (IRE)**[48] 1506 5-9-2 **96**.............................. RichardHughes 17 (R Hannon) *sn led: rdn over 2f out: hdd narrowly ent fnl f: sn edgd lft: r.o u.p: jst hld* **20/1**	107
/	**3**	*shd*	**Hitchcock (USA)**[34] 1868 4-9-2 **96**.............................. MJKinane 12 (A P O'Brien, Ire) *lw: hld up in midfield: hdwy over 4f out: styd on fr over 2f out: swtchd lft 1f out: pressed ldrs and ev ch ins fnl f: hld fnl strides* **9/2**[2]	107
0-04	**4**	*7*	**Ogee**[17] 2351 4-8-11 **91**.............................. KerrinMcEvoy 18 (Sir Michael Stoute) *lw: in tch: pushed along to chse ldrs over 3f out: one pce and no ch w front trio fnl f* **5/1**[3]	91
-005	**5**	*3*	**Futun**[38] 1767 4-9-1 **95**.............................. JamieSpencer 7 (L M Cumani) *lw: racd wd early: hld up: rdn and hdwy over 2f out: hung rt over 1f out: nvr able to trble ldrs* **12/1**	90
10-1	**6**	*shd*	**Scriptwriter (IRE)**[36] 1805 5-9-7 **101**.............................. LDettori 5 (Saeed Bin Suroor) *lw: broke wl: racd wd early: handy: rdn over 2f out: wknd over 1f out* **5/2**[1]	96
200	**7**	*¾*	**Kings Quay**[22] 2209 5-8-10 **90**.............................. (t) JHBowman 19 (J J Quinn) *hld up: rdn 3f out: hdwy over 1f out: no imp fnl f* **33/1**	83
2440	**8**	*5*	**Eva Soneva So Fast (IRE)**[35] 1844 5-8-9 **89**.............................. JimmyQuinn 14 (J L Dunlop) *midfield: clsd 7f out: effrt to chse ldrs 3f out: wknd over 1f out* **33/1**	74
213	**9**	*hd*	**Cedar Mountain (IRE)**[17] 2351 4-8-10 **90**.............................. JimmyFortune 11 (J H M Gosden) *lw: in tch: pushed along over 4f out: wknd over 2f out* **8/1**	75
1360	**10**	*1 ½*	**Weightless**[17] 2351 7-9-1 **95**.............................. JamesDoyle 9 (N P Littmoden) *prom: rdn and ev ch 3f out: wknd wl over 1f out* **40/1**	78
-534	**11**	*3*	**Acropolis (IRE)**[14] 2462 6-8-13 **93**.............................. (p) TomEaves 10 (I Semple) *swtg: racd keenly: midfield: lost pl 4f out: n.d after* **33/1**	71
3240	**12**	*3 ½*	**Nakheel**[21] 2236 4-9-3 **97**.............................. RHills 13 (M Johnston) *swtg: s.i.s: midfield: pushed along over 2f out: no imp whn n.m.r over 1f out: bhd after* **12/1**	69
10-2	**13**	*9*	**Mikao (IRE)**[35] 1844 6-8-8 **91**.............................. SaleemGolam(3) 15 (M H Tompkins) *s.s: hdwy into midfield after 4f: rdn and wknd over 3f out* **12/1**	49
5-42	**14**	*72*	**Bandama (IRE)**[17] 2351 4-9-4 **98**.............................. JimCrowley 4 (Mrs A J Perrett) *racd wd early: hld up in midfield: rdn and wknd over 5f out: eased whn btn over 2f out: t.o* **20/1**	—

2m 36.64s (3.64) **Going Correction** +0.60s/f (Yiel) **14** Ran SP% **129.5**

Speed ratings (Par 109):111,110,110,106,104 104,103,100,100,99 97,94,88,40

CSF £170.93 CT £830.53 TOTE £10.80: £3.50, £5.80, £2.20; EX 263.20 Trifecta £2021.80 Pool £5980.04 - 2.10 winning units..

Owner Dum Spiro Spero **Bred** Barronstown Stud & Orpendale **Trained** Settrington, N Yorks

■ The first winner at Royal Ascot for John Quinn.

■ Stewards' Enquiry : Graham Gibbons two-day ban: used whip with excessive frequency (Jul 4-5)

FOCUS

With five absentees due to the ground, this was not that competitive a renewal, but it was run at a decent pace and produced a stirring finish, with the first three clear. The form has been rated fairly positively but should not be taken too literally.

NOTEBOOK

Pevensey(IRE), 3lb higher than when winning a heritage handicap for Mark Buckley over course and distance last September, landed a gamble. Held up and kept wide in the first part of the contest before nipping through on the inside turning for home, he edged ahead with a furlong to run and held on gamely. He was given a fine ride and is another excellent advertisement for his trainer's skills. (tchd 9-1)

Solent(IRE) showed his Salisbury running to have been all wrong. Soon in front, he kicked once in line for home but was collared entering the final furlong. Refusing to fold, he rallied bravely under pressure. This was a fine effort and he will not mind a step back up in trip.

Hitchcock(USA) ◆ was sharper for his recent reappearance at Gowran Park over a shorter trip. Outpaced by the leaders going into the home turn, but soon starting to stay on, he was pulled off the rail to mount his challennge and just failed to peg back the first two. He could be interesting if going for the Ebor, a race his trainer won with Mediterranean in 2001. (op 6-1 tchd 7-2, 7-1 in a place and 13-2 in a place)

Ogee could not go with the leaders in the straight but plugged on to finish best of the rest, himself clear of the remainder. The return to this trip suited and he reversed Kempton form with Bandama and Cedar Mountain. (op 7-2)

Futun, held up and racing wide, settled better this time. Making his effort on the outside turning in, he soon began to hang and could only stick on at the same pace. (op 9-1)

Scriptwriter(IRE), 4lb higher than when landing a Listed handicap at Hamilton, was another to race wide in search of the best ground. He was close enough turning into the straight but was soon found wanting. (op 7-2 tchd 4-1 and 9-2 in places)

Kings Quay, a stablemate of the winner, ran respectably on ground that had gone against him. He has not won on the Flat since his two-year-old days with Richard Hannon, but is capable of putting that right.

Cedar Mountain(IRE) was encountering soft ground for the first time, on only his second run on turf. Under pressure with half a mile to run, he was soon on the retreat once into the home straight. (tchd 17-2)

Mikao(IRE) Official explanation: jockey said gelding slipped on leaving stalls

Bandama(IRE) Official explanation: jockey said colt did not handle the soft ground

2860 QUEEN ALEXANDRA STKS (CONDITIONS RACE) 2m 5f 159y

5:35 (5:36) (Class 2) 4-Y-O+

£34,276 (£10,263; £5,131; £2,568; £1,281; £643) **Stalls** High

Form				RPR
-030	**1**		**Enjoy The Moment**[4] 2736 4-9-0 92.............................. JamieSpencer 4 (J A Osborne) *hld up: gd hdwy 5f out: led over 2f out: edgd lft ins fnl f: styd on wl and in command after* **6/1**[3]	106
0-20	**2**	*3*	**Baddam**[2] 2787 5-9-5 108.............................. IanMongan 8 (M R Channon) *hld up in midfield: hdwy over 5f out: rdn to chal over 2f out: wnt 2nd 1f out: no imp on wnr ins fnl f* **4/1**[2]	106
06-3	**3**	*¾*	**Golden Quest**[14] 2462 6-9-2 103.............................. JoeFanning 9 (M Johnston) *lw: in tch: wnt 2nd 10f out: rdn and ev ch over 2f out: lost 2nd 1f out: kpt on at same pce after* **5/2**[1]	102
0-22	**4**	*10*	**Ned Ludd (IRE)**[42] 1654 4-9-0 83.............................. EddieAhern 5 (J G Portman) *hld up in midfield: hdwy over 8f out: led 3f out: rdn and hdd over 2f out: wknd fnl f* **12/1**	92
560-	**5**	*17*	**Vinando**[99] 5963 6-9-2 100.............................. (bt) LDettori 3 (C R Egerton) *reluctant and cajoled along leaving stalls: wnt 2nd after 3f: led 6f out: rdn and hdd 3f out: wknd over 2f out* **6/1**[3]	75
1	**6**	*hd*	**Secret Ploy**[49] 1479 7-9-2 77.............................. JimmyFortune 11 (H Morrison) *lw: handy tl rdn and wknd 4f out* **13/2**	75
64/4	**7**	*10*	**Mith Hill**[42] 1654 6-9-2 79.............................. JimCrowley 16 (Ian Williams) *midfield: rdn along and lost pl 8f out: rallied over 6f out: wknd over 4f out* **14/1**	65
1100	**8**	*9*	**Vanishing Dancer (SWI)**[2] 2800 10-9-2 62.............. (vt) DPMcDonogh 2 (K J Burke) *hld up: hdwy over 6f out: wknd over 5f out* **66/1**	56
/55-	**9**	*20*	**Corrib Eclipse**[282] 5318 8-9-2 99.............................. RyanMoore 17 (Ian Williams) *midfield tl rdn and wknd over 5f out: t.o* **20/1**	36
5606	**10**	*12*	**Flame Creek (IRE)**[7] 2675 11-9-2 76.............................. TQuinn 10 (E J Creighton) *led: hdd 6f out: rdn and wknd over 4f out: t.o* **50/1**	24
021-	**11**	*1 ½*	**Hue**[395] 1931 6-9-2 72.............................. (b) TomEaves 12 (B Ellison) *a bhd: rdn over 4f out: t.o* **10/1**	23
433/	**12**	*dist*	**Barati (IRE)**[92] 3238 6-9-2 85.............................. VinceSlattery 15 (B N Pollock) *midfield: sn niggled along: wknd 10f out: sn lost tch: t.o* **66/1**	—

4m 56.25s (8.05) **Going Correction** +0.60s/f (Yiel)

WFA 4 from 5yo+ 2lb **12** Ran SP% **123.6**

Speed ratings (Par 109):109,107,107,104,97 97,94,90,83,79 78,—

CSF £31.00 TOTE £5.90: £1.80, £1.90, £1.60; EX 24.90 Trifecta £45.50 Pool £6,188.83 - 96.41 winning units. Place 6 £ 212.54, Place 5 £ 126.11.

Owner Lynn Wilson And Martin Landau **Bred** Millsec Limited **Trained** Upper Lambourn, Berks

FOCUS

The usual assortment of smart stayers and no-hopers lined up for this unique event. Not many saw out the marathon trip in the conditions. Although the second and third were not at their very best, the form does seem sound enough, with Enjoy The Moment up 9lb on his previous best.

NOTEBOOK

Enjoy The Moment, badly hampered in the Ascot Stakes on the opening day of the meeting, had no problem with the underfoot conditions and gained compensation in ready fashion. Held up before making steady progress, he quickened up to lead once in the straight and was in no danger thereafter despite edging to his left. He will be interesting if taking up his entry in the Northumberland Plate at Newcastle next week under a 5lb penalty. (op 11-2)

Baddam, seventh in the Gold Cup just two days earlier, had less time to recover than when landing this race in 2006. A thorough stayer, he ran a solid race but could not match the winner, to whom he was conceding 5lb. (op 3-1 tchd 9-2 and 5-1 in places)

Golden Quest was not inconvenienced by the rain and ran a solid race, just lacking a change of gear in the last quarter-mile. He is running respectably but has not quite recaptured the sort of form he showed prior to his injury in 2005. (tchd 11-4 and 3-1 in places)

Ned Ludd(IRE), who missed the cut in the Ascot Stakes earlier in the week, briefly showed ahead going into the home turn but his stamina ebbed away before the final furlong. This was a good effort at the weights. (tchd 11-1 and 14-1 in places)

Vinando, third to Baddam last year, was appearing for the first time since the Cheltenham Festival. Reluctant to race early on but in second place by the end of the third furlong, he moved past the long-time leader with three-quarters of a mile to run but was headed on the home turn and soon on the retreat. (op 13-2 tchd 8-1)

Secret Ploy did not see out the trip on this ground but probably ran up to his mark. (op 8-1)

Corrib Eclipse, winner of this event in 2004 when trained by Jamie Poulton, was well beaten on this first run for nine months. Official explanation: jockey said gelding was unsuited by the good to soft ground (op 16-1)

Hue, off the track since winning a Goodwood handicap in May last year, was well backed for this return but, after travelling well in rear, was beaten with half a mile to run. (op 25-1)

T/Jkpt: Not won. T/Plt: £275.00 to a £1 stake. Pool: £408,422.25. 1,083.85 winning tickets. T/Qpdt: £159.00 to a £1 stake. Pool: £14,143.20. 65.80 winning tickets. SP

2818 AYR (L-H)

Saturday, June 23

OFFICIAL GOING: Good (good to firm in places)

Wind: Breezy, half against

2861 SCOTTISH NEWS OF THE WORLD H'CAP 1m 5f 13y

2:25 (2:25) (Class 3) (0-95,92) 4-Y-O+ **£11,658** (£3,468; £1,733; £865) **Stalls** Low

Form				RPR
4/42	**1**		**Misty Dancer**[21] 2236 8-8-10 **81**.............................. PaulFessey 1 (Miss Venetia Williams) *hld up on ins: qcknd to ld over 1f out: sn clr* **11/2**[2]	91+
10-5	**2**	*3 ½*	**Topjeu (IRE)**[29] 2002 4-9-4 **89**.............................. NickyMackay 12 (L M Cumani) *hld up in midfield: hdwy over 2f out: kpt on fnl f: no ch w wnr* **3/1**[1]	94
-430	**3**	*nk*	**Tilt**[21] 2236 5-8-11 **85**.............................. JamieMoriarty(3) 6 (B Ellison) *hld up: hdwy over 2f out: kpt on fnl f: nrst fin* **6/1**[3]	90
12/2	**4**	*½*	**Clueless**[19] 2314 5-9-1 **86**.............................. DavidAllan 9 (N G Richards) *prom: rdn over 2f out: one pce over 1f out* **9/1**	90
5416	**5**	*nk*	**La Estrella (USA)**[21] 2236 4-9-1 **86**.............................. PatCosgrave 2 (J G Given) *led to over 2f out: rallied and ev ch over 1f out: sn no ex fnl f* **8/1**	90
-263	**6**	*1*	**Lets Roll**[21] 2245 6-9-2 **92**.............................. PJMcDonald(5) 5 (C W Thornton) *hld up: hdwy over 4f out: rdn and no ex fr 2f out* **7/1**	94
1315	**7**	*1 ¾*	**Beldon Hill (USA)**[123] 507 4-8-3 **74**.............................. DaleGibson 3 (R A Fahey) *prom tl rdn and outpcd fr 2f out* **20/1**	73
-501	**8**	*1*	**Luna Landing**[19] 2314 4-8-10 **81**.............................. PaulEddery 10 (Jedd O'Keeffe) *pressed ldr: led over 2f out to over 1f out: sn btn* **25/1**	79+
-014	**9**	*1*	**Doctor Scott**[21] 2245 4-8-4 **78**.............................. GregFairley(3) 7 (M Johnston) *midfield: lost pl after 2f: rdn 4f out: n.d* **10/1**	74
10-6	**10**	*2 ½*	**Rationale (IRE)**[14] 2474 4-9-0 **85**.............................. DeanMcKeown 11 (S C Williams) *chsd ldrs tl wknd over 2f out* **9/1**	78
0255	**11**	*4*	**Kames Park (IRE)**[21] 2245 5-8-12 **86**.............................. (b) AndrewMullen(3) 8 (I Semple) *s.s: hld up: hdwy over 2f out: carried hd high: sn btn* **18/1**	73

2m 50.33s (-6.28) **Going Correction** -0.40s/f (Firm) **11** Ran SP% **121.2**

Speed ratings (Par 107):103,100,100,100,100 99,98,97,97,95 93

CSF £23.08 CT £105.94 TOTE £4.30: £1.90, £1.60, £3.40; EX 16.20.

Owner Pinks Gym & Leisure Wear Ltd **Bred** Mrs D O Joly **Trained** Kings Caple, H'fords

FOCUS

Mainly exposed sorts but a decent gallop and a ready winner. This form, rated around the third and fourth, should prove reliable.

NOTEBOOK

Misty Dancer, who developed into a useful chaser last term, had been running creditably on the Flat and turned in an improved effort on his first start over this trip. He will stay further still and, although the Handicapper will have his say, he may be capable of a bit better in this sphere. (op 6-1)

Topjeu(IRE), a lightly raced and fairly unexposed sort, bettered his reappearance run and left the impression that he would be worth a try over further. He is in good hands and appeals as the type to win more races. (op 4-1 tchd 11-4)

Tilt is 11lb higher than his last winning mark so has little margin for error against the better handicapped or more progressive rivals from this mark but he ran creditably and he should continue to give a good account around this distance. (op 15-2)
Clueless, who ran creditably at Thirsk on his previous start, was far from disgraced with the headgear left off over this extra furlong. He has little room for manoeuvre from his current mark, though. (op 14-1)
La Estrella(USA) looks high enough in the weights but is a consistent sort who may be a bit better than the bare form as he was up with decent pace throughout. He should continue to give a good account in this type of event.
Lets Roll, who beat three rivals in this race two years ago, had run creditably on his previous start at Musselburgh, ran creditably on ground that would have been plenty quick enough. A bit of cut would have been ideal but he is vulnerable to anything progressive from his current mark. (op 9-2)
Luna Landing Official explanation: jockey said saddle slipped
Kames Park(IRE) Official explanation: jockey said gelding missed the break

2862 SCOTTISH SUN STKS (H'CAP) 1m 1f 20y
2:55 (2:56) (Class 2) (0-100,90) 3-Y-O
£15,580 (£4,665; £2,332; £1,167; £582; £292) **Stalls** Low

Form | | | | RPR
1 **1** **Samira Gold (FR)**[15] [2433] 3-8-12 **81** NickyMackay 8 96+
(L M Cumani) *hld up: effrt and hdwy over 2f out: led appr fnl f: styd on strly: readily* **7/2**[2]
2111 **2** *3* **Jewelled Dagger (IRE)**[21] [2248] 3-8-5 **74** (b) PaulFessey 6 83
(I Semple) *chsd ldrs: wd st: led over 2f out to appr fnl f: kpt on same pce* **12/1**
-011 **3** *3 1/2* **Lacework**[26] [2092] 3-9-7 **90** JDSmith 3 92
(Sir Michael Stoute) *hld up: hdwy over 2f out: no ex appr fnl f* **11/4**[1]
50-4 **4** *1 1/4* **Domino Dancer (IRE)**[35] [1851] 3-8-10 **84** PJMcDonald(5) 9 83
(J Wade) *hld up: rdn and effrt over 2f out: no imp over 1f out* **14/1**
-436 **5** *1 1/2* **Plane Painter (IRE)**[18] [2340] 3-8-8 **80** AndrewMullen(3) 2 76
(M Johnston) *cl up: ev ch over 2f out: edgd lft: no ex over 1f out* **8/1**
00-6 **6** *3/4* **Prince Golan (IRE)**[37] [1790] 3-9-5 **88** DO'Donohoe 10 82
(K A Ryan) *bhd: drvn and struggling 1/2-way: sme late hdwy: nvr on terms* **20/1**
3230 **7** *1* **New World Order (IRE)**[28] [2045] 3-8-11 **80** PatCosgrave 7 72
(K R Burke) *in tch: drvn 3f out: btn over 1f out* **22/1**
32-6 **8** *shd* **Marriaj (USA)**[67] [1075] 3-8-2 **76** AhmedAjtebi(5) 1 68
(B Smart) *led to over 2f out: sn rdn and btn* **20/1**
-154 **9** *4* **Voodoo Moon**[28] [2037] 3-9-3 **89** GregFairley(3) 11 73
(M Johnston) *w ldr tl wknd over 2f out* **4/1**[3]
20-0 **10** *1 3/4* **Lemon Silk (IRE)**[36] [1827] 3-8-6 **75** PaulEddery 4 55
(T P Tate) *hld up: rdn 3f out: nvr on terms* **10/1**

1m 54.13s (-5.87) **Going Correction** -0.40s/f (Firm) **10** Ran SP% **117.3**
Speed ratings (Par 105):110,107,104,103,101 101,100,100,96,95
CSF £43.54 CT £132.43 TOTE £3.60: £1.80, £3.10, £1.60; EX 44.00.
Owner Jaber Abdullah **Bred** L L C Woodside Farms **Trained** Newmarket, Suffolk

FOCUS
A decent handicap and a solid gallop resulted in a good winning time for a race like this. The form is rated fairly positively through the third.

NOTEBOOK
Samira Gold(FR) ◆ looked to have a much stiffer task than when winning a maiden on her debut but she appreciated the good gallop and turned in an improved effort on this handicap debut. She will stay a mile and a quarter and appeals strongly as the type to win more races. (op 5-2)
Jewelled Dagger(IRE), a much-improved performer in blinkers in lesser company, was up in the weights and in grade but turned in his best effort yet and may be better than the bare form as he was up with the strong pace throughout. He looks sure to win again when allowed to dominate in lesser company. (op 10-1)
Lacework, up in the weights and in grade, looked one of the few progressive types in this race but, although not disgraced, may not have been suited by the drop in distance. She looked more of a stayer at Redcar on her previous start and is well worth a try over 1m4f. (op 9-4 tchd 3-1)
Domino Dancer(IRE), having his first run for his predominantely jumping-orientated stable, was not disgraced and, although leaving the impression that a stiffer overall test of stamina would have suited, he is likely to remain vulnerable from his current mark in handicaps. (op 12-1)
Plane Painter(IRE) was not far behind Lacework when running creditably on his reappearance but he was again below that level, though he may be a bit better than this bare form as he was up with the strong pace. He is not one to write off just yet. (op 11-1)
Prince Golan(IRE), tailed off behind Derby winner Authorized on his two previous starts, was back at a more realistic level but did not really show enough to suggest he is of much interest in the short term in similar handicap company. (op 25-1)

2863 MISS SCOTLAND EUROPEAN BREEDERS' FUND MAIDEN STKS 6f
3:25 (3:25) (Class 5) 2-Y-O **£3,886** (£1,156; £577; £288) **Stalls** High

Form | | | | RPR
2 **1** **Unilateral (IRE)**[17] [2364] 2-8-12 0 PaulEddery 4 72
(B Smart) *chsd ldrs: led 2f out: edgd rt: kpt on strly* **5/4**[1]
6 **2** *2* **Merchant Of Dubai**[10] [2575] 2-9-3 0 DeanMcKeown 5 71
(G A Swinbank) *led to 2f out: kpt on same pce fnl f* **6/1**
3 **3** *2* **Wotashirtfull (IRE)**[11] [2532] 2-9-3 0 DO'Donohoe 2 65
(K A Ryan) *cl up: ev ch fr 1/2-way: drvn whn n.m.r over 1f out: nt qckn* **7/2**[3]
0 **4** *2 1/2* **Powys Lad**[14] [2443] 2-9-3 0 PatCosgrave 1 58
(K R Burke) *wnt lft s: prom: nt clr run 1/2-way: rdn and no imp fr 2f out* **20/1**
5 *10* **Jerry Hamilton (USA)** 2-9-0 0 GregFairley(3) 3 28
(M Johnston) *chsd ldrs to 1/2-way: sn rdn and wknd* **11/4**[2]

1m 12.96s (-0.71) **Going Correction** -0.15s/f (Firm) **5** Ran SP% **112.4**
Speed ratings (Par 93):98,95,92,89,76
CSF £9.52 TOTE £2.20: £1.40, £2.00; EX 8.80.
Owner Prime Equestrian **Bred** Gaines-Gentry Thoroughbred & Tower Bloodstock **Trained** Hambleton, N Yorks

FOCUS
Little strength in depth but this could be a fair event.

NOTEBOOK
Unilateral(IRE) fully confirmed debut promise and justified some solid market support when opening her account in workmanlike fashion. Her stable has a strong hand in the juvenile department and this one may be capable of better. (op 11-8 tchd 6-4 in places)
Merchant Of Dubai ◆ took the eye beforehand as a strong sort with plenty of scope and, although he enjoyed the run of the race, he turned in an improved effort. He is open to plenty of improvement and is sure to win races in due course. (op 9-2)
Wotashirtfull(IRE), who shaped well on his reappearance, probably ran to a similar level but would have finished closer but for suffering interference at a crucial stage. He looks sure to win an ordinary event at some stage. (op 4-1)
Powys Lad, tailed off on his debut at Goodwood, fared better this time but, although likely to remain vulnerable in this type of event, may do better in nursery company granted a stiffer test of stamina.
Jerry Hamilton(USA), a $120,000 yearling and half-brother to the stable's former top juvenile Shamardal, was solid in the market but was soundly beaten on this racecourse debut. While he did not show much this time, he would not be one to write off by any means. (op 3-1 tchd 10-3 in places)

2864 MARGARET WYLLIE MEMORIAL H'CAP 6f
4:00 (4:00) (Class 5) (0-70,70) 3-Y-O+ **£3,238** (£963; £481; £240) **Stalls** High

Form | | | | RPR
0403 **1** **Inca Soldier (FR)**[3] [2762] 4-8-9 **51** oh2 PaulEddery 9 61
(R C Guest) *t.k.h: in tch: hdwy to ld ins fnl f: rdn out* **9/1**
0025 **2** *1/2* **John Keats**[12] [2509] 4-9-3 **59** NickyMackay 7 68
(J S Goldie) *trckd ldrs gng wl: led over 1f out to ins fnl f: kpt on* **11/4**[1]
4043 **3** *1 1/4* **Brigadore**[12] [2508] 8-9-9 **65** HayleyTurner 3 70
(J G Given) *stdd s: hld up: hdwy over 1f out: kpt on: nrst fin* **7/1**
4100 **4** *1 1/4* **Dorn Dancer (IRE)**[21] [2256] 5-9-3 **62** JamieMoriarty(3) 5 63
(D W Barker) *hld up: smooth hdwy and cl up over 1f out: no ex fnl f* **14/1**
063 **5** *1 1/4* **Regal Royale**[5] [2725] 4-9-9 **70** (b) RussellKennemore(5) 6 67
(Peter Grayson) *prom tl rdn and nt qckn over 1f out* **10/1**
0-10 **6** *1* **Hit's Only Money (IRE)**[10] [2561] 7-8-8 **57** GaryBartley(7) 10 51
(J S Goldie) *hld up: rdn whn nt clr run over 2f out: no imp fnl f* **6/1**[3]
3302 **7** *1 1/4* **Cross Of Lorraine (IRE)**[26] [2072] 4-9-6 **67** (b) PJMcDonald(5) 1 58
(I Semple) *led tl hdd over 1f out: sn btn* **11/2**[2]
0-30 **8** *1/2* **Word Perfect**[40] [1718] 5-9-9 **65** (b) DaleGibson 8 54
(M W Easterby) *cl up tl rdn and wknd over 1f out* **10/1**
3664 **9** *3* **Oeuf A La Neige**[5] [2711] 7-8-9 **51** oh3 (p) DO'Donohoe 2 31
(Miss L A Perratt) *cl up tl rdn and wknd wl over 1f out* **10/1**
30-3 **10** *1* **Markestino**[10] [2576] 4-8-9 **51** oh1 DavidAllan 4 28
(T D Easterby) *cl up to over 2f out: sn lost pl* **10/1**

1m 12.24s (-1.43) **Going Correction** -0.15s/f (Firm) **10** Ran SP% **121.9**
Speed ratings (Par 103):103,102,100,99,97 96,94,93,89,88
CSF £35.60 CT £195.89 TOTE £12.50: £3.10, £1.60, £2.60; EX 48.30.
Owner Philip Pinnington **Bred** Sheikh Sultan B K B Z Al Nahyan **Trained** Brancepeth, Co Durham

FOCUS
An ordinary handicap but one in which the pace was sound throughout and the form looks straightforward rated through the second.
Hit's Only Money(IRE) Official explanation: jockey said gelding was denied a clear run
Markestino Official explanation: jockey said gelding was unsuited by the good (good to firm places) ground

2865 DREAM TEAM H'CAP 1m 1f 20y
4:35 (4:35) (Class 5) (0-75,72) 4-Y-O+ **£4,533** (£1,348; £674; £336) **Stalls** Low

Form | | | | RPR
6423 **1** **Final Tune (IRE)**[39] [1751] 4-9-2 **72** RussellKennemore(5) 9 79
(Miss M E Rowland) *t.k.h: hld up: hdwy to ld over 1f out: kpt on strly fnl f* **3/1**[1]
26-2 **2** *1 1/4* **Shiitake**[30] [1967] 4-8-12 **63** DO'Donohoe 5 67
(Miss L A Perratt) *t.k.h: hld up: hdwy over 2f out: kpt on fnl f: nt rch wnr* **3/1**[1]
6000 **3** *3/4* **Bolton Hall (IRE)**[7] [2660] 5-8-6 **57** DavidAllan 2 59
(R A Fahey) *hld up: hdwy over 1f out: kpt on fnl f: no imp* **7/1**[3]
3-02 **4** *3/4* **Hawkit (USA)**[21] [2254] 6-9-3 **68** DaleGibson 3 69
(P Monteith) *chsd ldrs: effrt and ev ch 2f out: one pce fnl f* **3/1**[1]
0245 **5** *1 3/4* **Sforzando**[29] [1997] 6-8-8 **66** (b[1]) KristinStubbs(7) 1 63
(Mrs L Stubbs) *t.k.h: w ldr: led 1/2-way to over 2f out: no ex over 1f out* **6/1**[2]
0260 **6** *3* **Mandarin Rocket (IRE)**[1] [2820] 4-8-2 **53** oh2 ow3.. AndrewMullen(3) 10 46
(Miss L A Perratt) *led to 1/2-way: led over 2f out to over 1f out: sn wknd* **7/1**[3]

1m 58.3s (-1.70) **Going Correction** -0.40s/f (Firm) **6** Ran SP% **114.3**
Speed ratings (Par 103):91,89,89,88,87 84
CSF £12.36 CT £56.24 TOTE £4.70: £1.90, £1.70; EX 20.20.
Owner M Armstrong M Shirley HallFarm M Rowland **Bred** Shortgrove Manor Stud **Trained** Lower Blidworth, Notts

FOCUS
A run-of-the-mill handicap, decimated by withdrawals, and a steady early gallop resulted in a very moderate winning time, 4.17 seconds slower than the earlier handicap, so the form looks dubious.
Sforzando Official explanation: jockey said mare ran too free in first time blinkers
Mandarin Rocket(IRE) Official explanation: jockey said gelding had no more to give

2866 REAL RADIO H'CAP 5f
5:10 (5:10) (Class 4) (0-85,83) 4-Y-O+ **£3,781** (£3,781; £866; £432) **Stalls** High

Form | | | | RPR
3006 **1** **Garstang**[11] [2529] 4-8-3 **65** (b) HayleyTurner 1 74
(Peter Grayson) *s.i.s: bhd and outpcd: gd hdwy fnl f: kpt on wl to force dead-heat on line* **25/1**
-023 **1** *dht* **Gallery Girl (IRE)**[18] [2339] 4-9-6 **82** DavidAllan 8 91
(T D Easterby) *mde virtually all: hrd pressed fnl 2f: kpt on gamely: jnd on line* **7/1**[3]
6250 **3** *hd* **Welcome Approach**[13] [2494] 4-8-4 **66** DO'Donohoe 5 74
(J R Weymes) *bhd and sn outpcd: gd hdwy fnl f: fin wl* **16/1**
5000 **4** *shd* **Curtail (IRE)**[10] [2566] 4-9-4 **83** AndrewMullen(3) 10 91
(I Semple) *trckd ldrs: effrt over 1f out: ev ch ins fnl f: kpt on: jst hld* **5/1**[2]
6302 **5** *1/2* **Blazing Heights**[14] [2461] 4-9-0 **83** GaryBartley(7) 9 89
(J S Goldie) *t.k.h: w wnr: rdn 2f out: kpt on same pce ins fnl f* **5/1**[2]
-500 **6** *1 1/2* **Glasshoughton**[16] [2394] 4-8-10 **72** PaulFessey 3 72
(M Dods) *hld up: hdwy over 1f out: nvr trbld ldrs* **9/1**
2443 **7** *hd* **Bo McGinty (IRE)**[21] [2244] 6-8-12 **77** (p) JamieMoriarty(3) 6 77
(R A Fahey) *chsd ldrs tl rdn and no ex over 1f out* **7/2**[1]
5056 **8** *nk* **Ptarmigan Ridge**[14] [2461] 11-8-3 **68** GregFairley(3) 7 67
(Miss L A Perratt) *in tch: drvn over 2f out: nvr imp over 1f out* **9/1**
0514 **9** *1 1/2* **Raccoon (IRE)**[14] [2461] 7-8-12 **79** PJMcDonald(5) 4 72
(D W Chapman) *rrd s: sn chsng ldrs: drvn and wknd over 1f out* **5/1**[2]
1010 **10** *5* **Colorus (IRE)**[21] [2244] 4-9-2 **78** DaleGibson 2 53
(M W Easterby) *prom tl rdn and wknd over 1f out* **11/1**

59.23 secs (-1.21) **Going Correction** -0.15s/f (Firm) **10** Ran SP% **122.8**
Speed ratings (Par 105):103,103,102,102,101 99,99,98,96,88
WIN: Gallery Girl £4.10, Garstang £12.20. PL: GG £2.70, GA £4.30, Welcome Approach £5.10. EX: GG/GA £110.00, GA/GG £143.50. CSF: GG/GA £85.76, GA/GG £100.00. TRIC: GG/GA/WA £1,387.74, GA/GG/WA £1,495.03..
Owner Peter C Bourke **Bred** Dr D Crone And P Lafarge And P Johnston **Trained** Great Habton, N Yorks
Owner The Foulrice Twenty **Bred** Mrs S E Barclay **Trained** Formby, Lancs

FOCUS
Exposed performers in this ordinary sprint handicap, but the pace was sound throughout and the form looks solid.
Bo McGinty(IRE) Official explanation: jockey said gelding hung right-handed

2867 REID FURNITURE H'CAP 5f
5:45 (5:46) (Class 4) (0-85,85) 3-Y-O £5,829 (£1,734; £866; £432) Stalls High

Form RPR
6410 1 **The Nifty Fox**[16] 2395 3-9-4 **82**.......................... DavidAllan 6 83
(T D Easterby) *chsd ldrs: drvn and led ins fnl f: hld on wl* **11/4**[2]
636- 2 *shd* **Final Dynasty**[239] 6201 3-9-4 **85**.......................... JamieMoriarty(3) 3 86
(Mrs G S Rees) *prom: effrt over 1f out: ev ch fnl f: jst hld* **16/1**
3210 3 *hd* **Baileys Outshine**[12] 2513 3-8-12 **76**.......................... HayleyTurner 1 76
(J G Given) *led: rdn and hdd ins fnl f: edgd rt u.p: kpt on towards fin* **13/2**
2 4 *shd* **Aye Aye Definitely (IRE)**[1] 2821 3-8-7 **71**.......................... DaleGibson 5 71
(R A Fahey) *in tch: effrt over 1f out: kpt on fnl f* **6/1**[3]
31 5 *3/4* **Twosheetstothewind**[40] 1709 3-8-2 **66** oh2.......................... PaulFessey 8 63+
(M Dods) *trckd ldrs: effrt over 1f out: keeping on fnl f whn n.m.r towards fin* **9/4**[1]
3105 6 *1 1/4* **Fish Called Johnny**[12] 2518 3-8-6 **75**..............(b) RussellKennemore(5) 7 68
(Peter Grayson) *bhd: drvn 1/2-way: sme hdwy over 1f out: n.d* **13/2**
6000 7 *1 1/4* **Grange Lili (IRE)**[7] 2672 3-8-3 **70** ow1.......................... GregFairley(3) 4 58
(Peter Grayson) *dwlt and hmpd s: bhd: effrt over 1f out: no imp fnl f* **11/1**
30 8 *hd* **Just Joey**[33] 1900 3-9-5 **83**.......................... DO'Donohoe 2 71
(J R Weymes) *chsd ldrs tl rdn and wknd over 1f out* **16/1**

59.96 secs (-0.48) **Going Correction** -0.15s/f (Firm) 8 Ran SP% **118.5**
Speed ratings (Par 101):97,96,96,96,95 93,91,90
CSF £46.67 CT £270.49 TOTE £3.90: £1.70, £3.60, £1.70; EX 51.90 Place 6 £76.39, Place 5 £ 51.53.
Owner Roy Peebles **Bred** Mrs Norma Peebles **Trained** Great Habton, N Yorks

FOCUS
A fair handicap run at a good pace throughout and another triumph for the Handicapper with very little separating the first five home. The form looks sound enough.
Twosheetstothewind Official explanation: jockey said filly was denied a clear run
T/Plt: £100.60 to a £1 stake. Pool: £60,246.15. 436.80 winning tickets. T/Qpdt: £54.20 to a £1 stake. Pool: £2,391.85. 32.60 winning tickets. RY

2448 HAYDOCK (L-H)
Saturday, June 23

OFFICIAL GOING: Heavy (6.7)
After 24mm rain the previous day the ground had dried out and was described as 'genuine soft'. There were 13 non-runners on account of the ground.
Wind: Moderate, half-against Weather: overcast, occasional light showers

2868 MOUCHEL PARKMAN WATERAID APPRENTICE H'CAP 1m 2f 120y
6:45 (6:45) (Class 5) (0-75,70) 4-Y-0+ £2,817 (£838; £418; £209) Stalls High

Form RPR
3105 1 **Royal Flynn**[14] 2467 5-9-6 **66**.......................... NeilBrown 3 74
(M Dods) *s.s: hld up: hdwy over 2f out: squeezed through to ld last strides* **3/1**[1]
0025 2 *hd* **Dark Charm (FR)**[10] 2551 8-9-0 **65**..............(p) JamesRogers(5) 1 73
(R A Fahey) *w ldr: led 7f out: pushed clr over 5f out: hdd over 2f out: regained ld 1f out: rdr dropped whip ins fnl f: jst ct* **7/1**
6426 3 *1/2* **Suits Me**[52] 1416 4-9-7 **67**.......................... JamieHamblett 2 74
(T P Tate) *t.k.h: led: hdd 7f out: led over 2f out tl 1f out: no ex nr fin* **7/1**
1-14 4 *3* **Saluscraggie**[10] 2579 5-8-9 **55**.......................... DanielleMcCreery 8 56
(K G Reveley) *chsd ldrs: rdn over 3f out: one pce whn n.m.r over 1f out* **4/1**[3]
4656 5 *3/4* **Gallego**[14] 2467 5-8-13 **59**.......................... WilliamCarson 6 59
(R J Price) *hld up: hdwy on outer over 2f out: edgd lft over 1f out: one pce* **13/2**
0044 6 *5* **Ahlawy (IRE)**[26] 2095 4-9-5 **70**.......................... NSLawes(5) 7 60
(M W Easterby) *trckd ldrs: wknd 1f out* **9/1**
0035 7 *2* **Stravara**[5] 2721 4-8-7 **53**.......................... JackMitchell 4 39
(R Hollinshead) *hld up: effrt 4f out: wknd over 1f out* **7/2**[2]

2m 23.22s (7.08) **Going Correction** +0.55s/f (Yiel) 7 Ran SP% **115.6**
Speed ratings (Par 103):102,101,101,99,98 95,93
CSF £24.79 CT £135.45 TOTE £4.30: £2.20, £3.60; EX 36.50.
Owner J A Wynn-Williams **Bred** Highclere Stud Ltd **Trained** Denton, Co Durham
■ Stewards' Enquiry : James Rogers two-day ban: used whip with excessive frequency and from above shoulder height (Jul 4-5)

FOCUS
Just a steady pace for the first half-mile. The race has been rated around the winner and the third.

2869 BALFOUR BEATTY UTILITIES WATERAID MAIDEN AUCTION STKS 5f
7:15 (7:18) (Class 5) 2-Y-O £2,817 (£838; £418; £209) Stalls Centre

Form RPR
1 **Broken Applause (IRE)** 2-8-10 0.......................... TonyHamilton 10 82
(R A Fahey) *uns rdr and rn loose to s: s.i.s: gd hdwy over 1f out: hung lft: styd on strly to ld last 50yds* **11/1**
2 *1 1/2* **Foreign Rhythm (IRE)** 2-8-3 0.......................... DanielleMcCreery(7) 5 77
(N Tinkler) *dwlt: reminders after 1f: hdwy 3f out: led 1f out: hdd and no ex wl ins fnl f* **33/1**
P42 3 *1 1/2* **Look Busy (IRE)**[11] 2526 2-8-1 0.......................... PatrickMathers(3) 1 65
(A Berry) *led tl 1f out: no ex* **7/2**[3]
63 4 *6* **Eastern Romance**[24] 2134 2-8-10 0.......................... J-PGuillambert 6 50
(K A Ryan) *chsd ldrs: hung lft and wknd over 1f out* **11/4**[2]
00 5 *2* **Moonlight Gambler (IRE)**[30] 1963 2-8-9 0.......................... DuranFentiman(3) 8 44
(T D Easterby) *chsd ldrs: wknd over 1f out* **25/1**
32 6 *3* **Miss Firefly**[14] 2447 2-8-10 0.......................... DarryllHolland 4 32
(M R Channon) *chsd ldrs: lost pl over 1f out* **7/4**[1]
0 7 *1/2* **Jafra (IRE)**[18] 2337 2-8-10 0.......................... MichaelJStainton(5) 2 35
(R M Whitaker) *dwlt: sn chsng ldrs: lost pl 3f out* **20/1**
00 8 *7* **Chief Powderface (IRE)**[40] 1713 2-8-9 0.......................... MickyFenton 3 4
(Jedd O'Keeffe) *chsd ldrs: lost pl over 3f out: sn bhd* **50/1**
9 *13* **Madame Rio (IRE)** 2-8-10 0.......................... PatCosgrave 9 —
(K R Burke) *in rr-div: hung lft and lost pl 2f out: sn bhd* **9/1**

64.13 secs (4.01) **Going Correction** +0.40s/f (Good) 9 Ran SP% **117.1**
Speed ratings (Par 93):99,96,94,84,81 76,75,64,43
CSF £311.21 TOTE £12.90: £2.40, £8.60, £1.60; EX 434.60.
Owner Rob Lloyd Racing Limited **Bred** J Hanly **Trained** Musley Bank, N Yorks

FOCUS
An ordinary maiden auction race with the third the best guide to the overall value of the form.

NOTEBOOK
Broken Applause(IRE), a March foal, has size and scope. She dropped her rider going onto the course and ran loose to the start. Very inexperienced, in the end she won going away and this will have taught her plenty. (op 8-1)
Foreign Rhythm(IRE), a leggy March foal, missed the break and had to be put about her job. She came sailing through to take charge but in the end the winner proved much too strong. (op 25-1)
Look Busy(IRE) took them along but on this much slower ground was unable to last out. At least this time she ran in a straight line. (op 6-1 tchd 13-2)
Eastern Romance, third in a Listed event at Beverley, never looked that happy and showing a marked tendency to hang, she dropped right away coming to the final furlong. Official explanation: jockey said filly hung left-handed (op 5-2)
Moonlight Gambler(IRE), well beaten on his first two starts, shaped better and may now be nursery bound. (op 33-1)
Miss Firefly, on the leg and narrow, was dropping back in trip but seemed unsuited by the rain-soaked ground. Official explanation: jockey said filly was unsuited by the heavy ground (op 9-4 tchd 5-2 in a place)
Madame Rio(IRE) Official explanation: jockey said filly was unsuited by the heavy ground

2870 TELEWARE WATERAID RACEDAY FILLIES' H'CAP 6f
7:45 (7:47) (Class 5) (0-75,74) 3-Y-0+ £2,817 (£838; £418; £209) Stalls Centre

Form RPR
0530 1 **Misphire**[4] 2744 4-9-11 **71**..............(p) DarryllHolland 7 82
(M Dods) *in rr: effrt on wd outside 2f out: hrd rdn and styd on to ld nr fin* **10/1**
2314 2 *1 1/4* **Katie Boo (IRE)**[5] 2712 5-8-8 **57**.......................... PatrickMathers(3) 13 65
(A Berry) *mid-div: hdwy over 2f out: led over 1f out: hrd rdn: hdd and no ex wl ins fnl f* **5/2**[1]
4602 3 *1 3/4* **Mugeba**[9] 2608 6-8-9 **55** oh1..............(t) MickyFenton 1 57
(Miss Gay Kelleway) *s.i.s: hdwy over 2f out: upsides over 1f out: kpt on same pce* **8/1**
6502 4 *3* **Riquewihr**[7] 2657 7-9-5 **65**.......................... TonyHamilton 12 58
(J S Wainwright) *chsd ldrs: one pce fnl 2f* **5/1**[2]
6042 5 *2* **Jilly Why (IRE)**[11] 2529 6-9-0 **67**..............(b) JohnCavanagh(7) 14 54
(Paul Green) *w ldr: led over 2f out tl over 1f out: sn wknd* **7/1**[3]
0601 6 *1* **Limonia (GER)**[7] 2657 5-8-2 **55** oh3.......................... ThomasO'Brien(7) 8 39
(Mike Murphy) *led after 1f: hdd over 2f out: wknd over 1f out* **8/1**
36- 7 *2* **Joyeaux**[204] 6664 5-8-11 **60**.......................... DuranFentiman(3) 11 38
(J Hetherton) *mid-div: kpt on fnl 2f: nvr a threat* **10/1**
-020 8 *nk* **Choysia**[32] 1914 4-9-6 **66**..............(p) PatCosgrave 9 44
(D W Barker) *taken to r alone far side after 1f: sn chsng ldrs: wknd over 1f out* **8/1**
0000 9 *6* **Princess Arwen**[14] 2472 5-8-2 **55** oh10.......................... SoniaEaton(7) 4 15
(Mrs Barbara Waring) *led 1f: sn lost pl: bhd fnl 3f* **66/1**
24 10 *1/2* **Lady Aspen (IRE)**[7] 2657 4-9-5 **65**.......................... TPO'Shea 10 23
(Ian Williams) *sn outpcd and in rr: bhd fnl 2f* **8/1**

1m 17.76s (3.87) **Going Correction** +0.40s/f (Good)
WFA 3 from 4yo+ 7lb 10 Ran SP% **121.9**
Speed ratings (Par 100):96,94,92,88,85 84,81,80,72,72
CSF £36.90 CT £225.88 TOTE £10.40: £2.70, £1.30, £3.00; EX 47.00.
Owner The Cresswell Partnership **Bred** P T Tellwright **Trained** Denton, Co Durham
■ Stewards' Enquiry : Patrick Mathers five-day ban: used whip with excessive force and frequency (Jul 4--8)

FOCUS
Ordinary form with the first two running to their pre-race marks. A number of these failed to handle the conditions.
Misphire Official explanation: trainer said, regarding apparent improvement in form, that the filly was an inconsistent sort who was suited by a change of tactics.

2871 MWH WATERAID H'CAP 1m 30y
8:15 (8:16) (Class 3) (0-90,85) 3-Y-0+ £9,715 (£2,890; £1,444; £721) Stalls Low

Form RPR
2410 1 **Moody Tunes**[14] 2446 4-9-11 **83**.......................... PatCosgrave 1 91
(K R Burke) *chsd ldrs: styd on to ld jst ins fnl f: edgd rt: rdn rt out* **11/2**[2]
20 2 *1* **Vacation (IRE)**[38] 1767 4-9-13 **85**.......................... J-PGuillambert 8 91
(V Smith) *hmpd s: hld up in rr: stdy hdwy on outside over 2f out: hung lft: no ex ins fnl f* **15/2**[3]
0-50 3 *3/4* **Vicious Warrior**[17] 2374 8-9-11 **83**.......................... DeanMcKeown 4 87
(R M Whitaker) *chsd ldrs: effrt on ins to ld 2f out: hdd jst ins fnl f: no ex* **8/1**
-000 4 *4* **Campo Bueno (FR)**[11] 2528 5-8-9 **70**..............(b) PatrickMathers(3) 13 65
(A Berry) *hld up in rr: effrt over 3f out: kpt on fnl 2f: nvr rchd ldrs* **12/1**
-615 5 *nk* **Flighty Fellow (IRE)**[28] 2038 7-8-9 **70**..............(b) DuranFentiman(3) 3 64
(T D Easterby) *chsd ldrs: upsides 2f out: wknd appr fnl f* **9/1**
0-00 6 *3* **Advancement**[10] 2550 4-8-8 **66** oh1.......................... TonyHamilton 12 53
(R A Fahey) *in rr-div: effrt 4f out: wandered: nvr nr ldrs* **14/1**
13-5 7 *1 1/2* **Wheels In Motion (IRE)**[38] 1773 3-8-13 **81**.......................... MickyFenton 6 65
(T P Tate) *wnt rt s: led: t.k.h: hung rt and hdd 2f out: sn wknd* **3/1**[1]
0334 8 *6* **Emerald Bay (IRE)**[14] 2466 5-9-12 **84**.......................... PhillipMakin 5 54
(I Semple) *trckd ldrs: t.k.h: wknd 2f out* **3/1**[1]
5003 9 *2 1/2* **Tous Les Deux**[33] 1905 4-9-1 **73**.......................... TPO'Shea 2 37
(Peter Grayson) *hld up in rr: stdy hdwy on outside over 2f out: lost pl over 1f out* **12/1**

1m 48.16s (2.65) **Going Correction** +0.55s/f (Yiel)
WFA 3 from 4yo+ 10lb 9 Ran SP% **120.3**
Speed ratings (Par 107):108,107,106,102,101 98,97,91,88
CSF £48.27 CT £338.10 TOTE £5.20: £2.30, £2.80, £2.20; EX 55.50.
Owner Geoffrey Hamilton **Bred** Llety Stud **Trained** Middleham Moor, N Yorks

FOCUS
Ordinary form with the underfoot conditions suiting the winner and the third, who set the standard.

NOTEBOOK
Moody Tunes, 6lb higher than Yarmouth, is not easy to predict but this was one of his going days and he responded to strong pressure to come out on top. (tchd 5-1)
Vacation(IRE), in no hurry to join issue under his big weight, came there down the outside but he tended to hang in and was never doing quite enough. (op 7-1 tchd 8-1 in a place)
Vicious Warrior, 2lb lower than his last success, made his effort bang on the inner. After working hard to get his head in front he was edged out inside the last. He is happiest when able to dominate. (op 6-1)
Campo Bueno(FR), slipping right down the ratings, had the ground to suit. Ridden to get the trip, his best efforts in France came when he was allowed to make the running over shorter.
Flighty Fellow(IRE), 4lb higher than Pontefract, had the blinkers on again but he seemed to fold rather tamely. That success was his first for three years and he does not find the winning habit easy. (op 8-1)
Wheels In Motion(IRE), very keen to get on with it, hung away from the fence and dropped out in disappointing fashion. A change of tactics may be called for. (op 7-2 tchd 4-1)
Emerald Bay(IRE), 4lb higher than his last success, was keen to get on with it and his finishing effort had a tame look about it. (op 5-1)

2872 EC HARRIS WATERAID H'CAP 1m 30y
8:45 (8:46) (Class 4) (0-80,78) 3-Y-O £5,181 (£1,541; £770; £384) Stalls Low

Form RPR

3415 1 **Blue Monkey (IRE)**[43] [1634] 3-8-9 **69**.......................... AndrewElliott(3) 7 75
(M L W Bell) *trckd ldr: led on bit 2f out: shkn up 1f out: rdn and styd on wl* **7/2**[1]

1 2 1 1/4 **Champfleurie**[35] [1840] 3-9-5 **76**.......................... DeanMcKeown 4 83+
(G A Swinbank) *hld up wl in tch: hdwy on ins to trck ldrs over 3f out: nt clr run over 2f out tl 1f out: styd on wl* **7/2**[1]

1-60 3 1 1/2 **Spume (IRE)**[38] [1773] 3-9-6 **77**..........................(t) NickyMackay 2 77
(Sir Michael Stoute) *trckd ldrs: nt clr run over 2f out: swtchd rt over 1f out: styd on same pce* **9/2**[2]

3421 4 1/2 **Medici Pearl**[24] [2137] 3-9-1 **75**.......................... DuranFentiman(3) 5 74
(T D Easterby) *trckd ldrs: t.k.h: chal over 1f out: kpt on same pce* **7/1**

35-0 5 3 **Blue Madeira**[35] [1851] 3-9-4 **75**.......................... DarryllHolland 11 67?
(Mrs L Stubbs) *swvd rt s: in rr: sn drvn along: sme hdwy over 2f out: nvr nr ldrs* **15/2**

15 6 1 3/4 **Tutor (IRE)**[54] [1365] 3-9-7 **78**.......................... PaulMulrennan 3 66
(W J Haggas) *led: drvn over 3f out: hdd 2f out: wknd fnl f* **6/1**[3]

0134 7 1 **Snow Dancer (IRE)**[11] [2530] 3-8-10 **70**.......................... PatrickMathers(3) 9 55
(A Berry) *hld up in rr: effrt on outer over 2f out: wknd over 1f out* **8/1**

46-0 8 3 1/2 **Sonar Sound (GER)**[34] [1863] 3-8-9 **66**.......................... MickyFenton 8 43
(T P Tate) *t.k.h: trckd ldrs: lost pl over 1f out* **22/1**

1m 49.59s (4.08) **Going Correction** +0.55s/f (Yiel) **8** Ran SP% **116.6**

Speed ratings (Par 101):101,99,98,97,94 93,92,88

CSF £16.07 CT £56.25 TOTE £5.50: £1.60, £1.40, £2.50; EX 20.70.

Owner J A Barton And R P B Michaelson **Bred** Sweetmans Bloodstock **Trained** Newmarket, Suffolk

FOCUS

A tactical affair in which the form makes some sense at face value. The runner-up looked unlucky and has been rated a narrow winner.

Snow Dancer(IRE) Official explanation: jockey said filly was unsuited by the heavy ground

2873 UNITED UTILITIES WATERAID MAIDEN STKS 1m 30y
9:15 (9:17) (Class 5) 3-Y-O+ £2,817 (£838; £418; £209) Stalls Low

Form RPR

4- 1 **Mutajarred**[239] [6200] 3-9-2 0.......................... PaulMulrennan 7 78
(W J Haggas) *trckd ldrs: effrt over 3f out: carried hd high and led over 1f out: hung lft: drvn clr towards fin* **6/4**[1]

04 2 2 **Montrachet**[10] [2580] 3-8-11 0.......................... DarryllHolland 8 68
(M L W Bell) *chsd ldr: led 2f out: hdd over 1f out: kpt on same pce ins fnl f* **9/1**

3 3 9 **Areyaam (USA)**[15] [2429] 3-8-11 0.......................... NickyMackay 5 48
(L M Cumani) *hld up in midfield: effrt 3f out: kpt on to take modest 3rd nr line* **9/4**[2]

60 4 3/4 **New Year (IRE)**[16] [2393] 3-9-2 0.......................... MickyFenton 2 51
(T P Tate) *led: shkn up over 3f out: hdd over 2f out: wknd appr fnl f* **33/1**

0 5 3 1/2 **Ravenhill Ralph (IRE)**[11] [2542] 3-8-9 0.......................... NeilBrown(7) 13 43
(J G M O'Shea) *swvd bdly rt s: hdwy on outer over 3f out: nvr nr ldrs* **66/1**

2-0 6 9 **Beautiful Reward (FR)**[64] [1127] 3-8-11 0.......................... PhillipMakin 1 17
(J R Fanshawe) *chsd ldrs: drvn over 3f out: lost pl over 2f out* **10/3**[3]

0 7 1 1/4 **Come On Nellie (IRE)**[11] [2541] 3-8-11 0.......................... AdrianTNicholls 3 14
(J G M O'Shea) *in rr: sme hdwy 4f out: sn lost pl* **12/1**

8 3/4 **Pretty Posey** 3-8-4 0.......................... JamieHamblett(7) 9 13
(J G M O'Shea) *dwlt: wnt prom over 4f out: lost pl 3f out* **66/1**

U6 9 4 **Sky Chart (IRE)**[10] [2580] 3-9-2 0.......................... TonyHamilton 14 9
(N J Vaughan) *carried bdly rt s: swtchd lft after s: in rr: bhd fnl 2f* **33/1**

00- 10 2 **Chicamia**[250] [6013] 3-8-11 0.......................... DeanMcKeown 4 —
(M Mullineaux) *sn chsng ldrs: drvn over 4f out: lost pl over 3f out* **50/1**

1m 49.34s (3.83) **Going Correction** +0.55s/f (Yiel)

WFA 3 from 4yo 10lb **10** Ran SP% **122.4**

Speed ratings (Par 103):102,100,91,90,86 77,76,75,71,69

CSF £17.19 TOTE £2.60: £1.20, £2.40, £1.40; EX 17.50 Place 6 £100.16, Place 5 £41.80.

Owner Hamdan Al Maktoum **Bred** Floors Farming & Beckhampton Stables Ltd **Trained** Newmarket, Suffolk

FOCUS

An ordinary maiden and the first two finished some way clear. The exact worth is not easy to assess.

Sky Chart(IRE) Official explanation: jockey said colt hung left-handed

T/Plt: £237.30 to a £1 stake. Pool: £79,108.40. 243.35 winning tickets. T/Qpdt: £15.40 to a £1 stake. Pool: £5,216.60. 250.10 winning tickets. WG

2797 LINGFIELD (L-H)

Saturday, June 23

OFFICIAL GOING: Turf course - good (good to firm in places) changing to good after race 3 (7.00); all weather - standard

Wind: Moderate, half-behind Weather: showers

2874 PLATINUM ABBA LIVE AT LINGFIELDPARK.CO.UK (S) STKS 1m 4f (P)
5:55 (6:00) (Class 6) 3-Y-O+ £2,047 (£604; £302) Stalls Low

Form RPR

0552 1 **Treetops Hotel (IRE)**[12] [2511] 8-9-8 56.......................... RichardSmith 3 55
(B R Johnson) *s.i.s: sn in tch: hdwy over 3f out: led 2f out: rdn out* **6/4**[2]

0502 2 1 1/4 **Hathaal (IRE)**[85] [829] 8-9-8 77..........................(vt) EdwardCreighton 6 53
(E J Creighton) *hld up: hdwy over 4f out: led over 3f out: hdd 2f out: kpt on but no imp on wnr fnl f* **5/4**[1]

3 2 1/2 **Oscar Ireland (IRE)**[59] 6-9-8 0.......................... GeorgeBaker 5 49
(R M Beckett) *v.s.a: in rr: rdn 4f out: hdwy and kpt on one pce ins fnl 2f* **17/2**[3]

40-0 4 3/4 **Lady Korrianda**[118] [558] 6-9-3 42.......................... AlanDaly 7 43
(R Curtis) *trckd ldr to 3f out: rdn and one pce after* **25/1**

03/5 5 11 **Almavara (USA)**[11] [2544] 5-9-8 70..........................(b[1]) StephenCarson 1 30
(C P Morlock) *broke wl: sn hdd: rdn 5f out: wknd 3f out* **9/1**

0260 6 5 **Shannon Arms (USA)**[21] [2258] 6-9-3 48.......................... KevinGhunowa(5) 8 22
(R Brotherton) *sn led: hdd over 3f out: wknd qckly* **12/1**

2m 35.06s (0.67) **Going Correction** -0.025s/f (Stan)

WFA 3 from 5yo+ 14lb **6** Ran SP% **116.5**

Speed ratings (Par 101):96,95,93,93,85 82

CSF £3.95 TOTE £2.60: £1.20, £1.50; EX 3.50.There was no bid for the winner.

Owner Tann Racing **Bred** Miss Jill Finegan **Trained** Ashtead, Surrey

■ Barney's Dancer was withdrawn (12/1, bolted on way to start.) R4 applies, deduct 5p in the £. New market formed.

FOCUS

A moderate contest, even by selling standards, and the proximity of the fourth limits the form.

Oscar Ireland(IRE) Official explanation: jockey said gelding missed the break

2875 BANJO FURNITURE SERVICES H'CAP 1m 2f (P)
6:30 (6:30) (Class 6) (0-60,59) 4-Y-O+ £2,047 (£604; £302) Stalls Low

Form RPR

0-66 1 **Ile Michel**[15] [2423] 10-8-7 **53**.......................... WilliamBuick(5) 9 64
(Lady Herries) *w.w in mid-div: smooth hdwy to ld 2f out: sn clr: comf* **13/2**

-000 2 3 1/2 **Bowl Of Cherries**[7] [2667] 4-8-12 **53**..........................(v[1]) JamesDoyle 3 57
(I A Wood) *chsd ldrs to 3f out: kpt on but no ch w wnr fr over 1f out* **11/1**

0-00 3 1 **Bouzouki (USA)**[11] [2544] 4-9-0 **55**.......................... ChrisCatlin 2 57
(Karen George) *bhd: rdn over 3f out: hdwy over 2f out: styd on: nvr nrr* **33/1**

2050 4 2 1/2 **Ciccone**[133] [426] 4-9-2 **57**..........................(p) FergusSweeney 10 55
(G L Moore) *mid-div: rdn over 3f out: styd on ins fnl 2f* **8/1**

36-0 5 3 1/2 **The Iron Giant (IRE)**[24] [2141] 5-8-6 **50**..........(v[1]) RichardKingscote(3) 12 41
(B G Powell) *led for 1f and again over 4f out: hdd 2f out: wknd fnl f* **14/1**

-244 6 4 **Piano Man**[20] [2275] 5-9-2 **57**.......................... GeorgeBaker 13 40
(B G Powell) *s.i.s: bhd: effrt over 3f out: wknd over 1f out* **7/2**[1]

3631 7 2 1/2 **Kinsman (IRE)**[64] [1119] 10-8-7 **48**..........................(p) EdwardCreighton 5 27
(T D McCarthy) *mid-div: rdn over 3f out: sn btn* **20/1**

24/0 8 1 1/4 **Captain Marryat**[18] [2332] 6-8-11 **52**.......................... RobertMiles 6 28
(J Akehurst) *a bhd* **14/1**

0000 9 8 **Marbaa (IRE)**[22] [2214] 4-9-4 **59**.......................... JohnEgan 4 20
(S Dow) *in tch tl rdn and wknd over 2f out* **5/1**[2]

0160 10 nk **El Capitan (FR)**[10] [2582] 4-9-0 **55**.......................... NCallan 8 16
(Miss Gay Kelleway) *mid-div: rdn over 3f out: wknd over 1f out* **6/1**[3]

0031 11 13 **Danceinthevalley (IRE)**[10] [2557] 5-9-0 **55**.......................... AlanDaly 14 —
(D K Ivory) *trckd ldr: rdn over 4f out: sn wknd* **8/1**

0-65 12 33 **Twinned (IRE)**[148] [254] 4-8-9 **50**.......................... LPKeniry 1 —
(M J Wilkinson) *led after 1f: hdd over 4f out: wknd qckly* **33/1**

2m 6.28s (-1.51) **Going Correction** -0.025s/f (Stan) **12** Ran SP% **121.0**

Speed ratings (Par 101):105,102,101,99,96 93,91,90,84,83 73,46

CSF £76.01 CT £2193.79 TOTE £8.20: £2.80, £3.40, £12.90; EX 109.30.

Owner Lady Herries **Bred** Hascombe & Valiant Studs **Trained** Patching, W Sussex

FOCUS

A moderate handicap and the form is difficult to be confident about with few of the principals in form.

Piano Man Official explanation: jockey said gelding would not face the kickback

El Capitan(FR) Official explanation: jockey said gelding lost its action

Twinned(IRE) Official explanation: jockey said gelding ran too free

2876 DAVIDSON GREEN PARTNERSHIP MAIDEN AUCTION STKS 7f
7:00 (7:04) (Class 5) 2-Y-O £2,817 (£838; £418; £209) Stalls High

Form RPR

5 1 **Distant Charm (IRE)**[11] [2539] 2-8-13 0.......................... RichardHughes 12 70
(R Hannon) *led tl 3f out: styd cl up: rdn to ld 1f out: drvn out* **5/2**[1]

04 2 3/4 **Ruby Delta**[16] [2398] 2-8-9 0.......................... FergusSweeney 10 64
(P D Cundell) *chsd ldrs: kpt on same pce fnl f* **4/1**[3]

0 3 3 **Kintyre Lass (IRE)**[13] [2488] 2-8-6 0 ow1.......................... StephenCarson 11 54
(B R Millman) *w ldrs: led 3f out: rdn wl over 1f out: hdd 1f out: wknd ins fnl f* **40/1**

0 4 1 **Smith Esquire (USA)**[24] [2147] 2-8-11 0.......................... AdamKirby 2 56
(W R Swinburn) *in tch: hdwy 3f out: ev ch 2f out: rdn and wknd over 1f out* **18/1**

4 5 1/2 **Feasible**[14] [2447] 2-8-13 0.......................... FrankieMcDonald 3 57+
(J G Portman) *bhd: rdn 3f out: styd on over 1f out: nt rch ldrs* **10/1**

0 6 nk **Highland Homestead**[10] [2575] 2-8-9 0.......................... JHBowman 16 52+
(B R Millman) *s.i.s: bmpd rival after 1f: swtchd lft 3f out: kpt on fnl f: nt trble ldrs* **7/2**[2]

7 2 1/2 **Dancer's Legacy** 2-8-12 0.......................... KDarley 17 49
(E A L Dunlop) *s.i.s: bhd: rdn over 3f out: n.d* **10/1**

04 8 nk **Blandys Wood**[14] [2443] 2-8-4 0.......................... EdwardCreighton 1 40
(M R Channon) *in tch on outer: rdn over 2f out: sn wknd* **10/1**

5 9 1 1/2 **Sarah Park (IRE)**[10] [2569] 2-8-1 0.......................... KMay(7) 4 40
(B J Meehan) *racd in midfield on outer: rdn 3f out: sn no ch* **14/1**

0 10 3 1/2 **Tintorero**[39] [1743] 2-9-0 0.......................... NCallan 7 38
(M J Wallace) *t.k.h: hld up in tch: rdn over 2f out: sn wknd* **16/1**

0 11 1 1/4 **Honest Yankee (USA)**[10] [2569] 2-8-12 0.......................... LPKeniry 6 32
(Mrs L C Jewell) *a bhd: rdn over 3f out: sn wl bhd* **50/1**

0 12 shd **Lord's Bidding**[16] [2398] 2-8-12 0.......................... AmirQuinn 13 32
(R Ingram) *in tch: rdn over 3f out: no ch last 2f* **40/1**

13 1 **Air Chief** 2-9-1 0.......................... JimmyQuinn 5 33
(H J L Dunlop) *dwlt: a bhd: no ch last 3f* **33/1**

14 nk **Randama Bay (IRE)** 2-8-6 0.......................... TolleyDean(5) 9 28
(I A Wood) *in tch in midfield: rdn wl over 2f out: sn wknd* **66/1**

15 2 1/2 **It's Josr** 2-8-11 0.......................... JamesDoyle 18 22
(I A Wood) *s.i.s: hmpd after 1f: nvr on terms* **33/1**

0 16 5 **Rannoch**[45] [1586] 2-8-4 0.......................... BradleyRoper(7) 14 9
(Miss D A McHale) *s.i.s: t.k.h: sn chsng ldrs: rdn and wknd qckly over 2f out: t.o* **50/1**

17 11 **Llab Nala** 2-8-11 0.......................... ChrisCatlin 8 —
(M R Channon) *prom tl 1/2-way: sn wknd: t.o* **10/1**

1m 26.48s (2.27) **Going Correction** +0.125s/f (Good) **17** Ran SP% **141.1**

Speed ratings (Par 93):92,91,87,86,86 85,82,82,80,76 75,75,74,73,70 65,52

CSF £13.77 TOTE £3.30: £1.90, £2.30, £17.10; EX 20.60.

Owner A J Ilsley **Bred** Frank Prendergast **Trained** East Everleigh, Wilts

FOCUS

Plenty of runners, but this looked like just a modest maiden. They raced stands' side and a high draw was no disadvantage.

NOTEBOOK

Distant Charm(IRE) confirmed the promise he showed over 6f on his debut at Salisbury with a ready success. This was a weak race, despite the numbers, but he is open to improvement. (op 7-2)

Ruby Delta shaped quite well when dropped back to 5f at Sandown on his previous start, but he showed himself just as effective over this longer trip with a solid effort in defeat. (op 15-2)

Kintyre Lass(IRE) was no match for the front two, but she still improved significantly on the form she showed over an extended 5f at Bath first time up and is clearly going the right way.

Smith Esquire(USA) was far from ideally drawn, but he stepped up a fair bit on the form he showed when down the field over 6f on Fibresand on his debut and could find his level during the nursery season later in the year. (op 16-1)

Feasible was not ideally drawn in stall three and he failed to build on the form he showed on his debut at Goodwood. (op 11-1)

Highland Homestead hampered It's Josr after a furlong when trying to grab the stands' rail and lost his position when short of room himself not long after. He ultimately failed to get in a blow, but is better than he showed. (op 9-2)

Lord's Bidding Official explanation: jockey said colt ran green
It's Josr, a 8,000gns half-brother to multiple sprint winner Tartatartufata, out of a dual 7f scorer, was badly hampered after about a furlong and should be capable of a lot better.

2877 CGG VERITAS H'CAP 7f 140y
7:30 (7:33) (Class 5) (0-75,74) 3-Y-O+ **£2,817** (£838; £418; £209) **Stalls** Centre

Form RPR
33-4 **1** **Kasumi**^{42} [1666] 4-9-9 **74**.. TravisBlock(5) 1 83
(H Morrison) *in tch on outer: hdwy to chse ldr wl over 2f out: rdn to ld 1f out: drvn out* **7/1**
-000 **2** *3/4* **Life's A Whirl**^{42} [1673] 5-8-9 **55** oh10................................(p) DMylonas 12 62
(Mrs C A Dunnett) *chsd ldr tl led after 1f: rdn over 2f out: hdd 1f out: kpt on same pce* **66/1**
0016 **3** *1/2* **Glencalvie (IRE)**^{17} [2358] 6-9-13 **73**.........................(v) RichardHughes 15 79
(J Akehurst) *led for 1f: chsd ldr tl wl over 2f out: rdn and outpcd wl over 1f out: kpt on again u.p ins fnl f* **7/1**
-004 **4** *2* **Border Edge**^{10} [2568] 9-8-13 **62**..............................(b) MarcHalford(3) 14 63
(J J Bridger) *s.i.s: bhd: rdn over 3f out: styd on u.p last 2f: nrst fin* **20/1**
3513 **5** *3 1/2* **Takitwo**^{6} [2689] 4-9-4 **64**.. NCallan 3 56
(P D Cundell) *hld up wl bhd: hdwy and rdn wl over 2f out: no imp fnl f* **4/1**^{1}
1636 **6** *1 1/4* **Urban Warrior**^{8} [2635] 3-9-3 **73**.. JamesDoyle 7 62
(Mrs Norma Pook) *in tch in midfield: rdn over 3f out: kpt on u.p fnl f: nt trble ldrs* **14/1**
3341 **7** *3/4* **Napoletano (GER)**^{7} [2665] 6-8-9 **55**.................................(p) JohnEgan 9 42
(S Dow) *plld hrd: hld up in midfield: rdn and effrt over 2f out: sn btn* **6/1**
0/04 **8** *2 1/2* **Pivotal Era**^{23} [2175] 4-9-6 **66**.. IanMongan 11 47
(C F Wall) *trckd ldrs: rdn over 2f out: sn btn* **9/2**^{2}
5600 **9** *hd* **Seldemosa**^{17} [2358] 6-8-4 **55** oh10.................................. LukeMorris(5) 8 35
(M S Saunders) *t.k.h: chsd ldrs: rdn wl over 2f out: wknd wl over 1f out* **66/1**
-005 **10** *nk* **Lincolneurocruiser**^{14} [2458] 5-9-7 **72**......................... ColinHaddon(5) 5 52
(Mrs N Macauley) *hld up in rr: rdn and effrt wl over 2f out: sn no imp* **20/1**
6006 **11** *1 1/2* **Snark (IRE)**^{12} [2514] 4-9-4 **64**......................................(vt^{1}) FergusSweeney 10 40
(P J Makin) *bhd: rdn wl over 3f out: n.d after* **12/1**
-006 **12** *5* **Isphahan**^{37} [1787] 4-9-6 **66**...(p) LPKeniry 6 29
(A M Balding) *hld up towards outer: rdn and hdwy 3f out: wknd over 2f out* **10/1**
00-0 **13** *1/2* **Halfwaytoparadise**^{10} [2556] 4-8-4 **55** oh3...................(p) TolleyDean(5) 4 17
(W G M Turner) *racd on outer: in tch: rdn 4f out: wknd wl over 2f out* **66/1**
2211 **14** *2* **Charlie Delta**^{11} [2540] 4-9-9 **69**..(b) JHBowman 13 26
(J M Bradley) *trckd ldrs on rail: rdn wl over 2f out: sn wknd* **5/1**^{3}
6200 **15** *hd* **Raza Cab (IRE)**^{10} [2573] 5-9-9 **69**.. ChrisCatlin 2 26
(Karen George) *chsd ldrs for 3f: sn rdn and lost pl: no ch last 3f* **20/1**

1m 32.63s (1.17) **Going Correction** +0.125s/f (Good)
WFA 3 from 4yo+ 10lb **15** Ran SP% **136.3**
Speed ratings (Par 103):99,98,97,95,92 91,90,87,87,87 85,80,80,78,78
CSF £454.18 CT £3475.98 TOTE £9.50: £3.40, £12.10, £3.30; EX 684.30.
Owner Viscountess Trenchard **Bred** Fonthill Stud **Trained** East Ilsley, Berks

FOCUS
Just a modest handicap although the winner is generally progressive. The main action took place down the centre of the track.
Charlie Delta Official explanation: trainer said gelding was unsuited by the good ground

2878 LADIES NIGHT JULY 21ST MAIDEN STKS 6f
8:00 (8:03) (Class 5) 3-Y-O+ **£2,817** (£838; £418; £209) **Stalls** High

Form RPR
0 **1** **Pragmatist**^{15} [2428] 3-8-9 0... StephenCarson 8 58
(P Winkworth) *pressed ldr tl led over 3f out: hrd pressed and rdn 2f out: styd on gamely fnl f* **66/1**
5-00 **2** *1* **Make My Dream**^{10} [2576] 4-9-7 50.. JamesDoyle 15 62
(J Gallagher) *chsd ldrs: rdn 3f out: kpt on u.p: wnt 2nd nr fin* **18/1**
0- **3** *hd* **Raglan Copenhagen**^{302} [4781] 3-9-0 0.............................. JHBowman 11 59
(B R Millman) *s.i.s: t.k.h: sn chsng ldrs: ev ch and rdn 2f out: no ex last 100yds* **20/1**
2 **4** *1/2* **Jimmy Styles**^{16} [2393] 3-9-0 0.. KDarley 10 58
(C G Cox) *chsd ldrs: hdwy over 2f out: rdn wl over 1f out: kpt on same pce u.p fnl f* **1/1**^{1}
64- **5** *2* **Caught You Looking**^{229} [6377] 3-8-9 0.............................. AdamKirby 14 47
(W R Swinburn) *bhd: rdn and hdwy 3f out: kpt on fnl f: nt rch ldrs* **12/1**
3 **6** *1 1/4* **Gimme Some Lovin (IRE)**^{14} [2470] 3-8-9 0.................. FergusSweeney 12 43
(D W P Arbuthnot) *bhd: rdn and hdwy 3f out: styd on last 2f: nt rch ldrs* **5/1**^{2}
40-0 **7** *1 1/2* **Batchworth Fleur**^{23} [2175] 4-9-2 42...................................... LPKeniry 7 40
(E A Wheeler) *in tch: rdn wl over 2f out: edgd lft and no imp fnl f* **100/1**
0 **8** *1* **Reigning Monarch (USA)**^{24} [2153] 4-9-0 0............ JemmaMarshall(7) 4 42
(Miss Z C Davison) *racd in midfield off the pce: rdn 3f out: sn struggling* **100/1**
0 **9** *shd* **Confucius Classic (IRE)**^{14} [2470] 3-9-0 0................................ NCallan 5 40
(J R Boyle) *chsd ldrs: rdn wl over 2f out: wknd qckly over 1f out* **25/1**
35-6 **10** *1 1/4* **Path To Glory**^{15} [2415] 3-9-0 50.. IanMongan 9 36
(Mrs L J Mongan) *bhd: rdn 3f out: n.d* **40/1**
0-00 **11** *2 1/2* **Maiden Investor**^{39} [1749] 4-9-2 45.. ChrisCatlin 6 26
(M S Saunders) *led tl over 3f out: sn rdn: wknd over 1f out* **100/1**
6/3 **12** *2 1/2* **Exotic Venture**^{30} [1973] 4-9-2 0.. GeorgeBaker 18 18
(R M Beckett) *a bhd: no ch last 3f* **8/1**^{3}
00 **13** *2* **Egregius Max**^{35} [1838] 3-9-0 0.. JohnEgan 2 15
(C F Wall) *a bhd: no ch last 2f* **40/1**
4- **14** *nk* **Bonne D'Argent (IRE)**^{238} [6215] 3-8-9 0.............................. AmirQuinn 17 9
(J R Boyle) *racd in midfield off the pce: rdn 3f out: nvr on terms* **8/1**^{3}
2200 **15** *1/2* **Bertie Swift**^{52} [1403] 3-8-11 64.. JerryO'Dwyer(3) 16 13
(J Gallagher) *chsd ldrs tl 1/2-way: sn rdn and struggling* **20/1**
60 **16** *16* **Hello Nemo**^{14} [2470] 3-9-0 0.. JimmyQuinn 1 —
(T E Powell) *a bhd: no ch and eased wl over 1f out: t.o* **66/1**
04 **17** *dist* **Tamarack (IRE)**^{14} [2470] 3-9-0 0.................................... RichardHughes 3 —
(W R Muir) *chsd ldrs tl over 3f out: wknd rapidly: virtually p.u last 2f: t.o* **12/1**
0/00 **P** **Romantic Gift**^{52} [1400] 5-9-2 45... DMylonas 13 —
(Mrs C A Dunnett) *bhd: rdn and wkng whn p.u and dismntd 2f out* **66/1**

1m 11.88s (0.21) **Going Correction** +0.125s/f (Good)
WFA 3 from 4yo+ 7lb **18** Ran SP% **135.2**
Speed ratings (Par 103):103,101,101,100,98 96,94,93,92,91 87,84,81,81,80 59,—,—
CSF £1022.77 TOTE £136.50: £22.30, £5.30, £8.10; EX 2857.90.
Owner Mrs Jenny Willment **Bred** Mrs J A M Willment **Trained** Chiddingfold, Surrey

FOCUS
Some of the likelier types failed to run their races and this was a very moderate sprint maiden, limited by the presence of the runner-up. They were spread out all over the track at the line.
Exotic Venture Official explanation: trainer said filly was unsuited by the good ground
Hello Nemo Official explanation: jockey said colt had no more to give
Tamarack(IRE) Official explanation: trainer's rep said gelding failed to handle the rain softened ground

2879 THE GREAT PRETENDER LIVE AT LINGFIELDPARK.CO.UK H'CAP 5f
8:30 (8:34) (Class 5) (0-75,74) 3-Y-O+ **£2,817** (£838; £418; £209) **Stalls** High

Form RPR
4600 **1** **Caustic Wit (IRE)**^{60} [1212] 9-8-10 **57**.............................. FergusSweeney 5 66
(M S Saunders) *taken down early: chsd ldrs: led 2f out: sn rdn: hdd wl ins fnl f: led again on line* **12/1**
0621 **2** *shd* **Thoughtsofstardom**^{3} [2761] 4-8-4 **56** 6ex.................(be) LukeMorris(5) 4 65
(P S McEntee) *trckd ldrs: hdwy to chse wnr over 1f out: rdn to ld wl ins fnl f: hdd on line* **10/1**
6000 **3** *1 1/2* **Malapropism**^{15} [2411] 7-9-4 **65**.. JHBowman 8 69
(M R Channon) *chsd ldrs: rdn and effrt to chse ldng pair over 1f out: no ex last 100yds* **4/1**^{2}
4045 **4** *1 1/4* **Chinalea (IRE)**^{7} [2673] 5-9-5 **66**...(b) KDarley 6 65
(C G Cox) *chsd ldrs: rdn over 2f out: wknd ins fnl f* **11/4**^{1}
00-0 **5** *3/4* **Rare Cross (IRE)**^{15} [2411] 5-9-9 **70**.. ChrisCatlin 3 66
(R A Teal) *led tl 2f out: sn rdn: wknd fnl f* **25/1**
6-31 **6** *3/4* **Safari Mischief**^{15} [2411] 4-9-10 **74**.................................. SaleemGolam(3) 11 68
(P Winkworth) *chsd ldrs: rdn 2f out: wknd over 1f out* **9/2**^{3}
0041 **7** *1 1/2* **Charming Ballet (IRE)**^{7} [2664] 4-9-0 **61**........................(b) JamesDoyle 13 49
(N P Littmoden) *unruly in stalls: a bhd: rdn after 2f: n.d* **5/1**
-605 **8** *1/2* **Calabaza**^{14} [2479] 5-8-11 **58**..(b) AmirQuinn 14 45
(W Jarvis) *hld up in tch: rdn over 2f out: no imp fnl f* **11/2**
-000 **9** *4* **Kennington**^{43} [1640] 7-8-8 **55** oh3.......................................(b) DMylonas 12 27
(Mrs C A Dunnett) *s.i.s: a bhd: rdn and lost tch over 2f out* **14/1**
000 **10** *1 1/4* **Spinetail Rufous (IRE)**^{23} [2191] 9-8-8 **55** oh10............ JimmyQuinn 1 23
(Miss Z C Davison) *stdd s: hld up and bhd: nvr on terms* **50/1**
6-00 **11** *2* **Clipper Hoy**^{17} [2350] 5-8-6 **60**.. KylieManser(7) 9 20
(Mrs H Sweeting) *chsd ldrs: rdn over 2f out: wknd qckly over 1f out* **20/1**

58.35 secs (-0.59) **Going Correction** +0.125s/f (Good) **11** Ran SP% **130.9**
Speed ratings (Par 103):109,108,106,104,103 102,99,98,92,90 87
CSF £137.40 CT £585.10 TOTE £10.90: £2.30, £2.80, £2.20; EX 114.10 Place 6 £10,072.23, Place 5 £9,002.44.
Owner Mrs Sandra Jones **Bred** Gainsborough Stud Management Ltd **Trained** Green Ore, Somerset

FOCUS
A modest handicap, but the winning time was decent for the grade. The form is ordinary with the third the best guide to the level.
Caustic Wit(IRE) Official explanation: trainer said, regarding apparent improvement in form, that the gelding appeared better having been rested.
Charming Ballet(IRE) Official explanation: jockey said gelding became upset in the stalls
T/Plt: £43,580.50 to a £1 stake. Pool: £59,699.35. 0.75 winning tickets. T/Qpdt: £3,276.00 to a £1 stake. Pool: £4,427.05. 0.20 winning tickets. SP

2831

NEWMARKET (JULY) (R-H)
Saturday, June 23

OFFICIAL GOING: Good to soft
Wind: Light, across Weather: Cloudy with sunny spells

2880 PLAY BLACKJACK AT INTERCASINO.CO.UK MAIDEN STKS (DIV I) 1m
1:40 (1:41) (Class 4) 3-Y-O **£4,533** (£1,348; £674; £336) **Stalls** High

Form RPR
053 **1** **Novikov**^{28} [2046] 3-9-3 77.. RobertHavlin 4 88
(J H M Gosden) *a.p: chsd ldr over 5f out: led over 2f out: rdn out* **8/1**
2 *1 1/2* **Pillar Of Hercules (IRE)** 3-9-3 0.. TedDurcan 6 84
(H R A Cecil) *a.p: rdn to chse wnr over 1f out: no imp ins fnl f* **1/1**^{1}
20 **3** *3* **Sister Act**^{10} [2581] 3-8-12 0.. OscarUrbina 5 72
(J R Fanshawe) *chsd ldr over 2f: remained handy: rdn over 1f out: edgd rt and no ex ins fnl f* **4/1**^{2}
4 *1 1/4* **Insiyaabi (USA)** 3-9-3 0.. MartinDwyer 2 74
(J L Dunlop) *hld up: hdwy over 2f out: wknd over 1f out* **14/1**
6-62 **5** *1 1/2* **Saviour Sand (IRE)**^{28} [2046] 3-9-3 78................................ DaneO'Neill 7 71
(D R C Elsworth) *led over 5f: wkng whn nt clr run ins fnl f* **15/2**^{3}
4 **6** *2* **Honest Prospector (USA)**^{15} [2433] 3-9-3 0............. PhilipRobinson 10 66
(Sir Michael Stoute) *prom: rdn over 2f out: wknd over 1f out* **10/1**
0 **7** *nk* **My Spring Rose**^{14} [2477] 3-8-12 0................................ StephenCarson 3 61
(J R Jenkins) *hld up: a in rr* **100/1**
60 **8** *1/2* **Hot Diamond**^{19} [2320] 3-9-3 0.. AntonyProcter 8 65
(D R C Elsworth) *s.s: hld up: hdwy over 2f out: wknd over 1f out* **40/1**
9 *hd* **King Zeal (IRE)** 3-8-10 0.. MJMurphy(7) 9 64
(L M Cumani) *dwlt: hld up: plld hrd: rdn and wknd 2f out* **50/1**

1m 42.68s (2.25) **Going Correction** +0.275s/f (Good) **9** Ran SP% **114.0**
Speed ratings (Par 101):99,97,94,93,91 89,89,88,88
CSF £16.17 TOTE £11.10: £2.10, £1.10, £1.70; EX 26.00.
Owner George Strawbridge **Bred** The Duke Of Devonshire **Trained** Newmarket, Suffolk
■ Stewards' Enquiry : Oscar Urbina one-day ban: careless riding (Jul 4)

FOCUS
A fair first division of the maiden, run at an average pace in a time 0.91 seconds faster than the second. The form looks decent for the time of year and should work out.

2881 PLAY BLACKJACK AT INTERCASINO.CO.UK H'CAP 7f
2:10 (2:12) (Class 4) (0-85,83) 3-Y-O **£6,477** (£1,927; £963; £481) **Stalls** High

Form RPR
4-06 **1** **Steam Cuisine**^{21} [2243] 3-8-12 **77**.................................... JerryO'Dwyer(3) 4 90+
(M G Quinlan) *rdr lost iron sn after s: hld up: hdwy over 1f out: rdn to ld ins fnl f: r.o wl* **33/1**
0-11 **2** *2 1/2* **Zaahid (IRE)**^{16} [2400] 3-9-7 **83**.. MartinDwyer 8 89
(B W Hills) *chsd ldrs: led over 2f out: rdn over 1f out: edgd lft and hdd ins fnl f: styd on same pce* **5/2**^{1}
3114 **3** *1 1/4* **Kyle (IRE)**^{16} [2400] 3-9-7 **83**.. PatDobbs 5 86
(R Hannon) *mid-div: hdwy and n.m.r over 2f out: rdn over 1f out: nt clr run ins fnl f: styd on same pce* **10/1**^{3}
0-43 **4** *1/2* **Goodbye**^{24} [2137] 3-8-10 **72**.. PhilipRobinson 10 73+
(G A Swinbank) *hmpd sn after s: hld up: hdwy over 2f out: rdn over 1f out: no ex ins fnl f* **10/1**^{3}
-033 **5** *nk* **Salient**^{22} [2213] 3-9-0 **79**.. RichardKingscote(3) 11 79
(J Akehurst) *s.i.s and hmpd s: hld up: nt clr run and outpcd 1/2-way: nt clr run ent fnl f: r.o towards fin* **10/1**^{3}
1- **6** *hd* **Steady As A Rock (FR)**^{416} [1420] 3-9-5 **81**.......................... OscarUrbina 14 81
(M Johnston) *chsd ldrs: rdn and ev ch over 1f out: hung lft and wknd ins fnl f* **6/1**^{2}

0-35 **7** *1¾* **Okikoki**[28] 2045 3-9-3 **79**........ RichardMullen 13 — 74
(W R Muir) *prom: rdn 1/2-way: styd on same pce appr fnl f* **12/1**

3-10 **8** *nk* **Nadawat (USA)**[44] 1610 3-9-0 **76**........ DaneO'Neill 1 — 70
(J L Dunlop) *hld up: hdwy over 2f out: rdn over 1f out: sn wknd* **14/1**

-556 **9** *2½* **Sunnyside Tom (IRE)**[16] 2395 3-8-12 **74**........(v) TedDurcan 6 — 62
(R A Fahey) *mid-div: rdn over 2f out: wknd over 1f out* **20/1**

1-60 **10** *4* **Cat De Mille (USA)**[8] 2633 3-8-13 **75**........(b[1]) AdrianMcCarthy 7 — 52
(P W Chapple-Hyam) *chsd ldrs over 5f* **20/1**

-064 **11** *1¾* **Lunces Lad (IRE)**[22] 2213 3-9-5 **81**........ DarryllHolland 3 — 53
(M R Channon) *led over 4f: sn edgd rt: wknd over 1f out* **6/1**[2]

0400 **12** *3* **Dora Explora**[16] 2400 3-8-11 **73**........ StephenDonohoe 9 — 37
(P D Evans) *sn outpcd* **50/1**

0-14 **13** *6* **Double Bill (USA)**[10] 2570 3-9-2 **78**........ RobertHavlin 2 — 26
(P F I Cole) *chsd ldrs: rdn over 2f out: wknd over 1f out* **14/1**

3225 **14** *12* **Sheriff's Silk**[30] 1978 3-8-10 **72**........(b) FrancisNorton 12 — —
(B Smart) *wnt rt s: sn pushed along in rr: wknd 1/2-way* **25/1**

1m 27.21s (0.43) **Going Correction** +0.275s/f (Good) **14** Ran SP% **123.7**
Speed ratings (Par 101):108,105,103,103,102 102,100,100,97,92 90,87,80,66
CSF £112.22 CT £948.62 TOTE £45.50: £11.00, £1.50, £2.70; EX 169.90.
Owner Burns Farm Racing **Bred** Burns Farm Stud **Trained** Newmarket, Suffolk
■ Stewards' Enquiry : Pat Dobbs one-day ban: careless riding (Jul 4)

FOCUS
A fair three-year-old handicap. The winner did the job nicely and the form looks sound rated through the runner-up.
Salient Official explanation: jockey said colt was hampered on leaving stalls
Steady As A Rock(FR) Official explanation: jockey said colt hung left

2882 £600 FREE AT INTERCASINO.CO.UK H'CAP — 6f
2:40 (2:45) (Class 4) (0-80,80) 3-Y-O+ **£6,477** (£1,927; £963; £481) **Stalls** High

Form — RPR

-011 **1** **Osiris Way**[22] 2217 5-9-5 **73**........ PhilipRobinson 14 — 89
(P R Chamings) *racd stands' side: mde virtually all: rdn over 1f out: jst hld on* **5/2**[1]

2551 **2** *nk* **Barney McGrew (IRE)**[15] 2427 4-9-10 **78**........ OscarUrbina 9 — 93
(J A R Toller) *racd stands' side: a.p: rdn to chse wnr over 1f out: r.o* **11/2**[2]

2121 **3** *3* **Vegas Boys**[18] 2334 4-9-2 **70**........ BrettDoyle 4 — 76
(M Wigham) *racd stands' side: hld up in tch: rdn over 1f out: styd on same pce* **9/1**

2203 **4** *1* **Mr Cellophane**[24] 2155 4-9-6 **74**........ DarryllHolland 8 — 77
(J R Jenkins) *racd stands' side: hld up: hdwy over 1f out: nt rch ldrs* **14/1**

0-00 **5** *hd* **Capricorn Run (USA)**[32] 1915 4-9-5 **80**........(v[1]) MCGeran(7) 7 — 82
(A J McCabe) *racd stands' side: chsd ldrs: rdn over 1f out: no ex fnl f* **50/1**

1110 **6** *1¼* **Brunelleschi**[16] 2394 4-9-7 **80**........(b) LukeMorris(5) 5 — 79
(P L Gilligan) *racd stands' side: hld up in tch: rdn over 2f out: wknd fnl f* **16/1**

0000 **7** *shd* **Connect**[14] 2440 10-9-5 **78**........(b) PatrickHills(5) 1 — 76
(M H Tompkins) *racd stands' side: hld up: effrt over 1f out: nvr trbld ldrs* **25/1**

0-05 **8** *½* **Roman Quest**[16] 2399 4-9-4 **72**........ RobertHavlin 11 — 69
(H Morrison) *racd stands' side: chsd ldrs over 4f* **9/1**

4524 **9** *¾* **Who's Winning (IRE)**[7] 2655 6-9-9 **80**........ RichardKingscote(3) 2 — 75
(B G Powell) *racd alone far side: spd over 4f* **16/1**

450- **10** *nk* **Starlight Gazer**[238] 6221 4-9-6 **74**........ RichardThomas 10 — 68
(J A Geake) *racd stands' side: chsd ldrs tl rdn and wknd over 1f out* **33/1**

3263 **11** *hd* **Cornus**[4] 2744 5-9-4 **72**........(be) StephenDonohoe 16 — 65
(A J McCabe) *racd stands' side: hld up: rdn over 1f out: n.d* **11/1**

2066 **12** *2* **Guildenstern (IRE)**[11] 2546 5-8-13 **74**........(t) MarkCoumbe(7) 15 — 61
(P L Gilligan) *racd stands' side: mid-div: rdn over 2f out: sn wknd* **25/1**

0034 **13** *2* **Figaro Flyer (IRE)**[19] 2318 4-9-8 **76**........ AmirQuinn 13 — 57
(P Howling) *racd stands' side: hld up: rdn and wknd over 1f out* **25/1**

0003 **14** *nk* **Mine Behind**[6] 2688 7-9-10 **78**........ TedDurcan 12 — 58
(J R Best) *racd stands' side: hld up: hdwy over 2f out: rdn and edgd rt over 1f out: sn wknd* **13/2**[3]

4200 **15** *38* **River Kirov (IRE)**[4] 2744 4-9-12 **80**........ MartinDwyer 6 — —
(P W Chapple-Hyam) *reluctant to s: a t.o* **16/1**

1m 13.68s (0.33) **Going Correction** +0.275s/f (Good) **15** Ran SP% **126.4**
Speed ratings (Par 105):108,107,103,102,102 100,100,99,98,98 97,95,92,92,41
CSF £14.72 CT £116.99 TOTE £3.80: £1.80, £2.60, £2.70; EX 24.70.
Owner Mrs Alexandra J Chandris **Bred** Whitsbury Manor Stud **Trained** Baughurst, Hants

FOCUS
A decent sprint for the class run in a decent time suggesting the form is solid. The first pair came clear and both could rate higher.
Mr Cellophane Official explanation: jockey said gelding jumped awkwardly leaving stalls
River Kirov(IRE) Official explanation: jockey said gelding was slowly away on leaving stalls

2883 INTERCASINO.CO.UK EBF FILLIES' H'CAP — 1m
3:15 (3:16) (Class 4) (0-85,85) 3-Y-O+ **£6,477** (£1,927; £963; £481) **Stalls** High

Form — RPR

416- **1** **Tarteel (USA)**[238] 6217 3-9-3 **84**........ TedDurcan 11 — 97+
(J L Dunlop) *s.i.s: hld up: hdwy over 1f out: rdn to ld and hung rt ins fnl f: r.o* **7/1**

-501 **2** *2½* **Lavenham (IRE)**[14] 2472 4-9-5 **76**........ PatDobbs 2 — 79+
(R Hannon) *hld up: hdwy over 1f out: r.o* **4/1**[2]

216- **3** *nk* **Pearl's Girl**[294] 5024 4-9-4 **78**........ LiamJones(3) 1 — 80
(W J Haggas) *trckd ldr: racd keenly: led 2f out: rdn: edgd rt and hdd ins fnl f: styd on same pce* **10/1**

5231 **4** *½* **Bavarica**[9] 2603 5-8-9 **73**........ AmyBaker(7) 3 — 74
(Miss J Feilden) *chsd ldrs: racd keenly: rdn over 1f out: styd on* **14/1**

3312 **5** *shd* **Indian's Feather (IRE)**[10] 2568 6-9-5 **76**........ RichardMullen 8 — 77
(N Tinkler) *chsd ldrs: rdn over 2f out: styd on* **12/1**

1-0 **6** *nk* **Lady Stardust**[47] 1524 4-9-12 **83**........ OscarUrbina 9 — 83
(J R Fanshawe) *prom: outpcd over 3f out: rdn over 1f out: nt clr run ins fnl f: r.o* **10/1**

1-14 **7** *¾* **Manaal (USA)**[52] 1414 3-8-13 **80**........ MartinDwyer 5 — 76
(Sir Michael Stoute) *led 6f: sn rdn: wknd ins fnl f* **3/1**[1]

12- **8** *1½* **Dream Scheme**[239] 6204 3-9-3 **84**........ DaneO'Neill 4 — 77
(E A L Dunlop) *hld up: hdwy over 2f out: wknd over 1f out* **5/1**[3]

4141 **9** *nk* **Tender The Great (IRE)**[13] 2492 4-9-0 **74**........ RichardKingscote(3) 10 — 68
(B G Powell) *hld up: hdwy over 4f out: rdn over 1f out: wkng whn hmpd ins fnl f* **12/1**

0530 **10** *6* **Adventuress**[25] 2123 4-9-7 **85**........ KMay(7) 7 — 65
(B J Meehan) *hld up in tch: rdn over 3f out: wknd wl over 1f out* **12/1**

1m 41.61s (1.18) **Going Correction** +0.275s/f (Good)
WFA 3 from 4yo+ 10lb **10** Ran SP% **122.1**
Speed ratings (Par 102):105,102,102,101,101 101,100,99,98,92
CSF £36.93 CT £296.38 TOTE £8.40: £2.90, £1.90, £3.50; EX 46.60.
Owner Hamdan Al Maktoum **Bred** Shadwell Farm LLC **Trained** Arundel, W Sussex

FOCUS
A good fillies' handicap for the class, run at a sound pace. The winner should rate higher with the fifth setting the level.
Tender The Great(IRE) Official explanation: jockey said filly was unsuited by the good to soft ground

2884 INTERCASINO.CO.UK H'CAP — 5f
3:50 (3:51) (Class 2) (0-100,92) 3-Y-O
£12,464 (£3,732; £1,866; £934; £466; £234) **Stalls** High

Form — RPR

-011 **1** **Fathom Five (IRE)**[7] 2659 3-9-7 **92**........ PhilipRobinson 7 — 101
(B Smart) *chsd ldr: rdn to ld and hung lft fr 1f out: hdd wl ins fnl f: rallied to ld post* **3/1**[2]

2222 **2** *hd* **Sohraab**[25] 2114 3-8-9 **80**........ RobertHavlin 3 — 90
(H Morrison) *chsd ldrs: rdn to ld ins fnl f: sn hmpd and hdd post* **9/1**

2211 **3** *1¾* **Morinqua (IRE)**[24] 2135 3-9-7 **92**........ MickyFenton 6 — 95
(J G Given) *led: rdn edgd rt and hdd 1f out: unable qckn wl ins fnl f* **5/1**[3]

-050 **4** *1* **Lady Lily (IRE)**[28] 2044 3-8-13 **84**........ TedDurcan 2 — 83
(H R A Cecil) *hld up: rdn over 1f out: nt pce to chal* **14/1**

3000 **5** *2½* **Steelcut**[21] 2234 3-9-0 **85**........ DarryllHolland 4 — 75
(R A Fahey) *hld up: rdn over 1f out: nvr trbld ldrs* **20/1**

5-50 **6** *2* **Top Bid**[36] 1825 3-8-11 **82**........ RichardMullen 10 — 65
(T D Easterby) *chsd ldrs: rdn over 1f out: wknd fnl f* **20/1**

-425 **7** *hd* **Luscivious**[28] 2044 3-9-7 **92**........(b) StephenDonohoe 5 — 74
(A J McCabe) *s.i.s: hld up: effrt over 1f out: wknd ins fnl f* **8/1**

-611 **8** *nk* **Bertoliver**[16] 2399 3-9-4 **89**........ PatDobbs 9 — 70
(D K Ivory) *chsd ldrs: rdn over 1f out: wknd fnl f* **15/2**

10-1 **9** *nk* **Makshoof (IRE)**[42] 1658 3-9-0 **85**........ MartinDwyer 8 — 65
(M A Jarvis) *sn pushed along in mid-div: wknd over 1f out* **5/2**[1]

59.89 secs (0.33) **Going Correction** +0.275s/f (Good) **9** Ran SP% **119.3**
Speed ratings (Par 105):108,107,104,103,99 96,95,95,94
CSF £37.48 CT £153.14 TOTE £11.30: £2.40, £1.70, £1.70; EX 47.80.
Owner Hintlesham Racing **Bred** Eamonn Connolly **Trained** Hambleton, N Yorks
■ Stewards' Enquiry : Philip Robinson three-day ban: improper riding; one-day ban: careless riding (Jul 4-7)
Robert Havlin seven-day ban: improper riding, intentionally struck out with whip (Jul 4-10)

FOCUS
A decent three-year-old sprint handicap and sound form. The front two came clear and first past the post Fathom Five was demoted to second place by the Stewards. However the original result was reinstated following an appeal. The first two riders also fell foul of the Stewards.

NOTEBOOK
Fathom Five(IRE), bidding for the hat-trick from a 7lb higher mark, found the ground had come right for him here and just did enough to emerge on top of his battle with the runner-up. He was deemed by the Stewards to have caused interference to that rival, and was disqualified and placed second. However, his connections appealed successfully against the decision. He proved game when the chips were down and no doubt continues on an upwards curve at present. (tchd 7-2)
Sohraab, a runner-up on his four previous outings, again had to settle for second place as he just came out the worst in his battle with Fathom Five. He was awarded the race in the Stewards' room, as the interference was deemed enough to have cost him victory, only for the original result to be reinstated following an appeal. No doubt he deserves to win again as he has been so very consistent, but how he will cope with a likely hike in the weights now remains to be seen. (tchd 10-1)
Morinqua(IRE), up another 3lb for her Beverley success 24 days previously, showed her customary speed and led the field at a frantic early pace. She could not sustain her effort at the business end on this more taxing surface, but this was still another fine effort and she continues right at the top of her game. (op 9-2)
Lady Lily(IRE), back in trip, showed her best form of the current campaign. She can build on this when returning to suitably faster ground in due course. (op 16-1)
Steelcut posted a more encouraging effort in defeat and has now dropped to a fairer mark again. He looks to really need another furlong now, however. (op 25-1)
Luscivious Official explanation: jockey had no more to give
Makshoof(IRE), raised 6lb for winning nicely on his seasonal bow 42 days previously, was never really going the pace on this drop back to the minimum trip and disappointed. (tchd 9-4 and 11-4)

2885 INTERCASINO.CO.UK MAIDEN STKS — 7f
4:20 (4:23) (Class 4) 2-Y-O **£4,533** (£1,348; £674; £336) **Stalls** High

Form — RPR

0 **1** **Unnefer (FR)**[28] 2041 2-9-3 0........ TedDurcan 4 — 78+
(H R A Cecil) *chsd ldrs: led over 2f out: rdn and edgd rt ins fnl f: r.o* **9/4**[2]

2 *2½* **Mujaadel (USA)** 2-9-3 0........ MartinDwyer 3 — 72
(E A L Dunlop) *a.p: rdn over 2f out: chsd wnr over 1f out: styd on same pce ins fnl f* **8/1**

33 **3** *1¼* **Al Muheer (IRE)**[23] 2183 2-9-3 0........ RichardMullen 7 — 69
(C E Brittain) *chsd ldrs: rdn 1/2-way: styd on same pce fnl f* **2/1**[1]

0 **4** *1¼* **Excape (IRE)**[9] 2600 2-9-3 0........ AntonyProcter 6 — 66
(D R C Elsworth) *s.i.s: hld up: hdwy u.p over 1f out: no imp fnl f* **9/2**[3]

0 **5** *¾* **Titfer (IRE)**[38] 1762 2-9-3 0........ FrancisNorton 5 — 64
(A W Carroll) *led over 5f: wknd over 1f out* **50/1**

6 *1* **Formation (USA)** 2-9-3 0........ DaneO'Neill 2 — 61
(E A L Dunlop) *hld up: rdn over 1f out: n.d* **16/1**

7 *nk* **Timocracy** 2-9-3 0........ DarryllHolland 8 — 60
(M Johnston) *hld up in tch: rdn 1/2-way: wknd over 1f out* **8/1**

8 *5* **Dancing Dik** 2-9-3 0........ OscarUrbina 1 — 48
(Mrs A J Perrett) *s.i.s: sn chsng ldrs: wknd over 1f out* **20/1**

1m 30.0s (3.22) **Going Correction** +0.275s/f (Good) **8** Ran SP% **117.1**
Speed ratings (Par 95):92,89,87,86,85 84,83,78
CSF £21.34 TOTE £3.20: £1.20, £2.60, £1.20; EX 25.60.
Owner Niarchos Family **Bred** S Niarchos **Trained** Newmarket, Suffolk
■ Stewards' Enquiry : Darryll Holland caution: breach of Rule 158, prematurely eased mount

FOCUS
This could prove to be a decent maiden, taking the Listed-placed third as a guide. The winner is value for a bit further.

NOTEBOOK
Unnefer(FR) ◆, eighth in a decent maiden at this venue on his debut four weeks ago, was well backed to get off the mark and duly obliged in taking fashion. The easier ground on this step up in trip proved much to his liking and he could have been called the winner at the 3f marker. His trainer's first two-year-old winner of the season, he now fully deserves his place at a higher level and connections are mulling over a tilt at the Group 2 Superlative Stakes over course and distance next month. (op 11-4 tchd 2-1)
Mujaadel(USA) ◆, a 160,000 bred to get further in time, was always handy and turned in a pleasing debut effort. He was firmly put in his place by the winner, but should come on a bundle for the run and will take some beating next time out. (op 5-1)
Al Muheer(IRE), the National Stakes third, failed to raise his game on this drop in class over a longer trip. It may be that time will tell there was no disgrace in this defeat, however, and he should still find a winning opportunity before too long, perhaps when dropped back to 6f. (op 9-4 tchd 11-4)

Excape(IRE), as had been the case when well backed on debut at Newbury nine days previously, fell out of the gates and was always then playing catch-up. This was still an improved effort, however. (op 5-1)

2886 PLAY BLACKJACK AT INTERCASINO.CO.UK MAIDEN STKS (DIV II) 1m

4:55 (4:55) (Class 4) 3-Y-O **£4,533** (£1,348; £674; £336) **Stalls** High

Form RPR

4 **1** **Held Captive (USA)**[35] [1839] 3-8-12 0 StephenDonohoe 5 80
(E A L Dunlop) *hld up: hdwy over 3f out: rdn to ld 1f out: styd on wl* **5/1**[2]

-022 **2** *6* **Murbek (IRE)**[25] [2118] 3-9-3 82 MartinDwyer 9 72
(M A Jarvis) *led: clr 3f out: rdn and hdd 1f out: wknd ins fnl f* **8/11**[1]

3 *1 1/2* **Andmoreagain (USA)** 3-8-12 0 DarryllHolland 4 63+
(J Noseda) *rn green in rr: hdwy over 1f out: hung lft and no ex ins fnl f* **7/1**

00- **4** *3 1/2* **Sonning Star (IRE)**[254] [5914] 3-9-3 0 TedDurcan 7 60
(D R C Elsworth) *prom: rdn over 2f out: wknd over 1f out* **16/1**

0-0 **5** *7* **Sunburn (IRE)**[14] [2477] 3-9-3 0 PatDobbs 2 44
(Mrs A J Perrett) *hld up: rdn over 2f out: wknd over 1f out* **20/1**

6 *2 1/2* **Shela House** 3-9-3 0 OscarUrbina 8 38
(J R Fanshawe) *hld up: hdwy over 1f out: wknd fnl f* **12/1**

42 **7** *shd* **Zach's Harmoney (USA)**[33] [1904] 3-9-3 0 BrettDoyle 10 38
(B J Meehan) *chsd ldr: rdn over 2f out: wknd over 1f out* **6/1**[3]

0 **8** *58* **With Ease (IRE)**[9] [2606] 3-9-3 0 MickyFenton 1 —
(P W D'Arcy) *chsd ldrs: rdn 1/2-way: wknd over 2f out* **33/1**

1m 43.59s (3.16) **Going Correction** +0.275s/f (Good) **8** Ran SP% **122.6**
Speed ratings (Par 101):95,89,87,84,77 74,74,16
CSF £9.73 TOTE £6.10: £1.50, £1.10, £2.10; EX 9.70.
Owner Gainsborough **Bred** Gainsborough Farm Llc **Trained** Newmarket, Suffolk

FOCUS
A modest winning time for a race of its type, 0.91 seconds slower than the first division, and it has been rated the weaker of the pair, with the runner-up the best guide.
With Ease(IRE) Official explanation: jockey said gelding never travelled

2887 PLAY ROULETTE AT INTERCASINO.CO.UK H'CAP 1m 6f 175y

5:30 (5:33) (Class 5) (0-75,74) 4-Y-0+ **£3,886** (£1,156; £577; £288) **Stalls** High

Form RPR

2-10 **1** **Dhehdaah**[37] [1793] 6-9-0 **67** MickyFenton 7 75
(Mrs P Sly) *chsd ldrs: wnt far side ent st: rdn to ld over 1f out: all out* **5/1**[2]

1063 **2** *hd* **Muntami (IRE)**[34] [1668] 6-8-12 **65** StephenDonohoe 11 73
(John A Harris) *hld up: wnt far side ent st: hdwy over 2f out: rdn and ev ch fnl f: styd on* **12/1**

3442 **3** *2* **Apache Fort**[14] [2471] 4-8-8 **61** TedDurcan 10 66
(T Keddy) *hld up: wnt far side ent st: hdwy over 2f out: rdn over 1f out: styd on* **12/1**

5045 **4** *shd* **Rose Bien**[17] [2375] 5-8-8 **61** (p) RichardMullen 2 66
(P J McBride) *hld up: wnt far side ent st: hdwy over 5f out: outpcd 2f out: styd on u.p ins fnl f* **14/1**

/0-0 **5** *3/4* **Screenplay**[15] [2430] 6-8-12 **65** BrettDoyle 6 69
(G L Moore) *chsd ldr tl wnt far side and led that gp ent st: overall ldr 4f out: rdn and hdd over 1f out: no ex* **14/1**

1130 **6** *2 1/2* **Three Boars**[60] [1225] 5-8-13 **66** (b) DaneO'Neill 9 67
(S Gollings) *prom: wnt far side ent st: rdn over 2f out: wknd fnl f* **25/1**

25-1 **7** *1 3/4* **Gallileo Figaro (USA)**[21] [2252] 4-8-12 **68** JerryO'Dwyer(3) 5 66
(N B King) *chsd ldrs: wnt far side ent st: rdn and wknd over 1f out* **8/1**[3]

3556 **8** *nk* **Most Definitely (IRE)**[14] [2471] 7-9-2 **69** SimonWhitworth 1 67
(R M Stronge) *s.i.s: hld up: wnt far side ent st: nt clr run over 2f out: sn rdn: nt trble ldrs* **14/1**

-000 **9** *2 1/2* **Freddy (ARG)**[14] [2471] 8-9-0 **67** (bt) PatDobbs 4 62
(D K Ivory) *led: hdd over 8f out: wnt far side ent st: rdn over 2f out: sn wknd* **50/1**

2213 **10** *29* **Toparudi**[5] [2715] 6-9-1 **68** DarryllHolland 12 25
(M H Tompkins) *s.i.s: hld up: plld hrd: hdwy to ld over 8f out: racd alone in centre ent st: c stands' side over 5f out: hdd 4f out: sn wknd and eased* **5/1**[2]

0134 **11** *1* **Spring Dream (IRE)**[17] [2375] 4-8-13 **66** SamHitchcott 8 22
(M R Channon) *hld up: wnt far side ent st: hdwy over 6f out: wknd 3f out* **16/1**

5112 **12** *26* **Noble Minstrel**[30] [1959] 4-9-7 **74** (t) MartinDwyer 3 —
(S C Williams) *chsd ldrs: wnt far side ent st: wknd over 2f out: eased* **2/1**[1]

3m 17.9s (6.86) **Going Correction** +0.275s/f (Good) **12** Ran SP% **124.9**
Speed ratings (Par 103):92,91,90,90,90 89,88,87,86,71 70,56
CSF £67.64 CT £704.90 TOTE £6.50: £2.30, £4.70, £3.30; EX 83.80 Place 6 £ 31.72, Place 5 £ 25.56.
Owner D Bayliss, T Davies, G Libson & P Sly **Bred** Wickfield Farm Partnership **Trained** Thorney, Cambs

FOCUS
A modest handicap in which the first pair came clear and the form seems sound enough rated around the first three.
Toparudi Official explanation: jockey said gelding ran too free
Noble Minstrel Official explanation: trainer had no explanation for the poor form shown
T/Plt: £27.80 to a £1 stake. Pool: £82,028.70. 2,152.10 winning tickets. T/Qpdt: £11.60 to a £1 stake. Pool: £3,708.30. 235.50 winning tickets. CR

2838 REDCAR (L-H)

Saturday, June 23

OFFICIAL GOING: Soft
Wind: Nil Weather: Thunderstorms

2888 GISBOROUGH HALL HOTEL MAIDEN STKS (DIV I) 7f

1:50 (1:50) (Class 5) 2-Y-O **£2,169** (£645; £322; £161) **Stalls** Centre

Form RPR

5333 **1** **Runswick Bay**[21] [2251] 2-9-3 0 PhillipMakin 12 78
(G M Moore) *trckd ldrs: hdwy to ld 1/2-way: edgd rt 2f out: rdn wl over 1f out: drvn ins fnl f and kpt on wl* **5/2**[1]

40 **2** *hd* **Relinquished**[14] [2457] 2-8-12 0 SebSanders 3 73
(J Noseda) *hld up towards rr: gd hdwy 1/2-way: rdn to chse wnr wl over 1f out: drvn to chal and ev ch ins fnl f: nt qckn nr fin* **3/1**[2]

6 **3** *1/2* **Transmission (IRE)**[23] [2166] 2-9-3 0 TPO'Shea 6 76
(B Smart) *hld up towards rr: hdwy 1/2-way: effrt on outer over 2f out: rdn over 1f out: styd on strly ins fnl f* **4/1**[3]

4 *2 1/2* **Especially (IRE)** 2-8-12 0 J-PGuillambert 11 65+
(M Johnston) *hld up: hdwy to chse wnr over 3f out: rdn 2f out: swtchd lft and drvn wl over 1f out: sn one pce* **7/1**

0 **5** *5* **Marie Camargo**[17] [2364] 2-8-12 0 TonyHamilton 8 53
(R A Fahey) *towards rr: hdwy over 2f out: sn rdn and kpt on appr fnl f: nt rch ldrs* **11/1**

6 **6** *shd* **Cairnbrae**[15] [2432] 2-9-3 0 AdrianTNicholls 4 57
(Miss J A Camacho) *green and sn outpcd in rr: hdwy over 2f out: rdn and in tch whn hung lft wl over 1f out: kpt on same pce* **12/1**

00 **7** *1/2* **Premier Class (IRE)**[11] [2532] 2-9-0 0 MarkLawson(3) 9 56
(J S Wainwright) *led to 1/2-way: sn pushed along: rdn over 2f out and grad wknd* **80/1**

8 *11* **Panamar Besar (IRE)** 2-9-3 0 PaulMulrennan 7 29
(J Howard Johnson) *a towards rr* **12/1**

00 **9** *7* **Woodford**[9] [2604] 2-8-10 0 NSLawes(7) 1 11
(M W Easterby) *chsd ldrs: rdn along 3f out: sn wknd* **100/1**

0 **10** *hd* **Bollin Guil**[34] [1859] 2-9-0 0 DuranFentiman(3) 5 11
(T D Easterby) *midfield: rdn along 3f out: sn wknd* **33/1**

6 **11** *6* **Mujinda**[63] [1156] 2-8-12 0 DeanMernagh 10 —
(M Brittain) *cl up: rdn along 3f out: sn wknd* **50/1**

1m 27.21s (2.31) **Going Correction** +0.175s/f (Good) **11** Ran SP% **116.9**
Speed ratings (Par 93):93,92,92,89,83 83,82,70,62,62 55
CSF £9.81 TOTE £3.70: £1.10, £1.50, £1.70; EX 12.70.
Owner John Lishman **Bred** P D And Mrs Player **Trained** Middleham Moor, N Yorks
■ Stewards' Enquiry : Seb Sanders one-day ban: used whip with excessive frequency without giving filly time to respond (Jul 4)

FOCUS
An ordinary maiden run in a similar time to the second division.

NOTEBOOK
Runswick Bay had shown enough in his previous four starts to suggest a race of this quality was within his ability, and he finally got the job done, appreciating the extra furlong and coping well with the soft underfoot conditions. (op 9-2)
Relinquished, who ran better than her finishing position suggests at Lingfield last time, handled the easier ground well and was only narrowly denied. She has the ability to win a little race and will soon have the option of nurseries. (op 15-8 tchd 10-3)
Transmission(IRE), who is by Galileo and shaped as though he would be suited by this extra furlong on his debut at Ayr, stayed on well late and will get a mile in time. After one more run he will be eligible to run in nurseries. (op 9-2)
Especially(IRE), a half-sister to Esquire, a 7f winner at two, is out of a champion two-year-old filly in Argentina. She shaped alright on her debut, will improve for the experience, and will be suited by quicker ground. (op 13-2)
Marie Camargo is a half-sister to Anna Pavlova, a smart performer over 1m4f, but there is a bit more speed on the sire side of her pedigree. (op 9-1)

2889 GISBOROUGH HALL HOTEL MAIDEN STKS (DIV II) 7f

2:20 (2:20) (Class 5) 2-Y-O **£2,169** (£645; £322; £161) **Stalls** Centre

Form RPR

36 **1** **Borasco (USA)**[11] [2532] 2-8-12 0 PhillipMakin 6 74+
(T D Barron) *mde all: pushed clr 2f out: rdn ins fnl f and kpt on* **11/1**

64 **2** *1 1/4* **Dream Express (IRE)**[23] [2166] 2-9-3 0 PaulMulrennan 4 76
(M Dods) *prom: chsd wnr 1/2-way: rdn along 2f out: drvn over 1f out: styd on wl fnl f* **3/1**[2]

3 *5* **Phoenix Flight (IRE)** 2-9-3 0 SebSanders 7 63
(Sir Mark Prescott) *midfield and pushed along 1/2-way: hdwy 2f out: kpt on fnl f: nrst fin* **7/4**[1]

5 **4** *1 1/2* **Madison Heights (IRE)**[30] [1963] 2-9-3 0 TPO'Shea 5 60
(J Howard Johnson) *chsd wnr: pushed along 1/2-way: rdn over 2f out: drvn wl over 1f out and sn one pce* **17/2**

53 **5** *1 1/2* **Gulf Coast**[34] [1859] 2-9-3 0 J-PGuillambert 8 56
(M Johnston) *chsd ldrs: rdn along wl over 2f out: sn btn* **4/1**[3]

6 *2* **Elk Trail (IRE)** 2-9-3 0 AdrianTNicholls 11 51
(T P Tate) *sn outpcd and bhd tl sme late hdwy* **28/1**

7 *2 1/2* **Ras Laffan** 2-9-3 0 SilvestreDeSousa 10 45
(E S McMahon) *outpcd and bhd tl hdwy wl over 2f out: rdn and in tch whn hung lft wl over 1f out: no imp after* **16/1**

8 *5* **Ginger Pickle** 2-9-0 0 AndrewElliott(3) 3 32
(J R Weymes) *towards rr: effrt and sme hdwy 3f out: sn rdn along and nvr a factor* **33/1**

00 **9** *3/4* **Utrillo's Art (IRE)**[9] [2604] 2-8-5 0 NSLawes(7) 9 25
(M W Easterby) *a towards rr* **100/1**

10 *5* **Stateside (CAN)** 2-8-12 0 TonyHamilton 2 13
(R A Fahey) *sn outpcd and a in rr* **25/1**

11 *12* **Medici Time** 2-9-0 0 DuranFentiman(3) 1 —
(T D Easterby) *sn outpcd and bhd* **33/1**

1m 27.25s (2.35) **Going Correction** +0.175s/f (Good) **11** Ran SP% **120.3**
Speed ratings (Par 93):93,91,85,84,82 80,77,71,70,65 51
CSF £43.44 TOTE £14.80: £3.70, £1.80, £1.10; EX 69.70.
Owner Patrick Toes & R G Toes **Bred** Kidder, Cole & J K & Linda Griggs **Trained** Maunby, N Yorks

FOCUS
Run in a similar time to the first division, this looked another average maiden.

NOTEBOOK
Borasco(USA) appreciated the softer ground and put her experience to good use to make every yard. The form is only modest, but she is entitled to improve further. (op 9-1)
Dream Express(IRE), whose stable is in cracking form at present, has been crying out for this extra furlong and duly improved for it. He finished well clear of the rest and is now eligible to run in nurseries. (op 7-2 tchd 11-4)
Phoenix Flight(IRE), a 110,000euros purchase, is a half-brother to Grey Plover, a winner over 1m4f at three, and Lady Songbird, a 1m4f winner at four. Entered in the Group 1 National Stakes, he looked to have been found a low-key opening, but he was much too green and shaped as though the experience will do him the world of good. He will improve. (op 15-8 tchd 2-1)
Madison Heights(IRE), who ran with promise on his debut, was not obviously suited by the extra furlong, although the softer ground may have had a lot to do with that. (op 11-1 tchd 8-1)
Gulf Coast may have found the ground too soft. He has not really progressed so far but nurseries might bring about some improvement in form. (op 7-2)

2890 SGW CONSTRUCTION GROUP LTD ABIGAIL H'CAP 1m 6f 19y

3:00 (3:01) (Class 6) (0-60,60) 4-Y-0+ **£1,943** (£578; £288; £144) **Stalls** Low

Form RPR

26-0 **1** **Hi Dancer**[8] [733] 4-8-9 **51** LeeEnstone 14 63
(P C Haslam) *hld up in rr: stdy hdwy 4f out: trckd ldrs over 2f out: rdn to ld over 1f out: styd on wl fnl f* **15/2**[3]

0051 **2** *1 3/4* **Just Waz (USA)**[11] [2537] 5-8-8 **55** MichaelJStainton(5) 6 65
(R M Whitaker) *in tch: hdwy on outer over 3f out: rdn to chse wnr 1f out: drvn and kpt on fnl f* **10/1**

4635 **3** *5* **Let It Be**[15] [2434] 6-9-0 **56** PhillipMakin 9 59
(K G Reveley) *hld up in trr: hdwy on outer over 3f out: rdn to chse ldrs wl over 1f out: sn drvn and kpt on same pce fnl f* **15/2**[3]

0242 **4** *hd* **Qaasi (USA)**[3] [2764] 5-8-6 **55**.................................. PatrickDonaghy(7) 13 58
(M Brittain) *midfield: hdwy 1/2-way: trckd ldrs 4f out: rdn to ld 2f out: drvn and hdd over 1f out: wknd ins fnl f* **7/1**[2]

3623 **5** *½* **Theflyingscottie**[21] [2252] 5-8-5 **47**..............................(v) CatherineGannon 12 49
(D Shaw) *bhd tl hdwy over 2f out: sn rdn and styd on wl appr fnl f: nrst fin* **7/1**[2]

4320 **6** *3* **My Legal Eagle (IRE)**[9] [2595] 13-8-4 **46**.............................. NeilPollard 8 44
(E G Bevan) *hld up: hdwy and in tch over 3f out: rdn along over 2f out and kpt on same pce* **20/1**

4-32 **7** *½* **Generous Jem**[32] [1926] 4-9-4 **60**....................................... SebSanders 10 57
(G G Margarson) *trckd ldrs: hdwy to dispute ld over 2f out and sn rdn: drvn over 1f out and sn wknd* **3/1**[1]

0-00 **8** *12* **Wavertree One Off**[18] [2345] 5-8-4 **46**...........................(p) DeanMernagh 7 26
(J Ryan) *prom: effrt to dispute ld 3f out: sn rdn and wknd wl over 1f out* **80/1**

3-31 **9** *5* **Orchard House (FR)**[18] [2345] 4-8-6 **55**...................(b) GihanArnolda(7) 5 28
(J Jay) *chsd ldrs: rdn along over 3f out and grad wknd* **12/1**

0116 **10** *6* **Vice Admiral**[11] [2531] 4-9-4 **60**.. PaulMulrennan 4 25
(M W Easterby) *led: rdn along 4f out: sn drvn and hdd 3f out: wknd* **7/1**[2]

6-00 **11** *½* **Merchant Bankes**[25] [2106] 4-8-6 **55**................................... JackDean(7) 3 19
(W G M Turner) *stmbld s: a in rr* **25/1**

0060 **12** *3½* **Silent Street**[21] [2252] 4-7-11 **46** oh1...................... DanielleMcCreery(7) 11 5
(K G Reveley) *a in rr* **20/1**

5446 **13** *21* **Squirtle (IRE)**[13] [2493] 4-8-11 **56**................................ DuranFentiman(3) 2 —
(W M Brisbourne) *in tch: effrt to chse ldrs 5f out: rdn along over 3f out and sn btn* **14/1**

6644 **14** *4* **Piccolomini**[18] [2345] 5-8-4 **46** oh1.......................................(b) TPO'Shea 1 —
(E W Tuer) *prom: rdn along 4f out: sn wknd* **33/1**

3m 12.33s (7.31) **Going Correction** +0.55s/f (Yiel) **14** Ran SP% **127.0**
Speed ratings (Par 101):101,100,97,97,96 95,94,87,85,81 81,79,67,65
CSF £79.95 CT £601.03 TOTE £9.40: £2.80, £3.10, £3.00; EX 206.10.
Owner Middleham Park Racing & R Tocher **Bred** Mrs E Roberts **Trained** Middleham Moor, N Yorks
■ Stewards' Enquiry : Danielle McCreery two-day ban: used whip when out of contention (Jul 20-21)

FOCUS
Moderate handicap form. Hi Dancer has improved over hurdles and is entitled to rate at least this high on the Flat. The runner-up was back to his 3yo form.
Qaasi(USA) Official explanation: vet said gelding finished lame right-fore

2891 BETFAIR H'CAP 1m
3:35 (3:35) (Class 2) (0-100,94) 4-Y-0+ **£11,658** (£3,468; £1,733; £865) **Stalls** Centre

Form RPR

61 **1** **European Dream (IRE)**[34] [1860] 4-9-7 **94**.....................(p) PhillipMakin 1 105
(R C Guest) *trckd ldrs: hdwy over 2f out: rdn over 1f out: styd on u.p ins fnl f to ld nr fin* **3/1**[1]

5233 **2** *nk* **Baileborough (IRE)**[26] [2093] 8-9-0 **87**...................... SilvestreDeSousa 4 97
(B Ellison) *in tch on outer: hdwy over 3f out: rdn to ld wl over 1f out: edgd rt and drvn ins fnl f: hdd and no ex nr fin* **6/1**[3]

-033 **3** *5* **Granston (IRE)**[34] [1860] 6-9-0 **87**... SebSanders 6 86
(J D Bethell) *trckd ldrs: hdwy over 2f out: rdn and ev ch wl over 1f out: drvn and one pce ent fnl f* **7/2**[2]

3000 **4** *1¼* **Mezuzah**[34] [1860] 7-8-12 **85**... PaulMulrennan 5 81
(M W Easterby) *prom: effrt 3f out and ev ch tl rdn wl over 1f out and grad wknd* **8/1**

4500 **5** *hd* **Bolodenka (IRE)**[63] [1145] 5-9-6 **93**................................ TonyHamilton 8 88
(R A Fahey) *cl up: led over 3f out: rdn along and hdd wl over 1f out: sn drvn and wknd ent fnl f* **13/2**

0565 **6** *5* **Middlemarch (IRE)**[1] [2842] 7-7-13 **75** oh4............(b) DuranFentiman(3) 3 59
(J S Goldie) *prom: rdn along 3f out: sn wknd* **16/1**

0020 **7** *shd* **Wovoka (IRE)**[16] [2403] 4-8-12 **85**... TPO'Shea 2 68
(M R Channon) *a in rr* **6/1**[3]

5600 **8** *6* **Rain Stops Play (IRE)**[22] [2208] 5-8-5 **78**............................ NeilPollard 7 48
(M Quinn) *led: rdn along and hdd over 3f out: sn wknd* **9/1**

1m 39.57s (1.77) **Going Correction** +0.55s/f (Yiel) **8** Ran SP% **116.1**
Speed ratings (Par 109):111,110,105,104,104 99,99,93
CSF £21.74 CT £65.82 TOTE £3.40: £1.30, £1.60, £1.50; EX 21.60.
Owner You Trotters **Bred** Limetree Stud Ltd **Trained** Brancepeth, Co Durham

FOCUS
A decent handicap run at a proper gallop despite the worsening ground. Another step up from European Dream, with a fine run from Baileborough off a career-high mark, the pair clear.

NOTEBOOK
European Dream(IRE), who just keeps improving, loves to get his toe in, and conditions had very much come in his favour here. He defied a 7lb higher mark than when successful at Ripon, and could well take his chance at Newcastle on Thursday under a penalty, but the Cambridgeshire is the long-term aim. (op 11-4)
Baileborough(IRE), who has been a model of consistency this term, put up another sound effort in defeat. He came clear of the rest but was racing off a 10lb higher mark than when last successful, and is likely to go up another pound or two for this. (op 9-2)
Granston(IRE) has done all his winning on good ground or faster, but he has run well on soft before. Almost four lengths behind European Dream at Ripon last time out, he got beaten a little further this time, despite being 8lb better off at the weights. (op 9-2 tchd 5-1)
Mezuzah had conditions to suit but he has looked held this season off marks in the 80s. (op 10-1 tchd 11-1)
Bolodenka(IRE) ran quite well in Dubai back in February but he has failed to build on that since coming back to Britain. (op 6-1 tchd 7-1)

2892 BETFAIR MOBILE H'CAP 6f
4:10 (4:10) (Class 5) (0-70,70) 3-Y-0 **£2,817** (£838; £418; £209) **Stalls** Centre

Form RPR

6106 **1** **Poppy's Rose**[12] [2515] 3-8-11 **60**.. SebSanders 3 68
(I W McInnes) *cl up: effrt to dispute ld over 2f out: sn rdn: drvn ins fnl f: led and tried to bite rival nr fin* **9/4**[1]

0-66 **2** *hd* **Aussie Blue (IRE)**[22] [2206] 3-7-11 **51** oh3.........(b[1]) NataliaGemelova(5) 2 58
(R M Whitaker) *cl up: led 1/2-way: sn rdn: drvn and edgd rt over 1f out and ins fnl f: hdd and no ex nr fin* **16/1**

050 **3** *5* **Dendor**[19] [2312] 3-8-2 **51**.. CatherineGannon 7 43
(D W Barker) *prom: effrt to dispute ld wl over 2f out and sn rdn: drvn over 1f out and kpt on same pce* **9/1**

3-00 **4** *shd* **Charlie Tipple**[30] [1965] 3-9-2 **68**.................................... DuranFentiman(3) 9 60
(T D Easterby) *sn pushed along in rr: hdwy over 2f out: sn rdn and styd on fnl f: nrst fin* **8/1**

-000 **5** *4* **Prince Rossi (IRE)**[17] [2373] 3-8-8 **60**........................(p) AndrewElliott(3) 1 40
(J D Bethell) *led: rdn along and hdd 1/2-way: drvn and wknd wl over 1f out* **16/1**

5004 **6** *¾* **La Marmotte (IRE)**[22] [2205] 3-8-3 **55**....................... StephaneBreux(3) 10 32
(R E Barr) *chsd ldrs: rdn along 1/2-way: sn drvn and grad wknd* **7/1**

0-03 **7** *shd* **Bond Casino**[47] [1530] 3-8-6 **55**................................... AdrianTNicholls 5 32
(G R Oldroyd) *in tch: pushed along 1/2-way: rdn over 2f out and sn wknd* **11/2**[3]

4415 **8** *12* **Strathmore (IRE)**[17] [2363] 3-9-7 **70**................................ TonyHamilton 8 11
(R A Fahey) *hld up: pushed along 1/2-way: a in rr* **11/4**[2]

1m 14.25s (2.55) **Going Correction** +0.50s/f (Yiel) **8** Ran SP% **118.2**
Speed ratings (Par 99):103,102,96,95,90 89,89,73
CSF £40.92 CT £281.66 TOTE £3.60: £1.30, £2.20, £3.00; EX 46.20.
Owner Mrs Ann Morris **Bred** Mrs A Morris **Trained** Catwick, E Yorks
■ Stewards' Enquiry : Natalia Gemelova two-day ban: careless riding (Jul 4-5); two-day ban: used whip with excessive frequency (Jul 6, 8)

FOCUS
An ordinary handicap which is difficult to rate with the third and fourth having no form this year, although the first two were clear.

2893 SGW CONSTRUCTION GROUP LTD CLAIMING STKS 7f
4:45 (4:45) (Class 5) 3-Y-0+ **£2,817** (£838; £418; £209) **Stalls** Centre

Form RPR

6600 **1** **Petite Mac**[5] [2711] 7-8-6 57.. AndrewElliott(3) 1 53
(N Bycroft) *a.p: led 1/2-way: rdn wl over 1f out: edgd lft ins fnl f: kpt on wl* **13/2**[3]

6-00 **2** *1¾* **World At My Feet**[29] [2008] 5-8-9 42........................... SilvestreDeSousa 5 48
(N Bycroft) *hld up: hdwy wl over 2f out: rdn to chse wnr over 1f out: swtchd rt and drvn ins fnl f: kpt on* **33/1**

24-5 **3** *1¾* **Vanilla Delight (IRE)**[43] [1626] 4-9-6 70.......................... PaulMulrennan 2 54
(J Howard Johnson) *a.p: rdn along 3f out: drvn wl over 1f out and kpt on same pce* **7/2**[2]

0-00 **4** *nk* **Lewis Lloyd (IRE)**[26] [2091] 4-8-10 40..........................(t) MarkLawson(3) 3 46
(R E Barr) *s.i.s and bhd: hdwy on wd outside wl over 2f out: sn rdn along: drvn and kpt on same pce fr wl over 1f out* **50/1**

5-20 **5** *hd* **Zhitomir**[21] [2256] 9-9-1 55... PhillipMakin 6 48
(M Dods) *led: pushed along and hdd 1/2-way: rdn wl over 2f out and kpt on same pce* **7/2**[2]

2500 **6** *3½* **Methusaleh (IRE)**[32] [1933] 4-8-13 54......................... CatherineGannon 8 36
(D Shaw) *nvr bttr than midfield* **12/1**

0005 **7** *1¾* **Filey Buoy**[8] [2619] 5-8-7 43....................................(v) NataliaGemelova(5) 4 31
(R M Whitaker) *chsd ldrs: rdn along 3f out: sn drvn and wknd wl over 1f out* **40/1**

0-30 **8** *½* **Frimley's Matterry**[16] [2390] 7-8-11 47......................... StephaneBreux(3) 7 31
(R E Barr) *a towards rr* **33/1**

6-03 **9** *12* **Amazing King (IRE)**[22] [2200] 3-8-2 61............................... JackDean(7) 12 3
(W G M Turner) *chsd ldrs on outer: rdn along over 2f out and sn wknd* **14/1**

-000 **10** *4* **Jaassey**[15] [2431] 4-9-5 46... LeeEnstone 10 —
(P T Midgley) *a towards rr: bhd fr 1/2-way* **33/1**

-063 **11** *16* **Henry Bernstein (USA)**[11] [2535] 3-8-10 74......................(t) SebSanders 9 —
(H R A Cecil) *chsd ldrs: rdn along wl over 2f out and sn btn: eased* **2/1**[1]

00-0 **12** *12* **Sheriff Star**[29] [1995] 4-8-12 30.. TPO'Shea 11 —
(G P Kelly) *s.i.s: a bhd* **100/1**

1m 28.35s (3.45) **Going Correction** +0.50s/f (Yiel)
WFA 3 from 4yo+ 9lb **12** Ran SP% **119.7**
Speed ratings (Par 103):100,98,96,95,95 91,89,88,75,70 52,38
CSF £209.57 TOTE £10.30: £2.10, £8.70, £1.40; EX 141.60.
Owner Michael Marsh **Bred** T Umpleby **Trained** Brandsby, N Yorks

FOCUS
A poor claimer and moderate form, especially with the favourite running so poorly.
Jaassey Official explanation: trainer said gelding was unsuited by the soft ground
Henry Bernstein(USA) Official explanation: trainer's rep said colt was unsuited by the soft ground

2894 MARKET CROSS JEWELLERS MAIDEN STKS 6f
5:20 (5:22) (Class 5) 3-Y-0+ **£2,817** (£838; £418; £209) **Stalls** Centre

Form RPR

6523 **1** **Silca Elegance**[9] [2606] 3-9-0 73.. TPO'Shea 12 70+
(M R Channon) *hld up in tch: smooth hdwy 1/2-way: led 2 1/2f out: sn clr* **8/13**[1]

-324 **2** *4* **Miss Taboo (IRE)**[28] [2032] 3-8-9 45...................................... LeeEnstone 5 53
(P T Midgley) *in tch: rdn along 1/2-way: hdwy u.p over 1f out: kpt on wl u.p ins fnl f* **7/1**[2]

0 **3** *¾* **Celeb Style (IRE)**[43] [1620] 3-8-9 0.................................... DeanMernagh 1 51
(D Nicholls) *prom: effrt to ld briefly 1/2-way: hdd 2 1/2f out: sn rdn and kpt on same pce* **8/1**[3]

6- **4** *8* **Ardennes (IRE)**[197] [6749] 3-9-0 0...................................(t) NeilPollard 8 32
(M Botti) *s.i.s: hdwy 1/2-way: rdn over 2f out: kpt on u.p appr fnl f: nt rch ldrs* **10/1**

00 **5** *1* **Betteras Bertie**[58] [1259] 4-9-0 0.................................. PatrickDonaghy(7) 9 29
(M Brittain) *s.i.s and bhd: rdn along 1/2-way: sme late hdwy* **50/1**

0 **6** *3* **The Cube**[43] [1635] 3-9-0 0.. PaulMulrennan 2 20
(J Balding) *a in rr* **66/1**

00 **7** *nk* **Western Land**[32] [1913] 3-8-11 0... MarkLawson(3) 11 19
(B Smart) *chsd ldrs: rdn along wl over 2f out and sn wknd* **12/1**

00 **8** *1¾* **Archimage (USA)**[4] [2740] 3-9-0 0.. PhillipMakin 7 14
(T D Barron) *prom to 1/2-way: sn wknd* **14/1**

0 **9** *6* **Summer Gift**[10] [2554] 4-8-10 60 ow1.................................. JamesO'Reilly(7) 6 —
(J O'Reilly) *led to 1/2-way: sn wknd* **25/1**

4000 **10** *8* **Boppys Dream**[25] [2121] 5-9-2 42...............................(b) AdrianTNicholls 10 —
(P T Midgley) *chsd ldrs: rdn along 1/2-way: sn wknd* **33/1**

1m 14.96s (3.26) **Going Correction** +0.50s/f (Yiel)
WFA 3 from 4yo+ 7lb **10** Ran SP% **119.2**
Speed ratings (Par 103):98,92,91,81,79 75,75,72,64,54
CSF £5.44 TOTE £1.50: £1.02, £1.80, £2.80; EX 3.30.
Owner Aldridge Racing Partnership **Bred** G S Shropshire **Trained** West Ilsley, Berks

FOCUS
A weak, uncompetitive maiden with the winner scoring as ratings suggested but the form limited by the runner-up.
Ardennes(IRE) Official explanation: jockey said gelding was unsuited by the soft ground
Boppys Dream Official explanation: jockey said mare lost its action on the soft ground

2895 ARYM FLOWERS BEST DRESSED LADY H'CAP 5f
5:50 (5:51) (Class 6) (0-60,58) 3-Y-0 **£2,047** (£604; £302) **Stalls** Centre

Form RPR

-603 **1** **Baybshambles (IRE)**[26] [2094] 3-8-7 **50**......................... DominicFox(3) 11 54
(R E Barr) *towards rr and rdn along 1/2-way: hdwy wl over 1f out: drvn ent fnl f and styd on wl to ld nr line* **12/1**

2502 **2** *shd* **Moonlight Applause**[19] [2301] 3-8-7 **50**......................... AndrewElliott(3) 3 54
(T D Easterby) *trckd ldrs: hdwy 2f out: rdn to ld ent fnl f: hdd and no ex nr line* **11/4**[1]

2030 **3** 1 1/4 **Rue Soleil**[26] 2094 3-8-12 **55**.. MarkLawson(3) 5 54
(J R Weymes) *prom: effrt 2f out: sn rdn and led wl over 1f out: drvn and hdd ent fnl f: kpt on same pce* **12/1**

5055 **4** nk **Dotty's Daughter**[10] 2560 3-8-8 **48**....................(p) SilvestreDeSousa 8 46
(Mrs A Duffield) *racd wd: towards rr: hdwy 2f out: sn rdn and ch ent fnl f: drvn and kpt on same pce* **6/1**

U-30 **5** 1 1/2 **Fly Time**[28] 2029 3-8-10 **50**.. AdrianTNicholls 4 43
(Mrs L Williamson) *in tch on wd outside: effrt 2f out: sn rdn and ch tl drvn and one pce ent fnl f* **16/1**

-530 **6** 1 **Princess Ileana (IRE)**[12] 2515 3-9-4 **58**....................(v[1]) PaulMulrennan 7 47
(K R Burke) *cl up: rdn 2f out and ev ch tl drvn and one pce appr fnl f* **4/1**[2]

0-06 **7** 10 **Miss Capricorn**[22] 2205 3-8-5 **45**.............................. CatherineGannon 1 —
(K A Ryan) *led: rdn along 2f out: sn drvn and hdd: grad wknd* **14/1**

006- **8** 2 1/2 **By The Edge (IRE)**[298] 4913 3-8-12 **52**.............................. PhillipMakin 9 —
(P D Deegan, Ire) *a towards rr* **6/1**

-000 **9** 3/4 **Esprit De Nuit (IRE)**[51] 1426 3-8-6 **46** ow1....................(b[1]) VHalliday 2 —
(Mrs A Duffield) *prom: rdn along over 2f out: sn wknd* **33/1**

002 **10** 1 **Sharpattack**[26] 2094 3-8-13 **53**....................................(t) NeilPollard 10 —
(M Botti) *a towards rr* **5/1**[3]

61.69 secs (2.99) **Going Correction** +0.50s/f (Yiel) **10** Ran SP% **122.8**
Speed ratings (Par 97):96,95,93,93,90 89,73,69,68,66
CSF £47.58 CT £436.42 TOTE £13.80: £2.90, £1.80, £3.80; EX 47.00 Place 6 £ 69.90, Place 5 £ 56.35.
Owner Miss S Haykin **Bred** Mrs H F Mahr **Trained** Seamer, N Yorks
■ Stewards' Enquiry : Silvestre De Sousa three-day ban: used whip with excessive force and frequency (Jul 4-6)
Dominic Fox caution: used whip with excessive frequency

FOCUS
A weak handicap rated through the runner-up and third to this year's turf form.
Sharpattack Official explanation: vet said gelding returned distressed
T/Plt: £55.50 to a £1 stake. Pool: £49,798.00. 654.95 winning tickets. T/Qpdt: £35.50 to a £1 stake. Pool: £2,462.80. 51.20 winning tickets. JR

2896 - 2902a (Foreign Racing) - See Raceform Interactive

HAMBURG (R-H)
Saturday, June 23

OFFICIAL GOING: Soft

2903a JAXX-POKAL (HAMBURGER MEILE) (GROUP 3) 1m
3:30 (3:33) 3-Y-0+ **£21,622** (£6,757; £3,378; £2,027)

RPR

1 **Konig Turf (GER)**[41] 1699 5-9-2 .... TMundry 6 109
(C Sprengel, Germany) *hld up in 4th on outside: hdwy to ld 1 1/2f out: r.o strly* **3/1**[3]

2 1 **Aspectus (IRE)**[41] 1699 4-9-4 .... ADeVries 3 109
(H Blume, Germany) *hld up in last: swtchd outside over 1f out: r.o to take 2nd last 50yds: nt threaten wnr* **24/10**[2]

3 3/4 **Aviso (GER)**[48] 1516 3-8-8 .... ASuborics 2 108
(J Hirschberger, Germany) *led: set stdy pce: hdd 1 1/2f out: lost 2nd last 50yds* **7/10**[1]

4 1 1/4 **Madresal (GER)**[41] 1699 8-9-2 .... AStarke 1 103
(P Schiergen, Germany) *hld up in 3rd on ins: styd on at one pce fnl 2f* **7/1**

5 5 **Signum (GER)**[37] 1800 4-9-2 .... JiriPalik 5 93
(Frau A Glodde, Germany) *racd in 2nd: rdn to press ldr briefly 2f out: sn wknd* **13/1**

1m 45.3s (105.30)
WFA 3 from 4yo+ 10lb **5** Ran SP% **132.9**
(including 10 Euro stake): WIN 40; PL 18, 20; SF 124.
Owner Stall Route 66 **Bred** Gestut Elsetal **Trained** Germany

2504 PONTEFRACT (L-H)
Sunday, June 24

OFFICIAL GOING: Good to soft (5.5)
After 11/2" of rain over the previous five days the ground was described as 'genuine soft, the grass left longer than usual'.
Wind: Almost nil Weather: Light rain

2904 EBF TOTEPLACEPOT MAIDEN FILLIES' STKS 6f
2:10 (2:13) (Class 5) 2-Y-0 **£4,533** (£1,348; £674; £336) **Stalls** Low

Form RPR

1 **Salingers Star (IRE)** 2-9-0 0.. JimCrowley 9 77
(G A Swinbank) *mid-div: gd hdwy over 1f out: r.o wl to ld last 50yds* **25/1**

32 **2** 1 1/4 **Romantic Destiny**[16] 2432 2-9-0 0.. NCallan 4 73
(K A Ryan) *led tl over 1f out: kpt on wl ins fnl f* **9/2**[2]

3 nk **Tudor Court (IRE)** 2-9-0 0.. JoeFanning 5 75+
(M Johnston) *s.i.s: sn prom: rapid hdwy to ld over 1f out: sn 3 l clr: wknd and hdd wl ins fnl f* **10/1**

4 1 1/4 **Dark Tara** 2-9-0 0.. TonyHamilton 8 68
(R A Fahey) *chsd ldrs: kpt on ins fnl f* **8/1**

3 **5** shd **Threestoneburn (USA)**[29] 2039 2-9-0 0.. LeeEnstone 1 68
(P C Haslam) *chsd ldrs: kpt on same pce fnl 2f* **6/1**[3]

6 1 1/2 **Misplaced Fortune** 2-9-0 0.. TomEaves 2 64
(N Tinkler) *s.i.s: in rr: styd on fnl 2f: nt rch ldrs* **50/1**

7 4 **Lady Calido (USA)** 2-9-0 0.. SebSanders 3 52
(Sir Mark Prescott) *mid-div: sn drvn along: nvr nr ldrs* **9/1**

0 **8** 6 **Frammenti**[10] 2590 2-9-0 0.. StephenDonohoe 13 34
(A J McCabe) *s.s: sn prom on outer: hung rt and lost pl over 2f out* **80/1**

3 **9** 5 **Dea Caelestis (FR)**[30] 2000 2-9-0 0.. TedDurcan 10 19
(H R A Cecil) *w ldrs: lost pl over 2f out* **6/4**[1]

10 nk **Cottam Breeze** 2-9-0 0.. PaulMulrennan 7 18
(M W Easterby) *sn bhd* **50/1**

11 1/2 **Loose Caboose (IRE)** 2-9-0 0.. NeilPollard 6 16
(A J McCabe) *s.s: bhd fnl 2f* **100/1**

0 **12** 4 **Missabeat (IRE)**[18] 2364 2-9-0 0.. KDarley 12 4
(T D Easterby) *chsd ldrs: lost pl over 1f out* **40/1**

0 **13** 29 **Pussycat Bow**[33] 1919 2-9-0 0.. DaleGibson 11 —
(M W Easterby) *w ldrs: lost pl 3f out: sn wl bhd: t.o 2f out: virtually p.u* **50/1**

1m 20.62s (3.22) **Going Correction** +0.45s/f (Yiel) **13** Ran SP% **117.1**
Speed ratings (Par 90):96,94,93,92,92 90,84,76,70,69 69,63,25
CSF £129.66 TOTE £41.80: £7.50, £1.60, £3.40; EX 185.30.
Owner Hokey Cokey Partnership **Bred** G J King **Trained** Melsonby, N Yorks

FOCUS
An average maiden fillies' race rated through the runner-up and the fifth.

NOTEBOOK
Salingers Star(IRE), an April foal, is on the leg and narrow. Picking up ground once in line for home, she stayed on in willing fashion to show ahead near the line. A rare first-time-out two-year-old winner for this yard, she will be even better over 7f. (op 22-1)
Romantic Destiny, the most experienced in the line-up, took them along, only to be mugged near the line. (op 4-1 tchd 5-1)
Tudor Court(IRE) ◆, a May foal, is a half-sister to five winners including Group 1 winner Fly To The Stars. A close-coupled daughter of Cape Cross, after a tardy start she swept round on the outside to take it up once in line for home. She looked to have it in the bag but tied up near the line and was edged out. She showed a really bright turn of foot in the ground and is sure to have learnt plenty, so she looks a ready-made winner. (tchd 11-1)
Dark Tara, an April foal, looks on the immature side. She made a pleasing debut and there should be something better to come given a little more time.
Threestoneburn(USA), never far away, stuck to her task but did not look entirely at home in the soft ground. (op 11-2)
Misplaced Fortune, a leggy April foal, stayed on in good style after a tardy start. This should have taught her plenty. (op 66-1)
Dea Caelestis(FR), who is not that big, continually swished her tail in the paddock. She dropped right away going into the final turn and the soft ground was almost certainly against her. Official explanation: trainer's rep said filly was unsuited by the good to soft ground (op 15-8 tchd 2-1)

2905 TOTECOURSE TO COURSE FILLIES' H'CAP 1m 4y
2:40 (2:41) (Class 5) (0-70,70) 3-Y-0+ **£3,886** (£1,156; £577; £288) **Stalls** Low

Form RPR

-421 **1** **Froissee**[5] 2748 3-9-1 **67** 6ex.. JimmyFortune 2 73+
(N A Callaghan) *hld up towards rr: nt clr run over 2f out: swtchd rt over 1f out: str run to ld last 75yds* **4/6**[1]

0030 **2** 1 1/2 **The Mighty Ogmore**[12] 2538 3-8-2 **54** oh5 ow3......(p) RoystonFfrench 5 57
(R C Guest) *in rr: sn drvn along: gd hdwy over 1f out: styd on wl ins fnl f: tk 2nd nr line* **50/1**

2205 **3** 3/4 **Fortress**[11] 2564 4-9-3 **59**.. KDarley 9 62
(E J Alston) *chsd ldrs: styd on same pce ins fnl f* **14/1**

-510 **4** shd **Society Music (IRE)**[17] 2388 5-10-0 **70**....................(p) PhillipMakin 8 73
(M Dods) *hld up in rr: hdwy over 2f out: hung rt over 1f out: kpt on same pce* **15/2**[3]

3541 **5** 1 1/4 **Gee Ceffyl Bach**[38] 1782 3-8-2 **57**.............................. AndrewElliott(3) 4 55
(John A Harris) *led tl hdd ins fnl f: wknd towards fin* **14/1**

0-40 **6** 1 **Reflective Glory (IRE)**[11] 2552 3-7-6 **51** oh3..(p) DanielleMcCreery(7) 10 47
(J S Wainwright) *chsd ldrs: wknd fnl f* **66/1**

00-0 **7** 3 **Hazelhurst (IRE)**[34] 1892 4-9-11 **67**.............................. TomEaves 6 58
(J Howard Johnson) *hld up in rr: hdwy on ins 2f out: nvr rchd ldrs* **50/1**

0-62 **8** 3 1/2 **Convallaria (FR)**[25] 2154 4-9-6 **62**.............................. SteveDrowne 1 45
(G Wragg) *chsd ldrs: lost pl appr fnl f* **9/1**

00-0 **9** 7 **Ivana Illyich (IRE)**[11] 2554 5-8-9 **51** oh6.............................. TonyHamilton 11 18
(J S Wainwright) *w ldrs: lost pl over 1f out* **80/1**

123 **10** 1/2 **Stolen Glance**[4] 2760 4-9-12 **68**.............................. PaulMulrennan 7 33
(M W Easterby) *chsd ldrs: lost pl over 1f out* **7/1**[2]

2-40 **11** 17 **Princess Palatine (IRE)**[60] 1238 3-8-11 **63**....................(v[1]) NCallan 3 —
(K R Burke) *hld up in rr: hdwy over 3f out: sn rdn: lost pl 2f out: sn bhd: virtually p.u* **28/1**

1m 49.2s (3.50) **Going Correction** +0.45s/f (Yiel)
WFA 3 from 4yo+ 10lb **11** Ran SP% **117.7**
Speed ratings (Par 100):100,98,97,97,96 95,92,88,81,81 64
CSF £63.18 CT £300.71 TOTE £1.50: £1.10, £9.90, £2.50; EX 46.00.
Owner Mrs T A Foreman **Bred** Rosyground Stud **Trained** Newmarket, Suffolk

FOCUS
Ordinary form. The winner is value for further, a seemingly much improved effort from the runner-up who was 8lb 'wrong'.
Convallaria(FR) Official explanation: trainer's rep said filly had a breathing problem

2906 TOTEQUADPOT H'CAP 1m 2f 6y
3:10 (3:10) (Class 3) (0-90,90) 3-Y-0+
£9,348 (£2,799; £1,399; £700; £349; £175) **Stalls** Low

Form RPR

-606 **1** **Dunaskin (IRE)**[39] 1767 7-10-0 **87**....................................(p) RHills 4 100
(Karen McLintock) *mde all: styd on strly ins fnl f* **4/1**[1]

0004 **2** 2 1/2 **Blue Spinnaker (IRE)**[27] 2093 8-9-12 **85**................(b[1]) PaulMulrennan 1 93
(M W Easterby) *trckd wnr: effrt over 1f out: kpt on same pce ins fnl f* **4/1**[1]

-610 **3** 5 **Ballinteni**[37] 1822 5-9-13 **86**.. JimmyFortune 6 84
(D M Simcock) *chsd ldrs: effrt 3f out: kpt on same pce appr fnl f* **9/2**[2]

1155 **4** 3/4 **Fongs Gazelle**[13] 2506 3-8-11 **82**.. KDarley 10 79
(M Johnston) *chsd ldrs: drvn along over 5f out: kpt on same pce fnl 3f* **8/1**

0000 **5** shd **Lucayan Dancer**[35] 1862 7-9-8 **81**.............................. AdrianTNicholls 8 77
(D Nicholls) *chsd ldrs: one pce fnl 2f* **14/1**

-122 **6** 1/2 **Harvest Warrior**[19] 2338 5-9-0 **73**.............................. PhilipRobinson 11 68
(T D Easterby) *in rr: effrt on outside over 4f out: nvr nr ldrs* **13/2**[3]

-110 **7** 1 **William's Way**[18] 2351 5-9-12 **85**.............................. SebSanders 7 78
(I A Wood) *hld up in rr: effrt 2f out: kpt on: nvr nr ldrs* **14/1**

1-60 **8** 3 **Folio (IRE)**[48] 1543 7-10-0 **87**.............................. TedDurcan 9 74
(W J Musson) *hld up in rr: effrt over 2f out: wknd over 1f out* **16/1**

-006 **9** 3 **Krugerrand (USA)**[35] 1862 8-9-10 **83**.............................. NCallan 2 64
(W J Musson) *hld up in mid-div: effrt over 2f out: wknd over 1f out* **9/1**

-000 **10** 13 **Mulaazem**[17] 2397 4-9-0 **73**.............................. DaleGibson 5 28
(J Mackie) *chsd ldrs: drvn over 3f out: rdn and wknd wl over 1f out: sn bhd* **40/1**

2m 15.52s (1.44) **Going Correction** +0.45s/f (Yiel)
WFA 3 from 4yo+ 12lb **10** Ran SP% **114.3**
Speed ratings (Par 107):112,110,106,105,105 104,104,101,99,88
CSF £19.34 CT £73.72 TOTE £5.10: £1.90, £1.80, £2.10; EX 21.90 Trifecta £105.80 Pool: £328.00 - 2.20 winning units..
Owner Equiname Ltd **Bred** J P And Miss M Mangan **Trained** Ingoe, Northumberland

FOCUS
A good winning time for the class of contest. The winner deserves full marks and it was hard to make ground from off the pace. Fair form, the winner rated back to his best.

NOTEBOOK
Dunaskin(IRE), without a win for over two years, was having his first outing at this track. His rider judged the fractions to perfection and, finding another gear, he pulled clear inside the last. (op 11-2)
Blue Spinnaker(IRE), in first-time blinkers, had the winner in his sights and looked nailed on when still on the bridle turning in. When asked to go and win his race the response was limited, and he was very much second best at the line. (op 7-2)
Ballinteni, suited by the soft ground, was dropping back in trip but 5lb higher than Windsor. He had no excuse. (op 7-2 tchd 5-1)

Fongs Gazelle, very warm beforehand, was 7lb higher than her last success when completing a hat-trick at Beverley in May, and she continues to struggle. (tchd 17-2)
Lucayan Dancer, back after a five-week break, looked at his very best and is back on his last winning mark.
Harvest Warrior has run well here in the past but, ridden with one eye on his stamina, in this ground he never really figured. (tchd 6-1)

2907 TOTESPORT PONTEFRACT CASTLE STKS (LISTED RACE) 1m 4f 8y
3:40 (3:41) (Class 1) 4-Y-0+

£19,631 (£7,472; £3,741; £1,869; £934; £469) **Stalls** Low

Form				RPR
-631	**1**		**Ivy Creek (USA)**^{23} [2216] 4-9-4 110 SteveDrowne 6 (G Wragg) *hld up in rr: hdwy 5f out: drvn over 3f out: rdn over 2f out: upsides over 1f out: swvd rt jst ins fnl f: kpt on to ld last 75yds* **9/2**^{3}	115
4/5-	**2**	*1 1/2*	**The Geezer**^{401} [1833] 5-9-1 111 KerrinMcEvoy 7 (Saeed Bin Suroor) *trckd ldr: t.k.h: led after 2f tl wl ins fnl f: no ex* **4/1**^{2}	110
0141	**3**	*3*	**Peppertree Lane (IRE)**^{36} [1833] 4-9-4 105 KDarley 4 (M Johnston) *chsd ldrs: upsides and hung lft over 1f out: styd on same pce* **10/3**^{1}	108
/6-2	**4**	*1*	**Shahin (USA)**^{23} [2216] 4-9-1 109 RHills 3 (M P Tregoning) *hld up: effrt over 3f out: lost pl over 2f out: styd on wl fnl f* **11/2**	104
0-33	**5**	*1 1/4*	**Foxhaven**^{23} [2216] 5-9-4 110 JimCrowley 2 (P R Chamings) *led 2f: chsd ldr: upsides over 1f out: kpt on same pce* **10/1**	105
-052	**6**	*nk*	**Alfie Flits**^{15} [2462] 5-9-4 112 NCallan 5 (G A Swinbank) *t.k.h in midfield: hdwy on ins to chal over 1f out: kpt on same pce* **4/1**^{2}	104
3-32	**7**	*30*	**Camrose**^{37} [1805] 6-9-1 102 (b) JimmyFortune 1 (J L Dunlop) *in rr: drvn over 4f out: lost pl over 2f out: sn bhd and virtually p.u: wl t.o* **16/1**	53

2m 41.92s (1.62) **Going Correction** +0.45s/f (Yiel) 7 Ran SP% **111.6**
Speed ratings (Par 111):112,111,109,108,107 107,87
CSF £21.59 TOTE £5.60: £2.90, £2.80; EX 30.80.
Owner Mollers Racing **Bred** Eleanor Drake Rose Trust Et Al **Trained** Newmarket, Suffolk

FOCUS
A high-class renewal of this Listed race. Five in line over a furlong out and the third is probably the key to the overall value.

NOTEBOOK
Ivy Creek(USA), taken to post early, has presumably had problems with the stalls in the past. The first to come under serious pressure, he veered off a straight line before grabbing the prize near the line. (op 4-1)
The Geezer, having just his third start since finishing runner-up in the 2005 St Leger, has been absent since last year's Yorkshire Cup. Looking very fit and kept away from the running rail, he fought off three serious challengers but was mugged near the line. Basically a stayer, he has lost time to make up for. (op 9-2)
Peppertree Lane(IRE) had a bit to find and in the end the first two were simply too good for him. With him it is a case of the softer the ground the better. (op 4-1 tchd 3-1)
Shahin(USA), who had to have screws in a hind joint, was having just his sixth career start. Narrowly denied by the winner at Goodwood, he dropped right back going into the final turn but really found his stride late on and finished best of all. He is talented but may not be entirely straightforward. (op 9-2)
Foxhaven, closely matched with the winner and Shahin on Goodwood form, had no excuse. (op 12-1 tchd 14-1)
Alfie Flits, who took this a year ago, found this year's renewal much tougher. He is proven in soft ground, but in the end he was simply not up to the task. (op 7-2)
Camrose, without a win for almost two years, was very edgy beforehand and he does not want the ground as soft as this. Even so it was a poor effort. Official explanation: jockey said colt was unsuited by the good to soft ground

2908 TOTEPOOL PONTEFRACT CUP (H'CAP) 2m 1f 216y
4:10 (4:10) (Class 4) (0-85,85) 4-Y-0+ **£6,477** (£1,927; £963; £481) **Stalls** Low

Form				RPR
26-2	**1**		**Thewhirlingdervish (IRE)**^{18} [2375] 9-8-5 **68** ow1 KDarley 7 (T D Easterby) *chsd ldr: chal 6f out: led 4f out: hrd drvn: hld on towards fin* **7/1**^{3}	79
2121	**2**	*3/4*	**Great As Gold (IRE)**^{13} [2505] 8-8-12 **75** TomEaves 9 (B Ellison) *in rr: hdwy and prom 9f out: drvn over 5f out: styd on wl to go 2nd ins fnl f: kpt on wl towards fin* **3/1**^{1}	85
5010	**3**	*2 1/2*	**Kayf Aramis**^{31} [1959] 5-8-6 **72** MarcHalford$^{(3)}$ 1 (J L Spearing) *led tl 4f out: kpt on same pce fnl 2f* **3/1**^{1}	79
0-14	**4**	*3/4*	**Monolith**^{24} [2170] 9-9-5 **85** GregFairley$^{(3)}$ 10 (L Lungo) *chsd ldrs: styd on same pce fnl 2f* **8/1**	91
4050	**5**	*6*	**High Point (IRE)**^{31} [1959] 9-8-6 **69** RoystonFfrench 8 (G P Enright) *sn chsng ldrs: drvn over 4f out: wknd appr fnl f* **14/1**	69
-622	**6**	*1/2*	**Karlani (IRE)**^{27} [2095] 4-8-3 **67** JoeFanning 5 (G A Swinbank) *chsd ldrs: pushed along 10f out: wknd appr fnl f* **9/1**	66
0/54	**7**	*15*	**Turbo (IRE)**^{12} [2531] 8-8-7 **70** (t) PaulMulrennan 2 (M W Easterby) *hld up in last: hdwy on ins over 3f out: sn rdn: lost pl over 1f out: eased ins fnl f* **16/1**	53
54-1	**8**	*34*	**Tribe**^{75} [994] 5-9-3 **80** JimmyFortune 6 (P R Webber) *trckd ldrs: effrt 4f out: wknd 2f out: sn bhd: virtually p.u fnl f: t.o* **9/2**^{2}	25
30/6	**9**	*4*	**Astronomic**^{22} [2245] 7-9-5 **82** TonyHamilton 3 (J Howard Johnson) *hld up in rr: drvn 5f out: lost pl 3f out: sn bhd: virtually p.u fnl f: t.o* **40/1**	23

4m 9.44s (6.44) **Going Correction** +0.45s/f (Yiel)
WFA 4 from 5yo+ 1lb 9 Ran SP% **116.8**
Speed ratings (Par 105):103,102,101,101,98 98,91,76,74
CSF £28.65 CT £77.58 TOTE £6.80: £1.90, £1.50, £1.60; EX 24.20.
Owner Mrs M H Easterby **Bred** Yeomanstown Stud **Trained** Great Habton, N Yorks

FOCUS
A true test in the conditions and the form looks solid.
Tribe Official explanation: jockey said gelding was unsuited by the good to soft ground
Astronomic Official explanation: jockey said gelding had no more to give

2909 TOTEEXACTA MAIDEN STKS 1m 4f 8y
4:40 (4:41) (Class 5) 3-Y-0 **£4,533** (£1,348; £674; £336) **Stalls** Low

Form				RPR
54	**1**		**Flavius (IRE)**^{30} [2005] 3-9-3 0 KerrinMcEvoy 2 (Sir Michael Stoute) *hld up in mid-div: effrt over 4f out: wnt 2nd over 2f out: styd on to ld last 100yds: hld on towards fin* **6/4**^{1}	60+
000	**2**	*nk*	**Ja Myford**^{43} [1676] 3-9-3 50 PaulMulrennan 10 (P T Midgley) *mid-div: hdwy over 5f out: wnt 3rd over 2f out: hung lft and styd on fnl f: jst hld* **80/1**	59
	3	*1*	**Thorax** 3-9-3 0 JoeFanning 8 (M Johnston) *trckd ldrs: led over 3f out: drvn clr 2f out: wknd and hdd ins fnl f* **9/2**	57+
40	**4**	*9*	**Starr Flyer**^{47} [1566] 3-9-3 0 TomEaves 4 (A Bailey) *mid-div: hdwy to chse ldrs over 5f out: outpcd over 2f out: kpt on fnl f* **33/1**	39+
-00	**5**	*26*	**Hillside Smoki (IRE)**^{11} [2565] 3-8-12 35 StephenDonohoe 1 (A Berry) *in rr: sme hdwy 6f out: lost pl 4f out* **100/1**	—
00-0	**6**	*9*	**Finlay's Footsteps**^{54} [1375] 3-9-0 47 AndrewElliott$^{(3)}$ 6 (G M Moore) *chsd ldrs: drvn over 6f out: lost pl over 3f out* **66/1**	—
34	**7**	*7*	**Djalalabad (FR)**^{18} [2360] 3-8-12 0 PhilipRobinson 9 (M A Jarvis) *led: t.k.h: hdd over 3f out: wknd rapidly over 2f out: sn bhd* **4/1**^{3}	—
	8	*16*	**Ajzal (IRE)** 3-9-3 0 RHills 3 (M P Tregoning) *hld up in rr: hdwy on wd outside over 5f out: rdn and wknd rapidly 3f out: sn bhd* **9/4**^{2}	—
000	**9**	*8*	**Holiday Rock**^{20} [2308] 3-9-0 45 PatrickMathers$^{(3)}$ 7 (A J McCabe) *dwlt: sn chsng ldrs: drvn 7f out: lost pl over 4f out: t.o 2f out* **100/1**	—
0	**10**	*40*	**Ebn Zahr (UAE)**^{63} [1177] 3-9-0 0 MarcHalford$^{(3)}$ 5 (Miss J E Foster) *sn chsng ldrs: drvn and lost pl 5f out: hopelessly t.o 3f out* **100/1**	—

2m 45.68s (5.38) **Going Correction** +0.45s/f (Yiel) **10** Ran SP% **117.6**
Speed ratings (Par 99):100,99,99,93,75 69,65,54,49,22
CSF £139.88 TOTE £2.70: £1.10, £18.20, £2.40; EX 120.60.
Owner M Tabor, Mrs J Magnier & D Smith **Bred** Colbinstown Lodge Stud **Trained** Newmarket, Suffolk

FOCUS
A weak maiden. They came home well strung out, and with the runner-up rated just 50 the form needs treating with caution. The complexion changed late on.
Ajzal(IRE) Official explanation: jockey said gelding had breathing problems

2910 TOTESPORTCASINO.COM H'CAP 6f
5:10 (5:11) (Class 5) (0-75,69) 3-Y-0 **£3,886** (£1,156; £577; £288) **Stalls** Low

Form				RPR
-602	**1**		**Cheery Cat (USA)**^{23} [2203] 3-8-7 **55** ow1 (p) PaulMulrennan 1 (D W Barker) *w ldr: led 3f out: clr over 1f out: drvn rt out* **9/2**^{1}	63
4360	**2**	*2 1/2*	**Mangano**^{2} [2844] 3-7-9 **50** DanielleMcCreery$^{(7)}$ 6 (A Berry) *mid-div: hdwy 2f out: styd on to take 2nd towards fin* **14/1**	50
-616	**3**	*1/2*	**Multitude (IRE)**^{26} [2120] 3-9-7 **69** KDarley 5 (T D Easterby) *chsd ldrs: rdn over 2f out: kpt on fnl f* **9/2**^{1}	68
0036	**4**	*nk*	**Rainbow Fox**^{12} [2534] 3-9-4 **66** (v^{1}) TonyHamilton 10 (R A Fahey) *mid-div: hdwy over 2f out: kpt on fnl f* **11/2**^{2}	64
-000	**5**	*1 3/4*	**Mandy's Maestro (USA)**^{12} [2534] 3-8-7 **55** (b^{1}) DaleGibson 8 (R M Whitaker) *sn chsng ldrs: rdn over 2f out: kpt on fnl f* **14/1**	47
-600	**6**	*1/2*	**Milson's Point (IRE)**^{15} [2453] 3-9-1 **63** (b^{1}) TomEaves 2 (I Semple) *s.i.s: hld up: hdwy over 2f out: kpt on fnl f: nvr rchd ldrs* **12/1**	54
301	**7**	*3*	**Maia**^{29} [2032] 3-9-1 **63** AdrianTNicholls 9 (D Nicholls) *s.i.s: hdwy on outside and hung rt over 2f out: chsng ldrs over 1f out: sn wknd* **9/2**^{1}	45
100	**8**	*2*	**Jord (IRE)**^{18} [2363] 3-9-0 **62** StephenDonohoe 7 (A J McCabe) *led 3f: lost pl over 1f out* **8/1**	38
-431	**9**	*7*	**Ishibee (IRE)**^{11} [2560] 3-8-8 **56** (p) RoystonFfrench 4 (Mrs A Duffield) *s.i.s: in rr: rdn over 2f out: nvr on terms* **6/1**^{3}	11

1m 21.19s (3.79) **Going Correction** +0.45s/f (Yiel) 9 Ran SP% **116.4**
Speed ratings (Par 99):92,88,88,87,85 84,80,77,68
CSF £68.54 CT £302.36 TOTE £4.50: £1.70, £3.60, £2.00; EX 67.40 Place 6 £55.42, Place 5 £10.15.
Owner The Cataractonium Racing Syndicate **Bred** K L Ramsay & Sarah K Ramsay **Trained** Scorton, N Yorks

FOCUS
A moderate winning time for the type of race, 0.57 seconds slower than the two-year-old fillies in the opening maiden. Very modest form, rated through the second and third.
Maia Official explanation: jockey said filly hung right-handed
Ishibee(IRE) Official explanation: jockey said filly had no more to give
T/Plt: £54.80 to a £1 stake. Pool: £71,039.10. 945.55 winning tickets. T/Qpdt: £11.80 to a £1 stake. Pool: £4,494.20. 280.50 winning tickets. WG

2716 WARWICK (L-H)
Sunday, June 24

OFFICIAL GOING: Soft (heavy in places, 5.6)
This meeting marked the 300th year of racing at Warwick.
Wind: Light, behind Weather: Overcast with the odd shower

2911 TOTE TEXT BETTING 60021 MAIDEN AUCTION STKS 5f
2:30 (2:34) (Class 5) 2-Y-0 **£3,071** (£906; £453) **Stalls** Centre

Form				RPR
60	**1**		**Tamrai Dancer**^{39} [1762] 2-8-4 0 JamesDoyle 5 (R M Beckett) *led: hdd over 3f out: led over 1f out: rdn clr ins fnl f* **4/1**^{2}	72+
3233	**2**	*4*	**Shatter Resistant (IRE)**^{16} [2410] 2-8-12 0 JHBowman 4 (M R Channon) *prom: chsd wnr over 1f out: sn rdn: fnd nil* **8/11**^{1}	66
	3	*5*	**Towy Boy (IRE)** 2-8-12 0 AdamKirby 1 (I A Wood) *sn pushed along and prom: rdn and edgd rt over 1f out: sn wknd* **16/1**	48
	4	*3/4*	**Princely Green (IRE)** 2-8-9 0 RichardThomas 2 (I A Wood) *chsd wnr tl led over 3f out: swvd lft 2f out: sn hdd & wknd* **25/1**	42
	5	*6*	**Watch This Place** 2-9-1 0 RyanMoore 6 (K R Burke) *dwlt and swvd rt s: outpcd* **9/2**^{3}	26
	6	*2 1/2*	**Qwertyuiop (IRE)** 2-8-9 0 CatherineGannon 3 (K J Burke) *s.i.s: outpcd* **22/1**	11

63.67 secs (4.27) **Going Correction** +0.40s/f (Good) 6 Ran SP% **110.2**
Speed ratings (Par 93):81,74,66,65,55 51
CSF £7.04 TOTE £4.30: £2.10, £1.10; EX 7.50.
Owner Whitsbury Hopefuls **Bred** Beech Tree Stud **Trained** Whitsbury, Hants

FOCUS
A moderate maiden at best and the soft ground ensured they finished well strung out.

NOTEBOOK
Tamrai Dancer had not shaped without ability in two previous outings and this softer ground brought about an improved effort. Soon in front, she was headed before halfway, but rallied strongly under pressure and powered clear in the straight, ultimately winning with plenty in hand. There may be more to come from her in nurseries, especially later in the season when the ground rides similar. (tchd 10-3 and 9-2)

Shatter Resistant(IRE) brought a steady level of form into this whilst looking vulnerable to an improver at the same time, but his proven ability to act in soft ground was an obvious plus. He has been racing over 6f and was expected to see his race out strongly, but having gone in pursuit of the winner it soon became clear he had little left and he was left toiling in the final half a furlong. This was a great chance for him to break his duck and he is likely to remain vulnerable in maidens. (op 5-6)
Towy Boy(IRE), a half-brother to the yard's useful She's My Outsider, was pushed along to hold a prominent early position and he ran well for a long way, but the his lack of racecourse experience told in the conditions and he faded in the final furlong. This was quite a pleasing debut and he can be expected to come on appreciably for the experience. (tchd 20-1)
Princely Green(IRE), who is likely to prove effective at around this sort of distance, showed plenty of speed and would probably have prefered a faster surface, ending up on the slowest part of the track having veered left under pressure. He is entitled to come on for the experience. (tchd 28-1)
Watch This Place, whose stable have been enjoying a good time of it with their juveniles of late, did not show a lot on this racecourse debut, but is bred to appreciate a faster surface and deserves a chance to show this running to be all wrong. (op 4-1 tchd 7-2 and 5-1)

2912 TOTESPORT 0800 221 221 H'CAP — 6f
3:00 (3:00) (Class 4) (0-85,83) 3-Y-0+ **£6,477** (£1,927; £963; £481) **Stalls Centre**

Form RPR
-000 **1** **Paris Bell**^{13} 2508 5-8-13 **68** PaulQuinn 8 — 80
(T D Easterby) *s.i.s: hld up: hdwy over 1f out: rdn to ld and hung rt ins fnl f: r.o* **6/1**^{3}
0000 **2** 1 3/4 **Blessed Place**^{8} 2655 7-8-9 **64** oh5 (t) FergusSweeney 9 — 71
(D J S Ffrench Davis) *led: rdn over 1f out: hung lft and hdd ins fnl f: unable qckn* **50/1**
0-06 **3** 1 1/4 **Blue Aura (IRE)**^{15} 2479 4-9-3 **72** (b) JamesDoyle 3 — 75
(R M Beckett) *chsd ldr: rdn and ev ch fr over 1f out: styng on same pce whn hmpd ins fnl f* **14/1**
004- **4** 3/4 **Sea Salt**^{233} 6320 4-9-5 **77** JamieMoriarty$^{(3)}$ 6 — 78
(R A Fahey) *chsd ldrs: rdn over 1f out: edgd rt ins fnl f: styd on same pce* **12/1**
31 **5** 1 **Gilded Cove**^{8} 2655 7-8-7 **67** RussellKennemore$^{(5)}$ 10 — 65
(R Hollinshead) *dwlt: outpcd: swtchd lft and hdwy over 1f out: no imp ins fnl f* **6/1**^{3}
155 **6** nk **Balakiref**^{4} 2762 8-9-6 **75** DarryllHolland 7 — 72
(M Dods) *prom: shkn up over 1f out: styng on same pce whn nt clr run ins fnl f* **7/2**^{2}
6225 **7** hd **Chatshow (USA)**^{8} 2655 6-8-11 **71** KevinGhunowa$^{(5)}$ 4 — 68
(A W Carroll) *trckd ldrs: racd keenly: rdn over 1f out: no ex* **13/2**
54-0 **8** 14 **Hill Of Lujain**^{18} 2363 3-8-8 **70** ChrisCatlin 1 — 25
(Ian Williams) *chsd ldrs: lost pl 4f out: sn bhd* **33/1**
1-30 **9** 28 **Tender Process (IRE)**^{36} 1854 4-9-5 **74** GrahamGibbons 11 — —
(E S McMahon) *chsd ldrs: rdn 1/2-way: wknd 2f out: eased fnl f* **9/4**^{1}

1m 15.8s (1.52) **Going Correction** +0.40s/f (Good)
WFA 3 from 4yo+ 7lb **9** Ran SP% **114.2**
Speed ratings (Par 105):105,102,101,100,98 98,98,79,42
CSF £233.63 CT £3972.53 TOTE £5.20: £1.90, £7.30, £3.40; EX 146.40.
Owner Ryedale Partners No 8 **Bred** M H Easterby **Trained** Great Habton, N Yorks
■ Stewards' Enquiry : Paul Quinn one-day ban: careless riding (Aug 5)

FOCUS
Modest sprint handicap form and limited by the runner-up who was racing from out of the handicap.
Tender Process(IRE) Official explanation: vet said gelding finished lame

2913 TOTESPORTCASINO.COM MAIDEN STKS — 7f 26y
3:30 (3:37) (Class 5) 3-Y-0+ **£2,914** (£867; £433; £216) **Stalls Low**

Form RPR
25 **1** **Gleneagles (IRE)**^{34} 1904 3-9-0 0 LiamJones$^{(3)}$ 8 — 71
(W J Haggas) *chsd ldrs: rdn over 1f out: edgd rt and styd on to ld wl ins fnl f* **7/2**^{2}
45 **2** nk **Al Badeya (IRE)**^{16} 2429 3-8-12 0 RyanMoore 2 — 65
(Sir Michael Stoute) *led over 5f out: rdn over 1f out: hdd wl ins fnl f* **6/4**^{1}
3 1 1/4 **Paradise Dancer (IRE)** 3-8-12 0 DaneO'Neill 1 — 62
(Pat Eddery) *chsd ldrs: rdn and edgd lft over 1f out: edgd rt ins fnl f: styd on same pce* **5/1**^{3}
4 2 **Nassau Style** 3-9-3 0 AdamKirby 12 — 62
(J R Fanshawe) *hld up: hdwy over 1f out: nt rch ldrs* **16/1**
36 **5** 1/2 **Ionian**^{11} 2581 4-9-12 0 PatDobbs 13 — 63
(Pat Eddery) *chsd ldrs: rdn and hung lft over 1f out: styd on same pce* **14/1**
0 **6** 1 **Tavares (IRE)**^{11} 2580 4-9-9 0 SaleemGolam$^{(3)}$ 5 — 61
(P S McEntee) *s.s: hld up: hdwy u.p over 1f out: nt trble ldrs* **50/1**
06 **7** 2 **Arithmatix (USA)**^{15} 2477 3-9-3 0 JHBowman 6 — 52
(G A Butler) *prom: rdn over 2f out: wknd fnl f* **14/1**
00-0 **8** 4 **Hill Of Clare (IRE)**^{52} 1435 5-9-4 41 DominicFox$^{(3)}$ 4 — 40
(G H Jones) *hld up: rdn over 2f out: n.d* **80/1**
05- **9** 1 1/2 **Serene Dancer**^{413} 1513 4-9-0 0 NBazeley$^{(7)}$ 9 — 36
(Mrs P N Dutfield) *hld up: rdn over 2f out: n.d* **33/1**
0-0 **10** 1 1/2 **Aphrodisia**^{34} 1901 3-8-12 0 GrahamGibbons 10 — 29
(S C Williams) *s.i.s: hld up: hdwy over 2f out: wknd over 1f out* **12/1**
0 **11** 7 **Word Of Warning**^{28} 2059 3-9-3 0 ChrisCatlin 11 — 16
(G Wragg) *mid-div: rdn 1/2-way: wknd over 2f out* **16/1**
12 18 **Holyfield Warrior (IRE)** 3-9-3 0 JamesDoyle 14 — —
(I A Wood) *led: hdd over 5f out: rdn and wknd over 2f out* **33/1**

1m 30.22s (6.02) **Going Correction** +0.75s/f (Yiel)
WFA 3 from 4yo+ 9lb **12** Ran SP% **120.8**
Speed ratings (Par 103):95,94,93,90,90 89,86,82,80,78 70,50
CSF £9.08 TOTE £5.50: £1.50, £1.30, £2.30; EX 13.10.
Owner Wentworth Racing (pty) Ltd **Bred** Darley **Trained** Newmarket, Suffolk

FOCUS
Only a modest maiden and little solid form to go on. The form is limited by the poor eighth.

2914 TOTESPORT.COM ETERNAL STKS (LISTED RACE) (FILLIES) — 7f 26y
4:00 (4:03) (Class 1) 3-Y-0
£14,762 (£5,595; £2,800; £1,396; £699; £351) **Stalls Low**

Form RPR
-620 **1** **Ponty Rossa (IRE)**^{29} 2037 3-8-12 93 DavidAllan 1 — 96
(T D Easterby) *a.p: chsd ldr 3f out: rdn to chal whn hmpd over 1f out: styd on to ld wl ins fnl f: edgd lft nr fin* **6/1**
4414 **2** nk **Nans Joy (IRE)**^{23} 2207 3-8-12 100 ChrisCatlin 2 — 95
(E J O'Neill) *led: rdn and hung rt fr over 1f out: hdd wl ins fnl f: hmpd nr fin* **5/1**^{3}
10-5 **3** 1 3/4 **Mimisel**^{29} 2043 3-8-12 79 MartinDwyer 3 — 90
(Rae Guest) *hld up in tch: rdn over 1f out: styd on same pce ins fnl f* **20/1**
-023 **4** 2 1/2 **Whazzis**^{23} 2212 3-8-12 88 RyanMoore 6 — 83
(W J Haggas) *hld up: hdwy u.p over 1f out: no imp fnl f* **7/2**^{1}
10-3 **5** 2 **Pinkabout (IRE)**^{28} 2060 3-8-12 85 DavidKinsella 4 — 78
(J H M Gosden) *chsd ldr 4f: sn rdn: wknd fnl f* **16/1**
1646 **6** 1/2 **Knapton Hill**^{29} 2043 3-8-12 63 GrahamGibbons 5 — 77?
(R Hollinshead) *hld up: hdwy over 2f out: rdn over 1f out: wknd fnl f* **66/1**
011 **7** 3/4 **Look So**^{8} 2662 3-8-12 77 JamesDoyle 13 — 74
(R M Beckett) *hld up: rdn over 2f out: n.d* **7/1**
40-5 **8** 10 **Alovera (IRE)**^{53} 1391 3-8-12 95 DarryllHolland 12 — 47
(M R Channon) *hld up: effrt over 2f out: sn wknd* **22/1**
440- **9** nk **Zanida (IRE)**^{240} 6201 3-8-12 89 FergusSweeney 8 — 47
(K R Burke) *hld up: plld hrd: rdn adn wknd over 2f out* **33/1**
60-3 **10** 3 **Elusive Flash (USA)**^{64} 1146 3-8-12 102 PatDobbs 7 — 39
(P F I Cole) *chsd ldrs: rdn over 2f out: sn wknd* **6/1**
22-2 **11** 6 **Siamese Cat (IRE)**^{34} 1901 3-8-12 97 JamieMoriarty 14 — 22
(B J Meehan) *hld up: rdn 1/2-way: wknd over 2f out* **9/2**^{2}

1m 28.59s (4.39) **Going Correction** +0.75s/f (Yiel) **11** Ran SP% **117.6**
Speed ratings (Par 104):104,103,101,98,96 95,95,83,83,79 73
CSF £34.58 TOTE £8.20: £2.30, £2.30, £5.00; EX 38.60.
Owner The Lapin Blanc Racing Partnership **Bred** Jim McDonald **Trained** Great Habton, N Yorks

FOCUS
Not a strong Listed race and the testing ground conditions make the form questionable. The form is rated around the first two, but the third and sixth limit the form.

NOTEBOOK
Ponty Rossa(IRE) failed to stay 1m in a hot handicap at Haydock last time, but her early form at up to 7f gave her every chance in what was a weak race for the grade and she handled the testing going perfectly well to get up close home. She may have caused the runner-up some slight interference close home, but it made little difference to the result and she fully deserved the win. The form though is unlikely to be worth much and she may struggle to win again at this sort of level. (op 7-1 tchd 8-1)
Nans Joy(IRE) ran above herself when fourth in a Group 3 at Epsom on Oaks day and this run confirmed her to be an improved filly. She ran a bold race, being made plenty of use of on this drop in trip, and can probably find a race at this level. (op 15-2)
Mimisel struggled in a decent Listed contest at Newmarket last time, won by subsequent Jersey Stakes winner Tariq, and this lesser contest enabled her to run better, the daughter of Selkirk seeming to appreciate the return to soft ground. (tchd 22-1)
Whazzis, who ran well in a Listed contest at Epsom last time, looks to be progressing well and she ran another sound race on ground she handles. She looks worth a try at 1m now. (op 9-2 tchd 10-3)
Pinkabout(IRE), who ran well off this mark in a handicap on her return, was up in trip and did not see it out in this soft ground. She deserves another chance back on a faster surface. Official explanation: jockey said filly hung right throughout (tchd 14-1)
Look So, a progressive filly who fully deserved her chance at this level, was not quite ready for it yet and she struggled to get involved. There may be more to come from her back in handicaps. (op 9-2)
Elusive Flash(USA) set the standard on the form of her reappearance third behind Majestic Roi in the Fred Darling, but she had been off since and there had to be major doubts as to how she would handle this ground - well beaten once in heavy. Well positioned early on, she briefly threatened to get involved, but was in trouble two-out dropped away tamely. She deserves another chance back on a faster surface. (op 9-2)
Siamese Cat(IRE), although still a maiden, brought some good soft-ground form into this and it was disappointing she could not fare better, evidently failing to run her race. (op 11-2 tchd 4-1)

2915 TFS DERBY 25TH ANNIVERSARY H'CAP — 1m 2f 188y
4:30 (4:30) (Class 5) (0-75,67) 3-Y-0 **£3,238** (£963; £481; £240) **Stalls Low**

Form RPR
066 **1** **Jawaaneb (USA)**^{23} 2219 3-9-3 **63** RyanMoore 1 — 67
(J L Dunlop) *chsd ldrs: rdn to ld 1f out: edgd rt: styd on* **13/2**^{3}
5050 **2** 1 1/4 **Always Best**^{22} 2259 3-8-10 **59** AndrewMullen$^{(3)}$ 5 — 60
(M Johnston) *led: hdd 9f out: led again over 5f out: rdn and hdd 1f out: styd on same pce* **15/2**
5-00 **3** hd **Disintegration (IRE)**^{31} 1972 3-9-1 **61** FergusSweeney 3 — 62
(A King) *hld up: hdwy over 4f out: rdn and ev ch 1f out: styd on same pce* **11/2**^{2}
3-00 **4** 3 **Dark Energy**^{37} 1804 3-9-3 **66** MarkLawson$^{(3)}$ 4 — 62
(B Smart) *hld up in tch: plld hrd: rdn and hung lft over 1f out: sn ev ch: wknd wl ins fnl f* **11/2**^{2}
0-0P **5** 1 1/2 **Everyman**^{8} 2653 3-8-0 **51** KevinGhunowa$^{(5)}$ 9 — 44
(A W Carroll) *hld up: hdwy over 4f out: outpcd over 3f out: styd on u.p fnl f* **25/1**
-010 **6** 2 1/2 **Polyquest (IRE)**^{22} 2246 3-9-0 **60** JHBowman 2 — 48
(G A Butler) *chsd ldrs: lost pl 8f out: hdwy over 3f out: sn rdn: wknd fnl f* **4/1**^{1}
2014 **7** 4 **King Of The Beers (USA)**^{11} 2558 3-8-8 **57** (p) SaleemGolam$^{(3)}$ 8 — 38
(R A Harris) *chsd ldrs: lost pl over 8f out: hdwy over 4f out: wknd over 2f out* **7/1**
5-00 **8** 15 **Brouhaha**^{44} 1634 3-8-11 **57** (t) DaneO'Neill 10 — 11
(Miss Diana Weeden) *chsd ldrs: wnt far side in bk st: wknd over 2f out* **25/1**
0-30 **9** 44 **Tullythered (IRE)**^{15} 2453 3-8-8 **54** CatherineGannon 11 — —
(K R Burke) *chsd ldrs over 8f* **33/1**
-503 **10** 86 **Mujma**^{12} 2530 3-9-7 **67** (v) MartinDwyer 6 — —
(Sir Michael Stoute) *trckd ldr: plld hrd: led 9f out: sn clr: wnt far side in bk st: rdn: hdd & wknd over 5f out* **4/1**^{1}

2m 30.04s (10.64) **Going Correction** +0.95s/f (Soft) **10** Ran SP% **119.0**
Speed ratings (Par 99):99,98,97,95,94 92,89,79,47,—
CSF £54.36 CT £290.01 TOTE £5.60: £2.20, £3.20, £2.40; EX 43.50.
Owner Hamdan Al Maktoum **Bred** Shadwell Farm LLC **Trained** Arundel, W Sussex

FOCUS
Just an average handicap rated around the third.
Mujma Official explanation: jockey said colt ran too freely and then lost interest

2916 TOTEPOOL APPRENTICE H'CAP — 1m 22y
5:00 (5:00) (Class 6) (0-65,72) 3-Y-0 **£2,047** (£604; £302) **Stalls Low**

Form RPR
0-03 **1** **Palmetto Point**^{23} 2203 3-8-8 **52** (p) TravisBlock$^{(3)}$ 4 — 56
(H Morrison) *mde virtualy all: rdn and hung rt over 1f out: hung lft ins fnl f: r.o* **11/1**^{3}
0-00 **2** 3/4 **Lordship (IRE)**^{14} 2489 3-8-7 **55** MarkCoumbe$^{(7)}$ 1 — 57
(A W Carroll) *hld up: plld hrd: hdwy over 3f out: rdn and ev ch fr over 1f out: unable qckn wl ins fnl f* **50/1**
0006 **3** hd **Piano Key**^{7} 2697 3-8-0 **46** oh1 (v^{1}) MCGeran$^{(5)}$ 2 — 48
(M D I Usher) *hld up: hdwy over 2f out: rdn over 1f out: r.o* **20/1**
1300 **4** 1 1/2 **Mark Of Love (IRE)**^{27} 2079 3-9-5 **65** ThomasO'Brien$^{(5)}$ 16 — 63
(M R Channon) *s.i.s: hld up: hdwy over 1f out: edgd lft and styd on ins fnl f* **16/1**

1504 **5** *1* **Doctor Ned**[24] 2187 3-8-2 **50** .... BradleyRoper(7) 5 46
(N A Callaghan) *hld up: hdwy over 1f out: sn rdn: styd on same pce ins fnl f* **12/1**

2021 **6** *hd* **Susanna's Prospect (IRE)**[10] 2607 3-9-12 **72** .... KMay(5) 7 68
(B J Meehan) *trckd ldrs: racd keenly: rdn and swtchd rt over 1f out: no ex ins fnl f* **13/8**[1]

000 **7** *5* **Red Brick Road (IRE)**[27] 2077 3-8-6 **50** .... RussellKennemore(3) 8 34
(A J Lidderdale) *s.i.s: sn pushed along in rr: styd on u.p ins fnl f: nrst fin* **20/1**

4066 **8** *½* **Zelos (IRE)**[8] 2653 3-8-11 **59** .... SophieDoyle(7) 14 42
(J A Osborne) *chsd ldrs: rdn and hung lft 2f out: hmpd and wknd over 1f out* **16/1**

0636 **9** *1 ½* **Brean Dot Com (IRE)**[15] 2456 3-8-6 **54** .... NBazeley(7) 3 34
(Mrs P N Dutfield) *prom: chsd wnr over 2f out: rdn and wknd over 1f out* **12/1**

1640 **10** *4* **Homes By Woodford**[33] 1927 3-9-5 **63** .... MichaelJStainton(3) 17 33
(R A Harris) *prom: rdn over 3f out: wknd over 2f out* **25/1**

060 **11** *3* **Dark Druid (IRE)**[23] 2196 3-9-0 **55** .... JamesDoyle 12 18
(I A Wood) *prom over 4f* **25/1**

4400 **12** *nk* **Pajada**[7] 2697 3-8-5 **46** oh1 .... AlanCreighton 6 9
(M D I Usher) *chsd ldrs over 5f* **33/1**

0435 **13** *5* **Dee Jay Wells**[20] 2305 3-8-13 **61** .... (v[1]) JamesRogers(7) 10 12
(R A Fahey) *chsd ldrs: hmpd 2f out: sn wknd* **7/1**[2]

2004 **14** *3 ½* **Goose Green (IRE)**[10] 2601 3-9-9 **64** .... RichardKingscote 9 7
(R J Hodges) *chsd wnr: rdn over 3f out: wknd over 2f out* **7/1**[2]

-446 **15** *18* **Kassuta**[11] 2571 3-9-8 **63** .... SaleemGolam 15 —
(S C Williams) *mid-div: wknd over 3f out* **20/1**

1m 48.24s (8.64) **Going Correction** +0.95s/f (Soft) **15** Ran SP% **125.5**
Speed ratings (Par 97):94,93,93,91,90 90,85,84,83,79 76,76,71,67,49
CSF £493.05 CT £5716.25 TOTE £14.20: £3.70, £15.10, £7.70; EX 896.40 Place 6 £830.61, Place 5 £720.96.
Owner M T Bevan & H Scott-Barrett **Bred** Wyck Hall Stud Ltd **Trained** East Ilsley, Berks

FOCUS
A poor event that is unlikely to produce anything other than the occasional winner. The winner is rated as back to juvenile form but the third, from out of the handicap, limits things.
Goose Green(IRE) Official explanation: jockey said gelding was unsuited by the soft ground
Kassuta Official explanation: jockey said filly never travelled
T/Jkpt: Part won. £134,232.59 to a £1 stake. Pool: £189,060.00. 0.50 winning tickets. T/Plt: £2,283.90 to a £1 stake. Pool: £89,636.03. 28.65 winning tickets. T/Qpdt: £238.20 to a £1 stake. Pool: £9,690.13. 30.10 winning tickets. CR

2917 - 2923a (Foreign Racing) - See Raceform Interactive

2903 HAMBURG (R-H)
Sunday, June 24

OFFICIAL GOING: Heavy

2924a IDEE HANSA-PREIS (GROUP 2) 1m 3f
4:15 (4:20) 3-Y-0+ **£40,541** (£14,189; £7,432; £3,716; £1,689)

RPR

1 **Schiaparelli (GER)**[35] 1872 4-9-6 .... AStarke 4 119
(P Schiergen, Germany) *trckd clr ldr: led ent st: rdn clr wl over 1f out: r.o wl* **1/1**[1]

2 *2 ½* **Poseidon Adventure (IRE)**[35] 1872 4-9-2 .... AHelfenbein 3 111
(W Figge, Germany) *hld up: 5th st on outside: hdwy 2f out: r.o u.p to take 2nd wl ins fnl f* **136/10**

3 *nk* **Oriental Tiger (GER)**[273] 5561 4-9-2 .... (b) ASuborics 5 111
(U Ostmann, Germany) *hld up in rr: hdwy over 3f out: 4th on ins st: sn chsng wnr: rdn and hung lft below dist: lost 2nd wl ins fnl f* **26/10**[2]

4 *1 ¼* **Waleria (GER)**[14] 4-8-11 .... VSchulepov 6 104
(H J Groschel, Germany) *disp 3rd to 1/2-way: 3rd st: u.p whn sltly hmpd by 3rd 1f out: one pce* **46/10**

5 *9* **Arcadio (GER)**[35] 1872 5-9-2 .... THellier 7 94
(J Hirschberger, Germany) *led: sn plld his way clr: hdd ent st: wknd 2f out* **7/2**[3]

6 *1 ½* **Expensive Dream (GER)**[35] 1872 8-9-2 .... J-PCarvalho 1 92
(P Vovcenko, Germany) *disp 3rd to 1/2-way: last st: sn btn* **112/10**

2m 31.75s (7.05) **6** Ran SP% **132.9**
(including ten euro stakes): WIN 20; PL 15, 33; SF 305.
Owner Stall Blankenese **Bred** Gestut Karlshof **Trained** Germany

FOCUS
The race was started by flag owing to the heavy ground, and leading fancy Egerton was withdrawn for the same reason.

NOTEBOOK
Schiaparelli(GER) successfully returned to the scene of his Deutsches Derby win last July.

2649 SAINT-CLOUD (L-H)
Sunday, June 24

OFFICIAL GOING: Good to soft

2925a GRAND PRIX DE SAINT-CLOUD (GROUP 1) 1m 4f
2:50 (2:58) 4-Y-0+ **£154,432** (£61,784; £30,892; £15,432; £7,730)

RPR

1 **Mountain High (IRE)**[21] 2292 5-9-2 .... KFallon 5 123
(Sir Michael Stoute) *trckd ldr: chal ent st: led over 2f out: drvn out* **25/2**

2 *1 ½* **Mandesha (FR)**[25] 2165 4-8-13 .... CSoumillon 2 118
(A De Royer-Dupre, France) *s.i.s: hld up and sn pulling: settled in 5th after 4f: 5th st: hdwy 2f out and rdn over 1f out: r.o one pce* **4/5**[1]

3 *½* **Prince Flori (GER)**[35] 1872 4-9-2 .... JVictoire 1 120
(S Smrczek, Germany) *racd in 3rd to st: hdwy on outside to dispute 2nd fr wl over 1f out: no ex ins fnl f* **52/10**[3]

4 *2* **Irish Wells (FR)**[21] 2292 4-9-2 .... DBoeuf 4 117
(F Rohaut, France) *led to over 2f out: kpt on one pce* **10/1**

5 *1* **Youmzain (IRE)**[28] 2064 4-9-2 .... JamieSpencer 3 116
(M R Channon) *hld up in 5th: last after 4f: nvr a factor* **34/10**[2]

6 *3* **Ponte Tresa (FR)**[35] 1881 4-8-13 .... OPeslier 6 108
(Y De Nicolay, France) *disp 3rd: 4th st: sn btn* **13/1**

2m 29.7s (-10.70) **Going Correction** -0.50s/f (Hard) **6** Ran SP% **118.1**
Speed ratings: 115,114,113,112,111 109
PARI-MUTUEL: WIN 13.50; PL 3.10, 1.40; SF 28.30.
Owner Mrs John Magnier & M Tabor **Bred** Ballymacoll Stud Farm Ltd **Trained** Newmarket, Suffolk
■ Kieren Fallon's first Group 1 winner since returning from a six-month ban.

NOTEBOOK
Mountain High(IRE), a half-brother to Islington, was always beautifully placed just behind the leader. He was asked to quicken at the turn into the straight and stayed on well to hold off the challenge of the second. Much better suited going left handed and fitted with a cross noseband, there was no sign of him hanging this time. He is going from strength to strength and on a left-handed track he is a force to be reckoned with.
Mandesha(FR) was led into the paddock very late to avoid the temperament she showed last time. On her toes in the parade, she went nicely to the start but again sat back in the stalls when they opened and missed the break. She did not settle early on and, although rounding the turn she progressed up the inside rail and ran on well, she could make no impression in the last furlong. This was her first time racing against males and her trainer was not disappointed, but she could go for the Nassau Stakes back against fillies, although her main objective is an autumn campaign.
Prince Flori(GER) raced in third position for much of the race, settled well and when asked to make his move on the outside up the straight, he looked likely to threaten the winner. He was unable to quicken and eventually lost second place by half a length.
Irish Wells(FR), very warm in the preliminaries, led the field at a steady pace until the turn into the straight where he was passed by the eventual winner. He stayed on one paced up the straight and was again disappointing.
Youmzain(IRE), another who was very warm in the preliminaries, settled in fourth position but slipped on the first bend and dropped back last. He was never travelling afterwards.

2926a PRIX DE MALLERET - AIR MAURITIUS (GROUP 2) (FILLIES) 1m 4f
3:20 (3:28) 3-Y-O **£50,068** (£19,324; £9,223; £6,149; £3,074)

RPR

1 **Legerete (USA)**[22] 2270 3-8-9 .... OPeslier 4 103
(A Fabre, France) *racd in 4th to st: hdwy wl over 1f out: led 150yds out: pushed out and r.o wl* **22/10**[2]

2 *½* **Kaloura (IRE)**[18] 2384 3-8-9 .... CSoumillon 3 102
(A Fabre, France) *led: hrd rdn 2f out: hdd 150yds out: r.o one pce* **Evs**[1]

3 *¾* **Topka (FR)**[14] 2501 3-8-9 .... TJarnet 1 101
(F Doumen, France) *disp 2nd on ins: 3rd st: rdn and ev ch wl over 1f out: kpt on one pce* **12/1**

4 *¾* **La Hernanda (IRE)**[22] 2270 3-8-9 .... JVictoire 7 100
(H-A Pantall, France) *racd in 6th to st: moved to outside: styd on steadily fnl 2f: nvr nr to chal* **54/10**[3]

5 *nk* **Impetious**[31] 1958 3-8-9 .... KFallon 2 99
(Eamon Tyrrell, Ire) *broke wl: restrained in 5th: 5th st: rdn wl over 1f out: kpt on steadily* **12/1**

6 *1* **Fiumicino**[37] 1809 3-8-9 .... JamieSpencer 6 98
(M R Channon) *last most of way: rdn 2f out: nvr a factor* **17/1**

7 *½* **Daralara (FR)**[42] 1705 3-8-9 .... C-PLemaire 5 97
(J-C Rouget, France) *trckd ldr to st: tried to chal over 2f out: btn 1 1/2f out* **Evs**[1]

2m 33.0s (-7.40) **Going Correction** -0.50s/f (Hard) **7** Ran SP% **167.8**
Speed ratings: 104,103,103,102,102 101,101
PARI-MUTUEL: WIN 3.20; PL 1.70, 1.60; SF 8.40.
Owner Wertheimer Et Frere **Bred** Wertheimer Et Frere **Trained** Chantilly, France

NOTEBOOK
Legerete(USA), raced in fourth position, and was brought to the outside halfway up the straight and produced with a finely-timed run to sweep past the rest of the field to win cosily by half a length. She stayed the trip well and will now be given a break. She looks the perfect type for the Prix Vermeille.
Kaloura(IRE), quickly into the lead, she set a good pace and stayed on well up the straight although she could not quicken when the winner went past. Connections feel she will be better over further and she may go for a long-distance race at Deauville.
Topka(FR) raced in third position for much of the race and kept on well up the straight on the inside rail but was unable to quicken again in the closing stages. However, this was an improved performance.
La Hernanda(IRE) looked threatening in the straight and accelerated again at the furlong pole on the outside but was one paced thereafter.
Fiumicino, always near the tail of the field, was outpaced in the straight and at this level she did not have the ability to quicken with the others.

2618 CHEPSTOW (eve) (L-H)
Monday, June 25

2927 Meeting Abandoned - Waterlogged

2825 MUSSELBURGH (R-H)
Monday, June 25

OFFICIAL GOING: Good to soft
Wind: Fresh across Weather: Ocercast

2933 RECTANGLE GROUP FILLIES' H'CAP 5f
2:00 (2:02) (Class 5) (0-75,73) 4-Y-0+ **£3,238** (£963; £481; £240) **Stalls** Low

Form RPR

0533 **1** **Tilly's Dream**[4] 2805 4-8-13 **68** .... AndrewMullen(3) 2 78+
(P S McEntee) *hld up towards rr: gd hdwy 2f out: rdn ent fnl f: led last 100yds* **9/2**[1]

6063 **2** *1 ¾* **Rothesay Dancer**[3] 2830 4-7-10 **55** oh4 ow1 .... KellyHarrison(7) 1 59
(J S Goldie) *trckd ldrs: gd hdwy on outer 2f out: rdn to ld 1f out: drvn and hdd last 100yds* **12/1**

0041 **3** *2 ½* **Miacarla**[3] 2844 4-8-2 **54** 6ex oh3 .... PaulFessey 3 49
(A Berry) *trckd ldrs: hdwy to chal and ev ch wl over 1f out: sn rdn: edgd rt and one pce ent fnl f* **15/2**

0000 **4** *hd* **Toy Top (USA)**[17] 2418 4-8-10 **62** .... (b) PhillipMakin 9 56+
(M Dods) *cl up: led 2f out: sn rdn and hdd 1f out: edgd lft and one pce fnl f* **20/1**

2660 **5** *3* **Overwing (IRE)**[18] 2399 4-9-0 **73** .... MCGeran(7) 7 56
(R M H Cowell) *bmpd s and bhd tl styd on appr fnl f* **11/1**

0420 **6** *1 ½* **Princess Cleo**[4] 2805 4-8-8 **60** .... DavidAllan 4 38
(T D Easterby) *prom: rdn along 2f out: sn drvn and grad wknd* **11/2**[2]

3402 **7** *2* **Ashes (IRE)**[16] 2459 5-8-11 **63** .... PaulMulrennan 8 34
(K R Burke) *led: rdn along and hdd 2f out: grad wknd* **13/2**[3]

0056 **8** *nk* **Glenviews Youngone (IRE)**[23] 2244 4-8-12 **67** .. (b) PatrickMathers(3) 5 37
(Peter Grayson) *hld up: effrt and n.m.r 2f out: sn rdn and nvr a factor* **9/1**

-000 **9** *hd* **Smiddy Hill**[34] 1914 5-8-5 **57** .... RoystonFfrench 6 26
(R Bastiman) *prom: rdn along 1/2-way: sn wknd* **11/1**

0150 **10** 2 **Champagne Cracker**[12] 2553 6-8-6 **58** .... TomEaves 10 20
(M Dods) *prom on inner: rdn along 1/2-way and sn btn* **11/2**[2]

61.51 secs (1.01) **Going Correction** +0.275s/f (Good) **10** Ran SP% **113.2**
Speed ratings (Par 100):102,99,95,94,90 87,84,84,83,80
CSF £57.13 CT £313.83 TOTE £4.10: £1.70, £4.30, £2.10; EX 40.40.
Owner Richard Withers And Meddler Bloodstock **Bred** Southill Stud **Trained** Newmarket, Suffolk

FOCUS
A moderate sprint handicap. With the stalls on the far side, these drawn low proved at an advantage with the first pair coming down the centre. The winner is rated back to her best with the runner-up rated to her recent level from out of the weights.
Glenviews Youngone(IRE) Official explanation: jockey said filly bled from the nose

2934 RACING UK CHANNEL 432 MEDIAN AUCTION MAIDEN STKS 5f
2:30 (2:31) (Class 6) 2-Y-O £2,590 (£770; £385; £192) **Stalls** Low

Form RPR
42 **1** **Mazzanti**[21] 2297 2-9-3 0 .... NCallan 4 88+
(K A Ryan) *dwlt: squeezed out s and bhd: gd hdwy after 2f: led 2f out: sn rdn clr* **10/11**[1]

63 **2** 3 1/2 **Firewalker**[21] 2297 2-8-12 0 .... RoystonFfrench 5 65
(B Smart) *plld hrd: stdd s and sn bhd: swtchd outside and hdwy 2f out: sn rdn and styd on fnl f* **4/1**[3]

64 **3** shd **Maracana Boy (IRE)**[47] 1585 2-9-3 0 .... PhillipMakin 2 70
(M Dods) *chsd ldrs: hdwy 2f out: sn rdn and kpt on same pce* **10/3**[2]

4 4 **Whispering Desert** 2-8-12 0 .... LeeEnstone 7 51
(P T Midgley) *sn outpcd and bhd tl styd on appr fnl f: nvr a factor* **33/1**

00 **5** 3/4 **Caprima (IRE)**[40] 1772 2-8-12 0 .... DeanMernagh 3 48
(M Brittain) *led: rdn along 1/2-way: hdd 2f out: sn drvn and wknd* **14/1**

0 **6** nk **Firenza Bond**[49] 1528 2-8-10 0 .... SladeO'Hara(7) 8 52
(G R Oldroyd) *t.k.h: cl up: effort 2f out: sn rdn: wandered and wknd* **14/1**

5 **7** nk **Premium Port**[18] 2385 2-8-12 0 .... PBradley(5) 1 51
(A Berry) *wnt lft s: sn rdn along and bhd fr 1/2-way* **50/1**

62.95 secs (2.45) **Going Correction** +0.275s/f (Good) **7** Ran SP% **113.7**
Speed ratings (Par 91):91,85,85,78,77 77,76
CSF £4.84 TOTE £1.80: £1.30, £2.00; EX 4.50.
Owner Hambleton Racing Ltd II & T Fawcett **Bred** Jeremy Gompertz **Trained** Hambleton, N Yorks
■ Stewards' Enquiry : Dean Mernagh two-day ban: careless riding (Jul 6,8)

FOCUS
An ordinary juvenile maiden. There was little strength in depth and Mazzanti was in a different league. He was value for extra and there should be more to come. The form in behind is solid but modest.

NOTEBOOK
Mazzanti came right away from his rivals to score a decisive first success on this switch to a softer surface. He confirmed form with the runner-up and is clearly getting the hang of things now, with connections keen to have a go at the Newbury Super Sprint in July. No doubt he will have to improve again to figure there, but his versatility as regards underfoot conditions is a real plus and he should be high on confidence now. (tchd 11-8)
Firewalker took a pull early on and got unbalanced on more than one occasion, still looking distinctly green despite this being her third outing. She finished further behind today's winner than had been the case at Carlisle last time, but that was probably on account of this deeper surface and it is a good bet we have yet to see the best of her. (op 9-2)
Maracana Boy(IRE) had her chance and simply failed to find an extra gear when it mattered on this softer ground. This looks about as good as he is at this stage and he should appreciate the move into nurseries in due course. (op 3-1 tchd 2-1 and 7-2)
Whispering Desert, a half-sister to multiple 5-7f winner Desert Opal, took time to get the hang of things on this racecourse bow and was doing her best work too late in the day. She should prove sharper next time.
Caprima(IRE) Official explanation: jockey said filly was unsuited by the good to soft ground
Firenza Bond showed good speed to go with the eventual winner early on, but he paid for his early exertions and dropped right out soon after the 2f pole. (op 20-1 tchd 22-1)

2935 D&W H'CAP 1m 4f
3:00 (3:00) (Class 5) (0-70,72) 4-Y-0+ £3,238 (£963; £481; £240) **Stalls** High

Form RPR
3106 **1** **Sudden Impulse**[20] 2342 6-9-5 **65** .... SilvestreDeSousa 7 73+
(A D Brown) *trckd ldr: hdwy 3f out: rdn to ld over 2f out: sn edgd lft: styd on fnl f* **11/4**[1]

33-2 **2** 2 **Acuzio**[13] 2531 6-8-13 **59** .... DavidAllan 4 63
(W M Brisbourne) *led: rdn along 3f out: hdd over 2f out: sn drvn and hung lft: kpt on u.p fnl f* **3/1**[2]

525- **3** nk **Edas**[227] 6426 5-9-7 **67** .... GrahamGibbons 1 70
(J J Quinn) *chsd ldrs: rdn along over 3f out: sn drvn and kpt on same pce fnl 2f* **6/1**

0644 **4** 5 **Grey Outlook**[3] 2824 4-8-9 **55** .... RoystonFfrench 5 50
(Miss L A Perratt) *trckd ldrs: hdwy over 3f out: rdn along wl over 2f out and sn btn* **3/1**[2]

3500 **5** 4 **Northern Boy (USA)**[18] 2388 4-9-6 **66** .... PhillipMakin 8 55
(T D Barron) *hld up in tch: effrt and hdwy over 3f out: sn rdn and wknd over 2f out* **5/1**[3]

00 **6** 15 **My Causeway Dream (IRE)**[23] 2254 4-8-2 **48** ....(v) PaulQuinn 2 13
(J S Wainwright) *a in rr: bhd fnl 3f* **50/1**

2m 49.04s (12.14) **Going Correction** +0.375s/f (Good) **6** Ran SP% **109.6**
Speed ratings (Par 103):74,72,72,69,66 56
CSF £10.72 CT £39.32 TOTE £4.20: £2.20, £1.20.
Owner Mrs Glen E Salt **Bred** Sagittarius Bloodstock Associates Ltd **Trained** Pickering, York

FOCUS
A pedestrian winning time for the grade. Modest form. The winner won with a deal left up her sleeve and it is doubtful if she had to improve on her early-season wins, with the runner-up on a stiff enough mark.

2936 BARCLAYS WEALTH H'CAP 7f 30y
3:30 (3:30) (Class 4) (0-85,80) 4-Y-0+ £5,505 (£1,637; £818; £408) **Stalls** High

Form RPR
1-60 **1** **Carnivore**[37] 1845 5-9-2 **75** .... PaulFessey 9 84+
(T D Barron) *hld up in rr: hdwy 3f out: chal over 1f out: sn rdn and styd on to ld last 100yds* **5/2**[1]

3231 **2** nk **Il Castagno (IRE)**[13] 2536 4-9-7 **80** .... TomEaves 7 88
(B Smart) *led: rdn along and clr 3f out: drvn wl over 1f out: hdd and no ex last 100yds* **7/2**[2]

0000 **3** 1 1/4 **Stoic Leader (IRE)**[13] 2536 7-9-4 **77** .... PaulHanagan 8 82
(R F Fisher) *hld up in rr: hdwy wl over 2f out: sn rdn and kpt on u.p ins fnl f* **20/1**

4402 **4** 1 1/2 **Fiefdom (IRE)**[16] 2458 5-9-3 **76** .... RoystonFfrench 6 77
(I W McInnes) *trckd ldrs: hdwy 3f out: rdn to chal and ch 2f out: sn drvn and wknd appr fnl f* **6/1**

1104 **5** 4 **Violent Velocity (IRE)**[17] 2419 4-8-9 **68** .... GrahamGibbons 4 58
(J J Quinn) *chsd ldr: rdn along 3f out: wkng whn n.m.r 2f out* **8/1**

5340 **6** shd **Josh**[12] 2573 5-9-3 **76** ....(p) NCallan 5 66
(K A Ryan) *chsd ldr: rdn along 3f out: drvn 2f out and sn wknd* **5/1**

3341 **7** 10 **Tough Love**[6] 2741 8-8-11 **73** 6ex ....(p) DuranFentiman(3) 3 36
(T D Easterby) *hld up in tch: effrt 3f out: rdn over 2f out and sn btn* **9/2**[3]

1m 30.9s (0.96) **Going Correction** +0.375s/f (Good) **7** Ran SP% **115.8**
Speed ratings (Par 105):109,108,107,105,100 100,89
CSF £11.76 CT £139.80 TOTE £4.00: £2.30, £1.90; EX 19.70.
Owner The Meat Eaters **Bred** Lord Halifax **Trained** Maunby, N Yorks

FOCUS
A fair handicap, run at a solid pace. The form is sound and both the first two are on the upgrade.
Tough Love Official explanation: jockey said gelding was unsuited by the good to soft ground

2937 TURFTV H'CAP 7f 30y
4:00 (4:00) (Class 6) (0-50,50) 4-Y-0+ £2,590 (£770; £385; £192) **Stalls** High

Form RPR
4366 **1** **Guadaloup**[34] 1933 5-8-9 **47** .... DeanMernagh 9 56
(M Brittain) *hld up towards rr: gd hdwy 3f out: rdn along on outer over 1f out: styd on to ld ins fnl f* **6/1**[3]

504- **2** 3/4 **Dulce Sueno**[293] 5077 4-8-11 **49** .... TomEaves 10 56
(I Semple) *hld up in rr: hdwy 3f out: rdn over 1f out: styd on ins fnl f* **16/1**

230- **3** hd **Royal Pardon**[314] 4455 5-8-10 **48** ....(p) PhillipMakin 7 55
(M Dods) *prom: led over 2f out: sn rdn: drvn over 1f out: hdd ins fnl f: no ex* **17/2**

6600 **4** 2 1/2 **Cottam Eclipse**[24] 2203 6-8-8 **46** .... RoystonFfrench 12 46
(I W McInnes) *prom: rdn along over 2f out: drvn wl over 1f out: wknd ent fnl f* **14/1**

6640 **5** 3/4 **Oeuf A La Neige**[2] 2864 7-8-7 **48** .... GregFairley(3) 11 46
(Miss L A Perratt) *in rr: rdn along 1/2-way: hdwy 2f out: drvn and kpt on appr fnl f: nrst fin* **5/1**[1]

2004 **6** 1 1/2 **Penel (IRE)**[4] 2806 6-8-12 **50** ....(p) LeeEnstone 5 44
(P T Midgley) *chsd ldrs: rdn along over 2f out: grad wknd* **11/2**[2]

00-0 **7** 1/2 **Rondo**[41] 1753 4-8-11 **49** .... PaulFessey 8 42
(T D Barron) *in tch: rdn along over 2f out: sn drvn and kpt on same pce* **8/1**

-045 **8** 1 1/4 **Bandos**[95] 729 7-8-10 **48** .... DavidAllan 14 37
(M Smith) *chsd ldrs on inner: n.m.r 4f out: rdn along and ev ch 2f out: sn drvn and wknd over 1f out* **13/2**

0000 **9** 1/2 **Obe One**[12] 2561 7-8-5 **46** oh1 .... PatrickMathers(3) 3 34
(A Berry) *midfield: rdn along 1/2-way: sn no hdwy* **33/1**

-030 **10** 2 1/2 **Procrastinate (IRE)**[7] 2709 5-8-8 **49** ....(b) AndrewMullen(3) 4 30
(R F Fisher) *a towards rr* **22/1**

0063 **11** 8 **Astorygoeswithit**[34] 1933 4-8-8 **46** ....(be) PaulMulrennan 2 6
(P S McEntee) *led: rdn along and hdd over 2f out: sn wknd* **11/1**

4031 **12** 1/2 **Alucica**[11] 2592 4-8-12 **50** ....(v) NCallan 1 8
(D Shaw) *in tch: rdn along wl over 2f out: sn wknd* **10/1**

1m 32.96s (3.02) **Going Correction** +0.375s/f (Good) **12** Ran SP% **118.6**
Speed ratings (Par 101):97,96,95,93,92 90,89,88,87,85 75,75
CSF £98.07 CT £822.19 TOTE £8.30: £2.80, £5.30, £3.40; EX 76.30.
Owner Northgate Red **Bred** Cheveley Park Stud Ltd **Trained** Warthill, N Yorks

FOCUS
A very weak handicap which saw three come clear. The winner is rated close to last season's turf form.
Procrastinate(IRE) Official explanation: jockey said gelding never travelled
Astorygoeswithit Official explanation: jockey said gelding hung both right and left-handed

2938 TURFTV.CO.UK CLASSIFIED STKS 1m
4:30 (4:31) (Class 7) 3-Y-0+ £1,706 (£503; £252) **Stalls** High

Form RPR
-042 **1** **Catherines Cafe (IRE)**[7] 2714 4-9-4 44 ....(p) AndrewMullen(3) 14 59
(A C Whillans) *trckd ldrs: hdwy 3f out: rdn to ld over 1f out: edgd lft ins fnl f: drvn out* **3/1**[1]

05- **2** 3 **Linden's Lady**[305] 4729 7-9-7 45 ....(v) NCallan 9 52
(J R Weymes) *trckd ldrs: hdwy over 2f out: rdn to chse wnr ent fnl f: kpt on* **20/1**

-005 **3** 2 1/2 **Pepper Road**[68] 1086 8-9-7 45 .... RoystonFfrench 13 47
(R Bastiman) *in tch: hdwy over 2f out: sn rdn and styd on ins fnl f* **16/1**

-542 **4** nk **The Jailer**[12] 2559 4-9-0 45 ....(p) MCGeran(7) 11 46
(J G M O'Shea) *cl up: rdn to ld 2f out: drvn: edgd lft and hdd over 1f out: wknd fnlf* **9/1**

0-33 **5** 3/4 **Spring Time Girl**[7] 2716 5-9-7 44 .... PhillipMakin 8 44+
(B Ellison) *s.i.s and bhd tl styd on fnl 3f: nrst fin* **7/2**[2]

0-00 **6** 2 1/2 **Briery Blaze**[21] 2298 4-9-2 45 .... PJMcDonald(5) 7 39
(Mrs K Walton) *bhd: rdn along and hdwy over 2f out: kpt on u.p appr fnl f: nrst fin* **33/1**

-001 **7** 1 1/4 **Ignition**[5] 2760 5-9-13 45 .... PaulHanagan 2 42
(W M Brisbourne) *midfield: hdwy 3f out: rdn along 2f out and sn no imp* **4/1**[3]

0-00 **8** 1/2 **Suhezy (IRE)**[9] 2657 4-9-7 45 .... TonyHamilton 12 35
(J S Wainwright) *prom: hdwy on inner to ld 1/2-way: rdn along and hdd 2f out: grad wknd* **33/1**

0000 **9** 1 3/4 **Wizby**[24] 2214 4-9-4 45 ....(v[1]) JamieMoriarty(3) 3 30
(P D Evans) *nvr bttr than midfield* **16/1**

0-06 **10** 7 **The Salwick Flyer (IRE)**[53] 1426 4-9-7 45 .... TomEaves 1 14
(I Semple) *a midfield* **8/1**

00-4 **11** 2 1/2 **Churchtown**[25] 2167 3-8-11 45 .... LeeEnstone 6 9
(K R Burke) *in tch: rdn along wl over 2f out: sn wknd* **33/1**

0055 **12** 2 1/2 **Smart Pick**[17] 2422 4-9-4 45 .... GregFairley(3) 5 3
(Mrs L Williamson) *a in rr* **25/1**

00-0 **13** 9 **Only A Splash**[24] 2205 3-8-11 45 .... PaulMulrennan 10 —
(D W Chapman) *led to 1/2-way: sn rdn along and wknd 3f out* **66/1**

0-00 **14** 8 **Passionately Royal**[49] 1527 5-9-7 45 .... DeanMernagh 4 —
(M Brittain) *a in rr* **33/1**

1m 44.75s (2.25) **Going Correction** +0.375s/f (Good)
WFA 3 from 4yo+ 10lb **14** Ran SP% **122.0**
Speed ratings (Par 97):103,100,97,97,96 93,92,92,90,83 80,78,69,61
CSF £70.26 TOTE £4.20: £1.20, £6.20, £4.30; EX 79.50.
Owner Mrs L M Whillans **Bred** Michael Sexton **Trained** Newmill-On-Slitrig, Borders

FOCUS
Not much of a race, but Catherines Cafe did it well. The time was relatively good and the form seems sound at this very low level.
Spring Time Girl Official explanation: jockey said mare missed the break
Churchtown Official explanation: jockey said gelding was unsuited by the good to soft ground

2939 SCOTTISH RACING "YOUR BEST BET" H'CAP 5f

5:00 (5:00) (Class 6) (0-65,62) 3-Y-O £2,590 (£770; £385; £192) Stalls Low

Form				RPR
2-44	1		**Inspainagain (USA)**^{3} 2844 3-9-5 **60** ... PhillipMakin 3 (T D Barron) *cl up: rdn to ld over 1f out: kpt on wl u.p ins fnl f* **15/8**^{1}	68
0-00	2	1 ¾	**River Club**^{12} 2554 3-9-3 **58** ... NCallan 4 (G A Swinbank) *chsd ldrs: hdwy 2f out: sn rdn and styd on wl fnl f* **7/2**^{3}	59+
2500	3	shd	**Kilvickeon (IRE)**^{11} 2594 3-8-3 **47** ... PatrickMathers(3) 6 (Peter Grayson) *wnt lft s: sn outpcd and rdn along 1/2-way: hdwy wl over 1f out: styd on wl u.p ins fnl f* **16/1**	48
-306	4	nk	**Beechside (IRE)**^{52} 1453 3-8-6 **47** ... TomEaves 8 (W A Murphy, Ire) *hld up: hdwy 2f out: rdn over 1f out: swtchd rt and ch ins fnl f: sn drvn and one pce* **20/1**	47
3001	5	2 ½	**Come What May**^{3} 2837 3-9-1 **56** 6ex ... (bt) PaulMulrennan 7 (Rae Guest) *led: rdn along 2f out: hdd over 1f out: wknd ins fnl f* **3/1**^{2}	47
-350	6	3	**Billy Ruffian**^{19} 2363 3-9-7 **62** ... (p) DavidAllan 9 (T D Easterby) *cl up: rdn along 2f out: sn wknd* **7/1**	42
-630	7	3	**The Brat**^{46} 1595 3-8-5 **46** ... PaulHanagan 5 (J S Wainwright) *bmpd s: t.k.h and sn cl up: rdn along 1/2-way and sn wknd* **9/1**	15

61.70 secs (1.20) **Going Correction** +0.275s/f (Good) **7** Ran SP% **115.1**
Speed ratings (Par 97):101,98,98,97,93 88,83
CSF £8.84 CT £77.49 TOTE £2.90: £1.70, £2.30 Place 6 £59.28, Place 5 £24.57.
Owner Jim Beaumont & Douglas Pryde **Bred** L Millsap **Trained** Maunby, N Yorks
■ Stewards' Enquiry : Patrick Mathers two-day ban: used whip with excessive force and frequency (Jul 9-10)

FOCUS
The time compared favourably with the earlier two 5f races, but this time they raced on the stands' side. It was not much of a race but the form is sound rated through the third and fourth. The front pair are relatively unexposed.
The Brat Official explanation: jockey said filly was unsuited by the good to soft ground
T/Plt: £149.20 to a £1 stake. Pool: £68,199.05. 333.65 winning tickets. T/Qpdt: £45.10 to a £1 stake. Pool: £4,363.40. 71.50 winning tickets. JR

2722 WINDSOR (R-H)

Monday, June 25

OFFICIAL GOING: Soft (heavy in places; 6.8)
There were 23 non-runners due to the testing ground.
Wind: Almost nil, races 1-3; light behind, races 4-5; moderate behind, race 6
Weather: Fine becoming overcast

2940 MCGEE GROUP FILLIES' H'CAP 1m 2f 7y

6:40 (6:40) (Class 5) (0-70,69) 3-Y-O £3,238 (£963; £481; £240) Stalls Low

Form				RPR
304	1		**Etain (IRE)**^{24} 2219 3-9-5 **67** ... AdamKirby 2 (W R Swinburn) *led 1f: chsd ldr: clr in ldng trio 4f out: rdn to ld over 1f out against far rail: hrd drvn and kpt on* **9/2**^{2}	75
-004	2	1 ½	**Anthea**^{27} 2105 3-8-9 **57** ... TedDurcan 14 (B R Millman) *led after 1f: clr 1/2-way: hdd u.p over 1f out: kpt on* **15/2**	62
2325	3	5	**Spritza (IRE)**^{16} 2445 3-9-2 **64** ... JohnEgan 6 (M L W Bell) *hld up in last pair early: stdy prog gng wl fr over 3f out: chsd clr ldng pair 2f out: no imp* **4/1**^{1}	59
000	4	5	**Doubly Guest**^{7} 2727 3-9-7 **69** ... JHBowman 10 (G G Margarson) *settled in last pair: wl off the pce 1/2-way: stdy prog over 3f out: no imp 2f out: pushed along and plugged on* **6/1**	54
06-0	5	hd	**Barbs Pink Diamond (USA)**^{17} 2428 3-8-12 **60** ... JimCrowley 12 (Mrs A J Perrett) *chsd ldng pair and clr of rest: hanging lft fr 3f out: lost 3rd and wl btn 2f out* **20/1**	45
062	6	2	**Driving Miss Suzie**^{22} 2274 3-8-12 **65** ... WilliamBuick(5) 5 (A M Balding) *hld up off the pce: reminders over 5f out: reluctant and wl btn over 2f out: plugged on fnl f* **5/1**^{3}	46
2305	7	nk	**Miss Saafend Plaza (IRE)**^{16} 2475 3-9-2 **64** ... PatDobbs 1 (R Hannon) *hld up in rr and off the pce: effrt over 3f out: no prog 2f out: wknd* **14/1**	44
00-0	8	½	**Little Iris**^{23} 2262 3-8-5 **53** ... KerrinMcEvoy 13 (L M Cumani) *chsd clr ldng trio: tried to cl over 3f out: wknd over 2f out* **6/1**	32
5-50	9	21	**Little Miss Tara (IRE)**^{21} 2317 3-9-5 **67** ... SteveDrowne 7 (A B Haynes) *settled off the pce: clsd over 3f out: sn wknd rapidly: t.o* **16/1**	4
0-00	10	59	**Bali Belony**^{129} 484 3-7-11 **52** oh5 ow2 ... JosephWalsh(7) 8 (J R Jenkins) *plld hrd for 1f: sn dropped out: t.o bef 1/2-way: virtually p.u 2f out* **50/1**	—

2m 14.9s (6.60) **Going Correction** +0.75s/f (Yiel) **10** Ran SP% **114.5**
Speed ratings (Par 96):103,101,97,93,93 92,91,91,74,27
CSF £37.46 CT £145.11 TOTE £5.30: £1.90, £3.40, £1.70; EX 80.40.
Owner C J Collins **Bred** Thomas F Brennan **Trained** Aldbury, Herts

FOCUS
A modest fillies' handicap and essentially ordinary form. They tended to race towards the far side in the straight.
Little Iris Official explanation: jockey said saddle slipped
Little Miss Tara(IRE) Official explanation: jockey said filly had no more to give
Bali Belony Official explanation: jockey said filly was unsuited by the ground

2941 K & L GATES MAIDEN AUCTION STKS 6f

7:10 (7:11) (Class 5) 2-Y-O £3,238 (£963; £481; £240) Stalls High

Form				RPR
	1		**Dry Speedfit (IRE)** 2-9-2 0 ... TQuinn 7 (G G Margarson) *settled towards rr: taken to outer and prog fr 1/2-way: clsd to chal 1f out: led ins fnl f: pushed out* **16/1**	83+
00	2	½	**Silver Wind**^{74} 1007 2-8-13 0 ... (b^{1}) StephenDonohoe 10 (P D Evans) *pushed along to chse ldrs: prog on outer over 2f out: drvn to ld over 1f out: hdd ins fnl f: styd on but readily hld* **16/1**	79
06	3	6	**Fathsta (IRE)**^{18} 2398 2-8-4 0 ... WilliamBuick(5) 2 (S Kirk) *pressed ldrs: rdn 2f out: wnt 3rd but sn outpcd over 1f out* **15/2**	57
0	4	1 ½	**Synge Street**^{16} 2443 2-8-11 0 ... DaneO'Neill 11 (R Hannon) *mostly chsd ldr to over 2f out: sn outpcd* **10/1**	54
5	5	hd	**Farthermost (IRE)**^{16} 2447 2-8-9 0 ... PatDobbs 6 (R Hannon) *bmpd s: chsd ldrs: rdn over 2f out: outpcd over 1f out* **7/1**^{3}	51
0	6	2	**Relative Order**^{14} 2510 2-9-2 0 ... GeorgeBaker 16 (J R Best) *racd on outer in rr: pushed along and kpt on same pce fnl 2f: nvr nr ldrs* **9/2**^{2}	52+
0	7	shd	**We Have A Dream**^{11} 2596 2-8-11 0 ... KerrinMcEvoy 1 (W R Muir) *pressed ldrs tl 2f out: fdd* **16/1**	47
0	8	1	**Illusionary**^{13} 2539 2-8-9 0 ... AdamKirby 8 (J G Portman) *pushed along to chse ldrs: outpcd 2f out: n.d after* **33/1**	42
0	9	¾	**Bilboa**^{24} 2193 2-8-13 0 ... JimCrowley 13 (B R Millman) *mde most: racd on outer tl swtchd to far rail over 2f out: carried hd v high and hdd over 1f out: wknd* **16/1**	44
0	10	1 ¼	**Indian Days**^{12} 2575 2-9-2 0 ... TedDurcan 14 (J G Given) *restless stalls and rrd s: wl in rr: hung bdly lft 1/2-way: plugged on fnl f* **14/1**	43+
	11	2 ½	**Deckguard** 2-8-13 0 ... JohnEgan 12 (J S Moore) *dwlt: wl in rr: nvr a factor* **16/1**	33
00	12	½	**Tapas Lad (IRE)**^{11} 2604 2-8-8 0 ... JerryO'Dwyer(3) 4 (V Smith) *s.s: wl in rr and pushed along: effrt whn hmpd jst over 2f out: no prog after* **50/1**	29
43	13	2 ½	**L'Art Du Silence (IRE)**^{11} 2590 2-8-13 0 ... MartinDwyer 5 (J R Boyle) *bmpd s: nvr beyond midfield: rdn and struggling whn stmbld over 1f out: eased* **7/2**^{1}	24+
40	14	1 ¼	**Galley Slave (IRE)**^{21} 2303 2-9-2 0 ... MickyFenton 3 (Mrs P Sly) *chsd ldrs but stl rdn: wknd over 2f out* **16/1**	23
0	15	24	**City Wizzard**^{18} 2398 2-8-13 0 ... DarryllHolland 9 (M L W Bell) *w ldrs over 2f: sn wknd: no ch whn lost action over 1f out: t.o* **14/1**	—

1m 15.52s (1.85) **Going Correction** +0.20s/f (Good) **15** Ran SP% **127.3**
Speed ratings (Par 93):95,94,86,84,84 81,81,79,78,77 73,73,69,68,36
CSF £263.13 TOTE £22.40: £5.00, £6.20, £2.90; EX 571.30.
Owner John Guest **Bred** Yeomanstown Stud **Trained** Newmarket, Suffolk

FOCUS
Plenty of runners, but this was a weak maiden behind the first two. The winner is capable of better. They raced far side in the straight.

NOTEBOOK
Dry Speedfit(IRE) ◆, a 35,000gns purchase, out of a dual sprint winner at two to three in Italy, looked to take this a shade cosily on his racecourse debut. He was quite a way off the pace early on, but made smooth progress to get into a threatening position and only had to be pushed out to hold off Silver Wind's persistent challenge. This was a modest race, but he was a cut above his rivals. (op 14-1 tchd 20-1)
Silver Wind showed improved form in first-time blinkers, keeping the winner up to his work and finishing clear of the remainder. (op 25-1)
Fathsta(IRE) appreciated the step back up in trip, but he was no match for the front two. He is probably more of a nursery type. (op 8-1)
Synge Street is another who will probably find his level once handicapped. (op 9-1 tchd 11-1)
Farthermost(IRE) did not really improve on his debut running at Goodwood and, like his stablemate, may do better once handicapped. (op 15-2 tchd 6-1)
Relative Order failed to impove on the form he showed over course and distance on his debut and was a little disappointing. (op 5-1 tchd 6-1)
Indian Days Official explanation: jockey said colt reared leaving stalls
L'Art Du Silence(IRE) was well below the form of his two previous efforts, even allowing for a stumble over a furlong from the finish, and this soft ground clearly didn't suit. Official explanation: jockey said colt was unsuited by the ground (op 3-1 tchd 4-1 in places)
City Wizzard Official explanation: vet said gelding finished lame

2942 RAB CAPITAL H'CAP 6f

7:40 (7:40) (Class 4) (0-85,80) 3-Y-O £6,477 (£1,927; £963; £481) Stalls High

Form				RPR
326	1		**Kelamon**^{5} 2769 3-8-3 **67** ... WilliamBuick(5) 3 (M D I Usher) *settled in last pair: prog on outer over 2f out: rdn to ld over 1f out: styd on wl* **7/2**^{3}	77
1-	2	2	**Edge Closer**^{233} 6331 3-9-4 **77** ... PatDobbs 1 (R Hannon) *dwlt: hld up in last pair: prog 1/2-way: led briefly wl over 1f out: chsd wnr after: one pce fnl f* **7/4**^{1}	81+
1-34	3	1 ¾	**Sunoverregun**^{5} 2769 3-9-7 **80** ... AmirQuinn 7 (J R Boyle) *trckd ldr: led over 2f out gng wl: rdn and hdd wl over 1f out: nt qckn* **9/4**^{2}	79
-615	4	3	**Yerevan**^{17} 2435 3-9-7 **80** ... JohnEgan 6 (R T Phillips) *pressed ldrs: upsides ent fnl 2f: sn rdn: wknd fnl f* **6/1**	70
2-21	5	5	**Farefield Lodge (IRE)**^{19} 2366 3-9-3 **76** ... PhilipRobinson 8 (C G Cox) *w ldrs tl wknd wl over 1f out* **13/2**	51
4000	6	7	**Dora Explora**^{2} 2881 3-9-0 **73** ... (b^{1}) StephenDonohoe 9 (P D Evans) *drvn to ld: hdd & wknd over 2f out* **16/1**	27

1m 15.13s (1.46) **Going Correction** +0.20s/f (Good) **6** Ran SP% **122.9**
Speed ratings (Par 101):98,95,93,89,82 73
CSF £11.28 CT £17.23 TOTE £4.60: £2.70, £1.90; EX 12.60.
Owner Mr & Mrs Richard Hames And Friends **Bred** R And Mrs Hames **Trained** Upper Lambourn, Berks

FOCUS
Only six runners and this looked like an ordinary handicap for the grade. The third is the best guide to the form. Once again, they raced far side in the straight.

2943 PM QUINLAN H'CAP 1m 67y

8:10 (8:10) (Class 4) (0-85,85) 3-Y-O £5,181 (£1,541; £770; £384) Stalls High

Form				RPR
0-53	1		**Paceman (USA)**^{34} 1929 3-9-5 **83** ... TedDurcan 2 (R Hannon) *trckd ldng pair: led 2f out: sn rdn: drew clr ent fnl f: eased last 50yds* **7/2**^{1}	92+
14-4	2	2	**Nicada (IRE)**^{21} 2317 3-8-5 **69** ow2 ... (p) JohnEgan 5 (J S Moore) *in tch in midfield: effrt 3f out: rdn and nt qckn 2f out: kpt on u.p to take 2nd last stride* **10/1**	70
2010	3	shd	**Eau Good**^{18} 2400 3-9-7 **85** ... GeorgeBaker 6 (B G Powell) *hld up in last: prog on outer over 2f out: rdn to chse wnr over 1f out: no imp: lost 2nd last stride* **9/2**^{2}	86
0020	4	¾	**Highland Harvest**^{30} 2045 3-8-12 **76** ... TQuinn 8 (D R C Elsworth) *t.k.h: led after 2f: stdd after 3f: rdn and hdd 2f out: one pce* **7/2**^{1}	75
2-43	5	1	**Count Ceprano (IRE)**^{53} 1439 3-9-6 **84** ... (p) AdamKirby 9 (W R Swinburn) *hld up towards rr: effrt 3f out: hrd rdn and nt on terms wl over 1f out: kpt on* **9/2**^{2}	81
1-00	6	14	**Alfredian Park**^{32} 1956 3-8-3 **72** ... WilliamBuick(5) 1 (S Kirk) *t.k.h: led for 2f: chsd ldr to 3f out: sn wknd u.p* **22/1**	37
2-10	7	1 ½	**Sea Land (FR)**^{19} 2354 3-8-11 **75** ... (v^{1}) MartinDwyer 10 (M P Tregoning) *t.k.h: hld up in rr: awkward bnd over 5f out: rdn 3f out: wknd over 2f out* **5/1**^{3}	36
1-16	8	shd	**All Of Me (IRE)**^{53} 1439 3-9-4 **82** ... (b^{1}) DaneO'Neill 3 (T G Mills) *s.i.s: settled in rr: effrt 3f out: wknd over 2f out* **14/1**	43

1m 50.72s (6.02) **Going Correction** +0.75s/f (Yiel) **8** Ran SP% **117.6**
Speed ratings (Par 101):99,97,96,96,95 81,79,79
CSF £40.55 CT £161.91 TOTE £4.60: £1.80, £2.80, £1.80; EX 46.00.

Owner Highclere Thoroughbred Racing XLIII **Bred** R D Hubbard **Trained** East Everleigh, Wilts

FOCUS

Six non-runners but this was a reasonable handicap for the level. Paceman was value for further. The winning time was 0.59 seconds quicker than the following three-year-old maiden.

Highland Harvest Official explanation: jockey said colt ran too freely

Sea Land(FR) Official explanation: jockey said gelding ran too free and was unsuited by the ground

2944 CLIC SARGENT MAIDEN STKS — 1m 67y

8:40 (8:41) (Class 5) 3-Y-O — £3,238 (£963; £481; £240) Stalls High

Form — RPR

0-4 **1** **Just Two Numbers**[69] [1077] 3-9-3 0 ... DarryllHolland 9 — 79
(W Jarvis) *t.k.h early: trckd ldng pair: taken to outer and effrt over 2f out: pushed into ld wl over 1f out: rdn out fnl f* **11/1**

2-42 **2** 1 ½ **Castara Bay**[10] [2625] 3-9-3 77 ... DaneO'Neill 8 — 76
(R Hannon) *disp ld: def advantage over 2f out: drvn and hdd wl over 1f out: kpt on wl u.p: hld last 100yds* **3/1**[2]

30- **3** 1 ¼ **Limbo King**[240] [6214] 3-9-3 0 ... GeorgeBaker 1 — 73
(J R Fanshawe) *trckd ldrs: effrt 3f out: rdn 2f out: sn outpcd: kpt on fnl f* **11/4**[1]

4 **4** hd **Vincenzio (IRE)**[59] [1278] 3-9-3 0 ... TedDurcan 7 — 73
(C R Egerton) *trckd ldng pair: rdn and effrt over 2f out: kpt on same pce fr over 1f out* **7/1**

00 **5** 5 **Garden Party**[21] [2320] 3-9-3 0 ... JohnEgan 12 — 61
(Sir Michael Stoute) *restless stalls: dwlt: sn in tch in midfield: effrt 3f out: chsd ldng pair briefly over 1f out: sn wknd* **12/1**

43 **6** 2 ½ **Candy Mountain**[23] [2253] 3-8-12 0 ... MartinDwyer 6 — 50
(L M Cumani) *dwlt: towards rr: rdn and no prog 3f out: plugged on* **5/1**[3]

7 1 ¼ **Own Boss (USA)** 3-9-3 0 ... PhilipRobinson 5 — 53
(M A Jarvis) *dwlt: hld up towards rr: rn green fr 3f out: no prog* **6/1**

0 **8** ½ **Pulsate**[17] [2429] 3-8-12 0 ... JimCrowley 3 — 46
(Mrs A J Perrett) *w ldr to over 2f out: wknd* **33/1**

9 ¾ **Polish Prize** 3-9-3 0 ... AdamKirby 13 — 50
(W R Swinburn) *s.s: a in rr: pushed along and no prog over 2f out* **16/1**

0 **10** 5 **Nouveau (GER)**[47] [1587] 3-9-3 0 ... PatDobbs 10 — 38
(R Hannon) *hld up in last: pushed along and no prog over 2f out: wknd over 1f out* **33/1**

1m 51.31s (6.61) **Going Correction** +0.75s/f (Yiel) — **10** Ran SP% **122.9**

Speed ratings (Par 99):96,94,93,93,88 85,84,83,83,78

CSF £46.56 TOTE £11.90: £3.00, £1.70, £2.00; EX 54.60.

Owner Camsey, Folan, Lees & Heath **Bred** L T And M Foster **Trained** Newmarket, Suffolk

FOCUS

Just an ordinary maiden, but it should produce some winners. The runner-up is the obvious guide to the form's worth. The winning time was 0.59 seconds slower than the previous handicap won by the 83-rated Paceman.

2945 BGC H'CAP — 1m 3f 135y

9:10 (9:10) (Class 5) (0-75,75) 3-Y-O — £3,238 (£963; £481; £240) Stalls Low

Form — RPR

5-60 **1** **Polish Red**[11] [2602] 3-9-4 72 ... JohnEgan 2 — 81
(G G Margarson) *hld up in rr: prog to trck ldrs 3f out: rdn to ld wl over 1f out: edgd rt after: kpt on wl* **11/1**

0-42 **2** 1 ¾ **Cushat Law (IRE)**[12] [2552] 3-8-4 58 ... KerrinMcEvoy 14 — 64
(W Jarvis) *hld up towards rr: prog over 3f out: rdn to chal 2f out: kpt on but hld fnl f* **15/8**[1]

325 **3** 3 **Haarth Sovereign (IRE)**[27] [2127] 3-9-7 75 ... AdamKirby 5 — 76
(W R Swinburn) *chsd ldrs: rdn 4f out: effrt to press ldrs 2f out: racd against far rail and one pce over 1f out* **5/1**[3]

0-02 **4** ¾ **Pagan Rules (IRE)**[12] [2558] 3-8-8 62 ...(b) JimCrowley 11 — 62
(Mrs A J Perrett) *trckd ldrs: prog to ld over 3f out: hdd wl over 1f out: nt qckn* **4/1**[2]

31-0 **5** 2 **Mardi**[10] [2635] 3-9-5 73 ... DarryllHolland 1 — 70
(W J Haggas) *led for 4f: trckd ldr: led 4f out to over 3f out: sn btn* **7/1**

-000 **6** 17 **Chunky's Choice (IRE)**[10] [2627] 3-8-8 62 ... SebSanders 3 — 31
(J Noseda) *nvr gng wl: mostly in last pair: wl bhd over 3f out: t.o* **6/1**

4440 **7** 12 **Mango Masher (IRE)**[10] [2635] 3-8-13 67 ...(b[1]) DaneO'Neill 6 — 17
(C R Egerton) *pressed ldr: led after 4f to 4f out: wknd rapidly: t.o* **14/1**

-006 **8** 49 **Shine Like A Star**[19] [2359] 3-8-11 65 ... TedDurcan 10 — —
(J L Dunlop) *nvr gng wl: a in last pair: t.o fnl 3f* **10/1**

2m 38.54s (8.44) **Going Correction** +0.75s/f (Yiel) — **8** Ran SP% **122.3**

Speed ratings (Par 99):101,99,97,97,96 84,76,44

CSF £34.44 CT £124.86 TOTE £15.70: £3.40, £1.30, £2.00; EX 55.10 Place 6 £78.96, Place 5 £47.03..

Owner Norcroft Park Stud **Bred** Norcroft Park Stud **Trained** Newmarket, Suffolk

FOCUS

Despite the defections this was a fair handicap, and the form looks solid considering the ground. The promising Polish Red is a fine physical specimen and not one to underestimate.

Shine Like A Star Official explanation: jockey said filly had no more to give

T/Jkpt: Not won. T/Plt: £70.80 to a £1 stake. Pool £134,249.60 - 1,383.10 winning units. T/Qpdt: £3.70 to a £1 stake. Pool £9,109.50 - 1,819.50 winning units. JN

2516 WOLVERHAMPTON (A.W) (L-H)

Monday, June 25

OFFICIAL GOING: Standard

Wind: Fresh against Weather: Overcast, turning to rain from the 4th race onwards

2946 STAY AT THE WOLVERHAMPTON HOLIDAY INN AMATEUR RIDERS' (S) STKS — 1m 4f 50y(P)

2:15 (2:15) (Class 6) 4-Y-O+ — £1,977 (£608; £304) Stalls Low

Form — RPR

5603 **1** **Regency Red (IRE)**[5] [2764] 9-10-9 50 ... MrBenBrisbourne(5) 11 — 50
(W M Brisbourne) *hld up: hdwy 1/2-way: rdn and edgd lft over 1f out: styd on to ld nr fin* **3/1**[1]

5060 **2** ½ **Alexian**[16] [2467] 4-10-7 65 ... BrydieKilloran(7) 10 — 49
(D W P Arbuthnot) *s.i.s: hld up: plld hadr: hdwy over 6f out: led 5f out to 4f out: led ins fnl f: hdd nr fin* **10/3**[2]

0 **3** ½ **Callitquits (IRE)**[18] [1732] 5-10-9 49 ... MrPCollington(5) 12 — 48
(Jennie Candlish) *chsd ldrs: led 4f out: rdn over 1f out: hdd and unable qck ins fnl f* **40/1**

0000 **4** 1 ½ **Penwell Hill (USA)**[22] [789] 8-11-0 41 ...(b) MrSWalker 3 — 46
(Miss M E Rowland) *prom: racd keenly: outpcd over 2f out: styd on ins fnl f* **18/1**

640 **5** 1 ¾ **Itcanbedone Again (IRE)**[9] [2656] 8-11-0 52 ... MissSBrotherton 5 — 43
(Ian Williams) *hld up: hdwy u.p over 1f out: nt rch ldrs* **4/1**[3]

060/ **6** nk **Neckar Valley (IRE)**[646] [5298] 8-10-11 55 ow4 ... MrGWalters(7) 6 — 47
(J G Portman) *led 7f: rdn over 2f out: no ex fnl f* **10/1**

-040 **7** 3 **Integration**[112] [615] 7-11-0 40 ... MrMSeston 4 — 38
(Miss M E Rowland) *hld up: plld hrd: hdwy over 5f out: rdn and wknd over 1f out* **14/1**

-000 **8** 1 ½ **Yenaled**[9] [2656] 10-10-7 45 ... MissHDavies(7) 2 — 36
(J M Bradley) *s.i.s: hld up: n.d* **10/1**

635/ **9** 6 **Queen Excalibur**[18] [1917] 8-10-9 40 ... MissLHorner 1 — 21
(C Roberts) *trckd ldr: racd keenly: rdn over 3f out: wknd over 1f out* **33/1**

5500 **10** 6 **Undeterred**[4] [2802] 11-10-7 55 ... MrECookson(7) 8 — 16
(K J Burke) *hld up: rdn and wknd over 2f out* **9/1**

-00 **11** 4 **Roll Em Over**[31] [1998] 4-10-9 0 ... MrSDobson 7 — 5
(C W Thornton) *chsd ldrs over 8f* **25/1**

2m 49.37s (6.95) **Going Correction** -0.125s/f (Stan) — **11** Ran SP% **117.4**

Speed ratings (Par 101):71,70,70,69,68 67,65,64,60,56 54

CSF £12.68 TOTE £3.60: £1.10, £1.10, £14.60; EX 15.10 Trifecta £93.70 Pool £171.62 - 1.30 winning units..There was no bid for the winner. Alexian was claimed by G L Moore for £6,000.

Owner Hamerton, Twidle **Bred** Patrick J Burke **Trained** Great Ness, Shropshire

FOCUS

An already bad race was turned into a complete nonsense by a pedestrian gallop, hence the painfully slow winning time. Several of these ruined their chances by pulling like a train early and this form adds up to very little, with the first two some way off their best.

2947 WBX.COM WORLD BET EXCHANGE H'CAP — 7f 32y(P)

2:45 (2:45) (Class 6) (0-60,60) 3-Y-0+ — £2,388 (£705; £352) Stalls High

Form — RPR

0004 **1** **Benny The Bus**[24] [2225] 5-9-2 55 ... J-PGuillambert 7 — 63
(Mrs G S Rees) *chsd ldr: led over 2f out: rdn out* **14/1**

0-00 **2** ¾ **Boreana**[27] [2121] 4-8-13 57 ... TravisBlock(5) 9 — 63
(Jedd O'Keeffe) *hld up in tch: rdn to chse wnr over 1f out: styd on* **12/1**

4300 **3** ¾ **Royal Envoy (IRE)**[14] [2516] 4-9-4 57 ... JimmyQuinn 11 — 61+
(D Shaw) *s.i.s: hld up: r.o ins fnl f: nrst fin* **16/1**

2004 **4** shd **Green Pirate**[15] [2492] 5-9-4 57 ... GeorgeBaker 6 — 61+
(W M Brisbourne) *s.i.s: hld up: hdwy over 1f out: rdn and edgd lft ins fnl f: styd on* **11/2**[3]

1043 **5** ½ **Mistral Sky**[4] [2799] 8-9-6 59 ...(p) MickyFenton 1 — 61
(Stef Liddiard) *chsd ldrs: rdn and hung rt over 2f out: kpt on* **9/2**[1]

4305 **6** ¾ **Compton Plume**[17] [2421] 7-9-2 55 ... DaleGibson 10 — 55
(M W Easterby) *trckd ldrs: racd keenly: rdn over 2f out: styd on same pce fnl f* **33/1**

0020 **7** nk **Lucius Verrus (USA)**[9] [2665] 7-7-9 60 ...(v) DaneO'Neill 5 — 59
(D Shaw) *mid-div: rdn over 4f out: nt clr run over 1f out: nt trble ldrs* **12/1**

0601 **8** 1 **Royal Orissa**[24] [2225] 5-9-3 56 ... TedDurcan 2 — 53
(D Haydn Jones) *trckd ldrs: racd keenly: rdn over 2f out: wknd over 1f out* **5/1**[2]

1-06 **9** 3 **Ours (IRE)**[24] [2225] 4-9-4 57 ...(b) JoeFanning 8 — 46
(J D Bethell) *hld up: rdn 1/2-way: n.d* **9/1**

1206 **10** 1 **Grand Palace (IRE)**[4] [2799] 4-9-0 56 ...(v) SaleemGolam(3) 3 — 42
(D Shaw) *led over 4f: wknd fnl f* **9/1**

2600 **11** 2 **Musicmaestroplease (IRE)**[12] [2550] 4-9-4 60 ... DominicFox(3) 4 — 41
(S Parr) *s.i.s: hld up: n.d* **16/1**

3030 **12** 3 **Bessemer (JPN)**[3] [2823] 6-9-7 60 ... SebSanders 12 — 32
(I W McInnes) *hld up: effrt over 2f out: sn wknd* **5/1**[2]

1m 29.82s (-0.58) **Going Correction** -0.125s/f (Stan) — **12** Ran SP% **123.7**

Speed ratings (Par 101):98,97,96,96,95 94,94,93,89,88 86,82

CSF £178.89 CT £2732.92 TOTE £14.80: £4.50, £5.60, £7.60; EX 381.30 TRIFECTA Not won..

Owner I F Campbell **Bred** Capt J H Wilson **Trained** Sollom, Lancs

FOCUS

A moderate handicap in which the pace was no more than ordinary. The form probably adds up to very little, the winner rated to this year's form.

Mistral Sky Official explanation: jockey said gelding hung right-handed

Bessemer(JPN) Official explanation: jockey said gelding hung right-handed

2948 WBX.COM CLAIMING STKS — 5f 216y(P)

3:15 (3:16) (Class 6) 3-Y-O — £2,914 (£867; £433; £216) Stalls Low

Form — RPR

0404 **1** **Time Share (IRE)**[19] [2357] 3-8-3 48 ow3 ... MartinDwyer 2 — 56
(J A Osborne) *chsd ldrs: rdn over 2f out: sn hung rt: led 1f out: styd on wl* **5/1**[2]

4230 **2** 3 ½ **Strike Force**[18] [2387] 3-9-1 57 ...(p) DarryllHolland 5 — 57
(R A Harris) *chsd ldrs: outpcd over 2f out: rdn and hung lft over 1f out: styd on* **7/2**[1]

00 **3** nk **Lord Of The Reins (IRE)**[19] [2366] 3-8-3 0 ow1 ... SaleemGolam(3) 6 — 47
(D Shaw) *s.s: r.o ins fnl f: nrst fin* **50/1**

6016 **4** nk **Totally Free**[23] [2262] 3-8-8 62 ...(v) TravisBlock(5) 13 — 53
(M D I Usher) *sn outpcd: hdwy over 1f out: styd on* **5/1**[2]

0406 **5** nk **Pirner's Brig**[25] [2172] 3-8-4 63 ... NSLawes(7) 4 — 50
(M W Easterby) *led: rdn and hdd over 1f out: wknd ins fnl f* **11/2**[3]

4400 **6** hd **Head To Head (IRE)**[9] [2668] 3-8-6 52 ow1 ... LPKeniry 12 — 45
(Peter Grayson) *s.i.s: hld up: hdwy over 2f out: sn rdn: kpt on* **14/1**

3062 **7** nk **Eastern Princess**[24] [2195] 3-8-0 45 ...(v) RichardThomas 10 — 38
(J A Geake) *mid-div: hdwy over 2f out: sn rdn: one pce fnl f* **10/1**

00 **8** ½ **Altos Reales**[14] [2520] 3-8-5 0 ... PatrickHills(5) 9 — 46
(D Shaw) *s.i.s: outpcd: r.o ins fnl f: nvr nrr* **33/1**

0006 **9** 6 **Zaafira (SPA)**[9] [2668] 3-8-4 52 ... EdwardCreighton 11 — 22
(E J Creighton) *prom: rdn over 2f out: wknd over 1f out* **14/1**

045 **10** 2 ½ **Zil Up**[98] [711] 3-8-4 48 ...(b) LeeTopliss(7) 3 — 22
(S R Bowring) *s.i.s: hdwy 1/2-way: rdn and wknd over 1f out* **33/1**

11 2 ½ **Dark Mask (IRE)** 3-8-11 0 ... SebSanders 1 — 14
(J L Spearing) *prom: n.m.r and lost pl 4f out: sn bhd* **5/1**[2]

-033 **12** ¾ **Valeesha**[21] [2304] 3-8-3 45 ... LiamJones(3) 7 — 7
(W G M Turner) *chsd ldrs over 3f* **16/1**

1m 15.45s (-0.36) **Going Correction** -0.125s/f (Stan) — **12** Ran SP% **123.8**

Speed ratings (Par 97):97,92,91,91,91 90,90,89,81,78 75,74

CSF £23.65 TOTE £7.80: £2.90, £1.60, £23.00; EX 28.60 Trifecta £156.20 Pool £220.07 - 1.00 winning units..The winner was claimed by P McEntee for £5,000.

Owner J Palmer-Brown **Bred** Austin Lyons **Trained** Upper Lambourn, Berks

FOCUS

A poor claimer contested by some dubious types. The early pace was frantic and not many ever got involved.

Totally Free Official explanation: jockey said gelding hung right-handed

2949 EUROPEAN BREEDERS' FUND MAIDEN STKS — 5f 216y(P)
3:45 (3:46) (Class 5) 2-Y-O — £3,562 (£1,059; £529; £264) Stalls Low

Form — RPR

3 **1** **Ten Meropa (USA)**[18] 2398 2-9-3 0 .... MartinDwyer 6 — 86+
(J A Osborne) *trckd ldrs: racd keenly: rdn to ld ins fnl f: r.o: eased nr fin* **4/1**[2]

4 **2** 1 ½ **Bailey (IRE)**[17] 2424 2-9-3 0 .... TedDurcan 9 — 80
(B J Meehan) *trckd ldrs: rdn over 1f out: hung lft and r.o ins fnl f* **3/1**[1]

54 **3** shd **Menadha (USA)**[16] 2451 2-9-3 0 .... DarryllHolland 10 — 79
(M R Channon) *chsd ldr: rdn and ev ch 1f out: edgd lft and styd on same pce* **6/1**

46 **4** 2 ½ **Captain Esteem**[11] 2596 2-9-3 0 .... MichaelHills 8 — 72
(B W Hills) *led: rdn over 1f out: hdd and no ex ins fnl f* **11/1**

32 **5** 3 **Carrickmacross (IRE)**[32] 1975 2-9-3 0 .... RichardMullen 11 — 63
(E S McMahon) *chsd ldrs: rdn over 2f out: wknd over 1f out* **8/1**

00 **6** nk **Biased Opinion (IRE)**[12] 2575 2-9-3 0 .... JimmyQuinn 2 — 62
(H J L Dunlop) *hld up: effrt over 2f out: n.d* **66/1**

0 **7** hd **Spinning Ridge (IRE)**[26] 2138 2-9-0 0 .... LiamJones(3) 7 — 61
(R A Harris) *sn outpcd: hung lft and styd on ins fnl f* **66/1**

8 1 **Sourire** 2-8-12 0 .... SebSanders 4 — 53
(Sir Mark Prescott) *s.i.s: outpcd* **10/1**

0 **9** shd **Coachhouse Lady (USA)**[26] 2134 2-8-12 0 .... DO'Donohoe 12 — 53
(K A Ryan) *hld up: rdn 1/2-way: n.d* **12/1**

632 **10** 2 ½ **Swindon Town Flyer (IRE)**[31] 1989 2-9-3 0 .... DaneO'Neill 5 — 50+
(A B Haynes) *chsd ldrs: nt clr run over 3f out: rdn and wknd over 1f out* **11/2**[3]

11 2 **Monte Mayor Birdie (IRE)** 2-8-12 0 .... MickyFenton 1 — 39
(D Haydn Jones) *unruly to post: s.i.s: outpcd* **50/1**

12 1 ¼ **Lady Bower** 2-8-12 0 .... JoeFanning 13 — 36
(M Johnston) *mid-div: effrt 1/2-way: wknd wl over 1f out* **20/1**

13 7 **Just Puddie** 2-8-5 0 .... JackDean(7) 3 — 15
(W G M Turner) *sn pushed along in rr: bhd fr 1/2-way* **66/1**

1m 14.74s (-1.07) **Going Correction** -0.125s/f (Stan) — 13 Ran SP% **122.1**
Speed ratings (Par 93):102,100,99,96,92 92,91,90,90,87 84,82,73
CSF £16.31 TOTE £5.10: £2.00, £1.40, £2.30; EX 15.90 Trifecta £55.40 Pool £274.27 - 3.51 winning units..
Owner Mountgrange Stud **Bred** Desperado Stables, Inc **Trained** Upper Lambourn, Berks

FOCUS
Some big stables were represented here and this looked a decent maiden for the track, especially as the winning time was 0.71 seconds faster than the preceding three-year-old claimer. The form should work out well.

NOTEBOOK
Ten Meropa(USA) ◆, up a furlong from his very encouraging Sandown debut, raced much closer to the pace this time and, once unleashed, he powered right away from his rivals. He looks capable of going on to rather better things. (op 7-2)
Bailey(IRE) had every chance, but shaped as though he may need an extra furlong now and probably ran into a nice prospect. He is likely to progress again from this. (op 9-2 tchd 5-1)
Menadha(USA), whose American pedigree suggested he would be suited by this switch to sand, was always up with the pace over this extra furlong but could not match the finishing speed of the winner. He did have the edge in experience on the front pair and the imminent arrival of nurseries will give him a few more options.
Captain Esteem tried to make every yard and did his best, but the front three proved much too good. The Goodwood maiden he showed ability in on his debut has not worked out very well and he is another that may be better off in nurseries. (op 8-1)
Carrickmacross(IRE), placed in a couple of modest Fibresand maidens, dropped out after showing up prominently and it is more likely that the different surface did not suit him rather than the extra furlong. (op 9-1)
Sourire, a half-sister to four winners including Songerie and Souvenance, was always being taken along faster than she cared for. Her breeding suggests that trips of around 1m will suit her best and she looks the type that will come into her own once handicapped. (op 8-1)

2950 BET NOW AT WBX.COM H'CAP — 5f 20y(P)
4:15 (4:16) (Class 5) (0-70,70) 3-Y-O — £3,071 (£906; £453) Stalls Low

Form — RPR

4336 **1** **Feelin Foxy**[14] 2513 3-9-4 **67** ....(v) JimmyQuinn 6 — 70
(D Shaw) *trckd ldrs: rdn to ld ins fnl f: r.o* **8/1**[3]

5405 **2** ½ **Stoneacre Gareth (IRE)**[11] 2594 3-8-12 **61** ....(b) LPKeniry 7 — 62
(Peter Grayson) *trckd ldrs: rdn over 1f out: edgd lft and r.o ins fnl f* **11/1**

0305 **3** 1 ½ **The Geester**[34] 1932 3-8-5 **54** ....(b) PaulEddery 2 — 50
(S R Bowring) *led: rdn over 1f out: hdd ins fnl f: styd on same pce* **16/1**

3315 **4** nk **Diminuto**[22] 2276 3-8-12 **66** .... TravisBlock(5) 8 — 61
(M D I Usher) *chsd ldr: chal 1/2-way: rdn over 1f out: no ex wl ins fnl f* **8/1**[3]

1221 **5** shd **Drifting Gold**[16] 2444 3-9-7 **70** ....(b) DaneO'Neill 5 — 65+
(C G Cox) *sn outpcd: hdwy 1/2-way: rdn and hung lft over 1f out: swtchd rt ins fnl f: nt rch ldrs* **1/1**[1]

254 **6** ¾ **Ioweyou**[16] 2444 3-8-1 **55** ow2 ....(b) TolleyDean(5) 1 — 47
(J S Moore) *sn outpcd: rdn 1/2-way: styd on ins fnl f: nvr nrr* **8/1**[3]

000 **7** 1 ¼ **Stoneacre Donny (IRE)**[11] 2593 3-7-13 **51** oh4 .... LiamJones(3) 10 — 38
(Peter Grayson) *s.i.s: outpcd: r.o ins fnl f: nrst fin* **50/1**

0164 **8** hd **Charlotte Grey**[23] 2260 3-9-1 **64** .... EdwardCreighton 11 — 51
(C N Allen) *chsd ldrs: rdn 1/2-way: hung lft over 1f out: sn wknd* **16/1**

-054 **9** 2 **Durova (IRE)**[47] 1577 3-9-5 **68** .... SebSanders 9 — 47
(T D Easterby) *chsd ldrs: edgd rt 1/2-way: wknd over 1f out* **6/1**[2]

60-5 **10** 7 **Montemayorprincess (IRE)**[28] 2080 3-8-4 **53** .... DaleGibson 4 — 7
(D Haydn Jones) *s.i.s: outpcd* **14/1**

62.35 secs (-0.47) **Going Correction** -0.125s/f (Stan) — 10 Ran SP% **126.3**
Speed ratings (Par 99):98,97,94,94,94 92,90,90,87,76
CSF £100.05 CT £1406.76 TOTE £11.30: £2.40, £2.70, £6.00; EX 59.40 TRIFECTA Not won..
Owner Danethorpe Racing Ltd **Bred** Bearstone Stud **Trained** Danethorpe, Notts
■ Stewards' Enquiry : Jimmy Quinn caution: used whip with excessive frequency

FOCUS
A weakish sprint handicap dominated by those that raced handily. The winner is rated to her 2yo best with the runner-up to recent form.
Drifting Gold Official explanation: jockey said filly hung left-handed
Montemayorprincess(IRE) Official explanation: jockey said filly wouldn't face the kickback

2951 BOOK ONLINE AT WOLVERHAMPTON-RACECOURSE.CO.UK MEDIAN AUCTION MAIDEN STKS — 1m 141y(P)
4:45 (4:49) (Class 6) 3-Y-O — £2,266 (£674; £337; £168) Stalls Low

Form — RPR

0 **1** **Trans Siberian**[7] 2726 3-8-12 0 .... TolleyDean(5) 4 — 78+
(P F I Cole) *a.p: chsd ldr over 2f out: rdn to ld over 1f out: sn hung lft: hung rt ins fnl f: drvn out* **5/2**[1]

00-0 **2** 3 **View From The Top**[5] 2763 3-9-3 68 .... SebSanders 1 — 71
(Sir Mark Prescott) *led: rdn and hdd over 1f out: hung rt ins fnl f: styd on same pce* **9/2**

20 **3** ½ **Le Singe Noir**[34] 1920 3-9-3 73 .... RichardMullen 10 — 70
(D M Simcock) *chsd ldrs: rdn over 3f out: nt clr run over 1f out: styd on same pce ins fnl f* **4/1**[3]

4 **4** 10 **Derricks Dotty**[20] 2341 3-9-3 0 .... DO'Donohoe 8 — 48
(N J Vaughan) *prom: rdn over 2f out: wknd over 1f out* **12/1**

0-00 **5** 2 ½ **Pure Velvet (IRE)**[10] 2620 3-8-12 46 .... LPKeniry 9 — 37
(S Kirk) *hld up: hdwy over 2f out: wknd over 1f out* **40/1**

0- **6** 1 ½ **Memphis Marie**[317] 4373 3-8-12 0 .... EdwardCreighton 7 — 34
(C N Allen) *chsd ldrs 6f* **20/1**

00 **7** 3 ½ **Pugnacity**[37] 1841 3-8-9 0 .... SaleemGolam(3) 2 — 26
(S C Williams) *s.i.s: a in rr* **40/1**

8 ¾ **Star Of Angels** 3-9-3 0 .... JoeFanning 5 — 30
(M Johnston) *chsd ldr tl rdn and wknd over 2f out* **11/4**[2]

9 nk **Perry's Pride** 3-8-12 0 .... DaleGibson 6 — 24
(Mrs G S Rees) *s.s: sme hdwy over 3f out: sn wknd* **28/1**

0-40 **10** 1 ¾ **Cranworth Blaze**[24] 2206 3-8-7 47 .... RussellKennemore(5) 3 — 20
(T J Etherington) *mid-div: sn pushed along: wknd over 3f out* **50/1**

11 6 **Hayfield Flyer** 3-8-5 0 .... JohnCavanagh(7) 11 — 7
(Paul Green) *s.s: outpcd* **33/1**

1m 50.2s (-1.56) **Going Correction** -0.125s/f (Stan) — 11 Ran SP% **119.1**
Speed ratings (Par 97):101,98,97,89,86 85,82,81,81,79 74
CSF £12.80 TOTE £3.80: £1.10, £1.80, £1.50; EX 15.80 Trifecta £147.20 Pool £557.83 - 2.69 winning units. Place 6 £559.41, Place 5 £312.70..
Owner C Shiacolas **Bred** Lordship Stud Limited **Trained** Whatcombe, Oxon
■ Wassendale was withdrawn (12/1, unruly in stalls.) R4 applies, deduct 5p in the £.
■ Stewards' Enquiry : Russell Kennemore caution: used whip when out of contention

FOCUS
Just a moderate maiden.
T/Plt: £862.40 to a £1 stake. Pool: £56,472.20. 47.80 winning tickets. T/Qpdt: £28.40 to a £1 stake. Pool: £5,406.50. 140.80 winning tickets. CR

2751 LONGCHAMP (R-H)
Monday, June 25

OFFICIAL GOING: Soft

2952a PRIX DAPHNIS (GROUP 3) (C&G) — 1m 1f
2:20 (2:20) 3-Y-O — £27,027 (£10,811; £8,108; £5,405; £2,703)

RPR

1 **Loup Breton (IRE)**[22] 2293 3-8-11 .... C-PLemaire 5 — 109
(E Lellouche, France) *hld up: disputing last 1/2-way: hdwy on outside 2f out: rdn to chal appr fnl f: led 1f out: r.o wl* **59/10**

2 hd **Bleu Intense (FR)**[32] 3-8-11 .... KFallon 4 — 109
(J-M Beguigne, France) *hld up: disputing last 1/2-way: drvn and r.o 1 1/2f out: nrest at fin* **42/10**[2]

3 ½ **Tian Shan (IRE)**[39] 3-8-11 .... SPasquier 7 — 108
(A Fabre, France) *led 4f: 2nd and pushed along st: disputing ld and ev ch fnl f: styd on to line* **46/10**[3]

4 2 **No Dream (USA)**[22] 2293 3-8-11 .... OPeslier 3 — 104
(C Laffon-Parias, France) *hld up: 5th st: styd on fnl stages but n.d* **22/10**[1]

5 ¾ **Gris De Gris (IRE)**[39] 3-8-11 .... TThulliez 1 — 103
(J-M Capitte, France) *led after 4f: drvn and r.o whn pressed 1 1/2f out: hdd 1f out: no ex fnl stages* **10/1**

6 2 **Medicine Path**[22] 2293 3-8-11 .... CSoumillon 2 — 99
(E J O'Neill) *in tch: pushed along disputing 3rd st: hdwy on ins to press ldr 1 1/2f out: no ex u.p fnl f* **10/1**

7 6 **Hurricane Fly (IRE)**[47] 1593 3-8-11 .... F-XBertras 6 — 87
(J-L Pelletan, France) *prom: pushed along disputing 3rd st: rdn over 1 1/2f out: sn one pce* **53/10**

1m 51.1s (-7.80) — 7 Ran SP% **116.9**
PARI-MUTUEL: WIN 6.90; PL 3.10, 2.60; SF 32.60.
Owner Ecurie Wildenstein **Bred** Dayton Investments Ltd **Trained** Lamorlaye, France

NOTEBOOK
Loup Breton(IRE) thoroughly deserved this victory following his good performance in the French Derby. An improving colt, he was given a patient ride and did not make his effort until halfway up the straight. He took the advantage a furlong from home and held on gamely when challenged in the final stages. Further improvement can be expected and his targets now could be the Prix Eugene Adam and the Prix Guillaume d'Ornano.
Bleu Intense(FR) followed the winner throughout but was unable to quicken in the same way when pace was injected. He kept on really well inside the final furlong and only went down by a narrow margin. He should have a chance to take his revenge in the Prix Eugene Adam.
Tian Shan(IRE), who raced prominently, lengthened his stride from over a furlong out but could not hold the winner and runner-up inside the final furlong. A longer trip might be an advantage in the future.
No Dream(USA) did stretch out in the final stages but failed to quicken. An extra furlong or two might be an advantage for him.
Medicine Path, who was close to the leader throughout, made an effort up the straight but could make no further progress up the far rail.

2953a PRIX DE LA PORTE MAILLOT (GROUP 3) — 7f
2:50 (2:51) 3-Y-O+ — £27,027 (£10,811; £8,108; £5,405; £2,703)

RPR

1 **Marchand D'Or (FR)**[55] 1389 4-9-2 .... DBonilla 8 — 115
(F Head, France) *hld up: 7th st: hdwy over 2 1/2f out: wnt 2nd 2f out: r.o wl to ld 1f out: wnt clr ins fnl f: readily* **5/2**[1]

2 2 ½ **Bertranicus (FR)**[28] 2100 4-9-2 .... CSoumillon 5 — 108
(L Urbano-Grajales, France) *mid-div: 6th on rail st: rdn and hdwy 1 1/2f out: tk 2nd on line* **81/10**

3 nse **Ridaar (FR)**[28] 2100 7-9-2 .... JVictoire 1 — 108
(J-P Gallorini, France) *led and set gd pce: 4 l clr ent st: pushed along 2 1/2f out: hdd 1f out: lost 2nd on line* **41/10**[2]

4 2 ½ **Sabasha (FR)**[28] 2100 4-8-13 .... RMarchelli 4 — 98
(F Rohaut, France) *in tch: 4th st: drvn over 2f out: sn u.p and lost pl: rcvrd and styd on to take 4th ins fnl f* **17/1**

5 snk **Satri (IRE)**[323] 4191 5-9-2 .... OPeslier 6 — 101
(J-M Beguigne, France) *mid-div: 5th st: styd on at one pce fr over 1f out: nvr a threat* **5/2**[1]

6 nk **Trip To The Moon**[60] 1273 4-8-13 .... J-LMartinez 9 — 97
(M Delzangles, France) *hld up: last st: nvr a factor* **22/1**

7 3/4 **Ricine (IRE)**36 1876 5-8-13 .... F-XBertras 2 95
(F Rohaut, France) *racd in 2nd: drvn 2 1/2f out: lost pl 2f out: wknd* **24/1**
8 snk **Donatello (GER)**28 2100 6-9-2 .... DBoeuf 3 98
(W Baltromei, Germany) *prom: 3rd st: drvn 3f out: no ex fr 2f out* **66/10**3
9 8 **Princess Jones**28 2100 7-8-13 .... YGourraud 7 73
(J-L Guillochon, France) *towards rr: 8th st: n.d* **58/1**
1m 19.9s (-2.50) 9 Ran SP% **116.5**
PARI-MUTUEL: WIN 3.50; PL 1.70, 2.30, 1.60; DF 20.00.
Owner Mme J-L Giral **Bred** Mme Carla Giral **Trained** France

NOTEBOOK
Marchand D'Or(FR) outclassed his rivals and returned to form. Held up in seventh early on, he came with a devastating late run from a furlong and a half out and took the lead shortly after, coasting past the post with plenty in hand. He appears to be over his training problems and will now probably go for the July Cup, which could be then followed by another tilt at the Prix Maurice de Gheest.
Bertranicus(FR) ran a decent race but never looked like catching the winner. Sixth for much of the race, he could not quicken like the winner but still ran on to snatch second place on the line. He now heads for a Group 3 race in Germany.
Ridaar(FR) attempted to make all the running as usual. He was still at the head of affairs a furlong and a half out, but his stride began to shorten inside the final furlong and he was just caught for second place on the line.
Sabasha(FR) was always thereabouts on the rail and responded well when put under pressure halfway up the straight. He stayed on gamely to take fourth place.

2791 BEVERLEY (R-H)
Tuesday, June 26
2954 Meeting Abandoned - Waterlogged

2555 BRIGHTON (L-H)
Tuesday, June 26
OFFICIAL GOING: Good to soft (7.8)
After race 1, they stayed away from the far rail and only two came right across to the stands' rail, with the jockeys believing the middle path to be the best.
Wind: Light, half behind Weather: Cloudy and cool

2961 BRAKES FRESH IDEAS MAIDEN AUCTION STKS 5f 213y
2:30 (2:30) (Class 5) 2-Y-O £2,914 (£867; £433; £216) **Stalls Low**

Form RPR
1 **Miss Bootylishes** 2-8-1 .... KevinGhunowa(5) 1 65
(A B Haynes) *hld up and bhd: rdn and hdwy on rail 2f out: rn green: r.o to ld 100yds out: edgd rt: drvn out* **33/1**
032 2 1 **Maybe I Wont**9 2687 2-9-1 .... DaneO'Neill 5 71
(S Dow) *led: hrd rdn 2f out: hdd 100yds out: rdr dropped whip: nt qckn* **10/11**1
00 3 1/2 **Bid Art (IRE)**17 2473 2-8-9 .... WilliamBuick(5) 4 69+
(A M Balding) *hld up in 5th: effrt and hrd rdn 2f out: styd on fnl f* **15/2**3
60 4 3 **Purple Ransom (IRE)**12 2604 2-8-13 .... JimCrowley 6 59
(I A Wood) *pressed ldr: hrd rdn ins fnl 2f: no ex 1f out* **66/1**
032 5 1 **Ballinskelligs Boy**14 2539 2-8-11 .... RyanMoore 7 54
(R Hannon) *trckd ldrs gng wl on outside: rdn 2f out: wknd over 1f out* **7/4**2
6 2 1/2 **Easy Wonder (GER)** 2-8-9 .... JamesDoyle 2 44
(I A Wood) *s.i.s: towards rr: rdn 3f out: sn btn* **40/1**
0 7 15 **Llab Nala**3 2876 2-8-11 .... ChrisCatlin 3 —
(M R Channon) *chsd ldng pair tl wknd over 2f out* **25/1**
1m 12.61s (2.51) **Going Correction** +0.35s/f (Good) 7 Ran SP% **111.2**
Speed ratings (Par 93):97,95,95,91,89 86,66
CSF £61.66 TOTE £13.80: £7.10, £1.10; EX 41.70.
Owner Mrs Helen Adams **Bred** T P Young & D Hanson **Trained** Limpley Stoke, Bath

FOCUS
This was the only race in which the field stayed near the far rail. A weak maiden, but the unfancied winner made a successful debut and looks capable of improvement. The favourite was disappointing.

NOTEBOOK
Miss Bootylishes, a 10,500gns yearling, is a Mujahid half-sister to a couple of winners at 6f and 7f. Despite showing obvious signs of inexperience, she made it a winning debut over this tricky track and looks capable of improving quite a bit with the benefit of the run behind her.
Maybe I Wont has yet to win in four outings, but continues to run well enough to find a routine maiden at one of the smaller courses. The fact that his rider dropped his whip made no difference to the result, and in any case he was beaten by a filly who looked well up to standard for the track. (op 5-6 tchd Evens)
Bid Art(IRE) has improved steadily with racing, and this was by far his best effort in three attempts. This 22,000gns yearling, a son of Hawk Wing out of a mare who stayed up to 1m4f, will be even better at longer trips and is now qualified for nurseries, so there is every chance of an imminent success, especially over 7f. (op 12-1)
Purple Ransom(IRE) has shown minor ability in three outings to date, and nurseries will be his natural home from now on.
Ballinskelligs Boy was a bit disappointing on the final climb, having travelled well for a long way. He got this trip well enough on the stiff Salisbury track last time, where he looked ready to score soon, so maybe he is not as effective with a bit of cut. (tchd 13-8)
Easy Wonder(GER), a 40,000euro yearling and 24,000gns juvenile, is a half-sister to five winners in Germany over a variety of trips, her sire Royal Dragon having been a top-class miler in that country. However, more is needed to live up to her pedigree following this low-key debut. (op 33-1)

2962 SUSSEX NEWSPAPERS MEDIAN AUCTION MAIDEN STKS 7f 214y
3:00 (3:01) (Class 6) 3-4-Y-O £2,072 (£616; £308; £153) **Stalls Low**

Form RPR
0-56 1 **Expedience (USA)**24 2261 3-8-12 71 .... RyanMoore 2 72
(Sir Michael Stoute) *mde virtually all: hrd rdn and styd on wl fnl 2f: holding runner-up whn edgd rt 100yds out* **15/8**2
23 2 1 **Commandment (IRE)**15 2520 3-9-3 0 .... DaneO'Neill 7 75
(E A L Dunlop) *pressed wnr: drvn to chal fnl 2f: jst hld whn sltly hmpd 100yds out* **4/6**1
3 12 **Benellino**212 4-9-13 0 .... SimonWhitworth 1 47
(R M Stronge) *s.s: bhd: rdn to take modest 3rd ins fnl 2f* **33/1**
00-0 4 8 **Port Luanda (IRE)**35 1928 3-9-3 40 .... JamesDoyle 6 29
(R M Flower) *in tch: rdn 4f out: wknd 2f out* **66/1**
-000 5 nk **Fluters House**13 2560 3-9-3 43 .... JimCrowley 3 28
(S Woodman) *in tch on rail: rdn 4f out: wknd over 2f out* **66/1**
6 2 **Indiannie Moon** 3-8-12 0 .... TPO'Shea 4 18
(M R Channon) *chsd ldrs: rdn and wknd 2f out* **12/1**3
0000 7 37 **Mustard Benn**27 2141 4-9-6 37 .... JamieHamblett(7) 5 —
(Mouse Hamilton-Fairley) *prom tl wknd rapidly over 3f out: eased whn no ch fnl 2f* **66/1**
1m 37.71s (2.67) **Going Correction** +0.35s/f (Good)
WFA 3 from 4yo 10lb 7 Ran SP% **109.9**
Speed ratings (Par 101):100,99,87,79,78 76,39
CSF £3.14 TOTE £3.30: £1.20, £1.10; EX 4.30.
Owner J Wigan & G Strawbridge **Bred** George Strawbridge And London Thoroughbred Service **Trained** Newmarket, Suffolk

FOCUS
A weakish contest, dominated by two of the seven runners who came well clear. The form seems sound. The runners all came towards the middle of the track, with the first two home gradually edging even closer to the stands' rail.

2963 CLASSIC EVENT MARQUEES CLAIMING STKS 1m 1f 209y
3:30 (3:30) (Class 6) 3-Y-O+ £1,943 (£578; £288; £144) **Stalls High**

Form RPR
0050 1 **Lawyer To World**16 2490 3-7-12 44 .... WilliamBuick(5) 4 52
(N A Callaghan) *t.k.h: in tch: led wl over 1f out: edgd lft: rdn clr* **7/2**2
0432 2 3 **Shaheer (IRE)**16 2490 5-9-11 54 .... JimCrowley 6 56
(J Gallagher) *led and set slow pce 4f: chsd wnr over 1f out: hrd rdn: nt qckn* **8/11**1
2002 3 2 1/2 **Savoy Chapel**13 2557 5-8-12 40 .... KevinGhunowa(5) 3 43
(A W Carroll) *stdd s: t.k.h: in tch: effrt over 2f out: one pce* **12/1**
500 4 3 **Voice Mail**10 2656 8-9-5 50 ....(b) LPKeniry 5 39
(A M Balding) *trckd ldng pair tl wknd 2f out* **7/1**3
033/ 5 1/2 **Senor Bond (USA)**544 6683 6-9-2 55 .... JerryO'Dwyer(3) 8 38
(A M Hales) *chsd ldr: led and set modest pce after 4f: hdd wl over 1f out: sn wknd* **10/1**
206- 6 8 **Franky'N'Jonny**196 6794 4-8-7 42 ....(p) JosephWalsh(7) 1 17
(M J Attwater) *s.s: t.k.h in rr: rdn and no ch fnl 2f* **25/1**
2m 9.56s (6.96) **Going Correction** +0.35s/f (Good)
WFA 3 from 4yo+ 12lb 6 Ran SP% **113.3**
Speed ratings (Par 101):86,83,81,79,78 72
CSF £6.56 TOTE £5.00: £2.10, £1.10; EX 8.40 Trifecta £58.60 Pool £572.03 - 6.92 winning units.The winner was claimed by Christine Dunnett for £5,000.
Owner N A Callaghan **Bred** James M Egan **Trained** Newmarket, Suffolk

FOCUS
A weak race, run at a funereal pace. The winner has been disappointing, the favourite was below-par and the third was running his best race on turf for a long time. The runners came to the middle of the track, with the winner edging back towards the far side in the last two furlongs.

2964 WBX.COM H'CAP 1m 3f 196y
4:00 (4:01) (Class 5) (0-70,70) 4-Y-O+ £2,849 (£847; £423; £211) **Stalls High**

Form RPR
601 1 **Tiboucchina (IRE)**16 2491 4-9-0 63 .... JamesDoyle 8 70+
(R M Beckett) *hld up in 3rd: led 2f out: drvn clr: eased fnl 50yds* **11/8**1
5004 2 6 **Burgundy**6 2765 10-9-5 68 ....(b) GeorgeBaker 4 65
(P Mitchell) *s.s: bhd: hdwy and rdn to grab stands' rail over 2f out: chsd wnr over 1f out: nt qckn* **7/2**3
2100 3 5 **Recalcitrant**17 2471 4-8-4 58 .... WilliamBuick(5) 1 47
(S Dow) *edgy in stalls: led tl 2f out: sn outpcd* **5/2**2
-560 4 10 **And Again (USA)**22 2321 4-9-4 67 .... ChrisCatlin 3 40
(R A Teal) *pressed ldr tl wknd qckly 2f out* **5/1**
2m 37.33s (5.13) **Going Correction** +0.35s/f (Good) 4 Ran SP% **109.6**
Speed ratings (Par 103):96,92,88,82
CSF £6.44 TOTE £2.20; EX 5.20.
Owner James M Egan **Bred** Benedikt Fassbender **Trained** Whitsbury, Hants

FOCUS
A disappointing turnout, with half the original field of eight coming out because of the rain-softened ground. Run at a modest pace, and with the field strung out at the finish, it resembled a procession more than a race, and the form is poor. All four came towards the stands' rail.

2965 WBX.COM WORLD BET EXCHANGE H'CAP 6f 209y
4:30 (4:30) (Class 5) (0-75,74) 3-Y-O+ £2,849 (£847; £423; £211) **Stalls Low**

Form RPR
5031 1 **Purus (IRE)**18 2414 5-10-0 74 .... ChrisCatlin 6 89
(R A Teal) *chsd ldrs: led 2f out: rdn clr 1f out: styd on wl* **7/2**3
0011 2 5 **Magroom**23 2273 3-7-7 55 oh1 ....(v) KMay(7) 10 54
(R J Hodges) *led tl 2f out: one pce appr fnl f* **6/1**
0-00 3 2 1/2 **Landucci**13 2573 6-9-9 74 .... PatrickHills(5) 1 69
(J W Hills) *hld up in 6th: rdn to chse ldng pair ins fnl 2f: rdr dropped whip jst over 1f out: no ex* **11/4**1
0250 4 shd **Desert Dreamer (IRE)**22 2318 6-9-8 68 .... GeorgeBaker 7 62
(P R Chamings) *dwlt: hld up in tch: effrt over 2f out: one pce* **10/3**2
2300 5 hd **Postsprofit (IRE)**26 2177 3-8-6 66 .... WilliamBuick(5) 4 57
(N A Callaghan) *stdd sn after s: t.k.h in rr: rdn over 2f out: little rspnse: nvr rchd ldrs* **15/2**
0042 6 1 1/4 **Lady Edge (IRE)**13 2556 5-8-5 56 .... KevinGhunowa(5) 5 47
(A W Carroll) *in tch: hrd rdn and wknd over 2f out* **12/1**
0-05 7 16 **Vampyrus**13 2580 4-8-9 55 oh5 ....(v) DaneO'Neill 8 2
(H Candy) *w ldr 3f: wknd over 2f out* **20/1**
1m 23.54s (0.84) **Going Correction** +0.35s/f (Good)
WFA 3 from 4yo+ 9lb 7 Ran SP% **110.5**
Speed ratings (Par 103):109,103,100,100,100 98,80
CSF £22.73 CT £60.62 TOTE £5.10: £2.40, £2.60; EX 24.80 Trifecta £48.10 Pool £441.39 - 6.51 winning units..
Owner J Morton **Bred** K Nercessian **Trained** Headley, Surrey

FOCUS
A moderate contest, with the field coming to the middle. A solid effort from winner Purus and the time was very good, but nothing else ran to form.

2966 BET NOW AT WBX.COM H'CAP 5f 59y
5:00 (5:00) (Class 6) (0-65,65) 3-Y-O+ £2,072 (£616; £308; £153) **Stalls Low**

Form RPR
3622 1 **Harrison's Flyer (IRE)**5 2805 6-9-8 65 ....(p) KevinGhunowa(5) 13 75
(J M Bradley) *towards rr on outside: hrd rdn and hdwy whn edgd lft over 1f out: r.o to ld fnl 50yds* **15/8**1
-000 2 3/4 **Gone'N'Dunnett (IRE)**45 1673 8-8-9 47 ....(v) DMylonas 10 54
(Mrs C A Dunnett) *prom: hrd rdn and edgd rt over 1f out: kpt on: nt qckn nr fin* **12/1**

4531 **3** *nk* **Cosmic Destiny (IRE)**[13] [2555] 5-9-5 **57**........................... JimCrowley 1 63
(E F Vaughan) *rrd s: plld hrd in rr: hdwy to ld 1f out: hrd rdn: hdd and one pce fnl 50yds* **7/1**

4000 **4** *1 1/2* **Pulse**[36] [1885] 9-8-9 **50**..(p) RichardKingscote(3) 12 51
(Miss J R Tooth) *in tch: outpcd 2f out: styd on fnl f* **25/1**

0010 **5** *shd* **Majestical (IRE)**[15] [2509] 5-8-7 **50**..............................(p) WilliamBuick(5) 8 50
(V Smith) *t.k.h: in tch: drvn to press ldrs over 1f out: edgd lft: one pce fnl f* **8/1**

-303 **6** *1 1/4* **Rosie Cross (IRE)**[18] [2415] 3-8-8 **55**............................ JerryO'Dwyer(3) 6 51
(Eve Johnson Houghton) *in tch on rail: rdn to chse ldrs ins fnl 2f: no ex 1f out* **11/1**

50-0 **7** *3/4* **Talcen Gwyn (IRE)**[15] [2516] 5-9-5 **57**..........................(v) DavidKinsella 9 50
(M F Harris) *led after 1f: hrd rdn and hdd 1f out: wknd* **11/2**[2]

-000 **8** *3/4* **Decider (USA)**[15] [2516] 4-9-5 **57**....................................... GeorgeBaker 5 48
(J M Bradley) *led 1f: pressed ldr tl wknd 1f out* **6/1**[3]

00-0 **9** *1 1/4* **Whistler**[55] [1405] 10-9-0 **52**..(p) PaulFitzsimons 11 38
(Miss J R Tooth) *a outpcd in rr* **20/1**

63.64 secs (1.34) **Going Correction** +0.35s/f (Good)
WFA 3 from 4yo+ 6lb **9** Ran SP% **112.7**
Speed ratings (Par 101):103,101,101,98,98 96,95,94,92
CSF £25.64 CT £129.48 TOTE £3.00: £1.30, £3.10, £1.60; EX 22.10 Trifecta £98.30 Pool £688.13 - 4.97 winning units. Place 6 £18.53, Place 5 £10.30.
Owner racingshares.co.uk **Bred** Geoff Mulcahy **Trained** Sedbury, Gloucs

FOCUS
A modest but competitive sprint, with the runners racing middle to far side. Sound form, which should prove reliable amongst the principals
T/Plt: £8.40 to a £1 stake. Pool: £105,067.65. 9,033.80 winning tickets. T/Qpdt: £4.90 to a £1 stake. Pool: £6,241.90. 938.60 winning tickets. LM

2596 NEWBURY (L-H)
Tuesday, June 26

OFFICIAL GOING: Soft (good to soft in places; 5.8)
Wind: Fresh, across Weather: Bright but overcast

2967 PUMP TECHNOLOGY APPRENTICE H'CAP 1m 3f 5y
6:30 (6:30) (Class 5) (0-70,70) 4-Y-O+ **£3,238** (£963; £481; £240) **Stalls** High

Form RPR

-400 **1** **Duelling Banjos**[25] [2218] 8-8-8 **57**................................ JackMitchell(3) 7 66
(J Akehurst) *hld up in midfield: hdwy 4f out: rdn to ld over 2f out: styd on u.p fnl f* **13/2**

/153 **2** *nk* **Charmatic (IRE)**[22] [2321] 6-9-7 **70**............................ ThomasO'Brien(3) 3 78
(Andrew Turnell) *s.i.s: t.k.h: hld up in tch: rdn and hdwy 4f out: chsd wnr over 2f out: swtchd lft over 1f out: kpt on* **8/1**

0551 **3** *3* **Desert Hawk**[7] [2745] 6-8-6 **55** 6ex.............................. KirstyMilczarek(3) 5 58
(W M Brisbourne) *t.k.h: trckd ldrs: hdwy on inner 3f out: chsd ldng pair 2f out: kpt on same pce fnl f* **4/1**[2]

6004 **4** *3/4* **Kylkenny**[33] [1980] 12-8-5 **51** oh4.......................................(t) TravisBlock 1 53
(H Morrison) *chsd ldr tl over 2f out: kpt on one pce after* **4/1**[2]

0-03 **5** *10* **Sovietta (IRE)**[8] [2721] 6-8-6 **55**....................................(t) JamieHamblett(3) 9 40
(A G Newcombe) *stdd s: hld up in last trio: plld wd and rdn 4f out: no imp and wl hld last 2f* **11/2**[3]

4303 **6** *3* **Hatch A Plan (IRE)**[14] [2544] 6-9-5 **65**.................................. NicolPolli 8 45
(Mouse Hamilton-Fairley) *stdd s: dropped in last trio: hit rail 8f out: nt clr run over 3f out: sn swtchd rt: n.d* **12/1**

00 **7** *1* **Daring Racer (GER)**[63] [1222] 4-9-3 **63**............................... MarkFlynn 4 41
(S Dow) *chsd ldrs: rdn wl over 4f out: wknd 3f out: sn wl bhd* **33/1**

0046 **8** *10* **Rawaabet (IRE)**[12] [2603] 5-8-2 **51** oh4.......................... WilliamCarson(3) 10 12
(P W Hiatt) *stdd s: plld hrd: hld up in last trio tl rapid hdwy to ld 6f out: hdd over 2f out: sn btn: eased ins fnl f* **7/2**[1]

3020 **9** *13* **Makai**[13] [2572] 4-8-5 **51** oh1...(b) TolleyDean 6 —
(J J Bridger) *led at stdy pce tl 6f out: rdn 4f out: sn wknd: t.o and eased fnl f* **25/1**

2m 31.31s (9.04) **Going Correction** +0.675s/f (Yiel) **9** Ran SP% **116.5**
Speed ratings (Par 103):94,93,91,91,83 81,80,73,64
CSF £57.81 CT £235.99 TOTE £9.20: £2.60, £2.60, £2.00; EX 51.50.
Owner Tattenham Corner Racing 2 **Bred** L T And M Foster **Trained** Epsom, Surrey
■ Stewards' Enquiry : Tolley Dean four-day ban: careless riding (Jul 8-10,12)

FOCUS
A modest handicap restricted to apprentices who had not ridden more than 50 winners. Not many liked this ground. The winner is rated to his winter sand form, with the third to his latest start.

2968 WIN RACES WITH JONATHAN PORTMAN MAIDEN AUCTION FILLIES' STKS 6f 8y
7:05 (7:07) (Class 4) 2-Y-O **£6,477** (£1,927; £963; £481) **Stalls** High

Form RPR

5 **1** **Geestring (IRE)**[32] [2000] 2-8-8 0................................ RichardHughes 12 79
(R Hannon) *trckd ldrs: pressed wnr and ev ch over 1f out: carried lft ins fnl f and bmpd nr fin: jst hld: fin 2nd, shd: awrdd r* **5/1**[3]

2 *shd* **Edge Of Gold** 2-8-10 0...................................... CatherineGannon 14 81
(B Palling) *sn led: mde rest: rdn wl over 1f out: hung bdly lft ins fnl f: hld on: uns rdr after fin: fin 1st: disq: plcd 2nd* **22/1**

6 **3** *2 1/2* **Sakhacity**[32] [2000] 2-8-6 0.. KerrinMcEvoy 13 69
(J R Jenkins) *pressed wnr: ev ch and rdn wl over 1f out: wknd last 100yds* **11/2**

0 **4** *2 1/2* **Lady Nova (IRE)**[24] [2241] 2-8-10 0....................................... JohnEgan 4 66
(J S Moore) *in tch in midfield: rdn wl over 2f out: outpcd wl over 1f out: hung lft and plugged on same pce fnl f* **16/1**

5 *3* **Tina's Best (IRE)** 2-8-10 0.. RyanMoore 5 57
(R Hannon) *s.i.s: hld up in tch: rdn over 2f out: hung lft wl over 1f out: sn wknd* **4/1**[2]

6 *1 3/4* **Cosmea** 2-8-4 0... JimmyQuinn 2 45
(A King) *s.i.s: hld up in tch: hdwy 3f out: rdn 2f out: wknd over 1f out* **20/1**

7 *3* **Bikini** 2-8-4 0.. MartinDwyer 15 36
(H Candy) *towards rr in tch: rdn 3f out: sn bhd* **6/1**

8 *7* **Pay Pay Pay** 2-8-7 0 ow1.. StephenDonohoe 1 18
(P D Evans) *a outpcd: nvr on terms* **20/1**

5 **9** *shd* **Talamahana**[17] [2468] 2-8-8 0... LPKeniry 16 19
(S Kirk) *s.i.s: sn chsng ldrs: rdn 2f out: sn dropped out* **11/4**[1]

10 *3* **Her Name Is Rio (IRE)** 2-8-6 0.............................. SimonWhitworth 11 8
(J S Moore) *s.i.s: a outpcd* **33/1**

1m 15.72s (1.40) **Going Correction** +0.375s/f (Good) **10** Ran SP% **115.7**
Speed ratings (Par 92):104,105,101,98,94 91,87,78,78,74
CSF £104.39 TOTE £4.00: £1.70, £7.20, £1.70; EX 100.10.
Owner Mrs J K Powell **Bred** David John Brown **Trained** East Everleigh, Wilts
■ Tathkaar was withdrawn (12/1, refused to enter stalls.) R4 applies, deduct 5p in the £.

FOCUS
An ordinary fillies' maiden with a dramatic outcome. The form is pretty solid with both the promoted winner and the third coming from the same maiden, and the time was very smart for a race of its type.

NOTEBOOK
Geestring(IRE) was awarded the race in the Stewards' room having been carried left by the first past the post well inside the final furlong. That was probably the right decision strictly on the rule book, as her run was impeded, but one suspects Edge Of Gold was the better horse on the day, and the margin may have been more clear-cut had she stayed in a straight line. Whatever the case, she has lost her maiden tag and things are going to get tougher, but she gives the impression there is more improvement in her. (op 3-1)
Edge Of Gold ◆, a 25,000gns purchase who is closely related to the smart Bright Edge, a multiple 6f winner at two to three, passed the post in first place on her racecourse debut, but was demoted to second by the Stewards who felt she cost Geestring the race when carrying that one left inside the final furlong. Her supporters can probably feel a little hard done by, as she was easily the best filly in the race, looking set to win quite well without her rider having to resort to the whip at any stage, but she ran green and continually drifted to her left. There was not much room for Gannon to pull her whip through to her left hand and take corrective action, but there is little doubt she would have won had she stayed in a straight line. The drama did not end there, though, as she again showed her inexperience when dropping her rider soon after the line, Gannon sustaining a dislocated shoulder. The filly has clearly got a lot of growing up to do, but this experience will have taught her plenty and compensation surely awaits. (op 25-1)
Sakhacity was only a short head behind Geestring on her debut at Newmarket, and she was weighted to reverse to placings, but she has clearly not progressed as much as one might have hoped. (op 7-2)
Lady Nova(IRE) improved on the form she showed on her debut at Folkestone.
Tina's Best(IRE), a 35,000euros half-sister to 1m1f Phantom Lad, later a dual winner over hurdles, out of a dual 1m4f scorer, failed to justify a bit of a gamble on her racecourse debut, but she should be capable of a lot better with the benefit of this experience. (op 9-1)
Talamahana failed to confirm the promise she showed when fifth to a nice type over course and distance on her debut and this was disappointing. (op 10-3 tchd 7-2)

2969 ENJOY THE GAME AT TADLEY RUGBY CLUB MAIDEN FILLIES' STKS 7f (S)
7:35 (7:38) (Class 4) 2-Y-O **£6,477** (£1,927; £963; £481) **Stalls** High

Form RPR

1 **Muthabara (IRE)** 2-9-0 0.. MartinDwyer 9 83+
(J L Dunlop) *s.i.s: hld up in rr but wl in tch: swtchd lft over 1f out: led 1f out: sn pushed clr* **5/1**[3]

2 *5* **Isent She Rich (IRE)** 2-9-0 0.. TedDurcan 12 71
(M G Quinlan) *trckd ldrs: hdwy over 2f out: sn ev ch and rdn: outpcd by wnr fnl f: kpt on* **7/1**

3 *1 1/2* **Sayedati Elhasna (IRE)** 2-9-0 0.. RHills 13 67
(J L Dunlop) *hld up in tch: rdn wl over 1f out: styd on ins fnl f: no ch w wnr* **4/1**[2]

05 **4** *1 1/4* **Quick Sands (IRE)**[50] [1533] 2-9-0 0............................. RichardHughes 6 64
(R Hannon) *pressed ldrs: rdn and ev ch 2f out tl wknd jst ins fnl f* **8/1**

3 **5** *2 1/2* **Lush (IRE)**[33] [1960] 2-9-0 0... RyanMoore 8 58
(R Hannon) *s.i.s: sn w ldr: led 4f out: rdn wl over 1f out: hdd 1f out: wknd ins fnl f* **11/8**[1]

0 **6** *shd* **Compton Abbess**[28] [2122] 2-9-0 0............................. FergusSweeney 7 58
(B R Millman) *t.k.h: trckd ldrs: hdwy over 2f out: ev ch and rdn wl over 1f out: wknd jst ins fnl f* **25/1**

0 **7** *13* **New Minerton (IRE)**[70] [1079] 2-9-0 0............................ JHBowman 11 25
(B R Millman) *led tl 4f out: cl up tl rdn over 2f out: sn wknd: t.o fnl f* **33/1**

8 *33* **Ely Une (IRE)** 2-9-0 0.. PaulFitzsimons 14 —
(B W Duke) *s.i.s: sn in tch: rdn and wknd qckly over 2f out: t.o wl over 1f out* **40/1**

1m 30.71s (3.71) **Going Correction** +0.375s/f (Good) **8** Ran SP% **111.6**
Speed ratings (Par 92):93,87,85,84,81 81,66,28
CSF £36.90 TOTE £6.60: £1.80, £2.30, £1.50; EX 41.80.
Owner Hamdan Al Maktoum **Bred** Shadwell Estate Company Limited **Trained** Arundel, W Sussex

FOCUS
This would have been a fair test for these juvenile fillies on the soft ground. The winner was impressive and should rate higher.

NOTEBOOK
Muthabara(IRE) ◆, a half-sister to 9f winner Estiqraar and Aqmaar, a dual 7f-1m winner, got her career off to an impressive start and won this most decisively. She fell out of the gates and ran distinctly green early on, but once the penny dropped from halfway there was only going to be one outcome and she showed a nice turn of foot on this soft ground when asked to go clear. She looks a smart prospect and is well worthy of her place in better company now, perhaps in the same Listed race over this trip at Sandown in July that her stable won last year with Sudoor, who it should be noted also made a winning debut in this maiden. (op 9-2)
Isent She Rich(IRE) ◆, a half-sister to smart 6f-1m winner Kings Point and whose dam won in soft ground, was nibbled at in the betting ahead of this racecourse debut. She was given time to find her stride before being produced with every chance nearing two out, but she was firmly put in her place by the winner's turn of foot when that rival asserted. She kept on nicely thereafter and still finished clear in second, so should not be too long in going one better. (op 9-1)
Sayedati Elhasna(IRE) ◆, a half-sister to two 6f juvenile winners yet bred to appreciate further in time, would probably have been better off being allowed to stride on through the early parts as she was soon behind a wall of horses and had to wait longer than ideal for her challenge. She picked up nicely when switched to the rail and, while she would not have won, no doubt she would have given her winning stable companion more to think about with a clear run. She ought to learn a deal for this experience and clearly has a future. (op 11-2)
Quick Sands(IRE), up in trip, was given a positive ride and had her chance. She did not appear to really stay this far on such easy ground, but still rates a fair benchmark for this form and will fare better when switching to nurseries. Dropping back a furlong should also help. (op 15-2 tchd 9-1)
Lush(IRE), who set the standard on her debut third over 6f at Goodwood a month ago, was rushed up to join the early pace after a sluggish start and never really looked too happy on this soft surface. Her Group 1 entry indicates that she is well regarded and it would be folly to write her off on the back of this effort. (op 5-4 tchd 6-5 and 6-4)

2970 JUNG PUMPEN & PUMP TECHNOLOGY PARTNERSHIP MAIDEN FILLIES' STKS 1m 4f 5y
8:05 (8:05) (Class 4) 3-Y-O+ **£6,477** (£1,927; £963; £481) **Stalls** High

Form RPR

04-0 **1** **Mirin**[74] [1024] 3-8-12 63.. SteveDrowne 4 70
(G Wragg) *hld up in rr: smooth hdwy 3f out: led 2f out: sn rdn: hrd drvn fnl f: all out* **9/1**

3 **2** *nk* **Louviere**[32] [2005] 3-8-12 0.. RichardHughes 5 71+
(Pat Eddery) *chsd ldr for 3f: chsd ldrs after: rdn over 4f out: nt clr run 3f out tl 2f out: sn swtchd rt: chsd wnr over 1f out: clsd steadily u.p: nt quite rch wnr* **7/4**[1]

3 *2* **Propaganda (IRE)** 3-8-12 0... KerrinMcEvoy 2 67+
(L M Cumani) *hld up in rr: nt clr run 4f out tl swtchd rt wl over 1f out: styd on to chse ldng pair over 1f out: no imp last 100yds* **5/2**[2]

The Form Book, Raceform Ltd, Compton, RG20 6NL

4 15 **Bonchester Bridge**[23] 6-9-12 0 TQuinn 3 43
(N J Henderson) *led tl hdd wl over 3f out: sn rdn: wknd 1f out* **10/3**[3]

60 **5** *nk* **Hayward's Heath**[12] 2597 3-8-12 0 PaulFitzsimons 6 42
(B W Duke) *chsd ldr 9f out: rdn to ld wl over 3f out: hdd 2f out: wknd 1f out* **25/1**

00 **6** *7* **Moonfinder (IRE)**[20] 2359 3-8-12 0 IanMongan 7 31
(J L Dunlop) *hld up in tch: rdn 3f out: wknd over 1f out: eased whn wl btn ins fnl f* **10/1**

2m 42.34s (6.35) **Going Correction** +0.675s/f (Yiel)
WFA 3 from 6yo 14lb **6** Ran SP% **111.0**
Speed ratings (Par 102):105,104,103,93,93 88
CSF £24.71 TOTE £11.90: £4.10, £1.90; EX 32.10.

Owner B H Voak **Bred** B H Voak **Trained** Newmarket, Suffolk

FOCUS
A modest maiden, run at an ordinary gallop. The race has been rated around the runner-up, who was unfortunate not to win.

2971 JOIN LONDON IRISH AT MADJESKI STADIUM FILLIES' H'CAP 1m 2f 6y
8:40 (8:40) (Class 4) (0-85,85) 3-Y-0 **£4,857** (£1,445; £722; £360) **Stalls** High

Form RPR

-500 **1** **Sell Out**[20] 2354 3-8-11 **75** SteveDrowne 7 86
(G Wragg) *hld up in last trio: hdwy 3f out: hung lft fr 2f out: led jst over 1f out: flashed tail u.p: pushed out last 100yds* **10/1**

6-10 **2** *½* **Noojoom (IRE)**[33] 1974 3-8-11 **75** PatDobbs 1 85
(M P Tregoning) *led for 1f: chsd ldr tl led again 3f out: rdn wl over 1f out: hdd jst over 1f out: unable qck last 100yds* **15/2**

-262 **3** *1* **Gull Wing (IRE)**[24] 2246 3-9-2 **80** KerrinMcEvoy 5 88
(M L W Bell) *chsd ldrs: rdn over 2f out: sltly outpcd over 1f out: swtchd rt 1f out: kpt on u.p* **7/2**[1]

0-01 **4** *1 ½* **Maid To Believe**[43] 1722 3-8-10 **74** EddieAhern 9 79
(J L Dunlop) *t.k.h: hld up wl in tch: ev ch 3f out: sn rdn: hrd drvn and hanging lft over 1f out: one pce fnl f* **9/2**[2]

21- **5** *1 ½* **Perfect Star**[257] 5914 3-9-3 **81** AdamKirby 4 83
(C G Cox) *t.k.h: hld up in midfield: rdn 2f out: kpt on same pce* **7/2**[1]

6035 **6** *3* **La Roca (IRE)**[10] 2671 3-9-0 **78** SebSanders 10 74
(R M Beckett) *t.k.h: hdwy to chse ldrs over 2f out: sn rdn: btn over 1f out* **17/2**

-00U **7** *½* **Harvest Joy (IRE)**[9] 2691 3-9-7 **85** JHBowman 2 80
(B R Millman) *hld up in tch: rdn 3f out: n.d after* **40/1**

2-10 **8** *½* **Toccata (IRE)**[24] 2231 3-8-13 **77** MartinDwyer 11 71
(D M Simcock) *led after 1f: stdd pce 6f out: rdn and hdd 3f out: wknd over 2f out* **6/1**[3]

-333 **9** *5* **Aussie Cricket (FR)**[25] 2196 3-8-2 **66** EdwardCreighton 8 50
(D J Coakley) *plld hrd: hld up in rr: rdn and effrt on outer 3f out: sn btn* **14/1**

2m 14.15s (5.44) **Going Correction** +0.675s/f (Yiel) **9** Ran SP% **117.4**
Speed ratings (Par 98):105,104,103,102,101 99,98,98,94
CSF £83.75 CT £318.83 TOTE £10.70: £3.50, £2.70, £1.70; EX 129.10.

Owner T D Rootes **Bred** Shutford Stud **Trained** Newmarket, Suffolk

FOCUS
A decent fillies' handicap likely to produce its share of winners. Sound form for the level.

Perfect Star Official explanation: jockey said filly was unsuited by the soft (good to soft in places) ground

2972 PUMP TECHNOLOGY H'CAP 5f 34y
9:10 (9:10) (Class 5) (0-70,67) 3-Y-0+ **£3,562** (£1,059; £529; £264) **Stalls** High

Form RPR

0002 **1** **Blessed Place**[2] 2912 7-9-3 **59** (t) TQuinn 6 69
(D J S Ffrench Davis) *taken down early: w ldr tl led on bit over 1f out: rdn 1f out: hdd last 100yds: rallied gamely to ld on post* **9/2**[2]

0613 **2** *shd* **Monte Major (IRE)**[8] 2712 6-8-8 **55** (v) PatrickHills(5) 5 65
(D Shaw) *hld up wl in tch: hdwy 2f out: sn ev ch and rdn: led last 100yds: hdd on post* **10/3**[1]

0003 **3** *¾* **Malapropism**[3] 2879 7-9-9 **65** JHBowman 8 72
(M R Channon) *hld up in tch: hdwy and rdn 2f out: ev ch over 1f out: no ex last 100yds* **9/2**[2]

1600 **4** *1 ½* **Must Be Keen**[35] 1933 8-8-7 **49** oh3 ow1 (p) FergusSweeney 11 51
(P S McEntee) *s.i.s: bhd: swtchd lft over 2f out: r.o u.p fnl f: nrst fin* **33/1**

5000 **5** *nk* **Montzando**[10] 2652 4-8-6 **48** oh3 (v) JimmyQuinn 7 49
(B R Millman) *s.i.s: towards rr: rdn 1/2-way: kpt on u.p fnl f: nt trble ldrs* **9/1**

40-5 **6** *1 ¼* **Drumming Party (USA)**[36] 1885 5-9-4 **60** (t) LPKeniry 1 56
(A M Balding) *t.k.h: hld up in tch on outer: rdn 2f out: wknd 1f out* **11/2**[3]

0 **7** *2 ½* **Green Lagonda (AUS)**[18] 2418 5-9-9 **65** EddieAhern 12 52
(J G Given) *sn led: rdn 2f out: hdd over 1f out: wknd fnl f* **11/1**

-000 **8** *2* **Danjet (IRE)**[26] 2191 4-9-8 **64** StephenDonohoe 3 44
(J M Bradley) *taken down early: racd on outer: rdn and struggling 1/2-way: n.d after* **9/1**

0000 **9** *5* **Jayanjay**[27] 2139 8-9-11 **67** SebSanders 10 29
(P Mitchell) *towards rr and sn pushed along: rdn and btn 2f out: eased ins fnl f* **11/1**

0000 **10** *4* **Fancy You (IRE)**[11] 2622 4-8-1 **48** oh3 KevinGhunowa(5) 9 —
(A W Carroll) *s.i.s: sn in tch: rdn 1/2-way: no ch last 2f* **50/1**

63.95 secs (1.39) **Going Correction** +0.375s/f (Good) **10** Ran SP% **116.4**
Speed ratings (Par 103):103,102,101,99,98 96,92,89,81,75
CSF £19.85 CT £71.38 TOTE £5.20: £1.90, £1.60, £2.00; EX 21.70 Place 6 £117.37, Place 5 £45.44.

Owner S J Edwards **Bred** Mrs W H Gibson Fleming **Trained** Lambourn, Berks

FOCUS
Not a good sprint handicap, but it was at least fought out by the in-form runners. Straightforward form, rated through the third.

Danjet(IRE) Official explanation: jockey said filly missed the break

Jayanjay Official explanation: jockey said gelding lost its action

T/Jkpt: £262,558.19 to a £1 stake. Pool: £369,800.31. 1.00 winning ticket. T/Plt: £158.00 to a £1 stake. Pool: £124,840.20. 576.50 winning tickets. T/Qpdt: £31.10 to a £1 stake. Pool: £7,513.90. 178.45 winning tickets. SP

The Form Book, Raceform Ltd, Compton, RG20 6NL

2973 - 2975a (Foreign Racing) - See Raceform Interactive

[2924] HAMBURG (R-H)
Tuesday, June 26

OFFICIAL GOING: Heavy

2976a ALICE BUSINESS-CUP (LANGER HAMBURGER) (LISTED RACE) 2m
6:30 (6:41) 4-Y-0+ **£9,459** (£3,716; £2,027; £1,014; £676)

RPR

1 **El Tango (GER)**[11] 2649 5-8-9 AStarke 4 106
(P Schiergen, Germany) **3/5**[1]

2 *4* **Carus (GER)**[19] 2409 8-8-9 AHelfenbein 1 102
(D K Richardson, Germany) **88/10**

3 *12* **Mick Jerome (IRE)**[40] 6-8-9 JiriPalik 9 90
(Rune Haugen, Norway) **42/1**

4 *9* **Naukos (GER)**[19] 4-9-0 ADeVries 2 86
(H Blume, Germany) **39/10**[2]

5 *4* **Jump For You (FR)**[19] 2409 5-9-2 NRichter 11 84
(W Baltromei, Germany) **rn wout bets*

6 *22* **Jagodin (IRE)**[270] 7-8-9 (b) MSantos 7 55
(B Neuman, Sweden) **20/1**

7 *22* **Atamane (GER)**[268] 5709 4-8-9 (b) ASuborics 6 33
(Mario Hofer, Germany) **17/1**

8 *39* **All Spirit (GER)**[45] 1689 5-9-4 EPedroza 8 3
(N Sauer, Germany) **108/10**

9 *10* **Souvenance**[32] 2018 4-8-8 ow1 TMundry 10 —
(Sir Mark Prescott) *hld up disputing 2nd on outside for 7f: 5th 1/2-way: lost pl qckly in bk st: t.o fnl 4f* **42/10**[3]

3m 57.31s (237.31) **9** Ran SP% **133.5**
(including ten euro stakes): WIN 16; PL 12, 19, 30; SF 147.
Owner Stall Mydlinghoven **Bred** Gestut Wittekindshof **Trained** Germany

NOTEBOOK
Souvenance, whose trainer had found a couple of weak races in Ireland for her on her previous two starts, ran poorly on this step up in trip, but it was windy and the course was almost waterlogged, so she has her excuses.

[2650] BATH (L-H)
Wednesday, June 27

OFFICIAL GOING: Good (8.2)
Wind: Moderate against Weather: Fine

2977 M. J. CHURCH MAIDEN STKS 5f 161y
6:40 (6:43) (Class 5) 2-Y-0 **£2,849** (£847; £423; £211) **Stalls** Centre

Form RPR

53 **1** **Barbarossa**[19] 2424 2-9-3 0 RichardHughes 5 79
(R Hannon) *a.p: rdn to ld ins fnl f: r.o* **6/1**[3]

0 **2** *1 ¼* **Latin Scholar (IRE)**[33] 1989 2-9-3 0 SimonWhitworth 3 75
(A King) *s.i.s: hdwy over 2f out: rdn over 1f out: r.o ins fnl f: tk 2nd nr fin* **20/1**

22 **3** *hd* **Aaim For Applause**[12] 2624 2-9-3 0 JHBowman 6 74
(M R Channon) *led 1f: a.p: led wl over 1f out: rdn and hdd ins fnl f: nt qckn* **10/11**[1]

4 *4* **Lille Tuva** 2-8-12 0 HayleyTurner 9 56+
(B R Millman) *bhd: rdn over 3f out: hdwy fnl f: nvr nrr* **33/1**

0 **5** *1* **Polygraph (IRE)**[39] 1832 2-9-3 0 LPKeniry 1 58
(A M Balding) *s.i.s: sn chsng ldrs: rdn over 2f out: wknd over 1f out* **5/2**[2]

6 *1* **Champagne Dancer** 2-9-3 0 TQuinn 10 54+
(D J S Ffrench Davis) *s.s: rdn and sme hdwy fnl f: n.d* **20/1**

05 **7** *nk* **Ridge Wood Dani (IRE)**[18] 2451 2-9-3 0 DavidKinsella 12 53
(E J Alston) *led after 1f: rdn and hdd wl over 1f out: wknd ins fnl f* **20/1**

4 **8** *¾* **Sawpit Sunshine (IRE)**[19] 2416 2-8-9 0 MarcHalford(3) 4 46
(J L Spearing) *prom: rdn over 2f out: wknd over 1f out* **33/1**

0 **9** *nk* **Berties Goodenough**[29] 2103 2-9-0 0 RichardKingscote(3) 2 50
(Andrew Turnell) *hld up in tch: rdn over 2f out: wknd over 1f out* **50/1**

10 *1 ¾* **Mr Funshine** 2-8-10 0 NBazeley(7) 8 44
(Mrs P N Dutfield) *bhd fnl 3f* **50/1**

11 *3 ½* **Riorun (IRE)** 2-9-0 0 EmmettStack(3) 7 32
(J G Portman) *s.v.s and wnt rt: a in rr* **66/1**

12 *10* **Mouse White** 2-9-3 0 DaneO'Neill 11 —
(H Candy) *s.s: sn chsng ldrs: rdn and wknd 3f out* **20/1**

1m 13.2s (2.00) **Going Correction** +0.15s/f (Good) **12** Ran SP% **125.6**
Speed ratings (Par 93):92,90,90,84,83 82,81,80,80,77 73,59
CSF £116.13 TOTE £6.90: £1.90, £6.10, £1.20; EX 142.40.
Owner Michael Pescod & Justin Dowley **Bred** Helshaw Grange Stud Ltd **Trained** East Everleigh, Wilts

FOCUS
An ordinary maiden. The first three finished clear and the form is pretty sound, despite the favourite being disappointing.

NOTEBOOK
Barbarossa, who had shown enough in his first two starts to suggest he could win a race like this, showed plenty of pace, just like at Goodwood last time, and found plenty for pressure to get home in front. He will get further in time, and he should pay his way in nurseries. (tchd 13-2)
Latin Scholar(IRE), who cost 40,000gns and is a brother to multiple 5f winner Holbeck Ghyll, did not show the early pace he had on his debut at Goodwood, but he ran on well late on for second. He too looks likely to make his mark in nurseries, after one more outing. (op 16-1)
Aaim For Applause was sent off a short price to make it third time lucky. His last outing at Goodwood may have flattered him, but this was still a disappointing effort, even though he finished well clear of the rest. Official explanation: jockey said he eased down for a stride close home as colt baulked slightly at the winner (op 5-6 tchd Evens)
Lille Tuva, whose dam was a 6f winner at two and also useful over a mile in Norway later in her career, shaped with some promise against the boys on her debut. She should improve a bit for a longer trip. (op 25-1)
Polygraph(IRE), who ran with promise in a decent maiden at Newbury on his debut, had less on his plate here but was another who failed to improve. One more outing will give connections the option of nurseries. (op 4-1)
Champagne Dancer, a half-brother to Tuscany Rose, a moderate 1m6f winner at three, is bred to want middle distances next year, so this was not a bad start to his career. Official explanation: jockey said colt ran green (op 25-1 tchd 28-1)
Riorun(IRE) Official explanation: jockey said gelding was slowly away and ran green

2978 ARCTIC SPAS BATH.CO.UK (S) H'CAP — 1m 5y
7:10 (7:11) (Class 6) (0-60,54) 3-Y-O **£1,943** (£578; £288; £144) **Stalls** Low

Form RPR

55-0 **1** **Flying Grey (IRE)**[51] [1538] 3-8-11 **52**........................ KevinGhunowa(5) 11 55
(P A Blockley) *mid-div: hdwy 5f out: rdn to ld over 2f out: drvn out* **4/1**[2]

6006 **2** *½* **Kyllachy Storm**[12] [2622] 3-9-0 **50**..............................(b) RichardHughes 13 52
(R J Hodges) *a.p: swtchd rt over 2f out: hrd rdn over 1f out: kpt on ins fnl f* **7/2**[1]

0006 **3** *shd* **Flamestone**[11] [2661] 3-8-4 **45**.................................. LukeMorris(5) 9 47
(A E Price) *hld up: rdn and hdwy over 2f out: kpt on ins fnl f* **25/1**

5000 **4** *nk* **Tina's Ridge (IRE)**[51] [1538] 3-9-0 **50**..........................(p) DavidKinsella 12 51
(E J Alston) *s.i.s: hld up and bhd: rdn and hdwy over 1f out: swtchd rt ins fnl f: r.o* **9/2**[3]

-303 **5** *½* **Sad Times (IRE)**[8] [2747] 3-9-1 **54**...............................(v[1]) LiamJones(3) 15 54
(W G M Turner) *s.i.s: bhd: rdn and hdwy over 3f out: nt qckn ins fnl f* **6/1**

5005 **6** *½* **Cantique (IRE)**[6] [2800] 3-8-13 **49**............................... HayleyTurner 16 48
(Ms J S Doyle) *hld up in tch: ev ch over 2f out: sn rdn: one pce fnl f* **8/1**

0000 **7** *2* **Tizzydore (IRE)**[9] [2718] 3-8-9 **45**.. AmirQuinn 4 42+
(A G Newcombe) *bhd: rdn and hdwy over 1f out: no imp whn n.m.r and eased towards fin* **14/1**

-050 **8** *½* **Elmasong**[18] [2445] 3-8-4 **45**.. TolleyDean(5) 14 38
(J J Bridger) *led early: prom: led wl over 2f out: sn rdn and hdd: wknd ins fnl f* **20/1**

000- **9** *shd* **Bronco's Filly (IRE)**[320] [4334] 3-8-9 **45**.................................. LPKeniry 7 38
(J G M O'Shea) *s.v.s: rdn and sme hdwy whn nt clr run jst over 1f out: n.d after* **25/1**

00-0 **10** *nk* **Beshairt**[11] [2654] 3-8-9 **45**.. AlanDaly 1 37
(D Burchell) *bhd: rdn over 2f out: swtchd rt over 1f out: nvr nr ldrs* **20/1**

0060 **11** *4* **Spinning Dixie (IRE)**[96] [738] 3-9-4 **54**.....................(t) RichardThomas 2 37
(J A Geake) *mid-div: rdn over 4f out: wknd over 2f out* **14/1**

5-00 **12** *13* **Little Tiny Tom**[89] [832] 3-8-6 **49**.................................(p) PaulPickard(7) 8 2
(C N Kellett) *sn led: hdd 4f out: rdn and wknd over 2f out* **50/1**

36-6 **13** *nk* **Stars Above**[146] [322] 3-8-9 **45**.. DaneO'Neill 3 —
(M S Saunders) *sn w ldr: led 4f out tl wl over 2f out: sn wknd* **9/1**

1m 43.48s (2.38) **Going Correction** +0.15s/f (Good) **13** Ran SP% **128.3**

Speed ratings (Par 97):94,93,93,93,92 92,90,89,89,89 85,72,71

CSF £18.55 CT £330.87 TOTE £7.40: £2.20, £1.90, £7.60; EX 32.10.There was no bid for the winner. Kyllachy Storm was subject to a friendly claim. Tina's Ridge was claimed by John Marriott for £6,000.

Owner Market Avenue Racing Club Ltd **Bred** Swordlestown Stud **Trained** Lambourn, Berks

■ Stewards' Enquiry : Richard Hughes one-day ban: used whip with excessive frequency (Jul 8)
Kevin Ghunowa one-day ban: used whip above shoulder height (Jul 8)

FOCUS
A poor affair featuring only one previous winner. Weak form, and not too solid.

2979 BRISTOL PORT COMPANY H'CAP — 1m 5y
7:40 (7:41) (Class 5) (0-70,70) 4-Y-O+ **£2,914** (£867; £433; £216) **Stalls** Low

Form RPR

-300 **1** **Moves Goodenough**[37] [1886] 4-8-11 **60**.......................(b[1]) HayleyTurner 2 70
(Andrew Turnell) *a.p: rdn to ld 1f out: r.o* **20/1**

1642 **2** *1 ½* **Indian Edge**[9] [2722] 6-9-5 **68**... FergusSweeney 3 75
(B Palling) *led: rdn 2f out: hdd 1f out: nt qckn ins fnl f* **7/2**[1]

2003 **3** *¾* **Azreme**[6] [2809] 7-8-12 **61**... DaneO'Neill 11 66
(P Howling) *hld up and bhd: nt clr run 2f out: hdwy over 1f out: rdn and nt qckn ins fnl f* **7/1**[2]

0000 **4** *3* **Lizarazu (GER)**[12] [2619] 8-8-3 **55**.................................(p) LiamJones(3) 13 53
(R A Harris) *hld up and bhd: rdn and hdwy on outside over 1f out: edgd lft ins fnl f: one pce* **16/1**

3420 **5** *1 ½* **Merrymadcap (IRE)**[20] [2401] 5-9-7 **70**............................... JamieSpencer 5 64
(M Blanshard) *hld up and bhd: stdy hdwy 3f out: rdn over 1f out: wknd ins fnl f* **7/2**[1]

5160 **6** *nk* **Our Kes (IRE)**[11] [2665] 5-8-11 **60**.. AmirQuinn 10 54
(P Howling) *w ldr: ev ch over 2f out: rdn and wknd over 1f out* **25/1**

6020 **7** *nk* **Over To You Bert**[6] [2798] 8-8-4 **53**................................ RichardThomas 9 46
(R J Hodges) *hld up in tch: rdn over 2f out: wknd over 1f out* **14/1**

0005 **8** *¾* **Salvestro**[46] [1671] 4-8-0 **54** ow3.............................. KevinGhunowa(5) 7 45
(A W Carroll) *t.k.h in mid-div: hdwy on ins 3f out: rdn and wknd 2f out* **8/1**[3]

-561 **9** *nk* **Legal Lover (IRE)**[43] [1740] 5-8-10 **64**................... RussellKennemore(5) 6 55
(R Hollinshead) *prom: rdn over 2f out: wknd over 1f out* **7/1**[2]

0100 **10** *shd* **The Gaikwar (IRE)**[17] [2492] 8-9-0 **68**...........................(b) LukeMorris(5) 1 58
(R A Harris) *bhd: rdn over 3f out: nvr nr ldrs* **16/1**

0-01 **11** *shd* **Bahhmirage (IRE)**[9] [2716] 4-7-9 **51** 6ex.................... CharlotteKerton(7) 8 41
(C N Kellett) *s.s: a bhd* **25/1**

-031 **12** *1 ¼* **Drum Dance (IRE)**[23] [2304] 5-8-2 **51** oh1........................ ChrisCatlin 12 38
(M Hill) *hld up in mid-div: hdwy over 2f out: rdn over 1f out: wknd fnl f* **11/1**

1m 41.15s (0.05) **Going Correction** +0.15s/f (Good) **12** Ran SP% **119.8**

Speed ratings (Par 103):105,103,102,99,98 97,97,96,96,96 96,95

CSF £87.98 CT £561.95 TOTE £24.40: £5.30, £1.80, £3.20; EX 137.00.

Owner D Goodenough Removals & Transport **Bred** G Foster **Trained** Broad Hinton, Wilts

FOCUS
A modest handicap in which it paid to race fairly close to the pace. Ordinary but solid form.

Moves Goodenough Official explanation: trainer said, regarding apparent improvement in form, that the gelding had improved for wearing the first time blinkers

2980 HAYS & CIOB H'CAP — 1m 2f 46y
8:10 (8:12) (Class 6) (0-65,65) 4-Y-O+ **£2,184** (£644; £322) **Stalls** Low

Form RPR

2411 **1** **Drawback (IRE)**[11] [2656] 4-9-2 **65**...............................(p) LukeMorris(5) 8 74
(R A Harris) *t.k.h early: a.p: rdn to ld over 1f out: r.o* **3/1**[3]

03 **2** *½* **Oldrik (GER)**[12] [2621] 4-9-4 **62**... JamieSpencer 3 70
(P J Hobbs) *hld up: hdwy on ins over 1f out: sn rdn: ev ch whn hung lft ins fnl f: nt qckn* **15/8**[1]

-042 **3** *2 ½* **Ermine Grey**[9] [2716] 6-8-1 **50**.. KevinGhunowa(5) 7 53
(A W Carroll) *plld hrd: towards rr: hdwy over 4f out: rdn over 1f out: no ex ins fnl f* **11/4**[2]

0000 **4** *1 ¼* **Orpen Quest (IRE)**[21] [2370] 5-8-5 **49** oh1 ow3..........(p) PaulFitzsimons 2 50
(M J Attwater) *hld up and bhd: plld out 2f out: styd on ins fnl f: nt rch ldrs* **22/1**

0003 **5** *1 ½* **Corrib (IRE)**[11] [2654] 4-9-4 **62**.. FergusSweeney 1 60
(B Palling) *hld up and bhd: stdy hdwy over 2f out: rdn over 1f out: wknd ins fnl f* **12/1**

3-54 **6** *nk* **Musical Gift**[164] [129] 7-8-2 **46** oh1..................................... ChrisCatlin 9 43
(M Hill) *plld hrd: set slow pce: rdn and hdd over 1f out: wknd fnl f* **16/1**

50-0 **7** *6* **High Seasons**[172] [48] 4-9-3 **61**.. VinceSlattery 10 46
(A J Chamberlain) *prom: rdn over 2f out: wknd over 1f out* **20/1**

1060 **8** *11* **Play Up Pompey**[110] [651] 5-8-8 **57**................................ TolleyDean(5) 6 20
(J J Bridger) *prom: lost pl over 4f out: bhd fnl 3f: eased whn no ch fnl f* **14/1**

2m 12.68s (1.68) **Going Correction** +0.15s/f (Good) **8** Ran SP% **115.8**

Speed ratings (Par 101):99,98,96,95,94 94,89,80

CSF £9.18 CT £16.36 TOTE £4.00: £1.30, £1.30, £1.60; EX 10.70.

Owner B & T Hicks Transport Limited **Bred** Mrs H B Raw **Trained** Earlswood, Monmouths

■ Stewards' Enquiry : Jamie Spencer one-day ban: used whip with excessive force (Jul 8)

FOCUS
Not a very good race, and slowly run, but it was dominated by in-form runners. The winner improved by 5lb on his previous course-and-distance win, but the fourth limits the form.

2981 BET NOW AT WBX.COM MAIDEN STKS — 1m 3f 144y
8:40 (8:41) (Class 5) 3-Y-O+ **£2,849** (£847; £423; £211) **Stalls** Low

Form RPR

0-63 **1** **Mirthful (USA)**[23] [2308] 3-8-8 75.................................... RichardHughes 11 70
(B W Hills) *hld up and bhd: hdwy over 2f out: rdn to ld and edgd lft over 1f out: drvn clr ins fnl f: r.o wl* **3/1**[2]

2-04 **2** *5* **Dan Buoy (FR)**[29] [2113] 4-9-13 69................................... FergusSweeney 6 67
(A King) *a.p: led 3f out: rdn 2f out: hdd over 1f out: one pce* **6/1**[3]

25 **3** *3 ½* **Pugnacious Lady**[19] [2436] 3-8-9 0 ow1............................. JHBowman 10 57
(J W Hills) *hld up in mid-div: hdwy over 3f out: rdn over 2f out: wknd over 1f out* **7/1**

0065 **4** *4* **The Tinker Man**[10] [2697] 3-8-13 45.................................... HayleyTurner 4 54
(M D I Usher) *prom tl wknd over 2f out* **40/1**

0- **5** *2 ½* **Accumulus**[220] [5086] 7-9-13 0.. EdwardCreighton 3 50
(Noel T Chance) *dwlt: hld up and bhd: rdn whn plld out and hdwy over 2f out: edgd lft and wknd over 1f out* **22/1**

6 *½* **Pertemps Power** 3-8-13 0.. VinceSlattery 1 49
(A D Smith) *s.i.s: bhd: rdn 3f out: swtchd rt and sme hdwy over 1f out: n.d* **100/1**

0 **7** *5* **Burnley (IRE)**[50] [1560] 4-9-10 0............................. RichardKingscote(3) 12 40
(Mrs A L M King) *s.i.s: nvr nr ldrs* **100/1**

333 **8** *nk* **Orama's Ghost**[21] [2359] 3-8-8 74.. JamieSpencer 8 59+
(Sir Michael Stoute) *hld up in mid-div: hdwy 3f out: chsd ldr over 2f out: rdn and btn whn sltly hmpd over 1f out: sn wknd* **5/4**[1]

20 **9** *1 ¾* **Mercury Blue**[24] [2274] 3-8-8 0... LPKeniry 5 32
(S Kirk) *hld up and bhd: rdn over 4f out: hdwy over 3f out: nt clr run over 2f out: sn wknd* **12/1**

60/ **10** *4* **Mighty Mover (IRE)**[904] [20] 5-9-13 0............................... DavidKinsella 9 30
(B Palling) *led: hdd over 6f out: wknd over 2f out* **66/1**

0-0 **11** *½* **On Watch**[41] [1785] 3-8-8 0.. DaneO'Neill 7 24
(H Candy) *s.i.s: a bhd* **33/1**

0-0 **12** *7* **Elounda (IRE)**[71] [1077] 3-8-8 0..(b[1]) TQuinn 2 12
(H R A Cecil) *chsd ldr: sddle slipped: led over 6f out to 3f out: sn wknd* **12/1**

2m 31.16s (0.86) **Going Correction** +0.15s/f (Good)
WFA 3 from 4yo+ 14lb **12** Ran SP% **124.8**

Speed ratings (Par 103):103,99,97,94,93 92,89,89,87,85 84,80

CSF £21.91 TOTE £5.50: £2.00, £2.10, £2.50; EX 26.70.

Owner K Abdulla **Bred** Juddmonte Farms Inc **Trained** Lambourn, Berks

FOCUS
Not a strong maiden by any means, demonstrated by the close proximity to the leaders of the 45-rated The Tinker Man. The form could have been rated up to a stone higher, but the winner did not need to improve in the circumstances with the second and third below par.

Burnley(IRE) Official explanation: trainer said gelding finished distressed

Orama's Ghost Official explanation: jockey said filly lost its action; vet said filly returned distressed

Elounda(IRE) Official explanation: jockey said filly ran too keenly and saddle slipped

2982 HIGHER SOCIETY HATS FOR ALL OCCASIONS H'CAP — 5f 161y
9:10 (9:10) (Class 5) (0-75,75) 3-Y-O+ **£2,914** (£867; £433; £216) **Stalls** Centre

Form RPR

1116 **1** **Stamford Blue**[19] [2414] 6-9-8 **74**...................................(b) LukeMorris(5) 1 85
(R A Harris) *bhd: rdn over 2f out: hdwy and squeezed through jst over 1f out: led wl ins fnl f: r.o* **6/1**[3]

0-00 **2** *1 ½* **Goodenough Mover**[18] [2458] 11-9-1 **62**.....................(b[1]) HayleyTurner 7 68
(Andrew Turnell) *chsd ldr: led over 1f out: sn rdn: hdd and nt qckn wl ins fnl f* **14/1**

0005 **3** *1 ¾* **Nautical**[19] [2414] 9-9-6 **67**.. JHBowman 6 67
(A W Carroll) *hld up and bhd: hdwy on ins over 1f out: kpt on same pce ins fnl f* **15/2**

0-05 **4** *nk* **Jucebabe**[18] [2459] 4-8-6 **56** oh2.. MarcHalford(3) 2 55
(J L Spearing) *hld up in mid-div: rdn over 2f out: hdwy over 1f out: nt clr run briefly ent fnl f: one pce* **8/1**

0020 **5** *1 ¼* **Briannsta (IRE)**[15] [2546] 5-10-0 **75**.................................. RichardHughes 3 70
(C G Cox) *chsd ldrs: ev ch over 1f out: rdn and one pce fnl f* **7/1**

060- **6** *3 ½* **Cerulean Rose**[218] [6556] 8-8-9 **56** oh1................................ DaneO'Neill 4 40
(A W Carroll) *hld up: hdwy 2f out: sn rdn: wknd ins fnl f* **25/1**

5035 **7** *3* **Outer Hebrides**[9] [2725] 6-9-6 **72**..............................(bt[1]) KevinGhunowa(5) 5 46
(J M Bradley) *hld up towards rr: rdn over 2f out: no rspnse* **5/1**[2]

4220 **8** *¾* **Willhewiz**[11] [2673] 7-9-1 **62**.. TQuinn 8 33
(M S Saunders) *led: rdn and hdd over 1f out: wkng whn n.m.r briefly ent fnl f: eased* **3/1**[1]

0066 **9** *2* **Enjoy The Buzz**[14] [2555] 8-8-9 **56** oh11............................ PaulFitzsimons 10 21
(J M Bradley) *prom: rdn over 2f out: wknd over 1f out* **25/1**

543 **10** *3 ½* **Golden Brown (IRE)**[25] [2242] 3-8-12 **66**.......................... FergusSweeney 9 19
(David Pinder) *hld up towards rr: rdn 3f out: no rspnse* **13/2**

1m 11.35s (0.15) **Going Correction** +0.15s/f (Good)
WFA 3 from 4yo+ 7lb **10** Ran SP% **119.0**

Speed ratings (Par 103):105,103,100,100,98 93,89,88,86,81

CSF £87.98 CT £652.84 TOTE £8.20: £2.50, £2.60, £3.00; EX 92.60 Place 6 £59.23, Place 5 £43.72..

Owner Brian Hicks **Bred** Mrs Wendy Miller **Trained** Earlswood, Monmouths

■ Stewards' Enquiry : Luke Morris one-day ban: careless riding (Jul 8)

FOCUS
Just a modest sprint handicap. The form does not look that strong with the winner seemingly high enough in the weights and the runner-up having lost his form, although the latter was a lot better than this last year.

Outer Hebrides Official explanation: jockey said gelding never travelled

Willhewiz Official explanation: jockey said gelding suffered interference in running; vet said gelding returned lame right-hind

Golden Brown(IRE) Official explanation: jockey said gelding ran flat

T/Plt: £70.60 to a £1 stake. Pool: £78,406.25. 810.15 winning tickets. T/Qpdt: £26.80 to a £1 stake. Pool: £4,525.10. 124.90 winning tickets. KH

[2709] CARLISLE (R-H)

Wednesday, June 27

OFFICIAL GOING: Good to soft (good in places; 7.8)

Wind: Breezy, across Weather: Cloudy, fine

2983 EUROPEAN BREEDERS' FUND MAIDEN STKS 5f 193y

2:00 (2:00) (Class 5) 2-Y-O **£3,562** (£1,059; £529; £264) **Stalls** High

Form				RPR
	1		**Choose Your Moment** 2-9-3 0 .... LeeEnstone 8 (P C Haslam) *s.i.s: sn prom: led over 2f out: rdn and edgd lft ins fnl f: kpt on wl* **5/1**[3]	81
23	2	1 ¾	**Nawaaff**[26] [2215] 2-9-3 0 .... DarryllHolland 9 (M R Channon) *cl up: ev ch over 2f out: sn rdn: kpt on u.p fnl f* **11/8**[1]	76
2	3	hd	**Feisty Royale**[32] [2039] 2-8-12 0 .... J-PGuillambert 11 (M Johnston) *led to over 2f out: hung lft u.p: kpt on ins fnl f* **10/3**[2]	70
	4	1 ¾	**Chivola (IRE)** 2-9-3 0 .... RoystonFfrench 7 (B Smart) *prom: effrt over 2f out: one pce fnl f* **8/1**	70
0	5	3	**Duke Of Touraine (IRE)**[6] [2803] 2-9-3 0 .... PaulMulrennan 2 (P C Haslam) *cl up tl rdn and outpcd fr 2f out* **66/1**	60+
	6	½	**Terrasini (FR)** 2-9-3 0 .... TomEaves 5 (J Howard Johnson) *in tch tl rdn and outpcd fr over 2f out* **40/1**	59
	7	½	**Miss Skycat (USA)** 2-8-12 0 .... PhillipMakin 4 (T D Barron) *towards rr and sn drvn along: n.d* **16/1**	52
4	8	hd	**Baby Jack**[20] [2392] 2-9-3 0 .... AdrianTNicholls 1 (D Nicholls) *bhd and sn pushed along: nvr rchd ldrs* **14/1**	57
0	9	1 ¾	**Johnny Friendly**[47] [1622] 2-9-3 0 .... PatCosgrave 3 (K R Burke) *w ldr tl wknd fr 2f out* **66/1**	51
	10	1 ¼	**Kalhan Sands (IRE)** 2-9-3 0 .... DeanMcKeown 6 (G A Swinbank) *missed break: hung rt thrght: nvr on terms* **25/1**	47

1m 15.29s (1.68) **Going Correction** +0.10s/f (Good) **10 Ran SP% 114.8**

Speed ratings (Par 93):92,89,89,87,83 82,81,81,79,77

CSF £11.82 TOTE £6.10: £2.00, £1.40, £1.20; EX 17.70.

Owner Mr & Mrs Duncan Davidson **Bred** Alpha Bloodstock Limited **Trained** Middleham Moor, N Yorks

FOCUS

A decent event and one in which the pace was sound. The form looks solid and should prove reliable.

NOTEBOOK

Choose Your Moment ◆, a half-brother to a middle-distance winner, is a big individual with plenty of scope and he created a favourable impression after a tardy start when beating a fairly reliable yardstick on this racecourse debut. He should stay 7f and looks the type to progress again. (tchd 9-2 and 11-2)

Nawaaff, whose form entitled him to maximum respect in this company, looked fit and well but, although seemingly giving it his best shot, once again underlined his vulnerability to the better sorts in this grade. However he should stay 7f and looks sure to pick up a small event this summer. (op 13-8 tchd 7-4 in places)

Feisty Royale, a leggy sort who had shown ability in ordinary company on her debut at Haydock, ran to a similar level. She should have no problems with an extra furlong and is the sort to win a race for her leading stable. (op 3-1 tchd 11-4 and 7-2)

Chivola(IRE), who cost 45,000gns and is a half-brother to dual winner Sandrey, is not overly big but shaped creditably for a stable that has a strong hand in the juvenile department. He should come on for this experience and is likely to be placed to best advantage. (op 10-1)

Duke Of Touraine(IRE), soundly beaten after getting loose before the start on his debut, proved more tractable this time and showed he possesses ability. He should stay further but looks the type to fare better once handicapped.

Terrasini(FR), a not overly big son of Linamix, was not totally disgraced but shaped as though possessing more stamina than speed on this racecourse debut, and he may continue to look vulnerable in this type of event. (op 25-1)

Kalhan Sands(IRE) Official explanation: jockey said colt hung right-handed throughout

2984 EDMUNDSON ELECTRICAL MAIDEN AUCTION STKS 5f

2:30 (2:42) (Class 5) 2-Y-O **£2,817** (£838; £418; £209) **Stalls** High

Form				RPR
032	1		**Brixworth Scribe**[7] [2758] 2-8-9 0 .... RoystonFfrench 1 (B Smart) *chsd ldrs: drvn along 1/2-way: styd on wl fnl f to ld towards fin* **3/1**[1]	75
3	2	¾	**Liberty Ship**[33] [1992] 2-8-13 0 .... NCallan 5 (J D Bethell) *cl up: led and hung bdly rt over 1f out: kpt on u.p: hdd nr fin* **5/1**	76
	3	¾	**Quest For Success (IRE)** 2-9-2 0 .... PaulHanagan 3 (R A Fahey) *prom: drvn over 2f out: kpt on wl fnl f: nrst fin* **10/3**[2]	77
04	4	½	**Ponder Anew (IRE)**[29] [2109] 2-8-8 0 .... PhillipMakin 11 (K R Burke) *cl up: rdn and ev ch whn carried rt over 1f out: kpt on same pce* **20/1**	67
3	5	nk	**Elijah Pepper (USA)**[80] [952] 2-8-11 0 .... PaulFessey 12 (T D Barron) *led: hdd whn carried bdly rt appr fnl f: kpt on same pce* **9/2**[3]	69
	6	shd	**Coffee Cup (IRE)** 2-8-1 0 .... AndrewElliott[(3)] 4 (G A Swinbank) *bhd tl kpt on fnl f: nvr on terms* **33/1**	61+
	7	1	**Best Suited** 2-8-4 0 .... GrahamGibbons 7 (J J Quinn) *s.i.s: bhd tl kpt on fnl f: n.d* **25/1**	58+
55	8	nk	**Starlight Girl**[22] [2337] 2-8-11 0 .... DavidAllan 10 (T D Easterby) *in tch tl rdn and outpcd fr 2f out* **14/1**	64
	9	4	**Attribution** 2-8-11 0 .... KDarley 6 (K R Burke) *towards rr: effrt over 2f out: btn fnl f* **8/1**	49
40	10	shd	**Whiskey Creek**[23] [2297] 2-8-6 0 .... JamieMoriarty[(3)] 2 (R A Fahey) *hld up: shortlived effrt over 2f out: sn btn* **28/1**	47
0	11	nk	**Smilodon**[23] [2297] 2-8-2 0 ow1 .... (b[1]) PatrickMathers[(3)] 9 (A Berry) *s.i.s: nvr on terms* **200/1**	42
	12	dist	**Magnushomestwo (IRE)** 2-8-9 0 .... JoeFanning 8 (A Berry) *missed break: struggling whn hung bdly lft 1/2-way: virtually p.u* **50/1**	—

62.74 secs (1.24) **Going Correction** +0.10s/f (Good) **12 Ran SP% 118.2**

Speed ratings (Par 93):94,92,91,90,90 90,88,88,81,81 81,—

CSF £16.89 TOTE £4.30: £1.70, £1.80, £1.30; EX 21.40.

Owner White, Beesley, Mason **Bred** Mrs B A Matthews **Trained** Hambleton, N Yorks

■ Stewards' Enquiry : N Callan two-day ban: careless riding (Jul 8-9)

FOCUS

An ordinary bunch on looks, but this looks solid form and decent for the grade.

NOTEBOOK

Brixworth Scribe had lost ground at the start on his two previous starts when showing fair form, but jumped out on terms this time and, although down in distance, proved suited by the good gallop and this stiff track. The return to six will suit and, although lacking much in the way of scope, he should continue to give a good account. (op 11-4 tchd 5-2 and 10-3 in a place)

Liberty Ship, who had wandered when running creditably on his debut, ran at least as well this time but looked anything but straightforward on this easier ground. He has the ability to win a similar race but does not look one to place maximum faith in on this evidence. (op 4-1 tchd 11-2)

Quest For Success(IRE) ◆, who cost 25,000gns and is related to winners over sprint and middle distances, was well supported for this racecourse debut. He showed more than enough, despite showing his inexperience both before and during the race, to suggest that a similar event can be found. He will be suited by 6f and is one to keep an eye on. (op 11-2)

Ponder Anew(IRE) turned in her best effort, despite being hampered, and, although she is going to remain vulnerable to the more progressive sorts in this grade, she will be suited by the step up to 6f and looks sure to be placed to best advantage. (op 16-1)

Elijah Pepper(USA), who ran creditably in an ordinary event on his debut in April, bettered that form on this first run since and would have been closer but for being carried across the course in the closing stages. He will be suited by the step up to 6f and should do better. (op 5-1 tchd 11-2)

Coffee Cup(IRE), the first foal of a triple middle-distance winner in France, is not from a yard normally associated with debut winners in this grade, and, although not disgraced on this first run, shaped as though much more of a test of stamina would suit in due course. (op 25-1)

Magnushomestwo(IRE) Official explanation: jockey said colt lost its action

2985 AZURE CARLISLE BELL CONSOLATION RACE (H'CAP) 7f 200y

3:00 (3:07) (Class 5) 3-Y-O+ **£5,181** (£1,541; £770; £384) **Stalls** High

Form				RPR
05-2	1		**Webbow (IRE)**[15] [2536] 5-9-7 72 .... DavidAllan 13 (T D Easterby) *hld up in midfield: hdwy to ld over 1f out: pushed out: comf* **4/1**[1]	87+
3401	2	1 ½	**Gunfighter (IRE)**[20] [2390] 4-9-4 72 .... JamieMoriarty[(3)] 5 (J S Wainwright) *prom: effrt and ev ch over 1f out: kpt on fnl f: nt rch wnr* **12/1**	84
4111	3	2 ½	**Networker**[20] [2388] 4-9-7 72 .... NCallan 11 (P J McBride) *prom: effrt and ev ch wl over 1f out: sn rdn and hung lft: one pce ins fnl f* **6/1**[2]	78+
-505	4	1 ½	**Kirkby's Treasure**[9] [2714] 9-8-9 60 .... DeanMcKeown 6 (G A Swinbank) *hld up: shkn up and hdwy over 1f out: kpt on: nrst fin* **8/1**	63
6430	5	1 ½	**Champain Sands (IRE)**[23] [2311] 8-8-6 62 .... MichaelJStainton[(5)] 4 (E J Alston) *hld up: hdwy over 1f out: kpt on fnl f: nvr rchd ldrs* **16/1**	61+
/0-3	6	1 ¾	**Burley Flame**[60] [1287] 6-9-10 75 .... JoeFanning 14 (J G Given) *chsd ldrs: effrt over 2f out: no ex over 1f out* **17/2**	70
0-02	7	½	**Heureux (USA)**[23] [2311] 4-9-6 71 .... (b) TomEaves 2 (J Howard Johnson) *prom: outpcd 3f out: edgd rt and rallied over 1f out: no imp* **15/2**[3]	65
2-11	8	1 ¾	**Ballyhurry (USA)**[5] [2828] 10-9-0 72 6ex .... GaryBartley[(7)] 7 (J S Goldie) *hld up in midfield: outpcd over 2f out: n.d after* **18/1**	62
-230	9	nk	**Letham Island (IRE)**[40] [1827] 3-9-0 75 .... KDarley 12 (M Johnston) *led to 1/2-way: no ex fr over 2f out* **14/1**	64
0515	10	shd	**Franksalot (IRE)**[14] [2550] 7-9-6 71 .... RoystonFfrench 3 (I W McInnes) *prom tl rdn and wknd over 2f out* **22/1**	60
5342	11	1 ¼	**Spinning**[5] [2842] 4-9-1 66 .... (b[1]) PhillipMakin 10 (T D Barron) *sn rdn and disp ld: led 1/2-way to over 1f out: wknd* **11/1**	52
0000	12	1 ¼	**Choreography**[30] [2072] 4-9-1 66 .... SilvestreDeSousa 1 (D Nicholls) *towards rr: drvn 1/2-way: btn fnl 2f* **33/1**	49
-551	13	1 ¼	**Wasalat (USA)**[22] [2338] 5-9-7 72 .... PaulHanagan 9 (D W Barker) *in midfield: rdn and edgd rt 2f out: sn btn* **20/1**	53
06-0	14	12	**Lago D'Orta (IRE)**[36] [1915] 7-9-10 75 .... AdrianTNicholls 8 (D Nicholls) *hld up: rdn over 2f out: sn btn* **14/1**	28

1m 39.92s (-0.17) **Going Correction** +0.10s/f (Good)

WFA 3 from 4yo+ 10lb **14 Ran SP% 120.2**

Speed ratings (Par 103):104,102,100,98,97 95,94,93,92,92 91,90,88,76

CSF £51.24 CT £298.61 TOTE £5.60: £2.10, £4.50, £2.20; EX 82.60.

Owner Wentdale Limited **Bred** Joe O'Callaghan **Trained** Great Habton, N Yorks

FOCUS

The first running of this race, for horses which failed to make the cut in the historic Carlisle Bell. It was a competitive event for the grade, run at a sound pace, and the first three all look the sort to improve further. The form should work out.

2986 CARLING CARLISLE BELL (H'CAP) 7f 200y

3:30 (3:35) (Class 4) (0-80,80) 3-Y-O+ **£19,431** (£5,781; £2,889; £1,443) **Stalls** High

Form				RPR
5100	1		**Bold Marc (IRE)**[18] [2452] 5-9-4 80 .... AndrewElliott[(3)] 2 (K R Burke) *pressed ldr: led over 2f out: hld on gamely fnl f* **33/1**	91
1-53	2	½	**Prince Evelith (GER)**[5] [2822] 4-8-13 77 .... PJMcDonald[(5)] 11 (G A Swinbank) *hld up: hdwy over 2f out: sn rdn: ch ins fnl f: kpt on* **10/1**	87
3151	3	nk	**Daaweitza**[33] [1996] 4-9-7 80 .... TomEaves 14 (B Ellison) *t.k.h: chsd ldrs: rdn 3f out: rallied and ch ins fnl f: hld towards fin* **10/1**	89
0003	4	1	**Stoic Leader (IRE)**[2] [2936] 7-9-1 77 .... AndrewMullen[(3)] 17 (R F Fisher) *prom: effrt over 2f out: kpt on same pce fnl f* **20/1**	84
2221	5	2	**Veiled Applause**[9] [2722] 4-9-3 76 6ex .... JamesDoyle 5 (R M Beckett) *hld up: hdwy over 2f out: kpt on fnl f: no imp* **7/1**[2]	78
0-05	6	½	**Bajan Parkes**[21] [2374] 4-9-6 79 .... KDarley 9 (E J Alston) *bhd tl styd on fr 2f out: nrst fin* **20/1**	80
0-54	7	½	**Zennerman (IRE)**[39] [1845] 4-9-2 75 .... NCallan 16 (K A Ryan) *midfield: effrt and rdn over 2f out: no imp over 1f out* **10/1**	75
3122	8	1	**Exit Smiling**[21] [2374] 5-9-5 78 .... MickyFenton 15 (P T Midgley) *midfield: drvn over 2f out: no further imp* **11/1**	76
0031	9	1 ¼	**Regent's Secret (USA)**[9] [2714] 7-9-3 76 6ex .... (p) PaulHanagan 4 (J S Goldie) *hld up: drvn 3f out: nvr rchd ldrs* **7/2**[1]	71
-053	10	shd	**Rubenstar (IRE)**[19] [2427] 4-9-5 78 .... DarryllHolland 1 (M H Tompkins) *hld up: hmpd after 3f: sme hdwy over 1f out: n.d* **11/1**	74+
1304	11	nk	**Just Bond (IRE)**[18] [2452] 5-9-3 76 .... GrahamGibbons 8 (G R Oldroyd) *hld up: rdn over 2f out: nvr on terms* **14/1**	70
0-24	12	1	**United Nations**[20] [2397] 6-9-3 76 .... TonyHamilton 6 (N Wilson) *bhd: rdn over 3f out: nvr on terms* **50/1**	67
-011	13	hd	**Logsdail**[19] [2423] 7-9-3 76 .... (p) GeorgeBaker 10 (G L Moore) *hld up: rdn over 2f out: btn over 1f out* **8/1**[3]	67
4434	14	1 ¼	**Shot To Fame (USA)**[15] [2528] 8-9-5 78 .... (t) SilvestreDeSousa 13 (D Nicholls) *led to over 2f out: wknd wl over 1f out* **12/1**	66
2052	15	nk	**Blacktoft (USA)**[18] [2476] 4-9-4 77 .... (e) J-PGuillambert 3 (S C Williams) *prom tl rdn and wknd wl over 1f out* **20/1**	64
5-00	16	1 ½	**Hypnotic**[88] [842] 5-9-4 77 .... (t) AdrianTNicholls 12 (D Nicholls) *prom tl rdn and wknd over 2f out* **33/1**	61

1m 39.19s (-0.90) **Going Correction** +0.10s/f (Good) **16 Ran SP% 126.3**

Speed ratings (Par 105):108,107,107,106,104 103,103,102,100,100 100,99,99,98,97 96

CSF £325.27 CT £3702.71 TOTE £44.70: £8.50, £2.70, £3.00, £5.30; EX 689.80 TRIFECTA Not won..

Owner Market Avenue Racing Club Ltd **Bred** Eamon D Delany **Trained** Middleham Moor, N Yorks

FOCUS

Few progressive performers in this open handicap, but the form looks rock solid despite a couple of the market leaders disappointing. A slight career best from Bold Marc.

Bold Marc(IRE) Official explanation: trainer's rep had no explanation for the apparent improvement in form

2987 GROLSCH CUMBERLAND PLATE (H'CAP) 1m 3f 107y
4:00 (4:01) (Class 4) (0-80,79) 3-Y-O+ £19,431 (£5,781; £2,889; £1,443) Stalls Low

Form				RPR
6361	1		**Oddsmaker (IRE)**[18] 2465 6-9-6 75 (t) DeanMcKeown 11 (M A Barnes) mde all: rdn clr over 2f out: hung lft ins fnl f: hld on wl 12/1	84
-031	2	1	**Lady Songbird (IRE)**[40] 1813 4-9-3 72 AdamKirby 10 (W R Swinburn) hld up in midfield: effrt 3f out: chsd wnr over 1f out: kpt on ins fnl f 7/4[1]	79+
1114	3	4	**Court Of Appeal**[22] 2342 10-9-1 70 (tp) RoystonFfrench 1 (B Ellison) prom: effrt 3f out: no ex over 1f out 25/1	71
441	4	1 1/4	**Cotton Eyed Joe (IRE)**[9] 2715 6-8-12 72 6ex PJMcDonald(5) 12 (G A Swinbank) hld up: hdwy over 2f out: rdn and no imp fnl f 7/1[2]	71
-213	5	1/2	**Tcherina (IRE)**[23] 2314 5-9-7 79 DuranFentiman(3) 16 (T D Easterby) bhd tl styd on fnl 2f: nrst fin 10/1	77
0/24	6	nk	**Grizebeck (IRE)**[25] 2253 5-9-1 70 PhillipMakin 3 (R F Fisher) in tch: effrt over 2f out: sn one pce 80/1	68
3-02	7	3	**Fossgate**[22] 2342 6-9-7 76 NCallan 6 (J D Bethell) hld up: effrt whn hmpd 3f out: sn rdn and hung rt: nvr rchd ldrs 16/1	69
5500	8	nk	**Prince Charlemagne (IRE)**[33] 2003 4-9-5 74 JamesDoyle 7 (N P Littmoden) towards rr: rdn over 3f out: sme late hdwy: nvr on terms 18/1	66
0050	9	1	**Dium Mac**[15] 2536 6-9-7 76 GrahamGibbons 15 (N Bycroft) bhd: effrt u.p over 2f out: n.d 18/1	67
6-01	10	2 1/2	**Tsaroxy (IRE)**[47] 1627 5-9-6 75 TomEaves 8 (J Howard Johnson) in tch tl rdn and outpcd fr 3f out 16/1	62
021	11	1 1/4	**Pocketwood**[25] 2238 5-9-4 73 J-PGuillambert 9 (Jean-Rene Auvray) hld up: drvn 3f out: btn over 1f out 12/1	58
3252	12	7	**Sir Arthur (IRE)**[14] 2551 4-9-4 73 KDarley 5 (M Johnston) cl up tl rdn and wknd over 2f out 8/1[3]	47
4050	13	nk	**Wulimaster (USA)**[9] 2715 4-9-0 69 (v[1]) PatCosgrave 17 (D W Barker) hld up: shortlived effrt over 2f out: sn wknd 40/1	42
3-00	14	8	**Missoula (IRE)**[42] 1771 4-9-5 74 DarryllHolland 13 (M H Tompkins) bhd: rdn over 3f out: nvr on terms 14/1	34
2-00	15	7	**Magic Sting**[21] 2374 6-9-1 73 JamieMoriarty(3) 4 (B S Rothwell) t.k.h in midfield: rdn and wknd fr 3f out 100/1	22
304/	16	29	**Skylarker (USA)**[626] 5757 9-9-2 71 TonyHamilton 2 (T A K Cuthbert) cl up tl wknd over 3f out 100/1	—
0-11	17	1	**Diamonds And Dust**[35] 380 5-9-6 75 (b) PaulMulrennan 14 (F P Murtagh) sn towards rr: drvn over 4f out: nvr on terms 25/1	—

2m 25.6s (2.60) **Going Correction** +0.10s/f (Good) 17 Ran SP% **126.8**
Speed ratings (Par 105):94,93,90,89,89 88,86,86,85,83 83,77,77,71,66 45,44
CSF £32.97 CT £565.70 TOTE £15.70: £3.00, £1.30, £4.80, £2.50; EX 57.90 Trifecta £158.20 Pool £222.87 - 1.00 winning units..
Owner D Maloney **Bred** Margaret Conlon **Trained** Farlam, Cumbria
■ Stewards' Enquiry : Jamie Moriarty three-day ban: careless riding (Jul 8-10)

FOCUS
Mainly exposed sorts in this decent handicap but an improved effort from Oddsmaker to beat a progressive sort, with the pair clear of the remainder. However the winner was probably advantaged by having things his own way up front.
Magic Sting Official explanation: trainer said gelding was scoped after the race and had been found to have mud and grass in its nasal passage
Skylarker(USA) Official explanation: vet said gelding finished lame
Diamonds And Dust Official explanation: vet said gelding finished lame

2988 EUROPEAN BREEDERS' FUND FILLIES' H'CAP 6f 192y
4:30 (4:30) (Class 4) (0-85,79) 3-Y-O+ £6,477 (£1,927; £963; £481) Stalls High

Form				RPR
-200	1		**Inaminute (IRE)**[30] 2085 4-9-7 75 AndrewElliott(3) 1 (K R Burke) mde virtually all: rdn and hld on gamely fnl f 20/1	85
6033	2	1	**Passion Fruit**[5] 2742 6-10-0 79 DeanMcKeown 5 (C W Fairhurst) dwlt: hld up: hdwy to chse wnr ins fnl f: r.o 13/2[3]	86
0-02	3	1 1/4	**Damelza (IRE)**[19] 2422 4-9-5 70 (t) DavidAllan 9 (T D Easterby) hld up: hdwy over 1f out: kpt on fnl f: no imp 9/1	74
-525	4	nk	**Colchium (IRE)**[27] 2181 3-8-8 73 TravisBlock(5) 3 (H Morrison) prom: effrt over 2f out: one pce fnl f 7/2[1]	73
3-53	5	1	**Angel Voices (IRE)**[23] 2309 4-8-11 62 PhillipMakin 7 (K R Burke) hld up: hdwy and prom over 1f out: no ex fnl f 10/1	62
4631	6	3/4	**Coconut Queen (IRE)**[9] 2713 3-9-0 74 6ex (p) RoystonFfrench 12 (Mrs A Duffield) chsd ldrs: drvn 1/2-way: one pce over 1f out 8/1	69
0312	7	nk	**Dispol Isle (IRE)**[8] 2742 5-8-13 71 NeilBrown(7) 2 (T D Barron) trckd ldrs gng wl: rdn and edgd rt 2f out: sn no ex 9/2[2]	68
0102	8	2 1/2	**Flylowflylong (IRE)**[14] 2564 4-9-0 65 TomEaves 6 (I Semple) towards rr: drvn over 3f out: nvr on terms 9/1	56
-510	9	hd	**Kudbeme**[8] 2741 5-8-10 61 PaulFessey 10 (N Bycroft) s.i.s: nvr on terms 16/1	51
006-	10	1 1/4	**Ava's World (IRE)**[228] 6444 3-9-4 78 KDarley 13 (M Johnston) cl up tl rdn and wknd over 1f out 18/1	62
25-4	11	1 1/4	**Cassie's Choice (IRE)**[15] 2534 3-8-6 69 MarkLawson(3) 8 (B Smart) prom: rdn and hung rt over 2f out: btn over 1f out 9/1	49

1m 27.55s (0.45) **Going Correction** +0.10s/f (Good)
WFA 3 from 4yo+ 9lb 11 Ran SP% **119.8**
Speed ratings (Par 102):101,99,98,98,96 96,95,92,92,91 89
CSF £147.53 CT £1297.05 TOTE £23.40: £6.30, £2.40, £3.10; EX 99.60.
Owner Ray Bailey **Bred** R Bailey **Trained** Middleham Moor, N Yorks

FOCUS
Another run-of-the-mill handicap featuring mainly exposed sorts. Inaminute set just a fair pace and was the third consecutive winner to make virtually all. Pretty ordinary form, but sound enough.
Inaminute(IRE) Official explanation: trainer had no explanation for the apparent improvement in form

2989 PERSIMMON HOMES H'CAP 5f
5:00 (5:01) (Class 4) (0-85,82) 3-Y-O+ £5,181 (£1,541; £770; £384) Stalls High

Form				RPR
0040	1		**Deserted Dane (USA)**[18] 2461 3-9-3 80 DeanMcKeown 13 (G A Swinbank) prom: effrt centre over 1f out: led ins fnl f: r.o 20/1	91
4000	2	1	**First Order**[25] 2244 6-9-11 82 (v) TomEaves 8 (I Semple) led: c stands' side w main gp ent st: rdn and hdd ins fnl f: one pce 12/1	91
2503	3	3/4	**Welcome Approach**[4] 2866 4-8-9 66 DarryllHolland 5 (J R Weymes) bhd: hdwy stands' side over 1f out: kpt on: nrst fin 11/2[2]	72
4430	4	1/2	**Bo McGinty (IRE)**[4] 2866 6-9-6 77 (b) PaulHanagan 3 (R A Fahey) prom: effrt stands' side gp over 2f out: edgd rt over 1f out: r.o fnl f 9/2[1]	82
6162	5	3/4	**Namir (IRE)**[11] 2673 5-9-3 77 (vt) DuranFentiman(3) 9 (D Shaw) bhd: effrt stands' side gp over 1f out: r.o fnl f 6/1[3]	79
16/3	6	3/4	**Abientot (IRE)**[167] 97 5-8-13 70 TonyHamilton 7 (D W Barker) cl up: wnt far side w one other ent st: one pce over 1f out 14/1	69
-450	7	nk	**Ryedale Ovation (IRE)**[14] 2550 4-8-9 66 (b) DavidAllan 11 (T D Easterby) dwlt and early reminders in rr: effrt on far side over 2f out: one pce over 1f out 8/1	64
5006	8	1/2	**Glasshoughton**[4] 2866 4-9-1 72 PhillipMakin 2 (M Dods) in tch: effrt stands' side 2f out: sn outpcd 9/2[1]	68
0260	9	1 3/4	**Mr Rooney (IRE)**[6] 2805 4-8-3 67 (t) AdeleRothery(7) 12 (D Nicholls) in tch: effrt centre 2f out: edgd rt and sn outpcd 25/1	57
-000	10	2	**Circuit Dancer (IRE)**[39] 1854 7-9-8 79 AdrianTNicholls 1 (D Nicholls) chsd ldrs: rdn stands' side gp over 2f out: sn btn 16/1	62
/00-	11	3/4	**Artie**[413] 1597 8-9-8 79 KDarley 6 (T D Easterby) cl up stands' side gp tl wknd fr 2f out 28/1	59

61.26 secs (-0.24) **Going Correction** +0.10s/f (Good)
WFA 3 from 4yo+ 6lb 11 Ran SP% **109.4**
Speed ratings (Par 105):105,103,102,101,100 99,98,97,94,91 90
CSF £198.16 CT £1139.18 TOTE £19.50: £4.70, £4.00, £1.90; EX 224.70 Place 6 £118.78, Place 5 £96.58..
Owner A Flower & R H Hall **Bred** Skymarc Farm Et Al **Trained** Melsonby, N Yorks
■ Hypnosis was withdrawn (6/1, unruly in stalls.) R4 applies, deduct 10p in the £. The filly has been banned for six months.

FOCUS
A fair event in which the field raced far side, centre and stands' side in the straight. The pace was sound throughout. Solid form, the winner back to his 2yo best.
Deserted Dane(USA) ◆ Official explanation: trainer had no explanation for the apparent improvement in form
T/Jkpt: Not won. T/Plt: £69.70 to a £1 stake. Pool: £76,910.05. 805.40 winning tickets. T/Qpdt: £108.50 to a £1 stake. Pool: £3,917.10. 26.70 winning tickets. RY

2765 KEMPTON (A.W) (R-H)
Wednesday, June 27

OFFICIAL GOING: Standard
Continuing the theme of recent meetings, it proved hard to make up significant amounts of ground in most races.
Wind: Moderate, half behind, races 1-3; almost nil, races 4-7 Weather: Cloudy, heavy downpour after race 3

2990 WEATHERBYS VAT SERVICES APPRENTICE H'CAP (ROUND 4) 1m (P)
6:20 (6:21) (Class 6) (0-65,65) 4-Y-O+ £2,388 (£705; £352) Stalls High

Form				RPR
000-	1		**Fantasy Crusader**[187] 6904 8-8-1 47 JackDean(5) 7 (R M H Cowell) chsd ldrs: outpcd over 2f out: clsd fr over 1f out: rdn and r.o to ld last 75yds 50/1	55
320	2	3/4	**Shunkawakhan (IRE)**[119] 579 4-8-7 48 (p) AmyBaker 13 (G C H Chung) prom: wnt 2nd 3f out: led 2f out: bmpd along fr over 1f out: hdd and outpcd last 75yds 25/1	55
55-4	3	3/4	**Desert Island Miss**[28] 2154 4-9-5 60 (p) KirstyMilczarek 14 (W R Swinburn) led at decent pce: hdd 2f out: pressed ldr after: stl ch 100yds out: one pce 9/2[2]	65
-116	4	1	**Im Ova Ere Dad (IRE)**[123] 549 4-9-10 65 JamieHamblett 10 (D E Cantillon) prom: chsd ldng pair over 2f out: sn rdn: hanging and nt qckn: kpt on same pce 5/1[3]	68
2254	5	1	**Murrumbidgee (IRE)**[18] 2467 4-9-3 61 MCGeran(3) 6 (J W Hills) settled in midfield: outpcd wl over 2f out: styd on u.p fr over 1f out: nvr able to chal 6/1	61
0300	6	3/4	**Hansomelle (IRE)**[14] 2572 5-8-2 48 JosephWalsh(5) 12 (Miss Sheena West) hld up wl in rr: outpcd and plenty to do wl over 2f out: styd on u.p: nt rch ldrs 25/1	47
2446	7	hd	**Postmaster**[28] 2154 5-8-11 55 HarryPoulton(3) 8 (R Ingram) hld up wl in rr: rdn on inner over 2f out: styd on fr over 1f out: n.d 8/1	53
3533	8	1/2	**Rafferty (IRE)**[6] 2798 8-8-2 48 (p) ThomasBubb(5) 5 (S Dow) t.k.h: hld up wl in rr: outpcd wl over 2f out: kpt on fr over 1f out: no ch 12/1	45
0002	9	1 1/2	**Bowl Of Cherries**[4] 2875 4-8-12 53 (v) JackMitchell 3 (I A Wood) racd wd: hld up in midfield: outpcd wl over 2f out: effrt over 1f out: one pce fnl f 4/1[1]	47
23-6	10	1 3/4	**October Ben**[14] 2568 4-9-5 65 FrankiePickard(5) 4 (M D I Usher) stdd s: hld up in last: effrt on outer over 2f out: no real prog 14/1	55
0301	11	3 1/2	**Mamichor**[19] 2412 4-8-5 49 (p) JemmaMarshall(3) 11 (B R Johnson) chsd ldr to 3f out: sn wknd 14/1	31
0-00	12	2 1/2	**Klassen (USA)**[43] 1741 4-8-11 52 (b) KMay 9 (A King) stdd s: hld up wl in rr: rdn and effrt 3f out: wknd 2f out 25/1	28
003-	13	11	**Captain Darling (IRE)**[195] 6814 7-9-7 62 SCreighton 2 (R W Price) prom tl wknd rapidly 3f out: t.o 33/1	12

1m 39.31s (-1.49) **Going Correction** -0.15s/f (Stan) 13 Ran SP% **117.7**
Speed ratings (Par 101):101,100,99,98,97 96,96,96,94,92 89,86,75
CSF £946.49 CT £6799.27 TOTE £46.80: £15.80, £7.00, £1.60; EX 702.00.
Owner The Fantasy Fellowship **Bred** J R C And Mrs Wren **Trained** Six Mile Bottom, Cambs

FOCUS
A moderate handicap restricted to apprentices who had not ridden more than 25 winners. The pace was good, but the principals were never too far away, with those held up struggling to get involved. Solid form for the grade, rated through the winner.

2991 AUSTIN ALLISON BIRTHDAY MAIDEN STKS 7f (P)
6:50 (6:52) (Class 4) 2-Y-O £3,886 (£1,156; £577; £288) Stalls High

Form				RPR
5	1		**La Voile Rouge**[12] 2632 2-9-3 0 IanMongan 6 (B J Meehan) trckd ldrs gng wl: prog to ld jst over 2f out: in command over 1f out: pushed out 9/1	78+
4	2	1 1/4	**Ordinance (USA)**[10] 2687 2-8-12 0 WilliamBuick(5) 2 (T G Mills) prog on outer to trck ldrs 1/2-way: rdn and hdwy to chse wnr over 1f out: edgd rt: kpt on but no imp 11/2[3]	75
0	3	1 1/4	**Determind Stand (USA)**[18] 2473 2-9-3 0 RyanMoore 10 (Sir Michael Stoute) prom: rdn 3f out: sn lost pl: rn green 2f out: styd on again fr over 1f out to take 3rd ins fnl f 7/2[1]	72+

4 **4** *1* **Kyrie Eleison (IRE)**[13] 2600 2-9-3 0 PatDobbs 11 69
(R Hannon) *mde most to jst over 2f out: one pce after* **9/2**[2]

5 *hd* **Safari Sunup (IRE)** 2-9-3 0 AdamKirby 8 68+
(P Winkworth) *stdd s: hld up wl in rr: stdy prog on outer over 2f out: pushed along and styd on encouragingly* **16/1**

6 **6** *shd* **Bencorr (USA)**[13] 2590 2-9-3 0 JimmyQuinn 12 68
(M J Wallace) *towards rr on inner: prog and rdn over 2f out: styd on u.p: nvr trbld ldrs* **33/1**

05 **7** *3 1/2* **Seeking The Star (CAN)**[21] 2353 2-9-3 0 RichardMullen 13 59
(D M Simcock) *pressed ldrs: drvn 3f out: wknd rapidly over 1f out* **6/1**

0 **8** *2* **Isander (USA)**[25] 2241 2-9-3 0 JimCrowley 3 54
(Mrs A J Perrett) *nvr beyond midfield: rdn and outpcd over 2f out: no prog over 1f out* **20/1**

0 **9** *hd* **Cross Fell (USA)**[19] 2432 2-9-0 0 GregFairley(3) 9 53
(M Johnston) *pressed ldr: upsides over 2f out: sn wknd rapidly* **16/1**

10 *1 1/4* **Mandalay King (IRE)** 2-9-3 0 JohnEgan 4 50
(Jane Chapple-Hyam) *a towards rr: outpcd over 2f out: no ch after* **16/1**

11 *3/4* **Kaldoun Kingdom (IRE)** 2-9-3 0 StephenDonohoe 5 48
(E A L Dunlop) *rn green in rr: wandering and no prog over 2f out* **25/1**

12 *3/4* **Doctor Robert** 2-9-3 0 SteveDrowne 1 46
(R Charlton) *s.s: mostly last and rdn bef 1/2-way: nvr a factor* **11/1**

5 **13** *1 3/4* **Seconds Out (IRE)**[34] 1975 2-9-3 0 SebSanders 14 42
(Sir Mark Prescott) *a wl in rr: struggling over 2f out* **16/1**

1m 26.72s (-0.08) **Going Correction** -0.15s/f (Stan) **13** Ran SP% **123.5**
Speed ratings (Par 95):94,92,91,90,89 89,85,83,83,81 80,80,78
CSF £58.56 TOTE £12.50: £5.10, £2.30, £1.50; EX 68.60.
Owner Malcolm C Denmark **Bred** R C Bond **Trained** Manton, Wilts

FOCUS
A fair maiden that should produce some winners. Again, it proved hard to make up significant amounts of ground.

NOTEBOOK
La Voile Rouge confirmed the promise he showed when fifth in a reasonable Sandown maiden on his debut with a decisive victory. He is developing into a useful sort and should make his presence felt in nurseries. (op 11-2)
Ordinance(USA), just as when fourth on his debut at Folkestone, was forced to race wide, with a low draw proving far from ideal, but he stayed on well on the straight to show improved form. Granted a better in trip in future, he looks capable of winning a similar race, and is another who should find his level in nurseries. (op 9-2)
Determind Stand(USA) improved on the form he showed when down the field on his debut over 6f at Windsor and is clearly going the right way. (op 5-1)
Kyrie Eleison(IRE) tried to make full use of his good draw under a positive ride, but he did not improve significantly on the form he showed on his debut at Newbury. (op 4-1 tchd 6-1)
Safari Sunup(IRE) ◆, a 36,000gns half-brother to 6f winner Oi Vay Jo, multiple 7f scorer Mrs Evans, and 1m4f winner San Marco, who was later successful over hurdles, made a very pleasing debut. He was forced to try and move into a challenging position towards the outer on the home bend, but stayed on nicely in the straight and hinted at plenty of ability. This should have taught him plenty and he ought to go very close in similar company next time. (op 33-1)
Bencorr(USA) improved on the form he showed on his debut at Lingfield, but is probably more of a nursery type.
Seeking The Star(CAN) was disappointing on this step up in trip, but he is now eligible for nurseries and might do better back over shorter. (op 8-1)

2992 DIGIBET.COM E B F MAIDEN FILLIES' STKS 6f (P)
7:20 (7:21) (Class 5) 2-Y-O £3,562 (£1,059; £529; £264) Stalls High

Form RPR

0 **1** **Eva's Request (IRE)**[21] 2364 2-9-0 0 TPO'Shea 10 79+
(M R Channon) *cl up: rdn wl over 2f out and looked in trble: picked up over 1f out: r.o to ld last 100yds: won gng away* **6/1**[3]

32 **2** *1 1/2* **Primed And Poised (USA)**[18] 2443 2-9-0 0 EddieAhern 8 74
(J W Hills) *trckd ldrs: effrt 2f out: got through to ld jst ins fnl f: hdd and outpcd last 100yds* **6/4**[1]

3 *1 1/4* **Temple Of Thebes (IRE)** 2-9-0 0 JimmyFortune 1 70
(E A L Dunlop) *trckd ldrs: poised to chal gng wl 2f out: upsides 1f out: hung bdly lft and threw ch away* **12/1**

5 **4** *1* **Chatham Islands (USA)**[30] 2071 2-8-11 0 GregFairley(3) 7 67
(M Johnston) *pressed ldr: rdn to ld 2f out: hdd and outpcd jst ins fnl f* **8/1**

40 **5** *3/4* **Deal Flipper**[28] 2134 2-9-0 0 JimCrowley 5 67+
(P Winkworth) *towards rr: rdn and prog on inner to press ldrs whn no room and snatched up over 1f out: no ch after: kpt on* **10/1**

6 *1 1/4* **Altitude** 2-9-0 0 SebSanders 6 61
(Sir Mark Prescott) *dwlt: rn green in last pair: struggling fr 1/2-way: kpt on ins fnl f* **10/3**[2]

4 **7** *3/4* **Lavande**[11] 2663 2-9-0 0 StephenDonohoe 11 59
(M J Wallace) *led to 2f out: wknd fnl f* **12/1**

8 *1 3/4* **Ile Royale** 2-9-0 0 JimmyQuinn 2 54
(C N Allen) *dwlt: a struggling in last pair* **25/1**

1m 13.54s (-0.16) **Going Correction** -0.15s/f (Stan) **8** Ran SP% **116.8**
Speed ratings (Par 90):95,93,91,90,89 87,86,84
CSF £15.81 TOTE £7.50: £2.10, £1.10, £3.20; EX 19.90.
Owner Liam Mulryan **Bred** Ballylinch Stud **Trained** West Ilsley, Berks

FOCUS
A fair fillies' maiden. The principals all raced close to the pace.

NOTEBOOK
Eva's Request(IRE) ◆ did not show a great deal on her debut over 5f at Nottingham, but that run clearly taught her plenty and she produced a much-improved effort. She took a while to pick up when initially asked for her challenge, but she got the hang of things inside the final furlong and was well on top at the line. There should be better to come again. (op 10-1 tchd 5-1)
Primed And Poised(USA) has already shown herself to be a fair sort, but she does not seem to possess a change of pace and that again found her out. She is genuine, but perhaps the fitting of headgear might just sharpen her up. (op 7-4 tchd 2-1)
Temple Of Thebes(IRE) ◆, out of a triple 7f-1m winner, shaped very nicely on her racecourse debut. She looked the most likely winner inside the final two furlongs when moving into contention without having to be asked, but she was just found out by her inexperience, not knowing what to do when coming under pressure and drifting right the way over to the stands' rail. She should know a lot more next time. Official explanation: jockey said filly hung left (op 10-1 tchd 9-1)
Chatham Islands(USA) raced a little too freely for her own good, but this was still an improvement on her debut effort at Carlisle. She has bags of speed and would not be inconvenienced by a return to 5f. (op 9-1 tchd 12-1)
Deal Flipper ◆ would have finished a lot closer had she not had to be snatched up around a furlong from the finish, when just beginning to hit top stride, and she can be rated much better than the bare form suggests. (op 14-1)
Altitude, a half-sister to among others the top-class multiple 7f-10f winners Albanova and Alborada, out of a useful triple 1m-12f scorer, was too green to do herself justice. She should have learnt plenty, but it may be that she does not come into her own until sent handicapping over further. (op 5-2 tchd 4-1)

2993 DIGIBET SPORTS BETTING H'CAP 6f (P)
7:50 (7:51) (Class 4) (0-80,80) 3-Y-O+ £4,728 (£1,406; £702; £351) Stalls High

Form RPR

0500 **1** **Romany Nights (IRE)**[15] 2528 7-9-4 70 (bt) JohnEgan 10 80
(Miss Gay Kelleway) *chsd clr ldng pair: rdn over 2f out: clsd over 1f out: drvn and kpt on to ld last 50yds* **8/1**

200 **2** *1/2* **Dvinsky (USA)**[15] 2546 6-9-6 72 IanMongan 4 80
(P Howling) *chsd clr ldr: rdn over 2f out: clsd to ld jst ins fnl f: wknd and hdd fnl 50yds* **20/1**

4345 **3** *nk* **Go On Green (IRE)**[29] 2114 3-9-5 78 JimmyFortune 3 83+
(E A L Dunlop) *hld up in last pair and wl off the pce: prog and weaved through fr 2f out: styd on fnl f: gaining at fin* **15/2**

0501 **4** *shd* **China Cherub**[9] 2725 4-9-9 75 6ex (b) RyanMoore 1 82
(R Hannon) *wl in rr: rdn and nt qckn over 2f out: styd on fr over 1f out: gaining at fin* **6/1**[2]

-442 **5** *nk* **Seamus Shindig**[15] 2546 5-9-4 77 AmyScott(7) 7 83
(H Candy) *chsd ldrs but nt on terms: nudged along and styd on steadily fr over 1f out: nrst fin* **13/2**[3]

0006 **6** *3/4* **Hollow Jo**[7] 2771 7-8-12 69 WilliamBuick(5) 9 73
(J R Jenkins) *settled in midfield: outpcd over 2f out: rdn and styd on fr over 1f out: nt rch ldrs* **8/1**

6044 **7** *nk* **Mujood**[7] 2771 4-10-0 80 (b) SebSanders 5 83
(Eve Johnson Houghton) *sn pushed along in last pair and struggling to keep in tch on outer: styd on fr over 1f out: nrst fin* **11/4**[1]

4030 **8** *nk* **Peter Island (FR)**[34] 1971 4-9-12 78 (v) JimCrowley 11 80
(J Gallagher) *led and sn clr at furious pce: hdd jst ins fnl f: wknd rapidly last 100yds and lost many pls* **10/1**

166 **9** *3/4* **Linda Green**[18] 2472 6-9-1 74 ThomasO'Brien(7) 6 74
(M R Channon) *wl in rr: drvn over 2f out: kpt on same pce fnl f: n.d* **12/1**

0000 **10** *1* **Kingscross**[23] 2318 9-9-5 71 JimmyQuinn 12 68
(M Blanshard) *pushed up in inner to rch midfield after 2f: outpcd over 2f out: no real prog after* **20/1**

4226 **11** *1 1/4* **Black Oval**[88] 841 6-8-6 61 oh12 DominicFox(3) 8 54
(S Parr) *towards rr: shkn up and no prog 2f out: sn btn* **33/1**

003U **12** *shd* **Law Maker**[46] 1681 7-8-8 67 (v) MartinGuest(7) 2 60
(A Bailey) *prom to 1/2-way: wknd 2f out* **50/1**

1m 12.78s (-0.92) **Going Correction** -0.15s/f (Stan)
WFA 3 from 4yo+ 7lb **12** Ran SP% **119.5**
Speed ratings (Par 105):100,99,98,98,98 97,97,96,95,94 92,92
CSF £162.15 CT £1275.46 TOTE £11.00: £3.40, £6.10, £2.70; EX 188.60.
Owner C Peach T & Z Racing Club **Bred** The Lloyd Farm Stud **Trained** Exning, Suffolk

FOCUS
The early pace was frantic thanks to Peter Island, but he probably did too much too soon as the final time was ordinary. Several of these struggled with the early pace and did not get going until it was too late. Solid form, the first four within a length of their marks.

2994 DIGIBET CASINO H'CAP 1m 4f (P)
8:20 (8:22) (Class 4) (0-85,84) 4-Y-O+ £4,728 (£1,406; £702; £351) Stalls Centre

Form RPR

0321 **1** **Wild Fell Hall (IRE)**[15] 2544 4-9-0 77 AdamKirby 3 87+
(W R Swinburn) *mde all: set stdy pce tl kicked on wl over 2f out: hrd pressed fnl f and edgd lft briefly: fnd ex* **9/2**[2]

1405 **2** *hd* **I Have Dreamed (IRE)**[21] 2351 5-9-7 84 (b[1]) StephenDonohoe 5 94
(T G Mills) *hld up in midfield: smooth prog over 2f out: wnt 2nd jst over 1f out: sn chalng strly: r.o wl but jst hld* **10/1**

2053 **3** *2 1/2* **Turner's Touch**[28] 2156 5-8-8 71 (b) RyanMoore 11 77
(G L Moore) *hld up in last trio: prog over 2f out: wnt 3rd jst over 1f out: nt qckn and safely hld fnl f* **7/1**

13 **4** *2* **Rickety Bridge (IRE)**[49] 1591 4-8-7 70 JimCrowley 6 73
(P R Chamings) *dwlt: hld up towards rr: rdn 3f out: c rt across to nr side rail fr 2f out: styd on fnl f: nt pce to rch ldrs* **13/2**[3]

3102 **5** *1/2* **Fregate Island (IRE)**[25] 2238 4-9-6 83 JimmyFortune 2 85
(B J Meehan) *pressed ldr to wl over 1f out: hung lft and fdd fnl f* **7/2**[1]

00-4 **6** *nk* **Noora (IRE)**[15] 2543 6-9-0 77 (v) SebSanders 1 79
(C G Cox) *dwlt: hld up in last trio: rdn and nt looking keen over 2f out: c across to nr side and kpt on* **14/1**

-310 **7** *1/2* **Tromp**[49] 1591 6-8-11 74 JimmyQuinn 7 75
(D J Coakley) *hld up bhd ldrs: effrt over 2f out: disp 2nd wl over 1f out: fdd fnl f* **16/1**

00-6 **8** *nk* **Ringsider (IRE)**[7] 2765 6-8-5 75 MarkCoumbe(7) 12 75
(Declan Gillespie, Ire) *dwlt: hld up in last pair: rdn 3f out: sn outpcd: styd on fr over 1f out: no ch* **50/1**

6000 **9** *1 3/4* **Valance (IRE)**[109] 662 7-8-8 76 (t) WilliamBuick(5) 8 73
(C R Egerton) *trckd ldng pair: outpcd and lost pl over 2f out: one pce and n.d fnl 2f* **10/1**

00-0 **10** *shd* **Island Odyssey**[41] 1783 4-9-5 82 SteveDrowne 4 79
(E A L Dunlop) *trckd ldrs on outer: rdn over 2f out: edgd lft fr over 1f out: wknd* **12/1**

1344 **11** *nk* **Sgt Schultz (IRE)**[46] 1664 4-9-5 82 JohnEgan 9 79
(J S Moore) *t.k.h: hld up in midfield: effrt on inner over 2f out: disp 2nd wl over 1f out: wknd fnl f* **14/1**

0610 **12** *2 1/2* **Wild Pitch**[25] 2238 6-8-12 82 (b) JackMitchell(7) 10 75
(P Mitchell) *s.s: hld up in last: outpcd wl over 2f out: no prog after* **10/1**

2m 34.49s (-2.41) **Going Correction** -0.15s/f (Stan) **12** Ran SP% **122.4**
Speed ratings (Par 105):102,101,100,98,98 98,98,97,96,96 96,94
CSF £51.02 CT £319.83 TOTE £5.00: £1.80, £3.30, £2.10; EX 50.90.
Owner Mrs P W Harris **Bred** M H Dixon **Trained** Aldbury, Herts

FOCUS
A decent little handicap, but spoiled a little by an ordinary pace and it developed into something of a sprint up the home straight. They certainly used the whole width of the track in the straight, with some coming stands' side, a few making their efforts up the far rail whilst others, including the first two, stayed up the middle. An improved effort from Wild Fell Hall, who is capable of better still.

2995 TFM NETWORKS H'CAP (LONDON MILE QUALIFIER) 1m (P)
8:50 (8:51) (Class 4) (0-80,79) 3-Y-O+ £4,728 (£1,406; £702; £351) Stalls High

Form RPR

2410 **1** **Samarinda (USA)**[56] 1395 4-9-11 76 MickyFenton 4 85
(Mrs P Sly) *trckd ldr: rdn to ld narrowly jst over 1f out: hld on u.p* **8/1**

2501 **2** *hd* **Top Mark**[7] 2765 5-9-6 78 HarryPoulton(7) 9 87
(J R Boyle) *led: kicked on over 2f out: narrowly hdd jst over 1f out: battled on wl: jst hld* **7/2**[2]

25-0 **3** *2* **Don Pietro**[18] 2469 4-9-10 75 EddieAhern 8 79
(D J Coakley) *t.k.h: trckd ldng pair: rdn and outpcd over 2f out: styd on same pce fr over 1f out* **11/2**

-030 **4** *nk* **Bee Stinger**[19] 2427 5-10-0 **79**............(v) RyanMoore 6 82
(I A Wood) *dwlt: hld up in rr: outpcd over 2f out: drvn and styd on fr over 1f out: n.d* **8/1**

4034 **5** *1/2* **Katiypour (IRE)**[14] 2573 10-9-7 **72**............ SebSanders 2 74
(P Mitchell) *t.k.h: trckd ldng pair: rdn and outpcd over 2f out: pushed along and kpt on same pce fr over 1f out* **5/1**[3]

025- **6** *3/4* **Coleridge (AUS)**[191] 6863 8-9-7 **72**............ PatDobbs 7 72
(J C Fox) *hld up towards rr: outpcd over 2f out: rdn and kpt on same pce fnl 2f* **20/1**

0560 **7** *3* **Royal Amnesty**[11] 2665 4-9-7 **72**............ OscarUrbina 1 66
(G C H Chung) *hld up in last: outpcd over 2f out: reminders over 1f out: one pce and nvr nr ldrs* **10/1**

0-0 **8** *3* **Mulligans Pursuit (IRE)**[16] 2518 3-8-3 **64**............(v[1]) RichardSmith 3 51
(M D I Usher) *racd wd in tch: hung lft and reluctant over 2f out: sn no ch* **50/1**

-006 **9** *1* **Blues In The Night (IRE)**[14] 2573 4-9-11 **76**............ JimmyFortune 5 60
(P J Makin) *in tch in midfield: rdn over 2f out: wknd* **3/1**[1]

1m 38.94s (-1.86) **Going Correction** -0.15s/f (Stan)
WFA 3 from 4yo+ 10lb **9** Ran SP% **117.3**
Speed ratings (Par 105):103,102,100,100,100 99,96,93,92
CSF £36.77 CT £171.65 TOTE £9.50: £3.00, £1.60, £1.50; EX 32.20.
Owner D Bayliss, T Davies, G Libson & P Sly **Bred** Gainsborough Farm Llc **Trained** Thorney, Cambs

FOCUS
A fair handicap, but the pace was just ordinary and, yet again, those who raced handy were at an advantage. Fairly sound form, with the winner up another 4lb on his sand best.
Blues In The Night(IRE) Official explanation: trainer's rep said gelding never travelled

2996 BARRY BRAMLEY 70TH BIRTHDAY H'CAP 2m (P)
9:20 (9:20) (Class 6) (0-65,65) 4-Y-O+ **£2,047** (£604; £302) **Stalls** High

Form RPR

2-45 **1** **Sendinpost**[10] 2686 4-9-5 **63**............ JimCrowley 1 76
(S C Williams) *hld up wl in rr: stl in last pair of main gp 4f out: stdy prog 3f out: drvn and clsd fr 2f out: led last 150yds: styd on wl* **11/2**[3]

0321 **2** *3/4* **Bob's Your Uncle**[13] 2595 4-9-0 **58**............ SebSanders 2 70
(J G Portman) *hld up: last to 7f out: stl wl in rr 4f out: stdy prog on outer wl over 2f out: r.o to chal ins fnl f: a hld* **3/1**[1]

0506 **3** *2 1/2* **Synonymy**[30] 2089 4-9-6 **64**............(b) JimmyQuinn 8 73
(M Blanshard) *trckd ldrs: prog 4f out: led wl over 2f out and kicked on: hdd and outpcd last 150yds* **9/1**

1-04 **4** *2* **Montosari**[21] 2355 8-8-13 **64**............ JackMitchell(7) 9 71
(P Mitchell) *hld up in rr: prog over 4f out: rdn to chse ldng pair over 2f out: no imp over 1f out: outpcd after* **12/1**

4-60 **5** *shd* **Phoenix Hill (IRE)**[19] 2430 5-8-9 **53**............(t) SteveDrowne 6 59
(D R Gandolfo) *hld up in midfield: prog 5f out: chsd ldr over 2f out and tried to chal: wknd jst over 1f out* **11/1**

023- **6** *5* **That Look**[180] 6979 4-8-9 **53**............ StephenDonohoe 11 56+
(D E Cantillon) *dwlt: sn in tch on inner: cl up 4f out: rdn whn hmpd wl over 2f out: sn btn* **7/1**

1350 **7** *6* **Moon Emperor**[36] 1925 10-9-0 **58**............(b) RyanMoore 7 51
(J R Jenkins) *hld up in rr: in tch over 3f out: wknd over 2f out* **14/1**

0-06 **8** *5* **Our Monogram**[21] 2375 11-9-7 **65**............ AdamKirby 13 52
(R M Beckett) *pushed up to press ldr: clr of rest 1/2-way: led 7f out to over 5f out: sn lost pl and btn* **16/1**

00/0 **9** *1/2* **Cambo (FR)**[7] 2770 6-8-9 **56**............(bt[1]) NeilChalmers(3) 4 43
(Miss Sheena West) *hld up wl in rr: in tch to over 3f out: wknd over 2f out* **40/1**

0312 **10** *1/2* **Mister Completely (IRE)**[7] 2770 6-9-5 **63**............ JamesDoyle 3 49
(Ms J S Doyle) *dwlt: forced to r wd in rr: drvn and effrt on bnd over 4f out: struggling and btn over 2f out: wknd* **7/2**[2]

4220 **11** *6* **Bulberry Hill**[25] 2252 6-8-12 **56**............ SamHitchcott 10 35
(R W Price) *trckd ldrs: prog gng wl to ld over 5f out: hdd & wknd rapidly wl over 2f out* **14/1**

0/06 **12** *32* **Code (IRE)**[24] 2274 6-8-1 **50**............ WilliamBuick(5) 12 —
(Miss Z C Davison) *chsd ldng pair to 1/2-way: sn wknd u.p: t.o* **33/1**

4-10 **13** *12* **Dream Mountain**[149] 291 4-8-5 **56**............ SophieDoyle(7) 14 —
(Ms J S Doyle) *led to 7f out: wknd 5f out: t.o* **20/1**

3m 27.86s (-3.54) **Going Correction** -0.15s/f (Stan) **13** Ran SP% **130.5**
Speed ratings (Par 101):102,101,100,99,99 96,93,91,91,90 87,71,65
CSF £24.10 CT £158.27 TOTE £7.50: £3.40, £1.02, £6.30; EX 30.10 Place 6 £375.90, Place 5 £91.77..
Owner The Tipsy Fountain Partnership **Bred** K G Powter **Trained** Newmarket, Suffolk

FOCUS
Quite a competitive staying handicap with Dream Mountain and Our Monogram forcing the issue, but the pace was no more than ordinary and the front two came right from the back of the field. Solid-looking form.
Bulberry Hill Official explanation: jockey said gelding ran too free
T/Plt: £455.10 to a £1 stake. Pool: £60,072.50. 96.35 winning tickets. T/Qpdt: £23.00 to a £1 stake. Pool: £4,807.80. 154.50 winning tickets. JN

2692 SALISBURY (R-H)
Wednesday, June 27

OFFICIAL GOING: Good to soft (good in places; 8.3)
On easy ground, and with more rain around, the runners came across to the stands' side half of the course in all races.
Wind: Almost nil Weather: Showers

2997 NEW MILTON CONSTRUCTION EBF MAIDEN FILLIES' STKS 5f
2:10 (2:11) (Class 4) 2-Y-O **£4,533** (£1,348; £674; £336) **Stalls** Centre

Form RPR

1 **Edge Of Light** 2-9-0 0............ SteveDrowne 8 78
(B Palling) *s.s and wnt rt: pushed along and bhd: gd hdwy 2f out: led ins fnl f: drvn out* **25/1**

2 *1/2* **Royal Confidence** 2-9-0 0............ MichaelHills 6 77
(B W Hills) *bhd: rdn and hdwy 2f out: chal for 2nd ins fnl f: r.o* **12/1**

3 *shd* **Amylee (IRE)** 2-9-0 0............ PhilipRobinson 9 76
(C G Cox) *prom: drvn to ld over 1f out: hdd ins fnl f: r.o* **7/1**[3]

0 **4** *1 3/4* **Cosenza**[35] 1945 2-9-0 0............ EddieAhern 4 70
(H J L Dunlop) *hld up towards rr: rdn and hdwy over 1f out: nrst fin* **33/1**

66 **5** *2 1/2* **Cocabana**[17] 2488 2-9-0 0............ JimCrowley 2 69+
(J G Portman) *in tch: rdn and nt clr run 2f out: hmpd and lost pl over 1f out: gng on again nr fin* **12/1**

0 **6** *1/2* **Don't Tell Anna (IRE)**[37] 1896 2-9-0 0............ RichardHughes 3 59
(R Hannon) *led tl wknd over 1f out* **11/1**

052 **7** *2* **Flying Indian**[13] 2590 2-9-0 0............ LPKeniry 5 52
(A M Balding) *prom over 3f* **9/1**

2 **8** *1 1/2* **Drastic Measure**[29] 2109 2-9-0 0............ SebSanders 7 47
(Sir Mark Prescott) *mid-div: hrd rdn and outpcd 2f out: n.d after* **1/1**[1]

3 **9** *16* **Katrina Bee (IRE)**[11] 2651 2-9-0 0............ PatDobbs 1 —
(R Hannon) *chsd ldrs over 2f: eased whn no ch fnl f* **6/1**[2]

63.54 secs (1.95) **Going Correction** +0.375s/f (Good) **9** Ran SP% **117.3**
Speed ratings (Par 92):99,98,98,95,91 90,87,84,59
CSF £295.21 TOTE £34.30: £5.90, £3.40, £1.90; EX 270.90.
Owner Nigel Thomas and Christopher Mason **Bred** Christopher J Mason **Trained** Tredodridge, Vale Of Glamorgan
■ Stewards' Enquiry : Eddie Ahern caution: careless riding

FOCUS
They all came stands' side in the straight, as is the norm here on easy ground. Hard to weigh up, with little form to go on, but the gallop seemed to test these juveniles, with three of the first four staying on from the rear.

NOTEBOOK
Edge Of Light, a second daughter of the racemare Bright Edge, a decent sprinter on soft ground, is already a good deal better than her only previous foal. Despite looking green early on, she picked up really well to beat two fellow newcomers. (op 20-1)
Royal Confidence is by the top-class sprinter Royal Applause, and out of a Group 2 sprint winner, so she is bred to be quick. This was a promising debut and, though hard to assess with any degree of accuracy, it would be a surprise if she did not win her share of races. (op 10-1)
Amylee(IRE) did best of those who raced prominently, and impressed with the way she battled when headed. This 90,000euro daughter of Danehill Dancer is out of a useful miler, so should stay a bit farther before long, and has realistic prospects of paying her way. (tchd 8-1)
Cosenza, dropped to the minimum trip and held up this time, ran much better than on her debut. A daughter of top miler Bahri, she is bred to stay a bit farther and already looks as if she would get the sixth furlong with a repeat of these tactics.
Cocabana did not get an ideal passage, and caught the eye with nurseries in mind now she is qualified. (op 9-1)
Don't Tell Anna(IRE) was allowed to bowl along in front, but just ran herself into the ground on the rain-softened surface up this stiff climb. There will be better opportunities to put her pace to good use. (op 14-1)
Drastic Measure Official explanation: trainer's rep had no explanation for the poor form shown

2998 SMITH & WILLIAMSON MAIDEN FILLIES' STKS 6f 212y
2:40 (2:45) (Class 4) 3-Y-O **£4,857** (£1,445; £722; £360) **Stalls** Centre

Form RPR

64 **1** **Rustic Flame (IRE)**[10] 2693 3-9-0 0............ SteveDrowne 8 81
(C R Egerton) *dwlt: t.k.h in midfield: eased lft and effrt over 2f out: led ins fnl f: rdn out* **20/1**

43 **2** *nk* **Fondled**[28] 2153 3-9-0 0............ JamieSpencer 6 80
(J R Fanshawe) *s.s: in tch after 2f: effrt 2f out: led over 1f out tl ins fnl f: r.o: sddle slipped* **13/8**[1]

3 *3 1/2* **Plucky** 3-9-0 0............ RyanMoore 4 71
(J H M Gosden) *hld up in rr: hdwy to press ldrs ins fnl 2f: nt qckn fnl f* **14/1**

5 **4** *1 3/4* **Safwa (IRE)**[26] 2219 3-9-0 0............ RHills 9 66
(Sir Michael Stoute) *prom: rdn and rn green 2f out: wknd over 1f out* **13/8**[1]

-420 **5** *1 3/4* **Cape Velvet (IRE)**[15] 2541 3-9-0 **75**............ EddieAhern 2 61
(J W Hills) *t.k.h in rr of mid-div: rdn 3f out: nt pce to chal* **16/1**

0- **6** *1* **Decision Day**[235] 6331 3-9-0 0............ RichardThomas 5 58
(J A Geake) *in rr of mid-div: sltly hmpd 4f out: no imp whn hung rt over 1f out* **40/1**

220- **7** *shd* **Dragon Flower (USA)**[267] 5754 3-9-0 **75**............ MichaelHills 1 58
(B W Hills) *prom over 5f* **12/1**[3]

04 **8** *1 1/2* **Labor Day (IRE)**[37] 1901 3-9-0 0............ JimmyFortune 7 54
(J H M Gosden) *led and travelled wl tl hdd & wknd qckly over 1f out* **6/1**[2]

0-0 **9** *5* **Polish Prospect (IRE)**[50] 1560 3-9-0 0............ DaneO'Neill 10 41
(H S Howe) *w ldr 4f: sn rdn and wknd* **100/1**

10 *22* **Tagula Song (IRE)** 3-9-0 0............ LPKeniry 3 —
(J A Geake) *a bhd: rdn 1/2-way: no ch fnl 2f* **66/1**

1m 31.03s (1.97) **Going Correction** +0.375s/f (Good) **10** Ran SP% **120.4**
Speed ratings (Par 98):103,102,98,96,94 93,93,91,85,60
CSF £53.99 TOTE £24.70: £4.30, £1.20, £2.50; EX 79.40.
Owner Mrs Paul Shanahan **Bred** Swettenham Stud **Trained** Chaddleworth, Berks

FOCUS
They raced up the centre of the course before the first two, who pulled clear, ended up near the stands' side. Probably a fair maiden, but run at just a modest gallop. The form has been rated at face value, with a step up from the winner.
Fondled Official explanation: jockey said saddle slipped

2999 DOCCOMBE EUROPEAN BIBURY CUP (H'CAP) 1m 4f
3:10 (3:13) (Class 3) (0-95,87) 3-Y-O
£9,971 (£2,985; £1,492; £747; £372; £187) **Stalls** High

Form RPR

0-51 **1** **Hi Calypso (IRE)**[13] 2602 3-9-1 **81**............ RyanMoore 5 92
(Sir Michael Stoute) *dwlt: bhd: rdn 4f out: drvn along and gd hdwy over 1f out: styd on wl to ld on line* **8/1**

312 **2** *shd* **Mad Rush (USA)**[23] 2305 3-9-5 **85**............ TedDurcan 4 96+
(L M Cumani) *hdwy and prom 7f out: hrd rdn 2f out: led over 1f out and drvn 1 1/2 l ahd: ct on line* **11/2**[3]

1-62 **3** *2* **Eglevski (IRE)**[40] 1827 3-9-5 **85**............ EddieAhern 3 93
(J L Dunlop) *prom: hrd rdn 2f out: nt qckn fnl f* **5/1**[2]

1 **4** *1 3/4* **Moon Quest (IRE)**[23] 2320 3-9-7 **87**............ KerrinMcEvoy 7 92
(Saeed Bin Suroor) *hld up in tch: rdn to chse ldrs over 2f out: one pce appr fnl f* **10/3**[1]

21-2 **5** *3 1/2* **Algarade**[18] 2475 3-8-10 **76**............(t) SebSanders 1 76
(Sir Mark Prescott) *led at gd pce tl wknd wl over 1f out* **6/1**

2-21 **6** *1/2* **Latanazul**[40] 1816 3-9-3 **83**............ RHills 6 82
(J L Dunlop) *t.k.h: prom tl wknd 2f out* **16/1**

3-22 **7** *2* **Oakley Heffert (IRE)**[37] 1898 3-8-12 **78**............ RichardHughes 2 74
(R Hannon) *in rr: drvn along and mod effrt over 3f out: nt trble ldrs* **20/1**

2216 **8** *1/2* **Bergonzi (IRE)**[25] 2231 3-9-4 **84**............ JimmyFortune 9 79
(J H M Gosden) *chsd ldrs tl wknd over 2f out* **9/1**

0535 **9** *1/2* **Sweetheart**[27] 2185 3-8-9 **75** ow1............ SteveDrowne 10 69
(Jamie Poulton) *towards rr: rdn 4f out: nvr a factor* **33/1**

0-11 **10** *1/2* **Intiquilla (IRE)**[29] 2112 3-8-13 **79**............ JimCrowley 8 72
(Mrs A J Perrett) *mid-div: sme hdwy 4f out: wknd 3f out* **16/1**

11-3 **11** *dist* **Zoom One**^{19} [2426] 3-9-2 **82**.. MartinDwyer 11 —
(M P Tregoning) *plld hrd: in tch tl wknd rapidly over 4f out: sn bhd* **11/2**^{3}

2m 38.17s (1.81) **Going Correction** +0.375s/f (Good) **11** Ran SP% **125.4**
Speed ratings (Par 103):108,107,106,105,103 102,101,101,100,100 —
CSF £55.22 CT £252.03 TOTE £10.20: £3.40, £3.00, £2.10; EX 70.90.
Owner Philip Newton **Bred** Philip Newton **Trained** Newmarket, Suffolk

FOCUS
A competitive handicap in which they went a decent gallop, again coming to the stands' side half of the track. The form has been rated positively and should work out.

NOTEBOOK
Hi Calypso(IRE) handles soft ground well, but she needed every inch of the trip and looks as if she would be even more at home around 1m6f.
Mad Rush(USA) was 5lb higher, but is still improving and did everything but win. Though just pipped, he got the longer trip well enough to suggest that he is capable of winning over 1m4f on good ground. (op 5-1 tchd 9-2 and 6-1)
Eglevski(IRE), raised 6lb despite being beaten last time, suggested that the Handicapper was not far wrong with another good effort. He has done well since stepping up to 1m4f. (op 7-1)
Moon Quest(IRE), carrying topweight despite having had only one previous outing - when successful at Windsor - found the task beyond him. He should be suited by this longer trip, so maybe he just needs to drop a couple of pounds, but this was still a creditable effort considering his lack of experience. (op 11-4 tchd 4-1)
Algarade tried to make it a good test but, ridden like this, 1m2f would have suited her better on this testing track given the cut in the ground. Despite this setback, she remains a decent prospect in similarly competitive handicaps. (op 9-1 tchd 10-1)
Latanazul had been raised 6lb for winning a race that has not worked out well so far. Too keen on ground that required horses to settle to give them a serious chance of victory, she back-pedalled quickly in the last quarter-mile.
Zoom One was far too headstrong over this longer trip, giving himself no chance of lasting home. Official explanation: jockey said colt ran too free (op 6-1 tchd 7-1)

3000 WINTERTHUR LIFE FILLIES' H'CAP 6f
3:40 (3:42) (Class 5) (0-70,69) 3-Y-O **£3,238** (£963; £481; £240) **Stalls** Centre

Form RPR

0-00 **1** **Vivi Belle**^{161} [160] 3-8-5 **53**.. HayleyTurner 10 56
(M L W Bell) *in tch: drvn along and clsd on ldrs 2f out: slt ld fnl f: all out* **8/1**

44-2 **2** *shd* **Hucking Hope (IRE)**^{8} [2750] 3-9-2 **64**.............................. DaneO'Neill 5 67
(J R Best) *mid-div: hdwy and swtchd to stands' rail over 2f out: w wnr fnl f: kpt on wl nr fin* **5/2**^{1}

1435 **3** *1 3/4* **Dualagi**^{57} [1373] 3-9-0 **62**.. LPKeniry 3 60
(J S Moore) *stdd s: t.k.h in rr: hrd rdn and hdwy 2f out: styd on wl fnl f* **11/1**

06-0 **4** *1 1/2* **By The Edge (IRE)**^{4} [2895] 3-8-4 **52**..............................(v^{1}) ChrisCatlin 1 45
(P D Deegan, Ire) *sn led: rdn over 2f out: hdd and no ex 1f out* **20/1**

2-04 **5** *2 1/2* **Izabela Hannah**^{30} [2080] 3-9-1 **63**...............................(b^{1}) SebSanders 2 49
(R M Beckett) *chsd ldrs: hrd rdn 2f out: wknd over 1f out* **3/1**^{2}

-500 **6** *3/4* **Camissa**^{16} [2513] 3-9-5 **67**.. JimCrowley 8 51
(D K Ivory) *sn pushed along towards rr: mod hdwy and hrd rdn over 1f out: nt rch ldrs* **10/1**

-040 **7** *1 1/4* **Rubilini**^{84} [924] 3-8-9 **57**.. TPO'Shea 9 37
(M R Channon) *sn pushed along in midfield: drvn and nt pce to chal fnl 2f* **9/1**

00-6 **8** *8* **Nabra**^{58} [1346] 3-8-10 **58**...(b^{1}) RHills 4 14
(J H M Gosden) *pressed ldr tl wknd 2f out* **8/1**

2000 **9** *6* **Whipchord (IRE)**^{10} [2696] 3-8-12 **60**........................(b^{1}) RichardHughes 7 —
(R Hannon) *chsd ldrs: drvn along over 2f out: sn wknd: eased when no chance over 1f out* **7/1**^{3}

1m 17.73s (2.75) **Going Correction** +0.375s/f (Good) **9** Ran SP% **120.5**
Speed ratings (Par 96):96,95,93,91,88 87,85,74,66
CSF £29.65 CT £231.54 TOTE £10.20: £2.70, £1.30, £2.60; EX 27.70.
Owner Mr & Mrs Raymond Tooth **Bred** Jeremy Green And Sons **Trained** Newmarket, Suffolk
■ Stewards' Enquiry : Hayley Turner one-day ban: used whip with excessive frequency (Jul 8)
Dane O'Neill four-day ban: used whip with excessive frequency without giving filly time to respond (Jul 26-29)

FOCUS
A modest fillies' handicap, but run at a decent gallop, with the runners again coming stands' side. Weak form.

3001 NOEL CANNON MEMORIAL TROPHY H'CAP 1m
4:10 (4:17) (Class 2) (0-100,97) 3-Y-O+
£11,217 (£3,358; £1,679; £840; £419; £210) **Stalls** High

Form RPR

3353 **1** **Ordnance Row**^{18} [2446] 4-9-9 **92**.................................. RichardHughes 5 108+
(R Hannon) *trckd ldr: led on bit 2f out: shkn up and drew clr fnl f: comf* **7/4**^{1}

3-53 **2** *5* **Gaelic Princess**^{18} [2469] 7-8-11 **80**.............................. FergusSweeney 6 84
(A G Newcombe) *hmpd s: hld up in rr: rdn and hdwy whn hung rt over 1f out: styd on to take 2nd fnl 50yds* **10/1**

-120 **3** *3/4* **Apply Dapply**^{26} [2207] 4-8-9 **78** oh3................................. SteveDrowne 1 80
(H Morrison) *in tch: hrd rdn and outpcd 2f out: kpt on to take 3rd nr fin* **7/2**^{2}

1111 **4** *nk* **Apex**^{37} [1886] 6-9-2 **85**.. JamieSpencer 3 86
(M Hill) *t.k.h: in tch: jnd wnr 2f out: hrd rdn and no ex 1f out* **6/1**^{3}

0300 **5** *3 1/2* **Prince Of Thebes (IRE)**^{26} [2208] 6-9-6 **92**.......... RichardKingscote$^{(3)}$ 4 85
(J Akehurst) *led tl 2f out: hrd rdn and wknd over 1f out* **8/1**

66-0 **6** *3 1/2* **Prime Number (IRE)**^{11} [2670] 5-8-10 **79**............................. TQuinn 7 64
(J Akehurst) *wnt lft s: in tch tl wknd over 2f out* **33/1**

4060 **7** *3 1/2* **Pentecost**^{7} [2755] 8-9-9 **97**.. WilliamBuick$^{(5)}$ 2 74
(A M Balding) *hld up towards rr: hdwy 1/2-way: wknd 2f out: eased whn no ch fnl f* **6/1**^{3}

1m 45.75s (2.66) **Going Correction** +0.375s/f (Good) **7** Ran SP% **110.3**
Speed ratings (Par 109):101,96,95,94,91 87,84
CSF £18.84 TOTE £2.60: £1.50, £4.10; EX 17.70.
Owner Mrs P Good **Bred** Mrs P Good **Trained** East Everleigh, Wilts

FOCUS
A decent handicap, run on the stands' side of the track, but the pace was ordinary. The clear-cut winner improved by 5lb, but it may be wise not to take the form at face value.

NOTEBOOK
Ordnance Row goes on most ground, but he had shown in the past that he handles cut better than many horses. Always tanking along, he was a revelation when let down, and the only negative is the likely response of the Handicapper to this stylish victory. (op 2-1 tchd 9-4)
Gaelic Princess goes well on this track, and won here a slightly lower mark last year. A tough sort, she is in good form at present, and would have come out on top here but for an extraordinary performance by the winner. (tchd 8-1 and 11-1)
Apply Dapply did well from 3lb out of the handicap, and gave the impression that she would stay a bit farther these days. (op 4-1 tchd 9-2 and 10-3)
Apex, first past the post in his previous five races, had been raised a whopping 32lb in the process, although he was rated higher than this two years ago. He was without his regular partner Hadden Frost, who has been taking off a valuable 7lb, and ran another decent race. (op 7-2)
Prince Of Thebes(IRE) is theoretically on a winning mark at present, but he is not in top form. Fast ground, on which all four of his victories have been achieved, could well see him staging a return to form. (op 9-1)
Prime Number(IRE), reported to have slipped leaving the stalls, has not been at his best this season, but a return to his 2005 form would make him a live contender off his current mark. His three wins have all been on good or fast ground. Official explanation: jockey said gelding slipped on leaving stalls (op 40-1)
Pentecost needs a stronger gallop to bring out the best in him. Official explanation: jockey said gelding lost its action (op 9-2 tchd 13-2)

3002 J S GLEDHILL & ASSOCIATES SURVEYORS & VALUERS H'CAP 1m 1f 198y
4:40 (4:42) (Class 3) (0-95,93) 4-Y-O+ **£7,124** (£2,119; £1,059; £529) **Stalls** High

Form RPR

33-4 **1** **Celtic Spirit (IRE)**^{81} [940] 4-8-11 **83**.................................. SebSanders 5 99
(R M Beckett) *chsd clr ldrs: tk clsr order over 3f out: led 2f out: drvn out* **11/4**^{1}

10-0 **2** *1* **Oh Glory Be (USA)**^{25} [2236] 4-9-1 **87**.......................... RichardHughes 7 101
(R Hannon) *chsd clr ldrs: led 3f out tl 2f out: rdn and kpt on wl* **9/2**^{2}

203- **3** *6* **Ingratitude (IRE)**^{33} [5512] 4-8-13 **85**.............................. JamieSpencer 4 87
(N J Henderson) *hld up towards rr: rdn and hdwy 2f out: one pce appr fnl f* **11/2**^{3}

3152 **4** *2* **Full Victory (IRE)**^{6} [2807] 5-8-8 **80**.............................. FergusSweeney 6 78
(R A Farrant) *hld up towards rr: gd hdwy to join ldrs on stands' rail 3f out: wknd over 1f out* **13/2**

430/ **5** *1/2* **Mutawassel (USA)**^{48} 6-9-7 **93**.. MichaelHills 3 90
(B W Hills) *chsd clr ldrs: effrt over 3f out: rdn and btn 2f out* **20/1**

-012 **6** *3 1/2* **Nawaqees**^{18} [2469] 4-8-9 **81**.. RHills 8 71
(J L Dunlop) *hld up in rr: effrt over 3f out: wknd 2f out* **11/4**^{1}

-404 **7** *12* **Invention (USA)**^{29} [2123] 4-9-0 **86**.................................... MartinDwyer 1 52
(Miss E C Lavelle) *chsd tearaway ldr and clr of rest tl over 3f out: wknd over 2f out: eased whn no ch fnl f* **20/1**

310- **8** *18* **Invasian (IRE)**^{263} [5810] 6-9-0 **86**.................................... SteveDrowne 2 16
(A J Liddderdale) *led and set str pce tl hdd & wknd rapidly 3f out: eased whn no ch over 1f out* **16/1**

2m 10.42s (1.96) **Going Correction** +0.375s/f (Good) **8** Ran SP% **115.6**
Speed ratings (Par 107):107,106,101,99,99 96,87,72
CSF £15.56 CT £61.23 TOTE £3.90: £1.50, £1.60, £2.20; EX 22.60.
Owner Mrs H M Chamberlain **Bred** Genesis Green Stud Ltd **Trained** Whitsbury, Hants
■ Stewards' Enquiry : Richard Hughes caution: used whip with excessive frequency

FOCUS
A decent race, run at a fast pace, which suited the hold-up horses. As in previous races on the card, they came to the stands' side. Solid form, the progressive first pair finishing clear.

NOTEBOOK
Celtic Spirit(IRE), lightly raced but admirably consistent, is best on soft ground, and connections had been patient by not racing him since April. The front pair pulled well clear, suggesting that the form is solid, and this likeable sort may well be tried over 1m4f or even 1m6f before long. (op 7-2)
Oh Glory Be(USA), last year's Bibury Cup winner, goes particularly well at Salisbury, and showed she has trained on well with a sterling effort in defeat. She is at least as good over 1m4f, and has few miles on the clock, so she is one to consider for another decent handicap this season. (op 10-3 tchd 5-1)
Ingratitude(IRE) has been doing really well over hurdles, but he was 10lb above his winning Flat mark here, and the leading pair - both of whom are very useful sorts - were simply too good. (op 5-1 tchd 6-1)
Full Victory(IRE) found the final furlong a bit too far, particularly on this easy ground. He is higher in the weights these days, but should have finished closer, and the way he folded in the last 250 yards suggested it was lack of stamina. (tchd 15-2)
Mutawassel(USA), 15 times a winner in Qatar, was having his first run since returning to Britain and his original trainer. All his victories in the Middle East were on firm ground, so he deserves another chance on faster conditions before an assessment can be made of his handicap mark. (op 16-1 tchd 14-1)
Nawaqees petered out in the last two furlongs, and looks better suited by a mile. (op 7-2 tchd 5-2)
Invention(USA) tried to take on the leader, who was going far too fast, and both paid the penalty. (tchd 16-1)
Invasian(IRE) went off like a scalded cat, giving him no hope of lasting home on the easy ground. Official explanation: jockey said gelding ran too free (op 25-1)

3003 RODIN DEVELOPMENTS LTD H'CAP 1m 1f 198y
5:10 (5:11) (Class 5) (0-75,74) 3-Y-O **£3,238** (£963; £481; £240) **Stalls** High

Form RPR

4002 **1** **Rustic Gold**^{9} [2727] 3-8-1 **57**.. StephaneBreux$^{(3)}$ 2 64
(J R Best) *dwlt: hld up and bhd: hdwy over 2f out: led 1f out: drvn out* **3/1**^{2}

5-31 **2** *1 1/2* **Passing Hour (USA)**^{26} [2219] 3-9-6 **73**.......................... JamieSpencer 8 77
(G A Butler) *led and set slow pce 2f: chsd ldrs after: rdn to chal over 1f out: nt qckn fnl f* **11/2**^{3}

5050 **3** *nk* **Stagehand (IRE)**^{37} [1887] 3-8-11 **64**.................................. ChrisCatlin 3 67
(B R Millman) *led after 2f and increased tempo: hrd rdn and hdd 1f out: one pce* **9/1**

0521 **4** *1 1/2* **Yes One (IRE)**^{15} [2530] 3-9-7 **74**...................................... EddieAhern 1 75+
(J W Hills) *hdwy and in tch after 3f: promising effrt whn nt clr run over 2f out tl over 1f out: styd on same pce* **11/2**^{3}

0032 **5** *6* **Trump Call (IRE)**^{12} [2635] 3-9-3 **70**.........................(v^{1}) FergusSweeney 4 58
(R M Beckett) *plld hrd: chsd ldr after 2f tl wknd wl over 1f out* **11/4**^{1}

2400 **6** *1 3/4* **Tracer**^{23} [2317] 3-9-1 **68**... MartinDwyer 7 53
(R Hannon) *bhd: hrd rdn over 2f out: n.d* **14/1**

004 **7** *23* **Mr Grand Lodge (FR)**^{25} [2261] 3-9-1 **68**............................ TedDurcan 6 7
(L M Cumani) *plld hrd: in tch: rdn over 2f out: sn wknd: eased whn no ch fnl f* **15/2**

2m 13.9s (5.44) **Going Correction** +0.375s/f (Good) **7** Ran SP% **110.9**
Speed ratings (Par 99):93,91,91,90,85 84,65
CSF £18.45 CT £124.13 TOTE £3.90: £2.30, £3.40; EX 24.90 Place 6 £221.96, Place 5 £29.59..
Owner John Griffin Owen Mullen **Bred** Overbury Partnership **Trained** Hucking, Kent

FOCUS
A modest winning time for the type of contest, 3.48 seconds slower than the preceding handicap, with the runners again racing stands' side. The early pace was poor, but it stepped up after 2f and was respectable thereafter. Just an ordinary handicap, but sound form.
Trump Call(IRE) Official explanation: jockey said colt ran too free
T/Plt: £763.20 to a £1 stake. Pool: £58,182.50. 55.65 winning tickets. T/Qpdt: £11.60 to a £1 stake. Pool: £5,787.60. 366.30 winning tickets. LM

3004 - 3011a (Foreign Racing) - See Raceform Interactive

2758 HAMILTON (R-H)

Thursday, June 28

OFFICIAL GOING: Good to soft (good in places) changing to good to soft after race 4 (8.30)

Wind: Almost nil

3012 JOIN WBX.COM FOR £150 FREE BETS AMATEUR H'CAP — 1m 5f 9y

7:00 (7:01) (Class 6) (0-65,71) 4-Y-0+ — **£1,977** (£608; £304) — **Stalls** High

Form — RPR

2641 **1** **Charlotte Vale**[9] 2743 6-10-7 **71** 6ex ... MrsGHogg(7) 13 — 80
(Micky Hammond) *sn chsng ldr: led 5f out: hld on wl fnl f* — **8/1**[3]

-031 **2** ½ **Compton Dragon (USA)**[8] 2764 8-9-12 **55** ... MrsSBosley 14 — 63
(W M Brisbourne) *hld up: plenty to do 5f out: gd hdwy over 2f out: chsd wnr wl ins fnl f: r.o* — **4/1**[1]

1246 **3** nk **Ronsard (IRE)**[20] 2434 5-9-7 **53** ... MissEFolkes(3) 2 — 61
(P D Evans) *hld up: hdwy to chse wnr 2f out tl wl ins fnl f: no ex* — **10/1**

/002 **4** 2 **Reason (IRE)**[7] 2795 9-9-3 **46** oh1 ...(b) MissLEllison 8 — 51
(D W Chapman) *bhd tl styd on fr 2f out: nvr rchd ldrs* — **8/1**[3]

25-6 **5** 11 **Front Rank (IRE)**[20] 2431 7-9-10 **60** ... MissNSayer(7) 1 — 48
(Mrs Dianne Sayer) *prom: drvn and outpcd over 4f out: kpt on fnl f: no imp* — **11/1**

050- **6** shd **Red Sun**[30] 3522 10-10-4 **61** ...(t) MissFayeBramley 10 — 49
(R C Guest) *bhd: struggling 1/2-way: sme late hdwy: nvr on terms* — **33/1**

0/00 **7** 1½ **Kid'Z'Play (IRE)**[8] 2764 11-9-10 **53** ... MrsCBartley 6 — 39
(J S Goldie) *chsd ldrs tl wknd fr over 3f out* — **25/1**

4060 **8** 5 **Richtee (IRE)**[16] 2531 6-9-7 **50** ...(p) MissSBrotherton 7 — 28
(R A Fahey) *chsd ldrs: effrt and wnt 2nd over 4f out: wknd 2f out* — **6/1**[2]

45-0 **9** 3½ **Scurra**[166] 126 8-8-12 **46** oh1 ... MissHCuthbert(5) 12 — 19
(A C Whillans) *bhd: drvn over 4f out: nvr on terms* — **33/1**

1020 **10** 19 **Hugs Destiny (IRE)**[20] 2431 6-9-8 **56** ...(t) MissAngelaBarnes(5) 5 — —
(M A Barnes) *midfield: outpcd over 4f out: sn btn* — **8/1**[3]

1203 **11** 1½ **Al Moulatham**[29] 2148 8-9-9 **55** ...(bt) MissCarolineHurley(3) 4 — —
(R Ford) *sn led and set decent pce: hdd 5f out: sn wknd: t.o* — **11/1**

40-0 **12** ½ **Planters Punch (IRE)**[12] 665 6-9-2 **52** ... MissJRRichards(7) 3 — —
(N G Richards) *prom tl rdn and wknd over 3f out: t.o* — **12/1**

005- **13** 9 **Domesday (UAE)**[215] 6606 6-8-12 **46** oh1 ... MrsLHannity(5) 11 — —
(W G Harrison) *prom 4f: wl bhd fr 1/2-way: t.o* — **100/1**

506- **14** 7 **Bollin Thomas**[4] 1610 9-10-3 **63** ... JennyRiding(3) 9 — —
(R Allan) *midfield: struggling 1/2-way: t.o* — **25/1**

2m 58.98s (5.58) **Going Correction** +0.525s/f (Yiel) — **14** Ran SP% **115.6**

Speed ratings (Par 101):103,102,102,101,94 94,93,90,88,76 75,75,69,65

CSF £36.37 CT £326.65 TOTE £7.20: £2.60, £1.80, £3.60; EX 27.90.

Owner Peter J Davies **Bred** Snailwell Stud Co Ltd **Trained** Middleham Moor, N Yorks

■ A first winner for Gemma Hogg, and a final ride for former champion lady amateur Sarah Bosley.

■ Stewards' Enquiry : Mrs C Bartley one-day ban: entered wrong stall prior to race (Jul 14)

FOCUS

A typically moderate race of its type. The first three came clear and the form looks sound enough for the class.

3013 EUROPEAN BREEDERS FUND MAIDEN STKS — 6f 5y

7:30 (7:31) (Class 5) 2-Y-0 — **£3,562** (£1,059; £529; £264) — **Stalls** Low

Form — RPR

2 **1** **Red And White (IRE)**[12] 2658 2-8-12 0 ... JoeFanning 3 — 83+
(M Johnston) *cl up: led and edgd lft over 1f out: pushed clr fnl f* — **8/11**[1]

6 **2** 6 **Natmana**[19] 2473 2-9-3 0 ... JHBowman 2 — 70
(M R Channon) *t.k.h: led to over 1f out: no ex* — **11/4**[2]

3 1½ **Doon Haymer (IRE)** 2-9-3 0 ... TomEaves 5 — 66
(I Semple) *chsd ldrs: rn green: effrt and ev ch over 2f out: no ex over 1f out: bttr for r* — **10/3**[3]

4 16 **Elusive Lady (IRE)** 2-8-9 0 ... AndrewElliott(3) 1 — 13
(J R Weymes) *chsd ldrs tl rdn and wknd fr 2f out* — **50/1**

1m 14.34s (1.24) **Going Correction** +0.20s/f (Good) — **4** Ran SP% **109.6**

Speed ratings (Par 93):99,91,89,67

CSF £3.11 TOTE £1.90; EX 2.50.

Owner J Shack **Bred** Gainsborough Stud Management Ltd **Trained** Middleham Moor, N Yorks

FOCUS

A fair little juvenile maiden. The easy winner rates value for a bit further.

NOTEBOOK

Red And White(IRE) confirmed the promise of her debut second behind Highland Daughter and got off the mark with a clear-cut success. She proved much more professional this time, clearly goes well with some cut underfoot, and again did more than enough to suggest a seventh furlong would pose no problems. It will be interesting to see where she is pitched in next. (op 4-6 tchd 5-6 in places)

Natmana, sixth at Windsor on his debut 19 days previously, proved too free for his own good at the head of affairs and was made to look pedestrian when the winner swept past. He will need to learn to settle better, but is entitled to do so and could prove better again when reverting to a less taxing surface. (op 5-2)

Doon Haymer(IRE), whose sales price rose to 110,000euros and is related to a 7f juvenile winner, proved very popular in the betting ring ahead of this racecourse bow. He ultimately proved too green through the race, looking as though he is already in need of another furlong, and should get a deal closer next time out. (op 6-1)

Elusive Lady(IRE), bred to make her mark around this trip at two, showed early pace before tiring right out of it after the 2f pole. A drop back to 5f will help in the sort term. (op 20-1)

3014 RUTHVEN KEENAN SPRINT H'CAP — 5f 4y

8:00 (8:00) (Class 4) (0-80,78) 3-Y-0+ — **£6,477** (£1,927; £963; £481) — **Stalls** Low

Form — RPR

0-02 **1** **Elkhorn**[41] 1806 5-9-3 **72** ...(b) TomEaves 10 — 85+
(Miss J A Camacho) *in tch on outside: smooth hdwy 1/2-way: led over 1f out: pushed out fnl f* — **4/1**[1]

0511 **2** 1 **Compton Classic**[6] 2830 5-8-0 **62** 12ex ...(p) KellyHarrison(7) 1 — 71
(J S Goldie) *in tch: effrt over 1f out: chsd wnr ins fnl f: r.o* — **5/1**[3]

0560 **3** 1¼ **Ptarmigan Ridge**[5] 2866 11-8-13 **68** ... PaulHanagan 2 — 73
(Miss L A Perratt) *prom: effrt 2f out: kpt on u.p fnl f* — **8/1**

5540 **4** shd **Nusoor (IRE)**[12] 2673 4-8-9 **67** ...(b) PatrickMathers(3) 4 — 71
(Peter Grayson) *hmpd s: bhd: effrt on outside 2f out: kpt on fnl f: no imp* — **9/1**

0211 **5** 1 **Brut**[8] 2762 5-8-13 **68** 6ex ...(p) TonyHamilton 7 — 69
(D W Barker) *led to over 1f out: no ex ins fnl f* — **9/2**[2]

-040 **6** 1½ **Give Me The Night (IRE)**[9] 2744 4-9-9 **78** ... RoystonFfrench 6 — 73
(B Smart) *cl up: ev ch 1/2-way: one pce appr fnl f* — **7/1**

436 **7** 2 **Henry Hall (IRE)**[17] 2509 11-8-8 **63** ... KimTinkler 3 — 51
(N Tinkler) *prom: hung rt thrght: rdn and wknd fr over 1f out* — **25/1**

0-03 **8** 4 **Matty Tun**[12] 2673 8-9-1 **70** ...(p) SebSanders 5 — 44
(J Balding) *blkd s: sn cl up: hung rt thrght: rdn and ev ch 1/2-way: wknd over 1f out: eased whn no ch* — **4/1**[1]

61.50 secs (0.30) **Going Correction** +0.20s/f (Good) — **8** Ran SP% **112.3**

Speed ratings (Par 105):105,103,101,101,99 97,94,87

CSF £23.18 CT £150.60 TOTE £5.10: £1.40, £2.30, £2.70; EX 27.00.

Owner Lee Bolingbroke & Partners VI **Bred** George Strawbridge **Trained** Norton, N Yorks

■ Stewards' Enquiry : Seb Sanders one-day ban: used whip without giving gelding time to respond (Jul 9)

Tony Hamilton one-day ban: failed to ride to draw (Jul 9)

FOCUS

A modest sprint, run at a sound pace. The form looks straightforward enough.

3015 ATLAS INTERNATIONAL MAIDEN STKS — 1m 1f 36y

8:30 (8:31) (Class 5) 3-4-Y-0 — **£3,238** (£963; £481; £240) — **Stalls** High

Form — RPR

53 **1** **Gone Gold (USA)**[26] 2261 3-9-0 0 ...(v[1]) SebSanders 1 — 77
(J Noseda) *hld up in tch: smooth hdwy to ld over 2f out: edgd rt: rdn and kpt on wl fnl f* — **10/3**[1]

32- **2** 2½ **Cooperstown**[211] 5727 4-9-11 0 ... TomEaves 6 — 72
(I Semple) *cl up: led over 3f out to over 2f out: rallied: one pce ins fnl f* — **4/1**[3]

3242 **3** nk **Arena's Dream (USA)**[19] 2464 3-9-0 71 ... PaulHanagan 8 — 71
(R A Fahey) *trckd ldrs: rdn 3f out: kpt on u.p fnl f* — **7/2**[2]

22 **4** shd **Dolce Dovo**[61] 1312 4-9-6 74 ...(b) PaulMulrennan 2 — 66
(W J Haggas) *cl up: drvn over 2f out: kpt on u.p ins fnl f* — **7/2**[2]

5 7 **Sinatas (GER)**[46] 4-9-8 51 ... MarkLawson(3) 3 — 55
(P Monteith) *led to over 3f out: sn outpcd* — **50/1**

0-0 **6** ¾ **Forrest Flyer (IRE)**[24] 2312 3-9-0 0 ... RoystonFfrench 7 — 53
(Miss L A Perratt) *hld up: hmpd after 3f: n.d after* — **66/1**

4 **7** 4 **Lochiel**[41] 1804 3-8-7 0 ... NeilBrown(7) 9 — 43
(Mrs S C Bradburne) *prom: hit rail: stmbld bdly and lost pl after 3f: nt rcvr* — **12/1**

8 12 **Ancient Cross** 3-9-0 0 ... JoeFanning 4 — 16
(M Johnston) *hld up: hdwy over 4f out: rdn and wknd over 2f out* — **6/1**

9 15 **Quicuyo (GER)**[53] 4-9-11 0 ... DaleGibson 5 — —
(P Monteith) *s.i.s: hmpd after 3f: nvr on terms* — **33/1**

2m 3.70s (4.04) **Going Correction** +0.525s/f (Yiel)

WFA 3 from 4yo 11lb — **9** Ran SP% **115.9**

Speed ratings (Par 103):103,100,100,100,94 93,89,79,65

CSF £16.94 TOTE £4.40: £1.10, £1.80, £1.60; EX 21.00.

Owner Jayeff B Stables **Bred** Jayeff 'B' Stables **Trained** Newmarket, Suffolk

FOCUS

A fair maiden, run at an average pace. The form is rated through the third and fourth.

3016 EUROPEAN BREEDERS' FUND FILLIES' CONDITIONS STKS — 1m 65y

9:00 (9:00) (Class 3) 3-Y-0+ — **£9,348** (£2,799; £1,399; £700) — **Stalls** High

Form — RPR

0111 **1** **Just Lille (IRE)**[33] 2027 4-8-11 80 ...(p) RoystonFfrench 2 — 82
(Mrs A Duffield) *chsd ldr: rdn over 3f out: rallied to ld over 1f out: styd on strly* — **7/4**[2]

40-5 **2** 1½ **Home Sweet Home (IRE)**[17] 2507 4-8-11 92 ... NickyMackay 1 — 79
(L M Cumani) *chsd ldrs: effrt over 2f out: chsd wnr ins fnl f: kpt on* — **11/10**[1]

3222 **3** 3 **News Of The Day (IRE)**[21] 2389 3-8-1 67 ... DaleGibson 3 — 70
(P Monteith) *led to over 1f out: sn no ex* — **7/2**[3]

4- **4** 55 **Craig Y Nos**[360] 3143 3-8-2 0 ow4 ... PatrickMathers(3) 4 — —
(A Berry) *s.i.s: bhd: lost tch fr 1/2-way* — **100/1**

1m 52.56s (3.26) **Going Correction** +0.525s/f (Yiel)

WFA 3 from 4yo 10lb — **4** Ran SP% **107.2**

Speed ratings (Par 104):104,102,99,44

CSF £4.01 TOTE £3.00; EX 4.30.

Owner Miss Helen Wynne **Bred** Sweetmans Bloodstock **Trained** Constable Burton, N Yorks

FOCUS

An interesting fillies' conditions stakes, run at a solid pace. The winner remains on an upward curve but the proximity of the modest third limits the form.

NOTEBOOK

Just Lille(IRE), back in trip, maintained her winning sequence with another resolute effort despite another 6lb rise in the weights. She is in the form of her life at present, handles any ground, and further improvement cannot be ruled out yet. Another hike in the weights is now inevitable, however. (op 5-4 tchd 15-8)

Home Sweet Home(IRE) was unable to cope with the game winner at level weights, despite officially being rated 12lb her superior and could be deemed as disappointing. She has yet to reproduce her three-year-old form for her current connections, but this was a step in the right direction and she would have found this ground plenty soft enough. (tchd 10-11 tchd 6-5 in a place)

News Of The Day(IRE), runner-up on her previous three outings, was put in her place when the race became serious. She faced a difficult task at the weights, however, and deserves to get her head in front again. (op 6-1 tchd 13-2)

3017 BET NOW AT WBX.COM H'CAP — 6f 5y

9:30 (9:30) (Class 6) (0-65,65) 4-Y-0+ — **£2,388** (£705; £352) — **Stalls** Low

Form — RPR

0-50 **1** **Night In (IRE)**[47] 1675 4-9-0 **58** ...(t) KimTinkler 2 — 66
(N Tinkler) *dwlt: hdwy 1/2-way: styd on wl fnl f to ld nr fin* — **20/1**

6-21 **2** ½ **Dematraf (IRE)**[26] 2249 5-7-12 **49** ... BernadetteQuinn(7) 6 — 55
(P D Evans) *led: rdn 2f out: kpt on fnl f: hdd nr fin* — **14/1**

4-03 **3** ¾ **No Grouse**[15] 2561 7-8-10 **54** ... SebSanders 7 — 58
(E J Alston) *hld up: hdwy over 1f out: kpt on fnl f: nrst fin* — **5/1**[2]

3660 **4** shd **Digital**[15] 2576 10-8-13 **57** ... JHBowman 12 — 60
(M R Channon) *prom: effrt over 1f out: kpt on same pce fnl f* — **6/1**

0005 **5** ½ **Strawberry Patch (IRE)**[6] 2830 8-8-1 **52** ...(p) KellyHarrison(7) 4 — 54
(J S Goldie) *in tch: effrt over 2f out: hung rt over 1f out: nt qckn ins fnl f* — **12/1**

0005 **6** 1¾ **Alexia Rose (IRE)**[8] 2761 5-8-2 **46** oh1 ...(b) RoystonFfrench 5 — 43
(A Berry) *prom: effrt over 1f out: kpt on same pce* — **25/1**

6000 **7** 1½ **Drink To Me Only**[76] 1028 4-8-1 **48** oh1 ow2 ... AndrewElliott(3) 9 — 40
(J R Weymes) *bhd and rdn along: kpt on wl fnl f: nvr rchd ldrs* — **66/1**

4031 **8** ½ **Inca Soldier (FR)**[5] 2864 4-8-11 **55** 6ex ... PaulMulrennan 3 — 46
(R C Guest) *t.k.h: prom: outpcd 2f out: n.d after* — **9/2**[1]

0402 **9** nk **Shadow Jumper (IRE)**[23] 2343 6-8-3 **47** ow1 ...(v) JoeFanning 10 — 37
(J T Stimpson) *midfield: drvn over 2f out: sn no imp* — **12/1**

5001 **10** nk **Soto**[14] 2608 4-9-7 **65** ... DaleGibson 1 — 54
(M W Easterby) *prom tl rdn and wknd fr 2f out* — **7/1**

1365 **11** 2½ **Maison Dieu**[17] 2508 4-9-2 **60** ... TonyHamilton 11 — 41
(E J Alston) *hld up: hdwy over 2f out: wknd over 1f out* — **14/1**

4-00 **12** 2 1/2 **George The Best (IRE)**[10] 2711 6-9-2 **60** PaulHanagan 13 34
(Micky Hammond) *in tch: rdn and hung lft 2f out: sn btn* **11/2**[3]
04-0 **13** 2 1/2 **Quaker Boy**[24] 2298 4-8-7 **54** AndrewMullen(3) 8 20
(A C Whillans) *chsd ldrs tl wknd over 2f out* **50/1**
3036 **14** 3 1/2 **Newkeylets**[36] 1940 4-8-6 **50** ow1 (p) TomEaves 14 6
(I Semple) *racd alone far side: rdn and wknd fr over 2f out* **16/1**
1m 15.05s (1.95) **Going Correction** +0.20s/f (Good) **14** Ran SP% **123.7**
Speed ratings (Par 101):95,94,93,93,92 90,88,87,87,86 83,80,76,72
CSF £276.53 CT £1636.41 TOTE £27.30: £9.60, £3.70, £2.60; EX 478.30 Place 6 £148.00, Place 5 £62.90.
Owner Leeds Plywood And Doors Ltd **Bred** Churchtown Stud **Trained** Langton, N Yorks
FOCUS
A modest winning time, 0.71 seconds slower than the earlier two-year-old maiden, and the form is ordinary. There was not much between the first five at the finish.
T/Plt: £106.60 to a £1 stake. Pool: £97,070.35. 664.45 winning tickets. T/Qpdt: £61.80 to a £1 stake. Pool: £6,247.50. 74.70 winning tickets. RY

2657 LEICESTER (R-H)
Thursday, June 28
3018 Meeting Abandoned - Waterlogged

2251 NEWCASTLE (L-H)
Thursday, June 28
OFFICIAL GOING: Soft (good to soft in places; 5.9)
After 10mm rain the previous day the ground was described as 'soft, testing in the home straight, heavy in places on the round course'.
Wind: Blustery, half against Weather: Blustery, overcast, cool and rain race 6.

3024 GUINNESS MAIDEN AUCTION STKS 6f
2:30 (2:34) (Class 5) 2-Y-O £3,238 (£963; £481; £240) Stalls High

Form RPR
00 **1** **Allahor**[19] 2451 2-8-6 0 PatrickMathers(3) 3 72
(A Berry) *trckd ldrs far side: hdwy over 2f out: rdn to ld ent fnl f: styd on strly* **16/1**
023 **2** 1 **Rub Of The Relic (IRE)**[29] 2147 2-8-11 0 PaulHanagan 15 71
(P A Blockley) *cl up stands' side: led that gp 1/2-way: rdn wl over 1f out: sn drvn and styd on fnl f: 1st in gp* **3/1**[2]
3 hd **Low Flyer (USA)** 2-8-11 0 PaulFessey 16 70
(T D Barron) *trckd ldrs stands' side: effrt 2f out: rdn and kpt on ins fnl f: nrst fin* **12/1**
53 **4** 1 1/2 **Karky Schultz (GER)**[14] 2604 2-9-2 0 SebSanders 5 71
(J M P Eustace) *cl up far side: led and overall ldr 1/2-way: rdn along over 2f out: drvn and hdd ent fnl f: sn wknd: 2nd in gp* **5/2**[1]
5 1 1/2 **Hildegarde (IRE)** 2-8-6 0 DavidAllan 14 56
(T D Easterby) *hld up stands' side: swtchd lft and effrt wl over 1f out: styd on ins fnl f: nrst fin: 3rd in gp* **7/1**
0 **6** 3 1/2 **Stormy Journey**[24] 2297 2-8-11 0 TomEaves 13 51
(Mrs K Walton) *led stands' side gp: hdd 1/2-way: sn rdn along and wknd wl over 1f out: 4th in gp* **40/1**
62 **7** 1/2 **Our Sunnie**[7] 2804 2-8-11 0 AdrianTNicholls 4 49
(D Nicholls) *overall ldr far side: hdd 1/2-way: cl up tl rdn along wl over 1f out and sn wknd: 3rd in gp* **5/1**[3]
8 1 3/4 **Mister Christie** 2-9-2 0 KDarley 6 49
(N Tinkler) *in tch: far side: rdn along wl over 2f out: kpt on same pce: 4th in gp* **20/1**
00 **9** 3 **Big Slick (IRE)**[7] 2804 2-8-11 0 DeanMernagh 9 35
(M Brittain) *racd far side: sn rdn along and a towards rr: 5th in gp* **50/1**
046 **10** 2 1/2 **Limestone**[51] 1553 2-8-9 0 PhillipMakin 2 26
(J R Weymes) *chsd ldrs far side: rdn along wl over 2f out: sn wknd: 6th in gp* **66/1**
11 1 1/4 **Viscount Monty** 2-8-2 0 DanielleMcCreery(7) 7 22
(N Tinkler) *sn rdn along and a in rr far side: 7th in gp* **66/1**
4 **12** 3 **Personal Choice**[6] 2818 2-7-12 0 ow1 PatrickDonaghy(7) 10 9
(M Brittain) *in tch stands' side: rdn along 1/2-way: sn wknd: 5th in gp* **14/1**
13 7 **Paint Stripper** 2-8-6 0 AndrewElliott(3) 1 —
(W Storey) *uns rdr and bolted bef s: s.i.s and a bhd far side: last in gp* **66/1**
14 11 **Buju** 2-8-11 0 KimTinkler 11 —
(N Tinkler) *bmpd s: a outpcd stands' side: 6th in gp* **33/1**
2 **15** 1 1/4 **Geordie Girl**[69] 1130 2-8-3 0 ow2 RoryMoore(5) 12 —
(R C Guest) *chsd ldng pair stands' side: rdn along 1/2-way: wknd fnl 2f: last in gp* **12/1**
1m 20.1s (5.01) **Going Correction** +0.45s/f (Yiel) **15** Ran SP% **127.3**
Speed ratings (Par 93):84,82,82,80,78 73,73,70,66,63 61,57,48,33,32
CSF £64.61 TOTE £24.10: £4.70, £2.10, £4.60; EX 91.60 TRIFECTA Not won..
Owner H R H Prince of Saxe-Weimar **Bred** Jason Puckey **Trained** Cockerham, Lancs
FOCUS
A modest maiden auction race and the time was very moderate, 1.79 seconds slower than the following two-year-old novice event. The form looks sound at this level. Eight raced on the far side including the winner, but at the line there was little between the two groups.
NOTEBOOK
Allahor, slowly away on his first two starts, jumped off on level terms this time. He was first home on the far side and will now presumably take the nursery route. (op 18-1 tchd 20-1)
Rub Of The Relic(IRE), absent for four weeks, looked really fit and well. He dominated the stands'-side group but at the line the winner, racing out in the centre, held the upper hand. He deserves a change of luck. (op 7-2 tchd 11-4)
Low Flyer(USA), a robust, leggy January foal, missed a beat at the start. He put in some sterling late work and is sure to improve and find a race. (op 11-1)
Karky Schultz(GER), giving away weight to all bar one, came out second best on the far side. This was his third start and he is starting to look exposed. (op 10-3 tchd 7-2)
Hildegarde(IRE), a May foal out of a mare that has already produced five winners, is a small, close-coupled filly. She put in some pleasing work late on and this will have taught her plenty. (op 14-1)
Stormy Journey, a neat gelding, showed a lot more than on his debut three weeks earlier, showing good speed until tiring markedly.
Our Sunnie, who again gave a problem or two behind the stalls, showed plenty of toe racing quite keenly on the far side, but carried his head high and tired badly inside the last. (tchd 9-2)

3025 WEATHERBYS BANK NOVICE STKS 6f
3:00 (3:00) (Class 5) 2-Y-O £3,238 (£963; £481; £240) Stalls High

Form RPR
33 **1** **Montaquila**[28] 2166 2-8-12 0 TomEaves 4 85
(J Howard Johnson) *mde all: rdn and qcknd 2f out: styd on strly fnl f* **11/4**[2]
1 **2** 2 1/2 **Eternal Luck (IRE)**[17] 2510 2-9-2 0 PhilipRobinson 1 82
(M A Jarvis) *hld up in rr: swtchd outside and hdwy wl over 2f out: rdn to chse wnr over 1f out: sn drvn and no imp* **4/1**[3]
21 **3** 6 **Pelican Prince**[35] 1963 2-9-0 0 PatCosgrave 3 62
(K R Burke) *chsd ldrs: hdwy 1/2-way: rdn along 2f out and kpt on same pce appr fnl f* **9/2**
31 **4** 2 **Style Award**[20] 2416 2-8-6 0 AndrewMullen(3) 2 51
(W J H Ratcliffe) *trckd ldng pair: hdwy to chse wnr wl over 2f out: sn rdn and wknd wl over 1f out* **20/1**
1 **5** 1 **Mahusay (IRE)**[31] 2086 2-9-2 0 NickyMackay 6 61+
(L M Cumani) *trckd ldrs: hdwy on inner whn nt clr run wl over 1f out: sn swtchd lft and rdn: no imp and eased ins fnl f: sddle slipped* **2/1**[1]
10 **6** 1 3/4 **Lieutenant Pigeon**[26] 2232 2-9-5 0 RoystonFfrench 7 52
(B Smart) *chsd wnr: pushed along 1/2-way: sn rdn and wknd 2f out* **8/1**
0 **7** 10 **Peltre**[45] 1713 2-8-0 0 PatrickDonaghy(7) 5 10
(M Brittain) *s.i.s: sn rdn along and a outpcd in rr* **150/1**
1m 18.31s (3.22) **Going Correction** +0.45s/f (Yiel) **7** Ran SP% **114.7**
Speed ratings (Par 93):96,92,84,82,80 78,65
CSF £14.30 TOTE £3.90: £2.30, £2.10; EX 16.90.
Owner Transcend Bloodstock LLP **Bred** Ridgecourt Stud **Trained** Billy Row, Co Durham
FOCUS
The winner put a poor effort last time behind him and was confirming the promise he showed on his debut. The first two came right away from four previous winners with the winner setting the standard.
NOTEBOOK
Montaquila, on edge and swishing his tail in the paddock, was very keen to lead. He stepped up the pace from the front and in the end won going away. He may need careful handling if he is to progress. (op 7-2 tchd 4-1)
Eternal Luck(IRE), a good-bodied individual, took time to warm to his task. Racing on much slower ground, he went in pursuit of the winner but in the end was very much second best. (op 7-2 tchd 3-1)
Pelican Prince, encountering much softer ground, found this a lot tougher and in the end the first two left him for dead. Nurseries now beckon. (tchd 5-1)
Style Award was stepping up to 6f and racing on much softer ground. In the end she was simply not up to it. (op 16-1)
Mahusay(IRE) is not very big but very well put together. Inclined to be coltish in the paddock, he was tucked away on the inner. Left short of room and forced to switch, he was going nowhere when his saddle shifted and he had to be heavily eased, forfeiting fourth place near the line. It might be best to put a line through this. Official explanation: jockey said saddle slipped (op 5-2)
Lieutenant Pigeon, on the leg and narrow, was tackling a stiff task conceding weight all round. (op 7-1)

3026 GNER SEATON DELAVAL TROPHY H'CAP 1m 3y(S)
3:30 (3:30) (Class 2) (0-100,100) 4-Y-O+
£15,580 (£4,665; £2,332; £1,167; £582; £292) Stalls High

Form RPR
-250 **1** **Rio Riva**[27] 2208 5-9-5 **97** TomEaves 1 109
(Miss J A Camacho) *hld up in rr: gd hdwy 2f out: rdn and qcknd to ld ent fnl f: sn clr* **9/2**[3]
4101 **2** 5 **Moody Tunes**[5] 2871 4-8-11 **89** 6ex PatCosgrave 6 89
(K R Burke) *trckd ldng pair: hdwy 2f out: rdn and ev ch over 1f out: sn drvn and kpt on same pce ins fnl f* **5/1**
0-60 **3** 1 1/4 **St Andrews (IRE)**[19] 2446 7-9-0 **92** PhilipRobinson 4 89
(M A Jarvis) *hld up: hdwy 3f out: rdn along 2f out: styd on u.p ins fnl f* **8/1**
0040 **4** shd **Kings Point (IRE)**[42] 1791 6-9-2 **94** (p) PaulHanagan 2 91
(R A Fahey) *trckd ldr: hdwy to ld 2f out: sn rdn and hdd ent fnl f: drvn: edgd rt and wknd* **16/1**
-004 **5** 3 **Zero Tolerance (IRE)**[42] 1791 7-9-7 **99** PaulFessey 3 89
(T D Barron) *led: rdn along and edgd lft wl over 2f out: hdd 2f out: sn drvn and wknd* **11/4**[1]
-000 **6** 2 **Best Prospect (IRE)**[43] 1767 5-9-0 **92** PhillipMakin 7 77
(M Dods) *hld up towards rr: hdwy wl over 2f out: sn rdn and chsd ldrs: hld and n.m.r ent fnl f: sn wknd* **15/2**
/00- **7** 6 **Swing The Ring (IRE)**[251] 6093 4-9-1 **98** PBradley(5) 8 70
(A Berry) *a towards rr: rdn along 1/2-way and sn outpcd* **66/1**
11 **8** 7 **European Dream (IRE)**[5] 2891 4-9-3 **100** 6ex (p) RoryMoore(5) 5 55
(R C Guest) *stdd s: hld up in rr: hdwy to chse ldrs 1/2-way: rdn along wl over 2f out and sn wknd* **7/2**[2]
1m 44.12s (2.22) **Going Correction** +0.45s/f (Yiel) **8** Ran SP% **114.0**
Speed ratings (Par 109):106,101,99,99,96 94,88,81
CSF £27.00 CT £174.67 TOTE £5.90: £1.70, £2.20, £2.20; EX 29.50 Trifecta £303.50 Pool: £761.01 - 1.78 winning tickets..
Owner Rio Riva Partnership **Bred** Mrs S Camacho **Trained** Norton, N Yorks
FOCUS
Lincoln runner-up Rio Riva was back on song and turned this quite competitive handicap into a procession. The race has been rated through the in-form runner-up.
NOTEBOOK
Rio Riva, on the same mark as when runner-up in the Lincoln here, put two subsequent below-par efforts behind him. His rider left nothing to chance and as a result he will have a lot more on his plate when he next appears. (op 5-1)
Moody Tunes, under a penalty in a much tougher race, went down fighting and is clearly in very good heart. (op 11-2)
St Andrews(IRE), who has slipped to a lenient mark, had the ground he likes and had a senior rider aboard. He was making hard work of it at the halfway mark but to his credit kept going all the way to the line. (op 7-1)
Kings Point(IRE) is waging a war with the official assessor and all his best efforts have been on much quicker ground than he encountered here.
Zero Tolerance(IRE), racing wide, has slipped to a lenient mark but he carried his head high and did not look in the right frame of mind. (op 5-2 tchd 3-1)
Best Prospect(IRE) found this trip on the sharp side and he is still 7lb higher than the second his his two victories last year. (op 9-1)
Swing The Ring(IRE), a winner once from 15 starts in Germany, was having his first outing since October and never figured.
European Dream(IRE), making a quick return under a penalty, missed a beat at the start. He saw plenty of daylight and stopped to nothing. Hopefully he will bounce back after a short break. Official explanation: jockey said gelding ran flat (tchd 4-1)

3027 WEATHERBYS FINANCE H'CAP 2m 19y

4:00 (4:00) (Class 4) (0-80,80) 4-Y-O+ **£5,362** (£1,604; £802; £401; £199) **Stalls** Low

Form RPR

42 **1** **Nero West (FR)**[15] 2567 6-8-3 **62**....(b[1]) PaulFessey 5 74
(I Semple) *mde all: clr 1/2-way: rdn and qcknd 3f out: drvn over 1f out and styd on strly* **4/1**[2]

024 **2** *6* **Great Quest (IRE)**[20] 2434 5-8-8 **67**.... KDarley 4 72
(James Moffatt) *in tch: hdwy 6f out: chsd wnr over 3f out and sn rdn along: drvn 2f out and kpt on same pce ent fnl f* **8/1**

21-0 **3** *5* **Hue**[5] 2860 6-8-13 **72**....(b) TonyHamilton 7 71
(B Ellison) *hld up in rr: hdwy 5f out: rdn along to chse ldng pair over 2f out: drvn over 1f out: sn one pce* **5/2**[1]

-524 **4** *hd* **Balyan (IRE)**[33] 2031 6-9-3 **76**.... TomEaves 3 75
(J Howard Johnson) *hld up in rr: hdwy 4f out: rdn along 3f out: styd on fnl 2f: nrst fin* **6/1**

/00- **5** *10* **Double Deputy (IRE)**[4] 4990 6-9-4 **80**....(v) JamieMoriarty[(3)] 1 67
(J J Quinn) *prom: rdn along 6f out: wknd 4f out* **10/1**

142- **6** *12* **Prairie Sun (GER)**[381] 2501 6-9-2 **75**.... RoystonFfrench 2 47
(Mrs A Duffield) *trckd ldrs: effrt over 4f out: sn rdn along and wknd over 3f out* **8/1**

20-1 **7** *57* **Industrial Star (IRE)**[22] 2375 6-8-13 **72**....(p) PaulHanagan 6 —
(Micky Hammond) *prom: chsd wnr 1/2-way: rdn along over 4f out: sn wknd and eased* **9/2**[3]

3m 44.29s (9.09) **Going Correction** +0.75s/f (Yiel) **7** Ran SP% **112.4**
Speed ratings (Par 105):107,104,101,101,96 90,61
CSF £33.71 TOTE £5.10: £2.30, £3.80; EX 44.40.
Owner Mr & Mrs Charles Villiers **Bred** Ecurie Pelder **Trained** Carluke, S Lanarks

FOCUS
An ordinary staying handicap, but at least the winner made sure this was a true test of stamina and nothing else ever got into it. The form is rated at face value through the runner-up.
Industrial Star(IRE) Official explanation: jockey said gelding was unsuited by the soft (good to soft places) ground

3028 EUROPEAN BREEDERS' FUND/GNER GO RACING HOPPINGS STKS (LISTED RACE) (F&M) 1m 2f 32y

4:30 (4:31) (Class 1) 3-Y-O+

£17,034 (£6,456; £3,231; £1,611; £807; £405) **Stalls** Centre

Form RPR

-554 **1** **Mango Mischief (IRE)**[10] 2720 6-9-5 94.... KDarley 6 104
(M R Channon) *mde all: rdn along wl over 2f out: drvn over 1f out: styd on strly fnl f* **11/2**[3]

-125 **2** *7* **In Safe Hands (IRE)**[8] 2757 3-8-7 92.... PhilipRobinson 2 90
(C G Cox) *hld up in tch: hdwy over 3f out: rdn to chse wnr over 1f out: sn drvn and one pce* **9/4**[2]

-036 **3** *3* **Ransom Captive (USA)**[14] 2599 3-8-7 91.... PaulHanagan 3 84
(M A Magnusson) *chsd wnr: rdn along over 3f out: drvn along 2f out: wknd appr fnl f* **10/1**

12 **4** *12* **Promising Lead**[41] 1824 3-8-7 97.... RyanMoore 4 60
(Sir Michael Stoute) *trckd ldrs: hdwy to chse wnr over 3f out: rdn along wl over 2f out: sn btn* **1/1**[1]

520- **5** *1 3/4* **Flor Y Nata (USA)**[300] 5008 4-9-5 93.... SebSanders 1 57
(Sir Mark Prescott) *s.i.s and bhd: effrt and sme hdwy 4f out: rdn 3f out and sn btn* **14/1**

6 **6** *7* **Enforce (USA)**[54] 1472 4-9-5 91.... RoystonFfrench 5 43
(E A L Dunlop) *a in rr: rdn along over 4f out: drvn over 3f out and sn bhd* **20/1**

2m 17.08s (5.28) **Going Correction** +0.75s/f (Yiel)
WFA 3 from 4yo+ 12lb **6** Ran SP% **116.7**
Speed ratings (Par 111):108,102,100,90,89 83
CSF £19.21 TOTE £6.20: £2.40, £2.20; EX 19.70.
Owner Antoniades Family **Bred** A G Antoniades **Trained** West Ilsley, Berks

FOCUS
An ordinary fillies' Listed event run at a fair pace and once again the place to be was out in front. The winner sets the level for the form.

NOTEBOOK
Mango Mischief(IRE) may not have won for two years, but she has winning form in Group company and also on this sort of ground. With conditions appearing to be suiting front-runners, she was positive from the start and found more than enough to see off the challengers when they arrived. As meritorious as the victory was the way the race panned out, and with a couple of her rivals running below their best, does put a question mark against the form. (op 9-2)
In Safe Hands(IRE) travelled well enough off the pace and looked as though she might provide a stern test for the winner, but she failed to find as much off the bridle as had looked likely and merely plodded on to finish second at a respectful distance. This softer ground did not appear to suit her. (op 4-1)
Ransom Captive(USA), just behind In Safe Hands at Newbury last month, had every chance but failed to get home in this more testing ground. (tchd 9-1)
Promising Lead travelled well enough for much of the way, but when asked to go and pick up the winner she folded completely. She was stepping up a quarter of a mile in trip, but her dam won over 1m6f so it is more likely the testing ground found her out. Official explanation: jockey said filly was unsuited by the soft (good to soft places) ground; vet said filly returned lame (tchd 10-11 and 11-8)
Flor Y Nata(USA), reappearing from nine months off, drifted like a barge in the market and put in one of her trademark lethargic starts for good measure. The main objective was probably to get a run into her and when she gets the start right she will leave this form well behind. (op 8-1)
Enforce(USA) looked to be hating the ground and never figured. Official explanation: jockey said filly was unsuited by the soft (good to soft places) ground (tchd 16-1)

3029 JOIN WBX.COM FOR £150 FREE BETS H'CAP 7f

5:00 (5:00) (Class 5) (0-75,74) 3-Y-O **£3,886** (£1,156; £577; £288) **Stalls** High

Form RPR

3-54 **1** **Apache Dawn**[24] 2312 3-9-3 **70**.... KDarley 10 89
(K A Ryan) *mde all: rdn clr over 1f out: styd on strly* **5/1**[2]

464 **2** *11* **Chjimes (IRE)**[35] 1978 3-9-4 **71**.... PatCosgrave 11 64+
(K R Burke) *trckd ldrs on inner: hdwy to chse wnr over 1f out: sn rdn and no imp* **4/1**[1]

6021 **3** *3* **Cheery Cat (USA)**[4] 2910 3-8-4 **60** 6ex....(p) AndrewMullen[(3)] 2 41
(D W Barker) *hld up in rr: hdwy over 2f out: sn rdn and styd on ins fnl f* **4/1**[1]

-003 **4** *1/2* **Handsome Falcon**[22] 2373 3-9-7 **74**.... PaulHanagan 1 54
(R A Fahey) *hld up and bhd: hdwy over 2f out: styd on ins fnl f: nrst fin* **10/1**

0666 **5** *2* **Alavana (IRE)**[10] 2713 3-8-2 **55** oh1.... PaulQuinn 4 29
(D W Barker) *prom: rdn along over 2f out: grad wknd* **33/1**

-313 **6** *1 1/4* **Bid For Gold**[12] 2662 3-9-1 **68**.... PaulMulrennan 3 39
(Jedd O'Keeffe) *trckd ldrs on outer: hdwy 3f out: rdn along 2f out: wknd over 1f out* **8/1**

-036 **7** *5* **Bollin Fergus**[6] 2829 3-8-5 **58**.... DavidAllan 5 15
(T D Easterby) *hld up in midfield: swtchd outside and hdwy over 2f out: sn rdn and btn* **6/1**[3]

0-23 **8** *2 1/2* **Kunte Kinteh**[9] 2740 3-8-12 **65**.... AdrianTNicholls 8 16
(D Nicholls) *cl up: rdn along 3f out: drvn over 2f out and sn wknd* **6/1**[3]

-205 **9** *1* **Perfect Courtesy (IRE)**[19] 2453 3-9-1 **68**....(b) PhilipRobinson 7 16
(G A Swinbank) *t.k.h: trckd ldrs: effrt over 2f out: sn rdn and wknd wl over 1f out* **7/1**

00-0 **10** *1 1/2* **Averti Star**[16] 2535 3-8-7 **60**.... RoystonFfrench 6 —
(Mrs A Duffield) *a towards rr* **40/1**

1m 30.83s (2.81) **Going Correction** +0.45s/f (Yiel) **10** Ran SP% **123.3**
Speed ratings (Par 99):101,88,85,84,82 80,75,72,71,69
CSF £26.98 CT £92.77 TOTE £6.50: £2.10, £2.40, £1.90; EX 34.70 Trifecta £410.10 Pool: £618.13 - 1.07 winning tickets. Place 6 £169.96, Place 5 £56.93.
Owner Guy Reed **Bred** G Reed **Trained** Hambleton, N Yorks

FOCUS
A modest yet competitive handicap according to the market, but yet another race dominated by a front-runner who ended up routing his field. As a result the form, rated around the first two, has to be treated with some caution.
Perfect Courtesy(IRE) Official explanation: jockey said gelding was unsuited by the soft (good to soft places) ground
T/Jkpt: Not won. T/Plt: £447.50 to a £1 stake. Pool: £81,839.50. 133.50 winning tickets. T/Qpdt: £131.90 to a £1 stake. Pool: £4,172.00. 23.40 winning tickets. JR

2911 WARWICK (L-H)

Thursday, June 28

OFFICIAL GOING: Good to soft (soft in places; 6.0)
Wind: Fresh, behind Weather: Cloudy with sunny spells

3030 SYSTIMAX SOLUTIONS AND ABLE DATA MEDIAN AUCTION MAIDEN STKS 5f

2:20 (2:20) (Class 5) 2-Y-O **£3,238** (£963; £481; £240) **Stalls** Centre

Form RPR

6 **1** **Weet A Surprise**[45] 1728 2-8-12 0.... FergusSweeney 4 64
(R Hollinshead) *chsd ldr: rdn over 1f out: r.o to ld wl ins fnl f* **8/1**

4 **2** *1/2* **Lambrini Lace (IRE)**[12] 2651 2-8-7 0.... TolleyDean[(5)] 2 62
(Mrs L Williamson) *led: rdn over 1f out: hdd wl ins fnl f* **7/2**[3]

003 **3** *1 1/2* **A Wish For You**[12] 2663 2-8-12 0.... KerrinMcEvoy 1 57
(D K Ivory) *chsd ldrs: rdn whn lost action crossing path over 1f out: styd on same pce* **2/1**[2]

4 *1* **Know No Fear** 2-9-3 0.... GrahamGibbons 5 58
(J J Quinn) *wnt rt s: sn chsng ldrs: rdn over 1f out: no ex* **15/8**[1]

5 *2 1/2* **Avian Flew** 2-8-12 0.... ChrisCatlin 3 44
(J A Pickering) *s.s: sn in tch: bhd fnl 3f* **12/1**

61.59 secs (2.19) **Going Correction** 0.0s/f (Good) **5** Ran SP% **109.1**
Speed ratings (Par 93):82,81,78,77,73
CSF £34.13 TOTE £8.20: £4.50, £1.50; EX 31.60.
Owner Ed Weetman (haulage & Storage) Ltd **Bred** Longdon Stud Ltd **Trained** Upper Longdon, Staffs
■ Stewards' Enquiry : Tolley Dean one-day ban: used whip in incorrect place (Jul 14)

FOCUS
A moderate juvenile maiden and the form is pretty shaky rated through the third. The principals raced down the middle of the track in the straight.

NOTEBOOK
Weet A Surprise improved significantly on the form she showed when only sixth in a Wolverhampton claimer on her debut, even if this was a pretty weak maiden. She should not be too harshly treated for nurseries. (op 12-1)
Lambrini Lace(IRE) showed good early speed, but she soon looked vulnerable and did not really improve a great deal on the form she showed first time up at Bath. (op 10-3)
A Wish For You was the clear form pick beforehand and she looked the most likely winner until losing her action when attempting to jump the path around a furlong from the finish. Official explanation: jockey said filly stumbled a furlong out (op 13-8)
Know No Fear, a half-brother to multiple sprint winner Thoughtsofstardom, out of a 5f juvenile scorer, was heavily supported to make a winning debut, but he showed real signs on inexperience when veering right coming out of the stalls and never posed a serious threat. This represents very modest form, but he has presumably been showing something at home and is open to improvement. (op 2-1 after 9-4 in places, tchd 13-8)
Avian Flew, a 3,500gns first foal of a half-sister to six winners, showed just moderate form on her racecourse debut, but she can be expected to come on for the run. (op 16-1 tchd 20-1)

3031 SYSTIMAX SOLUTIONS AND BAILEY TESWAINE MAIDEN FILLIES' STKS 6f

2:50 (2:50) (Class 5) 3-Y-O+ **£3,238** (£963; £481; £240) **Stalls** Centre

Form RPR

4-22 **1** **Excessive**[26] 2242 3-8-12 64.... KerrinMcEvoy 2 54
(W Jarvis) *chsd ldr: led 4f out: rdn and hung rt over 1f out: styd on u.p* **4/6**[1]

06 **2** *1 1/2* **Navene (IRE)**[19] 2470 3-8-12 0.... IanMongan 5 49
(C F Wall) *hld up in tch: rdn over 2f out: styd on* **8/1**[3]

5 **3** *nk* **Bold Bobby**[14] 2606 3-8-12 0.... RichardHughes 6 49
(J M P Eustace) *led: hdd 4f out: rdn over 2f out: hung lft fr over 1f out: styd on same pce* **7/2**[2]

6000 **4** *1/2* **Task Complete**[38] 1899 4-9-5 44.... StephenCarson 1 49
(Jean-Rene Auvray) *chsd ldrs: outpcd 2f out: styd on ins fnl f* **25/1**

5 *1 1/4* **Lempicka** 3-8-12 0.... GrahamGibbons 4 43
(J J Quinn) *s.i.s and hmpd s: sn chsng ldrs: rdn and hung lft 2f out: no ex ins fnl f* **11/1**

-000 **6** *5* **Maiden Investor**[5] 2878 4-9-5 45.... FergusSweeney 3 30
(M S Saunders) *chsd ldrs 4f* **50/1**

1m 14.27s (-0.01) **Going Correction** 0.0s/f (Good)
WFA 3 from 4yo 7lb **6** Ran SP% **107.5**
Speed ratings (Par 100):100,98,97,96,95 88
CSF £6.07 TOTE £1.50: £1.10, £2.30; EX 4.20.
Owner Mrs Susan Davis **Bred** John And Susan Davis **Trained** Newmarket, Suffolk

FOCUS
A very weak fillies' maiden with the form limited by the proximity of the fourth. They raced down the middle of the track in the straight.

3032 SYSTIMAX SOLUTIONS AND COMUNICA MEDIAN AUCTION MAIDEN STKS 7f 26y
3:20 (3:21) (Class 5) 3-5-Y-0 £3,238 (£963; £481; £240) Stalls Low

Form RPR
000 1 Poppets Sweetlove[11] [2693] 3-8-12 0 .... RichardHughes 4 48
(A B Haynes) *chsd ldr: rdn to ld ins fnl f: jst hld on* 12/1
3-65 2 *nk* Risque Heights[14] [2601] 3-9-3 68 ....(bt) SteveDrowne 2 52
(G A Butler) *s.s: hld up: rdn over 1f out: swtchd lft and r.o wl ins fnl f: jst failed* 5/2[2]
0-50 3 1 1/2 Musical Chimes[29] [2137] 4-9-4 41 .... LiamJones(3) 3 46
(W M Brisbourne) *led: rdn over 1f out: hdd and unable qckn ins fnl f* 50/1
50- 4 3/4 Greyfriars Abbey[237] [6316] 3-9-0 0 .... GregFairley(3) 1 46
(M Johnston) *s.i.s: sn chsng ldrs: rdn over 2f out: styd on same pce fnl f* 11/2[3]
22 5 1/2 Taghreed (IRE)[14] [2606] 3-8-12 0 .... KerrinMcEvoy 5 40
(W Jarvis) *trckd ldrs: plld hrd: rdn and nt clr run wl over 1f out: no ex ins fnl f* 5/6[1]
000- 6 28 Tay Bridge (IRE)[216] [6584] 4-9-9 25 .... DominicFox(3) 7 —
(G F Bridgwater) *prom 3f* 100/1

1m 28.98s (4.78) **Going Correction** +0.60s/f (Yiel)
WFA 3 from 4yo 9lb 6 Ran SP% **109.2**
Speed ratings (Par 103):96,95,93,93,92 60
CSF £39.76 TOTE £10.30: £2.80, £1.70; EX 39.80.
Owner Graham Robinson **Bred** G And Mrs Robinson **Trained** Limpley Stoke, Bath
FOCUS
The third-placed horse came into this rated just 41 and so this was clearly a moderate maiden.
Taghreed(IRE) Official explanation: jockey said filly ran too free and hung right-handed

3033 SYSTIMAX SOLUTIONS AND PTC SYSTEMS H'CAP 2m 39y
3:50 (3:50) (Class 5) (0-70,67) 4-Y-0+ £3,238 (£963; £481; £240) Stalls Low

Form RPR
0-06 1 Squiffy[23] [2345] 4-8-2 48 .... ChrisCatlin 1 58
(P D Cundell) *chsd ldr 10f: remained handy: rdn to ld 1f out: styd on wl* 7/1
605- 2 1 1/2 To Arms[13] [2762] 5-8-8 57 .... EmmettStack(3) 6 65
(K J Burke) *hld up: hdwy 6f out: led over 2f out: rdn and hdd 1f out: styd on same pce* 13/2
510- 3 3 Picacho (IRE)[56] [6027] 4-9-7 67 .... RichardHughes 8 71
(P J Hobbs) *chsd ldrs: lost pl 6f out: hdwy over 3f out: rdn over 1f out: hung rt and no ex fnl f* 4/1[2]
0-00 4 3 Turn 'n Burn[110] [662] 6-9-3 63 .... AdamKirby 9 64
(C A Cyzer) *wnt rt s: hld up: rdn 7f out: hdwy u.p over 1f out: nt trble ldrs* 16/1
1404 5 2 Treason Trial[11] [2686] 6-8-2 53 .... TolleyDean(5) 2 51
(Stef Liddiard) *hld up: racd keenly: hdwy 6f out: rdn over 2f out: wknd over 1f out* 13/2
-054 6 1 1/4 Coda Agency[8] [2770] 4-8-6 52 .... KerrinMcEvoy 4 49
(D W P Arbuthnot) *prom: chsd ldr 6f out tl rdn 3f out: wknd over 1f out* 7/2[1]
4142 7 2 1/2 York Cliff[6] [2825] 9-8-11 60 .... LiamJones(3) 3 54
(W M Brisbourne) *hld up: rdn and wknd over 3f out* 5/1[3]
3516 8 3/4 Eforetta (GER)[29] [2148] 5-9-6 66 .... SamHitchcott 5 59
(D J Wintle) *led: rdn and hdd over 2f out: wknd over 1f out* 11/1

3m 39.78s (7.08) **Going Correction** +0.60s/f (Yiel) 8 Ran SP% **112.3**
Speed ratings (Par 103):106,105,103,102,101 100,99,99
CSF £49.54 CT £205.12 TOTE £10.00: £2.10, £2.30, £1.50; EX 48.30.
Owner Nigel Johnson-Hill **Bred** Roden House Stud **Trained** Compton, Berks
FOCUS
A modest staying handicap in which very few landed a telling blow, but the form looks sound rated around the placed horses. They raced middle to stands' side in the straight.
Turn 'n Burn Official explanation: jockey said gelding never travelled; trainer said gelding lost a shoe

3034 SYSTIMAX SOLUTIONS LEADS BY A MILE H'CAP 1m 22y
4:20 (4:20) (Class 5) (0-70,69) 3-Y-0+ £3,562 (£1,059; £529; £264) Stalls Low

Form RPR
4022 1 The Grey One (IRE)[7] [2809] 4-9-3 63 ....(p) KevinGhunowa(5) 4 70
(J M Bradley) *hld up: stmbld over 3f out: hdwy over 2f out: rdn over 1f out: r.o to ld post* 9/2[2]
2240 2 *shd* Danawi (IRE)[15] [2556] 4-8-10 51 .... ChrisCatlin 7 58
(M R Hoad) *led: rdn over 2f out: hdd post* 12/1
6520 3 1 1/4 Pelham Crescent (IRE)[47] [1666] 4-8-12 56 ......(b) RichardKingscote(3) 8 60
(B Palling) *s.s: outpcd: hdwy u.p over 1f out: r.o* 14/1
-003 4 *hd* Feeling Wonderful (IRE)[8] [2767] 3-8-11 65 .... GregFairley(3) 2 67
(M Johnston) *chsd ldrs: rdn over 2f out: ev ch ins fnl f: no ex towards fin* 9/2[2]
0006 5 3 1/2 Panshir (FR)[9] [2745] 6-8-6 50 oh4 ....(t) MarcHalford(3) 9 46
(Mrs C A Dunnett) *hld up in tch: lost pl and nt clr run over 3f out: hdwy over 2f out: sn rdn: wknd fnl f* 12/1
0001 6 1 3/4 Apache Nation (IRE)[7] [2809] 4-9-0 58 6ex .... LiamJones(3) 6 50
(M Dods) *chsd ldrs: rdn over 3f out: styd on same pce fnl 2f* 9/4[1]
1115 7 3/4 Very Well Red[21] [2388] 4-9-7 69 .... WilliamCarson(7) 3 59
(P W Hiatt) *chsd ldrs: rdn over 2f out: wknd over 1f out* 5/1[3]
0503 8 1 Attacca[6] [2827] 6-8-9 50 oh4 .... DO'Donohoe 5 38
(J R Weymes) *prom tl rdn and wknd over 1f out* 9/1

1m 43.12s (3.52) **Going Correction** +0.60s/f (Yiel)
WFA 3 from 4yo+ 10lb 8 Ran SP% **115.9**
Speed ratings (Par 103):106,105,104,104,100 99,98,97
CSF £56.60 CT £706.95 TOTE £6.70: £2.00, £2.30, £2.70; EX 55.80.
Owner R Miles **Bred** Blackdown Stud **Trained** Sedbury, Gloucs
FOCUS
A modest handicap that looks solid enough rated around the principals. They raced towards the stands' side in the straight.
Pelham Crescent(IRE) Official explanation: jockey said gelding missed the break

3035 SYSTIMAX SOLUTIONS AND ROYCE COMMUNICATIONS H'CAP 1m 2f 188y
4:50 (4:50) (Class 6) (0-60,60) 3-Y-0+ £2,730 (£806; £403) Stalls Low

Form RPR
3405 1 Cavendish[17] [2520] 3-8-11 57 ....(b) RichardHughes 11 65
(J M P Eustace) *led: hdd 8f out: led again over 3f out: hung lft 2f out: sn rdn clr: hung rt nr fin: all out* 14/1
0305 2 1/2 Key Partners (IRE)[17] [2519] 6-9-9 56 .... GeorgeBaker 1 64+
(J T Stimpson) *hld up in tch: nt clr run over 3f out: rdn to chse wnr over 1f out: r.o: hmpd nr fin* 9/2[1]
0-03 3 1 1/2 Marquee (IRE)[38] [1894] 3-8-4 55 .... KevinGhunowa(5) 7 60
(P A Blockley) *hld up: hdwy over 2f out: rdn and hung lft over 1f out: styd on same pce ins fnl f* 9/1
0004 4 10 Orpen Quest (IRE)[1] [2980] 5-8-13 46 oh1 ....(p) PaulFitzsimons 10 34
(M J Attwater) *chsd ldrs: rdn over 2f out: wknd over 1f out* 12/1
-032 5 *nk* Sharmy (IRE)[10] [2721] 11-9-9 56 .... TPO'Shea 9 43
(Ian Williams) *hld up: hdwy 1/2-way: nt clr run over 3f out: sn rdn: wknd over 1f out* 6/1[2]
-204 6 3 Justcallmehandsome[10] [2721] 5-8-7 47 .... LauraReynolds(7) 4 29
(D J S Ffrench Davis) *hld up: rdn over 1f out: nvr trbld ldrs* 11/1
0460 7 1 Rawaabet (IRE)[2] [2967] 5-8-7 47 .... WilliamCarson(7) 12 28
(P W Hiatt) *s.s: bhd: nvr nrr* 13/2[3]
5-66 8 2 English Archer[10] [2721] 4-8-10 46 oh1 .... LiamJones(3) 16 23
(W M Brisbourne) *hld up: hdwy u.p over 3f out: hung lft and wknd wl over 1f out* 14/1
-000 9 *nk* Makfly[16] [2531] 4-9-5 52 .... GrahamGibbons 13 29
(R Hollinshead) *hld up: rdn and wknd over 2f out* 12/1
5003 10 3 1/2 Snake Hips[31] [2084] 3-8-10 59 ....(b) RichardKingscote(3) 5 30
(B Palling) *hld up in tch: rdn and wknd over 2f out* 15/2
50/0 11 4 Don Jose (USA)[24] [2312] 4-9-12 59 .... DO'Donohoe 15 23
(N J Vaughan) *chsd ldrs: rdn over 4f out: wknd over 2f out* 33/1
0-00 12 3 Safari[16] [2540] 4-8-10 46 oh1 ....(b) EmmettStack(3) 6 5
(A J Chamberlain) *prom: chsd ldr over 2f out: rdn: hung lft and wknd over 1f out* 100/1
0-06 13 6 Hopeful Isabella (IRE)[38] [1894] 3-8-0 46 oh1 .... ChrisCatlin 14 —
(Sir Mark Prescott) *chsd ldr: led 8f out: hdd over 3f out: rdn and wknd over 2f out* 6/1[2]
000 14 *nk* Highbourne Lady[24] [2308] 3-7-11 46 oh1 .... DominicFox(3) 8 —
(B N Pollock) *bhd fnl 8f* 100/1

2m 23.93s (4.53) **Going Correction** +0.60s/f (Yiel)
WFA 3 from 4yo+ 13lb 14 Ran SP% **123.8**
Speed ratings (Par 101):107,106,105,98,98 95,95,93,93,90 88,85,81,81
CSF £77.87 CT £620.69 TOTE £13.00: £4.00, £3.00, £3.20; EX 147.70.
Owner The Cavendish Partnership **Bred** Mrs S Clifford **Trained** Newmarket, Suffolk
■ Stewards' Enquiry : Richard Hughes caution: careless riding
FOCUS
Just a moderate handicap and the form is not solid, although it was quite a decent winning time for a race of its class. They were spread out all over the track at the line, with Cavendish the first horse of the day to win racing against the far rail.
Rawaabet(IRE) Official explanation: jockey said gelding missed the break

3036 BOLLINGER CHAMPAGNE CHALLENGE SERIES H'CAP (FOR GENTLEMAN AMATEUR RIDERS) 1m 4f 134y
5:20 (5:20) (Class 5) (0-70,65) 4-Y-0+ £3,123 (£968; £484; £242) Stalls Low

Form RPR
1432 1 Trafalgar Day[6] [2824] 4-10-13 59 .... MrBenBrisbourne(5) 3 73
(W M Brisbourne) *hld up: hdwy 1/2-way: led over 2f out: rdn clr fnl f* 8/11[1]
2503 2 7 Scottish River (USA)[14] [2603] 8-11-8 63 .... MrLeeNewnes 4 66
(M D I Usher) *hld up: hdwy over 4f out: rdn to chse wnr fnl f: no imp* 4/1[2]
3540 3 5 Agilete[10] [2716] 5-11-0 58 .... MrSPearce(3) 8 53
(J Pearce) *hld up: hdwy over 7f out: ev ch over 2f out: sn rdn: wknd fnl f* 6/1[3]
-000 4 5 James Street (IRE)[14] [2603] 4-11-3 65 .... RyanHill(7) 2 52
(J R Best) *trckd ldrs: plld hrd: wknd over 3f out* 10/1
0005 5 3 Royal Sailor (IRE)[10] [2716] 5-9-11 45 ....(p) MrDavidMcMinn(7) 6 27
(J Ryan) *chsd ldrs 9f* 20/1
000/ 6 3 End Of An Error[21] [3576] 8-10-4 48 ow3 ....(v) MrMJJSmith(3) 7 25
(G F Bridgwater) *sn led: clr 10f out: wknd and hdd wl over 2f out: sn hung lft* 33/1
0/00 7 2 1/2 Chisel[6] [2825] 6-9-11 45 .... MrJPearce(7) 5 18
(M Wigham) *bhd fnl 8f* 50/1
0600 8 2 1/2 Bournonville[6] [2825] 4-9-13 45 .... MrSRees(5) 1 14
(M Wigham) *chsd ldrs: hmpd after 1f: rdn 7f out: rdn to ld wl over 2f out: sn hdd & wknd* 18/1

2m 54.37s (10.77) **Going Correction** +0.60s/f (Yiel) 8 Ran SP% **116.2**
Speed ratings (Par 103):90,85,82,79,77 75,74,72
CSF £3.86 CT £10.00 TOTE £1.60: £1.10, £1.40, £1.50; EX 4.90 Place 6 £557.79, Place 5 £111.05.
Owner Mrs C P Lees-Jones **Bred** Major W R Paton-Smith **Trained** Great Ness, Shropshire
FOCUS
Considering this was a handicap, it was a very uncompetitive race with five of the eight runners starting at double-figure prices and the red-hot favourite scoring as he liked, so the form is not solid and probably means very little. The early pace was strong, but those that helped force it eventually fell in a heap and, as in some of the earlier races, the runners mostly came up the middle of the track in the home straight.
T/Plt: £545.70 to a £1 stake. Pool: £42,201.45. 56.45 winning tickets. T/Qpdt: £175.70 to a £1 stake. Pool: £3,064.40. 12.90 winning tickets. CR

2745 YARMOUTH (L-H)
Thursday, June 28

OFFICIAL GOING: Good to soft (good in places in home straight; 7.3)
Wind: Almost nil Weather: Sunny

3037 EDP MEDIAN AUCTION MAIDEN STKS 6f 3y
2:10 (2:12) (Class 6) 2-Y-0 £2,914 (£867; £324; £324) Stalls High

Form RPR
4 1 Artsu[17] [2510] 2-9-3 0 .... JamieSpencer 2 73+
(M L W Bell) *prom: led wl over 1f out: racd awkwardly whn drvn but a jst holding rival* 13/8[1]
2 *hd* Harbour Blues 2-9-3 0 .... DarrylHolland 5 72
(C E Brittain) *s.s: prog 1/2-way: chsd wnr hrd fr over 1f out: rn green but kpt on wl* 11/1
0 3 5 Black Duke[53] [1498] 2-9-3 0 .... JimmyQuinn 6 57
(M G Quinlan) *prom: rdn and outpcd by ldng pair over 1f out* 11/1
3 *dht* Craggy Cat (IRE) 2-9-3 0 .... TedDurcan 4 57
(L M Cumani) *t.k.h: chsd ldrs: rn green and outpcd 2f out: kpt on ins fnl f but no threat* 4/1[2]
5 5 3/4 Metal Madness (IRE)[14] [2604] 2-9-0 0 .... JerryO'Dwyer(3) 3 55
(M G Quinlan) *chsd ldrs: rdn over 1f out: one pce and sn btn* 11/1
6 *nk* Vive Les Rouges 2-8-12 0 .... EddieAhern 8 49
(C F Wall) *got loose paddock: t.k.h in rr: outpcd 1/2-way: sme late prog* 7/1[3]

0 **7** *hd* **Race The Moon (IRE)**[32] [2056] 2-9-3 0 .... AntonyProcter 9 54
(V Smith) *taken down early: led tl rdn and hdd wl over 1f out: one pce fnl f* **8/1**

6 **8** *8* **Culzean Bay**[14] [2605] 2-8-12 0 .... MickyFenton 1 25
(A Bailey) *chsd ldrs tl rdn 1/2-way: sn struggling* **100/1**

9 *1/2* **Lunatico (GER)** 2-9-3 0 .... JimCrowley 10 28
(S C Williams) *towards rr: lost tch 1/2-way* **20/1**

0 **10** *hd* **Cobbold Point**[9] [2739] 2-8-10 0 .... NSLawes(7) 7 28
(M W Easterby) *chsd ldrs: rdn 1/2-way: sn struggling* **50/1**

1m 17.44s (3.74) **Going Correction** +0.50s/f (Yiel) **10** Ran SP% **114.4**

Speed ratings (Par 91):95,94,88,88,87 86,86,75,75,74

WIN: £2.30. PL: £1.02, £3.30, Black Duke £2.20, Craggy Cat £1.10. EX: £17.60. CSF: £20.59..

Owner Mrs Moira Gershinson **Bred** Lady Whent **Trained** Newmarket, Suffolk

FOCUS

An ordinary maiden which is hard to rate, but the first two came nicely clear.

NOTEBOOK

Artsu, who was the only one to make the first seven from a single-figure draw at Windsor on his debut, had less to do in this company, and both he and the runner-up came well clear in the closing stages. He looks a likely type for nurseries and his future lies in the hands of the Handicapper. (op 11-8 tchd 7-4 in a place)

Harbour Blues, who is a half-brother to Sparkling Eyes, a dual 5f winner at two and three, pulled clear with the more experienced winner, and with this run under his belt he should be able to win a race, if kept to a realistic level. (op 12-1)

Black Duke, a half-brother to Fairfield Princess, a 5f winner at two, showed more pace than on his debut, and the ground was probably of assistance to this son of Diktat. (op 10-3)

Craggy Cat(IRE), who cost 160,000euros, is a half-brother to Biens Nanti, a dual 1m2f winner at three and later a winner over jumps in France, and winning miler Striking. Showing signs of inexperience on his debut, he looks likely to derive plenty from this run, and another furlong is likely to suit him. (op 10-3)

Metal Madness(IRE) has now run twice on softish ground but, being by Acclamation, the suspicion is that he will be better when he gets to hear his hooves rattle. (op 8-1 tchd 12-1)

Vive Les Rouges, whose dam won three times between 7f and 1m1f, was keen enough on her debut and hails from a stable whose juveniles tend to need their debut outings. (op 8-1)

3038 NORFOLK AND NELSON MUSEUM H'CAP 6f 3y

2:40 (2:40) (Class 5) (0-75,75) 3-Y-O **£4,210** (£1,252; £625; £312) **Stalls** High

Form RPR

-450 **1** **Kind Of Fizzy**[13] [2622] 3-8-8 **62** .... TedDurcan 4 67
(Rae Guest) *chsd ldrs: drvn over 2f out: outpcd briefly: rallied ins fnl f: urged ahd cl home* **14/1**

-046 **2** *1/2* **Miss Ippolita**[15] [2570] 3-9-7 **75** .... DarryllHolland 6 78
(J R Jenkins) *plld hrd and disp 2nd: led over 1f out: hrd drvn and racd awkwardly: edgd lft and hdd 50yds out* **7/1**[3]

-000 **3** *3/4* **Disco Dan**[15] [2570] 3-9-4 **72** ....(p) JimmyQuinn 3 73
(D M Simcock) *t.k.h chsng ldrs: effrt to chal 1f out: rdn and one pce after* **17/2**

-001 **4** *1 3/4* **Kondakova (IRE)**[17] [2515] 3-9-6 **74** .... JamieSpencer 7 70
(M L W Bell) *t.k.h: hld up in last: effrt 2f out: racd awkwardly 1f out: sn no ex* **9/4**[1]

20-4 **5** *3/4* **Beautiful Madness (IRE)**[9] [2749] 3-8-9 **66** .... JerryO'Dwyer(3) 1 59
(M G Quinlan) *led tl rdn and hdd over 1f out: sn btn* **4/1**[2]

5-35 **6** *2 1/2* **Futuristic Dragon (IRE)**[48] [1635] 3-8-8 **62** .... FrankieMcDonald 2 48
(P A Blockley) *v excited in paddock: pressed ldrs tl rdn and wknd 1f out: eased cl home* **9/4**[1]

1m 16.25s (2.55) **Going Correction** +0.50s/f (Yiel) **6** Ran SP% **111.2**

Speed ratings (Par 99):103,102,101,99,98 94

CSF £99.83 TOTE £18.80: £3.20, £2.00; EX 132.80.

Owner The Luminaries **Bred** Theakston Stud **Trained** Newmarket, Suffolk

FOCUS

Modest handicap form but probably sound rated around the first two.

Futuristic Dragon(IRE) Official explanation: jockey said colt was very coltish

3039 GREAT YARMOUTH MERCURY H'CAP 1m 3y

3:10 (3:11) (Class 4) (0-85,82) 4-Y-O+ **£5,413** (£1,619; £809; £404; £201) **Stalls** High

Form RPR

000- **1** **Mineral Star (IRE)**[287] [5320] 5-8-9 **70** .... JimmyQuinn 7 79
(M H Tompkins) *stdd in rr: hdwy 2f out: led over 1f out: drvn and kpt on gamely after: all out* **9/1**

0003 **2** *shd* **Direct Debit (IRE)**[6] [2835] 4-9-7 **82** .... JamieSpencer 3 91
(M L W Bell) *stdd s: effrt 2f out: chsd wnr hrd and ev ch fr over 1f out: jst hld* **3/1**[1]

4-00 **3** *1* **Press The Button (GER)**[27] [2209] 4-9-3 **78** .... TedDurcan 5 85
(J R Boyle) *2nd tl led over 2f out: hdd over 1f out: drvn and kpt on ins fnl f* **4/1**[3]

1243 **4** *2 1/2* **Luckylover**[10] [2719] 4-9-0 **78** ....(t) JerryO'Dwyer(3) 2 79
(M G Quinlan) *led tl hrd rdn and hdd over 2f out: sn lost pl: btn over 1f out* **7/2**[2]

-650 **5** *1 1/4* **Daniel Thomas (IRE)**[20] [2427] 5-9-4 **79** ....(e) JimCrowley 1 77
(Mrs A J Perrett) *towards rr: n.d fnl 2f* **8/1**

6-44 **6** *1/2* **Boundless Prospect (USA)**[149] [308] 8-9-3 **78** .... DarryllHolland 8 75
(Miss Gay Kelleway) *chsd ldrs: u.p 2f out: sn btn* **12/1**

4162 **7** *hd* **Oscar Snowman**[17] [2512] 4-9-2 **77** ....(p) EddieAhern 6 74
(M P Tregoning) *chsd ldrs: effrt 2f out: sn rdn: nt run on fnl f* **5/1**

1m 42.89s (2.99) **Going Correction** +0.50s/f (Yiel) **7** Ran SP% **112.7**

Speed ratings (Par 105):105,104,103,101,100 99,99

CSF £35.06 CT £125.60 TOTE £11.00: £3.20, £3.10; EX 45.40.

Owner Mineral Star Partnership **Bred** Lee Valley Farm **Trained** Newmarket, Suffolk

FOCUS

Not a bad little handicap and the form looks sound enough.

Boundless Prospect(USA) Official explanation: jockey said gelding moved poorly

3040 SCROBY SANDS (S) H'CAP 1m 2f 21y

3:40 (3:41) (Class 6) (0-65,58) 3-Y-O **£1,943** (£578; £288; £144) **Stalls** Low

Form RPR

-004 **1** **Miss Havisham (IRE)**[10] [2709] 3-9-0 **45** .... DarryllHolland 5 51+
(J R Weymes) *stdd s: hld up in last tl 3f out: stdy run to ld ins fnl f: sn clr but idling w ears pricked* **5/1**[3]

0-00 **2** *2* **Roxy Singer**[7] [2801] 3-9-0 **45** ....(v[1]) DavidKinsella 4 46
(W J Musson) *stdd s: clsd 3f out to ld wl over 2f out: sn rdn: hdd ins fnl f: no ch w wnr* **8/1**

560 **3** *3 1/2* **Celtic Memories (IRE)**[7] [2793] 3-9-7 **52** ....(b) TedDurcan 3 46
(M W Easterby) *pressed ldr: hrd rdn over 2f out: nt keen after: wknd over 1f out* **11/2**

5-01 **4** *1 1/4* **Flying Grey (IRE)**[1] [2978] 3-9-10 **58** 6ex .... JerryO'Dwyer(3) 6 50
(P A Blockley) *settled towards rr: effrt 3f out: sn rdn: wknd over 1f out* **10/3**[1]

-350 **5** *1 1/2* **Three No Trumps**[37] [1928] 3-9-0 **45** .... JimmyQuinn 1 34
(P S Felgate) *pressed ldrs: drvn over 2f out: little rspnse and sn btn* **16/1**

00-0 **6** *5* **Rotation (IRE)**[28] [2192] 3-9-0 **45** .... EddieAhern 8 24
(J W Hills) *dwlt: sn chsng ldrs: hrd rdn 3f out: nt run on* **4/1**[2]

5052 **7** *shd* **Firebird Annie (IRE)**[9] [2747] 3-9-6 **51** ....(v[1]) MickyFenton 7 29
(A Bailey) *led: drvn and hdd wl over 2f out: nt keen and sn gave up* **6/1**

0-01 **8** *12* **Joint Expectations (IRE)**[9] [2747] 3-9-6 **51** 6ex ....(b) DMylonas 2 5
(Mrs C A Dunnett) *t.k.h early: chsd ldrs 6f: t.o and eased ins fnl f* **9/1**

2m 17.45s (9.35) **Going Correction** +0.50s/f (Yiel) **8** Ran SP% **116.4**

Speed ratings (Par 97):82,80,77,76,75 71,71,61

CSF £44.93 CT £228.79 TOTE £6.70: £1.80, £2.60, £2.20; EX 39.70.The winner was bought in for 5,800gns. Celtic Memories was subject to a friendly claim.

Owner High Moor Racing 1 **Bred** Downfield Cottage Stud **Trained** Middleham Moor, N Yorks

FOCUS

A weak race run in a very slow winning time, even for a seller. However, the form appears sound enough.

3041 EVENING NEWS MEDIAN AUCTION MAIDEN STKS 1m 3f 101y

4:10 (4:11) (Class 5) 3-4-Y-O **£3,238** (£963; £481; £240) **Stalls** Low

Form RPR

-204 **1** **Tempelstern (GER)**[28] [2185] 3-8-13 80 ....(b[1]) TedDurcan 1 86+
(H R A Cecil) *mde all at brisk pce: pushed clr 2f out: eased ins fnl f: unchal* **10/11**[1]

0436 **2** *8* **Natural Action**[10] [2727] 3-8-13 70 .... DarryllHolland 4 71+
(W Jarvis) *chsd ldrs: drvn to go 2nd 3f out: outpcd over 2f out: in hopeless pursuit of wnr after* **9/2**[3]

4 **3** *5* **Woolfall Rose**[22] [2359] 3-8-8 0 .... NeilPollard 7 54
(G G Margarson) *bhd: drvn 4f out: outpcd 3f out: plodded on ins fnl f* **12/1**

36 **4** *11* **Crispian (IRE)**[26] [2253] 3-8-13 0 .... JamieSpencer 6 40
(W J Haggas) *chsd wnr: hrd drvn 4f out: lost 2nd 3f out and fdd v bdly: t.o* **3/1**[2]

0306 **5** *10* **Fizzy Bella**[7] [2801] 3-8-8 65 .... EddieAhern 3 18
(M G Quinlan) *uns rdr at s: chsd ldrs: drvn 4f out: sn btn: fin v feebly and wl t.o* **12/1**

6 **6** *10* **Spring Creek**[16] [2535] 3-8-2 0 ow1 .... NSLawes(7) 2 2
(M W Easterby) *racd in last: t.o over 3f out* **50/1**

0-0 **7** *27* **Young Emma**[40] [1849] 4-9-7 0 ....(v[1]) MickyFenton 5 —
(G G Margarson) *towards rr: hopelessly t.o fnl 4f* **66/1**

2m 31.51s (4.01) **Going Correction** +0.50s/f (Yiel)

WFA 3 from 4yo 13lb **7** Ran SP% **114.4**

Speed ratings (Par 103):105,99,95,87,80 73,53

CSF £5.51 TOTE £1.80: £1.30, £3.10; EX 5.00.

Owner Ennismore Racing I **Bred** Dr O Herminghaus **Trained** Newmarket, Suffolk

FOCUS

An uncompetitive maiden in which the odds-on favourite dominated throughout and not a race to get carried away with.

3042 BBC RADIO NORFOLK H'CAP 1m 2f 21y

4:40 (4:40) (Class 5) (0-70,70) 4-Y-O+ **£3,238** (£963; £481; £240) **Stalls** Low

Form RPR

-004 **1** **Lady Romanov (IRE)**[6] [2833] 4-9-7 **70** .... JimmyQuinn 7 79
(M H Tompkins) *prom: led wl over 1f out: rdn and styd on wl fnl f: readily* **11/1**

0036 **2** *3* **Danzare**[12] [2656] 5-7-13 **53** .... WilliamBuick(5) 8 56
(J L Spearing) *cl up: tk slt ld over 3f out tl wl over 1f out: nt qckn after* **15/2**

000 **3** *1* **Grandad Bill (IRE)**[22] [2370] 4-8-2 **51** oh1 .... DavidKinsella 3 52+
(W J Musson) *bhd: stl last over 3f out: stdy prog after: kpt on wout threatening: snatched 3rd nr fin* **9/1**

34-4 **4** *nk* **Mitanni (USA)**[17] [2514] 4-9-4 **67** .... JimCrowley 5 67
(Mrs A J Perrett) *prom: rdn and ev ch fr 3f out tl over 1f out: fading ins fnl f* **10/3**[1]

0030 **5** *3 1/2* **Alsadaa (USA)**[7] [2810] 4-9-2 **65** .... TedDurcan 6 58
(M W Easterby) *towards rr: effrt over 2f out: sn rdn and no imp after* **12/1**

-054 **6** *3* **Rawdon (IRE)**[26] [2238] 6-9-7 **70** ....(v) HayleyTurner 4 57
(M L W Bell) *t.k.h early: midfield: rdn 4f out: little rspnse: btn 2f out* **7/2**[2]

0330 **7** *4* **Wee Charlie Castle (IRE)**[21] [2403] 4-8-6 **55** .... OscarUrbina 1 34
(G C H Chung) *midfield: drvn and btn 2f out* **9/2**[3]

/1-0 **8** *hd* **Sir Haydn**[8] [2765] 7-9-4 **67** .... EddieAhern 9 46
(J R Jenkins) *dwlt: towards rr: rdn 4f out: sn struggling* **20/1**

0060 **9** *31* **Faith And Reason (USA)**[17] [2512] 4-9-5 **68** ....(p) JamieSpencer 2 —
(B J Curley) *led tl hdd over 3f out: rapidly dropped out: t.o and eased* **13/2**

2m 14.56s (6.46) **Going Correction** +0.50s/f (Yiel) **9** Ran SP% **119.4**

Speed ratings (Par 103):94,91,90,90,87 85,82,82,57

CSF £93.38 CT £786.27 TOTE £17.00: £4.00, £3.20, £3.00; EX 108.60 Place 6 £1,232.04, Place 5 £897.13.

Owner P Heath, K Bowry, K Chapman **Bred** Rory Mathews **Trained** Newmarket, Suffolk

FOCUS

An ordinary handicap run in a moderate winning time for the grade but the form looks sound.

T/Plt: £619.80 to a £1 stake. Pool: £52,349.30. 61.65 winning tickets. T/Qpdt: £119.50 to a £1 stake. Pool: £3,585.70. 22.20 winning tickets. IM

2686 FOLKESTONE (R-H)

Friday, June 29

OFFICIAL GOING: Soft (6.3)

Wind: Strong, half behind Weather: cloudy and breezy

3043 SPEEDY MEDIAN AUCTION MAIDEN STKS 7f (S)

2:30 (2:33) (Class 5) 2-Y-O **£2,914** (£867; £433; £216) **Stalls** Low

Form RPR

22 **1** **Gypsy Baby (IRE)**[9] [2768] 2-8-12 0 .... RichardHughes 8 77+
(R Hannon) *trckd ldrs: gng wl: shkn up to ld and edgd rt 2f out: sn in command: easily* **11/10**[1]

44 **2** *5* **Midnite Blews (IRE)**[28] [2193] 2-9-3 0 .... DavidKinsella 12 66
(A B Haynes) *led: hdd and sltly hmpd 2f out: no ch w wnr after but hld on for 2nd* **12/1**

65 **3** *nk* **King Bathwick (IRE)**[25] [2303] 2-9-3 0 .... RobertHavlin 2 65
(B R Millman) *hld up in rr: rdn and effrt over 2f out: styd on fnl f: wnt 3rd nr fin: nvr nrr* **20/1**

4 *shd* **Carnival Queen** 2-8-12 0 .... JamieSpencer 5 60+
(J R Fanshawe) *hld up: hdwy 3f out: chsd ldrs and wandered 2f out: kpt on same pce* **7/1**[2]

5 hd **The Betchworth Kid** 2-9-3 0 .... HayleyTurner 6 64+
(M L W Bell) *s.i.s: bhd and pushed along after 2f: hdwy on far rail over 2f out: kpt on: nvr nrr* **7/1[2]**

0 6 5 **Redesdale**[7] 2832 2-9-3 0 .... DarryllHolland 11 52+
(P W D'Arcy) *s.i.s and bmpd s: racd in last pair: kpt on last 2f: nvr threatened ldrs* **7/1[2]**

05 7 ¾ **Marmite (IRE)**[24] 2344 2-8-12 0 .... SamHitchcott 9 45
(E F Vaughan) *in tch in midfield: rdn after 2f: outpcd 3f out: kpt on same pce* **40/1**

6 8 1¼ **Solent Ridge (IRE)**[17] 2539 2-9-3 0 .... JohnEgan 13 47
(J S Moore) *chsd ldr tl over 3f out: rdn and wknd wl over 2f out* **10/1[3]**

9 ¾ **Zen Factor** 2-9-3 0 .... JimCrowley 3 45
(J G Portman) *hld up towards rr: hdwy to chse ldrs over 3f out: rdn and wknd over 2f out* **50/1**

10 2½ **Birdsville** 2-8-7 0 .... PatrickHills[(5)] 7 33
(Rae Guest) *a bhd: no ch last 2f* **100/1**

11 5 **Totally Focussed (IRE)** 2-9-3 0 .... OscarUrbina 10 26
(S Dow) *chsd ldrs tl 3f out: sn wknd* **20/1**

00 12 shd **Hyper Viper (IRE)**[17] 2539 2-9-3 0 .... TPO'Shea 14 26
(J S Moore) *racd in midfield: rdn after 2f: wknd over 3f out* **33/1**

5 13 4 **Whatalotofbuts**[14] 2618 2-9-3 0 .... PatDobbs 4 16
(B De Haan) *chsd ldrs tl over 3f out: sn wknd* **66/1**

14 5 **Has To Be Abacus (IRE)** 2-9-3 0 .... DaneO'Neill 1 3
(A B Haynes) *s.i.s: a wl bhd* **20/1**

1m 32.29s (4.39) **Going Correction** +0.425s/f (Yiel) **14 Ran SP% 126.0**
Speed ratings (Par 93):91,85,84,84,84 78,78,76,75,72 67,67,62,56
CSF £15.45 TOTE £2.10: £1.20, £3.90, £4.90; EX 19.30 Trifecta £158.70 Pool: £270.52 - 1.21 winning tickets..
Owner M Sines **Bred** Harron Eakin Farms **Trained** East Everleigh, Wilts
■ Gypsy Baby was providing Richard Hannon with his 50th winner of the season.
■ Stewards' Enquiry : Richard Hughes caution: careless riding

FOCUS
An ordinary maiden won in good style by favourite, although she probably did not beat a great deal. The placed horses help set the standard.

NOTEBOOK
Gypsy Baby(IRE) has shown enough in two previous starts to suggest a race such as this was well within her capabilities, and she made short work of her rivals, handling the soft ground perfectly well and winning easily. She is clearly going the right way and it will be interesting to see what mark she gets for handicaps. (op 5-4 tchd 10-11)
Midnite Blews(IRE) comes from a yard which has been enjoying a fine run with its juveniles and he ran his best race to date, appreciating the step up to 7f and keeping on once headed. He is likely to find life easier in nurseries and still looks to be going the right way. Official explanation: jockey said gelding hung left (op 25-1)
King Bathwick(IRE) has progressed with each run as he has gone up in trip and this was another decent effort. He got going too late, having been in rear, but this was his third run and connections can now look forward to sending him handicapping.
Carnival Queen, her trainer's first juvenile runner of the season, was Spencer's only ride at the meeting, but her market drift suggested no fireworks were expected and she fell short. There was definite promise in the run though and normal improvement should see her getting more competitive in a similar heat next time. (op 9-2)
The Betchworth Kid ◆, a 31,000gns son of Tobougg and a good-looking colt, comes from a stable whose juveniles usually benefit from a run and he made quite a promising debut, keeping on well under pressure and finishing five lengths clear of the remainder. He looks sure to do better. (tchd 9-1)

3044 REDEC LTD MEDIAN AUCTION MAIDEN STKS 7f (S)
3:00 (3:02) (Class 5) 3-5-Y-0 **£3,071** (£906; £453) **Stalls Low**

Form RPR

6- 1 **Ventura (USA)**[246] 6186 3-8-9 0 .... RichardHughes 3 82
(Mrs A J Perrett) *hld up in midfield: hdwy to chse ldr 3f out: rdn to ld over 1f out: sn in command: rdn out* **11/10[1]**

0-5 2 8 **Orchestrator (IRE)**[14] 2625 3-9-0 0 .... DaneO'Neill 4 69+
(T G Mills) *led: clr after 2f: hdd over 1f out: no ch w wnr after* **15/8[2]**

2- 3 3 **The Cool Sandpiper**[313] 4624 3-9-0 0 .... JimCrowley 1 57
(P Winkworth) *chsd ldrs: rdn over 3f out: sn no imp* **7/1[3]**

0-60 4 7 **Straight Gal (IRE)**[70] 1120 4-8-13 47 .... PatrickHills[(5)] 6 33
(Mrs N Smith) *hld up in tch: rdn 3f out: sn wl outpcd* **12/1**

5 3 **Fine Art World (IRE)** 3-8-7 0 .... BradleyRoper[(7)] 7 30
(N A Callaghan) *stdd s: hld up: rdn over 3f out: sn t.o* **12/1**

0-04 6 7 **Port Luanda (IRE)**[3] 2962 3-9-0 40 .... JohnEgan 8 11
(R M Flower) *chsd ldr tl 3f out: sn wknd: t.o* **50/1**

00 7 9 **Vive La Chasse (IRE)**[39] 1901 4-8-11 0 .... (b[1]) ThomasO'Brien[(7)] 5 —
(Eve Johnson Houghton) *sn rdn and tk no interest: t.o after 2f* **33/1**

1m 30.01s (2.11) **Going Correction** +0.425s/f (Yiel)
WFA 3 from 4yo 9lb **7 Ran SP% 115.2**
Speed ratings (Par 103):104,94,91,83,80 72,61
CSF £3.40 TOTE £2.10: £1.40, £1.20; EX 4.50 Trifecta £9.90 Pool: £454.80 - 32.36 winning tickets..
Owner K Abdulla **Bred** Juddmonte Farms Inc **Trained** Pulborough, W Sussex

FOCUS
A weak maiden won in impressive fashion by the useful-looking Ventura. The form looks reasonable, rated through the runner-up, with the winner up 8lb.

3045 FORD THUNDER AT INVICTA MOTORS CLAIMING STKS 6f
3:30 (3:30) (Class 6) 3-Y-0+ **£2,730** (£806; £403) **Stalls Low**

Form RPR

0105 1 **Majestical (IRE)**[3] 2966 5-8-10 50 .... (p) DarryllHolland 9 48
(V Smith) *t.k.h: hld up: hdwy on outer 2f out: rdn to ld narrowly jst over 1f out: drvn out* **7/2[3]**

02-0 2 hd **Milton's Keen**[24] 2336 4-9-6 55 .... JohnEgan 4 57
(John Berry) *trckd ldrs: nt clr run over 1f out tl ins fnl f: r.o wl last 100yds: wnt 2nd nr fin* **11/4[1]**

4452 3 nk **Ever Cheerful**[98] 734 6-9-8 52 .... (p) DaneO'Neill 2 58
(A B Haynes) *led tl jst over 1f out: edgd rt u.p fnl f: kpt on same pce* **3/1[2]**

56-2 4 2½ **Danehill Stroller (IRE)**[13] 2652 7-8-9 48 .... JerryO'Dwyer[(3)] 5 41
(A M Hales) *hld up in tch: effrt and short of room briefly 2f out: sn rdn: wknd last 100yds* **11/4[1]**

0050 5 2 **Princess Kai (IRE)**[31] 2104 6-8-5 39 .... (b) DavidKinsella 6 28
(R Ingram) *t.k.h: chsd ldr tl wl over 1f out: sn rdn and hanging rt: wknd ins fnl f* **25/1**

0004 6 1¾ **Tantien**[25] 2304 5-8-5 38 .... (p) TPO'Shea 3 22
(T Keddy) *hld up in last pair: rdn over 2f out: swtchd rt wl over 1f out: no imp after* **12/1**

1m 16.53s (2.93) **Going Correction** +0.425s/f (Yiel) **6 Ran SP% 112.1**
Speed ratings (Par 101):97,96,96,93,90 88
CSF £13.48 TOTE £4.40: £2.20, £1.80; EX 12.90 Trifecta £58.00 Pool: £236.36 - 2.89 winning tickets..Milton's Keen was claimed by M. Salaman for £10,000.
Owner Raymond Tooth **Bred** Sean Beston **Trained** Exning, Suffolk

FOCUS
A weak claimer, run at a strong race, and the front three were covered by a head and neck at the line. The form is rated through the runner-up backed up by the third.

3046 MC TRUCK & BUS MAIDEN STKS 5f
4:00 (4:07) (Class 5) 3-Y-0+ **£2,914** (£867; £433; £216) **Stalls Low**

Form RPR

-525 1 **Castano**[14] 2631 3-9-0 70 .... DarryllHolland 6 74
(B R Millman) *chsd ldr: led 2f out: clr over 1f out: easily* **7/4[1]**

0-0 2 5 **Water Margin (IRE)**[15] 2606 3-9-0 0 .... DaneO'Neill 5 56
(T G Mills) *chsd ldrs: rdn and effrt 2f out: chsd wnr over 1f out: no imp* **9/1**

45 3 1¾ **Glencal**[36] 1973 3-8-9 0 .... RobertHavlin 12 45
(H Morrison) *hld up and bhd: hdwy wl over 2f out: plugged on to go 3rd ins fnl f: no ch w wnr* **8/1**

0-0 4 ¾ **Contentious (IRE)**[53] 1541 3-8-2 0 .... KirstyMilczarek[(7)] 4 42
(D M Simcock) *taken down early: led tl 2f out: hanging rt after: kpt on but no ch w wnr* **20/1**

5-53 5 ½ **Galipette**[22] 2393 3-8-9 72 .... RichardHughes 8 40
(H R A Cecil) *chsd ldrs: ev ch 2f out: sn rdn: wknd qckly 1f out* **15/8[2]**

00-6 6 2½ **Madam Patti**[45] 1737 4-9-1 38 .... DavidKinsella 1 31
(R Ingram) *sn wl bhd: sme late hdwy: n.d* **100/1**

7 nk **Lawdy Miss Clawdy** 3-8-9 0 .... JimCrowley 2 30
(D W P Arbuthnot) *s.i.s: wl bhd: sme modest late hdwy: n.d* **33/1**

-025 8 6 **Lady Lafitte (USA)**[27] 2242 3-8-4 65 .... PatrickHills[(5)] 11 9
(B W Hills) *racd alone in centre for 2f: chsd ldrs tl rdn and wknd qckly over 2f out* **5/1[3]**

9 ¾ **Withywood (USA)** 3-8-9 0 .... PatDobbs 9 6
(G L Moore) *v s.i.s: a wl bhd* **25/1**

0-00 10 ½ **Brief Engagement (IRE)**[56] 1452 4-8-12 35 .... MarcHalford[(3)] 7 4
(T D McCarthy) *t.k.h early: chsd ldrs for over 1f: sn struggling: no ch last 2f* **100/1**

61.89 secs (1.09) **Going Correction** +0.425s/f (Yiel)
WFA 3 from 4yo 6lb **10 Ran SP% 122.5**
Speed ratings (Par 103):108,100,97,96,95 91,90,81,79,79
CSF £18.64 TOTE £3.10: £1.40, £3.00, £1.90; EX 24.50 Trifecta £136.30 Pool: £514.86 - 2.68 winning tickets..
Owner H G Gooding & Mrs A A Gooding **Bred** Mrs V J Bjerke And Mrs E K Tope-Ottesen **Trained** Kentisbeare, Devon

FOCUS
Not a strong maiden and, of the front three in the betting, only Castano ran his race, so the form does not look solid.

3047 O'CONNELL'S DRYWALL H'CAP 1m 4f
4:30 (4:31) (Class 6) (0-60,60) 4-Y-0+ **£2,730** (£806; £403) **Stalls Low**

Form RPR

6050 1 **Icannshift (IRE)**[15] 2595 7-8-7 52 .... NeilChalmers[(3)] 5 63
(T M Jones) *mde all: rdn over 2f out: styd on wl* **16/1**

/025 2 ¾ **Selkirk Grace**[15] 2595 7-8-7 49 .... RobertHavlin 8 59
(K A Morgan) *chsd ldrs: wnt 2nd over 6f out tl over 3f out: chsd wnr again over 2f out: kpt on same pce u.p last 2f* **6/1[3]**

0-00 3 3 **First Boy (GER)**[9] 1570 8-8-4 46 oh1 .... DavidKinsella 12 51
(D J Wintle) *chsd ldng trio: rdn over 2f out: chsd ldng pair last 2f: no imp* **7/1**

-002 4 5 **Prince Zafonic**[8] 2810 4-9-1 60 .... (t) JerryO'Dwyer[(3)] 10 57
(Miss Gay Kelleway) *hld up and bhd: hdwy on outer 4f out: rdn and no imp on ldrs over 2f out: kpt on to go 4th fnl f* **3/1[2]**

-002 5 5 **Joy In The Guild (IRE)**[19] 2491 4-8-9 51 .... JimCrowley 11 40
(W S Kittow) *hld up towards rr: hdwy 5f out: effrt on inner 3f out: rdn and no hdwy over 2f out* **12/1**

0512 6 3½ **Adage**[30] 2142 4-8-13 55 .... (t) DaneO'Neill 6 39
(David Pinder) *s.i.s: hld up towards rr: pushed along and hdwy 6f out: rdn and btn wl over 2f out* **12/1**

-600 7 1½ **Mucho Loco (IRE)**[20] 2467 4-7-12 47 .... ThomasO'Brien[(7)] 3 28
(R Curtis) *hld up towards rr: rdn wl over 3f out: no real hdwy tl kpt on past btn horses fnl f* **33/1**

00-0 8 5 **Book Of Days (IRE)**[24] 2332 4-7-11 46 oh1 .... DanielleMcCreery[(7)] 9 19
(Evan Williams) *t.k.h: hld up in midfield: losing pl whn hmpd over 4f out: no ch after* **40/1**

3550 9 7 **Twilight Avenger (IRE)**[9] 2764 4-8-4 46 oh1 .... JohnEgan 2 8
(W M Brisbourne) *t.k.h: hld up in rr: n.d* **20/1**

2242 10 2 **Prince Des Neiges (FR)**[11] 2715 4-9-3 59 .... RichardHughes 1 18
(A M Hales) *chsd wnr tl 6f out and again over 3f out tl over 2f out: sn btn: eased fnl f* **5/2[1]**

0453 11 6 **General Flumpa**[10] 2745 6-8-11 53 .... DarryllHolland 7 —
(Miss Tor Sturgis) *stdd after s and hld up in rr: hdwy wl over 4f out: wknd wl over 3f out* **7/1**

/0-0 12 44 **Norman Norman**[18] 2519 5-8-4 46 oh1 .... TPO'Shea 4 —
(W S Kittow) *t.k.h: stdd and hld up in midfield: rdn and lost pl 7f out: t.o over 2f out* **66/1**

2m 48.8s (8.30) **Going Correction** +0.775s/f (Yiel) **12 Ran SP% 125.8**
Speed ratings (Par 101):103,102,100,97,93 91,90,87,82,81 77,47
CSF £112.68 CT £759.25 TOTE £16.00: £3.90, £2.20, £2.90; EX 136.20 Trifecta £247.20 Pool: £348.26 - 1.00 winning ticket..
Owner T M Jones **Bred** Piercetown Stud **Trained** Albury Heath, Surrey

FOCUS
Those who raced prominently appeared to be at an advantage in what was a poor handicap. The form looks sound enough rated through the runner-up, with Icannshift posting his best form since 2004.
Selkirk Grace Official explanation: jockey said gelding hung left
Prince Des Neiges(FR) Official explanation: jockey said gelding ran flat and in latter stages had no more to give
General Flumpa Official explanation: jockey said gelding was unsuited by the soft ground

3048 LIPSCOMB ISUZU H'CAP 1m 1f 149y
5:00 (5:00) (Class 5) (0-75,72) 3-Y-0+ **£3,238** (£963; £481; £240) **Stalls Low**

Form RPR

0033 1 **Kavachi (IRE)**[18] 2512 4-9-6 62 .... GeorgeBaker 2 68
(G L Moore) *hld up in midfield: hdwy to trck ldr 3f out: led 2f out: rdn over 1f out: hld on wl* **5/1[2]**

0230 2 hd **Lap Of Honour (IRE)**[17] 2530 3-8-11 65 .... DaneO'Neill 4 71
(N A Callaghan) *t.k.h: chsd ldr tl 5f out: styd in tch: hdwy to chse wnr wl over 1f out: ev ch over 1f out: kpt on u.p but a jst hld* **5/1[2]**

0021 **3** *1* **Rustic Gold**[2] 3003 3-8-9 **63** 6ex.. TPO'Shea 5 67+
(J R Best) *s.i.s: hld up in rr: hdwy on outer 2f out: rdn and hung rt over 1f out: chsd ldrs fnl f: no imp last 100yds* **11/4**[1]
3-61 **4** *3* **Colinca's Lad (IRE)**[7] 2831 5-9-1 **62**.............................. PJMcDonald(5) 3 60
(T T Clement) *hld up in midfield: hdwy to chse ldrs over 2f out: rdn 2f out: wknd over 1f out* **11/4**[1]
1140 **5** *23* **Nicomedia (IRE)**[16] 2579 3-9-4 **72**.............................. RichardHughes 6 24
(R Hannon) *led: rdn 3f out: hdd 2f out: sn wknd: eased fnl f* **11/1**
24-3 **6** *2 1/2* **Factual Lad**[26] 2275 9-9-6 **62**.. RobertHavlin 1 9
(B R Millman) *chsd ldrs tl wnt 2nd 5f out tl 3f out: sn wknd: eased fnl f* **16/1**
511 **7** *5* **Birkside**[13] 2667 4-10-0 **70**.. DarryllHolland 8 7
(S Dow) *hld up in rr: hdwy on outer over 2f out: sn rdn and btn: eased fnl f* **13/2**[3]
3000 **8** *3 1/2* **Titus Lumpus (IRE)**[8] 2802 4-9-1 **57**.............................. PatDobbs 7 —
(R M Flower) *chsd ldrs tl rdn and wknd wl over 3f out: eased fnl f* **28/1**

2m 12.56s (7.33) **Going Correction** +0.775s/f (Yiel)
WFA 3 from 4yo+ 12lb **8 Ran SP% 117.7**
Speed ratings (Par 103):101,100,100,97,79 77,73,70
CSF £31.08 CT £83.03 TOTE £6.90: £2.20, £1.80, £1.30; EX 30.10 Trifecta £377.60 Part won. Pool: £531.96 - 0.67 winning tickets. Place 6 £35.35, Place 5 £19.14.
Owner Bryan Pennick & Roy Martin **Bred** Gainsborough Stud Management Ltd **Trained** Woodingdean, E Sussex

FOCUS
Just a modest contest with the winner rated slightly below last season's best and the runner-up to form. The first four finished a long way clear.
Factual Lad Official explanation: jockey said gelding was unsuited by the soft ground
Birkside Official explanation: jockey said gelding was unsuited by the soft ground
T/Plt: £73.60 to a £1 stake. Pool: £66,608.60. 660.40 winning tickets. T/Qpdt: £53.40 to a £1 stake. Pool: £3,106.50. 43.00 winning tickets. SP

[3024] NEWCASTLE (L-H)
Friday, June 29

OFFICIAL GOING: Heavy (soft in places)
The testing ground led to 18 withdrawals.
Wind: Light, half-against Weather: Overcast

3049 GOSFORTH DECORATING & BUILDING SERVICES H'CAP 1m 2f 32y
6:45 (6:46) (Class 5) (0-70,69) 4-Y-0+ **£3,562** (£1,059; £529; £264) **Stalls** Centre

Form RPR
-024 **1** **Thornaby Green**[8] 2795 6-8-4 **52**.............................. FrancisNorton 11 61
(T D Barron) *led after 2f: mde rest: rdn 2f out: hld on wl fnl f* **12/1**
20-0 **2** *1/2* **Turn Of Phrase (IRE)**[27] 2254 8-8-10 **58**.............................. TonyHamilton 5 66
(B Ellison) *midfield: outpcd over 4f out: rallied over 1f out: wnt 2nd wl ins fnl f: r.o* **18/1**
1051 **3** *1 1/4* **Royal Flynn**[6] 2868 5-9-4 **66**.. PaulFessey 7 72
(M Dods) *t.k.h: hld up: hdwy over 2f out: kpt on ins fnl f* **7/2**[1]
-655 **4** *1 3/4* **Tidy (IRE)**[8] 2809 7-9-0 **62**.............................. (p) PatCosgrave 17 64
(Micky Hammond) *midfield: hdwy to chse wnr over 1f out to wl ins fnl f: no ex* **22/1**
3422 **5** *nk* **Mystical Ayr (IRE)**[7] 2823 5-8-11 **59**.............................. RoystonFfrench 13 60
(Miss L A Perratt) *cl up: effrt over 2f out: no ex ins fnl f* **11/2**[3]
-001 **6** *6* **Best Of The Lot (USA)**[27] 2254 5-9-4 **66**.............................. PaulHanagan 3 55
(R A Fahey) *prom: shkn up over 2f out: wknd over 1f out* **4/1**[2]
5-50 **7** *2* **Trouble Mountain (USA)**[38] 1922 10-9-7 **69**.............................. (t) DaleGibson 14 54
(M W Easterby) *hld up: drvn 3f out: no imp over 1f out* **12/1**
-024 **8** *3/4* **Hawkit (USA)**[6] 2865 6-9-6 **68**.. NCallan 4 52
(P Monteith) *hld up: rdn over 2f out: sn btn* **15/2**
0032 **9** *3/4* **Everest (IRE)**[11] 2709 10-9-5 **67**.. TomEaves 6 49
(B Ellison) *hld up: pushed along over 2f out: sn btn* **6/1**
5440 **10** *2 1/2* **Summer Lodge**[63] 1284 4-8-13 **61**.............................. (b) JHBowman 15 38
(A J McCabe) *in tch: drvn over 2f out: sn btn* **16/1**
3005 **11** *29* **Susiedil (IRE)**[8] 2795 6-8-4 **52** oh2 ow2.............................. (v) AdrianTNicholls 8 —
(S T Mason) *led 2f: cl up tl wknd over 2f out: eased whn no ch over 1f out* **40/1**

2m 22.86s (11.06) **Going Correction** +1.20s/f (Soft) **11 Ran SP% 117.0**
Speed ratings (Par 103):103,102,101,100,99 95,93,92,92,90 67
CSF £207.21 CT £919.92 TOTE £15.50: £4.30, £3.10, £1.70; EX 197.20.
Owner K J Alderson **Bred** Mrs S Broadhurst **Trained** Maunby, N Yorks

FOCUS
A run-of-the-mill handicap featuring exposed sorts. The pace was just fair, with the winner making most. Not many showed their form in the ground.
Summer Lodge Official explanation: jockey said gelding was unsuited by the heavy (soft in places) ground
Susiedil(IRE) Official explanation: jockey said mare lost its action

3050 NORTHERN ROCK GOSFORTH PARK CUP (H'CAP) 5f
7:15 (7:16) (Class 2) (0-105,104) 3-Y-0+
£18,696 (£5,598; £2,799; £1,401; £699; £351) **Stalls** High

Form RPR
0530 **1** **Green Park (IRE)**[20] 2440 4-8-11 **88**.............................. PaulHanagan 3 96
(R A Fahey) *bhd: rdn 1/2-way: hdwy 2f out: kpt on wl fnl f to ld towards fin* **11/2**[2]
-000 **2** *1/2* **Mecca's Mate**[55] 1474 6-9-7 **98**.............................. TonyHamilton 17 104
(D W Barker) *cl up: led 1f out: kpt on: hdd towards fin* **12/1**
-013 **3** *2* **Caribbean Coral**[27] 2234 8-9-2 **93**.............................. GrahamGibbons 14 92
(J J Quinn) *hld up: hdwy over 1f out: kpt on fnl f: nt rch first two* **5/1**[1]
2220 **4** *nk* **River Falcon**[20] 2463 7-9-6 **97**.............................. PhillipMakin 9 95
(J S Goldie) *cl up: rdn 1/2-way: kpt on same pce fnl f* **6/1**[3]
0-50 **5** *1* **Orientor**[20] 2463 9-8-13 **97**.............................. GaryBartley(7) 12 91
(J S Goldie) *hld up in midfield: drvn 1/2-way: no imp over 1f out* **8/1**
0420 **6** *1 1/4* **Prince Namid**[16] 2566 5-8-10 **87**.............................. RoystonFfrench 11 77
(Mrs A Duffield) *dwlt: bhd and rdn along: kpt on fnl f: nvr rchd ldrs* **6/1**[3]
1115 **7** *3* **Turn On The Style**[50] 1601 5-8-12 **92**.............................. (b) AndrewElliott(3) 5 71
(J Balding) *taken early to post: dwlt: sn led: hdd 1f out: sn wknd* **7/1**
4-00 **8** *2 1/2* **Overstayed (IRE)**[27] 2234 4-8-10 **87**.............................. TomEaves 1 57
(I Semple) *taken early to post: racd alone far side: outpcd fnl 2f* **20/1**
4006 **9** *3/4* **Tournedos (IRE)**[20] 2463 5-9-2 **93**.............................. FrancisNorton 2 60
(D Nicholls) *prom tl rdn and wknd over 2f out* **8/1**
2015 **10** *2 1/2* **Continent**[7] 2841 10-8-11 **88** 6ex.............................. AdrianTNicholls 7 46
(D Nicholls) *taken early to post: chsd ldrs tl wknd over 1f out* **14/1**
402- **11** *6* **Inter Vision (USA)**[258] 5957 7-8-9 **91**.............................. MichaelJStainton(5) 8 28
(A Dickman) *hld up: drvn 1/2-way: n.d* **22/1**

64.79 secs (3.29) **Going Correction** +0.90s/f (Soft) **11 Ran SP% 118.8**
Speed ratings (Par 109):109,108,105,104,102 100,96,92,90,86 77
CSF £70.56 CT £360.61 TOTE £6.80: £2.20, £4.60, £1.60; EX 73.60.
Owner G A Fixings Ltd **Bred** James Burns And A Moynan **Trained** Musley Bank, N Yorks

FOCUS
Mainly exposed sorts but a decent handicap in which all bar one raced on the stands' side. The winner returned to his best 3yo form, which came on heavy ground. Only the first two showed their form.

NOTEBOOK
Green Park(IRE), a proven performer in testing ground, looked better than the bare form of his previous start at Goodwood and he showed a good attitude in the closing stages to notch his first win for over a year. He may be the type that needs things to drop right but is capable of further success - especially in these conditions - when they do. (op 6-1 tchd 13-2 and 5-1)
Mecca's Mate had not been at her best this year but she returned to form having enjoyed the run of the race next to the stands' rail. Although effective on a sound surface, she seems ideally suited by give in the ground and, although she has little margin for error from her mark, she is capable of winning again this term granted suitable conditions. (op 15-2)
Caribbean Coral, who won this race in soft ground three years ago and has confirmed he retains all his ability this year, turned in another decent effort. He may be better suited by coming off a stronger pace on better ground. (tchd 9-2 and 11-2)
River Falcon not at his best over 5f on fast ground at Musselburgh last time, ran creditably in these more suitable conditions. He has been essentially consistent this term but is vulnerable to progressive or well handicapped sorts from his current mark. (tchd 13-2)
Orientor was again not disgraced but remains vulnerable from his current mark and, although he seems genuine enough, a losing run of nearly three years means he remains one to tread carefully with. (op 6-1)
Prince Namid is a proven performer in testing ground but, although not disgraced, was always fighting a losing battle after missing a beat at the start. Although vulnerable to the more progressive sorts from this mark, he should continue to give it his best shot. Official explanation: jockey said gelding reared leaving stalls (tchd 7-1)
Turn On The Style, an improved performer on artificial surfaces in winter, shaped a bit better than the bare form on this first run after a short break and will be one to keep an eye on back on a sound surface and back at a sharper course. (op 13-2 tchd 8-1)
Continent Official explanation: jockey said gelding hung left-handed

3051 PHOENIX SECURITY GROUP MAIDEN FILLIES' STKS 7f
7:45 (7:45) (Class 5) 3-Y-0+ **£3,886** (£1,156; £577; £288) **Stalls** High

Form RPR
0426 **1** **Eternal Legacy (IRE)**[11] 2711 5-9-7 52.............................. KDarley 7 58
(E J Alston) *mde all: rdn and kpt on strly to go clr fnl f* **5/1**[3]
2 *6* **Lan Kwai Fong** 3-8-12 0.............................. DavidAllan 11 43
(T D Easterby) *in tch: outpcd 1/2-way: rallied to chse wnr wl ins fnl f: kpt on* **12/1**
0-00 **3** *2 1/2* **Ivana Illyich (IRE)**[5] 2905 5-9-7 36.............................. PaddyAspell 6 36
(J S Wainwright) *prom: outpcd 1/2-way: rallied 2f out: kpt on same pce ins fnl f* **66/1**
02 **4** *1/2* **Wells Of Badr (IRE)**[21] 2433 3-8-12 0.............................. NCallan 5 35
(P W Chapple-Hyam) *cl up: drvn over 2f out: wknd ins fnl f* **7/2**[2]
6-00 **5** *3/4* **Waiheke Island**[11] 2713 3-8-12 55.............................. PatCosgrave 1 33
(B Mactaggart) *hld up: rdn 1/2-way: effrt 2f out: nvr rchd ldrs* **50/1**
020 **6** *2* **Hansomis (IRE)**[11] 2713 3-8-12 61.............................. RoystonFfrench 3 28
(B Mactaggart) *t.k.h: in tch: drvn over 2f out: sn no imp* **13/2**
4 **7** *4* **Haedi**[30] 2137 3-8-12 0.............................. (t) DO'Donohoe 2 17
(Saeed Bin Suroor) *t.k.h: chsd ldrs: rdn and edgd rt over 1f out: sn wknd* **11/2**
00 **8** *3 1/2* **Mary From Maryhill (IRE)**[34] 2032 3-8-12 0.............................. TomEaves 10 8
(Miss L A Perratt) *sn bhd: struggling 1/2-way: nvr on terms* **66/1**
3 **9** *16* **Red Blossom**[16] 2554 3-8-12 0.............................. PaulHanagan 8 —
(Sir Mark Prescott) *prom: drvn over 2f out: sn wknd* **13/8**[1]
000- **10** *18* **Axis Mundi (IRE)**[235] 6377 3-8-9 40.............................. GregFairley(3) 9 —
(T J Etherington) *bhd: drvn 1/2-way: sn btn* **100/1**

1m 37.36s (9.34) **Going Correction** +0.90s/f (Soft)
WFA 3 from 5yo 9lb **10 Ran SP% 119.3**
Speed ratings (Par 100):82,75,72,71,70 68,64,60,41,21
CSF £63.09 TOTE £6.60: £1.60, £3.10, £8.20; EX 76.20.
Owner Derrick Mossop **Bred** Colin Kennedy **Trained** Longton, Lancs

FOCUS
A weak event with four of the market leaders disappointing and with the proximity of the 36-rated third. The winner enjoyed the run of the race from the front on the rail but the form is far from solid.
Red Blossom Official explanation: jockey said filly was unsuited by the heavy (soft in places) ground

3052 DIGIBET H'CAP 1m 3y(S)
8:20 (8:20) (Class 4) (0-85,83) 3-Y-0+
£6,232 (£1,866; £933; £467; £233; £117) **Stalls** High

Form RPR
04-0 **1** **Wigwam Willie (IRE)**[17] 2536 5-9-11 **80**.............................. (p) NCallan 11 88
(K A Ryan) *prom: effrt and chsd wnr 2f out: sn rdn and edgd rt: kpt on wl fnl f to ld nr fin* **3/1**[1]
4340 **2** *3/4* **Shot To Fame (USA)**[2] 2986 8-9-9 **78**.............................. (t) AdrianTNicholls 5 85
(D Nicholls) *led: clr 2f out: rdn fnl f: hdd nr fin* **3/1**[1]
0410 **3** *8* **King Of The Moors (USA)**[24] 2338 4-9-4 **73**.............................. PhillipMakin 3 64+
(T D Barron) *hld up: pushed along over 2f out: kpt on fnl f: no ch w first two* **6/1**[3]
02P4 **4** *1 3/4* **Ammeyrr**[16] 2554 3-8-2 **70** ow3.............................. AndrewMullen(3) 10 57
(A Crook) *towards rr: rdn 1/2-way: effrt over 2f out: no imp* **16/1**
5-00 **5** *5* **Bayberry King (USA)**[11] 2711 4-8-9 **64** oh11.............................. TomEaves 7 41
(J S Goldie) *stdd in rr: shkn up over 2f out: n.d* **14/1**
4115 **6** *1 1/2* **Malinsa Blue (IRE)**[35] 2008 5-8-11 **66**.............................. RoystonFfrench 9 40
(B Ellison) *cl up tl rdn and wknd fr 2f out* **8/1**
-64 **7** *4* **Superior Star**[64] 1264 4-9-1 **70**.............................. (v) PaulHanagan 2 36
(R A Fahey) *chsd ldrs tl wknd over 2f out* **5/1**[2]
10-0 **8** *18* **Just Dust**[17] 2536 3-9-3 **82**.............................. DaleGibson 8 12
(M W Easterby) *prom: hung lft 1/2-way: sn wknd* **7/1**

1m 50.49s (8.59) **Going Correction** +0.90s/f (Soft)
WFA 3 from 4yo+ 10lb **8 Ran SP% 117.1**
Speed ratings (Par 105):93,92,84,82,77 76,72,54
CSF £12.08 CT £50.71 TOTE £3.40: £1.40, £1.70, £2.40; EX 9.10.
Owner Neil & Anne Dawson Partnership **Bred** Mrs Margaret Christie **Trained** Hambleton, N Yorks
■ Stewards' Enquiry : Adrian T Nicholls one-day ban: not riding to draw (Jul 10)

FOCUS
A fair handicap run at just an ordinary pace and one in which the first two did well to pull so far clear in the last quarter mile. They were the only two to show their form, with the rest below par in the conditions.
Just Dust Official explanation: jockey said gelding hung left-handed

3053 INTERSKY 50 CLUB H'CAP 6f
8:50 (8:51) (Class 5) (0-75,78) 3-Y-O+ **£3,886** (£1,156; £577; £288) **Stalls** High

Form RPR

0052 **1** **Prospect Court**[11] [2711] 5-8-7 **54**................................ AndrewMullen(3) 5 78
(A C Whillans) *prom far side: led that gp and overall ldr over 1f out: sn clr* **7/2**[1]

0000 **2** *7* **Funfair Wane**[11] [2711] 8-8-13 **57**................................ AdrianTNicholls 3 60
(D Nicholls) *cl up: effrt and chsd wnr over 1f out: sn no imp: 2nd of 6 in gp* **28/1**

2630 **3** *1/2* **Cornus**[6] [2882] 5-9-11 **72**..(be) AndrewElliott(3) 1 74
(A J McCabe) *in tch far side: hdwy over 1f out: kpt on fnl f: no imp: 3rd of 6 in gp* **16/1**

3020 **4** *2 1/2* **Cross Of Lorraine (IRE)**[6] [2864] 4-9-9 **67**......................(b) TomEaves 16 61+
(I Semple) *chsd stands' side ldr: led that gp ins fnl f: no ch w far side: 1st of 8 in gp* **12/1**

0004 **5** *2* **Breaking Shadow (IRE)**[10] [2741] 5-9-5 **63**................ FrancisNorton 12 51+
(M A Peill) *hld up stands' side: rdn over 2f out: kpt on fnl f: nrst fin: 2nd of 8 in gp* **13/2**[3]

3364 **6** *1 1/4* **Melalchrist**[46] [1718] 5-9-8 **66**..(p) NCallan 7 50
(K A Ryan) *led far side to over 1f out: sn no ex: 4th of 6 in gp* **9/1**

1004 **7** *3/4* **Dorn Dancer (IRE)**[6] [2864] 5-9-4 **62**.......................... RoystonFfrench 15 44+
(D W Barker) *hld up in tch stands' side: outpcd over 2f out: n.d after: 3rd of 8 in gp* **13/2**[3]

-400 **8** *3 1/2* **Newcastles Owen (IRE)**[18] [2509] 4-8-6 **53** oh8............ GregFairley(3) 6 25
(R Johnson) *trckd far side ldrs: ev ch over 1f out: sn no ex: 5th of 6 in gp* **66/1**

0642 **9** *hd* **High Reach**[10] [2744] 7-9-7 **72**.................................... DeanHeslop(7) 10 43+
(T D Barron) *led stands' side to ins fnl f: no ex: 4th of 8 in gp* **10/1**

0001 **10** *1* **Paris Bell**[5] [2912] 5-9-13 **74** 6ex................................ DuranFentiman(3) 11 42+
(T D Easterby) *hld up stands' side: rdn over 2f out: n.d: 5th of 8 in gp* **5/1**[2]

00-6 **11** *4* **Swiper Hill (IRE)**[107] [673] 4-9-12 **70**............................. TonyHamilton 2 26
(B Ellison) *hld up far side: rdn over 2f out: n.d: last of 6 in gp* **66/1**

05-0 **12** *10* **Red Chairman**[11] [2714] 5-8-9 **53** oh3.................................(b) DavidAllan 8 —
(R Johnson) *chsd stands' side ldrs tl wknd fr 1/2-way: 6th of 8 in gp* **33/1**

-501 **13** *7* **Highland Warrior**[8] [2805] 8-10-6 **78** 6ex.......................... MickyFenton 13 —
(P T Midgley) *prom stands' side: rdn over 2f out: sn wknd: 7th of 8 in gp* **10/1**

-030 **14** *3 1/2* **Ellens Academy (IRE)**[41] [1847] 12-10-0 **72**.......................... KDarley 17 —
(E J Alston) *hld up stands' side: drvn over 2f out: sn btn: last of 8 in gp* **16/1**

1m 19.74s (4.65) **Going Correction** +0.90s/f (Soft) **14 Ran SP% 122.6**
Speed ratings (Par 103):105,95,95,91,89 87,86,81,81,80 74,61,52,47
CSF £115.20 CT £1022.85 TOTE £5.20: £2.20, £6.30, £5.80; EX 88.70.

Owner Mrs L M Whillans **Bred** Mrs G Slater **Trained** Newmill-On-Slitrig, Borders

■ Stewards' Enquiry : Adrian T Nicholls one-day ban: careless riding (Jul 12); one-day ban: failed to ride to draw (Jul 14)

Dean Heslop one-day ban: failed to ride to draw (Jul 10)

FOCUS
An ordinary handicap in which the field split into two fairly even-sized groups. However the far-side bunch held the edge. A big step up on recent form from the wide-margin winner, but nothing really showed their form.

Ellens Academy(IRE) Official explanation: jockey said gelding was unsuited by the heavy (soft in places) ground

3054 PEOPLE PORTAL H'CAP 5f
9:20 (9:20) (Class 5) (0-75,75) 3-Y-O **£3,886** (£1,156; £577; £288) **Stalls** High

Form RPR

-440 **1** **Morristown Music (IRE)**[16] [2553] 3-8-8 **62**.................... TonyHamilton 1 69
(J S Wainwright) *chsd far side ldr: led and overall ldr over 1f out: kpt on wl fnl f* **14/1**

0116 **2** *2 1/2* **Darcy's Pride (IRE)**[14] [2631] 3-9-1 **72**......................... AndrewMullen(3) 2 70
(D W Barker) *racd w wnr far side: led to over 1f out: kpt on ins fnl f* **13/2**

0041 **3** *1 1/2* **La Vecchia Scuola (IRE)**[7] [2826] 3-8-1 **58** 6ex...(b[1]) DuranFentiman(3) 6 51
(R Johnson) *prom stands' side: drvn 1/2-way: kpt on fnl f to ld that gp cl home: no ch w far side* **25/1**

-111 **4** *shd* **Ishetoo**[21] [2435] 3-9-7 **75**... PaulHanagan 4 71+
(A Dickman) *prom stands' side: led that gp ins fnl f to nr fin: no ex* **10/3**[1]

-660 **5** *1 3/4* **Miss Daawe**[49] [1639] 3-8-2 **56** oh11.............................. RoystonFfrench 3 42
(B Ellison) *bhd stands' side: drvn 1/2-way: kpt on fnl f: nvr rchd ldrs* **22/1**

5-02 **6** *3 1/2* **Bollin Franny**[27] [2255] 3-8-11 **65**.. DavidAllan 7 38
(T D Easterby) *hld up stands' side: drvn over 2f out: kpt on: nvr rchd ldrs* **9/2**[2]

00-1 **7** *nk* **Hawaii Prince**[34] [2029] 3-9-1 **69**................................ SilvestreDeSousa 5 41
(S T Mason) *led stands' side to ins fnl f: sn btn* **12/1**

4562 **8** *2* **Ronnie Howe**[29] [2172] 3-8-13 **67**.. PhillipMakin 8 32
(M Dods) *in tch stands' side: drvn over 2f out: wknd over 1f out* **7/1**

00-3 **9** *2 1/2* **Triple Shadow**[31] [2120] 3-8-12 **66**..................................... PaulFessey 10 22
(T D Barron) *t.k.h to post: hld up stands' side: drvn over 2f out: btn over 1f out* **5/1**[3]

1063 **10** *6* **New York Oscar (IRE)**[7] [2837] 3-9-3 **71**...............................(b) NCallan 9 5
(A J McCabe) *w stands' side ldr tl wknd fr 2f out* **10/1**

66.49 secs (4.99) **Going Correction** +0.90s/f (Soft) **10 Ran SP% 115.4**
Speed ratings (Par 99):96,92,89,89,86 81,80,77,73,63
CSF £101.06 CT £2297.59 TOTE £19.70: £3.50, £2.20, £4.60; EX 111.50 Place 6 £1,149.65, Place 5 £364.04.

Owner J S Wainwright **Bred** J S Wainwright **Trained** Kennythorpe, N Yorks

■ Stewards' Enquiry : Andrew Mullen one-day ban: failed to ride to draw (Jul 10)

FOCUS
An ordinary handicap in which the two to race far side finished first and second. Ishetoo shaped much the best of the main bunch.

New York Oscar(IRE) Official explanation: jockey said gelding lost its action

T/Jkpt: Not won. T/Plt: £4,625.50 to a £1 stake. Pool: £122,609.35. 19.35 winning tickets. T/Qpdt: £362.50 to a £1 stake. Pool: £7,299.30. 14.90 winning tickets. RY

2880 NEWMARKET (JULY) (R-H)
Friday, June 29

OFFICIAL GOING: Good to soft (soft in places)
Wind: Light, half-behind Weather: Cloudy with sunny spells

3055 UNICORN ASSET MANAGEMENT JULY COURSE SERIES EBF MAIDEN FILLIES' STKS (QUALIFIER) 6f
6:00 (6:05) (Class 3) 2-Y-O **£6,477** (£1,927; £963; £481) **Stalls** Low

Form RPR

1 **Don't Forget Faith (USA)** 2-9-0 0.............................. PhilipRobinson 11 88+
(C G Cox) *leggy: scope: chsd ldr tl led over 1f out: rdn out* **11/4**[1]

2 *hd* **Visit** 2-9-0 0.. RyanMoore 9 87+
(Sir Michael Stoute) *gd sort: bit bkwd: chsd ldrs: rdn and swtchd rt 1f out: r.o wl* **8/1**

3 *1 1/2* **Honky Tonk Sally** 2-9-0 0.. JamieSpencer 2 83
(M L W Bell) *cmpt: led over 4f: styd on same pce towards fin* **14/1**

4 *1 3/4* **Crystany (IRE)** 2-9-0 0.. TedDurcan 7 78
(H R A Cecil) *wl grwn: chsd ldrs: rdn and ev ch over 1f out: wknd nr fin* **7/2**[2]

5 *1* **Lady Deauville (FR)** 2-9-0 0.................................... SimonWhitworth 5 75
(P A Blockley) *w'like: bit bkwd: mid-div: hdwy over 2f out: rdn over 1f out: styd on same pce* **50/1**

6 *1/2* **Lady Zabeen (IRE)** 2-9-0 0.. RichardMullen 14 73
(D M Simcock) *gd sort: bit bkwd: chsd ldrs: rdn over 2f out: styd on same pce appr fnl f* **20/1**

7 *shd* **Victoria Valentine** 2-9-0 0.. MichaelHills 1 73
(B W Hills) *w'like: bit bkwd: chsd ldrs: rdn over 2f out: no ex fnl f* **17/2**

8 *4* **Redeemed** 2-9-0 0.. SteveDrowne 12 61
(B J Meehan) *leggy: scope: hld up: rdn and hung lft over 2f out: n.d* **20/1**

9 *3 1/2* **Town And Gown** 2-9-0 0.. JimmyFortune 6 50
(J H M Gosden) *gd sort: mid-div: hung lft and wknd 2f out* **14/1**

10 *2* **Exodia** 2-9-0 0.. JimmyQuinn 3 44
(Jane Chapple-Hyam) *w'like: s.i.s: outpcd* **20/1**

11 *24* **Ochenvay** 2-9-0 0.. TQuinn 13 —
(M Quinn) *cmpt: bit bkwd: s.i.s: outpcd* **66/1**

P **Laureldean Dream (USA)** 2-9-0 0.......................... KerrinMcEvoy 8 —
(P W Chapple-Hyam) *neat: lw: p.u sn after s* **13/2**[3]

1m 14.56s (1.21) **Going Correction** +0.20s/f (Good) **12 Ran SP% 114.9**
Speed ratings (Par 94):99,98,96,94,93 92,92,86,82,79 47,—
CSF £22.38 TOTE £3.40: £1.60, £3.10, £2.30; EX 28.80.

Owner S R Hope And S W Barrow **Bred** Calumet Farm **Trained** Lambourn, Berks

FOCUS
Traditionally a decent maiden, and this year's renewal looks set to continue the trend of producing future winners.

NOTEBOOK
Don't Forget Faith(USA), who is by Belmont Stakes winner Victory Gallop, is a half-sister to three winners, including Hokko Beauty, who won three times in Japan, and She's Fine, a turf sprint winner at four in the US. Well backed throughout the day on the exchanges, she was supported on course as well, and clearly she was expected to show up well on her debut. Always up with the pace, she galloped on strongly once she hit the rising ground, and she should get another furlong as the season progresses. (op 7-2 tchd 4-1 in a place)

Visit ◆, who is closely related to Promising Lead, is out of a Listed-race winner who is also a half-sister to the dam of Banks Hill, Intercontinental, Dansili & Heat Haze, and to the dam of top-class Leroidesanimaux. From the stable that sent out Russian Rhythm and Enthused to win this race on their debuts, she ran a blinder to go so close, staying on really powerfully inside the final furlong. The chances are that this daughter of Oasis Dream is going to improve a great deal for both the experience and for faster ground, and she is likely to be contesting Pattern races before too long. A maiden should be a formality, and a seventh furlong will suit her, too, in time. (tchd 9-1)

Honky Tonk Sally, a half-sister to Group 3 winner Eco Friendly, Roaring Twenties, a 1m winner at three, Water Flower, a multiple 1m4f winner at three, and Eloquent Silence, a 1m winner at two, hails from a stable whose juveniles usually improve for their debuts, so in the circumstances this can be considered a highly promising effort. She looks likely to follow in the family tradition and will be winning soon.

Crystany(IRE) ◆, who cost 520,000euros, is out of Crystal Music, who won the Fillies' Mile at two and was runner-up in both the Irish 1000 Guineas and Coronation Stakes at three. Entered in the Moyglare Stud Stakes, she is clearly well regarded, and the only concern for backers beforehand was whether, being by Green Desert, she might find the ground too soft. Having travelled well for much of the contest, she did not really pick up as one might have hoped, but the underfoot conditions are probably a good excuse, and she could leave this form behind on quicker ground. (op 3-1)

Lady Deauville(FR), who is a half-sister to Fabulous La Fouine, a multiple winner at three in Japan, Croom Saint Pierre, a 1m2f winner in France, and Policalle, a 1m winner at two in France, has a real mix of speed and stamina in her pedigree, as she is by Fasliyev out of a staying mare who won eight races in France, including the Prix du Cadran. She seemed to handle the rather testing conditions well.

Lady Zabeen(IRE), whose dam is a sister to Machikane Sanshirem, a dual winner in Japan, saw her sales price increase significantly at the breeze-ups. She is bred for middle distances next year, though, and one would assume that she will be suited by a step up to 7f in due course. (op 25-1 tchd 28-1)

Victoria Valentine, who cost 125,000euros, is out of a mare who won at two in Germany and was placed in Group 2 company over a mile at three. Representing a stable that is not in the best of form at present, it is likely that she will appreciate quicker ground as she is by Royal Applause. (op 10-1)

Redeemed, whose dam was placed in Pattern-grade sprints, hails from a stable that tends not to have first-time-out two-year-old winners. She should improve for this experience.

Town And Gown, a half-sister to Mister Cosmi, a high-class 6f winner at two and later a useful miler at three, Auditorium, a useful dual 6f winner at two, and Princess Georgina, a 5f winner at two, is another by Oasis Dream. This ground would have been plenty soft enough for her, and in any case her trainer's two-year-olds usually need their debuts. (op 12-1)

Exodia, whose dam was a winner over 1m1f and placed in Listed company, and is also a half-sister to African Dream, who won a couple of Classic trials back in 2004, looks more of a longer-term prospect. Official explanation: jockey said filly was slowly away (op 25-1)

Laureldean Dream(USA), whose stable can do little wrong with its juveniles this term, cost $300,000 and is a half-sister to that top-class miler Ad Valorem. Pulled up very early on, it is to be hoped that whatever was the matter is not too serious. Official explanation: jockey said filly knocked itself coming out of stalls (op 6-1 tchd 11-2)

3056 LTM GROUP H'CAP 1m
6:30 (6:32) (Class 5) (0-75,75) 3-Y-O+ **£3,886** (£1,156; £577; £288) **Stalls** Low

Form RPR

3405 **1** **Encores**[20] [2456] 3-8-3 **60**.. RichardThomas 7 67+
(N A Callaghan) *chsd ldrs: led over 4f out: rdn out* **9/1**[3]

-355 **2** ½ **Dr Synn**[12] 2689 6-9-1 **62**....(p) JimmyQuinn 14 70
(J Akehurst) *b: b.hind: trckd ldrs: plld hrd: rdn and hung lft ins fnl f: nt run on* **16/1**

4000 **3** 1 ¾ **Sonny Parkin**[7] 2833 5-9-12 **73**....(v) SteveDrowne 4 77
(G A Huffer) *hld up: hdwy over 2f out: rdn over 1f out: no ex ins fnl f* **14/1**

3-40 **4** 5 **Chief Exec**[49] 1629 5-8-9 **56**.... RyanMoore 2 49
(C A Cyzer) *chsd ldrs: rdn and ev ch 2f out: wknd over 1f out* **10/1**

5040 **5** nk **Finsbury**[18] 2512 4-9-3 **71**.... AmyBaker(7) 12 63
(Miss J Feilden) *hmpd s: hld up: hdwy over 2f out: nt trble ldrs* **14/1**

0-05 **6** 1 ¾ **Veenwouden**[20] 2472 3-9-3 **74**.... JamieSpencer 1 60
(J R Fanshawe) *lw: hld up: hdwy over 3f out: rdn and wknd over 1f out* **5/1**[1]

-202 **7** 2 ½ **Gunner's View**[54] 1504 3-9-2 **73**....(t) JimmyFortune 16 53
(B J Meehan) *lw: chsd ldrs: rdn over 2f out: wknd fnl f* **10/1**

4-10 **8** 1 ¼ **Leptis Magna**[21] 2425 3-9-4 **75**.... TQuinn 11 52
(D R C Elsworth) *edgd rt s: hld up: racd keenly: hdwy over 2f out: rdn and wknd over 1f out* **11/2**[2]

0023 **9** 6 **Resplendent Nova**[9] 2771 5-9-12 **73**.... TedDurcan 9 38
(P Howling) *chsd ldrs: rdn 1/2-way: wknd wl over 1f out* **11/2**[2]

3601 **10** 1 **Wodhill Schnaps**[24] 2343 6-8-9 **56** oh6.... HayleyTurner 15 19
(D Morris) *hld up: rdn over 2f out: sn wknd* **16/1**

-344 **11** 4 **Lord Of Dreams (IRE)**[18] 2521 5-8-9 **56**....(b[1]) EddieAhern 3 10
(D W P Arbuthnot) *s.s: sn given reminders in rr: rdn: hung lft and wknd over 2f out* **10/1**

3623 **12** 1 ½ **Josr's Magic (IRE)**[30] 2146 3-8-5 **62**.... ChrisCatlin 10 10
(S W Hall) *plld hrd and prom: wknd over 2f out* **33/1**

0-03 **13** 3 **Jalamid (IRE)**[16] 2559 5-10-0 **75**....(t) MichaelHills 8 19
(G C Bravery) *chsd ldrs: led over 6f out: hdd over 4f out: wknd over 2f out* **20/1**

06-0 **14** 1 ¼ **Pink Bay**[24] 2331 5-8-2 **56** oh11.... JosephWalsh(7) 6 —
(K F Clutterbuck) *led: hdd over 6f out: rdn 1/2-way: wknd over 2f out* **50/1**

1-50 **15** 6 **Our Ruby**[42] 1815 3-8-12 **69**.... AdrianMcCarthy 13 —
(P W Chapple-Hyam) *lw: sn pushed along in mid-div: lost pl over 5f out: bhd fnl 3f* **20/1**

1m 41.4s (0.97) **Going Correction** +0.20s/f (Good)
WFA 3 from 4yo+ 10lb **15** Ran SP% **124.2**
Speed ratings (Par 103):103,102,100,95,95 93,91,89,83,82 78,77,74,73,67
CSF £142.44 CT £2067.67 TOTE £12.40: £4.20, £5.20, £3.90; EX 308.10.
Owner G C Hartigan **Bred** Chippenham Lodge Stud Ltd **Trained** Newmarket, Suffolk
■ Stewards' Enquiry : Richard Thomas caution: used whip with excessive frequency

FOCUS
Not a strongly-run contest, but the first three pulled well clear. Probably pretty ordinary form, and the second and third are not trustworthy types, but the winner can probably do better.
Resplendent Nova Official explanation: jockey said gelding was unsuited by the good to soft, soft in places ground
Lord Of Dreams(IRE) Official explanation: jockey said horse was slowly away
Josr's Magic(IRE) Official explanation: jockey said gelding ran too free

3057 NEWMARKET NIGHTS CLAIMING STKS 1m
7:05 (7:06) (Class 5) 3-Y-O **£3,886** (£1,156; £577; £288) **Stalls** Low

Form RPR

2612 **1** **Mick Is Back**[14] 2619 3-8-9 61....(p) EddieAhern 7 61
(J R Boyle) *racd centre: trckd ldr: led over 2f out: edgd lft ins fnl f: rdn out* **13/8**[1]

4300 **2** ¾ **Red Current**[15] 2607 3-8-8 60.... JamieSpencer 1 58
(J R Fanshawe) *racd centre: hld up: hdwy u.p over 1f out: styd on* **13/2**

5505 **3** 1 ¼ **Metropolitan Chief**[17] 2545 3-8-11 56.... RichardMullen 3 58
(D M Simcock) *lw: racd centre: s.i.s: hld up: hdwy over 3f out: rdn over 1f out: styd on same pce ins fnl f* **4/1**[3]

0 **4** ½ **Corkscrew Hill (IRE)**[7] 2836 3-8-4 0.... ChrisCatlin 2 50
(N A Callaghan) *racd centre: chsd ldrs: rdn over 1f out: styd on same pce* **7/1**

5-30 **5** 1 ½ **Fairly Honest**[15] 2598 3-9-6 70.... AntonyProcter 6 63
(D R C Elsworth) *lw: racd centre: s.i.s: hld up in tch: nt clr run over 2f out: sn rdn and hung lft: no ex fnl f* **3/1**[2]

000 **6** 4 **Pugnacity**[4] 2951 3-9-0 0.... SteveDrowne 4 48
(S C Williams) *racd alone far side: w ldrs: rdn over 2f out: wknd fnl f* **20/1**

400 **7** 16 **Above And Below (IRE)**[15] 2607 3-8-12 47.... NeilPollard 5 9
(M Quinn) *swtg: racd centre: led over 5f: sn hung lft and wknd* **33/1**

1m 42.22s (1.79) **Going Correction** +0.20s/f (Good) **7** Ran SP% **116.6**
Speed ratings (Par 99):99,98,97,96,95 91,75
CSF £13.59 TOTE £2.40: £1.20, £2.60; EX 7.00.The winner was subject to a friendly claim.
Owner M Khan X2 **Bred** J E Abbey **Trained** Epsom, Surrey

FOCUS
Modest claiming form. The first two were closely match on their form at Leicester in April (race 1297).
Fairly Honest Official explanation: jockey said gelding hung badly left

3058 NEWMARKETRACECOURSES.CO.UK H'CAP 1m 4f
7:35 (7:37) (Class 4) (0-80,78) 3-Y-O **£5,181** (£1,541; £770; £384) **Stalls** Centre

Form RPR

0203 **1** **Phreeze**[38] 1937 3-9-1 **72**.... JamieSpencer 3 82
(G A Swinbank) *lw: chsd ldrs: led 3f out: rdn over 1f out: hdd ins fnl f: rallied to ld nr fin* **11/2**[2]

4-14 **2** hd **Market Forces**[31] 2112 3-9-4 **75**.... TedDurcan 7 85
(H R A Cecil) *lw: hld up: hdwy over 2f out: rdn and edgd rt over 1f out: r.o* **7/1**[3]

1-01 **3** 1 **Encircled**[20] 2475 3-9-7 **78**.... MichaelHills 2 86
(D Haydn Jones) *s.i.s: hld up: hdwy over 2f out: rdn to ld ins fnl f: hung lft and hdd nr fin* **10/1**

51 **4** 1 ¼ **Pathos (GER)**[20] 2464 3-9-5 **76**.... AntonyProcter 8 82
(D R C Elsworth) *lw: s.i.s: hld up: hdwy over 3f out: nt clr run over 2f out: rdn: hung rt and ev ch over 1f out: no ex ins fnl f* **4/1**[1]

2304 **5** 1 ¼ **Norman The Great**[20] 2455 3-9-2 **73**.... JohnEgan 9 77
(Jane Chapple-Hyam) *prom: rdn over 2f out: styd on same pce appr fnl f* **20/1**

1202 **6** 1 **Its Moon (IRE)**[16] 2579 3-8-11 **68**.... ChrisCatlin 10 71
(T D Walford) *chsd ldrs: rdn over 2f out: hung lft and no ex fnl f* **7/1**[3]

0015 **7** 1 **Sir Duke (IRE)**[11] 2727 3-8-5 **62**.... JimmyQuinn 1 63+
(P W D'Arcy) *s.i.s: hld up: nt clr run over 2f out: styd on ins fnl f: nt trble ldrs* **10/1**

-616 **8** 1 ¾ **Wester Ross (IRE)**[31] 2126 3-9-6 **77**.... RyanMoore 5 75
(J M P Eustace) *chsd ldrs: rdn over 2f out: wkng whn nt clr run over 1f out* **17/2**

0-40 **9** 1 ¾ **Hope Road**[25] 2320 3-9-6 **77**.... KerrinMcEvoy 6 73
(J R Fanshawe) *chsd ldr: led over 3f out: sn hdd: wknd over 1f out* **8/1**

1-60 **10** 1 **Free Offer**[38] 1929 3-9-5 **76**.... EddieAhern 4 70
(J L Dunlop) *hld up: nt clr run over 3f out: sn rdn: wknd over 1f out* **16/1**

24-0 **11** 12 **Minnis Bay (CAN)**[22] 2402 3-9-6 **77**.... DarryllHolland 11 52
(E F Vaughan) *s.s: hld up: wknd over 2f out* **33/1**

510- **12** 15 **Lets Get Cracking (FR)**[216] 6609 3-9-2 **73**.... SteveDrowne 12 24
(A E Jones) *led over 8f: wknd over 2f out* **16/1**

2m 36.46s (3.55) **Going Correction** +0.20s/f (Good) **12** Ran SP% **119.7**
Speed ratings (Par 101):96,95,95,94,93 92,92,91,89,89 81,71
CSF £44.33 CT £381.71 TOTE £6.50: £2.20, £2.00, £3.60; EX 36.00.
Owner W J Gredley **Bred** Belgrave Bloodstock & Ocean Bstock **Trained** Melsonby, N Yorks

FOCUS
A competitive-looking handicap on paper, and that is how it turned out. Sound form, which should work out.
Minnis Bay(CAN) Official explanation: jockey said gelding was unsuited by the good to soft, soft in places ground
Lets Get Cracking(FR) Official explanation: jockey said colt had no more to give

3059 EUROPEAN BREEDERS' FUND FILLIES' CONDITIONS STKS 6f
8:10 (8:10) (Class 3) 3-Y-O+ **£7,772** (£2,312; £1,155; £577) **Stalls** Low

Form RPR

-401 **1** **Gloved Hand**[7] 2835 5-8-7 88.... KerrinMcEvoy 3 97
(R M Beckett) *lw: hld up in tch: led ins fnl f: hung lft: rdn out* **11/4**[1]

1-32 **2** 1 ¼ **Medley**[25] 2306 3-7-12 95.... WilliamBuick(5) 1 94
(R Hannon) *chsd ldrs: edgd rt over 3f out: rdn to ld over 1f out: hdd and unable qck ins fnl f* **3/1**[2]

-511 **3** ¾ **Pusey Street Lady**[23] 2363 3-8-0 77.... RichardThomas 5 89
(J Gallagher) *chsd ldrs: rdn and ev ch whn hmpd over 1f out: styng on same pce whn nt clr run wl ins fnl f* **12/1**

50-P **4** 5 **Daniella**[20] 2450 5-8-7 82....(p) TQuinn 6 76
(Rae Guest) *led: rdn: hung lft and hdd over 1f out: sn wknd* **20/1**

1-11 **5** 2 ½ **Para Siempre**[164] 147 3-8-0 99....(b) NickyMackay 2 66
(B Smart) *chsd ldrs: n.m.r and lost pl wl over 3f out: n.d after* **8/1**

-351 **6** 2 ½ **Diamond Diva**[18] 2518 3-8-0 90.... ChrisCatlin 4 59
(J W Hills) *lw: prom: racd keenly: rdn whn hmpd over 1f out: sn wknd* **7/2**[3]

6-00 **7** 11 **Dizzy Dreamer (IRE)**[47] 1704 4-8-7 97.... RyanMoore 7 28
(P W Chapple-Hyam) *chsd ldrs over 4f* **4/1**

1m 13.01s (-0.34) **Going Correction** +0.20s/f (Good)
WFA 3 from 4yo+ 7lb **7** Ran SP% **117.5**
Speed ratings (Par 104):110,108,107,100,97 94,79
CSF £11.86 TOTE £3.90: £2.10, £2.30; EX 12.30.
Owner Mrs M V Chaworth-Musters **Bred** Mrs M Chaworth Musters **Trained** Whitsbury, Hants

FOCUS
They went a decent pace considering the tiring ground in this conditions event. The form is a bit muddling, rated through the winner, with not much strength in depth.

NOTEBOOK
Gloved Hand, who is in foal to Cadeaux Genereux, won a handicap here over 7f last time out, so the fact that they went a good clip over this shorter distance suited her down to the ground. She picked up well from off the pace and won very cosily in the end, her rider not having to get too serious with her, and with four weeks or so to play with, connections will no doubt be hunting for an opportunity to gain some further black type with her. (op 5-2 tchd 10-3)
Medley did not get home over 7f last time but her previous third in a Listed race at Ascot gave her every chance in this company. She was perhaps a little unlucky to run into a rival at the top of her game in Gloved Hand, but she may also be more effective on a quicker surface. (op 9-2 tchd 11-2 and 5-1 in a place)
Pusey Street Lady had work to do to be competitive at this level according to the official ratings, but she has improved with every outing this season and took another step forward here. Her handicap mark is likely to take a battering after this, however, so things are not going to get any easier.
Daniella, pulled up on her previous outing this year when she lost a shoe, again hung left, and perhaps all is not well with her. Official explanation: jockey said mare hung badly left
Para Siempre, coming here off a hat-trick on Fibresand which was completed in January, was entitled to need this run. She has still to prove that she is as effective on turf as she is on the artificial surface at Southwell.
Diamond Diva is another who has only won on the All-Weather, in her case Polytrack, but she had decent form in soft ground as a two-year-old so was entitled to respect in this company. She was disappointing, though, and perhaps this rather tacky surface just did not suit her. Official explanation: jockey said filly suffered interference in running (op 4-1)
Dizzy Dreamer(IRE) has struggled in Pattern company this term and did not perform any better on this drop in class. She is becoming disappointing. (op 7-2)

3060 NEWMARKETRACECOURSES.CO.UK H'CAP 1m 2f
8:40 (8:44) (Class 4) (0-85,85) 3-Y-O+
£4,985 (£1,492; £746; £373; £186; £93) **Stalls** Centre

Form RPR

0212 **1** **Night Cru**[9] 2765 4-9-8 **81**.... GeorgeBaker 10 92+
(C F Wall) *lw: chsd ldr tl led over 2f out: rdn and hung rt over 1f out: r.o: eased nr fin* **7/2**[1]

0-03 **2** 2 ½ **Magicalmysterytour (IRE)**[20] 2474 4-9-11 **84**.... BrettDoyle 9 88
(W J Musson) *chsd ldrs: rdn over 1f out: styd on* **5/1**[3]

1100 **3** hd **William's Way**[5] 2906 5-9-12 **85**.... JamieSpencer 2 89
(I A Wood) *s.i.s: hld up: hdwy over 1f out: sn rdn: styd on* **11/1**

0-20 **4** ¾ **Bedizen**[64] 1259 4-9-4 **77**.... RyanMoore 4 79
(Sir Michael Stoute) *swtg: chsd ldrs: rdn and ev ch over 1f out: no ex ins fnl f* **9/2**[2]

3-50 **5** 5 **Bobby Charles**[23] 2351 6-9-2 **75**.... DarryllHolland 8 67
(Dr J D Scargill) *hld up: hdwy over 2f out: sn rdn: nt trble ldrs* **9/1**

-001 **6** 1 **Zaif (IRE)**[16] 2551 4-9-10 **83**.... AntonyProcter 3 73
(D R C Elsworth) *hld up: rdn over 3f out: n.d* **7/1**

005- **7** 2 **Jack Of Trumps (IRE)**[289] 5299 7-9-7 **80**.... SteveDrowne 1 66
(G Wragg) *lw: hld up: rdn over 1f out: n.d* **11/2**

0-60 **8** 3 ½ **Spanish Don**[28] 2208 9-9-9 **82**.... NeilPollard 11 61
(D R C Elsworth) *b: led: racd keenly: clr 1/2-way: hdd over 2f out: wknd over 1f out* **14/1**

1- **9** 8 **Shotfire Ridge**[276] 5598 4-9-6 **79**.... OscarUrbina 6 42
(M Wigham) *hld up: rdn and wknd over 2f out* **14/1**

440- **10** 9 **Archiestown (USA)**[393] 2175 4-9-2 **75**.... TQuinn 7 20
(J L Dunlop) *lw: hld up: wknd over 4f out* **20/1**

2m 9.10s (2.66) **Going Correction** +0.20s/f (Good) **10** Ran SP% **121.4**
Speed ratings (Par 105):97,95,94,94,90 89,87,85,78,71
CSF £21.87 CT £179.76 TOTE £3.70: £1.60, £2.30, £3.70; EX 24.30.
Owner Archangels 2 **Bred** Jeremy Green And Sons **Trained** Newmarket, Suffolk

FOCUS
They did not go a mad gallop here and the hold-up horses were at a big disadvantage. As a result it is hard to be too confident about the form, but the winner is improving and the third ran as well as ever.

3061 TURFTV H'CAP 5f

9:10 (9:11) (Class 4) (0-85,82) 3-Y-O £5,181 (£1,541; £770; £384) **Stalls** Low

Form RPR

-211 **1** **Sundae**[14] [2631] 3-9-4 **79** TedDurcan 4 94+
(C F Wall) *half-rrd and wnt rt s: outpcd: hdwy over 1f out: sn rdn: r.o to ld post* **4/5**[1]

-321 **2** *shd* **Obstructive**[18] [2513] 3-9-5 **80** JimCrowley 10 95
(D K Ivory) *chsd ldrs: led 1/2-way: rdn fnl f: hdd post* **7/1**[3]

1555 **3** *5* **Rocker**[14] [2629] 3-9-0 **75** (v) JohnEgan 6 72
(B R Johnson) *chsd ldrs: rdn over 1f out: wknd ins fnl f* **16/1**

2103 **4** *nk* **Baileys Outshine**[6] [2867] 3-8-10 **76** PatrickHills(5) 1 72
(J G Given) *led to 1/2-way: sn rdn: wknd ins fnl f* **12/1**

0436 **5** *1 1/2* **Prospect Place**[7] [2821] 3-9-2 **77** JamieSpencer 8 67
(M Dods) *s.i.s: nvr nrr* **13/2**[2]

63-3 **6** *1 3/4* **Star Strider**[18] [2513] 3-8-5 **71** WilliamBuick(5) 3 55
(A M Balding) *chsd ldrs: rdn and swtchd rt over 1f out: sn wknd* **8/1**

5-06 **7** *5* **Bridge It Jo**[33] [2060] 3-9-7 **82** TQuinn 5 48
(G G Margarson) *s.s: outpcd* **16/1**

116 **8** *3* **Daddy Cool**[49] [1616] 3-9-3 **81** LiamJones(3) 2 36
(W G M Turner) *chsd ldrs to 1/2-way* **14/1**

1-40 **9** *nk* **Frisky Talk (IRE)**[42] [1825] 3-9-6 **81** MichaelHills 9 35
(B W Hills) *lw: b.hind: chsd ldrs: rdn 1/2-way: hung lft and wknd over 1f out* **20/1**

59.73 secs (0.17) **Going Correction** +0.20s/f (Good) **9** Ran SP% **123.4**
Speed ratings (Par 101):106,105,97,97,94 92,84,79,78
CSF £7.85 CT £60.86 TOTE £1.80: £1.10, £2.30, £5.30; EX 9.30 Place 6 £209.19, Place 5 £102.46.
Owner Peter Gregory **Bred** Jeremy Green And Sons **Trained** Newmarket, Suffolk

FOCUS
An interesting handicap featuring a couple of progressive sprinters who came clear of the rest. The form looks solid.
Prospect Place Official explanation: jockey said gelding moved poorly
Bridge It Jo Official explanation: jockey said filly missed the break
T/Plt: £232.90 to a £1 stake. Pool: £64,720.65. 202.80 winning tickets. T/Qpdt: £6.10 to a £1 stake. Pool: £5,420.00. 655.85 winning tickets. CR

[2946] WOLVERHAMPTON (A.W) (L-H)

Friday, June 29

OFFICIAL GOING: Standard to fast
Wind: Moderate across becoming fresh behind Weather: Broken sunshine with threat of light showers

3062 SPONSOR A RACE BY CALLING 0870 220 2442 MAIDEN STKS 5f 216y(P)

2:20 (2:20) (Class 5) 3-Y-O+ £2,817 (£838; £418; £209) **Stalls** Low

Form RPR

03 **1** **Sugar Land**[66] [1215] 3-8-9 0 MartinDwyer 6 75
(C A Cyzer) *trckd ldrs: rdn and hdwy to ld ins fnl f: r.o wl* **14/1**

40-0 **2** *1 3/4* **Tarkamara (IRE)**[50] [1610] 3-8-4 78 TolleyDean(5) 4 70
(P F I Cole) *led tl rdn and hdd ins fnl f: kpt on one pce* **9/2**[2]

30-2 **3** *1 1/4* **Wolf River (USA)**[72] [1098] 3-9-0 80 FergusSweeney 11 71
(D M Simcock) *trckd ldr tl rdn over 1f out: kpt on one pce fnl f* **7/2**[1]

5 **4** *1 1/2* **Topflightcoolracer**[155] [237] 3-8-9 0 J-PGuillambert 12 62
(Mrs G S Rees) *trckd ldrs: rdn over 1f out: nt qckn* **14/1**

03 **5** *2* **Hartmann (USA)**[29] [2175] 3-8-11 0 JamieMoriarty(3) 1 61
(B J Meehan) *s.i.s: rdn over 2f out: sme hdwy over 1f out* **5/1**[3]

0 **6** *1/2* **Lithaam (IRE)**[54] [1501] 3-8-7 0 BarrySavage(7) 8 59
(J M Bradley) *hld up: kpt on one pce ins fnl 2f: nvr on terms* **50/1**

6 **7** *nk* **Dirty Dancing**[29] [2175] 3-9-0 0 MichaelHills 5 58
(B W Hills) *trckd ldrs tl rdn over 2f out: sn btn* **13/2**

0 **8** *1 1/4* **Le Riche**[20] [2470] 3-8-6 0 (p) RichardKingscote(3) 10 49
(Miss J R Gibney) *slowly away: nvr on terms* **40/1**

9 *shd* **Caravel (IRE)** 3-9-0 0 JimmyQuinn 9 54+
(Sir Mark Prescott) *slowly away: outpcd thrght* **7/1**

-050 **10** *3* **Land Ahoy**[14] [2631] 3-9-0 68 AdamKirby 2 45
(D W P Arbuthnot) *a bhd* **8/1**

11 *3/4* **Katie Coniston** 3-8-4 0 KevinGhunowa(5) 13 38
(Dr J R J Naylor) *mid-div: tl rdn after 2f: sn bhd* **50/1**

4 **12** *5* **Almost Married (IRE)**[46] [1716] 3-9-0 0 PaulMulrennan 3 28
(J D Bethell) *in tch to 1/2-way* **16/1**

1m 14.01s (-1.80) **Going Correction** -0.10s/f (Stan)
WFA 3 from 4yo 7lb **12** Ran SP% **119.6**
Speed ratings (Par 103):108,105,104,102,99 98,98,96,96,92 91,84
CSF £76.15 TOTE £13.50: £3.00, £2.40, £1.50; EX 89.70.
Owner Mrs Charles Cyzer **Bred** C A Cyzer **Trained** Maplehurst, W Sussex

FOCUS
An ordinary maiden, run at a strong early pace. The form is rated through the second and third. Big improvement from the winner.
Le Riche Official explanation: jockey said filly reared on leaving stalls
Caravel(IRE) Official explanation: jockey said gelding was slowly away and ran green

3063 RINGSIDE SUITE 700 THEATRE STYLE CONFERENCE CLAIMING STKS 1m 4f 50y(P)

2:50 (2:50) (Class 6) 4-Y-O+ £2,590 (£770; £385; £192) **Stalls** Low

Form RPR

0501 **1** **Champagne Shadow (IRE)**[8] [2800] 6-9-0 68 (p) FergusSweeney 8 64
(Miss Tor Sturgis) *chsd ldrs: rdn to go 2nd 2f out: edgd rt bef led jst ins fnl f: edgd lft: all out* **9/2**[2]

4315 **2** *nk* **Rudry World (IRE)**[59] [1376] 4-7-11 53 SophieDoyle(7) 9 53
(P A Blockley) *trckd ldrs: sltly checked ent fnl f: r.o to press wnr nr fin* **5/1**[3]

6405 **3** *1 1/2* **Itcanbedone Again (IRE)**[4] [2946] 8-8-1 52 WilliamBuick(5) 2 53
(Ian Williams) *t.k.h in mid-div: sltly hmpd over 3f out: hdwy over 1f out and kpt on one pce* **8/1**

0220 **4** *nk* **Brastar Jelois (FR)**[37] [1951] 4-8-4 64 RussellKennemore(5) 3 56
(R Hollinshead) *bhd tl rdn and hdwy on ins 2f out: kpt on one pce fnl f* **8/1**

1464 **5** *1 1/4* **Atlantic Gamble (IRE)**[8] [2810] 7-9-8 64 (p) PaulMulrennan 6 67
(K R Burke) *t.k.h: sn prom: wnt 2nd 6f out: led 3f out: rdn and hdd jst ins fnl f: fdd* **11/4**[1]

02-3 **6** *9* **North Walk (IRE)**[8] [2800] 4-9-10 70 LPKeniry 10 54
(Jennie Candlish) *led for 2f: chsd ldr to 6f out: styd in tch tl wknd over 1f out* **14/1**

0/0- **7** *4* **Lazzaz**[417] [1548] 9-7-11 46 MCGeran(7) 7 28
(P W Hiatt) *bhd: rdn and brief effrt 3f out: sn btn* **33/1**

0400 **8** *21* **Gala Jackpot (USA)**[23] [2372] 4-8-1 37 (b[1]) LiamJones(3) 5 —
(W M Brisbourne) *plld hrd: led after 2f: hdd 3f out: wknd qckly* **28/1**

-436 **9** *7* **Port 'n Starboard**[74] [1069] 6-9-0 62 MartinDwyer 4 —
(C A Cyzer) *hld up: lost tch over 2f out: eased fnl f* **5/1**[3]

2m 40.29s (-2.13) **Going Correction** -0.10s/f (Stan) **9** Ran SP% **113.5**
Speed ratings (Par 101):103,102,101,101,100 94,92,78,73
CSF £26.74 TOTE £5.00: £1.60, £1.50, £2.60; EX 30.50.Rudry World was claimed by Michael Mullineaux for £5,000.
Owner Miss Tor Sturgis **Bred** Mrs Kate Watson **Trained** Lambourn, Berks
■ Stewards' Enquiry : Fergus Sweeney one-day ban: using whip with excessive frequency (Jul 10)

FOCUS
A typically modest claimer. It was run at just an ordinary pace and the third is the best guide to the form.

3064 BOOK ONLINE AT WOLVERHAMPTON-RACECOURSE.CO.UK H'CAP 5f 216y(P)

3:20 (3:20) (Class 6) (0-60,63) 3-Y-O+ £2,730 (£806; £403) **Stalls** Low

Form RPR

3031 **1** **Mambazo**[8] [2799] 5-9-7 **63** 6ex (e) RichardKingscote(3) 4 74+
(S C Williams) *t.k.h: a.p: rdn over 1f out: led ins fnl f: won gng away* **3/1**[1]

6001 **2** *1 1/2* **Caustic Wit (IRE)**[6] [2879] 9-9-6 **59** 6ex FergusSweeney 9 65
(M S Saunders) *a.p: led wl over 1f out: rdn and hdd ins fnl f: nt pce of wnr* **9/1**

6010 **3** *1/2* **Royal Orissa**[4] [2947] 5-9-3 **56** AdamKirby 1 61
(D Haydn Jones) *slowly away: sn mid-div: rdn over 1f out: kpt on fnl f* **7/1**[3]

0066 **4** *hd* **Ebraam (USA)**[66] [1226] 4-9-4 **57** DeanMcKeown 12 61+
(D Shaw) *swtchd to ins fr outside draw: hdwy over 1f out: ev ch ins fnl f: nt qckn* **11/1**

0-05 **5** *hd* **Turkish Sultan (IRE)**[14] [2622] 4-8-13 **57** (p) KevinGhunowa(5) 2 60
(J M Bradley) *chsd ldrs: one pce fnl f* **18/1**

1250 **6** *nk* **Balerno**[8] [2799] 8-9-3 **56** IanMongan 10 58
(Mrs L J Mongan) *broke wl: c wd into st: nt qckn fnl f* **10/1**

00/0 **7** *3/4* **Dorchester**[29] [2190] 10-9-0 **60** AlanRutter(7) 11 60
(W J Musson) *in rr: sme late hdwy: n.d* **33/1**

0000 **8** *1* **Decider (USA)**[3] [2966] 4-9-4 **57** LPKeniry 3 54
(J M Bradley) *t.k.h: prom tl wknd ins fnl f* **14/1**

0435 **9** *hd* **Mistral Sky**[4] [2947] 8-9-1 **59** (v) WilliamBuick(5) 5 56
(Stef Liddiard) *bhd: rdn over 2f out: nvr on terms* **9/2**[2]

0-00 **10** *hd* **Canina**[17] [2527] 4-8-9 **55** JohnCavanagh(7) 8 51
(Paul Green) *led tl rdn and hdd wl over 1f out: wknd qckly ins fnl f* **50/1**

5530 **11** *1* **Musical Script (USA)**[17] [2546] 4-9-6 **59** MartinDwyer 6 52
(Mouse Hamilton-Fairley) *bhd: rdn over 2f out: nvr on terms* **15/2**

2060 **P** **Grand Palace (IRE)**[4] [2947] 4-9-3 **56** (v) J-PGuillambert 7 —
(D Shaw) *in rr whn lost action and p.u 1/2-way* **14/1**

1m 14.43s (-1.38) **Going Correction** -0.10s/f (Stan) **12** Ran SP% **118.4**
Speed ratings (Par 101):105,103,102,102,101 101,100,99,98,98 97,—
CSF £30.44 CT £180.06 TOTE £2.90: £1.60, £3.00, £3.00; EX 20.50.
Owner D G Burge **Bred** Barry Taylor **Trained** Newmarket, Suffolk
■ Stewards' Enquiry : John Cavanagh three-day ban: used whip with excessive force (Jul 10,12,14)

FOCUS
A moderate sprint, run at just an average early pace. The form still looks sound for the class, with the winner back to his best.
Mistral Sky Official explanation: jockey said gelding missed the break
Musical Script(USA) Official explanation: jockey said gelding hung right

3065 ENJOY EXECUTIVE HOSPITALITY AT WOLVERHAMPTON (S) STKS 7f 32y(P)

3:50 (3:50) (Class 6) 2-Y-O £2,047 (£604; £302) **Stalls** High

Form RPR

002 **1** **Never Sold Out (IRE)**[23] [2356] 2-8-4 0 MCGeran(7) 7 60
(J G M O'Shea) *in tch: c wd into st: edgd lft but sustained run to ld ins fnl f: pushed out* **5/1**[3]

540 **2** *1 3/4* **Ten On Line (IRE)**[11] [2723] 2-8-11 0 MartinDwyer 5 55
(J A Osborne) *towards rr: hdwy on ins 2f out: kpt on to chse wnr ins fnl f* **3/1**[1]

4313 **3** *2 1/2* **Miss Willoughby**[7] [2838] 2-8-12 0 J-PGuillambert 8 50
(J Ryan) *trckd ldr: rdn to ld wl over 1f out: hdd and lost 2nd ins fnl f* **11/2**

0 **4** *shd* **Little By Luck (IRE)**[13] [2651] 2-8-3 0 LiamJones(3) 10 44
(W G M Turner) *chsd ldrs: rdn 2f out: one pce fnl f* **17/2**

5 *2* **Riki Wiki Wheels** 2-8-6 0 RussellKennemore(5) 4 44
(P T Midgley) *s.i.s: in rr tl styd on fnl f: nvr nrr* **12/1**

04 **6** *shd* **Madam Zorro**[7] [2838] 2-8-3 0 DominicFox(3) 9 39
(S Parr) *mid-div: c wd into st: one pce fr over 1f out* **25/1**

5330 **7** *1 1/2* **Miss Antropist (IRE)**[18] [2517] 2-8-6 0 PaulMulrennan 6 35
(R A Harris) *prom: led 1/2-way: hdd wl over 1f out: wknd fnl f* **9/1**

065 **8** *3/4* **Fraamington**[15] [2605] 2-8-11 0 (v[1]) EdwardCreighton 3 38
(M R Channon) *prom: rdn 1/2-way: wknd over 1f out* **10/1**

000 **9** *1 1/4* **Adam Eterno (IRE)**[14] [2632] 2-8-8 0 (b[1]) JamieMoriarty(3) 2 35
(B J Meehan) *s.i.s: nvr bttr than mid-div* **9/2**[2]

06 **10** *10* **Misk Hills**[7] [2838] 2-8-11 0 LeeEnstone 1 10
(P T Midgley) *led to 1/2-way: wknd 2f out* **33/1**

1m 32.24s (1.84) **Going Correction** -0.10s/f (Stan) **10** Ran SP% **119.3**
Speed ratings (Par 91):85,83,80,80,77 77,75,75,73,62
CSF £20.91 TOTE £6.50: £2.20, £1.20, £2.20; EX 22.80.There was no bid for the winner. Ten On Line was claimed by J. G. M. O'Shea for £6,000.
Owner W R Baddiley **Bred** Victor Connolly **Trained** Elton, Gloucs

FOCUS
A poor juvenile affair. The form looks straightforward enough.

NOTEBOOK
Never Sold Out(IRE), making his debut for new connections, built on the promise of his second at Lingfield 23 days previously and duly went one better in ready fashion on this step up in trip. This is clearly his sort of level, but he should still have a little more to offer over this sort of distance. (op 6-1)
Ten On Line(IRE), behind today's winner at Lingfield on his penultimate outing, came through to show his best form to date and got the longer trip without much fuss. He was later claimed by the trainer of the winner and should win races in this type of grade. (op 9-2)
Miss Willoughby was always up with the pace and ran respectably under top weight, but again did enough to suggest that a drop to 6f is now in order. (op 7-2 tchd 6-1)
Little By Luck(IRE), up in trip, posted an improvement on the level of her Bath debut effort and is entitled to come on again a bit for the experience. (op 8-1 tchd 9-1)
Adam Eterno(IRE), down in grade and tried in first-time blinkers, never looked like justifying market support and is clearly very tricky. (op 5-1 tchd 11-2)

3066 **ENJOY THE HORIZONS RESTAURANT H'CAP** **7f 32y(P)**
4:20 (4:21) (Class 5) (0-70,70) 3-Y-O **£3,238** (£963; £481; £240) **Stalls** High

Form RPR

44-0 **1** **Lawyers Choice**^{18} 2515 3-9-4 **67** IanMongan 11 70
(Pat Eddery) *in tch: rdn over 2f out: r.o u.str.p to ld nr fin: all out* **16/1**

04-2 **2** *hd* **Pivotalia (IRE)**^{27} 2261 3-9-3 **66** AdamKirby 8 68
(W R Swinburn) *led tl hdd wl over 1f out: rdn and r.o fnl f to regain 2nd nr fin* **5/1^{2}**

5613 **3** *½* **Divertimenti (IRE)**^{36} 1978 3-9-4 **70** LiamJones(3) 5 71
(C R Dore) *t.k.h: hdwy 3f out: led wl over 1f out tl no ex nr fin whn hdd and lost 2nd* **5/1^{2}**

1446 **4** *hd* **Pietersen (IRE)**^{30} 2133 3-9-5 **68** (b) PaulMulrennan 12 68
(T D Barron) *trckd ldr to over 4f out: edgd lft over 3f out: rdn and kpt on one pce fnl f* **7/1**

-400 **5** *1 ½* **Royal Guest**^{65} 1247 3-9-1 **64** EdwardCreighton 9 60+
(M R Channon) *in rr: rdn over 1f out: r.o ins fnl f: nvr nrr* **17/2**

154 **6** *2* **Dressed To Dance (IRE)**^{18} 2515 3-9-3 **66** (v) J-PGuillambert 4 57+
(N Tinkler) *slowly away: bdly hmpd over 3f out: hdwy on outside over 1f out: no imp fnl f* **4/1^{1}**

130 **7** *2* **Still Crazy (IRE)**^{98} 744 3-8-12 **61** LPKeniry 6 46+
(E F Vaughan) *mid-div whn bmpd over 3f out: nvr on terms after* **6/1^{3}**

4300 **8** *hd* **Early Promise (IRE)**^{16} 2571 3-8-6 **60** LukeMorris(5) 7 45
(P L Gilligan) *t.k.h: 2nd over 4f out to over 1f out: wknd fnl f* **16/1**

005- **9** *6* **Berbatov**^{221} 6536 3-8-1 **57** JohnCavanagh(7) 10 26
(Paul Green) *slowly away: forced wd 3f out: sn btn* **33/1**

000 **10** *77* **Capping (IRE)**^{17} 2542 3-8-10 **59** (vt^{1}) FergusSweeney 3 —+
(W R Swinburn) *mid-div whn bdly hmpd and almost fell over 3f out: nt rcvr: t.o* **20/1**

253 **11** *shd* **Six Of Hearts**^{17} 2541 3-9-4 **67** MartinDwyer 2 —+
(J A Osborne) *trcking ldrs whn bdly hmpd over 3f out: nt rcvr: t.o* **7/1**

1m 29.85s (-0.55) **Going Correction** -0.10s/f (Stan) **11** Ran SP% **122.6**
Speed ratings (Par 99):99,98,98,97,96 93,91,91,84,— —
CSF £98.22 CT £482.72 TOTE £23.40: £5.30, £1.50, £1.80; EX 185.00.
Owner Raymond Tooth **Bred** Chippenham Lodge Stud & Rathbarry Stud **Trained** Nether Winchendon, Bucks
■ Stewards' Enquiry : Luke Morris caution: careless riding

FOCUS
A modest yet eventful handicap, run at a solid pace. A number of runners lost their chances when badly hampered going into the final bend but the first four stayed clear of the trouble. The form is pretty limited.

3067 **HOLD YOUR CHRISTMAS PARTY AT WOLVERHAMPTON AMATEUR RIDERS' H'CAP** **1m 141y(P)**
4:50 (4:50) (Class 6) (0-60,59) 4-Y-O+ **£2,307** (£709; £354) **Stalls** Low

Form RPR

-022 **1** **Turn Me On (IRE)**^{18} 2508 4-11-4 **59** MrMWalford(3) 1 68
(T D Walford) *led for 1f: styd in tch: led wl over 1f out: rdn and r.o wl fnl f* **4/1^{1}**

5450 **2** *1* **Hoh Wotanite**^{16} 2576 4-11-2 **59** (p) MrStephenHarrison(5) 7 68+
(R Hollinshead) *in rr: hdwy whn short of room over 2f out: swtchd rt over 1f out: nt clr run and swtchd lft ins fnl f: r.o to go 2nd post* **7/1**

0300 **3** *shd* **Golden Spectrum (IRE)**^{18} 2521 8-11-3 **55** (b) MrSDobson 8 62
(R A Harris) *in rr: hdwy on ins over 3f out: rdn over 2f out: chsd wnr ins fnl f tl lost 2nd post* **14/1**

653 **4** *1 ¼* **Trevian**^{19} 2492 6-10-7 **52** MissHDavies(7) 9 56
(J M Bradley) *mid-div: c v wd into st: hdwy over 1f out: r.o ins fnl f* **14/1**

2036 **5** *nk* **Machinate (USA)**^{16} 2550 5-10-10 **53** MrBenBrisbourne(5) 2 56
(W M Brisbourne) *s.i.s: hdwy over 2f out: rdn over 1f out: one pce after* **6/1^{3}**

5206 **6** *½* **Border Artist**^{20} 2458 8-11-0 **55** MrSPearce(3) 6 57
(J Pearce) *hld up in rr: hdwy on ins over 1f out: one pce fnl f* **12/1**

0020 **7** *1* **Bowl Of Cherries**^{2} 2990 4-11-1 **53** (v) MrSWalker 11 53
(I A Wood) *prom whn stmbld over 3f out: rdn over 2f out: no hdwy fr over 1f out* **13/2**

4001 **8** *1* **Ceredig**^{8} 2798 4-10-8 **53** 6ex MissLauraGray(7) 12 51
(Mrs L J Mongan) *t.k.h: prom: led over 2f out: hdd wl over 1f out: wknd fnl f* **16/1**

40-0 **9** *1 ¾* **Uhuru Peak**^{161} 179 6-11-2 **54** (bt) MissSBrotherton 3 48
(M W Easterby) *mid-div: c wd into st: no hdwy after* **20/1**

-204 **10** *1 ¼* **Rock Haven (IRE)**^{13} 2656 5-10-9 **54** MrSeanKerr(7) 4 45
(G F Bridgwater) *wnt prom 6f out: wknd over 1f out* **12/1**

04-0 **11** *¾* **Band**^{11} 2716 7-10-9 **54** MissEGeorge(7) 10 43
(E S McMahon) *trckd ldrs tl wknd wl over 1f out* **14/1**

0-00 **12** *3* **Gary's Indian (IRE)**^{21} 2433 4-10-12 **55** MrCPHuxley(5) 5 38
(B P J Baugh) *a bhd* **40/1**

05-1 **13** *1* **Coronado's Gold (USA)**^{21} 2431 6-11-5 **57** MissLEllison 13 38
(B Ellison) *led after 1f: hdd over 2f out: wknd over 1f out* **11/2^{2}**

1m 51.84s (0.08) **Going Correction** -0.10s/f (Stan) **13** Ran SP% **124.0**
Speed ratings (Par 101):95,94,94,92,92 92,91,90,88,87 87,84,83
CSF £32.62 CT £381.91 TOTE £4.20: £1.60, £2.70, £6.30; EX 45.30 Place 6 £72.02, Place 5 £40.33.
Owner Ms M Austerfield **Bred** Brendan Lavery **Trained** Sheriff Hutton, N Yorks

FOCUS
A moderate handicap, confined to amateur riders, run at a modest pace. Just ordinary pace, although the winner could build on this.
T/Plt: £44.70 to a £1 stake. Pool: £61,640.50. 1,004.60 winning tickets. T/Qpdt: £12.80 to a £1 stake. Pool: £3,028.00. 174.80 winning tickets. JS

3068 - 3070a (Foreign Racing) - See Raceform Interactive

2480 CURRAGH (R-H)
Friday, June 29

OFFICIAL GOING: Soft

3071a **SAOIRE STKS (LISTED RACE) (FILLIES)** **6f**
7:30 (7:30) 2-Y-O **£24,192** (£7,097; £3,381; £1,152)

RPR

1 **Listen (IRE)** 2-8-12 KFallon 7 100+
(A P O'Brien, Ire) *hld up towards rr: 6th 1/2-way: 4th and hdwy on outer 2f out: led 1 1/2f out: rdn clr ins fnl f* **7/2^{2}**

2 *1 ¼* **Tuscan Evening (IRE)**^{9} 2756 2-8-12 DMGrant 4 96
(John Joseph Murphy, Ire) *trckd ldrs: 5th 1/2-way: rdn 2f out: 2nd ins fnl f: kpt on wout threatening wnr* **7/1^{3}**

3 *½* **Charlotte Bronte** 2-8-12 WMLordan 3 95
(David Wachman, Ire) *hld up in rr: rdn and outpcd 1/2-way: styd on fr over 1f out* **11/1**

4 *1 ¼* **Porto Marmay (IRE)**^{25} 2325 2-8-12 DPMcDonogh 2 91
(K J Condon, Ire) *led: rdn 1/2-way: hdd 1 1/2f out: no ex ins fnl f* **25/1**

5 *1 ¼* **Saoirse Abu (USA)**^{25} 2325 2-8-12 KJManning 5 90+
(J S Bolger, Ire) *cl 2nd: rdn to chal 1/2-way: 3rd 1 1/2f out: sn no ex* **9/10^{1}**

6 *4 ½* **Fourpenny Lane**^{14} 2642 2-8-12 MJKinane 6 74
(Ms Joanna Morgan, Ire) *chsd ldrs in 3rd: rdn and wknd fr over 2f out* **20/1**

7 *1 ¾* **Invincible Woman (IRE)**^{28} 2226 2-8-12 PJSmullen 1 68
(Ms F M Crowley, Ire) *upset in stalls: trckd ldrs: 4th bef 1/2-way: wknd fr under 2f out* **7/1^{3}**

1m 15.4s (0.90) **Going Correction** +0.20s/f (Good) **7** Ran SP% **116.8**
Speed ratings: 102,100,99,98,96 90,88
CSF £28.74 TOTE £3.60: £2.10, £3.80; DF 31.30.
Owner Derrick Smith **Bred** Brittas House Stud **Trained** Ballydoyle, Co Tipperary

FOCUS
A very pleasing success for the well bred and well regarded newcomer Listen. The form seems soild enough.

NOTEBOOK
Listen(IRE) put up a pleasing debut performance and is primed to emulate her sister Sequoyah, mother of the unbeaten Coventry Stakes hero Henrythenavigator, later in the season, by going for Group 1 glory in the Moyglare Stud Stakes. Obviously well regarded, she quickened nicely to take up the running before the final furlong and kept on very well in the closing stages. A daughter of Sadler's Wells, she should be more at home over a trip, and the Debutante Stakes back here on August 12 is likely to be her next start, before she steps up to Group 1 company for the Moyglare. (op 7/2 tchd 9/2)
Tuscan Evening(IRE) was reappearing after her ninth place finish behind Elletelle in the Queen Mary. She appreciated this extra furlong when staying on in the closing stages and, based on this evidence, she should be more than capable of winning her maiden before long over this trip or even over a furlong further. (op 6/1)
Charlotte Bronte, who is from the family of Pas De Response and Storm Bird, made an encouraging debut and is open to improvement. (op 8/1 tchd 12/1)
Porto Marmay(IRE) broke smartly to lead but, once the race unfolded, she was soon struggling to maintain that early momentum.
Saoirse Abu(USA), whose stable won this race last year, was sent off a hot favourite but was very disappointing. She seemed to settle into a nice rhythm tracking the leader early on, but the distress signals went up after halfway and she soon dropped right out. This surely did not represent her true form, and perhaps the easier ground was her downfall. (op 1/1)

3072 - 3074a (Foreign Racing) - See Raceform Interactive

2976 HAMBURG (R-H)
Friday, June 29

OFFICIAL GOING: Soft

3075a **FAHRHOFER STUTENPREIS (GROUP 3) (F&M)** **1m 3f**
6:25 (6:26) 3-Y-O+ **£21,622** (£6,757; £3,378; £2,027)

RPR

1 **Avanti Polonia (GER)**^{26} 2294 3-8-5 DBonilla 5 108
(P Schiergen, Germany) *racd in 3rd to st: chal over 2f out: led wl over 1f out: drvn out* **5/2^{2}**

2 *hd* **Neele (IRE)**^{306} 3-8-5 AHelfenbein 8 108
(H Steinmetz, Germany) *racd in 4th to st: styd on fr over 1f out: hrd rdn and ev ch last 100yds: r.o* **42/10**

3 *6* **Fair Breeze (GER)**^{26} 2296 4-9-6 ASuborics 2 100
(Mario Hofer, Germany) *led 7f out to wl over 1f out: wknd appr fnl f* **26/10^{3}**

4 *hd* **Carolines Secret**^{23} 2384 3-8-5 NRichter 4 98
(Mario Hofer, Germany) *led 4f: lost pl qckly 4f out and last st: drvn to take 4th cl home* **147/10**

5 *hd* **Nordtanzerin (GER)**^{41} 4-9-6 AStarke 1 99
(P Schiergen, Germany) *hld up in rr: rapid hdwy wl over 3f out to go 2nd st: ev ch 2f out: sn btn* **1/1^{1}**

2m 26.28s (1.58)
WFA 3 from 4yo 13lb **9** Ran SP% **131.9**
(including ten euro stakes): WIN 35; PL 23, 29; SF 96.
Owner Gestut Ebbesloh **Bred** Gestut Ebbesloh **Trained** Germany

2526 CHESTER (L-H)
Saturday, June 30

OFFICIAL GOING: Soft (6.8)
After 3" rain over the previous six days and more ran in the day the ground was 'genuine soft, becoming heavy in places'.
Wind: light half-behind Weather: Persistent light showers, rain race 4 and 5

3076 **WARWICK INTERNATIONAL CLAIMING STKS** **1m 2f 75y**
2:15 (2:16) (Class 5) 3-Y-O+ **£3,432** (£1,021; £510; £254) **Stalls** High

Form RPR

00-0 **1** **Realism (FR)**^{35} 1583 7-9-10 **95** JamieMoriarty(3) 3 92+
(R A Fahey) *trckd ldrs: nt clr run on inner over 2f out: led 1f out: drvn clr* **9/2^{2}**

0-41 **2** *3 ½* **Yakimov (USA)**^{25} 2346 8-9-3 **85** VinceSlattery 1 75
(D J Wintle) *trckd ldrs: nt clr run 2f out: styd on to take 2nd ins fnl f: no imp* **13/8^{1}**

0000 **3** *1 ½* **Punta Galera (IRE)**^{19} 2512 4-9-0 **73** DuranFentiman(3) 7 72
(R Hannon) *led: hdd 1f out: wknd ins fnl f* **15/2**

5505 **4** *3* **Optimus (USA)**^{15} 2621 5-9-4 **70** AdamKirby 9 67
(B G Powell) *hld up in rr: effrt over 2f out: kpt on: nvr rchd ldrs* **8/1**

0-43 **5** *nk* **Telegonus**^{58} 1231 4-8-12 **68** PJMcDonald(5) 5 66
(D McCain Jnr) *chsd ldrs: chal 2f out: one pce fnl f* **16/1**

0030 **6** *½* **Tous Les Deux**^{7} 2871 4-9-0 **70** RussellKennemore(5) 4 67
(Peter Grayson) *s.s: hld up in rr: effrt over 2f out: nvr rchd ldrs* **8/1**

00-0 **7** *5* **Chancellor (IRE)**^{24} 2351 9-9-3 **87** (t) J-PGuillambert 8 55
(D K Ivory) *hld up: effrt on outer over 4f out: chsng ldrs over 2f out: wknd fnl f* **5/1^{3}**

04-0 **8** *17* **Strife (IRE)**^{8} 2820 4-9-3 **47** (v^{1}) RichardMullen 2 23
(W M Brisbourne) *s.s: sn chsng ldrs: lost pl 3f out: sn bhd* **16/1**

0-00 **9** *14* **Height Of Esteem**[32] [2121] 4-9-3 43..........(t) FrancisNorton 6 —
(W M Brisbourne) *hld up in last: effrt 3f out: sn lost pl and bhd* **40/1**

2m 18.78s (5.64) **Going Correction** +0.50s/f (Yiel) **9** Ran SP% **121.1**
Speed ratings (Par 103):97,94,93,90,90 89,85,72,61
CSF £12.88 TOTE £5.80: £1.90, £1.40, £2.40; EX 13.00.
Owner G H Leatham **Bred** Darley Stud Management Co Ltd **Trained** Musley Bank, N Yorks

FOCUS
Just a steady gallop in this fair claimer. The winner put his seal on this once he was left with racing room and the runner-up ought to have finished further ahead of the next four home judged on official ratings. The form makes sense around the third and fifth.

3077 ELEGANT RESORTS NOVICE STKS — 5f 16y
2:50 (2:51) (Class 4) 2-Y-O **£4,728** (£1,406; £702; £351) **Stalls** Low

Form RPR

623 **1** **Captain Gerrard (IRE)**[21] [2451] 2-8-12 0.......... RichardMullen 6 99+
(B Smart) *mde all: shkn up over 1f out: drvn clr* **7/2**[3]

136 **2** *5* **Kersaint (IRE)**[28] [2232] 2-9-2 0.......... FrancisNorton 4 85+
(K A Ryan) *trckd ldrs: nt clr run over 1f out: styd on to take 2nd ins fnl f: no ch w wnr* **11/4**[2]

P423 **3** *3/4* **Look Busy (IRE)**[7] [2869] 2-8-4 0.......... PatrickMathers(3) 2 74
(A Berry) *chsd ldrs on inner: nt clr run over 1f out: swtchd rt ins fnl f: kpt on wl* **5/1**

01 **4** *hd* **Grylls (USA)**[23] [2398] 2-9-2 0.......... PatDobbs 1 82
(R Hannon) *chsd wnr: rdn over 1f out: kpt on same pce* **9/4**[1]

0120 **5** *6* **Little Pete (IRE)**[11] [2737] 2-9-0 0.......... AdamKirby 7 58
(R A Farrant) *sn chsng ldrs: lost pl over 1f out* **17/2**

51 **6** *1 1/4* **Fitolini**[47] [1727] 2-8-11 0.......... J-PGuillambert 3 51
(Mrs G S Rees) *s.i.s: hdwy on outer to chse ldrs over 2f out: wknd over 1f out* **12/1**

63.07 secs (1.02) **Going Correction** +0.50s/f (Yiel) **6** Ran SP% **114.5**
Speed ratings (Par 95):111,103,101,101,91 89
CSF £13.94 TOTE £4.10: £2.10, £2.30; EX 15.50.
Owner R C Bond **Bred** Alan Dargan **Trained** Hambleton, N Yorks

FOCUS
A decent novice event with four previous winners in the line-up. The winner appreciated being given his head and streaked clear in the style of a useful juvenile. He looks Listed class at least.

NOTEBOOK
Captain Gerrard(IRE) ◆, allowed to get on with it this time, revelled in the soft ground and drew right away. He is all speed and should make his presence felt in even stronger company. (op 9-2)
Kersaint(IRE), back in trip, met traffic problems but would not have troubled the winner anyway. (op 9-4 tchd 3-1, 10-3 in places)
Look Busy(IRE), tucked away on the inner, had to switch for a run and would have taken second spot with a bit further to go. She can surely be found an easier opportunity to get off the mark. (op 8-1 tchd 9-2)
Grylls(USA), awkward to load, had the plum draw and this may be as good as he is. (op 7-4 tchd 5-2 in places)
Little Pete(IRE), out of his depth at Royal Ascot, had the worst of the draw but that was no real excuse. (op 12-1 tchd 8-1, 7-1 in a place)
Fitolini, on turf for the first time on her third career start, missed a beat at the start and was always going the long way round in this much stronger company. (op 11-1)

3078 WARWICK INTERNATIONAL H'CAP — 7f 2y
3:25 (3:25) (Class 3) (0-90,90) 3-Y-O **£9,463** (£2,832; £1,416; £708; £352) **Stalls** Low

Form RPR

-221 **1** **Vitznau (IRE)**[29] [2213] 3-9-1 **84**.......... PatDobbs 2 92
(R Hannon) *trckd ldrs: led over 1f out: hld on towards fin* **3/1**[1]

-361 **2** *hd* **White Deer (USA)**[26] [2313] 3-9-7 **90**.......... J-PGuillambert 1 97
(M Johnston) *led tl over 1f out: rallied ins fnl f: jst hld* **7/2**[2]

31 **3** *1/2* **Vainglory (USA)**[16] [2606] 3-8-11 **80**.......... RichardMullen 3 86+
(D M Simcock) *trckd ldrs: kpt on wl fnl f: no ex fnl 75yds* **3/1**[1]

4214 **4** *1 3/4* **Medici Pearl**[7] [2872] 3-8-1 **73**.......... DuranFentiman(3) 7 74
(T D Easterby) *hmpd s: sn chsng ldrs: kpt on same pce appr fnl f* **14/1**

16-0 **5** *3/4* **Tudor Prince (IRE)**[9] [2788] 3-9-0 **86**.......... JamieMoriarty(3) 6 85
(B J Meehan) *sn chsng ldrs: kpt on same pce appr fnl f* **8/1**

1166 **6** *1* **Arch Of Titus (IRE)**[36] [1994] 3-8-5 **77**..........(t) AndrewElliott(3) 4 73
(M L W Bell) *sn drvn along: kpt on fnl 2f: nvr trbld ldrs* **14/1**

5001 **7** *3/4* **Bold Indian (IRE)**[29] [2200] 3-7-11 **71** oh3.......... ColinHaddon(5) 5 65
(I Semple) *sn trcking ldrs: effrt on outer 2f out: hung lft: kpt on same pce* **25/1**

-445 **8** *7* **Dubai Magic (USA)**[29] [2213] 3-8-11 **80**..........(t) FrancisNorton 10 55
(C E Brittain) *in rr: effrt over 2f out: sn lost pl and bhd* **14/1**

0054 **9** *5* **Everymanforhimself (IRE)**[35] [2044] 3-8-13 **87**..........(b) PatrickHills(5) 9 49
(J G Given) *sn chsng ldrs: rdn over 2f out: sn lost pl* **7/1**[3]

1m 30.65s (2.18) **Going Correction** +0.50s/f (Yiel) **9** Ran SP% **119.7**
Speed ratings (Par 103):107,106,106,104,103 102,101,93,87
CSF £14.21 CT £34.48 TOTE £3.90: £1.60, £1.70, £1.70; EX 13.50.
Owner Louis Stalder **Bred** John McLoughlin **Trained** East Everleigh, Wilts

FOCUS
A competitive handicap with the first three home having the best of the draw. All three are progressive and the form looks very sound.

NOTEBOOK
Vitznau(IRE), 7lb higher than at Epsom, never left the inner. After taking a definite advantage, in the end he was screaming for the line. (op 5-2 tchd 10-3)
White Deer(USA), 6lb higher than Thirsk, had the plum draw. He let the winner up his inner and was hitting back hard at the line. He deserves plenty of credit for this game defeat. (tchd 4-1)
Vainglory(USA), having just his third career start and making his handicap debut over an extra furlong, ran a fine race and battled away all the way to the line. This should have made a man of him. (op 5-2 tchd 10-3 in a place)
Medici Pearl, 2lb lower, was squeezed out at the start. She ran with plenty orf credit and is still on a learning curve.
Tudor Prince(IRE), making a quick return after his reappearance at Royal Ascot, went down fighting but is at his very best when allowed to take them along. (op 9-1)
Arch Of Titus(IRE), now just 3lb higher than his last success, has his quirks and, though not beaten all that far in the end, he never got competitive. Official explanation: jockey said colt lost its action (op 20-1)

3079 ELEGANT RESORTS MAIDEN STKS — 1m 2f 75y
4:00 (4:01) (Class 4) 3-Y-O+ **£5,505** (£1,637; £818; £408) **Stalls** High

Form RPR

05 **1** **Bee Sting**[12] [2726] 3-9-1 0.......... AdamKirby 2 84+
(W R Swinburn) *led: qcknd over 3f out: forged clr over 1f out: eased towards fin* **7/2**[3]

03 **2** *4* **Soul Mountain (IRE)**[16] [2597] 3-8-10 0.......... PatDobbs 10 68
(B W Hills) *hld up towards rr: hdwy 4f out: wnt 2nd over 1f out: no ch w wnr* **15/8**[1]

00 **3** *nk* **New Star (UAE)**[28] [2261] 3-9-1 0.......... PaulQuinn 5 72
(W M Brisbourne) *in rr: hdwy on outer over 2f out: styd on to take 3rd 1f out: kpt on same pce* **33/1**

52 **4** *2 1/2* **Lady Friend**[12] [2726] 5-9-3 0.......... PatrickHills(5) 6 64+
(J W Hills) *chsd ldrs: one pce fnl 3f* **11/4**[2]

5 *3* **Ful Of Grace (IRE)** 3-8-10 0.......... J-PGuillambert 1 56
(M G Quinlan) *s.i.s: sn chsng ldrs: drvn 3f out: one pce* **7/1**

00-0 **6** *1 1/2* **Dubai Shadow (IRE)**[10] [2766] 3-8-10 62.......... FrancisNorton 7 53
(C E Brittain) *trckd ldrs: t.k.h: lost pl over 3f out: n.d after* **12/1**

03-0 **7** *1* **Four Tel**[26] [2312] 3-8-10 59.......... PJMcDonald(5) 9 56
(N J Vaughan) *mid-div: jnd wnr over 6f out: wknd over 1f out* **33/1**

8 *11* **Airman (IRE)**[12] 4-9-13 0.......... RichardMullen 8 34
(W M Brisbourne) *s.s: in rr: drvn over 4f out: sn bhd* **12/1**

00 **9** *1* **Zen Garden**[22] [2436] 6-9-5 0.......... DuranFentiman(3) 4 27
(W M Brisbourne) *trckd wnr: lost pl over 2f out: sn bhd* **50/1**

2m 20.38s (7.24) **Going Correction** +0.50s/f (Yiel)
WFA 3 from 4yo+ 12lb **9** Ran SP% **119.4**
Speed ratings (Par 105):91,87,87,85,83 81,81,72,71
CSF £10.77 TOTE £4.30: £1.50, £1.20, £7.10; EX 15.30.
Owner Mrs P W Harris **Bred** R And Mrs Watson & Mrs A J Ralli **Trained** Aldbury, Herts

FOCUS
A weak maiden and an improved effort from the all-the-way winner. The form has been rated a little negatively.

3080 WARWICK INTERNATIONAL GROUP STKS (H'CAP) — 5f 16y
4:30 (4:30) (Class 3) (0-90,90) 3-Y-O **£9,463** (£2,832; £1,416; £708; £352) **Stalls** Low

Form RPR

6414 **1** **Our Little Secret (IRE)**[9] [2805] 5-8-8 **71** oh1.......... FrancisNorton 10 87
(A Berry) *smartly away: mde all: clr over 1f out: drvn out: unchal* **12/1**

0223 **2** *2 1/2* **Coconut Moon**[18] [2529] 5-8-9 **72**.......... PaulQuinn 3 79+
(E J Alston) *dwlt: bhd: hdwy and c outside over 1f out: styd on wl: tk 2nd nr fin* **6/1**

6051 **3** *nk* **Hoh Hoh Hoh**[18] [2529] 5-9-9 **86**.......... J-PGuillambert 5 92
(R J Price) *trckd ldrs: effrt over 1f out: styd on same pce* **10/3**[1]

6531 **4** *1/2* **Efistorm**[14] [2673] 6-9-5 **85**.......... JamieMoriarty(3) 2 89
(C R Dore) *chsd ldrs: kpt on same pce fnl 2f* **7/2**[2]

3025 **5** *1/2* **Blazing Heights**[7] [2866] 4-9-3 **83**.......... DuranFentiman(3) 1 85
(J S Goldie) *chsd wnr: rdn 2f out: kpt on same pce* **5/1**[3]

0004 **6** *1* **Curtail (IRE)**[7] [2866] 4-9-3 **85**.......... PJMcDonald(5) 9 84
(I Semple) *sn bhd: hdwy over 1f out: styd on wl* **10/1**

0030 **7** *1* **Cashel Mead**[13] [2694] 7-9-7 **84**.......... AdamKirby 4 79
(J L Spearing) *in rr and sn drvn along: kpt on fnl f* **6/1**

3140 **8** *2 1/2* **Magic Glade**[21] [2463] 8-9-13 **90**.......... RichardThomas 7 76
(Tom Dascombe) *chsd ldrs: wknd over 1f out* **14/1**

-433 **9** *3 1/2* **Stoneacre Lad (IRE)**[46] [1754] 4-9-8 **88**..........(b) PatrickMathers(3) 6 62
(Peter Grayson) *prom: wknd appr fnl f* **12/1**

0040 **10** *5* **Total Impact**[61] [1363] 4-9-1 **83**.......... MarkFlynn(5) 8 39
(C A Cyzer) *chsd ldrs on outer: lost pl over 1f out* **33/1**

63.53 secs (1.48) **Going Correction** +0.50s/f (Yiel) **10** Ran SP% **124.6**
Speed ratings (Par 107):108,104,103,102,101 100,98,94,89,81
CSF £87.97 CT £311.17 TOTE £12.30: £2.70, £1.90, £1.70; EX 90.20.
Owner J Berry **Bred** Camogue Stud Ltd **Trained** Cockerham, Lancs

FOCUS
The winner had the worst of the draw yet was soon ahead against the running rail. She never looked like being caught and this was a clear career best.

NOTEBOOK
Our Little Secret(IRE), in effect 10lb higher than Catterick, had the worst of the draw yet incredibly was showing them a clean pair of heels hard against the running rail after only one hundred yards. This in-foal mare kept up the gallop all the way to the line and her and her rider deserve full marks. (op 16-1)
Coconut Moon, who likes it round here, is normally a quick starter but from her inside draw fluffed her lines this time. Making her final effort on the outer, she snatched second place near the line and is overdue a change of luck. Official explanation: jockey said mare was hampered on leaving stalls (op 11-2)
Hoh Hoh Hoh, 4lb higher than when winning over course and distance, lay a lot handier and saw a lot more daylight this time. Forced to go in pursuit of the winner, he was never going to land a blow. (op 13-2 tchd 7-1 in a place)
Efistorm, 6lb higher, was drawn one off the inside but he was always being asked to go one stride too quick. (op 4-1 tchd 9-2)
Blazing Heights, drawn hard against the rail, likes it here but is a bit of a tricky customer who needs everything to fall just right. He was in trouble soon after halfway but to his credit kept going all the way to the line. (op 9-2 tchd 6-1 in a place)
Curtail(IRE), drawn one from the outside, struggled badly to keep up but put in some sterling late work. Six furlongs on a more orthodox track surely plays more to his strengths. (tchd 11-1)
Cashel Mead, 1lb below her last winning mark, looks to be on the verge of regaining her best form. She has a marked preference for give in the ground. (op 5-1)
Stoneacre Lad(IRE) Official explanation: jockey said colt lost its action

3081 ELEGANT RESORTS H'CAP — 1m 4f 66y
5:00 (5:00) (Class 4) (0-85,85) 3-Y-O **£5,505** (£1,637; £818; £408) **Stalls** Low

Form RPR

1-36 **1** **Aureate**[22] [2426] 3-9-1 **79**.......... J-PGuillambert 2 93
(M Johnston) *chsd ldr: led over 6f out: clr 4f out: drvn rt out* **11/8**[1]

4-26 **2** *19* **Yossi (IRE)**[42] [1843] 3-8-13 **82**.......... PatrickHills(5) 4 66
(M H Tompkins) *hld up: wnt 2nd over 3f out: sn rdn: no ch w wnr* **2/1**[2]

5625 **3** *14* **Delta Shuttle (IRE)**[23] [2389] 3-8-0 **67** oh5 ow1..........(p) AndrewElliott(3) 1 28
(K R Burke) *sn last and pushed along: wnt 2nd over 5f out: wknd 3f out* **7/1**

0-31 **4** *43* **Baba Ganouge (IRE)**[15] [2620] 3-9-4 **85**.......... JamieMoriarty(3) 5 —
(B J Meehan) *led: hdd over 6f out: lost pl over 3f out: sn bhd: virtually p.u fnl f: t.o* **7/2**[3]

2m 46.87s (6.22) **Going Correction** +0.50s/f (Yiel) **4** Ran SP% **110.2**
Speed ratings (Par 101):99,86,77,48
CSF £4.51 TOTE £2.50; EX 4.70 Place 6 £24.96, Place 5 £16.41..
Owner Sheikh Mohammed **Bred** Darley **Trained** Middleham Moor, N Yorks

FOCUS
The ground had softened up a fair amount by now and the mud always accentuates the winning distance. The winner was the only one to show his form, but the race is impossible to rate accurately.
Baba Ganouge(IRE) Official explanation: vet said filly had lost an off-fore plate
T/Plt: £18.30 to a £1 stake. Pool: £70,506.30. 2,812.40 winning tickets. T/Qpdt: £5.30 to a £1 stake. Pool: £2,347.10. 323.60 winning tickets. WG

[2874] LINGFIELD (L-H)

Saturday, June 30

OFFICIAL GOING: All-weather - standard; turf course - soft

Wind: Moderate, behind Weather: Drizzly rain

3082 JUNE EASTWELL MEMORIAL H'CAP — 1m 4f (P)

5:45 (5:46) (Class 6) (0-60,60) 3-Y-O — £2,047 (£604; £302) Stalls Low

Form — RPR

00 **1** — **Ainama (IRE)**[105] 700 3-8-10 **52**........ NickyMackay 2 — 58
(M Wigham) *chsd ldrs: trckd ldng pair gng wl over 2f out: swtchd rt and rdn wl over 1f out: styd on u.p to ld nr fin* **5/1**[2]

0314 **2** shd **Featherlight**[21] 2456 3-9-0 **56**........ IanMongan 16 — 62
(Jamie Poulton) *hld up in tch: hdwy 5f out: chsd ldrs and rdn over 2f out: ev ch over 1f out: kpt on u.p* **13/2**[3]

0130 **3** hd **Lapina (IRE)**[12] 2727 3-9-3 **59**........(b) StephenCarson 7 — 65
(Pat Eddery) *t.k.h: hld up in tch: hdwy to chse ldrs wl over 2f out: ev ch over 1f out: hung lft and rt fnl f: r.o nr fin* **15/2**

5000 **4** shd **Western Point (IRE)**[10] 2759 3-9-0 **56**........ PatCosgrave 4 — 62
(Sir Mark Prescott) *chsd ldr tl led 4f out: hrd pressed and drvn: 3f out: hdd and lost 3 pls fnl strides* **16/1**

-020 **5** hd **Converti**[9] 2801 3-8-5 **52**........ TolleyDean(5) 10 — 57
(P F I Cole) *chsd ldrs: rdn 5f out: chsd ldr and ev ch fr 3f out: no ex nr fin* **18/1**

0-42 **6** 1 ½ **Alnwick**[9] 2801 3-8-13 **60**........ TravisBlock(5) 3 — 63
(P D Cundell) *racd in midfield: rdn over 3f out: no imp over 2f out: styd on ins fnl f: nt rch ldrs* **5/2**[1]

6-00 **7** 3 ½ **Dr Light (IRE)**[37] 1972 3-9-0 **56**........ LPKeniry 8 — 53
(S Kirk) *hld up towards rr: hdwy over 4f out: chsd ldrs and rdn wl over 2f out: kpt on same pce* **25/1**

6605 **8** 1 ¾ **Silca Key**[14] 2668 3-9-1 **57**........ EdwardCreighton 5 — 51
(M R Channon) *hld up bhd: rdn and hdwy 3f out: kpt on: nvr threatened ldrs* **12/1**

00-6 **9** ¾ **Susie May**[89] 884 3-8-13 **55**........ SamHitchcott 9 — 48
(C A Cyzer) *reluctant and rdn sn after s: bhd: sme late hdwy: n.d* **25/1**

56-3 **10** 4 **Papradon**[21] 2456 3-8-12 **54**........ SteveDrowne 11 — 41
(J R Best) *s.i.s: effrt and hdwy on outer over 4f out: no hdwy over 2f out* **7/1**

2000 **11** 5 **Royal Tender (IRE)**[21] 2456 3-8-13 **55**........ RichardSmith 12 — 34
(B G Powell) *t.k.h: hld up in rr: hdwy and rdn on outer over 3f out: sn no imp* **33/1**

-060 **12** ¾ **Black Mogul**[21] 2456 3-8-12 **54**........ DarryllHolland 1 — 32
(W R Muir) *racd in midfield: rdn 8f out: bhd last 3f* **14/1**

3-00 **13** 12 **Compton Charlie**[47] 1726 3-8-12 **57**........ EmmettStack(3) 13 — 15
(J G Portman) *hld up in rr: rdn on outer over 4f out: no ch last 3f* **50/1**

003- **14** hd **Atlantic Coast (IRE)**[231] 6447 3-9-0 **59**........ GregFairley(3) 15 — 17
(M Johnston) *racd in midfield: rdn 10f out: wl bhd last 3f* **16/1**

50-0 **15** 2 ½ **Vietnam**[14] 2653 3-8-12 **54**........ JDSmith 14 — 8
(S Kirk) *t.k.h: chsd ldrs: rdn and wknd 3f out: eased fnl f* **25/1**

-005 **16** 3 ½ **Super Nebula**[16] 2609 3-8-10 **55**........ JerryO'Dwyer(3) 6 — 3
(P L Gilligan) *led tl 4f out: sn rdn and wknd* **40/1**

2m 30.37s (-4.02) **Going Correction** -0.15s/f (Stan) **16** Ran SP% **133.1**

Speed ratings (Par 97):107,106,106,106,106 105,103,102,101,98 95,95,87,86,85 82

CSF £38.57 CT £258.88 TOTE £6.00: £1.70, £1.40, £2.60, £6.30; EX 63.10.

Owner D Morrison **Bred** Roundhill Stud And A Stroud **Trained** Newmarket, Suffolk

FOCUS

The first five finished in a heap and this is very moderate handicap form. The winning time was 6.08 seconds faster than the following seller, but that was a very muddling contest and it would be unwise to draw comparisons.

3083 PULSE FIXINGS SPECTACULAR (S) STKS — 1m 4f (P)

6:15 (6:15) (Class 6) 3-Y-O+ — £2,047 (£604; £302) Stalls Low

Form — RPR

3500 **1** — **Ravenna**[18] 2545 3-8-3 63........ HayleyTurner 1 — 61+
(M P Tregoning) *t.k.h: led for 1f: chsd ldr tl led again over 2f out: rdn and qcknd clr wl over 1f out: eased towards fin* **8/1**[3]

6630 **2** 2 **Chant De Guerre (USA)**[14] 2668 3-8-3 57........ NickyMackay 3 — 56
(H J L Dunlop) *t.k.h: chsd ldrs: rdn over 2f out: chsd wnr 2f out: kpt on same pce* **9/1**

5455 **3** 2 ½ **Laugh 'n Cry**[64] 1279 6-9-3 47........ SamHitchcott 8 — 52+
(C A Cyzer) *plld hrd: hld up in rr: nt clr run briefly jst over 2f out: hdwy wl over 1f out: hung lft fr over 1f out: wnt 3rd last 100yds: no ch w wnr* **16/1**

5521 **4** ¾ **Treetops Hotel (IRE)**[7] 2874 8-9-13 56........ RichardSmith 4 — 61
(B R Johnson) *hld up towards rr: rdn over 2f out: sn outpcd by ldrs: plugged on fnl f* **11/4**[1]

-005 **5** ½ **Kanonkop**[32] 2105 3-8-0 49........ DominicFox(3) 7 — 50
(Miss J R Gibney) *led: rdn and hdd over 2f out: wknd wl over 1f out* **20/1**

55-5 **6** 4 **Ocean Pride (IRE)**[19] 316 4-9-8 73........(p) PatCosgrave 9 — 49
(D E Pipe) *hld up in midfield: rdn and effrt 3f out: outpcd over 2f out* **11/4**[1]

0000 **7** hd **Yenaled**[5] 2946 10-9-8 45........ SteveDrowne 6 — 48
(J M Bradley) *hld up in tch: rdn over 2f out: wknd over 1f out* **20/1**

2631 **8** 1 ¼ **Right Option (IRE)**[21] 2454 3-8-13 55........ DarryllHolland 5 — 51
(S Dow) *stdd s: hld up in rr: hdwy on outer over 3f out: chsd ldrs and rdn over 2f out: sn btn* **7/2**[2]

0654 **9** 1 ¾ **Christmas Truce (IRE)**[17] 2559 8-9-5 46........(b) JerryO'Dwyer(3) 2 — 43
(M R Hoad) *t.k.h: hdwy on inner 4f out: rdn 3f out: sn bhd* **20/1**

2m 36.45s (2.06) **Going Correction** -0.15s/f (Stan)

WFA 3 from 4yo+ 14lb **9** Ran SP% **116.8**

Speed ratings (Par 101):87,85,84,83,83 80,80,79,78

CSF £74.92 TOTE £10.10: £2.60, £3.10, £2.70; EX 55.50.The winner was bought in for 12,000gns.

Owner Park Walk Racing **Bred** Whitsbury Manor Stud **Trained** Lambourn, Berks

FOCUS

Form to treat with real caution. The pace slowed dramatically at about halfway and this was a very muddling contest, as a winning time 6.08 seconds slower than the previous 46-60 three-year-old handicap suggests.

Laugh 'n Cry Official explanation: jockey said mare was denied a clear run

Treetops Hotel(IRE) Official explanation: jockey said gelding was denied a clear run

3084 RAY QUINN & BEN MILLS LIVE AT LINGFIELDPARK.CO.UK MEDIAN AUCTION MAIDEN STKS — 1m 2f (P)

6:45 (6:48) (Class 5) 3-4-Y-O — £2,817 (£838; £418; £209) Stalls Low

Form — RPR

0-64 **1** — **Vallemeldee (IRE)**[21] 2475 3-8-11 69........ DarryllHolland 12 — 68
(P W D'Arcy) *in tch: hdwy wl over 3f out: rdn to ld 2f out: styd on wl ins fnl f* **10/1**[3]

254- **2** ½ **Gordonsville**[322] 4374 4-10-0 82........ LPKeniry 4 — 72
(A M Balding) *w.w in tch: hdwy over 3f out: rdn and chsd ldng trio over 2f out: styd on to chse wnr ins fnl f: no imp last 50yds* **3/1**[2]

6 **3** 1 ½ **Eastwell Smiles**[21] 2455 3-8-11 0........(t) TravisBlock(5) 3 — 69
(R T Phillips) *t.k.h: chsd ldr tl over 2f out: kpt on same pce u.p fnl f* **14/1**

00 **4** nk **Nothingtodeclaire**[31] 2153 3-9-2 0........ SteveDrowne 7 — 68
(G A Huffer) *racd in midfield: hdwy wl over 3f out: outpcd over 2f out: styd on wl fnl f: nrst fin* **80/1**

2 **5** ½ **Cybersnow (USA)**[21] 2455 3-9-2 0........ RichardHughes 1 — 67
(Mrs A J Perrett) *sn led: rdn and hdd 2f out: ev ch tl wknd last 100yds* **4/7**[1]

05-0 **6** 6 **Split Briefs (IRE)**[24] 2369 3-8-8 69........ JerryO'Dwyer(3) 8 — 50
(D J Daly) *prom: rdn wl over 2f out: ev ch whn squeezed out jst over 2f out: wknd over 1f out* **20/1**

00 **7** ½ **Victory Mile (USA)**[21] 2477 3-9-2 0........ IanMongan 11 — 54
(B J Meehan) *bhd: rdn and hdwy on outer over 3f out: sn outpcd: no ch last 2f* **28/1**

00- **8** ½ **Jaufrette**[278] 5567 4-9-4 0........ KevinGhunowa(5) 5 — 48
(Dr J R J Naylor) *t.k.h: chsd ldrs: rdn 3f out: wknd jst over 2f out* **100/1**

0 **9** 6 **Slip Silver**[21] 2477 3-8-11 0........ AmirQuinn 2 — 36
(P J Makin) *t.k.h: trckd ldrs: rdn and struggling whn short of room 3f out: no ch after* **66/1**

05 **10** ¾ **Break Out**[17] 2581 3-8-9 0........ BarrySavage(7) 10 — 40
(J M Bradley) *s.i.s: hld up in rr: rdn over 3f out: sn lost tch* **100/1**

0- **11** 8 **Demolition**[231] 6434 3-9-2 0........ SamHitchcott 9 — 24
(C A Cyzer) *sn rdn: bhd: hdwy and in tch 4f out: sn wknd* **50/1**

12 32 **Hook Money (IRE)** 3-9-2 0........ TQuinn 6 — —
(D W P Arbuthnot) *s.i.s: sn bhd: lost tch 8f out: t.o last 5f* **33/1**

2m 5.36s (-2.43) **Going Correction** -0.15s/f (Stan)

WFA 3 from 4yo 12lb **12** Ran SP% **122.2**

Speed ratings (Par 103):103,102,101,101,100 95,95,95,90,89 83,57

CSF £39.89 TOTE £10.60: £1.80, £1.20, £3.50; EX 46.50.

Owner Mrs Dot Burlton **Bred** Celbridge Estates Ltd **Trained** Newmarket, Suffolk

■ Stewards' Enquiry : Darryll Holland two-day ban: careless riding (Jul 12,14)

FOCUS

A very ordinary maiden. It was falsely run and there are doubts over the form, with the winner probably not needing to improve on his latest handicap form.

Slip Silver Official explanation: jockey said filly hung left

Hook Money(IRE) Official explanation: jockey said gelding never travelled

3085 SOUTH ESSEX INSURANCE BROKERS EBF MAIDEN STKS — 5f

7:15 (7:16) (Class 5) 2-Y-O — £3,562 (£1,059; £529; £264) Stalls High

Form — RPR

3450 **1** — **Major Eazy (IRE)**[11] 2737 2-9-3 0........ JimmyFortune 6 — 93+
(B J Meehan) *taken down early: chsd ldr tl led over 2f out: rdn clr wl over 1f out: in n.d and pushed out fnl f* **11/10**[1]

220 **2** 5 **Magical Speedfit (IRE)**[11] 2737 2-9-3 0........ TQuinn 9 — 75
(G G Margarson) *chsd ldrs: rdn and chsd wnr over 2f out: sn outpcd: lost position ins fnl f: rallied to regain 2nd on line* **15/8**[2]

3 shd **Our Acquaintance** 2-9-3 0........ SteveDrowne 3 — 75
(W R Muir) *chsd ldrs: rdn and effrt 2f out: sn outpcd by wnr: wnt 2nd ins fnl f tl ct on line* **25/1**

6 **4** 2 ½ **Splash The Cash**[29] 2193 2-9-3 0........ StephenCarson 13 — 66
(P Winkworth) *chsd ldr on stands' rail: hdwy to chse ldrs over 2f out: rdn and wknd over 1f out* **16/1**

0 **5** 3 ½ **Lunar Limelight**[23] 2398 2-9-3 0........ EddieAhern 4 — 53
(P J Makin) *s.i.s: chsd ldrs on outer: rdn over 2f out: wknd wl over 1f out* **16/1**

6 shd **Sailor At Sea (USA)** 2-9-3 0........ RichardHughes 14 — 53+
(R Charlton) *s.i.s and wnt lft s: sn in tch: hdwy to chse ldrs over 2f out: wknd qckly 1f out* **7/1**[3]

0 **7** 1 ¼ **Pennyspider (IRE)**[12] 2724 2-8-12 0........ SamHitchcott 11 — 43
(M S Saunders) *led on stands' rail: hdd over 2f out: wknd qckly wl over 1f out* **33/1**

8 3 **Lady Of Passion (IRE)** 2-8-12 0........ EdwardCreighton 8 — 32
(M R Channon) *awkward leaving stalls and s.i.s: nvr on terms* **16/1**

0 **9** 4 **Lightning Lad**[54] 1540 2-9-3 0........ LPKeniry 7 — 23
(J R Jenkins) *t.k.h: chsd ldrs for 2f: sn struggling: no ch last 2f* **50/1**

10 13 **Starfinch** 2-8-9 0........ MarcHalford(3) 10 — —
(J J Bridger) *v s.i.s: sn wl outpcd: t.o after 2f* **50/1**

60.64 secs (1.70) **Going Correction** +0.45s/f (Yiel) **10** Ran SP% **123.3**

Speed ratings (Par 93):104,96,95,91,86 86,84,79,72,52

CSF £3.41 TOTE £2.10: £1.10, £1.40, £4.90; EX 4.00.

Owner The Comic Strip Heroes **Bred** Swettenham Stud **Trained** Manton, Wilts

FOCUS

This maiden lacked strength in depth. It looked a two-horse race on paper but, with Magical Speedfit failing to cope with the conditions, Major Easy came home alone. He could be rated a few pounds higher. The winning time was 0.70 seconds faster than the following 56-75 handicap for three-year-olds and upwards. The principals tended to race up towards the middle of the track.

NOTEBOOK

Major Eazy(IRE), who had run creditable races in both the National Stakes at Sandown and the Windsor Castle at Royal Ascot, benefited from the drop in class and gained a confidence-boosting success in good style. It will come as no surprise to see him stepped back up in grade. (op 5-4 tchd 6-4 and Evens)

Magical Speedfit(IRE) gives the strong impression he needs fast ground and he ran some way below his best. (op 3-1)

Our Acquaintance, a 12,000gns son of Bahamian Bounty, half-brother to among others multiple 6f-7f winner High Reach, showed a fair level of ability on his racecourse debut and newcomers from the Muir yard tend to improve. (op 20-1)

Splash The Cash, who showed good speed on his debut at Bath, raced more towards the stands' rail than most of his rivals and finished up well held. He seems to be going the right way, though, and could find his level in nurseries. (op 11-1 tchd 10-1)

Lunar Limelight, down the field on his debut at Sandown, again never really looked like taking a hand in the finish and he may be one for nurseries later down the line. (op 10-1)

Sailor At Sea(USA), a Mizzen Mast half-brother to dual 6f winner Como, was too green to do himself justice and will have learnt plenty. (op 8-1 tchd 9-1)

3086 PPL H'CAP 5f

7:45 (7:45) (Class 5) (0-75,74) 3-Y-0+ **£2,817** (£838; £418; £209) **Stalls** High

Form RPR

3043 **1** **Black Moma (IRE)**[15] 2631 3-9-6 **73**............................ RichardHughes 6 77
(R Hannon) *pressed ldr: led over 1f out: hrd rdn fnl f: hld on wl nr fin: all out* **3/1**[1]

0-05 **2** *hd* **Rare Cross (IRE)**[7] 2879 5-9-6 **67**...................................... EddieAhern 2 72
(R A Teal) *led: rdn and hdd over 1f out: ev ch after: unable qck nr fin* **11/2**

6003 **3** *nk* **Hythe Bay**[16] 2594 3-9-0 **67**.. GeorgeBaker 5 69
(J R Best) *s.i.s: racd wd: racd in midfield: rdn and hdwy over 1f out: kpt on u.p: hld fnl strides* **7/1**

1050 **4** *1* **Egyptian Lord**[36] 1991 4-8-10 **57**...................................(b) LPKeniry 4 57
(Peter Grayson) *bmpd s: chsd ldrs: rdn 2f out: swtchd rt 1f out: no imp last 50yds* **9/2**[3]

1316 **5** *1 3/4* **Matterofact (IRE)**[14] 2655 4-9-5 **66**... TQuinn 7 60
(M S Saunders) *chsd ldrs: rdn over 2f out: wknd 1f out* **10/3**[2]

0660 **6** *1/2* **Enjoy The Buzz**[3] 2982 8-8-2 **56** oh10 ow1...............(p) BarrySavage(7) 1 48
(J M Bradley) *v.s.a: sn outpcd and detached: rdn and styd on over 1f out: nrst fin* **10/1**

0000 **7** *3 1/2* **Danjet (IRE)**[4] 2972 4-8-12 **64**.................................. KevinGhunowa(5) 11 44
(J M Bradley) *chsd ldrs: rdn wl over 1f out: sn wknd: eased wl ins fnl f* **9/1**

0-00 **8** *6* **Don't Tell Sue**[50] 1630 4-9-13 **74**.................................... PaulFitzsimons 9 32
(Miss J R Tooth) *rrd and v.s.a: sn hrd drvn: hdwy and in tch over 2f out: wknd wl over 1f out* **20/1**

61.34 secs (2.40) **Going Correction** +0.45s/f (Yiel)
WFA 3 from 4yo+ 6lb **8** Ran SP% **118.0**
Speed ratings (Par 103):98,97,97,95,92 92,86,76
CSF £20.64 CT £107.79 TOTE £3.30: £1.40, £2.60, £1.60; EX 25.90.
Owner B Bull **Bred** Poulton Farm Stud **Trained** East Everleigh, Wilts
■ Stewards' Enquiry : Paul Fitzsimons five-day ban: used whip with excessive force and without giving gelding time to respond (Jul 11-15)

FOCUS
Just a modest sprint handicap, with the winner fairly exposed. The pace was plenty quick enough considering the conditions and the winning time was 0.70 seconds slower than the previous juvenile maiden. They tended to race down the middle of the track.
Hythe Bay Official explanation: jockey said filly suffered interference at start
Matterofact(IRE) Official explanation: jockey said filly got very tired on soft ground
Danjet(IRE) Official explanation: jockey said filly became unbalanced

3087 BEANBOY FILLIES' H'CAP 7f

8:15 (8:15) (Class 5) (0-75,75) 3-Y-0 **£2,817** (£838; £418; £209) **Stalls** High

Form RPR

3451 **1** **Baltic Belle (IRE)**[26] 2317 3-9-7 **75**............................ RichardHughes 10 79
(R Hannon) *a.p: rdn to ld 1f out: styd on wl* **4/1**[3]

-600 **2** *3/4* **Anthill**[22] 2425 3-8-7 **61** ow1... LPKeniry 1 63
(I A Wood) *t.k.h: prom: led 5f out: rdn 2f out: hdd 1f out: no ex last 100yds* **20/1**

344- **3** *2* **Princess Taylor**[221] 6558 3-9-2 **70**................................(t) SamHitchcott 9 67
(M Botti) *hld up wl in tch: rdn and hdwy over 2f out: hanging lft fr wl over 1f out: kpt on same pce fnl f* **10/1**

4-22 **4** *shd* **Hucking Hope (IRE)**[3] 3000 3-8-11 **65**............................. DaneO'Neill 2 62
(J R Best) *hld up in rr: hdwy 3f out: rdn and chsd ldrs over 1f out: no imp ins fnl f* **9/4**[1]

-010 **5** *1/2* **Princess Zada**[26] 2317 3-9-0 **68**...................................... SteveDrowne 5 63
(B R Millman) *hld up wl in tch: hdwy 3f out: rdn 2f out: wknd jst ins fnl f* **10/3**[2]

4-65 **6** *5* **Flying Encore (IRE)**[24] 2369 3-9-5 **73**......................(p) StephenCarson 8 55
(W R Swinburn) *hld up in tch: rdn wl over 2f out: sn btn* **11/2**

446- **7** *7* **Ishimagic**[194] 6853 3-7-9 **56** oh6.. KMay(7) 7 19
(J J Bridger) *prom: rdn wl over 3f out: wknd over 2f out: no ch after* **33/1**

035 **8** *29* **Appleby**[18] 2542 3-9-5 **73**... JimmyFortune 4 —
(J H M Gosden) *t.k.h: led for 2f: styd handy tl rdn and wknd qckly over 2f out: virtually p.u fnl f* **7/1**

1m 27.49s (3.28) **Going Correction** +0.45s/f (Yiel) **8** Ran SP% **118.5**
Speed ratings (Par 96):99,98,95,95,95 89,81,48
CSF £79.07 CT £761.56 TOTE £6.10: £1.80, £2.90, £3.00; EX 138.00 Place 6 £328.86, Place 5 £146.53..
Owner Thurloe Thoroughbreds Viii **Bred** Ocal Bloodstock **Trained** East Everleigh, Wilts

FOCUS
An ordinary fillies' handicap in which they raced down the middle of the track. Sound but limited form.
Appleby Official explanation: jockey said filly ran too free
T/Plt: £794.50 to a £1 stake. Pool: £56,818.15. 52.20 winning tickets. T/Qpdt: £21.70 to a £1 stake. Pool: £5,505.30. 187.10 winning tickets. SP

3049 NEWCASTLE (L-H)

Saturday, June 30

OFFICIAL GOING: Heavy (soft in places; 4.4)
There were 20 withdrawals owing to the testing ground.
Wind: Breezy, half behind Weather: Overcast

3088 NEWCASTLE BROWN ALE 80TH BIRTHDAY CHIPCHASE STKS (GROUP 3) 6f

2:10 (2:10) (Class 1) 3-Y-0+

£28,390 (£10,760; £5,385; £2,685; £1,345; £675) **Stalls** High

Form RPR

-250 **1** **Confuchias (IRE)**[35] 2051 3-9-0 0.. NCallan 2 114
(Francis Ennis, Ire) *chsd ldrs: rdn over 1f out: styd on to ld cl home* **12/1**

5400 **2** *1/2* **Appalachian Trail (IRE)**[7] 2857 6-9-3 108.....................(b) TomEaves 5 111
(I Semple) *cl up gng wl: rdn to ld appr fnl f: kpt on: hdd cl home* **14/1**

-300 **3** *1 1/4* **Fonthill Road (IRE)**[21] 2463 7-9-3 104.............................. TonyHamilton 3 107
(R A Fahey) *chsd ldrs: drvn along over 2f out: kpt on u.p fnl f* **11/1**

-140 **4** *1/2* **Rising Shadow (IRE)**[7] 2857 6-9-3 110................................ JimmyQuinn 1 106
(T D Barron) *in tch: rdn over 2f out: one pce over 1f out* **5/2**[1]

0111 **5** *2* **Sierra Vista**[30] 2184 7-9-6 110... PaulHanagan 7 103
(D W Barker) *led to appr fnl f: no ex ins fnl f* **9/2**[3]

153- **6** *1 1/4* **Misu Bond (IRE)**[381] 2559 4-9-3 110.............................. RoystonFfrench 8 96
(B Smart) *hld up in tch: drvn over 2f out: no imp over 1f out* **8/1**

0140 **7** *2 1/2* **Dhaular Dhar (IRE)**[28] 2237 5-9-3 98................................ PhillipMakin 9 88
(J S Goldie) *bhd: drvn 1/2-way: n.d* **50/1**

0220 **8** *7* **Excusez Moi (USA)**[30] 2184 5-9-3 103...........................(p) RyanMoore 4 67
(C E Brittain) *hld up: rdn 2f out: sn wknd* **10/1**

-121 **9** *nk* **Hoh Mike (IRE)**[14] 2672 3-8-10 110............................ JamieSpencer 10 64
(M L W Bell) *hld up: rdn 2f out: nvr on terms* **4/1**[2]

3060 **10** *52* **Fayr Jag (IRE)**[7] 2857 8-9-3 104... DavidAllan 6 —
(T D Easterby) *blindfold on whn stalls opened: missed break: wnt bdly rt and rdr lost iron: nt rcvr* **33/1**

1m 16.8s (1.71) **Going Correction** +0.60s/f (Yiel)
WFA 3 from 4yo+ 7lb **10** Ran SP% **114.5**
Speed ratings (Par 113):112,111,109,109,106 104,101,92,91,22
CSF £164.07 TOTE £11.50: £2.60, £5.00, £3.30; EX 186.20 TRIFECTA Not won..
Owner Annette O'Callaghan **Bred** Mrs Vanessa Hutch **Trained** the Curragh, Co Kildare

FOCUS
A fair event but just an ordinary pace in the conditions and those held up were at a disadvantage, meaning the form is not solid. The whole field raced far side.

NOTEBOOK
Confuchias(IRE), dropped to sprint distances and back on testing ground after a fair effort in the Irish 2000 Guineas, had the run of the race but showed a good attitude in the closing stages. He should be suited by the return to 7f and he should continue to give a good account in this type of event, especially when there is cut in the ground. (op 14-1)
Appalachian Trail(IRE), out of his depth in the Golden Jubilee last time, travelled in his customary fashion and returned to something like his best after enjoying the run of the race. Equally effective on a sound surface, he may be even better suited by being held onto for longer off a stronger pace and he is capable of winning a similar event. (op 16-1)
Fonthill Road(IRE), who was not at his best over 5f on quick ground last time, was another to enjoy the run of the race and he ran creditably, despite having a bit to find at the weights. He seems best with give in the ground and he is capable of winning in Listed company when he gets his conditions. (op 10-1)
Rising Shadow(IRE), better than ever when winning over course and distance on easy ground on his reappearance, was soundly beaten in the Golden Jubilee last time but returned to form in this company. A more strongly-run race would have been to his liking and he may be capable of winning in Listed or minor Group company granted a truly-run race with cut in the ground. (op 3-1 tchd 10-3)
Sierra Vista had looked better than ever this year with three straight wins, including in Group 2 company last time, but she proved a bit of a disappointment back up in trip after enjoying an uncontested lead. She may just be better over 5f these days and is worth another chance back over that trip in similar company. (tchd 4-1)
Misu Bond(IRE) looked in tremendous shape on this first run for over a year but ran as though this was not a stiff enough test of stamina. He should be all the better for this outing and this lightly-raced sort is well worth another try in this company, especially when returned to 7f. (op 15-2)
Dhaular Dhar(IRE) had plenty to find in this company, especially in a race that did not play to his strengths, but he was not disgraced in the face of a stiff task. The return to 7f in a more strongly-run race will see him in a better light. (op 40-1)
Hoh Mike(IRE), having his first run in ground as testing as this, seemed to flounder in the conditions. He will be worth another chance in similar company back on a sounder surface. Official explanation: jockey said colt was unsuited by the heavy (soft in places) ground (op 7-2)
Fayr Jag(IRE), who won this race on fast ground last year, lost all chance when the stalls opened when his blindfold was still on but it is debatable whether these conditions would have seen him in his best light. Official explanation: jockey said he was unable to remove blindfold due to losing irons in the stalls

3089 TOTESCOOP6 NORTHERN SPRINT (HANDICAP STKS) 6f

2:45 (2:45) (Class 2) (0-100,98) 3-Y-0+

£18,696 (£5,598; £2,799; £1,401; £699; £351) **Stalls** High

Form RPR

1000 **1** **Protector (SAF)**[7] 2858 6-9-9 **93**.. RyanMoore 8 108
(Miss Gay Kelleway) *hld up in midfield: hdwy to ld over 1f out: pushed clr fnl f* **12/1**

5022 **2** *5* **Zomerlust**[35] 2030 5-9-10 **94**...................................... GrahamGibbons 15 94
(J J Quinn) *hld up: hdwy 2f out: chsd wnr ins fnl f: kpt on: no imp* **10/1**

10-0 **3** *1 3/4* **Damika (IRE)**[8] 2841 4-9-4 **88**... JimCrowley 9 83
(R M Whitaker) *bhd tl hdwy over 1f out: kpt on fnl f: nrst fin* **40/1**

0061 **4** *hd* **Ice Planet**[8] 2841 6-9-9 **93**.. JoeFanning 10 87
(D Nicholls) *chsd ldrs: effrt and ev ch over 1f out: one pce fnl f* **9/1**

-030 **5** *3/4* **Gift Horse**[7] 2858 7-10-0 **98**... JamieSpencer 1 90
(D Nicholls) *w ldr: rdn and ev ch over 1f out: sn no ex* **12/1**

0002 **6** *2* **Mecca's Mate**[1] 3050 6-10-0 **98**...................................... TonyHamilton 4 84
(D W Barker) *trckd ldrs: drvn over 2f out: no ex over 1f out* **8/1**

-403 **7** *2* **King's Gait**[8] 2841 5-9-6 **90**..(b) DavidAllan 3 70
(T D Easterby) *t.k.h: led to over 1f out: sn btn* **9/2**[2]

5034 **8** *2 1/2* **Fullandby (IRE)**[21] 2463 5-9-9 **93**.............................. PaulMulrennan 14 65
(T J Etherington) *t.k.h early: trckd ldrs: effrt 2f out: sn no ex* **4/1**[1]

4100 **9** *1/2* **Dickie Le Davoir**[29] 2213 3-9-1 **92**................................... PhillipMakin 7 63
(K R Burke) *in midfield: outpcd over 2f out: sn btn* **20/1**

0052 **10** *1 1/2* **Turnkey**[8] 2841 5-9-7 **91**... AdrianTNicholls 11 57
(D Nicholls) *in midfield: drvn and outpcd 1/2-way: n.d after* **11/2**[3]

-200 **11** *3 1/2* **Mr Wolf**[8] 2841 6-9-4 **88**.. PaulHanagan 17 44
(D W Barker) *racd alone stands' side: rdn and hung bdly lft over 2f out: sn btn and eased whn no ch over 1f out* **14/1**

-500 **12** *4* **Sunderland Echo (IRE)**[8] 2841 4-9-4 **88**.......................... TomEaves 5 32
(B Ellison) *dwlt: bhd: drvn 1/2-way: nvr on terms* **11/1**

1m 16.65s (1.56) **Going Correction** +0.60s/f (Yiel)
WFA 3 from 4yo+ 7lb **12** Ran SP% **121.4**
Speed ratings (Par 109):113,106,104,103,102 100,97,94,93,91 86,81
CSF £129.65 CT £4669.54 TOTE £15.80: £4.60, £3.10, £12.00; EX 176.50 Trifecta £822.30 Part won. Pool £1,158.20 - 0.10 winning units..
Owner Joshua Snellings **Bred** Dr M Thomson **Trained** Exning, Suffolk

FOCUS
An open handicap in which all bar one raced far side but a ready winner in Protector, who may well be capable of better. However, the form is difficult to take at face value and is best rated through the runner-up.

NOTEBOOK
Protector(SAF) ◆, a 7f winner for Herman Brown at Nad Al Sheba in January who ran creditably in a visor in the Wokingham, had the headgear left off this time and he turned in a career-best effort on this second start for the stable. These conditions suited him ideally and he is the type to hold his own in stronger company for current connections. (op 11-1 tchd 14-1)
Zomerlust, who had been running well in defeat this term, had conditions to suit and got a decent gallop but, despite running right up to his best, was no match for the ready winner. The fact that he has not won for over a year and is the type that needs things to drop right remains a bit of a concern, though. (op 8-1)
Damika(IRE), a much-improved performer last year, shaped as though retaining much of his ability on this second start of the year. He will be suited by the return to a sound surface and he may well be capable of better this term. (tchd 33-1)
Ice Planet is a reliable sort who came here in good heart and ran another creditable race having enjoyed the rub of things. While vulnerable to the more progressive and better handicapped sorts, he should continue to give a good account, especially in less-testing conditions. (op 11-1)

Gift Horse has not won since landing the Stewards Cup nearly two years ago but he shaped as though better than the bare form on ground that would have been plenty soft enough. He travelled strongly for much of the way, is edging down the weights and is one to keep an eye on back on better ground. (op 11-1)
Mecca's Mate, turned out after her very creditable run in the Gosforth Park Cup at the same course the previous evening, had her limitations exposed over this trip. A strongly-run race over 5f with cut in the ground are her requirements. (op 10-1)
Fullandby(IRE) had won his only previous start in heavy ground but he was disappointing after failing to settle in the early stages back over this trip. While capable of winning a similar event, he has flattered to deceive on more than one occasion in the past and he is not really one to be lumping on at single-figure odds. (op 7-2 tchd 9-2)
Mr Wolf Official explanation: jockey said gelding hung left throughout

3090 JOHN SMITH'S NORTHUMBERLAND PLATE (HERITAGE H'CAP) 2m 19y
3:20 (3:21) (Class 2) 3-Y-0+

£123,320 (£37,120; £18,560; £9,260; £4,640; £2,340) **Stalls** Centre

Form RPR
1-02 **1** **Juniper Girl (IRE)**[11] 2736 4-8-11 **93** LukeMorris(5) 13 104+
(M L W Bell) *hld up: hdwy over 2f out: edgd lft: kpt on wl fnl f: led post* **5/1**[1]
-666 **2** *shd* **Macorville (USA)**[43] 1822 4-8-11 **88** DO'Donohoe 4 99
(G M Moore) *chsd ldrs: led gng wl over 2f out: sn rdn: kpt on wl fnl f: hdd post* **9/1**
4303 **3** *3* **Tilt**[7] 2861 5-8-8 **85** TomEaves 18 92
(B Ellison) *hld up: hdwy over 6f out: effrt and chsd ldr 2f out to ins fnl f: no ex* **12/1**
43/ **4** *7* **Al Eile (IRE)**[77] 6358 7-9-5 **96** NCallan 2 95
(John Queally, Ire) *hld up in tch: effrt over 2f out: hung lft over 1f out: one pce* **11/2**[2]
0-02 **5** *3½* **River Alhaarth (IRE)**[21] 2449 5-9-2 **93** (b[1]) AdrianMcCarthy 9 88
(P W Chapple-Hyam) *t.k.h in tch: drvn fr over 4f out: no ex fr 2f out* **16/1**
-000 **6** *10* **Winged D'Argent (IRE)**[11] 2736 6-8-8 **85** (b) PaulMulrennan 3 68
(B J Llewellyn) *sn cl up: led 1/2-way to over 2f out: sn btn* **40/1**
3314 **7** *7* **Gee Dee Nen**[37] 1959 4-8-7 **84** JimmyQuinn 19 58
(M H Tompkins) *in midfield: pushed along over 4f out: wknd 3f out* **20/1**
1505 **8** *2½* **Odiham**[11] 2736 6-8-13 **90** DaleGibson 1 61
(H Morrison) *bhd: rdn 5f out: nvr on terms* **33/1**
-006 **9** *4* **Dr Sharp (IRE)**[30] 2170 7-8-6 **83** AdrianTNicholls 8 50
(T P Tate) *in midfield: rdn over 4f out: sn no imp* **12/1**
0-10 **10** *1* **Cape Secret (IRE)**[28] 2236 4-8-10 **87** JamesDoyle 14 52
(R M Beckett) *led: swtchd wd and hdd 1/2-way: wknd over 3f out* **28/1**
1-11 **11** *1¾* **Nosferatu (IRE)**[28] 2236 4-9-1 **92** JimCrowley 16 55
(Mrs A J Perrett) *in tch: rdn 5f out: wknd 3f out* **6/1**[3]
-144 **12** *6* **Monolith**[6] 2908 9-8-8 **85** PhillipMakin 11 41
(L Lungo) *hld up: pushed along over 5f out: sn btn* **33/1**
3641 **13** *8* **Mustajed**[13] 2692 6-8-12 **89** 5ex GrahamGibbons 12 36
(B R Millman) *hld up ins: pushed along over 4f out: n.d* **40/1**
-230 **14** *35* **Mceldowney**[11] 2736 5-8-7 **84** JoeFanning 6 —
(M Johnston) *prom: rdn 5f out: wknd over 3f out* **33/1**
0-01 **15** *¾* **Colloquial**[21] 2449 6-9-1 **92** (v) FergusSweeney 17 —
(H Candy) *hld up: drvn over 5f out: sn btn* **33/1**
4165 **16** *1½* **La Estrella (USA)**[7] 2861 4-8-9 **86** RoystonFfrench 20 —
(J G Given) *racd wd: in tch to 1/2-way: sn lost pl* **66/1**
56-1 **17** *5* **Sentry Duty (FR)**[42] 1844 5-9-10 **101** BrettDoyle 5 —
(N J Henderson) *prom: rdn over 4f out: sn btn* **10/1**
-120 **18** *7* **Halla San**[43] 1822 5-9-4 **95** TonyHamilton 7 —
(R A Fahey) *t.k.h: in tch tl rdn and wknd over 3f out* **33/1**
05-1 **19** *41* **Greenwich Meantime**[52] 1582 7-9-8 **99** PaulHanagan 15 —
(R A Fahey) *hld up in tch: rdn 5f out: sn btn* **16/1**
11/4 **20** *27* **Leg Spinner (IRE)**[11] 2736 6-8-9 **86** JamieSpencer 10 —
(A J Martin, Ire) *hld up: pushed along over 6f out: sn struggling* **14/1**

3m 46.01s (10.81) **Going Correction** +0.925s/f (Soft) **20** Ran SP% **128.5**
Speed ratings (Par 109):109,108,107,103,102 97,93,92,90,89 89,86,82,64,64 63,60,57,36,23
CSF £45.42 CT £536.65 TOTE £5.10: £1.60, £2.60, £4.80, £2.00; EX 58.60 Trifecta £574.60 Pool £9,141.52 - 11.30 winning units..
Owner M B Hawtin **Bred** Mrs E Kent **Trained** Newmarket, Suffolk

FOCUS
Several exposed sorts and a few disappointments but a decent pace in the conditions. The first two look the types to progress again and the level looks sound enough, although the exaggerated distances behind the first two mean the form cannot be taken literally.

NOTEBOOK
Juniper Girl(IRE), who has come a long way in the last twelve months, turned in a career-best effort back in trip and back in heavy ground. She showed a fine attitude in the closing stages and at this stage the obvious target looks to be Cesarewitch at Newmarket in October.
Macorville(USA), a grand sort with a pronounced knee action, travelled strongly for much of the way in these ideal conditions and ran his best race yet. He was unfortunate to be nailed on the post having looked the most likely winner when taking up the running but did nothing wrong and, although he will be up in the weights for this, looks the type to win a decent handicap this season. (op 8-1)
Tilt, 11lb higher than when last successful over a year ago, proved well suited by the return to this trip and to testing ground. He did not get home as well as the first two but pulled well clear of the remainder and this versatile sort, who will be interesting if sent over hurdles later in the year, looks capable of better in this sphere
Al Eile(IRE), the winner of the Grade 1 Aintree Hurdle when last seen in April, has plenty of form in testing ground but he did not get home as well as the principals from this mark, showing a tendency to hang when getting tired after his break. However, he is a useful sort on the Flat and remains capable of winning more races. (op 6-1 tchd 13-2)
River Alhaarth(IRE), who has only won once, back in October 2004, ran second in this race on fast ground last year but failed to get home as well in these conditions equipped with first-time blinkers. The return to a sound surface will see him in a better light but he may not be one for maximum faith. (op 14-1)
Winged D'Argent(IRE), who has gone well in testing ground in the past, ran a bit better than the bare form suggests on this fourth start for current connections. He has slipped a fair way in the weights and will be interesting in a lesser event from a lower mark granted suitable conditions.
Gee Dee Nen, in fair form on a sound surface, did not get home on this first attempt on this testing ground and he will be well suited by the return to fast ground. (op 25-1)
Nosferatu(IRE), a lightly-raced and progressive performer over middle distances, failed to get home on this first start over this trip in these very testing conditions. He will be well worth another chance back on better ground back around 1m4f. (op 13-2)
Sentry Duty(FR) turned in a useful performance to win at Newmarket in May but floundered in these conditions back up in trip. He would not be one to write off in this sphere and will also be of interest if and when returned to hurdles later in the season. (op 8-1)
Leg Spinner(IRE) Official explanation: jockey said gelding was unsuited by the heavy (soft in places) ground

3091 JOURNAL 175 ANNIVERSARY H'CAP 7f
3:55 (3:56) (Class 2) (0-100,97) 3-Y-0+

£12,464 (£3,732; £1,866; £934; £466; £234) **Stalls** High

Form RPR
0000 **1** **Game Lad**[43] 1818 5-8-12 **81** DavidAllan 5 96
(T D Easterby) *hld up: hdwy over 2f out: led ins fnl f: r.o strly* **15/2**
0004 **2** *3½* **Mezuzah**[7] 2891 7-9-0 **83** PaulMulrennan 10 89
(M W Easterby) *led to ins fnl f: nt qckn* **6/1**[2]
-204 **3** *1* **Imperial Echo (USA)**[11] 2744 6-9-0 **83** PaulFessey 3 86
(T D Barron) *chsd ldrs: effrt over 2f out: kpt on fnl f* **8/1**
032- **4** *nk* **Red Romeo**[299] 5070 6-8-13 **82** DaleGibson 1 85
(N Wilson) *trckd ldrs: rdn over 1f out: kpt on same pce fnl f* **16/1**
3106 **5** *3½* **Glenbuck (IRE)**[50] 1619 4-8-11 **87** (v) NeilBrown(7) 8 81
(A Bailey) *cl up: rdn over 2f out: no ex over 1f out* **12/1**
1513 **6** *5* **Daaweitza**[3] 2986 4-8-11 **80** RoystonFfrench 11 61
(B Ellison) *towards rr: drvn 1/2-way: nvr rchd ldrs* **7/2**[1]
-020 **7** *5* **Yorkshire Blue**[17] 2566 8-8-5 **81** GaryBartley(7) 2 49
(J S Goldie) *towards rr: drvn 1/2-way: sn btn* **7/1**
040- **8** *14* **Tagula Sunrise (IRE)**[295] 5159 5-9-6 **89** PaulHanagan 6 20
(R A Fahey) *in tch: drvn over 2f out: btn over 1f out* **9/1**
6130 **9** *16* **Presumptive (IRE)**[18] 2528 7-9-8 **91** RyanMoore 4 —
(R Charlton) *sn t.o* **10/1**
5010 **10** *11* **Black Charmer (IRE)**[8] 2817 4-10-0 **97** JoeFanning 9 —
(M Johnston) *dwlt: hld up: rdn 1/2-way: sn btn* **13/2**[3]

1m 33.1s (5.08) **Going Correction** +0.90s/f (Soft) **10** Ran SP% **117.9**
Speed ratings (Par 109):106,102,100,100,96 90,85,69,50,38
CSF £52.63 CT £383.04 TOTE £10.10: £3.00, £2.50, £2.90; EX 57.10 Trifecta £425.80 Part won. Pool £599.72 - 0.30 winning units..
Owner T D Easterby **Bred** M H Easterby **Trained** Great Habton, N Yorks
■ Stewards' Enquiry : Neil Brown one-day ban: careless riding (Jul 12)

FOCUS
Mainly exposed performers for this valuable prize but, although the gallop was just fair, the winner won with plenty in hand and is the type to score again when there is cut in the ground. The form makes sense rated around the first four.

NOTEBOOK
Game Lad ◆, who had slipped to a decent mark, goes well in testing ground and turned in easily his best effort of the year for his in-form stable. In a race run at just an ordinary gallop, he powered clear having been dropped out and appeals as the type to win from a higher mark granted suitable underfoot conditions. (op 7-1)
Mezuzah, a noted mudlark, had the run of the race and ran up to the pick of his form from this season. Although 5lb higher than for his last win in October, he may be capable of picking up another race away from progressive or well-handicapped sorts in similar conditions this season. (op 7-1 tchd 11-2)
Imperial Echo(USA), back over 7f, is a consistent sort who ran creditably on this first start on heavy going. He may be best suited by less-testing ground and he should continue to give a good account over this trip in this sort of company. (op 13-2)
Red Romeo, easy to back, shaped as though retaining much of his ability on this first start since early September. Although effective with give in the ground, all his wins have been on a sound surface and he is one to keep an eye on from what looks a fair mark.
Glenbuck(IRE), an improved performer on a sound surface this term, was not disgraced back in testing ground. His current mark offers little room for manoeuvre, though. (tchd 11-1)
Daaweitza, who ran well over 1m at Carlisle on his previous outing, failed to reproduce that effort over this shorter trip and in these much more testing conditions. He is worth another chance on less-testing ground. (tchd 4-1)
Yorkshire Blue, a heavy-ground winner at Ayr last autumn, was soundly beaten on his first start of the year over this trip. A more strongly-run race on better ground may be more to his liking. (op 10-1)
Presumptive(IRE) Official explanation: jockey said gelding was unsuited by the heavy (soft in places) ground

3092 JOHN SMITH'S "EXTRA COLD" EBF MAIDEN STKS 6f
4:25 (4:25) (Class 4) 2-Y-0

£6,232 (£1,866; £933; £467; £233; £117) **Stalls** High

Form RPR
1 **Robscarvic (IRE)** 2-9-3 0 NCallan 12 81
(G A Swinbank) *towards rr: effrt and hdwy over 1f out: led ins fnl f: kpt on wl* **8/1**
2 *¾* **Harrison George (IRE)** 2-9-3 0 PaulHanagan 5 78
(R A Fahey) *prom: outpcd over 2f out: rallied over 1f out: chsd wnr ins fnl f: kpt on* **11/2**[3]
2242 **3** *1¾* **Fol Hollow (IRE)**[12] 2710 2-9-3 0 AdrianTNicholls 9 73
(D Nicholls) *t.k.h: led to ins fnl f: no ex* **5/2**[1]
4 *2* **Miss Solo** 2-8-12 0 LeeEnstone 8 62
(P C Haslam) *prom: effrt 2f out: nt qckn ins fnl f* **12/1**
5 *1½* **Climaxtackledotcom** 2-8-10 0 NSLawes(7) 7 63
(M W Easterby) *missed break: towards rr: effrt over 2f out: no imp fnl f* **28/1**
6 *nk* **When Yer Ready (IRE)** 2-9-3 0 GrahamGibbons 11 62
(T D Easterby) *dwlt: bhd: sme hdwy over 1f out: nvr on terms* **12/1**
00 **7** *3* **Note Perfect**[35] 2021 2-8-12 0 DaleGibson 10 48
(M W Easterby) *trckd ldrs tl rdn and wknd over 1f out* **25/1**
0 **8** *12* **Battlecruiser (IRE)**[59] 1390 2-9-3 0 JoeFanning 4 17
(M Johnston) *chsd ldrs tl wknd over 2f out* **3/1**[2]
66 **9** *1½* **Tikinheart (IRE)**[45] 1772 2-9-3 0 DavidAllan 14 12
(T D Easterby) *t.k.h: cl up: ev ch over 2f out: wknd qckly appr fnl f* **7/1**
10 *7* **Flower Appeal** 2-8-12 0 PaulMulrennan 3 —
(M W Easterby) *missed break: a struggling* **20/1**

1m 20.83s (5.74) **Going Correction** +0.90s/f (Soft) **10** Ran SP% **120.0**
Speed ratings (Par 95):97,96,93,91,89 88,84,68,66,57
CSF £51.81 TOTE £12.00: £3.30, £1.80, £1.50; EX 53.50.
Owner Adrian Butler **Bred** Peter McCutcheon **Trained** Melsonby, N Yorks

FOCUS
An ordinary maiden in which the pace was fair in the conditions. The whole field raced far side. The level of the form is guessy and is rated conservatively through the runner-up.

NOTEBOOK
Robscarvic(IRE), who cost 21,000 guineas and is a half-brother to a couple of middle-distance winners, created a favourable impression on this racecourse debut. He is bred to stay further and appeals as the type to win more races. (tchd 9-1)
Harrison George(IRE) ◆, a 45,000euro half-brother to several juvenile winners, attracted support on this racecourse debut and showed more than enough to suggest a similar event can be found, especially when upped to 7f. He is one to keep an eye on. (op 7-1)
Fol Hollow(IRE) is a headstrong sort who looked the best of those with previous form but he failed to settle in the conditions and again was turned over at shortish odds. While capable of picking up a race, he is likely to remain vulnerable to the more progressive sorts in this type of event. (tchd 11-4)

Miss Solo, the second foal of an unraced half-sister to a smart performer at around 1m in Hong Kong and to a useful sort over middle distances, ran creditably on this racecourse debut and is sure to win a race in ordinary company when upped to 7f. (op 14-1)
Climaxtackledotcom, the first foal of a half-sister to a classy sort up to 1m2f in Germany, was far from disgraced after losing ground at the start on this racecourse debut. He looks the sort to do better in nursery company in due course. (op 33-1 tchd 25-1)
When Yer Ready(IRE), a half-brother to ordinary handicapper Apache Nation, looked the yard's second string but finished ahead of his stable companion and may do better on a sounder surface once qualified for a handicap mark. (op 20-1)
Battlecruiser(IRE) was again well beaten but floundered in the conditions this time. He may well be better on a sound surface, is in very good hands and would not be one to write off just yet. (op 9-2)

3093 TOTESPORT.COM H'CAP 1m 2f 32y
4:55 (4:55) (Class 4) (0-85,86) 3-Y-0+
£6,232 (£1,866; £933; £467; £233; £117) Stalls Centre

Form RPR
0-44 1 **Domino Dancer (IRE)**[7] 2862 3-9-2 81 PaulMulrennan 7 89
(J Wade) *in midfield: hdwy to chal over 1f out: led ins fnl f: hld on wl* 10/1
4433 2 hd **Cleaver**[15] 2634 6-9-9 76 JamieSpencer 6 84
(Lady Herries) *t.k.h: hld up: stdy hdwy on bit over 2f out: rdn to ld appr fnl f: edgd lft and hdd ins fnl f: kpt on* 7/4[1]
4304 3 2 1/2 **Dzesmin (POL)**[28] 2236 5-9-9 81 (p) RoryMoore(5) 3 84+
(R C Guest) *hld up: hdwy on ins whn no room over 2f out: hdwy over 1f out: kpt on fnl f: nt rch first two* 9/2[2]
4225 4 1 1/4 **Tizzy May (FR)**[18] 2531 7-9-5 72 TomEaves 2 73
(B Ellison) *chsd ldrs: effrt and ev ch over 1f out: no ex ins fnl f* 11/2[3]
0446 5 6 **Ahlawy (IRE)**[7] 2868 4-9-1 68 DaleGibson 11 57
(M W Easterby) *prom: rdn over 2f out: wknd appr fnl f* 20/1
5-00 6 nk **Red Chairman**[1] 3053 5-8-10 63 oh15 (p) AdrianTNicholls 4 51
(R Johnson) *s.s: led after 2f: hdd appr fnl f: sn wknd* 66/1
-000 7 19 **Magic Sting**[3] 2987 6-9-6 73 DO'Donohoe 5 23
(B S Rothwell) *hld up: drvn over 2f out: sn wknd* 25/1
1261 8 6 **Torrens (IRE)**[18] 2527 5-9-12 79 PaulHanagan 9 17
(R A Fahey) *prom tl rdn and wknd 2f out* 7/1
00-6 9 7 **Abbondanza (IRE)**[38] 1939 4-9-10 77 TonyHamilton 8 —
(J Howard Johnson) *led 2f: cl up: effrt over 2f out: wknd over 1f out* 20/1
-665 10 23 **Kildare Sun (IRE)**[41] 1862 5-9-9 76 NCallan 1 —
(J Mackie) *in midfield: effrt 3f out: no imp whn checked 2f out: sn wknd* 9/1

2m 23.23s (11.43) **Going Correction** +1.225s/f (Soft)
WFA 3 from 4yo+ 12lb 10 Ran SP% **116.4**
Speed ratings (Par 105):103,102,100,99,95 94,79,74,69,50
CSF £26.73 CT £93.45 TOTE £10.10: £1.90, £1.30, £2.40; EX 31.40.
Owner John Wade **Bred** D And Mrs D Veitch **Trained** Mordon, Co Durham
■ John Wade's first winner on the Flat.
■ Stewards' Enquiry : Paul Mulrennan one-day ban: careless riding (Jul 12)

FOCUS
A run-of-the-mill handicap in which the pace was just fair. The placed horses set the level of the form.

3094 MILLER UK H'CAP 1m (R)
5:25 (5:26) (Class 4) (0-85,84) 3-Y-0 £6,232 (£1,866; £933; £467; £233) Stalls Centre

Form RPR
12 1 **Champfleurie**[7] 2872 3-9-3 80 NCallan 1 91+
(G A Swinbank) *trckd ldrs: led over 1f out: rdn clr* 5/4[1]
3-50 2 4 **Wheels In Motion (IRE)**[7] 2871 3-9-2 79 PaulHanagan 2 81
(T P Tate) *t.k.h early: hld up in tch: hdwy 2f out: chsd wnr 1f out: edgd lft: no imp* 6/1
1-6 3 5 **Steady As A Rock (FR)**[7] 2881 3-9-3 80 JoeFanning 9 71
(M Johnston) *led to over 1f out: sn btn* 9/4[2]
1-36 4 11 **Musca (IRE)**[24] 2373 3-9-7 84 TomEaves 6 49
(J Wade) *cl up tl rdn and wknd fr 2f out* 11/2[3]
0-00 5 70 **Mr Klick (IRE)**[8] 2821 3-8-7 70 DaleGibson 7 —
(N Wilson) *in tch tl rdn and wknd over 3f out* 16/1

1m 52.64s (9.16) **Going Correction** +1.225s/f (Soft) 5 Ran SP% **110.8**
Speed ratings (Par 101):103,99,94,83,13
CSF £9.26 TOTE £1.90: £1.30, £2.10; EX 9.20 Place 6 £2,534.18, Place 5 £156.12..
Owner Guy Reed **Bred** G Reed **Trained** Melsonby, N Yorks

FOCUS
Seven withdrawals meant this was not the competitive race it was at the 48-hour stage but nevertheless it went to a progressive performer, who won with plenty in hand and is the type to progress again. The form is rated at face value through the second.
T/Jkpt: Not won. T/Plt: £1,216.30 to a £1 stake. Pool: £181,953.09. 109.20 winning tickets.
T/Qpdt: £14.90 to a £1 stake. Pool: £11,745.80. 580.90 winning tickets. RY

3055
NEWMARKET (JULY) (R-H)
Saturday, June 30

OFFICIAL GOING: Soft
Wind: Light across Weather: Showery

3095 FAIRSTEAD HOMES MAIDEN STKS 7f
1:50 (1:54) (Class 4) 2-Y-0 £4,533 (£1,348; £674; £336) Stalls High

Form RPR
4 1 **Ghetto**[16] 2596 2-9-3 0 RichardHughes 7 84
(R Hannon) *s.i.s: hld up: hdwy over 2f: sn rdn: r.o u.p to ld towards fin* 10/3[1]
0 2 3/4 **Albaqaa**[36] 1990 2-9-3 0 RHills 8 82
(E A L Dunlop) *lw: chsd ldrs: rdn to ld 1f out: edgd rt: hdd towards fin* 16/1
3 1 3/4 **Cool Judgement (IRE)** 2-9-3 0 PhilipRobinson 13 78
(M A Jarvis) *cmpt: bit bkwd: led: rdn and hung lft over 1f out: sn hdd: styd on same pce* 5/1[2]
4 nk **Spinning Sound (IRE)** 2-9-3 0 ChrisCatlin 9 77+
(E J O'Neill) *gd sort: s.i.s: sn pushed along in rr: hdwy u.p over 1f out: r.o: nt rch ldrs* 14/1
5 shd **Jack Dawkins (USA)** 2-9-3 0 TedDurcan 10 76
(H R A Cecil) *w'like: scope: chsd ldrs: outpcd over 1f out: styd on ins fnl f* 13/2[3]
6 1/2 **Woolfall Treasure** 2-9-3 0 JohnEgan 5 75+
(G G Margarson) *leggy: scope: in rr whn hmpd over 4f out: nt clr run over 2f out: r.o ins fnl f: nrst fin* 22/1
0 7 3/4 **Prince Desire (IRE)**[22] 2424 2-9-3 0 MichaelHills 3 73
(B W Hills) *lw: hld up: racd keenly: shkn up over 1f out: nvr trbld ldrs* 13/2[3]
8 shd **Noble Citizen (USA)** 2-9-3 0 MartinDwyer 2 73
(D M Simcock) *w'like: scope: hld up: rdn over 2f out: nt trble ldrs* 14/1
2 9 1 **Crystal Reign (IRE)**[21] 2473 2-9-3 0 EddieAhern 11 70
(P W Chapple-Hyam) *s.i.s: sn chsng ldrs: rdn over 1f out: wknd fnl f* 10/3[1]
0 10 8 **Singer Of Songs (IRE)**[41] 1858 2-9-3 0 TPO'Shea 14 50
(P A Blockley) *bit bkwd: chsd ldrs: rdn over 2f out: wknd over 1f out* 50/1
11 2 1/2 **Valiant Vicar (USA)** 2-9-3 0 RobertHavlin 4 43
(B J Meehan) *wl grwn: bkwd: chsd ldrs over 4f* 20/1

1m 30.22s (3.44) **Going Correction** +0.50s/f (Yiel) 11 Ran SP% **119.8**
Speed ratings (Par 95):100,99,97,96,96 96,95,95,94,84 82
CSF £60.79 TOTE £3.80: £1.60, £4.70, £2.30; EX 60.70.
Owner Mrs J K Powell **Bred** Cothi Bloodstock **Trained** East Everleigh, Wilts

FOCUS
A fair maiden that should produce its share of winners. They all raced towards the stands'-side rail.

NOTEBOOK
Ghetto shaped nicely on his debut over 6f on quick ground at Newbury and confirmed that promise under these very different conditions. He was the slowest away from the stalls, and was a touch keen through the early stages, but he picked up in good style when asked to deliver his challenge to get up near the line. A horse with plenty of size, he is expected to get 1m and his connections may now look for a conditions race. (op 4-1, tchd 9-2 in a place)
Albaqaa looked all over the winner when sent on around a furlong from the finish, having travelled well close to the pace throughout, but he was just reeled in late on. This was a massive improvement on the form he showed on his debut at Goodwood and he is clearly well up to winning a maiden. (op 20-1)
Cool Judgement(IRE), a 70,000gns son of Pentire Celebre, out of a 1m4f winner, showed good early speed to lead the field against the stands' rail for much of the way, but he did not quite last home. This was a pleasing debut and he can be expected to come on for the outing. (op 6-1)
Spinning Sound(IRE) ◆, a 52,000euros Spinning World half-brother to sprint winners Glenmuir (5f winner on two-year-old debut) and Juniper Banks, out of a 1m4f winner, gave some trouble before the start, but shaped very nicely in the race itself. He was noted doing some good late work having started slowly and will have learnt plenty from this experience.
Jack Dawkins(USA), a 40,000gns Fantastic Light half-brother to useful dual 7f-1m two-year-old winner Manbala, showed a fair amount of ability on his racecourse debut and can be expected to come on for the run. (op 6-1)
Woolfall Treasure ◆, a 36,000gns son of Daylami and half-brother to among others multiple 6f-7f winner Zhitomir, was one of the real eye-catchers of the race. He was hampered half a mile from the finish and was denied a clear run when just beginning to find his stride, but he kept on very nicely when switched into the clear. This should have taught him plenty and it will be disappointing if he does not find a maiden.
Prince Desire(IRE) raced widest of all for much of the way and never posed a threat. One suspects he is better than he has shown so far. (op 9-1)
Noble Citizen(USA), a $190,000 son of Kentucky Derby runner-up Proud Citizen and half-brother to six winners, including high-class 7f-1m winner Mutaahab, was another caught wider than was probably ideal, but he showed ability. A faster surface will probably suit better and he looks to have plenty of potential. (op 16-1, tchd 18-1 in a place)
Crystal Reign(IRE) did not appear happy on the ground and was unable to confirm the promise he showed when second over 6f on his debut at Windsor. Official explanation: jockey said colt was unsuited by the good to soft (soft in places) ground (op 11-4 tchd 7-2)

3096 CLIPPER LOGISTICS EMPRESS STKS (LISTED RACE) (FILLIES) 6f
2:25 (2:26) (Class 1) 2-Y-0
£12,491 (£4,734; £2,369; £1,181; £591; £297) Stalls High

Form RPR
10 1 **Polar Circle (USA)**[10] 2756 2-9-1 0 JimmyFortune 13 94
(P W Chapple-Hyam) *lw: mde all: drvn out: hung lft wl ins fnl f* 9/2[3]
0 2 nk **Thought Is Free**[42] 1832 2-8-12 0 JohnEgan 4 90
(J S Moore) *hld up: rdn over 2f out: r.o wl ins fnl f* 66/1
1 3 1 1/4 **Highland Daughter (IRE)**[14] 2658 2-8-12 0 PhilipRobinson 6 86
(C G Cox) *stdd s: hdwy over 2f out: rdn and ev ch ins fnl f: edgd lft: no ex towards fin* 6/4[1]
1 4 hd **Yasinisi (IRE)**[32] 2115 2-8-12 0 ChrisCatlin 5 86
(E J O'Neill) *lw: chsd ldrs: rdn and ev ch over 1f out: styd on same pce* 9/1
1135 5 2 **Cake (IRE)**[10] 2756 2-9-1 0 RichardHughes 12 83
(R Hannon) *trckd ldrs: racd keenly: rdn over 1f out: edgd lft and no ex fnl f* 4/1[2]
41 6 1/2 **Dalkey Girl (IRE)**[11] 2746 2-8-12 0 MartinDwyer 11 78
(V Smith) *hld up: rdn over 2f out: nvr trbld ldrs* 14/1
1340 7 1/2 **Cristal Clear (IRE)**[10] 2756 2-8-12 0 RHills 8 77
(T D Easterby) *hld up: racd keenly: sme hdwy over 1f out: nvr trbld ldrs* 10/1
232 8 4 **Rebel Aclaim (IRE)**[21] 2460 2-8-12 0 TedDurcan 2 65
(M G Quinlan) *lw: chsd ldrs over 4f* 28/1
510 9 1 3/4 **Liberty Belle (IRE)**[8] 2812 2-8-12 0 TQuinn 1 60
(J R Best) *w wnr tl rdn and wknd over 1f out* 12/1

1m 16.33s (2.98) **Going Correction** +0.50s/f (Yiel) 9 Ran SP% **116.6**
Speed ratings (Par 98):100,99,97,97,95 94,93,88,86
CSF £224.69 TOTE £6.00: £2.00, £8.50, £1.30; EX 260.90 TRIFECTA Not won..
Owner Sangster Family **Bred** Swettenham Stud **Trained** Newmarket, Suffolk

FOCUS
An ordinary fillies' Listed contest. Unlike in the opening maiden, they raced down the middle of the track.

NOTEBOOK
Polar Circle(USA) could manage only 11th in the Queen Mary on her previous start, but her debut success in a conditions event at Newbury had been well advertised with the runner-up, Nijoom Dubai, winning the Group 3 Albany Stakes. She proved well suited by both the step up in trip and return to easy ground and made just about every yard of the running, battling on gamely when strongly pressed late on. She could return to the July course for the Cherry Hinton, or go for the Prix Robert Papin in France. (op 4-1, tchd 5-1 in places)
Thought Is Free ◆ finished down the field in a good Newbury maiden against the colts on her debut and this represents a big improvement, easily faring best of those held up. She finished very strongly, despite still displaying signs of greenness, and looks a smart prospect. She should hack up in her maiden next time before stepping back up in class.
Highland Daughter(IRE) landed the same Leicester maiden that her stable won with last year's winner of this race, Hope'n'charity, and the form of that success, gained on similarly soft ground, had already received a boost, so she looked to have plenty going for her. However, she gave trouble before the start, unshipping her jockey and proving very reluctant to enter the stalls, and she failed to make the anticipated improvement in the race itself. She was produced with every chance more towards the far side of the track than some of her rivals, but she never quite looked like getting there and one suspects her antics before the start may well have taken their toll. This still represents useful form strictly on the book, and there is no doubt she is a talented filly, but she probably has a bit of growing up to do yet. (op 2-1)

Yasinisi(IRE) improved on the form she showed when winning on her debut at Redcar and just missed out on some black type. (op 10-1)

Cake(IRE) had Polar Circle behind when fifth in the Queen Mary on her previous start, but she appeared to be unsuited by the soft ground. Official explanation: jockey said filly was unsuited by the soft ground (tchd 9-2 in places)

Dalkey Girl(IRE) stepped up on the bare form of her Yarmouth success, but she was still not quite good enough. (op 10-1)

Rebel Aclaim(IRE) Official explanation: jockey said filly had no more to give

Liberty Belle(IRE) Official explanation: filly was unsuited by the soft ground

3097 LADBROKES FRED ARCHER STKS (LISTED RACE) 1m 4f

3:00 (3:00) (Class 1) 4-Y-O+

£15,330 (£5,810; £2,907; £1,449; £726; £364) **Stalls** Centre

Form RPR

200- **1** **Classic Punch (IRE)**[275] 5641 4-9-0 102 TQuinn 2 111
(D R C Elsworth) *lw: led 10f out: hdd 6f out: rdn to ld and hung rt over 1f out: styd on* **12/1**

4-26 **2** *2 1/2* **Hard Top (IRE)**[36] 1985 5-9-0 110 EddieAhern 5 107
(Sir Michael Stoute) *lw: chsd ldrs: led 6f out: rdn and hdd over 1f out: styng on same pce whn rdr dropped reins wl ins fnl f* **6/1**[3]

-361 **3** *1 1/4* **Munsef**[21] 2441 5-9-0 110 (b) RHills 3 105
(J L Dunlop) *led: hdd 10f out: remained handy: rdn and ev ch over 1f out: no ex ins fnl f* **1/1**[1]

-346 **4** *1* **Under The Rainbow**[32] 2125 4-8-9 100 ChrisCatlin 1 98
(B W Hills) *hld up: rdn over 1f out: no imp fnl f* **7/1**

0224 **5** *1 3/4* **Grand Passion (IRE)**[54] 1550 7-9-0 104 TedDurcan 7 101
(G Wragg) *lw: hld up: rdn over 2f out: nvr trbld ldrs* **12/1**

0330 **6** *6* **Group Captain**[29] 2216 5-9-0 104 RichardHughes 4 91
(R Charlton) *hld up: rdn over 2f out: wknd over 1f out* **7/2**[2]

4640 **7** *1 1/4* **Amwell Brave**[8] 2833 6-9-0 59 WilliamBuick 6 89?
(J R Jenkins) *hld up: rdn and wknd 2f out* **150/1**

2m 35.74s (2.83) **Going Correction** +0.50s/f (Yiel) 7 Ran SP% **115.1**
Speed ratings (Par 111):110,108,107,106,105 101,100
CSF £81.20 TOTE £16.00: £4.60, £2.90; EX 91.20.

Owner J C Smith **Bred** Granham Farm **Trained** Newmarket, Suffolk

FOCUS
An ordinary Listed contest run at a steady pace and the bare form is not great for the grade and does not look that reliable. The field split into two groups when they turned into the straight a mile from the finish, with four horses, including the first two home, racing down the middle of the track, and the other three sticking towards the rail.

NOTEBOOK
Classic Punch(IRE) ◆ was highly tried after winning a hot maiden at Windsor on his reappearance last season but, although he failed to add to his tally, he often showed smart form in defeat. Gelded since he was last seen, he took this Listed contest in good style and looks to have to have improved from three to four, as he was entitled to being a half-brother to Persian Punch. He was allowed the run of the race out in front and, in racing down the centre of the track in the straight, he may have been on better ground than the favourite, so it would be unwise to get carried away with the form, but it was hard not to be impressed with the way he stayed on for pressure. This was the softest ground he has encountered to date, but he handled it without any problems at all. He gives the strong impression he will stay further and could be a decent middle-distance/stayer for years to come, keeping up the family tradition. (op 11-1)

Hard Top(IRE) has yet to rediscover his best form this season and, having raced a touch keenly early on, he proved no match for the winner. (tchd 5-1)

Munsef finally got his head back in front when dictating in a conditions event at Goodwood on his previous start, but he was unable to dominate this time and did not look to be putting it all in under pressure. This might not have been too bad an effort considering he raced towards the stands' rail in the straight, whereas the first two home came down the middle, and the ground was probably softer than he really cares for, but he still failed to inspire much confidence. (op 5-4 tchd 11-8)

Under The Rainbow was never a threat and she is proving hard to place at the moment. She may do better back against her own sex. (op 15-2)

Grand Passion(IRE) was having his first run over 1m4f and he was never a danger. (op 9-1)

Group Captain was well below his best and probably would have preferred a stronger end-to-end gallop. (op 4-1, tchd 9-2 in places)

3098 CHEVELEY PARK STUD CRITERION STKS (GROUP 3) 7f

3:35 (3:36) (Class 1) 3-Y-O+

£26,686 (£10,114; £5,061; £2,523; £1,264; £634) **Stalls** High

Form RPR

05-0 **1** **Silver Touch (IRE)**[35] 2050 4-9-0 107 TPO'Shea 5 110
(M R Channon) *hld up: rdn and r.o ins fnl f: hung lft: led nr fin* **10/1**

2-16 **2** *hd* **Major Cadeaux**[56] 1473 3-8-13 115 RichardHughes 10 114
(R Hannon) *trckd ldr: racd keenly: rdn to ld 1f out: hdd nr fin* **11/10**[1]

0232 **3** *3/4* **Fajr (IRE)**[8] 2817 5-9-3 95 JohnEgan 1 110
(Miss Gay Kelleway) *b: b.hind: chsd ldrs: rdn and ev ch ins fnl f: unable qckn towards fin* **12/1**

0-03 **4** *hd* **Welsh Emperor (IRE)**[28] 2233 8-9-3 111 MartinDwyer 4 109
(T P Tate) *led: rdn and hdd 1f out: styd on* **15/2**[3]

3-22 **5** *1/2* **Bahia Breeze**[29] 2207 5-9-0 106 ChrisCatlin 9 105
(Rae Guest) *chsd ldrs: nt clr run over 1f out: sn rdn: r.o* **9/1**

0-01 **6** *shd* **Mine (IRE)**[23] 2396 9-9-3 108 (v) TQuinn 2 108
(J D Bethell) *lw: s.i.s: hld up: hdwy over 1f out: rdn and ev ch ins fnl f: styd on same pce* **9/1**

1532 **7** *hd* **Levera**[32] 2111 4-9-3 105 RobertHavlin 8 107
(A King) *hld up: rdn over 1f out: r.o ins fnl f: nt trble ldrs* **16/1**

1121 **8** *3/4* **Munaddam (USA)**[49] 1656 5-9-3 112 RHills 11 105
(E A L Dunlop) *lw: hld up in tch: rdn over 1f out: no ex fnl f* **7/1**[2]

4-30 **9** *1* **Metropolitan Man**[114] 646 4-9-3 0 EddieAhern 6 103
(D M Simcock) *hld up: hdwy over 1f out: wknd ins fnl f* **66/1**

2543 **10** *3 1/2* **Mac Love**[49] 1656 6-9-3 104 TedDurcan 3 93
(J Noseda) *lw: trckd ldrs: plld hrd: rdn and wknd 1f out* **20/1**

1m 28.03s (1.25) **Going Correction** +0.50s/f (Yiel)
WFA 3 from 4yo+ 9lb 10 Ran SP% **120.8**
Speed ratings (Par 113):112,111,110,110,110 110,109,108,107,103
CSF £22.16 TOTE £16.20: £4.00, £1.30, £2.90; EX 47.30 Trifecta £571.40 Part won. Pool £804.87 - 0.10 winning units..

Owner Jaber Abdullah **Bred** Kildaragh Stud **Trained** West Ilsley, Berks

FOCUS
On paper this looked a quality renewal of this Group 3, but they went just an ordinary pace for much of the way and the first eight home were covered by less than three lengths, suggesting the bare form is nothing special and should not be taken too literally. They raced up the middle of the track.

NOTEBOOK
Silver Touch(IRE) was well below her best in a 6f Group 3 at the Curragh on her reappearance, but she left that form behind with a fine effort stepped up in trip and faced with her softest ground to date. She raced enthusiastically off the steady early gallop, but had plenty left when asked for her effort and picked up best of all. She should be capable of even better in a stronger-run race, and should prove versatile with regards trip, but whatever the case, soft ground is the key. (tchd 9-1)

Major Cadeaux, who made every yard of the running in the Greenham Stakes before running a highly-creditable sixth in the 2000 Guineas, was always in a handy position and only just failed. He seemed to have every chance, but seeing as the pace was just steady, and he has already proven himself under a forceful ride, he may just have been better served by putting more pressure on Welsh Emperor up front. Whatever way you look at it, this was a fine effort considering he was carrying a 5lb penalty against his elders, and he is one to keep on the right side of when he gets his favoured soft ground. He should also prove just as effective back over sprint trips. (op 7-4 tchd 15-8 and 2-1 in a place)

Fajr(IRE) ran a terrific race to take second in the Buckingham Palace at Royal Ascot and he confirmed himself an improved performer with another fine effort in defeat.

Welsh Emperor(IRE) was allowed to dictate at just a steady pace, but he has yet to find his best form so far this season and he just found a few too strong late on. (op 7-1, tchd 8-1 in places)

Bahia Breeze was denied a clear run when trying to stay on and would not have appreciated the steady gallop. She deserves to get her head back in front and could well do so when granted a strong pace on a stiff track. (op 10-1)

Mine(IRE) absolutely loves this track and came into this in great form having won a Listed race at Haydock on his previous start. However, he at as his best finishing off a frantic early pace and this race was simply not run to suit. (op 8-1, tchd 15-2 in places)

Levera has gained his five career wins from the front, so with the pace steady, he would surely have been better served by pressuring Welsh Emperor for the lead. (tchd 18-1)

Munaddam(USA) had never previously raced on ground this soft and it did not appear to suit.

3099 BARCLAYS EASTERN H'CAP 6f

4:10 (4:14) (Class 4) (0-80,80) 3-Y-O **£5,181** (£1,541; £770; £384) **Stalls** High

Form RPR

12 **1** **Big Noise**[17] 2570 3-9-0 73 TedDurcan 1 79
(Dr J D Scargill) *chsd ldrs: rdn to ld ins fnl f: r.o* **2/1**[1]

0255 **2** *shd* **King's Bastion (IRE)**[28] 2243 3-9-7 80 HayleyTurner 6 86
(M L W Bell) *led: rdn over 1f out: edgd rt and hdd ins fnl f: r.o* **6/1**

1 **3** *1/2* **Bee Eater (IRE)**[23] 2393 3-9-3 76 EddieAhern 7 80
(Sir Mark Prescott) *hld up: flashed tail thrght: effrt and nt clr run ins fnl f: swtchd lft: r.o* **4/1**[3]

2045 **4** *nk* **Comrade Cotton**[22] 2415 3-7-13 63 WilliamBuick(5) 8 66
(N A Callaghan) *chsd ldrs: rdn over 1f out: edgd lft ins fnl f: r.o u.p* **8/1**

5231 **5** *1* **Silca Elegance**[7] 2894 3-9-0 73 TPO'Shea 5 73
(M R Channon) *lw: chsd ldr: rdn and ev ch over 1f out: no ex wl ins fnl f* **11/4**[2]

3-05 **6** *4* **Usk Melody**[44] 1785 3-9-5 78 TQuinn 9 66
(G A Huffer) *b.hind: hld up: hdwy over 1f out: sn rdn: wknd ins fnl f* **12/1**

3400 **7** *9* **Leg Sweep**[73] 1098 3-8-2 68 TobyAtkinson(7) 3 29
(D R C Elsworth) *swtg: stdd s: a bhd* **22/1**

1m 15.76s (2.41) **Going Correction** +0.50s/f (Yiel) 7 Ran SP% **117.4**
Speed ratings (Par 101):103,102,102,101,100 95,83
CSF £15.36 CT £44.70 TOTE £3.20: £1.90, £3.30; EX 20.90.

Owner Theme Tune Partnership **Bred** F B B White **Trained** Newmarket, Suffolk

FOCUS
The principals finished in a bunch owing to a steady early pace, but this still looked like a fair sprint handicap and the form appears solid, rated through the fourth. They raced towards the stands' side, although most of these were happy to ignore the rail.

3100 EBF FORCE GROUP WORKING FOR RACING WELFARE FILLIES' H'CAP 1m

4:40 (4:41) (Class 3) (0-90,90) 3-Y-O+ **£8,096** (£2,408; £1,203; £601) **Stalls** High

Form RPR

1-06 **1** **Lady Stardust**[7] 2883 4-10-0 82 OscarUrbina 7 91
(J R Fanshawe) *b.hind: hld up: hdwy over 1f out: rdn to ld wl ins fnl f* **11/1**

4211 **2** *1/2* **Froissee**[6] 2905 3-8-7 76 6ex WilliamBuick(5) 9 82
(N A Callaghan) *trckd ldrs: rdn to ld 1f out: hdd ins fnl f: styd on* **5/2**[1]

5012 **3** *nk* **Lavenham (IRE)**[7] 2883 4-9-9 77 RichardHughes 6 84
(R Hannon) *hld up: hdwy over 1f out: rdn to ld ins fnl f: sn hdd and unable qckn* **10/3**[2]

1-31 **4** *2 1/2* **World Spirit**[14] 2654 3-8-12 76 ChrisCatlin 8 76
(Rae Guest) *led early: chsd ldrs: rdn over 1f out: no ex ins fnl f* **7/2**[3]

2314 **5** *1/2* **Bavarica**[7] 2883 5-8-12 73 AmyBaker(7) 2 73
(Miss J Feilden) *racd keenly: led over 6f out: rdn: edgd rt and hdd 1f out: styd on same pce* **14/1**

3246 **6** *1 1/4* **Neardown Beauty (IRE)**[19] 2507 4-10-0 82 EddieAhern 1 80
(I A Wood) *chsd ldrs: rdn and ev ch over 1f out: wknd ins fnl f* **10/1**

10-5 **7** *1/2* **Divine Right**[14] 2669 3-9-12 90 JimmyFortune 3 84
(B J Meehan) *sn led: hdd over 6f out: chsd ldrs tl rdn over 1f out: sn wknd* **7/1**

1m 44.39s (3.96) **Going Correction** +0.50s/f (Yiel)
WFA 3 from 4yo+ 10lb 7 Ran SP% **110.5**
Speed ratings (Par 104):100,99,99,96,96 94,94
CSF £36.13 CT £107.47 TOTE £13.20: £4.60, £1.90; EX 36.90.

Owner Mrs Martin Armstrong **Bred** Newsells Park Stud Limited **Trained** Newmarket, Suffolk

FOCUS
A fair fillies' handicap, in which there was no pace on early, but the form looks solid enough rated around the placed horses. They raced middle to stands' side, but nobody wanted to know the rail.

NOTEBOOK
Lady Stardust ◆ had struggled to make much impression in a couple of outings so far this year, including when not enjoying the best of trips behind both Lavenham and Bavarica over course and distance on her previous start, but those two runs clearly put her right. She was held up in last off just a steady early pace, but picked up best of all when switched to the inside with her challenge. Now she is back in form she appeals as one to very much keep on the right side of.

Froissee ran right up to her best under the penalty she picked up for her recent Pontefract success, but she was just unable to complete the hat-trick. (op 9-4)

Lavenham(IRE) was produced with every chance and was not beaten very far into third. (op 7-2)

World Spirit would have found this harder than the Bath handicap she won on her previous start and she could not defy a 6lb rise. (tchd 4-1 in places)

Bavarica was a touch keen in front and finished up well held.

3101 MORRIS ARMITAGE APPRENTICE H'CAP 7f

5:10 (5:11) (Class 5) (0-70,70) 4-Y-O+ **£3,886** (£1,156; £577; £288) **Stalls** High

Form RPR

6023 **1** **Mugeba**[7] 2870 6-8-5 54 (t) NicolPolli(3) 6 65
(Miss Gay Kelleway) *lw: s.i.s: hld up: racd centre: hdwy over 2f out: hung rt fr over 1f out: rdn to ld ins fnl f: styd on* **5/1**[2]

3060 **2** 3/4 **Joy And Pain**[14] 2665 6-8-0 **53**...(v) JosephWalsh(7) 3 62
(M J Attwater) *racd centre: hld up: hdwy over 2f out: rdn and ev ch ins fnl f: styd on* **16/1**

0060 **3** 3/4 **Whistleupthewind**[25] 2334 4-8-0 **51** oh1...(b) KMay(5) 13 58
(J M P Eustace) *racd alone stands' side: overall ldr: hung lft fr over 2f out: rdn over 1f out: hdd and unable qckn ins fnl f* **16/1**

00 **4** nk **Reigning Monarch (USA)**[7] 2878 4-8-1 **52** oh6 ow1 JemmaMarshall(5) 11 58
(Miss Z C Davison) *racd centre: trckd ldr tl led that gp 1/2-way: rdn and ev ch over 1f out: no ex ins fnl f* **33/1**

4001 **5** 1 1/2 **Out For A Stroll**[17] 2568 8-8-7 **60**... FLenclud(7) 1 62
(S C Williams) *swtg: s.i.s: racd centre: hld up: hdwy over 1f out: nt trble ldrs* **8/1**

1213 **6** nk **Vegas Boys**[7] 2882 4-9-10 **70**... SaleemGolam 8 71
(M Wigham) *racd centre: hld up: hdwy over 2f out: rdn over 1f out: no ex* **5/2**[1]

003 **7** nk **Pick A Nice Name**[17] 2553 5-9-1 **64**... MichaelJStainton(3) 9 64
(R M Whitaker) *racd centre: hld up: rdn over 2f out: hung lft over 1f out: no ex* **8/1**

6235 **8** 10 **Quantum Leap**[18] 2546 10-8-12 **65**...(p) ThomasBubb(7) 12 38
(S Dow) *racd centre: hld up: plld hrd: wknd 2f out* **8/1**

0065 **9** hd **Panshir (FR)**[2] 3034 6-8-5 **56** oh5 ow5...(t) AshleyHamblett(5) 4 29
(Mrs C A Dunnett) *lw: led centre to 1/2-way: rdn over 2f out: sn wknd* **7/1**[3]

450- **10** 7 **Patavium Prince (IRE)**[235] 6390 4-9-0 **65**... WilliamCarson(5) 5 19
(J R Best) *racd centre: chsd ldrs over 4f* **10/1**

-650 **11** 1 **Contemplation**[39] 1918 4-8-4 **55**...(bt[1]) JamieHamblett(5) 7 6
(J Balding) *racd centre: chsd ldrs: wkng whn hung lft over 2f out* **12/1**

1m 29.57s (2.79) **Going Correction** +0.50s/f (Yiel) **11** Ran SP% **122.6**
Speed ratings (Par 103):104,103,102,101,100 99,99,88,87,79 78
CSF £85.71 CT £1241.04 TOTE £6.80: £2.20, £4.50, £4.10; EX 112.00 Place 6 £118.23, Place 5 £55.50..
Owner M M Foulger **Bred** Broughton Bloodstock And M Billings **Trained** Exning, Suffolk

FOCUS
A moderate apprentices' handicap run at a sound pace and the form looks solid enough. The majority of these raced up the middle of the track, but the winner hugged the stands' rail in the closing stages.
T/Plt: £284.00 to a £1 stake. Pool: £98,121.20. 252.15 winning tickets. T/Qpdt: £123.30 to a £1 stake. Pool: £4,667.20. 28.00 winning tickets. CR

2940 WINDSOR (R-H)
Saturday, June 30

OFFICIAL GOING: Soft (heavy in places)
Wind: Almost nil Weather: Overcast

3102 TOTEPLACEPOT MAIDEN STKS 6f
2:30 (2:30) (Class 5) 3-4-Y-O **£3,238** (£963; £481; £240) **Stalls** High

Form RPR

42-5 **1** **Impromptu**[88] 899 3-9-3 77... GeorgeBaker 9 66+
(R M Beckett) *mde virtually all: gng much bttr than rest 2f out: drvn 1f out: sn clr* **11/4**[2]

0-00 **2** 1 1/2 **Batchworth Fleur**[7] 2878 4-9-5 42... StephenCarson 1 55
(E A Wheeler) *cl up: chsd wnr over 2f out: rdn and nt qckn wl over 1f out: readily hld after* **33/1**

04- **3** 3/4 **Titan Triumph**[304] 4928 3-9-3 0... IanMongan 7 56
(W J Knight) *hld up in tch: prog over 2f out: rdn to chse ldng pair over 1f out: kpt on one pce* **3/1**[3]

0-5 **4** 1/2 **Land's End (IRE)**[39] 1923 3-9-3 0... SteveDrowne 3 57+
(J Noseda) *dwlt: hld up in rr: prog 1/2-way: chsng ldrs 2f out: shkn up and one pce* **5/2**[1]

00 **5** 5 **Nouveau (GER)**[5] 2944 3-9-3 0... RichardSmith 6 39
(R Hannon) *dwlt: hld up in last trio: sme prog 2f out: sn outpcd and no ch w ldrs* **16/1**

6 6 **King Roy (IRE)** 3-8-10 0... KylieManser(7) 8 21
(N I M Rossiter) *dwlt: sn rcvrd to chse ldrs: rdn 2f out: green and wknd over 1f out* **25/1**

7 3 **Vogarth** 3-9-3 0... DaneO'Neill 5 12
(B R Millman) *dwlt: in tch tl wknd 2f out* **17/2**

0-24 **8** 5 **Dragon Flame (IRE)**[16] 2606 4-9-10 58...(v) DarryllHolland 2 —
(M Quinn) *pressed wnr to over 2f out: wknd rapidly: fin tired* **6/1**

0 **9** 5 **Watt A Will**[17] 2580 4-9-0 0... KevinGhunowa(5) 4 —
(J M Bradley) *dwlt: a last and sn struggling* **80/1**

1m 16.58s (2.91) **Going Correction** +0.50s/f (Yiel)
WFA 3 from 4yo 7lb **9** Ran SP% **119.0**
Speed ratings (Par 103):100,98,97,96,89 81,77,71,64
CSF £91.72 TOTE £3.40: £1.30, £9.20, £1.70; EX 140.30 Trifecta £68.70 Pool £96.80. - 1.00 winning unit..
Owner C F Colquhoun **Bred** Mrs S Joint **Trained** Whitsbury, Hants

FOCUS
A modest event that is unlikely to prove informative. The early gallop was very moderate and the form, which is anchored by the proximity of the rnunner-up, should be treated with caution.

3103 TOTEPOOL MIDSUMMER STKS (LISTED RACE) 1m 67y
3:05 (3:05) (Class 1) 3-Y-O+
£14,762 (£5,595; £2,800; £1,396; £699; £351) **Stalls** High

Form RPR

112/ **1** **Winged Cupid (IRE)**[616] 6019 4-9-4 105... KerrinMcEvoy 8 117+
(Saeed Bin Suroor) *chsd ldrs: pushed along over 3f out: str run on wd outside to ld over 1f out: sn rdn clr: eased nr fin* **7/4**[1]

-603 **2** 4 **Babodana**[21] 2442 7-9-4 100... GeorgeBaker 4 106
(M H Tompkins) *chsd ldrs: disp 2nd 1/2-way: hrd rdn and edgd lft 2f out whn cl up: kpt on ins fnl f: no ch w wnr* **9/2**[2]

40 **3** 3/4 **Vanderlin**[17] 2586 8-9-4 105... SteveDrowne 6 104
(A M Balding) *chsd ldr to 1/2-way: sn pushed along: renewed effrt to chal 2f out: sn brushed aside by wnr: one pce* **9/1**

-354 **4** 1 1/2 **Final Verse**[47] 1723 4-9-4 105... LPKeniry 7 101
(J S Moore) *hld up in 7th: stdy prog fr 3f out: chsng ldrs whn n.m.r and swtchd lft 2f out: sn rdn and one pce* **9/1**

3-54 **5** nk **Summer's Eve**[21] 2441 4-8-13 98... DaneO'Neill 1 95
(H Candy) *led at gd pce to over 1f out: wknd* **6/1**[3]

3-60 **6** 4 **Tell**[127] 544 4-9-4 0... StephenCarson 5 91
(J L Dunlop) *hld up in detached last: pushed along 1/2-way: nvr on terms* **25/1**

16-3 **7** 5 **Pearl's Girl**[7] 2883 4-8-13 78... IanMongan 3 74
(W J Haggas) *dwlt: sn in tch: pushed up to dispute 2nd 1/2-way: wknd 2f out* **20/1**

0-61 **8** 39 **Massive (IRE)**[32] 2124 3-8-11 105... DarryllHolland 2 —
(M R Channon) *chsd ldrs: wknd over 3f out: t.o whn virtually p.u fnl f* **9/2**[2]

1m 47.61s (2.91) **Going Correction** +0.65s/f (Yiel)
WFA 3 from 4yo+ 10lb **8** Ran SP% **115.6**
Speed ratings (Par 111):111,107,106,104,104 100,95,56
CSF £9.83 TOTE £2.60: £1.40, £1.60, £2.70; EX 12.10 Trifecta £113.60 Part won. Pool £160.10 - 0.80 winning units..
Owner Godolphin **Bred** Longfield Stud **Trained** Newmarket, Suffolk

FOCUS
This looked a decent field for the grade. The winner could prove to be even better than this level if progressing again, and Babodana is a solid yardstick to the form considering the underfoot conditions.

NOTEBOOK
Winged Cupid(IRE) ◆, off the track since a fine second in the 2005 Racing Post Trophy, when trained by Mark Johnston, showed all of his class to put matters beyond his rivals with a smart turn of foot. The stable won this race with Librettist last season, and there is no doubt Winged Cupid could be just as classy as that colt proved to be. He does, however, seem sure to be suited by further than a mile later in the season and it is worth remembering that he finished well in front of the likes of Dylan Thomas and Red Rocks as a juvenile. (op 2-1)
Babodana ◆, from a stable just starting to show some form, handles easy ground well and kept on strongly to just edge past Vanderlin late on. It has been a long time since he actually got his nose in front but is well handicapped if reproducing this effort next time. (op 5-1 tchd 11-2)
Vanderlin did not do a great deal wrong but just does not act that well in easy ground. It was heartening to see him run so well in the face of a stiff task and is worthy of consideration next time if finding a quicker surface. (op 15-2 tchd 7-1)
Final Verse, having his first run for the Stan Moore stable, never quite got on terms but did at least show a little bit more than he had done recently.
Summer's Eve, dropping down in trip, set a fair tempo in front but is struggling to find her form this season at the business end of a race. A drop in class might be required to get her head in front again. (tchd 11-2)
Pearl's Girl looked to hate the ground and was not given a hard time up the home straight. (op 25-1 tchd 18-1)
Massive(IRE) ran no sort of race and it is not hard to forgive this effort, as it was clearly not his true form. (op 5-1 tchd 11-2)

3104 TOTESPORT STKS (HERITAGE H'CAP) 6f
3:40 (3:41) (Class 2) (0-105,102) 3-Y-0+
£31,160 (£9,330; £4,665; £2,335; £1,165; £585) **Stalls** High

Form RPR

5115 **1** **Aahayson**[35] 2035 3-9-8 **102**... PatCosgrave 12 109
(K R Burke) *mde all: drvn over 1f out: styd on wl fnl f: a holding on* **16/1**

3002 **2** 1/2 **Phantom Whisper**[23] 2399 4-9-0 **87**... KerrinMcEvoy 7 94
(B R Millman) *trckd ldrs: rdn 2f out: styd on fr over 1f out: clsd on wnr nr fin: a hld* **9/1**[3]

0004 **3** nk **Idle Power (IRE)**[13] 2688 9-8-11 **84**... AmirQuinn 4 90
(J R Boyle) *cl up: chsd wnr over 2f out: rdn and no imp over 1f out: kpt on ins fnl f but lost 2nd nr fin* **11/1**

5020 **4** hd **Tony James (IRE)**[42] 1836 5-9-8 **95**... GeorgeBaker 15 101
(K O Cunningham-Brown) *trckd rival nr side: rdn to ld pair over 1f out: kpt on fnl f: nvr quite on terms* **50/1**

1560 **5** 1/2 **Beaver Patrol (IRE)**[7] 2858 5-9-8 **95**... StephenCarson 6 99
(Eve Johnson Houghton) *trckd ldrs: rdn and nt qckn 2f out: swtchd outside and styd on again ins fnl f* **13/2**[2]

6100 **6** shd **Lucayos**[13] 2688 4-8-7 **83**... RichardKingscote(3) 13 87
(Mrs H Sweeting) *dwlt: pushed up to ld nr side pair but nt on terms: drvn 1/2-way: hdd over 1f out: kpt on* **25/1**

2-06 **7** shd **Burning Incense (IRE)**[7] 2858 4-9-9 **96**... SteveDrowne 10 100
(R Charlton) *settled in last trio: pushed along 1/2-way: prog on outer 2f out: clsd on ldrs u.p 1f out: fdd* **9/4**[1]

0040 **8** 2 **Fantasy Believer**[21] 2463 9-9-10 **97**... DarryllHolland 2 95
(J J Quinn) *settled in last trio: prog and drvn over 1f out: keeping on but no ch whn nt clr run last 75yds* **13/2**[2]

3030 **9** 1 1/4 **Lethal**[28] 2237 4-9-2 **89**... IanMongan 9 83
(D K Ivory) *pressed wnr to over 2f out: fdd u.p* **33/1**

0000 **10** 3/4 **Bazroy (IRE)**[23] 2395 3-7-11 **84**... BernadetteQuinn(7) 11 74
(P D Evans) *racd on wd outside of far side gp: effrt u.p 2f out: wknd over 1f out* **66/1**

-230 **11** 1 3/4 **Kay Two (IRE)**[44] 1788 5-8-10 **88**... TolleyDean(5) 14 74
(R J Price) *chsd ldrs: drvn and effrt on outer 2f out: wknd fnl f* **14/1**

3241 **12** 3 1/2 **Adantino**[26] 2318 8-8-9 **82**...(b) DaneO'Neill 1 58
(B R Millman) *in tch tl wknd 2f out* **12/1**

0016 **13** 2 **Angus Newz**[30] 2184 4-9-6 **93**...(v) NeilPollard 5 63
(M Quinn) *dwlt: t.k.h and hld up wl in rr: rdn over 2f out: no real prog: wknd over 1f out* **16/1**

5512 **14** 6 **Barney McGrew (IRE)**[7] 2882 4-8-9 **85**... MarcHalford(3) 3 37
(J A R Toller) *reluctant to enter stalls and restless in them: dwlt: a in rr: struggling 2f out* **13/2**[2]

1m 15.19s (1.52) **Going Correction** +0.50s/f (Yiel)
WFA 3 from 4yo+ 7lb **14** Ran SP% **125.5**
Speed ratings (Par 109):109,108,107,107,107 106,106,104,102,101 99,94,91,83
CSF £156.18 CT £1733.10 TOTE £23.10: £5.00, £3.90, £4.40; EX 236.40 TRIFECTA Not won..
Owner Philip Richards **Bred** Whitsbury Manor Stud And Mrs M E Slade **Trained** Middleham Moor, N Yorks

FOCUS
A very solid handicap run at decent pace in the ground with the runner-up the best guide to the form. Tony James and Lucayos kept to the stands' side down the home straight and appeared to lose little ground taking that route. Aahayson, the highest-rated in the race, is progressive and did well to beat his elders but Burning Incense and Fantasy Believer could have finished a bit closer if given more prominent rides.

NOTEBOOK
Aahayson showed terrific pace from a modest draw to make all. One of only two three-year-olds in the race, his connections have some lofty plans for him this season, and will give him entries in the Stewards' Cup and Ayr Gold Cup later on in the year. His record shows that he appears to handle most ground but one would guess that he is at his best with some ease in the ground.
Phantom Whisper, who seems to run well at the track, kept on well in the final stages but could not trouble the winner in the final stages. He is still a touch high in the weights to have an obvious chance. (op 12-1)
Idle Power(IRE) ◆ is on a fair handicap mark again but looks better suited by quicker ground. He goes well at Goodwood, and is one to keep an eye on if entered in a race at that course in the coming month. (op 12-1)
Tony James(IRE) was one of only two that came down the stands' side and only just failed to get to those racing down the inside rail. He is far from consistent but so well handicapped now on his two-year-old form that he must be given respect wherever he turns up next time.

Beaver Patrol(IRE) got outpaced when the tempo increased before staying on well inside the final furlong. It was a good effort in ground he has no solid form in, but he remains quite high in the handicap after his success at Newmarket earlier in the season. (op 10-1)
Lucayos led the two horses that came down the stands' side and was not totally disgraced. However, he is still quite high in the weights and is not easy to seriously fancy until dropping a few pounds.
Burning Incense(IRE), making a fairly swift reappearance after running so well in the Wokingham Handicap at Royal Ascot, was probably not given the most advantageous of rides in the underfoot conditions and did not pose the principals any problems. (tchd 5-2 in a place)
Fantasy Believer, who was stepping back up to 6f, was another in the race probably not ridden to best advantage in the ground and is well worth another chance next time. Official explanation: jockey said gelding was denied a clear run (op 6-1 tchd 7-1)
Bazroy(IRE) did not run quite as badly as his finishing position suggests and hinted at a return to form.

3105 TOTESPORT 0800 221 221 H'CAP — 1m 3f 135y
4:15 (4:15) (Class 2) (0-100,89) 3-Y-0+
£12,464 (£3,732; £1,866; £934; £466; £234) Stalls Low

Form / RPR
04-2 1 **Castle Howard (IRE)**[36] [2002] 5-10-0 **89** .... DavidKinsella 4 — 99
(W J Musson) *t.k.h: hld up bhd ldng pair: taken towards far side over 3f out: led over 2f out: forged clr over 1f out* **7/2**[1]
5-10 2 5 **Dan Dare (USA)**[33] [2093] 4-9-12 **87** .... (v[1]) KerrinMcEvoy 7 — 88
(Sir Michael Stoute) *cl up: taken towards far side and rdn 3f out: plugged on to go 2nd ins fnl f: no ch w wnr* **4/1**[2]
10-0 3 1 **Philanthropy**[42] [1843] 3-8-9 **87** .... GregFairley[(3)] 2 — 86
(M Johnston) *led: hung lft towards far side over 3f out: hdd over 2f out: no ch w wnr after: lost 2nd ins fnl f* **4/1**[2]
3004 4 2 1/2 **Polish Power (GER)**[13] [2692] 7-9-4 **79** .... LPKeniry 8 — 74
(J S Moore) *stmbld bdly s and rdr nrly uns: hld up in last: rdn over 3f out: prog in centre to dispute 2nd over 1f out: no ex* **8/1**
-000 5 1 3/4 **Sienna Storm (IRE)**[42] [1844] 4-9-11 **86** .... DarryllHolland 3 — 79
(M H Tompkins) *t.k.h: sn trckd ldr: styd nr side fr 3f out: no worse than 2nd over 1f out: wknd rapidly* **7/1**[3]
0-35 6 11 **John Terry (IRE)**[29] [2209] 4-9-12 **87** .... SteveDrowne 5 — 62
(Mrs A J Perrett) *hld up towards rr: rdn 4f out: sn struggling: bhd fnl 3f* **7/2**[1]
2130 7 9 **Paktolos (FR)**[56] [1477] 4-10-0 **89** .... DaneO'Neill 6 — 50
(A King) *hld up in tch: rdn over 3f out: wknd and bhd fnl 2f* **12/1**

2m 36.38s (6.28) **Going Correction** +0.65s/f (Yiel)
WFA 3 from 4yo+ 14lb — 7 Ran SP% **115.7**
Speed ratings (Par 109):105,101,101,99,98 90,84
CSF £18.17 CT £57.73 TOTE £4.50: £2.60, £1.90; EX 8.70 Trifecta £43.00 Pool £181.90 - 3.00 winning units..
Owner The Square Table **Bred** Churchtown Bloodstock **Trained** Newmarket, Suffolk

FOCUS
A decent handicap although not that solid, but the winner looks to be on the upgrade. The early tempo was not strong, as one might expect in the ground.

NOTEBOOK
Castle Howard(IRE) ♦, who held an entry in the Northumberland Plate at the five-day stage, had shown plenty of promise on his seasonal debut and confirmed that effort with a smooth success. The imminent rise in the weights will test him but there is every chance that he is still on an upward curve, and could be good enough to go close in a decent handicap later in the season. (tchd 9-2)
Dan Dare(USA), a little keen in a first-time visor, seemed to see out the trip well enough in the ground but was not good enough to trouble the winner. He has made a decent start to his handicapping career and looks the sort to hold is form well in similar company.
Philanthropy took the field along early but the winner as he swept past him about two furlongs from home. A fine-looking sort, he has proved to be very disappointing since winning a conditions race last season, but is at least coming down the handicap as a result. (tchd 7-2)
Polish Power(GER) is probably just a shade high in the weights at the moment, although winning off a higher mark on the Fibresand in March, but kept on nicely enough after being hard at work rounding the final bend. Official explanation: jockey said horse stumbled on leaving stalls (op 15-2)
Sienna Storm(IRE) took a different route to almost all of his rivals down the home straight which did not pay off. (op 8-1 tchd 13-2)
John Terry(IRE) has some fair form in ground with ease in it, so this effort is not easy to explain as he was beaten at a very early stage of the race. (op 5-1)

3106 TOTEEXACTA H'CAP — 6f
4:50 (4:50) (Class 5) (0-70,67) 3-Y-0+
£3,238 (£963; £481; £240) Stalls High

Form / RPR
4102 1 **Makabul**[13] [2694] 4-9-13 **66** .... KerrinMcEvoy 5 — 75
(B R Millman) *in tch towards rr: rdn and effrt on outer 2f out: styd on wl fnl f to ld last stride* **7/2**[2]
4500 2 shd **Polar Force**[58] [1436] 7-8-11 **53** .... MarcHalford[(3)] 10 — 62
(Mrs C A Dunnett) *pressed ldrs: led jst over 2f out: hrd rdn and tired fnl f: hdd last stride* **8/1**[3]
4305 3 1/2 **Bens Georgie (IRE)**[9] [2799] 5-8-13 **52** .... DaneO'Neill 3 — 59
(D K Ivory) *awkward s and slowly away: hld up in rr: stdy prog over 2f out: drvn over 1f out: clsd fnl f: a hld* **10/1**
-055 4 3/4 **Turkish Sultan (IRE)**[1] [3064] 4-8-13 **57** .... (p) KevinGhunowa[(5)] 6 — 62
(J M Bradley) *chsd ldrs: pushed along bef 1/2-way: effrt u.p and cl up 1f out: hrd drvn and kpt on* **12/1**
1060 5 2 **Bobby Rose**[52] [1589] 4-9-3 **63** .... ChrisHough[(7)] 7 — 62
(D K Ivory) *trckd ldrs gng easily: chal 2f out: sn rdn and fnd nil* **25/1**
0065 6 3 **Dunn Deal (IRE)**[16] [2608] 7-8-6 **48** oh1 .... NeilChalmers[(3)] 4 — 38
(J Balding) *towards rr: rdn and no prog over 2f out: plugged on* **20/1**
0002 7 2 1/2 **Gone'N'Dunnett (IRE)**[4] [2966] 8-8-9 **48** oh1 .... (v) DMylonas 8 — 30
(Mrs C A Dunnett) *w ldrs: upsides and rdn over 2f out: wknd over 1f out* **8/1**[3]
0024 8 nk **Trinculo (IRE)**[23] [2386] 10-8-10 **56** .... (b) KylieManser[(7)] 9 — 38
(R A Harris) *dwlt: rcvrd and led after 2f to over 2f out: wandered and wknd* **14/1**
6403 9 2 1/2 **George The Second**[29] [2217] 4-9-6 **62** .... RichardKingscote[(3)] 2 — 36
(Mrs H Sweeting) *led for 2f: w ldrs: led over 2f out: sn hdd: wknd over 1f out* **9/1**
0021 10 nk **Looks Could Kill (USA)**[9] [2806] 5-10-0 **67** .... DavidKinsella 11 — 40
(A B Haynes) *nvr gng wl: sn pushed along on outer: drvn in rr 1/2-way: btn after* **11/4**[1]
4020 11 3 1/2 **North Fleet**[50] [1640] 4-8-4 **50** .... BarrySavage[(7)] 1 — 13
(J M Bradley) *chsd ldrs: rdn bef 1/2-way: lost pl and struggling over 2f out* **12/1**

1m 16.19s (2.52) **Going Correction** +0.50s/f (Yiel) — 11 Ran SP% **120.9**
Speed ratings (Par 103):103,102,102,101,98 94,91,90,87,87 82
CSF £32.91 CT £267.49 TOTE £5.20: £1.90, £2.50, £2.30; EX 49.90 Trifecta £43.40 Pool £287.40 - 4.70 winning units..
Owner M S T Partnership **Bred** D Lowe **Trained** Kentisbeare, Devon

FOCUS
A low-grade sprint that produced a very close finish. The form looks solid enough rated around the third and fourth.

3107 TOTESPORTCASINO.COM FILLIES' H'CAP — 1m 2f 7y
5:20 (5:20) (Class 5) (0-75,75) 3-Y-0+
£3,238 (£963; £481; £240) Stalls Low

Form / RPR
-463 1 **Sister Maria (USA)**[17] [2579] 3-9-0 **73** .... DaneO'Neill 6 — 79
(E A L Dunlop) *led after 2f: mde rest: rdn 2f out: hanging lft after but drew clr fr over 1f out* **2/1**[1]
0004 2 5 **Doubly Guest**[5] [2940] 3-8-10 **69** .... NeilPollard 1 — 65
(G G Margarson) *hld up in tch: effrt to chse wnr over 2f out: sn rdn and lft bhd: kpt on* **6/1**
332- 3 3 **Moon Valley**[278] [5567] 4-10-0 **75** .... GeorgeBaker 5 — 65
(W J Haggas) *s.i.s: cl up: rdn to dispute 2nd over 1f out: wknd ins fnl f* **3/1**[3]
-056 4 5 **Cortesia (IRE)**[24] [2361] 4-9-10 **71** .... KerrinMcEvoy 4 — 51
(P W Chapple-Hyam) *led for 2f: chsd wnr tl wknd over 2f out* **11/4**[2]
3205 5 5 **Fangorn Forest (IRE)**[14] [2654] 4-8-9 **63** .... (p) KylieManser[(7)] 2 — 33
(R A Harris) *hld up in tch: cl up 3f out: rdn over 2f out: sn wknd* **7/1**

2m 16.15s (7.85) **Going Correction** +0.65s/f (Yiel)
WFA 3 from 4yo 12lb — 5 Ran SP% **111.8**
Speed ratings (Par 100):94,90,87,83,79
CSF £14.19 TOTE £3.00: £1.60, £2.10; EX 10.10 Place 6 £199.93, Place 5 £95.73..
Owner Cliveden Stud **Bred** Cliveden Stud **Trained** Newmarket, Suffolk

FOCUS
A very modest affair that will probably have little impact of future races with the form looking weak for the grade.
T/Plt: £270.60 to a £1 stake. Pool: £70,484.55. 190.10 winning tickets. T/Qpdt: £74.10 to a £1 stake. Pool: £3,538.50. 35.30 winning tickets. JN

3062 WOLVERHAMPTON (A.W) (L-H)
Saturday, June 30

OFFICIAL GOING: Standard
Wind: Fresh, behind Weather: Overcast, light rain

3108 STEVE BADDELEY'S STAG NIGHT H'CAP — 5f 216y(P)
7:00 (7:02) (Class 4) (0-85,85) 3-Y-0+
£5,829 (£1,734; £866; £432) Stalls Low

Form / RPR
5560 1 **Westport**[11] [2744] 4-8-13 **71** .... FrancisNorton 8 — 82
(K A Ryan) *chsd ldrs: hdwy over 2f out: led 1f out: rdn out* **11/2**[3]
3010 2 1 1/4 **Matuza (IRE)**[26] [2318] 4-9-13 **85** .... RichardMullen 4 — 92
(W R Muir) *in tch: rdn and hdwy over 1f out: chsd wnr fnl f* **13/2**
0265 3 2 **Canadian Danehill (IRE)**[18] [2529] 5-9-6 **85** .... (p) JackDean[(7)] 7 — 86
(R M H Cowell) *t.k.h: led 2f out: rdn and hdd 1f out: no ex fnl f* **9/1**
-005 4 1/2 **Capricorn Run (USA)**[7] [2882] 4-9-7 **79** .... (v) AdamKirby 1 — 79
(A J McCabe) *s.i.s: hdwy appr fnl f: nvr nrr* **9/1**
6111 5 3 **Dramatic**[11] [2750] 3-8-11 **76** .... JimmyQuinn 5 — 65
(Sir Mark Prescott) *trckd ldrs: rdn and ev ch 2f out: hung lft and wknd ent fnl f* **9/4**[1]
5110 6 1 1/2 **Cool Sands (IRE)**[37] [1977] 5-8-11 **72** .... (v) DuranFentiman[(3)] 3 — 58
(D Shaw) *in rr: rdn wl over 1f out and nvr on terms* **12/1**
03U0 7 1 1/2 **Law Maker**[3] [2993] 7-8-9 **67** .... (v) RobertHavlin 2 — 49
(A Bailey) *led tl hdd 2f out: sn btn* **22/1**
-022 8 11 **Rosein**[25] [2347] 5-9-6 **78** .... J-PGuillambert 6 — 27
(Mrs G S Rees) *v.s.a and nvr got into r* **7/2**[2]

1m 14.47s (-1.34) **Going Correction** +0.025s/f (Slow)
WFA 3 from 4yo+ 7lb — 8 Ran SP% **113.7**
Speed ratings (Par 105):109,107,104,104,100 98,96,81
CSF £40.29 CT £318.17 TOTE £8.30: £2.50, £2.40, £2.10; EX 46.60.
Owner The C H F Partnership **Bred** Agricola Ficomontanino S R L **Trained** Hambleton, N Yorks

FOCUS
A fair handicap run 3.63sec faster than the following juvenile contest. It has been rated through the runner-up.
Rosein Official explanation: jockey said mare missed the break

3109 EUROPEAN BREEDERS' FUND MAIDEN FILLIES' STKS — 5f 216y(P)
7:30 (7:31) (Class 5) 2-Y-O
£3,562 (£1,059; £529; £264) Stalls Low

Form / RPR
1 **Green Oasis (USA)** 2-9-0 0 .... ChrisCatlin 8 — 75+
(E J O'Neill) *trckd ldr: led 2f out: rdn out: comf* **7/2**[3]
0 2 3 **Tenjack Queen (IRE)**[21] [2457] 2-9-0 0 .... AdamKirby 4 — 66
(J A Osborne) *hld up: hdwy 2f out: chsd wnr ins fnl f: no imp* **5/2**[2]
23 3 1 1/4 **Montiboli (IRE)**[32] [2115] 2-9-0 0 .... TedDurcan 3 — 62
(K A Ryan) *led tl hdd 2f out: one pce and lost 2nd ins fnl f* **2/1**[1]
0 4 3 **Lady Calido (USA)**[6] [2904] 2-9-0 0 .... JimmyQuinn 7 — 53
(Sir Mark Prescott) *in rr: hdwy 3f out: wknd over 1f out* **7/1**
00 5 nk **Frammenti**[6] [2904] 2-9-0 0 .... VHalliday 6 — 52
(A J McCabe) *chsd ldrs: rdn 3f out: wknd 2f out* **50/1**
6 1/2 **Rathmolyon** 2-9-0 0 .... RobertHavlin 1 — 51
(D Haydn Jones) *stdd s: hdwy on outside 1/2-way: wknd over 1f out* **14/1**
0 7 1 3/4 **Morforwyn**[18] [2539] 2-9-0 0 .... FrancisNorton 2 — 45
(J A Osborne) *in rr on ins: effrt 2f out: sn btn* **16/1**

1m 18.1s (2.29) **Going Correction** +0.025s/f (Slow) — 7 Ran SP% **111.1**
Speed ratings (Par 90):85,81,79,75,74 74,71
CSF £11.93 TOTE £4.70: £2.90, £1.40; EX 8.80.
Owner Michael Gerard Daly **Bred** W S Farish **Trained** Averham Park, Notts

FOCUS
An ordinary maiden run 3.63 sec slower than the opening handicap, but a decisive winner. He probably did not beat agreat deal, though.

NOTEBOOK
Green Oasis(USA), a $140,000 filly related to several American milers, is clearly well thought of as she is entered in the Moyglare Stud Stakes. From a yard that does well with its juveniles, she put up a decent performance to score with something in hand and, although the time was ordinary, looks capable of going on to better things. (op 3-1 tchd 4-1)
Tenjack Queen(IRE), who made an encouraging debut at the beginning of the month, chased the winner through but could make no impression in the last furlong. She is going the right way and could be one for nurseries after another run. (op 7-2)
Montiboli(IRE), who set the standard having been placed on her two previous starts on turf, set the pace but had nothing in reserve when taken on by the winner. She seems to lack a change of gear which means she may struggle to get her head in front. (op 15-8 tchd 7-4)
Lady Calido(USA), who is from the family of Machiavellian and related to several winners abroad, is bred to need a mile and never landed a blow at this trip. (op 6-1 tchd 15-2)

Frammenti had been well beaten in two previous outings and, along with the time, tends to limit the form. (tchd 40-1)
Rathmolyon, the first foal of a half-sister to Jack Dawson, also has speed in her pedigree and did not fare too badly considering she was slowly into her stride and then made ground around the outside on the bend. (op 28-1)

3110 HORIZONS RESTAURANT FILLIES' H'CAP 7f 32y(P)
7:55 (7:57) (Class 5) (0-70,70) 3-Y-O+ £3,238 (£963; £481; £240) Stalls High

Form RPR
3-45 1 **Cleide Da Silva (USA)**[26] 2317 3-9-11 69....................(v[1]) TedDurcan 12 81
(J Noseda) *in tch and gng wl: hdwy to ld 3f out: strly rdn fnl f: jst hld on* 5/1[2]
2151 2 *shd* **Nan Jan**[9] 2802 5-9-13 62..(t) RobertHavlin 11 76
(R Ingram) *mid-div: hdwy to go 2nd 2f out: pressed wnr strly ins fnl f: jst failed* 3/1[1]
2050 3 *5* **Dasheena**[19] 2516 4-8-10 52..(be) MCGeran[(7)] 8 53
(A J McCabe) *mid-div: styd on fr 2f out but no ch w first 2 fnl f* 12/1
-006 4 *1 3/4* **Isobel Rose (IRE)**[16] 2607 3-9-0 58.......................... J-PGuillambert 5 51
(E A L Dunlop) *in tch tl lost pl 3f out: effrt 2f out but n.d after* 16/1
-301 5 *1 3/4* **Fairdonna**[28] 2257 4-9-7 56.. AdamKirby 10 47
(D J Coakley) *towards rr: mde sme late hdwy* 7/1[3]
500- 6 *shd* **Dancing Storm**[273] 5690 4-9-5 54.................................... ChrisCatlin 4 45
(W S Kittow) *led tl hdd 3f out: wknd appr fnl f* 14/1
04-5 7 *2* **Gwyllion (USA)**[23] 2393 3-9-9 67.................................. JamieSpencer 1 50+
(J H M Gosden) *mid-div tl rdn and wknd 2f out* 3/1[1]
-405 8 *2 1/2* **Boogie Board**[16] 2592 3-8-4 51.......................... DuranFentiman[(3)] 3 27
(S Parr) *trckd ldrs: rdn 3f out: wknd over 1f out* 50/1
0-40 9 *1 1/4* **Cadi May**[31] 2137 3-8-7 51.. JimmyQuinn 7 24
(W M Brisbourne) *chsd ldr: rdn 3f out: wknd 2f out* 40/1
3516 10 *1 3/4* **Ridgewell (USA)**[16] 2598 3-9-9 70..........................(t) JamieMoriarty[(3)] 2 38
(B J Meehan) *s.i.s: a bhd* 8/1
5-00 11 *24* **To Party (IRE)**[37] 1973 3-9-7 65.................................... RichardMullen 6 —
(P D Evans) *slowly away: a bhd* 33/1
1m 29.08s (-1.32) **Going Correction** +0.025s/f (Slow)
WFA 3 from 4yo+ 9lb 11 Ran SP% 117.9
Speed ratings (Par 100):108,107,102,100,98 98,95,92,91,89 62
CSF £20.18 CT £156.13 TOTE £6.90: £2.50, £1.30, £4.20; EX 28.00.
Owner Sir Robert Ogden **Bred** K Smith **Trained** Newmarket, Suffolk

FOCUS
A modest fillies' handicap run at a sound gallop and the first two came clear. Solid form, the winner up 12lb.
Gwyllion(USA) Official explanation: jockey said filly hung right-handed

3111 E.ON ENERGY SERVICES H'CAP 1m 141y(P)
8:25 (8:25) (Class 4) (0-80,82) 3-Y-O+ £5,829 (£1,734; £866; £432) Stalls Low

Form RPR
3040 1 **Just Bond (IRE)**[3] 2986 5-9-3 76.................................. SladeO'Hara[(7)] 3 85
(G R Oldroyd) *in rr tl hdwy on outside over 3f out: led 2f out: hung lft appr fnl f: drvn out* 13/2
0-31 2 *3/4* **El Toreador (USA)**[13] 2693 3-9-2 79............................ JamieSpencer 7 86+
(G A Butler) *stdd s: hdwy over 2f out: r.o fnl f to go 2nd cl home* 5/2[1]
2152 3 *hd* **Scamperdale**[19] 2521 5-9-6 72................................(p) J-PGuillambert 9 79
(B P J Baugh) *in tch: hdwy over 2f out: chsd wnr fnl f tl lost 2nd nr fin* 5/1[3]
3310 4 *2* **Western Roots**[9] 2802 6-9-0 66...(p) JimmyQuinn 8 69
(M Appleby) *trckd ldr to over 1f out: rdn and one pce fnl f* 20/1
2332 5 *1/2* **Bailieborough (IRE)**[7] 2891 8-9-11 82............................ PJMcDonald[(5)] 4 83
(B Ellison) *towards rr: rdn over 2f out: kpt on one pce* 9/2[2]
3001 6 *1 3/4* **Carmenero (GER)**[24] 2358 4-9-10 76............................... RichardMullen 5 74
(W R Muir) *hld up: rdn 3f out: one pce and nvr on terms* 8/1
-041 7 *3/4* **Dante's Diamond (IRE)**[28] 2258 5-8-9 61 oh1......... FrankieMcDonald 2 57
(D Burchell) *in tch on ins tl rdn and wknd 2f out* 9/1
5500 8 *2 1/2* **Atlantic Quest (USA)**[24] 2351 8-9-10 79.................. LiamTreadwell[(3)] 6 69
(Miss Venetia Williams) *led tl hdd 2f out: wknd over 1f out* 8/1
3-06 9 *3* **Book Of Facts (FR)**[14] 2662 3-8-4 74 ow1.................. GihanArnolda[(7)] 1 58
(J McAuley) *in tch: rdn over 3f out: wknd over 2f out* 33/1
1m 50.52s (-1.24) **Going Correction** +0.025s/f (Slow)
WFA 3 from 4yo+ 11lb 9 Ran SP% 116.7
Speed ratings (Par 105):106,105,105,103,102 101,100,98,95
CSF £23.38 CT £89.91 TOTE £8.10: £2.70, £1.50, £1.60; EX 35.20.
Owner R C Bond **Bred** Schwindibode Ag **Trained** Brawby, N Yorks

FOCUS
A fair handicap in which the first two were held up out the back in the early stages. There was not much pace on and the form may not prove solid. The winner is rated to his winter best.

3112 REMEMBER FAMILY FUN DAYS AT WOLVERHAMPTON STAYERS' H'CAP 1m 5f 194y(P)
8:55 (8:56) (Class 4) (0-85,84) 4-Y-O+ £5,829 (£1,734; £866; £432) Stalls Low

Form RPR
0-03 1 **Corum (IRE)**[35] 2047 4-9-1 83....................................(p) WilliamBuick[(5)] 4 90
(Mrs K Waldron) *t.k.h early: a in tch: pushed along over 2f out: led 1f out: pushed out* 5/1[2]
441 2 *1 1/2* **Annambo**[21] 2471 7-9-1 78.. TedDurcan 1 83
(D Morris) *in tch: hdwy over 1f out: rdn to chse wnr ins fnl f* 11/2[3]
5003 3 *1 1/2* **Blue Hills**[24] 2367 6-8-2 65...(b) ChrisCatlin 5 68
(P W Hiatt) *pulld hrd: trckd ldr: led 3f out: hdd 1f out: one pce and lost 2nd ins fnl f* 7/1
0046 4 *1 1/4* **Quince (IRE)**[23] 2397 4-9-7 84.....................................(v) JimmyQuinn 2 85
(J Pearce) *trckd ldrs: rdn over 3f out: fdd appr fnl f* 11/2[3]
400- 5 *2 1/2* **Jack Dawson (IRE)**[253] 6075 10-8-7 70........................ JamieSpencer 7 68
(John Berry) *s.i.s: hld up: styd on ins fnl 2f: n.d* 8/1
2114 6 *2* **Penang Cinta**[32] 2106 4-8-9 72...................................... RobertHavlin 8 67
(P D Evans) *t.k.h: hld up: rdn over 2f out: sn btn* 6/1
4412 7 *1/2* **Mister Arjay (USA)**[21] 2465 7-8-4 67......................... RoystonFfrench 6 61
(B Ellison) *led tl rdn and hdd 3f out: sn btn* 7/2[1]
-200 8 *nk* **Billich**[21] 2449 4-9-3 80.. RichardMullen 3 74
(E J O'Neill) *t.k.h: hld up: rdn 3f out: no hdwy after* 7/1
3m 8.99s (1.62) **Going Correction** +0.025s/f (Slow) 8 Ran SP% 120.1
Speed ratings (Par 105):96,95,94,93,92 91,90,90
CSF £34.27 CT £196.81 TOTE £6.60: £2.00, £2.20, £2.30; EX 27.70.
Owner Nick Shutts **Bred** The Vallee Des Reves Syndicate **Trained** Stoke Bliss, Worcs

FOCUS
An ordinary staying handicap run at a steady gallop early on. The form makes sense among the first three.

3113 WOLVERHAMPTON RACECOURSE CONFERENCE CENTRE MAIDEN STKS 1m 1f 103y(P)
9:20 (9:20) (Class 4) 3-Y-O+ £5,829 (£1,734; £866; £432) Stalls Low

Form RPR
4502 1 **Gold Prospect**[10] 2767 3-9-3 80...................................... JamieSpencer 9 83
(M L W Bell) *slowly away: towards rr tl rdn and hdwy on outside over 2f out: led appr fnl f: sn clr* 10/11[1]
3 2 *3* **Pivotal Answer (IRE)**[17] 2581 3-8-12 0............................ TedDurcan 2 72+
(J Noseda) *mid-div: rdn and styd on wl fr over 1f out to go 2nd cl home* 8/1[3]
-322 3 *nk* **Ravarino (USA)**[24] 2360 3-8-5 74.............................. JamieHamblett[(7)] 6 71
(Sir Michael Stoute) *led after 1f: rdn and hdd appr fnl f: one pce and lost 2nd nr fin* 10/3[2]
5206 4 *3/4* **Super Cross (IRE)**[8] 2834 3-9-3 71............................ J-PGuillambert 8 74
(E A L Dunlop) *mid-div: rdn and hdwy over 2f out: hung lft appr fnl f: one pce* 12/1
5 *3 1/2* **Actilius (IRE)** 3-9-3 0.. OscarUrbina 12 67
(M Botti) *trckd ldrs: chsd ldr over 2f out tl wknd appr fnl f* 18/1
6-4 6 *1 1/4* **Saaratt**[22] 2429 3-8-7 0.. WilliamBuick[(5)] 7 59
(M P Tregoning) *trckd ldrs: rdn over 3f out: wknd wl over 1f out* 12/1
06 7 *6* **Cheeky Jack (USA)**[60] 1375 3-9-3 0............................ RichardMullen 4 52
(B J Meehan) *in tch: rdn over 3f out: wknd over 2f out* 33/1
8 *1* **Noble Plum (IRE)** 3-8-12 0.. JimmyQuinn 1 45
(Sir Mark Prescott) *v.s.a: a bhd* 20/1
4 9 *11* **Arctiz (USA)**[13] 2690 3-9-3 0... ChrisCatlin 13 27
(P F I Cole) *trckd ldr tl wknd qckly over 2f out* 25/1
0 10 *28* **Golden Peacock**[33] 2083 3-9-3 0.. AdamKirby 10 —
(M Appleby) *sn bhd: t.o* 100/1
00 11 *shd* **Jaffna**[46] 1749 5-9-9 0... RobertHavlin 5 —
(R T Phillips) *led for 1f: chsd ldrs tl wknd over 3f out: t.o* 150/1
2m 1.15s (-1.47) **Going Correction** +0.025s/f (Slow)
WFA 3 from 5yo 11lb 11 Ran SP% 120.4
Speed ratings (Par 105):107,104,104,103,100 99,93,92,83,58 58
CSF £9.03 TOTE £2.10: £1.30, £2.00, £1.50; EX 10.30 Place 6 £51.23, Place 5 £15.68..
Owner B J Warren **Bred** W And R Barnett Ltd **Trained** Newmarket, Suffolk

FOCUS
A fair but uncompetitive maiden in which they bet 12/1 bar three, and those three dominated the finish. The winner did not need to improve and the form looks pretty solid.
T/Plt: £119.30 to a £1 stake. Pool: £67,085.25. 410.45 winning tickets. T/Qpdt: £7.30 to a £1 stake. Pool: £5,672.90. 571.60 winning tickets. JS

3114 - 3116a (Foreign Racing) - See Raceform Interactive

3068 CURRAGH (R-H)
Saturday, June 30

OFFICIAL GOING: Soft

3117a AUDI PRETTY POLLY STKS (GROUP 1) (F&M) 1m 2f
3:45 (3:47) 3-Y-O+
£101,351 (£32,094; £15,202; £5,067; £3,378; £1,689)

RPR
1 **Peeping Fawn (USA)**[29] 2211 3-8-11 115.................................. KFallon 7 119+
(A P O'Brien, Ire) *hld up in 6th: 5th and hdwy on stands' side under 2f out: qcknd to ld ins fnl f: r.o wl: easily* 7/4[1]
2 *2* **Speciosa (IRE)**[42] 1834 4-9-9 .... MickyFenton 5 114
(Mrs P Sly) *led: rdn over 2f out: hdd ins fnl f: kpt on: nt pce of wnr* 8/1
3 *2* **West Wind**[20] 2501 3-8-11 .... JMurtagh 6 110
(H-A Pantall, France) *trckd ldrs in 4th: 3rd and prog 2f out: 2nd whn edgd lft 1 1/2f out: 3rd and no imp fnl f* 7/2[3]
4 *1 1/2* **Timarwa (IRE)**[34] 2069 3-8-11 .... MJKinane 4 108
(John M Oxx, Ire) *settled 3rd: 4th and rdn 2f out: no imp fr over 1f out: kpt on same pce* 10/3[2]
5 *4* **Truly Mine (IRE)**[24] 2377 3-8-11 101.............................. PJSmullen 8 101
(D K Weld, Ire) *trckd ldr in 2nd: rdn ent st: 3rd whn sltly hmpd 1 1/2f out: 5th and no ex over 1f out* 20/1
6 *6* **Echelon**[10] 2753 5-9-9 .... OPeslier 3 90
(Sir Michael Stoute) *hld up in 7th: rdn and no imp st: mod 6th whn eased fnl f* 12/1
7 *2* **Musical Way (FR)**[16] 2617 5-9-9 ....(p) RonanThomas 2 86
(P Van De Poele, France) *hld up in rr: no imp st* 20/1
8 *hd* **Luminous One (IRE)**[17] 2589 3-8-11 90..........................(p) KJManning 9 86
(J S Bolger, Ire) *towards rr: 8th and rdn bef st: sn no ex* 100/1
9 *14* **Dimenticata (IRE)**[34] 2065 3-8-11 110................................ CDHayes 1 61
(Kevin Prendergast, Ire) *trckd ldrs: 5th 1/2-way: rdn and wknd early st: eased fnl f* 16/1
2m 10.6s (1.30) **Going Correction** +0.50s/f (Yiel)
WFA 3 from 4yo+ 12lb 9 Ran SP% 116.9
Speed ratings: 114,112,110,109,106 101,100,99,88
CSF £16.83 TOTE £3.60: £1.50, £3.90, £1.10; DF 26.30.
Owner Michael Tabor **Bred** Barnett Enterprises **Trained** Ballydoyle, Co Tipperary

FOCUS
A race worthy of its Group 1 status that attracted a Classic winner from this year and last, two Classic-placed fillies from this season, as well as a less exposed three-year-old with a big reputation. The time was good considering the ground conditions, and the performances of the runner-up and fifth makes the form fairly easy to rate. The winner quickened up well and gave a solid boost to the Oaks form.

NOTEBOOK
Peeping Fawn(USA) was gaining a deserved Group 1 win after being placed in the Irish Guineas and English Oaks. The fact that she won her first race in May just goes to show how far she has come in such a short space of time. She grabbed the initiative on the near side inside the final furlong to win with authority, and is proving a real credit to her trainer. Though Kieren Fallon acknowledged that she did not have a particularly easy race on demanding ground, she looks the one they all have to beat in the Irish Oaks in a couple of weeks' time. Versatile in terms of distance, blessed with a fine temperament and a hardy constitution, she has all the attributes of a top-class filly. (op 9/4)
Speciosa(IRE) has failed to add to her tally since her Classic triumph, but is proving a very smart four-year-old, and her ability to handle soft ground was an asset. She had the excuse of being in season when contesting the Lockinge and this was more in keeping with her second behind the hugely talented Manduro in the Earl Of Sefton Stakes.

West Wind brought a high standard of French form to the contest having won the Prix de Diane on only her fourth start. Apart from the fact that she edged a little to the left when asked for her effort around a furlong and a half down, there was little to criticise about her display, and she should continue to hold her own in top middle-distance races. On this evidence, connections were probably right to supplement her for this rather than aim her at the Irish Oaks, since it did not look as if a longer trip would suit. (op 3/1 tchd 4/1)
Timarwa(IRE), making only the third appearance of her career, was facing a major step up in class from her maiden win at this venue in late May, but there was no shortage of confidence behind her chance. While she did not meet the higher range of expectation, she did enough to suggest that she has a bright future, and success at Group 3 level can be anticipated. (op 11/4)
Truly Mine(IRE) dropped away after being squeezed up a bit a furlong and a half down. (op 16/1)
Echelon, a moderate sixth, was eased after her chance had gone. A multiple Group 3 winner, she is better than this, but she is perhaps a little shy of genuine Group 1 standard. (op 10/1)
Musical Way(FR) was unable to impose her presence. (op 16/1)
Luminous One(IRE) was out of her depth. (op 66/1)
Dimenticata(IRE) was a major disappointment, though the market did not seem to take her chance very seriously in any case. The Irish 1000 Guineas second was struggling too far from home to suggest that this can be attributed to a failure to stay the extra two furlongs. (op 14/1)

3119a AT THE RACES CURRAGH CUP (GROUP 3) — 1m 6f
4:45 (4:47) 3-Y-0+ £31,418 (£9,628; £4,560; £1,520; £1,013)

RPR
1 **Peppertree Lane (IRE)**[6] [2907] 4-9-11 .... KDarley 4 112
(M Johnston) *mde all: strly pressed ent st: styd on wl fr 1 1/2f out* **1/1**[1]
2 3 **Nick's Nikita (IRE)**[13] [2702] 4-9-11 102................ JMurtagh 5 108
(M Halford, Ire) *trckd ldrs: 3rd 1/2-way: rdn st: impr into 2nd and chal over 1f out: no imp ins fnl f* **8/1**
3 1 **Alfie Flits**[6] [2907] 5-9-11 .... KFallon 3 107
(G A Swinbank) *hld up in 4th: prog after 1/2-way: 2nd 5f out: rdn to chal ent st: 3rd and no ex fnl f* **7/2**[2]
4 5 1/2 **All The Good (IRE)**[28] [2245] 4-9-11 .... MJKinane 1 104
(G A Butler) *bhd: prog into 4th early st: no ex fr under 2f out* **7/1**
5 25 **Mutakarrim**[31] [2161] 10-9-11 108................(b) PJSmullen 2 67+
(D K Weld, Ire) *racd keenly: 2nd bef 1/2-way: dropped to 4th 5f out: wknd ent st: eased over 1f out* **6/1**[3]
3m 10.9s (8.60) **Going Correction** +0.50s/f (Yiel) 5 Ran SP% 110.1
Speed ratings: 95,93,92,89,75
CSF £9.56 TOTE £1.70: £1.10, £2.30; DF 6.60.
Owner P D Savill **Bred** Gestut Wittekindshof **Trained** Middleham Moor, N Yorks

FOCUS
A disappointingly small field for this Group 3 race, and poorly supported by the Irish trainers, who could manage only two runners between them, one of them a ten-year-old. The form looks safe rated through the third.

NOTEBOOK
Peppertree Lane(IRE), whose victory over Day Flight at Newbury gave him the strongest credentials, was the one that punters wanted, and the four-year-old accomplished the task in professional fashion from the front. The early pace that he set was nothing startling but he was able to wind it up to see off a couple of challengers in the straight. A tough sort in the mould of so many of his trainer's horses, he handles soft ground well and can continue his ascent of the staying ladder. (op 1/1 tchd 9/10)
Nick's Nikita(IRE) justified her trainer's decision to step her up in trip following her win in a Group 3 race over two furlongs shorter at Cork with a spirited effort. This broadens the options for this tough and progressive filly. (op 6/1)
Alfie Flits tried to throw down a challenge in the straight, but it never really looked as if he would reverse recent Pontefract form with the winner. This former smart bumper performer is a capable stayer and should make a fine novice hurdler if connections opt to take that route. (op 7/2 tchd 4/1)
All The Good(IRE) looked a little short of the required standard on his British handicap form and that view was borne out as he failed to threaten seriously despite making some headway from the rear on the approach to the straight. (op 11/2)
Mutakarrim has had many good days over the course of an honourable career. This was not one of the them, and he was allowed to come home in his own time after dropping tamely out of contention. (op 5/1)

3118 - 3120a (Foreign Racing) - See Raceform Interactive

[3075]HAMBURG (R-H)
Saturday, June 30

OFFICIAL GOING: Soft

3121a CREDIT SUISSE-RENNEN - HAMBURGER STUTENPREIS (GROUP 3) (F&M) — 1m
3:05 (3:07) 3-Y-0+ £21,622 (£6,757; £3,378; £2,030)

RPR
1 **Touch My Soul (FR)**[82] 3-8-8 .... ASuborics 7 106
(P Schiergen, Germany) *a cl up: trckd ldr fr 1/2-way: led wl over 1f out: drvn out* **4/5**[1]
2 2 **Waky Love (GER)**[42] [1855] 3-8-8 .... AHelfenbein 5 103
(Frau J Meyer, Germany) *led after 2f to wl over 1f out: drvn and ev ch 1f out: no ex last 150yds* **62/10**
3 6 **The Spring Flower (GER)**[23] [2408] 5-9-6 .... CarinaFey 1 95
(Andreas Lowe, Germany) *led 2f: cl 3rd st: one pce fr wl over 1f out* **25/2**
4 3 **Hashbrown (GER)**[23] [2408] 3-8-8 .... J-PCarvalho 2 88
(C Sprengel, Germany) *hld up in rr: 4th st: nvr a factor* **18/10**[2]
5 6 **Directa (GER)**[215] 4-9-0 .... ADeVries 6 75
(Andreas Lowe, Germany) *racd in 4th tl taken v wd on fnl turn: last st: sn btn* **44/10**[3]
1m 45.1s (105.10)
WFA 3 from 4yo+ 10lb 5 Ran SP% 131.1
(including ten euro stakes): WIN 18; PL 14, 21; SF 93.
Owner Team Valor **Bred** Helmut Volz **Trained** Germany

3122a LOTTO-HAMBURG-TROPHY (GROUP 3) — 6f
4:45 (4:57) 3-Y-0+ £27,027 (£12,162; £6,081; £3,378; £2,027)

RPR
1 **Key To Pleasure (GER)**[401] [1973] 7-9-0 .... ASuborics 1 109
(Mario Hofer, Germany) *racd in 4th to st: rapid hdwy to ld over 2f out: drvn out* **56/10**
2 1 1/2 **Matrix (GER)**[48] [1704] 6-9-4 .... DBoeuf 5 108
(W Baltromei, Germany) *led to over 2f out: r.o same pce* **11/10**[1]
3 3 **Shinko's Best (IRE)**[20] 6-9-4 .... NRichter 4 99
(A Kleinkorres, Germany) *a in tch: 3rd st: one pce fr wl over 1f out* **22/10**[2]
4 3/4 **Slade (GER)**[44] [1800] 5-8-9 .... ADeVries 2 88
(M Trybuhl, Germany) *hld up: 5th st: nvr able to chal* **4/1**[3]
5 6 **Mharadono (GER)**[20] 4-9-4 .... JBojko 3 79
(P Hirschberger, Germany) *pressed ldr: 2nd st: rdn and btn wl over 1f out* **22/1**
6 2 1/2 **Saldario (GER)**[82] 5-9-0 .... J-PCarvalho 6 67
(P Vovcenko, Germany) *a in rr: last st: sn btn* **61/10**
1m 18.47s (5.78) 6 Ran SP% 132.5
WIN 66; PL 24, 17; SF 141.
Owner Stall Undosa **Bred** Stall Calluna **Trained** Germany

3123 - 3124a (Foreign Racing) - See Raceform Interactive

[2997]SALISBURY (R-H)
Sunday, July 1

3125 Meeting Abandoned - Waterlogged

[3102]WINDSOR (R-H)
Sunday, July 1

3132 Meeting Abandoned - Waterlogged

[3114]CURRAGH (R-H)
Sunday, July 1

OFFICIAL GOING: Soft changing to soft to heavy after race 2 (2.05)
Weather: Rain, easing before race 5

3138a BUDWEISER GUINNESS H'CAP (PREMIER HANDICAP) — 1m
1:30 (1:34) 3-Y-0+ £43,986 (£12,905; £6,148; £2,094)

RPR
1 **Jumbajukiba**[36] [2052] 4-9-3 91................(b[1]) FMBerry 13 104
(Mrs John Harrington, Ire) *mid-div: smooth hdwy 2 1/2f out: 3rd 1 1/2f out: led over 1f out: styd on wl* **14/1**
2 1 3/4 **Settigano (IRE)**[7] [2921] 4-8-5 79................(p) MCHussey 8 88
(Brian Nolan, Ire) *mid-div: hdwy under 3f out: rdn to chal 2f out: led 1 1/2f out: hdd over 1f out: kpt on u.p* **20/1**
3 2 **Ridge Boy (IRE)**[42] [1868] 6-8-10 84................(b[1]) DPMcDonogh 12 89
(Kevin Prendergast, Ire) *mid-div: hdwy over 2f out: 3rd over 1f out: kpt on* **14/1**
4 7 **King Of Tory (IRE)**[18] [2587] 5-9-7 95................(b) CDHayes 14 86
(Edward Lynam, Ire) *trckd ldrs: 5th 1/2-way: hdwy into 2nd over 2f out: led under 2f out: hdd 1 1/2f out: 4th and no ex fnl f* **14/1**
5 1 1/4 **My Paris**[11] [2755] 6-9-9 97................ NCallan 27 86
(K A Ryan) *led: rdn and hdd under 2f out: 5th and no ex fr over 1f out* **10/1**[2]
6 3 1/2 **Bawaader (IRE)**[36] [2052] 5-9-6 99................(b) SMGorey(5) 21 81
(D K Weld, Ire) *chsd ldrs: 4th 1/2-way: 3rd over 3f out: rdn and no imp fr over 2f out: one pce* **16/1**
7 1 **Fremen (USA)**[10] [2807] 7-8-6 80................ SilvestreDeSousa 5 60
(D Nicholls) *hld up: hdwy on outer under 3f out: 8th over 2f out: 7th and no ex fr over 1f out* **25/1**
8 3/4 **Propinquity**[27] [2323] 5-8-7 88................ MPFlanagan(7) 15 66
(Liam McAteer, Ire) *slowly away and bhd: kpt on wl fr 2f out* **50/1**
9 hd **Mooretown Lady (IRE)**[36] [2052] 4-8-7 81................ WJSupple 26 59
(H Rogers, Ire) *trckd ldrs: 6th 1/2-way: rdn and no imp fr over 2f out: one pce* **14/1**
10 3/4 **Crooked Throw (IRE)**[11] [2755] 8-9-6 94................ EddieAhern 2 70
(C F Swan, Ire) *s.i.s and hld up: rdn over 3f out: kpt on same pce* **12/1**[3]
11 3/4 **Hoffman (IRE)**[11] [2783] 5-8-11 88................ WJLee(3) 20 63
(T Stack, Ire) *mid-div: rdn over 2f out: 10th 1 1/2f out: no imp* **8/1**[1]
12 hd **Trefflich (GER)**[20] [5844] 6-8-9 93................ PTownend(10) 10 67
(Paul Nolan, Ire) *in rr of mid-div: kpt on same pce fr over 2f out* **25/1**
13 1 3/4 **Absolute Image (IRE)**[275] [5663] 5-9-4 92................(b[1]) PJSmullen 19 63
(D K Weld, Ire) *chsd ldrs: 7th 1/2-way: wknd fr over 2f out* **10/1**[2]
14 1 1/2 **Farinelli**[8] [2899] 4-9-9 97................ MJKinane 23 65
(John M Oxx, Ire) *bhd: trailing 3f out: sme late hdwy* **16/1**
15 5 1/2 **Bricks And Porter (IRE)**[18] [2587] 7-8-1 82................(bt) SMLevey(7) 6 39
(John A Quinn, Ire) *in rr of mid-div: no imp fr 2 1/2f out* **25/1**
16 1 3/4 **Akimbo (USA)**[18] [2587] 6-8-11 90................ CPGeoghegan(5) 3 43
(James Leavy, Ire) *mid-div on outer: effrt 2 1/2f out: sn no ex* **33/1**
17 shd **Royal Dignitary (USA)**[22] [2466] 7-9-2 90................ AdrianTNicholls 11 43
(D Nicholls) *chsd ldrs in 3rd: rdn after 1/2-way: wknd fr 2 1/2f out* **25/1**
18 7 **Natural Force (IRE)**[256] [6051] 4-8-10 84................ DMGrant 9 23
(R P Burns, Ire) *chsd ldrs: 9th 1/2-way: no ex fr 2 1/2f out* **33/1**
19 4 **Anna's Rock (IRE)**[98] [784] 3-8-4 90................(b[1]) DJMoran(3) 18 21
(J S Bolger, Ire) *cl 2nd: rdn to chal 3f out: wknd fr over 2f out* **14/1**
20 2 1/2 **Grisham**[56] [1514] 9-8-11 85................ KJManning 7 11
(Michael John Phillips, Ire) *chsd ldrs: 8th 1/2-way: rdn over 2f out: sn wknd* **25/1**
21 nk **Norther Bay (FR)**[238] [6360] 4-8-9 83................ PShanahan 24 8
(Eoin Griffin, Ire) *a bhd: trailing fr 3f out* **33/1**
22 2 **Rockie**[238] [6359] 4-9-3 91................(bt) WMLordan 16 12
(T Hogan, Ire) *nvr a factor* **25/1**
23 2 **Deerpark (IRE)**[14] [2701] 5-8-8 85................ PBBeggy(3) 4 2
(John F Gleeson, Ire) *rrd up leaving stalls: settled in mid-div: effrt 2 1/2f out: sn wknd* **14/1**
24 6 **Kyles Bay (IRE)**[27] [2322] 4-9-2 90................ JAHeffernan 1 —
(Ms Caroline Hutchinson, Ire) *in rr of mid-div: sme prog on outer 3f out: wknd fr under 2f out* **12/1**[3]
25 nk **Saintly Rachel (IRE)**[346] [3371] 9-9-7 95................ RPCleary 22 —
(C F Swan, Ire) *a bhd* **33/1**
26 2 **Film Festival (USA)**[49] [5799] 4-9-7 95................ JMurtagh 25 84
(M Halford, Ire) *alway towards rr* **14/1**
1m 43.8s (1.70) **Going Correction** +0.40s/f (Good)
WFA 3 from 4yo+ 9lb 27 Ran SP% 144.7
Speed ratings: 107,105,103,96,51 91,90,89,89,88 88,87,86,84,79 77,77,70,66,63 63,61,59,53,53 95
CSF £290.86 CT £4044.94 TOTE £20.20: £5.30, £5.80, £4.70, £2.30; DF 529.70.

Owner J P O'Flaherty **Bred** Woodcote Stud Ltd **Trained** Moone, Co Kildare
■ Stewards' Enquiry : Adrian T Nicholls four-day ban: careless riding (Jul 15-18); 200 euro fine: failed to keep straight from stalls

NOTEBOOK
Jumbajukiba travelled best from some way out in the first-time blinkers and won well. (op 12/1)
My Paris helped to force a strong pace that had the field well strung out, but he paid the price for those exertions in the closing stages. He may well prefer better ground and was well below the form he showed when sixth in the Royal Hunt Cup at Royal Ascot. (op 10/1 tchd 11/1)
Fremen(USA) ran respectably in what was a stronger race than several of those he has contested lately.
Royal Dignitary(USA) has done all his winning on good ground or faster.
Grisham Official explanation: jockey said gelding lost its action after 1 1/2f
Film Festival(USA) Official explanation: trainer said gelding ran very free going to post

3139a BUD LIGHT STKS (LISTED RACE) 5f
2:05 (2:06) 3-Y-O+ **£43,986** (£12,905; £6,148; £2,094)

RPR
1 **Snaefell (IRE)**[14] 2701 3-9-1 97 .... JMurtagh 6 109
(M Halford, Ire) *hld up: 5th and hdwy 2f out: chal between horses 1f out: led 150yds out: styd on wl* **16/1**
2 *1 3/4* **Tax Free (IRE)**[12] 2733 5-9-11 .... AdrianTNicholls 7 110
(D Nicholls) *a.p: 2nd 1/2-way: led 2f out: hdd 150yds out: kpt on* **11/4**[2]
3 *nk* **Grecian Dancer**[25] 2379 4-9-3 99 .... FMBerry 3 101
(Charles O'Brien, Ire) *sn outpcd: mod 8th and drvn along 1/2-way: 7th over 1f out: r.o strly cl home* **14/1**
4 *1 1/4* **Peace Offering (IRE)**[28] 2291 7-9-11 .... KFallon 5 104
(D Nicholls) *led: hdd 2f out: 3rd 1f out: no ex* **7/4**[1]
5 *nk* **City Of Tribes (IRE)**[15] 2672 3-9-1 103 .... EddieAhern 8 96
(G M Lyons, Ire) *cl up on outer: 3rd 1/2-way: chal 2f out: no ex fnl f* **10/1**
6 *1* **Green Manalishi**[12] 2733 6-9-6 .... NCallan 1 95
(K A Ryan) *chsd ldrs in 5th: kpt on same pce fr 1 1/2f out* **13/2**[3]
7 *nk* **Speed Dream (IRE)**[36] 2035 3-9-1 100 .... WMLordan 9 92
(David Wachman, Ire) *chsd ldrs: 6th 1/2-way: no imp fr 2f out* **12/1**
8 *4 1/2* **Regional Counsel**[85] 948 3-9-6 100 .... DPMcDonogh 4 80
(Kevin Prendergast, Ire) *a bhd: trailing 1/2-way: kpt on same pce* **25/1**
9 *1* **Flash McGahon (IRE)**[27] 2324 3-9-4 100 .... (b[1]) MJKinane 2 75
(John M Oxx, Ire) *chsd ldrs: cl 4th bef 1/2-way: wknd over 2f out* **16/1**

62.90 secs (1.60) **Going Correction** +0.60s/f (Yiel)
WFA 3 from 4yo+ 5lb **9** Ran SP% **115.4**
Speed ratings: 111,108,107,105,105 103,103,95,94
CSF £59.98 TOTE £18.30: £2.90, £1.60, £2.30; DF 92.30.
Owner Lady Clague **Bred** Newberry Stud Farm **Trained** the Curragh, Co Kildare
■ Stewards' Enquiry : K Fallon 200 euro fine: failed to keep straight from stalls

FOCUS
A fairly competitive Listed race rated through the runner-up and fifth.

NOTEBOOK
Snaefell(IRE) struck a blow for the three-year-old generation in reversing form with Tax Free, who had relegated him to fourth in a sprint at Naas early last month. Soundly beaten when favourite for a 6f contest at Cork after that, he stepped up considerably on that form, handling the ground well and asserting just over half a furlong down to capture a notable scalp. His trainer reckons that he is best suited by a strong-run 5f.
Tax Free(IRE), who had finished in midfield in the King's Stand since beating the top Irish sprinter Dandy Man at Naas, was always in the front rank in a race in which the pace was supplied by his shorter-priced stablemate. He took over two furlongs out but was mastered inside the last half furlong. (op 5/2)
Grecian Dancer, whose trainer chose this race in preference to Saturday's valuable fillies' handicap, was rewarded for aiming high with a third placing that looked improbable in the early stages when she got outpaced. She still had plenty to do a furlong out before staying on strongly. This daughter of Dansili has improved in leaps and bounds since gaining the first of four handicaps wins off a modest 66 over 7f at the same venue last year, and this performance, taken in conjunction with her fourth in a Group 3 race at Leopardstown, consolidates her status as an attractive broodmare prospect.
Peace Offering(IRE), who has performed with great credit in Pattern races in France since losing out narrowly to Tax Free in the Palace House Stakes, made the running until headed by his stablemate two furlongs out. He possibly went a bit fast for his own good in the conditions, though the ground should not have been a problem on the basis of form such as last season's Listed win at Tipperary. (op 7/4 tchd 2/1)
City Of Tribes(IRE) has been productively campaigned in Britain this season by his trainer. He ran his usual honest race, but is probably more effective on good ground.
Green Manalishi, who had finished a couple of places in front of Tax Free from a more favouable draw in the King's Stand, has shown his best form on quickish surfaces. (op 6/1)
Speed Dream(IRE) more or less reproduced last month's Haydock running relative to City Of Tribes. (op 14/1)

3140a JOHN ROARTY MEMORIAL SCURRY H'CAP (PREMIER HANDICAP) 6f 63y
2:40 (2:40) 3-Y-O+ **£43,986** (£12,905; £6,148; £2,094)

RPR
1 **Machinist (IRE)**[18] 2566 7-9-3 94 .... SilvestreDeSousa 12 106
(D Nicholls) *mid-div: prog 2f out: 4th 1 1/2f out: led under 1f out: sn clr: styd on wl* **14/1**
2 *4* **Nastrelli (IRE)**[27] 2322 4-8-10 87 .... JMurtagh 9 87
(M Halford, Ire) *hld up: prog on stands' side 2f out: mod 2nd and kpt on ins fnl f* **11/2**[1]
3 *shd* **Excelerate (IRE)**[27] 2322 4-8-3 85 .... SMGorey(5) 1 85
(Edward Lynam, Ire) *hld up: hdwy on stands' rail 2f out: 7th over 1f out: styd on* **20/1**
4 *1/2* **Bahamian Pirate (USA)**[9] 2817 12-9-1 92 .... AdrianTNicholls 11 90
(D Nicholls) *s.i.s and hld up towards rr: swtchd to centre over 2f out: hdwy 1 1/2f out: 3rd 1f out: kpt on u.p* **14/1**
5 *2* **Alone He Stands (IRE)**[27] 2322 7-8-4 81 .... CDHayes 18 73
(J C Hayden, Ire) *s.i.s and bhd: rdn over 2f out: styd on fr over 1f out* **25/1**
6 *shd* **Fit The Cove (IRE)**[98] 781 7-9-3 94 .... MJKinane 7 86
(H Rogers, Ire) *towards rr: last 1/2-way: styd on fr 1 1/2f out* **12/1**
7 *shd* **Tajneed (IRE)**[16] 2643 4-8-13 90 .... (bt) PJSmullen 13 82
(D K Weld, Ire) *hld up in mid-div: rdn and kpt on fr 1 1/2f out* **6/1**[2]
8 *2* **Lucky Kyllachy (USA)**[55] 1547 3-8-13 96 .... (b) WMLordan 16 82
(David Wachman, Ire) *chsd ldrs: prog into 3rd under 2f out: no ex fr over 1f out* **12/1**
9 *1* **Cheddar Island (IRE)**[63] 1324 5-9-2 93 .... DPMcDonogh 3 76
(Kevin Prendergast, Ire) *hld up: sme prog on stands' rail 2f out: no imp fr over 1f out* **14/1**
10 *1/2* **Majestic Times (IRE)**[36] 2050 7-10-0 105 .... NGMcCullagh 2 86
(Liam McAteer, Ire) *mid-div: no imp fr 2f out* **25/1**
11 *3/4* **Johnstown Lad (IRE)**[18] 2585 3-8-1 87 .... (t) DJMoran(3) 19 66
(Niall Moran, Ire) *cl up on outer: led under 2f out: hdd 1f out: no ex* **20/1**
12 *shd* **Desert Commander (IRE)**[26] 2339 5-8-12 89 .... (b) NCallan 21 68
(K A Ryan) *trckd ldrs on outer: 2nd and chal 1 1/2f out: wknd ins fnl f* **12/1**
13 *3/4* **Orpailleur**[18] 2587 6-8-10 87 .... PShanahan 15 63
(Ms Joanna Morgan, Ire) *led on outer: hdd under 2f out: sn no ex: eased ins fnl f* **25/1**
14 *1* **Benwilt Breeze (IRE)**[16] 2643 5-9-2 98 .... (t) CPGeoghegan(5) 10 71
(G M Lyons, Ire) *chsd ldrs: 7th 1/2-way: 6th and rdn 2f out: sn no ex* **20/1**
15 *2* **Holbien (IRE)**[39] 1955 4-8-5 82 .... DMGrant 4 49
(Liam Roche, Ire) *mid-div on stands' side: no ex fr 2f out* **14/1**
16 *1/2* **Ireland's Call (IRE)**[58] 1461 6-8-11 93 .... OCasey(5) 14 59
(Peter Casey, Ire) *prom: 4th 1/2-way: wknd over 2f out* **33/1**
17 *1 1/2* **Gradetime (IRE)**[46] 1775 3-8-4 87 .... RPCleary 8 48
(M Halford, Ire) *prom on stands' side: 5th appr 1/2-way: sn wknd* **20/1**
18 *3/4* **Slaney Time (IRE)**[9] 2849 3-7-8 87 .... (b) MHarley(10) 5 46
(J S Bolger, Ire) *a towards rr* **20/1**
19 *3* **Baggio (IRE)**[28] 2283 6-9-5 96 .... FMBerry 6 46
(Charles O'Brien, Ire) *a towards rr* **7/1**[3]
20 *1/2* **Mist And Stone (IRE)**[315] 4637 4-8-9 86 .... WJSupple 17 35
(G M Lyons, Ire) *prom: 3rd 1/2-way: wknd fr over 2f out* **16/1**

1m 20.2s (2.70) **Going Correction** +0.70s/f (Yiel)
WFA 3 from 4yo+ 6lb **21** Ran SP% **136.1**
Speed ratings: 110,104,104,103,101 101,100,98,96,96 95,95,94,92,90 89,87,86,82,81
CSF £82.73 CT £1648.73 TOTE £17.90: £3.90, £1.70, £4.40, £4.20; DF 222.10.
Owner Berry & Gould Partnership **Bred** Ballymacoll Stud Farm Ltd **Trained** Sessay, N Yorks

FOCUS
A strong pace up front in the early stages of this race played into the hands of those that were ridden patiently. It has been rated through the fifth.

NOTEBOOK
Machinist(IRE), a solid sprint handicapper in Britain, came here off a victory in a useful 6f event at Hamilton last month and shrugged off a 6lb rise for that success. He has done most of his winning on good ground or quicker, but he coped well with the prevailing conditions. After settling towards the rear of midfield in the centre of the track, he began a forward move after halfway that carried him to the front over a furlong from home, and he kept on well for a clear-cut success. It is quite possible that there are more good races to be won with him, and he will undoubtedly bolster his trainer's strong hand in top English sprint handicaps over the coming months.
Bahamian Pirate(USA) was putting in his best work at the finish. The former Nunthorpe Stakes winner is not as good as he used to be, but he has been running creditably in handicaps this season and could well be placed to further advantage. (op 12/1)
Desert Commander(IRE), who bounced back to form in first-time blinkers at Ripon, found these conditions too testing. (op 10/1)

3141a ANHEUSER-BUSCH ADVENTURE PARKS RAILWAY STKS (GROUP 2) 6f
3:10 (3:10) 2-Y-O **£54,898** (£16,047; £7,601; £2,533)

RPR
1 **Lizard Island (USA)**[11] 2778 2-9-1 .... JAHeffernan 2 103
(A P O'Brien, Ire) *mde all: rdn and qcknd clr 2f out: kpt on wl u.p fnl f* **10/3**[3]
2 *3/4* **South Dakota (IRE)**[12] 2732 2-9-1 .... KFallon 6 101
(A P O'Brien, Ire) *hld up in 4th: drvn along after 1/2-way: hdwy on outer 1 1/2f out: 2nd and kpt on ins fnl f* **7/4**[2]
3 *nk* **Irish Jig (IRE)**[14] 2699 2-9-1 .... JMurtagh 5 100
(G M Lyons, Ire) *trckd ldr in 2nd: rdn and outpcd 2f out: 3rd and kpt on ins fnl f* **13/8**[1]
4 *2 1/2* **Another Express (IRE)**[14] 2699 2-9-1 .... (b[1]) WMLordan 1 93
(T Stack, Ire) *trckd ldrs in 3rd: rdn and no imp 2f out: no ex fr over 1f out* **8/1**

1m 18.7s (4.20) **Going Correction** +0.70s/f (Yiel) **6** Ran SP% **108.6**
Speed ratings: 100,99,98,95
CSF £9.49 TOTE £4.10; DF 9.30.
Owner Michael Tabor **Bred** Eagle Holdings **Trained** Ballydoyle, Co Tipperary

FOCUS
Two defectors reduced this to a four-runner contest, and the outcome continued Aidan O'Brien's virtual monopoly of this important juvenile contest. Not easy to assess with the small field and lack of pace, but the third have been rated as running to form.

NOTEBOOK
Lizard Island(USA), who made all under a well-judged ride from Seamus Heffernan, did not look an obvious candidate for imminent Group race honours when second on his debut at Leopardstown, but he was clearly at home in the conditions and his rider's tactical awareness was a factor. As O'Brien acknowledged afterwards, he profited from getting a soft lead through the first half mile, and he stole a vital advantage when quickening the tempo around two furlongs down. Whatever the possible limitations of the form, it was a creditable display by a juvenile having only his second start, and he is clearly a useful prospect, though O'Brien's post-race reaction was of a low-key nature that hints at the fact that he may not be considered a potential star. (op 7/2 tchd 3/1)
South Dakota(IRE), who had finished in midfield behind stablemate Henrythenavigator in the Coventry at Royal Ascot, was held up and gave the impression of being unhappy on the ground. He was outpaced as Lizard Island raised his effort before staying on towards the finish. (op 6/4)
Irish Jig(IRE) was backed into favouritism, no doubt as a result of concerns about South Dakota's ability to go in the ground. He tracked the leader but was unable to match his acceleration when it mattered. (op 13/8 tchd 7/4)
Another Express(IRE), blinkered for the first time, found little when asked for his effort, though he seemed to run roughly to the same level of form as when third to Irish Jig at Cork. (op 7/1)

3142a BUDWEISER IRISH DERBY (GROUP 1) (ENTIRE COLTS & FILLIES) 1m 4f
3:50 (3:50) 3-Y-O
£572,635 (£194,594; £93,243; £32,432; £22,297; £12,162)

RPR
1 **Soldier Of Fortune (IRE)**[29] 2235 3-9-0 112 .... JAHeffernan 11 127
(A P O'Brien, Ire) *trckd ldrs in 5th: 3rd and hdwy ent st: led 2f out: sn rdn clr: styd on strly: impressive* **5/1**[2]
2 *9* **Alexander Of Hales (USA)**[28] 2293 3-9-0 107 .... MJKinane 9 114
(A P O'Brien, Ire) *trckd ldrs in 3rd: 5th early st: kpt on fr 2f out to go remote 2nd cl home* **33/1**
3 *shd* **Eagle Mountain**[29] 2235 3-9-0 117 .... KFallon 6 114+
(A P O'Brien, Ire) *hld up in 8th: prog on outer appr st: 3rd 2f out: mod 2nd fr 1 1/2f out: no imp: kpt on same pce* **6/4**[1]
4 *3 1/2* **Boscobel**[9] 2813 3-9-0 .... JoeFanning 2 109
(M Johnston) *settled 2nd: led ent st: rdn and hdd 2f out: sn outpcd: 4th and no ex fnl f* **8/1**

5 1/2 **Mores Wells**[49] [1693] 3-9-0 110......(t) DPMcDonogh 3 108
(Kevin Prendergast, Ire) *trckd ldrs in 4th: impr into 2nd travelling wl ent st: sn rdn: 5th and no ex fnl 1 1/2f out* **14/1**

6 2 1/2 **Prince Erik**[49] [1691] 3-9-0 ...... PJSmullen 7 105
(D K Weld, Ire) *hld up in 9th: 7th early st: no imp fr 2f out* **33/1**

7 1 1/2 **Al Shemali**[10] [2789] 3-9-0 ......(t) RyanMoore 8 103
(Sir Michael Stoute) *hld up: 7th 1/2-way: rdn and no imp st* **12/1**

8 18 **Royal And Regal (IRE)**[34] [2101] 3-9-0 ...... JMurtagh 4 77
(A Fabre, France) *chsd ldrs in 6th: drvn along 1/2-way: wknd appr st: eased 1 1/2f out* **7/1**[3]

9 3/4 **Shamdinan (FR)**[28] [2293] 3-9-0 ...... CSoumillon 5 76
(A De Royer-Dupre, France) *a towards rr: 10th 1/2-way: sme prog on outer early st: no ex whn heavily eased fnl f* **15/2**

10 1/2 **Spanish Harlem (IRE)**[35] [2066] 3-9-0 106...... FMBerry 1 76
(A P O'Brien, Ire) *sn led: hdd & wknd ent st: eased ins fnl f* **50/1**

11 17 **Striving Storm (USA)**[64] [1306] 3-9-0 ...... EddieAhern 10 52
(P W Chapple-Hyam) *a in rr: trailing whn eased 2f out* **28/1**

2m 36.0s (-2.90) **Going Correction** +0.20s/f (Good) 11 Ran SP% **117.7**
Speed ratings: 117,111,110,108,108 106,105,93,93,92 81
CSF £164.22 TOTE £6.70: £2.30, £6.60, £1.10; DF 122.90.
Owner Mrs John Magnier **Bred** J S Bolger **Trained** Ballydoyle, Co Tipperary

FOCUS
Without the impressive Epsom winner in the line-up, this needed to be won with authority in order to give the form a substance in keeping with the primacy that the race has achieved in recent years. Aidan O'Brien trained the first three home and the winner was impressive, but there remains a question mark over the value of the form given the testing conditions.

NOTEBOOK
Soldier Of Fortune(IRE) obliged in brilliant fashion, producing an irresistible surge a quarter of a mile out that ended with an extravagant winning margin that suggests a very high level of form. No doubt, the going played its part in determining the extent of his supremacy, but the winner had already proved himself amongst the best of his generation with a fifth placing at Epsom following a hard-earned win in the Chester Vase that proved his resolution. His form at Pattern level in France - second in a Group 1 last season and winner of this season's Prix Noailles - coupled with his relish for soft ground, would seem to make him a natural contender for the Arc. (op 6/1)
Alexander Of Hales(USA) bounced back from a poor run in the Prix du Jockey-Club in a manner reminiscent of Scorpion when second to Hurricane Run in 2005. Running over the trip for the first time, he was ridden in touch throughout and stayed on gamely to snatch the runner-up spot. Still quite lightly raced, he now has a solid foundation for the second half of the season. (op 25/1)
Eagle Mountain was fairly easy to back as a result of the softening ground. After being held up in midfield, he improved his position on the outside approaching the straight but was soon fighting a losing battle when Soldier Of Fortune kicked clear, and he ended up conceding the second position that he had held from a furlong and a half down. The obvious conclusion is that the ground brought about his undoing, and at least his performance underlines the overall solidity of the Epsom form. (op 7/4 tchd 15/8)
Boscobel, who beat the Derby fourth Lucarno in the King Edward VII Stakes last time out, was supplemented for this and fully entitled to his place in the line-up. He took up second place when the field sorted itself out and led two and a half furlongs down before being left for dead when Soldier Of Fortune struck for home. This display helps to illustrate again how far he has come since his successful forays in All-Weather handicaps early in the season.
Mores Wells, who finished second to Soldier Of Fortune in a Navan maiden as a two-year-old, was appearing for the first time since disappointing in the Derrinstown Stud Derby Trial, and was having a first attempt at the trip. It looked as if the Ballysax Stakes winner was set to be a major factor when moving up threateningly on the approach to the straight, but his effort was shortlived in the end. It is hard to be certain whether he failed to stay or is simply not quite up to Group 1 standard.
Prince Erik, whose defeat of Red Rock Canyon could hardly be interpreted as giving him a winning chance in a Group 1 contest, gave a perfectly respectable performance, and there could be a decent prize to be won him before the season is out.
Al Shemali at no stage gave rise to hopes that he could enhance his trainer's fine record in the race.
Royal And Regal(IRE) impressed with his appearance in the paddock but was beaten before the straight and was eased to finish a long way adrift. (op 15/2)
Shamdinan(FR), third in the Prix du Jockey-Club, put up a tame performance. (op 7/1)
Spanish Harlem(IRE) performed an effective task as pacemaker to pave the way for the stable's overall triumph.

3143a ARTHUR GUINNESS EUROPEAN BREEDERS FUND H'CAP (PREMIER HANDICAP) 1m 4f
4:35 (4:37) 3-Y-0+ **£43,986** (£12,905; £6,148; £2,094)

RPR

1 **Arc Bleu (GER)**[35] [6252] 6-8-5 74...... JamieSpencer 8 88+
(A J Martin, Ire) *s.i.s and hld up: 8th and hdwy on inner early st: 4th over 1f out: qckn d to ld 100yds out: comf* **7/2**[1]

2 3/4 **Jalwada**[76] [1070] 5-8-11 80...... JAHeffernan 17 92
(John Queally, Ire) *trckd ldrs in 6th: prog into 4th 1 1/2f out: led 1f out: hdd 100yds out: kpt on* **16/1**

3 3 1/2 **King Rama (USA)**[35] [2067] 6-9-10 93...... MJKinane 14 100
(John E Kiely, Ire) *hld up: 10th 2f out: 6th under 1f out: kpt on* **8/1**[2]

4 shd **My Arch**[29] [2236] 5-9-4 87...... NCallan 6 94
(K A Ryan) *led: hdd 5f out: 2nd and chal st: led 2f out: hdd 1f out: kpt on* **16/1**

5 3/4 **Harrington (IRE)**[77] [1050] 5-9-4 87...... PShanahan 5 92
(Noel Furlong, Ire) *trckd ldrs in 5th: rdn early st: no imp fnl f: kpt on same pce* **12/1**

6 hd **Red Lancer**[19] [2527] 6-8-12 81...... SilvestreDeSousa 15 86
(D Nicholls) *mid-div: prog on outer early st: 7th 1 1/2f out: kpt on* **14/1**

7 1 3/4 **Star Wood (IRE)**[9] [2852] 5-9-7 90...... PJSmullen 19 93
(Michael Joseph Fitzgerald, Ire) *cl up: 2nd to 1/2-way: led 5f out: rdn and hdd 2f out: sn no ex* **9/1**[3]

8 1 1/2 **Marikhar (IRE)**[16] [2644] 5-8-12 81...... EddieAhern 4 81
(Seamus Fahey, Ire) *trckd ldrs: 4th 1/2-way: 3rd 4f out: no ex early st* **9/1**[3]

9 2 1/2 **Grand Revival (IRE)**[77] [1051] 5-8-5 77...... PBBeggy(3) 10 74
(David P Myerscough, Ire) *chsd ldrs: 7th 1/2-way: sn rdn: outpcd ent st: kpt on same pce fr 2f out* **14/1**

10 nk **Whoneedswings (IRE)**[7] [2923] 5-9-4 87...... DPMcDonogh 18 83
(David Wachman, Ire) *chsd ldrs in 3rd: 4th and rdn 4f out: no ex st* **12/1**

11 14 **Princess Nala (IRE)**[8] [2899] 5-9-11 94...... JMurtagh 11 69
(M Halford, Ire) *towards rr: clipped heels appr st: no imp fr 2f out* **14/1**

12 6 **Mamlook (IRE)**[28] [2288] 3-8-4 86...... CDHayes 7 52
(Kevin Prendergast, Ire) *hld up: rdn and no imp st: eased ins fnl f* **16/1**

13 3 1/2 **Virginia Woolf**[21] [4822] 5-9-12 95......(b[1]) WMLordan 13 56
(D T Hughes, Ire) *hld up: prog into 7th appr st: no ex fr over 2f out* **50/1**

14 12 **Swiss Cottage**[35] [4852] 5-9-7 90...... FMBerry 2 33
(Niall Madden, Ire) *a towards rr: eased over 1f out* **16/1**

15 2 1/2 **Our Jaffa (IRE)**[16] [2644] 6-8-4 73...... WJSupple 12 —
(H Rogers, Ire) *a towards rr: eased fr under 2f out* **33/1**

16 21 **Grafton Street (IRE)**[12] [2736] 4-9-8 91...... KFallon 9 —
(A P O'Brien, Ire) *hld up: towards rr whn eased appr st: t.o* **10/1**

17 1/2 **Basra (IRE)**[36] [2054] 4-9-0 83......(p) KJManning 1 —
(J S Bolger, Ire) *mid-div: wknd 4f out: eased st: t.o* **33/1**

2m 40.07s (1.17) **Going Correction** +0.20s/f (Good)
WFA 3 from 4yo+ 13lb 19 Ran SP% **129.2**
Speed ratings: 104,103,101,101,100 100,99,98,96,96 87,83,80,72,71 57,56
CSF £62.95 CT £390.64 TOTE £3.80: £1.70, £4.90, £2.00, £7.20; DF 113.00.
Owner P J McGee **Bred** Frau J Mayer **Trained** Summerhill, Co. Meath

NOTEBOOK
Arc Bleu(GER), a multiple winner on the Flat in Germany who won over hurdles in May, did this well and should build on this. (op 4/1 tchd 11/4)
My Arch helped to force the pace and, given the conditions, he ran an honourable race in defeat. He showed enough to suggest that another handicap can come his way. (op 14/1)
Red Lancer seems to like some ease in the ground and ran respectably without ever looking as though he would mount a meaningful challenge. He has not won a race since capturing the 2004 Chester Vase.
Princess Nala(IRE) Official explanation: jockey said mare clipped heels on turn into straight

3144a NETJETS CELEBRATION STKS (LISTED RACE) 1m
5:10 (5:11) 3-Y-0+ **£43,986** (£12,905; £6,148; £2,094)

RPR

1 **Danehill Music (IRE)**[36] [2052] 4-9-6 100...... DMGrant 4 106
(David Wachman, Ire) *hld up: 6th into st: 5th and rdn 2f out: hdwy over 1f out: led 150yds out: styd on* **5/1**

2 1/2 **Hard Rock City (USA)**[18] [2586] 7-9-9 101...... JAHeffernan 9 108
(M J Grassick, Ire) *2nd and disp ld: rdn to chal st: led 2f out: hdd 150yds out: kpt on u.p* **14/1**

3 1 **Cougar Bay (IRE)**[25] [2381] 4-9-9 109...... WMLordan 2 106
(David Wachman, Ire) *trckd ldrs in 3rd: rdn and outpcd 2f out: 4th 1f out: styd on* **9/2**[3]

4 3 1/2 **Latino Magic (IRE)**[260] [5978] 7-9-9 107...... PJSmullen 1 99
(D K Weld, Ire) *settled 4th: rdn and outpcd 2f out: 5th over 1f out: kpt on same pce* **10/1**

5 6 **Finicius (USA)**[350] [3574] 3-9-0 ...... JMurtagh 7 87
(Eoin Griffin, Ire) *hld up in rr: 5th and effrt ent st: no imp fr under 2f out: one pce* **7/1**

6 1 1/4 **Chinese Whisper (IRE)**[10] [2789] 3-9-0 108...... KFallon 10 85
(A P O'Brien, Ire) *led and disp: rdn and strly pressed ent st: hdd 2f out: wknd ins fnl f* **9/4**[1]

7 hd **Ashaawes (USA)**[288] [5360] 4-9-9 110...... DPMcDonogh 3 84
(Kevin Prendergast, Ire) *hld up towards rr: bhd fr over 2f out: kpt on ins fnl f* **7/2**[2]

1m 43.9s (1.80) **Going Correction** +0.50s/f (Yiel)
WFA 3 from 4yo+ 9lb 10 Ran SP% **116.1**
Speed ratings: 111,110,109,106,100 98,98
CSF £69.43 TOTE £6.30: £2.50, £5.20; DF 76.20.
Owner Jack Of Trumps Racing Club **Bred** Patrick J Connolly **Trained** Goolds Cross, Co Tipperary

FOCUS
Despite being hit by several withdrawals this was still a useful Listed race.

NOTEBOOK
Danehill Music(IRE) returned to her best to prevail. The four-year-old was chasing her first success since winning a Group 3 here in April 2006, but had since run some creditable races in defeat. She had not been able to show her best on unsuitably quick ground on her last two starts, but conditions certainly came in her favour here. She improved to join Hard Rock City up front inside the final furlong and found plenty under pressure to edge out that rival. Trainer David Wachman reported that the ground and track were in her favour and that she would now be campaigned in similar events. (op 8/1)
Hard Rock City(USA) had not produced his best following a comeback victory at Gowran, but he came back to form here. He probably would not want the ground as soft as this, but does appreciate an easy surface. He has yet to win a Listed race, but victory at this level is within his reach.
Cougar Bay(IRE) made a bright start to his season when third to Quinmaster at Leopardstown last time and ran creditably on ground that was softer than he would like. He has just a Leopardstown maiden win to his name, but remains more than capable of making his mark at this level. (op 7/2)
Latino Magic(IRE) was not disgraced on his first run of the season and this confirmed quick-ground performer should derive significant benefit from this outing. On this evidence, he looks as good as ever and will command the utmost respect at this level when the ground dries out. (op 8/1)
Finicius(USA), a promising juvenile last term, was running for the first time in nearly a year and, although unable to land a telling blow, can be expected to make significant progress from this outing. (op 5/1 tchd 8/1)
Chinese Whisper(IRE), who started out his season with a couple of creditable placed efforts in French Derby Trials, was dropping back to this trip following an unplaced run in the French Derby and a sixth in a 1m2f Listed event at Royal Ascot. He helped to force the pace and still held every chance heading towards the final furlong but soon weakened under pressure. He is capable of better than he has shown lately. (op 5/2 tchd 11/4)
Ashaawes(USA) was disappointing on his Irish debut and could never land a blow. The Kingmambo colt was possibly undone by the ground and can show this run to be all wrong in due course. (op 3/1)

3145 - (Foreign Racing) - See Raceform Interactive

3121 HAMBURG (R-H)
Sunday, July 1

OFFICIAL GOING: Heavy

3146a BMW DEUTSCHES DERBY (GROUP 1) (C&F) 1m 4f
4:25 (4:30) 3-Y-0 **£257,432** (£85,811; £51,486; £25,743; £8,561)

RPR

1 **Adlerflug (GER)**[34] 3-9-2 ...... FJohansson 15 117
(J Hirschberger, Germany) *a in tch: 5th st: led wl over 1f out: drvn out* **11/2**[2]

2 7 **Antek (GER)**[21] [2502] 3-9-2 ...... ADeVries 12 106
(H Blume, Germany) *a in tch: wnt 2nd over 4f out: rdn and ev ch wl over 1f out: sn one pce* **106/10**

3 1 **Anton Chekhov**[29] [2235] 3-9-2 ...... CO'Donoghue 17 105
(A P O'Brien, Ire) *midfield: 8th and rdn st: 6th 1f out: drvn to take 3rd last strides* **62/10**[3]

4 nk **Appel Au Maitre (FR)**[21] [2502] 3-9-2 ...... JVictoire 8 104
(Wido Neuroth, Norway) *towards rr: stdy prog on outside fnl 2f: tk 4th on line* **125/10**

The Form Book, Raceform Ltd, Compton, RG20 6NL

5 nse **Davidoff (GER)**[34] [2102] 3-9-2 .... MartinDwyer 5 104
(P Schiergen, Germany) *hld up: hdwy 4f out: 7th st: 4th and hrd rdn whn hung lft appr fnl f: hung rt ins fnl f: lost 3rd cl home* **136/10**
6 3 1/2 **Persian Storm (GER)**[34] [2102] 3-9-2 .... THellier 4 99
(J Hirschberger, Germany) *led to wl over 1f out: no ex* **62/10**[3]
6 dht **Shrek (GER)**[42] [1875] 3-9-2 .... EPedroza 9 99
(A Wohler, Germany) *a in tch: 3rd st: rdn 2f out: one pce* **11/2**[2]
8 6 **Eiswind** 3-9-2 .... AStarke 13 90
(P Schiergen, Germany) *played up bef s: hld up in rr: nvr a factor* **39/10**[1]
9 1 1/2 **Sommersturm (GER)**[21] [2502] 3-9-2 .... DarryllHolland 1 87
(J Hirschberger, Germany) *a towards rr* **149/10**
10 5 **Byron (GER)**[34] 3-9-2 .... VSchulepov 16 80
(W Hefter, Germany) *trckd ldr to 4f out: 4th on ins st: sn btn* **32/1**
11 1 1/2 **Monreale (GER)**[14] 3-9-2 .... ABest 2 78
(T Horwart, Germany) *disp 3rd tl wknd over 4f out: bhd fnl 3f* **74/1**
12 1/2 **Lovely Tiger (GER)**[22] 3-9-2 .... DBonilla 14 77
(P Schiergen, Germany) *midfield tl wknd appr st* **29/1**
13 1 **Waldvogel (IRE)** 3-9-2 .... JBojko 19 75
(A Wohler, Germany) *disp 3rd: 6th st: sn btn* **20/1**
14 5 **Invincible Hero (FR)**[22] 3-9-2 .... AHelfenbein 6 68
(A Wohler, Germany) *a in rr: last st* **168/10**
15 15 **Global Dream (GER)**[21] [2502] 3-9-2 .... GBocskai 7 45
(U Ostmann, Germany) *in tch tl wknd 4f out* **212/10**
2m 36.57s (2.02) 15 Ran SP% **130.7**
(including 10 Euro stake): WIN 65; PL 25, 37, 30; SF 918.
Owner Gestut Schlenderhan **Bred** Gestut Schlenderhan **Trained** Germany

NOTEBOOK
Adlerflug(GER) was sent to the front inside the final quarter mile and forged clear for a runaway success. Conditions were very testing but he clearly revelled in them and ran out an impressive winner. The performance of Anton Chekhov in third helps give an indication of the level of form he achieved.
Anton Chekhov, having his final start for Aidan O'Brien before he joins his new trainer Uwe Ostmann, never really threatened to win, but he kept battling away and stayed on well to take third close home. He goes well in soft ground and will stay further than this.

1005 MAISONS-LAFFITTE (R-H)
Sunday, July 1

OFFICIAL GOING: Good to soft

3147a PRIX DU BOIS (GROUP 3) 5f
2:50 (2:53) 2-Y-0 £27,027 (£10,811; £8,108; £5,405; £2,703)

RPR
1 **Natagora (FR)**[17] [2616] 2-8-8 .... SPasquier 3 103
(P Bary, France) *a cl up: led wl over 2f out: rdn 1f out: r.o wl* **1/1**[1]
2 3/4 **Wilki (FR)**[33] 2-8-9 ow1 .... OPeslier 2 101
(J-M Sauve, France) *led to wl over 2f out: drvn appr fnl f: styd on same pce* **68/10**
3 2 1/2 **Faslen (USA)**[33] 2-8-8 .... C-PLemaire 1 91
(J-C Rouget, France) *6th at 1/2-way: styd on: no threat to first two* **39/10**[2]
4 1 1/2 **Garden City (FR)**[34] 2-8-8 .... TThulliez 5 86
(Y De Nicolay, France) *s.i.s and taken to rails: outpcd early: rdn 2f out: styd on: nvr a factor* **51/10**[3]
5 3/4 **Salut L'Africain (FR)**[17] [2616] 2-8-11 .... SMaillot 4 86
(Robert Collet, France) *outpcd tl sme late prog* **20/1**
6 hd **In Uniform**[27] [2316] 2-8-11 .... RichardMullen 7 85
(E S McMahon) *rrd up in stalls and fell: taken out and resddled: hdwy after 2f: rdn and disp 3rd 2f out: sn wknd* **17/1**
7 2 **City Roma (IRE)**[29] 2-8-11 .... IMendizabal 6 78
(A Peraino, Italy) *chsd ldrs on outside tl wknd 2f out* **34/1**
8 6 **Ashantee (GER)**[15] [2684] 2-8-8 .... DBoeuf 8 54
(M Rulec, Germany) *in tch on outside to 1/2-way: wknd qckly* **21/1**
57.20 secs (57.20) 8 Ran SP% **117.3**
PARI-MUTUEL: WIN 2.00; PL 1.10, 1.60, 1.50; DF 5.60.
Owner Stefan Friborg **Bred** Bertrand Gouin & Georges Duca **Trained** Chantilly, France

FOCUS
Solid form for the grade.
NOTEBOOK
Natagora(FR) is getting better with every outing and is already a thoroughly professional racehorse. Well away and always near the leaders, she took control at the furlong marker and won with plenty in hand. A longer trip might even be an advantage for this speedy individual. She will come back to this track for the Robert Papin next and then go on to Deauville for the Prix Morny.
Wilki(FR) tried to make every yard of the running and ran a thoroughly genuine race. Her jockey put up a pound overweight but it did not make much difference as the winner had plenty in hand at the post. She deserves a victory in this grade and is another who might be better suited by a longer trip.
Faslen(USA), never far from the leaders, could not accelerate from a furlong and a half out and just stayed on at the one pace. She has not lived up to her initial promise.
Garden City(FR) was well back and given a patient ride. She did make some late progress but never threatened the first three past the post. She will surely be suited by 6f plus in future.
In Uniform, who dived under the stall before the off, was not too quickly into his stride. Fifth early on, he was under strong pressure by the two-furlong marker. It was an unfortunate experience for the colt and the outing is best forgotten. His jockey felt an extra furlong would be to his advantage in future.

3148a PRIX CHLOE (GROUP 3) (FILLIES) 1m 1f
3:25 (3:29) 3-Y-0 £27,027 (£10,811; £8,108; £5,405; £2,703)

RPR
1 **Utrecht**[36] 3-8-12 .... SPasquier 9 107
(A Fabre, France) *hld up on outside: hdwy wl over 1f out: led ins fnl f: pushed out: r.o wl* **5/1**[3]
2 2 **Maria Gabriella (IRE)**[20] [2525] 3-8-12 .... MBlancpain 2 103
(C Laffon-Parias, France) *trckd ldrs: drvn to ld appr fnl f: hrd rdn and hdd ins fnl f: no ex last 100yds* **9/2**[2]
3 1 1/2 **Toque De Queda**[21] 3-8-12 .... WMongil 8 100
(M Delzangles, France) *hld up in last: hdwy on outside fr over 1f out: r.o to take 3rd ins fnl f* **71/1**
4 snk **Hapsburg (FR)**[27] 3-8-12 .... TJarnet 3 100
(E Libaud, France) *mid-div: styd on one pce fnl 2f* **35/1**
5 1 1/2 **Mayano Sophia (IRE)**[27] 3-8-12 .... OPeslier 7 97
(J E Hammond, France) *led or disp ld to wl over 1f out: one pce* **17/1**
6 1 1/2 **Scoubidou (GER)**[28] [2294] 3-9-1 .... DBoeuf 1 97
(H Blume, Germany) *hld up in rr: hdwy on rails over 2f out: rdn to dispute 3rd over 1f out: sn btn* **21/10**[1]
7 4 **Grande Rousse (FR)**[42] 3-8-12 .... TThulliez 10 87
(P Bary, France) *hld up: a bhd* **25/1**
8 nk **La Conseillante (USA)**[65] 3-8-12 .... C-PLemaire 6 86
(J-C Rouget, France) *disp ld tl wknd 2f out* **58/10**
9 hd **Nini De Paris (FR)**[31] 3-8-12 .... RonanThomas 86
(J-P Gallorini, France) *trckd ldrs tl wknd 2f out* **41/1**
10 **Sismix (IRE)**[25] [2384] 3-8-12 .... TGillet 4 —
(C Laffon-Parias, France) *prom on outside: jnd ldrs at 1/2-way: btn over 2f out* **17/2**
1m 47.1s (-12.00) 10 Ran SP% **108.3**
PARI-MUTUEL: WIN 6.00; PL 2.40, 2.00, 2.50; DF 11.70.
Owner Sheikh Mohammed **Bred** Darley **Trained** Chantilly, France

NOTEBOOK
Utrecht put up a most impressive performance and looks Group 1 material in the making. Since being equipped with cheekpieces, her mind has really been on the job. Towards the rear at the beginning, she made steady progress on the outside to lead at the furlong marker. It would be no surprise if this filly ended up in a race like the Group 1 Prix de l'Opera at the end of the season.
Maria Gabriella(IRE) put up a thoroughly genuine performance. She was settled just behind the leaders and took the advantage a furlong out, but could do nothing when the winner came sailing past. She thoroughly deserves a victory in this category.
Toque De Queda, equipped with cheekpieces for the first time, ran extremely well. Held up for the early part of the race, she began her run from a furlong and a half out and was staying on at the finish.
Hapsburg(FR) did not get the clearest of runs but kept on at the one pace in the straight. She is one to watch next time out.

2624 GOODWOOD (R-H)
Monday, July 2

OFFICIAL GOING: Good to soft (soft in places)
Wind: Half head wind across Weather: Very breezy and cloudy

3149 BOLLINGER CHAMPIONSHIP CHALLENGE SERIES H'CAP (FOR GENTLEMAN AMATEUR RIDERS) 1m
6:30 (6:31) (Class 6) (0-65,65) 4-Y-0+ £3,123 (£968; £484; £242) Stalls High

Form RPR
0600 1 **Mythical Charm**[15] [2696] 8-10-4 **50** ....(t) MrHHaynes(5) 10 63
(J J Bridger) *chsd ldrs tl wnt 2nd 6f out: led jst over 2f out: sn rdn clr: kpt on* **17/2**
2040 2 1 3/4 **Rock Haven (IRE)**[3] [3067] 5-10-6 **54** .... MrSeanKerr(7) 8 63
(G F Bridgwater) *hld up: hdwy wl over 1f out: styd on wl to chse wnr ins fnl f: nvr able to chal* **11/1**
3252 3 3 **Height Of Spirits**[117] [637] 5-10-2 **46** oh1 .... MrSPearce(3) 4 48
(T D McCarthy) *b. racd in midfield: rdn over 2f out: styd on steadily: wnt 3rd wl ins fnl f: nt trble wnr* **8/1**[3]
0606 4 1/2 **Prince Valentine**[33] [2141] 6-10-6 **50** ....(p) MrDHutchison(3) 3 51
(G L Moore) *racd in midfield: rdn and effrt 3f out: kpt on: nt pce to trble wnr* **14/1**
0654 5 2 1/2 **Bollywood (IRE)**[29] [2273] 4-10-5 **46** oh1 .... MrSDobson 5 41
(J J Bridger) *chsd ldrs: hdwy to chse ldng pair wl over 3f out tl over 1f out: kpt on same pce* **12/1**
4114 6 3/4 **Doctor's Cave**[14] [2719] 5-11-5 **60** ....(b) MrSWalker 13 53
(K O Cunningham-Brown) *led after 1f: clr 5f out: hdd jst over 2f out: no ch w wnr after: fdd last 100yds* **11/2**[1]
2403 7 5 **Lady Duxyana**[15] [2696] 4-10-7 **48** ....(v) MrLeeNewnes 1 30
(M D I Usher) *racd wd: hld up bhd: rdn and hung rt over 2f out: no prog* **7/1**[2]
0055 8 1/2 **Royal Sailor (IRE)**[4] [3036] 5-9-12 **46** oh1 .... MrDavidMcMinn(7) 7 27
(J Ryan) *lw: hld up bhd: rdn 3f out: n.d* **25/1**
0-05 9 3 1/2 **Red Rudy**[17] [2623] 5-11-5 **63** .... MrMJJSmith(3) 12 36
(A W Carroll) *v.s.a: a bhd: n.d* **11/2**[1]
06-0 10 nk **Three Ships**[50] [279] 6-10-10 **51** .... MrMatthewSmith 14 23
(Miss J Feilden) *a bhd: rdn over 3f out: n.d* **8/1**[3]
5000 11 1 3/4 **Love You Always (USA)**[14] [2716] 7-10-0 **46** ....(t) MrRBirkett(5) 11 14
(Miss J Feilden) *a wl bhd: nvr on terms* **20/1**
-004 12 2 **Parthenope**[18] [2592] 4-10-5 **46** oh1 .... MrDHDunsdon 6 9
(J A Geake) *led for 1f: chsd ldr tl 6f out: rdn and wknd over 3f out* **20/1**
330- 13 11 **Sekula Pata (NZ)**[213] [6661] 8-11-3 **65** .... MrDHannig(7) 9 —
(Christian Wroe) *chsd ldrs: c wd wl over 3f out: sn wknd: eased ins fnl f* **14/1**
1m 45.63s (5.36) **Going Correction** +0.575s/f (Yiel) 13 Ran SP% **118.7**
Speed ratings (Par 101): 96,94,91,90,88 87,82,82,78,78 76,74,63
CSF £95.11 CT £806.86 TOTE £8.00: £2.00, £4.50, £2.80; EX 151.90.
Owner Tommy Ware **Bred** B J And Mrs Crangle **Trained** Liphook, Hants
■ Stewards' Enquiry : Mr David McMinn three-day ban: careless riding (Jul 27, Aug 2,6)
FOCUS
A very modest event, run at a fair pace. They stayed on the far side in the straight. The form seems sound.

3150 CHEVIOT ASSET MANAGEMENT STKS (H'CAP) 1m 1f 192y
7:00 (7:00) (Class 6) (0-65,65) 3-Y-0 £3,238 (£963; £481; £240) Stalls High

Form RPR
0005 1 **Mandalay Prince**[11] [2796] 3-8-8 **52** .... BrettDoyle 14 62+
(W J Musson) *hld up wl bhd: gd hdwy over 2f out: led over 1f out: sn clr: r.o strly* **13/2**[3]
4402 2 4 **Red Flare (IRE)**[15] [2697] 3-8-1 **52** .... MatthewDavies(7) 9 54
(M R Channon) *hld up in rr: rdn and hdwy wl over 2f out: styd on fnl f: wnt 2nd last 100yds: no ch w wnr* **20/1**
112 3 1/2 **Jafaru**[23] [2445] 3-9-7 **65** .... JHBowman 6 66
(G A Butler) *lw: hld up in midfield: hdwy 4f out: ev ch and rdn over 2f out: kpt on same pce* **4/1**[1]
4051 4 3/4 **Cavendish**[4] [3035] 3-9-5 **63** 6ex ....(v[1]) KerrinMcEvoy 18 63
(J M P Eustace) *led for 2f: stdd and trckd ldrs: hdwy 4f out: ev ch and gng wl over 2f out: rdn and fnd nil over 1f out* **13/2**[3]
0040 5 1 1/4 **Paymaster General (IRE)**[14] [2727] 3-9-4 **62** .... DaneO'Neill 1 59
(M D I Usher) *hld up towards rr: hdwy wl over 2f out: swtchd rt over 1f out: styd on ins fnl f: nrst fin* **22/1**
060 6 shd **Beau Michael**[14] [2726] 3-9-7 **65** ....(e[1]) MartinDwyer 2 62
(W R Swinburn) *chsd ldrs: rdn 4f out: hrd rdn and swtchd rt over 1f out: no imp* **33/1**

-024 **7** 1¼ **Pagan Rules (IRE)**[7] 2945 3-9-4 **62**..............................(b) JimCrowley 11 56
(Mrs A J Perrett) *sn pushed along in rr: hdwy u.p wl over 2f out: no imp fnl f* **9/1**

6-43 **8** *nk* **Gib (IRE)**[14] 2727 3-9-4 **62**.. RHills 5 56+
(B W Hills) *hld up wl bhd: hdwy over 2f out: kpt on past btn horses fnl f: nvr nrr* **13/2**[3]

4062 **9** *1* **Spinal Tap (IRE)**[19] 2572 3-9-4 **62**......................................(b[1]) LDettori 3 54
(C R Egerton) *led after 2f: rdn over 4f out: hdd over 1f out: sn wknd* **6/1**[2]

3554 **10** *1* **Irish Dancer**[23] 2445 3-9-7 **65**.. EddieAhern 15 55
(J L Dunlop) *chsd ldrs: rdn over 3f out: sn lost pl: swtchd rt 1f out: kpt on same pce fnl f* **11/1**

000- **11** ½ **Double Banded (IRE)**[233] 6434 3-8-11 **55**.................... NickyMackay 13 44
(J L Dunlop) *hld up in tch: rdn over 3f out: wknd 2f out* **11/1**

034- **12** *4* **Good Effect (USA)**[220] 6581 3-9-4 **62**................................ PatDobbs 16 43
(A P Jarvis) *hld up towards rr: nt clr run over 2f out: bdly hmpd and stmbld 2f out: n.d* **20/1**

5-00 **13** *4* **Heights Of Golan**[23] 2445 3-9-4 **62**..........................(b[1]) RichardThomas 8 35
(I A Wood) *t.k.h: chsd ldr after 2f: ev ch and rdn 3f out: wknd wl over 1f out: no ch whn rdr dropped reins ins fnl f* **33/1**

0-35 **14** ¾ **Apache Chant (USA)**[19] 2558 3-8-9 **53** ow1................ SamHitchcott 17 24
(A W Carroll) *hld up in tch: hdwy to chse ldrs wl over 3f out: wknd over 2f out* **33/1**

0604 **15** *9* **Beckenham's Secret**[20] 2545 3-9-4 **62**............................... TPO'Shea 10 15
(B R Millman) *t.k.h: chsd ldrs tl rdn and wknd qckly over 3f out* **16/1**

0000 **16** *61* **Silver Surprise**[15] 2697 3-8-11 **55**.............................. StephenCarson 12 —
(J J Bridger) *virtually lft in stalls: a t.o: virtually p.u last 3f* **66/1**

2m 13.87s (6.12) **Going Correction** +0.575s/f (Yiel) **16 Ran SP% 131.0**
Speed ratings (Par 98):98,94,94,93,92 92,91,91,90,89 89,86,83,82,75 26
CSF £141.32 CT £607.95 TOTE £10.90: £2.80, £4.10, £2.10, £2.10; EX 349.40.
Owner McGregor Bloodstock and Gillings **Bred** Mrs D O Joly **Trained** Newmarket, Suffolk

FOCUS
A tight-knit handicap with only 3lb separating the top eleven in the weights. As is customary in soft ground here, they came over to the stands' side in the straight. Very ordinary form, but sound enough.
Silver Surprise Official explanation: jockey said filly planted and would not come out of stalls

3151 RENAULT TRAFIC MAIDEN STKS 1m 1f
7:30 (7:30) (Class 5) 3-Y-O+ **£3,400** (£1,011; £505; £252) **Stalls High**

Form RPR

22 **1** **Purple Emperor (USA)**[25] 2402 3-8-13 0..............................(t) LDettori 3 90+
(Saeed Bin Suroor) *lw: trckd ldr: rdn and upsides wl over 2f out: led over 1f out: drew clr fnl f* **1/3**[1]

2524 **2** *7* **Zifaaf (USA)**[18] 2597 3-8-8 76.. RHills 5 71+
(B W Hills) *led: jnd and rdn over 2f out: hdd over 1f out: wl btn 1f out* **10/3**[2]

0-0 **3** *7* **New Light**[39] 1973 3-8-8 0.. StephenCarson 1 53
(Eve Johnson Houghton) *t.k.h: stdd after s and hld up in last: rdn and outpcd 4f out: wnt modest 3rd over 3f out: no ch w ldrs* **25/1**

04 **4** 1¾ **Hot Property (IRE)**[20] 2542 3-8-13 0............................... JimmyFortune 2 54
(W R Muir) *t.k.h: hld up: rdn and outpcd by ldrs 4f out: no ch after* **14/1**[3]

00-0 **5** *31* **Better Off Red (USA)**[32] 2192 3-8-8 48........................ MartinDwyer 4 —
(D M Simcock) *w.w in 3rd: rdn and dropped last over 4f out: t.o and eased fnl f* **40/1**

2m 0.85s (3.99) **Going Correction** +0.575s/f (Yiel) **5 Ran SP% 111.0**
Speed ratings (Par 103):105,98,92,91,63
CSF £1.80 TOTE £1.30: £1.10, £1.20; EX 1.80.
Owner Godolphin **Bred** S E Brown II & Abbie S Wood **Trained** Newmarket, Suffolk

FOCUS
An uncompetitive maiden. They again raced on the stands' side in the straight and it was pretty easy for Purple Emperor. The runner-up has not really progressed.

3152 RENAULT MASTER MAIDEN AUCTION FILLIES' STKS 6f
8:00 (8:01) (Class 4) 2-Y-O **£6,477** (£1,927; £963; £481) **Stalls Low**

Form RPR

325 **1** **Shamrock Lady (IRE)**[25] 2398 2-8-4 0......................... MartinDwyer 11 77+
(Pat Eddery) *sn pushed along and outpcd: hdwy over 2f out: rdn to ld over 1f out: edgd lft 1f out: r.o strly* **9/2**[2]

0 **2** *3* **Her Name Is Rio (IRE)**[6] 2968 2-8-7 0 ow2............... StephenCarson 8 71
(J S Moore) *chsd ldrs: rdn over 2f out: carried rt briefly 1f out: kpt on same pce fnl f* **50/1**

3 *shd* **Minshar** 2-8-9 0.. NickyMackay 5 73+
(L M Cumani) *leggy: s.i.s: hdwy over 2f out: swtchd rt over 1f out: r.o wl fnl f: nrst fin* **12/1**

330 **4** *nk* **May Day Queen (IRE)**[10] 2812 2-8-9 0............................ DaneO'Neill 3 72
(R Hannon) *chsd ldr: ev ch over 2f out: kpt on same pce u.p fr over 1f out* **6/4**[1]

04 **5** 1¾ **Lady Nova (IRE)**[6] 2968 2-8-8 0.. JimCrowley 6 66
(J S Moore) *racd in midfield: pushed along 3f out: hdwy over 2f out: hung lft over 1f out: keeping on same pce whn sltly hmpd wl ins fnl f* **13/2**[3]

3202 **6** *hd* **Hucking Harmony (IRE)**[13] 2746 2-8-3 0............... StephaneBreux[(3)] 4 63
(J R Best) *led: rdn over 2f out: hdd over 1f out: sltly hmpd and swtchd rt 1f out: wknd ins fnl f* **8/1**

7 *shd* **Belle Bellino (FR)** 2-8-11 0... JHBowman 2 68+
(B R Millman) *w'like: s.i.s: outpcd wl in rr: hdwy and rn green 2f out: r.o strly ins fnl f: nrst fin* **18/1**

60 **8** 3½ **Tamara Moon (IRE)**[23] 2457 2-8-6 0..................................... TPO'Shea 7 53
(M R Channon) *taken down early: prom: rdn wl over 2f out: wknd wl over 1f out* **17/2**

0 **9** *11* **L'Orage**[12] 2756 2-8-1 0.. DominicFox[(3)] 9 18
(J Ryan) *sn outpcd in rr: no ch last 2f* **40/1**

003 **10** *4* **Seventh Cloud (IRE)**[54] 1586 2-8-10 0 ow3................ PatDobbs 1 12+
(A P Jarvis) *chsd ldrs for 2f: bhd and rdn wl over 2f out: no ch after* **20/1**

11 *nk* **Lenouska (IRE)** 2-8-6 0.. EddieAhern 10 7+
(B De Haan) *cmpt: sn outpcd in rr: sme hdwy 1/2-way: sn wknd* **16/1**

1m 16.28s (3.43) **Going Correction** +0.40s/f (Good) **11 Ran SP% 121.2**
Speed ratings (Par 93):93,89,88,88,86 85,85,81,66,61 60
CSF £221.18 TOTE £5.50: £1.80, £8.50, £3.20; EX 116.50.
Owner Mrs Irene Clifford **Bred** Mrs I L Clifford **Trained** Nether Winchendon, Bucks

FOCUS
A reasonable race of its type, with a couple of interesting debut performances. Shamrock Lady did it well and the form has been rated on the positive side.

NOTEBOOK
Shamrock Lady(IRE), who was poorly drawn last time, held a fine chance on the form of her previous run at Windsor where she finished ahead of May Day Queen, with whom she was 5lb better off here. Stepping up in trip, she could not go the early pace but came through on the outer to lead with over a furlong to run, scoring decisively despite edging towards the rail. A well regarded filly, she is obviously at home in soft conditions. (tchd 4-1 and 5-1)
Her Name Is Rio(IRE), last of ten after a slow start on her Newbury debut, showed the benefit of that experience and turned around the form with her stablemate Lady Nova. Carrying 2lb overweight, she was always in the front rank this time and stuck on for second after the winner had swept to the front.
Minshar ◆, whose dam was a smart performer at around a mile, is a half-sister to multiple winning sprinter Oeuf A La Neige. After missing the break, and running green towards the rear, she was switched out with over a furlong to run. With her rider not being at all hard on her, she ran on strongly and would have been second in another stride. She should be hard to beat in an ordinary maiden with this experience behind her. (op 10-1)
May Day Queen(IRE), well beaten in the Albany Stakes at Royal Ascot last time, was 5lb worse off with today's winner from their meeting at Windsor in May. She ran her race with no obvious excuses, and this looks a better guide to her ability than her third in a Naas Group 3 last month. (op 13-8 tchd 15-8)
Lady Nova(IRE), who had her stablemate Her Name Is Rio, today's runner-up, well behind her at Newbury last time, now has the option of contesting nurseries. (op 8-1 tchd 11-2)
Hucking Harmony(IRE), who displayed no wayward tendencies this time, showed pace to lead until past halfway and only faded out of the frame inside the last. (tchd 15-2)
Belle Bellino(FR) ◆, out of a very useful sprinter, made an eyecatching debut. Giving weight away all round, she looked set to finish at the back of the field after missing the kick, but really found her feet in the final furlong and came home in good style. Considerable improvement can be expected next time. (tchd 16-1)

3153 RENAULT VANS STKS (H'CAP) 1m 6f
8:30 (8:31) (Class 2) (0-100,91) 4-Y-O+ **£12,954** (£3,854; £1,926; £962) **Stalls High**

Form RPR

-044 **1** **Ogee**[9] 2859 4-9-7 **91**... LDettori 5 99+
(Sir Michael Stoute) *lw: trckd ldng pair: rdn to chal 2f out: led wl ins fnl f: drvn out* **15/8**[1]

-231 **2** *hd* **Swan Queen**[16] 2675 4-9-7 **91**... KerrinMcEvoy 6 99+
(J L Dunlop) *led at stdy pce: qcknd 4f out: hrd pressed fr 2f out: drvn 1f out: hdd and no ex wl ins fnl f* **2/1**[2]

0/0- **3** *3* **Caracciola (GER)**[51] 2013 10-9-3 **87**.................................. EddieAhern 2 91
(N J Henderson) *hld up wl in tch in last: effrt to chse ldng pair wl over 1f out: no imp u.p fnl f* **15/2**

1133 **4** *45* **Dundry**[46] 1794 6-8-11 **81**..(p) JimmyFortune 3 22
(G L Moore) *b. trckd ldr: rdn over 3f out: wknd 2f out: virtually p.u fnl f* **5/2**[3]

3m 17.66s (13.69) **Going Correction** +0.85s/f (Soft) **4 Ran SP% 108.5**
Speed ratings (Par 109):94,93,92,66
CSF £5.93 TOTE £2.80; EX 5.20.
Owner Sir Evelyn De Rothschild **Bred** Hesmonds Stud Ltd **Trained** Newmarket, Suffolk

FOCUS
A poor turnout for this valuable prize. They went no pace, resulting in very moderate time for a race of its value, even allowing for the ground. The runners raced under the trees down the back straight and came over to the stands' side once in line for home. The first two are progressive types.

NOTEBOOK
Ogee, fourth in the Duke Of Edinburgh Handicap at Royal Ascot last time, missed an engagement in the Northumberland Plate because of the heavy ground. Upped in trip, he threw it down to the leader with two to run and just got on top after a good duel. (op 7-4 tchd 2-1)
Swan Queen, raised 7lb for her Sandown win over this trip, set a sedate pace. Winding things up with half a mile to run, she was joined at the two pole and could find no extra well inside the last. (op 15-8 tchd 13-8)
Caracciola(GER), who is more familiar in his role as a hurdler, had not run on the Flat for over a year. Unable to quicken up with the leading pair, he was not knocked about when held and will be suited by a greater test of stamina. (op 6-1)
Dundry, who is high enough in the weights, was the first to come under pressure and was eased down when beaten. Official explanation: jockey said gelding ran flat (op 100-30 tchd 7-2)

3154 FEDERATION OF BLOODSTOCK AGENTS FILLIES' STKS (H'CAP) 7f
9:00 (9:00) (Class 4) (0-85,82) 3-Y-O+ **£6,477** (£1,927; £963; £481) **Stalls High**

Form RPR

30-1 **1** **Our Faye**[15] 2696 4-9-5 **73**.. JimmyFortune 5 85+
(S Kirk) *stdd s: hld up in last: hdwy 2f out: pushed into ld jst ins fnl f: r.o strly* **15/8**[1]

0-00 **2** 2½ **Pelican Key (IRE)**[12] 2769 3-8-11 **73**................................. MartinDwyer 2 73
(D M Simcock) *led at stdy pce: rdn over 2f out: hdd jst ins fnl f: nt pce of wnr* **14/1**

4311 **3** *1* **Ivory Lace**[17] 2626 6-10-0 **82**.. JimCrowley 3 82
(S Woodman) *t.k.h: hld up in last pair: hdwy 2f out: rdn over 1f out: kpt on same pce fnl f* **4/1**[3]

1660 **4** ½ **Linda Green**[5] 2993 6-9-6 **74**.. JHBowman 4 73
(M R Channon) *trckd ldr: rdn and ev ch 2f out: outpcd fnl f* **3/1**[2]

3120 **5** 1½ **Spring Goddess (IRE)**[24] 2427 6-9-7 **75**............................. PatDobbs 7 70
(A P Jarvis) *t.k.h: hld up in tch: rdn wl over 1f out: sn outpcd* **5/1**

323- **6** *3* **Towy Girl (IRE)**[210] 6697 3-8-8 **70**...................................... DaneO'Neill 6 54
(A W Carroll) *t.k.h: trckd ldrs: c to stands' rail and racd alone over 2f out: sn rdn: wknd over 1f out* **7/1**

1m 33.6s (5.56) **Going Correction** +0.85s/f (Soft)
WFA 3 from 4yo+ 8lb **6 Ran SP% 115.6**
Speed ratings (Par 102):102,99,98,97,95 92
CSF £29.11 TOTE £2.60: £1.70, £4.40; EX 28.40 Place 6 £229.98, Place 5 £40.49..
Owner J B J Richards **Bred** J B J Richards **Trained** Upper Lambourn, Berks

FOCUS
A steadily-run race in which most of the field raced down the centre of the track in the home straight. The form is not the strongest, but Our Faye continues to improve.
T/Plt: £258.50 to a £1 stake. Pool: £81,865.80. 231.10 winning tickets. T/Qpdt: £15.00 to a £1 stake. Pool: £4,310.20. 212.30 winning tickets. SP

2904 PONTEFRACT (L-H)
Monday, July 2

OFFICIAL GOING: Soft
Wind: Virtually nil Weather: Overcast and showers

3155 JOHN SMITH'S LADIES' H'CAP (LADY AMATEUR RIDERS) 1m 2f 6y
2:15 (2:15) (Class 5) (0-70,70) 3-Y-O+ **£3,747** (£1,162; £580; £290) **Stalls Low**

Form RPR

0/61 **1** **Gardasee (GER)**[11] 2810 5-9-4 **54**................................... MissARyan[(3)] 3 65
(T P Tate) *mde all: rdn along 2f out: drvn ins fnl f and hld on gamely* **4/1**[1]

0044 **2** *hd* **Kylkenny**[6] 2967 12-9-0 **52** oh4 ow1..................(t) MissZoeLilly[(5)] 14 63
(H Morrison) *a.p: effrt to chse wnr 2f out: rdn and ev ch ins fnl f: kpt on wl: jst hld* **11/2**[3]

0600 **3** *5* **Richtee (IRE)**[4] 3012 6-9-4 **51** oh1..................................(p) MissADeniel 11 53
(R A Fahey) *hld up: hdwy 3f out: rdn to chse ldrs wl over 1f out: kpt on on same pce ins fnl f* **10/1**

2560 **4** *2* **Thunderwing (IRE)**[24] 2431 5-9-8 **60**...................... MissKellyBurke(5) 9 58
(K R Burke) *hld up: gd hdwy on outer over 3f out: rdn to chse ldng pair 2f out: sn drvn and one pce appr fnl f* **16/1**

0045 **5** *1 1/4* **Great View (IRE)**[10] 2833 8-10-9 **70**..............................(p) MissLEllison 2 66
(Mrs A L M King) *hmpd s: sn trcking wnr: effrt 3f out: sn rdn along: one pce fr wl over 1f out* **9/2**[2]

-440 **6** *3 1/2* **Riguez Dancer**[20] 2530 3-9-10 **68**............................ MissFayeBramley 7 58+
(P C Haslam) *in tch: rdn along on inner 4f out: drvn over 2f out and plugged on same pce* **7/1**

0305 **7** *1* **Alsadaa (USA)**[4] 3042 4-9-11 **63**............................... MissJCoward(5) 10 51
(M W Easterby) *hld up towards rr: hdwy 3f out: rdn wl over 1f out: sn no imp* **14/1**

6/-0 **8** *2 1/2* **Moment Of Clarity**[20] 2531 5-8-13 **51** oh3.................... MrsLHannity(5) 1 35
(R C Guest) *wnt rt s: prog on inner and hanging rt thrght first firlong: trckd ldrs tl rdn along over 3f out and grad wknd* **80/1**

/540 **9** *1* **Turbo (IRE)**[8] 2908 8-10-2 **70**..........................(t) MissJoannaMason(7) 5 52
(M W Easterby) *hmpd sn after s: trckd ldrs: effrt 3f out: sn rdn and grad wknd fnl 2f* **14/1**

0050 **10** *1 3/4* **Global Traffic**[41] 1927 3-9-2 **63**..................................(b) MissEFolkes(3) 6 42
(P D Evans) *s.i.s: a bhd* **25/1**

400- **11** *1 1/2* **Gala Sunday (USA)**[202] 5889 7-10-5 **66**.................(t) MissSBrotherton 4 42
(M W Easterby) *a in rr* **16/1**

5005 **12** *nk* **Northern Boy (USA)**[7] 2935 4-10-5 **66**.......................... MrsCBartley 12 41
(T D Barron) *t.k.h: hld up in tch: effrt and rdn along over 3f out: sn btn* **11/1**

2m 23.22s (9.14) **Going Correction** +0.725s/f (Yiel)
WFA 3 from 4yo+ 11lb **12** Ran SP% **113.7**
Speed ratings (Par 103):92,91,87,86,85 82,81,79,78,77 76,76
CSF £24.35 CT £202.75 TOTE £4.00: £1.90, £2.10, £3.80; EX 28.60.
Owner A S Helaissi **Bred** Gestut Romerhof **Trained** Tadcaster, N Yorks
■ Stewards' Enquiry : Mrs L Hannity caution: careless riding

FOCUS
A competitive enough heat and the stronger jockey prevailed. The form has been rated through the higher and the winner is entitled to rate higher on his old jumps form.

3156 AEDAS ARCHITECTS FILLIES' H'CAP 1m 4y
2:45 (2:45) (Class 5) (0-70,70) 3-Y-O+ **£3,886** (£1,156; £577; £288) **Stalls** Low

Form RPR

4-05 **1** **Emily's Place (IRE)**[13] 2748 4-9-6 **62**.............................. JimmyQuinn 9 72
(J Pearce) *hld up towards rr: stdy hdwy 4f out: led over 2f out: rdn wl over 1f out: drvn and styd on wl fnl f* **14/1**

5104 **2** *3* **Society Music (IRE)**[8] 2905 5-9-7 **70**..........................(p) NeilBrown(7) 7 73
(M Dods) *trckd ldrs: hdwy 3f out: effrt and ev ch over 2f out: sn rdn: drvn and kpt on same pce ent fnl f* **4/1**[1]

0400 **3** *3/4* **Casablanca Minx (IRE)**[18] 2603 4-8-9 **51** oh5.........(b) DeanMcKeown 6 52
(P D Evans) *t.k.h: hld up in rr: gd hdwy over 3f out: chsd ldng pair over 1f out: sn rdn and hung lft ins fnl f: kpt on* **14/1**

1150 **4** *2* **Very Well Red**[4] 3034 4-9-6 **69**.......................... WilliamCarson(7) 4 66
(P W Hiatt) *chsd ldrs on inner: rdn along 4f out: drvn over 2f out: plugged on same pce* **7/1**[3]

4-51 **5** *7* **Keisha Kayleigh (IRE)**[65] 1301 4-9-0 **56**......................(b) TomEaves 12 37
(B Ellison) *dwlt: reminders and sn cl up on outer: effrt over 3f out: rdn along and ch over 2f out: sn drvn and wknd* **10/1**

5-44 **6** *1 3/4* **Nice To Know (FR)**[20] 2541 3-8-13 **64**.............................. TedDurcan 8 41
(E A L Dunlop) *towards rr: hdwy on outer over 3f out: rdn to chse ldrs over 2f out: sn drvn and btn* **13/2**[2]

1006 **7** *6* **Hostage**[23] 2475 3-9-5 **70**..(v1) KDarley 10 33
(M L W Bell) *a in rr* **11/1**

603 **8** *1 3/4* **Celtic Memories (IRE)**[4] 3040 3-8-0 **51** oh1.................(b) DaleGibson 5 10
(M W Easterby) *cl up: led 1/2-way: rdn along and hdd over 2f out: sn wknd* **16/1**

-040 **9** *6* **Apsara**[27] 2338 6-9-5 **61**.. MickyFenton 1 6
(G M Moore) *wnt rt s: reminders and sn led: rdn along and hdd 1/2-way: drvn 3f out and sn wknd* **4/1**[1]

-002 **10** *1 3/4* **World At My Feet**[9] 2893 5-8-9 **51** oh6.................... SilvestreDeSousa 2 —
(N Bycroft) *a bhd* **8/1**

1060 **11** *18* **Crush On You**[63] 1360 4-8-9 **51** oh6......................... GrahamGibbons 13 —
(R Hollinshead) *a towards rr: bhd and eased fnl 2f* **25/1**

1m 51.99s (6.29) **Going Correction** +0.725s/f (Yiel)
WFA 3 from 4yo+ 9lb **11** Ran SP% **117.4**
Speed ratings (Par 100):97,94,93,91,84 82,76,74,68,67 49
CSF £69.23 CT £817.35 TOTE £16.40: £5.60, £1.90, £4.40; EX 95.20.
Owner Macniler Racing Partnership **Bred** Bryan Ryan **Trained** Newmarket, Suffolk

FOCUS
Not much of a race, but it is likely to produce the odd winner at a similarly moderate level. The runner-up ran to her latest course form, but it is a long time since the winner rated this high so the form is slightly dubious.
Nice To Know(FR) Official explanation: trainer said filly was unsuited by the soft ground

3157 SPINDRIFTER CONDITIONS STKS 6f
3:15 (3:16) (Class 3) 2-Y-O **£6,477** (£1,927; £963; £481) **Stalls** Low

Form RPR

1 **1** **Easy Target (FR)**[19] 2575 2-9-1 0....................................... PaulEddery 3 93
(B Smart) *trckd ldrs: effrt and swtchd to stands' rail 2f out: sn rdn and led wl over 1f out: drvn ins fnl f and kpt on gamely* **6/1**

61 **2** *shd* **Nacho Libre**[23] 2473 2-9-1 0.. MichaelHills 1 93
(B W Hills) *hld up: smooth hdwy over 2f out: rdn to chal over 1f out and sn ev ch: drvn ins fnl f and kpt on wl: jst hld* **9/4**[1]

10 **3** *8* **Golan Knight (IRE)**[9] 2855 2-9-1 0.................................. DO'Donohoe 4 69
(K A Ryan) *led: rdn along over 2f out: drvn and hdd wl over 1f out: sn one pce* **3/1**[3]

01 **4** *3 1/2* **Captain Dunne (IRE)**[38] 1993 2-8-13 0.............................. DavidAllan 2 57
(T D Easterby) *tk keen hld: cl up: rdn along over 2f out: sn drvn and btn wl over 1f out* **11/4**[2]

10 **5** *4* **Bere Davis (FR)**[13] 2732 2-9-1 0.................................. DeanMcKeown 5 47
(P D Evans) *chsd ldrs: rdn along over 2f out and sn wknd* **13/2**

1m 20.58s (3.18) **Going Correction** +0.575s/f (Yiel) **5** Ran SP% **110.1**
Speed ratings (Par 98):101,100,90,85,80
CSF £19.73 TOTE £6.80: £3.30, £1.30; EX 16.40.
Owner Prime Equestrian **Bred** David Brown **Trained** Hambleton, N Yorks

FOCUS
A good little conditions race in which the front pair pulled eight lengths clear of the third. Neither of the front two would be out of place at Listed level, although the form has been rated conservatively with the bad ground in mind.

NOTEBOOK
Easy Target(FR), whose trainer has enjoyed a fine season so far with his juveniles, including a Royal Ascot winner, created a good impression when winning on fast ground at Nottingham on his debut, but he is by a sire whose progeny can handle some cut and he ran on strongly for pressure against the stands' rail to narrowly deny favourite Nacho Libre. His rider wanted to ensure he got to the rail and that was probably the telling factor in his victory. Reportedly a buzzy sort, he clearly has plenty of ability and is likely to be given a break now before having a crack at a Listed contest. (op 9-2)
Nacho Libre, bred to go in the ground, confirmed the promise of his Newbury debut success with a ready win at Windsor and he improved again on that here, just losing out in a close finish. He may well have won had he been able to race against the rail, but he was a long way clear of the rest and there should still be more to come. (op 5-2 tchd 11-4 in a place)
Golan Knight(IRE) ran out an easy winner in soft ground on his debut at Leicester, but failed to cope with the rise in grade when down the field in the Chesham at Royal Ascot, and this drop in grade was expected to yield a better effort. He took them along early, but it became clear as they started to turn for home that he was beaten and he ultimately finished well held. He may not be that easy to place. (op 7-2)
Captain Dunne(IRE) was quite impressive in winning at Haydock last time, but he raced far too keenly on this step back up in trip and failed to get home. He is worth another chance back at 5f. (op 4-1)
Bere Davis(FR), a winner on his debut, was outclassed behind Henrythenavigator in the Coventry at Royal Ascot and again struggled to make an impact here. He deserves another chance back on faster ground, but at the moment is not progressing. (op 9-2 tchd 7-1)

3158 EBF PARK SUITE FILLIES' H'CAP 6f
3:45 (3:45) (Class 3) (0-90,90) 3-Y-O+
£9,348 (£2,799; £1,399; £700; £349; £175) **Stalls** Low

Form RPR

030 **1** **Pick A Nice Name**[2] 3101 5-8-6 **72** oh5 ow3......... MichaelJStainton(5) 3 81
(R M Whitaker) *in tch: hdwy on inner over 2f out: rdn to ld over 1f out: styd on strly u.p fnl f* **13/2**

211- **2** *2 1/2* **Robema**[360] 3250 4-9-4 **79**.. GrahamGibbons 8 81
(J J Quinn) *trckd ldrs: hdwy on outer and cl up 1/2-way: rdn and ev ch 2f out: sn drvn and kpt on same pce u.p ins fnl f* **9/2**[2]

5301 **3** *nk* **Misphire**[9] 2870 4-9-1 **76**...(p) DarryllHolland 2 77
(M Dods) *hld up in rr: hdwy wl over 2f out: rdn to chse ldrs over 1f out: sn drvn and kpt on same pce* **3/1**[1]

2423 **4** *2 1/2* **Shes Minnie**[30] 2240 4-8-12 **73**.. KDarley 5 66
(J G M O'Shea) *led: rdn along wl over 2f out: drvn and hdd over 1f out: wknd ent fnl f* **6/1**[3]

-046 **5** *1/2* **Flying Valentino**[19] 2577 3-8-5 **75**................................ AndrewElliott(3) 7 66
(G A Swinbank) *in tch: hdwy over 2f out: sn rdn and no imp appr fnl f* **14/1**

24 **6** *shd* **Aye Aye Definitely (IRE)**[9] 2867 3-8-6 **73**..................... PaulHanagan 4 63
(R A Fahey) *t.k.h: trckd ldrs: effrt over 2f out: sn rdn and btn over 1f out* **9/2**[2]

0- **7** *nk* **El Soprano (IRE)**[288] 5408 3-9-9 **90**................................. DO'Donohoe 6 79
(K A Ryan) *midfield: effrt 3f out: sn rdn and no hdwy* **16/1**

0/0- **8** *2* **Queen's Lodge (IRE)**[403] 1949 7-9-2 **77**........................ TonyHamilton 1 61
(I W McInnes) *prom: rdn along over 2f out: drvn and wknd over 1f out* **33/1**

5000 **9** *22* **Sunderland Echo (IRE)**[2] 3089 4-9-13 **88**............................ TomEaves 9 6
(B Ellison) *dwlt: sn chsd along to join ldrs on outer: cl up tl rdn along 3f out and sn wknd* **10/1**

1m 20.16s (2.76) **Going Correction** +0.575s/f (Yiel)
WFA 3 from 4yo+ 6lb **9** Ran SP% **113.6**
Speed ratings (Par 104):104,100,100,96,96 96,95,93,63
CSF £35.19 CT £105.82 TOTE £9.60: £2.70, £1.90, £1.30; EX 74.00.
Owner John W Ford **Bred** J W Ford **Trained** Scarcroft, W Yorks

FOCUS
A decent sprint handicap. The winner was 8lb wrong at the weights and the form has an unreliable feel to it.

NOTEBOOK
Pick A Nice Name, all in all racing from 8lb wrong, failed to last home over 7f at Newmarket the previous weekend, but she was nibbled at in the market here and ran out a quite authoritative winner, relishing the ground well and powering home under pressure. This lightly raced five-year-old is in foal to Monsieur Bond and will be off to the paddocks shortly. (op 15-2 tchd 8-1)
Robema was returning from a year off, but she had shown when winning two of her three starts as a three-year-old that she is a decent filly and this has to go down as a highly positive return over what is an inadequate trip. Seemingly effective from 6f-1m on fast and soft ground, she remains open to a good deal of further improvement and is another to keep on side in future. (op 13-2)
Misphire likes a bit of cut in the ground and looked a leading contender following her heavy-ground Haydock victory. Up 5lb, she ran well, but bumped into a couple of less-exposed sorts. (op 5-2)
Shes Minnie is a consistent filly who seems versatile with regards to ground conditions, but in the end it proved to be too much of a test of stamina for her and she failed to see her race out. (op 7-1)
Flying Valentino, reverting from 1m, has yet to find her optimum trip and is likely to find winning hard whilst connections continue to experiment. (op 12-1)
Aye Aye Definitely(IRE) was cut off when trying to get across to the stands' rail, but did not pick up anyway. She has so far been a bit disappointing since coming from Ireland. (tchd 4-1, 5-1 in a place)
Sunderland Echo(IRE) Official explanation: trainer said filly finished lame behind

3159 BEST UK RACECOURSES ON TURFTV H'CAP 1m 4f 8y
4:15 (4:15) (Class 6) (0-65,63) 3-Y-O **£3,238** (£963; £481; £240) **Stalls** Low

Form RPR

-413 **1** **Bollin Felix**[41] 1917 3-9-5 **61**..(b) DavidAllan 12 81+
(T D Easterby) *hld up in midfield: stdy hdwy to trck ldrs 5f out: led 3f out: rdn clr over 2f out: styd on wl u.p ins fnl f* **7/2**[1]

0614 **2** *2* **Sadler's Kingdom (IRE)**[30] 2246 3-9-2 **58**.................... PaulHanagan 10 75+
(R A Fahey) *trckd ldrs: hdwy to ld over 4f out: rdn along and hdd 3f out: drvn and chsd wnr over 1f out: kpt on u.p fnl f* **9/2**[2]

0002 **3** *10* **Ja Myford**[8] 2909 3-8-8 **50**.. MickyFenton 4 51
(P T Midgley) *hld up: stdy hdwy on inner and cl up 4f out: rdn along 3f out: drvn over 1f out and sn one pce* **9/2**[2]

00-5 **4** *2 1/2* **Admiral Savannah (IRE)**[19] 2552 3-8-8 **50**..................(v1) TedDurcan 2 47
(T D Easterby) *hld up in rr: stdy hdwy on inner 5f out: rdn to chse ldrs 3f out: sn drvn and kpt on same pce* **16/1**

0000 **5** *shd* **Foxxy**[20] 2538 3-8-3 **52**... MCGeran(7) 7 49
(J R Norton) *towards rr: hdwy over 4f out: rdn along 3f out: kpt on fnl 2f: nrst fin* **33/1**

6061 **6** *9* **Mr Crystal (FR)**[19] 2552 3-8-11 **58**....................... MichaelJStainton(5) 11 40
(Micky Hammond) *chsd ldrs: rdn along over 3f out: sn drvn and btn over 2f out* **14/1**

6-00 **7** ½ **Currahee**[69] 1224 3-8-8 **50** TomEaves 3 31
(Miss J A Camacho) *hld up towards rr: hdwy over 3f out: sn rdn along and no imp* **25/1**

0060 **8** 15 **Malguru**[35] 2096 3-8-11 **56** AndrewElliott(3) 16 13
(G A Swinbank) *trckd ldrs: hdwy and cl up 4f out: rdn along 3f out and wknd over 2f out* **25/1**

30-0 **9** 22 **Miss Percy**[33] 2133 3-8-13 **62** JamesRogers(7) 17 —
(R A Fahey) *midfield: rdn along over 4f out: sn outpcd and bhd* **50/1**

2000 **10** 18 **Ingleby Hill (IRE)**[20] 2538 3-8-8 **50** PaulFessey 13 —
(T D Barron) *chsd ldrs: rdn along 4f out: sn wknd* **33/1**

5-12 **11** 4 **Raise The Goblet (IRE)**[18] 2609 3-9-7 **63** (v1) DarryllHolland 8 —
(W J Haggas) *hld up in rr: hdwy on outer to chse ldrs over 4f out: sn rdn along and wknd* **13/2**

0200 **12** 16 **Laughing Game**[18] 2610 3-9-0 **56** MichaelHills 9 —
(M L W Bell) *a in rr* **33/1**

40-6 **13** 32 **Danehill Silver**[20] 2530 3-9-6 **62** KDarley 14 —
(R Hollinshead) *cl up: rdn along over 4f out and sn wknd* **20/1**

50-0 **14** 91 **Remark (IRE)**[114] 661 3-8-8 **50** DaleGibson 6 —
(M W Easterby) *led: rdn along 5f out: hdd over 4f out and sn wknd* **6/1**3

0020 **15** 3 **Whodunit (UAE)**[11] 2801 3-8-3 **52** WilliamCarson(7) 15 —
(P W Hiatt) *prom: rdn along 1/2-way: sn wknd* **50/1**

2m 46.59s (6.29) **Going Correction** +0.725s/f (Yiel) **15 Ran SP% 124.0**
Speed ratings (Par 98):108,106,100,98,98 92,91,81,67,55 52,41,20,—,—
CSF £17.34 CT £74.44 TOTE £4.40: £1.60, £1.80, £2.10; EX 18.20.

Owner Sir Neil Westbrook **Bred** Sir & Exors Of Late Lady Westbrook **Trained** Great Habton, N Yorks

FOCUS
The progressive front pair drew ten lengths clear of the well-in third in what was a modest handicap. The winning time was decent for the grade considering the ground.

Danehill Silver Official explanation: jockey said gelding ran too freely

Remark(IRE) Official explanation: trainer said gelding had breathing problems

3160 WILFRED UNDERWOOD MEMORIAL MAIDEN FILLIES' STKS 1m 2f 6y
4:45 (4:46) (Class 5) 3-4-Y-O **£4,533** (£1,348; £674; £336) **Stalls** Low

Form RPR

33-2 **1** **Circle Of Love**[18] 2597 3-9-0 79 KDarley 4 83
(J L Dunlop) *trckd ldr: hdwy to ld wl over 2f out: sn rdn clr* **5/6**1

-24 **2** 10 **Hazarayna**[28] 2308 3-9-0 0 TedDurcan 1 63
(H R A Cecil) *trckd ldng pair: hdwy 3f out: rdn to chse wnr wl over 1f out: sn drvn and no imp* **7/2**2

05-4 **3** 2½ **Niqaab**[34] 2127 3-9-0 71 MichaelHills 5 58
(B W Hills) *led: rdn along 3f out: sn hdd & wknd fnl 2f* **7/2**2

4 3 **Ridge Rose** 3-8-9 0 AshleyHamblett(5) 6 52
(L M Cumani) *dwlt: hld up in rr: pushed along 4f out: rdn and green 3f out: nvr a factor* **10/1**3

2m 21.58s (7.50) **Going Correction** +0.725s/f (Yiel) **4 Ran SP% 108.1**
Speed ratings (Par 100):99,91,89,86
CSF £4.01 TOTE £1.60; EX 3.30.

Owner Hesmonds Stud **Bred** Hesmonds Stud Ltd **Trained** Arundel, W Sussex

FOCUS
Half the declared runners were absentees. This took little winning and Circle Of Love blew her rivals away. She was just about entitled to win by this far.

3161 WRAGBY H'CAP 1m 4y
5:15 (5:15) (Class 5) (0-75,70) 3-Y-0+ **£3,886** (£1,156; £577; £288) **Stalls** Low

Form RPR

3000 **1** **Magical Music**[10] 2831 4-9-2 **58** JimmyQuinn 2 63
(J Pearce) *hld up in tch: hdwy 3f out: rdn to ld over 1f out: drvn and kpt on ins fnl f* **7/1**3

640 **2** ¾ **Superior Star**[3] 3052 4-10-0 **70** (v) PaulHanagan 4 73
(R A Fahey) *t.k.h: trckd ldrs: hdwy 3f out: effrt and ev ch 2f out: sn rdn and hung lft: drvn and kpt on ins fnl f* **7/1**3

4455 **3** 1¼ **Ming Vase**[10] 2843 5-8-9 **51** oh6 (b1) MickyFenton 3 51
(P T Midgley) *led: rdn along 3f out: drvn 2f out: hdd over 1f out: kpt on same pce fnl f* **16/1**

31-0 **4** 6 **Moonstreaker**[27] 2338 4-8-12 **59** MichaelJStainton(5) 7 45
(R M Whitaker) *wnt rt s: hld up: hdwy on inner 3f out: rdn and ch 2f out: sn drvn and wknd* **7/1**3

000 **5** ½ **Dazzler Mac**[14] 2711 6-8-10 **52** (b1) SilvestreDeSousa 1 37
(N Bycroft) *prom: effrt and ev ch 3f out: sn rdn and wknd wl over 1f out* **9/2**1

4356 **6** 5 **General Feeling (IRE)**[13] 2741 6-8-10 **52** PatCosgrave 8 26
(K R Burke) *bmpd s: a in rr* **5/1**2

0-00 **7** 7 **Centenary (IRE)**[56] 1530 3-8-11 **62** GrahamGibbons 6 19
(J J Quinn) *prom: rdn along 3f out: sn wknd* **12/1**

3420 **8** 8 **Spinning**[5] 2985 4-9-10 **66** (b) PaulFessey 5 5
(T D Barron) *hld up towards rr: hdwy to chse ldrs 3f out: sn rdn and btn* **5/1**2

3165 **9** 19 **Blushing Prince (IRE)**[70] 1199 9-8-9 **51** oh1 (t) DarryllHolland 9 —
(R C Guest) *a in rr* **8/1**

1m 51.5s (5.80) **Going Correction** +0.725s/f (Yiel)
WFA 3 from 4yo+ 9lb **9 Ran SP% 113.7**
Speed ratings (Par 103):100,99,98,92,91 86,79,71,52
CSF £54.16 CT £753.11 TOTE £8.60: £2.90, £3.10, £4.10; EX 66.50 Place 6 £25.33, Place 5 £12.82..

Owner Killarney Glen & Mrs E M Clarke **Bred** Peter Taplin **Trained** Newmarket, Suffolk

FOCUS
Weak form, the sort of result that shows that form on this sort of ground should not be taken too literally.

Magical Music Official explanation: trainer said, regarding apparent improvement in form, that the filly benefited from softer ground and a more experienced jockey.

T/Plt: £25.80 to a £1 stake. Pool: £76,976.40. 2,171.80 winning tickets. T/Qpdt: £5.90 to a £1 stake. Pool: £4,693.00. 585.80 winning tickets. JR

3102 WINDSOR (R-H)
Monday, July 2

OFFICIAL GOING: Heavy
The meeting survived a morning inspection and conditions were testing. There were 18 non-runners due to the ground.
Wind: Moderate, across Weather: Raining

3162 TOTEPLACEPOT FILLIES' MEDIAN AUCTION MAIDEN STKS 5f 10y
6:40 (6:42) (Class 5) 2-Y-O **£3,886** (£1,156; £577; £288) **Stalls** High

Form RPR

032 **1** **Luscious Lips**[14] 2724 2-9-0 0 RichardHughes 5 76
(R Hannon) *mde all: shkn up and drew clr over 1f out: rdn out last 100yds* **8/11**1

0 **2** 1¾ **Meridian Line (IRE)**[23] 2468 2-9-0 0 TQuinn 2 70
(J G Portman) *chsd wnr after 1f: rdn and no imp wl over 1f out: kpt on towards fin* **14/1**

03 **3** 8 **Bahamarama (IRE)**[11] 2797 2-9-0 0 FergusSweeney 10 43
(J R Boyle) *chsd wnr for 1f: 3rd after: rdn 2f out: wknd over 1f out* **11/2**3

665 **4** ½ **Cocabana**[5] 2997 2-9-0 0 AdamKirby 1 41+
(J G Portman) *racd alone far side: nvr on terms after 2f: wl adrift over 1f out* **7/2**2

5 10 **La Varrosa** 2-8-7 0 NBazeley(7) 4 7
(Mrs P N Dutfield) *s.s: outpcd and sn t.o* **40/1**

6 6 **Night Robe** 2-9-0 0 StephenDonohoe 9 —
(P D Evans) *s.s: outpcd and sn t.o* **16/1**

7 15 **Seductive Witch** 2-9-0 0 HayleyTurner 3 —
(M D I Usher) *v restless stalls: s.s: sn t.o* **33/1**

63.45 secs (2.35) **Going Correction** +0.325s/f (Good) **7 Ran SP% 113.4**
Speed ratings (Par 91):94,91,78,77,61 52,28
CSF £13.07 TOTE £1.70: £1.20, £4.30; EX 12.60.

Owner Lady Caffyn-Parsons **Bred** Lady Caffyn-Parsons **Trained** East Everleigh, Wilts

FOCUS
An ordinary juvenile fillies' maiden in which the first pair came clear. The form could be rated 10lb better but a cautious view has been taken given the bad ground.

NOTEBOOK
Luscious Lips coped sufficiently with the testing surface and deservedly opened her account at the fourth attempt. She was given a no-nonsense ride by Hughes, could have been called the winner nearing 2f out, and this should have served her confidence well. Her immediate future lies over sprint trips in nurseries and there is no reason why she cannot make her mark in that sphere. (op 5-6 tchd 4-6, evens in a place and 10-11 in places)
Meridian Line(IRE) proved suited by the drop to this trip in the testing ground and showed the benefit of her Newbury debut, comfortably reversing form with the third in the process. Likely to prove happier on better ground in due course, she is clearly going the right way. (op 12-1)
Bahamarama(IRE) did not enjoy this testing ground and was treading water inside the final furlong. She now qualifies for a nursery mark and can find her feet in the arena. (op 9-2 tchd 6-1)
Cocabana, bred to be at home in the mud, tried to do it alone on the far side in the home straight and her fate was apparent from halfway. She is not one to judge too harshly on the back of this effort. (op 4-1)
Seductive Witch Official explanation: jockey said filly reared up and struck its head in the stalls; vet said filly had bled from the nose

3163 TOTESPORT 0800 221 221 (S) STKS 6f
7:10 (7:10) (Class 5) 3-Y-0+ **£3,886** (£1,156; £577; £288) **Stalls** High

Form RPR

0601 **1** **Mafaheem**[16] 2652 5-9-8 70 StephenDonohoe 6 65
(P D Evans) *pressed ldr: led over 2f out: hrd rdn fnl f: jst hld on* **11/8**1

4460 **2** nk **Kassuta**[8] 2916 3-8-3 63 (b1) SaleemGolam(3) 7 53
(S C Williams) *dwlt: pushed along in rr: prog u.p 1/2-way: wnt 2nd over 1f out: clsd on wnr fnl f: jst hld* **7/1**3

6540 **3** 5 **A Teen**[27] 2343 9-9-8 43 IanMongan 9 49
(P Howling) *hld up in tch: outpcd whn plld out and effrt 2f out: shkn up and kpt on to take 3rd fnl f: no imp* **20/1**

3051 **4** 6 **Mister Incredible**[11] 2791 4-9-1 52 (v) BarrySavage(7) 8 31
(J M Bradley) *t.k.h: trckd ldrs: cl 3rd whn hmpd and stmbld over 2f out: nt rcvr* **7/2**2

0504 **5** 1¾ **Saintly Place**[16] 2652 6-9-1 45 MarkCoumbe(7) 12 26
(A W Carroll) *dwlt: sn cl up: outpcd 2f out: fdd u.p* **8/1**

345- **6** 1 **Noddledoddle (IRE)**[186] 6963 3-8-4 50 ow1 MarcHalford(3) 16 13
(J Ryan) *led to over 2f out: wknd over 1f out* **12/1**

040- **7** 1 **Banana Belle**[420] 1542 3-7-13 45 MarvinCheung(7) 4 9
(J Ryan) *racd alone on far side: nvr on terms: bmpd along furiously and wl btn fnl 2f* **33/1**

00-0 **8** 6 **A One (IRE)**[18] 2603 8-9-3 48 RichardHughes 1 —
(H J Manners) *racd wd: in tch over 2f: sn outpcd and struggling* **14/1**

50-6 **9** 10 **Master Malarkey**[84] 978 4-9-3 43 (b) JohnEgan 5 —
(Mrs C A Dunnett) *t.k.h: cl up to 1/2-way: sn wknd: eased over 1f out* **25/1**

0-00 **10** 2 **Patitiri (USA)**[13] 2748 4-8-12 38 (tp) SteveDrowne 3 —
(Mrs C A Dunnett) *racd on outer: struggling over 3f out: sn bhd* **33/1**

4-05 **11** 2 **Canary Girl**[67] 1267 4-8-12 41 (v) DMylonas 14 —
(Mrs C A Dunnett) *w ldrs over 2f: sn lost pl and struggling: eased over 1f out* **25/1**

1m 17.3s (3.63) **Going Correction** +0.65s/f (Yiel)
WFA 3 from 4yo+ 6lb **11 Ran SP% 120.6**
Speed ratings (Par 103):101,100,93,85,83 82,80,72,59,56 54
CSF £10.98 TOTE £2.60: £1.30, £2.30, £5.40; EX 19.10.

Owner W Clifford **Bred** J H And J M Wall **Trained** Pandy, Monmouths

■ Stewards' Enquiry : Saleem Golam one-day ban: used whip with excessive frequency (Jul 14)

FOCUS
A very weak event. The first two came nicely clear, with the winner up 10lb on his recent Bath form.

Saintly Place Official explanation: jockey said gelding suffered interference in running

3164 TOTESPORT.COM H'CAP 6f
7:40 (7:40) (Class 4) (0-85,84) 3-Y-O **£6,477** (£1,927; £963; £481) **Stalls** High

Form RPR

261 **1** **Kelamon**[7] 2942 3-8-7 73 6ex SaleemGolam(3) 3 77
(M D I Usher) *chsd ldr: rdn over 2f out: clsd over 1f out: rdn to ld last 150yds: drvn out* **5/4**2

21-2 **2** ¾ **Gentle Guru**[17] 2631 3-8-12 75 SteveDrowne 6 77
(R T Phillips) *hld up in 3rd: rdn to cl 2f out: chal and edgd lft fnl f: nt qckn* **11/10**1

-000 **3** *shd* **Loves Bidding**[18] 2601 3-8-3 **66** .... DavidKinsella 2 67
(R Ingram) *awkward s: sn led at gd pce: rdn 2f out: hdd last 150yds: no ex* **18/1**

1014 **4** *7* **Goodbye Cash (IRE)**[28] 2306 3-8-12 **82** .... BernadetteQuinn(7) 7 62
(P D Evans) *a last: brought wd and effrt over 2f out: wknd over 1f out* **8/1**[3]

1m 16.89s (3.22) **Going Correction** +0.65s/f (Yiel) **4** Ran SP% **108.4**
Speed ratings (Par 102):104,103,102,93
CSF £2.97 TOTE £2.40; EX 3.60.
Owner Mr & Mrs Richard Hames And Friends **Bred** R And Mrs Hames **Trained** Upper Lambourn, Berks

FOCUS
A weakly contested handicap. The form looks worth treating with some caution as the first three were very closely bunched at the finish.

3165 TOTEEXACTA H'CAP 1m 2f 7y
8:10 (8:10) (Class 4) (0-80,80) 3-Y-0+ **£5,181** (£1,541; £770; £384) **Stalls** Low

Form RPR

-343 **1** **Mull Of Dubai**[47] 1771 4-9-9 **75** .... JohnEgan 8 83
(J S Moore) *hld up: t.k.h and prog 6f out to trck ldrs: effrt on outer over 2f out: led over 1f out: drvn out* **11/4**[2]

14-3 **2** *1 1/4* **Beverly Hill Billy**[55] 1563 3-8-13 **76** .... RichardHughes 11 82
(A King) *dwlt: last to 1/2-way: rdn in rr over 3f out: styd on fnl 2f to take 2nd nr fin* **13/2**

5124 **3** *1/2* **Mutual Friend (USA)**[12] 2767 3-9-0 **77** .... StephenDonohoe 10 82
(E A L Dunlop) *trckd ldrs: effrt to dispute 2nd 3f out: edgd lft and nt qckn sn after: chsd wnr over 1f out: no imp: lost 2nd nr fin* **8/1**

0213 **4** *2 1/2* **Russian Epic**[16] 2669 3-9-2 **79** .... PhilipRobinson 6 79
(M A Jarvis) *chsd ldr to over 5f out: effrt to dispute 2nd again 3f out to 2f out: wknd fnl f* **2/1**[1]

0055 **5** *3/4* **Transvestite (IRE)**[12] 2765 5-9-5 **76** .... WilliamBuick(5) 5 74
(J W Hills) *prom: chsd ldr over 5f out to 3f out: drvn and tried to rally 2f out: wknd fnl f* **6/1**[3]

650- **6** *6* **Petito (IRE)**[413] 1741 4-9-1 **67** .... AdamKirby 2 53
(J L Spearing) *led: gng wl enough over 3f out: hdd & wknd rapidly over 1f out* **16/1**

-400 **7** *23* **Nordic Affair**[24] 2426 3-8-12 **75** .... TQuinn 13 15
(D R C Elsworth) *a in last trio: nt gng wl fr 1/2-way: t.o* **12/1**

-300 **8** *1 1/4* **Red Somerset (USA)**[39] 1962 4-10-0 **80** .... SteveDrowne 4 18
(R J Hodges) *chsd ldrs tl dropped to last pair 1/2-way: sn rdn and struggling: t.o* **16/1**

2m 14.25s (5.95) **Going Correction** +0.725s/f (Yiel)
WFA 3 from 4yo+ 11lb **8** Ran SP% **118.2**
Speed ratings (Par 105):105,104,103,101,101 96,77,76
CSF £21.89 CT £129.62 TOTE £3.90: £1.40, £1.90, £2.60; EX 24.00.
Owner Mrs Fitri Hay **Bred** B Walters **Trained** Upper Lambourn, Berks
■ Stewards' Enquiry : John Egan caution: used whip with excessive frequency

FOCUS
A fair handicap, and straightforward to rate with the first three running pretty much to form.

3166 TOTE TEXT BETTING 60021 FILLIES' H'CAP 1m 3f 135y
8:40 (8:40) (Class 5) (0-70,70) 3-Y-0+ **£3,238** (£963; £481; £240) **Stalls** Low

Form RPR

055 **1** **Windbeneathmywings (IRE)**[11] 2793 3-7-13 **59** .... WilliamBuick(5) 5 65
(J W Hills) *chsd ldr to over 6f out: rdn to cl over 2f out: led wl over 1f out: drvn clr* **9/4**[1]

3-40 **2** *2 1/2* **Red**[52] 1637 3-8-7 **62** .... JamesDoyle 6 64
(R M Beckett) *hld up: rdn and effrt over 3f out: nt qckn 2f out: kpt on to take 2nd ins fnl f: no ch w wnr* **5/1**

41-6 **3** *3* **Pairumani Princess (IRE)**[52] 1628 3-8-8 **63** .... SteveDrowne 7 60
(E A L Dunlop) *dropped to last 1/2-way: plenty to do over 3f out: shkn up over 2f out: kpt on to take 3rd last strides* **11/4**[3]

0 **4** *1/2* **Hill Queen (IRE)**[32] 2177 3-9-1 **70** .... RichardHughes 1 66
(L M Cumani) *hld up tl chsd clr ldr over 6f out: clsd to ld over 2f out: hdd wl over 1f out: wknd ins fnl f* **5/2**[2]

43-0 **5** *10* **Hemispear**[63] 1355 3-8-7 **62** .... PaulFitzsimons 3 42
(Miss J R Tooth) *led: clr after 3f: hdd & wknd over 2f out* **16/1**

2m 40.52s (10.42) **Going Correction** +0.725s/f (Yiel)
WFA 3 from 6yo 13lb **5** Ran SP% **108.6**
Speed ratings (Par 100):94,92,90,90,83
CSF £13.04 TOTE £3.00: £1.40, £2.90; EX 13.80.
Owner Christopher Wright & Mrs J A Wright **Bred** Nawara Stud Co Ltd **Trained** Upper Lambourn, Berks

FOCUS
A modest fillies' handicap. The winner scored in good style but this is pretty weak form.

3167 TOTESPORTCASINO.COM H'CAP 1m 67y
9:10 (9:11) (Class 5) (0-70,70) 3-Y-0+ **£3,238** (£963; £481; £240) **Stalls** High

Form RPR

0033 **1** **Azreme**[5] 2979 7-10-0 **61** .... SteveDrowne 6 72
(P Howling) *hld up in tch: clsd on ldrs gng wl fr 3f out: rdn to ld over 1f out: styd on wl* **7/4**[1]

4450 **2** *3/4* **Valley Observer (FR)**[20] 2530 3-9-9 **65** .... (e[1]) AdamKirby 5 72
(W R Swinburn) *trckd ldr: clsd to ld 3f out: drvn and hdd over 1f out: kpt on but a hld fnl f* **4/1**[3]

25-2 **3** *3* **Corlough Mountain**[13] 2749 3-9-9 **70** .... WilliamBuick(5) 2 70
(N A Callaghan) *t.k.h: hld up in tch: effrt 3f out: rdn to chal 2f out: wandered and nt qckn sn after* **9/4**[2]

000 **4** *2 1/2* **Salisbury Plain**[10] 2831 6-8-11 **49** .... NicolPolli(5) 7 46
(N I M Rossiter) *t.k.h: hld up in last pair: hrd rdn 3f out: no imp: plugged on u.p* **16/1**

6-30 **5** *9* **Divine White**[37] 2033 4-9-5 **52** .... RichardHughes 1 28
(P Bowen) *led: rdn and hdd 3f out: wknd 2f out* **11/1**

3001 **6** *17* **Prince Of Charm (USA)**[20] 2545 3-10-0 **70** .... (p) GeorgeBaker 3 5
(R A Teal) *s.s: t.k.h and hld up in last: brief effrt over 2f out: wknd and heavily eased over 1f out* **7/1**

1m 49.86s (5.16) **Going Correction** +0.725s/f (Yiel)
WFA 3 from 4yo+ 9lb **6** Ran SP% **113.8**
Speed ratings (Par 103):103,102,99,96,87 70
CSF £9.41 TOTE £3.10: £1.70, £2.40; EX 12.20 Place 6 £48.45, Place 5 £32.09..
Owner Halcyon Partnership **Bred** Miss Helen Mary Ann Omersa **Trained** Newmarket, Suffolk

FOCUS
A moderate handicap, run at an uneven pace. The form is unlikely to prove all that solid.
Prince Of Charm(USA) Official explanation: jockey said gelding was unsuited by the heavy ground
T/Plt: £72.50 to a £1 stake. Pool: £82,614.05. 831.25 winning tickets. T/Qpdt: £23.00 to a £1 stake. Pool: £4,617.50. 148.20 winning tickets. JN

3108 WOLVERHAMPTON (A.W) (L-H)
Monday, July 2

OFFICIAL GOING: Standard
Wind: Fresh behind Weather: Cloudy with sunny spells

3168 WORLDWIDE SPORTS BETTING KNOWLEDGE AT PUNTERSLOUNGE.COM H'CAP 5f 216y(P)
2:30 (2:33) (Class 6) (0-65,65) 3-Y-0 **£2,388** (£705; £352) **Stalls** Low

Form RPR

4-25 **1** **Metal Guru**[31] 2198 3-9-1 **64** .... RussellKennemore(5) 13 70
(R Hollinshead) *hld up: hdwy over 1f out: rdn to ld wl ins fnl f: r.o* **25/1**

-302 **2** *1/2* **The Jay Factor (IRE)**[18] 2594 3-9-6 **64** .... JamieSpencer 3 69
(Pat Eddery) *s.i.s: hld up: rdn over 1f out: hung lft and r.o ins fnl f: nt rch wnr* **2/1**[1]

3400 **3** *hd* **Rann Na Cille (IRE)**[10] 2829 3-9-2 **60** .... (p) FrancisNorton 5 64
(K A Ryan) *led: rdn over 1f out: hdd wl ins fnl f* **14/1**

4643 **4** *1 1/4* **Comptonspirit**[14] 2718 3-9-1 **59** .... (p) J-PGuillambert 4 59
(B P J Baugh) *chsd ldrs: rdn over 1f out: no ex fnl f* **16/1**

0120 **5** *shd* **Scarlet Oak**[21] 2515 3-9-5 **63** .... LPKeniry 11 63
(D J S Ffrench Davis) *s.i.s: hld up: nt clr run over 2f out: r.o ins fnl f: nvr nrr* **9/1**[3]

0324 **6** *3/4* **Wadnagin (IRE)**[14] 2718 3-8-13 **57** .... JamesDoyle 10 54
(I A Wood) *chsd ldrs: rdn 1/2-way: styd on same pce appr fnl f* **11/1**

610- **7** *shd* **Theoretical**[191] 6926 3-9-2 **65** .... LukeMorris(5) 8 62
(A J McCabe) *plld hrd and prom: rdn over 1f out: no ex fnl f* **40/1**

0012 **8** *shd* **Nashharry (IRE)**[19] 2571 3-9-0 **63** .... WilliamBuick(5) 7 60
(S Kirk) *chsd ldrs: rdn over 1f out: styd on same pce* **6/1**[2]

00-3 **9** *1* **Call Me Rosy (IRE)**[30] 2260 3-9-4 **62** .... GeorgeBaker 1 55
(C F Wall) *mid-div: hdwy over 2f out: sn rdn: wknd ins fnl f* **9/1**[3]

4210 **10** *shd* **Pennyrock (IRE)**[39] 1965 3-9-0 **61** .... JamieMoriarty(3) 9 54
(J J Quinn) *hld up: nvr nrr* **12/1**

53 **11** *1 1/2* **Vadinka**[32] 2167 3-8-13 **57** .... KimTinkler 12 45
(N Tinkler) *mid-div: rdn 1/2-way: sn lost pl* **20/1**

6244 **12** *1* **Bentley**[10] 2837 3-9-4 **65** .... (v) DuranFentiman(3) 6 50
(D Shaw) *s.i.s: hdwy over 3f out: sn rdn: wknd over 1f out* **9/1**[3]

603 **13** *4* **Musical Parkes**[26] 2366 3-8-10 **57** .... AndrewMullen(3) 2 29
(W J H Ratcliffe) *prom: rdn 1/2-way: wknd over 1f out* **14/1**

1m 15.11s (-0.70) **Going Correction** -0.125s/f (Stan) **13** Ran SP% **123.9**
Speed ratings (Par 98):99,98,98,96,96 95,95,95,93,93 91,90,84
CSF £76.24 CT £814.90 TOTE £34.30: £10.30, £1.20, £6.60; EX 134.90 Trifecta £227.20 Part won. Pool £320.11 - 0.34 winning units..
Owner Moores Metals Ltd **Bred** R Hollinshead **Trained** Upper Longdon, Staffs

FOCUS
A very moderate contest and the way the race panned out rather confirmed the impression of the meetings here on Friday and Saturday that the middle of the track was riding quicker than the inside. The form is sound, if pretty ordinary.
Wadnagin(IRE) Official explanation: jockey said filly hung right

3169 BET NOW AT WBX.COM (S) STKS 5f 20y(P)
3:00 (3:01) (Class 6) 3-Y-0+ **£2,047** (£604; £302) **Stalls** Low

Form RPR

2250 **1** **Danish Blues (IRE)**[40] 1947 4-9-4 **55** .... (p) JamieSpencer 10 59
(D E Cantillon) *s.i.s: hld up: r.o ins fnl f: led nr fin* **5/2**[1]

5400 **2** *1/2* **Dysonic (USA)**[14] 2711 5-8-13 **48** .... (v) TolleyDean(5) 1 57
(J Balding) *chsd ldrs: rdn to ld ins fnl f: hdd nr fin* **6/1**[2]

3060 **3** *hd* **Ruby's Dream**[11] 2791 5-8-8 **44** .... (p) KevinGhunowa(5) 12 51
(J M Bradley) *chsd ldrs: rdn and ev ch ins fnl f: styd on* **20/1**

5446 **4** *1 1/2* **Lady Hopeful (IRE)**[11] 2791 5-8-8 **45** .... (b) RussellKennemore(5) 2 46
(Peter Grayson) *s.i.s: hdwy 1/2-way: rdn over 1f out: no ex wl ins fnl f* **7/1**[3]

2400 **5** *nk* **Beamsley Beacon**[12] 2761 6-9-4 **48** .... (bt) StephenDonohoe 3 50
(S T Mason) *chsd ldr: led 2f out: sn rdn: hdd and no ex ins fnl f* **7/1**[3]

0104 **6** *2* **Mystery Pips**[19] 2553 7-9-4 **50** .... (v) KimTinkler 8 43
(N Tinkler) *led 3f: sn rdn: wknd ins fnl f* **17/2**

-00 **7** *1/2* **Ballybunion (IRE)**[16] 2652 8-8-13 **52** .... LukeMorris(5) 13 41
(R A Harris) *mid-div: lost pl 3f out: n.d after* **20/1**

0010 **8** *2* **Sir Loin**[21] 2516 6-9-2 **55** .... (b) DanielleMcCreery(7) 11 39
(N Tinkler) *s.i.s: hdwy over 3f out: rdn and wknd over 1f out* **8/1**

00-0 **9** *nk* **Orpenlina (IRE)**[10] 2830 4-8-10 **44** .... PatrickMathers(3) 6 28
(Peter Grayson) *sn pushed along in rr: hmpd 4f out: n.d* **33/1**

0066 **10** *1 1/4* **Royal Dagger (IRE)**[10] 2826 3-8-13 **45** .... ChrisCatlin 5 26
(Rae Guest) *chsd ldrs over 3f* **16/1**

000- **11** *nk* **Von Wessex**[359] 3306 5-8-11 **43** .... JackDean(7) 7 27
(W G M Turner) *chsd ldrs to 1/2-way* **40/1**

1500 **12** *2 1/2* **Mustammer**[11] 2799 4-9-6 **50** .... DuranFentiman(3) 4 23
(D Shaw) *a in rr* **9/1**

62.07 secs (-0.75) **Going Correction** -0.125s/f (Stan)
WFA 3 from 4yo+ 5lb **12** Ran SP% **120.3**
Speed ratings (Par 101):101,100,99,97,97 93,93,89,89,87 86,82
CSF £16.24 TOTE £3.10: £1.30, £2.90, £7.80; EX 20.60 Trifecta £145.60 Pool £225.60 - 1.10 winning units..There was no bid for the winner.
Owner Mrs Catherine Reed **Bred** Tally-Ho Stud **Trained** Newmarket, Suffolk

FOCUS
A modest seller, but nothing was thrown in on adjusted official ratings with 12lb covering the 12 runners. Once again the winner made the most of the quicker strip down the middle of the track. The form seems solid.

3170 BETTING TIPS ARE FREE AT PUNTERSLOUNGE.COM H'CAP 1m 4f 50y(P)
3:30 (3:31) (Class 5) (0-75,75) 3-Y-0 **£3,238** (£963; £481; £240) **Stalls** Low

Form RPR

4-00 **1** **History Boy**[26] 2354 3-9-7 **75** .... JamieSpencer 1 89+
(D J Coakley) *hld up and bhd: hdwy over 1f out: led on bit wl ins fnl f: edgd lft towards fin: comf* **12/1**

000- **2** *1* **Crossing The Line (IRE)**[276] 5648 3-8-10 **64** .... ChrisCatlin 5 71
(Sir Mark Prescott) *chsd ldr tl led over 4f out: rdn over 1f out: hdd wl ins fnl f* **9/4**[1]

2050 **3** *shd* **My Secrets**[18] 2602 3-9-2 **70** .... J-PGuillambert 4 76
(M Johnston) *in rr: reminders thrght: hdwy over 4f out: rdn and ev ch fr over 1f out: styng on whn n.m.r and eased last strides* **11/2**[2]

05-1 **4** *6* **Abounding**[31] 2223 3-8-10 **64** .... JamesDoyle 6 61
(R M Beckett) *s.i.s: hld up: hdwy u.p over 2f out: wknd over 1f out* **9/4**[1]

45-5 **5** *1/2* **Private Reason (USA)**[23] 2464 3-9-2 **70** .... FrancisNorton 8 66
(K A Ryan) *chsd ldrs: rdn over 3f out: wknd over 1f out* **20/1**

060 **6** 2½ **Present**[32] 2192 3-7-11 **56** oh6....................(p) WilliamBuick(5) 3 48
(D Morris) *led 1f: chsd ldrs: rdn over 3f out: wknd 2f out* **40/1**
-223 **7** 1¼ **Bachnagairn**[33] 2132 3-9-0 **68**....................(b[1]) RobertHavlin 2 58
(R Charlton) *hld up: hdwy over 6f out: rdn over 2f out: sn wknd* **15/2**
151 **8** 13 **Stringsofmyheart**[19] 2565 3-9-2 **70**....................(b[1]) PaulMulrennan 7 39
(W J Haggas) *drvn to ld after 1f: clr 9f out: rdn over 6f out: hdd over 4f out: wknd over 2f out* **7/1**[3]

2m 40.09s (-2.33) **Going Correction** -0.125s/f (Stan) **8** Ran SP% **116.1**
Speed ratings (Par 100):102,101,101,97,96 95,94,85
CSF £40.01 CT £171.37 TOTE £15.20: £3.60, £1.30, £1.60; EX 58.50 Trifecta £431.60 Part won. Pool £607.94 - 0.84 winning units..
Owner Chris Van Hoorn **Bred** C T Van Hoorn **Trained** West Ilsley, Berks
■ Stewards' Enquiry : J-P Guillambert 14-day ban: failed to ride out for second place (Jul 13-26)

FOCUS
A modest middle-distance handicap was turned into a one-horse race by the winner who scored with embarrassing ease. This gave Spencer the ideal platform from which to show off, and he did not disappoint. The form is tricky to assess, but History Boy has been rated value for 5l.
History Boy Official explanation: trainer said, regarding apparent improvement in form, that the gelding was better suited by the strong early pace and longer trip.

3171 WORLD'S BEST BETTING FORUM AT PUNTERSLOUNGE.COM EBF MAIDEN STKS 7f 32y(P)
4:00 (4:01) (Class 5) 2-Y-O **£3,886** (£1,156; £577; £288) **Stalls** High

Form RPR
3 **1** **Phoenix Flight (IRE)**[9] 2889 2-9-3 0.................... PaulMulrennan 1 77
(Sir Mark Prescott) *mde all: rdn and edgd lft ins fnl f: jst hld on* **5/4**[1]
02 **2** nk **Non Sucre (USA)**[80] 1021 2-9-3 0.................... SimonWhitworth 11 76
(P A Blockley) *s.i.s: hdwy over 5f out: rdn over 2f out: nt clr run ins fnl f: r.o* **9/2**[3]
4 **3** ¾ **Casino Night**[19] 2562 2-8-12 0.................... J-PGuillambert 6 69
(M Johnston) *chsd wnr tl rdn over 1f out: styd on* **6/1**
4 3½ **Rockfield Lodge (IRE)** 2-9-3 0.................... JamieSpencer 2 66
(J A Osborne) *prom: rdn to chse wnr over 1f out: wknd ins fnl f* **4/1**[2]
5 5 **Yankee Storm** 2-8-12 0.................... KevinGhunowa(5) 12 53
(M J Wallace) *hld up: hdwy 1/2-way: rdn and hung rt over 2f out: wkng whn hung lft over 1f out* **14/1**
6 nk **Townkab (IRE)** 2-9-3 0.................... JamesDoyle 5 52+
(N P Littmoden) *in rr: effrt over 2f out: no ch whn nt clr run over 1f out* **14/1**
0 **7** 2½ **Loose Caboose (IRE)**[8] 2904 2-8-12 0.................... NeilPollard 9 41
(A J McCabe) *mid-div: hdwy 1/2-way: wknd over 2f out* **100/1**
0 **8** 2½ **Kay One (IRE)**[22] 2488 2-8-7 0.................... TolleyDean(5) 10 35
(R J Price) *s.i.s: a in rr* **125/1**
0 **9** 2½ **Naming Problems**[14] 2717 2-8-12 0.................... VinceSlattery 3 29
(K J Burke) *prom: rdn over 4f out: wknd 1/2-way* **50/1**
10 3½ **Viola Rosa (IRE)** 2-8-9 0.................... DuranFentiman(3) 4 20
(D Shaw) *s.s: outpcd* **25/1**
6 **11** 1¼ **Qwertyuiop (IRE)**[8] 2911 2-9-0 0....................(b[1]) EmmettStack(3) 7 22
(K J Burke) *sn pushed along and prom: wknd 1/2-way* **50/1**

1m 30.59s (0.19) **Going Correction** -0.125s/f (Stan) **11** Ran SP% **119.8**
Speed ratings (Par 94):93,92,91,87,82 81,78,76,73,69 67
CSF £7.07 TOTE £2.20: £1.10, £1.60, £1.60; EX 10.80 Trifecta £20.30 Pool £661.13 - 23.08 winning units..
Owner W E Sturt - Osborne House Iv **Bred** Airlie Stud And Sir Thomas Pilkington **Trained** Newmarket, Suffolk

FOCUS
A fairly weak and uncompetitive maiden in which very few ever got into the argument. The time does not read badly. Those outside the front three would need to improve considerably in order to win a race, though that is possible.

NOTEBOOK
Phoenix Flight(IRE), given his head this time, made every yard and, after being brought away from the inside rail turning in, battled on well to the line. He had precious little in hand though and does not look anything special at this stage. (op 15-8)
Non Sucre(USA) was the most experienced in the field though he had been off since April and was stepping up a quarter of a mile in trip. He did much the best of those held up and would have been closer still had he not had to be switched around the favourite in the last furlong. He could find a race like this, whilst nurseries give him another option. (op 7-2 tchd 5-1)
Casino Night, trying an extra furlong, was always there or thereabouts and probably improved a bit from her Hamilton debut. She should find a modest maiden and her pedigree suggests this will be just about as far as she wants. (op 9-2 tchd 4-1)
Rockfield Lodge(IRE), a 62,000euros colt out of a winning half-sister to Haydock Sprint Cup winner Lavinia Fontana, ran well for a long way and did much the best of the newcomers. (op 5-1)
Yankee Storm, a half-brother to three winners in the US, looked very green on this debut and should improve with racing. Official explanation: jockey said colt held its breath on leaving stalls (op 12-1)
Townkab(IRE), who fetched 40,000gns as a two-year-old, never got involved but there is plenty of stamina on the dam's side so he should improve as he goes up in trip. (op 16-1)

3172 WBX.COM APPRENTICE CLAIMING STKS 7f 32y(P)
4:30 (4:31) (Class 6) 4-Y-O+ **£2,730** (£806; £403) **Stalls** High

Form RPR
4203 **1** **Samuel Charles**[30] 2258 9-9-2 71....................(p) PJMcDonald 3 57
(C R Dore) *chsd ldrs: rdn over 2f out: nt clr run and swtchd lft over 1f out: led ins fnl f: styd on* **5/2**[1]
-006 **2** hd **Al Rayanah**[10] 2831 4-8-10 63.................... KirstyMilczarek(3) 10 54
(G Prodromou) *mid-div: hdwy and hung rt fr 1/2-way: rdn and ev ch ins fnl f: styd on* **6/1**[3]
1054 **3** nk **Le Chiffre (IRE)**[11] 2798 5-8-12 56....................(p) LukeMorris 5 52
(R A Harris) *mid-div: rdn 1/2-way: hdwy over 1f out: r.o* **7/2**[2]
0050 **4** 2 **Mister Benji**[31] 2225 8-8-9 54.................... SoniaEaton(5) 2 49
(B P J Baugh) *chsd ldr: led 1/2-way: rdn over 1f out: hdd and no ex ins fnl f* **14/1**
0-40 **5** nk **Seesawmilu (IRE)**[38] 2007 4-9-6 45.................... TravisBlock 7 54
(E J Alston) *chsd ldrs: rdn over 1f out: no ex fnl f* **12/1**
3300 **6** 1¾ **Memphis Man**[12] 2762 4-8-12 47....................(p) JackMitchell(3) 6 44
(W M Brisbourne) *dwlt: rdn over 1f out: nvr nrr* **11/1**
0500 **7** 3 **Shrine Mountain (USA)**[40] 1947 5-8-7 53.................... SCreighton(3) 1 32
(Miss J S Davis) *led to 1/2-way: rdn and wknd over 1f out* **14/1**
8 2 **Little Paso (FR)**[3] 7-9-6 0....................(v[1]) RussellKennemore 4 36
(B N Pollock) *mid-div: sn drvn along: wknd over 2f out* **50/1**
4060 **9** 1 **Blythe Spirit**[32] 2187 8-8-10 52....................(v) TolleyDean 9 24
(Mrs L Williamson) *hld up: hdwy over 2f out: rdn and wknd over 1f out* **16/1**

1m 29.31s (-1.09) **Going Correction** -0.125s/f (Stan) **9** Ran SP% **102.3**
Speed ratings (Par 101):101,100,100,98,97 95,92,90,88
CSF £13.83 TOTE £2.70: £1.30, £1.60, £1.50; EX 14.50 Trifecta £111.90 Pool £200.17 - 1.27 winning units..Le Chiffre was claimed by J. M. (Sean) Curran for £6,000.
Owner Chris Marsh **Bred** Sheikh Mohammed Obaid Al Maktoum **Trained** West Pinchbeck, Lincs
■ Italian-trained Fast Gate was withdrawn (6/1, unruly in stalls.) R4 applies, deduct 10p in the £.
■ Stewards' Enquiry : Kirsty Milczarek caution: used whip with excessive frequency

FOCUS
A wide range of abilities in this claimer and the result was pretty much as adjusted offcial ratings suggested it would be. The winner rather bucked the trend by winning up the inside rail, but he was best in at the weights so not too much should be read into that. The first three were probably below their best.
Al Rayanah Official explanation: jockey said filly hung right

3173 ALL POKER LEAGUES AT PUNTERSLOUNGE.COM H'CAP 1m 141y(P)
5:00 (5:00) (Class 6) (0-60,59) 3-Y-O+ **£2,388** (£705; £352) **Stalls** Low

Form RPR
3003 **1** **Golden Spectrum (IRE)**[3] 3067 8-9-1 **55**....................(b) LukeMorris(5) 9 64
(R A Harris) *s.i.s: sn pushed along in rr: hdwy over 2f out: led 1f out: edgd lft: rdn out* **13/2**[2]
4502 **2** ¾ **Hoh Wotanite**[3] 3067 4-9-10 **59**....................(p) JamieSpencer 2 66
(R Hollinshead) *hld up in tch: rdn and ev ch 1f out: edgd rt: styd on* **9/4**[1]
0044 **3** ¾ **Green Pirate**[7] 2947 5-9-8 **57**.................... GeorgeBaker 5 63
(W M Brisbourne) *stdd s: hld up: hdwy over 1f out: sn rdn: r.o* **7/1**[3]
-002 **4** ½ **Boreana**[7] 2947 4-9-3 **57**.................... TravisBlock(5) 6 62
(Jedd O'Keeffe) *chsd ldrs: rdn over 1f out: styd on same pce ins fnl f* **10/1**
0206 **5** shd **Burford Lass (IRE)**[18] 2592 4-9-6 **55**.................... J-PGuillambert 13 59
(D K Ivory) *hld up: racd keenly: hdwy over 6f out: led 2f out: hdd 1f out: styd on same pce* **16/1**
4460 **6** hd **Postmaster**[5] 2990 5-9-6 **55**.................... RobertHavlin 12 59
(R Ingram) *hld up: hdwy over 2f out: rdn over 1f out: r.o* **11/1**
6660 **7** 1½ **Reveur**[12] 2760 4-9-1 **50**.................... LeeEnstone 7 51
(K R Burke) *chsd ldrs: rdn over 1f out: no ex fnl f* **10/1**
0220 **8** 1¾ **King Of Knight (IRE)**[119] 612 6-9-5 **54**.................... AdrianMcCarthy 11 51
(G Prodromou) *trckd ldrs: racd keenly: rdn and ev ch over 1f out: wknd ins fnl f* **20/1**
1206 **9** shd **The City Kid (IRE)**[41] 1918 4-9-9 **58**....................(v) PaulMulrennan 1 55
(C R Dore) *hld up: rdn over 2f out: nvr trbld ldrs* **14/1**
-000 **10** 3½ **Entranced**[16] 2302 4-9-4 **56**.................... GregFairley(3) 10 45
(L Lungo) *sn rdn to ld: hdd 2f out: wknd fnl f* **16/1**
2544 **11** ¾ **Wodhill Gold**[49] 1720 6-9-2 **58**.................... GihanArnolda(7) 3 45
(D Morris) *hld up in tch: lost pl over 5f out: n.d after* **10/1**
-000 **12** ½ **Iced Diamond (IRE)**[48] 1739 8-9-4 **53**.................... ChrisCatlin 4 39
(S Wynne) *hld up: plld hrd: rdn over 2f out: sn wknd* **50/1**
5030 **13** ½ **Sun Bian**[14] 2716 5-9-1 **50**....................(p) LPKeniry 8 35
(L P Grassick) *chsd ldrs 6f* **33/1**

1m 51.37s (-0.39) **Going Correction** -0.125s/f (Stan) **13** Ran SP% **120.3**
Speed ratings (Par 101):96,95,94,94,94 93,92,91,90,87 87,86,86
CSF £21.10 CT £113.04 TOTE £6.70: £1.80, £1.70, £1.90; EX 24.40 Trifecta £40.20 Pool £553.34 - 9.75 winning units. Place 6 £10.78, Place 5 £4.34..
Owner Peter A Price **Bred** Orpendale And Global Investments **Trained** Earlswood, Monmouths

FOCUS
A moderate handicap run at an ordinary pace and the time was modest. They finished in a heap and the form seems to make sense.
Hoh Wotanite Official explanation: jockey said colt hung right in straight
Sun Bian Official explanation: jockey said gelding had no more to give
T/Jkpt: Not won. T/Plt: £13.00 to a £1 stake. Pool: £70,408.50. 3,927.30 winning tickets. T/Qpdt: £4.20 to a £1 stake. Pool: £4,869.80. 853.00 winning tickets. CR

2961 BRIGHTON (L-H)
Tuesday, July 3

OFFICIAL GOING: Good to soft (7.9)
Despite the softish ground, there was no obvious bias towards horses coming wide, with runners covering every inch of ground in the home straight.
Wind: Fresh, across Weather: Sunny spells

3174 TRENTON FIRE CLAIMING STKS 5f 213y
2:30 (2:30) (Class 6) 2-Y-O **£1,943** (£578; £288; £144) **Stalls** Low

Form RPR
1031 **1** **Artdeal**[20] 2549 2-8-12 0....................(p) WilliamBuick(5) 7 70+
(M J Wallace) *t.k.h: trckd ldr: drvn to ld 1f out: styd on wl: readily* **15/8**[1]
4053 **2** 1½ **Straight And Level (CAN)**[20] 2569 2-9-3 0....................(p) EddieAhern 2 65
(J W Hills) *hld up in tch gng wl: effrt and hung lft over 1f out: no imp tl r.o to take 2nd fnl 75yds* **9/4**[2]
1U5 **3** 1 **My Sheilas Dream (IRE)**[20] 2549 2-8-0 0.................... JackDean(7) 3 52
(W G M Turner) *led and restrained in front: set modest pce tl qcknd over 2f out: hrd rdn and hdd 1f out: one pce* **16/1**
20 **4** 3 **Giggling Monkey**[17] 2663 2-7-11 0.................... BernadetteQuinn(7) 8 40
(P D Evans) *chsd ldrs on outside: rdn and lost pl 2f out: styd on again fnl f* **8/1**
521 **5** ¾ **Caught In Paradise (IRE)**[26] 2392 2-9-3 0.................... DaneO'Neill 6 51
(A B Haynes) *dwlt: in rr: hrd rdn 2f out: nt trble ldrs* **5/1**[3]
00 **6** 1 **Goldhill Fair**[21] 2539 2-8-7 0.................... TolleyDean(5) 1 43
(W G M Turner) *in tch: rdn over 2f out: sn outpcd* **16/1**
0004 **7** 2½ **Bold Diva**[15] 2723 2-8-2 0.................... KevinGhunowa(5) 4 30
(A W Carroll) *dwlt: a in rr: rdn and n.d fnl 2f* **12/1**

1m 14.65s (4.55) **Going Correction** +0.70s/f (Yiel) **7** Ran SP% **112.8**
Speed ratings (Par 92):97,95,93,89,88 87,84
CSF £6.11 TOTE £2.20: £1.50, £1.40; EX 8.00 Trifecta £47.30 Pool £617.15 - 9.26 winning units..The winner was subject to a friendly claim. Straight And Level was claimed by Jamie Poulton for £15,000.
Owner Matthew Green **Bred** Miss A Shaykhutdinova **Trained** Newmarket, Suffolk

FOCUS
The runners stayed towards the far side in this routine juvenile claimer run at a weak early tempo. The form is modest but seems solid enough.

NOTEBOOK
Artdeal had no problem with the extra furlong - indeed, the farther he went, the better he looked. On breeding, he should stay 7f, and quite possibly a mile in due course. (op 6-4)
Straight And Level(CAN), wearing first-time cheekpieces, took a while to pick up after travelling comfortably. However, his stamina began to kick in up the final climb, and his new connections forked out £15,000 to claim him, so they must have spotted some potential. (op 4-1)
My Sheilas Dream(IRE), reported to have coughed after finishing last of five in her previous race, ran a more positive race this time. She has obvious limitations, but is capable enough at a modest level. (op 12-1)
Giggling Monkey needs at least this trip to show her potential, and might be the sort for a low-grade 7f claimer or nursery now she is qualified. (op 13-2)
Caught In Paradise(IRE), racing on softer ground than before, never really got going. It may have been that, rather than the return to 6f, which beat him. (op 9-2 tchd 4-1)

Goldhill Fair has not shown much in his three races to date. He is now qualified for nurseries, but improvement is needed for him to be competitive even though he will be lowly-weighted in that sphere. (op 25-1)
Bold Diva Official explanation: jockey said filly never travelled

3175 TRENTON CONSULTANTS (S) STKS 7f 214y
3:00 (3:00) (Class 6) 3-4-Y-0 **£1,943** (£578; £288; £144) **Stalls** Low

Form RPR
0-00 **1** **Kiss Chase (IRE)**[16] [2697] 3-8-8 52........................(b[1]) JimCrowley 6 58
(P Mitchell) *chsd ldrs: nt clr run on rail and swtchd rt 2f out: styd on dourly to wear down rivals ins fnl f* **14/1**
5350 **2** *4* **Razzano (IRE)**[27] [2362] 3-8-3 56........................ ChrisCatlin 8 44
(A M Hales) *in tch: drvn to ld over 2f out: hdd and no ex ins fnl f* **4/1**[2]
0-00 **3** *1 1/2* **Kastan**[36] [2077] 3-8-8 50........................ SteveDrowne 3 46
(B Palling) *led over 2f: prom tl wknd ins fnl f* **6/1**
06-6 **4** *4* **Franky'N'Jonny**[7] [2963] 4-8-5 42........................(p) JosephWalsh(7) 4 31
(M J Attwater) *lost 8 l s: t.k.h: hdwy to ld over 5f out: hdd over 2f out: wknd over 1f out* **16/1**
00-0 **5** *nk* **Porjenski**[23] [2489] 3-8-3 43........................ DavidKinsella 1 31
(A B Haynes) *hld up in 6th: hrd rdn over 2f out: nt pce to chal* **20/1**
050 **6** *19* **Martinet (IRE)**[15] [2726] 3-8-8 65........................ StephenDonohoe 7 —
(P D Evans) *t.k.h: prom: rdn over 4f out: wknd over 3f out* **9/2**[3]
5045 **7** *4* **Doctor Ned**[9] [2916] 3-8-8 50........................ WilliamBuick(5) 5 —
(N A Callaghan) *s.s: hld up in rr: effrt on outside over 3f out: edgd rt and wknd over 2f out: eased whn no ch 1f out* **6/4**[1]

1m 42.08s (7.04) **Going Correction** +0.70s/f (Yiel)
WFA 3 from 4yo 9lb **7** Ran SP% **109.8**
Speed ratings (Par 101):92,88,86,82,82 63,59
CSF £63.28 TOTE £18.40: £9.40, £3.00; EX 95.70 Trifecta £310.60 Part won. Pool £437.55 - 0.68 winning units..There was no bid for the winner. Doctor Ned was claimed by Miss Sheena West for £6,000.
Owner Horses For Causes (Chase) **Bred** Rathasker Stud **Trained** Epsom, Surrey

FOCUS
A poor contest, in which the runners finished slowly, having remained in the far half of the track. Dubious form, with the favourite not running his race.

3176 BUTLER & YOUNG APPROVED INSPECTORS MAIDEN STKS 1m 1f 209y
3:30 (3:32) (Class 5) 3-Y-0+ **£2,849** (£847; £423; £211) **Stalls** High

Form RPR
-242 **1** **Four Miracles**[13] [2763] 3-8-10 65........................ JimmyQuinn 2 71
(M H Tompkins) *in tch: effrt 2f out: swtchd to stands' rail and led 1f out: drvn clr* **4/1**[2]
5500 **2** *2 1/2* **Calculating (IRE)**[15] [2727] 3-9-1 70........................ JimmyFortune 5 71
(J H M Gosden) *w ldrs: drvn to ld over 1f out: sn hdd and nt qckn* **4/1**[2]
0 **3** *3* **Dabawiyah (IRE)**[19] [2597] 3-8-10........................ NickyMackay 12 60
(L M Cumani) *chsd ldrs: outpcd 3f out: rallied and hung lft over 1f out: no ex fnl f* **9/1**
06- **4** *1 1/2* **Magdalene**[244] [6297] 3-8-10........................ ChrisCatlin 7 57+
(Rae Guest) *dwlt: t.k.h in midfield: rdn 3f out: hdwy to chse ldrs over 1f out: no ex* **20/1**
3500 **5** *1 1/4* **Bajan Pride**[18] [2627] 3-9-1 70........................ RichardHughes 9 60
(R Hannon) *w ldrs: hrd rdn 2f out: wknd fnl f* **2/1**[1]
-033 **6** *1/2* **Ashmal (USA)**[18] [2620] 3-8-10 73........................ RHills 1 54
(J L Dunlop) *m most tl wknd over 1f out* **5/1**[3]
030 **7** *4* **Roxie Princess (IRE)**[18] [2625] 3-8-10 68........................ TPO'Shea 10 46
(J A R Toller) *in tch: hrd rdn over 2f out: wkng wn edged lft over 1f out* **20/1**
0 **8** *4* **Roymar**[16] [2693] 3-8-10........................ AdamKirby 6 38
(M Appleby) *dwlt: a bhd: no ch fnl 3f* **100/1**
9 *3 1/2* **Toga Party (IRE)**[28] 5-9-9........................ NeilChalmers(3) 11 36
(Miss Sheena West) *dwlt: bhd: rdn 1/2-way: no ch fnl 3f* **66/1**
00 **10** *4* **River Hunter (IRE)**[31] [2261] 3-8-10........................ LPKeniry 3 23
(S Kirk) *mid-div tl wknd 3f out* **50/1**
00 **11** *23* **Satwa Baron**[153] [311] 3-9-1........................ DaneO'Neill 8 —
(D J Daly) *dwlt: a in rr: wl bhd fnl 3f* **50/1**

2m 9.33s (6.73) **Going Correction** +0.70s/f (Yiel)
WFA 3 from 5yo 11lb **11** Ran SP% **115.9**
Speed ratings (Par 103):101,99,96,95,94 94,90,87,84,81 63
CSF £18.84 TOTE £5.10: £1.70, £1.70, £3.70; EX 24.30 Trifecta £58.50 Pool £782.86 - 9.49 winning units..
Owner Pat Swayne and Partners **Bred** A G Antoniades **Trained** Newmarket, Suffolk

FOCUS
This time the horses came to the stands'-side half of the track. A moderate maiden, but many of these will be at home in handicaps from now on. Sound form among the principals.

3177 BUTLER & YOUNG TRAINING H'CAP 1m 3f 196y
4:00 (4:00) (Class 5) (0-70,70) 3-Y-0+ **£2,849** (£847; £423; £211) **Stalls** High

Form RPR
1312 **1** **They All Laughed**[26] [2391] 4-9-10 66........................ ChrisCatlin 4 70
(P W Hiatt) *hld up in rr: rdn 4f out: hdwy over 2f out: led ins fnl f: drvn out* **10/3**[2]
6011 **2** *1/2* **Tibouchina (IRE)**[7] [2964] 4-9-13 69 6ex........................ JamesDoyle 2 73
(R M Beckett) *hld up in 6th: hdwy and grabbed stands' rail st: led 2f out tl ins fnl f: kpt on* **15/8**[1]
0633 **3** *shd* **King's Ransom**[22] [2511] 4-9-4 60........................ RichardHughes 5 63
(W R Muir) *hld up in rr: rdn and hdwy 3f out: chal over 1f out: kpt on* **8/1**
034 **4** *nk* **Proposal**[27] [2362] 3-7-7 53........................ WilliamBuick(5) 7 56
(A W Carroll) *prom: rdn to press ldrs wl over 1f out: kpt on* **7/1**[3]
-000 **5** *1/2* **Don'Tcallmeginger (IRE)**[13] [2770] 4-8-11 53........................ JimmyQuinn 8 55
(M H Tompkins) *led after 1f tl 2f out: hung lft over 1f out: nt qckn* **12/1**
232 **6** *1 1/4* **Generous Lad (IRE)**[32] [2194] 4-10-0 70........................(p) DaneO'Neill 9 70
(A B Haynes) *in tch: rdn over 2f out: styd on same pce* **8/1**
065 **7** *6* **Rainbow Flame**[29] [2308] 3-8-10 65........................(v[1]) AdamKirby 1 56
(W R Swinburn) *chsd ldrs: outpcd 4f out: n.d after* **16/1**
4620 **8** *5* **Theatre Royal**[25] [2430] 4-9-4 60........................ TQuinn 3 43
(Mouse Hamilton-Fairley) *led 1f: wknd 2f out: btn whn hung lft and eased over 1f out* **16/1**

2m 41.03s (8.83) **Going Correction** +0.70s/f (Yiel)
WFA 3 from 4yo 13lb **8** Ran SP% **112.0**
Speed ratings (Par 103):98,97,97,97,97 96,92,88
CSF £9.55 CT £43.05 TOTE £3.90: £1.10, £1.40, £1.90; EX 8.20 Trifecta £36.00 Pool £615.58 - 12.14 winning units..
Owner Clive Roberts **Bred** T G And B B Mills **Trained** Hook Norton, Oxon

FOCUS
A moderate handicap, with the runners spreading across the track - the winner near the far side and the runner-up under the stands' rail - so hard to weigh up with any conviction. Weak form in all probability, with the winner not needing to improve.

Theatre Royal Official explanation: jockey said filly was unsuited by the good to soft ground and hung left

3178 BUTLER & YOUNG RESIDENTIAL H'CAP 6f 209y
4:30 (4:31) (Class 5) (0-70,65) 3-Y-0 **£2,849** (£847; £423; £211) **Stalls** Low

Form RPR
036 **1** **Nelly's Glen**[16] [2693] 3-9-5 63........................ RichardHughes 2 70
(R Hannon) *hld up towards rr: hdwy towards ins 3f out and styd alone in centre: led wl over 1f out: hld on wl fnl f* **9/1**
0660 **2** *nk* **Zelos (IRE)**[9] [2916] 3-9-1 59........................(b) JimCrowley 7 65
(J A Osborne) *hld up towards rr: effrt and nt clr run over 2f out: hdwy to chse ldrs 1f out: kpt on wl: jst hld by wnr nr fin* **14/1**
-002 **3** *3/4* **Lordship (IRE)**[9] [2916] 3-8-4 55........................ MarkCoumbe(7) 8 59
(A W Carroll) *hld up in rr: hdwy 3f out: chal and hrd rdn over 1f out: kpt on* **14/1**
0112 **4** *hd* **Magroom**[7] [2965] 3-8-10 54........................ SteveDrowne 9 57
(R J Hodges) *hld up towards rr: hdwy to chse ldrs 1f out: kpt on* **7/2**[1]
-020 **5** *1 1/2* **Fun In The Sun**[21] [2545] 3-8-11 55........................ StephenDonohoe 6 54+
(P D Evans) *chsd ldrs: rdn and lost pl 3f out: rallied and styd on wl fnl f* **7/1**
6400 **6** *1/2* **Hucking Heat (IRE)**[28] [2335] 3-9-7 65........................ DaneO'Neill 1 63
(J R Best) *sn chsng ldrs: chal and hrd rdn over 1f out: no ex fnl f* **14/1**
0022 **7** *1* **Realy Naughty (IRE)**[20] [2560] 3-9-7 65........................ TQuinn 4 62
(B G Powell) *led: claimed stands' rail st: hdd wl over 1f out: sn wknd: eased whn wl btn ins fnl f* **10/1**
5444 **8** *1* **Baby Dordan (IRE)**[19] [2607] 3-9-4 62........................ EddieAhern 10 55
(H J L Dunlop) *prom 4f* **9/2**[3]
0454 **9** *1 1/2* **Comrade Cotton**[3] [3099] 3-9-0 63........................ WilliamBuick(5) 5 52
(N A Callaghan) *prom: hrd rdn 2f out: edgd lft and wknd over 1f out* **4/1**[2]
-023 **10** *12* **Lost All Alone**[20] [2560] 3-8-2 51 ow2........................ KevinGhunowa(5) 3 7
(D M Simcock) *prom over 4f: eased whn no ch fnl f* **20/1**

1m 26.95s (4.25) **Going Correction** +0.70s/f (Yiel) **10** Ran SP% **116.8**
Speed ratings (Par 100):103,102,101,101,99 99,98,97,95,81
CSF £126.99 CT £1793.92 TOTE £9.10: £2.50, £4.10, £3.80; EX 106.90 Trifecta £403.20 Part won. Pool £567.95 - 0.50 winning units..
Owner Lady Carolyn Warren & Mrs John Magnier **Bred** Highclere Stud Ltd **Trained** East Everleigh, Wilts

FOCUS
A modest handicap, with the winner staying in the middle and the others coming wider, though it is hard to say what difference that made. Sound form at an ordinary level, with the winner likely to do better.

3179 BUTLER & YOUNG GROUP H'CAP 5f 59y
5:00 (5:00) (Class 4) (0-80,78) 3-Y-0+ **£4,605** (£1,378; £689; £344; £171) **Stalls** Low

Form RPR
0-00 **1** **Talcen Gwyn (IRE)**[7] [2966] 5-8-7 58 oh1........................(v) DavidKinsella 1 64
(M F Harris) *hld up in 5th: rdn and hdwy over 1f out: rn to ld fnl 100yds: drvn out* **9/1**
6540 **2** *nk* **Gower**[22] [2513] 3-9-8 78........................ SteveDrowne 6 81
(R Charlton) *in tch: swtchd outside and effrt 2f out: drvn to chal fnl f: kpt on wl* **7/2**[2]
5553 **3** *1* **Rocker**[4] [3061] 3-9-5 75........................(v) JohnEgan 2 74
(B R Johnson) *led and set gd pce: hrd rdn fnl f: hdd and one pce fnl 100yds* **7/2**[2]
6036 **4** *3/4* **Puskas (IRE)**[17] [2673] 4-9-7 77........................ KevinGhunowa(5) 7 75
(J M Bradley) *towards rr: hrd rdn over 2f out: swtchd rt ins fnl f: nrst fin* **11/2**[3]
2653 **5** *nk* **Canadian Danehill (IRE)**[3] [3108] 5-9-5 77........................(p) JackDean(7) 3 74
(R M H Cowell) *prom: hrd rdn 2f out: no ex fnl f* **10/3**[1]
0425 **6** *shd* **Mr Loire**[13] [2769] 3-9-2 77........................(b) WilliamBuick(5) 5 72
(H J L Dunlop) *hld up in rr: rdn and hdwy on rail over 1f out: one pce ins fnl f* **14/1**
2400 **7** *1/2* **Azygous**[16] [2694] 4-9-5 70........................ JimmyQuinn 4 65
(J Akehurst) *chsd ldr most of way: rdn over 2f out: wknd fnl f* **6/1**

64.97 secs (2.67) **Going Correction** +0.70s/f (Yiel)
WFA 3 from 4yo+ 5lb **7** Ran SP% **113.9**
Speed ratings (Par 105):106,105,103,102,102 102,101
CSF £40.00 TOTE £14.10: £5.80, £2.20; EX 65.70 Place 6 £288.76, Place 5 £235.18..
Owner D K Watkins **Bred** Paul Smyth **Trained** Edgcote, Northants

FOCUS
A fair sprint, with Rocker setting a good pace and the field staying on the far side of the track. The form seems sound enough rated through the second and third.
Puskas(IRE) Official explanation: jockey said gelding hung left
T/Plt: £242.00 to a £1 stake. Pool: £80,089.60. 241.50 winning tickets. T/Qpdt: £42.90 to a £1 stake. Pool: £5,497.20. 94.70 winning tickets. LM

3012 HAMILTON (R-H)
Tuesday, July 3

OFFICIAL GOING: Soft (7.1)
Wind: Light, half against

3180 DAILY RECORD CLAIMING STKS 5f 4y
2:15 (2:15) (Class 6) 3-5-Y-0 **£2,047** (£604; £302) **Stalls** Centre

Form RPR
4000 **1** **Kenmore**[11] [2841] 5-9-2 80........................ PJMcDonald(5) 10 66
(D Nicholls) *hld up in midfield: drvn along 1/2-way: rallied over 1f out: led ins fnl f: kpt on wl* **7/4**[1]
4000 **2** *1/2* **Newcastles Owen (IRE)**[4] [3053] 4-8-11 44........................ AndrewElliott(3) 9 57
(R Johnson) *bhd: outpcd 1/2-way: edgd lft and gd hdwy fnl f: kpt on fin* **25/1**
3023 **3** *3/4* **Howards Tipple**[13] [2761] 3-8-11 62........................ TomEaves 4 54
(I Semple) *trckd ldrs gng wl: effrt over 1f out: ev ch ins fnl f: r.o* **5/1**[3]
3003 **4** *1 1/4* **Spiritual Peace (IRE)**[12] [2806] 4-9-7 73........................(p) DO'Donohoe 5 57
(K A Ryan) *cl up: led 2f out to ins fnl f: no ex* **15/2**
554 **5** *1 3/4* **Dotty's Daughter**[10] [2895] 3-8-2 48........................(p) RoystonFfrench 8 35
(Mrs A Duffield) *chsd ldrs: drvn 1/2-way: one pce fnl f* **14/1**
0350 **6** *1* **Lake Chini (IRE)**[13] [2762] 5-9-2 73........................(b) DaleGibson 6 42
(M W Easterby) *led to 2f out: sn no ex* **7/2**[2]
-405 **7** *3/4* **Seesawmilu (IRE)**[1] [3172] 4-9-2 45........................ PaulQuinn 3 39
(E J Alston) *in tch: effrt 1/2-way: no ex over 1f out* **20/1**
60-0 **8** *1/2* **Stanley Wolfe (IRE)**[15] [2711] 4-8-10 45........................ MarkLawson(3) 2 34
(Garry Moss) *chsd ldrs tl rdn and wknd appr fnl f* **50/1**
0000 **9** *1/2* **Following Flow (USA)**[20] [2563] 5-8-8 40........................(p) JamieMoriarty(3) 11 31
(R Allan) *bhd and sn struggling: sme late hdwy: nvr on terms* **66/1**

0-06 **10** *2* **Signor Whippee**[26] 2387 4-9-0 47..........(b) TonyHamilton 1 26
(A Berry) *dwlt: effrt 1/2-way: sn btn* **28/1**

2000 **11** *1 1/2* **Miss Mujahid Times**[20] 2553 4-8-6 45..........(b) SilvestreDeSousa 7 13
(A D Brown) *prom to 1/2-way: sn rdn and btn* **16/1**

62.46 secs (1.26) **Going Correction** +0.30s/f (Good)
WFA 3 from 4yo+ 5lb **11 Ran SP% 115.1**
Speed ratings (Par 101):101,100,99,97,94 92,91,90,89,86 84
CSF £57.50 TOTE £2.40: £1.10, £7.00, £1.50; EX 64.80.The winner was bought by J Given for £15,000.
Owner Alfi and Partners **Bred** Downclose Stud **Trained** Sessay, N Yorks

FOCUS
A modest claimer containing some useful but disappointing sorts. It was run at a sound pace. The winner made hard work of beating the 44-rated runner-up, whose proximity makes this form look shaky, and the third is the best guide.

3181 BELSTANE STABLES H'CAP 1m 65y
2:45 (2:46) (Class 5) (0-70,67) 3-Y-O **£3,238** (£963; £481; £240) **Stalls** High

Form RPR

4653 **1** **John Dillon (IRE)**[13] 2759 3-8-13 62..........(v[1]) AndrewElliott(3) 14 68
(P C Haslam) *s.i.s: bhd: hdwy over 3f out: led and edgd lft over 1f out: r.o wl* **7/1**[3]

3003 **2** *1 3/4* **Bivouac (UAE)**[21] 2538 3-8-7 53 ow1.......... PatCosgrave 5 55
(G A Swinbank) *hld up: hdwy 3f out: kpt on fnl f: nt rch wnr* **12/1**

0231 **3** *nk* **Rebel Pearl (IRE)**[11] 2829 3-9-3 66.......... JerryO'Dwyer(3) 3 67
(M G Quinlan) *chsd ldr: led 3f out: sn rdn and edgd towards stands rail: hdd over 1f out: kpt on ins fnl f* **6/1**[2]

6400 **4** *hd* **Tomorrow's Dancer**[29] 2300 3-8-4 50.......... DO'Donohoe 9 51
(K A Ryan) *dwlt: hld up: hdwy over 2f out: kpt on stands rail fnl f: nrst fin* **16/1**

2355 **5** *3/4* **Nota Liberata**[11] 2829 3-8-13 62.......... JamieMoriarty(3) 4 61
(G M Moore) *hld up: effrt over 3f out: edgd rt over 2f out: kpt on same pce fnl f* **8/1**

00-1 **6** *hd* **Surprise Pension (IRE)**[13] 2759 3-8-9 55.......... GrahamGibbons 7 54
(J J Quinn) *midfield: effrt over 3f out: kpt on same pce appr fnl f* **8/1**

4102 **7** *1 1/4* **Shandelight (IRE)**[13] 2759 3-8-5 51..........(p) RoystonFfrench 13 47
(Mrs A Duffield) *prom: drvn and effrt 3f out: one pce fnl f* **6/1**[2]

4030 **8** *6* **Colditz (IRE)**[13] 2759 3-8-7 56..........(p) MarkLawson(3) 1 38
(D W Barker) *chsd ldrs tl rdn and wknd fr 3f out* **33/1**

5-00 **9** *5* **One And Gone (IRE)**[57] 1531 3-8-7 53..........(p) TonyHamilton 6 23
(R A Fahey) *t.k.h: hld up: rdn over 3f out: sn btn* **33/1**

6-40 **10** *3/4* **Dilwin (IRE)**[11] 2844 3-9-5 65.......... AdrianTNicholls 8 34
(D Nicholls) *midfield: rdn 3f out: btn over 1f out: eased* **33/1**

450 **11** *1/2* **Morbick**[20] 2554 3-8-12 58.......... DeanMcKeown 2 25
(M Johnston) *towards rr: drvn over 3f out: sn btn* **14/1**

1006 **12** *2 1/2* **Chookie Hamilton**[31] 2246 3-9-7 67.......... TomEaves 12 29
(I Semple) *prom tl rdn and wknd fr 3f out* **17/2**

6000 **13** *5* **Grethel (IRE)**[15] 2713 3-8-2 48 oh1.......... PaulQuinn 11 —
(A Berry) *towards rr: drvn over 3f out: sn btn* **50/1**

0-02 **14** *8* **View From The Top**[8] 2951 3-9-0 60.......... J-PGuillambert 10 —
(Sir Mark Prescott) *t.k.h: led to 3f out: sn wknd* **11/2**[1]

1m 52.6s (3.30) **Going Correction** +0.45s/f (Yiel) **14 Ran SP% 120.2**
Speed ratings (Par 100):101,99,98,98,98 97,96,90,85,84 84,81,76,68
CSF £85.72 CT £553.88 TOTE £8.80: £2.50, £4.90, £2.30; EX 129.30.
Owner Michael Ryan & John Maguire **Bred** M Hosokawa **Trained** Middleham Moor, N Yorks
■ Stewards' Enquiry : D O'Donohoe four-day ban: used whip with excessive frequency (Jul 14-17)

FOCUS
An ordinary handicap but a decent gallop throughout. The bare form looks limited but sound and should stand up at a similar level.
View From The Top Official explanation: trainer had no explanation for the poor form shown

3182 TRADESTYLE CABINETS H'CAP (QUALIFIER FOR THE HAMILTON PARK TOTEPOOL HANDICAP SERIES FINAL) 1m 1f 36y
3:15 (3:15) (Class 5) (0-75,67) 3-Y-O+ **£3,238** (£963; £481; £240) **Stalls** High

Form RPR

6340 **1** **Mayadeen (IRE)**[20] 2564 5-8-13 52..........(b) TomEaves 4 59
(I Semple) *hld up: hdwy 3f out: led over 1f out: drvn and hld on wl* **11/2**[2]

2606 **2** *1/2* **Mandarin Rocket (IRE)**[10] 2865 4-8-11 50..........(p) J-PGuillambert 8 56
(Miss L A Perratt) *chsd ldr: led over 3f out to over 1f out: rallied and kpt on fnl f: hld towards fin* **16/1**

0302 **3** *6* **The Mighty Ogmore**[9] 2905 3-7-13 48 oh2..........(p) DaleGibson 2 42
(R C Guest) *towards rr: pushed along 1/2-way: hdwy over 2f out: kpt on fnl f: no ch w first two* **7/1**[3]

-003 **4** *1 1/4* **Topflight Wildbird**[53] 1627 4-9-5 61.......... AndrewElliott(3) 1 53
(Mrs G S Rees) *hld up in tch: effrt and cl up 3f out: no ex over 1f out* **7/1**[3]

3406 **5** *4* **Leprechaun's Gold (IRE)**[13] 2759 3-8-6 55.......... RoystonFfrench 3 39
(M Johnston) *prom: drvn and outpcd 3f out: n.d after* **8/1**

0252 **6** *1* **Dark Charm (FR)**[10] 2868 8-10-0 67..........(p) TonyHamilton 5 49
(R A Fahey) *trckd ldrs: effrt and ev ch 3f out: wknd over 1f out* **7/2**[1]

-402 **7** *1/2* **Dispol Veleta**[17] 2660 6-9-8 61.......... DeanMcKeown 6 42
(Miss T Spearing) *in tch: effrt over 2f out: edgd rt: sn wknd* **7/2**[1]

4030 **8** *24* **Jordans Elect**[26] 2391 7-9-5 61..........(v) MarkLawson(3) 7 —
(P Monteith) *led to 3f out: sn wknd* **8/1**

2m 5.04s (5.38) **Going Correction** +0.45s/f (Yiel)
WFA 3 from 4yo+ 10lb **8 Ran SP% 112.9**
Speed ratings (Par 103):94,93,88,87,83 82,82,60
CSF £83.45 CT £618.27 TOTE £6.60: £1.60, £5.00, £2.00; EX 69.30.
Owner Cheesie & The Quiet Men **Bred** Shadwell Estate Company Limited **Trained** Carluke, S Lanarks
■ Stewards' Enquiry : Tom Eaves three-day ban: used whip with excessive frequency (Jul 14-16)

FOCUS
A modest but open race run at just a fair gallop and a moderate winning time for the grade. The first two finished clear, but it is doubtful if they have suddenly improved.

3183 JOIN WBX.COM FOR £150 FREE BETS H'CAP 1m 4f 17y
3:45 (3:48) (Class 6) (0-65,63) 3-Y-O **£2,266** (£674; £337; £168) **Stalls** High

Form RPR

-002 **1** **Toboggan Lady**[25] 2420 3-8-3 45.......... RoystonFfrench 2 53
(Mrs A Duffield) *in tch: effrt 3f out: led ins fnl f: styd on wl* **16/1**

00-3 **2** *nk* **Kentucky Boy (IRE)**[31] 2259 3-8-2 47.......... AndrewElliott(3) 3 55
(Jedd O'Keeffe) *midfield on outside: effrt 3f out: sn outpcd: rallied over 1f out: edgd rt and chsd wnr ins fnl f: r.o* **14/1**

-033 **3** *3* **Marquee (IRE)**[5] 3035 3-8-13 55.......... GrahamGibbons 4 58
(P A Blockley) *hld up in tch: smooth hdwy to ld 3f out: rdn and hdd ins fnl f: no ex* **10/3**[1]

000- **4** *1 1/4* **Sangfroid**[281] 5570 3-7-13 46.......... LukeMorris(5) 7 47
(Sir Mark Prescott) *chsd ldrs: drvn fr 1/2-way: rallied and ev ch fr 3f out: one pce whn checked ins fnl f* **10/1**

0502 **5** *9* **Always Best**[9] 2915 3-9-0 59.......... MarkLawson(3) 13 46
(M Johnston) *towards rr: drvn 1/2-way: rallied u.p 2f out: nvr rchd ldrs* **9/2**[2]

-012 **6** *4* **Amanda Carter**[21] 2538 3-9-3 59.......... TonyHamilton 9 39
(R A Fahey) *hld up in midfield: drvn over 3f out: nvr rchd ldrs* **11/2**[3]

00-4 **7** *1* **Watch Out**[19] 2609 3-8-4 46 ow1.......... AdrianTNicholls 14 25
(M W Easterby) *bhd: drvn 1/2-way: nvr rchd ldrs* **40/1**

634 **8** *3* **Flagstone (USA)**[20] 2581 3-8-12 59.......... PJMcDonald(5) 8 33
(G A Swinbank) *hld up: effrt over 3f out: hung rt and sn outpcd* **11/2**[3]

6104 **9** *18* **Patavian (IRE)**[20] 2565 3-9-7 63..........(b[1]) TomEaves 6 8
(I Semple) *led to 3f out: sn rdn and btn* **12/1**

00 **10** *8* **Diamond Key (IRE)**[140] 449 3-8-6 51 ow1.......... JerryO'Dwyer(3) 5 —
(M G Quinlan) *bhd: rdn 4f out: nvr on terms* **16/1**

-064 **11** *2 1/2* **Caviar Heights (IRE)**[24] 2453 3-8-12 54..........(b) J-PGuillambert 1 —
(Miss L A Perratt) *in tch: effrt and chsng ldrs 4f out: wknd 3f out* **25/1**

50-0 **12** *2* **Glorious View**[4] 2609 3-8-3 45..........(b[1]) DaleGibson 10 —
(M W Easterby) *prom to 1/2-way: sn lost pl* **66/1**

2m 44.9s (5.72) **Going Correction** +0.45s/f (Yiel) **12 Ran SP% 115.0**
Speed ratings (Par 98):98,97,95,94,88 86,85,83,71,66 64,63
CSF £212.73 CT £930.64 TOTE £18.60: £5.30, £4.60, £1.60; EX 187.40.La Chesneraie was withdrawn. Price at time of withdrawal 33/1. Rule 4 does not apply.
Owner T P McMahon and D McMahon **Bred** Blenheim Bloodstock **Trained** Constable Burton, N Yorks

FOCUS
An ordinary handicap in which the pace was just fair. Just modest form, but improvement from the first two.
Caviar Heights(IRE) Official explanation: jockey said colt lost its action

3184 DAILY RECORD H'CAP 5f 4y
4:15 (4:15) (Class 5) (0-75,72) 3-Y-O+ **£4,533** (£1,348; £674; £336) **Stalls** Centre

Form RPR

3142 **1** **Katie Boo (IRE)**[10] 2870 5-9-0 60.......... TomEaves 8 69+
(A Berry) *w ldrs: rdn 2f out: led ins fnl f: hld on wl* **7/2**[1]

6-0 **2** *nk* **Joyeaux**[10] 2870 5-8-12 58..........(v) DaleGibson 2 66
(J Hetherton) *hld up in tch: smooth hdwy over 1f out: rdn and ev ch ins fnl f: kpt on towards fin* **8/1**[3]

2115 **3** *hd* **Brut**[5] 3014 5-9-2 67..........(p) PJMcDonald(5) 1 74
(D W Barker) *led to ins fnl f: kpt on: hld cl home* **9/1**

2040 **4** *2 1/2* **Kings College Boy**[15] 2712 7-9-6 66..........(b) TonyHamilton 6 64
(R A Fahey) *in tch: outpcd after 2f: rallied over 1f out: no imp* **8/1**[3]

6132 **5** *1 1/2* **Monte Major (IRE)**[7] 2972 6-8-10 61..........(v) PatrickHills(5) 3 54
(D Shaw) *chsd ldrs tl rdn and no ex over 1f out* **9/2**[2]

4006 **6** *shd* **River Thames**[14] 2744 4-9-9 72.......... RoystonFfrench(3) 7 64
(K A Ryan) *in tch: effrt 1/2-way: one pce over 1f out* **9/2**[2]

5112 **7** *7* **Compton Classic**[5] 3014 5-8-10 63..........(p) GaryBartley(7) 4 30
(J S Goldie) *t.k.h: cl up tl wknd over 1f out* **7/2**[1]

-000 **8** *10* **Mister Marmaduke**[24] 2461 6-8-8 57 oh8 ow4.......... MarkLawson(3) 5 —
(D A Nolan) *dwlt: sn in tch: rdnm and wknd fr 1/2-way* **150/1**

62.30 secs (1.10) **Going Correction** +0.30s/f (Good) **8 Ran SP% 113.7**
Speed ratings (Par 103):103,102,102,98,95 95,84,68
CSF £31.76 CT £231.56 TOTE £3.70: £1.40, £2.90, £3.00.
Owner The Early Doors Partnership **Bred** Michael McGlynn **Trained** Cockerham, Lancs

FOCUS
A run-of-the-mill handicap but several in-form types and the pace was sound. Straightforward form which should prove reliable.
Compton Classic Official explanation: jockey said gelding ran too free

3185 BET NOW AT WBX.COM H'CAP 6f 5y
4:45 (4:47) (Class 6) (0-65,63) 3-Y-O+ **£2,388** (£705; £352) **Stalls** Centre

Form RPR

-300 **1** **Word Perfect**[10] 2864 5-9-13 63..........(b) DaleGibson 8 75
(M W Easterby) *cl up: led gng wl 1/2-way: rdn and kpt on wl fnl f* **14/1**

5042 **2** *1 1/2* **Local Poet**[13] 2762 6-9-7 57..........(b) TomEaves 7 64
(I Semple) *hld up: hdwy over 1f out: edgd rt: kpt on fnl f: nt rch wnr* **7/1**[3]

000 **3** *1* **George The Best (IRE)**[5] 3017 6-9-3 58.......... PJMcDonald(5) 6 62
(Micky Hammond) *dwlt: bhd: hdwy 2f out: edgd rt and kpt on fnl f: nrst fin* **10/1**

1130 **4** *hd* **Megalo Maniac**[11] 2827 4-9-9 59.......... TonyHamilton 2 62
(R A Fahey) *in tch: effrt and ev ch over 1f out: no ex ins fnl f* **10/1**

0055 **5** *nk* **Strawberry Patch (IRE)**[5] 3017 8-8-7 50..........(p) GaryBartley(7) 1 53
(J S Goldie) *midfield: effrt stands' rail over 2f out: one pce fnl f* **11/1**

6-06 **6** *1* **Pitbull**[32] 2203 4-9-2 52.......... J-PGuillambert 9 52
(Mrs G S Rees) *in tch: effrt over 2f out: one pce appr fnl f* **10/1**

2440 **7** *5* **Throw The Dice**[15] 2712 5-9-2 52.......... RoystonFfrench 14 37
(D W Barker) *led to 1/2-way: wknd fr 2f out* **11/2**[1]

0002 **8** *1 1/4* **Funfair Wane**[4] 3053 8-9-0 50.......... AdrianTNicholls 11 31
(D Nicholls) *cl up: disp ld over 2f out: wknd over 1f out* **11/2**[1]

0246 **9** *2 1/2* **Wainwright (IRE)**[34] 2149 7-8-9 48..........(t) JerryO'Dwyer(3) 3 21
(P A Blockley) *bhd: effrt u.p 1/2-way: hung rt and no imp fnl 2f* **9/1**

30-3 **10** *3* **Royal Pardon**[8] 2937 5-8-7 48..........(p) LukeMorris(5) 5 12
(M Dods) *towards rr: drvn 1/2-way: nvr on terms* **6/1**[2]

-450 **11** *1 1/4* **Cut Ridge (IRE)**[20] 2553 8-8-12 48..........(p) PaulQuinn 13 9
(J S Wainwright) *bhd: drvn along 1/2-way: sn btn* **20/1**

000- **12** *1 3/4* **Vondova**[321] 4477 5-9-1 54.......... MarkLawson(3) 10 9
(D A Nolan) *chsd ldrs tl wknd over 2f out* **100/1**

-000 **13** *2* **Dukestreet**[32] 2221 6-8-9 50.......... PatrickHills(5) 12 —
(D Shaw) *bhd: rdn 1/2-way: sn btn* **33/1**

1m 15.3s (2.20) **Going Correction** +0.30s/f (Good) **13 Ran SP% 118.5**
Speed ratings (Par 101):97,95,93,93,93 91,85,83,80,76 74,72,69
CSF £106.44 CT £1039.39 TOTE £16.60: £4.40, £1.90, £3.70; EX 63.60 Place 6 £697.97, Place 5 £415.19..
Owner Mrs Jean Turpin **Bred** Mrs Jean Turpin **Trained** Sheriff Hutton, N Yorks

FOCUS
Another ordinary handicap in which the pace was sound throughout. Whether it was down to the ground or the good pace set by the winner, the first six were those to race nearest the stands'-side rail, with the seventh the best of those to race down the middle. The form looks sound among the principals.
Pitbull Official explanation: jockey said gelding hung left-handed throughout
Cut Ridge(IRE) Official explanation: jockey said mare was unsuited by the soft ground
T/Jkpt: Not won. T/Plt: £1,068.60 to a £1 stake. Pool: £74,953.40. 51.20 winning tickets. T/Qpdt: £215.40 to a £1 stake. Pool: £4,164.10. 14.30 winning tickets. RY

3082 LINGFIELD (L-H)

Tuesday, July 3

OFFICIAL GOING: Standard

Wind: Nil Weather: Sunshine and heavy showers

3186 FALKLANDS VETERANS CLASSIFIED STKS 1m 2f (P)

6:30 (6:32) (Class 7) 3-Y-0+ **£2,252** (£664; £332) **Stalls** Low

Form RPR

/004 **1** **Lytham (IRE)**[22] 2519 6-9-7 45 VinceSlattery 4 56
(D J Wintle) *hld up in midfield: prog wl over 2f out: rdn to ld over 1f out: sn clr* **7/2**[2]

0-00 **2** 3 **Slavonic Lake**[12] 2801 3-8-10 45 (t) JamesDoyle 1 50
(I A Wood) *led: drvn 2f out: hdd over 1f out: wknd ins fnl f but hld on for 2nd* **14/1**

0-00 **3** 1 1/4 **Royal Axminster**[33] 2176 12-9-0 45 NBazeley(7) 6 48
(Mrs P N Dutfield) *towards rr: lost pl and rdn over 3f out: prog on inner 2f out: styd on to take 3rd ins fnl f* **33/1**

0463 **4** nk **Veba (USA)**[22] 2519 4-9-7 45 HayleyTurner 7 47+
(M D I Usher) *hld up wl in rr: prog gng strly 3f out: nt clr run over 2f out: outpcd wl over 1f out: rdn and kpt on* **11/4**[1]

0350 **5** 3/4 **Tumble Jill (IRE)**[24] 2445 3-8-10 45 (p) JimCrowley 11 45
(J J Bridger) *hld up in last trio: effrt on outer 3f out: wd bnd 2f out and outpcd: styd on fnl f* **14/1**[3]

51 **6** hd **Mountain Climb (IRE)**[70] 1210 5-9-7 45 RichardHughes 12 45
(J D Frost) *hld up in rr: rdn and prog fr 3f out: chsd ldng pair over 1f out: one pce and lost pl fnl f* **7/1**

-060 **7** 1 1/2 **Beautiful Mover (USA)**[41] 1951 5-9-2 45 NataliaGemelova(5) 8 42
(J E Long) *hld up in midfield: effrt gng wl 3f out: nt clr run over 2f out: rdn and fnd nil wl over 1f out* **22/1**

0-00 **8** 2 1/2 **By Storm**[27] 2370 4-9-0 45 KirstyMilczarek(7) 14 37
(John Berry) *towards rr: rdn over 3f out: effrt u.p 2f out: wknd fnl f* **16/1**

0405 **9** nk **Kyburg**[17] 2661 3-8-10 45 TQuinn 2 36
(P F I Cole) *pressed ldr to wl over 1f out: wknd* **5/1**[3]

0500 **10** hd **Compton Express**[27] 2361 4-9-7 45 SimonWhitworth 13 36
(Jamie Poulton) *hld up: prog to press ldng pair 1/2-way: wknd wl over 1f out* **12/1**

6000 **11** 2 1/2 **Just An Angel (IRE)**[16] 2697 3-8-10 45 PatDobbs 3 31
(A P Jarvis) *prom tl wknd u.p on inner over 1f out* **20/1**

060- **12** 21 **Ernmoor**[461] 792 5-9-7 45 EddieAhern 10 —
(J R Jenkins) *trckd ldng pair to over 3f out: sn wknd: eased: t.o* **16/1**

43-0 **13** 7 **Oedipuss (IRE)**[15] 2520 3-8-7 45 (t) EmmettStack(3) 5 —
(K J Burke) *s.s: last tl rapid prog to press ldrs 4f out: wknd rapidly over 2f out: t.o* **25/1**

2m 6.12s (-1.67) **Going Correction** -0.15s/f (Stan)
WFA 3 from 4yo+ 11lb **13** Ran SP% **126.7**
Speed ratings (Par 97):100,97,96,96,95 95,94,92,92,92 90,73,67
CSF £52.80 TOTE £5.10: £1.10, £6.40, £13.10; EX 90.70.
Owner D J Wintle **Bred** Mrs A S O'Brien And Lars Pearson **Trained** Naunton, Gloucs

FOCUS
Obviously a moderate event, run at a fair pace, but the first two home both attracted support in the market and this did not look too bad a race for the grade. The form seems sound.
Ernmoor Official explanation: jockey said gelding hung left

3187 HIPHIPHOORAY.COM MAIDEN FILLIES' STKS 6f (P)

7:00 (7:01) (Class 5) 2-Y-0 **£3,238** (£963; £481; £240) **Stalls** Low

Form RPR

1 **Eat Pie (USA)** 2-9-0 0 EddieAhern 4 70+
(M J Wallace) *trckd ldr: led over 3f out: kicked on 2f out: rdn out and styd on wl fnl f* **8/1**

2 1 1/4 **Lille Ida** 2-9-0 0 MartinDwyer 11 67+
(M P Tregoning) *s.s: t.k.h: hld up and last to over 2f out: rapid prog over 1f out: wnt 2nd last 100yds: no imp on wnr* **9/2**[3]

32 **3** 1/2 **Rio Princess (IRE)**[27] 2349 2-9-0 0 SteveDrowne 5 65
(T G Mills) *trckd ldrs: effrt 2f out: chsd wnr over 1f out: fnd nil u.p* **85/40**[1]

2 **4** 1 **Nothing Likea Dame**[23] 2488 2-9-0 0 EdwardCreighton 2 62
(D J Coakley) *trckd ldrs: rdn and outpcd over 2f out: styd on to dispute 2nd fnl f: one pce last 100yds* **3/1**[2]

0 **5** 1/2 **Saoodah (IRE)**[18] 2630 2-9-0 0 MatthewHenry 7 61
(M A Jarvis) *s.i.s: sn rcvrd to trck ldng pair 4f out: chsd wnr over 2f out: wd bnd sn after: one pce* **10/1**

6 3 **Bauhaus Bourbon (USA)** 2-9-0 0 (t) TQuinn 1 52
(P F I Cole) *led to over 3f out: chsd wnr to 2f out: wknd over 1f out* **13/2**

7 1 1/4 **Todber** 2-9-0 0 PatDobbs 10 48
(M P Tregoning) *dwlt: towards rr: pushed along 1/2-way: sme prog whn swtchd to inner 1f out: wknd* **12/1**

8 3 1/2 **Enchanted Lady** 2-9-0 0 DaneO'Neill 12 37
(H J L Dunlop) *s.i.s: a in rr: last and outpcd 2f out: no ch after* **25/1**

0 **9** 1/2 **Spanish Heroine**[24] 2447 2-9-0 0 (p) JimCrowley 8 36
(P Winkworth) *rn green and rdn towards rr over 3f out: struggling over 2f out* **33/1**

1m 14.67s (1.86) **Going Correction** -0.15s/f (Stan) **9** Ran SP% **123.2**
Speed ratings (Par 91):81,79,78,77,76 72,71,66,65
CSF £46.96 TOTE £10.20: £2.40, £2.50, £1.20; EX 90.30.
Owner Hillen, McIntosh, Walsh And Partners **Bred** Ms K Bullitt **Trained** Newmarket, Suffolk

FOCUS
A very moderate winning time, even for a race like this, but that was mainly down to the lack of pace. The bare form is weak, rated through the third, although the first two did nothing wrong.

NOTEBOOK
Eat Pie(USA), a half-sister to very useful miler Millie's Quest, comes from a stable who can ready a newcomer and she landed something of a gamble, running on strongly once getting to the front and winning with a bit to spare. The runner-up was unquestionably unlucky, but this was a bright start to her career and she looks worth her place in a decent contest now. (op 14-1 tchd 16-1)
Lille Ida, a 95,000gns daughter of Hawk Wing who has reportedly been going well at home, was asleep at the stalls and, although not losing much ground, she was never able to obtain a good position. Still last two furlongs out, she came with a strong run in the straight to claim second, but the winner had gone beyond recall. This was a mighty fine effort considering the lack of pace on up front and winning races is not going to prove a problem for her. (op 7-2)
Rio Princess(IRE) had the form to go close and she looked likely to be suited by this extra furlong, but having gone in pursuit of the winner she did not find much under pressure and was run out of second close home. She has shown enough ability to win races, but her weak finishing effort here was disappointing. (op 9-4 tchd 5-2 and 2-1)
Nothing Likea Dame, a promising second on her debut at Bath, needed to improve to win this better contest and she was unable to do so, just keeping on at the one pace under pressure. It was still a fair effort, but she appeal as more of a nursery type now. (op 5-2)
Saoodah(IRE), never involved following a slow start on her debut at Sandown, was again not the quickest away, but she recovered to have every chance and was basically not good enough. She is another nursery type. (op 12-1)
Bauhaus Bourbon(USA) is related to several winners and her trainer's juveniles have enjoyed a good time of it so far this season, so she had to be respected on this racecourse debut. She knew her job and was soon in front, but having been pased at halfway it was apparent she was not going to win. (op 9-1 tchd 10-1)
Todber, whose dam won the King's Stand Stakes for the same connections and was a half-sister to useful sprinter Bowness, was slowly away and came under pressure well over two furlongs out. Her trainer expects her to improve a good deal for the experience and she may win an average maiden. (op 16-1)

3188 TINDLE NEWSPAPERS H'CAP 6f (P)

7:30 (7:30) (Class 4) (0-85,81) 3-Y-0+ **£5,181** (£1,541; £770; £384) **Stalls** Low

Form RPR

5014 **1** **China Cherub**[6] 2993 4-9-8 76 (b) RichardHughes 3 93+
(R Hannon) *t.k.h: trckd ldr: shkn up to ld over 1f out: pushed clr fnl f: comfortably* **7/2**[2]

664 **2** 3 **Louphole**[57] 1545 5-9-7 75 EddieAhern 1 81
(P J Makin) *dwlt: hld up in tch: smooth prog to go 3rd over 1f out: rdn and limited rspnse after: tk 2nd ins fnl f* **9/2**[3]

0311 **3** hd **Mambazo**[4] 3064 5-8-12 69 6ex (e) RichardKingscote(3) 9 74
(S C Williams) *t.k.h: racd wd: trckd ldrs: effrt 2f out: nt qckn over 1f out: kpt on* **9/4**[1]

0213 **4** 1/2 **Silent Storm**[108] 697 7-9-9 77 AdamKirby 4 81
(C A Cyzer) *trckd ldng pair: lost pl over 2f out: rdn and kpt on same pce fr over 1f out* **9/1**

500- **5** 1 **Tony The Tap**[288] 5420 6-9-11 79 MartinDwyer 5 80
(W R Muir) *chsd ldrs: rdn and outpcd over 2f out: n.d after: plugged on fnl f* **12/1**

4450 **6** 1/2 **Dubai Magic (USA)**[3] 3078 3-9-6 80 (t) TQuinn 2 78
(C E Brittain) *led: tried to kick on over 2f out: hdd over 1f out: wknd fnl f* **12/1**

04 **7** 1 1/4 **High Ridge**[23] 2494 8-8-10 69 (p) KevinGhunowa(5) 6 65
(J M Bradley) *settled in last pair: rdn and outpcd over 2f out: no prog after* **5/1**

1106 **8** nk **Cool Sands (IRE)**[3] 3108 5-9-4 72 (v) DaneO'Neill 7 67
(D Shaw) *dwlt: hld up in last: outpcd and pushed along sn after 1/2-way: nvr nr ldrs after* **12/1**

1m 12.18s (-0.63) **Going Correction** -0.15s/f (Stan)
WFA 3 from 4yo+ 6lb **8** Ran SP% **120.9**
Speed ratings (Par 105):98,94,93,93,91 91,89,89
CSF £21.00 CT £43.87 TOTE £4.30: £1.60, £1.80, £1.40; EX 14.20.
Owner J Connolly R Goward J Jenkins W Thornton **Bred** Wayne And Hilary Thornton **Trained** East Everleigh, Wilts

FOCUS
They did not go a strong pace in this sprint handicap in which they finished in a bit of a heap behind the comfortable winner. The second and third ran to their marks.
Mambazo Official explanation: jockey said gelding was unsuited by the slow early pace
Dubai Magic(USA) Official explanation: jockey said gelding lost near-fore shoe
High Ridge Official explanation: jockey said gelding never travelled

3189 BARCLAYS BUSINESS BANKING H'CAP 1m 5f (P)

8:00 (8:00) (Class 4) (0-80,80) 3-Y-0 **£4,857** (£1,445; £722; £360) **Stalls** Low

Form RPR

00-1 **1** **Raffaas**[24] 2445 3-9-2 75 MartinDwyer 1 93+
(M P Tregoning) *stdd s and hld up wl off the pce: wnt 3rd over 5f out: sn rdn: clsd as ldng pair tired fr 3f out: led wl over 1f out: sn clr: eased last 100yds* **11/2**

-426 **2** 6 **Alnwick**[3] 3082 3-8-2 61 oh1 ChrisCatlin 2 67
(P D Cundell) *hld up wl off the pce: last and drvn 5f out: styd on fr 3f out: wnt modest 2nd ins fnl f* **11/2**

6-05 **3** 6 **Old Romney**[24] 2448 3-9-4 80 GregFairley(3) 4 77
(M Johnston) *trckd ldr and clr of rest: moved up to chal 5f out: drvn to ld 3f out: hdd wl over 1f out: fin tired* **10/3**[2]

30-6 **4** 1 **Tivers Song (USA)**[24] 2445 3-8-8 67 JimCrowley 5 63
(Mrs A J Perrett) *hld up wl off the pce: rdn to go 4th over 4f out: one pce and n.d fnl 3f* **18/1**

-111 **5** 1 3/4 **Copernican**[12] 2808 3-9-7 80 PaulMulrennan 7 73
(Sir Mark Prescott) *led and spreadeagled field: pressed over 5f out: drvn and hdd 3f out: wknd 2f out: fin tired* **15/8**[1]

3033 **6** 1/2 **Dan Tucker**[20] 2574 3-9-2 75 RichardHughes 6 67
(B J Meehan) *hld up wl off the pce: rdn over 5f out: no prog and no ch* **4/1**[3]

-606 **7** 7 **Opera Crown (IRE)**[20] 2558 3-8-8 67 (t) TQuinn 3 49
(P F I Cole) *chsd clr ldng pair to over 5f out: sn wknd* **14/1**

2m 42.47s (-5.83) **Going Correction** -0.15s/f (Stan) course record **7** Ran SP% **120.6**
Speed ratings (Par 102):111,107,103,103,101 101,97
CSF £37.74 TOTE £6.80: £3.50, £3.30; EX 39.70.
Owner Sheikh Ahmed Al Maktoum **Bred** Darley **Trained** Lambourn, Berks

FOCUS
A fair three-year-old staying handicap, run at a frantic early pace, and it proved a massive advantage to come from behind. Raffaas took nearly half a second off the course record, set on the old Equitrack back in December 1994. The winner is improving and in view of the time the race has been rated fairly positively, although the second and third lend doubts to the form.

3190 SURREY POPPY SUPPORT H'CAP 5f (P)

8:30 (8:31) (Class 6) (0-65,65) 3-Y-0+ **£3,238** (£963; £481; £240) **Stalls** High

Form RPR

4030 **1** **George The Second**[3] 3106 4-9-8 65 RichardKingscote(3) 5 77
(Mrs H Sweeting) *pressed ldr: rdn 2f out: led jst over 1f out: drvn out and a holding rivals* **4/1**[2]

5313 **2** 3/4 **Cosmic Destiny (IRE)**[7] 2966 5-9-3 57 JimCrowley 8 66
(E F Vaughan) *dwlt: t.k.h and hld up on outside: prog 2f out: r.o to take 2nd last 75yds: nt rch wnr* **7/2**[1]

2060 **3** 1/2 **Quality Street**[32] 2217 5-9-9 63 (p) RichardThomas 4 70
(P Butler) *chsd ldrs: rdn and nt qckn 2f out: styd on fnl f to take 3rd last strides* **7/1**

0-40 **4** hd **Even Bolder**[17] 2673 4-9-8 62 (p) SimonWhitworth 6 68
(R Simpson) *s.i.s: t.k.h: hld up in rr: prog on inner over 1f out: looked dangerous ent fnl f: shkn up and one pce* **20/1**

0500 **5** 1/2 **Pride Of Joy**[27] 2350 4-9-4 58 RobertHavlin 10 63
(D K Ivory) *pressed ldng pair on outer: rdn 2f out: nt qckn over 1f out: one pce after* **12/1**

0000 **6** *nk* **Decider (USA)**[4] 3064 4-9-3 **57** .... LPKeniry 3 61
(J M Bradley) *t.k.h: hld up bhd ldrs: cl up jst over 1f out: rdn and nt qckn ent fnl f* **5/1**[3]

-044 **7** *½* **Bold Argument (IRE)**[21] 2546 4-9-8 **62** .... JamesDoyle 7 64
(Mrs P N Dutfield) *towards rr: pushed along 1/2-way: last 2f out: styd on ins fnl f: nrst fin* **14/1**

3000 **8** *nk* **Triskaidekaphobia**[43] 1885 4-9-2 **56** .... (t) DaneO'Neill 1 57
(Miss J R Tooth) *led to jst over 1f out: fdd and lost several pls last 100yds* **11/1**

6-50 **9** *½* **Sparkwell**[168] 154 5-9-8 **62** .... SteveDrowne 9 61
(D Shaw) *hld up in rr: plenty to do whn wd bnd 2f out: kpt on one pce and no ch after* **8/1**

1-0 **10** *2* **That's Blue Chip**[42] 1914 4-9-4 **58** .... PatDobbs 2 50
(P W D'Arcy) *hld up in rr: rdn and no prog 2f out: wknd fnl f* **6/1**

58.54 secs (-1.24) **Going Correction** -0.15s/f (Stan) **10** Ran SP% **124.2**
Speed ratings (Par 101):103,101,101,100,99 99,98,98,97,94
CSF £19.84 CT £99.66 TOTE £7.00: £2.00, £1.80, £3.30; EX 23.30.
Owner The Kennet Connection **Bred** R Withers **Trained** Lockeridge, Wilts

FOCUS
Modest sprint handicap form, rated through the fourth. The winner has a good record here.

3191 HICKMOTT H'CAP — 1m (P)
9:00 (9:01) (Class 6) (0-65,65) 3-Y-0+ **£3,238** (£963; £481; £240) **Stalls** High

Form RPR

1512 **1** **Nan Jan**[3] 3110 5-9-8 **62** .... (t) RobertHavlin 11 71+
(R Ingram) *restrained to rr after 1f: effrt and nt clr run briefly over 2f out: gd prog over 1f out: r.o wl to ld last 50yds* **13/8**[1]

6000 **2** *nk* **High Class Problem (IRE)**[15] 2721 4-9-6 **60** .... (t) TQuinn 10 68
(P F I Cole) *pressed ldr: led wl over 1f out: edgd rt: drvn and hdd last 50yds* **16/1**

-000 **3** *½* **Fateful Attraction**[15] 2716 4-9-8 **62** .... (b) JamesDoyle 5 69
(I A Wood) *hld up towards rr: gd prog wl over 1f out: styd on fnl f: nt quite pce to chal* **33/1**

0300 **4** *1 ¼* **Moon Bird**[80] 1038 5-9-2 **56** .... EddieAhern 1 60
(C A Cyzer) *trckd ldrs: poised to chal gng easily over 1f out: sn rdn and fnd nil* **16/1**

63-0 **5** *1 ½* **Greenmeadow**[32] 2194 5-9-7 **61** .... LPKeniry 2 62
(S Kirk) *hld up in midfield on inner: effrt 2f out: rdn and kpt on same pce fr over 1f out* **25/1**

0032 **6** *¾* **Scuba (IRE)**[12] 2802 5-8-13 **58** .... (b) TravisBlock[(5)] 9 57
(H Morrison) *hld up towards rr: plld wd and drvn 3f out: struggling after: kpt on fnl f* **10/3**[2]

2045 **7** *hd* **Capricho (IRE)**[18] 2626 10-9-8 **62** .... (b) PaulDoe 7 61
(J Akehurst) *hld up in rr: nt qckn 2f out: kpt on same pce after: n.d* **15/2**[3]

0014 **8** *1* **Crafty Fox**[28] 2331 4-9-5 **59** .... (v) PatDobbs 3 55
(A P Jarvis) *trckd ldng pair to over 2f out: lost pl: one pce u.p fr over 1f out* **16/1**

-063 **9** *1 ¾* **Material Witness (IRE)**[18] 2626 10-9-11 **65** .... MartinDwyer 12 57
(W R Muir) *led to wl over 1f out: wknd fnl f* **8/1**

1510 **10** *3* **Nikki Bea (IRE)**[13] 2771 4-9-11 **65** .... IanMongan 6 50
(Jamie Poulton) *t.k.h: prom: rdn and cl up over 2f out: wkng whn sltly hmpd over 1f out* **8/1**

000/ **11** *nk* **Nesnaas (USA)**[15] 3180 6-9-11 **65** .... JimCrowley 8 50
(M G Rimell) *hld up in last pair: outpcd over 2f out: no ch after* **20/1**

0-00 **12** *6* **And I**[24] 2472 4-9-9 **63** .... SimonWhitworth 4 34
(C A Horgan) *taken down early: s.s: plld hrd and hld up on outer: effrt 3f out: wknd 2f out* **50/1**

1m 38.13s (-1.30) **Going Correction** -0.15s/f (Stan) **12** Ran SP% **126.3**
Speed ratings (Par 101):100,99,99,97,96 95,95,94,92,89 89,83
CSF £33.36 CT £697.03 TOTE £2.70: £1.50, £3.70, £5.90; EX 60.10 Place 6 £148.71, Place 5 £30.44..
Owner The Waltons **Bred** Mrs S Ingram **Trained** Epsom, Surrey
■ Stewards' Enquiry : Eddie Ahern two-day ban: careless riding (Jul 14,15)

FOCUS
A modest but competitive handicap. Solid form, the winner not having to run to her recent Wolverhampton figure. The next three are all on fair marks.
T/Plt: £220.70 to a £1 stake. Pool: £74,070.85. 245.00 winning tickets. T/Qpdt: £21.60 to a £1 stake. Pool: £6,347.80. 217.40 winning tickets. JN

2738 THIRSK (L-H)
Tuesday, July 3

OFFICIAL GOING: Soft (heavy in places; 5.5)
After the meeting survived an inspection there were wholesale withdrawals, 28 in all. The ground was described as 'wet, very soft, heavy in places'.
Wind: moderate 1/2 behind Weather: mainly fine but becoming overcast

3192 HOUSE DESIGNER WEAR MAIDEN STKS — 6f
6:15 (6:15) (Class 5) 2-Y-0 **£3,238** (£963; £481; £240) **Stalls** High

Form RPR

1 **Sir Gerry (USA)** 2-9-3 0 .... JamieSpencer 11 92+
(J R Fanshawe) *stdd s: hdwy over 2f out: shkn up to ld jst ins fnl f: r.o strly* **2/1**[1]

2 *3* **Imperial Mint (IRE)** 2-9-3 0 .... DO'Donohoe 16 83+
(K A Ryan) *w ldrs: led 3f out tl jst ins fnl f: no ex* **3/1**[2]

022 **3** *hd* **Ink Spot**[29] 2303 2-9-3 0 .... JoeFanning 2 79+
(M L W Bell) *chsd ldrs: hmpd over 2f out: kpt on wl fnl f* **10/3**[3]

4 *3* **Annaliesse (IRE)** 2-8-9 0 .... JamieMoriarty[(3)] 8 65
(R A Fahey) *swvd lft s: mid-div: kpt on fnl 2f: nvr rchd ldrs* **14/1**

5 *1* **Red Delight (IRE)** 2-8-12 0 .... PaulFessey 1 62
(R A Fahey) *mid-div: styd on fnl 2f: nt rch ldrs* **28/1**

0 **6** *3 ½* **Straight (IRE)**[86] 952 2-9-3 0 .... DeanMernagh 13 57
(M Brittain) *mid-div: kpt on fnl 2f: nvr nr ldrs* **66/1**

0 **7** *1* **Paint Stripper**[5] 3024 2-8-12 0 .... MichaelJStainton[(5)] 4 54
(W Storey) *unruly and uns rdr on way to s: led: hung lft and hdd 3f out: hung bdly lft and lost pl over 1f out* **66/1**

8 *1 ¾* **Strictly Elsie (IRE)** 2-8-12 0 .... PaddyAspell 6 44+
(J R Norton) *hmpd s: nvr a factor* **66/1**

9 *nk* **Lady See (IRE)** 2-8-9 0 .... DuranFentiman[(3)] 17 43
(T D Easterby) *w ldrs: lost pl over 2f out* **40/1**

0 **10** *1* **Mimton (IRE)**[81] 1029 2-8-12 0 .... DavidAllan 18 40
(N Wilson) *w ldrs: wknd over 2f out* **40/1**

11 *10* **Resolute Defender (IRE)** 2-9-3 0 .... KDarley 20 15
(J Howard Johnson) *s.i.s: a bhd* **12/1**

04 **12** *1 ½* **Powys Lad**[10] 2863 2-9-3 0 .... PatCosgrave 12 10
(K R Burke) *s.s: a in rr* **18/1**

13 *2* **Weetfromthechaff** 2-8-12 0 .... RussellKennemore[(5)] 9 4
(R Hollinshead) *mid-div: hdwy over 2f out: sn edgd lft and lost pl* **28/1**

1m 15.61s (3.11) **Going Correction** +0.40s/f (Good) **13** Ran SP% **117.3**
Speed ratings (Par 94):95,91,90,86,85 80,79,77,76,75 62,60,57
CSF £7.22 TOTE £2.40: £1.60, £2.00, £1.10; EX 9.50.
Owner Mrs Gerry Galligan **Bred** Dr Catherine Wills **Trained** Newmarket, Suffolk

FOCUS
A fair maiden two-year-old race and a winner of real potential. A promising debut from the runner-up too, with the third the key to the overall value of the form.

NOTEBOOK
Sir Gerry(USA) ◆, a leggy, athletic newcomer, cost 100,000gns at the breeze-up sales. Dropped in at the start and making his way towards the stands'-side rail, he looked very inexperienced when asked to go and claim the prize but in the end he pulled clear. He looks potentially very useful. (op 7-4 tchd 13-8, 9-4 in places)
Imperial Mint(IRE), a lengthy, well-made newcomer, cost 52,000gns at the breeze-up sales. He knew his job but in the end the winner saw it out much the better in the conditions. He looks sure to go one better. (op 9-2)
Ink Spot, easily the most experienced in the line-up, stuck on strongly and will be suited by a step up to seven. (tchd 7-2)
Annaliesse(IRE), a neat April foal, stuck on in her own time after going sideways at the start. This will have opened her eyes. (tchd 16-1)
Red Delight(IRE), a late-April foal, is a close-coupled newcomer. She put in some solid late work and this will have taught her plenty. (op 25-1)

3193 RECTANGLE GROUP H'CAP — 2m
6:45 (6:46) (Class 6) (0-60,58) 4-Y-0+ **£2,218** (£654; £327) **Stalls** Low

Form RPR

6235 **1** **Theflyingscottie**[10] 2890 5-8-6 **46** ow1 .... (v) DavidAllan 6 57
(D Shaw) *hld up in mid-div: hdwy over 3f out: led over 1f out: styd on wl* **9/2**[1]

0512 **2** *3* **Just Waz (USA)**[10] 2890 5-8-13 **58** .... MichaelJStainton[(5)] 4 65
(R M Whitaker) *trckd ldrs: wnt 2nd over 1f out: sn rdn: no imp* **9/2**[1]

6-10 **3** *2 ½* **Singhalongtasveer**[31] 2252 5-8-9 **49** .... PaulEddery 19 53
(G A Charlton) *sn wl in tch: effrt on outer 3f out: kpt on same pce* **7/1**[2]

0024 **4** *1* **Reason (IRE)**[5] 3012 9-8-8 **48** .... (b) JoeFanning 14 51
(D W Chapman) *in rr: hdwy over 4f out: staye don down wd outside fnl 3f: nvr rchd ldrs* **9/2**[1]

323- **5** *3* **Golden Groom**[279] 5618 4-8-9 **49** .... DeanMcKeown 7 48
(C W Fairhurst) *trckd ldrs: effrt over 3f out: one pce fnl 2f* **15/2**[3]

00-0 **6** *shd* **Sweet Lavinia**[27] 2372 4-8-3 **45** ow1 .... AndrewElliott[(3)] 18 45
(J D Bethell) *trckd ldrs: drvn over 4f out: one pce fnl 2f* **20/1**

00-0 **7** *6* **Farne Isle**[20] 2567 8-8-11 **51** .... (v[1]) PaddyAspell 13 43
(G A Harker) *hld up in rr: hdwy over 7f out: led over 5f out: hdd over 1f out: sn wknd* **33/1**

00-0 **8** *4* **Matinee Idol**[18] 1554 4-8-2 **45** .... DuranFentiman[(3)] 10 32
(Mrs S Lamyman) *hld up in rr: nvr on terms* **16/1**

3-40 **9** *nk* **Lucky Find (IRE)**[40] 1968 4-8-5 **45** .... SilvestreDeSousa 15 32
(M Mullineaux) *mid-div: drvn 5f out: lost pl over 3f out* **22/1**

0053 **10** *1* **Compton Commander**[11] 2839 9-7-12 **45** .... (p) DanielleMcCreery[(7)] 9 31
(E W Tuer) *hld up in rr: nvr on terms* **12/1**

0-03 **11** *2* **High Frequency (IRE)**[25] 2417 6-8-5 **45** .... (p) PaulFessey 2 28
(A Crook) *sn drvn along: led after 2f: hdd over 5f out: wknd and eased over 1f out* **20/1**

4255 **12** *8* **Mystified (IRE)**[15] 2715 4-8-5 **45** .... (p) DO'Donohoe 5 19
(R F Fisher) *led 2f: drvn 5f out: lost pl over 3f out: sn bhd* **12/1**

3m 45.48s (14.28) **Going Correction** +0.55s/f (Yiel) **12** Ran SP% **116.9**
Speed ratings (Par 101):86,84,83,82,81 81,78,76,76,75 74,70
CSF £21.67 CT £140.72 TOTE £5.90: £1.30, £1.80, £3.00; EX 22.10.
Owner Roger Milward **Bred** Mrs Rosamund Lane **Trained** Danethorpe, Notts

FOCUS
A low-grade stayers' handicap run at a funereal pace, resulting in a very slow winning time. The race has been rated through the runner-up and the form though limited seems sound enough.
High Frequency(IRE) Official explanation: jockey said gelding had no more to give

3194 WEATHERBYS BLOODSTOCK INSURANCE H'CAP — 7f
7:15 (7:16) (Class 5) (0-75,74) 3-Y-0+ **£3,238** (£963; £481; £240) **Stalls** Low

Form RPR

6301 **1** **Skyelady**[11] 2827 4-9-5 **72** .... NeilBrown[(7)] 12 83
(T D Barron) *hld up in rr: stdy hdwy on outer over 2f out: led jst ins fnl f: r.o wl* **9/2**[2]

6/-0 **2** *1* **Zamalik (USA)**[39] 1995 4-9-5 **65** .... KDarley 16 73
(E J Alston) *mid-div: hdwy on outer over 2f out: chal jst ins fnl f: no ex* **25/1**

6615 **3** *2* **The Osteopath (IRE)**[14] 2741 4-9-13 **73** .... (p) JamieSpencer 15 76
(M Dods) *hld up in rr: hdwy on outside over 2f out: hung rt: kpt on wl fnl f* **4/1**[1]

25-6 **4** *shd* **Moonhawk**[46] 1804 4-9-6 **66** .... JoeFanning 10 69
(J Howard Johnson) *chsd ldrs: led over 1f out: hdd jst ins fnl f: no ex* **14/1**

0561 **5** *1 ¼* **Efidium**[11] 2842 9-9-0 **67** .... GihanArnolda[(7)] 1 66
(N Bycroft) *s.i.s: hdwy on outer 2f out: nvr rchd ldrs* **11/1**

2-05 **6** *nk* **Scotland The Brave**[15] 2719 7-9-7 **67** .... (v) PatCosgrave 5 66
(J D Bethell) *chsd ldrs: drvn over 3f out: one pce* **15/2**

6001 **7** *1* **Petite Mac**[10] 2893 7-8-8 **57** .... AndrewElliott[(3)] 2 53
(N Bycroft) *mid-div: effrt over 3f out: nvr nr ldrs* **11/1**

0040 **8** *nk* **Mozakhraf (USA)**[11] 2827 5-9-1 **61** .... DO'Donohoe 3 56
(K A Ryan) *t.k.h: trckd ldrs: drvn 3f out: fdd fnl f* **20/1**

6412 **9** *1* **Viva Volta**[24] 2466 4-10-0 **74** .... DavidAllan 9 67
(T D Easterby) *led tl over 1f out: sn wknd* **5/1**[3]

-003 **10** *1 ½* **Sake (IRE)**[11] 2842 5-9-8 **68** .... KimTinkler 4 57
(N Tinkler) *sn prom: effrt 3f out: fdd fnl f* **9/1**

0005 **11** *1 ¾* **Time To Regret**[29] 2311 7-8-9 **58** .... (p) SaleemGolam[(3)] 8 42
(I W McInnes) *chsd ldrs: hrd drvn over 3f out: lost pl over 1f out* **12/1**

5-30 **12** *11* **Rigat**[11] 2842 4-9-8 **68** .... PaulFessey 11 24
(T D Barron) *s.s: a last: detached fnl 2f* **20/1**

1m 30.32s (3.22) **Going Correction** +0.55s/f (Yiel) **12** Ran SP% **121.0**
Speed ratings (Par 103):103,101,99,99,98 97,96,96,95,93 91,78
CSF £118.33 CT £412.20 TOTE £6.00: £2.60, £12.60, £1.80; EX 186.10.
Owner David W Armstrong **Bred** Manor Farm Stud (rutland) **Trained** Maunby, N Yorks

FOCUS
A modest handicap run at a sound pace in the conditions. The form, though limited, should work out.
Rigat Official explanation: jockey said gelding missed the break

The Form Book, Raceform Ltd, Compton, RG20 6NL

3195 RECTANGLE H'CAP — 1m
7:45 (7:45) (Class 6) (0-55,55) 3-Y-0+ £2,047 (£604; £302) Stalls Low

Form				RPR
0040	1		**Top Dirham**[15] [2714] 9-9-4 53 DaleGibson 8 (M W Easterby) *trckd ldrs: led on bit 2f out: shkn up and qckned 1f out: jst hld on* **6/1**[2]	59+
0062	2	hd	**Apache Point (IRE)**[11] [2843] 10-9-2 51 KimTinkler 13 (N Tinkler) *mid-div: hdwy 3f out: chal over 1f out: kpt on wl ins fnl f* **10/1**	55
0-03	3	nk	**Emperor's Well**[15] [2714] 8-8-9 51 (b) NSLawes(7) 4 (M W Easterby) *w ldrs: n.m.r and dropped bk over 2f out: styd on strly ins fnl f* **7/1**	57+
-205	4	shd	**Zhitomir**[10] [2893] 9-9-3 52 TomEaves 12 (M Dods) *hld up in rr: hdwy on outside over 2f out: styd on strly fnl f* **8/1**	55
0504	5	shd	**Volaticus (IRE)**[11] [2820] 6-9-6 55 SilvestreDeSousa 1 (A D Brown) *s.i.s: sn prom: styd on wl fnl f* **13/2**[3]	58
-010	6	1 3/4	**Coalite (IRE)**[20] [2561] 4-9-3 52 (p) DO'Donohoe 14 (A D Brown) *t.k.h in rr: effrt on outer over 2f out: kpt on fnl f* **20/1**	51
5006	7	2	**Methusaleh (IRE)**[10] [2893] 4-9-3 52 DeanMcKeown 10 (D Shaw) *bhd: styd on fnl 2f: nvr nr ldrs* **12/1**	46
5234	8	nk	**Nevinstown (IRE)**[12] [2809] 7-9-3 52 TonyHamilton 11 (C Grant) *sn prom: one pce fnl 2f* **12/1**	46
3661	9	3 1/2	**Guadaloup**[8] [2937] 5-9-4 53 6ex DeanMernagh 16 (M Brittain) *in rr: sme hdwy on outer over 2f out: nvr on terms* **9/1**	38
0365	10	3	**Machinate (USA)**[4] [3067] 5-9-4 53 JamieSpencer 9 (W M Brisbourne) *hld up towards rr: effrt and hung rt over 2f out: nvr nr ldrs: eased ins fnl f* **5/1**[1]	32
0-00	11	42	**Red Contact (USA)**[11] [2827] 6-9-0 54 (p) MichaelJStainton(5) 3 (A Dickman) *led tl 3f out: sn lost pl: virtually p.u fnl f: t.o* **20/1**	—
-006	12	1 3/4	**Pianoforte (USA)**[12] [2809] 5-9-6 55 KDarley 7 (E J Alston) *sn w ldrs: led 3f out: hdd 2f out: sn wknd: virtually p.u: t.o* **10/1**	—

1m 45.91s (6.21) **Going Correction** +0.55s/f (Yiel) 12 Ran SP% **121.0**
Speed ratings (Par 101):90,89,89,89,89 87,85,85,81,78 36,35
CSF £66.31 CT £437.04 TOTE £8.70: £2.50, £2.40, £3.70; EX 90.50.
Owner Steve Hull **Bred** Whitsbury Manor Stud **Trained** Sheriff Hutton, N Yorks
■ Stewards' Enquiry : Kim Tinkler caution: used whip with excessive frequency
Dale Gibson caution: used whip without giving gelding time to respond

FOCUS
A low-grade handicap run at a very steady pace, resulting in a very moderate winning time for the grade. A bunch finish mostly involving older horses, and very ordinary form.
Guadaloup Official explanation: jockey said mare ran flat
Machinate(USA) Official explanation: jockey said gelding hung right

3196 CALVERTS CARPETS H'CAP — 1m
8:15 (8:15) (Class 4) (0-85,84) 3-Y-0 £4,857 (£1,445; £722; £360) Stalls Low

Form				RPR
2221	1		**Milla's Rocket (IRE)**[127] [569] 3-8-10 73 (b) DO'Donohoe 8 (K A Ryan) *t.k.h: trckd ldrs: led 2f out: edgd rt: styd on wl* **12/1**	81
0600	2	2 1/2	**Osteopathic Remedy (IRE)**[11] [2841] 3-9-3 80 TomEaves 4 (M Dods) *hld up in rr: hdwy over 4f out: styd on same pce fnl 2f: no imp* **10/3**[2]	82
452	3	1 1/4	**Jibajaba (USA)**[12] [2792] 3-8-11 74 TonyHamilton 1 (R A Fahey) *hld up in mid-div: effrt 3f out: kpt on same pce fnl 2f* **11/1**	73
2-41	4	1 1/2	**Sign Of The Cross**[20] [2580] 3-9-5 82 JamieSpencer 6 (J R Fanshawe) *t.k.h: trckd ldrs: rdn over 2f out: kpt on fnl f* **5/4**[1]	78
53-0	5	1/2	**Snowflight**[46] [1804] 3-8-2 65 DaleGibson 2 (R A Fahey) *trckd ldrs: t.k.h: outpcd over 4f out: kpt on fnl 2f* **22/1**	60
0140	6	3 1/2	**Flores Sea (USA)**[20] [2577] 3-9-0 77 PaulFessey 5 (T D Barron) *hld up in rr: effrt over 3f out: nvr nr ldrs* **5/1**[3]	63
1-43	7	4	**Tencendur (IRE)**[75] [1110] 3-8-13 76 AdrianTNicholls 3 (D Nicholls) *set mod pce: qcknd over 4f out: hdd 2f out: sn wknd* **8/1**	53

1m 45.56s (5.86) **Going Correction** +0.55s/f (Yiel) 7 Ran SP% **115.7**
Speed ratings (Par 102):92,89,88,86,86 82,78
CSF £52.82 CT £462.37 TOTE £11.80: £4.60, £2.20; EX 75.00.
Owner Trevor C Stewart **Bred** James F Hanly **Trained** Hambleton, N Yorks

FOCUS
A slowly-run race to past halfway, resulting in a modest winning time. The winner is progressive but the form does not look entirely reliable.
Sign Of The Cross Official explanation: jockey said colt ran too free in the early stages
Tencendur(IRE) Official explanation: jockey said gelding hung right

3197 LADIES EVENING H'CAP — 5f
8:45 (8:46) (Class 4) (0-85,86) 3-Y-0+ £4,857 (£1,445; £722; £360) Stalls High

Form				RPR
-121	1		**How's She Cuttin' (IRE)**[24] [2461] 4-9-9 80 (b) PaulFessey 13 (T D Barron) *w ldrs: led over 1f out: kpt on wl towards fin* **9/4**[1]	94
3000	2	3/4	**Bond Boy**[11] [2841] 10-8-11 75 (b) SladeO'Hara(7) 4 (G R Oldroyd) *sn chsng ldrs: hung lft over 1f out: no ex wl ins fnl f* **15/2**	86
2351	3	1 1/4	**Mimi Mouse**[29] [2315] 5-9-10 81 DavidAllan 1 (T D Easterby) *sn chsng ldrs on outer: kpt on same pce fnl f* **7/2**[2]	88
5010	4	3/4	**Highland Warrior**[4] [3053] 8-8-7 78 MickyFenton 6 (P T Midgley) *hld up in tch stands' rail: effrt 2f out: hung lft: kpt on fnl f* **9/1**	82
-030	5	shd	**Matty Tun**[5] [3014] 8-8-13 70 RoystonFfrench 7 (J Balding) *rrd s: hdwy and swtchd lft 2f out: kpt on same pce fnl f* **13/2**	74+
0100	6	4	**Colorus (IRE)**[10] [2866] 4-9-6 77 DaleGibson 5 (M W Easterby) *t.k.h: led tl over 1f out: sn wknd* **16/1**	66
-010	7	2 1/2	**Sahara Silk (IRE)**[17] [2657] 6-8-3 67 (v) KellyHarrison(7) 8 (D Shaw) *chsd ldrs: hung lft and lost pl over 1f out* **25/1**	47
1-10	8	3/4	**Valery Borzov (IRE)**[75] [1108] 3-9-6 82 AdrianTNicholls 3 (D Nicholls) *sn chsng ldrs: hung bdly and lost pl 1f out: eased* **4/1**[3]	60

61.52 secs (1.62) **Going Correction** +0.40s/f (Good)
WFA 3 from 4yo+ 5lb 8 Ran SP% **117.8**
Speed ratings (Par 105):103,101,99,98,98 92,88,86
CSF £20.79 CT £58.91 TOTE £2.90: £1.50, £2.30, £1.60; EX 24.10 Place 6 £56.82, Place 5 £50.30..
Owner Chris McHale **Bred** A M Burke **Trained** Maunby, N Yorks

FOCUS
A tight-knit sprint handicap and the progressive winner was helped by being able to race against the stands'-side rail. The form looks rock solid.
Valery Borzov(IRE) Official explanation: jockey said gelding hung left
T/Plt: £85.90 to a £1 stake. Pool: £80,557.10. 684.50 winning tickets. T/Qpdt: £89.80 to a £1 stake. Pool: £3,944.00. 32.50 winning tickets. WG

[2416] CATTERICK (L-H)
Wednesday, July 4

OFFICIAL GOING: Good to soft (soft in places; 6.5)
Wind: Breezy across Weather: Overcast

3199 EUROPEAN BREEDERS' FUND ZETLAND MEDIAN AUCTION MAIDEN STKS (DIV I) — 7f
2:35 (2:35) (Class 5) 2-Y-0 £2,590 (£770; £385; £192) Stalls Low

Form				RPR
0	1		**Sourire**[9] [2949] 2-8-12 0 PaulMulrennan 8 (Sir Mark Prescott) *cl up: rdn along and outpcd 2f out: styd on u.p ins fnl f to ld nr line* **5/1**[3]	81+
	2	nk	**Gothenburg (UAE)** 2-9-3 0 JoeFanning 1 (M Johnston) *led: pushed clr 2f out: rdn and idled ins fnl f: hdd nr fin* **11/4**[2]	85+
	3	6	**Midnight Muse (USA)** 2-9-3 0 PaulFessey 2 (T D Barron) *chsd ldrs on inner: rdn along 2f out: sn no imp* **9/1**	70
3	4	1 1/4	**Silk Drum (IRE)**[13] [2804] 2-9-3 0 TomEaves 3 (J Howard Johnson) *trckd ldrs: effrt 3f out: sn rdn and no hdwy fnl 2f* **2/1**[1]	67
342	5	7	**Demure Princess**[13] [2803] 2-8-5 0 JackDean(7) 6 (W G M Turner) *chsd ldrs: rdn along over 2f out: sn wknd* **8/1**	45
	6	2 1/2	**What's For Tea** 2-8-12 0 DavidAllan 7 (T D Easterby) *dwlt: hdwy 1/2-way: rdn along over 2f out and sn no imp* **25/1**	38
500	7	1/2	**Majigal**[23] [2504] 2-8-5 0 NSLawes(7) 4 (M W Easterby) *in tch: effrt 3f out: sn rdn and wknd 2f out* **33/1**	37
	8	4	**Sheer Fantastic** 2-9-3 0 KDarley 5 (P C Haslam) *s.i.s: a bhd* **11/1**	32
0	9	3 1/2	**Horologist**[15] [2739] 2-9-3 0 DaleGibson 10 (M W Easterby) *s.i.s: sme hdwy 1/2-way: sn rdn and wknd* **80/1**	23

1m 29.27s (1.91) **Going Correction** +0.25s/f (Good) 9 Ran SP% **114.1**
Speed ratings (Par 94):99,98,91,90,82 79,78,74,70
CSF £18.66 TOTE £6.80: £2.00, £1.90, £2.00; EX 26.80.
Owner Miss K Rausing **Bred** Miss K Rausing **Trained** Newmarket, Suffolk

FOCUS
Quite a good maiden for the track. The pace was strong and the winning time was 0.36 seconds faster than the second division. Improved form from the winner, the first two pulling clear.

NOTEBOOK
Sourire ◆ found 6f an inadequate test on her debut at Wolverhampton and this longer trip was much more suitable. Having chased the early leader Gothenburg from the start, she was outpaced when that one kicked for home off the final bend and looked booked for second at best, but she responded gamely to pressure in the straight, gradually grasping what was required to get up in the shadow of the post. This was a useful effort and she gives the impression she can take another significant step forward next time. (op 11-2 tchd 6-1)
Gothenburg(UAE) ◆, a half-brother to Just Do It, who was placed over 1m at two, out of a mare who placed over 1m1f, knew his job and was soon taking the field along at a strong pace, making full use of his inside draw. He looked to have the race in the bag at the top of the straight, but got tired late on and was just reeled in. This rates as a useful effort in defeat and, even if he is not open to as much basic improvement as some of these, that's not to say he can't progress with racing. He should be very hard to beat in similar company next time. (op 3-1 tchd 10-3 in a place)
Midnight Muse(USA), an $18,000 son of dual King George winner Swain, half-brother to useful 7f juvenile winner Holocene, out of a winner over 1m2f, made a pleasing debut in third. He was left behind by the front two in the straight, but kept on nicely for a fair third and should be able to build on this. (op 16-1)
Silk Drum(IRE) produced a laboured effort, making this look like real hard work, and was never going to justify his place at the head of the market. Perhaps headgear might sharpen him up. (tchd 9-4 in a place)
Demure Princess seemed to race a touch keenly on this step up in trip and she did not get home. (op 6-1)

3200 EUROPEAN BREEDERS' FUND MAIDEN FILLIES' STKS — 5f
3:05 (3:06) (Class 5) 2-Y-0 £3,562 (£1,059; £529; £264) Stalls Low

Form				RPR
46	1		**Bohobe (IRE)**[12] [2819] 2-9-0 0 JoeFanning 6 (J G Given) *in tch far side: hdwy 2f out: rdn to ld over 1f out: styd on strly* **14/1**	74
6	2	1 1/4	**Alabama Spirit (USA)**[40] [1992] 2-8-11 0 DuranFentiman(3) 10 (K R Burke) *trckd ldrs far side: hdwy 2f out: sn rdn and kpt on ins fnl f* **12/1**	70
06	3	1	**Linnet Park**[28] [2365] 2-9-0 0 KDarley 7 (J G Given) *cl up far side: rdn to ld that gp and overall ldr 2f out: drvn and hdd over 1f out: one pce* **20/1**	66
45	4	shd	**Choisette**[13] [2803] 2-9-0 0 TomEaves 2 (B Smart) *overall ldr far side: rdn along 1/2-way: sn hdd and kpt on same pce appr fnl f* **10/1**	66
634	5	1 1/2	**Eastern Romance**[11] [2869] 2-9-0 0 NCallan 12 (K A Ryan) *trckd ldr stands' side: hdwy 2f out sn rdn to ld stands' side over 1f out: kpt on same pce fnl f* **11/4**[2]	60+
	6	2 1/2	**Mey Blossom** 2-9-0 0 DeanMcKeown 13 (R M Whitaker) *led stands' side gp: rdn and ev ch 2f out: hdd & wknd over 1f out* **16/1**	51+
P	7	1 1/4	**Everything**[40] [1993] 2-9-0 0 LeeEnstone 8 (P T Midgley) *sn outpcd and a in rr* **100/1**	47
00	8	1 1/2	**Ephesian (IRE)**[51] [1727] 2-9-0 0 DO'Donohoe 5 (Mrs A Duffield) *s.i.s and a in rr* **66/1**	41
20	9	1 1/2	**Drastic Measure**[7] [2997] 2-9-0 0 DavidAllan 1 (Sir Mark Prescott) *prom far side: rdn along 2f out and sn wknd* **5/2**[1]	36
	10	3/4	**Maahe (IRE)** 2-9-0 0 TonyHamilton 4 (R A Fahey) *racd far side: a towards rr* **13/2**[3]	33
	11	5	**Bahamian Ballad** 2-9-0 0 PatCosgrave 3 (J D Bethell) *a in rr far side* **18/1**	15
0	12	2	**Miss Deeds (IRE)**[12] [2812] 2-9-0 0 PaulMulrennan 11 (N P Littmoden) *chsd ldrs far side: rdn along over 2f out and sn wknd* **8/1**	8

61.60 secs (1.00) **Going Correction** +0.10s/f (Good) 12 Ran SP% **121.5**
Speed ratings (Par 91):96,94,92,92,89 85,83,81,79,77 69,66
CSF £173.66 TOTE £15.50: £3.70, £3.70, £5.60; EX 173.20.
Owner P A Horton,M J Beadle & I Booth **Bred** Bryan Ryan **Trained** Willoughton, Lincs

FOCUS
A very modest fillies' maiden, but improved form from the first four. Both Eastern Romance and Mey Blossom tried their luck against the stands' rail in the straight, but the much larger group towards the far side held sway.

NOTEBOOK

Bohobe(IRE) stepped up on the form she showed in a couple of 6f maidens, proving suited by the drop back to the minimum trip. She was a clear-cut winner, but this was a modest contest and her connections will no doubt be hoping the Handicapper does not overreact.

Alabama Spirit(USA), whose debut sixth at Haydock represented just moderate form, has clearly gone the right way since then. She might find a weak maiden, but is probably more of a nursery type. (op 10-1 tchd 14-1)

Linnet Park, a stablemate of the winner, ran with credit in third and will have more options now she is eligible for nurseries. (op 16-1)

Choisette is another who may benefit from a switch to nurseries now she is eligible. (op 7-1)

Eastern Romance was taken over to the stands' side soon after the start, but she only had one other filly to race with and was seemingly on the slower ground. (op 3-1 tchd 10-3 and 7-2 in places)

Mey Blossom ◆, a Captain Rio half-sister to 1m winner Tahilah, and 7f scorer Paris Heights, had little chance as it turned out racing on the stands' side with only Eastern Romance to keep her company, but she showed ability. She just got tired late on and, with improvement likely, it would be unwise to underestimate her in similar company next time. (op 20-1)

Drastic Measure again failed to build on the form she showed when second in a weak maiden at Leicester on her debut. She is in danger of becoming disappointing, but it would be silly to underestimate a horse from the Prescott yard now qualified for handicaps. (op 11-4 tchd 7-2 and 4-1 in a place)

Miss Deeds(IRE) Official explanation: jockey said filly was unsuited by the track

3201 CATTERICKBRIDGE.CO.UK H'CAP 7f
3:35 (3:35) (Class 3) (0-90,86) 3-Y-O+ £7,124 (£2,119; £1,059; £529) Stalls Low

Form RPR

5654 **1** **Countdown**[12] [2841] 5-9-5 **77** ... DavidAllan 4 89
(T D Easterby) *in tch and pushed along 1/2-way: hdwy 2f out: sn rdn and styd on wl to ld ins fnl f: sn clr* **2/1**[1]

0506 **2** *2 1/2* **Wavertree Warrior (IRE)**[18] [2670] 5-10-0 **86** ... NCallan 8 91
(N P Littmoden) *trckd ldrs on outer: hdwy over 2f out: rdn to ld 1 1/2f out: hdd ins fnl f: kpt on same pce* **8/1**

0004 **3** *1 1/2* **Campo Bueno (FR)**[11] [2871] 5-8-10 **68** ...(b) JoeFanning 9 69
(A Berry) *hld up: hdwy on outer wl over 2f out: rdn and ch wl over 1f out: drvn and one pce ent fnl f* **10/1**

31-4 **4** *2* **Grand Opera (IRE)**[60] [1481] 4-9-2 **74** ... TomEaves 2 70
(J Howard Johnson) *s.i.s and bhd tl styd on u.p fnl 2f* **14/1**

1-61 **5** *shd* **Amy Louise (IRE)**[15] [2742] 4-9-9 **81** ... KDarley 5 76
(T D Barron) *cl up: led 3f out: sn rdn and hdd 1 1/2f out: wknd* **3/1**[2]

0-51 **6** *nk* **Secret Liaison**[14] [2771] 4-9-13 **85** ... PaulMulrennan 7 79
(Sir Mark Prescott) *trckd ldrs: effrt over 2f out: sn rdn and wknd wl over 1f out* **6/1**[3]

-020 **7** *1/2* **King Harson**[25] [2466] 8-9-5 **77** ... PatCosgrave 6 70
(J D Bethell) *led: rdn along and hdd 3f out: sn drvn and grad wknd* **12/1**

1005 **8** *1/2* **King Marju (IRE)**[26] [2419] 5-8-7 **68** ...(v) AndrewElliott(3) 3 60
(K R Burke) *t.k.h: chsd ldrs on inner: rdn along wl over 2f out: grad wknd* **10/1**

1m 27.89s (0.53) **Going Correction** +0.25s/f (Good) 8 Ran SP% **116.3**
Speed ratings (Par 107):106,103,101,99,99 98,98,97
CSF £19.29 CT £131.84 TOTE £2.80: £1.40, £2.50, £2.70; EX 24.40.
Owner David W Armstrong **Bred** Lady Fairhaven **Trained** Great Habton, N Yorks

FOCUS

A fair little handicap for the grade and sound enough form.

NOTEBOOK

Countdown has been crying out for a return to 7f and, with the ground suitably on the soft side, he returned to the scene of his last success to bounce back to winning ways. He won easily in the end, but he has struggled off marks in the 80s in the past so might not find things easy once reassessed. (op 5-2)

Wavertree Warrior(IRE) keeps slipping down the weights but he remains above his last winning turf mark. He ran well but might need to drop a little further in the ratings before he begins winning again.

Campo Bueno(FR), who ran quite well off marks in the 80s last autumn, ought to be competitive off his current rating, so this was only a fair effort. Soft ground does seem to be essential to him. (tchd 11-1)

Grand Opera(IRE) would not have found this sharp track ideal. He was staying on late in the day and will appreciate a return to a stiffer course. (op 12-1)

Amy Louise(IRE) normally contests weaker fillies-only handicaps, and she had more on her plate here against the boys. It would be dangerous to write her off back against her own sex off this sort of mark. Official explanation: trainer said filly ran too free early stages (op 5-2 tchd10-3 in a place)

Secret Liaison, 3lb higher than when winning on the Polytrack at Kempton last time, was a bit disappointing, even allowing for the softish ground. Official explanation: jockey said gelding never travelled (op 13-2 tchd 5-1)

3202 WE RACE AGAIN NEXT WEDNESDAY MEDIAN AUCTION MAIDEN STKS 5f 212y
4:05 (4:08) (Class 6) 3-4-Y-O £2,730 (£806; £403) Stalls Low

Form RPR

-220 **1** **Onatopp (IRE)**[22] [2534] 3-8-12 69 ... DavidAllan 9 59+
(T D Easterby) *sn led: rdn clr wl over 1f out: styd on wl* **1/1**[1]

-040 **2** *2 1/2* **Beaumont Boy**[41] [1964] 3-9-3 53 ... NCallan 3 54
(G A Swinbank) *in tch: hdwy over 2f out: sn rdn and styd on to chse wnr appr fnl f: no imp* **4/1**[2]

060- **3** *1/2* **Heidi Hi**[302] [5076] 3-8-12 55 ... PaulFessey 4 48
(J R Turner) *bhd hdwy over 2f out: n.m.r and swtchd lft wl over 1f out: styd on strly ins fnl f* **28/1**

0303 **4** *3/4* **Rue Soleil**[11] [2895] 3-8-9 55 ... JamieMoriarty(3) 7 45
(J R Weymes) *in tch: hdwy to chse ldrs over 2f out and sn rdn: drvn and kpt on same pce ins fnl f* **10/1**

056 **5** *3* **Caluba**[25] [2464] 3-8-12 65 ... PatCosgrave 12 36
(K R Burke) *in tch: hdwy to chse wnr wl over 2f out: drvn and wknd wl over 1f out* **8/1**

6 **6** *shd* **Red Barnet**[20] [2606] 3-9-3 0 ... DaleGibson 1 41
(M W Easterby) *rdn along to chse ldrs on inner: drvn over 2f out and plugged on same pce* **5/1**[3]

7 *5* **Very Wise Kid** 4-9-4 0 ... LeeEnstone 2 21
(P T Midgley) *sn outpcd and a bhd* **40/1**

00 **8** *1* **Recovery Mission**[30] [2312] 3-9-0 0 ... AndrewElliott(3) 5 23
(G M Moore) *a towards rr* **100/1**

0- **9** *2 1/2* **Whats Your Game (IRE)**[362] [3247] 3-9-3 0 ... TomEaves 11 15
(A Berry) *prom on outer: rdn along over 2f out: grad wknd* **20/1**

00 **10** *3* **Ducal Regancy Red**[39] [2032] 3-8-5 0 ... KellyHarrison(7) 10 1
(C J Teague) *a in rr* **100/1**

11 *9* **Bella Grande** 3-8-12 0 ... DO'Donohoe 6 —
(Garry Moss) *a bhd* **50/1**

1m 15.88s (1.88) **Going Correction** +0.25s/f (Good)
WFA 3 from 4yo 6lb 11 Ran SP% **121.5**
Speed ratings (Par 101):97,93,93,92,88 87,81,79,76,72 60
CSF £5.06 TOTE £1.90: £1.10, £1.80, £4.90; EX 8.80.
Owner David Lowrey **Bred** Mrs Kerstin Sundgren **Trained** Great Habton, N Yorks

FOCUS

A weak maiden in which the winner did not need to be at her best.

3203 TELEPHONE 01748 810165 FOR RACEDAY HOSPITALITY H'CAP 5f
4:35 (4:35) (Class 5) (0-70,70) 3-Y-O+ £3,238 (£963; £481; £240) Stalls Low

Form RPR

4-03 **1** **Dark Champion**[26] [2421] 7-8-6 **53** ...(v) MarkLawson(3) 13 65
(R E Barr) *in tch: hdwy on outer 2f out: rdn to chal ent fnl f: drvn and kpt on to ld nr fin* **7/1**

0632 **2** *hd* **Rothesay Dancer**[9] [2933] 4-8-0 **51** oh1 ... KellyHarrison(7) 14 62
(J S Goldie) *hld up towards rr: gd hdwy on outer 2f out: rdn ent fnl f: led fnl 100yds: edgd lft and hdd nr fin* **13/2**[3]

0413 **3** *1 1/4* **Miacarla**[9] [2933] 4-8-7 **51** oh1 ... TonyHamilton 5 58
(A Berry) *trckd ldrs: hdwy 1/2-way: rdn to ld jst ins fnl f: sn drvn: hdd and no ex fnl 100yds* **15/2**

0-06 **4** *1* **King Egbert (FR)**[29] [2334] 6-8-7 **51** ... JoeFanning 6 54+
(R J Price) *hmpd s: hdwy 2f out: rdn and styd on wl fnl f: nrst fin* **5/1**[1]

0656 **5** *3/4* **Dunn Deal (IRE)**[4] [3106] 7-8-7 **51** oh4 ... PaulQuinn 11 51
(J Balding) *bhd: hdwy wl over 1f out: rdn and styd on ins fnl f: nrst fin* **20/1**

3100 **6** *nk* **Whinhill House**[25] [2461] 7-9-1 **59** ...(p) PatCosgrave 8 58
(D W Barker) *cl up: led over 2f out: sn rdn: drvn and hdd jst ins fnl f: wknd* **10/1**

1235 **7** *1 3/4* **Spirit Of Coniston**[16] [2712] 4-8-8 **55** ...(b) DuranFentiman(3) 9 48
(C J Teague) *towards rr: effrt 2f out: sn rdn and kpt on u.p ins fnl f* **10/1**

0244 **8** *shd* **Sharp Hat**[12] [2830] 13-8-7 **51** oh2 ... DaleGibson 1 43
(D W Chapman) *led: rdn along and hdd over 2f out: drvn and wknd appr fnl f* **10/1**

5220 **9** *1 3/4* **Mulligan's Gold (IRE)**[16] [2712] 4-9-7 **65** ... DavidAllan 15 51
(T D Easterby) *a towards rr* **6/1**[2]

0500 **10** *1 1/4* **Taboor (IRE)**[23] [2509] 9-8-7 **51** oh1 ... AdrianTNicholls 2 33
(R M H Cowell) *a in rr* **12/1**

-000 **11** *1* **Vanadium**[37] [2088] 5-9-12 **70** ... TomEaves 10 48
(J G Given) *cl up: rdn along 1/2-way: sn wknd* **16/1**

0060 **12** *1 3/4* **Minimum Fuss (IRE)**[21] [2553] 3-7-11 **51** oh4 ...(b) NicolPolli(5) 12 23
(M C Chapman) *rrd s: t.k.h and a in rr* **66/1**

4065 **13** *6* **Pirner's Brig**[9] [2948] 3-9-0 **63** ...(b) PaulMulrennan 7 13
(M W Easterby) *cl up: rdn along 1/2-way: sn wknd* **25/1**

61.10 secs (0.50) **Going Correction** +0.10s/f (Good)
WFA 3 from 4yo+ 5lb 13 Ran SP% **119.5**
Speed ratings (Par 103):100,99,97,96,94 94,91,91,88,86 85,82,72
CSF £51.02 CT £368.39 TOTE £7.80: £2.50, £2.60, £2.70; EX 40.70 Trifecta £172.90 Pool £487.10. - 2 winning units.
Owner A Suddes **Bred** R G Percival **Trained** Seamer, N Yorks

FOCUS

A moderate sprint handicap, but the time was decent and the form should prove sound. The whole field raced towards the far side but the first two home were drawn high and raced towards the outside of the pack.

Mulligan's Gold(IRE) Official explanation: jockey said gelding hung left throughout

3204 STOCKTON H'CAP 1m 3f 214y
5:05 (5:06) (Class 6) (0-65,65) 4-Y-O+ £2,730 (£806; £403) Stalls Low

Form RPR

0-02 **1** **Turn Of Phrase (IRE)**[5] [3049] 8-9-0 **58** ...(b) TomEaves 13 68+
(B Ellison) *trckd ldrs: smooth hdwy to ld 4f out: rdn clr 2f out: comf* **3/1**[2]

-354 **2** *2* **William John**[16] [2715] 4-8-8 **55** ...(t) AndrewElliott(3) 6 61+
(P C Haslam) *midfield: hdwy 6f out: effrt 3f out: rdn 2f out: kpt on ins fnl f* **13/2**

/00- **3** *2* **Rifleman (IRE)**[32] [5972] 7-8-11 **55** ...(tp) PaulMulrennan 10 58
(D W Thompson) *led 1f: styd prom: effrt to chse wnr over 2f out: drvn wl over 1f out and kpt on same pce* **20/1**

3044 **4** *3 1/2* **Moyne Pleasure (IRE)**[18] [1934] 9-7-13 **46** oh1...(p) DuranFentiman(3) 12 43
(R Johnson) *hld up: towards rr: hdwy on outer 3f out: rdn along 2f out: styd on appr fnl f: nrst fin* **16/1**

6612 **5** *1* **Press Express (IRE)**[15] [2743] 5-9-1 **62** ... JamieMoriarty(3) 2 57
(R A Fahey) *hld up in rr: hdwy over 3f out: rdn along over 2f out: kpt on u.p appr fnl f: nt rch ldrs* **11/4**[1]

4262 **6** *1* **Dispol Peto**[53] [907] 7-8-5 **49** ...(tp) AdrianTNicholls 7 43
(R Johnson) *hld up towards rr: hdwy 3f out: rdn 2f out: kpt on: nt rch ldrs* **14/1**

0060 **7** *3/4* **Nesno (USA)**[26] [2434] 4-9-7 **65** ... PatCosgrave 1 58
(J D Bethell) *in tch: effrt over 3f out: sn rdn along and no imp* **40/1**

6411 **8** *1* **Don Pasquale**[13] [2795] 5-8-12 **56** ... NCallan 9 47
(J T Stimpson) *hld up: a in rr* **9/2**[3]

030- **9** *hd* **Explode**[27] [6238] 10-8-4 **48** ...(b) DO'Donohoe 11 39
(Miss L C Siddall) *prom: rdn along over 4f out: wknd 3f out* **80/1**

6005 **10** *nk* **Kristalchen**[26] [2417] 5-7-11 **46** oh1 ...(p) NicolPolli(5) 3 36
(D W Thompson) *nvr bttr than midfield* **33/1**

-650 **11** *1 3/4* **Waterloo Corner**[120] [631] 5-8-13 **57** ...(v) PaulFessey 5 44
(R Craggs) *s.i.s: a bhd* **16/1**

-006 **12** *7* **Briery Blaze**[9] [2938] 4-8-3 **47** oh1 ow1 ... JoeFanning 8 23
(Mrs K Walton) *prom: led after 1f: rdn along and hdd 4f out: sn drvn and wknd wl over 2f out* **20/1**

14-0 **13** *9* **Mister Fizzbomb (IRE)**[22] [2537] 4-8-11 **55** ...(v) TonyHamilton 4 17
(J S Wainwright) *prom: rdn along over 3f out and sn wknd* **22/1**

2m 42.1s (3.10) **Going Correction** +0.25s/f (Good) 13 Ran SP% **122.1**
Speed ratings (Par 101):99,97,96,94,93 92,92,91,91,91 90,85,79
CSF £21.38 CT £343.25 TOTE £4.00: £1.50, £2.90, £6.20; EX 25.90.
Owner Naughty Diesel Ltd **Bred** Moyglare Stud Farm Ltd **Trained** Norton, N Yorks

FOCUS

A moderate handicap, won in good style by Turn Of Phrase, who has a good strike-rate for a horse of his class. The runner-up sets the standard.

Don Pasquale Official explanation: jockey said gelding hung right throughout

Explode Official explanation: jockey said gelding had no more to give

Waterloo Corner Official explanation: jockey said gelding was denied a clear run

3205 EUROPEAN BREEDERS' FUND ZETLAND MEDIAN AUCTION MAIDEN STKS (DIV II) 7f
5:35 (5:35) (Class 5) 2-Y-0 £2,590 (£770; £385; £192) Stalls Low

Form RPR

5 1 **Serena's Storm (IRE)**[23] [2504] 2-8-12 0 PatCosgrave 3 79+
(J J Quinn) *trckd ldrs: smooth hdwy on inner to ld 2f out: sn rdn clr: easily* **9/2**[2]

54 2 7 **Madison Heights (IRE)**[11] [2889] 2-9-3 0 TomEaves 2 67
(J Howard Johnson) *pushed along and sn led: rdn 3f out: hdd 2f out: sn drvn and kpt on same pce* **9/1**

6 3 *hd* **Parliamentary (JPN)**[15] [2739] 2-9-3 0 JoeFanning 6 66
(M Johnston) *towards rr: hdwy over 2f out: sn rdn and styd on ins fnl f: nrst fin* **6/1**[3]

54 4 ½ **Carnival Dream**[23] [2504] 2-8-12 0 DeanMcKeown 10 60
(A Berry) *cl up: rdn along 3f out: drvn over 2f out and sn one pce* **22/1**

40 5 3½ **Hurstpierpoint (IRE)**[14] [2758] 2-8-9 0 JamieMoriarty(3) 8 51
(R A Fahey) *chsd ldrs: hdwy 3f out: sn rdn along and no prog fnl 2f* **14/1**

40 6 1¾ **Kingstyle (IRE)**[22] [2532] 2-9-3 0 DeanMernagh 5 52
(M Brittain) *a in rr* **66/1**

044 7 1¾ **Willyn (IRE)**[12] [2819] 2-8-12 0 NCallan 7 42
(J R Weymes) *in tch: rdn along 3f out: sn drvn and wknd* **14/1**

8 7 **Raines Boy** 2-9-3 0 PaulMulrennan 1 30+
(N P Littmoden) *dwlt: a in rr* **50/1**

000 9 2 **Utrillo's Art (IRE)**[11] [2889] 2-8-5 0 NSLawes(7) 9 20
(M W Easterby) *a bhd* **100/1**

032 10 17 **Fortuity (IRE)**[12] [2832] 2-9-3 0 KDarley 4 —
(J H M Gosden) *in tch: sn pushed along: rdn 3f out and sn wknd: eased* **10/11**[1]

1m 29.63s (2.27) **Going Correction** +0.25s/f (Good) 10 Ran SP% **117.0**
Speed ratings (Par 94):97,89,88,88,84 82,80,72,69,50
CSF £43.36 TOTE £5.40: £1.50, £2.00, £2.60; EX 61.00 Place 6 £305.82, Place 5 £162.52.
Owner Bobby Donworth **Bred** Round Hill Stud **Trained** Settrington, N Yorks

FOCUS
A reasonable enough maiden and the winning time was only 0.36 seconds slower than the first division, a decent-looking contest. A wide-margin winner, who should do better than the bare form.

NOTEBOOK
Serena's Storm(IRE) ♦ improved significantly on the form she showed when fifth over 6f on her debut at Pontefract, coming home a wide-margin winner in impressive fashion. It remains to be seen exactly what she has beaten, but she clearly deserves her chance in something better. (op 6-1)
Madison Heights(IRE) ran a respectable race in second, but the winner was in a different league.
Parliamentary(JPN), who showed just moderate form on his debut at Thirsk, did some good late work to claim a place, but he never looked like winning. He is progressing and could develop into a decent type in nurseries later in the season. (op 11-2)
Carnival Dream ran a respectable race stepped up in trip with the blinkers left off this time. Her yard is in fair form. (op 20-1 tchd 25-1)
Hurstpierpoint(IRE) again failed to confirm the promise she showed when fourth on her racecourse debut, although she is now qualified for nurseries. (tchd 16-1)
Fortuity(IRE), upped to his furthest trip to date, was never really travelling with any fluency and dropped out very tamely in the straight, running a mile below his best. Official explanation: jockey said colt never travelled (op 5-6 tchd 4-5, evens and 8-11 in places)
T/Plt: £1,307.00 to a £1 stake. Pool: £109,040.50. 60.90 winning tickets. T/Qpdt: £16.30 to a £1 stake. Pool: £9,652.60. 436.40 winning tickets. JR

2618 CHEPSTOW (L-H)
Wednesday, July 4 (eve)

3206 Meeting Abandoned - Waterlogged

2990 KEMPTON (A.W) (R-H)
Wednesday, July 4

OFFICIAL GOING: Standard
Wind: Strong, half behind Weather: Fine but cloudy

3212 INDEPENDENCE NIGHT H'CAP 5f (P)
6:20 (6:21) (Class 5) (0-75,75) 3-Y-0+ £2,817 (£838; £418; £209) Stalls High

Form RPR

2054 1 **Fromsong (IRE)**[18] [2673] 9-9-12 74 JimCrowley 6 83
(D K Ivory) *prom: rdn to chse ldr 2f out: styd on to ld fnl 75yds: sn in command* **11/4**[1]

2200 2 1¼ **Bookiesindex Boy**[12] [2837] 3-9-8 75 (b) DarryllHolland 3 78
(J R Jenkins) *led: 2 l clr over 1f out and gng wl: wknd and hdd fnl 75yds* **9/1**

0-56 3 *hd* **Drumming Party (USA)**[8] [2972] 5-8-12 60 (t) LPKeniry 9 64
(A M Balding) *off the pce in 7th: prog on inner 2f out: drvn and styd on to take 3rd nr fin* **6/1**[3]

-604 4 *nk* **Heavens Walk**[28] [2350] 6-9-6 68 (t) EddieAhern 5 71
(P J Makin) *chsd ldrs: wnt 3rd over 1f out: styd on fnl f: nvr able to chal* **7/2**[2]

0P40 5 *shd* **Xaluna Bay (IRE)**[16] [2725] 4-9-6 68 SteveDrowne 4 71
(W R Muir) *off the pce in 6th: rdn and gd prog jst over 1f out: kpt on same pce fnl 100yds* **11/1**

4060 6 1¾ **Supreme Kiss**[25] [2459] 4-8-2 55 oh3 WilliamBuick(5) 7 51
(Mrs N Smith) *off the pce in 8th: sme prog over 1f out: kpt on: nvr pce to rch ldrs* **16/1**

-160 7 1¾ **Macademy Royal (USA)**[40] [1999] 4-8-10 65 (t) FrankiePickard(7) 8 55
(H Morrison) *awkward s: detached in last most of way: kpt on u.p fnl f* **7/1**

4052 8 *nk* **Stoneacre Gareth (IRE)**[9] [2950] 3-8-8 61 (b) JamieSpencer 2 50
(Peter Grayson) *chsd ldr to 2f out: wknd over 1f out* **7/1**

000 9 1 **Spinetail Rufous (IRE)**[11] [2879] 9-8-7 55 oh10 (b) ChrisCatlin 1 40
(Miss Z C Davison) *chsd ldrs on outer tl wknd wl over 1f out* **66/1**

60.78 secs (0.38) **Going Correction** +0.05s/f (Slow)
WFA 3 from 4yo+ 5lb 9 Ran SP% **113.9**
Speed ratings (Par 103):98,96,95,95,95 92,89,88,87
CSF £27.90 CT £137.42 TOTE £3.90: £1.40, £2.90, £2.80; EX 38.90.
Owner Dean Ivory **Bred** Mrs Teresa Bergin **Trained** Radlett, Herts

FOCUS
The early pace was far from frantic in this sprint handicap and that favoured those that raced prominently, as is usually the case over this sharp 5f. Straightforward form to rate.

3213 EBF EDWIN COE MAIDEN FILLIES' STKS 7f (P)
6:50 (6:52) (Class 5) 2-Y-0 £3,886 (£1,156; £577; £288) Stalls High

Form RPR

4 1 **Kay Es Jay (FR)**[14] [2768] 2-9-0 0 RHills 3 77+
(B W Hills) *trckd ldrs: prog to ld wl over 1f out: sn in command: hung rt fnl f: rdn out* **5/4**[1]

2 1 **Georgie The Fourth (IRE)** 2-9-0 0 ChrisCatlin 4 72+
(E J O'Neill) *pushed along in midfield bef 1/2-way: gd prog fr 2f out: chsd wnr 1f out: clsd but nvr able to chal* **14/1**

4 3 1¾ **Narmeen**[28] [2365] 2-9-0 0 JHBowman 9 68
(M R Channon) *prom carrying hd to one side: effrt over 2f out: rdn to dispute 2nd jst over 1f out: styd on same pce* **9/2**[2]

4 ¾ **Rosaleen (IRE)** 2-9-0 0 SteveDrowne 1 66
(B J Meehan) *s.s: racd on wd outside: sn in midfield: shkn up and styd on wl over 1f out: nrst fin* **10/1**

5 ¾ **River Bounty** 2-9-0 0 RichardMullen 7 64
(A P Jarvis) *chsd ldr: led over 2f out to wl over 1f out: fdd fnl f* **40/1**

6 1 **Gower Belle** 2-9-0 0 EddieAhern 8 61
(W R Muir) *chsd ldrs: rdn and cl enough 2f out: one pce after* **33/1**

0 7 ½ **Lady Bower**[9] [2949] 2-9-0 0 J-PGuillambert 14 60
(M Johnston) *led: hdd over 2f out: hanging and green after: wknd fnl f* **25/1**

8 *nk* **Rosy Alexander** 2-8-9 0 WilliamBuick(5) 13 59+
(N A Callaghan) *lost pl and in rr after 2f: pushed along and kpt on steadily fnl 2f: n.d* **14/1**

9 1¼ **Fernlawn Hope (IRE)** 2-9-0 0 MartinDwyer 6 56+
(J A Osborne) *dwlt: wl in rr: shuffled along and sme prog 2f out: one pce and no hdwy fnl f* **14/1**

10 *hd* **Neve Lieve (IRE)** 2-9-0 0 LDettori 10 56
(M Botti) *nvr bttr than midfield on inner: shkn up and no prog over 2f out* **8/1**[3]

11 2½ **Aneebee (IRE)** 2-9-0 0 JimmyFortune 5 49
(R Hannon) *s.s: a wl in rr: shkn up and no prog over 2f out* **14/1**

40 12 3 **Bunty Malenoir**[25] [2468] 2-9-0 0 AdamKirby 2 41
(I A Wood) *chsd ldrs and racd on outer: rdn 3f out: wknd 2f out* **100/1**

13 ¾ **Jazamataz** 2-9-0 0 JimCrowley 12 39
(Tom Dascombe) *rn green in rr and reminder after 2f: nvr a factor* **66/1**

14 1 **A Dream Come True** 2-9-0 0 JohnEgan 11 37+
(D K Ivory) *s.s: a in last trio: wl bhd fnl 2f* **40/1**

1m 28.17s (1.37) **Going Correction** +0.05s/f (Slow) 14 Ran SP% **123.6**
Speed ratings (Par 91):94,92,90,90,89 88,87,87,85,85 82,79,78,77
CSF £21.36 TOTE £2.30: £1.20, £5.20, £1.60; EX 34.40.
Owner Steve Jenkins **Bred** Team Hogdala Ab **Trained** Lambourn, Berks

FOCUS
This looked a fair fillies' maiden in which the pace was ordinary. A few of these look capable of quite a bit of improvement, particularly the winner who created a nice impression.

NOTEBOOK
Kay Es Jay(FR), whose debut fourth over course and distance two weeks earlier had been boosted by the subsequent success of the runner-up, had obviously learnt a lot from that and picked up well when asked. She should have little difficulty in getting a mile and is likely to try and pick up some black type now. (op 2-1 tchd 6-5)
Georgie The Fourth(IRE) ♦, a 30,000euros filly out of a half-sister to two winners, has a speedy pedigree so it was a bit surprising that she took a while to pick up and was doing all her best work late. This was a fine debut considering she was conceding experience to the pair that finished either side of her and it should not be long before she goes one better.
Narmeen was stepping up two furlongs from her debut, but despite her sire and dam both being sprinters, there is still plenty of stamina on the distaff side. Even though she had previous experience, she still looked green early and though she stayed right in the thick of the action throughout, it was lack of finishing pace, rather than lack of stamina, that eventually found her out. (op 6-1 tchd 7-1 and 4-1)
Rosaleen(IRE) ♦, a 70,000gns half-sister to dual winner Rosbay, was forced to race wide from the outside stall but still posted a pleasing first effort and she can be expected to step up on this. (op 14-1 tchd 16-1)
River Bounty, a relatively cheap foal whose dam is from the family of Gryffindor and Midnight Legend, showed up for a long way on this debut and can be expected to improve. (op 33-1)
Gower Belle, a 16,000gns filly whose dam is closely related to the useful sprinters Danehurst and Humouresque, comes from a yard not noted for winning debutants so this was encouraging. She shaped as though she has inherited some of her sire's stamina and there should be races to be won with her in time.

3214 DIGIBET CASINO MAIDEN FILLIES' STKS 1m 3f (P)
7:20 (7:23) (Class 5) 3-Y-0+ £2,817 (£838; £418; £209) Stalls High

Form RPR

0-0 1 **Inchinata (IRE)**[19] [2625] 3-8-12 0 RHills 9 76+
(B W Hills) *dwlt: wl in rr: pushed along 1/2-way: effrt u.p but off the pce over 2f out: swtchd wd and r.o strly to ld last stride* **33/1**

0 2 *shd* **Noble Plum (IRE)**[4] [3113] 3-8-12 0 JimmyQuinn 8 76+
(Sir Mark Prescott) *towards rr: prog 4f out: rdn and effrt over 2f out: led ins fnl f: hdd last stride* **66/1**

2 3 1 **Salsa Verdi (USA)**[14] [2766] 3-8-12 0 LDettori 14 74
(Saeed Bin Suroor) *prom: led over 2f out: sn hung lft: drvn and hdd ins fnl f: nt qckn* **9/4**[1]

4-2 4 *nk* **Thinking Positive**[21] [2580] 3-8-12 0 JimmyFortune 5 74
(J H M Gosden) *in tch in midfield: trckd ldrs 3f out: rdn to chal over 1f out: one pce ins fnl f* **11/4**[2]

4203 5 1¾ **Best Selection**[25] [2445] 3-8-12 69 RichardMullen 6 71
(A P Jarvis) *racd on outer in midfield: pushed along and prog 4f out: rdn to chal 2f out: nrly upsides 1f out: fdd* **16/1**

0 6 4 **Sugarbush**[20] [2597] 3-8-12 0 JamieSpencer 13 64
(J R Fanshawe) *settled wl in rr: wl off the pce 3f out: nudged along and styd on steadily nvr nrr* **7/2**[3]

5 7 ½ **Meynell**[25] [2455] 3-8-12 0 KerrinMcEvoy 1 63
(M A Jarvis) *led after 3f to 4f out: styd pressing ldrs tl wknd jst over 1f out* **7/1**

0 8 ¾ **Spanish Diva**[40] [2005] 3-8-12 0 AdamKirby 4 62
(S C Williams) *dwlt: wl in rr tl gd prog on outer to ld 4f out: hdd over 2f out: wknd rapidly over 1f out* **10/1**

9 3½ **Blush On Cue (USA)** 3-8-12 0 MartinDwyer 12 56+
(J H M Gosden) *s.s: detached in last tl past 1/2-way: nudged along and kpt on steadily fr over 2f out: nvr nr ldrs* **50/1**

04 10 5 **Madam Vouvray**[14] [2766] 3-8-12 0 SteveDrowne 7 48
(B J Meehan) *prom but sn pushed along: lost pl 5f out: sn struggling* **25/1**

11 1½ **Passing True (IRE)** 3-8-12 0 J-PGuillambert 11 45
(M Johnston) *led for 3f: prom tl lost pl rapidly over 3f out* **33/1**

0 **12** *7* **Rhondda Valley**[28] 2360 3-8-12 0 .... JimCrowley 2 33
(Mrs A J Perrett) *nvr on terms w ldrs: struggling fr 3f out* **66/1**

0 **13** *10* **Boekenhoutskloof (IRE)**[19] 2620 3-8-12 0 .... EddieAhern 3 16
(E F Vaughan) *in tch: prog to pressed ldrs 1/2-way: wknd wl over 3f out* **66/1**

00 **14** *27* **Winforjoe (IRE)**[93] 884 3-8-9 0 .... MarcHalford(3) 10 —
(J J Bridger) *chsd ldrs 4f: sn wknd: t.o* **100/1**

2m 20.62s (-2.06) **Going Correction** +0.05s/f (Slow) **14** Ran SP% **124.3**
Speed ratings (Par 100):109,108,108,107,106 103,103,102,100,96 95,90,83,63
CSF £1376.93 TOTE £52.00: £8.90, £12.00, £1.50; EX 405.60.
Owner D M James **Bred** Derek Veitch & Saleh Ali Hammadi **Trained** Lambourn, Berks

FOCUS
They went off at some pace in this, probably too fast as things turned out as those that set it fell in a heap, but it did produce a very decent winning time for a race of its type. This was also a race of changing fortunes, as there were around eight different leaders in the last three furlongs. Fair maiden form, with the first two big improvers, but limited by the fifth.

3215 DIGIBET.COM LONDON MILE H'CAP (LONDON MILE QUALIFIER) 1m (P)
7:50 (7:53) (Class 4) (0-80,82) 3-Y-0+ **£4,728** (£1,406; £702; £351) **Stalls** High

Form RPR

4101 **1** **Samarinda (USA)**[7] 2995 4-10-2 **82** 6ex .... MickyFenton 3 93+
(Mrs P Sly) *mde all: set v stdy pce tl qcknd over 2f out: clr over 1f out: unchal* **13/2**

1113 **2** *1 1/2* **Networker**[7] 2985 4-9-1 **72** .... WilliamBuick(5) 13 81+
(P J McBride) *shuffled bk to last pair sn after s: prog fr 2f out: n.m.r 1f out: r.o to take 2nd nr fin: no ch w wnr* **9/2**[1]

3310 **3** *nk* **Eager Igor (USA)**[19] 2627 3-9-5 **80** .... StephenCarson 9 83
(Eve Johnson Houghton) *trckd ldrs: drvn on inner to chse wnr over 1f out: carried hd awkwardly and nt qckn: lost 2nd nr fin* **10/1**

2010 **4** *3/4* **Sailor King (IRE)**[14] 2771 5-9-12 **78** .... JimCrowley 10 82
(D K Ivory) *t.k.h: hld up in midfield: drvn and nt qckn 2f out: styd on to dispute 2nd 1f out: one pce* **8/1**

0220 **5** *3/4* **Crocodile Bay (IRE)**[15] 2748 4-9-6 **72** .... LDettori 7 74
(B J Meehan) *hld up in midfield: outpcd over 2f out: kpt on fr over 1f out: n.d* **10/1**

-021 **6** *nk* **Summer Dancer (IRE)**[20] 2601 3-9-0 **75** .... TQuinn 5 74
(D R C Elsworth) *free to post: plld hrd: hld up in last pair: prog 2f out: ch of a pl whn n.m.r 1f out and hmpd sn after* **11/2**[2]

31-0 **7** *1 3/4* **Esteem**[40] 2004 4-9-8 **74** .... DarryllHolland 14 71
(W Jarvis) *t.k.h: hld up bhd ldrs: chsd wnr over 2f out: hanging bdly and nt qckn: lost 2nd over 1f out: fdd* **16/1**

-345 **8** *nk* **Sky Quest (IRE)**[125] 594 9-8-8 **67** .... HarryPoulton(7) 11 63
(J R Boyle) *t.k.h: hld up in rr: effrt on outer but outpcd over 2f out: n.d after* **33/1**

4365 **9** *1* **Plane Painter (IRE)**[11] 2862 3-9-2 **77** .... J-PGuillambert 4 69
(M Johnston) *prom: outpcd over 2f out: wknd over 1f out* **12/1**

5150 **10** *1 1/4* **Genari**[25] 2452 4-9-13 **79** ....(t) JimmyFortune 12 70
(P F I Cole) *s.i.s: hld up in midfield on inner: effrt over 2f out: sn outpcd: no prog over 1f out* **6/1**[3]

000- **11** *nk* **Habanero**[27] 6313 6-9-8 **74** .... JamieSpencer 1 65
(A King) *trckd wnr to over 2f out: hanging bdly and wknd over 1f out* **12/1**

3310 **12** *2 1/2* **Northern Desert (IRE)**[61] 1446 8-9-4 **70** .... ChrisCatlin 6 55
(P W Hiatt) *hld up in midfield on outer: wknd 2f out* **25/1**

1056 **13** *4* **Binnion Bay (IRE)**[19] 2626 6-9-9 **75** ....(b) AmirQuinn 2 51
(J J Bridger) *s.s: t.k.h and in tch on outer: wknd over 2f out* **16/1**

1m 40.28s (-0.52) **Going Correction** +0.05s/f (Slow)
WFA 3 from 4yo+ 9lb **13** Ran SP% **124.4**
Speed ratings (Par 105):104,102,102,101,100 100,98,98,97,96 95,93,89
CSF £37.37 CT £310.79 TOTE £8.10: £2.80, £1.80, £3.90; EX 30.80.
Owner D Bayliss, T Davies, G Libson & P Sly **Bred** Gainsborough Farm Llc **Trained** Thorney, Cambs

FOCUS
A messy contest run at an early dawdle, but the tempo increased significantly down the home straight and the final time was perfectly acceptable. The way the race was run favoured the winner, who was in the ideal position to take advantage. The form may not prove all that reliable.
Summer Dancer(IRE) Official explanation: jockey said gelding was denied a clear run
Binnion Bay(IRE) Official explanation: jockey said gelding ran too free

3216 DIGIBET SPORTS BETTING H'CAP 2m (P)
8:20 (8:20) (Class 3) (0-90,87) 4-Y-0+
£6,855 (£2,052; £1,026; £513; £256; £128) **Stalls** High

Form RPR

1-13 **1** **Junior**[53] 1654 4-9-2 **82** .... JimmyFortune 5 94
(B J Meehan) *mde all: 6 l clr after 3f: kicked on 4f out: in n.d after: drvn out fnl f* **3/1**[1]

6-26 **2** *3* **Whispering Death**[56] 1582 5-9-1 **84** ....(v) LiamJones(3) 1 93
(W J Haggas) *hld up in last trio: rdn and prog to go 2nd 2f out: clsd fnl f but a hopeless pursuit of wnr* **11/2**[2]

-451 **3** *1/2* **Sendinpost**[7] 2996 4-7-11 **68** 6ex .... WilliamBuick(5) 7 76
(S C Williams) *hld up in 6th: prog to chse clr wnr briefly jst over 2f out: kpt on but nvr any ch* **3/1**[1]

1205 **4** *1 3/4* **Salute (IRE)**[59] 1506 8-9-4 **84** .... SteveDrowne 9 90
(P G Murphy) *hld up in 5th: rn into trble over 2f out: rdn and kpt on fr over 1f out: nvr in the r* **12/1**

120 **5** *shd* **Newnham (IRE)**[41] 1959 6-8-3 **76** .... JackMitchell(7) 2 82
(J R Boyle) *hld up in last rdn and styd on fnl 2f: nvr in the r* **7/1**[3]

02-0 **6** *5* **Simondiun**[47] 1822 4-9-7 **87** ....(v[1]) JamieSpencer 8 87
(W J Haggas) *hld up in last trio: rdn and no prog 3f out: nvr in the r* **8/1**

0-00 **7** *shd* **Establishment**[74] 1148 10-8-8 **74** ow1 .... EddieAhern 3 74
(C A Cyzer) *wnt 3rd over 6f out: rdn to chse clr wnr 3f out to jst over 2f out: wknd rapidly* **33/1**

0505 **8** *7* **High Point (IRE)**[10] 2908 9-8-7 **73** .... TQuinn 10 64
(G P Enright) *chsd clr wnr to 3f out: wknd* **14/1**

5-1 **9** *27* **Megaton**[28] 2367 6-8-10 **76** .... LDettori 6 35
(P Bowen) *chsd clr ldng pair to over 6f out: wknd rapidly 3f out: eased and t.o* **7/1**[3]

3m 27.39s (-4.01) **Going Correction** +0.05s/f (Slow) **9** Ran SP% **118.8**
Speed ratings (Par 107):112,110,110,109,109 106,106,103,89
CSF £20.36 CT £54.19 TOTE £4.50: £1.40, £2.30, £1.30; EX 18.00.
Owner Paul Green **Bred** P C Green **Trained** Manton, Wilts

FOCUS
This decent staying handicap was basically decided in the first couple of furlongs when the eventual winner went off at a decent pace and his rivals left him to it. He was probably the best horse anyway, but the riders of the beaten horses left it far too late before making their moves on what was plainly a speed-favouring track. Fair handicap form, rated through the placed horses.

NOTEBOOK
Junior, as when winning at Newbury two starts ago, was allowed his own way out in front. He still set what looked a decent tempo though and it was being kicked right away from his field rounding the home bend that removed any doubt over the result. He was gifted this to a large extent, but the winning time was very solid for the grade so it would be wrong to underestimate the performance. His trainer is keen to aim him at the Cesarewitch. (tchd 5-2 and 7-2)
Whispering Death, with the visor back on, stayed on to finish best of the rest and his jockey cannot really be blamed for this defeat as he has to be ridden this way. He is handicapped right up to his best, but will be suited by a return to a fast surface on turf if the ground ever dries out. (op 5-1 tchd 9-2)
Sendinpost, carrying a 6lb penalty for her course-and-distance victory seven days earlier, was given a similarly patient ride before making her move soon after turning in. She plugged on to prove that she does truly stay the trip, but this time the leader was not coming back. (op 10-3 tchd 7-2 and 11-4)
Salute(IRE), back on Polytrack after a couple of indifferent efforts on turf including when just over three lengths behind Junior at Newbury, was 6lb better off here but the way the track was riding suited his old rival especially and he could never extricate himself from the pack to throw down any sort of an challenge.
Newnham(IRE), another hold-up performer unsuited by the way the track was riding, tried to come from last and in this contest that was always likely to be an impossible task. (op 10-1)
Simondiun, beaten out of sight on his return to action, never got into the race on this sand debut in the first-time visor and is yet to prove himself for his new yard. Official explanation: jockey said gelding hung right (op 10-1 tchd 14-1)
Establishment had plenty to find with a couple of these on recent efforts and after trying to get on terms with the winner rounding the home bend, was duly left behind.
High Point(IRE), who has a good record over this course and distance, led the main bulk of the field for a long way but lacked the pace to bridge the gap to the winner and his efforts to do so eventually told. Official explanation: jockey said gelding had no more to give
Megaton, 8lb higher than when making a successful return to the Flat at Nottingham last month, had been in great form over hurdles prior to that but he had no previous experience of sand and he dropped out very tamely over the last half-mile. This was too bad to be true. Official explanation: jockey said gelding was struck into soon after start (op 11-2 tchd 15-2)

3217 REUTERS FIRST FOR NEWS H'CAP 1m 4f (P)
8:50 (8:50) (Class 6) (0-65,65) 3-Y-0+ **£2,047** (£604; £302) **Stalls** Centre

Form RPR

2220 **1** **Don't Mind Me**[21] 2582 4-9-5 **57** .... KerrinMcEvoy 1 64
(T Keddy) *quick move to go prom after 2f: rdn to chal 2f out: narrow ld 1f out: hld on wl* **14/1**

000 **2** *nk* **Daring Racer (GER)**[8] 2967 4-9-11 **63** .... TQuinn 9 70
(S Dow) *trckd ldr: rdn to ld 2f out: narrowly hdd 1f out: kpt on but jst hld nr fin* **40/1**

230 **3** *1/2* **Master'n Commander**[117] 651 5-9-8 **60** .... EddieAhern 2 66
(C A Cyzer) *sn prom: rdn and effrt over 2f out: pressed ldrs over 1f out: nt qckn and hld fnl f* **16/1**

6400 **4** *1/2* **Amwell Brave**[4] 3097 6-9-12 **64** .... JHBowman 6 69
(J R Jenkins) *t.k.h: hld up towards rr: stdy prog fr 4f out: rdn to chse ldrs 2f out: plld out over 1f out: nt qckn* **11/2**

1403 **5** *1* **Bienheureux**[20] 2595 6-9-2 **54** ....(t) JohnEgan 12 58
(Miss Gay Kelleway) *hld up and sn towards rr: prog over 2f out: drvn and hanging over 1f out: r.o fnl f: unable to chal* **4/1**[2]

0041 **6** *1* **Thorny Mandate**[23] 2519 5-9-9 **61** .... MartinDwyer 7 63
(W M Brisbourne) *s.s: hld up in rr: prog on inner over 2f out: drvn and one pce over 1f out* **5/1**[3]

0-16 **7** *3/4* **Stolen Hours (USA)**[17] 2692 7-9-13 **65** .... JimCrowley 14 66
(J Akehurst) *led at stdy pce: tried to kick on 3f out: hdd 2f out: outpcd* **14/1**

-100 **8** *2 1/2* **Dream Mountain**[7] 2996 4-8-11 **56** .... SophieDoyle(7) 4 53
(Ms J S Doyle) *prom tl outpcd fr over 2f out* **50/1**

3300 **9** *1/2* **Follow On**[26] 2430 5-9-10 **62** .... JamieSpencer 11 58
(A P Jarvis) *hld up in rr: rdn and modest prog over 2f out: nt keen and nvr a threat* **7/2**[1]

0046 **10** *3/4* **Hallings Overture (USA)**[21] 2572 8-9-5 **57** .... DarryllHolland 3 52
(C A Horgan) *s.s: hld up wl in rr: effrt 3f out: sn rdn and no rspnse* **15/2**

1232 **11** *hd* **Mighty Kitchener (USA)**[23] 2519 4-9-9 **61** .... IanMongan 8 55
(P Howling) *hld up wl in rr: last and rdn 3f out: nvr a factor* **10/1**

0063 **12** *5* **Swords**[31] 1730 5-9-3 **55** .... J-PGuillambert 5 41
(Heather Dalton) *hld up in rr: rdn and no prog 3f out* **8/1**

600- **13** *6* **Project Sunshine (GER)**[235] 4044 4-9-6 **58** .... StephenCarson 13 35
(C P Morlock) *prom tl wknd u.p 3f out* **66/1**

600- **14** *3* **Grand Sefton**[214] 6674 4-9-3 **55** .... MickyFenton 10 27
(Stef Liddiard) *plld hrd: trckd ldrs: wknd rapidly over 2f out* **40/1**

2m 38.46s (1.56) **Going Correction** +0.05s/f (Slow) **14** Ran SP% **133.8**
Speed ratings (Par 101):96,95,95,95,94 93,93,91,91,90 90,87,83,81
CSF £519.51 CT £8775.33 TOTE £13.50: £3.90, £8.80, £6.40; EX 423.20.
Owner Dynamic Duo **Bred** J Horgan And J Stevens **Trained** Newmarket, Suffolk

FOCUS
A moderate but competitive handicap, run at just an ordinary pace. The winner was less exposed than most, unlike the third through whom the form has been rated.
Daring Racer(GER) Official explanation: jockey said colt lost a near-fore shoe
Follow On Official explanation: jockey said horse missed the break
Swords Official explanation: jockey said gelding hung right throughout

3218 LONDON IRISH/WEATHERBYS APPRENTICE H'CAP (ROUND 5) 6f (P)
9:20 (9:20) (Class 5) (0-75,76) 3-Y-0+ **£2,817** (£838; £418; £209) **Stalls** High

Form RPR

3113 **1** **Mambazo**[1] 3188 5-9-6 **69** 6ex ....(e) FLenclud(3) 6 84
(S C Williams) *mde all: stretched field bef 1/2-way: drew rt away over 1f out: unchal* **11/4**[1]

5001 **2** *5* **Romany Nights (IRE)**[7] 2993 7-9-11 **76** 6ex ....(bt) MJMurphy(5) 4 76
(Miss Gay Kelleway) *chsd ldrs: outpcd fr 1/2-way: r.o over 1f out to take 2nd fnl 100yds: no ch w wnr* **7/2**[2]

0500 **3** *3/4* **Mine The Balance (IRE)**[19] 2619 4-8-9 **55** oh9 .... ThomasO'Brien 5 53
(H J Manners) *chsd ldrs: outpcd 1/2-way: styd on over 1f out: n.d to wnr* **33/1**

0-00 **4** *shd* **Young Bertie**[43] 1931 4-8-13 **62** ....(p) RyanBird(3) 3 59
(H Morrison) *hld up in rr: outpcd by 1/2-way: styd on fnl f: n.d* **8/1**

0220 **5** *1/2* **Wrighty Almighty (IRE)**[18] 2665 5-8-9 **55** .... WilliamCarson 8 51
(P R Chamings) *chsd wnr: outpcd fr 2f out: lost 2nd and wknd fnl 100yds* **11/4**[1]

3000 **6** *1 1/2* **Stir Crazy (IRE)**[43] 1912 3-7-12 **55** oh1 .... MatthewDavies(5) 2 55+
(M R Channon) *hld up in rr: effrt on inner whn trapped thrght fnl 2f: no ch* **16/1**

6004 **7** *5* **Must Be Keen**[8] 2972 8-8-9 **55** oh10 ....(p) JamieHamblett 1 31
(G C H Chung) *t.k.h: hld up on outer: outpcd 1/2-way: bhd whn wandered all over the trck in st* **14/1**

-006 8 3 **Scarlet Knight**[16] 2725 4-10-0 74 JackMitchell 7 41
(P Mitchell) *chsd ldng pair tl wknd rapidly 2f out* **11/2**[3]

1m 13.57s (-0.13) **Going Correction** +0.05s/f (Slow)
WFA 3 from 4yo+ 6lb 8 Ran SP% **117.5**
Speed ratings (Par 103):102,95,94,94,93 91,84,80
CSF £13.01 CT £258.86 TOTE £4.80: £1.80, £1.70, £4.20; EX 10.90 Place 6 £ 297.29, Place 5 £ 154.49.
Owner D G Burge **Bred** Barry Taylor **Trained** Newmarket, Suffolk

FOCUS
A modest apprentices' handicap that became a one-horse race. A clear career best from Mambazo, but he did enjoy the run of the race on a card which favoured front-runners.
Stir Crazy(IRE) Official explanation: jockey said gelding was denied a clear run
T/Jkpt: Not won. T/Plt: £310.80. Pool £10,4424.15. 245.25 winning units T/Qpdt: £212.50. Pool £7,324.20. 25.50 winning units JN

2778 LEOPARDSTOWN (L-H)
Wednesday, July 4

OFFICIAL GOING: Yielding to soft

3222a IRISH STALLION FARMS EUROPEAN BREEDERS FUND BROWNSTOWN STKS (GROUP 3) (F&M) 7f
7:30 (7:34) 3-Y-O+ **£39,527** (£11,554; £5,472; £1,824)

RPR
1 **Redstone Dancer (IRE)**[4] 3116 5-9-6 94 PShanahan 5 113+
(Miss S Collins, Ire) *s.i.s: sn chsd ldrs: 4th 1/2-way: impr to cl 3rd 2f out: rdn to chal 1f out: sn led: kpt on wl fnl f* **4/1**[3]
2 2 1/2 **She's Our Mark**[30] 2323 3-8-12 103 DMGrant 3 103
(Patrick J Flynn, Ire) *chsd ldrs: 3rd 1/2-way: rdn to chal 2f out: led 1 1/2f out: hdd under 1f out: no ex: kpt on* **7/1**
3 2 1/2 **Modeeroch (IRE)**[21] 2586 4-9-6 105 (t) KJManning 7 101+
(J S Bolger, Ire) *chsd ldrs: sn 2nd: impr to ld 2f out and strly pressed: hdd 1 1/2f out: 3rd and no ex fr 1f out* **7/2**[2]
4 1 **Wake Up Maggie (IRE)**[53] 1661 4-9-9 MichaelHills 1 100
(C F Wall) *hld up: hmpd after 1f: rdn in 5th bef st: kpt on to 4th under 2f out: no imp* **9/10**[1]
5 7 **Precocious Star (IRE)**[14] 2757 3-8-12 FMBerry 2 75+
(K R Burke) *hld up in rr: rdn in 5th under 2f out: no imp* **20/1**
6 hd **Sakkara Star (IRE)**[28] 2381 4-9-6 83 (b) RPCleary 8 77+
(M Halford, Ire) *led and sn clr: reduced advantage over 4f out: rdn and hdd 2f out: sn wknd* **50/1**

1m 32.56s (0.36) **Going Correction** +0.325s/f (Good)
WFA 3 from 4yo+ 8lb 8 Ran SP% **114.1**
Speed ratings: 110,107,104,103,95 94
CSF £31.29 TOTE £5.00: £2.60, £2.30; DF 26.90.
Owner K Lynch **Bred** Newberry Stud Company **Trained** the Curragh, Co Kildare

FOCUS
Not the strongest Group 3 for fillies. The pace was solid with the winner rated to her previous form.

NOTEBOOK
Redstone Dancer(IRE), back to winning ways at the Curragh four days previously, overcame a sluggish start and followed up with a comfortable success on this debut in Group company. She is clearly in the form of her life at present, but is already in foal to Refuse To Bend and is now likely to be retired as this will enhance her paddock value even further. (op 4/1 tchd 9/2)
She's Our Mark, just in front of the winner on her previous outing a month before, failed to confirm that form despite racing on 2lb better terms. This was still another solid effort in defeat and, nicely clear of the remainder at the finish, she remains on an upward curve. (op 6/1)
Modeeroch(IRE) was given a positive ride, but folded disappointingly when the gun was put to her head nearing the final furlong. The re-application of a tongue tie failed to have the desired effect and this was disappointing. (op 7/2 tchd 4/1)
Wake Up Maggie(IRE), just touched off in this event last year and impressive when winning in this grade on her seasonal bow 53 days previously, was never travelling with the same fluency. She was hampered early on, but still had enough time to recover and it may transpire that something was amiss. Official explanation: trainer said filly did not handle the yielding to soft ground (op 1/1)
Precocious Star(IRE) has not gone on from her Listed win at Kempton in March and was never in the hunt on this drop back from 1m. (op 16/1)

3223 - 3225a (Foreign Racing) - See Raceform Interactive

2868 HAYDOCK (L-H)
Thursday, July 5

3226 Meeting Abandoned - Waterlogged

2967 NEWBURY (L-H)
Thursday, July 5

OFFICIAL GOING: Heavy
Wind: Strong, ahead

3232 BATHWICK TYRES APPRENTICE H'CAP 1m 3f 5y
6:20 (6:21) (Class 5) (0-70,70) 4-Y-O+ **£3,238** (£963; £481; £240) **Stalls** High

Form RPR
0455 1 **Great View (IRE)**[3] 3155 8-9-7 70 (v) AshleyHamblett(3) 6 76
(Mrs A L M King) *hld up in rr: hdwy over 2f out: drvn to ld 1f out: styd on wl* **11/4**[2]
1106 2 1 3/4 **Street Life (IRE)**[13] 2833 9-9-3 68 AlanRutter(5) 8 71
(W J Musson) *hld up in rr: hdwy over 2f out: str chal fr over 1f out: kpt on same pce ins fnl f* **3/1**[3]
3222 3 nk **Augustine**[20] 2621 6-9-6 69 WilliamCarson(3) 2 72
(P W Hiatt) *led: rdn over 2f out: hdd 1f out: styd on same pce ins fnl f* **2/1**[1]
00/0 4 shd **Ashmolian (IRE)**[41] 1998 4-8-0 51 oh6 JemmaMarshall(5) 7 53?
(Miss Z C Davison) *in tch: rdn along and one pce over 2f out: kpt on u.p ins fnl f: gng on cl home* **33/1**
5032 5 2 1/2 **Scottish River (USA)**[7] 3036 8-8-12 63 FrankiePickard(5) 4 61
(M D I Usher) *towards rr but t.k.h and chsd ldrs 6f out: wnt 2nd 5f out: rdn 2f out: wknd ins fnl f* **7/1**
0000 6 22 **Atticus Trophies (IRE)**[19] 2656 4-8-0 51 oh6 SophieDoyle(5) 5 14
(Ms J S Doyle) *chsd ldr to 5f out: styd prom tl wknd qckly over 2f out* **16/1**
5022 7 3 1/2 **Hathaal (IRE)**[12] 2874 8-9-7 70 (vt) SCreighton(3) 3 28
(E J Creighton) *chsd ldrs to 3f out: wknd qckly* **12/1**

2m 34.03s (11.76) **Going Correction** +1.10s/f (Soft) 7 Ran SP% **114.0**
Speed ratings (Par 103):101,99,99,99,97 81,79
CSF £11.40 CT £18.85 TOTE £4.30: £2.40, £2.20; EX 13.50.
Owner All The Kings Horses **Bred** Terry McGrath **Trained** Wilmcote, Warwicks
■ Stewards' Enquiry : Jemma Marshall three-day ban: used whip with excessive frequency (Jul 16-18)

FOCUS
A modest contest, confined to apprentice riders. The form looks dubious and not solid.

3233 DREWEATT NEATE EBF MAIDEN STKS 6f 8y
6:50 (6:51) (Class 4) 2-Y-O **£6,477** (£1,927; £963; £481) **Stalls** Centre

Form RPR
3 1 **Legal Eagle (IRE)**[21] 2596 2-9-3 0 JimmyFortune 5 85+
(J H M Gosden) *mde all: forged clr appr fnl f: eased cl home* **4/5**[1]
0 2 2 **Binfield (IRE)**[17] 2724 2-8-12 0 TQuinn 7 68
(B G Powell) *chsd wnr thrght: no ch fnl 2f but kpt on wl for clr 2nd* **14/1**
3 3 1/2 **King Supreme (IRE)** 2-9-3 0 RichardHughes 8 63+
(R Hannon) *slowly away: bhd: rdn 1/2-way: styd on wl thrght fnl f: gng on cl home* **8/1**[2]
4 hd **Candle Sahara (IRE)** 2-8-12 0 JHBowman 4 57+
(M R Channon) *in tch tl rdn and outpcd 1/2-way: styd on fr over 1f out: green ins fnl f: gng on cl home* **10/1**[3]
5 1 **Castles In The Air** 2-9-3 0 PaulEddery 1 59
(Pat Eddery) *chsd ldrs in 3rd: no imp fr 2f out: wknd ins fnl f* **8/1**[2]
6 1 **Kara Tau** 2-9-3 0 PaulFitzsimons 6 56
(M P Tregoning) *sn in tch: rdn 1/2-way: wknd fr 2f out* **12/1**
7 1 3/4 **Dauberval (IRE)** 2-9-3 0 LPKeniry 2 51
(S Kirk) *chsd ldrs: rdn 3f out: wknd 2f out* **20/1**
8 19 **Caradoc Place** 2-9-3 0 MartinDwyer 3 —
(M P Tregoning) *in tch: rdn 1/2-way: wknd over 2f out* **8/1**[2]

1m 18.9s (4.58) **Going Correction** +0.675s/f (Yiel) 8 Ran SP% **117.1**
Speed ratings (Par 96):96,93,88,88,87 85,83,58
CSF £14.70 TOTE £1.90: £1.10, £2.20, £1.70; EX 15.90.
Owner H R H Princess Haya Of Jordan **Bred** J Cooke **Trained** Newmarket, Suffolk

FOCUS
Probably just an average juvenile maiden and somewhat guessy. The only two with previous experience came clear and the winner is value for further than the bare margin.

NOTEBOOK
Legal Eagle(IRE) confirmed the promise of his fast-ground debut over course and distance three weeks previously and opened his account with an easy success. Always front rank, he handled the much softer ground without fuss and could have been called the winner from halfway. He is value for further than his winning margin, left the impression he would get another furlong before long and should be high on confidence after this. (op 11-10 tchd 6-5 in places)
Binfield(IRE), seventh on her debut at Windsor 17 days previously, stepped up on that effort and kept on to finish a clear second best. Her previous experience was a distinct advantage and she is greatly flattered by her proximity to the easy winner, but connections will have been very pleased with this run all the same. (op 16-1)
King Supreme(IRE) ♦, a 38,000gns purchase, fell out of the gates and looked well held nearing the final furlong. However, he stayed on nicely under hands-and-heels riding thereafter and caught the eye. He will learn a deal for this debut experience and another furlong should suit. Official explanation: jockey said colt missed the break (op 9-1)
Candle Sahara(IRE), a half-sister to fast-ground 6f winner Kyle, was another who kept on inside the final furlong having been detached at the halfway stage. Faster ground should see her in a better light and she is entitled to improve a good deal for the run. (op 8-1)
Castles In The Air, bred to make his mark at around this trip at two, only tired out of contention inside the final furlong and turned in a respectable enough debut effort. He too will appreciate a less-taxing surface over this trip in the short term. (op 15-2)

3234 BURGES SALMON H'CAP 7f (S)
7:25 (7:25) (Class 4) (0-80,80) 3-Y-O+ **£4,857** (£1,445; £722; £360) **Stalls** Centre

Form RPR
50-0 1 **Starlight Gazer**[12] 2882 4-9-5 72 RichardThomas 3 81
(J A Geake) *in tch: rdn and hdwy over 2f out: chsd ldr 1f out: drvn to ld fnl 100yds: all out* **9/1**
5-22 2 1 1/4 **Blue Java**[20] 2626 6-9-2 74 (t) TravisBlock(5) 4 80
(H Morrison) *chsd ldrs: led 3f out: rdn over 1f out: hdd and no ex fnl 100yds* **3/1**[1]
00-4 3 hd **Sonning Star (IRE)**[12] 2886 3-8-4 65 MartinDwyer 6 67
(D R C Elsworth) *chsd ldrs: rdn 2f out: hung rt u.p ins fnl f: kpt on cl home* **12/1**
0030 4 6 **Bonnie Prince Blue**[15] 2771 4-9-12 79 MichaelHills 9 69
(B W Hills) *chsd ldrs: rdn over 2f out: wknd over 1f out* **6/1**
5560 5 1 **Gavarnie Beau (IRE)**[20] 2626 4-9-0 67 SebSanders 8 54
(M Blanshard) *in rr: rdn and sme hdwy over 2f out: nvr gng pce to rch ldrs* **4/1**[2]
0-14 6 8 **Grizedale (IRE)**[27] 2427 8-9-9 76 (t) PaulDoe 2 42
(J Akehurst) *led 4f: wknd over 2f out* **8/1**
0044 7 nk **Border Edge**[12] 2877 9-8-5 61 (b) MarcHalford(3) 7 27
(J J Bridger) *chsd ldrs: rdn over 3f out: sn wknd* **11/2**[3]
-006 8 11 **Akram (IRE)**[26] 2452 5-9-13 80 GeorgeBaker 1 17
(Jonjo O'Neill) *pressed ldrs to 1/2-way: sn wknd* **20/1**
00-0 9 10 **Alfie Tupper (IRE)**[31] 2318 4-9-8 75 JimmyFortune 5 —
(S Kirk) *prom early: bhd fr 1/2-way* **10/1**

1m 30.96s (3.96) **Going Correction** +0.675s/f (Yiel)
WFA 3 from 4yo+ 8lb 9 Ran SP% **117.3**
Speed ratings (Par 105):104,102,102,95,94 85,84,72,60
CSF £36.83 CT £333.36 TOTE £11.30: £3.40, £1.90, £3.00; EX 51.70.
Owner The Burning Stars **Bred** Dr J M Leigh **Trained** Kimpton, Hants

FOCUS
A fair handicap, run at a sound pace. The first three came clear and the form looks solid rated around the first three.
Alfie Tupper(IRE) Official explanation: jockey said gelding was unsuited by the heavy ground

3235 RIDGEWAY VOLKSWAGEN H'CAP 1m (S)
7:55 (7:59) (Class 4) (0-85,83) 3-Y-O **£4,857** (£1,445; £722; £360) **Stalls** Centre

Form RPR
3004 1 **Mark Of Love (IRE)**[11] 2916 3-7-10 65 MatthewDavies(7) 4 73
(M R Channon) *hld up in rr: stdy hdwy fr 3f out to ld jst ins fnl f: pushed out* **16/1**
4151 2 2 **Blue Monkey (IRE)**[12] 2872 3-8-7 74 LukeMorris(5) 5 78
(M L W Bell) *chsd ldrs: led over 2f out: sn rdn: hdd jst ins fnl f and kpt on same pce* **7/2**[2]

-102 **3** *1* **Rule Of Life**[21] 2598 3-9-1 **77**....................(b[1]) RichardHughes 7 79
(B W Hills) *in tch: rdn over 3f out: hrd drvn 2f out: styd on fnl f but nvr gng pce to trble ldng pair* **11/2**[3]
4-42 **4** *1 1/4* **Nicada (IRE)**[10] 2943 3-8-5 **67**....................(p) SimonWhitworth 9 67
(J S Moore) *chsd ldrs: rdn and effrt 2f out: styd on same pce fnl f* **16/1**
-300 **5** *4* **Mystery Ocean**[34] 2213 3-9-4 **80**.................... SebSanders 11 72
(R M Beckett) *in rr: rdn 3f out: hdwy fr 2f out but nvr gng pce to be competitive* **20/1**
-603 **6** *3* **Spume (IRE)**[12] 2872 3-9-1 **77**....................(t) MartinDwyer 8 63
(Sir Michael Stoute) *chsd ldrs: rdn and outpcd fr 3f out: n.d after* **7/1**
-541 **7** *nk* **Apache Dawn**[7] 3029 3-9-0 **76** 6ex.................... NCallan 2 61
(K A Ryan) *led main gp but jst hld by lone ldr on stands' rail: rdn and ev ch fr over 2f out: wknd over 1f out* **7/4**[1]
0-00 **8** *1 1/2* **Awwal Malika (USA)**[22] 2571 3-8-5 **67**.................... PaulDoe 1 49
(C E Brittain) *chsd ldrs: rdn and ev ch over 2f out: sn wknd* **40/1**
-420 **9** *6* **Curzon Prince (IRE)**[28] 2400 3-9-5 **81**.................... EddieAhern 14 51
(C F Wall) *racd along stands' side and led overall tl hdd over 2f out: sn wknd* **11/1**
1-20 **10** *1 1/2* **Aegean Prince**[42] 1956 3-9-7 **83**.................... JimmyFortune 3 50
(W R Muir) *chsd ldrs: rdn over 2f out and sn wknd* **16/1**
5-00 **11** *8* **Apollo Five**[28] 2400 3-8-12 **74**.................... TQuinn 13 25
(D J Coakley) *in tch 5f* **40/1**
-006 **12** *31* **Alfredian Park**[10] 2943 3-8-10 **72**.................... LPKeniry 6 —
(S Kirk) *early spd: wknd qckly fr 1/2-way: t.o* **66/1**

1m 45.18s (4.56) **Going Correction** +0.675s/f (Yiel) **12** Ran SP% **123.6**
Speed ratings (Par 102):104,102,101,99,95 92,92,90,84,83 75,44
CSF £72.79 CT £365.35 TOTE £17.70: £3.60, £1.60, £1.80; EX 103.70.
Owner Box 41 **Bred** G Swift **Trained** West Ilsley, Berks
■ The first winner for Matthew Davies.

FOCUS
A fair three-year-old handicap but not easy to be confident about the form, which is rated through the placed horses.
Aegean Prince Official explanation: jockey said colt was unsuited by the heavy ground

3236 GARDNER MECHANICAL SERVICES MAIDEN STKS 1m 4f 5y
8:30 (8:30) (Class 5) 3-Y-O+ **£4,533** (£1,348; £674; £336) **Stalls** High

Form RPR
03-4 **1** **Furmigadelagiusta**[42] 1974 3-9-0 78.................... JimmyFortune 6 84
(L M Cumani) *in tch: slt ld fr over 3f out: hrd rdn and hdd fnl 75yds: rallied u.p to ld again last stride* **5/2**[2]
2-4 **2** *shd* **Loulwa (IRE)**[60] 1499 3-8-9 0....................(t) SebSanders 4 79
(J Noseda) *mid-div: drvn along 5f out: hdwy to trck ldrs 4f out: hrd rdn to ld fnl 75yds: hdd last strides* **7/2**[3]
3535 **3** *3* **Sunley Peace**[13] 2816 3-9-0 85.................... MichaelHills 10 79
(D R C Elsworth) *s.i.s: sn mid-div: hdwy 5f out: w ldrs fr 3f out: rdn 2f out: outpcd ins fnl f* **7/4**[1]
6 **4** *1* **Hesivorthedriver (GER)**[103] 764 3-9-0 0.................... JimCrowley 11 77
(Mrs A J Perrett) *in rr: hdwy 6f out: pressed ldrs fr 3f out: outpcd fnl f* **10/1**
02 **5** *17* **Sadler's Leap (IRE)**[20] 2620 4-9-8 0.................... PaulEddery 1 45
(Pat Eddery) *chsd ldrs: hrd drvn 4f out: wknd fr 3f out* **9/1**
0-0 **6** *3* **By The River**[18] 2690 3-9-0 0.................... PaulDoe 5 45
(P Winkworth) *led tl hdd over 3f out: wknd sn after* **100/1**
7 *5* **Welsh Guard (USA)**[17] 4-9-13 0.................... TQuinn 3 37
(G P Enright) *slowly away: in tch w main gp 1/2-way: sn wknd* **33/1**
0/ **8** *1/2* **Pauls Plain**[21] 1552 6-9-13 0.................... VinceSlattery 2 37
(S Curran) *a in rr* **100/1**
9 *15* **Moonshine Vixen**[14] 6-9-1 0.................... WilliamCarson(7) 9 8
(P W Hiatt) *slowly away: in tch 1/2-way: sn bhd* **80/1**
0- **10** *28* **Tejareb (IRE)**[419] 1650 4-9-8 0.................... EddieAhern 7 —
(C E Brittain) *chsd ldrs: rdn 5f out: sn btn* **20/1**

2m 47.45s (11.46) **Going Correction** +1.10s/f (Soft)
WFA 3 from 4yo+ 13lb **10** Ran SP% **117.2**
Speed ratings (Par 103):105,104,102,102,90 88,85,85,75,56
CSF £11.46 TOTE £3.80: £1.60, £2.00, £1.50; EX 19.10.
Owner Scuderia Rencati Srl **Bred** Azienda Agricola Francesca **Trained** Newmarket, Suffolk

FOCUS
A fair maiden and the first pair came clear in a thrilling finish. The form looks pretty sound, rated around the winner and third to earlier form, backed up by the second.
Welsh Guard(USA) Official explanation: jockey said gelding missed the break
Moonshine Vixen Official explanation: jockey said mare missed the break

3237 ELECTROLUX H'CAP 6f 8y
9:00 (9:02) (Class 5) (0-75,74) 3-Y-O **£3,562** (£1,059; £529; £264) **Stalls** Centre

Form RPR
5656 **1** **Tipsy Prince**[21] 2601 3-9-3 **70**.................... JimmyFortune 5 72
(David Pinder) *chsd ldrs: hrd rdn fnl f to ld cl home: all out* **11/4**[1]
4353 **2** *nk* **Dualagi**[8] 3000 3-8-9 **62**.................... LPKeniry 9 63
(J S Moore) *t.k.h: hld up in rr: stdy hdwy over 2f out: rdn and r.o wl fnl f: gng on cl home but nvr quite gng pce of wnr* **8/1**
5105 **3** *nk* **Game Lady**[26] 2444 3-8-10 **68**.................... LukeMorris(5) 1 68
(I A Wood) *sn in narrow ld: hrd rdn and hung lft appr fnl f: hung rt u.p ins fnl f: hdd and no ex cl home* **11/1**
6102 **4** *7* **Jack Oliver**[19] 2662 3-9-7 **74**.................... RichardHughes 7 53
(B J Meehan) *stdd s and in rr: rdn over 2f out: effrt over 1f out but nvr gng pce to be competitive and wknd ins fnl f* **7/2**[2]
04 **5** *4* **Sherjawy (IRE)**[32] 2276 3-7-11 **55** oh6....................(b) NicolPolli(5) 3 22
(Miss Z C Davison) *w ldr to 1/2-way: wknd over 1f out* **33/1**
0000 **6** *1/2* **Lordswood (IRE)**[18] 2697 3-7-9 **55** oh1.................... KMay(7) 6 21
(J J Bridger) *chsd ldrs: rdn 1/2-way and sn outpcd* **33/1**
522 **7** *8* **Spiffing (IRE)**[36] 2144 3-9-1 **68**.................... SebSanders 2 10
(R M Beckett) *chsd ldrs tl wknd over 2f out* **7/2**[2]
-002 **8** *2 1/2* **The Skerret**[19] 2661 3-8-6 **59**....................(p) JimCrowley 8 —
(P Winkworth) *in tch: rdn over 3f out: sn btn* **9/2**[3]
35-4 **9** *1* **Pont Wood**[172] 128 3-8-10 **63**.................... NCallan 4 —
(M Blanshard) *chsd ldrs: rdn over 3f out: wknd qckly 2f out* **16/1**

1m 19.03s (4.71) **Going Correction** +0.675s/f (Yiel) **9** Ran SP% **120.5**
Speed ratings (Par 100):95,94,94,84,79 78,68,64,63
CSF £27.13 CT £213.35 TOTE £4.40: £1.50, £2.20, £2.50; EX 32.40 Place 6 £46.62, Place 5 £16.32..
Owner Ambermarley Partnership **Bred** Capt J H Wilson **Trained** Kingston Lisle, Oxon

FOCUS
A modest sprint in which the first three came well clear, although the placed horses do not look well treated.
T/Plt: £63.90 to a £1 stake. Pool: £88,915.80. 1,014.45 winning tickets. T/Qpdt: £23.50 to a £1 stake. Pool: £5,134.90. 161.60 winning tickets. ST

[3030]WARWICK (L-H)
Thursday, July 5

OFFICIAL GOING: Soft (heavy in places; 5.5)
Wind: Light, half-behind Weather: Showers

3238 EUROPEAN BREEDERS' FUND MEDIAN AUCTION MAIDEN STKS 7f 26y
6:30 (6:33) (Class 4) 2-Y-O **£4,857** (£1,445; £722; £360) **Stalls** Low

Form RPR
R4 **1** **Toto Skyllachy**[17] 2710 2-9-3 0.................... MickyFenton 2 81
(T P Tate) *led 6f out: rdn over 1f out: r.o* **7/1**[3]
2 **2** *4* **Billion Dollar Kid**[21] 2600 2-9-3 0.................... JamieSpencer 5 71
(R Hannon) *led 1f: chsd wnr: rdn over 2f out: hung lft over 1f out: no ex fnl f* **10/11**[1]
0 **3** *4* **Softly Killing Me**[26] 2468 2-8-12 0.................... FergusSweeney 7 56
(J Gallagher) *prom: rdn over 2f out: sn wknd* **33/1**
4 *1 1/2* **Janet's Delight** 2-8-12 0.................... JamesDoyle 1 52
(S Curran) *chsd ldrs: rdn over 2f out: sn hung lft and wknd* **50/1**
442 **5** *1 3/4* **Midnite Blews (IRE)**[6] 3043 2-9-3 0....................(p) SteveDrowne 3 53
(A B Haynes) *s.i.s: hdwy over 5f out: rdn over 2f out: sn wknd* **7/1**[3]
6 **6** *10* **Champagne Dancer**[8] 2977 2-9-3 0.................... DaneO'Neill 4 28
(D J S Ffrench Davis) *s.i.s: hdwy 4f out: rdn and wknd over 2f out* **12/1**
02 **7** *20* **Marning Star**[16] 2739 2-9-3 0.................... TPO'Shea 8 —
(M R Channon) *sn pushed along in rr: wknd 4f out* **9/2**[2]
5 **8** *3 1/2* **Prince's Decree**[46] 1859 2-9-3 0.................... TomEaves 6 —
(G M Moore) *s.i.s: sn prom: wknd 1/2-way* **12/1**

1m 31.9s (7.70) **Going Correction** +0.975s/f (Soft) **8** Ran SP% **115.9**
Speed ratings (Par 96):95,90,85,84,82 70,47,43
CSF £13.99 TOTE £9.40: £2.60, £1.02, £9.20; EX 21.00.
Owner Phil Martin and Richard Longley **Bred** Mrs G Slater **Trained** Tadcaster, N Yorks

FOCUS
Not many horses are suited by such testing conditions, let alone two-year-olds, and this was a weak maiden. The form is somewhat guess, rated around the principals.

NOTEBOOK
Toto Skyllachy refused to race on his intended debut at Ripon, but he shaped well when fourth at Carlisle next time and stepped forward again to get off the mark at the third attempt. Given a really positive ride, he was one of the few to really relish the conditions and ran out a clear-cut winner. (op 15-2 tchd 8-1)
Billion Dollar Kid could make little impression over 6f on quick ground on her debut at Newbury, but she showed some ability under these vastly different conditions. (op 11-10)
Softly Killing Me could make little impression over 6f on quick ground on her debut at Newbury, but she showed some ability under these vastly different conditions.
Janet's Delight, an Erhaab half-sister to Fields Of Green, who was placed over 1m at three, travelled quite nicely through the early stages and clearly has ability.
Midnite Blews(IRE) seemed to handle soft ground well enough when second at Folkestone on his previous start, but these conditions appeared even more testing and he failed to run his race, with the first-time cheekpieces clearly having little impact. (tchd 13-2 and 8-1)
Marning Star was never travelling at any stage and failed to run his race. This ground was seemingly too testing. Official explanation: jockey said colt never travelled (op 7-2)

3239 HEWDEN HIRE H'CAP 7f 26y
7:00 (7:00) (Class 4) (0-85,82) 3-Y-O+ **£5,181** (£1,541; £770; £384) **Stalls** Low

Form RPR
-131 **1** **Guilded Warrior**[20] 2623 4-9-10 **78**.................... FergusSweeney 1 92
(W S Kittow) *chsd ldr: led over 1f out: edgd lft and rdn clr* **11/4**[1]
0630 **2** *5* **Material Witness (IRE)**[2] 3191 10-9-7 **75**.................... JamieSpencer 2 78+
(W R Muir) *led: rdn and hdd over 1f out: sn outpcd: eased whn btn nr fin* **4/1**[3]
1360 **3** *5* **Hiccups**[23] 2528 7-10-0 **82**.................... DarryllHolland 5 69
(M Dods) *hld up: hdwy 1/2-way: wknd 2f out* **10/3**[2]
6466 **4** *1* **Knapton Hill**[11] 2914 3-7-10 **63**.................... WilliamBuick(5) 3 47
(R Hollinshead) *chsd ldrs: lost pl 1/2-way: n.d after* **11/4**[1]
220 **5** *12* **Barons Spy (IRE)**[26] 2469 6-9-5 **73**.................... JamesDoyle 4 24
(R J Price) *hld up: hdwy 1/2-way: wknd over 2f out* **7/1**

1m 28.76s (4.56) **Going Correction** +0.975s/f (Soft)
WFA 3 from 4yo+ 8lb **5** Ran SP% **108.9**
Speed ratings (Par 105):112,106,100,99,85
CSF £13.43 TOTE £3.80: £1.70, £2.00; EX 12.00.
Owner The Racing Guild **Bred** Manor Farm Packers Ltd **Trained** Blackborough, Devon

FOCUS
A very uncompetitive handicap, with the winner appearing the only one to show form, but the pace was strong and the winning time was decent for the grade allowing for the conditions.
Knapton Hill Official explanation: jockey said filly was unsuited by the soft ground
Barons Spy(IRE) Official explanation: jockey said gelding was unsuited by the soft ground

3240 COMPAIR COMPRESSORS H'CAP 6f
7:35 (7:36) (Class 3) (0-95,93) 3-Y-O+ **£7,124** (£2,119; £1,059; £529) **Stalls** Centre

Form RPR
2310 **1** **Nobilissima (IRE)**[20] 2629 3-8-1 **76**.................... LiamJones(3) 1 82
(J L Spearing) *led: hdd over 4f out: led over 1f out: sn hdd: rallied to ld post* **9/1**
5230 **2** *shd* **Pawan (IRE)**[18] 2688 7-8-6 **77**....................(b) AnnStokell(5) 7 84
(Miss A Stokell) *chsd ldrs: led 1f out: hdd post* **14/1**
0144 **3** *6* **Goodbye Cash (IRE)**[3] 3164 3-8-10 **82**.................... StephenDonohoe 3 70
(P D Evans) *chsd ldrs: outpcd 1/2-way: styd on ins fnl f* **12/1**
0160 **4** *1/2* **Angus Newz**[5] 3104 4-9-13 **93**....................(v) DarryllHolland 5 81
(M Quinn) *w ldr tl led over 4f out: rdn and hdd over 1f out: hung lft and wknd fnl f* **8/1**
10-0 **5** *1 1/4* **River Bravo (IRE)**[82] 1041 4-9-5 **92**.................... MCGeran(7) 2 76
(P W Chapple-Hyam) *s.i.s: hdwy over 2f out: sn rdn: wknd over 1f out* **10/3**[2]
0440 **6** *8* **Mujood**[8] 2993 4-9-9 **89**.................... StephenCarson 8 49
(Eve Johnson Houghton) *chsd ldrs over 3f* **13/2**
0-00 **7** *2* **Pacific Pride**[33] 2237 4-9-11 **91**.................... JamieSpencer 4 45
(J J Quinn) *chsd ldrs: rdn over 2f out: wknd over 1f out* **3/1**[1]
0040 **8** *dist* **Charles Darwin (IRE)**[30] 2339 4-9-5 **85**.................... TedDurcan 6 —
(M Blanshard) *chsd ldrs: rdn 1/2-way: sn wknd and eased* **11/2**[3]

1m 17.83s (3.55) **Going Correction** +0.775s/f (Yiel)
WFA 3 from 4yo+ 6lb **8** Ran SP% **112.3**
Speed ratings (Par 107):107,106,98,98,96 85,83,—
CSF £118.14 CT £1516.77 TOTE £4.80: £1.10, £3.10, £2.80; EX 53.00.
Owner Nine Traders Syndicate **Bred** Sea Syndicate **Trained** Kinnersley, Worcs

FOCUS
An ordinary sprint handicap for the grade rated around the first two, who were clear. They raced towards the stands' side in the straight.

The Form Book, Raceform Ltd, Compton, RG20 6NL

NOTEBOOK
Nobilissima(IRE) ran no sort of race at Goodwood last time, but she returned to the sort of form she showed when winning at Chepstow two starts previously to win very narrowly. She looked booked for second for most of the way inside the final furlong, but found reserves to get up on the line. Official explanation: trainer had no explanation for the apparent improvement in form (op 12-1)
Pawan(IRE) handled the conditions well and looked the most likely winner for most of the final furlong, but he was kept more towards the middle of the track than Nobilissima, who had the benefit of the stands' rail, and was reeled in literally on the line. He is quite a likable type and should have won more races over the years. (tchd 16-1)
Goodbye Cash(IRE) had conditions to suit, but she was no match for the front two and looks high enough in the weights. (tchd 11-1)
Angus Newz should not really have minded the ground, but she failed to sustain her challenge after showing good speed. (op 9-2 tchd 4-1)
River Bravo(IRE) is another who had the ground in his favour and he could have been expected to run much better. (op 7-2 tchd 5-1)
Pacific Pride has some form on testing ground, but his only win came on 'good to firm', and he will probably be happier when returned to a faster surface. (op 7-2 tchd 4-1 and 11-4)
Charles Darwin(IRE) Official explanation: jockey said colt was unsuited by the soft ground

3241 REG HARRIS MEMORIAL CLAIMING STKS — 1m 22y
8:05 (8:07) (Class 5) 3-Y-0+ — **£3,238** (£963; £481; £240) — **Stalls** Low

Form				RPR
5020	1		**Surwaki (USA)**[16] 2748 5-9-6 74 ... JamieSpencer 3 (R M H Cowell) *a.p: chsd ldr 3f out: styd far side ent st: rdn to ld over 1f out: styd on u.p* **15/8**[1]	68
5434	2	3 1/2	**Rowan Lodge (IRE)**[13] 2831 5-9-4 59 ...(v) JimmyQuinn 5 (M H Tompkins) *hld up: hdwy and styd far side ent st: rdn to chse wnr ins fnl f: no imp* **9/4**[2]	59
6056	3	2 1/2	**Kirkhammerton (IRE)**[24] 2519 5-8-12 41 ...(b) AdamKirby 4 (A J McCabe) *sn rdn to ld: c stands' side ent st: rdn and hdd over 1f out: edgd lft and wknd ins fnl f* **16/1**	48
0003	4	1/2	**Punta Galera (IRE)**[5] 3076 4-9-7 73 ... PatDobbs 6 (R Hannon) *hld up in tch: styd far side ent st: rdn and wknd over 1f out* **7/2**[3]	56
2050	5	1 1/4	**Tipsy Lad**[23] 2540 5-8-12 39 ...(t) FergusSweeney 1 (D J S Ffrench Davis) *hld up: styd far side ent st: hdwy u.p over 1f out: n.d* **18/1**	44
5330	6	6	**Rafferty (IRE)**[8] 2990 8-8-7 44 ...(p) ThomasBubb(7) 9 (S Dow) *prom: racd keenly: styd far side ent st: sn rdn and wknd* **12/1**	33
-000	7	4	**Safari**[7] 3035 4-8-4 36 ...(b) EmmettStack(3) 2 (A J Chamberlain) *hld up: styd far side ent st: rdn over 1f out: n.d* **66/1**	18
0000	8	9	**Wizby**[10] 2938 4-8-8 45 ow1 ... StephenDonohoe 7 (P D Evans) *hld up: rdn and c stands' side ent st: sn wknd* **9/1**	—
5206	9	nk	**Cape Of Storms**[63] 1435 4-9-5 45 ... TolleyDean(5) 8 (R Brotherton) *chsd ldr 5f: sn rdn: wkng whn hung rt over 1f out* **33/1**	16

1m 46.95s (7.35) **Going Correction** +0.975s/f (Soft) **9** Ran SP% **121.0**
Speed ratings (Par 103):102,98,96,95,94 88,84,75,74
CSF £6.66 TOTE £3.10: £1.50, £1.60, £4.40; EX 9.70.
Owner Tessona Racing **Bred** Airlie Stud **Trained** Six Mile Bottom, Cambs

FOCUS
A modest claimer with the form limited by the proximity of the third and fifth. Kirkhammerton, Wizby and Cape Of Storms raced towards the stands' side in the straight, but the much larger group on the far side of the track had the call.

3242 GEORGE WIMPEY CENTRAL CELEBRATION H'CAP — 1m 2f 188y
8:40 (8:41) (Class 4) (0-85,85) 3-Y-0+ — **£5,181** (£1,541; £770; £384) — **Stalls** Low

Form				RPR
3431	1		**Mull Of Dubai**[3] 3165 4-9-7 **81** 6ex ... JohnEgan 2 (J S Moore) *hld up: hdwy to chse ldr over 2f out: led over 1f out: sn rdn: jst hld on* **15/8**[1]	91
4332	2	nk	**Cleaver**[5] 3093 6-9-2 **76** ... JamieSpencer 4 (Lady Herries) *stdd s: hld up: hdwy to chse wnr over 1f out: r.o wl nr fin* **2/1**[2]	85
0001	3	6	**Peruvian Prince (USA)**[28] 2397 5-9-8 **85** ... JamieMoriarty(3) 5 (R A Fahey) *hld up: hdwy u.p over 2f out: wknd fnl f* **11/2**[3]	84
0001	4	9	**Prize Fighter (IRE)**[19] 2660 5-9-7 **81** ...(b) TedDurcan 3 (H R A Cecil) *led: clr over 2f out: hdd & wknd over 1f out* **6/1**	65
060-	5	5	**Artistic Style**[272] 5787 7-9-9 **83** ... TomEaves 6 (B G Powell) *chsd ldrs: rdn over 2f out: sn wknd* **14/1**	58
/10-	6	26	**Pound Sign**[440] 1108 4-9-11 **85** ... DaneO'Neill 1 (Evan Williams) *chsd ldr tl rdn and wknd over 2f out* **25/1**	16

2m 30.35s (10.95) **Going Correction** +0.975s/f (Soft) **6** Ran SP% **108.3**
Speed ratings (Par 105):99,98,94,87,84 65
CSF £5.45 TOTE £3.30: £1.70, £1.20; EX 5.30.
Owner Mrs Fitri Hay **Bred** B Walters **Trained** Upper Lambourn, Berks

FOCUS
Just the six runners and not the strongest of contests for the grade. The first two finished clear and the form is best rated around the runner-up to his latest mark.

3243 HYDROVANE COMPRESSORS H'CAP — 1m 4f 134y
9:10 (9:10) (Class 5) (0-75,74) 4-Y-0+ — **£3,238** (£963; £481; £240) — **Stalls** Low

Form				RPR
-021	1		**Olimpo (FR)**[20] 2621 6-9-7 **74** ... DaneO'Neill 2 (B R Millman) *chsd ldrs: rdn over 1f out: styd on u.p to ld post* **7/1**	83
-042	2	hd	**Dan Buoy (FR)**[8] 2981 4-9-2 **69** ... FergusSweeney 5 (A King) *trckd ldr: racd keenly: led over 2f out: sn rdn: hdd post* **6/1**[2]	78
4321	3	1 3/4	**Trafalgar Day**[7] 3036 4-9-1 **68** 6ex ... JamieSpencer 6 (W M Brisbourne) *s.i.s: hld up: hmpd after 1f: hdwy over 2f out: rdn over 1f out: styd on same pce fnl f* **11/4**[1]	74
313	4	3	**Broughtons Revival**[15] 2765 5-9-3 **70** ... BrettDoyle 9 (W J Musson) *prom: rdn over 3f out: styd on same pce fnl 2f* **7/1**	72
3001	5	4	**Mahmjra**[30] 2348 5-8-13 **66** ... EdwardCreighton 3 (C N Allen) *led: rdn and hdd over 2f out: wknd fnl f* **14/1**	62
6-00	6	7	**The Composer**[22] 2572 5-8-7 **60** ... TedDurcan 1 (M Blanshard) *hld up: rdn over 3f out: sn wknd* **12/1**	45
3150	7	10	**Beldon Hill (USA)**[12] 2861 4-9-3 **73** ... JamieMoriarty(3) 7 (R A Fahey) *hld up: hdwy over 3f out: rdn and wknd over 2f out* **14/1**	43
0350	8	12	**Stravara**[12] 2868 4-7-11 **55** oh3 ... WilliamBuick(5) 11 (R Hollinshead) *s.i.s: hld up: hdwy 5f out: rdn and wknd over 2f out* **14/1**	7
0041	9	40	**Lady Romanov (IRE)**[7] 3042 4-9-7 **74** 6ex ... JimmyQuinn 10 (M H Tompkins) *prom over 8f* **8/1**	—
3052	10	1/2	**Key Partners (IRE)**[7] 3035 6-8-3 **56** ... TPO'Shea 8 (J T Stimpson) *hld up: wknd 4f out* **13/2**[3]	—

2m 55.1s (11.50) **Going Correction** +0.975s/f (Soft) **10** Ran SP% **118.1**
Speed ratings (Par 103):103,102,101,99,97 93,87,79,55,54
CSF £49.32 CT £145.11 TOTE £8.90: £2.60, £2.50, £1.50; EX 42.40 Place 6 £66.34, Place 5 £47.39..
Owner Pot Black Racing **Bred** Ewar Stud Farm **Trained** Kentisbeare, Devon
■ Stewards' Enquiry : Dane O'Neill four-day ban: used whip with excessive frequency and without giving gelding time to respond (Jul 16-19)
Fergus Sweeney three-day ban: used whip with excessive frequency (Jul 16-18)

FOCUS
A modest handicap rated around the placed horses to recent form.
T/Plt: £28.60 to a £1 stake. Pool: £66,893.05. 1,706.45 winning tickets. T/Qpdt: £11.60 to a £1 stake. Pool: £4,192.60. 266.35 winning tickets. CR

3037 YARMOUTH (L-H)
Thursday, July 5

OFFICIAL GOING: Soft (6.4)
Wind: Half across Weather: Cloudy

3244 WEATHERBYS VAT SERVICES MAIDEN STKS (DIV I) — 1m 2f 21y
2:00 (2:03) (Class 5) 3-Y-0+ — **£2,145** (£641; £320; £160; £79) — **Stalls** Low

Form				RPR
0-0	1		**Miss Marvellous (USA)**[64] 1408 3-8-11 0 ... OscarUrbina 3 (J R Fanshawe) *trckd ldrs: effrt gng wl over 3f out: led over 2f out: kpt on wl fnl f: pushed out* **6/1**[2]	73+
0-	2	1/2	**Earl Marshal (USA)**[250] 6220 3-9-2 0 ... KerrinMcEvoy 8 (Sir Michael Stoute) *reluctant to enter stalls: towards rr: outpcd 4f out: styd on unwillingly fr over 1f out: wnt 2nd cl home: nvr gng to win* **4/5**[1]	76
	3	1	**Opal Haze (USA)** 3-8-11 0 ... KDarley 2 (J H M Gosden) *2nd tl led over 4f out: rdn and hdd over 2f out: one pce fnl f: lost 2nd cl home* **7/1**[3]	69
-004	4	11	**Brierley Lil**[132] 534 3-8-11 46 ... SamHitchcott 1 (J L Spearing) *settled in 3rd pl: 2nd briefly over 4f out: sn rdn: btn 2f out: plodded on* **22/1**	47
0	5	1 3/4	**Laurentian Lad**[17] 2726 3-9-2 0 ... ChrisCatlin 4 (Rae Guest) *hld up: sme prog over 4f out: rdn 3f out: sn struggling* **12/1**	49
0	6	11	**Wightgar**[43] 1950 3-9-2 0 ...(t) StephenDonohoe 7 (R A Kvisla) *dwlt: sn rdn: a bhd: t.o 3f out* **33/1**	27
	7	3 1/2	**Kaichou (IRE)** 3-8-4 0 ... BradleyRoper(7) 10 (N A Callaghan) *s.s: last tl 1/2-way: drvn 5f out: fnd nil: t.o fnl 3f* **20/1**	15
0006	8	17	**Feeling Peckish (USA)**[6] 2420 3-8-11 31 ... RussellKennemore(5) 5 (M C Chapman) *rdn to ld: reluctant to stay there and several reminders: hdd over 4f out: sn t.o* **100/1**	—
-000	9	8	**Three Half Crowns (IRE)**[14] 2796 3-9-2 50 ... IanMongan 9 (P Howling) *bhd: rdn 4f out: sn t.o: eased fnl 2f* **66/1**	—
0/0	10	12	**Black Wadi**[41] 1998 5-9-8 0 ...(t) JimmyQuinn 6 (T Keddy) *chsd ldrs tl 1/2-way: t.o fnl 4f: eased 2f out* **33/1**	—
	11	1/2	**Best One** 3-9-2 0 ... DarryllHolland 11 (C E Brittain) *s.s: hdwy to go 4th 1/2-way: virtually pulling himself up and hd on one side 3f out: t.o and eased fnl 2f* **10/1**	—

2m 18.33s (10.23) **Going Correction** +1.075s/f (Soft)
WFA 3 from 5yo 11lb **11** Ran SP% **116.6**
Speed ratings (Par 103):102,101,100,92,90 81,79,65,59,49 49
CSF £10.44 TOTE £8.00: £1.80, £1.20, £1.90; EX 15.70 Trifecta £17.90 Pool £568.81 - 22.45 winning units..
Owner Ali Saeed **Bred** Derry Meeting Farm Et Al **Trained** Newmarket, Suffolk

FOCUS
This developed into a war of attrition in the ground and the front three, who were the only ones that mattered according to the market anyway, pulled a mile clear of the others. The winning time was 0.7 seconds faster than the second division and the first two have been rated 12lb above previous form.

3245 EBF/GREAT YARMOUTH GLASS MAIDEN FILLIES' STKS — 6f 3y
2:30 (2:32) (Class 5) 2-Y-0 — **£3,562** (£1,059; £529; £264) — **Stalls** High

Form				RPR
	1		**Shaker (IRE)** 2-9-0 0 ... JamieSpencer 4 (M L W Bell) *s.s: hld up last early: effrt 2f out: burst ahd over 1f out: hld on wl* **7/2**[1]	80+
	2	1/2	**Gone Fast (USA)** 2-9-0 0 ... OscarUrbina 9 (J R Fanshawe) *towards rr: hdwy and rdn over 1f out: nt clr run briefly: stl 5th 200yds out: kpt on wl to snatch 2nd: promising* **7/1**[3]	80+
	3	shd	**Pivotal Queen (IRE)** 2-9-0 0 ... NickyMackay 6 (L M Cumani) *trckd ldrs: rdn and chsd wnr over 1f out: no imp: jst lost 2nd* **7/2**[1]	78+
	4	2	**Whiteoak Lady (IRE)** 2-9-0 0 ... StephenDonohoe 1 (J L Spearing) *pressed ldrs on outside: rdn over 2f out: one pce ins fnl f* **16/1**	72
	5	3	**Nylla** 2-9-0 0 ... JHBowman 8 (M R Channon) *led 1f: drvn and wknd over 1f out* **10/1**	63
	6	1/2	**Mayaar (USA)** 2-9-0 0 ... AdrianMcCarthy 5 (P W Chapple-Hyam) *led after 1f tl drvn and hdd over 1f out: sn wknd* **6/1**[2]	62
	7	1 3/4	**Floristry** 2-9-0 0 ... JDSmith 10 (Sir Michael Stoute) *midfield: pushed along and rn green 2f out: no ch after but kpt on steadily* **6/1**[2]	56+
0	8	4	**Weight In Gold**[13] 2832 2-9-0 0 ... JimmyQuinn 3 (P J McBride) *midfield: rdn over 2f out: sn btn* **50/1**	44
0	9	4	**Little Bones**[24] 2510 2-9-0 0 ... ChrisCatlin 12 (Rae Guest) *towards rr: rdn 1/2-way: struggling after* **33/1**	32
	10	1 1/4	**Queen Be** 2-9-0 0 ... DarryllHolland 14 (I W McInnes) *pressed ldrs 3f out: no ch and hanging bdly lft over 1f out* **14/1**	29
00	11	2 1/2	**Beyabi**[29] 2365 2-9-0 0 ... NCallan 13 (J R Jenkins) *midfield: rdn over 2f out: sn struggling* **25/1**	21

1m 17.89s (4.19) **Going Correction** +0.525s/f (Yiel) **11** Ran SP% **115.9**
Speed ratings (Par 91):93,92,92,89,85 84,82,77,71,70 66
CSF £27.33 TOTE £4.00: £1.60, £2.40, £1.70; EX 29.90 Trifecta £86.20 Pool £344.90 - 2.84 winning units..
Owner T G N Burrage **Bred** Ballylinch Stud **Trained** Newmarket, Suffolk

FOCUS
An ordinary maiden for juvenile fillies on paper and the time was only fair, just 0.11 seconds faster than the following two-year-old seller over the same trip. The form is rather shaky as there was little separating the front three at the line, but they are likely to improve and each should win races.

NOTEBOOK

Shaker(IRE) ◆, a 155,000euros half-sister to six winners including Coliseum and Homer, was given quite a bit to do but showed a nifty turn of foot to take her to the front and kept on well despite rather hanging away from the stands' rail under pressure. She can only improve and the Goffs Sales race is her main target. (op 100-30)

Gone Fast(USA) ◆, a $230,000 filly, is out of a multiple winner in the US who is from the same family as Awaasif, Lammtarra and Bosra Sham. Given a waiting ride, she tried to weave her way through the entire field and had to change direction a couple of times. Her rider did not get serious with her until well inside the last furlong, but by then it was too late and she could never quite get there in time. She was probably the best horse in this race and she looks a sure-fire future winner. (op 15-2 tchd 13-2)

Pivotal Queen(IRE) ◆, out of a mutiple winner in France and the US at up to 1m1f, showed a lot of promise on this debut and fared much the best of those that raced handily. She should not be hard to place. (op 4-1 tchd 100-30)

Whiteoak Lady(IRE), out of a multiple winner at up to 1m in Italy, was always up there and kept on pretty well in these testing conditions. She only cost 8,000euros and was probably beaten by three nice fillies, so connections should have been very encouraged by this. (op 25-1)

Nylla, a 10,000gns foal out of a multiple winner in Sweden, showed up well for a long way and should come on for the run. (op 12-1)

Mayaar(USA), a $130,000 filly, is closely related to winners in the US. She ran fast for a long way and should know more next time, especially on better ground. (tchd 13-2)

Floristry, a half-sister to Old Romney, raced quite keenly off the pace and did not seem to know what to do when the leaders started to get away, but she was by no means knocked about and should come on quite a bit for this. (op 4-1 tchd 7-1)

3246 PKF (UK) LLP (S) STKS — 6f 3y

3:00 (3:02) (Class 6) 2-Y-O — **£1,943** (£578; £288; £144) **Stalls** High

Form — RPR

4224 **1** — **Secret Meaning**[21] 2605 2-8-3 0 ... SaleemGolam(3) 7 — 60
(W G M Turner) *chsd ldrs: drvn over 2f out: impeded briefly 1f out: kpt on to ld 100yds out: sn clr* **8/1**

00 **2** 2 — **Mister Beano (IRE)**[13] 2832 2-8-11 0 ... NCallan 1 — 59
(V Smith) *racd freely on outside: edgd rt and drvn ahd wl over 1f out: hdd 100yds out and immediately outpcd* **9/4**[1]

3133 **3** 4 — **Miss Willoughby**[6] 3065 2-8-11 0 ... SebSanders 6 — 47
(J Ryan) *prom: led over 2f out tl wl over 1f out: fnd nil fnl f* **15/2**

4 1 — **Wicksy Creek** 2-8-8 0 ... JerryO'Dwyer(3) 5 — 44
(M G Quinlan) *stdd early: effrt 1/2-way: rdn over 2f out: no imp fnl f* **11/2**[3]

2 **5** 2 — **Liani (IRE)**[17] 2723 2-8-6 0 ... ChrisCatlin 8 — 33
(W M Brisbourne) *plld hrd: led tl over 2f out: wl btn whn hung lft over 1f out* **10/3**[2]

400 **6** ¾ — **Galley Slave (IRE)**[10] 2941 2-8-11 0 ... AdrianTNicholls 2 — 36
(Mrs P Sly) *cl up: rdn after 2f: hmpd 2f out: no imp fnl 2f* **15/2**

0 **7** 6 — **No Guilt (IRE)**[21] 2604 2-8-8 0 ow2 ... StephenDonohoe 3 — 15
(J L Spearing) *bhd: sn rdn: struggling over 2f out* **10/1**

00 **8** 25 — **Korcula**[46] 1857 2-8-11 0 ... JHBowman 10 — —
(M J Wallace) *pressed ldr 2f: lost pl 1/2-way and racd awkwardly: t.o and eased 1f out* **16/1**

60 **9** 8 — **Culzean Bay**[7] 3037 2-7-13 0 ... AmyBaker(7) 4 — —
(A Bailey) *missed break: bhd: struggling 1/2-way: t.o and eased over 1f out* **66/1**

1m 18.0s (4.30) **Going Correction** +0.525s/f (Yiel) — **9** Ran SP% **120.3**

Speed ratings (Par 92):92,89,84,82,80 79,71,37,27

CSF £27.55 TOTE £8.60: £2.30, £1.20, £2.00; EX 44.30 Trifecta £323.30 Pool £537.38 - 1.18 winning units..The winner was bought in for 7,200gns. Galley Slave was claimed by M. C. Chapman for £6,000. Mister Beano was claimed by Declan Carroll for £6,000.

Owner Sparsholt Stud **Bred** P C Hunt **Trained** Sigwells, Somerset

■ Stewards' Enquiry : N Callan caution: careless riding; one-day ban: careless riding (Jul 16)

FOCUS

A moderate seller in which the time was about right for the grade allowing for the conditions. The runner-up sets the level, bu the first two pulled right away and the future does not look particularly rosy for the others.

NOTEBOOK

Secret Meaning, well beaten behind Miss Willoughby in a similar contest here last time, was 5lb better off with her here. However, a bigger factor in the form turnaround was the drop in trip as it enabled her to settle just behind the leaders and, when asked to go and pick up the favourite, she found plenty. This is her grade, though nurseries are also an option for her. (op 9-1)

Mister Beano(IRE), taking a big drop in class, was well backed but probably saw too much daylight on the far side of the field. Despite that he still hit the front in plenty of time and pulled right away from the others, but the winner's finishing pace proved far too much for him. He was claimed by Declan Carroll for £6,000 and can probably pick up an ordinary seller. (op 3-1 tchd 7-2)

Miss Willoughby, who beat the winner over an extra furlong in similar ground here last month, had a 5lb penalty to contend with and, after holding every chance, was completely done for speed over the last furlong or so on this drop in trip. This was her tenth outing, so she has nothing in the way of scope. (op 6-1 tchd 11-2)

Wicksy Creek, out of a half-sister to the Flat/hurdles winner Waterwing, is obviously not considered anything special to be making his debut at this level. He did show a little bit, but will need to improve from this even to win a poor seller. (op 5-1 tchd 9-2 and 6-1)

Liani(IRE) did too much too soon in this ground and paid the penalty. Her Windsor debut shows that she is capable of better than this when she settles. (op 7-2)

Galley Slave(IRE), dropped in grade, was never travelling that well and does not seem to be progressing. He was claimed by Michael Chapman for £6,000. Official explanation: jockey said gelding hung right (op 8-1 tchd 7-1)

3247 BET365 BEST ODDS GUARANTEED ON EVERY RACE FILLIES' H'CAP — 7f 3y

3:30 (3:31) (Class 5) (0-75,75) 3-Y-O+ — **£2,849** (£847; £423; £211) **Stalls** High

Form — RPR

3125 **1** — **Indian's Feather (IRE)**[12] 2883 6-9-13 **75** ... KDarley 10 — 81
(N Tinkler) *chsd ldrs: drvn 2f out: sustained chal fnl f: r.o gamely to ld fnl stride* **9/1**

0-16 **2** hd — **What A Treasure (IRE)**[18] 2696 3-9-0 **70** ... NickyMackay 5 — 72
(L M Cumani) *prom: led 2f out: drvn and hrd pressed fnl f: pipped on post* **17/2**[3]

-630 **3** ½ — **Tilsworth Charlie**[22] 2553 4-8-9 **57** oh4 ow1 ... (v) NCallan 1 — 61
(J R Jenkins) *plld hrd and heavily restrained towards rr: effrt 2f out: ev ch thrght fnl f tl no ex cl home* **25/1**

0231 **4** 1½ — **Mugeba**[5] 3101 6-8-8 **56** oh2 ... (t) JimmyQuinn 2 — 56+
(Miss Gay Kelleway) *midfield: rdn and effrt 2f out: one pce and no imp fnl f* **9/4**[1]

263 **5** ½ — **Cassiara**[29] 2369 3-9-5 **75** ... SebSanders 13 — 71
(J Pearce) *last early: hdwy over 1f out: kpt on steadily wout threatening* **10/1**

0023 **6** 5 — **Mannello**[20] 2619 4-8-3 **56** oh5 ... (p) KevinGhunowa(5) 6 — 42
(Mrs C A Dunnett) *prom: drvn over 2f out: btn over 1f out* **20/1**

203 **7** nk — **Sister Act**[12] 2880 3-9-3 **73** ... OscarUrbina 4 — 55
(J R Fanshawe) *taken down early: dwlt: t.k.h and sn midfield: effrt to chse ldrs whn lost action wl over 1f out: no ch after* **10/3**[2]

0002 **8** 1½ — **Life's A Whirl**[12] 2877 5-8-8 **56** ... (p) DMylonas 3 — 37
(Mrs C A Dunnett) *plld hrd and pressed ldr: led 3f out: hdd 2f out: sn lost pl* **18/1**

0-00 **9** 4 — **Halfwaytoparadise**[12] 2877 4-8-5 **56** oh6 ... (p) SaleemGolam(3) 12 — 27
(W G M Turner) *plld hrd and led 4f: dropped out qckly* **66/1**

0066 **10** shd — **First Rhapsody (IRE)**[17] 2714 5-8-5 **56** oh9 ... DominicFox(3) 9 — 26
(T J Etherington) *drvn in rr 1/2-way: struggling after* **33/1**

0062 **11** 15 — **Al Rayanah**[3] 3172 4-8-3 **58** ... KirstyMilczarek(7) 11 — —
(G Prodromou) *s.s: plld hrd in rr: t.o 2f out: eased* **16/1**

050- **12** 20 — **Ashwell Rose**[50] 3998 5-8-8 **56** oh11 ... AdrianTNicholls 8 — —
(J R Jenkins) *drvn 1/2-way: struggling over 2f out: t.o and eased* **100/1**

1m 29.65s (3.05) **Going Correction** +0.525s/f (Yiel)

WFA 3 from 4yo+ 8lb — **12** Ran SP% **108.6**

Speed ratings (Par 100):103,102,102,100,99 94,93,92,87,87 70,47

CSF £64.81 CT £1364.97 TOTE £9.90: £2.90, £2.20, £4.70; EX 61.80 TRIFECTA Not won..

Owner James Marshall & Mrs Susan Marshall **Bred** The Duke Of Roxburghe's Stud, Beckhampton House St **Trained** Langton, N Yorks

■ Black Sea Pearl was withdrawn (9/1, vet's advice). R4 applies, deduct 10p in the £.

FOCUS

Quite a competitive fillies' handicap in which the front five came right away. The forrm looks ordinary but solid enough for the grade.

Halfwaytoparadise Official explanation: jockey said filly ran too free

Al Rayanah Official explanation: jockey said filly never travelled

Ashwell Rose Official explanation: jockey said mare had no more to give

3248 WEATHERBYS VAT SERVICES MAIDEN STKS (DIV II) — 1m 2f 21y

4:00 (4:01) (Class 5) 3-Y-O+ — **£2,145** (£641; £320; £160; £79) **Stalls** Low

Form — RPR

0-0 **1** — **Iceman George**[13] 2836 3-9-2 0 ... RichardMullen 9 — 68
(D Morris) *2nd tl drvn to ld over 2f out: hdd wl ins fnl f: battled bk to ld again fnl stride* **66/1**

2-22 **2** shd — **Dawn Sky**[18] 2690 3-9-2 85 ... NCallan 3 — 68
(M A Jarvis) *trckd ldng pair: gng wl 3f out tl rdn 2f out: racd idly but ev ch tl led wl ins fnl f: jst ct* **2/7**[1]

3 1¾ — **Dubai World** 3-9-2 0 ... (e[1]) ChrisCatlin 4 — 65
(Rae Guest) *hld up last tl over 3f out: effrt over 1f out: rdn and no imp fnl 100yds* **33/1**

P053 **4** 6 — **Feeling (IRE)**[27] 2436 3-9-2 76 ... AdrianMcCarthy 8 — 53
(P W Chapple-Hyam) *led: drvn and hdd over 2f out: wknd ins fnl f* **13/2**[2]

5 1½ — **Crystal Ball** 3-8-11 0 ... DarryllHolland 11 — 45
(Rae Guest) *towards rr: rdn 4f out: racd awkwardly: wl btn 2f out* **25/1**

6 **6** 1¼ — **Hannahbecc**[13] 2836 3-8-11 0 ... JimmyQuinn 6 — 42
(H R A Cecil) *towards rr: pushed along 4f out: wl btn 2f out* **8/1**[3]

2m 19.03s (10.93) **Going Correction** +1.075s/f (Soft) — **6** Ran SP% **110.5**

Speed ratings (Par 103):99,98,97,92,91 90

CSF £86.15 TOTE £30.60: £6.30, £1.10; EX 73.80 Trifecta £437.90 Part won. Pool £616.82 - 0.68 winning units..

Owner T J Wells **Bred** T J And J Wells **Trained** Newmarket, Suffolk

■ Stewards' Enquiry : N Callan one-day ban: used whip with excessive frequency (Jul 17)

FOCUS

This looked much the weaker of the two divisions, especially with the five non-runners due to the state of the ground, and the time was 0.7 seconds slower. This was a rather messy contest, which may have contributed to the demise of the red-hot favourite, and the form looks modest and not that solid.

3249 WEATHERBYS BLOODSTOCK INSURANCE H'CAP — 1m 2f 21y

4:30 (4:30) (Class 5) (0-70,69) 3-Y-O+ — **£2,914** (£867; £433; £216) **Stalls** Low

Form — RPR

5015 **1** — **Kingscape (IRE)**[19] 2660 4-9-12 **67** ... KerrinMcEvoy 11 — 77
(J R Fanshawe) *hld up towards rr: stdy prog on outside fr over 2f out: awkward hd carriage after but cajoled ahd cl home* **7/1**[3]

1-03 **2** ½ — **Salonga (IRE)**[24] 2521 4-9-9 **64** ... SebSanders 12 — 73
(C F Wall) *prom: hrd drvn 2f out: led 1f out: hdd and no ex nr fin* **11/1**

043 **3** 3 — **Arabiyah**[22] 2580 3-8-5 **57** ... NickyMackay 10 — 60
(L M Cumani) *chsd ldrs: briefly outpcd 4f out: kpt on fnl 2f but unable to chal* **11/1**

0504 **4** shd — **Magic Amigo**[16] 2745 6-8-12 **53** ... (v[1]) NCallan 13 — 56
(J R Jenkins) *stdd s: bhd: hdwy 2f out: hanging lft 1f out: plld outside: rdn and nt run on* **14/1**

2302 **5** shd — **Lap Of Honour (IRE)**[6] 3048 3-8-6 **65** ... KirstyMilczarek(7) 9 — 68
(N A Callaghan) *sn led: rdn 2f out: hdd 1f out: one pce and lost two pls nr fin* **5/2**[1]

2100 **6** 2 — **Mr Mischief**[37] 2117 7-9-2 **62** ... RussellKennemore(5) 7 — 61
(M C Chapman) *chsd ldrs: rdn over 4f out: kpt trying hrd and styd on steadily fnl f* **14/1**

0362 **7** 12 — **Danzare**[7] 3042 5-8-12 **53** ... SamHitchcott 6 — 28
(J L Spearing) *midfield: rdn and brief effrt over 3f out: sn btn* **10/1**

4-00 **8** nk — **Colton**[28] 2403 4-10-0 **69** ... DaleGibson 4 — 43
(J M P Eustace) *taken down early: a bhd: struggling 4f out* **33/1**

3434 **9** hd — **Paparaazi (IRE)**[40] 2023 5-9-11 **66** ... (p) DarryllHolland 1 — 40
(I W McInnes) *chsd ldrs: rdn 4f out: sn btn* **7/1**[3]

6024 **10** 13 — **A Mothers Love**[14] 2793 3-8-7 **59** ... EdwardCreighton 3 — 7
(P J McBride) *bhd: pushed along over 4f out: sn no ch: t.o* **6/1**[2]

1-00 **11** 3 — **Sir Haydn**[7] 3042 7-9-12 **67** ... AdrianTNicholls 2 — 9
(J R Jenkins) *bhd: struggling bdly over 2f out: t.o* **66/1**

5215 **12** 24 — **Watchmaker**[19] 2667 4-9-11 **66** ... IanMongan 8 — —
(W J Knight) *pressed ldr tl 1/2-way: lost pl 4f out: eased over 2f out: bdly t.o* **14/1**

2m 17.35s (9.25) **Going Correction** +1.075s/f (Soft)

WFA 3 from 4yo+ 11lb — **12** Ran SP% **118.0**

Speed ratings (Par 103):106,105,103,103,103 101,91,91,91,81 78,59

CSF £81.40 CT £845.05 TOTE £7.90: £2.70, £4.60, £3.00; EX 92.80 Trifecta £362.00 Part won. Pool £509.96 - 0.34 winning units..

Owner Mrs V Shelton **Bred** E Tynan **Trained** Newmarket, Suffolk

FOCUS

A fairly competitive handicap and thanks to the tactics on the favourite this race was run at a very solid pace, so the form looks reliable.

A Mothers Love Official explanation: jockey said filly was unsuited by the soft ground

Watchmaker Official explanation: jockey said gelding lost its action

3250 **PERTEMPS PEOPLE DEVELOPMENT "HANDS AND HEELS" APPRENTICE SERIES H'CAP** **1m 3f 101y**
5:00 (5:00) (Class 6) (0-65,65) 4-Y-0+ **£1,943** (£578; £288; £144) **Stalls** Low

Form RPR
4530 **1** **General Flumpa**[6] 3047 6-8-4 **50** LauraReynolds(3) 8 63
(Miss Tor Sturgis) *chsd tearaway ldng pair and clr of rest tl led over 3f out: sn in long ld and nvr looked like being ct* **11/2**[2]
0-06 **2** *8* **Kuster**[31] 2307 11-9-5 **65** HeatherMcGee(3) 1 65
(L M Cumani) *bhd: stl poor 7th 3f out: wnt poor 2nd wl over 1f out: nvr nr wnr* **11/2**[2]
5513 **3** *5* **Desert Hawk**[9] 2967 6-8-7 **55** Julie-AnneCumine(5) 6 47
(W M Brisbourne) *in rr gp and nvr gng pce of clr ldng trio: poor 4th st: plodded on* **2/1**[1]
-000 **4** *3* **Wavertree One Off**[12] 2890 5-7-12 **46** oh1 (b) MarvinCheung(5) 3 33
(J Ryan) *wnt furious pce w one rival: hdd over 3f out: bmpd along and sn no ch: lost 2nd wl over 1f out* **20/1**
6-05 **5** *6* **Dance World**[19] 2675 7-9-8 **65** AmyBaker 9 43
(Miss J Feilden) *set furious pce w one rival tl over 3f out: sn labouring: t.o* **8/1**
330- **6** *½* **Looks The Business (IRE)**[28] 5422 6-9-5 **62** JackDean 2 39
(W G M Turner) *in rr gp and wl off pce: rdn 4f out: no ch after: t.o* **13/2**[3]
0030 **7** *1 ¼* **Longhill Tiger**[13] 2833 4-9-3 **60** JamieHamblett 4 35
(G G Margarson) *in rr gp and wl off pce: struggling 4f out: hanging lft after* **9/1**
06-6 **8** *27* **Siegfrieds Night (IRE)**[107] 716 6-8-1 **49** ow2 PaulPickard(5) 7 —
(M C Chapman) *in rr gp and no ch w clr ldng trio: t.o fnl 4f* **16/1**
-550 **9** *63* **Shaika**[16] 2745 4-8-3 **49** (b[1]) BradleyRoper(3) 10 —
(G Prodromou) *ref to come out of stalls tl eventually tugged out by stalls handler: continued wl over a f bhd* **12/1**

2m 38.97s (11.47) **Going Correction** +1.075s/f (Soft) **9** Ran SP% **116.9**
Speed ratings (Par 101):101,95,91,89,85 84,83,64,18
CSF £36.25 CT £81.07 TOTE £7.80: £2.30, £2.70, £1.40; EX 56.00 Trifecta £303.00 Pool £836.58 - 1.96 winning units. Place 6 £76.15, Place 5 £66.40..
Owner Steven Astaire **Bred** Chippenham Lodge Stud Ltd **Trained** Lambourn, Berks

FOCUS
Not a race that will live long in the memory, and the leaders went off far too quickly in the conditions. The margins separating the runners at the line were more akin to a 3m chase and the form looks highly dubious.
General Flumpa Official explanation: trainer's rep said, regarding apparent improvement in form, that the gelding was better suited by the drying ground and left-handed track.
T/Jkpt: Not won. T/Plt: £54.20 to a £1 stake. Pool: £106,114.50. 1,426.95 winning tickets. T/Qpdt: £32.30 to a £1 stake. Pool: £5,635.90. 128.90 winning tickets. IM

3251 - 3255a (Foreign Racing) - See Raceform Interactive

2791 BEVERLEY (R-H)
Friday, July 6

OFFICIAL GOING: Heavy
After three weeks' rain resulting in local flooding the meeting had to survive two inspections. 'Very wet, very heavy' was the riders' verdict. Last race abandoned.
Wind: fresh 1/2 against Weather: fine but breezy and very cool

3256 **EUROPEAN BREEDERS' FUND NOVICE STKS** **5f**
6:45 (6:45) (Class 4) 2-Y-0 **£5,181** (£1,541; £770; £384) **Stalls** High

Form RPR
314 **1** **Style Award**[8] 3025 2-8-6 0 AndrewMullen(3) 1 71+
(W J H Ratcliffe) *sn pushed along in last: hdwy and nt clr run 2f out: styd on o ld last 100yds: edgd rt: hld on towards fin* **7/1**
51 **2** *¾* **Lady Rangali (IRE)**[64] 1422 2-8-11 0 SaleemGolam 3 70
(Mrs A Duffield) *chsd ldrs: hung lft over 2f out: styd on towards fin* **7/2**[3]
32 **3** *¾* **Select Committee**[39] 2090 2-8-12 0 TomEaves 6 69
(J J Quinn) *trckd ldrs: chal jst ins fnl f: kpt on same pce* **2/1**[1]
4 **4** *1 ½* **Whispering Desert**[11] 2934 2-8-4 0 DuranFentiman(3) 7 58+
(P T Midgley) *led 1f: chsd ldrs: led briefly jst ins fnl f: hld whn sltly hmpd towards fin* **11/1**
001 **5** *1 ½* **Gin Genereux**[16] 2758 2-8-11 0 GregFairley(3) 5 60
(M Johnston) *led after 1f: hdd jst ins fnl f: wknd* **9/4**[2]
00 **6** *7* **Johnny Friendly**[9] 2983 2-8-12 0 PaulMulrennan 2 33
(K R Burke) *sn chsng ldrs: lost pl 2f out* **22/1**

1m 10.09s (6.09) **Going Correction** +0.95s/f (Soft) **6** Ran SP% **111.5**
Speed ratings (Par 96):89,87,86,84,81 70
CSF £30.85 TOTE £8.60: £3.40, £1.50; EX 34.20.
Owner Bolton Hall Partnership 1 **Bred** Mrs S F Dibben **Trained** Wensley, N Yorks

FOCUS
A weak novice race and the first five seemed to get in each others way in the bad ground. The form looks solid though at this level.

NOTEBOOK
Style Award, back in trip, made hard work of it and came off a straight line once in front. With two wins under her belt, nurseries presumably beckon now. (tchd 15-2)
Lady Rangali(IRE), absent for two months, hung under pressure but was hauling in the winner at the line. (op 3-1)
Select Committee, weighted to turn Catterick tables on the runner-up, threw down a strong challenge but was just found lacking near the line. (op 9-4 tchd 11-4)
Whispering Desert stepped up a good deal on her debut effort a week earlier. After taking a narrow advantage just inside the last she was held when squeezed for room near the line. (tchd 10-1)
Gin Genereux, down in trip, took them along but on this much softer ground he did not see it out. (op 5-2 tchd 15-8)
Johnny Friendly, well beaten on his first two starts, walked stiff behind in the paddock and dropped right away. (tchd 20-1)

3257 **WESTWOOD (S) STKS** **7f 100y**
7:15 (7:16) (Class 6) 3-Y-0+ **£2,914** (£867; £433; £216) **Stalls** High

Form RPR
0-00 **1** **Scotty's Future (IRE)**[95] 891 9-8-10 47 AdamCarter(7) 2 54
(A Berry) *sn detached in last: t.o after 3f: hdwy alone in centre over 2f out: styd on wl to ld last 75yds* **6/1**[3]
060 **2** *1* **Little Nipper**[34] 2253 3-8-6 45 AndrewMullen(3) 8 49
(W J H Ratcliffe) *in rr: hdwy and swtchd rt over 1f out: styd on wl ins fnl f* **16/1**
0046 **3** *½* **Penel (IRE)**[11] 2937 6-9-0 50 (p) DuranFentiman(3) 7 50
(P T Midgley) *sn prom: hung lft over 1f out: led jst ins fnl f: sn hdd and no ex* **4/1**[1]
5060 **4** *2 ½* **Mister Maq**[18] 2709 4-9-3 47 (b) DO'Donohoe 9 44
(A Crook) *s.i.s: bhd: hdwy and swtchd rt over 1f out: styd on* **11/1**
0050 **5** *1 ¾* **Filey Buoy**[13] 2893 5-8-12 43 (b[1]) MichaelJStainton(5) 11 40
(R M Whitaker) *trckd ldrs: led appr fnl f: hdd jst ins fnl f: sn fdd* **8/1**
-400 **6** *2 ½* **Didactic**[14] 2829 3-8-9 45 (b) DavidAllan 12 30
(A J McCabe) *chsd ldrs: hrd rdn and wknd over 1f out* **8/1**
0600 **7** *¾* **O'Dwyer (IRE)**[22] 2591 3-8-9 39 PaulMulrennan 6 29
(A D Brown) *in rr: kpt on appr fnl f: nvr nr ldrs* **16/1**
100/ **8** *2* **Cadogen Square**[540] 6082 5-8-12 44 (be) DaleGibson 14 22
(D W Chapman) *led tl hdd & wknd appr fnl f* **20/1**
0400 **9** *¾* **Mister Minty (IRE)**[33] 2023 5-9-3 45 TomEaves 3 25
(Mrs S Lamyman) *mid-div: effrt over 2f out: nvr a threat* **12/1**
0-00 **10** *1 ¾* **Hows That**[15] 2809 5-8-5 40 (p) KellyHarrison(7) 10 15
(K R Burke) *chsd ldrs: edgd rt and lost pl 2f out* **5/1**[2]
0-06 **11** *6* **Dutch Key Card (IRE)**[73] 1221 6-9-0 48 GregFairley(3) 13 5
(C Smith) *trckd ldrs: rdn and lost pl over 2f out* **10/1**

1m 43.32s (9.01) **Going Correction** +1.05s/f (Soft)
WFA 3 from 4yo+ 8lb **11** Ran SP% **114.8**
Speed ratings (Par 101):90,88,88,85,83 80,79,77,76,74 67
CSF £95.08 TOTE £6.90: £2.30, £4.10, £1.30; EX 75.40.There was no bid for the winner.
Owner Alan Berry **Bred** William J Hamilton **Trained** Cockerham, Lancs
■ A first career winner for 20-year-old Adam Carter.

FOCUS
A weak seller that could be higher rated through the placed horses. The winner was tailed off at one stage and was the only one to come up the centre of the track.

3258 **AUNT BESSIE'S YORKSHIRE PUDDING H'CAP** **1m 100y**
7:45 (7:45) (Class 4) (0-85,85) 4-Y-0+ **£6,477** (£1,927; £963; £481) **Stalls** High

Form RPR
1226 **1** **Harvest Warrior**[12] 2906 5-8-9 **73** DavidAllan 2 85
(T D Easterby) *in rr: sn pushed along: hdwy over 3f out: rdn to ld over 1f out: drew clr: eased towards fin* **9/4**[1]
40-0 **2** *5* **Riley Boys (IRE)**[24] 2536 6-9-7 **85** TomEaves 8 87
(J G Given) *hld up in rr: hdwy over 2f out: kpt on wl to take 2nd ins fnl f* **7/1**[3]
64-0 **3** *nk* **Rodeo**[14] 2822 4-8-11 **75** (b[1]) DeanMcKeown 9 76
(C W Thornton) *led 1f: chsd ldrs: edgd lft and styd on same pce fnl f* **12/1**
0200 **4** *½* **Wovoka (IRE)**[13] 2891 4-9-5 **83** EdwardCreighton 4 83
(M R Channon) *trckd ldrs: led over 2f out tl over 1f out: kpt on same pce* **9/2**[2]
6-16 **5** *1* **Nuit Sombre (IRE)**[25] 2511 7-8-11 **75** (p) PaulMulrennan 7 73
(G A Harker) *t.k.h: in tch: hmpd over 2f out: kpt on fnl f* **20/1**
06-4 **6** *19* **Kamanda Laugh**[15] 2807 6-9-7 **85** DO'Donohoe 5 43
(K A Ryan) *in tch: effrt over 3f out: lost pl over 1f out: heavily eased* **9/2**[2]
6312 **7** *6* **Baylaw Star**[46] 1892 6-8-8 **72** TonyHamilton 3 17
(I W McInnes) *led after 1f: hdd over 2f out: wknd and heavily eased over 1f out* **9/2**[2]

1m 54.1s (6.70) **Going Correction** +1.05s/f (Soft) **7** Ran SP% **110.3**
Speed ratings (Par 105):108,103,102,102,101 82,76
CSF £17.18 CT £141.24 TOTE £4.20: £2.40, £2.40; EX 22.20.
Owner Swanland Racing **Bred** Campbell Stud **Trained** Great Habton, N Yorks

FOCUS
They went off at a very strong gallop in the conditions and the pacesetters paid the price. The winner was back to his very best form but overall it does not look that solid.
Kamanda Laugh Official explanation: trainer's rep said gelding scoped dirty

3259 **WESTBRIDGE HOMES CLASSIC H'CAP** **5f**
8:15 (8:15) (Class 6) (0-65,65) 3-Y-0+ **£3,238** (£963; £481; £240) **Stalls** High

Form RPR
0521 **1** **Prospect Court**[7] 3053 5-9-4 **60** 6ex AndrewMullen(3) 15 80
(A C Whillans) *racd far side: sn chsng ldrs: led ins fnl f: styd on strly* **5/4**[1]
0223 **2** *2* **El Potro**[104] 766 5-8-10 **49** GrahamGibbons 12 62
(J R Holt) *racd far side: chsd ldr: led 1f out: sn hdd and no ex* **14/1**
0253 **3** *2* **She's Our Beauty (IRE)**[15] 2791 4-8-4 **46** oh1 (p) DuranFentiman(3) 16 52
(S T Mason) *overall ldr far side: hdd 1f out: kpt on same pce* **12/1**
0033 **4** *9* **Malapropism**[10] 2972 7-9-12 **65** EdwardCreighton 8 38
(M R Channon) *chsd ldrs far side: lost pl over 1f out* **7/1**[2]
5024 **5** *1 ¾* **Riquewihr**[13] 2870 7-9-6 **64** (p) PJMcDonald(5) 14 31
(J S Wainwright) *racd far side: chsd ldrs: wknd 2f out* **7/1**[2]
0-00 **6** *3 ½* **Lovers Kiss**[14] 2829 3-8-5 **49** (b) DaleGibson 9 —
(N Wilson) *racd far side: sn outpcd and drvn along: nvr on terms* **33/1**
0056 **7** *1 ¼* **Alexia Rose (IRE)**[8] 3017 5-8-7 **46** oh1 (b) PaulMulrennan 10 —
(A Berry) *racd far side: in rr: rdn and hung rt over 2f out: rdn and wknd after* **12/1**
0-00 **8** *5* **The Thrifty Bear**[14] 2827 4-8-0 **46** oh1 KellyHarrison(7) 2 —
(C W Fairhurst) *racd stands' side: chsd ldrs: kpt on to ld that gp nr fin* **40/1**
4500 **9** *nk* **Cut Ridge (IRE)**[3] 3185 8-8-9 **48** (p) TonyHamilton 3 —
(J S Wainwright) *racd stands' side: chsd ldr: led that gp 2f out: hdd that gp nr fin: 2nd of 5 that gp* **20/1**
202- **10** *11* **Yorke's Folly (USA)**[309] 4948 6-8-7 **46** oh1 DeanMcKeown 1 —
(C W Fairhurst) *racd stands' side: mid-div: wknd over 1f out: 3rd of 5 that gp* **16/1**
0020 **11** *1* **Paddywack (IRE)**[18] 2712 10-9-2 **62** (b) DanielleMcCreery(7) 5 —
(D W Chapman) *racd far side: hdwy over 2f out: edgd rt and lost pl over 1f out: 4th of 5 in that gp* **8/1**[3]
0-00 **12** *2* **Tombalina**[34] 2249 4-8-2 **46** oh1 ColinHaddon(5) 7 —
(C J Teague) *led stands' side: hdd & wknd 2f out: last of 5 that gp* **40/1**

67.79 secs (3.79) **Going Correction** +0.95s/f (Soft)
WFA 3 from 4yo+ 5lb **12** Ran SP% **121.1**
Speed ratings (Par 101):107,103,100,86,83 77,75,67,67,49 48,44
CSF £20.96 CT £154.33 TOTE £2.30: £1.20, £4.10, £3.60; EX 21.30.
Owner Mrs L M Whillans **Bred** Mrs G Slater **Trained** Newmill-On-Slitrig, Borders

FOCUS
A low-grade sprint handicap with the high-drawn horses dominating and the winner not needing to be at his best to score. The runner-up sets the standard backed up by the third. Five chose the stands' side headed home by the eighth-placed The Thrifty Bear.
Alexia Rose(IRE) Official explanation: jockey said mare hung right-handed

3260 **FERGUSON FAWSITT ARMS H'CAP** **1m 4f 16y**
8:45 (8:45) (Class 5) (0-70,71) 3-Y-0+ **£3,886** (£1,156; £577; £288) **Stalls** High

Form RPR
0001 **1** **Red River Rebel**[39] 2089 9-8-11 **53** oh2 PaulMulrennan 3 59
(J R Norton) *led: qcknd 6f out: styd on wl fnl 2f* **7/2**[3]
3152 **2** *1 ½* **Rudry World (IRE)**[7] 3063 4-8-4 **53** SophieDoyle(7) 2 57
(M Mullineaux) *hld up in rr: hdwy on outer 3f out: rdr lost whip 1f out: styd on to take 2nd last 75yds* **8/1**

25-3 **3** *1 ½* **Edas**[11] [2935] 5-9-11 **67**.. GrahamGibbons 5 68
(J J Quinn) *trckd wnr: t.k.h: hung rt over 1f out: kpt on same pce* **5/2**[2]

1061 **4** *9* **Sudden Impulse**[11] [2935] 6-9-10 **71** 6ex........................ PJMcDonald(5) 1 58
(A D Brown) *trckd ldrs: effrt over 2f out: wknd over 1f out* **9/4**[1]

000- **5** *2* **Pertemps Networks**[326] [4433] 3-8-3 **58**............................. DaleGibson 6 42
(M W Easterby) *t.k.h in last: effrt 3f out: edgd lft and lost pl over 2f out* **16/1**

6155 **6** *2 ½* **Boppys Dancer**[43] [1966] 4-8-11 **53** oh4.........................(b) MickyFenton 8 33
(P T Midgley) *trckd ldrs: drvn over 5f out: wknd over 2f out* **6/1**

2m 51.86s (11.65) **Going Correction** +1.05s/f (Soft)
WFA 3 from 4yo+ 13lb **6** Ran SP% **112.8**
Speed ratings (Par 103):103,102,101,95,93 92
CSF £30.17 CT £80.19 TOTE £3.40: £1.90, £3.60; EX 23.30 Place 6 £232.81, Place 5 £35.30..
Owner Jeff Slaney **Bred** J Slaney **Trained** High Hoyland, S Yorks

FOCUS
A low-grade stayers' handicap run at a very steady pace and the game winner wound it up from the halfway mark. The placed horses set the level and the race could be higher.

3261 WILLIAM JACKSON BAKERY FILLIES' H'CAP 1m 1f 207y
() (Class 5) (0-70,) 3-Y-O £

T/Plt: £64.00 to a £1 stake. Pool: £69,604.55. 792.80 winning tickets. T/Qpdt: £10.20 to a £1 stake. Pool: £5049.60. 364.40 winning tickets. WG

2868 HAYDOCK (L-H)
Friday, July 6 (eve)

3262 Meeting Abandoned - Waterlogged.

2669 SANDOWN (R-H)
Friday, July 6

OFFICIAL GOING: Round course - good to soft (soft in places; 7.0); sprint course - soft (6.1)
The course was drying out and conditions were nothing like as testing as had seemed likely earlier in the week.
Wind: Strong, against Weather: Fine but cloudy

3268 BRITISH LAND H'CAP 5f 6y
2:05 (2:06) (Class 3) (0-95,95) 3-Y-O+ **£7,772** (£2,312; £1,155; £577) **Stalls** High

Form RPR

0300 **1** **Cashel Mead**[6] [3080] 7-9-1 **84**.. FrancisNorton 9 94
(J L Spearing) *chsd ldrs: wnt 2nd 1f out: drvn to ld last 100yds: hld on* **10/1**

0031 **2** *nk* **Golden Dixie (USA)**[19] [2694] 8-9-5 **88**............................. RyanMoore 11 97
(R A Harris) *b. s.i.s: settled in rr: gd prog on inner jst over 1f out: r.o wl to take 2nd nr fin and gaining on wnr* **17/2**

0022 **3** *hd* **Phantom Whisper**[6] [3104] 4-9-4 **87**.................................... JHBowman 2 95
(B R Millman) *hld up in rr: prog fr over 1f out: plld out and r.o fnl f: gaining at fin* **4/1**[2]

0050 **4** *½* **Cape Royal**[34] [2234] 7-9-4 **92**.................................(bt) KevinGhunowa(5) 10 98
(J M Bradley) *w ldr: led after 1f: gng strly over 1f out: drvn and hdd last 100yds: run out of 2 pls nr fin* **14/1**

-030 **5** *nk* **Out After Dark**[13] [2858] 6-9-12 **95**...(p) LDettori 5 100
(C G Cox) *settled in last: stl last over 1f out: rapid prog ent fnl f: r.o but no ch whn short of room nr fin: hopeless task* **11/4**[1]

115- **6** *1 ½* **Little Edward**[217] [6660] 9-9-3 **86**.. JimCrowley 3 86
(R J Hodges) *taken down early: hld up in rr: prog on outer 2f out: one pce and no hdwy fnl f* **33/1**

6625 **7** *1 ½* **Talbot Avenue**[42] [1986] 9-9-4 **87**...................................... JimmyFortune 8 82
(M Blanshard) *b. prom: drvn to chse ldr 2f out to 1f out: wknd ins fnl f* **12/1**

0-00 **8** *3 ½* **Texas Gold**[27] [2440] 9-9-10 **93**... MartinDwyer 4 75
(W R Muir) *nvr bttr than midfield: struggling over 1f out: no ch whn n.m.r briefly 1f out* **33/1**

-044 **9** *¾* **Zowington**[19] [2694] 5-9-0 **83**..(b[1]) GeorgeBaker 12 62
(C F Wall) *led 1f: pressed ldr to 2f out: wknd over 1f out* **6/1**[3]

0300 **10** *3* **Diane's Choice**[27] [2440] 4-9-0 **83**... NCallan 6 51
(J Akehurst) *prom: rdn bef 1/2-way: wknd over 1f out* **16/1**

1040 **11** *1 ¾* **Lady Livius (IRE)**[27] [2450] 4-9-7 **90**............................. RichardHughes 7 52
(R Hannon) *lw: chsd ldrs: u.p and in trble by 1/2-way* **14/1**

0-30 **12** *15* **Come Out Fighting**[48] [1836] 4-9-11 **94**.......................... TPO'Shea 1 2
(P A Blockley) *nt wl away on outer: rcvrd to chse ldrs: wknd u.p over 2f out: t.o* **14/1**

63.31 secs (1.10) **Going Correction** +0.425s/f (Yiel) **12** Ran SP% **120.0**
Speed ratings (Par 107):108,107,107,106,105 103,101,95,94,89 86,62
CSF £93.57 CT £406.40 TOTE £11.20: £2.60, £3.00, £2.00; EX 131.50.
Owner Masonaires **Bred** D R Tucker **Trained** Kinnersley, Worcs
■ Stewards' Enquiry : J H Bowman one-day ban: careless riding (Jul 17); caution: used whip without giving gelding time to respond

FOCUS
A typically competitive sprint for the course and there were a fair amount of contenders for being unluckiest loser. However, the form looks reasonably solid, rated around the first three.

NOTEBOOK
Cashel Mead, 1lb lower than when last successful at Newmarket in August of last year, had a decent draw and the ground in her favour, so it was no surprise to see her return to winning ways, getting up in the final half a furlong to deny the fast-finishing Golden Dixie. She is always a danger when the going is slow, but will need to progress further to defy a rise. (op 15-2)
Golden Dixie(USA), raised 5lb for his recent Salisbury victory, did himself no favours with a slow start and, judging by the way he finished, it cost him the race. He was closing on Cashel Mead with every stride as they flashed past the post and is clearly capable of scoring off this mark. (op 9-1 tchd 8-1)
Phantom Whisper has been running well in defeat and this was another sound effort without any reward, also looking slightly unlucky. He flashed home once getting into the clear, and is another who looks capable of defying this mark. (op 11-2)
Cape Royal tends to blow hot and cold and he took up his customary position towards the head of affairs, but unsurprisingly proved vulnerable on the climb to the line and he was run out of the placings.
Out After Dark was another who had strong claims for having a hard-luck story. Last early on, he came with a storming late run, but ran into trouble and finished his race with half a tank of gas. This was far from a vintage ride by Dettori, but the six-year-old is surely not too far off a win. Official explanation: jockey said gelding was denied a clear run (op 10-3 tchd 7-2)
Talbot Avenue Official explanation: jockey said gelding hung right

Zowington showed plenty of zip from a good draw in the first-time blinkers, but he went a little too quickly and faded right out in the end. Official explanation: jockey said horse hung right (op 5-1)

3269 AAIM DRAGON STKS (LISTED RACE) 5f 6y
2:40 (2:41) (Class 1) 2-Y-O
£12,207 (£4,626; £2,315; £1,154; £578; £290) **Stalls** High

Form RPR

2 **1** **Western Art (USA)**[45] [1919] 2-9-2 0................................ JimmyFortune 1 99+
(P W Chapple-Hyam) *strong: lw: s.i.s: hld up last: prog on outer wl over 1f out: r.o wl to ld last 50yds* **11/2**[3]

4214 **2** *1* **New Jersey (IRE)**[36] [2183] 2-9-2 0... NCallan 4 95
(K A Ryan) *lw: cl up: led wl over 1f out and sn 2l clr: drvn ent fnl f: swished tail: faltered and hdd fnl 50yds* **7/2**[1]

230 **3** *½* **Miss Versatile (IRE)**[14] [2812] 2-8-11 0................................... JohnEgan 5 88
(J S Moore) *pushed along over 3f out in midfield: prog 2f out: disp 2nd u.p jst over 1f out: kpt on* **16/1**

32 **4** *2 ½* **Cute Ass (IRE)**[18] [2717] 2-8-11 0.. MartinDwyer 2 79
(K R Burke) *w'like: t.k.h: hld up bhd ldrs: effrt to dispute 2nd jst over 1f out: wknd ins fnl f* **14/1**

10 **5** *¾* **Regal Step**[16] [2756] 2-8-11 0... RyanMoore 6 77
(R M H Cowell) *trckd ldr: led 1/2-way to wl over 1f out: wknd fnl f* **4/1**[2]

0514 **6** *2 ½* **Sirjoshua Reynolds**[20] [2684] 2-9-2 0.. LDettori 7 73
(N A Callaghan) *sn in last pair: pushed along bef 1/2-way: struggling 2f out: no prog* **11/1**

201 **7** *2 ½* **Presto Levanter**[38] [2122] 2-8-11 0................................. RichardHughes 3 59
(R Hannon) *lw: dwlt: a in last trio: pushed along 3f out: no prog* **7/1**

10 **8** *nk* **Vhujon (IRE)**[17] [2737] 2-9-2 0.............................. StephenDonohoe 8 62
(P D Evans) *taken steadily to post: led to 1/2-way: sn wknd* **4/1**[2]

64.07 secs (1.86) **Going Correction** +0.425s/f (Yiel) **8** Ran SP% **111.0**
Speed ratings (Par 102):102,100,99,95,94 90,86,85
CSF £23.54 TOTE £6.60: £2.20, £1.60, £4.20; EX 25.90.
Owner Matthew Green & Ben Sangster **Bred** Ms N M Cox & Rose Retreat Farm **Trained** Newmarket, Suffolk

FOCUS
A pretty weak Listed event with maidens filling three of the first four placings and the runner-up coming into this having been readily held in the National Stakes over course and distance in May. The form however, looks pretty solid.

NOTEBOOK
Western Art(USA), a beaten favourite on his debut at Leicester when the Chapple-Hyam juveniles were flying, still shaped with promise that day and better was expected here despite the rise in grade. This was not a good race by Listed standards, but he managed to overcome a slow start from a poor draw to win going away, really running on strongly once asked for his effort. He looks another useful juvenile for his trainer to go war with, and his next possible target is the Prix Robert Papin over half a furlong extra at Maisons-Laffitte. (op 9-2 tchd 4-1)
New Jersey(IRE) was comfortably held when a beaten-favourite in this grade over course and distance in May, but this was better and he looked the winner until flashing his tail and tying up close home. He is certainly no better than this level and may benefit from racing over 6f on better ground. (op 9-2)
Miss Versatile(IRE) finished midfield in the Albany at Royal Ascot and this obviously represented a drop in grade. She was being ridden before halfway, but kept on well in the testing conditions to earn black type, and can lose her maiden tag when stepped back up to 6f. (tchd 20-1)
Cute Ass(IRE), just touched off in similar conditions at Warwick last time, was taking a big rise in class and she ran well without suggesting she is capable of winning at this level. She can win her maiden before going handicapping. (op 12-1)
Regal Step, a ready winner on her Nottingham debut, was found to be heavily in season when disappointing in the Queen Mary and, although she deserved another chance, as a daughter of Royal Applause there was always going to be a doubt as to how she would handle this soft going. It is probably fair to give her another chance on faster ground, but she certainly has it all to prove now. Official explanation: jockey said filly ran too free (tchd 9-2)
Sirjoshua Reynolds came into this having finished a one-paced fourth in a 6f Group 3 at San Siro, but that probably amounts to little and he was always struggling for pace on this return to the minimum distance. (op 10-1 tchd 9-1)
Presto Levanter won her maiden in the style of a decent filly when making all over course and distance back in May, but she was forced to settle in the rear here following a sluggish start and she never featured. It is likely she requires further than 5f. (op 13-2 tchd 6-1)
Vhujon(IRE), although running well in the Windsor Castle at Royal Ascot, was unable to build on his highly-impressive winning debut at Bath and this was a step in the wrong direction. He took them along early, but was in trouble well over two furlongs out and ultimately dropped out tamely. It is probable the ground was too soft, but he is going to be tough to place from now on. (tchd 9-2)

3270 CUSHMAN & WAKEFIELD EBF MAIDEN STKS 7f 16y
3:15 (3:16) (Class 4) 2-Y-O **£6,477** (£1,927; £963; £481) **Stalls** High

Form RPR

50 **1** **Scintillo**[13] [2855] 2-9-3 0... RichardHughes 10 90
(R Hannon) *pressed ldr gng wl: led over 1f out: shkn up and wl in command fnl f* **6/4**[1]

2 *1 ¾* **Better Hand (IRE)** 2-9-3 0.. JHBowman 7 86
(M R Channon) *w'like: strong: lw: led: rdn and hdd over 1f out: styd on but no ch w wnr* **8/1**

3 *1 ½* **Mut'Ab (USA)** 2-9-3 0.. RyanMoore 2 82+
(C E Brittain) *w'like: scope: strong: trckd ldng trio: clsd to chal 2f out: rn green and one pce over 1f out* **10/1**

0 **4** *2* **Tayarat (IRE)**[50] [1781] 2-9-3 0.. RHills 6 77+
(M P Tregoning) *w'like: s.i.s: sn trckd ldrs: clsd 2f out: rn green and wknd 1f out* **9/2**[2]

5 *2* **Calistos Quest** 2-9-3 0.. JoeFanning 9 72
(M Johnston) *w'like: lw: trckd ldng pair: rdn to chal 2f out: wknd and hanging lft fnl f* **5/1**[3]

6 *1 ¼* **Aaim To Succeed (IRE)** 2-8-12 0.. TPO'Shea 1 64+
(M R Channon) *leggy: scope: stdd s and v.s.a: nvr on terms: pushed along and kpt on steadily fnl 2f* **16/1**

00 **7** *1* **Race The Moon (IRE)**[8] [3037] 2-9-3 0........................... AntonyProcter 4 66+
(V Smith) *dwlt: off the pce towards rr: kpt on steadily fnl 2f: n.d* **25/1**

8 *5* **Dancing Marabout (IRE)** 2-9-3 0.................................... JohnEgan 11 54
(C R Egerton) *w'like: cmpt: rdn in last pair 1/2-way: bhd after* **14/1**

60 **9** *4* **Wooden King (IRE)**[29] [2398] 2-9-3 0......................... StephenDonohoe 5 44
(P D Evans) *chsd ldrs to 1/2-way: sn wknd* **40/1**

00 **10** *3 ½* **Honest Yankee (USA)**[13] [2876] 2-9-3 0.......................... SamHitchcott 8 35
(Mrs L C Jewell) *rdn in last pair 1/2-way: bhd after* **100/1**

1m 32.84s (3.50) **Going Correction** +0.425s/f (Yiel) **10** Ran SP% **114.9**
Speed ratings (Par 96):97,95,93,91,88 87,86,80,75,71
CSF £13.91 TOTE £2.20: £1.10, £2.80, £2.10; EX 14.00.
Owner White Beech Farm **Bred** Woodcote Stud Ltd **Trained** East Everleigh, Wilts
■ Stewards' Enquiry : J H Bowman one-day ban: careless riding (Jul 17)

FOCUS
They all came stands' side for what was the first race of the day on the round course. This is usually a decent contest and it can produce the odd high-class performer, but there did not appear to be any stars on show this year, with the winner rated to his Chesham form.

NOTEBOOK
Scintillo set a decent standard on the evidence of his close-up seventh in the Chesham at Royal Ascot, but that was not much of a contest and he looked potentially vulnerable to a decent newcomer. Thankfully for him though there was nothing on show that could match him first time up and he stayed on dourly under pressure to win with a bit to spare. His trainer expects further progress and has him pencilled in for either the Washington Singer at Newbury or Solario Stakes back at this course. (op 11-8 tchd 13-8 and 7-4 in places)

Better Hand(IRE) ♦, a 100,000gns son of Montjeu, comes from a stable whose juveniles often benefit from a run, so it was pleasing to see him show so much ability first time up. He certainly knew his job, attempting to make all the running, but the winner's previous experience gave him the upper hand and he was forced to settle for second. He can win his maiden, possibly over 1m, before stepping up in grade. (op 5-1)

Mut'Ab(USA) ♦, a fine-looking son of Alhaarth, was representing a yard that rarely has a juvenile ready to go first time up and as a result he has to be the one to take from the race. Always well positioned, he came to challenge in the final quarter mile, but was uncertain of what was required and in the end his effort flattened out. The fact there was good money for him beforehand suggests he is thought a bit of at home and he should have little trouble landing an ordinary maiden, with significant improvement anticipated. (op 25-1)

Tayarat(IRE), always outpaced over 5f behind the useful Sweepstake on his debut at Salisbury, is bred to appreciate this sort of this distance and he started a run over two furlongs out, but could not sustain it and faded in the final furlong. It is possible the son of Noverre requires a faster surface and he deserves another chance with his stable hardly firing at present. Will be qualified for nurseries after one more run.

Calistos Quest, whose trainer is always to be feared in 7f-plus two-year-old events, was not particularly strong in the market and all the signs were that he was going to need the experience. He did not see his race out as well as one would have liked, hanging under pressure and looking green, but is entitled to come on for the experience and will appreciate 1m in time. It is worth noting though that Johnston's two-year-olds have not been improving anywhere near as much from their first to second start in what has so far been a quiet year for the Middleham trainer with his youngsters. (op 9-2 tchd 4-1)

Aaim To Succeed(IRE) ♦, the only filly in the field, is a nicely-bred daughter of Montjeu and she shaped really promisingly following a very slow start, keeping on nicely in the straight for a never-nearer sixth. She is going to relish an extra furlong in time and looks a ready-made maiden winner. (op 20-1 tchd 25-1)

3271 WILLIAM EWART PROPERTIES GALA STKS (LISTED RACE) 1m 2f 7y
3:50 (3:50) (Class 1) 3-Y-O+

£14,762 (£5,595; £2,800; £1,396; £699; £351) **Stalls** High

Form				RPR
5-10	**1**		**Harland**[14] 2813 3-8-8 101 ... NCallan 1 (M A Jarvis) *led at slow pce to over 7f out: chsd clr ldr: clsd to chal 2f out: sn drvn: gained narrow upper hand last 100yds* **10/3**[3]	117
12-6	**2**	*hd*	**Tam Lin**[36] 2182 4-9-5 115 ... LDettori 5 (Saeed Bin Suroor) *lw: dwlt: hld up tl led over 7f out: racd wd and sn clr: jnd 2f out: cajoled along and disp ld w much tail waving tl nt qckn last 100yds* **3/1**[2]	117
5125	**3**	*1 3/4*	**Blue Bajan (IRE)**[13] 2856 5-9-5 111 ... MichaelHills 6 (Andrew Turnell) *chsd clr ldng pair over 6f out: tried to cl fr 3f out: styd on but nvr quite on terms* **9/4**[1]	113
0-21	**4**	*9*	**Topatoo**[50] 1789 5-9-6 105 ... JimmyQuinn 2 (M H Tompkins) *outpcd in 4th bef 1/2-way: rdn and no imp fnl 3f* **5/1**	96
3034	**5**	*1*	**New Beginning (IRE)**[25] 2506 3-8-8 79 ... JoeFanning 7 (Mrs S Lamyman) *outpcd in last pair bef 1/2-way: no ch fnl 3f* **100/1**	93?
4/60	**6**	*nk*	**Kong (IRE)**[35] 2216 5-9-5 93 ... (b) JimmyFortune 3 (J L Dunlop) *hld up in rr: wl outpcd in 6th bef 1/2-way: rdn and no rspnse over 2f out* **14/1**	92
6044	**7**	*3/4*	**Fann (USA)**[16] 2753 4-9-0 104 ... RyanMoore 4 (C E Brittain) *trckd ldr to over 7f out: sn lost pl: wl outpcd in 5th 1/2-way: nudged along and no prog* **12/1**	86

2m 16.55s (6.31) **Going Correction** +0.425s/f (Yiel)
WFA 3 from 4yo+ 11lb **7** Ran SP% **110.9**
Speed ratings (Par 111):91,90,89,82,81 81,80
CSF £12.87 TOTE £4.00: £2.20, £1.90; EX 17.80.
Owner Sheikh Mohammed **Bred** Darley **Trained** Newmarket, Suffolk

FOCUS
A decent contest in which three smart performers pulled clear, but the time was very moderate in comparison with the following handicap, which raises doubts about the form. This event has now gone to a three-year-old in five of its six runnings.

NOTEBOOK
Harland was allowed to take his chance in the King Edward VII at Royal Ascot, having thrashed the useful Eradicate in his maiden, but the 1m4f trip proved beyond him there and better was expected returned to 1m2f. He led until Tam Lin got lit up and went charging past, but homed in on that rival turning into the straight and it soon became clear he had those in behind beaten. Callan was taken a bit by surprise though as the runner-up pulled out more, but he always just looked to be getting on top and edged ahead close home. A soft surface is viewed as being imperative by his trainer and he may look towards a race at Deauville next. (op 7-2 tchd 3-1, 4-1 in places)

Tam Lin managed to win his share last season for Sir Michael Stoute, despite looking awkward on more than one occasion, but his recent debut for connections in the Brigadier Gerard saw a new side to him as he got very worked up and raced far too freely in the lead. More relaxed before the race here, everything appeared to be going smoothly early on, but as soon as the pace slackened he got lit up and Dettori allowed him to stride on, taking up a clear lead and racing someway wide of runners down the back straight. He looked cooked when they closed in on him soon after turning for home, but Dettori had managed to store some energy on the gelding and did not ask him for his effort until the winner drew alongside. He very nearly pulled off a remarkable win, and despite flashing his tail under pressure he does appear to give it his all in a finish. Dettori must receive much credit for what was an excellent ride in defeat. He is clearly tricky, but there is serious ability there and, if connections can get him to settle, he could take high rank amongst the middle-distance performers. (op 5-2 tchd 7-2, 4-1 in places)

Blue Bajan(IRE) has progressed into a Listed/Group 3 performer this season and he set a decent standard on the evidence of his two most recent runs behind Maraahel. However, having turned into the straight with every chance, he could not quicken under pressure and never looked like threatening the front two in the final furlong. This was a bit disappointing, but he would have preferred a faster gallop. (op 2-1 tchd 5-2 in places)

Topatoo, last seen winning the Group 3 Middleton Stakes at York back in May, faced a stiffer task here under her 6lb penalty against the boys, but she should still have done a lot better. (op 6-1 tchd 13-2)

New Beginning(IRE) was racing out of his grade and he did well to beat not one, but two rivals.

Kong(IRE) has lost the plot and the first-time blinkers did little to spark him back to life. (op 16-1 tchd 20-1 in a place)

Fann(USA) has been running above herself in decent contests, but this was not such a good effort and she failed to last home having raced keenly. (op 16-1)

3272 HELICAL BAR H'CAP 1m 2f 7y
4:25 (4:26) (Class 2) (0-100,100) 3-Y-O+

£9,971 (£2,985; £1,492; £747; £372; £187) **Stalls** High

Form				RPR
21-	**1**		**Mariotto (USA)**[323] 4534 3-9-1 98 ... (t) LDettori 3 (Saeed Bin Suroor) *led or disp: rdn and narrowly hdd jst over 1f out: kpt on wl and forced ahd again last stride* **9/4**[1]	108
6103	**2**	*hd*	**Ballinteni**[12] 2906 5-9-0 86 ... NCallan 4 (D M Simcock) *w ldr: rdn to ld narrowly jst over 1f out: looked like holding on fnl f: collared last stride* **7/1**[3]	96
110-	**3**	*2*	**Spanish Hidalgo (IRE)**[272] 5805 3-8-7 90 ... TPO'Shea 7 (J L Dunlop) *lw: hld up in last pair: prog to chse ldng pair over 1f out: drvn and kpt on but nvr able to chal* **10/1**	96
0006	**4**	*2 1/2*	**Counsel's Opinion (IRE)**[30] 2351 10-9-3 89 ... GeorgeBaker 5 (C F Wall) *lw: t.k.h: trckd ldng pair: cl enough 2f out: rdn and nt qckn after* **16/1**	90
131	**5**	*1*	**One Hour**[20] 2669 3-8-10 93 ... MartinDwyer 2 (M P Tregoning) *lw: trckd ldrs: rdn over 2f out: no imp and btn fnl 2f* **9/4**[1]	92
650-	**6**	*shd*	**Before You Go (IRE)**[244] 6337 4-10-0 100 ... MichaelHills 6 (T G Mills) *hld up in last pair: rdn and effrt over 2f out: no imp over 1f out: fdd* **12/1**	99
0-46	**7**	*1 3/4*	**Star Of Light**[14] 2815 6-9-11 97 ... RichardHughes 9 (B J Meehan) *t.k.h: hld up towards rr: rdn and no prog over 2f out: struggling after* **13/2**[2]	92
1400	**8**	*2 1/2*	**Art Modern (IRE)**[42] 2002 5-8-9 81 ... RyanMoore 1 (G L Moore) *racd wd: trckd ldrs: lost pl and struggling 4f out: sn btn* **20/1**	71

2m 12.85s (2.61) **Going Correction** +0.425s/f (Yiel)
WFA 3 from 4yo+ 11lb **8** Ran SP% **114.8**
Speed ratings (Par 109):106,105,104,102,101 101,99,97
CSF £19.18 CT £130.39 TOTE £3.30: £1.20, £2.20, £2.10; EX 25.10.
Owner Godolphin **Bred** Darley **Trained** Newmarket, Suffolk

FOCUS
They again came towards the stands' side in what was a decent handicap. The time was pretty good, especially in comparison with the preceding contest over the same trip, and the first three look to be improving.

NOTEBOOK
Mariotto(USA) ♦, a highly-promising two-year-old when with Mark Johnston last season, won in the style of a smart performer on his second and final outing as a juvenile at this course and was subsequently moved to Godolphin. Having his first run of the season, like many of the Godolphin runners he was sporting a tongue-tie and Dettori was intent on making plenty of use of the son of Swain. He looked vulnerable when being joined and briefly headed over a furlong out, but battled back doggedly and regained the lead in the final strides. Bred to relish 1m4f, he looks the type to continue to progress and connections will no doubt have high hopes that he can make up into a Group performer. (op 9-2, tchd 5-1 in a place)

Ballinteni, who himself used to be a Godolphin inmate, has not yet built on May's Windsor victory, but this was a much more respectable effort and he was probably unfortunate to bump into such a smart performer. A faster surface suits better and, as this was only the eighth start of his career, it is reasonable to expect further improvement. (tchd 6-1)

Spanish Hidalgo(IRE) ♦, a progressive juvenile who scored in a soft-ground nursery off a mark of 84, ran poorly on his final outing in the Royal Lodge, but it was possible he was over the top by then and he looked a fascinating contender on this seasonal bow. In rear early, he became outpaced early in the straight, but ran on really well in the final quarter mile and did best of those attempting to come from behind. There is a decent race in him this season, probably over further, and he is entitled to improve for the outing. (op 11-1 tchd 14-1)

Counsel's Opinion(IRE) is a grand old performer, but he struggles to win these days and this was as good a run as he could have hoped for.

One Hour, a recent winner at the course over a furlong shorter, looked a three-year-old to keep on side that day, but he was unable to dominate as he did on that occasion and fell short off a 4lb higher mark. This was disappointing, but his stable are hardly flying at present and he may warrant another chance. (op 11-8)

Before You Go(IRE), returning from a lengthy absence, was always going to struggle under top weight and this was probably as good a run as connections could have hoped for. (op 14-1 tchd 16-1)

Star Of Light ran just reasonably at Royal Ascot, but this effort further suggested he is firmly in the Handicapper's grip at present. (op 11-2)

3273 CONSENSUS H'CAP 1m 6f
5:00 (5:03) (Class 4) (0-85,85) 3-Y-O+ **£6,477** (£1,927; £963; £481) **Stalls** Centre

Form				RPR
2130	**1**		**Toparudi**[13] 2887 6-8-12 68 ... JimmyQuinn 6 (M H Tompkins) *stdd s: hld up in last mostly: pushed along over 3f out then smooth prog to ld wl over 1f out: sn drvn: in command fnl f* **12/1**	79
1-04	**2**	*1 3/4*	**Desert Sea (IRE)**[27] 2449 4-9-9 79 ... JimmyFortune 4 (D W P Arbuthnot) *hld up in 8th: prog and barging match w rival 6f out: hrd rdn over 2f out: chsd ldng pair over 1f out: kpt on to take 2nd last strides* **17/2**	87
4P-2	**3**	*nk*	**Sphinx (FR)**[50] 1794 9-10-0 84 ... (b) JohnEgan 5 (Jamie Poulton) *b. lw: hld up in 7th: prog and barging match w rival 6f out: rdn to chal 2f out: pressed wnr: hld fnl f: lost 2nd last strides* **13/2**[2]	92
10-3	**4**	*3*	**Picacho (IRE)**[8] 3033 4-8-11 67 ... RichardHughes 9 (P J Hobbs) *mostly pressed ldr: hrd rdn 3f out: lost pl and btn wl over 1f out* **15/2**[3]	71
-361	**5**	*nk*	**Aureate**[6] 3081 3-9-0 85 6ex ... JoeFanning 1 (M Johnston) *lw: led at decent pce: rdn and hdd wl over 1f out: sn btn* **5/4**[1]	88
6-00	**6**	*1/2*	**Stoop To Conquer**[43] 1959 7-9-7 77 ... FrancisNorton 3 (A W Carroll) *chsd clr ldng trio: rdn wl over 2f out: no imp and btn wl over 1f out* **8/1**	80
1243	**7**	*4*	**Dark Parade (ARG)**[40] 2055 6-8-9 65 oh1 ... StephenDonohoe 2 (P D Evans) *settled in 6th: rdn 3f out: no prog and btn 2f out: eased fnl f* **15/2**[3]	62
1-00	**8**	*12*	**Mostarsil (USA)**[19] 2692 9-9-0 70 ... (p) RyanMoore 7 (G L Moore) *mostly in 5th tl dropped to last over 4f out: sn bhd* **20/1**	50
-005	**9**	*15*	**Brigadore (USA)**[57] 1598 4-8-12 68 ... DavidKinsella 8 (E J Alston) *mostly chsd ldng pair and clr of rest: drvn 3f out: sn wknd rapidly: t.o* **25/1**	27

3m 8.03s (3.52) **Going Correction** +0.425s/f (Yiel)
WFA 3 from 4yo+ 15lb **9** Ran SP% **119.2**
Speed ratings (Par 105):106,105,104,103,102 102,100,93,84
CSF £112.45 CT £731.76 TOTE £13.00: £3.00, £2.60, £1.80; EX 137.20 Place 6 £208.72, Place 5 £69.74..
Owner M P Bowring **Bred** M P Bowring **Trained** Newmarket, Suffolk
■ Stewards' Enquiry : John Egan seven-day ban: carless riding (Jul 16-23)

FOCUS
A race that played into the hands of the hold-up performers, with Aureate, being egged on by Picacho, setting too fast a gallop. the form is rated around the winner and third and the form appears reasonably solid.
T/Jkpt: £28,980.20 to a £1 stake. Pool: £346,946.81. 8.50 winning tickets. T/Plt: £159.60 to a £1 stake. Pool: £106,652.40. 487.70 winning tickets. T/Qpdt: £30.90 to a £1 stake. Pool: £4,854.70. 116.00 winning tickets. JN

3238 WARWICK (L-H)
Friday, July 6

OFFICIAL GOING: Heavy (soft in places)
Wind: Fresh, half-behind Weather: Overcast

3274 ENTERTAIN CLIENTS AT WARWICK RACECOURSE (S) STKS 1m 2f 188y
2:20 (2:23) (Class 6) 3-Y-O £2,047 (£604; £302) Stalls Low

Form RPR
000 1 **Diamond Key (IRE)**[3] 3183 3-8-8 50 (b[1]) TedDurcan 5 49
(M G Quinlan) *wnt lft s: hld up: hdwy over 3f out: rdn to ld over 1f out: styd on u.p* 8/1
0006 2 ½ **Pugnacity**[7] 3057 3-8-8 0 SteveDrowne 1 48
(S C Williams) *wnt rt s: hld up: hdwy over 3f out: rdn and ev ch fr over 1f out: styd on* 5/2[1]
6555 3 2½ **Gertie (IRE)**[27] 2454 3-8-5 42 AlanCreighton(3) 12 44
(E J Creighton) *hld up: hdwy over 2f out: sn rdn: styd on* 12/1
-000 4 2½ **Wingsinmotion (IRE)**[39] 2096 3-8-5 40 (p) MarcHalford(3) 6 40
(Miss Tracy Waggott) *prom: led over 3f out: rdn and hdd over 1f out: wknd ins fnl f* 9/1
-014 5 2½ **Flying Grey (IRE)**[8] 3040 3-9-4 52 (p) GrahamGibbons 7 45
(P A Blockley) *hld up in tch: plld hrd: rdn over 1f out: wknd fnl f* 10/3[2]
00 6 3½ **Augustus Caeser (IRE)**[27] 2454 3-8-6 0 SCreighton(7) 10 34
(E J Creighton) *chsd ldrs: rdn and ev ch 2f out: sn wknd* 20/1
0056 7 15 **Cantique (IRE)**[9] 2978 3-8-8 47 JamesDoyle 13 4
(Ms J S Doyle) *chsd ldrs: rdn and wknd 3f out* 6/1[3]
0-6 8 11 **Cocobean**[15] 2800 3-8-13 0 (b) ChrisCatlin 11 —
(M Appleby) *led over 7f: sn wknd* 33/1
00- 9 3 **Hurricane Dennis**[386] 2588 3-8-13 0 LPKeniry 2 —
(Mike Murphy) *hmpd s: hld up: rdn over 6f out: wknd 5f out* 80/1
00-0 10 1¾ **Miss Silver Spurs**[107] 720 3-8-8 40 (v[1]) RichardSmith 8 —
(M D I Usher) *prom over 7f* 10/1
11 11 **Clare Park** 3-8-1 0 ThomasO'Brien(7) 9 —
(H J Manners) *s.s: a in rr: wknd over 4f out* 40/1
-000 12 46 **Little Tiny Tom**[9] 2978 3-8-13 49 (p) MickyFenton 14 —
(C N Kellett) *prom: lost pl 7f out: wknd over 4f out* 28/1

2m 31.7s (12.30) **Going Correction** +0.875s/f (Soft) 12 Ran SP% 118.7
Speed ratings (Par 98):90,89,87,86,84 81,70,62,60,59 51,17
CSF £27.01 TOTE £9.40: £3.70, £1.30, £4.10; EX 32.60.The winner was bought in for 6,000gns. Flying Grey was claimed by Mrs L M Edwards for £6,000. Pugnacity was claimed by Auldyn Stud Ltd for £6,000.
Owner Mrs J Quinlan **Bred** Michael Dalton **Trained** Newmarket, Suffolk
FOCUS
A very poor race even for a seller, run at a fair pace.

3275 MIDSUMMER NOVICE AUCTION STKS 7f 26y
2:55 (2:57) (Class 5) 2-Y-O £3,238 (£963; £481; £240) Stalls Low

Form RPR
51 1 **Distant Charm (IRE)**[13] 2876 2-9-1 0 PatDobbs 4 82
(R Hannon) *led 3f: rdn to ld over 1f out: edgd rt ins fnl f: styd on* 7/2[3]
601 2 1½ **Tamrai Dancer**[12] 2911 2-8-8 0 JamesDoyle 5 71
(R M Beckett) *w wnr tl led 4f out: rdn: edgd rt and hdd over 1f out: no ex wl ins fnl f* 13/8[2]
0232 3 ½ **Rub Of The Relic (IRE)**[8] 3024 2-8-9 0 GrahamGibbons 6 71
(P A Blockley) *chsd ldrs: rdn over 1f out: styd on same pce ins fnl f* 11/8[1]
0 4 1½ **Pay Pay Pay**[10] 2968 2-7-11 0 BernadetteQuinn(7) 3 62
(P D Evans) *dwlt: hld up: effrt and hung lft over 1f out: styd on same pce* 16/1

1m 30.37s (6.17) **Going Correction** +0.875s/f (Soft) 4 Ran SP% 108.3
Speed ratings (Par 94):99,97,96,95
CSF £9.52 TOTE £3.40; EX 8.40.
Owner A J Ilsley **Bred** Frank Prendergast **Trained** East Everleigh, Wilts
FOCUS
Just the four runners, but still an interesting novice event. The second and third were close to their pre-race marks but the bare form may not turn out quite this good.
NOTEBOOK
Distant Charm(IRE), a winner over this trip on good ground at Lingfield last month, successfully gave weight away all round. After being taken on up front by the runner-up, he railed the better but edged across the track once in the straight. Getting well on top inside the last, he was still green and should be capable of further improvement. He should stay a bit further too. (op 9-4)
Tamrai Dancer, who proved her liking for a soft surface when making all over 5f here last month, ran another sound race on this step up in trip, only giving best in the final furlong. She looks a nursery type. (op 7-4 tchd 6-4)
Rub Of The Relic(IRE), upped in trip after some sound efforts over shorter, had already proven he could handle soft ground, but he was unable to make his presence felt despite keeping on. (op 15-8 tchd 2-1)
Pay Pay Pay, well beaten on her recent debut at Newbury, still looked green and brought up the rear throughout, but she was by no means disgraced in this company. (tchd 14-1)

3276 RACING UK MAIDEN STKS 7f 26y
3:30 (3:32) (Class 5) 3-4-Y-O £3,238 (£963; £481; £240) Stalls Low

Form RPR
4 1 **Nassau Style**[12] 2913 3-9-3 0 OscarUrbina 1 76
(J R Fanshawe) *chsd ldrs: rdn to ld and edgd lft ins fnl f: r.o* 5/2[1]
2 2 ½ **Trees Of Green (USA)**[17] 2740 3-9-3 0 KerrinMcEvoy 12 75
(Saeed Bin Suroor) *chsd ldr: rdn to ld over 1f out: edgd lft and hdd ins fnl f: styd on* 5/2[1]
-650 3 3 **Optical Illusion (USA)**[31] 2335 3-9-3 70 TedDurcan 2 67
(E A L Dunlop) *led: rdn and hdd over 1f out: no ex ins fnl f* 11/2[3]
0- 4 2 **Cow Girl (IRE)**[350] 3700 3-8-12 0 MickyFenton 4 57
(Miss Gay Kelleway) *s.i.s: hld up: hmpd 2f out: r.o ins fnl f: nvr nrr* 14/1
3 5 2 **Paradise Dancer (IRE)**[12] 2913 3-8-12 0 PatDobbs 11 52
(Pat Eddery) *chsd ldrs: rdn over 2f out: wknd over 1f out* 9/2[2]
0 6 3½ **Sea Willow (IRE)**[22] 2606 3-9-3 0 TQuinn 3 48
(D R C Elsworth) *s.i.s: sn mid-div: n.m.r 1/2-way: sn wknd* 50/1
4 7 ½ **Istead Rise (IRE)**[67] 1348 3-9-3 0 FrankieMcDonald 6 46
(P A Blockley) *s.s: hld up: n.d* 40/1
8 2½ **And Your Point Is (USA)** 3-9-3 0 SteveDrowne 10 40
(C R Egerton) *prom to 1/2-way* 22/1
006- 9 1½ **Numerical (IRE)**[330] 4290 3-9-3 61 ChrisCatlin 5 36
(J L Dunlop) *prom to 1/2-way* 25/1
4-0 10 ¾ **Swing On A Star (IRE)**[19] 2693 3-8-12 0 AdamKirby 8 29
(W R Swinburn) *hld up: wknd 1/2-way* 20/1
0 11 1¾ **Caravel (IRE)**[7] 3062 3-9-3 0 J-PGuillambert 9 29
(Sir Mark Prescott) *dwlt: hld up: wknd 1/2-way* 22/1
0 12 3 **Dark Mask (IRE)**[11] 2948 3-9-0 0 MarcHalford(3) 7 22
(J L Spearing) *chsd ldrs: rdn over 2f out: sn wknd* 66/1

1m 29.19s (4.99) **Going Correction** +0.875s/f (Soft) 12 Ran SP% 120.6
Speed ratings (Par 103):106,105,102,99,97 93,92,90,88,87 85,82
CSF £7.74 TOTE £4.30: £1.40, £1.80, £1.80; EX 13.30.
Owner The N S Partnership **Bred** A B Barraclough **Trained** Newmarket, Suffolk
FOCUS
A reasonable maiden, with the third the obvious guide to the form, which should work out. An improved effort from Nassau Style.
Cow Girl(IRE) Official explanation: jockey said, regarding running and riding, that his orders were to settle the filly down to post and get it settled and covered up in the race, adding that he had reported at scales that he was denied a clear run entering straight; trainer confirmed adding that the filly was difficult to train, and is in foal.

3277 CHURCHILL OFFICE SOLUTIONS LTD FILLIES' H'CAP 5f 110y
4:05 (4:05) (Class 5) (0-70,69) 3-Y-O+ £3,238 (£963; £481; £240) Stalls Centre

Form RPR
-212 1 **Dematraf (IRE)**[8] 3017 5-8-6 **49** BernadetteQuinn(7) 1 64
(P D Evans) *chsd ldr: led and edgd rt 1f out: drvn clr* 11/4[1]
0312 2 5 **Ocean Blaze**[25] 2513 3-9-13 **69** KerrinMcEvoy 5 65
(B R Millman) *led: hung rt and hdd 1f out: sn wknd* 3/1[2]
3154 3 2 **Diminuto**[11] 2950 3-9-3 **66** FrankiePickard(7) 3 55
(M D I Usher) *chsd ldrs: rdn 1/2-way: wknd fnl f* 9/1
5650 4 1¼ **Safranine (IRE)**[31] 2343 10-8-9 **50** AnnStokell(5) 6 36
(Miss A Stokell) *dwlt: hdwy 1/2-way: rdn and wknd over 1f out* 12/1
-003 5 3 **Zimbali**[23] 2555 5-8-2 **45** KirstyMilczarek(7) 2 21
(J M Bradley) *chsd ldrs over 3f* 6/1[3]
-503 6 3½ **Musical Chimes**[8] 3032 4-8-6 **45** LiamJones(3) 9 8
(W M Brisbourne) *prom: hung rt and wknd 1/2-way* 9/1
-006 7 ½ **She Whispers (IRE)**[21] 2619 4-8-9 **45** LPKeniry 8 7
(R Hollinshead) *hld up in tch: rdn and wknd over 1f out* 16/1
630- 8 1¾ **Jessica Wigmo**[277] 5729 4-8-13 **49** JamesDoyle 4 5
(A W Carroll) *mid-div: rdn 1/2-way: sn wknd* 16/1
240 9 15 **Lady Aspen (IRE)**[13] 2870 4-9-13 **63** ChrisCatlin 7 —
(Ian Williams) *mid-div: wknd 1/2-way* 17/2
0000 10 2 **Redflo**[35] 2195 3-7-12 **47** ow2 SophieDoyle(7) 10 —
(Ms J S Doyle) *bhd fnl 3f* 66/1

67.99 secs (2.10) **Going Correction** +0.125s/f (Good)
WFA 3 from 4yo+ 5lb 10 Ran SP% 117.4
Speed ratings (Par 100):91,84,81,80,76 71,70,68,48,45
CSF £11.16 CT £64.91 TOTE £4.30: £1.40, £1.30, £3.40; EX 13.00.
Owner T V Cullen **Bred** Edward Ryan **Trained** Pandy, Monmouths
FOCUS
Few got into this very modest fillies' handicap, in which they finished well strung out. The winner is rated back to her best but it is doubtful if anything else showed their form.
Safranine(IRE) Official explanation: jockey said mare missed the break

3278 1707 RESTAURANT H'CAP 6f
4:40 (4:41) (Class 4) (0-80,80) 3-Y-O £6,477 (£1,927; £963; £481) Stalls Centre

Form RPR
13 1 **Bee Eater (IRE)**[6] 3099 3-9-3 **76** J-PGuillambert 6 83
(Sir Mark Prescott) *flashed tail: a.p: chsd ldr over 2f out: shkn up to ld ins fnl f: r.o* 2/1[1]
0462 2 1¼ **Miss Ippolita**[8] 3038 3-9-2 **75** KerrinMcEvoy 5 78
(J R Jenkins) *led: rdn and hdd ins fnl f: unable qckn nr fin* 15/2
2552 3 ¾ **King's Bastion (IRE)**[6] 3099 3-9-4 **80** LiamJones(3) 1 81
(M L W Bell) *w ldr over 3f: sn outpcd: swtchd rt over 1f out: r.o wl towards fin* 11/4[2]
2611 4 5 **Kelamon**[4] 3164 3-9-1 **79** 12ex WilliamBuick(3) 3 65
(M D I Usher) *chsd ldrs: rdn over 2f out: wknd fnl f* 7/2[3]
4365 5 ½ **Prospect Place**[7] 3061 3-9-4 **77** SteveDrowne 4 61
(M Dods) *hld up in tch: rdn over 2f out: wknd over 1f out* 5/1
5120 6 10 **Rebel Duke (IRE)**[49] 1820 3-9-6 **79** (t) BrettDoyle 8 33
(M G Quinlan) *hld up: hung rt over 2f out: sn wknd* 16/1

1m 14.28s **Going Correction** +0.125s/f (Good) 6 Ran SP% 116.5
Speed ratings (Par 102):105,103,102,95,95 81
CSF £18.37 CT £41.85 TOTE £2.90: £1.90, £2.80; EX 16.90.
Owner Sir Edmund Loder **Bred** Sir E J Loder **Trained** Newmarket, Suffolk
■ Stewards' Enquiry : Brett Doyle two-day ban: improper riding - appeared to strike colt across the face (Jul 17-18)
FOCUS
A decent handicap but only the first three showed anything like their form. It has been rated through the runner-up.

3279 SPONSOR AT WARWICK RACECOURSE H'CAP 2m 39y
5:10 (5:12) (Class 5) (0-75,74) 3-Y-O+ £3,238 (£963; £481; £240) Stalls Low

Form RPR
-062 1 **Last Flight (IRE)**[22] 2610 3-8-4 **67** KerrinMcEvoy 7 76
(J L Dunlop) *chsd ldrs: rdn to ld 1f out: styd on* 11/8[1]
0103 2 1¾ **Kayf Aramis**[12] 2908 5-9-11 **72** MarcHalford(3) 6 79
(J L Spearing) *hld up: hdwy 1/2-way: rdn and ev ch 1f out: styd on same pce* 2/1[2]
2463 3 1¼ **Ronsard (IRE)**[8] 3012 5-8-9 **53** SteveDrowne 2 59
(P D Evans) *hld up: hdwy 5f out: led over 2f out: rdn and hdd 1f out: no ex* 11/2[3]
3621 4 1¼ **Sand Repeal (IRE)**[19] 2686 5-9-1 **66** (v) AmyBaker(7) 9 70
(Miss J Feilden) *led: hdd 5f out: led again over 3f out: hdd over 2f out: no ex fnl f* 8/1
3120 5 4 **Mister Completely (IRE)**[9] 2996 6-9-7 **65** JamesDoyle 1 64?
(Ms J S Doyle) *chsd ldrs: outpcd over 4f out: rallied over 2f out: wknd over 1f out* 14/1
6060 6 10 **Flame Creek (IRE)**[13] 2860 11-9-11 **72** AlanCreighton(3) 8 59
(E J Creighton) *chsd ldrs: led 5f out: hdd over 3f out: rdn and wknd 2f out* 33/1

3m 45.98s (13.28) **Going Correction** +0.875s/f (Soft)
WFA 3 from 5yo+ 19lb 6 Ran SP% 111.5
Speed ratings (Par 103):101,100,99,98,96 91
CSF £4.28 CT £9.22 TOTE £2.20: £1.50, £1.80; EX 5.00.

The Form Book, Raceform Ltd, Compton, RG20 6NL

Owner Windflower Overseas Holdings Inc **Bred** Windflower Overseas Holdings Inc **Trained** Arundel, W Sussex

■ Stewards' Enquiry : Kerrin McEvoy three-day ban: used whip with excessive frequency and down the neck in the forehand position (Jul 17-19)

FOCUS

This stamina test was run at a sensible pace. Modest if sound form, the unexposed winner up 6lb.

3280 RACING UK APPRENTICE H'CAP 1m 4f 134y

5:40 (5:40) (Class 6) (0-60,60) 4-Y-0+ **£2,047** (£604; £302) **Stalls** Low

Form RPR

/0-5 **1** **Raffish**[33] 1924 5-9-3 **58** JackDean 2 67
(M Scudamore) *chsd ldr: led over 1f out: sn rdn clr: styd on u.str.p* **16/1**

-035 **2** *1 1/2* **Sovietta (IRE)**[10] 2967 6-8-13 **54** (t) AlanRutter 3 61
(A G Newcombe) *hld up: hdwy over 2f out: rdn and hung rt ins fnl f: styd on* **6/1**[3]

6-01 **3** *hd* **Hi Dancer**[13] 2890 4-8-13 **57** WJCafferty(3) 12 64
(P C Haslam) *broke wl: stdd and sn dropped to rr: hdwy 2f out: sn rdn: hung rt ins fnl f: too much to do* **11/10**[1]

-550 **4** *8* **Always Baileys (IRE)**[40] 515 4-9-1 **59** (b) JosephWalsh(3) 5 55
(T Wall) *led: clr 10f out: hdd & wknd over 1f out* **14/1**

30-0 **5** *3* **Amnesty**[22] 2595 8-8-13 **57** (b) JemmaMarshall(3) 8 48
(G L Moore) *hld up in tch: rdn and wknd 3f out* **11/1**

/060 **6** *2* **Code (IRE)**[9] 2996 6-8-2 **50** (p) PaulPickard(7) 7 39
(Miss Z C Davison) *chsd ldrs tl wknd over 2f out* **50/1**

0044 **7** *nk* **Orpen Quest (IRE)**[8] 3035 5-8-0 **46** oh1 (p) BradleyRoper(5) 9 34
(M J Attwater) *hld up: rdn over 4f out: n.d* **8/1**

5500 **8** *3* **Twilight Avenger (IRE)**[7] 3047 4-7-9 **46** oh1 (p) Julie-AnneCumine(10) 10 30
(W M Brisbourne) *chsd ldrs: rdn and wknd over 2f out* **33/1**

030- **9** *5* **Summer Bounty**[246] 6067 11-8-10 **56** ChrisHough(5) 11 33
(F Jordan) *s.i.s: hld up: wknd over 3f out* **20/1**

4110 **10** *3* **Don Pasquale**[2] 3204 5-8-12 **56** SoniaEaton(3) 4 29
(J T Stimpson) *hld up: racd keenly: hdwy 9f out: wknd over 2f out* **5/1**[2]

2m 55.13s (11.53) **Going Correction** +0.875s/f (Soft) **10** Ran SP% **120.2**

Speed ratings (Par 101):99,98,97,93,91 89,89,87,84,83

CSF £110.27 CT £197.70 TOTE £15.70: £3.60, £1.50, £1.20; EX 116.90 Place 6 £39.65, Place 5 £18.47..

Owner I J Anderson **Bred** P And Mrs Venner **Trained** Bromsash, Herefordshire

FOCUS

A moderate apprentice handicap in which the first three finished clear. Again not many showed their form, with the winner the best guide.

T/Plt: £41.80 to a £1 stake. Pool: £47,182.20. 822.90 winning tickets. T/Qpdt: £2.80 to a £1 stake. Pool: £3,549.70. 905.80 winning tickets. CR

3168 WOLVERHAMPTON (A.W) (L-H)

Friday, July 6

OFFICIAL GOING: Standard

Wind: Moderately strong behind

3281 WOLVERHAMPTON-RACECOURSE.CO.UK H'CAP 5f 20y(P)

2:30 (2:30) (Class 6) (0-65,64) 3-Y-0 **£2,388** (£705; £352) **Stalls** Low

Form RPR

3036 **1** **Rosie Cross (IRE)**[10] 2966 3-8-12 **55** StephenCarson 7 59
(Eve Johnson Houghton) *a chsng ldr: rdn wl over 1f out: drvn and styd on wl fnl f to ld nr line* **8/1**

1640 **2** *hd* **Charlotte Grey**[11] 2950 3-9-7 **64** EdwardCreighton 12 67
(C N Allen) *led: rdn wl over 1f out: drvn ins fnl f: hdd nr line* **15/2**[3]

5022 **3** *1 1/4* **Moonlight Applause**[13] 2895 3-8-11 **54** DavidAllan 1 53
(T D Easterby) *trckd ldrs: hdwy over 2f out: sn rdn and styd on ins fnl f: nrst fin* **11/4**[1]

-305 **4** *1 1/2* **Fly Time**[13] 2895 3-8-2 **50** ow2 TolleyDean(5) 2 43
(Mrs L Williamson) *midfield: hdwy over 2f out: sn rdn and styd on ent fnl f: nrst fin* **16/1**

3053 **5** *3/4* **The Geester**[11] 2950 3-8-11 **54** (b) PaulEddery 10 44
(S R Bowring) *chsd ldrs: rdn wl over 1f out: sn drvn and kpt on same pce ins fnl f* **15/2**[3]

0606 **6** *nk* **Hephaestus**[69] 1313 3-8-7 **50** DeanMcKeown 4 39
(A J Chamberlain) *hld up: hdwy 2f out: sn rdn and kpt on same pce ent fnl f* **6/1**[2]

0-50 **7** *hd* **Compton Special**[44] 1943 3-8-7 **50** HayleyTurner 5 39
(J G Given) *hld up in rr: effrt 2f out: sn rdn and kpt on ins fnl f: nrst fin* **20/1**

0-60 **8** *1/2* **Shantina's Dream (USA)**[35] 2205 3-8-10 **58** (t) TravisBlock(5) 11 45
(H Morrison) *s.i.s: a in rr* **25/1**

5003 **9** *nk* **Kilvickeon (IRE)**[11] 2939 3-8-4 **47** AdrianMcCarthy 9 33
(Peter Grayson) *chsd ldrs on outer: rdn along wl over 1f out: sn drvn and wknd 1f out* **12/1**

0463 **10** *shd* **Temtation (IRE)**[14] 2826 3-8-0 **48** LukeMorris(5) 6 33
(Peter Grayson) *chsd ldrs: rdn along 1/2-way: wknd wl over 1f out* **15/2**[3]

4006 **11** *1/2* **Head To Head (IRE)**[11] 2948 3-8-4 **52** RussellKennemore(5) 3 36
(Peter Grayson) *sn rdn along and a in rr* **14/1**

6-56 **12** *3 1/2* **Millsini**[34] 2242 3-8-12 **55** SebSanders 8 26
(Rae Guest) *sn rdn along and a in rr* **6/1**[2]

62.08 secs (-0.74) **Going Correction** -0.225s/f (Stan) **12** Ran SP% **130.5**

Speed ratings (Par 98):96,95,93,91,90 89,89,88,88,87 87,81

CSF £73.92 CT £218.84 TOTE £13.00: £5.10, £3.10, £1.80; EX 114.30 Trifecta £87.90 Pool £158.58 - 1.20 winning units..

Owner Eden Racing (II) **Bred** Century Farms **Trained** Blewbury, Oxon

FOCUS

A very moderate race that is unlikely to prove informative with the first three pretty exposed. However, the form appears sound enough.

3282 ENJOY THE AIR-CONDITIONED HORIZONS RESTAURANT CLAIMING STKS 1m 4f 50y(P)

3:05 (3:05) (Class 6) 3-Y-0+ **£2,184** (£644; £322) **Stalls** Low

Form RPR

5011 **1** **Champagne Shadow (IRE)**[7] 3063 6-9-8 **68** (p) FergusSweeney 1 68
(Miss Tor Sturgis) *trckd ldrs: hdwy 4f out: rdn along over 2f out: swtchd wd over 1f out: styd on strly u.p to ld wl ins fnl f* **2/1**[2]

3255 **2** *1* **Chiff Chaff**[15] 2801 3-7-13 **61** LukeMorris(5) 10 62
(M L W Bell) *led tl rn wd bnd over 7f out: remained prom: rdn to ld wl over 1f out: drvn and hdd wl ins fnl f: no ex* **6/4**[1]

2204 **3** *1 1/4* **Brastar Jelois (FR)**[7] 3063 4-9-3 **64** JamieSpencer 5 60
(R Hollinshead) *hld up towards rr: smooth hdwy 5f out: trckd ldrs 3f out: effrt over 1f out: rdn and ev ch ins fnl f: sn one pce* **7/1**[3]

1034 **4** *1* **Bethanys Boy (IRE)**[66] 1368 6-9-4 **57** SimonWhitworth 7 59
(P A Blockley) *hld up: gd hdwy 4f out: rdn and ev ch over 1f out: sn drvn and kpt on same pce ins fnl f* **8/1**

3 **5** *9* **Oscar Ireland (IRE)**[13] 2874 6-9-3 0 SebSanders 12 44
(R M Beckett) *a.p: effrt to ld 3f out and sn rdn: drvn and hdd wl over 1f out: sn wknd and eased* **12/1**

6400 **6** *3* **Reaching Out (IRE)**[35] 2214 5-9-8 **62** (b) EddieAhern 9 44
(N P Littmoden) *a in rr* **10/1**

/0-0 **7** *7* **Lazzaz**[7] 3063 9-8-10 **46** WilliamCarson(7) 6 28
(P W Hiatt) *prom: lft in ld bnd over 7f out: rdn along and hdd 3f out: sn wknd* **33/1**

5050 **8** *44* **Barzak (IRE)**[37] 2145 7-8-12 **39** (t) LeeTopliss(7) 2 —
(S R Bowring) *chsd ldrs: rdn along 1/2-way: lost pl 5f out and sn bhd* **50/1**

03 **9** *1 1/2* **Callitquits (IRE)**[11] 2946 5-9-4 **49** HayleyTurner 8 —
(Jennie Candlish) *chsd ldrs: rdn along over 4f out: sn wknd* **33/1**

10 *106* **Little Darlin** 3-8-0 0 AdrianMcCarthy 11 —
(G J Smith) *s.i.s: a in rr: wl bhd fnl 4f* **50/1**

-003 **R** **Bouzouki (USA)**[13] 2875 4-9-5 **54** JerryO'Dwyer(3) 4 —
(Karen George) *ref to r: tk no part* **20/1**

2m 40.08s (-2.34) **Going Correction** -0.225s/f (Stan)

WFA 3 from 4yo+ 13lb **11** Ran SP% **128.3**

Speed ratings (Par 101):94,87,86,85,84 77,75,75,72,64 49,—

CSF £58.42 TOTE £2.90: £1.10, £5.80, £1.30; EX 101.30 TRIFECTA Not won..

Speed ratings (Par 101):98,97,96,95,89 87,83,53,52,— —

CSF £5.72 TOTE £3.60: £1.40, £1.10, £2.90; EX 9.90 Trifecta £22.20 Pool £372.72 - 11.92 winning units..Chiff Chaff was claimed by Andrew Page for £10,000.

Owner Miss Tor Sturgis **Bred** Mrs Kate Watson **Trained** Lambourn, Berks

FOCUS

A very moderate affair run in a time much slower than the maiden later on the card.

3283 SPONSOR A RACE BY CALLING 0870 220 2442 MEDIAN AUCTION MAIDEN STKS 5f 216y(P)

3:40 (3:40) (Class 6) 2-Y-0 **£2,184** (£644; £322) **Stalls** Low

Form RPR

62 **1** **Cosmic Art**[23] 2569 2-9-3 0 DaneO'Neill 2 78+
(E A L Dunlop) *mde all: rdn clr wl over 1f out: easily* **6/4**[1]

0 **2** *5* **Kaystar Ridge**[21] 2630 2-9-3 0 AdrianMcCarthy 5 60
(D K Ivory) *cl up: chsd wnr fr 1/2-way: rdn along 2f out and kpt on same pce* **25/1**

4 **3** *nk* **Cobo Bay**[15] 2803 2-9-3 0 JamieSpencer 1 59
(K A Ryan) *chsd ldng pair: effrt 2f out: sn swtchd rt and rdn: edgd lft and no imp* **9/2**[3]

4 *1 1/4* **Wreningham** 2-9-0 0 JerryO'Dwyer(3) 6 55+
(T Keddy) *towards rr: gd hdwy on outer over 2f: sn rdn and kpt on ins fnl f: nrst fin* **25/1**

4 **5** *1/2* **Siberian Tiger (IRE)**[28] 2432 2-9-3 0 DarryllHolland 8 54
(M R Channon) *in tch: effrt 3f out: rdn over 2f out: styd on ins fnl f* **11/4**[2]

6 *5* **Sultan Of The Sand** 2-9-3 0 DeanMcKeown 7 39
(C C Bealby) *prom: rdn along over 2f out: wknd wl over 1f out* **25/1**

02 **7** *1 1/2* **Distant Noble**[22] 2605 2-8-12 0 TolleyDean(5) 9 34
(R Brotherton) *a towards rr* **25/1**

0 **8** *nk* **Amber Ridge**[25] 2517 2-9-3 0 PaulEddery 4 33
(B P J Baugh) *chsd ldrs: rdn along 3f out: sn wknd* **33/1**

9 *2 1/2* **Don Picolo** 2-9-3 0 SimonWhitworth 3 26
(P A Blockley) *s.i.s: a in rr* **14/1**

03 **10** *6* **Black Duke**[8] 3037 2-9-3 0 SebSanders 11 8
(M G Quinlan) *chsd ldrs on outer: rdn along 3f out: sn wknd* **7/1**

11 *11* **Running Buck (USA)** 2-9-3 0 EddieAhern 12 —
(N P Littmoden) *sn outpcd and a in rr* **16/1**

12 *38* **Dawn Storm (IRE)** 2-9-3 0 LeeEnstone 10 —
(K R Burke) *s.i.s: a in rr* **14/1**

1m 15.33s (-0.48) **Going Correction** -0.225s/f (Stan) **12** Ran SP% **134.9**

Speed ratings (Par 92):94,87,86,85,84 77,75,75,72,64 49,—

CSF £58.42 TOTE £2.90: £1.10, £5.80, £1.30; EX 101.30 TRIFECTA Not won..

Owner Byculla Thoroughbreds **Bred** Hellwood Stud Farm **Trained** Newmarket, Suffolk

FOCUS

A modest contest won easily by the favourite. It does not appear to be strong form.

NOTEBOOK

Cosmic Art blasted out from the stalls and never saw a rival. He was far too good for any of his opponents but will be faced with much stiffer tasks from now on, probably in nursery company. (op 9-4)

Kaystar Ridge was always thereabouts and only just hung on for second. It was a big improvement from his initial effort and can win an ordinary maiden if maintaining this level of ability.

Cobo Bay had come on for his first effort but still looked in need of the experience. Another furlong will probably suit him in the future. Official explanation: jockey said colt ran green throughout (op 4-1)

Wreningham was never going the pace early, but kept plugging away and finished fairly well as a result. He seems sure to be better for the experience.

Siberian Tiger(IRE) looked ill at ease on the track and probably resented the kick back. He has something to prove now. (op 3-1)

Sultan Of The Sand was far too green to do himself justice but shaped with enough promise to suggest he will be winning races in time. Official explanation: jockey said colt hung badly right throughout

Black Duke never looked that happy racing wide of the pack and was eased once his chance had gone. He is possibly the sort for nurseries now, if this run can be excused. Official explanation: jockey said colt moved poorly throughout (tchd 15-2)

Running Buck(USA) was not quickly away and the jockey did not appear to give him a hard time as a result. Official explanation: jockey said colt didn't face the kickback

3284 CELEBRATE AT WOLVERHAMPTON RACECOURSE MAIDEN STKS 1m 4f 50y(P)

4:15 (4:16) (Class 5) 3-Y-0+ **£2,968** (£876; £438) **Stalls** Low

Form RPR

00-3 **1** **Chord**[55] 1665 3-9-0 **69** (v[1]) DaneO'Neill 6 79
(Sir Michael Stoute) *trckd ldrs: hdwy 5f out: chsd ldr 3f out: rdn to chal wl over 1f out: styd on to ld ins fnl f* **14/1**

54 **2** *4* **Golden Wave (IRE)**[38] 2118 3-8-9 0 DarryllHolland 5 68
(J Noseda) *led: rdn and qcknd 3f out: jnd and drvn over 1f out: hdd ins fnl f: no ex* **12/1**

3 **3** *3* **Alma Mater**[16] 2766 4-9-8 0 SebSanders 2 63
(Sir Mark Prescott) *hld up: hdwy over 4f out: rdn to chse ldng pair wl over 2f out: sn drvn and btn wl over 1f out* **1/2**[1]

2302 **4** *10* **Guardian Of Truth (IRE)**[21] 2628 3-9-0 77........................ EddieAhern 4 52
(W J Knight) *chsd ldng pair: effrt over 4f out: sn rdn along and wknd 3f out* **4/1**[2]

0/6 **5** *shd* **This Way That Way**[28] 602 6-9-13 0........................ FergusSweeney 1 52
(Ian Williams) *chsd ldr: pushed along and lost pl 1/2-way: drvn along 3f out and no prog* **25/1**

6 **6** *3/4* **Kwazulu (USA)**[18] 2726 3-9-0 0.. KDarley 3 51
(J H M Gosden) *hld up in rr: hdwy on outer 5f out: rdn along to chse ldrs 4f out: drvn and wknd 3f out* **5/1**[3]

2m 37.57s (-4.85) **Going Correction** -0.225s/f (Stan)
WFA 3 from 4yo+ 13lb **6** Ran SP% **121.5**
Speed ratings (Par 103):107,104,102,95,95 95
CSF £160.57 TOTE £13.00: £4.70, £6.80; EX 81.60.
Owner Cheveley Park Stud **Bred** Cheveley Park Stud Ltd **Trained** Newmarket, Suffolk

FOCUS
An ordinary maiden that lacked any early pace and the form is not strong. The favourite could not get on terms after being held up, and is probably better than the bare result suggests.

3285 BOOK YOUR CHRISTMAS PARTY NOW H'CAP 7f 32y(P)
4:50 (4:50) (Class 5) (0-70,70) 3-Y-0+ £3,071 (£906; £453) Stalls High

Form RPR

6010 **1** **Wodhill Schnaps**[7] 3056 6-8-9 51 oh1..................(b) AdrianMcCarthy 10 60
(D Morris) *in tch on outer: hdwy to chse ldrs 3f out: rdn along 2f out: styd on to chal ent fnl f: drvn and led nr fin* **14/1**

1-06 **2** *nk* **Ochre Bay**[18] 2719 4-9-9 70.................................. RussellKennemore(5) 7 78
(R Hollinshead) *trckd ldrs: hdwy 4f out: rdn to ld ins fnl f: sn drvn: hdd and no ex nr fin* **14/1**

0041 **3** *1* **Benny The Bus**[11] 2947 5-9-5 61 6ex................................ EddieAhern 9 66
(Mrs G S Rees) *prom: hdwy to ld 3f out: rdn and hdd wl over 1f out: sn drvn and ev ch tl one pce wl ins fnl f* **9/1**

6133 **4** *nk* **Divertimenti (IRE)**[7] 3066 3-9-6 70................................ JamieSpencer 4 71
(C R Dore) *hld up in rr: gd hdwy on outer 3f out: rdn to chse ldrs ins fnl f: sn drvn and one pce* **5/2**[1]

6033 **5** *1 3/4* **Xpres Maite**[23] 2550 4-9-13 69... PaulEddery 1 69
(S R Bowring) *hld up: hmpd over 4f out: hdwy wl over 2f out: sn rdn and styd on ins fnl f: nt rch ldrs* **13/2**

5434 **6** *3 1/2* **Norcroft**[55] 1678 5-9-6 62..(p) DMylonas 8 52
(Mrs C A Dunnett) *sn prom: led over 4f out: rdn along and hdd 3f out: drvn and grad wknd fnl 2f* **12/1**

0553 **7** *1 1/2* **Soviet Sound (IRE)**[20] 2661 3-7-10 51......................... LukeMorris(5) 2 34
(Jedd O'Keeffe) *hld up: effrt and sme hdwy 1/2-way: rdn along wl over 2f out and no further prog* **14/1**

6022 **8** *shd* **Lii Najma**[20] 2654 4-9-11 67... SebSanders 11 53
(C E Brittain) *sn trcking ldrs on outer: effrt over 3f out: rdn along over 2f out: sn drvn and btn wl over 1f out* **3/1**[2]

3003 **9** *shd* **Royal Envoy (IRE)**[11] 2947 4-9-1 57........................... DeanMcKeown 6 43
(D Shaw) *a towards rr* **5/1**[3]

604 **10** *nk* **Stagnite**[24] 2540 7-8-9 51 oh2.. DarryllHolland 3 36
(Karen George) *trckd ldrs on inner: n.m.r and snatched up over 4f out: n.d after* **16/1**

040- **11** *hd* **The Crooked Ring**[240] 6396 5-9-3 59............................... DaneO'Neill 12 43
(A G Newcombe) *midfield: hdwy on outer to chse ldrs over 3f out: sn rdn and wknd* **20/1**

0000 **12** *3* **Kennington**[13] 2879 7-8-5 52..(b) TolleyDean(5) 5 28
(Mrs C A Dunnett) *led: hdd over 4f out: rdn along over 3f out and sn wknd* **33/1**

1m 29.14s (-1.26) **Going Correction** -0.225s/f (Stan)
WFA 3 from 4yo+ 8lb **12** Ran SP% **134.8**
Speed ratings (Par 103):98,97,96,96,94 90,88,88,88,87 87,84
CSF £221.36 CT £1906.80 TOTE £20.20: £5.90, £5.60, £3.40; EX 216.50 Trifecta £496.30 Part won. Pool £699.06 - 0.99 winning units..
Owner Miss S Graham **Bred** Wodhill Stud **Trained** Newmarket, Suffolk
■ Stewards' Enquiry : D Mylonas four-day ban: careless riding (Jul 17-20)

FOCUS
The early gallop was not strong, which probably helped to produce a close finish. Apart from the winner, who was scoring off a mark of 51, the form makes sense for the grade rated around those in the frame behind the winner.

3286 STAY AT THE WOLVERHAMPTON HOLIDAY INN H'CAP 1m 141y(P)
5:20 (5:20) (Class 6) (0-65,65) 3-Y-0+ £2,388 (£705; £352) Stalls Low

Form RPR

5022 **1** **Hoh Wotanite**[4] 3173 4-9-8 59.....................................(b) JamieSpencer 5 72
(R Hollinshead) *hld up in rr: gd hdwy wl over 2f out: rdn over 1f out: styd on to chal and hung bdly rt ent fnl f: drvn to ld last 150yds* **13/8**[1]

4003 **2** *1 1/4* **Casablanca Minx (IRE)**[4] 3156 4-8-9 46...................(v[1]) PaulEddery 7 56
(P D Evans) *midfield: hdwy over 3f out: rdn to chal over 1f out: drvn to ld ent fnl f: hdd and nt qckn last 150yds* **6/1**[3]

0034 **3** *3* **Feeling Wonderful (IRE)**[8] 3034 3-9-4 65.......................... KDarley 8 67
(M Johnston) *cl up: led over 2f out: sn rdn and hung bdly right over 1f out: drvn and hdd whn n.m.r ent fnl f: kpt on same pce* **6/1**[3]

5304 **4** *1/2* **Majehar**[15] 2802 5-9-7 58.. DaneO'Neill 3 60
(A G Newcombe) *hld up: stdy hdwy 3f out: rdn to chse ldrs wl over 1f out: kpt on same pce* **4/1**[2]

0403 **5** *3 1/2* **Fire At Will**[28] 2412 5-8-2 46 oh1................................ MarkCoumbe(7) 10 40
(A W Carroll) *hld up: hdwy 3f out: rdn wl over 1f out: kpt on ins fnl f* **25/1**

033 **6** *1/2* **Mister Jingles**[31] 2343 4-8-4 46 oh1.............................. LukeMorris(5) 2 39
(R M Whitaker) *hld up: hdwy on inner over 2f out: styd far rails and rdn over 1f out: kpt on same pce ins fnl f* **8/1**

0-06 **7** *1/2* **Day By Day**[17] 2740 3-8-13 60....................................(b[1]) DarryllHolland 4 51
(B J Meehan) *chsd ldrs: effrt over 2f out: rdn along over 1f out: drvn and wknd ent fnl f* **16/1**

0300 **8** *3/4* **Major League (USA)**[17] 2748 5-10-0 65.......................... SebSanders 13 55
(D Morris) *trckd ldrs: hdwy 3f out: rdn to chse ldr 2f out: drvn and hld whn n.m.r over 1f out: wknd* **14/1**

1004 **9** *1 1/2* **Grand Lucre**[28] 2422 3-9-2 63... EddieAhern 1 48
(J W Hills) *led: rdn along over 3f out: hdd over 2f out and grad wknd* **12/1**

2060 **10** *3* **Mid Valley**[36] 2179 4-8-12 49.......................................(v) StephenCarson 6 29
(J R Jenkins) *a towards rr* **33/1**

2440 **11** *19* **Marist Madame**[22] 2591 3-8-5 52................................. AdrianMcCarthy 9 —
(D K Ivory) *a towards rr* **33/1**

1m 49.64s (-2.12) **Going Correction** -0.225s/f (Stan)
WFA 3 from 4yo+ 10lb **11** Ran SP% **127.7**
Speed ratings (Par 101):100,98,96,95,92 92,91,91,89,87 70
CSF £12.81 CT £51.85 TOTE £2.60: £1.30, £2.00, £3.30; EX 15.30 Trifecta £48.50 Pool £316.31 - 4.63 winning units. Place 6 £985.62, Place 5 £425.78.
Owner The Three R'S **Bred** Dunchurch Lodge Stud Co **Trained** Upper Longdon, Staffs
■ Stewards' Enquiry : Jamie Spencer caution: careless riding

FOCUS
A race full of varying abilities and not one that is likely to produce too many winners in the short term. The form looks sound overall, rated around the third and fourth.
Feeling Wonderful(IRE) Official explanation: jockey said filly hung right
T/Plt: £265.90 to a £1 stake. Pool: £54,800.05. 150.40 winning tickets. T/Qpdt: £72.90 to a £1 stake. Pool: £3,430.30. 34.80 winning tickets. JR

3287 - 3295a (Foreign Racing) - See Raceform Interactive

3256 BEVERLEY (R-H)
Saturday, July 7

OFFICIAL GOING: Heavy
Wind: Slight half against Weather: Sunny

3296 HALL PLUMBING AND HEATING CLAIMING STKS 7f 100y
2:15 (2:20) (Class 5) 2-Y-0 £3,238 (£963; £481; £240) Stalls High

Form RPR

00 **1** **Pequeno Dinero (IRE)**[70] 1302 2-7-11 0 ow4........... KellyHarrison(7) 1 55
(C W Fairhurst) *t.k.h: trckd ldrs: hdwy over 2f out: swtchd rt and rdn wl over 1f out: styd on ins fnl f to ld last 50yds* **12/1**[3]

0031 **2** *1 1/2* **Indecision**[15] 2838 2-8-11 0.. PaulMulrennan 4 58
(M W Easterby) *t.k.h: chsd ldr: hdwy over 2f out: rdn to chal wl over 1f out: drvn to ld ent fnl f: hdd and no ex last 50yds* **2/1**[2]

0 **3** *3* **La Belle Joannie**[98] 845 2-7-13 0 ow2........................ LiamJones(3) 8 42
(P T Midgley) *led: rdn along over 2f out: jnd and drvn wl over 1f out: hdd ent fnl f: wknd* **16/1**

00 **4** *1 1/4* **Friction**[19] 2723 2-8-2 0... DaleGibson 3 39
(J G Portman) *hmpd s: in tch: pushed along 3f out: rdn over 2f out and plugged on same pce* **12/1**[3]

45 **5** *nk* **Arabian Fern**[15] 2838 2-8-1 0 ow2................................ AndrewMullen(3) 5 40
(M E Sowersby) *chsd ldrs: rdn along wl over 2f out: no imp whn n.m.r over 1f out* **16/1**

0060 **6** *14* **Welcome Inn**[15] 2838 2-7-10 0...............................(t) DuranFentiman(3) 2 2
(M E Sowersby) *sn outpcd and a bhd* **66/1**

4452 **P** **Alpen Adventure (IRE)**[15] 2819 2-8-11 0...............(p) RoystonFfrench 6 —
(Mrs L Stubbs) *cl up whn stmbld after 1f: sn p.u: dead* **10/11**[1]

1m 42.16s (7.85) **Going Correction** +0.925s/f (Soft) **7** Ran SP% **114.4**
Speed ratings (Par 94):92,90,86,85,85 69,—
CSF £36.46 TOTE £15.50: £4.90, £1.20; EX 75.10.The winner was the subject of a friendly claim.
Owner France, Turner and Friends **Bred** John J Cosgrave **Trained** Middleham Moor, N Yorks
■ Stewards' Enquiry : Kelly Harrison one-day ban: careless riding (Jul 18)

FOCUS
A very moderate race that is unlikely to have much impact in the coming months, with the runner-up the best guide to the level.

NOTEBOOK
Pequeno Dinero(IRE), stepping up in trip and getting a stone from the runner-up, kept on to really good effect to stay on past Indecision and win going away. She seem sure to stay a bit further. (op 16-1 tchd 20-1)
Indecision was not in the best of moods before the start but had every chance once taking up the lead about a furlong from home despite being keen throughout. He gives the form shape, however limited that is. (op 7-4)
La Belle Joannie was not the quickest away but still managed to take them along soon afterwards.This was a lot better than her last-place finish in the Brocklesby back in March, and a race in this grade or a seller can be won with her. (op 33-1)
Friction was pushed along rounding the home bend before staying on moderately up the hill. She does not look about to win a race quite yet. (op 11-1)
Alpen Adventure(IRE) ran wide at the first bend and was sadly put down due to injuries incurred. (op Evens)

3297 BATTY JOINERY MANUFACTURERS MAIDEN STKS 5f
2:45 (2:54) (Class 4) 2-Y-0 £3,886 (£1,156; £577; £288) Stalls High

Form RPR

1 **Soopacal (IRE)** 2-8-13 0.. RoystonFfrench 2 77+
(B Smart) *t.k.h: trckd ldrs: hdwy to ld over 1f out: sn pushed clr* **4/1**[2]

4 **2** *5* **Know No Fear**[9] 3030 2-9-3 0...................................... GrahamGibbons 7 66+
(J J Quinn) *rrd and lost many ls: hdwy 1/2-way: nt clr run on inner over 1f out: sn swtchd lft and styd on ins fnl f* **9/4**[1]

3 *1 1/2* **Lekin Sedona (IRE)** 2-8-13 0.. TonyHamilton 9 54
(J M Saville) *led 2f: cl up: rdn along wl over 1f out: kpt on u.p fnl f* **11/1**

60 **4** *1 1/4* **Rich James (IRE)**[31] 2371 2-9-3 0.. TPO'Shea 5 53
(J D Bethell) *cl up: led after 2f: rdn along and hdd over 1f out: wknd ins fnl f* **13/2**[3]

00 **5** *10* **Pussycat Bow**[13] 2904 2-8-12 0...............................(b[1]) DaleGibson 8 12
(M W Easterby) *chsd ldrs: rdn along 1/2-way: sn outpcd* **14/1**

6 *7* **Penny Arcade** 2-8-5 0...................................... AndrewMullen(3) 6 —
(M E Sowersby) *chsd ldrs: rdn along bef 1/2-way and sn wknd* **18/1**

7 *20* **Doubtless** 2-8-1 0...................................... DanielleMcCreery(7) 4 —
(D W Chapman) *fly j. and veered bdly rt s: a wl bhd: t.o* **28/1**

1m 10.47s (6.47) **Going Correction** +0.975s/f (Soft) **7** Ran SP% **87.8**
Speed ratings (Par 96):87,79,76,74,58 47,15
CSF £7.81 TOTE £3.70: £2.20, £1.80; EX 8.10.
Owner Brian Grieve & Jeff Evans **Bred** Paul Trainor **Trained** Hambleton, N Yorks
■ Pay Parade (5/2, ref to enter stalls) & Dawn Whisper (40/1, unruly in stalls) were withdrawn. R4, applies, deduct 25p in the £.

FOCUS
A race that appeared to involve quite a few overly-green horses. The winner and probably the second apart, the form looks moderate.

NOTEBOOK
Soopacal(IRE), descibed by his trainer as a runaway at home, was always ideally positioned throughout and won going away. There is no doubt this race took little winning but he is entitled to improve from the run and hold his own against better sorts. Another furlong will be within his scope as long as he can be kept relaxed during a race. (op 11-4)
Know No Fear, who was one of many in the race that appeared to have quirks, did exceptionally well to get second place and with a clearer run would have finished a couple of lengths closer at least. If overcoming his 'problems', he can win an ordinary maiden somewhere. Official explanation: jockey said gelding reared on leaving stalls losing many lengths (op 3-1 tchd 7-2)
Lekin Sedona(IRE) set the early pace but looked to be doing it on sufferance. It would be dangerous to take his third place as a promising effort. (op 12-1 tchd 14-1 and 9-1)
Rich James(IRE) had every chance but once again came up short. (op 5-1 tchd 9-2)
Pussycat Bow did not make any significant improvement for having the blinkers fitted for the first time. (op 33-1)
Doubtless, who was walked part of the way to the start, looked a real lunatic leaving the stalls and the jockey did really well just to keep the partnership together. (op 50-1)

3298 HALL CONSTRUCTION H'CAP 5f
3:20 (3:26) (Class 3) (0-90,86) 3-Y-O+ £7,772 (£2,312; £1,155; £577) Stalls High

Form RPR
0060 1 **Glasshoughton**[10] [2989] 4-8-9 **69**...................................... PhillipMakin 13 84
(M Dods) *cl up: led after 2f: rdn clr over 1f out: styd on wl* **8/1**
0002 2 1 3/4 **Bond Boy**[4] [3197] 10-8-10 **75**.......................................(b) SladeO'Hara(5) 12 84
(G R Oldroyd) *hld up: effrt and nt clr run on inner over 2f out: gd hdwy over 1f out: rdn to chse wnr ins fnl f: no imp towards fin* **9/4**[1]
6141 3 2 1/2 **Desert Opal**[46] [1914] 7-8-9 **72**.......................................(p) LiamJones(3) 1 72
(C R Dore) *in midfield: gd hdwy on outer 2f out: rdn to chse wnr ent fnl f: kpt on same pce* **10/1**
4304 4 2 1/2 **Bo McGinty (IRE)**[10] [2989] 6-8-9 **76**..........................(v) JamesRogers(7) 5 67+
(R A Fahey) *in tch: effrt whn bdly bmpd 2f out: sn rdn and styd on ins fnl f: nrst fin* **8/1**
0200 5 nk **Monashee Brave (IRE)**[18] [2744] 4-8-11 **71**................ GrahamGibbons 9 61
(J J Quinn) *cl up: rdn along 2f out: drvn and wknd appr fnl f* **16/1**
0-10 6 1 1/4 **Wanchai Lad**[18] [2744] 6-9-10 **84**... DavidAllan 8 69
(T D Easterby) *trckd ldrs: effrt and swtchd lft over 2f out: sn rdn and kpt on same pce ent fnl f* **8/1**
4206 7 nk **Prince Namid**[8] [3050] 5-9-11 **85**...............................(v[1]) RoystonFfrench 6 69
(Mrs A Duffield) *swtchd to far rail and hld up in rr: hdwy 2f out: sn rdn and no imp* **11/2**[2]
1625 8 1/2 **Namir (IRE)**[10] [2989] 5-9-0 **77**..................................(vt) DuranFentiman(3) 2 59
(D Shaw) *stdd s: hld up: a towards rr* **16/1**
00-0 9 hd **Artie**[10] [2989] 8-9-0 **74**... TonyHamilton 14 56
(T D Easterby) *led 2f: rdn along 1/2-way: grad wknd* **20/1**
5314 10 2 1/2 **Efistorm**[7] [3080] 6-9-10 **84**.. DaleGibson 4 57
(C R Dore) *chsd ldrs: rdn along 2f out: sn drvn and wknd over 1f out* **7/1**[3]
0400 11 2 1/2 **Steel Blue**[18] [2744] 7-9-1 **75**.. DeanMcKeown 3 39
(R M Whitaker) *a towards rr* **12/1**

67.64 secs (3.64) **Going Correction** +0.975s/f (Soft)
WFA 3 from 4yo+ 5lb **11** Ran SP% **125.3**
Speed ratings (Par 107):109,106,102,98,97 95,95,94,94,90 86
CSF £28.08 CT £198.34 TOTE £10.90: £2.80, £1.80, £4.10; EX 43.60.
Owner J N Blackburn **Bred** Theakston Stud **Trained** Denton, Co Durham

FOCUS
A good and competitive handicap just about dominated by the draw. The form is a bit messy and best rated through the first two.

NOTEBOOK
Glasshoughton did not get the clearest of passages last time when making a challenge, but was soon to the fore from a decent draw, and kept on well for pressure. He should to be capable of going close again next time, even after being reassessed. (tchd 17-2)
Bond Boy did not have an untroubled run when the race started to take shape, but he never really looked like reeling in the winner. An admirable sort for his age, he is nicely handicapped and should remain competitive with his younger rivals. (op 11-4)
Desert Opal had a lot to do from his draw and did well to finish where he did. Even though he has won on ground with ease in it, he is probably better suited by quicker going. (op 12-1)
Bo McGinty(IRE) got badly baulked when making an effort and can be counted unlucky not to have finished closer. (op 12-1)
Monashee Brave(IRE) raced keenly and was never far away from the front before weakening late on. It was a fair effort and his turn should not be far away now, considering his favourable handicap mark. (tchd 14-1)
Wanchai Lad caused a bit of trouble a couple of furlongs from home and never really got involved. Better ground would suit him, but he remains plenty high enough in the weights now. (op 11-1)
Prince Namid, wearing a first-time visor, did not shape without some promise and probably ran slightly better than his finishing position suggests. Official explanation: jockey said gelding was hampered at start and denied a clear run (op 9-2)

3299 HALL BUILDING SERVICES H'CAP 1m 100y
3:55 (4:01) (Class 4) (0-80,80) 3-Y-O £5,181 (£1,541; £770; £384) Stalls High

Form RPR
5-11 1 **The Grey Berry**[15] [2834] 3-9-3 **76**................................ GrahamGibbons 4 93+
(T D Walford) *hld up: smooth hdwy 3f out: chal on bit over 1f out: led ins fnl f: cleverly* **2/1**[1]
0051 2 1/2 **Smugglers Bay (IRE)**[16] [2796] 3-8-8 **67**....................(b) PaulMulrennan 5 78
(T D Easterby) *prom on outer: effrt to chal over 2f out and sn rdn: drvn to ld briefly 1f out: sn hdd and kpt on: no ch w wnr* **7/2**[2]
0-00 3 7 **Lemon Silk (IRE)**[14] [2862] 3-8-12 **71**.......................... MickyFenton 3 67
(T P Tate) *led: rdn along over 2f out: drvn and hdd 1f out: one pce* **15/2**
0034 4 nk **Handsome Falcon**[9] [3029] 3-9-1 **74**.................................... TonyHamilton 9 70
(R A Fahey) *hld up in rr: hdwy over 2f out: rdn wl over 1f out: kpt on ins fnl f: nrst fin* **6/1**[3]
3-10 5 5 **Rabbit Fighter (IRE)**[79] [1106] 3-9-7 **80**.................................. TPO'Shea 6 65
(P A Blockley) *bmpd s and hld up in rr: stdy hdwy on outer 3f out: rdn to chse ldrs 2f out: sn drvn and wknd* **12/1**
3001 6 2 1/2 **Leonard Charles**[32] [2331] 3-8-13 **72**................................(b) DaleGibson 8 52
(C R Dore) *wnt lft s: sn prom: rdn along 3f out: drvn over 2f out and sn wknd* **20/1**
-302 7 3 **Laish Ya Hajar (IRE)**[28] [2453] 3-9-1 **74**.......................... SamHitchcott 2 48
(M R Channon) *t.k.h: chsd ldrs: rdn along over 2f out and sn wknd* **8/1**
1112 8 1 1/4 **Jewelled Dagger (IRE)**[14] [2862] 3-9-5 **78**...................... PhillipMakin 1 49
(I Semple) *chsd ldrs: rdn along wl over 2f out: wknd wl over 1f out* **8/1**

1m 52.26s (4.86) **Going Correction** +0.925s/f (Soft) **8** Ran SP% **116.3**
Speed ratings (Par 102):112,111,104,104,99 96,93,92
CSF £9.16 CT £42.74 TOTE £2.90: £1.40, £1.50, £2.10; EX 9.90.
Owner N J Maher **Bred** G Deacon **Trained** Sheriff Hutton, N Yorks

FOCUS
A fair handicap run in a very good time for the grade and rated positively with the first two clear. The winner is improving and won easily.
Laish Ya Hajar(IRE) Official explanation: jockey said gelding ran too free early stages
Jewelled Dagger(IRE) Official explanation: jockey said gelding was unsuited by the heavy ground

3300 HALL CIVIL ENGINEERING H'CAP 2m 35y
4:25 (4:30) (Class 5) (0-70,68) 3-Y-O+ £3,886 (£1,156; £577; £288) Stalls High

Form RPR
5-10 1 **Gallileo Figaro (USA)**[14] [2887] 4-9-11 **68**.................... JerryO'Dwyer(3) 1 74
(N B King) *hld up: stdy hdwy 5f out: effrt to ld 2f out and sn rdn: drvn ins fnl f and hld on gamely* **8/1**
1342 2 shd **Rocknest Island (IRE)**[15] [2839] 4-9-3 **60**...............(p) AndrewMullen(3) 7 66
(P D Niven) *hld up in rr: hdwy 3f out: rdn over 1f out: drvn and styd on wl fnl f: jst failed* **4/1**[2]
-061 3 nk **Squiffy**[9] [3033] 4-8-12 **52**.. FergusSweeney 2 58
(P D Cundell) *prom: effrt to ld 3f out: rdn and hdd 2f out: drvn and rallied ins fnl f: kpt on* **7/4**[1]
02/3 4 10 **Princess Kiotto**[58] [1598] 6-9-13 **67**.. DavidAllan 6 61
(W M Brisbourne) *chsd ldrs: rdn along over 3f out: sn drvn and outpcd fnl 2f* **13/2**[3]
3400 5 1 3/4 **Crimson Monarch (USA)**[22] [2628] 3-8-7 **66**..................(b) DaleGibson 3 58
(Mrs A J Perrett) *chsd ldrs: rdn along over 3f out: sn drvn and wknd over 2f out* **7/1**
20-4 6 1 1/4 **Figaro's Quest (IRE)**[15] [2839] 5-9-2 **56**........................ RoystonFfrench 4 46
(C N Kellett) *a in rr: rdn along 1/2-way: nvr a factor* **22/1**
3335 7 2 1/2 **Patavium (IRE)**[16] [2810] 4-9-2 **56**.................................. PaulMulrennan 5 43
(E W Tuer) *t.k.h: trckd ldrs: effrt 3f out: sn rdn and wknd qckly over 2f out* **11/1**
000- 8 1/2 **Michaels Dream (IRE)**[38] [4960] 8-8-9 **49** oh4.............(b) TonyHamilton 8 35
(N Wilson) *led: rdn along and hdd 3f out: sn wknd* **17/2**

3m 52.7s (13.20) **Going Correction** +0.925s/f (Soft)
WFA 3 from 4yo+ 19lb **8** Ran SP% **116.5**
Speed ratings (Par 103):104,103,103,98,97 97,96,95
CSF £40.77 CT £82.04 TOTE £13.10: £2.80, £1.70, £1.50; EX 56.60.
Owner The Not Over Big Partnership **Bred** Finger Rock Farm **Trained** Newmarket, Suffolk
■ Stewards' Enquiry : Fergus Sweeney two-day ban: used whip with excessive frequency (Jul 19-20)

FOCUS
A modest staying event that produced a great finish and is rated through the third to his latest mark.
Figaro's Quest(IRE) Official explanation: jockey said gelding never travelled
Patavium(IRE) Official explanation: jockey said gelding ran too freely

3301 HALL SPECIAL PROJECTS H'CAP 1m 1f 207y
5:00 (5:05) (Class 5) (0-75,73) 3-Y-O+ £3,886 (£1,156; £577; £288) Stalls High

Form RPR
0513 1 **Royal Flynn**[8] [3049] 5-9-7 **68**.. PaulFessey 6 76
(M Dods) *hld up: hdwy on inner 2f out: rdn over 1f out: styd on strly to ld ins fnl f* **11/8**[1]
-006 2 nk **Advancement**[14] [2871] 4-9-2 **63**.. TonyHamilton 8 70
(R A Fahey) *chsd ldr to 1/2-way: rdn along and ev ch 2f out: drvn and sltly outpcd ent fnl f: styd on wl towards fin* **14/1**
2520 3 2 1/2 **Sir Arthur (IRE)**[10] [2987] 4-9-9 **73**.................................... GregFairley(3) 7 75
(M Johnston) *led: rdn along over 2f out: drvn over 1f out: hdd and no ex ins fnl f* **7/2**[3]
2223 4 1/2 **Augustine**[2] [3232] 6-9-8 **69**.. MickyFenton 1 70
(P W Hiatt) *chsd ldrs: effrt 3f out: rdn along over 2f out: drvn and one pce appr fnl f* **3/1**[2]
12-3 5 1 1/4 **Princess Cocoa (IRE)**[16] [2794] 4-9-3 **71**..................... JamesRogers(7) 3 70
(R A Fahey) *bhd and pushed along 1/2-way: rdn wl over 2f out: swtchd rt and hdwy u.p over 1f out: kpt on ins fnl f: nrst fin* **7/1**
5 6 8 **Gloucester**[18] [2743] 4-9-11 **72**.. GrahamGibbons 5 55
(J J Quinn) *trckd ldrs: hdwy to trck ldr 1/2-way: eased 2f out and sn in rr* **20/1**

2m 16.26s (8.96) **Going Correction** +0.925s/f (Soft) **6** Ran SP% **113.3**
Speed ratings (Par 103):101,100,98,98,97 90
CSF £22.24 CT £57.34 TOTE £2.70: £1.60, £5.20; EX 26.90.
Owner J A Wynn-Williams **Bred** Highclere Stud Ltd **Trained** Denton, Co Durham

FOCUS
A modest event won by a horse in form and the form seems sound enough. The runner-up was trying the trip for the first time and seemed to improve for it.
Gloucester Official explanation: jockey said gelding ran too free

3302 YORKSHIRE PLANT MAIDEN STKS 5f
5:35 (5:41) (Class 5) 3-Y-O+ £3,238 (£963; £481; £240) Stalls High

Form RPR
30- 1 **Vesuvio**[246] [6324] 3-9-3 0... FergusSweeney 10 63
(C W Thornton) *trckd ldrs: hdwy 2f out: rdn over 1f out: styd on to ld ins fnl f: drvn out* **9/2**[3]
0- 2 3/4 **Moheebb (IRE)**[351] [3701] 3-9-0 0...................................... LiamJones(3) 4 60
(D W Chapman) *in rr: pushed along and rn green 2f out: rapid hdwy over 1f out: rdn to chse wnr ins fnl f: kpt on* **16/1**
5 3 2 **Lempicka**[9] [3031] 3-8-12 0.. GrahamGibbons 5 48
(J J Quinn) *trckd ldrs: hdwy 2f out: rdn to ld 1f out: sn drvn: hdd and one pce ins fnl f* **14/1**
4- 4 1 1/4 **Staked A Claim (IRE)**[297] [5288] 3-9-3 0.............................. PhillipMakin 9 49
(T D Barron) *towards rr: hdwy on inner 2f out: sn rdn and kpt on ins fnl f: nrst fin* **4/1**[2]
-052 5 hd **Orotund**[15] [2844] 3-9-0 45... DuranFentiman(3) 2 48
(T D Easterby) *cl up: led 1/2-way: rdn and hdd 1f out: sn drvn and wknd ins fnl f* **8/1**
0-55 6 1 **Gap Princess (IRE)**[24] [2553] 3-8-9 62.............................. JamieMoriarty(3) 3 39
(R A Fahey) *trckd ldrs: rdn along 2f out: hld whn rdr dropped whip ins fnl f* **3/1**[1]
06 7 1 **The Cube**[14] [2894] 3-9-3 0..(b[1]) MickyFenton 6 41
(J Balding) *chsd ldrs: rdn along 2f out: sn drvn and no imp fnl f* **33/1**
0/-0 8 8 **Princess Charlmane (IRE)**[24] [2554] 4-9-3 0.................. PaddyAspell 11 7
(C J Teague) *led: rdn along and hdd 1/2-way: sn wknd* **50/1**
9 4 **White's Ruby** 3-8-12 0.. RoystonFfrench 8 —
(B Smart) *dwlt: a bhd* **3/1**[1]
6- 10 6 **College Land Boy**[330] [4323] 3-9-3 0.. TPO'Shea 7 —
(J J Quinn) *s.i.s: a bhd* **14/1**
0005 11 4 **Mandy's Maestro (USA)**[13] [2910] 3-8-12 52......(b) MichaelJStainton(5) 1 —
(R M Whitaker) *chsd ldrs: swtchd towards stands' side 1/2-way: sn rdn and wknd* **16/1**

68.49 secs (4.49) **Going Correction** +0.975s/f (Soft)
WFA 3 from 4yo 5lb **11** Ran SP% **129.3**
Speed ratings (Par 103):103,101,98,96,96 94,93,80,73,64 57
CSF £82.25 TOTE £7.60: £1.80, £3.70, £2.90; EX 102.10 Place 6 £16.74, Place 5 £4.77..
Owner Guy Reed **Bred** G Reed **Trained** Middleham Moor, N Yorks

FOCUS
A typically moderate three-year-old plus sprint maiden. The form looks sound rated through the fifth.
The Cube Official explanation: jockey said gelding was denied a clear run
T/Plt: £20.20 to a £1 stake. Pool: £122,255.55. 4,402.35 winning tickets. T/Qpdt: £4.90 to a £1 stake. Pool: £6,863.70. 1,032.90 winning tickets. JR

2983 CARLISLE (R-H)

Saturday, July 7 (eve)

3303 Meeting Abandoned - Waterlogged.

2868 HAYDOCK (L-H)

Saturday, July 7

3309 Meeting Abandoned - Waterlogged.

2657 LEICESTER (R-H)

Saturday, July 7

3316 Meeting Abandoned - Waterlogged.

2575 NOTTINGHAM (L-H)

Saturday, July 7 (eve)

3322 Meeting Abandoned - Waterlogged.

3268 SANDOWN (R-H)

Saturday, July 7

OFFICIAL GOING: Good to soft (soft in places on sprint course) changing to good after race 5 (4.20pm) (round:7.5) (sprint: 6.4)

Wind: Moderate, against Weather: Fine

3329 LAURENT-PERRIER CHAMPAGNE SPRINT STKS (GROUP 3) 5f 6y

2:05 (2:07) (Class 1) 3-Y-0+

£28,390 (£10,760; £5,385; £2,685; £1,345; £675) **Stalls** High

Form			Horse	RPR
1210	**1**		**Hoh Mike (IRE)**[7] 3088 3-8-12 110 ..... JamieSpencer 8 (M L W Bell) *lw: dwlt: hld up in last: plenty to do whn swtchd to outer over 1f out: rapid prog fnl f: r.o wl to ld nr fin* **9/2**[3]	112+
2-50	**2**	½	**Wi Dud**[14] 2857 3-8-12 113 ..... NCallan 4 (K A Ryan) *trckd ldng pair gng wl: led jst over 1f out: rdn and styd on: hdd and outpcd nr fin* **13/2**	110+
3003	**3**	1 ¼	**Bond City (IRE)**[28] 2463 5-9-3 103 ..... ChrisCatlin 10 (G R Oldroyd) *settled in rr: rdn over 2f out and no prog: n.m.r jst over 1f out: r.o wl fnl f to snatch 3rd on line* **14/1**	106
3150	**4**	shd	**The Tatling (IRE)**[18] 2733 10-9-3 100 ..... DarryllHolland 2 (J M Bradley) *dwlt: rcvrd grad to chse ldrs 1/2-way: drvn and effrt over 1f out: styd on same pce* **16/1**	106
112-	**5**	1 ¼	**Reverence**[279] 5712 6-9-11 117 ..... KDarley 5 (E J Alston) *b.bkwd: pressed ldr: led wl over 1f out to jst over 1f out: outpcd fnl f* **5/2**[1]	109
1400	**6**	1	**Dhaular Dhar (IRE)**[7] 3088 5-9-3 98 ..... JimmyFortune 3 (J S Goldie) *wl in rr: drvn and struggling 2f out: bmpd jst over 1f out: plugged on* **33/1**	98
5410	**7**	hd	**Dazed And Amazed**[18] 2733 3-8-12 101 ..... RyanMoore 9 (R Hannon) *chsd ldrs: lost pl 1/2-way and drvn: struggling after: kpt on fnl f* **25/1**	96
1115	**8**	1 ¼	**Sierra Vista**[7] 3088 7-9-6 110 ..... LDettori 7 (D W Barker) *led at str pce to wl over 1f out: wknd ins fnl f* **11/4**[2]	95
043	**9**	½	**Sand Cat**[106] 4-9-3 95 ..... EddieAhern 6 (G L Moore) *nvr bttr than midfield: struggling fnl 2f* **100/1**	91
5-46	**10**	1 ¼	**The Trader (IRE)**[20] 2695 9-9-3 102 ..... (b) SebSanders 1 (M Blanshard) *lw: chsd ldrs to 1/2-way: wknd wl over 1f out* **14/1**	86

61.89 secs (-0.32) **Going Correction** +0.275s/f (Good)

WFA 3 from 4yo+ 5lb **10** Ran SP% **113.7**

Speed ratings (Par 113):113,112,110,110,108 106,106,104,103,101

CSF £32.43 TOTE £5.00: £1.70, £2.20, £3.00; EX 29.00 Trifecta £411.40 Pool £1,564.60. - 2.70 winning units..

Owner M Lynch & the late D Allport **Bred** John Malone **Trained** Newmarket, Suffolk

■ Stewards' Enquiry : Jamie Spencer two-day ban: careless riding (Jul 18-19)

FOCUS

Two three-year-olds finished to the fore in a race run at a blistering pace. The exposed third and fourth just hold down the form, but the winner impressed.

NOTEBOOK

Hoh Mike(IRE) was well beaten at Newcastle a week earlier, but a line could be drawn under that performance as the ground was very wet that day and he showed his true colours here where the fast pace and stiff finish suited him. Held up at the back, he was pulled out for his effort with over a furlong to run and made rapid headway to get up close home, actually scoring a shade readily. An improving sprinter, he could go for the Nunthorpe next. (op 5-1 tchd 11-2)

Wi Dud could never get into the Golden Jubilee at Ascot after stumbling leaving the stalls, but this was better and he returned to something like his juvenile form. After tracking the two leaders, he went on going well but was cut down by the late thrust of his fellow three-year-old. He loses nothing in defeat. (tchd 7-1)

Bond City(IRE), under pressure when short of room approaching the furlong pole, really found his stride inside the last and grabbed third on the line. He is smart but exposed, and has now been placed six times since his last win. (op 12-1)

The Tatling(IRE), who won the last running of this race as a Listed event four years ago, retains plenty of ability and was just mugged on the line for third. (op 20-1)

Reverence, last year's Nunthorpe and Haydock Sprint Cup hero, looked just in need of this reappearance. Well at home in the underfoot conditions, but saddled with a Group 1 penalty, he briefly showed ahead before lack of race sharpness told. With this race under his belt he should enjoy a rewarding second half of the season. (op 7-4, tchd 11-4 in places)

Dhaular Dhar(IRE), in rear when inconvenienced by the winner over a furlong out, ran on quite nicely inside the last without ever posing a threat. He is more effective over further.

Dazed And Amazed ran his race but does not quite look up to this level. (op 33-1)

Sierra Vista, who finished in front of today's winner in bad ground at Newcastle, carried a 6lb penalty for her win over course and distance in the Temple Stakes. Showing her customary blazing pace, she was collared with over a furlong to run and faded out of the placings inside the last. (op 7-2)

Sand Cat, returning to action after a winter campaign in the UAE, was by no means disgraced in this warm company.

The Trader(IRE), who was third in this last year, raced handier than is usually the case before dropping away in the latter stages.

3330 TOTESCOOP6 STKS (HERITAGE H'CAP) 1m 14y

2:35 (2:42) (Class 2) 3-Y-0+

£62,320 (£18,660; £9,330; £4,670; £2,330; £1,170) **Stalls** High

Form			Horse	RPR
3531	**1**		**Ordnance Row**[10] 3001 4-9-5 100 ..... RyanMoore 12 (R Hannon) *lw: wl plcd bhd ldrs: effrt 2f out: rdn to ld jst over 1f out: styd on wl* **11/1**	111
1310	**2**	½	**Colorado Rapid (IRE)**[16] 2788 3-8-3 93 ..... JoeFanning 6 (M Johnston) *lw: settled in rr: stl at bk of main gp 2f out: gd prog over 1f out: chsd wnr last 100yds: clsd but nvr able to chal* **13/2**[3]	101+
0-21	**3**	1	**Unshakable (IRE)**[36] 2208 8-8-10 91 ..... PaulEddery 15 (Bob Jones) *prom: rdn over 2f out: no imp on ldrs tl over 1f out: styd on wl fnl f* **14/1**	99
3-36	**4**	nk	**Pride Of Nation (IRE)**[15] 2817 5-9-4 99 ..... JamieSpencer 1 (L M Cumani) *wl in rr: eased to outside and prog fr 2f out: hanging rt but styd on fnl f* **5/1**[2]	106
3-11	**5**	1	**Mutanaseb (USA)**[21] 2671 3-8-5 95 ..... RHills 8 (M A Jarvis) *lw: trckd ldr gng wl: led wl over 1f out: hdd jst over 1f out: fdd ins fnl f* **9/2**[1]	98
4060	**6**	½	**Lundy's Lane (IRE)**[17] 2755 7-9-0 95 ..... FrancisNorton 10 (A M Balding) *lw: settled in midfield: rdn over 2f out: sn lost pl: swtchd lft over 1f out: styd on: nrst fin* **25/1**	99
2-15	**7**	1	**Yeaman's Hall**[41] 2066 3-8-13 103 ..... LDettori 16 (A M Balding) *lw: t.k.h: trckd ldrs: edgd rt over 2f out and u.p over 1f out: one pce* **10/1**	103
0100	**8**	1	**Plum Pudding (IRE)**[17] 2755 4-9-2 97 ..... JimmyFortune 14 (R Hannon) *settled in midfield: effrt 2f out and swtchd to inner: nt clr run 1f out and swtchd lft: styd on: nvr rchd ldrs* **50/1**	96
-413	**9**	½	**Killena Boy (IRE)**[30] 2401 5-8-11 92 ..... PaulDoe 9 (W Jarvis) *lw: prom: rdn over 2f out: losing pl and btn whn n.m.r jst ins fnl f* **12/1**	90
0120	**10**	½	**Montpellier (IRE)**[17] 2755 4-8-8 89 ..... KerrinMcEvoy 17 (E A L Dunlop) *hld up in midfield: effrt on inner and nt clr run over 2f out: effrt again and bdly hmpd over 1f out: nt rcvr* **10/1**	86+
1001	**11**	1 ¼	**Bold Marc (IRE)**[10] 2986 5-8-8 89 ow5 ..... EddieAhern 13 (K R Burke) *led to wl over 1f out: wknd fnl f* **25/1**	83
2501	**12**	shd	**Rio Riva**[9] 3026 5-9-10 105 ..... TomEaves 11 (Miss J A Camacho) *wl in rr: rdn and no prog wl over 2f out: plugged on fr over 1f out: no ch* **16/1**	99
3005	**13**	hd	**Prince Of Thebes (IRE)**[10] 3001 6-8-5 89 ..... RichardKingscote(3) 5 (J Akehurst) *swtg: prom: rdn to chse ldng pair over 2f out: wknd over 1f out* **33/1**	82
02	**14**	nk	**Vacation (IRE)**[14] 2871 4-8-0 86 ..... WilliamBuick(5) 7 (V Smith) *a wl in rr: hrd rdn and no prog over 2f out* **22/1**	79
151	**15**	1	**Laa Rayb (USA)**[22] 2633 3-8-5 95 ..... KDarley 2 (M Johnston) *swtg: a wl in rr and racd wd: no prog over 2f out* **9/1**	83
1012	**16**	3	**Moody Tunes**[9] 3026 4-8-7 88 ..... PatCosgrave 4 (K R Burke) *racd wd in midfield: no prog over 2f out: struggling after* **20/1**	72
130-	**17**	10	**Blue Trojan (IRE)**[324] 4535 7-8-4 85 ..... ChrisCatlin 3 (S Kirk) *a wl in rr: detached 2f out: t.o* **100/1**	46

1m 40.86s (-3.09) **Going Correction** +0.025s/f (Good)

WFA 3 from 4yo+ 9lb **17** Ran SP% **127.6**

Speed ratings (Par 109):116,115,114,114,113 112,111,110,110,109 108,108,108,107,106 103,93

CSF £78.23 CT £1075.58 TOTE £14.10: £3.20, £2.20, £3.30, £1.90; EX 120.00 Trifecta £2678.10 Part won. Pool £3,772.02. - 0.90 winning units..

Owner Mrs P Good **Bred** Mrs P Good **Trained** East Everleigh, Wilts

■ Stewards' Enquiry : L Dettori three-day ban: careless riding (Jul 27,29-30)

FOCUS

A strong handicap run at a decent pace, and solid form. Plenty of winners should come out of the race.

NOTEBOOK

Ordnance Row impressed when winning on similar ground at Salisbury and the 8lb rise was insufficient to stop him following up. Always in a good position, he went for home over a furlong out and found plenty for pressure. This was a smart performance and he deserves another crack at something better now. (op 12-1)

Colorado Rapid(IRE) ◆, who failed to get much cover in the Britannia at Ascot, was settled two-thirds of the way down the field. Weaving his way through in the final quarter-mile, he chased the winner in the last half-furlong but could not quite get to him. He does not look the finished article yet and there is a nice prize waiting for him. (op 8-1)

Unshakable(IRE), who finished in front of today's winner when successful at Epsom, was actually 3lb better off with that rival but could not confirm the form. That said, he ran a cracking race, racing prominently from the off and staying on willingly. (op 16-1)

Pride Of Nation(IRE), back over a more suitable trip after a run over 7f at Ascot, stayed on from the rear of the field despite wanting to hang. This was a solid effort from his disadvantageous draw. (op 6-1)

Mutanaseb(USA) was raised 7lb for his win over a furlong shorter here last time. After showing ahead travelling well, he could not hold on into the final furlong and might have paid for tracking the fast pace set by Bold Marc. Although he probably stays this far, he will not mind a drop back to 7f on this evidence. (tchd 4-1 and 5-1)

Lundy's Lane(IRE), who made an encouraging return to Britain in the Royal Hunt Cup, lost his pitch with two to run but rallied and came home in good style. He stays 1m2f and could be worth stepping up in trip again. (op 33-1)

Yeaman's Hall was back down in trip and grade after finishing fifth to Alexander Of Hales in a Curragh Group 3 over 1m2f. Racing keenly on the inside, he had his chance but was unable to find a turn of foot when required. (op 12-1)

Plum Pudding(IRE), currently 4lb above his last winning mark, ran respectably considering he did not enjoy an entirely clear run. His three wins have all come over this trip on the Rowley Mile.

Killena Boy(IRE) likes it here and gave his running, but is struggling with a career-high mark at present. (op 11-1)

Montpellier(IRE), 2lb higher than when disappointing in the Hunt Cup, was attempting to stay on up the inside when almost put over the rail by Yeaman's Hall over a furlong out. He would certainly have finished closer, but should not be classed as unlucky. (op 12-1)

Bold Marc(IRE), with the overweight, was 9lb higher than when landing the Carlisle Bell. After setting a strong pace, he was collared with over a furlong to run and eventually faded right out of it inside the last.

Rio Riva, put up 8lb for his Newcastle win, was never in the hunt off topweight.

Prince Of Thebes(IRE) ran a fair race on ground that did not suit.

Laa Rayb(USA), raised nearly a stone for beating horses his own age over course and distance, was trapped out wide from his low draw and was never seen with a chance. (op 15-2)

3331 CORAL-ECLIPSE STKS (GROUP 1) 1m 2f 7y
3:15 (3:20) (Class 1) 3-Y-0+

£259,314 (£98,281; £49,186; £24,524; £12,285; £6,165) **Stalls** High

Form RPR

-413 **1** **Notnowcato**[17] 2754 5-9-7 122 RyanMoore 1 124
(Sir Michael Stoute) *b. hld up: trckd ldr 1/2-way: c alone to nr side in st: def advantage fr at least over 1f out: drvn out* **7/1**[3]

1-11 **2** 1 1/2 **Authorized (IRE)**[35] 2235 3-8-10 126 LDettori 6 121
(P W Chapple-Hyam) *lw: hld up in last pair: prog on outer 2f out: sn drvn: led main gp ent fnl f: jst hld on but nt on terms w wnr* **4/7**[1]

16-4 **3** hd **George Washington (IRE)**[18] 2735 4-9-7 0 JAHeffernan 8 120
(A P O'Brien, Ire) *lw: swtg and fractious to post: hld up in last pair: prog 2f out: hanging rt over 1f out: rdn to chal main gp ldr last 100yds: jst hld* **4/1**[2]

0203 **4** 1 1/4 **Yellowstone (IRE)**[15] 2813 3-8-10 0 FMBerry 4 118+
(A P O'Brien, Ire) *rousted to chse ldr for 2f then restrained: cl up 4f out: led main gp 3f out tl ent fnl f: hld whn n.m.r nr fin* **50/1**

-010 **5** 4 **Admiralofthefleet (USA)**[35] 2235 3-8-10 0 MJKinane 2 110
(A P O'Brien, Ire) *hld up off the pce: effrt over 3f out: drvn to chse ldrs wl over 1f out: wknd fnl f* **12/1**

1635 **6** 1 1/4 **Kandidate**[48] 1877 5-9-7 112 (t) EddieAhern 7 108
(C E Brittain) *hld up off the pce: clsd 1/2-way: rdn to chal 2f out: wknd jst over 1f out* **50/1**

10 **7** 5 **Archipenko (USA)**[35] 2235 3-8-10 0 CO'Donoghue 3 98
(A P O'Brien, Ire) *rousted to chse ldr for 2f then restrained: hrd rdn 3f out: sn btn* **16/1**

2310 **8** shd **Champery (USA)**[16] 2789 3-8-10 107 JoeFanning 5 97
(M Johnston) *led: lft clr after 2f: hdd 3f out: wknd 2f out* **150/1**

2m 5.85s (-4.39) **Going Correction** +0.025s/f (Good)
WFA 3 from 4yo+ 11lb **8** Ran SP% **114.3**
Speed ratings (Par 117):118,116,116,115,112 111,107,107
CSF £11.46 TOTE £7.70: £2.10, £1.02, £1.80; EX 14.60 Trifecta £53.00 Pool £25,709.79. - 344.05 winning units..
Owner Anthony & David de Rothschild **Bred** Southcourt Stud **Trained** Newmarket, Suffolk
■ The highlight of a 2,375/1 four-timer for Ryan Moore.
■ Stewards' Enquiry : L Dettori three-day ban: careless riding (Jul 31, Aug 2-3)

FOCUS
A high-class renewal, and tactically fascinating, but unsatisfactory from a form perspective. The clash between Authorized and George Washington did materialise, but they were both beaten by Notnowcato who ploughed a lone furrow in the straight. He is rated to form, but Authorized was 6lb off his Derby form and George Washington 8lb below his 3yo best. The fourth finished closer than expected too, rated up 9lb.

NOTEBOOK
Notnowcato, twice a winner at the top level since finishing second to David Junior in last year's renewal, upset the big pair to underline that he is a top-notch performer at this trip. Tracking the pacemaker from halfway, he was brought right over to the stands' side once in the straight, racing a few horse widths off the fence and wide apart from the remainder of the field who opted to stay on the inside. Maintaining the gallop, it was apparent well inside the last that he was on top overall. It is debatable whether he gained an advantage by coming to the near side, but Moore deserves great credit for being brave enough to carry out the manoeuvre in such an important event. (tchd 8-1 in places)
Authorized(IRE) was brilliant at Epsom but, tackling older rivals and stepping back in trip, he became the fourth Derby winner since Nashwan scored in 1989 to be beaten in this event. Held up in rear, in company with George Washington, things went awry tactically when his pacemaker was left isolated up front and of no use to him. Improving on the outer of the main group once into the straight, he showed in front on his side a furlong out and battled on well, despite edging right, to hold off the third, but Notnowcato had his measure on the opposite side of the track. A little below his best here, he is well capable of making amends, although he may miss the King George now to allow him more time to recover from what was quite a hard race. (op 8-13, tchd 4-6 in places)
George Washington(IRE), ridden by his regular gallops partner, behaved well in the preliminaries until threatening to go through the rails on the way to post. Held up at the back of the field in company with his big rival, he improved in the straight but not for the first time hung fire when asked to really go forward. Running on inside the last, he would have got to Authorized in a couple more strides, but the winner was in command on the opposite flank in any case. He has still to prove he retains all his old brilliance, but he certainly stays this trip and it would not be a surprise to see him win at the top level again. (tchd 9-2 in places)
Yellowstone(IRE), eighth in the Derby prior to finishing third in the King Edward VII Stakes, appeared to excel himself in fourth. Together with stablemate Archipenko, he was rousted along from the stalls to bustle up Authorized's pacemaker before being restrained to race prominently in the main group. Sticking to the inside in the straight, he kept on well and was only headed entering the last, but was just held when tightened up on the rail by Authorized near the finish. (op 66-1)
Admiralofthefleet(USA), who failed to stay the trip in the Derby, ran as if a stiff test at 1m2f was beyond him too and failed to get in a telling blow.
Kandidate travelled well into the straight and was close enough with a quarter of a mile to run, but once more was found wanting at this level. (op 66-1)
Archipenko(USA), who finished last in the Derby, for which he was sent off third favourite, was bustled up with stablemate Yellowstone to chase pacesetter Champery before the brakes were applied after two furlongs. Under pressure again turning for home, he shaped as if he did not stay. (op 20-1)
Champery(USA) was supplemented for £20,000 by Sheikh Mohammed and leased to Authorized's owners in order to act as pacemaker, but he was left stranded out in front after two furlongs and was not of much use to the favourite from then on. (tchd 100-1)

3332 ADDLESHAW GODDARD (REGISTERED AS THE DISTAFF STKS) (LISTED RACE) 1m 14y
3:45 (3:50) (Class 1) 3-Y-0

£14,762 (£5,595; £2,800; £1,396; £699; £351) **Stalls** High

Form RPR

1-02 **1** **Selinka**[17] 2757 3-9-1 103 RyanMoore 7 105
(R Hannon) *lw: hld up in last pair: gd prog on outer fr 2f out: led jst over 1f out: sn drvn clr* **9/2**

1501 **2** 1 3/4 **Barshiba (IRE)**[17] 2757 3-9-1 103 TQuinn 5 101
(D R C Elsworth) *s.i.s: hld up in last: rdn and effrt on outer over 2f out: styd on wl fr over 1f out to take 2nd last 100yds: no ch w wnr* **3/1**[1]

-464 **3** 1 1/4 **Treat**[23] 2599 3-8-12 108 JHBowman 2 95
(M R Channon) *led: drvn and hdd jst over 1f out: one pce* **4/1**[3]

3-10 **4** 1/2 **Cliche (IRE)**[17] 2757 3-8-12 96 LDettori 8 94
(Sir Michael Stoute) *hld up in midfield: rdn to cl on ldrs 2f out: one pce over 1f out* **7/2**[2]

42-1 **5** 1 **Contentious (USA)**[29] 2429 3-8-12 80 IanMongan 4 92
(J L Dunlop) *lw: hld up in 7th: rdn and effrt over 2f out: no imp on ldrs 1f out: eased last 75yds* **10/1**

1410 **6** nk **Chantilly Tiffany**[17] 2757 3-8-12 91 JimmyFortune 1 91
(E A L Dunlop) *mostly trckd ldr: chal over 2f out: upsides over 1f out: wknd fnl f* **16/1**

-042 **7** 1 **Russian Rosie (IRE)**[23] 2599 3-8-12 97 EddieAhern 3 89
(J G Portman) *cl up: rdn over 2f out: lost pl and struggling over 1f out* **20/1**

0-53 **8** nk **Mimisel**[13] 2914 3-8-12 79 SebSanders 6 88
(Rae Guest) *cl up: rdn over 2f out: wknd over 1f out* **20/1**

33- **9** 12 **Guarantia**[280] 5672 3-8-12 0 (t) JoeFanning 9 60
(C E Brittain) *t.k.h: cl up: rdn over 2f out: wknd rapidly over 1f out: t.o* **20/1**

1m 42.35s (-1.60) **Going Correction** +0.025s/f (Good) **9** Ran SP% **114.7**
Speed ratings (Par 108):109,107,106,105,104 104,103,102,90
CSF £17.63 TOTE £5.60: £1.80, £1.60, £1.70; EX 20.90 Trifecta £40.70 Pool £1,854.15. - 32.30 winning units..
Owner R Barnett **Bred** W And R Barnett Ltd **Trained** East Everleigh, Wilts

FOCUS
The runners followed Notnowcato's lead and all came over to the stands' side in the home straight. The pace was not strong and the race was somewhat messy, Selinka reversing Royal Ascot form with runner-up Barshiba. The form is rated through the sixth.

NOTEBOOK
Selinka ♦, runner-up to Barshiba in the Sandringham at Ascot, reversed the form on these 3lb better terms. Held up at the back and sticking to the outside of the bunch in the straight, she showed a smart turn of foot to sweep into the lead and stayed on well once in front despite edging left. She should stay a bit further and can handle a step up in grade. (op 4-1)
Barshiba(IRE) beat Selinka in the Sandringham Handicap at Ascot last time but could not confirm the form on 3lb worse terms. Held up at the back of the field, she ran on well down the outside but the winner had taken first run and was not going to be caught. A more end-to-end gallop would have suited her and she remains a smart filly. (op 4-1)
Treat, adopting different tactics on this drop back to a mile, set just a moderate pace and led the field over to the stands' side in the straight. Unable to counter when headed by the winner, she stuck on but remains below her Guineas form. (op 3-1)
Cliche(IRE), ridden less prominently than at Ascot, could only stick on at the same pace when the pressure was on but did finish closer to Selinka and Barshiba than she had at Ascot. (op 4-1)
Contentious(USA), whose maiden win was gained on fast ground, faced a stiff task on this first venture into Listed company and ran a creditable race in the circumstances. (op 12-1 tchd 9-1)
Chantilly Tiffany, another to have run in the Sandringham last time, was having her first run on an easy surface. She had her chance but looks to be held by the Handicapper at present.

3333 WEATHERBYS VAT SERVICES STKS (REGISTERED AS THE ESHER STAKES) (LISTED RACE) 2m 78y
4:20 (4:21) (Class 1) 4-Y-0+ **£14,762** (£5,595; £2,800; £1,396) **Stalls** Centre

Form RPR

-321 **1** **Balkan Knight**[28] 2462 7-9-3 108 JohnEgan 3 113
(D R C Elsworth) *hld up in last pair: effrt 3f out: swtchd rt over 1f out: r.o to ld jst ins fnl f: sn in command: idled and drvn out nr fin* **11/4**[3]

13-2 **2** 1/2 **Alambic**[26] 2505 4-8-9 82 SebSanders 2 104
(Sir Mark Prescott) *lw: hld up in last pair: effrt over 2f out: drvn to chal over 1f out: upsides ent fnl f: sn outpcd: kpt on nr fin* **9/1**

-344 **3** hd **Finalmente**[16] 2787 5-9-0 105 JimmyFortune 1 109
(N A Callaghan) *led: kicked on 3f out: hrd rdn and pressed fr 2f out: hdd jst ins fnl f: kpt on* **9/4**[2]

/5-2 **4** 3 **The Geezer**[13] 2907 5-9-0 111 LDettori 4 105
(Saeed Bin Suroor) *trckd ldr: gng easily over 2f out: rdn to chal over 1f out: nt qckn: btn fnl f* **11/8**[1]

3m 38.72s (0.49) **Going Correction** +0.025s/f (Good) **4** Ran SP% **109.5**
Speed ratings (Par 111):99,98,98,97
CSF £20.89 TOTE £3.80; EX 21.90.
Owner Raymond Tooth **Bred** Sheikh Mohammed Bin Rashid Al Maktoum **Trained** Newmarket, Suffolk

FOCUS
Again the runners made their way over to the near side in the home straight. The third set a rather stop-start pace and this became a tactical affair. The form is rated through the winner.

NOTEBOOK
Balkan Knight, successful in this grade at Musselburgh last time, followed up under a good ride. Turning for home in third place, he was switched outside for his run and showed a decent turn of foot to seal the race before idling in front. He will win more races when things drop right for him. (op 10-3, tchd 7-2 in a place)
Alambic, who raced a bit keenly through the early parts, was relegated to last place as the field entered the home straight. She soon improved to throw down her challenge, but lacked the pace of the winner. This was a much-improved effort from this big filly, who faced a stiff task at the weights and would have been suited by a stronger gallop. (tchd 8-1 and 10-1)
Finalmente ran the race of his life when fourth in the Gold Cup and was a little off that form here. Able to dictate the pace on this drop back to 2m, he tried to kick away in the straight but was soon collared and unable to hit back. (op 5-2 tchd 11-4)
The Geezer, the pick on official figures, had every chance with over a furlong to run but was the first of the four to crack. This longer trip may have been to blame but this was still a little diappointing. (op 6-5, tchd 6-4 in places)

3334 UB40 ON 19TH JULY H'CAP 7f 16y
4:55 (4:57) (Class 3) (0-95,95) 3-Y-0

£8,724 (£2,612; £1,306; £653; £326; £163) **Stalls** High

Form RPR

1-21 **1** **Danehillsundance (IRE)**[24] 2577 3-8-11 **85** RyanMoore 4 90
(R Hannon) *lw: cl up: led wl over 1f out: hrd pressed after: drvn and hld on wl* **7/2**[2]

642 **2** 1/2 **Chjimes (IRE)**[9] 3029 3-7-13 **76** oh5 AndrewElliott(3) 2 79
(K R Burke) *trckd ldr: upsides 2f out: pressed wnr over 1f out: kpt on wl fnl f: a hld* **14/1**

4511 **3** shd **Baltic Belle (IRE)**[7] 3087 3-8-1 **80** LukeMorris(5) 6 83
(R Hannon) *chsd ldrs: drvn wl over 1f out: kpt on wl fnl f: a hld* **6/1**[3]

1100 **4** shd **Regal Parade**[16] 2788 3-9-4 **92** KDarley 7 95
(M Johnston) *lw: led: rdn and hdd wl over 1f out: kpt on wl fnl f: a hld* **7/2**[2]

4-12 **5** 1 **Endiamo (IRE)**[21] 2671 3-9-3 **91** PatDobbs 3 91
(M P Tregoning) *lw: hld up in rr but wl in tch: effrt against nr side rail over 2f out gng wl: drvn over 1f out: kpt on same pce* **11/4**[1]

016- **6** 1/2 **Regal Quest (IRE)**[280] 5676 3-8-7 **81** JohnEgan 10 80
(S Kirk) *plld hrd: hld up in rr but in tch: clsd on ldrs over 1f out: sn rdn and nt qckn* **16/1**

3-20 **7** 1/2 **Ravi River (IRE)**[79] 1110 3-8-9 **83** MichaelHills 8 81
(B W Hills) *hld up in rr but in tch: effrt on outer over 2f out: nt qckn over 1f out: no imp after* **7/1**

0500 **8** *nk* **Cheap Street**[21] 2669 3-8-8 **82**..(b[1]) EddieAhern 9 79
(J G Portman) *t.k.h: hld up in rr: taken to outer and shkn up 2f out: no real prog* **25/1**

136- **9** *5* **Prince Of Elegance**[343] 3924 3-9-7 **95**............................ JimCrowley 1 79
(Mrs A J Perrett) *in tch: rdn over 2f out: wknd over 1f out* **20/1**

1m 30.2s (0.86) **Going Correction** +0.025s/f (Good) **9** Ran SP% **119.1**
Speed ratings (Par 104):96,95,95,95,94 93,92,92,86
CSF £52.84 CT £290.73 TOTE £4.40: £1.80, £3.60, £1.90; EX 55.60.
Owner J P Hardiman **Bred** J P Hardiman **Trained** East Everleigh, Wilts

FOCUS
A competitive heat but the field finished well-bunched at the line and the form may not prove that reliable.

NOTEBOOK
Danehillsundance(IRE), hard-fought winner of a decent 1m handicap at Nottingham, was up just 3lb and the red-hot Moore wisely made plenty of use of the gelding on this drop in trip. He went on racing into the final quarter mile and battled on gamely to hold his many persistent challengers. Evidently tough, he seems to be progressing well and will relish the return to 1m. (op 9-2)
Chjimes(IRE), trounced by the subsequently disappointing Apache Dawn at Newcastle last time, was having to race from 5lb out of the handicap and he put up a fine effort considering, keeping on well to just sneak second in a bunch finish. A soft surface suits him well, and he would be entitled to respect if turned out quickly off his correct mark, but may find things tougher off a higher mark in the long run. (op 18-1)
Baltic Belle(IRE), on a hat-trick following hard-fought wins at Windsor and Lingfield, was up another 5lb and looked a major player with the ground immaterial to her. Always well positioned, she emerged to have every chance racing into the final furlong and a half and stuck on well, but her stable companion proved too strong for her. She continues to progress. (op 7-1)
Regal Parade has been held off a similar mark in a couple of competitive handicaps of late, but he was reverting to 7f and racing on a slightly slower surface was expected to suit. He was soon in front, but was passed over a furlong out and could only plug on at the same pace. His improvement has levelled out for the time being. (op 3-1, tchd 4-1 in a place)
Endiamo(IRE), second to the progressive Mutanaseb over course and distance on his return from a break, was ridden with more restraint on this occasion and he came there travelling strongly on the stands' rail, but was unable to quicken sufficiently and could only keep on at the one pace. This was slightly disappointing, but it is possible he will improve for an extra furlong. (tchd 10-3)
Regal Quest(IRE), readily held off a 1lb higher mark on her handicap debut last September, reappeared with a fine effort and is certainly one to be interested in for the future. She is bred to appreciate further than this and is entitled to come on for the outing. (tchd 20-1)
Ravi River(IRE) was one of the main disappointments and seems to be heading the wrong way. (op 9-1)
Prince Of Elegance, a good-looking colt, was reappearing off a stiff mark and it may take a few runs before he is ready to win again.

3335 SANDOWN PARK'S ONE BIG SATURDAY CONCERT H'CAP — 1m 2f 7y
5:30 (5:30) (Class 4) (0-85,85) 3-Y-O **£7,772** (£2,312; £1,155; £577) **Stalls** High

Form RPR

-120 **1** **Soft Morning**[49] 1835 3-9-0 **78**... SebSanders 2 86
(Sir Mark Prescott) *mde all: styd alone against far side rail in st: def advantage over 1f out: drvn out* **5/1**[2]

3410 **2** *1* **Sahrati**[16] 2790 3-9-7 **85**... EddieAhern 6 91
(C E Brittain) *mounted on crse: hld up in midfield: effrt whn hmpd over 2f out: rallied jst over 1f out: r.o to ld nr side gp nr fin* **6/1**[3]

-133 **3** *nk* **Monte Alto (IRE)**[22] 2633 3-8-13 **77**................................. RyanMoore 11 83
(L M Cumani) *lw: trckd ldrs: effrt and bmpd over 2f out: led gp 2f out: nt on terms w wnr: hdd nr fin* **11/4**[1]

51-0 **4** *½* **Ajaan**[39] 2126 3-9-0 **78**... TedDurcan 5 83
(H R A Cecil) *dwlt: hld up in rr: rdn over 2f out: no prog tl styd on wl fnl f: nrst fin* **6/1**[3]

6366 **5** *1 ½* **Urban Warrior**[14] 2877 3-8-8 **72**.. JohnEgan 8 74
(Mrs Norma Pook) *trckd ldrs: bmpd over 2f out: drvn and one pce over 1f out* **20/1**

146 **6** *¾* **Woodcraft**[22] 2627 3-9-2 **80**... MichaelHills 10 80
(B W Hills) *lw: cl up: led nr side gp 3f out to 2f out: wknd fnl f* **7/1**

00-6 **7** *½* **Bring It On Home**[22] 2625 3-8-6 **70**................................. JoeFanning 7 69
(G L Moore) *hld up in rr: rdn over 2f out: no prog and struggling after: plugged on fnl f* **12/1**

0103 **8** *3* **Eau Good**[12] 2943 3-9-6 **84**.. StephenDonohoe 4 77
(B G Powell) *hld up and sn last: shkn up over 2f out: no prog after* **14/1**

1554 **9** *2* **Fongs Gazelle**[13] 2906 3-9-2 **80**.. KDarley 3 69
(M Johnston) *trckd ldr: c to nr side in st and disp gp ld: veered lft over 2f out: wknd over 1f out* **6/1**[3]

5-05 **10** *22* **Blue Madeira**[14] 2872 3-8-8 **72**.. TomEaves 9 17
(Mrs L Stubbs) *s.i.s: in tch tl wknd u.p 3f out: t.o* **25/1**

2m 8.88s (-1.36) **Going Correction** +0.025s/f (Good) **10** Ran SP% **121.7**
Speed ratings (Par 102):106,105,104,104,103 102,102,99,98,80
CSF £36.82 CT £101.31 TOTE £6.90: £2.40, £2.40, £1.60; EX 46.70 Place 6 £127.74, Place 5 £48.79..
Owner Miss K Rausing **Bred** Miss K Rausing **Trained** Newmarket, Suffolk

FOCUS
A good three-year-old handicap likely to produce its share of winners and has been rated slightly positively, although it is hard to tell whether Soft Morning would have won had she stayed stands' side with the main pack.
Soft Morning Official explanation: trainer's rep had no explanation for the apparent improvement in form
T/Jkpt: Not won. T/Plt: £110.10 to a £1 stake. Pool: £238,939.15. 1,583.45 winning tickets. T/Qpdt: £13.30 to a £1 stake. Pool: £11,027.95. 612.80 winning tickets. JN

3336 - 3340a (Foreign Racing) - See Raceform Interactive

2861 AYR (L-H)
Sunday, July 8

OFFICIAL GOING: Good (good to soft in places; 6.8)
With races on the round course continuing to use the hurdles track, the times were much quicker in comparison to those on the traditional straight track.
Wind: Fresh, against Weather: Cloudy, fine

3341 SLATER MENSWEAR MEDIAN AUCTION MAIDEN STKS — 6f
2:20 (2:20) (Class 5) 2-Y-O **£3,238** (£963; £481; £240) **Stalls** Low

Form RPR

1 **Danzig Fox** 2-9-3 0... RichardMullen 11 72+
(M Mullineaux) *missed break and blkd s: towards rr: hdwy over 2f out: led ins fnl f: r.o wl* **50/1**

2323 **2** *1 ¾* **Rub Of The Relic (IRE)**[2] 3275 2-9-3 0.................. SimonWhitworth 13 67
(P A Blockley) *led to ins fnl f: kpt on same pce* **11/4**[1]

3 *¾* **Paddy Jack** 2-9-3 0... PhillipMakin 8 65
(J R Weymes) *prom: effrt 2f out: kpt on same pce fnl f* **14/1**

0 **4** *¾* **Mister Christie**[10] 3024 2-9-3 0... KDarley 5 63
(N Tinkler) *chsd ldrs: effrt and ev ch over 1f out to ins fnl f: r.o* **6/1**[3]

0 **5** *1 ¾* **Caribbean Cruiser**[16] 2819 2-9-3 0.. PaulMulrennan 6 57
(Garry Moss) *towards rr: drvn and hdwy over 2f out: kpt on fnl f: nrst fin* **100/1**

003 **6** *½* **Handsinthemist (IRE)**[25] 2549 2-8-12 0.......................... MickyFenton 9 51
(P T Midgley) *t.k.h in midfield: drvn over 2f out: kpt on fnl f: no imp* **20/1**

50 **7** *shd* **Premium Port**[13] 2934 2-8-12 0... PBradley[(5)] 7 55
(A Berry) *cl up tl rdn and wknd over 1f out* **66/1**

8 *1 ¾* **Abbey Express** 2-9-3 0... PaulFessey 2 50
(M Dods) *cl up tl rdn and wknd over 1f out* **8/1**

9 *hd* **Dareios (GER)** 2-9-3 0... PatCosgrave 4 50
(G A Swinbank) *s.i.s: sn rdn in rr: n.d* **9/2**[2]

4 **10** *hd* **Kamal**[45] 1975 2-9-3 0... DO'Donohoe 3 49
(K A Ryan) *bhd and sn drvn: hung lft 1/2-way: n.d* **15/2**

11 *1 ¼* **Miss Sunshine** 2-8-5 0... GaryBartley[(7)] 10 40
(J S Goldie) *wnt rt s: a bhd* **12/1**

3543 **12** *3* **La Guancha**[26] 2533 2-8-9 0 ow2.. PJMcDonald[(5)] 1 33
(D A Nolan) *cl up tl rdn and wknd over 1f out* **28/1**

13 *10* **Social Height (IRE)** 2-9-3 0... FrancisNorton 12 6
(A Berry) *bhd: rdn 1/2-way: nvr on terms* **16/1**

1m 16.39s (2.72) **Going Correction** +0.10s/f (Good) **13** Ran SP% **114.9**
Speed ratings (Par 94):85,82,81,80,78 77,77,75,74,74 73,69,55
CSF £174.73 TOTE £41.70: £8.60, £1.60, £3.00; EX 264.20.
Owner Michael Mullineaux **Bred** R S And Mrs S H Kitching **Trained** Alpraham, Cheshire
■ Stewards' Enquiry : Simon Whitworth one-day ban: careless riding (Jul 19)

FOCUS
This looked a weak maiden and the time was very moderate, so not a race to be with.

NOTEBOOK
Danzig Fox, a Foxhound colt, half-brother to Nee Lemon Left, who was placed over 5f at two, overcame a slow start to make a winning debut. He soon had a few lengths to find on the pacesetters, but showed good mid-race speed to move into a challenging position and kept responding to pressure in the closing stages to get up and win going away. This was a modest race, but he displayed a likeable attitude and could make his mark in nurseries. (op 33-1)
Rub Of The Relic(IRE) had a very tough task turned out just two days after running over 7f on heavy ground at Warwick and he failed to produce his best. He is clearly a tough sort, but such a hard campaign so early in his career could leave its mark. (op 9-4 tchd 3-1 and 100-30 in places)
Paddy Jack, a gelded son of 1999 Palace House winner Rambling Bear, brother to Baysgarth Park, who was placed over 5f at two, made a satisfactory debut. He was keeping on at the finish and could improve. (op 16-1)
Mister Christie, mid-division on his debut at Newcastle, looked the one to beat approaching the final furlong, but he could not sustain his challenge. (op 7-1)
Caribbean Cruiser finished tailed off over course and distance on his debut, so this was much better. (op 80-1)
Dareios(GER), a 20,000euros half-brother to Desert Princess, a 1m winner in Italy, has been given a Derby entry, but he was never seen with a chance after starting slowly. (op 4-1 tchd 7-2)

3342 RACE FOR LIFE H'CAP — 6f
2:50 (2:51) (Class 6) (0-60,60) 3-Y-O **£2,590** (£770; £385; £192) **Stalls** Low

Form RPR

-563 **1** **Exit Strategy (IRE)**[26] 2545 3-9-1 **57**.......................(b) PaulMulrennan 14 70
(W J Haggas) *prom: led over 2f out: rdn clr over 1f out: comf* **5/1**[1]

3602 **2** *5* **Mangano**[14] 2910 3-8-7 **49**... JoeFanning 2 47
(A Berry) *a.p: rdn along over 2f out: kpt on u.p fnl f* **16/1**

5600 **3** *½* **Stormburst (IRE)**[20] 2718 3-8-10 **52**..........................(v[1]) PhillipMakin 9 49
(M Dods) *chsd ldrs: hdwy over 2f out: sn rdn and styd on ins fnl f* **12/1**

0213 **4** *nk* **Cheery Cat (USA)**[10] 3029 3-9-4 **60**...........................(p) TonyHamilton 3 56
(D W Barker) *led 2f: cl up tl rdn along and styd on one pce fnl 2f* **7/1**[3]

6605 **5** *¾* **Miss Daawe**[9] 3054 3-8-3 **48**.. GregFairley[(3)] 1 41
(B Ellison) *towards rr: hdwy 2f out: sn rdn: swtchd rt and styd on ins fnl f: nrst fin* **16/1**

6031 **6** *½* **Baybshambles (IRE)**[15] 2895 3-8-10 **55**.................. MarkLawson[(3)] 15 47
(R E Barr) *towards rr: hdwy over 2f out: sn rdn and styd on ins fnl f: nrst fin* **16/1**

-060 **7** *nk* **Ocean Of Champagne**[20] 2713 3-8-6 **48**......................(b[1]) PaulFessey 7 39
(A Dickman) *bhd tl hdwy on inner 2f out: sn rdn and styd on ins fnl f: nrst fin* **28/1**

-002 **8** *1 ¼* **River Club**[13] 2939 3-9-2 **58**... PatCosgrave 5 45
(G A Swinbank) *chsd ldrs: rdn along over 2f out: sn drvn and one pce* **8/1**

-000 **9** *nk* **Only A Grand**[36] 2255 3-8-8 **50**..................................(b) FrancisNorton 18 36
(R Bastiman) *towards rr: hdwy on outer 1/2-way: sn rdn along and no imp fr wl over 1f out* **12/1**

0301 **10** *hd* **Karmest**[20] 2718 3-9-2 **58**... GrahamGibbons 11 44
(E S McMahon) *cl up: led after 2f: rdn along and hdd over 2f out: sn drvn and grad wknd* **11/2**[2]

3242 **11** *shd* **Miss Taboo (IRE)**[15] 2894 3-8-10 **52**............................ MickyFenton 6 37
(P T Midgley) *towards rr: rdn along and hdwy 2f out: no imp u.p ent fnl f* **16/1**

530 **12** *2 ½* **Vadinka**[6] 3168 3-9-1 **57**... KimTinkler 13 35
(N Tinkler) *s.i.s: a in rr* **22/1**

0-00 **13** *2* **Spectacular Joy (IRE)**[55] 1712 3-8-11 **53**...............(p) J-PGuillambert 10 25
(Mrs A Duffield) *a towards rr* **66/1**

0-32 **14** *2* **Beat The Bully**[22] 2665 3-9-3 **59**.................................... JamesDoyle 12 25
(I A Wood) *chsd ldrs: rdn along 1/2-way: sn wknd* **7/1**[3]

225- **15** *1 ¼* **Wee Ellie Coburn**[197] 6927 3-9-2 **58**............................ TomEaves 17 20
(I Semple) *prom: rdn along over 2f out and sn wknd* **16/1**

40-0 **16** *2* **Warm Tribute (USA)**[91] 954 3-8-6 **55**.......................... GaryBartley[(7)] 16 11
(J S Goldie) *a towards rr* **20/1**

1m 13.73s (0.06) **Going Correction** +0.10s/f (Good) **16** Ran SP% **127.0**
Speed ratings (Par 98):103,96,95,95,94 93,93,91,91,90 90,87,84,82,80 77
CSF £85.32 CT £980.17 TOTE £7.50: £2.10, £3.00, £2.90, £2.10; EX 123.50.
Owner Shortgrove Manor Stud **Bred** Shortgrove Manor Stud **Trained** Newmarket, Suffolk
■ Stewards' Enquiry : Micky Fenton caution: careless riding

FOCUS
A moderate sprint handicap won in decisive style and the form is best rated through the runner-up.
Karmest Official explanation: trainer had no explanation for the poor form shown
Wee Ellie Coburn Official explanation: jockey said filly hung right-handed in straight

3343 CAMPBELTOWN BAR STEWART SCOTT MEMORIAL H'CAP — 1m 1f 20y
3:20 (3:22) (Class 6) (0-65,64) 4-Y-O+ **£2,590** (£770; £385; £192) **Stalls** Low

Form RPR

4620 **1** **Neil's Legacy (IRE)**[18] 2760 5-8-9 **55**............................ GregFairley[(3)] 6 64
(Miss L A Perratt) *chsd ldrs: led over 1f out: kpt on strly fnl f* **12/1**

4225 **2** *2 ½* **Mystical Ayr (IRE)**[9] 3049 5-9-3 **60**.................................. DO'Donohoe 7 64
(Miss L A Perratt) *in tch: drvn over 2f out: rallied over 1f out: chsd wnr ins fnl f: r.o* **11/2**[2]

-001 **3** *nk* **Zabeel Tower**[16] 2820 4-8-11 **54** TomEaves 8 57
(R Allan) *pressed ldr: led over 2f out to over 1f out: no ex and lost 2nd ins fnl f* **8/1**

0502 **4** *3/4* **Royal Citadel (IRE)**[16] 2820 4-8-4 **54** KellyHarrison(7) 12 55
(Mrs L B Normile) *chsd ldrs on outside: effrt over 2f out: nt qckn fnl f* **16/1**

0421 **5** *1* **Catherines Cafe (IRE)**[13] 2938 4-8-6 **52** (p) AndrewMullen(3) 2 51
(A C Whillans) *midfield: drvn over 2f out: kpt on same pce fnl f* **11/4**[1]

0300 **6** *1 1/2* **Jordans Elect**[5] 3182 7-9-1 **61** MarkLawson(3) 4 57
(P Monteith) *led to over 2f out: no ex over 1f out* **14/1**

/0-6 **7** *nk* **Tiger King (GER)**[16] 2823 6-9-1 **63** PJMcDonald(5) 9 58
(P Monteith) *hld up: rdn over 3f out: sme late hdwy: nvr on terms* **8/1**

-400 **8** *hd* **Fair Shake (IRE)**[54] 1747 7-9-5 **62** (v) PaulMulrennan 3 57
(Karen McLintock) *hld up: rdn 3f out: kpt on fnl f: nvr on terms* **12/1**

-601 **9** *1 1/4* **Rotuma (IRE)**[16] 2843 8-8-10 **53** (b) PhillipMakin 5 45
(M Dods) *towards rr: drvn 3f out: n.d* **8/1**

6113 **10** *4* **Bijou Dan**[16] 2823 6-9-7 **64** (b) TonyHamilton 1 47
(D W Thompson) *sn drvn along to chse ldrs: drvn and wknd fr 2f out* **7/1**[3]

500- **11** *3* **Awaken**[294] 5403 6-8-13 **56** PatCosgrave 11 33
(Miss Tracy Waggott) *bhd: rdn over 3f out: sn btn* **40/1**

1m 55.32s (-4.68) **Going Correction** -0.45s/f (Firm) 11 Ran SP% **118.3**
Speed ratings (Par 101):102,99,99,98,97 96,96,96,95,91 88
CSF £77.16 CT £570.91 TOTE £16.00: £4.40, £1.90, £2.90; EX 48.20.
Owner Terry & Mrs Linda Pardoe **Bred** Patrick M Ryan **Trained** Ayr, S Ayrshire

FOCUS
A moderate handicap with the third and fourth close to recent course form.
Neil's Legacy(IRE) Official explanation: trainer had no explanation for the apparent improvement in form

3344 EBF LAND O'BURNS FILLIES' STKS (LISTED RACE) 5f
3:50 (3:51) (Class 1) 3-Y-0+
£15,898 (£6,025; £3,015; £1,503; £753; £189) **Stalls** Low

Form RPR

0026 **1** **Mecca's Mate**[8] 3089 6-9-3 98 TonyHamilton 11 100
(D W Barker) *stdd s and swtchd to ins rail: in tch: swtchd rt and hdwy wl over 1f out: rdn ent fnl f: qcknd to ld last 100yds: r.o* **8/1**

36-2 **2** *hd* **Final Dynasty**[15] 2867 3-8-12 87 JoeFanning 1 97
(Mrs G S Rees) *cl up on inner: hdwy 2f out: rdn to chal ent fnl f and ev ch tl drvn and nt qckn towards fin* **50/1**

2113 **3** *1 3/4* **Morinqua (IRE)**[15] 2884 3-8-12 92 MickyFenton 3 91
(J G Given) *led: rdn and qcknd over 1f out: drvn ent fnl f: hdd and no ex last 100yds* **11/1**

3-15 **4** *hd* **Enticing (IRE)**[19] 2733 3-9-2 113 PaulMulrennan 9 94
(W J Haggas) *trckd ldrs on outer: hdwy 2f out: rdn over 1f out: drvn ent fnl f and sn one pce* **5/4**[1]

4141 **5** *1 3/4* **Our Little Secret (IRE)**[8] 3080 5-9-3 70 FrancisNorton 6 86
(A Berry) *cl up: effrt 2f out and ev ch tl rdn and wknd appr fnl f* **25/1**

3-11 **6** *1 1/4* **Pivotal's Princess (IRE)**[43] 2022 5-9-3 102 GrahamGibbons 7 81
(E S McMahon) *in tch towards outer: effrt 2f out: sn rdn and no imp appr fnl f* **3/1**[2]

2232 **6** *dht* **Coconut Moon**[8] 3080 5-9-3 72 KDarley 5 81
(E J Alston) *in tch: effrt over 2f out: sn rdn and kpt on u.p appr fnl f* **33/1**

-431 **8** *hd* **Terentia**[52] 1788 4-9-3 102 RichardMullen 8 80
(E S McMahon) *prom: rdn along 2f out: sn drvn and wknd* **7/1**[3]

0-60 **9** *2 1/2* **Bowness**[36] 2240 5-9-3 75 TomEaves 2 71
(J G Given) *midfield: effrt 2f out: sn rdn and no hdwy* **100/1**

1-36 **10** *1 3/4* **Ishi Adiva**[22] 2672 3-8-12 85 JamesDoyle 10 63
(Tom Dascombe) *chsd ldrs towards outer: rdn along over 2f out and sn wknd* **33/1**

00-0 **11** *1/2* **Vondova**[5] 3185 5-9-3 54 MarkLawson 4 63?
(D A Nolan) *a towards rr* **500/1**

59.44 secs (-1.00) **Going Correction** +0.10s/f (Good)
WFA 3 from 4yo+ 5lb 11 Ran SP% **114.3**
Speed ratings (Par 108):112,111,108,108,105 103,103,103,99,96 95
CSF £340.65 TOTE £10.10: £2.20, £5.30, £2.50; EX 127.80.
Owner David T J Metcalfe **Bred** Miss C Tagart **Trained** Scorton, N Yorks
■ Stewards' Enquiry : Graham Gibbons three-day ban: dropped hands and lost outright sixth place (Jul 19-21)

FOCUS
A Listed sprint for fillies run at a good pace. The form is not entirely solid and is best rated through the fifth and Coconut Moon.

NOTEBOOK
Mecca's Mate, who won this race two years ago, needs a good pace to be seen at her best, and that is what she got here. Best over 5f with some cut in the ground, conditions were ideal for her, and she ran on well to record her eighth career success. Her trainer plans to turn her out quickly for a Group 3 fillies' sprint at York on Friday. (tchd 9-1)
Final Dynasty only has an official rating of 87, but she was placed in a Listed race last autumn, was in form following a good second in a handicap last time, and does like a bit of cut in the ground, so arguably she should not have been as big a price as she was. In any case, she increased her paddock value again with this solid effort in defeat. (op 40-1)
Morinqua(IRE), a natural front-runner, set a good pace in front and seemed to run her race. She has the ability to win another little conditions event when allowed the run of the race. (op 9-1)
Enticing(IRE) held outstanding claims on the ratings, but she is well known to need it rattling underfoot to show her best, and conditions were probably on the easy side for her. She simply did not pick up like she can, but should be a different proposition back on fast ground. (op 10-11)
Our Little Secret(IRE) has been in great form of late, showing great speed to win from the widest stall at Chester on her previous start, but that still left her with plenty to find at this level. She ran well to claim fifth and has clearly improved a bundle for being in-foal.
Pivotal's Princess(IRE) was well below form with little clear excuse. (op 5-1)
Coconut Moon, runner-up to Our Little Secret at Chester last time out, ran close to that form in this higher grade. (op 5-1)
Terentia, like her stablemate, a leading contender on ratings, was also below her best. Perhaps all is not 100 per cent with the stable. (op 15-2)

3345 LADIES NIGHT ON SATURDAY 11 AUGUST H'CAP 6f
4:20 (4:22) (Class 5) (0-70,68) 3-Y-0+ **£3,238** (£963; £481; £240) **Stalls** Low

Form RPR

-303 **1** **Quicks The Word**[20] 2711 7-8-5 **49** oh4 GregFairley(3) 5 57
(T A K Cuthbert) *mde all far side: clr over 1f out: hld on wl fnl f* **18/1**

6006 **2** *1/2* **Milson's Point (IRE)**[14] 2910 3-8-13 **60** PhillipMakin 16 66
(I Semple) *led stands' side quartet: rdn over 2f out: kpt on: nt rch far side wnr* **16/1**

2015 **3** *hd* **Wiltshire (IRE)**[65] 1459 5-9-0 **55** MickyFenton 15 61
(P T Midgley) *chsd stands' side ldr: effrt and edgd lft over 1f out: kpt on fnl f: no ex nr fin* **20/1**

0045 **4** *3/4* **Charles Parnell (IRE)**[16] 2827 4-9-5 **60** PaulMulrennan 17 64
(M Dods) *chsd stands' side ldrs: effrt that gp over 1f out: edgd lft: kpt on same pce wl ins fnl f* **10/1**

0040 **5** *1/2* **Dorn Dancer (IRE)**[9] 3053 5-9-5 **60** TonyHamilton 9 62
(D W Barker) *midfield far side: rdn over 2f out: styd on wl fnl f: nrst fin* **10/1**

0433 **6** *1/2* **Brigadore**[15] 2864 8-9-10 **65** JoeFanning 12 66
(J G Given) *dwlt: hld up far side: effrt over 2f out: no imp wl ins fnl f* **9/2**[1]

6405 **6** *dht* **Oeuf A La Neige**[13] 2937 7-8-8 **49** oh3 DO'Donohoe 6 50
(Miss L A Perratt) *hld up far side: effrt and hdwy over 1f out: kpt on: nrst fin* **16/1**

-000 **8** *1* **Regal Raider (IRE)**[31] 2390 4-9-11 **66** TomEaves 8 64
(I Semple) *bhd far side tl styd on fr 2f out: n.d* **14/1**

-004 **9** *1* **Lewis Lloyd (IRE)**[15] 2893 4-8-7 **51** oh4 ow2 (t) MarkLawson(3) 7 46
(R E Barr) *dwlt: bhd far side: hdwy over 1f out: no imp* **40/1**

400- **10** *1/2* **Indian Spark**[373] 3041 13-9-4 **66** KellyHarrison(7) 18 59
(J S Goldie) *chsd stands' side ldrs tl rdn and no ex ent fnl f* **16/1**

0252 **11** *nk* **John Keats**[15] 2864 4-9-0 **62** GaryBartley(7) 1 54
(J S Goldie) *hld up far side: effrt 2f out: no imp ins fnl f* **11/2**[2]

501 **12** *1* **Night In (IRE)**[10] 3017 4-9-7 **62** (t) KimTinkler 3 51
(N Tinkler) *in tch far side: rdn over 2f out: no ex over 1f out* **8/1**[3]

4261 **13** *1 1/2* **Eternal Legacy (IRE)**[9] 3051 5-9-6 **61** KDarley 2 46
(E J Alston) *chsd far side ldrs to 2f out: sn btn* **9/1**

0-00 **14** *1/2* **Stanley Wolfe (IRE)**[5] 3180 4-8-5 **49** oh4 AndrewMullen(3) 10 32
(Garry Moss) *midfield far side: pushed along over 2f out: btn over 1f out* **50/1**

26-0 **15** *1/2* **Fern House (IRE)**[20] 2712 5-8-9 **50** oh4 ow1 PatCosgrave 4 32
(Garry Moss) *chsd far side ldrs tl wknd fr 2f out* **66/1**

5060 **16** *nk* **Sir Orpen (IRE)**[19] 2741 4-9-6 **68** (b) NeilBrown(7) 13 49
(T D Barron) *prom far side: rdn over 2f out: sn wknd* **10/1**

0000 **17** *1 1/2* **Drury Lane (IRE)**[25] 2556 7-8-6 **52** oh4 ow3 (b) AnnStokell(5) 11 28
(Miss A Stokell) *chsd far side ldrs tl wknd over 2f out* **66/1**

0606 **18** *dist* **Crux**[25] 2554 5-8-11 **57** PJMcDonald(5) 14 —
(R E Barr) *bhd far side: drvn 1/2-way: sn struggling: t.o* **33/1**

1m 13.89s (0.22) **Going Correction** +0.10s/f (Good)
WFA 3 from 4yo+ 6lb 18 Ran SP% **126.6**
Speed ratings (Par 103):102,101,101,100,99 98,98,97,96,95 95,93,91,91,90 89,87,—
CSF £275.49 CT £5884.74 TOTE £24.70: £4.80, £4.40, £5.30, £3.20; EX 638.50.
Owner W Hurst **Bred** Roy Matthews **Trained** Little Corby, Cumbria

FOCUS
A moderate but competitive handicap and the form seems sound overall. The field split into two, with the much larger group racing on the far side of the track, but three of the four horses who raced stands' side finished in the first four, and there did not appear to be any bias.
Crux Official explanation: jockey said gelding bled from the nose

3346 BLACK BOTTLE H'CAP 1m 1f 20y
4:50 (4:53) (Class 4) (0-80,80) 3-Y-0+ **£5,829** (£1,734; £866; £432) **Stalls** Low

Form RPR

2254 **1** **Tizzy May (FR)**[8] 3093 7-9-1 **70** GregFairley(3) 11 76
(B Ellison) *trckd ldrs: hdwy to ld over 2f out: sn rdn: drvn and edgd lft ins fnl f: styd on gamely towards fin* **8/1**[3]

4103 **2** *1* **King Of The Moors (USA)**[9] 3052 4-9-0 **73** NeilBrown(7) 7 77
(T D Barron) *trckd ldrs: hdwy 3f out: rdn along wl over 1f out: drvn and styd on ins fnl f* **10/1**

-056 **3** *shd* **Bajan Parkes**[11] 2986 4-9-11 **77** KDarley 5 81
(E J Alston) *hld up in rr: hdwy on inner over 2f out: rdn wl over 1f out: n.m.r ins fnl f: styd on wl* **7/1**[2]

050- **4** *shd* **Given A Choice (IRE)**[258] 6148 5-9-7 **73** PatCosgrave 4 76
(M Todhunter) *a.p: effrt and rdn wl over 1f out: ev ch tl drvn and no ex wl ins fnl f* **25/1**

231 **5** *1 1/4* **Final Tune (IRE)**[15] 2865 4-9-5 **76** RussellKennemore(5) 10 77
(Miss M E Rowland) *hld up in rr: hdwy 3f out: rdn to chse ldrs over 1f out: sn drvn and one pce ins fnl f* **11/1**

1552 **6** *2* **Shy Glance (USA)**[16] 2822 5-9-10 **76** DaleGibson 3 72
(P Monteith) *in tch: hdwy 3f out: rdn to chse ldrs over 2f out: drvn and one pce appr fnl f* **8/1**[3]

1505 **7** *1/2* **Frank Crow**[16] 2822 4-8-13 **72** GaryBartley(7) 6 67
(J S Goldie) *hld up and bhd tl styd on fnl 2f: nvr a factor* **28/1**

-532 **8** *1/2* **Prince Evelith (GER)**[11] 2986 4-9-9 **80** PJMcDonald(5) 8 74
(G A Swinbank) *hld up in midfield: hdwy 3f out: rdn along over 2f out: drvn to chse ldrs wl over 1f out: wknd ent fnl f* **11/4**[1]

6-22 **9** *2 1/2* **Shiitake**[15] 2865 4-8-12 **64** DO'Donohoe 2 53
(Miss L A Perratt) *hld up and bhd: hdwy over 2f out: swtchd rt and rdn wl over 1f out: sn no imp* **12/1**

6510 **10** *2* **Stargazer Jim (FR)**[16] 2831 5-9-9 **75** (v) PaulMulrennan 9 59
(W J Haggas) *cl up: rdn along 3f out: drvn and wknd over 2f out* **7/1**[2]

0034 **11** *shd* **Bright Sun (IRE)**[33] 2338 6-9-0 **66** KimTinkler 12 50
(N Tinkler) *midfield: rdn along 3f out and sn wknd* **16/1**

1604 **12** *5* **Primo Way**[16] 2828 6-9-5 **71** (b) TomEaves 1 44
(I Semple) *led: rdn along and hdd over 2f out: sn wknd* **22/1**

1m 55.23s (-4.77) **Going Correction** -0.45s/f (Firm) 12 Ran SP% **116.5**
Speed ratings (Par 105):103,102,102,101,100 99,98,98,95,94 94,89
CSF £81.85 CT £590.80 TOTE £9.90: £3.00, £4.30, £2.30; EX 118.10 TRIFECTA Not won..
Owner S Hawe **Bred** John Cullinan **Trained** Norton, N Yorks
■ Stewards' Enquiry : Gary Bartley one-day ban: careless riding (Jul 19)

FOCUS
An ordinary handicap best rated around the winner and runner-up and sound form.
Shiitake Official explanation: jockey said filly had breathing problems

3347 KIDZPLAY AMATEUR RIDERS' H'CAP 5f
5:20 (5:23) (Class 6) (0-65,64) 4-Y-0+ **£2,637** (£811; £405) **Stalls** Low

Form RPR

0000 **1** **The History Man (IRE)**[27] 2516 4-10-7 **55** (b) MissMMullineaux(5) 4 69
(M Mullineaux) *mde all far side: clr over 1f out: unchal* **25/1**

-005 **2** *3* **Conjecture**[30] 2418 5-10-7 **55** MissRBastiman(5) 5 58
(R Bastiman) *chsd wnr far side: rdn over 2f out: kpt on: 2nd of 9 in gp* **8/1**

0100 **3** *nk* **Sir Loin**[6] 3169 6-10-12 **55** (v) MrSWalker 13 56
(N Tinkler) *chsd stands' side ldrs: rdn to ld that gp ins fnl f: nt rch far side: 1st of 8 in gp* **20/1**

5550 **4** *nk* **Legal Set (IRE)**[25] 2555 11-9-11 **45** (b) MissLAllan(5) 17 45
(Miss A Stokell) *prom stands' side: effrt over 1f out: kpt on fnl f: nrst fin: 2nd of 8 in gp* **28/1**

0-00 **5** *shd* **Highland Song (IRE)**[59] 1597 4-10-12 **55** ow3 MrMSeston 12 55
(R F Fisher) *w stands' side ldr: ev ch to ins fnl f: kpt on same pce: 3rd of 8 in gp* **50/1**

0312 **6** ¾ **Whozart (IRE)**[25] [2561] 4-10-6 **49** MrSDobson 16 46
(A Dickman) *led stands' side: rdn: hung lft and hdd ins fnl f: kpt on same pce: 4th of 8 in gp* **10/3**[1]

6322 **7** 1 **Rothesay Dancer**[4] [3203] 4-10-11 **54** MissSBrotherton 18 48
(J S Goldie) *chsd stands' side ldrs: effrt over 1f out: nt qckn fnl f: 5th of 8 in gp* **9/2**[2]

0000 **8** ½ **Rosie's Result**[16] [2830] 7-9-11 **45** MrHHaynes(5) 7 37
(M Todhunter) *prom far side: rdn over 2f out: edgd lft over 1f out: no imp fnl f: 3rd of 9 in gp* **25/1**

1120 **9** 1¼ **Compton Classic**[5] [3184] 5-11-7 **64** MrsCBartley 10 51
(J S Goldie) *towards rr far side: rdn and hdwy over 1f out: nvr rchd ldrs: 4th of 9 in gp* **8/1**

-060 **10** nk **Signor Whippee**[5] [3180] 4-9-13 **47** (b) MrBenBrisbourne(5) 6 33
(A Berry) *towards rr far side: drvn 1/2-way: n.d: 5th of 9 in gp* **33/1**

0-00 **11** nk **Fairgame Man**[66] [1423] 9-9-9 **45** (p) MissFRodmell(7) 1 30
(J S Wainwright) *towards rr far side: drvn 1/2-way: nvr on terms: 6th of 9 in gp* **100/1**

0555 **12** nk **Strawberry Patch (IRE)**[5] [3185] 8-10-4 **50** (p) MrMJJSmith(3) 11 34
(J S Goldie) *hld up stands' side: effrt and edgd lft over 1f out: sn btn: 6th of 8 in gp* **6/1**[3]

-00 **13** ½ **Seafield Towers**[48] [1892] 7-10-8 **51** MissLEllison 8 33
(Miss L A Perratt) *chsd far side ldrs tl wknd over 1f out: 7th of 9 in gp* **22/1**

0560 **14** ¾ **Alexia Rose (IRE)**[2] [3259] 5-9-9 **45** (b) MissWGibson(7) 3 24
(A Berry) *bhd far side: drvn 1/2-way: sn btn: 8th of 9 in gp* **33/1**

0000 **15** ½ **Polish Emperor (USA)**[27] [2509] 7-10-9 **55** (tp) MissARyan(3) 15 33
(D W Barker) *bhd stands' side: drvn 1/2-way: nvr on terms: 7th of 8 in gp* **33/1**

430 **16** 1 **Desert Dust**[48] [1902] 4-9-9 **45** MrsRCaudillo(7) 14 19
(R M H Cowell) *t.k.h: in tch stands' side to 2f out: sn wknd: last of 8 in gp* **16/1**

4-00 **17** 3 **Quaker Boy**[10] [3017] 4-10-0 **50** MrCWhillans(7) 9 13
(A C Whillans) *sn bhd far side: struggling fr 1/2-way: last of 9 in gp* **16/1**

60.81 secs (0.37) **Going Correction** +0.10s/f (Good) **17** Ran SP% **121.6**
Speed ratings (Par 101):101,96,95,95,95 93,92,91,89,89 88,88,87,86,85 83,78
CSF £194.85 CT £4220.12 TOTE £26.00: £5.20, £3.10, £3.90, £5.40; EX 223.20 Place 6 £2,618.89, Place 5 £921.94..
Owner D E Simpson & R Farrington-Kirkham **Bred** J Beckett **Trained** Alpraham, Cheshire
■ Stewards' Enquiry : Miss S Brotherton one-day ban: failed to ride to draw (Jul 27)

FOCUS
Moderate sprint form. The field split in two and there appeared little draw bias.
Seafield Towers Official explanation: jockey said gelding lost a front shoe
T/Jkpt: Not won. T/Plt: £2,357.10 to a £1 stake. Pool: £77,174.05. 23.90 winning tickets. T/Qpdt: £886.30 to a £1 stake. Pool: £4,312.00. 3.60 winning tickets. RY

3174 BRIGHTON (L-H)
Sunday, July 8

OFFICIAL GOING: Good to firm (9.2)
With the ground firming up again, the runners - with the exception of a few with wayward steering - all stayed on the far side of the track.
Wind: Moderate, half against Weather: Fine

3348 EBF 123RACING.COM MEDIAN AUCTION MAIDEN STKS 6f 209y
2:30 (2:31) (Class 6) 2-Y-O £2,590 (£770; £385; £192) **Stalls** Low

Form RPR

5 **1** **The Betchworth Kid**[9] [3043] 2-9-3 0 TedDurcan 7 79
(M L W Bell) *in tch: drvn to chse ldr over 1f out: led ins fnl f: sn clr: styd on strly* **7/2**[2]

2 **2** 5 **Harbour Blues**[10] [3037] 2-9-3 0 DarryllHolland 9 66
(C E Brittain) *w ldrs: led 2f out tl ins fnl f: nt pce of wnr* **15/8**[1]

60 **3** 2½ **Bellalatino (IRE)**[16] [2812] 2-8-12 0 JimCrowley 4 54
(Mrs Norma Pook) *sn bhd: rdn and styd on fnl 2f: nt trble ldng pair* **25/1**

046 **4** nk **Alfredtheordinary**[49] [1858] 2-9-3 0 EddieAhern 8 58
(M R Channon) *w ldrs tl outpcd fnl 2f* **33/1**

650 **5** 3½ **Star In The East**[17] [2797] 2-8-7 0 WilliamBuick(5) 2 44
(A M Balding) *mde most tl 2f out: sn wknd* **8/1**

363 **6** 2 **Sheik'N'Knotsterd**[29] [2447] 2-9-3 0 SebSanders 3 44
(J Akehurst) *in tch: effrt over 2f out: wknd wl over 1f out* **8/1**

00 **7** 5 **Tiger's Rocket (IRE)**[30] [2424] 2-9-3 0 RyanMoore 5 31
(R Hannon) *sn outpcd and bhd* **4/1**[3]

8 ¾ **Woodcote Wildcat (USA)** 2-8-12 0 SteveDrowne 6 24
(N A Callaghan) *s.s: hdwy on outside 4f out: wknd 2f out: wl btn whn hung lft over 1f out* **16/1**

1m 24.52s (1.82) **Going Correction** +0.20s/f (Good) **8** Ran SP% **111.9**
Speed ratings (Par 92):97,91,88,88,84 81,76,75
CSF £9.98 TOTE £4.40: £1.20, £1.40, £5.60; EX 8.60 Trifecta £322.10 Part won. Pool £453.67 - 0.50 winning units..
Owner W H Ponsonby **Bred** R P Williams **Trained** Newmarket, Suffolk

FOCUS
An ordinary maiden, but the winner looked above average for the track and can progress.

NOTEBOOK
The Betchworth Kid coped well with the faster ground, though his rider reported that he was not entirely comfortable on the downhill run into the straight. Likely to be even more effective on a more conventional track, he will stay a mile no problem and looks an above-average juvenile winner at this track. (op 11-4)
Harbour Blues ran a fair enough race, only to be well outpointed by a progressive sort. He is good enough to find a little race over 6f or 7f. (tchd 13-8)
Bellalatino(IRE) got the trip well enough, and gave encouragement for the future back at this more realistic level. She is now qualified for nurseries, and should be a lively contender when making the switch. (op 20-1)
Alfredtheordinary is falling short in maidens, and would be more at home in nurseries, though his best trip has yet to be established. (tchd 28-1)
Star In The East did not stay the longer trip, and her best chance at the moment would be in 6f nurseries. (op 9-1)
Sheik'N'Knotsterd looks best at 6f at present, and now deserves a crack at nursery company. (op 10-1)
Tiger's Rocket(IRE), who started a short price on what he had achieved before this, was never going the pace, and looks more suited to nurseries now he is qualified. (op 6-1 tchd 7-1)

3349 SDS GROUP MAIDEN STKS 7f 214y
3:00 (3:00) (Class 5) 3-Y-O £2,744 (£821; £410; £205; £102) **Stalls** Low

Form RPR

02 **1** **Cactus Rose**[29] [2477] 3-9-3 0 SteveDrowne 7 82
(R Charlton) *hld up in midfield: hdwy over 2f out: led over 1f out: rdn out* **7/2**[3]

0 **2** ¾ **Own Boss (USA)**[13] [2944] 3-9-3 0 PhilipRobinson 13 80
(M A Jarvis) *prom: led 2f out tl over 1f out: r.o* **7/1**

02 **3** 2½ **Know The Law**[25] [2554] 3-9-3 0 SebSanders 5 75
(D R C Elsworth) *in tch on rail: effrt and swtchd wd 2f out: styd on wl: nt rch ldng pair* **10/3**[2]

02-4 **4** 1¼ **High 'n Dry (IRE)**[80] [1105] 3-8-12 75 EddieAhern 4 67
(C A Cyzer) *plld hrd: led after 3f tl 2f out: no ex over 1f out* **5/2**[1]

5-23 **5** 1½ **Corlough Mountain**[6] [3167] 3-9-3 70 PatDobbs 1 68
(N A Callaghan) *chsd ldrs: rdn and one pce fnl 2f* **9/2**

-000 **6** 2½ **Motarjm (USA)**[49] [1863] 3-9-0 0 (t) JerryO'Dwyer(3) 8 62
(H J Collingridge) *t.k.h in rr: rdn and styd on fnl 2f: nvr nrr* **50/1**

0 **7** 1¼ **King Of Legend (IRE)**[41] [2083] 3-9-0 0 TinaSmith(3) 6 60
(Miss Gay Kelleway) *plld hrd and prom early: stdd in tch after 2f: rdn and no hdwy fnl 2f* **66/1**

8 1 **Final Overture (FR)** 3-8-12 0 TedDurcan 11 52
(H R A Cecil) *hld up in rr: sme hdwy and hung lft over 1f out: eased whn no imp fnl f* **20/1**

0500 **9** 4 **Elmasong**[11] [2978] 3-8-12 41 JimCrowley 10 43
(J J Bridger) *led 3f: prom tl wknd 2f out* **100/1**

10 13 **Half A Tsar (IRE)** 3-8-10 0 JackDean(7) 14 18
(Mark Gillard) *mid-div on outside: wknd over 2f out* **100/1**

0 **11** 26 **Best One**[3] [3244] 3-9-3 0 DarryllHolland 3 —
(C E Brittain) *a bhd: no ch fnl 2f* **40/1**

1m 36.71s (1.67) **Going Correction** +0.20s/f (Good) **11** Ran SP% **117.2**
Speed ratings (Par 100):99,98,95,94,93 90,89,88,84,71 45
CSF £26.70 TOTE £4.20: £1.80, £2.00, £1.40; EX 26.60 Trifecta £113.60 Pool £448.15 - 2.80 winning units..
Owner Exors Of The Late A J Yemm **Bred** Langton Stud **Trained** Beckhampton, Wilts

FOCUS
A decent maiden for the track, run at an ordinary gallop, but several of these lacked experience and can do better.
Final Overture(FR) Official explanation: jockey said filly hung left
Best One Official explanation: trainer's rep said gelding had a breathing problem

3350 SDS GROUP H'CAP 6f 209y
3:30 (3:30) (Class 4) (0-80,79) 3-Y-O+ **£4,605** (£1,378; £689; £344; £171) **Stalls** Low

Form RPR

2504 **1** **Desert Dreamer (IRE)**[12] [2965] 6-9-4 **66** JimCrowley 12 79
(P R Chamings) *hld up in tch: effrt and briefly nt clr run over 2f out: led over 1f out: drvn out* **6/1**

0230 **2** 1½ **Resplendent Nova**[9] [3056] 5-9-8 **70** SteveDrowne 5 79
(P Howling) *in tch: drvn to chse ldrs over 1f out: kpt on* **6/1**

0014 **3** shd **Scarlet Flyer (USA)**[23] [2626] 4-9-11 **73** (b) GeorgeBaker 8 82
(G L Moore) *mid-div: gd hdwy on outside over 1f out: hung lft: nt qckn fnl 75yds* **9/2**[2]

0220 **4** 1¼ **Realy Naughty (IRE)**[5] [3178] 3-8-4 **65** WilliamBuick(5) 14 67
(B G Powell) *chsd ldrs: hrd rdn and slt ld 2f out: hdd over 1f out: hung lft: one pce* **11/1**

-140 **5** hd **Manaal (USA)**[15] [2883] 3-9-9 **79** MartinDwyer 9 81
(Sir Michael Stoute) *mid-div on rail: effrt and hrd rdn over 1f out: styd on same pce* **4/1**[1]

4024 **6** hd **Fiefdom (IRE)**[13] [2936] 5-10-0 **76** SebSanders 2 80
(I W McInnes) *t.k.h: disp ld tl 2f out: hrd rdn over 1f out: 5th and btn whn carried lft ins fnl f* **5/1**[3]

-004 **7** nk **Russian Symphony (USA)**[21] [2689] 6-9-13 **75** TedDurcan 10 78
(C R Egerton) *stdd s: hld up in midfield: hrd rdn 2f out: nt clr run and swtchd rt ins fnl f: styd on* **14/1**

1060 **8** 1¾ **Proper (IRE)**[36] [2243] 3-9-8 **78** ChrisCatlin 11 74
(M R Channon) *t.k.h: prom tl wknd over 1f out* **33/1**

0/0- **9** nk **Sagunt (GER)**[371] 4-9-7 **69** PaulDoe 6 67
(S Curran) *hld up towards rr: shkn up and stayed on stdly fnl 2f, nvr rchd chal position* **50/1**

-000 **10** ½ **Imperial Gain (USA)**[20] [2725] 4-9-1 **70** BarrySavage(7) 4 67
(J M Bradley) *towards rr: rdn 3f out: hung lft ins fnl 2f: nvr trbld ldrs* **16/1**

2350 **11** 4 **Quantum Leap**[8] [3101] 10-9-2 **64** (p) DarryllHolland 7 50
(S Dow) *rdn 3f out: a bhd* **16/1**

0440 **12** 1¼ **Border Edge**[3] [3234] 9-8-13 **61** (b) EddieAhern 13 43
(J J Bridger) *disp ld tl wknd 2f out* **16/1**

1m 22.92s (0.22) **Going Correction** +0.20s/f (Good)
WFA 3 from 4yo+ 8lb **12** Ran SP% **121.0**
Speed ratings (Par 105):106,104,104,102,102 102,101,99,99,99 94,93
CSF £42.85 CT £184.15 TOTE £7.90: £2.20, £2.80, £1.70; EX 54.10 Trifecta £284.10 Part won. Pool £400.23 - 0.60 winning units..
Owner Patrick Chamings Sprint Club **Bred** Gainsborough Stud Management Ltd **Trained** Baughurst, Hants

FOCUS
A typical Brighton handicap, modest in quality but competitive enough, and solid form for the grade with the third to sixth close to their marks.
Fiefdom(IRE) ◆ Official explanation: jockey said gelding hung right

3351 G & S MECHANICAL SERVICES H'CAP 1m 1f 209y
4:00 (4:02) (Class 5) (0-70,70) 3-Y-O £2,744 (£821; £410; £205; £102) **Stalls** High

Form RPR

1404 **1** **Beau Sancy**[22] [2653] 3-9-1 **67** LiamJones(3) 12 70
(R A Harris) *hld up in rr: hdwy on outside over 3f out: drvn to ld over 1f out: styd on* **12/1**

0020 **2** 1¼ **Iolanthe**[48] [1887] 3-9-4 **67** SteveDrowne 13 67
(B J Meehan) *chsd ldrs: led 2f out tl over 1f out: nt qckn fnl f* **25/1**

3-06 **3** shd **Penny From Heaven (IRE)**[41] [2079] 3-9-4 **67** DaneO'Neill 7 67
(E A L Dunlop) *hld up in midfield: n.m.r over 4f out: hrd rdn over 2f out: styd on wl fnl f* **10/1**

0-35 **4** ½ **Montjeu's Melody (IRE)**[18] [2766] 3-9-7 **70** EddieAhern 6 69
(J W Hills) *prom: sltly outpcd whn squeezed for room ins fnl 2f: rallied and styd on wl fnl 100yds* **14/1**

0-03 **5** nk **She's So Pretty (IRE)**[28] [2490] 3-9-2 **65** (v[1]) AdamKirby 5 63
(W R Swinburn) *led tl 2f out: one pce* **5/1**[2]

343 **6** 2 **Summer Of Love (IRE)**[22] [2653] 3-9-0 **63** RyanMoore 10 57
(P F I Cole) *hld up in midfield: hdwy over 3f out: 4th and rdn whn n.m.r ins fnl 2f: sn btn* **7/2**[1]

4403 **7** 1 **Brave Jack (IRE)**[28] 2489 3-7-13 **51** oh1.................. StephaneBreux(3) 8 43
(J R Best) *towards rr: rdn and sme hdwy over 1f out: nvr nr to chal* **9/1**[3]

0-64 **8** shd **La Cuvee**[28] 2489 3-7-11 **51** oh3.................................. WilliamBuick(5) 2 43
(B G Powell) *bhd: rdn after 2f: nvr rchd ldrs* **12/1**

4523 **9** 3 **Dana Music (USA)**[24] 2610 3-9-7 **70**.................................. TPO'Shea 3 56
(M R Channon) *dwlt: sn in tch: rdn over 4f out: wknd over 3f out* **7/2**[1]

0-04 **10** ½ **Tykie Two**[26] 2535 3-8-11 **60**.. ChrisCatlin 4 45
(E J O'Neill) *prom 7f* **11/1**

000- **11** ¾ **Eridani (IRE)**[191] 6976 3-8-2 **51** oh6.............................. AdrianMcCarthy 9 35
(M L W Bell) *prom 7f* **10/1**

2m 4.96s (2.36) **Going Correction** +0.20s/f (Good) **11** Ran SP% **123.5**
Speed ratings (Par 100):98,97,96,96,96 94,93,93,91,91 90
CSF £286.45 CT £3110.22 TOTE £16.70: £4.50, £7.40, £3.10; EX 425.80 TRIFECTA Not won..
Owner S & A Mares **Bred** Mrs J Keegan **Trained** Earlswood, Monmouths

FOCUS
A fairly moderate race and few progressive runners, but some of these were lightly-raced and can improve a little.

3352 SPEND A DAY AT BUTLINS H'CAP 7f 214y
4:30 (4:34) (Class 6) (0-65,65) 3-Y-0+ **£1,943** (£578; £288; £144) **Stalls** Low

Form RPR

0-50 **1** **Blue Mistral (IRE)**[38] 2178 3-8-10 **58**..............................(vt¹) PaulDoe 11 66
(W J Knight) *bhd: drvn along and hdwy on outside 3f out: led over 1f out: hld on wl fnl 100yds* **50/1**

3001 **2** ½ **Moves Goodenough**[11] 2979 4-9-11 **64**......................(b) SebSanders 13 73
(Andrew Turnell) *stdd s: t.k.h towards rr: hrd rdn and hdwy over 1f out: pressed wnr fnl 100yds: jst hld* **7/2**[1]

6534 **3** 1 ½ **Trevian**[9] 3067 6-9-1 **54**.. DarryllHolland 9 60
(J M Bradley) *hld up in tch: drvn to chse ldrs over 1f out: nt qckn fnl f* **13/2**[2]

4460 **4** 1 ½ **Trifti**[85] 1036 6-8-9 **48**.. AdamKirby 7 50
(C A Cyzer) *bhd: rdn and swtchd outside over 1f out: styd on wl fnl f* **16/1**

5025 **5** shd **Call My Bluff (FR)**[16] 2831 4-9-7 **65**............................ PatrickHills(5) 14 67
(Rae Guest) *towards rr: effrt and hmpd over 2f out: styd on u.p: nt rch ldrs* **7/1**[3]

2402 **6** 1 ½ **Danawi (IRE)**[10] 3034 4-9-0 **53**.. ChrisCatlin 12 51
(M R Hoad) *prom: rdn and one pce fnl 2f* **10/1**

6064 **7** 1 ¾ **Prince Valentine**[6] 3149 6-8-11 **50**.............................(p) JimCrowley 10 44
(G L Moore) *towards rr: sme hdwy and hrd rdn ins fnl 2f: no imp* **10/1**

4040 **8** 2 **Valart**[29] 2467 4-9-2 **55**...(tp) SteveDrowne 5 45
(A J Lidderdale) *sn outpcd towards rr on rail: swtchd rt over 1f out: sme late hdwy* **50/1**

0504 **9** 2 **Ciccone**[15] 2875 4-9-2 **55**..(b¹) RyanMoore 3 40
(G L Moore) *dwlt: sn prom: wknd and coasted in fnl 2f* **7/1**[3]

4040 **10** 1 ¼ **Sopran Gath (ITY)**[17] 2802 4-9-11 **64**.............................(t) EddieAhern 4 46
(J W Hills) *led at gd pce tl wknd over 1f out: eased whn btn fnl f* **16/1**

5050 **11** 1 ¼ **Ellen's Girl (IRE)**[38] 2179 4-8-10 **49**................................(p) PatDobbs 6 28
(B G Powell) *chsd ldrs tl hrd rdn and wknd 2f out* **33/1**

0200 **12** 1 ¼ **Makai**[12] 2967 4-8-4 **48**...(b) WilliamBuick(5) 8 25
(J J Bridger) *prom over 5f* **25/1**

0004 **13** 3 **Lizarazu (GER)**[11] 2979 8-8-11 **53**...............................(p) LiamJones(3) 2 23
(R A Harris) *mid-div tl wknd over 2f out* **9/1**

4000 **14** 1 ¼ **Todlea (IRE)**[27] 2514 7-9-10 **63**.................................(b) DaneO'Neill 15 30
(Jean-Rene Auvray) *chsd ldrs 5f: bhd fnl 2f* **33/1**

0002 **15** ¾ **High Class Problem (IRE)**[5] 3191 4-9-7 **60**....................(t) TedDurcan 1 25
(P F I Cole) *in tch on rail: hrd rdn over 2f out: sn wknd: eased whn no ch fnl f* **7/1**[3]

1m 36.06s (1.02) **Going Correction** +0.20s/f (Good)
WFA 3 from 4yo+ 9lb **15** Ran SP% **126.7**
Speed ratings (Par 101):102,101,100,98,98 96,95,93,91,89 88,87,84,83,82
CSF £223.46 CT £1357.53 TOTE £50.10: £10.60, £1.70, £2.40; EX 423.80 TRIFECTA Not won..
Owner Angmering Park Thoroughbreds **Bred** Blue Bloodstock Limited **Trained** Patching, W Sussex

FOCUS
A modest race, but a strong gallop set it up for the come-from-behind performers. The form looks sound rated around the placed horses.
Trifti Official explanation: jockey said gelding was unbalanced throughout
Valart Official explanation: jockey said filly was denied a clear run
High Class Problem(IRE) Official explanation: jockey said gelding ran flat

3353 123SPORT.COM H'CAP 5f 59y
5:00 (5:09) (Class 6) (0-65,60) 3-Y-0 **£1,943** (£578; £288; £144) **Stalls** Low

Form RPR

0-04 **1** **Contentious (IRE)**[9] 3046 3-8-4 **50**.......................... KirstyMilczarek(7) 7 54
(D M Simcock) *dwlt and hmpd s: hld up in 5th: hdwy 2f out: led ins fnl f: bmpd nr fin: drvn out* **7/2**[3]

0006 **2** ½ **Stir Crazy (IRE)**[4] 3218 3-8-8 **54**............................... MatthewDavies(7) 4 56
(M R Channon) *hld up in rr: effrt and nt clr run ins fnl 2f: swtchd wd and hung rt: r.o wl fnl f: jst hld* **10/3**[2]

40-0 **3** hd **Banana Belle**[6] 3163 3-8-3 **45**... DominicFox(3) 3 46
(J Ryan) *chsd ldng pair: rdn to join ldrs over 1f out: kpt on* **25/1**

6546 **4** hd **Billy Red**[24] 2594 3-9-4 **57**..(b) RyanMoore 8 58
(J R Jenkins) *led: hung bdly rt 2f out: hdd and veered lft ins fnl f: nt rcvr* **5/2**[1]

46-0 **5** 2 ½ **Ishimagic**[8] 3087 3-8-11 **50**... JimCrowley 1 42
(J J Bridger) *hld up in 4th: effrt 2f out: hrd rdn over 1f out: no ex* **12/1**

000 **6** 1 ¾ **Stravinsky's Art (USA)**[16] 2837 3-8-6 **45**................. FrankieMcDonald 2 30
(D R C Elsworth) *chsd ldr over 3f* **11/2**

63.86 secs (1.56) **Going Correction** +0.20s/f (Good) **6** Ran SP% **100.8**
Speed ratings (Par 98):95,94,93,93,89 86
CSF £12.27 CT £156.21 TOTE £3.90: £2.60, £2.40; EX 16.00 Trifecta £88.10 Pool £481.80 - 3.88 winning units. Place 6 £351.56, Place 5 £215.44..
Owner S R Hope & D J Erwin **Bred** John O Browne **Trained** Newmarket, Suffolk
■ Croeso Bach was withdrawn (15/2, broke out of stalls). R4 applies, deduct 10p in the £.

FOCUS
A weak race, but run at a good pace, and the lightly-raced winner, who sets the standard, can improve more than most.
Billy Red Official explanation: jockey said gelding hung badly left
T/Plt: £350.00 to a £1 stake. Pool: £85,118.70. 177.50 winning tickets. T/Qpdt: £161.40 to a £1 stake. Pool: £4,015.20. 18.40 winning tickets. LM

3354 - 3360a (Foreign Racing) - See Raceform Interactive

[2811]CHANTILLY (R-H)
Sunday, July 8

OFFICIAL GOING: Good to soft

3361a PRIX PELLEAS (LISTED RACE) (C&G) 1m 2f
2:50 (2:50) 3-Y-0 **£17,568** (£7,027; £5,270; £3,514)

RPR

1 **El Comodin (IRE)**[38] 3-8-11 .... SPasquier 5 104
(A Fabre, France)

2 ¾ **Binocular (FR)**[24] 3-8-11 .... OPeslier 4 103
(E Lellouche, France)

3 nse **Big Robert**[17] 2789 3-8-11 .... KFallon 1 103
(W R Muir) *racd in cl 2nd on rail: led after 3 1/2f: pushed along st: jnd 2f out: rdn and stl ev ch 1f out: r.o to line* **32/10**[1]

4 1 **Silverlord (FR)**[30] 3-8-11 .... C-PLemaire 2 101
(Mme C Head-Maarek, France)

2m 4.90s (-1.90) **Going Correction** +0.025s/f (Good) **4** Ran SP% **23.8**
Speed ratings: 108,107,107,106
PARI-MUTUEL: WIN 1.40; PL 1.10, 1.50; SF 4.70.
Owner Baron G Von Ullmann **Bred** Wittekindshof Stud **Trained** Chantilly, France

NOTEBOOK
Big Robert, slowly out of the stalls, was pushed up to make the running. He battled on gamely in the straight, but looked tapped for speed in the final 100 metres and lost second on the line. This was a reasonable effort considering he was reported to have been unsuited by the ground. His connections are considering a possible tilt at the Gordon Stakes at Goodwood.

3362a PRIX JEAN PRAT (GROUP 1) (C&F) 1m
3:20 (3:22) 3-Y-0 **£154,432** (£61,784; £30,892; £15,432; £7,730)

RPR

1 **Lawman (FR)**[35] 2293 3-9-2 .... OPeslier 5 118
(J-M Beguigne, France) *sn led: r.o st: qcknd clr over 1 1/2f out: easily* **15/8**[2]

2 3 **Stoneside (IRE)**[28] 2499 3-9-2 .... TGillet 2 112
(Rod Collet, France) *first to show and prom: cl 3rd 1/2-way: wnt 2nd early st: rdn and styd on fr 1 1/2f out but no ch w wnr* **16/1**

3 1 ½ **Golden Titus (IRE)**[70] 1336 3-9-2 .... CSoumillon 1 109
(A Renzoni, Italy) *in tch: 5th 1/2-way: pushed along st: hdwy over 1 1/2f out: rdn and wnt 3rd over 1f out: styd on* **14/1**

4 4 **Astronomer Royal (USA)**[19] 2734 3-9-2 .... KFallon 4 101
(A P O'Brien, Ire) *hld up in last: drvn 2f out: styd on fr 1 1/2f out but nvr in contention* **13/8**[1]

5 snk **Tobosa**[43] 2037 3-9-2 .... MichaelHills 3 101
(W Jarvis) *hld up: 6th 1/2-way: pushed along on outside over 2f out: rdn over 1 1/2f out to dispute 3rd briefly: sn no ex* **8/1**[3]

6 1 **Asperity (USA)**[28] 2499 3-9-2 .... JimmyFortune 6 99
(J H M Gosden) *mid-div: 4th 1/2-way: drvn 2f out: one pce* **8/1**[3]

7 snk **Grand Vista**[28] 2499 3-9-2 .... SPasquier 7 98
(A Fabre, France) *sn racing in 2nd: u.p ent st: sn rdn and wknd* **14/1**

1m 41.2s (0.90) **Going Correction** +0.025s/f (Good) **7** Ran SP% **114.3**
Speed ratings: 96,93,91,87,87 86,86
PARI-MUTUEL: WIN 2.30; PL 1.70, 3.30; SF 13.50.
Owner C Marzocco & E Ciampi **Bred** Petra Bloodstock Agency **Trained** France

NOTEBOOK
Lawman(FR), quickly out of the stalls, gave another brilliant front-running performance, controlling things at a steady pace until the turn into the straight. When asked to quicken, the response was electric and he galloped away from his six rivals, leaving them toiling in the mud. The rain-softened ground seemed to have no effect on him and his trainer is contemplating sending him next to the Jacques le Marois at Deauville in August, followed by the Irish Champion Stakes, and then a possible tilt at the Arc.
Stoneside(IRE), wearing his habitual cheekpieces, he tracked the winner throughout and stayed on gamely up the straight, making a little late headway near the line. He is improving with every race and is a tough and durable sort. His trainer is thinking of giving him a break following a string of races in quite a short space of time.
Golden Titus(IRE), the Italian Guineas winner, put up a gutsy performance in defeat. Held up at the back for much of the race, he made steady headway up the straight to take third with the rest of the field finishing four lengths behind him. His jockey reported that he will improve on better ground.
Astronomer Royal(USA), held up at the back for much of the race, he never looked happy on the ground and was toiling in the straight. His jockey reported that this was not his true form and a faster surface should suit better.
Tobosa raced behind the leaders on the outside for much of the race, but he never really picked up in the ground. He is another who was reported to hate the going.
Asperity(USA) lost ground turning into the straight and was always struggling on the soft ground. It is probably best to ignore this.

[2977]BATH (L-H)
Monday, July 9

OFFICIAL GOING: Good to soft
Wind: Brisk ahead

3363 EUROPEAN BREEDERS' FUND/FORD BROTHERS MAIDEN STKS 5f 11y
2:15 (2:15) (Class 5) 2-Y-0 **£3,238** (£963; £481; £240) **Stalls** Centre

Form RPR

6 **1** **Little Knickers**[33] 2349 2-8-12 0... MartinDwyer 2 79
(D K Ivory) *racd far side: rdn and hdwy over 2f out: styd on u.p to ld wl ins fnl f* **33/1**

40 **2** 1 ¼ **Perfect Paula (USA)**[19] 2756 2-8-12 0............................ SteveDrowne 9 75
(B J Meehan) *racd far side: trckd ldrs: led travelling wl ins fnl 2f: rdn 1f out: hdd wl ins fnl f* **4/1**[3]

6 **3** ½ **Art Sale**[31] 2424 2-9-3 0... RyanMoore 15 78
(G L Moore) *racd stands' side: chsd ldrs: led that gp 1f out but 3rd overall: edgd lft and one pce ins fnl f* **3/1**[2]

0 **4** 1 ¼ **Gross Prophet**[33] 2349 2-9-3 0.................................... RichardThomas 11 73
(Tom Dascombe) *racd stands' side: chsd ldrs and ev ch 2f out tl one pce fnl f: fin 2nd in gp* **100/1**

2 **5** 1 ½ **Royal Confidence**[12] 2997 2-8-12 0................................. MichaelHills 13 63+
(B W Hills) *racd stands' side: chsd ldrs: led 2f out but nvr quite gng pce of far side: hdd 1f out: btn whn hmpd ins fnl f: fin 3rd in gp* **11/4**[1]

0 **6** *1* **Flying Applause**[46] 1970 2-9-3 0 DaneO'Neill 10 64
(A King) *chsd ldrs and c towards stands' side 1/2-way: rdn and one pce fnl f: fin 4th in gp* **25/1**

7 *1* **Mandarinka** 2-9-3 0 StephenCarson 7 61
(P Winkworth) *s.i.s: c stands' side and hdwy to chse ldrs over 2f out: wknd fnl f: fin 5th in gp* **33/1**

00 **8** *1 1/2* **Pennyspider (IRE)**[9] 3085 2-8-12 0 FergusSweeney 6 50
(M S Saunders) *racd far side and sn led overall: hdd ins fnl 2f: wknd fnl f: fin 3rd in gp* **100/1**

9 *hd* **Harry Gee** 2-9-3 0 RichardMullen 12 54
(W R Muir) *c to stands' side after 2f: towards rr tl rdn 2f out: r.o fnl f: fin 6th in gp* **40/1**

05 **10** *3/4* **Altercation**[27] 2526 2-8-12 0 DarryllHolland 1 47
(W Jarvis) *racd far side: chsd ldrs and t.k.h: outpcd over 2f out: kpt on ins fnl f: fin 4th in gp* **28/1**

326 **11** *nk* **Advertisement**[28] 2510 2-9-3 0 (b[1]) PhilipRobinson 4 51
(C G Cox) *racd far side: chsd ldrs: rdn over 2f out: wknd over 1f out: fin 5th in gp* **8/1**

12 *nk* **Rich Kid (IRE)** 2-9-3 0 RichardHughes 5 50
(R Hannon) *v.s.a: styd towards far side: mod late prog: fin 6th in gp* **18/1**

03 **13** *3/4* **Hadaf (IRE)**[34] 2337 2-9-3 0 RHills 16 47
(M P Tregoning) *racd stands' side and slt ld that gp tl narrowly hdd 2f out: wknd over 1f out: fin 7th in gp* **8/1**

14 *1* **Mandelieu (IRE)** 2-9-0 0 (b[1]) LiamJones(3) 8 43
(W J Haggas) *racd far side and chsd ldrs tl wknd ins fnl 2f: fin 7th in gp* **20/1**

05 **15** *3 1/2* **Titfer (IRE)**[16] 2885 2-9-3 0 FrancisNorton 14 31
(A W Carroll) *racd stands' side: sn outpcd: fin 8th and last in gp* **40/1**

0 **16** *16* **Mr Funshine**[12] 2977 2-9-3 0 JamesDoyle 3 —
(Mrs P N Dutfield) *bmpd s: racd far side: sn outpcd: fin 8th and last in gp* **100/1**

63.34 secs (0.84) **Going Correction** +0.225s/f (Good) **16** Ran SP% **124.9**
Speed ratings (Par 94):102,100,99,97,94 93,91,89,88,87 87,86,85,83,78 52
CSF £157.34 TOTE £17.60: £3.30, £1.50, £2.00; EX 211.50 Trifecta £202.20 Pool £284.87, 1 winning units.
Owner A S Reid **Bred** A S Reid **Trained** Radlett, Herts

FOCUS
There was a major difference of opinion amongst the jockeys as to where the best ground was and they used the whole width of the track. Eventually there was a perfect split with eight coming stands' side and eight staying far side. Although the first two home raced towards the far side, the next five all came down the nearside so it is hard to be sure whether there was a major advantage. Either way, the time was very good for a race like this and was 0.37 seconds faster than the handicap for older horses later on the card. Big improvement from the winner, but the second was 8lb below her Ascot level.

NOTEBOOK
Little Knickers, who showed a small amount of ability on her Kempton debut, a meeting at which it was impossible to come from off the pace, had no such problem here and saw her race out well. She has a speedy pedigree, but would get another furlong on this evidence and should develop into a fair sprint handicapper.
Perfect Paula(USA), totally out of her depth in the Queen Mary, was contesting her first maiden in her third outing. She had every chance over on the far side of the track, but the winner saw her race out that much better. She is obviously not anything special, but should be up to winning an ordinary maiden or nursery. (op 7-2 tchd 10-3)
Art Sale, well backed, stepped up from his Goodwood debut and emerged best of the stands'-side group, but unfortunately the front pair on the other side always had his measure. He is likely to step forward again from this and ought to find an ordinary sprint maiden before too long. (op 7-2 tchd 4-1, 9-2 in a place)
Gross Prophet, just over two lengths behind Little Knickers on his Kempton debut, like that filly had no chance in that contest given the way the track was riding on the day and ran very close to form with her here, despite racing on the opposite flank. Despite his huge price, it is probably best to give him the benefit of the doubt and there should be a small race in him judged on this performance.
Royal Confidence had every chance in the stands'-side group and though the front pair were on the opposite flank, the fact that she did not win the race on her side suggests she did not step up from her promising Salisbury debut. Nurseries may be her best option after one more run. (op 7-2)
Flying Applause showed a lot more than on his Salisbury debut and this half-brother to six winners seems to be going the right way. (op 20-1)
Advertisement Official explanation: jockey said colt suffered interference at start
Rich Kid(IRE) Official explanation: jockey said colt missed the break

3364 AVENANCE (S) STKS 5f 11y
2:45 (2:47) (Class 6) 2-Y-O **£1,943** (£578; £288; £144) **Stalls** Centre

Form RPR

0 **1** **Attribution**[12] 2984 2-9-0 0 KDarley 2 64
(K R Burke) *sn led: rdn over 2f out: hdd ent fnl f: rallied gamely: led again nr fin* **9/4**[1]

4404 **2** *nk* **Mama Leo**[40] 2152 2-8-9 0 (v[1]) StephenDonohoe 3 58
(P D Evans) *trckd ldrs: rdn to chal over 2f out: tk narrow advantage ent fnl f: no ex whn hdd nr fin* **5/1**[3]

00 **3** *6* **Planet Paradise (IRE)**[33] 2349 2-8-9 0 DaneO'Neill 4 36
(D Shaw) *t.k.h early: hld up: outpcd over 2f out: r.o ins fnl f to go 3rd fnl 50yds* **22/1**

053 **4** *1 1/2* **Sailing By**[21] 2723 2-9-0 0 (b) RyanMoore 8 36
(B R Millman) *chsd ldrs: rdn and effrt over 2f out: sn one pce* **11/4**[2]

5 *shd* **Careenya (IRE)** 2-8-9 0 JamesDoyle 5 31
(R M Beckett) *chsd ldrs: rdn wl over 2f out: one pce fr over 1f out* **6/1**

0366 **6** *1 3/4* **O'Casey (IRE)**[42] 2078 2-8-7 0 (p) MCGeran(7) 1 29
(J G M O'Shea) *w wnr: rdn over 2f out: wknd ent fnl f* **15/2**

04 **7** *2* **Little By Luck (IRE)**[10] 3065 2-8-2 0 (p) JackDean(7) 7 17
(W G M Turner) *wnt lft s: towards rr: rdn 3f out: no imp* **11/1**

8 *15* **Tombas Legacy** 2-8-11 0 JerryO'Dwyer(3) 6 —
(Mark Gillard) *squeezed out s: sn outpcd in rr* **28/1**

65.86 secs (3.36) **Going Correction** +0.225s/f (Good) **8** Ran SP% **116.3**
Speed ratings (Par 92):82,81,71,69,69 66,63,39
CSF £14.26 TOTE £3.50: £1.20, £1.70, £6.90; EX 16.90 Trifecta £368.40 Part won. Pool £518.91 - 0.40 winning units..The winner was sold to Andrew Haynes for 10,000gns. Mama Leo was claimed by K R Burke for £6,000.
Owner Joy And Valentine Feerick **Bred** Bloomsbury Stud **Trained** Middleham Moor, N Yorks

FOCUS
A pretty strong seller overall, run in a time 2.52 seconds slower than the earlier maiden. The first two pulled clear, and the future looks far from rosy for those adrift of the front pair.

NOTEBOOK
Attribution was very well backed on this step down in class from his debut, but he was forced to dig very deep to get the better of the runner-up and having the rail to run against may have made the difference, though to be fair his attitude could not be faulted. He was subsequently sold for 10,000gns at the subsequent auction, which looks very generous. (op 4-1)
Mama Leo, sporting a first-time visor, ran a lot better than on her debut at this level at Yarmouth last time. She gave the winner quite a fright too, pressing him right to the line and pulling a mile clear of the others. The trainer of the winner was impressed enough to claim her for £6,000, but she does not have much in the way of scope and there must be a danger that this performance was largely influenced by the first-time headgear. (op 7-2)
Planet Paradise(IRE), who had only managed to beat one horse in two Polytrack maidens, emerged best of the rest but the likelihood is that she achieved nothing. (tchd 20-1)
Sailing By improved for the fitting of blinkers at Windsor last time, but they did not have the same effect here. (tchd 3-1, 7-2 in places)
Careenya(IRE), a 16,000euros filly out of a winning half-sister to Caradak and Caraman, was obviously not considered to be anything special by making her debut at this level and connections were right about that. (op 5-1)

3365 LEADENT MAIDEN STKS (DIV I) 1m 2f 46y
3:15 (3:18) (Class 5) 3-Y-O+ **£2,266** (£674; £337; £168) **Stalls** Low

Form RPR

42 **1** **Fantastic Morning**[33] 2376 3-9-3 0 KDarley 8 83+
(M Johnston) *trckd ldrs: led 7f out: drvn along 2f out: forged clr appr fnl f: readily* **4/1**[3]

0-3 **2** *3 1/2* **Abyla**[30] 2455 3-8-12 0 MartinDwyer 14 69+
(M P Tregoning) *chsd ldrs: rdn over 2f out: styd on to chse wnr ins fnl f but a wl hld* **4/1**[3]

0 **3** *1* **Muqadam (IRE)**[72] 1303 3-9-3 0 RHills 7 71
(Sir Michael Stoute) *chsd ldrs: hdwy 3f out: chsd wnr ins fnl 2f but no imp: one pce and lost 2nd ins fnl f* **3/1**[2]

0 **4** *2* **Adorabella (IRE)**[19] 2766 4-9-9 0 DaneO'Neill 6 62
(A King) *sn chsng ldrs: rdn fr 3f out: styd on same pce fnl 2f* **25/1**

4-33 **5** *2* **Binocular**[68] 1412 3-9-3 71 RichardHughes 15 63
(B W Hills) *chsd ldrs: rdn and outpcd 3f out: styd on same pce fnl 2f* **11/4**[1]

00 **6** *5* **Surprise Act**[35] 2320 3-9-3 0 PaulDoe 10 53
(P R Chamings) *hdwy 6f out: drvn to press ldrs ins fnl 3f: wknd ins fnl 2f* **50/1**

0654 **7** *1 1/2* **The Tinker Man**[12] 2981 3-9-3 53 RichardSmith 5 50
(M D I Usher) *prom: chsd wnr over 3f out but nvr any ch: lost 2nd ins fnl 2f and wknd qckly* **20/1**

40 **8** *nk* **Istead Rise (IRE)**[3] 3276 3-9-3 0 FrankieMcDonald 2 49
(P A Blockley) *stdd s: bhd tl styd on fnl 2f: nvr in contention* **40/1**

66 **9** *1 3/4* **Glenisland**[19] 2763 3-8-7 0 RussellKennemore(5) 9 41
(Mrs L Williamson) *towards rr: rdn over 4f out: mod prog fr 2f out* **66/1**

0 **10** *nk* **Princess Aimee**[36] 1560 7-9-2 0 (p) HaddenFrost(7) 1 40
(D Burchell) *a towards rr* **33/1**

0-00 **11** *2* **Polish Prospect (IRE)**[12] 2998 3-8-12 50 SteveDrowne 11 36
(H S Howe) *chsd ldrs over 6f* **100/1**

006/ **12** *1* **Inchcape Rock**[19] 5670 5-9-7 40 (v) SophieDoyle(7) 16 39
(W K Goldsworthy) *t.k.h: racd wd and hung rt on bnd over 4f out: sn wknd* **33/1**

0-0 **13** *1/2* **Galloise (IRE)**[33] 2359 3-8-12 0 PhilipRobinson 13 33
(C G Cox) *led 3f: wknd fr 3f out* **25/1**

05 **14** *3 1/2* **Ravenhill Ralph (IRE)**[16] 2873 3-9-3 0 FergusSweeney 12 31
(J G M O'Shea) *a towards rr* **100/1**

60- **15** *1/2* **Dreams Jewel**[357] 2220 7-10-0 0 AdrianScholes 4 30
(C Roberts) *in tch early: sn bhd* **66/1**

00 **U** **Come On Nellie (IRE)**[16] 2873 3-8-5 0 MCGeran(7) 3 —
(J G M O'Shea) *towards rr whn clipped heels and uns rdr 7f out* **66/1**

2m 12.42s (1.42) **Going Correction** +0.225s/f (Good)
WFA 3 from 4yo+ 11lb **16** Ran SP% **120.9**
Speed ratings (Par 103):103,100,99,97,96 92,91,90,89,89 87,86,86,83,83 —
CSF £18.00 TOTE £3.70: £1.80, £1.20, £1.50; EX 19.00 Trifecta £35.10 Pool £340.55 - 6.88 winning units..
Owner Gainsborough **Bred** Gainsborough Stud Management Ltd **Trained** Middleham Moor, N Yorks

FOCUS
Plenty of dead wood in this maiden and not as competitive as the numbers would suggest. Only four of the 16 runners started at less than 25-1 and the winning time was 0.68 seconds slower than the second division. Sound maiden form. The race was dominated by those that raced handily, but the winner did it well and the front four all probably have some sort of future.
Istead Rise(IRE) ◆ Official explanation: jockey said gelding hung left-handed
Galloise(IRE) Official explanation: jockey said filly lost its action

3366 LEADENT MAIDEN STKS (DIV II) 1m 2f 46y
3:45 (3:49) (Class 5) 3-Y-O+ **£1,470** (£1,470; £337; £168) **Stalls** Low

Form RPR

4-20 **1** **Ideally (IRE)**[34] 2340 3-9-3 70 MichaelHills 1 80
(B W Hills) *sn led: rdn over 2f out: kpt on gamely u.p: jnd on line* **6/1**[3]

32 **1** *dht* **Pivotal Answer (IRE)**[9] 3113 3-8-12 0 EddieAhern 9 75
(J Noseda) *trckd ldrs: rdn 2f out: wnt 2nd and edgd lft ent fnl f: r.o strly to join ldr on line* **7/4**[1]

30 **3** *3 1/2* **Compton Falcon**[31] 2436 3-9-3 0 (t) RichardHughes 8 73
(G A Butler) *trckd ldr: rdn over 2f out: edgd lft over 1f out: kpt on same pce* **8/1**

06 **4** *1 3/4* **Esclarmonde (IRE)**[24] 2620 3-8-12 0 NickyMackay 4 65
(L M Cumani) *trckd ldrs: rdn over 2f out: kpt on same pce* **14/1**

00 **5** *2 1/2* **Kings Story (IRE)**[32] 2402 3-9-3 0 AdamKirby 10 68+
(W R Swinburn) *mid-div: outpcd over 2f out: styd on again ins fnl f* **14/1**

44 **6** *3/4* **Vincenzio (IRE)**[14] 2944 3-9-3 0 TedDurcan 14 63
(C R Egerton) *mid-div: rdn and hdwy over 2f out: wnt 4th over 1f out: one pce fnl f* **9/2**[2]

3 **7** *2 1/2* **Torba (IRE)**[62] 1560 3-8-12 0 DaneO'Neill 6 53
(Evan Williams) *mid-div: hdwy 3f out: sn rdn: one pce fr over 1f out* **6/1**[3]

8 *3/4* **Tweed River (USA)** 3-9-3 0 FrancisNorton 13 57+
(A M Balding) *s.i.s: towards rr: sme late prog but nvr a danger* **20/1**

00- **9** *1 3/4* **Always Sparkle (CAN)**[296] 5381 3-9-3 0 SteveDrowne 5 53
(B Palling) *in tch: rdn over 2f out: wknd ent fnl f* **33/1**

3-02 **10** *2 1/2* **Storm Path (IRE)**[38] 2206 3-9-3 51 StephenCarson 11 48
(Eve Johnson Houghton) *a towards rr* **20/1**

0005 **11** *8* **Fluters House**[13] 2962 3-9-3 40 StephenDonohoe 15 32
(S Woodman) *s.i.s: sn rcvrd to trck ldrs: rdn over 2f out: wknd over 1f out* **200/1**

0 **12** *1* **Pretty Posey**[16] 2873 3-8-12 0 FergusSweeney 12 25
(J G M O'Shea) *mainly towards rr* **100/1**

3 **13** *5* **Benellino**[13] 2962 4-10-0 0 SimonWhitworth 7 20
(R M Stronge) *stdd s: a towards rr* **66/1**

14 13 **Fine Edge**[32] 6-9-4 0 NicolPolli(5) 3 —
(H E Haynes) *a bhd* **100/1**

2m 11.74s (0.74) **Going Correction** +0.225s/f (Good)
WFA 3 from 4yo+ 11lb **14 Ran SP% 124.0**
Speed ratings (Par 103):106,106,103,101,99 99,97,96,95,93 86,86,82,71
, £2.50 TRIFECTA Win: I 3.80, PA 1.10; Pl I 2.40, PA 1.50; Ex I-PA 9.00, PA-I 12.30; CSF I-PA 8.33, PA-I 16.07 TF: I-PA-CF 21.60, PA-I-CF 55.40.
Owner Gainsborough **Bred** Gainsborough Stud Ltd **Trained** Lambourn, Berks
Owner Tom Ludt **Bred** Pontchartrain Stud **Trained** Newmarket, Suffolk

FOCUS
As in the first division, there was some dead wood here and again the principals were all up there from the start, but the betting suggested that this was the more competitive division and the time was 0.68 seconds quicker. The form is of a similar standard to that of division one, rated around the principals.

3367 WATERAID MAIDEN H'CAP 1m 3f 144y
4:15 (4:16) (Class 5) (0-75,75) 3-Y-0 **£2,979** (£886; £442; £221) **Stalls** Low

Form RPR

0-20 **1** **Hypoteneuse (IRE)**[19] 2766 3-9-4 **72** RyanMoore 12 81
(Sir Michael Stoute) *hld up in rr: hdwy over 4f out: drvn and styd on fr over 2f out: hung lft and led jst ins fnl f: drvn out* **9/1**

4-54 **2** 1 1/4 **Duty Free (IRE)**[18] 2801 3-9-2 **70** SteveDrowne 17 77
(H Morrison) *chsd ldr: rdn to ld jst ins fnl 2f: hdd ins fnl f: kpt on but a hld by wnr* **8/1**[3]

000 **3** 3 **Irish Quest (IRE)**[21] 2726 3-9-2 **70** PhilipRobinson 14 73
(M A Jarvis) *led tl hdd jst ins fnl 2f: outpcd fr over 1f out* **12/1**

-223 **4** 1 **Snake's Head**[23] 2666 3-9-4 **72** EddieAhern 5 73
(J L Dunlop) *chsd ldrs: rdn 3f out: one pce fnl 2f* **10/1**

000- **5** 1 **Franchoek (IRE)**[285] 5622 3-8-2 **56** DavidKinsella 7 55+
(A King) *in rr: drvn and styd on fr 3f out: kpt on wl fnl f but nvr gng pce to rch ldrs* **16/1**

605 **6** nk **Hayward's Heath**[13] 2970 3-8-5 **59** PaulFitzsimons 16 58
(B W Duke) *chsd ldrs: rdn 3f out: wknd fnl f* **66/1**

2245 **7** 3/4 **Vanquisher (IRE)**[24] 2627 3-9-7 **75** (v) TedDurcan 15 73
(W J Haggas) *slowly away and sn pushed along: rdn over 3f out: kpt on fnl 2f but nvr in contention* **5/1**[1]

0200 **8** nk **Up In Arms (IRE)**[21] 2727 3-9-0 **68** StephenCarson 9 70+
(P Winkworth) *in rr: effrt whn hmpd over 4f out: sme prog u.p fnl 2f: nvr in contention* **28/1**

003 **9** 1 1/4 **Muraco**[21] 2726 3-9-2 **70** GeorgeBaker 6 65
(R M Beckett) *sn chsng ldrs: rdn 3f out: wknd fr 2f out* **5/1**[1]

0-36 **10** 3 1/2 **Colonel Flay**[46] 1974 3-9-0 **68** JamesDoyle 13 58
(Mrs P N Dutfield) *in rr: drvn and sme hdwy fr 4f out: nvr in contention* **14/1**

606 **11** 29 **A Little More (IRE)**[50] 1863 3-8-13 **67** SimonWhitworth 4 10
(P A Blockley) *s.i.s: in rr tl sme prog 4f out: sn wknd* **33/1**

-035 **12** 1 **Baldovina**[22] 2691 3-8-9 **63** RichardThomas 2 5
(Tom Dascombe) *chsd ldrs: rdn over 3f out: sn wknd* **20/1**

0426 **13** hd **Mowadeh (IRE)**[22] 2690 3-9-4 **72** DarryllHolland 8 13
(M R Channon) *chsd ldrs tl rdn and wknd 3f out* **8/1**[3]

003 **14** 1/2 **Sister Agnes (IRE)**[22] 2690 3-9-2 **70** OscarUrbina 3 11
(J R Fanshawe) *in tch tl outpcd over 5f out: grad lost pl: eased fnl 2f* **12/1**

33-0 **15** 16 **Spartan Dance**[56] 1724 3-8-7 **61** (v[1]) MartinDwyer 11 —
(J A Geake) *a in rr* **33/1**

4-64 **16** 61 **Spice Bar**[29] 2490 3-8-8 **62** FrancisNorton 1 —
(A M Balding) *hdwy to chse ldrs 6f out: wknd qckly 4f out: eased fnl 3f: t.o* **7/1**[2]

2m 31.34s (1.04) **Going Correction** +0.225s/f (Good) **16 Ran SP% 130.7**
Speed ratings (Par 100):105,104,102,101,100 100,100,99,99,96 77,76,76,76,65 24
CSF £81.05 CT £901.73 TOTE £10.80: £3.40, £2.60, £3.20, £1.80; EX 105.90 Trifecta £262.40 Part won. Pool £369.66 - 0.49 winning units..
Owner The Queen **Bred** The Queen **Trained** Newmarket, Suffolk

FOCUS
By its very nature this was a modest race, but the form is not bad for the grade and looks pretty sound. The pace was solid enough and the principals may have a bit more to offer.
Sister Agnes(IRE) Official explanation: jockey said filly was in season
Spartan Dance Official explanation: jockey said gelding hung right-handed
Spice Bar Official explanation: vet said gelding returned lame behind

3368 GARDINERS GROUNDS MAINTENANCE H'CAP 5f 11y
4:45 (4:46) (Class 6) (0-65,63) 3-Y-0+ **£2,072** (£616; £308; £153) **Stalls** Centre

Form RPR

4650 **1** **Sands Crooner (IRE)**[21] 2712 4-9-4 **55** (v) DaneO'Neill 7 66
(D Shaw) *mid-div: hdwy over 2f out: rdn to ld ent f: drvn out* **16/1**

0012 **2** nk **Caustic Wit (IRE)**[10] 3064 9-9-11 **62** FergusSweeney 4 72
(M S Saunders) *prom: led over 2f out: rdn and hdd ent f: rallied gamely: hld nr fin* **5/1**[2]

-002 **3** 2 **Goodenough Mover**[12] 2982 11-9-9 **63** (b) RichardKingscote(3) 15 66
(Andrew Turnell) *mid-div: sn pushed along: rdn 3f out: r.o fr over 1f out: wnt 3rd ins fnl f* **10/1**

0-00 **4** nk **Summer Recluse (USA)**[29] 2494 8-9-11 **62** (t) SteveDrowne 14 64+
(J M Bradley) *towards rr: hdwy over 2f out: sn rdn: styd on fnl f* **14/1**

-054 **5** nk **Jucebabe**[12] 2982 4-9-3 **54** FrancisNorton 12 55
(J L Spearing) *t.k.h in tch: rdn over 2f out: kpt on fnl f* **8/1**[3]

6606 **6** 1 1/4 **Enjoy The Buzz**[5] 3086 8-8-13 **50** (p) StephenDonohoe 17 46
(J M Bradley) *hld up towards rr: rdn and hdwy fr 2f out: kpt on ins fnl f* **25/1**

0-00 **7** nk **Whistler**[13] 2966 10-8-13 **50** (p) PaulFitzsimons 6 45
(Miss J R Tooth) *mid-div: rdn over 2f out: styd on ins fnl f* **33/1**

0440 **8** 1 **Bold Argument (IRE)**[6] 3190 4-9-11 **62** JamesDoyle 3 53+
(Mrs P N Dutfield) *mid-div: rdn over 2f out: styng on whn hmpd ins fnl f: no further imp* **25/1**

4032 **9** nk **Luloah**[19] 2761 4-8-5 **49** (p) MCGeran(7) 11 39
(J G M O'Shea) *hld up bhd: nt clr run fr over 1f out: nvr able to chal* **20/1**

0013 **10** nk **Seven No Trumps**[32] 2386 10-9-1 **52** DarryllHolland 13 41
(J M Bradley) *prom: rdn over 2f out: one pce fr over 1f out* **10/1**

60-5 **11** hd **Peruvian Style (IRE)**[26] 2555 6-9-1 **52** EddieAhern 16 41
(J M Bradley) *towards rr: hdwy 3f out: effrt 2f out: one pce fnl f* **14/1**

0060 **12** 1 **Hello Roberto**[18] 2799 6-9-3 **57** (b) LiamJones(3) 8 42
(R A Harris) *s.i.s: a towards rr* **28/1**

0514 **13** 1/2 **Mister Incredible**[7] 3163 4-8-8 **52** (v) BarrySavage(7) 5 35
(J M Bradley) *led tl over 2f out: sn rdn: grad fdd* **16/1**

-000 **14** nk **Ballybunion (IRE)**[7] 3169 8-9-1 **52** PaulDoe 1 34+
(R A Harris) *chsd ldrs: rdn over 2f out: in tch whn hmpd ins fnl f: nt rcvr* **40/1**

2121 **15** 3/4 **Dematraf (IRE)**[3] 3277 5-8-13 **57** 6ex BernadetteQuinn(7) 2 36+
(P D Evans) *mid-div on rails: rdn over 2f out: styng on whn bdly hmpd ins fnl f: nt rcvr* **9/4**[1]

0240 **U** **Trinculo (IRE)**[9] 3106 10-8-13 **55** (p) LukeMorris(5) 9 —
(R A Harris) *uns rdr leaving stalls* **14/1**

63.71 secs (1.21) **Going Correction** +0.225s/f (Good) **16 Ran SP% 129.8**
Speed ratings (Par 101):99,98,95,94,94 92,91,90,89,89 89,87,86,86,84 —
CSF £92.77 CT £911.39 TOTE £17.60: £4.10, £1.70, £2.60, £4.10; EX 166.70 TRIFECTA Not won..
Owner Danethorpe Racing Ltd **Bred** Peter Molony **Trained** Danethorpe, Notts

FOCUS
A competitive sprint handicap in which they whole field stayed towards the far side, but the quality was poor and the winning time was 0.37 seconds slower than the opening two-year-old maiden. Straightforward form.

3369 ADECCO RECRUITMENT H'CAP 5f 161y
5:15 (5:16) (Class 5) (0-75,72) 3-Y-0 **£2,979** (£886; £442; £221) **Stalls** Centre

Form RPR

1543 **1** **Diminuto**[3] 3277 3-8-7 **65** FrankiePickard(7) 8 72
(M D I Usher) *mde all: rdn and kpt on wl fr over 1f out* **10/1**

005 **2** 1 **Nouveau (GER)**[9] 3102 3-7-11 **53** oh3 LukeMorris(5) 10 57
(R Hannon) *in rr: rdn and hdwy 2f out: r.o u.p to go 2nd ins fnl f but nvr quite gng pce to rch wnr* **14/1**

1205 **3** 1 **Scarlet Oak**[7] 3168 3-8-3 **61** BillyCray(7) 2 61
(D J S Ffrench Davis) *in rr: rdn 3f out: hdwy u.p and edgd lft over 1f out: styd on ins fnl f but nvr quite gng pce to rch ldrs* **14/1**

0016 **4** shd **Mr Forthright**[33] 2363 3-8-1 **55** LiamJones(3) 9 55
(J M Bradley) *in rr: hdwy on outside fr 2f out: styd on u.p to chse ldrs ins fnl f: sn one pce* **12/1**

2440 **5** 3/4 **Bentley**[7] 3168 3-9-0 **65** (v) DaneO'Neill 1 62
(D Shaw) *s.i.s: in rr: rdn over 2f out: kpt on ins fnl f: nt rch ldrs* **20/1**

5306 **6** 3/4 **Princess Ileana (IRE)**[16] 2895 3-8-5 **56** JamesDoyle 7 51
(K R Burke) *chsd ldrs: rdn 1/2-way: wknd fnl f* **16/1**

-110 **7** hd **No Worries Yet (IRE)**[38] 2198 3-9-1 **66** FrancisNorton 6 60
(J L Spearing) *pressed wnr: rdn over 2f out: wknd ins fnl f* **15/2**

-005 **8** 2 **Aaron's Way**[21] 2718 3-8-12 **63** SteveDrowne 3 50
(A W Carroll) *in tch: sme hdwy on ins 2f out: n.m.r over 1f out: sn btn* **10/1**

3-36 **9** 2 **Star Strider**[10] 3061 3-9-1 **71** WilliamBuick(5) 12 51
(A M Balding) *chsd ldrs: rdn over 2f out: wknd over 1f out* **9/2**[2]

4-20 **10** 3/4 **Russian Gift (IRE)**[28] 2515 3-9-4 **69** AdamKirby 4 47
(C G Cox) *in rr: effrt over 2f out: sn wknd* **6/1**[3]

20-1 **11** 18 **Maysarah (IRE)**[59] 1625 3-9-1 **66** NickyMackay 11 —
(G A Butler) *t.k.h: trckd ldrs: rdn over 2f out: sn wknd* **7/2**[1]

1m 13.48s (2.28) **Going Correction** +0.225s/f (Good) **11 Ran SP% 116.3**
Speed ratings (Par 100):93,91,90,90,89 88,87,85,82,81 57
CSF £139.84 CT £1986.26 TOTE £12.90: £3.80, £5.70, £5.30; EX 185.30 TRIFECTA Not won. Place 6 £74.94, Place 5 £42.60.
Owner R H Brookes **Bred** B Minty **Trained** Upper Lambourn, Berks
■ Stewards' Enquiry : Billy Cray caution: careless riding

FOCUS
A very moderate handicap and the winning time was modest, even for a race like this. A slight career best from Diminuto, but there are doubts over what she actually achieved.
Maysarah(IRE) Official explanation: jockey said filly stopped very quickly
T/Plt: £106.50 to a £1 stake. Pool: £70,100.90. 480.25 winning tickets. T/Qpdt: £19.80 to a £1 stake. Pool: £4,846.90. 180.60 winning tickets. TM

[2933] MUSSELBURGH (R-H)
Monday, July 9

OFFICIAL GOING: Good (good to soft in places; 7.8)
Wind: Slight across Weather: Sunny

3370 GUINNESS MEDIAN AUCTION MAIDEN STKS 5f
2:30 (2:30) (Class 6) 2-Y-0 **£2,590** (£770; £385; £192) **Stalls** High

Form RPR

2423 **1** **Fol Hollow (IRE)**[9] 3092 2-9-3 0 AdrianTNicholls 5 84
(D Nicholls) *chsd ldrs: swtchd rt and gd hdwy to ld 2f out: rdn clr ent fnl f* **5/2**[1]

632 **2** 2 1/2 **Rievaulx Valentino**[17] 2818 2-9-3 0 DO'Donohoe 2 75+
(K A Ryan) *in tch and sn rdn along: hdwy 2f out: styd on ins fnl f* **3/1**[2]

34 **3** 3 **Rocheport**[27] 2532 2-9-3 0 TomEaves 6 64
(J Howard Johnson) *cl up: ev ch 2f out: sn rdn and kpt on same pce 1f out* **12/1**

2332 **4** 3/4 **Shatter Resistant (IRE)**[15] 2911 2-9-3 0 DavidAllan 3 62
(M R Channon) *cl up: ev ch 2f out: sn rdn and wknd appr fnl f* **13/2**

052 **5** 1 1/2 **Grudge**[42] 2071 2-9-3 0 PatCosgrave 8 56
(D W Barker) *led: rdn along and hdd 2f out: grad wknd* **14/1**

5430 **6** 3/4 **La Guancha**[1] 3341 2-8-9 0 ow2 PJMcDonald(5) 7 50
(D A Nolan) *in tch: rdn along 1/2-way: no imp* **100/1**

7 3/4 **Wild Bill Tracey** 2-9-3 0 JamieSpencer 4 51
(M J Wallace) *s.i.s: rdn along and sme hdwy 1/2-way: m green and hung rt 2f out: nvr a factor* **7/2**[3]

000 **8** 6 **Woodford**[16] 2888 2-9-3 0 PaulMulrennan 9 29
(M W Easterby) *sn rdn along: a in rr* **200/1**

0 **U** **Mill Creek**[41] 2115 2-8-9 0 MarkLawson(3) 1 —
(B Smart) *bucked and uns rdr shortly after s* **18/1**

61.90 secs (1.40) **Going Correction** +0.175s/f (Good) **9 Ran SP% 113.1**
Speed ratings (Par 92):95,91,86,85,82 81,80,70,—
CSF £9.86 TOTE £3.60: £1.20, £1.70, £2.30; EX 11.40.
Owner Middleham Park Racing Iii **Bred** Dan O'Brien **Trained** Sessay, N Yorks

FOCUS
An ordinary juvenile maiden. The form is not easy assess with everything bar the winner and the last horse below par, and the form could worth 6lb more.

NOTEBOOK
Fol Hollow(IRE) finally gained reward for a string of consistent efforts and broke his duck at the sixth time of asking. He came right away from his rivals inside the final furlong, and should be high on confidence now, so may have a little more to offer when switching to a nursery. However, considering he had been placed on all but one of his previous outings, the Handicapper will likely know all about him. (op 7-2)
Rievaulx Valentino could not cope with the winner's turn of foot and was always held by that rival. He still finished a clear second best, however, and did more than enough to suggest he is now ready for a sixth furlong. (tchd 11-4 and 10-3 in places)
Rocheport was ridden positively and had every chance on this drop back to the minimum trip. He looks more of a nursery type and can get closer again when returned to a sixth furlong. (op 8-1 tchd 9-1)

Shatter Resistant(IRE) showed early dash before dropping out tamely entering the final furlong. This was the first time he has finished out of the first three in seven starts, but he is fully exposed now and probably needs to drop into plating company to get off the mark. (op 6-1 tchd 7-1)

Grudge Official explanation: jockey said colt hung left-handed throughout

Wild Bill Tracey, a May foal related to winners over further, was never a factor after falling out of the gates and proved very green. He was popular in the betting for this racecourse bow and is presumably thought capable of a lot better. Official explanation: jockey said colt ran green throughout and hung right in final furlong (op 3-1)

3371 WILLIAM HILL H'CAP — 1m 6f

3:00 (3:01) (Class 5) (0-70,70) 4-Y-0+ — **£3,238** (£963; £481; £240) **Stalls** High

Form — RPR

324 **1** — **Artless (USA)**[36] 2274 4-9-7 **70** .... PaulMulrennan 8 — 81+
(Sir Mark Prescott) *trckd ldng pair: hdwy over 4f out: rdn to ld over 2f out: clr over 1f out: kpt on wl* — **7/2**[2]

0-05 **2** *1* — **Nimra (USA)**[24] 2620 4-9-7 **70** ....(b[1]) DavidAllan 9 — 80
(G A Butler) *in tch: hdwy to trck ldrs over 4f out: rdn and n.m.r on inner 2f out: sn swtchd lft and chsd wnr ins fnl f: styd on wl towards fin* — **14/1**

414 **3** *6* — **Cotton Eyed Joe (IRE)**[12] 2987 6-9-7 **70** .... JamieSpencer 2 — 72
(G A Swinbank) *hld up in rr: hdwy 3f out: rdn wl over 1f out: kpt on ins fnl f: nrst fin* — **9/4**[1]

2255 **4** *½* — **Danzatrice**[17] 2824 5-8-12 **61** .... TomEaves 5 — 62
(C W Thornton) *trckd ldrs: effrt 3f out and sn rdn along: drvn wl over 1f out and plugged on same pce* — **9/2**[3]

50-6 **5** *5* — **Red Sun**[11] 3012 10-8-9 **58** ....(t) PaulEddery 3 — 52
(R C Guest) *cl up: led 5f out: rdn along and hdd over 2f out: sn drvn and grad wknd* — **25/1**

62-0 **6** *1 ¼* — **Rossin Gold (IRE)**[15] 2764 5-8-2 **51** oh6........ DO'Donohoe 11 — 43
(P Monteith) *hld up: hdwy over 3f out: rdn along to chse ldrs 2f out: sn drvn and wknd* — **10/1**

0-13 **7** *5* — **Fenners (USA)**[34] 2342 4-9-2 **65** .... DaleGibson 10 — 50
(M W Easterby) *trckd ldrs: rdn along 3f out: drvn over 2f out and sn wknd* — **7/2**[2]

0-00 **8** *7* — **On Every Street**[17] 2825 6-7-13 **51** oh6........(v) DuranFentiman(3) 4 — 26
(R Bastiman) *hld up: a in rr* — **80/1**

0-20 **9** *53* — **Slavonic (USA)**[26] 2563 6-8-1 **53** oh1 ow2........(p) AndrewMullen(3) 7 — —
(B Storey) *led: rdn along and hdd 5f out: sn wknd* — **50/1**

3m 5.44s (-0.26) **Going Correction** +0.175s/f (Good) — **9** Ran SP% **116.2**

Speed ratings (Par 103):107,106,103,102,99 99,96,92,62

CSF £49.96 CT £133.26 TOTE £4.70: £1.60, £3.20, £1.20; EX 39.20.

Owner Dr Catherine Wills **Bred** Dr Catherine Wills **Trained** Newmarket, Suffolk

■ Stewards' Enquiry : Paul Eddery caution: careless riding

FOCUS

A modest staying handicap, run at an uneven gallop. The idling winner is value for further than the bare margin, with the second back to form in the blinkers, the pair clear.

Slavonic(USA) Official explanation: jockey said gelding lost its action

3372 RAILS BOOKMAKERS MEDIAN AUCTION MAIDEN STKS — 7f 30y

3:30 (3:31) (Class 6) 3-5-Y-0 — **£2,266** (£674; £337; £168) **Stalls** High

Form — RPR

5-00 **1** — **Tommy Tobougg**[52] 1804 3-9-3 65........ TomEaves 5 — 54
(I Semple) *chsd ldng pair: hdwy 3f out: rdn to ld wl over 1f out: drvn ins fnl f and kpt on* — **4/1**[2]

/500 **2** *2* — **Sydneyroughdiamond**[24] 2622 5-9-11 37........(b) ChrisCatlin 7 — 52
(M Mullineaux) *cl up: rdn along 3f out: ev ch 2f out and sn drvn: kpt on gamely ins fnl f* — **33/1**

0-55 **3** *shd* — **Takanewa (IRE)**[21] 2711 4-9-6 48........ PaulMulrennan 9 — 47
(J Howard Johnson) *led: rdn along 3f out: drvn 2f out: sn hdd: no ex ins fnl f* — **6/1**

4 *3* — **Papa's Princess** 3-8-5 0........ GaryBartley(7) 2 — 36
(J S Goldie) *bhd tl styd on fr over 2f out: fin wl* — **16/1**

0-34 **5** *1* — **Sparky Vixen**[49] 1894 3-8-12 56........ PatCosgrave 3 — 33
(G A Swinbank) *in tch: hdwy over 3f out: rdn along to chse ldrs over 2f out: sn drvn and no imp* — **9/2**[3]

-003 **6** *5* — **Ivana Illyich (IRE)**[10] 3051 5-9-6 49........ PaddyAspell 1 — 22
(J S Wainwright) *in tch: rdn along 3f out: no imp* — **25/1**

-652 **7** *½* — **Risque Heights**[11] 3032 3-9-3 67........(b) JamieSpencer 6 — 35
(G A Butler) *s.i.s: hdwy 4f out: rdn over 3f out: drvn over 2f out: nt rch ldrs: btn and eased over 1f out* — **5/4**[1]

60 **8** *24* — **Harts In Mo Shun (IRE)**[45] 2012 3-8-12 0........(b[1]) PBradley(5) 4 — —
(A Berry) *t.k.h: a in rr* — **50/1**

1m 32.14s (2.20) **Going Correction** +0.175s/f (Good)

WFA 3 from 4yo+ 8lb — **8** Ran SP% **111.5**

Speed ratings (Par 101):94,91,91,88,87 81,80,53

CSF £114.36 TOTE £5.70: £1.60, £6.40, £1.70; EX 120.50.

Owner Northmore Stud **Bred** Elsdon Farms **Trained** Carluke, S Lanarks

FOCUS

A very weak maiden. The placed horses sum up the low level of the form.

Risque Heights Official explanation: jockey said gelding lost its action and hung badly right throughout

Harts In Mo Shun(IRE) Official explanation: jockey said gelding lost its action

3373 STRATSTONE LANDROVER NURSERY — 7f 30y

4:00 (4:00) (Class 5) 2-Y-0 — **£3,238** (£963; £481; £240) **Stalls** High

Form — RPR

41 **1** — **Apollo Shark (IRE)**[20] 2739 2-9-0 **75**........ TomEaves 6 — 83+
(J Howard Johnson) *t.k.h: led 1f: cl up: rdn to ld over 1f out: styd on strly* — **5/4**[1]

030 **2** *4* — **Suite Francaise**[19] 2768 2-7-13 **60**........ AdrianMcCarthy 4 — 58
(Sir Mark Prescott) *sn pushed along to ld after 1f: rdn along over 2f out: drvn and hdd over 1f out: wknd ins fnl f* — **9/4**[2]

001 **3** *2 ½* — **Allahor**[11] 3024 2-8-12 **78**........ PBradley(5) 3 — 70
(A Berry) *trckd ldrs: hdwy 3f out: rdn along wl over 1f out and sn no imp* — **11/2**[3]

600 **4** *½* — **Dhaka Dazzle**[46] 1963 2-8-1 **62**........ ChrisCatlin 5 — 53
(M R Channon) *in rr: hdwy on outer wl over 2f out: sn rdn and kpt on u.p ins fnl f: nrst fin* — **8/1**

6345 **5** *2 ½* — **Varinia (IRE)**[50] 1858 2-7-13 **67**........ PatrickDonaghy(7) 1 — 52
(M Brittain) *chsd ldng pair: rdn along wl over 2f out: sn drvn and one pce* — **14/1**

1m 32.86s (2.92) **Going Correction** +0.175s/f (Good) — **5** Ran SP% **108.4**

Speed ratings (Par 94):90,85,82,82,79

CSF £4.12 TOTE £1.90: £1.10, £1.50; EX 4.70.

Owner Transcend Bloodstock LLP **Bred** Churchtown House Stud **Trained** Billy Row, Co Durham

FOCUS

Due to abandoned meetings this was the first nursery of the current season, and the official ratings shown next to each horse are estimated and for information purposes only. The winner did the job nicely and is progressive but this was a weak race of its type.

NOTEBOOK

Apollo Shark(IRE), despite taking time to settle, followed up his Thirsk maiden success 20 days previously on this nursery bow and ultimately did the job comfortably. He will get an extra furlong and is clearly progressive, but the Handicapper will have his say now all the same. (op 11-8 tchd 6-4 in places)

Suite Francaise, making her nursery debut after the mandatory three outings in maiden company, showed improved form under a positive ride yet was eventually firmly put in her place by the winner. She was nicely clear in second and, still learning her trade, can find a winning opportunity when upped to 1m. (op 7-4 tchd 5-2 in places)

Allahor, off the mark on easy ground at Newcastle 11 days previously, travelled nicely enough until appearing to run out of stamina over this extra furlong. (tchd 5-1 and 6-1)

Dhaka Dazzle, who showed just moderate form in three previous outings in maidens, failed to raise his game for the step up in distance and is not a betting proposition at present. (op 11-1)

3374 RACECOURSE BOOKMAKERS LE GARCON D'OR H'CAP — 5f

4:30 (4:30) (Class 4) (0-80,76) 3-Y-0+ — **£5,181** (£1,541; £770; £384) **Stalls** High

Form — RPR

3220 **1** — **Rothesay Dancer**[1] 3347 4-8-0 **57** oh3........ KellyHarrison(7) 6 — 66+
(J S Goldie) *hld up: gd hdwy 2f out: rdn to chal ent fnl f: kpt on to ld fnl 100yds* — **5/1**[2]

5603 **2** *nk* — **Ptarmigan Ridge**[11] 3014 11-9-3 **67**........ DO'Donohoe 3 — 75
(Miss L A Perratt) *trckd ldrs: hdwy to chal 2f out: rdn to ld wl over 1f out: drvn ins fnl f: hdd and nt qckn fnl 100yds* — **5/1**[2]

1200 **3** *1 ¾* — **Compton Classic**[1] 3347 5-8-7 **64**........ GaryBartley(7) 8 — 66
(J S Goldie) *chsd ldrs: hdwy 2f out: sn rdn and kpt on fnl f* — **11/2**[3]

5331 **4** *½* — **Tilly's Dream**[14] 2933 4-9-6 **73**........ AndrewMullen(3) 1 — 73
(Miss K B Boutflower) *in tch: hdwy on outer 2f out: sn rdn and kpt on same pce ins fnl f* — **5/1**[2]

04-4 **5** *1* — **Sea Salt**[15] 2912 4-9-12 **76**........ DaleGibson 9 — 73+
(R A Fahey) *a.p: rdn along 2f out: styd on u.p ins fnl f* — **7/2**[1]

1162 **6** *1 ¼* — **Darcy's Pride (IRE)**[10] 3054 3-9-2 **71**........ TomEaves 4 — 61
(D W Barker) *prom: rdn along 2f out: sn drvn and grad wknd* — **7/1**

00-0 **7** *½* — **Mutayam**[17] 2830 7-8-9 **64** oh12 ow7........(t) PJMcDonald(5) 11 — 54?
(D A Nolan) *a in rr* — **150/1**

0004 **8** *nk* — **Toy Top (USA)**[14] 2933 4-8-9 **59**........(b) PaulMulrennan 5 — 48
(M Dods) *sn led: rdn along 2f out: sn hdd & wknd ins fnl f* — **8/1**

0000 **9** *1* — **Mister Marmaduke**[6] 3184 6-8-5 **60** oh12 ow3... MichaelJStainton(5) 10 — 46?
(D A Nolan) *a in rr* — **150/1**

-000 **10** *5* — **Alfie Lee (IRE)**[37] 2249 10-8-4 **57** oh12........(t) GregFairley(3) 2 — 25?
(D A Nolan) *chsd ldrs: rdn along 1/2-way: sn wknd* — **200/1**

60.79 secs (0.29) **Going Correction** +0.175s/f (Good)

WFA 3 from 4yo+ 5lb — **10** Ran SP% **113.0**

Speed ratings (Par 105):104,103,100,99,98 96,95,95,93,85

CSF £29.38 CT £140.61 TOTE £5.10: £2.10, £1.50, £2.60; EX 37.30.

Owner Highland Racing **Bred** Frank Brady **Trained** Uplawmoor, E Renfrews

FOCUS

A modest sprint. The first pair came clear and the form looks straightforward enough among the principals, although the three no-hopers were not beaten that far from a long way out of the weights.

3375 LADBROKES H'CAP — 7f 30y

5:00 (5:01) (Class 6) (0-65,62) 4-Y-0+ — **£2,266** (£674; £337; £168) **Stalls** High

Form — RPR

5030 **1** — **Attacca**[11] 3034 6-8-7 **48**........ DO'Donohoe 13 — 57
(J R Weymes) *chsd ldng pair: swtchd ins over 2f out: swtchd lft 2f out: rdn to ld wl over 1f out: drvn ins fnl f and kpt on* — **11/1**

6604 **2** *½* — **Digital**[11] 3017 10-9-2 **57**........ ChrisCatlin 4 — 65
(M R Channon) *hld up in rr: hdwy whn nt clr run 2f out: swtchd lft wl over 1f out: styd onstrly ins fnl f* — **6/1**

-010 **3** *1 ½* — **Barataria**[21] 2714 5-9-3 **58**........ PaulMulrennan 6 — 62
(R Bastiman) *hld up in rr: gd hdwy whn n.m.r 2f out: sn swtchd lft and rdn: styd on wl fnl f* — **12/1**

0-00 **4** *hd* — **Rondo**[14] 2937 4-8-3 **47**........ AndrewMullen(3) 8 — 50
(T D Barron) *in tch: hdwy over 3f out: chsd ldrs whn n.m.r 2f out: sn rdn and kpt on ins fnl f* — **5/1**[2]

4020 **5** *1* — **Shadow Jumper (IRE)**[11] 3017 6-8-2 **46**........(v) DominicFox(3) 11 — 46
(J T Stimpson) *cl up: rdn along over 2f out: drvn wl over 1f out and grad wknd* — **25/1**

0-51 **6** *½* — **Bold Haze**[21] 2711 5-8-12 **58**........(v) MichaelJStainton(5) 14 — 57+
(Miss S E Hall) *trckd ldrs: hdwy and ev ch whn nt clr run on inner over 2f out and again over 1f out: kpt on ins fnl f* — **4/1**[1]

0052 **7** *1 ¼* — **Sands Of Barra (IRE)**[17] 2827 4-9-2 **62**........(p) PJMcDonald(5) 1 — 58
(I W McInnes) *in tch: hdwy whn n.m.r 2f out: sn rdn and hung rt ins fnl f: no imp* — **9/1**

04-2 **8** *1 ½* — **Dulce Sueno**[14] 2937 4-8-10 **51**........ TomEaves 12 — 43
(I Semple) *led: rdn along 3f out: drvn 2f out: sn hdd & wknd* — **11/2**[3]

-034 **9** *¾* — **Pay Time**[17] 2842 8-9-0 **58**........(t) DuranFentiman(3) 10 — 48
(R E Barr) *chsd ldrs: rdn along over 2f out: solon drvn and wknd over 1f out* — **14/1**

30-0 **10** *1 ¾* — **Newsround**[60] 1596 5-8-6 **47**........(b) DaleGibson 2 — 32
(D W Chapman) *s.i.s: a in rr* — **20/1**

6610 **11** *½* — **Guadaloup**[6] 3195 5-8-3 **51**........ PatrickDonaghy(7) 9 — 34
(M Brittain) *nvr bttr than midfield* — **10/1**

-005 **12** *½* — **Bayberry King (USA)**[10] 3052 4-8-8 **49**........ JamieSpencer 7 — 31
(J S Goldie) *s.i.s: a in rr* — **18/1**

0-00 **13** *2* — **Crosby Hall**[58] 1675 4-8-6 **50**........(t) GregFairley(3) 3 — 27
(N Tinkler) *chsd ldrs: rdn along wl over 2f out and sn wknd* — **50/1**

1m 31.6s (1.66) **Going Correction** +0.175s/f (Good) — **13** Ran SP% **124.0**

Speed ratings (Par 101):97,96,94,94,93 92,91,89,88,86 86,85,83

CSF £77.06 CT £855.58 TOTE £11.50: £3.30, £2.90, £4.60; EX 107.10.

Owner High Moor Racing 2 **Bred** Pigeon House Stud **Trained** Middleham Moor, N Yorks

■ Stewards' Enquiry : D O'Donohoe two-day ban: careless riding (Jul 20-21)

FOCUS

A moderate handicap, and fairly sound form, although plenty were hampered at around the 2f marker.

Attacca Official explanation: trainer's rep could offer no explanation regarding apparent improvement in form

Bold Haze Official explanation: jockey said gelding was denied a clear run

Newsround Official explanation: jockey said gelding hung right-handed in straight

3376 COUNTRY REFRESHMENTS H'CAP 1m

5:30 (5:31) (Class 6) (0-65,65) 3-Y-0+ **£2,590** (£770; £385; £192) **Stalls** High

Form RPR

0000 **1** **Drink To Me Only**[11] [3017] 4-9-1 **45**.................................. ChrisCatlin 12 56
(J R Weymes) *hld up towards rr on inner: swtchd outside and hdwy wl over 2f out: rdn to chal over 1f out: drvn and kpt on ins fnl f to ld fnl 100yds* **33/1**

-033 **2** *hd* **Emperor's Well**[6] [3195] 8-9-7 **51**..................................(b) PaulMulrennan 7 62
(M W Easterby) *trckd ldrs gng wl: smooth hdwy over 2f out: led over 1f out: rdn ins fnl f: hdd and no ex fnl 100yds* **7/2**[2]

5054 **3** *shd* **Kirkby's Treasure**[12] [2985] 9-10-0 **58**.............................. JamieSpencer 14 68
(G A Swinbank) *dwlt: hld up in rr: hdwy over 2f out: swtchd rt and rdn ent fnl f: sn drvn and styd on wl* **5/2**[1]

0003 **4** *4* **Ho Pang Yau**[26] [2563] 9-8-12 **49**......................................(p) GaryBartley(7) 1 50
(J S Goldie) *bhd: hdwy 3f out: rdn wl over 1f out: styd on ins fnl f: nrst fin* **33/1**

5-2 **5** *nk* **Linden's Lady**[14] [2938] 7-9-2 **46**......................................(v) DO'Donohoe 11 46
(J R Weymes) *in tch: hdwy 3f out: effrt 2f out: sn rdn and n.m.r ent fnl f: kpt on u.p* **7/1**[3]

0533 **6** *shd* **Borodinsky**[20] [2741] 6-9-3 **50**.. DuranFentiman(3) 4 50
(R E Barr) *midfield: hdwy 3f out: rdn to chse ldrs 2f out: sn drvn and kpt on same pce* **14/1**

6004 **7** *5* **Cottam Eclipse**[14] [2937] 6-8-8 **45**..................................... NeilBrown(7) 10 34
(I W McInnes) *chsd ldrs: rdn along 3f out: drvn over 2f out and grad wknd over 1f out* **14/1**

05-0 **8** *nk* **Domesday (UAE)**[11] [3012] 6-8-12 **45**.............................. DominicFox(3) 9 33
(W G Harrison) *bhd tl sme late hdwy* **150/1**

2-04 **9** *½* **Akiyama (IRE)**[20] [2740] 3-9-12 **65**... TomEaves 8 52
(J Howard Johnson) *in tch on inner: effrort 3f out: rdn along over 2f out and sn btn* **9/1**

0050 **10** *1* **Time To Regret**[6] [3194] 7-9-9 **58**..................................(p) PJMcDonald(5) 13 43
(I W McInnes) *prom: led 1/2-way: rdn along over 2f out: drvn and hdd wl over 1f out: wknd* **12/1**

5034 **11** *1 ¼* **Anthemion (IRE)**[17] [2827] 10-9-10 **57**......................... AndrewMullen(3) 2 39
(Mrs J C McGregor) *led to 1/2-way: cl up tl rdn along over 2f out and grad wknd* **14/1**

0450 **12** *4* **Bandos**[14] [2937] 7-9-2 **46**... PatCosgrave 3 18
(M Smith) *cl up: rdn along 3f out: drvn over 2f out and sn wknd* **25/1**

0050 **13** *16* **Jordans Spark**[17] [2820] 6-9-1 **45**..............................(b) AdrianMcCarthy 6 —
(P Monteith) *a towards rr* **20/1**

00-0 **14** *2 ½* **Double Precedent**[70] [1361] 3-8-3 **45**................................ GregFairley(3) 5 —
(M Johnston) *in tch: effrt over 3f out: sn rdn along and wknd* **16/1**

1m 43.04s (0.54) **Going Correction** +0.175s/f (Good)
WFA 3 from 4yo+ 9lb **14** Ran SP% **122.0**
Speed ratings (Par 101):104,103,103,99,99 99,94,94,93,92 91,87,71,68
CSF £142.95 CT £424.90 TOTE £25.50: £4.70, £2.00, £1.30; EX 195.60 Place 6 £ 89.81, Place 5 £ 57.1.
Owner Lovely Bubbly Racing **Bred** Mrs Deborah O'Brien **Trained** Middleham Moor, N Yorks
■ Stewards' Enquiry : Chris Catlin one-day ban: careless riding (Jul 29)

FOCUS
Another weak handicap, run at a sound enough pace. The first three came clear in a bobbing finish and the form seems sound enough.
Linden's Lady Official explanation: jockey said mare was denied a clear run
Akiyama(IRE) Official explanation: jockey said gelding was denied a clear run
T/Plt: £169.00 to a £1 stake. Pool: £70,051.55. 302.45 winning tickets. T/Qpdt: £48.00 to a £1 stake. Pool: £3,453.90. 53.20 winning tickets. JR

2803 RIPON (R-H)

Monday, July 9

OFFICIAL GOING: Heavy
After a downpour and 8mm rain at lunchtime the ground was 'very heavy, holding, desperate conditions'.
Wind: light 1/2 behind Weather: Fine, dry and warm

3377 MARKET PLACE (S) STKS 1m 1f 170y

6:55 (6:57) (Class 6) 3-Y-0 **£2,730** (£806; £403) **Stalls** High

Form RPR

4646 **1** **Danalova**[38] [2223] 3-8-7 41.. PaulFessey 11 49
(R A Fahey) *trckd ldrs: led 3f out: rdr lost whip: edgd rt ins fnl f: hld on wl* **15/2**

5-04 **2** *¾* **Bret Maverick (IRE)**[19] [2763] 3-8-12 57..................... GrahamGibbons 12 52
(J R Weymes) *chsd ldrs: hrd rdn and kpt on to take 2nd ins fnl f: no ex* **4/1**[1]

3040 **3** *2 ½* **Irish Relative (IRE)**[18] [2796] 3-8-12 48............................ PhillipMakin 13 47
(T D Barron) *w ldrs: led 7f out tl 3f out: one pce* **5/1**[2]

0300 **4** *½* **Colditz (IRE)**[6] [3181] 3-8-12 56....................................(p) JoeFanning 4 46
(D W Barker) *w ldrs: hung rt thrght: styd on same pce fnl 2f* **4/1**[1]

66-3 **5** *2 ½* **Ellies Faith**[41] [2116] 3-8-7 45.................................... SilvestreDeSousa 6 36
(N Bycroft) *sn prom: edgd rt and one pce fnl 2f* **6/1**[3]

0602 **6** *4* **Little Nipper**[3] [3257] 3-8-12 45.....................................(p) HayleyTurner 1 33
(W J H Ratcliffe) *in rr: sme hdwy 3f out: nvr nr ldrs* **6/1**[3]

000- **7** *3* **Soundasapound**[227] [6576] 3-8-4 40.......................... AndrewElliott(3) 8 22
(I W McInnes) *mid-div: drvn 4f out: sn btn* **80/1**

0004 **8** *5* **Play Straight**[26] [2557] 3-8-2 40............................... NataliaGemelova(5) 9 12
(I W McInnes) *in rr: hdwy over 3f out: lost pl 2f out* **33/1**

-000 **9** *nk* **Shotley Mac**[17] [2840] 3-8-12 43.. DeanMcKeown 7 16
(N Bycroft) *led tl 7f out: wl lft over 3f out: lost pl over 2f out* **33/1**

-060 **10** *20* **Xaar Too Busy**[21] [2713] 3-8-7 50...(v) MickyFenton 2 —
(Mrs A Duffield) *in tch: lost pl over 2f out: sn bhd and eased* **14/1**

-005 **11** *13* **Hillside Smoki (IRE)**[15] [2909] 3-8-2 20........................ KevinGhunowa(5) 5 —
(A Berry) *in tch: hung bdly lft over 3f out: sn lost pl and bhd* **100/1**

-606 **12** *40* **Inflagrantedelicto (USA)**[87] [1030] 3-8-12 50..........(p) AdrianTNicholls 10 —
(D W Chapman) *sn wl bhd: t.o 7f out: virtually p.u* **22/1**

2m 14.87s (9.87) **Going Correction** +0.80s/f (Soft) **12** Ran SP% **116.1**
Speed ratings (Par 98):92,91,89,89,87 83,81,77,77,61 50,18
CSF £35.59 TOTE £10.40: £2.80, £1.50, £2.50; EX 51.90.There was no bid for the winner
Owner Galaxy Racing **Bred** Cheveley Park Stud Ltd **Trained** Musley Bank, N Yorks
■ Stewards' Enquiry : Graham Gibbons three-day ban: used whip with excessive frequency (Jul 22-24)

FOCUS
A rock-bottom seller rated through the third, with an improved effort from the winner.
Inflagrantedelicto(USA) Official explanation: jockey said gelding was never travelling

3378 RIPON SPA HOTEL CENTENARY MAIDEN AUCTION FILLIES' STKS 5f

7:25 (7:26) (Class 5) 2-Y-0 **£3,238** (£963; £481; £240) **Stalls** High

Form RPR

1 **Cheshire Rose** 2-8-4 0... PaulFessey 1 77+
(T D Barron) *mde all: drvn clr over 1f out: eased nr fin* **7/1**

0 **2** *5* **Best Suited**[12] [2984] 2-8-4 0... GrahamGibbons 4 59
(J J Quinn) *chsd wnr: kpt on to take 2nd ins fnl f* **4/1**[1]

5 **3** *1* **Revue Princess (IRE)**[44] [2021] 2-8-7 0.................................. DavidAllan 6 58
(T D Easterby) *chsd wnr: kpt on same pce fnl 2f* **4/1**[1]

6554 **4** *nk* **Turn And River (IRE)**[19] [2758] 2-8-4 0........................ AdrianTNicholls 7 54
(M Brittain) *sn chsng ldrs: edgd lft 2f out: kpt on same pce* **13/2**[3]

5 **5** *½* **Avian Flew**[11] [3030] 2-8-2 0 ow3.................................. KevinGhunowa(5) 9 56
(J A Pickering) *chsd ldrs: outpcd 2f out: kpt on ins fnl f* **16/1**

0 **6** *14* **Wizzy Izzy (IRE)**[100] [845] 2-8-10 0...................................... PhillipMakin 8 8
(N Wilson) *in rr: effrt over 2f out: sn lost pl and bhd* **22/1**

0 **7** *10* **Filthygorgeous (IRE)**[20] [2739] 2-8-7 0.................................. JoeFanning 3 —
(J R Weymes) *sn hopelessly detached in last: t.o 2f out* **33/1**

4 **8** *3 ½* **Erin Thomas (IRE)**[18] [2797] 2-8-4 0.. TPO'Shea 2 —
(M G Quinlan) *sn chsng ldrs: lost pl over 1f out: sn bhd* **5/1**[2]

64.16 secs (3.96) **Going Correction** +0.80s/f (Soft) **8** Ran SP% **95.7**
Speed ratings (Par 91):100,92,90,89,89 66,50,45
CSF £24.08 TOTE £6.20: £2.30, £1.30, £1.90; EX 18.60.
Owner D C Rutter P J Huntbach **Bred** Northcombe Stud **Trained** Maunby, N Yorks
■ Coffee Cup was withdrawn (4/1, refused to enter stalls.) R4 applies, deduct 20p in the £.

FOCUS
A very decent winning time for the type of contest given the conditions. They looked a weak bunch beforehand but take nothing away from the winner, although the bad ground tempers enthusiasm for the form.

NOTEBOOK
Cheshire Rose, a February foal, half-sister to useful sprinter Peopleton Brook, has size and scope. Worst drawn, she knew her job and came right away, value for at least eight lengths. (op 8-1)
Best Suited, a moderate walker, improved on her debut effort and will be suited by a step up to six. (op 6-1)
Revue Princess(IRE), absent for six weeks, still looks on the immature side. She will improve further given more time. (op 11-2)
Turn And River(IRE), easily the most experienced in the line-up, looks to have lost her chance of winning outside claiming or selling company. (op 6-1)
Avian Flew, last of five on her debut, looks as though she needs a step up to 6f. (op 14-1)
Erin Thomas(IRE) dropped right out and seemed unsuited by the testing conditions. Official explanation: jockey said filly was unsuited by the heavy ground (op 7-2)

3379 WORK INTERIORS H'CAP 1m 4f 10y

7:55 (7:55) (Class 5) (0-75,74) 3-Y-0 **£5,181** (£1,541; £770; £384) **Stalls** High

Form RPR

4131 **1** **Bollin Felix**[7] [3159] 3-9-0 **67** 6ex.......................................(b) DavidAllan 3 80+
(T D Easterby) *trckd ldrs: rdn to ld over 2f out: clr over 1f out: eased towards fin* **10/11**[1]

534 **2** *7* **Music Review**[17] [2840] 3-8-12 **65**.................................... JamieSpencer 4 68
(R A Fahey) *hld up in rr: hdwy 7f out: wnt 2nd over 1f out: no ch w wnr* **12/1**

0006 **3** *1 ½* **Pagan Starprincess**[18] [2793] 3-8-0 **56** ow1................. AndrewElliott(3) 9 57
(G M Moore) *led 2f: w ldr: led over 3f out: hdd over 2f out: kpt on same pce* **14/1**

0000 **4** *5* **Firestorm (IRE)**[17] [2840] 3-8-2 **55** oh10..............................(b) PaulFessey 6 49
(C W Fairhurst) *bhd and pushed along: hdwy over 4f out: nvr trbld ldrs* **80/1**

01-0 **5** *6* **Act Sirius (IRE)**[52] [1827] 3-9-7 **74**.. MickyFenton 10 60
(J Howard Johnson) *in rr and sn pushed along: kpt on fnl 2f: nvr a factor* **25/1**

4-13 **6** *2* **Ballet Boy (IRE)**[18] [2801] 3-9-3 **70**..................................... PatCosgrave 8 53
(Sir Mark Prescott) *led after 2f: rdn 4f out: hdd over 3f out: wknd 2f out* **3/1**[2]

5322 **7** *3 ½* **Honorable Love**[18] [2808] 3-9-4 **71**...................................... PhillipMakin 1 49
(M Dods) *trckd ldrs: quite keen: lost pl over 2f out* **7/1**[3]

4065 **8** *13* **Leprechaun's Gold (IRE)**[6] [3182] 3-8-2 **55**........................ JoeFanning 5 15
(M Johnston) *in rr: hdwy 8f out: lost pl over 2f out: sn bhd* **16/1**

0005 **9** *1* **Foxxy**[7] [3159] 3-7-11 **55** oh3... ColinHaddon(5) 2 13
(J R Norton) *in rr: bhd fnl 3f* **33/1**

2m 43.97s (6.97) **Going Correction** +0.80s/f (Soft) **9** Ran SP% **118.1**
Speed ratings (Par 100):108,103,102,99,95 93,91,82,82
CSF £14.43 CT £101.83 TOTE £1.90: £1.10, £2.80, £3.20; EX 15.30.
Owner Sir Neil Westbrook **Bred** Sir & Exors Of Late Lady Westbrook **Trained** Great Habton, N Yorks

FOCUS
A decent winning time for the type of contest. They went a fair gallop and the fast-improving winner came right away, but it was not a strong contest by any means, with the winner's market rivals not running their races.

3380 COMMERCIAL FIRST MORTGAGES H'CAP 6f

8:25 (8:25) (Class 2) (0-100,94) 3-Y-0 **£10,363** (£3,083; £1,540; £769) **Stalls** High

Form RPR

0313 **1** **El Bosque (IRE)**[32] [2395] 3-9-7 **94**.................................. GrahamGibbons 7 106
(B R Millman) *w ldr: led over 2f out: clr over 1f out: r.o strly* **7/1**

-506 **2** *7* **Top Bid**[16] [2884] 3-8-6 **79**.. DavidAllan 6 70
(T D Easterby) *led tl over 2f out: rallied to take 2nd ins fnl f* **10/1**

6-05 **3** *1* **Tudor Prince (IRE)**[9] [3078] 3-8-12 **85**............................. JamieSpencer 5 73
(B J Meehan) *wnt lft s: chsd ldrs: kpt on same pce appr fnl f* **11/4**[1]

0401 **4** *¾* **Deserted Dane (USA)**[12] [2989] 3-8-13 **86**.................... DeanMcKeown 1 72
(G A Swinbank) *racd wd: sn chsng ldrs: wnt 2nd over 1f out: fdd ins fnl f* **7/1**

5060 **5** *1* **Danum Dancer**[17] [2841] 3-8-10 **83**.............................. SilvestreDeSousa 8 66
(N Bycroft) *sn outpcd and in rr: kpt on fnl 2f: nvr nr ldrs* **13/2**[3]

-006 **6** *1 ¼* **College Scholar (GER)**[44] [2044] 3-9-2 **89**............................ JoeFanning 4 68
(E A L Dunlop) *sltly hmpd s: sn chsng ldrs: wknd over 1f out* **7/2**[2]

1000 **7** *1 ½* **Dickie Le Davoir**[9] [3089] 3-9-3 **90**....................................... PatCosgrave 2 65
(K R Burke) *sn in rr: sme hdwy over 2f out: sn wknd* **16/1**

0310 **8** *1 ¾* **Heywood**[38] [2212] 3-9-5 **92**... TPO'Shea 3 61
(M R Channon) *dwlt and sn sltly hmpd: bhd and drvn along: nvr on terms* **15/2**

1m 17.91s (4.91) **Going Correction** +0.80s/f (Soft) **8** Ran SP% **114.0**
Speed ratings (Par 106):99,89,88,87,86 84,82,80
CSF £72.64 CT £237.95 TOTE £7.20: £2.60, £3.50, £1.30; EX 160.80.

Owner Wessex Racing **Bred** Mrs M Campbell-Andenaes **Trained** Kentisbeare, Devon

FOCUS

What looked a tight sprint handicap beforehand was turned into a one-horse race by El Bosque. He won so easily and showed such improved form there must be a serious question mark over the exact value of the race, with his rivals below-par in the ground.

NOTEBOOK

El Bosque(IRE), a winner at up to 7f, had yet to show he could handle soft ground. He took what looked a competitive handicap beforehand by a wide margin and might be able to take a Listed race now. (op 6-1 tchd 8-1)

Top Bid, who has slipped to a lenient mark, looked in tip-top shape beforehand. After matching strides with the winner, he found plenty to regain second spot inside the last. (op 12-1)

Tudor Prince(IRE) couldn't dominate. He is proven in soft ground but might just appreciate a return to seven. (op 7-2 tchd 5-2)

Deserted Dane(USA), 6lb higher, raced wide and may well have been on the slower part of the track. (op 13-2 tchd 15-2)

Danum Dancer, well backed, was without the usual blinkers and he never fired. (op 9-1 tchd 6-1)

College Scholar(GER), who has changed stables, had the visor left off. (tchd 10-3 and 4-1 in a place)

3381 BONDGATE H'CAP — 1m

8:55 (8:55) (Class 5) (0-70,68) 3-Y-O+ — **£3,238** (£963; £481; £240) **Stalls** High

Form	Pos	Dist	Horse / details	RPR
0331	1		**Azreme**[7] 3167 7-10-0 **67** 6ex .... AmirQuinn 11 (P Howling) *mid-div: hdwy 3f out: styd on to ld appr fnl f: hld on wl* **4/1**[2]	75
402	2	½	**Superior Star**[7] 3161 4-10-0 **67** .... (v) JamieSpencer 13 (R A Fahey) *hld up towards rr: hdwy and nt clr run over 2f out: kpt on to chse wnr wl ins fnl f* **10/3**[1]	74
0016	3	¾	**Apache Nation (IRE)**[11] 3034 4-9-7 **60** .... PhillipMakin 5 (M Dods) *trckd ldrs: chal 1f out: no ex* **13/2**[3]	65
600-	4	¾	**Lauro**[268] 5972 7-8-13 **59** .... DawnRankin(7) 9 (Miss J A Camacho) *mid-div: hdwy on outer 3f out: kpt on wl fnl f* **16/1**	63
1000	5	1 ¼	**Kadia**[48] 1933 4-8-9 **48** oh3 .... PaulFessey 16 (P T Midgley) *w ldr: led over 2f out: hdd appr fnl f: one pce* **50/1**	49
5615	6	½	**Efidium**[6] 3194 9-9-7 **67** .... GihanArnolda(7) 15 (N Bycroft) *hld up in rr: styd on fnl 2f: nt rch ldrs* **11/1**	67
1640	7	4	**Pigeon Flight**[27] 2530 3-9-2 **64** .... HayleyTurner 4 (M L W Bell) *mid-div: hdwy on outer to chse ldrs over 2f out: wknd over 1f out* **11/1**	56
300-	8	8	**Libre**[263] 6069 7-9-7 **60** .... PaddyAspell 10 (F Jordan) *chsd ldrs: lost pl wl over 1f out* **33/1**	35
005	9	1	**Dazzler Mac**[7] 3161 6-8-13 **52** .... SilvestreDeSousa 8 (N Bycroft) *chsd ldrs: lost pl over 1f out* **17/2**	25
4553	10	6	**Ming Vase**[7] 3161 5-8-9 **48** oh3 .... (b) JoeFanning 6 (P T Midgley) *sn w ldrs: wkng whn sltly hmpd and eased over 1f out* **8/1**	8
604	11	5	**New Year (IRE)**[16] 2873 3-8-9 **57** .... MickyFenton 12 (T P Tate) *led tl over over 2f out: sn lost pl* **14/1**	7
0336	12	1 ½	**Mister Jingles**[3] 3286 4-8-9 **48** oh3 .... DeanMcKeown 1 (R M Whitaker) *hld up in rr: bhd whn hmpd 1f out* **25/1**	—
0/06	13	16	**Pre Eminance (IRE)**[17] 2843 6-8-5 **49** .... ColinHaddon(5) 7 (J S Wainwright) *s.i.s: t.k.h in rr: bhd whn hmpd over 1f out* **66/1**	—
0-00	S		**Orphan (IRE)**[32] 2390 5-9-10 **63** .... (b1) DavidAllan 2 (E J Alston) *s.i.s: swtchd rt after s: mid-div whn stmbld and fell 1f out* **22/1**	—
0000	U		**Whithorn**[17] 2844 4-8-6 **48** oh3 .... AndrewElliott(3) 3 (J Balding) *in rr: hmpd and uns rdr 1f out* **80/1**	—

1m 46.7s (5.60) **Going Correction** +0.80s/f (Soft)

WFA 3 from 4yo+ 9lb — **15** Ran SP% **123.1**

Speed ratings (Par 103):104,103,102,102,100 100,96,88,87,81 76,74,58,—,—

CSF £16.97 CT £90.11 TOTE £5.80: £2.10, £2.00, £2.60; EX 13.60.

Owner Halcyon Partnership **Bred** Miss Helen Mary Ann Omersa **Trained** Newmarket, Suffolk

FOCUS

A low-grade handicap and little between the first four at the line. The race has been rated through the third with the fifth, running from out of the handicap, limiting the form, which is otherwise sound.

Dazzler Mac Official explanation: trainer said gelding was unsuited by the heavy ground

3382 KIRKGATE MAIDEN STKS — 1m

9:25 (9:25) (Class 5) 3-Y-O+ — **£3,238** (£963; £481; £240) **Stalls** High

Form	Pos	Dist	Horse / details	RPR
65	1		**Getrah**[51] 1841 3-9-3 0 .... JoeFanning 5 (W J Haggas) *trckd ldrs: styd on to ld fnl 100yds* **11/4**[2]	74
33	2	2	**Ducal Pip Squeak**[19] 2763 3-8-12 0 .... PhillipMakin 10 (M Dods) *led: hdd and no ex ins fnl f* **8/1**[3]	65
4	3	3	**Axiom**[51] 1840 3-9-3 0 .... JamieSpencer 4 (E A L Dunlop) *hld up: quite keen: hdwy 3f out: chal and hung rt over 1f out: eased whn hld fnl 50yds* **11/10**[1]	64
0	4	6	**Treasure Isle**[20] 2740 3-8-12 0 .... DaleGibson 3 (R A Fahey) *in rr and sn pushed along: styd on fnl 2f: tk modest 4th nr fin* **50/1**	46+
5	5	¾	**Actilius (IRE)**[9] 3113 3-9-3 0 .... NeilPollard 9 (M Botti) *sn chsng ldrs: wknd over 1f out* **11/1**	50
6-0	6	½	**Topazleo (IRE)**[50] 1863 3-9-3 0 .... PatCosgrave 6 (J Wade) *chsd ldrs: wknd over 1f out* **20/1**	48
0-2	7	2 ½	**Moheebb (IRE)**[2] 3302 3-8-12 0 .... MichaelJStainton(5) 2 (D W Chapman) *uns rdr gng to s: hld up in rr: hdwy 4f out: rdn and wknd 2f out* **10/1**	43
6	8	5	**Julian Joachim (USA)**[45] 2012 3-9-3 0 .... DeanMcKeown 1 (G A Swinbank) *s.s: hdwy over 3f out: shkn up and lost pl over 2f out* **20/1**	33
	9	14	**Oriental Gift (FR)** 3-9-3 0 .... PaddyAspell 7 (J R Norton) *s.i.s: in rr and sn pushed along: bhd fnl 3f* **66/1**	—
00-0	10	33	**Skodger (IRE)**[58] 1676 4-9-12 32 .... PaulFessey 8 (G Woodward) *dwlt: sn prom: lost pl 3f out: sn bhd: t.o: lame* **150/1**	—

1m 46.92s (5.82) **Going Correction** +0.80s/f (Soft)

WFA 3 from 4yo 9lb — **10** Ran SP% **116.5**

Speed ratings (Par 103):102,100,97,91,90 89,87,82,68,35

CSF £23.46 TOTE £3.50: £1.40, £2.10, £1.30; EX 31.00 Place 6 £ 8.68, Place 5 £ 4.50.

Owner B Haggas **Bred** J B Haggas **Trained** Newmarket, Suffolk

FOCUS

A modest and uncompetitive maiden in which the first three finished clear. The favourite did not run up to his previous mark and the race has been rated round the first two.

Skodger(IRE) Official explanation: vet said colt finished lame in front

T/Plt: £10.30 to a £1 stake. Pool: £67,695.90. 4,773.20 winning tickets. T/Qpdt: £4.00 to a £1 stake. Pool: £4,621.90. 853.25 winning tickets. WG

[3162] WINDSOR (R-H)

Monday, July 9

OFFICIAL GOING: Good to soft (good in places)

Race times suggested the ground was much quicker than the official description.

Wind: Moderate, across, races 1-3; almost nil, races 4-6 Weather: Heavy thunderstorms before racing. Fine during meeting.

3383 PERTEMPS E B F MAIDEN STKS — 6f

6:35 (6:36) (Class 5) 2-Y-O — **£3,238** (£963; £481; £240) **Stalls** High

Form	Pos	Dist	Horse / details	RPR
	1		**Sharp Nephew** 2-9-3 0 .... RichardHughes 5 (B J Meehan) *reluctant to enter stalls: chsd ldrs: prog to go 2nd over 1f out: rdn to ld fnl 100yds: r.o wl* **8/1**	87+
22	2	2	**Wolgan Valley (USA)**[30] 2451 2-9-3 0 .... LDettori 8 (Saeed Bin Suroor) *fast away: led: rdn over 1f out: hdd and outpcd fnl 100yds* **11/10**[1]	81
	3	1 ½	**Oasis Wind** 2-9-3 0 .... JimmyFortune 4 (P F I Cole) *chsd ldr to over 1f out: one pce* **9/2**[2]	77
04	4	nk	**Golden Penny**[40] 2138 2-9-3 0 .... EdwardCreighton 11 (H Morrison) *chsd ldrs: shkn up and outpcd 2f out: styd on ins fnl f: pressed for 3rd nr fin* **20/1**	76
0	5	1 ¼	**Tobogganist**[17] 2832 2-9-3 0 .... TedDurcan 13 (W Jarvis) *settled towards rr: pushed along and styd on steadily fr 2f out: nrst fin* **33/1**	72
02	6	1 ¾	**Latin Scholar (IRE)**[12] 2977 2-9-3 0 .... MartinDwyer 7 (A King) *prom: shkn up and outpcd 2f out: fdd* **13/2**[3]	67
	7	1 ¼	**Smokey Rye** 2-8-12 0 .... RichardMullen 14 (G L Moore) *a in midfield: shkn up over 2f out: one pce* **33/1**	58
	8	1 ¼	**Our Chairman (IRE)** 2-9-3 0 .... PatDobbs 2 (R Hannon) *settled in rr: sme prog fr 2f out: pushed along and kpt on steadily fnl f* **33/1**	59
	9	hd	**Spent** 2-9-3 0 .... GeorgeBaker 10 (R M Beckett) *prom tl pushed along and grad wknd fr 2f out* **33/1**	59
0	10	8	**Ledgerwood**[53] 1781 2-9-3 0 .... J-PGuillambert 15 (J W Hills) *sn in midfield: struggling over 2f out: wknd* **66/1**	35
	11	1 ¼	**Holy Storm (IRE)** 2-9-3 0 .... StephenCarson 6 (Eve Johnson Houghton) *reluctant to enter stalls: dwlt: rn green and a bhd* **50/1**	31
0	12	½	**Lunatico (GER)**[11] 3037 2-9-3 0 .... SaleemGolam 16 (S C Williams) *a in rr: rdn and struggling 1/2-way: sn no ch* **100/1**	29
	13	hd	**Westwood** 2-9-3 0 .... BrettDoyle 3 (D Haydn Jones) *dwlt: towards rr: sme prog and pushed along over 2f out: eased over 1f out* **66/1**	29
	14	9	**Mileaminutemurphy** 2-9-3 0 .... RyanMoore 12 (R Hannon) *s.s and awkwardly: a bhd: t.o* **10/1**	—

1m 11.49s (-2.18) **Going Correction** -0.375s/f (Firm) — **14** Ran SP% **121.8**

Speed ratings (Par 94):99,96,94,93,92 89,88,86,86,75 74,73,73,61

CSF £16.27 TOTE £10.50: £2.20, £1.40, £2.00; EX 22.20.

Owner Saleh Al Homeizi & Imad Al Sagar **Bred** Keith Wills **Trained** Manton, Wilts

FOCUS

This looked like quite a good juvenile maiden and the winning time was 0.38 seconds quicker than the later 51-70 three-year-old and upwards handicap. The runner-up is the guide to the form.

NOTEBOOK

Sharp Nephew, a 155,000gns son of Dr Fong, half-brother to triple sprint winner Handsome Cross, and 6f juvenile scorer Snip Snap, out of a quite useful 5f winner at two, created a good impression on his racecourse debut. He had to be niggled along to keep tabs on the early leaders, but gradually got the hang of things in the straight and was able to reel in the favourite, who had gone off plenty quick enough. Using Wolgan Valley as a guide, this represents useful form and his trainer is confident he is a pattern-class performer in the making. There is tons of speed in his pedigree, but he is expected to get further - he certainly ran as though he will stay beyond sprint trips - and a 7f Listed race at Ascot is under consideration. (op 7-1 tchd 9-1 and 10-1 in places)

Wolgan Valley(USA), stepping up in trip, was soon taking these along at a good clip and looked the most likely winner when still holding a healthy advantage approaching the furlong pole, but he failed to see out his race. He failed to improve on his two previous efforts and does not appear to be progressing, but a return to 5f should suit. (op 11-8)

Oasis Wind, a 95,000gns Oasis Dream colt, first foal of an unraced half-sister to 1m2f winner Sarabande, and 1m scorer Reel Style, was not without support in the market and he made a pleasing debut back in third. He should find a similar race with normal improvement. (op 7-2 tchd 11-2)

Golden Penny had shown ability on his two previous starts, but this represented a much-improved performance. He is now qualified for nurseries and could be dangerous in that sphere. (op 28-1)

Tobogganist was continually denied a clear run when trying to stay on in the straight and probably could have finished a length or two closer. This represents improvement on the form he showed on his debut at Newmarket.

Latin Scholar(IRE) could not quite match the form he showed when second at Bath on his previous start, but he will have more options now he is qualified for a handicap mark. (op 8-1 tchd 6-1)

Spent Official explanation: jockey said colt hung right

Westwood Official explanation: jockey said colt hung right

3384 RAB CAPITAL H'CAP — 1m 67y

7:05 (7:05) (Class 5) (0-70,71) 3-Y-O — **£3,238** (£963; £481; £240) **Stalls** High

Form	Pos	Dist	Horse / details	RPR
6210	1		**Cnoc Moy (IRE)**[17] 2834 3-9-6 **69** .... GeorgeBaker 1 (C F Wall) *trckd ldr gng easily: led wl over 1f out: pressed and shkn up ent fnl f: readily* **7/1**	75+
34-0	2	1	**Distiller (IRE)**[80] 1117 3-9-6 **69** .... RichardMullen 6 (W R Muir) *chsd ldng trio: rdn over 3f out: prog u.p to press wnr ent fnl f: kpt on but no imp nr fin* **33/1**	73
4051	3	1 ¾	**Encores**[10] 3056 3-9-1 **64** .... RichardThomas 14 (N A Callaghan) *led to wl over 1f out: one pce u.p* **5/1**[3]	64
5415	4	¾	**Gee Ceffyl Bach**[15] 2905 3-8-8 **57** .... EdwardCreighton 11 (G Woodward) *chsd ldng pair: nt qckn over 2f out: one pce after* **14/1**	55
-603	5	nk	**The King And I (IRE)**[22] 2697 3-9-4 **67** .... RichardHughes 9 (J S Moore) *a abt same pce: outpcd by ldrs over 3f out: plugged on* **8/1**	65
-005	6	½	**Our Herbie**[24] 2633 3-9-4 **67** .... (t) RyanMoore 8 (J W Hills) *hld up in midfield: rdn over 2f out and off the pce: nt clr run briefly over 1f out: kpt on* **9/1**	63+
0041	7	¾	**Mark Of Love (IRE)**[4] 3235 3-9-1 **71** 6ex .... MatthewDavies(7) 13 (M R Channon) *stdd s: hld up in last trio and wl off the pce: sme prog on outer fr 3f out: pushed along and kpt on: nvr nr ldrs* **9/2**[2]	66+
054-	8	nk	**Carlitos Spirit (IRE)**[296] 5382 3-8-13 **62** .... DarrylHolland 12 (B R Millman) *chsd ldrs but nvr on terms: one pce and no prog fnl 2f* **12/1**	56

0-02 **9** 3/4 **The Fifth Member (IRE)**[34] 2335 3-9-3 **66**.............................. LDettori 3 60+
(J R Boyle) *chsd ldrs: lost pl 1/2-way: rdn over 2f out: no imp* **4/1**[1]
3-30 **10** 1 **Lady Alize (USA)**[53] 1784 3-9-7 **70**..............................(t) MartinDwyer 7 60
(R A Kvisla) *s.s: detached in last: rdn and kpt on fnl 2f: no ch* **40/1**
035- **11** 1 3/4 **Hope Your Safe**[219] 6669 3-8-10 **59**.............................. TedDurcan 10 45
(J R Best) *s.s: mostly in last trio: pushed along and kpt on fr over 2f out: no ch* **33/1**
1-02 **12** 1/2 **Sularno**[40] 2150 3-9-2 **70**.............................. TravisBlock(5) 2 55
(H Morrison) *a in rr: rdn 3f out: no prog* **14/1**
00-0 **13** 5 **Addictive**[17] 2834 3-8-13 **62**.............................. SaleemGolam 4 35
(S C Williams) *rdn in rr 1/2-way: sn struggling* **33/1**
5225 **14** 5 **First Princess (IRE)**[40] 2150 3-8-13 **62**..............................(p) JohnEgan 5 24
(J S Moore) *wl in rr: brief effrt over 3f out: sn btn: heavily eased over 1f out* **20/1**

1m 40.79s (-3.91) **Going Correction** -0.375s/f (Firm) **14** Ran SP% **125.5**
Speed ratings (Par 100):104,103,101,100,100 99,98,98,97,96 95,94,89,84
CSF £236.61 CT £1309.78 TOTE £8.10: £2.70, £10.50, £2.20; EX 598.00.
Owner Peter Botham **Bred** Miss Gemma Cunningham **Trained** Newmarket, Suffolk

FOCUS
A race lacking strength in depth and, despite the gallop appearing good throughout, nothing got involved from off the pace. The winner looks capable of better. The winning time was 0.78 seconds quicker than the later fillies' maiden.
Encores Official explanation: trainer said gelding was unsuited by the track

3385 TOTESPORT.COM E B F H'CAP 1m 3f 135y
7:35 (7:35) (Class 4) (0-80,78) 3-Y-0+ **£6,477** (£1,927; £963; £481) **Stalls** Centre

Form RPR
-601 **1** **Polish Red**[14] 2945 3-8-12 **75**.............................. JohnEgan 6 83+
(G G Margarson) *hld up in last pair: stdy prog on outer over 3f out: rdn 2f out: led jst ins fnl f: styd on wl* **3/1**[1]
0244 **2** 3/4 **Prince Nureyev (IRE)**[24] 2634 7-10-0 **78**.............................. SteveDrowne 1 85
(B R Millman) *dwlt: hld up in last trio: prog 4f out: clsd and drvn to ld over 1f out: hdd jst ins fnl f: styd on* **15/2**
4-04 **3** 1 1/4 **Dove Cottage (IRE)**[24] 2621 5-9-4 **68**.............................. FergusSweeney 8 73
(W S Kittow) *taken down early: led: rdn and hdd 2f out: kpt on same pce* **9/1**
-220 **4** 3/4 **Oakley Heffert (IRE)**[12] 2999 3-9-0 **77**..............................(b[1]) RichardHughes 3 81
(R Hannon) *chsd ldrs: hrd drvn and nt qckn over 2f out: kpt on u.str.p fnl f* **7/2**[2]
6400 **5** 1/2 **Prime Powered (IRE)**[38] 2218 6-9-7 **71**.............................. GeorgeBaker 2 74
(R M Beckett) *trckd ldng trio: smooth prog over 3f out: rdn to ld 2f out: idled and edgd lft: hdd and fnd nil over 1f out* **25/1**
-000 **6** 4 **Tender Falcon**[46] 1959 7-9-1 **72**.............................. HaddenFrost(7) 9 68
(R J Hodges) *chsd ldrs: rdn 3f out: lost tch 2f out: n.d after* **16/1**
1006 **7** 1/2 **Mr Mischief**[4] 3249 7-8-7 **62**.............................. RussellKennemore(5) 11 57
(M C Chapman) *sn trckd ldng pair: rdn wl over 3f out: outpcd wl over 2f out: one pce after* **16/1**
5103 **8** 5 **Medieval Maiden**[26] 2572 4-9-3 **67**.............................. BrettDoyle 10 54
(W J Musson) *in tch: rdn and lost pl over 3f out: sn struggling* **16/1**
-025 **9** 1 1/4 **Cavallini (USA)**[30] 2474 5-9-6 **70**..............................(b[1]) RyanMoore 5 55
(G L Moore) *pressed ldr: rdn 4f out: wknd over 2f out* **6/1**[3]
210 **10** 6 **Pocketwood**[12] 2987 5-9-9 **73**.............................. StephenCarson 7 48
(Jean-Rene Auvray) *chsd ldrs: u.p and losing pl 4f out: sn btn* **14/1**
020/ **11** 5 **Classic Role**[34] 106 8-9-4 **68**..............................(v) JimmyFortune 4 35
(L Wells) *a last: rdn over 3f out: sn bhd* **14/1**

2m 24.82s (-5.28) **Going Correction** -0.375s/f (Firm)
WFA 3 from 4yo+ 13lb **11** Ran SP% **118.1**
Speed ratings (Par 105):102,101,100,100,99 97,96,93,92,88 85
CSF £26.02 CT £184.47 TOTE £3.20: £1.70, £2.90, £2.50; EX 30.10.
Owner Norcroft Park Stud **Bred** Norcroft Park Stud **Trained** Newmarket, Suffolk

FOCUS
A fair handicap. Straightforward to rate, with the second, third and fourth all to form.
Pocketwood Official explanation: jockey said gelding ran flat

3386 CHEVIOT ASSET MANAGEMENT H'CAP 1m 2f 7y
8:05 (8:05) (Class 4) (0-85,83) 3-Y-0+ **£6,477** (£1,927; £963; £481) **Stalls** Centre

Form RPR
2142 **1** **Emerald Wilderness (IRE)**[24] 2627 3-9-0 **80**.............................. LDettori 3 91+
(E A L Dunlop) *led after 2f and qcknd clr: stdd bnd over 6f out: shkn up and drew clr again fr 2f out: comf* **9/4**[1]
2140 **2** 2 1/2 **Can Can Star**[41] 2106 4-9-5 **74**.............................. RichardHughes 10 77
(A W Carroll) *hld up in last trio: prog 3f out: got through 2f out: drvn to chse wnr ins fnl f: no imp* **8/1**
-122 **3** 1/2 **Nightspot**[32] 2397 6-9-6 **75**.............................. StephenCarson 7 77
(Eve Johnson Houghton) *led for 2f: chsd wnr: outpcd fr 2f out: lost 2nd ins fnl f: kpt on* **6/1**[3]
0060 **4** hd **Krugerrand (USA)**[15] 2906 8-9-10 **79**.............................. BrettDoyle 5 81
(W J Musson) *hld up in last trio: stdy prog on outer over 2f out: shkn up over 1f out: disp 2nd ins fnl f: nt qckn* **8/1**
0520 **5** 1 1/2 **Blacktoft (USA)**[12] 2986 4-9-7 **76**..............................(e) J-PGuillambert 9 75
(S C Williams) *plld hrd: hld up bhd ldrs: rdn wl over 2f out: one pce and no real prog* **14/1**
50-5 **6** 1/2 **Baan (USA)**[18] 2807 4-10-0 **83**.............................. JimmyFortune 6 81
(M Johnston) *hld up in last trio: rdn over 3f out: plugged on one pce: n.d* **7/1**
0-43 **7** nk **Parnassian**[32] 2403 7-8-13 **68**..............................(v) RichardThomas 8 65
(J A Geake) *sltly hmpd after 2f: chsd ldrs: rdn over 3f out: no imp on ldrs 2f out: edgd rt fnl f* **11/2**[2]
2342 **8** 1 **Orpen Wide (IRE)**[17] 2835 5-9-8 **82**..............................(b) RussellKennemore(5) 1 77
(M C Chapman) *prom 3f: lost pl: last and rdn 3f out: keeping on but no ch whn hmpd fnl 100yds* **11/1**
60-5 **9** 11 **Artistic Style**[4] 3242 7-10-0 **83**.............................. GeorgeBaker 4 56
(B G Powell) *prog to chse ldng pair after 3f: wknd wl over 2f out: t.o* **20/1**
0-00 **10** 17 **Chancellor (IRE)**[9] 3076 9-9-10 **79**..............................(t) IanMongan 2 18
(D K Ivory) *in tch tl wknd rapidly on outer over 2f out: wl t.o* **33/1**

2m 4.90s (-3.40) **Going Correction** -0.375s/f (Firm)
WFA 3 from 4yo+ 11lb **10** Ran SP% **117.9**
Speed ratings (Par 105):98,96,95,95,94 93,93,92,84,70
CSF £21.15 CT £97.51 TOTE £3.20: £1.60, £3.00, £1.70; EX 37.00.
Owner Mohammed Jaber **Bred** Mrs Joan Murphy **Trained** Newmarket, Suffolk

FOCUS
Ordinary form for the grade with the front two both racing off career-high ratings, and the improved winner set a stop-start gallop.

3387 COOLMORE AUSSIE RULES MAIDEN FILLIES' STKS 1m 67y
8:35 (8:36) (Class 5) 3-4-Y-O **£3,238** (£963; £481; £240) **Stalls** High

Form RPR
23 **1** **Duchess Royale (IRE)**[22] 2693 3-9-3 0..............................(v[1]) RyanMoore 1 78
(Sir Michael Stoute) *trckd ldrs: pushed along and effrt over 2f out: rdn to ld ent fnl f: edgd rt but sn in command* **5/1**
2-20 **2** 1 3/4 **Siamese Cat (IRE)**[15] 2914 3-9-3 95.............................. JimmyFortune 10 76+
(B J Meehan) *trckd ldr after 2f: rdn to chal 2f out: upsides 1f out: hld whn n.m.r briefly ins fnl f* **3/1**[2]
524 **3** shd **Angel Kate (IRE)**[31] 2428 3-9-3 75.............................. TedDurcan 9 74
(H R A Cecil) *hld up in ldrs: rdn to ld then settled pce after 2f: kicked on over 2f out: drvn and hdd ent fnl f: kpt on* **7/1**
42- **4** 2 **Salsa Steps (USA)**[256] 6186 3-9-3 0.............................. SteveDrowne 14 69
(H Morrison) *n.m.r after 2f: trckd ldrs: 4th and rdn whn nt clr run over 1f out: one pce after* **5/2**[1]
0 **5** 1 3/4 **Idesia (IRE)**[22] 2693 3-9-3 0.............................. AdamKirby 6 65
(W R Swinburn) *chsd ldrs: pushed along over 2f out: rdn and edgd lft 1f out: kpt on but no imp on ldrs* **25/1**
6- **6** 4 **Auntie Mame**[205] 6840 3-9-3 0.............................. EdwardCreighton 3 56
(D J Coakley) *towards rr: pushed along over 3f out: outpcd sn after but plugged on* **50/1**
3 **7** nk **Rolexa**[31] 2428 3-9-3 0.............................. PhilipRobinson 11 55
(C G Cox) *chsd ldr for 2f: shuffled bk on bnd sn after: effrt on outer over 3f out: wknd 2f out* **4/1**[3]
00- **8** 1 **Edgefour (IRE)**[261] 6098 3-9-0 0.............................. RichardKingscote(3) 13 53
(B I Case) *n.m.r after 2f: nvr beyond midfield: outpcd fr 3f out* **100/1**
04 **9** 2 **Bundle Up**[23] 2666 4-9-12 0.............................. IanMongan 7 49
(Mrs L J Mongan) *nvr beyond midfield: wl outpcd fr 3f out: no ch fnl 2f* **33/1**
00 **10** nk **My Spring Rose**[16] 2880 3-9-3 0.............................. StephenCarson 8 48
(J R Jenkins) *stdd s: a towards rr: outpcd fr 3f out* **66/1**
11 nk **Princess Danehill (IRE)** 3-9-3 0.............................. LDettori 5 47
(P F I Cole) *wl in tch: prog to press ldrs over 3f out: wknd over 2f out* **10/1**
0 **12** 1 3/4 **Dance Steps**[164] 257 3-9-3 0.............................. AntonyProcter 2 43
(Miss K B Boutflower) *s.s: sn in tch in rr: wknd wl over 2f out* **100/1**
00 **13** nk **Panda Power**[17] 2836 3-9-3 0.............................. J-PGuillambert 12 42
(S C Williams) *hld up in rr: pushed along and steadily lost tch fr 3f out* **33/1**
0- **14** 14 **Iceni Princess**[201] 6879 3-9-3 0.............................. JimmyQuinn 4 10
(P Howling) *rn green and sn last: t.o* **66/1**

1m 41.57s (-3.13) **Going Correction** -0.375s/f (Firm)
WFA 3 from 4yo 9lb **14** Ran SP% **128.5**
Speed ratings (Par 100):100,98,98,96,94 90,90,89,87,86 86,84,84,70
CSF £21.14 TOTE £6.50: £2.10, £1.90, £2.80; EX 18.00.
Owner Mrs Elizabeth Moran **Bred** Mrs E Moran **Trained** Newmarket, Suffolk
■ Stewards' Enquiry : Ryan Moore caution: careless riding

FOCUS
Just a fair fillies' maiden, as is to be expected for the time of year. The third, who caused trouble for several in behind when slowing up the pace into the bend, looks the best guide to the form. The winning time was 0.78 seconds slower than the earlier 51-70 three-year-old handicap.

3388 BET AT LADBROKES NOW ON 0800 777888 H'CAP 6f
9:05 (9:05) (Class 5) (0-70,70) 3-Y-0+ **£3,238** (£963; £481; £240) **Stalls** High

Form RPR
1021 **1** **Makabul**[9] 3106 4-9-13 **69**.............................. DarryllHolland 16 81
(B R Millman) *trckd ldrs: effrt over 1f out: edgd lft but r.o to ld fnl 50yds* **7/2**[1]
5002 **2** nk **Polar Force**[9] 3106 7-8-13 **55**.............................. JohnEgan 15 66
(Mrs C A Dunnett) *racd against nr side rail: mde most: drvn over 1f out: hung lft and hdd fnl 50yds* **5/1**[2]
0605 **3** 2 **Bobby Rose**[9] 3106 4-8-13 **62**..............................(p) ChrisHough(7) 5 67
(D K Ivory) *racd towards centre: trckd ldrs: smooth prog over 2f out: rdn to chal 1f out and upsides: folded tamely fnl 50yds* **14/1**
/000 **4** shd **Registrar**[58] 1675 5-9-1 **57**.............................. DMylonas 13 62
(Mrs C A Dunnett) *dwlt: hld up in rr: stdy prog 2f out: hanging lft after: urged along and kpt on but nvr able to chal* **25/1**
0602 **5** 1 **Joy And Pain**[9] 3101 6-8-13 **55**..............................(v) PaulFitzsimons 14 57
(M J Attwater) *dwlt: sn rcvrd to press ldr: fdd fnl f* **7/1**[3]
0053 **6** shd **Nautical**[12] 2982 9-9-10 **66**.............................. JamesDoyle 10 67
(A W Carroll) *hld up wl in rr: prog 2f out: looked dangerous jst over 1f out: effrt petered out* **7/1**[3]
0-00 **7** 3/4 **Fisberry**[21] 2725 5-9-13 **69**.............................. FergusSweeney 11 68
(M S Saunders) *dwlt: detached in last: pushed along beofre 1/2-way: hanging lft but styd on fnl 2f: n.d* **16/1**
1060 **8** 1 3/4 **Cool Sands (IRE)**[6] 3188 5-8-13 **55**..............................(v) JimmyQuinn 4 49
(D Shaw) *settled wl in rr: rdn and effrt 2f out: nt pce to threaten ldrs* **14/1**
0103 **9** 3/4 **Royal Orissa**[10] 3064 5-9-0 **56**.............................. AdamKirby 9 48
(D Haydn Jones) *towards rr: effrt but little prog whn hmpd over 1f out: no ch after* **8/1**
00-0 **10** 3 1/2 **Proud Killer**[21] 2719 4-9-11 **67**.............................. J-PGuillambert 8 48
(J R Jenkins) *chsd ldrs: lost pl 2f out: sn struggling* **40/1**
-100 **11** nk **Sea Land (FR)**[14] 2943 3-9-8 **70**..............................(v) MartinDwyer 2 50
(M P Tregoning) *racd towards far side: wl on terms tl wknd over 1f out* **11/1**
0021 **12** 1 1/2 **Blessed Place**[13] 2972 7-9-9 **65**..............................(t) JimmyFortune 1 41
(D J S Ffrench Davis) *racd towards far side: wl on terms tl wknd over 1f out* **8/1**
-002 **13** 5 **Batchworth Fleur**[9] 3102 4-9-2 **58**.............................. StephenCarson 12 19
(E A Wheeler) *reluctant to go bhd stalls: prom over 3f: wknd rapidly* **33/1**
000/ **14** 12 **Al Qudra (IRE)**[599] 5-10-0 **70**.............................. TedDurcan 6 —
(J R Jenkins) *in tch to 1/2-way: wknd and eased: t.o* **50/1**

1m 11.87s (-1.80) **Going Correction** -0.375s/f (Firm)
WFA 3 from 4yo+ 6lb **14** Ran SP% **124.8**
Speed ratings (Par 103):97,96,93,93,92 92,91,89,88,83 82,80,74,58
CSF £20.19 CT £234.47 TOTE £4.70: £1.90, £2.30, £4.10; EX 17.50 Place 6 £ 57.09, Place 5 £ 45.07.
Owner M S T Partnership **Bred** D Lowe **Trained** Kentisbeare, Devon

FOCUS
Very few of these came into this in any sort of form and this looked a weak sprint handicap for the grade, although the first three tie in well on previous C/D form. They were spread out across the track at the line.
T/Jkpt: Not won. T/Plt: £39.60 to a £1 stake. Pool: £113.036.45. 2,080.45 winning tickets. T/Qpdt: £13.30 to a £1 stake. Pool: £4,961.40. 274.20 winning tickets. JN

3389 - 3391a (Foreign Racing) - See Raceform Interactive

3186 LINGFIELD (L-H)

Tuesday, July 10

OFFICIAL GOING: Standard

Wind: Virtually nil Weather: Cloudy

3392 LINGFIELD PARK GOLF CLUB (S) STKS — 5f (P)
2:30 (2:33) (Class 6) 2-Y-O — **£2,184** (£644; £322) **Stalls** High

Form — RPR

1 **Only A Game (IRE)** 2-8-11 0 .... RichardMullen 7 — 60+
(E J O'Neill) *chsd ldng pair: rdn and outpcd 3f out: rallied over 1f out: styd on to ld towards fin* **4/6**[1]

0031 2 *nk* **Areweplayingout (IRE)**[29] [2517] 2-8-11 0 .... LPKeniry 5 — 59
(Peter Grayson) *chsd ldr: rdn to ld jst over 1f out hdd and no ex towards fin* **4/1**[3]

4 3 *3* **Princely Green (IRE)**[16] [2911] 2-8-11 0 .... SebSanders 6 — 48
(I A Wood) *led: rdn over 2f out: hdd jst over 1f out: wknd fnl f* **11/4**[2]

00 4 *4* **Rannoch**[17] [2876] 2-8-6 0 .... KevinGhunowa(5) 3 — 34
(Miss D A McHale) *in tch for 2f: sn outpcd and rdn: no ch last 2f* **20/1**

0650 5 *1* **Fraamington**[11] [3065] 2-8-11 0 .... (v) TPO'Shea 8 — 30
(M R Channon) *s.i.s: a bhd: no ch last 2f* **10/1**

6 *2 ½* **Goldacre** 2-8-7 0 ow1 .... AlanDaly 1 — 17+
(Miss D A McHale) *v s.i.s: a wl bhd* **25/1**

600 7 *45* **Culzean Bay**[5] [3246] 2-8-6 0 .... (b[1]) FrancisNorton 4 — —
(A Bailey) *planted in stalls and lft many l: continued t.o* **33/1**

60.89 secs (1.11) **Going Correction** -0.05s/f (Stan) — **7 Ran SP% 127.3**

Speed ratings (Par 92):89,88,83,77,75 71,—

CSF £4.62 TOTE £1.90: £1.10, £1.90; EX 5.10 Trifecta £13.20 Pool: £513.89 - 27.53 winning units..The winner was bought in for 9,800gns. Areweplayingout was claimed by I. W. McInnes for £6,000.

Owner Ballard Campbell,JC Fretwell & C Evans **Bred** Maggie And Eric Hemming **Trained** Averham Park, Notts

FOCUS

An already very ordinary seller was made even more so when a few of the runners blew it at the start. This was also a race where money talked and the form looks very moderate.

NOTEBOOK

Only A Game(IRE), out of a half-sister to a couple of winning juveniles, was expected to go in at the first time of asking according to the market, but his supporters must have been nervous as he was off the bridle a long way out and was not travelling as well as the front pair turning for home. However, once into the straight and with the leaders starting to wilt, he made full use of the faster strip down the middle of the track to snatch the race out of the fire. He was bought in for 9,800gns at the subsequent auction, but will do well to find another race as weak as this. (op 5-4)

Areweplayingout(IRE), the most experienced in the field and carrying a penalty for her Wolverhampton win, was without the blinkers she had on then. She was involved in a speed duel with Princely Green from the start, but although she dourly got the better of that private battle, she then found herself vulnerable to the favourite's late flurry. She was claimed by Ian McInnes for £6,000. (op 7-2)

Princely Green(IRE) tried to make every yard, but was given no peace by Areweplayingout and, sticking to the inside rail throughout which can be a disadvantage here, eventually ran out of puff entering the last furlong. He may need an even sharper 5f than this to help him see out the trip. (op 3-1 tchd 7-2)

Rannoch, back to the minimum trip, was always in about the same place and was always struggling to stay in touch. (op 16-1)

Fraamington, trying the minimum trip for the first time in his fifth outing, was outpaced from the start. He had already been well beaten in a couple of sellers and must be near the bottom of the yard's juveniles.

Goldacre, a half-sister to a dual winner over 7f, blew the start completely. (op 22-1)

Culzean Bay virtually refused to race. (op 25-1)

3393 LINGFIELD PARK FOR CONFERENCES MAIDEN FILLIES' H'CAP — 1m (P)
3:00 (3:02) (Class 6) (0-65,65) 3-Y-O+ — **£2,388** (£705; £352) **Stalls** High

Form — RPR

3404 1 **Dansil In Distress**[23] [2697] 3-9-9 **64** .... LPKeniry 8 — 70
(S Kirk) *hld up towards rr: stl plenty to do over 2f out: hdwy and rdn over 1f out: str run to ld last 100yds: r.o wl* **7/1**[2]

-000 2 *1 ½* **Puissant Princess (IRE)**[31] [2472] 3-9-9 **64** .... EddieAhern 11 — 67
(J W Hills) *hld up in last trio: hdwy on outer over 2f out: ev ch jst ins fnl f: outpcd by wnr last 100yds* **12/1**

0550 3 *1 ¾* **Cat Six (USA)**[19] [2801] 3-9-5 **60** .... RichardHughes 3 — 59
(B J Meehan) *stdd s: hld up in rr: swtchd rt wl over 1f out: r.o wl fnl f: wnt 3rd nr fin: nvr nrr* **9/1**

2065 4 *1* **Burford Lass (IRE)**[8] [3173] 4-9-9 **55** .... DaneO'Neill 9 — 53
(D K Ivory) *s.i.s: t.k.h: sn chsng ldrs: hdwy over 3f out: led narrowly over 1f out tl and last 100yds: wknd* **9/2**[1]

-306 5 *hd* **Run For Ede'S**[23] [2691] 3-9-9 **64** .... IanMongan 12 — 60
(P M Phelan) *trckd ldrs: led wl over 2f out: sn rdn: ev ch tl wknd last 100yds* **14/1**

00-5 6 *2 ½* **Split The Wind (USA)**[69] [1409] 3-9-8 **63** .... StephenCarson 10 — 53
(Eve Johnson Houghton) *in tch: rdn over 2f out: wknd over 1f out* **10/1**

4053 7 *½* **Inscribed (IRE)**[105] [798] 4-9-6 **52** .... J-PGuillambert 2 — 43
(G A Huffer) *t.k.h: chsd ldrs: rdn jst over 2f out: wknd over 1f out* **14/1**

/32- 8 *5* **Ya Late Maite**[403] [2195] 4-9-9 **55** .... SebSanders 1 — 35
(E S McMahon) *s.i.s: sn rdn to press ldrs: led over 6f out: rdn and hdd wl over 2f out: wknd qckly over 1f out* **8/1**[3]

6-05 9 *shd* **Barbs Pink Diamond (USA)**[15] [2940] 3-9-2 **57** .... (b[1]) JimCrowley 6 — 34
(Mrs A J Perrett) *racd in midfield: rdn wl over 3f out: sn struggling* **16/1**

04-6 10 *1 ¼* **Storm Petrel**[28] [2542] 3-9-10 **65** .... GeorgeBaker 7 — 39
(N P Littmoden) *hld up in rr: rdn and effrt wl over 2f out: no hdwy: eased ins fnl f* **12/1**

020 11 *½* **Spinneret**[26] [2606] 3-9-10 **65** .... PhilipRobinson 5 — 38
(M A Jarvis) *in tch: pushed along wl over 3f out: outpcd wl over 2f out: no ch after* **9/2**[1]

3000 12 *4* **Verone (USA)**[26] [2607] 3-9-5 **60** .... (v[1]) OscarUrbina 4 — 24
(M Botti) *sn chsng ldr: rdn 3f out: wknd qckly over 2f out: eased fnl f* **20/1**

1m 38.37s (-1.06) **Going Correction** -0.05s/f (Stan)

WFA 3 from 4yo 9lb — **12 Ran SP% 118.4**

Speed ratings (Par 98):103,101,99,98,98 96,95,90,90,89 88,84

CSF £88.13 CT £780.08 TOTE £9.40: £2.80, £7.00, £3.50; EX 145.70 TRIFECTA Not won..

Owner Willie And The Good Boys **Bred** Stratford Place Stud **Trained** Upper Lambourn, Berks

■ Stewards' Enquiry : Dane O'Neill two-day ban: used whip with excessive frequency without allowing time to respond (Jul 21-22)

FOCUS

A maiden fillies' handicap is never going to be the classiest of events, but this one was quite competitive and the first two showed improved form. A solid pace suited those that were held up and the winning time was 0.91 seconds quicker than the following claimer.

Storm Petrel Official explanation: jockey said filly was affected by the kickback down the back straight

Spinneret Official explanation: vet said filly bled from the nose

3394 LINGFIELD PARK FOR WEDDINGS CLAIMING STKS — 1m (P)
3:30 (3:30) (Class 5) 3-Y-O — **£2,968** (£876; £438) **Stalls** High

Form — RPR

3002 1 **Red Current**[11] [3057] 3-8-10 58 .... SebSanders 6 — 57
(J R Fanshawe) *racd in midfield: rdn over 3f out: sltly hmpd and swtchd lft 2f out: hrd rdn after: styd on fnl f to ld on post* **5/2**[1]

51-0 2 *shd* **Gifted Heir (IRE)**[19] [2798] 3-8-9 55 .... JamesDoyle 4 — 56
(I A Wood) *led for 1f: chsd ldr tl led again over 2f out: hung rt ins fnl f: hdd on post* **5/1**[3]

3 *1* **Foxy Diplomat** 3-8-4 0 .... KevinGhunowa(5) 5 — 54
(I A Wood) *chsd ldrs: swtchd rt and rdn jst over 2f out: ev ch whn carried rt jst ins fnl f: one pce* **20/1**

0000 4 *1 ¼* **Bubbly Girl**[22] [2727] 3-8-6 59 .... EddieAhern 10 — 48
(P J McBride) *t.k.h: hld up: hdwy wl over 3f out: chsd ldng trio and sltly hmpd 2f out: kpt on same pce fr over 1f out* **5/1**[3]

5006 5 *2* **Camissa**[13] [3000] 3-8-12 65 .... (p) DaneO'Neill 11 — 49
(D K Ivory) *s.i.s: bhd: reminder 4f out: hdwy to chse ldrs over 2f out: no hdwy u.p after* **4/1**[2]

0406 6 *½* **Camp Counsellor**[31] [2454] 3-9-1 55 .... (b) JimCrowley 1 — 51
(J A Osborne) *s.i.s: sn pushed up and led after 1f: hdd over 2f out: sn rdn: wknd 1f out* **10/1**

7 *nk* **Hugo Quick** 3-9-0 0 .... NeilChalmers(3) 2 — 52
(T M Jones) *s.i.s: bhd: sme hdwy u.p on outer over 2f out: kpt on: nvr able to chal* **50/1**

0000 8 *½* **Bathwick Fancy (IRE)**[29] [2511] 3-8-8 47 .... (b[1]) DavidKinsella 7 — 46+
(J G Portman) *s.i.s: bhd: rdn 4f out: styng on but no ch whn short of room ins fnl f* **16/1**

0-05 9 *2 ½* **Sew In Character**[39] [2223] 3-9-1 47 .... FrancisNorton 12 — 43
(M Blanshard) *t.k.h: prom on outer: rdn over 3f out: sn wknd* **16/1**

04L 10 *hd* **Hester Brook (IRE)**[27] [2557] 3-8-3 65 .... (p) MCGeran(7) 3 — 38
(J G M O'Shea) *s.i.s: t.k.h and sn in midfield: lost pl over 3f out: no ch last 2f* **20/1**

-000 11 *1 ¾* **Millyjean**[26] [2607] 3-8-4 49 .... (b[1]) TPO'Shea 8 — 28
(John Berry) *chsd ldrs: rdn over 3f out: sn wknd* **20/1**

1m 39.28s (-0.15) **Going Correction** -0.05s/f (Stan) — **11 Ran SP% 119.0**

Speed ratings (Par 100):98,97,96,95,93 93,92,92,89,89 87

CSF £14.25 TOTE £2.80: £1.10, £2.40, £6.40; EX 13.60 Trifecta £374.80 Part won. Pool: £528.02 - 0.68 winning units..Red Current was claimed by R. A. Harris for £9,000. Foxy Diplomat was claimed by Raymond Tooth for £6,000.

Owner Mrs Denis Haynes **Bred** Wretham Stud **Trained** Newmarket, Suffolk

■ Stewards' Enquiry : James Doyle one-day ban: careless riding (Jul 21)

FOCUS

A modest claimer in which the pace was ordinary and the winning time was nearly a second slower than the preceding maiden fillies' handicap. The winner did not need to run to her best, with the second the best guide to the form's worth.

3395 LINGFIELDPARK.CO.UK MAIDEN STKS — 6f (P)
4:00 (4:02) (Class 5) 3-4-Y-O — **£2,968** (£876; £438) **Stalls** Low

Form — RPR

2- 1 **Marozi (USA)**[256] [6200] 3-9-3 0 .... PhilipRobinson 11 — 72+
(M A Jarvis) *t.k.h: sn pressing ldr on outer: led over 2f out: sn rdn: clr over 1f: r.o strly* **1/2**[1]

2 *2* **Sweetsformysweet (USA)** 3-8-12 0 .... SebSanders 4 — 61+
(J Noseda) *t.k.h: chsd ldrs: rdn and hdwy 2f out: chsd wnr jst over 1f out: kpt on* **5/1**[2]

3 *1 ¾* **Winning Show** 3-9-0 0 .... LiamJones(3) 5 — 61
(R A Harris) *plld hrd: chsd ldrs: rdn 2f out: kpt on same pce fnl f* **50/1**

0-2 4 *½* **Six Of Trumps (IRE)**[47] [1976] 3-9-3 0 .... JimCrowley 8 — 59
(J A Osborne) *wnt lft s: t.k.h: hld up towards rr: hdwy over 1f out: kpt on fnl f: n.d* **12/1**

5 *½* **Blackat Blackitten (IRE)** 3-9-3 0 .... StephenCarson 7 — 58
(G A Butler) *s.i.s: t.k.h: hld up in last: pushed along and effrt on inner over 1f: kpt on past btn horse fnl f: n.d* **16/1**

0- 6 *1 ¾* **Mirko**[260] [6145] 3-9-3 0 .... DaneO'Neill 6 — 52
(B R Millman) *plld hrd: hld up in tch: rdn 2f out: no hdwy after* **33/1**

6 7 *½* **Regal Cheer**[91] [998] 3-8-12 0 .... IanMongan 12 — 46
(C F Wall) *plld hrd: hld up in rr: c wd bnd 2f out: no hdwy u.p after* **25/1**

53 8 *nk* **Bold Bobby**[12] [3031] 3-8-12 0 .... RichardHughes 3 — 45
(J M P Eustace) *led at stdy pce: hdd over 2f out: wknd over 1f out* **10/1**[3]

0 9 *1 ½* **Withywood (USA)**[11] [3046] 3-8-12 0 .... PatDobbs 9 — 40
(G L Moore) *stdd s: t.k.h: hld up in last pair: rdn over 2f out: no imp* **100/1**

00 10 *shd* **Shortcake**[133] [574] 3-8-12 0 .... LPKeniry 10 — 40
(M R Hoad) *chsd ldrs: rdn over 2f out: sn outpcd* **100/1**

1m 13.76s (0.95) **Going Correction** -0.05s/f (Stan)

WFA 3 from 4yo 6lb — **10 Ran SP% 116.7**

Speed ratings (Par 103):91,88,86,85,84 82,81,81,79,79

CSF £3.12 TOTE £1.50: £1.10, £1.50, £10.60; EX 4.80 Trifecta £123.10 Pool: £832.75 - 4.80 winning units..

Owner Sheikh Mohammed **Bred** Gaines-Gentry Thoroughbreds **Trained** Newmarket, Suffolk

FOCUS

A most uncompetitve maiden, dominated by the two market leaders, was spoiled by a pedestrian early pace with several pulling hard as a result. The winning time was very moderate, 2.26 seconds slower than the following handicap, but the front two are still likely to go on to better things.

Blackat Blackitten(IRE) Official explanation: jockey said colt missed the break

Regal Cheer Official explanation: jockey said filly was not moving well

3396 ARENALEISUREPLC.COM H'CAP — 6f (P)
4:30 (4:30) (Class 5) (0-70,71) 3-Y-O+ — **£3,071** (£906; £453) **Stalls** Low

Form — RPR

0603 1 **Quality Street**[7] [3190] 5-9-3 **63** .... (p) RichardThomas 8 — 74
(P Butler) *chsd ldng pair: wnt 2nd over 1f out: styd on u.p to ld wl ins fnl f: sn in command* **12/1**

0301 2 *1 ¼* **George The Second**[7] [3190] 4-9-8 **71** 6ex .... RichardKingscote(3) 2 — 78
(Mrs H Sweeting) *led for 2f: led again over 2f out: rdn and clr over 1f out: hdd wl ins fnl f: fdd cl home* **13/2**[3]

0000 3 *¾* **Brandywell Boy (IRE)**[17] [1969] 4-9-7 **67** .... EddieAhern 6 — 72
(D J S Ffrench Davis) *racd in midfield: hdwy to chse ldng trio over 2f out: kpt on same pce u.p fnl f* **13/2**[3]

0635 4 *½* **Regal Royale**[17] [2864] 4-9-5 **65** .... (b) GeorgeBaker 11 — 69
(Peter Grayson) *hld up in rr: hdwy and rdn wl over 1f out: r.o fnl f: nvr nrr* **10/1**

4346 **5** ½ **Norcroft**[4] 3285 5-9-2 **62** (p) DMylonas 4 64
(Mrs C A Dunnett) *sn outpcd towards rr: rdn and hdwy over 1f out: r.o fnl f: nvr nrr* **12/1**

106 **6** 1 **Imperium**[30] 2492 6-9-3 **63** DaneO'Neill 1 62
(Jean-Rene Auvray) *racd in midfield: rdn and hdwy on inner over 2f out: no imp fnl f* **12/1**

1131 **7** ½ **Mambazo**[6] 3218 5-9-9 **69** (e) JamesDoyle 9 67
(S C Williams) *hld up off the pce: effrt on outer 3f out: sn rdn: no imp wl over 1f out* **2/1**[1]

3U00 **8** 1 ¼ **Law Maker**[10] 3108 7-9-4 **64** (v) FrancisNorton 12 58
(A Bailey) *sn drvn up to press ldr: led after 2f tl over 2f out: sn wknd* **33/1**

0066 **9** 2 **Hollow Jo**[13] 2993 7-9-7 **67** J-PGuillambert 3 55
(J R Jenkins) *outpcd and bhd after 2f: no ch after* **5/1**[2]

2000 **10** 8 **Stoneacre Boy (IRE)**[63] 1565 4-9-2 **62** LPKeniry 10 26
(Peter Grayson) *a outpcd in rr* **25/1**

000- **11** 1 ¼ **Empire Dancer (IRE)**[242] 6426 4-9-9 **69** OscarUrbina 7 29
(C N Allen) *chsd ldrs tl 1/2-way: sn wknd* **33/1**

1m 11.5s (-1.31) **Going Correction** -0.05s/f (Stan) **11** Ran SP% **118.6**
Speed ratings (Par 103):106,104,103,102,102 100,100,98,95,85 83
CSF £87.09 CT £565.66 TOTE £12.50: £3.40, £2.70, £2.90; EX 86.30 Trifecta £341.10 Part won. Pool: £480.50 - 0.54 winning units..
Owner E H Whatmough **Bred** S R Hope **Trained** East Chiltington, E Sussex

FOCUS
An ordinary sprint handicap, but they went a cracking gallop and not many could make any impression from off the pace. Straightforward form.

3397 BOOK ONLINE FOR A DISCOUNT H'CAP 1m 5f (P)
5:00 (5:00) (Class 6) (0-65,64) 4-Y-0+ **£2,388** (£705; £352) **Stalls** Low

Form RPR

1246 **1** **Josh You Are**[21] 2748 4-9-0 **57** PatCosgrave 9 67
(D E Cantillon) *awkward leaving stalls: dropped in bhd: hdwy over 4f out: rdn to chse wnr 2f out: edgd rt but r.o fnl f to ld towards fin* **4/1**[2]

0252 **2** ¾ **Selkirk Grace**[11] 3047 7-8-11 **54** JimCrowley 7 63
(K A Morgan) *in tch: hdwy gng wl over 3f out: rdn to ld 2f out: hung rt jst ins fnl f: hdd and no ex towards fin* **7/1**

3212 **3** 3 ½ **Bob's Your Uncle**[13] 2996 4-9-4 **61** EddieAhern 14 65
(J G Portman) *hld up in midfield: hdwy over 4f out: rdn wl over 2f out: chsd ldng pair 1f out: no imp* **5/1**[3]

4004 **4** 2 ½ **Amwell Brave**[6] 3217 6-9-7 **64** J-PGuillambert 3 64
(J R Jenkins) *t.k.h: hld up in rr: hdwy on wd outside over 3f out: chsd ldrs over 2f out: kpt on same pce after* **9/1**

42 **5** ½ **Super Sensation (GER)**[26] 2595 6-8-10 **53** (b) PatDobbs 11 52
(G L Moore) *stdd s: hld up in rr: hdwy wl over 4f out: chsd ldrs and rdn over 2f out: sn btn* **7/2**[1]

6314 **6** 1 ½ **Missie Baileys**[19] 2800 5-8-5 **48** (p) StephenCarson 8 45
(Mrs L J Mongan) *chsd ldrs: rdn to ld 3f out: hdd 2f out: wknd over 1f out* **14/1**

0/00 **7** 1 **Silver Dreamer (IRE)**[57] 1730 5-8-2 **45** DavidKinsella 13 41
(H S Howe) *hld up bhd: rdn over 4f out: sn outpcd: styd on past btn horse over 1f out: nt trble ldrs* **50/1**

6-05 **8** 1 ¼ **The Iron Giant (IRE)**[17] 2875 5-8-3 **49** ow1 RichardKingscote(3) 6 43
(B G Powell) *t.k.h: hld up in midfield: rdn and struggling over 4f out: n.d after* **20/1**

0646 **9** 4 **Bobsleigh**[32] 2430 8-8-2 **45** (b) FrancisNorton 12 33
(H S Howe) *sn drvn up to chse ldr after 2f: led after 3f: clr 10f out: hdd over 4f out: sn wknd* **14/1**

5604 **10** 3 ½ **And Again (USA)**[14] 2964 4-9-5 **62** (p) GeorgeBaker 10 44
(R A Teal) *led for 3f: chsd ldr tl led again over 4f out: rdn and hdd 3f out: wknd qckly over 2f out* **22/1**

4/00 **11** 7 **Captain Marryat**[17] 2875 6-8-4 **47** RobertMiles 1 19
(J Akehurst) *t.k.h: hld up in midfield: rdn and lost pl wl over 4f out: no ch last 3f* **25/1**

0-00 **12** 2 ½ **Sonny Mac**[55] 1761 4-9-3 **60** (t) RichardHughes 4 28
(M J McGrath) *hld up in rr: rdn over 4f out: sn lost tch: eased whn no ch fnl f* **33/1**

-006 **13** *dist* **Inchloss (IRE)**[19] 2810 6-8-2 **45** RichardThomas 5 —
(S Parr) *chsd ldr for 2f: chsd ldrs tl rdn and wknd over 4f out: t.o and eased last 2f* **33/1**

-044 **14** 15 **Montosari**[13] 2996 8-8-12 **62** JackMitchell(7) 2 —
(P Mitchell) *hld up in rr: hdwy on outer 6f out: rdn and btn wl over 3f out: virtually p.u ins fnl f: dismntd: lame* **9/1**

2m 45.55s (-2.75) **Going Correction** -0.05s/f (Stan) **14** Ran SP% **125.5**
Speed ratings (Par 101):106,105,103,101,101 100,100,99,96,94 90,88,—,—
CSF £30.87 CT £149.43 TOTE £5.70: £1.80, £2.50, £1.80; EX 55.40 Trifecta £124.80 Pool: £552.17 - 3.14 winning units. Place 6 £63.10, Place 5 £49.69.
Owner Exors of the late Mrs Edward Cantillon **Bred** Phil Jen Racing **Trained** Newmarket, Suffolk

FOCUS
A moderate handicap, but thanks to Bobsleigh this was run at a decent pace and that was a big help to those that were held up. Solid form for the grade, the winner up another 5lb.
Montosari Official explanation: jockey said gelding finished lame
T/Plt: £91.40 to a £1 stake. Pool: £62,181.30. 496.55 winning tickets. T/Qpdt: £13.30 to a £1 stake. Pool: £3,861.80. 214.60 winning tickets. SP

3155 PONTEFRACT (L-H)
Tuesday, July 10

OFFICIAL GOING: Good (good to soft in places; 6.3)
Wind: Slight, half behind Weather: Sunny

3398 DIANNE NURSERY 6f
2:45 (2:46) (Class 4) 2-Y-0 **£6,477** (£1,927; £963; £481) **Stalls** Low

Form RPR

3331 **1** **Runswick Bay**[17] 2888 2-9-3 **79** TomEaves 4 85
(G M Moore) *mde most: rdn wl over 1f out: drvn ins fnl f and kpt on gamely* **11/2**[2]

241 **2** 1 **Lady Benjamin**[33] 2385 2-8-3 **68** AndrewElliott(3) 7 71
(P C Haslam) *chsd ldrs: rdn along and outpcd 1/2-way: gd hdwy over 1f out: styd on strly ins fnl f* **7/1**

002 **3** *nk* **Silver Wind**[15] 2941 2-9-1 **77** (b) StephenDonohoe 9 79
(P D Evans) *chsd ldrs: hdwy over 2f out: rdn to chal ent fnl f and ev ch tl drvn: edgd lft and no ex last 100yds* **10/1**

15 **4** 1 ¾ **Mahusay (IRE)**[12] 3025 2-9-6 **82** NickyMackay 11 79
(L M Cumani) *bhd and sn rdn along: hdwy 1/2-way: rdn wl over 1f out: kpt on u.p ins fnl f: nrst fin* **13/2**[3]

13 **5** *nk* **Rubirosa (IRE)**[41] 2151 2-9-7 **83** PhillipMakin 6 79
(M Dods) *trckd ldrs on inner: effrt 2f out: sn rdn and kpt on same pce ins fnl f* **11/1**

445 **6** *nk* **Berrymead**[38] 2251 2-8-3 **65** DaleGibson 10 60
(M W Easterby) *midfield: hdwy 2f out: sn rdn and kpt on u.p ins fnl f: nrst fin* **16/1**

616 **7** *nk* **Stage Acclaim (IRE)**[36] 2316 2-9-7 **83** RyanMoore 2 77
(B R Millman) *towards rr: rdn along over 2f out: swtchd outside over 1f out: styd on ins fnl f: nrst fin* **11/2**[2]

4310 **8** 2 ½ **Barraland**[45] 2049 2-9-3 **79** JHBowman 13 66
(M R Channon) *prom: rdn along over 2f out: sn drvn and grad wknd* **9/1**

4143 **9** 2 **Bahama Baileys**[45] 2024 2-9-5 **81** JoeFanning 5 62
(M Johnston) *cl up: rdn along 2f out and ev ch tl drvn and wknd ent fnl f* **9/2**[1]

004 **10** 4 **Zaplamation (IRE)**[33] 2385 2-7-12 **60** oh4 PaulQuinn 1 29
(D W Barker) *in tch on inner: rdn along 2f out: sn wknd* **33/1**

000 **11** *hd* **Eboracum Dream**[21] 2739 2-7-9 **60** oh2 (b[1]) DuranFentiman(3) 8 28
(T D Easterby) *a towards rr* **40/1**

0440 **12** ¾ **Willyn (IRE)**[6] 3205 2-8-2 **64** ow1 (p) ChrisCatlin 3 30
(J R Weymes) *a towards rr* **33/1**

1045 **13** 22 **Little Finch (IRE)**[28] 2533 2-7-12 **60** oh12 (b) PaulFessey 12 —
(R C Guest) *bhd fr 1/2-way* **100/1**

1m 18.6s (1.20) **Going Correction** +0.125s/f (Good) **13** Ran SP% **117.4**
Speed ratings (Par 96):97,95,95,92,92 92,91,88,85,80 80,79,49
CSF £42.05 CT £378.41 TOTE £6.40: £2.80, £2.60, £3.40; EX 53.90.
Owner John Lishman **Bred** P D And Mrs Player **Trained** Middleham Moor, N Yorks

FOCUS
A fair, competitive nursery, and the form seems solid. The official ratings shown next to each horse are estimated and for information purposes only.

NOTEBOOK
Runswick Bay took a few runs to get off the mark, but he is progressing nicely now and followed up his Redcar maiden success, coping well with the drop in trip and quicker ground. He is a tough sort and could well go in again. (op 13-2 tchd 7-1)
Lady Benjamin ♦, successful in a Hamilton maiden on her previous start, looked a touch unlucky not to follow up on this switch to nursery company. Racing freely through the first furlong, she seemed to almost clip the heels of one of the leaders and stumble, forcing her to come off the bridle. She was always playing catch-up thereafter and there was plenty to like about the way she stayed on for second. (op 10-1)
Silver Wind was always well placed and kept on in the straight. This looks as good as he is. (op 7-1)
Mahusay(IRE) stayed on from an unpromising position to claim fourth in the straight. A more positive ride should suit better in future and he ought to stay 7f. (op 5-1)
Rubirosa(IRE) had no easy task off joint top weight, but this was a respectable effort. (op 12-1)
Stage Acclaim(IRE), up a furlong in trip on his nursery debut, did no enjoy the clearest of runs in the straight, but he did not look unlucky. (op 6-1 tchd 13-2 and 9-2)
Barraland Official explanation: trainer said gelding was unsuited by the good, good to soft in places ground
Bahama Baileys, stepped up in trip and switched to nursery company, showed good speed from the outset, but he failed to see out his race. (tchd 5-1)

3399 MARTYN WINDSOR - A LIFETIME IN RACING MAIDEN STKS 1m 2f 6y
3:15 (3:16) (Class 5) 3-Y-0+ **£3,886** (£1,156; £577; £288) **Stalls** Low

Form RPR

52 **1** **Dar Es Salaam**[18] 2836 3-9-1 0 JimmyFortune 5 86
(E A L Dunlop) *hld up: hdwy to trck ldrs 1/2-way: effrt over 2f out: rdn to ld wl over 1f out: sn clr and styd on wl* **7/2**[2]

4/2- **2** 3 **Fisher Bridge (IRE)**[324] 4625 4-9-12 0 AdamKirby 6 80
(W R Swinburn) *hld up: stdy hdwy 1/2-way: effrt and nt clr run 2f out: swtchd rt and rdn to chse wnr over 1f out: sn edgd lft and no imp ins fnl f* **6/1**

4-5 **3** 5 **Top Tiger**[101] 849 3-8-10 0 PatrickHills(5) 2 70
(M H Tompkins) *prom: led over 7f out: rdn along 3f out: drvn and hdd wl over 1f out: kpt on same pce* **11/2**

032 **4** 2 ½ **Soul Mountain (IRE)**[10] 3079 3-8-10 77 MichaelHills 1 60
(B W Hills) *led over 2f: trckd ldr tl chal 3f out: sn rdn and ev ch tl drvn 2f out and grad wknd* **5/2**[1]

5 **5** 5 **Legend Erry (IRE)**[18] 2836 3-9-1 0 JimmyQuinn 4 55
(Jane Chapple-Hyam) *in tch: effrt over 3f out: sn rdn along and no further prog* **14/1**

6 *shd* **Pom Pom** 3-8-11 0 ow1 JHBowman 8 51
(J G Given) *hld up: hdwy and in tch 4f out: sn rdn along and wknd 3f out* **33/1**

3 **7** 10 **Thorax**[16] 2909 3-9-1 0 JoeFanning 10 35
(M Johnston) *prom: effrt and ev ch 3f out: rdn over 2f out: sn drvn and wknd wl over 1f out* **4/1**[3]

00- **8** ¾ **Glenridding**[220] 6675 3-9-1 0 DaleGibson 9 33
(J G Given) *a towards rr* **100/1**

-000 **9** 17 **Silver Sail**[19] 2795 4-9-7 41 (p) TomEaves 7 —
(J S Wainwright) *chsd ldrs on outer: rdn along 4f out: sn wknd* **100/1**

10 4 **The Borderer**[33] 4-9-12 0 PaulMulrennan 3 —
(M W Easterby) *s.i.s: a towards rr* **100/1**

2m 14.9s (0.82) **Going Correction** +0.125s/f (Good)
WFA 3 from 4yo 11lb **10** Ran SP% **113.0**
Speed ratings (Par 103):101,98,94,92,88 88,80,79,66,63
CSF £23.76 TOTE £3.60: £1.50, £2.40, £2.10; EX 19.60.
Owner Andy Macdonald **Bred** Cliveden Stud Ltd **Trained** Newmarket, Suffolk

FOCUS
A fair maiden, with the winner up 11lb on his previous form. The winning time 2.57 seconds quicker than the following 56-75 handicap, and 0.32 seconds faster than the closing 51-70 apprentice race.

3400 HARWORTH ESTATES H'CAP 1m 2f 6y
3:45 (3:46) (Class 5) (0-75,74) 3-Y-0 **£3,886** (£1,156; £577; £288) **Stalls** Low

Form RPR

5-06 **1** **Tebee**[20] 2766 3-9-6 **73** JimmyFortune 1 81
(J H M Gosden) *mde all: set stdy pce: qcknd 3f out: rdn clr wl over 1f out: styd on strly* **8/1**

-651 **2** 2 **Seeking The Buck (USA)**[32] 2413 3-9-6 **73** (t) ChrisCatlin 5 77+
(M A Magnusson) *trckd ldrs: pushed along and sltly outpcd 1/2-way: hdwy over 2f out: rdn wl over 1f out: styd on ins fnl f: nt rch wnr* **13/2**[3]

1-00 **3** *hd* **Milliegait**[34] 2369 3-9-7 **74** DavidAllan 6 78
(T D Easterby) *hld up in rr: gd hdwy 2f out: sn rdn and styd on wl fnl f: nrst fin* **9/1**

3023 **4** 2 ½ **The Mighty Ogmore**[7] 3182 3-8-3 **56** ow1 (p) PaulEddery 3 55
(R C Guest) *prom: hdwy to trck wnr 6f out: rdn over 2f out: drvn wl over 1f out and kpt on same pce* **12/1**

0051 **5** *1* **Mandalay Prince**[8] [3150] 3-8-5 **58** 6ex........................ GrahamGibbons 8 55
(W J Musson) *trckd ldrs: hdwy 4f out: rdn along over 2f out: sn drvn and one pce* **11/10**[1]

5062 **6** *6* **Professor Twinkle**[21] [2748] 3-9-4 **71**........................(v) PaulDoe 2 56
(W J Knight) *hld up: hdwy to chse ldrs 4f out: rdn along 3f out and sn wknd* **5/1**[2]

0-60 **7** *1 3/4* **Grand Dream (IRE)**[47] [1964] 3-8-7 **60**........................ JoeFanning 4 42
(J G Given) *t.k.h: cl up: rdn along over 4f out: wknd 3f out* **16/1**

2m 17.47s (3.39) **Going Correction** +0.125s/f (Good) **7** Ran SP% **112.3**
Speed ratings (Par 100):91,89,89,87,86 81,80
CSF £55.60 CT £474.95 TOTE £7.40: £3.20, £2.80; EX 39.60.
Owner George Strawbridge **Bred** Nawara Stud Co Ltd **Trained** Newmarket, Suffolk

FOCUS
A fair handicap, but Tebee was allowed the run of the race and set just a steady pace. She and the runner-up are progressive. The winning time was 2.57 seconds slower than the maiden, and 2.25 seconds off the time recorded in the later 51-70 apprentice handicap.
Professor Twinkle Official explanation: jockey said colt ran too free in the early stages

3401 KING RICHARD III H'CAP 6f
4:15 (4:15) (Class 3) (0-90,90) 3-Y-0+
£9,348 (£2,799; £1,399; £700; £349; £175) **Stalls** Low

Form RPR

0520 **1** **Turnkey**[10] [3089] 5-9-6 **90**........................ AdeleRothery(7) 2 101
(D Nicholls) *hld up in rr: gd hdwy on outer over 1f out: str run ent fnl f to ld last 100yds* **10/1**

0-03 **2** *1 1/4* **Damika (IRE)**[10] [3089] 4-9-5 **87**........................ MichaelJStainton(5) 5 94
(R M Whitaker) *chsd ldrs: hdwy 2f out: sn rdn: styd on to chal ins fnl f and ev ch tl drvn and nt qckn last 100yds* **13/2**[2]

0000 **3** *hd* **Stonecrabstomorrow (IRE)**[28] [2528] 4-8-9 **72**........................ TonyHamilton 4 78
(R A Fahey) *midfield: hdwy 2f out: rdn to chse ldrs over 1f out: sn drvn and kpt on ins fnl f* **10/1**

6006 **4** *1 3/4* **Coeur Courageux (FR)**[46] [1996] 5-9-0 **77**........................(t) PhillipMakin 1 78
(D Nicholls) *trckd ldrs on inner: hdwy 2f out: rdn over 1f out: kpt on same pce ins fnl f* **11/1**

2000 **5** *1/2* **Mr Wolf**[10] [3089] 6-9-11 **88**........................(p) TomEaves 6 88
(D W Barker) *led: rdn wl over 1f out: drvn ins fnl f: hdd & wknd last 100yds* **7/1**[3]

0010 **6** *3/4* **Paris Bell**[11] [3053] 5-8-10 **73**........................ PaulQuinn 15 70
(T D Easterby) *s.i.s and bhd: hdwy 2f out: sn rdn and styd on ins fnl f: nrst fin* **14/1**

5600 **7** *shd* **The Snatcher (IRE)**[24] [2670] 4-9-7 **84**........................(v[1]) RyanMoore 9 81
(R Hannon) *in tch: rdn along and sltly outpcd over 2f out: drvn and styd on on outer fr over 1f out: nrst fin* **9/1**

-226 **8** *nk* **Angaric (IRE)**[31] [2466] 4-8-11 **74**........................ RoystonFfrench 10 70
(B Smart) *chsd ldrs: rdn wl over 1f out: drvn and wknd ins fnl f* **8/1**

4336 **9** *nk* **Brigadore**[2] [3345] 8-8-8 **71** oh6........................ HayleyTurner 7 66
(J G Given) *dwlt and rr: hdwy 2f out: rdn over 1f out and sn no imp* **16/1**

4030 **10** *6* **King's Gait**[10] [3089] 5-9-12 **89**........................(b) GrahamGibbons 11 66
(T D Easterby) *a towards rr* **5/1**[1]

0043 **11** *2* **Campo Bueno (FR)**[6] [3201] 5-8-8 **71** oh3........................(b) JoeFanning 3 42
(A Berry) *chsd ldr on inner: rdn along and wkng whn n.m.r 2f out* **12/1**

0150 **12** *2 1/2* **Continent**[11] [3050] 10-9-8 **85**........................ SilvestreDeSousa 12 49
(D Nicholls) *chsd ldrs: rdn 2f out: sn drvn and wknd over 1f out* **12/1**

1m 16.48s (-0.92) **Going Correction** +0.125s/f (Good)
WFA 3 from 4yo+ 6lb **12** Ran SP% **118.1**
Speed ratings (Par 107):111,109,109,106,106 105,104,104,104,96 93,90
CSF £73.35 CT £676.54 TOTE £13.20: £3.80, £2.20, £3.90; EX 78.60.
Owner Middleham Park Racing Xxiii **Bred** Mrs E M Charlton **Trained** Sessay, N Yorks
■ Stewards' Enquiry : Adele Rothery caution: used whip with excessive frequency

FOCUS
A good sprint handicap, the winner taking advantage of a reduced mark and the runner-up running to his best. The leaders seemed to go off a little too quickly.

NOTEBOOK
Turnkey was given a well-judged ride by Adele Rothery, who took a pull coming out of the stalls and held her mount up in last, well off the strong early pace. He was switched widest of all in the straight and took off to ultimately win very convincingly. There was clearly enough juice in the ground for him and a fast-run race on a stiff track suits him well. (op 11-1 tchd 12-1)
Damika(IRE) returned to form when third at Newcastle on his previous start, when he had three of today's rivals behind, including Turnkey, and this was another good effort. He raced much closer to the pace than the eventual winner, but was still sensibly ridden a little way off the leaders. (op 7-1)
Stonecrabstomorrow(IRE) ◆ was able to race off a career-low mark and shaped very encouragingly back in third. He will be able to get into much lower-grade contests off his current rating and must be followed. (op 15-2)
Coeur Courageux(FR) is a generally disappointing sort, but he offered a little more off a career-low rating. (tchd 12-1)
Mr Wolf, with the cheekpieces re-fitted, looked to go off too fast and did not last out. (op 11-2)
King's Gait never landed a blow and proved rather disappointing. Official explanation: trainer said gelding was unsuited by the good, good to soft in places ground (tchd 6-1)

3402 SOUTHDALE HOMES AND CIRCA MAIDEN STKS 1m 4f 8y
4:45 (4:46) (Class 5) 3-Y-0+ **£4,533** (£1,348; £674; £336) **Stalls** Low

Form RPR

-634 **1** **Rhaam**[46] [1998] 3-8-13 80........................ RHills 9 77
(B W Hills) *hld up: hdwy 1/2-way: rdn to chal over 1f out: drvn ins fnl f: styd on to ld last stride* **2/1**[1]

-262 **2** *shd* **Yossi (IRE)**[10] [3081] 3-8-13 81........................ JimmyQuinn 1 77
(M H Tompkins) *trckd ldrs: hdwy 3f out: led wl over 1f out and sn rdn: drvn ins fnl f: no ex and hdd on line* **5/2**[2]

646 **3** *1 1/2* **Ancient Culture**[36] [2308] 3-8-13 78........................(t) RyanMoore 5 74
(Sir Michael Stoute) *hld up in rr: stdy hdwy 1/2-way: rdn along to chse ldrs 3f out: drvn wl over 1f out: kpt on same pce u.p ins fnl f* **5/2**[2]

420/ **4** *5* **Oniz Tiptoes (IRE)**[11] [4710] 6-9-7 0........................(v) PJMcDonald(5) 8 66
(J S Wainwright) *chsd clr ldr: led 1/2-way: rdn along 3f out: drvn and hdd wl over 1f out: grad wknd* **14/1**[3]

5 *15* **Guerilla (AUS)**[38] 7-9-12 0........................ PaulEddery 4 42
(R C Guest) *bhd: pushed along 1/2-way: sme late hdwy* **25/1**

0004 **6** *4* **Wingsinmotion (IRE)**[4] [3274] 3-8-5 40........................(p) AndrewElliott(3) 7 31
(Miss Tracy Waggott) *chsd ldrs: rdn along over 3f out: sn drvn and wknd* **100/1**

0 **7** *1* **Star Of Angels**[15] [2951] 3-8-13 0........................ JoeFanning 2 34
(M Johnston) *chsd ldrs: rdn along 4f out: wknd 3f out* **20/1**

05 **8** *2* **Arabian Sun**[23] [2690] 3-8-13 0........................ PaulFitzsimons 6 31
(M J Attwater) *chsd ldrs: rdn along over 4f out: snw eakened* **33/1**

04F0 **9** *3/4* **Arcangela**[18] [2825] 4-9-7 40........................ SilvestreDeSousa 3 25
(Miss Tracy Waggott) *a towards rr* **100/1**

00-0 **10** *35* **Dandys Hurricane**[57] [1715] 4-9-12 46........................ DaleGibson 11 —
(M W Easterby) *a towards rr* **66/1**

66 **11** *56* **Spring Creek**[12] [3041] 3-8-8 0........................ PaulMulrennan 10 —
(M W Easterby) *led and sn clr: hdd 1/2-way and sn wknd* **66/1**

2m 39.61s (-0.69) **Going Correction** +0.125s/f (Good)
WFA 3 from 4yo+ 13lb **11** Ran SP% **113.7**
Speed ratings (Par 103):107,106,105,102,92 89,89,87,87,64 26
CSF £6.50 TOTE £3.00: £1.10, £1.40, £1.50; EX 6.70.
Owner Hamdan Al Maktoum **Bred** Shadwell Estate Company Limited **Trained** Lambourn, Berks
■ Stewards' Enquiry : Jimmy Quinn two-day ban: used whip with excessive frequency (Jul 21-22)

FOCUS
Just an ordinary maiden, as one would expect for the time of year. The first three are fairly exposed and not really progressing.

3403 BETFAIR.COM APPRENTICE SERIES (ROUND 3) H'CAP 1m 2f 6y
5:15 (5:19) (Class 5) (0-70,68) 4-Y-0+ **£3,886** (£1,156; £577; £288) **Stalls** Low

Form RPR

-021 **1** **Turn Of Phrase (IRE)**[6] [3204] 8-9-6 **68** 6ex........................(b) LanceBetts(5) 5 77
(B Ellison) *prom: effrt 2f out: rdn to ld ent fnl f: edgd lft and sn clr* **15/2**

0005 **2** *2 1/2* **Don'Tcallmeginger (IRE)**[7] [3177] 4-8-3 **53**........................ AshleyMorgan(7) 2 57
(M H Tompkins) *chsd ldrs: rdn along over 2f out: kpt on u.p fnl f* **7/1**

/-00 **3** *nk* **Moment Of Clarity**[8] [3155] 5-8-5 **48**........................ DanielleMcCreery 1 51
(R C Guest) *hld up in rr: stdy hdwy over 3f out: rdn wl over 1f out: kpt on ins fnl f: nrst fin* **22/1**

0442 **4** *nk* **Kylkenny**[8] [3155] 12-8-2 **48** oh1........................(t) FrankiePickard(3) 3 51
(H Morrison) *cl up: led 4f out: rdn wl over 1f out: hdd ent fnl f: wknd* **5/2**[1]

-001 **5** *3* **Scotty's Future (IRE)**[4] [3257] 9-8-5 **53** 6ex........................ AdamCarter(5) 6 50
(A Berry) *midfield on outer: rdn along over 2f out: no imp appr fnl f* **20/1**

0500 **6** *1* **Wulimaster (USA)**[13] [2987] 4-9-3 **65**........................(v) NSLawes(5) 9 60
(D W Barker) *in tch on inner: rdn along over 2f out: plugged on same pce* **25/1**

/611 **7** *3 1/2* **Gardasee (GER)**[8] [3155] 5-9-3 **60** 6ex........................ JamieHamblett 10 48
(T P Tate) *led: rdn along and hdd 4f out: drvn 2f out and sn wknd* **9/2**[2]

000/ **8** *hd* **Forzacurity**[22] [5821] 8-8-0 **48**........................ BernadetteQuinn(5) 7 35
(P D Evans) *chsd ldrs: rdn along over 4f out: sn wknd* **14/1**

6554 **9** *3* **Tidy (IRE)**[11] [3049] 7-9-4 **61**........................(p) WilliamCarson 8 42
(Micky Hammond) *s.i.s: a towards rr* **13/2**[3]

2526 **10** *hd* **Dark Charm (FR)**[7] [3182] 8-9-7 **67**........................ JamesRogers(3) 4 48
(R A Fahey) *hld up: hdwy to chse ldrs over 3f out: sn rdn and wknd* **15/2**

2m 15.22s (1.14) **Going Correction** +0.125s/f (Good) **10** Ran SP% **115.7**
Speed ratings (Par 103):100,98,97,97,95 94,91,91,88,88
CSF £56.80 CT £1105.11 TOTE £9.30: £2.70, £2.70, £4.70; EX 77.20 Place 6 £684.16, Place 5 £239.62.
Owner Naughty Diesel Ltd **Bred** Moyglare Stud Farm Ltd **Trained** Norton, N Yorks

FOCUS
A modest handicap restricted to apprentices who, at the start of the 2007 Turf season, had not ridden more than ten winners. The winning time was 2.25 seconds quicker than the earlier 56-75 handicap, but 0.32 seconds slower than the maiden. A career best from Turn Of Phrase, but the two favourites were below their recent C/D form.
T/Jkpt: £36,268.60 to a £1 stake. Pool: £51,082.59. 1.00 winning ticket. T/Plt: £387.10 to a £1 stake. Pool: £86,764.25. 163.60 winning tickets. T/Qpdt: £59.40 to a £1 stake. Pool: £4,671.30. 58.10 winning tickets. JR

3281 WOLVERHAMPTON (A.W) (L-H)
Tuesday, July 10

OFFICIAL GOING: Standard
Wind: Light across Weather: Fine

3404 HORIZONS RESTAURANT MAIDEN AUCTION STKS 7f 32y(P)
6:50 (6:51) (Class 5) 2-Y-0 **£3,071** (£906; £453) **Stalls** High

Form RPR

1 **Semah Harold** 2-8-9 0........................ RichardMullen 1 75
(E S McMahon) *a.p: rdn over 2f out: led over 1f out: jst hld on* **20/1**

2 *shd* **Without A Prayer (IRE)** 2-8-11 0........................ SebSanders 7 77
(R M Beckett) *a.p: rdn and ev ch over 1f out: hung lft wl ins fnl f: r.o: jst failed* **11/4**[1]

3 *3* **Quick Off The Mark** 2-8-8 0........................ JamieSpencer 6 66
(J G Given) *led: rdn and hdd over 1f out: no ex ins fnl f* **4/1**[2]

4 *nk* **Lady Rochbonne** 2-8-6 0 ow2........................ DeanMcKeown 4 63
(Mrs G S Rees) *mid-div: rdn over 3f out: hdwy and edgd lft over 1f out: kpt on towards fin* **20/1**

45 **5** *3* **Feasible**[17] [2876] 2-8-12 0........................ ChrisCatlin 9 62
(J G Portman) *chsd ldrs: rdn over 3f out: wknd over 2f out* **7/1**

6 *3/4* **Bozeman Trail** 2-8-13 0........................ JHBowman 5 61
(M R Channon) *hld up and bhd: pushed along over 3f out: swtchd rt over 1f out: nvr nr ldrs* **10/1**

0 **7** *2* **Agon Eyes (USA)**[31] [2468] 2-8-7 0........................ EdwardCreighton 8 50
(D J Coakley) *sn w ldr: rdn over 3f out: wknd over 2f out* **5/1**[3]

8 *1/2* **Agglestone Rock** 2-8-2 0........................ JackDean(7) 11 51
(W G M Turner) *s.i.s: bhd: hung lft wl over 1f out: n.d* **33/1**

0 **9** *9* **Ely Une (IRE)**[14] [2969] 2-8-5 0 ow1........................ AlanDaly 3 24
(B W Duke) *hld up in mid-div: rdn over 3f out: wknd 2f out* **50/1**

10 *1* **Strong Market** 2-8-9 0........................ MickyFenton 10 26
(H J L Dunlop) *rdn over 5f out: a bhd* **14/1**

11 *12* **Pembo** 2-8-11 0........................ SteveDrowne 2 —
(B Palling) *a bhd* **7/1**

1m 30.18s (-0.22) **Going Correction** -0.175s/f (Stan) **11** Ran SP% **118.5**
Speed ratings (Par 94):94,93,90,90,86 85,83,82,72,71 57
CSF £72.87 TOTE £26.50: £6.00, £1.60, £1.80; EX 140.30.
Owner J P Hames **Bred** J P Hames **Trained** Lichfield, Staffs

FOCUS
A modest-looking event with little previous form to go on and the first four home were all newcomers. Probably not strong form.

NOTEBOOK
Semah Harold only cost 800gns and has been slow to come to hand particularly mentally according to his trainer, who thinks he will be better suited to a mile. (op 25-1)
Without A Prayer(IRE) ◆ probably would have prevailed had he kept straight in the closing stages. He seems perfectly capable of taking a similar contest. (op 3-1)
Quick Off The Mark, a half-sister to seven and nine-furlong winner Market Trend, lived up to her name but had nothing more to offer in the final 200 yards. (op 5-1 tchd 7-2)
Lady Rochbonne is a half-sister to a 2m4f winner over hurdles in Ireland. She shaped as though she is going to need further. (op 16-1)
Feasible did not find a switch to the sand the answer. (op 5-1 tchd 15-2)

3405 BOOK ONLINE AT WOLVERHAMPTON-RACECOURSE.CO.UK (S) H'CAP 1m 141y(P)
7:20 (7:21) (Class 6) (0-65,65) 3-Y-O+ **£2,047** (£604; £302) **Stalls** Low

Form RPR
0543 **1** **Le Chiffre (IRE)**[8] 3172 5-9-11 **56**....(p) SebSanders 2 71
(S Curran) *led early: a.p: rdn to ld wl over 1f out: drew clr u.p fnl f: r.o wl* **6/1**[3]
0200 **2** *5* **Over To You Bert**[13] 2979 8-8-13 **51**.... HaddenFrost(7) 4 55
(R J Hodges) *sn chsng ldr: lost 2nd over 3f out: rdn over 1f out: kpt on ins fnl f: no ch w wnr* **9/1**
0600 **3** *½* **Crush On You**[8] 3156 4-8-11 **47**.... RussellKennemore(5) 10 50
(R Hollinshead) *hld up in mid-div: rdn and hdwy 2f out: kpt on ins fnl f* **20/1**
2105 **4** *½* **Mademoiselle**[87] 1038 5-9-8 **58**.... LukeMorris(5) 6 60
(R A Harris) *hld up in mid-div: rdn and hdwy 2f out: kpt on same pce fnl f* **13/2**
-610 **5** *½* **Bond Diamond**[46] 2007 10-9-8 **53**.... MickyFenton 8 54
(P T Midgley) *stdd and n.m.r s: hld up and bhd: hdwy on outside 2f out: sn hung lft: one pce fnl f* **12/1**
036 **6** *1* **Feelin Irie (IRE)**[19] 2798 4-9-10 **55**....(p) JHBowman 13 54
(J R Boyle) *sn led: hdd wl over 1f out: sn rdn: wknd ins fnl f* **7/1**
5354 **7** *4* **Dexileos (IRE)**[25] 2619 8-9-1 **46**.... ChrisCatlin 11 36
(David Pinder) *hld up in tch: lost pl over 3f out: wknd wl over 1f out* **16/1**
0 **8** *¾* **Little Paso (FR)**[8] 3172 7-9-2 **47**....(v) StephenDonohoe 3 35
(B N Pollock) *hld up in mid-div: hdwy 4f out: sn rdn: wknd wl over 1f out* **40/1**
-005 **9** *nk* **Cove Mountain (IRE)**[24] 2656 5-9-5 **50**.... SteveDrowne 5 37
(S Kirk) *prom: rdn over 3f out: wknd over 2f out* **7/2**[1]
0205 **10** *3 ½* **Scroll**[19] 2798 4-9-7 **52**....(v) JamieSpencer 7 32
(P Howling) *a bhd* **9/2**[2]
-554 **11** *3* **Chateau (IRE)**[18] 2843 5-9-2 **47**....(t) TomEaves 1 20
(M E Sowersby) *hld up in mid-div: rdn 4f out: wknd 3f out* **10/1**
00-0 **12** *8* **Bellini Star**[29] 1368 4-9-2 **47**.... AlanDaly 9 —
(G A Ham) *rdn 4f out: a bhd* **33/1**
3600 **13** *nk* **L'Oiseau De Feu (USA)**[22] 2079 3-9-10 **65**....(p) VinceSlattery 12 20
(Mrs K Waldron) *s.i.s: rdn over 4f out: a bhd* **22/1**

1m 49.57s (-2.19) **Going Correction** -0.175s/f (Stan)
WFA 3 from 4yo+ 10lb **13** Ran SP% **127.7**
Speed ratings (Par 101):102,97,97,96,96 95,91,91,90,87 85,77,77
CSF £60.87 CT £1086.19 TOTE £5.60: £2.80, £2.40, £5.20; EX 55.90.The winner was bought in for 5,500gns.
Owner L M Power **Bred** Agricola Del Parco **Trained** Faringdon, Oxon

FOCUS
An ordinary seller with little solid form to go on. The winner came clear and is rated back to his winter best.

3406 STAY AT THE WOLVERHAMPTON HOLIDAY INN MEDIAN AUCTION MAIDEN STKS 1m 141y(P)
7:50 (7:51) (Class 6) 3-4-Y-O **£2,388** (£705; £352) **Stalls** Low

Form RPR
0-2 **1** **Muhannak (IRE)**[71] 1343 3-9-3 0.... NickyMackay 1 71+
(G A Butler) *hld up in mid-div: reminder 4f out: hdwy on ins whn nt clr run over 2f out: rdn over 1f out: led ins fnl f: drvn out* **5/2**[1]
06 **2** *1 ¼* **Mega Dame (IRE)**[29] 2520 3-8-12 0.... BrettDoyle 3 63
(D Haydn Jones) *hld up in mid-div: hdwy over 2f out: ev ch over 1f out: kpt on towards fin* **33/1**
03 **3** *1 ¼* **Le Singe Noir**[15] 2951 3-9-3 73.... RichardMullen 2 65
(D M Simcock) *a.p: rdn and ev ch ins fnl f: nt qckn* **9/2**[3]
5-06 **4** *hd* **Split Briefs (IRE)**[10] 3084 3-8-12 66.... JamieSpencer 8 60
(D J Daly) *hld up and bhd: rdn and hdwy on outside wl over 1f out: kpt on ins fnl f* **7/1**
44 **5** *nk* **Derricks Dotty**[15] 2951 3-9-3 0.... DO'Donohoe 12 64
(N J Vaughan) *prom: led 3f out: hdd ins fnl f: no ex* **33/1**
0- **6** *1 ¼* **Sweet Peak (IRE)**[37] 2285 3-8-12 0.... KDarley 13 56
(Eamon Tyrrell, Ire) *a.p: rdn and ev ch over 2f out: fdd ins fnl f* **4/1**[2]
54 **7** *2 ½* **Topflightcoolracer**[11] 3062 3-8-12 0.... DeanMcKeown 7 51
(Mrs G S Rees) *hld up in mid-div: hdwy whn nt clr run briefly jst over 2f out: sn rdn: wknd ins fnl f* **16/1**
4050 **8** *½* **Boogie Board**[10] 3110 3-8-9 50.... DominicFox(3) 6 50
(S Parr) *hld up towards rr: short-lived effrt over 2f out* **66/1**
9 *½* **Coppergirl (IRE)** 3-8-12 0.... MickyFenton 5 48
(G A Huffer) *a bhd* **16/1**
-020 **10** *1 ¼* **View From The Top**[7] 3181 3-9-3 73.... SebSanders 4 51
(Sir Mark Prescott) *led: rdn and hdd 3f out: wknd over 1f out* **4/1**[2]
0-00 **11** *2 ½* **Tora Warning**[36] 2304 3-9-3 38.... StephenDonohoe 11 45
(John A Harris) *a bhd* **66/1**
0 **12** *11* **Perry's Pride**[15] 2951 3-8-12 0.... DaleGibson 9 16
(Mrs G S Rees) *t.k.h: sn w ldr: wknd 3f out* **66/1**
00-0 **13** *29* **Danjoe**[43] 2083 3-8-12 47.... LukeMorris(5) 10 —
(R Brotherton) *a bhd: lost tch fnl 2f: t.o* **66/1**

1m 50.26s (-1.50) **Going Correction** -0.175s/f (Stan) **13** Ran SP% **122.9**
Speed ratings (Par 101):99,97,96,96,96 95,93,92,92,91 88,79,53
CSF £102.63 TOTE £3.80: £1.50, £7.30, £2.10; EX 101.00.
Owner Fawzi Abdulla Nass **Bred** Mount Coote Stud **Trained** Blewbury, Oxon

FOCUS
A moderate maiden, and hugely dubious form with the field finishing far too bunched and some poor performers not beaten far. The form could otherwise have been rated higher.
Split Briefs(IRE) Official explanation: jockey said filly hung right in home straight
Sweet Peak(IRE) Official explanation: trainer said filly was in season
Danjoe Official explanation: jockey said gelding would not face the kickback

3407 APOLLO 2000 SUMMER SALE H'CAP 1m 4f 50y(P)
8:20 (8:20) (Class 5) (0-75,81) 3-Y-O+ **£3,238** (£963; £481; £240) **Stalls** Low

Form RPR
0406 **1** **Broughtons Folly**[36] 2321 4-9-6 **64**.... BrettDoyle 6 74
(W J Musson) *hld up and bhd: rdn and hdwy 3f out: r.o u.p to ld towards fin* **10/1**
0503 **2** *1 ½* **My Secrets**[8] 3170 3-8-13 **70**....(b[1]) JoeFanning 5 78
(M Johnston) *led 1f: w ldr: rdn 2f out: led over 1f out: hdd and no ex towards fin* **11/4**[2]
310- **3** *2 ½* **Mexican Pete**[361] 3497 7-10-0 **72**.... DaneO'Neill 8 76
(A King) *hld up in mid-div: hdwy over 5f out: rdn 3f out: one pce fnl f* **14/1**
1623 **4** *1 ½* **Chia (IRE)**[30] 2491 4-9-9 **67**.... SimonWhitworth 7 68
(D Haydn Jones) *t.k.h: prom: rdn 2f out: one pce* **12/1**
-406 **5** *shd* **Majestic Chief**[49] 1936 3-8-3 **60**....(p) JimmyQuinn 2 61
(P D Niven) *t.k.h: set modest pce after 1f: rdn and hdd over 1f out: wknd ins fnl f* **33/1**
30-6 **6** *½* **Looks The Business (IRE)**[5] 3250 6-9-8 **66**.... SaleemGolam 10 66
(W G M Turner) *prom: rdn over 3f out: wknd over 2f out* **20/1**
0416 **7** *nk* **Thorny Mandate**[6] 3217 5-9-3 **61**.... EddieAhern 4 61
(W M Brisbourne) *hld up in mid-div: lost pl over 4f out: rdn and sme hdwy wl over 1f out: n.d* **6/1**[3]
-001 **8** *¾* **History Boy**[8] 3170 3-9-10 **81** 6ex.... JamieSpencer 9 80
(D J Coakley) *hld up in rr: rdn and hdwy on outside over 2f out: wknd wl over 1f out* **11/8**[1]
0/0- **9** *1 ½* **Rosecliff**[111] 5792 5-10-0 **72**....(b[1]) J-PGuillambert 1 68
(Heather Dalton) *prom tl rdn and wknd over 3f out* **16/1**
6-00 **10** *3 ½* **Top Seed (IRE)**[28] 2527 6-9-4 **62**.... DeanMcKeown 3 53
(A J Chamberlain) *plld hrd in mid-div: bhd fnl 4f* **33/1**
000/ **11** *8* **Gumlayloy**[33] 4687 8-8-8 **55** oh10.... DominicFox(3) 11 33
(G H Jones) *hld up and bhd: hdwy on outside 5f out: rdn 4f out: sn wknd* **100/1**

2m 41.42s (-1.00) **Going Correction** -0.175s/f (Stan)
WFA 3 from 4yo+ 13lb **11** Ran SP% **124.0**
Speed ratings (Par 103):96,95,93,92,92 91,91,91,90,87 82
CSF £38.85 CT £407.40 TOTE £13.50: £4.30, £1.80, £4.70; EX 41.30.
Owner Broughton Thermal Insulation **Bred** Broughton Bloodstock **Trained** Newmarket, Suffolk

FOCUS
A slow pace resulted in a moderate winning time for the grade, and the form may not prove solid. The winner is rated to his best.

3408 RINGSIDE SUITE 700 THEATRE STYLE CONFERENCE H'CAP 5f 216y(P)
8:50 (8:51) (Class 6) (0-60,60) 3-Y-O+ **£2,388** (£705; £352) **Stalls** Low

Form RPR
0664 **1** **Ebraam (USA)**[11] 3064 4-9-5 **57**.... JimmyQuinn 4 66
(D Shaw) *t.k.h towards rr: stdy hdwy over 3f out: rdn over 1f out: r.o wl to ld last stride* **9/2**[2]
0020 **2** *hd* **Silver Prelude**[27] 2555 6-9-3 **55**.... SteveDrowne 13 63
(D K Ivory) *led: rdn and hdd last stride* **20/1**
0454 **3** *1 ½* **Ryedane (IRE)**[29] 2516 5-9-7 **59**.... DavidAllan 8 62
(T D Easterby) *chsd ldr: ev ch over 2f out: rdn wl over 1f out: one pce fnl f* **7/2**[1]
0-02 **4** *2 ½* **Berti Bertolini**[19] 2799 4-9-4 **56**.... ChrisCatlin 7 51
(Rae Guest) *hld up in tch: rdn over 2f out: one pce*
0-00 **5** *½* **Playtotheaudience**[43] 2072 4-9-8 **60**.... TonyHamilton 9 54
(R A Fahey) *hld up in mid-div: lost pl 3f out: sn rdn: kpt on fnl f* **33/1**
0504 **6** *1 ¼* **Duke Of Milan (IRE)**[19] 2799 4-9-4 **56**.... SebSanders 12 46
(G C Bravery) *hld up: sn bhd: sme hdwy on outside over 2f out: hung lft over 1f out: sn wknd* **10/1**
00 **7** *½* **Green Lagonda (AUS)**[14] 2972 5-9-8 **60**.... EddieAhern 2 48
(J G Given) *hld up in mid-div: hdwy on ins over 2f out: sn hung rt and rdn: no rspnse* **14/1**
0/00 **8** *1* **Dorchester**[11] 3064 10-9-6 **58**.... BrettDoyle 6 43
(W J Musson) *prom: rdn over 1f out: wknd fnl f* **12/1**
5452 **9** *½* **Union Jack Jackson (IRE)**[19] 2806 5-9-6 **58**....(b) StephenDonohoe 5 41
(John A Harris) *a towards rr* **8/1**
4401 **10** *shd* **Desert Light (IRE)**[73] 1309 6-9-8 **60**....(v) DeanMcKeown 3 43
(D Shaw) *hld up in mid-div: btn whn hung lft 1f out* **8/1**
5406 **11** *1 ¼* **Formidable Will (FR)**[29] 2516 5-9-2 **54**....(vt) DaneO'Neill 11 33
(D Shaw) *a bhd* **16/1**
0002 **12** *5* **Falmassim**[27] 2576 4-9-6 **58**....(p) TomEaves 1 21
(Miss J A Camacho) *s.s: a bhd* **13/2**[3]

1m 13.81s (-2.00) **Going Correction** -0.175s/f (Stan) **12** Ran SP% **124.1**
Speed ratings (Par 101):106,105,103,100,99 98,97,96,95,95 93,86
CSF £95.64 CT £366.42 TOTE £6.40: £2.80, £4.40, £1.80; EX 109.80.
Owner The Circle Bloodstock I Limited **Bred** Shadwell Farm LLC **Trained** Danethorpe, Notts

FOCUS
A decent pace led to a fair winning time for the class. Solid form.
Green Lagonda(AUS) Official explanation: jockey said gelding hung right
Desert Light(IRE) Official explanation: jockey said gelding was denied a clear run
Falmassim Official explanation: jockey said gelding missed the break

3409 SPONSOR A RACE BY CALLING 0870 220 2442 H'CAP 7f 32y(P)
9:20 (9:20) (Class 6) (0-65,65) 3-Y-O+ **£2,388** (£705; £352) **Stalls** High

Form RPR
2150 **1** **Sedge (USA)**[27] 2550 7-9-8 **61**....(b) MickyFenton 10 70
(P T Midgley) *hld up: hdwy over 2f out: swtchd lft wl over 1f out: rdn to ld ins fnl f: r.o* **9/1**
0443 **2** *1 ¼* **Green Pirate**[8] 3173 5-9-4 **57**....(p) DavidAllan 1 63+
(W M Brisbourne) *s.i.s: hld up in rr: hdwy on ins whn swtchd rt over 1f out: rdn and r.o ins fnl f: nt rch wnr* **5/1**[2]
0350 **3** *1 ½* **Plateau**[31] 2458 8-9-12 **65**.... EddieAhern 4 67
(C R Dore) *led 1f: a.p: rdn and hung rt over 1f out: ev ch ins fnl f: one pce* **8/1**
0413 **4** *1* **Benny The Bus**[4] 3285 5-9-6 **59**.... J-PGuillambert 3 58
(Mrs G S Rees) *w ldrs: led 3f out: rdn over 1f out: hdd ins fnl f: no ex* **3/1**[1]
5-46 **5** *nk* **Bajeel (IRE)**[76] 1236 3-9-4 **65**....(t) NickyMackay 2 63
(G A Butler) *hld up: rdn and hdwy on ins wl over 1f out: one pce fnl f* **8/1**
6/30 **6** *1* **Exotic Venture**[17] 2878 4-9-4 **57**.... SebSanders 12 53
(R M Beckett) *prom: rdn over 2f out: wknd over 1f out* **16/1**
0200 **7** *¾* **Lucius Verrus (USA)**[15] 2947 7-9-6 **59**....(v) DeanMcKeown 7 53
(D Shaw) *hld up: rdn wl over 1f out: no rspnse* **10/1**
3246 **8** *hd* **Moon Forest (IRE)**[25] 2623 5-9-2 **55**....(p) SteveDrowne 9 48
(J M Bradley) *hld up: rdn over 2f out: sn bhd* **9/1**
-020 **9** *hd* **Antigoni (IRE)**[26] 2592 4-9-10 **63**....(v) JimmyQuinn 8 56
(A M Balding) *led after 1f: hdd 3f out: wknd ins fnl f* **6/1**[3]
3650 **10** *shd* **Maison Dieu**[12] 3017 4-9-4 **57**.... DavidKinsella 11 49
(E J Alston) *hld up: short-lived effrt on outside over 2f out* **12/1**

1m 28.7s (-1.70) **Going Correction** -0.175s/f (Stan)
WFA 3 from 4yo+ 8lb **10** Ran SP% **120.8**
Speed ratings (Par 101):102,100,98,97,97 96,95,95,94,94
CSF £55.63 CT £393.52 TOTE £12.40: £1.80, £1.80, £3.20; EX 45.90 Place 6 £228.82, Place 5 £139.22..
Owner Peter Mee **Bred** Twin Creeks Farm **Trained** Westow, N Yorks

FOCUS
An open-looking, low-grade affair. Ordinary form, the winner basically running to his best.
Plateau Official explanation: jockey said gelding hung right
T/Plt: £341.70 to a £1 stake. Pool: £69,499.30. 148.45 winning tickets. T/Qpdt: £43.30 to a £1 stake. Pool: £5,241.20. 89.40 winning tickets. KH

3199 CATTERICK (L-H)

Wednesday, July 11

OFFICIAL GOING: Good to firm (9.1)

The ground had dried out and was described as 'genuine good to firm'.

Wind: light half-against Weather: overcast but becoming fine and warm

3410 ARNIE ROBINSON LIFETIME IN RACING (S) STKS 5f
2:20 (2:23) (Class 6) 2-Y-O **£2,730** (£806; £403) **Stalls** Low

Form RPR

1 **Genethni** 2-8-6 0 ... DO'Donohoe 3 56
(K A Ryan) *w ldrs: led over 2f out: edgd rt 1f out: hld on wl towards fin* **3/1**[2]

45 2 ¾ **Tanley**[34] [2392] 2-8-11 0 ... RoystonFfrench 1 58
(James Moffatt) *chsd ldrs: chal 1f out: edgd lft: no ex wl ins fnl f* **11/4**[1]

6523 3 1½ **Next Best**[22] [2738] 2-8-6 0 ...(p) TomEaves 6 48
(A Berry) *led over 2f out: edgd rt 1f out: kpt on same pce* **7/2**[3]

4 ½ **Dark Queen** 2-8-6 0 ... SilvestreDeSousa 5 46
(D W Thompson) *dwlt: reminders and hdwy to chse ldrs 3f out: keeping on same pce whn n.m.r ins fnl f* **11/2**

000 5 10 **Chief Powderface (IRE)**[18] [2869] 2-8-11 0 ...(b[1]) PaulMulrennan 2 15
(Jedd O'Keeffe) *w ldrs: wandered and wknd wl over 1f out* **8/1**

0060 6 2½ **Blazing Bullet (IRE)**[30] [2517] 2-8-4 0 ... LanceBetts(7) 8 —
(N Wilson) *chsd ldrs: lost pl 2f out: sn bhd* **14/1**

0 7 7 **Doubtless**[4] [3297] 2-7-13 0 ...(b[1]) DanielleMcCreery(7) 7 —
(D W Chapman) *s.s: a detached in last* **14/1**

61.52 secs (0.92) **Going Correction** 0.0s/f (Good) 7 Ran SP% **113.7**

Speed ratings (Par 92):92,90,88,87,71 67,56

CSF £11.57 TOTE £4.70: £2.70, £1.50; EX 14.30.The winner was bought in for 8,800gns. Dark Queen was claimed by Declan Carroll for £6,000.

Owner H B Hughes **Bred** H B Hughes **Trained** Hambleton, N Yorks

FOCUS

A poor race even by selling standards. The race has been rated through the exposed third.

NOTEBOOK

Genethni, a home-bred half-sister to Guto, a winner three times, is not the best of walkers and a moderate mover. She knew her job and, after edging towards the centre, in the end she did enough. (op 9-4 tchd 7-2 and 4-1 in a place)

Tanley, awkward to load, had the rail to help but in the end was only second best despite being matched at 1.25 on the exchanges. (op 7-2 tchd 5-2 and 4-1 in a place)

Next Best, down in trip, was on her toes in the paddock and quite keen to post. (op 11-4)

Dark Queen, a close-coupled newcomer, missed a beat at the start and had to be put about her job. She was going nowhere when tightened up against the running rail. She was claimed. (op 15-2)

Chief Powderface(IRE), dropped in class and fitted with blinkers, was keen to post and duck and dived as he dropped away. (op 12-1 tchd 14-1 and 7-1)

3411 BOOK TICKETS ON-LINE AT CATTERICKBRIDGE.CO.UK H'CAP 7f
2:55 (2:55) (Class 5) (0-75,75) 3-Y-O **£3,238** (£963; £481; £240) **Stalls** Low

Form RPR

2443 1 **Musical Beat**[24] [2691] 3-9-7 75 ... PaulMulrennan 14 83
(Miss V Haigh) *trckd ldrs: chal over 1f out: led towards fin* **9/1**

0005 2 shd **Prince Rossi (IRE)**[18] [2892] 3-8-3 57 ...(p) PaulFessey 4 65
(J D Bethell) *led: kpt on wl fnl 2f: hdd nr fin* **25/1**

4003 3 2 **Rann Na Cille (IRE)**[9] [3168] 3-8-6 60 ... DO'Donohoe 5 63
(K A Ryan) *chsd ldrs: styd on same pce appr fnl f* **16/1**

2144 4 ½ **Medici Pearl**[11] [3078] 3-9-5 73 ... DavidAllan 1 74+
(T D Easterby) *hld up in rr: hdwy on inner over 2f out: kpt on same pce appr fnl f* **7/2**[1]

0201 5 ½ **Toms Laughter**[26] [2622] 3-8-6 60 ... DaleGibson 6 60
(B Palling) *chsd ldrs: kpt on same pce fnl 2f* **8/1**

50-3 6 ¾ **Harry The Hawk**[20] [2796] 3-8-6 60 ... GrahamGibbons 2 58
(T D Walford) *chsd ldrs: effrt on inner over 2f out: styd on same pce* **4/1**[2]

2100 7 ¾ **Falcon's Fire (IRE)**[19] [2829] 3-8-3 60 ...(p) AndrewMullen(3) 10 56
(Mrs A Duffield) *s.i.s: effrt and c outside over 2f out: kpt on: nvr trbld ldrs* **22/1**

-400 8 shd **Dilwin (IRE)**[8] [3181] 3-8-11 65 ...(v[1]) AdrianTNicholls 13 61
(D Nicholls) *mid-div: effrt on outer over 2f out: hung rt: kpt on same pce* **25/1**

0010 9 1 **Bold Indian (IRE)**[11] [3078] 3-9-0 68 ... TomEaves 12 61
(I Semple) *sn prom: effrt on outer over 2f out: nvr rchd ldrs* **15/2**[3]

6316 10 ½ **Coconut Queen (IRE)**[14] [2988] 3-9-7 75 ...(p) RoystonFfrench 3 67
(Mrs A Duffield) *mid-div: effrt over 2f out: nvr a factor* **15/2**[3]

503- 11 3 **Captain Nemo (USA)**[268] [6012] 3-9-0 68 ... PhillipMakin 9 51
(T D Barron) *in rr: bhd fnl 2f* **10/1**

6060 12 8 **Inflagrantedelicto (USA)**[2] [3377] 3-7-9 56 oh6(b) DanielleMcCreery(7) 7 18
(D W Chapman) *s.s: a last* **50/1**

1m 24.75s (-2.61) **Going Correction** -0.225s/f (Firm) 12 Ran SP% **115.8**

Speed ratings (Par 100):105,104,102,102,101 100,99,99,98,97 94,85

CSF £216.94 CT £3538.35 TOTE £10.40: £2.60, £6.70, £4.20; EX 248.20.

Owner R J Budge **Bred** Juddmonte Farms Ltd **Trained** Wiseton, Notts

FOCUS

A modest handicap and the first three home raced bang up with the pace throughout. Only the fourth made any significant ground from off the pace. Few of these are progressive but the form seems sound enough.

3412 "TURMERIC" H'CAP 1m 7f 177y
3:30 (3:30) (Class 4) (0-85,82) 3-Y-O+ **£5,181** (£1,541; £770; £384) **Stalls** Low

Form RPR

2-00 1 **Inchnadamph**[22] [2736] 7-9-11 79 ...(t) PaulMulrennan 8 87+
(T J Fitzgerald) *trckd ldrs: wnt 2nd 2f out: shkn up: edgd lft and qcknd to ld last 75yds* **15/2**

26-2 2 1¾ **Falpiase (IRE)**[41] [2170] 5-10-0 82 ... TomEaves 2 88
(J Howard Johnson) *trckd ldrs: t.k.h: led over 2f out: hdd and hmpd last 75yds* **5/1**[2]

6-21 3 nk **Thewhirlingdervish (IRE)**[17] [2908] 9-9-4 72 ... DavidAllan 5 78
(T D Easterby) *in rr: drvn along and hdwy over 3f out: chsng ldrs 1f out: keeping on same pce whn no room wl ins fnl f* **11/2**[3]

4-23 4 1½ **Indonesia**[30] [2505] 5-9-7 75 ... GrahamGibbons 1 81+
(T D Walford) *in rr: pushed along 7f out: hdwy and n.m.r 1f out: 4th and styng on same pce whn bdly hmpd wl ins fnl f* **5/2**[1]

0140 5 1 **Doctor Scott**[18] [2861] 4-9-7 75 ... J-PGuillambert 7 78
(M Johnston) *mid-div: hdwy over 3f out: kpt on fnl 2f: nvr able to chal* **6/1**

6226 6 1 **Karlani (IRE)**[17] [2908] 4-8-10 64 ...(b[1]) DeanMcKeown 6 66
(G A Swinbank) *s.i.s: shkn up over 5f out: hdwy over 3f out: one pce* **12/1**

-020 7 1¼ **Fossgate**[14] [2987] 6-9-5 76 ... JamieMoriarty(3) 9 76
(J D Bethell) *hld up in rr: hdaway on outer over 2f out: kpt on: nvr rchd ldrs* **16/1**

42-6 8 2 **Prairie Sun (GER)**[13] [3027] 6-9-5 73 ... RoystonFfrench 3 71
(Mrs A Duffield) *chsd ldrs: effrt on inner over 2f out: wknd over 1f out* **10/1**

4120 9 2½ **Mister Arjay (USA)**[11] [3112] 7-9-3 76 ... PJMcDonald(5) 10 71
(B Ellison) *led tl over 7f out: rdn over 3f out: lost pl over 1f out* **12/1**

0 10 18 **Samizdat (FR)**[61] [1152] 4-8-9 63 oh1 ...(v[1]) DO'Donohoe 4 36
(James Moffatt) *trckd ldr: t.k.h: led and qcknd clr over 7f out: hdd over 2f out: sn lost pl and bhd* **66/1**

3m 25.03s (-6.37) **Going Correction** -0.225s/f (Firm) 10 Ran SP% **118.5**

Speed ratings (Par 105):106,105,104,104,103 103,102,101,100,91

CSF £45.64 CT £226.78 TOTE £7.90: £3.00, £2.10, £2.00; EX 42.30.

Owner R N Cardwell **Bred** Bloomsbury Stud & R & A Craddock **Trained** Malton, N Yorks

■ Stewards' Enquiry : Paul Mulrennan four-day ban: careless riding (Jul 22-25)

FOCUS

A decent stayers' handicap but the pace was just steady to halfway. The winner caused a domino effect when edging left late on. Solid form, the winner taking advantage of a good mark and the next three close to form.

3413 CALL 01748 810165 TO BOOK RACEDAY HOSPITALITY H'CAP 5f 212y
4:05 (4:07) (Class 5) (0-75,75) 3-Y-O **£3,238** (£963; £481; £240) **Stalls** Low

Form RPR

3010 1 **Maia**[17] [2910] 3-8-9 63 ... SilvestreDeSousa 8 67
(D Nicholls) *awkward to load: s.i.s: hdwy on inner over 2f out: squeezed through to ld wl insde fnl f* **15/2**[3]

0413 2 nk **La Vecchia Scuola (IRE)**[12] [3054] 3-8-3 57 oh2 ow1(v) AdrianTNicholls 4 60
(R Johnson) *chsd ldrs: effrt on outer over 2f out: hung lft and kpt on wl fnl f: jst hld* **16/1**

5-40 3 hd **Cassie's Choice (IRE)**[14] [2988] 3-8-11 65 ... RoystonFfrench 5 67
(B Smart) *mid-div: hdwy on outside over 2f out: styd on wl fnl f: jst hld* **17/2**

2325 4 1 **Mundo's Magic**[35] [2373] 3-8-13 72 ... PJMcDonald(5) 2 71
(G M Moore) *s.i.s: hdwy over 2f out: upsides whn hung lft ins fnl f: no ex: fin 5th, nk, hd, 3/4 & hd: plcd 4th* **11/2**[2]

4015 5 ½ **Distant Sun (USA)**[19] [2821] 3-8-11 65 ... TomEaves 6 63
(I Semple) *in rr: lost pl bnd over 4f out: hung lft and styd on fnl 2f: nt rch ldrs: fin 6th: plcd 5th* **17/2**

0364 6 2 **Rainbow Fox**[17] [2910] 3-8-8 65 ...(b[1]) JamieMoriarty(3) 1 57
(R A Fahey) *chsd ldrs: outpcd over 2f out: wknd fnl f: fin 7th: plcd 6th* **10/1**

-026 7 ½ **Bollin Franny**[12] [3054] 3-8-10 64 ... DavidAllan 10 60+
(T D Easterby) *led 1f: chsd ldrs: chal over 2f out: keeping on same pce whn hmpd and eased wl ins fnl f: fin 8th: plcd 7th* **12/1**

1114 8 4 **Ishetoo**[12] [3054] 3-9-2 75 ... MichaelJStainton(5) 7 53+
(A Dickman) *in rr: rt-hand rein became unbuckled and lost pl over 4f out: sme hdwy on ins whn hmpd 1f out: eased: fin 9th: plcd 8th* **2/1**[1]

4563 D **Pegasus Dancer (FR)**[19] [2821] 3-9-5 73 ... DO'Donohoe 3 73
(K A Ryan) *led after 1f: hdd and no ex wl ins fnl f: fin 4th, nk, hd & ¾l: disq & plcd last* **17/2**

1m 12.64s (-1.36) **Going Correction** -0.225s/f (Firm) 9 Ran SP% **114.7**

Speed ratings (Par 100):100,99,99,98,97 94,94,88,98

CSF £116.85 CT £1042.32 TOTE £8.50: £2.40, £4.20, £3.30; EX 130.30.

Owner Racegoers Club Owners Group **Bred** L C And Mrs A E Sigsworth **Trained** Sessay, N Yorks

■ Stewards' Enq: Pegasus Dancer disq: D O'Donohoe 3-day ban: failed to weigh-in (Jul 22-24)

FOCUS

Quite a rough race, with the first six on top of each other at the line. Improvement from the winner, but modest form, with the second casting doubts.

Ishetoo Official explanation: jockey said buckle on rein became undone

3414 TURFTV.CO.UK H'CAP 7f
4:40 (4:40) (Class 6) (0-65,65) 3-Y-O+ **£2,730** (£806; £403) **Stalls** Low

Form RPR

0200 1 **Choysia**[18] [2870] 4-10-0 65 ... TomEaves 6 76
(D W Barker) *trckd ldrs: led over 2f out: styd on wl fnl f* **14/1**

0310 2 1¾ **Inca Soldier (FR)**[13] [3017] 4-9-4 55 ... DO'Donohoe 15 61
(R C Guest) *trckd ldrs: t.k.h: kpt on same pce fnl f* **9/1**

-066 3 ½ **Pitbull**[8] [3185] 4-9-1 52 ... DeanMcKeown 11 57
(Mrs G S Rees) *s.i.s: bhd tl hdwy on outer over 2f out: kpt on wl ins fnl f* **14/1**

3162 4 shd **Another Genepi (USA)**[65] [1534] 4-9-10 64 ...(b) AndrewMullen(3) 4 68
(K A Ryan) *trckd ldrs: effrt over 2f out: kpt on same pce fnl f* **4/1**[2]

-060 5 1¼ **Ours (IRE)**[16] [2947] 4-9-1 55 ...(p) JamieMoriarty(3) 14 56
(J D Bethell) *slowly intro stride: bhd tl hdd 2f out: n.m.r and edgd rt 1f out: fin wl* **18/1**

6500 6 ¾ **Contemplation**[11] [3101] 4-9-1 52 ... DavidAllan 3 51
(J Balding) *hld up towards rr: hdwy on inner over 2f out: nvr rchd ldrs* **12/1**

0000 7 ½ **Iced Diamond (IRE)**[9] [3173] 8-8-13 50 ... LPKeniry 10 48
(S Wynne) *prom: effrt over 2f out: kpt on: nvr rchd ldrs* **50/1**

2054 8 1 **Zhitomir**[8] [3195] 9-9-1 52 ... PhillipMakin 5 47
(M Dods) *led tl over 2f out: wknd fnl f* **7/1**

0520 9 hd **Sands Of Barra (IRE)**[2] [3375] 4-9-6 62 ...(p) PJMcDonald(5) 1 56
(I W McInnes) *trckd ldrs: chal over 2f out: wknd fnl f* **7/2**[1]

5100 10 nk **Kudbeme**[14] [2988] 5-9-2 60 ... GihanArnolda(7) 12 54
(N Bycroft) *s.i.s: effrt on outer over 2f out: nvr nr ldrs* **20/1**

5440 11 ¾ **Cabourg (IRE)**[43] [2121] 4-9-5 56 ...(b) RoystonFfrench 2 48
(R Bastiman) *trckd ldrs: effrt on inner over 2f out: wknd appr fnl f* **6/1**[3]

0-30 12 2 **Royal Pardon**[8] [3185] 5-8-13 50 ...(p) PaulFessey 13 36
(M Dods) *s.i.s: in rr and drvn along: sme hdwy over 2f out: sltly hmpd and lost pl over 1f out* **18/1**

3550 13 8 **Vibrato (USA)**[150] [431] 5-8-10 50 ...(v) DuranFentiman(3) 9 15
(C J Teague) *prom: drvn over 2f out: sn lost pl and bhd* **33/1**

1m 25.74s (-1.62) **Going Correction** -0.225s/f (Firm) 13 Ran SP% **120.2**

Speed ratings (Par 101):100,98,97,97,95 95,94,93,93,92 91,89,80

CSF £133.06 CT £1863.23 TOTE £13.60: £3.80, £2.50, £5.60; EX 131.80.

Owner Mrs J D Trotter **Bred** Mrs John Trotter **Trained** Scorton, N Yorks

FOCUS

A low-grade handicap with the placed horses both drawn in double figures. The form seems sound.

3415 RACINGUK.TV MEDIAN AUCTION MAIDEN STKS 1m 5f 175y
5:15 (5:16) (Class 5) 3-4-Y-O £3,238 (£963; £481; £240) Stalls Low

Form RPR

0-00 **1** **Blue Jet (USA)**[57] 1746 3-8-11 45 DeanMcKeown 3 59
(R M Whitaker) *trckd ldrs: wnt 2nd over 1f out: hrd rdn and edgd lft: led towards fin* **33/1**

54-2 **2** *shd* **Gordonsville**[11] 3084 4-9-12 82 LPKeniry 5 59
(A M Balding) *trckd ldrs: led over 2f out: tightened up and hdd last strides* **4/6**[1]

40-4 **3** *11* **Hunting Haze**[48] 1968 4-9-7 57 MichaelJStainton(5) 6 44
(Miss S E Hall) *t.k.h: effrt over 3f out: sn chsng ldrs: wknd over 1f out* **15/2**[3]

4 *3 1/2* **Polish Myth** 3-8-11 0 TomEaves 4 39
(J G Given) *sn w ldr: rn wd bnd after 5f: chal over 5f out: lost pl over 2f out* **10/1**

00-0 **5** *1/2* **Bishop Auckland (IRE)**[28] 2554 3-8-11 45 RoystonFfrench 1 38
(Mrs A Duffield) *led tl over 2f out: wknd fnl f* **40/1**

0-4 **6** *18* **El Dottore**[32] 2477 3-8-11 0 HayleyTurner 2 13
(M L W Bell) *hld up in rr: effrt over 4f out: lost pl 3f out: sn bhd and eased* **7/2**[2]

0 **7** *dist* **After Nine**[33] 2420 3-8-3 0 AndrewMullen(3) 7 —
(F Watson) *in tch: rdn 7f out: lost pl over 5f out: sn t.o: rn wd bnd 3f out: virtually p.u* **150/1**

3m 3.47s (-1.03) **Going Correction** -0.225s/f (Firm)
WFA 3 from 4yo 15lb 7 Ran SP% **109.1**
Speed ratings (Par 103):93,92,86,84,84 74,—
CSF £51.53 TOTE £51.70: £9.40, £1.10; EX 95.20 Place 6 £1313.14, Place 5 £826.00..
Owner Country Lane Partnership **Bred** Latitude 27, Llc **Trained** Scarcroft, W Yorks
■ Stewards' Enquiry : Dean McKeown four-day ban: used whip with excessive frequency (Jul 22-25)

FOCUS
What looked a formality for 82-rated Gordonsville, matched a 1.03 on the exchanges, didn't work out that way as he put in his worst performance yet. The winner is rated up a stone. The winning time was modest.
Blue Jet(USA) Official explanation: trainer said, regarding apparent improvement in form, that the gelding was better suited by the step up in trip
El Dottore Official explanation: vet said colt returned suffering from pelvic discomfort
T/Plt: £1,277.90 to a £1 stake. Pool: £45,342.15. 25.90 winning tickets. T/Qpdt: £110.10 to a £1 stake. Pool: £3,363.10. 22.60 winning tickets. WG

3212 KEMPTON (A.W) (R-H)
Wednesday, July 11

OFFICIAL GOING: Standard
Wind: Light, half against Weather: Fine, warm

3416 REDACTIVE MEDIA GROUP H'CAP 1m 2f (P)
6:20 (6:27) (Class 4) (0-80,78) 3-Y-0+ £4,728 (£1,406; £702; £351) Stalls High

Form RPR

10-5 **1** **Crossbow Creek**[30] 2512 9-9-9 78 LukeMorris(5) 9 88+
(M G Rimell) *towards rr: n.m.r over 6f out: rdn over 3f out: prog and nt clr run over 1f out: r.o wl to ld last 100yds: sn clr* **12/1**

0042 **2** *1 1/4* **Burgundy**[15] 2964 10-8-9 66 (b) JackMitchell(7) 1 73
(P Mitchell) *hld up in last trio: rdn 3f out: rapid prog on outer 1f out: r.o to take 2nd nr fin* **20/1**

2065 **3** *1* **Star Of Canterbury (IRE)**[32] 2471 4-9-1 65 SimonWhitworth 10 70
(A P Jarvis) *led: pressed and rdn 3f out: hdd & wknd last 100yds* **13/2**[2]

1523 **4** *hd* **Scamperdale**[11] 3111 5-9-9 73 (p) FrancisNorton 8 78
(B P J Baugh) *hld up in last trio: swtchd ins and gd prog jst over 1f out: r.o: nt rch ldrs* **9/1**

2365 **5** *nk* **Magic Warrior**[28] 2568 7-9-3 67 PatDobbs 12 71
(J C Fox) *trckd ldrs: gng wl enough over 2f out: rdn over 1f out: kpt on but nt pce to chal* **20/1**

326- **6** *1/2* **Mexican Bob**[237] 4842 4-9-1 65 FergusSweeney 11 68+
(A King) *lost pl and towards rr over 6f out: rdn 3f out: prog and nt clr run over 1f out: styd on: nt rch ldrs* **20/1**

2205 **7** *1 1/2* **Crocodile Bay (IRE)**[7] 3215 4-9-8 72 PaulEddery 2 72
(B J Meehan) *chsd ldrs: rdn 3f out: tried to cl over 1f out: one pce* **12/1**

0533 **8** *nk* **Turner's Touch**[14] 2994 5-9-7 71 (b) GeorgeBaker 6 70
(G L Moore) *stdd s: hld up and racd wd in midfield: rdn 3f out: nt qckn and no imp over 1f out* **9/1**

044 **9** *1/2* **Eastern Emperor**[19] 2836 3-8-13 74 AdamKirby 4 72
(W R Swinburn) *hld up: rapid prog to trck ldr after 3f: tried to chal 3f out: hanging bnd 2f out: wknd fnl f* **15/2**[3]

0230 **10** *hd* **Love Brothers**[54] 1827 3-9-0 75 JHBowman 5 73
(M R Channon) *chsd ldr for 3f: styd prom tl wknd over 1f out* **12/1**

-040 **11** *2 1/2* **Dream Catcher (SWE)**[132] 587 4-10-0 78 (t) DaneO'Neill 13 71
(R A Kvisla) *prom: 3rd and rdn over 2f out: eased and lost pls over 1f out* **22/1**

14-0 **12** *1 3/4* **Where's Broughton**[54] 1819 4-9-1 72 AlanRutter(7) 14 62
(W J Musson) *hld up in last trio: prog on inner wl over 1f out: hld whn hmpd 1f out: eased* **25/1**

000- **13** *13* **Mystic Storm**[325] 4634 4-9-6 70 SebSanders 7 34
(Lady Herries) *t.k.h: prog to chse ldrs 1/2-way: rdn 4f out: wknd rapidly: t.o* **4/1**[1]

10 **14** *14* **Seleet (IRE)**[50] 1920 3-9-2 77 IanMongan 3 13
(M A Jarvis) *dwlt: chsd ldrs on outer: wknd over 4f out: t.o* **8/1**

2m 7.45s (-1.55) **Going Correction** -0.10s/f (Stan)
WFA 3 from 4yo+ 11lb 14 Ran SP% **121.8**
Speed ratings (Par 105):102,101,100,100,99 99,98,97,97,97 95,94,83,72
CSF £238.93 CT £1707.85 TOTE £14.50: £4.80, £3.50, £2.70; EX 265.10.
Owner Mark Rimell **Bred** Mrs M R T Rimell **Trained** Leafield, Oxon
■ Stewards' Enquiry : Dane O'Neill caution: careless riding

FOCUS
A competitive-looking handicap. Pretty straightforward form, the winner up 5lb on his maiden win last year.
Mystic Storm Official explanation: jockey said gelding had no more to give
Seleet(IRE) Official explanation: vet said colt returned lame

3417 EUROPEAN BREEDERS' FUND MEDIAN AUCTION MAIDEN FILLIES' STKS 6f (P)
6:50 (6:57) (Class 5) 2-Y-O £3,886 (£1,156; £577; £288) Stalls High

Form RPR

1 **Reel Gift** 2-9-0 0 RichardHughes 6 76+
(R Hannon) *t.k.h: trckd ldrs: led over 1f out: rdn and r.o wl* **11/2**[3]

3 **2** *2* **Temple Of Thebes (IRE)**[14] 2992 2-9-0 0 JimmyFortune 7 70
(E A L Dunlop) *hld up in midfield: prog over 2f out: rdn to chse wnr fnl f: hanging lft and nt qckn: fin weakly* **7/4**[1]

5 **3** *1/2* **Nylla**[6] 3245 2-9-0 0 JHBowman 8 69+
(M R Channon) *trckd ldrs: lost pl and pushed along over 2f out: no prog tl over 1f out: styd on wl fnl f* **9/1**

4 *1 1/2* **Maramba (USA)** 2-9-0 0 RyanMoore 4 64
(Sir Michael Stoute) *restless stalls and dwlt: at the bk of main gp: prog over 2f: shkn up and styd on fnl f: nvr able to chal* **11/1**

5 *nk* **River Gleam (IRE)** 2-9-0 0 RichardMullen 11 63
(A P Jarvis) *chsd ldrs: pushed along over 2f out: one pce and no imp* **33/1**

02 **6** *1 3/4* **Tenjack Queen (IRE)**[11] 3109 2-9-0 0 SebSanders 10 58
(J A Osborne) *trckd ldng pair: effrt to chal on inner and upsides over 1f out: wknd rapidly fnl f* **5/1**[2]

7 *3/4* **Hennalaine (IRE)** 2-9-0 0 TQuinn 5 56
(P F I Cole) *dwlt: rn green at bk of main gp: effrt over 2f out: pushed along and no hdwy over 1f out* **33/1**

323 **8** *nk* **Rio Princess (IRE)**[8] 3187 2-9-0 0 SteveDrowne 1 55
(T G Mills) *pressed ldr to 2f out: wknd rapidly* **11/2**[3]

0 **9** *1 1/4* **Far Song (IRE)**[23] 2724 2-9-0 0 FrancisNorton 3 51
(A M Balding) *led at decent pce to over 1f out: wknd rapidly* **50/1**

0 **10** *4* **Starfinch**[11] 3085 2-8-7 0 KMay(7) 9 39
(J J Bridger) *dwlt: outpcd and a wl bhd* **100/1**

11 *3 1/2* **Red Amaryllis** 2-9-0 0 DaneO'Neill 12 28
(H J L Dunlop) *dwlt: v green and hung across crse sn after s: a t.o* **20/1**

12 *3* **Tournevr (IRE)** 2-9-0 0 IanMongan 2 19
(Jane Chapple-Hyam) *dwlt: rcvrd to chse ldrs after 2f: wknd rapidly over 2f out* **33/1**

1m 14.0s (0.30) **Going Correction** -0.10s/f (Stan) 12 Ran SP% **118.7**
Speed ratings (Par 91):94,91,90,88,88 85,84,84,82,77 72,68
CSF £14.66 TOTE £8.60: £2.30, £1.10, £2.80; EX 17.90.
Owner G Battocchi & Mrs Anna Doyle **Bred** Mrs M Holdcroft And Mrs M Forsyth **Trained** East Everleigh, Wilts

FOCUS
Not a bad juvenile event and Reel Gift looks a promising filly. Not much form to go on, and the race could have been rated up to 8lb higher.

NOTEBOOK
Reel Gift, a half-sister to a couple of sprint winners, is by the stable's formerly high-class miler Reel Buddy and it was no surprise to see her prove good enough to make a winning debut. Always well positioned, she found plenty when sent to the front over a furlong out and ran out a ready winner. She is in most of the big sales races later in the season, and it would not surprise to see her take her chance in Newbury's Super Sprint later in the month, a race her trainer has a fine record in. (op 11-4 tchd 6-1)
Temple Of Thebes(IRE), who would have gone close on her course-and-distance debut but for hanging away to the left and wandering under pressure, went in pursuit of the winner racing into the final furlong, but again threw her chance away by hanging. She clearly has ability, but cannot be backed with any confidence on the evidence of her first two starts. (tchd 11-8 and 15-8)
Nylla improved on her initial Yarmouth effort and stayed on in the manner of a filly who is going to benefit from trips beyond this in time. She is more of a nursery type. (op 12-1)
Maramba(USA), bred to appreciate further in time, gave some trouble at the start and was edgy in the stalls. After breaking sluggishly, she made some good late headway to claim a never-nearer fourth and looks likely to come on appreciably for the outing. Winning an ordinary maiden should prove within her capabilities. (op 9-1 tchd 12-1)
River Gleam(IRE), a daughter of Trans Island, showed signs of greenness on this debut and could only keep on at the one pace under pressure. Her stable are capable with their juveniles and she is going to appreciate an extra furlong in future.
Tenjack Queen(IRE) failed to build on her Wolverhampton second and stopped worryingly quickly in the final furlong. She is now qualified for handicaps, but has a bit to prove now. (op 8-1)

3418 DIGIBET POKER H'CAP 6f (P)
7:20 (7:25) (Class 4) (0-85,85) 3-Y-O £4,728 (£1,406; £702; £351) Stalls High

Form RPR

1201 **1** **King's Apostle (IRE)**[35] 2373 3-9-1 82 LiamJones(3) 7 90+
(W J Haggas) *trckd ldrs: nt clr run over 2f out: prog wl over 1f out: drvn to ld last 100yds: jst hld on* **6/1**[3]

104 **2** *hd* **Mambo Spirit (IRE)**[25] 2659 3-9-7 85 RyanMoore 11 92
(J G Given) *t.k.h: trckd ldng pair: led on inner 2f out: drvn and hdd last 100yds: styd on wl: jst hld* **14/1**

1143 **3** *1* **Kyle (IRE)**[18] 2881 3-9-6 84 RichardHughes 10 89+
(R Hannon) *hld up in midfield: nt clr run and swtchd lft over 2f out: swtchd bk ins and drvn to chse ldng pair 1f out: r.o but no imp* **5/1**[1]

-113 **4** *3* **Rasaman (IRE)**[30] 2518 3-9-6 84 PhilipRobinson 9 79
(M A Jarvis) *led for 1f: pressed ldr to over 2f out: styd cl up tl wknd ins fnl f* **13/2**

1-26 **5** *nk* **Golden Desert (IRE)**[54] 1817 3-9-4 82 SteveDrowne 8 79+
(T G Mills) *t.k.h early: hld up in midfield: effrt whn hmpd over 2f out: styd on fr over 1f out: nt pce to trble ldrs* **12/1**

2-14 **6** *3/4* **Shustraya**[26] 2629 3-9-6 84 EddieAhern 2 76
(P J Makin) *hld up in last trio: taken to wd outside over 2f out: rdn and kpt on: no ch* **16/1**

11-6 **7** *1/2* **Bateleur**[26] 2629 3-9-5 83 EdwardCreighton 4 73
(M R Channon) *sn last: rdn over 2f out and struggling: plugged on fr over 1f out* **14/1**

3453 **8** *1/2* **Go On Green (IRE)**[14] 2993 3-9-1 79 JimmyFortune 6 68
(E A L Dunlop) *hld up in last trio: effrt on inner and sme prog 2f out: no hdwy 1f out: fdd* **11/2**[2]

-451 **9** *nk* **Cleide Da Silva (USA)**[11] 3110 3-8-11 75 (v) JohnEgan 5 63
(J Noseda) *trckd ldng pair: rdn and nt qckn over 2f out: sn lost pl and btn* **5/1**[1]

140 **10** *1 1/4* **Double Bill (USA)**[18] 2881 3-8-13 77 TQuinn 3 61
(P F I Cole) *settled towards rr: rdn over 2f out: no prog* **20/1**

-140 **11** *1/2* **Our Blessing (IRE)**[34] 2395 3-9-5 83 RichardMullen 1 66
(A P Jarvis) *trckd ldrs on outer tl wknd 2f out* **33/1**

-120 **12** *1/2* **High Tribute**[21] 2769 3-8-10 74 (t) SebSanders 12 55
(Sir Mark Prescott) *led after 1f to 2f out: wknd rapidly and tamely* **14/1**

1m 12.44s (-1.26) **Going Correction** -0.10s/f (Stan) 12 Ran SP% **117.6**
Speed ratings (Par 102):104,103,102,98,98 97,96,95,95,93 92,92
CSF £86.42 CT £454.05 TOTE £7.10: £2.40, £3.50, £2.00; EX 109.70.

Owner Wentworth Racing (pty) Ltd **Bred** Wentworth Racing **Trained** Newmarket, Suffolk

FOCUS
A good, competitive handicap likely to produce winners. The winner progressed a bit further and the form is sound.

Rasaman(IRE) Official explanation: jockey said gelding hung right in straight

3419 DIGIBET SPORTS BETTING H'CAP 1m (P)
7:50 (7:52) (Class 6) (0-58,62) 3-Y-0+ **£2,047** (£604; £302) **Stalls** High

Form RPR

0-1 **1** **Bucharest**[28] 2556 4-9-5 **55** SteveDrowne 3 64
(M Wigham) *mde virtually all: jnd over 3f out to over 2f out: drew clr over 1f out: pushed out: a holding on* **3/1**[1]

0031 **2** ¾ **Golden Spectrum (IRE)**[9] 3173 8-9-7 **62** 6ex (b) LukeMorris(5) 12 69
(R A Harris) *s.s: mostly in last trio: swtchd outside over 2f out: r.o wl fr over 1f out: tk 2nd last 100yds: nt rch wnr* **12/1**

00-1 **3** 1 ¼ **Fantasy Crusader**[14] 2990 8-9-1 **51** DaneO'Neill 11 55
(R M H Cowell) *chsd ldrs: rdn over 3f out: nt qckn over 2f out: styd on to dispute 2nd ins fnl f: nt pce to chal* **14/1**

202 **4** ¾ **Shunkawakhan (IRE)**[14] 2990 4-8-7 **50** (p) AmyBaker(7) 1 52
(G C H Chung) *trckd wnr: chal and upsides over 3f out to over 2f out: hld after: wknd ins fnl f* **16/1**

0301 **5** *hd* **Blue Quiver (IRE)**[27] 2591 7-9-6 **56** SimonWhitworth 13 58
(C A Horgan) *dwlt: mostly in last trio tl prog over 2f out: drvn and styd on: nvr able to rch ldrs* **25/1**

0200 **6** *nk* **Bowl Of Cherries**[12] 3067 4-9-2 **52** (b) RichardHughes 9 53
(I A Wood) *towards rr: rdn and prog fr 3f out: chsd ldrs over 1f out: no imp after* **4/1**[2]

0450 **7** *hd* **Bold Cross (IRE)**[23] 2721 4-9-5 **55** PaulDoe 7 56+
(E G Bevan) *s.i.s: wl in rr: nt clr run and swtchd lft over 2f out: hmpd sn after: nt rcvr: kpt on* **14/1**

-406 **8** 1 ¾ **Moyoko (IRE)**[161] 313 4-9-5 **55** FrancisNorton 6 52
(M Blanshard) *nvr bttr than midfield: rdn and no real prog over 2f out* **14/1**

2506 **9** *hd* **Balerno**[12] 3064 8-9-5 **55** IanMongan 8 51
(Mrs L J Mongan) *towards rr: rdn and hanging lft fr over 2f out: modest prog over 1f out: wknd fnl f* **16/1**

2200 **10** ½ **King Of Knight (IRE)**[9] 3173 6-9-4 **54** AdrianMcCarthy 14 49
(G Prodromou) *mostly chsd ldng pair: outpcd 3f out: tried to cl 2f out: wknd over 1f out* **25/1**

5440 **11** 1 ½ **Wodhill Gold**[9] 3173 6-9-8 **58** (b) RichardMullen 4 50
(D Morris) *prom: rdn wl over 3f out: lost pl and btn over 2f out* **25/1**

0030 **12** ½ **Royal Envoy (IRE)**[5] 3285 4-9-4 **57** LiamJones(3) 2 47
(D Shaw) *s.i.s: hld up in last pair: taken to outer and brief effrt over 2f out: sn no prog and btn* **8/1**

2066 **13** ½ **Border Artist**[12] 3067 8-9-4 **54** (v[1]) JimmyQuinn 5 43
(J Pearce) *chsd ldrs: n.m.r over 2f out whn rdn: sn wknd* **20/1**

3410 **14** 6 **Napoletano (GER)**[18] 2877 6-9-5 **55** (p) SebSanders 10 30
(S Dow) *t.k.h: hld up bhd ldrs: wknd rapidly over 2f out* **7/1**[3]

1m 40.04s (-0.76) **Going Correction** -0.10s/f (Stan) **14** Ran SP% **124.4**
Speed ratings (Par 101):99,98,97,96,96 95,95,93,93,93 91,91,90,84
CSF £39.58 CT £451.66 TOTE £3.30: £2.00, £4.50, £2.80; EX 33.00.

Owner D T L Limited **Bred** Juddmonte Farms Ltd **Trained** Newmarket, Suffolk

■ Stewards' Enquiry : Luke Morris caution: raised whip arm above shoulder height

FOCUS
A moderate handicap run at a fair pace. The winner is well in on sand and was 5lb off his latest turf win, with the runner-up posted his best figure for three years.

Bold Cross(IRE) Official explanation: jockey said gelding was denied a clear run

Moyoko(IRE) Official explanation: jockey said filly hung left

Balerno Official explanation: jockey said gelding did not face the kickback

3420 DIGIBET LONDON MILE H'CAP (LONDON MILE QUALIFIER) 1m (P)
8:20 (8:22) (Class 4) (0-80,80) 3-Y-0+ **£4,728** (£1,406; £702; £351) **Stalls** High

Form RPR

5002 **1** **Electric Warrior (IRE)**[21] 2771 4-9-13 **79** FergusSweeney 13 91
(K R Burke) *hld up in midfield: gd prog on inner over 2f out: drvn to ld narrowly jst over 1f out: kpt on and a holding on* **7/2**[1]

5164 **2** ½ **Shot Gun**[35] 2354 3-9-2 **77** JHBowman 3 86
(M R Channon) *trckd ldr after 3f: led 3f out: tried to kick on but limited rspnse: hdd jst over 1f out: pressed wnr but nt qckn after* **5/1**[3]

0060 **3** 1 ¼ **Alfresco**[21] 2767 3-9-3 **78** (b) DaneO'Neill 7 84
(Pat Eddery) *s.s: hld up in rr: prog 3f out: rdn to chse ldng pair over 1f out: nt qckn and readily hld fnl f* **16/1**

0-31 **4** ½ **Rambling Light**[123] 655 3-9-4 **79** FrancisNorton 5 84
(A M Balding) *hld up in midfield: prog on outer over 2f out: clsd on ldrs and looked dangerous over 1f out: effrt petered out fnl f* **9/2**[2]

1205 **5** 2 **Spring Goddess (IRE)**[9] 3154 6-9-9 **75** RichardMullen 2 77+
(A P Jarvis) *hld up in last: stl last 2f out: effrt whn carried rt over 1f out: styd on fnl f: no ch* **14/1**

0345 **6** ½ **Katiypour (IRE)**[14] 2995 10-8-11 **70** JackMitchell(7) 4 71
(P Mitchell) *wl in rr: styd on fnl 2f at one pce: n.d* **7/1**

0340 **7** 1 **Music Note (IRE)**[53] 1842 4-10-0 **80** (t) JohnEgan 9 79
(Miss Gay Kelleway) *led to 3f out: pressed ldr to 2f out: wknd rapidly fnl f* **14/1**

25-6 **8** 1 ½ **Coleridge (AUS)**[14] 2995 8-9-4 **70** GeorgeBaker 12 71+
(J C Fox) *wl in tch: effrt to chse ldrs over 2f out: hld whn hmpd over 1f out and eased* **18/1**

5410 **9** 3 ½ **Chattan Clan**[72] 1359 3-9-0 **75** (t) EddieAhern 10 60
(R A Kvisla) *s.i.s: hld up in rr: brief effrt over 2f out: sn no prog* **50/1**

2020 **10** 1 ¼ **Gunner's View**[12] 3056 3-8-11 **72** (t) RichardHughes 11 54
(B J Meehan) *towards rr: rdn and hung rt over 1f out: no prog* **12/1**

-625 **11** 4 **Saviour Sand (IRE)**[18] 2880 3-9-2 **77** TQuinn 14 50
(D R C Elsworth) *pressed ldr for 3f: sn lost pl: wknd over 2f out* **14/1**

0163 **12** 3 ½ **Glencalvie (IRE)**[18] 2877 6-9-7 **73** (v) SebSanders 1 40
(J Akehurst) *chsd ldrs: rdn over 3f out: sn wknd and bhd* **8/1**

1m 38.98s (-1.82) **Going Correction** -0.10s/f (Stan)
WFA 3 from 4yo+ 9lb **12** Ran SP% **121.5**
Speed ratings (Par 105):105,104,103,102,100 100,99,97,94,93 89,85
CSF £21.02 CT £257.77 TOTE £5.20: £1.80, £2.10, £5.20; EX 28.30.

Owner Market Avenue Racing Club Ltd **Bred** Limestone Stud **Trained** Middleham Moor, N Yorks

■ Stewards' Enquiry : Francis Norton four-day ban: careless riding (Jul 22-25)

FOCUS
A fair handicap, run at a solid pace. The form is sound, rated through the placed horses.

3421 LEONARD CURTIS FILLIES' H'CAP 1m 3f (P)
8:50 (8:54) (Class 5) (0-75,75) 3-Y-0 **£2,817** (£838; £418; £209) **Stalls** High

Form RPR

5001 **1** **Ravenna**[11] 3083 3-8-4 **63** WilliamBuick(5) 6 72+
(M P Tregoning) *settled in midfield: pushed along over 3f out: prog to chse clr ldr over 1f out: sn clsd and led 1f out: wl in command fnl f* **11/2**[2]

5523 **2** 1 ½ **Silver Mitzva (IRE)**[27] 2609 3-8-7 **61** ow1 (v) MickyFenton 2 67
(M Botti) *trckd ldrs: prog to ld over 4f out: drew at least 4 l clr over 2f out: wknd and hdd 1f out* **10/1**

6306 **3** ¾ **Dansimar**[61] 1624 3-8-11 **65** JHBowman 8 70
(M R Channon) *trckd ldrs: rdn 3f out: chsd clr ldr 2f out to over 1f out: kpt on* **12/1**

-641 **4** ¾ **Vallemeldee (IRE)**[11] 3084 3-9-4 **72** JohnEgan 10 76
(P W D'Arcy) *settled in rr: outpcd and rdn over 3f out: prog u.p over 2f out: kpt on: nrst fin* **8/1**[3]

-532 **5** 4 **Kailasha (IRE)**[25] 2666 3-9-4 **72** EddieAhern 9 69
(C F Wall) *dwlt: sn in midfield: prog to chse ldr over 3f out to 2f out: wknd over 1f out* **11/2**[2]

2035 **6** 2 ½ **Best Selection**[7] 3214 3-9-1 **69** FrancisNorton 4 62
(A P Jarvis) *hld up in last: outpcd over 3f out: rdn wl over 2f out: plugged on: no ch* **8/1**[3]

36-0 **7** *hd* **Rosie's Glory (USA)**[32] 2472 3-9-4 **72** PaulEddery 7 64
(B J Meehan) *s.s: mostly in last pair: outpcd over 3f out: kpt on fnl 2f: no ch* **25/1**

43-1 **8** 2 **Starparty (USA)**[26] 2635 3-9-5 **73** JimCrowley 11 62
(Mrs A J Perrett) *s.i.s: sn in midfield: rdn over 3f out: no prog: struggling over 2f out* **11/2**[2]

-312 **9** ¾ **Passing Hour (USA)**[14] 3003 3-9-7 **75** RichardHughes 5 63
(G A Butler) *racd wd towards rr: u.p over 5f out: sn struggling: no ch fnl 3f* **4/1**[1]

606 **10** 8 **Present**[9] 3170 3-8-2 **56** oh6 (p) AdrianMcCarthy 13 30
(D Morris) *led at gd pce to over 4f out: wkng whn hmpd on inner over 2f out* **40/1**

40-6 **11** 11 **Wishing On A Star**[19] 2840 3-9-4 **72** (tp) RichardMullen 14 27
(E J O'Neill) *prom: pushed along 1/2-way: wknd 4f out: t.o* **25/1**

12 5 **Ashleigh Anderson (FR)**[18] 2901 3-8-9 **63** ow1 PatDobbs 3 10
(Eamon Tyrrell, Ire) *trckd ldr to over 4f out: stl gng wl enough over 3f out: sn rdn and wknd rapidly* **20/1**

0 **13** 6 **Palanoverre (IRE)**[26] 2647 3-9-0 **68** AdamKirby 1 5
(D J S Ffrench Davis) *racd wd in midfield: rdn 5f out: sn wknd: t.o* **33/1**

2m 20.06s (-2.62) **Going Correction** -0.10s/f (Stan) **13** Ran SP% **123.0**
Speed ratings (Par 97):105,103,103,102,99 98,97,96,95,90 82,78,74
CSF £57.25 CT £649.48 TOTE £8.20: £2.80, £3.20, £4.70; EX 70.10.

Owner Park Walk Racing **Bred** Whitsbury Manor Stud **Trained** Lambourn, Berks

FOCUS
A modest handicap but the form is sound, rated through the placed horses. The pace was fair, even if it did slow a touch at halfway.

Passing Hour(USA) Official explanation: jockey said filly had no more to give

3422 WEATHERBYS BLOODSTOCK INSURANCE APPRENTICE H'CAP (ROUND 6) 7f (P)
9:20 (9:20) (Class 5) (0-70,70) 4-Y-0+ **£2,817** (£838; £418; £209) **Stalls** High

Form RPR

0025 **1** **Motafarred (IRE)**[19] 2823 5-9-0 **60** ThomasO'Brien 8 69
(Micky Hammond) *trckd ldrs: prog on inner 2f out: sustained effrt to ld last 100yds: kpt on* **12/1**

0044 **2** ½ **Reeling N' Rocking (IRE)**[32] 2472 4-9-0 **65** ChrisGlenister(5) 4 73
(B W Hills) *led: rdn 2f out: worn down last 100yds* **4/1**[1]

2013 **3** ½ **Million Percent**[36] 2331 8-9-10 **70** WilliamCarson 7 77
(C R Dore) *pushed along in midfield 1/2-way: prog on inner fr 2f out: styd on but nvr quite able to chal* **15/2**[3]

-004 **4** ½ **Young Bertie**[7] 3218 4-8-11 **62** (p) RyanBird(5) 3 67
(H Morrison) *mostly chsd ldr to jst over 1f out: nt qckn* **14/1**

3552 **5** 1 ¼ **Dr Synn**[12] 3056 6-9-5 **65** JackMitchell 14 67
(J Akehurst) *wnt lft s and bmpd rival: n.m.r on inner 1st 2f and dropped to rr: styd on fnl 2f: no ch* **8/1**

3-60 **6** *nk* **October Ben**[14] 2990 4-8-12 **63** FrankiePickard(5) 11 64
(M D I Usher) *bmpd and hmpd s: wl in rr: styd on wl fr over 1f out: nrst fin* **25/1**

4-00 **7** *hd* **Gifted Flame**[37] 2302 8-8-8 **54** NeilBrown 12 55
(T D Barron) *bmpd and hmpd s: wl in rr: kpt on fr over 1f out: no ch* **7/1**[2]

0600 **8** 1 **Greenwood**[48] 1969 9-8-12 **63** JosephWalsh(5) 5 61
(P G Murphy) *wl in rr: last pair 3f out: kpt on fr over 1f out: n.d* **20/1**

5600 **9** *hd* **Royal Amnesty**[14] 2995 4-9-3 **70** MarvinCheung(7) 10 67
(G C H Chung) *chsd ldrs: bmpd along furiously 2f out: hld whn rdr dropped reins and unbalanced ins fnl f* **18/1**

0236 **10** ½ **Mannello**[6] 3247 4-8-5 **51** (p) HaddenFrost 13 47
(Mrs C A Dunnett) *bmpd and wnt lft s: rcvrd into midfield 1/2-way: no imp on ldrs over 1f out: wknd* **16/1**

5135 **11** *hd* **Takitwo**[18] 2877 4-9-5 **65** JamieHamblett 9 60
(P D Cundell) *chsd ldrs early: lost pl bef 1/2-way: struggling in rr over 2f out* **4/1**[1]

6001 **12** *nk* **Mythical Charm**[9] 3149 8-8-10 **56** 6ex (t) KMay 2 51
(J J Bridger) *pressed ldrs tl wknd 2f out* **10/1**

-400 **13** 1 **Only If I Laugh**[106] 800 6-8-5 **51** oh3 MCGeran 6 43
(M J Attwater) *pushed along in midfield 1/2-way: struggling over 2f out: wknd* **33/1**

6545 **14** 4 **Bollywood (IRE)**[9] 3149 4-8-0 **51** oh6 (p) LauraReynolds(5) 1 32
(J J Bridger) *a bhd* **28/1**

1m 25.95s (-0.85) **Going Correction** -0.10s/f (Stan) **14** Ran SP% **125.0**
Speed ratings (Par 103):100,99,98,98,96 96,96,95,94,94 94,93,92,88
CSF £59.21 CT £402.90 TOTE £15.80: £4.10, £2.30, £2.30; EX 93.10 Place 6 £321.69, Place 5 £51.41..

Owner R D Bickenson **Bred** Shadwell Estate Company Limited **Trained** Middleham Moor, N Yorks

■ Stewards' Enquiry : Ryan Bird one-day ban: failed to ride to draw (Jul 22); four-day ban: careless riding (Jul 23-26)

FOCUS
Quite a rough contest, which is to be expected in a race restricted to apprentices who had not ridden more than 25 winners. Little got into it from the rear. The pace was good and the form, although only modest, looks fairly reliable.

October Ben Official explanation: jockey said filly was hampered at start

T/Plt: £411.70 to a £1 stake. Pool: £85,490.75. 151.55 winning tickets. T/Qpdt: £90.50 to a £1 stake. Pool: £6,941.20. 56.70 winning tickets. JN

[3392]LINGFIELD (L-H)

Wednesday, July 11

OFFICIAL GOING: All-weather - standard; turf course - good (good to firm in places; 8.6)

Wind: moderate across

3423 THE REAL THING LIVE AT LINGFIELDPARK.CO.UK MAIDEN AUCTION STKS (DIV I) 6f (P)

1:40 (1:40) (Class 6) 2-Y-O **£2,047** (£604; £302) **Stalls** Low

Form RPR

5 **1** **Maddy**[25] 2663 2-8-4 0 JamesDoyle 4 64
(R M Beckett) *in tch and sn drvn along: hdwy over 1f out: str run u.p ins fnl f to ld fnl 50yds* **15/2**

350 **2** *nk* **Bookiebasher Dude**[36] 2333 2-9-1 0 RobertHavlin 9 74
(M Quinn) *mde most: rdn and styd on whn strly chal fr 2f out: hdd and no ex fnl 50yds* **14/1**

3 *nk* **Honey Monster (IRE)** 2-8-10 0 ColinHaddon(5) 3 73
(Miss V Haigh) *s.i.s: t.k.h and sn upsides ldr: ev ch fr 2f out and tendency to run wd bnd ins fnl 2f: no ex fnl half f* **25/1**

042 **4** *shd* **Ruby Delta**[18] 2876 2-8-9 0 FergusSweeney 6 67
(P D Cundell) *chsd ldrs: rdn 2f out: styd on wl fnl f but nvr gng pce to press ldrs* **2/1**[1]

046 **5** *2* **Replicator**[51] 1882 2-8-12 0 DaneO'Neill 12 64
(Pat Eddery) *s.i.s: sn in tch: rdn and hdwy over 1f out: kpt on ins fnl f but nt rch ldrs* **11/2**[2]

55 **6** *shd* **Southwest Star (IRE)**[91] 999 2-8-9 0 SimonWhitworth 1 61
(J S Moore) *chsd ldrs: rdn and ev ch over 1f out: wknd ins fnl f* **6/1**[3]

6 **7** *1 1/4* **Cosmea**[15] 2968 2-8-4 0 JimmyQuinn 5 52
(A King) *s.i.s: sn outpcd and drvn along: kpt on fr over 1f out but nvr gng pce to trble ldrs* **13/2**

5 **8** *1 3/4* **Mac Dalia**[22] 2746 2-8-7 0 TPO'Shea 8 50
(M G Quinlan) *rrd stalls: t.k.h and sn chsng ldrs: rn wd bnd ins fnl 2f: wknd fnl f* **11/1**

00 **9** *1* **We Have A Dream**[16] 2941 2-8-12 0 RichardMullen 11 52
(W R Muir) *outpcd tl sme hdwy fnl f* **16/1**

006 **10** *3* **Goldhill Fair**[8] 3174 2-8-2 0 JackDean(7) 10 40
(W G M Turner) *chsd ldrs tl wknd over 1f out* **33/1**

00 **11** *1 1/2* **Morforwyn**[11] 3109 2-8-7 0 JimCrowley 7 33
(J A Osborne) *s.i.s: a bhd* **40/1**

12 *28* **Help (IRE)** 2-8-4 0 (b[1]) PaulEddery 2 —
(Mrs P N Dutfield) *slowly away: sn wl bhd* **40/1**

1m 13.44s (0.63) **Going Correction** -0.075s/f (Stan) **12** Ran SP% **120.6**

Speed ratings (Par 92):92,91,91,91,88 88,86,84,82,78 76,39

CSF £105.37 TOTE £7.90: £2.20, £4.30, £3.30; EX 140.50 TRIFECTA Not won..

Owner P K Gardner **Bred** P K Gardner **Trained** Whitsbury, Hants

■ Stewards' Enquiry : Robert Havlin one-day ban: used whip with excessive frequency (Jul 22)

FOCUS

A real mixed bag of talents and shapes went to post, and only four of them had experience of an All-Weather surface, so the race probably took little winning. A few of the horses in both divisions had raced against each other already, so the form is probably fairly sound for this sort of moderate level.

NOTEBOOK

Maddy was very green in the early stages on her debut here on the turf, but slowly got the hang of things and stayed on well in the final stages. Running much the same way again, the further she went the better she looked and another furlong should be within her scope. (op 8-1 tchd 9-1)

Bookiebasher Dude had not obviously progressed since his fair debut effort and was trying a sixth furlong for the first time. He showed plenty of dash from an early stage and was just edged out of it close to home. (op 16-1)

Honey Monster(IRE), who was wearing a sheepskin noseband, shaped really well on his debut, showing little sign of inexperience. An ordinary affair is within his compass.

Ruby Delta did not really benefit from the drop in trip and was doing all of his best work late on. (op 9-4)

Replicator had shown signs of ability in the past but was inconvenienced by a wide draw and a bit of trouble early. He kept on reasonably well and is worth a chance at 7f. (op 6-1 tchd 13-2 and 7-1 in a place)

Southwest Star(IRE) was never far away but did not get home as well as some others and will surely come on for the run. (op 11-2 tchd 13-2)

Mac Dalia was far too keen and never had a chance of getting home. (op 12-1 tchd 10-1)

3424 THE REAL THING LIVE AT LINGFIELDPARK.CO.UK MAIDEN AUCTION STKS (DIV II) 6f (P)

2:10 (2:12) (Class 6) 2-Y-O **£2,047** (£604; £302) **Stalls** Low

Form RPR

4 **1** **Afram Blue**[29] 2539 2-9-1 0 DaneO'Neill 8 75+
(W J Knight) *chsd ldrs: slt ld appr fnl 2f: drvn out ins fnl f: in command whn edgd rt cl home* **5/2**[1]

60 **2** *1* **Solent Ridge (IRE)**[12] 3043 2-8-12 0 JamesDoyle 10 69+
(J S Moore) *in tch: hdwy 2f out: rdn to chse wnr and hung bdly lft fr 1f out: no imp whn pushed rt nr fin* **6/1**

55 **3** *3* **Farthermost (IRE)**[16] 2941 2-8-9 0 PatDobbs 7 57
(R Hannon) *prom: rdn and outpcd appr fnl 2f: rn in again ins fnl f but nt rch ldrs* **5/1**[3]

00 **4** *3/4* **Tintorero**[18] 2876 2-9-1 0 TPO'Shea 3 61
(M J Wallace) *chsd ldrs tl outpcd 2f out: rdn and styd on again fnl f but nvr gng pce to be competitive* **16/1**

5 *nk* **Elizabeth's Quest** 2-7-11 0 SophieDoyle(7) 9 49
(R Simpson) *s.i.s: in rr whn bmpd after 1f: stl wl in rr tl r.o strly ins fnl f: gng on cl home* **33/1**

6 *nk* **Magical Song** 2-8-9 0 RichardMullen 12 53
(E J O'Neill) *sn chsng ldr: rdn over 2f out: wknd fnl f* **12/1**

5 **7** *3/4* **La Varrosa**[9] 3162 2-8-4 0 JimmyQuinn 6 52+
(Mrs P N Dutfield) *s.i.s: wnt rt after 1f: styd in rr tl styd on fnl f but nvr gng pce to be competitive* **40/1**

034 **8** *nk* **Pretty Bonnie**[22] 2746 2-8-7 0 JimCrowley 1 48
(J G Portman) *chsd ldrs tl wknd over 1f out* **7/1**

033 **9** *1 3/4* **Bahamarama (IRE)**[9] 3162 2-8-7 0 FergusSweeney 5 43
(J R Boyle) *led tl hdd appr fnl 2f: wknd appr fnl f* **9/2**[2]

10 *3/4* **Hucking Hero (IRE)** 2-8-6 0 StephaneBreux(3) 4 42
(J R Best) *s.i.s: outpcd most of way* **12/1**

11 *7* **Ataensic** 2-8-4 0 (be[1]) FrancisNorton 2 16
(C N Allen) *s.i.s: t.k.h and sn chsng ldrs: wknd fr 2f out* **33/1**

1m 13.42s (0.61) **Going Correction** -0.075s/f (Stan) **11** Ran SP% **119.8**

Speed ratings (Par 92):92,90,86,85,85 84,83,83,81,80 70

CSF £17.71 TOTE £3.70: £1.30, £2.90, £2.10; EX 17.10 Trifecta £156.60 Part won. Pool £220.70 - 0.78 winning units..

Owner Mr & Mrs I H Bendelow **Bred** Mrs J A M Willment **Trained** Patching, W Sussex

■ Stewards' Enquiry : James Doyle two-day ban: careless riding (Jul 22-23)

FOCUS

There was even less All-Weather form to go on in this division and, like the first race, it is difficult to gauge the true worth of the form.

NOTEBOOK

Afram Blue gained enough of an advantage off the home bend to hold the late challenge of Solent Ridge. It is interesting that the Knight stable won this race with their only previous representative, but quite how good he will turn out to be is still open to question. (op 11-4 tchd 3-1)

Solent Ridge(IRE), who finished behind Afram Blue on his debut, was well beaten at Folkestone last time over 7f but came back to something like his debut promise. He needed every yard of this trip, and was slightly hampered as the winner jinked close to the line, so the ground must have been the excuse last time. (op 10-1)

Farthermost(IRE) was not far from the leaders during the race but never really got going until inside the final furlong. (tchd 4-1)

Tintorero was fancied on his debut in May but ran poorly and finished last. He improved only slightly on his next run and this was better, but he does not look like winning a race yet, even though he was short of room on the inside at one stage. (tchd 20-1)

Elizabeth's Quest was going nowhere off the final bend before picking up well in the latter stages. She seems sure to get at least another furlong.

Magical Song showed plenty of promise despite falling out of the stalls. The run will have done him good mentally.

La Varrosa stayed on quite nicely but still looked in need of the experience. Official explanation: jockey said filly was hampered leaving stalls (tchd 50-1)

3425 JASON DONOVAN LIVE AT LINGFIELDPARK.CO.UK MEDIAN AUCTION MAIDEN STKS 6f (P)

2:45 (2:48) (Class 6) 3-4-Y-O **£2,730** (£806; £403) **Stalls** Low

Form RPR

00-4 **1** **Shaded Edge**[116] 700 3-9-3 55 JamesDoyle 12 63
(D W P Arbuthnot) *chsd ldrs: qcknd to chal wl ins fnl f: late burst to ld last stride* **12/1**

0-03 **2** *shd* **Siesta (IRE)**[41] 2186 3-8-7 50 (e) PatrickHills(5) 8 57
(J R Fanshawe) *hld up in rr but in tch: hdwy over 1f out and qcknd to ld wl ins fnl f: ct last stride* **9/1**

3 **3** *3/4* **Affrettando (IRE)**[27] 2593 3-9-3 0 TPO'Shea 9 60
(J A R Toller) *s.i.s: sn in tch: drvn and outpcd over 2f out: styd on ell fnl f: gng on cl home* **9/2**[2]

-200 **4** *3/4* **Support Fund (IRE)**[58] 1731 3-8-12 65 StephenCarson 10 53
(Eve Johnson Houghton) *chsd ldrs: pushed along 1/2-way: outpcd 2f out: kpt on again fnl f but nvr gng pce to chal* **7/2**[1]

20- **5** *shd* **Luck Will Come (IRE)**[242] 6433 3-8-12 0 DaneO'Neill 7 52
(M J Wallace) *slt ld tl kicked off home turn and 3 l up over 1f out: hdd & wknd wl ins fnl f* **7/2**[1]

3000 **6** *1/2* **Double Valentine**[25] 2665 4-9-4 45 RobertHavlin 2 52
(R Ingram) *in rr: rdn over 2f out: kpt on fr over 1f out: nvr gng pce to be competitive* **8/1**[3]

0066 **7** *1* **Chingford (IRE)**[51] 1883 3-8-12 50 (b[1]) JimCrowley 11 47
(J G Portman) *w ldr tl over 2f out: styd in 2nd tl wknd ins fnl f* **25/1**

0 **8** *3 1/2* **Katie Coniston**[12] 3062 3-8-7 0 KevinGhunowa(5) 4 36
(Dr J R J Naylor) *chsd ldrs tl rdn and outpcd 1/2-way: styd on same pce fnl f* **33/1**

00 **9** *2* **Pixie Princess (IRE)**[44] 2083 3-8-7 0 ColinHaddon(5) 6 30
(Miss V Haigh) *s.i.s: sn chsng ldrs and running freely: wknd over 1f out* **66/1**

10 *6* **Pathway To Glory** 3-9-3 0 FrancisNorton 3 16
(M Quinn) *a towards rr* **14/1**

L05- **11** *2* **Linkslade Lad**[289] 5570 3-9-3 65 (b) RichardMullen 5 9
(W R Muir) *slowly away: rdn and rel to r early: tacked in to main gp after 2f but a in rr* **16/1**

1m 12.83s (0.02) **Going Correction** -0.075s/f (Stan)

WFA 3 from 4yo 6lb **11** Ran SP% **112.3**

Speed ratings (Par 101):96,95,94,93,93 93,91,87,84,76 73

CSF £103.14 TOTE £16.20: £4.20, £2.80, £1.80; EX 100.00 TRIFECTA Not won..

Owner Lady Whent And Friends **Bred** Lady Whent **Trained** Compton, Berks

■ Ardennes (12/1, refused to enter stalls) was withdrawn. Rule 4 applies, deduct 5p in the £.

FOCUS

It seems highly unlikely that anything of last year's winner Al Qasi's considerable talent was hiding away in this bunch and the form looks only modest. However, it was interesting that a couple in the line-up spurned the chance of running in a handicap after having the requisite three runs, and it was those horses that fought out a really tight finish.

3426 TOWERGATE UNDERWRITING NURSERY 5f (P)

3:20 (3:20) (Class 5) 2-Y-O **£3,238** (£963; £481; £240) **Stalls** High

Form RPR

2321 **1** **Concertmaster**[35] 2349 2-9-4 **82** GeorgeBaker 10 83
(R M Beckett) *in rr: rdn and outpcd early: swtchd rt and str run fnl f: led last stride* **9/2**[3]

41 **2** *nk* **Victorian Bounty**[32] 2460 2-8-11 **75** RichardMullen 4 75
(E J O'Neill) *chsd ldrs: led jst ins fnl f: kpt narrow ld u.p tl ct last stride* **7/2**[1]

2335 **3** *hd* **Ben**[32] 2443 2-8-13 **77** RobertHavlin 3 76
(P G Murphy) *chsd ldrs: drvn and qcknd to chal fr ins fnl f: no ex last strides* **10/1**

0322 **4** *hd* **Maybe I Wont**[15] 2961 2-8-10 **74** DaneO'Neill 5 72
(S Dow) *s.i.s: bhd: rdn over 2f out: str run thrght fnl f: finshed wl but nt quite rch ldrs* **4/1**[2]

050 **5** *nk* **Choisky (IRE)**[26] 2630 2-8-5 **69** JimmyQuinn 8 66
(J Akehurst) *in rr: rdn along fr 1/2-way: styd on u.p thrght fnl f but nvr gng pce to chal ldrs* **12/1**

0520 **6** *3/4* **Flying Indian**[14] 2997 2-8-4 **68** FrancisNorton 6 63
(A M Balding) *chsd ldrs: n.m.r 3f out: styd on u.p fr over 1f out but nvr gng pce to be competitive* **8/1**

2154 **7** *hd* **Ten Down**[40] 2199 2-9-7 **85** JimCrowley 9 79
(J A Osborne) *sn chsng ldr: rdn over 2f out: wknd over 1f out: btn whn n.m.r wl ins fnl f* **6/1**

0033 **8** *nk* **A Wish For You**[13] 3030 2-8-5 **69** DavidKinsella 1 62
(D K Ivory) *chsd ldrs: rdn over 2f out: styng on whn nt clr run wl ins fnl f: nt rcvr: kpt on again last strides* **14/1**

2026 **9** *1* **Hucking Harmony (IRE)**[9] 3152 2-8-1 **68**............... StephaneBreux(3) 7 57
(J R Best) *sn led: hdd jst ins fnl f and sn btn* **11/1**

59.76 secs (-0.02) **Going Correction** -0.075s/f (Stan) **9** Ran SP% **117.6**
Speed ratings (Par 94):97,96,96,95,95 94,93,93,91
CSF £21.08 CT £151.85 TOTE £4.50: £1.60, £1.80, £3.50; EX 18.80 Trifecta £165.90 Pool £317.97 - 1.36 winning units..
Owner The Millennium Madness Partnership **Bred** B Whitehouse **Trained** Whitsbury, Hants

FOCUS
The early pace looked to be sound but the main body of the field were only covered by a few lengths passing the line, so the form could well be unreliable. The official ratings shown next to each horse are estimated and for information purposes only.

NOTEBOOK
Concertmaster always appears to run well, at a modest level, and importantly, he had All-Weather experience. Towards the rear early, he came with a really strong run to get up close to the line under a trademark George Baker ride, and possibly win with a little bit in hand. He is most progressive at his level and his in-form trainer has done very well with him. (tchd 4-1 and 5-1)
Victorian Bounty ◆ had less experience than most in this field and kept on really well under pressure. With more time, he may well emerge the best of these, and he is going the right way. (op 4-1 tchd 5-1)
Ben is a consistent sort and has run up against a few promising performers who went on to run in big races. However, he had seen the rear end of Concertmaster twice already, including over this course and distance in the first juvenile race of the season, and had to settle for that view once again. (op 12-1)
Maybe I Wont was without a success coming into the race but had shaped like a horse capable of winning. He did not help his chances with a slow start but finished strongly to look a little unlucky. Official explanation: jockey said colt missed the break (op 13-2)
Choisky(IRE) was not going that well early but put his head down under pressure to finish on the heels of the leading bunch. (op 16-1 tchd 10-1)
Flying Indian had every chance off the final bend but got involved in some scrimmaging there and lost her position. She did keep on nicely enough but never proved a threat. (tchd 15-2)
Ten Down, who obviously had the best form considering the weight he carried, was bang there rounding the final bend but weakened under his weight. (op 9-2)
A Wish For You ◆ was an unlucky horse once again, meeting trouble at least twice during the race and seemingly having plenty still to give crossing the line. (op 12-1)
Hucking Harmony(IRE), who set the early pace, looked to go off far too quickly. (op 8-1)

3427 LADIES NIGHT JULY 21ST FILLIES' H'CAP — 1m 3f 106y
3:55 (3:55) (Class 5) (0-70,70) 3-Y-O+ **£2,817** (£838; £418; £209) **Stalls** High

Form RPR
0430 **1** **Tranquilizer**[23] 2720 5-10-0 **70**..(t) TPO'Shea 9 77
(D J Coakley) *trckd ldrs: wnt 2nd 1m out: led over 4f out: hrd rdn whn chal thrght fnl 2f: hld on all out* **6/1**[3]
0661 **2** *shd* **Jawaaneb (USA)**[17] 2915 3-9-0 **68**...................................... IanMongan 6 75
(J L Dunlop) *chsd ldrs: wnt 2nd 4f out: hrd drvn to chal fr 2f out: kpt on wl cl home but a jst hld* **10/3**[1]
1-63 **3** *2 1/2* **Pairumani Princess (IRE)**[9] 3166 3-8-9 **63**.................... JimmyQuinn 3 66
(E A L Dunlop) *led 1f: styd trcking ldrs tl rdn and outpcd over 3f out: styd on u.p fnl 2f: styd on cl home but nvr gng pce to chal* **5/1**[2]
51 **4** *1 1/4* **Windbeneathmywings (IRE)**[9] 3166 3-8-6 **65** 6ex..... PatrickHills(5) 11 66
(J W Hills) *led after 2f: hdd over 4f out: styd prom: rdn over 2f out: wknd fnl f* **7/1**
/60- **5** *3/4* **Spunger**[218] 6712 4-9-6 **62**..(v[1]) DaneO'Neill 4 62
(H J L Dunlop) *in rr: rdn and hdwy over 2f out: sn hung lft and styd on same pce* **25/1**
3-50 **6** *1 1/4* **Over Ice**[40] 2194 4-9-0 **59**.. JerryO'Dwyer(3) 1 57
(Karen George) *rrd s and slowly away: bhd: rdn over 3f out: kpt on fr over 1f out: n.d* **20/1**
0626 **7** *nk* **Driving Miss Suzie**[16] 2940 3-8-10 **64**......................... FrancisNorton 10 61
(A M Balding) *led after 1f: sn hdd: styd chsng ldrs: rdn over 3f out: wknd ins fnl 2f* **12/1**
0025 **8** *1 3/4* **Sweet Request**[28] 2579 3-8-6 **60**...................................... JamesDoyle 8 55
(R M Beckett) *chsd ldrs: rdn 4f out: wknd over 2f out* **5/1**[2]
006 **9** *1 3/4* **Hermanita**[35] 2360 3-8-11 **65**.. RobertHavlin 7 57
(G Wragg) *in tch: rdn and hdwy 4f out: wknd over 2f out* **10/1**
305 **10** *12* **Anne Bonney**[48] 1964 3-7-9 **56**.......................................(t) MCGeran(7) 2 29
(E J O'Neill) *v.s.a: a towards rr* **12/1**

2m 31.26s (1.34) **Going Correction** -0.025s/f (Good)
WFA 3 from 4yo+ 12lb **10** Ran SP% **116.3**
Speed ratings (Par 100):94,93,92,91,90 89,89,88,86,78
CSF £26.22 CT £108.31 TOTE £7.80: £2.10, £1.80, £1.80; EX 22.30 Trifecta £21.40 Pool £413.97 - 13.72 winning units..
Owner Count Calypso Racing **Bred** Highclere Stud Ltd **Trained** West Ilsley, Berks

FOCUS
The jockeys reported that ground was riding good, with a couple of softer patches. A modest handicap run at a steady early pace. The form is unlikely to prove too solid.
Over Ice Official explanation: jockey said filly missed the break
Sweet Request Official explanation: jockey said filly was denied a clear run
Anne Bonney Official explanation: jockey said filly missed the break

3428 BRIEFCASE BLUES BROTHERS LIVE AT LINGFIELDPARK.CO.UK (S) STKS — 1m 2f
4:30 (4:31) (Class 6) 3-Y-O+ **£2,047** (£604; £302) **Stalls** Low

Form RPR
6302 **1** **Chant De Guerre (USA)**[11] 3083 3-8-4 54.................... JimmyQuinn 12 62+
(H J L Dunlop) *chsd ldrs: rdn 3f out: led 2f out: drvn clr fnl f* **5/1**[1]
500- **2** *5* **Princely Ted (IRE)**[226] 6628 6-9-6 49............................. DaneO'Neill 1 57
(R A Farrant) *chsd ldrs: drvn and effrt 2f out: outpcd by wnr over 1f out but styd on wl for clr 2nd* **6/1**[2]
2060 **3** *2 1/2* **The City Kid (IRE)**[9] 3173 4-9-7 58...............................(v) RobertHavlin 5 53+
(C R Dore) *in rr: rdn over over 3f out: styd on fnl 2f but nvr in contention w ldng pair* **7/1**
5300 **4** *1/2* **Star Berry**[27] 2595 4-8-8 48.. KMay(7) 9 46
(B J Meehan) *led: rdn and hdd 2f out: sn btn* **13/2**[3]
0023 **5** *4* **Savoy Chapel**[15] 2963 5-9-6 42...................................... FrancisNorton 6 43
(A W Carroll) *in rr: rdn fr 4f out: sme hdwy fnl 2f* **14/1**
005- **6** *shd* **Grangehurst**[263] 6098 3-8-3 58 ow2.................(t) RichardKingscote(3) 8 40
(Miss J R Gibney) *chsd ldrs: rdn 4f out: wknd qckly 2f out* **10/1**
000- **7** *hd* **Littleton Aldor (IRE)**[303] 5248 7-8-13 37........................ JackDean(7) 10 42
(Mark Gillard) *w ldr: rdn 4f out: wknd 2f out* **40/1**
0006 **8** *1 1/4* **Atticus Trophies (IRE)**[6] 3232 4-8-13 45.............(e[1]) SophieDoyle(7) 14 40
(Ms J S Doyle) *nvr bttr than mid-div* **25/1**
4035 **9** *1* **Fire At Will**[5] 3286 5-8-13 42.. MarkCoumbe(7) 7 38
(A W Carroll) *slowly away: in rr tl mod hdwy fnl 2f* **9/1**
-000 **10** *3/4* **By Storm**[8] 3186 4-8-8 45... KirstyMilczarek(7) 3 31
(John Berry) *in tch 6f* **14/1**
000- **11** *nk* **Sprouston (FR)**[34] 6855 4-9-3 40................................ JerryO'Dwyer(3) 4 36
(Karen George) *a towards rr* **40/1**
0000 **12** *nk* **Marbaa (IRE)**[18] 2875 4-9-6 55... PaulDoe 2 35
(S Dow) *a towards rr* **6/1**[2]
3306 **13** *3/4* **Rafferty (IRE)**[6] 3241 8-8-13 44.............................(p) ThomasBubb(7) 13 34
(S Dow) *slowly away: t.k.h: a in rr* **12/1**
0600 **14** *105* **Kitchen Sink (IRE)**[36] 2334 5-9-12 48.....................(e) StephenCarson 11 —
(Jean-Rene Auvray) *chsd ldrs tl wknd qckly 4f out: virtually p.u fnl 2f* **20/1**

2m 8.33s (-1.39) **Going Correction** -0.025s/f (Good)
WFA 3 from 4yo+ 11lb **14** Ran SP% **124.7**
Speed ratings (Par 101):104,100,98,97,94 94,94,93,92,91 91,91,90,—
CSF £33.91 TOTE £4.40: £2.00, £2.60, £2.70; EX 40.50 Trifecta £138.50 Part won. Pool £195.18 - 0.50 winning units..The winner was sold to P Mitchell for 7,600gns.
Owner M Vickers **Bred** Shadwell Farm LLC **Trained** Lambourn, Berks
■ Stewards' Enquiry : Stephen Carson three-day ban: careless riding (Jul 22-24)

FOCUS
Very much the sort of field you would expect to see in a seller, and some old favourites too. The race took very little winning and Chant De Guerre did not need to improve despite the wide margin.

3429 PLATINUM ABBA LIVE AT LINGFIELDPARK.CO.UK H'CAP — 1m 1f
5:05 (5:05) (Class 6) (0-65,65) 3-Y-O **£2,047** (£604; £302) **Stalls** Low

Form RPR
00-4 **1** **Sun Of The Sea**[19] 2834 3-9-6 **64**...................................... GeorgeBaker 2 80+
(N P Littmoden) *hld up in mid-div: stdy hdwy fr 3f out to ld on bit over 1f out: sn clr: v easily* **15/8**[1]
6050 **2** *7* **Silca Key**[11] 3082 3-9-7 **65**.. TPO'Shea 13 70
(M R Channon) *in tch: hdwy 5f out: drvn to chal fr 2f out: nt ch w wnr fnl f but styd on wl fr 2nd* **16/1**
6-50 **3** *1 1/4* **April Fool**[58] 1726 3-9-0 **58**.......................................(v[1]) StephenCarson 10 60
(J A Geake) *chsd ldrs: wnt 2nd 7f out: drvn to take slt ld 2f out: hdd and edgd lft over 1f out: kpt on same pce* **25/1**
-031 **4** *shd* **Palmetto Point**[17] 2916 3-8-7 **56**................................(p) TravisBlock(5) 3 58
(H Morrison) *chsd ldrs: rdn and hung lft over 1f out: kpt on same pce* **8/1**[3]
6400 **5** *1 1/4* **Homes By Woodford**[17] 2916 3-8-13 **60**........................ LiamJones(3) 1 60
(R A Harris) *chsd ldrs: rdn and hmpd ins fnl 2f: no imp after* **22/1**
6602 **6** *nk* **Zelos (IRE)**[8] 3178 3-8-13 **57**...(b) JimCrowley 12 56
(J A Osborne) *in rr: rdn over 3f out: styd on fnl f: nvr in contention* **8/1**[3]
030 **7** *1 1/4* **White Moss (IRE)**[39] 2253 3-9-4 **62**.................................. JimmyQuinn 14 58
(M H Tompkins) *in rr tl rdn styd on fnl 2f: nvr rchd ldrs* **16/1**
50-0 **8** *3/4* **Law Of The Land (IRE)**[37] 2317 3-9-2 **60**...................... RichardMullen 6 55
(W R Muir) *chsd ldrs: rdn 3f out: wknd fr 2f out* **25/1**
0042 **9** *nk* **Anthea**[16] 2940 3-9-2 **60**.. DaneO'Neill 7 54
(B R Millman) *sn led: hdd 2f out: sn wknd* **9/2**[2]
30-0 **10** *5* **The Bronx**[113] 713 3-8-11 **55**..(p) PaulDoe 11 39
(M J Wallace) *chsd ldrs: rdn over 3f out: wknd 2f out* **8/1**[3]
0060 **11** *1/2* **Shouldntbethere (IRE)**[23] 2727 3-9-0 **58**...................... RobertHavlin 9 41
(Mrs P N Dutfield) *s.i.s: a towards rr* **33/1**
30-0 **12** *nk* **Serene Highness (IRE)**[24] 2693 3-9-2 **60**......................... IanMongan 8 42
(J L Dunlop) *a in rr* **16/1**
00-0 **13** *1 1/4* **Kimono My House**[27] 2607 3-8-7 **56**.......................... ColinHaddon(5) 5 35
(J G Given) *in tch to 1/2-way* **40/1**
4P00 **14** *14* **Lights Of Vegas**[27] 2598 3-9-7 **65**... PatDobbs 4 15
(B J Meehan) *a towards rr* **33/1**

1m 55.46s (0.17) **Going Correction** -0.025s/f (Good) **14** Ran SP% **124.3**
Speed ratings (Par 98):98,97,96,95,94 94,93,92,92,88 87,87,86,73
CSF £34.51 CT £628.86 TOTE £3.30: £1.50, £4.40, £6.30; EX 35.10 Trifecta £163.30 Part won. Pool £230.04 - 0.30 winning units. Place 6 £190.40, Place 5 £18.84..
Owner Miss Vanessa Church **Bred** Red House Stud **Trained** Newmarket, Suffolk

FOCUS
Winning form was very thin on the ground and virtually all of the unexposed runners had a smidgen of a chance on their one and only piece of good form. The trick beforehand was guessing which one it would be. The winner was value for fruther and the form, although not strong, makes sense.
Kimono My House Official explanation: trainer said filly was found to have injured her off-fore during the race
T/Plt: £255.30 to a £1 stake. Pool: £39,241.60. 112.20 winning tickets. T/Qpdt: £6.10 to a £1 stake. Pool: £3,882.25. 470.20 winning tickets. ST

3095 NEWMARKET (JULY) (R-H)
Wednesday, July 11

OFFICIAL GOING: Good (8.1) changing to good to firm after race 6 (4.20)
Wind: Light, behind Weather: overcast

3430 RACING POST BLOODSTOCK E B F FILLIES' H'CAP — 7f
1:30 (1:34) (Class 2) (0-100,92) 3-Y-O
£18,696 (£5,598; £2,799; £1,401; £699; £351) **Stalls** Low

Form RPR
16-1 **1** **Tarteel (USA)**[18] 2883 3-9-5 **90**.. RHills 13 99+
(J L Dunlop) *gng wl in midfield on stands' side: clsd to ld over 1f out: edgd rt and lft: r.o strly* **8/1**[2]
3130 **2** *1 1/2* **Graduation**[21] 2757 3-9-7 **92**.. JimmyFortune 12 97
(E A L Dunlop) *lw: midfield on stands' side: rdn and outpcd over 2f out: kpt on wl ins fnl f: nt rch wnr* **16/1**
-322 **3** *3/4* **Medley**[12] 3059 3-9-7 **92**... RichardHughes 15 95
(R Hannon) *stdd s: drvn and outpcd 3f out: kpt on wl ins fnl f but unable to chal* **9/1**[3]
-061 **4** *hd* **Steam Cuisine**[18] 2881 3-8-12 **86**............................. JerryO'Dwyer(3) 19 88+
(M G Quinlan) *stdd s: last on stands' side tl over 2f out: swtchd to centre and r.o strly fnl f: too much to do* **8/1**[2]
512 **5** *hd* **Telltime (IRE)**[26] 2629 3-8-0 **76**.................................. WilliamBuick(5) 11 78
(A M Balding) *prom stands' side: rdn and ev ch over 1f out: kpt on same pce* **16/1**
022 **6** *3/4* **Medicea Sidera**[33] 2428 3-8-8 **79**...................................... MartinDwyer 5 79+
(E F Vaughan) *led far side: no ch w stands' side gp fnl f but kpt on* **25/1**
0-0 **7** *3/4* **El Soprano (IRE)**[9] 3158 3-9-5 **90**... NCallan 17 88
(K A Ryan) *cl up stands' side: rdn 3f out: one pce over 1f out* **40/1**
121 **8** *1/2* **Champfleurie**[11] 3094 3-9-3 **88**...................................... JamieSpencer 1 84+
(G A Swinbank) *prom far side: outpcd by stands' side gp over 1f out but kpt on steadily* **7/1**[1]
40-0 **9** *3/4* **Zanida (IRE)**[17] 2914 3-9-2 **87**..................................... PatCosgrave 18 81
(K R Burke) *led stands' side: drvn 2f out: hdd over 1f out: nt qckn* **50/1**

0234 **10** *nk* **Whazzis**[17] 2914 3-9-3 **88**......(v1) KerrinMcEvoy 2 82+
(W J Haggas) *swtg: nt clr passage early and again 1/2-way on far side: racd w awkward hd carriage: kpt on ins fnl f but no ch* **12/1**

1540 **11** *3/4* **Voodoo Moon**[18] 2862 3-9-1 **89**...... GregFairley(3) 14 81
(M Johnston) *swtg: prom stands' side: drvn over 2f out: no ex over 1f out* **33/1**

1005 **12** *1/2* **Precocious Star (IRE)**[7] 3222 3-9-2 **90**...... AndrewElliott(3) 16 80
(K R Burke) *stands' side and chsng ldrs: rdn 3f out: btn over 1f out* **33/1**

10-1 **13** *shd* **Folly Lodge**[53] 1837 3-9-2 **87**...... MichaelHills 8 77+
(B W Hills) *stdd s: t.k.h: racd far side: rdn and btn over 1f out* **7/1**[1]

50-0 **14** *1 1/4* **Millestan (IRE)**[28] 2578 3-9-2 **87**...... TedDurcan 3 74+
(H R A Cecil) *chsd ldr far side early: btn wl over 1f out* **25/1**

641 **15** *3/4* **Rustic Flame (IRE)**[14] 2998 3-8-11 **82**...... SteveDrowne 10 67+
(C R Egerton) *racd far side: rdn and btn over 1f out* **20/1**

0110 **16** *nk* **Look So**[17] 2914 3-8-10 **81**...... RyanMoore 6 65+
(R M Beckett) *last and drvn on far side 1/2-way: nvr on terms* **14/1**

6124 **17** *nk* **Fealeview Lady (USA)**[26] 2623 3-7-11 **73** oh3...... LukeMorris(5) 7 56+
(H Morrison) *spd far side to 1/2-way* **33/1**

2116 **18** *1/2* **Truly Enchanting (IRE)**[21] 2757 3-9-6 **91**...... LDettori 9 73+
(J Noseda) *lw: towards rr far side: btn 2f out* **7/1**[1]

06-0 **19** *nk* **Miss Jenny (IRE)**[35] 2369 3-8-1 **79**...... KMay(7) 20 60
(B J Meehan) *lw: chsd ldrs stands' side 4f* **40/1**

1m 23.82s (-2.96) **Going Correction** -0.20s/f (Firm) **19** Ran SP% **124.0**
Speed ratings (Par 103):108,106,105,105,104 104,103,102,101,101 100,100,99,98,97 97,96,96,96
CSF £115.12 CT £1194.96 TOTE £8.20: £2.20, £4.90, £2.30, £2.70; EX 199.80 Trifecta £547.10 Part won. Pool £770.68 - 0.50 winning units..
Owner Hamdan Al Maktoum **Bred** Shadwell Farm LLC **Trained** Arundel, W Sussex
■ Stewards' Enquiry : Luke Morris three-day ban: careless riding (Jul 22-24)

FOCUS
The first of many races where runners split into two groups and overall it looked an advantage to race stands' side. Not much early pace on for what was a good fillies' handicap, and that makes the performance of the smart Tarteel all the more impressive. She looks Listed class, and the race should produce its share of winners. The form seems solid, although the far-side group could be rated 10lb higher.

NOTEBOOK
Tarteel(USA) ◆, who scoped dirty when proving a disappointing favourite in a Listed contest on the Rowley Mile course on her final start at two, reappeared with an impressive display off a most favourable mark of 84 over 1m here last month, and she showed sufficient speed that day to suggest the drop in trip would pose no problems. Dropped in early, she was always travelling strongly and there was only ever going to be one result once she hit the front a furlong out. A filly going places, she is at least Listed class and better can be expected of her as she goes back up to 1m. (op 7-1)
Graduation shows plenty of speed for a horse bred to appreciate further than 1m, but she came into this with it all to prove following a dismal effort behind Barshiba at Royal Ascot. Even though she was dropped 2lb for that effort, she still had her share of weight and it was surprising to see her run so well, sticking on for pressure without troubling the winner. It is probable that trips beyond 1m will suit her best in the long run. (op 20-1)
Medley ran well dropped back to an inadequate 6f here last time and it was no surprise to see her better that effort with a keeping-on third. She picked up well once switched towards the centre of the track, but is likely to remain vulnerable to improvers off her current mark. (op 12-1)
Steam Cuisine readily disposed of a lesser field over course and distance last time and, although she had a lot more to do off a 9lb higher mark, she gave a good account of herself, looking unfortunate not to get second having been given far too much to do. She is clearly capable of winning off this mark and, as she is already a winner at 1m, it may be an idea to step her back up in trip. (op 9-1 tchd 10-1)
Telltime(IRE) had never gone this far before and she stuck on well having held a prominent position from the off. She was passed by several classier rivals when it mattered, but at least connections have a few more options now with the daughter of Danetime.
Medicea Sidera, placed in a couple of modest maidens, was making her handicap debut off a stiffish-looking mark, but she surpassed expectations and, having taken them along early, she kept on well to 'win' the race on the far side. She is likely to find easier opportunities whilst remaining vulnerable off this sort of mark at the same time. (op 28-1)
El Soprano(IRE), formerly with Kevin Prendergast in Ireland, did not offer a great deal on her recent debut for connections at Pontefract, but she was up to a more suitable distance here and gave a better account of herself. She is not going to be easy to win with off this sort of mark, but clearly has a decent level of ability. (op 66-1)
Champfleurie handles testing ground well, as she showed when readily scoring off a mark of 80 at Newcastle last time, and it was easy to see why she was prominent in the betting, but she was tackling a furlong less, on faster ground, and also had an 8lb hike to deal with. She ran reasonably well, but this trio of factors, along with her racing on the 'wrong' side, means she can be given another chance. (op 13-2)
Zanida(IRE) Official explanation: trainer said filly finished distressed
Whazzis is clearly a bit quirky, but there is no denying that she received little fortune in her run here and she rates a good bit better than her placing. Official explanation: jockey said filly was denied a clear run
Folly Lodge reappeared with a fine winning effort over this distance at Newbury in May, but she had not been seen since and had 10lb more on her back in a much stronger contest. On the disadvantageous far side, she never really figured, but can be given another chance and may benefit from 1m. (op 11-2 tchd 8-1 in a place)
Millestan(IRE) Official explanation: jockey said filly suffered interference shortly after start
Look So had been most progressive, winning her maiden and a handicap off a mark of 71, but she found the rise to Listed level too much for her at Warwick last time and it was clear after a couple of furlongs she was not going to be winning here. This ground may have been a shade lively for her.
Truly Enchanting(IRE) was the main disappointment of the race, never getting into it having been held up on the far side, and running way below the level of form she showed in defeat at Royal Ascot. (tchd 15-2 and 8-1 in a place)

3431 TOTESPORT.COM STKS (HERITAGE H'CAP) 6f
2:00 (2:04) (Class 2) (0-105,103) 3-Y-O
£56,088 (£16,794; £8,397; £4,203; £2,097; £1,053) **Stalls** Low

Form RPR
-110 **1** **Shmookh (USA)**[20] 2788 3-8-7 **89**...... RHills 10 104+
(J L Dunlop) *racd stands' side: hld up: hdwy over 2f out: rdn to ld 1f out: r.o:* **12/1**

-111 **2** *nk* **Off The Record**[57] 1754 3-8-7 **89**...... KDarley 18 103
(J G Given) *racd stands' side: chsd ldr: rdn and ev ch over 1f out: r.o: 2nd of 12 in gp* **9/1**[3]

11-0 **3** *1* **Utmost Respect**[32] 2440 3-8-8 **90**...... TonyHamilton 13 101+
(R A Fahey) *lw: racd stands' side: s.i.s and hmpd s: hdwy over 2f out: sn rdn: r.o: 3rd of 12 in gp* **5/1**[1]

0-43 **4** *1 1/4* **Celtic Sultan (IRE)**[46] 2044 3-8-13 **95**...... MickyFenton 19 102
(T P Tate) *racd stands' side: overall ldr tl rdn and hdd 1f out: edgd lft: styd on same pce: 4th of 12 in gp* **12/1**

4-24 **5** *1/2* **Siren's Gift**[25] 2672 3-8-8 **95**...... WilliamBuick(5) 20 101
(A M Balding) *lw: racd stands' side: chsd ldrs: rdn over 1f out: styd on same pce: 5th of 12 in gp* **14/1**

2211 **6** *1 1/4* **Vitznau (IRE)**[11] 3078 3-8-8 **90**...... RichardHughes 14 92
(R Hannon) *racd stands' side: prom: rdn over 1f out: styd on same pce: 6th of 12 in gp* **10/1**

4404 **7** *1 1/4* **Mastership (IRE)**[40] 2212 3-9-4 **100**......(b) EddieAhern 1 98+
(C E Brittain) *lw: racd far side: hld up: hdwy and nt clr run over 1f out: led that gp 1f out: r.o: 1st of 7 in gp* **33/1**

10-1 **8** *1/2* **Longquan (IRE)**[54] 1817 3-9-1 **97**...... TedDurcan 9 94
(P J Makin) *racd stands' side s.i.s: sn prom: lost pl over 4f out: styd on ins fnl f: 7th of 12 in gp* **14/1**

1256 **9** *3/4* **Annemasse**[20] 2788 3-8-10 **92**...... JoeFanning 15 86
(M Johnston) *racd stands' side: chsd ldrs over 4f: 8th of 12 in gp* **10/1**

-211 **10** *nk* **Express Wish**[34] 2395 3-8-7 **89**...... JohnEgan 11 82
(J Noseda) *racd stands' side: chsd ldrs: rdn over 2f out: wknd over 1f out: 9th of 12 in gp* **7/1**[2]

20-0 **11** *hd* **Rainbow Mirage (IRE)**[34] 2395 3-8-7 **89**...... TQuinn 2 82+
(E S McMahon) *racd far side: prom: nt clr run and lost pl over 1f out: n.d after: 2nd of 7 in gp* **40/1**

1-10 **12** *3/4* **Sandrey (IRE)**[46] 2044 3-8-6 **88**...... RyanMoore 5 79+
(P W Chapple-Hyam) *racd far side: chsd ldrs: rdn whn n.m.r 1f out: sn wknd: 3rd of 7 in gp* **14/1**

4250 **13** *hd* **Luscivious**[18] 2884 3-8-9 **91**......(b) AdamKirby 6 81+
(A J McCabe) *racd far side: dwlt: hdwy and hung rt over 1f out: wknd fnl f: 10th of 12 in gp* **66/1**

5420 **14** *hd* **Solid Rock (IRE)**[21] 2752 3-8-13 **95**...... MJKinane 8 84+
(T G Mills) *racd far side: trckd ldrs: racd keenly: rdn and edgd lft over 1f out: sn wknd: 4th of 7 in gp* **28/1**

10-6 **15** *shd* **Pretty Majestic (IRE)**[84] 1096 3-8-8 **90**...... MartinDwyer 12 79
(M R Channon) *racd stands' side: s.i.s and edgd rt s: a in rr: 11th of 12 in gp* **16/1**

53-1 **16** *3 1/2* **He's A Humbug (IRE)**[90] 1009 3-8-10 **92**...... NCallan 3 71+
(K A Ryan) *racd far side: disp ld 5f: sn wknd: 5th of 7 in gp* **25/1**

0-12 **17** *1/2* **Lipocco**[46] 2044 3-9-4 **100**...... KerrinMcEvoy 4 77+
(R M Beckett) *racd far side: disp ld 5f: sn wknd: 6th of 7 in gp* **14/1**

6100 **18** *1 3/4* **Fares (IRE)**[21] 2752 3-9-1 **97**......(b) JimmyFortune 16 69
(C E Brittain) *racd stands' side: prom 4f: last of 12 in gp* **50/1**

1325 **19** *4* **City Of Tribes (IRE)**[10] 3139 3-9-7 **103**...... JMurtagh 7 63+
(G M Lyons, Ire) *racd far side: hld up: plld hrd: wknd over 1f out: last of 7 in gp* **20/1**

69.93 secs (-3.42) **Going Correction** -0.20s/f (Firm) **19** Ran SP% **126.2**
Speed ratings (Par 106):114,113,112,110,109 108,106,105,104,104 104,103,103,102,102 97,97,94,89
CSF £110.29 CT £643.06 TOTE £14.20: £3.30, £3.60, £2.10, £4.20; EX 198.60 Trifecta £752.10 Pool £1,059.32 - 1.00 winning units..
Owner Hamdan Al Maktoum **Bred** Shadwell Farm LLC **Trained** Arundel, W Sussex

FOCUS
The suspected advantage towards the stands'-side runners was confirmed here with the first six home coming from high berths. Mastership 'won' the far side race readily and would have gone close had he been able to race stands' side. The winning time was good for a race like this. A strong handicap, with the first three unexposed and the fourth a good guide. The form has been rated positively.

NOTEBOOK
Shmookh(USA), a dual winner over 7f earlier in the season, managed to beat only one of his 29 rivals home in the Brittannia at Royal Ascot and connections clearly felt the 1m stretched him. He had a bit to prove at this trip, but having been restrained in the rear of the stands'-side group, he came with a telling challenge to lead a furlong out and ran on well once getting there to hold the persistent runner-up. Despite recording a very smart time, it is still likely that 7f is his trip, but he at least proved he can be versatile. Official explanation: trainer said, regarding apparent improvement in form, that the colt failed to stay over the extended distance previously. (op 14-1)
Off The Record ◆ has made a name for himself at Southwell, winning all four starts there in the style of a useful sprinter, and he had run well enough on his debut on turf to suggest he would prove effective here. Always well positioned to strike, he held every chance racing into the final furlong and stuck on willingly, but Shmookh always just had him covered. There could be even more to come returned to a slower surface and he remains one to keep on side. (op 10-1 tchd 11-1)
Utmost Respect ◆, two from two as a juvenile, including when winning a nursery off a mark of 81, looked slightly unlucky off this mark on his reappearance at Goodwood against older horses, and it was easy to see why he headed the market. However, lady luck once again deserted him as he was slowly away and impeded soon after the start, meaning he had to do plenty of running just to reach a challenging position. This was a fine effort from a clearly promising sprinter and it would not surprise to see him claim a nice prize at some stage this term. (op 11-2 tchd 6-1)
Celtic Sultan(IRE) has the makings of a solid handicapper and he ran another sound race from his good draw. Soon in front, he could not repel the front pair when challenged a furlong out, but kept plugging away for a good fourth. He will not be easy to win with off his current mark, but may well be ready for another go at 7f now. (op 14-1)
Siren's Gift, whose connections won this with recent Wokingham winner Dark Missile a year ago, was one of only two fillies in the race and she showed improved form on the step back up to 6f. She had previously been held in stakes races, most recently behind Hoh Mike, and could do with a few more pounds off her back before being of real interest. (op 12-1)
Vitznau(IRE), on a hat-trick following wins at Epsom and Chester, was down in trip and up another 6lb, but still looked a player from a decent draw and he ran well without suggesting sprinting is his game. (op 11-1 tchd 12-1 in a place)
Mastership(IRE) ◆, a very easy winner when last racing at this distance, has gone up 18lb in the ratings since that last win as a result of some creditable efforts in Group contests, and he was unlucky on two counts not to have gone very close on this return to handicap company. Firstly he had to race on the 'wrong' side and, even though he 'won' that race, he got little luck in running and was value for a good bit better than his finishing position suggests. He would have gone very close had he been drawn high and this is evidently his best trip.
Longquan(IRE), who got a bit warm beforehand, came across from stall nine to race stands' side and he kept on well late to suggest he will come on for this first run since May. (op 12-1)
Annemasse has been tried from 6f-1m in recent weeks and he continues to run as though winning off this mark is beyond him. (op 14-1)
Express Wish, although coming into this on a hat-trick and representing a highly respectable trainer/jockey duo, struggled to defy a mark of 84 at Haydock last time and he needed to have improved a good deal to defy a 5lb higher mark. He was not up to it and may struggle for the time being. (op 13-2 tchd 15-2 in a place)
Rainbow Mirage(IRE), a useful sprinter at two, faced a very stiff task off a mark of 89, but he emerged second best of those to race far side and he could be of interest once dropped a few pounds.
Pretty Majestic(IRE), having her first start since the Nell Gywn, was disappointing on this drop back to sprinting and is not going to be easy to place. (op 14-1)

3432 IRISH THOROUGHBRED MARKETING CHERRY HINTON STKS (GROUP 2) (FILLIES) 6f

2:35 (2:39) (Class 1) 2-Y-O

£39,746 (£15,064; £7,539; £3,759; £1,883; £945) **Stalls** Low

Form RPR

212 **1** **You'resothrilling (USA)**[19] 2812 2-8-12 0 MJKinane 13 103
(A P O'Brien, Ire) *led stands' side gp of four 3f out: drvn 2f out: styd on to ld wl ins fnl f: burst clr* **6/4**[1]

10 **2** *1* **Festoso (IRE)**[19] 2812 2-8-12 0 PhilipRobinson 6 100
(H J L Dunlop) *chsd ldrs centre: str run fnl f: ev ch 50yds out: kpt on wl but no match for wnr* **40/1**

1 **3** *nk* **Elletelle (IRE)**[21] 2756 2-9-1 0 JMurtagh 5 102+
(G M Lyons, Ire) *missed break and lost several l: sn pulling hrd: stl last 2f out: rapid run fnl f: fin wl* **9/2**[2]

1610 **4** *hd* **Loch Jipp (USA)**[19] 2812 2-8-12 0 KDarley 4 98
(J S Wainwright) *led centre: jnd far side ldr and drvn 1f out: no ex wl ins fnl f: game effrt* **33/1**

04 **5** *shd* **Francesca D'Gorgio (USA)**[21] 2756 2-8-12 0 (v[1]) LDettori 1 98+
(J Noseda) *lw: racd alone far side and overall ldr: jnd 1f out: ev ch tl no ex fnl 50yds* **7/1**[3]

10 **6** *¾* **Kylayne**[21] 2756 2-8-12 0 TedDurcan 14 96
(P W D'Arcy) *led stands' side 3f: sn rdn: one pce fnl f* **50/1**

1 **7** *¾* **Eat Pie (USA)**[8] 3187 2-8-12 0 EddieAhern 15 94
(M J Wallace) *stands' side: drvn and outpcd 2f out: kpt on again ins fnl f* **25/1**

1 **8** *shd* **Green Oasis (USA)**[11] 3109 2-8-12 0 ChrisCatlin 7 93
(E J O'Neill) *w'like: t.k.h: prom in centre: rdn over 1f out: kpt on steadily* **14/1**

4614 **9** *nk* **Aide Memoir (IRE)**[19] 2812 2-8-12 0 MartinDwyer 12 92
(S Kirk) *in last pair of stands' quartet: drvn over 2f out: no ex over 1f out* **12/1**

02 **10** *2* **Thought Is Free**[11] 3096 2-8-12 0 JohnEgan 11 86
(J S Moore) *midfield in centre: rdn 1/2-way: no imp fnl 2f* **16/1**

35 **11** *shd* **Cute**[19] 2812 2-8-12 0 RyanMoore 9 86
(C E Brittain) *bhd in centre gp: drvn over 2f out: no ex over 1f out* **14/1**

12 *hd* **Nahoodh (IRE)** 2-8-12 0 JamieSpencer 3 86
(M R Channon) *w'like: leggy: t.k.h: in rr of centre gp: effrt 1/2-way: rn green and hung lft: no ex ins fnl f: promising* **12/1**

210 **13** *2½* **Eileen's Violet (IRE)**[19] 2812 2-8-12 0 StephenDonohoe 2 78
(P D Evans) *prom in centre tl 1/2-way: sn drvn: wavered wl over 1f out* **66/1**

310 **14** *hd* **Waveline (USA)**[19] 2812 2-8-12 0 JimmyFortune 10 77
(B J Meehan) *dwlt: rdn 3f out: btn 2f out* **20/1**

1m 11.66s (-1.69) **Going Correction** -0.20s/f (Firm) **14** Ran SP% **122.7**
Speed ratings (Par 103):103,101,101,101,100 99,98,98,98,95 95,95,91,91
CSF £96.10 TOTE £2.30: £1.30, £13.50, £1.80; EX 79.20 Trifecta £391.20 Pool £1,311.42 - 2.38 winning units..
Owner Michael Tabor **Bred** Pacelco **Trained** Ballydoyle, Co Tipperary

FOCUS
A race with a mixed history, Attraction being the best winner since the Millennium, and although the promising You'resothrilling justified favouritism, it was a performance that lacked star quality and she would probably have been beaten had penalised Queen Mary winner Elletelle broken on terms. The winner was one of only four to race on the apparently advantageous stands' side. The fourth limits the form, as does the compressed field at the line.

NOTEBOOK
You'resothrilling(USA), who would undoubtedly have given shock winner Nijoom Dubai more to do had she not been squeezed by that rival in the Albany at Royal Ascot, looked in need of a seventh furlong that day and it was no surprise to see her made plenty of use of in the small group that raced towards the favoured stands' side. Asked for her effort well over two furlongs out, she kept finding like a filly who needs further and ground it out under a strong ride from Kinane, forging ahead close home. She would probably have been beaten had Elletelle broken on terms, but being a sister to Giant's Causeway she is going to relish a greater test of stamina and the Moyglare is the next obvious step, albeit the stable have another contender in the shape of Listen. (tchd 5-4)
Festoso(IRE) failed to see it out having come to hold every chance behind today's winner at Royal Ascot on softer ground, but she kept on with much more purpose on this occasion and was simply beaten by a better filly on the day. She is now likely to take her chance in the Lowther, where she will get her chance to try and reverse form with Albany victor Nijoom Dubai. (op 50-1)
Elletelle(IRE) would surely have become only the second filly in the last 21 years to do the Queen Mary/Cherry Hinton double had she broken on terms. A surprise winner at Royal Ascot, she faced no easy task with her 3lb penalty and did herself few favours by racing so keenly at the rear, but manged to drag herself into contention with a smart change of pace down the centre of the track, only to find the line coming too soon. Connections rightly felt she was the best filly in the race and she deserves to take her chance in the Group 1 Phoenix Stakes. (op 11-2 tchd 13-2)
Loch Jipp(USA), a surprise winner of the Hilary Needler earlier in the season, could make no impression in the Albany at Royal Ascot, but she ran the race of her life here and momentarily looked the winner when quickening to nose ahead over a furlong out. The trip may have stretched her in the end and this tall, scopey filly remains capable of a good deal better. (op 25-1)
Francesca D'Gorgio(USA), who moved very well to post, must be held in high regard to have run at Ascot after beating only one home on her debut at Nottingham, and she ran mightily well behind Elletelle in the Queen Mary. Representing last year's winning connections, she raced solo against the far rail in the first-time visor and led overall until just a over a furlong out. In the end she failed to last home, but it is not hard to see her winning her maiden now before no doubt stepping back up in grade. (op 6-1)
Kylayne ran a bit better than her finishing position implied behind Elletelle in the Queen Mary and she showed bright speed in leading You'resothrilling on the stands' side, but could not race on in the final furlong and looks in need of a drop in grade. She is worth her place at Listed level. (op 66-1)
Eat Pie(USA), who got first run when winning on her debut at Lingfield, was always likely to struggle faced with such a rise in grade and seventh was about as good as she could have hoped for. (op 22-1)
Green Oasis(USA), one of the better-looking fillies, was another stepping up from humble beginnings and she acquitted herself creditably without suggesting she is ever going to be up to this level. She has scope to improve and will be suited by a seventh furlong. (op 16-1 tchd 18-1 and 20-1 in a place)
Aide Memoir(IRE), keen going to post, was entitled to finish a bit closer on the form of her Albany fourth and was one of the main disappointments. (op 14-1)
Thought Is Free only just failed to spring a 66/1 shock in a Listed event over course and distance recently, but she was unable to build on that and it is probable she requires a softer surface. She should be given another chance in maiden company. (op 25-1)
Cute ran well for a maiden behind a couple of these at Ascot, but she was unable to build on that here and is another who needs to be given another chance back in maiden company. (op 25-1)
Nahoodh(IRE), withdrawn from a couple of maidens recently because of soft ground, could hardly have been given a tougher introduction and it was bizarre how she was as short as 12/1. She struggled to make an impact, but definitely hinted at ability and she will no doubt appreciate being dropped into maiden company. (op 10-1)
Waveline(USA) was very free going to post.

3433 UAE HYDRA PROPERTIES FALMOUTH STKS (GROUP 1) (F&M) 1m

3:10 (3:13) (Class 1) 3-Y-O+

£113,560 (£43,040; £21,540; £10,740; £5,380; £2,700) **Stalls** Low

Form RPR

1-36 **1** **Simply Perfect**[40] 2211 3-8-10 111 JMurtagh 4 116
(J Noseda) *sn led: rdn over 1f out: r.o* **6/1**

4-30 **2** *1* **Irridescence (SAF)**[102] 862 6-9-5 0 WCMarwing 2 116
(M F De Kock, South Africa) *chsd wnr tl over 6f out: rdn to go 2nd fnl f: r.o* **11/2**

1204 **3** *nk* **Arch Swing (USA)**[19] 2814 3-8-10 0 MJKinane 1 113+
(John M Oxx, Ire) *lw: prom: swtchd rt 2f out: sn rdn: r.o* **10/3**[2]

5-31 **4** *2* **Nannina**[21] 2753 4-9-5 115 JimmyFortune 3 111
(J H M Gosden) *lw: chsd ldrs: rdn over 1f out: no ex ins fnl f* **5/2**[1]

-020 **5** *nk* **Sweet Lilly**[31] 2501 3-8-10 105 JHBowman 5 108
(M R Channon) *lw: hld up: rdn over 1f out: n.d* **25/1**

-225 **6** *1½* **Bahia Breeze**[11] 3098 5-9-5 106 NCallan 6 107
(Rae Guest) *chsd ldr over 6f out: rdn over b1f out: wknd ins fnl f* **14/1**

5-10 **7** *1* **Red Evie (IRE)**[22] 2735 4-9-5 115 JamieSpencer 8 104
(M L W Bell) *b.hind: hld up: hrd rdn fr over 1f out: wknd ins fnl f* **7/2**[3]

1m 37.14s (-3.29) **Going Correction** -0.20s/f (Firm)
WFA 3 from 4yo+ 9lb **7** Ran SP% **114.1**
Speed ratings (Par 117):108,107,106,104,104 102,101
CSF £38.10 TOTE £8.80: £3.50, £2.90; EX 44.70 Trifecta £162.30 Pool £4,042.61 - 17.68 winning units..
Owner D Smith, M Tabor & Mrs J Magnier **Bred** Trehedyn Stud And Quarry Bloodstock **Trained** Newmarket, Suffolk

FOCUS
This looked a quality renewal of the Falmouth Stakes on paper, with some high-class three-year-olds taking on some of the best older fillies and mares but, for the third year in succession, they went just a steady gallop for much of the way. That obviously suited those who raced handily and the bare form needs treating with real caution. They raced towards the far rail throughout. All-the-way winner Simply Perfect produced a slight career best. The second and fourth were below their best, with the third better than the bare form.

NOTEBOOK
Simply Perfect failed to see out 1m4f in the Oaks last time, but she had previously shown herself to be high-class over 1m when winning both the May Hill and the Fillies' Mile last year, and again when running third in the 1000 Guineas on her reappearance. This success, though, owes as much to the drop in trip as it does to a wonderful front-running ride from Johnny Murtagh, who used his initiative when it was clear the only other potential front-runner, Irridescence, was happy to take a lead. He set a very steady pace through the first few furlongs, before gradually winding up the pace, and the filly proved a willing partner, keeping on strongly in the closing stages to prove far too strong for those trying to make up ground from off the speed. According to her trainer, she is now likely to go for the Prix d'Astarte. (op 8-1)
Irridescence(SAF) did not seem keen to go to post, but has done that before. A winner at the highest level in both South Africa and Hong Kong, has shown herself well suited to making the running several times in the past, so it was a surprise she did not put more pressure on Simply Perfect. She ended up racing a little keenly just in behind the early leader and found that rival too strong when let down with her effort. This was still a good performance in defeat, though, and she may now be aimed at the Beverly D. at Arlington. (op 5-1 tchd 6-1)
Arch Swing(USA) ◆ has not had things go her way since finishing second in the 1000 Guineas at Newmarket, picking up a knock coming out of the stalls in the Irish version before being stopped in her run in the Coronation Stakes, and things again failed to go her way. The steady early pace would not have suited and she finished about as close as could have been expected in the circumstances. She deserves a change of fortune and it could take a good one to beat her if things go her way in the Matron Stakes (op 7-2 tchd 3-1)
Nannina was totally unsuited by the steady pace and she could not match the form of her stunning Windsor Forest success. This campaign is already proving remarkably similar to last year's, for she was beaten on unsuitably soft ground on her reappearance, just as she was last season, then bolted up at Ascot, as she did in the Coronation Stakes the year before, and was then totally unsuited by a slow early gallop in this race, as she was a year earlier. Her profile could be more consistent considering how good she is at her best, and it would be interesting know whether her connections have ever been tempted to run a pacemaker to ensure a more suitable gallop. Whatever the case, though, she can be forgiven this and remains one of the best older fillies in training. It would be no surprise to see her now try and improve on last season's third in the Nassau Stakes. (op 2-1)
Sweet Lilly could make no impression in the French Oaks on her previous start, but she was worth another try over 1m and this was a sound effort, especially considering she was held up off the steady gallop. She flashed her tail, but it didn't seem to slow her down. (op 33-1)
Bahia Breeze needs a strongly-run race. (op 25-1 tchd 33-1)
Red Evie(IRE) was poorly positioned considering the lack of early pace and was found out when the leaders quickened. That said, she hardly picked up at all and her hard-fought Lockinge success may have left its mark. (tchd 4-1)

3434 HBLB LANCASHIRE OAKS (F&M) (GROUP 2) 1m 4f

3:45 (3:45) (Class 1) 3-Y-O+

£34,068 (£12,912; £6,462; £3,222; £1,614; £810) **Stalls** Centre

Form RPR

1 **1** **Turbo Linn**[33] 2420 4-9-5 0 NCallan 13 110+
(G A Swinbank) *lw: chsd ldrs: rdn 3f out: looked outpcd briefly: clsd to ld 1f out and stormed clr* **6/1**[3]

3464 **2** *4* **Under The Rainbow**[11] 3097 4-9-5 100 MJKinane 6 103
(B W Hills) *t.k.h in rr: pushed along and prog on outside fnl 3f: flattered briefly 1f out: no ch w wnr* **12/1**

5-3P **3** *nk* **Portal**[23] 2720 4-9-5 104 JamieSpencer 12 102
(J R Fanshawe) *lw: midfield: rdn over 2f out: styd on ins fnl f: unable to chal* **9/2**[2]

2210 **4** *shd* **Brisk Breeze (GER)**[19] 2816 3-8-6 94 TedDurcan 5 102
(H R A Cecil) *pressed ldr: led over 2f out: rdn and hdd 1f out: one pce after* **12/1**

40-2 **5** *½* **Mont Etoile (IRE)**[30] 2507 4-9-5 107 MichaelHills 9 101
(W J Haggas) *lw: bhd: effrt over 2f out: plld outside and tried to chal jst ins fnl f: sn no imp* **7/2**[1]

0-61 **6** *1* **Dash To The Front**[23] 2720 4-9-5 94 OscarUrbina 10 100
(J R Fanshawe) *cl up: rdn 3f out: no ex over 1f out* **16/1**

6-10 **7** *nk* **Trick Or Treat**[24] 2702 4-9-5 101 LDettori 11 99
(J G Given) *prom: drvn and ev ch 2f out: no ex fnl f* **15/2**

230 **8** *1¼* **Dont Dili Dali**[56] 1777 4-9-5 100 RyanMoore 4 97
(J S Moore) *t.k.h in rr: nvr able to chal* **20/1**

-040 **9** *¾* **Rising Cross**[20] 2787 4-9-8 108 MartinDwyer 3 99
(J R Best) *bhd: urged along over 2f out: sn no rspnse* **8/1**

13 **10** *½* **Scatina (IRE)**[24] 2707 3-8-9 0 ASuborics 8 98
(Mario Hofer, Germany) *cl up: rdn 3f out: wknd over 1f out: eased fnl 100yds* **6/1**[3]

2546 **11** *1 1/4* **Fiumicino**[17] [2926] 3-8-6 100 .... JohnEgan 2 93
(M R Channon) *plld hrd in last: effrt outside wl over 1f out: wknd ins fnl f* **50/1**

5216 **12** *1 1/4* **Wassfa**[23] [2720] 4-9-5 66 .... KerrinMcEvoy 7 91?
(C E Brittain) *led tl over 2f out: qckly lost pl: hmpd over 1f out* **100/1**

2m 31.34s (-1.57) **Going Correction** -0.20s/f (Firm)
WFA 3 from 4yo 13lb **12** Ran SP% **120.8**
Speed ratings: 97,94,94,94,93 93,92,91,91 90,89
CSF £76.46 TOTE £6.10: £2.10, £4.20, £2.10; EX 82.10.
Owner J Nelson **Bred** James Nelson **Trained** Melsonby, N Yorks

FOCUS

This Group 2 was re-routed from Haydock's abandoned card four days earlier. The early pace was only ordinary, the winning time was very slow, and it looked a modest event for the class. It still produced a taking winner in the unbeaten Turbo Linn, and although this bare form is only ordinary she can rate higher still.

NOTEBOOK

Turbo Linn, who was only entered for this after it was re-routed from Haydock's abandoned meeting on account of the better ground, maintained her remarkable winning sequence and produced an impressive display to score. Not that surprisingly she hit a flat spot passing the 2f pole, but with the benefit of the stands' rail she found a neat turn of foot when the gun was put to her head and eventually came right away from her rivals in the final furlong. She is now unbeaten in five bumpers and two starts in this sphere, is clearly still improving, and remains somewhat of an unknown quantity. While this was not a strong race for the grade she surely now deserves to be tested in Group 1 company. That may be in the Yorkshire Oaks next month and her trainer also indicated a possible crack at the Irish St Leger in September could also be on the cards - she would need to be supplemented for both of those, however. (op 8-1)

Under The Rainbow did not help her chances by refusing to settle early on and needed to be ridden after a mile. As the tempo got serious she picked up for rider's urgings, however, and was not that surprisingly doing her best work towards the finish. This sounder surface suited and she deserves to find another opening, but she ideally wants a stiffer test and opportunities are not that simple to find for her.

Portal left her previous effort well behind with a solid effort in defeat on this first outing over this longer trip. A sound surface looks key to her, she is certainly capable of landing a Group 3 on this evidence, and it is unlikely we have yet to quite see the best of her. (op 6-1 tchd 13-2)

Brisk Breeze(GER), a non-stayer in the Queen's Vase last time, enjoyed the run of the race and showed her true colours over this shorter distance. She is possibly a touch flattered, but she fared by far the best of the three-year-olds and can regain the winning thread when dropping back into Listed company. (tchd 14-1)

Mont Etoile(IRE) looked to have plenty in her favour on this return to her last winning distance, but she proved very disappointing and her fate was apparent before the final furlong. A stronger early pace may have helped her, but she again clearly failed to run near to her lofty rating here and now has a lot to prove. (op 3-1)

Dash To The Front was given a positive ride on this step up in trip and class, but was put in her place when the race became serious. She needs to drop back in grade and ideally prefers softer ground.

Rising Cross was never really going on this drop back to a more suitable trip and was probably still feeling the effects of her previous outing in the Gold Cup. (op 13-2)

Scatina(IRE) did little for the form of the Italian Oaks and failed to run near her previous best. (op 13-2 tchd 15-2)

3435 IAN MACNICOL MEMORIAL STRUTT & PARKER EBF MAIDEN STKS 7f

4:20 (4:22) (Class 2) 2-Y-O **£9,715** (£2,890; £1,444; £721) **Stalls** Low

Form RPR

3 **1** **Rio De La Plata (USA)**[19] [2832] 2-9-3 0 .... LDettori 18 99+
(Saeed Bin Suroor) *lw: mde all: shkn up over 1f out: r.o wl: eased nr fin* **11/4**[2]

2 *5* **Fifteen Love (USA)** 2-9-3 0 .... RichardHughes 8 85+
(R Charlton) *w'like: trckd ldrs: rdn over 1f out: styd on same pce* **12/1**

3 *hd* **Exhibition (IRE)** 2-9-3 0 .... JamieSpencer 15 84+
(N A Callaghan) *unf: scope: hld up in tch: rdn and hung lft fr over 1f out: styd on same pce* **7/1**[3]

2 **4** *1 3/4* **Mujaadel (USA)**[18] [2885] 2-9-3 0 .... RHills 19 80
(E A L Dunlop) *lw: chsd wnr: rdn over 1f out: no ex* **8/1**

5 *nk* **King Of Westphalia (USA)**[28] [2584] 2-9-3 0 .... MJKinane 14 79
(A P O'Brien, Ire) *lengthy: chsd ldrs: rdn over 1f out: no ex* **9/4**[1]

3 **6** *4* **Strategic Mission (IRE)**[26] [2632] 2-9-3 0 .... TQuinn 2 72+
(P F I Cole) *lw: sn pushed along in rr: hdwy over 2f out: nt trble ldrs* **12/1**

7 *1/2* **Upton Grey (IRE)** 2-9-3 0 .... JimmyFortune 20 68+
(J H M Gosden) *w'like: bit bkwd: mid-div: hdwy over 5f out: rdn and n.m.r over 1f out: sn wknd* **12/1**

8 *3/4* **Talayeb** 2-9-3 0 .... MartinDwyer 7 66+
(M P Tregoning) *w'like: scope: prom: hung rt and wknd over 1f out* **40/1**

9 *hd* **Sheer Bluff (IRE)** 2-9-3 0 .... AntonyProcter 4 65+
(D R C Elsworth) *w'like: bit bkwd: dwlt: nvr nrr* **100/1**

26 **10** *1/2* **Boomtown**[20] [2803] 2-9-3 0 .... JoeFanning 11 64
(M Johnston) *chsd ldrs over 5f* **40/1**

11 *1* **Visconti** 2-9-3 0 .... AdrianMcCarthy 5 62
(P W Chapple-Hyam) *str: mid-div: hdwy 1/2-way: edgd rt over 2f out: wknd over 1f out* **28/1**

44 **12** *1/2* **Kyrie Eleison (IRE)**[14] [2991] 2-9-3 0 .... RyanMoore 3 60
(R Hannon) *mid-div: rdn 1/2-way: wknd over 2f out* **33/1**

13 *1 3/4* **Bavarian Nordic (USA)** 2-9-3 0 .... KerrinMcEvoy 6 56
(E A L Dunlop) *w'like: bit bkwd: mid-div: hdwy over 2f out: wknd over 1f out* **66/1**

14 *1 3/4* **Mubher** 2-9-3 0 .... KDarley 12 52
(J L Dunlop) *str: hld up: a in rr* **33/1**

04 **15** *nk* **Excape (IRE)**[18] [2885] 2-9-3 0 .... JohnEgan 10 51
(D R C Elsworth) *unruly in stalls: s.i.s: a in rr* **33/1**

16 *1* **Soggy Dollar** 2-9-3 0 .... TedDurcan 16 48
(M H Tompkins) *w'like: sn pushed along in rr: bhd fr 1/2-way* **100/1**

17 *2* **Dubai Samurai** 2-9-3 0 .... EddieAhern 1 43
(J W Hills) *w'like: bit bkwd: hld up: a in rr* **66/1**

18 *nk* **Dream Bee** 2-8-12 0 .... SteveDrowne 13 38
(E A L Dunlop) *str: bit bkwd: mid-div: rdn 1/2-way: wknd over 2f out* **66/1**

19 *1 1/4* **Jabal Tariq** 2-9-3 0 .... MichaelHills 9 39+
(B W Hills) *tall: lengthy: lw: s.s: a bhd* **20/1**

1m 24.2s (-2.58) **Going Correction** -0.20s/f (Firm) **19** Ran SP% **132.5**
Speed ratings (Par 100):106,100,100,98,97 93,92,91,91,90 89,89,87,85,84 83,81,81,79
CSF £35.23 TOTE £4.20: £1.80, £4.20, £3.00; EX 61.80.
Owner Godolphin **Bred** J De Camargo, Robert N Clay Et Al **Trained** Newmarket, Suffolk
■ Stewards' Enquiry : Adrian McCarthy two-day ban: careless riding (Jul 22-23)

FOCUS

This looked like a very good maiden, with several leading trainers and owners represented, and the race should produce plenty of winners. They all raced towards the stands' side. Rio De La Plata impressed and looks Group-class.

NOTEBOOK

Rio De La Plata(USA) ◆ ran green when only third on his debut over 6f here nearly three weeks previously, but that experience clearly taught him plenty and this was a much-improved effort. Soon taking the field along, he was not exactly left alone, with some of his main rivals keeping him honest up front, but he was always travelling extremely well within himself and bounded clear when asked for his effort to win very impressively. The clock confirms this was a quality performance, for he recorded a time that was just 0.04 seconds off the juvenile course record set by My Hansel in 1999. He looks a Group horse in the making and definitely deserves his chance in a good race. It is guesswork as to where he will go next, but David Loder sent out Dubai Destination to win this maiden in 2001 before saddling him to win the Champagne Stakes on his next start, and the Doncaster Group 2 could be a suitable target. (tchd 7-2)

Fifteen Love(USA), an athletic type, is a good walker. A Point Given colt and half-brother to five winners, including 7f juvenile winner Expected Bonus, out of high-class 7f scorer Nidd, proved no match for the impressive winner, but he kept on well for second and this was a pleasing introduction. He should win his maiden next time before stepping up in class. (op 10-1)

Exhibition(IRE), a 225,000euros son of Invincible Spirit, first foal of a quite useful triple 1m2f-1m4f winner, was extremely well backed and made a highly satisfactory debut. He is clearly well regarded and is another who should win his maiden before going for something better. (op 11-1)

Mujaadel(USA) confirmed the promise he showed when second in a smaller-field maiden over course and distance on his debut and his proximity helps give the form a solid look. (op 7-1)

King Of Westphalia(USA), out of triple Classic runner-up Quarter Moon, could not repeat the form of his recent Leopardstown second and was disappointing. (op 10-3)

Strategic Mission(IRE), third on his debut at Sandown, is better than he was able to show as he was caught out wide early on and was then crossed by Visconti when trying to stay on. (tchd 14-1)

Upton Grey(IRE), a 66,000gns Dalakhani colt, half-brother to 7f winner Lasso, out of a dual 7f scorer, showed up well for a long way, but he could produce only a short-lived effort and should be better for the outing. (op 10-1 tchd 14-1 in a place)

Talayeb, a nice type, became the first son of Nayef to represent Marcus Tregoning and Hamdan Al Maktoum. A 65,000gns first foal of a mare who was placed over 7f-1m4f, he looked in need of this experience and should do better in time.

Sheer Bluff(IRE), a close-coupled Indian Ridge colt, out of a 1m juvenile winner, was never a danger and is another who will know more next time.

Boomtown did not run badly and will have more options now he is eligible for nurseries. (op 33-1)

Visconti, by Medicean and a 45,000gns brother to 1m juvenile winner Hohlethelonely, showed ability and can improve on this. (op 25-1)

Soggy Dollar was coltish beforehand.

Jabal Tariq Official explanation: jockey said colt became unsettled in stalls and was slowly away

3436 RACING POST MAIDEN STKS 1m 2f

4:55 (4:59) (Class 3) 3-Y-O **£9,715** (£2,890; £1,444; £721) **Stalls** Centre

Form RPR

2-55 **1** **Urban Spirit**[62] [1605] 3-9-3 86 .... RichardHughes 9 83
(B W Hills) *lw: t.k.h early: pressed ldng pair: qcknd to chal over 1f out: veered lft after but sn led ins fnl f: drvn out* **8/1**

6-20 **2** *nk* **Jack Junior (USA)**[22] [2734] 3-9-3 110 .... JamieSpencer 2 82
(B J Meehan) *pressed ldr: rdn wl over 1f out: led 1f out: sn hdd: r.o* **11/8**[1]

0- **3** *2 1/2* **Sugar Ray (IRE)**[299] [5339] 3-9-3 0 .... RyanMoore 4 77
(Sir Michael Stoute) *chsd ldrs: pushed along over 4f out: rdn over 2f out: one pce fnl f but wnt 3rd cl home* **11/2**[2]

5- **4** *nk* **Denbera Dancer (USA)**[336] [4260] 3-9-3 0 .... JoeFanning 3 77
(M Johnston) *set str gallop: drvn and hdd 1f out: one pce* **25/1**

05 **5** *3/4* **Silver Suitor (IRE)**[34] [2402] 3-9-3 0 .... JohnEgan 8 76+
(D R C Elsworth) *lw: t.k.h in 4th pl: outpcd over 2f out and looked wl btn: rallied and styd on wl tl snatched up cl home: promising* **7/1**[3]

5 **6** *12* **Ful Of Grace (IRE)**[11] [3079] 3-8-12 0 .... TedDurcan 5 46
(M G Quinlan) *stdd s: bhd: rdn 3f out: wl btn 2f out* **100/1**

7 *3/4* **Lord Of The Lake** 3-9-3 0 .... NCallan 6 50
(P J McBride) *w'like: leggy: s.s: bhd: shkn up over 3f out: wl btn 2f out* **100/1**

2m 6.83s (0.39) **Going Correction** -0.20s/f (Firm) **7** Ran SP% **86.9**
Speed ratings (Par 104):90,89,87,87,86 77,76
CSF £10.99 TOTE £5.10: £2.10, £1.30; EX 10.90.
Owner K Abdulla **Bred** Juddmonte Farms Ltd **Trained** Lambourn, Berks
■ Spring City (3/1, uns rdr & bolted going to post) was withdrawn. Rule 4 applies, deduct 25p in the £.

FOCUS

A fascinating maiden and the form looks useful, although the favourite was well below his best. The pace was fair.

NOTEBOOK

Urban Spirit ◆ could only manage fifth at Chester on his previous start, but that maiden is working out very well - the runner-up, Heron Bay, went on to win the King George V Handicap at Royal Ascot - and he proved good enough to get off the mark at the fourth attempt, despite hanging all the way across to the far rail close home. Having travelled as well as anything just off the pace for much of the way, he went left almost as soon as he was switched into the clear, but he clearly didn't lose much momentum. His waywardness could well be put down to greenness, as his connections reported he had never done anything like that home, and he is very much still maturing. He looks the type to improve physically and appeals as one to keep on side. (op 13-2)

Jack Junior(USA) had been highly tried on his last three starts, running sixth in the Somerville Tattersall Stakes on his final outing at two, before finishing second in the UAE Derby and running creditably in the St James's Palace Stakes. On the form of those three runs, he should have broken his maiden, but he ran some way below form. This was his first try beyond 1m and it's possible his stamina gave out, but whatever the case this was a major disappointment. There is no doubt he is smart on his day and he may well be worth another try on dirt. (op 5-4)

Sugar Ray(IRE), off the track since showing ability in a 7f maiden at Newbury last September, looked a bit ring rusty and this should have sharpened him up. (op 15-2)

Denbera Dancer(USA) had not been seen since running fifth in a 6f maiden at Pontefract the best part of a year ago and this was a pleasing return to action. He can be expected to improve plenty for the outing. (op 22-1)

Silver Suitor(IRE) ◆ struggled to land a telling blow, but he kept on for pressure. He is now qualified for handicaps and could make his mark over 1m4f plus. (op 8-1)

3437 CLASSIC FM H'CAP 1m

5:30 (5:31) (Class 3) (0-90,90) 3-Y-O+ **£9,715** (£2,890; £1,444; £721) **Stalls** Low

Form RPR

-020 **1** **Third Set (IRE)**[19] [2817] 4-9-9 **85** .... SteveDrowne 17 100+
(R Charlton) *chsd ldrs: nt clr run over 2f out: rdn to ld over 1f out: hung lft: r.o* **12/1**

-315 **2** *2* **Ashes Regained**[32] [2469] 4-9-6 **82** .... MJKinane 4 92
(B W Hills) *led centre duo tl jnd stands' side 1/2-way: rdn over 1f out: styd on same pce ins fnl f* **10/1**

5500 **3** *1 3/4* **Marajaa (IRE)**[34] [2401] 5-9-8 **84** .... BrettDoyle 9 90+
(W J Musson) *hld up: hdwy over 1f out: styd on same pce ins fnl f* **12/1**

1132 **4** *1 1/4* **Networker**[7] 3215 4-8-5 **72** .... WilliamBuick(5) 10 75+
(P J McBride) *lw: hld up: hdwy over 1f out: edgd lft ins fnl f: nt rch ldrs* **8/1**

1110 **5** *1/2* **Ektimaal**[102] 840 4-9-13 **89** .... (t) RyanMoore 8 91
(E A L Dunlop) *lw: chsd ldrs: rdn over 1f out: no ex ins fnl f* **16/1**

00 **6** *3/4* **Voliere**[19] 2835 4-9-0 **76** .... SaleemGolam 6 76
(S C Williams) *fly-leapt leaving stalls: hld up: hdwy over 1f out: nt trble ldrs* **66/1**

0015 **7** *nk* **South Cape**[19] 2817 4-9-3 **86** .... MatthewDavies(7) 3 86
(M R Channon) *swtchd to r stands' side 7f out: chsd ldrs: rdn over 1f out: btn whn hmpd ins fnl f* **15/2**[3]

1600 **8** *hd* **Bobski (IRE)**[19] 2835 5-9-7 **83** .... MickyFenton 2 82+
(G A Huffer) *hld up plld hrd: styd on ins fnl f: nvr nr to chal* **33/1**

0-40 **9** *nk* **Adaptation**[28] 2577 3-8-11 **82** .... JoeFanning 18 78
(M Johnston) *lw: sn led: hdd 2f out: wknd ins fnl f* **20/1**

-603 **10** *shd* **St Andrews (IRE)**[13] 3026 7-9-7 **90** .... MartinGuest(7) 16 88
(M A Jarvis) *chsd ldr: led 2f out: sn hdd: wknd ins fnl f* **20/1**

-061 **11** *nk* **Lady Stardust**[11] 3100 4-9-9 **85** .... JamieSpencer 12 82
(J R Fanshawe) *lw: hld up: nt clr run fr over 1f out: nvr nr to chal* **11/2**[2]

-532 **12** *1 1/4* **Gaelic Princess**[14] 3001 7-9-3 **79** .... ChrisCatlin 5 74
(A G Newcombe) *mid-div: rdn over 2f out: wknd over 1f out* **14/1**

4-01 **13** *1/2* **Wigwam Willie (IRE)**[12] 3052 5-9-7 **83** .... (p) NCallan 7 76
(K A Ryan) *hld up in tch: rdn over 2f out: wknd over 1f out* **20/1**

451- **14** *shd* **Tommy Toogood (IRE)**[264] 6076 4-9-8 **84** .... MichaelHills 11 77
(B W Hills) *hld up: nt clr run over 1f out: nvr nr to chal* **16/1**

0126 **15** *1 3/4* **Nawaqees**[14] 3002 4-9-5 **81** .... RHills 15 70
(J L Dunlop) *lw: s.i.s: hld up: effrt and edgd rt over 1f out: no ch whn nt clr run and eased ins fnl f* **5/1**[1]

6-06 **16** *3* **Prime Number (IRE)**[14] 3001 5-8-13 **75** .... RobertMiles 13 57
(J Akehurst) *chsd ldrs: rdn over 2f out: sn wknd* **50/1**

4-04 **17** *1 1/2* **Tumbleweed Glory (IRE)**[34] 2401 4-9-1 **77** .... LDettori 1 56
(B J Meehan) *chsd ldr in centre tl jnd stands' side 1/2-way: rdn over 1f out: wknd fnl f* **8/1**

1m 38.61s (-1.82) **Going Correction** -0.20s/f (Firm)
WFA 3 from 4yo+ 9lb **17** Ran SP% **129.6**
Speed ratings (Par 107):101,99,97,96,95 94,94,94,93,93 93,92,91,91,89 86,85
CSF £124.15 CT £1556.42 TOTE £15.90: £3.60, £3.30, £3.70, £2.50; EX 258.10 Place 6 £325.79, Place 5 £132.21.
Owner John Livock **Bred** A Stroud & J Hanly **Trained** Beckhampton, Wilts

FOCUS
A competitive handicap for the class, run at a sound enough pace. All bar two of the runners elected to come stands' side. The first two were always prominent and the form has been rated around the second and third.

NOTEBOOK
Third Set(IRE), having his first outing over this far, overcame a troubled passage nearing the 2f marker and, despite tending to hang left when in front, eventually came home to score in ready fashion. He has always had an engine, but has been hard to predict since winning at Kempton last term and this has to rate a career-best effort. The faster ground enabled him to show his true colours and he remains open to further improvement over this trip, so could well defy a higher future mark as he does not have many miles on the clock. His yard also appears to be back in form again now. (op 14-1 tchd 16-1)
Ashes Regained ◆ elected to race down the centre from his unfavourably low draw and emerges with plenty of credit. He too is still relatively unexposed and, on this evidence, is now ready to tackle 10f. (op 11-1 tchd 12-1)
Marajaa(IRE) is an in-and-out performer on all surfaces and posted one of his better efforts in defeat. He remains 4lb higher than his last winning mark, but deserves to be ridden a little more prominently in the future. (op 14-1)
Networker got going too late from off the pace, but still ran close to his recent level and has developed into a consistent performer. He will likely go up again in the weights for this, however. (tchd 17-2)
Ektimaal ◆ just left the impression this first outing for 102 days was needed and ran a perfectly respectable race. He has yet to win on turf, but the drop back to 7f could see him end that drought. (op 14-1)
Voliere ◆, who had shown very little in two starts since joining connections from Ireland, lost ground when jumping badly from the gates and should be rated better than the bare form. She showed the ability is still there this time, but probably wants a slightly stiffer test and is definitely one to keep an eye on.
Bobski(IRE), despite taking a strong hold early on, finished his race with some purpose and would have been seen to better effect under a more positive ride. He is back to his last winning mark now and can be found another race on one of the smaller tracks.
Lady Stardust, 3lb higher than when scoring on easy ground over course and distance 11 days previously, would have been closer with a clearer passage nearing the final furlong. She may just prefer racing in smaller fields and is not one to abandon on the back of this effort. (op 4-1 tchd 6-1 and 7-1 in a place)
Tommy Toogood(IRE), making his seasonal bow, shaped better than his finishing position would suggest as he met trouble on the rail after passing the 2f pole. He can build on this. (op 20-1)
Nawaqees, back in trip, was another who endured a troubled passage and was not given a hard time when his chance had gone. (op 6-1)
T/Jkpt: Not won. T/Plt: £689.70 to a £1 stake. Pool: £161,755.30. 171.20 winning tickets. T/Qpdt: £153.70 to a £1 stake. Pool: £8,477.35. 40.80 winning tickets. CR

3004 NAAS (L-H)
Wednesday, July 11

OFFICIAL GOING: Soft (soft to heavy in places)

3438a IRISH STALLION FARMS EUROPEAN BREEDERS FUND MAIDEN 6f
6:00 (6:00) 2-Y-O **£7,937** (£1,849; £815; £470)

RPR

1 **Famous Name** 2-9-3 .... PJSmullen 14 101+
(D K Weld, Ire) *trckd ldrs: hdwy to 4th 1f out: sn led and clr: easily* **8/1**

2 *7* **Pastellrosa (IRE)** 2-8-9 .... WJLee(3) 10 75
(Timothy Doyle, Ire) *in rr of mid-div: hdwy to 8th 1f out: r.o strly fnl f* **25/1**

3 *3/4* **Queen Jock (USA)**[14] 3008 2-8-12 .... PShanahan 2 72
(Tracey Collins, Ire) *chsd ldrs on far side: rdn in 6th 1f out: kpt on* **6/1**

4 *nk* **Linsalata (IRE)**[11] 3115 2-8-12 .... KJManning 7 73
(J S Bolger, Ire) *cl up: impr to ld 2f out: rdn and hdd under 1f out: kpt on* **10/3**[2]

5 *shd* **Leandros (FR)**[32] 2481 2-9-3 .... WJSupple 8 77
(G M Lyons, Ire) *cl up: chal in 2nd under 2f out: no ex fr 1f out* **9/4**[1]

6 *1* **Lime Tree Valley (IRE)**[42] 2158 2-9-3 .... DPMcDonogh 6 74
(Kevin Prendergast, Ire) *sn disp: hdd 2f out: sn rdn: no ex fnl f* **5/1**[3]

7 *1 3/4* **Icemancometh (IRE)**[80] 1182 2-9-3 .... CDHayes 3 68
(Edward Lynam, Ire) *chsd ldrs on far side: rdn to 5th 1f out: no ex fnl f* **14/1**

8 *1/2* **Le Citadel (USA)**[14] 3005 2-9-3 .... WMLordan 5 67
(P D Deegan, Ire) *mid-div: kpt on same pce fr 2f out* **20/1**

9 *1 1/4* **Northgate (IRE)**[55] 1796 2-9-3 .... JAHeffernan 12 63
(Joseph G Murphy, Ire) *led and disp: hdd 2f out: wknd over 1f out* **10/1**

10 *3* **Panamericano (IRE)** 2-9-3 .... NGMcCullagh 17 54
(Enda Kelly, Ire) *mid-div: rdn and no imp 2f out* **25/1**

11 *2 1/2* **Love Boat Captain**[12] 3068 2-9-3 .... FranciscoDaSilva 9 47
(John A Quinn, Ire) *s.i.s and a towards rr* **50/1**

12 *nk* **Lady Marquet (IRE)** 2-8-7 .... SMGorey(5) 4 41
(Jarlath P Fahey, Ire) *nvr a factor* **50/1**

13 *3 1/2* **Stop The Power (GER)**[12] 3068 2-8-10 .... SERyder(7) 1 35
(Ruaidhri Joseph Tierney, Ire) *a towards rr on far side* **100/1**

14 *1/2* **Aah Haa**[81] 1170 2-9-3 .... CO'Donoghue 15 34
(John Joseph Murphy, Ire) *chsd ldrs: rdn and wknd 1/2-way* **20/1**

15 *3 1/2* **Tiger Tee (IRE)**[32] 2481 2-9-3 .... MCHussey 13 23
(John A Quinn, Ire) *cl up: rdn and wknd bef 1/2-way* **40/1**

16 *1* **Quetzalcoatl (IRE)** 2-9-3 .... DMGrant 11 20
(John Joseph Murphy, Ire) *a towards rr* **33/1**

17 *3 1/2* **Dont Denie It (IRE)**[6] 3251 2-8-12 .... FMBerry 16 5
(H Rogers, Ire) *s.i.s and a bhd* **33/1**

1m 14.8s (1.60) **17** Ran SP% **142.1**
CSF £213.49 TOTE £8.60: £1.80, £15.30, £1.10, £2.10; DF 335.40.
Owner K Abdulla **Bred** Juddmonte Farms Ltd **Trained** The Curragh, Co Kildare

NOTEBOOK
Famous Name ◆ made an impressive winning debut, making short work of his rivals, several of whom had previously shown useful form. The son of Dansili improved to hold every chance heading towards the final furlong and hit the front inside the distance before storming clear for an emphatic victory, which was achieved without him ever coming under maximum pressure. A stakes race will be next and he looks as though he will be a force to be reckoned with at a higher level, and he should only get better as he moves up in trip. (op 6/1)

3439 - 3444a (Foreign Racing) - See Raceform Interactive

3339 DEAUVILLE (R-H)
Wednesday, July 11

OFFICIAL GOING: Turf course - soft; all-weather - standard

3445a PRIX DE RIS-ORANGIS (GROUP 3) 6f
2:35 (2:47) 3-Y-0+ **£27,027** (£10,811; £8,108; £5,405; £2,703)

RPR

1 **Tiza (SAF)**[102] 860 5-9-0 .... CSoumillon 12 111
(A De Royer-Dupre, France) *hld up in 13th on outside: hdwy 2f out: led jst ins fnl f: r.o wl* **198/10**

2 *1* **Garnica (FR)**[44] 2100 4-9-4 .... C-PLemaire 3 112
(J-C Rouget, France) *hld up in 12th: hdwy 1 1/2f out: squeezed through narrow gap in centre to go 2nd 150yds out: r.o: nt rch wnr* **1/1**[1]

3 *1* **Val Jaro (FR)**[38] 2291 4-9-0 .... THuet 7 105
(S Morineau, France) *pressed ldr in centre tl led 1/2-way: hrd rdn over 1 1/2f out: hdd jst ins fnl f: kpt on u.p* **42/1**

4 *1/2* **Kourka (FR)**[59] 1704 5-8-10 .... RonanThomas 10 100
(J-M Beguigne, France) *in tch in midfield: chsng ldrs appr fnl f: kpt on at one pce u.p fnl f* **13/1**[3]

5 *shd* **Law Lord**[44] 2100 3-8-8 .... SPasquier 6 103
(A Fabre, France) *in tch in 9th: hrd rdn over 1 1/2f out: kpt on* **13/1**[3]

6 *snk* **Mednaya (IRE)**[39] 4-8-10 .... (p) FSpanu 8 99
(R Gibson, France) *prom in 4th: hrd rdn and ev ch 1f out: one pce* **44/1**

7 *1 1/2* **Rakiza (IRE)**[20] 2811 3-8-5 .... DBonilla 13 95
(F Head, France) *led in centre to 1/2-way: lost 2nd appr fnl f: wknd* **15/1**

8 *1 1/2* **Matrix (GER)**[11] 3122 6-9-0 .... DBoeuf 11 94
(W Baltromei, Germany) *racd in 3rd: outpcd fr over 1f out* **86/10**[2]

9 *nk* **Chopastair (FR)**[39] 6-9-0 .... JAuge 5 93
(T Lemer, France) *racd in 10th: nvr a factor* **32/1**

10 *snk* **Presto Shinko (IRE)**[18] 2857 6-9-0 .... (p) TThulliez 14 92
(R Hannon) *racd in 11th on wd outside: nvr a factor* **14/1**

11 **Docksil**[25] 3-8-9 .... JVictoire 9 93
(B Grizzetti, Italy) *racd in 5th: wknd over 1f out* **42/1**

12 **Sacho (GER)**[20] 2811 9-9-0 .... AlxiBadel 1 92
(W Kujath, Germany) *pressed nr side ldr in 7th overall: wknd over 1 1/2f out* **15/1**

13 **Tycoon's Hill (IRE)**[20] 2811 8-9-0 .... OPeslier 4 92
(Robert Collet, France) *led nr side in 6th overall: wknd over 1 1/2f out* **13/1**[3]

14 **Manzila (FR)**[22] 2733 4-8-10 .... TGillet 2 88
(F Head, France) *a bhd* **44/1**

1m 11.2s (-1.80)
WFA 3 from 4yo+ 6lb **14** Ran SP% **117.9**
PARI-MUTUEL: WIN 20.80; PL 4.50, 1.40, 7.50; DF 19.40.
Owner J L Atkinson **Bred** Wilgerbosdrift **Trained** Chantilly, France

NOTEBOOK
Tiza(SAF), an ex-South African-trained gelding, took this race well. Held up out the back on the outside, he started to make headway from the two-furlong pole, and burst through to take the lead just inside the final furlong. He kept on well to win by a length, and is likely to be seen out next in the Prix Maurice de Gheest, before a tilt at the Prix de l'Abbaye in October.
Garnica(FR), held up at the back of the field, improved a furlong and a half out and squeezed through a narrow gap to go second inside the final furlong. From there he never looked like passing the winner, but he ran on to take second.
Val Jaro(FR), quickly up with the leaders, took the lead at halfway. Hard ridden to keep his position, he stayed on bravely.
Kourka(FR), who raced on the outside in midfield, produced a good effort to make some headway after the two-furlong marker, but she received a bump inside the final furlong and could only run on at one pace to take fourth.
Presto Shinko(IRE), last year's winner, never looked happy on the ground. She was always towards the rear on the outside, and connections felt that this race might have come a bit soon after Ascot.

[3043]FOLKESTONE (R-H)

Thursday, July 12

OFFICIAL GOING: Good to firm (9.5)

Those who raced on the far side of the track on the straight course were at a huge advantage over those who raced near side.

Wind: Moderate, behind

3446 EUROPEAN BREEDERS FUND MEDIAN AUCTION MAIDEN FILLIES' STKS 7f (S)

6:20 (6:22) (Class 5) 2-Y-O £3,238 (£963; £481; £240) Stalls Low

Form				RPR
	1		**Step Softly** 2-9-0 0 SteveDrowne 12	75+
			(R Hannon) *racd far side: led 2f out: r.o wl promising* **8/1**[3]	
054	**2**	*3*	**Quick Sands (IRE)**[16] 2969 2-9-0 0 TedDurcan 9	68
			(R Hannon) *racd far side: chsd wnr over 1f out: kpt on* **9/2**[2]	
6	**3**	*3½*	**Heavenly Saint**[26] 2663 2-9-0 0 JHBowman 11	59
			(M R Channon) *led far side to 2f out: no ex fnl f* **14/1**	
0	**4**	*1½*	**Rosy Dawn**[30] 2539 2-9-0 0 PaulDoe 10	55
			(H J L Dunlop) *chsd ldr far side tl 2f out: kpt on one pce* **50/1**	
0	**5**	*shd*	**Spectrana**[33] 2468 2-9-0 0 JimCrowley 7	60+
			(Mrs A J Perrett) *racd nr side: led that gp whn wl btn cl home* **20/1**	
5	**6**	*shd*	**Pampas (USA)**[22] 2768 2-9-0 0 RichardHughes 2	60+
			(R Charlton) *sn led on nr side: wl hld whn lost that position cl home* **11/8**[1]	
000	**7**	*2½*	**Bantham Bay**[32] 2488 2-9-0 0 RobertHavlin 4	53+
			(B J Meehan) *in tch on nr side: rdn over 2f out and nvr nr to chal* **50/1**	
	8	*3*	**Milanollo** 2-9-0 0 JamieSpencer 1	48+
			(M L W Bell) *towards rr on nr side: rdn 2f out: n.d* **9/2**[2]	
0	**9**	*1*	**Jazamataz**[8] 3213 2-8-9 0 TravisBlock(5) 5	43+
			(Tom Dascombe) *in tch on nr side tl wknd 2f out* **50/1**	
0	**10**	*4*	**Lady Of Passion (IRE)**[12] 3085 2-9-0 0 SamHitchcott 13	28
			(M R Channon) *swvd lft s: a bhd far side* **25/1**	
000	**11**	*5*	**In Decorum**[30] 2539 2-8-7 0 HaddenFrost(7) 8	21+
			(J A Geake) *prom on nr side tl wknd over 2f out* **40/1**	
0	**12**	*6*	**Miss Bouggy Wouggy**[47] 2039 2-9-0 0 SebSanders 3	6+
			(M Blanshard) *a bhd on nr side* **25/1**	
0	**13**	*2*	**Whistful Miss**[84] 1101 2-9-0 0 AmirQuinn 6	—
			(P Howling) *slowly away: a bhd on stands' side* **66/1**	

1m 26.12s (-1.78) **Going Correction** -0.375s/f (Firm) **13** Ran SP% **118.5**

Speed ratings (Par 91):95,91,87,85,85 85,82,79,78,73 67,61,58

CSF £40.31 TOTE £8.20: £2.20, £1.80, £2.80; EX 48.50.

Owner The Queen **Bred** The Queen **Trained** East Everleigh, Wilts

FOCUS

The field split into two groups and those who raced on the far side of the track were at a huge advantage over those who raced near side. As a result, the bare form of this maiden, rated through the runner-up, needs treating with real caution.

NOTEBOOK

Step Softly, a daughter of Golan, and a half-sister to dual 6f winner Free Lift, sprint winner Bright And Breezy, and 7f scorer Chief Yeoman, out of a 1m2f winner, attracted some support in the market and ran out a clear-cut winner on her racecourse debut, leading home a one-two for the Hannon yard. It would be unwise to get carried away with the form, as over half the field raced on slower ground on the opposite side of the track, but she took care of those on her side in good style. (op 10-1 tchd 12-1)

Quick Sands(IRE) did not seem to have too many excuses; her stablemate was basically too good. She might do better when switched to nurseries. (op 10-3)

Heavenly Saint never landed a blow over 5f on her debut at Lingfield, but this was better. She is by a sprinter, but there is lots of stamina on the dam's side and it remains to be seen what her optimum trip will be. (op 12-1)

Rosy Dawn improved on the form she showed in a 6f maiden at Salisbury on her debut and is going the right way. (op 40-1)

Spectrana never featured in a 6f maiden on her debut at Newbury, but the step up in trip clearly suited and she led home the group on the unfavoured near side of the track. She should continue to progress. (op 25-1)

Pampas(USA) raced on the unfavoured side of the track, so she obviously had no chance of winning, but she still only managed second on her side and did not really step forward as one might have hoped from her promising debut effort at Kempton. Not all horses take to a track like Folkestone though, and she can definitely be given another chance on a more galloping course. (tchd 15-8)

Milanollo, a 105,000gns Soviet Star filly, half-sister to among others the quite useful pair Nice Tune, multiple 7f-1m2f winner, and 7f scorer Play That Tune, had no chance racing on the near side of the track and can be given another opportunity. (op 6-1 tchd 4-1)

3447 FOLKESTONE-RACECOURSE.CO.UK MAIDEN STKS 7f (S)

6:50 (6:52) (Class 5) 3-Y-O £2,914 (£867; £433; £216) Stalls Low

Form				RPR
2-3	**1**		**Flying Goose (IRE)**[38] 2312 3-9-3 0 NickyMackay 12	79+
			(L M Cumani) *a.p: chal over 1f out bef led ins fnl f: rdn out* **2/1**[1]	
6	**2**	*1¾*	**Shela House**[19] 2886 3-9-3 0 JamieSpencer 9	74
			(J R Fanshawe) *sn chsd ldrs: rdn to ld over 1f out: hdd ins fnl f: kpt on one pce* **12/1**	
0-23	**3**	*1½*	**Wolf River (USA)**[13] 3062 3-9-3 80 RichardHughes 2	70
			(D M Simcock) *led after 1f: rdn and hdd over 1f out: one pce after* **9/2**[2]	
	4	*nk*	**Twilight Star (IRE)** 3-9-3 0 (t) TedDurcan 13	69+
			(Saeed Bin Suroor) *mid-div: rdn and hdwy 2f out: kpt on but nvr nr to chal* **9/2**[2]	
	5	*2*	**War Anthem** 3-9-3 0 SteveDrowne 6	64+
			(C R Egerton) *hld up in rr: mde sme late hdwy* **33/1**	
00	**6**	*1*	**Caravel (IRE)**[6] 3276 3-9-3 0 SebSanders 8	61+
			(Sir Mark Prescott) *towards rr: rdn 3f out: nvr nr to chal* **25/1**	
30-	**7**	*3*	**Clouded Leopard (USA)**[243] 6433 3-8-12 0 RobertHavlin 4	48
			(J H M Gosden) *in rr: mde sme late hdwy* **12/1**	
2-3	**8**	*hd*	**The Cool Sandpiper**[13] 3044 3-9-3 0 IanMongan 3	52
			(P Winkworth) *chsd ldrs tl wknd over 2f out* **20/1**	
452	**9**	*½*	**Al Badeya (IRE)**[18] 2913 3-8-5 72 JamieHamblett(7) 5	46
			(Sir Michael Stoute) *t.k.h: sn chsd ldr: wknd wl over 1f out* **5/1**[3]	
00	**10**	*7*	**Pulsate**[17] 2944 3-8-12 JimCrowley 11	27
			(Mrs A J Perrett) *led for 1f: wknd 2f out* **50/1**	
	11	*hd*	**Soul Angel** 3-8-10 0 HaddenFrost(7) 7	32
			(R Hannon) *a bhd* **33/1**	
0-6	**12**	*19*	**Decision Day**[15] 2998 3-8-7 0 TravisBlock(5) 10	—
			(J A Geake) *slowly away: sn prom: wknd 1/2-way* **40/1**	

1m 24.79s (-3.11) **Going Correction** -0.375s/f (Firm) **12** Ran SP% **120.6**

Speed ratings (Par 100):102,100,98,97,95 94,91,90,90,82 82,60

CSF £27.22 TOTE £3.20: £1.10, £3.20, £1.70; EX 32.20.

Owner Bruce Corman **Bred** Top Of The Form Syndicate **Trained** Newmarket, Suffolk

FOCUS

Some big stables were represented, but this was just an ordinary maiden. This time they all opted to race far side and with the time reasonable the form is probably sound.

Caravel(IRE) ◆ Official explanation: jockey said gelding lost a front shoe

The Cool Sandpiper Official explanation: jockey said gelding hung left

3448 HOBBS PARKER TELECOM H'CAP 2m 93y

7:20 (7:20) (Class 6) (0-60,60) 4-Y-O+ £2,730 (£806; £403) Stalls Low

Form				RPR
2131	**1**		**Colwyn Bay (IRE)**[22] 2770 5-9-3 59 (p) JamieSpencer 12	67
			(Jane Chapple-Hyam) *mid-div: hdwy to go 3rd 3f out: wnt 2nd over 1f out bef veered rt u.p: kpt on to ld fnl 50yds* **9/4**[1]	
2	**2**	*nk*	**Power Again (GER)**[57] 1764 6-8-11 53 PaulDoe 10	61
			(P R Chamings) *trckd ldrs: wnt 2nd 3f out: led over 2f out: rdn and hdd fnl 50yds* **12/1**	
/40-	**3**	*1¾*	**French Opera**[109] 3075 4-9-2 58 RichardHughes 8	64
			(N J Henderson) *hld up: rdn 3f out: styd on to go 3rd ins fnl f: nvr nrr* **7/2**[2]	
15-2	**4**	*½*	**Sharaab (USA)**[32] 2493 6-8-8 50 (t) LPKeniry 14	55
			(D E Cantillon) *towards rr on ins: styd on fnl 2f but nvr nr to chal* **11/2**[3]	
23-6	**5**	*1¼*	**That Look**[15] 2996 4-8-11 53 ow2 JHBowman 1	57
			(D E Cantillon) *led tl hdd over 2f out: rdn and no hdwy after* **12/1**	
6333	**6**	*5*	**King's Ransom**[9] 3177 4-9-4 60 SebSanders 11	58
			(W R Muir) *slowly away: hld up: nvr on terms* **14/1**	
00	**7**	*1½*	**Leonardo's Friend**[46] 212 4-9-4 60 (t) GeorgeBaker 9	56
			(B G Powell) *hld up: a bhd* **33/1**	
242	**8**	*3½*	**Madiba**[25] 2686 8-8-8 50 SteveDrowne 5	42
			(P Howling) *sn trckd ldr: wknd over 2f out* **16/1**	
0120	**9**	*¾*	**Ganymede**[22] 2770 6-9-0 56 IanMongan 4	47
			(Mrs L J Mongan) *a bhd* **16/1**	
65-0	**10**	*6*	**Almizan (IRE)**[40] 16 7-9-4 60 (b) TedDurcan 3	44
			(G L Moore) *trckd ldrs tl wknd over 2f out* **9/1**	
5-40	**11**	*15*	**Equilibria (USA)**[146] 482 5-8-7 49 SamHitchcott 6	15
			(G L Moore) *mid-div on outside: rdn over 6f out: wknd over 3f out: eased ins fnl 2f* **25/1**	
-106	**12**	*15*	**Himba**[25] 2686 4-8-13 55 JimCrowley 2	3
			(Mrs A J Perrett) *trckd ldrs: rn in snatches: wknd over 4f out: t.o* **25/1**	

3m 35.8s (-4.90) **Going Correction** -0.375s/f (Firm) **12** Ran SP% **122.8**

Speed ratings (Par 101):97,96,95,95,95 92,91,90,89,86 79,71

CSF £32.06 CT £97.85 TOTE £3.50: £1.70, £3.50, £1.60; EX 29.70.

Owner Philip M Hickey **Bred** Tower Bloodstock **Trained** Newmarket, Suffolk

FOCUS

Hand-timed. A moderate staying handicap run at an even tempo and the form looks straightforward and sound, with the third, fourth and fifth close to their marks.

3449 GO WEST LIVE AFTER RACING JULY 26TH H'CAP 5f

7:50 (7:52) (Class 5) (0-70,69) 3-Y-O+ £3,238 (£963; £481; £240) Stalls Low

Form				RPR
0122	**1**		**Caustic Wit (IRE)**[3] 3368 9-9-5 62 RichardHughes 7	72
			(M S Saunders) *a.p far side: wnt 2nd 2f out: rdn to ld ins fnl f* **7/4**[1]	
0334	**2**	*nk*	**Malapropism**[6] 3259 7-9-10 67 JHBowman 8	76
			(M R Channon) *racd far side: led for 1f: styd prom: rdn over 1f out: kpt on go go 2nd ins fnl f* **11/2**[3]	
-001	**3**	*1*	**Talcen Gwyn (IRE)**[9] 3179 5-9-3 60 6ex (v) DavidKinsella 4	65
			(M F Harris) *swtchd to far side: hld up: hdwy over 1f out r.o to go 3rd towards fin* **11/2**[3]	
0620	**4**	*hd*	**Desperate Dan**[33] 2479 6-9-12 69 (b) JamieSpencer 9	74
			(J A Osborne) *s.i.s on far side: led after 1f: rdn over 1f out: hdd and lost 2nd ins fnl f* **5/1**[2]	
0033	**5**	*3*	**Hythe Bay**[12] 3086 3-9-7 69 GeorgeBaker 2	61
			(J R Best) *chsd ldr nr side tl rdn and led that gp wl ins fnl f* **9/1**	
000-	**6**	*shd*	**Valiant Romeo**[233] 6548 7-8-2 50 oh5 KevinGhunowa(5) 5	43
			(R Bastiman) *led stands' side gp: rdn 2f out and no ex ins fnl f* **40/1**	
0000	**7**	*¾*	**Smiddy Hill**[17] 2933 5-8-11 54 JimCrowley 6	45
			(R Bastiman) *chsd ldrs stands' side: rdn over 2f out and no ch w far side after* **11/1**	
6066	**8**	*5*	**Enjoy The Buzz**[3] 3368 8-8-7 50 (p) SteveDrowne 1	23
			(J M Bradley) *a in rr on stands' side* **14/1**	
P405	**9**	*nk*	**Xaluna Bay (IRE)**[8] 3212 4-9-11 68 SebSanders 10	40
			(W R Muir) *racd on far side: in tch tl wknd 2f out* **12/1**	

58.61 secs (-2.19) **Going Correction** -0.375s/f (Firm) course record

WFA 3 from 4yo+ 5lb **9** Ran SP% **118.9**

Speed ratings (Par 103):102,101,99,99,94 94,93,85,84

CSF £11.98 CT £45.86 TOTE £3.10: £1.10, £2.40, £2.60; EX 13.40.

Owner Mrs Sandra Jones **Bred** Gainsborough Stud Management Ltd **Trained** Green Ore, Somerset

FOCUS

Despite it being quite obvious from the first race that the quickest ground was on the far side of the track, four horses were kept towards the near side, and were duly well beaten. This was just a modest sprint handicap and, with the field splitting into two groups, the form appears solid rated around the winner and third but wants treating with some caution.

Xaluna Bay(IRE) Official explanation: vet said filly bled

3450 FOLKESTONE-RACECOURSE.CO.UK H'CAP 1m 4f

8:20 (8:20) (Class 5) (0-70,65) 3-Y-O £3,238 (£963; £481; £240) Stalls Low

Form				RPR
0606	**1**		**Beau Michael**[10] 3150 3-9-7 65 (b[1]) TedDurcan 10	71
			(W R Swinburn) *led for 2f: styd prom: hmpd 3f out but rcvrd to ld 2f out: rdn out* **20/1**	
0065	**2**	*2*	**Shine And Rise (IRE)**[28] 2602 3-9-7 65 SteveDrowne 1	68
			(C G Cox) *racd keenly on outside: prom whn lft in ld 3f out: rdn and hdd 2f out: kpt on but no imp fnl f* **7/1**[3]	
4022	**3**	*¾*	**Red Flare (IRE)**[10] 3150 3-8-1 52 MatthewDavies(7) 9	54
			(M R Channon) *hld up in rr: styd on fnl 2f to go 3rd 1f out* **10/1**	
3253	**4**	*7*	**Spritza (IRE)**[17] 2940 3-9-5 63 JamieSpencer 5	54+
			(M L W Bell) *in tch: btn whn eased ins fnl f* **7/1**[3]	
0213	**5**	*5*	**Rustic Gold**[13] 3048 3-9-2 63 StephaneBreux(3) 3	46
			(J R Best) *hld up: nvr on terms* **8/1**	
0-06	**6**	*25*	**Acosta**[45] 2081 3-8-3 52 ow4 (be) KevinGhunowa(5) 8	—
			(Dr J R J Naylor) *towards rr whn sltly hmpd over 3f out: sn btn* **66/1**	
0-00	**7**	*140*	**Abbotts Account (USA)**[45] 2096 3-8-9 53 ow1 (b[1]) RichardHughes 4	—
			(Mrs A J Perrett) *towards rr: effrt 3f out: wknd rapidly 2f out: t.o* **10/1**	
00-2	**P**		**Crossing The Line (IRE)**[10] 3170 3-9-6 64 SebSanders 2	—
			(Sir Mark Prescott) *t.k.h: led over 7f out tl broke down 3f out: p.u and dismntd* **2/1**[1]	

123 **P** **Jafaru**[10] 3150 3-9-7 **65**.......................(b) JHBowman 6 —
(G A Butler) *led after 2f: hdd over 7f out: virtually p.u over 3f out and c bk in own time* **10/3**[2]

2m 36.77s (-3.73) **Going Correction** -0.375s/f (Firm) **9** Ran SP% **117.0**
Speed ratings (Par 100):97,95,95,90,87 70,—,—,—
CSF £154.48 CT £1500.84 TOTE £26.90: £5.40, £3.10, £2.10; EX 126.70.
Owner Mrs A M Richards **Bred** Berkshire Equestrian Services Ltd **Trained** Aldbury, Herts

FOCUS
Not an enjoyable race to watch, with two horses pulling up and another finishing tailed off, and it remains to be seen what the form is worth. The pace was very strong early on, suggesting it is sound enough.
Acosta Official explanation: jockey said colt hung left
Abbotts Account(USA) Official explanation: jockey said gelding stopped very quickly in straight
Jafaru Official explanation: jockey said gelding lost its action

3451 FOLKESTONE RACECOURSE FOR WEDDINGS FILLIES' H'CAP 1m 1f 149y
8:50 (8:50) (Class 5) (0-70,68) 3-Y-0+ **£3,238** (£963; £481; £240) **Stalls** Low

Form RPR

3405 **1** **Mystery River (USA)**[30] 2530 3-9-5 **67**.......................RichardHughes 6 74
(B J Meehan) *mde all: rdn clr 2f out: in command after but kpt up to work* **2/1**[1]

6630 **2** *5* **Central Force**[24] 2727 3-9-6 **68**.......................TedDurcan 5 65
(E A L Dunlop) *chsd wnr thrght: rdn 2f out: no imp after* **8/1**

3104 **3** *hd* **Princess Lavinia**[30] 2544 4-9-12 **63**.......................SteveDrowne 1 60
(G Wragg) *in rr tl hdwy on outside over 5f out: wnt 3rd over 2f out: kpt on one pce* **5/2**[2]

3-05 **4** *5* **Greenmeadow**[9] 3191 5-9-4 **55**.......................LPKeniry 3 42
(S Kirk) *s.i.s: hld up in tch: one pce fnl 2f* **4/1**[3]

0-00 **5** *3/4* **Sunny Afternoon**[32] 1507 7-8-6 **50**.......................RichardRowe(7) 4 35
(R Rowe) *plld hrd: trckd ldrs tl wknd over 2f out* **20/1**

-500 **6** *2* **Zameliana**[32] 2489 3-7-5 **46** oh1.......................FrankiePickard(7) 8 27
(Dr J R J Naylor) *a bhd* **50/1**

-305 **7** *1* **Divine White**[10] 3167 4-9-1 **52**.......................SebSanders 7 31
(P Bowen) *plld hrd: chsd ldrs tl wknd over 2f out* **6/1**

2m 2.56s (-2.67) **Going Correction** -0.375s/f (Firm)
WFA 3 from 4yo+ 11lb **7** Ran SP% **114.0**
Speed ratings (Par 100):95,91,90,86,86 84,83
CSF £18.68 CT £40.80 TOTE £2.90: £1.90, £4.20; EX 16.00 Place 6 £120.21, Place 5 £28.29.
Owner F C T Wilson **Bred** W Hamilton **Trained** Manton, Wilts

FOCUS
Not much of a contest and, although impressive, Mystery River was able to dominate and the form needs treating with caution.
T/Plt: £229.70 to a £1 stake. Pool: £64,971.55. 206.40 winning tickets. T/Qpdt: £33.10 to a £1 stake. Pool: £5,496.30. 122.80 winning tickets. JS

3423 LINGFIELD (L-H)
Thursday, July 12

OFFICIAL GOING: Standard
Wind: Slight, behind Weather: Cool and cloudy

3452 LINGFIELDPARK.CO.UK H'CAP 5f (P)
2:10 (2:10) (Class 5) (0-75,75) 3-Y-0+ **£3,071** (£906; £453) **Stalls** High

Form RPR

-316 **1** **Safari Mischief**[19] 2879 4-9-6 **74**.......................LiamJones(3) 7 85
(P Winkworth) *cl up: led jst ins fnl f: drvn out* **6/1**[3]

3012 **2** *1/2* **George The Second**[2] 3396 4-8-13 **71** 6ex.......................KylieManser(7) 4 80
(Mrs H Sweeting) *prom: drvn to chal and ev ch 1f out: no imp cl home* **2/1**[1]

0661 **3** *1 1/4* **Calypso King**[36] 2357 4-9-2 **67**.......................AdrianMcCarthy 10 72
(Peter Grayson) *cl up: rdn and wanting to edge lft fr over 1f out: no ex fnl f* **7/1**

0306 **4** *hd* **Tous Les Deux**[12] 3076 4-9-7 **72**.......................BrettDoyle 5 76
(Peter Grayson) *t.k.h in rr early: rdn 3f out: effrt 1f out: nt clr run and swtchd rt ins fnl f: kpt on* **14/1**

0504 **5** *nk* **Egyptian Lord**[12] 3086 4-9-9 **74**.......................(b) J-PGuillambert 2 77
(Peter Grayson) *pressed ldr tl 1/2-way: lost pl sltly: rallied on ins 1f out: nt qckn after* **12/1**

04-0 **6** *1* **After The Show**[151] 432 6-9-4 **74**.......................PatrickHills(5) 8 73
(Rae Guest) *towards rr: rdn over 2f out: no imp after* **7/1**

2002 **7** *1/2* **Bookiesindex Boy**[8] 3212 3-9-5 **75**.......................(b) RobertHavlin 6 72
(J R Jenkins) *led tl hdd jst ins fnl f: gave up qckly* **8/1**

6044 **8** *4* **Heavens Walk**[8] 3212 6-9-3 **68**.......................(t) SebSanders 1 51
(P J Makin) *a bhd* **3/1**[2]

9 *6* **Millenium Sun (IRE)**[57] 1775 3-8-13 **72**.......................AlanCreighton(3) 9 33
(E J Creighton) *sn drvn: bhd: drvn and btn 2f out* **33/1**

58.59 secs (-1.19) **Going Correction** -0.15s/f (Stan)
WFA 3 from 4yo+ 5lb **9** Ran SP% **126.0**
Speed ratings (Par 103):103,102,100,99,99 97,97,90,81
CSF £20.25 CT £93.05 TOTE £7.50: £2.20, £1.10, £2.30; EX 28.00 Trifecta £110.70 Pool: £183.99 - 1.18 winning units..
Owner P Winkworth **Bred** Bearstone Stud **Trained** Chiddingfold, Surrey

FOCUS
A fair sprint handicap and straightforward form, rated around the first three.

3453 LINGFIELD PARK FOR WEDDINGS MAIDEN FILLIES' STKS 7f (P)
2:45 (2:45) (Class 5) 2-Y-O **£2,968** (£876; £438) **Stalls** Low

Form RPR

1 **Dusty Moon** 2-9-0 0.......................PaulDoe 10 81+
(W J Knight) *last away: bhd tl rapid prog on outside over 2f out: led 1f out: sn in command: pushed out* **16/1**

6 **2** *1 1/4* **Altitude**[15] 2992 2-9-0 0.......................SebSanders 7 77
(Sir Mark Prescott) *prom: rdn over 2f out: led briefly over 1f out: chsd wnr vainly fnl f* **9/4**[1]

0 **3** *3* **Moonlight Angel**[33] 2457 2-9-0 0.......................SaleemGolam 6 69+
(W R Swinburn) *midfield: rdn over 3f out: wnt 3rd 1f out: unable to cl after* **3/1**[3]

0 **4** *3* **A Dream Come True**[8] 3213 2-9-0 0.......................RobertHavlin 4 61
(D K Ivory) *stdd and plld hrd briefly: rdn over 4f out: sn outpcd: effrt outside fnl f: styd on* **50/1**

5 **5** *2 1/2* **Astania**[20] 2832 2-9-0 0.......................StephenDonohoe 2 55
(P W D'Arcy) *chsd ldrs: rdn 1/2-way: struggling over 2f out* **7/1**

43 **6** *1 1/2* **Narmeen**[8] 3213 2-9-0 0.......................SamHitchcott 1 51
(M R Channon) *led tl rdn and hdd over 1f out: sn btn* **5/1**

0 **7** *shd* **Dawn Wind**[22] 2768 2-9-0 0.......................NickyMackay 9 50
(I A Wood) *s.i.s: nvr on terms* **50/1**

0 **8** *3/4* **Victorian Princess (IRE)**[22] 2758 2-8-7 0.......................MCGeran(7) 5 49
(E J O'Neill) *wnt lft s: t.k.h: cl up: w ldr briefly over 1f out: sn fdd* **25/1**

00 **9** *hd* **Kay One (IRE)**[10] 3171 2-8-11 0.......................LiamJones(3) 3 48
(R J Price) *awkward s: a wanting to hang rt in rr: no ch fnl 3f* **50/1**

63 **10** *3* **Polite Society (IRE)**[29] 2575 2-9-0 0.......................J-PGuillambert 8 40
(M Johnston) *rdn after 2f: sn floundering bdly* **11/4**[2]

1m 25.14s (-0.75) **Going Correction** -0.15s/f (Stan) **10** Ran SP% **127.2**
Speed ratings (Par 91):98,96,93,89,86 85,85,84,83,80
CSF £56.36 TOTE £26.20: £4.80, £1.30, £1.20; EX 79.10 Trifecta £253.30 Part won. Pool: £356.90 - 0.64 winning units..
Owner Hesmonds Stud **Bred** Hesmonds Stud Ltd **Trained** Patching, W Sussex

FOCUS
This looked an ordinary maiden, especially as those that had shown some form previously proved disappointing but they were well spread out behind the winner.

NOTEBOOK
Dusty Moon ◆, who was conceding experience to all her rivals, was given plenty to do but came from way off the pace to catch Altitude and eventually win pretty tidily. A sister to the high-class Spotlight and half-sister to two other winners, she can only improve and looks a nice prospect.
Altitude, who never got into the race after missing the break on her Kempton debut, was more organised this time and looked as though she might win when leading the field into the straight. However, although she beat the rest well enough, she could not match the winner's finishing pace. She is likely to carry on improving with racing. (op 5-2)
Moonlight Angel, who showed ability on her debut on turf here last month, raced wide all the way and stayed on to finish a clear third. She is another likely to improve with experience.
A Dream Come True, last on her Kempton debut earlier this month, was never a threat but did make up some late ground from well off the pace and is not without hope.
Astania, well backed, was off the bridle a long way out and did not step up from her Newmarket debut. (op 10-1)
Narmeen, who improved when stepped up to this trip at Kempton last time, dropped away after making the early running. (tchd 9-2)
Victorian Princess(IRE) Official explanation: jockey said filly ran too free early
Polite Society(IRE) was a major disappointment on this All-Weather debut, her rider reporting that she was never travelling. Official explanation: jockey said filly never travelled (op 5-2 tchd 3-1)

3454 BOOK TICKETS ON LINE MAIDEN STKS 1m (P)
3:20 (3:21) (Class 5) 3-Y-0+ **£2,968** (£876; £438) **Stalls** High

Form RPR

22 **1** **Classira (IRE)**[54] 1841 3-8-12 0.......................PhilipRobinson 6 74
(M A Jarvis) *t.k.h and cl up: rdn and hung rt over 1f out: styd on to master ldr 120yds out* **8/11**[1]

46 **2** *1 1/4* **Honest Prospector (USA)**[19] 2880 3-9-3 0.......................J-PGuillambert 1 76
(Sir Michael Stoute) *led at mod pce: drvn over 2f out: hdd 120yds out: nt qckn* **10/1**

33 **3** *3/4* **Areyaam (USA)**[19] 2873 3-8-12 0.......................NickyMackay 3 69
(L M Cumani) *t.k.h: pressed ldr: drvn over 2f out: one pce fnl f* **6/1**[3]

03 **4** *nk* **Emperor Court (IRE)**[30] 2542 3-9-3 0.......................AmirQuinn 2 73
(P J Makin) *t.k.h: prom: drvn wl over 1f out: a hld fnl f* **16/1**

30 **5** *shd* **Red Blossom**[13] 3051 3-8-12 0.......................SebSanders 8 68
(Sir Mark Prescott) *plld hrd on outside: looked awkward ride: hanging bdly lft fr over 1f out: no imp tl styd on wl ins fnl f* **14/1**

0 **6** *7* **Holyfield Warrior (IRE)**[18] 2913 3-9-3 0.......................StephenDonohoe 7 57?
(I A Wood) *bhd: rdn 1/2-way: nvr gng wl* **50/1**

0 **7** *3 1/2* **Polish Prize**[17] 2944 3-9-3 0.......................SaleemGolam 5 49
(W R Swinburn) *towards rr: rdn 3f out: struggling after* **33/1**

00- **8** *12* **Tivers Jewel (USA)**[275] 5891 3-9-3 0.......................BrettDoyle 9 21
(Mrs A J Perrett) *t.k.h in midfield: drvn over 3f out: sn lost pl: eased and t.o fnl f* **25/1**

U **Colourful Score (USA)** 3-9-3 0.......................(t) RobertHavlin 4 —
(Saeed Bin Suroor) *put hd down and uns rdr leaving stalls* **7/2**[2]

1m 38.42s (-1.01) **Going Correction** -0.15s/f (Stan) **9** Ran SP% **124.8**
Speed ratings (Par 103):99,97,97,96,96 89,86,74,—
CSF £10.87 TOTE £1.60: £1.10, £4.10, £1.10; EX 10.80 Trifecta £20.40 Pool: £313.07 - 10.85 winning units..
Owner N R A Springer **Bred** Barronstown Stud And Orpendale **Trained** Newmarket, Suffolk

FOCUS
After the expensive Godolphin newcomer Colourful Score had disgraced himself soon after the start, Classira was faced with a straightforward task and accomplished it in workmanlike fashion. The form is somewhat muddling behind her.

3455 LINGFIELD PARK GOLF CLUB FILLIES' H'CAP 1m (P)
3:55 (3:55) (Class 5) (0-70,70) 3-Y-0+ **£3,071** (£906; £453) **Stalls** High

Form RPR

3-26 **1** **Furbeseta**[29] 2579 3-9-8 **70**.......................NickyMackay 4 82+
(L M Cumani) *cl up and a gng wl: wnt 2nd 2f out: led over 1f out: immediately rdn clr* **10/3**[1]

1606 **2** *3 1/2* **Our Kes (IRE)**[15] 2979 5-9-10 **63**.......................AmirQuinn 12 69
(P Howling) *sn led: rdn and hdd over 1f out: immediately outpcd* **10/1**

4-22 **3** *2* **Pivotalia (IRE)**[13] 3066 3-9-5 **67**.......................SaleemGolam 5 66
(W R Swinburn) *chsd ldrs: rdn 3f out: effrt to dispute 2nd sn after: chsd ldng pair vainly fnl 2f* **7/2**[2]

4030 **4** *3/4* **Lady Duxyana**[10] 3149 4-8-9 **48** oh3.......................(v) RobertHavlin 7 47
(M D I Usher) *s.i.s: rn in snatches and drvn at several stages: effrt over 2f out: fnd little wl over 1f out* **12/1**

120 **5** *1/2* **Black Sea Pearl**[119] 686 4-9-11 **64**.......................StephenDonohoe 8 62
(P W D'Arcy) *bhd: effrt on outside wl over 2f out: kpt on but nvr looked like chalng: sddle slipped* **13/2**

1-00 **6** *1* **Ravinia (USA)**[46] 2061 3-8-11 **66**.......................KMay(7) 10 60
(B J Meehan) *sn bhd: last over 2f out: kpt on but nvr nr ldrs* **12/1**

0003 **7** *2* **Fateful Attraction**[9] 3191 4-9-9 **62**.......................(b) SebSanders 1 53
(I A Wood) *broke wl but sn lost pl: struggling after 1/2-way* **6/1**[3]

1300 **8** *shd* **Still Crazy (IRE)**[13] 3066 3-8-7 **58**.......................LiamJones(3) 9 47
(E F Vaughan) *s.i.s: t.k.h in rr: short lived effrt 3f out* **7/1**

-260 **9** *1/2* **My Tiger Lilly**[29] 2560 3-8-4 **52**.......................PaulDoe 11 40
(W J Knight) *nvr bttr than midfield: effrt over 3f out: faltered wl over 1f out: eased fnl f* **12/1**

20-0 **10** *8* **For Eileen**[176] 162 3-8-1 **49** ow1.......................FrankieMcDonald 3 18
(G C H Chung) *chsd ldrs: rdn 1/2-way: sn btn* **33/1**

0410 **11** *1 1/4* **Lunar River (FR)**[29] 2579 4-9-7 **67**.......................(t) HaddenFrost(7) 2 36
(David Pinder) *sn chsng ldr: lost pl 3f out: t.o* **12/1**

1m 37.75s (-1.68) **Going Correction** -0.15s/f (Stan)
WFA 3 from 4yo+ 9lb **11** Ran SP% **128.2**
Speed ratings (Par 100):102,98,96,95,95 94,92,92,91,83 82
CSF £41.30 CT £133.99 TOTE £4.40: £1.50, £3.40, £1.50; EX 59.30 TRIFECTA Not won..

The Form Book, Raceform Ltd, Compton, RG20 6NL

Owner Scuderia Rencati Srl **Bred** Azienda Agricola Francesca **Trained** Newmarket, Suffolk

FOCUS

Only a modest fillies' handicap, but the pace was decent and not many got into it. The form looks sound, rated around the placed horses.

Black Sea Pearl Official explanation: jockey said saddle slipped

3456 WORLD BET EXCHANGE H'CAP — 1m 2f (P)

4:30 (4:30) (Class 5) (0-70,70) 3-Y-O — **£3,071** (£906; £453) **Stalls** Low

Form — RPR

0440 **1** **Personal Column**[28] 2610 3-9-4 **67** J-PGuillambert 6 — 73
(T G Mills) *pressed ldr: rdn 3f out: styd on to ld fnl 100yds: r.o gamely* **9/2**[3]

0004 **2** ½ **Western Point (IRE)**[12] 3082 3-8-7 **56** SebSanders 3 — 61
(Sir Mark Prescott) *led: hrd drvn 3f out: hdd 100yds out: kpt on* **13/8**[1]

00 **3** 1 ¼ **Aypeeyes (IRE)**[49] 1974 3-9-2 **65** FrankieMcDonald 2 — 68
(S Kirk) *t.k.h early: bhd and rn in stages: rdn over 4f out: last over 2f out: racd v lazily ent st tl kpt on strly cl home* **12/1**

0520 **4** 1 ¼ **Kindlelight Blue (IRE)**[28] 2601 3-9-0 **63** (e) NickyMackay 7 — 63
(N P Littmoden) *pushed along early: chsd ldrs: rdn 3f out: one pce wl over 1f out* **8/1**

05-0 **5** 1 ¼ **Wickedish**[34] 2429 3-7-13 **51** oh1 (t) LiamJones(3) 1 — 49
(C F Wall) *prom: rdn over 4f out: no ex wl over 1f out: wknd to lose two pls ins fnl f* **25/1**

0601 **6** 1 ¾ **Cavallo Di Ferro (IRE)**[32] 2178 3-9-0 **63** AntonyProcter 5 — 57
(M J Gingell) *bhd: rdn wl over 2f out: n.d after* **12/1**

-005 **7** 3 ½ **Buckthorn**[59] 1722 3-9-7 **70** RobertHavlin 4 — 57
(G Wragg) *midfield: rdn over 4f out: struggling wl over 2f out* **7/2**[2]

0-05 **8** 14 **Sunburn (IRE)**[19] 2886 3-8-13 **62** BrettDoyle 8 — 21
(Mrs A J Perrett) *lost 6l at s: sn taking t.k.h and chsng ldrs: dropped bk to last 2f out: eased and t.o* **8/1**

2m 5.77s (-2.02) **Going Correction** -0.15s/f (Stan) — **8** Ran SP% **120.0**

Speed ratings (Par 100):102,101,100,99,98 97,94,83

CSF £12.92 CT £84.51 TOTE £7.30: £1.40, £1.60, £4.10; EX 16.80 Trifecta £134.60 Pool: £663.66 - 3.50 winning units..

Owner Mrs L M Askew **Bred** Cheveley Park Stud Ltd **Trained** Headley, Surrey

FOCUS

A modest handicap and not many runners, but they went a decent pace and the first two home occupied those positions throughout. The form looks solid, rated around the first three.

3457 BOOK A HOSPITALITY PACKAGE HERE APPRENTICE H'CAP — 1m 4f (P)

5:05 (5:05) (Class 6) (0-65,61) 4-Y-O+ — **£2,388** (£705; £352) **Stalls** Low

Form — RPR

1522 **1** **Rudry World (IRE)**[6] 3260 4-8-9 **51** SophieDoyle(5) 6 — 61
(M Mullineaux) *midfield and a gng wl: effrt over 1f out: led ins fnl f: pushed out* **4/1**[2]

4423 **2** 1 **Apache Fort**[19] 2887 4-9-5 **61** JamesRogers(5) 7 — 69
(T Keddy) *prom: wnt 2nd over 4f out: led 3f out: edgd rt ent st: rdn and hdd ins fnl f: nt qckn* **11/4**[1]

6565 **3** 1 ¾ **Gallego**[19] 2868 5-9-2 **53** WilliamCarson 1 — 59
(R J Price) *t.k.h: midfield tl stdd to rr 4f out: hdwy on outside 3f out: chal and carried sltly rt over 1f out: ev ch briefly: wknd cl home* **9/2**[3]

4035 **4** 1 ½ **Bienheureux**[8] 3217 6-9-1 **55** (t) HarryPoulton(3) 2 — 58
(Miss Gay Kelleway) *stdd in last: effrt on ins wl over 1f out: no imp ins fnl f* **4/1**[2]

3300 **5** 3 ½ **Wee Charlie Castle (IRE)**[14] 3042 4-9-10 **61** JackMitchell 8 — 59
(G C H Chung) *mounted crse and taken down early: bhd and t.k.h: effrt 3f out: wnt 2nd briefly 2f out: wknd over 1f out* **9/1**

000 **6** 1 ½ **Dream Mountain**[8] 3217 4-8-10 **54** MJMurphy(7) 3 — 49
(Ms J S Doyle) *2nd tl led over 7f out: rdn and hdd 3f out: wknd 2f out* **20/1**

-000 **7** 4 **Wellington Hall (GER)**[136] 568 9-9-4 **55** MCGeran 4 — 44
(M Wigham) *cl up: rdn 3f out: sn btn* **7/1**

50-0 **8** 11 **Corviglia**[27] 2620 4-8-9 **46** KMay 5 — 17
(C E Longsdon) *led tl over 7f out: wknd over 3f out: eased fnl f: t.o* **33/1**

2m 32.92s (-1.47) **Going Correction** -0.15s/f (Stan) — **8** Ran SP% **115.1**

Speed ratings (Par 101):98,97,96,95,92 91,89,81

CSF £15.56 CT £50.63 TOTE £4.90: £1.30, £1.40, £1.70; EX 12.80 Trifecta £44.30 Pool: £428.52 - 6.86 winning units. Place 6 £7.81, Place 5 £4.66.

Owner Bellflower Racing Ltd **Bred** Richard Leonard **Trained** Alpraham, Cheshire

■ A winner on her 21st birthday for jockey Sophie Doyle.

FOCUS

A very modest apprentice handicap, in which they did not go a great pace early and a couple raced keenly as a result. The lead changed hands a few times and the form is modest.

T/Plt: £12.90 to a £1 stake. Pool: £44,344.40. 2,490.65 winning tickets. T/Qpdt: £2.40 to a £1 stake. Pool: £2,776.10. 838.10 winning tickets. IM

3430 NEWMARKET (JULY) (R-H)

Thursday, July 12

OFFICIAL GOING: Good to firm

Good ground that was quickening all the time, and there was an advantage throughout the day towards those who raced stands' side.

Wind: Fresh, across Weather: Overcast, with rain for the last

3458 BAHRAIN TROPHY (LISTED RACE) — 1m 5f

1:30 (1:33) (Class 1) 3-Y-O

£17,034 (£6,456; £3,231; £1,611; £807; £405) **Stalls** Centre

Form — RPR

-215 **1** **Tranquil Tiger**[21] 2789 3-9-0 101 RichardHughes 4 — 107
(H R A Cecil) *lw: a.p: chsd ldr over 5f out: led over 3f out: drvn out* **11/4**[1]

41 **2** ¾ **Wing Express (IRE)**[38] 2308 3-9-0 90 KerrinMcEvoy 2 — 106
(L M Cumani) *lw: chsd ldrs: rdn and n.m.r over 1f out: styd on* **5/1**[3]

0-32 **3** nk **Samuel**[48] 1998 3-9-0 92 EddieAhern 5 — 106
(J L Dunlop) *lw: hld up: rdn over 2f out: hdwy over 1f out: styd on* **9/1**

0115 **4** shd **Spice Route**[20] 2813 3-9-0 108 JamieSpencer 3 — 105
(M L W Bell) *hld up: hdwy over 2f out: sn swtchd rt: n.m.r fr over 1f out: kpt on* **3/1**[2]

3010 **5** 1 ½ **Halicarnassus (IRE)**[39] 2293 3-9-3 110 JHBowman 8 — 106
(M R Channon) *hld up: hdwy over 4f out: rdn and ev ch fr over 1f out: no ex wl ins fnl f* **11/2**

4320 **6** 6 **Duke Of Tuscany**[40] 2231 3-9-0 98 RyanMoore 7 — 94
(R Hannon) *prom: rdn over 2f out: wknd over 1f out* **7/1**

-460 **7** 2 ½ **Shimoni**[20] 2816 3-8-9 86 MartinDwyer 1 — 85
(W J Knight) *lw: chsd ldr over 7f: rdn over 3f out: wknd over 1f out* **33/1**

031 **8** 1 ¾ **Galianna (IRE)**[34] 2436 3-8-9 80 MJKinane 6 — 83
(Pat Eddery) *hld up: rdn over 3f out: wknd wl over 1f out* **20/1**

-314 **9** 20 **Baba Ganouge (IRE)**[12] 3081 3-8-9 83 KDarley 9 — 53
(B J Meehan) *lw: led over 9f: wknd 2f out* **50/1**

2m 42.11s (-9.89) — **9** Ran SP% **115.9**

CSF £16.62 TOTE £3.60: £1.50, £1.60, £2.20; EX 19.50 Trifecta £76.50 Pool: £754.70 - 7.00 winning units..

Owner K Abdulla **Bred** Juddmonte Farms Ltd **Trained** Newmarket, Suffolk

FOCUS

A good renewal of this staying Listed prize and well known St Leger trial. The form looks more solid than it often does, with the winner to his Royal Ascot form and the first four coming clear.

NOTEBOOK

Tranquil Tiger ◆, as expected, relished the step up in trip and showed a determined attitude to score. He was hanging somewhat in the home straight, perhaps suggesting he would ideally prefer an easier surface in the future, and still looked a little green. This imposing son of Selkirk has more to offer and looks worth stepping up in grade now to further test his St Leger credentials. However, his trainer considers him a likely Ebor type and, while he will probably go up a touch in the ratings for this, it should be noted connections won the race in 1998 with the filly Tuning, who ran off a mark of 101 there and had very similar credentials. (op 4-1)

Wing Express(IRE) ◆, winner of a Leicester maiden 38 days previously, stepped up again on that effort and ran a perfectly respectable race in this much higher grade. He is a relentless galloper and is the type his trainer tends to excel with, so providing he does not go up too much in the ratings for this, he could be a likely sort for the Melrose Handicap at York next month. (tchd 9-2 and 11-2)

Samuel ◆, another stepping up from maiden company, was doing his best work towards the finish and turned in by far his best effort to date. He has improved with every start this term, is still clearly learning his trade, and looks the one to take from the race with the immediate future in mind. He should not remain a maiden for long. (op 8-1 tchd 7-1)

Spice Route, a bit warm beforehand, looked a big threat when making up his ground from off the pace yet was done no favours when the winner shut the door on him as he tried to sneak past that rival on the rail. Surely he would have been better off making his challenge wide of the pack, but still he was not disgraced on this quicker surface and just ran out of stamina in the end over this extra furlong. He is not going to prove easy to place from his current rating, but the return to easier ground in the future can only help. Official explanation: trainer said colt failed to stay (op 2-1)

Halicarnassus(IRE), whose stable took this last year with Youmzain, held every chance under his penalty yet ran out of steam entering the final furlong and failed to convince he wants this far. A drop back in trip could pay off. (op 13-2 tchd 5-1)

3459 TNT JULY STKS (GROUP 2) (C&G) — 6f

2:00 (2:02) (Class 1) 2-Y-O

£39,746 (£15,064; £7,539; £3,759; £1,883; £945) **Stalls** Low

Form — RPR

11 **1** **Winker Watson**[21] 2785 2-9-1 0 JimmyFortune 1 — 116+
(P W Chapple-Hyam) *lw: s.i.s: hld up and bhd: hdwy over 1f out: rdn to ld nr fin* **11/4**[1]

1 **2** shd **River Proud (USA)**[28] 2600 2-8-12 0 TQuinn 7 — 111+
(P F I Cole) *chsd ldrs: rdn to ld and edgd rt ins fnl f: hdd nr fin* **3/1**[2]

3122 **3** 1 ½ **Swiss Franc**[23] 2732 2-8-12 0 TedDurcan 2 — 107+
(D R C Elsworth) *lw: hld up: hdwy over 1f out: rdn and swtchd lft ins fnl f: r.o* **5/1**[3]

210 **4** ½ **Dark Angel (IRE)**[23] 2737 2-8-12 0 MichaelHills 9 — 105
(B W Hills) *lw: led: rdn over 1f out: hdd and unable qck ins fnl f* **20/1**

10 **5** 1 ½ **Bobs Surprise**[23] 2732 2-8-12 0 RHills 5 — 100
(B W Hills) *lw: prom: rdn over 1f out: hmpd and wknd ins fnl f* **14/1**

324 **6** 1 ½ **Dream Eater (IRE)**[23] 2737 2-8-12 0 LPKeniry 12 — 96
(A M Balding) *trckd ldr: plld hrd: rdn over 1f out: wknd fnl f* **33/1**

106 **7** ½ **Fat Boy (IRE)**[23] 2737 2-8-12 0 RichardHughes 6 — 94
(R Hannon) *s.i.s: hld up: rdn over 2f out: nvr trbld ldrs* **33/1**

113 **8** ¾ **Spirit Of Sharjah (IRE)**[21] 2785 2-8-12 0 MJKinane 8 — 92
(Miss J Feilden) *trckd ldrs: rdn and ev ch over 1f out: wknd ins fnl f* **7/1**

11 **9** 1 ¾ **Gaspar Van Wittel (USA)**[27] 2618 2-8-12 0 JamieSpencer 4 — 87
(N A Callaghan) *hld up: rdn over 2f out: nt clr run over 1f out: n.d* **8/1**

11 **10** 1 ¼ **Spitfire**[43] 2151 2-8-12 0 RyanMoore 10 — 83
(J R Jenkins) *s.i.s: racd keenly: hdwy over 4f out: edgd rt and wknd over 1f out* **20/1**

20 **11** shd **Atheer Dubai (IRE)**[23] 2732 2-8-12 0 EddieAhern 11 — 82
(C E Brittain) *hld up: rdn over 2f out: no ch whn n.m.r over 1f out* **100/1**

1016 **12** 2 ½ **Carleton**[21] 2785 2-8-12 0 JHBowman 3 — 75
(M R Channon) *hld up: rdn over 2f out: sn wknd* **50/1**

21 **13** 2 ½ **King's Icon (IRE)**[34] 2424 2-8-12 0 MartinDwyer 13 — 67
(M P Tregoning) *prom: racd keenly: rdn over 2f out: wknd whn hmpd over 1f out* **14/1**

1m 11.56s (-1.79) **Going Correction** -0.05s/f (Good) — **13** Ran SP% **123.6**

Speed ratings (Par 106):109,108,106,106,104 102,101,100,98,96 96,93,89

CSF £10.61 TOTE £3.90: £1.50, £1.80, £2.30; EX 17.10 Trifecta £28.50 Pool: £1,158.06 - 28.80 winning units..

Owner The Comic Strip Heroes & Mrs J D Trotter **Bred** Mrs John Trotter **Trained** Newmarket, Suffolk

FOCUS

A strong renewal of this Group 2 contest and the winning time was very creditable, even for a race of this stature. The form looks solid rated through the sixth and seventh, among others, and the winner looks sure to be rated one of the leading juveniles at the end of the season.

NOTEBOOK

Winker Watson, the Norfolk Stakes winner, defied a 3lb penalty to justify favouritism, but only just. Having missed the break and been held up towards the back of the field, he needed every yard of this 6f to get in front, but it helped that the leaders set a decent pace and he was not put at a tactical disadvantage. The extra furlong certainly seemed to suit him and he picked up in taking style once Fortune got going on him. He looks set to take high rank amongst this season's juveniles and Group 1 races beckon, with the Prix Morny and Middle Park the obvious races for him. His pedigree suggests he will struggle to get a mile next year, but the bookmakers still have him as second-favourite, generally 10-1, in the ante-post market. (op 9-4)

River Proud(USA) ◆, who created a good impression when running away with a Newbury maiden on his debut, was strong in the market despite the huge rise in class. He did his connections proud, never far off the pace and only denied by the classy winner in the final strides. He looks sure to win in Group company before long, and he is being aimed at Goodwood's Vintage Stakes, which his stable won last year with their July Stakes winner Strategic Prince. (op 4-1)

Swiss Franc, runner-up in the Coventry Stakes, was held up towards the back of the field like the winner. He finished almost as well, but was forced to switch at a crucial moment inside the final furlong and lost a little momentum. Arguably, he prefers a bit more give in the ground, and it will not be a surprise to see him take on the winner again in France for the Prix Morny. (op 9-2 tchd 6-1 in a place)

Dark Angel(IRE) failed to run his race when fancied in the Windsor Castle Stakes last time, but his trainer was of the firm belief that this extra furlong would be very much in his favour. Considering that he set a good pace in front, he galloped on really well and put up a solid effort. On this evidence it looks as though he might even get 7f. (op 33-1)

Bobs Surprise, seventh in the Coventry, was neglected by Michael Hills in favour of Dark Angel, but there was not too much between them on the track, and a bump from Swiss Franc inside the final furlong did him no favours. (op 20-1)

Dream Eater(IRE), fourth in the Windsor Castle Stakes, looked sure to appreciate this extra furlong having finished with some purpose at Ascot. He did not help his chance by failing to settle, though, and weakened inside the last. He deserves a chance to get off the mark in a maiden before returning to Pattern company.
Fat Boy(IRE), not far behind Dream Eater at Ascot, appears to have run to a similar level here and helps set the level of the form.
Spirit Of Sharjah(IRE), third behind Winker Watson at Ascot, did not settle well enough on this occasion to have any chance of seeing out the extra furlong. (op 8-1)
Gaspar Van Wittel(USA) had made a good impression in winning his first two starts, but this was a step up in class for him and he was found out. It is, however, possible that the ground was faster than ideal. (op 10-1 tchd 12-1)
Spitfire, another coming here on the back of two wins in lesser company, was also a bit too keen in the early stages.

3460 KLEINWORT BENSON STKS (HERITAGE H'CAP) 1m 2f

2:35 (2:37) (Class 2) (0-105,104) 3-Y-O

£43,624 (£13,062; £6,531; £3,269; £1,631; £819) **Stalls** Centre

Form RPR
1230 **1** **Hearthstead Maison (IRE)**[20] [2816] 3-9-4 **104**............ GregFairley(3) 8 113
(M Johnston) *hld up: hdwy 6f out: led over 3f out: rdn over 1f out: styd on* **25/1**
2110 **2** *1 1/4* **Man Of Vision (USA)**[21] [2790] 3-8-4 **87**............ TPO'Shea 17 94+
(M R Channon) *lw: hld up: hdwy and nt clr run over 1f out: swtchd rt and r.o ins fnl f: nt rch wnr* **9/1**
1-30 **3** *1 3/4* **Ladies Best**[21] [2790] 3-8-8 **91**............ RyanMoore 15 94
(Sir Michael Stoute) *mid-div: hdwy over 2f out: rdn over 1f out: styd on same pce ins fnl f* **15/2**[3]
611 **4** *1/2* **Pipedreamer**[31] [2506] 3-8-10 **93**............ JimmyFortune 12 95
(J H M Gosden) *trckd ldrs: racd keenly: rdn over 1f out: no ex fnl f* **6/1**[2]
4540 **5** *shd* **Buccellati**[21] [2788] 3-8-1 **84**............ FrancisNorton 13 86
(A M Balding) *hld up: hdwy over 2f out: nt clr run over 1f out: nt rch ldrs* **10/1**
0-15 **6** *1/2* **Overrule (USA)**[68] [1476] 3-8-7 **90** ow1............ MJKinane 4 91
(J Noseda) *hld up: hdwy over 2f out: rdn over 1f out: edgd lft and no ex fnl f* **16/1**
-145 **7** *1/2* **Many Volumes (USA)**[47] [2042] 3-9-2 **99**............ RichardHughes 6 99+
(H R A Cecil) *stdd s: hld up: rdn: swtchd lft and hdwy over 1f out: no imp ins fnl f* **25/1**
-331 **8** *1/2* **Black Rock (IRE)**[26] [2674] 3-8-3 **86**............ RichardMullen 11 85
(M A Jarvis) *lw: chsd ldrs: rdn over 2f out: edgd lft and wknd ins fnl f* **10/1**
1-42 **9** *1/2* **King Charles**[45] [2092] 3-8-7 **90**............ JamieSpencer 9 88
(E A L Dunlop) *prom: rdn over 2f out: wknd fnl f* **16/1**
-331 **10** *shd* **Northern Jem**[53] [1863] 3-8-2 **85**............ JohnEgan 20 83
(G G Margarson) *hld up: hdwy over 2f out: rdn: nt clr run and hung lft over 1f out: wknd fnl f* **8/1**
1-55 **11** *3* **Ekhtiaar**[21] [2788] 3-8-8 **91**............ RHills 10 83
(J H M Gosden) *lw: hld up: hdwy over 3f out: rdn and wknd over 1f out* **9/2**[1]
0120 **12** *1* **Noticeable (IRE)**[21] [2790] 3-8-4 **87**............ JoeFanning 16 77
(M R Channon) *hld up in tch: racd keenly: rdn over 2f out: hung lft and wknd over 1f out* **33/1**
0030 **13** *1/2* **Golden Dagger (IRE)**[21] [2790] 3-8-3 **86**............(p) DO'Donohoe 1 75
(K A Ryan) *chsd ldrs over 7f* **66/1**
3-12 **14** *3 1/2* **Gremlin**[55] [1810] 3-8-2 **85**............ MartinDwyer 5 67
(A King) *hld up: hdwy over 3f out: wknd 2f out* **20/1**
6-5 **15** *5* **Vorteeva (USA)**[48] [2001] 3-8-5 **95**............ KellyHarrison(7) 7 67
(K R Burke) *hld up: bhd fnl 4f* **100/1**
4-21 **16** *2* **Bid For Glory**[29] [2578] 3-8-12 **95**............ TedDurcan 18 63
(H J Collingridge) *lw: hld up: rdn over 3f out: bhd whn eased over 1f out* **10/1**
1230 **17** *hd* **Dubai Twilight**[21] [2788] 3-8-9 **92**............ MichaelHills 19 59
(B W Hills) *hld up: rdn and wknd over 2f out* **14/1**
4300 **18** *2 1/2* **Habalwatan (IRE)**[21] [2789] 3-8-12 **95**............(b) EddieAhern 2 57
(C E Brittain) *led over 6f: wknd over 2f out* **50/1**
1252 **19** *6* **In Safe Hands (IRE)**[14] [3028] 3-8-9 **92**............ KDarley 14 42
(C G Cox) *mid-div: wknd over 2f out* **25/1**

2m 3.37s (-3.07) **Going Correction** -0.05s/f (Good) **19** Ran SP% **134.7**
Speed ratings (Par 106):110,109,107,107,107 106,106,105,105,105 103,102,101,99,95 93,93,91,86
CSF £241.25 CT £1906.24 TOTE £31.60: £4.40, £2.70, £2.00, £2.00; EX 328.30 Trifecta £925.30 Pool: £1,954.98 - 1.50 winning units..
Owner Hearthstead Homes Ltd **Bred** T Nakata **Trained** Middleham Moor, N Yorks

FOCUS
A very decent handicap run at a sound pace. While it was slightly surprising that the winner was able to win off a mark of 104, the form in behind looks solid so the race should produce its fair share of winners.

NOTEBOOK
Hearthstead Maison(IRE), dropping back in distance and running in handicap company for the first time since beating his stablemate Boscobel on the Rowley Mile in May, bounced back to form in great style, picking up well off the solid pace and galloping on strongly for a decisive win. This performance confirms that he is a Pattern-class performer and that this trip is probably his optimum. (op 20-1)
Man Of Vision(USA) did too much early at Ascot and ran better this time under more patient tactics. He got less than a clear run when asked to challenge, and flew once he hit the rising ground, but the line was always going to come too soon. He clearly has the ability to win a decent handicap, and when ridden this way, he should have no trouble getting 1m4f. (op 11-1 tchd 8-1)
Ladies Best, who did not get the best of runs at Ascot, looked likely to appreciate the drop back to 1m2f, and he ran a solid race in defeat. His two wins to date have come on easier ground but he is clearly fairly versatile on that score. (op 7-1 tchd 8-1 in a place)
Pipedreamer, who got a bit warm beforehand, raced far too keen for his own good, so it is to his credit that he kept on so well for fourth. He remains lightly raced and has the ability to rate higher as he gains further experience. (op 11-2)
Buccellati, steadily progressive before finding the drop back to a mile too short at Royal Ascot, returned to his consistent best, and only just missed out on a placing. He remains vulnerable to more progressive rivals, though. (op 12-1)
Overrule(USA), whose rider put up 1lb overweight, briefly looked a threat towards the far side as they raced towards the final furlong, but he could not go through with his effort. It is possible that he was racing on slightly slower ground on that part of the track. Another who does not have that many miles on the clock, he can do better. (op 14-1)
Many Volumes(USA) is now on a pretty stiff mark, and he seemed to have a task on his plate reversing form with Hearthstead Maison based on his previous two starts. That indeed proved the case, but at least he is another peg on which to hang the form. (op 20-1)
Black Rock(IRE), who finally got off the mark in a four-runner affair at Sandown last time, does not appear to be particularly well handicapped at present, but he could benefit from a drop back to a mile.
King Charles, who bumped into a progressive filly at Redcar last time, was racing off 3lb higher, and simply looks to be held off a mark of 90.
Northern Jem did not get the clearest of runs inside the final two furlongs, but he hung under pressure when asked to challenge, and perhaps he needs easier ground. (op 11-1)
Ekhtiaar ◆ was a well-backed favourite on the back of his fifth in the Britannia, but he was returning to a longer distance and it appeared to find him out. He travelled like the winner to two furlongs out but then fell in a hole. Official explanation: jockey said gelding failed to stay 1m 2f (op 7-1 tchd 15-2 in a place)
Noticeable(IRE), just like at Ascot, failed to settle in the early stages, and he paid the price.
Vorteeva(USA) Official explanation: trainer said gelding finished distressed

3461 PRINCESS OF WALES'S WBX.COM STKS (GROUP 2) 1m 4f

3:10 (3:15) (Class 1) 3-Y-O+

£51,102 (£14,530; £14,530; £4,833; £2,421; £1,215) **Stalls** Centre

Form RPR
5-45 **1** **Papal Bull**[42] [2182] 4-9-2 111............ RyanMoore 8 119
(Sir Michael Stoute) *hld up: rdn over 3f out: hdwy over 2f out: hung lft over 1f out: rdn to ld and hung rt ins fnl f: styd on* **11/1**
-250 **2** *2 1/2* **Laverock (IRE)**[103] [861] 5-9-7 118............ KerrinMcEvoy 3 119
(Saeed Bin Suroor) *hld up: hdwy over 2f out: rdn over 1f out: styd on* **12/1**
6-24 **2** *dht* **Shahin (USA)**[18] [2907] 4-9-2 109............(v[1]) MartinDwyer 4 114
(M P Tregoning) *led: hdd 1/2-way: led again over 3f out: rdn and edgd lft over 1f out: hdd and no ex ins fnl f* **25/1**
1142 **4** *hd* **Lucarno (USA)**[20] [2813] 3-8-3 113............ FrancisNorton 9 114
(J H M Gosden) *lw: chsd ldr tl led 1/2-way: hdd over 3f out: rdn and edgd lft fr over 1f out: styd on same pce* **10/3**[2]
6311 **5** *5* **Ivy Creek (USA)**[18] [2907] 4-9-2 110............ SteveDrowne 11 106
(G Wragg) *s.i.s: hld up: rdn over 2f out: n.d* **7/1**[3]
-335 **6** *1/2* **Foxhaven**[18] [2907] 5-9-2 110............ JimCrowley 12 105
(P R Chamings) *chsd ldrs: rdn over 3f out: wknd over 1f out* **50/1**
-130 **7** *2* **Steppe Dancer (IRE)**[41] [2216] 4-9-2 105............ EddieAhern 7 102
(D J Coakley) *lw: s.i.s: hld up: hdwy over 4f out: rdn and wknd over 1f out* **25/1**
4-23 **8** *5* **Mashaahed**[42] [2182] 4-9-2 112............ RHills 6 94
(B W Hills) *trckd ldrs tl wknd over 2f out* **14/1**
-524 **9** *6* **Admiral's Cruise (USA)**[19] [2856] 5-9-2 112............ JimmyFortune 5 84
(B J Meehan) *s.i.s: hld up: hdwy over 3f out: rdn: hung lft and wknd 2f out* **16/1**
0-10 **10** *9* **Sixties Icon**[41] [2210] 4-9-7 122............ JMurtagh 10 75
(J Noseda) *lw: hld up in tch: rdn and wknd over 2f out* **7/4**[1]
-500 **11** *16* **Corriolanus (GER)**[139] [545] 7-9-2 0............ RichardHughes 1 44
(A M Balding) *hld up: bhd fnl 3f* **100/1**
1214 **12** *20* **Eradicate (IRE)**[21] [2790] 3-8-3 100............ JoeFanning 2 12
(M Johnston) *sn prom: rdn over 3f out: wknd over 2f out* **8/1**

2m 28.73s (-4.18) **Going Correction** -0.05s/f (Good)
WFA 3 from 4yo+ 13lb **12** Ran SP% **122.3**
Speed ratings (Par 115):111,109,109,109,105 105,104,100,96,90 80,66
PL: Papal Bull £2.80, Laverock £3.40, Shahin £7.70; EX: Laverock £80.40, Shahin £102.50; CSF: Laverock £67.97 Shahin £132.54 TOTE £12.50 TRIFECTA Not won..
Owner Mrs J Magnier, D Smith & M Tabor **Bred** B H And C F D Simpson **Trained** Newmarket, Suffolk

FOCUS
This was not strongly run and resulted in a modest winning time for a Group 2 race. Favourite Sixties Icon disappointed, and it has been rated around Laverock, who has plenty of Group-race form, including at the top level, and the fourth to his Derby mark.

NOTEBOOK
Papal Bull had not looked straightforward in his previous two starts this season, but he has always had the talent to be a threat at this sort of level, and while he once again looked far from an easy ride, coming off the bridle a fair way out before running on and then hanging both ways once seeing daylight, his rider did a great job of getting him home in front. He will probably get further, and he might be worth trying out in one of the Cup races. (op 10-1 tchd 12-1)
Laverock(IRE), who was last seen in this country finishing fifth in last year's International Stakes at York, has victories in Group 1 company in France (beating Manduro no less) and Italy to his name, and he had run with credit in Dubai in the spring. Saddled with a 5lb penalty for his successes at the top level, he looked to face a stiff task, but he ran with credit, especially as the ground might have been on the fast side for him. (op 16-1)
Shahin(USA), like the winner, is not the easiest of rides, but he was visored for the first time here and, in a race in which nothing else really wanted to go on, he found himself being able to dictate a fairly steady early gallop. Quickening from the front, he looked to have his rivals in trouble two furlongs out, but in the end the winner proved too classy. This was a sound effort, and connections are apparently considering a Cup campaign for him now. (op 16-1)
Lucarno(USA), who only made his debut on 21st April, has had a few hard races of late and was having his sixth start of the campaign, so it is to his credit that he ran as well as he did. Benefiting from not being too far off the pace in a race not run at a strong gallop, he had every chance in the closing stages, although he did make his challenge on what was arguably slightly slower ground towards the far side. (op 4-1 tchd 9-2)
Ivy Creek(USA), who got warm beforehand, has been making up for lost time this year, scoring in good style in Listed company on his last two starts, and he deserved another chance to prove himself in Group company. The ground had dried up more than he would have probably wanted, though, and he is a hold-up performer seen at his best in a race run at a proper gallop. He did not get that here and was not seen at his best. (op 9-2)
Foxhaven has been held in lesser company this year and faced a tough task on all known form. He ran a creditable race in the circumstances, but he looks likely to remain a difficult horse to place.
Steppe Dancer(IRE), who ran his best race to date when third to Ask and Scorpion at Chester, was well enough positioned with three furlongs to run but could not pick up.
Mashaahed, who was reshod at the start, is at his best over 1m2f and is not really up to winning at Group 2 level. (tchd 16-1)
Admiral's Cruise(USA) came into the race with form figures at Newmarket (both courses) reading 210112, but he disappointed, even allowing for the steady gallop being against him.
Sixties Icon failed to give his running at Epsom last time but the punters gave him another chance and sent him off a well-backed 7-4 shot. He disappointed again, though, and it would appear that he has a problem of some description. The vet said that the colt was in distress afterwards. Official explanation: vet said colt finished distressed (op 9-4 tchd 13-8)
Corriolanus(GER) Official explanation: jockey said horse had no more to give
Eradicate(IRE), whose trainer won this race last year with another three-year-old in Soapy Danger, was sent off a surprisingly short price given that he was beaten in a handicap last time and was taking on proven Group-class performers here. Nevertheless, this was too bad to be true, as he raced wide and was too keen in the early stages, and as a result he hit the wall with three furlongs to run.

3462 TURF ITALIA EBF NOVICE STKS 6f

3:45 (3:45) (Class 2) 2-Y-O **£9,715** (£2,890; £1,444; £721) **Stalls** Low

Form RPR
012 **1** **Spanish Bounty**[26] [2650] 2-9-5 0............ EddieAhern 10 90+
(J G Portman) *chsd ldr tl led over 3f out: drvn out* **14/1**
2 *3/4* **Captain Brilliance (USA)** 2-8-8 0............ MJKinane 2 77+
(J Noseda) *str: w'like: scope: hld up: hdwy over 1f out: r.o* **7/4**[1]

	3	1 3/4	**Hunt The Bottle (IRE)** 2-8-8 0 ... MichaelHills 8 (B W Hills) *w'like: lengthy: s.s: hdwy over 1f out: r.o* **18/1**		72+
4120	4	nk	**Aaim To Storm (USA)**[23] 2732 2-9-0 0 ... JHBowman 5 (M R Channon) *led: hdd over 3f out: rdn over 1f out: styd on same pce* **8/1**		77
10	5	1/2	**Lindoro**[23] 2732 2-9-2 0 ... AdamKirby 9 (W R Swinburn) *swtg: hld up: nt clr run over 1f out: r.o ins fnl f: nt trble ldrs* **7/1**		77
	6	1/2	**Harald Bluetooth (IRE)** 2-8-8 0 ... JamieSpencer 11 (J R Fanshawe) *hld up: hdwy over 2f out: rdn and edgd lft over 1f out: no ex ins fnl f* **13/2**[3]		68+
100	7	nk	**Feeling Proud (USA)**[43] 2134 2-9-0 0 ... JimmyQuinn 1 (Jane Chapple-Hyam) *chsd ldrs: rdn over 1f out: no ex* **25/1**		73
	8	1/2	**City Of The Kings (IRE)** 2-8-8 0 ... RichardHughes 6 (R Hannon) *w'like: prom: rdn over 1f out: styd on same pce* **11/2**[2]		65+
	9	hd	**Traphalgar (IRE)** 2-8-8 0 ... TQuinn 14 (P F I Cole) *w'like: chsd ldrs: hung lft 2f out: wknd fnl f* **20/1**		65+
01	10	3/4	**Ellemujie**[29] 2569 2-9-2 0 ... JimmyFortune 7 (D K Ivory) *prom over 4f* **14/1**		73+
	11	4	**Tasleya** 2-8-8 0 ... RHills 3 (B W Hills) *w'like: s.s: hld up: wknd over 1f out* **9/1**		50+

1m 14.33s (0.98) **Going Correction** -0.05s/f (Good) **11** Ran SP% **125.9**
Speed ratings (Par 100):91,90,87,87,86 85,85,84,84,83 78
CSF £41.53 TOTE £13.00: £3.00, £1.50, £3.60; EX 64.00.
Owner The Farleigh Court Racing Partnership **Bred** Farleigh Court Racing Partnership **Trained** Compton, Berks

FOCUS
A fair novice stakes. However, it produced a moderate winning time for a race like this, due to the ordinary early pace, and the form should be treated with a degree of caution.

NOTEBOOK
Spanish Bounty, warm and free to post, improved again on his latest effort at Bath and scored in resolute fashion under his penalty. This fast ground seems to suit him particularly well, but he looks to need all of this trip now. It would not be a surprise to see him upped to Listed class after this. Whether he is up to that sort of company remains to be seen, however. (op 16-1)
Captain Brilliance(USA) ◆, a $160,000 purchase and bred to make his mark at this trip as a two-year-old, was very well touted for this racecourse bow and proved very popular in the betting ring. The penny did not drop with him until halfway and he got going too late, but he showed he has an engine by finishing best of all from off the pace. It is likely he would have won with a stronger early pace and he will be hard to beat next time with this experience under his belt. (op 15-8 tchd 9-4)
Hunt The Bottle(IRE), bred to be effective over this trip at two, was not helped by a sluggish start and was another who would have enjoyed a stronger early pace. He kept on nicely inside the final furlong and looks sure to improve for this debut experience. (op 20-1 tchd 16-1)
Aaim To Storm(USA), the most experienced runner in the field, proved at an advantage in being up with the modest early pace and was put in his place when the tempo increased. He was below his previous best here, but still confirmed his Coventry form with the fifth. (op 9-1)
Lindoro, outclassed when behind the fourth in the Coventry last time, got worked up before the race and then ran keenly through the early parts due to the ordinary pace. He is better than this, but is clearly still learning his trade. (tchd 15-2)
Harald Bluetooth(IRE) ◆, an athletic type who cost 525,000euros, briefly threatened to play a part in the finish yet failed to sustain his effort when it really mattered. He is bred to stay further, would have been seen in a better light off a stronger pace, and deserves to be ridden more positively next time. (tchd 6-1 and 7-1)
Traphalgar(IRE) showed plenty of knee action on the way to post. (op 14-1)
Ellemujie got a bit warm beforehand. (op 25-1)
Tasleya, a well-bred 180,000gns purchase, lost his chance after missing the break and was always playing catch-up thereafter. (tchd 10-1)

3463 XPLOR CONDITIONS STKS 1m
4:20 (4:21) (Class 2) 3-Y-0
£12,464 (£3,732; £1,866; £934; £466; £234) **Stalls** Low

Form				RPR
2604	1		**Traffic Guard (USA)**[22] 2752 3-8-12 105 ... (p) JohnEgan 12 (J S Moore) *lw: racd centre: chsd ldr: overall ldr over 3f out: rdn out* **9/2**[2]	105
130-	2	1 1/2	**Drumfire (IRE)**[264] 6104 3-9-6 103 ... JoeFanning 11 (M Johnston) *racd centre: hld up: hdwy over 2f out: sn rdn: styd on* **13/2**[3]	110
615-	3	1 3/4	**Mesbaah (IRE)**[306] 5176 3-8-12 96 ... RHills 7 (M A Jarvis) *racd centre: led that gp tl over 3f out: outpcd over 2f out: styd on ins fnl f* **14/1**	98
133	4	3/4	**Lone Wolfe**[35] 2400 3-8-12 82 ... JimmyFortune 9 (Jane Chapple-Hyam) *racd centre: chsd ldrs: rdn over 1f out: no ex ins fnl f* **20/1**	96
130-	5	1 1/2	**Cumin (USA)**[284] 5714 3-8-7 100 ... MichaelHills 8 (B W Hills) *racd centre: hld up: hdwy over 2f out: sn rdn: edgd rt and wknd ins fnl f* **15/2**	88
0340	6	hd	**Jo'Burg (USA)**[21] 2788 3-8-12 97 ... RyanMoore 1 (Mrs A J Perrett) *racd centre: chsd ldrs: rdn and hung lft over 1f out: wknd fnl f* **12/1**	92
-331	7	3	**Eddie Jock (IRE)**[21] 2788 3-9-3 111 ... JamieSpencer 6 (M L W Bell) *racd centre: hld up: hdwy u.p over 1f out: wknd and eased ins fnl f* **5/4**[1]	90
300	8	6	**Norisan**[21] 2788 3-8-12 95 ... (t) RichardHughes 4 (R Hannon) *racd far side: chsd ldr of that pair tl wknd over 1f out* **33/1**	71
22-1	9	6	**First Buddy**[29] 2581 3-8-12 82 ... NCallan 10 (W J Haggas) *racd far side: led that pair tl rdn and hung rt 3f out: wknd 2f out* **16/1**	58
-002	10	1/2	**Go On Be A Tiger (USA)**[48] 2001 3-8-12 92 ... TPO'Shea 2 (M R Channon) *racd alone stands' side: overall ldr tl hdd over 3f out: wknd over 1f out* **20/1**	56

1m 38.47s (-1.96) **Going Correction** -0.05s/f (Good) **10** Ran SP% **120.4**
Speed ratings (Par 106):107,105,103,103,101 101,98,92,86,85
CSF £34.12 TOTE £5.40: £1.90, £2.50, £4.90; EX 30.90.
Owner Mrs Fitri Hay **Bred** F Penn And John R Penn **Trained** Upper Lambourn, Berks

FOCUS
Rather muddling form, with the field spread across the track. The winner did not need to run to his best, and although the second and fourth looked to improve the form ought to be treated with caution.

NOTEBOOK
Traffic Guard(USA), fourth in the Group 3 Jersey Stakes at Royal Ascot on his previous outing, ran out a decisive winner on this drop in class and step back up to 1m. His stable are back in decent form again now and he has no doubt been improved for the recent application of cheekpieces. On his day he is Group class, and this now looks to be his optimum trip. His trainer outlined a plan that includes two races in September on the Polytrack in the US before going back to the Dubai carnival next year. (tchd 5-1)
Drumfire(IRE) ◆, who looked fit, turned in a very pleasing return to action under his 8lb penalty and was keeping on stoutly towards the finish. His action suggests he ideally needs an easier surface and he should come on a bundle for the run. He looks ready to tackle a longer trip and there could be a valuable prize within his compass before too long. (op 15-2 tchd 8-1 in a place and 6-1 in another)
Mesbaah(IRE), gelded during the off season, looked fit and was another to register a pleasing return to the track, keeping on steadily inside the final furlong under a considerate ride. He proved free through the early parts, but that was probably due to it being his first run of the season and it would not be a surprise to see him do better as he steps up in distance. Official explanation: jockey said gelding ran too freely (op 12-1 tchd 16-1)
Lone Wolfe faced a difficult task at the weights and, holding every chance, posted a personal-best effort in defeat. His official rating will likely shoot up as a result of this, but he is lightly raced and there is little reason to think it was a fluke.
Cumin(USA) left the clear impression she would come on for this seasonal bow and can be expected to prove sharper next time. However, she will not be easy to place from her official mark. (op 8-1)
Jo'Burg(USA), a bit warm beforehand, continues to struggle this term and remains one to avoid. (tchd 14-1)
Eddie Jock(IRE), rightly popular in the betting ring after his success under top weight in the Britannia last time, simply failed to spark in this smaller field and was never travelling. This was the first time he has finished out of the frame since winning at two and something may have been amiss. Official explanation: jockey said gelding never travelled (op 6-4 tchd 13-8)
Norisan Official explanation: jockey said colt had no more to give

3464 VOUTE SALES H'CAP 5f
4:55 (4:55) (Class 3) (0-95,93) 3-Y-0+ **£9,715** (£2,890; £1,444; £721) **Stalls** Low

Form				RPR
3220	1		**Moorhouse Lad**[23] 2733 4-10-0 93 ... JamieSpencer 12 (B Smart) *swtg: b.hind: chsd ldr: led over 1f out: rdn out* **7/2**[1]	106
1150	2	nk	**Turn On The Style**[13] 3050 5-9-11 90 ... (b) JimmyFortune 13 (J Balding) *chsd ldrs: rdn and edgd lft over 1f out: r.o* **15/2**[3]	102
320-	3	1 1/4	**Judd Street**[243] 6445 5-10-0 93 ... StephenCarson 7 (Eve Johnson Houghton) *chsd ldrs: rdn over 1f out: styd on* **11/1**	100
0046	4	nk	**Curtail (IRE)**[12] 3080 4-9-5 84 ... TomEaves 17 (I Semple) *hld up: nt clr run over 1f out: r.o ins fnl f: nt rch ldrs* **12/1**	90
0532	5	nk	**Forest Dane**[25] 2688 7-9-4 83 ... JohnEgan 4 (Mrs N Smith) *hld up: hdwy u.p over 1f out: styd on* **12/1**	88
1060	6	nk	**Harry Up**[33] 2463 6-9-8 87 ... NCallan 3 (K A Ryan) *led over 3f: no ex ins fnl f* **25/1**	91
5-20	7	nk	**Loch Verdi**[40] 2234 4-9-2 86 ... WilliamBuick(5) 2 (A M Balding) *chsd ldrs: hung lft 1/2-way: sn rdn: styd on same pce fnl f* **8/1**	89
0100	8	nk	**Dig Deep (IRE)**[29] 2566 5-9-4 83 ... EddieAhern 10 (W J Haggas) *lw: hld up: running on whn hmpd ins fnl f: n.d* **15/2**[3]	85
-000	9	1/2	**Woodcote (IRE)**[48] 1986 5-10-0 93 ... (be1) KDarley 16 (C G Cox) *hld up: hdwy 1/2-way: rdn and edgd lft over 1f out: no ex* **12/1**	93
1400	10	nk	**Magic Glade**[12] 3080 8-9-9 88 ... RichardThomas 6 (Tom Dascombe) *sn pushed along in rr: running on whn hmpd ins fnl f: nt trble ldrs* **33/1**	87
4200	11	hd	**Handsome Cross (IRE)**[33] 2463 6-9-7 86 ... SilvestreDeSousa 14 (D Nicholls) *chsd ldrs: rdn over 1f out: wknd ins fnl f* **10/1**	84
1303	12	2 1/2	**Distinctly Game**[104] 828 5-9-8 87 ... DO'Donohoe 15 (K A Ryan) *mid-div: hdwy 1/2-way: rdn over 1f out: sn wknd* **16/1**	76
0104	13	nk	**Highland Warrior**[9] 3197 8-8-13 78 ... MickyFenton 1 (P T Midgley) *s.i.s: n.d* **40/1**	66
5000	14	2 1/2	**Matsunosuke**[23] 2733 5-8-9 74 oh1 ... RyanMoore 5 (A B Coogan) *chsd ldrs over 3f* **11/2**[2]	53
0300	15	3 1/2	**Lethal**[12] 3104 4-9-8 87 ... MartinDwyer 9 (D K Ivory) *chsd ldrs 3f: eased ins fnl f* **20/1**	53
45-6	16	3/4	**Noddledoddle (IRE)**[10] 3163 3-8-1 74 oh24 ... (t) DominicFox(3) 8 (J Ryan) *sn outpcd* **100/1**	38

58.37 secs (-1.19) **Going Correction** -0.05s/f (Good)
WFA 3 from 4yo+ 5lb **16** Ran SP% **133.6**
Speed ratings (Par 107):107,106,104,104,103 103,102,102,101,100 100,96,96,92,86 85
CSF £30.80 CT £284.95 TOTE £5.00: £1.90, £2.20, £3.80, £3.90; EX 38.00 Place 6 £357.57, Place 5 £158.68.
Owner Ron Hull **Bred** P Onslow **Trained** Hambleton, N Yorks

FOCUS
A competitive sprint handicap, run at a strong pace, and the form is solid. The first pair finished nicely clear of the pack.

NOTEBOOK
Moorhouse Lad, who posted a career-best when outclassed in the King's Stand at the Royal Meeting, was given his usual positive ride and was always doing enough to repel the runner-up at the business end. This success was much deserved and it should have served his confidence well. (op 5-1)
Turn On The Style, despite playing up at the start, enjoyed the return to a sounder surface and showed his true colours with a narrow defeat. He was nicely clear in second and evidently has a similar race within his compass on turf from this mark. (op 8-1)
Judd Street, having his first outing since last November, had previously won first time up the last two years and was nibbled at in the betting ring. He ran a perfectably respectable race, keeping on well inside the final furlong, and cleary retains his ability. However, for a horse that has such a decent record when fresh it remains to be seen if he will now build on this and he remains 10lb higher than his last winning mark. (op 12-1)
Curtail(IRE) was doing his best work towards the finish and would have been a little closer with a clearer run nearing the final furlong. He is on a two-year losing run, but may just get closer to ending that drought when upped to 6f. (tchd 14-1)
Forest Dane was another noted doing his best work towards the finish on this drop back to the minimum trip. He really needs to be ridden more positively over this distance, but remains in decent form and helps to set the level of this form.
Harry Up showed up well enough on the far rail under his usual front-running ride, but not that surprisingly proved vulnerable up the rising finish.
Loch Verdi did not help her rider by hanging left from halfway, but still posted a much better effort in defeat. (op 13-2)
Dig Deep(IRE) was done no favours when hampered inside the final furlong and can be rated better than the bare form. This was just about his most encouraging effort on turf since winning at Newbury in 2005. (op 11-1 tchd 7-1)
Woodcote(IRE), a bit warm beforehand, failed to raise his game for the application of different headgear and again looked tricky. He probably also needs some respite from the Handicapper.
Handsome Cross(IRE), second in this event last year from a 1lb lower mark, saw too much daylight from his high draw and proved one paced when it mattered. He is very hard to catch right, but is capable of better than this on his day. (op 9-1)
Matsunosuke, who took this race last year from a 1lb lower mark, was edgy beforehand. He has not really been in the same sort of form this time around and ideally needs more cover in his races. (op 5-1)
Lethal was very edgy going to the start. Official explanation: jockey said saddle slipped
T/Jkpt: Not won. T/Plt: £679.90 to a £1 stake. Pool: £159,924.95. 171.70 winning tickets. T/Qpdt: £161.70 to a £1 stake. Pool: £8,260.35. 37.80 winning tickets. CR

2575 NOTTINGHAM (L-H)

Thursday, July 12

OFFICIAL GOING: Soft (heavy patches on straight course; 7.1)

The meeting on the previous Saturday was lost to waterlogging. After a storm and 6mm rain before racing 'soft, heavy patches in the home straight'.

Wind: Almost nil Weather: Fine and sunny

3465 BET NOW AT WBX.COM MAIDEN AUCTION STKS 6f 15y

6:40 (6:41) (Class 5) 2-Y-O £3,238 (£963; £481; £240) Stalls High

Form RPR

35 1 **Hansinger (IRE)**[31] 2510 2-9-2 0 ChrisCatlin 9 77+
(B I Case) *chsd ldrs: rdn to ld appr fnl f: forged clr* 11/4[1]

0 2 5 **Jastaanhi**[24] 2717 2-7-13 0 ColinHaddon(5) 4 50
(J A Pickering) *led tl appr fnl f: no ch w wnr* 80/1

40 3 1 **Sawpit Sunshine (IRE)**[15] 2977 2-8-5 0 MarcHalford(3) 11 51
(J L Spearing) *in rr: swtchd outside after 1f: hdwy 3f out: kpt on wl fnl f* 28/1

6 4 hd **Greystoke Prince**[45] 2086 2-9-2 0 AdamKirby 1 58
(W R Swinburn) *mid-div: hdwy over 2f out: styd on fnl f* 7/1[3]

5 nk **Farsighted** 2-8-6 0 HayleyTurner 5 51+
(J M P Eustace) *s.i.s: hdwy on ins over 2f out: nt clr run on inner jst ins fnl f: styd on wl towards fin* 16/1

053 6 1 **Bazguy**[31] 2510 2-9-2 0 NeilPollard 2 55
(P D Evans) *chsd ldr: wknd fnl f* 4/1[2]

7 3 **Gipsy Prince** 2-8-13 0 JimmyQuinn 6 43+
(M G Quinlan) *s.i.s: sme hdwy 2f out: nvr nr ldrs* 10/1

0040 8 3 **Una Auroraborealis**[20] 2812 2-7-13 0 LukeMorris(5) 10 25
(J Ryan) *chsd ldrs: wknd 2f out* 11/1

9 19 **Barbossa** 2-8-9 0 VHalliday 3 —
(A J McCabe) *s.i.s: sn prom: lost pl over 2f out* 28/1

03 10 1 3/4 **Kintyre Lass (IRE)**[19] 2876 2-8-4 0 AdrianMcCarthy 8 —
(B R Millman) *mid-div: lost pl over 2f out* 11/1

6 11 shd **Mr Lu**[45] 2071 2-8-9 0 DeanMcKeown 13 —
(G A Swinbank) *prom: lost pl over 2f out* 9/1

000 12 14 **Virtual Paddy**[33] 2443 2-8-11 0 DaleGibson 12 —
(M Blanshard) *in rr: bhd fnl 2f* 66/1

13 3 1/2 **Oronsay** 2-8-6 0 JamesDoyle 7 —
(B R Millman) *s.i.s: in rr: bhd fnl 2f* 25/1

1m 19.3s (4.30) **Going Correction** +0.575s/f (Yiel) 13 Ran SP% **114.3**

Speed ratings (Par 94):94,87,86,85,85 84,80,76,50,48 48,29,24

CSF £279.55 TOTE £3.70: £1.10, £12.30, £6.90; EX 271.50.

Owner Lovely Bubbly Racing **Bred** Tom Radley **Trained** Edgcote, Northants

FOCUS

They raced in one group towards the stands' side. A weak maiden auction race but the winner did his job well and could be underestimated.

NOTEBOOK

Hansinger(IRE), out of luck at Windsor, has a pronounced knee action and proved suited by the testing conditions. His rider left nothing to chance. (op 5-2 tchd 3-1)

Jastaanhi showed a lot more than on her debut three weeks earlier but in the end the winner ran right away from her. (op 100-1)

Sawpit Sunshine(IRE), lightly made and sweating up badly beforehand, was drawn two off the rail yet made her way to the wide outside. She was putting in her best work at the finish and seller or claimer over seven looks a likely option.

Greystoke Prince, an April foal, was the biggest in the line-up but he looks immature as yet. Staying on in his own time at the death, he looks a likely type for a nursery over further later in the year. (op 8-1 tchd 6-1)

Farsighted, a March foal, is a close-coupled, good-bodied filly. After a tardy start and left short of room on the inner, she finished with quite a flourish. This will have taught her plenty.

Bazguy, two places ahead of the winner at Windsor, was racing on much more testing ground and he did not get home this time. (op 3-1)

Kintyre Lass(IRE) Official explanation: jockey said filly was unsuited by the soft (heavy patches) ground

Mr Lu Official explanation: jockey said colt hung left-handed throughout

3466 JOIN WBX.COM NOW FOR £150 FREE BETS FILLIES' H'CAP 6f 15y

7:10 (7:10) (Class 4) (0-80,74) 3-Y-O+ £5,505 (£1,637; £818; £408) Stalls High

Form RPR

4234 1 **Shes Minnie**[10] 3158 4-9-13 73 FergusSweeney 8 81
(J G M O'Shea) *hld up in rr: hdwy over 2f out: led 1f out: hld on wl* 9/1

301 2 1/2 **Pick A Nice Name**[10] 3158 5-9-5 70 6ex MichaelJStainton(5) 5 76
(R M Whitaker) *trckd ldrs: t.k.h: led over 2f out tl 1f out: no ex last 75yds* 11/4[1]

434 3 1 **Goodbye**[19] 2881 3-9-6 72 DeanMcKeown 3 75
(G A Swinbank) *trckd ldrs: t.k.h: kpt on same pce fnl f* 11/2[3]

2314 4 shd **Mugeba**[7] 3247 6-8-12 58 (tp) AdamKirby 4 61
(Miss Gay Kelleway) *dwlt: in rr: hdwy and swtchd outside over 1f out: styd on wl towards fin* 11/2[3]

-02 5 1 1/4 **Joyeaux**[9] 3184 5-8-12 58 (v) DavidAllan 1 57
(J Hetherton) *trckd ldrs: kpt on same pce appr fnl f* 7/2[2]

3001 6 5 **Word Perfect**[9] 3185 5-9-9 69 6ex (b) DaleGibson 2 53
(M W Easterby) *led tl hdd over 2f out: lost pl over 1f out* 11/2[3]

231- 7 10 **Juncea**[257] 6222 3-9-8 74 ChrisCatlin 7 28
(H Morrison) *w ldr: wknd 2f out: sn bhd* 16/1

1m 17.57s (2.57) **Going Correction** +0.575s/f (Yiel)

WFA 3 from 4yo+ 6lb 7 Ran SP% **110.9**

Speed ratings (Par 102):105,104,103,102,101 94,81

CSF £31.93 CT £144.17 TOTE £10.10: £5.60, £1.40; EX 44.20.

Owner S G Martin **Bred** Stewart Martin And Alan Purvis **Trained** Elton, Gloucs

FOCUS

They raced in one group down the far side this time. The gallop was not strong yet the two pacesetters dropped right away and finished in the last two places. The race has been rated to the winner's best pre-race mark.

3467 SIMPLY CARTONS LTD JUMP JOCKEYS H'CAP (TO BE RIDDEN BY NATIONAL HUNT JOCKEYS) 1m 6f 15y

7:40 (7:40) (Class 4) (0-80,80) 4-Y-O+ £6,477 (£1,927; £963; £481) Stalls Low

Form RPR

0006 1 **Winged D'Argent (IRE)**[12] 3090 6-11-5 75 (b) ChristianWilliams 12 78
(B J Llewellyn) *sn chsng ldrs: 2nd ldr 9f out: led over 3f out: edgd lft and styd on strly to draw clr fnl f* 7/2[1]

0-51 2 3 1/2 **Raffish**[6] 3280 5-10-5 61 oh3 (p) TomScudamore 4 59
(M Scudamore) *trckd ldrs: wnt 2nd 2f out: no imp* 13/2

4633 3 nk **Ronsard (IRE)**[6] 3279 5-10-6 62 oh4 ow1 TonyEvans 13 60
(P D Evans) *hld up in rr: hdwy 3f out: styd on fnl f* 10/1

16 4 1/2 **Secret Ploy**[19] 2860 7-11-5 75 TimmyMurphy 2 72
(H Morrison) *led tl over 3f out: one pce fnl 2f* 4/1[2]

5-60 5 1 1/2 **Top Trees**[23] 2493 9-10-5 61 oh16 RJGreene 5 56
(W S Kittow) *in rr: hdwy u.p over 5f out: one pce fnl 3f* 22/1

5122 6 3 1/2 **Just Waz (USA)**[9] 3193 5-10-5 61 oh3 PadgeWhelan 6 51
(R M Whitaker) *hld up in rr: effrt on outer over 3f out: nvr nr ldrs* 11/2[3]

4560 7 5 **Mighty Moon**[48] 2011 4-11-10 80 (bt) AndrewThornton 9 63
(J O'Reilly) *hld up in rr: effrt on outside over 3f out: nvr nr ldrs* 15/2

0/ 8 4 **Adjami (IRE)**[55] 766 6-11-0 70 JamieMoore 1 47
(John A Harris) *chsd ldrs: lost pl over 1f out* 28/1

5160 9 nk **Eforetta (GER)**[14] 3033 5-10-9 65 PaulMoloney 10 42
(D J Wintle) *mid-div: rdn over 3f out: nvr a factor* 20/1

450/ 10 1 1/2 **Atlantic Rhapsody (FR)**[22] 5103 10-11-1 71 (p) TJO'Brien 7 46
(B J Llewellyn) *prom: hrd drvn 4f out: lost pl over 2f out* 25/1

020 11 1 **Debord (FR)**[26] 2675 4-10-5 61 oh2 RobertWalford 11 34
(Jamie Poulton) *jnd ldrs after 4f: rdn 4f out: sn lost pl* 16/1

12 17 **Sharbasia (IRE)**[91] 4-10-9 65 VinceSlattery 8 15
(H J Evans) *in tch: rdn over 3f out: sn lost pl and bhd* 25/1

3m 14.46s (7.36) **Going Correction** +0.325s/f (Good) 12 Ran SP% **117.9**

Speed ratings (Par 105):91,89,88,88,87 85,82,80,80,79 78,69

CSF £23.86 CT £210.29 TOTE £5.60: £2.00, £2.90, £2.80; EX 42.70.

Owner Terry Warner **Bred** Daniel A Couper And George Hosie **Trained** Fochriw, Caerphilly

FOCUS

A novelty jumps jockeys' handicap and modest form with four of the first six racing from out of the handicap. The winner was recording his first success since taking a Listed race here over two years ago.

3468 JOIN WBX.COM NOW FOR £150 FREE BETS CONDITIONS STKS 1m 1f 213y

8:10 (8:10) (Class 3) 3-Y-O+ £7,478 (£2,239; £1,119; £560) Stalls Low

Form RPR

5/1- 1 **Perfectperformance (USA)**[328] 4576 5-9-0 104 KerrinMcEvoy 3 109+
(Saeed Bin Suroor) *led 1f: trckd ldrs: smooth hdwy to ld over 2f out: pushed out towards fin* 4/5[1]

0-40 2 1/2 **Tucker**[20] 2815 5-9-0 102 (p) AdamKirby 1 107
(W R Swinburn) *hld up: hung lft and carried hd high: wnt 2nd over 1f out: kpt on wl towards fin* 7/2[3]

2400 3 17 **Nakheel**[19] 2859 4-9-0 96 KDarley 2 93+
(M Johnston) *s.i.s: shkn up after s: led after 1f: hdd after 2f: led over 3f out: hdd over 2f out: lost pl and eased over 1f out* 5/2[2]

4 4 **Air Guitar (IRE)**[50] 7-8-13 0 ow4 (v[1]) MarkFlynn(5) 4 69?
(J Ryan) *s.i.s: hdwy to ld after 2f: hdd over 3f out: sn lost pl and bhd* 80/1

2m 12.37s (2.67) **Going Correction** +0.325s/f (Good) 4 Ran SP% **107.6**

Speed ratings (Par 107):102,101,88,84

CSF £3.92 TOTE £1.10; EX 2.70.

Owner Godolphin **Bred** Brushwood Stable **Trained** Newmarket, Suffolk

FOCUS

The winner was easily the best horse on the day but the ground nearly found him out late on. The pace was very steady and the form is dubious.

NOTEBOOK

Perfectperformance(USA), who suffered a suspensory injury when winning his sole start at four at Newmarket in August, looked fit. He took it up travelling easily best but he tired late on in the ground. Hopefully he will come out of this in good shape. (op 8-11 tchd 4-6)

Tucker, friendless on the morning line, is without a win for over two years. He travelled sweetly in last but when asked to tackle the winner he hung and carried his head at an awkward angle. He was only closing the gap at the line because the winner was tiring. (op 9-2 tchd 5-1)

Nakheel regained the lead and stepped up the pace but he found little when tackled and his high promise at two before his pelvic injury is in the history books now sadly. (op 11-4 tchd 3-1)

Air Guitar(IRE), a winning hurdler, picked up nearly a monkey for just turning up. (op 50-1)

3469 BET WITH BOOKIES H'CAP 1m 1f 213y

8:40 (8:41) (Class 5) (0-70,71) 3-Y-O £3,238 (£963; £481; £240) Stalls Low

Form RPR

6142 1 **Sadler's Kingdom (IRE)**[10] 3159 3-8-9 58 TonyHamilton 4 67+
(R A Fahey) *trckd ldrs: wnt 3rd over 2f out: wnt 2nd 1f out: hung lft: styd on to ld last 75yds* 6/4[1]

5-60 2 1 **Path To Glory**[19] 2878 3-8-2 51 oh3 AdrianMcCarthy 5 58
(Miss Z C Davison) *led 1f: chsd clr ldr: led over 2f out: hdd and no ex wl ins fnl f* 100/1

0035 3 2 **Down The Brick (IRE)**[26] 2653 3-8-8 57 (b) FergusSweeney 10 60
(B R Millman) *led after 1f: clr over 5f out: hdd over 2f out: kpt on same pce* 14/1

5550 4 6 **Tifernati**[20] 2834 3-9-2 68 LiamJones(3) 6 59
(W J Haggas) *hld up in rr: effrt over 3f out: kpt on fnl 2f: nvr on terms* 6/1[2]

0405 5 4 **Paymaster General (IRE)**[10] 3150 3-8-13 62 HayleyTurner 1 45
(M D I Usher) *in rr: drvn 4f out: kpt on: nvr on terms* 14/1

0325 6 shd **Trump Call (IRE)**[15] 3003 3-9-7 70 JamesDoyle 3 53
(R M Beckett) *in rr: kpt on fnl 2f: nvr nr ldrs* 15/2[3]

0004 7 1 1/4 **Tina's Ridge (IRE)**[15] 2978 3-7-11 51 oh1 (p) WilliamBuick(5) 7 31
(R Hollinshead) *chsd ldrs: rdn over 3f out: wknd over 2f out* 16/1

00-0 8 1 1/2 **Bold Adventure**[42] 2192 3-8-2 51 oh1 PaulEddery 8 28
(W J Musson) *hld up in rr: effrt over 3f out: nvr a factor* 12/1

2421 9 1 3/4 **Four Miracles**[9] 3176 3-9-8 71 6ex JimmyQuinn 2 45
(M H Tompkins) *s.i.s: hdwy into mid-div after 3f: wknd over 2f out* 6/1[2]

0042 10 7 **Doubly Guest**[12] 3107 3-9-4 67 NeilPollard 9 27
(G G Margarson) *mid-div: effrt over 3f out: wknd over 2f out* 25/1

0462 11 12 **Giovanni D'Oro (IRE)**[21] 2796 3-8-5 54 ChrisCatlin 11 —
(Miss M E Rowland) *chsd ldrs: lost pl over 3f out: sn bhd* 33/1

2m 11.8s (2.10) **Going Correction** +0.325s/f (Good) 11 Ran SP% **115.0**

Speed ratings (Par 100):104,103,101,96,93 93,92,91,89,84 74

CSF £237.29 CT £1581.53 TOTE £2.30: £1.10, £19.00, £4.60; EX 186.90.

Owner J J Staunton **Bred** Tower Bloodstock **Trained** Musley Bank, N Yorks

■ Stewards' Enquiry : Adrian McCarthy five-day ban: used whip with excessive frequency (Jul 24-28)

FOCUS

A modest handicap run at a breakneck pace and the heavily-supported winner benefited from a well-judged ride. The form is rated through the third to this year's best.

3470 WBX.COM WORLD BET EXCHANGE H'CAP 1m 54y

9:10 (9:11) (Class 4) (0-85,84) 3-Y-O+ £5,505 (£1,637; £818; £408) Stalls Centre

Form RPR

21 1 **Gongidas**[33] 2477 3-9-7 84 KerrinMcEvoy 8 94+
(Saeed Bin Suroor) *hld up: hdwy on outside 3f out: hung bdly lft: swtchd ins over 1f out: led ins fnl f: drvn out* 11/8[1]

1512 **2** ½ **Blue Monkey (IRE)**[7] 3235 3-8-6 **74** LukeMorris(5) 3 80
(M L W Bell) *trckd ldrs: edgd rt over 1f out: no ex wl ins fnl f* **9/4**[2]

6153 **3** 1 **The Osteopath (IRE)**[9] 3194 4-9-5 **73** (p) PhillipMakin 6 79
(M Dods) *hld up: hdwy over 3f out: led over 2f out: hung rt over 1f out: hdd and no ex ins fnl f* **6/1**[3]

-502 **4** 2 ½ **Wheels In Motion (IRE)**[12] 3094 3-9-2 **79** MickyFenton 1 77
(T P Tate) *trckd ldrs: t.k.h: effrt 3f out: one pce appr fnl f* **6/1**[3]

-165 **5** 2 ½ **Nuit Sombre (IRE)**[6] 3258 7-9-2 **75** PJMcDonald(5) 5 70
(G A Harker) *s.s: hld up in last: kpt on fnl 2f: nvr nr ldrs* **25/1**

3003 **6** 10 **Pawn In Life (IRE)**[114] 715 9-8-2 **61** oh16 (v) ColinHaddon(5) 2 33
(G Woodward) *reluctant and led to s: led: t.k.h: qcknd over 3f out: hdd over 2f out: sn lost pl* **100/1**

2050 **7** 3 **Rebellious Spirit**[66] 1543 4-9-12 **80** ChrisCatlin 7 45
(P W Hiatt) *trckd ldrs: chal over 3f out: wknd over 2f out: sn bhd* **25/1**

1m 50.23s (3.83) **Going Correction** +0.325s/f (Good)
WFA 3 from 4yo+ 9lb 7 Ran SP% **110.1**
Speed ratings (Par 105):93,92,91,89,86 76,73
CSF £4.21 CT £10.73 TOTE £2.30: £1.10, £2.30; EX 5.70 Place 6 £38.00, Place 5 £13.05.
Owner Godolphin **Bred** Karl-Dieter Ellerbracke **Trained** Newmarket, Suffolk

FOCUS
A very sedate gallop resulting in a moderate winning time for the grade. The race has been rated through the third.
The Osteopath(IRE) Official explanation: jockey said gelding hung right closing stages
T/Plt: £16.10 to a £1 stake. Pool: £53,753.00. 2,422.95 winning tickets. T/Qpdt: £7.60 to a £1 stake. Pool: £3,357.80. 326.90 winning tickets. WG

3274 WARWICK (L-H)
Thursday, July 12

OFFICIAL GOING: Good (7.1)
Wind: Moderate, behind Weather: Fine

3471 GREEN 4 CRM SOLUTIONS MAIDEN AUCTION STKS 7f 26y
2:20 (2:22) (Class 5) 2-Y-O £2,914 (£867; £433; £216) Stalls Low

Form RPR

1 **Hobby** 2-8-4 0 JamesDoyle 2 73
(R M Beckett) *a.p: rdn to ld over 2f out: r.o* **12/1**

2 1 ¼ **Art Master** 2-8-13 0 PatDobbs 7 81+
(S Kirk) *s.i.s and n.m.r s: hld up: hdwy on ins over 3f out: rdn over 2f out: edgd lft 1f out: r.o* **9/2**[3]

0 **3** nk **Benhavis**[41] 2215 2-9-1 0 IanMongan 3 80
(J L Dunlop) *t.k.h in tch: rdn 2f out: nt qckn ins fnl f* **11/1**

4 1 ½ **Weet By Far** 2-8-4 0 PaulEddery 5 66
(R Hollinshead) *a.p: rdn and one pce fnl 2f* **33/1**

43 **5** 5 **Casino Night**[10] 3171 2-8-8 0 RoystonFfrench 10 57
(M Johnston) *mid-div: rdn over 3f out: hdwy 2f out: no further prog* **4/1**[2]

04 **6** 2 **Smith Esquire (USA)**[19] 2876 2-8-9 0 GrahamGibbons 4 53
(W R Swinburn) *hld up in mid-div: rdn and hdwy 3f out: wknd wl over 1f out* **5/2**[1]

7 1 ¾ **Anabaa's Secret (IRE)** 2-8-13 0 VinceSlattery 6 53
(J A Osborne) *hld up towards rr: stdy hdwy 3f out: nvr trbld ldrs* **18/1**

8 nk **Victorian Cape (IRE)** 2-8-11 0 ChrisCatlin 12 50
(E J O'Neill) *chsd ldr tl rdn and wknd over 2f out* **8/1**

0 **9** 1 ¾ **Dancer's Legacy**[19] 2876 2-8-11 0 HayleyTurner 13 46
(E A L Dunlop) *hld up in tch: rdn and wknd over 2f out* **14/1**

10 1 ½ **Millennium Storm (GER)** 2-8-11 0 DavidKinsella 9 42
(M F Harris) *hld up and bhd: rdn and hdwy on ins 2f out: wknd fnl f* **66/1**

11 2 ½ **Paul The Carpet (UAE)** 2-8-9 0 EdwardCreighton 1 34
(P F I Cole) *s.i.s: a bhd* **14/1**

12 3 **Ovthenight (IRE)** 2-8-11 0 FergusSweeney 14 28
(Mrs P Sly) *hld up towards rr: rdn over 3f out: no rspnse* **33/1**

0 **13** 1 ¾ **I Certainly May**[30] 2539 2-8-13 0 DaneO'Neill 8 26
(S Dow) *a towards rr* **28/1**

0 **14** 10 **Days Of Thunder (IRE)**[61] 1680 2-8-4 0 MarkCoumbe(7) 11 —
(G F Bridgwater) *led: rdn and hdd over 2f out: wknd qckly* **100/1**

1m 26.72s (2.52) **Going Correction** +0.20s/f (Good) 14 Ran SP% **124.3**
Speed ratings (Par 94):93,91,91,89,83 81,79,79,77,75 72,69,67,55
CSF £65.64 TOTE £18.40: £4.90, £2.40, £3.10; EX 111.80.
Owner Larksborough Stud Limited **Bred** Larksborough Stud Limited **Trained** Whitsbury, Hants

FOCUS
There was little previous form to go on in this minor maiden and it will take a while for the form to settle down.

NOTEBOOK
Hobby has a sister who won on her debut as a juvenile over 5f in the Czech Republic. Her trainer thought she was rather green and is hoping that there may be some improvement to come. (op 14-1)
Art Master ◆ is a half-brother to Faraway Lady who scored four times at around two miles. Shaping promisingly on his debut, he should have little difficulty opening his account in similar company and will stay further in time. (op 5-1)
Benhavis ◆, quite a well-bred colt, again raced freely but stepped up on his debut in this lower grade. There are races to be won with him. (op 16-1)
Weet By Far is a half-sister to a dual mile winner at three and a 12f winner who also scored twice over hurdles. Connections have every reason to be delighted with this debut given that she only cost 800 guineas.
Casino Night was rather disappointing and never really posed a threat when the chips were down. (op 7-2 tchd 10-3)
Smith Esquire(USA) was another to run below expectations having halved in price in the ring. (op 5-1 tchd 11-2)

3472 MITIE H'CAP 6f
2:55 (2:55) (Class 4) (0-85,82) 3-Y-O+
£6,232 (£1,866; £933; £467; £233; £117) Stalls High

Form RPR

1161 **1** **Stamford Blue**[15] 2982 6-9-8 **80** (b) LukeMorris(5) 6 92+
(R A Harris) *t.k.h: mde all: rdn whn sddle slipped bdly 1f out: drvn out* **11/2**

0141 **2** ¾ **China Cherub**[9] 3188 4-10-1 **82** 6ex (b) PatDobbs 4 90
(R Hannon) *chsd wnr: rdn over 2f out: nt qckn ins fnl f* **5/1**[3]

31-2 **3** ¾ **Observatory Star (IRE)**[34] 2421 4-8-13 **66** (b) GrahamGibbons 1 72
(T D Easterby) *hld up: rdn and hdwy 2f out: kpt on ins fnl f* **5/2**[1]

4425 **4** 1 **Seamus Shindig**[15] 2993 5-9-3 **77** AmyScott(7) 7 79
(H Candy) *wnt sltly rt s: hld up: hdwy whn hung lft 1f out: one pce* **13/2**

315 **5** 2 **Gilded Cove**[18] 2912 7-8-9 **67** RussellKennemore(5) 8 63
(R Hollinshead) *s.i.s: bhd: rdn over 2f out: nvr trbld ldrs* **17/2**

-262 **6** 2 ½ **Rydal Mount (IRE)**[24] 2725 4-9-6 **73** (v[1]) FergusSweeney 2 61
(W S Kittow) *hld up in tch: rdn 3f out: wknd over 1f out* **4/1**[2]

0350 **7** 3 **Outer Hebrides**[15] 2982 6-8-12 **70** (t) KevinGhunowa(5) 5 48
(J M Bradley) *prom: pushed along over 3f out: rdn whn rdr dropped whip 2f out: wknd over 1f out* **12/1**

1m 10.94s (-3.34) **Going Correction** -0.425s/f (Firm) course record 7 Ran SP% **112.2**
Speed ratings (Par 105):105,104,103,101,99 95,91
CSF £31.43 CT £84.11 TOTE £6.40: £2.80, £1.90; EX 15.00.
Owner Brian Hicks **Bred** Mrs Wendy Miller **Trained** Earlswood, Monmouths

FOCUS
An ordinary if eventful handicap, and with the time decent and the placed horses to their marks, the form looks sound.

3473 ACCURATES H'CAP 1m 6f 213y
3:30 (3:31) (Class 5) (0-75,70) 3-Y-O+ £2,914 (£867; £433; £216) Stalls Low

Form RPR

-052 **1** **Nimra (USA)**[3] 3371 4-10-0 **70** (b) DavidAllan 6 78
(G A Butler) *hld up in mid-div: rdn over 4f out: hdwy on ins 3f out: wnt 2nd jst over 1f out: styd on u.p to ld last strides* **7/2**[1]

-535 **2** shd **I Predict A Riot (IRE)**[27] 2628 3-8-9 **68** JamesDoyle 9 76
(J W Hills) *led after 1f: clr whn rdn over 2f out: edgd rt wl over 1f out: wandered u.p ins fnl f: ct last strides* **7/1**

4460 **3** 3 **Squirtle (IRE)**[19] 2890 4-8-6 **53** LukeMorris(5) 1 57
(W M Brisbourne) *s.s: hld up in rr: hdwy over 4f out: rdn over 3f out: one pce fnl f* **9/1**

2000 **4** shd **Into Action**[27] 2628 3-8-3 **62** RichardSmith 3 66
(R Hannon) *led 1f: chsd ldr tl 8f out: rdn and wnt 2nd again 3f out: one pce fnl f* **22/1**

2631 **5** 4 **Garnett (IRE)**[20] 2839 6-10-0 **70** (b) HayleyTurner 7 69
(D E Cantillon) *hld up towards rr: rdn over 3f out: sme hdwy 2f out: n.d* **4/1**[2]

0606 **6** 40 **Code (IRE)**[6] 3280 6-8-9 **51** oh4 (p) PatDobbs 2 —
(Miss Z C Davison) *dwlt: a in rr: t.o* **66/1**

-263 **7** nk **Adversane**[27] 2628 3-8-11 **70** IanMongan 8 16
(J L Dunlop) *prom: chsd ldr 8f out tl rdn 3f out: wknd 2f out: t.o* **7/2**[1]

-003 **8** 5 **Disintegration (IRE)**[18] 2915 3-8-3 **62** ChrisCatlin 4 2
(A King) *hld up in tch: rdn 4f out: wknd over 2f out: t.o* **5/1**[3]

040- **9** 2 ½ **First Slip**[123] 5478 4-9-9 **65** GrahamGibbons 5 2
(Jonjo O'Neill) *hld up in mid-div: rdn 5f out: bhd fnl 4fout: t.o* **25/1**

3m 18.45s (2.55) **Going Correction** +0.20s/f (Good)
WFA 3 from 4yo+ 17lb 9 Ran SP% **113.3**
Speed ratings (Par 103):101,100,99,99,97 75,75,73,71
CSF £27.21 CT £200.56 TOTE £5.60: £1.80, £2.40, £2.80; EX 35.00.
Owner Sheikh Nasser Bin Hamad **Bred** Mueller Farms Inc **Trained** Blewbury, Oxon
■ Stewards' Enquiry : David Allan five-day ban: used whip with excessive frequency (Jul 23-27)
James Doyle two-day ban: used whip with excessive frequency without giving gelding time to respond (Jul 24-25)

FOCUS
Just a modest staying handicap and rated through the third and fourth, although not particularly solid.
Squirtle(IRE) Official explanation: jockey said filly missed the break
Adversane Official explanation: trainer's rep had no explanation for the poor form shown

3474 E.B.F./MITIE FILLIES' H'CAP 7f 26y
4:05 (4:05) (Class 4) (0-80,78) 3-Y-O+ £6,477 (£1,927; £963; £481) Stalls Low

Form RPR

4-1 **1** **Rhuepunzel**[21] 2792 3-9-3 **73** HayleyTurner 5 79
(G A Butler) *a.p: hrd rdn over 1f out: r.o to ld nr fin* **6/1**[3]

-643 **2** nk **Kashmir Lady (FR)**[29] 2571 3-8-11 **67** DaneO'Neill 6 72
(H Candy) *led: rdn over 1f out: hdd nr fin* **6/1**[3]

6342 **3** nk **Angel Sprints**[33] 2472 5-9-9 **76** LukeMorris(5) 4 83
(C J Down) *hld up: rdn and hdwy on outside 2f out: r.o ins fnl f* **5/2**[2]

6504 **4** 1 **Safranine (IRE)**[6] 3277 10-8-4 **57** oh7 AnnStokell(5) 1 61?
(Miss A Stokell) *chsd ldr: rdn and ev ch over 1f out: nt qckn ins fnl f* **22/1**

-535 **5** ¾ **Angel Voices (IRE)**[15] 2988 4-8-13 **61** PhillipMakin 7 63
(K R Burke) *hld up: rdn and hdwy on ins wl over 1f out: one pce fnl f* **13/2**

1-10 **6** 2 ½ **Supa Sal**[54] 1837 3-9-2 **75** JerryO'Dwyer(3) 3 68
(P F I Cole) *hld up in tch: rdn and wknd over 1f out* **9/4**[1]

4501 **7** 8 **Kind Of Fizzy**[14] 3038 3-8-9 **65** ChrisCatlin 8 36
(Rae Guest) *hld up and bhd: rdn over 2f out: sn struggling* **10/1**

1m 24.53s (0.33) **Going Correction** +0.20s/f (Good)
WFA 3 from 4yo+ 8lb 7 Ran SP% **114.7**
Speed ratings (Par 102):106,105,105,104,103 100,91
CSF £41.25 CT £112.70 TOTE £6.00: £2.70, £2.70; EX 19.20.
Owner The Fairy Story Partnership **Bred** Deepwood Farm Stud **Trained** Blewbury, Oxon
■ Stewards' Enquiry : Luke Morris one-day ban: used whip with excessive frequency (Jul 25)
Dane O'Neill three-day ban: used whip with excessive frequency (Jul 23-25)

FOCUS
A modest fillies' handicap and there was little between the front three at the line. The third and fifth set the level but the proximity of the fourth raises doubts.

3475 WARWICKRACECOURSE.CO.UK H'CAP 7f 26y
4:40 (4:40) (Class 5) (0-75,75) 3-Y-O £2,914 (£867; £433; £216) Stalls Low

Form RPR

0023 **1** **Lordship (IRE)**[9] 3178 3-7-11 **56** LukeMorris(5) 1 64
(A W Carroll) *a.p: rdn over 1f out: edgd rt and led jst ins fnl f: r.o wl* **7/2**[2]

-200 **2** 3 ½ **Emma Jean Lad (IRE)**[30] 2545 3-8-4 **58** SimonWhitworth 9 57
(J S Moore) *hld up: hdwy on ins 2f out: sn rdn: kpt on same pce fnl f* **14/1**

-143 **3** 1 ½ **Fuschia**[36] 2363 3-9-6 **74** PatDobbs 3 69
(R Charlton) *hld up in tch: rdn over 2f out: one pce fnl f* **3/1**[1]

-140 **4** hd **Pickering**[75] 1286 3-9-7 **75** DavidAllan 2 69
(E J Alston) *led after 1f: rdn and edgd rt over 1f out: hdd jst ins fnl f: sn btn* **5/1**

6121 **5** 3 ½ **Mick Is Back**[13] 3057 3-8-7 **61** (p) FergusSweeney 7 46
(J R Boyle) *prom: rdn and wknd wl over 1f out* **9/2**[3]

-242 **6** 1 **Doyles Lodge**[28] 2601 3-9-6 **74** DaneO'Neill 5 56
(H Candy) *hld up in mid-div: rdn over 2f out: no rspnse* **7/1**

000- **7** 5 **Global Guest**[285] 5686 3-8-11 **72** MarkCoumbe(7) 4 41
(A J Chamberlain) *a bhd* **50/1**

2530 **8** nk **Six Of Hearts**[13] 3066 3-8-10 **67** RichardKingscote(3) 8 35
(J A Osborne) *bhd fnl 4f* **12/1**

300- **9** ½ **Ron In Ernest**[299] 5372 3-8-9 **63** (p) ChrisCatlin 6 30
(J A Geake) *led 1f: chsd ldr tl rdn and wknd 2f out* **20/1**

1m 25.03s (0.83) **Going Correction** +0.20s/f (Good) 9 Ran SP% **115.7**
Speed ratings (Par 100):103,99,97,97,93 91,86,85,85
CSF £51.14 CT £164.16 TOTE £4.80: £1.60, £3.40, £1.60; EX 56.90.

Owner Group 1 Racing (1994) Ltd **Bred** John Costello **Trained** Cropthorne, Worcs
FOCUS
A weak handicap, but Lordship won readily and the form appears sound enough.
Six Of Hearts Official explanation: jockey said colt never travelled

3476 RACING UK MAIDEN STKS — 1m 2f 188y
5:15 (5:16) (Class 5) 3-Y-0+ — **£2,914** (£867; £433; £216) **Stalls** Low

Form				RPR
3-32	**1**		**Font**[20] 2840 4-9-12 89 ... OscarUrbina 4 (J R Fanshawe) *a.p: rdn to ld and edgd lft wl over 1f out: edgd lft cl home: r.o* **13/8**[1]	81+
0-5	**2**	*nk*	**Unreachable Star**[28] 2597 3-8-9 0 ... PatDobbs 3 (Mrs A J Perrett) *a.p: rdn and ev ch 2f out: r.o ins fnl f* **9/2**	75+
32	**3**	*7*	**Louviere**[16] 2970 3-8-4 0 ... PatrickHills(5) 11 (Pat Eddery) *s.i.s: sn prom: jnd ldr over 6f out: rdn over 2f out: wkng whn rdr dropped whip jst over 1f out* **11/4**[2]	62
U60	**4**	*6*	**Sky Chart (IRE)**[19] 2873 3-9-0 0 ... TonyHamilton 8 (N J Vaughan) *led: rdn and hdd wl over 1f out: sn wknd* **66/1**	57
00	**5**	*5*	**Roymar**[9] 3176 3-8-6 0 ... NeilChalmers(3) 2 (M Appleby) *hld up and bhd: sme hdwy on ins whn nt clr run briefly 3f out: nvr nr ldrs* **100/1**	43+
06	**6**	*2 1/2*	**Wightgar**[7] 3244 3-9-0 0 ... (t) FergusSweeney 10 (R A Kvisla) *w ldr tl over 6f out: rdn and wknd 3f out* **66/1**	43
5	**7**	*2 1/2*	**Tahdeed**[47] 2046 3-9-0 0 ... DaneO'Neill 6 (Sir Michael Stoute) *hld up in mid-div: hdwy over 6f out: rdn over 2f out: sn wknd* **10/3**[3]	39
00	**8**	*1 1/4*	**Burnley (IRE)**[15] 2981 4-9-9 0 ... RichardKingscote(3) 1 (Mrs A L M King) *hld up in mid-div: rdn over 3f out: sn struggling* **100/1**	36
	9	*9*	**Sir Jake** 3-9-0 0 ... PhillipMakin 7 (T T Clement) *hld up: rdn 4f out: bhd fnl 3f* **66/1**	20
	10	*nk*	**Beths Choice**[47] 6-9-5 0 ... BarrySavage(7) 9 (J M Bradley) *a bhd* **80/1**	20
40	**11**	*10*	**Arctiz (USA)**[12] 3113 3-9-0 0 ... EdwardCreighton 12 (P F I Cole) *t.k.h early: in tch: rdn and wknd over 4f out* **20/1**	2
00	**12**	*26*	**Golden Peacock**[12] 3113 3-9-0 0 ... SimonWhitworth 5 (M Appleby) *a bhd: eased whn no ch fnl 3f: t.o* **100/1**	—

2m 21.56s (2.16) **Going Correction** +0.20s/f (Good)
WFA 3 from 4yo+ 12lb — **12** Ran SP% **119.5**
Speed ratings (Par 103):100,99,94,90,86 84,83,82,75,75 68,49
CSF £9.46 TOTE £2.40: £1.20, £2.10, £1.30; EX 11.60 Place 6 £237.20, Place 5 £70.75.
Owner Cheveley Park Stud **Bred** Cheveley Park Stud Ltd **Trained** Newmarket, Suffolk
FOCUS
The front two drew clear in what was just a modest maiden. The time was ordinary and the form looks dubious.
Louviere Official explanation: trainer said filly lost a shoe during the race
Burnley(IRE) Official explanation: jockey said gelding finished distressed
Arctiz(USA) Official explanation: jockey said colt hung left-handed
T/Plt: £1,097.90 to a £1 stake. Pool: £50,386.65. 33.50 winning tickets. T/Qpdt: £23.60 to a £1 stake. Pool: £3,321.70. 103.90 winning tickets. KH

2855 ASCOT (R-H)
Friday, July 13

OFFICIAL GOING: Good to firm
All the races took place on the straight track, with two events scheduled for the round course abandoned and the 2yo maiden divided to ensure a six-race card.
Wind: Mild Weather: Dry and overcast

3477 LIVERPOOL VETS H'CAP — 1m 2f
() (Class 3) (0-90,) 3-Y-0+ — £

3478 ICAP EBF MAIDEN STKS (DIV I) — 6f
1:50 (1:53) (Class 4) 2-Y-0 — **£6,477** (£1,927; £963; £481) **Stalls** Low

Form				RPR
533	**1**		**Master Chef (IRE)**[37] 2353 2-9-3 0 ... (b1) FrancisNorton 4 (J H M Gosden) *lw: mde all: sn clr: unchal* **3/1**[2]	92
05	**2**	*4*	**Polygraph (IRE)**[16] 2977 2-8-12 0 ... WilliamBuick(5) 10 (A M Balding) *lw: chsd wnr early: rdn 3f out: regained 2nd over 1f out but no ch w wnr* **8/1**	80
	3	*3 1/2*	**Funny Me** 2-9-3 0 ... IanMongan 5 (P W Chapple-Hyam) *cmpt: str: scope: lw: dwlt bdly: bhd: swtchd rt and hdwy over 2f out: styd on to go 3rd ins fnl f: n.d* **8/1**	70
	4	*1/2*	**Sir Ike (IRE)** 2-9-3 0 ... (t) FergusSweeney 9 (W S Kittow) *neat: lw: s.i.s: sn in tch: rdn over 2f out: kpt on same pce* **14/1**	68
62	**5**	*1*	**Natmana**[15] 3013 2-9-3 0 ... DarryllHolland 3 (M R Channon) *chsd wnr after 1f: rdn and hung rt fr over 2f out: wknd fnl f* **8/1**	65
0	**6**	*1 1/2*	**Deckguard**[18] 2941 2-9-3 0 ... SimonWhitworth 8 (J S Moore) *lw: bmpd sn after s: in tch: rdn 3f out: sn one pce* **33/1**	61
	7	*hd*	**Mr Keppel (IRE)** 2-9-3 0 ... JimCrowley 6 (J A Osborne) *w'like: str: bmpd sn after s: in tch: rdn 3f out: wknd over 1f out* **5/1**[3]	60
00	**8**	*2 1/2*	**Flash Of Fire (USA)**[34] 2473 2-8-12 0 ... LukeMorris(5) 1 (J M P Eustace) *sn struggling and a towards rr* **40/1**	52
	9	*1*	**Hustle (IRE)** 2-9-3 0 ... EddieAhern 2 (R Hannon) *str: bit bkwd: mid-div: rn green u.p fr 3f out: wknd 2f out* **11/4**[1]	49

1m 14.88s (-0.02) **Going Correction** +0.05s/f (Good) — **9** Ran SP% **113.7**
Speed ratings (Par 96):102,96,92,91,90 88,87,84,83
CSF £26.82 TOTE £3.00: £1.50, £2.90, £2.00; EX 29.40 Trifecta £95.40 Pool £449.12 - 3.34 winning units..
Owner H R H Princess Haya Of Jordan **Bred** Mountgrange Stud Ltd, T Stewart And A Stroud **Trained** Newmarket, Suffolk
■ Stewards' Enquiry : William Buick three-day ban: careless riding (Jul 24-26)
FOCUS
Even with the recent heavy rainfall, and the abandonment of the two races on the round course, the ground on the straight track was riding fast. This first division of the two-year-old maiden looked marginally weaker of the two overall, but the time was good for the grade and the race has therefore been rated positively.
NOTEBOOK
Master Chef(IRE), the most experienced of these, had finished behind some decent juveniles in his first three runs. Fitted with blinkers for the first time, he bowled along in front and, soon several lengths to the good, never looked in danger of being caught. It will be interesting to see whether the headgear works so well next time. (op 5-2)
Polygraph(IRE) was a little disappointing at Bath on his second start but this was better. He raced prominently throughout and, although never able to get on terms with the winner, he was clearly best of the rest. He should get 1m in time. (op 9-1)
Funny Me, whose dam was quite a useful winner over this trip at two, dwelt at the start but kept on in the closing stages and did well to reach his final position. He will be all the better for this experience. (op 6-1)
Sir Ike(IRE), who comes from a good family, was tongue tied for this debut. He showed ability despite appearing a little green and should improve for this experience. (op 16-1)
Natmana never looked like repeating his Hamilton second against this tougher competition. Connections have the option of nurseries now. (op 15-2 tchd 9-1)
Hustle(IRE), a half-brother to the useful 6f-1m winner Six Hitter, holds some big-race entries and this was a disappointing debut, although he can be expected to improve considerably with this outing under his belt. (op 4-1)

3479 LIVERPOOL VETS MAIDEN STKS (DIV II OF 1.50) — 6f
2:25 (2:26) (Class 4) 2-Y-0 — **£6,477** (£1,927; £963; £481) **Stalls** Low

Form				RPR
	1		**Sporting Art (USA)** 2-9-3 0 ... FergusSweeney 8 (G L Moore) *cmpt: str: hld up: hdwy 3f out: shkn up to chal over 1f out: tk narrow advantage ins fnl f: pushed out* **66/1**	85
3	**2**	*nk*	**Red Alert Day**[48] 2041 2-9-3 0 ... EddieAhern 2 (N A Callaghan) *lw: led: rdn over 1f out: hdd ins fnl f: kpt on* **8/11**[1]	84
223	**3**	*shd*	**Aaim For Applause**[16] 2977 2-9-3 0 ... DarryllHolland 9 (M R Channon) *hld up: hdwy and nt clr run briefly and swtchd lft 2f out: sn rdn: r.o ins fnl f: wandered fnl 50yds: nt quite get up* **11/4**[2]	84
	4	*1*	**Eastern Gift** 2-9-3 0 ... RichardSmith 4 (R Hannon) *w'like: s.i.s: bhd: swtchd lft and hdwy 2f out: sn rdn: racd alone but r.o ins fnl f: nrst fin* **25/1**	81+
6	**5**	*4*	**Jasmines Hero (USA)**[29] 2600 2-9-3 0 ... SimonWhitworth 10 (J S Moore) *lw: chsd ldrs: rdn to chal 2f out: wknd fnl f* **20/1**	69
	6	*1 1/4*	**Jaadull** 2-9-0 0 ... GregFairley(3) 1 (M Johnston) *wll grwn: prom: rdn 3f out: one pce and edgd rt fnl 2f* **11/1**[3]	65
5	**7**	*1*	**Tina's Best (IRE)**[17] 2968 2-8-12 0 ... PatDobbs 6 (R Hannon) *lw: prom: rdn over 2f out: grad fdd* **16/1**	57
	8	*1 1/2*	**Just Jimmy (IRE)** 2-9-3 0 ... JamesDoyle 5 (P D Evans) *w'like: mid-div: rdn over 2f out: wknd over 1f out* **50/1**	58
0	**9**	*1/2*	**Little Wing (IRE)**[35] 2424 2-9-3 0 ... JimCrowley 3 (J A Osborne) *t.k.h bhd ldng gp: rdn 2f out: wknd ent fnl f* **12/1**	56
50	**10**	*14*	**Amwell House**[52] 1919 2-9-0 0 ... PatrickMathers(3) 7 (J R Jenkins) *stdd and awkward sn after s: hld up: effrt 3f out: wknd 2f out* **66/1**	14

1m 14.95s (0.05) **Going Correction** +0.05s/f (Good) — **48** Ran SP% **120.0**
Speed ratings (Par 96):101,100,100,99,93 92,90,88,88,69
CSF £117.43 TOTE £84.80: £11.20, £1.10, £1.50; EX 181.70 TRIFECTA Not won..
Owner R A Green **Bred** Frank Penn & John R Penn **Trained** Woodingdean, E Sussex
■ Stewards' Enquiry : Eddie Ahern two-day ban: used whip in an incorrect place (Jul 24-25)
FOCUS
Probably the stronger of the two divisions overall, but just an ordinary event that produced a close finish and a shock winner. The form should be reasonable with slight improvement by the placed horses.
NOTEBOOK
Sporting Art(USA) is out of an unraced half-sister to the smart middle-distance performer Defensive Play. Racing towards the rear on the far side of the bunch, he improved with three furlongs to run and responded to pressure to get on top near the finish. A rare first-time out juvenile winner from this yard, he should get another furlong in due course. (op 50-1)
Red Alert Day, third in a decent Newmarket maiden on his debut last month, ran another solid race and only gave best well inside the last. An ordinary maiden should come his way. (op 4-5)
Aaim For Applause came home in good style and was fast closing on the two ahead of him at the line. Placed on each of his four starts now, he might be ready for a step up to 7f. (op 3-1 tchd 10-3)
Eastern Gift ◆, out of a winning half-sister to high-class performer La-Faah, was slow to break and still at the back of the field entering the final two furlongs. Beginning to find his stride, he came with a steady run towards the near side but was held inside the last. He should be capable of building on this promising debut. (op 20-1)
Jasmines Hero(USA), sixth behind subsequent July Stakes runner-up River Proud on his debut a month back, ran to a similar level here. (op 16-1)
Jaadull is closely related to 7f juvenile winner Manntab, out of a smart 1m-1m2f winer. Thought highly enough of to hold an entry in the Group 1 Phoenix Stakes, he is unlikely to reach those heights but should come on for this debut effort. (op 10-1 tchd 12-1)

3480 LBC H'CAP — 7f
3:00 (3:01) (Class 3) (0-90,89) 3-Y-0 — **£9,715** (£2,890; £1,444; £721) **Stalls** Low

Form				RPR
2132	**1**		**Docofthebay (IRE)**[30] 2577 3-8-12 **85** ... WilliamBuick(5) 4 (J A Osborne) *lw: hld up bhd ldrs: crept clsr over 1f out: sn rdn: led ins fnl f and drifted lft: kpt on: rdn out* **9/4**[1]	91
0640	**2**	*nk*	**Lunces Lad (IRE)**[20] 2881 3-8-11 **79** ... DarryllHolland 2 (M R Channon) *s.i.s: bhd: rdn and gd hdwy over 1f out: r.o: snatched 2nd fnl stride* **15/2**	84
5003	**3**	*hd*	**Princess Valerina**[39] 2306 3-9-0 **82** ... FrancisNorton 9 (B W Hills) *lw: t.k.h: prom: led 2f out: sn rdn: hdd ins fnl f: sn carried lft: no ex and lost 2nd fnl stride nr fin* **16/1**	87
31	**4**	*2 1/2*	**Shadow The Wind (IRE)**[34] 2470 3-8-6 **74** ... FergusSweeney 1 (E F Vaughan) *lw: led tl over 3f out: rdn and ev ch over 1f out: kpt on same pce* **4/1**[2]	72
-143	**5**	*1/2*	**Bold Abbott (USA)**[27] 2671 3-9-0 **82** ... (b1) JimCrowley 7 (Mrs A J Perrett) *hld up: hdwy 3f out: chalng whn bmpd 2f out: sn rdn: kpt on same pce* **10/1**	79
0-10	**6**	*2*	**Rudry Dragon (IRE)**[48] 2045 3-8-12 **80** ... SimonWhitworth 8 (P A Blockley) *hld up bhd ldrs: rdn and ev ch over 1f out: one pce fnl f* **13/2**[3]	72
-314	**7**	*1*	**Teen Ager (FR)**[52] 1930 3-8-9 **77** ... JamesDoyle 10 (J S Moore) *lw: racd freely: prom: led over 3f out: rdn and hdd whn wnt rt 2f out: one pce after* **14/1**	66
-400	**8**	*1 3/4*	**Opera Music**[22] 2788 3-9-7 **89** ... FrankieMcDonald 6 (S Kirk) *n.m.r sn after s: chsd ldrs: rdn over 2f out: wknd over 1f out* **12/1**	74
-203	**9**	*1 3/4*	**Love On Sight**[48] 2040 3-9-1 **83** ... EddieAhern 3 (A P Jarvis) *hld up bhd ldrs: effrt over 2f out: wknd ent fnl f* **7/1**	63
140-	**10**	*6*	**Diamond Hurricane (IRE)**[297] 5447 3-8-6 **74** ... SaleemGolam 5 (P D Evans) *in tch: rdn and effrt wl over 2f out: sn wknd* **40/1**	38

1m 27.62s (-0.48) **Going Correction** +0.05s/f (Good) — **10** Ran SP% **120.1**
Speed ratings (Par 104):104,103,103,100,100 97,96,94,92,85
CSF £20.53 CT £229.43 TOTE £3.30: £1.50, £2.90, £4.40; EX 26.00 Trifecta £299.70 Part won. Pool £442.15 - 0.34 winning units..

Owner Paul J Dixon **Bred** G And Mrs Middlebrook **Trained** Upper Lambourn, Berks

FOCUS

A fair handicap and sound form with the placed horses to their marks. The action took place down the centre again. The winner edged to his left late on and there was a lengthy enquiry before the result was allowed to stand.

NOTEBOOK

Docofthebay(IRE), a consistent if not entirely straightforward individual, was tackling this trip for the first time having done all his racing at around a mile. Waited with, he was produced to lead inside the final furlong before drifting to his left, inconveniencing the third horse in the process. There could be a bit of improvement still to come from him. (op 3-1 tchd 10-3)

Lunces Lad(IRE), who had made the running on his previous start at Windsor, missed the break and found himself in rear. After being switched to race on the near side with two furlongs to run, he finished well but the line just beat him. (op 17-2)

Princess Valerina showed in a definite lead two furlongs out but was cut down by inside the last by the winner, who then carried her left and probably cost her second place. This was more encouraging.

Shadow The Wind(IRE), back up in trip for this handicap debut, showed with a slight lead to halfway and stuck on at the same pace in the latter stages. (op 3-1 tchd 9-2)

Bold Abbott(USA), tried in first-time blinkers, was challenging Teen Ager for the lead when that rival veered right and bumped him, ending what chance he may have had. (op 12-1)

Teen Ager(FR), having his first run on turf since his racecourse debut, had not been in front for long when he suddenly veered to his right, bumping Bold Abbott in the process. Held from that point, he looks one to be wary of. (op 16-1)

Diamond Hurricane(IRE) Official explanation: jockey said gelding hung badly right

3481 RUFFLER BANK H'CAP 6f

3:35 (3:37) (Class 3) (0-90,90) 3-Y-O+ £9,715 (£2,890; £1,444; £721) Stalls Low

Form				RPR
0-11	1		**Orpsie Boy (IRE)**[50] 1971 4-9-6 **88** LukeMorris(5) 13 (N P Littmoden) *hld up towards rr: rdn and gd hdwy over 1f out: led ins fnl f: r.o wl* **9/2**[1]	98
4015	2	1 1/4	**Roman Maze**[31] 2528 7-9-10 **87** JamesDoyle 1 (W M Brisbourne) *hld up towards rr: rdn and stdy prog 2f out: r.o wl to take 2nd ins fnl f: nt rch wnr* **14/1**	93
0000	3	3/4	**Indian Trail**[21] 2817 7-9-10 **90** (v) LiamTreadwell(3) 15 (D Nicholls) *t.k.h: sn plld way into mid-div: rdn and hdwy 2f out: ev ch ent fnl f: no ex* **5/1**[2]	94+
4-56	4	nk	**Swinbrook (USA)**[26] 2688 6-9-5 **82** (v) EddieAhern 16 (J A R Toller) *mid-div: switchd to far side rails w one other over 4f out: clsd on ldr 3f out: ev ch 1f out: kpt on* **9/2**[1]	85
0400	5	3/4	**Lady Livius (IRE)**[7] 3268 4-9-13 **90** (b[1]) PatDobbs 14 (R Hannon) *lw: led tl 3f out: regained led 2f out: sn rdn: hdd ins fnl f: kpt on same pce* **25/1**	91
220	6	nk	**His Master's Voice (IRE)**[30] 2573 4-8-13 **76** IanMongan 12 (D W P Arbuthnot) *mid-div: rdn and effrt 2f out: kpt on same pce fnl f* **14/1**	76
4000	7	nk	**Obe Gold**[62] 1653 5-9-10 **87** (v) DarryllHolland 6 (M R Channon) *mid-div: rdn 3f out: hung rt and styd on fnl f* **16/1**	86
5240	8	hd	**Who's Winning (IRE)**[20] 2882 6-8-10 **80** KylieManser(7) 3 (B G Powell) *b: prom: rdn over 2f out: wknd ent fnl f* **33/1**	78
1006	9	hd	**Lucayos**[13] 3104 4-9-3 **83** RichardKingscote(3) 5 (Mrs H Sweeting) *chsd ldrs: rdn over 2f out: wknd ent fnl f* **16/1**	81
0-P4	10	1/2	**Daniella**[14] 3059 5-9-2 **79** (b[1]) SaleemGolam 11 (Rae Guest) *wnt rt s: sn prom: swtchd to far side rails w one other over 4f out: led 3f out tl 2f out: grad fdd* **33/1**	75
-050	11	hd	**Roman Quest**[20] 2882 4-8-8 **71** oh1 FrancisNorton 2 (H Morrison) *lw: mid-div for 4f* **10/1**	67
4115	12	1/2	**Rainbow Bay**[33] 2494 4-8-1 **71** oh1 (v) MCGeran(7) 10 (P D Evans) *crashed through rails on way to s: t.k.h trcking ldrs: rdn over 2f out: wknd over 1f out* **25/1**	65
-010	13	shd	**Dingaan (IRE)**[21] 2817 4-9-5 **87** WilliamBuick(5) 8 (A M Balding) *s.i.s: bhd: hdwy and short lived effrt 2f out* **10/1**	81
-501	14	1/2	**Pearly Wey**[26] 2688 4-9-13 **90** JimCrowley 4 (C G Cox) *lw: a towards rr* **7/1**[3]	82
2410	15	nk	**Adantino**[13] 3104 8-9-5 **82** (b) FergusSweeney 9 (B R Millman) *mid-div tl squeezed out and lost pl over 2f out: nvr a threat after* **33/1**	74

1m 14.69s (-0.21) **Going Correction** +0.05s/f (Good) 15 Ran SP% 125.3
Speed ratings (Par 107):103,101,100,99,98 98,98,97,97,96 96,96,95,95,94
CSF £66.71 CT £337.65 TOTE £4.80: £2.40, £4.40, £2.60; EX 87.30 Trifecta £354.10 Pool £48.70 - 1.10 winning units..
Owner Miss Vanessa Church **Bred** Minch Bloodstock **Trained** Newmarket, Suffolk

FOCUS

A decent contest with the winner on the upgrade and the runner-up rated to recent form, suggesting this form is solid. Once they had sorted themselves out, the majority of the field raced up the centre but two elected to go down the far side.

NOTEBOOK

Orpsie Boy(IRE) ◆, a progressive sprinter, landed the hat-trick in ready fashion. He was 11lb higher than when scoring on the Lingfield Polytrack two starts previously and in this sort of form he could shrug off a further rise in the weights. The Stewards' Cup and Ayr Gold Cup are possible targets, as is the Hong Kong Sprint over 5f here. (op 5-1 tchd 11-2)

Roman Maze, back down in trip to 6f and eased a couple of pounds, got the cover he needs and ran on well inside the last without troubling the progressive winner.

Indian Trail had not finished closer than tenth in any of his last eight outings, but the application of a visor had produced much better efforts than his final placing would suggest on his last two starts. This was another creditable run and he is certainly on an attractive mark now. (op 4-1 tchd 11-2)

Swinbrook(USA) was taken to race on the far rail after a furlong and a half, tracking Daniella who was the only other runner to take that route. Ridden with two furlongs to run, he could only stick on at the same pace but this was a fair run in the circumstances. (op 6-1 tchd 13-2)

Lady Livius(IRE), returned to 6f after a run over the minimum at Sandown, showed a bit more dash in the headgear.

His Master's Voice(IRE) is yet to win on turf, but this was a creditable effort. Official explanation: jockey said colt was hampered at start (op 20-1)

3482 FAIRFX.COM CHALLENGE (CLAIMING STKS) 1m (S)

4:10 (4:11) (Class 4) 3-4-Y-O £6,477 (£1,927; £963; £481) Stalls Low

Form				RPR
0032	1		**Direct Debit (IRE)**[15] 3039 4-9-7 85 LukeMorris(5) 3 (M L W Bell) *lw: wnt rt s: trckd ldr: led on bit over 2f out: kpt on gamely whn chal ins fnl f: drvn out* **11/10**[1]	85+
2004	2	3/4	**Wovoka (IRE)**[7] 3258 4-9-9 83 DarryllHolland 5 (M R Channon) *hld up 6th: hdwy to trck ldr over 1f out: rdn to chal ins fnl f: kpt on but a hld* **3/1**[2]	80+
05-0	3	8	**Serene Dancer**[19] 2913 4-8-11 48 FergusSweeney 1 (Mrs P N Dutfield) *hld up 5th: rdn over 2f out: kpt on to go 3rd ent fnl f but nt pce of ldng pair* **33/1**	50
5-00	4	1/2	**Silver Blue (IRE)**[72] 1395 4-9-2 72 PatDobbs 2 (R Hannon) *lw: trckd ldr: rdn 3f out: hung rt and one pce fr over 1f out* **8/1**	54
0-00	5	1/2	**Law Of The Land (IRE)**[2] 3429 3-8-9 60 EddieAhern 4 (W R Muir) *led: rdn and hdd over 2f out: sn one pce* **25/1**	55
2440	6	3	**Tufton**[37] 2351 4-9-9 89 (t) SamHitchcott 6 (M Botti) *t.k.h trcking ldr: rdn and ev ch over 2f out: grad fdd* **7/2**[3]	53

1m 42.39s (0.59) **Going Correction** +0.05s/f (Good)
WFA 3 from 4yo 9lb 6 Ran SP% 112.7
Speed ratings (Par 105):99,98,90,89,89 86
CSF £4.70 TOTE £2.10: £1.60, £1.80; EX 4.00.
Owner Billy Maguire **Bred** Hawthorn Villa Stud **Trained** Newmarket, Suffolk

FOCUS

They raced down the centre of the track and the pace was only steady. The first two finished well clear but the time was modest and the form is limited by the third and fifth.

Tufton Official explanation: jockey said colt hung right closing stages

3483 EQUISHARE H'CAP 6f

4:45 (4:45) (Class 4) (0-80,79) 3-Y-O £6,477 (£1,927; £963; £481) Stalls Low

Form				RPR
1-2	1		**Edge Closer**[18] 2942 3-9-5 77 PatDobbs 9 (R Hannon) *lw: mde virtually all: 1l clr and in command whn wandered u.p ins fnl f: rdn out* **5/4**[1]	85+
2315	2	1 1/2	**Silca Elegance**[13] 3099 3-9-0 72 SamHitchcott 6 (M R Channon) *trckd ldrs: rdn and ev ch over 1f out: kpt on but a hld ins fnl f* **9/2**[3]	75
-343	3	hd	**Sunoverregun**[18] 2942 3-9-7 79 AmirQuinn 4 (J R Boyle) *lw: trckd wnr: rdn 2f out: 1l 2nd whn sltly hmpd ins fnl f: no ex* **3/1**[2]	81
6623	4	1 1/4	**Buckie Massa**[29] 2601 3-9-2 74 FrankieMcDonald 8 (S Kirk) *trckd ldrs: jnd ldrs 3f out: sn rdn: kpt on same pce fr over 1f out* **7/1**	73
4405	5	1	**Bentley**[4] 3369 3-8-6 64 (v) FrancisNorton 3 (D Shaw) *t.k.h: hld up bhd ldng quartet: rdn over 2f out: no imp* **11/1**	60
0006	6	1 3/4	**Lordswood (IRE)**[8] 3237 3-7-11 60 oh8 NicolPolli(5) 5 (J J Bridger) *s.i.s: hld up 6th: rdn over 2f out: no imp* **33/1**	50

1m 14.98s (0.08) **Going Correction** +0.05s/f (Good) 6 Ran SP% 111.4
Speed ratings (Par 102):101,99,98,97,95 93
CSF £7.16 CT £12.82 TOTE £1.90: £1.50, £2.20; EX 4.10 Trifecta £21.20 Pool £852.82 - 28.45 winning units. Place 6 £14.71, Place 5 £9.78.
Owner Lady Whent And Friends **Bred** Caroline Wilson **Trained** East Everleigh, Wilts
■ Stewards' Enquiry : Pat Dobbs caution: careless riding

FOCUS

A fair handicap in which the pace was only steady and the race turned into something of a sprint. The winner is progressive and the form could be rated slightly higher.

3484 EQUISHARE APPRENTICE H'CAP 1m 4f

() (Class 4) (0-85,) 4-Y-O+ £

T/Plt: £15.10 to a £1 stake. Pool: £52,743.80. 2,535.85 winning tickets. T/Qpdt: £5.70 to a £1 stake. Pool: £2,031.00. 261.40 winning tickets. TM

[2618] CHEPSTOW (L-H)

Friday, July 13

OFFICIAL GOING: Soft (good to soft in places) changing to soft after race 2 (7.00)

A wet afternoon and evening meant the ground was changed both before and during racing.

Wind: Virtually nil Weather: Raining

3485 THE CROWN AT WHITEBROOK APPRENTICE H'CAP 1m 4f 23y

6:30 (6:30) (Class 5) (0-70,65) 4-Y-O+ £2,849 (£847; £423; £211) Stalls Low

Form				RPR
360/	1		**Master Wells (IRE)**[520] 5903 6-9-7 **62** HaddenFrost 10 (J D Frost) *chsd ldr: rdn to ld wl over 1f out: r.o* **4/1**[2]	68
3206	2	1/2	**My Legal Eagle (IRE)**[20] 2890 13-8-5 **46** oh1 JamieHamblett 8 (E G Bevan) *hld up and bhd: hdwy over 3f out: rdn 2f out: r.o ins fnl f* **9/2**[3]	51
4400	3	2	**Padre Nostro (IRE)**[66] 1570 8-8-2 **46** oh1 FrankiePickard(3) 4 (M Sheppard) *sn led: set modest pce: qcknd over 6f out: rdn and hdd wl over 1f out: one pce fnl f* **5/1**	48
0/04	4	1 1/2	**Ashmolian (IRE)**[8] 3232 4-8-2 **46** oh1 JemmaMarshall(3) 3 (Miss Z C Davison) *chsd ldrs: one pce fnl 2f* **6/1**	46
-062	5	3/4	**Kuster**[8] 3250 11-9-3 **65** (b) MJMurphy(7) 9 (L M Cumani) *hld up and bhd: rdn over 3f out: swtchd lft over 2f out: styd in ins fnl f: n.d* **3/1**[1]	64
006-	6	3/4	**Rashida**[142] 6380 5-8-6 **52** (t) SophieDoyle(5) 1 (S Lycett) *led early: chsd ldrs: rdn over 1f out: fdd fnl f* **9/1**	50
004-	7	4	**Smart John**[309] 5132 7-9-10 **65** ThomasO'Brien 7 (H J Evans) *s.i.s: hld up: hdwy over 4f out: rdn and btn 2f out* **10/1**	57
5504	8	30	**Always Baileys (IRE)**[7] 3280 4-8-13 **59** (b) JosephWalsh(5) 5 (T Wall) *t.k.h: sn towards rr: rdn over 3f out: sn struggling: t.o* **6/1**	6

2m 52.64s (13.92) **Going Correction** +1.25s/f (Soft) 8 Ran SP% 127.5
Speed ratings (Par 103):103,102,101,100,99 99,96,76
CSF £25.30 CT £97.43 TOTE £6.20: £2.20, £2.00, £2.30; EX 27.60.
Owner Cloud Nine-Premier Six **Bred** Barronstown Stud And Orpendale **Trained** Scorriton, Devon
■ Go Free (11/2), Mighty Mover (25/1) & Ruggtah (25/1) were withdrawn. R4 applies, deduct 15p in the £. New market formed.
■ Stewards' Enquiry : Jamie Hamblett one-day ban: used whip with excessive frequency (Jul 24)

FOCUS

A modest handicap with three late withdrawals because their apprentice riders did not arrive in time and there were no suitable replacements. The form is moderate and, although sound, is limited by the placed horses.

Always Baileys(IRE) Official explanation: jockey said gelding never travelled

3486 EUROPEAN BREEDERS' FUND NOVICE STKS 5f 16y

7:00 (7:01) (Class 4) 2-Y-O £4,533 (£1,348; £674; £336) Stalls High

Form				RPR
4331	1		**Brassini**[31] 2526 2-9-5 JimCrowley 2 (B R Millman) *led over 1f: led again over 2f out: rdn over 1f out: r.o wl* **7/2**[2]	84
1	2	1 3/4	**Little Big Boy (IRE)**[49] 1992 2-8-9 HaddenFrost(7) 1 (R Hannon) *w ldrs: ev ch over 1f out: rdn and nt qckn ins fnl f* **5/1**[3]	75
6	3	2 1/2	**Night Robe**[11] 3162 2-8-7 PaulEddery 4 (P D Evans) *sn outpcd: late hdwy: r.o* **40/1**	57

2324 **4** 1 1/4 **Silver Guest**[22] [2785] 2-8-12 DarryllHolland 3 61+
(M R Channon) *w ldr: led over 3f out tl over 2f out: rdn over 1f out: wknd wl ins fnl f* **1/2**[1]

65.09 secs (5.49) **Going Correction** +1.00s/f (Soft) **4** Ran SP% **108.0**
Speed ratings (Par 96):96,93,89,87
CSF £18.20 TOTE £5.70; EX 21.50.
Owner The Links Partnership **Bred** B N And Mrs Toye **Trained** Kentisbeare, Devon

FOCUS
None of these were proven on soft ground and this is not a race to be confident about. The form horse finished last.

NOTEBOOK
Brassini handled the conditions and saw it out well under the stands' rail. (tchd 4-1)
Little Big Boy(IRE) had narrowly beaten a subsequent winner on his debut at Haydock. He was eventually forced to concede defeat on this totally different surface. (op 3-1)
Night Robe ◆ left the form of her heavy-ground debut at Windsor behind. She took a long time to get going and would appear to be crying out for further. (op 33-1)
Silver Guest had by far the best form of these but seemed to be the one who got found out by the rain-softened ground. (op 4-6)

3487 PETESMITHCARSALES.CO.UK SOMETHING FOR EVERYONE H'CAP 1m 14y
7:30 (7:33) (Class 5) (0-71,69) 3-Y-0+ **£3,886** (£1,156; £577; £288) **Stalls** High

Form RPR
6422 **1** **Indian Edge**[16] [2979] 6-9-9 **69** TolleyDean(5) 10 79+
(B Palling) *led centre: overall ldr wl over 2f out: sn rdn: drvn out* **3/1**[1]
2-02 **2** 1 **Milton's Keen**[14] [3045] 4-8-6 **54** HaddenFrost(7) 14 61
(M Salaman) *racd stands' side: carried lft wl over 2f out: sn chsng wnr: rdn over 1f out: kpt on ins fnl f* **7/1**[3]
60- **3** nk **Measured Response**[254] [6294] 5-8-5 **53** ThomasO'Brien(7) 7 59
(J G M O'Shea) *s.i.s: sn chsng ldrs: swtchd rt over 1f out: rdn and r.o ins fnl f* **33/1**
5013 **4** 1 1/4 **Top Jaro (FR)**[25] [2709] 4-9-11 **69** LiamTreadwell(3) 2 72
(Jennie Candlish) *a.p: rdn 3f out: one pce fnl f* **9/1**
1000 **5** 1 1/4 **The Gaikwar (IRE)**[16] [2979] 8-9-6 **66** (b) LukeMorris(5) 9 67
(R A Harris) *chsd ldrs: rdn over 2f out: one pce fnl f* **14/1**
0221 **6** 1 **The Grey One (IRE)**[15] [3034] 4-9-6 **66** (p) KevinGhunowa(5) 3 64
(J M Bradley) *s.i.s: rdn and hdwy over 3f out: no ex ins fnl f* **11/2**[2]
00-0 **7** 1 **Marker**[24] [2217] 7-9-0 **55** (b[1]) SimonWhitworth 6 51
(J D Frost) *wnt lft s: prom: rdn over 2f out: wknd ins fnl f* **14/1**
6-60 **8** 1 **Jamaahir (USA)**[42] [2218] 4-9-6 **61** (t) AdamKirby 13 55
(S Lycett) *rrd s: racd stands' side: rdn over 3f out: styd on fnl f* **10/1**
3/0- **9** 6 **Ardent Prince**[405] [2244] 4-9-5 **60** JimCrowley 5 41
(Heather Dalton) *nvr nr ldrs* **33/1**
4205 **10** 1 **Merrymadcap (IRE)**[16] [2979] 5-9-13 **68** FrancisNorton 1 47
(M Blanshard) *bhd: rdn and sme hdwy 2f out: n.d* **8/1**
0205 **11** hd **Fun In The Sun**[10] [3178] 3-8-5 **55** PaulEddery 8 33
(P D Evans) *dwlt: rdn 3f out: a bhd* **10/1**
004 **12** 1 3/4 **Salisbury Plain**[11] [3167] 6-8-5 **53** oh1 ow3 (p) KylieManser(7) 15 27
(N I M Rossiter) *racd stands' side: rdn over 4f out: sn bhd* **25/1**
0603 **13** 3/4 **Whistleupthewind**[13] [3101] 4-8-3 **51** (b) KMay(7) 16 24
(J M P Eustace) *racd stands' side: led: rdn and hung lft wl over 2f out: sn hdd & wknd* **10/1**
00-0 **14** 4 **Sparkbridge (IRE)**[44] [1893] 4-8-9 **50** oh5 FrankieMcDonald 4 14
(S C Burrough) *a towards rr* **66/1**
0035 **15** 11 **Corrib (IRE)**[16] [2980] 4-9-5 **60** DarryllHolland 12 —
(B Palling) *racd stands' side: chsd ldrs: rdn 3f out: sn wknd* **14/1**
050- **16** 3 **Croft (IRE)**[295] [5098] 4-9-0 **55** FergusSweeney 11 —
(M S Saunders) *mid-div: rdn over 3f out: sn wknd* **33/1**

1m 42.14s (6.14) **Going Correction** +1.00s/f (Soft)
WFA 3 from 4yo+ 9lb **16** Ran SP% **135.4**
Speed ratings (Par 103):109,108,107,106,105 104,103,102,96,95 95,93,92,88,77 74
CSF £25.17 CT £664.36 TOTE £4.20: £1.60, £2.00, £11.00, £2.70; EX 29.90.
Owner Nigel Thomas and Christopher Mason **Bred** Christopher J Mason **Trained** Tredodridge, Vale Of Glamorgan
■ Stewards' Enquiry : Kevin Ghunowa one-day ban: used whip with excessive frequency (Jul 24)

FOCUS
A modest event but run at a good gallop and the form could rate slightly higher. The five highest drawn runners raced on the stands' side until merging at halfway with the rest who were in the centre.
Whistleupthewind Official explanation: jockey said filly hung left-handed
Corrib(IRE) Official explanation: jockey said filly was unsuited by the soft ground

3488 THE CROWN AT WHITEBROOK H'CAP 7f 16y
8:00 (8:06) (Class 3) (0-95,86) 3-Y-0 **£7,570** (£2,265; £1,132; £566; £282) **Stalls** High

Form RPR
1311 **1** **Guilded Warrior**[8] [3239] 4-9-8 **84** 6ex FergusSweeney 7 92
(W S Kittow) *hld up in tch: rdn to ld wl over 1f out: drvn out* **7/4**[1]
0-01 **2** hd **Starlight Gazer**[8] [3234] 4-8-11 **78** 6ex TravisBlock(5) 6 86
(J A Geake) *hld up and bhd: rdn whn swtchd rt and hdwy 1f out: r.o ins fnl f* **3/1**[2]
0024 **3** 3 **Compton's Eleven**[21] [2835] 6-9-9 **85** DarryllHolland 3 85
(M R Channon) *led early: hld up: hdwy 2f out: sn rdn and ev ch: no ex towards fin* **8/1**
0123 **4** 1 **Lavenham (IRE)**[13] [3100] 4-9-2 **78** PatDobbs 2 76
(R Hannon) *hld up: rdn and hdwy 2f out: one pce fnl f* **11/2**[3]
-030 **5** 11 **Woodcote Place**[23] [2755] 4-9-10 **86** JimCrowley 4 56
(P R Chamings) *sn chsng ldr: rdn and ev ch 2f out: wknd over 1f out* **12/1**
0304 **6** 1 1/4 **Bonnie Prince Blue**[8] [3234] 4-9-3 **79** (b[1]) JamieSpencer 5 56+
(B W Hills) *sn led: rdn and hdd wl over 1f out: sn wknd* **17/2**

1m 29.24s (5.94) **Going Correction** +1.00s/f (Soft) **6** Ran SP% **106.1**
Speed ratings (Par 107):106,105,102,101,88 87
CSF £6.29 TOTE £2.20: £1.60, £1.90; EX 7.80.
Owner The Racing Guild **Bred** Manor Farm Packers Ltd **Trained** Blackborough, Devon
■ Glenbuck was withdrawn (10/1, burst out of stalls). R4 applies, deduct 5p in the £.

FOCUS
The top weight was only rated 86 in this 76-95 handicap but the first two were at home in the conditions and ran to form.

NOTEBOOK
Guilded Warrior continues to defy the Handicapper and made it four wins from five starts despite having gone up a total of 19lb. He would have had another pound to carry had his new rating been in force. (tchd 11-8)
Starlight Gazer confirmed his liking for give in the ground. In contrast to the winner, he would have had 2lb less in future handicaps and lost nothing in defeat. (op 9-2 tchd 6-1)
Compton's Eleven has run well several times on this sort of surface although he has only won on ground good or softer. (op 10-1)
Lavenham(IRE) has a very similar profile to the third in that he seems to handle the soft but his wins have come on a sound surface. (op 9-2)
Bonnie Prince Blue Official explanation: jockey said gelding ran too freely

3489 THE CROWN AT WHITEBROOK SPRINT STKS (H'CAP) 6f 16y
8:30 (8:33) (Class 2) (0-100,96) 3-Y-0+
£12,464 (£3,732; £1,866; £934; £466; £234) **Stalls** High

Form RPR
2-40 **1** **Viking Spirit**[34] [2440] 5-9-11 **94** AdamKirby 1 108
(W R Swinburn) *hld up and bhd: hdwy 2f out: hrd rdn to ld jst over 1f out: hung rt wl ins fnl f: r.o* **4/1**[2]
0204 **2** 3 **Tony James (IRE)**[13] [3104] 5-9-13 **96** GeorgeBaker 5 101
(K O Cunningham-Brown) *hld up: hdwy over 2f out: rdn and edgd rt wl over 1f out: kpt on towards fin: nt trble wnr* **14/1**
0111 **3** 2 1/2 **Osiris Way**[20] [2882] 5-8-12 **81** JimCrowley 6 79
(P R Chamings) *chsd ldr: led wl over 2f out: hrd rdn and hdd jst over 1f out: one pce* **4/1**[2]
-055 **4** nk **Greenslades**[21] [2835] 8-9-11 **94** PatDobbs 3 91
(P J Makin) *sn prom: rdn and ev ch 2f out: one pce* **10/1**[3]
0000 **5** shd **The Kiddykid (IRE)**[47] [2058] 7-9-13 **96** (v[1]) StephenDonohoe 4 92
(P D Evans) *prom: rdn and lost pl over 3f out: styd on towards fin* **12/1**
11-1 **6** 13 **Braddock (IRE)**[59] [1747] 4-8-9 **78** JamieSpencer 7 35+
(T D Barron) *led: hdd wl over 2f out: sn wknd* **5/4**[1]
4-05 **7** 3 1/2 **Mango Music**[54] [1861] 4-9-1 **84** DarryllHolland 8 31
(M R Channon) *prom tl wknd wl over 1f out* **16/1**

1m 17.04s (4.64) **Going Correction** +1.00s/f (Soft) **7** Ran SP% **113.8**
Speed ratings (Par 109):109,105,101,101,101 83,79
CSF £54.25 CT £236.45 TOTE £5.40: £2.30, £5.10; EX 29.50.
Owner The Masterminds **Bred** Bearstone Stud **Trained** Aldbury, Herts

FOCUS
An interesting little handicap for some decent prizemoney and, with the time decent, the form is rated positively through the runner-up.

NOTEBOOK
Viking Spirit had ground conditions to suit and made amends for an unlucky run last time by registering his first victory since his two-year-old days. (tchd 7-2)
Tony James(IRE), who has not won since landing the Gimcrack in similar conditions, was never going to peg back the winner. (tchd 12-1)
Osiris Way could not overcome having been raised a total of 23lb for completing a hat-trick in what was admittedly softer ground than at Newmarket last time. (op 10-3)
Greenslades should have appreciated both the testing conditions and a drop back to six. (op 7-1 tchd 12-1)
The Kiddykid(IRE) looked in deep trouble in the first-time visor at halfway but he did find something of a second wind late on. (op 9-1)
Braddock(IRE), raised 7lb, was bitterly disappointing and was beaten so early that the drop back in distance was not an excuse. Official explanation: trainer had no explanation for the poor form shown (op 2-1)

3490 REUSSIR BRICKWORK CONTRACTORS FILLIES' H'CAP 1m 14y
9:00 (9:00) (Class 5) (0-70,68) 3-Y-0 **£3,886** (£1,156; £577; £288) **Stalls** High

Form RPR
042 **1** **Montrachet**[20] [2873] 3-9-7 **68** JamieSpencer 5 74
(M L W Bell) *hld up: hdwy over 3f out: wnt 2nd over 2f out: sn rdn: edgd lft and led ins fnl f: r.o* **5/2**[1]
0105 **2** 2 **Princess Zada**[13] [3087] 3-9-6 **67** FergusSweeney 4 69
(B R Millman) *a.p: led 4f out: rdn over 1f out: hdd and no ex ins fnl f* **11/4**[2]
-035 **3** 2 1/2 **Bidable**[46] [2079] 3-8-12 **62** RichardKingscote(3) 9 59
(B Palling) *prom: rdn over 3f out: outpcd over 2f out: styd on ins fnl f* **7/1**
0400 **4** 7 **Rubilini**[16] [3000] 3-8-8 **55** SamHitchcott 6 36
(M R Channon) *bhd: rdn over 3f out: nvr nr ldrs* **18/1**
5-05 **5** 4 **Inimical**[33] [2489] 3-8-6 **53** (v) FrancisNorton 2 25
(W S Kittow) *t.k.h: stmbld over 6f out: hdwy over 4f out: rdn over 3f out: wknd over 2f out* **14/1**
003- **6** 1 1/2 **Vanatina (IRE)**[315] [4986] 3-8-9 **56** ow1 StephenDonohoe 7 25
(Heather Dalton) *prom tl rdn and wknd over 2f out* **33/1**
2250 **7** 4 **First Princess (IRE)**[4] [3384] 3-8-10 **62** (p) TolleyDean(5) 3 22
(J S Moore) *rdn over 3f out: a bhd* **8/1**
2313 **8** 10 **Rebel Pearl (IRE)**[10] [3181] 3-9-2 **66** JerryO'Dwyer(3) 10 4
(M G Quinlan) *led: hdd 4f out: rdn and wknd over 2f out* **7/2**[3]
0-00 **9** 14 **Miss Silver Spurs**[7] [3274] 3-8-2 **49** oh4 (v) FrankieMcDonald 8 —
(M D I Usher) *bhd: rdn over 4f out: lost tch 3f out* **50/1**

1m 44.63s (8.63) **Going Correction** +1.00s/f (Soft) **9** Ran SP% **117.9**
Speed ratings (Par 97):96,94,91,84,80 79,75,65,51
CSF £9.82 CT £42.50 TOTE £2.60: £1.70, £1.70, £3.10; EX 9.30 Place 6 £168.37, Place 6 £77.34..
Owner Mr & Mrs G Middlebrook **Bred** G And Mrs Middlebrook **Trained** Newmarket, Suffolk
■ Stewards' Enquiry : Frankie McDonald one-day ban: used whip when out of contention (Jul 24)

FOCUS
The first three finished clear in this minor fillies' handicap but not the most solid contest.
Rebel Pearl(IRE) Official explanation: jockey said filly hung left-handed
T/Plt: £414.00 to a £1 stake. Pool: £58,881.30. 103.80 winning tickets. T/Qpdt: £29.10 to a £1 stake. Pool: £4,469.70. 113.48 winning tickets. KH

3076 CHESTER (L-H)
Friday, July 13

OFFICIAL GOING: Heavy
Wind: Moderate, behind Weather: Wet

3491 ETHEL AUSTIN PROPERTIES H'CAP 7f 122y
6:40 (6:41) (Class 4) (0-80,81) 3-Y-0 **£5,829** (£1,734; £866; £432) **Stalls** Low

Form RPR
6-54 **1** **Thunderousapplause**[36] [2395] 3-9-3 **75** DO'Donohoe 2 85
(K A Ryan) *hld up: gd hdwy to ld over 2f out: rdn clr over 1f out: drifted rt ins fnl f: wl in command and r.o wl after* **5/1**[3]
0025 **2** 8 **Just Oscar (GER)**[23] [2759] 3-8-1 **62** LiamJones(3) 1 54
(W M Brisbourne) *dwlt: racd keenly: hld up: hdwy on outside over 2f out: wnt 2nd over 1f out: sn hung lft and no ch w wnr* **6/1**
-350 **3** nk **Okikoki**[20] [2881] 3-9-6 **78** RichardMullen 7 70
(W R Muir) *chsd ldrs: nt clr run over 2f out: plugged on to take 3rd ent fnl f: kpt on to chal for 2nd wout threatening wnr* **7/2**[2]
1-63 **4** 6 **Steady As A Rock (FR)**[13] [3094] 3-9-7 **79** DeanMcKeown 5 58
(M Johnston) *sn led: rdn and hdd over 2f out: wknd over 1f out* **7/4**[1]
6163 **5** 6 **Multitude (IRE)**[19] [2910] 3-8-7 **68** DuranFentiman(3) 3 33
(T D Easterby) *chsd ldrs tl pushed along and wknd over 2f out* **5/1**[3]

5-00 **6** *2 1/2* **Chin Wag (IRE)**[55] 1851 3-9-7 **79**.. LeeEnstone 6 39
(K R Burke) *prom: rdn and ev ch 3f out: wknd over 2f out: eased whn btn ins fnl f* **10/1**

1m 41.35s (6.60) **Going Correction** +0.725s/f (Yiel) **6** Ran SP% **115.3**
Speed ratings (Par 102):96,88,87,81,75 73
CSF £34.78 TOTE £4.70: £2.10, £3.40; EX 40.40.
Owner Paul J Dixon **Bred** Mrs Yvette Dixon **Trained** Hambleton, N Yorks

FOCUS
An ordinary handicap and they finished well strung out in the very testing conditions, so it is not easy to be confident the winner is value for the winning margin.

3492 OWEN ELLIS ARCHITECTS CONDITIONS STKS 5f 16y
7:10 (7:11) (Class 2) 2-Y-O **£9,148** (£2,737; £1,368; £684; £340) **Stalls** Low

Form RPR

6231 **1** **Captain Gerrard (IRE)**[13] 3077 2-9-0 0........................ RichardMullen 7 99
(B Smart) *chsd ldng pair: bmpd whn burst through gap to ld over 1f out: r.o* **5/4**[1]

1 **2** *1 1/2* **Broken Applause (IRE)**[20] 2869 2-8-6 0...................... TonyHamilton 1 86+
(R A Fahey) *midfield: pushed along and outpced over 3f out: dropped to rr 2f out: hdwy over 1f out: fin strly: nt rch wnr* **2/1**[2]

1362 **3** *1 1/2* **Kersaint (IRE)**[13] 3077 2-8-11 0.......................... DO'Donohoe 5 86
(K A Ryan) *sn outpcd and pushed along: hdwy over 2f out: pressed ldrs over 1f out: no ex towards fin* **11/2**[3]

014 **4** *2 1/2* **Only In Jest**[27] 2650 2-8-9 0...........................(t) LiamJones 4 75
(W G M Turner) *pressed ldr: led wl over 1f out: sn rdn and hdd: wknd wl ins fnl f* **18/1**

2663 **5** *nk* **Cayman Fox**[25] 2717 2-8-6 0.......................... DeanMcKeown 2 71
(James Moffatt) *led: rdn and hdd wl over 1f out: hung lft whn wkng ins fnl f* **10/1**

3141 **6** *2 1/2* **Style Award**[7] 3256 2-8-9 0.................................... PatrickHills 8 65
(W J H Ratcliffe) *midfield: effrt over 1f out: sn btn* **14/1**

56 **7** *4* **Planet Queen**[23] 2758 2-8-6 0.................................. HayleyTurner 3 48
(K R Burke) *in rr: nt clr run 3f out: sn swtchd rt: no imp wl over 1f out* **33/1**

61 **8** *4* **Weet A Surprise**[15] 3030 2-8-6 0.......................... DuranFentiman 6 34
(R Hollinshead) *a outpcd and bhd* **20/1**

65.56 secs (3.51) **Going Correction** +0.725s/f (Yiel) **8** Ran SP% **121.9**
Speed ratings (Par 100):100,97,95,91,90 86,80,73
CSF £4.26 TOTE £2.20: £1.10, £1.20, £1.70; EX 4.50.
Owner R C Bond **Bred** Alan Dargan **Trained** Hambleton, N Yorks

FOCUS
Not a bad little race and it was run at a good pace considering the testing ground. The form looks pretty sound rated around the first three.

NOTEBOOK
Captain Gerrard(IRE), who bolted up in a little novice event over the course and distance last time out, was proven in soft ground and showed good speed from the traps to track the two pace-setters in third. He nipped through on the inside entering the straight and ran on well, and he will now probably take a step up in grade. His trainer has some nice two-year-olds this season and this speedy sort deserves to take his chance at Pattern level. (op 6-4 tchd 13-8)
Broken Applause(IRE) ◆, who overcame greenness to win on her debut, struggled to go the early pace but she found her stride in the latter stages, followed the winner through on the inside and was making up ground strongly at the finish. She will relish another furlong, is clearly well suited to soft ground and is capable of improving further. (tchd 15-8)
Kersaint(IRE), who was runner-up to Captain Gerrard here last time out, had five lengths to find with that rival and a 7lb pull in the weights resulted in him cutting that advantage down to three lengths. However, whether he wants the ground this soft is open to question. (tchd 5-1)
Only In Jest showed good early speed to press Cayman Fox for the lead, but she simply helped set things up for those ridden a bit more patiently. (op 20-1 tchd 16-1)
Cayman Fox, the most experienced runner in the line-up, probably set too strong a pace given the testing conditions and did not get home. (op 14-1)
Style Award, who had a 3lb penalty to carry for her win in a novice event at Beverley, had the race run to suit but could only find the one pace in the straight. (op 16-1)
Weet A Surprise Official explanation: trainer said filly was unsuited by the heavy ground

3493 8TH KATHLEEN B. CORBETT MEMORIAL H'CAP 5f 16y
7:40 (7:41) (Class 3) (0-95,92) 3-Y-O **£9,148** (£2,737; £1,368; £684; £340) **Stalls** Low

Form RPR

3212 **1** **Obstructive**[14] 3061 3-8-9 **85**.. PatrickHills(5) 3 96
(D K Ivory) *mde all: rdn and hung lft over 1f out: r.o: pushed out towards fin* **11/4**[1]

1133 **2** *1 3/4* **Morinqua (IRE)**[5] 3344 3-9-2 **92**.............................. ColinHaddon(5) 7 97
(J G Given) *chsd ldrs: wnt 2nd wl over 2f out: sn pressed wnr: nt qckn over 1f out: a hld after* **7/2**[3]

4101 **3** *1* **The Nifty Fox**[20] 2867 3-9-0 **85**............................... DO'Donohoe 2 86
(T D Easterby) *chsd ldrs: effrt whn sltly checked over 1f out: kpt on same pce ins fnl f* **3/1**[2]

2330 **4** *1 3/4* **Foxy Music**[31] 2529 3-8-8 **79**.............................. DeanMcKeown 6 74
(E J Alston) *racd keenly and pressed wnr: lost 2nd wl over 2f out: hung rt wl over 1f out: sn btn* **12/1**

1056 **5** *shd* **Fish Called Johnny**[20] 2867 3-8-2 **73**.......................... HayleyTurner 1 68
(Peter Grayson) *s.i.s: outpcd and bhd: styd on fnl f: nt pce to trble ldrs* **13/2**

3361 **6** *2 1/2* **Feelin Foxy**[18] 2950 3-7-13 **73**...............................(v) LiamJones(3) 5 59
(D Shaw) *hld up bhd ldrs: rdn over 2f out: wknd over 1f out* **10/1**

0-02 **7** *16* **Ice Mountain**[45] 2119 3-9-0 **85**.............................. RichardMullen 4 15
(B Smart) *sn outpcd: wl bhd fr 3f out: eased ins fnl f* **13/2**

64.83 secs (2.78) **Going Correction** +0.725s/f (Yiel) **7** Ran SP% **117.3**
Speed ratings (Par 104):106,103,101,98,98 94,69
CSF £13.29 TOTE £3.20: £2.00, £2.40; EX 13.30.
Owner A S Reid **Bred** A S Reid **Trained** Radlett, Herts

FOCUS
A decent race and, as there were one or two improving sprinters here, the form should work out alright.

NOTEBOOK
Obstructive, who was unlucky to run into a quickly improving rival at Newmarket last time, was put up 5lb for that effort. To deal with that, his trainer booked Patrick Hills, who can claim 5lb, and the partnership proved successful. Fast out of the gates, he made every yard for a comfortable win which confirmed his progressive profile. Versatile with regard to ground conditions, he looks sure to continue improving as he strengthens up. (op 15-8)
Morinqua(IRE), who began the year on a mark of 70, has improved considerably over the past few months, so much so that she placed in Listed company last time. Although denied her favoured front-running role, she ran a perfectly respectable race but could make no impression on the well-handicapped winner in the straight. (op 3-1 tchd 4-1)
The Nifty Fox also ran a sound race considering that the ground was probably softer than ideal. (op 9-2)
Foxy Music clearly wanted to make the running but he was denied that role by the favourite and ended up racing too keenly for his own good. He has plenty of speed. Official explanation: jockey said bit slipped through gelding's mouth (tchd 11-1)
Fish Called Johnny, whose two career wins have come over 6f, was slowly away and badly outpaced for much of the race. He will appreciate a return to further. (op 10-1)
Feelin Foxy, 6lb higher following her win on Polytrack last time, is still searching for her first win on turf. (op 11-1)
Ice Mountain was outpaced throughout and probably needs faster ground. Official explanation: trainer said gelding was unsuited by the heavy ground (op 8-1)

3494 ASTBURY WREN NURSERY 6f 18y
8:10 (8:10) (Class 4) 2-Y-O **£5,440** (£1,618; £808; £404) **Stalls** Low

Form RPR

021 **1** **La Chicaluna**[32] 2504 2-8-13 **77**.................................. RoystonFfrench 4 77+
(J G Given) *mde all: rdn over 1f out: hld on gamely towards fin* **11/8**[1]

310 **2** *nk* **Russian Reel**[24] 2737 2-9-7 **85**.. DO'Donohoe 3 85+
(K A Ryan) *chsd wnr: rdn over 1f out: ev ch and str chal ins fnl f but a hld* **15/8**[2]

2201 **3** *3 1/2* **Rio Taffeta**[25] 2723 2-8-1 **65**... HayleyTurner 6 54
(Peter Grayson) *in rr: pushed along 3f out: sn hung rt: chsd front pair wl over 1f out but no imp* **3/1**[3]

0050 **4** *13* **Thomas Malory (IRE)**[41] 2251 2-7-11 **66**...................... ColinHaddon(5) 7 16
(Miss V Haigh) *hung rt most of way: chsd ldrs: rn v wd and wknd ent st wl over 1f out* **8/1**

1m 21.94s (6.29) **Going Correction** +1.05s/f (Soft) **4** Ran SP% **113.0**
Speed ratings (Par 96):100,99,94,77
CSF £4.52 TOTE £1.90; EX 3.30.
Owner The Living Legend Racing Partnership **Bred** Gainsborough Stud Ltd **Trained** Willoughton, Lincs

■ Stewards' Enquiry : Royston Ffrench two-day ban: used whip with excessive frequency (Jul 24-25)
D O'Donohoe two-day ban: used whip with excessive frequency (Jul 24-25)

FOCUS
There was an ordinary gallop to this nursery and the winner dominated throughout. The form looks sound with the first two improving. The official ratings shown next to each horse are estimated and for information purposes only.

NOTEBOOK
La Chicaluna, although successful on fast ground last time, is a daughter of Cadeaux Genereux, so the conditions were probably not a concern to connections. She enjoyed the run of the race in being able to dictate a pretty ordinary gallop and, when she quickened from the front, she was always going to hold the challenge of Russian Reel. (op 5-6)
Russian Reel, last seen running at Royal Ascot, raced in second throughout and, although he edged closer to the winner in the closing stages, he was always being held. (op 9-4 tchd 5-2)
Rio Taffeta, who finally got off the mark in a seller last time out, was too keen for his own good and never seriously threatened the front two. (op 6-1)
Thomas Malory(IRE) did not cope with the track very well, running wide throughout and hanging badly right off the bend into the straight, giving away lots of ground in the process. Official explanation: jockey said colt hung right (tchd 7-1)

3495 SHELL UK H'CAP 1m 2f 75y
8:40 (8:40) (Class 4) (0-85,84) 3-Y-O **£5,829** (£1,734; £866; £432) **Stalls** High

Form RPR

0-43 **1** **Rosbay (IRE)**[58] 1773 3-9-1 **81**.............................. DuranFentiman(3) 2 89+
(T D Easterby) *midfield: pushed along over 3f out: hdwy over 2f out: carried wd ent st wl over 1f out: hung lft and led 1f out: styd on wl* **3/1**[1]

2211 **2** *3* **Milla's Rocket (IRE)**[10] 3196 3-9-2 **79** 6ex.......................... DO'Donohoe 8 81
(K A Ryan) *a.p: led over 2f out: rdn and hdd 1f out: one pce ins fnl f* **9/2**[3]

12-6 **3** *nk* **Sagredo (USA)**[30] 2574 3-9-7 **84**.......................... PaulMulrennan 7 85
(Sir Mark Prescott) *stdd s: sn swtchd lft: hld up: hdwy whn nt clr run over 2f out: rdn over 1f out: styd on towards fin* **7/1**

2300 **4** *3/4* **New World Order (IRE)**[20] 2862 3-8-12 **75**...................... LeeEnstone 1 75
(K R Burke) *trckd ldrs: rdn over 1f out: kpt on same pce* **12/1**

3311 **5** *6* **Magic Echo**[22] 2794 3-9-1 **78**.. PhillipMakin 4 67
(M Dods) *led: rdn and hdd over 2f out: plld out ent st wl over 1f out: sn wknd* **7/2**[2]

-014 **6** *3* **Radical Views**[30] 2577 3-9-0 **77**................................... DaneO'Neill 9 61
(B W Hills) *towards rr: pushed along over 4f out: no imp fr 2f out: eased whn btn ins fnl f* **9/2**[3]

-020 **7** *28* **Sir Sandicliffe (IRE)**[137] 569 3-8-1 **67**........................ LiamJones(3) 5 —
(W M Brisbourne) *hld up: rdn over 4f out: sn lost tch* **16/1**

0-66 **8** *11* **Prince Golan (IRE)**[20] 2862 3-9-5 **82**........................(p) RoystonFfrench 3 —
(K A Ryan) *racd keenly: in tch: pushed along over 4f out: wknd 3f out: lost tch over 2f out* **8/1**

2m 23.0s (9.86) **Going Correction** +1.05s/f (Soft) **8** Ran SP% **120.8**
Speed ratings (Par 102):102,99,99,98,93 91,69,60
CSF £17.93 CT £89.64 TOTE £4.90: £1.70, £1.30, £2.20; EX 18.60.
Owner Croft, Taylor, Stone & Hebdon **Bred** Alan Dargan **Trained** Great Habton, N Yorks

FOCUS
A fairly competitive little handicap run at a fair pace and a decisive winner from two in-form rivals, which gives the form a solid feel.
Prince Golan(IRE) Official explanation: jockey said colt had no more to give

3496 CHESHIRE YEOMANRY H'CAP 1m 4f 66y
9:10 (9:11) (Class 5) (0-75,75) 3-Y-O+ **£3,617** (£1,067; £534) **Stalls** Low

Form RPR

5010 **1** **Prelude**[22] 2810 6-8-8 **58** oh3.. LiamJones(3) 1 66
(W M Brisbourne) *s.i.s: in tch: niggled along 5f out: clsd to chse ldr over 3f out: led over 1f out: styd on wl to draw clr ins fnl f* **4/1**[3]

1143 **2** *5* **Court Of Appeal**[16] 2987 10-9-9 **70**...........................(t) RoystonFfrench 4 71
(B Ellison) *chsd ldr: led over 3f out: rdn 2f out: hdd over 1f out: one pce ins fnl f* **5/2**[1]

3 *8* **Command Marshal (FR)**[31] 4-9-9 **75**............................ PatrickHills(5) 3 64
(M Scudamore) *chsd ldrs: rdn 3f out: lost tch w front pair over 1f out* **10/1**

0312 **4** *shd* **Compton Dragon (USA)**[15] 3012 8-8-5 **59**................... KirstyMilczarek(7) 5 47
(W M Brisbourne) *s.i.s: bhd: pushed along after 4f: sme hdwy over 2f out: no imp on ldrs* **3/1**[2]

4160 **5** *18* **Thorny Mandate**[3] 3407 5-9-0 **61**...................................... RichardMullen 6 22
(W M Brisbourne) *s.s: racd keenly: hld up: pushed along 3f out: sn btn* **8/1**

0015 **6** *1 1/4* **Mahmjra**[8] 3243 5-9-5 **66**... EdwardCreighton 2 25
(C N Allen) *led: rdn and hdd over 3f out: sn wknd* **9/2**

2m 54.35s (13.70) **Going Correction** +1.05s/f (Soft) **6** Ran SP% **112.0**
Speed ratings (Par 103):96,92,87,87,75 74
CSF £14.32 CT £89.39 TOTE £6.20: £2.50, £1.70; EX 18.70 Place 6 £59.43, Place 5 £7.98..
Owner A P Burgoyne **Bred** Cheveley Park Stud Ltd **Trained** Great Ness, Shropshire

FOCUS
A modest handicap which turned into quite a stamina test. The first two home were the two previous course and distance winners in the race, and the form is solid but limited.
Thorny Mandate Official explanation: trainer said gelding was unsuited by the heavy ground

Mahmjra Official explanation: trainer said gelding was unsuited by the heavy ground and lost a near-fore shoe
T/Plt: £24.20 to a £1 stake. Pool: £64,255.00. 1,935.95 winning tickets. T/Qpdt: £4.60 to a £1 stake. Pool: £3,378.30. 536.35 winning tickets. DO

3180 HAMILTON (R-H)

Friday, July 13

OFFICIAL GOING: Good to soft (7.7)
Wind: Virtually nil Weather: Raining

3497 JOHN SMITH'S EXTRA COLD H'CAP 1m 65y
6:50 (6:54) (Class 6) (0-60,58) 3-Y-0+ **£2,914** (£867; £433; £216) **Stalls** High

Form RPR
03-1 **1** **Whittinghamvillage**[21] 2823 6-8-8 **50** LanceBetts(7) 11 58
(D W Whillans) *chsd ldrs: led over 2f out: hld on gamely fnl f* **7/1**[3]
6062 **2** *hd* **Mandarin Rocket (IRE)**[10] 3182 4-8-12 **50** AndrewMullen(3) 12 58
(Miss L A Perratt) *in tch: drvn and outpcd over 2f out: kpt on fnl f: jst hld* **5/1**[2]
6106 **3** *nk* **Muncaster Castle (IRE)**[72] 1410 3-8-9 **53** SilvestreDeSousa 14 58
(R F Fisher) *chsd clr ldr: ev ch over 2f out: kpt on fnl f: hld towards fin* **10/1**
-515 **4** *nk* **Keisha Kayleigh (IRE)**[11] 3156 4-9-2 **56** (v) PJMcDonald(5) 8 63
(B Ellison) *hld up: rdn over 3f out: hdwy wl over 1f out: kpt on fnl f: nrst fin* **12/1**
0543 **5** *1/2* **Kirkby's Treasure**[4] 3376 9-9-9 **58** PatCosgrave 7 63
(G A Swinbank) *hld up: rdn over 3f out: kpt on fnl f* **5/1**[2]
3401 **6** *1 1/4* **Mayadeen (IRE)**[10] 3182 5-9-9 **58** 6ex (b) TomEaves 2 61
(I Semple) *bhd tl styd on fr 2f out: nrst fin* **9/2**[1]
0205 **7** *1/2* **Shadow Jumper (IRE)**[4] 3375 6-8-8 **46** (v) DominicFox(3) 5 47
(J T Stimpson) *led and clr: hdd over 2f out: sn rdn: kpt on same pce over 1f out* **20/1**
-506 **8** *1 3/4* **Lambency (IRE)**[21] 2827 4-8-7 **49** KellyHarrison(7) 9 46
(J S Goldie) *towards rr: rdn 4f out: rallied 2f out: no imp fnl f* **12/1**
-000 **9** *1* **Newcorp Lad**[49] 2007 7-8-10 **45** DaleGibson 6 40
(Mrs G S Rees) *prom tl rdn and outpcd fr 2f out* **25/1**
0001 **10** *2 1/2* **Drink To Me Only**[4] 3376 4-8-13 **51** 6ex JamieMoriarty(3) 3 40
(J R Weymes) *hld up: rdn over 3f out: sn btn* **9/1**
-406 **11** *3* **Musical Giant (USA)**[38] 2348 4-8-12 **47** PaulFessey 13 29+
(J Wade) *prom: drvn over 3f out: sn outpcd* **20/1**
0034 **12** *11* **Ho Pang Yau**[4] 3376 9-8-7 **49** GaryBartley(7) 1 6
(J S Goldie) *hld up outside: drvn over 3f out: sn wknd* **20/1**
-000 **13** *6* **Pachello (IRE)**[45] 2108 5-8-8 **50** (p) BarrySavage(7) 4 —
(J M Bradley) *s.i.s: smooth hdwy and in tch 1/2-way: wknd over 2f out* **50/1**
006/ **14** *4* **Penmon Point (IRE)**[701] 4294 4-8-7 **45** AlanCreighton(3) 10 —
(R Johnson) *towards rr: rdn 4f out: sn btn* **100/1**

1m 47.31s (-1.99) **Going Correction** -0.20s/f (Firm)
WFA 3 from 4yo+ 9lb **14 Ran SP% 119.6**
Speed ratings (Par 101):101,100,100,100,99 98,97,96,95,92 89,78,72,68
CSF £37.95 CT £280.90 TOTE £8.10: £2.50, £2.00, £3.60; EX 49.40.
Owner Flex Racing **Bred** T And M A Bibby **Trained** Hawick, Borders

FOCUS
A run-of-the-mill handicap in which the pace was sound throughout. This bare form looks solid and should stand up at a similar level.

3498 NO NONSENSE (S) STKS 5f 4y
7:20 (7:22) (Class 6) 3-Y-0+ **£2,266** (£674; £337; £168) **Stalls** Centre

Form RPR
0020 **1** **Funfair Wane**[10] 3185 8-9-0 56 AdrianTNicholls 7 64
(D Nicholls) *mde all: rdn and r.o wl fnl f* **11/2**[2]
-005 **2** *1 1/4* **Highland Song (IRE)**[5] 3347 4-9-0 52 PatCosgrave 9 59
(R F Fisher) *cl up: ev ch over 1f out: kpt on ins fnl f* **13/2**
3506 **3** *2 1/2* **Lake Chini (IRE)**[10] 3180 5-9-0 73 (p) DaleGibson 12 50
(M W Easterby) *midfield: drvn 1/2-way: kpt on fnl f: nt rch first two* **9/2**[1]
0130 **4** *nk* **Seven No Trumps**[4] 3368 10-9-6 52 TomEaves 2 55
(J M Bradley) *prom: drvn over 2f out: kpt on same pce fnl f* **7/1**
4200 **5** *nk* **Blackheath (IRE)**[23] 2761 11-9-6 49 SilvestreDeSousa 11 54
(D Nicholls) *in tch centre: drvn over 2f out: one pce over 1f out* **10/1**
4056 **6** *2* **Oeuf A La Neige**[5] 3345 7-9-0 46 PaulFessey 4 41
(Miss L A Perratt) *prom: edgd rt thrght: rdn over 2f out: no ex appr fnl f* **9/2**[1]
5600 **7** *1* **Alexia Rose (IRE)**[5] 3347 5-8-6 45 (b) JamieMoriarty(3) 1 32
(A Berry) *bhd tl styd on fr over 1f out: nrst fin* **25/1**
5140 **8** *3/4* **Mister Incredible**[4] 3368 4-8-13 52 (v) BarrySavage(7) 8 40
(J M Bradley) *chsd ldrs tl rdn and wknd over 1f out* **12/1**
0000 **9** *1 1/4* **Alfie Lee (IRE)**[4] 3374 10-8-11 33 (t) AndrewMullen(3) 5 30
(D A Nolan) *towards rr: drvn 1/2-way: nvr on terms* **150/1**
0002 **10** *5* **Newcastles Owen (IRE)**[10] 3180 4-8-11 44 AlanCreighton(3) 13 12
(R Johnson) *racd in centre: drvn towards rr 1/2-way: nvr on terms* **6/1**[3]
0000 **11** *4* **Mister Marmaduke**[4] 3374 6-8-11 38 (p) DominicFox(3) 3 —
(D A Nolan) *missed break: nvr on terms* **100/1**
0-00 **12** *3* **Pays D'Amour (IRE)**[36] 2390 10-8-9 38 (t) PJMcDonald(5) 10 —
(D A Nolan) *sn bhd and outpcd: nvr on terms* **125/1**

60.46 secs (-0.74) **Going Correction** +0.025s/f (Good) **12 Ran SP% 114.9**
Speed ratings (Par 101):106,104,100,99,99 95,94,93,91,83 76,71
CSF £39.48 TOTE £6.60: £2.30, £2.80, £2.20; EX 58.80.There was no bid for the winner.
Owner The Wayward Lads **Bred** J K Keegan **Trained** Sessay, N Yorks

FOCUS
A moderate event but a decent gallop and this form looks reliable for the grade.

3499 JOHN SMITH'S EXTRA SMOOTH NURSERY 6f 5y
7:50 (7:51) (Class 4) 2-Y-0 **£5,181** (£1,541; £770; £384) **Stalls** Centre

Form RPR
2412 **1** **Lady Benjamin**[3] 3398 2-8-4 **67** AndrewElliott(3) 3 70
(P C Haslam) *mde all: rdn 2f out: edgd rt ins fnl f: hld on wl* **6/4**[1]
322 **2** *1/2* **Romantic Destiny**[19] 2904 2-8-13 **73** TomEaves 5 74
(K A Ryan) *chsd ldrs: drvn and outpcd over 2f out: rallied to chse wnr ins fnl f: kpt on* **4/1**[3]
620 **3** *1 3/4* **Our Sunnie**[15] 3024 2-8-8 **68** AdrianTNicholls 4 64
(D Nicholls) *t.k.h: chsd ldrs: effrt and ev ch over 1f out: no ex and lost 2nd ins fnl f* **9/1**
261 **4** *1 1/2* **Charlotti Carlotti (IRE)**[21] 2818 2-9-7 **81** PaulFessey 2 72
(T D Barron) *w wnr: drvn over 2f out: wknd over 1f out* **13/8**[2]
0460 **5** *2 1/2* **Limestone**[15] 3024 2-7-12 **58** oh4 (b1) DaleGibson 1 42
(J R Weymes) *sn bhd and outpcd: sme late hdwy: nvr on terms* **40/1**

1m 14.3s (1.20) **Going Correction** +0.025s/f (Good) **5 Ran SP% 110.5**
Speed ratings (Par 96):93,92,90,88,84
CSF £7.92 TOTE £2.60: £1.30, £2.00; EX 9.90.
Owner Geoffrey Lampard & S A B Dinsmore **Bred** Llety Stud **Trained** Middleham Moor, N Yorks

FOCUS
An ordinary contest and, although Charlotti Carlotti disappointed, the winner is a reliable yardstick and along with the third helps set the level. The official ratings shown next to each horse are estimated and for information purposes only.

NOTEBOOK
Lady Benjamin, who attracted plenty of support, is a consistent sort who showed a determined attitude to notch his second win over this course and distance. She should have no problems with 7f and should continue to give a good account. (op 2-1)
Romantic Destiny has shown a fair level of form in all four starts and, although yet to win a race, she shaped as though the step up to 7f would be in her favour. She looks sure to win an ordinary event. (op 10-3)
Our Sunnie looked to have a bit to find from a stiffish mark on his nursery debut but, although showing improved form, he did not look the most straightforward of individuals. However, he looks set to win an ordinary event. (op 12-1)
Charlotti Carlotti(IRE), a half-sister to multiple winners Rancho Cucamonga and Raccoon, looked the type to progress in nursery company over this trip but she proved a disappointment on this occasion. She may be better on a sound surface and is worth another chance in ordinary company. (op 11-8, tchd 7-4 in place)
Limestone, tried in blinkers, was not totally disgraced from 4lb out of the handicap but he will have to show more before he is a solid betting proposition. (tchd 33-1)

3500 JOHN SMITH'S SCOTTISH STEWARDS CUP H'CAP 6f 5y
8:20 (8:21) (Class 2) (0-105,105) 3-Y-0+
£21,812 (£6,531; £3,265; £1,634; £815; £409) **Stalls** Centre

Form RPR
2-60 **1** **Knot In Wood (IRE)**[20] 2858 5-9-0 **95** JamieMoriarty(3) 7 110+
(R A Fahey) *prom gng wl: smooth hdwy to ld over 1f out: rdn clr fnl f* **4/1**[1]
0001 **2** *3* **Protector (SAF)**[13] 3089 6-9-11 **103** PatCosgrave 6 109
(Miss Gay Kelleway) *prom: effrt and ch over 1f out: kpt on fnl f: nt pce of wnr* **4/1**[1]
5330 **3** *1 1/2* **Ingleby Arch (USA)**[21] 2817 4-8-12 **90** PaulFessey 2 92
(T D Barron) *in tch: drvn and outpcd over 2f out: r.o wl fnl f* **13/2**[2]
0614 **4** *1 1/4* **Ice Planet**[13] 3089 6-8-11 **92** AndrewMullen(3) 13 90
(D Nicholls) *in tch: effrt and rdn over 2f out: one pce fnl f* **12/1**
2304 **5** *1 1/2* **Bahamian Pirate (USA)**[12] 3140 12-9-0 **92** AdrianTNicholls 10 85
(D Nicholls) *bhd tl hdwy over 1f out: nrst fin* **18/1**
5201 **6** *hd* **Turnkey**[3] 3401 5-8-11 **96** 6ex AdeleRothery(7) 5 89
(D Nicholls) *sn wl bhd: hdwy centre over 2f out: no imp fnl f* **7/1**[3]
3-60 **7** *nk* **Hartshead**[162] 331 8-9-0 **95** AndrewElliott(3) 8 87
(G A Swinbank) *midfield: outpcd over 2f out: r.o fnl f* **33/1**
0002 **8** *1 1/4* **First Order**[16] 2989 6-8-5 **86** oh2 (v) DominicFox(3) 4 74
(I Semple) *led and sn clr: hdd over 1f out: sn btn* **20/1**
301 **9** *3/4* **Eisteddfod**[45] 2111 6-9-11 **103** SebSanders 14 89
(P F I Cole) *in tch tl rdn and wknd over 1f out: eased whn btn* **7/1**[3]
0160 **10** *1* **Wyatt Earp (IRE)**[21] 2817 6-9-0 **92** DaleGibson 1 75
(R A Fahey) *hld up: rdn over 2f out: n.d* **12/1**
-110 **11** *1 1/2* **King Orchisios (IRE)**[24] 2733 4-9-8 **105** (p) PJMcDonald(5) 3 83
(K A Ryan) *cl up tl rdn and wknd fr 2f out* **22/1**
-014 **12** *shd* **Sunrise Safari (IRE)**[30] 2566 4-8-8 **86** oh3 (v) TomEaves 12 64
(I Semple) *racd alone far side: nvr on terms* **20/1**

1m 11.76s (-1.34) **Going Correction** +0.025s/f (Good) **12 Ran SP% 115.8**
Speed ratings (Par 109):109,105,103,101,99 99,98,97,96,94 92,92
CSF £16.96 CT £103.20 TOTE £5.50: £1.70, £1.80, £3.00; EX 19.70.
Owner Rhodes, Kenyon & Gill **Bred** Rathbarry Stud **Trained** Musley Bank, N Yorks

FOCUS
A decent handicap and a sound pace throughout and the winner could be rated higher. The action unfolded towards the stands' side.

NOTEBOOK
Knot In Wood(IRE) ◆, who was not totally disgraced in first-time blinkers in the Wokingham, had the headgear left off this time and he turned in a career-best effort. Always travelling supremely well, he won with more in hand than the official margin suggests and he will be interesting in the Stewards Cup at Goodwood under only a 3lb penalty. (tchd 9-2)
Protector(SAF), 10lb higher than when bolting up in testing ground at Newcastle last time, did not have underfoot conditions as testing this time but still ran a sound race. Life may be tougher against the more progressive sorts from this mark but he will be one to keep an eye on in decent handicap company if the ground comes up really testing. (tchd 7-2 and 9-2)
Ingleby Arch(USA), who ran creditably over course and distance last month, had looked better than the bare form of his Royal Ascot run but, although turning in another fair effort, he left the impression that the return to 7f would be more to his liking. (op 8-1)
Ice Planet has been running creditably and fared best of those drawn in double figures. He should continue to give a good account but is likely to remain vulnerable from this mark in this type of event. (op 14-1 tchd 11-1)
Bahamian Pirate(USA), dropped in distance, fared the best of those that attempted to come from off the pace and was anything but disgraced. However, he is the type that needs things to drop right and may continue to look vulnerable against the younger and more progressive types from his current mark in the 90s. (op 16-1)
Turnkey, who made up a considerable amount of ground to win at Pontefract earlier in the week, found it much tougher to do the same thing at this course in this much stronger event under his penalty. He looks the type that needs things to drop perfectly.
Hartshead, having his first run for over five months, was not totally disgraced dropped in distance and left the strong impression that the return to 7f and 1m would be much more to his liking. (op 28-1)
Eisteddfod Official explanation: vet said gelding was slightly lame left hind

3501 JOHN SMITH'S STAYERS H'CAP 1m 5f 9y
8:50 (8:51) (Class 4) (0-85,82) 3-Y-0+ **£7,772** (£2,312; £1,155; £577) **Stalls** High

Form RPR
16 **1** **Bogside Theatre (IRE)**[32] 2506 3-8-8 **79** AndrewElliott(3) 1 89+
(G M Moore) *prom: rdn to ld over 2f out: styd on strly to go clr over 1f out* **10/1**
6411 **2** *6* **Charlotte Vale**[15] 3012 6-9-3 **76** PJMcDonald(5) 7 78
(Micky Hammond) *chsd ldr: led over 3f to over: nt pce of wnr fr over 1f out* **5/1**[3]
2300 **3** *3 1/2* **Mceldowney**[13] 3090 5-10-0 **82** AdrianTNicholls 5 79
(M Johnston) *chsd ldrs: drvn 1/2-way: rallied and ev ch over 3f out: no ex fr 2f out* **9/2**[2]
25-4 **4** *1 3/4* **White Lightening (IRE)**[55] 1849 4-9-6 **77** AndrewMullen(3) 4 72
(J Wade) *hld up in tch: effrt over 3f out: outpcd fr 2f out* **28/1**

The Form Book, Raceform Ltd, Compton, RG20 6NL

3-22 **5** 2 1/2 **Alambic**[6] 3333 4-10-0 **82** SebSanders 6 73+
(Sir Mark Prescott) *hld up: pushed along over 4f out: shortlived effrt over 3f out: wknd fr 2f out* **1/1**[1]
2223 **6** 13 **News Of The Day (IRE)**[15] 3016 3-8-0 **68** ow1 PaulFessey 2 41
(P Monteith) *t.k.h: prom: ev ch over 3f out: wknd over 2f out* **12/1**
06-0 **7** 5 **Bollin Thomas**[15] 3012 9-8-7 **64** oh3 ow1 JamieMoriarty(3) 3 30
(R Allan) *hld up: struggling 1/2-way: nvr on terms* **40/1**
-120 **8** 11 **Danish Rebel (IRE)**[56] 1827 3-8-10 **78** TomEaves 8 29
(G A Charlton) *led to over 3f out: sn lost tch* **12/1**
2m 55.28s (1.88) **Going Correction** +0.25s/f (Good)
WFA 3 from 4yo+ 14lb 8 Ran SP% **115.2**
Speed ratings (Par 105):104,100,98,97,95 87,84,77
CSF £59.53 CT £259.37 TOTE £19.10: £3.40, £1.40, £1.80; EX 108.90.
Owner B Lappin **Bred** Crone Stud Farms Ltd **Trained** Middleham Moor, N Yorks
■ Stewards' Enquiry : Paul Fessey one-day ban: careless riding (Jul 24)

FOCUS
A fair handicap but, with the market leader disappointing, this race did not take as much winning as seemed likely beforehand. The pace was only modest in the first half of the contest but the form appears reasonably solid.
Alambic Official explanation: jockey said filly was unsuited by the good to soft ground

3502 JOHN SMITH'S H'CAP (QUALIFIER FOR THE HAMILTON PARK TOTEPOOL HANDICAP SERIES FINAL) 1m 1f 36y
9:20 (9:20) (Class 5) (0-70,70) 3-Y-0+ **£3,238** (£963; £481; £240) **Stalls** High

Form RPR
-006 **1** **Red Chairman**[13] 3093 5-8-9 **51** oh3 (p) AdrianTNicholls 13 64
(R Johnson) *mde all: sn clr: kpt on wl fnl 2f: unchal* **11/1**
0034 **2** 5 **Topflight Wildbird**[10] 3182 4-9-2 **61** AndrewElliott(3) 4 64
(Mrs G S Rees) *hld up: rdn and hdwy over 2f out: chsd wnr ins fnl f: no imp* **17/2**
0240 **3** 1 1/4 **Hawkit (USA)**[14] 3049 6-9-11 **67** DaleGibson 9 68
(P Monteith) *hld up: rdn over 3f out: sn outpcd: rallied over 1f out: no imp* **11/1**
324- **4** 1 **Hurricane Thomas (IRE)**[252] 6318 3-9-4 **70** SebSanders 10 69
(M Johnston) *bhd: pushed along 1/2-way: rallied 2f out: no ex ins fnl f* **3/1**[2]
2252 **5** 1/2 **Mystical Ayr (IRE)**[5] 3343 5-9-1 **60** JamieMoriarty(3) 11 58
(Miss L A Perratt) *prom: effrt and edgd rt 2f out: sn one pce* **11/4**[1]
2626 **6** 3 1/2 **Dispol Peto**[9] 3204 7-8-6 **51** oh2 (vt) DominicFox(3) 12 42
(R Johnson) *hld up ins: drvn 4f out: rallied and hung rt 2f out: no imp* **20/1**
0106 **7** 1/2 **Polyquest (IRE)**[19] 2915 3-8-3 **58** AndrewMullen(3) 5 48
(G A Butler) *hld up: drvn over 3f out: nvr rchd ldrs* **6/1**[3]
1156 **8** 2 1/2 **Malinsa Blue (IRE)**[14] 3052 5-9-5 **66** PJMcDonald(5) 3 51
(B Ellison) *midfield: drvn over 3f out: no imp fr 2fout* **14/1**
20-0 **9** 2 1/2 **Penzo (IRE)**[41] 2256 4-9-7 **63** PatCosgrave 6 43
(J Wade) *cl up tl wknd fr 2f out* **25/1**
5020 **10** 4 **Defi (IRE)**[30] 2563 5-9-11 **67** (b) TomEaves 1 39
(I Semple) *cl up: rdn 2f out: sn wknd* **12/1**
2P44 **11** 5 **Ammeyrr**[14] 3052 3-9-1 **67** PaulFessey 7 35+
(A Crook) *midfield: drvn and outpcd over 3f out: n.d after* **33/1**
2m 1.16s (1.50) **Going Correction** +0.25s/f (Good)
WFA 3 from 4yo+ 10lb 11 Ran SP% **119.1**
Speed ratings (Par 103):103,98,97,96,96 93,92,90,88,84 80
CSF £99.87 CT £1065.46 TOTE £18.30: £4.10, £2.80, £3.60; EX 144.70 Place 6 £174.03, Place 5 £56.08.
Owner Graham D Brown **Bred** Newsells Park Stud Limited **Trained** Newburn, Tyne & Wear

FOCUS
A fair pace but a race in which only the winner featured, and he is rated to the best of last year's form.
Red Chairman Official explanation: trainer had no explanation for the apparent improvement in form
Ammeyrr Official explanation: jockey said colt lost its action
T/Plt: £477.00 to a £1 stake. Pool: £62,994.25. 96.40 winning tickets. T/Qpdt: £70.00 to a £1 stake. Pool: £3,693.40. 39.00 winning tickets. RY

3458
NEWMARKET (JULY) (R-H)
Friday, July 13

OFFICIAL GOING: Good to firm
Wind: Fresh across Weather: Overcast

3503 RITZ CLUB H'CAP 1m
1:30 (1:31) (Class 2) (0-100,97) 3-Y-0 **£18,696** (£5,598; £2,799; £1,401; £699; £351) **Stalls** Low

Form RPR
-260 **1** **Tybalt (USA)**[48] 2037 3-9-1 **91** JimmyFortune 20 108
(J H M Gosden) *hld up in rr: stdy hdwy fr 2f out: drvn and qcknd to ld jst ins fnl f: sn in command: readily* **9/1**
-414 **2** 1 3/4 **Artimino**[22] 2788 3-9-3 **93** (t) JamieSpencer 3 106
(J R Fanshawe) *lw: hld up in tch: travelling wl appr fnl 2f: drvn to take narrow ld appr fnl f: hdd jst ins fnl f: kpt on but nt pce of wnr* **6/1**[2]
2-21 **3** hd **We'll Come**[44] 2153 3-8-9 **85** PhilipRobinson 2 97
(M A Jarvis) *lw: in tch: hdwy over 2f out: drvn to chal over 1f out: kpt on same pce last half f* **8/1**
3-30 **4** 4 **Furnace (IRE)**[22] 2788 3-9-1 **91** JMurtagh 4 94
(M L W Bell) *in rr: rdn and hdwy over 2f out: styd on wl fnl f but nvr gng pce to rch ldrs* **12/1**
2213 **5** nk **Soccerjackpot (USA)**[31] 2536 3-8-6 **82** DeanMcKeown 6 84
(G A Swinbank) *chsd ldrs: drvn along fr 6f out: slt ld 2f out: hdd appr fnl f: wknd ins fnl f* **12/1**
-112 **6** nk **Zaahid (IRE)**[20] 2881 3-8-10 **86** RHills 8 88
(B W Hills) *chsd ldrs: rdn to press ldrs 2f out: wknd ins fnl f* **10/1**
-162 **7** 1/2 **Ea (USA)**[22] 2788 3-9-6 **96** RyanMoore 5 96
(Sir Michael Stoute) *lw: mid-div: rdn and sme hdwy fr 3f out but nvr gng pce to be competitive* **4/1**[1]
0-66 **8** nk **The Illies (IRE)**[30] 2578 3-8-4 **80** ChrisCatlin 7 80
(B W Hills) *lw: sn outpcd: pushed along over 2f out: kpt on fnl f but nvr gng pce to be competitive* **66/1**
0103 **9** 1 **Lazy Darren**[34] 2452 3-8-8 **84** TedDurcan 12 81
(R Hannon) *lw: towards rr: rdn and sme hdwy 3f out: kpt on fnl f but nvr in contention* **25/1**
-410 **10** 1 **Yaroslav (USA)**[48] 2045 3-8-9 **85** (b[1]) SteveDrowne 13 80
(R Charlton) *in tch: rdn to chse ldrs over 2f out: wknd fnl f* **16/1**
-012 **11** hd **Mr Aviator (USA)**[35] 2426 3-8-9 **85** RichardHughes 19 80
(R Hannon) *hld up towards rr: rdn and sme hdwy 3f out: nvr rchd ldrs* **7/1**[3]
1510 **12** 1 1/4 **Laa Rayb (USA)**[6] 3330 3-9-5 **95** JoeFanning 1 87
(M Johnston) *swtg: w ldr tl slt ld 5f out: rdn 3f out: hdd 2f out: wknd over 1f out* **14/1**
-410 **13** nk **Aqmaar**[48] 2037 3-9-3 **93** MartinDwyer 18 84
(J L Dunlop) *pressed ldrs: ev ch over 2f out: wknd qckly over 1f out* **25/1**
2220 **14** 3 1/2 **Captain Jacksparra (IRE)**[42] 2213 3-8-9 **85** NCallan 16 68
(K A Ryan) *swtg: t.k.h: chsd ldrs tl wknd over 2f out* **33/1**
3604 **15** 8 **Karoo Blue (IRE)**[27] 2671 3-8-6 **82** (b) JohnEgan 9 47
(C E Brittain) *slt ld tl hdd 5f out: wknd fr 3f out: eased whn no ch ins fnl f* **66/1**
230- **16** 10 **Always Fruitful**[384] 2844 3-9-7 **97** MichaelHills 11 39
(M Johnston) *prom early: bhd fr 1/2-way: eased whn no ch ins fnl f* **33/1**
1220 **17** 2 **Lady Gloria**[23] 2757 3-9-2 **92** SebSanders 14 29
(J G Given) *s.i.s: sn rcvrd to press ldrs 1/2-way: wknd qckly 2f out: eased whn no ch fnl f* **25/1**
1m 38.04s (-2.39) **Going Correction** +0.025s/f (Good) 17 Ran SP% **125.3**
Speed ratings (Par 106):112,110,110,106,105 105,104,104,103,102 102,101,100,97,89 79,77
CSF £59.55 CT £477.63 TOTE £12.80: £3.10, £2.20, £2.20, £4.00; EX 91.90 Trifecta £618.90 Pool £958.90 - 1.10 winning units..
Owner Stoneside Stable Llc **Bred** Stoneside Stable **Trained** Newmarket, Suffolk

FOCUS
A strong handicap in which the first three came nicely clear. The form looks solid. The winner was showing the form he was thought capable of earlier this season, while the runner-up has been raised 5lb and the third's form was in line with the Yarmouth maiden win which is working out better than expected. All three remain of interest.

NOTEBOOK
Tybalt(USA), who had excuses on his previous two starts, again attracted support in the market, and this time he delivered. He travelled sweetly throughout and quickened up in the manner of a smart horse. He was well on top at the finish and is likely to make up into a Pattern-class performer in time. The totesport Mile at Goodwood looks a likely next stop provided the ground is quick enough, but he is likely to head to the US before the season is done to contest Graded races out there. (op 11-1)
Artimino, sent off favourite for the Britannia, in which he finished fourth, only had a 2lb higher mark to contend with here and ran another solid race. He could not match the winner's turn of foot but he kept on well enough, although his connections now believe he will be more effective dropped back to 7f. (op 7-1)
We'll Come had seen the form of his maiden success boosted by the subsequent victories of the second and fourth, and he did not look too badly treated off a mark of 85. Just pipped for second, he finished nicely clear of the rest and clearly remains on the upgrade. (op 15-2)
Furnace(IRE), four places behind Artimino in the Britannia, had a 3lb pull at the weights with that rival this time, but he was unable to reverse the form with the progressive Fanshawe colt. His form seems to have plateaued somewhat. (op 14-1)
Soccerjackpot(USA) did not look to have been done any favours by the Handicapper, who put him up 5lb for getting beaten at Redcar last time. He ran well in the circumstances.
Zaahid(IRE), who got a bit warm beforehand, was stepping up a furlong in distance but his pedigree suggested he could well improve for it. He was brought to have every chance inside the last quarter mile, but the first three quickened away from him inside the last. It is unlikely that it was the longer trip that found him out, though, and that it was more a case of them just being better treated. (op 11-1)
Ea(USA), whose second in the Britannia gave him every chance here, failed to confirm form with Artimino or Furnace, and was a shade disappointing. He did not get the clearest of runs, though, and looks the type who needs a very strongly-run race over this distance to bring his finishing effort into play. (op 7-2)
The Illies(IRE) struggled to go the early pace and simply stayed on past beaten horses. He hails from a stable returning to form, though, which is encouraging.
Lazy Darren had no easy task, up in class off what has looked a difficult mark of late. He was another who just stayed on past horses that had already cried enough. (tchd 28-1)
Yaroslav(USA), the least experienced runner in the line-up, was wearing blinkers for the first time and did not get home. A son of Danzig, he might benefit from dropping back to his winning distance of 7f.
Mr Aviator(USA) should not have had a problem with this shorter trip but he failed to get involved from off the pace. (op 15-2)
Laa Rayb(USA), who sweated up beforehand, has not gone on from his handicap win at Sandown, although to be fair he was put up a whopping 13lb for that success. Perhaps he just needs time to strengthen up.
Aqmaar, a keen-going sort, is another who has not progressed on his last two starts. (op 20-1)
Karoo Blue(IRE) Official explanation: jockey said colt moved poorly latter stages

3504 WEATHERBYS SUPERLATIVE STKS (GROUP 2) 7f
2:00 (2:00) (Class 1) 2-Y-0
£39,746 (£15,064; £7,539; £3,759; £1,883; £945) **Stalls** Low

Form RPR
513 **1** **Hatta Fort**[24] 2737 2-9-0 0 JHBowman 9 105
(M R Channon) *lw: hld up: hdwy over 1f out: rdn to ld ins fnl f: r.o* **4/1**[2]
110 **2** nk **Declaration Of War (IRE)**[24] 2732 2-9-0 0 RobertHavlin 4 105
(P W Chapple-Hyam) *lw: chsd ldrs: n.m.r over 1f out: rdn and ev ch ins fnl f: r.o* **4/1**[2]
1 **3** 1 3/4 **Ellmau**[44] 2147 2-9-0 0 ChrisCatlin 2 100
(E J O'Neill) *unf: led: rdn over 1f out: hdd and unable qck ins fnl f* **25/1**
3 **4** 1/2 **Let Us Prey**[47] 2056 2-9-0 0 JamieSpencer 5 99+
(N A Callaghan) *lw: s.s: hld up: rdn over 1f out: r.o wl ins fnl f: nt rch ldrs* **8/1**[3]
1 **5** 1/2 **Mutabayen (USA)**[31] 2532 2-9-0 0 RoystonFfrench 8 98
(B Smart) *leggy: mid-div: rdn over 2f out: styd on ins fnl f* **16/1**
13 **6** hd **Feared In Flight (IRE)**[20] 2855 2-9-0 0 MJKinane 6 97
(B W Hills) *hld up in tch: rdn over 2f out: styd on same pce fnl f* **15/8**[1]
1 **7** 1 1/2 **Dry Speedfit (IRE)**[18] 2941 2-9-0 0 TQuinn 7 93
(G G Margarson) *w'like: prom: rdn over 2f out: wknd fnl f* **16/1**
51 **8** 1/2 **La Voile Rouge**[16] 2991 2-9-0 0 RichardHughes 10 92
(B J Meehan) *hld up in tch: rdn and ev ch whn edgd lft over 1f out: wknd ins fnl f* **16/1**
5210 **9** 3 **Jebel Tara**[22] 2785 2-9-0 0 KerrinMcEvoy 11 84
(C E Brittain) *chsd ldr: rdn over 2f out: wkng whn hmpd over 1f out* **33/1**
331 **10** 6 **Montaquila**[15] 3025 2-9-0 0 RyanMoore 1 68
(J Howard Johnson) *chsd ldrs: rdn over 2f out: wknd over 1f out* **11/1**
1m 25.91s (-0.87) **Going Correction** +0.025s/f (Good) 10 Ran SP% **118.7**
Speed ratings (Par 106):105,104,102,102,101 101,99,99,95,88
CSF £20.85 TOTE £4.50: £1.90, £1.80, £7.40; EX 22.80 Trifecta £429.10 Pool £664.92 - 1.10 winning units..
Owner Sheikh Ahmed Al Maktoum **Bred** Wellsummers Farm **Trained** West Ilsley, Berks
■ Stewards' Enquiry : M J Kinane two-day ban: failed to ride out for fifth place (Jul 24-25)

FOCUS
This did not look a strong renewal on paper, and that appeared to be borne out by events on the track, with the third improving greatly on a win in an ordinary maiden on his debut. The early pace was not that fast.

NOTEBOOK
Hatta Fort, third in the Windsor Castle Stakes at Royal Ascot, was taking a two-furlong step up in trip, but on pedigree he should get a mile this year so it was no surprise to see him show improved form over the distance. He only won by a neck but he did so a shade comfortably, and he could be the type for the Champagne Stakes at Doncaster later in the season. (tchd 7-2)
Declaration Of War(IRE) disappointed in the Coventry Stakes, but his previous success in the Woodcote at Epsom suggestsed he was destined for Group-race success. This was more like it, but it is possible that the ground had firmed up a bit more than he would have liked, and in the end he found one too good. (op 7-2)
Ellmau looked to have plenty on his plate in this company, having only won a fairly ordinary Fibresand maiden on his debut, but he had apparently been working well at home and he ran a blinder, dominating from the start and keeping on well to secure some black type. He did get the run of the race, but he has already proved a bargain buy at only 8,000gns. (op 20-1)
Let Us Prey, third in a decent maiden over 5f on the Rowley Mile course on his debut, looked sure to improve greatly for this step up in trip, as he is bred to get a mile this year, and he duly stepped up on that effort. A stronger pace would have suited him and he should have no trouble getting off the mark back in maiden company. (op 10-1)
Mutabayen(USA) did not beat a great deal on his debut at Redcar but he hails from a stable that won the Chesham Stakes at Royal Ascot (beating this race's favourite into third) and his home work had encouraged connections to have a go at a big prize. He is another who could have done with a stronger pace, but all in all it was a sound effort. (op 12-1)
Feared In Flight(IRE), who did not enjoy the best of luck in running when only third in the Chesham Stakes, was another unsuited by the way the race was run. He is better than this and a stronger pace is likely to see him to better effect, but, perhaps more importantly, the ground looked plenty quick enough for him. (op 2-1 tchd 9-4)
Dry Speedfit(IRE) made a good impression when successful in soft ground on his debut, but conditions were very different here for this step up in class.
La Voile Rouge was outclassed here but remains the sort who should pay his way in nurseries. (op 22-1)
Jebel Tara was tiring when badly squeezed out approaching the final furlong and was then eased down.

3505 LADBROKES BUNBURY CUP (HERITAGE H'CAP) 7f
2:35 (2:35) (Class 2) 3-Y-0+

£62,320 (£18,660; £9,330; £4,670; £2,330; £1,170) **Stalls** Low

Form				RPR
-143	**1**		**Giganticus (USA)**[31] 2528 4-8-8 **94** PhilipRobinson 3 (B W Hills) *chsd ldrs: chal fr ins fnl 2f tl led jst ins fnl f: drvn out* **16/1**	104
3101	**2**	*nk*	**King Of Argos**[34] 2446 4-8-12 **98** JamieSpencer 4 (E A L Dunlop) *lw: in tch: hdwy and swtchd lft ins fnl 2f: r.o strly u.p fnl f: gng on cl home but a jst hld by wnr* **10/1**[3]	107
0-34	**3**	*nk*	**Something (IRE)**[20] 2858 5-9-4 **104** JMurtagh 11 (T G Mills) *pressed ldrs tl slt ld 2f out: kpt narrow advantage tl hdd jst ins fnl f: styd on ell* **7/1**[2]	112
4006	**4**	*shd*	**Dhaular Dhar (IRE)**[6] 3329 5-8-11 **97** ChrisCatlin 13 (J S Goldie) *hld up in rr: hdwy over 2f out: str run fnl f: fin wl* **33/1**	105
6-30	**5**	*shd*	**Racer Forever (USA)**[21] 2817 4-9-3 **103** (b[1]) JimmyFortune 6 (J H M Gosden) *t.k.h: in tch: hdwy over 2f out: styd on wl to chse ldrs fnl f: no ex cl home* **20/1**	111
54/0	**6**	*1*	**Fantastic View (USA)**[23] 2755 6-8-11 **97** SebSanders 12 (J Noseda) *in rr: rdn and hdwy over 2f out: r.o wl fnl f but nvr quite gng pce to rch ldrs* **14/1**	102
1265	**7**	*nk*	**My Paris**[12] 3138 6-8-11 **97** (b[1]) NCallan 5 (K A Ryan) *slt ld tl hdd 2f out: styd pressing ldrs tl outpcd last half f* **28/1**	101
	8	*1 ½*	**Fixboard**[35] 6-8-11 **97** KerrinMcEvoy 8 (F Poulsen, France) *w'like: lw: chsd ldrs: rdn over 2f out: styd on same pce ins fnl f* **33/1**	97
1435	**9**	*shd*	**Grantley Adams**[20] 2858 6-9-4 **104** JHBowman 7 (M R Channon) *in tch: rdn to chse ldrs over 2f out: wknd last 100yds* **10/1**[3]	104
2303	**10**	*hd*	**Vortex**[23] 2755 8-9-7 **107** (t) RichardHughes 10 (Miss Gay Kelleway) *mid-div: rdn 2f out: sme hdwy over 1f out: nvr gng pce to rch ldrs* **14/1**	106
0305	**11**	*½*	**Gift Horse**[13] 3089 7-8-11 **97** StephenDonohoe 17 (D Nicholls) *towards rr: rdn 1/2-way: sme prog fr over 1f out but nvr in contention* **25/1**	95
-016	**12**	*½*	**Mine (IRE)**[13] 3098 9-9-8 **108** (v) TQuinn 19 (J D Bethell) *s.i.s: bhd: sme hdwy on rails whn hmpd ins fnl 2f: nt rcvr but r.o strly last 100yds* **7/1**[2]	105
3-03	**13**	*½*	**Dabbers Ridge (IRE)**[21] 2817 5-9-0 **100** MichaelHills 18 (B W Hills) *chsd ldrs: rdn over 2f out: wknd fnl f* **6/1**[1]	95
-020	**14**	*shd*	**Bentong (IRE)**[20] 2858 4-8-11 **102** (t) TolleyDean(5) 2 (P F I Cole) *swtg: t.k.h: chsd ldrs: rdn over 2f out: wknd fnl f* **33/1**	97
0222	**15**	*½*	**Zomerlust**[13] 3089 5-8-8 **94** GrahamGibbons 16 (J J Quinn) *s.i.s: bhd tl styd on fnl f but nvr in contention* **20/1**	88
2323	**16**	*2*	**Fajr (IRE)**[13] 3098 5-9-7 **107** (t) JohnEgan 20 (Miss Gay Kelleway) *lw: mid-div: rdn 1/2-way and nvr in contention: no ch whn hmpd 1f out* **14/1**	95
-222	**17**	*¾*	**Intrepid Jack**[20] 2858 5-9-4 **104** SteveDrowne 9 (H Morrison) *mid-div and rdn 1/2-way: sn btn* **6/1**[1]	90
0-00	**18**	*1 ½*	**Jedburgh**[36] 2396 6-9-0 **100** (b) MJKinane 15 (J L Dunlop) *a in rr: no ch whn edgd rt to stands' rail ins fnl 2f* **16/1**	82

1m 24.54s (-2.24) **Going Correction** +0.025s/f (Good) **18** Ran SP% **129.2**
Speed ratings (Par 109):113,112,112,112,112 110,110,108,108,108 107,107,106,106,106 103,103,101
CSF £161.27 CT £1277.70 TOTE £23.40: £4.70, £2.50, £2.50, £6.00; EX 261.90 Trifecta £1850.20 Part won. Pool £2,605.96 - 0.50 winning units..
Owner DM James,Cavendish Inv Ltd,Matthew Green **Bred** Gaines-Gentry Thoroughbreds Et Al **Trained** Lambourn, Berks

FOCUS
A typically competitive renewal, although they did not go that quick early and the first five home finished in something of a heap. The form looks solid, with the first two up a couple of pounds and the next three all to form.

NOTEBOOK
Giganticus(USA), who was rejected by Michael Hills in favour of stable companion Dabbers Ridge, had been given a nice break since his last outing at Chester and did not go unsupported on the exchanges. Never too far off the pace, he found plenty for pressure and was always just holding on as the pack closed in at the line. He looks like a real 7f specialist, and connections will no doubt now be eyeing the valuable totesport.com Internationl Handicap at Ascot later in the month, but that will be tougher under a penalty.
King Of Argos ◆ has won over as far as 1m2f so the fact that they did not go that fast early was against him, but he still travelled well on his favoured fast ground - he was previously unbeaten in three starts on good to firm - and stayed on strongly up the hill to be beaten only narrowly. He wants a mile really, and the totesport Mile at Goodwood, a venue where he won last time out, looks the ideal race for him. (tchd 11-1)
Something(IRE), fourth in the Wokingham on ground that would have been softer than ideal, has done all his winning over this distance and was given every chance, ridden prominently throughout. He goes for the Stewards' Cup next, but it will be a surprise if he does not once again run into one or two better handicapped rivals there.
Dhaular Dhar(IRE), who challenged nearest the far-side rail, picked up really well from the back of the field to get involved in the blanket finish for the places. He has done all his winning on good ground or softer but he coped with these conditions admirably.
Racer Forever(USA) ◆, eighth in the Buckingham Palace Stakes on ground that was probably too soft for him, travelled strongly in the first-time blinkers and kept on well once he hit the rising ground. A stronger early pace would have suited him and he has the ability to win a decent race - the obvious one being the totesport.com Internationl Handicap at Ascot on 28th July. Official explanation: jockey said gelding ran too free (op 22-1)
Fantastic View(USA), who ran really well to finish ninth in the Hunt Cup on his return from a lengthy absence, did not find the combination of a fairly steady early pace and drop back in distance playing to his strengths. He wants a mile, and the totesport Mile at Goodwood should be more his cup of tea, over a course and distance which he has been successful over in the past. (op 12-1)
My Paris, another wearing blinkers for the first time, is at his best when he can get his toe in a bit so conditions were not ideal. While to a certain extent he got the run of the race, he was also a shade too keen in front. (tchd 33-1)
Fixboard, a multiple winner between 7f and 1m1f in France, was a bit of an unknown quantity on his debut in this country. He ran well enough, having been near the front throughout, but his trainer expressed the view beforehand that the gelding is ideally suited by further, so a step up in trip is likely to suit him.
Grantley Adams has been an unlucky horse this season, running well from poor draws the last twice, and this looked a good opportunity to gain compensation. The seventh furlong was not sure to suit him, though, and in the end he ran like a non-stayer. (op 8-1)
Vortex, who ran such a good race in the Hunt Cup last time, was not seen at his very best here off a steadier gallop, and he looks likely to remain vulnerable off his current stiff mark.
Gift Horse, who last ran over a distance further than a sprint trip over two years ago, is dropping slowly down the handicap, but looks to need a little further help on this evidence.
Mine(IRE), winner of this race three times before, including the last two renewals, was racing off a 6lb higher mark than when successful in it last year. Things did not go his way this time, though, as the race was not as strongly run as he would have liked and he was just getting going when hampered two furlongs out.
Dabbers Ridge(IRE), third in the Buckingham Palace Stakes when the ground had more give in it, was well backed, but conditions were not as much in his favour this time. (op 15-2)
Fajr(IRE) was hampered by Intrepid Jack next to the rail a furlong out but he was not really going anywhere at the time anyway. He is very high in the handicap now.
Intrepid Jack, runner-up in the Wokingham, and also second here last year, was being pushed along a fair way out and made little headway. He was very disappointing and this was clearly not his true form. His rider later said that he was never travelling. Official explanation: jockey said horse never travelled (op 15-2 tchd 8-1 in places)

3506 DARLEY JULY CUP (GROUP 1) 6f
3:10 (3:10) (Class 1) 3-Y-0+

£212,925 (£80,700; £40,387; £20,137; £10,087; £5,062) **Stalls** Low

Form				RPR
-111	**1**		**Sakhee's Secret**[26] 2695 3-8-13 108 SteveDrowne 16 (H Morrison) *hld up: hdwy and nt clr run 2f out: rdn to ld and hung lft ins fnl f: r.o* **9/2**[2]	126+
-234	**2**	*½*	**Dutch Art**[24] 2734 3-8-13 118 JimmyFortune 11 (P W Chapple-Hyam) *chsd ldrs: n.m.r and lost pl 1/2-way: hdwy over 1f out: r.o wl* **5/1**[3]	124+
-204	**3**	*1 ¼*	**Red Clubs (IRE)**[20] 2857 4-9-5 114 MichaelHills 7 (B W Hills) *lw: hld up: hdwy over 2f out: rdn and ev ch 1f out: sn edgd lft: styd on same pce* **16/1**	121
-001	**4**	*nk*	**Marchand D'Or (FR)**[18] 2953 4-9-5 0 DBonilla 1 (F Head, France) *lw: w'like: strong: hld up: nt clr run over 2f out: swtchd lft and hdwy over 1f out: styd on* **25/1**	120
-122	**5**	*½*	**Dandy Man (IRE)**[24] 2733 4-9-5 0 PShanahan 9 (Tracey Collins, Ire) *trckd ldrs: plld hrd: led over 1f out: hdd and unable qck ins fnl f* **8/1**	119
2-13	**6**	*shd*	**Asset (IRE)**[20] 2857 4-9-5 113 RichardHughes 5 (R Hannon) *lw: chsd ldrs: outpcd over 2f out: rdn over 1f out: r.o* **4/1**[1]	118
-220	**7**	*1*	**Borderlescott**[20] 2857 5-9-5 109 RoystonFfrench 18 (R Bastiman) *chsd ldrs: rdn over 1f out: styd on same pce* **50/1**	115
124-	**8**	*½*	**Hellvelyn**[287] 5656 3-8-13 112 TedDurcan 4 (B Smart) *s.i.s: hld up: hdwy over 2f out: rdn over 1f out: no ex ins fnl f* **33/1**	113
	9	*shd*	**Mutawaajid (AUS)**[125] 4-9-5 0 JHBowman 3 (M R Channon) *gd sort: chsd ldrs: rdn and ev ch over 1f out: wknd ins fnl f* **16/1**	113
0	**10**	*shd*	**Bentley Biscuit (AUS)**[24] 2733 6-9-5 0 RyanMoore 8 (Mrs Gai Waterhouse, Australia) *mid-div: hdwy over 2f out: rdn and ev ch over 1f out: wknd ins fnl f* **10/1**	113
-405	**11**	*½*	**Drayton (IRE)**[20] 2857 3-8-13 0 WCMarwing 13 (M F De Kock, South Africa) *led: rdn and hdd over 1f out: wknd ins fnl f* **33/1**	111
5-10	**12**	*shd*	**Amadeus Wolf**[20] 2857 4-9-5 114 NCallan 20 (K A Ryan) *hld up: hdwy over 2f out: rdn over 1f out: wknd ins fnl f* **17/2**	111
1012	**13**	*1 ¾*	**Prime Defender**[26] 2695 3-8-13 111 RHills 19 (B W Hills) *lw: chsd ldrs: rdn and hung lft over 1f out: wknd fnl f* **33/1**	105
/15-	**14**	*1 ¾*	**Electric Beat**[33] 4-9-5 0 AHelfenbein 14 (Andreas Lowe, Germany) *prom: lost pl over 3f out: rdn and wknd over 1f out* **100/1**	101
1404	**15**	*2*	**Rising Shadow (IRE)**[13] 3088 6-9-5 110 JimmyQuinn 10 (T D Barron) *dwlt: hld up: effrt 1/2-way: wknd wl over 1f out* **100/1**	95
6040	**16**	*¾*	**Quito (IRE)**[20] 2857 10-9-5 108 (b) PhilipRobinson 6 (D W Chapman) *hld up: a in rr* **100/1**	93
4053	**17**	*¾*	**Balthazaar's Gift (IRE)**[20] 2858 4-9-5 106 MJKinane 2 (L M Cumani) *hld up: hdwy 1/2-way: hung lft and wknd over 1f out* **33/1**	90
1-20	**18**	*10*	**Sander Camillo (USA)**[61] 1702 3-8-10 111 (v[1]) SebSanders 17 (J Noseda) *s.i.s: hld up: rdn and wknd over 2f out* **20/1**	56

1m 10.77s (-2.58) **Going Correction** +0.025s/f (Good)
WFA 3 from 4yo+ 6lb **20** Ran SP% **122.6**
Speed ratings (Par 117):118,117,115,115,114 114,113,112,112,112 111,111,109,106,104 103,102,88
CSF £24.69 TOTE £7.00: £3.30, £2.60, £5.00; EX 22.50 Trifecta £278.40 Pool £3,607.76 - 9.20 winning units.

Owner Miss B Swire **Bred** Miss B Swire **Trained** East Ilsley, Berks

FOCUS

A good renewal rated through the fairly reliable third to his Ascot run. The winner has not been rated as highly as the likes of Mozart or Stravinsky, who got RPRs in the 130s for their wins, but he is unexposed and has plenty of scope to improve to that sort of level.

NOTEBOOK

Sakhee's Secret, while impressive in winning a Listed race at Salisbury last time, still had a bit to prove moving into this company for the first time, and by the off he had lost his position as market favourite, but he showed what a class act he is in the race itself, showing a smart turn of foot to quicken past his rivals before holding off fellow three-year-old Dutch Art a shade comfortably. He can already be regarded the best sprinter in Europe, yet he is still quite inexperienced and has further scope for improvement, so he is going to be hard to beat this year. A grand sort, he should make up into an even more imposing four-year-old. (tchd 5-1 in places)

Dutch Art, third in the 2000 Guineas and fourth at Ascot, was dropping back to sprinting for the first time since he ran away with the Middle Park Stakes last autumn. Well positioned until losing his place around halfway, he allowed the winner to get first run on him, but he stayed on strongly once he hit the rising ground and showed that he can be a proper force in the sprinting division. While the winner's effectiveness in softer ground is not certain, we know he handles it very well, and races like the Prix Maurice de Gheest at Deauville and the Sprint Cup at Haydock could see him record a well deserved Group 1 success at three. (op 9-2)

Red Clubs(IRE), fourth in the Golden Jubilee, looks to have run close to that form. He tends to find a few too good at the top level, and he hung left under pressure late on, but he still came out best of the older horses and deserves plenty of credit for that.

Marchand D'Or(FR), who won last year's Prix Maurice de Gheest, was one of four Group 1 winners in the field, but he was by far the biggest price of the quartet despite having won his prep race in good style last month. It is true that he had not run on ground as quick as this before, but he showed he can handle it well and ran a fine race to finish fourth, after being walked to post very early. Deauville will no doubt be on his agenda again now, and he will be deserving of maximum respect back on his own patch. (op 33-1)

Dandy Man(IRE), unlucky with the draw in the King's Stand, had another furlong to run this time and that was the big worry for his supporters. He raced plenty keen enough but was still going well a furlong and a half out. He could only find the one pace thereafter, though, and it now seems clear that he is a 5f horse through and through. His big chance at this level will be the Nunthorpe, providing the ground remains on the fast side. (op 9-1)

Asset(IRE), a splendid third in the Golden Jubilee on unsuitably easy ground, was well backed and assumed favouritism near the off, with his supporters expecting him to improve again on this faster surface. Although he ran well enough in sixth, it was surprising to see him get outpaced before running on again, and this has to go down as a bit disappointing, as his success in the Abernant on the Rowley Mile in the spring looked like that of a top-class sprinter in the making. Perhaps he needs a longer break between his races. (op 9-2 tchd 5-1)

Borderlescott showed good speed and improved one place on his eighth in the Golden Jubilee, but he again looked just short of the standard required in this company.

Hellvelyn, last year's Coventry Stakes winner, was making a belated seasonal reappearance having suffered with bruised feet. In the circumstances he ran a very encouraging race, and one would expect him to come on a bit for this.

Mutawaajid(AUS), formerly trained by Gai Waterhouse in Australia, where he won five of his six races, had not raced since March and was entitled to come on for the run. His new trainer expects him to do better as he steps him up to 7f, and the Prix de la Foret has been mentioned.

Bentley Biscuit(AUS), who found the ground too fast at Ascot, presumably would not have appreciated these drying conditions on the July course either. He has yet to show his best in this country but, if he gets to stay here until the autumn, then races like the Sprint Cup at Haydock may provide him with that opportunity. (tchd 9-1, 11-1 in places)

Drayton(IRE), ridden differently from how he was at Ascot, showed good speed, but he has a preference for easier ground.

Amadeus Wolf scoped dirty after Ascot so could be excused that poor run, but he again failed to run to his best here and now has a few questions to answer. (op 8-1 tchd 9-1)

Prime Defender showed early speed but weakened out of it once the race began in earnest. He is not up to this class but should taste further success at Listed/Group 3 level.

Electric Beat, a German raider who won over 7f last time out, lost his position at halfway and looks likely to appreciate a return to a longer trip on this evidence.

Rising Shadow(IRE) looked up against it in this company and was not helped by the quickening ground conditions as his best form is undoubtedly with give.

Quito(IRE) finished sixth in this race last year but it looks as though age is finally beginning to catch up with him now.

Balthazaar's Gift(IRE) ran well under a big weight in the Wokingham last time out but he never looked like threatening on this return to the top flight.

Sander Camillo(USA), visored for the first time, had always threatened to be a sprinter at three rather than a miler, and this was her chance to prove it. Ground conditions had come right for her, too, but she never looked like getting involved. She appears not to have trained on. (tchd 18-1)

3507 XPLOR EBF MAIDEN FILLIES' STKS — 6f

3:45 (3:45) (Class 2) 2-Y-O — **£9,715** (£2,890; £1,444; £721) **Stalls** Low

Form				RPR
	1		**Laureldean Gale (USA)** 2-9-0 0 ... JimmyFortune 19 (P W Chapple-Hyam) *w'like: scope: in rr: hdwy 2f out: drvn and qcknd between horses ins fnl f to ld fnl 100yds: readily* **2/1**[1]	90+
5	**2**	1 ½	**Kashoof**[37] [2364] 2-9-0 0 ... RHills 4 (J L Dunlop) *leggy: trckd ldrs: chal fr 2f out and stl upsides ins fnl f: nt pce of wnr fnl 100yds but kpt on wl* **8/1**	83
	3	hd	**Sweet Kiss (USA)** 2-9-0 0 ... MJKinane 8 (B J Meehan) *w'like: chsd ldrs: drvn along fr 3f out: edgd lft over 1f out: kpt on wl fnl f and gng on cl home but nvr gng pce to chal* **20/1**	82+
	4	hd	**Albabilia (IRE)** 2-9-0 0 ... JohnEgan 17 (C E Brittain) *strong: in tch: drvn along fr 1/2-way: kpt on wl fnl f but nvr quite gng pce to trble ldrs* **50/1**	81+
3	**5**	shd	**Honky Tonk Sally**[14] [3055] 2-9-0 0 ... JamieSpencer 12 (M L W Bell) *lw: led: rdn over 1f out: styd disputing ld tl hdd fnl 100yds: one pce* **3/1**[2]	81
3	**6**	2 ½	**Tudor Court (IRE)**[19] [2904] 2-9-0 0 ... JoeFanning 14 (M Johnston) *w'like: lw: chsd ldrs: rdn to chal fr over 1f out: wknd ins fnl f* **5/1**[3]	74+
	7	¾	**Top Vision** 2-9-0 0 ... JHBowman 18 (M R Channon) *athletic: hld up in rr: pushed along and hdwy fr 2f out: styd on wl cl home* **25/1**	71+
	8	¾	**Baraari (USA)** 2-9-0 0 ... MartinDwyer 2 (J L Dunlop) *w'like: scope: bit bkwd: in rr: pushed along 1/2-way: styd on fr over 1f out: kpt on nr fin but nvr in contention* **33/1**	69+
	9	½	**Izzibizzi** 2-9-0 0 ... StephenDonohoe 16 (E A L Dunlop) *unf: bit bkwd: in rr: rdn 1/2-way: styd on ins fnl f but nvr in contention* **25/1**	68
	10	hd	**Politeia (USA)** 2-9-0 0 ... RyanMoore 10 (R Hannon) *w'like: bit bkwd: in rr: sn mid-div: chsd ldrs 1/2-way but nvr gng pce to be competitive: one pce fnl 2f* **20/1**	67
20	**11**	1 ¾	**Geordie Girl**[15] [3024] 2-9-0 0 ... GrahamGibbons 20 (R C Guest) *s.i.s: bhd: pushed along 2f out: hdwy fnl f but nvr in contention* **40/1**	62
	12	1 ¼	**Rockellio (IRE)** 2-9-0 0 ... MichaelHills 7 (B W Hills) *w'like: bit bkwd: in rr: sme hdwy 1/2-way: sn bhd* **20/1**	58
	13	nk	**Superduper** 2-9-0 0 ... RichardHughes 11 (R Hannon) *neat: slowly away: bhd tl styd on fnl f* **40/1**	57
	14	hd	**Brave Mave** 2-9-0 0 ... KerrinMcEvoy 13 (W Jarvis) *leggy: a towards rr* **40/1**	56
24	**15**	2	**Nothing Likea Dame**[10] [3187] 2-9-0 0 ... TQuinn 6 (D J Coakley) *chsd ldrs: rdn over 2f out: sn btn* **16/1**	50
0	**16**	5	**Amazing Spirit**[66] [1553] 2-9-0 0 ... AdrianMcCarthy 1 (Miss V Haigh) *w'like: in tch: rdn 1/2-way: sn wknd* **100/1**	35
	17	nk	**Siryena** 2-9-0 0 ... TedDurcan 3 (E A L Dunlop) *w'like: scope: s.i.s: a bhd* **66/1**	35

1m 13.29s (-0.06) **Going Correction** +0.025s/f (Good) **17** Ran SP% **128.7**

Speed ratings (Par 97):101,99,98,98,98 95,94,93,92,92 89,88,87,87,84 78,77

CSF £16.83 TOTE £3.60: £1.60, £2.00, £5.70; EX 21.00.

Owner D Brennan **Bred** And Mrs Robert David Randal **Trained** Newmarket, Suffolk

FOCUS

This looked a decent fillies' maiden, and they went a proper pace. Solid form.

NOTEBOOK

Laureldean Gale(USA) ◆, who cost $325,000, is a half-sister to that smart filly Secret History, who was a multiple winner between 7f and 1m2f and won the Musidora Stakes at three, and Costume Designer, a smart multiple winner at around 6f to 1m in the US. A well-backed favourite for this debut, word had clearly got out that she had her fair share of ability, and the way she picked up from off the pace and quickened between horses to take this fairly comfortably in the end suggests that she has a bright future. No better than 16-1 for the 1000 Guineas already, her next outing, presumably in Pattern company, is eagerly awaited. (op 7-4 tchd 9-4 in places)

Kashoof improved on her debut effort at Nottingham and just edged the battle for second place. She might well have run into a smart rival in the winner, and should not be long in going one better. (tchd 15-2)

Sweet Kiss(USA), whose dam was a multiple sprint winner at in the US, did not attract a tremendous amount of support beforehand and hails from a stable not known for having first-time-out juvenile winners. She ran pretty green, and all in all this was a promising debut. She should improve. (op 25-1)

Albabilia(IRE), a half-sister to Brainy Benny, who won over a mile at two, is out of a mare who won over 1m6f. Bred to get a bit further than this, she was staying on in taking fashion late on and, providing her sights are not set too high too soon, she should be able to win a race before going on to take on better opposition. (op 40-1)

Honky Tonk Sally tried to put her experience to good use and set a decent pace in front. She can have few excuses, but a reproduction of this effort will probably be good enough to win most fillies' maidens. (op 7-2)

Tudor Court(IRE) ran a promising race on her debut at Pontefract and looked sure to take the beating next time on that evidence, but this was a hot maiden and, after showing good speed, she found a few too good late on. She was eased down in the closing stages but would probably have finished on the heels of the fifth filly had she been kept up to her work. (op 8-1)

Top Vision, a half-sister to Molly Dancer, a moderate 6f winner at four, stayed on late in the day from off the pace, benefiting from the decent gallop that had been set by the leaders. She looks likely to appreciate a step up to 7f. (op 33-1)

Baraari(USA) ◆ is out of a mare who placed over 6f on her only start at three, but more importantly is a half-sister to the Derby winner Erhaab. Running in the second colours of her owner, she was another staying on late from off the pace, and this daughter of Nayef looks the type to do a lot better as she gains experience and steps up in distance.

Izzibizzi, whose dam was a multiple winner over 1m4f to 2m, will not come into her own until she steps up in distance.

Politeia(USA), whose dam was unraced but is a half-sister to Tree Line, a triple sprint winner in the US, looks likely to derive plenty from this debut experience. (tchd 22-1)

Geordie Girl is now eligible to run in nurseries and might have more luck in that sphere. (op 33-1)

Nothing Likea Dame Official explanation: jockey said filly hung left throughout

3508 UNICORN ASSET MANAGEMENT JULY COURSE SERIES NURSERY (QUALIFIER) — 7f

4:20 (4:20) (Class 2) 2-Y-O — **£12,954** (£3,854; £1,926; £962) **Stalls** Low

Form				RPR
3150	**1**		**Dan Tucket**[37] [2353] 2-8-6 76 ... TPO'Shea 7 (M R Channon) *hld up: hmpd 1/2-way: hdwy over 1f out: hung lft ins fnl f: r.o u.p to ld nr fin* **16/1**	82+
333	**2**	½	**Al Muheer (IRE)**[20] [2885] 2-9-7 91 ... RichardHughes 8 (C E Brittain) *lw: led: rdn over 1f out: hdd nr fin* **15/2**	96
402	**3**	2	**Relinquished**[20] [2888] 2-8-3 73 ... JimmyQuinn 2 (J Noseda) *lw: hld up in tch: rdn over 1f out: styd on same pce ins fnl f* **11/2**[1]	73
416	**4**	½	**Dalkey Girl (IRE)**[13] [3096] 2-8-10 80 ... NCallan 4 (V Smith) *hmpd sn after s: hld up: hdwy 2f out: sn rdn: styd on* **15/2**	78
6254	**5**	½	**Avertitop**[37] [2349] 2-8-6 76 ... TedDurcan 9 (R Hannon) *hld up: pushed along over 2f out: r.o ins fnl f: nrst fin* **18/1**	73
653	**6**	¾	**King Bathwick (IRE)**[14] [3043] 2-7-13 69 ... AdrianMcCarthy 5 (B R Millman) *s.i.s: sn prom: rdn over 2f out: styd on same pce appr fnl f* **20/1**	64
045	**7**	hd	**Rough Rock (IRE)**[57] [1781] 2-8-2 72 ... MartinDwyer 6 (B J Meehan) *lw: chsd ldr: rdn over 2f out: ev ch over 1f out: wknd ins fnl f* **11/1**	66
10	**8**	nk	**Monaazalah (IRE)**[23] [2756] 2-9-3 87 ... RHills 3 (B W Hills) *hld up: hdwy 2f out: wknd ins fnl f* **11/2**[1]	81
003	**9**	2	**Bid Art (IRE)**[17] [2961] 2-8-1 71 ow2 ... RichardThomas 11 (A M Balding) *lw: prom: rdn over 2f out: wknd over 1f out* **12/1**	59
041	**10**	½	**Ramblin Bob**[31] [2539] 2-8-1 71 ... NickyMackay 10 (R M Beckett) *hld up in tch: racd keenly: lost pl over 4f out: swtchd lft 1/2-way: rdn and wknd over 1f out* **13/2**[3]	58
222	**11**	1	**Irving Place**[48] [2021] 2-8-6 76 ... JamieSpencer 15 (M L W Bell) *lw: hld up: plld hrd: hdwy over 4f out: rdn over 1f out: sn wknd* **6/1**[2]	61
002	**12**	hd	**Vigano (IRE)**[28] [2630] 2-8-5 75 ... JohnEgan 12 (S Kirk) *trckd ldrs: plld hrd: rdn over 1f out: sn wknd* **10/1**	59

1m 27.73s (0.95) **Going Correction** +0.025s/f (Good) **12** Ran SP% **122.9**

Speed ratings (Par 100):95,94,92,91,91 90,89,89,87,86 85,85

CSF £136.07 CT £772.06 TOTE £20.90: £4.80, £3.00, £2.10; EX 246.30.

Owner Box 41 **Bred** Grasshopper 2000 Ltd **Trained** West Ilsley, Berks

FOCUS

The official ratings shown next to each horse are estimated and for information purposes only. This was a competitive nursery full of unexposed sorts, but the early pace was not hectic. Solid form, and it could be rated a bit higher.

NOTEBOOK

Dan Tucket had not progressed from his maiden win in May, but this was the first time he had had the opportunity to race on fast ground since then, and he relished conditions. Settling well off what was not a strong pace, he picked up in grand style when asked to challenge, and clearly appreciated the step up in trip. He should not go up too much in the weights for this and can improve again while the ground remains on the fast side. A mile will be within his compass later in the season.

Al Muheer(IRE), who had to give weight away all round, got the run of the race out in front, being able to dictate a fairly ordinary gallop and kick from the front. He looked the likely winner until the winner surged by close home, and he deserves to get his head in front after a series of creditable efforts. (op 8-1)

Relinquished, who was thought worthy of an entry in the Phoenix Stakes, is clearly not up to that class, but this was a solid effort. (op 6-1)

Dalkey Girl(IRE), not disgraced in Listed company last time out, got the extra furlong well and kept on stoutly for fourth. She should remain a threat in nurseries, as not all will be as competitive as this one. (tchd 8-1)

Avertitop, whose pedigree suggests he should be a sprinter, had previously only raced over the minimum trip, but he showed here that without question he wants 7f, as he was staying on better than anything in the closing stages. (op 16-1 tchd 20-1)

King Bathwick(IRE), who has improved with every outing in maiden company, was racing on quick ground for the first time and performed with credit. (op 16-1)

Rough Rock(IRE), another stepping up to 7f for the first time having run exclusively over the minimum trip in maiden company, did not seem to get home. (tchd 12-1)

Monaazalah(IRE) created a good impression on her debut at Haydock but ran no race in the Queen Mary (apparently she was struck into). This looked an easier assignment, but the step up to 7f was not sure to suit her as she has plenty of speed in her pedigree, and it looked as though she did not last home, an opinion supported later by her rider. Official explanation: jockey said filly failed to stay 7f trip (op 5-1 tchd 6-1)

Bid Art(IRE), whose rider put up 2lb overweight, was expected to improve for the step up to 7f for the first time, but he proved a bit disappointing, getting outpaced from over two furlongs out and dropping out tamely. (op 14-1 tchd 11-1, 16-1 in places)

Ramblin Bob refused to settle in the early stages off the steady pace and paid the price in the latter part of the race. (op 10-1)

Irving Place also failed to settle off the ordinary gallop. Official explanation: jockey said gelding ran too free and was eased final furlong

Vigano(IRE) Official explanation: vet noted colt was eased final furlong and finished sore

3509 EGERTON HOUSE STABLES H'CAP — 1m 4f

4:55 (4:57) (Class 3) (0-90,89) 3-Y-O+ **£9,715** (£2,890; £1,444; £721) **Stalls** Centre

Form				RPR
-356	**1**		**John Terry (IRE)**[13] 3105 4-9-11 **86** .... JMurtagh 6 (Mrs A J Perrett) *mde all: shkn up over 1f out: hung lft ins fnl f: styd on* **16/1**	96
6-21	**2**	*shd*	**Samurai Way**[55] 1849 5-9-12 **87** .... NickyMackay 12 (L M Cumani) *hld up: rdn over 3f out: hdwy and n.m.r 2f out: rdn and ev ch ins fnl f: styd on* **2/1**[1]	97
330	**3**	*1/2*	**Nawamees (IRE)**[48] 1244 9-9-5 **80** ....(p) JimmyFortune 14 (G L Moore) *hld up in tch: rdn over 1f out: edgd lft ins fnl f: r.o* **16/1**	89
5-15	**4**	*hd*	**Hernando Royal**[41] 2236 4-9-11 **86** .... SteveDrowne 3 (H Morrison) *lw: a.p: rdn over 1f out: styd on same pce ins fnl f* **14/1**	95
4052	**5**	*3 1/2*	**I Have Dreamed (IRE)**[16] 2994 5-9-9 **84** ....(b) JoeFanning 5 (T G Mills) *hld up: hdwy over 7f out: rdn over 1f out: styd on same pce* **14/1**	87
46-2	**6**	*3/4*	**Ameeq (USA)**[53] 587 5-9-7 **82** .... RyanMoore 15 (G L Moore) *hld up: outpcd over 2f out: r.o ins fnl f* **14/1**	84+
-032	**7**	*1/2*	**Magicalmysterytour (IRE)**[14] 3060 4-9-10 **85** .... BrettDoyle 2 (W J Musson) *lw: hld up: nt clr run over 1f out: nvr nr to chal* **16/1**	86+
3043	**8**	*1*	**Dzesmin (POL)**[13] 3093 5-9-6 **81** ....(p) JohnEgan 10 (R C Guest) *hld up: hdwy 3f out: rdn over 1f out: wknd ins fnl f* **15/2**[3]	80
2/24	**9**	*nk*	**Clueless**[20] 2861 5-9-11 **86** .... RichardHughes 18 (N G Richards) *chsd ldrs: rdn over 2f out: wknd over 1f out* **12/1**	85
-321	**10**	*3/4*	**High Treason (USA)**[56] 1822 5-9-12 **87** .... TedDurcan 16 (W J Musson) *lw: hld up: effrt over 2f out: wknd over 1f out* **9/2**[2]	85
0006	**11**	*1/2*	**Best Prospect (IRE)**[15] 3026 5-10-0 **89** ....(t) JamieSpencer 1 (M Dods) *lw: hld up: swtchd lft and hdwy 2f out: wknd ins fnl f* **14/1**	86
4400	**12**	*shd*	**Eva Soneva So Fast (IRE)**[20] 2859 5-9-10 **85** .... MichaelHills 17 (J L Dunlop) *hld up: hdwy u.p over 2f out: wknd over 1f out* **16/1**	82
6234	**13**	*3 1/2*	**Active Asset (IRE)**[39] 2314 5-9-12 **87** .... MartinDwyer 4 (M Quinn) *chsd ldrs: rdn over 2f out: wknd over 1f out* **33/1**	78+
0104	**14**	*12*	**My Arch**[12] 3143 5-9-12 **87** ....(p) NCallan 11 (K A Ryan) *chsd ldrs 9f* **20/1**	59+

2m 33.12s (0.21) **Going Correction** +0.025s/f (Good) **14** Ran SP% **128.9**

Speed ratings (Par 107):100,99,99,99,97 96,96,95,95,94 94,94,92,84

CSF £51.28 CT £574.25 TOTE £19.70: £4.90, £1.50, £6.20; EX 76.80 Place 6 £261.24, Place 5 £114.13..

Owner A D Spence **Bred** Dr T A Ryan **Trained** Pulborough, W Sussex

■ Stewards' Enquiry : Nicky Mackay four-day ban: careless riding (Jul 24-27); three-day ban: used whip with excessive frequency, above shoulder height, without giving horse time to respond (Jul 29-31)

FOCUS

Mostly exposed handicappers contested this and the form looks fairly reliable rated through those that placed fifth to eighth. Much improved form from the first two.

NOTEBOOK

John Terry(IRE), who got a bit warm beforehand, is usually held up and has been kept to racing mainly on good ground or softer in his career so far, but he showed here that he can be just as effective on a quick surface, and he ran better for a change of riding tactics. Making every yard, he looked sure to succomb to Samurai Way's challenge in the closing stages, but he rallied well and just held on. (op 14-1 tchd 20-1)

Samurai Way, one of the least exposed in the line-up, was a very well-backed favourite. He came there to have every chance inside the last and was upsides the winner as they crossed the line, but John Terry's nose was just in front where it mattered. This was much improved form, nevertheless. (op 4-1 tchd 9-2 in places)

Nawamees(IRE), last seen running over hurdles in May, last won on the Flat when he was racing in the French Provinces in 2001, but it cannot be argued that he is on a favourable mark at present. Whether he is a win-only betting proposition is another question, though.

Hernando Royal, whose fifth at Epsom last time out is solid form, has a steadily progressive profile, and he once again gave the impression that he will get further than this. (op 16-1 tchd 20-1)

I Have Dreamed(IRE) perhaps did not run quite as well as he did on the All-Weather last time out, but this looked a stronger contest than that Polytrack event.

Ameeq(USA), who has yet to win on the Flat on turf, got outpaced but found his feet in the latter stages and stayed on well past beaten horses for a never nearer sixth. He has never been tried over further than 1m4f on the Flat but could be interesting over a staying distance. (tchd 12-1)

Magicalmysterytour(IRE) was back up to his ideal trip, but the ground had probably gone against him this time.

High Treason(USA) has looked progressive this term, but a 6lb rise for his latest success at York was enough to stop him here. (tchd 5-1 in places)

Best Prospect(IRE), who won this race last year off an 8lb lower mark, was wearing the tongue tie for the first time this year. He travelled well and looked a big danger over a furlong out, but he did not see his race out, weakening as they hit the rising ground. They did not go a great pace when he won this race last year and perhaps a truly-run 1m4f places a little too much emphasis on stamina for his liking.

T/Jkpt: Not won. T/Plt: £349.60 to a £1 stake. Pool: £179,039.50. 373.80 winning tickets. T/Qpdt: £139.70 to a £1 stake. Pool: £9,025.30. 47.80 winning tickets. CR

[1821]YORK (L-H)

Friday, July 13

OFFICIAL GOING: Soft (good to soft and heavy in places) changing to soft (heavy in places) after race 4 (3.55)

A revamped two-day meeting as parts of the back straight were waterlogged and races could not be staged over further than 1m1f.

Wind: Mod hlf bhd Weather: Dull and rain

3510 HOVIS MAIDEN STKS — 7f

2:15 (2:20) (Class 3) 2-Y-O **£6,541** (£1,946; £972; £485) **Stalls** Low

Form				RPR
2	**1**		**Donegal (USA)**[28] 2632 2-9-3 0........ LPKeniry 10 (A M Balding) *a.p: swtchd rt to centre and hdwy to ld 2f out: clr over 1f out: styd on wl* **11/4**[1]	92
63	**2**	*6*	**Transmission (IRE)**[20] 2888 2-9-3 0........ KDarley 9 (B Smart) *chsd ldrs: swtchd rt towards stands' rail 4f out and cl up: rdn and ev ch 2f out: swtchd lft to chse wnr over 1f out: sn drvn and no imp* **11/4**[1]	77
	3	*13*	**Manuka Bee** 2-9-3 0........ TonyHamilton 7 (J Howard Johnson) *hmpd s: sn rdn along and bhd: hdwy 2f out: styd on wl appr fnl f* **25/1**	45
	4	*1/2*	**Inspector Clouseau (IRE)** 2-9-3 0........ MickyFenton 5 (T P Tate) *towards rr: hdwy to chse ldrs 1/2-way: sn rdn along and outpcd 2f out: plugged on one pce* **10/1**[3]	43
	5	*1 3/4*	**Hold The Gold (IRE)** 2-9-3 0........ DaneO'Neill 6 (E J O'Neill) *wnt rt s: sn led: hdd 2f out and sn rdn: drvn and wknd over 1f out: tired whn hung lft ins fnl f* **10/3**[2]	39+
5	**6**	*1 1/2*	**Flop (IRE)**[24] 2739 2-8-12 0........ DeanMernagh 2 (M Brittain) *chsd ldrs: rdn along 1/2-way: sn wknd* **16/1**	30
000	**7**	*1 1/2*	**Lady Grantley**[38] 2344 2-8-5 0........ NSLawes(7) 4 (M W Easterby) *a towards rr* **150/1**	26
	8	*7*	**Jemima's Art** 2-8-12 0........ PhillipMakin 11 (M W Easterby) *s.i.s: a wl bhd* **33/1**	9+
6	**9**	*3*	**Terrasini (FR)**[16] 2983 2-9-3 0........ TomEaves 1 (J Howard Johnson) *chsd ldrs: rdn along 3f out: sn drvn and wknd 2f out* **14/1**	6
	10	*12*	**Flaxton (UAE)** 2-8-10 0........ PatrickDonaghy(7) 8 (M Brittain) *cl up: rdn along after 3f: sn wknd and bhd* **66/1**	—

1m 27.15s (1.75) **Going Correction** +0.20s/f (Good) **10** Ran SP% **107.0**

Speed ratings (Par 98):98,91,76,75,73 72,70,62,58,45

CSF £8.43 TOTE £3.60: £1.30, £1.30, £6.20; EX 7.00.

Owner The Donegal Partnership **Bred** A B Hancock III **Trained** Kingsclere, Hants

■ Climaxtackledotcom was withdrawn (9/1, broke out of stalls). R4 applies, deduct 10p in the £.

FOCUS

No strength in depth here. The field finished well strung out and the winner looks capable of rating higher, with the runner-up setting the level.

NOTEBOOK

Donegal(USA) confirmed the promise of his debut second in a much better race at Sandown and went one better with a commanding display. He clearly stays well as he was always prominent and was not stopping at the finish on this taxing surface. A step up in class now looks in order. (tchd 3-1)

Transmission(IRE) got warm beforehand and that cannot have helped his cause. His rider elected to come towards the stands' side in the home straight and that probably proved an advantage, but it was clear from two out that he was playing second fiddle to the winner. He too stays well and looks a likely type for nurseries. (op 5-2 tchd 9-4, 3-1 in places)

Manuka Bee, who cost 40,000euros, got himself well behind early on after being hampered and did well to finish third. His trainer's juvenile mostly come on a good deal for their debut experience and he should know more next time.

Inspector Clouseau(IRE), a half-brother to a juvenile debut winner over this trip, was another who got behind early before plugging on from 2f out. A sounder surface should help him and he can be expected to come on for this debut experience. Official explanation: jockey said gelding hung right throughout (tchd 11-1)

Hold The Gold(IRE), whose trainer had won the last two runnings of this event, cost 75,000euros and proved very popular in the betting ring. He clearly knew his job as he was quick to lead, and looked most likely to play a part in the finish 2f out, but he started to tread water nearing the final furlong and finished legless. He is capable of better, but he will know he has had a race and may need some time to recover. (op 9-2)

3511 CUISINE DE FRANCE SUMMER STKS (GROUP 3) (F&M) — 6f

2:45 (2:48) (Class 1) 3-Y-O+

£28,390 (£10,760; £5,385; £2,685; £1,345; £675) **Stalls** Centre

Form				RPR
0350	**1**		**Theann**[23] 2752 3-8-10 0........ JAHeffernan 1 (A P O'Brien, Ire) *in tch: hdwy over 2f out: rdn to ld appr fnl f: styd on strly* **5/1**[3]	108+
4011	**2**	*2 1/2*	**Gloved Hand**[14] 3059 5-9-2 99........ GeorgeBaker 4 (R M Beckett) *in tch: hdwy to trck ldrs over 2f out: rdn wl over 1f out: styd on to chse wnr ins fnl f: no imp towards fin* **8/1**	101
4-10	**3**	*1 1/2*	**Lady Grace (IRE)**[23] 2757 3-8-10 98........ PaulMulrennan 7 (W J Haggas) *trckd ldrs: hdwy 2f out: sn rdn and styd on ent fnl f: nrst fin* **8/1**	96
1-30	**4**	*1 1/2*	**Blue Echo**[40] 2291 3-8-10 93........ KDarley 2 (M A Jarvis) *cl up: rdn to ld 2f out: drvn and hdd appr fnl f: grad wknd* **14/1**	92
0261	**5**	*hd*	**Mecca's Mate**[5] 3344 6-9-2 100........ TonyHamilton 3 (D W Barker) *stdd s and hld up in rr: hdwy on inner wl over 1f out: sn rdn and styd on ins fnl f: nrst fin* **9/1**	91
-130	**6**	*3/4*	**Firenze**[20] 2857 6-9-2 105........ OscarUrbina 10 (J R Fanshawe) *hld up in rr: hdwy over 2f out: sn rdn and no imp* **2/1**[1]	89
6-66	**7**	*3*	**Sesmen**[61] 1702 3-8-10 105........(t) MickyFenton 11 (M Botti) *in tch: rdn along 1/2-way: sn btn* **18/1**	80
2200	**8**	*nk*	**Perfect Story (IRE)**[21] 2835 5-9-2 85........(v1) HayleyTurner 8 (J A R Toller) *midfield: rdn along 1/2-way: nvr a factor* **66/1**	79

0-41 **9** *2 1/2* **Dark Missile**[20] [2858] 4-9-2 101 LPKeniry 5 71
(A M Balding) *cl up: effrt and ev ch over 2f out: sn rdn and wknd wl over 1f out* **9/2**[2]

1604 **10** *2 1/2* **Angus Newz**[8] [3240] 4-9-2 91 (v) DaneO'Neill 9 64
(M Quinn) *led: rdn along 1/2-way: hdd 2f out and sn wknd* **40/1**

1m 13.27s (0.71) **Going Correction** +0.375s/f (Good)
WFA 3 from 4yo+ 6lb **21** Ran SP% **116.3**
Speed ratings (Par 113):110,106,104,102,102 101,97,97,93,90
CSF £44.57 TOTE £5.60: £2.10, £2.60, £2.70; EX 50.70.
Owner Mrs E M Stockwell **Bred** T Stewart **Trained** Ballydoyle, Co Tipperary
■ Seamie Heffernan's first winner in Britain.

FOCUS
No more than a fair Group 3 for fillies. The winner went well on the deep ground and produced a career-best effort to score. The form could rate higher but the form is rated conservatively with the market leaders not running their races.

NOTEBOOK
Theann, seventh in the Group 3 Jersey Stakes at the Royal Meeting last time, was perfectly positioned before finding a turn of foot when asked to win her race and eventually coming away from her rivals to score. She has faced some stiff tasks since resuming as a three-year-old, the drop into this grade helped, and clearly she goes well on a deep surface. This will have nicely enhanced her all-important paddock potential and she also ought to be high on confidence now. (op 6-1)
Gloved Hand ◆, bidding for the hat-trick, came through to run another improved race on this step up in class. She would have found this ground plenty soft enough, has been a revelation since getting in-foal to Cadeaux Genereux, and there is no reason why she cannot find another opening in her current mood when reverting a sounder surface. (op 9-1)
Lady Grace(IRE), ninth in the Sandringham at the Royal Meeting last time, hit a flat spot before picking up again under maximum pressure passing the final furlong marker. She found this too sharp a test despite the taxing surface and deserves to find another race when faced with a stiffer test again.
Blue Echo, outclassed in Group 2 company in France 40 days previously, showed her customary early pace yet proved a sitting duck for the winner and tired inside the final 100 yards. This was much more like her true form. (op 12-1)
Mecca's Mate, back to winning ways in this grade at Ayr five days previously, was given a fair amount to do from off the pace and basically got going too late on this return to the extra furlong. She remains in good heart. (op 8-1)
Firenze, ninth from a desperate draw in the Golden Jubilee 20 days previously, was another who was given a lot to do from off the pace. However, she was having to be niggled after two furlongs and this lacklustre showing was most likely down to the very soft ground. Official explanation: jockey said mare never travelled (op 9-4 tchd 5-2 in places)
Dark Missile, the Wokingham winner, was given a positive ride yet was in trouble as soon as she was pressed for the lead and has to rate disappointing on this step up in class. (op 4-1)

3512 HEARTHSTEAD HOMES STKS (H'CAP) 7f
3:20 (3:20) (Class 4) (0-85,82) 3-Y-0+ **£6,800** (£2,023; £1,011; £505) **Stalls** Low

Form RPR
0245 **1** **Riquewihr**[7] [3259] 7-8-10 64 (p) PaddyAspell 5 72
(J S Wainwright) *hld up in rr: c stands' side 1/2-way: smooth hdwy over 2f out: rdn to ld over 1f out: drvn ins fnl f and hld on gamely* **20/1**

0030 **2** *shd* **Sake (IRE)**[10] [3194] 5-9-0 68 KimTinkler 4 76
(N Tinkler) *chsd ldrs: styd far side home st: rdn over 2f out: swtchd rt to centre and drvn over 1f out: styd on u.p ins fnl f: jst hld* **20/1**

3240 **3** *nk* **Neon Blue**[31] [2536] 6-8-11 70 MichaelJStainton[(5)] 1 77
(R M Whitaker) *in tch: styd far side st: hdwy over 2f out and sn rdn: swtchd rt and drvn to chse ldng pair over 1f out: styd on wl u.p fnl f* **10/1**

3120 **4** *4* **Dispol Isle (IRE)**[16] [2988] 5-9-4 72 PhillipMakin 6 69
(T D Barron) *in tch: styd far side st: rdn along 2f out and kpt on same pce* **12/1**

4012 **5** *4* **Gunfighter (IRE)**[16] [2985] 4-9-7 75 TonyHamilton 3 62
(J S Wainwright) *trckd ldrs: styd far side st: swtchd rt to centre and hdwy to ld 2f out: sn rdn and hdd over 1f out: one pce* **7/2**[1]

4120 **6** *6* **Viva Volta**[10] [3194] 4-9-6 74 DavidAllan 7 46
(T D Easterby) *prom: c stands' side st: rdn along wl over 2f out and grad wknd* **8/1**

1501 **7** *5* **Sedge (USA)**[3] [3409] 7-8-13 67 6ex (b) MickyFenton 9 27
(P T Midgley) *in tch: hdwy to chse ldrs stands' side: over 2f out: sn rdn and wknd* **8/1**

3402 **8** *1/2* **Shot To Fame (USA)**[14] [3052] 8-9-11 79 (t) AdrianTNicholls 2 38
(D Nicholls) *led: c to stands' side 1/2-way: sn rdn: hdd 2f out and sn wknd* **9/2**[2]

32-4 **9** *2* **Red Romeo**[13] [3091] 6-10-0 82 PaulMulrennan 8 36
(N Wilson) *prom: c stands' side: rdn along 3f out: sn drvn and wknd* **6/1**[3]

0332 **10** *17* **Passion Fruit**[16] [2988] 6-9-13 81 KDarley 10 —
(C W Fairhurst) *hld up: c stands' side: rdn along wl over 2f out and a in rr* **13/2**

1m 27.58s (2.18) **Going Correction** +0.45s/f (Yiel) **10** Ran SP% **116.6**
Speed ratings (Par 105):105,104,104,99,95 88,82,82,79,60
CSF £360.78 CT £4185.05 TOTE £30.00: £4.50, £5.10, £3.80; EX 675.70.
Owner S Enwright **Bred** G B Partnership **Trained** Kennythorpe, N Yorks
■ Stewards' Enquiry : Kim Tinkler two-day ban: used whip with excessive frequency (Jul 24-25)

FOCUS
A modest handicap, run at a sound pace but just average form. A tight finish but the first three came clear.

3513 JOHN WEST TUNA STKS (H'CAP) 1m 208y
3:55 (3:55) (Class 2) (0-100,98) 3-Y-0+ **£11,658** (£3,468; £1,733; £865) **Stalls** Low

Form RPR
10 **1** **European Dream (IRE)**[15] [3026] 4-9-7 98 (p) NeilBrown[(7)] 4 107
(R C Guest) *hld up: stdy hdwy 3f out: trckd ldrs wl over 1f out: swtchd lft and rdn to chal ent fnl f: sn led and styd on wl* **12/1**

50-1 **2** *nk* **Greek Envoy**[39] [2305] 3-8-13 93 MickyFenton 3 100
(T P Tate) *trckd ldrs: effrt over 2f out: rdn to chal over 1f out and ev ch: drvn ent fnl f and kpt on* **9/2**[1]

-230 **3** *1 1/4* **Benandonner (USA)**[46] [2093] 4-9-0 84 TonyHamilton 2 90
(R A Fahey) *cl up: led after 1f: rdn along wl over 2f out: drvn over 1f out: hdd ins fnl f: no ex last 100yds* **13/2**

2261 **4** *4* **Harvest Warrior**[7] [3258] 5-8-9 79 3ex oh4 DavidAllan 5 77
(T D Easterby) *led 1f: cl up: rdn 2f out and ev ch tl drvn and wknd appr fnl f* **9/2**[1]

1200 **5** *2 1/2* **Goodbye Mr Bond**[23] [2755] 7-9-8 92 KDarley 1 85
(E J Alston) *trckd ldrs: hdwy wl over 2f out: swtchd rt and ch whn rdn over 1f out: sn drvn and btn* **8/1**

020 **6** *2* **Vacation (IRE)**[6] [3330] 4-9-2 86 DaneO'Neill 9 75
(V Smith) *hld up: a in rr* **9/1**

0604 **7** *3* **Krugerrand (USA)**[4] [3386] 8-8-9 79 DavidKinsella 6 62
(W J Musson) *hld up in rr: hdwy 3f out: rdn along 2f out and sn no imp* **11/2**[2]

0042 **8** *nk* **Blue Spinnaker (IRE)**[19] [2906] 8-9-2 86 (b) PaulMulrennan 7 68
(M W Easterby) *prom: rdn along 2f out: drvn over 1f out and sn wknd* **6/1**[3]

0060 **9** *18* **Boo**[104] [846] 5-8-12 85 AndrewElliott[(3)] 8 31
(K R Burke) *s.i.s: hdwy over 4f out: rdn along 3f out: sn wknd and bhd* **16/1**

1m 54.83s (3.84) **Going Correction** +0.55s/f (Yiel)
WFA 3 from 4yo+ 10lb **9** Ran SP% **114.1**
Speed ratings (Par 109):104,103,102,99,96 95,92,92,76
CSF £64.43 CT £386.08 TOTE £15.60: £3.50, £1.80, £2.70; EX 50.50.
Owner You Trotters **Bred** Limetree Stud Ltd **Trained** Carburton, Notts

FOCUS
A good handicap in which it proved hard to come from off the pace, so the winner deserves plenty of credit. The third sets a solid level for the form.

NOTEBOOK
European Dream(IRE) bounced back to form and ran out a game winner. He does go well on this sort of ground and has had an excellent season so far, this being his fourth win of the current campaign. His performance is made more meritorious as he was the only one to come from off the pace and no doubt he is still on an upward curve. It would not be a surprise to see him aimed at the Cambridgeshire. (op 11-1)
Greek Envoy, 9lb higher than when scoring on his seasonal return 39 days previously, did nothing wrong in defeat from his new mark and was only just thwarted. He can expect to go up again for this, but he was nicely clear of the remainder and also remains on an upward curve. (op 4-1)
Benandonner(USA) ran one of his better race in defeat, but had very much the run of the race and looks in need of respite from the Handicapper. (op 7-1 tchd 6-1)
Harvest Warrior was given a positive ride and held every chance under his penalty. He should not be too harsly judged on this effort as he probably found it coming a bit too soon. (op 4-1)
Blue Spinnaker(IRE) ran below his recent level and continues to prove hard to get right this term, although this ground was probably too soft even for him. (tchd 13-2)

3514 MR KIPLING EXCEEDINGLY GOOD STKS (H'CAP) 1m
4:30 (4:30) (Class 3) (0-90,90) 3-Y-0 **£9,715** (£2,890; £1,444; £721) **Stalls** Low

Form RPR
4-1 **1** **Mutajarred**[20] [2873] 3-8-9 78 PaulMulrennan 4 97+
(W J Haggas) *sn led: hdd briefly over 3f out: sn led again: rdn clr wl over 1f out: easily* **9/4**[1]

0531 **2** *9* **Novikov**[20] [2880] 3-9-1 84 KDarley 5 83
(J H M Gosden) *trckd ldng pair: swtchd rt and hdwy 3f out: effrt and ev ch over 2f out: rdn and chsd wnr over 1f out: sn drvn and no imp* **5/2**[2]

0-15 **3** *4* **Darfour**[43] [2171] 3-8-8 77 ow1 OscarUrbina 3 67
(J S Goldie) *hld up in rr: swtchd wd 3f out: rdn 2f out: styd on ins fnl f* **10/1**

41 **4** *1 3/4* **Held Captive (USA)**[20] [2886] 3-8-13 82 DaneO'Neill 7 69
(E A L Dunlop) *cl up: swtchd rt and led over 3f out: rdn and hdd wl over 2f out: sn drvn and wknd wl over 1f out* **5/1**[3]

25 **5** *6* **Dream Lodge (IRE)**[30] [2577] 3-8-8 77 MickyFenton 2 50
(J G Given) *chsd ldrs: rdn along over 3f out and sn wknd* **11/2**

6300 **6** *3 1/2* **Thunder Storm Cat (USA)**[22] [2788] 3-9-7 90 PhillipMakin 6 56
(P F I Cole) *hld up: a in rr* **8/1**

1m 42.18s (2.68) **Going Correction** +0.55s/f (Yiel) **6** Ran SP% **111.6**
Speed ratings (Par 104):108,99,95,93,87 83
CSF £8.06 TOTE £2.70: £1.80, £1.90; EX 5.90.
Owner Hamdan Al Maktoum **Bred** Floors Farming & Beckhampton Stables Ltd **Trained** Newmarket, Suffolk

FOCUS
An interesting three-year-old handicap which saw a clear-cut winner on the testing surface. The form should be treated with a little caution in view of the conditions.

NOTEBOOK
Mutajarred simply hacked up on this handicap bow. He still looked a touch green when asked for his effort, but when hitting full stride he came right away from the runner-up and has clearly been underestimated by an official mark of 78. It may have been a case of him handling the underfoot conditions best of all, and a hike in the weights is now inevitable, but this lightly-raced son of Alhaarth should still be given a chance to prove his worth in better company now. (op 2-1)
Novikov, off the mark on easy ground at Newmarket 20 days previously, came through to have his chance yet was firmly put in his place by the impressive winner. He still finished a clear second-best, however, and should pick up a handicap from this sort of mark when reverting to slightly less-taxing ground. (op 7-2)
Darfour found this first try at 1m beyond him on such taxing ground, but was not disgraced and the suspicion is that he can defy this mark when getting his optimum conditions. (op 12-1)
Held Captive(USA) had no more to give nearing the 2f marker and finished very tired. She is worthy of another chance when racing on better ground as she created a decent impression when scoring at Newmarket on her previous outing. (op 3-1)
Dream Lodge(IRE) found this deep surface against him and ran well below his previous best. (op 15-2)
Thunder Storm Cat(USA) was another who looked all at sea on this testing surface and remains out of sorts. (op 10-1)

3515 FIT AS A BUTCHER'S DOG STKS (H'CAP) 5f
5:05 (5:06) (Class 3) (0-90,89) 3-Y-0+ **£8,096** (£2,408; £1,203; £601) **Stalls** Centre

Form RPR
1040 **1** **Highland Warrior**[1] [3464] 8-9-3 78 MickyFenton 3 88
(P T Midgley) *hld up in rr: stdy hdwy on outer 2f out: rdn to ld ent fnl f: drvn out* **8/1**

0255 **2** *1* **Blazing Heights**[13] [3080] 4-9-7 82 OscarUrbina 1 88
(J S Goldie) *hld up in tch: swtchd rt and hdwy 2f out: rdn and styd wl fnl f* **6/1**[3]

0425 **3** *3/4* **Jilly Why (IRE)**[20] [2870] 6-8-5 71 oh4 ow1 (b) RussellKennemore[(5)] 9 75
(Paul Green) *cl up: rdn to ld over 2f out: drvn over 1f out: hdd ent fnl f and kpt on same pce* **12/1**

0022 **4** *1 1/2* **Bond Boy**[6] [3298] 10-8-9 75 (b) SladeO'Hara[(5)] 7 73
(G R Oldroyd) *prom: rdn along 2f out: swtchd rt and drvn over 1f out: sn one pce* **9/4**[1]

3513 **5** *2* **Mimi Mouse**[10] [3197] 5-9-6 81 DavidAllan 8 72
(T D Easterby) *led: hdd over 2f out: sn rdn and ev ch tl drvn and wknd appr fnl f* **4/1**[2]

5404 **6** *3 1/2* **Nusoor (IRE)**[15] [3014] 4-8-9 70 oh4 (b) LPKeniry 5 49
(Peter Grayson) *chsd ldrs: rdn 2f out: grad wknd* **14/1**

0005 **7** *3 1/2* **Steelcut**[20] [2884] 3-9-2 82 (b[1]) PhillipMakin 10 48
(R A Fahey) *chsd ldng pair: rdn along 2f out: grad wknd* **14/1**

02-0 **8** *nk* **Inter Vision (USA)**[14] [3050] 7-9-9 89 MichaelJStainton[(5)] 6 54
(A Dickman) *dwlt: a towards rr* **20/1**

0305 **9** *shd* **Matty Tun**[10] 3197 8-8-10 **71** ow1 .... DaneO'Neill 2 35
(J Balding) *towards rr: hdwy on stands' rail 1/2-way: rdn to chse ldrs wl over 1f out: sn drvn and btn* **7/1**

0-00 **10** *1 1/2* **Artie**[6] 3298 8-8-13 **74** .... PaddyAspell 4 33
(T D Easterby) *hood stl in pl whn stalls opened and s.i.s: a towards rr* **16/1**

61.58 secs (2.26) **Going Correction** +0.65s/f (Yiel)
WFA 3 from 4yo+ 5lb **10** Ran SP% **120.3**
Speed ratings (Par 107):107,105,104,101,98 93,87,86,86,84
CSF £57.26 CT £595.08 TOTE £10.50: £2.50, £2.40, £4.30; EX 74.40 Place 6 £959.44, Place 5 £582.53..
Owner Frank & Annette Brady **Bred** Rowcliffe Stud **Trained** Westow, N Yorks

FOCUS
A fair sprint handicap which was run at a solid pace in the taxing ground and the form looks solid rated around the placed horses.

NOTEBOOK
Highland Warrior, well beaten off at Newmarket 24 hours previously, again advertised his liking for soft ground and showed his true colours with a ready success. He found the race run to suit, but should at least remain competitive after being reassessed and is clearly one to be interested in when the ground is testing.
Blazing Heights posted one of his better efforts in defeat and was another who enjoyed the decent early tempo. He is not one for win-only purposes, but still helps to set the level of this form. (op 5-1 tchd 13-2)
Jilly Why(IRE), 4lb out of the weights, fared best of those to race up with the early pace and stuck to her task when headed. This rates as her best effort of the current campaign, but her optimum trip is not that clear at present and she has not won since 2005. (tchd 14-1)
Bond Boy, a runner-up the last twice, is proven on this sort of ground and helps to set the level of the form. He is just proving hard to actually win with. (op 11-4 tchd 3-1 in places)
Mimi Mouse paid for her early exertions and finished tired. She is a little better than this. (op 5-1 tchd 7-2)
T/Plt: £2,851.40 to a £1 stake. Pool: £83,003.10. 21.25 winning tickets. T/Qpdt: £182.60 to a £1 stake. Pool: £3,850.90. 15.60 winning tickets. JR

3516 - 3521a (Foreign Racing) - See Raceform Interactive

3478 ASCOT (R-H)
Saturday, July 14

OFFICIAL GOING: Straight course - good to firm (11.6); old mile - good (good to firm in places; 10.1)
Wind: Mild Weather: dry

3522 EURO EARTHWORKS NOVICE STKS — 7f
2:15 (2:17) (Class 4) 2-Y-O **£6,477** (£1,927; £963; £481) **Stalls** Low

Form RPR

6 **1** **Il Warrd (IRE)**[56] 1832 2-8-12 0 .... PatDobbs 9 90+
(M P Tregoning) *lw: w ldr: led after 2f: shkn up over 1f out: r.o strly: comf* **8/1**

2 *3* **Yahrab (IRE)** 2-8-8 0 .... KerrinMcEvoy 1 78
(C E Brittain) *hld up: hdwy 3f out: rdn to chal over 1f out: wnt narrow 2nd ent fnl f: nt pce of wnr* **40/1**

42 **3** *shd* **Ordinance (USA)**[17] 2991 2-8-12 0 .... TQuinn 4 82
(T G Mills) *s.i.s: sn mid-div: edgd clsr 3f out: rdn to chal 2f out: kpt on but nt pce of wnr* **14/1**

410 **4** *7* **Ruff Diamond (USA)**[25] 2732 2-9-2 0 .... GeorgeBaker 8 68
(J R Best) *lw: trckd ldrs: rdn to chal 2f out: hung rt and wknd ent fnl f* **10/1**

1 **5** *nk* **Dixey**[24] 2768 2-9-0 0 .... PhilipRobinson 6 65
(M A Jarvis) *lw: plld hrd bhd ldrs: rdn 2f out: sn hung rt and wknd* **7/2**[2]

13 **6** *hd* **Baffled (USA)**[22] 2812 2-9-0 0 .... JamieSpencer 2 64
(J Noseda) *hld up: rdn and no imp whn hung rt over 1f out* **5/4**[1]

10 **7** *1 1/4* **Yem Kinn**[25] 2732 2-9-5 0 .... JHBowman 7 66
(M R Channon) *neat: led for 2f: remained prom: rdn 2f out: sn btn* **13/2**[3]

3 **8** *15* **King Supreme (IRE)**[9] 3233 2-8-12 0 .... RichardHughes 3 20
(R Hannon) *chsd ldrs for 3f: sn bhd* **14/1**

1m 28.77s (0.67) **Going Correction** 0.0s/f (Good) **8** Ran SP% **116.0**
Speed ratings (Par 96):96,92,92,84,84 83,82,65
CSF £246.62 TOTE £12.40: £2.60, £5.00, £3.60; EX 366.90 TRIFECTA Not won..
Owner Sheikh Ahmed Al Maktoum **Bred** Castleton Group **Trained** Lambourn, Berks

FOCUS
A decent contest on paper and the first three finished well clear of the rest. The value of the form is open to question, though, on account of the ground being watered overnight and producing what looked like a bias towards racing up the middle of the track. The field was also pretty strung out at the finish, which was strange considering the ground was supposed to be good to firm.

NOTEBOOK
Il Warrd(IRE), who did not run up to expectations on his debut, had clearly come on a good deal for that outing and ran out an impressive winner. Well regarded by his trainer, he is likely to go to Goodwood next in a bid to emulate the stable's Derby winner Sir Percy in winning the Vintage Stakes. (op 12-1)
Yahrab(IRE), who is by Arc winner Dalakhani out of an unraced sister to Arc winner Carnegie, is clearly bred to make up into a decent middle-distance colt in time, but this sort of trip should be fine for him for the time being. Although drawn in stall one, he ended up racing widest of all towards the far side, which could have been an advantage, but this was still a most encouraging debut and, knowing his trainer, he is likely to be soon taking on Pattern-class opposition.
Ordinance(USA) kept on well for third and finished a long way clear of the rest. He will now be eligible to run in nurseries and could well win one if he keeps improving. (op 12-1)
Ruff Diamond(USA), who could be excused his Coventry run as he got hampered early on, was one of the most experienced runners in the line-up but had to give weight away to most of his rivals. Although fourth, he was beaten a long way in the end, but perhaps he can be excused this effort on watered ground. (tchd 9-1)
Dixey, a winner on Polytrack on her debut, did not help her chances of getting home by failing to settle in the early stages. By Diktat, she probably needs a bit of give in the ground to be seen at her best. Official explanation: jockey said filly was unsuited by the good to firm ground (tchd 4-1, 9-2 in places)
Baffled(USA), whose third in the Albany Stakes looked smart form in the context of this race, was very disappointing, although it is tempting to excuse her as she raced on the stands'-side of the pack and may not have been suited by the watered ground. Official explanation: trainer had no explanation for the poor form shown (tchd 11-10 and 7-4)
Yem Kinn, who never got in a blow in the Coventry Stakes, had to give weight away all round and did not look at all suited by the step up to 7f. (tchd 7-1)

3523 SONY SUMMER MILE STKS (GROUP 2) — 1m (R)
2:50 (2:52) (Class 1) 4-Y-O+
£48,263 (£18,292; £9,154; £4,564; £2,286; £1,147) **Stalls** High

Form RPR

5-15 **1** **Cesare**[25] 2735 6-9-1 115 .... JamieSpencer 1 121+
(J R Fanshawe) *lw: hld up in last: gd hdwy over 2f out: nt clr run on rails and swtchd lft over 1f out: r.o strly to ld ins fnl f: readily* **11/4**[2]

-201 **2** *1 1/4* **Royal Oath (USA)**[24] 2755 4-9-1 109 .... (b) JimmyFortune 7 116
(J H M Gosden) *sltly s.i.s: sn in mid-div: gd hdwy on ins 3f out: rdn and edgd rt over 1f out: led ent fnl f: kpt on but no ex whn hdd sn after* **13/2**

3122 **3** *1 1/4* **Heaven Sent**[22] 2815 4-8-12 106 .... RyanMoore 6 110
(Sir Michael Stoute) *lw: hld up: pushed along fr over 3f out: hdwy over 2f out: sltly hmpd over 1f out: styd on to take 3rd nr fin* **6/1**[3]

110- **4** *1/2* **Echo Of Light**[252] 6342 5-9-4 116 .... KerrinMcEvoy 9 115
(Saeed Bin Suroor) *swtg: led: hung lft and rdn fr over 2f out: bmpd rival over 1f out: hdd ent fnl f: 4th and hld whn jinked lft again nr fin* **2/1**[1]

-031 **5** *1* **Dunelight (IRE)**[35] 2442 4-9-1 111 .... (v) PhilipRobinson 8 110
(C G Cox) *lw: trckd ldrs: wnt 2nd 3f out: rdn to chal whn bmpd over 1f out: ev ch ins fnl f: 5th and hld whn bmpd again nr fin* **9/1**

-112 **6** *2 1/2* **Banknote**[27] 2705 5-9-1 108 .... FrancisNorton 3 104
(A M Balding) *t.k.h bhd ldrs: rdn wl over 2f out: one pce fr over 1f out* **16/1**

-116 **7** *1/2* **Racinger (FR)**[25] 2735 4-9-4 0 .... DBonilla 4 106
(F Head, France) *hung rt thrght: trckd ldr tl 3f out: sn rdn and btn* **10/1**

0413 **8** *3 1/2* **Charlie Cool**[22] 2815 4-9-1 106 .... (v) JHBowman 2 95
(W J Haggas) *mid-div: rdn over 2f out: sn btn* **25/1**

110- **9** *1* **Dark Islander (IRE)**[230] 6613 4-9-4 112 .... MichaelHills 5 95
(J W Hills) *plld hrd towards rr: rdn over 2f out: no imp* **33/1**

1m 40.65s (-1.45) **Going Correction** +0.20s/f (Good) **9** Ran SP% **119.4**
Speed ratings (Par 115):115,113,112,112,111 108,108,104,103
CSF £22.02 TOTE £3.30: £1.40, £2.90, £1.70; EX 20.50 Trifecta £81.60 Pool: £1,529.12 - 13.29 winning units..
Owner Cheveley Park Stud **Bred** Cheveley Park Stud Ltd **Trained** Newmarket, Suffolk

FOCUS
The first running as a Group 2 event of this race, back at Ascot after two runnings on the Lingfield Polytrack. They did not go a great gallop early but the winner showed a smart turn of foot to win having been held up in last in the early part of the race. Strong form for the level, and the winner deserves another crack at the top grade.

NOTEBOOK
Cesare, who was a little disappointing in the Queen Anne even allowing for it being a big step up in class for him, appreciated the slightly easier ground this time and showed a smart turn of foot to quicken to the front after being switched off the rail. He seems to be still improving, and the Celebration Mile looks an ideal race for him to take in prior to a return to the top flight in something like the QEII here in September. (op 15-8 tchd 3-1 in places)
Royal Oath(USA), an impressive winner of the Royal Hunt Cup last time out (interestingly, a race won by Cesare the previous year), ran a fine race on this step up in class. While the winner's turn of foot saw him off on this occasion, he beat the rest well enough and, considering that this was only his ninth career start, he is open to further improvement. Official explanation: jockey said colt hung right (op 7-1)
Heaven Sent, who ran with credit in a Listed handicap over 1m2f at Royal Ascot, had a bit to find at this level and the pretty steady early pace did not suit her. Outpaced when the leaders quickened, she kept on steadily to take the minor placing, but at this distance it would appear that she needs a proper gallop. (tchd 13-2)
Echo Of Light won this race last year on his seasonal reappearance when it was transferred to Polytrack and only had Group 3 status. He looked sure to be a strong candidate again on his seasonal return, and the market spoke in his favour, but having been gifted an uncontested lead and enjoyed the run of the race out in front, he carried his head to one side and was a bit too keen for his own good. Hanging badly left inside the final quarter mile, he threw away any chance he had, and he remains something of a frustrating character. Official explanation: jockey said horse hung badly left in home straight (op 11-4)
Dunelight(IRE), a winner in Listed company last time out, likes to make the running, but presumably connections had decided that, with more than one other front-runner in the race, it was prudent not to get into a war for the lead. Bumped twice by the eventual fourth inside the final two furlongs, he ran a bit better than his finishing position suggests. (op 12-1)
Banknote won in Group 3 company earlier in the year, but that was in Germany and this competition was tougher. He raced keenly, which did not help his cause either. (op 33-1)
Racinger(FR), one place behind Cesare in the Queen Anne, should have appreciated the watering that had taken place at the track as he likes to get his toe in, but he probably needs it properly soft. He hung right throughout this race. (op 11-1 tchd 12-1 and 9-1)
Charlie Cool was one place behind Heaven Sent here at the Royal meeting. Perhaps the effectiveness of the visor is beginning to wear off.
Dark Islander(IRE), who won a Grade 2 race in the US last autumn, pulled too hard at the back of the field on this belated seasonal reappearance. Official explanation: jockey said colt lost a front shoe (op 25-1)

3524 RUDDY NURSERY — 6f
3:25 (3:30) (Class 4) 2-Y-O **£6,477** (£1,927; £963; £481) **Stalls** Low

Form RPR

213 **1** **Pelican Prince**[16] 3025 2-9-0 **78** .... JimCrowley 10 81
(K R Burke) *wnt rt s: hld up: swtchd rt and hdwy 3f out: rdn 2f out: led 1f out: drifted lft ins fnl f: jst hld on* **13/2**[3]

31 **2** *hd* **Shifting Star (IRE)**[22] 2832 2-9-0 **78** .... AdamKirby 7 80
(W R Swinburn) *lw: wnt rt s: cl up: rdn over 2f out: swtchd rt over 1f out: str run ins fnl f: jst failed* **2/1**[1]

032 **3** *1/2* **Romany Princess (IRE)**[45] 2138 2-8-10 **74** .... RichardHughes 1 75
(R Hannon) *prom: led 2f out: sn rdn: hdd 1f out: kpt on* **8/1**

21 **4** *1* **Archived (IRE)**[27] 2687 2-9-7 **85** .... PatDobbs 4 83
(M G Quinlan) *hld up: hdwy 3f out: effrt 2f out: kpt on same pce fnl f* **9/1**

6320 **5** *1 1/4* **Swindon Town Flyer (IRE)**[19] 2949 2-8-6 **75** .... KevinGhunowa(5) 5 69
(A B Haynes) *hung lft thrght: chsd ldrs: outpcd over 2f out: kpt on again ins fnl f* **33/1**

531 **6** *3 1/2* **Barbarossa**[17] 2977 2-9-5 **83** .... RyanMoore 9 67
(R Hannon) *bhd: hdwy 3f out: rdn to press wnr 2f out: wknd fnl f* **9/2**[2]

41 **7** *1/2* **Artsu**[16] 3037 2-8-11 **75** .... JamieSpencer 8 57
(M L W Bell) *swtg: b.hind: hld up: hdwy over 3f out to join ldrs: sn rdn and hung rt: ev ch 2f out: wknd ent fnl f* **7/1**

361 **8** *2* **Borasco (USA)**[21] 2889 2-8-6 **70** .... FrancisNorton 2 46
(T D Barron) *lw: led tl 2f out: grad fdd* **7/1**

540 **9** *3 1/2* **New Balls Please (IRE)**[58] 1781 2-7-12 **62** .... NickyMackay 6 28
(P M Phelan) *bmpd s: cl up: rdn over 3f out: sn btn* **50/1**

1m 15.11s (0.21) **Going Correction** 0.0s/f (Good) **9** Ran SP% **115.9**
Speed ratings (Par 96):98,97,97,95,94 89,88,86,81
CSF £19.96 CT £107.60 TOTE £9.00: £2.30, £1.40, £2.40; EX 27.30 Trifecta £340.10 Pool: £1,159.23 - 2.42 winning units..

Owner Market Avenue Racing Club Ltd **Bred** S H And Mrs A M Bayless **Trained** Middleham Moor, N Yorks

■ Stewards' Enquiry : Kevin Ghunowa two-day ban: used whip with excessive frequency (Jul 25-26)

FOCUS

Not a bad nursery, featuring five last-time-out winners, and the form should work out. The 'official' ratings shown next to each horse are estimated and for information purposes only.

NOTEBOOK

Pelican Prince, unsuited by the soft ground at Newcastle last time, was far more effective on this quicker ground, and he arguably raced on the best ground up the centre of the track. His advantage over the runner-up was diminishing as they hit the line but he just held on. The big Sales race at York in August is his target. (tchd 15-2)

Shifting Star(IRE) had to be switched when Romany Princess cut across him inside the final two furlongs, but he stayed on strongly late on and only narrowly failed to get up. It is open to question whether he was racing on the best ground towards the stands'-side, and he looks capable of winning a similar race before long. (op 7-4)

Romany Princess(IRE) showed speed throughout but was another potentially at a disadvantage racing nearer to the stands'-side rail. She is building up a solid portfolio of form and should win a similar race in the next few weeks. (op 7-1 tchd 13-2, 9-1 in places)

Archived(IRE) looked to have been given plenty to do under top weight and was not disgraced in the circumstances. He might struggle to win unless eased a bit by the Handicapper, though. (tchd 8-1)

Swindon Town Flyer(IRE) stayed on well up the stands' side after getting outpaced when the leaders quickened. He hung throughout and softer ground is likely to suit this son of Captain Rio. (tchd 28-1)

Barbarossa, who challenged wide, like the winner, did not get home but was not knocked about when his chance had gone. He is surely better than this run suggests. (op 13-2)

Artsu, who got warm beforehand, may need easier ground to be seen at his best. He was another who hung. (tchd 8-1)

Borasco(USA) looked well treated, but having shown early pace shecould not sustain it over this shorter trip on quicker ground. She could be worth another chance. (tchd 15-2)

3525 SONY UNITED H'CAP 7f

4:00 (4:02) (Class 4) (0-85,85) 3-Y-O+ **£6,477** (£1,927; £963; £481) **Stalls** Low

Form				RPR
2500	**1**		**Bomber Command (USA)**[56] 1845 4-8-13 70....(v[1]) TQuinn 13 (J W Hills) *mde all: sn 5 l clr: kpt on gamely: drvn out* **16/1**	82
0544	**2**	½	**Moonlight Man**[28] 2670 6-10-0 85.... RyanMoore 4 (R Hannon) *lw: chsd wnr thrght: rdn wl over 2f out: no imp on wnr tl r.o ins fnl f* **5/1**[2]	96
0311	**3**	2 ½	**Purus (IRE)**[18] 2965 5-9-12 83.... GeorgeBaker 3 (R A Teal) *t.k.h early: mid-div: hdwy 3f out: sn rdn: wnt 3rd over 1f out: hung bdly lft and no ex ins fnl f* **8/1**	88
2524	**4**	shd	**Cross The Line (IRE)**[35] 2469 5-9-11 82.... JamieSpencer 7 (A P Jarvis) *lw: hld up bhd: rdn and hdwy wl over 1f out: styd on to take 4th ins fnl f: nt rch ldrs* **3/1**[1]	86
1032	**5**	nk	**Harare**[35] 2452 6-9-6 77....(v) PhilipRobinson 6 (R J Price) *hld up bhd: rdn and hdwy 2f out: styd on fnl f: nrst fin* **15/2**[3]	80+
3011	**6**	2	**Skylady**[11] 3194 4-9-0 78.... NeilBrown(7) 5 (T D Barron) *hld up towards rr: hdwy over 2f out: rdn and drifted rt over 1f out: styd on* **8/1**	76
0054	**7**	1 ¼	**Capricorn Run (USA)**[14] 3108 4-9-7 78....(v) AdamKirby 2 (A J McCabe) *trckd ldrs: effrt over 2f out: wknd fnl f* **25/1**	73
2-02	**8**	7	**Venir Rouge**[47] 2079 3-8-1 71 ow2.... KevinGhunowa(5) 14 (M Salaman) *a towards rr* **16/1**	48
0-00	**9**	1 ¾	**Jamieson Gold (IRE)**[28] 2670 4-10-0 85.... MichaelHills 8 (B W Hills) *mid-div: rdn 3f out: wknd over 1f out* **8/1**	57
0560	**10**	1 ¾	**Binnion Bay (IRE)**[10] 3215 6-8-10 67....(b) AmirQuinn 1 (J J Bridger) *chsd ldrs tl 3f out* **25/1**	35
0050	**11**	2 ½	**Lincolneurocruiser**[21] 2877 5-8-7 69.... LukeMorris(5) 9 (Mrs N Macauley) *b: hung rt fr over 1f out: mainly towards rr* **20/1**	30
1000	**12**	1	**Lopinot (IRE)**[35] 2469 4-9-7 78.... PatDobbs 10 (P J Makin) *b.hind: mid-div: rdn 3f out: wknd over 1f out* **20/1**	37
0060	**13**	14	**Blues In The Night (IRE)**[17] 2995 4-9-3 74.... JimmyFortune 12 (P J Makin) *mid-div tl wknd over 1f out* **12/1**	—
0-30	**14**	nk	**Rumbled**[48] 2061 3-8-3 68.... FrancisNorton 11 (J A Geake) *chsd ldrs: rdn and hung rt over 2f out: sn wknd* **33/1**	—

1m 27.79s (-0.31) **Going Correction** 0.0s/f (Good)
WFA 3 from 4yo+ 8lb **14** Ran SP% **126.4**
Speed ratings (Par 105):101,100,97,97,97 94,93,85,83,81 78,77,61,61
CSF £92.23 CT £736.87 TOTE £16.70: £4.20, £2.40, £2.90; EX 89.30 Trifecta £547.80 Part won. Pool: £771.67 - 0.30 winning units..

Owner Gary Woodward **Bred** J B Feins **Trained** Upper Lambourn, Berks

FOCUS

A fair handicap dominated by the front-running Bomber Command, who was allowed a lot of rope in what became a tactical race.

Purus(IRE) Official explanation: jockey said gelding hung left closing stages

Jamieson Gold(IRE) Official explanation: jockey said gelding suffered interference in running

Blues In The Night(IRE) Official explanation: jockey said gelding never travelled

Rumbled Official explanation: jockey said filly hung right

3526 NORMAN COURT STUD H'CAP 5f

4:35 (4:37) (Class 2) (0-105,104) 3-Y-O+

£9,971 (£2,985; £1,492; £747; £372; £187) **Stalls** Low

Form				RPR
0404	**1**		**Border Music**[38] 2352 6-8-7 85 oh4....(b) FrancisNorton 6 (A M Balding) *lw: travelled wl in tch: smooth hdwy fr 2f out: trckd ldrs ent fnl f: qcknd up to ld fnl 100yds: pushed out* **8/1**	98
0513	**2**	¾	**Hoh Hoh Hoh**[14] 3080 5-8-8 86.... JamieSpencer 1 (R J Price) *in tch: rdn and hdwy over 1f out: edgd rt ent fnl f: led sn after: no ex whn hdd fnl 100yds* **6/1**[3]	96
2400	**3**	2 ½	**Corridor Creeper (FR)**[21] 2858 10-9-4 96....(p) JHBowman 3 (J M Bradley) *lw: chsd clr ldr: rdn wl over 1f out: lost 2nd and n.m.r ent fnl f: no ex* **16/1**	97
101-	**4**	1 ¾	**The Jobber (IRE)**[299] 5433 6-9-7 99.... JimmyFortune 8 (M Blanshard) *chsd ldrs: rdn wl over 2f out: kpt on to go 4th ins fnl f* **11/1**	94
0504	**5**	½	**Cape Royal**[8] 3268 7-8-9 92....(bt) KevinGhunowa(5) 2 (J M Bradley) *led and set gd pce: sn 5 l clr: rdn over 1f out: hdd ins fnl f: wknd* **12/1**	85
-400	**6**	nk	**Sweet Afton (IRE)**[35] 2450 4-8-10 88.... FergusSweeney 5 (M S Saunders) *slowly away: sn ni mid-div: rdn wl over 2f out: styd on ins fnl f* **33/1**	80
0305	**7**	¾	**Out After Dark**[8] 3268 6-9-3 95....(p) RyanMoore 4 (C G Cox) *lw: towards rr: rdn 3f out: sme late hdwy: nvr a factor* **3/1**[1]	84
0312	**8**	½	**Golden Dixie (USA)**[8] 3268 8-8-7 90.... LukeMorris(5) 9 (R A Harris) *pumped along fr over 3f out: nvr bttr than mid-div* **11/2**[2]	77
15-6	**9**	1	**Little Edward**[8] 3268 9-8-7 85 oh1.... JimCrowley 7 (R J Hodges) *nvr bttr than mid-div* **16/1**	69
26-0	**10**	1	**One Putra (IRE)**[21] 2858 5-9-12 104.... PhilipRobinson 11 (M A Jarvis) *in tch: rdn over 2f out: wknd over 1f out* **11/2**[2]	84
-000	**11**	42	**Texas Gold**[8] 3268 9-8-11 89.... KerrinMcEvoy 10 (W R Muir) *sprawled leaving stalls: nvr rcvrd and a bhd* **12/1**	—

60.50 secs (-0.90) **Going Correction** 0.0s/f (Good) **11** Ran SP% **119.6**
Speed ratings (Par 109):107,105,101,99,98 97,96,95,94,92 25
CSF £56.44 CT £773.28 TOTE £12.10: £3.60, £2.10, £4.70; EX 74.10 Trifecta £1051.80 Part won. Pool: £1,481.46 - 0.34 winning units..

Owner Kingsclere Stud **Bred** Mrs I A Balding **Trained** Kingsclere, Hants

FOCUS

A decent sprint handicap run at a furious early gallop. Solid form.

NOTEBOOK

Border Music, racing from 4lb out of the weights but still nearly 20lb lower than on the All Weather, travelled well off the strong pace set by Cape Royal and picked up in good style to fight out the finish with Hoh Hoh Hoh. Although he was breaking his maiden tag on turf at the 25th attempt, he deserved this and, in this sort of form, would have to come into the reckoning if turning up for one of the handicaps at the Glorious Goodwood meeting. (op 11-1 tchd 12-1)

Hoh Hoh Hoh, who needs a strong pace to be seen at his best, certainly got that here, and he came clear in the closing stages with the winner, who was equally favoured by the way the race was run. He confirmed himself a progressive sprinter who seems to go on any ground. (op 13-2 tchd 11-2)

Corridor Creeper(FR), back over his best trip having failed to get home in the Wokingham, returned to form and would have been a touch closer but for getting squeezed for room inside the final furlong. He retains his enthusiasm despite his advancing years. (op 14-1)

The Jobber(IRE) had conditions to suit and has gone well fresh in the past, so it was not such a great concern that he had not been seen since last September. However, the stable has not had a great time of it this year, its only winner coming on the All-Weather back in March, so this was a promising effort in the circumstances. Official explanation: jockey said gelding hung left (op 12-1)

Cape Royal showed great early speed but he went too fast really and it was always going to be difficult for him to hang on having blazed at such a pace. A sharper track will suit him, although he will have to drop a couple of pounds to get into the 5f handicap at Glorious Goodwood. (tchd 14-1)

Sweet Afton(IRE), who has been trying to grab some black type in fillies' Listed races lately, stayed on late in the day but never really threatened. She looks held off her current mark. (op 25-1)

Out After Dark, who was unlucky in running at Sandown last time, ran poorly and continues to prove expensive to follow. (op 11-4 tchd 10-3)

Golden Dixie(USA) had an excuse as he lost a shoe. Official explanation: jockey said gelding never travelled and lost a front shoe (op 4-1)

One Putra(IRE) Official explanation: jockey said horse was unsuited by the good to firm ground

Texas Gold Official explanation: jockey said gelding stumbled on leaving stalls

3527 KELTBRAY CUP H'CAP 1m (R)

5:10 (5:11) (Class 3) (0-95,95) 3-Y-O+ **£7,772** (£2,312; £1,155; £577) **Stalls** High

Form				RPR
40-0	**1**		**River Tiber**[111] 783 4-9-12 95.... NickyMackay 7 (L M Cumani) *lw: trckd ldrs: nt clr run on rails and swtchd lft 1f out: sn rdn: r.o: led on line* **6/1**[3]	103
0006	**2**	shd	**Waterside (IRE)**[35] 2446 8-9-4 87.... GeorgeBaker 3 (G L Moore) *led: rdn and hrd pressed fr over 2f out: battled on: hdd on line* **7/2**[1]	95
0600	**3**	¾	**Pentecost**[17] 3001 8-9-10 93....(p) JimmyFortune 4 (A M Balding) *lw: hld up in last: swtchd lft over 2f out: sn rdn and hdwy: wnt 3rd ent fnl f: kpt on* **4/1**[2]	99
3000	**4**	1 ¼	**Red Somerset (USA)**[12] 3165 4-8-7 76 oh2.... SteveDrowne 1 (R J Hodges) *trckd ldr: rdn to chal over 2f out: no ex ins fnl f* **8/1**	79
1114	**5**	½	**Apex**[17] 3001 6-8-8 84.... HaddenFrost(7) 5 (M Hill) *cl up: rdn to chal over 2f out: no ex ins fnl f* **7/2**[1]	86
00-2	**6**	nk	**Cape Of Luck (IRE)**[42] 2239 4-9-1 91.... JackMitchell(7) 2 (P Mitchell) *cl up: rdn to chal over 2f out: no ex ins fnl f* **6/1**[3]	93
	7	7	**Florista Gg (URU)**[314] 4-9-2 90.... TolleyDean(5) 6 (J S Moore) *awkward leaving stalls: hld up: rdn 3f out: wknd over 1f out* **8/1**	75

1m 42.45s (0.35) **Going Correction** +0.20s/f (Good) **7** Ran SP% **115.2**
Speed ratings (Par 107):106,105,105,103,103 103,96
CSF £27.62 TOTE £8.30: £4.00, £2.90; EX 36.40.

Owner R J Baines **Bred** D G Hardisty Bloodstock **Trained** Newmarket, Suffolk

FOCUS

A fairly steadily-run handicap that has been rated through the runner-up and third.

NOTEBOOK

River Tiber was trapped on the rail until getting the chance to switch and make his challenge inside the last. It looked as though he might not get there in time but in the end his rider just got him up. He is probably deserving of rating a bit better than the bare form suggests and looks capable of further improvement now that he his new yard have got him back to form. A possible for the totesport Mile at Goodwood, he only picks up a 3lb penalty for this win. (op 15-2)

Waterside(IRE) was granted an uncontested lead and his rider proceeded to set a steady pace. He did everything right and only got done in the very last stride by a rival who is a bit better than his current mark suggests. (op 4-1)

Pentecost got a clear run down the outside and stayed on well, but he was not really suited by the way this race was run and is more effective off a stronger pace. (op 5-1 tchd 11-2)

Red Somerset(USA), who raced from 2lb out of the handicap, tracked the fairly steady pace set by Waterside so was well positioned throughout. He has yet to take advantage of a continually declining mark. (op 12-1)

Apex was reunited with Hadden Frost, but he gives the impression that he is now held by the Handicapper. (tchd 4-1)

Cape Of Luck(IRE) has yet to prove he truly stays a mile. (op 7-2)

Florista Gg(URU), twice a winner in Uruguay last year, including in their 1000 Guineas, was having her first race in this country and her first since September, so she is entitled to improve for the run. Whether she is deserving of her current rating of 90 remains to be seen. (op 15-2 tchd 7-1)

3528 CITYWIDE H'CAP 5f

5:40 (5:41) (Class 4) (0-85,85) 3-Y-O+ **£6,477** (£1,927; £963; £481) **Stalls** Low

Form				RPR
1000	**1**		**Dig Deep (IRE)**[2] 3464 5-9-12 83.... NickyMackay 6 (W J Haggas) *s.i.s: sn in mid-div: swtchd rt and hdwy 2f out: led over 1f out: sn hung lft: r.o wl: rdn out* **3/1**[1]	96+
2222	**2**	1 ¾	**Sohraab**[21] 2884 3-9-9 85.... SteveDrowne 1 (H Morrison) *lw: chsd ldrs: rdn and ev ch over 1f out: nt pce of wnr ins fnl f: edgd rt nr fin* **9/2**[2]	90
2-06	**3**	nk	**Don Pele (IRE)**[44] 2187 5-8-13 75.... LukeMorris(5) 4 (R A Harris) *b: bmpd s: mid-div: hdwy 2f out: rdn and ev ch over 1f out: nt pce of wnr* **12/1**	81
1413	**4**	1 ¾	**Desert Opal**[7] 3298 7-9-1 72....(p) JamieSpencer 10 (C R Dore) *hld up bhd: rdn whn swtchd lft to stands' side 2f out: r.o ins fnl f: nt rch ldrs* **6/1**[3]	72

0340 **5** *nk* **Figaro Flyer (IRE)**[21] 2882 4-9-4 **75** AmirQuinn 12 74
(P Howling) *hld up: swtchd rt and hdwy over 1f out: styd on* **20/1**

0210 **6** *1 1/2* **Blessed Place**[5] 3388 7-8-4 **66** ow1 AshleyHamblett(5) 2 59
(D J S Ffrench Davis) *led: rdn over 2f out: hdd over 1f out: wknd ins fnl f* **14/1**

12 **7** *1/2* **Gwilym (GER)**[35] 2479 4-9-1 **72** GeorgeBaker 9 63
(D Haydn Jones) *lw: mid-div: hdwy and effrt 2f out: wknd fnl f* **8/1**

-300 **8** *3/4* **Fairfield Princess**[34] 2494 3-9-3 **79** FergusSweeney 8 66
(M S Saunders) *hld up: rdn over 2f out: no imp* **33/1**

0454 **9** *shd* **Chinalea (IRE)**[21] 2879 5-8-8 **65** (p) PhilipRobinson 3 53
(C G Cox) *wnt rt s: chsd ldrs: rdn and hung rt fr 2f out: wknd ent fnl f* **13/2**

0300 **10** *1/2* **Peter Island (FR)**[17] 2993 4-9-1 **77** (v) TolleyDean(5) 5 64
(J Gallagher) *prom: rdn 2f out: wknd fnl f* **16/1**

6-12 **11** *2* **Ken's Girl**[48] 2060 3-9-0 **76** StephenCarson 7 53
(W S Kittow) *chsd ldrs: rdn over 2f out: sn wknd* **17/2**

60.48 secs (-0.92) **Going Correction** 0.0s/f (Good)
WFA 3 from 4yo+ 5lb **11 Ran SP% 120.4**
Speed ratings (Par 105):107,104,103,100,100 98,97,96,95,95 91
CSF £16.38 CT £147.98 TOTE £4.80: £1.80, £1.90, £4.70; EX 19.90 Trifecta £332.90 Pool: £1,444.51 - 3.08 winning units. Place 6 £1,028.42, Place 5 £113.15.
Owner G Roberts/F Green/Tessona Racing **Bred** Sir Eric Parker **Trained** Newmarket, Suffolk

FOCUS
A fair sprint which was run at a solid pace. Sound form for the class, and there is a good chance the winner will go on again from here, as he is more highly rated on the All Weather..
T/Plt: £2,284.80 to a £1 stake. Pool: £135,839.34. 43.40 winning tickets. T/Qpdt: £121.50 to a £1 stake. Pool: £8,508.50. 51.80 winning tickets. TM

3491 CHESTER (L-H)

Saturday, July 14

OFFICIAL GOING: Soft (good to soft in places)
No false rail. There were 15 non-runners because of the ground.
Wind: Fresh, across Weather: Sunny

3529 TOTESCOOP6 CONDITIONS STKS 7f 2y
2:25 (2:25) (Class 2) 3-Y-0+ **£13,248** (£3,964; £1,982; £991; £493) **Stalls** Low

Form RPR

531P **1** **Song Of Passion (IRE)**[22] 2817 4-8-8 98 DavidKinsella 4 104
(R Hannon) *mde all: rdn whn abt 3 l clr 1f out: a holding on towards fin* **13/2**

3003 **2** *3/4* **Fonthill Road (IRE)**[14] 3088 7-8-13 104 JimmyQuinn 3 107+
(R A Fahey) *midfield: hdwy whn nt clr run 2f out: wnt 2nd jst ins fnl f: r.o and gaining at fin* **7/2**[2]

403 **3** *3 1/2* **Vanderlin**[14] 3103 8-8-13 102 LPKeniry 9 98
(A M Balding) *chsd wnr: rdn whn hung rt ent st wl over 1f out: lost 2nd jst ins fnl f: one pce after* **8/1**

53-6 **4** *3/4* **Misu Bond (IRE)**[14] 3088 4-8-13 109 RoystonFfrench 1 97
(B Smart) *chsd ldrs: rdn over 2f out: kpt on same pce fr over 1f out* **3/1**[1]

3/0- **5** *2* **Opera Cape**[434] 1486 4-8-13 113 (t) PatrickHills 5 92
(Saeed Bin Suroor) *s.i.s: racd keenly: hld up: rdn whn c wd ent st wl over 1f out: nt trble ldrs* **5/1**

644- **6** *3/4* **Somnus**[259] 6218 7-8-13 111 RichardMullen 8 90
(T D Easterby) *chsd ldrs: rdn over 2f out: wknd over 1f out* **4/1**[3]

0-00 **7** *2 1/2* **Invincible Force (IRE)**[49] 2035 3-8-8 98 SamHitchcott 6 86
(Paul Green) *racd keenly early on: hld up: rdn over 2f out: nvr on terms* **33/1**

00-0 **8** *7* **Swing The Ring (IRE)**[16] 3026 4-8-13 94 PatrickMathers 7 66
(A Berry) *hld up: pushed along 3f out: edgd lft whn n.d wl over 1f out* **25/1**

1m 29.3s (0.83) **Going Correction** +0.375s/f (Good)
WFA 3 from 4yo+ 8lb **8 Ran SP% 115.1**
Speed ratings (Par 109):110,109,105,104,102 101,98,90
CSF £29.73 TOTE £7.20: £1.50, £1.90, £2.20; EX 34.30.
Owner Thurloe Thoroughbreds XVI **Bred** Mrs Stephanie Hanly **Trained** East Everleigh, Wilts

FOCUS
A decent conditions event. It was run at an uneven pace and the first pair came clear. The winner basically ran to his Leicester form, with the runner-up the key to the level.

NOTEBOOK
Song Of Passion(IRE) again showed her liking for a turning track and bounced back to form with a career-best effort to score. She had very much the run of the race out in front, but found extra when asked for maximum effort off the final bend and enjoyed the easy ground. (op 7-1 tchd 15-2 in a place)
Fonthill Road(IRE) gave his all in defeat and can be considered a little unfortunate as he met trouble around 2f out and finished clear of the remainder. He is back in top form again now and, providing the draw is kind, should run another big race if taking his place in the Stewards' Cup at Goodwood next month. (op 4-1)
Vanderlin, who won this race in 2004 and finished second in it last year, lost his chance when hanging wide into the home straight. This was still a decent effort in defeat from his outside stall, however, and he will appreciate the return to faster ground in due course. (op 13-2)
Misu Bond(IRE) proved disappointingly one-paced when it mattered. This was still an improvement on this seasonal bow, however. (op 7-2)
Opera Cape, having his first outing since flopping on his debut for Godolphin in the 2000 Guineas last year, proved keen under restraint and never seriously threatened to get involved from off the pace. He should come on a deal for the run, but needs to significantly up his game to prove he is still worthy of his current rating. (op 4-1)
Somnus left the impression he would benefit for this seasonal bow and will be seen to better effect when returning to a more galloping circuit.

3530 TOTECOURSE TO COURSE H'CAP 1m 2f 75y
3:00 (3:00) (Class 4) (0-80,80) 4-Y-0+ **£5,829** (£1,734; £866; £432) **Stalls** High

Form RPR

0005 **1** **Lucayan Dancer**[20] 2906 7-9-6 **79** SilvestreDeSousa 1 86
(D Nicholls) *in tch: rdn 2f out: led over 1f out: r.o wl and in command ins fnl f* **5/2**[1]

53-4 **2** *2* **Barbirolli**[183] 110 5-8-8 **67** RichardMullen 12 70
(W M Brisbourne) *midfield: hdwy over 3f out: rdn over 2f out: wnt 2nd ins fnl f and hung lft: styd on: no imp on wnr* **7/1**

3500 **3** *1/2* **Stravara**[9] 3243 4-8-2 **61** oh10 RoystonFfrench 2 63+
(R Hollinshead) *hld up: nt clr run 2f out and again over 1f out: hdwy ent fnl f: fin wl* **14/1**

0563 **4** *3/4* **Bajan Parkes**[6] 3346 4-9-4 **77** DavidKinsella 8 78
(E J Alston) *racd keenly: prom: lost pl over 2f out: rallied whn chsd ldrs ent fnl f: one pce sn after* **6/1**

0034 **5** *1* **Punta Galera (IRE)**[9] 3241 4-8-13 **72** SamHitchcott 13 71
(Paul Green) *sn led: rdn and hdd over 1f out: no ex ins fnl f* **16/1**

2610 **6** *1 3/4* **Torrens (IRE)**[14] 3093 5-9-6 **79** JimmyQuinn 7 75
(R A Fahey) *hld up: effrt and hdwy 2f out: wknd ins fnl f* **4/1**[2]

-646 **7** *3/4* **Royal Indulgence**[22] 2820 7-7-13 **61** oh7 LiamJones(3) 5 55
(W M Brisbourne) *hld up: hdwy over 3f out: rdn 2f out: sn rn wd and wknd ent st wl over 1f out* **12/1**

2500 **8** *1/2* **Credential**[32] 2531 5-8-2 **61** oh3 AdrianMcCarthy 11 54
(John A Harris) *prom: rdn and hung rt whn pressed ldr 3f out: wknd over 1f out* **25/1**

0401 **9** *33* **Just Bond (IRE)**[14] 3111 5-9-1 **74** ChrisCatlin 4 5
(G R Oldroyd) *hld up: hung rt 3f out: sn btn and lost tch: eased fnl f* **5/1**[3]

2m 18.48s (5.34) **Going Correction** +0.375s/f (Good) **9 Ran SP% 116.1**
Speed ratings (Par 105):93,91,91,90,89 88,87,87,60
CSF £20.71 CT £204.50 TOTE £3.40: £1.50, £2.10, £3.60; EX 21.80.
Owner James E Greaves **Bred** The National Stud Owner Breeders Club Ltd **Trained** Sessay, N Yorks

FOCUS
A pretty weak handicap, run at a fair pace. The form is fairly solid, although the third was 10lb out of the handicap.
Stravara Official explanation: jockey said gelding was denied a clear run
Credential Official explanation: jockey said horse had hung right
Just Bond(IRE) Official explanation: jockey said bit had pulled through gelding's mouth

3531 TOTESPORT.COM CITY WALL STKS (LISTED RACE) 5f 16y
3:35 (3:36) (Class 1) 3-Y-0+ **£14,762** (£5,595; £2,800; £1,396; £699) **Stalls** Low

Form RPR

1415 **1** **Our Little Secret (IRE)**[6] 3344 5-8-9 79 LPKeniry 8 100
(A Berry) *mde all: rdn and abt 3 l clr 1f out: hld on wl towards fin* **7/1**

0111 **2** *1/2* **Fathom Five (IRE)**[21] 2884 3-8-9 98 RoystonFfrench 6 103
(B Smart) *swtg: n.m.r s: racd in 4th pl: pushed along 3f out: hdwy over 1f out: chsd wnr ins fnl f: r.o and gaining towards fin* **3/1**[2]

0033 **3** *1 1/2* **Bond City (IRE)**[7] 3329 5-9-0 103 ChrisCatlin 7 98
(G R Oldroyd) *bmpd s: outpcd: hdwy 1f out: r.o to take 3rd wl ins fnl f: nvr gng pce to rch front pair but nrst fin* **10/3**[3]

2124 **4** *1* **Peace Offering (IRE)**[13] 3139 7-9-7 108 SilvestreDeSousa 3 101
(D Nicholls) *wnt rt s: chsd ldrs: wnt 2nd 3f out: rdn over 1f out: lost 2nd ins fnl f: no ex* **6/4**[1]

0/0- **5** *6* **Steve's Champ (CHI)**[27] 7-9-4 0 (bt) MLarsen 2 77
(Rune Haugen, Norway) *chsd wnr to 3f out: rdn and wknd 2f out* **13/2**

62.53 secs (0.48) **Going Correction** +0.375s/f (Good)
WFA 3 from 5yo+ 5lb **5 Ran SP% 113.9**
Speed ratings (Par 111):111,110,107,106,96
CSF £28.49 TOTE £6.40: £1.90, £2.10; EX 25.50.
Owner J Berry **Bred** Camogue Stud Ltd **Trained** Cockerham, Lancs

FOCUS
A modest contest for the class, weakened by three non-runners. The winner is progressing well and the form looks solid enough.

NOTEBOOK
Our Little Secret(IRE) again showed her customary early speed and, at a track she clearly loves, made all in game fashion. She does go well in this sort of ground and has improved no end since being in foal, with her all important paddock value now significantly enhanced. (op 10-1 tchd 13-2)
Fathom Five(IRE), who got warm beforehand, did not handle the track early on and should be rated better than the bare form. He is still on an upwards curve judging by the way he ran on in the home straight here and could well find a race at this level before the season's end. (op 11-4)
Bond City(IRE) got himself behind after taking a bump at the start and is another who can be rated a little better than the bare form. He ideally wants better ground and does deserve a change of fortune. (op 11-4 tchd 7-2)
Peace Offering(IRE) proved somewhat disappointing, even allowing for the fact he was carrying a penalty, and may be feeling the effects of some hard races now. (op 11-8 tchd 13-8 and 7-4 in places)
Steve's Champ(CHI) won at this level at Taby in May. (op 8-1 tchd 11-2)

3532 TOTEEXACTA MAIDEN AUCTION STKS 5f 16y
4:10 (4:11) (Class 5) 2-Y-0 **£3,562** (£1,059; £529; £264) **Stalls** Low

Form RPR

06 **1** **Firenza Bond**[19] 2934 2-8-9 0 ChrisCatlin 4 78
(G R Oldroyd) *dwlt: sn rcvrd to press ldr: led over 3f out: rdn over 1f out: hdd narrowly jst ins fnl f: rallied gamely: led fnl 100yds* **10/1**

2 **2** *nk* **Foreign Rhythm (IRE)**[21] 2869 2-8-8 0 RoystonFfrench 8 76
(N Tinkler) *carried sltly rt s: chsd ldrs: wnt 2nd 2f out: rdn over 1f out: nosed ahd ins fnl f: hdd and nt qckn fnl 100yds* **11/8**[1]

6 **3** *4* **Rightcar Ellie (IRE)**[23] 2797 2-8-7 0 ow1 LPKeniry 10 61
(Peter Grayson) *sltly hmpd shortly after s: towards rr: rdn over 3f out: kpt on to take 3rd cl home: nvr gng pce of ldrs* **12/1**

06 **4** *shd* **Our Kally**[29] 2630 2-7-11 0 FrankiePickard(7) 1 57
(M D I Usher) *led: hdd over 3f out: rdn and wknd over 1f out* **11/4**[2]

5 **5** *7* **Hildegarde (IRE)**[16] 3024 2-8-4 0 RichardMullen 9 32
(T D Easterby) *s.i.s and wnt rt s: a outpcd and bhd* **11/2**[3]

03 **6** *6* **Richardthesecond (IRE)**[22] 2819 2-8-6 0 LiamJones(3) 7 15
(W M Brisbourne) *wnt rt s: hung rt thrght: chsd ldrs tl over 3f out: wl bhd fr 1/2-way* **6/1**

64.37 secs (2.32) **Going Correction** +0.475s/f (Yiel) **6 Ran SP% 115.2**
Speed ratings (Par 94):100,99,93,92,81 72
CSF £25.28 TOTE £12.20: £3.90, £1.40; EX 27.50.
Owner R C Bond **Bred** R C Bond **Trained** Brawby, N Yorks

FOCUS
An ordinary juvenile maiden. The first pair came clear and the form is pretty solid, rated through the runner-up.

NOTEBOOK
Firenza Bond dug deep to get back on top inside the final furlong and just did enough to break his duck at the third attempt. This was by far his best effort to date, he does look suited by this sort of ground, and further improvement still should be on the cards. Another furlong should also be within his compass. (op 16-1)
Foreign Rhythm(IRE) came there with every chance inside the final furlong and looked poised to score, but having just got her head in front she was eventually outbattled by the rallying winner. She was well clear of the remainder and her turn should still not be too far off. (tchd 15-8 and 2-1 in places)
Rightcar Ellie(IRE) failed to go the early pace after being slightly hampered at the start, but was noted staying on with a degree of promise on this turf debut and left the impression a switch to a more galloping track can see her finish closer. (tchd 10-1)
Our Kally, well backed, showed a deal of early speed but proved a sitting duck for the principals and needs to be ridden with more restraint in the future. Official explanation: jockey said filly hung right (op 7-2 tchd 4-1)
Richardthesecond(IRE) Official explanation: jockey said gelding hung right

3533 TOTESPORT 0800 221 221 H'CAP 1m 7f 195y
4:45 (4:45) (Class 4) (0-85,85) 3-Y-0+ £5,829 (£1,734; £866; £432) Stalls Low

Form RPR
421 1 **Nero West (FR)**[16] 3027 6-8-13 69..........................(b) AndrewMullen(3) 8 76
(I Semple) *sn chsd clr ldr: led 7f out: clr 6f out: carried hd high & tried to stop 2f out: hrd pressed: styd on & in command wl ins fnl f* **7/2**[2]
1420 2 1 3/4 **York Cliff**[16] 3033 9-8-6 62 oh4.. LiamJones(3) 1 67
(W M Brisbourne) *hld up: hdwy over 6f out: rdn over 4f out: clsd to take 2nd 2f out: sn pressed wnr: one pce ins fnl f* **10/1**
0060 3 2 **Dr Sharp (IRE)**[14] 3090 7-10-0 81.. LPKeniry 7 84
(T P Tate) *chsd clr ldrs: rdn and outpcd 6f out: styd on fnl f: nt rch front pair* **5/1**[3]
3-22 4 2 **Acuzio**[19] 2935 6-8-9 62 oh4.. RichardMullen 9 62
(W M Brisbourne) *hld up: hdwy over 6f out: sn chsd clr ldr: rdn over 4f out: lost 2nd but cl up in 3rd pl 2f out: wknd ins fnl f* **7/1**
3141 5 28 **Madaarek (USA)**[44] 2185 3-8-13 85................................ MartinDwyer 6 52
(E A L Dunlop) *hld up: rdn over 5f out: toiling after: eased whn wl btn over 1f out* **2/1**[1]
-000 6 3/4 **Establishment**[10] 3216 10-9-1 68.................................. SamHitchcott 2 34
(John A Harris) *hld up: rdn wl over 7f out: bhd over 6f out: eased whn wl btn over 1f out* **8/1**
2030 7 22 **Al Moulatham**[16] 3012 8-8-6 62 oh11....................(bt) PatrickMathers(3) 5 —
(R Ford) *sn led: clr tl over 9f out: hdd 7f out: wknd 6f out: eased whn wl btn over 1f out: t.o* **33/1**
60/5 8 3/4 **Hello It's Me**[33] 2505 6-9-9 76..(p) PaddyAspell 3 14
(D McCain Jnr) *hld up: niggled along 1/2-way: bhd fnl 6f: eased whn wl btn over 1f out: t.o* **7/1**

3m 39.05s (5.45) **Going Correction** +0.475s/f (Yiel)
WFA 3 from 5yo+ 19lb 8 Ran SP% **120.4**
Speed ratings (Par 105):105,104,103,102,88 87,76,76
CSF £40.04 CT £179.05 TOTE £4.20: £1.80, £2.60, £2.20; EX 45.70.
Owner Mr & Mrs Charles Villiers **Bred** Ecurie Pelder **Trained** Carluke, S Lanarks

FOCUS
A modest staying handicap, run at a decent enough gallop. The form is limited and could be worth treating with a degree of caution.
Madaarek(USA) Official explanation: jockey said colt finished distressed

3534 TOTESPORTCASINO.COM APPRENTICE H'CAP 7f 122y
5:15 (5:16) (Class 5) (0-70,70) 4-Y-0+ £3,562 (£1,059; £529; £264) Stalls Low

Form RPR
00/0 1 **Cadogen Square**[8] 3257 5-8-0 51 oh6............... DanielleMcCreery(5) 6 56
(D W Chapman) *mde all: rdn over 1f out: hrd pressed ins fnl f: jst hld on* **20/1**
0550 2 shd **Smart Pick**[19] 2938 4-8-5 51 oh6.. LiamJones 10 56+
(Mrs L Williamson) *s.i.s: midfield: niggled along 5f out: hdwy over 2f out: wnt 2nd over 1f out: pressed wnr and r.o u.p ins fnl f* **20/1**
0221 3 1/2 **Hoh Wotanite**[8] 3286 4-9-3 66...........................(b) RussellKennemore(3) 3 70
(R Hollinshead) *hld up: hdwy 2f out: rdn and swtchd lft over 1f out: r.o u.p to press ldrs ins fnl f* **9/2**[2]
2053 4 2 1/2 **Fortress**[20] 2905 4-8-9 58...................................... PatrickHills(3) 8 56
(E J Alston) *chsd ldrs: wnt 2nd over 4f out tl rdn over 1f out: one pce ins fnl f* **3/1**[1]
5150 5 1 3/4 **Franksalot (IRE)**[17] 2985 7-9-10 70.............................. PatrickMathers 4 64
(I W McInnes) *in tch: lost pl 2f out: sn rdn: no imp on ldrs fnl f* **5/1**[3]
-005 6 4 **Jabraan (USA)**[77] 1311 5-8-0 51 oh6.............................. FrankiePickard(5) 9 36
(D W Chapman) *racd keenly: chsd ldrs: rdn 2f out: wknd over 1f out* **33/1**
0504 7 4 **Mister Benji**[12] 3172 8-7-12 51 oh4...................................... SoniaEaton(7) 16 26
(B P J Baugh) *racd keenly: hld up: rdn over 1f out: nvr trbld ldrs* **12/1**
0000 8 2 1/2 **Iced Diamond (IRE)**[3] 3414 8-8-2 51 oh3........................... NicolPolli(3) 1 20
(S Wynne) *chsd wnr tl over 4f out: rdn and wknd 2f out* **15/2**
0600 9 7 **Blythe Spirit**[12] 3172 8-8-5 51 oh4...............................(v) AndrewMullen 15 4
(Mrs L Williamson) *a bhd* **10/1**
-000 10 4 **Wee Ziggy**[46] 2108 4-8-2 51 oh6...........................(p) SCreighton(3) 13 —
(M Mullineaux) *midfield tl rdn and wknd over 2f out* **16/1**
2000 11 4 **Sir Bond (IRE)**[22] 2842 6-8-8 57 ow3.............................. SladeO'Hara(3) 2 —
(G R Oldroyd) *midfield: pushed along 3f out: wknd over 2f out* **9/2**[2]

1m 38.95s (4.20) **Going Correction** +0.475s/f (Yiel) 11 Ran SP% **124.9**
Speed ratings (Par 103):98,97,97,94,93 89,85,82,75,71 67
CSF £372.80 CT £2166.36 TOTE £34.10: £5.80, £5.00, £1.80; EX 306.80 Place 6 £ 297.45, Place 5 £ 125.52.
Owner Michael Hill **Bred** D W Chapman **Trained** Stillington, N Yorks

FOCUS
A very weak handicap. The form is suspect with the first pair racing from 6lb out of the handicap and the winner producing a career best on his 26th start.
T/Plt: £240.50 to a £1 stake. Pool: £100,208.95. 304.05 winning tickets. T/Qpdt: £28.80 to a £1 stake. Pool: £4,562.60. 116.90 winning tickets. DO

3497 HAMILTON (R-H)
Saturday, July 14

OFFICIAL GOING: Soft (heavy in places)
Wind: Fresh, across Weather: Cloudy, fine

3535 LORD ADVOCATE APPRENTICE RIDERS' H'CAP (ROUND 2) 6f 5y
6:50 (6:52) (Class 6) (0-60,60) 3-Y-0+ £2,388 (£705; £352) Stalls Centre

Form RPR
-004 1 **Rondo**[5] 3375 4-8-11 47.. DeanHeslop(5) 1 55
(T D Barron) *dwlt: hld up: hdwy over 2f out: led and edgd rt over 1f out: r.o strly* **11/2**[2]
-044 2 1 **Fistral**[24] 2759 3-8-10 47.. KirstyMilczarek 6 50
(J Hetherton) *prom: effrt and hung lft over 1f out: kpt on wl fnl f: tk 2nd towards fin* **25/1**
0554 3 nk **Turkish Sultan (IRE)**[14] 3106 4-9-7 57.......................(p) BarrySavage(5) 7 61
(J M Bradley) *trckd ldrs: effrt 2f out: kpt on same pce wl ins fnl f* **6/1**[3]
0566 4 3/4 **Oeuf A La Neige**[1] 3498 7-8-10 46................................ JamesRogers(5) 5 48
(Miss L A Perratt) *plld hrd: chsd ldrs: drvn and hung rt over 1f out: no ex ins fnl f* **6/1**[3]
-033 5 1 1/4 **No Grouse**[16] 3017 7-9-9 54.. KellyHarrison 10 52
(E J Alston) *towards rr: drvn 1/2-way: hdwy over 1f out: no imp ins fnl f* **6/1**[3]
1304 6 1 3/4 **Seven No Trumps**[1] 3498 10-9-0 52.................................. JakePayne(7) 13 45
(J M Bradley) *t.k.h: led to over 1f out: sn no ex* **11/1**
/00- 7 1/2 **Toberogan (IRE)**[14] 3114 6-9-0 48...................................... SJGray(3) 9 39
(W A Murphy, Ire) *bhd: drvn 1/2-way: sme late hdwy: nvr on terms* **16/1**
003 8 shd **George The Best (IRE)**[11] 3185 6-9-12 57................... ThomasO'Brien 8 48
(Micky Hammond) *missed break: sn towards rr: effrt 1/2-way: btn fnl f* **4/1**[1]
5550 9 1/2 **Strawberry Patch (IRE)**[6] 3347 8-9-4 49......................(p) GaryBartley 11 38
(J S Goldie) *t.k.h: cl up tl hung rt and wknd over 1f out* **9/1**
2260 10 5 **Black Oval**[17] 2993 6-8-11 49.. GaryEdwards(7) 12 23
(S Parr) *bhd: struggling 1/2-way: nvr on terms* **20/1**
30-0 11 7 **Fly So Free (IRE)**[22] 2844 3-9-6 60................................... AlanRutter(3) 3 13
(D Nicholls) *bhd: drvn 1/2-way: nvr on terms* **66/1**
4450 12 2 **Phinerine**[31] 2576 4-9-4 52 ow2..................................(b) PJBenson(3) 14 —
(Miss J E Foster) *t.k.h: chsd ldrs tl rdn and wknd over 2f out* **66/1**

1m 14.99s (1.89) **Going Correction** +0.15s/f (Good)
WFA 3 from 4yo+ 6lb 12 Ran SP% **114.1**
Speed ratings (Par 101):93,91,91,90,88 86,85,85,84,78 68,66
CSF £137.68 CT £843.99 TOTE £6.50: £2.30, £5.40, £2.90; EX 125.80.
Owner Orchard Partnership **Bred** Wyck Hall Stud Ltd **Trained** Maunby, N Yorks
■ Stewards' Enquiry : Dean Heslop three-day ban: careless riding (Jul 25-27)

FOCUS
A modest event but a decent gallop and the winner won with more in hand than the winning margin suggested. He sets the level along with the third to his recent mark.
Toberogan(IRE) Official explanation: trainer said gelding was found to have an injury to its hind leg after the race

3536 JOHN BANKS H'CAP 5f 4y
7:20 (7:20) (Class 5) (0-70,70) 3-Y-0+ £3,886 (£1,156; £577; £288) Stalls Centre

Form RPR
3646 1 **Melalchrist**[15] 3053 5-9-6 64..(b[1]) PatCosgrave 2 76
(K A Ryan) *mde all: rdn 2f out: hld on wl fnl f* **4/1**[2]
2201 2 1 1/4 **Rothesay Dancer**[5] 3374 4-8-9 60 6ex......................... KellyHarrison(7) 7 68
(J S Goldie) *hld up in tch: hdwy appr fnl f: kpt on: nt rch wnr* **6/1**
1421 3 hd **Katie Boo (IRE)**[11] 3184 5-9-3 64............................... JamieMoriarty(3) 8 71
(A Berry) *chsd ldrs: effrt and swtchd rt over 1f out: edgd rt ins fnl f: no ex nr fin* **3/1**[1]
6032 4 nk **Ptarmigan Ridge**[5] 3374 11-9-6 67.................................. GregFairley(3) 3 73+
(Miss L A Perratt) *prom: nt clr run over 1f out: kpt on fnl f* **4/1**[2]
6221 5 hd **Harrison's Flyer (IRE)**[18] 2966 6-9-5 70.....................(p) BarrySavage(7) 6 75
(J M Bradley) *t.k.h: in tch: effrt outside over 1f out: no imp ins fnl f* **5/1**[3]
0061 6 3/4 **Garstang**[21] 2866 4-9-9 67..(b) GrahamGibbons 13 69
(Peter Grayson) *bhd tl hdwy over 1f out: nrst fin* **13/2**
5504 7 3/4 **Legal Set (IRE)**[6] 3347 11-8-2 51 oh6.............................(b) AnnStokell(5) 11 51
(Miss A Stokell) *chsd ldrs: ev ch and hung rt over 1f out: no ex ins fnl f* **25/1**
00-0 8 4 **Compton Lad**[65] 1594 4-8-4 51 oh6.................................. MarcHalford(3) 9 36
(D A Nolan) *chsd ldrs: edgd lft over 1f out: sn wknd* **100/1**

61.52 secs (0.32) **Going Correction** +0.15s/f (Good) 8 Ran SP% **114.1**
Speed ratings (Par 103):103,101,100,100,99 98,97,91
CSF £27.98 CT £81.54 TOTE £5.20: £1.60, £2.40, £1.50; EX 38.10.
Owner T G S Wood **Bred** A C M Spalding **Trained** Hambleton, N Yorks

FOCUS
An ordinary handicap in which the field raced stands' side. The form is fair, rated through the third to her recent mark.
Legal Set(IRE) Official explanation: jockey said gelding hung right-handed final 2f
Compton Lad Official explanation: jockey said gelding hung left-handed final 2f

3537 THE SUNDAY MAIL MEDIAN AUCTION MAIDEN STKS 5f 4y
7:50 (7:50) (Class 5) 3-Y-0 £2,914 (£867; £433; £216) Stalls Centre

Form RPR
3034 1 **Rue Soleil**[10] 3202 3-8-9 55.. JamieMoriarty(3) 5 59
(J R Weymes) *trckd ldrs: rdn to ld ins fnl f: hld on wl* **10/1**
0233 2 nk **Howards Tipple**[11] 3180 3-9-3 64..............................(p) PaulMulrennan 4 63
(I Semple) *w ldr: led 1/2-way to ins fnl f: kpt on: hld cl home* **2/1**[1]
53 3 hd **Lempicka**[7] 3302 3-8-12 0... GrahamGibbons 1 57+
(J J Quinn) *trckd ldrs: effrt whn nt clr run over 2f out: effrt 1f out: kpt on fnl f* **11/4**[2]
0 4 1 3/4 **Invincible Lad (IRE)**[37] 2393 3-8-10 0.............................. GaryBartley(7) 6 56
(E J Alston) *bhd: drvn 1/2-way: kpt on fnl f: nrst fin* **28/1**
03 5 2 **Celeb Style (IRE)**[21] 2894 3-8-12 0..................................... DeanMernagh 8 44
(D Nicholls) *wnt rt and bmpd s: hld up in tch on outside: rdn and hung rt over 1f out: kpt on same pce fnl f* **8/1**
-465 6 2 **Bajeel (IRE)**[4] 3409 3-8-12 60.......................................(b[1]) PJMcDonald(5) 9 42
(G A Butler) *hmpd s: bhd: effrt over 2f out: hung lft and wknd 1f out* **4/1**[3]
6030 7 shd **Musical Parkes**[12] 3168 3-8-9 55..................................... GregFairley(3) 3 36
(W J H Ratcliffe) *led to 1/2-way: wknd over 1f out* **11/1**
0-00 8 6 **Senora Lenorah**[22] 2826 3-8-9 35...................................... DominicFox(3) 2 15
(D A Nolan) *prom: rdn 1/2-way: sn btn* **125/1**
0-0 9 1/2 **Whats Your Game (IRE)**[10] 3202 3-9-3 0............................. PatCosgrave 10 18
(A Berry) *wnt lft and bmpd s: racd wd towards rr: effrt and wnt lft over 2f out: wknd over 1f out* **40/1**

61.85 secs (0.65) **Going Correction** +0.15s/f (Good) 9 Ran SP% **115.2**
Speed ratings (Par 100):100,99,99,96,93 90,89,80,79
CSF £30.16 TOTE £14.60: £2.30, £1.40, £1.70; EX 32.40.
Owner Ray Burton **Bred** Carlton Consultants Ltd **Trained** Middleham Moor, N Yorks

FOCUS
A weak event in which things unfolded against the stands' rail. The pace was fair but the form is moderate, rated around the first two.
Celeb Style(IRE) Official explanation: jockey said filly hung right-handed throughout

3538 LEAD THE FIELD VIRGIN MEDIA CLAIMING STKS 1m 3f 16y
8:20 (8:21) (Class 6) 3-5-Y-0 £2,730 (£806; £403) Stalls High

Form RPR
00-0 1 **Simply St Lucia**[37] 1350 5-9-1 53................................... GrahamGibbons 4 47
(J R Weymes) *chsd ldr: led 1/2-way: hld on gamely fnl f* **2/1**[2]
/050 2 1/2 **Frith (IRE)**[68] 1532 5-9-6 60.. PaulMulrennan 10 51
(Mrs L B Normile) *hld up in tch: drvn and outpcd 3f out: rallied over 1f out: kpt on u.p fnl f* **13/2**
1040 3 1 1/2 **Patavian (IRE)**[11] 3183 3-8-7 62 ow1........................(p) JamieMoriarty(3) 1 51
(I Semple) *t.k.h: prom: effrt over 2f out: edgd rt over 1f out: no ex wl ins fnl f* **15/8**[1]
5 4 8 **Raguany (IRE)**[22] 2828 5-8-11 38...................................... GregFairley(3) 9 30
(B Mactaggart) *prom tl rdn and wknd 2f out* **12/1**
-000 5 2 1/2 **Roll Em Over**[19] 2946 4-8-8 32 ow1.............................(b[1]) PJMcDonald(5) 6 25
(C W Thornton) *chsd ldrs tl rdn and wknd over 2f out* **16/1**
-006 6 14 **Coronation Flight**[60] 1744 4-9-2 46.................................. PatCosgrave 8 6
(F P Murtagh) *hld up: drvn over 3f out: sn wknd* **6/1**[3]
00P/ 7 15 **Kinfayre Boy**[650] 5487 5-9-2 0... AnnStokell(5) 7 —
(K W Hogg) *led to 1/2-way: sn lost tch* **40/1**

00-0 **P** **Welcome Spirit**[22] [2825] 4-8-10 18................................. GaryBartley(7) 5 —
(J S Haldane) *t.k.h: in tch tl wknd 1/2-way: p.u over 1f out: lame* **100/1**

2m 30.38s (4.12) **Going Correction** +0.325s/f (Good)
WFA 3 from 4yo+ 12lb **8** Ran SP% **112.7**
Speed ratings (Par 101):98,97,96,90,88 78,67,—
CSF £15.08 TOTE £2.90: £1.10, £2.00, £1.30; EX 17.50.
Owner Mrs M Ashby **Bred** Tattersalls Ltd **Trained** Middleham Moor, N Yorks

FOCUS
A moderate event, even for this grade. The early pace was steady and the form is weak, rated through the third.

3539 THE SUNDAY MAIL H'CAP 1m 65y
8:50 (8:51) (Class 5) (0-75,73) 3-Y-0+ **£4,533** (£1,348; £674; £336) **Stalls** High

Form RPR
230 **1** **Stolen Glance**[20] [2905] 4-9-9 **68**................................. PaulMulrennan 6 78
(M W Easterby) *in tch: pushed along briefly 1/2-way: effrt over 2f out: led over 1f out: sn clr* **5/1**
6201 **2** *5* **Neil's Legacy (IRE)**[6] [3343] 5-8-13 **61** 6ex..................... GregFairley(3) 3 60
(Miss L A Perratt) *trckd ldrs: led gng wl 3f out: rdn and hdd over 1f out: nt pce of wnr* **11/4**[2]
0/6- **3** *nk* **Howards Rocket**[207] [6482] 6-8-2 **54** oh9...................... KellyHarrison(7) 8 52
(J S Goldie) *t.k.h: stdd in rr: effrt over 2f out: kpt on fnl f: no imp* **28/1**
344- **4** *3* **Sarraaf (IRE)**[395] [2546] 11-8-12 **60**............................. JamieMoriarty(3) 5 52
(I Semple) *led to 3f out: no ex fr 2f out* **8/1**
50-4 **5** *2½* **Greyfriars Abbey**[16] [3032] 3-8-8 **62**................................. JoeFanning 9 48
(M Johnston) *s.i.s: effrt fr rr 3f out: btn over 1f out* **9/2**[3]
00-0 **6** *hd* **Gala Sunday (USA)**[12] [3155] 7-9-0 **66**........................(t) NSLawes(7) 2 52
(M W Easterby) *cl up: rdn over 3f out: wknd over 2f out* **20/1**
1020 **7** *13* **Flylowflylong (IRE)**[17] [2988] 4-9-6 **65**........................... PatCosgrave 10 22
(I Semple) *trckd ldrs tl rdn and wknd qckly over 2f out* **9/4**[1]
300/ **8** *11* **Magic Box**[363] [3804] 9-8-8 **58** oh9 ow4........................(t) PJMcDonald(5) 4 —
(A M Crow) *in tch: drvn 1/2-way: wknd over 3f out* **50/1**

1m 50.31s (1.01) **Going Correction** +0.325s/f (Good)
WFA 3 from 4yo+ 9lb **8** Ran SP% **113.6**
Speed ratings (Par 103):107,102,101,98,96 96,83,72
CSF £18.65 CT £346.44 TOTE £5.40: £1.80, £1.50, £3.40; EX 15.90.
Owner R S Cockerill (Farms) Ltd **Bred** R S Cockerill (farms) Ltd **Trained** Sheriff Hutton, N Yorks

FOCUS
An ordinary handicap in which the early pace was on the steady side. The form is reasonable but limited by the proximity of the third.
Flylowflylong(IRE) Official explanation: vet said filly hung right-handed throughout

3540 HAMILTON PARK H'CAP 1m 65y
9:20 (9:20) (Class 6) (0-60,60) 3-Y-0 **£2,730** (£806; £403) **Stalls** High

Form RPR
4033 **1** **Ice Box (IRE)**[43] [2224] 3-8-13 **55**.. JoeFanning 4 69
(M Johnston) *midfield: hdwy to ld over 2f out: pushed clr* **4/1**[3]
0062 **2** *7* **Milson's Point (IRE)**[6] [3345] 3-8-11 **60**......................... GaryBartley(7) 14 59
(I Semple) *led to over 2f out: edgd lft over 1f out: no ch w wnr* **9/4**[1]
0063 **3** *3* **Flamestone**[17] [2978] 3-8-1 **46**.................................... DominicFox(3) 12 38
(A E Price) *chsd ldrs: ev ch over 3f out: one pce fr 2f out* **12/1**
6-00 **4** *1* **Cornell Precedent**[32] [2538] 3-8-6 **48**..................... GrahamGibbons 1 38
(J J Quinn) *towards rr: rdn over 3f out: sme late hdwy: n.d* **25/1**
4004 **5** *1¾* **Tomorrow's Dancer**[11] [3181] 3-8-8 **50**............................ PatCosgrave 9 36
(K A Ryan) *hld up in midfield: effrt over 3f out: no ex fr 2f out* **7/2**[2]
0565 **6** *3* **Storm Mission (USA)**[46] [2110] 3-8-6 **48**......................... DeanMernagh 6 27
(J Mackie) *hld up: rdn over 3f out: sn btn* **11/1**
-005 **7** *5* **Waiheke Island**[15] [3051] 3-8-6 **51** ow3..................... GregFairley(3) 8 19
(B Mactaggart) *hld up: drvn over 3f out: nvr able to chal* **16/1**
1034 **8** *2* **Heaven's Gates**[141] [535] 3-8-8 **55**.............................. PJMcDonald(5) 7 19
(K A Ryan) *chsd ldrs tl wknd over 2f out* **7/1**
00-0 **9** *shd* **Mr Wall Street**[15] [2538] 3-8-8 **50**............................ PaulMulrennan 10 14
(M W Easterby) *cl up tl wknd over 2f out* **33/1**
-606 **P** **Cape Dancer (IRE)**[23] [2796] 3-8-10 **55**...................... JamieMoriarty(3) 2 —
(J S Wainwright) *prom tl wknd qckly 4f out: t.o whn p.u over 1f out* **16/1**

1m 52.12s (2.82) **Going Correction** +0.325s/f (Good) **10** Ran SP% **120.1**
Speed ratings (Par 98):98,91,88,87,85 82,77,75,75,—
Place 6 £ 33.75, Place 5 £ 7.67 CSF £13.85 CT £103.59 TOTE £3.30: £1.30, £1.70, £3.30; EX 11.70.
Owner Mrs Catherine O'Flynn **Bred** Old Carhue Stud **Trained** Middleham Moor, N Yorks

FOCUS
A modest event in which the pace was fair and the form behind the clear-cut winner is weak and not that solid.
Mr Wall Street Official explanation: jockey said gelding had a breathing problem
Cape Dancer(IRE) Official explanation: jockey said filly pulled up lame but returned sound
T/Plt: £40.30 to a £1 stake. Pool: £68,812.50. 1,245.10 winning tickets. T/Qpdt: £4.50 to a £1 stake. Pool: £4,345.80. 714.10 winning tickets. RY

3465 NOTTINGHAM (L-H)
Saturday, July 14
3541 Meeting Abandoned - Waterlogged

2997 SALISBURY (R-H)
Saturday, July 14
OFFICIAL GOING: Good to firm (good in places; 9.1)
Wind: Nil Weather: Fine

3549 BATHWICK TYRES LADY RIDERS' SERIES H'CAP 6f
6:05 (6:05) (Class 5) (0-75,75) 3-Y-0+ **£3,123** (£968; £484; £242) **Stalls** High

Form RPR
5043 **1** **Tamino (IRE)**[28] [2665] 4-9-4 **60**...............................(t) MissVCartmel(5) 13 71
(H Morrison) *chsd ldrs: r.o to ld wl ins fnl f* **9/2**[1]
-031 **2** *1¼* **Roman Quintet (IRE)**[37] [2394] 7-9-10 **66**.................. MissABevan(5) 10 73
(R J Price) *a.p: led over 2f out: hdd and no ex wl ins fnl f* **5/1**[2]
0001 **3** *1¾* **The History Man (IRE)**[6] [3347] 4-9-5 **61** 6ex..(b) MissMMullineaux(5) 14 63
(M Mullineaux) *led: hdd over 2f out: sn rdn: one pce fnl f* **7/1**
0410 **4** *1* **Dante's Diamond (IRE)**[14] [3111] 5-9-7 **65** ow5 MissIsabelTompsett(7) 4 64
(D Burchell) *chsd ldrs: rdn over 2f out: one pce fnl f* **16/1**
3406 **5** *¾* **Josh**[19] [2936] 5-10-7 **75**...(p) MissARyan(3) 9 72
(K A Ryan) *mid-div: rdn over 2f out: no real prog fnl f* **11/2**[3]
4523 **6** *hd* **Ever Cheerful**[15] [3045] 6-9-5 **56** oh4................................(p) MrsSMoore 5 52
(A B Haynes) *chsd ldrs: no imp whn stmbld ins fnl f* **12/1**
5060 **7** *nk* **Balerno**[3] [3419] 8-8-12 **56** oh1....................................... MissLauraGray(7) 2 51
(Mrs L J Mongan) *hld up towards rr: swtchd lft 2f out: kpt on fnl f: n.d* **20/1**
-260 **8** *1¾* **The Cayterers**[43] [2197] 5-10-3 **75**................................ MissHDavies(7) 6 65
(J M Bradley) *s.i.s: bhd: hdwy over 2f out: rdn over 1f out: wknd ins fnl f* **13/2**
3500 **9** *5* **Outer Hebrides**[2] [3472] 6-10-0 **70**..........................(t) MissSBradley(5) 12 45
(J M Bradley) *a towards rr* **12/1**
0205 **10** *1¼* **Briannsta (IRE)**[17] [2982] 5-10-4 **74**......................... MissJFerguson(5) 7 45
(C G Cox) *a bhd* **12/1**
5046 **11** *nk* **Slipasearcher (IRE)**[36] [2421] 3-9-0 **60**.......................(b) MissEFolkes(3) 3 30
(P D Evans) *a bhd* **22/1**
000 **12** *7* **Miss Wolf**[100] [936] 7-9-7 **65** oh11 ow9......... MissSarah-JayneDavies(7) 1 14
(G H Jones) *outpcd* **100/1**

1m 14.08s (-0.90) **Going Correction** -0.075s/f (Good)
WFA 3 from 4yo+ 6lb **12** Ran SP% **115.1**
Speed ratings (Par 103):103,101,99,97,96 96,96,93,87,85 84,75
CSF £25.06 CT £136.51 TOTE £6.00: £1.90, £1.70, £3.10; EX 27.30.
Owner H Scott-Barrett & Lord Margadale **Bred** Century Bloodstock **Trained** East Ilsley, Berks
■ Stewards' Enquiry : Miss S Bradley caution: used whip when out of contention
Miss E Folkes caution: used whip when out of contention

FOCUS
Just a moderate contest overall, but an above-average race of its type. The winner is rated back to his best.

3550 MILFORD HALL HOTEL NOVICE AUCTION STKS 6f
6:35 (6:38) (Class 4) 2-Y-0 **£4,210** (£1,252; £625; £312) **Stalls** High

Form RPR
100 **1** **Vhujon (IRE)**[8] [3269] 2-9-6 0.....................................(t) StephenDonohoe 3 87
(P D Evans) *mde all: rdn wl over 1f out: r.o wl* **8/1**
0001 **2** *2* **Ocean Transit (IRE)**[47] [2078] 2-8-1 0.......................... JackDean(7) 13 69
(W G M Turner) *chsd ldrs: rdn whn swtchd rt 2f out: kpt on ins fnl f: nt trble wnr* **40/1**
1 **3** *shd* **Wigram's Turn (USA)**[47] [2090] 2-9-3 0.......................... FrancisNorton 6 78
(A M Balding) *hld up in mid-div: rdn 3f out: hdwy over 1f out: sn edgd lft: kpt on ins fnl f* **9/4**[1]
1 **4** *1½* **Miss Bootylishes**[18] [2961] 2-8-7 0.......................... KevinGhunowa(5) 1 68
(A B Haynes) *hld up on outside in mid-div: rdn and hdwy whn hung lft to stands' side 2f out: kpt on same pce fnl f: sddle slipped* **14/1**
0 **5** *¾* **Ezthegezza**[30] [2596] 2-8-11 0.. JohnEgan 10 65
(J S Moore) *s.s: outpcd: rdn over 2f out: late hdwy: nvr nrr* **25/1**
514 **6** *½* **Taurian**[49] [2024] 2-9-1 0... DaneO'Neill 14 67
(Mrs L Stubbs) *a.p: rdn 3f out: fdd ins fnl f* **6/1**
50 **7** *½* **Sarah Park (IRE)**[21] [2876] 2-7-13 0.. KMay(7) 12 57
(B J Meehan) *bhd: rdn and struggling over 2f out: sme late prog* **80/1**
0 **8** *nk* **El Fuser**[32] [2539] 2-8-11 0.. PatDobbs 9 61
(P J Makin) *mid-div: rdn 3f out: no hdwy fnl 2f* **40/1**
04 **9** *½* **Synge Street**[19] [2941] 2-8-11 0...................................... RichardHughes 5 60
(R Hannon) *nvr nr ldrs* **16/1**
02 **10** *½* **Meridian Line (IRE)**[12] [3162] 2-8-7 0.. TQuinn 2 54
(J G Portman) *prom: rdn over 1f out: wknd ins fnl f* **16/1**
1 **11** *hd* **Swallow Star**[39] [2333] 2-8-10 0.. SebSanders 8 56
(R M Beckett) *prom: rdn wl over 1f out: wknd ins fnl f* **11/2**[3]
12 *4* **Ogmore Junction (IRE)** 2-8-11 0.................................... JHBowman 7 45
(P D Cundell) *s.s: a bhd* **66/1**
13 *1¼* **Billy Hot Rocks (IRE)** 2-8-11 0.. JamesDoyle 4 42
(R M Beckett) *s.v.s: a in rr* **40/1**
021 **14** *nk* **Supermassive Muse (IRE)**[28] [2651] 2-8-13 0.............. JimCrowley 11 43
(E S McMahon) *prom: rdn 3f out: wknd 1f out* **5/1**[2]

1m 14.24s (-0.74) **Going Correction** -0.075s/f (Good) **14** Ran SP% **120.5**
Speed ratings (Par 96):101,98,98,96,95 94,93,93,92,92 91,86,84,84
CSF £310.18 TOTE £9.70: £3.40, £10.90, £1.70; EX 525.20.
Owner Nick Shutts **Bred** Robert Berns **Trained** Pandy, Monmouths

FOCUS
Containing several previous winners, and run at a strong pace, so probably a decent race of its type at this track. The winner returned to something like the form of his debut.

NOTEBOOK
Vhujon(IRE), disappointing on soft ground in a Listed race last time, bounced back to form impressively in a first-time tongue-tie. He seemed to be going plenty fast enough in mid-race but, when his rivals tried to attack, he shrugged them off and scorched home. This looked a smart performance, and it will be interesting to see if he can repeat it in better company.
Ocean Transit(IRE), bought in for 10,000gns after winning a Chepstow seller last time, showed that she is better than that level with a good effort. Though never going to beat the impressive winner, she got much closer than when they previously met, and looks a much improved performer.
Wigram's Turn(USA) still looked rather green, needing to be ridden to post and taking an age to pick up depiste being niggled along by halfway. Though he won over 5f on his debut, this trip should suit him well these days, and 7f should also be within reach, so there is better to come. (op 11-4)
Miss Bootylishes was handicapped by a slipping saddle, which meant her rider was unable to prevent her drifting badly towards the stands' rail, where she raced alone. That said, this was still a good follow-up to her debut at Brighton, and she can do even better with more luck. Official explanation: jockey said saddle slipped (op 12-1 tchd 16-1)
Ezthegezza ran more encouragingly than on his debut, and is beginning to look like an interesting type for nurseries after one more run, with 7f likely to suit.
Taurian should have been suited by this extra furlong, but ran as if a flatter 6f or stiff 5f would be ideal at present. (tchd 7-1)
Sarah Park(IRE) is now qualified for nurseries, and has shown enough to be worth looking at over this trip or 7f. (op 66-1)
El Fuser was never going the strong gallop, but nurseries will be his scene after one more run. (op 50-1)
Swallow Star showed plenty of pace, but ran as if failing to stay this stiffish 6f. (op 13-2 tchd 7-1)

3551 BATHWICK TYRES /EBF MAIDEN STKS (DIV I) 6f 212y
7:05 (7:10) (Class 4) 2-Y-0 **£3,886** (£1,156; £577; £288) **Stalls** Centre

Form RPR
6 **1** **Flawed Genius**[22] [2832] 2-9-3 0.. RyanMoore 12 78
(Sir Michael Stoute) *mde all: rdn over 1f out: rdn ent fnl f: r.o* **11/10**[1]
0 **2** *1* **Mymumsaysimthebest**[43] [2215] 2-9-3 0............................ PatDobbs 14 75
(R Hannon) *hld up: hdwy on ins 4f out: rdn over 2f out: r.o ins fnl f* **12/1**
3 *¾* **Pha Mai Blue** 2-9-3 0.. SebSanders 13 73
(W J Knight) *a.p: rdn and edgd lft 2f out and 1f out: nt qckn* **5/1**[3]
26 **4** *1* **Legendary Guest**[77] [1291] 2-9-3 0.................................... JHBowman 7 71
(M R Channon) *a.p: rdn over 1f out: nt qckn ins fnl f* **9/2**[2]

5 3 ½ **Lobby** 2-9-3 0 RichardHughes 4 62+
(Mrs A J Perrett) *stdd s: hld up and bhd: rdn and hdwy 2f out: no imp fnl f* **10/1**

0 6 1 **Air Chief**[21] 2876 2-9-3 0 DaneO'Neill 11 59
(H J L Dunlop) *mid-div: rdn over 4f out: no hdwy fnl 2f* **66/1**

7 nk **Hawk House** 2-9-3 0 MichaelHills 3 58
(B W Hills) *hld up and bhd: hdwy over 3f out: wknd over 1f out* **20/1**

8 hd **Meer Kat (IRE)** 2-9-0 0 RichardKingscote(3) 6 58
(R Charlton) *s.i.s: rdn over 2f out: nvr nr ldrs* **16/1**

9 5 **Nikolaievich (IRE)** 2-9-3 0 TQuinn 10 45
(P F I Cole) *t.k.h early: w wnr: rdn and wkng whn sltly hmpd 2f out* **33/1**

03 10 2 ½ **Kristal Glory (IRE)**[29] 2624 2-9-3 0 IanMongan 9 38
(J L Dunlop) *t.k.h in mid-div: rdn over 2f out: sn struggling* **33/1**

0 11 hd **Kryptonite (IRE)**[50] 1989 2-9-3 0 KerrinMcEvoy 2 38
(J W Hills) *plld hrd: sn prom: wknd over 3f out* **50/1**

12 ½ **Ride A White Swan** 2-9-3 0 FrankieMcDonald 8 37
(P A Blockley) *walked to s: plld hrd: a in rr* **40/1**

13 ¾ **Banjo Bandit (IRE)** 2-9-3 0 JohnEgan 5 35
(J S Moore) *hld up in tch: lost pl 4f out* **40/1**

1m 29.25s (0.19) **Going Correction** -0.075s/f (Good) **13** Ran SP% **124.1**
Speed ratings (Par 96):95,93,93,91,87 86,86,86,80,77 77,76,75
CSF £16.47 TOTE £2.10: £1.40, £2.80, £2.20; EX 21.40.
Owner Gainsborough **Bred** Darley **Trained** Newmarket, Suffolk

FOCUS
Little experience on show, and not easy to rate, but probably a typical Salisbury maiden containing several with some potential. The pace was, however, disappointing, with the winning favourite having to do the donkey work, and the time keeps the level of the form down.

NOTEBOOK
Flawed Genius, made hot favourite after showing promise on his debut over 6f, was forced to make the running and, despite having the run of the race, had to work harder than expected to stay on top. He should be even more effective when one of his rivals sets a decent gallop, so can step up quite a bit on this. (op 7-4 after 2-1 in places)
Mymumsaysimthebest ran much better than on his debut, and should be able to find a maiden over this trip. If not, he will be a strong competitor in decent nurseries after one more run. (op 8-1)
Pha Mai Blue ◆, the fourth foal of a mare whose previous three offspring were all winners, made a fine debut which suggests he will follow in the footsteps of his family. He travelled comfortably behind the winner and battled well in the closing stages, so has a bright future. (op 9-2 tchd 6-1)
Legendary Guest has run well in two of his three maidens and still looks capable of finding one. Nurseries are also an option now, though much will rest on how the Handicapper reacts to his second behind the high-class Winker Watson on his debut. (op 5-1 tchd 6-1)
Lobby ◆, the first foal of the Listed-quality 6f-1m French performer Real Trust, is by the top-class miler Dr Fong, so 7f or a mile looks his most likely trip this season. Making a promising debut despite never quite getting into a challenging position, he should improve and win races. (op 9-1 tchd 15-2)
Air Chief has winners in the family, including two successful juveniles in Europe, but he does not look precocious himself. Though soon struggling with the pace, he ran better than on his debut and looks one for nurseries when qualified. (op 50-1)
Hawk House, a 60,000euro Alhaarth half-brother to two winners, had a satisfactory introduction, and should be more competitive next time.
Meer Kat(IRE) was never going after a slow start, but this 90,000gns first foal of a juvenile 7f winner can do better with racing. (op 14-1)
Nikolaievich(IRE) Official explanation: jockey said colt suffered interference in running
Banjo Bandit(IRE) Official explanation: jockey said colt was keen early stages

3552 BATHWICK TYRES /EBF MAIDEN STKS (DIV II) 6f 212y
7:35 (7:41) (Class 4) 2-Y-O **£3,886** (£1,156; £577; £288) **Stalls** Centre

Form RPR

1 **Fast Company (IRE)** 2-9-3 0 RyanMoore 10 82+
(B J Meehan) *hld up towards rr: rdn and hdwy over 1f out: led ins fnl f: pushed clr* **11/2**[3]

2 3 **Redolent (IRE)** 2-9-3 0 RichardHughes 3 74
(R Hannon) *chsd ldr: rdn and ev ch 1f out: one pce* **10/1**

45 3 nk **Siberian Tiger (IRE)**[8] 3283 2-9-3 0 JHBowman 7 73
(M R Channon) *led: rdn over 1f out: hdd ins fnl f: one pce* **16/1**

40 4 1 **Huzzah (IRE)**[56] 1832 2-9-3 0 MichaelHills 2 71
(B W Hills) *a.p: rdn and ev ch over 1f out: one pce fnl f* **7/2**[2]

4 5 1 ¼ **By Command**[29] 2632 2-9-3 0 KerrinMcEvoy 9 68
(J L Dunlop) *hld up in tch: rdn and one pce fnl 2f* **6/5**[1]

6 hd **Barliffey (IRE)** 2-9-3 0 TPO'Shea 8 67
(D J Coakley) *s.s: hdwy on outside 3f out: edgd rt over 1f out: wknd fnl f* **66/1**

0 7 ½ **Dancing Dik**[21] 2885 2-9-3 0 JimCrowley 4 66
(Mrs A J Perrett) *hld up in mid-div: rdn over 2f out: wknd over 1f out* **50/1**

8 ½ **Black Jacari (IRE)** 2-9-3 0 FergusSweeney 5 64
(A King) *hld up in mid-div: rdn 2f out: wknd fnl f* **50/1**

9 1 ¼ **Home** 2-9-3 0 DaneO'Neill 6 61
(E A L Dunlop) *s.i.s: nvr trbld ldrs* **16/1**

10 2 **Cool The Heels (IRE)** 2-9-3 0 JohnEgan 1 56
(J S Moore) *hld up: rdn and hdwy 3f out: wknd over 1f out* **50/1**

11 5 **Seventh Hill** 2-9-3 0 FrancisNorton 13 43
(M Blanshard) *hld up in mid-div: rdn over 3f out: bhd fnl 2f* **50/1**

12 ½ **Grimes Hope (IRE)** 2-9-3 0 PatDobbs 14 42
(R Hannon) *prom: rdn 3f out: wknd 2f out* **33/1**

13 3 **Lancaster Lad (IRE)** 2-9-3 0 SebSanders 11 34
(A B Haynes) *dwlt: a bhd* **40/1**

0 14 8 **Aries Magic**[46] 2103 2-8-12 0 FrankieMcDonald 12 8
(S C Burrough) *s.i.s: a bhd* **100/1**

1m 29.09s (0.03) **Going Correction** -0.075s/f (Good) **14** Ran SP% **119.6**
Speed ratings (Par 96):96,92,92,91,89 89,88,88,86,84 78,78,74,65
CSF £56.39 TOTE £7.30: £1.70, £2.90, £3.00; EX 35.80.
Owner Earle I Mack **Bred** Limetree Stud Ltd And Aerial Bloodstock **Trained** Manton, Wilts

FOCUS
Like division one, little previous form, but run at a better tempo. The third and fifth help set the level of the form. The winner looked potentially smart and there will be other future winners behind.

NOTEBOOK
Fast Company(IRE) ◆, a 140,000gns son of Danehill Dancer out of a well-bred unraced mare with only moderate success to date, made an impressive debut. Though taking a while to get going, this strong, good-looking sort powered clear stylishly in the last furlong, and would not be out of place in better company. (op 4-1)
Redolent(IRE), a 120,000euro son of the high-class 7f-1m performer Redback, is out a mare who won over a mile, so he should be capable of finding races. This was a good debut behind a useful-looking sort, so he can soon go one better. (op 17-2 tchd 8-1)
Siberian Tiger(IRE) got the extra furlong well enough, only to be beaten by two decent debutants. He is good enough to win a maiden, but is now also qualified for nurseries. (op 14-1)
Huzzah(IRE) looked more comfortable over this longer trip, and can win a maiden, though nurseries are now also a possibility. (op 9-2)
By Command, though never far away, was not speedy enough to get into contention in the last quarter-mile. He looks more a staying type, so should come into his own when racing at a mile and beyond. (op 11-8 tchd 6-4)
Barliffey(IRE), a Bahri colt, is out of an unraced mare, but she hails from a family of successful juveniles. Considering his starting price, he ran really well after a very slow start, and is worth keeping an eye on.
Dancing Dik, a 41,000gns Diktat half-brother to a couple of winners at around a mile, has shown some ability in his two races to date, but will be more at home in nurseries after one more outing.
Black Jacari(IRE), a 31,000gns son of Black Sam Bellamy out of an unraced mare, made a satisfactory debut, but looks a nursery sort in the making.
Home, a first foal of a non-winning mare, missed the break, and looks to be heading for nurseries in due course. (op 20-1 tchd 12-1)

3553 SOVEREIGN WINDOWS UK H'CAP 1m
8:05 (8:11) (Class 4) (0-85,84) 3-Y-O **£5,181** (£1,541; £770; £384) **Stalls** High

Form RPR

-200 1 **Hunting Tower**[28] 2669 3-9-5 **82** RyanMoore 6 89
(R Hannon) *hld up towards rr: hdwy and squeezed through over 1f out: swtchd lft jst ins fnl f: rdn to ld fnl strides* **7/1**

0335 2 hd **Salient**[21] 2881 3-9-2 **79** PaulDoe 4 86
(J Akehurst) *hld up in tch: rdn to ld over 2f out: hdd fnl strides* **14/1**

0216 3 ½ **Summer Dancer (IRE)**[10] 3215 3-8-12 **75** TQuinn 7 80
(D R C Elsworth) *hld up in rr: hdwy on outside 2f out: rdn and edgd rt over 1f out: ev ch ins fnl f: nt qckn* **6/1**[3]

221 4 1 ¾ **Cape Hawk (IRE)**[38] 2354 3-9-4 **81** RichardHughes 11 82
(R Hannon) *hld up and bhd: hdwy 2f out: sn rdn: one pce fnl f* **5/2**[1]

3103 5 ¾ **Eager Igor (USA)**[10] 3215 3-9-3 **80** StephenCarson 14 80
(Eve Johnson Houghton) *hld up in rr: rdn and hdwy over 1f out: one pce fnl f* **8/1**

0-13 6 nk **Oceana Gold**[30] 2598 3-8-12 **75** FrancisNorton 2 74
(A M Balding) *hld up: hdwy over 3f out: rdn over 2f out: n.m.r over 1f out: one pce* **7/2**[2]

1-06 7 ¾ **Russki (IRE)**[29] 2633 3-9-2 **79** (b[1]) JimCrowley 8 76
(Mrs A J Perrett) *chsd ldr: rdn over 2f out: wknd fnl f* **25/1**

5-00 8 1 **Kilburn**[23] 2788 3-9-7 **84** JHBowman 10 79
(C G Cox) *hld up in mid-div: rdn over 2f out: wknd 1f out* **33/1**

-435 9 nk **Count Ceprano (IRE)**[19] 2943 3-9-5 **82** AdamKirby 5 76
(W R Swinburn) *prom: rdn over 2f out: wknd 1f out* **9/1**

0000 10 4 **Bazroy (IRE)**[14] 3104 3-9-5 **82** StephenDonohoe 13 67
(P D Evans) *led: swvd rt at entrnce to rnd crse over 3f out: rdn and hdd over 2f out: sn wknd* **50/1**

4300 11 3 ½ **Bed Fellow (IRE)**[42] 2231 3-9-2 **79** JohnEgan 3 56
(A P Jarvis) *bhd: rdn over 2f out: eased whn no ch ins fnl f* **16/1**

1m 42.18s (-0.91) **Going Correction** -0.075s/f (Good) **11** Ran SP% **120.0**
Speed ratings (Par 102):101,100,100,98,97 96,96,95,95,91 87
CSF £100.39 CT £630.56 TOTE £8.90: £2.80, £3.50, £1.70; EX 96.20.
Owner The Queen **Bred** The Queen **Trained** East Everleigh, Wilts
■ Stewards' Enquiry : Ryan Moore two-day ban: used whip with excessive frequency and without giving colt time to respond (July 25-26)

FOCUS
A competitive and decent-quality race, the field soon being stretched out at a solid, but not breakneck, gallop.

3554 HANDSTON GROUP H'CAP 1m 4f
8:35 (8:37) (Class 5) (0-75,75) 3-Y-0+ **£3,238** (£963; £481; £240) **Stalls** High

Form RPR

11-0 1 **Rehearsed (IRE)**[68] 1526 4-9-6 **67** SteveDrowne 1 75
(H Morrison) *hld up: hdwy over 2f out: rdn to ld over 1f out: r.o* **15/2**

326 2 nk **Generous Lad (IRE)**[11] 3177 4-9-7 **68** (p) DaneO'Neill 8 75
(A B Haynes) *hld up and bhd: rdn and hdwy over 1f out: r.o ins fnl f* **8/1**

06-4 3 2 ½ **Strong Survivor (USA)**[57] 1813 4-9-4 **65** RyanMoore 9 68
(P R Webber) *hld up: rdn and hdwy over 2f out: ev ch over 1f out: one pce ins fnl f* **7/2**[2]

0112 4 hd **Tibouchina (IRE)**[11] 3177 4-9-9 **70** SebSanders 7 73
(R M Beckett) *hld up: hdwy over 2f out: rdn and one pce whn flashed tail ins fnl f* **10/3**[1]

-414 5 2 ½ **Vale De Lobo**[38] 2361 5-10-0 **75** JHBowman 3 74
(B R Millman) *t.k.h early: hld up: swtchd lft and hdwy 2f out: sn rdn: fdd ins fnl f* **7/1**[3]

-301 6 2 ½ **Ocean Avenue (IRE)**[40] 2321 8-10-0 **75** SimonWhitworth 6 70
(C A Horgan) *led 2f: chsd ldr: led 6f out: clr 3f out: rdn and hdd over 1f out: wknd fnl f* **15/2**

3036 7 hd **Hatch A Plan (IRE)**[18] 2967 6-8-12 **64** TravisBlock(5) 5 59
(Mouse Hamilton-Fairley) *hld up and bhd: rdn and sme hdwy over 2f out: no further prog* **16/1**

134 8 11 **Rickety Bridge (IRE)**[17] 2994 4-9-9 **70** JimCrowley 2 47
(P R Chamings) *hld up and bhd: rdn over 4f out: eased whn no ch ins fnl f* **15/2**

006/ 9 14 **Shire (IRE)**[752] 2829 5-9-1 **62** TQuinn 4 17
(D R C Elsworth) *plld hrd: led after 2f to 6f out: wknd qckly over 2f out* **20/1**

2m 36.8s (0.44) **Going Correction** +0.125s/f (Good) **9** Ran SP% **114.9**
Speed ratings (Par 103):103,102,101,101,99 97,97,90,80
CSF £65.38 CT £247.23 TOTE £10.40: £2.80, £2.10, £1.80; EX 107.00.
Owner Mrs G C Maxwell & J D N Tillyard **Bred** J C Condon **Trained** East Ilsley, Berks

FOCUS
A fair contest, run at a good gallop, with Shire and Ocean Avenue going 10 lengths clear of the others. Solid, but limited form.

3555 EUROPEAN BREEDERS' FUND LADIES EVENING FILLIES' H'CAP 1m
9:05 (9:08) (Class 3) (0-95,88) 3-Y-O
£9,348 (£2,799; £1,399; £700; £349; £175) **Stalls** High

Form RPR

21-5 1 **Perfect Star**[18] 2971 3-8-12 **79** AdamKirby 5 86
(C G Cox) *hld up: rdn over 2f out: hdd ins fnl f: led fnl strides* **6/1**[3]

-132 2 hd **Gyroscope**[29] 2633 3-9-1 **82** RyanMoore 8 89
(Sir Michael Stoute) *hld up: rdn and hdwy 2f out: led ins fnl f: hdd fnl strides* **1/1**[1]

-020 3 1 ¾ **Ronaldsay**[32] 2543 3-8-13 **80** RichardHughes 9 86+
(R Hannon) *hld up and bhd: nt clr run over 1f out tl swtchd rt jst ins fnl f: r.o wl: unlucky* **25/1**

3003 4 1 ¼ **Going To Work (IRE)**[35] 2475 3-8-7 **74** TQuinn 2 74
(D R C Elsworth) *hld up and bhd: rdn and hdwy on outside over 1f out: kpt on same pce fnl f* **12/1**

0-50 5 nk **Divine Right**[14] 3100 3-9-7 **88** DaneO'Neill 3 87
(B J Meehan) *hld up in tch: rdn over 2f out: one pce fnl f* **16/1**

5254 **6** *nk* **Colchium (IRE)**[17] 2988 3-8-7 **74** ow1............................ SteveDrowne 6 73
(H Morrison) *plld hrd: prom: rdn and ev ch wl over 1f out: wknd ins fnl f* **11/1**

2110 **7** *1* **Graceful Steps (IRE)**[32] 2547 3-8-9 **76**.................... StephenDonohoe 7 72
(E J O'Neill) *hld up: rdn over 3f out: shortlived effrt over 2f out* **9/1**

22-1 **8** *2 1/2* **Zonta Zitkala**[50] 2012 3-8-9 **76**.. SebSanders 1 67
(R M Beckett) *hld up: hdwy over 3f out: rdn and ev ch wl over 1f out: wknd fnl f* **11/2**[2]

3330 **9** *shd* **Aussie Cricket (FR)**[18] 2971 3-8-2 **69** oh4............... EdwardCreighton 4 59
(D J Coakley) *plld hrd: prom: rdn and ev ch over 2f out: wknd wl over 1f out* **50/1**

1m 43.49s (0.40) **Going Correction** -0.075s/f (Good) **9** Ran SP% **117.4**
Speed ratings (Par 101):95,94,93,91,91 91,90,87,87
Place 6 £ 193.91, Place 5 £ 100.02 CSF £12.57 CT £145.17 TOTE £7.40: £2.20, £1.30, £3.90; EX 19.10.
Owner Dr Bridget Drew & E E Dedman **Bred** Mrs A M Jenkins And E D Kessly **Trained** Lambourn, Berks

FOCUS
A decent race with good prize money, but the pace was weak early on, and only ordinary after that. However, there were several potential improvers in the field and the form has been rated on the positive side.

NOTEBOOK
Perfect Star is reported to be happier on faster ground than she met at Newbury last time, and she deserves the utmost credit for a game performance which got her back up to beat the hot favourite. Though suited by this stiffish mile, she should stay a bit farther given decent conditions. (op 4-1 tchd 15-2)
Gyroscope came to win the race, only to be touched off again by the game winner. She can find compensation off a similar mark. (op 11-8)
Ronaldsay ◆ stays 1m2f, but showed she is capable of winning over a mile with better luck in running after being stopped in her tracks several times here. A stronger pace would also have helped, so she is one to consider strongly next time. Official explanation: jockey said filly was denied a clear run (op 20-1)
Going To Work(IRE) stays 1m2f, so the modest gallop over this shorter trip would not have brought out the best in her. (tchd 11-1)
Divine Right looks the sort to win more races, and is worth a try at 7f. (op 14-1)
Colchium(IRE) ran with credit, but less-exposed rivals had her measure in the final furlong. (tchd 12-1)
Zonta Zitkala, backed down to second favourite, would be better suited by a more strongly-run 6f or 7f. (op 8-1 tchd 5-1)
T/Plt: £246.50 to a £1 stake. Pool: £51,811.85. 153.40 winning tickets. T/Qpdt: £57.80 to a £1 stake. Pool: £3,763.20. 48.10 winning tickets. KH

3510 YORK (L-H)
Saturday, July 14

OFFICIAL GOING: Heavy
After 14mm rain in the previous 24 hours and a morning inspection, the ground was 'very testing, patchy' but it did dry out during the afternoon.
Wind: Fresh, half against Weather: Dry and breezy becoming sunny and warm

3556 JOHN SMITH'S CASK STKS (H'CAP) 1m
2:10 (2:11) (Class 3) (0-90,86) 3-Y-O+ **£9,715** (£2,890; £1,444; £721) **Stalls** Low

Form RPR

-503 **1** **Vicious Warrior**[21] 2871 8-9-11 **83**................................ DeanMcKeown 7 91
(R M Whitaker) *chsd ldr: lft in ld 6f out: hld on gamely* **10/1**

6156 **2** *3/4* **Efidium**[5] 3381 9-8-9 **67**.. PaulFessey 4 73
(N Bycroft) *hld up in rr: hdwy on ins over 2f out: kpt on wl fnl f: no ex towards fin* **20/1**

1524 **3** *nk* **Full Victory (IRE)**[17] 3002 5-9-11 **83**..................................... KDarley 10 89
(R A Farrant) *hld up: hdwy outside over 3f out: upsides over 1f out: kpt on same pce ins fnl f* **7/1**[3]

5-21 **4** *nk* **Webbow (IRE)**[17] 2985 5-9-7 **79**... DavidAllan 3 84
(T D Easterby) *s.i.s: hdwy over 2f out: chal over 1f out: kpt on same pce* **9/4**[2]

1032 **5** *3/4* **King Of The Moors (USA)**[6] 3346 4-9-1 **73**.................... PhillipMakin 5 76
(T D Barron) *chsd ldrs: edgd lft and outpcd over 2f out: kpt on fnl f* **12/1**

-111 **6** *shd* **The Grey Berry**[7] 3299 3-9-5 **86**................................. GrahamGibbons 8 89
(T D Walford) *hld up in tch: chal over 2f out: styd on same pce* **7/4**[1]

1220 **7** *3 1/2* **Exit Smiling**[17] 2986 5-9-5 **77**.. MickyFenton 2 72
(P T Midgley) *trckd ldrs: wknd fnl f* **14/1**

-105 **8** *4* **Rabbit Fighter (IRE)**[7] 3299 3-8-10 **77**......................... PaulMulrennan 9 64
(P A Blockley) *chsd ldrs: n.m.r on wd outside and lost pl 2f out* **25/1**

4-03 **9** *89* **Rodeo**[8] 3258 4-9-2 **74**..(b) DarryllHolland 11 —
(C W Thornton) *racd wd: led: hung bdly rt and hdd after 2f: reluctant: t.o 4f out* **20/1**

1m 44.24s (4.74) **Going Correction** +0.80s/f (Soft)
WFA 3 from 4yo+ 9lb **9** Ran SP% **116.5**
Speed ratings (Par 107):108,107,106,106,105 105,102,98,9
CSF £187.97 CT £1502.43 TOTE £9.90: £2.00, £5.20, £2.40; EX 243.00 Trifecta £424.90 Part won. Pool: £598.56 - 0.10 winning units..
Owner James Marshall & Mrs Susan Marshall **Bred** Hellwood Stud Farm **Trained** Scarcroft, W Yorks

FOCUS
Half-a-dozen in line coming to the final furlong. Sound enough form, but nothing really to take out of the race for the future.

NOTEBOOK
Vicious Warrior, left in charge, handles testing conditions better now and in the end did enough. (tchd 9-1, 11-1 in a place)
Efidium, making his ground up the centre, stuck on in brave fashion and in the end was just held at bay. (op 28-1)
Full Victory(IRE), still nearly a stone higher than his last victory, made his effort hard against the stands' side rail. In the end he was just found lacking. (op 13-2)
Webbow(IRE), 7lb higher, looked a serious threat coming to the final furlong but in the end was not quite good enough. (op 7-2)
King Of The Moors(USA) stuck on in the closing stages after edging towards the centre and being tapped for toe. A slight step up in distance will play to his strengths. (op 14-1)
The Grey Berry, hoisted 10lb, didn't seem to enjoy the very testing conditions. Even so he ran with plenty of credit. Official explanation: jockey said gelding was unsuited by the heavy ground (op 11-8)
Rodeo Official explanation: jockey said gelding cocked its jaw and failed to handle bend

3557 JOHN SMITH'S EXTRA COLD STKS (H'CAP) 6f
2:40 (2:40) (Class 3) (0-95,87) 3-Y-O+ **£9,715** (£2,890; £1,444; £721) **Stalls** Centre

Form RPR

5211 **1** **Prospect Court**[8] 3259 5-8-8 **68**.................................... PaulMulrennan 8 78
(A C Whillans) *w ldr gng wl: led on bit over 2f out: shkn up 1f out: hld on towards fin* **15/8**[1]

0106 **2** *hd* **Paris Bell**[4] 3401 5-8-13 **73**... PaulQuinn 4 84+
(T D Easterby) *hld up: effrt and nt clr run over 2f out: swtchd outside over 1f out: styd on wl: jst hld* **6/1**[2]

3044 **3** *1 1/2* **Bo McGinty (IRE)**[7] 3298 6-9-1 **75**..............................(b) TonyHamilton 6 80
(R A Fahey) *led tl over 2f out: styd on same pce* **9/1**

2060 **4** *1 1/4* **Prince Namid**[7] 3298 5-9-9 **83**...(p) KDarley 1 84
(Mrs A Duffield) *trckd ldrs on outer: edgd rt over 1f out: kpt on same pce* **6/1**[2]

012 **5** *2 1/2* **Pick A Nice Name**[2] 3466 5-8-12 **77**..................... MichaelJStainton(5) 5 71
(R M Whitaker) *trckd ldrs: effrt over 2f out: edgd lft over 1f out: sn fdd* **13/2**[3]

26-4 **6** *3* **Ingleby Princess**[63] 1658 3-8-11 **77**.................................. PaulFessey 7 62
(T D Barron) *in tch: effrt over 3f out: wknd fnl f* **14/1**

0506 **7** *nk* **High Curragh**[22] 2841 4-9-13 **87**.. NCallan 2 71
(K A Ryan) *chsd ldrs: wkng whn hmpd over 1f out* **10/1**

0001 **8** *3 1/2* **Kenmore**[11] 3180 5-9-4 **78**... MickyFenton 3 51
(J G Given) *rrd s: a detached in last* **8/1**

1m 17.74s (5.18) **Going Correction** +0.675s/f (Yiel)
WFA 3 from 4yo+ 6lb **8** Ran SP% **113.6**
Speed ratings (Par 107):92,91,89,88,84 80,80,75
CSF £13.08 CT £79.84 TOTE £2.80: £1.50, £2.00, £2.00; EX 13.60 Trifecta £145.70 Pool: £657.00 - 3.20 winning units..
Owner Mrs L M Whillans **Bred** Mrs G Slater **Trained** Newmill-On-Slitrig, Borders
■ Stewards' Enquiry : K Darley caution: careless riding
Michael J Stainton caution: careless riding

FOCUS
Not a strong pace but the right horses were to the fore at the end. The winner has been rated to his recent level, and the unlucky runner-up to his best.

NOTEBOOK
Prospect Court, 8lb higher, travelled as sweet as a nut. In the end it was a close call but he should continue to give a good account of himself with give in the ground. (op 9-4 tchd 5-2)
Paris Bell, who in the past has won from a 7lb higher mark, loves this ground. He had to make his way to the outside and, with his rider getting in a tangle with his whip and his reins, in the end he just missed out. (op 13-2 tchd 11-2)
Bo McGinty(IRE) is on a lengthy losing run but basically he does little wrong. He really prefers tracks with an uphill finish. (op 10-1)
Prince Namid, tried in cheekpieces this time, was drawn on the outside and tended to edge in. He seems to have lost the winning habit.
Pick A Nice Name, making a quick return, was racing from a 7lb higher mark. (op 5-1)
Ingleby Princess, tackling older sprinters, may not appreciate the ground as soft as this. (op 12-1)
Kenmore Official explanation: jockey said gelding reared on leaving stalls

3558 48TH JOHN SMITH'S CUP (HERITAGE H'CAP) 1m 208y
3:15 (3:16) (Class 2) 3-Y-O+
£93,480 (£27,990; £13,995; £7,005; £3,495; £1,755) **Stalls** Low

Form RPR

0124 **1** **Charlie Tokyo (IRE)**[66] 1583 4-8-9 **92**..................(b) JamieMoriarty(3) 4 104
(R A Fahey) *hld up in tch: smooth hdwy and edgd rt over 2f out: led on bit 1f out: shkn up and edgd rt: hld on towards fin* **11/1**

1220 **2** *1/2* **Flying Clarets (IRE)**[42] 2236 4-8-8 **88**................................... KDarley 5 99
(R A Fahey) *led tl 1f out: kpt on gamely towards fin* **16/1**

5053 **3** *3 1/2* **Collateral Damage (IRE)**[23] 2807 4-8-7 **87**..................(t) DavidAllan 14 91
(T D Easterby) *hld up in rr: hdwy and nt clr run over 2f out: styd on wl fnl f* **11/1**

2611 **4** *3/4* **Greek Well (IRE)**[29] 2634 4-8-1 **86**............................ WilliamBuick(5) 6 89
(Sir Michael Stoute) *trckd ldrs: effrt and sltly hmpd over 2f out: kpt on same pce* **6/1**[1]

3-45 **5** *4* **Smart Instinct (USA)**[49] 2037 3-8-9 **99** ow1......................... NCallan 12 94
(R A Fahey) *in tch: effrt over 3f out: kpt on same pce fnl 2f* **9/1**[3]

23-3 **6** *hd* **Resonate (IRE)**[43] 2209 9-8-6 **86**.............................. DeanMcKeown 13 80
(A G Newcombe) *mid-div: hdwy on outside over 3f out: kpt on same pce: nvr rchd ldrs* **16/1**

350 **7** *1/2* **Speedy Sam**[112] 761 4-8-10 **93**................................ AndrewElliott(3) 2 86
(K R Burke) *in tch: drvn 4f out: one pce fnl 2f* **22/1**

3-40 **8** *1/2* **Kyoto Summit**[57] 1822 4-8-7 **87**.................................... PaulMulrennan 9 79
(M W Easterby) *chsd ldrs: one pce fnl 2f* **20/1**

5-01 **9** *1 1/2* **Pevensey (IRE)**[21] 2859 5-9-1 **95** 5ex...................... GrahamGibbons 1 84
(J J Quinn) *s.i.s: sn drvn along: styd on fnl 3f: nvr nr ldrs* **8/1**[2]

-166 **10** *13* **Hassaad**[37] 2401 4-8-6 **86**.. RHills 20 49
(W J Haggas) *s.i.s: in rr: drvn over 4f out: sn bhd* **14/1**

4112 **11** *1 1/2* **Flipando (IRE)**[24] 2755 6-9-6 **100**... PaulFessey 7 60
(T D Barron) *chsd ldrs: lost pl over 2f out* **18/1**

3325 **12** *3/4* **Bailieborough (IRE)**[14] 3111 8-8-4 **87**.................... GregFairley(3) 10 46
(B Ellison) *chsd ldrs: drvn over 6f out: lost pl over 2f out* **25/1**

0211 **13** *1/2* **Fortunate Isle (USA)**[23] 2807 5-8-12 **92** 5ex...............(p) DaleGibson 17 50
(R A Fahey) *racd wd 1st 2f: w ldr: lost pl over 2f out* **12/1**

/3 **14** *1* **Hitchcock (USA)**[21] 2859 4-9-2 **96**............................. DarryllHolland 8 52
(A P O'Brien, Ire) *in rr: drvn over 5f out: no rspnse: sn bhd* **6/1**[1]

-600 **15** *15* **Folio (IRE)**[20] 2906 7-8-7 **87**... BrettDoyle 11 13
(W J Musson) *chsd ldrs: lost pl over 2f out: eased* **40/1**

0100 **16** *81* **Luberon**[57] 1805 4-9-10 **104**.. JoeFanning 16 —
(M Johnston) *sn bhd and drvn along: lost tch over 3f out: hopelessly t.o* **50/1**

32-1 **R** **Avoriaz (IRE)**[22] 2822 4-8-8 **88** 5ex............................... TonyHamilton 3 —
(R A Fahey) *ref to r: lft at s* **9/1**[3]

1m 56.61s (5.62) **Going Correction** +0.80s/f (Soft)
WFA 3 from 4yo+ 10lb **20** Ran SP% **125.1**
Speed ratings (Par 109):107,106,103,102,99 99,98,98,96,85 83,83,82,81,68 —,—
CSF £168.73 CT £2065.72 TOTE £14.70: £2.80, £4.10, £2.30, £2.60; EX 174.90 Trifecta £2511.90 Pool: £38,564.11 - 10.90 winning units..
Owner S L Tse **Bred** J Donnelly **Trained** Musley Bank, N Yorks
■ A one-two for Richard Fahey, successful with Vintage Premium in 2002. This year it had to be run over 1m76y less than normal.
■ Stewards' Enquiry : Jamie Moriarty two-day ban: careless riding (July 25-26)

FOCUS
This did not look quite up to its usual high standard. The first four finished clear, but the form is not that convincing and the winner was very much suited by the way the race panned out.

NOTEBOOK
Charlie Tokyo(IRE) travelled as sweet as a nut under his highly promising apprentice, but he got into a barging match with Greek Well and once in front he edged right and did just enough. (tchd 12-1)
Flying Clarets(IRE) put a poor effort at Epsom last time behind her. Running from a career high-mark, she fought off all but her stablemate and to her credit was coming back for more at the line.
Collateral Damage(IRE), who looked at his very best, is still 6lb higher than his last win, here over a year ago. He was denied racing room at a crucial stage and the first two were gone beyond recall. He really needs the full mile and a quarter and is well worth a try over a mile and a half. (op 12-1)
Greek Well(IRE), bidding to end his trainer's hoodoo since he landed the prize in 1989, was bumped by the winner halfway up the straight. He could only keep on in his own time and would have preferred the race to have been run over its normal mile and a quarter and on much less testing ground. (tchd 13-2)
Smart Instinct(USA) made laboured headway in the testing ground. He deserves to find a good prize.
Resonate(IRE), the old boy of the party, made his effort on the wide outside but over this trip he could never summon the pace to land a blow. He stays a mile and a half.
Speedy Sam ran with credit on his return to turf and his first outing since the Winter Derby in March. (op 20-1)
Kyoto Summit ran much better but this trip is on the sharp side for him.
Pevensey(IRE), under a 5lb penalty for his Royal Ascot success, was always being taken off his feet over this three furlong shorter trip. To his credit he never gave up the fight. (op 9-1)
Hassaad Official explanation: jockey said gelding hit false bit of ground after leaving stalls and never travelled thereafter
Hitchcock(USA), who had two handlers in the paddock, never went a yard and it was not just the drop back in trip. Official explanation: trainer's rep said colt needed further and never travelled (op 11-2 tchd 5-1)
Avoriaz(IRE), who gave serious problems before his win at Ayr, refused point blank to race and deserves to be a gelding when he next appears.

3559 JOHN SMITH'S EXTRA SMOOTH STKS (H'CAP) 7f
3:50 (3:53) (Class 2) (0-100,98) 3-Y-O+
£12,464 (£3,732; £1,866; £934; £466; £234) Stalls Low

Form			Horse	Jockey	RPR
6541	1		**Countdown**^{10} [3201] 5-8-10 **83**	DavidAllan 2	93
			(T D Easterby) *hdwy to chse ldrs 4f out: styd on wl fnl f: led towards fin*	6/1^{3}	
2043	2	½	**Imperial Echo (USA)**^{14} [3091] 6-8-10 **83**	PaulFessey 1	92
			(T D Barron) *trckd ldrs: led over 1f out: edgd rt: hdd towards fin*	12/1	
020	3	1¾	**Skhilling Spirit**^{24} [2755] 4-9-11 **98**	PhillipMakin 8	102
			(T D Barron) *s.s: hdwy over 2f out: kpt on wl fnl f*	5/1^{1}	
40-0	4	1¾	**Tagula Sunrise (IRE)**^{14} [3091] 5-8-13 **86**	DaleGibson 5	86
			(R A Fahey) *mid-div: kpt on fnl 2f: nvr rchd ldrs*	14/1	
0001	5	1¼	**Game Lad**^{14} [3091] 5-9-2 **89**	TedDurcan 10	86
			(T D Easterby) *in rr: effrt over 2f out: edgd rt over 1f out: kpt on: nvr nr ldrs*	11/2^{2}	
0042	6	1¾	**Mezuzah**^{14} [3091] 7-8-12 **85**	PaulMulrennan 9	78
			(M W Easterby) *led tl over 1f out: one pce*	10/1	
5300	7	4	**Billy Dane (IRE)**^{23} [2788] 3-8-7 **88**	TonyHamilton 4	71
			(R A Fahey) *trckd ldrs: wknd appr fnl f*	18/1	
-520	8	nk	**Trafalgar Bay (IRE)**^{22} [2817] 4-9-4 **91**	NCallan 11	73
			(K R Burke) *s.i.s: sn chsng ldrs: wkng whn sltly hmpd over 1f out*	6/1^{3}	
-032	9	nk	**Damika (IRE)**^{4} [3401] 4-8-9 **87**	MichaelJStainton$^{(5)}$ 14	68
			(R M Whitaker) *chsd ldrs on outside: lost pl over 1f out*	8/1	
3612	10	18	**White Deer (USA)**^{14} [3078] 3-9-0 **95**	JoeFanning 12	31
			(M Johnston) *chsd ldrs: hung lft and lost pl over 2f out: sn bhd*	15/2	
0100	11	27	**Black Charmer (IRE)**^{14} [3091] 4-9-10 **97**	KDarley 13	—
			(M Johnston) *chsd ldrs: wnt bdly lft and lost pl 3f out: sn bhd and eased*	16/1	

1m 28.39s (2.99) **Going Correction** +0.675s/f (Yiel)
WFA 3 from 4yo+ 8lb **11** Ran SP% **118.1**
Speed ratings (Par 109):109,108,106,104,103 101,96,95,75 44
CSF £76.18 CT £390.02 TOTE £6.50: £2.00, £4.50, £2.30; EX 100.00 Trifecta £353.00 Pool: £1,392.26 - 2.80 winning units..
Owner David W Armstrong **Bred** Lady Fairhaven **Trained** Great Habton, N Yorks

FOCUS
Rock solid form, and the winner looks better than ever.

NOTEBOOK
Countdown, 6lb higher, appreciates a strong run race and showed a good attitude to put his head in front where it really matters. He is in the form of his life. (tchd 11-2 and 13-2)
Imperial Echo(USA) continues in cracking form and, coming off a straight line once in front, in the end he just missed out. (tchd 14-1)
Skhilling Spirit, who gave away ground at the start, loves this type of ground and did really well under his big weight. (op 11-2 tchd 6-1)
Tagula Sunrise(IRE), just one pound higher than her last success at this track a year ago, stuck on in pleasing fashion. She should be cherry ripe next time. (op 11-1)
Game Lad, 8lb higher, found himself towards the rear. He stuck on in his own time but never entered the argument. (tchd 9-2)
Mezuzah, meeting Game Lad on 6lb better terms, took them along at a sound gallop but this trip at this track proved an insufficient test.
White Deer(USA) ran as if something had gone amiss. (op 17-2 tchd 7-1)
Black Charmer(IRE)again ran badly and this time something looked to have gone badly wrong. (op 14-1)

3560 JOHN SMITH'S MEDIAN AUCTION MAIDEN STKS 6f
4:25 (4:25) (Class 4) 2-Y-O £6,800 (£2,023; £1,011; £505) Stalls Centre

Form			Horse	Jockey	RPR
4	1		**Dark Tara**^{20} [2904] 2-8-12 0	TonyHamilton 5	76+
			(R A Fahey) *trckd ldrs: shkn up to ld appr fnl f: sn drew clr*	11/4^{1}	
05	2	5	**Complete Frontline (GER)**^{72} [1422] 2-9-0 0	AndrewElliott$^{(3)}$ 4	66
			(K R Burke) *w ldrs: led over 3f out: hdd appr fnl f: no ch w wnr*	16/1	
64	3	shd	**Daring Dream (GER)**^{23} [2804] 2-9-3 0	DavidAllan 9	66
			(T D Easterby) *led tl over 3f out: kpt on same pce fnl f*	11/2^{3}	
050	4	6	**Ridge Wood Dani (IRE)**^{17} [2977] 2-9-3 0	KDarley 11	48
			(E J Alston) *trckd ldrs: wknd appr fnl f*	11/1	
05	5	4	**Invincible Rose (IRE)**^{22} [2818] 2-8-5 0	PatrickDonaghy$^{(7)}$ 8	31
			(M Brittain) *sn chsng ldrs: wknd over 1f out*	33/1	
00	6	1¾	**Astrol**^{25} [2739] 2-8-12 0	TedDurcan 12	25
			(T D Easterby) *sn chsng ldrs: rdn along over 3f out: wknd over 1f out* 33/1		
66	7	10	**Bencorr (USA)**^{17} [2991] 2-9-3 0	RobertHavlin 2	—
			(M J Wallace) *sn outpcd and in rr: bhd fnl 3f*	10/1	
	8	6	**Bertie Vista** 2-9-3 0	BrettDoyle 7	—
			(T D Easterby) *s.i.s: a bhd*	11/1	
	9	1½	**Nothing To Add** 2-9-3 0	NCallan 1	—
			(K A Ryan) *dwlt and swvd lft s: a bhd*	11/2^{3}	
	10	5	**Cordon Bleu (IRE)** 2-9-3 0	JoeFanning 6	—
			(M Johnston) *w ldrs: lost pl over 2f out: sn bhd*	7/2^{2}	

1m 17.32s (4.76) **Going Correction** +0.675s/f (Yiel) **10** Ran SP% **117.2**
Speed ratings (Par 96):95,88,88,80,74 72,59,51,49,42
CSF £49.58 TOTE £3.50: £1.50, £5.00, £1.90; EX 70.80.
Owner J E M Hawkins Ltd **Bred** J E M Hawkins Ltd **Trained** Musley Bank, N Yorks

FOCUS
A very ordinary median auction race but a winner of some potential.

NOTEBOOK
Dark Tara had clearly learnt plenty from her debut three weeks earlier, for she travelled best and forged clear. Her trainer has given her a Lowther Stakes entry. (op 3-1)
Complete Frontline(GER), absent for ten weeks, appreciated the extra furlong and the testing ground. This opens up the nursery route for him. (op 14-1)
Daring Dream(GER) is improving with each outing and he too is now qualified for nurseries. (op 13-2 tchd 5-1)
Ridge Wood Dani(IRE) showed plenty of toe but the sixth furlong found him out. He would have a much more realistic chance in nursery company. (tchd 12-1)
Invincible Rose(IRE) showed plenty of dash but in the end was beaten a fair way. (tchd 28-1)
Cordon Bleu(IRE), a rangy, well-made newcomer, dropped right away in most disappointing fashion. He can surely do a lot better than this. (op 4-1)

3561 JOHN SMITH'S "NO NONSENSE RACING" MAIDEN FILLIES' STKS 7f
5:00 (5:01) (Class 4) 3-4-Y-O £6,800 (£2,023; £1,011; £505) Stalls Low

Form			Horse	Jockey	RPR
64	1		**Sweet Clover**^{50} [1995] 3-8-11 0	AndrewElliott$^{(3)}$ 5	65
			(K R Burke) *w ldrs: led over 3f out: kpt on wl fnl f*	5/2^{2}	
0-4	2	2	**Cow Girl (IRE)**^{8} [3276] 3-9-0 0	MickyFenton 9	60
			(Miss Gay Kelleway) *sn trcking ldrs: chal over 1f out: sn rdn and fnd little*	9/4^{1}	
4000	3	1¼	**Jentris Girl (IRE)**^{23} [2796] 3-9-0 52	TonyHamilton 4	57
			(T D Easterby) *led tl over 4f out: kpt on same pce fnl 2f*	8/1	
2	4	8	**Lan Kwai Fong**^{15} [3051] 3-9-0 0	DavidAllan 2	37
			(T D Easterby) *trckd ldrs: drvn 4f out: hung lft: wknd over 1f out*	3/1^{3}	
0	5	14	**Very Wise Kid**^{10} [3202] 4-9-8 0	LeeEnstone 1	2
			(P T Midgley) *chsd ldrs: edgd bdly lft over 2f out: sn bhd*	11/1	
	6	2½	**Final Desire** 4-9-1 0	PatrickDonaghy$^{(7)}$ 10	—
			(M Brittain) *s.i.s: hdwy to ld over 4f out: hdd over 3f out: wknd over 2f out*	7/1	

1m 30.97s (5.57) **Going Correction** +0.675s/f (Yiel)
WFA 3 from 4yo 8lb **6** Ran SP% **116.3**
Speed ratings (Par 102):95,92,91,82,66 63
CSF £9.02 TOTE £4.00: £2.00, £1.70; EX 10.70.
Owner Brian Walsh (Co Kildare) **Bred** Darley **Trained** Middleham Moor, N Yorks

FOCUS
A very weak maiden indeed for York after the certain two market leaders were withdrawn on account of the ground. The third is rated just 52.

3562 JOHN SMITH'S "PREMIER CLUB" STKS (NURSERY H'CAP) 5f
5:30 (5:31) (Class 3) 2-Y-O £7,772 (£2,312; £1,155; £577) Stalls Centre

Form			Horse	Jockey	RPR
512	1		**Lady Rangali (IRE)**^{8} [3256] 2-8-6 **69**	KDarley 4	79
			(Mrs A Duffield) *chsd ldrs: led over 1f out: edgd rt: styd on strly*	2/1^{1}	
15	2	2½	**Rose Siog**^{45} [2134] 2-8-11 **74**	TonyHamilton 5	75
			(R A Fahey) *trckd ldrs: effrt over 1f out: sn chsng wnr: no real imp*	3/1^{2}	
014	3	3½	**Captain Dunne (IRE)**^{12} [3157] 2-9-7 **84**	DavidAllan 6	72
			(T D Easterby) *wnt rt s: trckd ldrs: kpt on same pce appr fnl f*	4/1	
215	4	4	**Diademas (USA)**^{47} [2090] 2-9-0 **82**	WilliamBuick$^{(5)}$ 2	56
			(J A Osborne) *led: hdd over 1f out: hung lft and sn wknd*	7/2^{3}	
643	5	5	**Dalarossie**^{32} [2526] 2-8-6 **69**	DaleGibson 1	25
			(E J Alston) *bucked: swvd rt and sddle slipped sn after s: hdwy to chse ldrs over 3f out: lost pl 2f out*	7/1	

62.67 secs (3.35) **Going Correction** +0.675s/f (Yiel) **5** Ran SP% **113.1**
Speed ratings (Par 98):100,96,90,84,76
CSF £8.53 TOTE £2.40: £1.40, £1.90; EX 5.50 Place 6 £82.86, Place 5 £14.06.
Owner Mrs Sarah E Woodhead **Bred** Mrs C Hartery **Trained** Constable Burton, N Yorks

FOCUS
The 'official' ratings shown next to each horse are estimated and for information purposes only. The winner is going the right away and the second was regarded as well treated, but even so this was a pretty modest affair for a card like this. The riders reported the ground had dried out during the afternoon on a breezy and warm day.

NOTEBOOK
Lady Rangali(IRE), who had two handlers in the paddock, has a good attitude and, despite getting in the way of the runner-up, in the end won going away. (op 9-4 tchd 7-4)
Rose Siog, potentially well treated, went in pursuit of the winner but in the end was very much second best. She should have little difficulty going one better. (op 13-8 tchd 7-2)
Captain Dunne(IRE), a decent type, was back in trip but was unable to trouble two potentially well treated fillies. (op 7-1)
Diademas(USA), a sharp type, took them along but in the end dropped right away. (op 5-1)
Dalarossie, on his toes beforehand, bucked and reared soon after leaving the stalls and it transpired he was troubled by a slipped saddle. Official explanation: jockey said saddle slipped (op 9-1)
T/Jkpt: Not won. T/Plt: £159.20 to a £1 stake. Pool: £194,971.16. 894.00 winning tickets. T/Qpdt: £15.20 to a £1 stake. Pool: £9,927.00. 481.65 winning tickets. WG

2952 LONGCHAMP (R-H)
Saturday, July 14

OFFICIAL GOING: Good to soft

3564a PRIX DE THIBERVILLE (LISTED RACE) (FILLIES) 1m 4f
6:15 (6:18) 3-Y-O £17,568 (£7,027; £5,270; £3,514; £1,757)

		Horse	Jockey	RPR
1		**Van Gosh**^{38} 3-8-11	JVictoire 3	96
		(A Fabre, France)		
2	½	**Mahara (USA)**^{26} 3-8-11	TGillet 9	95
		(J E Hammond, France)	15/1^{3}	
3	snk	**Light Impact (IRE)**^{23} 3-8-11	MBlancpain 4	95
		(C Laffon-Parias, France)		
4	1½	**Red Diva**^{27} [2707] 3-8-11	ASuborics 8	93
		(Mario Hofer, Germany)		
5	hd	**Scotch Bonnet (IRE)**^{29} 3-8-11	TThulliez 1	92
		(R Gibson, France)		

6 3/4 **Synopsis (IRE)**[100] 3-8-11 SPasquier 11 91
(A Fabre, France) 1/1[1]
7 3 **Claire Et Bleu (FR)**[38] [2384] 3-8-11 AlxiBadel 2 87
(Mme M Bollack-Badel, France)
8 1 1/2 **Shawhill**[32] [2547] 3-8-11 CSoumillon 5 84
(Tom Dascombe) *led: pushed along st: hdd 1 1/2f out: no ex and eased fnl 100yds* 66/10[2]
9 2 **Une Pivoine (FR)**[32] [2547] 3-8-11 C-PLemaire 7 81
(J E Pease, France)
10 2 **Gare Du Nord (IRE)**[23] 3-8-11 OPeslier 6 78
(E Lellouche, France)
2m 31.1s (-3.90) **Going Correction** +0.05s/f (Good) **10** Ran SP% **69.4**
Speed ratings: 115,114,114,113,113 112,110,109,108,107
PARI-MUTUEL: WIN 18.30; PL 3.90, 4.60, 7.20; DF 66.80.
Owner G Reed **Bred** G Reed **Trained** Chantilly, France

NOTEBOOK
Shawhill attempted to make all the running, her jockey setting a very steady pace in front. When asked to quicken she did not find much and her jockey did not make much effort once she was passed.

3565a PRIX MAURICE DE NIEUIL (GROUP 2) 1m 6f
6:45 (6:49) 4-Y-O+ **£50,068** (£19,324; £9,223; £6,149; £3,074)

RPR
1 **Bussoni (GER)**[63] [1689] 6-8-11 CSoumillon 6 112
(H Blume, Germany) *mde all: pushed along st: rdn fnl f: r.o gamely to jst hold runner-up* 34/10[3]
2 nse **Champs Elysees**[41] [2292] 4-8-11 SPasquier 3 112
(A Fabre, France) *racd in 4th: cl 3rd st: rdn and r.o 1 1/2f out: chal cl home: jst failed* 5/2[1]
3 2 **Macleya (GER)**[45] [2165] 5-8-8 JVictoire 4 109
(A Fabre, France) *racd in 2nd: chsd ldr 2f out: styd on but no imp on ldr* 5/1
4 shd **Ponte Tresa (FR)**[20] [2925] 4-8-8 OPeslier 5 109
(Y De Nicolay, France) *towards rr: 6th 1/2-way: pushed along 3 1/2f out: disputing last st: hrd rdn 1 1/2f out: styd on fnl f to take 4th* 15/2
5 3 **Marend (FR)**[43] [2330] 6-8-11 KFallon 1 112
(D Sepulchre, France) *racd in 5th on ins: rdn 2f out: nvr in chalng position* 23/1
6 hd **Dragon Fly (GER)**[37] [2409] 5-8-11 ASuborics 2 112
(Frau Jutta Mayer, Germany) *racd in last: n.d* 18/1
7 1 1/2 **Le Miracle (GER)**[23] [2787] 6-8-11 DBoeuf 7 112
(W Baltromei, Germany) *racd in 3rd: 4th and pushed along st: u.p 1 1/2f out: btn over 1f out* 26/10[2]
2m 58.1s (178.10) **7** Ran SP% **116.9**
PARI-MUTUEL: WIN 4.40; PL 2.00, 2.10; SF 22.00.
Owner Stall Kaiserberg **Bred** Gestut Karlshof **Trained** Germany
■ Stewards' Enquiry : C Soumillon four-day ban: whip abuse (Jul 23-26)

NOTEBOOK
Bussoni(GER), a German raider, went from pillar to post under a well-judged ride. He quickened well up the straight and held off the late challenge of the second by a nose.
Champs Elysees, who raced in fourth for much of the race, moved up to third at the beginning of the straight and conjured up a late dash to go down narrowly. He proved his stamina at his first attempt over this distance and will be aimed at further races at this level and trip.
Macleya(GER) raced prominently in behind the leader and tried gamely to stay with the winner up the straight, but was rather one paced and passed by the eventual second close home. This was her first attempt at this longer distance and it may have stretched her stamina.
Ponte Tresa(FR), held up out the back of the field for much of the race, took a while to settle, but she made up ground well under hard urging from her jockey to take fourth.

3566a JUDDMONTE GRAND PRIX DE PARIS (GROUP 1) (C&F) 1m 4f
7:20 (7:24) 3-Y-O **£231,649** (£92,676; £46,338; £23,149; £11,595)

RPR
1 **Zambezi Sun**[41] [2293] 3-9-2 SPasquier 5 119+
(P Bary, France) *racd in 4th: disputing 3rd st: pushed along and r.o to ld over 1 1/2f out: drvn clr fnl f: impressive* 19/10[1]
2 5 **Axxos (GER)**[34] [2502] 3-9-2 AStarke 6 110
(P Schiergen, Germany) *led: pushed along st: hdd over 1 1/2f out: rdn and styd on to hold 2nd fnl f* 12/1
3 nk **Sagara (USA)**[41] [2293] 3-9-2 TGillet 8 109+
(J E Pease, France) *racd in 2nd: pushed along on rail 2f out: nt qckn fr 1 1/2f out: styd on to take 3rd fnl f* 71/10
4 3/4 **Airmail Special (IRE)**[25] [2751] 3-9-2 JVictoire 7 108
(A Fabre, France) *hld up: last 1/2-way: disputing 3rd towards outside st: wnt 3rd 1 1/2f out: no ex fnl f* 31/10[3]
5 1 1/2 **Ashkazar (FR)**[22] [2813] 3-9-2 CSoumillon 1 105
(A De Royer-Dupre, France) *missed break: racd in last: 5th 1/2-way: last again st: rdn 2f out: no imp* 11/1
6 nse **Prinz (GER)**[27] 3-9-2 EPedroza 2 105
(A Wohler, Germany) *settled towards rr: 3rd 1/2-way: drvn appr st: 5th st: unable qckn fr 2f out* 31/1
U **Eagle Mountain**[13] [3142] 3-9-2 KFallon 4 —
(A P O'Brien, Ire) *settled in 3rd: clipped heels of Sagara and uns rdr after 3f* 28/10[2]
2m 31.6s (-3.40) **Going Correction** +0.05s/f (Good) **7** Ran SP% **116.7**
Speed ratings: 113,109,109,108,107 107,—
PARI-MUTUEL: WIN 2.90; PL 1.70, 4.20; SF 16.20.
Owner K Abdulla **Bred** Juddmonte Farms **Trained** Chantilly, France

FOCUS
Zambesi Sun impressed and can do better, but it is doubtful if the form is worth any more than this. There was a lengthy stewards' enquiry into the winning jockey's riding and his part in Fallon's fall before the result was confirmed.

NOTEBOOK
Zambezi Sun ◆, raced on the outside in fourth position in a contest that was run at a crawl early on, was involved in a barging match with Eagle Mountain three and a half furlongs into the race which resulted in Fallon being ejected from the saddle. After this incident he was always travelling well and moved up to within the reach of the leader before rounding the final turn. When asked to quicken up the straight, he did so with ease, seeming to revel in the longer distance. He will now take the Rail Link route of the Prix Niel in September followed by the Prix de l'Arc de Triomphe and at this stage looks a leading contender.
Axxos(GER), an unwilling pace-setter for much of the race, was asked to quicken turning in and was still leading halfway up the straight. He leaned into the rail thus doing no favours to the eventual third, and the jockey stated that he was distracted by the loose horse. The Stewards unusually took no action with regards to his run and he was lucky to keep second. He could go for the Rheinland-Pokal der Sparkasse Kolnbonn at Cologne on August 12 followed by the Grosser Preis Von Baden on September 2 at Baden-Baden.
Sagara(USA), prominent in second for much of the race, followed the leader and, when asked to quicken, the eventual second closed the door on him. His momentum was interfered with, and when he found some room but was again impeded by the loose horse. Once a gap became available, he ran on strongly but the line came to soon. When this colt has some luck in running, he will surely pick up a big race and should have finished second here.
Airmail Special(IRE), held up out the back for much of the race, moved up to fourth position running down the false straight. When the pace quickened dramatically in the straight he was brought wide up the outside, but had no answer and was the disappointment of the race.
Eagle Mountain was hampered and put out of the race early on, coming back with cuts and giving Falon a nasty fall.

[2868]HAYDOCK (L-H)
Sunday, July 15

OFFICIAL GOING: Heavy (soft in places on back straight)
Football Furlong day. Jockeys wore the colours of Premiership clubs and took part in a points competition.
Wind: Fresh, behind Weather: Wet

3567 IG INDEX FOOTBALL FURLONG H'CAP 1m 2f 120y
2:20 (2:21) (Class 5) (0-75,74) 3-Y-O+ **£3,886** (£1,156; £577; £288) **Stalls High**

Form RPR
5131 1 **Royal Flynn**[8] [3301] 5-9-6 **73** NeilBrown(7) 6 82
(M Dods) *hld up: swtchd lft and hdwy 2f out: led over 1f out: edgd lft ins fnl f: styd on wl and pushed out towards fin* 3/1[1]
4551 2 2 1/2 **Great View (IRE)**[10] [3232] 8-9-9 **74** (v) AshleyHamblett(5) 7 79
(Mrs A L M King) *hld up: rdn and hdwy over 2f out: wnt 2nd ins fnl f: no imp on wnr* 8/1
-400 3 3/4 **Hope Road**[16] [3058] 3-9-1 **73** JoeFanning 1 76
(J R Fanshawe) *trckd ldrs: ev ch 2f out: styd on same pce fnl f* 5/1[3]
2456 4 1 1/2 **Mae Cigan (FR)**[29] [2660] 4-9-0 **60** FrancisNorton 3 61
(M Blanshard) *racd keenly: hld up: hdwy over 2f out: rdn over 1f out: one pce ins fnl f* 10/3[2]
030 5 hd **Blockley (USA)**[31] [2609] 3-8-0 **58** ow1 PaulFessey 5 58
(Ian Williams) *led: shkn up over 4f out: rdn 2f out: hdd over 1f out: sn hung lft: no ex ins fnl f* 16/1
4111 6 1 **Drawback (IRE)**[18] [2980] 4-9-5 **70** (p) LukeMorris(5) 10 69
(R A Harris) *prom: rdn and lost pl over 2f out: hung lft over 1f out: one pce ins fnl f* 6/1
-500 7 nk **Trouble Mountain (USA)**[16] [3049] 10-9-6 **66** (t) DaleGibson 2 64
(M W Easterby) *midfield: rdn whn n.m.r and hmpd over 2f out: n.d after* 9/1
0/0- 8 2 1/2 **Kingkohler (IRE)**[56] [250] 8-9-5 **65** JohnEgan 4 59
(K A Morgan) *midfield tl rdn and wknd over 2f out* 14/1
0000 9 15 **Drury Lane (IRE)**[7] [3345] 7-8-10 **56** oh11 (b) DeanMcKeown 9 23
(Miss A Stokell) *trckd ldrs: chal 3f out: ev ch over 2f out: wknd over 1f out* 66/1
2m 25.41s (9.27) **Going Correction** +0.775s/f (Yiel)
WFA 3 from 4yo+ 12lb **9** Ran SP% **114.2**
Speed ratings (Par 103):103,101,100,99,99 98,98,96,85
CSF £27.21 CT £115.31 TOTE £3.70: £1.20, £2.00, £2.40; EX 17.60.
Owner J A Wynn-Williams **Bred** Highclere Stud Ltd **Trained** Denton, Co Durham
■ Stewards' Enquiry : Ashley Hamblett two-day ban: used whip in forehand position and with excessive frequency (Jul 26-27)
Luke Morris two-day ban: careless riding (Jul 26-27)

FOCUS
Just a modest contest, but Royal Flynn loves these conditions and he revelled in the mud for a ready victory.

3568 SPORTS SPREAD BETTING WITH IG INDEX H'CAP 5f
2:50 (2:56) (Class 4) (0-80,79) 3-Y-O **£6,477** (£1,927; £963; £481) **Stalls High**

Form RPR
3304 1 **Foxy Music**[2] [3493] 3-9-7 **79** DeanMcKeown 6 85
(E J Alston) *mde all: shkn up over 1f out: r.o ins fnl f: a in command* 11/2[3]
0002 2 2 **Silly Gilly (IRE)**[23] [2826] 3-8-2 **60** oh12 FrancisNorton 5 59
(K R Burke) *chsd ldrs: rdn to take 2nd 1f out: no imp on wnr* 14/1
0565 3 nk **Fish Called Johnny**[2] [3493] 3-8-12 **73** LiamJones(3) 8 71
(Peter Grayson) *midfield: rdn and hdwy 2f out: edgd lft and chsd ldrs fr over 1f out: kpt on ins fnl f* 11/4[2]
1022 4 8 **Windjammer**[23] [2837] 3-9-2 **74** DavidAllan 3 43
(T D Easterby) *chsd wnr tl 1f out: wknd fnl f* 7/4[1]
0000 5 5 **Grange Lili (IRE)**[22] [2867] 3-8-9 **67** (b) LPKeniry 2 18
(Peter Grayson) *dwlt: bhd: rdn 2f out: nvr on terms w ldrs* 11/1
1-00 6 3 1/2 **Crow's Nest Lad**[51] [1994] 3-8-10 **68** PaulMulrennan 4 6
(T D Easterby) *in tch: rdn and wknd over 2f out* 6/1
-005 7 11 **Mr Klick (IRE)**[15] [3094] 3-8-0 **65** (p) LanceBetts(7) 1 —
(N Wilson) *in tch: rdn and wknd over 2f out* 16/1
64.41 secs (4.29) **Going Correction** +0.525s/f (Yiel) **7** Ran SP% **113.6**
Speed ratings (Par 102):102,98,98,85,77 71,54
CSF £72.87 CT £254.52 TOTE £6.70: £2.50, £3.40; EX 65.70.
Owner Springs Equestrian, G M & C Baillie **Bred** G M And Mrs C Baillie And Springs Equestrian Lt **Trained** Longton, Lancs

FOCUS
A pretty uneventful race with Foxy Music bounding out in front and staying there. Nothing threatened to come from behind and, with the runner-up racing from 12lb out of the handicap, the form needs treating with caution.
Crow's Nest Lad Official explanation: jockey said colt never travelled

3569 QUIT WHILE YOU'RE AHEAD WITH EXTRABET H'CAP 6f
3:20 (3:25) (Class 4) (0-85,86) 4-Y-O+ **£6,477** (£1,927; £963; £481) **Stalls High**

Form RPR
1556 1 **Balakiref**[21] [2912] 8-8-12 **74** DarryllHolland 7 79+
(M Dods) *bhd: rdn whn swtchd lft and hdwy 1f out: r.o to ld towards fin: comf* 9/2[3]
0003 2 hd **Stonecrabstomorrow (IRE)**[5] [3401] 4-8-10 **72** TonyHamilton 10 76
(R A Fahey) *a.p: rdn to ld over 1f out: sn edgd lft: hdd and hld towards fin* 5/2[1]
5040 3 1 1/2 **Legal Set (IRE)**[1] [3536] 11-8-2 **64** oh19 (b) JimmyQuinn 4 64?
(Miss A Stokell) *racd keenly: trckd ldrs: rdn 2f out: nt qckn ins fnl f* 50/1
4213 4 1 **Katie Boo (IRE)**[1] [3536] 5-8-2 **64** FrancisNorton 1 61
(A Berry) *prom: rdn over 2f out: styd on same pce fr over 1f out* 11/2
0000 5 hd **Kingscross**[18] [2993] 9-8-7 **69** FergusSweeney 8 65
(M Blanshard) *hld up: pushed along 2f out: styd on ins fnl f: nt pce of ldrs* 12/1

4253 **6** *shd* **Jilly Why (IRE)**[2] 3515 6-8-1 **66**....................(b) LiamJones(3) 2 62
(Paul Green) *in tch: rdn and chsd ldrs whn carried lft ent fnl f: kpt on same pce after* **8/1**
1611 **7** *1* **Stamford Blue**[3] 3472 6-9-5 **86** 6ex....................(b) LukeMorris(5) 9 79
(R A Harris) *midfield: pushed along over 3f out: no real imp on ldrs whn hmpd ent fnl f: one pce after* **7/2**[2]
4133 **8** *½* **Miacarla**[11] 3203 4-7-13 **64** oh14.................... DuranFentiman(3) 5 56
(A Berry) *racd keenly: led: rdn and hdd over 1f out: fdd ins fnl f* **33/1**
0300 **9** *4* **Ellens Academy (IRE)**[16] 3053 12-8-8 **70**.................... DavidAllan 3 50
(E J Alston) *towards rr: pushed along 3f out: swtchd rt whn n.m.r and no imp ent fnl f: n.d after* **25/1**
000- **10** *2 ½* **Imperial Sword**[326] 4707 4-9-7 **83**.................... PaulFessey 6 55
(T D Barron) *racd keenly: prom tl lost pl over 3f out: n.d after* **9/1**
1m 18.69s (4.80) **Going Correction** +0.625s/f (Yiel) **10** Ran SP% **121.9**
Speed ratings (Par 105):99,98,96,95,95 95,93,93,87,84
CSF £16.76 CT £523.38 TOTE £5.90: £1.30, £1.50, £8.30; EX 21.00.
Owner Septimus Racing Group **Bred** S R Hope And D Erwin **Trained** Denton, Co Durham
■ Stewards' Enquiry : Francis Norton one-day ban: not riding to draw (Jul 26)
FOCUS
Just an ordinary sprint handicap and the close proximity of 11-year-old Legal Set, who was racing from 19lb out of the handicap, cast huge doubts over the form.

3570 TIGER'S OPEN? WOODS 10-3 WITH EXTRABET H'CAP 1m 30y
3:50 (3:51) (Class 5) (0-70,73) 3-Y-O **£3,886** (£1,156; £577; £288) **Stalls** Low

Form RPR
4041 **1** **Beau Sancy**[7] 3351 3-9-7 **73** 6ex.................... LiamJones(3) 4 79
(R A Harris) *hld up: hdwy over 2f out: led over 1f out: r.o wl* **16/1**
0410 **2** *3* **Mark Of Love (IRE)**[6] 3384 3-9-8 **71**.................... DarryllHolland 6 70
(M R Channon) *plld hrd: midfield: rdn and hdwy 2f out: wnt 2nd ins fnl f: no imp on wnr* **10/3**[1]
0231 **3** *1* **Lordship (IRE)**[3] 3475 3-8-8 **62** 6ex.................... LukeMorris(5) 2 59
(A W Carroll) *midfield: rdn and hdwy 2f out: kpt on ins fnl f: nt pce to chal ldrs* **7/2**[2]
601 **4** *½* **Distant Pleasure**[33] 2535 3-9-3 **66**.................... PaulFessey 8 62
(M Dods) *led: rdn and hdd over 1f out: no ex ins fnl f* **16/1**
-424 **5** *2 ½* **Nicada (IRE)**[10] 3235 3-9-4 **67**....................(p) JohnEgan 9 57
(J S Moore) *prom: rdn over 2f out: wknd ins fnl f* **7/2**[2]
3-05 **6** *3 ½* **Snowflight**[12] 3196 3-9-0 **63**.................... TonyHamilton 3 46
(R A Fahey) *chsd ldr to 3f out: rdn over 2f out: wknd over 1f out* **12/1**
05-0 **7** *½* **Berbatov**[16] 3066 3-8-4 **53**.................... JimmyQuinn 5 34
(Paul Green) *racd keenly: hld up: struggling 3f out: nvr on terms w ldrs* **33/1**
2040 **8** *1 ¾* **Chip N Pin**[24] 2793 3-8-0 **52**.................... DuranFentiman(3) 10 30
(T D Easterby) *racd keenly: in tch: rdn over 2f out: wknd over 1f out* **10/1**
-004 **9** *½* **Dark Energy**[21] 2915 3-9-2 **65**.................... RoystonFfrench 7 41
(B Smart) *racd keenly: in tch: rdn 3f out: wknd over 1f out* **7/1**[3]
1340 **10** *2 ½* **Snow Dancer (IRE)**[22] 2872 3-9-1 **69**.................... PBradley(5) 1 40
(A Berry) *a bhd* **20/1**
1m 52.02s (6.51) **Going Correction** +0.875s/f (Soft) **10** Ran SP% **116.3**
Speed ratings (Par 100):102,99,98,97,95 91,91,89,88,86
CSF £68.75 CT £236.16 TOTE £17.30: £3.40, £1.70, £1.50; EX 74.10.
Owner S & A Mares **Bred** Mrs J Keegan **Trained** Earlswood, Monmouths
FOCUS
They went a fair gallop taking the ground into consideration, and Beau Sancy ran out a ready winner of this moderate handicap.
Berbatov Official explanation: jockey said gelding ran too freely

3571 BET TO THE 90TH MINUTE WITH EXTRABET H'CAP 1m 30y
4:20 (4:23) (Class 6) (0-65,71) 4-Y-0+ **£3,238** (£963; £481; £240) **Stalls** Low

Form RPR
0423 **1** **Ermine Grey**[18] 2980 6-8-5 **54**.................... LukeMorris(5) 2 62
(A W Carroll) *racd keenly: midfield: rdn and hdwy 2f out: led over 1f out: r.o u.p: all out nr fin* **6/1**[3]
0163 **2** *hd* **Apache Nation (IRE)**[6] 3381 4-9-2 **60**.................... RoystonFfrench 3 68
(M Dods) *chsd ldr tl rdn over 2f out: str chal and ev ch ins fnl f: r.o* **4/1**[1]
0401 **3** *1 ¼* **Top Dirham**[12] 3195 9-8-11 **55**.................... DaleGibson 7 60
(M W Easterby) *trckd ldrs: led gng wl 2f out: rdn and hdd over 1f out: nt qckn ins fnl f* **7/1**
3311 **4** *hd* **Azreme**[6] 3381 7-9-13 **71** 6ex.................... AmirQuinn 8 75
(P Howling) *midfield: hdwy over 2f out: rdn and ev ch over 1f out: kpt on u.p ins fnl f: hld towards fin* **5/1**[2]
-051 **5** *hd* **Emily's Place (IRE)**[13] 3156 4-9-9 **67**.................... JimmyQuinn 4 71
(J Pearce) *chsd ldrs: rdn 2f out: ev ch ent fnl f: no ex towards fin* **4/1**[1]
0253 **6** *½* **Gracie's Gift (IRE)**[23] 2831 5-9-4 **62**.................... DeanMcKeown 5 65
(A G Newcombe) *hld up: rdn and hdwy 2f out: kpt on ins fnl f: nt pce of ldrs* **13/2**
0050 **7** *4* **Northern Boy (USA)**[13] 3155 4-9-4 **62**.................... PhillipMakin 9 56
(T D Barron) *racd keenly: hld up: rdn over 2f out: nvr trbld ldrs* **12/1**
-000 **8** *hd* **First Show**[34] 2514 5-9-4 **65**....................(bt[1]) LiamJones(3) 6 59
(R A Harris) *midfield: rdn over 2f out: no imp fnl f* **20/1**
0015 **9** *nk* **Scotty's Future (IRE)**[5] 3403 9-8-9 **53** ow1.......... StephenDonohoe 10 46
(A Berry) *bhd: rdn over 2f out: nvr on terms* **14/1**
600 **10** *11* **Blue Bird's Dream**[64] 1679 4-8-13 **57**.................... DavidAllan 1 26
(E J Alston) *led: rdn and hdd 2f out: wknd over 1f out* **20/1**
1m 52.56s (7.05) **Going Correction** +0.875s/f (Soft) **10** Ran SP% **120.7**
Speed ratings (Par 101):99,98,97,97,97 96,92,92,92,81
CSF £31.40 CT £176.12 TOTE £8.00: £2.30, £2.20, £2.50; EX 40.50.
Owner L M Baker **Bred** D Brocklehurst **Trained** Cropthorne, Worcs
FOCUS
A moderate but competitive contest and any amount held a chance racing into the final furlong and a half.
Blue Bird's Dream Official explanation: jockey said gelding hung left

3572 FREEPHONE EXTRABET 0800 3777171 H'CAP 7f 30y
4:50 (4:51) (Class 5) (0-70,70) 4-Y-0+ **£3,886** (£1,156; £577; £288) **Stalls** Low

Form RPR
-056 **1** **Scotland The Brave**[12] 3194 7-9-3 **66**....................(v) DarryllHolland 1 76
(J D Bethell) *mde all: rdn over 1f out: r.o ins fnl f* **5/1**[2]
3006 **2** *1 ¼* **Coup D'Etat**[30] 2621 5-9-3 **66**....................(b[1]) JohnEgan 10 73
(R A Harris) *hld up: hdwy 2f out: rdn and edgd lft to take 2nd over 1f out: no imp on wnr nr fin* **14/1**
/-02 **3** *2* **Zamalik (USA)**[12] 3194 4-9-6 **69**.................... DavidAllan 3 71
(E J Alston) *in tch: outpcd 2f out: rallied to chse ldrs ins fnl f: styd on* **4/1**[1]
6042 **4** *½* **Digital**[6] 3375 10-8-1 **57**.................... MatthewDavies(7) 7 58
(M R Channon) *hld up: hdwy over 2f out: rdn over 1f out: kpt on ins fnl f: hld towards fin* **4/1**[1]
0045 **5** *5* **Breaking Shadow (IRE)**[16] 3053 5-9-3 **66**.................... JimmyQuinn 9 54
(M A Peill) *racd keenly: in tch: rdn over 1f out: wknd ins fnl f* **15/2**
140- **6** *1 ½* **Middleton Grey**[233] 6580 9-9-7 **70**....................(b) FergusSweeney 5 54
(A G Newcombe) *hld up: rdn over 1f out: nvr on terms w ldrs* **16/1**
0301 **7** *¾* **Attacca**[6] 3375 6-8-2 **54** 6ex.................... AndrewElliott(3) 6 37
(J R Weymes) *in tch: rdn over 1f out: wknd ins fnl f* **12/1**
1304 **8** *4* **Megalo Maniac**[12] 3185 4-8-9 **58**.................... TonyHamilton 4 31
(R A Fahey) *hld up: rdn 2f out: nvr on terms* **6/1**[3]
9 *½* **Takaamul**[441] 1323 4-9-4 **67**.................... AdrianScholes 2 38
(K A Morgan) *prom tl rdn and wknd over 1f out* **40/1**
0430 **10** *6* **Campo Bueno (FR)**[5] 3401 5-9-3 **66**....................(b) StephenDonohoe 8 22
(A Berry) *prom tl rdn and wknd over 2f out* **15/2**
1m 37.65s (5.59) **Going Correction** +0.875s/f (Soft) **10** Ran SP% **117.2**
Speed ratings (Par 103):103,101,99,98,93 91,90,85,85,78
CSF £72.78 CT £315.33 TOTE £6.70: £2.40, £2.40, £2.00; EX 71.20 Place 6 £114.23, Place 5 £63.57..
Owner Robert Gibbons **Bred** R F Gibbons **Trained** Middleham Moor, N Yorks
■ Stewards' Enquiry : Matthew Davies two-day ban: used whip above shoulder height (Jul 25-26)
FOCUS
Just an ordinary contest.
Coup D'Etat Official explanation: jockey said gelding hung badly left
T/Plt: £177.70 to a £1 stake. Pool: £77,163.50. 316.95 winning tickets. T/Qpdt: £27.10 to a £1 stake. Pool: £4,217.70. 115.10 winning tickets. DO

3138 CURRAGH (R-H)
Sunday, July 15
OFFICIAL GOING: Straight course - heavy; round course - soft to heavy

3573a LADBROKES ROCKINGHAM H'CAP (PREMIER HANDICAP) 5f
1:55 (1:55) 3-Y-0+
£48,729 (£15,486; £7,378; £2,513; £1,702; £891)

RPR
1 **Rainbow Rising (IRE)**[16] 3073 5-8-9 87.................... DPMcDonogh 1 100
(Adrian McGuinness, Ire) *trckd ldrs: rdn to ld 1f out: kpt on wl u.p* **15/2**
2 *½* **Lidanski (IRE)**[15] 3116 4-8-4 82.................... CDHayes 2 93
(W P Mullins, Ire) *in rr of mid-div: 12th 2f out: hdwy and short of room 1 1/2f out: wnt 2nd ins fnl f: kpt on wl* **20/1**
3 *1* **Senor Benny (USA)**[58] 1829 8-9-3 95.................... MJKinane 4 103
(M McDonagh, Ire) *in rr tl 2f out: prog on outer fnl f: kpt on wl: nvr nrr* **16/1**
4 *hd* **Hogmaneigh (IRE)**[22] 2858 4-9-12 104.................... KJManning 5 111
(S C Williams) *in rr: 13th 1/2-way: 9th and rdn 1f out: styd on wl: nvr nrr* **7/1**[3]
5 *1 ¾* **Nanotech (IRE)**[10] 3252 3-8-4 87.................... MCHussey 12 88
(Jarlath P Fahey, Ire) *prom: rdn and no ex fr 1 1/2f out* **14/1**
6 *shd* **Snaefell (IRE)**[14] 3139 3-9-9 106.................... JMurtagh 3 106
(M Halford, Ire) *trckd ldrs: no ex fr 2f out* **5/1**[2]
7 *shd* **If Paradise**[16] 3073 6-8-6 84....................(b) RPCleary 9 84
(M Halford, Ire) *prom: rdn and no ex fr 1 1/2f out* **20/1**
8 *nk* **Green Park (IRE)**[16] 3050 4-9-1 93.................... PaulHanagan 8 92
(R A Fahey) *mid-div: rdn 1 1/2f out: checked sltly 1f out: no ex* **4/1**[1]
9 *shd* **Shinko Dancer (IRE)**[16] 3073 4-8-1 82.................... DJMoran(3) 6 80
(H Rogers, Ire) *sn led: rdn and hdd 1f out: sn wknd* **16/1**
10 *hd* **Tajneed (IRE)**[14] 3140 4-8-12 90....................(bt) PJSmullen 15 88
(D K Weld, Ire) *in rr of mid-div: rdn and no ex fr 1 1/2f out* **8/1**
11 *hd* **Johnstown Lad (IRE)**[9] 3289 3-8-5 88....................(t) WJSupple 14 85
(Niall Moran, Ire) *chsd ldrs on outer: rdn and no ex fr 1 1/2f out* **12/1**
12 *1 ½* **Kingsdale Ocean (IRE)**[266] 6112 4-9-5 97....................(b[1]) JAHeffernan 11 89
(Ms Florence Mills, Ire) *mid-div: rdn and wknd fr 1 1/2f out* **20/1**
13 *hd* **King Of Swords (IRE)**[30] 2643 3-8-4 90.................... PBBeggy(3) 7 81
(Tracey Collins, Ire) *mid-div: wknd fr 2f out* **16/1**
14 *3* **Miss Donovan**[58] 1829 4-8-3 86.................... OCasey(5) 10 66
(Patrick J Moloney, Ire) *trckd ldrs: wknd fr 2f out* **16/1**
63.90 secs (2.60) **Going Correction** +0.75s/f (Yiel)
WFA 3 from 4yo+ 5lb **15** Ran SP% **124.2**
Speed ratings: 109,108,106,106,103 103,103,102,102,102 101,99,99,94
CSF £156.20 CT £1456.51 TOTE £8.90: £2.60, £6.30, £4.70; DF 175.30.
Owner Goose Syndicate **Bred** John Osbourne & Edgeridge Ltd **Trained** Lusk, Co Dublin
■ This race was salvaged from the waterlogged card on Saturday.
FOCUS
Solid form despite the bunch finish.
NOTEBOOK
Rainbow Rising(IRE), a progressive gelding, was sharper for his recent reappearance. (op 8/1)
Hogmaneigh(IRE) faced no easy task under topweight and was putting in his best work in the closing stages. (op 9/1)
Green Park(IRE) was switched out to challenge nearing the final furlong but didn't help his chances by drifting right.

3574a DUBAI DUTY FREE ANGLESEY STKS (GROUP 3) 6f 63y
2:25 (2:26) 2-Y-0 **£32,989** (£9,679; £4,611; £1,570)

RPR
1 **Myboycharlie (IRE)**[15] 3115 2-9-1.................... WMLordan 1 114+
(T Stack, Ire) *hld up and t.k.h early: hdwy travelling wl into 3rd 2f out: led over 1f out: sn qcknd clr: impressive* **2/1**[2]
2 *7* **Tuscan Evening (IRE)**[16] 3071 2-8-12.................... DMGrant 5 91
(John Joseph Murphy, Ire) *racd in cl 2nd: pushed along 1/2-way: led briefly 1 1/2f out: sn hdd: no imp on wnr: kpt on same pce fnl f* **11/2**[3]
3 *½* **Chun Tosaigh (USA)** 2-9-1.................... KJManning 7 93
(J S Bolger, Ire) *hld up: rdn fr 2f out: wnt mod 3rd 1f out: kpt on* **16/1**
4 *3 ½* **South Dakota (IRE)**[14] 3141 2-9-1.................... JAHeffernan 4 83
(A P O'Brien, Ire) *sn led: rdn 2f out: hdd 1 1/2f out: wknd ins fnl f* **6/4**[1]
5 *2* **Abolition (USA)**[43] 2251 2-9-1.................... KDarley 6 77
(M Johnston) *racd in cl 3rd: rdn and wknd fr 2f out* **6/1**
1m 21.7s (4.20) **Going Correction** +0.75s/f (Yiel) **8** Ran SP% **108.9**
Speed ratings: 102,92,92,87,84
CSF £12.51 TOTE £2.70: £1.40, £1.90; DF 11.60.
Owner Hammersboy - I.R.S.com Syndicate **Bred** Denis Noonan **Trained** Golden, Co Tipperary
FOCUS
The winner was very impressive having travelled all over the opposition from some way out. The race has been rated through the runner-up.

NOTEBOOK

Myboycharlie(IRE), who created a favourable impression when winning over this course on his debut on Irish Derby weekend, is clearly going the right way to judge by this impressive victory. Held up, he was travelling much better than his rivals two furlongs out and quickened approaching the final furlong to surge clear under hands-and-heels riding. His trainer feared that the heavy ground might prove the colt's undoing but that was certainly not the case, although connections expect him to be suited by drier ground. William Hill go 25-1 for the 2000 Guineas, for which the winner is quoted at 20-1 by the sponsors Stan James and Boylesports. The Gimcrack Stakes might be the next stop followed by either the National Stakes back at the Curragh in September or the Dewhurst. (op 7/4)

Tuscan Evening(IRE), twice placed at Listed level, remains a maiden, but she produced another solid performance. She disputed the early lead and kept on under pressure two furlongs out, although easily outpaced by the winner. (op 7/1)

Chun Tosaigh(USA), making his debut, lost his place after halfway but was coming back in the closing stages. He should not have much difficulty winning a maiden. (op 14/1)

South Dakota(IRE) had experience on his side. He had performed creditably on his three runs since winning at Tipperary on his debut and had finished well when second to stablemate Lizard Island in a slowly-run Railway Stakes here last month. However, he was disappointing here and, after making much of the running, he weakened quickly well over a furlong out. The ground was hardly ideal for him, although it was soft to heavy when he ran second here on his previous start. (op 7/4 tchd 11/8)

Abolition(USA), a beaten favourite on his two previous starts, was encountering heavy ground for the first time and was the first beaten fully two furlongs out. (op 11/2)

3575a EMIRATES AIRLINE MINSTREL STKS (GROUP 3) 7f

2:55 (2:55) 3-Y-0+ **£35,135** (£10,270; £4,864; £1,621)

RPR

1 **Redstone Dancer (IRE)**[11] [3222] 5-9-7 110 .... PShanahan 1 — 113
(Miss S Collins, Ire) *trckd ldrs in 3rd: pushed along to dispute ld 1 1/2f out: led narrowly over 1f out: kpt on wl ins fnl f* **9/4**[2]

2 *3/4* **Hard Rock City (USA)**[14] [3144] 7-9-7 106 .... JAHeffernan 3 — 111
(M J Grassick, Ire) *led: rdn along 2f out: jnd 1 1/2f out: hdd over 1f out: kpt on same pce fnl f* **7/2**[3]

3 *1 1/4* **Evening Time (IRE)**[280] [5850] 3-8-10 107 .... DPMcDonogh 4 — 105
(Kevin Prendergast, Ire) *hld up in 4th: prog to dispute ld briefly 1 1/2f out: hdd over 1f out: no ex fnl f* **1/1**[1]

4 *3* **Majestic Times (IRE)**[14] [3140] 7-9-7 102 .... NGMcCullagh 2 — 100
(Liam McAteer, Ire) *trckd ldr in 2nd: rdn along 2f out: no imp fr 1 1/2f out* **16/1**

1m 32.7s (5.20) **Going Correction** +0.75s/f (Yiel)
WFA 3 from 5yo+ 8lb — **4** Ran SP% **108.9**
Speed ratings: 100,99,97,94
CSF £9.89 TOTE £2.90; DF 8.40.
Owner K Lynch **Bred** Newberry Stud Company **Trained** the Curragh, Co Kildare

FOCUS

A small field but still a competitive renewal of this Group 3 event. It has been rated through the runner-up.

NOTEBOOK

Redstone Dancer(IRE), who is in foal to Refuse To Bend, landed a hat-trick in what might have been her final start. She had won a similar race over this trip at Leopardstown on her previous run and, while she handles all types of going, she is very effective on the type of ground she encountered here. She was asked to raise her effort well over a furlong out and responded to lead soon afterwards, running on well to the line. Whether she has one more run before being retired within the next few weeks has yet to be decided. (op 5/4)

Hard Rock City(USA), another who appears adaptable for ground, had been a model of consistency until putting two ordinary runs together following a successful reappearance at Gowran Park. He ran back to form when beaten half a length by Danehill Music in a 1m Listed event here on his previous start and produced another solid effort, making the running and keeping on under pressure when headed. (op 11/2)

Evening Time(IRE), a wide-margin winner on testing ground on both her starts last season, was making a delayed start to her campaign, having suffered muscle problems in the spring. Held up, she ranged up on the outside of her rivals two furlongs out but was unable to pick up when the winner went about her business and could find no extra inside the final furlong. She was possibly a bit rusty. (op 5/4)

Majestic Times(IRE), more effective over shorter distances, was far from disgraced, although unable to trouble the principals over the last two furlongs.

3576a DARLEY IRISH OAKS (GROUP 1) (FILLIES) 1m 4f

3:30 (3:32) 3-Y-0

£189,527 (£64,527; £30,743; £10,472; £7,094; £3,716)

RPR

1 **Peeping Fawn (USA)**[15] [3117] 3-9-0 118 .... JMurtagh 4 — 123+
(A P O'Brien, Ire) *mid-div: 6th 3f out: pushed along to ld over 1f out: kpt on wl fnl f: comf* **3/1**[2]

2 *3 1/2* **Light Shift (USA)**[44] [2211] 3-9-0 .... TedDurcan 5 — 117
(H R A Cecil) *trckd ldrs: 4th 3f out: rdn to ld briefly 1 1/2f out: hdd over 1f out: kpt on same pce fnl f* **9/4**[1]

3 *2* **All My Loving (IRE)**[24] [2786] 3-9-0 109 .... JAHeffernan 2 — 114
(A P O'Brien, Ire) *a.p: 2nd 3f out: rdn 2f out: kpt on same pce in 3rd fnl f* **5/1**[3]

4 *3* **Timarwa (IRE)**[15] [3117] 3-9-0 109 .... MJKinane 6 — 109
(John M Oxx, Ire) *trckd ldrs: 6th 4f out: rdn and kpt on wout threatening fr 2f out* **7/1**

5 *2* **Profound Beauty (IRE)**[41] [2328] 3-9-0 .... PJSmullen 1 — 106
(D K Weld, Ire) *trckd ldrs: 3rd 3f out: rdn and no ex fr 2f out* **10/1**

6 *4* **Uimhir A Haon (IRE)**[23] [2851] 3-9-0 90 .... CO'Donoghue 10 — 99
(A P O'Brien, Ire) *hld up: rdn along in 9th 4f out: mod 7th 2f out: kpt on one pce* **20/1**

7 *4 1/2* **Four Sins (GER)**[44] [2211] 3-9-0 106 .... FMBerry 12 — 92
(John M Oxx, Ire) *led: rdn 2f out: hdd 1 1/2f out: sn no imp* **10/1**

8 *16* **Vonne Owen (IRE)**[11] [3219] 3-9-0 68 .... DMGrant 11 — 67
(John Joseph Murphy, Ire) *dwlt and in rr: rdn along 5f out: no imp st* **300/1**

9 *3 1/2* **Maid Of Lorn (USA)**[4] [3440] 3-9-0 70 .... PShanahan 9 — 61
(Tracey Collins, Ire) *a towards rr* **200/1**

10 *8* **Athenian Way (IRE)**[23] [2851] 3-9-0 100 .... NGMcCullagh 8 — 48
(John M Oxx, Ire) *towards rr early: prog to trck ldrs after 2f: 2nd 5f out: rdn and wknd fr 4f out* **40/1**

11 *8* **Aqraan**[21] [2918] 3-9-0 95 .... DPMcDonogh 7 — 35
(Kevin Prendergast, Ire) *mid-div tl 1/2-way: rdn and no imp fr 4f out: sn wknd: eased fnl f* **33/1**

12 *dist* **Gaudeamus (USA)**[49] [2065] 3-9-0 103 .... KJManning 3 — —
(J S Bolger, Ire) *mid-div: rdn and wknd fr 4f out: sn bhd: eased fr 2f out: t.o* **80/1**

2m 39.1s (0.20) **Going Correction** +0.375s/f (Good) — **12** Ran SP% **115.3**
Speed ratings: 114,111,110,108,107 104,101,90,88,83 77,—
CSF £9.47 TOTE £3.30: £1.30, £1.10, £1.50; DF 10.50.
Owner Michael Tabor **Bred** Barnett Enterprises **Trained** Ballydoyle, Co Tipperary

■ Johnny Murtagh came in for the ride on Peeping Fawn after Kieren Fallon was injured at Longchamp the day before.

FOCUS

An excellent renewal, featuring the first four from Epsom as well as a couple of promising, lightly raced fillies. Silkwood was missing after scoping badly. Very solid form on paper, despite the ground, and the winner has now produced three top-class efforts in a row. The third is probably the best guide to the level.

NOTEBOOK

Peeping Fawn(USA) has made remarkable progress in the past two months. Already placed in two Classics and a Group 1 winner over 1m2f in that period, she was produced in outstanding shape and ran out a most impressive winner, leading over a furlong out and staying on strongly. Those who had feared after Epsom that the rigours of her campaign might start to take a toll have been shown to be well wide of the mark and she has proved herself a top-class filly over a range of distances, making her a broodmare prospect of the highest calibre. Official explanation: jockey said filly was showing signs of being in season prior to the running of this race (op 4/1)

Light Shift(USA), who had beaten Peeping Fawn fair and square at Epsom, lost nothing in defeat on ground that was possibly not quite as demanding as might have been anticipated but was clearly tougher than anything she had encountered before. She was given every chance, but her spell in the lead from a furlong and a half out always looked like being shortlived, with the winner perfectly placed to cover her move to the front. In all fairness, a third clash between the two on better ground will be needed to form a definitive judgement on their relative merits. (op 7/4)

All My Loving(IRE) was expected by many to cope better than most with the ground but failed to improve on her Epsom showing. Although always well placed, she never seemed to be travelling as well as might have been hoped and could not find a change of gear when it mattered. She is an admirable filly, only just below the very best of her generation over 1m4f. (op 9/2)

Timarwa(IRE) went into the race as a filly with the potential to upgrade her reputation. She gave an honest performance in confirming maiden form with the similarly unexposed Profound Beauty, but did not give the impression of being happy on the ground and was beaten further by Peeping Fawn than in the Pretty Polly. On better ground she can be rated a potential Group 3 winner.

Profound Beauty(IRE) may also have found the ground too soft, but she can yet make up into a Group race-winning filly. (op 12/1 tchd 14/1)

Uimhir A Haon(IRE) did enough to suggest she could prosper if her sights are lowered again.

Four Sins(GER) made much of the running, but her preference for fast ground is well documented. (op 10/1 tchd 12/1)

3577a THALGO LADIES DERBY H'CAP 1m 4f

4:05 (4:05) (60-100,88) 3-Y-0+ **£11,876** (£3,484; £1,660; £565) **Stalls** Far side

RPR

1 **Do The Trick (AUS)**[16] [3070] 6-9-11 69 .... MissLBoswell(5) — 86+
(M Halford, Ire) *trckd ldrs: mod 4th 1/2-way: prog to cl 2nd 4f out: led 3f out: clr 1 1/2f out: kpt on wl: easily* **10/1**

2 *4 1/2* **Always The Groom (IRE)**[10] [3254] 5-10-0 67 .... MissAFoley — 74
(Patrick J Flynn, Ire) *in rr of mid-div: prog into 8th 4f out: rdn in mod 4th 1 1/2f out: kpt on wl to 2nd cl home: no ch w wnr* **12/1**

3 *1/2* **Jalwada**[14] [3143] 5-11-3 84 .... MsKWalsh — 90
(John Queally, Ire) *in rr of mid-div: stdy prog into 6th 4f out: rdn and wnt 2nd 1 1/2f out: no ex and dropped to 3rd cl home* **7/2**[2]

4 *1/2* **Baron De'L (IRE)**[14] [3145] 4-10-2 76 .... MissKAMartin(7) — 82
(Edward P Harty, Ire) *in rr: mod 12th 2f out: r.o wl fnl f: nvr nrr* **25/1**

5 *1* **Polish Power (GER)**[15] [3105] 7-10-11 78 .... MrsSMoore — 82
(J S Moore) *mid-div: prog into 4th 4f out: rdn in mod 3rd 1 1/2f out: no ex fnl f* **14/1**

6 *hd* **Baron De Feypo (IRE)**[10] [3254] 9-9-10 70 .... MissHIMullen(7) — 74
(Patrick O Brady, Ire) *led after 1f: sn clr: reduced advantage 4f out: hdd 3f out: sn no imp* **16/1**

7 *2 1/2* **Kalmez (IRE)**[51] [4941] 4-11-2 88 .... (t) MissNadineForde(5) — 88
(D Broad, Ire) *towards rr: kpt on wout threatening fr 3f out* **33/1**

8 *4 1/2* **Hearthstead Dream**[169] [6268] 6-10-0 74 .... MissJWalsh(7) — 67
(D K Weld, Ire) *mid-div: 9th 4f out: kpt on same pce fr 2f out* **9/1**[3]

9 *hd* **Mutadarek**[22] [2899] 6-10-10 77 .... MissEALalor — 70
(Eoin Griffin, Ire) *hld up: rdn and no imp st* **10/1**

10 *nk* **Very Green (FR)**[39] [2383] 5-9-8 66 .... MissKFerris(5) — 58
(D T Hughes, Ire) *trckd ldrs: 5th 4f out: no imp fr 3f out* **25/1**

11 *3/4* **Loyal Focus (IRE)**[14] [3145] 6-10-2 76 .... MissSCiccone(7) — 67
(D K Weld, Ire) *led early: prom after 1f: rdn and wknd fr 4f out* **16/1**

12 *1 3/4* **Sendar (FR)**[29] [2615] 6-9-8 66 .... MissLLynch(5) — 55
(John Joseph Murphy, Ire) *mid-div: wknd fr 4f out* **33/1**

13 *4 1/2* **Hue**[17] [3027] 6-10-3 70 .... (b) MissLEllison — 52
(B Ellison) *mid-div: wknd fr 4f out* **10/1**

14 *1/2* **Rhythm 'N' Blues (IRE)**[35] [2498] 4-10-4 78 .... MsSQuirke(7) — 59
(John M Oxx, Ire) *a bhd* **25/1**

15 *3* **Right Or Wrong (IRE)**[15] [3118] 3-10-7 87 .... MissNCarberry — 64
(Noel Meade, Ire) *trckd ldrs: 3rd 4f out: sn rdn and wknd: eased fnl f* **5/2**[1]

16 *7* **All Sorts Star (IRE)**[258] [6268] 7-10-11 78 .... MrsALee — 44
(Andrew Lee, Ire) *a towards rr* **20/1**

17 *dist* **Winter Footprints (IRE)**[16] [3072] 3-9-3 76 ow3 .... MissGRyan(7) — —
(William Hayes, Ire) *mid-div: wknd 5f out: eased under 2f out: t.o* **66/1**

2m 47.8s (8.90) **Going Correction** +0.375s/f (Good)
WFA 3 from 4yo+ 13lb — **17** Ran SP% **137.9**
Speed ratings: 85,82,81,81,80 80,78,75,75,75 75,73,70,70,68 63,—
CSF £130.80 TOTE £13.60: £2.70, £2.40, £1.50, £7.50; DF 196.10.
Owner Paul Rooney **Bred** Jasmine Park **Trained** the Curragh, Co Kildare

FOCUS

A decent handicap.

NOTEBOOK

Polish Power(GER), a reliable British-based handicapper, was not disgraced and only gave best in the battle for minor money in the closing stages. (op 16/1)

Hue was a bit disappointing as he is proven in these conditions, but the likelihood is that the trip was just too sharp.

Right Or Wrong(IRE) Official explanation: vet said colt was found to be blowing hard post race

3578a KILBOY ESTATE STKS (LISTED RACE) (F&M) 1m 1f

4:35 (4:35) 3-Y-0+ **£26,391** (£7,743; £3,689; £1,256)

RPR

1 **Alexander Tango (IRE)**[49] [2065] 3-9-2 106 .... WMLordan 11 — 109
(T Stack, Ire) *trckd ldrs: 3rd 3f out: led 2f out: rdn and jnd fnl f: regained ld cl home: all out* **4/1**[2]

2 *1/2* **She's Our Mark**[11] [3222] 3-8-11 105 .... DMGrant 5 — 103
(Patrick J Flynn, Ire) *stmbld leaving stalls: hld up early: mid-div on outer 1/2-way: 8th 3f out: r.o wl fr 1 1/2f out: disp ld fnl f: hdd & no ex cl home* **9/2**[3]

3 *1 3/4* **Cherry Hinton**[23] [2814] 3-8-11 100 .... JAHeffernan 7 — 100
(A P O'Brien, Ire) *trckd ldrs: 4th 3f out: rdn in 3rd 2f out: kpt on one pce* **9/2**[3]

4 1 1/4 **Dani's Girl (IRE)**[15] [3116] 4-9-7 94 FMBerry 6 99
(P A Fahy, Ire) *dwlt and in rr: prog into 6th 3f out: rdn and kpt on one pce fr 1 1/2f out* **20/1**
5 shd **You're Beautiful (USA)**[28] [2702] 3-8-11 92 CO'Donoghue 10 97
(David Wachman, Ire) *trckd ldr in 2nd: rdn 3f out: no ex fr 1 1/2f out* **20/1**
6 shd **Deauville Vision (IRE)**[50] [2053] 4-9-7 104 JMurtagh 4 98
(M Halford, Ire) *hld up in rr: kpt on wout threatening fr 3f out* **2/1**[1]
7 shd **Dawla**[18] [3007] 3-8-11 92 DPMcDonogh 1 97
(Kevin Prendergast, Ire) *mid-div: 5th 3f out: no imp fr 2f out* **10/1**
8 3/4 **Mistress Bailey (IRE)**[11] [3223] 4-9-7 83 WJSupple 8 97
(Nicholas Cox, Ire) *hld up: rdn and no imp fr 3f out* **50/1**
9 4 **Jalmira (IRE)**[21] [2918] 6-9-7 88 WJLee 9 89
(C F Swan, Ire) *led taking t.k.h: rdn and hdd 2f out: sn wknd* **14/1**
10 7 **In The Fashion (IRE)**[30] [2645] 4-9-7 85 CDHayes 2 76
(H Rogers, Ire) *dwlt: sn trckd ldrs: 7th 3f out: sn rdn and wknd* **33/1**
11 9 **Dapple Grey (IRE)**[387] [2840] 4-9-7 85 PJSmullen 3 59
(T Stack, Ire) *mid-div: rdn and wknd fr 3f out* **33/1**

2m 3.50s (5.40) **Going Correction** +0.675s/f (Yiel)
WFA 3 from 4yo+ 10lb 11 Ran SP% **122.8**
Speed ratings: 103,102,101,99,99 99,99,98,95,89 81
CSF £22.02 TOTE £5.00: £1.90, £1.80, £2.20; DF 23.40.
Owner Noel O'Callaghan **Bred** Philip Brady **Trained** Golden, Co Tipperary

FOCUS
Solid enough Listed form rated through the third and fourth.

NOTEBOOK
Alexander Tango(IRE), a Group 3 winner over 1m at Leopardstown and fourth in the Irish 1000 Guineas on her previous start, had shown her best form on fast ground but she coped with the testing conditions here in a race run at an ordinary pace. She took advantage of a big gap on the inside to deliver her challenge and lead well over a furlong out. She was hard pressed inside the final furlong but was always doing enough to hold on. Her trainer that she could run in the Nassau Stakes at Goodwood next. (op 7/2)
She's Our Mark, winner of a maiden and a handicap, had finished second to the smart Redstone Dancer in a 7f Group 3 event at Leopardstown on her previous start. Stepping up in trip, she seemed to stumble leaving the stalls and was held up before coming with a determined effort on the outside in the straight. She looked a danger to the winner early in the final furlong but, although she kept on, she was being held near the finish. (op 9/2 tchd 4/1)
Cherry Hinton, beaten 11 lengths when stepped up in class and trip in the Vodafone Oaks, tracked the leaders and kept on without making much impression on the first two inside the final furlong. She is capable of success at up to 1m2f on better ground than she encountered here. (op 9/2 tchd 5/1)
Dani's Girl(IRE), winner of a maiden and a fillies' handicap over 7f last season, had performed in Group 3 events here this season and had just lost out in a handicap at Naas two runs back. Slowly away, she stayed on steadily in the straight and it will be no surprise to see her add to her tally at around this distance. (op 20/1 tchd 25/1)
You're Beautiful(USA), dropping back in trip, having been well beaten after racing prominently in a 1m4f Group 3 event at Cork last month, raced in second place for much of the journey and had every chance before finding no extra from well over a furlong out.
Deauville Vision(IRE), suited by this sort of ground, had run well below her best on firm ground here last time and again failed to show what she is capable of. She stayed on in the straight but never posed a threat. (op 5/2)

3579a KEENELAND INTERNATIONAL STKS (GROUP 3) 1m 1f
5:05 (5:05) 3-Y-0+ £35,135 (£10,270; £4,864; £1,621)

RPR
1 **Decado (IRE)**[63] [1696] 4-9-7 111 DPMcDonogh 4 114
(Kevin Prendergast, Ire) *trckd ldr in 2nd: narrowly led travelling wl 2 1/2f out: rdn and strly pressed fr 1 1/2f out: drvn out and kpt on wl ins fnl f* **11/8**[1]
2 2 **Cougar Bay (IRE)**[14] [3144] 4-9-7 107 MJKinane 3 110
(David Wachman, Ire) *led: rdn and hdd 2 1/2f out: strly pressed wnr fr 1 1/2f out: no ex ins fnl f* **3/1**[3]
3 3 1/2 **Danehill Music (IRE)**[14] [3144] 4-9-4 104 WMLordan 5 100
(David Wachman, Ire) *hld up in 4th: rdn and disp 3rd fr 3f out: kpt on same pce fr 2f out* **5/2**[2]
4 1/2 **Trinity College (USA)**[24] [2789] 3-8-11 107 JAHeffernan 1 101
(A P O'Brien, Ire) *racd in 3rd: rdn 3f out: no imp fr 2f out* **7/1**

2m 1.20s (3.10) **Going Correction** +0.675s/f (Yiel)
WFA 3 from 4yo+ 10lb 5 Ran SP% **108.2**
Speed ratings: 113,111,108,107
CSF £5.70 TOTE £1.80; DF 5.60.
Owner Mrs Catherine O'Flynn **Bred** Stonehorn Stud Farms Ltd **Trained** Friarstown, Co Kildare
■ This was carried forward from the abandoned card on Saturday.

FOCUS
A small field and only the first two can be said to have run to their best.

NOTEBOOK
Decado(IRE), last season's Irish 2000 Guineas third, made the most of a good opportunity to record his first success since the early part of his three-year-old career. As expected, the Danehill Dancer colt proved at home on the ground, though after travelling well he made fairly heavy weather of things. (op 11/10 tchd 13/8)
Cougar Bay(IRE) emerged with credit with a third successive placed effort, reversing form in the process with his stablemate Danehill Music, who had relegated him to third when winning a Listed contest at the venue two weeks previously. (op 5/1 tchd 11/4)
Danehill Music(IRE) was possibly feeling the effects of a hard race here a fortnight earlier and was below her best. She never really threatened the first two, though she did get the better of a private battle for third with Trinity College. (op 9/4 tchd 2/1)
Trinity College(USA) looked unsuited by the ground. (op 8/1)

3580 - (Foreign Racing) - See Raceform Interactive

2408 FRANKFURT (L-H)
Sunday, July 15

OFFICIAL GOING: Good

3581a GROSSE HESSEN MEILE - FRAPORT AG POKAL (GROUP 3) 1m
3:50 (4:03) 3-Y-0+ £21,622 (£6,757; £3,378; £2,027)

RPR
1 **Aspectus (IRE)**[22] [2903] 4-9-6 FJohansson 3 111
(H Blume, Germany) *3rd early: wnt 2nd after 2f: led 1 1/2f out: drvn out* **6/5**[1]
2 1/2 **Trip To The Moon**[20] [2953] 4-8-12 J-LMartinez 2 102
(M Delzangles, France) *hld up in 4th: 5th st: wnt 2nd ins fnl f: r.o* **32/10**[3]
3 1 1/2 **Konig Turf (GER)**[22] [2903] 5-9-4 THellier 6 105
(C Sprengel, Germany) *5th early: disputing 3rd on outside ent st: hrd rdn ins fnl f: styd on to take 3rd cl home* **51/10**
4 hd **Alaska River (GER)**[95] [1005] 3-8-6 ow1 AStarke 1 102
(P Schiergen, Germany) *2nd early: disputing 3rd on ins ent st: lost 3rd cl home* **43/10**
5 1/2 **Apollo Star (GER)**[42] [2295] 5-9-6 ASuborics 4 106
(Mario Hofer, Germany) *led to 1 1/2f out: one pce* **28/10**[2]
6 6 **Diable (GER)**[59] [1800] 8-9-0 ADeVries 5 88
(H Hesse, Germany) *last thrght* **30/1**

1m 34.5s (94.50)
WFA 3 from 4yo+ 9lb 6 Ran SP% **134.1**
(including 10 Euro stake): WIN 22; PL 12, 12; SF 216.
Owner Gestut Rottgen **Bred** Gestut Roettgen **Trained** Germany

3341 AYR (L-H)
Monday, July 16

OFFICIAL GOING: Good to soft
Once again the runners were using the hurdles track on the round course.
Wind: Breezy, half against Weather: Cloudy

3582 E B F JOIN WBX.COM FOR £150 FREE BETS MAIDEN STKS 6f
2:00 (2:02) (Class 4) 2-Y-O £3,886 (£1,156; £577; £288) Stalls High

Form RPR
62 1 **Merchant Of Dubai**[23] [2863] 2-9-3 0 JamieSpencer 5 78
(G A Swinbank) *midfield: sn drvn along: hdwy 2f out: styd on wl fnl f to ld nr fin* **11/4**[1]
42 2 nk **Atabaas Pride**[46] [2166] 2-9-3 0 KDarley 11 77
(M Johnston) *cl up: rdn to ld over 1f out: edgd rt ent fnl f: edgd lft and hdd nr fin* **3/1**[2]
3 3 **Cathedral Walk (USA)** 2-9-3 0 PatCosgrave 10 68+
(K R Burke) *in tch: effrt over 2f out: kpt on fnl f: nt rch first 2* **20/1**
4 3/4 **Diamond Lass (IRE)** 2-8-12 0 PaulHanagan 15 61
(R A Fahey) *chsd ldrs: effrt and ev ch 2f out: one pce fnl f* **9/1**
5 1 **Howards Hope** 2-9-3 0 PhillipMakin 6 63
(I Semple) *midfield: sn pushed along: effrt 2f out: no imp* **20/1**
6 6 nk **Rio Rocket (IRE)**[39] [2392] 2-8-12 0 PaulQuinn 8 57
(G A Swinbank) *prom: effrt and ev ch over 2f out: no ex fnl f* **33/1**
7 5 **Joinedupwriting** 2-9-3 0 DeanMcKeown 16 47
(R M Whitaker) *dwlt: sn midfield: drvn and outpcd fr over 2f out* **28/1**
05 8 hd **Marie Camargo**[23] [2888] 2-8-9 0 JamieMoriarty(3) 7 41
(R A Fahey) *hld up: pushed along 3f out: nvr rchd ldrs* **25/1**
9 nk **Senorita Parkes** 2-8-12 0 PaulMulrennan 1 46+
(K A Ryan) *swtchd to stands' side sn after s: led to over 1f out: sn btn* **9/1**
10 3 **Jazz Stick (IRE)**[74] [1441] 2-9-3 0 TonyHamilton 3 36
(I Semple) *missed break: nvr on terms* **16/1**
11 2 **Call For Liberty (IRE)** 2-9-3 0 PaulEddery 12 30
(B Smart) *prom tl rdn and wknd over 2f out* **9/2**[3]
12 3/4 **Killer Class** 2-8-5 0 GaryBartley(7) 13 23
(J S Goldie) *s.s: nvr on terms* **50/1**
0 13 1 **Miss Sunshine**[8] [3341] 2-8-5 0 KellyHarrison(7) 2 20
(J S Goldie) *bhd on outside: sn pushed along: struggling fr 1/2-way* **100/1**
0 14 nk **Magnushomestwo (IRE)**[19] [2984] 2-9-3 0 FrancisNorton 14 24
(A Berry) *bhd: pushed along 1/2-way: sn btn* **100/1**

1m 15.9s (2.23) **Going Correction** +0.20s/f (Good) 14 Ran SP% **119.4**
Speed ratings (Par 96): 93,92,88,87,86 85,79,78,78,74 71,70,69,69
CSF £9.79 TOTE £3.70: £1.50, £1.30, £5.80; EX 10.10.
Owner Highland Racing 2 **Bred** A Smith **Trained** Melsonby, N Yorks

FOCUS
Little strength in depth but the first two, who pulled clear of the remainder, are fair sorts capable of better still. The pace was sound.

NOTEBOOK
Merchant Of Dubai ◆, a fair sort with plenty of scope, has improved with every start and turned in his best effort yet. Victory looked unlikely for much of the way on this first run on easy ground but he showed a determined attitude to beat a fair sort, with the pair clear of the rest. He should stay 7f and appeals as the sort to win more races. (op 7-2)
Atabaas Pride had shown fair form on his first two starts on a sound surface and ran equally as well on this first run on easy ground. His tendency to wander both ways was less marked than it was on his previous start and he may prefer this sort of ground and, given the way he went through this race, he looks sure to win a similar race at the very least. (op 5-2 tchd 4-1 in a place)
Cathedral Walk(USA), from a stable that has done well in the juvenile department this term, looked green for this racecourse debut but showed more than enough to suggest an ordinary race can be found, especially when upped to 7f.
Diamond Lass(IRE) cost 75,000gns earlier this year and is out of a half-sister to a couple of very smart sprinters. She was relatively easy to back but she showed enough on this racecourse debut, despite having the run of the race, to suggest an ordinary event can be found. (op 12-1)
Howards Hope, out of a triple 7-9f winner at three years, was easy to back but showed ability on this racecourse debut. He left the impression that the step up to 7f would be very much to his liking and he is likely to be placed to best advantage. (op 25-1)
Rio Rocket(IRE), the lesser fancied of the Swinbank pair, fared a good deal better than on her debut in a Haydock claimer last month. She finished clear of the remainder but looks the sort to do better in ordinary nursery company in due course.
Senorita Parkes, a half-sister to a couple of juvenile winners, shaped better than the bare form after being switched from the widest draw on this racecourse debut and is entitled to improve a fair bit for the experience. (op 14-1)
Jazz Stick(IRE) Official explanation: jockey said colt reared as stalls opened
Call For Liberty(IRE), from a stable that has done very well with its juveniles this term, attracted plenty of support but proved a disappointment on this racecourse debut. He had obviously been showing a fair bit at home and he is well worth another chance, especially on a sound surface. (op 7-2)

3583 GILES INSURANCE CHARITIES H'CAP 6f
2:30 (2:31) (Class 5) (0-70,65) 3-Y-O £3,886 (£1,156; £577; £288) Stalls High

Form RPR
35-0 1 **Equuleus Pictor**[45] [2197] 3-9-8 64 FrancisNorton 5 71
(J L Spearing) *cl up on stands' side: led over 2f out: edgd lft ins fnl f: hld on wl* **12/1**
546 2 nk **Dressed To Dance (IRE)**[17] [3066] 3-9-9 65 (v) KDarley 12 71
(N Tinkler) *dwlt: bhd on stands' side: hdwy over 2f out: chsd wnr ins fnl f: jst hld* **13/2**[3]
0-30 3 2 1/2 **Triple Shadow**[17] [3054] 3-9-9 65 PhillipMakin 7 64
(T D Barron) *cl up on stands' side: effrt 2f out: kpt on same pce fnl f* **10/1**
2134 4 1/2 **Cheery Cat (USA)**[8] [3342] 3-9-4 60 (p) TonyHamilton 8 57
(D W Barker) *chsd stands' side ldrs: drvn 1/2-way: one pce over 1f out* **5/1**[1]

4-04 **5** 1 ½ **Davaye**[24] 2821 3-9-6 **65** .... AndrewElliott(3) 10 58
(K R Burke) *trckd stands' side ldrs: drvn 1/2-way: no ex over 1f out* **9/1**
-662 **6** 2 **Aussie Blue (IRE)**[23] 2892 3-8-8 **55** .... (v[1]) MichaelJStainton(5) 9 42
(R M Whitaker) *prom on stands' side: effrt over 2f out: sn no ex* **11/2**[2]
6003 **7** hd **Smash N'Grab (IRE)**[28] 2713 3-8-10 **52** .... PatCosgrave 13 38
(K A Ryan) *led on stands' side to over 2f out: wknd over 1f out* **12/1**
6022 **8** 2 ½ **Mangano**[8] 3342 3-8-0 **49** .... DanielleMcCreery(7) 11 28
(A Berry) *towards rr on stands' side: pushed along and hdwy over 1f out: nvr nrr* **8/1**
5530 **9** shd **Soviet Sound (IRE)**[10] 3285 3-8-9 **51** .... (b[1]) PaulMulrennan 14 29
(Jedd O'Keeffe) *bhd on stands' side: pushed along 1/2-way: n.d* **14/1**
1025 **10** 1 ¾ **Almora Guru**[46] 2172 3-9-2 **61** .... LiamJones(3) 1 34
(W M Brisbourne) *in tch stands' side: hung lft thrght: wknd over 2f out* **16/1**
4000 **11** ¾ **Meridian Grey (USA)**[30] 2661 3-8-5 **50** .... (b) AndrewMullen(3) 4 21+
(K A Ryan) *chsd far side ldrs: led that trio over 1f out: no ch w stands' side* **40/1**
5001 **12** 7 **Mambomoon**[42] 2300 3-8-11 **53** .... (b) DavidAllan 2 —+
(T D Easterby) *led far side trio to over 2f out: sn no ex* **12/1**
0000 **13** 4 **Stoneacre Donny (IRE)**[21] 2950 3-8-6 **48** ow1 .... LPKeniry 6 —
(Peter Grayson) *bhd stands' side: no ch fr 1/2-way* **66/1**
206 **14** 2 ½ **Hansomis (IRE)**[17] 3051 3-8-13 **55** .... (p) PaulHanagan 3 —+
(B Mactaggart) *pressed far side ldr: led that trio over 2f out to over 1f out: wknd* **16/1**

1m 14.6s (0.93) **Going Correction** +0.20s/f (Good) **14** Ran SP% **121.0**
Speed ratings (Par 100):101,100,97,96,94 91,91,88,88,85 84,75,70,66
CSF £88.45 CT £849.13 TOTE £17.00: £4.80, £2.30, £3.70; EX 175.90.
Owner Masonaires **Bred** A J And Mrs L Brazier **Trained** Kinnersley, Worcs

FOCUS
A run-of-the-mill handicap in which the majority came stands' side. The pace was sound and the form looks solid, if very ordinary.
Soviet Sound(IRE) Official explanation: jockey said gelding never travelled

3584 GILES INSURANCE PREMIER H'CAP 1m 5f 13y
3:00 (3:00) (Class 5) (0-70,76) 4-Y-0+ **£3,886** (£1,156; £577; £288) **Stalls** Low

Form RPR
3241 **1** **Artless (USA)**[7] 3371 4-10-1 **76** 6ex .... SebSanders 4 89+
(Sir Mark Prescott) *prom in chsng gp: effrt 3f out: led over 1f out: styd on wl* **13/8**[1]
-311 **2** 2 ½ **Rare Coincidence**[75] 1406 6-9-1 **62** .... (p) PaulHanagan 5 70+
(R F Fisher) *led and clr: rdn and hdd over 1f out: kpt on same pce fnl f* **7/1**
6461 **3** 1 **Kyber**[24] 2824 6-8-0 **54** .... KellyHarrison(7) 10 60
(J S Goldie) *hld up: hdwy 2f out: kpt on fnl f: nrst fin* **15/2**
2/34 **4** ¾ **Princess Kiotto**[9] 3300 6-9-4 **65** .... DavidAllan 1 70
(W M Brisbourne) *prom in chsng gp: drvn 3f out: one pce over 1f out* **13/2**[3]
-144 **5** 3 **Saluscraggie**[23] 2868 5-8-7 **54** .... JamieSpencer 3 54
(K G Reveley) *hld up in midfield: effrt over 2f out: no imp over 1f out* **7/2**[2]
5 **6** shd **Sinatas (GER)**[18] 3015 4-8-6 **53** .... PaulFessey 2 53
(P Monteith) *chsd clr ldr: drvn 3f out: sn one pce* **14/1**
0000 **7** 9 **City Miss**[24] 2823 4-8-4 **51** oh6 .... SilvestreDeSousa 6 39
(Miss L A Perratt) *prom in chsng gp tl wknd over 3f out* **100/1**
-004 **8** 1 ¼ **Fantastic Delight**[53] 1966 4-8-1 **51** oh6 .... DuranFentiman(3) 7 37
(G M Moore) *hld up: rdn over 3f out: sn btn* **14/1**
5000 **9** 40 **Borsch (IRE)**[24] 2825 5-8-1 **51** oh6 .... AndrewMullen(3) 9 —
(Miss L A Perratt) *bhd: lost tch over 4f out: t.o* **100/1**

2m 55.95s (-0.66) **Going Correction** -0.10s/f (Good) **9** Ran SP% **113.2**
Speed ratings (Par 103):98,96,95,95,93 93,87,87,62
CSF £13.44 CT £64.75 TOTE £2.50: £1.10, £2.10, £2.30; EX 6.10.
Owner Dr Catherine Wills **Bred** Dr Catherine Wills **Trained** Newmarket, Suffolk

FOCUS
An ordinary event run at a fair pace. The one progressive performer won with a bit to spare, with the next three close to their marks.

3585 GILES INSURANCE CORPORATE H'CAP 6f
3:30 (3:30) (Class 4) (0-80,80) 3-Y-0+ **£6,477** (£1,927; £963; £481) **Stalls** High

Form RPR
0066 **1** **River Thames**[13] 3184 4-9-2 **70** .... JamieSpencer 2 88+
(K A Ryan) *confidently rdn: hld up: smooth hdwy to ld over 1f out: sn clr: v easily* **6/1**[3]
0204 **2** 4 **Cross Of Lorraine (IRE)**[17] 3053 4-8-12 **66** .... (b) PatCosgrave 13 72
(J Wade) *dwlt: sn in midfield: effrt whn nt clr run over 1f out: kpt on fnl f: no ch w wnr* **6/1**[3]
6420 **3** ½ **High Reach**[17] 3053 7-8-12 **73** .... DeanHeslop(7) 5 78
(T D Barron) *mde most to over 1f out: kpt on same pce* **12/1**
0034 **4** hd **Stoic Leader (IRE)**[19] 2986 7-9-6 **77** .... AndrewMullen(3) 9 81
(R F Fisher) *cl up: drvn 1/2-way: no ex over 1f out* **10/1**
0200 **5** 1 ½ **Yorkshire Blue**[16] 3091 8-9-5 **80** .... GaryBartley(7) 11 79
(J S Goldie) *bhd tl kpt on fr 2f out: nvr rchd ldrs* **5/1**[2]
-021 **6** shd **Elkhorn**[18] 3014 5-9-10 **78** .... (b) TonyHamilton 8 77
(Miss J A Camacho) *hld up in tch: hdwy and ev ch 2f out: sn rdn and nt qckn* **11/4**[1]
0404 **7** hd **Kings College Boy**[13] 3184 7-8-10 **64** .... (b) PaulHanagan 4 63
(R A Fahey) *hld up in tch: effrt over 2f out: no ex over 1f out* **14/1**
-106 **8** 2 **Hit's Only Money (IRE)**[23] 2864 7-8-4 **61** oh4 .... DuranFentiman(3) 12 54
(J S Goldie) *bhd: pushed along 1/2-way: n.d* **14/1**
4000 **9** 2 ½ **Steel Blue**[9] 3298 7-8-13 **72** .... MichaelJStainton(5) 3 57
(R M Whitaker) *prom: drvn over 2f out: sn wknd* **16/1**
6354 **10** 8 **Regal Royale**[6] 3396 4-9-0 **68** .... (b) LPKeniry 1 29+
(Peter Grayson) *racd alone on far side: no ch fr 1/2-way* **22/1**
00 **11** 13 **Seafield Towers**[8] 3347 7-8-7 **61** oh10 .... (p) RoystonFfrench 14 —
(Miss L A Perratt) *cl up: wkng whn hmpd over 1f out: eased whn no ch* **28/1**

1m 13.97s (0.30) **Going Correction** +0.20s/f (Good) **11** Ran SP% **115.7**
Speed ratings (Par 105):106,100,100,99,97 97,97,94,91,80 63
CSF £41.18 CT £428.31 TOTE £7.40: £2.50, £2.10, £4.50; EX 57.20.
Owner Whitestonecliffe Racing Partnership **Bred** G And Mrs Middlebrook **Trained** Hambleton, N Yorks
■ Stewards' Enquiry : Jamie Spencer one-day ban: careless riding (Jul 27)

FOCUS
A fair handicap but a much improved effort from River Thames, who won without coming off the bridle and was arguably right back to his 2yo best. The form is rated through the placed horses. The pace was sound and all bar one raced stands side.

3586 GILES INSURANCE 40TH ANNIVERSARY HERITAGE H'CAP 5f
4:00 (4:01) (Class 2) 3-Y-0+ **£29,146** (£8,671; £4,333; £2,164) **Stalls** High

Form RPR
0340 **1** **Fullandby (IRE)**[16] 3089 5-8-13 **93** .... KDarley 12 104
(T J Etherington) *sn pushed along in midfield on stands' side: effrt on outside of that gp over 1f out: led ins fnl f: r.o wl* **5/1**[2]
0231 **2** ¾ **Gallery Girl (IRE)**[23] 2866 4-8-5 **85** .... DavidAllan 1 93
(T D Easterby) *cl up on stands' side: led that gp 1/2-way to ins fnl f: kpt on* **20/1**
-505 **3** ½ **Orientor**[17] 3050 9-9-1 **95** .... SebSanders 7 102
(J S Goldie) *prom on stands' side: effrt over 1f out: kpt on u.p ins fnl f* **14/1**
1502 **4** hd **Turn On The Style**[4] 3464 5-8-10 **90** .... (b) DarryllHolland 10 96
(J Balding) *cl up on stands' side: drvn over 2f out: kpt on ins fnl f* **9/2**[1]
0400 **5** shd **Fantasy Believer**[16] 3104 9-9-2 **96** .... JimmyQuinn 4 101+
(J J Quinn) *hld up in tch centre: effrt over 1f out: edgd rt ins fnl f: one pce wl ins fnl f* **12/1**
2204 **6** ¾ **River Falcon**[17] 3050 7-9-2 **96** .... PaulHanagan 13 99
(J S Goldie) *in tch on stands' side: lost pl over 3f out: rallied over 1f out: nrst fin* **11/1**
3030 **7** ½ **Distinctly Game**[4] 3464 5-8-7 **87** .... PaulMulrennan 11 88
(K A Ryan) *prom on stands' side tl rdn and nt qckn over 1f out* **33/1**
3001 **8** shd **Cashel Mead**[10] 3268 7-8-7 **87** .... FrancisNorton 16 88
(J L Spearing) *t.k.h: hld up on stands' side: hdwy over 1f out: nvr rchd ldrs* **12/1**
4330 **9** ½ **Stoneacre Lad (IRE)**[16] 3080 4-8-7 **87** .... (b) LPKeniry 14 86
(Peter Grayson) *bhd on stands' side tl hdwy over 1f out: n.d* **40/1**
0452 **10** 1 ½ **Celtic Mill**[37] 2463 9-9-10 **104** .... PatCosgrave 9 97
(D W Barker) *led on stands' side to 1/2-way: no ex over 1f out* **16/1**
0606 **11** hd **Harry Up**[4] 3464 6-8-4 **87** .... AndrewMullen(3) 8 80
(K A Ryan) *gd spd and clr of centre rivals: no ex ent fnl f* **28/1**
0133 **12** shd **Caribbean Coral**[17] 3050 8-8-13 **93** .... GrahamGibbons 2 85
(J J Quinn) *stdd and swtchd to stands' side s: pushed along over 2f out: n.d* **12/1**
60-6 **13** 2 **Chookie Heiton (IRE)**[51] 2022 9-9-0 **94** .... PhillipMakin 6 79
(I Semple) *prom in centre tl wknd fr 2f out* **33/1**
0464 **14** ¾ **Curtail (IRE)**[4] 3464 4-8-4 **84** .... RoystonFfrench 3 66
(I Semple) *prom in centre: drvn over 2f out: sn btn* **11/1**
1211 **15** 1 ½ **How's She Cuttin' (IRE)**[13] 3197 4-8-6 **86** .... (b) PaulFessey 17 63
(T D Barron) *in tch on stands' side: rdn over 2f out: sn btn* **11/2**[3]
0010 **16** ½ **Desert Commander (IRE)**[15] 3140 5-8-9 **89** .... (b) JamieSpencer 5 64
(K A Ryan) *hld up on stands' side: pushed along over 2f out: nvr on terms* **16/1**

60.69 secs (0.25) **Going Correction** +0.20s/f (Good) **16** Ran SP% **124.9**
Speed ratings (Par 109):106,104,104,103,103 102,101,101,100,98 97,97,94,93,90 90
CSF £111.68 CT £1400.72 TOTE £5.80: £2.20, £4.30, £2.50, £1.80; EX 160.90 TRIFECTA Not won..
Owner Miss M Greenwood **Bred** Mrs A Haskell Ellis **Trained** Norton, N Yorks
■ Stewards' Enquiry : Pat Cosgrave two-day ban: careless riding (Jul 27,29)

FOCUS
A good quality sprint, run at a decent pace and one in which the larger stands'-side group held an advantage over those that raced in the centre of the track. Solid form.

NOTEBOOK
Fullandby(IRE) was disappointing in very testing ground on his previous start but he looked a different horse back over the shorter trip and turned in a career best effort to notch his first win over this trip. He should not mind the return to 6f but a further rise in the weights may leave him vulnerable to the more progressive or better handicapped rivals. (op 13-2 tchd 7-1)
Gallery Girl(IRE) ◆, a course-and-distance winner in a lesser grade on her previous start, fared better from this 3lb higher mark and deserves extra credit as she came from stall 1. She will be of interest in decent company over either sprint distance when better drawn. (op 18-1)
Orientor ran as well as he has done all year but he is unlikely to be getting any respite from the handicapper for this creditable run and, as he has not won for three years, will not be one to get too carried away with next time. (op 16-1)
Turn On The Style, who turned in an improved effort at Newmarket on his previous start, ran creditably and left the impression that he would be even more effective given more of a test of speed. He remains the sort to win a decent handicap on turf. (op 6-1)
Fantasy Believer ◆, better than ever last year, has slipped back to a fair mark and fared easily the best of those that raced in the centre. He comes to hand at this time of year, will be suited by the return to 6f and appeals strongly as the sort to return to winning ways in the near future.
River Falcon has little room for manoeuvre from his current mark but ran creditably and again left the impression that the return to 6f would be in his favour. However the fact he has not won for some time remains a concern. (op 12-1)
Distinctly Game, who broke a losing run over 6f at Kempton in January, bettered the form of his recent reappearance. He should be spot on next time, will be suited by the return to 6f and is one to keep an eye on away from progressive sorts. (op 40-1)
How's She Cuttin'(IRE), up in the weights and in grade, had the run of the race against the inside rail but proved a disappointment on this occasion. She should have run better than this and, given her record, is worth another chance. Official explanation: jockey said filly hung right-handed throughout (tchd 9-2)

3587 JOIN WBX.COM FOR £150 FREE BETS H'CAP 1m 1f 20y
4:30 (4:31) (Class 6) (0-65,62) 3-Y-0 **£3,238** (£963; £481; £240) **Stalls** Low

Form RPR
3555 **1** **Nota Liberata**[13] 3181 3-9-4 **62** .... (t) PJMcDonald(5) 9 66
(G M Moore) *hld up in tch: smooth hdwy to chse ldr over 1f out: sn rdn: kpt on wl fnl f: led nr fin* **9/1**[3]
3004 **2** hd **Colditz (IRE)**[7] 3377 3-9-1 **54** .... (p) TonyHamilton 5 58
(D W Barker) *led: rdn over 2f out: kpt on wl fnl f: hdd nr fin* **16/1**
6461 **3** 2 ½ **Danalova**[7] 3377 3-8-9 **51** 6ex .... JamieMoriarty(3) 7 50
(R A Fahey) *chsd ldrs: outpcd over 2f out: rallied over 1f out: kpt on: nt rch first 2* **9/1**[3]
1020 **4** 1 ¼ **Shandelight (IRE)**[13] 3181 3-8-12 **51** .... (p) KDarley 12 47
(Mrs A Duffield) *prom: effrt and edgd lft wl over 1f out: no ex* **11/1**
5032 **5** shd **Cheshire Prince**[34] 2530 3-9-9 **62** .... DavidAllan 2 58
(W M Brisbourne) *hld up: hdwy over 2f out: kpt on fnl f: nvr rchd ldrs* **6/1**[2]
0640 **6** 2 ½ **Caviar Heights (IRE)**[13] 3183 3-9-0 **53** .... (b) PaulFessey 8 44
(Miss L A Perratt) *bhd tl styd on fr 2f out: nrst fin* **40/1**
1510 **7** hd **Skye But N Ben**[34] 2530 3-9-2 **62** .... (b) NeilBrown(7) 11 53
(T D Barron) *t.k.h: cl up: rdn and hung lft over 2f out: no ex whn hmpd wl over 1f out* **14/1**
0032 **8** 3 ½ **Bivouac (UAE)**[13] 3181 3-9-1 **54** .... JamieSpencer 1 38
(G A Swinbank) *hld up: drvn over 2f out: n.d* **7/4**[1]
0041 **9** 4 **Miss Havisham (IRE)**[18] 3040 3-8-12 **51** .... DarryllHolland 10 27
(J R Weymes) *missed break: a bhd* **9/1**[3]

0-06 **10** 5 **Forrest Flyer (IRE)**[18] 3015 3-9-3 **56**................ SebSanders 6 22
(Miss L A Perratt) *midfield: drvn 3f out: sn btn* **12/1**

0-06 **11** nk **Jane Of Arc (FR)**[56] 1898 3-9-8 **61**................ PaulHanagan 3 26
(J S Goldie) *hld up in tch: rdn 3f out: sn btn* **12/1**

1m 58.63s (-1.37) **Going Correction** -0.10s/f (Good) **11** Ran SP% **119.4**
Speed ratings (Par 98):102,101,99,98,98 96,96,92,89,84 84
CSF £145.52 CT £1341.84 TOTE £10.90: £2.80, £4.80, £3.20; EX 221.10.
Owner The Liberators **Bred** A C Birkle **Trained** Middleham Moor, N Yorks
■ Stewards' Enquiry : David Allan one-day ban: careless riding (Jul 29)

FOCUS
A low-grade handicap in which the pace was just fair. The form is sound but limited.
Bivouac(UAE) Official explanation: jockey said gelding never travelled

3588 BETRESCUE ANTEPOSTMAG.COM H'CAP 5f

5:00 (5:00) (Class 6) (0-65,63) 3-Y-O
£2,492 (£746; £373; £186; £93; £46) **Stalls** High

Form RPR

0130 **1** **Northern Dare (IRE)**[53] 1965 3-9-9 **63**................ SilvestreDeSousa 9 82+
(D Nicholls) *chsd ldrs: rdn and hung lft over 2f out: rallied to ld appr fnl f: drew clr ins fnl f* **11/4**[1]

6-04 **2** 3 **By The Edge (IRE)**[19] 3000 3-8-8 **48**................(v) PhillipMakin 7 53
(T D Barron) *led to appr fnl f: kpt on same pce* **11/2**

0525 **3** 2½ **Orotund**[9] 3302 3-8-2 **45**................ DuranFentiman(3) 5 41
(T D Easterby) *chsd ldrs tl drvn and one pce fr 2f out* **3/1**[2]

0520 **4** 1 **Stoneacre Gareth (IRE)**[12] 3212 3-9-8 **62**................(b) LPKeniry 3 55
(Peter Grayson) *t.k.h in rr: hdwy 2f out: nrst fin* **16/1**

0206 **5** nk **Ensign's Trick**[27] 2750 3-9-5 **62**................ LiamJones(3) 6 54
(W M Brisbourne) *hld up in tch: drvn 1/2-way: no imrpession over 1f out* **12/1**

0223 **6** 5 **Moonlight Applause**[10] 3281 3-9-0 **54**................ DavidAllan 4 28
(T D Easterby) *bhd: rdn 1/2-way: n.d* **4/1**[3]

5545 **7** 5 **Dotty's Daughter**[13] 3180 3-8-8 **48**................(p) KDarley 1 —
(Mrs A Duffield) *chsd ldrs: drvn 1/2-way: sn btn* **17/2**

6064 **8** ½ **Splendidio**[49] 2094 3-8-5 **45**................ PaulQuinn 10 —
(Mrs Marjorie Fife) *in tch: rdn 1/2-way: sn btn* **33/1**

60.93 secs (0.49) **Going Correction** +0.20s/f (Good) **8** Ran SP% **114.1**
Speed ratings (Par 98):104,99,95,93,93 85,77,76
CSF £18.22 CT £47.17 TOTE £3.60: £1.50, £2.00, £1.50; EX 19.30 Place 6 £ 222.93, Place 5 £ 151.66.
Owner Jim Dale **Bred** Frank Moynihan **Trained** Sessay, N Yorks

FOCUS
An ordinary event in which the pace was sound and this form should stand up at a similar level. The time was good but the placed horses do limit enthusiasm for the form.
T/Jkpt: Not won. T/Plt: £260.10 to a £1 stake. Pool: £89,474.00. 251.05 winning tickets. T/Qpdt: £59.30 to a £1 stake. Pool: £4,842.90. 60.35 winning tickets. RY

3383 WINDSOR (R-H)

Monday, July 16

OFFICIAL GOING: Good to firm (good in places; 8.7)
Wind: Virtually nil Weather: fine

3589 LADBROKES IN COMMUNITY CHARITABLE TRUST EBF MEDIAN AUCTION MAIDEN STKS 5f 10y

6:30 (6:30) (Class 4) 2-Y-O **£4,210** (£1,252; £625; £312) **Stalls** High

Form RPR

2 **1** **Imperial Mint (IRE)**[13] 3192 2-9-3 0................ TedDurcan 8 85
(K A Ryan) *chsd ldrs: drvn to chal 2f out: slt ld appr fnl f: hld on wl* **15/8**[1]

3 **2** 1 **Zippi Jazzman (USA)**[28] 2724 2-9-3 0................ GeorgeBaker 13 81
(R M Beckett) *sn led: rdn 2f out: narrowly hdd appr fnl f: one pce last half f but hld on wl for 2nd* **3/1**[3]

63 **3** nk **Art Sale**[7] 3363 2-9-3 0................ RyanMoore 11 80
(G L Moore) *chsd ldrs: drvn to challnge ins fnl 2f: styd on same pce ins fnl f* **5/2**[2]

0 **4** 2 **Piscean (USA)**[24] 2832 2-9-3 0................ MickyFenton 10 73+
(T Keddy) *s.i.s: bhd: hdwy towards outside and green over 2f out: r.o wl fnl f: gng on cl home* **20/1**

0 **5** 1¼ **Mistress Cooper**[31] 2630 2-8-12 0................ BrettDoyle 7 64
(W J Musson) *pressed ldr to 1/2-way: stl chalng 2f out: wknd ins fnl f* **80/1**

6 ¾ **Wise Son** 2-9-3 0................ KerrinMcEvoy 14 66
(W J Haggas) *chsd ldrs: rdn along over 2f out: wknd fnl f* **12/1**

7 hd **Mesmerize Me** 2-9-3 0................ RichardMullen 2 65+
(E S McMahon) *s.i.s: sn chsng ldrs: rdn over 2f out: wknd ins fnl f* **25/1**

0 **8** ½ **Connor's Choice**[40] 2349 2-9-0 0................ RichardKingscote(3) 12 63
(Andrew Turnell) *s.i.s: bhd: rdn over 2f out: styd on ins fnl f but nvr gng pce to be competitive* **100/1**

00 **9** ¾ **Mr Funshine**[7] 3363 2-9-3 0................ RobertHavlin 5 61
(Mrs P N Dutfield) *chsd ldrs tl wknd qckly fnl f* **100/1**

10 1½ **Joss Stick** 2-9-3 0................ EddieAhern 6 61+
(P J Makin) *in tch tl wknd fnl f: eased nr fin* **66/1**

11 4 **Tallulah Sunrise** 2-8-12 0................ RichardSmith 4 36+
(M D I Usher) *in tch: rdn halfway: wknd fr 2f out* **66/1**

25 **12** 1 **Valhillen**[63] 1713 2-9-3 0................ JimCrowley 9 37
(M J Wallace) *in rr: pushed along 1/2-way: mod prog ins fnl f* **25/1**

0 **13** 3 **Woodcote Wildcat (USA)**[8] 3348 2-8-12 0................ JohnEgan 15 22
(N A Callaghan) *slowly away: a outpcd* **50/1**

14 5 **High Standing (USA)** 2-9-3 0................ VinceSlattery 1 9
(N A Callaghan) *a in rr* **100/1**

15 9 **Tomba Maestro** 2-9-3 0................ SteveDrowne 3 —
(J L Spearing) *slowly away: hanging and v green thrght* **66/1**

59.63 secs (-1.47) **Going Correction** -0.30s/f (Firm) **15** Ran SP% **119.1**
Speed ratings (Par 96):99,97,96,93,91 90,90,89,88,85 79,77,73,65,50
CSF £6.87 TOTE £2.90: £2.40, £1.90, £1.60; EX 13.20.
Owner David Fravigar, Kathy Dixon **Bred** Paul Starr **Trained** Hambleton, N Yorks

FOCUS
A decent sprint maiden likely to produce winners. Strong form for the grade, and sound.

NOTEBOOK
Imperial Mint(IRE), who showed plenty of speed when second to the useful-looking Sir Gerry over 6f on his debut at Thirsk, was not expected to have any trouble with this drop in trip and he ran on strongly once getting to the front. He clearly has the makings of a decent juvenile, and boasts a Gimcrack entry, but will need to progress a fair bit before being considered for such a contest. (op 7-4 tchd 2-1)
Zippi Jazzman(USA), who shaped promisingly when third over course and distance behind Rocking on debut, had a good draw here and, with the faster ground expected to suit, he looked a major player. However, having got to the front he could not fend off the winner's challenge and simply lacked his speed. There is a small maiden in him. (tchd 11-4 and 10-3)
Art Sale, who may well have won at Bath last time had he stayed far side, was up there throughout and again gave his running, but the winner proved a bit too classy and he looks ready for a return to 6f now. He could be the sort to do well in nurseries. (op 3-1 tchd 7-2 in places)
Piscean(USA), quite an expensive purchase, stepped up on his initial effort, overcoming a sluggish start to claim a never-nearer fourth, and he will be qualified for nurseries following one more run. (op 16-1)
Mistress Cooper showed bright speed for a long way and is clearly not without ability. This was an improvement on her initial effort and she too could be of interest for nurseries once qualifying for a mark.
Wise Son, whose stable are capable of readying a newcomer, is bred for speed and he made a pleasing introduction despite still looking green under pressure. Standard improvement should see him winning an average maiden. (op 11-1)
Mesmerize Me, a 33,000gns purchase, comes from a yard who can ready a newcomer and he was another to shape with promise. (op 33-1)

3590 ROYAL BANK OF SCOTLAND H'CAP 1m 3f 135y

7:00 (7:00) (Class 4) (0-85,83) 3-Y-O **£5,047** (£1,510; £755; £377; £188) **Stalls** Low

Form RPR

3-13 **1** **Camps Bay (USA)**[31] 2627 3-9-3 **79**................ JimCrowley 8 86
(Mrs A J Perrett) *hld up in tch: drvn and hdwy over 2f out: led over 1f out: pushed clr: comf* **11/4**[1]

21 **2** 2 **Fourteenth**[28] 2726 3-9-4 **80**................ RyanMoore 6 84
(Sir Michael Stoute) *chsd ldrs in 3rd: pushed along over 3f out: drvn to ld over 2f out: hdd over 1f out: no ch w wnr ins fnl f but kpt on wl for 2nd* **11/4**[1]

-014 **3** 1½ **Maid To Believe**[20] 2971 3-8-11 **73**................ EddieAhern 7 75
(J L Dunlop) *in rr but in tch: drvn and hdwy fr 2f out to take 3rd ins fnl f but nvr gng pce to rch ldrs* **11/1**

-413 **4** nk **Fretwork**[42] 2305 3-9-7 **83**................ TedDurcan 5 84
(R Hannon) *sn led: rdn 3f out: hdd over 2f out: one pce ins fnl f* **9/2**[2]

4-6P **5** hd **Amazing Request**[68] 1584 3-9-6 **82**................ RichardHughes 3 83
(R Charlton) *chsd ldrs: rdn 3f out: one pce ins fnl f* **13/2**[3]

00U0 **6** 4 **Harvest Joy (IRE)**[20] 2971 3-9-6 **82**................ JHBowman 2 77
(B R Millman) *in rr tl sme hdwy 3f out: nvr rchd ldrs: wknd fr 2f out* **40/1**

4-32 **7** 3 **Beverly Hill Billy**[14] 3165 3-9-4 **80**................ RobertHavlin 4 70
(A King) *stdd s: t.k.h and hld up in rr: rdn over 3f out and nvr in contention* **8/1**

4140 **8** 2½ **Dee Cee Elle**[25] 2808 3-8-8 **70**................ TQuinn 1 56
(M Johnston) *chsd ldr: rdn to chal fr 5f out: wknd ins fnl 3f* **12/1**

2m 26.42s (-3.68) **Going Correction** -0.30s/f (Firm) **8** Ran SP% **114.4**
Speed ratings (Par 102):100,98,97,97,97 94,92,91
CSF £10.12 CT £69.09 TOTE £7.80: £1.80, £1.80, £2.00; EX 15.50.
Owner Mr & Mrs R Scott **Bred** Kidder,Cole,Marnakos,Graves & Beck **Trained** Pulborough, W Sussex
■ Stewards' Enquiry : Jim Crowley two-day ban: careless riding (Jul 27,29)

FOCUS
A decent three-year-old handicap likely to produce winners. The form looks sound enough.
Dee Cee Elle Official explanation: jockey said filly suffered interference in running

3591 SUNLEY FILLIES' H'CAP 1m 67y

7:30 (7:30) (Class 4) (0-85,80) 3-Y-O+ **£6,309** (£1,888; £944; £472; £235) **Stalls** High

Form RPR

25 **1** **Fragrancy (IRE)**[53] 1956 3-9-2 **76**................ PhilipRobinson 1 85+
(M A Jarvis) *mde all: rdn and edgd lft over 1f out: styd on grimly whn chal ins fnl f* **4/1**[2]

6-1 **2** hd **Ventura (USA)**[17] 3044 3-9-6 **80**................ RichardHughes 6 89+
(Mrs A J Perrett) *trckd ldrs: hdwy and swtchd lft over 1f out: nt clr run and swtchd rt sn after: r.o strly fnl f but a jst hld by wnr* **4/1**[2]

1410 **3** 3½ **Tender The Great (IRE)**[23] 2883 4-9-5 **74**................ RichardKingscote(3) 2 77+
(B G Powell) *in rr: hdwy 5f out: sn chsng ldrs: rdn to chal 2f out: wknd fnl f* **16/1**

-300 **4** 1¾ **Rakata (USA)**[65] 1649 5-9-9 **80**................ TolleyDean(5) 3 78
(P F I Cole) *chsd ldrs: rdn to chal over 2f out: wknd over 1f out* **25/1**

1203 **5** nk **Apply Dapply**[19] 3001 4-9-9 **75**................ SteveDrowne 7 73
(H Morrison) *chsd ldrs: drvn along 5f out: wknd over 1f out* **9/2**[3]

-614 **6** 1¼ **Arabian Treasure (USA)**[40] 2369 3-9-1 **75**................ RyanMoore 8 69
(Sir Michael Stoute) *in rr: sme hdwy 3f out: wknd over 2f out* **5/2**[1]

205 **7** ½ **Black Sea Pearl**[4] 3455 4-8-12 **64**................ TedDurcan 5 58
(P W D'Arcy) *in rr: rdn 3f out: nvr gng pce to get into contention* **12/1**

521 **8** 6 **Royal Secrets (IRE)**[31] 2625 3-9-3 **77**................ JimmyFortune 4 55
(E A L Dunlop) *chsd ldr to 3f out: wknd sn after* **10/1**

1m 41.72s (-2.98) **Going Correction** -0.30s/f (Firm)
WFA 3 from 4yo+ 8lb **8** Ran SP% **113.3**
Speed ratings (Par 102):102,101,98,96,96 95,94,88
CSF £19.97 CT £227.67 TOTE £7.20: £2.70, £1.40, £3.70; EX 14.40.
Owner Mohammed Al Nabouda **Bred** Darley **Trained** Newmarket, Suffolk

FOCUS
A fair fillies' handicap, run at an uneven pace. A positive view has been taken of the form. The first pair came clear and the runner-up looked unlucky.
Royal Secrets(IRE) Official explanation: jockey said filly was not suited by the way race was run

3592 LITTLEWOODS POOLS MAIDEN STKS 6f

8:00 (8:01) (Class 5) 2-Y-O **£3,886** (£1,156; £577; £288) **Stalls** High

Form RPR

63 **1** **Lady Aquitaine (USA)**[26] 2768 2-8-12 0................ RyanMoore 12 86+
(B J Meehan) *trckd ldrs: n.m.r 2f out: squeezed through to ld appr fnl f: sn clr: easily* **4/5**[1]

0 **2** 6 **Kaldoun Kingdom (IRE)**[19] 2991 2-9-3 0................ JimmyFortune 10 70
(E A L Dunlop) *pressed ldrs: rdn to ld jst ins fnl 2f: hdd appr fnl f: sn no ch w wnr but kpt on wl for clr 2nd* **33/1**

04 **3** 1¼ **Palm Court**[37] 2473 2-9-3 0................ SteveDrowne 13 66+
(R Charlton) *chsd ldrs: rdn and styd on same pce fnl 2f* **4/1**[2]

0 **4** ¾ **Caradoc Place**[11] 3233 2-9-3 0................ PatDobbs 4 64
(M P Tregoning) *sn led: rdn 3f out: hdd jst ins fnl 2f: styd on same pce* **16/1**

5 ¾ **Polar Annie** 2-8-12 0................ MickyFenton 16 57
(M S Saunders) *s.i.s: in rr: n.m.r over 2f out: kpt on fnl f: fin wl but nvr gng pce to rch ldrs* **33/1**

6 nk **Aye Aye Digby (IRE)** 2-9-3 0................ KerrinMcEvoy 14 61
(H Candy) *chsd ldrs: outpcd 1/2-way: kpt on again fnl f* **5/1**[3]

7 hd **Ambrose Princess (IRE)** 2-8-12 0................ JohnEgan 8 55
(J S Moore) *in rr: swtchd lft and styd on fr 2f out: nvr in contention* **50/1**

0 **8** *hd* **Riorun (IRE)**[19] 2977 2-9-3 0 EddieAhern 2 60
(J G Portman) *pressed ldrs: rdn 3f out: wknd over 1f out* **50/1**
9 *1 1/2* **Mystic Art (IRE)** 2-9-3 0 TedDurcan 7 55
(C R Egerton) *in rr: sme hdwy towards outside 1/2-way: nvr gng pce to be competitive* **22/1**
10 *2 1/2* **Restless Genius (IRE)** 2-9-3 0 RichardMullen 3 48
(A M Balding) *s.i.s: sn rdn: styd on to chse ldrs 1/2-way: wknd ins fnl 2f* **40/1**
11 *1* **Harlequinn Danseur (IRE)** 2-9-3 0 KimTinkler 1 45
(N Tinkler) *chsd ldrs: rdn 1/2-way: wknd fr 2f out* **40/1**
00 **12** *8* **Ledgerwood**[7] 3383 2-9-3 0 JHBowman 15 21
(J W Hills) *in rr: sme prog into mid-div 1/2-way: n.d after and sn bhd* **40/1**
13 *3 1/2* **Diamond Flute** 2-8-12 0 TQuinn 11 —
(Mouse Hamilton-Fairley) *s.i.s: a in rr* **33/1**
14 *1 1/4* **Pasta Prayer** 2-9-3 0 VinceSlattery 6 6
(N A Callaghan) *in tch over 3f* **20/1**

1m 12.39s (-1.28) **Going Correction** -0.30s/f (Firm) **14** Ran SP% **127.3**
Speed ratings (Par 94):96,88,86,85,84 83,83,83,81,78 76,66,61,59
CSF £48.26 TOTE £2.30: £1.40, £4.50, £1.30; EX 55.70.
Owner Sangster Family **Bred** Swettenham Stud **Trained** Manton, Wilts

FOCUS
An average juvenile maiden, run at a fair pace. The easy winner, the pre-race form pick, showed improvement and was value for further. The form looks solid enough.

NOTEBOOK
Lady Aquitaine(USA) ◆, very well backed, did the job easily in the end and lost her maiden tag at the third time of asking. The drop back to this trip proved no problem and she should be rated for around double her winning margin, as she had to wait for her challenge around the 2f pole and was not fully extended when in the clear. It would not be a surprise to see her rate higher now she has got her head in front and she will most likely go in search of valuable black type now. (op 11-8 tchd 6-4 in places)
Kaldoun Kingdom(IRE) was given a positive ride on this switch to turf and drop back in trip. He posted a much-improved effort, showing the clear benefit of his previous experience, and finished nicely clear in second. In time he will need further, but he looks worth another try over this distance and is evidently progressing.
Palm Court was on his toes in the preliminaries and proved very easy to back. He could not find an extra gear when it mattered around the 2f pole, but still kept on to run his race and performed very close to the level of his previous outing over course and distance. He should be of greater interest now he is qualified for a nursery mark and is still very much learning his trade. (op 7-2)
Caradoc Place put a tame effort at Newbury well behind him with a fair run from the front from his low draw. He proved much more happy on this fast ground and should come on again for this experience, with another furlong likely to suit before too long. (op 12-1)
Polar Annie, whose dam won over 7f at three, was always playing catch-up after a slow start yet caught the eye staying on when the race was all but over. She has an engine and should know a lot more next time. Official explanation: jockey said filly was denied a clear run
Aye Aye Digby(IRE), a good-looking colt, left the clear impression he would benefit for this debut experience and was not disgraced. He also did enough to suggest he will relish another furlong, and his pedigree backs that up, as his dam scored on her debut over 7f at two. Softer ground may also prove more in his favour. (tchd 13-2, 7-1 in places)
Harlequinn Danseur(IRE) Official explanation: trainer said gelding had a breathing problem because tongue strap came adrift and could not be refitted

3593 RITZ CLUB TROPHY (S) STKS 1m 3f 135y
8:30 (8:30) (Class 5) 3-4-Y-O **£3,238** (£963; £481; £240) **Stalls** Low

Form RPR
0205 **1** **Converti**[16] 3082 3-8-9 55 TQuinn 7 53
(P F I Cole) *trckd ldrs: drvn to ld ins fnl 2f: hung lft u.p ins fnl f: drvn out* **9/4**[1]
-000 **2** *3/4* **Compton Charlie**[16] 3082 3-8-9 57 (p) EddieAhern 6 52
(J G Portman) *mid-div: hdwy fr 3f out: rdn over 2f out: pressed wnr ins fnl f: no ex whn pushed lft* **9/1**
4300 **3** *3/4* **Ranavalona**[17] 1412 3-8-5 51 ow1 (t) JohnEgan 10 49+
(C Smith) *in tch: hdwy to chse ldrs 2f out: nt clr run over 1f out: swtchd lft to chal between horses whn n.m.r ins fnl f: pushed lft: nt rcvr* **16/1**
006 **4** *1/2* **Ceol Eile (IRE)**[47] 2140 4-9-2 45 (p) RobertHavlin 5 45
(D Haydn Jones) *chsd ldrs: led 3f out: hdd ins fnl 2f: wknd ins fnl f* **15/2**
0-06 **5** *1* **By The River**[11] 3236 3-8-9 52 PaulDoe 8 48
(P Winkworth) *chsd ldrs: rdn to chal fr 2f out: wknd ins fnl f* **10/1**
6310 **6** *shd* **Right Option (IRE)**[16] 3083 3-9-0 53 RyanMoore 2 53
(S Dow) *in rr: rdn and hdwy over 2f out: swtchd lft and styd on to chse ldrs over 1f out: no imp and sn one pce* **5/2**[2]
0006 **7** *8* **All Talk**[27] 2747 3-7-11 30 LauraReynolds(7) 9 31
(M J Gingell) *plld hrd and stdd in rr: sme prog and hung lft over 2f out: nvr in contention* **100/1**
-000 **8** *3* **Night Reveller (IRE)**[110] 807 4-8-9 28 GihanArnolda(7) 4 26
(M C Chapman) *in tch: rdn and effrt over 3f out: nvr in contention and sn btn* **66/1**
-000 **9** *2 1/2* **Cool Isle**[50] 2055 4-9-2 46 (b) IanMongan 3 22
(P Howling) *in rr: mod prog 3f out: sn btn* **5/1**[3]
0-00 **10** *1/2* **Young Emma**[18] 3041 4-9-2 20 (t) NeilPollard 11 21
(G G Margarson) *chsd ldrs: rdn 3f out: sn wknd* **33/1**
11 *9* **Camellia's Girl** 4-8-13 0 (t) MarcHalford(3) 12 8
(J J Bridger) *s.i.s: a in rr* **50/1**
12 *1/2* **Parbyblos (FR)**[36] 4-9-7 0 MickyFenton 1 12+
(John Allen) *led tl hdd 3f out: sn wknd: in rr whn hmpd over 2f out* **20/1**

2m 29.86s (-0.24) **Going Correction** -0.30s/f (Firm)
WFA 3 from 4yo 12lb **12** Ran SP% **124.9**
Speed ratings (Par 103):88,87,87,86,86 85,80,78,76,76 70,70
CSF £24.28 TOTE £3.10: £1.40, £2.20, £3.40; EX 32.90.The winner was sold to John Manners for 9,600gns
Owner The Fairy Story Partnership **Bred** Deepwood Farm Stud **Trained** Whatcombe, Oxon

FOCUS
A very moderate winning time, even for a seller, and the form is weak, rated around the principals.
Cool Isle Official explanation: jockey said filly had no more to give

3594 BDO STOY HAYWARD FINANCIAL SERVICES GROUP H'CAP 5f 10y
9:00 (9:00) (Class 5) (0-75,75) 3-Y-O+ **£3,238** (£963; £481; £240) **Stalls** High

Form RPR
3342 **1** **Malapropism**[4] 3449 7-9-1 65 JHBowman 9 77+
(M R Channon) *trckd ldrs: swtchd rt to stands' side 1f out: str run ins fnl f to ld fnl 50yds: readily* **9/2**[1]
-500 **2** *1 1/4* **Our Fugitive (IRE)**[52] 1999 5-8-12 62 JohnEgan 11 70
(A W Carroll) *led: rdn and carried hd high fr 2f out: kpt on whn strly chal: hdd and no ex fnl 50yds* **8/1**[3]
20 **3** *1/2* **Gwilym (GER)**[2] 3528 4-9-8 72 RobertHavlin 13 78
(D Haydn Jones) *chsd ldrs: rdn and str chal fr 1f out: no ex nr fin* **13/2**[2]
1221 **4** *nk* **Caustic Wit (IRE)**[4] 3449 9-9-4 68 6ex RichardHughes 4 73
(M S Saunders) *chsd ldrs: chal and edgd rt ins fnl f: no ex nr fin* **13/2**[2]
0-00 **5** *nk* **Endless Summer**[30] 2664 10-8-6 56 oh1 DavidKinsella 12 60
(A W Carroll) *in rr: hdwy and swtchd lft to outside 2f out: styd on u.p fnl f but nvr quite gng pce to press ldrs* **11/1**
2215 **6** *1/2* **Harrison's Flyer (IRE)**[2] 3536 6-8-13 70 (p) BarrySavage(7) 7 72+
(J M Bradley) *chsd ldrs: rdn and one pce whn n.m.r jst ins fnl f: n.d after* **12/1**
2106 **7** *3/4* **Blessed Place**[2] 3528 7-9-1 65 (t) TQuinn 6 64+
(D J S Ffrench Davis) *chsd ldrs: chal over 1f out: styng on at one pce whn hmpd ins fnl f: nt rcvr* **16/1**
4000 **8** *1/2* **Azygous**[13] 3179 4-9-3 67 RyanMoore 5 64
(J Akehurst) *hdwy to chse ldrs 1/2-way: ev ch over 1f out: wknd ins fnl f* **13/2**[2]
013 **9** *1/2* **Talcen Gwyn (IRE)**[4] 3449 5-8-12 62 (v) SteveDrowne 8 57
(M F Harris) *nvr gng pce to trble ldrs* **9/1**
6066 **10** *nk* **Prettilini**[30] 2657 4-8-5 58 oh11 ow2 RichardKingscote(3) 14 52
(A W Carroll) *sn outpcd* **33/1**
-250 **11** *shd* **Jakeini (IRE)**[34] 2529 4-9-8 72 (p) JimmyFortune 1 66
(E S McMahon) *in rr: hdwy to press ldrs over 2f out: wknd fnl f* **12/1**
0364 **12** *1/2* **Puskas (IRE)**[13] 3179 4-9-8 75 LiamTreadwell(3) 10 67
(J M Bradley) *nvr gng pce to be competitive* **12/1**
0/00 **13** *5* **Avoca Dancer (IRE)**[56] 1885 4-8-7 57 BrettDoyle 15 31
(M Wigham) *a in rr* **22/1**

59.02 secs (-2.08) **Going Correction** -0.30s/f (Firm) **13** Ran SP% **123.9**
Speed ratings (Par 103):104,102,101,100,100 99,98,97,96,96 96,95,87
CSF £41.37 CT £241.62 TOTE £4.10: £1.40, £4.20, £2.60; EX 57.40 Place 6 £ 16.33, Place 5 £ 15.00.
Owner Michael A Foy **Bred** Michael A Foy **Trained** West Ilsley, Berks

FOCUS
Just a modest sprint handicap, but solid enough form backed up by the third and fourth.
Talcen Gwyn(IRE) Official explanation: jockey said gelding missed the break and hung right
T/Plt: £18.30 to a £1 stake. Pool: £99,534.70. 3,956.55 winning tickets. T/Qpdt: £12.90 to a £1 stake. Pool: £3,676.60. 209.60 winning tickets. ST

3404 WOLVERHAMPTON (A.W) (L-H)
Monday, July 16

OFFICIAL GOING: Standard
Wind: Light behind Weather: Overcast

3595 P D FINANCIAL MANAGEMENT FIELD OF DREAMS CLASSIFIED CLAIMING STKS 1m 4f 50y(P)
6:50 (6:50) (Class 6) 3-Y-O+ **£2,730** (£806; £403) **Stalls** Low

Form RPR
0402 **1** **Birthday Star (IRE)**[45] 2222 5-9-6 57 AdamKirby 7 63
(A G Juckes) *hld up: hdwy over 2f out: rdn to ld wl ins fnl f* **4/1**[2]
0344 **2** *hd* **Bethanys Boy (IRE)**[10] 3282 6-9-5 57 TPO'Shea 9 62
(P A Blockley) *s.i.s: hld up: nt clr run over 3f out: hdwy over 2f out: rdn over 1f out: r.o* **11/4**[1]
2043 **3** *1/2* **Brastar Jelois (FR)**[10] 3282 4-9-3 58 RussellKennemore(5) 11 64
(R Hollinshead) *hld up: hdwy over 3f out: rdn to ld over 1f out: hdd wl ins fnl f* **7/1**
1642 **4** *3 1/2* **Bridgewater Boys**[108] 825 6-9-6 59 (b) ChrisCatlin 10 57+
(K A Ryan) *s.i.s: hld up: hdwy over 5f out: led over 2f out: rdn and hdd over 1f out: wknd ins fnl f* **11/2**[3]
4053 **5** *3 1/2* **Itcanbedone Again (IRE)**[17] 3063 8-8-12 53 WilliamBuick(5) 3 48
(Ian Williams) *prom: rdn over 2f out: wknd over 1f out* **4/1**[2]
0440 **6** *1 1/4* **Orpen Quest (IRE)**[10] 3280 5-9-6 43 PaulFitzsimons 4 50
(M J Attwater) *s.i.s: hld up: hdwy 6f out: rdn and wknd over 1f out* **14/1**
0-00 **7** *1* **Beshairt**[19] 2978 3-8-6 40 FrankieMcDonald 6 46
(D Burchell) *chasd ldrs tl rdn and wknd over 2f out* **40/1**
030 **8** *9* **Callitquits (IRE)**[10] 3282 5-8-11 48 (p) HaddenFrost(7) 12 33
(Jennie Candlish) *chsd ldr: led over 3f out: rdn and hdd over 2f out: wknd over 1f out* **25/1**
3-00 **9** *3 1/2* **Oedipuss (IRE)**[13] 3186 3-8-4 41 ow1 (t) EdwardCreighton 1 25
(K J Burke) *hld up: plld hrd: hdwy 6f out: wknd 3f out* **20/1**
000- **10** *2 1/2* **Spy Game (IRE)**[6] 1772 7-9-8 52 (v) SamHitchcott 5 28
(Jennie Candlish) *led after 1f: rdn and hdd over 3f out: wknd over 2f out* **50/1**
0-00 **11** *1 1/2* **Wicked Lady (UAE)**[77] 1344 4-8-13 45 KevinGhunowa(5) 2 21
(J M Bradley) *led 1f: remained handy: rdn over 3f out: sn wknd* **33/1**

2m 41.41s (-1.01) **Going Correction** -0.10s/f (Stan)
WFA 3 from 4yo+ 12lb **11** Ran SP% **117.2**
Speed ratings (Par 101):99,98,98,96,93 93,92,86,84,82 81
CSF £14.45 TOTE £4.70: £2.20, £1.10, £2.00; EX 15.30.Bethanys Boy was claimed by D. J. Daly for £7,000. Birthday Star was the subject of a friendly claim
Owner P K R N Recycling Limited **Bred** Woodhouse Syndicate **Trained** Abberley, Worcs
■ Stewards' Enquiry : Hadden Frost one-day ban: careless riding (Jul 27)

FOCUS
A claimer restricted to horses rated 60 or lower, so moderate stuff. The form has been rated through the winner.

3596 GEORGE GREEN LLP FIELD OF DREAMS MAIDEN AUCTION STKS 5f 216y(P)
7:20 (7:21) (Class 5) 2-Y-O **£3,071** (£906; £453) **Stalls** Low

Form RPR
6 **1** **Maryolini**[34] 2526 2-8-6 0 ChrisCatlin 10 64
(N J Vaughan) *mid-div: hung rt thrght: rdn over 2f out: styd on u.p to ld nr fin* **20/1**
6 **2** *1/2* **Mudhish (IRE)**[44] 2241 2-8-11 0 HayleyTurner 5 68
(C E Brittain) *a.p: chsd ldr over 3f out: rdn to ld ins fnl f: hdd nr fin* **8/1**
5 **3** *1/2* **Cracking Nick (IRE)**[32] 2590 2-9-1 0 AdamKirby 4 70
(W R Swinburn) *led: rdn over 1f out: hdd and unable qck ins fnl f* **6/4**[1]
4 *hd* **Nice Wee Girl (IRE)** 2-8-3 0 WilliamBuick(5) 6 62
(S Kirk) *hld up in tch: racd keenly: rdn over 1f out: sn hung lft: r.o* **6/1**[2]
5 *shd* **Intersky Melody (USA)** 2-8-11 0 DeanMcKeown 1 68+
(K A Ryan) *s.i.s: hdwy over 3f out: shkn up over 1f out: styd on* **14/1**
00 **6** *3/4* **Spinning Ridge (IRE)**[21] 2949 2-8-6 0 LukeMorris(5) 12 63
(R A Harris) *s.i.s: hld up: hdwy over 2f out: rdn over 1f out: styd on same pce ins fnl f* **13/2**[3]
30 **7** *2* **Carry On Cleo**[25] 2797 2-8-4 0 SimonWhitworth 9 50
(P D Evans) *chsd ldrs: rdn over 1f out: wknd ins fnl f* **20/1**
40 **8** *3 1/2* **Shabnaam**[28] 2710 2-8-10 0 SamHitchcott 11 45
(K A Ryan) *s.i.s: hld up: rdn and hung rt over 2f out: edgd lft and wknd over 1f out* **11/1**

	9	shd	**Rewski (IRE)** 2-8-9 0 EdwardCreighton 2		44
			(Ms Deborah J Evans) *s.i.s: hld up: hdwy over 1f out: wknd fnl f*	33/1	
0	10	1/2	**Anabaa's Secret (IRE)**[4] [3471] 2-9-1 0 StephenDonohoe 8		49
			(J A Osborne) *hld up: rdn over 2f out: a in rr*	8/1	
55	11	5	**Avian Flew**[7] [3378] 2-7-13 0 ColinHaddon(5) 3		23
			(J A Pickering) *chsd ldrs: rdn over 2f out: wknd over 1f out*	25/1	
	12	hd	**Imaginemysurprise** 2-8-4 0 ow7 HaddenFrost(7) 4		29
			(J A Geake) *mid-div: effrt over 2f out: sn wknd*	40/1	

1m 16.08s (0.27) **Going Correction** -0.10s/f (Stan) 12 Ran SP% **123.6**
Speed ratings (Par 94):94,93,92,92,92 91,88,83,83,83 76,76
CSF £169.24 TOTE £51.10: £5.80, £2.20, £1.10; EX 273.10.
Owner A Charlton P Jones I Smith K Warth **Bred** Ms M A Rowlands **Trained** Malpas, Cheshire
■ The first winner for Nicky Vaughan, whose stables are owned by football star Michael Owen.

FOCUS
A modest contest.

NOTEBOOK
Maryolini could make little impression on her debut in a 5f maiden at Chester, but she was carrying a lot of condition that day and ran very green. She knew more this time and was able to get off the mark at the second attempt, despite hanging right under pressure. This looked like a modest race, but she is open to further improvement. (op 14-1)
Mudhish(IRE), whose debut sixth at Folkestone could hardly have worked out any better, produced a respectable effort in second. (op 6-1)
Cracking Nick(IRE) failed to build on the form he showed on his debut at Lingfield and this could be considered a touch disappointing. (op 9-4)
Nice Wee Girl(IRE), a 20,000gns half-sister to among others the useful Riddlesdown, a prolific 1m-1m6f US winner, out of a smart 6f winner, was not without support on her racecourse debut and she showed ability. She was a touch keen and also hung in the straight, but she should know more next time. (op 4-1)
Intersky Melody(USA), a $15,000 Sky Mesa gelding, half-brother to Maya, a dual winner at 1m plus in the US, proved easy to back and will have learnt plenty from this. He could be one to keep an eye on. (op 7-1)

3597 WESTFIELD MERRY HILL SUPPORTING THE COMMUNITY (S) STKS 5f 20y(P)
7:50 (7:50) (Class 6) 3-4-Y-0 **£2,047** (£604; £302) **Stalls** Low

Form					RPR
000	1		**Bee Magic**[42] [2304] 4-9-4 39 (b) ChrisCatlin 7		54
			(C N Kellett) *chsd ldrs: rdn over 1f out: led and edgd lft ins fnl f: styd on u.p*	33/1	
0332	2	nk	**Nawayea**[25] [2791] 4-8-6 45 KirstyMilczarek(7) 5		48
			(C N Allen) *chsd ldrs: rdn over 1f out: hung lft and r.o ins fnl f*	7/1	
2501	3	hd	**Danish Blues (IRE)**[14] [3169] 4-9-9 55 (p) JamieSpencer 12		57
			(D E Cantillon) *hld up: hdwy over 1f out: rdn and hung lft ins fnl f: r.o*	11/10[1]	
0200	4	3/4	**City For Conquest (IRE)**[35] [2509] 4-8-8 48 (b) LukeMorris(5) 8		45
			(John A Harris) *s.i.s: outpcd: hdwy u.p over 1f out: hit over hd by rival's whip ins fnl f: styd on same pce*	6/1[3]	
3006	5	2	**Memphis Man**[14] [3172] 4-9-4 45 (p) JamesDoyle 3		42
			(W M Brisbourne) *s.i.s: outpcd: r.o ins fnl f: nrst fin*	11/2[2]	
1645	6	shd	**Mind The Style**[45] [2195] 3-8-12 58 JackDean(7) 1		47
			(W G M Turner) *prom: rdn over 2f out: no ex fnl f*	13/2	
4630	7	1/2	**Temtation (IRE)**[10] [3281] 3-8-10 47 ow1 AdamKirby 9		36
			(Peter Grayson) *sn pushed along in rr: hdwy over 1f out: sn rdn: no ex ins fnl f*	16/1	
0-00	8	nk	**Orpenlina (IRE)**[14] [3169] 4-8-8 41 RussellKennemore(5) 10		34
			(Peter Grayson) *led: rdn over 1f out: hdd & wknd ins fnl f*	33/1	
00-0	9	1	**Our Archie**[34] [2541] 3-9-0 33 (v[1]) PaulFitzsimons 11		35
			(M J Attwater) *chsd ldrs: rdn over 1f out: wknd ins fnl f*	40/1	
-00	10	4	**Afric Star**[28] [2718] 3-8-4 40 ColinHaddon(5) 2		16
			(John A Harris) *sn outpcd*	50/1	
000/	11	3/4	**Danehill Folly (IRE)**[635] [5969] 4-8-13 25 KevinGhunowa(5) 4		18
			(J M Bradley) *chsd ldrs: rdn 1/2-way: wknd over 1f out*	50/1	

62.82 secs **Going Correction** -0.10s/f (Stan)
WFA 3 from 4yo 4lb 11 Ran SP% **121.2**
Speed ratings (Par 101):96,95,95,94,90 90,89,89,87,81 80
CSF £249.78 TOTE £55.90: £10.70, £1.10, £1.20; EX 152.60.There was no bid for the winner. Danish Blues (IRE) was claimed by D. Nicholls for £6,000
Owner G C Chipman **Bred** W Meah **Trained** Woodlane, Staffs
■ Stewards' Enquiry : Kirsty Milczarek one-day ban: careless riding (Jul 27)

FOCUS
A very moderate contest, even by selling standards, won by a horse with an official rating of only 39.
City For Conquest(IRE) Official explanation: jockey said filly was struck across nose by a whip

3598 WEST BROM SUPPORTING TIMBERTREE PRIMARY SCHOOL H'CAP 1m 5f 194y(P)
8:20 (8:21) (Class 6) (0-65,65) 4-Y-0+ **£2,388** (£705; £352) **Stalls** Low

Form					RPR
5126	1		**Adage**[17] [3047] 4-8-10 54 (t) ChrisCatlin 4		65+
			(David Pinder) *hld up: hmpd over 3f out: hdwy over 2f out: rdn to ld over 1f out: styd on*	15/2	
2120	2	1 1/2	**Diktatorship (IRE)**[32] [1966] 4-8-11 55 TPO'Shea 9		64
			(Jennie Candlish) *mid-div: hmpd over 3f out: hdwy over 2f out: rdn and ev ch over 1f out: hung lft and no ex ins fnl f*	14/1	
1020	3	5	**Pentasilea**[26] [2770] 4-9-6 64 JimmyQuinn 3		66
			(H J L Dunlop) *prom: chsd ldr over 2f out: rdn and ev ch over 1f out: wknd ins fnl f*	7/1[3]	
0033	4	3/4	**Blue Hills**[16] [3112] 6-9-0 65 (b) WilliamCarson(7) 1		66
			(P W Hiatt) *chsd ldrs: rdn over 2f out: wknd over 1f out*	5/1[2]	
40-6	5	1	**Malibu (IRE)**[98] [39] 6-7-11 46 oh1 LukeMorris(5) 12		45
			(S Lycett) *hld up: hdwy u.p over 2f out: hung lft over 1f out: nt trble ldrs*	7/1[3]	
00-0	6	shd	**Explosive Fox (IRE)**[57] [665] 6-8-8 52 (p) AlanDaly 7		51
			(S Curran) *hld up: hdwy u.p over 1f out: n.d*	20/1	
-605	7	1 3/4	**Phoenix Hill (IRE)**[19] [2996] 5-8-8 52 (t) JamieSpencer 2		49
			(D R Gandolfo) *hld up: rdn whn hmpd over 3f out: hdwy and nt clr run over 1f out: swtchd lft: nt trble ldrs*	11/4[1]	
0000	8	3 1/2	**Freddy (ARG)**[23] [2887] 8-9-4 62 (bt) AdrianMcCarthy 11		54
			(D K Ivory) *chsd ldrs: led 5f out: rdn and hdd over 1f out: sn wknd*	25/1	
2-22	9	4	**Stagecoach Emerald**[167] [302] 5-9-4 62 EdwardCreighton 6		48
			(R W Price) *hld up: dropped to rr over 5f out: n.d*	9/1	
0200	10	5	**Hugs Destiny (IRE)**[18] [3012] 6-8-11 55 (t) DeanMcKeown 5		34
			(M A Barnes) *sn led: hdd over 11f out: chsd ldrs: rdn and edgd lft over 3f out: wknd 2f out*	8/1	
1205	11	22	**Mister Completely (IRE)**[10] [3279] 6-9-5 63 (b[1]) JamesDoyle 13		12
			(Ms J S Doyle) *chsd ldrs: led 11f out: hdd over 8f out: led again over 6f out: hdd 5f out: hmpd over 3f out: sn wknd*	14/1	
0-	12	2 1/2	**Brave Hiawatha (FR)**[35] [3547] 5-9-2 65 KevinGhunowa(5) 10		10
			(G J Smith) *chsd ldrs: rdn 7f out: hung lft over 3f out: sn wknd*	50/1	
0004	13	8	**Penwell Hill (USA)**[15] [2946] 8-8-1 48 (b) DominicFox(3) 8		—
			(Miss M E Rowland) *chsd ldrs: led over 8f out: hdd over 6f out: wknd over 4f out*	66/1	

3m 3.79s (-3.58) **Going Correction** -0.10s/f (Stan) **13** Ran SP% **126.6**
Speed ratings (Par 101):106,105,102,101,101 101,100,98,95,93 80,79,74
CSF £110.62 CT £787.54 TOTE £12.40: £3.60, £6.30, £4.40; EX 126.60.
Owner Ms L Burns **Bred** Side Hill Stud **Trained** Kingston Lisle, Oxon
■ Adage completed a 6,068-1 treble for jockey Chris Catlin.

FOCUS
A moderate staying handicap, but the pace was decent and the winning time was good. The first two finished clear and the form looks sound.
Penwell Hill(USA) Official explanation: jockey said gelding hung right-handed throughout

3599 PERTEMPS PEOPLE DEVELOPMENT GROUP H'CAP 7f 32y(P)
8:50 (8:50) (Class 5) (0-75,73) 3-Y-0+ **£3,562** (£1,059; £529; £264) **Stalls** High

Form					RPR
-540	1		**Zennerman (IRE)**[19] [2986] 4-9-12 71 (b[1]) JamieSpencer 5		79+
			(K A Ryan) *s.i.s: hld up: nt clr run over 1f out: rdn to ld ins fnl f: r.o*	15/8[1]	
3010	2	1 1/4	**Attacca**[1] [3572] 6-8-9 54 6ex StephenDonohoe 2		59
			(J R Weymes) *chsd ldrs: rdn over 1f out: hung lft ins fnl f: r.o*	8/1	
4104	3	nk	**Dante's Diamond (IRE)**[2] [3549] 5-9-1 60 FrankieMcDonald 3		64
			(D Burchell) *hld up: nt clr run over 2f out: hdwy over 1f out: r.o*	8/1	
0024	4	1 1/4	**Boreana**[14] [3173] 4-8-8 58 LukeMorris(5) 9		59
			(Jedd O'Keeffe) *chsd ldrs: rdn to ld over 1f out: hdd and no ex ins fnl f*	10/1	
3564	5	nk	**Nou Camp**[27] [2750] 3-7-11 54 oh6 WilliamBuick(5) 10		54
			(N A Callaghan) *s.i.s: hld up: hdwy over 1f out: hung lft: styd on*	20/1	
00-0	6	nk	**Empire Dancer (IRE)**[6] [3396] 4-9-3 69 KirstyMilczarek(7) 6		69
			(C N Allen) *led: hdd over 5f out: led again over 2f out: rdn and hdd over 1f out: no ex ins fnl f*	50/1	
-062	7	1/2	**Ochre Bay**[10] [3285] 4-9-9 73 RussellKennemore(5) 8		71
			(R Hollinshead) *chsd ldrs: rdn 1/2-way: outpcd whn hmpd over 1f out: n.d after*	4/1[2]	
6303	8	1 3/4	**Cornus**[17] [3053] 5-9-11 70 (be) AdamKirby 4		64
			(A J McCabe) *hld up: rdn over 2f out: n.d*	6/1[3]	
0660	9	5	**Guildenstern (IRE)**[23] [2882] 5-9-13 72 AmirQuinn 1		54
			(P Howling) *w ldr: racd keenly: led over 5f out: rdn and hdd over 2f out: wknd over 1f out*	8/1	

1m 29.42s (-0.98) **Going Correction** -0.10s/f (Stan)
WFA 3 from 4yo+ 7lb 9 Ran SP% **118.2**
Speed ratings (Par 103):101,99,99,97,97 97,96,94,88
CSF £18.44 CT £100.52 TOTE £2.10: £1.20, £1.70, £3.70; EX 23.90.
Owner Zen Racing **Bred** Eurostrait Ltd **Trained** Hambleton, N Yorks

FOCUS
An ordinary sprint handicap in which the leaders probably went off too quick and paid for it late on. Pretty weak overall and the winner did not need to be at his best.
Cornus Official explanation: jockey said gelding never travelled

3600 EATON ELECTRIC FIELD OF DREAMS H'CAP 1m 141y(P)
9:20 (9:20) (Class 6) (0-65,65) 3-Y-0+ **£2,388** (£705; £352) **Stalls** Low

Form					RPR
0040	1		**Mr Grand Lodge (FR)**[19] [3003] 3-9-6 65 NickyMackay 7		77+
			(L M Cumani) *chsd ldrs: swtchd rt over 2f out: sn led: rdn out*	7/1	
3440	2	3/4	**Lord Of Dreams (IRE)**[17] [3056] 5-9-11 61 JamesDoyle 2		69
			(D W P Arbuthnot) *s.i.s: hld up: hdwy and edgd lft over 2f out: rdn to chse wnr over 1f out: styd on*	8/1	
0312	3	1 3/4	**Golden Spectrum (IRE)**[5] [3419] 8-9-4 59 (b) LukeMorris(5) 9		64+
			(R A Harris) *s.s: hld up: hdwy over 2f out: rdn and edgd lft over 1f out: nt rch ldrs*	11/4[1]	
5343	4	2 1/2	**Trevian**[8] [3352] 6-9-2 52 StephenDonohoe 1		52
			(J M Bradley) *prom: rdn over 3f out: hmpd and lost pl over 2f out: rallied over 1f out: no ex ins fnl f*	7/1	
0034	5	3	**Music Celebre (IRE)**[28] [2716] 7-8-11 54 (b) WilliamCarson(7) 12		47
			(S Curran) *hld up: hmpd over 2f out: hdwy over 1f out: nvr nrr*	14/1	
0325	6	2 1/2	**Scottish River (USA)**[11] [3232] 8-9-13 63 HayleyTurner 4		51
			(M D I Usher) *s.s: hld up: hdwy over 1f out: nvr nrr*	13/2[3]	
-105	7	1 3/4	**The Bonus King**[47] [2154] 7-9-11 61 ChrisCatlin 13		45
			(J Jay) *chsd ldrs: rdn whn hmpd over 2f out: sn lost pl*	3/1[2]	
2-36	8	1	**North Walk (IRE)**[17] [3063] 4-9-12 62 TPO'Shea 8		44
			(Jennie Candlish) *chsd ldrs: rdn over 3f out: hmpd over 2f out: sn wknd*	25/1	
4-00	9	1 1/4	**Haneen (USA)**[47] [2154] 4-9-5 55 EdwardCreighton 5		35
			(R W Price) *s.i.s: hld up: a in rr*	66/1	
00-0	10	1	**Regal Sunset (IRE)**[24] [2833] 4-9-5 55 (b[1]) JimmyQuinn 10		32
			(D E Cantillon) *hld up in tch: rdn whn hmpd over 2f out: sn wknd*	15/2	
0000	11	4	**Golden Square**[36] [2492] 5-9-2 57 KevinGhunowa(5) 6		26
			(A W Carroll) *led: rdn and hdd over 2f out: sn wknd*	33/1	
150-	12	5	**Compton Eclipse**[36] [1325] 7-9-8 58 (b) JamieSpencer 3		17+
			(J J Lambe, Ire) *chsd ldrs: rdn and ev ch over 2f out: wkng whn eased over 1f out*	13/2[3]	

1m 49.77s (-1.99) **Going Correction** -0.10s/f (Stan)
WFA 3 from 4yo+ 9lb 12 Ran SP% **141.2**
Speed ratings (Par 101):104,103,101,99,96 94,93,92,91,90 86,82
CSF £73.66 CT £206.14 TOTE £8.50: £2.80, £4.90, £2.10; EX 115.80 Place 6 £ 60.88, Place 5 £ 37.76.
Owner Ahmed Jaber **Bred** Gainsborough Stud Management Ltd **Trained** Newmarket, Suffolk

FOCUS
An ordinary handicap, but the pace was decent and they finished well spread out. The race went to the only 3yo in the field. Quite a few of these were backed, so the form should stand up.
Golden Square Official explanation: jockey said gelding lost its action
Compton Eclipse Official explanation: jockey said gelding had no more to give
T/Plt: £77.10 to a £1 stake. Pool: £70,091.75. 663.25 winning tickets. T/Qpdt: £30.40 to a £1 stake. Pool: £3,796.30. 92.20 winning tickets. CR

[3296]BEVERLEY (R-H)

Tuesday, July 17

OFFICIAL GOING: Heavy

Wind: Moderate, half against Weather: Heavy shower at first but soon becoming fine but breezy

3605 RACING UK ON SKY 432 CLAIMING STKS 7f 100y

2:15 (2:15) (Class 5) 3-Y-O £2,914 (£867; £433; £216) Stalls High

Form RPR

251 **1** **Gleneagles (IRE)**[23] [2913] 3-9-1 78................................ LiamJones(3) 1 66+
(W J Haggas) hld up in mid-div: hdwy over 2f out: hung rt and led ins fnl f: drvn out **11/8**[1]

0000 **2** 1 1/4 **Shotley Mac**[8] [3377] 3-8-11 43..................................(b[1]) PaulFessey 11 56
(N Bycroft) chsd ldr: led 1f out: sn hdd and no ex **66/1**

0066 **3** 5 **Superjain**[46] [2220] 3-8-1 48.. PaulHanagan 8 34
(J M Jefferson) prom: outpcd and lost pl over 2f out: styd on wl fnl f **16/1**

6000 **4** 1 3/4 **Flushed**[49] [2110] 3-8-6 47..(be) DavidAllan 12 35
(A J McCabe) led: hung lft over 3f out: hdd & wknd 1f out **33/1**

0033 **5** 5 **Rann Na Cille (IRE)**[6] [3411] 3-8-8 62......................... AndrewMullen(3) 2 28
(K A Ryan) hld up in rr: hdwy over 2f out: wknd over 1f out **4/1**[2]

0-00 **6** 2 1/2 **Mr Wall Street**[3] [3540] 3-8-7 50...................................... PaulMulrennan 7 18
(M W Easterby) prom: drvn over 3f out: hung rt and wknd over 1f out **40/1**

000 **7** 1 1/4 **Recovery Mission**[13] [3202] 3-8-2 40......................... AndrewElliott(3) 3 13
(G M Moore) in tch: effrt on outer over 2f out: nvr trbld ldrs **50/1**

4602 **8** 3/4 **Kassuta**[15] [3163] 3-7-13 58...(b) DuranFentiman(3) 4 9
(S C Williams) hld up in rr: effrt on outer over 2f out: nvr a factor **5/1**[3]

6-00 **9** 2 **Sonar Sound (GER)**[24] [2872] 3-8-8 60................................ MickyFenton 6 10
(T P Tate) hld up in rr: drvn 3f out: swtchd lft 1f out: nvr on terms **17/2**

-400 **10** 6 **Princess Palatine (IRE)**[23] [2905] 3-8-2 58.................(t) FrancisNorton 5 —
(K R Burke) s.i.s: a in rr **12/1**

U000 **11** 2 1/2 **Spinning Game**[46] [2200] 3-7-7 36.....................(be) DanielleMcCreery(7) 9 —
(D W Chapman) chsd ldrs: wknd qckly over 1f out **50/1**

1m 39.24s (4.93) **Going Correction** +0.825s/f (Soft) 11 Ran SP% **113.7**

Speed ratings (Par 100):104,102,96,94,89 86,84,84,81,74 72

CSF £139.02 TOTE £2.20: £1.10, £6.30, £3.80; EX 89.90.Gleneagles was claimed by N. Wilson for £17,000.

Owner Wentworth Racing (pty) Ltd **Bred** Darley **Trained** Newmarket, Suffolk

FOCUS

A poor claimer with the runner-up rated just 43. The winner did not have to run anywhere near his official rating of 78.

3606 MEDIEVAL NIGHT HERE NEXT MONDAY MAIDEN AUCTION STKS 5f

2:45 (2:46) (Class 4) 2-Y-O £3,886 (£1,156; £577; £288) Stalls High

Form RPR

0 **1** **Ginger Pickle**[24] [2889] 2-8-10 0.. PhillipMakin 3 77+
(J R Weymes) swvd lft s: swtchd rt after s: hdwy over 2f out: led appr fnl f: styd on strly **33/1**

44 **2** 5 **Whispering Desert**[11] [3256] 2-7-13 0...................... DuranFentiman(3) 6 51
(P T Midgley) in tch: effrt over 2f out: kpt on wl fnl f **9/1**

5544 **3** nk **Turn And River (IRE)**[8] [3378] 2-8-2 0................................... DaleGibson 5 50
(M Brittain) mid-div: hdwy over 1f out: styd on wl **11/1**

02 **4** shd **Jastaanhi**[5] [3465] 2-7-11 0.. ColinHaddon(5) 13 50
(J A Pickering) led 1f: led over 2f out: edgd lft and wandered over 1f out: sn hdd and no ex **9/2**[3]

5 hd **Scanno (IRE)** 2-8-13 0... PatCosgrave 11 60
(K R Burke) prom: hdwy over 1f out: kpt on wl **11/2**

40 **6** shd **Destinys Dream (IRE)**[59] [1848] 2-8-5 0......................... RoystonFfrench 8 51
(Mrs A Duffield) sn outpcd and in rr: hung lft over 2f out and chsd ldr stands' side: led that gp jst ins fnl f: kpt on wl **16/1**

323 **7** 1 1/2 **Select Committee**[11] [3256] 2-8-10 0.......................... GrahamGibbons 1 51
(J J Quinn) chsd ldrs: sn drvn along: c stands' side over 2f out: wknd 1f out **3/1**[1]

063 **8** 3 1/2 **Discanti (IRE)**[26] [2803] 2-8-10 0...(t) DavidAllan 7 38+
(T D Easterby) sn chsng ldrs: t.k.h: wknd fnl f **4/1**[2]

00 **9** 5 **Mimton (IRE)**[14] [3192] 2-8-0 0 ow5.................................... LanceBetts(7) 9 17
(N Wilson) prom: lost pl over 1f out **80/1**

0 **10** 1 1/2 **Maahe (IRE)**[13] [3200] 2-8-8 0... PaulHanagan 12 13
(R A Fahey) chsd ldrs: lost pl over 1f out **12/1**

0 **11** nk **Rope Bridge (IRE)**[106] [890] 2-8-7 0...................................... TomEaves 10 11
(T D Easterby) w ldr: led after 1f tl over 2f out: wknd rapidly 1f out **28/1**

0 **12** 26 **Northwest**[29] [2710] 2-8-10 0.. FrancisNorton 4 —
(A Berry) s.s: sn detached in rr: edgd lft over 2f out: sn t.o **100/1**

68.46 secs (4.46) **Going Correction** +0.825s/f (Soft) 12 Ran SP% **119.1**

Speed ratings (Par 96):97,89,88,88,88 87,85,79,71,69 69,27

CSF £304.34 TOTE £29.60: £10.20, £2.70, £3.20; EX 448.20.

Owner Mrs R Morley **Bred** L Lawson & Partners **Trained** Middleham Moor, N Yorks

FOCUS

Easy for the winner, who is capable of better, but the placed form is weak and the time was poor.

NOTEBOOK

Ginger Pickle, a rangy January foal, overcame a poor draw. He took this going right away and should improve again.

Whispering Desert stuck to her task in willing fashion and was rewarded with second spot near the line. Six furlongs in nursery company will suit her well. (op 17-2 tchd 8-1 and 11-1)

Turn And River(IRE), who gets no respite, stuck on in game fashion in the closing stages. (op 9-1)

Jastaanhi showed bags of toe but wandered and left the running rail. (op 6-1)

Scanno(IRE), a strongly-made, robust newcomer, showed ability and will do better when fully fit. (op 5-1)

Destinys Dream(IRE) drifted towards the stands' side at halfway and made up an appreciable amount of late ground. There was just a suspicion she was racing on the quicker part of the track. (op 12-1)

Select Committee, drawn one, elected to come to the stands' side at halfway. He never really threatened and in the end was only second home on that side. (tchd 4-1)

Discanti(IRE), inclined to run with the choke out, did not see it out in the tersting conditions despitre dropping back a furlong in trip. Official explanation: jockey said colt ran too free (op 13-2 tchd 3-1)

3607 JOHN SMITH'S H'CAP 7f 100y

3:15 (3:15) (Class 4) (0-85,85) 3-Y-O £7,772 (£2,312; £1,155; £577) Stalls High

Form RPR

1444 **1** **Medici Pearl**[6] [3411] 3-8-9 73.. DavidAllan 4 79+
(T D Easterby) hld up in rr: nt clr run over 2f out: burst between horses to ld 1f out: styd on strly: readily **11/4**[1]

635 **2** 1 3/4 **Cassiara**[12] [3247] 3-8-10 74.. FrancisNorton 3 74
(J Pearce) hld up: hdwy over 2f out: edgd rt over 1f out: wnt 2nd 1f out: no imp **5/1**[3]

-003 **3** 5 **Lemon Silk (IRE)**[10] [3299] 3-8-5 69.................................. PaulHanagan 8 57
(T P Tate) led: hdd 1f out: one pce **7/2**[2]

-364 **4** 1 **Musca (IRE)**[17] [3094] 3-9-4 82... TomEaves 2 68
(J Wade) trckd ldrs: sltly hmpd over 1f out: one pce **14/1**

-160 **5** 3/4 **Gazboolou**[62] [1768] 3-8-13 77.. PatCosgrave 5 61
(K R Burke) trckd ldrs: effrt over 2f out: kpt on same pce appr fnl f **9/1**

5410 **6** shd **Apache Dawn**[12] [3235] 3-9-4 85.................................. AndrewMullen(3) 1 69
(K A Ryan) sn trcking ldrs: effrt 3f out: styd on same pce appr fnl f **6/1**

0-10 **7** 1 1/2 **Packers Hill (IRE)**[50] [2092] 3-8-8 75........................... AndrewElliott(3) 6 55
(G A Swinbank) rrd s: in rr: effrt on outer over 3f out: wknd over 1f out **13/2**

3160 **8** 11 **Coconut Queen (IRE)**[6] [3411] 3-8-11 75...................(p) RoystonFfrench 7 29
(Mrs A Duffield) trckd ldrs: drvn over 3f out: lost pl 2f out: sn bhd **18/1**

1m 38.61s (4.30) **Going Correction** +0.825s/f (Soft) 8 Ran SP% **115.1**

Speed ratings (Par 102):108,106,100,99,98 98,96,83

CSF £16.91 CT £48.93 TOTE £3.40: £1.40, £2.00, £1.40; EX 13.00.

Owner Ryedale Partners No 3 **Bred** Larkwood Stud **Trained** Great Habton, N Yorks

FOCUS

A decent winning time for a race of its type. Not the strongest of contests, but Medici Pearl won well.

3608 NICK WILMOT-SMITH MEMORIAL H'CAP 5f

3:45 (3:45) (Class 6) (0-65,70) 3-Y-O+ £2,914 (£867; £433; £216) Stalls High

Form RPR

0013 **1** **The History Man (IRE)**[3] [3549] 4-9-5 61 6ex.............(b) LiamJones(3) 16 73+
(M Mullineaux) hmpd s: hdwy over 2f out: wnt 2nd 1f out: hand drvn and styd on wl to ld towards fin **5/1**[2]

2232 **2** nk **El Potro**[11] [3259] 5-8-11 50.. GrahamGibbons 6 61
(J R Holt) led: clr over 1f out: hdd nr fin **8/1**

0322 **3** 1 3/4 **Divine Spirit**[25] [2830] 6-9-6 59.................................. RoystonFfrench 17 64
(M Dods) rrd s: hdwy over 2f out: kpt on wl fnl f **13/2**[3]

6461 **4** 1/2 **Melalchrist**[3] [3536] 5-9-12 70 6ex.................................(b) PJMcDonald(5) 15 75+
(K A Ryan) lost pl after 1f: nt clr run over 2f out: styd on wl fnl f **4/1**[1]

-031 **5** shd **Dark Champion**[13] [3203] 7-8-11 57.................................(v) NeilBrown(7) 12 60
(R E Barr) chsd ldrs: hung rt and wnt 2nd over 1f out: kpt on same pce **14/1**

0200 **6** 1 3/4 **Paddywack (IRE)**[11] [3259] 10-9-0 60...................(b) DanielleMcCreery(7) 7 56
(D W Chapman) dwlt: bhd tl r.o fnl 2f **16/1**

0034 **7** 2 1/2 **Viewforth**[36] [2509] 9-8-11 50..(b) PaulHanagan 11 37
(M A Buckley) chsd ldrs: wknd fnl f **8/1**

0410 **8** 1 **Mujart**[29] [2718] 3-8-5 53.. ColinHaddon(5) 4 37
(J A Pickering) sn bhd on outer: sme hdwy over 2f out: kpt on fnl f **50/1**

-000 **9** hd **Greek Secret**[66] [1675] 4-9-2 55.......................................(b) TomEaves 2 38
(J O'Reilly) swtchd rt after s: in rr tl styd on appr fnl f **50/1**

-000 **10** 1 3/4 **Making Music**[29] [2711] 4-8-6 48................................ DuranFentiman(3) 10 25
(T D Easterby) mid-div: drvn over 2f out: nvr a factor **33/1**

4620 **11** 1/2 **Favouring (IRE)**[25] [2831] 5-8-6 48...............................(v) DominicFox(3) 8 23
(M C Chapman) prom: rdn 2f out: sn lost pl **50/1**

0335 **12** 2 1/2 **Xpres Maite**[11] [3285] 4-9-8 61... PaulEddery 5 27
(S R Bowring) mid-div: effrt over 2f out: lost pl over 1f out **20/1**

1003 **13** 1 1/2 **Sir Loin**[9] [3347] 6-8-11 53......................................(v) JamieMoriarty(3) 13 13
(N Tinkler) chsd ldrs: wknd appr fnl f **16/1**

1126 **14** 1/2 **Count Cougar (USA)**[54] [1977] 7-9-2 60.............. MichaelJStainton(5) 14 19
(S P Griffiths) chsd ldrs: wkng whn n.m.r over 1f out **8/1**

1330 **15** 7 **Miacarla**[2] [3569] 4-8-11 50.. LeeEnstone 1 —
(A Berry) in rr-div: eased whn no ch fnl f **20/1**

67.80 secs (3.80) **Going Correction** +0.825s/f (Soft)

WFA 3 from 4yo+ 4lb 15 Ran SP% **120.1**

Speed ratings (Par 101):102,101,98,97,97 94,90,89,89,86 85,81,79,78,67

CSF £41.02 CT £268.68 TOTE £6.50: £2.10, £3.10, £2.40; EX 60.50.

Owner D E Simpson & R Farrington-Kirkham **Bred** J Beckett **Trained** Alpraham, Cheshire

FOCUS

A moderate handicap and a messy race in which several were better than the bare facts.

3609 122ND YEAR OF THE WATT MEMORIAL H'CAP 2m 35y

4:15 (4:15) (Class 4) (0-80,80) 3-Y-O+ £5,181 (£1,541; £770; £384) Stalls High

Form RPR

-213 **1** **Thewhirlingdervish (IRE)**[6] [3412] 9-9-6 72......................... DavidAllan 3 81
(T D Easterby) trckd ldr: led 1f out: edgd rt: styd on gamely **7/2**[3]

4204 **2** 2 **Serpentaria**[33] [2602] 3-8-9 78....................................... PaulHanagan 1 85
(Sir Mark Prescott) led: qcknd over 3f out: hdd 1f out: styd on same pce **4/1**

1212 **3** 3 **Great As Gold (IRE)**[23] [2908] 8-9-7 78......................... PJMcDonald(5) 6 81
(B Ellison) chsd ldrs: effrt over 3f out: kpt on to take 3rd nr fin **11/4**[2]

1032 **4** nk **Kayf Aramis**[11] [3279] 5-9-5 74....................................... MarcHalford(3) 4 77
(J L Spearing) hld up: hdwy to chse ldrs over 4f out: wnt 3rd over 1f out: one pce **5/2**[1]

5600 **5** 17 **Mighty Moon**[5] [3467] 4-9-7 80.................................(bt) JamesO'Reilly(7) 5 62
(J O'Reilly) s.i.s: hdwy to chse ldrs after 2f: lost pl over 2f out **16/1**

40-5 **6** 15 **Graham Island**[30] [2692] 6-9-11 77................................... TonyHamilton 2 41
(G Wragg) in rr: drvn over 3f out: sn lost tch **12/1**

3m 52.67s (13.17) **Going Correction** +0.825s/f (Soft)

WFA 3 from 4yo+ 17lb 6 Ran SP% **111.0**

Speed ratings (Par 105):100,99,97,97,88 81

CSF £17.25 TOTE £4.00: £1.90, £3.00; EX 17.90.

Owner Mrs M H Easterby **Bred** Yeomanstown Stud **Trained** Great Habton, N Yorks

FOCUS

Solid but limited form, the winner fractionally up on his best recent form.

3610 LADY JANE BETHELL MEMORIAL LADY RIDERS H'CAP (FOR LADY AMATEUR RIDERS) 1m 4f 16y

4:45 (4:45) (Class 6) (0-65,58) 3-Y-O+ £2,810 (£871; £435; £217) Stalls High

Form RPR

00/3 **1** **Grey Samurai**[26] [2810] 7-10-2 50.. MissLEllison 6 66+
(B Ellison) trckd ldrs: led 3f out: hrd rdn and wnt rt over 1f out: sn wl clr **7/2**[2]

0011 **2** 11 **Red River Rebel**[11] [3260] 9-10-7 55............................ MissSBrotherton 9 54
(J R Norton) led 2f: chsd ldrs: kpt on to take 2nd 1f out: no ch w wnr **5/4**[1]

0/00 **3** 1 3/4 **Don Jose (USA)**[19] [3035] 4-9-13 54.................................. MrsJEPugh(7) 2 50
(N J Vaughan) led after 2f: hdd 3f out: one pce **33/1**

5045 **4** 1 1/2 **Volaticus (IRE)**[14] [3195] 6-10-2 55.............................. MissJAKidd(5) 8 49
(A D Brown) hld up in rr: hdwy over 4f out: nt clr run and swtchd lft over 1f out: nvr nrr **11/1**

30-6 **5** 1 1/4 **Parchment (IRE)**[52] 2027 5-10-7 **58**............................(b) MissARyan(3) 5 50
(A J Lockwood) *in rr: styd on fnl 2f: nvr nr ldrs* **9/1**[3]
0-00 **6** 1 1/2 **Bollin Freddie**[34] 2552 3-9-7 **53**...................................... MissADeniel 11 43
(A J Lockwood) *in rr: effrt over 3f out: edgd lft 1f out: nvr nr ldrs* **16/1**
6003 **7** 3/4 **Richtee (IRE)**[15] 3155 6-10-1 **49**............................(p) MissFayeBramley 4 38
(I W McInnes) *mid-div: effrt 3f out: nvr nr ldrs* **10/1**
035- **8** nk **Lawaaheb (IRE)**[41] 568 6-9-10 **49**................................ MissLAllan(5) 12 37
(M J Gingell) *trckd ldrs: chal 3f out: hung rt and wknd over 1f out* **25/1**
1600 **9** 3 **El Capitan (FR)**[24] 2875 4-9-11 **52**..........................(p) MissOMaylam(7) 7 36
(Miss Gay Kelleway) *in rr: hdwy over 4f out: nvr a factor* **33/1**
550/ **10** 1 **Rojabaa**[16] 5791 8-9-9 **48**.. MissMMullineaux(5) 1 30
(M Mullineaux) *dwlt: a towards rr* **12/1**
0/0- **11** 1 1/4 **Southern Bazaar (USA)**[32] 4229 6-9-4 **45**.................. MissSEilbeck(7) 3 26
(M C Chapman) *in rr: effrt over 3f out: nvr on terms* **40/1**
6-60 **12** 15 **Siegfrieds Night (IRE)**[12] 3250 6-9-8 **45**.................. JennyRiding(3) 10 3
(M C Chapman) *prom: drvn over 3f out: sn lost pl and bhd* **33/1**

2m 52.01s (11.80) **Going Correction** +0.825s/f (Soft)
WFA 3 from 4yo+ 12lb **40** Ran SP% **122.8**
Speed ratings (Par 101):93,85,84,83,82 81,81,80,78,78 77,67
CSF £8.10 CT £128.80 TOTE £4.60: £1.50, £1.30, £10.20; EX 12.20.
Owner Robert E Cook **Bred** R E And Mrs G M Cook **Trained** Norton, N Yorks
■ Stewards' Enquiry : Miss L Ellison caution: used whip when clearly winning
Mrs J E Pugh caution: careless riding

FOCUS
A low-grade ladies' event. The winner improved to the tune of 15lb but there seemed no fluke about it.

3611 STARS OF THE FUTURE APPRENTICE H'CAP 1m 100y
5:15 (5:17) (Class 6) (0-65,60) 3-Y-O **£2,914** (£867; £433; £216) **Stalls** High

Form RPR
4350 **1** **Dee Jay Wells**[23] 2916 3-9-7 **60**.................................... PJMcDonald(3) 3 65
(B Ellison) *trckd ldrs: led 2f out: hrd rdn and hld on towards fin* **7/1**
6-4 **2** hd **Magdalene**[14] 3176 3-9-7 **60**.. PatrickHills(3) 2 65
(Rae Guest) *s.i.s: hdwy over 2f out: chal ins fnl f: edgd rt: no ex nr fin* **4/1**[2]
-346 **3** 5 **Chasing Memories (IRE)**[27] 2760 3-9-3 **58**.................... NeilBrown(5) 1 52
(B Smart) *hld up in mid-div: hdwy over 3f out: kpt on same pce appr fnl f* **6/1**
00 **4** 3 **King Of Tricks**[49] 2108 3-8-9 **50**.............................. FrankiePickard(5) 5 38
(M D I Usher) *trckd ldrs: one pce appr fnl f* **33/1**
60-0 **5** 1/2 **Namarian (IRE)**[46] 2224 3-8-12 **48**.............................. DuranFentiman 11 35
(T D Easterby) *trckd ldrs: one pce fnl 2f* **11/1**
0063 **6** 1 **Piano Key**[23] 2916 3-8-6 **47**...(v) MCGeran(5) 9 32
(M D I Usher) *prom: effrt over 2f out: one pce* **7/2**[1]
00-0 **7** 1/2 **Presque Perdre**[34] 2580 3-8-4 **45**......................... DanielleMcCreery(5) 6 29
(K G Reveley) *s.i.s: in rr: detached over 2f out: sme late hdwy* **40/1**
000 **8** nk **Grethel (IRE)**[14] 3181 3-8-4 **45**....................................... AdamCarter(5) 4 28
(A Berry) *in rr-div: t.k.h: drvn 3f out: nvr a factor* **33/1**
256 **9** nk **Prince Noel**[45] 2248 3-8-10 **51**.. LanceBetts(5) 12 33
(N Wilson) *prom: effrt over 2f out: sn fdd* **5/1**[3]
-400 **10** 1 1/2 **Sangreal**[25] 2829 3-9-10 **60**... AndrewElliott 10 39
(K R Burke) *led tl 2f out: sn wknd* **16/1**
-000 **11** 1 1/2 **Sofia Royale**[29] 2727 3-9-10 **60**... LiamJones 8 36
(B Palling) *hld up in rr: effrt on outer over 2f out: nvr a factor* **14/1**
00-5 **12** 7 **Forsters Plantin**[42] 2341 3-8-9 **45**.................................. JamieMoriarty 7 6
(J J Quinn) *mid-div: effrt over 3f out: sn lost pl and bhd* **12/1**

1m 55.04s (7.64) **Going Correction** +0.825s/f (Soft) **12** Ran SP% **122.6**
Speed ratings (Par 98):94,93,88,85,85 84,83,83,83,81 80,73
CSF £35.90 CT £161.71 TOTE £8.60: £3.00, £2.10, £2.50; EX 41.10 Place 6 £182.06, Place 5 £87.47.
Owner Keith Middleton **Bred** Wallhouse And Ballyhane Stud **Trained** Norton, N Yorks

FOCUS
A fairly weak race. The winner was well in on eaerlier form and the runner-up improved on this handicap debut.
T/Plt: £190.30 to a £1 stake. Pool: £72,298.55. 277.20 winning tickets. T/Qpdt: £10.00 to a £1 stake. Pool: £5,223.40. 385.30 winning tickets. WG

3348 BRIGHTON (L-H)
Tuesday, July 17

OFFICIAL GOING: Good
A 15 minute downpour an hour before racing turned the going from "good to firm, firm in places" to "good".
Wind: Almost nil Weather: Heavy downpour 1 hour before racing, then sunny

3612 MATTHEW CLARK MEDIAN AUCTION MAIDEN STKS 5f 213y
2:30 (2:30) (Class 6) 3-4-Y-O **£2,072** (£616; £308; £153) **Stalls** Low

Form RPR
2004 **1** **Support Fund (IRE)**[6] 3425 3-8-12 65......................... StephenCarson 5 64
(Eve Johnson Houghton) *sn rdn along in 4th: hdwy to chse ldrs over 1f out: drvn to ld 75yds out: styd on* **5/1**
-002 **2** 1 1/4 **Make My Dream**[24] 2878 4-9-8 60.................................... JamesDoyle 1 65
(J Gallagher) *led: hrd rdn 2f out: hdd and no ex fnl 75yds* **7/2**[2]
-353 **3** 2 1/2 **Oh So Saucy**[33] 2592 3-8-12 58.. IanMongan 4 51
(C F Wall) *dwlt: hld up in 5th: effrt on outside 2f out: hrd rdn: no imp* **4/1**[3]
5 **4** 3 **Strut The Stage (IRE)**[37] 2196 3-9-3 70.........................(b) SebSanders 2 46
(B W Duke) *pressed ldr 3f: hung lft and wknd over 1f out* **7/1**
2245 **5** 1 **Welsh Auction**[45] 2260 3-8-12 65.................................. WilliamBuick(5) 3 43
(G A Huffer) *trckd ldng pair: hrd rdn and wknd over 1f out* **13/8**[1]
0000 **6** 2 1/2 **Fancy You (IRE)**[21] 2972 4-8-12 40.........................(p) KevinGhunowa(5) 7 31
(A W Carroll) *s.s: a bhd: hrd rdn and n.d fnl 2f* **50/1**

1m 12.81s (2.71) **Going Correction** +0.475s/f (Yiel)
WFA 3 from 4yo 5lb **6** Ran SP% **111.4**
Speed ratings (Par 101):100,98,95,91,89 86
CSF £22.23 TOTE £5.70: £2.40, £2.20; EX 19.20.
Owner Fighttheban Partnership II **Bred** W Maxwell Ervine **Trained** Blewbury, Oxon

FOCUS
A poor race, run at an ordinary gallop. The runners stayed far side.

3613 3663 FIRST FOR FOOD SERVICE H'CAP 5f 213y
3:00 (3:00) (Class 5) (0-75,75) 3-Y-O+ **£2,775** (£830; £415; £207; £103) **Stalls** Low

Form RPR
0000 **1** **Jayanjay**[21] 2972 8-8-11 **60**.. TQuinn 1 72+
(P Mitchell) *trckd ldrs: led 1f out: rdn out* **16/1**
004 **2** 1 1/4 **Summer Recluse (USA)**[8] 3368 8-8-13 **62**..........................(t) LPKeniry 8 70
(J M Bradley) *hld up towards rr: hdwy and nt best of runs fnl 2f: styd on to chse wnr fnl 150yds* **12/1**
05-4 **3** 2 **Perfect Treasure (IRE)**[39] 2411 4-9-1 **64**........................ EddieAhern 3 66
(J A R Toller) *towards rr: hdwy and hrd rdn over 1f out: styd on* **15/2**
642 **4** 3/4 **Loophole**[14] 3188 5-9-12 **75**.. SebSanders 9 75
(P J Makin) *hld up in rr: rdn and hdwy 2f out: styd on same pce* **9/2**[2]
2150 **5** 1/2 **What Do You Know**[31] 2655 4-9-9 **72**............................ ChrisCatlin 2 70
(A M Hales) *led: hrd rdn and hdd 1f out: no ex* **8/1**
2250 **6** 1 1/2 **Chatshow (USA)**[23] 2912 6-9-2 **70**................................ LukeMorris(5) 4 64
(A W Carroll) *trckd ldrs gng wl: effrt 2f out: no ex over 1f out* **5/1**[3]
1-24 **7** 3/4 **Buy On The Red**[178] 198 6-9-6 **69**..................................(p) JamesDoyle 7 61
(W R Muir) *prom tl wknd over 1f out* **4/1**[1]
44-3 **8** 1 1/4 **Unlimited**[35] 2546 5-8-9 **58**..(p) RobertHavlin 11 46
(R Simpson) *stdd s: plld hrd: sn in tch: outpcd fnl 2f* **8/1**
6553 **9** 3/4 **Piddies Pride (IRE)**[31] 2657 5-8-7 **56**................................(v) TPO'Shea 6 42
(Miss Gay Kelleway) *dwlt: a bhd* **11/1**
5300 **10** 3 **Musical Script (USA)**[18] 3064 4-8-8 **57**........................... JimmyQuinn 13 34
(Mouse Hamilton-Fairley) *prom on outside: hrd rdn 2f out: sn wknd* **16/1**
0 **11** 13 **Millenium Sun (IRE)**[5] 3452 3-9-1 **72**......................... AlanCreighton(3) 10 10
(E J Creighton) *prom to 1/2-way: wknd qckly: eased whn no ch over 1f out* **50/1**

1m 12.38s (2.28) **Going Correction** +0.475s/f (Yiel)
WFA 3 from 4yo+ 5lb **11** Ran SP% **118.6**
Speed ratings (Par 103):103,101,98,97,97 95,94,92,91,87 70
CSF £195.91 CT £1597.57 TOTE £10.80: £3.20, £4.00, £2.00; EX 135.70 Trifecta £147.70 Part won. Pool: £208.16 - 0.70 winning units..
Owner Peter Crate **Bred** P D Crate **Trained** Epsom, Surrey
■ Sweet Pickle was withdrawn (10/1, unsuitable ground). Rule 4 applies, deduct 5p in the £. New market formed.

FOCUS
A moderate contest, but run at a reasonable gallop. The runners raced middle to far side. The winner was very well in on old form and the standard looks solid enough.
Piddies Pride(IRE) Official explanation: jockey said mare was never travelling

3614 GAYMERS CIDER (S) STKS 6f 209y
3:30 (3:30) (Class 6) 2-Y-O **£1,943** (£578; £288; £144) **Stalls** Low

Form RPR
050 **1** **Marmite (IRE)**[18] 3043 2-8-6 0..(b1) LPKeniry 2 53
(E F Vaughan) *cl up in 4th: swtchd outside and effrt 2f out: styd on u.p to ld nr fin* **15/8**[2]
5402 **2** nk **Ten On Line (IRE)**[18] 3065 2-8-11 0................................ SebSanders 1 57
(J G M O'Shea) *cl up in 3rd: fnd gap on rail and led 2f out: hrd rdn fnl f: hdd and nt qckn nr fin* **11/10**[1]
040 **3** 3 **Little By Luck (IRE)**[8] 3364 2-8-1 0............................... LukeMorris(5) 4 44
(W G M Turner) *led: rdn and hdd 2f out: one pce fnl f* **6/1**[3]
00 **4** 1 1/4 **Poppy Perfect**[29] 2723 2-8-6 0.. JimmyQuinn 3 41
(J M P Eustace) *chsd ldr 5f: sn outpcd* **8/1**

1m 27.22s (4.52) **Going Correction** +0.475s/f (Yiel) **4** Ran SP% **107.8**
Speed ratings (Par 92):93,92,89,87
CSF £4.31 TOTE £3.00; EX 4.10.There was no bid for the winner. Ten On Line was claimed by Miss V. Haigh for £6,000.
Owner Hungerford Park Stud **Bred** Mrs E L Hunter **Trained** Newmarket, Suffolk
■ Stewards' Enquiry : L P Keniry three-day ban: used whip with excessive frequency and without giving filly time to respond (Jul 29-31)

FOCUS
A weak race, and low on numbers too. The winner stayed far side. The second and third were close to their marks.

NOTEBOOK
Marmite(IRE), blinkered for the first time for this drop into selling company, just got there in time, and should stay farther in due course. However, the form does not amount to much. (op 9-4)
Ten On Line(IRE), running for a new stable after being claimed last time, may yet be good enough to find a weak 7f seller, having responded gamely to some strong driving. However, he is beginning to look rather exposed, even at this level. (tchd Evens and 5-4)
Little By Luck(IRE) looks best at this trip, but will have to be kept to this sort of company to have any chance of success. (op 5-1 tchd 13-2)
Poppy Perfect has looked very modest in her three runs to date, but there was a little more encouragement over this additional furlong. (op 7-1 tchd 17-2)

3615 PIPER HEIDSIECK CHAMPAGNE H'CAP 7f 214y
4:00 (4:00) (Class 6) (0-60,64) 3-Y-O+ **£2,072** (£616; £308; £153) **Stalls** Low

Form RPR
00-6 **1** **Dancing Storm**[17] 3110 4-9-1 **51**.. ChrisCatlin 9 61
(W S Kittow) *mde most: rdn over 2f out: styd on wl and wnt clr fnl f* **8/1**
2205 **2** 2 1/2 **Wrighty Almighty (IRE)**[13] 3218 5-9-5 **55**.......................... PaulDoe 8 59
(P R Chamings) *in tch: c to stands' rail and jnd wnr 3f out tl 2f out: nt qckn fnl f* **15/2**[3]
655 **3** nk **Jools**[29] 2722 9-9-3 **53**... RobertHavlin 13 56
(D K Ivory) *in tch: effrt over 2f out: hrd rdn over 1f out: styd on same pce* **16/1**
0640 **4** 1/2 **Prince Valentine**[9] 3352 6-8-12 **48**........................(p) StephenCarson 3 50
(G L Moore) *hld up in rr: shkn up and hdwy over 1f out: nt rch chalng position* **12/1**
0000 **5** nk **Goodwood Spirit**[32] 2619 5-9-3 **53**...............................(v1) LPKeniry 7 54
(J M Bradley) *hld up in midfield: effrt and c to stands' rail over 1f out: styd on wl fnl f* **20/1**
00-0 **6** nk **Ten To The Dozen**[29] 2716 4-8-9 **52**......................... WilliamCarson(7) 14 53
(P W Hiatt) *in tch: effrt over 2f out: one pce appr fnl f* **40/1**
4100 **7** nk **Napoletano (GER)**[6] 3419 6-9-5 **55**...................................(p) TQuinn 6 55
(S Dow) *plld hrd in midfield: outpcd and struggling over 2f out: rallied and r.o fnl f* **14/1**
4330 **8** 1/2 **Foolish Groom**[29] 2716 6-9-0 **55**......................(p) RussellKennemore(5) 15 54
(R Hollinshead) *chsd ldrs tl wknd over 1f out* **12/1**
5054 **9** 1 1/4 **Blue Empire (IRE)**[42] 2336 6-9-5 **55**................................. EddieAhern 1 51
(C R Dore) *prom tl wknd wl over 1f out* **10/1**
2545 **10** 1 1/4 **Murrumbidgee (IRE)**[20] 2990 4-9-10 **60**........................ SebSanders 2 53
(J W Hills) *hld up towards rr: hdwy towards inner 2f out: wknd 1f out* **7/2**[1]
501 **11** 2 **Blue Mistral (IRE)**[9] 3352 3-9-1 **64** 6ex..................(vt) WilliamBuick(5) 12 53
(W J Knight) *a in rr: rdn and n.d fnl 3f* **9/2**[2]
0304 **12** 2 1/2 **Lady Duxyana**[5] 3455 4-8-12 **48**.............................(v) RichardSmith 10 31
(M D I Usher) *in tch: hrd rdn 2f out: sn wknd* **14/1**
-604 **13** 2 1/2 **Straight Gal (IRE)**[18] 3044 4-9-0 **50**............................... JamesDoyle 5 27
(Mrs N Smith) *hrd rdn over 2f out: a bhd* **80/1**

0426 **14** *shd* **Lady Edge (IRE)**[21] 2965 5-9-1 **56** .... KevinGhunowa(5) 4 — 33
(A W Carroll) *chsd ldrs: hrd rdn over 2f out: sn wknd* **16/1**

1m 38.88s (3.84) **Going Correction** +0.475s/f (Yiel)
WFA 3 from 4yo+ 8lb — **14** Ran SP% **121.3**
Speed ratings (Par 101):99,96,96,95,95 95,94,94,93,91 89,87,84,84
CSF £66.45 CT £954.32 TOTE £10.50: £2.70, £2.80, £4.30; EX 73.30 TRIFECTA Not won..
Owner The Quintet Partnership **Bred** D R Tucker **Trained** Blackborough, Devon

FOCUS
A very modest race, but a competitive one. The winner was back to his best, with the third to form. Most of the runners headed for the middle of the track, with Wrighty Almighty coming all the way over to the stands' rail, and the favourite Murrumbidgee closest to the far rail.
Blue Mistral(IRE) Official explanation: jockey said filly was unsuited by the good ground

3616 BLAKES BUTCHERS H'CAP — 1m 1f 209y
4:30 (4:32) (Class 6) (0-65,65) 3-Y-0+ — **£2,072** (£616; £308; £153) **Stalls** High

Form — RPR

006- **1** **Cheveley Flyer**[90] 6630 4-8-9 **46** oh1 .... JimmyQuinn 8 — 55
(J Pearce) *mid-div: hdwy 3f out: drvn to ld ins fnl f* **13/2**[3]

6040 **2** *5½* **And Again (USA)**[7] 3397 4-9-11 **62** .... (p) ChrisCatlin 12 — 62
(R A Teal) *in tch: jnd ldr over 3f out: hrd rdn over 1f out: wknd fnl f: fin 3rd, ½l & 5l: plcd 2nd* **8/1**

2645 **3** *3* **Surdoue**[28] 2745 7-8-10 **47** .... AdrianMcCarthy 9 — 41
(D Morris) *led tl over 2f out: cl 4th but hld whn n.m.r jst ins fnl f: fin 4th: plcd 3rd* **16/1**

2446 **4** *¾* **Piano Man**[24] 2875 5-9-4 **55** .... TQuinn 4 — 47
(B G Powell) *bhd: sme hdwy over 3f out: sn rdn: nt pce to chal fnl 2f: fin 5th: plcd 4th* **9/2**[2]

0000 **5** *3* **Didnt Tell My Wife**[26] 2795 8-8-4 **46** oh1 .... NataliaGemelova(5) 16 — 33
(Miss K B Boutflower) *bhd: mod effrt over 3f out: n.d: fin 6th: plcd 5th* **25/1**

3010 **6** *5* **Mamichor**[20] 2990 4-8-11 **48** .... (p) RichardSmith 2 — 25
(B R Johnson) *in tch: rdn 3f out: sn wknd: fin 7th: plcd 6th* **9/1**

00 **7** *17* **Minstrel Flyer (IRE)**[45] 2257 5-8-6 **46** oh1 .... AlanCreighton(3) 3 — —
(E J Creighton) *stdd and wnt lft s: midfield tl wknd 5f out: sn bhd: fin 8th: plcd 7th* **66/1**

5-00 **8** *15* **Fortune Point (IRE)**[37] 2490 9-8-8 **50** .... (v) KevinGhunowa(5) 15 — —
(A W Carroll) *prom: drvn along over 4f out: wknd over 3f out: eased whn no ch fnl 2f: fin 9th: plcd 8th* **12/1**

00-0 **9** *3½* **Chart Express**[47] 2175 3-7-12 **48** .... StephaneBreux(3) 5 — —
(J R Best) *a bhd: t.o fr 1/2-way: fin 10th: plcd 9th* **25/1**

020- **10** *7* **Ground Patrol**[188] 2862 6-9-9 **60** .... GeorgeBaker 1 — —
(W G M Turner) *trckd ldrs on rail: wknd 5f out: eased whn no ch fnl 3f: fin 11th: plcd 10th* **14/1**

00-0 **11** *3* **Brogue Lanterns (IRE)**[184] 129 5-8-2 **46** oh1 .... SCreighton(7) 11 — —
(E J Creighton) *dwlt: a bhd: t.o fr 1/2-way: fin 12th: plcd 11th* **50/1**

00-2 **D** *½* **Princely Ted (IRE)**[6] 3428 6-8-7 **49** .... WilliamBuick(5) 10 — 44
(R A Farrant) *prom: led over 2f out: edgd to stands' rail over 1f out: hrd rdn and hdd ins fnl f: kpt on: fin 2nd, 1/2l: disq: failed to draw correct weight (carried 7st 9lb)* **3/1**[1]

2m 7.26s (4.66) **Going Correction** +0.475s/f (Yiel)
WFA 3 from 4yo+ 10lb — **12** Ran SP% **109.0**
Speed ratings (Par 101):100,95,93,92,90 86,72,60,57,52 49,99
CSF £46.22 CT £587.12 TOTE £6.80: £1.90, £2.90, £3.90; EX 57.30 TRIFECTA Not won..
Owner The Cheveley Red Lion Partnership **Bred** Lady Jennifer Green **Trained** Newmarket, Suffolk
■ Golden Platitude was withdrawn (8/1, refused to enter stalls.) R4 applies, deduct 10p in the £.
■ Stewards' Enq: Buick two-day ban: used whip with excessive frequency (Jul 29-30)

FOCUS
A weak race, but a fair gallop. The winner should be capable of better on his jumps form. For the first time at the meeting, the principals all came to the stands' rail, though Princely Ted came across later than the other leaders. R. Farrant fined £1,000 (failed to put weight cloth on).
Fortune Point(IRE) Official explanation: jockey said gelding was never travelling
Ground Patrol Official explanation: jockey said gelding lost its action

3617 CATERING SERVICES INTERNATIONAL APPRENTICE H'CAP — 1m 3f 196y
5:00 (5:02) (Class 6) (0-65,65) 4-Y-0+ — **£1,943** (£578; £288; £144) **Stalls** High

Form — RPR

0354 **1** **Bienheureux**[5] 3457 6-8-10 **54** .... (t) NicolPolli(3) 8 — 64
(Miss Gay Kelleway) *hld up and bhd: hdwy 4f out: swtchd lft 3f out: drvn to ld 1f out: styd on wl* **7/1**[3]

5502 **2** *3½* **Eldorado**[35] 2544 6-9-5 **65** .... HarryPoulton(5) 5 — 70
(G L Moore) *mid-div: effrt and hrd rdn over 2f out: styd on to take 2nd ins fnl f: nt pce to trble wnr* **2/1**[1]

050- **3** *shd* **Constant Cheers (IRE)**[383] 3017 4-9-2 **57** .... (p) SaleemGolam 10 — 62
(W R Swinburn) *chsd ldrs on outside: led briefly on stands' rail over 1f out: one pce fnl f* **20/1**

203 **4** *7* **Moonshine Creek**[41] 2370 5-8-6 **52** .... WilliamCarson(5) 12 — 46
(P W Hiatt) *t.k.h: trckd ldr: led over 3f out tl wknd over 1f out* **4/1**[2]

1003 **5** *1* **Recalcitrant**[21] 2964 4-8-12 **56** .... WilliamBuick(3) 11 — 49
(S Dow) *chsd ldrs: rdn 4f out: wknd over 1f out* **7/1**[3]

0010 **6** *shd* **Blackmail (USA)**[33] 2595 9-8-11 **57** .... (b) JackMitchell(5) 4 — 49
(P Mitchell) *in tch: hrd rdn and outpcd over 3f out: sme hdwy alone towards inner whn rdr dropped reins over 2f out: wknd over 1f out* **12/1**

-060 **7** *hd* **Phone In**[50] 2089 4-8-4 **48** .... TolleyDean(3) 7 — 40
(R Brotherton) *led tl over 3f out: wknd 2f out* **16/1**

0050 **8** *7* **Salvestro**[20] 2979 4-8-10 **51** .... JamesDoyle 2 — 33
(A W Carroll) *dwlt: hld up and bhd: hrd rdn and no ch over 2f out* **12/1**

0220 **9** *12* **Hathaal (IRE)**[12] 3232 8-9-0 **60** .... (vt) SCreighton(5) 9 — 24
(E J Creighton) *t.k.h towards rr: hmpd on outside rail 7f out: hdwy 4f out: wknd 3f out* **25/1**

2000 **10** *7* **Ariodante**[35] 2531 5-9-5 **60** .... StephenDonohoe 3 — 13
(J M P Eustace) *dwlt: sn prom on ins: wknd 3f out* **7/1**[3]

2m 36.02s (3.82) **Going Correction** +0.475s/f (Yiel) — **10** Ran SP% **120.7**
Speed ratings (Par 101):106,103,103,98,98 98,98,93,85,80
CSF £22.15 CT £279.98 TOTE £8.00: £2.60, £1.40, £5.30; EX 24.80 Trifecta £76.70 Pool: £181.59 - 1.68 winning units. Place 6 £1,523.24, Place 5 £536.33.
Owner Mr & Mrs I Henderson **Bred** N R Shields **Trained** Exning, Suffolk

FOCUS
A moderate race, but a good gallop which helped the hold-up winner. Limited form.
Ariodante Official explanation: jockey said gelding was unsuited by the good ground
T/Plt: £3,570.50 to a £1 stake. Pool: £73,613.00. 15.05 winning tickets. T/Qpdt: £370.00 to a £1 stake. Pool: £5,050.30. 10.10 winning tickets. LM

3416 KEMPTON (A.W) (R-H)
Tuesday, July 17

OFFICIAL GOING: Standard
Wind: Moderate, half against Weather: Sunny spells

3618 DIGIBET.COM H'CAP — 5f (P)
6:15 (6:15) (Class 6) (0-50,50) 3-Y-0+ — **£2,047** (£604; £302) **Stalls** High

Form — RPR

044 **1** **Piccostar**[30] 2696 4-9-4 **50** .... (v1) SamHitchcott 3 — 57
(A B Haynes) *towards rr: rdn and stl plenty to do ins fnl 2f: styd on strly thrght fnl f: led last stride* **7/1**

0000 **2** *hd* **Ballybunion (IRE)**[8] 3368 8-8-12 **49** .... LukeMorris(5) 10 — 55
(R A Harris) *towards rr: rdn and hdwy over 1f out: styd on str to take slt advantage fnl 30yds: ct last stride* **11/1**

0310 **3** *nk* **Drum Dance (IRE)**[20] 2979 5-8-11 **50** .... (b1) HaddenFrost(7) 5 — 55
(M Hill) *trckd ldrs: led travelling smoothly ins fnl f: ct fnl 30yds and no ex* **10/1**

1051 **4** *nk* **Majestical (IRE)**[18] 3045 5-9-4 **50** .... (p) DarryllHolland 11 — 54
(V Smith) *towards rr: hdwy whn nt clr run and swtchd lft 1f out: fin strly: gng on cl home* **7/2**[1]

0010 **5** *nk* **Arfinnit (IRE)**[34] 2555 6-9-2 **48** .... (p) SebSanders 4 — 51
(Mrs A L M King) *chsd ldrs tl led wl over 1f out: hdd ins fnl f: one pce fnl 100yds* **5/1**[2]

0-06 **6** *½* **Parkside Pursuit**[40] 2386 9-8-9 **48** .... BarrySavage(7) 2 — 49
(J M Bradley) *towards rr: rdn and hdwy over 1f out: kpt on fnl f but nvr quite gng pce to chal* **16/1**

0-04 **7** *nk* **Willofcourse**[32] 2622 6-8-11 **50** .... AmyScott(7) 9 — 50
(H Candy) *towards rr: pushed along and hdwy appr fnl f: kpt on but nvr in contention* **11/1**

0-00 **8** *¾* **Hard To Catch (IRE)**[42] 2334 9-9-4 **50** .... LPKeniry 7 — 47
(Mike Murphy) *chsd ldrs: drvn to chal appr fnl f: wknd fnl 100yds* **33/1**

6-24 **9** *1¾* **Danehill Stroller (IRE)**[18] 3045 7-8-13 **48** .... JerryO'Dwyer(3) 6 — 39
(A M Hales) *hdwy whn hmpd over 1f out: n.d after* **6/1**[3]

0020 **10** *2* **Gone'N'Dunnett (IRE)**[17] 3106 8-9-3 **49** .... (v) AmirQuinn 1 — 33
(Mrs C A Dunnett) *nvr gng pce to rch ldrs* **10/1**

1000 **11** *3* **Borzoi Maestro**[31] 2652 6-8-11 **50** .... (p) MarkCoumbe(7) 12 — 23
(G F Bridgwater) *chsd ldrs tl wknd ins fnl 2f* **12/1**

-000 **12** *¾* **Meikle Barfil**[53] 1991 5-9-4 **50** .... (b1) SteveDrowne 8 — 20
(J M Bradley) *led tl wknd wl over 1f out: sn wknd* **10/1**

60.93 secs (0.53) **Going Correction** -0.175s/f (Stan) — **12** Ran SP% **126.1**
Speed ratings (Par 101):88,87,87,86,86 85,84,83,80,77 72,71
CSF £87.25 CT £800.39 TOTE £8.50: £1.80, £4.30, £4.20; EX 186.70.
Owner K Corke & M L Brett **Bred** Catridge Farm Stud Ltd **Trained** Limpley Stoke, Bath

FOCUS
A very moderate winning time for a race like this and most of the field finished within about 5l of the winner. Limited form.
Meikle Barfil Official explanation: jockey said gelding ran too free

3619 DIGIBET CLAIMING STKS — 7f (P)
6:45 (6:48) (Class 5) 3-Y-0+ — **£2,914** (£867; £433; £216) **Stalls** High

Form — RPR

5041 **1** **Desert Dreamer (IRE)**[9] 3350 6-9-11 72 .... JimCrowley 7 — 83+
(P R Chamings) *hld up in rr: hdwy on bit fr 2f out to ld over 1f out: sn clr: v easily* **9/4**[2]

2031 **2** *3½* **Samuel Charles**[15] 3172 9-9-1 70 .... (p) EddieAhern 5 — 64
(C R Dore) *chsd ldrs: rdn and hung lft fr 2f out: styd on to chse wnr ins fnl f but nvr any ch* **5/4**[1]

0140 **3** *5* **Crafty Fox**[14] 3191 4-9-3 58 .... (v) SebSanders 12 — 53
(A P Jarvis) *led tl hdd over 1f out: sn no ch* **6/1**[3]

-030 **4** *1¼* **Amazing King (IRE)**[24] 2893 3-8-4 61 .... JackDean(7) 3 — 51
(W G M Turner) *towards rr: rdn 3f out: mod prog fnl f* **33/1**

5003 **5** *2½* **Mine The Balance (IRE)**[13] 3218 4-8-7 49 .... (b) ThomasO'Brien(7) 8 — 40
(H J Manners) *chsd ldr: chal 3f out to 2f out: wknd over 1f out* **20/1**

00-0 **6** *1¼* **Grand Sefton**[13] 3217 4-9-0 52 .... AmirQuinn 9 — 37
(Stef Liddiard) *chsd ldrs: rdn 3f out: wknd 2f out* **20/1**

0/0 **7** *1¼* **Princess Zaha**[43] 2307 5-9-0 0 .... LPKeniry 6 — 34
(A G Newcombe) *a in rr* **50/1**

0010 **8** *nk* **Ceredig**[18] 3067 4-9-5 50 .... IanMongan 4 — 38
(Mrs L J Mongan) *chsd ldrs tl wknd ins fnl 3f* **12/1**

-000 **9** *2* **Polish Prospect (IRE)**[8] 3365 3-8-2 50 .... JimmyQuinn 11 — 23
(H S Howe) *a in rr* **33/1**

0000 **10** *4* **Li Shih Chen**[66] 1666 4-9-3 58 .... SimonWhitworth 1 — 20
(A P Jarvis) *chsd ldrs to 1/2-way* **11/1**

1m 25.93s (-0.87) **Going Correction** -0.175s/f (Stan)
WFA 3 from 4yo+ 7lb — **10** Ran SP% **122.9**
Speed ratings (Par 103):97,93,87,85,83 81,80,79,77,72
CSF £5.40 TOTE £3.40: £1.10, £1.20, £2.10; EX 8.30.Desert Dreamer was claimed by G. A. Butler for £18,000.
Owner Patrick Chamings Sprint Club **Bred** Gainsborough Stud Management Ltd **Trained** Baughurst, Hants

FOCUS
A very moderate race dominated by the 'form' horses. The winner did it well, but the form may not prove very informative in the coming weeks.

3620 DIGIBET SPORTS BETTING H'CAP — 1m (P)
7:15 (7:16) (Class 6) (0-65,65) 3-Y-0 — **£2,047** (£604; £302) **Stalls** High

Form — RPR

-510 **1** **Mountain Cat (IRE)**[25] 2834 3-9-6 **64** .... TPO'Shea 4 — 76
(W J Musson) *mde virtually all: hrd drvn 2f out: styd on wl and in control fnl f* **7/2**[2]

4006 **2** *1¼* **Hucking Heat (IRE)**[14] 3178 3-9-6 **64** .... GeorgeBaker 6 — 73
(J R Best) *in tch: hdwy 3f out: chsd wnr over 2f out: win half a l and rdn over 1f out: no imp fnl f* **8/1**

34-0 **3** *1* **Good Effect (USA)**[15] 3150 3-9-4 **62** .... SebSanders 12 — 69+
(A P Jarvis) *towards rr: rdn over 2f out: styd on wl fr over 1f out to go 3rd ins fnl f but nvr gng pce of ldng pair* **9/1**

0040 **4** *2* **Goose Green (IRE)**[23] 2916 3-9-5 **63** .... SteveDrowne 10 — 65
(R J Hodges) *in tch: rdn and hdwy over 2f out: kpt on same pce fnl f* **14/1**

06-5 **5** *5* **Whaxaar (IRE)**[47] 2178 3-8-9 **58** .... WilliamBuick(5) 11 — 49
(S Kirk) *towards rr: sn pushed along: sme hdwy over 1f out: mod late prog ins fnl f* **9/2**[3]

0442 **6** *hd* **Inquisitress**[31] [2668] 3-8-11 **60** .... TolleyDean(5) 9 50
(J J Bridger) *in tch: sme hdwy whn nt clr run and swtchd lft over 2f out: nvr in contention after* **12/1**

3021 **7** *1 1/2* **Winged Farasi**[30] [2697] 3-9-0 **63** .... LukeMorris(5) 14 50
(R A Harris) *towards rr: rdn 3f out: mod prog fnl f* **5/2**[1]

-000 **8** *hd* **Heights Of Golan**[15] [3150] 3-9-1 **59** .... (b) JamesDoyle 3 45
(I A Wood) *towards rr: rdn over 3f out: mod late prog* **25/1**

3300 **9** *1 1/4* **Citrus Chief (USA)**[49] [2105] 3-8-5 **54** .... (b) KevinGhunowa(5) 2 37
(R A Harris) *sn chsng ldr: wknd over 2f out* **20/1**

6-30 **10** *1 1/2* **Geordie's Pool**[47] [2177] 3-9-7 **65** .... EddieAhern 1 45
(J W Hills) *a in rr* **20/1**

0-00 **11** *3/4* **Twenty Percent**[56] [1928] 3-9-2 **60** .... PaulDoe 13 38
(P R Chamings) *a in rr* **50/1**

6040 **12** *1* **Beckenham's Secret**[15] [3150] 3-9-2 **60** .... JimCrowley 7 36
(B R Millman) *chsd ldrs tl wknd 3f out* **16/1**

0-00 **13** *8* **Korty**[74] [1447] 3-8-13 **57** .... PatDobbs 5 14
(W J Musson) *chsd ldrs 5f* **50/1**

1m 40.3s (-0.50) **Going Correction** -0.175s/f (Stan) **13** Ran SP% **127.6**
Speed ratings (Par 98):95,93,92,90,85 85,84,83,82,81 80,79,71
CSF £32.16 CT £251.68 TOTE £5.50: £2.50, £3.60, £3.20; EX 40.70.
Owner S Rudolf **Bred** Mrs Mary Gallagher **Trained** Newmarket, Suffolk

FOCUS
Not the strongest of 3yo handicaps, this was run at a reasonable gallop.

3621 ROBERT DYAS KEY SUPPLIERS MEDIAN AUCTION MAIDEN STKS 1m 4f (P)
7:45 (7:48) (Class 6) 3-5-Y-0 **£2,047** (£604; £302) **Stalls** Centre

Form RPR

3 **1** **Opal Haze (USA)**[12] [3244] 3-8-7 0 .... RobertHavlin 3 76
(J H M Gosden) *trckd ldrs: wnt 3rd 5f out: drvn to take narrow ld 2f out: rdn clr fnl f* **6/1**[3]

-22 **2** *4* **Wicked Daze (IRE)**[25] [2833] 4-9-10 76 .... SebSanders 2 75
(Sir Mark Prescott) *sn led: rdn over 3f out: narrowly hdd 2f out: no ch w wnr fnl f* **4/5**[1]

0-3 **3** *4* **Harry Tricker**[40] [2402] 3-8-12 0 .... JimCrowley 4 69
(Mrs A J Perrett) *chsd ldrs: wnt 2nd 6f out: rdn and outpcd over 2f out* **2/1**[2]

6 **4** *12* **Pertemps Power**[20] [2981] 3-8-12 0 .... JimmyQuinn 6 51
(A D Smith) *towards rr: rdn 1/2-way: mod prog fr 2f out* **40/1**

3 **5** *1* **Blue Eyed Eloise**[78] [1342] 5-9-0 0 .... KevinGhunowa(5) 5 45
(J M Bradley) *chsd ldrs tl wknd 5f out* **16/1**

00 **6** *25* **Glentimon (IRE)**[64] [1725] 3-8-12 0 .... LPKeniry 1 12
(S Kirk) *towards rr: rdn 5f out: no rspnse* **66/1**

7 *10* **Running Rings** 3-8-0 0 .... JCorrigan(7) 8 —
(P W D'Arcy) *dropped jockey bef s: slowly away: a in rr* **50/1**

20 **8** *1* **Alexander Guru**[64] [1725] 3-8-12 0 .... SteveDrowne 7 —
(M Blanshard) *chsd ldrs tl wknd 5f out* **16/1**

2m 32.08s (-4.82) **Going Correction** -0.175s/f (Stan)
WFA 3 from 4yo+ 12lb **8** Ran SP% **120.8**
Speed ratings (Par 101):109,106,103,95,95 78,71,71
CSF £11.93 TOTE £5.00: £1.40, £1.10, £1.10; EX 11.00.
Owner K Abdulla **Bred** Juddmonte Farms Inc **Trained** Newmarket, Suffolk

FOCUS
A decent if rather uncompetitive maiden in which only three mattered in the market and they dominated the race. The pace was decent though, the time was exactly a second quicker than the later three-year-old handicap, and they finished very well spread out.
Pertemps Power Official explanation: jockey said gelding ran green
Glentimon(IRE) Official explanation: jockey said gelding had no more to give
Alexander Guru Official explanation: jockey said gelding moved poorly

3622 DIGIBET POKER H'CAP 1m (P)
8:15 (8:17) (Class 5) (0-70,70) 3-Y-0 **£3,238** (£963; £481; £240) **Stalls** High

Form RPR

5005 **1** **Bajan Pride**[14] [3176] 3-9-4 **67** .... PatDobbs 9 78+
(R Hannon) *chsd ldrs: led appr fnl 2f: drvn clr fnl f: comf* **5/1**[3]

3300 **2** *1 1/4* **Henry The Seventh**[43] [2317] 3-9-6 **69** .... EddieAhern 8 77+
(J W Hills) *in tch: hdwy 3f out: chsd wnr appr fnl f and kpt on but a readily hld* **20/1**

2-60 **3** *7* **Marriaj (USA)**[24] [2862] 3-9-7 **70** .... IanMongan 14 62
(B Smart) *chsd ldrs tl outpcd 5f out: drvn and styd on fr 2f out to take mod 3rd fnl f* **10/1**

1013 **4** *1 1/2* **Sweet World**[92] [1059] 3-9-2 **65** .... JimCrowley 12 54
(A P Jarvis) *rr: rdn 3f out: sme prog fnl 2f but nvr in contention* **16/1**

1-00 **5** *1/2* **Galaxy Stars**[34] [2570] 3-9-7 **70** .... (t) AmirQuinn 10 57+
(P J Makin) *in tch: sme hdwy on ins whn nt clr run over 2f out: n.d after* **20/1**

4502 **6** *1 1/2* **Valley Observer (FR)**[15] [3167] 3-9-6 **69** .... (e) DarryllHolland 4 53
(W R Swinburn) *chsd ldrs: wd bnd 3f out: sn btn* **3/1**[1]

0513 **7** *nk* **Encores**[8] [3384] 3-8-10 **64** .... WilliamBuick(5) 11 47+
(N A Callaghan) *slt advantage tl hdd over 2f out: wknd qckly over 1f out* **7/2**[2]

0021 **8** *1/2* **My Mentor (IRE)**[31] [2668] 3-9-3 **66** .... SebSanders 6 48
(Sir Mark Prescott) *w ldr tl over 2f out: sn wknd* **11/2**

-000 **9** *1/2* **Poyle Ruby**[104] [924] 3-8-3 **52** .... JimmyQuinn 3 33
(M Blanshard) *a towards rr* **50/1**

4005 **10** *3* **Royal Guest**[18] [3066] 3-8-13 **62** .... TPO'Shea 13 36
(M R Channon) *chsd ldrs to 3f out: sn wknd* **8/1**

5430 **11** *5* **Golden Brown (IRE)**[20] [2982] 3-9-3 **66** .... ChrisCatlin 5 29
(David Pinder) *a in rr* **33/1**

6360 **12** *hd* **Brean Dot Com (IRE)**[23] [2916] 3-8-7 **56** ow2 .... RobertHavlin 2 18
(Mrs P N Dutfield) *a in rr* **33/1**

1m 39.52s (-1.28) **Going Correction** -0.175s/f (Stan) **12** Ran SP% **122.7**
Speed ratings (Par 100):99,97,90,89,88 87,86,86,85,82 77,77
CSF £108.47 CT £997.17 TOTE £7.30: £2.90, £3.70, £5.00; EX 55.20.
Owner Terry Neill **Bred** Plantation Stud **Trained** East Everleigh, Wilts
■ Stewards' Enquiry : William Buick two-day ban: careless riding (Jul 31,Aug 2)

FOCUS
An ordinary handicap which did look quite competitive beforehand, but in the end the front pair routed the rest and this looks a race that was lacking strength in depth. The form of the first two is strong on the face of things.
Golden Brown(IRE) Official explanation: trainer said gelding scoped dirty after the race

3623 DIGIBET CASINO H'CAP 6f (P)
8:45 (8:46) (Class 4) (0-85,85) 3-Y-0+ **£6,477** (£1,927; £963; £481) **Stalls** High

Form RPR

130 **1** **Misaro (GER)**[31] [2655] 6-9-0 **78** .... (b) LukeMorris(5) 12 92+
(R A Harris) *mde all at gd pce: drvn along and edgd lft over 1f out: drew clr: readily* **9/1**

0043 **2** *4* **Idle Power (IRE)**[17] [3104] 9-9-3 **76** .... AmirQuinn 2 78
(J R Boyle) *in tch: rdn 3f out: styd on to dispute 2nd fnl f: no ch w wnr* **6/1**[3]

002 **3** *shd* **Dvinsky (USA)**[20] [2993] 6-9-1 **74** .... IanMongan 3 76
(P Howling) *prom: rdn over 3f out: disp 2nd fnl f but nt pce of wnr* **14/1**

1111 **4** *3/4* **Whitbarrow (IRE)**[54] [1977] 8-9-3 **81** ow2 .... (b) JamesMillman(5) 4 80
(B R Millman) *chsd wnr tl 1f out: no ex fnl f* **11/2**[2]

-000 **5** *nk* **Royal Storm (IRE)**[24] [2858] 8-9-1 **74** .... JimCrowley 10 73
(Mrs A J Perrett) *chsd ldrs: hrd rdn over 2f out: one pce* **13/2**

3063 **6** *1/2* **Marko Jadeo (IRE)**[32] [2623] 9-8-9 **73** .... KevinGhunowa(5) 9 70
(R A Harris) *s.i.s: towards rr tl styd on u.p fnl 2f: nvr nrr* **16/1**

102 **7** *nk* **Matuza (IRE)**[17] [3108] 4-9-12 **85** .... GeorgeBaker 5 81
(W R Muir) *bhd: rdn and hung rt fnl 2f: nvr rchd ldrs* **5/1**[1]

0012 **8** *1 1/2* **Romany Nights (IRE)**[13] [3218] 7-9-1 **74** .... (bt) SebSanders 8 66
(Miss Gay Kelleway) *a in mid-div: rdn and no imp fnl 2f* **7/1**

0450 **9** *1/2* **Tara Too (IRE)**[32] [2626] 4-9-2 **75** .... (b[1]) EddieAhern 11 65
(J G Portman) *in tch on rail: hmpd and snatched up bnd after 1f: n.d after* **10/1**

2034 **10** *1/2* **Mr Cellophane**[24] [2882] 4-9-0 **73** .... DarryllHolland 6 62
(J R Jenkins) *rrd s: a bhd* **11/2**[2]

0541 **11** *1 1/4* **Fromsong (IRE)**[13] [3212] 9-9-7 **80** .... RobertHavlin 7 65
(D K Ivory) *in tch: rdn to chse ldrs over 2f out: wknd over 1f out* **14/1**

1m 11.8s (-1.90) **Going Correction** -0.175s/f (Stan) **11** Ran SP% **125.9**
Speed ratings (Par 105):105,99,99,98,98 97,97,95,94,93 92
CSF £66.73 CT £789.57 TOTE £12.40: £4.00, £2.40, £5.00; EX 196.80.
Owner Messrs Criddle Davies Dawson & Villa **Bred** Wilhelm Fasching **Trained** Earlswood, Monmouths
■ Stewards' Enquiry : Jim Crowley two-day ban: careless riding (Jul 30-31)

FOCUS
This competitive-looking sprint handicap was turned into a one-horse race by Misaro and nothing else ever got into it. A career-best effort from the winner at the age of six.
Dvinsky(USA) Official explanation: jockey said gelding finished distressed
Marko Jadeo(IRE) Official explanation: jockey said gelding missed the break
Mr Cellophane Official explanation: jockey said gelding broke awkwardly

3624 DIGITOTE H'CAP 1m 4f (P)
9:15 (9:17) (Class 6) (0-65,65) 3-Y-0 **£2,047** (£604; £302) **Stalls** Centre

Form RPR

-542 **1** **Duty Free (IRE)**[8] [3367] 3-9-7 **65** .... SteveDrowne 9 78+
(H Morrison) *prom: rdn to ld wl over 1f out: sn clr: comf* **6/4**[1]

3063 **2** *4* **Dansimar**[6] [3421] 3-9-7 **65** .... TPO'Shea 7 72
(M R Channon) *mid-div: rdn and hdwy over 2f out: styd on to take 2nd ins fnl f: no ch w wnr* **9/1**

0514 **3** *2 1/2* **Cavendish**[15] [3150] 3-8-13 **62** .... (b) LukeMorris(5) 5 65
(J M P Eustace) *in tch: effrt on outside to press ldrs 3f out: no ex over 1f out* **16/1**

0-01 **4** *shd* **Strobe**[26] [2801] 3-9-7 **65** .... JimCrowley 6 68
(J A Osborne) *jnd ldr after 2f and disp ld after: rdn 5f out: hdd wl over 1f out: sn wknd* **3/1**[2]

0150 **5** *nk* **Sir Duke (IRE)**[18] [3058] 3-9-3 **61** .... DarryllHolland 8 64
(P W D'Arcy) *hld up on rail in midfield: effrt over 2f out: kpt on but nvr rchd ldrs* **9/1**

2000 **6** *3/4* **Laughing Game**[15] [3159] 3-8-9 **53** .... HayleyTurner 11 55
(M L W Bell) *t.k.h early: disp ld tl wknd wl over 1f out* **33/1**

-050 **7** *1/2* **Composing (IRE)**[33] [2602] 3-9-7 **65** .... (t) EdwardCreighton 12 66
(H Morrison) *awkward s: hld up in rr: rdn over 3f out: sme late hdwy* **33/1**

6-02 **8** *1 3/4* **Alleviate (IRE)**[26] [2793] 3-8-13 **57** .... SebSanders 14 55
(Sir Mark Prescott) *prom on rail: n.m.r bnd after 2f: rdn 3f out: sn outpcd* **4/1**[3]

0000 **9** *2* **Royal Tender (IRE)**[17] [3082] 3-8-8 **52** .... JimmyQuinn 10 47
(B G Powell) *s.i.s: towards rr: drvn along 3f out: nt pce to chal* **50/1**

-046 **10** *3* **Galingale (IRE)**[48] [2132] 3-8-13 **57** .... EddieAhern 2 48
(Mrs P Sly) *bhd: hrd rdn 3f out: nvr nr ldrs* **33/1**

6025 **11** *6* **Conny Nobel (IRE)**[37] [2490] 3-8-3 **52** ow2 .... (p) KevinGhunowa(5) 13 34
(J L Flint) *in tch: wd bnd into strt and hung rt 3f out: rdn and n.d after* **20/1**

-500 **12** *2 1/2* **The Graig**[38] [2456] 3-8-9 **53** .... JamesDoyle 1 31
(C Drew) *towards rr: modest effrt 5f out: wknd over 3f out* **66/1**

0-44 **13** *32* **Marlyn Ridge**[29] [2727] 3-9-6 **64** .... RobertHavlin 3 —
(D K Ivory) *sn prom on outside: wknd over 3f out* **20/1**

2m 33.08s (-3.82) **Going Correction** -0.175s/f (Stan) **13** Ran SP% **132.7**
Speed ratings (Par 98):105,102,100,100,100 99,99,98,97,95 91,89,68
CSF £18.02 CT £184.87 TOTE £3.30: £1.30, £2.70, £3.80; EX 19.80 Place 6 £314.08, Place 5 £65.94.
Owner De La Warr Racing **Bred** Mervyn Stewkesbury **Trained** East Ilsley, Berks

FOCUS
Despite the winning time being a second slower than the earlier maiden, there was still a solid pace for this quite decent middle-distance handicap. The winner looks a nice sort and has further improvement in him.
Marlyn Ridge Official explanation: jockey said gelding ran flat
T/Jkpt: £70,415.40 to a £1 stake. Pool: £148,765.00. 1.50 winning tickets. T/Plt: £308.10 to a £1 stake. Pool: £73,213.25. 173.45 winning tickets. T/Qpdt: £47.50 to a £1 stake. Pool: £5,955.10. 92.70 winning tickets. ST

3244 YARMOUTH (L-H)
Tuesday, July 17

OFFICIAL GOING: Good to firm (good in places; 8.1)
Wind: Almost nil Weather: black clouds

3625 EBF TOTEPLACEPOT MAIDEN STKS 7f 3y
6:25 (6:31) (Class 5) 2-Y-0 **£3,886** (£1,156; £577; £288) **Stalls** High

Form RPR

1 **Raven's Pass (USA)** 2-9-3 0 .... DavidKinsella 16 81
(J H M Gosden) *sn prom: rdn to ld ins fnl f: styd on wl* **20/1**

03 **2** *1 1/4* **Always Ready**[43] [2303] 2-8-12 0 .... AhmedAjtebi(5) 9 78
(C E Brittain) *prom: led over 2f out: hdd ins fnl f: rdn and nt qckn* **25/1**

3 3/4 **Centennial (IRE)** 2-9-3 0 .... RichardMullen 11 76+
(J H M Gosden) *rdn and outpcd early: rn green: stl 9th ent fnl f: fin strly to snatch 3rd: promising* **33/1**

4 1/2 **Copywriter** 2-9-3 0 .... JimmyFortune 6 75+
(J H M Gosden) *plld hrd and off pce early: rn green and prog over 1f out: kpt on wl: promising* **14/1**

03 5 1 **Determind Stand (USA)**[20] 2991 2-9-3 0 .... RyanMoore 17 72
(Sir Michael Stoute) *prom: rdn over 1f out: nt qckn after* **9/2**[3]

6 nk **Taken (IRE)** 2-9-3 0 .... JamieSpencer 7 71+
(J R Fanshawe) *s.s: plld hrd in rr: rdn over 2f out: prog to chal briefly 1f out: sn btn: bttr for experience* **16/1**

02 7 1 **Albaqaa**[17] 3095 2-9-3 0 .... RHills 10 69
(E A L Dunlop) *chsd ldrs: rdn 2f out: one pce fnl f* **4/1**[2]

5 8 1 **Jack Dawkins (USA)**[17] 3095 2-9-3 0 .... TedDurcan 4 66
(H R A Cecil) *t.k.h: prom: ev ch 2f out: sn drvn: fdd over 1f out* **11/4**[1]

6 9 1 **Woolfall Treasure**[17] 3095 2-9-3 0 .... NeilPollard 14 64
(G G Margarson) *s.i.s: nvr bttr than midfield: btn wl over 1f out* **7/1**

00 10 1 1/2 **Asian Power (IRE)**[25] 2832 2-9-3 0 .... OscarUrbina 12 60
(P J O'Gorman) *outpcd in rr: sme late prog* **80/1**

60 11 1 1/4 **Fyodorovich (USA)**[52] 2021 2-9-3 0 .... DeanMcKeown 3 56+
(J S Wainwright) *hmpd s: t.k.h and sn chsng ldrs: btn wl over 1f out* **100/1**

5 12 3/4 **Yankee Storm**[15] 3171 2-9-3 0 .... AdamKirby 13 54
(M J Wallace) *t.k.h: led tl hdd over 2f out: btn wl over 1f out* **66/1**

13 1 **Whodouthinkur (IRE)** 2-9-0 0 .... NeilChalmers(3) 8 52
(Mrs C A Dunnett) *chsd ldrs to 1/2-way* **80/1**

14 6 **Ski School (IRE)** 2-9-3 0 .... MichaelHills 15 36
(W J Haggas) *plld hrd in midfield: wknd wl over 2f out* **12/1**

15 3 **Always Brave** 2-9-3 0 .... JoeFanning 2 28
(M Johnston) *bdly hmpd s and wnt rt: struggling fr 1/2-way* **20/1**

0 16 1/2 **It's My Day (IRE)**[34] 2569 2-9-3 0 .... NickyMackay 5 27+
(Jane Chapple-Hyam) *drvn after 3f: wanting to hang lft after: sn btn: t.o and eased* **80/1**

17 4 **Rory Boy (USA)** 2-9-3 0 .... KDarley 1 17+
(E A L Dunlop) *wnt rt s and bdly hmpd two rivals: struggling 1/2-way: t.o and eased* **33/1**

1m 26.35s (-0.25) **Going Correction** -0.05s/f (Good) **17** Ran SP% **123.0**
Speed ratings (Par 94):99,97,96,96,95 94,93,92,91,89 88,87,86,79,75 75,70
CSF £425.98 TOTE £31.30: £9.70, £6.00, £10.40; EX 1136.70.
Owner Stoneside Stable Llc **Bred** Stoneside Stable **Trained** Newmarket, Suffolk

FOCUS
An interesting juvenile maiden, run at a fair pace. The form can be rated through the runner-up and it should produce future winners. John Gosden saddled the first, third and fourth.

NOTEBOOK
Raven's Pass(USA), whose dam was a dual 1m winner on the turf in the US, belied market weakness and got his career off to the best possible start with a ready display. He clearly knew his job as he was always in a handy position before lengthening clear of his rivals and looked right at home on the quick surface. While his pedigree does not obviously suggest a longer trip will be to his liking, he did more than enough here to suggest he should stay further in time and has the scope to rate higher. It should also be noted this was his trainer's first two-year-old debut winner of the current campaign. (op 33-1 tchd 40-1)
Always Ready was given a positive ride and posted another sound effort in defeat. He got the extra furlong without much fuss, seems versatile as regards underfoot conditions, and helps to set the level of this form. He also now has the option of nurseries. (tchd 28-1)
Centennial(IRE) ◆, a well-bred 360,000gns purchase whose dam scored over this trip at three, looked clueless through the early parts and seemed set to finish out the back. However, he picked up strongly and made up a lot of ground inside the final furlong, really catching the eye. Sure to improve a bundle for this, he clearly has an engine and a longer trip should be well within his compass before the season's end.
Copywriter ◆, bred to make his mark at two, was the seemingly best-fancied of his trainer's three runners with Fortune up. He did not help his cause through the early parts by refusing to settle and ran distinctly green, but he too stayed on takingly when the penny dropped. This debut experience ought to sharpen him up nicely and he looks sure to be placed to strike in the coming weeks. (op 10-1 tchd 9-1)
Determind Stand(USA) was given a positive ride on this return to the turf and held every chance when it mattered, but lacked a change of gear inside the final furlong. He now has the option of handicaps and, while he is no star, it is unlikely we have yet to see the best of him. (op 11-2 tchd 4-1)
Taken(IRE), from a decent family and whose yard has done well with its juveniles to date this term, had two handlers in the paddock and took time to get into the stalls. It was not that surprising therefore to see him pull hard early on, but he still showed ability when asked for an effort and should learn a deal for this debut run. (op 14-1)
Albaqaa, very easy to back, confirmed his Newmarket form with the eighth and ninth and simply lacked the pace to really threaten here. He may prefer easier ground again in the future and now qualifies for a handicap mark. (op 11-4)
Jack Dawkins(USA), well backed, did himself no favours by refusing to settle through the race and was cooked nearing the final furlong. He still ran close to his debut form with Albaqaa and is another who may prefer easier ground in the future, but will need to learn to settle if he is to progress. (op 3-1 tchd 9-4)
Woolfall Treasure was always playing catch-up after a sluggish start and proved somewhat disappointing. He still ran very close to his debut form with the seventh and eighth, however, and he too could prefer easier ground than this. (op 12-1)
Fyodorovich(USA) Official explanation: jockey said colt suffered interference at start
Always Brave Official explanation: jockey said colt suffered interference at start
It's My Day(IRE) Official explanation: jockey said colt hung left

3626 TOTEEXACTA (S) NURSERY 5f 43y
6:55 (6:56) (Class 6) 2-Y-O **£1,943** (£578; £288; £144) **Stalls** High

Form RPR

5215 1 **Caught In Paradise (IRE)**[14] 3174 2-9-7 **60** .... JamieSpencer 2 60
(A B Haynes) *pressed ldr: drvn over 2f out: looked reluctant 1f out: forced ahd fnl stride* **8/11**[1]

4042 2 shd **Mama Leo**[8] 3364 2-9-2 **58** .... (v) EmmettStack(3) 3 58
(K J Burke) *racd awkwardly in last: clsd to ld ins fnl f: bmpd along u.str.p: jst ct* **7/2**[2]

6000 3 1/2 **Culzean Bay**[7] 3392 2-8-6 **45** .... RichardMullen 4 43
(A Bailey) *t.k.h in 3rd: led over 2f out: rdn and hdd ins fnl f: kpt on wout finding much* **25/1**[3]

1333 4 5 **Miss Willoughby**[12] 3246 2-8-13 **52** .... RyanMoore 1 32
(J Ryan) *sn led: hdd over 2f out: gave up v tamely over 1f out* **7/2**[2]

64.75 secs (1.95) **Going Correction** -0.05s/f (Good) **4** Ran SP% **106.2**
Speed ratings (Par 92):82,81,81,73
CSF £3.42 TOTE £1.60; EX 2.90.The winner was bought in for 10,200gns. Mama Leo was claimed by W. R. Baddiley for £6,000.
Owner Ms C Berry **Bred** G Swift **Trained** Limpley Stoke, Bath

FOCUS
A weak event in which all the runners looked tricky. It was a very slow time, even for a juvenile seller. The 'official' ratings shown next to each horse are estimated and for information purposes only.

NOTEBOOK
Caught In Paradise(IRE), very well supported, was not at all helping his rider under maximum pressure yet still just did enough to edge it near the line. He was giving away weight to all of his rivals, so this was still a fair effort, and it may well be that some headgear in the future will see his attitude improve. Connections bought him back in for 10,200gns. (op 11-10)
Mama Leo, having her first outing for connections, would probably have scored with slightly stronger handling. However, she is another whose attitude is not convincing and she was getting weight here. (op 9-4)
Culzean Bay, with the blinkers abandoned, put in an improved effort and ran with credit at the weights on this return to turf. However, she paid for refusing to settle and is yet another who is not at all straightforward. (op 20-1)
Miss Willoughby spat out the dummy when headed and, while she probably wants softer ground, she could now be going backwards. (op 3-1)

3627 TOTESPORT.COM H'CAP 5f 43y
7:25 (7:25) (Class 5) (0-70,70) 3-Y-O+ **£3,238** (£963; £481; £240) **Stalls** High

Form RPR

0202 1 **Silver Prelude**[7] 3408 6-8-10 **55** .... KDarley 12 67
(D K Ivory) *mde all: rdn fnl f: a holding rival: gamely* **11/2**[3]

504 2 1/2 **Multahab**[34] 2555 8-8-13 **58** .... (t) AdamKirby 11 68
(Miss D A McHale) *handy: drvn to chse wnr over 1f out: kpt on but a hld* **20/1**

0052 3 1 3/4 **Conjecture**[9] 3347 5-8-10 **55** .... JoeFanning 4 59
(R Bastiman) *taken down early: prom: drvn 1/2-way: chsd wnr 2f out tl over 1f out: one pce* **4/1**[2]

5000 4 nk **Taboor (IRE)**[13] 3203 9-8-6 **51** oh2 .... RichardMullen 9 54
(R M H Cowell) *s.s: rdn over 2f out: effrt 1f out: no imp after* **16/1**

033 5 3/4 **Welcome Approach**[20] 2989 4-9-8 **67** .... JimmyFortune 3 67+
(J R Weymes) *last and rdn over 2f out: swtchd towards stands' side over 1f out: passed btn rivals but nvr looked like chalng ldrs* **7/2**[1]

6501 6 1 1/2 **Sands Crooner (IRE)**[8] 3368 4-9-2 **61** 6ex .... (v) DeanMcKeown 6 56
(D Shaw) *chsd ldrs: rdn 2f out: btn over 1f out* **12/1**

360 7 hd **Henry Hall (IRE)**[19] 3014 11-9-1 **60** .... KimTinkler 5 55
(N Tinkler) *midfield: rdn wl over 1f out: sn no imp* **10/1**

6605 8 1 1/2 **Overwing (IRE)**[22] 2933 4-9-11 **70** .... JamieSpencer 10 59+
(R M H Cowell) *pressed wnr 3f: sn lost pl and eased* **14/1**

4056 9 nk **Russian Rocket (IRE)**[69] 1589 5-9-5 **67** .... NeilChalmers(3) 1 55
(Mrs C A Dunnett) *chsd ldrs: drvn over 2f out: sn btn* **8/1**

6050 10 1 **Calabaza**[24] 2879 5-8-10 **55** .... (b) RyanMoore 8 40+
(W Jarvis) *chsd ldrs: rdn 2f out: sn btn: eased* **7/1**

0-03 11 3 **Banana Belle**[9] 3353 3-7-9 **51** oh6 .... KMay(7) 2 25
(J Ryan) *struggling in rr 1/2-way* **50/1**

4-00 12 2 1/2 **Kindallachan**[26] 2791 4-8-3 **51** oh6 .... EmmettStack(3) 7 16
(G C Bravery) *struggling 2f out* **40/1**

62.14 secs (-0.66) **Going Correction** -0.05s/f (Good)
WFA 3 from 4yo+ 4lb **12** Ran SP% **119.7**
Speed ratings (Par 103):103,102,99,98,97 95,95,92,92,90 85,81
CSF £113.40 CT £499.69 TOTE £6.00: £2.20, £5.70, £2.30; EX 70.70.
Owner Mrs A Shone **Bred** Bearstone Stud **Trained** Radlett, Herts

FOCUS
A moderate sprint in which it proved hard to come from off the pace. The winner was right back to his turf best and the form looks sound.
Overwing(IRE) Official explanation: jockey said saddle slipped

3628 EUROPEAN BREEDERS' FUND VIRGINIA STKS (LISTED RACE) (F&M) 1m 2f 21y
7:55 (7:56) (Class 1) 3-Y-O+
£14,583 (£5,551; £2,779; £1,388; £694; £348) **Stalls** Low

Form RPR

-160 1 **Yaqeen**[25] 2814 3-8-8 107 .... RHills 6 103+
(M A Jarvis) *a gng wl: midfield: clsd to ld 2f out: sn rdn clr: readily* **5/4**[1]

11 2 1 1/4 **Samira Gold (FR)**[24] 2862 3-8-8 92 .... NickyMackay 1 97+
(L M Cumani) *chsd ldrs: pushed along 4f out: n.m.r 3f out: drvn and bdly outpcd over 2f out: str run ins fnl f: snatched 2nd: no ch w wnr* **9/2**[2]

5-10 3 shd **Dance Of Light (USA)**[46] 2211 3-8-8 92 .... RyanMoore 4 96
(Sir Michael Stoute) *prom: rdn and outpcd over 3f out: rallied to chse wnr 1f out: no imp: jst lost 2nd* **11/2**[3]

22-0 4 1 **Sexy Lady (GER)**[44] 2296 4-9-4 0 .... TMundry 5 95
(P Rau, Germany) *midfield: rdn 3f out: styng on same pce whn swtchd rt 1f out* **16/1**

403 5 1/2 **Glitter Baby (IRE)**[29] 2720 4-9-4 89 .... TedDurcan 8 94
(M G Quinlan) *cl up: rdn over 2f out: nt qckn over 1f out* **25/1**

615 6 1 1/2 **Marzelline (IRE)**[26] 2786 3-8-8 102 .... AdamKirby 9 91
(W R Swinburn) *settled in rr: last over 3f out: sme prog 2f out: btn whn swtchd outside and sltly hmpd 1f out* **17/2**

5541 7 hd **Mango Mischief (IRE)**[19] 3028 6-9-7 102 .... KDarley 3 93
(M R Channon) *led 2f: 2nd tl led again 3f out: hdd 2f out: sn drvn: wknd ins fnl f* **10/1**

20-5 8 5 **Flor Y Nata (USA)**[19] 3028 4-9-4 93 .... JimmyFortune 2 81
(Sir Mark Prescott) *led after 2f tl drvn and hdd 3f out: qckly lost pl* **50/1**

300 9 1 1/2 **Dont Dili Dali**[6] 3434 4-9-4 100 .... (p) JamieSpencer 7 78
(J S Moore) *bhd: n.m.r whn disputing last 3f out: taken wd over 2f out: immediately struggling: eased 1f out* **12/1**

2m 7.55s (-0.55) **Going Correction** +0.175s/f (Good)
WFA 3 from 4yo+ 10lb **9** Ran SP% **117.0**
Speed ratings (Par 111):109,108,107,107,106 105,105,101,100
CSF £7.02 TOTE £2.00: £1.10, £2.70, £2.70; EX 7.70.
Owner Hamdan Al Maktoum **Bred** Brookdale And Dr Ted Folkerth **Trained** Newmarket, Suffolk
■ Stewards' Enquiry : T Mundry one-day ban: careless riding (Jul 29)

FOCUS
A good Listed contest likely to produce winners at this level and beyond. The front two are better than the bare form.

NOTEBOOK
Yaqeen, who is clearly held in the highest of regard at home, has had to tackle Group 1 assignments on each of her two starts since losing her maiden, but she has coped reasonably well on each occasion, not liking the ground at Ascot latest though, and this step up to 1m2f was expected to suit. Appreciating the drop in class, she was always travelling strongly back on this faster surface and improved going well racing into the final quarter mile. Soon on top once asked for her effort, she saw the trip out well and looks well worth her place back in Group company now she has gained a confidence-boosting victory. The Group 1 Nassau Stakes over 1m2f at Glorious Goodwood would appear to be the most obvious target. (op 11-8 tchd 7-4)

Samira Gold(FR) has improved with each race, winning well on her handicap debut last time, and although unable to make it three wins from three, this was easily her best effort to date. This trip and beyond is clearly required as having been tapped for toe and blocked with nowhere to go, she stuck on really well to snatch second off Dance Of Light. She would not have been far away had she got a clean run through and looks capable of winning races at Listed/Group 3 level. (tchd 7-2)

Dance Of Light(USA) was soon thrown into the deep end having won her maiden, being asked to contest the Oaks, where she did not run badly at all considering how uneasy she looked on the track. Off since, she did not neccessarily look likely to be suited by this drop in trip, but it certainly represented a drop in grade and she ran a fine race, sticking on gamely having been outpaced as the race for the line began. She looks capable of winning races at this level and will be suited by a return to further. (op 6-1 tchd 5-1)

Sexy Lady(GER), a Group 3 winner in her homeland, did not offer a great deal on her recent reappearance at San Siro, but with that run under her belt and back on better ground she was able to post a significantly improved effort, faring best of the older fillies. (op 14-1 tchd 20-1)

Glitter Baby(IRE), although third in this grade at Warwick last time, had a bit to find with the best of these and she ran as well as could have been expected. (op 33-1 tchd 40-1 and 20-1)

Marzelline(IRE), outclassed in the Ribblesdale latest, was not made enough use of on this drop in trip/grade and she could make only limited headway in the straight. This was disappointing. (op 11-1 tchd 12-1)

Mango Mischief(IRE), who stole a soft-ground Listed race from the front at Newcastle last time, was always likely to struggle under her penalty and she was found out in this stronger contest. (tchd 11-1)

Dont Dili Dali Official explanation: jockey said filly hung left-handed in straight

3629 TOTESPORT 0800 221 221 CLAIMING STKS — 1m 2f 21y

8:25 (8:44) (Class 6) 3-Y-O+ £1,943 (£578; £288; £144) Stalls Low

Form				RPR
0423	1		**Bronze Star**[25] 2833 4-9-6 65 ... JamieSpencer 5 (J R Fanshawe) *mde all: rdn clr fnl f* 1/1[1]	63+
3065	2	2 1/2	**Fizzy Bella**[19] 3041 3-8-7 57 ... TedDurcan 3 (M G Quinlan) *trckd wnr tl 4f out: rdn over 2f out: kpt on to take 2nd post* 16/1	55
-563	3	shd	**Desert Lightning (IRE)**[25] 2820 5-8-9 52 ... DeclanCannon[(7)] 2 (K R Burke) *t.k.h: in tch: nt clr run: swtchd sharply rt over 2f out: chsd wnr 1f out: lost 2nd post* 8/1	54
-500	4	1 1/4	**Monachello (USA)**[39] 2426 3-8-12 70 ... (b[1]) RyanMoore 4 (Mrs A J Perrett) *trckd ldrs: chsd wnr 4f out: rdn over 2f out: kpt on fnl f* 7/2[2]	58
-305	5	3/4	**Fairly Honest**[18] 3057 3-9-1 68 ... JimmyFortune 9 (D R C Elsworth) *t.k.h: in tch: rdn to chse wnr briefly over 1f out: no ex fnl f* 9/2[3]	59
04	6	2 1/2	**Corkscrew Hill (IRE)**[18] 3057 3-7-13 ow1 ... KirstyMilczarek[(7)] 8 (N A Callaghan) *s.i.s: hld up: rdn: hdwy 3f out: wknd over 1f out* 16/1	46
0000	7	1	**The London Gang**[47] 2174 4-9-1 43 ... (v) AdamKirby 1 (Miss D A McHale) *hld up in rr: rdn 3f out: nt trbld ldrs* 50/1	43
0003	8	2	**Coffin Dodger**[34] 2557 4-8-10 38 ... RichardMullen 7 (C N Allen) *reluctant to s: bhd: n.d* 25/1	34

2m 11.21s (3.11) **Going Correction** +0.175s/f (Good)
WFA 3 from 4yo+ 10lb — 8 Ran SP% 119.1
Speed ratings (Par 101):94,92,91,90,90 88,87,85
CSF £22.04 TOTE £2.10: £1.10, £3.50, £2.80; EX 31.20.Bronze Star was claimed by I McInnes for £15,000. Desert Lightning was claimed by I McInnes for £6,000.

Owner J M Greetham **Bred** J M Greetham **Trained** Newmarket, Suffolk

FOCUS
Bronze Star dominated throughout in what was an uncompetitive contest. She was below her recent form in this weak race.

Corkscrew Hill(IRE) Official explanation: jockey said filly lost its action

3630 TOTESPORTCASINO.COM H'CAP — 1m 6f 17y

8:55 (9:07) (Class 5) (0-70,70) 3-Y-O+ £3,238 (£963; £481; £240) Stalls High

Form				RPR
60/0	1		**Fourth Dimension (IRE)**[43] 2321 8-9-13 **65** ... AdamKirby 8 (Miss T Spearing) *hld up: rdn and hdwy over 1f out: sn chsd ldr: styd on to ld towards fin* 13/2	73
50	2	1/2	**Mabel (IRE)**[31] 2675 4-9-8 **60** ... JamieSpencer 4 (S C Williams) *sn led: rdn 3f out: drvn and edgd lft ins fnl f: hdd towards fin* 4/1[2]	67
1-56	3	1	**Sa Nau**[41] 2367 4-9-4 **56** ... NickyMackay 5 (T Keddy) *cl up: rdn 3f out: sltly outpcd ent fnl 2f: drvn and styd on towards fin* 13/2	62
6214	4	1 3/4	**Sand Repeal (IRE)**[11] 3279 5-9-7 **66** ... (v) AmyBaker[(7)] 7 (Miss J Feilden) *chsd ldr tl over 3f out: rdn and kpt on one pce fr over 1f out* 5/1[3]	70
2351	5	3/4	**Theflyingscottie**[14] 3193 5-9-0 **52** ... (v) DeanMcKeown 9 (D Shaw) *t.k.h: hld up in tch: effrt over 2f out: no ex ins fnl f* 11/2	55
20/4	6	1 1/4	**Oniz Tiptoes (IRE)**[7] 3402 6-8-12 **50** oh5 ... (v) PaddyAspell 2 (J S Wainwright) *t.k.h: trckd ldrs: chsd ldr over 3f out: tl over 1f out: wknd fnl f* 2/1[1]	51
400	7	13	**Lord Laing (USA)**[64] 1732 4-9-0 **52** ... RichardMullen 6 (H J Collingridge) *in rr: rdn and wknd over 2f out* 25/1	36

3m 9.88s (4.58) **Going Correction** +0.175s/f (Good)
WFA 3 from 4yo+ 14lb — 7 Ran SP% 115.9
Speed ratings (Par 103):93,92,92,91,90 90,82
CSF £33.34 CT £177.20 TOTE £11.70: £3.40, £2.00; EX 46.00 Place 6 £744.67, Place 5 £24.79.

Owner Advantage Chemicals Holdings Ltd **Bred** Milton Park Stud Partnership **Trained** Alcester, Warwicks

■ The first training success for Teresa Spearing, daughter of trainer John Spearing.

FOCUS
A moderate winning time and pretty weak form. The third and fourth help set the standard.

T/Plt: £7,927.30 to a £1 stake. Pool: £74,930.00. 6.90 winning tickets. T/Qpdt: £24.70 to a £1 stake. Pool: £7,990.00. 239.30 winning tickets. IM

3631 - 3634a (Foreign Racing) - See Raceform Interactive

3410 CATTERICK (L-H)

Wednesday, July 18

OFFICIAL GOING: Good (good to soft in places; 6.9)
Wind: Virtually nil Weather: Fine and showers

3635 RACING UK LIVE ON 432 NOVICE AUCTION STKS — 7f

2:30 (2:31) (Class 5) 2-Y-O £3,238 (£963; £481; £240) Stalls Low

Form				RPR
	1		**Montagne D'Or (IRE)** 2-8-13 0 ... JoeFanning 6 (M Johnston) *s.i.s: hdwy on outer 1/2-way: qcknd on outer to ld wl over 1f out: sn clr: comf* 6/1[3]	89+
05	2	1 1/2	**Shannersburg (IRE)**[35] 2575 2-8-13 0 ... ChrisCatlin 3 (E J O'Neill) *chsd ldrs: rdn along 1/2-way: hdwy 2f out: sn drvn and kpt on ins fnl f* 11/4[2]	80
1	3	2	**Robscarvic (IRE)**[18] 3092 2-9-5 0 ... NCallan 1 (G A Swinbank) *trckd ldng pair: effrt over 2f out and ev ch tl rdn and one pce fr wl over 1f out* 4/5[1]	81
0013	4	5	**Allahor**[9] 3373 2-8-12 0 ... PatrickMathers[(3)] 7 (A Berry) *t.k.h: cl up: rdn along over 2f out and sn btn* 11/1	65
4	5	2 1/2	**Elusive Lady (IRE)**[20] 3013 2-8-1 0 ... AndrewElliott[(3)] 4 (J R Weymes) *t.k.h: led: rdn along 3f out: hdd wl over 1f out and sn wknd* 80/1	47
6	6	1 1/2	**What's For Tea**[14] 3199 2-8-6 0 ow2 ... DavidAllan 2 (T D Easterby) *in tch: rdn along 3f out: outpcd fnl 2f* 25/1	46
0	7	12	**Lady See (IRE)**[15] 3192 2-8-1 0 ... DuranFentiman[(3)] 5 (T D Easterby) *a in rr: wl outpcd fr 1/2-way* 40/1	14

1m 31.57s (4.21) **Going Correction** +0.45s/f (Yiel) — 7 Ran SP% 112.4
Speed ratings (Par 94):93,91,89,83,80 78,65
CSF £21.94 TOTE £8.40: £3.30, £1.80; EX 24.50.

Owner Syndicate 2006 **Bred** Aylesfield Farms Stud Ltd **Trained** Middleham Moor, N Yorks

FOCUS
Just a fair race. The winner was not fancied in the market on his debut and could be a decent sort in the making.

NOTEBOOK
Montagne D'Or(IRE), who was weak in the market before the off, missed the break slightly but was soon travelling smoothly just off the pace before striding right away from his rivals once asked to quicken. It was a good performance, considering the juvenile form of the stable, and he is likely to hold his own in better company. (op 5-1 tchd 7-1)

Shannersburg(IRE) stayed on strongly in the final furlong and looks like a horse that will appreciate a test of stamina. He will find his level in nursery company. (op 9-2)

Robscarvic(IRE), who got checked over at the start after breaking through the stall once loaded, had every chance rounding the final bend but could not match the winner for a turn of pace. This was almost certainly a fair effort giving weight to the promising winner, and he can win more races as a juvenile. Official explanation: jockey said gelding stumbled on home turn (tchd 8-11 and 5-6 and 10-11 in a place)

Allahor raced very keenly throughout and failed to get home as a result. One suspects 6f is more his sort of trip. (op 10-1 tchd 12-1)

Elusive Lady(IRE), who was surprisingly stepped up in trip after showing tons of pace on her debut over 6f, was another in the race that raced far too keenly in the early stages to really see out the trip. She is probably one to watch out for in a sprint nursery later in the year. (op 66-1)

What's For Tea probably ran a tiny bit better than her final position suggests, but is not one that looks about to win any time soon. (op 20-1 tchd 16-1)

Lady See(IRE) ran really badly and could not be seriously fancied to go close at any level. (op 33-1)

3636 TURFTV BETTING SHOP SERVICE (S) STKS — 5f 212y

3:00 (3:01) (Class 6) 3-Y-O+ £2,730 (£806; £403) Stalls Low

Form				RPR
2302	1		**Strike Force**[23] 2948 3-8-12 57 ... (p) LiamJones[(3)] 1 (R A Harris) *towards rr: hdwy 2f out: sn pushed along: swtchd outside and rdn over 1f out: styd on u.p ins fnl f to ld nr line* 8/1	65
310	2	1/2	**Ishibee (IRE)**[24] 2910 3-8-10 56 ... (p) RoystonFfrench 5 (Mrs A Duffield) *chsd ldrs: rdn along 2f out: styd on u.p to ld last 100yds: hdd and no ex nr line* 14/1	58
3056	3	1 1/2	**Compton Plume**[23] 2947 7-9-0 57 ... DaleGibson 11 (M W Easterby) *chsd ldr: rdn to chal over 1f out: drvn and ev ch ins fnl f: one pce towards fin* 6/1[3]	54
0201	4	nk	**Funfair Wane**[5] 3498 8-8-13 55 ... OliveGaule[(7)] 10 (D Nicholls) *led: clr over 2f out: rdn over 1f out: hdd & wknd last 100yds* 4/1[1]	59
0560	5	1 1/4	**Jun Fan (USA)**[37] 2509 5-9-0 49 ... PatCosgrave 9 (B Ellison) *dwlt: hdwy 2f out: rdn to chse ldrs over 1f out: kpt on same pce ins fnl f* 9/1	49
2005	6	shd	**Blackheath (IRE)**[5] 3498 11-9-6 49 ... SilvestreDeSousa 3 (D Nicholls) *chsd ldrs: rdn along 2f out: kpt on same pce u.p ent fnl f* 13/2	54
-205	7	3	**Princely Vale (IRE)**[27] 2806 5-8-7 49 ... (p) JackDean[(7)] 2 (W G M Turner) *prom: rdn along 2f out: grad wknd* 7/1	39
-000	8	3	**Halfwaytoparadise**[13] 3247 4-8-9 50 ... (p) SaleemGolam 8 (W G M Turner) *a in rr* 50/1	24
0620	9	5	**Jellytot (USA)**[53] 2033 4-8-9 55 ... (b) TomEaves 12 (J O'Reilly) *midfield: hdwy on outer to chse ldrs 2f out: sn rdn and wknd over 1f out* 11/2[2]	8
0600	10	1	**Ocean Of Champagne**[10] 3342 3-8-4 48 ... (v) PaulHanagan 6 (A Dickman) *s.i.s: a bhd* 20/1	4
0005	11	5	**Meathop (IRE)**[47] 2200 3-8-6 50 ... AndrewElliott[(3)] 4 (R F Fisher) *a towards rr* 22/1	—

1m 16.77s (2.77) **Going Correction** +0.45s/f (Yiel)
WFA 3 from 4yo+ 5lb — 11 Ran SP% 114.4
Speed ratings (Par 101):99,98,96,95,94 94,90,86,79,78 71
CSF £107.74 TOTE £5.40: £2.10, £3.70, £2.50; EX 95.90.The winner was bought in for 9,500gns. Funfair Wane and Ishibee were subject to friendly claims.

Owner Mrs Ruth M Serrell **Bred** Cheveley Park Stud Ltd **Trained** Earlswood, Monmouths

FOCUS
A fairly sound race for the grade run at a decent gallop. The winner ran up to his best form this year.

Compton Plume Official explanation: jockey said gelding was unsuited by the good (good to soft places) ground

3637 5TH REGIMENT ROYAL ARTILLERY H'CAP 5f
3:30 (3:30) (Class 4) (0-85,85) 3-Y-O **£5,181** (£1,541; £770; £384) **Stalls** Low

Form RPR

5431 **1** **Diminuto**^{9} [3369] 3-8-0 **71** 6ex........ FrankiePickard$^{(7)}$ 8 78+
(M D I Usher) *in tch: gd hdwy on outer 2f out: rdn and qcknd to ld ins fnl f: styd on* **15/2**^{3}

1042 **2** *1* **Mambo Spirit (IRE)**^{7} [3418] 3-9-7 **85**........ TomEaves 2 88
(J G Given) *hld up: hdwy 1/2-way: rdn to ld briefly ent fnl f: sn hdd: drvn and one pce* **4/1**^{1}

0-10 **3** *2 1/2* **Hawaii Prince**^{19} [3054] 3-8-5 **69**........ SilvestreDeSousa 6 63
(S T Mason) *led: rdn wl over 1f out: drvn and hdd ent fnl f: kpt on same pce* **7/1**^{2}

-400 **4** *1 1/2* **Frisky Talk (IRE)**^{19} [3061] 3-8-13 **77**........ DaleGibson 11 66
(B W Hills) *prom on outer: rdn along 2f out: drvn and one pce appr fnl f* **11/1**

1626 **5** *1/2* **Darcy's Pride (IRE)**^{9} [3374] 3-8-7 **71**........ TonyHamilton 9 58
(D W Barker) *cl up: rdn along 2f out: sn drvn and one pce appr fnl f* **7/1**^{2}

00 **6** *1 1/4* **Just Joey**^{25} [2867] 3-9-2 **80**........ NCallan 7 62
(J R Weymes) *chsd ldrs: rdn along 2f out: sn drvn and wknd over 1f out* **7/1**^{2}

5620 **7** *3 1/2* **Ronnie Howe**^{19} [3054] 3-8-2 **66**........ PaulFessey 13 36
(M Dods) *a midfield* **10/1**

2223 **8** *2* **Valley Of The Moon (IRE)**^{32} [2659] 3-8-11 **75**........ PaulHanagan 1 38
(R A Fahey) *chsd ldrs: hdwy on inner ansd cl up 1/2-way: sn rdn and wknd wl over 1f out* **4/1**^{1}

5-00 **9** *15* **Winning Spirit (IRE)**^{69} [1604] 3-8-6 **70**........ JoeFanning 4 —
(D Nicholls) *dwlt: a in rr* **18/1**

61.03 secs (0.43) **Going Correction** +0.15s/f (Good) **9** Ran SP% **112.0**
Speed ratings (Par 102):102,100,96,94,93 91,85,82,58
CSF £36.03 CT £218.82 TOTE £8.40: £1.90, £2.70, £2.20; EX 33.80.
Owner R H Brookes **Bred** B Minty **Trained** Upper Lambourn, Berks

FOCUS
A fair sprint run at a good pace and a step up from Diminuto under her penalty. The winner and runner-up came from well of the pace, so the leaders probably went just a bit too quickly.
Valley Of The Moon(IRE) Official explanation: trainer had no explanation for the poor form shown
Winning Spirit(IRE) Official explanation: jockey said gelding lost its action

3638 SEE MORE ON RACING UK CLAIMING STKS 1m 3f 214y
4:00 (4:01) (Class 6) 3-Y-O+ **£2,730** (£806; £403) **Stalls** Low

Form RPR

2-50 **1** **Campbells Lad**^{58} [1907] 6-9-7 47........ PatrickMathers$^{(3)}$ 8 62+
(Mrs G S Rees) *dwlt: hld up in rr: smooth hdwy 5f out: trckd ldrs 3f out: led wl over 1f out: rdn and styd on fnl f* **22/1**

6424 **2** *2 1/2* **Bridgewater Boys**^{2} [3595] 6-10-0 64........(b) NCallan 7 62+
(K A Ryan) *hld up to trck ldrs 5f out: effrt over 2f out: sn rdn and ev ch tl drvn and one pce ins fnl f* **3/1**^{1}

30-0 **3** *7* **Explode**^{14} [3204] 10-9-6 46........(b) JoeFanning 6 43
(Miss L C Siddall) *in tch: hdwy to ld over 4f out: rdn along 3f out: drvn and hdd wl over 1f out: kpt on same pce* **33/1**

0063 **4** *3* **Time Marches On**^{36} [2537] 9-9-1 44........ DanielleMcCreery$^{(7)}$ 15 40
(K G Reveley) *hld up and bhd: hdwy 5f out: rdn along 3f out: kpt on fnl 2f: nrst fin* **8/1**

4-42 **5** *1/2* **Tiltili (IRE)**^{40} [2417] 4-8-11 48........(b^{1}) LeeEnstone 14 29
(P C Haslam) *chsd ldrs: rdn along over 4f out and sn one pce* **11/2**^{3}

300- **6** *hd* **Rocket Force (USA)**^{363} [3686] 7-9-7 70........ LanceBetts$^{(7)}$ 13 45
(N Wilson) *prom: disp ld over 5f out: rdn along 4f out and ev ch tl drvn 2f out and sn wknd* **9/2**^{2}

-200 **7** *hd* **Slavonic (USA)**^{9} [3371] 6-9-5 50........(p) PJMcDonald$^{(5)}$ 1 41
(B Storey) *hld up towards rr: hdwy over 4f out: chsd ldrs 3f out: sn rdn and wknd wl over 1f out* **40/1**

65 **8** *1 3/4* **Square Dealer**^{19} [2420] 6-10-0 0........(b) PaddyAspell 4 42
(J R Norton) *midfield on inner: rdn along over 4f out and nvr a factor* **18/1**

0050 **9** *8* **Susiedil (IRE)**^{19} [3049] 6-9-9 45........(p) SilvestreDeSousa 2 25
(S T Mason) *nvr bttr than midfield* **20/1**

5/0- **10** *6* **Verstone (IRE)**^{67} [1766] 5-9-3 33........ PaulHanagan 11 10
(R F Fisher) *prom: rdn along over 4f out and sn wknd* **12/1**

00-3 **11** *2* **Rifleman (IRE)**^{14} [3204] 7-10-0 55........(tp) PaulMulrennan 5 17
(D W Thompson) *prom: rdn along over 4f out and grad wknd* **11/2**^{3}

0005 **12** *7* **Roll Em Over**^{4} [3538] 4-8-11 32........(b) TomEaves 10 —
(C W Thornton) *a bhd: t.o fr 1/2-way* **50/1**

04/1 **13** *7* **Cadeaux Rouge (IRE)**^{40} [2417] 6-9-5 49........(tp) TonyHamilton 9 —
(D W Thompson) *sn led: rdn along and hdd over 4f out: sn drvn and wknd* **16/1**

0P/0 **14** *25* **Kinfayre Boy**^{4} [3538] 5-9-9 44........ AnnStokell$^{(5)}$ 12 —
(K W Hogg) *midfield tl rdn along and lost pl over 5f out* **200/1**

2m 44.19s (5.19) **Going Correction** +0.45s/f (Yiel)
WFA 3 from 4yo+ 12lb **14** Ran SP% **120.8**
Speed ratings (Par 101):100,98,93,91,91 91,91,89,84,80 79,74,69,53
CSF £84.17 TOTE £32.70: £10.00, £2.20, £6.80; EX 206.00.Tiltili was claimed by Tim Corby for £2,000.
Owner PCB Racing **Bred** J And Mrs Berry **Trained** Sollom, Lancs

FOCUS
A very weak affair, run at a fair pace. The first pair came clear and the winner produced a career-best effort. the third and fourth do keep the level of the form down.
Rifleman(IRE) Official explanation: jockey said gelding was unsuited by the good (good to soft places) ground

3639 TURFTV MEDIAN AUCTION MAIDEN STKS 7f
4:30 (4:33) (Class 6) 3-Y-O **£2,730** (£806; £403) **Stalls** Low

Form RPR

230 **1** **Kunte Kinteh**^{20} [3029] 3-9-3 65........ JoeFanning 8 58
(D Nicholls) *mde all: rdn along 2f out: drvn ent fnl f and styd on wl* **15/8**^{1}

2420 **2** *1/2* **Miss Taboo (IRE)**^{10} [3342] 3-8-12 52........ PaulMulrennan 11 52
(P T Midgley) *chsd ldrs: rdn along and hdwy 3f out: drvn wl over 1f out: kpt on ins fnl f* **12/1**

0402 **3** *1* **Beaumont Boy**^{14} [3202] 3-9-3 60........ NCallan 6 54
(G A Swinbank) *in tch: hdwy 1/2-way: rdn to chse wnr over 1f out: drvn and kpt on same pce ins fnl f* **9/2**^{2}

-40 **4** *1/2* **Lady Valentino**^{76} [1425] 3-8-12 0........ PhillipMakin 15 48
(M Dods) *towards rr: hdwy over 2f out: rdn to chse ldrs over 1f out: kpt on ins fnl f: nrst fin* **22/1**

000 **5** *1/2* **Hello Nod**^{54} [2012] 3-9-3 51........ TomEaves 4 52+
(Miss J A Camacho) *s.i.s and bhd: hdwy 1/2-way: styd on fnl 2f: nrst fin* **28/1**

5 **6** *shd* **March Mate**^{100} [968] 3-9-3 0........ PatCosgrave 1 52+
(B Ellison) *in tch: hdwy on inner to chse ldrs 2f out: sn rdn and kpt on same pce appr fnl f* **7/1**

0003 **7** *1* **Jentris Girl (IRE)**^{4} [3561] 3-8-12 52........ DavidAllan 13 44
(T D Easterby) *chsd ldrs: hdwy on outer to chal over 2f out: ev ch tl drvn and wknd wl over 1f out* **5/1**^{3}

600 **8** *3 1/2* **Harts In Mo Shun (IRE)**^{9} [3372] 3-9-0 0........(b) PatrickMathers$^{(3)}$ 12 40
(A Berry) *nvr nr ldrs* **125/1**

60-3 **9** *5* **Heidi Hi**^{14} [3202] 3-8-12 55........ PaulFessey 3 22
(J R Turner) *chsd ldrs: rdn along over 2f out and sn wknd* **10/1**

0- **10** *3* **King's Attitude**^{341} [4333] 3-9-0 0........ LiamJones$^{(3)}$ 7 19
(R A Harris) *a towards rr* **12/1**

0-00 **11** *7* **Averti Star**^{20} [3029] 3-9-3 55........ RoystonFfrench 9 1
(Mrs A Duffield) *a towards rr* **33/1**

0 **12** *5* **Scruffy (IRE)**^{29} [2740] 3-9-3 0........ PaddyAspell 2 —
(C J Teague) *a in rr* **100/1**

0 **13** *7* **Flying Princess (IRE)**^{53} [2032] 3-8-5 0........ AdamCarter$^{(7)}$ 5 —
(A Berry) *a in rr: bhd fr 1/2-way* **150/1**

14 *dist* **Betterlatethanever (IRE)** 3-9-3 0........ PaulQuinn 10 —
(C J Teague) *fly j. after s and sn wl bhd* **150/1**

1m 30.66s (3.30) **Going Correction** +0.45s/f (Yiel) **14** Ran SP% **120.5**
Speed ratings (Par 98):99,98,97,96,96 96,94,90,85,81 73,68,60,—
CSF £26.67 TOTE £2.80: £1.40, £3.20, £2.00; EX 36.10.
Owner Ian Guise & Warren Smith **Bred** S Cohn **Trained** Sessay, N Yorks

FOCUS
A poor three-year-old maiden, in which the second and fourth help set the standard.
Kunte Kinteh Official explanation: trainer said, regarding apparent improvement in form, that the gelding was suited by the drop in class and the better ground

3640 CATTERICKBRIDGE.CO.UK H'CAP 1m 3f 214y
5:00 (5:00) (Class 5) (0-70,66) 3-Y-O **£3,238** (£963; £481; £240) **Stalls** Low

Form RPR

0021 **1** **Toboggan Lady**^{15} [3183] 3-8-6 **51**........ RoystonFfrench 5 56
(Mrs A Duffield) *midfield: pushed along and hdwy on inner to chse ldrs 4f out: rdn 2f out: drvn and styd appr fnl f to ld last 100yds* **3/1**^{1}

305 **2** *1 3/4* **Blockley (USA)**^{3} [3567] 3-8-12 **57**........(v^{1}) TomEaves 2 59
(Ian Williams) *midfield: rdn along and outpcd 1/2-way: hdwy on inner 2f out: sn drvn and styd on ins fnl f: nrst fin* **12/1**

0560 **3** *shd* **Top Rocker**^{41} [2389] 3-8-4 **49**........ PaulFessey 7 51
(E W Tuer) *hld up in rr: gd hdwy on outer over 3f out: rdn 2f out: styd on to ld jst ins fnl f: sn drvn: hdd and one pce last 100yds* **50/1**

5025 **4** *1 3/4* **Always Best**^{15} [3183] 3-9-1 **60**........ JoeFanning 1 59
(M Johnston) *prom: rdn along and lost pl bnd 4f out: drvn and styd on to have ev ch over 1f out: wknd ins fnl f* **6/1**^{3}

4005 **5** *1/2* **Homes By Woodford**^{7} [3429] 3-8-12 **60**........ LiamJones$^{(3)}$ 14 59
(R A Harris) *hld up in rr: hdwy 4f out: rdn to ld wl over 1f out: drvn and hdd ins fnl f: wknd* **14/1**

6-35 **6** *2 1/2* **Ellies Faith**^{9} [3377] 3-8-2 47 oh2........ SilvestreDeSousa 10 42
(N Bycroft) *chsd ldrs: rdn along over 2f out: sn drvn and grad wknd* **33/1**

-003 **7** *5* **Lightning Queen (USA)**^{35} [2558] 3-8-5 **50**........ ChrisCatlin 9 37
(B W Hills) *chsd ldrs: hdwy over 4f out: rdn along and ch over 2f out: sn drvn and one pce* **13/2**

5-40 **8** *7* **Monsieur Dumas (IRE)**^{37} [2506] 3-9-3 **62**........ PaulMulrennan 3 39
(T P Tate) *led: rdn along over 3f out: drvn 2f out: sn hdd and grad wknd* **18/1**

033 **9** *8* **Still Dreaming**^{26} [2840] 3-9-7 **66**........ PhillipMakin 11 31
(M Dods) *hld up in rr: hdwy on outer 4f out: rdn along 3f out and sn btn* **9/1**

5-55 **10** *7* **Private Reason (USA)**^{16} [3170] 3-9-7 **66**........(p) NCallan 6 20
(K A Ryan) *prom: rdn along 3f out and sn wknd* **11/1**

00-4 **11** *1* **Jardines Bazaar**^{36} [2538] 3-8-8 **53**........ DavidAllan 4 6
(T D Easterby) *midfield: rdn along 1/2-way: sn wknd* **4/1**^{2}

000- **12** *1 1/2* **Kyrhena**^{223} [6737] 3-8-0 **48** oh2 ow1........ AndrewElliott$^{(3)}$ 8 —
(C W Thornton) *a in rr* **66/1**

2m 43.73s (4.73) **Going Correction** +0.45s/f (Yiel) **12** Ran SP% **117.0**
Speed ratings (Par 100):102,100,100,99,99 97,94,89,84,79 78,77
CSF £39.74 CT £1493.15 TOTE £3.50: £1.50, £3.60, £11.30; EX 50.40 Place 6 £279.56, Place 5 £72.87..
Owner T P McMahon and D McMahon **Bred** Blenheim Bloodstock **Trained** Constable Burton, N Yorks

FOCUS
A weak handicap, rated around the placed horses. The winner is progressive.
Jardines Bazaar Official explanation: trainer's rep had no explanation for the poor form shown
T/Jkpt: Not won. T/Plt: £269.70 to a £1 stake. Pool: £56,384.30. 152.60 winning tickets. T/Qpdt: £6.70 to a £1 stake. Pool: £3,767.75. 411.20 winning tickets. JR

3618 KEMPTON (A.W) (R-H)
Wednesday, July 18

OFFICIAL GOING: Standard
Wind: Light, half-against Weather: Sunny, warm

3641 WEATHERBYS BLOODSTOCK INSURANCE APPRENTICE H'CAP (ROUND 7) 1m 3f (P)
6:20 (6:20) (Class 4) (0-80,80) 4-Y-O+ **£4,728** (£1,406; £702; £351) **Stalls** High

Form RPR

0555 **1** **Transvestite (IRE)**^{16} [3165] 5-9-5 **75**........(v) MCGeran 1 84
(J W Hills) *mde all: set stdy pce tl qcknd 4f out: clr over 2f out: kpt on: unchal* **9/2**^{2}

150- **2** *1 1/2* **Masterofthecourt (USA)**^{366} [3589] 4-9-5 **80**........ RyanBird$^{(5)}$ 2 87+
(H Morrison) *lw: t.k.h: hld up in last pair: lft bhd fr 4f out: effrt over 2f out: r.o to take 2nd last 50yds: hopeless task* **10/3**^{1}

0422 **3** *3/4* **Burgundy**^{7} [3416] 10-8-10 **66**........(b) JackMitchell 6 71
(P Mitchell) *s.s: hld up in last tl prog to trck wnr after 5f: rdn 4f out: no imp over 2f out: lost 2nd last 50yds* **9/2**^{2}

5330 **4** *1* **Turner's Touch**^{7} [3416] 5-9-1 **71**........(b) HaddenFrost 4 75
(G L Moore) *stdd s: hld up in tch: outpcd and rdn over 3f out: nt qckn after: plugged on one pce fnl 2f* **9/2**^{2}

1224 **5** *10* **Cinematic (IRE)**^{37} [2512] 4-9-2 **75**........ HarryPoulton$^{(3)}$ 7 63
(J R Boyle) *t.k.h: trckd wnr for 5f: rdn and outpcd over 3f out: sn no ch* **10/3**^{1}

0400 **6** *1* **Dream Catcher (SWE)**^{7} [3416] 4-9-8 **78**........ ThomasO'Brien 3 64
(R A Kvisla) *t.k.h: trckd ldng pair: outpcd and rdn over 3f out: sn no ch* **16/1**^{3}

0600 **7** *shd* **Play Up Pompey**[21] 2980 5-8-5 **61** oh4 KMay 5 47
(J J Bridger) *s.s: t.k.h and hld up: hmpd after 2f: last after: struggling 4f out* **28/1**

2m 23.35s (0.67) **Going Correction** -0.05s/f (Stan) **7** Ran SP% **110.0**
Speed ratings (Par 105):95,93,93,92,85 84,84
CSF £18.28 TOTE £5.00: £2.20, £2.30; EX 20.80.
Owner Nigel Howlett Partnership **Bred** Rathasker Stud **Trained** Upper Lambourn, Berks
■ Stewards' Enquiry : Ryan Bird three-day ban: careless riding (Jul 29-31)
Thomas O'Brien caution: careless riding

FOCUS
A lot of familiar faces in this, and plenty of hold-up performers involved. The winner got the run of the race and the form is suspect.

3642 SUNRISE UK'S TOP ASIAN RADIO STATION NURSERY 7f (P)
6:50 (6:51) (Class 5) 2-Y-0 **£2,817** (£838; £418; £209) **Stalls** High

Form RPR

0320 **1** **Fortuity (IRE)**[14] 3205 2-8-13 **75** JimmyFortune 2 79+
(J H M Gosden) *s.i.s: racd wd but sn in midfield: rdn over 2f out: gd prog over 1f out: r.o to ld last 100yds* **5/1**[2]

01 **2** *1* **Sourire**[14] 3199 2-9-4 **80** SebSanders 7 81
(Sir Mark Prescott) *led: drvn and pressed over 2f out: flashed tail but styd on wl: hdd and outpcd last 100yds* **9/2**[1]

535 **3** *1 1/4* **Gulf Coast**[25] 2889 2-8-3 **68** GregFairley(3) 12 66+
(M Johnston) *lw: s.i.s: rchd midfield after 3f: effrt over 2f out: swtchd rt over 1f out: styd on wl fnl f: nt pce to chal* **9/1**

01 **4** *1/2* **Eva's Request (IRE)**[21] 2992 2-9-7 **83** JHBowman 11 80
(M R Channon) *cl up: rdn to chse ldr over 2f out: sn chalng: nt qckn and hld 1f out: one pce* **9/2**[1]

430 **5** *nk* **Lady Sandicliffe (IRE)**[32] 2658 2-8-8 **70** MichaelHills 9 66
(B W Hills) *t.k.h: trckd ldrs: swtchd lft over 2f out: nt qckn over 1f out: styd on ins fnl f* **14/1**

054 **6** *2 1/2* **Insomnitas**[33] 2618 2-7-13 **61** JimmyQuinn 10 51
(M G Quinlan) *trckd ldrs: rdn and cl up wl over 1f out: one pce* **33/1**

0450 **7** *1/2* **Rough Rock (IRE)**[5] 3508 2-8-9 **71** (b[1]) RyanMoore 5 59
(B J Meehan) *t.k.h: trckd ldrs: effrt to chal 2f out: fnd nil: wknd fnl f* **5/1**[2]

41 **8** *1* **Yes Meg**[44] 2310 2-7-7 **60** LukeMorris(5) 4 46
(P F I Cole) *lw: chsd ldng gp: drvn and nt on terms fr over 2f out: no imp* **9/1**

064 **9** *3/4* **Nathan Dee**[37] 2517 2-7-9 **60** oh5 DominicFox(3) 3 44
(Mrs H Sweeting) *dwlt: wl in rr and wd: detached in last quartet 1/2-way: plugged on steadily fnl 2f: no ch* **33/1**

0030 **10** *nk* **Seventh Cloud (IRE)**[16] 3152 2-8-6 **68** RichardMullen 6 51
(A P Jarvis) *pressed ldr to over 2f out: sn wknd* **40/1**

056 **11** *1 1/4* **Talk Of Saafend (IRE)**[56] 1945 2-7-10 **63** WilliamBuick(5) 13 43
(R Hannon) *wl in rr: reminder over 5f out: detached in last quartet 1/2-way: no ch after: styd on fnl f* **8/1**[3]

020 **12** *10* **Distant Noble**[12] 3283 2-8-0 **62** oh2 ow2 HayleyTurner 1 16
(R Brotherton) *chsd ldrs tl wknd rapidly wl over 2f out* **66/1**

30 **13** *11* **L'Art Du Silence (IRE)**[23] 2941 2-8-11 **73** EddieAhern 14 —
(J R Boyle) *shuffled bk to rr sn after s: detached in last quartet 1/2-way: eased whn no ch over 1f out: t.o* **12/1**

054 **14** *1 1/4* **Rubytwosox (IRE)**[40] 2410 2-8-3 **65** MartinDwyer 8 —
(W R Muir) *a in rr: detached in last quartet 1/2-way: t.o* **50/1**

1m 27.13s (0.33) **Going Correction** -0.05s/f (Stan) **14** Ran SP% **126.9**
Speed ratings (Par 94):96,94,93,92,92 89,89,87,87,86 85,73,61,59
CSF £28.57 CT £212.53 TOTE £8.70: £2.50, £2.00, £3.20; EX 43.70.
Owner H R H Princess Haya Of Jordan **Bred** John G Boohan **Trained** Newmarket, Suffolk

FOCUS
A tough nursery full of unexposed sorts. The winning time was much slower than the older-horse handicaps at the end of the card. The official ratings shown next to each horse are estimated and for information purposes only.

NOTEBOOK
Fortuity(IRE) put a dismal effort at Catterick well behind him on this nursery bow and lost his maiden tag at the fifth time of asking. He evidently goes well on this surface, stays this trip without fuss now, and showed his true colours on this return to a more conventional track. He looks one of his yard's lesser lights in the juvenile department, but should be high on confidence now and can strike again in this sphere. (op 13-2 tchd 8-1)
Sourire, off the mark in resolute fashion at Catterick last time, was not surprisingly again ridden positively and posted a sound enough effort in defeat. She did leave the impression a stiffer test would now suit, however. (op 4-1)
Gulf Coast, making his nursery and All-Weather debut after three outings in maiden company, showed his best form to date in defeat. He still looked green and will be seen to better effect when able to race more handily over this trip. (op 10-1)
Eva's Request(IRE) did not do a great deal wrong in defeat under top weight over this extra furlong and posted a slightly improved effort. She helps to set the level of this form and has now found her level. (op 7-2 tchd 10-3)
Lady Sandicliffe(IRE) proved keen early on and, having taken time to find her stride, kept on without seriously threatening at the business end. She may not be the most straightforward. (op 12-1)
Rough Rock(IRE) paid the price for refusing to settle and it remains to be seen which way he goes now. Official explanation: jockey said gelding hung right throughout (op 12-1)
Nathan Dee Official explanation: jockey said colt suffered interference at start
Talk Of Saafend(IRE), up in trip, ran below her previous level on this switch to handicap company and looked tricky. (op 11-1)

3643 REUTERS FIRST FOR NEWS E B F MAIDEN FILLIES' STKS 7f (P)
7:20 (7:23) (Class 4) 2-Y-0 **£4,533** (£1,348; £674; £336) **Stalls** High

Form RPR

64 **1** **Maybe I Will (IRE)**[34] 2590 2-9-0 0 RyanMoore 4 70
(R Hannon) *lw: mostly chsd ldr: hanging over 2f out: drvn to ld over 1f out: hld on wl* **7/2**[1]

2 *nk* **Spiritofthetiger (USA)** 2-9-0 0 EddieAhern 6 69
(R A Teal) *w'like: scope: bit bkwd: chsd ldrs: effrt over 2f out: wnt 2nd jst over 1f out: hrd rdn to chal: jst hld* **33/1**

3 *1 1/4* **Dream Sea** 2-9-0 0 JHBowman 7 66
(M R Channon) *athletic: lw: trckd ldrs: n.m.r over 2f out: effrt over 1f out: styd on to take 3rd ins fnl f* **13/2**

02 **4** *1 1/4* **Binfield (IRE)**[13] 3233 2-9-0 0 TQuinn 12 63
(B G Powell) *led and sn clr: drvn and hdd over 1f out: fdd* **5/1**[3]

5 *1 1/4* **Challow Hills (USA)** 2-9-0 0 SebSanders 2 59+
(B W Hills) *w'like: strong: scope: bit bkwd: wl in rr and off the pce: sme prog 3f out: rdn and styd on fr over 1f out: nrst fin* **11/1**

6 *1* **Hamalka (IRE)** 2-9-0 0 MichaelHills 13 59+
(B W Hills) *w'like: s.s: trying to rcvr on inner whn n.m.r over 4f out: effrt to chse ldrs over 2f out: wknd fnl f* **4/1**[2]

00 **7** *1/2* **Dawn Wind**[6] 3453 2-9-0 0 LPKeniry 9 56
(I A Wood) *chsd ldrs: rdn and nt on terms fr wl over 2f out: no imp after* **50/1**

8 *nk* **Rhode Island Red (USA)** 2-9-0 0 JimmyFortune 11 55
(B J Meehan) *chsd ldrs: lost pl bdly over 4f out: wl in rr over 2f out: plugged on again fnl f* **7/1**

9 *6* **Golddigging (IRE)** 2-8-11 0 EmmettStack(3) 10 39
(J G Portman) *w'like: bit bkwd: s.s: t.o in last pair after 2f: sme late prog* **50/1**

10 *1/2* **Angel Pie** 2-8-11 0 RichardKingscote(3) 8 38
(R Charlton) *w'like: lw: dwlt: wl in rr and off the pce: effrt 1/2-way: no prog over 2f out: wknd* **12/1**

11 *1* **Medici Gold** 2-9-0 0 SteveDrowne 3 35
(B J Meehan) *w'like: racd wd and nvr on terms: struggling fr 3f out* **12/1**

12 *1* **April's Quest (IRE)** 2-9-0 0 PatDobbs 1 33
(David Pinder) *w'like: bit bkwd: stdd s: hld up wl in rr: sme prog into midfield 3f out but nvr nr ldrs: eased over 1f out* **50/1**

13 *1/2* **Miss Cruisecontrol** 2-9-0 0 MartinDwyer 5 31
(J R Best) *w'like: leggy: s.s: t.o in last pair after 2f* **25/1**

1m 27.8s (1.00) **Going Correction** -0.05s/f (Stan) **13** Ran SP% **121.1**
Speed ratings (Par 93):92,91,90,88,87 86,85,85,78,77 76,75,75
CSF £132.95 TOTE £4.60: £1.70, £9.70, £2.90; EX 220.90.
Owner J R May **Bred** Cheval Court Stud **Trained** East Everleigh, Wilts

FOCUS
An open-looking maiden with a mix of horses who had run and those who were making their debuts. Probably just fair form, rated through the likes of the fourth and seventh.

NOTEBOOK
Maybe I Will(IRE) showed her true colours on this step up to the extra furlong and proved game to get off the mark at the third attempt. Open to further improvement over this trip, she is out of a sister to Alexander Of Hales and half-sister to 1000 Guineas winner Virginia Waters, and this win will have significantly enhanced her potential paddock value now. (tchd 4-1 in a place)
Spiritofthetiger(USA), bred to make her mark at around this trip, made a very pleasing start to her career and went down fighting. She clearly has ability and should be placed to strike in this sort of company.
Dream Sea, whose dam scored over 1m6f at three, was noted keeping on nicely after meeting a little trouble at the top of the home straight. A Group 1 Moyglare Stud Stakes entry, she ought to benefit for this debut experience and can be expected to find a race before too long. (op 5-1)
Binfield(IRE), making her All-Weather debut, had very much the run of the race out in front over this extra furlong. She may be best dropping back to 6f for the short term and now qualifies for a nursery mark. (op 13-2)
Challow Hills(USA), whose dam was a 1m2f winner at three, ran distinctly green through the early stages yet the penny dropped nearing the 2f pole and she left the clear impression she would learn for this debut experience. (op 9-1 tchd 12-1)
Hamalka(IRE), a 60,000euros purchase bred to appreciate 1m plus next year, was always playing catch up after a slow start and then met a little trouble when trying to make up her ground. She looks sure to improve for this. (op 11-2)

3644 DIGIBET.COM LONDON MILE H'CAP (LONDON MILE QUALIFIER) 1m (P)
7:50 (7:52) (Class 5) (0-70,69) 3-Y-0+ **£2,817** (£838; £418; £209) **Stalls** High

Form RPR

5121 **1** **Nan Jan**[15] 3191 5-10-0 **67** (t) RobertHavlin 6 79
(R Ingram) *towards rr: clsd on ldng gp 3f out: drvn and r.o fr over 1f out: led last stride* **7/2**[2]

0251 **2** *hd* **Motafarred (IRE)**[7] 3422 5-9-0 **60** ThomasO'Brien(7) 3 72
(Micky Hammond) *pushed along in midfield 1/2-way: prog on inner over 2f out: drvn to cl over 1f out: led last 75yds: hdd fnl stride* **3/1**[1]

5431 **3** *shd* **Le Chiffre (IRE)**[8] 3405 5-9-8 **61** 6ex (p) SebSanders 14 72
(S Curran) *b. prom: drvn to dispute 2nd wl over 1f out: hanging after: clsd and upsides 75yds out: nt qckn* **11/2**[3]

052 **4** *1 1/2* **Nouveau (GER)**[9] 3369 3-7-12 **50** WilliamBuick(5) 5 58
(R Hannon) *sn pressed ldr: led over 4f out: drvn and 2 l clr over 1f out: wknd and hdd last 75yds* **8/1**

6000 **5** *3 1/2* **Greenwood**[7] 3422 9-9-10 **63** SteveDrowne 7 63
(P G Murphy) *wl in rr: prog whn nt clr run over 2f out: swtchd ins and clsd on ldrs wl over 1f out: outpcd sn after* **16/1**

3655 **6** *1/2* **Magic Warrior**[7] 3416 7-10-0 **67** PatDobbs 9 66
(J C Fox) *hld up in midfield: sme prog over 2f out: rdn and no hdwy whn nt clr run briefly over 1f out* **9/1**

4305 **7** *1 1/4* **Champain Sands (IRE)**[21] 2985 8-9-5 **58** StephenDonohoe 2 54
(E J Alston) *hld up towards rr: stdy prog on outer fr halfway: chsd ldrs 2f out: wknd tamely over 1f out* **10/1**

-606 **8** *nk* **October Ben**[7] 3422 4-9-10 **63** HayleyTurner 11 58
(M D I Usher) *b. s.s: hld up in last trio: drvn and effrt over 2f out: no imp whn edgd rt 1f out* **11/1**

-000 **9** *1 1/2* **Megalala (IRE)**[49] 2143 6-8-9 **48** oh2 FrankieMcDonald 12 40
(J J Bridger) *t.k.h: hld up in last pair: hmpd after 3f: last and struggling 1/2-way: no ch after* **40/1**

3503 **10** *shd* **Plateau**[8] 3409 8-9-12 **65** EddieAhern 4 62+
(C R Dore) *prom: pressed ldr 4f: no imp and hld 2f out: losing pl whn n.m.r 1f out: eased* **14/1**

/50- **11** *3* **Pertemps Green**[335] 4527 4-9-12 **65** MickyFenton 8 50
(M S Saunders) *stdd s: hld up in rr: sme prog on outer 3f out: no imp on ldrs 2f out: wknd over 1f out* **50/1**

0650 **12** *3/4* **Panshir (FR)**[18] 3101 6-8-4 **48** oh2 KevinGhunowa(5) 1 31
(Mrs C A Dunnett) *t.k.h: prom: wnt 3rd over 3f out: wknd rapidly over 2f out* **33/1**

4134 **13** *shd* **Blue Line**[32] 2654 5-9-4 **60** MarcHalford(3) 10 43
(M Madgwick) *wl in rr: rdn 5f out: struggling after: brief effrt on inner 2f out: no prog whn n.m.r 1f out* **16/1**

-650 **14** *10* **Ede's Dot Com (IRE)**[33] 2629 3-9-8 **69** IanMongan 13 29
(P M Phelan) *led to over 4f out: lost pl: wknd rapidly over 2f out: t.o* **50/1**

1m 39.5s (-1.30) **Going Correction** -0.05s/f (Stan)
WFA 3 from 4yo+ 8lb **14** Ran SP% **128.9**
Speed ratings (Par 103):104,103,103,102,98 98,96,96,95,95 92,91,91,81
CSF £15.28 CT £62.09 TOTE £4.90: £2.00, £2.00, £1.90; EX 21.00.
Owner The Waltons **Bred** Mrs S Ingram **Trained** Epsom, Surrey
■ Stewards' Enquiry : Thomas O'Brien six-day ban: used whip with excessive frequency (Jul 29-Aug 3)

FOCUS
A fair race for the level and the form looks very solid.
Blue Line Official explanation: jockey said mare suffered interference in running
Ede's Dot Com(IRE) Official explanation: jockey said gelding suffered interference in running

3645 DIGIBET CASINO FILLIES' H'CAP 1m (P)

8:20 (8:22) (Class 4) (0-85,83) 3-Y-O £4,728 (£1,406; £702; £351) Stalls High

Form RPR

1-50 **1** **Les Fazzani (IRE)**[55] 1958 3-9-4 **80**.................................... EddieAhern 2 89+
(M J Wallace) *lw: hld up: prog to chse ldrs 3f out: rdn over 2f out: effrt to chal fnl f: led last 100yds: r.o wl* **6/1**

620- **2** ½ **Comma (USA)**[263] 6215 3-8-8 **70**.. RyanMoore 8 78+
(Sir Michael Stoute) *settled in tch: lost pl and in last pair 3f out: dashed through on inner over 2f out: led over 1f out: r.o but hdd and hld last 100yds* **5/2**[2]

21-0 **3** 5 **Sunlight (IRE)**[67] 1663 3-9-7 **83**.................................... PhilipRobinson 1 79
(M A Jarvis) *led after 2f: rdn and hdd over 1f out: wknd fnl f* **9/4**[1]

4431 **4** nk **Musical Beat**[7] 3411 3-9-7 **83** 6ex....................................... SebSanders 3 78
(Miss V Haigh) *swtg: hld up: prog to trck ldr over 3f out: stl cl up over 1f out: wknd fnl f* **8/1**

46-0 **5** 1 ¾ **Guacamole**[42] 2369 3-9-6 **82**.. MichaelHills 4 73
(B W Hills) *swtg: trckd ldrs: clsd 3f out: stl chsng over 1f out: wknd* **12/1**

5-13 **6** 1 **Cherie's Dream**[40] 2425 3-8-9 **71**.. LPKeniry 7 60
(A M Balding) *led for 2f: styd cl up tl wknd over 1f out* **10/1**

-312 **7** nk **El Toreador (USA)**[18] 3111 3-9-4 **80**................................ JHBowman 6 68
(G A Butler) *settled in last: no prog over 2f out: one pce* **5/1**[3]

1m 37.97s (-2.83) **Going Correction** -0.05s/f (Stan) 7 Ran SP% **118.2**
Speed ratings (Par 99):112,111,106,106,104 103,103
CSF £22.48 CT £44.61 TOTE £7.80: £2.70, £2.10; EX 33.00.
Owner Mike & Denise Dawes **Bred** J Erhardt & Mrs J Schonwalder **Trained** Newmarket, Suffolk

FOCUS
A really good race run at a sound gallop. The winning time was very quick. The first two finished clear and a positive view has been taken of the form.

3646 DIGIBET SPORTS BETTING H'CAP 7f (P)

8:50 (8:50) (Class 5) (0-75,74) 3-Y-O £2,817 (£838; £418; £104; £104) Stalls High

Form RPR

0600 **1** **Proper (IRE)**[10] 3350 3-8-12 **65**... JHBowman 10 71+
(M R Channon) *swtg: chsd ldrs: prog to go 2nd wl over 1f out: rdn to cl fnl f: led nr fin: shade cleverly* **6/1**[3]

-060 **2** nk **Day By Day**[12] 3286 3-8-2 **55**..(b) MartinDwyer 2 60
(B J Meehan) *b.hind: led: drvn and pressed 2f out: styd on wl fr over 1f out: collared nr fin* **33/1**

4635 **3** 2 **Ask Yer Dad**[29] 2749 3-8-12 **65**.......................................(p) MickyFenton 1 65
(Mrs P Sly) *mostly chsd ldr: rdn 4f out: nt qckn and hanging 2f out: kpt on* **16/1**

0-40 **4** ¾ **Take To The Skies (IRE)**[95] 1037 3-8-12 **65**............. RichardMullen 11 63
(A P Jarvis) *lw: t.k.h: hld up bhd ldrs: rdn and nt qckn 2f out: kpt on fnl f* **8/1**

-000 **4** dht **Awwal Malika (USA)**[13] 3235 3-8-4 **62**........................ AhmedAjtebi(5) 4 60
(C E Brittain) *lw: hld up towards rr: effrt over 2f out: styd on fr over 1f out: nt rch ldrs* **66/1**

4-00 **6** shd **Minnis Bay (CAN)**[19] 3058 3-9-7 **74**.................................... TedDurcan 5 72
(E F Vaughan) *racd wd and wl in rr: drvn over 2f out: styd on fr over 1f out: nrst fin* **20/1**

3022 **7** 1 **The Jay Factor (IRE)**[16] 3168 3-8-13 **66**........................... RyanMoore 7 61
(Pat Eddery) *wl in rr: last and struggling 4f out: taken to wd outside and drvn over 2f out: styd on fnl f: no ch* **10/3**[1]

0-52 **8** shd **Orchestrator (IRE)**[19] 3044 3-9-6 **73**............................ SteveDrowne 13 68
(T G Mills) *t.k.h: hld up bhd ldrs: disp 2nd 2f out to jst over 1f out on inner: wknd* **11/2**[2]

1200 **9** ¾ **High Tribute**[7] 3418 3-9-7 **74**...(t) SebSanders 6 67
(Sir Mark Prescott) *awkward s and sn in last trio: urged along and kpt on one pce fnl 2f: n.d* **14/1**

6561 **10** ¾ **Tipsy Prince**[13] 3237 3-9-6 **73**.. PatDobbs 8 64
(David Pinder) *dwlt: hld up in rr: sme prog over 2f out: wknd over 1f out* **8/1**

2204 **11** hd **Realy Naughty (IRE)**[10] 3350 3-8-12 **65**................................ TQuinn 12 56
(B G Powell) *t.k.h: hld up in midfield on inner: chsng ldrs 2f out: fdd over 1f out* **12/1**

0016 **12** 1 **Prince Of Charm (USA)**[16] 3167 3-9-3 **70**................(p) GeorgeBaker 14 58
(R A Teal) *s.s: wl in rr: brief effrt over 2f out: sn no hdwy: wknd and eased* **15/2**

06-0 **13** 2 **Queen Noverre (IRE)**[34] 2601 3-9-4 **71**............................ EddieAhern 3 54
(J W Hills) *chsd ldrs: shuffled along and lost pl steadily fr over 2f out* **22/1**

02-0 **14** ¾ **Tokyo Jo (IRE)**[135] 624 3-8-9 **62**.................................. SamHitchcott 9 43
(T T Clement) *chsd ldrs tl wknd over 2f out* **66/1**

1m 26.44s (-0.36) **Going Correction** -0.05s/f (Stan) 14 Ran SP% **122.0**
Speed ratings (Par 100):100,99,97,96,96 96,95,95,94,93 93,92,89,88
CSF £204.27 CT £3092.51 TOTE £7.60: £2.60, £7.30, £5.20; EX 215.10.
Owner Billy Parish **Bred** Sean Finnegan **Trained** West Ilsley, Berks

FOCUS
An ordinary handicap. The winner has been rated to his previous All-Weather best and could have a bit more to offer.

3647 TFM NETWORKS H'CAP 7f (P)

9:20 (9:21) (Class 6) (0-65,65) 3-Y-O+ £2,047 (£604; £302) Stalls High

Form RPR

0505 **1** **Tipsy Lad**[13] 3241 5-8-12 **49**...(t) TQuinn 12 57
(D J S Ffrench Davis) *wl detached after 2f and nt gng wl: prog on outer 2f out: str run fnl f: won on the nod* **33/1**

11 **2** shd **Bucharest**[7] 3419 4-9-10 **61** 6ex...................................... SteveDrowne 8 69
(M Wigham) *w ldr at fast pce: led wl over 2f out: shkn up to repel chalr fnl f: hdd on the post* **6/5**[1]

153 **3** 1 ¼ **Wiltshire (IRE)**[10] 3345 5-9-4 **55**...................................... MickyFenton 7 59
(P T Midgley) *in tch: prog to chse ldr 2f out: drvn to chal fnl f: jst hld and lost 2nd nr fin* **5/1**[2]

0-34 **4** ½ **Desert Hunter (IRE)**[40] 2421 4-9-0 **51**............................ JimmyQuinn 2 54
(Micky Hammond) *lw: in tch: drvn to cl fr over 2f out: nt qckn over 1f out: kpt on* **10/1**

-001 **5** 4 **On The Map**[35] 2571 3-9-3 **61**...(v) PatDobbs 4 54
(A P Jarvis) *lw: led at fast pce to wl over 2f out: fdd over 1f out* **25/1**

2002 **6** 1 **Over To You Bert**[8] 3405 8-8-7 **51**.................................... HaddenFrost(7) 3 41
(R J Hodges) *forced to r wd: nvr bttr than midfield: effrt 2f out: one pce* **20/1**

-005 **7** 1 ½ **Playtotheaudience**[8] 3408 4-9-6 **60**........................ JamieMoriarty(3) 13 46
(R A Fahey) *outpcd and detached after 2f: effrt u.p over 2f out: sn no prog* **14/1**

062 **8** nk **Navene (IRE)**[20] 3031 3-9-0 **58**... TedDurcan 9 44
(C F Wall) *lw: chsd ldrs: losing pl u.p whn squeezed out 2f out* **12/1**

2360 **9** hd **Mannello**[7] 3422 4-8-9 **51**.......................................(v[1]) KevinGhunowa(5) 10 36
(Mrs C A Dunnett) *t.k.h: hld up bhd ldrs: drvn and wknd over 2f out* **50/1**

16-0 **10** 1 ½ **Sovereignty (JPN)**[195] 32 5-10-0 **65**................................. RobertHavlin 14 46
(D K Ivory) *prom in chsng gp: wnt 3rd 1/2-way: wknd 2f out* **14/1**

1006 **11** 29 **Monashee River (IRE)**[30] 2716 4-8-11 **48**........................ JHBowman 5 —
(Miss V Haigh) *prom to 1/2-way: sn lost pl: t.o* **25/1**

5605 **12** 34 **Gavarnie Beau (IRE)**[13] 3234 4-9-11 **62**..........................(b) LPKeniry 11 —
(M Blanshard) *lft 100yds s: allowed to amble arnd* **8/1**[3]

1m 26.16s (-0.64) **Going Correction** -0.05s/f (Stan)
WFA 3 from 4yo+ 7lb 12 Ran SP% **120.7**
Speed ratings (Par 101):101,100,99,98,94 93,91,91,90,89 56,17
CSF £71.43 CT £267.00 TOTE £42.70: £7.40, £1.10, £1.90; EX 152.40 Place 6 £215.44, Place 5 £89.23..
Owner S J Edwards **Bred** Mrs R J Mitchell **Trained** Lambourn, Berks

FOCUS
Another ordinary handicap best rated through the in-form second and consistent third.
Over To You Bert Official explanation: jockey said gelding hung right
Gavarnie Beau(IRE) Official explanation: jockey said gelding sat down as stalls opened
T/Plt: £447.90 to a £1 stake. Pool: £74,717.00. 121.75 winning tickets. T/Qpdt: £97.00 to a £1 stake. Pool: £7,068.60. 53.90 winning tickets. JN

3452 LINGFIELD (L-H)

Wednesday, July 18

OFFICIAL GOING: All-weather - standard; turf course - good to firm (good in places)
Wind: brisk behind

3648 EUROPEAN BREEDERS' FUND MAIDEN FILLIES' STKS 6f (P)

2:20 (2:21) (Class 5) 2-Y-O £3,562 (£1,059; £529; £264) Stalls Low

Form RPR

3304 **1** **May Day Queen (IRE)**[16] 3152 2-9-0 0............................ SteveDrowne 3 78
(R Hannon) *trckd ldrs: led ins fnl 2f: drvn and styd on wl fnl f* **7/2**[2]

2 ½ **Fashion Rocks (IRE)** 2-9-0 0...................................... JimmyFortune 12 77+
(B J Meehan) *in rr: pushed along and stl plenty to do ins fnl 2f: str run fr over 1f out to take 2nd ins fnl f: fin wl but nt rch wnr* **6/1**[3]

05 **3** 1 ½ **Fidelias Dance**[61] 1814 2-8-11 0.................................... GregFairley(3) 8 72
(M Johnston) *sn chsng ldrs: rdn over 2f out: chsd wnr ins fnl f but no imp: wknd into 3rd cl home* **20/1**

26 **4** 1 **High Days (IRE)**[32] 2658 2-9-0 0... RyanMoore 5 70+
(Sir Michael Stoute) *chsd ldrs: outpcd over 2f out: sn rdn: styd on again fnl f but nvr gng pce to be competitive* **7/2**[2]

0 **5** 1 **Betty Burke**[54] 1993 2-9-0 0.. EddieAhern 4 66
(H J L Dunlop) *led: rdn and hdd ins fnl 2f: wknd jst ins fnl f* **100/1**

0350 **6** 1 ½ **Evenstorm (USA)**[28] 2756 2-9-0 0.. TQuinn 6 62
(B Gubby) *chsd ldrs: rdn over 2f out: saddle slipped & eased fnl f: wknd fnl f: dismntd after fin* **25/1**

0 **7** nk **Princess India (IRE)**[32] 2658 2-9-0 0................................ JimCrowley 10 61
(P Winkworth) *in rr: rdn 1/2-way: styd on fnl f but nvr gng pce to be competitive* **50/1**

5 **8** shd **Bermacha**[55] 1960 2-9-0 0.. MartinDwyer 9 60
(W R Muir) *rdn and outpcd 1/2-way: kpt on fr over 1f out but nvr gng pce to be competitive* **22/1**

00 **9** 1 ¾ **Orbital Orchid**[38] 2488 2-9-0 0.. LPKeniry 2 55
(W S Kittow) *s.i.s: sn chsng ldrs: wknd 2f out* **66/1**

02 **10** 2 ½ **Dresden Doll (USA)**[39] 2478 2-9-0 0.................................. HayleyTurner 1 48
(M L W Bell) *chsd ldr tl rdn and wknd 2f out* **13/8**[1]

0 **11** ¾ **Nisbah**[37] 2504 2-9-0 0.. SebSanders 11 45
(C E Brittain) *slowly into strie: a struggling: rn wd bnd ins fnl 2f and hung rt* **33/1**

1m 12.34s (-0.47) **Going Correction** -0.15s/f (Stan) 11 Ran SP% **117.2**
Speed ratings (Par 91):97,96,94,93,91 89,89,89,86,83 82
CSF £22.77 TOTE £4.30: £1.60, £2.00, £3.40; EX 23.50 TRIFECTA Part won. Pool £245.47 - 0.44 winning units..
Owner J R May **Bred** Martyn J McEnery **Trained** East Everleigh, Wilts

FOCUS
This looked a reasonable fillies' maiden. A better effort from the winner, although still below her Irish form, and the standard looks pretty solid.

NOTEBOOK
May Day Queen(IRE) again ran below the form she showed when third to subsequent Cherry Hinton winner You'resothrilling in a Group 3 at Naas, but she was still good enough to get off the mark at the fifth attempt. Always in a good position just in behind the leaders, she picked up well when asked for her effort and was always going to hold on from the fast-finishing Fashion Rocks. She has plenty of size and is expected to get better as she gets older. She could be aimed at a Listed race at either Goodwood or Sandown, but her connections will also consider nurseries. (op 4-1 tchd 9-2)
Fashion Rocks(IRE) ◆, a 200,000euros daughter of Rock Of Gibraltar, out of a smart dual 1m winner, made an eye-catching debut in second. She was last at about halfway, looking in need of the experience, but she stayed on in taking fashion when switched into the clear in the straight. She should improve plenty and ought to go very close in similar company next time.
Fidelias Dance ◆ had not been seen for two months, but this must rate as a pleasing return to action. She was forced to race a little wide for some of the way, but kept on in the straight and gave the impression she can improve. She is now eligible for nurseries and could be one to keep on side. Official explanation: jockey said filly hung left-handed (op 16-1)
High Days(IRE) does not seem to be progressing, but she is now qualified for a nursery mark and will have more options. She should be suited by a step up in trip. Official explanation: jockey said filly was denied a clear run (op 11-4)
Betty Burke showed bags of speed and would not mind a return to 5f on this evidence. (op 66-1)
Evenstorm(USA) Official explanation: jockey said saddle slipped
Dresden Doll(USA) seemed well enough placed, but she found nothing when asked for her effort and was very disappointing. Official explanation: trainer had no explanation for the poor form shown (op 15-8)

3649 RYDON GROUP H'CAP 6f (P)

2:50 (2:50) (Class 5) (0-75,75) 3-Y-O £2,817 (£838; £418; £209) Stalls Low

Form RPR

4 **1** **Expensive Art (IRE)**[64] 1737 3-8-0 **57**......................... WilliamBuick(5) 6 70+
(N A Callaghan) *trckd ldrs: led ins fnl 2f: drvn clr fnl f: readily* **11/4**[1]

16-0 **2** 3 ½ **Lay The Cash (USA)**[34] 2594 3-8-11 **63**......................(b) MartinDwyer 3 66+
(J S Moore) *chsd ldrs: rdn 1/2-way: hmpd and lost position on ins 2f out: rallied and r.o to chse wnr ins fnl f but nvr any ch* **25/1**

35-5 **3** 1 ½ **Millisecond**[55] 1961 3-9-8 **74**.. PhilipRobinson 2 72
(M A Jarvis) *led tl hdd ins fnl 2f: no ch w wnr over 1f out: wknd and lost 2nd ins fnl f* **10/3**[2]

14-0 **4** 1/2 **Hucking Hill (IRE)**[31] 2689 3-9-9 **75** GeorgeBaker 8 71
(J R Best) *in rr: rdn and hdwy to chse ldrs 3f out: wknd ins fnl f* **8/1**
1615 **5** 3/4 **Scarlett Heart (IRE)**[37] 2515 3-8-13 **65** JimCrowley 4 59
(J Gallagher) *in rr: rdn over 2f out: sme prog fnl f but nvr in contention* **13/2**[3]
6402 **6** 1 **Charlotte Grey**[12] 3281 3-9-2 **68** EdwardCreighton 5 59
(C N Allen) *chsd ldrs: rdn 3f out: wknd fnl f* **16/1**
0361 **7** 1 **Rosie Cross (IRE)**[12] 3281 3-8-8 **60** StephenCarson 1 48
(Eve Johnson Houghton) *chsd ldrs: rdn 1/2-way: wknd over 1f out* **8/1**
0062 **8** 2 **Stir Crazy (IRE)**[10] 3353 3-7-11 **56** oh2 MatthewDavies(7) 9 38
(M R Channon) *a outpcd in rr* **9/1**
0014 **9** 3 1/2 **Kondakova (IRE)**[20] 3038 3-9-8 **74** HayleyTurner 7 45
(M L W Bell) *s.i.s: a outpcd* **15/2**
1m 11.0s (-1.81) **Going Correction** -0.15s/f (Stan) 9 Ran SP% **116.8**
Speed ratings (Par 100):106,101,99,98,97 96,95,92,87
CSF £73.35 CT £242.27 TOTE £4.00: £1.70, £5.50, £1.80; EX 125.90 Trifecta £205.00 Part won Pool £288.78 - 0.50 winning units..
Owner Matthew Green **Bred** Stone Ridge Farm **Trained** Newmarket, Suffolk
■ Stewards' Enquiry : William Buick one-day ban: careless riding (Aug 3); one-day ban: careless riding (Aug 5)

FOCUS
This looked like a competitive, if modest sprint handicap, but nothing could live with the well-backed Expensive Art. She can win again and the form should work out.
Hucking Hill(IRE) Official explanation: jockey said gelding lost an off-fore shoe

3650 E B F PAUL KELLEWAY MEMORIAL CLASSIFIED STKS 1m (P)
3:20 (3:22) (Class 3) 3-Y-0+
£9,348 (£2,799; £1,399; £700; £349; £175) Stalls High

Form RPR
1011 **1** **Samarinda (USA)**[14] 3215 4-9-3 88 MickyFenton 6 97
(Mrs P Sly) *in rr but in tch: hdwy 4f out: led over 1f out: hung rt thrght fnl f: all out* **8/1**
1200 **2** hd **Montpellier (IRE)**[11] 3330 4-9-3 89 JimmyFortune 8 97+
(E A L Dunlop) *in rr: hdwy 3f out: drvn to press wnr ins fnl f: carried rt thrght: fin wl: nt rcvr* **15/8**[1]
-142 **3** 1 1/2 **Hazzard County (USA)**[44] 2313 3-8-9 85 EddieAhern 10 91+
(D M Simcock) *in rr: hdwy over 1f out: kpt on wl fnl f but nt pce to rch ldng pair* **16/1**
0002 **4** 3/4 **Gallantry**[36] 2528 5-9-3 85 DeanMcKeown 5 91
(D Shaw) *chsd ldrs: rdn over 2f out: styd on fnl f but nvr a danger* **14/1**
1400 **5** shd **Players Please (USA)**[27] 2788 3-8-6 88 GregFairley(3) 11 89
(M Johnston) *in rr: rdn and hdwy fr 2f out and wd into st: kpt on fnl f but nvr gng pce to rch ldrs* **7/2**[2]
1106 **6** 1 **Phluke**[36] 2528 6-9-3 83 StephenCarson 7 89
(Eve Johnson Houghton) *chsd ldrs: wnt 2nd 3f out: led 2f out: hdd over 1f out: wknd fnl f* **20/1**
6000 **7** 2 1/2 **Bobski (IRE)**[7] 3437 5-9-3 83 AdamKirby 3 83
(G A Huffer) *s.i.s: sn rcvrd to chse ldrs: wknd over 1f out* **20/1**
4-04 **8** 3/4 **Mina A Salem**[83] 1268 5-9-3 87 TQuinn 4 81
(C E Brittain) *chsd ldr: led appr fnl 4f: hdd 2f out: sn btn* **12/1**
5062 **9** 5 **Wavertree Warrior (IRE)**[14] 3201 5-9-3 90 RyanMoore 9 70
(N P Littmoden) *a towards rr* **11/2**[3]
-463 **10** 1 **Irony (IRE)**[32] 2670 8-8-12 86 (p) WilliamBuick(5) 1 68
(A M Balding) *led tl hdd appr fnl 4f: wknd ins fnl 4f* **16/1**
1m 36.67s (-2.76) **Going Correction** -0.15s/f (Stan)
WFA 3 from 4yo+ 8lb 10 Ran SP% **119.1**
Speed ratings (Par 107):107,106,105,104,104 103,100,100,95,94
CSF £23.87 TOTE £8.90: £2.40, £1.30, £4.10; EX 29.60 Trifecta £248.50 Pool £388.53 - 1.11 winning units..
Owner D Bayliss, T Davies, G Libson & P Sly **Bred** Gainsborough Farm Llc **Trained** Thorney, Cambs

FOCUS
A good classified event and, with just 7lb separating the entire field at the weights, it was very competitive. The runner-up was done no favours by the winner.

NOTEBOOK
Samarinda(USA) came into this off the back of a couple of wins in slightly lesser company over this trip at Kempton and continued his improvement to complete the hat-trick. He was sticking his neck out under pressure, certainly displaying a good attitude, but he also drifted right throughout the final furlong and clearly intimidated the eventual runner-up. The stewards duly held an inquiry, but they felt the interference was accidental and did not improve Samarinda's placing. Things are going to get really tough from now on, but he is in the form of his life and should not be underestimated when bidding for the four-timer. His trainer said he will need fast ground if switching to turf. (op 6-1)
Montpellier(IRE) was carried right by the eventual winner inside the final furlong, but it is impossible to know for sure if he would have won had both horses stayed straight. This was a good effort in defeat and he remains one to keep on the right side of in similar company. (op 2-1 tchd 7-4, 9-4 in places)
Hazzard County(USA) never looked like getting to the front two, but he responded well to strong pressure late on to take third.
Gallantry returned to form when runner-up at Chester on his previous start and this was another decent effort in defeat. (op 10-1)
Players Please(USA) ◆ was asked to make his effort very wide and can be rated a fair bit better than the bare form. (op 9-2)
Bobski(IRE) Official explanation: jockey said gelding had no more to give
Wavertree Warrior(IRE) was another caught very wide, but he basically just looked to have an off day. (op 6-1 tchd 13-2)

3651 BELLWAY MEDIAN AUCTION MAIDEN STKS 1m 1f
3:50 (3:51) (Class 6) 3-4-Y-0 £2,730 (£806; £403) Stalls Low

Form RPR
4 **1** **Elegant Hawk**[69] 1606 3-8-12 0 PaulDoe 8 64+
(W J Knight) *in tch: hdwy 3f out: drvn to chal 1f out: led ins fnl f: hung lft cl home* **2/1**[1]
50-0 **2** 1 1/2 **Dancing Jest (IRE)**[89] 1117 3-8-12 55 MickyFenton 4 61
(Rae Guest) *chsd ldr: chal fr 4f out: led over 2f out: hdd ins fnl f: styd on same pce* **33/1**
0 **3** 1 **Blue Space**[40] 2428 3-8-12 0 AmirQuinn 2 59+
(P J Makin) *s.i.s: sn drvn to chse ldrs: outpcd over 2f out: styd on again ins fnl f but nvr gng pce to rch ldng pair* **4/1**[2]
0-6 **4** 6 **Memphis Marie**[23] 2951 3-8-12 0 MartinDwyer 1 46
(C N Allen) *led tl hdd over 2f out: wknd over 1f out* **33/1**
5 1 **Power Player** 3-9-3 0 TPO'Shea 11 48
(D J Coakley) *slowly away: in rr: drvn along over 3f out: styd on fnl 2f and fin wl but nvr in contention* **9/1**
0000 **6** shd **Bathwick Fancy (IRE)**[8] 3394 3-8-12 47 DavidKinsella 3 43
(J G Portman) *in tch: hdwy 3f out but nvr gng pce to be competitive: wknd fr 2f out* **25/1**
43 **7** 2 **Woolfall Rose**[20] 3041 3-8-12 0 NeilPollard 10 39
(G G Margarson) *chsd ldrs tl wknd 3f out* **7/1**
8 8 **Quidor Way (GR)** 3-9-3 0 JimCrowley 9 26
(P R Chamings) *slowly away: a in rr* **11/1**
5-0 **9** 3 **Rangali Belle**[40] 2429 3-8-12 0 SteveDrowne 7 15
(C A Horgan) *green whn rdn 3f out: a in rr* **20/1**
004 **10** 2 **Nothingtodeclaire**[18] 3084 3-9-3 72 (b[1]) AdamKirby 5 15
(G A Huffer) *chsd ldrs over 5f* **11/2**[3]
1m 56.68s (1.39) **Going Correction** +0.175s/f (Good) 10 Ran SP% **114.0**
Speed ratings (Par 101):100,98,97,92,91 91,89,82,79,78
CSF £84.69 TOTE £2.70: £1.20, £8.60, £2.00; EX 75.90 Trifecta £222.00 Part won. Pool £312.81 - 0.34 winning units..
Owner Hesmonds Stud **Bred** Hesmonds Stud Ltd **Trained** Patching, W Sussex

FOCUS
A weak, uncompetitive maiden.
Bathwick Fancy(IRE) Official explanation: jockey said filly had no more to give
Nothingtodeclaire Official explanation: jockey said colt lost its action

3652 REAL THING LIVE AT LINGFIELDPARK.CO.UK H'CAP 1m 2f
4:20 (4:21) (Class 6) (0-65,65) 3-Y-0 £2,047 (£604; £302) Stalls Low

Form RPR
-430 **1** **Gib (IRE)**[16] 3150 3-9-6 62 MichaelHills 10 77+
(B W Hills) *mde virtually all: drvn and forged clr ins fnl 2f* **13/2**[3]
0503 **2** 5 **Stagehand (IRE)**[21] 3003 3-9-9 65 RyanMoore 2 68
(B R Millman) *in tch: hrd drvn over 3f out: styd on u.p fnl 2f to take 2nd last strides but nvr any ch w clr wnr* **3/1**[1]
344 **3** shd **Proposal**[15] 3177 3-8-11 53 JamesDoyle 13 56
(A W Carroll) *chsd wnr 6f out: rdn 3f out: outpcd fr 2f out: lost 2nd last stride* **10/1**
0-50 **4** 1 1/4 **Restless Soul**[79] 1364 3-8-10 52 AdamKirby 3 52
(C A Cyzer) *in rr: hdwy 4f out: kpt on fnl 2f: gng on ins fnl f but nvr a danger* **33/1**
0223 **5** nk **Red Flare (IRE)**[6] 3450 3-8-10 52 JHBowman 5 52
(M R Channon) *chsd ldrs: rdn over 3f out: styd on fnl 2f but nvr gng pce to be competitive* **10/3**[2]
00-0 **6** 1 1/4 **Like To Golf (USA)**[39] 2456 3-9-1 57 (p) JimCrowley 1 54
(Mrs A J Perrett) *chsd wnr to 6f out: rdn over 3f out: wknd appr fnl f* **20/1**
0501 **7** hd **Lawyer To World**[22] 2963 3-8-2 49 (p) WilliamBuick(5) 11 46
(Mrs C A Dunnett) *towards rr: rdn and hdwy over 3f out: styd on fnl 2f but nvr nr ldrs* **12/1**
0000 **8** 1/2 **Red Brick Road (IRE)**[24] 2916 3-8-6 48 (p) SimonWhitworth 4 44
(A J Lidderdale) *rr: rdn and hdwy 4f out: styd on fnl 2f but nvr in contention* **16/1**
0063 **9** 3/4 **A Nod And A Wink (IRE)**[113] 794 3-8-6 48 BThomas 6 43
(J C Fox) *hld up in rr on ins: swtchd rt to wd outside and stdy hdwy fr 3f out but nvr in contention* **50/1**
00-0 **10** nk **Double Banded (IRE)**[16] 3150 3-8-11 53 EddieAhern 12 47
(J L Dunlop) *n.m.r 5f out: a towards rr* **14/1**
0600 **11** nk **Black Mogul**[18] 3082 3-8-9 51 MartinDwyer 14 45
(W R Muir) *nvr bttr than mid-div* **20/1**
4030 **12** 5 **Brave Jack (IRE)**[10] 3351 3-8-8 50 TQuinn 9 34
(J R Best) *slowly away: a towards rr* **14/1**
0600 **13** 1 **Dark Druid (IRE)**[24] 2916 3-8-10 52 LPKeniry 7 34
(I A Wood) *rr: sme hdwy 4f out: wknd 2f out* **66/1**
4-05 **14** 30 **Dramatic Touch**[31] 2693 3-9-9 65 SteveDrowne 8 —
(G Wragg) *sn pushed along: drvn fr mid-div to chse ldrs 4f out: wknd over 3f out* **10/1**
2m 10.66s (0.94) **Going Correction** +0.175s/f (Good) 14 Ran SP% **122.4**
Speed ratings (Par 98):103,99,98,97,97 96,96,96,95,95 95,91,90,66
CSF £25.25 CT £201.83 TOTE £7.40: £2.30, £1.70, £2.90; EX 35.10 Trifecta £203.80 Part won. Pool £287.14 - 0.30 winning units..
Owner Jeremy Gompertz & Patrick Milmo **Bred** Denis Brosnan & Patsy Byrne **Trained** Lambourn, Berks

FOCUS
This looked like a very moderate handicap. The winenr proved something of a revelation with a change of tactics and the placed form looks sound.
A Nod And A Wink(IRE) Official explanation: jockey said, regarding running and riding, his orders were to settle the filly to enable it to get home, as in the past it has run very free and took a long time to settle, adding that having come down the hill he tried to improve position at 3f, but he had become very tired and was unable to give meaningful assistance; vet said; filly was lame near-fore
Double Banded(IRE) Official explanation: trainer said gelding had put its foot in a hole during the race
Brave Jack(IRE) Official explanation: jockey said gelding missed the break and never travelled
Dramatic Touch Official explanation: jockey said filly never travelled

3653 RAY QUINN & BEN MILLS LIVE AT LINGFIELDPARK.CO.UK H'CAP 2m
4:50 (4:50) (Class 5) (0-75,72) 3-Y-0+ £2,817 (£838; £418; £209) Stalls Low

Form RPR
2050 **1** **Mister Completely (IRE)**[2] 3598 6-9-5 63 (v[1]) JamesDoyle 10 70
(Ms J S Doyle) *in rr but in tch: hdwy to chse ldr 5f out: drivn to ld jst ins fnl 2f: edgd rt cl home: all out* **14/1**
0004 **2** 1/2 **Into Action**[6] 3473 3-7-10 62 WilliamBuick(5) 1 68
(R Hannon) *sn chsng ldr: rdn and outpcd 3f out: rallied u.p fr 2f out: styd on wl cl home but nt quite rch wnr* **9/2**[2]
4230 **3** 1/2 **Noddies Way**[53] 2026 4-8-12 61 LukeMorris(5) 8 67
(J F Panvert) *in rr: rdn and hdwy over 2f out: styd on wl fnl f: swtchd lft and gng on cl home* **9/2**[2]
-022 **4** 2 **Tavalu (USA)**[34] 1526 5-9-7 65 (b) RyanMoore 6 68
(G L Moore) *sn led: rdn over 3f out: hdd jst ins fnl 2f: sn one pce* **7/4**[1]
00-5 **5** 2 1/2 **Jack Dawson (IRE)**[18] 3112 10-10-0 72 GeorgeBaker 9 72
(John Berry) *hld up in tch: hdwy to chse ldrs over 3f out: one pce fnl 2f* **15/2**
30-0 **6** 6 **Liberman (IRE)**[86] 1196 9-9-7 65 EddieAhern 4 58
(R Curtis) *in rr but in tch: hdwy 5f out: rdn 3f out: sn btn* **25/1**
0120 **7** 4 **Red Petal**[65] 1724 3-8-11 72 (t) SebSanders 5 60
(Sir Mark Prescott) *hld up in rr: rdn and brief effrt over 3f out: nvr a danger and sn wknd* **6/1**[3]
000/ **8** 53 **Ruggtah**[45] 1822 6-8-9 53 oh3 JimCrowley 3 —
(M G Rimell) *chsd ldr tl wknd rapidly 6f out: virtually p.u fnl 3f* **33/1**
3m 34.83s (1.57) **Going Correction** +0.175s/f (Good)
WFA 3 from 4yo+ 17lb 8 Ran SP% **112.2**
Speed ratings (Par 103):103,102,102,101,100 97,95,68
CSF £72.86 CT £331.92 TOTE £13.00: £2.70, £2.10, £1.50; EX 73.90 Trifecta £260.40 Part won. Pool £366.83 - 0.60 winning units. Place 6 £59.30, Place 5 £16.23..

Owner Ms J S Doyle **Bred** Eamonn Griffin **Trained** Upper Lambourn, Berks
FOCUS
Just a modest staying handicap. Sound but limited form.
T/Plt: £121.60 to a £1 stake. Pool: £59,422.10. 356.60 winning tickets. T/Qpdt: £21.90 to a £1 stake. Pool: £4,551.70. 153.40 winning tickets. ST

3654 - 3658a (Foreign Racing) - See Raceform Interactive

3219 LEOPARDSTOWN (L-H)
Wednesday, July 18
OFFICIAL GOING: Soft (soft to heavy in places)

3659a IRISH STALLION FARMS EUROPEAN BREEDERS FUND SILVER FLASH STKS (LISTED RACE) (FILLIES) 7f
6:30 (6:31) 2-Y-O **£21,993** (£6,452; £3,074; £1,047)

				RPR
1		**Triskel**[10] 3354 2-8-12	WMLordan 4	100+
		(T Stack, Ire) *trckd ldrs on inner: 5th into st: led 1 1/2f out: clr ins fnl f: r.o wl: comf*	**14/1**	
2	2	**Mad About You (IRE)**[35] 2583 2-8-12	PJSmullen 5	95
		(D K Weld, Ire) *trckd ldrs: 5th bef 1/2-way: 4th appr st: impr into 2nd 1f out: kpt on wout threatening wnr*	**11/4**[1]	
3	½	**Saoirse Abu (USA)**[19] 3071 2-8-12	DJMoran 3	94
		(J S Bolger, Ire) *cl 3rd: rdn to chal ent st: 2nd 1 1/2f out: 3rd and no imp ins fnl f*	**8/1**	
4	4 ½	**Kayd Kodaun (IRE)**[21] 3008 2-8-12	KJManning 1	83
		(J S Bolger, Ire) *led and disp: slt advantage ent st: hdd 1 1/2f out: sn outpcd and no ex*	**9/2**[3]	
5	2	**Rainbow Crossing**[10] 3354 2-8-12	CDHayes 6	78
		(Kevin Prendergast, Ire) *sn 4th: lost pl over 3f out: kpt on same pce st*	**4/1**[2]	
6	hd	**Porto Marmay (IRE)**[19] 3071 2-8-12	DPMcDonogh 7	77
		(K J Condon, Ire) *chsd ldrs on outer: 5th after 1/2-way: effrt ent st: no ex fr 1 1/2f out*	**20/1**	
7	1 ¼	**Soinlovewithyou (USA)**[21] 3008 2-8-12	JAHeffernan 2	74
		(A P O'Brien, Ire) *cl 2nd and disp ld: hdd appr st: sn no ex*	**4/1**[2]	
8	nk	**I'm Well (IRE)**[87] 1182 2-8-12	PShanahan 9	73
		(Tracey Collins, Ire) *hld up towards rr: no imp st*	**33/1**	
9	nk	**Paint The Town (IRE)** 2-8-12	CO'Donoghue 8	72
		(A P O'Brien, Ire) *hld up in rr: no imp st*	**20/1**	

1m 36.8s (4.60) **Going Correction** +0.80s/f (Soft) **9** Ran SP% **115.1**
Speed ratings: 105,102,102,97,94 94,93,92,92
CSF £51.17 TOTE £15.40: £2.60, £1.50, £2.70; DF 94.80.
Owner Mrs W L O'Toole **Bred** Matthews Breeding & Racing Ltd **Trained** Golden, Co Tipperary

NOTEBOOK
Triskel continued the outstanding run of form of her stable's juveniles, showing considerable improvement on this ground to run out a convincing winner of what may turn out to be a very decent contest. Held up towards the rear, she stuck to the inner as the majority of the field drifted towards the centre of the track in the straight and quickened up well to lead a furlong out, drawing clear to score by a couple of lengths. The ease in the ground was important to her and she looks as though she will get further and appreciate middle distances in time.
Mad About You(IRE) is held in very high regard by her trainer and, despite the fact that the winner was just too good on the night, she did not do a whole lot to belie her trainer's opinion. She was in a good position but could not quicken on the ground like the winner, staying on inside the final furlong to be second. A step up in trip should be no problem for her and a return to better ground will see her improve on this effort. (op 5/2)
Saoirse Abu(USA) was the stable second-string, but improved significantly on her poor effort on a similar surface at the Curragh last time. She ran quite free early on but stuck to her task well inside the final furlong as the first three pulled well clear of the remainder.
Kayd Kodaun(IRE) was at the head of the group at a muddling early pace, but disappointingly found little when the race began in earnest early in the straight. She is better than this, though, and should prove that on better ground. (op 7/2)
Rainbow Crossing found herself a little tapped for speed early in the straight before keeping on at one pace inside the final furlong. (op 3/1)
Porto Marmay(IRE) made good progress on the outside to get into a challenging position early in the straight before weakening. She patently failed to stay but showed enough to suggest she could win a nice race over 6f.
Soinlovewithyou(USA) was in the front rank before weakening in the straight. She was not knocked about when beaten, though, and there should be a race or two to be won with her. (op 11/2 tchd 6/1)

3664a JOCKEY CLUB OF TURKEY CHALLENGE STKS (LISTED RACE) 1m 6f
9:00 (9:01) 3-Y-O+ **£21,993** (£6,452; £3,074; £1,047)

				RPR
1		**Galistic (IRE)**[38] 2498 4-9-6 94	DMGrant 4	105
		(Patrick J Flynn, Ire) *hld up in rr: hdwy 4f out: led ent st: sn rdn: styd on wl fnl f*	**10/1**	
2	1	**Reform Act (USA)**[31] 2702 4-9-9 101	PJSmullen 5	107
		(D K Weld, Ire) *hld up: 4th 5f out: hdwy 3f out: cl 2nd ent st: sn rdn to chal: swtchd lft 1f out: kpt on u.p*	**2/1**[2]	
3	5 ½	**Princess Nala (IRE)**[9] 3391 5-9-9 95	JMurtagh 1	100
		(M Halford, Ire) *led: clr early: rdn and strly pressed 3f out: hdd and dropped to 4th ent st: kpt on same pce*	**5/2**[3]	
4	shd	**Temlett (IRE)**[25] 2899 3-8-10 104	MJKinane 3	101
		(W P Mullins, Ire) *settled 2nd: pushed along briefly over 4f out: cl 3rd ent st: sn outpcd: no ex fr over 1f out*	**7/4**[1]	
5	dist	**Yellow Ridge (IRE)**[47] 2230 4-9-9 55	FranciscoDaSilva 2	—
		(Luke Comer, Ire) *chsd ldrs to 5f out: rdn and wknd qckly: t.o st*	**100/1**	
D	18	**Sandymount Earl (IRE)**[17] 3145 4-9-9 76	CO'Donoghue 6	78
		(Mrs John Harrington, Ire) *trckd ldrs in mod 3rd: tk clsr order after 1/2-way: rdn 4f out: no ex ent st: sn eased: fin 6th, disq*	**11/1**	

3m 9.00s (3.10) **Going Correction** +0.55s/f (Yiel)
WFA 3 from 4yo+ 14lb **6** Ran SP% **116.7**
Speed ratings: 113,112,109,109,— 98
CSF £31.89 TOTE £14.10: £4.10, £1.70; DF 40.50.
Owner Sir Michael Smurfit **Bred** Cathal Ryan **Trained** Carrick-On-Suir, Co Waterford
■ Stewards' Enquiry : C O'Donoghue caution: failed to weigh-in
FOCUS
The winner is better than ever this term and the form is sound.

NOTEBOOK
Galistic(IRE) was running over this trip for the first time and there seemed to be little fluke about her surprise success. The pace was a little stop-start and, having been happy to sit towards the rear, she was sent to the front over a furlong out and showed plenty of battling qualities as the runner-up was a persistent threat. The improvement she has shown in the last 12 months is amply shown by the fact that she was running off a mark of 55 a year ago. This was undoubtedly a career-best effort and the fact that she saw out the extra quarter mile so well here opens up plenty of possibilities. Her trainer mentioned that she might be seen over hurdles at Galway. (op 7/1)
Reform Act(USA) ran well in the ground and was the only one to threaten the winner at the business end. She had run well on a soft surface previously but not on ground as testing as this, adding another layer of versatility to her profile and opening up more options for her too. (op 11/4 tchd 100/30)
Princess Nala(IRE) attempted similar tactics to those that worked so brilliantly at Roscommon last week, but she could never dominate to the same extent. She was headed two furlongs out but plugged on reasonably well to finish third. (op 5/2 tchd 3/1)
Temlett(IRE) was exposed on his first try at this level. He tracked the leader and had every chance at the top of the straight before finishing a one-paced fourth. Stamina was probably an issue to some degree, but not enough to make any real difference. (op 6/4 tchd 11/8)
T/Jkpt: @2,500.00. Pool of @10,000.00 - 3 winning units. T/Plt: @305.80. Pool of @14,571.75. II

3660 - 3664a (Foreign Racing) - See Raceform Interactive

VICHY
Wednesday, July 18
OFFICIAL GOING: Good to soft

3665a GRAND PRIX DE VICHY - AUVERGNE (GROUP 3) 1m 2f
8:45 (9:06) 3-Y-O+ **£27,027** (£9,459; £9,459; £5,405; £2,703)

				RPR
1		**Atlantic Air (FR)**[34] 2617 5-9-2	TThulliez 2	109
		(Y De Nicolay, France) *held up, 7th on inside straight, switched outside 2f out, hard ridden and headway over 1f out, led 100y out, driven out*	**138/10**	
2	½	**Kentucky Dynamite (USA)**[38] 2500 4-9-2	CSoumillon 4	108
		(A De Royer-Dupre, France) *held up, 12th straight, headway over 2f out, disputed lead 150y out to 100y out, kept on*	**59/10**[3]	
2	dht	**Balius (IRE)**[53] 4-9-2	MBlancpain 1	108
		(C Laffon-Parias, France) *close up, 4th straight, hard ridden to disputed lead 150y out, headed 100y out, kept on*	**9/1**	
4	1	**Kocab**[25] 5-9-2	SPasquier 12	106
		(A Fabre, France) *held up, 11th straight, 9th 1f out, finished well*	**5/1**[2]	
5	shd	**Elasos (FR)**[21] 3011 5-9-2	DBonilla 11	106
		(D Sepulchre, France) *held up, 8th straight, 10th 1f out, finished well*	**9/1**	
6	½	**Kilometre Neuf (FR)**[34] 2617 4-9-2	DBoeuf 8	105
		(F Doumen, France) *held up, 9th straight, 8th 1f out, kept on*	**19/1**	
7	nk	**Bedaly (FR)**[21] 3011 4-9-2	JVictoire 13	105
		(A Bonin, France) *in touch on inside, 3rd straight, every chance 150y out, weakened*	**34/1**	
8	1	**Mohandas (FR)**[10] 6-9-2	AlxiBadel 7	103
		(W Hefter, Germany) *pulled hard in 2nd, 5th and pushed along straight, hard ridden and still 5th approaching final f, weakened*	**100/1**	
9	1 ½	**Blushing King (FR)**[34] 2617 5-9-2	YGourraud 14	100
		(J-L Guillochon, France) *last straight, always in rear*	**100/1**	
10	2	**Quijano (GER)**[109] 861 5-9-6	AStarke 5	100
		(P Schiergen, Germany) *in touch, 6th straight, ridden 1 1/2f out, no impression*	**13/10**[1]	
11		**Willywell (FR)**[34] 2617 5-9-2	IMendizabal 10	96
		(J-P Gauvin, France) *prominent, 2nd straight, travelling well 2f out, ridden 1 1/2f out, not much room and weakened inside final f*	**83/10**	
12		**Aquaturbo (FR)**[49] 4-9-2	(b) EAntoinat 3	96
		(J-P Gauvin, France) *always in rear*	**83/10**	
13		**Vol De Nuit**[31] 2706 6-9-2	MDemuro 6	96
		(L Brogi, Italy) *set steady pace, ridden 2 1/2f out, headed 150y out, weakened and eased*	**14/1**	

2m 35.15s (26.55) **13** Ran SP% **139.4**
PARI-MUTUEL (including 1 Euro stake): WIN 14.80; PL 3.90, 2.40 (Kentucky Dynamite), 3.50 (Balius); DF 24.00 (B), 16.40 (KD).
Owner Mrs Henri Devin **Bred** Mme H Devin **Trained** France

NOTEBOOK
Atlantic Air(FR) gained well-deserved victory at a course he goes very well at. Dropped out early on, he was not asked for his effort until two furlongs out, but he picked up well up the centre of the track and took the advantage running into the final furlong. He now heads for the Prix Gontaut-Biron at Deauville.
Kentucky Dynamite(USA), towards the tail of the field early on, ran on from two furlongs out and then had a battle royal before sharing second place. This was a good effort considering the ground was probably softer than he would have liked.
Balius(IRE), never far from the leaders, was just a little one paced when it mattered.
Kocab, another who was given a waiting ride, shaped as though he may need a little further.

3446 FOLKESTONE (R-H)
Thursday, July 19
OFFICIAL GOING: Good to firm
Wind: Virtually nil Weather: sunny and bright

3667 FOLKESTONE HERALD APPRENTICE H'CAP 5f
5:55 (5:55) (Class 6) (0-60,60) 3-Y-O+ **£2,047** (£604; £302) **Stalls** Low

Form					RPR
6040	1		**He's A Rocket (IRE)**[70] 1594 6-8-2 **46** oh1	(b) DeclanCannon(5) 10	54
			(K R Burke) *chsd overall ldr on far side: rdn to ld over 1f out: kpt on wl fnl f*	**12/1**	
0603	2	1	**Ruby's Dream**[17] 3169 5-8-1 **46** oh1	(p) PietroRomeo(6) 7	50
			(J M Bradley) *chsd stands' side ldr: rdn and hung rt fr 2f out: chsd wnr ins fnl f: kpt on*	**10/1**	
0-02	3	hd	**Water Margin (IRE)**[20] 3046 3-8-12 **55**	ChrisGlenister 6	57
			(T G Mills) *led stands' side gp and handy overall: rdn wl over 1f out: kpt on same pce u.p*	**10/3**[1]	
5-05	4	1	**Monashee Prince (IRE)**[183] 158 5-8-13 **60**	AmeliaHegarty(8) 9	60
			(J R Best) *led far side trio and overall ldr tl over 1f out: kpt on same pce fnl f*	**9/1**[3]	

0530 **5** *nk* **Inscribed (IRE)**[9] 3393 4-8-10 **52**..............................(b) BradleyRoper(3) 4 51
(G A Huffer) *awkward leaving stalls: chsd ldrs on stands' side: rdn wl over 1f out: kpt on same pce* **20/1**

00-6 **6** *1 1/4* **Valiant Romeo**[7] 3449 7-8-4 **46** oh1.................................. NSLawes(3) 8 41
(R Bastiman) *prom on far side: rdn and hung lft fr wl over 1f out: wknd last 100yds* **12/1**

1310 **7** *shd* **Mambazo**[9] 3396 5-8-7 **52**...(e) FLenclud(6) 5 46
(S C Williams) *chsd ldrs on stands' side: rdn and hanging rt 2f out: lost pl and rdr dropped whip 1f out: styd on towards fin* **7/2**[2]

-000 **8** *1* **Queensgate**[64] 1766 3-8-4 **50**.................................... LauraReynolds(3) 1 41
(M Blanshard) *t.k.h: hld up on stands' side: rdn wl over 1f out: no hdwy* **25/1**

0330 **9** *3/4* **Tibinta**[33] 2664 3-8-4 **53**.. BernadetteQuinn(6) 3 41
(P D Evans) *s.i.s: bhd on stands' side: effrt 2f out: n.d* **12/1**

-066 **10** *1 1/4* **Parkside Pursuit**[2] 3618 9-8-8 **50**...................................... BarrySavage(3) 2 33
(J M Bradley) *bhd on stands' side: rdn 2f out: no imp* **7/2**[2]

60.43 secs (-0.37) **Going Correction** -0.125s/f (Firm)
WFA 3 from 4yo+ 4lb **10** Ran SP% **118.3**
Speed ratings (Par 101):97,95,95,93,93 91,90,89,88,86
CSF £127.54 CT £496.21 TOTE £14.00: £3.30, £2.10, £1.80; EX 151.90.
Owner J C S Wilson **Bred** Lemongrove Stud **Trained** Middleham Moor, N Yorks
■ Declan Cannon's first winner in Britain.

FOCUS
A moderate sprint handicap although sound enough at a low level. The field ended up spread out all over the track at the line but, following the trend from the previous week's meeting, the winner raced far side throughout.

3668 FOLKESTONE RACECOURSE FOR CONFERENCES NOVICE FILLIES' STKS 5f
6:25 (6:26) (Class 4) 2-Y-O **£3,886** (£1,156; £577; £288) **Stalls** Low

Form RPR
4226 **1** **Littlemisssunshine (IRE)**[29] 2756 2-8-5 0.................(p) TolleyDean(5) 2 72+
(J S Moore) *mde all: shkn up over 1f out: in command fnl f* **4/7**[1]

0 **2** *1 1/4* **Ronsai (USA)**[40] 2468 2-8-10 0....................................... RichardSmith 5 68
(R Hannon) *s.i.s: hld up in 3rd: swtchd rt and effrt 1f out: chsd wnr and edgd lft ins fnl f: no imp* **20/1**[3]

41 **3** *3/4* **Rocking**[31] 2724 2-9-3 0... MichaelHills 1 72
(W J Haggas) *w ldr: rdn and hanging rt fr over 1f out: lost 2nd ins fnl f* **7/4**[2]

4 *2 1/2* **Kinlochard** 2-8-6 0... StephenCarson 6 52+
(Eve Johnson Houghton) *s.i.s: sn detached and rdn w much tail swishing: nvr on terms* **33/1**

60.66 secs (-0.14) **Going Correction** -0.125s/f (Firm) **4** Ran SP% **107.7**
Speed ratings (Par 93):96,94,92,88
CSF £11.33 TOTE £1.40; EX 10.90.
Owner Albert Conneally **Bred** Swordlestown Stud **Trained** Upper Lambourn, Berks

FOCUS
Littlemisssunshine looked to run well below the pick of her form, despite winning this modest affair. Just the four runners and they all stayed stands' side.

NOTEBOOK
Littlemisssunshine(IRE), tried in cheekpieces for the first time, was only workmanlike and ran some way below the form she showed when sixth in the Queen Mary on her previous start. She might just be the type who only really does what she has to. (op 8-11)
Ronsai(USA) stayed on nicely for second and this represents significant improvement on the form she showed on her debut at Newbury. (op 12-1 tchd 11-1)
Rocking showed good early speed, but she offered disappointingly little at the business end and was well below the form she showed when winning at Windsor on her previous start. (tchd 13-8)
Kinlochard, a 10,000gns daughter of Efisio out of a winner over 1m5f, showed ability in a close-up fourth, but she flashed her tail from the word go and hardly inspired much confidence for the future. (op 16-1)

3669 JEWSON NOVICE STKS 6f
7:00 (7:00) (Class 4) 2-Y-O **£3,886** (£1,156; £577; £288) **Stalls** Low

Form RPR
0023 **1** **Silver Wind**[9] 3398 2-8-11 0....................................(v1) StephenDonohoe 3 82
(P D Evans) *a pressing ldr on stands' side: rdn over 2f out: led last 100yds: styd on wl* **3/1**[3]

1204 **2** *hd* **Aaim To Storm (USA)**[7] 3462 2-8-13 0.................................. JHBowman 1 83
(M R Channon) *led on stands' side and overall ldr: rdn wl over 1f out: hdd last 100yds: no ex* **6/4**[1]

00 **3** *3* **Howdigo**[34] 2632 2-8-8 0... StephaneBreux(3) 6 72+
(J R Best) *w ldr in far side pair: carried lft and outpcd over 1f out: nudged into 3rd nr fin* **20/1**

06 **4** *hd* **Relative Order**[24] 2941 2-8-11 0....................................... MichaelHills 7 72
(J R Best) *led far side pair: shkn up and hanging lft wl over 1f out: outpcd over 1f out: lost 3rd nr fin* **8/1**

41 **5** *nk* **Sofia's Star**[40] 2443 2-9-1 0... JimCrowley 4 75
(P Winkworth) *in tch on stands' side: rdn and effrt jst over 2f out: wknd 1f out* **9/4**[2]

0 **6** *18* **Captain Jack Black**[38] 2510 2-8-11 0................................(t) LPKeniry 2 17
(M R Bosley) *v s.i.s: bhd on stands' side: rdn 1/2-way: sn wl bhd: t.o* **66/1**

1m 12.71s (-0.89) **Going Correction** -0.125s/f (Firm) **6** Ran SP% **113.1**
Speed ratings (Par 96):100,99,95,95,95 71
CSF £8.07 TOTE £4.00: £1.70, £1.20; EX 9.20.
Owner Silver Wind Partnership **Bred** W H R John And Partners **Trained** Pandy, Monmouths
■ Stewards' Enquiry : Stephane Breux ten-day ban: in breach of Rule 158 (Jul 30-Aug 8)

FOCUS
An ordinary novice event rated through the winner, with the time reasonable. The majority of these stayed stands' side and that proved the place to be.

NOTEBOOK
Silver Wind, with a visor replacing blinkers, improved on the form he showed when third on his nursery debut at Pontefract to narrowly deny the favourite. He is tough and progressive. (op 7-2 tchd 4-1)
Aaim To Storm(USA) was the clear form pick, but he did not seem to handle the track, appearing to hit the ground quite hard on occasions, and he was unable to justify favouritism. (op 5-4 tchd 7-4)
Howdigo raced on the far side of the track for much of the way, but he was carried left by his stablemate and ended up towards the stands' side. This was his best effort yet, but he was not given a hard time in the latter stages and the Stewards took action against his rider. The colt will have to run again before he is given a nursery mark. Official explanation: jockey said, regarding running and riding, that his orders were to jump out and do his best, adding that the colt was hanging and he was unable to push it out final 2f; trainer said, he instructed the jockey to go onto the far side where it was quicker ground and he wanted him to get a lead from his other runner, Relative Order. (op 16-1)
Relative Order was taken over to the far side of the track, which may not have been a bad idea judging by the result of the first race, but he compromised his chance by hanging left. Official explanation: jockey said colt hung left (op 14-1 tchd 15-2)
Sofia's Star was some way below the form he showed when winning at Goodwood on his previous start and was pretty disappointing. (op 5-2 tchd 7-4)

3670 WBX.COM WORLD BET EXCHANGE FILLIES' H'CAP 7f (S)
7:30 (7:30) (Class 3) (0-95,90) 3-Y-O+
£6,855 (£2,052; £1,026; £513; £256; £128) **Stalls** Low

Form RPR
3516 **1** **Diamond Diva**[20] 3059 3-9-10 **90**.. EddieAhern 5 97+
(J W Hills) *trckd ldrs gng wl: rdn to ld over 1f out: r.o wl* **4/1**[2]

0-21 **2** *1 1/4* **Yandina (IRE)**[32] 2689 4-9-5 **78**... MichaelHills 6 85
(B W Hills) *hld up in tch: hdwy and nt clr run briefly wl over 1f out: chsd wnr and hung lft 1f out: no imp fnl f* **15/8**[1]

3113 **3** *nk* **Ivory Lace**[17] 3154 6-9-9 **82**.. JimCrowley 3 88
(S Woodman) *stdd s: hld up in last pair: rdn and effrt over 1f out: swtchd lft 1f out: edgd rt but r.o fnl f: nt trble wnr* **8/1**

1210 **4** *4* **Keyaki (IRE)**[32] 2688 6-9-9 **87**.. PatrickHills(5) 7 82
(C F Wall) *hld up in tch in last: hdwy on outer 2f out: sn chsng ldrs: rdn and wknd 1f out* **5/1**[3]

2001 **5** *2 1/2* **Inaminute (IRE)**[22] 2988 4-9-3 **79**................................ AndrewElliott(3) 4 68
(K R Burke) *pressed ldr: ev ch and bmpd wl over 1f out: sn rdn: wknd over 1f out* **8/1**

-002 **6** *1 3/4* **Pelican Key (IRE)**[17] 3154 3-8-2 **73**............................ WilliamBuick(5) 2 57
(D M Simcock) *led: rdn and edgd rt briefly wl over 1f out: sn hdd & wknd* **10/1**

660 **7** *3/4* **Waterline Twenty (IRE)**[37] 2536 4-9-2 **75**............... StephenDonohoe 1 57
(P D Evans) *chsd ldrs: rdn over 2f out: wknd wl over 1f out* **8/1**

1m 25.96s (-1.94) **Going Correction** -0.125s/f (Firm)
WFA 3 from 4yo+ 7lb **7** Ran SP% **113.9**
Speed ratings (Par 104):106,104,104,99,96 94,93
CSF £11.84 TOTE £5.60: £2.50, £2.30; EX 11.30.
Owner Mrs L Meagher and Donald M Kerr **Bred** Glebe Stud And Mrs F Woodd **Trained** Upper Lambourn, Berks

FOCUS
A good fillies' handicap and the form looks reasonable, rated around the first three. They all stayed far side.

NOTEBOOK
Diamond Diva proved a little disappointing in a conditions event at Newmarket on her previous start, but that run came on tacky ground and this faster surface clearly suited much better. She ran out a decisive winner, confirming she is very useful when things go her way. (op 11-2 tchd 7-2)
Yandina(IRE) was only 3lb higher than when winning over course and distance on her previous start, but the winner was just too good. She was a little bit short of room over a furlong out, but did not look unlucky. (op 7-4 tchd 6-4 and 2-1)
Ivory Lace stayed on well once switched to the inside and continues in the form of her life. (op 6-1 tchd 11-2)
Keyaki(IRE), back up in trip, tried to make a move more towards the middle of the track and could make little impression. (op 7-1)
Inaminute(IRE) could not dominate and she was unable to show her best. (op 6-1 tchd 17-2)

3671 JOIN WBX.COM £150 FREE BETS H'CAP 1m 4f
8:05 (8:05) (Class 4) (0-80,84) 3-Y-O+ **£4,857** (£1,445; £722; £360) **Stalls** Low

Form RPR
1-02 **1** **Pentatonic**[37] 2543 4-9-13 **79**.. NickyMackay 8 89+
(L M Cumani) *t.k.h: chsd ldr tl led over 2f out: rdn and fnd ex over 1f out: readily* **6/5**[1]

0-51 **2** *2* **Crossbow Creek**[8] 3416 9-9-13 **84** 6ex......................... LukeMorris(5) 4 89
(M G Rimell) *w.w in midfield: hdwy wl over 2f out: rdn 2f out: styd on to chse wnr ins fnl f: nt pce to trble wnr* **9/1**[3]

211/ **3** *1 1/4* **Rustler**[148] 5974 5-9-9 **75**... MichaelHills 5 78
(N J Henderson) *w.w in midfield: rdn and hdwy on outer over 2f out: chsd wnr 2f out: kpt on same pce fnl f* **9/1**[3]

10-0 **4** *4* **Sualda (IRE)**[86] 1208 8-9-10 **76**................................... StephenDonohoe 3 73
(P D Evans) *stdd s: hld up in last trio: hdwy over 2f out: rdn 2f out: no hdwy wl over 1f out* **20/1**

0312 **5** *3/4* **Lady Songbird (IRE)**[22] 2987 4-9-12 **78**.............................. AdamKirby 9 74
(W R Swinburn) *chsd ldrs: nt clr run and lost pl over 2f out: swtchd lft 2f out: sn rdn and no imp* **11/4**[2]

-410 **6** *1/2* **Del Mar Sunset**[42] 2403 8-9-11 **80**................................... LiamJones(3) 2 75
(W J Haggas) *stdd s: t.k.h: hld up in last pair: slipped wl over 3f out: hdwy on outer over 2f out: rdn 2f out: sn btn* **12/1**

5000 **7** *3* **Atlantic Quest (USA)**[19] 3111 8-9-4 **73** ow1............ LiamTreadwell(3) 1 63
(Miss Venetia Williams) *hld up in last pair: shkn up over 2f out: no hdwy* **28/1**

0156 **8** *1 3/4* **Mahmjra**[6] 3496 5-9-0 **66**... EdwardCreighton 6 53
(C N Allen) *led: clr after 2f: rdn and hdd over 2f out: sn wknd* **28/1**

4-63 **9** *3 1/2* **Top Spec (IRE)**[171] 297 6-9-8 **74**....................................... EddieAhern 7 56
(J Pearce) *s.i.s: sn chsng ldrs: rdn wl over 2f out: wknd over 2f out* **9/1**[3]

2m 35.84s (-4.66) **Going Correction** -0.30s/f (Firm) **9** Ran SP% **121.5**
Speed ratings (Par 105):103,101,100,98,97 97,95,94,91
CSF £14.04 CT £71.70 TOTE £2.20: £1.40, £4.10, £1.80; EX 12.10.
Owner Helena Springfield Ltd **Bred** Meon Valley Stud **Trained** Newmarket, Suffolk

FOCUS
A fair handicap run at a good pace with the winner on the upgrade and sound enough with the placed horses close to recent form.
Del Mar Sunset Official explanation: jockey said gelding slipped on bend

3672 THE RACECOURSE OF KENT H'CAP 1m 1f 149y
8:35 (8:35) (Class 4) (0-85,86) 3-Y-O+ **£4,857** (£1,445; £722; £360) **Stalls** Low

Form RPR
1421 **1** **Emerald Wilderness (IRE)**[10] 3386 3-9-5 **86** 6ex............. JHBowman 3 95
(E A L Dunlop) *chsd ldr tl led 2f out: sn rdn: jst hld on* **7/4**[1]

/13- **2** *hd* **Tears Of A Clown (IRE)**[428] 1781 4-9-11 **85**....... RichardKingscote(3) 4 96+
(J A Osborne) *hld up in last pair: stl last wl over 1f out: weaved through and rapid hdwy jst ins fnl f: jst failed* **14/1**

-003 **3** *1 1/4* **Press The Button (GER)**[21] 3039 4-9-8 **79**....................... EddieAhern 5 85
(J R Boyle) *chsd ldrs: rdn over 2f out: kpt on u.p: one pce ins fnl f* **8/1**

-041 **4** *nk* **Rose Of Petra (IRE)**[32] 2691 3-8-11 **85**................... JamieHamblett(7) 9 91
(Sir Michael Stoute) *t.k.h: hld up wl in tch: lost pl 3f out: rallied and rdn 2f out: kpt on same pce ins fnl f* **5/1**[2]

-600 **5** *nk* **Spanish Don**[20] 3060 9-9-1 **77**...................................... WilliamBuick(5) 8 82
(D R C Elsworth) *plld hrd: hld up in tch: hdwy to chse ldrs over 2f out: rdn 2f out: one pce* **8/1**

4020 **6** *nk* **Pagan Sword**[42] 2397 5-9-13 **84**... JimCrowley 6 89
(Mrs A J Perrett) *hld up towards rr: hdwy on outer over 2f out: rdn 2f out: kpt on one pce* **7/1**[3]

5664 **7** ¾ **Robustian**[43] 2374 4-9-12 **83**.. StephenCarson 2 86
(Eve Johnson Houghton) *hld up in last pair: c wd and effrt 2f out: no hdwy fr 1f out* **7/1**[3]

01 **8** 2 **Siena Star (IRE)**[39] 2490 9-8-12 **69**.................................. MickyFenton 7 68
(Stef Liddiard) *w.w in midfield: rdn 3f out: nt pce to trble ldrs* **16/1**

100 **9** 1¼ **General Knowledge (USA)**[42] 2401 4-9-9 **80**..............(t) MichaelHills 1 77
(B G Powell) *sn led: rdn and hdd 2f out: wknd 1f out* **25/1**

2m 0.63s (-4.60) **Going Correction** -0.30s/f (Firm)
WFA 3 from 4yo+ 10lb **9** Ran SP% **116.6**
Speed ratings (Par 105):106,105,104,104,104 104,103,101,100
CSF £29.77 CT £161.18 TOTE £2.80: £1.30, £4.70, £2.60; EX 51.60 Place 6 £14.90, Place 5 £5.38.
Owner Mohammed Jaber **Bred** Mrs Joan Murphy **Trained** Newmarket, Suffolk

FOCUS
Not a bad little handicap and, despite not a great deal separating the main bulk of the field at the line, the pace was decent too and the form is rated positively.
T/Plt: £14.80 to a £1 stake. Pool: £47,883.40. 2,354.40 winning tickets. T/Qpdt: £7.50 to a £1 stake. Pool: £4,750.10. 466.80 winning tickets. SP

3535 HAMILTON (R-H)

Thursday, July 19

OFFICIAL GOING: Good to soft (6.6)
Wind: Fresh, across Weather: Overcast

3673 HAMILTON PARK IS IN BLOOM MAIDEN AUCTION STKS — 5f 4y
2:20 (2:21) (Class 6) 2-Y-O **£2,388** (£705; £352) **Stalls** Centre

Form RPR

1 **Anosti** 2-8-7 0 ow1.. NCallan 8 80+
(K A Ryan) *s.i.s: sn prom: led over 1f out: pushed out fnl f* **5/1**[3]

35 **2** 3 **Elijah Pepper (USA)**[22] 2984 2-8-10 0.................................. PaulFessey 7 69
(T D Barron) *led: hung rt thrght: hdd over 1f out: kpt on same pce* **7/4**[1]

06 **3** nk **Stormy Journey**[21] 3024 2-8-10 0.. TomEaves 9 68
(Mrs K Walton) *chsd ldrs: effrt and ev ch over 1f out: nt qckn* **9/1**

5 **4** 1¼ **Red Delight (IRE)**[16] 3192 2-8-6 0.................................... PaulHanagan 2 59
(R A Fahey) *bhd and outpcd: hdwy over 1f out: nrst fin* **11/4**[2]

500 **5** ½ **Premium Port**[11] 3341 2-8-6 0.............................. PatrickMathers(3) 3 61
(A Berry) *chsd ldrs to 2f out: sn rdn and outpcd* **33/1**

530 **6** nk **Natural Rhythm (IRE)**[56] 1963 2-8-12 0.................... RoystonFfrench 1 63
(Mrs A Duffield) *towards rr: hung rt thrght: rdn and wknd wl over 1f out* **6/1**

000 **7** 1¾ **Ephesian (IRE)**[15] 3200 2-8-6 0.. KDarley 4 50
(Mrs A Duffield) *unruly bef s: dwlt: sn in tch: rdn and wknd fr 2f out* **25/1**

61.07 secs (-0.13) **Going Correction** -0.075s/f (Good) **7** Ran SP% **110.8**
Speed ratings (Par 92):98,93,92,90,89 89,86
CSF £13.28 TOTE £6.60: £2.20, £1.40; EX 16.10.
Owner Theobalds Stud **Bred** Theobalds Stud **Trained** Hambleton, N Yorks

FOCUS
An ordinary bunch on looks and the third and fifth hold the form down but a fair pace and a ready winner, who is the type to improve again.

NOTEBOOK
Anosti ◆, a half-sister to two winners, looked as though the race would do her good in the preliminaries but she created a favourable impression when pulling clear in the closing stages to beat a rival that had shown fair form on his first two starts. She is open to plenty of improvement and appeals as the type to win more races. (op 7-2)
Elijah Pepper(USA), who had shown fair form on his two previous starts, had the run of the race and ran creditably, despite hanging. He looks a good guide to the worth of this form and will be suited by the step up to 6f. He is sure to win a small event. (op 9-4)
Stormy Journey, had shown ability at a modest level on his first two starts and his proximity holds this form down to some extent. He is likely to continue to look vulnerable in this grade and may do better in ordinary nursery company. (op 14-1)
Red Delight(IRE), a leggy, unfurnished type, had shaped with a bit of promise on her debut but was not suited by the drop to this trip. She is in very good hands and may do better granted a much stiffer test of stamina in ordinary nursery company in due course. (op 5-2 tchd 3-1)
Premium Port had improved steadily at a modest level with each of his three previous starts but, although not totally disgraced, again underlined his vulnerability in this type of event. A drop in grade is required. (op 28-1)
Natural Rhythm(IRE) fared better than at Newcastle on his previous start but, just as he had done over course and distance in May, ruined his chance by hanging badly throughout. He looks one to tread carefully with at present. Official explanation: jockey said colt hung right-handed throughout (op 13-2)

3674 TRADESTYLE CABINETS CLAIMING STKS — 6f 5y
2:50 (2:53) (Class 6) 3-Y-O+ **£2,266** (£674; £337; £168) **Stalls** Centre

Form RPR

0034 **1** **Spiritual Peace (IRE)**[16] 3180 4-9-8 70...............................(p) NCallan 2 64
(K A Ryan) *chsd ldrs: led over 1f out: hld on wl* **11/4**[2]

0000 **2** shd **Regal Raider (IRE)**[11] 3345 4-9-3 66.................................. TomEaves 1 59
(I Semple) *prom: effrt over 2f out: swtchd lft ins fnl f: kpt on wl: jst hld* **11/4**[2]

-060 **3** ½ **The Salwick Flyer (IRE)**[24] 2938 4-9-0 41............... JamieMoriarty(3) 9 57
(I Semple) *loose bef s: chsd ldr: ev ch over 1f out to ins fnl f: hld towards fin* **20/1**

4400 **4** 1¾ **Throw The Dice**[16] 3185 5-8-12 50..............................(v) RoystonFfrench 8 47
(D W Barker) *t.k.h: led to over 1f out: kpt on same pce* **5/2**[1]

5664 **5** shd **Oeuf A La Neige**[5] 3535 7-9-1 46...................................... PaulHanagan 4 49
(Miss L A Perratt) *hld up: hdwy 2f out: no imp fnl f* **6/1**[3]

0000 **6** 1 **Following Flow (USA)**[16] 3180 5-8-12 40..................(p) PaulMulrennan 3 43
(R Allan) *bhd and sn drvn along: sme late hdwy: nvr on terms* **40/1**

6000 **7** 2 **Blythe Spirit**[5] 3534 8-8-13 47...(v) ChrisCatlin 6 38
(Mrs L Williamson) *in tch: drvn along 1/2-way: sn btn* **25/1**

0660 **8** 7 **Telepathic (IRE)**[70] 1594 7-9-0 44.. KDarley 5 18
(A Berry) *dwlt and checked s: bhd and rdn: struggling fr 1/2-way* **25/1**

1m 12.83s (-0.27) **Going Correction** -0.075s/f (Good) **8** Ran SP% **111.1**
Speed ratings (Par 101):98,97,97,94,94 93,90,81
CSF £9.81 TOTE £3.30: £1.30, £1.50, £4.10; EX 12.30.Throw The Dice was claimed by E. Nisbet for £5,000.
Owner M P Burke **Bred** M P B Bloodstock Ltd **Trained** Hambleton, N Yorks
■ Stewards' Enquiry : N Callan three-day ban: used whip with excessive frequency without giving gelding time to respond (Jul 30-31, Aug 2)
Jamie Moriarty one-day ban: failed to ride to draw (Jul 30)

FOCUS
A mixed bag and the third - rated only 41 - holds this form down. The pace was sound and the form looks solid enough at a low level.

3675 BILL AND DAVID MCHARG MEMORIAL H'CAP — 1m 65y
3:25 (3:25) (Class 6) (0-65,59) 3-Y-O+ **£2,266** (£674; £337; £168) **Stalls** High

Form RPR

0010 **1** **Ignition**[24] 2938 5-9-9 **54**.. PaulHanagan 7 64
(W M Brisbourne) *set stdy pce: mde all: rdn over 1f out: kpt on wl* **9/2**[3]

0422 **2** 1½ **Local Poet**[16] 3185 6-9-13 **58**..(b) TomEaves 9 65
(I Semple) *towards rr: hdwy and ev ch over 1f out: edgd rt: kpt on ins fnl f* **4/1**[2]

/6-3 **3** nk **Howards Rocket**[5] 3539 6-8-7 **45**................................ KellyHarrison(7) 2 51
(J S Goldie) *hld up: hdwy to press ldrs over 1f out: no ex wl ins fnl f* **5/1**

0056 **4** 4 **Jabraan (USA)**[5] 3534 5-9-0 **45**.. KDarley 1 42
(D W Chapman) *in tch: effrt over 2f out: no ex over 1f out* **12/1**

3100 **5** 4 **Northern Desert (IRE)**[15] 3215 8-10-0 **59**......................... ChrisCatlin 10 47
(P W Hiatt) *t.k.h: trckd ldrs: effrt over 2f out: wknd over 1f out* **5/1**

/00- **6** 1¾ **Flaming Cat (IRE)**[412] 2198 4-9-2 **47**.........................(p) PaulMulrennan 6 32
(F Watson) *t.k.h: prom: outpcd over 2f out: sn btn* **50/1**

-300 **7** shd **Royal Pardon**[8] 3414 5-9-5 **50**...(p) PaulFessey 3 34
(M Dods) *midfield: rdn over 2f out: sn outpcd* **12/1**

000 **8** shd **Maysridge Ofkuwait**[29] 2761 3-8-6 **45**................................ PaulQuinn 8 29
(A Berry) *t.k.h: trckd ldrs tl wknd 2f out* **66/1**

0622 **9** ¾ **Mandarin Rocket (IRE)**[6] 3497 4-9-10 **55**................ RoystonFfrench 4 38
(Miss L A Perratt) *prom: rdn over 2f out: sn btn* **7/2**[1]

0-00 **10** 4 **Fadansil**[47] 2254 4-8-9 **45**...(b[1]) PJMcDonald(5) 5 19
(J Wade) *hld up: rdn over 3f out: sn btn* **25/1**

1m 50.99s (1.69) **Going Correction** +0.25s/f (Good)
WFA 3 from 4yo+ 8lb **10** Ran SP% **116.4**
Speed ratings (Par 101):101,99,99,95,91 89,89,89,88,84
CSF £22.58 CT £95.10 TOTE £6.50: £2.20, £2.00, £2.10; EX 29.80.
Owner M F Hyman **Bred** M F Hyman **Trained** Great Ness, Shropshire

FOCUS
A low-grade event with a steady pace but the bare form looks solid enough.
Mandarin Rocket(IRE) Official explanation: vet said gelding returned lame right-fore

3676 DOROTHY AND ARTHUR BALDING STKS (H'CAP) — 6f 5y
4:00 (4:00) (Class 5) (0-75,72) 3-Y-O+ **£3,238** (£963; £481; £240) **Stalls** Centre

Form RPR

0400 **1** **Mozakhraf (USA)**[16] 3194 5-8-12 **58**.. NCallan 6 67+
(K A Ryan) *trckd ldrs: led over 1f out: hrd pressed fnl f: hld on wl* **7/1**

-000 **2** ½ **Richelieu**[40] 2482 5-9-12 **72**.. CDHayes 2 79
(J J Lambe, Ire) *hld up: hdwy and swtchd rt over 1f out: ev ch ins fnl f: kpt on: hld nr fin* **9/2**[2]

025 **3** 1¼ **Joyeaux**[7] 3466 5-9-0 **60**...(v) DavidAllan 8 63
(J Hetherton) *hld up in tch: hdwy to chse ldrs over 1f out: swtchd lft and kpt on ins fnl f* **7/2**[1]

0030 **4** 1¼ **George The Best (IRE)**[5] 3535 6-8-11 **57**........................ PaulHanagan 1 57
(Micky Hammond) *w ldr tl rdn and one pce fnl f* **13/2**

4014 **5** 1 **Winthorpe (IRE)**[29] 2762 7-9-1 **64**.............................. JamieMoriarty(3) 4 61
(J J Quinn) *in tch: effrt whn nt clr run over 1f out: sn no imp* **6/1**[3]

6613 **6** 5 **Calypso King**[7] 3452 4-9-7 **67**.. SebSanders 7 49
(Peter Grayson) *hld up in tch: hdwy over 2f out: wknd over 1f out* **8/1**

0-00 **7** nk **Vondova**[11] 3344 5-8-9 **55** oh5 ow2..................................... PaulMulrennan 3 36
(D A Nolan) *chsd ldrs tl wknd over 2f out* **33/1**

1153 **8** nk **Brut**[16] 3184 5-9-4 **69**...(p) PJMcDonald(5) 5 49
(D W Barker) *led to over 1f out: sn btn* **9/2**[2]

1m 12.18s (-0.92) **Going Correction** -0.075s/f (Good) **8** Ran SP% **112.8**
Speed ratings (Par 103):103,102,100,99,97 91,90,90
CSF £37.31 CT £129.19 TOTE £8.10: £2.30, £1.80, £2.00; EX 54.60.
Owner John Coke **Bred** Audley Farm Inc **Trained** Hambleton, N Yorks
■ Stewards' Enquiry : Paul Hanagan one-day ban: not riding to draw (Jul 30)
P J McDonald one-day ban: not riding to draw (Jul 30)

FOCUS
A run-of-the-mill handicap in which the pace was sound and this form should stand up at a similar level.

3677 GRIFFITHS AND ARMOUR H'CAP — 1m 5f 9y
4:35 (4:37) (Class 5) (0-70,69) 3-Y-O+ **£3,886** (£1,156; £577; £288) **Stalls** High

Form RPR

03-0 **1** **Atlantic Coast (IRE)**[19] 3082 3-8-0 **54**...................(b[1]) RoystonFfrench 6 60
(M Johnston) *in tch: reminders after 2f: drvn and bdly outpcd 4f out: gd hdwy over 1f out: led ins fnl f: hung lft: sn clr* **18/1**

2 4 **Balakar (IRE)**[49] 4854 11-9-0 **55**..(p) CDHayes 5 55
(J J Lambe, Ire) *hld up in tch: rdn over 3f out: ev ch ins fnl f: kpt on: no ch w wnr* **8/1**

23-5 **3** nk **Golden Groom**[16] 3193 4-8-11 **52** oh4......................... DeanMcKeown 4 52
(C W Fairhurst) *cl up: led over 3f out to ins fnl f: kpt on same pce* **9/2**[2]

2424 **4** 1½ **Qaasi (USA)**[26] 2890 5-8-10 **58**................................ PatrickDonaghy(7) 8 55
(M Brittain) *hld up in tch: hdwy and chsng ldrs after 2f: smooth hdwy over 2f out: effrt and ev ch ins fnl f: sn no ex* **5/1**[3]

3121 **5** 2½ **They All Laughed**[16] 3177 4-10-0 **69**...................................... ChrisCatlin 7 63
(P W Hiatt) *hld up: effrt and rdn 3f out: no imp over 1f out* **7/2**[1]

06/6 **6** nk **Rightful Ruler**[27] 2825 5-8-12 **53**.. TomEaves 3 47
(N Wilson) *led to over 3f out: wknd over 1f out* **7/1**

2-04 **7** 9 **Peintre's Wonder (IRE)**[29] 2760 3-8-12 **66**.................. PaulHanagan 1 47
(E J O'Neill) *t.k.h: chsd ldrs: effrt 3f out: edgd rt and wknd 2f out* **7/2**[1]

400/ **8** 2 **My Portfolio (IRE)**[43] 2383 5-8-12 **53**.......................... PaulMulrennan 2 31
(J J Lambe, Ire) *cl up tl rdn and wknd over 3f out* **14/1**

2m 55.38s (1.98) **Going Correction** +0.25s/f (Good)
WFA 3 from 4yo+ 13lb **8** Ran SP% **114.8**
Speed ratings (Par 103):103,100,100,99,97 97,92,90
CSF £152.42 CT £767.06 TOTE £21.90: £5.20, £3.20, £1.80; EX 152.00.
Owner Atlantic Racing Limited **Bred** Gigginstown House **Trained** Middleham Moor, N Yorks

FOCUS
A modest event and weak form, but a decent gallop and a remarkable performance from the winner, who looks a fair bit better than his current mark.

3678 DAILY RECORD MAIDEN STKS — 1m 3f 16y
5:10 (5:14) (Class 5) 3-Y-O+ **£3,238** (£963; £481; £240) **Stalls** High

Form RPR

2-42 **1** **Loulwa (IRE)**[14] 3236 3-8-11 82...(t) SebSanders 4 62+
(J Noseda) *in tch: hdwy to ld over 2f out: pushed out fnl f* **1/3**[1]

40 **2** 1¾ **Lochiel**[21] 3015 3-9-2 0.. PaulMulrennan 8 64+
(Mrs S C Bradburne) *hld up: hdwy over 2f out: chsd wnr over 1f out: kpt on fnl f* **14/1**[3]

00 **3** 3½ **Star Of Angels**[9] 3402 3-8-13 0.................................... GregFairley(3) 2 58
(M Johnston) *led to over 2f out: outpcd over 1f out* **22/1**

0 **4** *14* **Quicuyo (GER)**[21] [3015] 4-9-8 0 .... PJMcDonald(5) 9 36
(P Monteith) *bhd: rdn and sme hdwy over 2f out: sn n.d* **66/1**
5 *½* **Beauty Shine** 3-8-11 0 .... KDarley 3 30
(M Johnston) *chsd ldrs: green and outpcd over 4f out: no ch after* **5/1**[2]
6 *2* **Rourke Star**[155] 5-9-10 0 .... JamieMoriarty(3) 5 32
(B Storey) *w ldr to over 3f out: rdn and wknd over 2f out* **100/1**
7 *nk* **Simba's Pride** 3-9-2 0 .... RoystonFfrench 6 32
(Miss L A Perratt) *prom tl rdn and wknd over 3f out* **80/1**
8 *¾* **Nasrawy**[257] 5-9-13 0 .... CDHayes 7 30
(J J Lambe, Ire) *hld up: rdn over 3f out: sn btn* **100/1**
9 *6* **Sierras Future** 3-9-2 0 .... (b[1]) TomEaves 1 21
(I Semple) *hld up: rdn over 3f out: sn btn* **25/1**

2m 27.93s (1.67) **Going Correction** +0.25s/f (Good)
WFA 3 from 4yo+ 11lb **9** Ran SP% **111.3**
Speed ratings (Par 103):103,101,99,89,88 87,86,86,82
CSF £5.29 TOTE £1.30: £1.02, £2.50, £3.40; EX 6.30.
Owner Saleh Al Homeizi & Imad Al Sagar **Bred** W Maxwell Ervine **Trained** Newmarket, Suffolk

FOCUS
A most uncompetitive event, run at just a fair gallop and a workmanlike display from the clear form pick, with little form to go on behind the winner.

3679 RECTANGLE GROUP APPRENTICE SERIES H'CAP (ROUND 3) 1m 3f 16y
5:40 (5:40) (Class 6) (0-65,62) 4-Y-0+ **£2,388** (£705; £352) **Stalls** High

Form RPR
-660 **1** **English Archer**[21] [3035] 4-8-3 **46** ow1 .... DeanHeslop(5) 2 54
(W M Brisbourne) *hld up in tch: outpcd and plenty to do over 4f out: rallied 2f out: styd on wl fnl f to ld nr fin* **11/1**
3112 **2** *¾* **Rare Coincidence**[3] [3584] 6-9-5 **62** .... (p) PatrickDonaghy(5) 6 69
(R F Fisher) *led to over 2f out: rallied and ev ch ins fnl f: kpt on nr fin* **10/11**[1]
0- **3** *hd* **Relocation (IRE)**[23] [2975] 6-8-2 **45** .... JamesRogers(5) 3 52
(J J Lambe, Ire) *chsd ldrs: effrt and ev ch over 2f out: led ins fnl f: hdd nr fin* **6/1**[3]
0150 **4** *¾* **The Pen**[56] [1967] 5-9-6 **58** .... KellyHarrison 4 63
(C W Fairhurst) *cl up: led over 2f out to ins fnl f: no ex* **4/1**[2]
/000 **5** *5* **Kid'Z'Play (IRE)**[4] [3012] 11-8-6 **49** .... (v[1]) LanceBetts(5) 1 46
(J S Goldie) *t.k.h early: cl up tl wknd fr 2f out* **15/2**
5000 **6** *32* **Twilight Avenger (IRE)**[13] [3280] 4-8-0 **45** .... (p) Julie-AnneCumine(7) 5 —
(W M Brisbourne) *missed break: t.k.h and sn prom: lost tch fr 1/2-way* **33/1**

2m 26.62s (0.36) **Going Correction** +0.25s/f (Good) **6** Ran SP% **109.7**
Speed ratings (Par 101):108,107,107,106,103 79
CSF £20.80 TOTE £12.20: £4.30, £1.10; EX 27.40 Place 6 £40.65, Place 5 £23.17.
Owner M F Hyman **Bred** M F Hyman **Trained** Great Ness, Shropshire
■ English Archer is a full brother to Ignition who won earlier on the card.
■ Stewards' Enquiry : James Rogers one-day ban: careless riding (Jul 30)

FOCUS
A moderate event but a fair pace and a decent winning time for a race like this, 1.31 seconds faster than the preceding maiden. The form looks weak with the runner-up the best guide.
English Archer Official explanation: trainer said, regarding apparent improvement in form, that the gelding was better suited by the pace
T/Plt: £59.00 to a £1 stake. Pool: £53,588.70. 662.60 winning tickets. T/Qpdt: £35.80 to a £1 stake. Pool: £2,610.10. 53.90 winning tickets. RY

[2657] LEICESTER (R-H)
Thursday, July 19

OFFICIAL GOING: Soft (heavy in dip in straight)
Wind: Almost nil Weather: Cloudy with sunny spells

3680 LADBROKES.COM NURSERY 5f 218y
2:10 (2:17) (Class 4) 2-Y-0 **£4,533** (£1,348; £674; £336) **Stalls** High

Form RPR
4164 **1** **Sauze D'Oulx**[59] [1882] 2-9-2 **84** .... JamesMillman(5) 1 84
(B R Millman) *chsd ldrs: rdn and hung rt fr over 1f out: styd on to ld nr fin* **15/2**
2241 **2** *hd* **Secret Meaning**[14] [3246] 2-7-7 **61** oh1 .... (p) LukeMorris(5) 5 60
(W G M Turner) *rn loose prior to s: sn chsng ldrs: rdn to ld 1f out: edgd lft: carried rt and hdd nr fin* **8/1**
000 **3** *1* **Hyper Viper (IRE)**[20] [3043] 2-7-7 **61** oh7 .... (p) WilliamBuick(5) 4 57
(J S Moore) *mid-div: rdn 1/2-way: hdwy over 1f out: styd on same pce ins fnl f* **9/1**
325 **4** *hd* **Carrickmacross (IRE)**[24] [2949] 2-8-2 **65** .... RichardMullen 6 61
(E S McMahon) *sn led: hung rt fr 1/2-way: rdn and hdd 1f out: nt run on* **7/2**[2]
0505 **5** *4* **Choisky (IRE)**[8] [3426] 2-8-0 **63** .... JimmyQuinn 2 47
(J Akehurst) *chsd ldrs: rdn over 1f out: wknd fnl f* **5/1**[3]
643 **6** *1 ¼* **Maracana Boy (IRE)**[24] [2934] 2-8-10 **73** .... PhillipMakin 8 53
(M Dods) *hld up: rdn over 1f out: sn wknd* **15/2**
045 **7** *1 ¼* **Lady Nova (IRE)**[17] [3152] 2-8-4 **67** .... MartinDwyer 3 43
(J S Moore) *dwlt: rdn 1/2-way: a in rr* **3/1**[1]
600 **8** *¾* **Happy Hacker (IRE)**[39] [2488] 2-7-9 **61** oh4 .... DuranFentiman(3) 7 35
(P D Evans) *chsd ldrs: rdn over 2f out: wknd over 1f out* **16/1**

1m 15.49s (2.29) **Going Correction** +0.425s/f (Yiel) **8** Ran SP% **114.4**
Speed ratings (Par 96):101,100,99,99,93 92,90,89
CSF £65.16 CT £551.03 TOTE £7.90: £2.50, £2.30, £3.60; EX 39.50 Trifecta £344.10 Part won. Pool: £484.71 - 0.34 winning tickets..
Owner Mrs L S Millman **Bred** Knight's Bloodstock **Trained** Kentisbeare, Devon
■ Stewards' Enquiry : James Millman one-day ban: careless riding (Jul 30)

FOCUS
A decent winning time for a nursery, fractionally quicker than the later older-horse handicap over the same trip. Solid nursery form, rated through the second and third. The 'official' ratings shown next to each horse are estimated and for information purposes only.

NOTEBOOK
Sauze D'Oulx, making his nursery bow, had done all his previous racing over 5f and this was his first try on a soft surface. After becoming slightly outpaced by the leaders going to the final furlong, he drifted off the rail but cut down the filly close home. He should stay another furlong. (op 9-2)
Secret Meaning, winner of a seller last time, had the cheekpieces back on here. She was mulish in the paddock and unshipped Morris out on the course, doing a circuit of the track before she was caught. Only claimed late on after showing ahead entering the last, in the circumstances this was a creditable effort. (op 7-1 tchd 6-1 and 9-1)
Hyper Viper(IRE), who finished unplaced in each of his first three starts, had cheekpieces on for the first time on this debut in handicap company. Racing from 7lb out of the weights, he was keeping on at the end and maybe a return to 7f will suit him. (op 16-1)
Carrickmacross(IRE), having his first run on turf, looked a difficult ride. After sweating up in the preliminaries, he showed pace to lead for five furlongs but was hanging to his right from halfway and not giving his jockey any help. (op 5-1 tchd 10-3)
Choisky(IRE), who halved in price in the betting ring, did not really see out this longer trip but looks better on Polytrack in any case. (op 11-1)
Lady Nova(IRE) proved disappointing on this nursery debut, missing the break and always struggling in rear. (tchd 9-2)

3681 LADBROKES.COM (S) STKS 5f 2y
2:40 (2:42) (Class 6) 2-Y-0 **£2,590** (£770; £385; £192) **Stalls** High

Form RPR
00 **1** **Drumalee Lass (IRE)**[11] [3359] 2-8-6 0 .... RichardMullen 5 67+
(P M Mooney, Ire) *wnt rt s: sn led: rdn over 1f out: sn clr: eased wl ins fnl f* **3/1**[1]
0 **2** *3 ½* **Just Puddie**[24] [2949] 2-8-1 0 .... LukeMorris(5) 7 53
(W G M Turner) *chsd wnr: rdn over 1f out: styd on same pce* **9/1**
5026 **3** *1* **Shipboard Romance (IRE)**[31] [2723] 2-8-6 0 .... PaulEddery 2 49
(P D Evans) *chsd ldrs: rdn 1/2-way: styd on same pce appr fnl f* **3/1**[1]
4 *½* **Silver Deal** 2-8-1 0 .... ColinHaddon(5) 3 47
(J A Pickering) *dwlt: hld up: hdwy over 1f out: sn rdn: wknd ins fnl f* **8/1**
5 *1* **Tiara Princess (IRE)** 2-8-6 0 .... MartinDwyer 1 44
(Rae Guest) *hld up: hdwy over 1f out: wknd ins fnl f* **13/2**[3]
0 **6** *shd* **Help (IRE)**[8] [3423] 2-8-4 0 ow5 .... (b) NBazeley(7) 6 48
(Mrs P N Dutfield) *s.s: outpcd: nvr nrr* **28/1**
00 **7** *9* **Rye Beau (IRE)**[66] [1728] 2-8-11 0 .... (p) TPQueally 4 16
(Mrs A Duffield) *chsd ldr: rdn 1/2-way: wknd over 1f out* **11/1**
0 **8** *3* **Queen Be**[14] [3245] 2-8-3 0 .... DuranFentiman(3) 10 —
(I W McInnes) *prom over 3f* **11/2**[2]

63.40 secs (2.50) **Going Correction** +0.425s/f (Yiel) **8** Ran SP% **111.6**
Speed ratings (Par 92):97,91,89,89,87 87,72,68
CSF £29.64 TOTE £4.20: £1.50, £3.40, £1.20; EX 44.40 Trifecta £189.90 Pool: £310.39 - 1.16 winning tickets..The winner was bought in for 4,600gns.
Owner Dominic Tully **Bred** Peter Mooney **Trained** Duleek, Co. Meath

FOCUS
A weak seller apart from the Irish-trained winner, who looks a bit better than this grade.

NOTEBOOK
Drumalee Lass(IRE) had never previously been placed in five starts, but had run a fair race at Naas in May and the drop to this grade saw her get off the mark with a very comfortable success. Back down in trip after a run over a mile last time, she was soon in front against the stands' rail, travelling much the best, and was value for a wider margin of victory. (op 7-2)
Just Puddie, well beaten in a Wolverhampton maiden on her one previous start, was no match for the winner who is a decent sort for this grade. The way she was plugging on, a return to 6f may suit her. (op 12-1)
Shipboard Romance(IRE), back over the minimum trip, was unproven in soft ground but ran up to form. She has an exposed look about her now. (op 5-2)
Silver Deal is out of a mare who was placed over this trip at two and who was a half-sister to Flying Childers Stakes winner Poker Chip. Outpaced early, she did pick up on the outside of the field but could not sustain her momentum inside the last. (op 12-1 tchd 7-1)
Tiara Princess(IRE), a cheaply-bought yearling, is out of a mare who showed little herself but who was a half-sister to the smart A-To-Z. (op 9-2 tchd 7-1)

3682 LADBROKESCASINO.COM H'CAP 7f 9y
3:15 (3:15) (Class 4) (0-80,80) 3-Y-0+ **£6,309** (£1,888; £944; £472; £235) **Stalls** High

Form RPR
-012 **1** **Starlight Gazer**[6] [3488] 4-9-3 **76** .... TravisBlock(5) 8 87+
(J A Geake) *hld up: swtchd rt 1/2-way: hdwy over 1f out: r.o to ld wl ins fnl f* **2/1**[1]
0104 **2** *1* **Sailor King (IRE)**[15] [3215] 5-9-9 **77** .... RobertHavlin 4 86
(D K Ivory) *chsd ldrs: led over 1f out: sn rdn: edgd lft and hdd wl ins fnl f* **8/1**
1533 **3** *1* **The Osteopath (IRE)**[7] [3470] 4-9-5 **73** .... (p) PhillipMakin 2 79
(M Dods) *s.i.s: hld up: hdwy over 2f out: rdn over 1f out: edgd rt: styd on* **9/2**[2]
3423 **4** *3 ½* **Angel Sprints**[7] [3474] 5-9-3 **76** .... LukeMorris(5) 12 73
(C J Down) *mid-div: hdwy 1/2-way: rdn over 1f out: wknd ins fnl f* **7/1**[3]
0450 **5** *1* **Capricho (IRE)**[16] [3191] 10-8-4 **65** .... (b) KirstyMilczarek(7) 11 60
(J Akehurst) *hld up: hdwy over 1f out: wknd fnl f* **14/1**
0200 **6** *2 ½* **King Harson**[15] [3201] 8-9-7 **75** .... PatCosgrave 5 64
(J D Bethell) *led: hdd over 4f out: led again over 2f out: rdn and hdd over 1f out: sn wknd* **12/1**
3400 **7** *3 ½* **Music Note (IRE)**[8] [3420] 4-9-9 **80** .... (t) JerryO'Dwyer(3) 6 60
(Miss Gay Kelleway) *chsd ldrs 5f* **12/1**
-000 **8** *½* **Fisberry**[10] [3388] 5-9-1 **69** .... TedDurcan 7 48
(M S Saunders) *s.i.s: hld up: racd keenly: rdn 1/2-way: wknd over 2f out* **14/1**
6302 **9** *3 ½* **Material Witness (IRE)**[14] [3239] 10-9-7 **75** .... MartinDwyer 3 45
(W R Muir) *w ldr tl led over 4f out: rdn and hdd over 2f out: sn wknd* **10/1**
00-0 **10** *1 ¼* **Global Guest**[7] [3475] 3-8-4 **72** .... MarkCoumbe(7) 10 39
(A J Chamberlain) *chsd ldrs over 4f* **100/1**
0-00 **11** *12* **Just Dust**[20] [3052] 3-9-4 **79** .... DaleGibson 1 16
(M W Easterby) *sn outpcd* **25/1**

1m 28.21s (2.11) **Going Correction** +0.425s/f (Yiel)
WFA 3 from 4yo+ 7lb **11** Ran SP% **117.8**
Speed ratings (Par 105):104,102,101,97,96 93,89,89,85,83 70
CSF £18.52 CT £67.27 TOTE £2.60: £1.20, £3.60, £1.60; EX 25.90 Trifecta £127.80 Pool: £487.99 - 2.71 winning tickets..
Owner The Burning Stars **Bred** Dr J M Leigh **Trained** Kimpton, Hants

FOCUS
A fair race and solid handicap form. The winner was well in and could have more improvement in him.
Material Witness(IRE) Official explanation: jockey said gelding lost its action
Just Dust Official explanation: jockey said gelding never travelled

3683 LADBROKES.COM MELTON MOWBRAY CONDITIONS STKS 1m 1f 218y
3:50 (3:54) (Class 3) 3-Y-0 **£7,790** (£2,332; £1,166) **Stalls** Low

Form RPR
6403 **1** **Big Robert**[11] [3361] 3-9-3 103 .... (t) MartinDwyer 1 102
(W R Muir) *chsd ldr 8f out: rdn over 1f out: styd on to ld wl ins fnl f* **11/10**[2]
-334 **2** *1* **Railying Cry (USA)**[110] [859] 3-9-7 114 .... (t) TedDurcan 2 104
(Saeed Bin Suroor) *led: rdn over 1f out: hdd wl ins fnl f* **8/11**[1]
0 **3** *62* **Little Darlin**[13] [3282] 3-8-12 0 .... SamHitchcott 3 —
(G J Smith) *chsd ldr 2f: lost tch fnl 4f: t.o* **150/1**[3]

2m 13.2s (4.90) **Going Correction** +0.425s/f (Yiel) **3** Ran SP% **106.2**
Speed ratings (Par 104):97,96,46
CSF £2.24 TOTE £2.00; EX 2.10.

Owner Martin P Graham **Bred** Deerfield Farm **Trained** Lambourn, Berks

FOCUS

A match in all but name, this did produce a decent scrap between the first two, a smart pair who both ran to this year's marks. However, the time was slow and the form should not be relied upon.

NOTEBOOK

Big Robert, down in grade after contesting Listed and Group races this term, had the tongue tie reapplied. After tracking his rival, he eventually got on top inside the last. He will be happier back on a sound surface and should have no problem with 1m4f. (op 5-4)

Rallying Cry(USA), who was sixth to Teofilo in last year's Dewhurst, had not run since a spring campaign in Dubai. Equipped with a tongue strap, he tried to make all but finally had to give best well inside the last. He is entitled to come on for the run. (op 4-6 tchd 4-5)

Little Darlin, tailed off last in a Wolverhampton claimer on her only previous start, seems devoid of ability, but her connections deserve a bit of credit for placing her to collect more than £1,100 here. (op 80-1)

3684 LADBROKESCASINO.COM CLAIMING STKS — 1m 3f 183y

4:25 (4:26) (Class 5) 4-Y-0+ — **£3,238** (£963; £481; £240) **Stalls Low**

Form				RPR
4645	1		**Atlantic Gamble (IRE)**[20] [3063] 7-9-7 65 ....(p) PatCosgrave 2 — (K R Burke) *chsd ldrs: led over 2f out: rdn clr over 1f out: eased towards fin* **5/6**[1]	65+
2200	2	1	**Hathaal (IRE)**[2] [3617] 8-8-6 60 ....(vt) SCreighton(7) 9 — (E J Creighton) *hld up: hdwy over 2f out: sn chsng wnr: rdn over 1f out: edgd rt and no imp fnl f* **7/2**[2]	53
0-00	3	2 ½	**Dandys Hurricane**[9] [3402] 4-8-5 46 ....(p) DaleGibson 6 — (M W Easterby) *led 2f: chsd ldr: rdn and ev ch over 2f out: no ex fr over 1f out* **12/1**	41
00	4	4	**Long Gone**[52] [2084] 4-8-4 0 ....(p) AdrianMcCarthy 3 — (John A Harris) *prom: rdn over 2f out: wknd over 1f out* **40/1**	34
	5	½	**Mustang Du Gueslan (FR)**[753] 7-8-7 0 .... TonyHamilton 8 — (D W Thompson) *hld up in tch: rdn over 2f out: wknd over 1f out* **15/2**[3]	36
0500	6	2	**Orphir (IRE)**[27] [2843] 4-8-12 33 ....(v[1]) ColinHaddon(5) 7 — (Mrs N Macauley) *s.i.s: hld up: rdn over 3f out: n.d* **28/1**	43
005-	7	15	**Rythm N Rhyme (IRE)**[382] [1572] 8-8-5 35 .... JimmyQuinn 1 — (John A Harris) *led 10f out: rdn and hdd over 2f out: sn wknd* **8/1**	8

2m 40.92s (6.42) **Going Correction** +0.425s/f (Yiel) — **7** Ran SP% **113.2**

Speed ratings (Par 103):95,94,92,90,89 88,78

CSF £3.84 TOTE £1.70: £1.30, £1.80; EX 4.70 Trifecta £14.50 Pool: £471.99 - 23.00 winning tickets..

Owner R G Greaney **Bred** Larry Ryan **Trained** Middleham Moor, N Yorks

FOCUS

An uncompetitive claimer that proved easy pickings for the favourite and has been rated negatively.

3685 LADBROKES.COM MOUNTSORREL MAIDEN STKS — 1m 1f 218y

5:00 (5:01) (Class 5) 3-4-Y-0 — **£3,238** (£963; £481; £240) **Stalls Low**

Form				RPR
0-	1		**Alaghiraar (IRE)**[264] [6214] 3-9-0 0 .... RHills 9 — (J L Dunlop) *mid-div: outpcd over 3f out: rallied: swtchd lft and hmpd over 1f out: styd on to ld wl ins fnl f* **3/1**[2]	83+
0-2	2	nk	**Earl Marshal (USA)**[14] [3244] 3-9-0 0 ....(v[1]) JDSmith 12 — (Sir Michael Stoute) *led after 1f: hdd 7f out: led again over 5f out: rdn over 1f out: edgd lft and hdd wl ins fnl f* **5/2**[1]	82
	3	1 ½	**Longspur** 3-9-0 0 .... TedDurcan 11 — (Saeed Bin Suroor) *dwlt: hld up: hdwy over 4f out: sn rdn: hung rt fr over 3f out: styd on same pce fnl f* **4/1**[3]	80
46	4	1	**Dig Gold (USA)**[82] [1290] 3-9-0 0 .... MatthewHenry 10 — (M A Jarvis) *trckd ldrs: plld hrd: rdn and ev ch over 2f out: no ex ins fnl f* **6/1**	78
4	5	1 ¼	**Ridge Rose**[17] [3160] 3-8-4 0 .... AshleyHamblett(5) 1 — (L M Cumani) *broke wl: stdd and lost pl after 1f: hdwy over 2f out: sn rdn and hung rt: styd on same pce fnl f* **16/1**	71
0	6	7	**Scripted (USA)**[54] [2046] 3-9-0 0 .... TPQueally 8 — (L M Cumani) *chsd ldrs: rdn over 3f out: nt clr run over 1f out: sn wknd* **5/1**	63+
60	7	30	**Tri Chara (IRE)**[55] [1998] 3-9-0 0 .... PaulEddery 13 — (R Hollinshead) *hld up: hdwy over 3f out: wknd over 2f out* **66/1**	9
0	8	7	**Southside Star**[55] [2005] 3-8-9 0 .... JimmyQuinn 2 — (H J L Dunlop) *led 1f: led again 7f out: hdd over 5f out: wknd over 2f out* **50/1**	—
0-	9	26	**Squirrel Tail**[447] [1274] 4-9-10 0 .... SamHitchcott 3 — (E S McMahon) *hld up: rdn 1/2-way: bhd fnl 4f* **66/1**	—

2m 10.3s (2.00) **Going Correction** +0.425s/f (Yiel)

WFA 3 from 4yo 10lb — **9** Ran SP% **115.4**

Speed ratings (Par 103):109,108,107,106,105 100,76,70,49

CSF £10.90 TOTE £4.00: £1.40, £1.70, £1.50; EX 10.60 Trifecta £30.30 Pool: £424.35 - 9.94 winning tickets..

Owner Hamdan Al Maktoum **Bred** Shadwell Estate Company Limited **Trained** Arundel, W Sussex

FOCUS

A decent winning time for a race of its type. There were some interesting sorts in this maiden, which has been rated through the second and fourth.

Southside Star Official explanation: jockey said filly ran too freely

Squirrel Tail Official explanation: jockey said gelding lost its action

3686 LADBROKES.COM APPRENTICE H'CAP — 5f 218y

5:30 (5:30) (Class 5) (0-70,70) 3-Y-0+ — **£3,886** (£1,156; £577; £288) **Stalls High**

Form				RPR
0621	1		**Dakota Rain (IRE)**[36] [2576] 5-9-10 70 .... JackDean(3) 7 — (Jennie Candlish) *chsd ldrs: rdn to ld over 1f out: r.o* **7/2**[1]	78+
0306	2	¾	**Bel Cantor**[28] [2805] 4-9-12 69 .... SladeO'Hara 11 — (W J H Ratcliffe) *chsd ldrs: rdn and ev ch fr over 1f out: styd on same pce wl ins fnl f* **7/2**[1]	75
3-00	3	nk	**John O'Groats (IRE)**[70] [1594] 9-8-8 51 oh6 ....(p) AmyBaker 4 — (T T Clement) *hld up in tch: rdn over 1f out: r.o* **40/1**	56
0536	4	nk	**Nautical**[10] [3388] 9-9-6 66 .... MarkCoumbe(3) 15 — (A W Carroll) *hld up: hdwy 2f out: rdn and n.m.r ins fnl f: styd on* **9/1**[3]	70
6016	5	1 ¼	**Limonia (GER)**[26] [2870] 5-8-9 52 .... ThomasO'Brien 17 — (Mike Murphy) *racd alone in centre: w ldrs: led 2f out: hung lft and hdd over 1f out: no ex ins fnl f* **10/1**	52
0000	6	1 ½	**Tag Team (IRE)**[48] [2220] 6-8-8 51 oh2 .... WilliamCarson 8 — (John A Harris) *led 4f: rdn and swtchd rt over 1f out: wknd ins fnl f* **33/1**	47
/0-0	7	hd	**Queen's Lodge (IRE)**[17] [3158] 7-9-13 70 .... NeilBrown 2 — (I W McInnes) *hld up: styd on ins fnl f: nvr trbld ldrs* **28/1**	65
5002	8	3	**Sydneyroughdiamond**[10] [3372] 5-8-8 51 oh6 ....(b) SCreighton 9 — (M Mullineaux) *unruly in stalls: mid-div: rdn over 2f out: no imp* **20/1**	37
-001	9	nk	**Vivi Belle**[22] [3000] 3-8-6 57 .... ChrisHough(3) 16 — (M L W Bell) *s.i.s: outpcd* **10/1**	42
-410	10	1 ¾	**Gold Flame**[31] [2725] 4-9-8 70 .... AmyScott(5) 3 — (H Candy) *hld up: rdn and wknd over 2f out* **16/1**	50
4400	11	nk	**Bold Argument (IRE)**[10] [3368] 4-9-0 60 .... NBazeley(3) 13 — (Mrs P N Dutfield) *unruly in stalls: s.i.s: outpcd* **12/1**	39
0065	12	3	**Memphis Man**[3] [3597] 4-8-8 51 oh1 .... KirstyMilczarek 1 — (W M Brisbourne) *swvd rt s and rel to r: bhd whn hung rt fr 1/2-way* **11/2**[2]	21
-030	13	32	**Iced Tango**[32] [2697] 3-8-0 51 oh3 .... MatthewDavies(3) 10 — (F Jordan) *chsd ldrs: stmbld and wknd over 2f out* **50/1**	—

1m 15.69s (2.49) **Going Correction** +0.425s/f (Yiel)

WFA 3 from 4yo+ 5lb — **13** Ran SP% **117.1**

Speed ratings (Par 103):100,99,98,98,96 94,94,90,89,87 87,83,40

CSF £13.34 CT £416.88 TOTE £5.00: £1.50, £1.80, £10.60; EX 20.20 TRIFECTA Not won. Place 6 £40.92, Place 5 £4.64.

Owner P and Mrs G A Clarke **Bred** Islanmore Stud **Trained** Basford Green, Staffs

FOCUS

A modest handicap, with the proximity of the third holding down the form, although the winner is on the up. The main action took place on the stands' side.

Tag Team(IRE) Official explanation: jockey said gelding was unsuited by the soft ground

Memphis Man Official explanation: jockey said gelding refused to race

T/Plt: £19.00 to a £1 stake. Pool: £47,791.20. 1,831.50 winning tickets. T/Qpdt: £5.10 to a £1 stake. Pool: £2,510.70. 358.40 winning tickets. CR

3329 SANDOWN (R-H)

Thursday, July 19

OFFICIAL GOING: Good (good to firm in places on round course)

Wind: Almost nil Weather: Muggy, shower before racing, some late sunshine

3687 CHERWELL GROUP SUPPORTING THE CHILDREN'S TRUST E B F MEDIAN AUCTION MAIDEN STKS — 5f 6y

6:10 (6:14) (Class 5) 2-Y-O — **£4,533** (£1,348; £674; £336) **Stalls High**

Form				RPR
6	1		**Sailor At Sea (USA)**[19] [3085] 2-9-3 0 .... JoeFanning 2 — (R Charlton) *w'like: scope: lw: prom and gng wl: led over 1f out: rdn clr: readily* **9/2**[2]	87+
3353	2	3	**Ben**[8] [3426] 2-9-3 0 .... GeorgeBaker 10 — (P G Murphy) *hld up in midfield: smooth hdwy 2f out: styd on to take 2nd jst ins fnl f: nt pce of wnr* **6/1**[3]	76+
	3	1	**Rash Judgement** 2-9-3 0 .... FrancisNorton 12 — (W S Kittow) *w'like: bit bkwd: s.i.s: bhd: sme hdwy whn hmpd 3f out: running on whn swtchd lft ins fnl f: tk 3rd on line: improve* **20/1**	75+
3	4	shd	**Our Acquaintance**[19] [3085] 2-9-3 0 .... SteveDrowne 14 — (W R Muir) *w'like: strong: lw: prom: rdn 3f out: one pce appr fnl f* **2/1**[1]	72
0	5	1 ½	**Totally Focussed (IRE)**[20] [3043] 2-9-3 0 .... IanMongan 9 — (S Dow) *w'like: bit bkwd: sn towards rr: hmpd 3f out: styd on wl appr fnl f: nrst fin* **50/1**	67
003	6	¾	**The Name Is Frank**[37] [2539] 2-9-3 0 .... JamesDoyle 5 — (J W Mullins) *swtg: outpcd in rr: rdn and r.o fnl 2f: nvr nrr* **14/1**	64
33	7	hd	**Sandy Par**[32] [2687] 2-9-3 0 .... PaulDoe 6 — (P Winkworth) *lt-fr: led tl wknd over 1f out* **8/1**	63
	8	1 ½	**Too Grand** 2-8-9 0 .... NeilChalmers(3) 4 — (A M Balding) *leggy: lt-fr: s.i.s: rn green and pushed along in rr: styd on fnl f: nt rch ldrs* **50/1**	53
00	9	1 ¼	**Ballyhealy Lady**[35] [2590] 2-8-12 0 .... RichardThomas 3 — (D K Ivory) *in tch: hmpd 3f out: n.d whn hung rt and hmpd jst ins fnl 2f* **50/1**	48
00	10	shd	**Transcendent (IRE)**[28] [2804] 2-9-3 0 .... TQuinn 7 — (J D Bethell) *swtg: prom: hrd rdn 2f out: sn wknd* **50/1**	53
06	11	2	**Don't Tell Anna (IRE)**[22] [2997] 2-8-12 0 .... RyanMoore 8 — (R Hannon) *lw: in tch tl wknd 2f out* **7/1**	41
0	12	½	**Memphis Kate**[33] [2663] 2-8-12 0 .... HayleyTurner 11 — (M L W Bell) *b.hind: in tch tl wknd jst over 2f out* **20/1**	39
	13	½	**Jal Music** 2-9-3 0 .... NickyMackay 13 — (L M Cumani) *w'like: towards rr on far rail: hmpd and snatched up 3f out: nt rcvr: sn wl bhd* **10/1**	42

61.02 secs (-1.19) **Going Correction** -0.325s/f (Firm) — **13** Ran SP% **122.5**

Speed ratings (Par 94):96,91,89,89,87 85,85,83,81,80 77,76,76

CSF £30.47 TOTE £5.90: £2.10, £2.20, £5.10; EX 33.10.

Owner K Abdulla **Bred** Juddmonte Farms Inc **Trained** Beckhampton, Wilts

FOCUS

An ordinary maiden, best rated through the runner-up, and the form should work out.

NOTEBOOK

Sailor At Sea(USA), who ran with promise on his debut at Lingfield, appreciated the better ground and travelled well before going clear in the closing stages. He looks a promising type for decent nurseries. (op 7-2 tchd 5-1)

Ben is pretty exposed but his third in a nursery last time out still gave him a solid chance in this company. He could not cope with the easy winner but ran another sound race and is probably a good guide to the level of the form. (op 7-1)

Rash Judgement, a 38,000gns half-brother to Tabulate, a 1m winner at four, showed his inexperience with a slow start, but he was staying on well at the finish after overcoming trouble in running, and looks very much the type who will improve when stepped up another furlong or two. (op 16-1)

Our Acquaintance finished in front of the winner at Lingfield on his debut, but the ground was soft that day and these different conditions clearly favoured Sailor At Sea more than him. (op 3-1)

Totally Focussed(IRE), whose dam was placed over 6f and 7f and is a sister to Premier Property, a three-time winning two-year-old sprinter in the US, showed a lot more than on his debut over 7f and was keeping on well late. He seems to be going the right way. (op 66-1)

The Name Is Frank, who led at Salisbury last time out over 6f, struggled to go the early pace on this occasion. (op 16-1)

Sandy Par showed early pace and will appreciate a return to 5f in nursery company. (op 17-2 tchd 9-1)

Too Grand, a cheap purchase, is a half-sister to three winners and was not disgraced despite showing definite signs of inexperience on this debut. She can improve. (op 66-1)

Ballyhealy Lady Official explanation: jockey said filly ran green

Transcendent(IRE) Official explanation: jockey said colt suffered interference in running

Jal Music, a half-brother to Piccatune and Coco De Mer, both 5f juvenile winners, is bred to be effective over this trip. Hampered three furlongs out, that more or less ended his chance, but he is likely to prove better in time. (op 12-1)

3688 HALBREN HOMES SUPPORTING THE CHILDREN'S TRUST H'CAP 5f 6y
6:40 (6:44) (Class 4) (0-80,78) 3-Y-O £5,181 (£1,541; £770; £384) Stalls High

Form				RPR
1-22	1		**Gentle Guru**[17] 3164 3-9-6 75 SteveDrowne 2	81
			(R T Phillips) *lw: chsd ldrs: hrd rdn 2f out: styd on wl to ld nr fin* 4/1[2]	
-103	2	½	**Pretty Miss**[40] 2444 3-9-1 70 RyanMoore 5	74
			(H Candy) *led and travelled strly in front: rdn clr ins fnl 2f: hung rt over 1f out: tired and hdd nr fin* 6/1	
0431	3	¾	**Black Moma (IRE)**[19] 3086 3-9-1 77 HaddenFrost(7) 9	79
			(R Hannon) *pressed ldr tl outpcd wl over 1f out: kpt on fnl f* 13/2	
1400	4	hd	**Our Blessing (IRE)**[8] 3418 3-9-9 78 TQuinn 10	79
			(A P Jarvis) *prom: hrd rdn fnl 2f: kpt on fnl f* 16/1	
041	5	shd	**Time Share (IRE)**[24] 2948 3-7-11 59 oh5 (be[1]) MCGeran(7) 6	59
			(J Ryan) *bmpd s: towards rr: rdn and r.o fnl 2f: nrst fin* 25/1	
-360	6	1 ¼	**Star Strider**[10] 3369 3-9-2 71 (p) FrancisNorton 3	67
			(A M Balding) *dwlt: in rr: rdn 1/2-way: styd on fnl f: nvr nrr* 12/1	
2215	7	1 ¼	**Drifting Gold**[24] 2950 3-9-1 70 (b) PhilipRobinson 8	61+
			(C G Cox) *t.k.h in midfield: effrt and hrd rdn 2f out: 6th and no imp whn n.m.r ins fnl f* 11/2[3]	
13-4	8	nk	**Fluttering Rose**[180] 188 3-9-0 69 JamesDoyle 1	59
			(R M Beckett) *prom tl hrd rdn and btn 2f out* 20/1	
5251	9	1 ½	**Castano**[20] 3046 3-9-1 70 JoeFanning 4	58+
			(B R Millman) *s.s: in rr: hmpd on far rail 3f out: sn rdn and n.d: eased whn no ch fnl 150yds* 10/3[1]	
4622	10	1	**Miss Ippolita**[13] 3278 3-9-8 77 RichardHughes 11	58
			(J R Jenkins) *mid-div: outpcd 3f out: n.d fnl 2f* 9/1	

60.48 secs (-1.73) **Going Correction** -0.325s/f (Firm) 10 Ran SP% **118.3**
Speed ratings (Par 102):100,99,98,97,97 95,93,93,90,89
CSF £28.80 CT £157.92 TOTE £5.40: £1.70, £2.00, £2.20; EX 38.20.
Owner Flying Tiger Partnership **Bred** R Phillips & Tweenhills Farm & Stud **Trained** Adlestrop, Gloucs

FOCUS
A competitive sprint handicap and pretty solid form for the grade.
Castano Official explanation: jockey said gelding missed the break

3689 DEVINE HOMES SUPPORTING THE CHILDREN'S TRUST H'CAP 1m 14y
7:15 (7:15) (Class 4) (0-80,80) 3-Y-O £6,477 (£1,927; £963; £481) Stalls High

Form				RPR
2101	1		**Cnoc Moy (IRE)**[10] 3384 3-9-4 75 6ex GeorgeBaker 1	83+
			(C F Wall) *lw: prom: shkn up 2f out: rdn w hands and heels to ld fnl 25yds* 4/1[2]	
3025	2	nk	**Lap Of Honour (IRE)**[14] 3249 3-8-9 66 JoeFanning 11	72
			(N A Callaghan) *led: rdn over 2f out: hdd fnl 25yds: kpt on wl* 8/1[3]	
4-00	3	hd	**Effigy**[27] 2834 3-8-8 65 TQuinn 12	71
			(H Candy) *prom: rdn to chal 2f out: kpt on wl* 33/1	
-106	4	2 ½	**Rudry Dragon (IRE)**[6] 3480 3-9-4 80 KevinGhunowa(5) 4	80
			(P A Blockley) *mid-div: drvn along 2f out: styd on* 20/1	
-616	5	nk	**Aegis (IRE)**[45] 2305 3-9-4 75 PatDobbs 10	74
			(B W Hills) *prom: rdn over 2f out: one pce* 16/1	
0-41	6	1 ¼	**Just Two Numbers**[24] 2944 3-9-9 80 DarryllHolland 7	77+
			(W Jarvis) *chsd ldrs: swtchd rt over 3f out: hrd rdn and one pce fnl 2f: 6th and btn whn snatched up nr fin* 12/1	
14-0	7	3 ½	**Tom Paris**[35] 2598 3-9-2 73 SteveDrowne 5	61
			(W R Muir) *in rr: effrt over 2f out: nt pce to chal* 33/1	
-461	8	1 ½	**Murrin (IRE)**[41] 2425 3-9-9 80 RyanMoore 9	65
			(T G Mills) *lw: s.s: bhd: mod effrt on rail over 2f out: sn btn* 7/2[1]	
005	9	2	**Monkey Glas (IRE)**[41] 2425 3-9-1 72 FrancisNorton 3	52
			(K R Burke) *t.k.h: sn stdd towards rr: rdn 3f out: n.d* 9/1	
2-20	10	9	**Waymark (IRE)**[55] 2005 3-9-6 77 PhilipRobinson 2	36
			(M A Jarvis) *swtg: settled in rr: rdn over 2f out: no rspnse* 4/1[2]	
-422	11	8	**Castara Bay**[24] 2944 3-9-6 77 RichardHughes 8	18
			(R Hannon) *towards rr: rdn 1/2-way: bhd fnl 2f: b.b.v* 8/1[3]	

1m 42.41s (-1.54) **Going Correction** -0.025s/f (Good) 11 Ran SP% **118.7**
Speed ratings (Par 102):106,105,105,103,102 101,97,96,94,85 77
CSF £35.64 CT £935.34 TOTE £4.40: £1.90, £2.40, £7.50; EX 36.40.
Owner Peter Botham **Bred** Miss Gemma Cunningham **Trained** Newmarket, Suffolk
■ Stewards' Enquiry : Pat Dobbs one-day ban: careless riding (Jul 30)

FOCUS
Not the strongest of handicaps, although the time was reasonable, and rated around the placed horses, with the winner value for more that the official margin.
Castara Bay Official explanation: jockey said colt bled from the nose

3690 THE CHILDREN'S TRUST CLAIMING STKS 1m 14y
7:45 (7:45) (Class 5) 3-Y-O+ £3,886 (£1,156; £577; £288) Stalls High

Form				RPR
5054	1		**Optimus (USA)**[19] 3076 5-9-7 70 TQuinn 11	71+
			(B G Powell) *b. chsd ldrs: drvn to ld over 1f out: sn clr* 4/1[2]	
4505	2	2 ½	**Smart Cat (IRE)**[32] 2696 4-9-2 53 (v[1]) RichardMullen 7	60
			(A P Jarvis) *in tch: effrt over 2f out: styd on u.p to take 2nd nr fin* 12/1	
3006	3	shd	**Hansomelle (IRE)**[22] 2990 5-8-7 46 (p) NeilChalmers(3) 4	54
			(Miss Sheena West) *prom: hrd rdn 2f out: kpt on same pce* 14/1	
630	4	2	**Copper King**[54] 2040 3-8-13 80 (v) SteveDrowne 6	60
			(P D Evans) *hld up in midfield travelling strly: effrt and hrd rdn 2f out: styd on same pce* 5/1[3]	
-004	5	¾	**Silver Blue (IRE)**[6] 3482 4-9-8 72 (b) RyanMoore 3	59
			(R Hannon) *prom: led wl over 1f out: hung rt and sn hdd: wknd fnl f* 5/1[3]	
-412	6	shd	**Yakimov (USA)**[19] 3076 8-9-7 81 VinceSlattery 5	58
			(D J Wintle) *hld up in tch: rdn and hung bdly rt fnl 3f: styd on fnl f* 11/4[1]	
0-00	7	3 ½	**A One (IRE)**[17] 3163 8-8-5 45 HaddenFrost(7) 9	41
			(H J Manners) *led tl wl over 1f out: sn wknd* 50/1	
3502	8	1	**Razzano (IRE)**[16] 3175 3-7-8 54 NicolPolli(5) 12	34
			(A M Hales) *in rr: drvn along and sme hdwy on rail over 2f out: wknd wl over 1f out* 16/1	
4604	9	1 ¾	**Trifti**[11] 3352 6-9-2 48 MartinDwyer 8	39
			(C A Cyzer) *t.k.h: a in last pair: rdn 1/2-way: lost tch over 2f out* 8/1	
00-0	10	5	**Da Bookie (IRE)**[55] 1629 7-8-13 67 (t) AlanCreighton(3) 10	27
			(E J Creighton) *stdd s: plld hrd towards rr: rdn wl over 2f out: no rspnse and sn bhd* 25/1	

1m 43.55s (-0.40) **Going Correction** -0.025s/f (Good) 10 Ran SP% **117.2**
WFA 3 from 4yo+ 8lb
Speed ratings (Par 103):101,98,98,96,95 95,92,91,89,84
CSF £51.51 TOTE £5.80: £1.80, £2.80, £4.10; EX 64.90.
Owner Andrew P Wyer **Bred** Strategy Bloodstock **Trained** Lambourn, Berks

FOCUS
The placed horses help set and limit the level for this modest claimer, and the winner probably did not have to run up to his official mark of 70 to win.
Da Bookie(IRE) Official explanation: jockey said gelding ran too free

3691 1 YEAR, 20 SHOPS, THAT'S BETTER H'CAP 1m 2f 7y
8:20 (8:20) (Class 4) (0-85,84) 3-Y-O £5,042 (£5,042; £1,155; £577) Stalls High

Form				RPR
3-21	1		**Malt Or Mash (USA)**[34] 2627 3-9-9 84 PatDobbs 11	92
			(R Hannon) *lw: hld up in tch: effrt 2f out: nt clr run on rail ins fnl f: swtchd lft and r.o to share on line* 11/4[1]	
4414	1	dht	**Six Of Diamonds (IRE)**[34] 2627 3-9-3 78 MartinDwyer 3	86
			(J A Osborne) *prom: led 6f out: rdn 2l ahd ins fnl f: jnd on line* 7/1	
2-14	3	1 ½	**Coeur De Lionne (IRE)**[53] 2057 3-9-6 81 SteveDrowne 7	86+
			(R Charlton) *mid-div: rdn and sltly outpcd 3f out: styd on fnl 2f: tk 3rd fnl 100yds* 20/1	
2132	4	nk	**Warm Embraces (IRE)**[56] 1974 3-8-13 77 MarcHalford(3) 10	81
			(D R C Elsworth) *in rr: rdn 3f out: styd on wl along rail fnl 2f: nvr nrr* 13/2[3]	
020	5	1	**Officer**[42] 2402 3-8-12 73 (v[1]) RyanMoore 6	76
			(Sir Michael Stoute) *led after 1f tl 6f out: w ldrs after: drvn 2f out: disputing 2nd and btn whn bmpd and wknd ins fnl f* 8/1	
-021	6	shd	**Rock Anthem (IRE)**[41] 2426 3-9-2 77 TQuinn 9	79
			(J L Dunlop) *hld up and bhd: effrt on outside over 2f out: hung rt over 1f out: nrst fin* 3/1[2]	
-000	7	nk	**Strikeen (IRE)**[34] 2627 3-9-0 75 DarryllHolland 1	77
			(T G Mills) *prom: rdn 3f out: outpcd fnl 2f* 20/1	
-013	8	shd	**Encircled**[20] 3058 3-9-6 81 RobertHavlin 8	83
			(D Haydn Jones) *hld up in rr: rdn and sme hdwy over 2f out: no imp over 1f out* 10/1	
4-02	9	2	**Distiller (IRE)**[10] 3384 3-8-8 69 RichardMullen 2	67
			(W R Muir) *in tch: rdn 3f out: sn outpcd* 14/1	
0-60	10	29	**Frosty Night (IRE)**[47] 2231 3-9-6 81 JoeFanning 5	24
			(M Johnston) *prom to 1/2-way: bhd fnl 3f* 20/1	
156	11	15	**Tutor (IRE)**[26] 2872 3-9-0 75 (b[1]) RichardHughes 4	—
			(W J Haggas) *lw: led 1f: t.k.h and stdd in rr of midfield: rdn 3f out: nt run on* 16/1	

2m 9.20s (-1.04) **Going Correction** -0.025s/f (Good) 11 Ran SP% **124.5**
Speed ratings (Par 102):103,103,101,101,100 100,100,100,98,75 63
WIN: Malt Or Mash £2.10, Six Of Diamonds £4.30. PL: MOM £1.60, SOD £2.10, Coeur de Lionne £5.60. EX: MOM/SOD £16.30, SOD/MOM £12.60. CSF: MOM/SOD £11.67, SOD/MOM £13.69. TRIC: MOM/SOD/CDL £159.38, SOD/MOM/CDL £184.91..
Owner A P Patey **Bred** Delahanty Stock Farm **Trained** East Everleigh, Wilts
Owner Booth,Durkan,Mountgrange&Wood Hall Studs **Bred** Tally-Ho Stud **Trained** Upper Lambourn, Berks

FOCUS
A fair, competitive-looking handicap that has been rated positively as those towards the fore look progressive types. That said, they finished in something of a heap after going a steady pace early.
Encircled Official explanation: trainer said filly was in season

3692 DIGITALANDDIRECT.COM H'CAP 1m 6f
8:50 (8:52) (Class 4) (0-80,79) 4-Y-0+ £5,181 (£1,541; £770; £384) Stalls Centre

Form				RPR
0211	1		**Olimpo (FR)**[14] 3243 6-9-4 79 JamesMillman(5) 3	86
			(B R Millman) *mde all: rdn clr over 2f out: r.o strly and a holding rivals* 9/4[1]	
0002	2	2	**Daring Racer (GER)**[15] 3217 4-8-8 64 TQuinn 5	68
			(S Dow) *chsd ldng pair: rdn 3f out: styd on same pce: tk 2nd nr fin* 6/1	
2002	3	nk	**Love Always**[32] 2692 5-9-2 72 RyanMoore 4	76
			(S Dow) *lw: hld up in 4th: effrt on outside over 2f out: chsd wnr 1f out: no imp: lost 2nd nr fin* 11/4[3]	
0-05	4	2 ½	**Screenplay**[26] 2887 6-8-8 64 JoeFanning 2	65
			(G L Moore) *chsd wnr: rdn to chal 3f out: btn 2f out: lost 2nd 1f out and wknd fnl f* 5/2[2]	
-000	5	8	**Mostarsil (USA)**[13] 3273 9-8-11 67 (p) SteveDrowne 1	57
			(G L Moore) *hld up in rr: pushed along 3f out: nvr threatened* 8/1	

3m 8.32s (3.81) **Going Correction** -0.025s/f (Good) 5 Ran SP% **111.4**
Speed ratings (Par 105):88,86,86,85,80
CSF £15.61 TOTE £3.40: £2.00, £1.80; EX 16.20 Place 6 £302.43, Place 5 £129.35.
Owner Pot Black Racing **Bred** Ewar Stud Farm **Trained** Kentisbeare, Devon

FOCUS
They went a very steady pace in this uncompetitive staying handicap, which played right into the hands of the favourite. As a result the time was very slow and the form is ordinary, although the winner remains in good form.
T/Plt: £431.50 to a £1 stake. Pool: £79,218.60. 134.00 winning tickets. T/Qpdt: £130.70 to a £1 stake. Pool: £6,024.90. 34.10 winning tickets. LM

3693 - 3696a (Foreign Racing) - See Raceform Interactive

3232 NEWBURY (L-H)
Friday, July 20
3697 Meeting Abandoned - waterlogged

3503 NEWMARKET (JULY) (R-H)
Friday, July 20

OFFICIAL GOING: Good
Wind: Light, half-behind Weather: Cloudy

3705 BASS SMOOTH H'CAP 1m 2f
5:45 (5:48) (Class 5) (0-70,73) 3-Y-0+ £3,886 (£1,156; £577; £288) Stalls Centre

Form				RPR
031-	1		**Hazelnut**[280] 5946 4-9-5 60 JamieSpencer 9	68
			(J R Fanshawe) *stdd s: hld up: hdwy over 2f out: rdn to ld ins fnl f: edgd rt: styd on* 7/1[3]	
3450	2	nk	**Sky Quest (IRE)**[16] 3215 9-9-3 65 HarryPoulton(7) 5	72
			(J R Boyle) *hld up: hdwy 1/2-way: led and edgd rt over 3f out: rdn over 1f out: hdd ins fnl f: styd on* 20/1	
3005	3	nk	**Postsprofit (IRE)**[24] 2965 3-8-13 64 NCallan 11	70
			(N A Callaghan) *s.i.s: hld up: hdwy over 2f out: sn rdn: styd on* 20/1	
600	4	shd	**Hot Diamond**[27] 2880 3-8-10 64 MarcHalford(3) 19	75+
			(D R C Elsworth) *hld up: nt clr run fr over 2f out tl r.o wl ins fnl f* 11/1	
0060	5	¾	**Mr Mischief**[11] 3385 7-9-0 60 RussellKennemore(5) 20	65
			(M C Chapman) *chsd ldrs: rdn over 1f out: styd on* 18/1	
-206	6	shd	**Piper's Song (IRE)**[49] 2194 4-9-13 68 DaneO'Neill 4	73
			(H Candy) *chsd ldrs: rdn over 1f out: styd on same pce ins fnl f* 10/1	

7 1 **Mr Napoleon (IRE)**42 2439 5-8-8 56 .... CharlotteKerton(7) 15 60+
(G Prodromou) *hld up in tch: racd keenly: lost pl over 4f out: hmpd over 2f out: swtchd lft and r.o ins fnl f* **50/1**
3100 8 1 **Montchara (IRE)**35 2621 4-9-9 64 .... SteveDrowne 3 65
(G Wragg) *prom: rdn over 2f out: no ex fnl f* **10/1**
4400 9 ¾ **Summer Lodge**21 3049 4-9-2 60 ....(v) JerryO'Dwyer(3) 16 59
(A J McCabe) *hld up: hdwy 2f out: no ex fnl f* **33/1**
0331 10 nk **Kavachi (IRE)**21 3048 4-9-10 65 .... RyanMoore 18 63
(G L Moore) *hld up in tch: racd keenly: rdn over 2f out: wknd ins fnl f* **7/2**1
1062 11 nk **Street Life (IRE)**15 3232 9-10-0 69 .... BrettDoyle 17 67
(W J Musson) *hld up: effrt over 1f out: n.d* **15/2**
35-0 12 6 **Lawaaheb (IRE)**3 3610 6-8-10 51 oh1 ow1 .... OscarUrbina 14 37
(M J Gingell) *prom: rdn over 3f out: wknd over 1f out* **25/1**
0340 13 hd **Bright Sun (IRE)**12 3346 6-9-11 66 ....(t) KimTinkler 10 51
(N Tinkler) *trckd ldr: plld hrd: rdn over 3f out: wknd 2f out* **16/1**
4051 14 hd **Mystery River (USA)**8 3451 3-9-8 73 6ex .... RichardHughes 6 58
(B J Meehan) *led over 6f: wknd fnl f* **13/2**2
00-0 15 1 ½ **Dado Mush**37 2556 4-8-9 50 .... JimCrowley 13 32
(T T Clement) *hld up: rdn and wknd over 2f out* **50/1**
420- 16 3 **Roya**322 4982 4-9-5 63 .... TinaSmith(3) 8 39
(Miss Gay Kelleway) *chsd ldrs 8f* **33/1**
2320 17 7 **Mighty Kitchener (USA)**16 3217 4-9-5 60 .... IanMongan 12 22
(P Howling) *hld up: a in rr: wknd over 2f out* **25/1**

2m 5.90s (-0.54) **Going Correction** 0.0s/f (Good)
WFA 3 from 4yo+ 10lb **17 Ran SP% 124.5**
Speed ratings (Par 103):102,101,101,101,100 100,99,99,98,98 98,93,93,92,91 89,83
CSF £147.40 CT £2685.10 TOTE £5.90: £1.60, £5.40, £4.80, £2.80; EX 263.80.
Owner The Hon William Vestey **Bred** Stowell Park Stud **Trained** Newmarket, Suffolk
■ Stewards' Enquiry : Jamie Spencer one-day ban: careless riding (Jul 31)

FOCUS
An ordinary handicap, but a very competitive one due to the large field. The pace was solid enough, but there were a couple that met trouble in running and can be considered unlucky not to have finished closer. However, with the leaders finishing in a heap, the form is probably average at best.
Hot Diamond ◆ Official explanation: jockey said gelding was denied a clear run
Mystery River(USA) Official explanation: jockey said filly lost a shoe

3706 HILLS DRINKS DISTRIBUTORS MAIDEN FILLIES' STKS 7f
6:15 (6:20) (Class 4) 2-Y-O **£4,533** (£1,348; £674; £336) **Stalls** High

Form RPR
1 **Queen Scarlet (IRE)** 2-9-0 0 .... SteveDrowne 8 80
(B J Meehan) *chsd ldrs: rdn over 2f out: led over 1f out: r.o gamely* **14/1**
2 2 **Badalona** 2-9-0 0 .... JamieSpencer 12 75+
(M L W Bell) *prom tl stdd after 3f: chsd ldrs: n.m.r fr wl over 1f out tl weaved through and r.o wl to go 2nd cl home: nt rch wnr* **20/1**
3 nk **Marwah** 2-9-0 0 .... DaneO'Neill 1 74
(E A L Dunlop) *hmpd s: t.k.h and sn prom: led 4f out tl over 2f out: ev ch over 1f out: nt qckn* **16/1**
0 4 1 **Close To Paradise (IRE)**28 2832 2-9-0 0 .... KerrinMcEvoy 3 72
(E A L Dunlop) *wnt lft s: sn cl up: rdn and ev ch 1f out: one pce* **8/1**3
5 nk **Tomorrow's World (IRE)** 2-9-0 0 .... RyanMoore 11 71
(Sir Michael Stoute) *wnt rt s: towards rr: rdn 1/2-way: styd on steadily fnl f: bttr for experience* **6/1**2
0 6 shd **Rosy Alexander**16 3213 2-9-0 0 .... FrancisNorton 9 71+
(N A Callaghan) *only had one bhd after 3f: pushed along fnl 2f: styng on v wl cl home: promising* **33/1**
7 ½ **Kashmina** 2-9-0 0 .... DarryllHolland 5 70
(M R Channon) *prom: rdn over 2f out: no ex over 1f out* **25/1**
0 8 hd **Victoria Valentine**21 3055 2-9-0 0 .... MichaelHills 4 69
(B W Hills) *sn prom: led over 2f out: hung rt and hdd over 1f out: qckly lost pl* **8/1**3
9 ½ **Free Fallin** 2-9-0 0 .... JimmyFortune 16 68
(P W Chapple-Hyam) *led at modest pce for 3f: rdn and no ex 2f out* **10/1**
2 10 nk **Isent She Rich (IRE)**24 2969 2-9-0 0 .... TedDurcan 6 67
(M G Quinlan) *stdd s: nvr trbld ldrs* **6/1**2
11 1 ½ **Beat The Rain** 2-9-0 0 .... RichardHughes 17 63
(J H M Gosden) *hld up: n.d fr 1/2-way* **11/2**1
0 12 nk **Exodia**21 3055 2-9-0 0 .... JimmyQuinn 14 63
(Jane Chapple-Hyam) *plld hrd: midfield: btn 2f out* **50/1**
13 ½ **Presbyterian Nun (IRE)** 2-9-0 0 .... SebSanders 18 61
(J L Dunlop) *sn outpcd: pushed along 1/2-way: n.d* **20/1**
14 1 ½ **Time Control** 2-9-0 0 .... NickyMackay 13 58
(L M Cumani) *s.s: a bhd: rn green* **10/1**
15 3 ½ **Miss Delila (USA)** 2-9-0 0 .... NCallan 15 49
(K A Ryan) *chsd ldrs: rdn over 2f out: rn green and sn btn* **16/1**
16 ½ **Luminous Gold** 2-9-0 0 .... IanMongan 19 48
(C F Wall) *s.s: plld hrd: rdn wl over 2f out: sn btn* **33/1**
17 10 **Sophies Secret** 2-8-11 0 .... JerryO'Dwyer(3) 10 23
(J R Holt) *drvn and struggling bdly 1/2-way: t.o* **100/1**
18 23 **Chrystal Venture (IRE)** 2-9-0 0 .... EddieAhern 7 —
(A J McCabe) *veered wildly lft s: a t.o* **66/1**

1m 27.91s (1.13) **Going Correction** 0.0s/f (Good) **18 Ran SP% 126.5**
Speed ratings (Par 93):93,90,90,89,88 88,88,87,87,87 85,85,84,82,78 78,66,40
CSF £280.53 TOTE £20.60: £4.90, £6.00, £9.60; EX 301.50.
Owner F C T Wilson **Bred** Tally-Ho Stud **Trained** Manton, Wilts

FOCUS
This may not have been the strongest fillies' maiden ever run here with the standard difficult to be confident about, but quite a few of these are likely to improve a good deal. The stalls stretched right across the track, but the action all eventually took place centre to stands' side.

NOTEBOOK
Queen Scarlet(IRE) ◆, a 270,000gns half-sister to three winners including the top-class Nannina, was always close to the pace and showed a good attitude to win in some style. The stable's youngsters often come on for their first run, which makes the future that much brighter for her. (op 10-1)
Badalona ◆, a half-sister to eight winners including the smart pair Badminton and Cala, had to switch positions a few times in order to see daylight, but she came home in most pleasing style and it should not be long before she goes one better.
Marwah ◆, out of a winning dam from the family of Rainbow Quest and Slightly Dangerous, was done no favours at all by Close To Paradise at the start, but nonetheless showed up prominently for a long way down the wide outside and was eventually not beaten far. This was a very pleasing introduction and there should be races to be won with her. (tchd 20-1)
Close To Paradise(IRE), despite having had the advantage of a previous outing, went badly out to her left after exiting the stalls, hampering her stable-companion Marwah in the process. Despite that she had every chance and certainly stepped up from her debut effort over this extra furlong. (op 10-1)
Tomorrow's World(IRE) ◆, a half-sister to Desert Dreamer out of a winner over 1m4f, looked in need of the experience but was noted staying on quite nicely out towards the centre of the track. There is quite a bit of stamina on the dam's side, so she should get further and can be expected to build on this debut effort. (op 9-1)
Rosy Alexander ◆ ran a similar race to her Kempton Polytrack debut, keeping on in eye-catching style from well off the pace to be nearest at the finish. She obviously possesses quite a lot of ability and just where and when that ability will eventually be unleashed may well be indicated by the market.
Kashmina, a 57,000gns half-sister to Dualagi, ran well for a long way and should improve from this. (tchd 33-1)
Victoria Valentine, who ran adequately on her debut here last month, was always up there but did not get home and this extra furlong did not seem to be the answer. (op 13-2)
Isent She Rich(IRE), who ran so well on soft ground at Newbury on her debut, never got into this and did little for the form of that contest. Although this ground was by no means fast, she may need genuinely testing condtions in order to show her best. (tchd 5-1)
Beat The Rain, a half-sister to both Quenched and Raincoat, never really got into this but was not given a hard race and should repay the kindness in due course. (op 9-2 tchd 6-1)
Chrystal Venture(IRE) Official explanation: jockey said filly missed the break and veered left

3707 ROUTE COLCHESTER NIGHT CLUB H'CAP 7f
6:45 (6:47) (Class 4) (0-85,85) 3-Y-O **£5,181** (£1,541; £770; £384) **Stalls** High

Form RPR
0301 1 **Samsons Son**31 2749 3-8-10 72 .... DaneO'Neill 7 84
(J R Best) *hld up in tch: rdn over 1f out: r.o to ld wl ins fnl f* **16/1**
1334 2 ½ **Lone Wolfe**8 3463 3-9-6 82 .... JimmyFortune 6 93
(Jane Chapple-Hyam) *led: hdd over 5f out: led again over 1f out: sn rdn clr: hdd wl ins fnl f* **9/2**2
-213 3 2 **We'll Come**7 3503 3-9-9 85 .... PhilipRobinson 8 91
(M A Jarvis) *chsd ldrs: rdn over 1f out: styd on same pce* **10/11**1
6402 4 2 **Lunces Lad (IRE)**7 3480 3-9-3 79 .... DarryllHolland 2 79
(M R Channon) *hld up: rdn over 2f out: styd on ins fnl f: nt trble ldrs* **9/1**3
0-54 5 ½ **Soviet Palace (IRE)**55 2040 3-9-9 85 .... NCallan 14 84
(K A Ryan) *led over 5f out: rdn and hdd over 1f out: wknd ins fnl f* **16/1**
1044 6 1 **Ambrosiano**35 2633 3-8-12 74 .... AdamKirby 9 70
(C G Cox) *hld up: racd keenly: hdwy over 2f out: wknd fnl f* **20/1**
5063 7 nk **Jawaab (IRE)**31 2749 3-8-7 69 ow1 ....(p) SteveDrowne 4 64
(M A Buckley) *s.i.s: hld up: sme hdwy over 1f out: sn rdn and wknd* **22/1**
12-0 8 3 **Greyt Big Stuff (USA)**88 1205 3-8-7 74 .... NicolPolli(5) 11 61
(Miss Gay Kelleway) *s.i.s: hld up: racd keenly: hdwy 4f out: n.m.r and wknd over 2f out* **50/1**
01 9 4 **Pagan Belief**38 2541 3-8-13 75 .... EddieAhern 5 51
(J A R Toller) *chsd ldrs: rdn over 2f out: wknd over 1f out* **14/1**
1406 10 1 **Flores Sea (USA)**17 3196 3-8-13 75 .... RyanMoore 1 49
(T D Barron) *s.i.s: hld up: rdn over 2f out: sn wknd* **14/1**
-430 11 19 **Tencendur (IRE)**17 3196 3-8-12 74 .... RichardHughes 12 —
(D Nicholls) *hld up: wknd over 2f out* **25/1**

1m 25.25s (-1.53) **Going Correction** 0.0s/f (Good) **11 Ran SP% 120.6**
Speed ratings (Par 102):108,107,105,102,102 101,100,97,92,91 69
CSF £85.22 CT £135.86 TOTE £13.20: £2.90, £2.00, £1.30; EX 81.40.
Owner M Folan **Bred** J R Best **Trained** Hucking, Kent

FOCUS
Quite a decent handicap run at a solid pace, but very few ever got into it and the form is rated around the placed horses. The action all took place down the middle of the course.
Tencendur(IRE) Official explanation: jockey said gelding lost its action

3708 ESTRELLA DAMM AT TALK NIGHTCLUB SOUTHEND CONDITIONS STKS 5f
7:15 (7:17) (Class 3) 3-Y-O+
£8,724 (£2,612; £1,306; £653; £326; £163) **Stalls** High

Form RPR
4520 1 **Celtic Mill**4 3586 9-9-0 104 .... JimmyFortune 14 97
(D W Barker) *racd alone stands' side: chsd ldrs: sustained chal fnl f: r.o gamely to ld fnl stride* **9/2**3
060 2 shd **Tabaret**65 1770 4-8-9 97 .... DeanMcKeown 4 92
(R M Whitaker) *prom: led 1/2-way: rdn fnl f: pipped on post* **13/2**
-004 3 nk **Masta Plasta (IRE)**55 2022 4-8-9 93 .... JamieSpencer 3 91
(D Nicholls) *stdd s: bhd tl prog 2f out: tried to chal ins fnl f: kpt on but a jst hld* **8/1**
-460 4 1 ¾ **The Trader (IRE)**13 3329 9-8-9 100 ....(b) TedDurcan 12 85
(M Blanshard) *outpcd early: tending to go lft most of way: effrt over 1f out: kpt on but unable to chal* **15/2**
2220 5 hd **Bounty Quest**111 860 5-8-9 105 .... NCallan 1 84
(K A Ryan) *chsd ldrs: drvn 1/2-way: no imp fnl f* **16/1**
0260 6 ½ **Baron's Pit**27 2858 7-8-9 101 ....(v) DarryllHolland 8 82
(E F Vaughan) *midfield: rdn 1/2-way: no ex 1f out* **4/1**2
0300 7 ¾ **Presto Shinko (IRE)**9 3445 6-9-1 104 ....(v1) RichardHughes 5 85
(R Hannon) *prom: rdn 2f out: btn 1f out* **7/2**1
3314 8 1 ½ **Tilly's Dream**11 3374 4-8-4 73 .... HayleyTurner 10 69
(Miss K B Boutflower) *midfield: drvn 2f out: btn over 1f out: eased ins fnl f* **25/1**
112- 9 ¾ **Vale Of Belvoir (IRE)**335 4594 3-8-0 96 .... FrancisNorton 7 65+
(K R Burke) *chsd ldrs tl 1/2-way* **10/1**
6165 10 5 **Classic Encounter (IRE)**44 2352 4-8-9 94 .... EddieAhern 6 53
(D M Simcock) *set fast pce tl 1/2-way: drvn and fdd over 1f out* **16/1**
-030 11 nk **Banana Belle**3 3627 3-7-9 45 .... NicolPolli(5) 9 46
(J Ryan) *sn outpcd* **100/1**
0050 12 shd **Axis Shield (IRE)**122 715 4-8-1 40 .... DominicFox(3) 13 47
(M C Chapman) *prom tl rdn and racd awkwardly 1/2-way: struggling over 1f out* **100/1**
5-60 13 7 **Noddledoddle (IRE)**8 3464 3-8-0 47 ....(t) DavidKinsella 2 21
(J Ryan) *sn bdly outpcd* **100/1**
4 14 8 **Air Guitar (IRE)**8 3468 7-8-6 0 ....(v) MarcHalford(3) 11 —
(J Ryan) *immediately hopelessly outpcd* **66/1**

58.47 secs (-1.09) **Going Correction** 0.0s/f (Good)
WFA 3 from 4yo+ 4lb **14 Ran SP% 125.8**
Speed ratings (Par 107):108,107,107,104,104 103,102,99,98,90 90,90,78,66
CSF £35.24 TOTE £6.60: £2.30, £3.10, £3.10; EX 65.00.
Owner P Asquith **Bred** P Asquith **Trained** Scorton, N Yorks

FOCUS
A good, competitive conditions contest and, with the time decent, the form is fair for the level. The majority of these raced up the middle of the track, but the winner hugged the stands' rail throughout.

NOTEBOOK
Celtic Mill was soon showing his customary early dash racing alone against the stands' rail, albeit not leading outright, and he responded most willing to pressure to deny those who raced up the middle of the track. A real credit to his connections, this was his 17th career-success and he should continue to go well in good sprint company. (tchd 5-1, 11-2 in places)

Tabaret was outclassed in the Duke Of York Stakes at York when last seen over two months previously, but this was more realistic and he put up a fine effort in defeat, winning the race of those who came up the middle of the track. He is smart on his day, as he showed when winning a Listed race at two, and he could have another decent prize in him. (op 6-1 tchd 11-2 and 7-1)
Masta Plasta(IRE) ◆ has not win since taking the 2005 Norfolk Stakes, but this was a good effort considering he had a little bit to find with the front two at the weights. He is starting to show a bit of his old sparkle and, able to run in the Stewards' Cup off a mark of 93, it might be worth snapping up a bit of 33/1 ante-post. (op 10-1)
The Trader(IRE) had every chance at the weights, but he has not really been at his best this year and did not help his chance by edging left for much of the way. (op 8-1 tchd 7-1)
Bounty Quest ◆, a triple winner on the dirt in Dubai and placed in Group 3 company for Doug Watson since leaving Richard Hannon's yard after his juvenile campaign, made a respectable debut for the Kevin Ryan yard. He was upwards of 4lb clear at the weights, so he was obviously not quite at his best, but he is entitled to be sharper next time considering this was his first run in nearly four months, and a Nunthorpe entry suggests his connections have high hopes for him. (op 14-1 tchd 12-1)
Baron's Pit could not match the form he showed when ninth of 26 in the Wokingham on his previous start. (op 11-2 tchd 6-1, 7-1 in a place)
Presto Shinko(IRE) was not at his best in a French Group 3 on his previous start and this was another below-par effort. He should appreciate a return to 5f. (tchd 4-1, 9-2 in places)
Tilly's Dream had loads to find at the weights, but she ran right up to her best and looks to be improving. (op 28-1)
Vale Of Belvoir(IRE) ◆, a triple winner and Listed place at two, was making a belated reappearance. She was by no means knocked about once her chance had gone and she should improve a fair bit on this. (op 8-1)

3709 JBR LEISURE LTD H'CAP — 1m 2f

7:50 (7:50) (Class 3) (0-95,90) 3-Y-O

£8,724 (£2,612; £1,306; £653; £326; £163) **Stalls** Centre

Form — RPR

1 **1** **Winter Sunrise**[52] 2127 3-9-6 **87** .... RyanMoore 1 — 97+
(Sir Michael Stoute) *sn led: c centre ent st: rdn over 1f out: hdd ins fnl f: rallied to ld post* **7/2**[1]

514 **2** *shd* **Pathos (GER)**[21] 3058 3-8-9 **79** .... MarcHalford(3) 10 — 89+
(D R C Elsworth) *hld up: wnt centre ent st: hdwy over 2f out: sn rdn and hung rt: led ins fnl f: hdd post: 2nd of 8 in gp* **13/2**

13- **3** *1* **Cold Quest (USA)**[321] 5020 3-9-9 **90** .... JimmyFortune 2 — 98
(J H M Gosden) *chsd ldrs: wnt centre ent st: ev ch and hung lft ins fnl f: styd on same pce: 3rd of 8 in gp* **9/1**

6122 **4** *1* **Tetouan**[45] 2340 3-9-0 **81** .... SteveDrowne 3 — 87
(R Charlton) *hld up: wnt centre ent st: hdwy 2f out: rdn over 1f out: styd on: 4th of 8 in gp* **4/1**[2]

1030 **5** *1 ½* **Eau Good**[13] 3335 3-9-2 **83** .... SebSanders 11 — 86
(B G Powell) *hld up: wnt centre ent st: hdwy over 2f out: rdn over 1f out: no ex ins fnl f: 5th of 8 in gp* **16/1**

-011 **6** *1 ½* **Calabash Cove (USA)**[45] 2340 3-9-3 **84** .... (t) KerrinMcEvoy 6 — 84+
(Saeed Bin Suroor) *chsd ldr tl styd stands' side ent st: led that pair: rdn over 2f out: no ex fr over 1f out: 1st of 2 that side* **4/1**[2]

5021 **7** *10* **Gold Prospect**[20] 3113 3-9-1 **82** .... JamieSpencer 7 — 62
(M L W Bell) *dwlt: hld up: wnt centre ent st: effrt over 2f out: wknd over 1f out: 6th of 8 in gp* **5/1**[3]

5560 **8** *nk* **Troialini**[41] 2448 3-8-7 **77** .... JerryO'Dwyer(3) 5 — 56
(S W Hall) *chsd ldrs: wnt centre ent st: rdn and wknd over 2f out: 7th of 8 in gp* **50/1**

-053 **9** *¾* **Old Romney**[17] 3189 3-8-11 **78** .... AdamKirby 4 — 56
(G A Huffer) *s.i.s: sn prom: chsd wnr and wnt centre ent st: rdn over 2f out: wknd over 1f out: last of 8 in gp* **14/1**

0-01 **10** *30* **Iceman George**[15] 3248 3-9-0 **81** .... TedDurcan 8 — —
(D Morris) *prom: chsd ldr and styd stands' side ent st: rdn and wknd over 2f out: last of 2 that side* **20/1**

2m 4.99s (-1.45) **Going Correction** 0.0s/f (Good) — **10** Ran SP% **121.5**
Speed ratings (Par 104):105,104,104,103,102 100,92,92,92,68
CSF £27.98 CT £194.92 TOTE £3.90: £1.90, £2.10, £3.20; EX 36.60.
Owner K Abdulla **Bred** Juddmonte Farms Ltd **Trained** Newmarket, Suffolk

FOCUS
A good three-year-old handicap with the first four all progressive and the form is rated fairly positively, only limited by the proximity of the fifth. The majority of these raced towards the middle of the track, and they held sway over the pair who stayed stands' side.

NOTEBOOK
Winter Sunrise was made to work extremely hard to follow up her debut success in a Sandown maiden, but she responded gamely to strong driving to win on the nod. She should have learnt plenty from this and ought to be able to step forward again. (tchd 9-2)
Pathos(GER) ◆ was a beaten favourite over 1m4f here on his previous start, but the drop in trip suited and he was just denied. He looks the type who can keep improving. (tchd 7-1)
Cold Quest(USA), who showed useful form in two runs over 7f as a juvenile, shaped nicely on his belated reappearance. He is entitled to come on a fair bit for this and looks one to keep on the right side of. (op 14-1 tchd 17-2)
Tetouan could not defy a career-high mark, but this was a respectable effort in defeat. (op 9-2)
Eau Good is fully exposed and he basically just found a few of these too good. (tchd 14-1)
Calabash Cove(USA) had Tetouan a neck away in second when winning at Ripon on his previous start, but he was well below that form this time. There looked to be at least two possible excuses; he may have resented the first-time tongue-tie, or have been at a disadvantage racing away from the main group on the stands' side. However, it is worth remembering Celtic Mill took a similar path when winning the previous race, albeit over a shorter distance. (tchd 9-2 in places)
Gold Prospect was well below the form he showed when winning at Wolverhampton on his previous start. (op 9-2)
Old Romney Official explanation: jockey said colt ran too free

3710 ATKINS MAIDEN STKS — 1m

8:20 (8:22) (Class 4) 3-Y-O

£5,181 (£1,541; £770; £384) **Stalls** High

Form — RPR

3- **1** **Lang Shining (IRE)**[281] 5914 3-9-3 0 .... RyanMoore 1 — 84+
(Sir Michael Stoute) *prom: rdn to ld ins fnl f: hld on wl* **11/8**[1]

2 *½* **Alo Pura** 3-8-12 0 .... PhilipRobinson 6 — 78+
(M A Jarvis) *towards rr early: hdwy 2f out: edgd rt and tried to chal u.p ins fnl f: no imp fnl 100yds* **16/1**

3 *1 ¾* **Time Over** 3-8-12 0 .... EddieAhern 13 — 74+
(J L Dunlop) *s.i.s: prog 2f out: nt clr run over 1f out: kpt on same pce fnl 100yds* **33/1**

22 **4** *1* **Trees Of Green (USA)**[14] 3276 3-9-3 0 .... KerrinMcEvoy 9 — 76
(Saeed Bin Suroor) *led: drvn and hdd ins fnl f: nt qckn* **5/1**[2]

0-43 **5** *shd* **Sonning Star (IRE)**[15] 3234 3-9-3 66 .... JimmyFortune 10 — 76
(D R C Elsworth) *chsd ldrs: drvn wl over 1f out: one pce fnl f* **13/2**[3]

6 *3 ½* **Double Doors** 3-9-3 0 .... RichardHughes 3 — 68
(J H M Gosden) *wnt rt s: sn drvn: effrt 1/2-way: no ch w ldrs over 1f out* **14/1**

53- **7** *½* **Not Another Cat (USA)**[263] 6257 3-9-3 0 .... NCallan 12 — 67
(K R Burke) *midfield: drvn 2f out: sn btn* **25/1**

4 **8** *hd* **Insiyaabi (USA)**[27] 2880 3-9-3 0 .... RHills 15 — 66
(J L Dunlop) *t.k.h and prom: rdn and fdd wl over 1f out* **7/1**

5 **9** *1* **Dream Of Fortune (IRE)**[74] 1522 3-9-3 0 .... SebSanders 16 — 64
(J Noseda) *cl up: rdn 2f out: btn over 1f out* **8/1**

00 **10** *½* **King Of Legend (IRE)**[12] 3349 3-9-3 0 .... DarrylIHolland 18 — 63
(Miss Gay Kelleway) *chsd ldrs: drvn 2f out: sn btn* **100/1**

11 *1* **Amichi** 3-8-12 0 .... DaneO'Neill 17 — 55
(G L Moore) *dwlt: rdn and a struggling: v green* **66/1**

0- **12** *½* **The Flying Cowboy (IRE)**[304] 5460 3-9-3 0 .... TedDurcan 11 — 59
(Jane Chapple-Hyam) *chsd ldrs: rdn and btn 2f out* **100/1**

56 **13** *shd* **Ful Of Grace (IRE)**[9] 3436 3-8-9 0 .... JerryO'Dwyer(3) 2 — 54
(M G Quinlan) *nvr on terms* **100/1**

14 *6* **Pagan Rose (IRE)** 3-8-9 0 .... MarcHalford(3) 5 — 40
(J A R Toller) *t.k.h early: chsd ldrs tl hrd drvn over 2f out: sn wknd* **100/1**

15 *nk* **Nutkin** 3-8-12 0 .... JamieSpencer 8 — 39
(J R Fanshawe) *stdd s: a wl bhd* **16/1**

0060 **16** *5* **Feeling Peckish (USA)**[15] 3244 3-8-12 31 .... RussellKennemore(5) 7 — 33
(M C Chapman) *t.k.h and prom early: struggling bdly 1/2-way: t.o* **100/1**

4-0 **17** *5* **Bonne D'Argent (IRE)**[27] 2878 3-8-12 0 .... AmirQuinn 4 — 16
(J R Boyle) *prom tl fdd qckly wl over 1f out: racd awkwardly and eased: t.o* **66/1**

1m 40.64s (0.21) **Going Correction** 0.0s/f (Good) — **17** Ran SP% **128.9**
Speed ratings (Par 102):98,97,95,94,94 91,90,90,89,88 87,87,87,81,81 76,71
CSF £29.33 TOTE £2.70: £1.30, £6.30, £8.80; EX 49.30.
Owner Ballymacoll Stud **Bred** Ballymacoll Stud Farm Ltd **Trained** Newmarket, Suffolk

FOCUS
Plenty of high-profile connections and this looked a good maiden, but the fifth home, rated just 66, tempers the enthusiasm somewhat. They raced down the middle for much of the way, before tending to edge towards the stands' rail late on.

3711 ANTICA CLASSIC SAMBUCA H'CAP — 1m

8:50 (8:51) (Class 5) (0-75,74) 4-Y-0+

£3,886 (£1,156; £577; £288) **Stalls** High

Form — RPR

40-0 **1** **Archiestown (USA)**[21] 3060 4-9-6 **71** .... EddieAhern 18 — 80
(J L Dunlop) *racd stands' side: prom: chsd ldr over 2f out: rdn over 1f out: styd on to ld nr fin* **20/1**

6000 **2** *½* **Rain Stops Play (IRE)**[27] 2891 5-9-8 **73** .... FrancisNorton 14 — 81
(M Quinn) *racd stands' side: overall ldr tl ins fnl f: styd on: 2nd of 5 in gp* **10/1**

4-44 **3** *¾* **Mitanni (USA)**[22] 3042 4-9-1 **66** .... (b[1]) JimCrowley 7 — 72+
(Mrs A J Perrett) *racd far side: prom: led that gp over 2f out: rdn to ld overall ins fnl f: hdd nr fin: 1st of 9 in gp* **10/1**

0003 **4** *½* **Sonny Parkin**[21] 3056 5-9-8 **73** .... (v) AdamKirby 15 — 78
(G A Huffer) *racd stands' side: hld up: hdwy over 1f out: styd on: 3rd of 5 in gp* **7/1**

0015 **5** *3 ½* **Out For A Stroll**[20] 3101 8-8-2 **60** .... FLenclud(7) 20 — 57
(S C Williams) *chsd ldr stands' side over 5f: hung lft and wknd ins fnl f: 4th of 5 in gp* **12/1**

0255 **6** *1 ¾* **Call My Bluff (FR)**[12] 3352 4-9-0 **65** .... NCallan 19 — 58
(Rae Guest) *racd stands' side: hld up: hdwy u.p over 1f out: hmpd and wknd ins fnl f: last of 5 in gp* **7/1**

365 **7** *½* **Ionian**[26] 2913 4-9-5 **70** .... DaneO'Neill 11 — 62
(Pat Eddery) *racd far side: chsd ldrs: rdn and ev ch over 2f out: wknd fnl f: 2nd of 9 in gp* **20/1**

4200 **8** *1 ¼* **Spinning**[18] 3161 4-8-13 **64** .... RyanMoore 9 — 53
(T D Barron) *racd far side: prom: lost pl over 4f out: n.d after: 3rd of 9 in gp* **10/1**

0201 **9** *1 ¼* **Surwaki (USA)**[15] 3241 5-9-9 **74** .... JamieSpencer 16 — 60
(R M H Cowell) *racd far side: led that gp over 3f: remained handy tl rdn and wknd over 1f out: 4th of 9 in gp* **11/2**[1]

-614 **10** *shd* **Colinca's Lad (IRE)**[21] 3048 5-8-12 **68** .... PJMcDonald(5) 17 — 54
(T T Clement) *racd far side: chsd ldrs: led that side over 4f out: hdd over 3f out: wknd 2f out: 5th of 9 in gp* **13/2**[3]

00-5 **11** *1 ¼* **Pirouetting**[38] 2527 4-9-7 **72** .... MichaelHills 6 — 55
(B W Hills) *racd far side: chsd ldrs: rdn and ev ch over 2f out: wknd over 1f out: 6th of 9 in gp* **14/1**

1164 **12** *¾* **Im Ova Ere Dad (IRE)**[23] 2990 4-9-0 **65** .... RichardHughes 12 — 46
(D E Cantillon) *racd far side: trckd ldrs: led that side over 3f out: hdd over 2f out: wknd over 1f out: 7th of 9 in gp* **6/1**[2]

4420 **13** *nk* **Arctic Desert**[97] 1036 7-8-13 **67** .... (t) JerryO'Dwyer(3) 1 — 48
(Miss Gay Kelleway) *racd far side: dwlt: hld up: rdn over 2f out: sn wknd: 8th of 9 in gp* **20/1**

0001 **14** *1 ¾* **Magical Music**[18] 3161 4-8-11 **62** .... JimmyQuinn 8 — 38
(J Pearce) *racd far side: hld up: hdwy over 2f out: wknd over 1f out: last of 9 in gp* **12/1**

1m 40.11s (-0.32) **Going Correction** 0.0s/f (Good) — **14** Ran SP% **131.6**
Speed ratings (Par 103):101,100,99,99,95 94,93,92,91,90 89,88,88,86
CSF £220.79 CT £2193.85 TOTE £34.90: £9.10, £3.30, £4.00; EX 225.60 Place 6 £365.79, Place 5 £98.98.
Owner D K Thorpe (Susan Abbott Racing) **Bred** N Cole & Charles Kidder **Trained** Arundel, W Sussex

FOCUS
Having been all over the place through the first furlong or two, the field eventually split into two groups and those that raced in the smaller group towards the stands' side looked to be at an advantage. This looked a fair handicap, but the form probably wants treating with some caution.
Archiestown(USA) Official explanation: trainer said he had no explanation for the apparent improvement in form
Surwaki(USA) Official explanation: jockey said gelding stopped quickly
Im Ova Ere Dad(IRE) Official explanation: jockey said gelding stopped quickly

T/Jkpt: Not won. T/Plt: £815.70 to a £1 stake. Pool: £86,772.80. 77.65 winning tickets. T/Qpdt: £15.70 to a £1 stake. Pool: £6,116.60. 287.50 winning tickets. CR

3465 NOTTINGHAM (L-H)
Friday, July 20

OFFICIAL GOING: Heavy (soft in places in back straight; 6.1) (abandoned after race 4 (3.55) due to torrential rain)

Heavy rain arrived before the start and it was just a question of time before a halt was called. The outside rail up the home straight was moved in 15 yards.
Weather: Persistent heavy rain

3712 EUROPEAN BREEDERS' FUND MAIDEN STKS — 6f 15y
2:15 (2:19) (Class 5) 2-Y-O — £3,562 (£1,059; £529; £264) Stalls Low

Form — RPR

3 **1** **Exhibition (IRE)**[9] [3435] 2-9-3 0 .... JamieSpencer 3 — 81+
(N A Callaghan) *trckd ldrs: shkn up to ld 2f out: hung lft: kpt on wl* **4/7**[1]

3232 **2** 2 **Rub Of The Relic (IRE)**[12] [3341] 2-9-3 0 .... TPO'Shea 10 — 75
(P A Blockley) *chsd ldrs: kpt on to take 2nd nr fin* **6/1**[3]

362 **3** ½ **Lake Sabina**[39] [2504] 2-8-12 0 .... RichardMullen 5 — 69
(E S McMahon) *led tl 2f out: wkng whn hmpd 1f out: lost 2nd nr line* **5/1**[2]

00 **4** nk **Indian Days**[25] [2941] 2-9-3 0 .... TPQueally 7 — 73
(J G Given) *chsd ldrs: sn drvn along: kpt on same pce fnl 2f* **20/1**

5 11 **Jonny Lesters Hair (IRE)** 2-9-3 0 .... DavidAllan 6 — 40
(T D Easterby) *s.i.s: nvr on terms* **12/1**

0 **6** 1 **Don Picolo**[14] [3283] 2-9-3 0 .... FrankieMcDonald 2 — 37
(P A Blockley) *sn outpcd and in rr* **33/1**

6 **7** ¾ **Sultan Of The Sand**[14] [3283] 2-9-3 0 .... PhillipMakin 8 — 34
(C C Bealby) *chsd ldrs: sn rdn along: lost pl over 2f out* **33/1**

00 **8** 2 **Anabaa's Secret (IRE)**[4] [3596] 2-9-3 0 .... VinceSlattery 1 — 28
(J A Osborne) *outpcd and in rr after 2f* **28/1**

9 1 ¾ **Night Mystery** 2-9-3 0 .... MickyFenton 9 — 23
(T D Easterby) *s.i.s: a bhd* **28/1**

1m 19.44s (4.44) **Going Correction** +0.60s/f (Yiel) — **9** Ran SP% **119.8**
Speed ratings (Par 94):94,91,90,90,75 74,73,70,68
CSF £4.31 TOTE £1.60: £1.10, £1.10, £1.70; EX 4.50.
Owner Mrs J Magnier M Tabor D Smith M Green **Bred** Mrs Mary Rose Hayes **Trained** Newmarket, Suffolk

FOCUS
The winner looked easily the best in the line-up but struggled in the bad conditions. The level seems reasonable, despite a big step up from the fourth.

NOTEBOOK
Exhibition(IRE), who had shown promise in much stronger company on his debut a week earlier, struggled in the bad ground but was firmly in command at the line. (op 8-13 tchd 4-6 in a place)
Rub Of The Relic(IRE) is standing up well to a busy first campaign. He snatched second spot near the line but the winner would most likely have made short work of him in less-testing ground. (tchd 13-2)
Lake Sabina showed plenty of toe but tired in the very testing conditions. She looked second best on the day.
Indian Days broke on terms this time and kept going all the way to the line. This was a much improved effort and opens up the nursery route for him. (op 25-1)
Jonny Lesters Hair(IRE), up in the air and narrow, was nibbled at on his debut but he was never a factor. (op 18-1)

3713 TURFTV.CO.UK H'CAP — 6f 15y
2:50 (2:51) (Class 5) (0-70,69) 3-Y-O — £2,914 (£867; £433; £216) Stalls Low

Form — RPR

-004 **1** **Charlie Tipple**[27] [2892] 3-9-3 **65** .... MickyFenton 12 — 78
(T D Easterby) *dwlt: sn chsng ldrs: led over 1f out: drvn clr* **13/2**

0052 **2** 4 **Prince Rossi (IRE)**[9] [3411] 3-8-9 **57** .... (p) PaulFessey 10 — 58
(J D Bethell) *led tl over 1f out: kpt on same pce* **11/2**[3]

0050 **3** 3 **Aaron's Way**[11] [3369] 3-9-1 **63** .... JamesDoyle 9 — 55
(A W Carroll) *t.k.h in rr: bmpd after 1f: hdwy on outside 3f out: sn chsng 1st 2: one pce fnl 2f* **10/1**

5631 **4** 2 ½ **Exit Strategy (IRE)**[12] [3342] 3-9-1 **63** 6ex .... (b) JamieSpencer 2 — 48
(R A Harris) *mid-div: hmpd on inner over 4f out: kpt on fnl 2f: nvr a threat* **11/4**[1]

-221 **5** 1 ¾ **Excessive**[22] [3031] 3-9-2 **64** .... KerrinMcEvoy 5 — 43
(W Jarvis) *in rr whn n.m.r over 4f out: kpt on fnl 2f: nvr a factor* **7/2**[2]

6060 **6** 1 **Avoncreek**[46] [2300] 3-8-2 **50** oh1 .... RoystonFfrench 1 — 26
(B P J Baugh) *chsd ldrs: wknd over 1f out* **33/1**

0164 **7** 4 **Totally Free**[25] [2948] 3-8-8 **61** ow1 .... (v) TravisBlock(5) 4 — 25
(M D I Usher) *prom: lost pl over 2f out* **14/1**

0043 **8** 8 **Cornerstone**[31] [2750] 3-8-3 **51** oh5 ow1 .... (b) SaleemGolam 8 — —
(S C Williams) *chsd ldrs: hmpd after 1f: lost pl over 2f out* **11/2**[3]

5-00 **9** 11 **Mootamaress (IRE)**[59] [1923] 3-9-7 **69** .... VinceSlattery 7 — —
(Mrs A L M King) *t.k.h: wandered 1st 2f: sn lost pl: bhd fnl 2f* **25/1**

1m 19.26s (4.26) **Going Correction** +0.725s/f (Yiel) — **9** Ran SP% **115.5**
Speed ratings (Par 100):100,94,90,87,85 83,78,67,53
CSF £42.08 CT £286.45 TOTE £7.80: £1.90, £1.90, £2.90; EX 38.30.
Owner Norman Jackson **Bred** P Wyatt And Ranby Hall **Trained** Great Habton, N Yorks

FOCUS
A modest handicap but doubtful form despite the winner being back to his very best. There was plenty of bumping and barging towards the rear in the first two furlongs.

3714 TURFTV BETTING SHOP SERVICE (S) STKS — 1m 1f 213y
3:20 (3:21) (Class 6) 3-Y-O+ — £2,388 (£705; £352) Stalls Low

Form — RPR

0400 **1** **Giddywell**[37] [2579] 3-8-4 55 .... PaulEddery 14 — 54
(R Hollinshead) *chsd ldrs: wnt 2nd over 3f out: led over 2f out: clr over 1f out: shkn up ins fnl f: rdn out: jst hld on* **15/2**

0330 **2** hd **Ruby Legend**[28] [2843] 9-9-5 55 .... (b) JamieSpencer 6 — 59
(K G Reveley) *in rr: hdwy over 3f out: wnt 6 l 2nd over 1f out: styd on wl towards fin: jst failed* **6/1**

/00- **3** 11 **Travelling Band (IRE)**[426] [1422] 9-9-5 55 .... (p) RoystonFfrench 16 — 37
(J Mackie) *chsd ldrs: wnt 2nd over 2f out: wknd over 1f out* **10/1**

0603 **4** 5 **The City Kid (IRE)**[9] [3428] 4-9-5 55 .... (v) TPQueally 9 — 27
(C R Dore) *sn pushed along in rr: hdwy over 3f out: nvr on terms* **5/1**[3]

-406 **5** 5 **Viable**[53] [2084] 5-9-5 55 .... MickyFenton 3 — 17
(Mrs P Sly) *led after 1f: hdd over 2f out: sn wknd* **3/1**[1]

0003 **6** 4 **Jiminor Mack**[29] [2795] 4-8-11 45 .... (b) AndrewMullen(3) 2 — 4
(W J H Ratcliffe) *s.i.s: nvr on terms* **9/2**[2]

5400 **7** 8 **Alloro**[33] [2697] 3-8-9 49 .... StephenDonohoe 7 — —
(D J S Ffrench Davis) *mid-div: drvn over 3f out: sn lost pl* **9/1**

0563 **8** 3 ½ **Kirkhammerton (IRE)**[15] [3241] 5-9-5 48 .... (b) DavidAllan 15 — —
(A J McCabe) *led 1f: chsd ldr: wknd over 3f out* **8/1**

3000 **9** 5 **Rose Muwasim**[29] [2795] 4-8-11 43 .... (v) DominicFox(3) 4 — —
(S Parr) *s.s: a in rr* **28/1**

000- **10** 4 **Marryl**[359] [3831] 3-8-9 35 .... PaulMulrennan 10 — —
(M W Easterby) *chsd ldrs: reminders over 5f out: stmbld on bnd over 4f out: sn lost pl* **40/1**

4000 **11** nk **Mi Odds**[59] [1934] 11-8-12 30 .... KellyHarrison(7) 12 — —
(Mrs N Macauley) *mid-div: sn drvn along: lost pl over 3f out* **33/1**

2m 21.59s (11.89) **Going Correction** +1.225s/f (Soft)
WFA 3 from 4yo+ 10lb — **11** Ran SP% **124.9**
Speed ratings (Par 101):101,100,92,88,84 80,74,71,67,64 64
CSF £54.68 TOTE £12.30: £3.80, £2.00, £3.20; EX 67.80.There was no bid for the winner
Owner The Giddy Gang **Bred** R Hollinshead **Trained** Upper Longdon, Staffs

FOCUS
A weak seller and the winner was fully entitled to take this with the form rated through the runner-up to this year's mark.

3715 GOLDER ASSOCIATES H'CAP — 1m 54y
3:55 (3:55) (Class 4) (0-85,85) 3-Y-O+ — £5,608 (£1,679; £839; £420) Stalls Centre

Form — RPR

4-11 **1** **Mutajarred**[7] [3514] 3-9-4 **84** 6ex .... RHills 3 — 105+
(W J Haggas) *trckd ldr: led over 3f out: shkn up and wnt clr appr fnl f: easily* **4/9**[1]

0426 **2** 6 **Mezuzah**[6] [3559] 7-9-13 **85** .... PaulMulrennan 4 — 89
(M W Easterby) *hld up in last but wl in tch: effrt over 2f out: wnt 2nd over 1f out: no ch w wnr* **5/1**[2]

1251 **3** 1 ½ **Indian's Feather (IRE)**[15] [3247] 6-9-4 **76** .... KDarley 5 — 77
(N Tinkler) *trckd ldrs: chal over 2f out: kpt on same pce* **5/1**[2]

0060 **4** 34 **Akram (IRE)**[15] [3234] 5-9-3 **75** .... (t) JamieSpencer 2 — 8
(Jonjo O'Neill) *led: hdd over 3f out: lost pl and eased over 1f out: virtually p.u* **20/1**[3]

1m 59.97s (13.57) **Going Correction** +1.825s/f (Heav)
WFA 3 from 4yo+ 8lb — **4** Ran SP% **107.3**
Speed ratings (Par 105):105,99,97,63
CSF £2.99 TOTE £1.50; EX 3.10 Place 6 £ 24.51, Place 5 £ 21.76.
Owner Hamdan Al Maktoum **Bred** Floors Farming & Beckhampton Stables Ltd **Trained** Newmarket, Suffolk

FOCUS
A steady gallop in the ever-deteriorating conditions and in the end a very easy winner who will have a lot more on his plate in future. The runner-up sets the standard.

3716 JOHN SMITH'S MAIDEN FILLIES' STKS — 1m 1f 213y
() (Class 5) 3-Y-O — £

3717 TURFTV A MATTER OF COURSE H'CAP — 1m 54y
() (Class 6) (0-60,) 3-Y-O+ — £

T/Plt: £16.10 to a £1 stake. Pool £82,133. 3,719.40 winning tickets T/Qpdt: £5.00 to a £1 stake. Pool £5,370.00. 784.10 winning tickets WG

3398 PONTEFRACT (L-H)
Friday, July 20

OFFICIAL GOING: Soft

Conditions worsened through the evening.
Wind: Moderate, half against Weather: Raining

3718 CORAL BET BY FREEPHONE 0800 242 232 MAIDEN AUCTION STKS — 6f
6:35 (6:35) (Class 4) 2-Y-O — £4,533 (£1,348; £674; £336) Stalls Low

Form — RPR

34 **1** **Let Us Prey**[7] [3504] 2-9-2 0 .... StephenDonohoe 12 — 91+
(N A Callaghan) *midfield: stdy hdwy to trck ldrs over 2f out: effrt over 1f out: sn swtchd rt and rdn: styd on strly to ld wl ins fnl f* **4/6**[1]

2 1 ¼ **Kiwi Bay** 2-8-9 0 .... PhillipMakin 5 — 77
(M Dods) *trckd ldrs: hdwy over 2f out: rdn to chal over 1f out and ev ch tl drvn and nt qckn ins fnl f* **33/1**

43 **3** nk **In Honour (IRE)**[77] [1454] 2-8-13 0 .... RichardMullen 7 — 80
(E S McMahon) *led: rdn along 2f out: drvn over 1f out: hdd and no ex ins fnl f* **7/1**[2]

4 6 **Thompsons Walls (IRE)** 2-9-2 0 .... LeeEnstone 17 — 65
(P C Haslam) *in tch on outer: hdwy over 2f out: sn rdn and styd on appr fnl f* **50/1**

0 **5** 1 **Bourbon Highball (IRE)**[58] [1938] 2-8-11 0 .... KDarley 4 — 57
(P C Haslam) *towards rr: hdwy over 2f out: styd on fnl f: nrst fin* **33/1**

6 1 ¼ **Marlena (IRE)** 2-8-7 0 ow1 .... DavidAllan 3 — 50
(T D Easterby) *dwlt: in rr tl hdwy over 2f out: rdn and styd on wl appr fnl f: nrst fin* **50/1**

4 **7** nk **Miss Solo**[20] [3092] 2-8-5 0 .... AndrewElliott(3) 1 — 50
(P C Haslam) *chsd ldrs: rdn along over 2f out: kpt on same pce* **11/1**[3]

8 1 **Highland Love** 2-8-11 0 .... PaulMulrennan 2 — 50
(Jedd O'Keeffe) *in tch on inner: rdn along 2f out: sn no imp* **100/1**

40 **9** 2 **Personal Choice**[22] [3024] 2-7-13 0 ow2 .... PatrickDonaghy(7) 8 — 39
(M Brittain) *prom: rdn along over 2f out: sn drvn and wknd over 1f out* **80/1**

02 **10** 1 ¼ **Her Name Is Rio (IRE)**[18] [3152] 2-8-4 0 .... AdrianMcCarthy 15 — 33
(J S Moore) *chsd ldrs on outer: rdn along 1/2-way: grad wknd* **12/1**

11 nk **Hasty Lady** 2-8-5 0 .... AndrewMullen(3) 16 — 36
(K A Ryan) *dwlt: a towards rr* **16/1**

12 2 **Trip The Light** 2-8-11 0 .... PaulHanagan 9 — 33
(R A Fahey) *in tch: rdn along over 2f out and grad wknd* **33/1**

13 5 **Sand Maiden (IRE)** 2-8-1 0 .... DuranFentiman(3) 14 — 11
(T D Easterby) *dwlt and a towards rr* **100/1**

14 1 ½ **Honeycott (IRE)** 2-8-8 0 ow2 .... TomEaves 10 — 11
(J D Bethell) *s.i.s: a in rr* **100/1**

15 shd **Sistos Fascination** 2-8-13 0 .... GregFairley(3) 13 — 18
(M Botti) *chsd ldrs towards outer: rdn along 3f out and grad wknd* **28/1**

16 3 ½ **Castlebury (IRE)** 2-8-11 0 .... PatCosgrave 6 — 3
(G A Swinbank) *a towards rr* **33/1**

1m 21.11s (3.71) **Going Correction** +0.525s/f (Yiel) — **16** Ran SP% **117.7**
Speed ratings (Par 96):96,94,93,85,84 82,82,81,78,76 76,73,67,65,65 60
CSF £37.40 TOTE £1.70: £1.30, £7.70, £2.10; EX 44.90.
Owner SP Racing Investments S A **Bred** Plantation Stud **Trained** Newmarket, Suffolk
■ Stewards' Enquiry : Richard Mullen one-day ban: not riding to draw (Jul 31)

FOCUS
No real strength in depth here and the first three came clear. The winner did not have to run near to his previous best to score.

NOTEBOOK

Let Us Prey, fourth at Newmarket in the Group 2 Superlative Stakes a week previously, did not have to run up to that form to score here and duly opened his account at the third attempt. He coped well with the softer ground, which helped to negate the drop back in trip, and was well on top at the finish. 7f looks to be his optimum trip at present, but 1m should be well within his compass before the season's end, and a step back up in grade now looks on the cards. (op 8-11 tchd 8-13)

Kiwi Bay ◆, half-brother to a 7f juvenile winner, posted a very pleasing debut effort and held every chance. Not surprisingly he lacked the speed of the winner inside the final furlong, but he acted without fuss on the deep surface and looks a sure-fire winner of a similar event in the coming weeks.

In Honour(IRE), returning from a 77-day break, had his chance from the front and only gave way to the first pair entering the final furlong. He should get this trip without much fuss before the season is out, but he may just be better off reverting to 5f while the ground remains soft. He now also has the option of nurseries. Official explanation: one-day ban: failed to ride to draw (Jul 31) (op 9-1)

Thompsons Walls(IRE), bred to make his mark over this sort of distance as a juvenile, shaped with a degree of promise and left the impression he would come on a deal for this debut run. A sounder surface may be more to his liking. (op 33-1)

Bourbon Highball(IRE), last of eight on his debut in May, showed improved form and looks to have benefited from his break. He appeals as much more of a nursery type and should enjoy another furlong before too long. (op 40-1)

3719 TOTESPORT.COM FILLIES' H'CAP — 1m 4f 8y

7:05 (7:05) (Class 5) (0-75,78) 3-Y-0+ — **£4,533** (£1,348; £674; £336) **Stalls** Low

Form — RPR

2026 **1** **Its Moon (IRE)**[21] 3058 3-8-8 **67** .... KDarley 5 — 76
(T D Walford) *in tch: pushed along over 3f out: hdwy 2f out: swtchd outside and rdn ent fnl f: styd on to ld last 100yds: sn clr* — **6/1**

0101 **2** 2 ½ **Prelude**[7] 3496 6-8-11 **61** 6ex .... LiamJones(3) 2 — 66
(W M Brisbourne) *led: jnd and rdn along 3f out: hdd 2f out: drvn and rallied to ld ent fnl f: hdd and no ex last 100yds* — **9/2**[2]

-201 **3** 5 **Hypoteneuse (IRE)**[11] 3367 3-9-5 **78** 6ex .... TomEaves 6 — 76
(Sir Michael Stoute) *trckd ldng pair: smooth hdwy on inner to ld 2f out: sn rdn and hdd wl over 1f out: wknd ent fnl f* — **3/1**[1]

5342 **4** ½ **Music Review**[11] 3379 3-8-6 **65** .... PaulHanagan 7 — 62
(R A Fahey) *in tch: rdn along and outpcd over 4f out: swtchd ins and drvn over 1f out: kpt on ins fnl f* — **5/1**[3]

354- **5** shd **Blushing Hilary (IRE)**[284] 5875 4-9-4 **65** .... PaulMulrennan 4 — 62
(Miss J A Camacho) *hld up in tch: effrt 3f out and sn rdn along: drvn and plugged on same pce* — **22/1**

4112 **6** 2 ½ **Charlotte Vale**[7] 3501 6-9-11 **75** .... GregFairley(3) 8 — 69
(Micky Hammond) *trckd ldr: effrt to chal 3f out: sn rdn and wknd wl over 1f out* — **6/1**

1445 **7** 1 ½ **Saluscraggie**[4] 3584 5-8-10 **57** oh3 ....(p) DavidAllan 3 — 49
(K G Reveley) *hld up: a in rr* — **9/1**

0614 **8** 6 **Sudden Impulse**[14] 3260 6-9-7 **68** .... SilvestreDeSousa 1 — 51
(A D Brown) *hld up in tch: hdwy 4f out: rdn along over 2f out and sn btn* — **10/1**

2m 48.11s (7.81) **Going Correction** +0.75s/f (Yiel)
WFA 3 from 4yo+ 12lb — 8 Ran SP% **111.9**
Speed ratings (Par 100):103,101,98,97,97 95,94,90
CSF £31.57 CT £94.96 TOTE £7.70: £1.90, £1.80, £1.60; EX 53.00.
Owner Jaass One Racing **Bred** Darley **Trained** Sheriff Hutton, N Yorks

FOCUS
A modest fillies' handicap, run at a sound pace in the deep ground and rated through the runner-up to recent form.

3720 ANTONIA DEUTERS H'CAP — 5f

7:35 (7:35) (Class 3) (0-90,90) 3-Y-0+

£11,217 (£3,358; £1,679; £840; £419; £210) **Stalls** Low

Form — RPR

6-22 **1** **Final Dynasty**[12] 3344 3-9-4 **87** .... PaulHanagan 8 — 98
(Mrs G S Rees) *trckd ldrs: hdwy wl over 1f out: rdn to ld ins fnl f: sn drvn: edgd lft and kpt on wl* — **10/1**

6250 **2** ¾ **Namir (IRE)**[13] 3298 5-8-7 **75** ....(vt) DuranFentiman(3) 13 — 83+
(D Shaw) *towards rr: hdwy 2f out: rdn over 1f out: styd on strly ins fnl f* — **20/1**

0005 **3** 2 **Mr Wolf**[10] 3401 6-9-9 **88** ....(p) TomEaves 2 — 89
(D W Barker) *led: rdn wl over 1f out: drvn and hdd ins fnl f: kpt on u.p* — **11/2**[2]

0601 **4** hd **Glasshoughton**[13] 3298 4-8-11 **76** .... PhillipMakin 10 — 76
(M Dods) *hld up in tch: hdwy 2f out: rdn to chse ldrs over 1f out: kpt on ins fnl f* — **8/1**[3]

2326 **5** 1 ½ **Coconut Moon**[12] 3344 5-8-7 **72** .... DavidAllan 7 — 67
(E J Alston) *cl up: rdn and ev ch over 1f out tl drvn and wknd ins fnl f* **12/1**

0000 **6** nk **Geojimali**[28] 2841 5-9-4 **83** .... SaleemGolam 11 — 77
(J S Goldie) *dwlt and sn outpcd in rr: rdn along 1/2-way: hdwy over 1f out: styd on strly ins fnl f: nrst fin* — **14/1**

0003 **7** nk **Indian Trail**[7] 3481 7-9-11 **90** ....(v) AdrianTNicholls 9 — 83
(D Nicholls) *hld up: gd hdwy 1/2-way: chsd ldrs 2f out: sn rdn and one pce fnl f* — **9/1**

0443 **8** ¾ **Bo McGinty (IRE)**[6] 3557 6-8-6 **76** ow1 ....(b) JamieMoriarty(3) 12 — 66
(R A Fahey) *chsd ldrs on outer: rdn along 1/2-way and sn wknd* — **14/1**

0401 **9** ½ **Highland Warrior**[7] 3515 8-9-4 **83** 6ex .... MickyFenton 6 — 71
(P T Midgley) *a towards rr* — **14/1**

1112 **10** 1 **Off The Record**[9] 3431 3-9-6 **89** .... TPQueally 4 — 73
(J G Given) *chsd ldrs: rdn along over 2f out: sn drvn and wknd* — **6/4**[1]

2-00 **11** 1 ¾ **Inter Vision (USA)**[7] 3515 7-9-5 **89** .... MichaelJStainton(5) 3 — 67
(A Dickman) *a in rr* — **50/1**

1006 **12** 9 **Colorus (IRE)**[17] 3197 4-8-10 **75** .... DaleGibson 1 — 21
(M W Easterby) *chsd ldrs: rdn along 2f out: sn drvn and wknd: eased fnl f* — **50/1**

67.42 secs (3.62) **Going Correction** +0.95s/f (Soft)
WFA 3 from 4yo+ 4lb — 12 Ran SP% **122.0**
Speed ratings (Par 107):109,107,104,104,101 101,100,99,98,97 94,80
CSF £197.98 CT £1235.40 TOTE £14.20: £3.40, £6.70, £2.10; EX 440.40.
Owner TBN Racing **Bred** Capt J H Wilson **Trained** Sollom, Lancs
■ Stewards' Enquiry : Duran Fentiman one-day ban: used whip with excessive frequency (Jul 31)

FOCUS
A decent sprint for the class. The first pair came clear and the form looks sound rated through the placed horses.

NOTEBOOK

Final Dynasty, a runner-up on both his previous outings this term, ran out a most deserving winner on this return to handicap company. This was her last opportunity to race from this mark, as she was already due to go up 12lb in the future and, while she is a relatively lightly-raced filly, her life is obviously going to be plenty tougher now. (op 8-1)

Namir(IRE) enjoyed this return to a track he does go well at and was doing some decent late work from his wide draw. He really deserves to go one better again and could well do so when returning to a sounder surface, but will probably go up a few pounds again for this. (op 16-1)

Mr Wolf, back down in trip, is another who does go really well at this venue and he did nothing wrong from the front. He ran very close to his official mark in defeat and is a decent benchmark for the form. (op 5-1 tchd 6-1)

Glasshoughton, 7lb higher, performed with credit from his double-figure stall and probably ran right up to his new mark in defeat. He does enjoy this ground. (tchd 17-2)

Geojimali got going all too late after a sluggish start and can be rated a touch better than the bare form. This was his most encouraging effort for a little while.

Indian Trail failed to find much when push came to shove from off the pace and ideally needs a sounder surface. This was no disgrace under top weight. (op 17-2 tchd 8-1)

Off The Record, due to race from a 6lb higher future mark, ran well below his previous level and surely got found out by the soft ground. Official explanation: jockey said colt was unsuited by the soft ground (op 5-2)

3721 COLSTROPE CUP H'CAP — 1m 4y

8:10 (8:10) (Class 5) (0-70,70) 3-Y-0+ — **£4,533** (£1,348; £674; £336) **Stalls** Low

Form — RPR

6155 **1** **Flighty Fellow (IRE)**[27] 2871 7-9-13 **69** ....(b) DavidAllan 2 — 83
(T D Easterby) *in tch: hdwy 3f out: rdn to chse ldr over 1f out: drvn to chal ins fnl f: styd on wl to ld nr fin* — **6/1**[3]

0061 **2** nk **Red Chairman**[7] 3502 5-8-12 **54** 6ex ....(p) AdrianTNicholls 6 — 67
(R Johnson) *led: rdn 2f out: drvn ent fnl f: hdd and no ex towards fin* **6/1**[3]

0-36 **3** 8 **Harry The Hawk**[9] 3411 3-8-10 **60** .... TomEaves 10 — 57
(T D Walford) *chsd ldrs on outer: hdwy 2f out: sn rdn and kpt on ins fnl f* — **8/1**

0040 **4** 1 ¼ **Komreyev Star**[50] 2168 5-8-9 **51** oh2 ....(p) SilvestreDeSousa 5 — 46
(R E Peacock) *in tch: hdwy 3f out: rdn along wl over 1f out: kpt on ins fnl f: nrst fin* — **11/1**

0500 **5** ¾ **Time To Regret**[11] 3376 7-8-13 **55** ....(p) TonyHamilton 11 — 48
(I W McInnes) *chsd ldr: rdn 2f out: drvn over 1f out and grad wknd* **16/1**

0000 **6** 1 ½ **Newcorp Lad**[7] 3497 7-8-6 **51** oh6 .... AndrewElliott(3) 15 — 41
(Mrs G S Rees) *towards rr: hdwy on outer 2f out: sn rdn and styd on ins fnl f* — **25/1**

7 1 **Beaver (AUS)**[428] 8-9-9 **65** .... VinceSlattery 9 — 53
(J G M O'Shea) *bhd tl styd on fnl 2f: nrst fin* — **40/1**

1042 **8** 1 **Society Music (IRE)**[18] 3156 5-9-9 **70** ....(p) NeilBrown(5) 8 — 56
(M Dods) *prom: rdn along 2f out: sn drvn and wknd over 1f out* — **9/2**[1]

006- **9** 6 **Ali D**[261] 6289 9-8-8 **55** .... ColinHaddon(5) 3 — 29
(G Woodward) *bhd: sme hdwy 2f out: sn rdn and nvr a factor* — **16/1**

5540 **10** 8 **Tidy (IRE)**[10] 3403 7-9-5 **61** ....(p) PatCosgrave 16 — 19
(Micky Hammond) *towards rr: rdn along 1/2-way: nvr a factor* — **11/1**

6000 **11** 3 ½ **Blue Bird's Dream**[5] 3571 4-9-1 **57** .... StephenDonohoe 12 — 8
(E J Alston) *chsd ldrs: rdn along 1/2-way: sn wknd* — **33/1**

3010 **12** 2 **Steel Grey**[85] 1260 6-8-2 **51** oh2 .... PatrickDonaghy(7) 7 — —
(M Brittain) *s.i.s: a bhd* — **33/1**

5604 **13** 14 **Thunderwing (IRE)**[18] 3155 5-9-2 **58** .... PaulHanagan 14 — —
(K R Burke) *in tch: rdn along over 3f out and sn wknd* — **11/2**[2]

0-56 **14** 10 **Moving Story**[29] 2795 4-8-9 **51** oh4 .... MickyFenton 4 — —
(P T Midgley) *chsd ldrs on inner: rdn along 3f out and sn wknd* — **9/1**

1m 52.44s (6.74) **Going Correction** +0.95s/f (Soft)
WFA 3 from 4yo+ 8lb — 14 Ran SP% **123.8**
Speed ratings (Par 103):104,103,95,94,93 92,91,90,84,76 72,70,56,46
CSF £41.78 CT £307.15 TOTE £5.80: £2.50, £2.50, £2.60; EX 44.10.
Owner David W Armstrong **Bred** F Hinojosa **Trained** Great Habton, N Yorks

FOCUS
A typically moderate handicap for the grade. The first pair came well clear and the form in behind looks suspect.

Society Music(IRE) Official explanation: trainer said mare was unsuited by the soft ground
Thunderwing(IRE) Official explanation: jockey said gelding hung left
Moving Story Official explanation: trainer said gelding was unsuited by the soft ground

3722 FRONTLINE BATHROOMS MAIDEN H'CAP — 1m 2f 6y

8:40 (8:41) (Class 5) (0-70,70) 3-Y-0+ — **£3,238** (£963; £481; £240) **Stalls** Low

Form — RPR

0502 **1** **Silca Key**[9] 3429 3-9-4 **65** .... TPO'Shea 13 — 74
(M R Channon) *in tch: hdwy to chse ldrs 3f out: rdn 2f out: drvn ent fnl f: styd on to ld last 75yds* — **9/2**[3]

0-63 **2** 1 ¼ **Fire In Cairo (IRE)**[164] 373 3-8-2 **49** .... DaleGibson 8 — 55
(P C Haslam) *in tch: hdwy on outer 3f out: rdn 2f out: styd on u.p to chal over 1f out and ev ch tl drvn and no ex last 100yds* — **25/1**

03-3 **3** hd **Monsoon Wedding**[76] 1479 3-9-4 **68** .... GregFairley(3) 2 — 74
(M Johnston) *prom: led over 3f out: rdn 2f out: drvn over 1f out: edgd lft ins fnl f: hdd and no ex last 75yds* — **4/1**[2]

22-0 **4** 5 **Lord Oroko**[186] 141 3-9-9 **70** .... VinceSlattery 5 — 66
(J G M O'Shea) *bhd: hdwy over 3f out: rdn 2f out: styd on wl fnl f: nrst fin* — **22/1**

-003 **5** nk **Moment Of Clarity**[10] 3403 5-8-10 **47** .... PaulEddery 7 — 42
(R C Guest) *in tch: hdwy to trck ldrs 3f out: rdn to chse ldr wl over 1f out and ev ch tl drvn and wknd ent fnl f* — **9/1**

3223 **6** 9 **Sofie Tucker**[29] 2792 3-9-4 **65** .... DavidAllan 1 — 42
(T D Easterby) *hld up: hdwy on inner 3f out: rdn 2f out: sn drvn and no imp* — **10/1**

50-6 **7** 11 **Petito (IRE)**[18] 3165 4-9-12 **63** .... StephenDonohoe 12 — 18
(J L Spearing) *hld up: gd hdwy 5f out: chal 3f out: sn rdn and wknd wl over 1f out* — **11/1**

6500 **8** 25 **Waterloo Corner**[16] 3204 5-9-4 **55** .... PaulHanagan 16 — —
(R Craggs) *prom: effrt to ld over 4f out: rdn and hdd over 3f out: sn wknd* — **25/1**

0432 **9** 13 **Falimar**[46] 2299 3-9-1 **62** ....(p) PaulMulrennan 6 — —
(Miss J A Camacho) *sson led: pushed along and hdd over 4f out: sn rdn and wknd* — **9/1**

5006 **10** 4 **Wulimaster (USA)**[10] 3403 4-10-0 **65** ....(v) PatCosgrave 15 — —
(D W Barker) *a towards rr* — **16/1**

24-4 **11** 2 **Hurricane Thomas (IRE)**[7] 3502 3-9-9 **70** .... KDarley 3 — —
(M Johnston) *sn pushed along in rr: rn in snatches: hdwy on outer and in tch 1/2-way: drvn and wknd 3f out: sn eased* — **3/1**[1]

-600 **12** ½ **Grand Dream (IRE)**[10] 3400 3-8-13 **60** .... TPQueally 10 — —
(J G Given) *prom: rdn along 4f out and sn wknd* — **28/1**

2m 25.4s (11.32) **Going Correction** +0.95s/f (Soft)
WFA 3 from 4yo+ 10lb — 12 Ran SP% **122.0**
Speed ratings (Par 103):92,91,90,86,86 79,70,50,40,37 35,35
CSF £120.75 CT £497.55 TOTE £5.50: £2.30, £7.50, £2.00; EX 147.90.
Owner Aldridge Racing Partnership **Bred** Genesis Green Stud Ltd **Trained** West Ilsley, Berks
■ Stewards' Enquiry : T P O'Shea two-day ban: used whip with excessive frequency (Jul 31-Aug 1)

FOCUS
A typically weak maiden handicap. The first three were clear at the finish but the form is modest.
Hurricane Thomas(IRE) Official explanation: jockey said gelding lost its action

3723 COUNTRYWIDE FREIGHT H'CAP — 6f
9:10 (9:10) (Class 5) (0-75,75) 3-Y-0+ **£3,886** (£1,156; £577; £288) **Stalls** Low

Form — RPR

3136 **1** **Bid For Gold**[22] 3029 3-8-13 **67** PaulMulrenan 16 — 76
(Jedd O'Keeffe) *in tch: hdwy to chse ldrs 2f out: rdn to chal over 1f out: led jst ins fnl f and sn clr* **12/1**

0424 **2** *3* **Digital**[5] 3572 10-8-8 **57** TPO'Shea 5 — 58
(M R Channon) *hld up: hdwy on inner 2f out: sn rdn and styd on ins fnl f* **4/1**[1]

0040 **3** *1 1/2* **Guest Connections**[31] 2744 4-9-12 **75** (v) AdrianTNicholls 2 — 72
(D Nicholls) *trckd ldrs: hdwy 2f out: rdn to chal wl over 1f out and ev ch tl drvn and one pce ins fnl f* **10/1**

0455 **4** *hd* **Breaking Shadow (IRE)**[5] 3572 5-8-10 **66** DeanHeslop(7) 6 — 62
(M A Peill) *led: rdn along 2f out: jnd and drvn over 1f out: hdd jst ins fnl f and wknd* **4/1**[1]

0010 **5** *2 1/2* **Soto**[22] 3017 4-9-2 **65** DaleGibson 14 — 53
(M W Easterby) *racd wd: cl up: rdn 2f out and ev ch tl wknd appr fnl f* **12/1**

3102 **6** *1/2* **Inca Soldier (FR)**[9] 3414 4-8-7 **56** oh1 PaulEddery 17 — 43
(R C Guest) *trckd ldrs: hdwy 2f out: rdn and ch over 1f out: wknd ins fnl f* **17/2**[3]

3360 **7** *3 1/2* **Brigadore**[10] 3401 8-9-2 **65** TPQueally 9 — 41
(J G Given) *s.i.s: a in rr* **9/2**[2]

2451 **8** *1* **Riquewihr**[7] 3512 7-9-5 **68** 6ex (p) PaddyAspell 11 — 41
(J S Wainwright) *chsd ldrs: effrt 2f out: sn rdn and wknd over 1f out* **9/2**[2]

0-60 **9** *1 1/2* **Swiper Hill (IRE)**[21] 3053 4-9-4 **67** TonyHamilton 4 — 36
(B Ellison) *a in rr* **25/1**

000- **10** *1/2* **Lord Conyers (IRE)**[223] 6756 8-8-2 **56** oh11 ColinHaddon(5) 13 — 23
(G Woodward) *prom: rdn along 1/2-way and sn wknd* **100/1**

1m 22.77s (5.37) **Going Correction** +0.95s/f (Soft)
WFA 3 from 4yo+ 5lb — **10** Ran SP% **116.2**
Speed ratings (Par 103):102,98,96,95,92 91,87,85,83,83
CSF £59.40 CT £521.26 TOTE £16.70: £3.20, £1.60, £3.50; EX 46.00 Place 6 £135.70, Place 5 £110.02.
Owner Paul Chapman And Ba'Tat Investments **Bred** B Minty **Trained** Middleham Moor, N Yorks
FOCUS
A modest sprint handicap. The winner rates value for slightly further than his winning margin.
Inca Soldier(FR) Official explanation: jockey said gelding had no more to give
Brigadore Official explanation: jockey said gelding was unsuited by the soft ground
T/Plt: £143.90 to a £1 stake. Pool: £71,183.50. 361.05 winning tickets. T/Qpdt: £76.30 to a £1 stake. Pool: £4,253.60. 41.20 winning tickets. JR

3567 HAYDOCK (L-H)
Saturday, July 21 (eve)
3724 Meeting Abandoned - Waterlogged

3648 LINGFIELD (L-H)
Saturday, July 21
OFFICIAL GOING: All-weather - standard; turf course - soft (heavy in places)
58mm of rain fell the previous day, 44mm of it in 1 hour, changing the going from the fast side of good. There were many withdrawals from the turf races.
Wind: modest behind Weather: overcast with bright spells

3730 GALLAGHER AGGREGATES (S) STKS — 1m 2f (P)
5:55 (5:55) (Class 6) 3-Y-0+ **£2,047** (£604; £302) **Stalls** Low

Form — RPR

0000 **1** **Takes Tutu (USA)**[38] 2582 8-9-2 48 LiamJones(3) 13 — 61
(C R Dore) *hld up wl bhd: stdy hdwy 4f out: hmpd over 2f out: pushed along over 1f out: led ins fnl f: comf* **9/2**[3]

3-5 **2** *1 1/2* **Scar Tissue**[61] 1901 3-8-4 0 NeilPollard 8 — 53
(Tom Dascombe) *prom: hmpd after 1f: chsd ldrs: rdn and effrt on inner over 2f out: led jst over 1f out: hdd ins fnl f: nt pce of wnr* **9/4**[1]

0106 **3** *1* **Blackmail (USA)**[4] 3617 9-9-11 57 (b) TQuinn 6 — 62
(P Mitchell) *chsd ldrs: hdwy over 3f out: led over 2f out: sn rdn: hdd jst over 1f out: nt qckn* **3/1**[2]

0640 **4** *3 1/2* **Fulvio (USA)**[30] 2798 7-9-5 46 (v) AmirQuinn 14 — 49
(P Howling) *w.w in midfield: hdwy over 4f out: led over 3f out: rdn and hdd over 2f out: wknd over 1f out* **16/1**

0000 **5** *3* **Marbaa (IRE)**[10] 3428 4-9-5 52 ChrisCatlin 12 — 43
(S Dow) *sn pushed along in rr: hdwy on outer 6f out: drvn to chse ldng pair over 2f out: wknd wl over 1f out* **6/1**

0350 **6** *3/4* **Kilmeena Magic**[35] 2656 5-9-0 41 PaulFitzsimons 11 — 37
(J C Fox) *racd in midfield: hdwy over 3f out: rdn over 2f out: sn outpcd* **16/1**

0000 **7** *5* **Rose Muwasim**[1] 3714 4-8-11 43 (v) DominicFox(3) 2 — 27
(S Parr) *s.i.s: hdwy over 4f out: rdn and no prog fr wl over 2f out* **25/1**

2/00 **8** *2 1/2* **Keynes (JPN)**[51] 2176 5-8-12 40 SCreighton(7) 9 — 27
(E J Creighton) *racd in midfield tl lost pl and rdn wl over 4f out: no ch after* **66/1**

00-6 **9** *1 1/4* **Royalties**[50] 2222 5-9-0 38 PaulDoe 1 — 19
(M A Allen) *hld up in midfield: lost pl and rdn over 4f out: no ch after* **66/1**

3540 **10** *2* **Dexileos (IRE)**[11] 3405 8-9-5 45 AdamKirby 10 — 20
(David Pinder) *t.k.h: led for 1f: prom: rdn 3f out: wkng whn hmpd bnd over 2f out: eased ins fnl f* **20/1**

3060 **11** *hd* **Rafferty (IRE)**[10] 3428 8-8-12 48 (p) ThomasBubb(7) 5 — 20
(S Dow) *t.k.h: prom tl wl over 3f out: wkng whn nt clr run 3f out: wl bhd after* **16/1**

0-00 **12** *8* **Tamworth (IRE)**[49] 2258 5-9-2 44 (v) AlanCreighton(3) 7 — 4
(E J Creighton) *led after 1f: clr 7f out: stopped to nil and hdd over 3f out: sn wl bhd: t.o* **33/1**

2m 7.47s (-0.32) **Going Correction** -0.025s/f (Stan)
WFA 3 from 4yo+ 10lb — **12** Ran SP% **120.4**
Speed ratings (Par 101):100,98,98,95,92 92,88,86,85,83 83,77
CSF £14.54 TOTE £6.70: £2.10, £1.40, £1.60; EX 23.60.The winner was bought in for 5,200gns. Scar Tissue was claimed by Edward Creighton for £6,000.

Owner Page, Ward, Marsh **Bred** Harbor View Farm **Trained** West Pinchbeck, Lincs
■ Stewards' Enquiry : Alan Creighton two-day ban: careless riding (Aug 2-3)
FOCUS
An ordinary seller, with two handicappers and a lightly-raced runner in the first three. The form is best rated around the third and fourth.

3731 ALLDERS OF CROYDON FILLIES' H'CAP — 1m 2f (P)
6:30 (6:31) (Class 5) (0-75,75) 3-Y-0+ **£2,817** (£838; £418; £209) **Stalls** Low

Form — RPR

3223 **1** **Ravarino (USA)**[21] 3113 3-9-0 **71** RHills 6 — 85+
(Sir Michael Stoute) *led for 1f: chsd ldr after tl led again wl over 2f out: sn rdn clr: unchal after* **4/1**[1]

321 **2** *1 1/4* **Pivotal Answer (IRE)**[12] 3366 3-9-3 **74** EddieAhern 8 — 85+
(J Noseda) *trckd ldrs: rdn to chse wnr over 2f out: kpt on u.p fnl f* **4/1**[1]

4100 **3** *6* **Lunar River (FR)**[9] 3455 4-9-4 **65** (t) FergusSweeney 11 — 65
(David Pinder) *stdd s: hld up in rr: hdwy to chse ldrs over 2f out: sn outpcd: kpt on u.p to go 3rd ins fnl f* **20/1**

224 **4** *1* **Dolce Dovo**[23] 3015 4-9-8 **72** (b) LiamJones(3) 7 — 70
(W J Haggas) *hld up towards rr: hdwy over 2f out: c v wd 2f out: kpt on: nvr trbld ldrs* **13/2**[3]

0202 **5** *shd* **Iolanthe**[13] 3351 3-8-11 **68** SteveDrowne 9 — 66
(B J Meehan) *hld up towards rr: hdwy wl over 3f out: rdn to chse ldng pair 2f out: sn no ch: lost 2 pls fnl f* **8/1**

1405 **6** *2 1/2* **Nicomedia (IRE)**[22] 3048 3-9-0 **71** (b[1]) RichardHughes 1 — 64
(R Hannon) *t.k.h: trckd ldrs: rdn over 2f out: sltly hmpd jst over 2f out: sn wknd* **11/2**[2]

0-46 **7** *1 1/4* **Noora (IRE)**[24] 2994 6-10-0 **75** (v) AdamKirby 4 — 66
(C G Cox) *s.i.s: hld up in rr: rdn 4f out: no ch last 2f* **9/1**

0162 **8** *1 3/4* **Cavort (IRE)**[34] 2691 3-9-2 **73** RichardMullen 5 — 60
(Pat Eddery) *in tch: rdn over 3f out: wknd over 2f out* **14/1**

0350 **9** *11* **Baldovina**[12] 3367 3-8-7 **64** ow1 (b[1]) JimCrowley 10 — 31
(Tom Dascombe) *led after 1f tl rdn and hdd over 2f out: sn wknd: eased ins fnl f* **25/1**

0021 **10** *77* **Red Current**[11] 3394 3-7-10 **58** LukeMorris(5) 3 — —
(R A Harris) *hld up towards rr: rdn and dropped to rr over 4f out: virtually p.u last 2f* **7/1**

2m 5.18s (-2.61) **Going Correction** -0.025s/f (Stan)
WFA 3 from 4yo+ 10lb — **10** Ran SP% **117.6**
Speed ratings (Par 100):109,108,103,102,102 100,99,97,89,27
CSF £19.56 CT £287.22 TOTE £5.00: £1.80, £2.00, £4.30; EX 14.90.
Owner Gainsborough **Bred** Gainsborough Farm Llc **Trained** Newmarket, Suffolk
FOCUS
A fair handicap in which the first two home looked a cut above the others, with the winner recording a decent time for a race like this, 2.29 seconds quicker than the seller. The form looks sound overall.
Red Current Official explanation: jockey said filly never travelled

3732 GALLAGHER GROUP CLAIMING STKS — 1m (P)
7:00 (7:00) (Class 6) 3-5-Y-0 **£2,047** (£604; £302) **Stalls** High

Form — RPR

6026 **1** **Zelos (IRE)**[10] 3429 3-8-9 63 (b) JimCrowley 6 — 56
(J A Osborne) *hld up: hdwy 3f out: trckd ldrs over 2f out: swtchd lft 1f out: shkn up to ld ins fnl f: pushed out* **5/1**[3]

0056 **2** *2* **Our Herbie**[12] 3384 3-8-12 65 (v[1]) RHills 11 — 54
(J W Hills) *hld up towards rr: hdwy over 3f out: rdn to ld 1f out: hdd ins fnl f: sn btn* **5/2**[2]

000P **3** *3* **Winds Of Kildare (IRE)**[38] 2559 4-8-13 43 (t) RichardMullen 5 — 42
(C N Allen) *chsd ldr tl rdn to ld 2f out: hdd 1f out: no ex* **66/1**

060 **4** *1 1/2* **Miss Invincible**[45] 2360 3-8-4 49 ChrisCatlin 3 — 36
(A P Jarvis) *t.k.h: chsd ldrs: rdn 3f out: kpt on one pce* **20/1**

0020 **5** *5* **High Class Problem (IRE)**[13] 3352 4-9-5 64 (p) TQuinn 7 — 33
(P F I Cole) *led tl rdn and hdd 2f out: wknd qckly over 1f out* **6/1**

6 *1 3/4* **Correy** 3-7-9 0 LukeMorris(5) 1 — 16
(B Palling) *s.i.s: rn green and sn detached: sme modest late hdwy* **40/1**

7 *2* **Lady Bid** 3-7-11 0 LiamJones(3) 12 — 12
(B Palling) *rn green and sn wl outpcd: nvr on terms* **50/1**

0-06 **8** *2 1/2* **Grand Sefton**[4] 3619 4-9-1 52 AmirQuinn 2 — 15
(Stef Liddiard) *hld up towards rr: effrt over 3f: sn struggling: eased ins fnl f* **33/1**

9 *40* **Aaliyah (IRE)**[538] 4-8-7 0 AlanCreighton(3) 4 — —
(E J Creighton) *in tch: tl rdn 5f out: sn bhd: t.o last 2f* **66/1**

1-0 **U** **Shotfire Ridge**[22] 3060 4-9-5 76 OscarUrbina 8 — —
(M Wigham) *hld up in tch: 5th and rdn whn lost action and veered bdly rt unseating rdr over 2f out: dead* **11/8**[1]

1m 38.98s (-0.45) **Going Correction** -0.025s/f (Stan)
WFA 3 from 4yo 8lb — **10** Ran SP% **116.7**
Speed ratings (Par 101):101,99,96,94,89 87,85,83,43,—
CSF £17.14 TOTE £5.60: £1.10, £1.90, £9.10; EX 13.70.
Owner Cavendish Racing **Bred** Dermot Brennan And Associates Ltd **Trained** Upper Lambourn, Berks
FOCUS
A routine claimer, with the first two, neither of whom was particularly favoured by the weights, looking much the best and the form appears weak. The race was marred by the demise of the favourite, who crashed off the track after suffering a fatal heart-attack.
Lady Bid Official explanation: vet said filly had bled from the nose

3733 GALLAGHER PROPERTIES EBF MAIDEN STKS — 7f
7:30 (7:33) (Class 5) 2-Y-0 **£3,562** (£1,059; £529; £264) **Stalls** High

Form — RPR

5 **1** **Safari Sunup (IRE)**[24] 2991 2-9-3 0 JimCrowley 4 — 75
(P Winkworth) *in tch: rdn and hdwy 3f out: rdn to ld wl over 1f out: styd on wl* **6/1**[3]

0 **2** *1 1/2* **Monte Mayor Birdie (IRE)**[26] 2949 2-8-12 0 AdamKirby 12 — 66
(D Haydn Jones) *walked to s: chsd ldr for 2f: lft in ld and rdn 3f out: hdd wl over 1f out: kpt on same pce fnl f* **25/1**

3 *2* **Alan Devonshire** 2-9-3 0 EddieAhern 2 — 66+
(M H Tompkins) *hld up wl in tch: hdwy 3f out: rdn and ch 2f out: no ex ins fnl f* **10/1**

0 **4** *3* **Enactment**[47] 2303 2-9-3 0 RyanMoore 1 — 59+
(Sir Michael Stoute) *cl up: chsd ldr 5f out tl rdn over 2f out: wknd 1f out* **9/2**[2]

4 **5** *1 3/4* **Eastern Gift**[8] 3479 2-9-3 0 RichardHughes 5 — 54+
(R Hannon) *in tch: hdwy over 3f out: rdn and ev ch 2f out: wknd qckly 1f out* **4/5**[1]

6 15 **Bridge Of Fermoy (IRE)** 2-8-12 0........................... WilliamBuick(5) 16 17
(N A Callaghan) *sn pushed along: bhd and j. path 5f out: t.o fr 1/2-way* **12/1**

0 7 *shd* **Safiyeh**[31] [2768] 2-8-12 0.. PaulFitzsimons 8 12
(M J Attwater) *s.i.s: a bhd: lost tch 4f out: t.o last 3f* **40/1**

8 14 **Southwark Newsboy (IRE)** 2-9-3 0................................ DMylonas 13 —
(Mrs C A Dunnett) *t.k.h: led: j. path 5f out: sddle slipped and hdd 3f out: virtually p.u after: t.o* **25/1**

1m 26.24s (2.03) **Going Correction** +0.10s/f (Good) 8 Ran SP% **114.9**
Speed ratings (Par 94):92,90,88,84,82 65,65,49
CSF £133.67 TOTE £6.80: £1.50, £6.30, £1.70; EX 174.00.
Owner P Winkworth **Bred** Lars Pearson **Trained** Chiddingfold, Surrey

FOCUS
The change in the going resulted in ten withdrawals from the original declaration of 18. Hard to weigh up, particularly in the soft ground, and rated slightly cautiously, but any of the first five home could probably win at this level.

NOTEBOOK
Safari Sunup(IRE), who had made a promising debut on the All-Weather, stayed on best to win the race in the centre of the track. Connections reported that they expected him to handle the soft ground, which he did, and that they believe him to be a nice horse in the making. (op 7-1)
Monte Mayor Birdie(IRE) had been difficult on the way to post on her debut, and this occasion she was walked to the start - not a promising sign. However, when the stalls opened she proved a revelation, showing lots of speed throughout. She can win a maiden if temperament does not get the better of her. (tchd 33-1)
Alan Devonshire, a 47,000gns Mtoto colt from a winning family over a wide range of trips, is bred to come into his own over middle distances, being the son of a mare who won over 1m2f. In the circumstances, this was a promising debut, and his former West Ham namesake, after whom he was named, must have been pleased he made the effort to turn up to witness this debut. (op 14-1)
Enactment, a Pivotal colt out of a mare who won in the USA as a juvenile, is bred to be speedy, and 6f would have suited better in this ground. Though fading out of it in the final furlong, he should improve enough to win a race or two.
Eastern Gift had given the impression that 7f would suit last time, but the extra furlong in soft ground stretched his stamina. He can be given another chance. (op Evens tchd 11-10 and 8-11)
Bridge Of Fermoy(IRE), a 28,000gns Danetime son out of an unraced mare who has produced a couple of decent performers up to a mile, was struggling from the word go, and deserves a chance to show what he can do on better ground. Official explanation: jockey said colt ran green (op 5-1)
Southwark Newsboy(IRE) Official explanation: jockey said saddle slipped

3734 GALLAGHER CONTRACTORS NURSERY 6f
8:00 (8:00) (Class 5) 2-Y-O **£3,238** (£963; £481; £240) **Stalls** High

Form RPR
000 1 **We Have A Dream**[10] [3423] 2-7-11 **55** ow2.................... LiamJones(3) 13 58
(W R Muir) *led tl over 3f out: pressed ldr tl rdn to ld again jst over 1f out: styd on wl nr fin* **9/2**[3]

100 2 1 1/2 **Barraland**[11] [3398] 2-9-6 **75**.. JHBowman 9 73
(M R Channon) *w ldr tl led over 3f out: hdd and rdn jst over 1f out: ev ch tl fdd nr fin* **4/1**[2]

14 3 *shd* **Miss Bootylishes**[7] [3550] 2-9-2 **71**.................................. SteveDrowne 4 69
(A B Haynes) *in tch: rdn and wanting to hang lft over 3f out: styd on over 1f out: chalng for 2nd whn stmbld nr fin* **5/4**[1]

103 4 6 **Nestor Protector (IRE)**[36] [2618] 2-8-5 **65**.............. KevinGhunowa(5) 14 45
(A B Haynes) *s.i.s: sn in tch: rdn 3f out: sn hung lft: wknd over 1f out* **16/1**

0465 5 7 **Replicator**[10] [3423] 2-8-12 **67**... RichardMullen 12 26
(Pat Eddery) *trckd ldrs: rdn and effrt 3f out: hung lft and wknd qckly over 1f out* **11/2**

3636 6 8 **Sheik'N'Knotsterd**[13] [3348] 2-8-9 **64**...............................(b[1]) ChrisCatlin 3 —
(J Akehurst) *nvr gng wl: drvn after 1f: no ch last 3f* **8/1**

1m 13.07s (1.40) **Going Correction** +0.10s/f (Good) 6 Ran SP% **115.0**
Speed ratings (Par 94):94,92,91,83,74 63
CSF £23.22 CT £34.80 TOTE £6.40: £1.90, £3.10; EX 37.70.
Owner The Dreaming Squires **Bred** Whitsbury Manor Stud **Trained** Lambourn, Berks

FOCUS
There were eight withdrawals from the original 14 because of the rain-softened ground, but it turned out to be competitive enough if lacking in numbers for a nursery with the winner rated below previous form. The 'official' ratings shown next to each horse are estimated and for information purposes only.

NOTEBOOK
We Have A Dream had never finished better than seventh in his three maidens, but consequently came into this first nursery off clear bottom-weight and battled well after disputing the lead throughout against the stands' rail. A half-brother to nine winners, this son of July Cup winner Oasis Dream probably has quite a bit more to offer. (op 11-1)
Barraland handled the testing ground well, even though connections reported him to have been unsuited by good to soft last time. Though not quite good enough, he had a protracted battle with the winner and made a brave effort to concede so much weight to him. (op 11-4)
Miss Bootylishes was well backed to make up for her defeat at Salisbury a week earlier, when hampered by a slipping saddle. She was never quite going fast enough to get there, but runs as if 7f should suit. Official explanation: jockey said filly hung left (op 6-4 tchd 13-8)
Nestor Protector(IRE) was not good enough on this handicap debut, though to be fair his best effort to date was on fast going. However, he again showed a tendency to hang, something that was probably accentuated as he tired in the soft ground. (op 14-1)
Replicator did not look happy when asked to pick up on the squelchy ground, and can do better in more suitable conditions. Official explanation: jockey said colt was unsuited by the soft (heavy in places) ground (op 5-1 tchd 9-2 and 6-1)
Sheik'N'Knotsterd never went a yard, and in all probability hated the ground. (tchd 15-2)

3735 CONTICAP H'CAP 6f
8:30 (8:30) (Class 6) (0-65,65) 3-Y-O+ **£2,047** (£604; £302) **Stalls** High

Form RPR
022 1 **Polar Force**[12] [3388] 7-9-11 **59**... DMylonas 18 69
(Mrs C A Dunnett) *mde all: gng best fr 2f out: pushed along and in command fr over 1f out* **10/3**[2]

3053 2 1 1/4 **Bens Georgie (IRE)**[21] [3106] 5-9-5 **53**............................. RobertHavlin 8 59
(D K Ivory) *hld up: rdn 3f out: hdwy and hung lft over 1f out: plugged on u.p to go 2nd ins fnl f: nt trble wnr* **3/1**[1]

4350 3 3/4 **Mistral Sky**[22] [3064] 8-9-10 **58**...(v) AmirQuinn 14 62
(Stef Liddiard) *chsd wnr: rdn wl over 2f out: one pce and lost 2nd ins fnl f* **7/1**

6025 4 5 **Joy And Pain**[12] [3388] 6-9-7 **55**..................................(v) PaulFitzsimons 15 44
(M J Attwater) *stdd s: hld up in tch: effrt and rdn over 2f out: sn btn* **9/2**[3]

01 5 3 1/2 **Pragmatist**[28] [2878] 3-9-5 **58**.. StephenCarson 10 36
(P Winkworth) *cl up on outer: rdn 3f out: wknd over 1f out* **5/1**

1030 6 7 **Royal Orissa**[12] [3388] 5-9-5 **53**.. AdamKirby 17 10
(D Haydn Jones) *taken down early: t.k.h: hld up in last: swtchd lft 4f out: sn rdn and struggling: no ch fr 1/2-way* **9/2**[3]

1m 11.56s (-0.11) **Going Correction** +0.10s/f (Good)
WFA 3 from 4yo+ 5lb 6 Ran SP% **113.6**
Speed ratings (Par 101):104,102,101,94,90 80
CSF £14.00 CT £63.73 TOTE £4.50: £2.30, £2.20; EX 14.30 Place 6 £94.84, Place 5 £75.22..
Owner Mrs Christine Dunnett **Bred** Cheveley Park Stud Ltd **Trained** Hingham, Norfolk

FOCUS
From an original line-up of 18, only six were left in this moderate handicap after the change in the going. However, the form seems sound enough rated around the first two.
Royal Orissa Official explanation: jockey said gelding never travelled
T/Plt: £316.90 to a £1 stake. Pool: £72,294.65. 166.50 winning tickets. T/Qpdt: £74.90 to a £1 stake. Pool: £5,718.90. 56.50 winning tickets. SP

3232 NEWBURY (L-H)
Saturday, July 21

3736 Meeting Abandoned - Waterlogged

Card due to feature the Weatherbys Super Sprint.

3705 NEWMARKET (JULY) (R-H)
Saturday, July 21

OFFICIAL GOING: Good (8.5)
Wind: Light, half-behind Weather: Cloudy with sunny spells

3743 LETTERGOLD PLASTICS MAIDEN STKS 7f
2:00 (2:05) (Class 4) 3-Y-O **£5,181** (£1,541; £770; £384) **Stalls** High

Form RPR
0226 1 **Medicea Sidera**[10] [3430] 3-8-12 **79**...................................... JoeFanning 7 78
(E F Vaughan) *racd centre: led that gp: rdn to ld overall 1f out: r.o* **11/4**[1]

3 2 *nk* **Plucky**[24] [2998] 3-8-12 0.. JimmyFortune 11 78
(J H M Gosden) *racd centre: hld up in tch: rdn over 1f out: r.o* **5/1**[3]

02 3 2 **Own Boss (USA)**[13] [3349] 3-9-3 0................................ PhilipRobinson 2 77
(M A Jarvis) *racd centre: w wnr: rdn and ev ch fr over 1f out: edgd lft and no ex ins fnl f* **11/2**

0 4 1 **Luck Be A Lady (IRE)**[93] [1105] 3-8-12 0.......................... SebSanders 6 69
(J Noseda) *racd centre: stdd s: hld up: plld hrd: hdwy and hung lft over 1f out: nt rch ldrs* **3/1**[2]

-056 5 *hd* **Usk Melody**[21] [3099] 3-8-12 **74**......................................(b[1]) EddieAhern 10 69
(G A Huffer) *racd alone on stands' side: overall ldr 6f: no ex* **20/1**

3 6 1 1/2 **Winning Show**[11] [3395] 3-9-0 0.. LiamJones(3) 3 70
(R A Harris) *racd centre: plld hrd and prom: rdn over 1f out: wknd ins fnl f* **50/1**

6- 7 *nk* **Timber Treasure (USA)**[393] [2821] 3-9-3 0........................... TPQueally 5 69
(H R A Cecil) *w ldrs in centre: rdn and ev ch over 1f out: edgd rt and wknd ins fnl f* **12/1**

00 8 3/4 **Spanish Diva**[17] [3214] 3-8-12 0.. SaleemGolam 1 62
(S C Williams) *racd centre: hld up: racd keenly: rdn and wknd over 1f out* **50/1**

40 9 2 1/2 **Pivotal Truth**[58] [1961] 3-8-12 0... MichaelHills 9 55
(B W Hills) *racd centre: prom: rdn over 2f out: sn wknd* **25/1**

10 1 **Ezdiyaad (IRE)** 3-9-3 0.. RHills 8 58
(M P Tregoning) *s.s: racd centre: hld up: rdn over 2f out: sn wknd* **7/1**

06 11 1/2 **Sea Willow (IRE)**[15] [3276] 3-9-3 0.. NeilPollard 4 56
(D R C Elsworth) *racd centre: hld up: bhd fr 1/2-way* **66/1**

1m 24.79s (-1.99) **Going Correction** -0.025s/f (Good) 11 Ran SP% **117.9**
Speed ratings (Par 102):110,109,107,106,106 104,103,103,100,99 98
CSF £16.08 TOTE £4.70: £1.60, £1.60, £2.10; EX 19.40 Trifecta £33.70 Pool: £440.78. 9.27 winning units.
Owner M A Whelton **Bred** Broughton Bloodstock **Trained** Newmarket, Suffolk

FOCUS
Probably a decent maiden as the winning time was smart for a race like this. The bulk of the field made for the centre of the track whilst just one decided to come down the stands' rail. The form is rated through the third, backed up by the fifth and eighth.

3744 PLANTATION STUD STKS (REGISTERED AS THE APHRODITE STAKES) (LISTED RACE) 1m 4f
2:35 (2:36) (Class 1) 3-Y-O+
£15,330 (£5,810; £2,907; £1,449; £726; £364) **Stalls** Centre

Form RPR
11 1 **Turbo Linn**[10] [3434] 4-9-9 **108**...................................... NCallan 10 113+
(G A Swinbank) *hld up: hdwy over 2f out: hung rt over 1f out: rdn to ld ins fnl f: styd on wl* **6/5**[1]

-030 2 1 3/4 **Green Room (FR)**[34] [2702] 4-9-5 **96**........................... SebSanders 11 106
(J L Dunlop) *sn led: hdd after 1f: chsd clr ldr to over 5f out: wnt 2nd again over 2f out: rdn to ld and hung rt over 1f out: hdd and unable qckn ins fnl f: hung lft nr fin* **12/1**

4642 3 2 **Under The Rainbow**[10] [3434] 4-9-2 **100**.......................... PhilipRobinson 2 100
(B W Hills) *hld up: hdwy over 2f out: rdn over 1f out: styd on same pce ins fnl f* **8/1**

-3P3 4 3 1/2 **Portal**[10] [3434] 4-9-2 **104**.. JamieSpencer 8 94
(J R Fanshawe) *hmpd s: hld up: hdwy u.p over 1f out: no ex ins fnl f* **10/3**[2]

-135 5 3 1/2 **La Spezia (IRE)**[55] [2070] 3-8-4 **95**................................... HayleyTurner 9 89
(M L W Bell) *plld hrd: led after 1f: sn wl clr: wknd and hdd over 1f out* **25/1**

-S35 6 1 3/4 **Impetious**[27] [2926] 3-8-5 0 ow1.. EddieAhern 7 87
(Eamon Tyrrell, Ire) *chsd ldrs: rdn over 3f out: hung rt and wknd over 1f out* **14/1**

5336 7 *nk* **Majounes Song**[30] [2786] 3-8-4 **97**.................................... JoeFanning 4 86
(M Johnston) *s.i.s: sn prom: chsd clr ldr over 5f out tl rdn over 2f out: wknd over 1f out* **13/2**[3]

2m 28.83s (-4.08) **Going Correction** -0.025s/f (Good)
WFA 3 from 4yo+ 12lb 7 Ran SP% **111.2**
Speed ratings (Par 111):112,110,109,107,104 103,103
CSF £16.32 TOTE £2.00: £1.40, £4.10; EX 13.80 Trifecta £90.40 Pool: £739.10, 5.80 winning units.

Owner J Nelson **Bred** James Nelson **Trained** Melsonby, N Yorks

FOCUS
Something of a re-run of the Lancashire Oaks, run here ten days earlier, with the first three home in that contest re-opposing. The result was similar despite the revised terms, though the third and fourth here did swap places with the former the best guide. After there threatened to be no pace on early, the race was eventually run at a very strong gallop thanks to La Spezia, though the bulk of the field were happy to ignore her. The field made for the centre of the track on reaching the home straight.

NOTEBOOK
Turbo Linn, 7lb worse off with both Portal and Under The Rainbow compared with the Lancashire Oaks, was buried away in the pack for much of the way and had to work quite hard to get to the front, but once she reached the stands' rail she always looked to have matters under control and maintained her unbeaten record. The fact that she managed to confirm the Lancashire Oaks form with her two old rivals on these revised terms so convincingly suggests she is still improving, and it will be fascinating to see how she copes if she is sent over to Deauville for the Prix de Pomone in a couple of weeks' time. (op 10-11)
Green Room(FR) probably found the ground has eased enough for her and returned to something like her best. Near the front of the main bulk of the field throughout, she had every chance and never stopped trying after the favourite had gone past her. She has winning form at this level and she will not always bump into such a smart rival as the winner.
Under The Rainbow, 7lb better off with Turbo Linn for a four-length beating in the Lancashire Oaks, managed to narrow the gap, but only fractionally and she seems to lack finishing pace where it matters. She is consistent at this sort of level, but achieving another victory to add to her pair in the autumn of her juvenile season is proving elusive. (op 10-1)
Portal, also 7lb better off with Turbo Linn for a beating of just over four lengths in the Lancashire Oaks, never managed to land an effective blow from off the pace and ended up being beaten further this time. To be fair, all her best form has been achieved on genuinely fast ground so the recent rain would not have done her any favours. (op 9-2)
La Spezia(IRE) went tearing off in front as though her tail was on fire and there was nothing her rider could do about it. The outcome was inevitable and because of the way the race was run, the evidence as to whether she stays this longer trip is inconclusive. Official explanation: jockey said filly ran too free (tchd 28-1)
Impetious, an Irish challenger not beaten far in a Saint-Cloud Group 2 last time, did not seem to see out the trip in this strongly-run event. (tchd 16-1)
Majounes Song, who has made the running herself in the past, was content to let the tearaway La Spezia do the donkey-work this time, but the fact that she could not even overhaul her shows how below-par this effort was. (op 7-1 tchd 15-2)

3745 COOLUS AIR CONDITIONING H'CAP — 1m

3:05 (3:08) (Class 2) (0-100,92) 3-Y-O

£12,464 (£3,732; £1,866; £934; £466; £234) **Stalls** High

Form				RPR
15-2	1		**Al Khaleej (IRE)**[58] 1956 3-9-1 **84** ... SebSanders 11 (E A L Dunlop) *hld up: hdwy over 1f out: rdn to ld ins fnl f: r.o wl* **7/2**[1]	92+
2560	2	2	**Annemasse**[10] 3431 3-9-9 **92** ... JoeFanning 3 (M Johnston) *chsd ldr: led 2f out: sn rdn: hdd and unable qckn ins fnl f* **9/1**[3]	96
221	3	shd	**Classira (IRE)**[9] 3454 3-8-9 **78** ... PhilipRobinson 2 (M A Jarvis) *hld up in tch: rdn and ev ch ins fnl f: edgd rt and styd on same pce* **10/1**	81
-660	4	1	**The Illies (IRE)**[8] 3503 3-8-9 **78** ... RHills 4 (B W Hills) *s.i.s: hld up: hdwy over 2f out: rdn over 1f out: no ex ins fnl f* **10/1**	79
-531	5	½	**Paceman (USA)**[26] 2943 3-9-5 **88** ... PatDobbs 9 (R Hannon) *led to 1/2-way: rdn and ev ch over 1f out: no ex ins fnl f* **13/2**[2]	88
0-10	6	nk	**Folly Lodge**[10] 3430 3-9-3 **86** ... MichaelHills 8 (B W Hills) *hld up in tch: plld hrd: rdn over 2f out: sn hung lft: no ex fnl f* **12/1**	85
1642	7	hd	**Shot Gun**[10] 3420 3-8-11 **80** ... DarryllHolland 1 (M R Channon) *hld up: rdn and nt clr run over 1f out: wknd wl ins fnl f* **14/1**	79
1030	8	8	**Lazy Darren**[8] 3503 3-8-9 **83** ... WilliamBuick(5) 10 (R Hannon) *mid-div: rdn over 2f out: wknd over 1f out* **10/1**	63
-414	9	2	**Sign Of The Cross**[18] 3196 3-8-11 **80** ... JamieSpencer 5 (J R Fanshawe) *trckd ldrs: racd keenly: led 1/2-way: hdd 2f out: sn rdn and wknd* **9/1**[3]	56

1m 39.18s (-1.25) **Going Correction** -0.025s/f (Good) **9** Ran SP% **97.2**
Speed ratings (Par 106):105,103,102,101,101 101,100,92,90
CSF £22.76 CT £125.81 TOTE £3.40: £1.40, £2.30, £2.10; EX 24.10 Trifecta £255.90 Part won. Pool: £360.50, 0.40 winning units..
Owner Mayoof Sultan **Bred** A Stroud And J Hanly **Trained** Newmarket, Suffolk
■ Escape Route (3/1) was withdrawn (refused to enter stalls). Rule 4 applies, deduction 25p in £.

FOCUS
The race lost some of its competitiveness when the favourite Escape Route refused to enter the stalls, but this still looked up to par for the grade. The field did race down the middle of the track for the most part, though a trio did experiment with the far rail for a couple of furlongs.

NOTEBOOK
Al Khaleej(IRE), for whom the ground appeared to have come just right, won this with quite an impressive turn of foot and was still going away at the line. He seems to be improving and looks capable of winning some more decent handicaps over this trip or a bit further. (op 4-1 tchd 9-2 in places)
Annemasse, back over a more suitable trip, was always up with the pace and kept battling right to the line. He cannot be expected to get much leniency from the Handicapper for this, but he looks a tough sort and there will be other days. (op 10-1 tchd 12-1)
Classira(IRE), back on turf and making her handicap debut following her victory in a maiden on the Lingfield Polytrack, put in a determined late effort up the far rail and emerged with a lot of credit. She still has a little scope and could do even better in handicaps confined to her own sex.
The Illies(IRE) ran a similar race to here last time, staying on from off the pace without ever looking likely to get there. He is a bit more exposed than many of these, but is dropping back to a more feasible mark now and seems to be returning to some sort of form. (op 14-1)
Paceman(USA), raised 5lb for his Windsor victory, was given a positive ride but lacked the necessary speed over the last furlong or so. He is on a stiff mark now, but could probably have done with even more rain. (op 6-1)
Folly Lodge, whose previous outings have all been over 7f, did not help her chances of seeing out the extra furlong by taking a grip. In any case she remains 9lb above her last winning mark and needs a lot more leniency from the Handicapper. (op 9-1)
Shot Gun did not really transfer his recent solid Polytrack form back onto grass. (op 16-1)
Lazy Darren may have seen more daylight than ideal, but he is more exposed than these rivals in any case. (op 14-1 tchd 16-1)
Sign Of The Cross, up there from the start, tried something different by edging towards the far rail at around halfway, taking two of his rivals with him, but he did not persist with that route and after he had joined back up with the bulk of the field, the writing was soon on the wall. He is not helping himself by racing too keenly at the moment. Official explanation: jockey said colt ran too free (op 10-1)

3746 INVESCO PERPETUAL EBF FILLIES' H'CAP — 6f

3:35 (3:37) (Class 3) (0-95,94) 3-Y-O+

£8,724 (£2,612; £1,306; £653; £326; £163) **Stalls** High

Form				RPR
131	1		**Bee Eater (IRE)**[15] 3278 3-8-10 **82** ... SebSanders 1 (Sir Mark Prescott) *hld up: hdwy over 2f out: rdn and hung rt over 1f out: sn led: swished tail: r.o wl* **5/2**[1]	95+
1412	2	1 ¾	**China Cherub**[9] 3472 4-9-4 **85** ... (b) RHills 8 (R Hannon) *w ldr: led 4f out: rdn: hmpd and hdd 1f out: styd on same pce* **8/1**	94
-P40	3	¾	**Daniella**[8] 3481 5-8-9 **76** ... (b) DarryllHolland 2 (Rae Guest) *hld up: hdwy and nt clr run over 1f out: swtchd lft: styd on u.p* **25/1**	83
-245	4	nk	**Siren's Gift**[10] 3431 3-9-3 **94** ... WilliamBuick(5) 7 (A M Balding) *chsd ldrs: rdn whn hmpd over 1f out: styd on* **5/1**[3]	99
1250	5	1 ¼	**Sparkling Eyes**[42] 2450 3-8-8 **80** ... JoeFanning 3 (C E Brittain) *hld up: hdwy over 1f out: nt trble ldrs* **40/1**	81
5113	6	¾	**Pusey Street Lady**[22] 3059 3-8-13 **85** ... JimCrowley 10 (J Gallagher) *chsd ldrs: rdn over 2f out: hmpd and no ex over 1f out* **14/1**	84
2341	7	½	**Shes Minnie**[9] 3466 4-8-10 **77** ... FergusSweeney 11 (J G M O'Shea) *hld up: hdwy over 1f out: no ex fnl f* **16/1**	75
1-65	8	1 ¼	**Cape**[34] 2688 4-9-5 **86** ... MichaelHills 6 (J R Fanshawe) *hld up: hdwy over 1f out: wknd ins fnl f* **11/4**[2]	81
215-	9	1 ½	**Blades Girl**[300] 5550 4-9-12 **93** ... (p) NCallan 4 (K A Ryan) *led 2f: rdn and edgd lft 2f out: wknd fnl f* **16/1**	83
-200	10	2 ½	**Folga**[45] 2379 5-9-12 **93** ... TPQueally 12 (J G Given) *prom: rdn over 2f out: sn hung lft and wknd* **16/1**	76
0640	11	1 ¼	**Woodnook**[42] 2450 4-9-9 **90** ... EddieAhern 5 (J A R Toller) *hood stl on whn lft stalls: hld up: rdn and wknd over 1f out* **25/1**	69

1m 11.06s (-2.29) **Going Correction** -0.025s/f (Good)
WFA 3 from 4yo+ 5lb **11** Ran SP% **117.5**
Speed ratings (Par 104):114,111,110,110,108 107,106,105,103,99 98
CSF £22.67 CT £418.30 TOTE £3.00: £1.40, £2.40, £5.30; EX 23.70 Trifecta £366.00 Part won. Pool: £515.50, 0.60 winning units..
Owner Sir Edmund Loder **Bred** Sir E J Loder **Trained** Newmarket, Suffolk

FOCUS
They went a serious pace in this decent fillies' handicap and as a result recorded a very smart winning time for a race of its type, so the form looks solid and should work out. They eventually used the full width of the track, but again the centre seemed the place to be.

NOTEBOOK
Bee Eater(IRE) ◆, for whom the rain would not have been a problem, travelled like a dream just behind the leaders and, despite the trademark whirling of the tail, powered away from her rivals when asked for a comprehensive success. She is beginning to look useful and, with the scope for further improvement, is likely to seek some black type on the continent next. (op 11-4)
China Cherub, now on a career-high mark and 16lb above her last winning mark on turf, helped force a strong pace and, despite hanging around under pressure, kept on very well if unable to cope with the progressive winner. This shows that she remains capable despite her rise up the weights.
Daniella ◆, given plenty to do, has shown a marked tendency to hang left and did so again, but on this occasion it looked more a case of her being manoeuvred that way in order to get a run. The way she stayed on very well towards the end suggests she has the ability to win again provided she remains sound, and may be worth stepping back up to 7f. (op 28-1)
Siren's Gift, gradually edging down the weights, was always in a good position but was done no favours by the hanging China Cherub inside the last quarter-mile. Having said that, she would not have bothered the winner even with an uninterrupted run. (op 13-2)
Sparkling Eyes, back at a more realistic level after being found out in a couple of Listed events, did not run at all badly but is 8lb above her last winning mark and probably needs to drop a bit more.
Pusey Street Lady had been severely punished by the Handicapper who raised her 8lb for running above herself in a conditions event here last time. Never far away, she rather got caught in the backwash started by the hanging China Cherub a furlong out, but she was not really going anywhere at the time. She is going to find life very tough off this sort of mark.
Cape had no excuses this time and was just disappointing. (op 5-2 tchd 3-1)
Blades Girl was given a very positive ride on this return from ten months off and not surprisingly she appeared to blow up. Better can be expected with this outing under her belt.
Woodnook would not have been helped by taking a couple of strides out of the stalls with the blindfold still in place. (op 20-1)

3747 UNICORN ASSET MANAGEMENT JULY COURSE SERIES MAIDEN STKS (QUALIFIER) — 6f

4:10 (4:10) (Class 3) 2-Y-O **£6,477** (£1,927; £963; £481) **Stalls** High

Form				RPR
	1		**Legislation** 2-9-3 0 ... JimmyFortune 2 (J H M Gosden) *hld up: hdwy over 1f out: rdn to ld ins fnl f: edgd rt: r.o* **15/2**[3]	83+
6	2	½	**Calmdownmate (IRE)**[30] 2804 2-9-3 0 ... FrancisNorton 12 (K R Burke) *trckd ldrs: plld hrd: rdn to ld 1f out: hung lft and hdd ins fnl f: styd on* **14/1**	82
	3	1	**Shallal** 2-9-3 0 ... JoeFanning 3 (P W Chapple-Hyam) *chsd ldrs: ev ch over 1f out: hmpd ins fnl f: styd on same pce* **9/2**[1]	79
4	4	½	**Cordell (IRE)**[68] 1721 2-9-3 0 ... PatDobbs 6 (R Hannon) *w ldr tl led over 2f out: rdn and hdd 1f out: hmpd and no ex ins fnl f* **12/1**	77
43	5	1 ½	**Cat Whistle**[33] 2710 2-8-12 0 ... TonyHamilton 5 (R A Fahey) *plld hrd and prom: rdn over 1f out: no ex fnl f* **15/2**[3]	68+
0	6	1	**Valentino Sky (USA)**[42] 2478 2-9-3 0 ... IanMongan 4 (N P Littmoden) *chsd ldrs: rdn and ev ch over 1f out: wknd ins fnl f* **66/1**	70
00	7	nk	**Aberavon**[42] 2473 2-8-12 0 ... SebSanders 14 (D R C Elsworth) *led over 3f: wknd ins fnl f* **20/1**	64
	8	½	**Andaman Sunset** 2-9-3 0 ... DarryllHolland 16 (G Wragg) *hld up: nvr trbld ldrs* **25/1**	67+
	9	nk	**Unbreak My Heart (IRE)** 2-9-3 0 ... FergusSweeney 10 (R Charlton) *s.i.s hld up: rdn and hung lft ins fnl f: nvr trbld ldrs* **14/1**	66
	10	¾	**Tevez** 2-9-3 0 ... SaleemGolam 8 (M H Tompkins) *hld up: rdn over 1f out: n.d* **33/1**	64
5	11	½	**Castles In The Air**[16] 3233 2-9-3 0 ... PaulEddery 7 (Pat Eddery) *prom over 4f* **9/2**[1]	62
	12	shd	**Imperial Decree** 2-8-12 0 ... StephenDonohoe 9 (John Berry) *hld up: n.d* **66/1**	57
	13	hd	**Kiss The Ring (USA)** 2-8-12 0 ... EddieAhern 18 (B J Meehan) *s.i.s: hld up: rdn and wknd over 1f out* **11/1**	57
	14	shd	**St Jean Cap Ferrat** 2-9-3 0 ... DeanMcKeown 1 (G Wragg) *dwlt and swvd lft s: a in rr* **33/1**	61

15 ¾ **Classical World (USA)** 2-9-3 0 .... RHills 19 59+
(Sir Michael Stoute) *prom 4f* **11/2**[2]
16 1 ½ **Pret A Tout** 2-8-12 0 .... MichaelHills 13 50
(P J McBride) *s.i.s: a in rr* **66/1**

1m 14.28s (0.93) **Going Correction** -0.025s/f (Good) **16** Ran SP% **123.6**
Speed ratings (Par 98):92,91,90,89,87 86,85,84,84,83 82,82,82,82,81 79
CSF £103.40 TOTE £10.10: £2.90, £5.10, £2.20; EX 152.90.
Owner H R H Princess Haya Of Jordan **Bred** Elsdon Farms **Trained** Newmarket, Suffolk

FOCUS
This maiden was won by subsequent dual Guineas winner Cockney Rebel last year and some decent stables were represented, but the bare form is not easy to assess and at present looks no more than fair. The early pace was ordinary and the winning time was modest.

NOTEBOOK
Legislation, a 140,000gns Oasis Dream half-brother to 1m2f winner Daylami Dreams, proved good enough to make a winning debut. The bare form does not look anything special, but he displayed a likeable attitude and should progress. (op 8-1)
Calmdownmate(IRE) ◆ did not show a great deal on his debut at Ripon, but he was sent off favourite that day and, taken to Newmarket for his next outing, he is seemingly well thought of. This was a much better performance, especially considering he took a bit of a grip early on, and he looks capable of progressing into a useful sort. (op 16-1 tchd 12-1)
Shallal, by Cape Cross, is a half-brother to, among others, multiple sprint winner Gimasha out of a top-class triple 6f winner at two in France. This was a pleasing introduction and he is open to improvement. (op 11-4 tchd 5-2)
Cordell(IRE) was quite well backed in a four-runner novice event on his debut at Windsor back in May, but he did not seem happy on the ground and failed to beat a rival. Stepped up in trip on his return from over two months off, he showed plenty of early dash and this was a lot better. He could come on again for this. (op 16-1)
Cat Whistle was too keen for her own good and she failed to confirm the promise of her two previous efforts. A more stronglyr-run race will suit much better and she is now qualified for nurseries. (op 9-1)
Valentino Sky(USA) stepped up on the form he showed on his debut at Windsor and could be one for nurseries later in the season.
Castles In The Air failed to build on the promise he showed on his debut at Newbury and his breeding suggests he will probably be better suited by a quicker surface. (op 7-1)
St Jean Cap Ferrat Official explanation: jockey said colt missed the break
Classical World(USA), by 1991 National Stakes winner El Prado, is a half-brother to dual 1m1f-1m2f winner Otranto. He did not show much on his racecourse debut, but attracted support and can be given another chance. (op 7-1)

3748 DUKE GRIME MEMORIAL H'CAP 1m 6f 175y
4:45 (4:46) (Class 4) (0-85,83) 4-Y-0+ **£5,181** (£1,541; £770; £384) **Stalls** Centre

Form RPR
00-0 **1** **Nobelix (IRE)**[32] 2736 5-9-4 **83** .... WilliamBuick(5) 4 92
(J R Fanshawe) *hld up: wnt centre ent st: swtchd rt and hdwy over 2f out: rdn to ld 1f out: edgd lft: styd on* **6/1**
3-04 **2** ½ **Velvet Heights (IRE)**[35] 2675 5-9-9 **83** .... IanMongan 3 91
(J L Dunlop) *hld up: wnt centre ent st: hdwy over 2f out: edgd rt over 1f out: sn rdn and ev ch: styd on u.p* **11/2**[3]
1321 **3** 2 **Osolomio (IRE)**[46] 2342 4-9-6 **80** .... NCallan 6 86
(G A Swinbank) *led: wnt centre ent st: hdd over 6f out: rdn to ld over 1f out: sn edgd rt and hdd: no ex ins fnl f* **7/2**[1]
2054 **4** 3 **Salute (IRE)**[17] 3216 8-9-9 **83** .... RobertHavlin 5 84
(P G Murphy) *chsd ldrs: wnt centre ent st: lost pl over 3f out: rallied over 1f out: wknd ins fnl f* **16/1**
3140 **5** 1 ¼ **Gee Dee Nen**[21] 3090 4-9-9 **83** .... EddieAhern 9 83
(M H Tompkins) *hld up: wnt centre ent st: hdwy over 3f out: rdn and wknd over 1f out* **7/1**
0-60 **6** nk **Rationale (IRE)**[28] 2861 4-9-9 **83** ....(t) SaleemGolam 8 82
(S C Williams) *hld up: racd alone on stands' side ent st: overall ldr over 6f out: sn clr: rdn: edgd lft and hdd over 1f out: sn wknd* **16/1**
4-10 **7** ½ **Tribe**[27] 2908 5-9-5 **79** .... JimmyFortune 1 77
(P R Webber) *hld up: wnt centre ent st: hdwy over 4f out: rdn and wknd fnl f* **8/1**
-234 **8** 1 ¼ **Indonesia**[10] 3412 5-9-1 **75** .... TonyHamilton 7 72
(T D Walford) *chsd ldrs: wnt centre ent st: rdn and wknd over 1f out* **4/1**[2]
21/3 **9** 3 ½ **Bull Market (IRE)**[34] 2692 4-9-7 **81** .... PhilipRobinson 2 73
(J A Osborne) *wnt lft s: plld hrd: trckd ldr after 2f: wnt centre ent st: rdn and wknd over 1f out* **8/1**

3m 12.57s (1.53) **Going Correction** -0.025s/f (Good) **9** Ran SP% **118.4**
Speed ratings (Par 105):94,93,92,91,90 90,89,87
CSF £39.97 CT £134.86 TOTE £8.10: £2.70, £1.80, £1.80; EX 47.50.
Owner Rupert Hambro **Bred** Horst Rapp And Dieter Burkle **Trained** Newmarket, Suffolk

FOCUS
The pace was very steady for much of the way, resulting in a sprint finish, and although the form looks solid it may need treating with caution. Unsurprisingly, the winning time was moderate for the grade.
Indonesia Official explanation: jockey said gelding ran too free
Bull Market(IRE) Official explanation: jockey said gelding did not get the trip

3749 TURFTV H'CAP 5f
5:15 (5:15) (Class 3) (0-95,93) 3-Y-0+ **£9,067** (£2,697; £1,348; £673) **Stalls** High

Form RPR
-360 **1** **Ishi Adiva**[13] 3344 3-8-12 **85** .... RichardKingscote(3) 15 93
(Tom Dascombe) *hld up: hung lft and r.o ins fnl f: led post* **14/1**
00-5 **2** shd **Tony The Tap**[18] 3188 6-9-0 **80** .... SaleemGolam 1 88
(W R Muir) *hld up: hdwy to ld 1f out: sn rdn and hung rt: hdd post* **14/1**
6535 **3** 1 ¼ **Canadian Danehill (IRE)**[18] 3179 5-8-9 **75** ....(p) DarryllHolland 6 79
(R M H Cowell) *trckd ldrs: rdn ins fnl f: styd on* **9/1**
0403 **4** nk **Holbeck Ghyll (IRE)**[34] 2694 5-8-7 **78** ....(p) WilliamBuick(5) 9 80
(A M Balding) *hld up: pushed along 1/2-way: hdwy and n.m.r over 1f out: styd on* **7/2**[1]
5140 **5** shd **Raccoon (IRE)**[28] 2866 7-8-12 **78** .... IanMongan 13 80
(D W Chapman) *chsd ldrs: rdn over 1f out: kpt on* **10/1**
4014 **6** 1 ¾ **Deserted Dane (USA)**[12] 3380 3-9-1 **85** .... DeanMcKeown 8 80
(G A Swinbank) *chsd ldrs: rdn and ev ch over 1f out: no ex ins fnl f* **5/1**[3]
3211 **7** 1 ¼ **Mac Gille Eoin**[31] 2769 3-9-6 **90** .... JoeFanning 3 80
(J Gallagher) *chsd ldr: rdn and ev ch over 1f out: wknd and eased ins fnl f* **9/2**[2]
6040 **8** ½ **Angus Newz**[8] 3511 4-9-10 **90** .... FrancisNorton 12 79
(M Quinn) *chsd ldrs over 3f* **9/1**
04-0 **9** 1 ½ **Nigella**[44] 2399 4-9-0 **80** .... PatDobbs 2 64
(E S McMahon) *chsd ldrs: rdn over 1f out: wknd ins fnl f* **14/1**
6500 **10** ½ **Merlin's Dancer**[28] 2858 7-9-13 **93** .... PhilipRobinson 4 75
(S Dow) *led: rdn and hdd 1f out: btn whn hmpd sn after* **12/1**
3-10 **11** 2 **He's A Humbug (IRE)**[10] 3431 3-9-6 **90** .... NCallan 10 65
(K A Ryan) *sn pushed along in rr: hdwy over 1f out: wkng whn hmpd ins fnl f* **11/1**

58.88 secs (-0.68) **Going Correction** -0.025s/f (Good)
WFA 3 from 4yo+ 4lb **11** Ran SP% **122.2**
Speed ratings (Par 107):104,103,101,101,101 98,96,95,93,92 89
CSF £202.07 CT £1915.28 TOTE £20.10: £4.90, £3.50, £3.00; EX 258.50 Place 6 £38.88, Place 5 £19.03..
Owner Stephen Bayless **Bred** S H And Mrs A M Bayless **Trained** Lambourn, Berks

FOCUS
A good sprint handicap and straightforward form rated through the runner-up. They raced middle to stands' side.

NOTEBOOK
Ishi Adiva would have been an unlucky loser had she not got up, for she travelled very sweetly off the pace for much of the way, but was denied a clear run against the stands' rail a furlong from the finish and had to be switched with her effort. This was a useful performance and she may be capable of even better again on easier ground. She is entered in the Hong Kong Jockey Club sprint at Ascot and could go well in such a race, but she is by no means guaranteed to make the cut, even with a penalty.
Tony The Tap improved on the form he showed on his reappearance/debut for this yard at Lingfield and only just failed. He was given a pretty hard ride though, and it remains to be seen which way he will go from this. (op 12-1)
Canadian Danehill(IRE) has been kept very busy this year, but he confirmed he is still at the top of his game with a solid effort in defeat. (op 12-1)
Holbeck Ghyll(IRE) kept on for pressure without ever looking like doing enough. He has won a few races in the past, but is proving rather frustrating this term, producing solid efforts in defeat without managing to force his head back in front. (tchd 4-1)
Raccoon(IRE) looks high enough in the weights now. (tchd 11-1)
Deserted Dane(USA) failed to run up to his best and was a touch disappointing. (op 4-1)
Mac Gille Eoin came into this chasing a hat-trick, but he was no less than 18lb higher than when winning at Goodwood two starts back, and 8lb higher than when successful at Kempton last time, and that proved enough to stop him. (op 13-2)
He's A Humbug(IRE) Official explanation: jockey said colt suffered interference in running
T/Jkpt: £14,385.40 to a £1 stake. Pool: £20,261.19. 1.00 winning ticket. T/Plt: £19.90 to a £1 stake. Pool: £158,629.59. 5,818.95 winning tickets. T/Qpdt: £12.20 to a £1 stake. Pool: £5,668.10. 343.10 winning tickets. CR

3377 RIPON (R-H)
Saturday, July 21

OFFICIAL GOING: Heavy
The ground was pretty testing.
Wind: Virtually nil Weather: Rain

3750 EBF DOBSONS GASKETS MAIDEN FILLIES' STKS 5f
2:30 (2:30) (Class 4) 2-Y-0 **£4,210** (£1,252; £625; £312) **Stalls** Low

Form RPR
53 **1** **Nylla**[10] 3417 2-9-0 0 .... TPO'Shea 4 72+
(M R Channon) *trckd ldrs: effrt 2f out and sn pushed along: swtchd rt and rdn ent fnl f: styd on strly to ld last 100yds* **11/4**[1]
53 **2** 1 **Revue Princess (IRE)**[12] 3378 2-9-0 0 .... DavidAllan 5 68
(T D Easterby) *led: rdn over 1f out: drvn ins fnl f: hdd and no ex last 100 yds* **5/1**[2]
6 **3** hd **Mayaar (USA)**[16] 3245 2-9-0 0 .... AdrianMcCarthy 8 68
(P W Chapple-Hyam) *sn prom: effrt and ev ch over 1f out: sn rdn and kpt on same pce ins fnl f* **11/4**[1]
30 **4** 5 **Elusive Deal (USA)**[56] 2039 2-9-0 0 .... PaulHanagan 2 50+
(R A Fahey) *towards rr tl styd on fnl 2f: nrst fin* **7/1**[3]
40 **5** 1 ¾ **Dawn Light (IRE)**[89] 1193 2-9-0 0 .... RoystonFfrench 9 43
(Mrs A Duffield) *chsd ldrs: rdn along wl over 1f out: sn wknd* **10/1**
6 6 **Fu Wa (USA)** 2-9-0 0 .... PaulMulrennan 1 22
(M W Easterby) *hung rt thrght: cl up: rdn along 1/2-way: sn wknd* **8/1**
7 5 **Falcon Speed** 2-9-0 0 .... MickyFenton 12 4
(P T Midgley) *dwlt: a in rr* **25/1**
00 **8** nk **Smilodon**[24] 2984 2-8-7 0 .... AdamCarter(7) 10 —
(A Berry) *a in rr* **66/1**
9 11 **Joint Agency (IRE)** 2-8-11 0 .... LeeEnstone(3) 11 —
(N Wilson) *dwlt: a towards rr* **16/1**

65.82 secs (5.62) **Going Correction** +1.075s/f (Soft) **9** Ran SP% **113.9**
Speed ratings (Par 93):98,96,96,88,85 75,67,67,49
CSF £16.37 TOTE £3.70: £1.50, £1.40, £1.40; EX 13.40 Trifecta £23.00 Pool: £349.89, 10.79 winning units.
Owner Jaber Abdullah **Bred** Ian Emes **Trained** West Ilsley, Berks

FOCUS
Just a modest maiden although the form seems sound enough. Few got into it and the first three finished clear.

NOTEBOOK
Nylla was dropping a furlong in trip, but that was not a problem in these testing conditions. She was still only third entering the final furlong, but came with a strong run to sweep into the lead. A return to 6f will suit her. (op 3-1)
Revue Princess(IRE) was third in a similar event here last time. Securing the lead against the stands' fence, she battled on and was only cut down in the last half-furlong. (tchd 9-2)
Mayaar(USA), down a furlong in trip from her debut, in which she finished just behind today's winner, was a bit slow to break. Soon recovering, she had her chance inside the last but could not force her head in front. Her turn should not be long in coming. (op 3-1 tchd 7-2)
Elusive Deal(USA), another who ran over 6f last time, was doing some decent late work. Now eligible for nurseries, she will be suited by a return to further. (op 6-1 tchd 11-2)
Dawn Light(IRE), a modest performer, was not disgraced in the heavy conditions. (op 14-1)

3751 CLOTHERHOLME (S) STKS 6f
3:00 (3:04) (Class 6) 2-Y-0 **£2,590** (£770; £385; £192) **Stalls** Low

Form RPR
04 **1** **Jane's Delight (IRE)**[68] 1728 2-8-3 0 ....(v[1]) AndrewElliott(3) 10 66+
(P C Haslam) *cl up: led 1/2-way: clr wl over 1f out: unchal* **4/1**[2]
02 **2** 8 **Lavender Moon (IRE)**[32] 2738 2-8-3 0 ....(p) AndrewMullen(3) 4 42
(K A Ryan) *chsd ldrs: rdn along to chse wnr wl over 1f out: sn drvn and no imp* **3/1**[1]
0312 **3** ½ **Indecision**[14] 3296 2-9-2 0 .... PaulMulrennan 3 51
(M W Easterby) *prom: rdn along wl over 2f out: drvn wl over 1f out: plugged on same pce* **3/1**[1]
4 nk **Freudian Slip** 2-8-6 0 .... PaulQuinn 9 43+
(W M Brisbourne) *s.i.s and bhd: hdwy over 2f out: styd on ins fnl f: nrst fin* **14/1**

03 **5** *4* **La Belle Joannie**[14] 3296 2-8-6 0 MickyFenton 8 28
(P T Midgley) *sn led: pushed along and hdd 1/2-way: sn rdn and grad wknd* **8/1**[3]

0 **6** *1 1/4* **Viscount Monty**[23] 3024 2-8-11 0 PhillipMakin 5 29
(N Tinkler) *s.i.s: rdn along and sme hdwy 1/2-way: nvr a factor* **18/1**

455 **7** *3* **Arabian Fern**[14] 3296 2-8-8 0 ow2 TomEaves 7 17
(M E Sowersby) *a in midfield* **20/1**

0 **8** *2 1/2* **Social Height (IRE)**[13] 3341 2-8-8 0 PatrickMathers(3) 2 12
(A Berry) *a towards rr* **33/1**

00 **9** *1 1/2* **Lay Down Darling**[29] 2838 2-8-6 0 KimTinkler 6 3
(N Tinkler) *chsd ldrs: rdn along wl over 2f out and sn wknd* **33/1**

0 **10** *20* **King Of Dalyan (IRE)**[114] 814 2-8-11 0 AdrianTNicholls 1 —
(D Nicholls) *prom: rdn along after 2f out: sn lost pl and bhd* **8/1**[3]

000 **11** *2 1/2* **Rye Beau (IRE)**[2] 3681 2-8-11 0 (p) RoystonFfrench 12 —
(Mrs A Duffield) *a towards rr* **14/1**

1m 21.81s (8.81) **Going Correction** +1.075s/f (Soft) **11** Ran SP% **121.5**
Speed ratings (Par 92):84,73,72,72,66 65,61,57,55,29 25
CSF £16.66 TOTE £5.70: £1.90, £1.40, £1.50; EX 25.10 Trifecta £74.70 Pool: £293.87, 2.79 winning units.The winner was sold to R C Bond for 12,800gns. Lavendar Moon was claimed by K. Burke for £6,000. Freudian Slip was the subject of a friendly claim

Owner Middleham Park Racing XXXIX **Bred** Brownstown Stud **Trained** Middleham Moor, N Yorks

■ Stewards' Enquiry : Andrew Elliott one-day ban: improper riding - used whip when clearly winning (Aug 2)

FOCUS
A moderate winning time, even for a seller. The winner routed the opposition but the bad ground had plenty to do with that. Not form to take at face value.

NOTEBOOK
Jane's Delight(IRE), fitted with a first-time visor, was stepping up in trip and down in grade on this third run. After shaking off the only opponent able to match strides with her, she came well clear before the final furlong and was driven out to score by a wide margin. She now changes stables. (op 6-1 tchd 7-2)

Lavender Moon(IRE), a temperamental filly, tried in cheekpieces, unseated her rider coming out onto the course and then slipped up. Runner-up in this grade at Thirsk last time, she again finished best of the rest but the winner was in a different league. (op 11-4 tchd 7-2)

Indecision, runner-up in a similar event at Beverley, lacked the pace over this shorter trip to grab the lead and was soon being ridden along, but did plug on for a fairly distant third. (tchd 9-4 and 10-3)

Freudian Slip, a cheap yearling, showed a bit of promise on her debut. She missed the break quite badly and was still at the back of the field at halfway, but made steady progress past toiling opponents and would probably have been second had things gone her way. She could derive plenty of improvement from this debut experience. (op 12-1)

La Belle Joannie again showed early pace and held a narrow lead from the eventual winner, the pair soon clear, before being steadily left behind as her opponent turned the screw. (tchd 15-2)

King Of Dalyan(IRE) Official explanation: jockey said colt had no more to give

Rye Beau(IRE) Official explanation: jockey said gelding had no more to give

3752 NICK MACKAREL 40TH BIRTHDAY MAIDEN H'CAP 6f
3:30 (3:31) (Class 5) (0-70,70) 3-Y-O+ **£3,886** (£1,156; £577; £288) **Stalls** Low

Form RPR

5253 **1** **Orotund**[5] 3588 3-7-13 **46** oh1 DuranFentiman(3) 15 56
(T D Easterby) *led far side gp: rdn along 2f out: drvn ins fnl f: styd on and overall ldr nr line* **11/2**[2]

-332 **2** *shd* **Swift Princess (IRE)**[33] 2718 3-8-13 **57** PatCosgrave 2 67+
(K R Burke) *cl up stands' side: led that gp and overall ldr 1/2-way: rdn and hung bdly rt fr wl over 1f out: drvn ins fnl f: hdd nr line* **5/1**[1]

0220 **3** *3* **Mangano**[5] 3583 3-8-3 **50** ow1 PatrickMathers(3) 19 51
(A Berry) *chsd ldrs far side: rdn along 2f out: kpt on u.p ins fnl f* **10/1**

6320 **4** *2* **Missus Molly Brown**[29] 2844 3-8-3 **47** (b) PaulHanagan 17 42
(R A Fahey) *chsd ldrs far side: hdwy over 2f out: sn rdn and kpt on ins fnl f* **7/1**[3]

000- **5** *4* **First Valentini**[280] 5956 3-8-7 **51** SilvestreDeSousa 16 34
(N Bycroft) *in tch far side: rdn along over 2f out: kpt on ins fnl f* **33/1**

50-0 **6** *1 3/4* **Miss Sure Bond (IRE)**[49] 2256 4-8-10 **54** SladeO'Hara(5) 1 32
(G R Oldroyd) *towards rr stands' side: hdwy over 2f out: rdn to ld that gp over 1f out: kpt on: but no ch w far side* **16/1**

-000 **7** *3/4* **Immaculate Red**[50] 2206 4-8-4 **46** oh1 (b) AndrewElliott(3) 9 22
(R Bastiman) *prom stands' side: rdn along 1/2-way: grad wknd fnl 2f* **20/1**

0050 **8** *1 1/2* **Mandy's Maestro (USA)**[14] 3302 3-7-13 **48** (b) NataliaGemelova(5) 18 19
(R M Whitaker) *chsd wnr far side: rdn along over 2f out: grad wknd* **20/1**

000- **9** *1/2* **Julatten (IRE)**[355] 3994 3-8-6 **50** NickyMackay 3 20
(D J Murphy) *chsd ldrs stands' side: rdn along over 2f out and grad wknd* **16/1**

5300 **10** *3* **Soviet Sound (IRE)**[5] 3583 3-8-7 **51** DaleGibson 12 12
(Jedd O'Keeffe) *prom far side: rdn along over 2f out and sn wknd* **11/1**

-030 **11** *1 1/4* **Bond Casino**[28] 2892 3-8-11 **55** PaulMulrennan 11 12
(G R Oldroyd) *a in rr stands' side* **20/1**

2002 **12** *1 3/4* **Emma Jean Lad (IRE)**[9] 3475 3-8-7 **58** JosephLoveridge(7) 7 10
(J S Moore) *racd stands' side: bhd fr 1/2-way* **17/2**

5050 **13** *3* **Danethorpe (IRE)**[29] 2844 4-8-7 **46** oh1 (v) AdrianMcCarthy 5 —
(D Shaw) *a towards rr stands' side* **16/1**

-235 **14** *1 1/2* **Corlough Mountain**[13] 3349 3-9-5 **70** BradleyRoper(7) 8 8
(N A Callaghan) *s.i.s and in rr stands' side: sme hdwy 1/2-way: sn rdn and wknd* **7/1**[3]

0-00 **15** *4* **Fly So Free (IRE)**[7] 3535 3-8-11 **55** AdrianTNicholls 10 —
(D Nicholls) *overall ldr stands' side: rdn along and hdd 1/2-way: sn wknd* **33/1**

1m 19.06s (6.06) **Going Correction** +1.075s/f (Soft)
WFA 3 from 4yo+ 5lb **15** Ran SP% **122.8**
Speed ratings (Par 103):102,101,97,95,89 87,86,84,83,79 78,75,71,69,64
CSF £30.87 CT £278.92 TOTE £6.80: £2.30, £1.50, £2.90; EX 30.60 Trifecta £164.70 Pool: £348.07. 1.50 winning units.

Owner Habton Farms **Bred** D R Botterill **Trained** Great Habton, N Yorks

■ Stewards' Enquiry : Natalia Gemelova one-day ban: used whip with excessive frequency (Aug 2)
Duran Fentiman one-day ban: failed to keep straight from the stalls (Aug 2)

FOCUS
A low-grade event. The field split into two groups with six, including four of the first five, racing on the far side. The unlucky runner-up drifted right over from the stands' rail to the far side in the latter stages and the first two finished clear. The form seems sound enough.

Fly So Free(IRE) Official explanation: jockey said filly was unsuited by the heavy ground

3753 RIPON BELL-RINGER H'CAP 1m 4f 10y
4:00 (4:03) (Class 3) (0-90,90) 3-Y-O+
£11,217 (£3,358; £1,679; £840; £419; £210) **Stalls** High

Form RPR

10-3 **1** **Spanish Hidalgo (IRE)**[15] 3272 3-9-3 **90** TPO'Shea 11 104+
(J L Dunlop) *hld up in rr: smooth hdwy on outer 3f out: led 2f out: rdn over 1f out: drvn ins fnl f and styd on wl* **9/2**[2]

230- **2** *1 1/4* **Wing Collar**[385] 3078 6-9-12 **87** DavidAllan 8 98
(T D Easterby) *hld up in rr: hdwy and nt clr run 2f out and again over 1f out: swtchd rt and rdn to chal ins fnl f: no ex towards fin* **20/1**

-400 **3** *3* **Kyoto Summit**[7] 3558 4-9-8 **83** PaulMulrennan 9 89
(M W Easterby) *a.p: ev ch 2f out: sn rdn and kpt on same pce ins fnl f* **10/1**

-060 **4** *2 1/2* **Nelsons Column (IRE)**[57] 2011 4-9-1 **79** AndrewElliott(3) 2 81
(G M Moore) *led after 2f: rdn along 3f out: hdd 2f out and sn drvn: wknd ent fnl f* **14/1**

1 **5** *3* **Speed Gifted**[34] 2690 3-9-2 **89** NickyMackay 4 87
(L M Cumani) *trckd ldrs: hdwy 3f out: rdn 2f out and ev ch: drvn over 1f out and sn one pce* **5/1**[3]

0-13 **6** *nk* **Stretton (IRE)**[42] 2465 9-9-7 **82** PatCosgrave 13 79
(J D Bethell) *trckd ldrs on inner: effrt over 2f out: sn rdn and kpt on same pce fnl f* **25/1**

2636 **7** *2* **Lets Roll**[28] 2861 6-9-9 **89** PJMcDonald(5) 1 83
(C W Thornton) *in tch on outer: effrt 3f out: sn rdn and one pce fnl 2f* **8/1**

143 **8** *shd* **Cotton Eyed Joe (IRE)**[12] 3371 6-8-10 **71** oh1 DaleGibson 7 65
(G A Swinbank) *in tch: effrt 3f out: sn rdn along and wknd wl over 1f out* **8/1**

3322 **9** *9* **Cleaver**[16] 3242 6-8-12 **80** WilliamCarson(7) 6 61
(Lady Herries) *hld up in rr: hdwy on outer 3f out: rdn wl over 1f out and sn btn* **7/2**[1]

/60- **10** *3 1/2* **Annibale Caro**[110] 3431 5-9-2 **77** PhillipMakin 12 52
(Grant Tuer) *in tch on inner: rdn along wl over 2f out and sn wknd* **66/1**

-441 **11** *7* **Domino Dancer (IRE)**[21] 3093 3-8-13 **86** TomEaves 5 51
(J Wade) *led 2f: prom tl rdn along 3f out and sn wknd* **17/2**

2m 47.41s (10.41) **Going Correction** +1.075s/f (Soft)
WFA 3 from 4yo+ 12lb **11** Ran SP% **115.7**
Speed ratings (Par 107):108,107,105,103,101 101,99,99,93,91 86
CSF £96.85 CT £867.14 TOTE £4.80: £2.10, £7.90, £3.20; EX 121.00 Trifecta £636.80 Part won. Pool: £897.02, 0.94 winning units..

Owner Windflower Overseas Holdings Inc **Bred** Windflower Overseas Holdings Inc **Trained** Arundel, W Sussex

FOCUS
A good handicap run at a decent pace in the ground and sound form. The winner improved by 6lb and could do better still.

NOTEBOOK
Spanish Hidalgo(IRE), upped in trip, travelled smoothly throughout before being let down to lead with a quarter of a mile to run. The runner-up looked a threat inside the last, but he found more when challenged. There could be more to come from him. (op 4-1 tchd 5-1)

Wing Collar, who has recorded all three of his wins on fast ground, ran well in these very different conditions. Held up as usual, he had to wait for a run but looked set to claim the leader when pulled out to challenge inside the last, only to find less than he had promised. This was an encouraging effort on his first start for a year, and the return of cheekpieces could sharpen him up next time. (op 16-1)

Kyoto Summit ran a solid race on this return to a more suitable trip and stuck on willingly for third.

Nelsons Column(IRE) managed to get over from his low stall to lead after a couple of furlongs and eventually faded after being collared entering the last quarter mile. He seems best at slightly shorter.

Speed Gifted, making his handicap debut after an easy win in a maiden on his debut, travelled well for much of the way but did not find much in the testing conditions when asked for his effort. (op 9-2 tchd 4-1)

Lets Roll is still 3lb above his last wining mark, and 13lb higher than when winning this race three years ago. (op 6-1)

Cleaver, who was well backed, was racing from a career-high mark and could make little impression after being asked to improve in the straight. Official explanation: trainer's rep had no explanation for the poor form shown (op 6-1)

Annibale Caro Official explanation: jockey said gelding was unsuited by the heavy ground

3754 BIRCHALL CATERING SUPPLIES H'CAP 1m
4:35 (4:36) (Class 5) (0-70,70) 3-Y-O+ **£3,886** (£1,156; £577; £288) **Stalls** High

Form RPR

0332 **1** **Emperor's Well**[12] 3376 8-8-9 **51** PaulMulrennan 14 68
(M W Easterby) *mde all: rdn clr 2f out: styd on strly* **11/4**[2]

-150 **2** *6* **Jeu D'Esprit (IRE)**[45] 2361 4-9-11 **67** RoystonFfrench 2 72
(J G Given) *chsd ldrs: rdn along over 2f out: n.m.r over 1f out: styd on ins fnl f* **25/1**

1632 **3** *1 3/4* **Apache Nation (IRE)**[6] 3571 4-9-4 **60** PhillipMakin 5 62
(M Dods) *hld up in tch: pushed along and outpcd over 3f out: rdn over 2f out: kpt on u.p appr fnl f* **9/4**[1]

4013 **4** *1 3/4* **Top Dirham**[6] 3571 9-8-13 **55** DaleGibson 1 53
(M W Easterby) *hld up in rr: hdwy over 2f out: rdn over 1f out: styd on ins fnl f: nrst fin* **15/2**

-023 **5** *hd* **Damelza (IRE)**[24] 2988 4-9-11 **70** DuranFentiman(3) 13 68
(T D Easterby) *hld up in rr: hdwy on inner 3f out: rdn and n.m.r over 1f out: swtchd lft and styd on same pce* **10/1**

0400 **6** *3 1/2* **Apsara**[19] 3156 6-9-0 **59** AndrewElliott(3) 3 50
(G M Moore) *chsd wnr: rdn along 3f out: drvn 2f out: wkng whn hmpd over 1f out* **14/1**

0-00 **7** *nk* **Newsround**[12] 3375 5-8-2 **51** oh6 (b) FrankiePickard(7) 6 41
(D W Chapman) *s.i.s and bhd: gd hdwy on outer 3f out: rdn to chse wnr whn hung bdly rt over 1f out: wknd ins fnl f* **40/1**

1562 **8** *4* **Efidium**[7] 3556 9-9-12 **68** PaulFessey 4 50
(N Bycroft) *hld up in rr: hdwy on outer 3f out: rdn to chse ldrs 2f out: sn drvn and wknd* **13/2**[3]

4300 **9** *1/2* **Campo Bueno (FR)**[6] 3572 5-9-7 **66** (b) PatrickMathers(3) 11 47
(A Berry) *chsd ldng pair on inner: rdn along 3f out: wknd 2f out* **16/1**

0005 **10** *1* **Kadia**[12] 3381 4-8-9 **51** oh6 MickyFenton 12 30
(P T Midgley) *midfield: rdn along 3f out: sn wknd* **25/1**

0046 **11** *8* **Tantien**[22] 3045 5-8-4 **51** oh6 (p) ColinHaddon(5) 9 14
(T Keddy) *chsd ldrs: rdn along 3f out and sn wknd* **80/1**

0660 **12** *19* **First Rhapsody (IRE)**[16] 3247 5-8-9 **51** oh4 NickyMackay 8 —
(T J Etherington) *a towards rr* **25/1**

1m 48.92s (7.82) **Going Correction** +1.075s/f (Soft) **12** Ran SP% **119.4**
Speed ratings (Par 103):103,97,95,93,93 89,89,85,85,84 76,57
CSF £79.14 CT £185.53 TOTE £4.10: £1.70, £4.80, £1.50; EX 85.30 Trifecta £650.80 Part won. Pool: £916.62, 0.64 winning units..

The Form Book, Raceform Ltd, Compton, RG20 6NL

Owner M W Easterby **Bred** M W Easterby & K Hodgson **Trained** Sheriff Hutton, N Yorks
FOCUS
The winner made all and nothing was able to seriously challenge him. He probably did not need to improve on his latest effort, and this is pretty weak form.
Newsround Official explanation: jockey said gelding hung right final 3f
First Rhapsody(IRE) Official explanation: jockey said mare was unsuited by the heavy ground

3755 BISHOPTON H'CAP — 1m 1f 170y
5:05 (5:05) (Class 4) (0-85,84) 3-Y-O+ **£6,309** (£1,888; £944; £472; £235) **Stalls** High

Form — RPR
4263 **1** **Suits Me**[28] 2868 4-8-11 **67** .... MickyFenton 7 — 76
(T P Tate) *mde virtually all: rdn 2f out: drvn ent fnl f: styd on gamely towards fin* **9/4**[2]
0512 **2** *nk* **Smugglers Bay (IRE)**[14] 3299 3-8-1 **70** .... DuranFentiman(3) 6 — 78
(T D Easterby) *chsd ldrs: effrt over 2f out and sn rdn: chal over 1f out and ev ch tl drvn ins fnl f and no ex towards fin* **13/8**[1]
5634 **3** *3* **Bajan Parkes**[7] 3530 4-9-7 **77** .... AdrianTNicholls 5 — 79
(E J Alston) *hld up: hdwy on inner 3f out: rdn along 2f out: drvn over 1f out and kpt on same pce* **9/2**[3]
0-06 **4** *9* **Gala Sunday (USA)**[7] 3539 7-8-9 **65** oh1 .... (t) DaleGibson 4 — 49
(M W Easterby) *prom: rdn along 3f out: drvn 2f out and sn one pce* **16/1**
111 **5** *6* **Just Lille (IRE)**[23] 3016 4-10-0 **84** .... (p) RoystonFfrench 2 — 56
(Mrs A Duffield) *trckd ldrs: rdn along and lost pl 1/2-way: drvn and hdwy on outer 3f out: wknd over 1f out* **5/1**
0000 **6** *26* **Magic Sting**[21] 3093 6-8-8 **67** .... JamieMoriarty(3) 3 — —
(B S Rothwell) *dwlt: sn cl up: rdn along 3f out and sn wknd* **14/1**

2m 14.56s (9.56) **Going Correction** +1.075s/f (Soft)
WFA 3 from 4yo+ 10lb — **6** Ran SP% **116.3**
Speed ratings (Par 105):104,103,101,94,89 68
CSF £6.66 CT £14.07 TOTE £3.70: £1.90, £1.40; EX 8.50 Trifecta £37.00 Pool: £859.55, 16.46 winning units. Place 6 £16.57, Place 5 £12.94..
Owner D E Cook **Bred** R S A Urquhart **Trained** Tadcaster, N Yorks
FOCUS
The slowest of the three races on the round course. Sound form, the winner up 3lb on his latest mark and the runner-up to his recent mark.
Just Lille(IRE) Official explanation: jockey said filly was unsuited by the heavy ground
T/Plt: £14.30 to a £1 stake. Pool: £84,338.70. 4,277.65 winning tickets. T/Qpdt: £11.20 to a £1 stake. Pool: £3,468.40. 227.60 winning tickets. JR

3756 - 3759a (Foreign Racing) - See Raceform Interactive

2888
REDCAR (L-H)
Sunday, July 22

OFFICIAL GOING: Good to soft (soft in places; 8.0)
The ground was described as 'mainly good to soft but with some soft patches'.
Wind: Moderate, half-behind Weather: Overcast, showers

3760 EUROPEAN BREEDERS' FUND MAIDEN STKS (DIV I) — 7f
2:20 (2:21) (Class 5) 2-Y-O **£2,817** (£838; £418; £209) **Stalls** Centre

Form — RPR
3 **1** **Midnight Muse (USA)**[18] 3199 2-9-3 0 .... PaulFessey 4 — 82
(T D Barron) *chsd ldr: led 3f out: hld on towards fin* **7/2**[1]
2 *nk* **The Oil Magnate** 2-9-3 0 .... PhillipMakin 11 — 81
(M Dods) *mid-div: hdwy over 2f out: chal 1f out: no ex towards fin* **20/1**
3 *1* **Tarkheena Prince (USA)** 2-9-3 0 .... JamieSpencer 14 — 79+
(G A Swinbank) *s.s: sn drvn along in rr: edgd rt over 2f out: chsng ldrs 1f out: kpt on: improve* **6/1**
20 **4** *3 1/2* **Isent She Rich (IRE)**[2] 3706 2-8-12 0 .... KDarley 2 — 65
(M G Quinlan) *trckd ldrs: effrt over 3f out: wknd fnl f* **9/2**[2]
5 *3* **Thunderstruck** 2-9-3 0 .... PatCosgrave 10 — 63
(K A Ryan) *sn chsng ldrs: kpt on same pce fnl 2f* **8/1**
6 **6** *3/4* **Rapidity**[38] 2604 2-9-3 0 .... ChrisCatlin 5 — 61
(E J O'Neill) *chsd ldrs: kpt on same pce fnl 2f* **11/1**
0 **7** *1* **Just Jimmy (IRE)**[9] 3479 2-9-3 0 .... StephenDonohoe 6 — 58
(P D Evans) *led tl 3f out: one pce* **16/1**
8 *2* **Grecian Slave** 2-9-3 0 .... PaulEddery 7 — 53
(B Smart) *swvd rt s: sn chsng ldrs: rdn over 2f out: sn fdd* **8/1**
0 **9** *6* **Cottam Breeze**[28] 2904 2-8-12 0 .... DaleGibson 15 — 33
(M W Easterby) *in rr: rdn 3f out: sn bhd* **40/1**
10 *2* **Step This Way (USA)** 2-8-12 0 .... JoeFanning 9 — 38+
(M Johnston) *dwlt and hmpd s: in rr: hdwy 3f out: edgd lft: wknd and eased over 1f out* **5/1**[3]
0 **11** *1 1/4* **Carlton Mac**[63] 1859 2-9-3 0 .... (b[1]) SilvestreDeSousa 1 — 30
(N Bycroft) *swvd lft s: in rr: rdn over 3f out: sn bhd* **66/1**
0 **12** *hd* **Viola Rosa (IRE)**[20] 3171 2-8-9 0 .... DuranFentiman(3) 13 — 25
(D Shaw) *mid-div: drvn over 3f out: sn lost pl* **100/1**
00 **13** *1* **Motherwell**[33] 2739 2-8-5 0 .... PatrickDonaghy(7) 12 — 22
(M Brittain) *mid-div: rdn and lost pl 3f out* **66/1**

1m 27.25s (2.35) **Going Correction** +0.30s/f (Good) — **13** Ran SP% **119.0**
Speed ratings (Par 94):98,97,96,92,89 88,87,84,77,75 74,74,72
CSF £79.29 TOTE £4.30: £1.50, £7.60, £2.00; EX 68.90.
Owner Clive Washbourn **Bred** Flaxman Holdings Ltd **Trained** Maunby, N Yorks
■ Eton Rifles (10/1) was withdrawn on vet's advice. R4 deduction 5p in the £. New market formed.
FOCUS
The quicker and almost certainly stronger division of this maiden and the form appears reasonable.
NOTEBOOK
Midnight Muse(USA), quite keen to post, knew his job this time and showed a gritty attitude to fight off the runner-up's sustained challenge. Nurseries now beckon. (old market op 5-1)
The Oil Magnate, a leggy, narrow March foal, did not go unbacked on his debut. He worked his way upsides entering the final furlong and in the end only just missed out. He looks a ready-made winner. (old market op 33-1)
Tarkheena Prince(USA) ◆, a May foal, is a lengthy, decent type. He fell out of the traps and showed his inexperience in the closing stages. He looks sure to improve a good deal. (old market op 13-2 tchd 7-1)
Isent She Rich(IRE), having her second outing in three days, lacks size and scope and was on her toes beforehand. In the end she did not see it out. (old market op 7-2)
Thunderstruck, who stands over a fair amount of ground, has quite a round action. He will improve for the outing. (old market op 9-1)
Rapidity, a moderate mover, showed a fair bit more than he had done on his debut five weeks earlier. (old market op 12-1)
Step This Way(USA), a rangy filly, is a lazy walker and showed a choppy action. Interfered with at the start, she was soon making hard work of it and in the end dropped right away. She can surely do a fair bit better than this. (old market op 6-1, new market tchd 9-2)

3761 EUROPEAN BREEDERS' FUND MAIDEN STKS (DIV II) — 7f
2:50 (2:51) (Class 5) 2-Y-O **£2,817** (£838; £418; £209) **Stalls** Centre

Form — RPR
4 **1** **Annaliesse (IRE)**[19] 3192 2-8-12 0 .... PaulHanagan 1 — 68
(R A Fahey) *chsd ldrs: effrt over 2f out: edgd rt over 1f out: styd on to ld last 150yds* **5/1**[3]
2 *1* **Mangham (IRE)** 2-9-3 0 .... RoystonFfrench 13 — 71
(B Smart) *mid-div: effrt over 2f out: sn chsng ldrs: styd on wl ins fnl f* **17/2**
3 **3** *1* **Red Cauldron**[33] 2739 2-9-3 0 .... ChrisCatlin 8 — 68
(E J O'Neill) *w ldrs: hrd rdn and edgd lft fnl f: kpt on same pce* **11/4**[1]
5 **4** *hd* **Zabougg**[40] 2532 2-9-3 0 .... JamieSpencer 3 — 68
(G A Swinbank) *hld up: hdwy and edgd rt over 2f out: sn chsng ldrs: hung lft: no ex fnl f* **3/1**[2]
0 **5** *3/4* **Strictly Elsie (IRE)**[19] 3192 2-8-12 0 .... PaddyAspell 2 — 61
(J R Norton) *led tl ins fnl f: wknd towards fin* **66/1**
6 *1 1/4* **Zakhaaref** 2-9-3 0 .... JoeFanning 15 — 63+
(M Johnston) *chsd ldrs: chal 2f out: fdd last 150yds* **11/2**
46 **7** *3 1/2* **Lady Of Kintyre (IRE)**[34] 2717 2-8-12 0 .... SaleemGolam 4 — 49
(E J Alston) *swvd lft s: hdwy to chse ldrs over 3f out: wknd over 1f out* **16/1**
0 **8** *4* **Flower Appeal**[22] 3092 2-8-12 0 .... DaleGibson 12 — 39
(M W Easterby) *mid-div: outpcd 3f out: no threat after* **80/1**
9 *1 1/2* **Kalanda Kurl (IRE)** 2-8-12 0 .... PatCosgrave 10 — 35
(J J Quinn) *dwlt: sme hdwy 3f out: sn wknd* **33/1**
66 **10** *3* **Cairnbrae**[29] 2888 2-9-3 0 .... TomEaves 5 — 33
(Miss J A Camacho) *hld up in rr: nvr a factor* **20/1**
00 **11** *2 1/2* **Cobbold Point**[24] 3037 2-8-10 0 .... NSLawes(7) 9 — 26
(M W Easterby) *chsd ldrs: lost pl 3f out* **100/1**
12 *1 3/4* **Barashi** 2-9-3 0 .... TonyHamilton 11 — 22
(J Howard Johnson) *sn chsng ldrs: lost pl over 2f out* **25/1**
13 *8* **Scarlet Royal** 2-8-12 0 .... PaulQuinn 6 — —
(Mrs Marjorie Fife) *mid-div: wknd 3f out* **66/1**
14 *41* **Fellrunner (IRE)** 2-9-3 0 .... StephenDonohoe 14 — —
(A Berry) *s.v.s: a t.o in last* **100/1**

1m 28.71s (3.81) **Going Correction** +0.30s/f (Good) — **14** Ran SP% **117.9**
Speed ratings (Par 94):90,88,87,87,86 85,81,76,74,71 68,66,57,10
CSF £43.41 TOTE £6.70: £2.00, £2.60, £1.50; EX 61.40.
Owner Dr Anne J F Gillespie **Bred** Dr A Gillespie **Trained** Musley Bank, N Yorks
FOCUS
The slower division, and much the weaker too, rated around the principals.
NOTEBOOK
Annaliesse(IRE) had clearly learned from her debut. She made hard work of it but was firmly in command at the line. (op 6-1)
Mangham(IRE), a February-foaled son of Montjeu, looked to be carrying plenty of condition. He took a while to grasp the nettle but finished to some purpose to claim second spot. This will have taught him plenty. (op 6-1)
Red Cauldron, keen to post, came off a straight line under severe pressure and in the end was simply not good enough. (op 3-1 tchd 10-3 and 5-2)
Zabougg, who looked really well, hung under pressure and never looked to be putting his best foot forward. (op 11-4 tchd 10-3)
Strictly Elsie(IRE), nothing much at all to look at, was a lot sharper this time and took them along only to fold completely near the line.
Zakhaaref, a February foal, stands over plenty of ground. He showed ability first time but tired in the closing stages. Hopefully the outing will bring him on a fair bit. (op 13-2)

3762 REDCAR SPRINT H'CAP — 6f
3:20 (3:20) (Class 4) (0-85,82) 3-Y-O+ **£6,477** (£1,927; £963; £481) **Stalls** Centre

Form — RPR
420- **1** **Tamagin (USA)**[204] 6986 4-9-7 **77** .... PatCosgrave 4 — 84
(K A Ryan) *mde all: hld on wl* **28/1**
422 **2** *3/4* **Chjimes (IRE)**[15] 3334 3-8-13 **77** .... AndrewElliott(3) 2 — 81
(K R Burke) *chsd wnr: no ex ins fnl f* **10/1**
0604 **3** *1/2* **Prince Namid**[8] 3557 5-9-12 **82** .... RoystonFfrench 8 — 85
(Mrs A Duffield) *chsd two clr ldrs: kpt on wl fnl f* **8/1**[3]
0661 **4** *shd* **River Thames**[6] 3585 4-9-6 **76** 6ex .... JamieSpencer 9 — 79
(K A Ryan) *stdd s: effrt and shkn up 2f out: edgd lft: sn chsng ldrs: fdd towards fin* **5/6**[1]
6011 **5** *1/2* **Mafaheem**[20] 3163 5-9-0 **70** .... StephenDonohoe 1 — 71
(P D Evans) *prom: lost pl over 3f out: hdwy and edgd rt 2f out: kpt on ins fnl f* **14/1**
1062 **6** *1 1/4* **Paris Bell**[8] 3557 5-9-7 **77** .... PaulQuinn 3 — 74
(T D Easterby) *s.s: t.k.h in rr: hdwy over 2f out: rdn and wknd over 1f out* **6/1**[2]
0010 **7** *1* **Petite Mac**[19] 3194 7-8-7 **63** oh8 .... (b) SilvestreDeSousa 6 — 57
(N Bycroft) *mid-div: rdn and outpcd 3f out: styd on fnl f* **40/1**
4203 **8** *6* **High Reach**[6] 3585 7-8-10 **73** .... DeanHeslop(7) 10 — 49
(T D Barron) *chsd two clr ldrs towards stands' side: wknd over 1f out* **12/1**
3030 **9** *hd* **Cornus**[6] 3599 5-9-0 **70** .... (be) DavidAllan 12 — 46
(A J McCabe) *chsd two clr ldrs: rdn over 2f out: sn lost pl* **16/1**
102- **10** *4* **Sir Nod**[254] 6428 5-9-8 **78** .... TomEaves 7 — 42
(Miss J A Camacho) *t.k.h in rr: effrt over 2f out: sn wknd* **22/1**

1m 14.0s (2.30) **Going Correction** +0.45s/f (Yiel)
WFA 3 from 4yo+ 5lb — **10** Ran SP% **119.5**
Speed ratings (Par 105):102,101,100,100,99 97,96,88,88,82
CSF £285.29 CT £2514.63 TOTE £37.70: £8.80, £2.70, £2.10; EX 296.70 TRIFECTA Not won..
Owner Tariq Al Nisf **Bred** Stonehaven Farm Llc **Trained** Hambleton, N Yorks
FOCUS
A fair handicap in which the first two were one-two throughout in what looked a strongly-run race. The form is not totally convincing and best rated through the runner-up.

3763 BOOK EARLY FOR GROUP DISCOUNTS H'CAP — 5f
3:50 (3:51) (Class 5) (0-70,69) 3-Y-O **£2,817** (£838; £418; £209) **Stalls** Centre

Form — RPR
0022 **1** **Silly Gilly (IRE)**[7] 3568 3-7-13 **50** oh2 .... AndrewElliott(3) 8 — 58
(K R Burke) *chsd ldr: led over 1f out: styd on wl* **4/1**[1]
-042 **2** *1 3/4* **By The Edge (IRE)**[6] 3588 3-8-2 **50** oh2 .... (v) PaulFessey 7 — 52
(T D Barron) *led tl over 1f out: kpt on same pce* **11/2**[3]
4036 **3** *3/4* **Princess Ellis**[34] 2718 3-8-12 **60** .... KDarley 3 — 59
(E J Alston) *s.s: racd w one other far side: t.k.h: led that side over 3f out: no ex ins fnl f* **5/1**[2]
060 **4** *1 1/2* **The Cube**[15] 3302 3-8-2 **50** oh5 .... (b) PaulHanagan 10 — 44
(J Balding) *swvd rt s: in rr: kpt on wl fnl f* **25/1**
0260 **5** *1/2* **Bollin Franny**[11] 3413 3-9-1 **63** .... (e[1]) DavidAllan 5 — 55
(T D Easterby) *chsd ldrs: effrt over 2f out: kpt on same pce* **7/1**

0316 **6** 1/2 **Baybshambles (IRE)**14 3342 3-8-4 **55** DominicFox(3) 11 45
(R E Barr) *s.i.s: in rr: hit over hd by rival rdr's whip 1f out: styd on wl* **8/1**
003 **7** 1 1/4 **Lord Of The Reins (IRE)**27 2948 3-8-3 **51** oh2 ow1.. SaleemGolam 14 37
(D Shaw) *prom: rdn over 2f out: one pce* **25/1**
415 **8** 1/2 **Time Share (IRE)**3 3688 3-8-6 **54** (be) HayleyTurner 13 38
(J Ryan) *chsd ldrs: outpcd fnl 2f* **6/1**
4132 **9** 1 1/4 **La Vecchia Scuola (IRE)**11 3413 3-8-11 **59** (b) AdrianTNicholls 9 39
(R Johnson) *mid-div: sn drvn along: nvr a threat* **15/2**
4055 **10** 2 **Bentley**9 3483 3-9-0 **62** (v) TomEaves 12 34
(D Shaw) *outpcd and a in rr* **11/1**
-000 **11** 1 1/2 **To Party (IRE)**22 3110 3-8-12 **60** StephenDonohoe 4 27
(P D Evans) *racd w one other far side: lost pl over 2f out: eased whn no ch fnl f* **25/1**

60.65 secs (1.95) **Going Correction** +0.45s/f (Yiel) **11** Ran SP% **121.6**
Speed ratings (Par 100):102,99,98,95,94 94,92,91,89,86 83
CSF £26.10 CT £110.77 TOTE £4.50: £1.80, £3.00, £2.40; EX 30.20.
Owner Gary Williams **Bred** Barronstown Stud **Trained** Middleham Moor, N Yorks

FOCUS
A low-grade handicap and the first two home dominated. The form looks sound rated around the first three.
La Vecchia Scuola(IRE) Official explanation: trainer said filly was in season

3764 JOURNEY SOUTH H'CAP 1m
4:20 (4:20) (Class 5) (0-75,77) 3-Y-0+ **£3,886** (£1,156; £577; £288) **Stalls** Centre

Form RPR
5622 **1** **Celtic Change (IRE)**30 2834 3-9-1 **71** JamieSpencer 7 78+
(M Dods) *hld up in rr: effrt over 2f out: hung rt and led 1f out: idled: rdn out* **11/8**1
5-64 **2** 3/4 **Moonhawk**19 3194 4-9-4 **66** TomEaves 9 73
(J Howard Johnson) *bmpd s: sn pushed along: hdwy over 3f out: styd on to take 2nd ins fnl f: no ex* **8/1**
-030 **3** 1 1/4 **Rodeo**8 3556 4-9-7 **74** (b) PJMcDonald(5) 4 78
(C W Thornton) *chsd ldrs: kpt on same pce fnl f* **25/1**
1000 **4** 1 1/2 **Kudbeme**11 3414 5-8-11 **59** PaulFessey 6 60
(N Bycroft) *s.i.s: bhd: hdwy over 2f out: styd on fnl f* **25/1**
6040 **5** nk **Thunderwing (IRE)**2 3721 5-8-7 **58** AndrewElliott(3) 2 58
(K R Burke) *w ldr: led over 2f out: hdd 1f out: n.m.r and wknd ins fnl f* **11/2**3
0325 **6** 7 **King Of The Moors (USA)**8 3556 4-9-11 **73** PhillipMakin 3 57
(T D Barron) *chsd ldrs: lost pl over 1f out* **4/1**2
30-0 **7** 3 **Queen's Composer (IRE)**68 1747 4-9-8 **70** RoystonFfrench 1 47
(B Smart) *sn drvn along: sn chsng ldrs: wknd 2f out* **12/1**
301 **8** 3 **Stolen Glance**8 3539 4-10-1 **77** DaleGibson 11 47
(M W Easterby) *chsd ldrs stands' side: wknd 2f out* **10/1**
0040 **9** 3 **Lewis Lloyd (IRE)**14 3345 4-8-5 **56** oh11 (t) DuranFentiman(3) 8 19
(R E Barr) *dwlt: a in rr: bhd fnl 2f* **50/1**
40-2 **10** 9 **Hiats**138 627 5-8-8 **56** oh9 PatCosgrave 10 —
(R Craggs) *swvd lft s: led: hdd over 2f out: wknd qckly* **33/1**

1m 41.33s (3.53) **Going Correction** +0.575s/f (Yiel)
WFA 3 from 4yo+ 8lb **10** Ran SP% **118.0**
Speed ratings (Par 103):105,104,103,101,101 94,91,88,85,76
CSF £12.97 CT £196.08 TOTE £2.40: £1.30, £2.40, £5.10; EX 14.70.
Owner P Taylor **Bred** Wardstown Stud Ltd **Trained** Denton, Co Durham

FOCUS
A modest handicap and the winner, who looks his own worst enemy, did not need to improve on previous form with the second setting the level.

3765 CLEVELAND HUNT H'CAP 1m
4:50 (4:50) (Class 6) (0-65,63) 3-Y-0+ **£1,943** (£578; £288; £144) **Stalls** Centre

Form RPR
00-4 **1** **Lauro**13 3381 7-9-3 **59** DawnRankin(7) 15 65
(Miss J A Camacho) *hld up: hdwy stands' side 3f out: styd on fnl f: led post* **7/1**2
4000 **2** shd **Fair Shake (IRE)**14 3343 7-9-10 **59** (v) FTahir 2 65
(Karen McLintock) *mid-div: effrt over 2f out: led 1f out: hung lft: hdd post* **12/1**
2610 **3** 1 **Eternal Legacy (IRE)**14 3345 5-9-5 **54** DavidAllan 13 58
(E J Alston) *w ldrs: led 3f out tl 1f out: kpt on same pce* **8/1**3
0042 **4** shd **Colditz (IRE)**6 3587 3-8-7 **50** (p) TonyHamilton 4 51
(D W Barker) *chsd ldrs: chal 2f out: kpt on same pce fnl f* **4/1**1
0-00 **5** hd **Miss Percy**20 3159 3-9-1 **58** PaulHanagan 12 59
(R A Fahey) *sn in rr and drvn along: hdwy over 2f out: styd on wl ins fnl f* **14/1**
5336 **6** 1 3/4 **Borodinsky**13 3376 6-9-1 **50** TomEaves 1 49
(R E Barr) *sn w ldrs: wknd ins fnl f* **11/1**
005 **7** 1 3/4 **Betteras Bertie**29 2894 4-8-10 **45** KDarley 11 40
(M Brittain) *swvd lft s: hdwy far side over 3f out: sn chsng ldrs: wknd last 150yds* **16/1**
0150 **8** 3 1/2 **Lobengula (IRE)**167 363 5-10-0 **63** RoystonFfrench 3 50
(I W McInnes) *led tl 3f out: lost pl over 1f out* **16/1**
0622 **9** 1 1/2 **Apache Point (IRE)**19 3195 10-9-3 **52** KimTinkler 5 35
(N Tinkler) *chsd ldrs: sn drvn along: edgd lft and lost pl over 2f out* **4/1**1
/50- **10** 2 **Young Scotton**417 1123 7-9-11 **60** PatCosgrave 9 39
(J D Bethell) *in rr-div: drvn 4f out: nvr on terms* **25/1**
0050 **11** 8 **Dazzler Mac**13 3381 6-9-0 **49** PaulFessey 10 9
(N Bycroft) *in rr-div: drvn over 3f out: bhd fnl 2f* **9/1**
0100 **12** 3/4 **Steel Grey**2 3721 6-9-0 **49** AdrianTNicholls 8 8
(M Brittain) *chsd ldrs: sn rdn and lost pl over 3f out: sn bhd* **33/1**
0-00 **13** nk **Uhuru Peak**23 3067 6-9-4 **53** (bt) DaleGibson 14 11
(M W Easterby) *s.i.s: hld up in rr: hdwy over 3f out: lost pl over 2f out* **11/1**

1m 42.59s (4.79) **Going Correction** +0.575s/f (Yiel)
WFA 3 from 4yo+ 8lb **13** Ran SP% **123.2**
Speed ratings (Par 101):99,98,97,97,97 95,94,90,89,87 79,78,78
CSF £91.29 CT £720.18 TOTE £9.70: £2.50, £5.60, £2.90; EX 109.60 Place 6 £202.29, Place 5 £75.39..
Owner Miss Julie Camacho **Bred** Mrs S Camacho **Trained** Norton, N Yorks

FOCUS
Another low-grade handicap and it was very much a case of the runner-up throwing it away. the form is moderate and does not look that strong.
Apache Point(IRE) Official explanation: jockey said gelding lost its action
Dazzler Mac Official explanation: jockey said gelding lost its action
T/Jkpt: Not won. T/Plt: £557.40 to a £1 stake. Pool: £84,763.60. 111.00 winning tickets. T/Qpdt: £65.90 to a £1 stake. Pool: £4,637.10. 52.00 winning tickets. WG

3766 - 3767a (Foreign Racing) - See Raceform Interactive

FAIRYHOUSE (R-H)
Sunday, July 22

OFFICIAL GOING: Heavy

3768a BELGRAVE STKS (LISTED RACE) 6f
3:05 (3:05) 3-Y-0+ **£21,993** (£6,452; £3,074; £1,047)

RPR
1 **Haatef (USA)**25 3009 3-9-1 116 DPMcDonogh 2 107+
(Kevin Prendergast, Ire) *hld up in tch: impr into 3rd on outer ent st: led 1 1/2f out: rdn and kpt on wl* **1/2**1
2 1 1/2 **Moone Cross (IRE)**306 5462 4-9-3 95 PJSmullen 3 98
(Mrs John Harrington, Ire) *hld up in rr: hdwy on outer early st: 2nd under 1f out: kpt on wl* **20/1**
3 1 1/4 **Majestic Times (IRE)**7 3575 7-9-6 100 PShanahan 7 97
(Liam McAteer, Ire) *chsd ldrs in 5th: outpcd ent st: 6th 1f out: styd on wl cl home* **12/1**
4 1 **Lidanski (IRE)**7 3573 4-9-3 86 JAHeffernan 4 91
(W P Mullins, Ire) *trckd ldrs: 4th and rdn early st: kpt on same pce fr over 1f out* **9/1**3
5 1 1/4 **Senor Benny (USA)**7 3573 8-9-6 97 MJKinane 1 91
(M McDonagh, Ire) *cl 2nd: rdn to ld 2f out: hdd 1 1/2f out: no ex fnl f* **6/1**2
6 1 **Kingsdale Ocean (IRE)**7 3573 4-9-6 97 (b) WJSupple 6 88
(Ms Florence Mills, Ire) *sn led: rdn and hdd 2f out: no ex fr over 1f out* **20/1**
7 4 1/2 **Lucky Kyllachy (USA)**21 3140 3-9-1 95 WMLordan 8 74
(David Wachman, Ire) *chsd ldrs: 3rd early: 5th after 1/2-way: no ex st* **14/1**

1m 18.6s (6.10)
WFA 3 from 4yo+ 5lb **8** Ran SP% **114.8**
CSF £13.74 TOTE £1.40: £1.10, £12.50; DF 20.40.
Owner Hamdan Al Maktoum **Bred** Shadwell Farm LLC **Trained** Friarstown, Co Kildare

FOCUS
The form has been rated through the third. The winner was value for a little further.

NOTEBOOK
Haatef(USA) was encountering what was by the some way the worst ground with which he has had to contend. The answer was that he coped with conditions well enough, travelling quite well before being asked to go for his race well over 1f out. He is now likely to head for Goodwood where the 7f Betfair Lennox Stakes is a likely alternative to the Sussex Stakes. (op 4/9)
Moone Cross(IRE), having her first run of the season, ran on from behind to take second without troubling the winner. She might go to Leopardstown at the weekend for the Sweet Mimosa Stakes. (op 16/1)
Majestic Times(IRE), last of four but far from disgraced in a 7f Group 3 on similar ground at the Curragh on his previous start, was back to a more suitable trip and he ran on well when switched to the outside and finished best of all. (op 9/1)
Lidanski(IRE), runner-up in the Rockingham Handicap at the Curragh on her previous start, was up against it at the weights. She performed creditably in the circumstances and managed to confirm Curragh placings with Senor Benny despite meeting that rival on far less favourable terms. (op 8/1 tchd 10/1)

3769 - 3777a (Foreign Racing) - See Raceform Interactive

2294 DUSSELDORF (R-H)
Sunday, July 22

OFFICIAL GOING: Good

3778a DEUTSCHLANDPREIS (GROUP 1) 1m 4f
3:35 (3:47) 3-Y-0+ **£60,811** (£23,649; £11,486; £5,743; £3,041)

RPR
1 **Schiaparelli (GER)**28 2924 4-9-6 AStarke 3 119
(P Schiergen, Germany) *first to show: trckd ldr tl led after 5f: rdn over 1f out: all out* **29/10**2
2 hd **Conillon (GER)**42 2502 3-8-6 TedDurcan 4 117
(A Wohler, Germany) *sn led: hdd after 5f: 2nd st: one l to make up 1f out: ev ch u.p wl ins fnl f: jst failed* **19/10**1
3 3 1/2 **First Stream (GER)**55 2102 3-8-6 ASuborics 5 111
(Mario Hofer, Germany) *a in tch: 4th st: kpt on one pce fr over 1f out* **9/2**
4 1/2 **Dickens (GER)**35 2706 4-9-6 FJohansson 1 113
(H Blume, Germany) *racd keenly early and hld up in 5th: effrt wl over 1f out on ins: disp 3rd 1f out: one pce* **92/10**
5 1/2 **Egerton (GER)**63 1872 6-9-6 TMundry 2 112
(P Rau, Germany) *disp 3rd to 3f out: 5th st: sn one pce* **34/10**3
6 1 1/4 **Oriental Tiger (GER)**28 2924 4-9-6 ABoschert 6 110
(U Ostmann, Germany) *hld up in rr: hdwy 3f out: 3rd st: btn over 1f out* **7/2**

2m 31.26s (1.72)
WFA 3 from 4yo+ 12lb **6** Ran SP% **133.1**
(including ten euro stakes): WIN 39; PL 20, 21; SF 95.
Owner Stall Blankenese **Bred** Gestut Karlshof **Trained** Germany

NOTEBOOK
Schiaparelli(GER) confirmed last year's Deutsches Derby form with Dickens and Oriental Tiger, ridden more prominently here and just holding off his younger rival.
Conillon(GER), taken out of the Deutsches Derby because of the testing ground, just missed out. He may take on Schiaparelli, and Derby winner Adlerflug, in the Grosser Preis Von Baden.

3147 MAISONS-LAFFITTE (R-H)
Sunday, July 22

OFFICIAL GOING: Good

3779a PRIX ROBERT PAPIN (GROUP 2) (C&F) 5f 110y
2:50 (2:52) 2-Y-O **£50,068** (£19,324; £9,223; £6,149; £3,074)

RPR
1 **Natagora (FR)**21 3147 2-8-13 C-PLemaire 1 108+
(P Bary, France) *mde all: pushed out: r.o wl* **9/10**1
2 3/4 **Magritte (ITY)**36 2684 2-8-13 CFiocchi 3 106
(R Menichetti, Italy) *pressed wnr: rdn and ev ch 1f out: no ex last 150yds* **44/10**2
3 3 **Strike The Deal (USA)**31 2785 2-9-2 CSoumillon 6 99+
(J Noseda) *s.i.s: hld up: last to 1f out: r.o to take 3rd cl home* **73/10**

The Form Book, Raceform Ltd, Compton, RG20 6NL

4 *nk* **Rey Davis (IRE)**[15] 2-9-2 .... J-BHamel 5 98
(Robert Collet, France) *hld up in 6th: styd on at one pce on outside fr over 1f out* **17/1**

5 *nk* **Art Advisor (IRE)**[31] 2785 2-9-2 .... SebSanders 2 97
(J Howard Johnson) *trckd wnr on rails while disputing 4th: rdn wl over 1f out: one pce* **47/10**[3]

6 *1 ½* **New Jersey (IRE)**[16] 3269 2-9-2 .... NCallan 4 92
(K A Ryan) *disp 4th: rdn wl over 1f out: one pce* **13/1**

7 *nk* **Major Eazy (IRE)**[22] 3085 2-9-2 .... JimmyFortune 7 91
(B J Meehan) *spd on outside while racing wd of first two: wknd wl over 1f out* **19/1**

63.02 secs (-3.05) **Going Correction** -0.35s/f (Firm) **7** Ran SP% **118.4**
Speed ratings: 106,105,101,100,100 98,97
PARI-MUTUEL: WIN 1.90; PL 1.40, 2.10; SF 6.10.
Owner Stefan Friborg **Bred** Bertrand Gouin & Georges Duca **Trained** Chantilly, France

FOCUS
The winner broke the course record by over a second.

NOTEBOOK
Natagora(FR), a very mature individual both physically and mentally, looked a picture in the paddock. Starting from the number one draw, she was smartly out of the stalls and when asked for a final effort at the furlong marker, quickened away and won with something in hand. She broke the course record by over a second and is unbeaten in her last four races. She now goes for the Prix Morny at Deauville and has already won over the trip.
Magritte(ITY), a fine-looking individual, tracked the winner virtually throughout and looked extremely dangerous at the furlong marker. She kept on right to the line and will try and take her revenge in the Morny.
Strike The Deal(USA) did not have the best of runs. He finally had some space running into the final furlong and was putting in his best work at the finish, but never looked like pegging back the front two. He is now a likely runner in the Richmond Stakes at Goodwood.
Rey Davis(IRE) was given a waiting race and came with his run on the outside. He just missed out on third and his performance might have been better than it looked as his jockey fell after the finish when his saddle slipped.
Art Advisor(IRE) looked in fine condition in the paddock and was raced just behind the winner. He could not quicken when things warmed up at the furlong marker and connections felt he did not like the lively ground.
New Jersey(IRE), given every possible chance, was settled behind the leaders in the stages, but was not a force to be reckoned with during the final furlong.
Major Eazy(IRE) raced on the outside and could not get cover. He was under pressure over a furlong out and gradually dropped out of contention.

3780a PRIX MESSIDOR (GROUP 3) (STRAIGHT) 1m (S)
3:20 (3:22) 3-Y-0+ **£27,027** (£10,811; £8,108; £5,405; £2,703)

RPR

1 **Stormy River (FR)**[63] 1879 4-9-1 .... TThulliez 7 116
(N Clement, France) *hld up in rr: hdwy on outside over 1f out: led 150yds out: pushed out and r.o wl* **2/1**[1]

2 *1 ½* **Satri (IRE)**[27] 2953 5-9-1 .... OPeslier 5 113
(J-M Beguigne, France) *trckd ldr: led 1 1/2f to 150yds out: one pce* **7/2**[3]

3 *hd* **Multiplex**[42] 2500 4-9-1 .... SPasquier 4 113
(A Fabre, France) *hld up: rdn over 1f out: styd on one pce* **22/10**[2]

4 *snk* **Echoes Rock (GER)**[25] 3011 4-9-1 .... JVictoire 3 112
(A Fabre, France) *pressed ldr: led 2f out to 1 1/2f out: sn one pce* **64/10**

5 *4* **Miles Gloriosus (USA)**[35] 4-9-1 .... CFiocchi 2 104
(R Menichetti, Italy) *hld up on rails: btn 2f out* **17/1**

6 *1 ½* **Notability (IRE)**[33] 2735 5-9-1 .... KerrinMcEvoy 1 101
(Saeed Bin Suroor) *racd on rails: disp 2nd tl wkng 2f out* **17/2**

7 *5* **Palafamix (FR)**[63] 1879 4-9-1 .... J-MBreux 6 91
(N Clement, France) *led to 2f out* **2/1**[1]

1m 33.9s (-9.70) **Going Correction** -0.90s/f (Hard) **7** Ran SP% **149.7**
Speed ratings: 112,110,110,110,106 104,99
PARI-MUTUEL: WIN 3.00 (coupled with Palafamix); PL 1.90, 2.30; SF 12.30.
Owner Ecurie Mister Ess A S **Bred** J Collet & Mlle M I Collet **Trained** Chantilly, France

NOTEBOOK
Stormy River(FR), wearing cheekpieces for the first time, was right back to his best and certainly appreciated the good ground and also being back to a mile for the first time this season. Waited with on the outside of the pack, he was not asked for an effort until the furlong marker. He then quickened impressively and won with plenty in hand. He will come on for this outing and should be spot on for the Prix Jacques-le-Marois next month.
Satri(IRE), racing for just the second time this season, put up a decent effort. Never far from the pacemaker, he went to the head of affairs a furlong out, but could not quicken over a distance slightly beyond his best. Connections were well pleased with this effort and he now heads for the Prix Maurice de Gheest at Deauville.
Multiplex, always up there, was given every possible chance but was unable to quicken with the front pair towards the end.
Echoes Rock(GER), never far away, had no excuses although he did pull a little in the early stages. Virtually in the lead a furlong out, he could only stay on at one pace towards the end.
Notability(IRE) led the small group that decided to hug the rail. Everything went well until over a furlong out when his stride shortened and he dropped out of contention. His rider felt the horse was not happy on the fastish ground.

3582 AYR (L-H)
Monday, July 23

OFFICIAL GOING: Good (7.0)
Wind: Fresh, half against Weather: Fine

3781 WILLIAM & MANDY MURDOCH MEDIAN AUCTION MAIDEN STKS 6f
2:15 (2:15) (Class 5) 2-Y-O **£3,238** (£963; £481; £240) **Stalls** High

Form RPR

2 **1** **Gothenburg (UAE)**[19] 3199 2-9-3 0 .... JoeFanning 4 84+
(M Johnston) *mde all: rdn and hung lft ent fnl f: styd on strly* **10/11**[1]

232 **2** *2* **Nawaaff**[26] 2983 2-9-3 0 .... JHBowman 8 78
(M R Channon) *chsd ldrs: effrt and swtchd lft wl over 1f out: kpt on fnl f: no ch w wnr* **3/1**[2]

3 **3** *hd* **Quest For Success (IRE)**[26] 2984 2-9-3 0 .... PaulHanagan 2 77
(R A Fahey) *t.k.h early: pressed wnr: effrt and chal over 1f out: no ex wl ins fnl f* **7/2**[3]

4 *1 ¼* **Another Decree** 2-9-3 0 .... PhillipMakin 9 73+
(M Dods) *t.k.h: hld up: nt clr run over 2f out: kpt on steadily fnl f: bttr for r* **20/1**

5 *5* **Geezers Colours** 2-9-3 0 .... PatCosgrave 3 58
(K R Burke) *stdd in tch: shkn up over 2f out: sn outpcd* **40/1**

0 **6** *shd* **Abbey Express**[15] 3341 2-9-3 0 .... DaleGibson 7 58
(M Dods) *prom tl rdn and wknd wl over 1f out* **50/1**

00 **7** *nk* **Miss Sunshine**[7] 3582 2-8-5 0 .... GaryBartley(7) 6 52
(J S Goldie) *prom to 1/2-way: sn rdn and wknd* **150/1**

0 **8** *6* **Killer Class**[7] 3582 2-8-12 0 .... TomEaves 1 34
(J S Goldie) *sn bhd: no ch fr 1/2-way* **125/1**

1m 15.01s (1.34) **Going Correction** +0.025s/f (Good) **8** Ran SP% **110.2**
Speed ratings (Par 94): 92,89,89,87,80 80,80,72
CSF £3.46 TOTE £1.70: £1.02, £1.20, £1.60; EX 3.40.
Owner Sheikh Mohammed **Bred** Darley **Trained** Middleham Moor, N Yorks

FOCUS
A fair event and a fair gallop. The winner looks a potentially useful prospect but did not need to improve on his debut effort. The second and third help set the level.

NOTEBOOK
Gothenburg(UAE) ◆, who very much took the eye in the paddock, had the run of the race against the inside rail and showed a good attitude once pressed to win dropped in distance. He will be suited by the return to 7f and appeals strongly as the sort to win more races. (op 8-11 tchd evens in places)
Nawaaff has had a few chances but once again seemed to give his running and he looks a good guide to the worth of this form. He looks worth a try over 7f and remains capable of winning an ordinary event. (tchd 7-2)
Quest For Success(IRE), who shaped pleasingly on his debut at Carlisle, looked in good shape and ran to a similar level but he is going to have to settle better than he did this time if he is to progress. However he looks sure to win a modest event. (op 9-2)
Another Decree ◆, who took the eye in the paddock, turned in a pleasing debut effort. He looks to have a fair bit more stamina than his half-sister Empress Jain, he will stay 7f and looks capable of winning races. (op 16-1)
Geezers Colours, noisy and green in the paddock, is from a stable that has had debut winners in this sphere this year but, although not disgraced on this first run and open to improvement, is likely to remain vulnerable in this type of event. (op 28-1)
Miss Sunshine, who hinted at ability on her racecourse debut, ran to a similar level and she is going to continue to look vulnerable in this type of race. (op 200-1)

3782 KAREN KAYE 50 TODAY H'CAP 5f
2:45 (2:46) (Class 6) (0-65,64) 3-Y-O+ **£2,590** (£770; £385; £192) **Stalls** High

Form RPR

2003 **1** **Compton Classic**[14] 3374 5-9-4 **64** .... (p) GaryBartley(7) 2 78
(J S Goldie) *hld up in tch far side: hdwy to ld that gp over 1f out: sn clr that side: hld on wl* **10/1**

3223 **2** *shd* **Divine Spirit**[6] 3608 6-9-6 **59** .... RoystonFfrench 14 73
(M Dods) *hld up on stands' side: hdwy to ld that gp over 1f out: kpt on strly fnl f: jst hld by far side wnr: 1st of 9 in gp* **9/2**[1]

0040 **3** *2 ½* **Toy Top (USA)**[14] 3374 4-9-4 **57** .... (b) PhillipMakin 3 62
(M Dods) *chsd far side ldrs: effrt and ev ch over 1f out: kpt on u.p fnl f: 2nd of 7 in gp* **14/1**

2520 **4** *½* **John Keats**[15] 3345 4-9-9 **62** .... PaulHanagan 9 65
(J S Goldie) *hld up on stands' side: hdwy 2f out: kpt on fnl f: nrst fin: 2nd of 9 in gp* **15/2**[3]

2350 **5** *hd* **Spirit Of Coniston**[19] 3203 4-8-8 **54** .... (b) KellyHarrison(7) 8 56
(C J Teague) *prom far side: effrt 2f out: hung lft: kpt on same pce fnl f: 3rd of 7 in gp* **12/1**

4020 **6** *nk* **Ashes (IRE)**[28] 2933 5-9-6 **62** .... AndrewElliott(3) 4 63
(K R Burke) *chsd far side ldrs: briefly led that gp over 1f out: kpt on same pce fnl f: 4th of 7 in gp* **14/1**

0403 **7** *2* **Legal Set (IRE)**[8] 3569 11-8-4 **48** ow2 .... (b) AnnStokell(5) 18 42
(Miss A Stokell) *bhd stands' side tl kpt on fr over 1f out: no imp: 3rd of 9 in gp* **11/1**

1500 **8** *¾* **Champagne Cracker**[28] 2933 6-9-3 **56** .... TomEaves 1 48
(M Dods) *led far side to over 1f out: no ex: 5th of 7 in gp* **16/1**

2440 **9** *½* **Sharp Hat**[19] 3203 13-8-10 **49** .... DaleGibson 6 39
(D W Chapman) *prom far side to over 2f out: sn outpcd: n.d after: 6th of 7 in gp* **18/1**

000 **10** *shd* **Seafield Towers**[7] 3585 7-8-12 **51** .... (p) JoeFanning 17 40
(Miss L A Perratt) *chsd stands' side ldrs tl no ex over 1f out: 4th of 9 in gp* **12/1**

0000 **11** *1* **Town House**[41] 2529 5-7-13 **45** .... SoniaEaton(7) 15 31
(B P J Baugh) *led stands' side to over 1f out: sn btn: 5th of 9 in gp* **33/1**

0000 **12** *½* **Rosie's Result**[15] 3347 7-8-8 **47** ow2 .... PatCosgrave 7 31
(M Todhunter) *dwlt: sn in tch far side: rdn and wknd fr 2f out: last of 7 in gp* **14/1**

0-00 **13** *nk* **Mutayam**[14] 3374 7-8-3 **45** .... (t) LiamJones(3) 16 28
(D A Nolan) *chsd stands' side ldrs tl wknd 2f out: 6th of 9 in gp* **100/1**

3126 **14** *nk* **Whozart (IRE)**[15] 3347 4-8-5 **49** .... MichaelJStainton(5) 11 31
(A Dickman) *prom far side: rdn and hung lft 2f out: sn wknd: 7th of 9 in gp* **5/1**[2]

0-00 **15** *2 ½* **Hebenus**[35] 2711 8-8-3 **45** .... (p) GregFairley(3) 10 18
(T A K Cuthbert) *in tch on outside of stands' side gp tl wknd fr 2f out: 8th of 9 in gp* **50/1**

0-00 **16** *2 ½* **Compton Lad**[9] 3536 4-8-1 **45** .... ColinHaddon(5) 13 9
(D A Nolan) *chsd stands' side ldrs tl wknd fr over 2f out: last of 9 in gp* **100/1**

60.40 secs (-0.04) **Going Correction** +0.025s/f (Good)
WFA 3 from 4yo+ 4lb **16** Ran SP% **117.4**
Speed ratings (Par 101): 101,100,96,96,95 95,92,90,90,89 88,87,87,86,82 78
CSF £51.74 CT £665.89 TOTE £9.10: £2.20, £1.20, £3.10, £3.80; EX 55.30.
Owner Jim Goldie Racing Club **Bred** James Thom And Sons And Peter Orr **Trained** Uplawmoor, E Renfrews

FOCUS
An ordinary handicap in which the form is not rock-solid. The field divided into two similar-sized groups and there was no advantage on either side.
Whozart(IRE) Official explanation: jockey said gelding never travelled

3783 WEATHERBYS PRINTING H'CAP 1m 1f 20y
3:15 (3:15) (Class 5) (0-70,68) 3-Y-O+ **£4,533** (£1,348; £674; £336) **Stalls** Low

Form RPR

2012 **1** **Neil's Legacy (IRE)**[9] 3539 5-9-4 **61** .... GregFairley(3) 6 72
(Miss L A Perratt) *prom: led and edgd lft 2f out: r.o strly fnl f* **5/1**[2]

-110 **2** *3* **Ballyhurry (USA)**[26] 2985 10-9-5 **66** .... GaryBartley(7) 2 71
(J S Goldie) *hld up: hdwy over 2f out: chsd wnr ins fnl f: r.o* **12/1**

0241 **3** *nk* **Thornaby Green**[24] 3049 6-8-11 **58** .... DeanHeslop(7) 9 62
(T D Barron) *t.k.h: cl up: led after 4f to over 3f out: one pce over 1f out* **5/1**[2]

525 **4** *½* **Mystical Ayr (IRE)**[10] 3502 5-9-6 **60** .... RoystonFfrench 1 63
(Miss L A Perratt) *prom: rdn over 2f out: kpt on same pce fnl f* **8/1**

0234 **5** *½* **The Mighty Ogmore**[13] 3400 3-8-4 **53** .... (p) PaulHanagan 5 54
(R C Guest) *rn in snatches: midfield: outpcd 3f out: rallied over 1f out: kpt on* **14/1**

220 **6** *nk* **Sedgwick**[31] 2822 5-10-0 **68**.. TPQueally 12 69
(J G Given) *t.k.h: cl up: led over 3f out to 2f out: no ex over 1f out* **4/1**[1]

64-0 **7** *3/4* **Andre Chenier (IRE)**[67] 1042 6-8-13 **58**........................ PJMcDonald(5) 8 57
(P Monteith) *hld up: hdwy 2f out: kpt on fnl f: nrst fin* **12/1**

2403 **8** *3 1/2* **Hawkit (USA)**[10] 3502 6-9-11 **65**.. DaleGibson 11 57
(P Monteith) *hld up: pushed along 3f out: nvr rchd ldrs* **7/1**[3]

500- **9** *8* **Insubordinate**[277] 5579 6-8-5 **52**.................................. KellyHarrison(7) 3 26
(J S Goldie) *s.i.s: nvr on temrs* **20/1**

0-00 **10** *3* **Penzo (IRE)**[10] 3502 4-9-5 **59**.. PatCosgrave 10 27
(J Wade) *hld up: rdn over 3f out: sn btn* **20/1**

41-0 **11** *6* **Roman History (IRE)**[51] 2254 4-9-1 **55**............................. TomEaves 7 9
(Miss Tracy Waggott) *led 4f: cl up tl wknd qckly over 3f out* **33/1**

4500 **12** *64* **Morbick**[20] 3181 3-8-7 **56**.. JoeFanning 4 —
(M Johnston) *bhd: lost tch fr 1/2-way: virtually p.u* **11/1**

1m 54.89s (-5.11) **Going Correction** -0.50s/f (Hard)
WFA 3 from 4yo+ 9lb **12** Ran SP% **119.8**
Speed ratings (Par 103):102,99,99,98,98 97,97,94,87,84 79,22
CSF £62.65 CT £320.56 TOTE £5.50: £1.70, £4.10, £2.60; EX 65.40.
Owner Terry & Mrs Linda Pardoe **Bred** Patrick M Ryan **Trained** Ayr, S Ayrshire
■ Stewards' Enquiry : T P Queally two-day ban: used whip with excessive force (Aug 3,5)

FOCUS
A run-of-the-mill event but one in which the pace was soon sound. The form seems sound enough, with a career best rom the winner.
Andre Chenier(IRE) Official explanation: jockey said gelding was unsuited by the good ground
Insubordinate Official explanation: jockey said gelding missed the break
Penzo(IRE) Official explanation: jockey said gelding hung left throughout
Morbick Official explanation: jockey said colt lost its action

3784 WEATHERBYS BANK FILLIES' H'CAP — 6f
3:45 (3:45) (Class 4) (0-85,76) 3-Y-0+
£6,232 (£1,866; £933; £467; £233; £117) **Stalls** High

Form RPR

0405 **1** **Dorn Dancer (IRE)**[15] 3345 5-8-10 **60**.............................. PatCosgrave 1 66
(D W Barker) *hld up in tch: hdwy to ld ent fnl f: hld on wl* **7/2**[1]

6604 **2** *hd* **Linda Green**[21] 3154 6-9-8 **72**.. JHBowman 8 77
(M R Channon) *chsd ldrs: squeezed through to chal 1f out: kpt on wl fnl f: jst hld* **9/2**[3]

2012 **3** *1* **Rothesay Dancer**[9] 3536 4-8-4 **61**.............................. KellyHarrison(7) 3 63+
(J S Goldie) *hld up: nt clr run fr 1/2-way to ins fnl f: swtchd lft: kpt on but no imp nr fin* **6/1**

2134 **4** *1* **Katie Boo (IRE)**[8] 3569 5-9-1 **65**...................................... TomEaves 4 64
(A Berry) *led tl hdd ent fnl f: kpt on same pce* **9/2**[3]

3013 **5** *1/2* **Misphire**[21] 3158 4-9-12 **76**..(b[1]) PhillipMakin 7 73+
(M Dods) *in tch: repeatedly denied room fr 2f out to ins fnl f: nt rcvr* **4/1**[2]

5044 **6** *3 1/2* **Safranine (IRE)**[11] 3474 10-8-4 **59** oh3 ow2.................... AnnStokell(5) 2 45
(Miss A Stokell) *cl up tl rdn and wknd over 1f out* **25/1**

246 **7** *1/2* **Aye Aye Definitely (IRE)**[21] 3158 3-9-3 **72**.................... PaulHanagan 5 56
(R A Fahey) *plld hrd: cl up tl wknd appr fnl f* **11/2**

1m 13.9s (0.23) **Going Correction** +0.025s/f (Good)
WFA 3 from 4yo+ 5lb **7** Ran SP% **112.1**
Speed ratings (Par 102):99,98,97,96,95 90,90
CSF £18.62 CT £88.82 TOTE £4.90: £2.60, £3.10; EX 26.00.
Owner The Ebor Partnership **Bred** Timothy Coughlan **Trained** Scorton, N Yorks
■ Stewards' Enquiry : Kelly Harrison two-day ban: careless riding (Aug 3,5)

FOCUS
An ordinary sprint in which the field raced against the stands' rail. There was not much pace on and a couple met trouble. The form has been rated through the winner.
Misphire Official explanation: jockey said filly was denied a clear run

3785 BETFAIR TODAY H'CAP — 1m 1f 20y
4:15 (4:15) (Class 5) (0-75,75) 3-Y-0
£3,238 (£963; £481; £240) **Stalls** Low

Form RPR

5021 **1** **Silca Key**[3] 3722 3-9-5 **73** 6ex.. JHBowman 7 77
(M R Channon) *chsd clr ldr after 2f: effrt over 2f out: led appr fnl f: sn hrd pressed: hld on wl towards fin* **5/1**[2]

4523 **2** *hd* **Jibajaba (USA)**[20] 3196 3-9-4 **72**.................................. PaulHanagan 8 75
(R A Fahey) *hld up: hdwy over 2f out: kpt on u.p fnl f: jst hld* **9/2**[1]

255 **3** *nk* **Dream Lodge (IRE)**[10] 3514 3-9-7 **75**...............................(v[1]) TPQueally 2 78
(J G Given) *chsd ldrs: effrt over 2f out: hung lft: disp ld ins fnl f: hld cl home* **5/1**[2]

0424 **4** *1 1/4* **Colditz (IRE)**[1] 3765 3-7-13 **56** oh6............................(p) AndrewElliott(3) 5 56
(D W Barker) *led after 2f and sn clr: hdd appr fnl f: kpt on same pce* **6/1**[3]

3220 **5** *2 1/2* **Honorable Love**[14] 3379 3-9-2 **70**.................................... TomEaves 4 65
(M Dods) *in tch: effrt over 2f out: no imp over 1f out* **5/1**[2]

620 **6** *9* **Run Free**[44] 2453 3-9-1 **69**.. PhillipMakin 1 44
(N Wilson) *led 2f: chsd ldrs tl wknd over 2f out* **12/1**

0-33 **7** *8* **He's Mine Too**[62] 1913 3-8-10 **64**................................ PatCosgrave 6 21
(J D Bethell) *hld up: struggling 3f out: sn btn* **9/2**[1]

40-2 **8** *3 1/2* **Judge Neptune**[77] 1531 3-8-7 **61**............................. RoystonFfrench 3 10
(J S Goldie) *hld up: struggling over 4f out: nvr on terms* **16/1**

1m 55.45s (-4.55) **Going Correction** -0.50s/f (Hard) **8** Ran SP% **114.2**
Speed ratings (Par 100):100,99,99,98,96 88,81,78
CSF £27.64 CT £117.47 TOTE £5.70: £1.20, £1.70, £2.30; EX 16.00.
Owner Aldridge Racing Partnership **Bred** Genesis Green Stud Ltd **Trained** West Ilsley, Berks

FOCUS
A run-of-the-mill handicap in which the pace was soon sound. Just ordinary form, anchored by the fourth.
He's Mine Too Official explanation: jockey said gelding never travelled
Judge Neptune Official explanation: jockey said gelding never travelled

3786 RECTANGLE GROUP H'CAP — 6f
4:45 (4:46) (Class 6) (0-65,69) 3-Y-0
£2,590 (£770; £385; £192) **Stalls** High

Form RPR

3640 **1** **Rainbow Fox**[12] 3413 3-9-5 **63**.. PaulHanagan 9 70
(R A Fahey) *towards rr outside of far side gp: sn pushed along: hdwy to ld wl over 1f out: kpt on wl* **12/1**

0503 **2** *1* **Dendor**[30] 2892 3-8-3 **50** ow1.. GregFairley(3) 17 53+
(D W Barker) *cl up stands' side: led that gp over 2f out: hung lft ins fnl f: kpt on: nt rch far side: 1st of 8 in gp* **12/1**

1301 **3** *nk* **Northern Dare (IRE)**[7] 3588 3-9-11 **69** 6ex................ AdrianTNicholls 2 71
(D Nicholls) *in tch far side: effrt and ev ch wl over 1f out: kpt on ins fnl f: 2nd of 8 in gp* **13/8**[1]

102 **4** *3/4* **Ishibee (IRE)**[5] 3636 3-8-12 **56**...............................(p) RoystonFfrench 18 56
(Mrs A Duffield) *led stands' side to over 2f out: hung lft and kpt on u.p ins fnl f: 2nd of 8 in gp* **10/1**

0-20 **5** *3/4* **Moheebb (IRE)**[14] 3382 3-8-12 **59**................................ LiamJones(3) 15 57
(D W Chapman) *bhd stands' side: drvn 1/2-way: kpt on wl fnl f: nrst fin: 3rd of 8 in gp* **7/1**[2]

0341 **6** *3/4* **Rue Soleil**[9] 3537 3-9-2 **60**.. PhillipMakin 12 55
(J R Weymes) *prom stands' side: drvn 1/2-way: kpt on same pce fnl f: 4th of 8 in gp* **20/1**

00-0 **7** *nk* **Chicamia**[30] 2873 3-7-9 **46** oh1...................................... SophieDoyle(7) 16 40
(M Mullineaux) *bhd stands' side tl styd on fnl f: n.d: 5th of 8 in gp* **100/1**

3246 **8** *1 1/4* **Wadnagin (IRE)**[21] 3168 3-8-12 **56**................................... TPQueally 7 46
(I A Wood) *in tch far side: ev ch that gp wl over 1f out: sn no ex: 3rd of 8 in gp* **8/1**[3]

0000 **9** *1 3/4* **Only A Grand**[15] 3342 3-8-4 **48**...(b) JoeFanning 5 33
(R Bastiman) *hld up far side: effrt and swtchd rt 2f out: no imp fnl f: 4th of 8 in gp* **20/1**

00-0 **10** *3* **My Maite Mickey**[31] 2844 3-8-2 **46** oh1.............................. PaulQuinn 14 21
(R C Guest) *in tch stands' side: rdn 1/2-way: no imp fr 2f out: 6th of 8 in gp* **50/1**

0620 **11** *shd* **Stir Crazy (IRE)**[5] 3649 3-8-11 **55**...................................... JHBowman 8 30
(M R Channon) *prom far side: ev ch that gp 2f out: sn rdn and btn: 5th of 8 in gp* **8/1**[3]

06-0 **12** *2* **Ancient Site (USA)**[178] 253 3-7-9 **46** oh1.................. SoniaEaton(7) 11 14
(B P J Baugh) *in tch on outside of stands' side gp: rdn and wknd fr 1/2-way: 7th of 8 in gp* **100/1**

0-00 **13** *1* **Only A Splash**[28] 2938 3-7-13 **46** oh1......................... AndrewElliott(3) 6 11
(D W Chapman) *led far side gp to wl over 1f out: sn btn: 6th of 8 in gp* **100/1**

006 **14** *2* **Lovers Kiss**[17] 3259 3-8-3 **47**...(b) DaleGibson 3 6
(N Wilson) *chsd far side ldrs to 2f out: sn btn: 7th of 8 in gp* **50/1**

-054 **15** *2 1/2* **Nufoudh (IRE)**[49] 2301 3-9-1 **59**.................................... PatCosgrave 13 10
(Miss Tracy Waggott) *cl up stands' side tl hung lft and wknd wl over 1f out: last of 8 in gp* **20/1**

6400 **16** *8* **Suntan Lady (IRE)**[93] 1164 3-7-13 **48**.......................(v) ColinHaddon(5) 1 —
(Miss V Haigh) *cl up far side to over 2f out: wknd: last of 8 in gp* **66/1**

1m 13.84s (0.17) **Going Correction** +0.025s/f (Good) **16** Ran SP% **120.0**
Speed ratings (Par 98):99,97,97,96,95 94,93,92,89,85 85,83,81,79,75 65
CSF £134.37 CT £373.83 TOTE £14.10: £2.30, £3.20, £1.10, £1.80; EX 183.50.
Owner Kevin Lee & David Barlow **Bred** Ms R A Myatt **Trained** Musley Bank, N Yorks

FOCUS
Another ordinary sprint in which the field divided into two equal groups, and there was no real advantage in the draw. Moderate form, the winner back to his 2yo best but the well-in favourite disappointing.

3787 KIDZPLAY H'CAP — 6f
5:15 (5:15) (Class 6) (0-65,64) 3-Y-0+
£2,730 (£806; £403) **Stalls** High

Form RPR

0454 **1** **Charles Parnell (IRE)**[15] 3345 4-9-8 **60**.......................... PhillipMakin 15 72
(M Dods) *hld up in tch stands' side: effrt 2f out: kpt on wl fnl f: led nr fin* **7/1**[3]

2014 **2** *nk* **Funfair Wane**[5] 3636 8-9-5 **57**................................ AdrianTNicholls 13 68+
(D Nicholls) *cl up stands' side: rdn whn hmpd over 2f out: rallied to ld that gp ent fnl f: hdd cl home: 2nd of 11 in gp* **15/2**

0041 **3** *1 1/4* **Rondo**[9] 3535 4-8-6 **51**.. DeanHeslop(7) 18 58
(T D Barron) *midfield stands' side: rdn over 2f out: styd on wl fnl f: nrst fin: 3rd of 11 in gp* **13/2**[2]

1060 **4** *2 1/2* **Hit's Only Money (IRE)**[7] 3585 7-9-5 **57**........................ TPQueally 4 56
(J S Goldie) *swtchd stands' side sn after s: bhd tl hdwy over 1f out: nrst fin: 4th of 11 in gp* **14/1**

4050 **5** *hd* **Seesawmilu (IRE)**[20] 3180 4-8-8 **53**............................ GaryBartley(7) 14 51
(E J Alston) *prom stands' side: drvn over 2f out: kpt on same pce fnl f: 5th of 11 in gp* **50/1**

0000 **6** *nk* **Polish Emperor (USA)**[15] 3347 7-9-0 **52**.......................... PatCosgrave 17 49
(D W Barker) *missed break: bhd stands' side tl kpt on over 1f out: n.d: 6th of 11 in gp* **33/1**

4242 **7** *nk* **Digital**[3] 3723 10-9-8 **60**... JHBowman 3 56+
(M R Channon) *chsd far side ldrs: led that gp 2f out: kpt on fnl f: no ch w stands' side: 1st of 6 in gp* **11/2**[1]

3031 **8** *nk* **Quicks The Word**[15] 3345 7-8-12 **53**............................. GregFairley(3) 9 48
(T A K Cuthbert) *led stands' side to ent fnl f: kpt on same pce: 7th of 11 in gp* **10/1**

000 **9** *1 1/2* **Newsround**[2] 3754 5-8-4 **45**...(b) LiamJones(3) 16 36
(D W Chapman) *bhd stands' side tl sme late hdwy: nvr on terms: 8th of 11 in gp* **7/1**[3]

-516 **10** *hd* **Bold Haze**[14] 3375 5-9-1 **58**.......................................(v) MichaelJStainton(5) 1 48+
(Miss S E Hall) *cl up far side: ev ch in that gp 2f out: one pce fnl f: 2nd of 6 in gp* **13/2**[2]

500- **11** *nk* **Ulysees (IRE)**[257] 6405 8-9-9 **61**.................................. RoystonFfrench 12 50
(J Barclay) *midfield stands' side: drvn and hung lft over 2f out: sn btn: 9th of 11 in gp* **50/1**

6645 **12** *nk* **Oeuf A La Neige**[4] 3674 7-8-8 **46**................................... PaulHanagan 7 34+
(Miss L A Perratt) *carried rt sn after s: swtchd to far side gp after 1f: in tch tl rdn and outpcd fr 2f out: 3rd of 6 in gp* **12/1**

-000 **13** *2 1/2* **Vondova**[4] 3676 5-8-12 **55**.. PJMcDonald(5) 8 35
(D A Nolan) *w stands' side ldr tl wknd over 1f out: 10th of 11 in gp* **100/1**

6000 **14** *2* **Alexia Rose (IRE)**[10] 3498 5-8-7 **45**.................................(b) JoeFanning 11 19
(A Berry) *a bhd stands' side: last of 11 in gp* **66/1**

00-0 **15** *5* **Indian Spark**[15] 3345 13-9-5 **64**................................ KellyHarrison(7) 2 22
(J S Goldie) *led far side to 2f out: sn btn: 4th of 6 in gp* **20/1**

5500 **16** *3 1/2* **Vibrato (USA)**[12] 3414 5-8-7 **45**......................................(v) PaulQuinn 6 —
(C J Teague) *s.s: a bhd far side: 5th of 6 in gp* **66/1**

4-20 **17** *1 1/4* **Dulce Sueno**[14] 3375 4-8-12 **50**...................................... TomEaves 5 —
(I Semple) *dwlt: sn cl up far side: rdn over 2f out: sn wknd: last of 6 in gp* **16/1**

1m 13.65s (-0.02) **Going Correction** +0.025s/f (Good) **17** Ran SP% **123.7**
Speed ratings (Par 101):101,100,98,95,95 94,94,94,92,91 91,91,87,85,78 73,72
Place 6 £ 23.07, Place 5 £ 21.58 CSF £56.88 CT £282.26 TOTE £8.10: £2.00, £2.00, £2.40, £3.80; EX 83.30.
Owner C A Lynch **Bred** R And Mrs R Hodgins **Trained** Denton, Co Durham
■ Stewards' Enquiry : Greg Fairley three-day ban: careless riding (Aug 3,5,6)
T P Queally three-day ban: careless riding (Aug 24-26)
Gary Bartley one-day ban: careless riding (Aug 3)

FOCUS
A run-of-the-mill sprint in which the best pace was in the larger stands'-side group, who held a decisive advantage this time. The winner was up 6lb on this year's form but was still the same amount off last year's best.
Newsround Official explanation: jockey said gelding was denied a clear run
T/Jkpt: Not won. T/Plt: £20.80 to a £1 stake. Pool: £71,134.00. 2,493.05 winning tickets. T/Qpdt: £14.30 to a £1 stake. Pool: £3,319.40. 171.70 winning tickets. RY

3605 BEVERLEY (R-H)

Monday, July 23

OFFICIAL GOING: Soft (heavy in places)

Wind: Virtually nil Weather: Fine

3788 WILLIAM GEORGE PEDERSON 80TH BIRTHDAY CLAIMING STKS 5f

6:30 (6:30) (Class 5) 2-Y-O **£3,071** (£906; £453) **Stalls** High

Form RPR

04 **1** **Mister Christie**[15] [3341] 2-9-2 0 .... KDarley 9 65
(N Tinkler) *trckd ldrs: hdwy 2f out: rdn to ld ent fnl f: drvn out* **2/1**[1]

522 **2** *4* **Prigsnov Dancer (IRE)**[46] [2392] 2-9-5 0 .... LeeEnstone 6 54
(P C Haslam) *chsd ldrs on outer: hdwy 2f out: rdn over 1f out: chsd wnr ins fnl f: kpt on* **9/4**[2]

00 **3** *1* **Rope Bridge (IRE)**[6] [3606] 2-8-13 0 .... DuranFentiman(3) 10 47+
(T D Easterby) *rrd s: sn cl up: led after 2f: rdn wl over 1f out: hdd and drvn ent fnl f: one pce* **14/1**

003 **4** *1 1/2* **Planet Paradise (IRE)**[14] [3364] 2-8-5 0 .... TPO'Shea 3 31
(D Shaw) *sn outpcd and bhd: rdn along 1/2-way: hdwy wl over 1f out: styd on ins fnl f: nrst fin* **16/1**

1U53 **5** *shd* **My Sheilas Dream (IRE)**[20] [3174] 2-8-2 0 .... JackDean(7) 5 34
(W G M Turner) *led 2f: cl up: rdn along 2f out: grad wknd* **7/1**

0036 **6** *1 1/4* **Handsinthemist (IRE)**[15] [3341] 2-8-9 0 .... MickyFenton 8 30
(P T Midgley) *chsd ldrs: rdn along 2f out: sn drvn and wknd* **11/2**[3]

5233 **7** *10* **Next Best**[12] [3410] 2-8-7 0 .... TonyHamilton 1 —
(A Berry) *prom: rdn along 1/2-way: rdr dropped whip 2f out and sn wknd* **14/1**

00 **8** *13* **Filthygorgeous (IRE)**[14] [3378] 2-8-4 0 .... AndrewMullen(3) 2 —
(J R Weymes) *dwlt: a outpcd and bhd* **40/1**

69.30 secs (5.30) **Going Correction** +0.925s/f (Soft) 8 Ran SP% **113.6**
Speed ratings (Par 94):94,87,86,83,83 81,65,44
CSF £6.60 TOTE £2.60: £1.30, £1.10, £4.30; EX 5.70.The winner was claimed by J. G. Given for £12,000
Owner Mrs Janis Macpherson **Bred** Llety Stud **Trained** Langton, N Yorks

FOCUS

A routine juvenile claimer in which the whole field stayed towards the inside early, though several, including the front two, hung out towards the centre as the race progressed. The market got it right, but the form outside of the winner looks very modest, albeit pretty solid.

NOTEBOOK

Mister Christie, down in class and also down to the minimum trip for the first time on his third outing, got a nice tow early and though he drifted out to his left when brought with his effort, he had little trouble in destroying this bunch. He may not have beaten much, but did it easily and still has a bit of scope. He was subsequently claimed by James Given for £12,000. (tchd 15-8 and 9-4)

Prigsnov Dancer(IRE), narrowly beaten a couple of times in similar company on faster ground, was always towards the outside of the field and plugged on to snatch second but never had a prayer with the winner. He can probably pick up a moderate event back on a quicker surface. (op 3-1)

Rope Bridge(IRE), beaten out of sight twice in slightly better company, was always up with the pace and stuck close to the far rail whilst his rivals all tended to hang out towards the centre. He looks very moderate, but may be capable of finding a moderate race on a less-demanding track. (op 16-1)

Planet Paradise(IRE) made a little late headway but, as at Bath, probably achieved very little. (op 14-1 tchd 18-1)

My Sheilas Dream(IRE), who has tended to struggle for her new yard since winning a seller on her debut, showed up for a while but did not get home and the drop back in trip did not compensate for the stiffer track and testing ground. (op 5-1)

Handsinthemist(IRE), just over two lengths behind Mister Christie at Ayr last time and 2lb better off, found this softer ground exposing a lack of stamina. (op 6-1 tchd 5-1)

3789 ROLLITS SOLICITORS AND PETER STOCKHILL LTD H'CAP 1m 100y

7:00 (7:01) (Class 6) (0-60,60) 3-Y-O+ **£3,238** (£963; £481; £240) **Stalls** High

Form RPR

3463 **1** **Chasing Memories (IRE)**[6] [3611] 3-8-12 **58** .... NeilBrown(5) 12 62
(B Smart) *in tch: hdwy towards inner 3f out: rdn and hung bdly lft 2f out: styd on to chal over 1f out: drvn to ld wl ins fnl f: hld on gamely* **9/1**

0036 **2** *hd* **Jiminor Mack**[3] [3714] 4-8-12 **45** .... (p) LeeEnstone 11 51
(W J H Ratcliffe) *hld up: hdwy 3f out: rdn wl over 1f out: styd on strly ins fnl f: jst failed* **20/1**

0150 **3** *3/4* **Scotty's Future (IRE)**[8] [3571] 9-8-12 **52** .... AdamCarter(7) 4 56
(A Berry) *bhd: hdwy on inner over 2f out: styd on wl appr fnl f: nrst fin* **16/1**

42 **4** *1 1/4* **Magdalene**[6] [3611] 3-9-5 **60** .... SebSanders 6 60
(Rae Guest) *in tch: wd st and hdwy on stands' rails over 2f out: led wl over 1f out and sn rdn: drvn and hdd wl ins fnl f: no ex* **3/1**[2]

4020 **5** *11* **Dispol Veleta**[20] [3182] 6-9-13 **60** .... NCallan 16 39
(Miss T Spearing) *trckd ldrs on inner: effrt over 2f out: sn rdn and wknd appr fnl f* **8/1**[3]

00-0 **6** *1 1/2* **Chilsdown**[40] [2554] 4-8-12 **45** .... TonyHamilton 2 21
(J G Given) *hld up: hdwy wl over 2f out: sn rdn and plugged on same pce* **50/1**

6323 **7** *nk* **Apache Nation (IRE)**[2] [3754] 4-9-13 **60** .... PaulFessey 14 35
(M Dods) *prom: rdn along wl over 2f out: drvn wl over 1f out and sn wknd* **5/2**[1]

0463 **8** *nk* **Penel (IRE)**[17] [3257] 6-9-1 **48** .... (p) MickyFenton 8 22
(P T Midgley) *nvr bttr than in midfield* **12/1**

0604 **9** *1/2* **Mister Maq**[17] [3257] 4-8-11 **47** .... (b) JamieMoriarty(3) 5 20
(A Crook) *hld up in rr: hdwy 3f out: rdn along 2f out: sn no imp* **40/1**

000 **10** *3 1/2* **Silver Sail**[13] [3399] 4-8-12 **45** .... (v[1]) PaddyAspell 9 11
(J S Wainwright) *chsd ldrs: rdn along wl over 2f out and sn wknd* **50/1**

6026 **11** *5* **Little Nipper**[14] [3377] 3-8-5 **49** .... (b[1]) AndrewMullen(3) 3 2
(W J H Ratcliffe) *in tch on inner: rdn along wl over 2f out: sn btn* **28/1**

-060 **12** *4* **The Diamond Bond**[60] [1964] 3-8-3 **47** .... DuranFentiman(3) 15 —
(G R Oldroyd) *led: rdn along and hdd 3f out: sn wknd* **20/1**

2050 **13** *10* **Shadow Jumper (IRE)**[10] [3497] 6-8-12 **45** .... (v) TPO'Shea 13 —
(J T Stimpson) *prom: led 3f out and wd st: rdn 2f out: sn hdd & wknd* **9/1**

0060 **14** *hd* **Abadia**[37] [2661] 3-8-4 **45** .... JimmyQuinn 1 —
(J G Given) *t.k.h: hld up: a in rr* **28/1**

1m 54.93s (7.53) **Going Correction** +0.975s/f (Soft)
WFA 3 from 4yo+ 8lb 14 Ran SP% **121.0**
Speed ratings (Par 101):101,100,100,98,87 86,86,85,85,81 76,72,62,62
CSF £180.16 CT £2899.44 TOTE £12.60: £2.90, £9.10, £3.00; EX 232.90.
Owner Bryan Smart, George And Us **Bred** Mrs V R Smart **Trained** Hambleton, N Yorks

FOCUS

A moderate handicap, but quite a competitive one nonetheless. The winner is rated back to her best. The runners used the full width of the track in the home straight and it was those that came closest to the stands' rail that just appeared to hold the advantage. The front four pulled miles clear of the others.

Dispol Veleta Official explanation: jockey said mare hung right-handed throughout
Chilsdown Official explanation: jockey said gelding ran too free

3790 NATWEST AGRICULTURAL TEAM H'CAP 7f 100y

7:30 (7:30) (Class 4) (0-80,80) 3-Y-O+ **£5,181** (£1,541; £770; £384) **Stalls** High

Form RPR

0344 **1** **Handsome Falcon**[16] [3299] 3-9-2 **72** .... TonyHamilton 6 79
(R A Fahey) *stdd s: rapid prog to trck ldrs after 1f: effrt over 2f out: sn rdn: styd on to ld ent fnl f: drvn out* **4/1**[3]

0303 **2** *2* **Rodeo**[1] [3764] 4-9-11 **74** .... (b) NCallan 4 78
(C W Thornton) *cl up: rdn to ld wl over 1f out: drvn and hdd ent fnl f: kpt on same pce* **11/2**

1204 **3** *nk* **Dispol Isle (IRE)**[10] [3512] 5-9-3 **71** .... NeilBrown(5) 1 74
(T D Barron) *hld up: hdwy over 2f out: rdn wl over 1f out: kpt on u.p fnl f* **9/2**

0302 **4** *3 1/2* **Sake (IRE)**[10] [3512] 5-9-5 **68** .... KimTinkler 3 63
(N Tinkler) *prom: pushed along 1/2-way: rdn over 2f out and sn no imp* **11/4**[1]

0561 **5** *4* **Scotland The Brave**[8] [3572] 7-9-9 **72** 6ex .... (v) SebSanders 7 57
(J D Bethell) *led: rdn along over 2f out: hdd wl over 1f out: sn drvn and wknd ent ins fnl f* **10/3**[2]

3410 **6** *10* **Tough Love**[28] [2936] 8-9-4 **70** .... (p) DuranFentiman(3) 2 30
(T D Easterby) *hld up: a in rr* **12/1**

1m 41.71s (7.40) **Going Correction** +1.20s/f (Soft)
WFA 3 from 4yo+ 7lb 6 Ran SP% **111.0**
Speed ratings (Par 105):105,102,102,98,93 82
CSF £24.85 TOTE £5.20: £2.00, £3.60; EX 30.00.
Owner B Shaw **Bred** Miss D Fleming **Trained** Musley Bank, N Yorks

FOCUS

A fair little handicap, but it developed into a war of attrition in the testing condtions over the last couple of furlongs and they were virtually walking home. Not form to be confident about. All six runners came over to the stands' rail once into the straight.

3791 REVVED UP RACEDAY ON 16 AUGUST H'CAP 5f

8:00 (8:00) (Class 4) (0-80,77) 3-Y-O+ **£4,857** (£1,445; £722; £360) **Stalls** High

Form RPR

4614 **1** **Melalchrist**[6] [3608] 5-9-2 **68** .... (b) NCallan 1 81
(K A Ryan) *qckly away: mde all: rdn wl over 1f out: styd on wl* **10/3**[1]

4040 **2** *1 3/4* **Kings College Boy**[7] [3585] 7-8-9 **64** .... (b) JamieMoriarty(3) 6 71
(R A Fahey) *a.p: chsd wnr 2f out: rdn over 1f out: drvn ins fnl f and kpt on same pce* **8/1**

4-06 **3** *1 1/2* **After The Show**[11] [3452] 6-9-6 **72** .... SebSanders 7 73
(Rae Guest) *hld up stands' side: hdwy 2f out: swtchd rt and rdn over 1f out: drvn and kpt on ins fnl f* **10/1**

016 **4** *1* **Hotham**[35] [2712] 4-8-11 **63** .... JimmyQuinn 4 61
(N Wilson) *chsd ldrs stands' side: rdn along 2f out: sn drvn and kpt on same pce* **8/1**

2006 **5** *1/2* **Paddywack (IRE)**[6] [3608] 10-8-1 **60** .... (b) DanielleMcCreery(7) 8 56
(D W Chapman) *in rr stands' side: hdwy over 1f out: sn rdn and kpt on ins fnl f: nrst fin* **13/2**

4500 **6** *nk* **Ryedale Ovation (IRE)**[26] [2989] 4-8-8 **63** .... DuranFentiman(3) 9 58+
(T D Easterby) *trckd ldr far side: hdwy 2f out: sn rdn and kpt on same pce* **11/2**[3]

0224 **7** *1 1/2* **Bond Boy**[10] [3515] 10-9-6 **77** .... (b) SladeO'Hara(5) 10 66+
(G R Oldroyd) *led far side gp of 2: rdn wl over 1f out: sn drvn and wknd* **9/2**[2]

0010 **8** *3/4* **Kenmore**[9] [3557] 5-9-9 **75** .... TonyHamilton 3 62
(J G Given) *chsd wnr stands' side: rdn along 2f out: sn drvn and wknd* **8/1**

3650 **9** *1* **Bond Playboy**[152] [516] 7-8-7 **62** .... (v) AndrewMullen(3) 5 45
(G R Oldroyd) *chsd ldrs stands' side: rdn along over 2f out: sn wknd* **22/1**

67.94 secs (3.94) **Going Correction** +0.925s/f (Soft) 9 Ran SP% **116.8**
Speed ratings (Par 105):105,102,99,98,97 96,94,93,91
CSF £30.91 CT £244.11 TOTE £3.80: £1.80, £2.80, £2.60; EX 32.50.
Owner T G S Wood **Bred** A C M Spalding **Trained** Hambleton, N Yorks

FOCUS

A modest sprint which saw all bar two of the field come stands' side. An improved effort from the winner, the form rated through the runner-up.

3792 SAILORS FAMILIES SOCIETY MAIDEN H'CAP 2m 35y

8:30 (8:31) (Class 6) (0-65,62) 3-Y-O **£2,590** (£770; £385; £192) **Stalls** High

Form RPR

0-32 **1** **Kentucky Boy (IRE)**[20] [3183] 3-8-11 **52** .... TonyHamilton 15 57
(Jedd O'Keeffe) *trckd ldrs on inner: hdwy 3f out: rdn to ld wl over 1f out: drvn ins fnl f and kpt on wl* **7/1**[2]

0005 **2** *1/2* **Tobougg Welcome (IRE)**[39] [2610] 3-8-4 **45** .... SaleemGolam 4 49
(S C Williams) *a.p: hdwy 3f out: led 2f out: sn rdn and hdd wl over 1f out: drvn and ev ch ins fnl f tl no ex towards fin* **7/1**[2]

2460 **3** *3/4* **Serhaaphim**[32] [2793] 3-9-1 **56** .... NCallan 11 59
(M L W Bell) *hld up: hdwy to chse ldrs over 3f out: rdn over 2f out: drvn over 1f out and kpt on ins fnl f* **12/1**

-063 **4** *nk* **Lady Traill**[32] [2793] 3-8-9 **50** .... KDarley 5 53
(B W Hills) *chsd ldrs: rdn along and outpcd 1/2-way: hdwy to chse ldrs 3f out: drvn 2f out: kpt on u.p fnl f* **9/2**[1]

-504 **5** *hd* **Sky Beam (USA)**[40] [2552] 3-8-9 **50** .... TPO'Shea 16 52
(J L Dunlop) *hld up in rr: gd hdwy over 4f out: rdn wl over 1f out and ev ch tl drvn and no ex ins fnl f* **9/1**[3]

0-40 **6** *2 1/2* **Watch Out**[20] [3183] 3-8-1 **45** .... (b[1]) AndrewMullen(3) 17 44
(M W Easterby) *hld up in rr: stdy hdwy 4f out: rdn to chse ldrs 2f out: sn drvn and no imp* **28/1**

00-4 **7** *6* **Sangfroid**[20] [3183] 3-8-7 **48** ow2 .... SebSanders 3 40
(Sir Mark Prescott) *led: rdn along 1/2-way: drvn along 3f out: hdd 2f out and grad wknd* **9/2**[1]

-000 **8** *5* **Currahee**[21] [3159] 3-8-9 **50** ow2 .... PaddyAspell 13 36
(Miss J A Camacho) *in tch on inner: rdn along to chse ldrs 3f out: drvn over 2f out and sn wknd* **33/1**

0023 **9** *19* **Ja Myford**[21] [3159] 3-9-3 **58** .... MickyFenton 10 21
(P T Midgley) *hld up: effrt and sme hdwy over 4f out: sn rdn along and nvr a factor* **10/1**

0004 **10** *2 1/2* **Firestorm (IRE)**[14] [3379] 3-8-4 **45** .... PaulFessey 1 5
(C W Fairhurst) *midfield: lost pl 1/2-way and sn bhd* **16/1**

-655 **11** *8* **Sendali (FR)**[32] 2808 3-9-0 **55** .... JimmyQuinn 9 — 6
(J D Bethell) *in tch: hdwy to chse ldrs 4f out: rdn along over 2f out and grad wknd* **28/1**

0-54 **12** *4* **Admiral Savannah (IRE)**[21] 3159 3-8-4 **48** .... DuranFentiman(3) 14 —
(T D Easterby) *chsd ldres: rdn along over 4f out and sn wknd* **11/1**

000- **13** *19* **Italstar (IRE)**[215] 6879 3-8-7 **48** .... DavidKinsella 8 —
(H Morrison) *a bhd* **20/1**

-356 **14** *4* **Ellies Faith**[5] 3640 3-8-4 **45** .... SilvestreDeSousa 6 —
(N Bycroft) *chsd ldrs: rdn along 6f out and sn wknd* **25/1**

066 **15** *19* **Wightgar**[11] 3476 3-8-8 **52** ow4 .... (t) JamieMoriarty(3) 2 —
(R A Kvisla) *chsd ldrs: rdn along over 3f out and sn wknd* **66/1**

0-62 **16** *dist* **Attila's Peintre**[40] 2565 3-9-7 **62** .... LeeEnstone 12 —
(P C Haslam) *bhd fr 1/2-way* **16/1**

00-0 **17** *dist* **Soundasapound**[14] 3377 3-7-13 **45** .... NataliaGemelova(5) 7 —
(I W McInnes) *a bhd* **50/1**

3m 58.86s (19.36) **Going Correction** +1.20s/f (Soft) **17** Ran SP% **130.1**
Speed ratings (Par 98):99,98,98,98,98 96,93,91,81,80 76,74,65,63,53 —,—
CSF £54.94 CT £605.82 TOTE £7.20: £1.60, £2.40, £2.70, £1.70; EX 69.50.
Owner A Walker **Bred** Eclipse Thoroughbreds Inc **Trained** Middleham Moor, N Yorks

FOCUS
A very moderate three-year-old handicap, which would have represented a real test of stamina. The first five were closely covered at the finish, and the first two are at least going the right way.

3793 MEDIEVAL NIGHT H'CAP — 1m 100y
9:00 (9:00) (Class 5) (0-75,75) 3-Y-0+ — **£3,238** (£963; £481; £240) **Stalls** High

Form — RPR

0252 **1** **Lap Of Honour (IRE)**[4] 3689 3-8-11 **66** .... NCallan 2 — 76
(N A Callaghan) *mde all: rdn over 2f out: drvn clr appr fnl f and styd on strly* **7/4**[1]

2541 **2** *5* **Tizzy May (FR)**[15] 3346 7-9-9 **73** .... JamieMoriarty(3) 4 — 74
(B Ellison) *trckd ldrs: effrt over 2f out: sn rdn and styd ent fnl f: no ch w wnr* **7/2**[3]

5530 **3** *3/4* **Ming Vase**[14] 3381 5-8-9 **56** oh7 .... MickyFenton 3 — 55
(P T Midgley) *chsd wnr: rdn along over 2f out: drvn wl over 1f out and kpt on same pce* **25/1**

022 **4** *nk* **Superior Star**[14] 3381 4-9-9 **70** .... (b) TonyHamilton 1 — 69
(R A Fahey) *trckd ldrs: hdwy 3f out: rdn over 2f out: drvn over 1f out and sn one pce* **5/1**

0515 **5** *nk* **Emily's Place (IRE)**[8] 3571 4-9-6 **67** .... JimmyQuinn 5 — 65
(J Pearce) *hld up in tch: effrt 3f out: rdn 2f out and sn btn* **3/1**[2]

0004 **6** *2* **Kudbeme**[1] 3764 5-8-12 **59** .... PaulFessey 7 — 53
(N Bycroft) *hld up: rapid hdwy on outer over 3f out: rdn to chal over 2f out: sn drvn and wknd wl over 1f out* **8/1**

1m 56.23s (8.83) **Going Correction** +1.20s/f (Soft)
WFA 3 from 4yo+ 8lb **6** Ran SP% **115.2**
Speed ratings (Par 103):103,98,97,96,96 94
CSF £8.55 CT £108.19 TOTE £2.60: £1.70, £2.50; EX 8.10 Place 6 £ 417.74, Place 5 £ 295.04.
Owner Michael Tabor **Bred** Ben Sangster **Trained** Newmarket, Suffolk

FOCUS
A moderate handicap, the winner dictating an ordinary gallop. It is doubtful whether he had to improve much despite the wide-margin victory.
T/Plt: £267.10 to a £1 stake. Pool: £68,711.15. 187.75 winning tickets. T/Qpdt: £13.60 to a £1 stake. Pool: £4,723.50. 255.60 winning tickets. JR

3589 WINDSOR (R-H)
Monday, July 23

OFFICIAL GOING: Good to soft (soft in places) changing to soft after race 3 (7.20)
As is usually the case when the ground is on the soft side at Windsor, the far side proved the place to be in the straight.
Wind: Virtually nil Weather: rain

3794 PLAY IN THE CARIBBEAN WITH LITTLEWOODSPOKER.COM MAIDEN STKS — 1m 2f 7y
6:20 (6:20) (Class 5) 3-4-Y-0 — **£3,238** (£963; £481; £240) **Stalls** Centre

Form — RPR

22 **1** **Spring City (GER)**[37] 2674 3-9-3 0 .... KerrinMcEvoy 8 — 80+
(Saeed Bin Suroor) *hld up in rr but in tch: stdy hdwy fr 5f out to ld ins fnl 2f: clr ins fnl f: easily* **1/5**[1]

30 **2** *4* **Torba (IRE)**[14] 3366 3-8-12 0 .... LPKeniry 7 — 67
(Evan Williams) *in rr: stdy hdwy fr 4f out: chal 2f out: chsd wnr wl over 1f out: sn no ch but kpt on wl for 2nd* **20/1**

54 **3** *1 1/2* **Berry Hill Lass (IRE)**[38] 2620 3-8-12 0 .... RobertHavlin 5 — 64
(J G M O'Shea) *chsd ldrs: rdn 3f out: styd on fnl 2f but nvr gng pce to be competitive* **33/1**

4 *1 1/2* **Tropical Strait (IRE)**[107] 4-9-13 0 .... PhilipRobinson 1 — 66
(D W P Arbuthnot) *chsd ldrs: drvn and slt ld appr fnl 2f: hdd sn after: wknd ins fnl f* **9/1**[2]

50 **5** *shd* **Looktheotherway (IRE)**[38] 2620 3-8-12 0 .... FergusSweeney 6 — 61
(J G M O'Shea) *in rr: hdwy 3f out: kpt on u.p fnl 2f: nvr gng pce to rch ldrs* **66/1**

-600 **6** *5* **Jamaahir (USA)**[10] 3487 4-9-13 **59** .... AdamKirby 12 — 56
(S Lycett) *s.i.s: bhd: rdn and sme hdwy over 4f out: nvr gng pce to be competitive* **16/1**[3]

7 *shd* **Borita (IRE)**[171] 4-9-1 0 .... ThomasO'Brien(7) 9 — 51
(M Scudamore) *s.i.s: nvr gng pce to rch ldrs* **100/1**

04-0 **8** *3* **Sagassa**[113] 869 3-8-12 **49** .... SamHitchcott 11 — 45
(W De Best-Turner) *wnt lft s: led after 2f: hdd over 2f out and wknd rapidly* **66/1**

00U **9** *1/2* **Come On Nellie (IRE)**[14] 3365 3-8-5 0 .... HaddenFrost(7) 10 — 44
(J G M O'Shea) *hmpd s: mod prog over 3f out: nvr in contention* **100/1**

0- **10** *17* **Pink Notes**[310] 5379 3-9-3 0 .... SteveDrowne 2 — 15
(R J Hodges) *chsd ldrs over 6f* **100/1**

00 **11** *7* **Pretty Posey**[14] 3366 3-8-12 0 .... VinceSlattery 4 —
(J G M O'Shea) *chsd ldrs to 1/2-way* **200/1**

0 **12** *7* **Half A Tsar (IRE)**[15] 3349 3-8-12 0 .... TolleyDean(5) 3 —
(Mark Gillard) *sn led: hdd after 2f: wknd 4f out* **150/1**

2m 9.61s (1.31) **Going Correction** +0.175s/f (Good)
WFA 3 from 4yo 10lb **12** Ran SP% **114.0**
Speed ratings (Par 103):101,97,96,95,95 91,91,88,88,74 69,63
CSF £9.59 TOTE £1.30: £1.02, £2.90, £3.20; EX 6.00.

Owner Godolphin **Bred** Stiftung Gestut Fahrhof **Trained** Newmarket, Suffolk

FOCUS
An uncompetitive maiden, but the pace was strong. They all raced far side in the straight. The winner was a class above his rivals, but the form is modest overall.
Jamaahir(USA) Official explanation: jockey said gelding hung left

3795 LITTLEWOODS CASINO - THE TRUSTED NAME (S) STKS — 1m 3f 135y
6:50 (6:50) (Class 5) 3-Y-0+ — **£3,238** (£963; £481; £240) **Stalls** Centre

Form — RPR

2002 **1** **Hathaal (IRE)**[4] 3684 8-9-4 60 .... (v) AlanCreighton(3) 6 — 48
(E J Creighton) *in tch: hdwy over 4f out: drvn to ld over 1f out: edgd lft u.p wl ins fnl f: all out* **11/2**[3]

00-0 **2** *1/2* **Littleton Aldor (IRE)**[12] 3428 7-9-2 42 .... TolleyDean(5) 1 — 47
(Mark Gillard) *sn slt ld: hdd 7f out: led again 4f out: rdn 3f out: hdd over 1f out: rallied u.p ins fnl f: no ex cl home* **20/1**

3106 **3** *nk* **Right Option (IRE)**[7] 3593 3-9-0 53 .... RyanMoore 8 — 52
(S Dow) *in tch: hdwy over 3f out: drvn to chal over 1f out: stl ev ch wl ins fnl f: one pce cl home* **3/1**[1]

3040 **4** *6* **Tiegs (IRE)**[123] 730 5-9-4 41 .... MarcHalford(3) 12 — 36
(P W Hiatt) *w ldr 4f: styd front rnk: rdn over 3f out: wknd over 1f out* **8/1**

0064 **5** *13* **Ceol Eile (IRE)**[7] 3593 4-9-2 45 .... (p) RobertHavlin 13 — 9
(D Haydn Jones) *led 7f out: hdd 4f out and sn rdn: wknd over 2f out* **7/1**

0560 **6** *2 1/2* **Cantique (IRE)**[17] 3274 3-8-4 46 .... HayleyTurner 11 — 5
(Ms J S Doyle) *in tch: rdn and effrt over 3f out: nvr in contention: sn wknd* **25/1**

000/ **7** *1 1/2* **Killala (IRE)**[637] 6079 7-9-7 30 .... VinceSlattery 4 — 8
(D J Wintle) *s.i.s: nvr bttr than in mid-div* **66/1**

400/ **8** *4* **Ren's Magic**[547] 9-9-0 50 .... (t) SCreighton(7) 7 — 1
(E J Creighton) *a towards rr* **33/1**

0 **9** *6* **Parbyblos (FR)**[7] 3593 4-9-4 0 .... JerryO'Dwyer(3) 10 —
(John Allen) *in rr: sme hdwy 5f out: sn wknd* **40/1**

514/ **10** *1 1/4* **Victory Sign (IRE)**[48] 4529 7-9-7 58 .... RichardThomas 5 —
(P Butler) *chsd ldrs tl wknd over 3f out* **25/1**

11 *1* **Anko (POL)**[34] 8-9-0 0 .... HaddenFrost(7) 2 —
(J D Frost) *in rr: brief effrt 5f out: sn wknd* **11/1**

50-0 **12** *2 1/2* **Majestas (IRE)**[43] 1672 3-8-9 60 .... (t) FergusSweeney 9 —
(Evan Williams) *a in rr* **9/1**

-310 **13** *nk* **Orchard House (FR)**[30] 2890 4-9-12 54 .... (b) JamieSpencer 3 —
(J Jay) *rdn over 4f out: a bhd* **4/1**[2]

2m 32.76s (2.66) **Going Correction** +0.175s/f (Good)
WFA 3 from 4yo+ 12lb **13** Ran SP% **121.7**
Speed ratings (Par 103):98,97,97,93,84 83,82,79,75,74 73,72,72
CSF £118.61 TOTE £5.00: £1.90, £6.90, £1.20; EX 146.10.The winner was sold to Jim Best for £8,800. Right Option was claimed by J. L. Flint for £6,000
Owner The Vixens **Bred** Airlie Stud **Trained** East Garston, Berks
■ The first winner in Britain for Alan Creighton, a former champion jockey in Spain and son of winning trainer Eddie.

FOCUS
A weak seller and very moderate form. They raced middle to far side in the straight.
Majestas(IRE) Official explanation: jockey said gelding had no more to give
Orchard House(FR) Official explanation: jockey said gelding never travelled

3796 MILLIONS PAID OUT AT LITTLEWOODSCASINO.COM E B F MAIDEN FILLIES' STKS — 6f
7:20 (7:20) (Class 4) 2-Y-0 — **£5,181** (£1,541; £770; £384) **Stalls** High

Form — RPR

2 **1** **Gone Fast (USA)**[18] 3245 2-9-0 0 .... JamieSpencer 8 — 92+
(J R Fanshawe) *hld up in tch: stdy hdwy over 2f out to ld over 1f out: sn clr: easily* **2/1**[1]

1 **2** *5* **Edge Of Gold**[27] 2968 2-9-0 0 .... SteveDrowne 10 — 77
(B Palling) *chsd ldrs: rdn and styd on to chse wnr 1f out: nvr any ch but kpt on wl for clr 2nd* **3/1**[2]

3 *1 1/2* **Jazz Jam** 2-9-0 0 .... TQuinn 3 — 72
(P F I Cole) *chsd ldrs tl rdn and outpcd over 2f out: kpt on fnl f but nvr a threat to ldng pair* **6/1**[3]

6 **4** *2* **Gower Belle**[19] 3213 2-9-0 0 .... RichardHughes 13 — 66
(W R Muir) *slt ld 2f: styd chalng tl led again over 2f out: hdd over 1f out: wknd ins fnl f* **25/1**

0 **5** *hd* **Infinite Patience**[33] 2768 2-9-0 0 .... LPKeniry 7 — 65
(J S Moore) *s.i.s: in rr: pushed along over 3f out: kpt on fr over 1f out but nvr gng pce to be competitive* **15/2**

6 **6** *nk* **Rathmolyon**[23] 3109 2-9-0 0 .... RobertHavlin 5 — 65
(D Haydn Jones) *prssed ldr: slt ld after 2f: hdd over 2f out: wknd over 1f out* **100/1**

7 *hd* **Xaravella (IRE)** 2-9-0 0 .... FergusSweeney 14 — 64
(J G M O'Shea) *s.i.s: sn in mid-div: styd on fnl 2f but nvr nr ldrs* **100/1**

0 **8** *3/4* **Danamight (IRE)**[59] 2000 2-9-0 0 .... EddieAhern 6 — 66+
(G G Margarson) *s.i.s: bhd tl r.o fr over 1f out* **33/1**

0 **9** *1 1/4* **Belle Bellino (FR)**[21] 3152 2-9-0 0 .... KerrinMcEvoy 12 — 58
(B R Millman) *early spd: sn outpcd: sme prog fnl f* **9/1**

4 **10** *hd* **Lille Tuva**[26] 2977 2-9-0 0 .... HayleyTurner 9 — 57
(B R Millman) *chsd ldrs: rdn 1/2-way: wknd ins fnl 2f* **33/1**

0 **11** *2* **Treacle Noir (IRE)**[48] 2333 2-8-11 0 .... RichardKingscote(3) 15 — 51+
(Tom Dascombe) *racd stands' side and chsd sole opponent that side tl ins fnl f but a wl off pce of main gp far side fr 1/2-way* **66/1**

46 **12** *1* **Lowry's Art**[44] 2468 2-9-0 0 .... AdamKirby 11 — 48+
(R M Beckett) *led sole opponent stands' side tl ins fnl f but wl off pce of main gp far side fr 1/2-way* **7/1**

13 *nk* **Liz Long** 2-9-0 0 .... IanMongan 4 — 47
(P Howling) *s.i.s: a in rr* **100/1**

1m 14.84s (1.17) **Going Correction** +0.175s/f (Good) **13** Ran SP% **121.1**
Speed ratings (Par 93):99,92,90,87,87 87,86,85,84,83 81,79,79
CSF £7.65 TOTE £3.20: £1.40, £1.40, £2.00; EX 6.40.
Owner Dr Ali Ridha **Bred** James Heyward **Trained** Newmarket, Suffolk

FOCUS
This looked like a pretty decent fillies' maiden, and the winner is destined for Group races. Two of these stayed near side in the straight, but they were a mile behind the main group on the far side.

NOTEBOOK
Gone Fast(USA) ◆ probably would have won under a better ride on her debut at Yarmouth, but Spencer was taking over from Urbina, and she made no mistake this time, scoring most impressively. She looks pattern-class in the making and could now take her chance in the Group 3 Sweet Solera Stakes. (op 15-8 tchd 9-4)
Edge Of Gold looked the best horse in the race when disqualified from first place in an ordinary maiden at Newbury on her debut, but there were no excuses this time; she just ran into a potential Group horse. She deserves to win her maiden. (op 5-2)
Jazz Jam ◆, a Pivotal half-sister to dual 1m-1m2f winner Framboise, and 5f juvenile winner Reebal, out of high-class Cherry Hinton winner Applaud, made a pleasing introduction. (op 5-1)

Gower Belle, who showed ability on her debut over 6f at Kempton, showed speed on this drop in trip and looks to be coming along nicely. (op 20-1)
Infinite Patience ◆ showed next to nothing on her debut over 7f at Kempton, but this was a lot better. She should be suited by a return to further in time and looks a nice prospect in the making. (op 20-1 tchd 25-1)
Treacle Noir(IRE) had no chance racing on the near side of the track and is better than she showed. (op 50-1)
Lowry's Art was at a huge disadvantage racing away from the main pack on the near side of the track and can be forgiven this. (op 12-1)

3797 HIGH ROLLERS CHOOSE LITTLEWOODSCASINO.COM H'CAP 6f
7:50 (7:55) (Class 4) (0-85,85) 3-Y-O £6,477 (£1,927; £963; £481) Stalls High

Form RPR
3121 **1** **Royal Rock**[40] [2570] 3-9-6 **84** GeorgeBaker 12 99+
(C F Wall) *in tch: smooth hdwy fr 3f out to ld on bit over 1f out: sn clr: eased cl home* **3/1**[2]
110 **2** *3 1/2* **Crystal Gazer (FR)**[65] [1837] 3-9-0 **78** RichardHughes 10 77
(R Hannon) *in rr: hdwy 2f out: styd on to go 2nd ins fnl f but no ch w eased down wnr* **11/1**
2-51 **3** *2* **Impromptu**[23] [3102] 3-8-13 **77** AdamKirby 9 70
(R M Beckett) *chsd ldrs: rdn over 2f out: styd on same pce fnl f* **14/1**
2-1 **4** *nk* **Marozi (USA)**[13] [3395] 3-9-2 **80** PhilipRobinson 3 72
(M A Jarvis) *trckd ldrs: led 3f out rdn and hdd over 1f out: wknd ins fnl f* **13/8**[1]
3101 **5** *1 1/4* **Nobilissima (IRE)**[18] [3240] 3-8-13 **80** MarcHalford(3) 8 68
(J L Spearing) *slt ld to 3f out: sn rdn: wknd over 1f out* **10/1**
12-0 **6** *1/2* **Dream Scheme**[30] [2883] 3-9-4 **82** SteveDrowne 4 69
(E A L Dunlop) *in rr: rdn 1/2-way: mod hdwy fnl f* **12/1**
0-30 **7** *hd* **Pango's Legacy**[48] [2335] 3-8-8 **72** RobertHavlin 6 58
(H Morrison) *chsd ldrs: rdn 1/2-way: wknd fr 2f out* **28/1**
5523 **8** *5* **King's Bastion (IRE)**[17] [3278] 3-9-4 **82** JamieSpencer 7 53
(M L W Bell) *chsd ldrs: rdn 1/2-way: wknd 2f out* **11/2**[3]
211- **9** *1 1/4* **Benllech**[209] [6937] 3-9-7 **85** EddieAhern 1 53
(S Kirk) *in tch: rdn and effrt 1/2-way: sn wknd* **33/1**

1m 13.44s (-0.23) **Going Correction** +0.175s/f (Good) **9** Ran SP% **116.7**
Speed ratings (Par 102):108,103,100,100,98 97,97,91,89
CSF £36.32 CT £332.42 TOTE £4.50: £1.60, £2.40, £2.30; EX 42.70.
Owner S Fustok **Bred** Deerfield Farm **Trained** Newmarket, Suffolk

FOCUS
The looked like a good sprint handicap beforehand, but nothing could go with the impressive Royal Rock who posted another improved effort. The placed form has not been rated too positively.
King's Bastion(IRE) Official explanation: jockey said gelding had no more to give

3798 $400,000 FREEROLL AT LITTLEWOODSPOKER.COM FILLIES' H'CAP 1m 67y
8:20 (8:20) (Class 5) (0-75,74) 3-Y-O £3,238 (£963; £481; £240) Stalls High

Form RPR
0421 **1** **Montrachet**[10] [3490] 3-9-6 **73** JamieSpencer 11 83+
(M L W Bell) *chsd ldrs: hrd rdn fr 2f out to ld jst ins fnl f: drvn out* **5/4**[1]
6432 **2** *1* **Kashmir Lady (FR)**[11] [3474] 3-9-1 **68** FergusSweeney 9 76
(H Candy) *led: stl travelling wl 2f out: rdn over 1f out and hdd jst ins fnl f: kpt on but a hld by wnr* **11/2**[3]
0353 **3** *2 1/2* **Bidable**[10] [3490] 3-8-4 **60** RichardKingscote(3) 2 62
(B Palling) *chsd ldrs: rdn 3f out: styd on same pce fnl 2f* **15/2**
520- **4** *2* **Seaflower Reef (IRE)**[348] [4246] 3-8-8 **66** WilliamBuick(5) 7 63
(A M Balding) *in rr: drvn along 4f out: mod prog fr 2f out: kpt on ins fnl f but nvr gng pce to rch ldrs* **20/1**
6-15 **5** *3/4* **Keidas (FR)**[31] [2834] 3-9-7 **74** EddieAhern 6 70
(C F Wall) *chsd ldrs: rdn over 2f out: wknd fnl f* **4/1**[2]
4-01 **6** *nk* **Lawyers Choice**[24] [3066] 3-9-2 **69** IanMongan 1 64
(Pat Eddery) *in tch: rdn and sme prog 2f out: nt rch ldrs: wknd fnl f* **12/1**
400- **7** *1/2* **Maid Of Ale (IRE)**[304] [5503] 3-8-10 **62** ow1 AdamKirby 10 57
(A King) *in tch: rdn over 3f out: n.d after: wknd fr 2f out* **33/1**
10-0 **8** *3 1/2* **Sylvan (IRE)**[65] [1837] 3-9-6 **73** GeorgeBaker 8 59
(S Kirk) *in tch: rdn over 3f out: sn btn* **14/1**

1m 45.67s (0.97) **Going Correction** +0.175s/f (Good) **8** Ran SP% **113.7**
Speed ratings (Par 97):102,101,98,96,95 95,94,91
CSF £8.34 CT £36.01 TOTE £2.10: £1.20, £1.50, £2.20; EX 7.30.
Owner Mr & Mrs G Middlebrook **Bred** G And Mrs Middlebrook **Trained** Newmarket, Suffolk

FOCUS
Just a modest fillies' handicap, but pretty sound form and there could be more to come from the winner. They all raced far side in the straight.
Maid Of Ale(IRE) Official explanation: jockey said filly hung left throughout

3799 ARENA LEISURE H'CAP 1m 2f 7y
8:50 (8:50) (Class 5) (0-70,70) 3-Y-O+ £3,238 (£963; £481; £240) Stalls Centre

Form RPR
524 **1** **Lady Friend**[23] [3079] 5-9-9 **70** PatrickHills(5) 8 80+
(J W Hills) *in rr: rdn and hdwy over 2f: styd on to ld appr fnl f: hung lft ins fnl f: drvn out* **7/2**[1]
003 **2** *1 1/4* **Aypeeyes (IRE)**[11] [3456] 3-8-13 **65** LPKeniry 7 73
(S Kirk) *in rr: hdwy 3f out: n.m.r and swtchd rt over 2f out: styd on to chse wnr ins fnl f but a hld* **15/2**[3]
4005 **3** *1 3/4* **Prime Powered (IRE)**[14] [3385] 6-9-13 **69** GeorgeBaker 9 73
(R M Beckett) *chsd ldrs: rdn 3f out: styd on same pce fr over 1f out* **11/2**[2]
0012 **4** *nk* **Moves Goodenough**[15] [3352] 4-9-11 **67** (b) HayleyTurner 4 70
(Andrew Turnell) *plld hrd: chsd ldrs tl led 2f out: hdd over 1f out: rdn and hung bdly rt sn after and wknd* **11/2**[2]
30-0 **5** *3* **Summer Bounty**[17] [3280] 11-8-13 **55** OscarUrbina 5 52
(F Jordan) *in rr: hdwy fr 2f out: kpt on cl home* **25/1**
0546 **6** *1/2* **Rawdon (IRE)**[25] [3042] 6-9-11 **67** JamieSpencer 11 63
(M L W Bell) *chsd ldrs: rdn over 3f out: wknd fr 2f out* **7/2**[1]
00-0 **7** *nk* **Libre**[14] [3381] 7-9-1 **57** SteveDrowne 1 53
(F Jordan) *in rr: rdn and sme prog fnl 2f: nvr rchd ldrs* **25/1**
5450 **8** *1/2* **Bollywood (IRE)**[12] [3422] 4-8-9 **51** oh6 FrankieMcDonald 6 46
(J J Bridger) *led tl hdd 5f out: ev ch 2f out: wkng whn hmpd 1f out* **50/1**
4400 **9** *1 3/4* **Border Edge**[15] [3350] 9-9-2 **58** FergusSweeney 3 49
(J J Bridger) *chsd ldrs: rdn 3f out: wknd fr 2f out* **16/1**
5406 **10** *nk* **Ganache (IRE)**[32] [2802] 5-9-4 **60** PaulDoe 2 51
(P R Chamings) *in tch: hdwy 5f out: drvn to chal over 2f out: wknd qckly over 1f out* **16/1**
0-00 **11** *8* **Mixing**[52] [2214] 5-8-4 **51** oh6 (b) WilliamBuick(5) 12 26
(W Jarvis) *led 5f out: hdd 2f out: btn whn hmpd 1f out* **8/1**
4500 **12** *2 1/2* **Bold Cross (IRE)**[12] [3419] 4-8-12 **54** PaulFitzsimons 10 24
(E G Bevan) *in tch: effrt 4f out: wknd 3f out* **16/1**

2m 10.41s (2.11) **Going Correction** +0.175s/f (Good)
WFA 3 from 4yo+ 10lb **12** Ran SP% **125.4**
Speed ratings (Par 103):98,97,95,95,92 92,92,91,90,90 83,81
CSF £31.76 CT £149.03 TOTE £4.90: £1.70, £2.40, £2.20; EX 29.70 Place 6 £ 15.16, Place 5 £ 12.83.
Owner Mrs P De W Johnson **Bred** Mrs P De W Johnson **Trained** Upper Lambourn, Berks

FOCUS
A modest handicap, not run at a strong pace. An improved effort from the unexposed winner, but just fair form overall, if reasonably sound.
Bollywood(IRE) Official explanation: jockey said gelding suffered interference in running
T/Plt: £19.50 to a £1 stake. Pool: £82,563.40. 3,084.90 winning tickets. T/Qpdt: £7.00 to a £1 stake. Pool: £5,063.00. 531.10 winning tickets. ST

3625 YARMOUTH (L-H)
Monday, July 23

OFFICIAL GOING: Good to firm (8.3)
Wind: Fresh across Weather: Showers

3800 GREAT YARMOUTH MERCURY MEDIAN AUCTION MAIDEN STKS 1m 1f
2:30 (2:31) (Class 6) 3-4-Y-O £1,943 (£578; £288; £144) Stalls Low

Form RPR
-325 **1** **Grand Art (IRE)**[51] [2248] 3-9-3 66 SebSanders 6 67
(M H Tompkins) *a.p: led over 2f out: drvn out* **13/8**[1]
0-56 **2** *3/4* **Split The Wind (USA)**[13] [3393] 3-8-12 63 EddieAhern 4 61
(Eve Johnson Houghton) *chsd ldrs: ev ch fr over 2f out: styd on* **17/2**
00 **3** *1 1/4* **Dot's Delight**[31] [2836] 3-8-12 0 JimmyQuinn 2 58
(M H Tompkins) *chsd ldrs: led over 3f out: rdn and hdd over 2f out: sn outpcd: styd on ins fnl f* **25/1**
-242 **4** *3* **Hazarayna**[21] [3160] 3-8-12 66 TedDurcan 11 51
(H R A Cecil) *hld up: hdwy over 2f out: sn rdn: styng on same pce whn edgd lft over 1f out* **2/1**[2]
3 **5** *nk* **Dubai World**[18] [3248] 3-9-3 0 (e) ChrisCatlin 5 56
(Rae Guest) *hld up: rdn over 3f out: nt trble ldrs* **7/1**[3]
0040 **6** *12* **Nothingtodeclaire**[5] [3651] 3-9-3 72 JDSmith 3 29
(G A Huffer) *hld up: effrt over 3f out: wknd over 2f out* **14/1**
60 **7** *4* **Littlemissdynamite**[33] [2766] 4-9-7 0 PaulEddery 1 16
(J McAuley) *prom over 6f* **50/1**
-000 **8** *19* **Bali Belony**[28] [2940] 3-8-9 39 PatrickMathers(3) 7 —
(J R Jenkins) *hld up: bhd fnl 5f: hung rt fnl 3f* **100/1**
0-0 **9** *5* **Iceni Princess**[14] [3387] 3-8-12 0 AmirQuinn 8 —
(P Howling) *sn led: hdd over 7f out: rdn over 3f out: sn wknd* **100/1**
34-0 **10** *5* **Penmara**[45] [2431] 4-9-4 48 (b[1]) MarcHalford(3) 9 —
(Miss J E Foster) *dwlt: rdn to ld over 7f out: hdd over 3f out: wknd over 2f out* **50/1**

1m 55.12s (115.12)
WFA 3 from 4yo 9lb **10** Ran SP% **110.9**
CSF £14.90 TOTE £2.20: £1.10, £2.50, £4.70; EX 15.40 Trifecta £123.50 Pool: £431.66, 2.48 winning units.
Owner Matthew Green **Bred** Mrs Teresa Bergin And Mrs Anne Fitzgerald **Trained** Newmarket, Suffolk
■ The first race to be run over 1m1f at Yarmouth.

FOCUS
Amodest maiden. With the fourth disappointing it is doubtful if the winner had to improve.

3801 BET NOW AT WBX.COM (S) STKS 6f 3y
3:00 (3:01) (Class 6) 2-Y-O £1,943 (£578; £288; £144) Stalls High

Form RPR
1 **1** **Only A Game (IRE)**[13] [3392] 2-9-4 0 RichardMullen 1 69+
(E J O'Neill) *chsd ldrs: led over 2f out: rdn and edgd rt ins fnl f: r.o* **4/5**[1]
4 **2** *3* **Wicksy Creek**[18] [3246] 2-8-12 0 EddieAhern 5 54
(M G Quinlan) *led over 3f out: rdn over 1f out: no ex ins fnl f* **7/2**[2]
0263 **3** *1 3/4* **Shipboard Romance (IRE)**[4] [3681] 2-8-9 0 ow2 StephenDonohoe 6 46
(P D Evans) *chsd ldrs: rdn 1/2-way: styd on same pce fnl 2f* **4/1**[3]
0 **4** *3/4* **Birdsville**[24] [3043] 2-8-7 0 JimmyQuinn 3 42
(Rae Guest) *dwlt: outpcd: styd on ins fnl f: nvr nrr* **20/1**
5 **5** *2 1/2* **Sharps Gold**[53] [2188] 2-8-7 0 (t) TedDurcan 7 34
(P J McBride) *sn pushed along in rr: hdwy over 3f out: rdn and wknd over 1f out* **20/1**
0 **6** *2* **Emily's Dens Joy (IRE)**[95] [1101] 2-8-4 0 PatrickMathers(3) 2 28
(Miss D A McHale) *chsd ldrs to 1/2-way* **22/1**
004 **7** *nk* **Rannoch**[13] [3392] 2-8-7 0 KevinGhunowa(5) 8 32
(Miss D A McHale) *chsd ldrs: rdn and hung rt over 2f out: hung lft and wknd over 1f out* **66/1**

1m 15.44s (1.74) **Going Correction** +0.075s/f (Good) **7** Ran SP% **113.1**
Speed ratings (Par 92):91,87,84,83,80 77,77
CSF £3.59 TOTE £1.60: £1.10, £2.40; EX 4.10 Trifecta £6.90 Pool: £766.41, 78.14 winning units.The winner was bought-in for 15,000gns. Wicksy Creek was the subject of a friendly claim
Owner Ballard Campbell,JC Fretwell & C Evans **Bred** Maggie And Eric Hemming **Trained** Averham Park, Notts

FOCUS
Obviously just a modest race, but the winner is better than this grade.

NOTEBOOK
Only A Game(IRE), a narrow winner in this grade on his debut at Lingfield, only had to reproduce the effort to follow up and he saw the extra furlong out well to score with ease. He may well prove to be a bit better than this grade and the fact connections went to 15,000gns to keep him suggests they too are hopeful of further progress. (op 4-6)
Wicksy Creek improved on his initial effort in a similar contest over course and distance, attempting to make all and seemingly appreciating the faster surface. There is one of these in him and a drop to 5f may help. (op 9-2)
Shipboard Romance(IRE) is fully exposed, even at this level, and she is likely to continue to find at least one too good. Perhaps 6f in soft ground would be her ideal conditions. (tchd 5-1)
Birdsville struggled to make an impact on her debut at Folkestone, but that was in a maiden and the combination of a drop in trip and grade brought about a more prominent showing. (op 25-1)
Sharps Gold has not offered a lot in two starts now and winning races is clearly going to prove difficult. (op 25-1 tchd 28-1)

3802 JOIN WBX.COM FOR £150 FREE BETS H'CAP 6f 3y
3:30 (3:30) (Class 4) (0-85,85) 3-Y-O+ £4,857 (£1,445; £722; £360) Stalls High

Form RPR
2414 **1** **Everygrainofsand (IRE)**[44] [2458] 4-8-13 **72** TedDurcan 6 83
(J R Best) *mde all: rdn and edgd rt ins fnl f: r.o* **6/1**[3]

-063 **2** 1 1/4 **Don Pele (IRE)**[9] 3528 5-9-2 **75** ..... RichardMullen 8 82
(R A Harris) *chsd ldrs: rdn and ev ch ins fnl f: nt qckn* **4/1**[1]

0000 **3** 2 1/2 **Connect**[30] 2882 10-8-12 **76** ..... (b) PatrickHills(5) 7 75
(M H Tompkins) *hld up: hdwy over 1f out: no imp fnl f* **17/2**

6600 **4** 1/2 **Guildenstern (IRE)**[7] 3599 5-8-13 **72** ..... ChrisCatlin 1 69
(P Howling) *chsd ldrs: rdn over 1f out: styd on same pce* **14/1**

4100 **5** 3/4 **Adantino**[10] 3481 8-9-2 **80** ..... (b) JamesMillman(5) 2 75
(B R Millman) *chsd ldrs: rdn over 2f out: styd on same pce appr fnl f* **7/1**

0000 **6** 1 1/4 **Obe Gold**[10] 3481 5-9-12 **85** ..... (v) DarryllHolland 5 76
(M R Channon) *broke wl: sn lost pl: rdn 1/2-way: nvr trbld ldrs* **5/1**[2]

040 **7** 5 **High Ridge**[20] 3188 8-8-3 **67** ..... (p) KevinGhunowa(5) 4 42
(J M Bradley) *edgd lft s: sn pushed along in rr: n.d* **20/1**

30-6 **8** 6 **Ten Shun**[111] 902 4-8-12 **71** ..... StephenDonohoe 3 27
(P D Evans) *hmpd s: sn outpcd* **10/1**

3405 **9** 3 **Figaro Flyer (IRE)**[9] 3528 4-9-1 **74** ..... AmirQuinn 9 20
(P Howling) *stdd s: hld up plld hrd: swtchd to stands' side to r alone over 3f out: wknd over 1f out* **8/1**

00 **10** 4 **Two Step Kid (USA)**[149] 550 6-9-11 **84** ..... SebSanders 10 17
(J Noseda) *chsd ldrs over 4f: eased ins fnl f* **10/1**

1m 13.15s (-0.55) **Going Correction** +0.075s/f (Good) **10** Ran SP% **114.7**
Speed ratings (Par 105):106,104,101,100,99 97,91,83,79,73
CSF £29.70 CT £203.93 TOTE £5.60: £1.70, £1.90, £3.10; EX 25.30 Trifecta £422.30 Part won. Pool: £594.90, 0.74 winning units..
Owner John Mayne **Bred** Mrs C Hartery **Trained** Hucking, Kent

FOCUS
Just an ordinary sprint handicap. The pace was not over strong but the form seems sound enough.
High Ridge Official explanation: jockey said gelding was never travelling
Ten Shun Official explanation: jockey said gelding lost its action
Figaro Flyer(IRE) Official explanation: jockey said gelding hung right
Two Step Kid(USA) Official explanation: jockey said horse lost its action

3803 LETHEBY & CHRISTOPHER FILLIES' H'CAP 1m 3f 101y
4:00 (4:11) (Class 6) (0-65,65) 3-Y-O+ **£2,137** (£635; £317; £158) **Stalls** Low

Form RPR

0011 **1** **Ravenna**[12] 3421 3-8-0 **53** ..... WilliamBuick(5) 3 65+
(M P Tregoning) *chsd ldrs: led over 2f out: sn clr: eased ins fnl f* **9/4**[1]

54-6 **2** 6 **Tafiya**[42] 2521 4-10-0 **65** ..... ChrisCatlin 7 65
(J W Hills) *chsd ldrs: led wl over 2f out: sn rdn and hdd: styd on same pce* **9/1**

300 **3** 3/4 **White Moss (IRE)**[12] 3429 3-8-12 **60** ..... JimmyQuinn 6 59
(M H Tompkins) *hld up: hdwy over 3f out: sn rdn: styd on same pce fnl 2f* **9/1**

0-06 **4** 1/2 **Dubai Shadow (IRE)**[23] 3079 3-8-7 **60** ..... AhmedAjtebi(5) 9 58
(C E Brittain) *chsd ldrs: rdn over 3f out: styd on same pce fnl 2f* **33/1**

0001 **5** 1 1/4 **Diamond Key (IRE)**[17] 3274 3-7-9 **50** ..... (b) MCGeran(7) 10 46
(M G Quinlan) *s.s: hld up: styd on u.p fnl 2f: nvr trbld ldrs* **25/1**

1030 **6** 3 1/2 **Medieval Maiden**[14] 3385 4-9-11 **62** ..... TedDurcan 1 52
(W J Musson) *hld up: hdwy over 3f out: wknd over 1f out* **8/1**

50-0 **7** 3 **Ashwell Rose**[18] 3247 5-8-6 **46** oh1 ..... (b[1]) PatrickMathers(3) 12 31
(J R Jenkins) *s.i.s: hld up: nvr nrr* **100/1**

3124 **8** 3 1/2 **Snake Skin**[40] 2572 4-9-10 **61** ..... JimCrowley 5 40
(J Gallagher) *prom: lost pl 7f out: hdwy over 2f out: sn rdn and wknd* **11/2**[2]

2552 **9** 2 1/2 **Chiff Chaff**[17] 3282 3-8-13 **61** ..... DarryllHolland 11 36
(C R Dore) *hld up in tch: rdn over 3f out: wknd over 2f out* **13/2**[3]

00-0 **10** 1 3/4 **Eridani (IRE)**[15] 3351 3-7-13 **47** oh1 ow1 ..... FrankieMcDonald 2 19
(M L W Bell) *chsd ldrs over 8f* **33/1**

2455 **11** shd **Sforzando**[30] 2865 6-9-7 **65** ..... KristinStubbs(7) 8 36
(Mrs L Stubbs) *s.s: rdn over 4f out: hdwy over 2f out: sn hung lft and wknd* **12/1**

0-64 **12** 22 **Gigi Glamor**[43] 2491 5-8-12 **49** ..... StephenDonohoe 15 —
(W M Brisbourne) *hld up: rdn over 4f out: sn lost tch* **12/1**

-000 **13** 3/4 **Grand Court (IRE)**[54] 2157 4-8-4 **46** oh1 ..... KevinGhunowa(5) 4 —
(Evan Williams) *sn led: rdn over 3f out: wknd and hdd wl over 2f out* **25/1**

2m 26.76s (-0.74) **Going Correction** +0.075s/f (Good)
WFA 3 from 4yo+ 11lb **13** Ran SP% **120.5**
Speed ratings (Par 98):105,100,100,99,98 96,94,91,89,88 88,72,71
CSF £22.24 CT £160.10 TOTE £2.80: £1.20, £3.20, £3.10; EX 24.80 Trifecta £137.70 Pool: £587.69, 3.03 winning units.
Owner Park Walk Racing **Bred** Whitsbury Manor Stud **Trained** Lambourn, Berks

FOCUS
A weakish fillies' handicap. Ravenna did not need to reproduce her recent sand form despite winning easily.
Diamond Key(IRE) Official explanation: jockey said filly missed the break
Grand Court(IRE) Official explanation: jockey said filly ran too free

3804 WBX.COM WORLD BET EXCHANGE H'CAP 1m 2f 21y
4:30 (4:39) (Class 6) (0-65,65) 3-Y-O **£2,137** (£635; £317; £158) **Stalls** Low

Form RPR

00-0 **1** **Smirfy's Silver**[89] 1236 3-8-7 **51** ow1 ..... DarryllHolland 10 60+
(E S McMahon) *sn led: shkn up over 1f out: styd on wl: eased nr fin* **28/1**

0305 **2** 3/4 **Mutoon (IRE)**[77] 1538 3-8-8 **52** ..... RichardMullen 9 59
(S C Williams) *a.p: rdn to chse wnr fnl f: styd on* **12/1**

030- **3** 4 **Born West (USA)**[234] 6658 3-9-0 **65** ..... MCGeran(7) 15 64
(P W Chapple-Hyam) *s.s: hld up: hdwy over 3f out: rdn and edgd lft over 1f out: styd on same pce* **10/1**

0-00 **4** 1 **Bold Adventure**[11] 3469 3-8-5 **49** ..... PaulEddery 2 46
(W J Musson) *hld up: hdwy over 1f out: nvr nr to chal* **7/1**[2]

000- **5** 1 1/4 **Persian Fox (IRE)**[307] 5461 3-9-5 **63** ..... JDSmith 14 58
(G A Huffer) *hld up in tch: plld hrd: trckd wnr 1/2-way: rdn over 1f out: sn wknd* **16/1**

3-00 **6** 1/2 **Etoile D'Or (IRE)**[31] 2834 3-9-2 **60** ..... JimmyQuinn 3 54+
(M H Tompkins) *chsd ldrs: lost pl over 3f out: n.d after* **12/1**

0055 **7** shd **Homes By Woodford**[5] 3640 3-9-1 **59** ..... (p) AmirQuinn 16 52
(R A Harris) *hld up: hdwy over 3f out: rdn and wknd over 1f out* **17/2**

6-06 **8** nk **Terry Molloy (IRE)**[40] 2565 3-9-4 **62** ..... StephenDonohoe 8 55
(K R Burke) *hld up: hdwy u.p over 3f out: wknd fnl f* **17/2**

0-03 **9** 1 1/2 **New Light**[21] 3151 3-8-10 **54** ..... JimCrowley 13 44
(Eve Johnson Houghton) *hld up: rdn over 2f out: n.d* **11/1**

0652 **10** 2 1/2 **Fizzy Bella**[6] 3629 3-8-13 **57** ..... TedDurcan 7 42
(M G Quinlan) *hld up: hdwy over 2f out: wknd over 1f out* **8/1**

3052 **11** 1 3/4 **Blockley (USA)**[5] 3640 3-8-10 **57** ..... (v) PatrickMathers(3) 5 38
(Ian Williams) *prom: lost pl over 4f out: sn rdn and no rspnse* **6/1**[1]

0-05 **12** 3 **Bishop Auckland (IRE)**[12] 3415 3-7-13 **50** ..... KMay(7) 12 25
(Mrs A Duffield) *s.i.s: hld up: hdwy 1/2-way: wknd over 3f out* **40/1**

006- **13** 1 1/4 **Golden Folly**[251] 6475 3-8-11 **55** ..... SebSanders 11 28
(Lady Herries) *hld up: hdwy over 3f out: wknd over 2f out* **15/2**[3]

050 **14** 4 **Break Out**[23] 3084 3-8-1 **50** ..... KevinGhunowa(5) 6 15
(J M Bradley) *hld up: wknd 3f out* **66/1**

006- **15** 41 **Little Rutland**[249] 6498 3-8-13 **57** ..... ChrisCatlin 4 —
(E J O'Neill) *chsd ldrs: hung rt 1/2-way: wknd over 3f out* **25/1**

2m 9.41s (1.31) **Going Correction** +0.075s/f (Good) **15** Ran SP% **120.6**
Speed ratings (Par 98):97,96,93,92,91 91,90,90,89,87 86,83,82,79,46
CSF £326.37 CT £3590.51 TOTE £35.10: £10.30, £3.80, £5.60; EX 774.40 TRIFECTA Not won..
Owner Mrs Dian Plant **Bred** G S Shropshire **Trained** Lichfield, Staffs

FOCUS
Just a modest handicap, but the form looks solid enough for the grade and it should produce winners at a similar level.
Blockley(USA) Official explanation: jockey said colt was never travelling from 3f out

3805 NORFOLK NELSON MUSEUM APPRENTICE RIDERS' H'CAP 1m 2f 21y
5:00 (5:06) (Class 6) (0-60,60) 4-Y-O+ **£2,137** (£635; £317; £158) **Stalls** Low

Form RPR

3620 **1** **Danzare**[18] 3249 5-8-11 **52** ..... JamieHamblett 1 58
(J L Spearing) *a.p: chsd ldr over 2f out: styd on to ld wl ins fnl f* **7/1**[3]

5040 **2** hd **Ciccone**[15] 3352 4-8-9 **53** ..... JemmaMarshall(3) 4 58
(G L Moore) *chsd ldrs: rdn over 1f out: r.o* **14/1**

5301 **3** 1 **General Flumpa**[18] 3250 6-8-12 **58** ..... LauraReynolds(5) 8 61
(Miss Tor Sturgis) *led over 8f out: slipped over 4f out: hdd wl ins fnl f* **9/2**[2]

5133 **4** 3/4 **Desert Hawk**[18] 3250 6-8-13 **54** ..... KirstyMilczarek 10 56
(W M Brisbourne) *prom: rdn over 2f out: styd on* **7/2**[1]

1100 **5** shd **Don Pasquale**[17] 3280 5-9-0 **55** ..... JamesO'Reilly 11 56+
(J T Stimpson) *s.i.s: hld up: rdn over 3f out: hdwy over 2f out: nt rch ldrs* **11/1**

3434 **6** 2 **Trevian**[7] 3600 6-8-8 **54** ..... BarrySavage(5) 5 51
(J M Bradley) *s.s: hld up: plld hrd: rdn over 2f out: styd on ins fnl f: nvr nrr* **15/2**

540- **7** 2 **Polish Welcome**[307] 5445 4-8-5 **46** oh1 ..... MCGeran 7 39
(S C Williams) *chsd ldrs: rdn and hung lft over 2f out: wknd over 1f out* **15/2**

300- **8** 1 **Hogan's Heroes**[31] 2849 4-9-0 **60** ..... BradleyRoper(5) 12 51
(Eoin Doyle, Ire) *mid-div: effrt over 2f out: n.d* **33/1**

4634 **9** 1/2 **Veba (USA)**[20] 3186 4-8-2 **46** oh1 ..... FrankiePickard(3) 6 36
(M D I Usher) *hld up: rdn and hung lft over 1f out: n.d* **8/1**

-000 **10** 3 1/2 **Sir Haydn**[18] 3249 7-9-5 **60** ..... (v) WilliamCarson 3 43
(J R Jenkins) *led: hdd over 8f out: chsd ldrs tl rdn and wknd over 1f out* **25/1**

0-00 **11** 2 1/2 **Classic Hall (IRE)**[61] 1950 4-8-5 **46** oh1 ..... KMay 2 24
(T Keddy) *hld up: racd keenly: wknd over 2f out* **14/1**

030/ **12** hd **C'Est La Vie**[64] 5366 5-8-9 **50** ..... (t) AmyBaker 13 28
(Miss J E Foster) *hld up: wknd over 2f out* **66/1**

2m 11.66s (3.56) **Going Correction** +0.075s/f (Good) **12** Ran SP% **117.5**
Speed ratings (Par 101):88,87,87,86,86 84,83,82,81,79 77,77
CSF £98.21 CT £492.59 TOTE £9.20: £2.50, £5.00, £2.10; EX 45.40 Trifecta £335.40 Part won. Pool: £472.52 - 0.50 winning units. Place 6 £ 188.33, Place 5 £ 90.43.
Owner Masonaires **Bred** A Seelbinder **Trained** Kinnersley, Worcs
■ Stewards' Enquiry : William Carson one-day ban: used whip when gelding was out of contention and showing no repsonse (Aug 3)
Barry Savage caution: used whip down the shoulder in the forehand position

FOCUS
A moderate event in which the first four were always prominent. Pretty limited form.
Desert Hawk Official explanation: jockey said gelding was unsuited by the good to firm ground
T/Plt: £417.30 to a £1 stake. Pool: £69,171.95. 121.00 winning tickets. T/Qpdt: £90.00 to a £1 stake. Pool: £4,452.50. 36.60 winning tickets. CR

3806 - 3809a (Foreign Racing) - See Raceform Interactive

2487 BELMONT PARK (L-H)
Saturday, July 21

OFFICIAL GOING: Fast

3810a COACHING CLUB AMERICAN OAKS (GRADE 1) (FILLIES) (DIRT) 1m 2f (D)
9:44 (9:45) 3-Y-O
£91,837 (£30,612; £15,306; £7,653; £4,592; £1,531)

RPR

1 **Octave (USA)**[21] 3-8-9 ..... JRVelazquez 5 113
(T Pletcher, U.S.A) **1/2**[1]

2 1/2 **Lear's Princess (USA)**[20] 3-8-9 ..... ECoa 6 112
(K McLaughlin, U.S.A) **43/10**[3]

3 3/4 **Folk (USA)**[112] 859 3-8-9 ..... MLuzzi 7 111
(Saeed Bin Suroor) **73/20**[2]

4 3 1/4 **Humble Janet (USA)**[22] 3-8-9 ..... AGarcia 2 105
(S Asmussen, U.S.A) **207/10**

5 1 1/4 **Wow Me Free (USA)** 3-8-9 ..... (b) JCastellano 3 103
(R Jenkins, U.S.A) **61/1**

6 12 **Coy Coyote (USA)**[294] 3-8-9 ..... FJara 1 81
(M Dickinson, U.S.A) **29/1**

7 6 **Rosie's Attitude (USA)** 3-8-9 ..... (b) RBejarano 4 70
(T Bush, U.S.A) **56/1**

2m 2.17s (1.55) **7** Ran SP% **118.3**
PARI-MUTUEL (including $2 stakes): WIN 3.00; PL (1-2) 2.10, 3.30; SHOW(1-2-3) 2.10, 2.50, 2.50; SF 8.50.
Owner Starlight Stables & D Lucarelli **Bred** Mr & Mrs Martin J Wygood **Trained** USA

NOTEBOOK
Octave(USA), runner-up five times in a row before winning the Mother Goose Stakes here last month, proved a fine substitute for star stablemate Rags To Riches, getting to the front a furlong out and holding on well.
Lear's Princess(USA), on her dirt debut, ran on late for second.
Folk(USA), off the track since the UAE Derby in March, made the running to the furlong pole.

[3370]MUSSELBURGH (R-H)

Tuesday, July 24

OFFICIAL GOING: Good (good to soft in places on straight course; good to firm in places on round course; 8.1)

Wind: Almost nil Weather: Cloudy

3811 TURFTV.CO.UK APPRENTICE H'CAP — 5f 2y

6:50 (6:50) (Class 6) (0-65,62) 3-Y-O — £2,590 (£770; £385; £192) Stalls Low

Form — RPR

3422 1 **Nomoreblondes**[53] 2205 3-9-8 **60**....(p) JamieMoriarty 4 — 66
(P T Midgley) *mde all: rdn over 1f out: hld on wl fnl f* **9/2[3]**

0000 2 hd **Spinning Game**[7] 3605 3-8-2 **45**....(b) DanielleMcCreery(5) 10 — 50
(D W Chapman) *racd alone centre: in tch: effrt 2f out: ev ch ins fnl f: jst hld* **100/1**

0221 3 1 1/2 **Silly Gilly (IRE)**[2] 3763 3-9-2 **54** 6ex.... AndrewElliott 1 — 54
(K R Burke) *cl up: effrt over 1f out: kpt on same pce fnl f* **5/2[2]**

0422 4 3/4 **By The Edge (IRE)**[2] 3763 3-8-3 **48**....(v) DeanHeslop(7) 8 — 45
(T D Barron) *prom: effrt over 1f out: kpt on same pce fnl f* **7/4[1]**

5204 5 1 **Stoneacre Gareth (IRE)**[8] 3588 3-9-7 **62**....(b) RussellKennemore(3) 5 — 56
(Peter Grayson) *prom: drvn 2f out: kpt on same pce* **8/1**

6300 6 hd **The Brat**[29] 2939 3-8-7 **45**.... AndrewMullen 6 — 38
(J S Wainwright) *chsd ldrs: drvn 1/2-way: one pce over 1f out* **20/1**

0-00 7 3 **Warm Tribute (USA)**[16] 3342 3-8-7 **50**.... GaryBartley(5) 9 — 32
(J S Goldie) *bhd: drvn 1/2-way: n.d* **20/1**

-000 8 1 1/4 **Senora Lenorah**[10] 3537 3-8-0 **45**.... PaulPickard(7) 3 — 23
(D A Nolan) *bhd: rdn and edgd rt 1/2-way: nvr on terms* **100/1**

6300 9 3/4 **Temtation (IRE)**[8] 3597 3-8-9 **47**.... PatrickMathers 7 — 22
(Peter Grayson) *t.k.h: prom tl wknd 2f out* **16/1**

61.27 secs (0.77) **Going Correction** -0.025s/f (Good) — 9 Ran SP% **111.6**

Speed ratings (Par 98): **92,91,89,88,86 86,81,79,78**

CSF £375.76 CT £1333.86 TOTE £4.40: £1.30, £14.80, £1.30; EX 149.40.

Owner Anthony D Copley **Bred** P John And Redmyre Bloodstock **Trained** Westow, N Yorks

FOCUS

A moderate sprint best rated around the first two.

3812 MORTON FRASER MAIDEN AUCTION STKS — 5f 2y

7:20 (7:21) (Class 6) 2-Y-O — £2,590 (£770; £385; £192) Stalls Low

Form — RPR

4233 1 **Look Busy (IRE)**[24] 3077 2-8-3 0.... PatrickMathers(3) 6 — 78
(A Berry) *mde all: drew clr fr over 1f out: unchal* **2/1[1]**

6203 2 6 **Our Sunnie**[11] 3499 2-8-13 0.... AdrianTNicholls 8 — 63
(D Nicholls) *chsd wnr: rdn: carried hd high and edgd rt over 1f out: kpt on same pce* **6/1**

3 2 1/2 **Emef Princess** 2-8-7 0 ow1.... NCallan 7 — 48
(K A Ryan) *chsd ldrs: effrt 2f out: sn one pce* **9/2[3]**

P0 4 1/2 **Everything**[20] 3200 2-8-7 0 ow3.... MickyFenton 1 — 47
(P T Midgley) *prom: drvn and outpcd 1/2-way: kpt on fnl f* **25/1**

5 nk **Red Wings (IRE)** 2-8-8 0.... PatCosgrave 5 — 47
(G A Swinbank) *sn bhd and outpcd: kpt on fnl f: n.d* **11/1**

45 6 hd **Elusive Lady (IRE)**[6] 3635 2-8-1 0.... AndrewElliott(3) 3 — 42
(J R Weymes) *midfield: drvn 1/2-way: no imp over 1f out* **50/1**

03 7 shd **The Magic Blanket (IRE)**[35] 2746 2-8-11 0.... TomEaves 9 — 48
(Mrs L Stubbs) *prom tl rdn and no ex wl over 1f out* **8/1**

0 8 nk **Red River Boy**[49] 2337 2-8-4 0.... KellyHarrison(7) 2 — 47
(C W Fairhurst) *cl up: hung rt fr 1/2-way: wknd wl over 1f out* **100/1**

3 9 1 3/4 **Honey Monster (IRE)**[13] 3423 2-9-1 0.... PaulHanagan 4 — 52+
(Miss V Haigh) *dwlt: outpcd and bhd: hung rt 1/2-way: nvr on terms* **4/1[2]**

4306 10 1 1/2 **La Guancha**[15] 3370 2-8-1 0.... AndrewMullen(3) 11 — 29
(D A Nolan) *bhd and outpcd: no ch fr 1/2-way* **80/1**

06 11 15 **Frizzini**[32] 2818 2-9-1 0....(b[1]) PhillipMakin 10 — —
(N Tinkler) *squeezed out s: a outpcd* **40/1**

60.64 secs (0.14) **Going Correction** -0.025s/f (Good) — 11 Ran SP% **115.7**

Speed ratings (Par 92): **97,87,83,82,82 81,81,81,78,75 51**

CSF £13.77 TOTE £3.40: £1.20, £2.00, £2.40; EX 14.00.

Owner A Underwood **Bred** Tom And Hazel Russell **Trained** Cockerham, Lancs

FOCUS

This was nothing more than a modest maiden, but the form looks reasonable through the runner-up and fourth and it should produce the odd winner at a similar level.

NOTEBOOK

Look Busy(IRE) has been running well enough to suggest a race of this nature was within her capabilities and she led throughout for an easy victory. She could be the type to progress further in nurseries for her in-form stable. (op 5-2 tchd 11-4 and 3-1 in places)

Our Sunnie, third off a mark of 69 on his recent handicap debut, was entitled to run well and he had his chance, but found the winner far too pacey for him and did not overly impress with the way he carried himself under pressure. (op 11-2)

Emef Princess, an 8,000gns daughter of Mind Games, is clearly no star, but this was a promising-enough start and she is in the right hands to win races. (tchd 5-1)

Everything looks to be getting a little better with every run and she could be the type to improve for a move into handicaps, especially when tackling an extra furlong or so. (tchd 28-1)

Red Wings(IRE), who is related to several winners, showed her inexperience early on, but was noted putting in some good late headway and she is going to relish an extra furlong or so in time. (op 13-2 tchd 12-1)

Honey Monster(IRE) was unable to improve on his initial effort, but he was again sluggish from the gate and looks another more likely to make an impact in nurseries. (op 5-1 tchd 3-1)

3813 EDINBURGH EVENING NEWS H'CAP — 1m

7:50 (7:50) (Class 3) (0-90,87) 3-Y-O+ — £7,772 (£2,312; £1,155; £577) Stalls High

Form — RPR

2060 1 **Fremen (USA)**[23] 3138 7-7-9 **78**.... AdrianTNicholls 2 — 92
(D Nicholls) *hld up bhd: hdwy whn nt clr run 3f and 2f out: swtchd lft and qcknd to ld 1f out: edgd rt: r.o strly* **14/1**

0344 2 1 3/4 **Stoic Leader (IRE)**[8] 3585 7-9-3 **77**.... AndrewMullen(3) 9 — 87
(R F Fisher) *towards rr: hdwy 3f out: kpt on fnl f: nt rch wnr* **17/2[3]**

2303 3 2 **Benandonner (USA)**[11] 3513 4-10-0 **85**.... PaulHanagan 6 — 91
(R A Fahey) *prom: rdn over 3f out: rallied and disp ld over 1f out: one pce ins fnl f* **7/2[1]**

-010 4 nk **Wigwam Willie (IRE)**[13] 3437 5-9-12 **83**....(p) NCallan 8 — 88
(K A Ryan) *midfield: pushed along over 3f out: rallied: one pce ins fnl f* **10/1**

0246 5 1 1/2 **Fiefdom (IRE)**[16] 3350 5-9-0 **76**.... NeilBrown(5) 13 — 78
(I W McInnes) *chsd ldrs: edgd lft and led briefly over 1f out: sn one pce* **22/1**

5400 6 3/4 **Voodoo Moon**[13] 3430 3-9-5 **87**.... GregFairley(3) 11 — 85
(M Johnston) *chsd ldrs: pushed along 3f out: one pce appr fnl f* **10/1**

5050 7 3/4 **Frank Crow**[16] 3346 4-9-0 **71**.... PatCosgrave 12 — 69
(J S Goldie) *hld up: hdwy whn nt clr run 2f out: no imp appr fnl f* **12/1**

0310 8 2 **Regent's Secret (USA)**[27] 2986 7-8-9 **73**....(p) GaryBartley(7) 4 — 67
(J S Goldie) *bhd and sn drvn along: hdwy over 2f out: sn no imp* **11/1**

0043 9 1 1/2 **Nevada Desert (IRE)**[49] 2346 7-9-2 **78**.... MichaelJStainton(5) 5 — 68
(R M Whitaker) *prom tl rdn and wknd wl over 1f out* **12/1**

0314 10 shd **Hula Ballew**[35] 2742 7-9-10 **81**.... PhillipMakin 3 — 71
(M Dods) *midfield: pushed along 1/2-way: wknd over 2f out* **16/1**

3340 11 1 3/4 **Emerald Bay (IRE)**[31] 2871 5-9-11 **82**.... TomEaves 1 — 68
(I Semple) *bhd: drvn over 3f out: n.d* **20/1**

2312 12 1/2 **Il Castagno (IRE)**[29] 2936 4-9-7 **83**.... PJMcDonald(5) 7 — 68
(B Smart) *t.k.h: cl up: led over 2f out to over 1f out: sn btn* **11/2[2]**

1311 13 8 **H Harrison (IRE)**[42] 2528 7-9-8 **82**.... AndrewElliott(3) 10 — 48
(I W McInnes) *led to over 2f out: wknd over 1f out* **10/1**

1m 39.42s (-3.08) **Going Correction** -0.20s/f (Firm)

WFA 3 from 4yo+ 8lb — **13** Ran SP% **120.8**

Speed ratings (Par 107): **107,105,103,102,101 100,99,97,96,96 94,94,86**

CSF £129.61 CT £537.71 TOTE £16.90: £4.60, £3.00, £1.50; EX 195.60.

Owner Miss C King Mrs A Seed Ms Finola Devaney **Bred** Flaxman Holdings Ltd **Trained** Sessay, N Yorks

■ Stewards' Enquiry : Neil Brown three-day ban: careless riding (Aug 5-7)

FOCUS

A fair contest but a race full of exposed handicappers. The form looks solid with the first four close to their best recent marks.

NOTEBOOK

Fremen(USA) had looked to have lost his form, but efforts from earlier in the season entitled him to some respect and he bounced right back to his best to win with something to spare. He overcame trouble in running to win, but will need to progress again if he is to defy a rise. (op 12-1)

Stoic Leader(IRE) has been running well off this mark and he recorded another fine effort in defeat, but gives the impression he is going to remain vulnerable to an improver. (op 8-1 tchd 9-1)

Benandonner(USA) gives his running more often than not and he stuck on willingly under his big weight, but could make no impression in the final furlong. His consistency is likely to be rewarded sooner rather than later and he may benefit from returning to 1m2f. (op 4-1)

Wigwam Willie(IRE), a winner at Newcastle on his penultimate outing, is not the most consistent, but this was certainly better than his last effort and he kept on well enough to suggest he is up to winning off this mark. (op 12-1)

Fiefdom(IRE) is on a lengthy losing run, but he has not been running badly and there was no disgrace in this effort either. (op 20-1 tchd 25-1)

3814 LANDSBANKI CLAIMING STKS — 7f 30y

8:20 (8:20) (Class 6) 3-Y-O+ — £2,590 (£770; £385; £192) Stalls High

Form — RPR

3360 1 **Mister Jingles**[15] 3381 4-8-13 42....(v[1]) MichaelJStainton(5) 6 — 59
(R M Whitaker) *chsd ldrs: effrt and hung bdly lft over 1f out: styd on wl to ld cl home* **66/1**

1102 2 1/2 **Ballyhurry (USA)**[1] 3783 10-8-9 66.... GaryBartley(7) 8 — 55+
(J S Goldie) *hld up: effrt over 2f out: drvn and outpcd whn n.m.r over 1f out: styd on wl fnl f* **11/4[1]**

3566 3 hd **General Feeling (IRE)**[22] 3161 6-9-0 52.... PatCosgrave 13 — 53
(K R Burke) *midfield: rdn 3f out: led ins fnl f: hdd nr fin* **7/1**

-440 4 1 **Andorran (GER)**[41] 2563 4-9-2 47....(tp) PaulHanagan 11 — 52
(A Dickman) *bhd: rdn over 3f out: styd on wl fnl 2f: nrst fin* **16/1**

4500 5 shd **Fairy Monarch (IRE)**[64] 1893 8-9-0 50....(b) MickyFenton 7 — 50
(P T Midgley) *hld up: hdwy over 2f out: kpt on ins fnl f* **20/1**

003 6 1 3/4 **Wahoo Sam (USA)**[32] 2828 7-9-9 70.... NCallan 4 — 54
(K A Ryan) *led 1f: led again over 2f out to ins fnl f: no ex* **9/2[2]**

3120 7 1 1/2 **Baylaw Star**[18] 3258 6-9-4 72.... PJMcDonald(5) 3 — 50
(I W McInnes) *chsd ldrs: effrt over 2f out: one pce whn carried lft over 1f out: no ex* **5/1[3]**

0002 8 1 1/4 **Regal Raider (IRE)**[5] 3674 4-9-4 64.... TomEaves 1 — 42
(I Semple) *prom: effrt over 2f out: no ex over 1f out* **5/1[3]**

0000 9 hd **Miss Mujahid Times**[21] 3180 4-8-8 45....(p) SilvestreDeSousa 10 — 31
(A D Brown) *led after 1f to over 2f out: wknd over 1f out* **66/1**

0340 10 1 1/4 **Ho Pang Yau**[11] 3497 9-8-13 44....(p) PhillipMakin 9 — 33
(J S Goldie) *towards rr: drvn 1/2-way: nvr rchd ldrs* **25/1**

0006 11 2 **Following Flow (USA)**[5] 3674 5-8-10 40....(p) AndrewElliott(3) 5 — 27
(R Allan) *bhd: drvn over 3f out: nvr on terms* **20/1**

-000 12 3 1/2 **Suhezy (IRE)**[29] 2938 4-8-8 43.... TonyHamilton 2 — 13
(J S Wainwright) *chsd ldrs to 1/2-way: sn rdn and btn* **66/1**

0000 13 12 **Mister Marmaduke**[11] 3498 6-8-10 38....(p) PatrickMathers(3) 12 — —
(D A Nolan) *s.i.s: bhd: rdn 3f out: wknd 2f out* **150/1**

1m 29.75s (-0.19) **Going Correction** -0.20s/f (Firm) — 13 Ran SP% **115.1**

Speed ratings (Par 101): **93,92,92,91,90 88,87,85,85,84 81,77,64**

CSF £227.02 TOTE £35.40: £5.60, £1.60, £2.70; EX 270.20.Ballyhurry was claimed by Jason Parfitt for £8,000. General Feeling was claimed by S. T. Mason for £6,000.

Owner James Marshall & Mrs Susan Marshall **Bred** Catridge Farm Stud Ltd **Trained** Scarcroft, W Yorks

■ Stewards' Enquiry : Michael J Stainton four-day ban: careless riding (Aug 5-8)

FOCUS

A modest winning time, even for a claimer and the form is limited by the proximity of the fourth with several behind below par.

3815 TURFTV A MATTER OF COURSE H'CAP — 1m 4f

8:50 (8:50) (Class 6) (0-65,62) 4-Y-O+ — £2,590 (£770; £385; £192) Stalls Low

Form — RPR

-222 1 **Light Sentence**[71] 1730 4-9-2 **62**.... PJMcDonald(5) 2 — 72+
(G A Swinbank) *hld up: smooth hdwy over 3f out: rdn to ld over 1f out: edgd rt: hld on wl fnl f* **7/4[1]**

-4U5 2 1/2 **Collette's Choice**[64] 1890 4-9-6 **61**....(p) PaulHanagan 1 — 68
(R A Fahey) *hld up in tch: effrt 3f out: chsd wnr ins fnl f: r.o* **15/2**

2000 3 1/2 **Hugs Destiny (IRE)**[5] 3598 6-8-9 **55**.... NeilBrown(5) 7 — 61
(M A Barnes) *led to over 1f out: rallied: kpt on same pce ins fnl f* **9/1**

0454 4 1 **Volaticus (IRE)**[7] 3610 6-9-0 **55**.... SilvestreDeSousa 11 — 59
(A D Brown) *midfield: effrt over 2f out: kpt on same pce fnl f* **13/2[3]**

54-0 5 shd **Abstract Folly (IRE)**[44] 623 5-9-7 **62**.... TomEaves 8 — 66
(J D Bethell) *towards rr: drvn over 3f out: styd on fnl f: n.d* **14/1**

0-00 6 4 **Touch Of Ivory (IRE)**[69] 1488 4-9-2 **57**.... PhillipMakin 4 — 55
(P Monteith) *towards rr: drvn over 3f out: sme late hdwy: n.d* **33/1**

0-00 7 1 3/4 **Kyle Of Lochalsh**[9] 2764 7-8-5 **49**.... AndrewMullen(3) 13 — 44
(Miss Lucinda V Russell) *s.i.s: bhd: rdn 4f out: n.d* **16/1**

0005 8 3 **Kid'Z'Play (IRE)**[5] 3679 11-8-1 **49**.... KellyHarrison(7) 9 — 39
(J S Goldie) *chsd ldrs tl wknd over 2f out* **16/1**

330/ 9 nk **Rossall Point**[723] 2649 6-9-1 **56**.... TonyHamilton 14 — 46
(Karen McLintock) *prom: bdly hmpd after 1f: lost pl after 4f: n.d after* **33/1**

1556 10 1 1/2 **Boppys Dancer**[18] 3260 4-8-7 **48**....(b) MickyFenton 6 — 35
(P T Midgley) *t.k.h: cl up: hung rt and wknd over 2f out* **12/1**

00/0 **11** *2* **Erte**[56] [64] 6-8-1 **45**......(v) AndrewElliott(3) 3 29
(W Storey) *towards rr: drvn 1/2-way: n.d* **50/1**

334- **12** *2* **English City (IRE)**[77] [4255] 4-9-0 **55**...... PatCosgrave 5 36
(Mrs L B Normile) *hld up: shortlived effrt 3f out: sn btn* **11/2**[2]

1-00 **13** *14* **Missouri (USA)**[77] [1559] 4-8-4 **48** ow3...... GregFairley(3) 12 7
(M A Barnes) *chsd ldrs: bmpd after 1f: cl up tl wknd over 2f out* **50/1**

0000 **P** **Wee Ziggy**[10] [3534] 4-8-3 **47** ow2...... PatrickMathers(3) 10 —
(M Mullineaux) *plld hrd in midfield: sddle slipped and p.u after 3f* **100/1**

2m 37.43s (0.53) **Going Correction** -0.20s/f (Firm) 14 Ran SP% **123.8**
Speed ratings (Par 101): **90,89,89,88,88 85,84,82,82,81 80,78,69,—**
CSF £15.05 CT £100.85 TOTE £2.60: £1.10, £2.50, £3.20; EX 17.80.
Owner Mrs J Porter **Bred** Brook Stud Bloodstock Ltd **Trained** Melsonby, N Yorks
■ Stewards' Enquiry : Neil Brown three-day ban: used whip with excessive frequency (Aug 8-10)
Micky Fenton six-day ban: careless riding (Aug 4-9)

FOCUS
A moderate winning time for this modest handicap but the form appears sound enough.
Wee Ziggy Official explanation: jockey said saddle slipped

3816 HIGH SUMMER H'CAP 1m
9:20 (9:20) (Class 5) (0-70,70) 3-Y-0+ **£3,238** (£963; £481; £240) **Stalls** High

Form RPR

114 **1** **Sam's Secret**[41] [2550] 5-9-4 **60**...... NCallan 9 78
(G A Swinbank) *t.k.h in midfield: smooth hdwy to ld over 1f out: pushed out fnl f* **11/2**[3]

0003 **2** *4* **Bolton Hall (IRE)**[31] [2865] 5-9-1 **57**...... PaulHanagan 10 66
(R A Fahey) *hld up: hdwy over 2f out: chsd wnr ins fnl f: no imp* **7/2**[1]

0340 **3** *3 1/2* **Anthemion (IRE)**[15] [3376] 10-8-12 **57**...... AndrewMullen(3) 6 58
(Mrs J C McGregor) *cl up: drvn and outpcd 2f out: kpt on u.p fnl f* **33/1**

5604 **4** *hd* **Cool Ebony**[32] [2822] 4-10-0 **70**...... PhillipMakin 11 70
(M Dods) *chsd ldrs tl rdn and nt qckn over 1f out* **4/1**[2]

013 **5** *nk* **Zabeel Tower**[16] [3343] 4-8-9 **54**...... AndrewElliott(3) 14 54
(R Allan) *led to over 1f out: kpt on same pce* **12/1**

5024 **6** *3/4* **Royal Citadel (IRE)**[16] [3343] 4-8-4 **53**...... KellyHarrison(7) 12 51
(Mrs L B Normile) *chsd ldrs tl no ex fr 2f out* **33/1**

0044 **7** *1 1/2* **Esoterica (IRE)**[32] [2823] 4-9-1 **57**......(b) PatCosgrave 5 51
(J S Goldie) *bhd: drvn over 3f out: nvr rchd ldrs* **12/1**

-000 **8** *shd* **It's Unbelievable (USA)**[43] [2508] 4-9-1 **57**...... MickyFenton 4 51
(P T Midgley) *plld hrd in rr: rdn 3f out: n.d* **50/1**

0033 **9** *1 1/2* **Grand Diamond (IRE)**[32] [2829] 3-8-5 **62**......(p) GaryBartley(7) 8 53
(J S Goldie) *bhd: rdn 3f out: nvr rchd ldrs* **12/1**

3501 **10** *1 1/2* **Dee Jay Wells**[7] [3611] 3-8-6 **61** ow1...... PJMcDonald(5) 3 48
(B Ellison) *prom: effrt over 2f out: sn wknd* **15/2**

1505 **11** *1 1/4* **Franksalot (IRE)**[10] [3534] 7-9-8 **69**...... NeilBrown(5) 2 53
(I W McInnes) *hld up outside: rdn over 3f out: btn 2f out* **20/1**

0/01 **12** *7* **Cadogen Square**[10] [3534] 5-8-4 **53**...... DanielleMcCreery(7) 7 21
(D W Chapman) *t.k.h: chsd ldrs tl wknd fr 2f out* **33/1**

4016 **13** *nk* **Mayadeen (IRE)**[11] [3497] 5-8-13 **55**......(b) TomEaves 1 23
(I Semple) *hld up: rdn over 3f out: sn btn* **9/1**

-000 **R** **Gifted Flame**[13] [3422] 8-8-11 **60**...... DeanHeslop(7) 13 —
(T D Barron) *hld up: n.m.r and wnt through rail over 4f out* **12/1**

1m 40.13s (-2.37) **Going Correction** -0.20s/f (Firm)
WFA 3 from 4yo+ 8lb 14 Ran SP% **125.7**
Speed ratings (Par 103): **103,99,95,95,95 94,92,92,91,89 88,81,81,—**
CSF £24.89 CT £610.04 TOTE £6.20: £2.00, £2.30, £9.30; EX 29.50 Place 6 £45.13, Place 5 £15.78..
Owner Copskam Partnership **Bred** Dandy's Farm **Trained** Melsonby, N Yorks

FOCUS
An ordinary handicap and things got very tight around the home bend, but the winner finally dotted up and looks a bit better than this grade. The form looks decent and has been rated fairly positively.
It's Unbelievable(USA) Official explanation: jockey said gelding ran too free early stages
T/Plt: £90.90 to a £1 stake. Pool: £81,654.90. 655.65 winning tickets. T/Qpdt: £17.40 to a £1 stake. Pool: £4,561.85. 193.90 winning tickets. RY

3549 SALISBURY (R-H)
Tuesday, July 24
3817 Meeting Abandoned - waterlogged

3800 YARMOUTH (L-H)
Tuesday, July 24

OFFICIAL GOING: Good (good to firm in places) changing to good to soft (good in places) after race 3 (3.00) changing to soft after race 6 (4.30)
Wind: Fresh, half-behind Weather: Cloudy with sunny spells, turning to showers after race 3

3823 EUROPEAN BREEDERS' FUND/CARLSBERG UK MAIDEN STKS 5f 43y
2:00 (2:05) (Class 5) 2-Y-0 **£3,562** (£1,059; £529; £264) **Stalls** High

Form RPR

3 **1** **Speed Song**[48] [2364] 2-8-12 0...... MichaelHills 6 79+
(W J Haggas) *chsd ldr: led over 1f out: sn rdn: r.o: eased nr fin* **4/5**[1]

0 **2** *2* **Mandelieu (IRE)**[15] [3363] 2-9-0 0......(b) LiamJones(3) 4 74
(W J Haggas) *led: rdn and hdd over 1f out: no ex ins fnl f* **25/1**

2202 **3** *3/4* **Magical Speedfit (IRE)**[24] [3085] 2-9-3 0...... SebSanders 11 71
(G G Margarson) *chsd ldrs: rdn over 1f out: styd on same pce* **9/4**[2]

0 **4** *4* **Bury Treasure (IRE)**[32] [2832] 2-9-3 0...... JohnEgan 2 57
(Miss Gay Kelleway) *chsd ldrs over 3f* **33/1**

5 *1/2* **Faber Hall Flyer** 2-9-3 0......(t) DMylonas 9 55
(Mrs C A Dunnett) *outpcd: hdwy and hung lft 1/2-way: rdn over 1f out: n.d* **100/1**

03 **6** *1 3/4* **Hold That Call (USA)**[39] [2630] 2-9-3 0...... TedDurcan 5 49
(R Hannon) *chsd ldrs over 3f* **7/1**[3]

7 *6* **Maccabeus** 2-9-0 0...... JerryO'Dwyer(3) 12 27
(P J O'Gorman) *s.s: outpcd* **66/1**

0 **8** *nk* **High Standing (USA)**[8] [3589] 2-9-3 0...... JamieSpencer 8 26
(N A Callaghan) *s.i.s: outpcd* **33/1**

5 **9** *4* **Day Shift (IRE)**[46] [2416] 2-8-12 0...... ChrisCatlin 10 7
(Rae Guest) *chsd ldrs 3f* **66/1**

00 **10** *3 1/2* **Lightning Lad**[24] [3085] 2-9-3 0...... RichardMullen 7 —
(J R Jenkins) *prom to 1/2-way* **100/1**

11 *2* **Me Me Me** 2-9-3 0...... TPQueally 3 —
(M J Wallace) *s.s: outpcd* **25/1**

0 **P** **Ataensic**[13] [3424] 2-8-12 0......(be) StephenDonohoe 1 —
(C N Allen) *chsd ldrs tl p.u and dismntd 1/2-way* **100/1**

62.32 secs (-0.48) **Going Correction** -0.225s/f (Firm) 12 Ran SP% **118.4**
Speed ratings (Par 94): **94,90,89,83,82 79,70,69,63,57 54,—**
CSF £31.41 TOTE £1.80: £1.10, £7.90, £1.20; EX 35.30 Trifecta £91.70 Pool £768.69 - 5.95 winning units..
Owner Lael Stable **Bred** Lael Stables **Trained** Newmarket, Suffolk

FOCUS
An ordinary juvenile maiden, run at a sound-enough pace. The winner can rate higher but the third is not progressing.

NOTEBOOK
Speed Song confirmed the promise of her debut third in a fair maiden at Nottingham 48 days previously and opened her account with a straightforward display. She still looked green here, and was noted changing her legs under pressure, so further improvement looks assured for this confidence-boosting experience. Her trainer knows this family inside out and now intends to step up her to Listed company, with the St Hugh's Stakes at Newbury next month a possibility. (op 8-11 tchd 4-6 and 5-6 in a place)
Mandelieu(IRE) stepped up greatly on the form of his debut at Bath 15 days previously and showed much better speed on this switch to a straight track. He is clearly not straightforward and is likely to be gelded before long, but this effort still shows he has an engine. The faster ground was also much more to his liking. (op 33-1)
Magical Speedfit(IRE) proved too free through the early parts and was never really travelling with any real fluency. He is looking exposed now, but does possess some scope and deserves to find an opening all the same. He also helps to set the standard of this form. (op 5-2 tchd 3-1)
Bury Treasure(IRE) was another to step up on his debut form and showed he is going the right way. He will need another furlong or so to shine and is one to note when qualifying for nurseries.
Ataensic Official explanation: vet said filly pulled up lame

3824 PETTITTS ANIMAL ADVENTURE PARK AT REEDHAM (S) STKS 1m 2f 21y
2:30 (2:31) (Class 6) 3-Y-0 **£1,943** (£578; £288; £144) **Stalls** Low

Form RPR

0 **1** **Coppergirl (IRE)**[14] [3406] 3-8-7 0...... ChrisCatlin 3 65+
(G A Huffer) *chsd ldrs: led over 2f out: sn clr: eased towards fin* **5/1**

0650 **2** *6* **Rainbow Flame**[21] [3177] 3-8-12 63......(b) AdamKirby 7 54
(W R Swinburn) *hld up: hdwy over 3f out: no ch w wnr* **9/2**[3]

0-60 **3** *1 1/2* **Lady Pickpocket**[34] [2759] 3-8-7 56......(v[1]) JimmyQuinn 10 46
(M H Tompkins) *prom: outpcd over 4f out: styd on u.p fnl 2f: n.d* **7/1**

3055 **4** *3/4* **Fairly Honest**[7] [3629] 3-8-12 68......(b[1]) SebSanders 9 50
(D R C Elsworth) *plld hrd: led over 8f out: sn clr: hdd over 2f out: wknd over 1f out* **5/2**[1]

042 **5** *1* **Bret Maverick (IRE)**[15] [3377] 3-8-12 55...... DarryllHolland 8 48
(J R Weymes) *chsd ldrs: pushed along over 6f out: outpcd 1/2-way: styd on ins fnl f* **4/1**[2]

0000 **6** *1 1/2* **Elizabeth Garrett**[25] [900] 3-8-9 38 ow2...... StephenDonohoe 4 42
(M J Gingell) *s.s: n.d* **100/1**

-060 **7** *2 1/2* **Book Of Facts (FR)**[24] [3111] 3-8-12 69......(b[1]) PaulEddery 2 40
(J McAuley) *hld up: rdn over 3f out: n.d* **16/1**

-600 **8** *4* **Noddledoddle (IRE)**[4] [3708] 3-8-7 47......(t) DavidKinsella 1 27
(J Ryan) *hld up: hdwy over 3f out: wknd over 1f out* **20/1**

0004 **9** *8* **Bubbly Girl**[14] [3394] 3-8-2 53...... PatrickHills(5) 5 11
(P J McBride) *hld up: hdwy u.p and hung lft over 2f out: sn wknd* **6/1**

0060 **10** *3* **All Talk**[8] [3593] 3-8-4 30...... LiamJones(3) 6 5
(M J Gingell) *plld hrd: led: hdd over 8f out: wknd over 2f out* **100/1**

2m 10.92s (2.82) **Going Correction** +0.10s/f (Good) 10 Ran SP% **116.2**
Speed ratings (Par 98): **92,87,86,85,84 83,81,78,71,69**
CSF £27.42 TOTE £5.80: £2.20, £2.00, £4.10; EX 47.70 Trifecta £155.00 Pool £497.83 - 2.28 winning units..The winner was bought in for 22,000gns. Fairly Honest was claimed by P. W. Hiatt for £5,000. Rainbow Flame was claimed by T. Dascombe for £5,000.
Owner D Hanafin **Bred** Mrs E M Burke **Trained** Newmarket, Suffolk

FOCUS
A moderate winning time, even for a seller and the form is limited by the sixth, but the winner is a cut above this class and rates value for around double the winning margin.

3825 SOUTH PIER LEISURE COMPLEX (LOWESTOFT) H'CAP 1m 3f 101y
3:00 (3:02) (Class 6) (0-65,65) 3-Y-0 **£1,943** (£578; £288; £144) **Stalls** Low

Form RPR

001 **1** **Ainama (IRE)**[24] [3082] 3-8-9 **53**...... OscarUrbina 8 70+
(M Wigham) *hld up: swtchd rt and hdwy over 2f out: led over 1f out: shkn up and r.o wl* **5/1**[3]

-122 **2** *5* **Potentiale (IRE)**[38] [2653] 3-8-11 **60**...... PatrickHills(5) 13 65
(J W Hills) *hld up: hdwy over 2f out: rdn over 1f out: sn outpcd* **11/4**[1]

604- **3** *1 1/2* **Tonnante**[302] [5580] 3-9-4 **62**...... SebSanders 12 64
(Sir Mark Prescott) *dwlt: hdwy over 7f out: led over 3f out: rdn and hdd over 1f out: sn outpcd* **11/1**

4-33 **4** *1 1/2* **Hatton Flight**[57] [2096] 3-9-2 **60**......(p) JamieSpencer 2 60
(A M Balding) *hld up: styd on fnl 2f: nvr trbld ldrs* **6/1**

4400 **5** *5* **Mango Masher (IRE)**[29] [2945] 3-9-7 **65**......(p) TedDurcan 15 56
(C R Egerton) *hld up: hdwy over 3f out: sn rdn and edgd lft: wknd over 1f out* **66/1**

0-00 **6** *1/2* **Kimono My House**[13] [3429] 3-8-12 **56**...... TPQueally 14 47
(J G Given) *chsd ldrs: rdn 1/2-way: wknd over 1f out* **100/1**

1420 **7** *3 1/2* **Sonara (IRE)**[36] [2727] 3-9-7 **65**...... JimmyQuinn 5 50
(M H Tompkins) *hld up in tch: stmbld 5f out: rdn and wknd over 1f out* **9/2**[2]

4050 **8** *3* **Kingsmead (USA)**[40] [2610] 3-8-1 **52**......(b[1]) AmyBaker(7) 3 32
(Miss J Feilden) *hld up in tch: racd keenly: rdn over 2f out: wknd over 1f out* **25/1**

000 **9** *4* **Boz**[78] [1522] 3-8-6 **50**...... DarryllHolland 1 23
(L M Cumani) *chsd ldrs: pushed along over 6f out: wknd over 2f out* **11/2**

5010 **10** *1/2* **Lawyer To World**[6] [3652] 3-8-5 **49**......(v[1]) DMylonas 9 21
(Mrs C A Dunnett) *s.i.s: hld up: hmpd over 4f out: n.d* **33/1**

0401 **11** *1* **Bathwick Breeze**[38] [2653] 3-9-2 **60**...... DavidKinsella 16 30
(A B Haynes) *chsd ldrs 9f* **10/1**

-040 **12** *3* **Tykie Two**[16] [3351] 3-8-11 **55**...... ChrisCatlin 7 20
(E J O'Neill) *led 2f: chsd ldrs tl wknd 3f out* **40/1**

-050 **13** *34* **Bishop Auckland (IRE)**[1] [3804] 3-8-6 **50**...... KDarley 4 —
(Mrs A Duffield) *led over 9f out: hdd over 3f out: sn wknd* **50/1**

2m 27.74s (0.24) **Going Correction** +0.10s/f (Good) 13 Ran SP% **122.3**
Speed ratings (Par 98): **103,99,98,97,93 93,90,88,85,85 84,82,57**
CSF £18.87 CT £150.48 TOTE £7.50: £2.20, £1.50, £3.30; EX 26.50 Trifecta £89.30 Pool £572.46 - 4.55 winning units..
Owner D Morrison **Bred** Roundhill Stud And A Stroud **Trained** Newmarket, Suffolk

FOCUS
A modest three-year-old handicap, run at a solid pace. The winner is progressive and the form looks sound for the grade.

Bishop Auckland(IRE) Official explanation: jockey said race came too soon for gelding

3826 WELLINGTON PIER / WINTER GARDENS FILLIES' H'CAP 1m 3y

3:30 (3:34) (Class 5) (0-70,70) 3-Y-0+ **£2,849** (£847; £423; £211) **Stalls** High

Form RPR
0020 **1** **Life's A Whirl**[19] 3247 5-9-4 **56**...(p) DMylonas 9 65
(Mrs C A Dunnett) *wnt lft s: chsd ldrs: led over 2f out: rdn out* **14/1**
4205 **2** *2* **Astroangel**[40] 2607 3-8-12 **63**... PatrickHills(5) 4 66
(M H Tompkins) *mid-div: hdwy over 3f out: rdn and ev ch over 1f out: styd on same pce ins fnl f* **8/1**
0220 **3** *1 1/4* **Lii Najma**[18] 3285 4-9-9 **66**... AhmedAjtebi(5) 10 68
(C E Brittain) *led: hdd over 6f out: led again over 3f out: hdd over 2f out: rdn over 1f out: hung rt ins fnl f: styd on same pce* **14/1**
0032 **4** *nk* **Casablanca Minx (IRE)**[18] 3286 4-8-12 **50**...(v) StephenDonohoe 6 51
(P D Evans) *hld up: rdn over 2f out: hdwy over 1f out: nt rch ldrs* **13/2**[3]
500- **5** *1* **Royal Tavira Girl (IRE)**[297] 5690 4-9-0 **55**... JerryO'Dwyer(3) 12 54
(M G Quinlan) *hld up: hdwy over 1f out: nrst fin* **28/1**
0620 **6** *1/2* **Al Rayanah**[19] 3247 4-8-10 **55**... CharlotteKerton(7) 15 53
(G Prodromou) *hld up: styd on ins fnl f: nvr nrr* **33/1**
-500 **7** *3/4* **Little Miss Tara (IRE)**[29] 2940 3-9-7 **67**...(v[1]) SebSanders 16 61
(A B Haynes) *chsd ldrs: rdn over 1f out: edgd lft and no ex* **33/1**
3236 **8** *3 1/2* **Hessian (IRE)**[35] 2749 3-9-5 **65**... JamieSpencer 8 51
(M L W Bell) *hmpd s: hld up: swtchd rt over 2f out: rdn and hung lft over 1f out: n.d* **11/2**[2]
-035 **9** *1* **She's So Pretty (IRE)**[16] 3351 3-9-5 **65**... AdamKirby 5 49
(W R Swinburn) *hld up: rdn 1/2-way: n.d* **7/1**
00-0 **10** *shd* **Peppermint Green**[37] 2693 3-9-10 **70**... DarryllHolland 11 54
(L M Cumani) *led over 6f out: hdd over 3f out: sn rdn: wknd over 1f out* **5/1**[1]
05-0 **11** *nk* **Baarrij**[83] 1403 3-8-8 **54**... JDSmith 13 37
(G A Huffer) *chsd ldrs 6f* **20/1**
050 **12** *1/2* **Apolina**[40] 2606 3-7-8 **47** oh2...(be[1]) MCGeran(7) 14 29
(Miss K B Boutflower) *sn outpcd* **100/1**
0000 **13** *nk* **Charlottebutterfly**[119] 800 7-8-9 **47** oh2... KDarley 3 30
(P J McBride) *hld up in tch: rdn and wknd over 1f out* **25/1**
2055 **14** *1* **Fangorn Forest (IRE)**[24] 3107 4-9-5 **60**...(p) LiamJones(3) 7 41
(R A Harris) *mid-div: lost pl 1/2-way: sn bhd* **12/1**
-300 **15** *1/2* **Lady Alize (USA)**[15] 3384 3-9-7 **67**...(t) ChrisCatlin 2 45
(R A Kvisla) *s.i.s: hld up: hdwy over 3f out: wknd 2f out* **16/1**
2-00 **16** *1/2* **Tokyo Jo (IRE)**[6] 3646 3-9-2 **62**... SamHitchcott 1 38
(T T Clement) *hld up: hdwy over 2f out: sn wknd* **50/1**
6350 **17** *1/2* **Wodhill Be**[33] 2798 7-8-9 **47** oh2... HayleyTurner 17 24
(D Morris) *hld up in tch: racd keenly: rdn and wknd over 1f out* **25/1**

1m 41.88s (1.98) **Going Correction** +0.225s/f (Good)
WFA 3 from 4yo+ 8lb **17** Ran SP% **120.6**
Speed ratings (Par 100): **99,97,95,95,94 93,93,89,88,88 88,87,87,86,86 85,85**
CSF £109.47 CT £1618.48 TOTE £19.30: £3.70, £2.40, £3.20, £1.80; EX 178.50 Trifecta £364.10 Part won. Pool £512.85 - 0.50 winning units..
Owner Life's a Whirl Partnership **Bred** The Queen **Trained** Hingham, Norfolk

FOCUS
A moderate handicap. The form is ordinary rated around the placed horses and fourth.

3827 WALTON PIER / WALTON ON NAZE MAIDEN STKS 7f 3y

4:00 (4:03) (Class 5) 3-4-Y-0 **£2,849** (£847; £423; £211) **Stalls** High

Form RPR
435 **1** **Jacaranda Ridge**[46] 2428 3-8-12 79... KDarley 4 83
(M A Jarvis) *led: rdn and hdd over 1f out: rallied to ld post* **6/1**[3]
2 **2** *shd* **Pillar Of Hercules (IRE)**[31] 2880 3-9-3 0... TedDurcan 1 88
(H R A Cecil) *chsd wnr: rdn to ld over 1f out: hdd post* **10/11**[1]
00 **3** *5* **Best One**[16] 3349 3-9-3 0... HayleyTurner 9 74
(C E Brittain) *chsd ldrs: rdn and hung lft fr over 1f out: styd on same pce* **150/1**
04 **4** *2 1/2* **Atayeb (USA)**[39] 2625 3-8-12 0... RHills 3 62
(M P Tregoning) *chsd ldrs: rdn 1/2-way: sn outpcd: rallied over 1f out: wknd fnl f* **14/1**
3 **5** *3/4* **Andmoreagain (USA)**[31] 2886 3-8-12 0... SebSanders 6 60
(J Noseda) *hld up in tch: rdn over 2f out: wknd over 1f out* **9/1**
2- **6** *3* **Reballo (IRE)**[457] 1165 4-9-10 0... JamieSpencer 7 67+
(J R Fanshawe) *hld up in tch: rdn over 2f out: wknd over 1f out: eased ins fnl f* **10/3**[2]
64 **7** *1* **Art Professor (IRE)**[136] 655 3-8-12 0... PatrickHills(5) 8 55
(J W Hills) *dwlt: outpcd: effrt over 2f out: sn edgd lft and wknd* **20/1**
00 **8** *9* **Polish Prize**[12] 3454 3-9-3 0... AdamKirby 5 30
(W R Swinburn) *hld up: wknd over 2f out* **100/1**
5 **9** *8* **Black Meyeden (FR)**[40] 2593 3-8-5 0... JCorrigan(7) 2 4
(S W Hall) *trckd ldrs: plld hrd: wknd 3f out* **100/1**

1m 27.02s (0.42) **Going Correction** +0.225s/f (Good)
WFA 3 from 4yo 7lb **9** Ran SP% **113.8**
Speed ratings (Par 103): **106,105,100,97,96 93,91,81,72**
CSF £11.63 TOTE £7.40: £1.80, £1.10, £12.80; EX 16.00 Trifecta £638.30 Part won. Pool £899.05 - 0.87 winning units..
Owner P D Savill **Bred** P D Savill **Trained** Newmarket, Suffolk

FOCUS
No more than a fair maiden, but the form looks sound enough with the first pair coming well clear and the time reasonable. Both can rate higher still.

3828 STANLEY M THREADWELL MEMORIAL H'CAP 7f 3y

4:30 (4:31) (Class 5) (0-75,74) 3-Y-0+ **£2,914** (£867; £433; £216) **Stalls** High

Form RPR
2302 **1** **Resplendent Nova**[16] 3350 5-10-0 **72**... JamieSpencer 10 82+
(P Howling) *chsd ldrs: rdn and swtchd lft over 1f out: r.o to ld nr fin* **7/2**[1]
0050 **2** *nk* **Kaveri (USA)**[52] 2240 4-9-4 **67**... AhmedAjtebi(5) 4 76
(C E Brittain) *racd keenly: led: hdd 5f out: led again over 2f out: hdd over 1f out: led again ins fnl f: hdd nr fin* **14/1**
0660 **3** *1 3/4* **Border Artist**[13] 3419 8-8-12 **56**...(v) JimmyQuinn 14 60+
(J Pearce) *hld up: nt clr run over 1f out: r.o ins fnl f: nt rch ldrs* **20/1**
0062 **4** *1/2* **Coup D'Etat**[9] 3572 5-9-8 **66**...(b) JohnEgan 7 69
(R A Harris) *hld up: hdwy over 2f out: led over 1f out: hung lft and hdd ins fnl f: no ex* **9/2**[2]
0101 **5** *1 1/2* **Wodhill Schnaps**[18] 3285 6-8-9 **53**...(b) HayleyTurner 12 52
(D Morris) *mid-div: hdwy over 1f out: styd on* **20/1**
5000 **6** *hd* **Outer Hebrides**[10] 3549 6-9-6 **67**...(vt) LiamJones(3) 5 65
(J M Bradley) *hld up in tch: plld hrd: rdn and ev ch over 1f out: wknd ins fnl f* **16/1**
0431 **7** *1/2* **Tamino (IRE)**[10] 3549 4-9-1 **64**... TravisBlock(5) 15 61
(H Morrison) *trckd ldrs: rdn over 1f out: wknd ins fnl f* **5/1**[3]
0000 **8** *1* **Imperial Gain (USA)**[16] 3350 4-9-9 **67**...(b[1]) StephenDonohoe 16 61
(J M Bradley) *chsd ldrs: led 4f out: rdn and hdd over 2f out: wknd ins fnl f* **18/1**
2403 **9** *1* **Neon Blue**[11] 3512 6-9-12 **70**... TedDurcan 3 62
(R M Whitaker) *chsd ldrs: lost pl 4f out: n.d after* **5/1**[3]
0 **10** *3/4* **Nans Lady (IRE)**[129] 702 4-9-8 **66**... ChrisCatlin 6 56
(E J O'Neill) *hld up: rdn over 2f out: n.d* **33/1**
0060 **11** *nk* **Isphahan**[31] 2877 4-9-5 **63**...(p) DarryllHolland 11 52
(A M Balding) *chsd ldrs: led 5f out to 4f out: n.m.r over 2f out: rdn and wknd over 1f out* **14/1**
0-00 **12** *3* **Marshman (IRE)**[60] 1984 8-8-7 **72**... AshleyMorgan(7) 2 53
(M H Tompkins) *s.i.s: hld up: rdn over 2f out: a in rr* **16/1**
-606 **13** *1 1/4* **Capistrano**[40] 1083 4-9-7 **65**... TPQueally 9 42
(Mrs P Sly) *hld up: rdn 1/2-way: a in rr* **25/1**
0500 **14** *3* **Lincolneurocruiser**[10] 3525 5-9-3 **66**...(p) ColinHaddon(5) 1 35
(Mrs N Macauley) *chsd ldrs over 4f* **40/1**
6500 **15** *8* **Panshir (FR)**[6] 3644 6-8-9 **53** oh7... RichardMullen 8 —
(Mrs C A Dunnett) *hld up: rdn 1/2-way: wknd over 2f out* **22/1**

1m 27.95s (1.35) **Going Correction** +0.275s/f (Good)
WFA 3 from 4yo+ 7lb **15** Ran SP% **127.2**
Speed ratings (Par 103): **103,102,100,100,98 98,97,96,95,94 94,90,89,85,76**
CSF £52.13 CT £919.82 TOTE £4.30: £1.50, £5.20, £4.90; EX 69.00 Trifecta £298.90 Part won. Pool £421.03 - 0.20 winning units..
Owner Resplendent Racing Limited **Bred** A Turner **Trained** Newmarket, Suffolk

FOCUS
A modest handicap that saw those racing on the stands' side at an advantage. The form looks fair with the first pair coming clear late on and could work out at a similar level.
Panshir(FR) Official explanation: jockey said gelding had a breathing problem

3829 BRITANNIA PIER THEATRE SUMMER SEASON H'CAP 5f 43y

5:00 (5:04) (Class 6) (0-60,60) 4-Y-0+ **£2,047** (£604; £302) **Stalls** High

Form RPR
0514 **1** **Majestical (IRE)**[7] 3618 5-8-8 **50**...(p) DarryllHolland 3 59
(V Smith) *hld up: hdwy 1/2-way: rdn to ld towards fin* **8/1**[3]
40 **2** *hd* **Briery Lane (IRE)**[41] 2576 6-8-11 **53**... StephenDonohoe 14 61
(J M Bradley) *chsd ldrs: rdn to ld and hung lft fr over 1f out: hdd towards fin* **15/2**[2]
0004 **3** *1* **Registrar**[15] 3388 5-9-1 **57**... DMylonas 10 62
(Mrs C A Dunnett) *mid-div: hdwy 1/2-way: rdn and ev ch ins fnl f: no ex nr fin* **11/1**
0523 **4** *1 1/4* **Conjecture**[7] 3627 5-8-13 **55**... SebSanders 5 55
(R Bastiman) *chsd ldrs: rdn 1/2-way: styd on same pce fnl f* **7/2**[1]
0340 **5** *hd* **Viewforth**[7] 3608 9-8-8 **50**...(b) KDarley 16 49
(M A Buckley) *awkward leaving stalls: sn led: hdd wl over 1f out: nt clr run 1f out: styd on* **8/1**[3]
0-60 **6** *1 1/4* **Master Malarkey**[22] 3163 4-8-4 **46** oh1...(b) ChrisCatlin 12 41
(Mrs C A Dunnett) *chsd ldr: led wl over 1f out: sn rdn and hdd: no ex ins fnl f* **40/1**
3322 **7** *nk* **Nawayea**[8] 3597 4-7-13 **48** oh1 ow2... KirstyMilczarek(7) 7 42
(C N Allen) *prom: rdn over 1f out: kpt on* **14/1**
0002 **8** *nk* **Ballybunion (IRE)**[7] 3618 8-8-4 **49**... LiamJones(3) 1 42
(R A Harris) *mid-div: hdwy 1/2-way: rdn over 1f out: wknd ins fnl f* **16/1**
0200 **9** *hd* **Gone'N'Dunnett (IRE)**[7] 3618 8-8-7 **49**...(v) JohnEgan 9 41
(Mrs C A Dunnett) *chsd ldrs: outpcd 1/2-way: r.o ins fnl f* **15/2**[2]
4560 **10** *1 1/2* **Muktasb (USA)**[71] 1729 6-8-6 **48**...(v) JimmyQuinn 17 35
(D Shaw) *hdwy over 3f out: rdn and hung lft 2f out: wknd over 1f out* **22/1**
6260 **11** *hd* **Jabbara (IRE)**[70] 1748 4-8-5 **47**...(b) HayleyTurner 13 33
(C E Brittain) *sn outpcd* **14/1**
0000 **12** *3* **Kennington**[18] 3285 7-8-4 **49** ow2...(b) MarcHalford(3) 11 24
(Mrs C A Dunnett) *s.i.s: sn outpcd* **22/1**
-000 **13** *3/4* **Rare Breed**[63] 1914 4-9-4 **60**... JamieSpencer 15 32
(Mrs L Stubbs) *sn outpcd* **12/1**
0004 **14** *1* **Taboor (IRE)**[7] 3627 9-8-7 **49**... RichardMullen 4 18
(R M H Cowell) *s.s: outpcd* **10/1**

63.95 secs (1.15) **Going Correction** +0.275s/f (Good) **14** Ran SP% **123.4**
Speed ratings (Par 101): **101,100,99,97,96 94,94,93,93,91 90,85,84,83**
CSF £67.17 CT £694.06 TOTE £8.60: £2.90, £3.30, £3.90; EX 93.10 TRIFECTA Not won..
Owner Raymond Tooth **Bred** Sean Beston **Trained** Exning, Suffolk

FOCUS
A competitive handicap due to the size of the field, but a very modest sprint full of exposed performers. The form looks solid enough at a low level, rated around the first three.
Viewforth Official explanation: jockey said he was injured on leaving stalls and was unable to ride out
Rare Breed Official explanation: jockey said gelding was unsuited by the soft ground
Taboor(IRE) Official explanation: jockey said gelding missed the break
T/Jkpt: £12,906.70 to a £1 stake. Pool: £18,178.50. 0.50 winning tickets. T/Plt: £51.40 to a £1 stake. Pool: £105,126.35. 1,491.40 winning tickets. T/Qpdt: £10.40 to a £1 stake. Pool: £7,077.80. 499.10 winning tickets. CR

3830 - 3832a (Foreign Racing) - See Raceform Interactive

3635 CATTERICK (L-H)

Wednesday, July 25

OFFICIAL GOING: Good to soft (good in places; 6.0)
After 3/4" rain over the previous week the ground was described as 'genuine soft'.
Wind: Moderate, across Weather: Overcast and blustery

3833 EAT, SLEEP AT THE NAGS HEAD, PICKHILL MAIDEN STKS (DIV I) 5f 212y

2:20 (2:21) (Class 5) 2-Y-0 **£2,590** (£770; £385; £192) **Stalls** Low

Form RPR
5 **1** **The Game**[46] 2460 2-9-3 0... PatCosgrave 4 76+
(J R Boyle) *trckd ldrs: t.k.h: led over 1f out: edgd rt: styd on* **5/1**[2]
225 **2** *2 1/2* **Ramatni**[67] 1848 2-8-9 0... GregFairley(3) 2 64
(M Johnston) *chsd ldrs: drvn over 3f out: chal over 1f out: kpt on same pce* **1/1**[1]
63 **3** *1* **Woodford Regen**[103] 1029 2-8-5 0... NSLawes(7) 7 61
(M W Easterby) *led 2f: led over 2f out tl over 1f out: kpt on same pce* **25/1**
4 *5* **Novestar (IRE)** 2-9-3 0... TPQueally 1 51+
(Mrs A Duffield) *outpcd and lost pl over 4f out: hdwy over 1f out: styd on towards fin* **8/1**
5 *1/2* **Tactical Move** 2-8-12 0... ColinHaddon(5) 6 49
(Miss V Haigh) *outpcd and lost pl over 4f out: hdwy over 2f out: nvr nr ldrs* **40/1**
3 **6** *1* **Lekin Sedona (IRE)**[18] 3297 2-9-3 0... TonyHamilton 3 46
(J M Saville) *w ldr: led 4f out tl over 2f out: wknd over 1f out* **6/1**[3]

50 7 1/2 **Prince's Decree**[20] 3238 2-9-0 0 .... AndrewElliott(3) 8 45
(G M Moore) *chsd ldrs: hung lft and lost pl over 1f out* **12/1**
8 12 **Flashy Max** 2-9-3 0 .... PaulHanagan 9 9
(Jedd O'Keeffe) *s.s: outpcd and lost pl over 4f out: sn bhd* **20/1**
00 9 6 **Doubtless**[14] 3410 2-8-5 0 ....(b) DanielleMcCreery(7) 5 —
(D W Chapman) *s.v.s: a detached in rr* **150/1**
10 3 1/2 **Lunar Lass** 2-8-12 0 .... NCallan 10 —
(D J Murphy) *swvd rt s: hdwy over 4f out: sn chsng ldrs: hung rt and wknd 2f out* **18/1**

1m 17.6s (3.60) **Going Correction** +0.475s/f (Yiel) **10** Ran SP% **116.7**
Speed ratings (Par 94): **95,91,90,83,83 81,81,65,57,52**
CSF £10.06 TOTE £6.20: £1.80, £1.10, £5.50; EX 11.60.
Owner M Khan X2 **Bred** Aston House Stud **Trained** Epsom, Surrey

FOCUS
The winning time was close to par for the type of race, despite being 1.19 seconds slower than the second division. With the runner-up again not at her best it probably took little winning.

NOTEBOOK
The Game, a leggy type, was again very keen. He came off a straight line but in the end won going away. (op 11-2 tchd 9-2)
Ramatni, fresh and well after a two-month break, was under pressure before the home turn. She was upsides coming to the final furlong but again proved a very weak finisher. (op 5-6 tchd 11-10 tchd 6-5 in a place)
Woodford Regen, absent since April, seemed to show improved form on her first outing on turf. This opens up the nursery route for her. (tchd 28-1)
Novestar(IRE), a February foal, is a strongly-made, close-coupled type. He was clueless but put in some sterling late work and this will have taught him plenty. (op 16-1)
Tactical Move, a robust newcomer, looks to have a twisted off-fore. He showed ability on his debut and ought to improve. (op 33-1)
Lekin Sedona(IRE) did not improve for the step up in trip. (op 15-2 tchd 11-2)
Prince's Decree Official explanation: jockey said colt hung left
Doubtless Official explanation: jockey said filly missed the break
Lunar Lass Official explanation: jockey said filly hung right throughout

3834 EAT, SLEEP AT THE NAGS HEAD, PICKHILL MAIDEN STKS (DIV II) 5f 212y

2:50 (2:50) (Class 5) 2-Y-O **£2,590** (£770; £385; £192) **Stalls** Low

Form RPR
0 1 **Kalhan Sands (IRE)**[28] 2983 2-9-3 0 .... TPO'Shea 7 80
(G A Swinbank) *hld up: effrt over 2f out: led over 1f out: styd on wl* **40/1**
23 2 1 3/4 **Feisty Royale**[28] 2983 2-8-9 0 .... GregFairley(3) 8 70
(M Johnston) *chsd ldrs: drvn over 2f out: kpt on same pce fnl f* **7/4**[1]
05 3 nk **Duke Of Touraine (IRE)**[28] 2983 2-9-3 0 .... LeeEnstone 5 74
(P C Haslam) *trckd ldrs: led 2f out: sn hdd and no ex* **33/1**
4 hd **Van Bossed (CAN)** 2-9-3 0 .... AdrianTNicholls 10 74+
(D Nicholls) *chsd ldrs: drvn and outpcd over 4f out: hdwy over 1f out: kpt on wl* **6/1**[3]
66 5 7 **Leading Edge (IRE)**[74] 1680 2-8-12 0 .... EdwardCreighton 9 47
(M R Channon) *sn chsng ldrs: edgd lft and one pce appr fnl f* **16/1**
6 shd **Toolittleyourlate (USA)** 2-9-3 0 .... NCallan 6 52+
(K A Ryan) *trckd ldrs: chal 2f out: wkng whn sltly hmpd over 1f out* **2/1**[2]
343 7 6 **Rocheport**[16] 3370 2-9-3 0 .... TomEaves 3 34
(J Howard Johnson) *led: edgd rt and hdd 2f out: sn wknd* **8/1**
8 1/2 **Green's Delight** 2-8-12 0 .... DaleGibson 1 28
(M W Easterby) *s.v.s: nvr on terms* **100/1**
06 9 2 **Straight (IRE)**[22] 3192 2-8-10 0 .... PatrickDonaghy(7) 4 27
(M Brittain) *chsd ldrs: wkng whn bmpd 2f out* **66/1**
04 10 12 **Lady Calido (USA)**[25] 3109 2-8-12 0 .... PatCosgrave 2 —
(Sir Mark Prescott) *s.s: a detached in rr* **20/1**

1m 16.41s (2.41) **Going Correction** +0.475s/f (Yiel) **10** Ran SP% **113.6**
Speed ratings (Par 94): **102,99,99,99,89 89,81,80,78,62**
CSF £105.79 TOTE £57.10: £8.80, £1.30, £8.00; EX 181.50.
Owner Elsa Crankshaw & Gordon Allan **Bred** Ronnie Boland **Trained** Melsonby, N Yorks

FOCUS
A very decent winning time for the type of contest, 1.19 seconds faster than the first division and only 1/100th of a second slower than the later handicap for older horses. The first four finished clear and it looked much the better division.

NOTEBOOK
Kalhan Sands(IRE), last of ten first time at Carlisle, did absolutely nothing wrong here and scored in decisive fashion. He should improve again. (tchd 50-1)
Feisty Royale made hard work of it and in the end the winner proved simply too good. She might appreciate much better ground than she encounted here and at Carlisle. (op 15-8 tchd 13-8 and 2-1 in places)
Duke Of Touraine(IRE), a close-coupled type, improved again and looks a likely nursery type. (tchd 28-1)
Van Bossed(CAN), a March foal, is a sturdy type. Drawn on the wide outside, he stayed on when it was all over and this should have taught him plenty. (op 8-1)
Leading Edge(IRE), an edgy type, continually swished her tail beforehand. This was her first outing for ten weeks and she can now try her hand in nursery company. (op 14-1)
Toolittleyourlate(USA), a lengthy newcomer, has quite a round action. She came in for plenty of support and travelled strongly but her chance had gone when slightly impeded. She has presumably been showing much better at home ahead of this debut run. (op 7-4 tchd 9-4 in a place)

3835 SUBSCRIBE ONLINE AT RACINGUK.TV (S) STKS 7f

3:20 (3:20) (Class 6) 2-Y-O **£2,730** (£806; £403) **Stalls** Low

Form RPR
2013 1 **Rio Taffeta**[12] 3494 2-9-3 0 .... NCallan 1 64
(Peter Grayson) *led early: trckd ldrs: led 2f out: hung rt: styd on ins fnl f* **6/4**[1]
4 2 1 1/4 **Freudian Slip**[4] 3751 2-8-6 0 .... PaulQuinn 8 50
(W M Brisbourne) *s.i.s: in rr: hdwy over 2f out: styd on wl to take 2nd wl ins fnl f: fin lame* **15/2**
66 3 3/4 **What's For Tea**[7] 3635 2-8-7 0 ow1 .... TomEaves 9 49
(T D Easterby) *s.i.s: hdwy to chse ldrs over 4f out: effrt on wd outside over 2f out: kpt on same pce fnl f* **11/2**[3]
3123 4 3/4 **Indecision**[4] 3751 2-9-3 0 .... DaleGibson 11 57
(M W Easterby) *w ldrs: c wd and led over 2f out: sn hdd and no ex* **5/1**[2]
4022 5 3 **Ten On Line (IRE)**[8] 3614 2-8-6 0 .... ColinHaddon(5) 7 46+
(Miss V Haigh) *mid-div: outpcd over 3f out: edgd lft 2f out: one pce* **15/2**
045 6 4 **Amy Lionheart**[36] 2738 2-7-13 0 .... DanielleMcCreery(7) 6 28
(N Tinkler) *sn led: hdd over 2f out: hung rt and wknd over 1f out* **25/1**
0 7 nk **Brilliantsensation (IRE)**[43] 2532 2-8-11 0 .... TPQueally 10 32
(J G Given) *trckd ldrs: hung bdly lft over 2f out: nt rcvr* **14/1**
00 8 1 3/4 **King Of Dalyan (IRE)**[4] 3751 2-8-11 0 ....(v[1]) AdrianTNicholls 2 27
(D Nicholls) *t.k.h: trckd ldrs: rdn over 2f out: wknd and eased over 1f out* **20/1**
0 9 18 **Tombas Legacy**[16] 3364 2-8-4 0 .... JackDean(7) 3 —
(Mark Gillard) *mid-div: hmpd and lost pl after 2f: bhd and eased over 1f out* **66/1**

1m 32.99s (5.63) **Going Correction** +0.475s/f (Yiel) **9** Ran SP% **112.3**
Speed ratings (Par 92): **86,84,83,82,79 74,74,72,51**
CSF £12.58 TOTE £2.40: £1.10, £2.90, £1.90; EX 12.30.The winner was bought in for 10,200gns. Freudian Slip was claimed by M. J. Gingell for £6,000. Ten On Line was claimed by J. G. M. O'Shea for £6,000. What's For Tea was claimed by T. Dascombe for £6,000.
Owner Richard Teatum **Bred** And Mrs P Trant & Mrs **Trained** Formby, Lancs

FOCUS
A modest time, even for a juvenile seller and the form is typical of the grade. A weak event but winning connections had to dig deep at the auction and three horses were claimed.

NOTEBOOK
Rio Taffeta, on his toes and with two handlers, is by no means straightforward but he always looked in command here. In the end the extra furlong did not prove a problem at least on a sharp track like this, and in any cae he is bred to get it on the dam's side of his pedigree. (tchd 11-8 and 13-8)
Freudian Slip improved on her debut effort and relished the extra furlong. She finished lame behind but was claimed. Official explanation: vet said filly returned lame right-hind (op 9-1)
What's For Tea, dropped in grade on her third start, made her effort on the outer and stayed on all the way to the line. She too was claimed. (op 13-2)
Indecision, who had something to find with the winner on Ripon running, had the worst of the draw. He is holding his form really well. (op 9-2 tchd 11-2)
Ten On Line(IRE), with his third trainer, was claimed back by John O'Shea, rather a case of pass the parcel! (tchd 8-1)
Amy Lionheart Official explanation: jockey said filly hung right in straight

3836 BOOK ONLINE AT CATTERICKBRIDGE.CO.UK H'CAP 5f

3:50 (3:51) (Class 4) (0-85,85) 3-Y-O+ **£5,181** (£1,541; £770; £384) **Stalls** Low

Form RPR
-031 1 **Bahamian Ballet**[46] 2479 5-9-3 77 .... NCallan 7 91+
(E S McMahon) *w ldr gng wl: shkn up to ld over 1f out: rdn and hld on wl* **10/3**[1]
1150 2 3/4 **Rainbow Bay**[12] 3481 4-8-4 69 ....(v) MichaelJStainton(5) 8 76
(P D Evans) *mid-div: hdwy and swtchd rt over 1f out: styd on to take 2nd last 75yds* **17/2**
4- 3 2 **Coseadrom (IRE)**[48] 2407 5-9-3 77 .... TonyHamilton 1 77
(M F Harris) *in rr: hdwy over 1f out: styd on strly ins fnl f* **13/2**
1006 4 3/4 **Whinhill House**[21] 3203 7-8-7 67 oh9 ow1 ....(v) TomEaves 4 64
(D W Barker) *wnt lft s: led: hung lft: carried hd high and hdd over 1f out: no ex* **20/1**
2005 5 1 **Monashee Brave (IRE)**[18] 3298 4-8-8 68 .... PatCosgrave 2 62
(J J Quinn) *chsd ldrs: kpt on same pce fnl 2f* **6/1**[3]
4046 6 3/4 **Nusoor (IRE)**[12] 3515 4-8-3 66 ....(b) PatrickMathers(3) 6 57
(Peter Grayson) *chsd ldrs: one pce fnl 2f* **12/1**
0-02 7 nk **Strensall**[47] 2418 10-8-6 66 oh3 .... PaulHanagan 9 56
(R E Barr) *sn chsng ldrs: edgd lft and kpt on same pce appr fnl f* **12/1**
6500 8 2 1/2 **Bond Playboy**[2] 3791 7-8-3 66 oh4 ....(v) DuranFentiman(3) 5 47
(G R Oldroyd) *in rr: nvr on terms* **28/1**
-052 9 3/4 **Rare Cross (IRE)**[25] 3086 5-8-3 70 .... KellyHarrison(7) 10 48
(D Shaw) *chsd ldrs: lost pl over 1f out* **10/1**
2000 10 2 **Handsome Cross (IRE)**[13] 3464 6-9-11 85 .... AdrianTNicholls 3 56
(D Nicholls) *hmpd s: sn mid-div: effrt over 2f out: hung lft and lost pl over 1f out* **4/1**[2]

61.99 secs (1.39) **Going Correction** +0.475s/f (Yiel) **10** Ran SP% **113.9**
Speed ratings (Par 105): **107,105,102,101,99 98,98,94,92,89**
CSF £31.28 CT £176.82 TOTE £3.60: £1.30, £3.10, £2.50; EX 35.50.
Owner B N Toye **Bred** B N And Mrs Toye **Trained** Lichfield, Staffs

FOCUS
A modest handicap and the form looks sound enough. They raced in one group down the stands' side and the winner travelled easily best and is value for a bit more.
Handsome Cross(IRE) Official explanation: jockey said gelding hung left throughout

3837 GO RACING AT YORK TOMORROW NIGHT CLAIMING STKS 5f

4:20 (4:21) (Class 6) 3-Y-O+ **£2,730** (£806; £403) **Stalls** Low

Form RPR
2533 1 **She's Our Beauty (IRE)**[19] 3259 4-8-4 45 ....(p) DuranFentiman(3) 2 56
(S T Mason) *racd alone far side: led overall: swtchd stands' side over 3f out: clr appr fnl f: hld on wl* **5/1**[3]
5013 2 1 1/2 **Danish Blues (IRE)**[9] 3597 4-8-13 58 .... AdrianTNicholls 10 57
(D Nicholls) *mid-div: hdwy to chse wnr over 1f out: kpt on: no real imp* **6/1**
6565 3 3 1/2 **Dunn Deal (IRE)**[21] 3203 7-8-13 46 .... PaulQuinn 9 44+
(J Balding) *in rr: hdwy and nt clr run over 1f out: kpt on wl fnl f* **10/1**
0341 4 1/2 **Spiritual Peace (IRE)**[6] 3674 4-9-7 70 ....(p) NCallan 8 50
(K A Ryan) *chsd ldrs: edgd lft and kpt on same pce ins fnl f* **5/2**[1]
-000 5 1 1/4 **Stanley Wolfe (IRE)**[17] 3345 4-8-13 45 .... PaulHanagan 6 41+
(Garry Moss) *mid-div: effrt over 2f out: keeping one same pce whn n.m.r jst ins fnl f* **66/1**
-000 6 nk **Westbrook Blue**[34] 2805 5-8-9 65 ....(t) JackDean(7) 4 40
(W G M Turner) *mid-div: sn hrd rdn: edgd rt 1f out: kpt on* **6/1**
5063 7 nk **Lake Chini (IRE)**[12] 3498 5-9-0 66 ....(p) DaleGibson 11 37
(M W Easterby) *in rr: hdwy over 1f out: styd on towards fin* **9/2**[2]
0060 8 3 1/2 **She Whispers (IRE)**[19] 3277 4-8-7 41 .... PaulEddery 7 17
(R Hollinshead) *s.i.s: sme hdwy whn hmpd 1f out: nvr a factor* **40/1**
0-00 9 nk **Underthemistletoe (IRE)**[47] 2422 5-8-7 44 ow1 ....(b[1]) TomEaves 14 16
(R E Barr) *hld up in rr: hmpd 2f out: nvr on terms* **66/1**
-120 10 2 1/2 **Maromito (IRE)**[33] 2830 10-8-13 52 .... TPQueally 12 13
(R Bastiman) *chsd wnr: edgd lft and wknd over 1f out* **20/1**
3506 11 1 1/4 **Billy Ruffian**[30] 2939 3-8-12 60 .... PatCosgrave 3 11
(T D Easterby) *mid-div: wknd 2f out* **20/1**
-000 12 3/4 **Tombalina**[19] 3259 4-8-0 43 .... KellyHarrison(7) 13 —
(C J Teague) *chsd ldrs: lost pl over 1f out* **100/1**
0-04 13 3/4 **Northern Candy**[33] 2826 3-8-7 45 ....(p) MichaelJStainton(5) 15 6
(A Dickman) *chsd ldrs over 2f: sn lost pl* **66/1**

62.86 secs (2.26) **Going Correction** +0.475s/f (Yiel)
WFA 3 from 4yo+ 4lb **13** Ran SP% **118.5**
Speed ratings (Par 101): **100,97,92,91,89 88,88,82,82,78 76,74,73**
CSF £32.96 TOTE £6.00: £2.20, £1.90, £3.30; EX 48.20.Danish Blues was the subject of a friendly claim for £7,000. She's Our Beauty was the subject of a friendly claim for £6,000
Owner Tarn Lads Syndicate **Bred** R N Auld **Trained** Lanchester, Co. Durham
■ Stewards' Enquiry : N Callan caution: careless riding

FOCUS
A typical mixed-bag claimer in which the winner raced alone in the early stages but was able to cross over to join the others on the stands' side. She was never really threatened and is rated to her best recent mark, although the proximity of the fifth limits things.

Maromito(IRE) Official explanation: jockey said gelding was unsuited by the good to soft (soft in places) ground

3838 TURFTV A MATTER OF COURSE NURSERY 7f
4:50 (4:51) (Class 5) 2-Y-O £3,238 (£963; £481; £240) Stalls Low

Form RPR

600 1 **Tamara Moon (IRE)**[23] 3152 2-8-7 **66** .... TPO'Shea 5 70+
(M R Channon) *mde all: styd on gamely fnl f* **12/1**

41 2 *1* **Nine Stories (IRE)**[63] 1938 2-9-9 **82** .... TomEaves 2 83
(J Howard Johnson) *trckd ldrs: drvn over 3f out: chal over 1f out: no ex* **7/4**[1]

001 3 *2* **Pequeno Dinero (IRE)**[18] 3296 2-7-11 **63** ow4.......... KellyHarrison[(7)] 1 59
(C W Fairhurst) *sn trcking ldrs: styd far side over 2f out: kpt on same pce fnl f* **20/1**

3222 4 *shd* **Romantic Destiny**[12] 3499 2-9-2 **75** .... NCallan 8 71
(K A Ryan) *trckd ldrs: kpt on same pce fnl f* **7/2**[2]

243 5 *9* **Mission Impossible**[49] 2371 2-9-3 **76** .... LeeEnstone 7 49
(P C Haslam) *s.s: hld up in rr: hdwy over 2f out: sn chsng ldrs: wknd and eased fnl f* **7/2**[2]

200 6 *6* **Drastic Measure**[21] 3200 2-8-13 **72** ....(t) PatCosgrave 6 30
(Sir Mark Prescott) *s.i.s: hdwy to chse ldrs over 4f out: c wd over 2f out: edgd lft and lost pl over 1f out* **9/1**

405 7 *15* **Hurstpierpoint (IRE)**[21] 3205 2-8-4 **63** .... PaulHanagan 4 —
(R A Fahey) *trckd ldrs: rdn and lost pl over 3f out: sn bhd: virtually p.u* **7/1**[3]

1m 31.26s (3.90) **Going Correction** +0.475s/f (Yiel) 7 Ran SP% **115.8**
Speed ratings (Par 94): **96,94,92,92,82 75,58**
CSF £34.39 CT £433.50 TOTE £19.60: £5.90, £1.50; EX 61.00.
Owner Jaber Abdullah **Bred** Ms Sheila Lavery **Trained** West Ilsley, Berks

FOCUS
A fair nursery rated through the runner-up. The 'official' ratings shown next to each horse are estimated and for information purposes only.

NOTEBOOK
Tamara Moon(IRE), stepping up in trip for this handicap debut, looked very fit and relished the extra yardage, holding on bravely to get off the mark. (tchd 14-1)
Nine Stories(IRE), struggling to keep up at halfway, carried his head rather high and in the end the winner proved simply too tough. (tchd 6-4)
Pequeno Dinero(IRE) appreciates soft ground and, sticking to the far side, kept on and will be suited by a mile. (op 16-1)
Romantic Destiny keeps running with credit but that first success is proving highly elusive. The extra furlong was not a problem. (op 9-2 tchd 5-1)
Mission Impossible, who missed a beat at the start, in the end dropped right away and the seventh furlong seemed beyond him at this stage. (op 4-1)
Drastic Measure, who finished ahead of Romantic Destiny when runner-up on her debut at Leicester, is a very lean type. Fitted with a tongue strap for the first time, she again ran poorly. (op 13-2)

3839 RACING UK FOR £15 PER MONTH H'CAP 5f 212y
5:20 (5:20) (Class 6) (0-60,66) 3-Y-O+ £2,590 (£770; £385; £192) Stalls Low

Form RPR

4541 1 **Charles Parnell (IRE)**[2] 3787 4-10-1 **66** 6ex.................. PhillipMakin 10 78
(M Dods) *mid-div: smooth hdwy over 2f out: shkn up to ld over 1f out: edgd rt: kpt on wl* **3/1**[1]

4543 2 *¾* **Ryedane (IRE)**[15] 3408 5-9-4 **58** ....(b) DuranFentiman[(3)] 6 68
(T D Easterby) *w ldrs: styd far side over 2f out: no ex ins fnl f* **7/2**[2]

3366 3 *2½* **Borodinsky**[3] 3765 6-8-13 **50** .... PaulHanagan 4 52
(R E Barr) *mid-div: effrt over 2f out: kpt on fnl f* **6/1**[3]

5502 4 *1* **Smart Pick**[11] 3534 4-9-1 **52** .... TonyHamilton 5 51
(Mrs L Williamson) *s.s: hdwy on wd outside 2f out: styd on fnl f* **25/1**

0505 5 *½* **Seesawmilu (IRE)**[2] 3787 4-9-2 **53** .... AdrianTNicholls 2 50
(E J Alston) *chsd ldrs kpt on same pce appr fnl f* **14/1**

1-00 6 *nk* **Laphonic (USA)**[65] 1892 4-9-0 **51** .... LeeEnstone 3 47
(T J Etherington) *s.s: hdwy on inner over 2f out: nvr ldrs* **25/1**

3021 7 *¾* **Strike Force**[7] 3636 3-9-7 **63** 6ex....................(p) TPQueally 1 57
(R A Harris) *hld up in mid-div: effrt 2f out: nvr trbld ldrs* **8/1**

0-30 8 *1¾* **Markestino**[32] 2864 4-8-13 **50** .... TPO'Shea 7 38
(T D Easterby) *in rr: sme hdwy 2f out: nvr a factor* **14/1**

0052 9 *¾* **Highland Song (IRE)**[12] 3498 4-9-2 **53** .... PatCosgrave 8 39
(R F Fisher) *led tl hdd & wknd over 1f out* **7/1**

-344 10 *5* **Butterfly Bud (IRE)**[54] 2206 4-9-2 **53** .... TomEaves 12 23
(J O'Reilly) *w ldrs: lost pl over 1f out* **9/1**

1m 16.4s (2.40) **Going Correction** +0.475s/f (Yiel)
WFA 3 from 4yo+ 5lb 10 Ran SP% **116.1**
Speed ratings (Par 101): **103,102,98,97,96 96,95,92,91,85**
CSF £13.32 CT £58.09 TOTE £4.60: £2.20, £1.40, £2.40; EX 17.60.
Owner C A Lynch **Bred** R And Mrs R Hodgins **Trained** Denton, Co Durham

FOCUS
A moderate sprint handicap in which all but the runner-up headed for the stands' side once in line for home. The time was reasonable and the form looks sound rated around the winner and third.

3840 WILLIE CARSON - PINKER'S POND APPRENTICE H'CAP 1m 3f 214y
5:50 (5:50) (Class 6) (0-65,62) 3-Y-O+ £2,730 (£806; £403) Stalls Low

Form RPR

6266 1 **Dispol Peto**[12] 3502 7-8-13 **47** ....(v) TobyAtkinson 8 54+
(R Johnson) *t.k.h: sn trcking ldrs: wnt 2nd over 4f out: led 1f out: edgd rt: hld on* **12/1**

0444 2 *1* **Moyne Pleasure (IRE)**[21] 3204 9-8-11 **45** ....(p) GaryWales 13 50
(R Johnson) *hld up in rr: gd hdwy on outer 5f out: wnt 3rd over 3f out: w wnr jst ins fnl f: carried rt and no ex* **11/1**

1122 3 *1* **Rare Coincidence**[6] 3679 6-10-0 **62** ....(p) PaulPickard 6 66
(R F Fisher) *led: hdd 1f out: edgd rt and kpt on same pce* **10/3**[1]

0-65 4 *nk* **Red Sun**[16] 3371 10-9-7 **55** ....(t) MartinGuest 2 58
(R C Guest) *trckd ldrs: outpcd over 5f out: edgd lft over 2f out: styd on same pce* **14/1**

5603 5 *1¼* **Top Rocker**[7] 3640 3-8-3 **49** .... Julie-AnneCumine 7 50
(E W Tuer) *hld up in rr: hdwy 5f out: styd on same pce fnl f* **8/1**

0003 6 *1½* **Hugs Destiny (IRE)**[1] 3815 6-9-7 **55** ....(p) AshleyMorgan 3 54
(M A Barnes) *chsd ldrs: outpcd over 5f out: styd on same pce fnl 2f* **13/2**

2422 7 *5* **Eijaaz (IRE)**[47] 2431 6-9-8 **56** ....(p) GaryEdwards 12 47
(G A Harker) *chsd ldrs: wknd appr fnl f* **5/1**[3]

63/0 8 *1¼* **Top Tenor (IRE)**[81] 62 7-9-4 **52** ....(t) AndrewHeffernan 11 41
(W Storey) *hld up in rr: hdwy over 3f out: edgd lft and wknd over 1f out* **28/1**

056 9 *8* **Dream On Dreamers (IRE)**[10] 2842 3-7-13 **45** ....(p) CharlesEddery 4 21
(R C Guest) *t.k.h: trckd ldrs: lost pl and c wd over 2f out: sn bhd* **25/1**

064/ 10 *5* **Jackadandy (USA)**[593] 4998 5-9-12 **60** .... PNolan 9 28
(B Storey) *chsd ldrs: drvn 6f out: lost pl 4f out* **66/1**

0400 11 *20* **Scuzme (IRE)**[55] 2176 4-8-11 **45** .... JosephLoveridge 1 —
(M A Barnes) *s.i.s: bhd: drvn over 5f out: a detached* **9/2**[2]

0000 L **By Storm**[14] 3428 4-8-11 **45** .... BillyCray 14 —
(Miss J E Foster) *rrd in stalls: uns rdr and tk no part* **40/1**

2m 46.0s (7.00) **Going Correction** +0.475s/f (Yiel)
WFA 3 from 4yo+ 12lb 12 Ran SP% **116.3**
Speed ratings (Par 101): **95,94,93,93,92 91,88,87,82,78 65,—**
CSF £130.15 CT £543.15 TOTE £18.20: £4.20, £4.60, £1.30; EX 62.70 Place 6 £44.82, Place 5 £31.63..
Owner Tim Forbes **Bred** B N And Mrs Toye **Trained** Newburn, Tyne & Wear

■ A race confined to apprentices who had not ridden a winner. Toby Atkinson was having only his second ride.

■ Stewards' Enquiry : Toby Atkinson two-day ban: caereless riding (Aug 5-6)

FOCUS
A low-grade contest and a modest winning time, even for the grade and the form, rated around the runner-up and fifth, is weak.
T/Plt: £40.30 to a £1 stake. Pool: £60,187.35. 1,089.95 winning tickets. T/Qpdt: £19.10 to a £1 stake. Pool: £3,475.40. 134.00 winning tickets. WG

3680 LEICESTER (R-H)
Wednesday, July 25

OFFICIAL GOING: Soft (heavy in places between 6f and 7f markers)
Wind: Fresh, behind Weather: Overcast

3841 LEICESTER ANNUAL MEMBERSHIP NURSERY 5f 218y
6:15 (6:17) (Class 4) 2-Y-O £3,886 (£1,156; £577; £288) Stalls High

Form RPR

403 1 **Sawpit Sunshine (IRE)**[13] 3465 2-7-12 **60** oh3.............. DavidKinsella 7 65
(J L Spearing) *s.i.s: hld up: nt clr run over 2f out: swtchd lft and hdwy over 1f out: hung rt and r.o to ld wl ins fnl f* **7/1**

063 2 *¾* **Fathsta (IRE)**[30] 2941 2-7-6 **61** oh2 ow1.................... KMay[(7)] 3 64
(S Kirk) *chsd ldrs: led over 2f out: sn hung rt: hdd wl ins fnl f* **4/1**[2]

103 3 *1¼* **Golan Knight (IRE)**[23] 3157 2-9-1 **80** .... AndrewMullen[(3)] 1 79
(K A Ryan) *chsd ldrs: rdn over 1f out: styd on same pce ins fnl f* **7/2**[1]

2322 4 *3* **Rub Of The Relic (IRE)**[5] 3712 2-8-12 **74** .... FrankieMcDonald 6 64
(P A Blockley) *chsd ldrs: rdn over 2f out: wknd ins fnl f* **4/1**[2]

0504 5 *2* **Thomas Malory (IRE)**[12] 3494 2-7-11 **66** ow6.................. MCGeran[(7)] 2 50
(Miss V Haigh) *s.i.s: hld up: rdn over 2f out: nvr trbld ldrs* **16/1**

544 6 *1¼* **Angle Of Attack (IRE)**[46] 2460 2-8-8 **70** ow3.................. MickyFenton 9 50
(R A Fahey) *chsd ldrs: rdn over 2f out: wknd over 1f out* **6/1**

4006 7 *nk* **Galley Slave (IRE)**[20] 3246 2-7-5 **60** oh8................ CharlotteKerton[(7)] 5 39+
(M C Chapman) *prom: rdn whn stmbld over 2f out: sn wknd* **80/1**

000 8 *shd* **Kay One (IRE)**[13] 3453 2-7-9 **60** oh5.................... DominicFox[(3)] 8 39
(R J Price) *s.i.s: hld up: rdn over 2f out: sn wknd* **40/1**

10 9 *2* **Double Attack (FR)**[32] 2855 2-9-4 **83** .... GregFairley[(3)] 4 56
(M Johnston) *led: rdn and hdd over 2f out: wknd over 1f out* **5/1**[3]

1m 14.24s (1.04) **Going Correction** +0.075s/f (Good) 9 Ran SP% **115.2**
Speed ratings (Par 96): **96,95,93,89,86 85,84,84,81**
CSF £35.06 CT £115.84 TOTE £8.70: £2.70, £2.50, £2.00; EX 48.70.
Owner David A Hunt **Bred** A Brosnan **Trained** Kinnersley, Worcs

FOCUS
A competitive little nursery. The 'official' ratings shown next to each horse are estimated and for information purposes only.

NOTEBOOK
Sawpit Sunshine(IRE), who ran quite well in soft ground at Nottingham last time, had to race from 3lb out of the weights for this handicap debut, but it did not prevent her winning and she looked good value for at least a length, as she did not get the clearest of runs through and tended to hang under pressure. She should not be put up too much for this and can probably win another of these. (op 6-1)
Fathsta(IRE), quietly progressive in maidens, was always going to do better once contesting nurseries and he ran an improved race in second, just finding the one too good. He was another racing from out of the weights and it is possible the return to a faster surface will help. (op 13-2)
Golan Knight(IRE), down in grade for this nursery debut having contested a couple of decent races at Ascot and Pontefract, is already a winner in soft ground and he ran well, but found two lightly-weighted rivals too strong on the day. He looks ready for another try at 7f. (op 4-1 tchd 3-1)
Rub Of The Relic(IRE), who finished either second or third in six of his seven starts in maidens, looked set to run his race whilst looking vulnerable at the same time and he failed to see it out having held every chance over two furlongs out. Official explanation: jockey said colt hung right throughout (tchd 7-2)
Thomas Malory(IRE), whose rider effectively lost his claim through overweight, shaped a little better than when beaten a long way on his nursery debut, running on steadily under pressure, but he may require some assistance from the Handicapper before he is winning. (op 20-1 tchd 25-1)
Double Attack(FR), behind Golan Knight at Royal Ascot, has not built on her debut win and this effort suggested there may be a physical problem. Official explanation: jockey said filly ran too freely early stages (op 4-1 tchd 11-2)

3842 "EAT IN THE NELSON RESTAURANT" MAIDEN AUCTION STKS 7f 9y
6:45 (6:45) (Class 4) 2-Y-O £4,210 (£1,252; £625; £312) Stalls High

Form RPR

2 1 **Art Master**[13] 3471 2-8-12 0.................................. JamieSpencer 7 88+
(S Kirk) *hld up in tch: led over 1f out: shkn up and r.o wl: eased nr fin* **5/4**[1]

0424 2 *3* **Ruby Delta**[14] 3423 2-8-8 0.................................. JohnEgan 6 73
(P D Cundell) *chsd ldrs: rdn and ev ch over 1f out: styd on same pce fnl f* **13/2**[3]

632 3 *hd* **Transmission (IRE)**[12] 3510 2-8-12 0........................ TedDurcan 2 77
(B Smart) *chsd ldrs: led 2f out: rdn and hdd over 1f out: no ex ins fnl f* **2/1**[2]

03 4 *3½* **Softly Killing Me**[20] 3238 2-8-3 0........................ ChrisCatlin 1 59
(J Gallagher) *chsd ldrs: rdn over 2f out: wknd over 1f out* **20/1**

0 5 *2½* **Paddy Rielly (IRE)**[114] 890 2-8-6 0........................ DominicFox[(3)] 3 59
(P D Evans) *sn pushed along in rr: bhd fr 1/2-way: hung rt over 1f out* **25/1**

0 6 *9* **Ovthenight (IRE)**[13] 3471 2-8-11 0........................ MickyFenton 9 38
(Mrs P Sly) *sn pushed along in rr: wknd 1/2-way* **66/1**

0 7 *1¾* **Mouse White**[28] 2977 2-8-9 0....................(b[1]) FrankieMcDonald 4 32
(H Candy) *hmpd s: a in rr: wknd 1/2-way* **50/1**

00 8 *5* **Lunatico (GER)**[16] 3383 2-8-10 0........................ DavidKinsella 8 20
(S C Williams) *chsd ldrs over 4f* **66/1**

9 *7* **Terracos Do Pinhal** 2-8-13 0 GregFairley(3) 5 24
(M Johnston) *led: rdn and hdd 2f out: sn wknd* **9/1**

1m 28.8s (2.70) **Going Correction** +0.30s/f (Good) 9 Ran SP% **114.7**
Speed ratings (Par 96): **96,92,92,88,85 75,73,67,66**
CSF £9.54 TOTE £2.30: £1.20, £2.10, £1.10; EX 11.20.

Owner Lady Davis **Bred** A G Antoniades **Trained** Upper Lambourn, Berks

FOCUS
Just an ordinary maiden, but Art Master looks a useful performer in the making.

NOTEBOOK
Art Master, nibbled at on his debut when second at Warwick, comes from a stable that can produce the odd decent juvenile and he looks a bright prospect. Restrained early, he was brought to challenge racing into the final quarter mile and readily came clear once hitting the front. An extra furlong will hold no fears for the son of Peintre Celebre and he looks one to keep on-side. (op 6-4 tchd 11-10)

Ruby Delta came into this with a little to find on some of the principals and in finishing second to the useful-looking winner he recorded a personal best. He is becoming exposed now, but can pick up a race before long. (op 10-1)

Transmission(IRE) came into this looking to hold every chance following sound placed efforts at Redcar and York, but having gone to the front over two furlongs out, he could not find any more when the winner swept past and was claimed close home for second. This was a bit disappointing and it remains to be seen what the son of Galileo's best trip is. (op 7-4)

Softly Killing Me, the only filly in the field, has improved a little with each start and she is the type to do better in nurseries, for which she is now qualified. (op 18-1)

Paddy Rielly(IRE) improved on his initial effort over 5f at Southwell and is another likely to improve a little once contesting nurseries. (op 28-1)

Terracos Do Pinhal, whose stable's juveniles have not been firing all season, failed to get home having showed up prominently in the early stages and the son of Selkirk will need to leave this well behind if he is to be winning this season. (op 7-1)

3843 NEWTON HARCOURT (S) STKS — 1m 60y
7:20 (7:21) (Class 6) 3-Y-O — **£2,590** (£770; £385; £192) **Stalls High**

Form / RPR

0040 **1** **Tina's Ridge (IRE)**[13] 3469 3-8-11 50 (p) JamieSpencer 7 51
(R Hollinshead) *hld up in tch: led over 1f out: rdn out* **7/4[1]**

4605 **2** *1 3/4* **Dr Dream (IRE)**[39] 2662 3-8-8 60 JerryO'Dwyer(3) 2 47
(D M Simcock) *a.p: rdn over 2f out: chsd wnr and edgd rt fnl f: styd on same pce* **11/4[2]**

6600 **3** *2 1/2* **Homecroft Boy**[37] 2298 3-8-11 38 (b) JohnEgan 6 42
(P D Evans) *chsd ldrs: led over 2f out: rdn and hdd over 1f out: n.m.r and no ex sn after* **7/1**

000- **4** *7* **Alice Howe**[228] 6768 3-8-6 40 HayleyTurner 5 22
(W R Muir) *chsd ldrs: led 3f out: sn rdn and hdd: wknd over 1f out* **16/1**

0600 **5** *hd* **Mr Mini Scule**[70] 1763 3-8-11 45 VinceSlattery 1 27
(S Wynne) *led over 5f: sn rdn: wknd over 1f out* **20/1**

0000 **6** *1 1/4* **Espejo (IRE)**[54] 2200 3-8-11 62 MickyFenton 4 24
(W J Musson) *hld up: rdn over 2f out: sn wknd* **7/2[3]**

00-0 **7** *4* **Soylent Green**[42] 2581 3-8-6 25 PaulEddery 3 11
(S Parr) *s.i.s: hld up: rdn and wknd over 2f out* **50/1**

1m 51.14s (5.84) **Going Correction** +0.70s/f (Yiel) 7 Ran SP% **110.4**
Speed ratings (Par 98): **98,96,93,86,86 85,81**
CSF £6.20 TOTE £2.60: £2.20, £1.40; EX 7.90.The winner was bought in for 7,200gns. Dr Dream was claimed by Gary Roberts for £6,000.

Owner John L Marriott **Bred** Mrs Chris Harrington **Trained** Upper Longdon, Staffs

FOCUS
A very weak contest, even for the grade with the form rated through the winner and third.

3844 PROLOGIS JIM ANDERSON MEMORIAL H'CAP — 1m 3f 183y
7:50 (7:50) (Class 4) (0-85,85) 4-Y-O+ — **£4,857** (£1,445; £722; £360) **Stalls High**

Form / RPR

134 **1** **Broughtons Revival**[20] 3243 5-8-5 **69** HayleyTurner 1 76
(W J Musson) *chsd ldr: rdn over 1f out: styd on to ld wl ins fnl f* **11/4[2]**

10-P **2** *1/2* **Fear To Tread (USA)**[77] 1591 4-8-13 **77** MickyFenton 3 83
(Mrs P Sly) *led: qcknd over 3f out: rdn and edgd rt over 1f out: hdd wl ins fnl f* **20/1**

20-3 **3** *4* **Candle**[69] 1783 4-9-3 **81** JohnEgan 2 81
(H Candy) *hld up: hdwy over 2f out: rdn over 1f out: styd on same pce* **9/4[1]**

402 **4** *1 3/4* **Can Can Star**[16] 3386 4-8-10 **74** TedDurcan 5 71
(A W Carroll) *hld up: hdwy over 2f out: sn rdn: wknd ins fnl f* **7/2[3]**

0/0 **5** *14* **Adjami (IRE)**[13] 3467 6-8-3 **67** ChrisCatlin 6 41
(John A Harris) *chsd ldrs: rdn over 2f out: sn wknd* **18/1**

510- **6** *23* **Chocolate Caramel (USA)**[397] 2817 5-9-7 **85** JamieSpencer 4 23
(Mrs A J Perrett) *chsd ldrs: rdn over 3f out: wknd and eased fnl 2f* **7/2[3]**

2m 41.6s (7.10) **Going Correction** +0.70s/f (Yiel) 6 Ran SP% **111.9**
Speed ratings (Par 105): **104,103,101,99,90 75**
CSF £47.24 TOTE £4.40: £1.80, £4.70; EX 57.40.

Owner Broughton Thermal Insulation **Bred** Broughton Bloodstock And M Billings **Trained** Newmarket, Suffolk

FOCUS
A fair handicap in which it proved hard to come from off the pace and which saw the first pair come clear. The form does not look that strong.

Chocolate Caramel(USA) Official explanation: trainer's rep said gelding appeared to feel the effects of testing ground after 13 months absence

3845 EUROPEAN BREEDERS' FUND WATERLOO FILLIES' H'CAP — 7f 9y
8:25 (8:25) (Class 4) (0-80,80) 3-Y-O — **£6,232** (£1,866; £933; £467) **Stalls High**

Form / RPR

-162 **1** **What A Treasure (IRE)**[20] 3247 3-8-11 **70** JamieSpencer 3 75
(L M Cumani) *trckd ldr: led over 1f out: sn rdn: r.o* **8/15[1]**

16-6 **2** *1 3/4* **Regal Quest (IRE)**[18] 3334 3-9-7 **80** JohnEgan 2 80
(S Kirk) *a.p: rdn to chse wnr over 1f out: no imp* **6/1[3]**

3005 **3** *13* **Mystery Ocean**[20] 3235 3-9-5 **78** GeorgeBaker 1 44
(R M Beckett) *reluctant to s: bhd: sme hdwy 1/2-way: rdn and wknd over 1f out* **11/4[2]**

0040 **4** *3 1/2* **Retaliate**[36] 2750 3-8-2 **61** oh11 ChrisCatlin 4 18
(M Quinn) *led: rdn over 2f out: hdd & wknd over 1f out* **25/1**

1m 29.44s (3.34) **Going Correction** +0.55s/f (Yiel) 4 Ran SP% **110.0**
Speed ratings (Par 99): **102,100,85,81**
CSF £4.38 TOTE £1.40; EX 3.70.

Owner Scuderia Archi Romani **Bred** Serpentine Bloodstock Et Al **Trained** Newmarket, Suffolk

FOCUS
A modest turnout for the prize. The first pair came a long way clear and set the level for the form.

Mystery Ocean Official explanation: jockey said filly was slowly away

3846 BOSWORTH FIELD MEDIAN AUCTION MAIDEN STKS — 5f 2y
8:55 (8:56) (Class 5) 3-Y-O — **£3,562** (£1,059; £529; £264) **Stalls High**

Form / RPR

0030 **1** **Lord Of The Reins (IRE)**[3] 3763 3-9-3 48 TedDurcan 6 55
(D Shaw) *chsd ldrs: rdn over 1f out: qcknd to ld ins fnl f: sn clr: eased nr fin* **6/1[3]**

04 **2** *3* **Invincible Lad (IRE)**[11] 3537 3-9-3 0 JamieSpencer 4 44
(E J Alston) *chsd ldr: rdn to ld 1f out: sn hdd and unable qckn* **5/6[1]**

6- **3** *3* **Midnight Sky**[243] 6575 3-8-12 0 ChrisCatlin 1 28
(Rae Guest) *hld up in tch: rdn over 1f out: wknd fnl f* **3/1[2]**

4 *1 1/2* **Champagne Mindy** 3-8-9 0 NeilChalmers(3) 3 23
(Garry Moss) *s.s: hdwy over 3f out: led over 1f out: sn rdn and hdd: wknd ins fnl f* **33/1**

2 **5** *3/4* **Lula (IRE)**[111] 934 3-8-5 0 MCGeran(7) 5 20
(M Quinn) *led: rdn and hdd over 1f out: wknd ins fnl f* **8/1**

6 *3* **Collematteo (IRE)** 3-9-3 0 VinceSlattery 2 15
(D J Wintle) *s.s: plld hrd and sn prom: wknd wl over 1f out* **28/1**

64.33 secs (3.43) **Going Correction** +0.70s/f (Yiel) 6 Ran SP% **111.3**
Speed ratings (Par 100): **100,95,90,88,86 82**
CSF £11.34 TOTE £7.80: £1.90, £1.40; EX 9.30 Place 6 £13.38, Place 5 £7.23..

Owner Danethorpe Racing Ltd **Bred** C Farrell **Trained** Danethorpe, Notts

FOCUS
A dire three-year-old maiden. The winner is value for around double the winning margin but the form is far from solid.

T/Plt: £26.70 to a £1 stake. Pool: £60,110.15. 1,643.15 winning tickets. T/Qpdt: £7.50 to a £1 stake. Pool: £4,206.80. 413.50 winning tickets. CR

3730 LINGFIELD (L-H)
Wednesday, July 25

OFFICIAL GOING: Turf course - soft; all-weather - standard
Wind: Strong, behind Weather: Overcast

3847 WBX.COM WE'LL MATCH YOUR COMMISSION RATE MAIDEN STKS — 1m 3f 106y
2:05 (2:07) (Class 5) 3-Y-O+ — **£2,817** (£838; £418; £209) **Stalls High**

Form / RPR

-222 **1** **Dawn Sky**[20] 3248 3-9-2 85 PhilipRobinson 4 76
(M A Jarvis) *trckd ldng pair: effrt to ld over 1f out: in command whn edgd lft ins fnl f: rdn out* **7/4[1]**

0 **2** *1* **Precept**[37] 2726 3-8-11 0 FergusSweeney 6 69
(H Candy) *trckd ldrs: effrt over 2f out: rdn and styd on to take 2nd wl ins fnl f: unable to chal* **20/1**

00 **3** *nk* **Two Timer (IRE)**[33] 2836 3-9-2 0 AntonyProcter 7 74
(D R C Elsworth) *led: rdn and hdd over 1f out: keeping on but hld whn n.m.r and lost 2nd last 75yds* **33/1**

2622 **4** *nk* **Yossi (IRE)**[15] 3402 3-9-2 80 JimmyQuinn 13 73
(M H Tompkins) *settled in midfield: effrt 3f out: rdn and styd on fr over 2f out: nt rch ldrs* **9/4[2]**

3 **5** *2 1/2* **Propaganda (IRE)**[29] 2970 3-8-11 0 JamieSpencer 11 64
(L M Cumani) *t.k.h: mostly trckd ldr to 2f out: eased whn btn last 75yds* **7/2[3]**

5 **6** *2 1/2* **Act Three**[92] 1217 3-8-8 0 NeilChalmers(3) 3 60
(Mouse Hamilton-Fairley) *hld up towards rr: shkn up over 2f out: kpt on steadily fr over 1f out: nrst fin* **50/1**

7 *3/4* **Aquamarine Beauty (FR)** 3-8-11 0 RHills 1 58
(Sir Michael Stoute) *wl in tch: shkn up 2f out: grad wknd* **11/1**

340 **8** *8* **Just Julie (USA)**[38] 2690 3-8-11 65 SteveDrowne 2 45
(N A Callaghan) *sn lost pl and hld up towards rr: reminder 2f out: nvr nr ldrs: eased fnl f* **20/1**

0 **9** *2* **Hook Money (IRE)**[25] 3084 3-9-2 0 JimCrowley 8 46
(D W P Arbuthnot) *mostly in last trio: rdn and no prog 3f out: plugged on* **66/1**

10 *4* **Kitebrook**[609] 6-9-8 0 VinceSlattery 14 34
(Mrs Mary Hambro) *dwlt: a wl in rr: rdn and struggling 3f out: no ch* **66/1**

5500 **11** *3/4* **Wally Barge**[65] 1906 4-9-13 48 RobertHavlin 12 38
(D K Ivory) *prom tl wknd rapidly wl over 2f out* **66/1**

0/ **12** *14* **Satan's Sister**[1146] 2647 6-9-8 0 ChrisCatlin 5 9
(Ian Williams) *detached in last after 4f: struggling after: t.o* **66/1**

50- **13** *1/2* **Kimpton Carer**[210] 6950 3-9-2 0 (t) StephenCarson 15 14
(J A Geake) *s.s: a in last trio: wknd over 3f out: t.o* **66/1**

2m 37.62s (7.70) **Going Correction** +0.75s/f (Yiel)
WFA 3 from 4yo+ 11lb 13 Ran SP% **119.6**
Speed ratings (Par 103): **102,101,101,100,99 97,96,90,89,86 85,75,75**
CSF £43.65 TOTE £2.40: £1.10, £5.00, £5.40; EX 52.50 Trifecta £526.00 Part won. Pool £740.91 - 0.44 winning units..

Owner Saif Ali **Bred** Darley **Trained** Newmarket, Suffolk

FOCUS
A modest maiden, lacking in strength in depth, and dominated by those that raced handily. Very few ever got into it from off the pace. The race has been rated largely on the time, with the placed horses both improvers.

Just Julie(USA) Official explanation: vet said filly had lost a shoe

3848 AUTOGRAPH H'CAP — 1m 3f 106y
2:35 (2:36) (Class 5) (0-75,77) 3-Y-O — **£2,817** (£838; £418; £209) **Stalls High**

Form / RPR

1 **1** **Hazy Days**[44] 2520 3-9-4 **71** SebSanders 4 79
(Sir Mark Prescott) *spooked at rival after 1f: settled in 5th: prog to chse ldr jst over 2f out: hrd rdn and sustained chal over 1f out: led last strides* **5/1[3]**

6612 **2** *nk* **Jawaaneb (USA)**[14] 3427 3-9-5 **72** RHills 2 79
(J L Dunlop) *trckd ldng pair: led over 2f out: drvn over 1f out: hdd last strides* **9/4[2]**

0411 **3** *1 3/4* **Beau Sancy**[10] 3570 3-9-7 **77** 6ex LiamJones(3) 8 81
(R A Harris) *hld up in last trio: prog on outer 3f out: sn rdn: hanging and nt qckn fnl 2f: wnt 3rd over 1f out but nvr gng pce to chal* **7/1**

5504 **4** *1 1/2* **Tifernati**[13] 3469 3-8-12 **65** JamieSpencer 10 66
(W J Haggas) *s.i.s: t.k.h: hld up in last pair: prog wl over 2f out: chsd ldrs over 1f out: rdn and nt qckn* **2/1[1]**

4260 **5** *3* **Mowadeh (IRE)**[16] 3367 3-9-3 **70** JHBowman 11 66
(M R Channon) *hld up in last: prog over 2f out: reminders wl over 1f out: and jst over 1f out: nt rch ldrs: eased ins fnl f* **12/1**

The Form Book, Raceform Ltd, Compton, RG20 6NL

050 **6** *16* **Arabian Sun**[15] [3402] 3-9-3 **70**.. PaulFitzsimons 9 39
(M J Attwater) *w ldr: reminders after 5f: wknd wl over 2f out: t.o* **33/1**

3-00 **7** *hd* **Spartan Dance**[16] [3367] 3-8-5 **58**..............................(v) RichardThomas 1 27
(J A Geake) *prom: lost pl u.p sn after 1/2-way: struggling 3f out: t.o* **25/1**

-220 **8** *3* **Stark Contrast (USA)**[46] [2464] 3-9-6 **73**..................(b[1]) StephenCarson 6 37
(G A Butler) *led to over 2f out: wknd rapidly: t.o* **16/1**

0-60 **9** *½* **Cocobean**[19] [3274] 3-8-2 **55** oh10.......................................(tp) ChrisCatlin 7 18
(M Appleby) *dropped to last and struggling over 4f out: t.o over 3f out* **66/1**

2m 37.83s (7.91) **Going Correction** +0.75s/f (Yiel) **9** Ran SP% **115.1**
Speed ratings (Par 100): **101,100,99,98,96 84,84,82,81**
CSF £16.39 CT £78.43 TOTE £6.00: £2.00, £1.20, £1.50; EX 14.30 Trifecta £29.00 Pool £664.80. - 16.27 winning units..
Owner Lordship Stud **Bred** Lordship Stud Limited **Trained** Newmarket, Suffolk

FOCUS
A fair three-year-old handicap for the grade and the pace was fair. The first two remain progressive and the form seems sound.
Tifernati Official explanation: jockey said gelding hung right

3849 EUROPEAN BREEDERS FUND MEDIAN AUCTION MAIDEN STKS (DIV I) 7f (P)
3:05 (3:06) (Class 5) 2-Y-O **£2,266** (£674; £337; £168) **Stalls** Low

Form RPR

2 **1** **Without A Prayer (IRE)**[15] [3404] 2-9-3 0........................... SebSanders 6 79+
(R M Beckett) *trckd ldrs: prog over 2f out: led wl over 1f out: sn rdn wl clr* **5/4**[1]

4 **2** *4* **Rockfield Lodge (IRE)**[23] [3171] 2-9-3 0........................ JamieSpencer 9 69
(J A Osborne) *t.k.h: hld up: prog to trck ldrs 2f out: wnt 2nd 1f out but wnr already gone: plugged on* **13/2**[3]

440 **3** *shd* **Kyrie Eleison (IRE)**[14] [3435] 2-9-3 0........................... RichardHughes 3 69
(R Hannon) *trckd ldr to 3f out: styd cl up: outpcd wl over 1f out: pressed for 2nd fnl f* **7/2**[2]

0 **4** *1 ½* **Resplendent Light**[32] [2855] 2-9-3 0................................ SaleemGolam 1 65
(W R Muir) *trckd ldrs: outpcd and pushed along over 2f out: styd on again ins fnl f* **16/1**

5 **5** *1 ½* **River Bounty**[21] [3213] 2-8-12 0...................................... RichardMullen 10 56
(A P Jarvis) *prom: led over 2f out to wl over 1f out: wknd on inner fnl f* **10/1**

00 **6** *3* **Kryptonite (IRE)**[11] [3551] 2-9-3 0..................................... MichaelHills 11 53
(J W Hills) *hld up in rr: prog on outer 1/2-way: chsd ldrs over 2f out: hanging lft and wknd over 1f out* **50/1**

3205 **7** *1 ¾* **Swindon Town Flyer (IRE)**[11] [3524] 2-9-3 0................. SamHitchcott 8 49
(A B Haynes) *led to over 2f out: wknd rapidly over 1f out* **12/1**

8 *1* **Arniecoco** 2-9-3 0.. SteveDrowne 2 46
(B J Meehan) *pushed along to chse ldrs: wknd fr over 2f out* **12/1**

9 *½* **Up The Wycombe** 2-9-3 0... TQuinn 7 45
(S Dow) *hld up: a in last trio: no ch after being outpcd over 2f out* **33/1**

00 **10** *nk* **Weight In Gold**[20] [3245] 2-8-12 0.................................... HayleyTurner 4 39
(P J McBride) *hld up in last trio: outpcd over 2f out: no ch whn rdn over 1f out* **66/1**

11 *½* **Honest Value (IRE)** 2-9-3 0... LPKeniry 5 43
(Mrs L C Jewell) *hld up: a in last trio: wl outpcd over 2f out: no ch after* **66/1**

1m 26.75s (0.86) **Going Correction** -0.175s/f (Stan) **11** Ran SP% **118.2**
Speed ratings (Par 94): **88,83,83,81,79 76,74,73,72,72 71**
CSF £9.78 TOTE £2.00: £1.10, £1.80, £1.60; EX 10.90 Trifecta £21.80 Pool £773.27 - 25.16 winning units..
Owner McDonagh Murphy And Nixon **Bred** Brownstown Stud **Trained** Whitsbury, Hants

FOCUS
This looked like an ordinary juvenile maiden and the winning time was 1.46sec slower than the second division.

NOTEBOOK
Without A Prayer(IRE), just pipped on his debut at Wolverhampton, made no mistake this time, taking several lengths out of his rivals in a matter of strides when asked to go and win his race at the top of the straight. His trainer is confident he can prove at least as effective on turf and he is likely to be given entries in some early-closing races. He certainly deserves his chance in better company. (op 6-4 tchd 13-8)
Rockfield Lodge(IRE) looked likely to give the winner a race when moving into contention quite easily approaching the turn into the straight, but he was left behind at the business end. He probably ran into quite a nice type and looks capable of winning an ordinary maiden, although he only needs one more run for a nursery mark. (op 6-1 tchd 11-2)
Kyrie Eleison(IRE) would have found this easier than the hot Newmarket maiden he contested on his previous start and posted a respectable effort in defeat. His proximity helps give the form a solid look, but he may just be worth a try in nurseries. (op 4-1 tchd 10-3 and 9-2 in a place)
Resplendent Light was thought good enough to contest the Chesham Stakes on his debut and this was a reasonable effort switched to maiden company. He looks the type who will progress with time. (op 14-1 tchd 20-1)
River Bounty showed ability on her debut at Kempton and this was another reasonable effort. (op 14-1)
Kryptonite(IRE) raced widest of all early on and may be a little bit better than he showed. He could be one to look out for in nursery company a little later down the line. Official explanation: jockey said colt hung left final bend

3850 EUROPEAN BREEDERS FUND MEDIAN AUCTION MAIDEN STKS (DIV II) 7f (P)
3:35 (3:35) (Class 5) 2-Y-O **£2,266** (£674; £337; £168) **Stalls** Low

Form RPR

4 **1** **Spinning Sound (IRE)**[25] [3095] 2-9-3 0.............................. ChrisCatlin 3 78
(E J O'Neill) *prom: rdn to chse ldr 3f out: sustained chal u.p fr over 1f out: led last stride* **7/2**[2]

553 **2** *shd* **Farthermost (IRE)**[14] [3424] 2-9-3 0................................. RichardHughes 8 78
(R Hannon) *led: hrd rdn over 1f out: kpt on u.p: hdd last stride* **16/1**

602 **3** *1 ½* **Solent Ridge (IRE)**[14] [3424] 2-9-3 0.................................... JohnEgan 5 74
(J S Moore) *chsd ldrs: rdn 3f out: kpt on u.p to take 3rd ins fnl f* **12/1**

05 **4** *½* **Tobogganist**[16] [3383] 2-9-3 0.. TedDurcan 2 73
(W Jarvis) *chsd ldr to 3f out: lost pl sltly over 2f out and rdn: kpt on again fnl f* **11/1**[3]

4 **5** *nk* **Copywriter**[8] [3625] 2-9-3 0.. JimmyFortune 4 72
(J H M Gosden) *trckd ldrs: squeezed through on inner to go 3rd over 2f out: rdn and tried to chal 1f out: nt qckn* **5/6**[1]

0 **6** *3 ½* **Hawk House**[11] [3551] 2-9-3 0.. MichaelHills 9 63
(B W Hills) *pressed ldrs on outer: rdn over 2f out: wknd over 1f out* **12/1**

5 **7** *3* **Elizabeth's Quest**[14] [3424] 2-8-5 0.................................. SophieDoyle(7) 6 50
(R Simpson) *restless stalls and dwlt: rcvrd into midfield 1/2-way: chsd ldrs and in tch 2f out: rdn and wknd over 1f out* **25/1**

8 *1 ¾* **Distant Diamond (IRE)** 2-9-3 0....................................... AdamKirby 11 50
(W R Swinburn) *sn pushed along in last pair and off the pce: no ch fr 3f out* **25/1**

9 *nk* **Casa Catalina (IRE)** 2-8-12 0.. JoeFanning 7 45
(M Johnston) *sn pushed along: a wl in rr* **20/1**

6 **10** *1* **Townkab (IRE)**[23] [3171] 2-9-3 0... IanMongan 10 47
(N P Littmoden) *dwlt: rcvrd into midfield after 2f: struggling sn after 1/2-way* **66/1**

00 **11** *5* **Jermajesty (IRE)**[41] [2590] 2-8-10 0............................... HarryPoulton(7) 1 34
(J R Boyle) *mostly last and a off the pce: wl bhd fr 3f out* **100/1**

1m 25.29s (-0.60) **Going Correction** -0.175s/f (Stan) **11** Ran SP% **121.3**
Speed ratings (Par 94): **96,95,94,93,93 89,85,83,83,82 76**
CSF £55.22 TOTE £3.80: £1.20, £3.10, £2.70; EX 59.40 Trifecta £415.80 Pool £591.62. - 1.01 winning units..
Owner Miss A H Marshall **Bred** Frank Dunne **Trained** Averham Park, Notts

FOCUS
An ordinary but competitive maiden. The winning time was 1.46sec quicker than the first division, most likely due to the stronger early pace.

NOTEBOOK
Spinning Sound(IRE) had shaped very well when fourth on his debut in a 7f maiden on the July course and showed he has gone the right way since with a game effort to get off the mark at the second attempt. He was made to work hard to reel in the long-timer leader, but should come on again for the experience. It remains to be seen where he will go next, but he may be best off going down the nursery route for the time being. (op 4-1)
Farthermost(IRE) ran a terrifically game race from the front and deserved more than to be nailed on the line. He managed to reverse recent course placings with Solent Ridge, though, and is clearly progressing. (op 20-1 tchd 22-1)
Solent Ridge(IRE) ran a respectable race in defeat, but he was unable to confirm recent form with Farthermost. He might just prove best back over shorter. (op 14-1 tchd 16-1)
Tobogganist shaped quite nicely and could be one to keep in mind now he is eligible for nurseries.
Copywriter failed to build on the promise he showed when fourth on his debut at Yarmouth the previous week and was a little disappointing. This could easily have come a bit too soon, or perhaps he was not ideally suited to the Polytrack, but whatever the case it is too early to be giving up on him. (op 4-6 tchd 10-11 and evens in places)

3851 PLATINUM ABBA LIVE AT LINGFIELDPARK.CO.UK H'CAP 7f (P)
4:05 (4:05) (Class 5) (0-70,71) 3-Y-O+ **£2,817** (£838; £418; £209) **Stalls** Low

Form RPR

0442 **1** **Reeling N' Rocking (IRE)**[14] [3422] 4-9-6 **66**..................... MichaelHills 7 76
(B W Hills) *trckd ldrs: prog over 2f out: shkn up to ld jst ins fnl f: pressed last 75yds but r.o wl* **5/1**[2]

0133 **2** *nk* **Million Percent**[14] [3422] 8-9-7 **70**...................................... LiamJones(3) 5 79
(C R Dore) *hld up in midfield: prog over 2f out: clsd over 1f out: drvn to chse wnr wl ins fnl f: r.o and gaining at fin* **8/1**[3]

04-3 **3** *1 ¾* **Titan Triumph**[25] [3102] 3-9-3 **70**... PaulDoe 14 71+
(W J Knight) *fast away fr wd draw: t.k.h and w ldrs: led 4f out: gng wl 2f out: hdd and folded jst ins fnl f* **3/1**[1]

6001 **4** *1 ½* **Proper (IRE)**[7] [3646] 3-9-4 **71** 6ex... JHBowman 2 68
(M R Channon) *wl in tch: prog to chse ldr briefly over 1f out: fdd ins fnl f* **8/1**[3]

6000 **5** *1* **Royal Amnesty**[14] [3422] 4-9-9 **69**... OscarUrbina 4 67
(G C H Chung) *hld up in midfield: trckd ldrs gng wl enough 2f out: already outpcd and no ch whn reminders ins fnl f* **16/1**

0210 **6** *1 ¼* **Looks Could Kill (USA)**[25] [3106] 5-9-7 **67**................... RichardHughes 8 61
(A B Haynes) *stdd s: hld up wl in rr: styd on fr 2f out on outer: nvr nrr* **10/1**

6003 **7** *hd* **Special Place**[34] [2802] 4-9-2 **62**... SebSanders 9 56
(J A R Toller) *hld up in last pair: prog over 2f out: swtchd to inner and clsd over 1f out: fdd ins fnl f* **5/1**[2]

0000 **8** *nk* **Fisberry**[6] [3682] 5-9-6 **66**.. FergusSweeney 12 59
(M S Saunders) *dwlt: wl in rr: rdn 1/2-way: hanging and wandering wl over 1f out: kpt on fnl f* **25/1**

50-0 **9** *¾* **Soizic (NZ)**[200] [48] 5-9-5 **65**.. JimCrowley 1 56
(L A Dace) *wl in rr: struggling fr 1/2-way: modest late prog* **100/1**

0060 **10** *hd* **Meditation**[142] [614] 5-9-6 **66**... RichardThomas 6 56
(I A Wood) *prom: lost pl and rdn wl over 2f out: sn btn* **50/1**

5100 **11** *nk* **Nikki Bea (IRE)**[22] [3191] 4-9-3 **63**................................ SimonWhitworth 13 53
(Jamie Poulton) *w ldrs tl wknd over 2f out* **25/1**

0-00 **12** *1 ½* **Alfie Tupper (IRE)**[20] [3234] 4-9-10 **70**............................ GeorgeBaker 10 56
(S Kirk) *taken steadily to post: trckd ldrs: lost pl and rdn 1/2-way: sn struggling in rr* **16/1**

6-00 **13** *hd* **Zabeel House**[46] [2452] 4-9-9 **69**..................................... JamieSpencer 11 54
(J A R Toller) *towards rr: pushed along on outer over 3f out: brief effrt over 2f out: sn wknd* **12/1**

062 **14** *10* **Our Kes (IRE)**[13] [3455] 5-9-3 **63**.. AmirQuinn 3 21
(P Howling) *led to 4f out: sn gave up: t.o* **14/1**

1m 24.51s (-1.38) **Going Correction** -0.175s/f (Stan)
WFA 3 from 4yo+ 7lb **14** Ran SP% **126.4**
Speed ratings (Par 103): **100,99,97,95,94 93,93,92,91,91 91,89,89,78**
CSF £46.13 CT £150.08 TOTE £6.50: £2.00, £3.30, £2.20; EX 41.60 Trifecta £219.80 Pool £662.74. - 2.14 winning units..
Owner D M James **Bred** Richard F Barnes **Trained** Lambourn, Berks

FOCUS
A modest but competitive handicap run at a strong pace. Sound form.
Titan Triumph Official explanation: jockey said colt ran too free
Alfie Tupper(IRE) Official explanation: jockey said gelding hung right
Zabeel House Official explanation: jockey said gelding had no more to give

3852 JOIN WBX.COM £150 OF FREE BETS H'CAP 6f (P)
4:35 (4:35) (Class 5) (0-70,70) 3-Y-O+ **£2,817** (£838; £418; £209) **Stalls** Low

Form RPR

6031 **1** **Quality Street**[15] [3396] 5-9-12 **69**.............................(p) RichardThomas 11 79
(P Butler) *chsd ldrs: effrt on outer over 1f out: rdn and r.o to ld ins fnl f: styd on wl* **9/1**

6641 **2** *nk* **Ebraam (USA)**[15] [3408] 4-9-5 **62**...................................... JimmyQuinn 4 71
(D Shaw) *t.k.h: hld up in last trio: prog on outer over 1f out: r.o wl to cl on wnr ins fnl f: nt get up* **6/1**[3]

2214 **3** *nk* **Caustic Wit (IRE)**[9] [3594] 9-9-3 **60**............................ FergusSweeney 3 68
(M S Saunders) *taken down early: hld up in last trio: rapid prog on wd outside over 1f out: gaining at fin* **11/2**[2]

0006 **4** *1* **Tag Team (IRE)**[6] [3686] 6-9-1 **58**.................................... JamieSpencer 6 63
(John A Harris) *disp ld at fast pce: upsides ent fnl f: fdd* **13/2**

-404 **5** *shd* **Even Bolder**[22] [3190] 4-8-13 **63**...................................(p) SophieDoyle(7) 5 68
(R Simpson) *t.k.h: hld up bhd ldrs: effrt on inner over 1f out: upsides ent fnl f: sn outpcd* **20/1**

4502 **6** *nk* **Methaaly (IRE)**[56] [2155] 4-9-9 **66**....................................... JohnEgan 8 70
(Jane Chapple-Hyam) *disp ld at fast pce: upsides ent fnl f: sn wknd* **4/1**[1]

0560 **7** 1 1/4 **Russian Rocket (IRE)**[8] 3627 5-9-10 **67**.......................... DMylonas 12 67
(Mrs C A Dunnett) *t.k.h: sn pressed ldng pair fr wd draw: rdn over 1f out: wknd ins fnl f* **16/1**
5236 **8** 1/2 **Ever Cheerful**[11] 3549 6-9-6 **63**..................................(p) SteveDrowne 10 62
(A B Haynes) *hld up towards rr: rdn and no prog 2f out* **14/1**
-656 **9** 1 1/4 **Flying Encore (IRE)**[25] 3087 3-9-8 **70**................................ AdamKirby 9 65
(W R Swinburn) *s.i.s: a in last trio: rdn and no prog 2f out* **14/1**
3540 **10** 1 1/4 **Regal Royale**[9] 3585 4-9-7 **64**..(b) LPKeniry 7 55
(Peter Grayson) *chsd ldrs: rdn bef 1/2-way: wknd 2f out* **11/1**
0003 **11** 2 1/2 **Brandywell Boy (IRE)**[15] 3396 4-9-10 **67**................................ TQuinn 1 51
(D J S Ffrench Davis) *nvr bttr than midfield: rdn and struggling over 2f out: wknd over 1f out* **7/1**

1m 11.38s (-1.43) **Going Correction** -0.175s/f (Stan)
WFA 3 from 4yo+ 5lb **11** Ran SP% **117.8**
Speed ratings (Par 103): **102,101,101,99,99 99,97,97,95,93 90**
CSF £62.31 CT £336.54 TOTE £8.70: £2.40, £2.50, £2.00; EX 39.90 Trifecta £85.10 Pool £680.26. - 5.67 winning units..
Owner E H Whatmough **Bred** S R Hope **Trained** East Chiltington, E Sussex

FOCUS
A very competitive sprint handicap and the pace was strong. Solid form, although only modest.

3853 THE REAL THING LIVE AT LINGFIELDPARK.CO.UK FILLIES' H'CAP 5f (P)
5:05 (5:06) (Class 6) (0-65,62) 3-Y-O+ **£2,047** (£604; £302) **Stalls** High

Form RPR
-041 **1** **Contentious (IRE)**[17] 3353 3-8-5 **53**.......................... KirstyMilczarek(7) 3 64
(D M Simcock) *taken down early: mde all: rdn and hung rt over 1f out: kpt on wl fnl f* **14/1**
3132 **2** 1 **Cosmic Destiny (IRE)**[22] 3190 5-9-8 **59**.......................... JimCrowley 2 67
(E F Vaughan) *hld up bhd ldrs gng wl: effrt over 1f out: wnt 2nd ins fnl f: nt qckn and hld after* **4/1**[2]
453 **3** nk **Glencal**[26] 3046 3-8-11 **52**.. SteveDrowne 7 58
(H Morrison) *chsd ldrs on outer: rdn and nt qckn over 1f out: kpt on ins fnl f* **3/1**[1]
2536 **4** 3/4 **Jilly Why (IRE)**[10] 3569 6-8-13 **50**................................(b) SamHitchcott 8 54
(Paul Green) *pushed along in rr: no prog tl styd on wl fnl f: nt rch ldrs* **4/1**[2]
2004 **5** nk **City For Conquest (IRE)**[9] 3597 4-8-11 **48**.................(b) JimmyQuinn 5 51
(John A Harris) *s.i.s: wl in rr: rdn and styd on fnl f: nrst fin* **16/1**
/005 **6** hd **Lake Hero**[160] 465 4-9-11 **62**.. SebSanders 9 64
(M J Wallace) *mostly chsd wnr tl jst ins fnl f: wknd* **6/1**[3]
0600 **7** nk **Hello Roberto**[16] 3368 6-9-1 **55**..................................(p) LiamJones(3) 6 56
(R A Harris) *chsd ldrs: rdn and no ex over 1f out* **20/1**
0606 **8** 1/2 **Supreme Kiss**[21] 3212 4-8-8 **52**................................ SophieDoyle(7) 4 52
(Mrs N Smith) *s.i.s: a in last trio: shkn up and kpt on fnl f: no ch* **33/1**
0250 **9** 1 3/4 **Lady Lafitte (USA)**[26] 3046 3-9-5 **60**..........................(bt[1]) MichaelHills 10 52
(B W Hills) *racd wd: hld up: effrt over 2f out: wknd over 1f out* **16/1**
5005 **10** 2 1/2 **Pride Of Joy**[22] 3190 4-9-7 **58**.. TQuinn 1 42
(M A Buckley) *prom on inner early: wknd over 1f out* **15/2**

58.54 secs (-1.24) **Going Correction** -0.175s/f (Stan)
WFA 3 from 4yo+ 4lb **10** Ran SP% **117.2**
Speed ratings (Par 98): **102,100,99,98,98 97,97,96,93,89**
CSF £69.73 CT £222.33 TOTE £17.20: £3.70, £1.60, £1.90; EX 36.60 Trifecta £96.60 Pool £605.64. - 4.45 winning units. Place 6 £59.28, Place 5 £26.01..
Owner D J Erwin **Bred** John O Browne **Trained** Newmarket, Suffolk

FOCUS
A moderate but competitive fillies' sprint. Sound form, rated through the runner-up.
City For Conquest(IRE) Official explanation: jockey said filly missed the break
Pride Of Joy Official explanation: jockey said filly never travelled
T/Jkpt: £2,800.20 to a £1 stake. Pool: £15,776.25. 4.00 winning tickets. T/Plt: £24.60 to a £1 stake. Pool: £75,325.40. 2,234.70 winning tickets. T/Qpdt: £9.70 to a £1 stake. Pool: £4,973.70. 377.40 winning tickets. JN

3687 SANDOWN (R-H)
Wednesday, July 25

OFFICIAL GOING: Round course - good (good to soft in places; 7.7); sprint course - good to soft (7.2)
Wind: Virtually nil.

3854 PANMURE GORDON INSTITUTIONAL EQUITIES APPRENTICE H'CAP 1m 2f 7y
6:05 (6:05) (Class 5) (0-75,75) 4-Y-O+ **£3,238** (£963; £481; £240) **Stalls** High

Form RPR
4223 **1** **Burgundy**[7] 3641 10-8-10 **66**......................................(b) JackMitchell(5) 1 76
(P Mitchell) *s.i.s: hld up in rr: hdwy 2f out: drvn to ld 1f out: edgd lft u.p: styd on strly* **8/1**
2215 **2** 2 1/2 **Veiled Applause**[28] 2986 4-9-6 **74**................................ PJMcDonald(3) 6 79
(R M Beckett) *in tch: hdwy 4f out: led appr fnl 2f: hrd rdn and hdd 1f out: kpt on same pce* **11/4**[2]
/2-2 **3** 1 1/4 **Fisher Bridge (IRE)**[15] 3399 4-9-10 **75**.......................... SaleemGolam 4 78
(W R Swinburn) *lw: chsd ldrs: stdd in rr but in tch 5f out: hdwy 2f out: swtchd rt and effrt over 1f out: kpt on but nvr gng pce to trble ldng pair* **15/8**[1]
2234 **4** 1 3/4 **Augustine**[18] 3301 6-8-13 **67**......................................(b) TravisBlock(3) 5 66
(P W Hiatt) *t.k.h: hld up in rr: hdwy 5f out: chsd ldr 4f out: drvn to chal 2f out: wknd fnl f* **6/1**
66-0 **5** 3 **Pinch Of Salt (IRE)**[46] 2474 4-9-5 **73**.......................... JamesMillman(3) 3 66
(A M Balding) *t.k.h: chsd ldrs: rdn 2f out: wknd over 1f out* **14/1**
2556 **6** 1/2 **Call My Bluff (FR)**[5] 3711 4-8-11 **65**............................ PatrickHills(3) 7 57
(Rae Guest) *sn chsng ldrs: led 6f out: hdd over 2f out: wknd qckly wl over 1f out* **11/2**[3]
2000 **7** 57 **Makai**[17] 3352 4-8-2 **56** oh11..(b) TolleyDean(3) 2 —
(J J Bridger) *led to 6f out: wknd over 3f out: virtually p.u fnl 2f: t.o* **50/1**

2m 10.75s (0.51) **Going Correction** +0.15s/f (Good) **7** Ran SP% **110.9**
Speed ratings (Par 103): **103,101,100,98,96 95,50**
CSF £28.41 TOTE £8.20: £2.90, £2.00; EX 28.00.
Owner Mrs S Sheldon **Bred** Cheveley Park Stud Ltd **Trained** Epsom, Surrey
■ Stewards' Enquiry : Saleem Golam two-day ban: careless riding (Aug 5-6); two-day ban: careless riding (Aug 7-8)

FOCUS
A modest handicap, but at least the pace was decent. Even so one or two managed to find traffic problems, in the only race of the night in which the runners stayed on the far rail in the straight. The winner is rated back to last year's turf form.

3855 PANMURE GORDON LOUDWATER H'CAP 1m 14y
6:35 (6:35) (Class 4) (0-80,78) 3-Y-O+ **£6,477** (£1,927; £963; £481) **Stalls** High

Form RPR
5122 **1** **Blue Monkey (IRE)**[13] 3470 3-8-13 **76**.......................... TravisBlock(5) 3 82
(M L W Bell) *lw: trckd ldrs: qcknd to chal 1f out: drvn to ld fnl half f: readily* **9/4**[1]
5012 **2** 1/2 **Top Mark**[28] 2995 5-9-3 **74**.. HarryPoulton(7) 4 81
(J R Boyle) *sn led: styd on wl whn strly chal fnl 3f: hdd and no ex last half f* **4/1**[3]
2112 **3** 1 3/4 **Froissee**[25] 3100 3-9-6 **78**.. JimmyFortune 1 79
(N A Callaghan) *lw: chsd ldr: str chal fr 3f out: hrd drvn fr over 2f out tl outpcd ins fnl f* **11/4**[2]
2216 **4** 3/4 **The Grey One (IRE)**[12] 3487 4-9-2 **66**..........................(p) JHBowman 7 67
(J M Bradley) *chsd ldrs: rdn over 2f out: styd on same pce fr over 1f out* **8/1**
3114 **5** 1/2 **Azreme**[10] 3571 7-9-7 **71**.. SteveDrowne 5 71
(P Howling) *in rr but in tch: rdn and sme hdwy over 2f out: nvr gng pce to trble ldrs* **15/2**
2050 **6** 1 1/2 **Merrymadcap (IRE)**[12] 3487 5-9-1 **65**................................ TQuinn 2 62
(M Blanshard) *in rr: rdn 3f out: styd on fr over 1f out but nvr in contention* **14/1**
-446 **7** 1/2 **Boundless Prospect (USA)**[27] 3039 8-9-12 **76**.......... DarryllHolland 6 72
(Miss Gay Kelleway) *in rr: rdn 3f out: styd on fnl 2f but nvr in contention* **22/1**

1m 44.66s (0.71) **Going Correction** +0.15s/f (Good)
WFA 3 from 4yo+ 8lb **7** Ran SP% **111.3**
Speed ratings (Par 105): **102,101,99,99,98 97,96**
CSF £10.90 TOTE £3.30: £1.80, £2.30; EX 11.50.
Owner J A Barton And R P B Michaelson **Bred** Sweetmans Bloodstock **Trained** Newmarket, Suffolk

FOCUS
A fair little handicap in which the early pace was modest and it developed into something of a sprint, which suited those that raced handily whilst those that were dropped our never got involved. The jockeys decided to switch to the stands'-side hedge on reaching the home straight. The form looks sound enough.

3856 PANMURE GORDON CORPORATE FINANCE EBF MAIDEN STKS 7f 16y
7:05 (7:07) (Class 5) 2-Y-O **£5,181** (£1,541; £770; £384) **Stalls** High

Form RPR
2 **1** **Better Hand (IRE)**[19] 3270 2-9-3 0.................................... JHBowman 3 88+
(M R Channon) *lw: mde all: drvn along fr 2f out: styd on strly and asserted thrght fnl f* **7/4**[1]
5 **2** 2 1/2 **Jedediah**[32] 2855 2-9-3 0.. MartinDwyer 6 80
(A M Balding) *b.hind: trckd ldrs: drvn to dispute 2nd fr 2f out but nvr quite gng pce to press wnr: no imp thrght fnl f* **2/1**[2]
3 nk **McCartney (GER)** 2-9-3 0.. JoeFanning 5 79
(M Johnston) *unf: scope: in rr: gd hdwy fr 3f out to dispute 2nd 2f out: nvr quite gng pce to press wnr: one pce fnl f* **9/1**
4 3/4 **Sainglend** 2-9-3 0.. FergusSweeney 8 77
(H Candy) *w'like: cl cpld: in rr but in tch: hdwy 3f out: chsd ldrs and rdn 2f out: kpt on same pce ins fnl f* **16/1**
5 2 **Dr Faustus (IRE)** 2-9-3 0.. KerrinMcEvoy 2 72+
(Sir Michael Stoute) *str: trckd wnr: rdn over 2f out: sn hanging lft: wknd ins fnl f* **5/1**[3]
6 10 **Al Azy (IRE)** 2-9-3 0.. RHills 10 47
(J L Dunlop) *str: scope: bit bkwd: s.i.s: a in rr* **10/1**
00 **7** nk **Starfinch**[14] 3417 2-8-7 0.. TolleyDean(5) 4 41
(J J Bridger) *chsd ldrs: rdn 3f out: wknd over 2f out* **100/1**
8 3 1/2 **Peer Pressure** 2-8-10 0.. JackMitchell(7) 1 38
(P Mitchell) *neat: bit bkwd: v.s.a: a in rr* **50/1**

1m 30.53s (1.19) **Going Correction** +0.15s/f (Good) **8** Ran SP% **114.3**
Speed ratings (Par 94): **99,96,95,94,92 81,80,76**
CSF £5.45 TOTE £2.80: £1.10, £1.20, £2.40; EX 4.50.
Owner Wood Street Syndicate II **Bred** Sandro Garavelli **Trained** West Ilsley, Berks

FOCUS
This was probably quite a fair maiden as the pace was solid and the first two home were at the sharp end throughout. Once again the runners all came over to the stands' side in the home straight.

NOTEBOOK
Better Hand(IRE) ◆, so promising on his debut over course and distance earlier in the month, adopted forcing tactics once again and this time he proved far too good for his rivals with a powerful front-running display. He is bred to get further and now looks ready for a step up in class. (op 2-1)
Jedediah, down in class after finishing fifth in the Chesham on his debut, was brought through to hold every chance over the last couple of furlongs, but could never get to the winner. He almost certainly bumped into a smart rival here, but he probably needs further already and will get the chance to run over a mile fairly soon. (op 7-4)
McCartney(GER) ◆, a 90,000euros half-brother to a winner over 1m out of a winning sprinter, faced a tough task on this debut against a couple of rivals that had already shown a decent level of form, having been edgy in the paddock. However, having been given a much more patient ride than the front pair, he was produced to hold every chance against the hedge and emerged from this with plenty of credit. There is a mixture of stamina and speed in his pedigree and he should not take long in getting off the mark. (op 8-1 tchd 12-1)
Sainglend ◆, who fetched 40,000gns as a two-year-old, is a half-brother to five winners in the US including the smart Monkey Puzzle. Brought with his effort more towards the centre of the track than the principals, he never stopped trying and recorded a very promising debut, especially as he comes from a yard not renowned for rushing its juveniles. He is likely to come on for this and looks capable of winning races. (op 14-1)
Dr Faustus(IRE), a half-brother to winning juvenile Desert Flora out of a dam who is from the same family as the likes of Alleluia, Arrikala, Last Second and Alouette, ran well for a long way but just hinted at signs of greenness in the latter stages of the contest. He should have learnt plenty from this debut. (op 6-1 tchd 9-2)
Al Azy(IRE), a half-brother to a couple of decent types out of a three-time winner at up to 1m2f, was never in the race but his family have all tended to come into their own when stepped up to middle distances so he almost certainly needs more time.

3857 LORD MCGOWAN H'CAP 7f 16y
7:40 (7:40) (Class 3) (0-90,87) 3-Y-O **£7,772** (£2,312; £1,155; £577) **Stalls** High

Form RPR
-321 **1** **Shevchenko (IRE)**[51] 2312 3-8-13 **79**.................................... SebSanders 8 93+
(J Noseda) *lw: trckd ldrs: qcknd to ld wl over 1f out: c clr fnl f: easily* **7/4**[1]

1-51 **2** 2 **Perfect Star**[11] 3555 3-9-2 **82** AdamKirby 5 91
(C G Cox) *lw: chsd ldrs: rdn to go 2nd 1f out: kpt on wl but a readily hld* **4/1**[2]

-006 **3** 3 **Don't Panic (IRE)**[54] 2213 3-9-2 **82** KerrinMcEvoy 2 83
(P W Chapple-Hyam) *in tch: hdwy over 2f out: rdn to chse ldrs sn after: outpcd ins fnl f* **8/1**

-541 **4** 2 ½ **Thunderousapplause**[12] 3491 3-9-7 **87** SteveDrowne 3 81
(K A Ryan) *in rr: rdn and hdwy over 2f out: nvr gng pce to trble ldrs: wknd fnl f* **6/1**

053 **5** nk **Tudor Prince (IRE)**[16] 3380 3-9-3 **83** RichardHughes 4 76
(B J Meehan) *lw: sn led: rdn over 2f out: hdd wl over 1f out: sn btn* **5/1**[3]

-200 **6** 2 **Ravi River (IRE)**[18] 3334 3-9-2 **82** JimmyFortune 7 70
(J R Boyle) *b.hind: in rr: n.m.r after 1f: shkn up and sme hdwy 2f out: nvr in contention* **10/1**

-160 **7** 11 **All Of Me (IRE)**[30] 2943 3-8-11 **77** (b) JoeFanning 6 35
(T G Mills) *chsd ldr tl wknd 2f out: hung lft and nt run on* **20/1**

1m 29.05s (-0.29) **Going Correction** +0.15s/f (Good) **7** Ran SP% **112.3**
Speed ratings (Par 104): **107,104,101,98,98 95,83**
CSF £8.48 CT £41.67 TOTE £2.20: £1.40, £2.90; EX 8.30.
Owner M Tabor, Mrs J Magnier & D Smith **Bred** Jim Fleming **Trained** Newmarket, Suffolk

FOCUS
A funny race in that the riders did not seem to know whether they wanted to stay on the inside or come over to the stands' side in the home straight. In the event they did neither and came up the middle. This was another strongly-run race, but on this occasion the leaders may have gone off too quick as the pair responsible for the early pace ended up unplaced. The first two may well be better than therir marks and the form has been rated positively.

NOTEBOOK
Shevchenko(IRE) ◆, gelded since winning a Thirsk maiden on his most recent start - the trio that followed him home have all won since - was making his handicap debut, but despite his recent operation he took a very strong hold in the early stages. It made no difference though, as he found more than enough when asked for his effort and, with his confidence now sky-high, he looks capable of adding to this. (op 6-4 tchd 15-8 and 2-1 in places)
Perfect Star ◆, raised 3lb for her Salisbury win, had every chance down the outside but the drop in trip probably did not do her many favours and she lacked the finishing pace of the winner. She is still open to a bit more improvement and a return to further should see her winning again. (op 7-2 tchd 3-1)
Don't Panic(IRE), like the winner gelded since he was last seen, raced handily but could never really land an effective blow. He is more exposed than most, but he might just come on a bit for this first run in nearly two months. (tchd 9-1)
Thunderousapplause, raised a massive 12lb for her Chester romp in very testing conditions earlier this month, was never able to get competitive. Form shown on extremes of going is often unreliable and the Handicapper surely overreacted. (op 11-2)
Tudor Prince(IRE) gained his only win on soft ground, but he has enough form on quick ground to suggest these drying conditions would not bother him. Despite getting his own way out in front, he was rather easily brushed off and lacks the scope of a few of these. (op 8-1)
Ravi River(IRE), making his debut for his new yard, could never land a blow. The stable often finds opportunities with horses they get from other yards and there may be a race in him further down the line, but he probably needs his mark to drop a bit first. Official explanation: jockey said colt never travelled and hung left (op 12-1)
All Of Me(IRE) is yet to reproduce his Polytrack form on turf and, after showing up for much of the way, eventually dropped right out. (op 16-1)

3858 PANMURE GORDON H'CAP 1m 6f
8:10 (8:13) (Class 4) (0-85,86) 4-Y-O+ **£6,477** (£1,927; £963; £481) **Stalls** Centre

Form RPR

5162 **1** **Takafu (USA)**[39] 2675 5-9-1 **81** JamesMillman(5) 2 88
(W S Kittow) *chsd ldrs: led over 2f out r.o gamely whn chal thrght fnl f* **9/4**[1]

0024 **2** ½ **Prince Zafonic**[26] 3047 4-8-0 **66** (t) NicolPolli(5) 6 72
(Miss Gay Kelleway) *b: b.hind: chsd ldrs: rdn and styd on to press wnr ins fnl f and dispute 2nd: no ex cl home* **15/2**[3]

0250 **3** 1 **Cavallini (USA)**[16] 3385 5-8-6 **67** FergusSweeney 1 72
(G L Moore) *in tch: hdwy 3f out: rdn to dispute 2nd and press wnr 1f out: sn hung rt and fnd no ex* **9/1**

0022 **4** 1 ½ **Daring Racer (GER)**[6] 3692 4-8-4 **65** oh1 KerrinMcEvoy 8 68
(S Dow) *chsd ldr: led 5f out: hdd over 2f out: wknd ins fnl f* **8/1**

1301 **5** nk **Toparudi**[19] 3273 6-8-12 **73** JimmyQuinn 5 75
(M H Tompkins) *t.k.h: hld up towards rr: pushed along and effrt over 2f out: sn one pce and no imp on ldrs* **9/4**[1]

6100 **6** 2 **Wild Pitch**[28] 2994 6-8-10 **78** (b) JackMitchell(7) 3 77
(P Mitchell) *hld up in rr: racd alone far side and rdn 3f out: kpt on but nvr gng pce to rch ldrs* **20/1**

006- **7** 3 ½ **Michabo (IRE)**[37] 4560 6-9-9 **84** JimmyFortune 4 78
(P Bowen) *led tl hdd 5f out: wknd ins fnl 2f* **6/1**[2]

3m 9.24s (4.73) **Going Correction** +0.15s/f (Good) **7** Ran SP% **113.5**
Speed ratings (Par 105): **92,91,91,90,90 88,86**
CSF £19.96 CT £125.81 TOTE £3.20: £1.60, £4.50; EX 29.30.
Owner Midd Shire Racing **Bred** G W Humphrey Jr **Trained** Blackborough, Devon

FOCUS
Another moderately-run staying handicap at this track and that did not help a few. Again the runners came up the centre of the track starting up the home straight and it may be significant that the first three home raced closest to the stands' side. Pretty sound form.
Cavallini(USA) Official explanation: jockey said gelding hung right
Toparudi Official explanation: jockey said gelding ran too free

3859 PANMURE GMP SECURITIES H'CAP 5f 6y
8:45 (8:45) (Class 5) (0-75,75) 4-Y-O+ **£4,533** (£1,348; £674; £336) **Stalls** High

Form RPR

4134 **1** **Desert Opal**[11] 3528 7-9-5 **71** (p) PhilipRobinson 2 80
(C R Dore) *in rr: str run fr over 1f out: fin wl but hung rt bef ldng cl home* **7/2**[1]

-063 **2** ½ **Blue Aura (IRE)**[31] 2912 4-9-6 **72** (b) SebSanders 1 79
(R M Beckett) *in rr: stl plenty to do 2f out: str run fnl f: fin strly to take 2nd nr fin but nt rch wnr* **6/1**[2]

0632 **3** ½ **Don Pele (IRE)**[2] 3802 5-9-6 **75** LiamJones(3) 7 80
(R A Harris) *b: chsd ldrs: rdn 2f out: kpt on wl fnl f but nvr quite gng pce of ldng pair* **7/2**[1]

1060 **4** ½ **Blessed Place**[9] 3594 7-8-11 **63** (t) DarryllHolland 10 66
(D J S Ffrench Davis) *led: sn 4l clr: wknd ins fnl f and hdd cl home* **8/1**

1055 **5** 2 **Exponential (IRE)**[34] 2805 5-8-9 **61** SteveDrowne 6 57
(J M Bradley) *chsd ldr: rdn 2f out: no imp fnl f and wkng whn hmpd cl home* **8/1**

0545 **6** hd **Jucebabe**[16] 3368 4-8-4 **56** oh3 RichardThomas 8 51
(J L Spearing) *slowly away: bhd: rdn and hdwy over 1f out: kpt on cl home but nvr gng pce to rch ldrs* **12/1**

4540 **7** 2 **Chinalea (IRE)**[11] 3528 5-8-12 **64** (p) AdamKirby 4 52
(C G Cox) *chsd ldrs: rdn 1/2-way: wknd ins fnl f* **7/1**

0001 **8** 2 ½ **Jayanjay**[8] 3613 8-9-0 **66** 6ex TQuinn 9 45
(P Mitchell) *chsd ldrs: rdn 1/2-way: wknd fnl f* **13/2**[3]

-500 **9** ¾ **Sparkwell**[22] 3190 5-8-8 **60** JimmyQuinn 5 37
(D Shaw) *outpcd most of way* **25/1**

2-05 **10** 4 **Devine Dancer**[81] 1465 4-9-6 **72** FergusSweeney 3 34
(H Candy) *outpcd most of way* **20/1**

62.04 secs (-0.17) **Going Correction** +0.05s/f (Good) **10** Ran SP% **123.1**
Speed ratings (Par 103): **103,102,101,100,97 97,93,89,88,82**
CSF £26.13 CT £83.11 TOTE £4.30: £1.50, £1.80, £2.20; EX 14.60 Place 6 £18.98, Place 5 £4.81..
Owner Page, Ward, Marsh **Bred** Juddmonte Farms **Trained** West Pinchbeck, Lincs

FOCUS
Unusually for the sprint track here, the stalls were placed on the stands' side, but that did not stop the entire field from crossing straight over to the far rail. Blessed Place made sure this was run at a true gallop, but that played into the hands of the strong finishers such as the front pair, who in theory had furthest to travel to get across early on. Sound form, rated through the third, with the winner up 8lb.
Jucebabe Official explanation: jockey said filly missed the break
Jayanjay Official explanation: jockey said gelding never travelled
T/Plt: £36.20 to a £1 stake. Pool: £70,087.55. 1,411.30 winning tickets. T/Qpdt: £5.10 to a £1 stake. Pool: £5,266.30. 763.40 winning tickets.

3860 - 3865a (Foreign Racing) - See Raceform Interactive

3363 BATH (L-H)
Thursday, July 26

OFFICIAL GOING: Soft
Wind: Strong, against Weather: Raining

3866 RENAULT TRAFIC MEDIAN AUCTION MAIDEN STKS 5f 161y
2:20 (2:25) (Class 6) 2-Y-O **£2,072** (£616; £308; £153) **Stalls** Centre

Form RPR

0 **1** **Mesmerize Me**[10] 3589 2-9-3 0 RichardMullen 15 84
(E S McMahon) *sn prom: racd alone on stands' side tl jnd by main gp 3f out: led 2f out: drvn out* **9/2**[3]

020 **2** 1 ¼ **Meridian Line (IRE)**[12] 3550 2-8-12 0 ChrisCatlin 7 75
(J G Portman) *mid-div: rdn over 3f out: styd on to chse wnr 1f out but a hld* **4/1**[2]

55 **3** 2 ½ **Mizooka**[40] 2658 2-8-12 0 RichardHughes 16 67
(R M Beckett) *mid-div: rdn 4f out: styd on fr over 1f out: wnt 3rd ins fnl f* **7/2**[1]

5 **4** 2 **Polar Annie**[10] 3592 2-8-12 0 MickyFenton 12 61
(M S Saunders) *led: rdn and hdd 2f out: one pce after* **15/2**

0 **5** 5 **Too Grand**[7] 3687 2-8-9 0 NeilChalmers(3) 8 45
(A M Balding) *mid-div: rdn 3f out: kpt on same pce fnl 2f* **16/1**

00 **6** ½ **Amber Ridge**[20] 3283 2-9-3 0 PatDobbs 6 48
(B P J Baugh) *prom: rdn over 2f out: kpt on same pce fr over 1f out* **100/1**

7 2 **Nezami (IRE)** 2-9-3 0 SteveDrowne 4 42
(B J Meehan) *mid-div: rdn and effrt 2f out: wknd fnl f* **7/1**

0 **8** 1 ¼ **Holy Storm (IRE)**[17] 3383 2-9-3 0 VinceSlattery 5 38
(Eve Johnson Houghton) *chsd ldrs: rdn over 3f out: wknd over 1f out* **25/1**

00 **9** nk **Treacle Noir (IRE)**[3] 3796 2-8-9 0 RichardKingscote(3) 2 32
(Tom Dascombe) *prom and racd alone on far side rails: rdn 3f out: wknd 1f out* **20/1**

10 1 ¼ **Little Toto** 2-9-3 0 LPKeniry 3 33
(C G Cox) *mid-div: rdn 3f out: wknd over 1f out* **25/1**

11 7 **Marchpane** 2-8-12 0 HayleyTurner 17 —
(R M Beckett) *a towards rr* **20/1**

50 **12** 12 **La Varrosa**[15] 3424 2-8-12 0 JimmyQuinn 11 —
(Mrs P N Dutfield) *a towards rr* **66/1**

00 **13** 10 **Llab Nala**[30] 2961 2-9-3 0 (v[1]) TPO'Shea 1 —
(M R Channon) *s.i.s: a bhd* **25/1**

14 1 ¼ **Jimmy Dean** 2-9-0 0 EmmettStack(3) 10 —
(M Wellings) *s.i.s: a bhd* **100/1**

1m 18.23s (7.03) **Going Correction** +0.975s/f (Soft) **14** Ran SP% **115.1**
Speed ratings (Par 92): **92,90,87,84,77 77,74,72,72,70 61,45,31,30**
CSF £18.71 TOTE £5.70: £2.20, £2.10, £1.50; EX 27.30 Trifecta £41.50 Pool: £193.41 - 2.74 winning units..
Owner J C Fretwell **Bred** Mrs R Pease **Trained** Lichfield, Staffs
■ Blue Zenith was withdrawn (12/1, unruly at start). Deduct 5p in the £ under Rule 4.

FOCUS
Just an ordinary juvenile maiden. The field came stands' side the home straight and the form is rated through the second.

NOTEBOOK
Mesmerize Me, seventh at Windsor on his debut ten days previously, broke much better this time and had clearly learned from his previous experience. He was in the right place when the field came stands' side in the home straight, and grabbing the rail helped his cause, but he could still have been called the winner shortly after hitting the front. This much softer ground was evidently to his liking, as was the greater emphasis on stamina. (op 4-1 tchd 5-1)
Meridian Line(IRE) gave her all in defeat on this drop back in class and finished a clear second best. She helps to set the level of this form and may be better off in nurseries.
Mizooka, well backed, took too long to find her full stride and left the impression a more prominent ride would have seen her to slightly better effect. She also looks to need all of 6f now. (op 9-2)
Polar Annie showed the benefit of her Windsor debut experience and showed decent early pace this time. She was not as happy on this much easier ground however, and remains capable of winning one of these when reverting to a sounder surface. (op 6-1)
Too Grand ran close to the level of her Sandown debut and looks to need more time. (op 20-1)

3867 A.K.S. YEOVIL/E.B.F. NOVICE STKS 5f 11y
2:55 (2:57) (Class 5) 2-Y-O **£3,886** (£1,156; £577) **Stalls** Centre

Form RPR

61 **1** **Sailor At Sea (USA)**[7] 3687 2-9-2 0 RichardHughes 2 87+
(R Charlton) *trckd ldng pair: led ins fnl f: pushed clr* **4/6**[1]

002 **2** 3 ½ **Barraland**[5] 3734 2-9-5 0 TPO'Shea 3 73
(M R Channon) *prom: rdn over 2f out: led over 1f out: hdd ins fnl f: no ex* **11/2**[2]

000 **3** 37 **Pennyspider (IRE)**[17] 3363 2-8-7 0 MickyFenton 5 —
(M S Saunders) *wnt rt s: led: rdn and hdd over 1f out: wknd qckly* **33/1**[3]

68.22 secs (5.72) **Going Correction** +0.975s/f (Soft) **3** Ran SP% **78.3**
Speed ratings (Par 94): **93,87,28**
CSF £1.52 TOTE £1.20; EX 1.40.
Owner K Abdulla **Bred** Juddmonte Farms Inc **Trained** Beckhampton, Wilts
■ Secret Asset was withdrawn (5/2, refused to enter stalls). Deduct 25p in the £ under Rule 4.

FOCUS
No strength in depth here, but the progressive winner did the job easily and should rate much higher.

NOTEBOOK
Sailor At Sea(USA) ◆, comfortably off the mark at Sandown a week previously, followed with a similarly ready effort and had no trouble with the softer ground. He is clearly learning fast, evidently handles most ground, and should be rated value for at least double his winning margin. Another furlong should also be within his compass and it would be no surprise to see him upped to Listed company after this. (op 4-7)
Barraland did nothing wrong in defeat, but he was a sitting duck for the winner throughout and is flattered by his proximity to that rival at the finish. He goes some way to helping set the level of this form and would have probably found this ground plenty soft enough. (op 13-2 tchd 15-2)
Pennyspider(IRE) was predictably outclassed and looked uneasy on the deep surface. She will be much better off in low-grade nuseries, especially when faced with fast ground. Official explanation: jockey said filly lost its action

3868 BRIDGES MOTOR GROUP (S) STKS — 1m 2f 46y
3:30 (3:30) (Class 6) 4-Y-0+ — **£1,943** (£578; £288; £144) **Stalls** Low

Form — RPR
4406 **1** **Orpen Quest (IRE)**[10] 3595 5-9-3 43 ... AlanDaly 6 — 56
(M J Attwater) *trckd ldrs: rdn over 2f out: styd on to ld jst ins fnl f: rdn out* **12/1**
-060 **2** *2* **Grand Sefton**[5] 3732 4-9-3 52 ...(t) HayleyTurner 8 — 52
(Stef Liddiard) *stdd s: bhd: stdy prog fr 3f out: rdn 2f out: styd on ins fnl f: wnt 2nd nr fin* **25/1**
100- **3** *nk* **Miss Porcia**[211] 6955 6-8-5 52 ... ManavNem(7) 13 — 46
(P A Blockley) *plld hrd: trckd ldrs: outpcd over 2f out: styd on fr over 1f out: chsd wnr ins fnl f: lost 2nd nr fin* **9/1**[3]
3506 **4** *2 1/2* **Kilmeena Magic**[5] 3730 5-8-12 41 ... PatDobbs 15 — 41
(J C Fox) *trckd ldrs: rdn and effrt fr 2f out: kpt on same pce fnl f* **9/1**[3]
5633 **5** *hd* **Desert Lightning (IRE)**[9] 3629 5-9-3 52 ... LeeEnstone 2 — 46
(I W McInnes) *mid-div: hdwy 3f out: sn rdn: ch ent fnl f: no ex* **7/2**[1]
0005 **6** *1 1/4* **Marbaa (IRE)**[5] 3730 4-9-3 52 ...(v[1]) JimmyQuinn 3 — 44
(S Dow) *sn led: rdn 2f out: hdd jst ins fnl f: fdd* **15/2**[2]
0-00 **7** *5* **Sparkbridge (IRE)**[13] 3487 4-9-3 45 ...(b) FrankieMcDonald 5 — 34
(S C Burrough) *towards rr: rdn 3f out: styd on fr over 1f out: nvr trbld ldrs* **80/1**
350 **8** *nk* **Fire At Will**[15] 3428 5-9-3 40 ...(b[1]) RichardThomas 11 — 33
(A W Carroll) *s.i.s: sn mid-div: rdn and hdwy fr over 2f out: wknd fnl f* **20/1**
0235 **9** *1 1/2* **Savoy Chapel**[15] 3428 5-9-3 42 ...(v) JamesDoyle 17 — 30
(A W Carroll) *mid-div tl 3f out* **16/1**
0000 **10** *1 1/4* **Yenaled**[26] 3083 10-9-3 47 ... SamHitchcott 16 — 27
(J M Bradley) *nvr bttr than mid-div* **20/1**
4465 **11** *5* **Piano Man**[9] 3616 5-9-3 55 ...(b) VinceSlattery 10 — 17
(B G Powell) *dwlt: a towards rr* **7/2**[1]
6-64 **12** *2* **Franky'N'Jonny**[23] 3175 4-8-9 38 ...(p) EmmettStack(3) 4 — 8
(M J Attwater) *slowly away: steadily rcvrd to trck ldrs after 2f: rdn over 2f out: wknd over 1f out* **33/1**
005 **13** *2* **Katie Lawson (IRE)**[57] 2142 4-8-12 51 ...(p) DavidKinsella 14 — 4
(D Haydn Jones) *in tch: rdn 3f out: sn wknd* **15/2**[2]
0000 **14** *34* **Mustard Benn**[30] 2962 4-9-3 37 ... RichardMullen 9 — —
(Mouse Hamilton-Fairley) *s.i.s: sn mid-div: bhd fnl 4f* **100/1**
2m 22.8s (11.80) **Going Correction** +1.125s/f (Soft) — **14** Ran SP% **120.1**
Speed ratings (Par 101): **97,95,95,93,93 92,88,87,86,85 81,79,78,51**
CSF £291.46 TOTE £16.60: £4.30, £9.10, £3.00; EX 290.80 TRIFECTA Not won..The winner was bought in for 5,000gns.
Owner Mrs J Osbaldeston **Bred** Pursuit Of Truth Syndicate **Trained** Epsom, Surrey

FOCUS
A typically weak seller rated through the winner.
Piano Man Official explanation: jockey said gelding missed the break

3869 CITY MOTORS AND S.J. COOK & SONS CLAIMING STKS — 5f 11y
4:05 (4:11) (Class 6) 3-Y-0+ — **£2,072** (£616; £308; £153) **Stalls** Centre

Form — RPR
1100 **1** **No Worries Yet (IRE)**[17] 3369 3-8-12 64 ... JimmyQuinn 11 — 60
(J L Spearing) *prom: rdn to ld 2f out: kpt on gamely: drvn out* **13/2**[2]
3046 **2** *3/4* **Seven No Trumps**[12] 3535 10-9-1 51 ... SteveDrowne 6 — 57
(J M Bradley) *mid-div: rdn and hdwy over 2f out: chsd wnr over 1f out: kpt on* **11/1**
0-50 **3** *1 1/4* **Peruvian Style (IRE)**[17] 3368 6-9-2 50 ... RichardKingscote(3) 2 — 56
(J M Bradley) *trckd ldrs: rdn over 2f out: kpt on ins fnl f* **22/1**
0620 **4** *nk* **Eastern Princess**[31] 2948 3-8-2 49 ...(v) DavidKinsella 7 — 41
(J A Geake) *prom: led 3f out: rdn and hdd 2f out: no ex ins fnl f* **25/1**
0115 **5** *hd* **Mafaheem**[4] 3762 5-9-7 70 ... StephenDonohoe 13 — 56
(P D Evans) *s.i.s: sn pushed along in rr: rdn wl over 2f out: styd on fr over 1f out: nrst fin* **11/8**[1]
0-50 **6** *1 1/2* **Montemayorprincess (IRE)**[31] 2950 3-8-2 50 ... HayleyTurner 4 — 35
(D Haydn Jones) *chsd ldrs: rdn 3f out: kpt on same pce fnl 2f* **33/1**
0006 **7** *1* **Westbrook Blue**[1] 3837 5-9-9 65 ...(t) AmirQuinn 15 — 49
(W G M Turner) *mid-div: nt clr run briefly wl over 1f out: sn rdn: styd on* **8/1**
2000 **8** *1 1/4* **Devon Flame**[96] 1165 8-8-13 59 ... OscarUrbina 12 — 35
(R J Hodges) *nvr bttr than mid-div* **8/1**
0035 **9** *1/2* **Mine The Balance (IRE)**[9] 3619 4-8-10 49 ... ThomasO'Brien(7) 5 — 37
(H J Manners) *a mid-div* **50/1**
064 **10** *2 1/2* **King Egbert (FR)**[22] 3203 6-9-3 50 ... TolleyDean(5) 9 — 33
(R J Price) *s.i.s: a towards rr* **7/1**[3]
0320 **11** *9* **Luloah**[17] 3368 4-9-4 49 ...(p) ChrisCatlin 16 — —
(J G M O'Shea) *prom: rdn over 2f out: sn wknd* **14/1**
-000 **12** *15* **Auction Oasis**[40] 2652 3-8-6 50 ... TPO'Shea 17 — —
(B Palling) *led tl 3f out: sn wknd* **50/1**
66.85 secs (4.35) **Going Correction** +0.975s/f (Soft)
WFA 3 from 4yo+ 4lb — **12** Ran SP% **120.2**
Speed ratings (Par 101): **104,102,100,100,100 97,96,94,93,89 74,50**
CSF £72.41 TOTE £6.40: £1.90, £2.70, £7.80; EX 47.90 Trifecta £191.50 Pool: £291.32 - 1.08 winning units..Eastern Princess was claimed by Paul Morrison for £3,000. No Worries Yet was the subject of a friendly claim.
Owner J Spearing **Bred** Mark Donohoe **Trained** Kinnersley, Worcs

FOCUS
This claimer was run at a fair pace and the form looks sound enough for the class.
Westbrook Blue Official explanation: jockey said horse was denied a clear run
King Egbert(FR) Official explanation: jockey said gelding missed the break
Luloah Official explanation: vet said filly returned lame

3870 PLATINUM GROUP H'CAP — 5f 11y
4:40 (4:40) (Class 5) (0-70,70) 3-Y-0 — **£3,044** (£905; £452; £226) **Stalls** Centre

Form — RPR
0164 **1** **Mr Forthright**[17] 3369 3-8-7 56 ow1 ... SteveDrowne 8 — 56
(J M Bradley) *chsd ldng trio: rdn wl over 2f out: r.o u.p ins fnl f: tk narrow advantage towards fin* **10/3**[3]
3054 **2** *shd* **Fly Time**[20] 3281 3-8-2 51 oh3 ... ChrisCatlin 4 — 51
(Mrs L Williamson) *chsd ldng pair: rdn wl over 2f out: r.o w wnr and ev ch ins fnl f: jst hld* **11/1**
1053 **3** *hd* **Game Lady**[21] 3237 3-9-6 69 ... JamesDoyle 9 — 68
(I A Wood) *w ldr: rdn to chal 2f out: tk narrow advantage ent fnl f: ct nr fin* **3/1**[2]
3122 **4** *1 1/2* **Ocean Blaze**[20] 3277 3-9-1 69 ... JamesMillman(5) 3 — 63
(B R Millman) *stmbld leaving stalls: sn led: rdn wl over 1f out: hdd ent fnl f: no ex* **11/10**[1]
1640 **5** *3* **Totally Free**[6] 3713 3-8-11 60 ...(v) HayleyTurner 6 — 43
(M D I Usher) *sn struggling bhd ldrs: rdn 3f out: no imp* **14/1**
69.01 secs (6.51) **Going Correction** +0.975s/f (Soft) — **5** Ran SP% **110.7**
Speed ratings (Par 100): **86,85,85,83,78**
CSF £33.39 TOTE £4.10: £1.50, £3.80; EX 39.90 Trifecta £51.60 Pool: £201.52 - 2.77 winning units..
Owner E A Hayward **Bred** C D Shore **Trained** Sedbury, Gloucs

FOCUS
A moderate handicap, run at a strong early pace. The first three were bunched at the finish and form looks somewhat suspect.
Ocean Blaze Official explanation: jockey said filly hung right-handed

3871 RENAULT MASTER FILLIES' H'CAP — 1m 2f 46y
5:10 (5:10) (Class 5) (0-70,69) 3-Y-0 — **£3,044** (£905; £452; £226) **Stalls** Low

Form — RPR
4301 **1** **Gib (IRE)**[8] 3652 3-9-6 68 6ex ... ChrisCatlin 9 — 72
(B W Hills) *led: rdn and hrd pressed fr 2f out: hdd ins fnl f: rallied gamely to regain ld fnl strides* **2/1**[1]
0250 **2** *hd* **Sweet Request**[15] 3427 3-8-7 58 ... RichardKingscote(3) 6 — 62
(R M Beckett) *trckd ldrs: drvn to chal 2f out: tk narrow advantage ins fnl f: hdd fnl strides* **5/1**[2]
4001 **3** *4* **Giddywell**[6] 3714 3-8-8 61 6ex ... RussellKennemore(5) 7 — 57
(R Hollinshead) *trckd ldr: rdn to chal over 2f out: kpt on same pce fr over 1f out* **5/1**[2]
00 **4** *3/4* **Palanoverre (IRE)**[15] 3421 3-8-4 59 ...(t) BillyCray(7) 8 — 54
(D J S Ffrench Davis) *trckd ldr: rdn 3f out: sn drifted lft to centre of crse: kpt on same pce* **22/1**
0636 **5** *1 1/2* **Piano Key**[9] 3611 3-8-2 50 oh3 ... HayleyTurner 1 — 42
(M D I Usher) *trckd ldr: rdn over 2f out: kpt on same pce fr over 1f out* **14/1**[3]
0-01 **6** *shd* **Miss Marvellous (USA)**[21] 3244 3-9-7 69 ... OscarUrbina 3 — 60
(J R Fanshawe) *hld up: hdwy 3f out: effrt 2f out: wknd fnl f* **2/1**[1]
0000 **7** *33* **Tizzydore (IRE)**[29] 2978 3-8-2 50 oh5 ... FrankieMcDonald 5 — —
(A G Newcombe) *hld up: rdn 3f out: sn wknd: t.o fnl 2f* **40/1**
2m 21.37s (10.37) **Going Correction** +1.125s/f (Soft) — **7** Ran SP% **113.5**
Speed ratings (Par 97): **103,102,99,99,97 97,71**
CSF £12.51 CT £42.65 TOTE £2.50: £1.70, £2.90; EX 15.70 Trifecta £77.10 Pool: £229.37 - 2.11 winning units. Place 6 £568.24, Place 5 £390.38.
Owner Jeremy Gompertz & Patrick Milmo **Bred** Denis Brosnan & Patsy Byrne **Trained** Lambourn, Berks

FOCUS
A moderate fillies' handicap which saw the first pair come clear but the form is limited.
T/Jkpt: Not won. T/Plt: £979.80 to a £1 stake. Pool: £59,531.95. 44.35 winning tickets. T/Qpdt: £291.30 to a £1 stake. Pool: £2,677.20. 6.80 winning tickets. TM

3667 FOLKESTONE (R-H)
Thursday, July 26

OFFICIAL GOING: Good to soft (good in places; 7.4)
Wind: Gale Force, half behind Weather: Overcast; heavy shower race 4

3872 FOLKESTONE-RACECOURSE.CO.UK APPRENTICE H'CAP — 6f
6:10 (6:10) (Class 5) (0-70,70) 3-Y-0 — **£2,914** (£867; £433; £216) **Stalls** Low

Form — RPR
0524 **1** **Nouveau (GER)**[8] 3644 3-8-4 55 ... HaddenFrost(5) 4 — 70
(R Hannon) *prom nr side: led wl over 2f out: clr over 1f out: rdn out* **5/2**[2]
1 **2** *3* **Expensive Art (IRE)**[8] 3649 3-8-12 63 6ex ... KirstyMilczarek(5) 2 — 68
(N A Callaghan) *rrd and s.s: racd nr side: prog fr rr 1/2-way: chsd wnr over 1f out: no imp* **11/8**[1]
-224 **3** *2 1/2* **Hucking Hope (IRE)**[26] 3087 3-9-7 67 ... StephaneBreux 9 — 64
(J R Best) *chsd rival far side: rdn to ld pair over 2f out: nt on terms w nr side ldrs after* **6/1**[3]
6314 **4** *1* **Exit Strategy (IRE)**[6] 3713 3-9-9 69 ...(b) LiamJones 8 — 63
(R A Harris) *led far side pair to over 2f out: one pce* **6/1**[3]
024 **5** *3* **Wells Of Badr (IRE)**[27] 3051 3-9-5 70 ... MCGeran(5) 1 — 54
(P W Chapple-Hyam) *dwlt: chsd nr side ldrs: rdn over 2f out: sn btn* **14/1**
-000 **6** *3 1/2* **Spirit Rising**[46] 2489 3-8-5 51 oh6 ... GregFairley 7 — 24
(J M Bradley) *prom nr side over 3f: sn wknd* **66/1**
6-05 **7** *hd* **Ishimagic**[18] 3353 3-8-2 51 oh3 ... NicolPolli(3) 5 — 23
(J J Bridger) *led nr side gp to wl over 2f out: edgd rt and wknd* **40/1**
0-00 **8** *4* **Victory Spirit**[51] 2335 3-9-0 65 ... KMay(5) 6 — 25
(H J L Dunlop) *chsd nr side ldrs: rdn wl over 2f out: sn edgd rt and wknd* **16/1**
1m 11.22s (-2.38) **Going Correction** -0.40s/f (Firm) — **8** Ran SP% **115.7**
Speed ratings (Par 100): **99,95,91,90,86 81,81,76**
CSF £6.39 CT £17.17 TOTE £3.20: £1.20, £1.20, £1.60; EX 10.70.
Owner Jenny Powell & Sue Jensen **Bred** W Bischoff **Trained** East Everleigh, Wilts

FOCUS
A moderate apprentice handicap run in a similar time to the following seller over the same trip with the first two unexposed and likely to go on from this. The main group stuck to the stands' side, although the two who went to the far rail finished third and fourth.

3873 INVICTA MOTORS (S) STKS — 6f
6:40 (6:40) (Class 6) 3-Y-0+ — **£2,388** (£705; £352) **Stalls** Low

Form — RPR
0654 **1** **Burford Lass (IRE)**[16] 3393 4-8-9 54 ... RobertHavlin 3 — 58
(D K Ivory) *chsd nr side ldrs: prog to go 2nd wl over 1f out: rdn to ld jst ins fnl f: styd on wl* **9/2**[2]

5002 **2** 1 1/2 **Calloff The Search**[35] 2798 3-8-9 53 (v) SaleemGolam 11 57
(W G M Turner) *pressed nr side ldr: led over 2f out: drvn and hdd jst ins fnl f: one pce* **14/1**

40-0 **3** 1/2 **The Crooked Ring**[20] 3285 5-9-0 56 AdamKirby 1 57
(A G Newcombe) *chsd nr side ldrs: reminder 1/2-way: rdn and kpt on same pce against rail fnl 2f* **11/1**

4650 **4** 1 **Ocean Gift**[38] 2725 5-9-0 64 JamieSpencer 2 54
(P D Evans) *hld up in rr nr side: rdn and prog 2f out: chsd ldrs 1f out: no imp after* **6/4**[1]

0040 **5** 3 **Lizarazu (GER)**[18] 3352 8-8-11 51 (p) LiamJones(3) 10 45
(R A Harris) *hld up in last trio nr side: effrt over 2f out: hrd rdn and modest prog over 1f out: nvr on terms* **8/1**

00-0 **6** 3/4 **Von Wessex**[24] 3169 5-8-7 42 JamieHamblett(7) 9 43
(W G M Turner) *w nr side ldrs over 3f: fdd* **50/1**

-030 **7** 1/2 **Jalamid (IRE)**[27] 3056 5-9-0 68 (t) SebSanders 7 42
(G C Bravery) *settled in last trio nr side: shkn up over 2f out: plugged on one pce: no ch* **6/1**[3]

0300 **8** 1 3/4 **Banana Belle**[6] 3708 3-7-13 45 NicolPolli(5) 13 30
(J Ryan) *led far side pair and clr of rival: no ch w nr side gp fnl 2f* **28/1**

546- **9** 1 1/4 **Gaudalpin (IRE)**[210] 6962 5-8-9 42 (v[1]) PaulEddery 6 28
(J McAuley) *led nr side gp to over 2f out: sn wknd* **33/1**

3030 **10** 3 **Sham Ruby**[43] 2556 5-8-5 46 ow3 (t) HaddenFrost(7) 8 22
(M R Bosley) *stdd s: trckd nr side ldrs on outer: wknd 2f out* **20/1**

0-00 **11** 7 **For Eileen**[14] 3455 3-7-11 45 (t) MCGeran(7) 14 —
(G C H Chung) *sn lft bhd by far side rival* **40/1**

0505 **12** 1 1/4 **Full Spate**[40] 2652 12-8-11 47 GregFairley(3) 5 —
(J M Bradley) *s.v.s and swvd rt: a last of nr side gp: bhd fr 1/2-way* **20/1**

1m 11.42s (-2.18) **Going Correction** -0.40s/f (Firm)
WFA 3 from 4yo+ 5lb **12** Ran SP% **118.9**
Speed ratings (Par 101): **98,96,95,94,90 89,88,86,84,80 71,69**
CSF £58.57 TOTE £5.80: £1.70, £2.90, £3.00; EX 52.60.There was no bid for the winner. Ocean Gift was claimed by Nigel Tinkler for £6,000.
Owner Martin Bourke and Kevin Forde **Bred** Peter Mooney **Trained** Radlett, Herts

FOCUS
A moderate seller run in a slightly faster time than the opening handicap and the form is sound despite the winner being below par. Two went to the far side but were well beaten and the first four came clear.

3874 EUROPEAN BREEDERS' FUND MAIDEN FILLIES' STKS 7f (S)
7:10 (7:12) (Class 5) 2-Y-O **£4,210** (£939; £939; £312) **Stalls** Low

Form RPR

05 **1** **Night Skier (IRE)**[47] 2457 2-9-0 0 IanMongan 4 80+
(J L Dunlop) *racd against nr side rail: trckd ldrs: wnt 2nd 2f out: shkn up to ld jst over 1f out: sn clr* **14/1**

0 **2** 5 **Izzibizzi**[13] 3507 2-9-0 0 JamieSpencer 3 67
(E A L Dunlop) *led: gng strly over 2f out: edgd rt and hdd jst over 1f out: no ch w wnr* **9/2**[3]

2 dht **Winter Bloom (USA)** 2-9-0 0 RichardHughes 9 67+
(H R A Cecil) *trckd ldrs: shkn up over 2f out: outpcd over 1f out: kpt on fnl f* **7/2**[2]

62 **4** 3/4 **Altitude**[14] 3453 2-9-0 0 SebSanders 12 65
(Sir Mark Prescott) *pressed ldrs: pushed along 1/2-way: rdn and one pce fr over 2f out* **11/8**[1]

50 **5** 1 1/2 **Tina's Best (IRE)**[13] 3479 2-8-7 0 HaddenFrost(7) 14 61
(R Hannon) *racd on wd outside: sn chsng ldrs: rdn over 2f out: one pce after* **16/1**

6 1 3/4 **Lyrical Symphony** 2-9-0 0 PaulEddery 1 57
(W J Knight) *off the pce towards rr: shkn up and rchd midfield 3f out: plugged on but n.d* **20/1**

7 2 **In A Pickle** 2-9-0 0 PhilipRobinson 10 52
(H J L Dunlop) *dwlt: wl off the pce: detached in last trio 1/2-way: styng on steadily whn rn green over 1f out: kpt on: bttr for experience* **40/1**

8 hd **Khibraat** 2-9-0 0 AdamKirby 2 52
(E A L Dunlop) *dwlt: last early: rchd rr of main gp after 3f: shkn up over 2f out: kpt on one pce* **25/1**

0 **9** 2 1/2 **Starfala**[36] 2768 2-9-0 0 TQuinn 11 45
(P F I Cole) *nvr on terms w ldrs: struggling 3f out: eased fnl f* **16/1**

00 **10** 1 **Lady Bower**[22] 3213 2-8-11 0 GregFairley(3) 8 43
(M Johnston) *chsd ldr to 2f out: wknd* **33/1**

4 **11** 2 **Janet's Delight**[21] 3238 2-9-0 0 RobertHavlin 6 38
(S Curran) *nvr bttr than midfield: tried to cl on ldrs 3f out: wknd over 1f out* **40/1**

05 **12** 3 1/2 **Spectrana**[14] 3446 2-9-0 0 JimCrowley 7 29
(Mrs A J Perrett) *chsd ldrs tl wknd 3f out* **22/1**

0 **13** 2 **Miss Cruisecontrol**[8] 3643 2-8-11 0 StephaneBreux(3) 13 24
(J R Best) *dwlt: a in last trio: wl bhd fr 1/2-way* **66/1**

14 16 **Modhana (IRE)** 2-8-11 0 JerryO'Dwyer(3) 5 —
(M G Quinlan) *sn struggling: t.o* **66/1**

1m 26.46s (-1.44) **Going Correction** -0.40s/f (Firm) **14** Ran SP% **124.7**
Speed ratings (Par 91): **92,86,86,85,83 81,79,79,76,75 72,68,66,48**
PL: Night Skier £3.00, Izzibizzi £2.00, Winter Bloom £2.00; EX: Izzibizzi £36.10, Winter Bloom £37.60; CSF: Izzibizzi £36.58; Winter Bloom £30.19 TOTE £14.50.
Owner Windflower Overseas Holdings Inc **Bred** Windflower Overseas Holdings Inc **Trained** Arundel, W Sussex

FOCUS
An interesting maiden with some nicely bred sorts from major yards, but a surprise winner. The field all raced on the stands' side and the time was nearly a second faster than the following handicap for three-year-olds.

NOTEBOOK
Night Skier(IRE), who had shown a measure of promise in two outings over 6f on fast ground, appreciated the longer trip and handled the ground really well to score in fine style. She should get further in time but this clear-cut success could mean she will not get a favourable handicap mark.
Izzibizzi, who is bred to get middle-distances at least, built on her debut effort under a positive ride but was brushed aside by the winner in the closing stages. (op 11-4)
Winter Bloom(USA) ◆, a half-sister to Phoenix Tower and from the family of Day Flight, showed promise on this debut having taken a while to comprehend what was required. She should be better for the experience and looks capable of winning a maiden at least. (op 11-4)
Altitude, a well-bred filly, had shown promise in two maidens on Polytrack. However, she looked ill-at-ease on this soft ground on her turf debut and received a reminder before halfway. She did keep on to get involved before being left behind by the winner in the closing stages. She should not be written off as, being by Green Desert, she may be far happier on a sound surface. (op 15-8 tchd 2-1 and 9-4 in a place)
Tina's Best(IRE) ◆, had shown signs of ability in two runs and showed why she had been backed on her debut with this effort. She ran really well from the highest stall and forced to race on the outside of her field, only fading late on. She now qualifies for a handicap mark and is one to watch out for in that sphere.
Lyrical Symphony, a 50,000gns first foal who is related to several decent performers, never really got into contention but hinted at ability and the experience should bring her on. (op 16-1 tchd 22-1)
In A Pickle, a cheaply-bought first foal, has plenty of winners in her family and showed promise on this debut without getting seriously involved. (op 33-1)
Khibraat is bred to appreciate middle-distances in time and was clearly unfancied on this debut. She should come on for the outing. (tchd 22-1)

3875 BET NOW AT WBX.COM H'CAP 7f (S)
7:40 (7:41) (Class 6) (0-65,65) 3-Y-O **£2,388** (£705; £352) **Stalls** Low

Form RPR

62 **1** **Dressed To Dance (IRE)**[10] 3583 3-9-7 65 (v) SebSanders 2 71
(N Tinkler) *settled wl in rr: prog over 2f out: rdn and jinked over 1f out: drvn and styd on to ld nr fin* **2/1**[1]

0404 **2** hd **Goose Green (IRE)**[9] 3620 3-9-5 63 GeorgeBaker 10 68
(R J Hodges) *trckd ldrs: smooth prog over 2f out: led wl over 1f out: drvn fnl f: hdd last strides* **8/1**

0252 **3** 2 **Just Oscar (GER)**[13] 3491 3-9-4 62 JamieSpencer 3 62
(W M Brisbourne) *hld up and last early: plenty to do over 2f out: swtchd and gd prog to press ldng pair over 1f out: rdn and fnd nil* **9/2**[2]

0160 **4** 8 **Dance Of Dreams**[113] 931 3-9-2 60 IanMongan 8 38
(N P Littmoden) *wl in rr: pushed along 1/2-way: n.d after: passed wkng rivals fr over 1f out* **14/1**

-320 **5** 1/2 **Beat The Bully**[18] 3342 3-9-1 59 (b) AdamKirby 4 36
(I A Wood) *dwlt: rousted along and sn ld: hdd & wknd wl over 1f out* **16/1**

6000 **6** 2 **Becharm**[34] 2834 3-9-1 59 FergusSweeney 7 30
(A G Newcombe) *pressed ldng pair to over 2f out: wknd* **9/2**[2]

0050 **7** 2 1/2 **Royal Guest**[9] 3622 3-9-0 58 JHBowman 6 23
(M R Channon) *chsd ldr to over 2f out: wknd* **6/1**[3]

-300 **8** 1 1/4 **Rumbled**[12] 3525 3-9-6 64 (v[1]) RobertHavlin 12 25
(J A Geake) *chsd ldrs: u.p and losing pl 1/2-way: sn btn* **25/1**

0-00 **9** 8 **Sunley Gift**[34] 2837 3-9-7 65 TQuinn 14 5
(B G Powell) *chsd ldrs on outer over 4f: wknd rapidly* **33/1**

5-50 **10** 23 **Danehill Kikin (IRE)**[56] 2173 3-9-1 59 MartinDwyer 1 —
(B W Hills) *rdn and wknd after 3f: sn t.o* **14/1**

1m 27.43s (-0.47) **Going Correction** -0.40s/f (Firm) **10** Ran SP% **121.1**
Speed ratings (Par 98): **86,85,83,74,73 71,68,67,58,31**
CSF £19.98 CT £69.75 TOTE £2.50: £1.80, £3.20, £1.30; EX 26.70.
Owner W K Syndicate **Bred** J Doyle **Trained** Langton, N Yorks

FOCUS
A modest handicap run in a very moderate time, nearly a second slower than the preceding fillies' maiden and the form is ordinary. The field all stayed on the stands' side and the first three came clear.
Just Oscar(GER) Official explanation: jockey said gelding hung badly right
Sunley Gift Official explanation: jockey said filly slipped on leaving stalls

3876 WBX.COM WORLD BET EXCHANGE H'CAP 1m 4f
8:10 (8:10) (Class 6) (0-65,65) 3-Y-O **£2,388** (£705; £352) **Stalls** Low

Form RPR

4060 **1** **President Dan**[35] 2801 3-8-8 52 PaulDoe 5 59
(M R Channon) *towards rr: reminder over 6f out: prog and prom 5f out: outpcd 3f out: drvn and styd on to ld jst over 1f out: hld on* **33/1**

1303 **2** nk **Lapina (IRE)**[26] 3082 3-9-2 60 (b) IanMongan 1 67
(Pat Eddery) *hld up in rr: prog on outer over 3f out: drvn to ld 2f out and racd awkwardly in front: hdd jst over 1f out: kpt on but a hld* **8/1**

00-5 **3** 1 **Franchoek (IRE)**[17] 3367 3-8-12 56 AdamKirby 10 61+
(A King) *settled bhd ldrs: trapped on inner over 3f out: outpcd wl over 2f out: effrt to cl over 1f out: nt quite able to chal* **11/4**[1]

-633 **4** 5 **Pairumani Princess (IRE)**[15] 3427 3-9-5 63 JamieSpencer 6 60
(E A L Dunlop) *hld up in rr: prog over 3f out: sn drvn: chsd ldng pair over 1f out: wknd fnl f* **5/1**[2]

0042 **5** 3 1/2 **Western Point (IRE)**[14] 3456 3-8-13 57 SebSanders 4 49
(Sir Mark Prescott) *pressed ldr: carried wd bnd after 2f: reminder over 5f out: drvn to ld over 3f out: hdd & wknd 2f out* **5/1**[2]

5143 **6** 12 **Cavendish**[9] 3624 3-9-4 62 (b) RichardHughes 2 35
(J M P Eustace) *trckd ldrs tl wknd over 2f out* **15/2**

000 **7** 3 1/2 **Almahaza (IRE)**[52] 2320 3-8-12 56 (b[1]) TQuinn 9 23
(Mrs A J Perrett) *led: rn wd bnd after 2f: hdd over 3f out: wknd* **20/1**

0-00 **8** 3 1/2 **On Watch**[29] 2981 3-9-2 60 FergusSweeney 12 21
(H Candy) *a in rr: struggling fr 4f out* **25/1**

6056 **9** 11 **Hayward's Heath**[17] 3367 3-8-11 55 PaulFitzsimons 7 —
(B W Duke) *a in rr: t.o over 3f out* **20/1**

0-06 **10** 1/2 **Like To Golf (USA)**[8] 3652 3-8-13 57 (b[1]) JimCrowley 8 —
(Mrs A J Perrett) *prom: carried wd bnd after 2f: wknd rapidly 4f out* **25/1**

3021 **U** **Chant De Guerre (USA)**[15] 3428 3-8-7 58 JackMitchell(7) 11 —
(P Mitchell) *sn in rr: rdn and effrt over 3f out: 8th and trying to cl on ldrs whn stmbld and uns rdr wl over 2f out* **6/1**[3]

-504 **P** **Restless Soul**[8] 3652 3-8-8 52 MartinDwyer 3 —
(C A Cyzer) *v restless in stalls: s.s: immediately t.o: p.u 3f out* **14/1**

2m 41.96s (1.46) **Going Correction** +0.175s/f (Good) **12** Ran SP% **124.0**
Speed ratings (Par 98): **102,101,101,97,95 87,85,82,75,75 —,—**
CSF £273.28 CT £989.22 TOTE £42.50: £6.20, £3.20, £1.60; EX 569.90.
Owner N Martin **Bred** W And R Barnett Ltd **Trained** West Ilsley, Berks

FOCUS
A moderate handicap but quite a rough race with a couple of hard-luck stories and a surprise winner. Despite that the form is rated slightly positively.
Lapina(IRE) Official explanation: jockey said filly hung both ways
Almahaza(IRE) Official explanation: jockey said colt ran too free and hung left on 1st bend
Hayward's Heath Official explanation: trainer said filly coughed post-race and was found to have a temperature
Restless Soul Official explanation: vet said filly cut both hind legs; jockey said filly got upset in stalls

3877 BOOK TICKETS ONLINE FOR DISCOUNTED PRICES H'CAP 1m 1f 149y
8:40 (8:40) (Class 4) (0-85,85) 3-Y-O **£4,857** (£1,445; £722; £360) **Stalls** Low

Form RPR

1333 **1** **Monte Alto (IRE)**[19] 3335 3-9-1 79 JamieSpencer 5 86+
(L M Cumani) *hld up in last trio: gd prog on inner 2f out: dream run through to ld jst ins fnl f: sn clr: eased nr fin* **2/1**[1]

3310 **2** 1 1/4 **Northern Jem**[14] 3460 3-9-6 84 SebSanders 4 87
(G G Margarson) *hld up in last trio: prog on outer over 3f out to chse ldrs: drvn to ld over 1f out to jst ins fnl f: outpcd* **5/2**[2]

1064 **3** 1 **Rudry Dragon (IRE)**[7] 3689 3-9-0 78 FergusSweeney 7 79
(P A Blockley) *t.k.h: trckd ldrs: rdn to chal over 1f out: nt qckn* **11/1**

0626 **4** 1 **Professor Twinkle**[16] 3400 3-8-7 71 (v) PaulDoe 6 70
(W J Knight) *hld up in 3rd tl jnd ldr over 4f out to over 1f out: one pce* **22/1**

3650 **5** 1/2 **Plane Painter (IRE)**[22] 3215 3-8-8 **75**.............................. GregFairley(3) 8 73
(M Johnston) *trckd ldr to 1/2-way: cl up over 2f out: lost pl and outpcd sn after* **14/1**

21 **6** *nk* **Wise Little Girl**[50] 2359 3-8-13 **77**................................ PhilipRobinson 3 74
(M A Jarvis) *led and set stdy pce tl forced to qckn over 4f out: hdd & wknd over 1f out* **7/1**

-560 **7** 1 1/4 **Fascinatin Rhythm**[35] 2786 3-9-4 **82**.............................. MartinDwyer 1 76
(V Smith) *hld up in last trio: rdn and struggling 3f out* **33/1**

1200 **8** 2 1/2 **Noticeable (IRE)**[14] 3460 3-9-7 **85**.............................. JHBowman 2 74
(M R Channon) *hld up in rr: rdn over 2f out: no prog and sn btn* **9/2**[3]

2m 7.54s (2.31) **Going Correction** +0.175s/f (Good) **8 Ran SP% 114.9**
Speed ratings (Par 102): **97,96,95,94,94 93,92,90**
CSF £7.18 CT £41.24 TOTE £3.20: £1.30, £1.70, £2.60; EX 7.90 Place 6 £47.92, Place 5 £38.92.
Owner Timothy Steel **Bred** C H Wacker Iii **Trained** Newmarket, Suffolk

FOCUS
A fair and interesting handicap in which the pace was steadied before developing into something of a sprint from the home turn. The form is unlikely to prove solid although the winner can build on this.
T/Plt: £54.10 to a £1 stake. Pool: £64,817.35. 873.50 winning tickets. T/Qpdt: £20.20 to a £1 stake. Pool: £4,927.60. 180.00 winning tickets. JN

3854 SANDOWN (R-H)

Thursday, July 26

OFFICIAL GOING: Good (good to soft in places) changing to good to soft after race 3 (3.20) changing to soft after race 4 (3.55)
Wind: Strong, ahead

3878 EUROPEAN BREEDERS' FUND MAIDEN STKS — 5f 6y
2:10 (2:12) (Class 4) 2-Y-O — **£4,533** (£1,348; £674; £336) **Stalls** Low

Form — RPR

0 **1** **Royal Intruder**[47] 2478 2-9-3 0.............................. EddieAhern 6 80
(R Hannon) *str: lw: sn led: rdn over 1f out: r.o strly thrght fnl f* **16/1**

2 1 3/4 **Effingham (IRE)** 2-9-3 0.............................. RHills 7 74
(B W Hills) *leggy: cl cpld: s.i.s: bhd: hdwy 2f out: drvn to chse wnr ins fnl f: kpt on but a hld* **14/1**

3 **3** *nk* **Hunt The Bottle (IRE)**[14] 3462 2-9-3 0.............................. MichaelHills 3 73
(B W Hills) *lw: chsd ldrs: rdn and effrt over 1f out: kpt on same pce ins fnl f* **8/11**[1]

4 *nk* **Hitchens (IRE)** 2-9-3 0.............................. GeorgeBaker 4 72
(G L Moore) *w'like: scope: s.i.s: bhd: rdn and hdwy over 1f out: kpt on wl fnl f but nvr quite gng pce to rch ldrs* **5/1**[2]

0 **5** 1 1/2 **Dancing Marabout (IRE)**[20] 3270 2-9-3 0.............................. TedDurcan 9 66
(C R Egerton) *lw: in tch: rdn along fr 1/2-way: styd on fnl f but nvr gng pce to be competitive* **25/1**

00 **6** 1 1/2 **Little Wing (IRE)**[13] 3479 2-9-3 0.............................. JamieSpencer 1 61+
(J A Osborne) *s.i.s: bhd: hdwy into mid-div 2f out: nvr gng pce to be competitive* **8/1**[3]

0 **7** 1 1/4 **Running Buck (USA)**[20] 3283 2-9-3 0.............................. IanMongan 8 56
(N P Littmoden) *neat: leggy: chsd ldrs: rdn 1/2-way: wknd appr fnl f* **66/1**

0 **8** 1 1/2 **Tell Me What (FR)**[64] 1945 2-8-12 0.............................. JimmyFortune 2 46
(R Hannon) *chsd ldrs: rdn 1/2-way: wknd over 1f out* **14/1**

9 *17* **Wynberg (IRE)** 2-9-3 0.............................. JMurtagh 5 —
(N A Callaghan) *unf: noisy in paddock: sn struggling in rr* **14/1**

63.56 secs (1.35) **Going Correction** +0.15s/f (Good) **9 Ran SP% 116.9**
Speed ratings (Par 96): **95,92,91,91,88 86,84,82,54**
CSF £218.65 TOTE £20.00: £4.70, £2.80, £1.10; EX 188.10.
Owner Thurloe Thoroughbreds XX **Bred** Farmers Hill Stud **Trained** East Everleigh, Wilts

FOCUS
Just a fair maiden. The runners stayed on the stands' side, where the stalls were positioned.

NOTEBOOK
Royal Intruder, a half-brother to several winners, notably French Group 3 winner Ziria, out of a mare who won over jumps in France, has the make and shape of a sprinter and showed the benefit of his debut experience over a furlong further at Windsor, where connections thought he had tried to do everything on one breath. Making virtually all, he was pushed clear for a pretty comfortable success. There should be more to come from him, and he looks a nice type for nurseries. (op 20-1)
Effingham(IRE), an attractive son of Celtic Swing, is the first foal of a dam who was placed over 1m2f at three. After a tardy start, he stayed on nicely down the outside and, although no match for the winner, did get the better of his odds-on stablemate for second.
Hunt The Bottle(IRE), down in grade after a promising third on his debut at Newmarket's July festival, was unable to build on that performance over this shorter trip and on this easier ground. (op 4-6 tchd 4-5 in places)
Hitchens(IRE), a half-brother to Listed winner Grand Marque, more than doubled his yearling price when resold this year. After a slow start he was keeping on quite nicely in the latter stages and the experience should not be lost on him. (op 8-1)
Dancing Marabout(IRE) built on his debut effort over 7f here earlier in the month, and perhaps 6f could prove his trip in the short term.
Tell Me What(FR), a stablemate of the winner, again showed good early pace but, as on her debut on the Polytrack, she failed to get home. (op 16-1)

3879 TWM WOMEN IN BUSINESS H'CAP — 5f 6y
2:45 (2:47) (Class 5) (0-75,75) 3-Y-O — **£4,533** (£1,348; £674; £336) **Stalls** Low

Form — RPR

5464 **1** **Billy Red**[18] 3353 3-8-7 **61** ow4.............................. (b) JohnEgan 6 66
(J R Jenkins) *towards rr: rdn 2f out: hdwy u.p over 1f out: styd on to ld fnl 50yds: styd on wl* **9/1**

3152 **2** 1 1/4 **Silca Elegance**[13] 3483 3-9-4 **72**.............................. JHBowman 2 73
(M R Channon) *lw: sn led: shkn up and stl gng wl 1f out: hdd and no ex fnl 50yds* **4/5**[1]

4026 **3** 1 1/4 **Charlotte Grey**[8] 3649 3-9-0 **68**.............................. EdwardCreighton 4 64
(C N Allen) *w ldrs: rdn 1/2-way: one pce ins fnl f* **20/1**

0335 **4** 1/2 **Hythe Bay**[14] 3449 3-9-1 **69**.............................. GeorgeBaker 3 63
(J R Best) *in tch: rdn and hdwy over 1f out: sn one pce* **4/1**[2]

0003 **5** *5* **Loves Bidding**[24] 3164 3-8-12 **66**.............................. RobertHavlin 5 42
(R Ingram) *pressed ldrs to 1/2-way: sn rdn: appr fnl f* **7/1**[3]

4256 **6** *8* **Mr Loire**[23] 3179 3-9-7 **75**.............................. (b) EddieAhern 7 22
(H J L Dunlop) *lw: racd towards centre of crse: wknd 2f out* **8/1**

045 **R** **Sherjawy (IRE)**[21] 3237 3-7-11 **56** oh7.............................. (b) NicolPolli(5) 1 —
(Miss Z C Davison) *ref to r* **40/1**

62.84 secs (0.63) **Going Correction** +0.15s/f (Good) **7 Ran SP% 116.4**
Speed ratings (Par 100): **100,98,96,95,87 74,—**
CSF £17.31 TOTE £10.10: £3.60, £1.30; EX 20.40.
Owner Mrs Irene Hampson **Bred** D R Tucker **Trained** Royston, Herts

FOCUS
An ordinary handicap in which again they raced on the near side. The form is pretty solid rated through the runner-up.
Mr Loire Official explanation: jockey said gelding never travelled

3880 BEAT CHARITY STAR STKS (LISTED RACE) (FILLIES) — 7f 16y
3:20 (3:22) (Class 1) 2-Y-O
£12,491 (£4,734; £2,369; £1,181; £591; £297) **Stalls** High

Form — RPR

1 **1** **Muthabara (IRE)**[30] 2969 2-8-12 0.............................. RHills 11 97+
(J L Dunlop) *lw: s.i.s: hld up in rr: stdy hdwy fr 2f out: drvn and qcknd to ld fnl 50yds: easily* **11/4**[1]

5 **2** 3/4 **Lady Deauville (FR)**[27] 3055 2-8-12 0.............................. SimonWhitworth 3 92
(P A Blockley) *chsd ldrs: rdn to ld appr fnl 2f: kpt on tl hdd and outpcd fnl 50yds* **33/1**

1 **3** *2* **Hobby**[14] 3471 2-8-12 0.............................. AdamKirby 10 87
(R M Beckett) *w'like: pressed ldrs: led 5f out: rdn 3f out: hdd appr fnl 2f: one pce u.p fnl f* **20/1**

350 **4** *hd* **Cute**[15] 3432 2-8-12 0.............................. KerrinMcEvoy 6 86
(C E Brittain) *lw: sn led: hdd 5f out: styd pressing ldrs: one pce fnl 2f* **9/1**

41 **5** 1 3/4 **Kay Es Jay (FR)**[22] 3213 2-8-12 0.............................. MichaelHills 12 82
(B W Hills) *lw: towards rr: hdwy and rdn over 2f out: chsd ldrs 1f out and sn one pce* **9/1**

14 **6** *2* **Yasinisi (IRE)**[26] 3096 2-8-12 0.............................. JMurtagh 4 77
(E J O'Neill) *chsd ldrs: rdn over 2f out: wknd fnl f* **6/1**

221 **7** 1/2 **Gypsy Baby (IRE)**[27] 3043 2-8-12 0.............................. JimmyFortune 7 75
(R Hannon) *lw: bmpd after 1f: sn in tch: rdn 3f out: n.d after* **11/2**[3]

4164 **8** 1/2 **Dalkey Girl (IRE)**[13] 3508 2-8-12 0.............................. EddieAhern 9 74
(V Smith) *towards rr: rdn over 2f out: kpt on ins fnl f but nvr in contention* **50/1**

3251 **9** 1 1/2 **Shamrock Lady (IRE)**[24] 3152 2-8-12 0.............................. MartinDwyer 8 70
(Pat Eddery) *plld hrd: chsd ldrs: rdn 3f out: wknd over 1f out* **25/1**

1 **10** 2 1/2 **Rescue Me**[80] 1519 2-8-12 0.............................. TedDurcan 1 64
(R Hannon) *s.i.s: towards rr tl drvn and effrt 3f out: nvr rchd ldrs: wknd fr 2f out* **25/1**

1 **11** 1 1/2 **Shaker (IRE)**[21] 3245 2-8-12 0.............................. JamieSpencer 2 60
(M L W Bell) *w'like: s.i.s: towards rr: rdn 3f out and nvr got beyond mid-div: sn wknd* **5/1**[2]

012 **12** *5* **Sourire**[8] 3642 2-8-12 0.............................. SebSanders 5 47+
(Sir Mark Prescott) *bmpd after 1f: nvr bttr than mid-div* **12/1**

1m 30.35s (1.01) **Going Correction** +0.20s/f (Good) **12 Ran SP% 118.1**
Speed ratings (Par 99): **102,101,98,98,96 94,93,93,91,88 86,81**
CSF £115.55 TOTE £3.50: £1.50, £6.10, £6.50; EX 112.60.
Owner Hamdan Al Maktoum **Bred** Shadwell Estate Company Limited **Trained** Arundel, W Sussex
■ Stewards' Enquiry : Simon Whitworth two-day ban: careless riding (Aug 6-7)

FOCUS
The runners came over to the stands' side in the home straight although they ended up some way off the rail. The winner apart, nothing got involved from the rear. Muthabara won well and looks a decent prospect.

NOTEBOOK
Muthabara(IRE) ◆ emulated her connections' Sudoor by winning the same Newbury maiden before following up here. Again slow to find her stride, she had plenty to do early in the home straight but came with a strong run towards the inside to win in good style. She looks a nice prospect, and could be interesting in races like the May Hill Stakes later in the season. (op 9-4)
Lady Deauville(FR), upped in trip on this second start, was responsible for some early scrimmaging. After showing in front going to the two pole, she could not match the winner's pace inside the last, but she loses nothing in defeat and is clearly a useful filly.
Hobby, always in the front rank, stepped up on the form of her debut win over this trip in modest company at Warwick and earned some valuable black type.
Cute, who has been highly tried since her debut, hung at Newmarket and was tried on a round course as a result. Up there all the way, she was staying on again in the latter stages over this longer trip. (op 11-1 tchd 12-1)
Kay Es Jay(FR), who holds an entry in the Group 1 Moyglare Stud Stakes, was running on turf for the first time. She kept on from the rear down the outside and should get a bit further than this. (tchd 11-1)
Yasinisi(IRE) did not see out the seventh furlong in this rain-affected ground. (op 8-1)
Gypsy Baby(IRE), a winner in soft ground at Folkestone, was one of several involved in some early bumping and could never make her presence felt. (op 7-1)
Shaker(IRE), an attractive daughter of Key Of Luck whose maiden win has been working out well, was disappointing on this rise in grade but an excuse soon came to light. Official explanation: trainer said filly had become upset prior to race (op 4-1)

3881 FIM SERVICES MAIDEN STKS — 1m 14y
3:55 (3:57) (Class 5) 3-4-Y-O — **£3,886** (£1,156; £577; £288) **Stalls** High

Form — RPR

43 **1** **Viva La Flag (USA)**[41] 2625 3-8-11 0.............................. TedDurcan 8 80+
(J L Dunlop) *chsd ldrs: hrd drvn fr 3f out: styd on strly fr over 1f out to ld fnl 100yds: kpt on wl* **8/1**

023 **2** 3 1/2 **Know The Law**[18] 3349 3-9-2 79.............................. TQuinn 14 77
(D R C Elsworth) *lw: towards rr: rdn over 3f out: styd on fr over 1f out: fin wl to take 2nd last strides but no ch w wnr* **7/2**[1]

62 **3** *hd* **Shela House**[14] 3447 3-9-2 0.............................. JamieSpencer 13 80+
(J R Fanshawe) *lw: led tl hdd 5f out: led again over 2f out and stl travelling wl appr fnl f: sn rdn: rn green: wknd and hdd fnl 100yds: lost 2nd last strides* **9/2**[2]

4 3/4 **Amarna (USA)** 3-9-2 0.............................. KerrinMcEvoy 12 75
(Saeed Bin Suroor) *w'like: towards rr: rdn over 3f out: styd on fnl 2f and gng on cl home but nvr gng pce to rch ldrs* **9/2**[2]

0- **5** 1 3/4 **Daweyrr (USA)**[322] 5125 3-9-2 0.............................. (b[1]) PaulFitzsimons 3 71
(M P Tregoning) *h.d.w: towards rr: pushed along over 3f out: styd on wl fr over 1f out but nvr gng pce to rch ldrs* **20/1**

56 **6** *1* **Willow Dancer (IRE)**[79] 1560 3-9-2 0.............................. AdamKirby 7 68
(W R Swinburn) *in tch: rdn to chse ldrs 3f out: one pce fnl 2f* **33/1**

06 **7** *5* **Tavares (IRE)**[32] 2913 4-9-10 0.............................. SaleemGolam 15 59
(J Jay) *towards rr: rdn 4f out: styd on fnl 2f but nvr in contention* **50/1**

8 *1* **Mini Mosa**[307] 3-8-11 0.............................. JimmyFortune 4 50
(J H M Gosden) *w'like: chsd ldrs: rdn over 3f out: wknd fr 2f out* **14/1**

00-0 **9** *hd* **Little Carmela**[80] 1541 3-8-11 40.............................. JimCrowley 10 49?
(S C Williams) *chsd ldrs: rdn 4f out: wknd fr 2f out* **50/1**

32-3 **10** *hd* **Moon Valley**[26] 3107 4-9-5 72.............................. MichaelHills 11 51
(W J Haggas) *slowly away: sn rcvrd to chse ldrs: rdn 3f out: wknd qckly 2f out* **7/1**[3]

66 **11** 1 3/4 **Hannahbecc**[21] 3248 3-8-11 0.............................. EddieAhern 2 45
(H R A Cecil) *chsd ldrs: rdn 4f out: wknd fr 3f out* **33/1**

0 **12** *nk* **Hugo Quick**[16] 3394 3-9-2 0.............................. JohnEgan 1 49
(T M Jones) *a towards rr* **66/1**

The Form Book, Raceform Ltd, Compton, RG20 6NL

-05 **13** *hd* **Woodins Way**[44] 2541 3-9-2 0 SebSanders 6 49
(P J Makin) *led 5f out: hdd over 2f out and sn btn* **16/1**
50 **14** *3/4* **Tahdeed**[14] 3476 3-9-2 0 RHills 5 47
(Sir Michael Stoute) *chsd ldrs: rdn 3f out: wknd over 2f out* **9/1**
1m 45.04s (1.09) **Going Correction** +0.20s/f (Good)
WFA 3 from 4yo 8lb **14** Ran SP% **120.8**
Speed ratings (Par 103): **102,98,98,97,95 94,89,88,88,88 86,86,86,85**
CSF £34.32 TOTE £8.50: £2.70, £1.90, £1.90; EX 37.20.
Owner Phipps Stable **Bred** Phipps Stable **Trained** Arundel, W Sussex

FOCUS
A reasonable maiden and the form is fair and sound. They avoided the inside rail down the far side and again made their way to the stands' side in the straight.

3882 ZYCKO H'CAP 1m 2f 7y
4:30 (4:33) (Class 3) (0-90,90) 3-Y-O+ **£7,772** (£2,312; £1,155; £577) **Stalls** High

Form RPR
1-46 **1** **Cabinet (IRE)**[47] 2448 3-8-10 **82** SebSanders 8 93+
(Sir Michael Stoute) *lw: towards rr: hdwy 4f out: rdn to take narrow ld over 2f out: hrd drvn and styd on strly fnl f* **4/1**[2]
3600 **2** *1 3/4* **Weightless**[33] 2859 7-10-0 **90** IanMongan 3 97
(N P Littmoden) *chsd ldr 7f out: styd alone far side and upside w ldrs stands' side tl outpcd by wnr jst ins fnl f* **25/1**
/21- **3** *1/2* **Seabow (USA)**[295] 5768 4-9-13 **89** (t) KerrinMcEvoy 7 95+
(Saeed Bin Suroor) *towards rr: hdwy fr 3f out: styd on wl fr over 1f out but nvr gng pce to rch wnr* **9/4**[1]
2121 **4** *hd* **Night Cru**[27] 3060 4-9-13 **89** GeorgeBaker 4 95
(C F Wall) *lw: chsd ldrs: rdn to chal over 2f out: styd on same pce fnl f* **4/1**[2]
0445 **5** *4* **Polish Power (GER)**[11] 3577 7-9-2 **78** JohnEgan 1 76
(J S Moore) *towards rr and rdn fr 6f out: styd on u.p fnl 2f but nvr gng pce to be a danger* **12/1**
6002 **6** *1 3/4* **Brief Goodbye**[41] 2634 7-9-4 **80** TedDurcan 11 74
(John Berry) *s.i.s: bhd: sme hdwy 3f out: nvr gng pce to rch ldrs and wknd fnl 2f* **12/1**
0604 **7** *hd* **Fabrian**[40] 2660 9-8-9 **71** TQuinn 2 65
(R J Price) *led tl hdd over 2f out: sn btn* **18/1**
0016 **8** *1/2* **Zaif (IRE)**[27] 3060 4-9-7 **83** AntonyProcter 10 76
(D R C Elsworth) *s.i.s: towards rr: pushed along over 4f out: nvr in contention* **16/1**
31-5 **9** *5* **Clear Sailing**[41] 2634 4-9-8 **84** JimCrowley 5 67
(Mrs A J Perrett) *lw: chsd ldrs: rdn over 3f out: wknd over 2f out* **20/1**
31 **10** *14* **Manbar (USA)**[77] 1611 3-8-11 **83** RHills 12 38
(Sir Michael Stoute) *chsd ldrs: rdn over 3f out and sn wknd* **8/1**[3]
2m 11.98s (1.74) **Going Correction** +0.30s/f (Good)
WFA 3 from 4yo+ 10lb **10** Ran SP% **117.0**
Speed ratings (Par 107): **105,103,103,103,99 98,98,97,93,82**
CSF £97.29 CT £278.66 TOTE £5.70: £2.10, £4.70, £1.60; EX 180.00.
Owner The Royal Ascot Racing Club **Bred** Hascombe & Valiant Studs **Trained** Newmarket, Suffolk

FOCUS
A decent handicap and again they stayed away from the inside rail in the back straight. The bulk of the field came over to the stands' side once in the home straight, the expection being the runner-up who stayed on the inside. The time was reasonable and the form is sound.

NOTEBOOK
Cabinet(IRE), who failed to stay 1m4f at Haydock, was much happier with this give underfoot. Taking it up nearest the rail and soon establishing a decisive advantage over the rest of the stands'-side group, he battled on well to get the better of the runner-up who was racing alone on the inside rail. This will have boosted his confidence and there should be further improvement in him now. (op 11-2 tchd 13-2)
Weightless, winner of the Group 3 Gordon Richards Stakes over course and distance two seasons ago, has been given a chance by the Handicapper and nearly took advantage. Sticking to the far side of the track once in the home straight, he kept galloping but found one too good on the opposite wing. (op 20-1)
Seabow(USA), off the track since winning a Nottingham maiden last October, made a promising return to action and there should be races to be won with him this year, perhaps over 1m4f. (op 5-2)
Night Cru has enjoyed a successful season, but an 8lb rise for his recent Newmarket success means he has gone up 20lb in the space of a year and the Handicapper looks to have him now. (op 7-2 tchd 3-1)
Polish Power(GER) had not run over a trip this short for nearly two years and he could never get close enough to land a blow. (op 14-1 tchd 16-1)
Brief Goodbye Official explanation: jockey said gelding was not suited by the soft ground
Manbar(USA), off the track since landing his maiden in May, was down in trip for this handicap debut and ran a lacklustre race. Official explanation: jockey said colt had a breathing problem (op 6-1)

3883 LANGHAM HOTEL H'CAP 1m 6f
5:00 (5:05) (Class 3) (0-95,94) 3-Y-O **£9,067** (£2,697; £1,348; £673) **Stalls** Centre

Form RPR
2041 **1** **Tempelstern (GER)**[28] 3041 3-8-9 **82** (b) TedDurcan 1 96
(H R A Cecil) *mde all: rdn clr fnl 2f: unchal* **7/1**[3]
1230 **2** *8* **Dansant**[35] 2790 3-9-3 **90** StephenCarson 5 93
(G A Butler) *lw: sn prom: rdn over 3f out: chsd wnr over 1f out but nvr any ch: hld on wl for 2nd* **17/2**
3-41 **3** *3/4* **Furmigadelagiusta**[21] 3236 3-9-0 **87** JimmyFortune 7 89
(L M Cumani) *towards rr: rdn and styd on fr 3f out: kpt on fnl 2f but nvr nr easy wnr* **15/2**
-146 **4** *nk* **Metaphoric (IRE)**[34] 2816 3-9-7 **94** JMurtagh 2 96
(M L W Bell) *towards rr: rdn over 3f out: styd on fnl 2f and gng on cl home but nvr nr clr wnr* **5/1**[2]
2215 **5** *1 1/4* **Elyaadi**[75] 1663 3-8-12 **85** JHBowman 9 85
(M R Channon) *towards rr: drvn along 4f out: styd on fr over 1f out but nvr gng pce to be competitive* **20/1**
-623 **6** *1/2* **Eglevski (IRE)**[29] 2999 3-8-12 **85** EddieAhern 10 84
(J L Dunlop) *lw: chsd ldrs: wnt 2nd over 2f out but nvr any ch w clr wnr: wknd fnl f* **4/1**[1]
61 **7** *1 1/2* **Horseford Hill**[34] 2836 3-8-6 **79** KerrinMcEvoy 6 76
(D R C Elsworth) *lw: towards rr: stl wl bhd over 3f out and rdn: styd on fnl f and gng on cl home: nvr in contention* **7/1**[3]
2031 **8** *hd* **Phreeze**[27] 3058 3-8-6 **79** ow1 JamieSpencer 3 76
(G A Swinbank) *hld up in rr: rdn and effrt over 3f out: nvr in contention and sn wknd* **5/1**[2]
-332 **9** *1/2* **Coyote Creek**[42] 2602 3-8-6 **79** MartinDwyer 8 75
(E F Vaughan) *chsd ldrs: rdn and outpcd 5f out: effrt again 3f out: sn btn* **8/1**
4600 **10** *15* **Shimoni**[14] 3458 3-8-13 **86** PaulDoe 4 61
(W J Knight) *sn chsng wnr: rdn 4f out: wknd 3f out* **25/1**
3m 6.57s (2.06) **Going Correction** +0.30s/f (Good) **10** Ran SP% **120.3**
Speed ratings (Par 104): **106,101,101,100,100 99,98,98,98,90**
CSF £67.31 CT £467.20 TOTE £8.70: £2.20, £3.40, £3.00; EX 102.10 Place 6 £58.47, Place 5 £42.01.
Owner Ennismore Racing I **Bred** Dr O Herminghaus **Trained** Newmarket, Suffolk

FOCUS
Another good handicap in which the runners again shunned the inside rail in the back straight and came to the stands' side once in line for home. The winner enjoyed something of a soft lead but the form looks sound with the third, fourth and fifth close to their marks..

NOTEBOOK
Tempelstern(GER), off the mark in first-time blinkers at Yarmouth, followed up on this return to handicap company back up in trip. Getting over from his low draw to lead, he was able to dictate the pace and had little trouble pulling away in the last two furlongs to score by a wide margin. He looks a stayer on the up. (op 6-1 tchd 11-2)
Dansant, who finished in midfield in Ascot's King George V Handicap last time, kept on to finish best of the rest without threatening the dominant winner. He had no problem with the softening ground and stayed this longer trip well enough. (op 16-1 tchd 8-1)
Furmigadelagiusta was 10lb higher than when previously in a handicap, having landed a Newbury maiden in the interim. Upped in trip, he stayed on near the stands' rail but was never a threat to the all-the-way winner. (op 13-2)
Metaphoric(IRE), making his handicap bow after being found wanting in a couple of Group 3 events, was staying on quite well at the end and would probably not mind a return to 2m. (op 11-2 tchd 13-2)
Elyaadi, off the track since finishing fifth in the Lingfield Oaks Trial in May, was another who plugged on in the latter stages without ever posing a threat to the winner.
Eglevski(IRE) faded after racing prominently and the conclusion has to be that he failed to stay this longer trip in the soft ground. (op 9-2 tchd 5-1 in places)
T/Plt: £67.50 to a £1 stake. Pool: £73,644.25. 795.30 winning tickets. T/Qpdt: £60.50 to a £1 stake. Pool: £3,446.00. 42.10 winning tickets. ST

3556 YORK (L-H)
Thursday, July 26

OFFICIAL GOING: Heavy (soft in places; 5.2)
The ground was described as 'desperate, patchy and very testing'. The track was narrowed, with the rail down the middle of the home straight.
Wind: Moderate, half behind Weather: Overcast, changeable

3884 MINSTER JAGUAR MAIDEN AUCTION FILLIES' STKS 7f
6:00 (6:00) (Class 4) 2-Y-O **£6,541** (£1,946; £972; £485) **Stalls** Low

Form RPR
5 **1** **Farsighted**[14] 3465 2-8-5 0 DaleGibson 5 70
(J M P Eustace) *mde all: kpt on fnl 2f: jst hld on* **11/2**[3]
2 *nk* **Graceful Descent (FR)** 2-8-6 0 PaulHanagan 2 71
(R A Fahey) *dwlt: hdwy on ins over 4f out: wnt 2nd over 1f out: styd on wl towards fin* **8/1**
56 **3** *5* **Flop (IRE)**[13] 3510 2-8-4 0 JoeFanning 4 55
(M Brittain) *hld up: effrt on outer over 3f out: kpt on to take 3rd ins fnl f* **16/1**
3 **4** *2* **Minshar**[24] 3152 2-8-9 0 DarryllHolland 6 55
(L M Cumani) *trckd ldrs: drvn over 2f out: hung lft: fdd and lost 3rd ins fnl f* **10/11**[1]
5 *2 1/2* **Grand Value (USA)** 2-8-5 0 PaulFessey 3 44
(T D Barron) *sn trcking ldrs: fdd fnl 2f* **11/1**
026 **6** *13* **Welcome Return (IRE)**[45] 2504 2-8-5 0 KDarley 7 9
(T D Easterby) *chsd wnr: drvn over 4f out: lost pl and eased over 1f out* **5/1**[2]
00 **7** *12* **Amazing Spirit**[13] 3507 2-8-1 0 ColinHaddon[(5)] 1 —
(Miss V Haigh) *chsd ldrs: drvn over 3f out: sn lost pl and bhd* **66/1**
1m 30.92s (5.52) **Going Correction** +0.75s/f (Yiel) **7** Ran SP% **111.3**
Speed ratings (Par 93): **98,97,91,89,86 71,58**
CSF £44.80 TOTE £6.90: £2.90, £2.20; EX 54.80.
Owner Blue Peter Racing 7 **Bred** Manor Farm Stud (rutland) **Trained** Newmarket, Suffolk

FOCUS
A steady gallop in the testing conditions. With the favourite unable to handle the ground it took little winning.

NOTEBOOK
Farsighted, a slip of a thing, seized the favoured far-side rail. She looked likely to run out a decisive winner entering the final furlong but in the end was crying out for the line. (op 5-1 tchd 9-2)
Graceful Descent(FR), an April foal, is on the leg and narrow. After a tardy start she went in pursuit of the winner and was closing her down all the way to the line.
Flop(IRE), well beaten in similar ground here three weeks earlier, did just enough to secure third spot. (op 14-1)
Minshar, a good-quartered filly, never looked that happy in the ground and tired badly. She is much better than she was able to show here. Official explanation: jockey said filly was unsuited by the heavy (soft in places) ground (op 5-6 tchd Evens and 4-5 in places)
Grand Value(USA), an April foal, had to be handled very gently in the paddock. The outing should at least have helped her confidence. (op 12-1 tchd 14-1)
Welcome Return(IRE) looked all at sea in the very testing conditions. (op 7-1)

3885 FIRST TRANSPENNINE EXPRESS STKS (H'CAP) 6f
6:30 (6:30) (Class 4) (0-80,80) 3-Y-O **£6,477** (£1,927; £963; £481) **Stalls** Centre

Form RPR
3013 **1** **Northern Dare (IRE)**[3] 3786 3-8-10 **69** 6ex AdrianTNicholls 6 88
(D Nicholls) *led after 1f: kpt on wl fnl 2f: readily* **9/2**[1]
1140 **2** *2 1/2* **Ishetoo**[15] 3413 3-8-11 **75** MichaelJStainton[(5)] 2 87
(A Dickman) *led 1f: chsd ldrs: wnt 2nd over 1f out: kpt on same pce* **16/1**
5653 **3** *6* **Fish Called Johnny**[11] 3568 3-8-12 **71** (b) NCallan 9 65
(Peter Grayson) *chsd ldrs: one pce fnl 2f* **9/1**
0041 **4** *3/4* **Charlie Tipple**[6] 3713 3-8-12 **71** 6ex PaulMulrennan 10 62
(T D Easterby) *chsd ldrs: one pce fnl 2f* **9/2**[1]
6002 **5** *3* **Osteopathic Remedy (IRE)**[23] 3196 3-9-7 **80** TomEaves 4 62
(M Dods) *in rr: kpt on fnl 2f: nvr nr ldrs* **6/1**[2]
30-1 **6** *7* **Vesuvio**[19] 3302 3-8-4 **63** DeanMcKeown 3 24
(C W Thornton) *chsd ldrs: wknd fnl 2f* **9/2**[1]
5-01 **7** *5* **Equuleus Pictor**[10] 3583 3-8-11 **70** 6ex TPQueally 8 16
(J L Spearing) *chsd ldrs: edgd lft and wknd appr fnl f* **8/1**[3]
0540 **8** *4* **Nufoudh (IRE)**[3] 3786 3-8-2 **61** oh2 RoystonFfrench 11 —
(Miss Tracy Waggott) *stall failed to open properly: v.s.a: nvr on terms* **50/1**

3655 **9** 2 **Prospect Place**[20] 3278 3-9-0 **73** DarryllHolland 5 —
(M Dods) *a in rr* **11/1**

000- **10** 16 **Kerry's Dream**[314] 5335 3-9-4 **80** DuranFentiman(3) 1 —
(T D Easterby) *in rr: bhd fnl 2f* **25/1**

1404 **11** 6 **Pickering**[14] 3475 3-9-1 **74** KDarley 7 —
(E J Alston) *mid-div: lost pl over 2f out: sn bhd* **14/1**

1m 16.42s (3.86) **Going Correction** +0.75s/f (Yiel) **11** Ran SP% **116.6**
Speed ratings (Par 102): **104,100,92,91,87 78,71,66,63,42 34**
CSF £79.02 CT £635.88 TOTE £6.00: £2.20, £3.70, £2.40; EX 100.50.
Owner Jim Dale **Bred** Frank Moynihan **Trained** Sessay, N Yorks

FOCUS
The first two raced nearest to the favoured far side rail and in the end came clear. The race has been rated through the runner-up to his mark.
Nufoudh(IRE) Official explanation: jockey said gelding missed break after gate sprung back

3886 SMITH BROTHERS STKS (H'CAP) 5f 89y
7:00 (7:22) (Class 4) (0-80,77) 3-Y-O+ **£6,477** (£1,927; £963; £481) **Stalls** Centre

Form RPR
2111 **1** **Prospect Court**[12] 3557 5-9-4 **73** AndrewMullen(3) 7 83+
(A C Whillans) *trckd ldrs: shkn up to ld 1f out: idled: drvn out* **6/5**[1]

430 **2** ½ **Bo McGinty (IRE)**[6] 3720 6-9-9 **75** (b) PaulHanagan 4 82
(R A Fahey) *mde most: hdd 1f out: kpt on* **9/2**[2]

4030 **3** 1¾ **Legal Set (IRE)**[3] 3782 11-8-3 **60** oh12 ow2 (b) AnnStokell(5) 1 61
(Miss A Stokell) *w ldrs: outpcd over 2f out: styd on fnl f: tk 3rd nr line* **25/1**

0031 **4** nk **Compton Classic**[3] 3782 5-8-11 **70** 6ex (p) GaryBartley(7) 2 70
(J S Goldie) *trckd ldrs: drvn 3f out: kpt on same pce fnl f* **7/1**

0131 **5** 1½ **The History Man (IRE)**[9] 3608 4-8-10 **69** 6ex (b) SophieDoyle(7) 8 64
(M Mullineaux) *half rrd s: jnd ldr after 1f: wknd over 1f out* **11/2**[3]

3140 **6** 2 **Tilly's Dream**[6] 3708 4-9-7 **73** NCallan 10 61
(Miss K B Boutflower) *trckd ldrs: lost pl over 1f out* **9/1**

11-0 **7** 5 **Minnow**[45] 2508 3-8-6 **62** RoystonFfrench 9 33
(S C Williams) *a detached in last* **16/1**

69.83 secs (4.83)
WFA 3 from 4yo+ 4lb **7** Ran SP% **111.2**
CSF £6.36 CT £78.03 TOTE £2.50: £1.60, £2.20; EX 8.50.
Owner Mrs L M Whillans **Bred** Mrs G Slater **Trained** Newmill-On-Slitrig, Borders

FOCUS
The course was inspected before this race before the go-ahead was given to continue, causing a delay. This was a fair handicap in which Prospect Court completed the four-timer from a much stiffer mark. He was pushed hard in the end by luckless Bo McGinty who seized the favoured far-side rail. The proximity of the veteran third, a stone out of the handicap, limits the form.
Minnow Official explanation: jockey said filly was unsuited by the heavy (soft in places) ground

3887 SKYBET.COM STKS (CONDITIONS RACE) 1m
7:30 (7:42) (Class 3) 4-Y-O+ **£10,363** (£3,083; £1,540; £769) **Stalls** Low

Form RPR
-364 **1** **Pride Of Nation (IRE)**[19] 3330 5-8-9 99 JoeFanning 3 111
(L M Cumani) *trckd ldrs: effrt over 2f out: led appr fnl f: edgd lft: styd on strly* **11/4**[1]

15-2 **2** 2½ **Shumookh (IRE)**[50] 2368 4-8-9 102 NCallan 5 106
(M A Jarvis) *led: qcknd over 2f out: hdd appr fnl f: styd on same pce* **3/1**[2]

5010 **3** 3 **Rio Riva**[19] 3330 5-8-9 104 TomEaves 6 99
(Miss J A Camacho) *swtchd lft after s: trckd ldrs: effrt over 3f out: kpt on same pce fnl 2f* **9/2**[3]

/0-5 **4** 3 **Opera Cape**[12] 3529 4-8-9 111 (t) DarryllHolland 2 93
(Saeed Bin Suroor) *t.k.h in rr: nt clr run 3f out: wknd over 1f out* **14/1**

0-03 **5** 6 **Hinterland (IRE)**[50] 2368 5-8-9 100 KDarley 4 81
(Saeed Bin Suroor) *trckd ldrs: chal 3f out: wknd over 1f out* **10/1**

5-04 **6** 14 **Secret World (IRE)**[68] 1834 4-8-9 111 TPQueally 1 51
(J Noseda) *stdd s: hld up in last: effrt over 3f out: nvr a threat: lost pl and eased over 1f out* **3/1**[2]

1m 44.07s (4.57) **Going Correction** +0.75s/f (Yiel) **6** Ran SP% **110.6**
Speed ratings (Par 107): **107,104,101,98,92 78**
CSF £10.93 TOTE £3.40: £1.90, £2.30; EX 11.00.
Owner Equibreed S.R.L. **Bred** Deni S R L **Trained** Newmarket, Suffolk

FOCUS
A tactical race with the first two both having something to find on official ratings. The bad ground obviously had its say but the race looks pretty solid, and has been rated through the runner-up.

NOTEBOOK
Pride Of Nation(IRE), who had the least chance on official ratings, wore earplugs. Proven on heavy ground, in the end he ran out a decisive winner and this will have ended his handicap days. (op 9-4)
Shumookh(IRE) set a sensible pace in the conditions. He wound it up halfway up the home straight but in the end the winner simply proved too strong. (op 11-4 tchd 10-3)
Rio Riva, who had a better chance on official ratings than either of the first two, had the outside draw. In the end he had to settle for third spot with no obvious excuse. (op 15-2)
Opera Cape, who had 12lb in hand of the winner on official ratings, looked at his very best but his smart two-year-old form is a long way behind him now. (op 11-1)
Hinterland(IRE), winner of four of his first six starts, has gone downhill since joining his present stable. (op 12-1)
Secret World(IRE), who is clearly difficult to train, was dropped out at the start. Making his effort away from the running rail, he never entered the argument and in the end his rider gave up. He has plenty to pove now. Official explanation: jockey said colt was unsuited by the heavy (soft in places) ground (op 5-2)

3888 GNER.CO.UK STKS (H'CAP) 1m 4f
8:00 (8:05) (Class 5) (0-75,71) 3-Y-O+ **£5,181** (£1,541; £770; £384) **Stalls** Low

Form RPR
-512 **1** **Raffish**[14] 3467 5-8-10 **60** (p) JackDean(7) 3 71
(M Scudamore) *hld up wl in tch: effrt on ins and nt clr run over 2f out: swtchd rt: led jst ins fnl f: styd on wl* **11/4**[1]

0211 **2** 13½ **Turn Of Phrase (IRE)**[16] 3403 8-10-0 **71** (b) TomEaves 5 63
(B Ellison) *trckd ldrs: led ov 3f out tl ov 2f out: wknd fnl f: fin 3rd 3½l, 10l: plcd 2nd* **4/1**[2]

3-01 **3** 2½ **Atlantic Coast (IRE)**[7] 3677 3-8-5 **60** 6ex (b) RoystonFfrench 6 49
(M Johnston) *trckd ldrs: led after 2f: hdd over 7f out: drvn 4f out: edgd rt and lost pl over 1f out: fin 4th, plcd 3rd* **4/1**[2]

0062 **4** 13 **Advancement**[19] 3301 4-9-9 **66** PaulHanagan 9 36
(R A Fahey) *trckd ldrs: led ov 7f out tl ov 3f out: wknd over 1f out: fin 5th, plcd 4th* **7/1**

4244 **5** 17 **Qaasi (USA)**[7] 3677 5-9-1 **58** KDarley 8 5
(M Brittain) *hld up: jnd ldrs over 6f out: drvn over 4f out: wknd and eased over 2f out: fin 6th, plcd 5th* **5/1**[3]

-130 **6** 5 **Fenners (USA)**[17] 3371 4-9-7 **64** DaleGibson 4 4
(M W Easterby) *led 2f: drvn over 5f out: lost pl 4f out: sn bhd: fin 7th, plcd 6th* **10/1**

000 **D** 3½ **Red Wine**[43] 2572 8-8-10 **60** RobbieEgan(7) 2 66
(A J McCabe) *hld up: smooth hdwy on outside 4f out: led on bit over 2f out: hdd jst ins fnl f: no ex: fin 2nd, 3½l : subs disq: rdr not licensed* **9/1**

2m 45.93s (11.33) **Going Correction** +0.75s/f (Yiel)
WFA 3 from 4yo+ 12lb **7** Ran SP% **114.9**
Speed ratings (Par 103): **84,75,73,64,53 50,81**
CSF £28.35 CT £98.02 TOTE £4.10: £2.50, £3.10; EX 38.20.
Owner I J Anderson **Bred** P And Mrs Venner **Trained** Bromsash, Herefordshire

FOCUS
A very steady gallop and in the end just a two-horse race. Modest form rated round the first two.

3889 SAWFISH SOFTWARE STKS (H'CAP) 1m 208y
8:30 (8:30) (Class 4) (0-85,86) 3-Y-O **£5,181** (£1,541; £770; £384) **Stalls** Low

Form RPR
-501 **1** **Les Fazzani (IRE)**[8] 3645 3-9-13 **86** 6ex PaulHanagan 1 97
(M J Wallace) *sn pushed along in rr: hdwy on outer over 3f out: led appr fnl f: drew clr* **5/1**[3]

5122 **2** 4 **Smugglers Bay (IRE)**[5] 3755 3-8-11 **70** (b) PaulMulrennan 4 73
(T D Easterby) *t.k.h: led tl appr fnl f: sn btn* **9/4**[1]

651 **3** 2½ **Getrah**[17] 3382 3-9-3 **76** JoeFanning 2 74
(W J Haggas) *drvn along to chse ldr: chal over 3f out: edgd rt over 1f out: one pce* **9/4**[1]

5232 **4** 9 **Jibajaba (USA)**[3] 3785 3-8-13 **72** TonyHamilton 3 51
(R A Fahey) *hld up: hdwy to trck ldrs 4f out: nt clr run over 2f out tl over 1f out: sn wknd* **6/1**

1100 **5** 18 **Look So**[15] 3430 3-9-7 **80** KDarley 5 21
(R M Beckett) *sn chsng ldrs: effrt over 4f out: edgd lft and wknd over 1f out: sn bhd and eased* **4/1**[2]

1m 58.09s (7.10) **Going Correction** +0.75s/f (Yiel) **5** Ran SP% **112.5**
Speed ratings (Par 102): **98,94,92,84,68**
CSF £16.93 TOTE £7.90: £3.10, £1.70; EX 18.40 Place 6 £158.49, Place 5 £18.59.
Owner Mike & Denise Dawes **Bred** J Erhardt & Mrs J Schonwalder **Trained** Newmarket, Suffolk

FOCUS
The hard-pulling leader seemed to go too fast and the winner, who was soon struggling, came from last to first. Not easy to rate with the third the best guide for now.
Look So Official explanation: jockey said filly was unsuited by the heavy (soft in places) ground
T/Plt: £301.50 to a £1 stake. Pool: £63,473.60. 153.65 winning tickets. T/Qpdt: £12.00 to a £1 stake. Pool: £6,068.15. 371.85 winning tickets. WG

3890 - 3892a (Foreign Racing) - See Raceform Interactive

3361 CHANTILLY (R-H)
Thursday, July 26

OFFICIAL GOING: Good

3893a PRIX LA MOSKOWA (LISTED RACE) 1m 7f
3:05 (3:13) 4-Y-O+ **£17,568** (£7,027; £5,270; £3,514; £1,757)

RPR
1 **King Luna (FR)**[37] 4-8-8 SPasquier 3 101
(A Fabre, France)

2 ½ **Varevees**[41] 2649 4-9-1 TJarnet 7 107
(J Boisnard, France) **2/1**[1]

3 4 **Latin Mood (FR)**[21] 4-8-11 RonanThomas 8 98
(P Demercastel, France)

4 nk **Milongo (FR)**[55] 2330 5-8-11 BrigitteRenk 4 98
(Brigitte Renk, Switzerland)

5 ¾ **Water Dragon**[17] 6-8-11 GBenoist 6 97
(Mlle C Cardenne, France)

6 3 **El Biba D'Or (IRE)**[33] 8-8-11 JVictoire 1 93
(P Giannotti, Italy)

7 10 **Ivory Gala (FR)**[70] 1789 4-8-8 TThulliez 2 78
(B J Meehan) *racd in 3rd: hdwy on outside to press ldr 6f out: 2nd st: sn wknd* **81/10**[2]

8 1 **Arnuide (SPA)**[49] 4-8-11 C-PLemaire 5 80
(R Martin-Vidania, Germany)

3m 10.6s (-5.80) **8** Ran SP% **44.3**
PARI-MUTUEL: WIN 2.60; PL 1.10, 1.10, 1.20; DF 2.90.
Owner H H Aga Khan **Bred** Snc Lagardere Elevage **Trained** Chantilly, France

NOTEBOOK
Ivory Gala(FR), who finished runner-up in similar company over 12f last season, was ridden positively and did not seem to get home.

3522 ASCOT (R-H)
Friday, July 27

OFFICIAL GOING: Straight course - good to soft (9.8); round course - soft (7.4) (overall 8.4)
Wind: moderate behind

3894 H.B.L.B. HACKWOOD STKS (GROUP 3) 6f
1:35 (1:36) (Class 1) 3-Y-O+
£19,873 (£7,532; £3,769; £1,879; £941; £472) **Stalls** Centre

Form RPR
0530 **1** **Balthazaar's Gift (IRE)**[14] 3506 4-9-3 108 JoeFanning 5 119+
(L M Cumani) *lw: hld up in rr: hdwy and nt clr run appr fnl f: swtchd rt and rapid hdwy to ld wl ins fnl f: easily* **15/2**

1-60 **2** 1½ **Al Qasi (IRE)**[34] 2857 4-9-3 107 KerrinMcEvoy 9 112
(P W Chapple-Hyam) *b: s.i.s: sn in tch: chsd ldrs 1/2-way: rdn to chal ins fnl f: kpt on but readily outpcd by wnr* **4/1**[1]

-206 **3** ½ **Sonny Red (IRE)**[37] 2752 3-8-12 109 RyanMoore 8 109
(R Hannon) *lw: in tch: hdwy over 1f out: drvn to chal ins fnl f: kpt on same pce nr fin* **8/1**

2510 **4** nk **Assertive**[34] 2857 4-9-3 106 (b[1]) RichardHughes 10 109
(R Hannon) *led 1f: styd pressing ldr tl led again wl over 1f out: hdd and outpcd wl ins fnl f* **10/1**

-400 **5** 2 **Baltic King**[34] 2857 7-9-3 107 (t) JimmyFortune 6 103
(H Morrison) *in rr but in tch: rdn 1/2-way: kpt on fnl f but nvr gng pce to rch ldrs* **6/1**[3]

12-5 **6** shd **Reverence**[20] 3329 6-9-11 116 KDarley 1 111
(E J Alston) *pressed ldrs: rdn over 2f out: wknd fnl f* **6/1**[3]

0032 **7** *nk* **Fonthill Road (IRE)**[13] 3529 7-9-3 104 PaulHanagan 4 102
(R A Fahey) *in rr: sn drvn along: kpt on ins fnl f but nvr gng pce to be competitive* **12/1**

4002 **8** *nk* **Appalachian Trail (IRE)**[27] 3088 6-9-3 106 (b) TomEaves 3 101
(I Semple) *in tch and rdn 1/2-way: nvr quite gng pce to be competitive* **16/1**

4050 **9** *2* **Drayton (IRE)**[14] 3506 3-8-12 0 (e1) SteveDrowne 11 94
(M F De Kock, South Africa) *led after 1f tl hdd wl over 1f out: sn btn* **5/1**[2]

0600 **10** *1 3/4* **Fayr Jag (IRE)**[27] 3088 8-9-3 103 DarryllHolland 2 89
(T D Easterby) *chsd ldrs: rdn 1/2-way: n.d after* **33/1**

4550 **11** *nk* **Ashdown Express (IRE)**[34] 2858 8-9-3 103 (v1) GeorgeBaker 7 88
(C F Wall) *in rr: sme prog 1/2-way: sn wknd* **33/1**

1m 14.31s (-0.59) **Going Correction** +0.30s/f (Good)
WFA 3 from 4yo+ 5lb **11** Ran SP% **116.7**
Speed ratings: **115,113,112,111,109 109,108,108,105,103 102**
CSF £37.24 TOTE £9.40: £2.60, £2.10, £1.90; EX 48.50 Trifecta £284.90 Pool £1,123.78 - 2.80 winning units..
Owner Ryder Racing Ltd **Bred** Pat Beirne **Trained** Newmarket, Suffolk

FOCUS
A competitive Group 3 sprint transferred from the recent abandoned meeting at Newbury. The form looks straighforward with the first three to their marks.

NOTEBOOK
Balthazaar's Gift(IRE) was nearly last in the July Cup last time but in two previous runs on this track had finished runner-up in the 2006 Golden Jubilee and third in this year's Wokingham. He found this contest right up his street and, having been held up, produced an irresistible burst of pace to settle things inside the final furlong. It looks as if his trainer has found the key to him, and he could well prove a force for the rest of the season, with the Diadem back here an obvious target. (tchd 7-1, 9-1 in a place and 8-1 in places)
Al Qasi(IRE), who progressed so well in handicaps last season, had found things tougher in top sprints so far this season. However, this slight drop in grade proved suitable and he ran very well, only to find the running him down late on. He looks well up to winning races at Group level.
Sonny Red(IRE), dropping in trip after decent efforts in the Craven, the 2000 Guineas and the Jersey Stakes, showed what he is capable of. Although unable to find an extra gear late on, this was no disgrace against older rivals. (tchd 17-2 and 9-1 in places)
Assertive, fitted with blinkers for the first time, tended to race keenly early up with the pace, so in the circumstances did well to keep going and finish as close as he did. (op 17-2)
Baltic King has won at Listed level but has still to pick up a Group race despite numerous attempts. He ran on late but is probably better off in handicaps from his current mark. (tchd 11-2)
Reverence, having just his second race of the season, was weak in the market but showed plenty of pace until fading approaching the final furlong. He would have preferred softer ground and will be hoping to get it when he bids to repeat last year's success in the Nunthorpe next month. He will need to improve on what he has done so far if he is to succeed though. (op 5-1)
Fonthill Road(IRE) has run well at this level before but is ideally suited by carrying big weights in the top handicaps. This was another fair effort, and the Stewards Cup next week and an attempt at a repeat win in the Ayr gold Cup are likely to be on his agenda once again. (op 16-1)
Appalachian Trail(IRE), who has run well on this track in the past, travelled well in the slipstream of Reverence but could not quicken and will be ideally served by an extra furlong. (op 20-1)
Drayton(IRE) fitted with the eyeshield for the first time, showed plenty of speed before fading. (op 6-1)

3895 CENKOS SECURITIES OCTOBER CLUB MAIDEN FILLIES' CHARITY STKS 6f
2:10 (2:12) (Class 4) 2-Y-O **£6,477** (£1,927; £963; £481) **Stalls** Centre

Form RPR

4 **1** **Albabilia (IRE)**[14] 3507 2-9-0 0 KerrinMcEvoy 8 94
(C E Brittain) *lw: sn led: kpt slt advantage and r.o wl whn strly chal fr over 2f out: asserted wl ins fnl f* **9/2**[2]

2 *hd* **Naomh Geileis (USA)** 2-9-0 0 JoeFanning 9 93
(M Johnston) *str: scope: lw: sn w wnr and strly chal fr over 2f out: styd on wl but no ex cl home* **22/1**

0 **3** *shd* **Nahoodh (IRE)**[16] 3432 2-9-0 0 JHBowman 13 93+
(M R Channon) *hld up in rr: n.m.r over 2f out and sn swtchd rt: qcknd to chse ldrs 1f out: styd on wl cl home but a jst hld* **11/4**[1]

4 *5* **Rinterval (IRE)** 2-9-0 0 PatDobbs 16 78
(R Hannon) *str: bit bkwd: chsd ldrs: rdn 2f out: outpcd by ldng trio fnl f but hld on wl for 4th* **13/2**[3]

5 *1/2* **Double On Red** 2-9-0 0 HayleyTurner 12 77
(J M P Eustace) *neat: cmpt: mid-div and sn drvn along: kpt on wl thrght fnl f but nvr gng pce to be competitive* **12/1**

6 *3/4* **Acquifer** 2-9-0 0 IanMongan 4 74
(J L Dunlop) *cmpt: in rr: rdn 3f out: styd on fr over 1f out and gng on cl home but nvr a danger* **25/1**

7 *nk* **Mullein** 2-9-0 0 GeorgeBaker 6 73
(R M Beckett) *neat: lw: s.i.s: bhd: stl plenty to do and rdn over 2f out: r.o strly thrght fnl f: gng on cl home* **11/1**

8 *1/2* **Joffe's Run (USA)** 2-9-0 0 JimmyFortune 5 72
(B J Meehan) *unf: chsd ldrs: rdn over 2f out and kpt on same pce* **16/1**

9 *hd* **Totem Flower (IRE)** 2-9-0 0 SteveDrowne 3 71+
(R Charlton) *tall: lw: in rr: sn drvn along: plenty to do 2f out: r.o wl appr fnl f: kpt on wl cl home* **25/1**

10 *1/2* **Manhattan Dream (USA)** 2-9-0 0 MichaelHills 2 70
(B W Hills) *str: lw: chsd ldrs: pushed along 3f out: one pce fnl 2f* **25/1**

11 *nk* **Ballora (FR)** 2-9-0 0 KDarley 14 69
(S Kirk) *leggy: in rr: pushed along 1/2-way: kpt on fnl f but nvr in contention* **33/1**

4 **12** *shd* **Patio**[41] 2658 2-9-0 0 RichardHughes 1 69
(Mrs A J Perrett) *chsd ldrs: rdn over 2f out: wknd fnl f* **11/1**

3 **13** *1 3/4* **Amylee (IRE)**[30] 2997 2-9-0 0 PhilipRobinson 11 63
(C G Cox) *chsd ldrs: pushed along over 2f out: wknd fnl f* **7/1**

0 **14** *1/2* **Jelly Mo**[55] 2241 2-9-0 0 RHills 10 62
(J W Hills) *chsd ldrs: rdn over 2f out: wknd over 1f out* **80/1**

15 *1 1/2* **La Columbina** 2-9-0 0 RyanMoore 15 57
(R Hannon) *str: lw: outpcd most of way* **16/1**

16 *2* **Tea Cake (IRE)** 2-9-0 0 MartinDwyer 17 51
(H J L Dunlop) *w'like: scope: wnt rt s: a outpcd* **40/1**

1m 16.35s (1.45) **Going Correction** +0.30s/f (Good) **16** Ran SP% **129.3**
Speed ratings (Par 93): **102,101,101,94,94 93,92,92,91,91 90,90,88,87,85 83**
CSF £111.07 TOTE £5.60: £2.10, £12.20, £1.80; EX 177.00 Trifecta £273.40 Part won. Pool £385.21 - 0.50 winning units..
Owner Saif Ali **Bred** Paul And Eilidh Hyland **Trained** Newmarket, Suffolk

FOCUS
An interesting fillies' maiden run 2.04 sec slower than the earlier Group 3, but still a respectable time for the grade, and the first three pulled clear. The form looks quite strong.

NOTEBOOK
Albabilia(IRE), who made her debut in a decent-looking Newmarket maiden earlier in the month, boosted that form with a game display. She had clearly learnt a lot from her debut and made virtually all up the centre of the track. She kept finding for pressure and the stamina on her dam's side proved a valuable asset. No doubt her trainer will be looking to secure some black type now. (op 6-1 tchd 13-2)
Naomh Geileis(USA) ◆, a $90,000 yearling who is related to several speedy types, knew her job on this debut and really stuck to her task, having kept the winner company all the way. She had a hard race here, but her trainer specialises in tough sorts and he should be able to find her a maiden before going on to better things (op 16-1 tchd 25-1)
Nahoodh(IRE) ◆, who made her debut in the Cherry Hinton Stakes, is clearly well thought of and went off favourite. However, she was held up off the pace and found herself with a fair amount of ground to make up from the halfway mark. She ran on well in the final furlong and only just failed to catch the two fillies who had disputed the lead from the start. She should not be long getting off the mark. (op 5-2 tchd 10-3)
Rinterval(IRE), who is from a good family of milers, ran well on this debut, despite being left behind by the first three. She is the type to progress a fair amount with racing and is likely to be placed to score before too long.
Double On Red, a half-sister to Rapscallion and Orcadian, both of whom showed Group-race form as juveniles, made an encouraging start to her career. The race will definitely bring her on. (tchd 11-1)
Acquifer, a half-sister to six winners from an excellent family, was another to run a decent first race and she will appreciate a little further in time. (tchd 28-1)
Mullein ◆ ran really well having missed the break and was a couple of lengths last at the intersection with the round course. However, she responded to pressure to pick up and run past a number of her rivals in the last furlong to finish as well as anything. There looks to be more to come from this half-sister to the multiple winners Illustrious Blue and Romany Nights. (op 14-1 tchd 16-1)

3896 JOHN GUEST EBF MAIDEN STKS 7f
2:45 (2:47) (Class 3) 2-Y-O **£6,800** (£2,023; £1,011; £505) **Stalls** Centre

Form RPR

1 **City Leader (IRE)** 2-9-3 0 KDarley 7 84+
(B J Meehan) *tall: unf: scope: in tch: drvn and rapid hdwy over 1f out: hung bdly rt ins fnl f and led fnl 100yds: readily* **33/1**

2 *1 1/4* **Bold Choice (IRE)** 2-9-3 0 PhilipRobinson 13 81+
(M A Jarvis) *w'like: chsd ldrs tl led over 2f out: rdn over 1f out: edgd lft ins fnl f: hdd and one pce fnl 100yds* **9/2**[3]

3 *shd* **Missioner (USA)** 2-9-3 0 JoeFanning 10 81
(M Johnston) *gd sort: lengthy: lw: sn w ldr: stl upsides and rdn fr 2f out: kpt on same pce wl ins fnl f* **14/1**

0 **4** *1* **Dubai Samurai**[16] 3435 2-9-3 0 JHBowman 12 78
(J W Hills) *chsd ldrs: rdn over 2f out: styd on same pce ins fnl f* **66/1**

5 *1/2* **Bencoolen (IRE)** 2-9-3 0 SteveDrowne 14 77
(R Charlton) *neat: sn chsng ldrs: rdn to chal 2f out: no ex ins fnl f* **14/1**

423 **6** *shd* **Ordinance (USA)**[13] 3522 2-9-3 0 JimmyFortune 8 80+
(T G Mills) *lw: slt advantage tl hdd over 2f out: styng on same pce whn bdly hmpd and lost 4th ins fnl f* **4/1**[2]

7 *shd* **Majestic Marauder (USA)** 2-9-3 0 RyanMoore 5 76
(Sir Michael Stoute) *wl grwn: b.hind: in rr: rdn over 2f out: styd on wl fnl f but nvr in contention* **7/4**[1]

8 *2* **Yathreb (USA)** 2-9-3 0 RHills 2 71+
(J L Dunlop) *str: scope: lw: in rr: rdn and green 3f out: stl plenty to do over 1f out: kpt on ins fnl f* **7/1**

9 *shd* **Morestead (IRE)** 2-9-3 0 GeorgeBaker 9 71+
(B G Powell) *str: bit bkwd: in rr: pushed along 1/2-way: kpt on fr over 1f out but nvr a danger* **33/1**

10 *shd* **Moville (IRE)** 2-9-3 0 MichaelHills 6 71+
(B W Hills) *leggy: lw: in rr: shkn up 2f out: kpt on fnl f: gng on cl home* **50/1**

5 **11** *2 1/2* **Lobby**[13] 3551 2-9-3 0 RichardHughes 11 65
(Mrs A J Perrett) *in rr: rdn and hdwy over 2f out: nvr quite gng pce to rch ldrs: sn one pce* **16/1**

12 *shd* **Perks (IRE)** 2-9-3 0 EddieAhern 1 64
(J L Dunlop) *str: scope: bit bkwd: chsd ldrs: rdn over 2f out: wknd over 1f out* **33/1**

0 **13** *3/4* **Traphalgar (IRE)**[15] 3462 2-9-3 0 TQuinn 4 63
(P F I Cole) *chsd ldrs: rdn over 2f out: wknd over 1f out* **50/1**

14 *nk* **Red Merlin (IRE)** 2-9-3 0 AdamKirby 3 62
(C G Cox) *unf: lw: s.i.s: a outpcd* **40/1**

1m 31.01s (2.91) **Going Correction** +0.30s/f (Good) **14** Ran SP% **122.9**
Speed ratings (Par 98): **95,93,93,92,91 91,91,89,89,89 86,86,85,84**
CSF £175.69 TOTE £18.60: £4.50, £2.40, £3.50; EX 226.30 Trifecta £580.30 Part won. Pool £817.34 - 0.20 winning units..
Owner Sangster Family **Bred** Swettenham Stud **Trained** Manton, Wilts
■ Stewards' Enquiry : K Darley three-day ban: careless riding (Aug 7-9)

FOCUS
An interesting maiden featuring several well-bred sorts from major stables but a surprise result and a controversial finish. The early pace was not that strong and those in the frame were always near the front, but the form is reasonably solid.

NOTEBOOK
City Leader(IRE), a half-brother to top performers Lit De Justice, Commander Collins and Colonel Collins, was from a yard whose juveniles usually benefit for their first outing and was unfancied in the market. However, he produced a change of gear despite running green to take the lead in last side the last and won in the style of a colt with a decent future. He did go sharply right under pressure causing interference to Ordinance in particular, and with his jockey persisting in using his whip in his left hand a ban was inevitable. His trainer has entered him in a couple of Group races in the autum, but he is likely to look for a conditions event first. (op 25-1)
Bold Choice(IRE) ◆, a half-brother to three winners including a triple juvenile winner and from the family of Oath, has been entered in the Derby. He made a particularly encouraging debut, having raced up with the pace throughout, and only getting run out of it late on. He should have no trouble winning his maiden and he shapes as if he will appreciate further in due course.
Missioner(USA) ◆, a big, strapping son of Rahy, was another to run a race full of promise. Up with the pace from the start, he kept going in resolute fashion despite looking as if the experience will not be lost on him. He has an entry at Goodwood next week, but that is likely to come too soon, and he seems more likely to be aimed at a maiden before stepping up in grade and has the scope to develop into a decent performer.
Dubai Samurai, who was well beaten on his debut at Newmarket, had clearly benefited from that outing as he performed much better this time. He should continue to progress and looks capable of winning races. (op 80-1)
Bencoolen(IRE), a 110,000gns half-brother to the useful Puggy, from a family full of high-class middle-distance performers, made a satisfactory debut having seen plenty of daylight. He looks sure to come on for the run. (op 22-1)

Ordinance(USA), the most experienced runner in the line-up, came into this with some fair form, including over course and distance. He had every chance but just appeared to be held when squeezed out badly between the eventual winner and the third. He would probably have finished a length or two closer with a clear run and gives a fair indicator of the level of the form. (tchd 9-2 and 5-1 in a place)

Majestic Marauder(USA) ◆, a $200,000 half-brother to several winners at 7f-1m, went off favourite but was held up and could not get a clear run when he needed it. He ran on to do best of those coming from behind without ever threatening to get involved and a lot better can be expected next time. (op 6-4 tchd 11-8 and 2-1 in places)

Yathreb(USA), a half-brother to Sakhee among others, looked in need of the experience despite being supported in the market, but as the race worked out being held up at the back was not the place to be. (op 14-1)

Moville(IRE), a half-brother to the stayer Sweetness Herself but also to sprinters, missed the break slightly and was held up at the back. He was noted keeping on quite nicely under considerate handling and should come on considerably with this under his belt. (op 40-1)

3897 EUROPEAN BREEDERS' FUND VALIANT STKS (LISTED RACE) (F&M) 1m (S)

3:20 (3:21) (Class 1) 3-Y-0+

£17,034 (£6,456; £3,231; £1,611; £807; £405) **Stalls** Centre

Form RPR

2340 **1** **Whazzis**[16] 3430 3-8-7 87 ....(v) KerrinMcEvoy 4 107
(W J Haggas) *hld up in mid-div: rapid hdwy 2f out to ld wl over 1f out: c clr ins fnl f: easily* **16/1**

0440 **2** *6* **Fann (USA)**[21] 3271 4-9-1 104 .... RyanMoore 14 95
(C E Brittain) *in rr: hdwy fr 2f out: bmpd over 1f out: styng on but no ch w wnr whn bmpd again ins fnl f: kpt on* **16/1**

0610 **3** *½* **Lady Stardust**[16] 3437 4-9-1 85 .... OscarUrbina 9 94
(J R Fanshawe) *in rr: rdn 3f out: styd on fr over 1f out and kpt on cl home to take 3rd* **10/1**

401- **4** *¾* **Wagtail**[307] 5525 4-9-5 95 .... JimmyFortune 11 96
(E A L Dunlop) *chsd ldrs: rdn and effrt to chse wnr 1f out but no imp: hung lft ins fnl f: sn one pce* **8/1**

0-22 **5** *1 ¼* **Sudoor**[64] 1958 3-8-7 102 .... MartinDwyer 8 87
(J L Dunlop) *t.k.h: sn led: hdd 4f out: rdn 3f out: stl upsides 2f out: one pce fnl f* **4/1**[1]

12-0 **6** *nk* **Smart Ass (IRE)**[189] 185 4-9-1 72 .... RichardHughes 7 89
(J S Moore) *in rr: rdn 1/2-way: kpt on fr over 1f out: gng on cl home* **66/1**

4643 **7** *hd* **Treat**[20] 3332 3-8-7 104 .... DarryllHolland 6 86
(M R Channon) *lw: chsd ldrs: rdn over 2f out: one pce fnl f* **4/1**[1]

/55- **8** *hd* **Tiana**[307] 5525 4-9-1 98 .... SteveDrowne 13 88
(Mrs A J Perrett) *in tch: rdn along 3f out: kpt on but nvr gng pce to be competitive* **20/1**

-545 **9** *½* **Summer's Eve**[27] 3103 4-9-1 96 .... FergusSweeney 12 87
(H Candy) *plld hrd: led 4f out: hdd wl over 1f out and sn wknd* **12/1**

5-15 **10** *3 ½* **Harvest Queen (IRE)**[56] 2207 4-9-5 105 .... EddieAhern 3 83
(P J Makin) *in tch: stdy hdwy to trck ldrs over 2f out: sn rdn: edgd lft over 1f out and sn btn* **13/2**[3]

30-5 **11** *5* **Cumin (USA)**[15] 3463 3-8-7 100 .... PaulHanagan 10 65
(B W Hills) *b.hind: chsd ldrs: rdn 3f out: wknd fr 2f out* **12/1**

0-40 **12** *8* **Kaseema (USA)**[82] 1496 3-8-7 97 .... RHills 5 47
(Sir Michael Stoute) *swtg: chsd ldrs: rdn 3f out: wknd over 2f out* **6/1**[2]

4664 **13** *5* **Knapton Hill**[22] 3239 3-8-7 82 .... JoeFanning 1 35
(R Hollinshead) *in tch 5f* **100/1**

-600 **14** *31* **Bowness**[19] 3344 5-9-1 75 .... KDarley 2 —
(J G Given) *lw: a towards rr: lost tch fnl 3f: t.o* **100/1**

1m 42.31s (0.51) **Going Correction** +0.30s/f (Good)
WFA 3 from 4yo+ 8lb **14** Ran SP% **123.2**
Speed ratings (Par 111): **109,103,102,101,100 100,100,99,99,95 90,82,77,46**
CSF £251.68 TOTE £21.40: £5.50, £5.50, £4.30; EX 253.60 Trifecta £651.50 Part won. Pool £917.74 - 0.10 winning units..
Owner W Gredley & The Hon Mrs Peter Stanley **Bred** Eurostrait Ltd **Trained** Newmarket, Suffolk
■ Stewards' Enquiry : Jimmy Fortune three-day ban: careless riding (Aug 7-9)

FOCUS
An ordinary fillies' Listed race but a runaway winner. The form looks dubious with the third and sixth raising doubts.

NOTEBOOK

Whazzis, who was unlucky in running in the first-time visor at Newmarket last time, had not such problems in this higher grade and over a longer trip and absolutely sluiced up. Her handicap mark will shoot up now, but that may not be a problem, as connections are looking to find a Group race for her.

Fann(USA), who did not appear to get 10f last time, had been rated only 77 before running well behind Nannina over course and distance at the Royal meeting. She came from well back to earn black type despite not getting the best of passages, and although she beat the rest well enough the winner was long gone.

Lady Stardust, earned black type at the first attempt, having been racing in handicaps prior to this. She came from the rear and got a clear-enough run, so probably represents the best guide to the level of the form.

Wagtail, having her first outing since winning a Listed handicap here last September and, with the usual tongue tie left off, ran well until getting very tired and wandering in the final furlong, earning her rider a three-day ban. (op 10-1)

Sudoor, both of whose races this season have been over 10f, was too keen early and evidence suggests she is better suited by a sounder surface. (op 5-1)

Smart Ass(IRE), a four-time Fibresand winner, has never won on turf and is rated just 72. She ran on well from the rear on this return from a six-month break but her proximity limits the form. (op 100-1)

Treat, runner-up in the Fillies' Mile last year and fourth in the 1000 Guineas on her return, has been running well below that form recently and did so again on ground that has suited in the past. Connections must be scratching their heads wondering where they go with her from here. (op 5-1)

Harvest Queen(IRE) travelled well but then did not find a lot when asked. Her profile suggests she is a filly who goes well fresh and is possibly a spring filly. (op 15-2 tchd 8-1)

Kaseema(USA), not seen since being well beaten in the 1000 Guineas having run well in the Nell Gwyn previously, was quite keen early but dropped out very tamely and has a good deal to prove now. (op 4-1)

3898 JOHN GUEST BROWN JACK STKS (H'CAP) 2m

3:55 (3:56) (Class 2) (0-100,97) 3-Y-0+ **£12,954** (£3,854; £1,926; £962) **Stalls** High

Form RPR

5050 **1** **Odiham**[27] 3090 6-9-6 89 ....(v) SteveDrowne 10 96
(H Morrison) *swtg: set modest pce: drvn and qcknd fr 2f out: styd on wl whn strly chal fr over 1f out* **7/1**[3]

2131 **2** *½* **Thewhirlingdervish (IRE)**[10] 3609 9-8-9 78 6ex .... KDarley 6 84
(T D Easterby) *lw: chsd ldrs: rdn and qcknd to chal wnr 1f out: outstyd wl ins fnl f* **8/1**

100- **3** *¾* **Mirjan (IRE)**[153] 6319 11-9-7 90 ....(b) PaulHanagan 5 96
(L Lungo) *lw: t.k.h: stdd mid-div 1/2-way: rdn and hdwy fr 3f out: styd on to chse ldrs ins fnl f but a hld* **20/1**

0441 **4** *½* **Ogee**[25] 3153 4-9-11 94 .... RyanMoore 8 99
(Sir Michael Stoute) *trckd ldrs: rdn and effrt whn n.m.r over 2f out: hung rt sn after and styd on same pce* **6/1**[2]

-063 **5** *nk* **Mudawin (IRE)**[69] 1844 6-9-12 95 .... KerrinMcEvoy 7 100
(Jane Chapple-Hyam) *chsd ldrs: rdn 3f out: styd on same pce fnl 2f* **7/1**[3]

1440 **6** *½* **Monolith**[27] 3090 9-9-1 84 .... TomEaves 2 88
(L Lungo) *chsd wnr: rdn 3f out: outpcd appr fnl f* **33/1**

-042 **7** *nk* **Desert Sea (IRE)**[21] 3273 4-8-13 82 .... FergusSweeney 1 86+
(D W P Arbuthnot) *hld up in rr: rdn and hdwy on outside over 2f out: kpt on but nvr gng pce to rch ldrs* **14/1**

0301 **8** *shd* **Enjoy The Moment**[34] 2860 4-10-0 97 .... MartinDwyer 3 100+
(J A Osborne) *hld up in rr: stl last and nt clr run ins fnl 3f: kpt on ins fnl f but nvr in contention* **7/2**[1]

3033 **9** *hd* **Tilt**[27] 3090 5-9-3 86 .... JimmyFortune 9 89+
(B Ellison) *hld up in rr: hdwy on ins over 2f out: kpt on but nvr nr ldrs* **7/2**[1]

P-23 **10** *3* **Sphinx (FR)**[21] 3273 9-9-2 85 ....(b) IanMongan 4 85
(Jamie Poulton) *in rr: rdn and effrt 3f out: nvr nr ldrs and sn btn* **14/1**

3m 40.09s (9.93) **Going Correction** +0.55s/f (Yiel) **10** Ran SP% **115.9**
Speed ratings (Par 109): **97,96,96,96,95 95,95,95,95,93**
CSF £61.45 CT £1069.02 TOTE £10.30: £2.60, £1.70, £5.20; EX 62.10 Trifecta £869.30 Part won. Pool £1,224.38 - 0.20 winning units..
Owner D L Brooks, J F Dean, Mrs J Scott **Bred** Glebe Stud **Trained** East Ilsley, Berks

FOCUS
A decent staying handicap in which the winner dictated a steady pace and the field finished closely bunched, with three lengths separating the first nine and the finish dominated by the older generation. The form appears sound enough but slightly limited.

NOTEBOOK

Odiham, who had not won on turf for over three years, had the visor back on and dictated a steady pace. He responded well to pressure to hold off the runner-up and is likely to come back here in a fortnight for the stayers' event at the Shergar Cup meeting. (op 12-1)

Thewhirlingdervish(IRE), who has rediscovered his form in the last year after dropping down the handicap, ran really well in an attempt to repeat his win in this race back in 2002 off his highest mark since early 2005. He looked sure to win when throwing down his challenge at the furlong pole, but the winner would not be denied. He will not find things easy from now on. (tchd 15-2)

Mirjan(IRE), not seen since pulling up over hurdles in February, was quite keen held up off the steady pace and in the circumstances ran really well. He can be expected to build on this and connections will presumably be aiming him at the Cesarewitch once again. (op 18-1 tchd 16-1)

Ogee, who just got home over 1m6f last time, was racing over this trip for the first time since the Royal meeting last season and was always close to the pace. Although he did not have much room at one point, seemed to have every chance and did not pick up as might have been expected. He is in the Ebor next month and the return to 1m6f and a likely good pace should suit him better. (op 11-2 tchd 13-2)

Mudawin(IRE) ◆, a shock winner of the Ebor last season, was quite keen under restraint and then could not pick up when the pace quickened, just keeping on at the one pace. This was his first run for ten weeks however, and it should have set him up nicely for a repeat success in the big York handicap. (op 8-1)

Monolith ran a reasonable race but could not quicken on this ground and is best suited by a sound surface. (op 28-1)

Desert Sea(IRE), who has yet to win on turf, is clearly in good form at present through and was not helped by being held up off a steady pace. (op 12-1)

Enjoy The Moment, winner of the Queen Alexandra at the Royal Meeting, was held up as he has been in recent races, but in view of the funereal gallop would surely have been better ridden more positively. In the event he did not get a clear-enough run and then could not pick up well enough anyway. This run can be ignored and he is sure to get a stronger pace if returning here for the Shergar Cup meeting. Official explanation: jockey said gelding was denied a clear run (op 11-4)

Tilt, another who is well suited by a strong gallop, was held up and, like the other joint favourite, would have been much better off ridden closer to the pace. (op 4-1 tchd 9-2 in places)

3899 SODEXHO H'CAP 1m 2f

4:30 (4:30) (Class 2) (0-105,101) 3-Y-0+

£9,971 (£2,985; £1,492; £747; £372; £187) **Stalls** High

Form RPR

13-2 **1** **Tears Of A Clown (IRE)**[8] 3672 4-8-12 85 .... MartinDwyer 2 95+
(J A Osborne) *in rr: stl last 3f out: plld to outside and str run fr 2f out: led wl ins fnl f: edgd rt cl home: drvn out* **7/2**[2]

43-1 **2** *nk* **Familiar Territory**[51] 2351 4-10-0 101 .... KerrinMcEvoy 1 112+
(Saeed Bin Suroor) *lw: hld up in rr: hdwy and nt clr run 2f out and again over 1f out: swtchd rt: styd on strly ins fnl f but nt quite rch wnr* **4/1**[3]

6061 **3** *nk* **Dunaskin (IRE)**[33] 2906 7-9-6 93 .... RHills 6 101
(Karen McLintock) *led over 7f out: styd trcking ldr tl led again over 2f out: sn hrd drvn and kpt on: hdd and no ex wl ins fnl f: lost 2nd cl home* **17/2**

500 **4** *1 ¾* **Speedy Sam**[13] 3558 4-9-3 90 .... JimmyFortune 7 95
(K R Burke) *chsd ldrs: rdn 2f out: styd on to chal 1f out: wknd ins fnl f* **10/1**

/21- **5** *½* **Galactic Star**[282] 6053 4-8-10 83 .... RyanMoore 3 87
(Sir Michael Stoute) *lw: trckd ldrs: rdn and effrt over 2f out: nvr quite gng pce to chal: wknd fnl f* **7/4**[1]

10-0 **6** *3 ½* **Invasian (IRE)**[30] 3002 6-8-12 85 ....(e[1]) DarryllHolland 4 82
(P W D'Arcy) *plld hrd: led 7f out: rdn and hdd over 2f out: wknd over 1f out* **25/1**

4050 **7** *nk* **Impeller (IRE)**[83] 1477 8-9-6 98 .... TolleyDean[(5)] 8 94
(J S Moore) *lw: mid-div: rdn and hdwy on ins over 2f out and sn chsng ldrs: no imp: wknd ins fnl f* **25/1**

-460 **8** *¾* **Star Of Light**[21] 3272 6-9-8 95 .... RichardHughes 5 90
(B J Meehan) *in rr: rdn and sme hdwy over 2f out: nvr in contention and sn wknd* **10/1**

2m 11.02s (3.02) **Going Correction** +0.55s/f (Yiel) **8** Ran SP% **115.0**
Speed ratings (Par 109): **109,108,108,107,106 103,103,103**
CSF £18.06 CT £106.71 TOTE £4.20: £1.70, £1.70, £2.20; EX 15.10 Trifecta £45.60 Pool £839.33 - 13.04 winning units..
Owner Mountgrange Stud **Bred** A Stroud & J Hanly **Trained** Upper Lambourn, Berks

FOCUS
A good handicap featuring several unexposed sorts and run at a good early pace that slowed mid-race, and producing a close finish. The form is rated through the third to his latest mark.

NOTEBOOK

Tears Of A Clown(IRE), who is very lightly raced, was making a quick reappearance after running well on his return from a 14-month absence last time. He showed no signs of the 'bounce factor' as he ran on gamely under strong pressure to get the upper hand near the line. He should not go up too much for this but may now need a little while to recover, and looks the sort who could go well in the John Smith's Handicap at Newbury next month. (op 11-4 tchd 4-1 in places)

Familiar Territory ◆, another lightly-raced sort who was a winner on Polytrack on his return to action, looked somewhat unlucky as he was impeded more than once in the straight before staying on really well near the line. He deserves compensation and is one to bear in mind as his yard hits top form. (op 9-2 tchd 5-1)

Dunaskin(IRE), who won in first-time cheekpieces last time, had them left off on this occasion. He was up with the pace from the start and and showed a good attitude when tackled, only just being run out of it late on. He does not look that favourably handicapped but is running well at present. (op 10-1 tchd 8-1)
Speedy Sam, who ran well on his retun from a break in the John Smith's Cup at York last time, again performed with credit and could well pick up a decent handicap before long. (op 9-1)
Galactic Star, another unexposed colt, was made favourite despite having not run since October last year. He has given the impression in the past that he has a little temperament and he did not look the easiest of rides here, but that said he ran respectably, only fading in the closng stages. (op 15-8 tchd 2-1)
Invasian(IRE) had the 'pacifier' on for the first time, but it had a negative effect as he pulled really hard until getting to the front, whereupon he settled. It was no surprise he had nothing in reserve for the business end of the race.
Impeller(IRE), another returning from a break, having raced in Dubai in the winter, would have been suited by a better gallop but ran well enough until appearing to blow up in the last furlong or so. He will be interesting with this behind him back on a switchback track. (op 33-1)
Star Of Light is gradually slipping down the handicap but did not offer a lot this time. He may be a different proposition if aimed at the John Smith's Cup at Newbury, a race he won last season, on a track that suits him better. (op 12-1)

3900 JOHN GUEST H'CAP 1m (S)
5:05 (5:05) (Class 4) (0-85,84) 3-Y-0+ £6,477 (£1,927; £963; £481) Stalls Centre

Form RPR
0042 1 **Wovoka (IRE)**[14] 3482 4-9-11 **81** DarryllHolland 4 89
(M R Channon) *hld up in rr: swtchd rt and gd hdwy fr 2f out: str run u.p to ld cl home* **9/1**
-100 2 *nk* **Leptis Magna**[28] 3056 3-8-10 **74** JoeFanning 10 79
(D R C Elsworth) *t.k.h: chsd ldrs: rdn to ld appr fnl 2f: kpt on u.p tl ct cl home* **8/1**
132- 3 *¾* **Baylini**[220] 6866 3-8-12 **83** SophieDoyle(7) 7 86
(Ms J S Doyle) *in rr: rdn over 2f out: hdwy over 1f out and styd on wl to chse ldrs ins fnl f: one pce nr fin* **33/1**
-110 4 *1* **Golden Prospect**[43] 2598 3-8-7 **71** RHills 6 72
(J W Hills) *in rr: gd hdwy over 2f out to chse ldrs over 1f out: nvr quite gng pce to chal and sn no ex* **14/1**
0325 5 *1¼* **Harare**[13] 3525 6-9-2 **77** (v) TolleyDean(5) 2 77
(R J Price) *lw: in tch: smooth hdwy to trck ldrs 2f out: rdn over 1f out: wknd ins fnl f* **14/1**
5243 6 *4* **Full Victory (IRE)**[13] 3556 5-9-8 **83** PatrickHills(5) 8 74
(R A Farrant) *lw: chsd ldrs: hrd drven 3f out: wknd qckly ins fnl 2f* **11/2**[3]
10-5 7 *3½* **Personify**[94] 1209 5-9-4 **74** (p) AdamKirby 1 57
(C G Cox) *swtg: racd alone stands' side: wl in tch whn rdn over 3f out: wknd qckly fr 2f out* **16/1**
2-1 8 *2* **Fifty Cents**[63] 1995 3-9-4 **82** SteveDrowne 3 58
(R Charlton) *lw: led after 1f and t.k.h: hdd over 4f out: wknd 2f out* **2/1**[1]
4625 9 *3½* **Master Pegasus**[37] 2771 4-10-0 **84** GeorgeBaker 9 54
(C F Wall) *swtg: chsd ldrs tl wknd qckly 2f out* **4/1**[2]
-040 10 *3½* **Tumbleweed Glory (IRE)**[16] 3437 4-8-13 **76** KMay(7) 11 38
(B J Meehan) *lw: led 1f: styd w ldr tl led again over 4f out: hdd appr fnl 2f and wknd qckly* **14/1**

1m 44.22s (2.42) **Going Correction** +0.30s/f (Good)
WFA 3 from 4yo+ 8lb **10** Ran SP% **118.7**
Speed ratings (Par 105): **99,98,97,96,95 91,88,86,82,79**
CSF £80.33 CT £2317.90 TOTE £9.20: £2.40, £2.90, £4.10; EX 77.30 TRIFECTA Not won. Place 6 £2437.42, Place 5 £930.43..
Owner Mrs T Burns **Bred** Rathasker Stud **Trained** West Ilsley, Berks

FOCUS
Just an ordinary handicap for the track and the pace was modest, resulting in a time 1.91 sec slower than the earlier Listed race. The form does not look that solid.
Fifty Cents Official explanation: jockey said colt ran too free early
T/Jkpt: Not won. T/Plt: £5,422.20 to a £1 stake. Pool: £101,016.80. 13.60 winning tickets. T/Qpdt: £471.40 to a £1 stake. Pool: £6,561.90. 10.30 winning tickets. ST

3485 CHEPSTOW (L-H)
Friday, July 27

OFFICIAL GOING: Heavy
The ground was testing after the meeting survived a morning inspection.
Wind: Almost nil Weather: Fine

3901 TOTEPLACEPOT AMATEUR RIDERS' H'CAP 1m 4f 23y
6:20 (6:20) (Class 6) (0-65,65) 3-Y-0+ £1,998 (£619; £309; £154) Stalls Low

Form RPR
0500 1 **Global Traffic**[25] 3155 3-10-1 **60** MissEFolkes(3) 4 66
(P D Evans) *s.s: hld up in rr: swtchd rt over 4f out: hdwy over 3f out: led wl over 1f out: drvn out* **25/1**
130 2 *½* **Pocket Too**[62] 677 4-10-9 **58** MrAshleePrice(5) 12 63
(M Salaman) *chsd ldr: led over 3f out: sn rdn: hdd wl over 1f out: r.o ins fnl f* **9/1**
6351 3 *2½* **Raquel White**[36] 2793 3-9-13 **62** MrRPFlint(7) 16 64
(J L Flint) *hld up in mid-div: hdwy over 5f out: ev ch over 2f out: sn rdn: one pce fnl f* **8/1**[3]
0352 4 *1* **Sovietta (IRE)**[21] 3280 6-10-9 **53** (t) MissCHannaford 8 53
(A G Newcombe) *s.i.s: hld up and bhd: hdwy on ins over 3f out: edgd rt over 1f out: styd on ins fnl f* **7/1**[2]
0/31 5 *2* **Grey Samurai**[10] 3610 7-10-12 **56** 6ex MissLEllison 7 53
(B Ellison) *hld up in tch: rdn 3f out: wknd 2f out* **13/8**[1]
000- 6 *1¾* **Dovedale**[262] 5971 7-10-5 **52** MrNScholfield(3) 1 47
(Mrs S D Williams) *s.i.s: sn prom: rdn 4f out: wknd over 2f out* **16/1**
2062 7 *1* **My Legal Eagle (IRE)**[14] 3485 13-9-12 **49** MissIPickard(7) 10 42
(E G Bevan) *hld up and bhd: hdwy over 3f out: no further prog* **12/1**
5221 8 *1* **Rudry World (IRE)**[15] 3457 4-10-6 **55** MissMMullineaux(5) 5 47
(M Mullineaux) *prom: rdn 4f out: wknd over 2f out* **8/1**[3]
4003 9 *7* **Padre Nostro (IRE)**[14] 3485 8-9-11 **46** MrLRPayter(5) 9 28
(M Sheppard) *hld up in tch: rdn over 3f out: wknd 2f out* **16/1**
46-0 10 *1* **River Gypsy**[123] 134 6-9-11 **48** MrSTPayne(7) 11 29
(J D Frost) *led: hdd over 3f out: sn wknd* **40/1**
11 *¾* **Mancebo (GER)**[117] 4-10-2 **46** oh1 MissFayeBramley 13 26
(R Curtis) *hld up in mid-div: wknd over 3f out* **33/1**
/044 12 *1¼* **Ashmolian (IRE)**[14] 3485 4-10-0 **49** MissGDGracey-Davison(5) 6 27
(Miss Z C Davison) *mid-div: rdn over 3f out: sn struggling* **25/1**
0140 13 *21* **King Of The Beers (USA)**[33] 2915 3-9-11 **53** MissLHorner 2 2
(C Roberts) *a bhd* **20/1**
00 14 *18* **Investment Pearl (IRE)**[39] 2721 4-9-13 **50** MissCBoxall(7) 15 —
(D R Gandolfo) *a bhd* **66/1**
500- 15 *134* **Magnum Opus (IRE)**[211] 5513 5-11-7 **65** (p) MrsSMoore 3 —
(J S Moore) *t.k.h in mid-div: lost pl over 5f out: eased whn no ch fnl 2f* **28/1**

2m 51.23s (12.51) **Going Correction** +1.075s/f (Soft)
WFA 3 from 4yo+ 12lb **15** Ran SP% **125.0**
Speed ratings (Par 101): **101,100,99,98,97 95,95,94,89,89 88,87,73,61,—**
CSF £230.23 CT £1996.74 TOTE £39.70: £10.20, £3.90, £2.60; EX 641.80.
Owner Mrs Folkes, Mrs Madden & Mrs Prendergast **Bred** P F I Cole **Trained** Pandy, Monmouths

FOCUS
A poor amateurs' handicap rated around the first three.
Global Traffic Official explanation: trainer had no explanation for the apparent improvement in form
Magnum Opus(IRE) Official explanation: jockey said gelding had a breathing problem

3902 TOTESPORT 0800 221 221 MAIDEN AUCTION STKS 6f 16y
6:50 (6:50) (Class 5) 2-Y-0 £2,849 (£847; £423; £211) Stalls High

Form RPR
4 1 **Whiteoak Lady (IRE)**[22] 3245 2-8-4 0 FrancisNorton 8 69
(J L Spearing) *w ldr: rdn 2f out: led 1f out: r.o* **11/4**[2]
2 2 *¾* **Baronovici (IRE)**[46] 2510 2-8-11 0 PatDobbs 7 74
(R Hannon) *led: rdn 2f out: hdd 1f out: kpt on* **5/2**[1]
05 3 *2½* **Ezthegezza**[13] 3550 2-8-9 0 LPKeniry 4 64
(J S Moore) *a.p: rdn 2f out: no ex ins fnl f* **7/2**[3]
0 4 *½* **Observatory Ridge**[83] 1469 2-8-4 0 RichardSmith 2 58+
(M D I Usher) *wnt lft s: sn in tch: rdn and outpcd over 3f out: styd on fr over 1f out: nt rch ldrs* **16/1**
5 *¾* **Lady Jinks** 2-8-4 0 HayleyTurner 9 56
(M D I Usher) *s.i.s: rdn over 3f out: outpcd over 2f out: styd on fnl f* **14/1**
00 6 *½* **Singer Of Songs (IRE)**[27] 3095 2-8-13 0 TPO'Shea 6 63
(P A Blockley) *chsd ldrs: rdn and wknd 2f out* **11/1**
63 7 *5* **Night Robe**[14] 3486 2-8-4 0 SimonWhitworth 10 39
(P D Evans) *prom tl rdn and wknd 2f out* **8/1**
00 8 *8* **Illusionary**[32] 2941 2-8-9 0 StephenCarson 1 20
(J G Portman) *carried lft s: a bhd* **25/1**

1m 17.78s (5.38) **Going Correction** +0.825s/f (Soft) **8** Ran SP% **113.3**
Speed ratings (Par 94): **97,96,92,92,91 90,83,73**
CSF £9.86 TOTE £3.20: £1.10, £1.50, £1.70; EX 8.10.
Owner Leonard Kinsella **Bred** Thomas J Reid **Trained** Kinnersley, Worcs

FOCUS
A fair contest of its type and the form looksreliable enough, rated around the principals.

NOTEBOOK
Whiteoak Lady(IRE) built on the promise of her Yarmouth debut and should stay further. (op 5-2 tchd 9-4)
Baronovici(IRE) ◆ handled this totally different surface and did not do much wrong. He is certainly knocking on the door and is another who should get a longer trip. (op 2-1 tchd 15-8, 3-1 and 10-3 in a place)
Ezthegezza was by no means disgraced on this testing surface after a couple of outings on good to firm. (tchd 10-3 and 9-2)
Observatory Ridge shaped like one who is crying out for a longer distance after being done no favours at the start and getting caught flat-footed before halfway. (tchd 20-1)
Lady Jinks, who only cost 2,000 guineas, is a half-sister to seven furlong and mile winner Aperitif. She was another who ran as if she would benefit for a step up in distance. (op 16-1 tchd 12-1)
Singer Of Songs(IRE) fared a little better in this lower grade. (op 22-1)

3903 TOTEQUADPOT CLAIMING STKS 2m 49y
7:20 (7:22) (Class 6) 3-Y-0+ £2,072 (£616; £308; £153)

Form RPR
6333 1 **Ronsard (IRE)**[15] 3467 5-9-12 61 StephenDonohoe 6 55+
(P D Evans) *hld up in rr: hdwy over 6f out: rdn to ld wl over 1f out: drvn out* **4/11**[1]
000- 2 *¾* **Dansilver**[12] 6522 3-8-11 53 EdwardCreighton 1 54
(D J Wintle) *hld up in tch: rdn and outpcd over 4f out: rallied over 1f out: styd on ins fnl f* **8/1**[3]
0250 3 *1* **Conny Nobel (IRE)**[10] 3624 3-8-6 50 (p) KevinGhunowa(5) 2 53
(J L Flint) *chsd ldr: led over 3f out: rdn and hdd wl over 1f out: nt qckn ins fnl f* **10/1**
-065 4 *9* **By The River**[11] 3593 3-8-5 52 PaulDoe 3 36
(P Winkworth) *set modest pce: qcknd 7f out: hdd over 3f out: sn rdn: wknd over 1f out* **15/2**[2]
0/0- 5 *14* **Hunting Lodge (IRE)**[211] 3203 6-9-3 80 JackMitchell(7) 4 21
(H J Manners) *hld up and bhd: short-lived effrt over 5f out* **14/1**
0 6 *26* **Clare Park**[21] 3274 3-7-11 0 DominicFox(3) 5 —
(H J Manners) *a bhd: lost tch fnl 5f: t.o* **66/1**

4m 14.2s (34.80) **Going Correction** +1.075s/f (Soft)
WFA 3 from 5yo+ 17lb **6** Ran SP% **113.4**
Speed ratings (Par 101): **56,55,55,50,43 30**
CSF £4.25 TOTE £1.40: £1.20, £2.40; EX 4.00.Conny Nobel was claimed by C. Roberts for £10,000.
Owner Mrs I M Folkes **Bred** Liscannor Stud Ltd **Trained** Pandy, Monmouths
■ Stewards' Enquiry : Kevin Ghunowa one-day ban: used whip with whip arm above shoulder height (Aug 7)

FOCUS
A flip start was used and the race was hand-timed. They went no gallop until past halfway in this weak affair and tentatively rated around the placed horses.

3904 TOTESPORT.COM EBF FILLIES' H'CAP 7f 16y
7:50 (7:53) (Class 5) (0-70,69) 3-Y-0+ £3,562 (£1,059; £529; £264) Stalls High

Form RPR
60-0 1 **Kims Rose (IRE)**[175] 337 4-8-2 **50** oh5 MCGeran(7) 3 59
(R J Price) *mde all: rdn over 2f out: clr whn edgd rt ins fnl f: drvn out* **33/1**
1052 2 *5* **Princess Zada**[14] 3490 3-9-6 **68** FergusSweeney 8 63
(B R Millman) *s.i.s: sn chsng ldrs: wnt 2nd over 3f out: rdn and edgd lft over 1f out: no imp* **11/8**[1]
0361 3 *7* **Nelly's Glen**[24] 3178 3-9-4 **66** PatDobbs 2 42
(R Hannon) *hld up and bhd: hdwy over 2f out: rdn and wknd over 1f out* **4/1**[2]
000- 4 *2½* **Primeshade Promise**[258] 6436 6-8-8 **54** KevinGhunowa(5) 7 23
(J L Flint) *prom tl wknd 3f out* **8/1**
4060 5 *hd* **Moyoko (IRE)**[16] 3419 4-8-13 **54** FrancisNorton 6 23
(M Blanshard) *hld up and bhd: rdn and hdwy over 3f out: edgd lft and wknd over 2f out* **5/1**[3]
500- 6 *2½* **Celtic Spa (IRE)**[216] 6934 5-10-0 **69** StephenDonohoe 5 31
(P D Evans) *hld up and bhd: rdn 3f out: sn struggling* **9/1**
3300 7 *12* **It's No Problem (IRE)**[57] 2181 3-8-5 **53** StephenCarson 1 —
(M Salaman) *prom tl wknd 3f out* **8/1**
6-60 8 *1* **Stars Above**[30] 2978 3-8-2 **50** oh5 RichardThomas 4 —
(M S Saunders) *prom: rdn over 3f out: sn wknd* **50/1**

-600 **9** *shd* **Lady Shirley Hunt**[40] 2696 3-7-13 **50** oh5 LiamJones(3) 9 —
(A D Smith) *prom: rdn over 4f out: wknd over 3f out* **50/1**

1m 28.66s (5.36) **Going Correction** +0.825s/f (Soft)
WFA 3 from 4yo+ 7lb **9** Ran SP% **117.9**
Speed ratings (Par 100): **102,96,88,85,85 82,68,67,67**
CSF £80.32 CT £241.41 TOTE £39.40: £6.10, £1.40, £1.80; EX 123.50.
Owner John Richards **Bred** Lucayan Stud Ltd **Trained** Ullingswick, H'fords

FOCUS
A minor handicap and they came home well strung out, but the form looks somewhat suspect.
Primeshade Promise Official explanation: jockey said mare became unbalanced
Moyoko(IRE) Official explanation: jockey said filly had no more to give

3905 TOTEEXACTA H'CAP 7f 16y
8:25 (8:25) (Class 5) (0-75,75) 3-Y-0+ **£3,368** (£1,002; £500; £250) **Stalls** High

Form RPR
-003 **1** **John O'Groats (IRE)**[8] 3686 9-8-2 **56** oh11 (p) AmyBaker(7) 4 62
(T T Clement) *mde virtually all: rdn and edgd lft to far rail over 1f out: r.o* **9/1**
-022 **2** *hd* **Milton's Keen**[14] 3487 4-8-4 **56** oh1 KevinGhunowa(5) 7 61
(M Salaman) *w ldrs: ev ch over 2f out: rdn over 1f out: r.o ins fnl f* **15/8**[1]
2015 **3** *3* **Toms Laughter**[16] 3411 3-8-6 **60** RichardThomas 2 54+
(B Palling) *hld up: rdn and outpcd over 2f out: styd on wl ins fnl f* **5/2**[2]
004 **4** *3* **Reigning Monarch (USA)**[27] 3101 4-8-9 **56** oh4 SamHitchcott 3 45
(Miss Z C Davison) *s.i.s: rdn and hdwy over 3f out: wknd over 1f out* **9/1**
1116 **5** *2* **Drawback (IRE)**[12] 3567 4-9-6 **70** (p) LiamJones(3) 6 53
(R A Harris) *w wnr: rdn over 3f out: wknd 1f out* **5/1**[3]
2605 **6** *4* **Sun Catcher (IRE)**[44] 2573 4-10-0 **75** (b) PatDobbs 5 48
(R Hannon) *hld up: rdn 3f out: sn struggling* **13/2**

1m 28.94s (5.64) **Going Correction** +0.825s/f (Soft)
WFA 3 from 4yo+ 7lb **6** Ran SP% **113.4**
Speed ratings (Par 103): **100,99,96,92,90 86**
CSF £26.84 TOTE £10.60: £3.20, £1.80; EX 42.70.
Owner Miss E Johnston **Bred** Paul Traynor **Trained** Newmarket, Suffolk

FOCUS
Half the field were out of the handicap proper in this low-grade contest. The form is rated through the runner-up.

3906 TOTESPORTCASINO.COM H'CAP 5f 16y
8:55 (8:55) (Class 5) (0-70,70) 3-Y-0+ **£3,368** (£1,002; £500; £250) **Stalls** High

Form RPR
5002 **1** **Our Fugitive (IRE)**[11] 3594 5-9-3 **62** (b1) FrancisNorton 5 69
(A W Carroll) *mde all: clr over 2f out: rdn and edgd rt ins fnl f: drvn out* **10/3**[1]
2156 **2** *nk* **Harrison's Flyer (IRE)**[11] 3594 6-9-6 **70** (p) KevinGhunowa(5) 8 76
(J M Bradley) *mid-div: rdn over 2f out: hdwy over 1f out: r.o ins fnl f* **8/1**
0122 **3** *nk* **George The Second**[15] 3452 4-9-3 **65** RichardKingscote(3) 1 70
(Mrs H Sweeting) *chsd wnr: rdn wl over 1f out: kpt on ins fnl f* **9/2**[3]
2143 **4** *3/4* **Caustic Wit (IRE)**[2] 3852 9-9-7 **66** FergusSweeney 4 68
(M S Saunders) *chsd ldrs: rdn over 1f out: kpt on ins fnl f* **7/2**[2]
6050 **5** *3/4* **Gavarnie Beau (IRE)**[9] 3647 4-9-5 **64** (b) PatDobbs 11 64
(M Blanshard) *mid-div: rdn over 2f out: hdwy fnl f: nt rch ldrs* **16/1**
-000 **6** *1/2* **Whistler**[18] 3368 10-8-6 **51** oh3 (p) PaulFitzsimons 13 49
(Miss J R Tooth) *bhd: hdwy over 1f out: edgd lft ins fnl f: no ex* **20/1**
5543 **7** *nk* **Turkish Sultan (IRE)**[13] 3535 4-8-12 **57** (p) StephenDonohoe 10 54
(J M Bradley) *chsd ldrs: rdn over 1f out: no hdwy fnl f* **5/1**
0060 **8** *shd* **Scarlet Knight**[23] 3218 4-9-2 **68** JackMitchell(7) 3 65
(P Mitchell) *chsd ldrs: rdn wl over 1f out: one pce* **9/1**
0305 **9** *nk* **Spy Gun (USA)**[52] 2343 7-8-3 **51** oh6 (p) LiamJones(3) 6 47
(T Wall) *s.i.s: n.d* **40/1**
1600 **10** *7* **Macademy Royal (USA)**[23] 3212 4-8-12 **62** (t) TravisBlock(5) 2 34
(H Morrison) *prom: rdn over 2f out: wknd over 1f out* **16/1**
0040 **11** *nk* **Must Be Keen**[23] 3218 8-7-13 **51** oh3 (p) MCGeran(7) 9 22
(Miss K B Boutflower) *fly-jmpd s: a bhd* **20/1**
000/ **12** *14* **Our Sion**[611] 1067 7-8-0 **52** oh6 ow1 BradleyRoper(7) 7 —
(G C H Chung) *rdn over 2f out: a bhd* **66/1**

63.19 secs (3.59) **Going Correction** +0.825s/f (Soft) **12** Ran SP% **126.5**
Speed ratings (Par 103): **104,103,103,101,100 99,99,99,98,87 87,64**
CSF £31.66 CT £129.44 TOTE £5.30: £1.90, £2.40, £2.60; EX 56.90 Place 6 £28.57, Place 5 £4.31.
Owner Serafino Agodino **Bred** Dr Paschal Carmody **Trained** Cropthorne, Worcs

FOCUS
A modest sprint handicap rated through the runner-up to his recent best.
T/Plt: £26.10 to a £1 stake. Pool: £61,989.55. 1,727.20 winning tickets. T/Qpdt: £3.20 to a £1 stake. Pool: £5,909.80. 1,325.90 winning tickets. KH

3743
NEWMARKET (JULY) (R-H)
Friday, July 27

OFFICIAL GOING: Good to firm (9.8)
Wind: Fresh, behind Weather: Cloudy with sunny spells

3907 BOLLINGER CHAMPAGNE CHALLENGE SERIES H'CAP (FOR GENTLEMAN AMATEUR RIDERS) 1m 2f
5:40 (5:42) (Class 5) (0-70,69) 3-Y-0+ **£3,747** (£1,162; £580; £290) **Stalls** Centre

Form RPR
440/ **1** **Jacaranda (IRE)**[313] 5940 7-10-8 **58** MrJGuerriero(5) 3 67
(P J Hobbs) *s.i.s: hld up: hdwy and swtchd rt over 1f out: rdn to ld ins fnl f: r.o* **11/2**[1]
4065 **2** *1 1/4* **Majestic Chief**[17] 3407 3-10-0 **60** (p) MrBMcHugh(5) 6 66
(P D Niven) *hld up: hdwy over 4f out: n.m.r over 1f out: rdn and ev ch ins fnl f: edgd rt: styd on same pce* **22/1**
0145 **3** *2* **Wait For The Will (USA)**[84] 1451 11-11-7 **69** (b) MrDHutchison(3) 4 71
(G L Moore) *hld up: hdwy 1/2-way: rdn and edgd rt over 1f out: styd on same pce* **16/1**
0060 **4** *hd* **Snark (IRE)**[34] 2877 4-11-2 **61** MrSWalker 18 63
(P J Makin) *chsd ldrs: rdn over 1f out: styd on* **9/1**
0054 **5** *hd* **Pactolos Way**[41] 2667 4-10-12 **64** MrSGoswell(7) 13 65
(P R Chamings) *chsd ldr: rdn and ev ch over 1f out: styd on same pce fnl f* **12/1**
3-42 **6** *nk* **Barbirolli**[13] 3530 5-11-3 **67** MrBenBrisbourne(5) 11 68
(W M Brisbourne) *hld up: hdwy over 2f out: rdn over 1f out: styd on same pce fnl f* **6/1**[2]
0-13 **7** *nk* **Fantasy Crusader**[16] 3419 8-10-3 **53** MrCPHuxley(5) 20 53
(R M H Cowell) *trckd ldrs: racd keenly: rdn to ld over 1f out: hdd and no ex ins fnl f* **14/1**
0015 **8** *3/4* **Diamond Key (IRE)**[4] 3803 3-9-5 **51** ow1 (b) MrHHaynes(5) 1 50
(M G Quinlan) *hld up: hdwy over 2f out: rdn and hmpd over 1f out: no ex fnl f* **20/1**
4231 **9** *nk* **Ermine Grey**[12] 3571 6-10-12 **60** 6ex MrMJJSmith(3) 15 58
(A W Carroll) *s.i.s: hdwy over 6f out: rdn over 1f out: wknd ins fnl f* **8/1**[3]
3256 **10** *2* **Scottish River (USA)**[11] 3600 8-11-4 **63** MrLeeNewnes 14 57
(M D I Usher) *dwlt: hld up: rdn over 1f out: wknd ins fnl f* **10/1**
0000 **11** *hd* **Dancewiththestars (USA)**[43] 2610 3-9-4 **50** MrPCollington(5) 19 44
(Miss J Feilden) *led: rdn and hdd over 1f out: wknd ins fnl f* **33/1**
-055 **12** *3* **Dance World**[22] 3250 7-10-12 **62** (b1) MrRBirkett(5) 10 50
(Miss J Feilden) *hld up: a in rr* **25/1**
40-0 **13** *1/2* **Alasil (USA)**[161] 278 7-10-3 **55** MrMPrice(7) 12 42
(R J Price) *chsd ldrs: ev ch over 2f out: hmpd and wknd over 1f out* **22/1**
0402 **14** *1 1/4* **Rock Haven (IRE)**[25] 3149 5-10-4 **56** MrSeanKerr(7) 5 40
(G F Bridgwater) *s.s: hld up: sddle slipped sn after s: swtchd lft and hdwy over 3f out: wknd over 1f out* **12/1**
1020 **15** *hd* **Government (IRE)**[51] 2370 6-10-0 **50** oh1 MrStephenHarrison(5) 8 34
(M C Chapman) *chsd ldrs: rdn over 3f out: wknd over 1f out* **66/1**
1650 **16** *1/2* **Blushing Prince (IRE)**[25] 3161 9-10-2 **50** oh1 (t) MrPCallaghan(3) 2 33
(R C Guest) *hld up: rdn over 2f out: n.d* **22/1**
06/0 **17** *2 1/2* **Shire (IRE)**[13] 3554 5-10-12 **57** MrDHDunsdon 7 35
(D R C Elsworth) *hld up: hdwy over 6f out: wknd over 2f out* **12/1**
450- **18** *shd* **Dance Spirit (IRE)**[42] 4249 4-11-1 **67** MrBJToomey(7) 17 44
(C J Mann) *hld up: a in rr* **40/1**
3-30 **19** *9* **Sol Rojo**[43] 2603 5-11-5 **67** (v) MrSPearce(3) 16 26
(J Pearce) *trckd ldrs: plld hrd: rdn and wknd 2f out* **10/1**

2m 7.65s (1.21) **Going Correction** -0.10s/f (Good)
WFA 3 from 4yo+ 10lb **19** Ran SP% **133.1**
Speed ratings (Par 103): **91,90,88,88,88 87,87,87,86,85 85,82,82,81,81 80,78,78,71**
CSF £135.95 CT £1895.06 TOTE £7.30: £2.50, £7.40, £2.40, £3.40; EX 281.00.
Owner Pot Black Racing **Bred** The Near Miracle Syndicate **Trained** Withycombe, Somerset
■ A first Flat winner for Josh Guerriero.

FOCUS
A moderate amateurs' handicap run at a modest early pace but straightforward form rated around the placed horses and the fifth.
Rock Haven(IRE) Official explanation: jockey said saddle slipped

3908 NEWMARKETRACECOURSES.CO.UK MAIDEN STKS 1m 4f
6:05 (6:09) (Class 4) 3-Y-0 **£5,181** (£1,541; £770; £384) **Stalls** Centre

Form RPR
055 **1** **Silver Suitor (IRE)**[16] 3436 3-9-3 80 TQuinn 3 88+
(D R C Elsworth) *prom: rdn over 4f out: led 1f out: styd on wl* **10/3**[2]
6463 **2** *3 1/2* **Ancient Culture**[17] 3402 3-9-3 78 (v1) RyanMoore 10 82
(Sir Michael Stoute) *dwlt: sn drvn along and prom: rdn to ld over 1f out: sn hdd: hung lft and no ex ins fnl f* **9/4**[1]
66 **3** *1 1/4* **Kwazulu (USA)**[21] 3284 3-9-3 0 (b1) JimmyFortune 4 80
(J H M Gosden) *chsd ldrs: rdn over 1f out: no ex fnl f* **16/1**
02 **4** *4* **Demisemiquaver**[51] 2359 3-8-12 0 TPQueally 7 69
(J Noseda) *led: rdn: hung lft and hdd over 1f out: wknd ins fnl f* **11/1**
2 **5** *3* **Take The Gold (IRE)**[35] 2836 3-8-12 0 PhilipRobinson 5 64
(M A Jarvis) *hld up: effrt over 2f out: sn wknd* **11/2**
64 **6** *2* **Hesivorthedriver (GER)**[22] 3236 3-9-3 0 JHBowman 6 66
(Mrs A J Perrett) *chsd ldr: rdn and ev ch over 1f out: wknd fnl f* **4/1**[3]
00 **7** *14* **Boekenhoutskloof (IRE)**[23] 3214 3-8-12 0 RichardMullen 9 38
(E F Vaughan) *hld up: rdn over 3f out: sn wknd* **80/1**
0600 **8** *1 1/4* **Feeling Peckish (USA)**[7] 3710 3-8-10 31 MJMurphy(7) 1 41
(M C Chapman) *mid-div: rdn and wknd over 3f out* **150/1**
0 **9** *1 1/4* **Running Rings**[10] 3621 3-8-5 0 JCorrigan(7) 2 34
(P W D'Arcy) *s.s: bhd and rdn over 6f out: wknd over 3f out: sn hung lft* **100/1**
0534 **10** *91* **Feeling (IRE)**[22] 3248 3-9-3 74 RichardHughes 8 —
(P W Chapple-Hyam) *hld up: pushed along 1/2-way: wknd and eased over 3f out* **8/1**

2m 29.08s (-3.83) **Going Correction** -0.10s/f (Good) **10** Ran SP% **117.4**
Speed ratings (Par 102): **108,105,104,102,100 98,89,88,87,27**
CSF £11.39 TOTE £4.60: £1.50, £1.60, £4.00; EX 15.20.
Owner J C Smith **Bred** Tallyho Stud, J Delahooke & P Twoomey **Trained** Newmarket, Suffolk

FOCUS
A decent pace for what was just an ordinary maiden, and although the winner is value for more the placed horses both wore headgear already and give rise to slight reservations.
Take The Gold(IRE) Official explanation: jockey said filly was unsuited by the good to firm ground
Hesivorthedriver(GER) Official explanation: jockey said colt was unsuited by the good to firm ground
Feeling(IRE) Official explanation: jockey said colt moved poorly

3909 UNICORN ASSET MANAGEMENT JULY COURSE SERIES NURSERY (QUALIFIER) 7f
6:35 (6:35) (Class 3) 2-Y-0 **£6,477** (£1,927; £963; £481) **Stalls** Low

Form RPR
321 **1** **Elna Bright**[49] 2410 2-9-0 **78** RyanMoore 1 84
(R Hannon) *hld up in tch: rdn over 1f out: styd on u.p to ld wl ins fnl f* **6/1**
0560 **2** *nk* **Talk Of Saafend (IRE)**[9] 3642 2-7-13 **63** DavidKinsella 7 69
(R Hannon) *hld up: hdwy over 2f out: rdn to ld over 1f out: hung lft and hdd wl ins fnl f* **25/1**
1501 **3** *2 1/2* **Dan Tucket**[14] 3508 2-9-4 **82** JHBowman 2 81
(M R Channon) *hld up: hmpd over 2f out: hdwy over 1f out: sn rdn: no imp ins fnl f* **9/2**
3311 **4** *1 1/2* **Runswick Bay**[17] 3398 2-9-2 **85** PJMcDonald(5) 6 80
(G M Moore) *led: rdn and hdd over 1f out: wknd ins fnl f* **7/2**[2]
052 **5** *9* **Polygraph (IRE)**[14] 3478 2-8-9 **78** WilliamBuick(5) 5 50
(A M Balding) *chsd ldrs: rdn over 2f out: wknd over 1f out* **4/1**[3]
000 **6** *1/2* **Race The Moon (IRE)**[21] 3270 2-8-1 **65** SilvestreDeSousa 4 35
(V Smith) *chsd ldr tl rdn over 2f out: sn edgd rt and wknd* **11/1**
154 **7** *6* **Mahusay (IRE)**[17] 3398 2-9-3 **81** JimmyFortune 8 36
(L M Cumani) *chsd ldrs: rdn over 2f out: sn wknd* **11/4**[1]
0134 **8** *3/4* **Allahor**[9] 3635 2-8-8 **75** PatrickMathers(3) 3 28
(A Berry) *s.s: outpcd* **50/1**

1m 25.26s (-1.52) **Going Correction** -0.10s/f (Good) **8** Ran SP% **115.5**
Speed ratings (Par 98): **104,103,100,99,88 88,81,80**
CSF £133.83 CT £742.52 TOTE £6.60: £2.00, £4.90, £1.90; EX 87.90.
Owner David Mort **Bred** D R Tucker **Trained** East Everleigh, Wilts

FOCUS
An ordinary nursery but a decent time and the form looks solid, rated through the third. The 'official' ratings shown next to each horse are estimated and for information purposes only.

NOTEBOOK

Elna Bright came into this having got off the mark in a 6f maiden at Brighton last time and it took every yard of this 7f trip for him to get on top, just edging out his much longer-priced stable companion Talk Of Saafend. This was not the strongest of nurseries, but he saw the trip out well, although that was not cast-iron on pedigree, and looks capable of further improvement. (tchd 11-2 and 13-2)

Talk Of Saafend(IRE), never involved having got behind early on her recent nursery debut at Kempton, showed that running to be all wrong with a gallant effort in second, just failing to hold on from her better-fancied stable companion. Racing off a mark of 64, she is likely to go up a little for this, but it will be both disappointing and surprising if she cannot win races in this sphere.

Dan Tucket, a winner over course and distance on his recent nursery debut, was up 7lb, but still looked a major player and he was arguably a little unlucky not to finish a shade closer. He is clearly progressing the right way. (tchd 4-1)

Runswick Bay, on a hat-trick following wins at Redcar and Pontefract, latterly on his handicap debut, was up 7lb in the weights, but he gave it a good go from the front and it was only in the final furlong he began to struggle. It is possible 6f is his preferred trip. (op 11-4)

Polygraph(IRE) was certainly one of the more interesting ones on this handicap debut, but it is possible the son of Pivotal found the ground a shade faster than he would prefer and he failed to see his race out. His stable is hardly firing and he may do better later in the season. (op 7-1)

Race The Moon(IRE), who qualified for this with three down-the-field runs in decent maidens, failed to improve as anticipated for the switch to handicaps and it is probable this trip stretches his stamina. (op 9-1 tchd 12-1)

Mahusay(IRE) has been getting outpaced over 6f, having made a winning debut of 5f, but he appeared not to see this seventh furlong out and was most disappointing. He is not that big and winning more races is not going to be easy for him. Official explanation: trainer's rep said colt may have been unsuited by the good to firm ground (tchd 5-2 and 3-1)

3910 EUROPEAN BREEDERS' FUND CONDITIONS STKS — 6f

7:10 (7:10) (Class 3) 2-Y-O — **£7,772** (£2,312; £1,155; £577) **Stalls** Low

Form — RPR

1060 **1** **Fat Boy (IRE)**[15] 3459 2-9-5 0 .... RichardHughes 5 — 98
(R Hannon) *mde all: qcknd over 2f out: rdn over 1f out: sn edgd lft: r.o* — **8/1**[3]

1 **2** ¾ **Philario (IRE)**[53] 2297 2-8-13 0 .... PhillipMakin 6 — 90
(K R Burke) *plld hrd and prom: trckd wnr 1/2-way: rdn over 1f out: r.o* — **10/1**

1016 **3** 1 **Cee Bargara**[38] 2732 2-9-9 0 .... RyanMoore 4 — 97
(J A Osborne) *plld hrd: trckd wnr to 1/2-way: rdn and nt clr run over 1f out: styd on same pce* — **11/2**[2]

1 **4** ½ **Sir Gerry (USA)**[24] 3192 2-9-5 0 .... OscarUrbina 2 — 91+
(J R Fanshawe) *bmpd sn after s: hld up: hdwy over 1f out: sn rdn: no imp ins fnl f* — **8/11**[1]

136 **5** 5 **In Uniform**[26] 3147 2-8-13 0 .... RichardMullen 3 — 70
(E S McMahon) *hld up: plld hrd: rdn and wknd over 1f out* — **11/2**[2]

421 **6** 2 **Mazzanti**[32] 2934 2-8-13 0 .... NCallan 1 — 68+
(K A Ryan) *chsd ldrs over 4f* — **16/1**

1m 12.65s (-0.70) **Going Correction** -0.10s/f (Good) — **6** Ran SP% **114.8**
Speed ratings (Par 98): **100,99,97,97,90 87**
CSF £79.20 TOTE £6.00: £2.00, £4.00; EX 56.50.
Owner M Sines **Bred** Peter Mooney **Trained** East Everleigh, Wilts

FOCUS

A tricky contest to weigh-up with Fat Boy getting run of the race. The third and fourth set the level.

NOTEBOOK

Fat Boy(IRE) has faced some tough tasks since making a winning debut at Kempton, finishing midfield in the Group 2 July Stakes latest, and he found the nature of this race much more to his liking. Soon at the head of affairs, he quickened the tempo running into the final quarter mile before sticking on too strongly for the runner-up. There was no doubting he had the run of the race and he is going to find life tougher once more returned to Pattern level, but this should at least act as a confidence booster. (op 11-1)

Philario(IRE), a narrow victor over Mazzanti on his debut at Carlisle, coped well with the combination of a rise in class on faster ground and he saw the extra furlong out with no trouble. The winner was always holding him, but his trainer feels there is more to come from the son of Captain Rio and the Doncaster Sales race later in the season is his next likely target. (op 12-1 tchd 8-1)

Cee Bargara, fresh into this off the back of a career-best behind Henrythenavigator in the Coventry at Royal Ascot, made the running that day and it was clear from an early stage here he wanted to go a shade quicker than Moore would allow. He could not quicken sufficiently to mount a serious challenge, just keeping on at the one pace under pressure, and looks well worth a try at 7f now. Official explanation: jockey said colt ran too free (tchd 5-1 and 13-2)

Sir Gerry(USA) created quite an impression when giving subsequent winner Imperial Mint a good beating on his debut at Thirsk, so it was no surprise to see him head the market here, but odds of 8/11 were short enough under the penalty and, having travelled well, he could not quicken from a furlong out. He made his winning debut in soft ground and perhaps the return to a slower surface will help. (tchd 4-5)

In Uniform shows plenty of speed and he was wanting to go faster the second he came out of the stalls. This experiment with a new trip evidently failed to work. (op 6-1 tchd 7-1)

3911 PORTLAND PLACE PROPERTIES H'CAP — 6f

7:40 (7:42) (Class 3) (0-90,90) 3-Y-O+ — **£7,772** (£2,312; £1,155; £577) **Stalls** Low

Form — RPR

6-60 **1** **Signor Peltro**[35] 2817 4-9-7 85 .... (b[1]) TQuinn 10 — 93
(H Candy) *hld up: swtchd rt and hdwy over 2f out: rdn to ld over 1f out: hung lft: r.o* — **10/1**

0152 **2** ¾ **Roman Maze**[14] 3481 7-9-11 89 .... RyanMoore 6 — 95
(W M Brisbourne) *hld up: swtchd rt and hdwy over 1f out: sn rdn: edgd lft ins fnl f: r.o wl* — **6/1**[2]

5010 **3** hd **Pearly Wey**[14] 3481 4-9-12 90 .... PhilipRobinson 1 — 95+
(C G Cox) *hld up: hdwy over 2f out: nt clr run over 1f out and ins fnl f: r.o* — **11/1**

301 **4** hd **Misaro (GER)**[10] 3623 6-8-13 84 6ex .... (b) JamieHamblett(7) 14 — 89
(R A Harris) *chsd ldr: led 4f out: rdn and hdd over 1f out: edgd lft: styd on same pce* — **11/2**[1]

4254 **5** 1 **Seamus Shindig**[15] 3472 5-8-6 77 .... AmyScott(7) 13 — 79
(H Candy) *led 2f: rdn and ev ch over 1f out: no ex ins fnl f* — **14/1**

0300 **6** shd **King's Gait**[17] 3401 5-9-10 88 .... RichardMullen 2 — 89
(T D Easterby) *hld up: pushed along 1/2-way: r.o ins fnl f: nrst fin* — **16/1**

-564 **7** 1¾ **Swinbrook (USA)**[14] 3481 6-9-4 82 .... (v) EddieAhern 12 — 78
(J A R Toller) *prom: rdn over 1f out: edgd lft and no ex fnl f* — **11/2**[1]

0403 **8** hd **Guest Connections**[7] 3723 4-8-11 75 .... (v) SilvestreDeSousa 9 — 70
(D Nicholls) *hld up: effrt over 1f out: edgd lft: nvr trbld ldrs* — **14/1**

0223 **9** shd **Phantom Whisper**[21] 3268 4-9-6 89 .... JamesMillman(5) 15 — 84
(B R Millman) *prom: rdn over 2f out: wknd ins fnl f* — **7/1**[3]

2400 **10** shd **Who's Winning (IRE)**[14] 3481 6-8-7 78 .... KylieManser(7) 3 — 73
(B G Powell) *chsd ldrs: rdn over 1f out: wknd ins fnl f* — **20/1**

-000 **11** nk **Captain Hurricane**[48] 2440 5-9-9 87 .... RichardHughes 7 — 81
(B J Meehan) *trckd ldrs: racd keenly: rdn over 2f out: wknd fnl f* — **10/1**

0-00 **12** 1 **Swing The Ring (IRE)**[13] 3529 4-9-9 90 .... PatrickMathers(3) 11 — 81
(A Berry) *mid-div: rdn and lost pl over 3f out: n.d after* — **66/1**

0300 **13** 2 **Distinctly Game**[11] 3586 5-9-8 86 .... NCallan 4 — 71
(K A Ryan) *chsd ldrs over 4f* — **14/1**

0030 **14** nk **Mine Behind**[34] 2882 7-9-2 80 .... GeorgeBaker 8 — 64
(J R Best) *hld up: rdn over 2f out: wknd over 1f out* — **14/1**

2000 **15** 49 **River Kirov (IRE)**[34] 2882 4-9-0 78 .... (b[1]) JimmyFortune 5 — —
(P W Chapple-Hyam) *rel to r: a t.o* — **14/1**

1m 11.76s (-1.59) **Going Correction** -0.10s/f (Good) — **15** Ran SP% **129.5**
Speed ratings (Par 107): **106,105,104,104,103 103,100,100,100,100 99,98,95,95,30**
CSF £73.62 CT £715.88 TOTE £12.80: £3.70, £2.70, £4.10; EX 119.10.
Owner First Of Many Partnership **Bred** R D And J S Chugg & The Overbury Partnership **Trained** Kingston Warren, Oxon

FOCUS

A fair sprint handicap rated around the first two and likely to produce future winners.

NOTEBOOK

Signor Peltro, fitted with blinkers for this drop in distance, ran reasonably well in a big-field handicap at Royal Ascot latest and he received a peach of a ride from Quinn to win for the first time this season. He is clearly not straightforward though and will be doing well to defy a rise, with the headgear far from certain to have the same effect next time. (op 12-1)

Roman Maze's good run of recent form continued with another spirited effort in defeat, getting going too late to reach the winner. He is clearly capable of winning more races off this mark. (op 7-1)

Pearly Wey was unable to build on his Folkestone win when down the field at Ascot latest, but this was a much better effort and he was another a shade unlucky not to give the winner more to think about. Consistency is not his strong point, but he is clearly smart on his day. (op 10-1 tchd 12-1)

Misaro(GER) has had a profitable time of it this season, winning four times already, and he again ran well under his 6lb penalty. This drop in trip was probably not in his favour and there is no reason why he cannot continue to run well. (op 13-2 tchd 4-1)

Seamus Shindig remains winless since his two-year-old debut three years back, but he has run several good races of late and is surely not too far off a welcome return to winning ways.

King's Gait remains on a bit of a losing run and not for the first time this season he looked a shade unfortunate. That said, he is talented on his day and it surely will not be long before he wins again. (tchd 20-1)

3912 TURFTV CONDITIONS STKS — 1m 4f

8:15 (8:15) (Class 3) 3-Y-O+

£9,971 (£2,985; £1,492; £747; £372; £187) **Stalls** Centre

Form — RPR

00-1 **1** **Classic Punch (IRE)**[27] 3097 4-9-11 110 .... TQuinn 6 — 114+
(D R C Elsworth) *led to 1/2-way: led over 2f out: rdn over 1f out: hung lft ins fnl f: styd on* — **10/3**[3]

0345 **2** ½ **New Beginning (IRE)**[21] 3271 3-8-3 80 .... JimmyQuinn 3 — 103?
(Mrs S Lamyman) *hld up: hdwy over 2f out: rdn and ev ch fr over 1f out: styd on* — **20/1**

2245 **3** 2½ **Grand Passion (IRE)**[27] 3097 7-9-1 104 .... SteveDrowne 4 — 99
(G Wragg) *a.p: rdn over 1f out: styd on same pce fnl f* — **10/1**

5-24 **4** 3 **The Geezer**[20] 3333 5-9-1 107 .... KerrinMcEvoy 5 — 94
(Saeed Bin Suroor) *chsd wnr to 1/2-way: rdn over 3f out: wknd over 1f out* — **11/8**[1]

-262 **5** ½ **Hard Top (IRE)**[27] 3097 5-9-1 106 .... RyanMoore 2 — 94
(Sir Michael Stoute) *s.i.s: sn chsng ldrs: led 1/2-way: rdn and hdd over 2f out: wknd fnl f* — **2/1**[2]

0044 **6** 42 **Amwell Brave**[17] 3397 6-9-1 54 .... EddieAhern 1 — 26
(J R Jenkins) *hld up: bhd fnl 4f: t.o* — **100/1**

2m 29.85s (-3.06) **Going Correction** -0.10s/f (Good)
WFA 3 from 4yo+ 12lb — **6** Ran SP% **113.4**
Speed ratings (Par 107): **106,105,104,102,101 73**
CSF £57.26 TOTE £4.30: £2.40, £3.60; EX 54.60.
Owner J C Smith **Bred** Granham Farm **Trained** Newmarket, Suffolk

FOCUS

A fair conditions stakes but the proximity of the runner-up suggests this is suspect form, although there was once again a lot to like about the way Classic Punch got the job done.

NOTEBOOK

Classic Punch(IRE) ◆ made a most pleasing return to the action when taking the Listed Fred Archer Stakes over course and distance on his seasonal reappearance and, despite the large penalty, he looked set to take all the beating. Soon bowling along in front, he was forced to fight off numerous challengers, none more so than outsider New Beginning, but in a style reminescent of his illustrious half-brother Persian Punch he battled battled on doggedly to assert close home. The form is clearly worth little, but he has been brought along steadily by Elsworth and now looks ready for another try at further. Connections mentioned a few possible targets, namely the Prix Kergorlay at Deauville next month and the Geoffrey Freer at Newbury. (op 7-2 tchd 3-1)

New Beginning(IRE), although receiving plenty of weight from the winner, still had something to find and he ran a remarkable race in second, travelling easily the best, but not being able to get the better of the determined winner. Only three, he remains capable of further improvement, although it remains to be seen how the Handicapper acts on this effort. (op 25-1)

Grand Passion(IRE) is not the horse he once was and remains winless since February of last year. He is likely to continue to pick up bits of place money without winning. (op 15-2)

The Geezer, a pleasing second to Ivy Creek on his reappearance at Pontefract, failed to build on that when finding little for pressure at Sandown last time over 1m6f, and the combination of a drop in trip on this faster ground was not enough to see him return to winning ways, again finding little for pressure. He looks one to tread carefully with for the time being. (op 7-4)

Hard Top(IRE) has long been a disappointing sort and, although weighted to reverse recent form with Classic Punch, it was no surprise to see the gelding fail to do so. Consistency is not his strong point and he is likely to continue to struggle to get his head in front. (op 15-8 tchd 9-4)

3913 NGK SPARK PLUGS H'CAP — 1m

8:45 (8:46) (Class 5) (0-75,78) 3-Y-O — **£3,886** (£1,156; £577; £288) **Stalls** Low

Form — RPR

0051 **1** **Bajan Pride**[10] 3622 3-9-6 73 6ex .... RichardHughes 14 — 82+
(R Hannon) *mde all: qcknd over 1f out: eased nr fin* — **7/1**[3]

0004 **2** 1 **Awwal Malika (USA)**[9] 3646 3-8-4 62 .... AhmedAjtebi(5) 5 — 68
(C E Brittain) *a.p: rdn to chse wnr over 1f out: styd on* — **33/1**

3011 **3** hd **Samsons Son**[7] 3707 3-9-11 78 6ex .... GeorgeBaker 8 — 84+
(J R Best) *hld up: hdwy over 1f out: sn rdn: hung lft ins fnl f: styd on* — **5/2**[2]

20-2 **4** 4 **Comma (USA)**[9] 3645 3-9-3 70 .... RyanMoore 7 — 66
(Sir Michael Stoute) *hld up in tch: rdn over 1f out: no ex fnl f* — **1/1**[1]

-000 **5** ¾ **Brouhaha**[33] 2915 3-8-2 55 oh2 .... (t) JimmyQuinn 13 — 50
(Miss Diana Weeden) *chsd wnr tl rdn over 1f out: wknd fnl f* — **66/1**

3064 **6** 2 **Kalasam**[49] 2425 3-9-5 72 .... RichardMullen 9 — 62
(W R Muir) *hld up in tch: rdn over 2f out: wknd over 1f out* — **12/1**

0-00 **7** ½ **Elounda (IRE)**[30] 2981 3-8-12 65 .... TedDurcan 4 — 54
(H R A Cecil) *hld up: nt clr run over 2f out: swtchd rt over 1f out: nvr trbld ldrs* — **25/1**

-000 **8** ½ **Stanley George (IRE)**[35] 2834 3-8-12 65 .... MatthewHenry 2 — 53
(M A Jarvis) *chsd ldrs over 6f* — **25/1**

2313 **9** *3* **Lordship (IRE)**[12] 3570 3-8-9 **62**............ TQuinn 15 43
(A W Carroll) *plld hrd and prom: rdn over 2f out: wknd over 1f out* **11/1**
0-00 **10** *1 1/2* **Barley Moon**[70] 1815 3-8-2 **55**............ ChrisCatlin 11 32
(T Keddy) *s.i.s: hld up: a in rr* **50/1**
326- **11** *7* **Bay Of Light**[314] 5380 3-9-5 **72**............ SteveDrowne 10 33
(P W Chapple-Hyam) *hld up: wknd 2f out* **25/1**
1m 41.07s (0.64) **Going Correction** -0.10s/f (Good) **11** Ran SP% **125.0**
Speed ratings (Par 100): **92,91,90,86,86 84,83,83,80,78 71**
CSF £222.55 CT £761.77 TOTE £7.60: £2.30, £7.70, £1.50; EX 140.80 Place 6 £9,140.75, Place 5 £2,635.69.
Owner Terry Neill **Bred** Plantation Stud **Trained** East Everleigh, Wilts
FOCUS
Only a modest handicap, but the first three are going the right way and it should produce the odd winner.
Lordship(IRE) Official explanation: jockey said gelding ran too free
T/Plt: £3,204.50 to a £1 stake. Pool: £62,993.75. 14.35 winning tickets. T/Qpdt: £205.80 to a £1 stake. Pool: £4,923.40. 17.70 winning tickets. CR

3192 THIRSK (L-H)
Friday, July 27

OFFICIAL GOING: Good (good to soft in places; 8.5)
The ground had dried out and was described as 'just on the easy side of good'.
Wind: fresh half-behind Weather: overcast and breezy

3914 IRISH RACEGOERS CLUB MAIDEN STKS (DIV I) 7f
1:25 (1:28) (Class 5) 3-Y-0+ **£3,238** (£963; £481; £240) **Stalls** Low

Form RPR
343 **1** **Goodbye**[15] 3466 3-8-12 72............ TedDurcan 3 64+
(G A Swinbank) *trckd ldrs: wnt 2nd over 2f out: led over 1f out: sn wnt clr: eased towards fin* **9/4**[2]
0222 **2** *4* **Murbek (IRE)**[34] 2886 3-9-3 79............ NCallan 2 56
(M A Jarvis) *led: qcknd clr over 3f out: hdd over 1f out: no ch w wnr* **4/5**[1]
20-0 **3** *3/4* **Double Carpet (IRE)**[88] 1349 4-9-10 55............ TGMcLaughlin 8 57
(G Woodward) *chsd ldrs: kpt on same pce fnl 2f* **50/1**
04 **4** *1 1/4* **Treasure Isle**[18] 3382 3-8-9 0............ JamieMoriarty(3) 13 46+
(R A Fahey) *swvd rt s: sn in tch: styd on fnl 2f* **33/1**
6-20 **5** *nk* **Crosby Jemma**[67] 1894 3-8-12 50............ PhillipMakin 15 45
(J R Weymes) *in tch on outer: outpcd over 3f out: kpt on fnl 2f* **22/1**
-256 **6** *1* **Acapulco Bay**[73] 1746 3-9-3 47............ TonyHamilton 1 47
(Miss J A Camacho) *trckd ldrs: t.k.h: outpcd fnl 2f* **25/1**
0035 **7** *hd* **Musette (IRE)**[45] 2535 4-9-5 47............ RoystonFfrench 5 45
(R E Barr) *chsd ldrs: one pce fnl 2f* **50/1**
0036 **8** *1* **Ivana Illyich (IRE)**[18] 3372 5-9-5 42............(p) PaddyAspell 6 42
(J S Wainwright) *in rr: styd on fnl 2f: nvr nr ldrs* **66/1**
0 **9** *hd* **Lady Johanna (USA)**[38] 2740 3-8-9 0............ AndrewElliott(3) 4 42+
(K R Burke) *dwlt: sn in tch: one pce fnl 2f* **28/1**
20- **10** *4* **Laura's Best (IRE)**[273] 6201 3-8-12 0............ PaulMulrennan 7 28
(W J Haggas) *in tch: t.k.h: lost pl over 1f out* **9/1**[3]
0 **11** *6* **Hayfield Flyer**[32] 2951 3-8-12 0............ AdrianTNicholls 9 11
(Paul Green) *a towards rr* **100/1**
5-00 **12** *3 1/2* **Cumberland Road**[156] 518 4-9-5 45............(v[1]) MichaelJStainton(5) 14 10
(C A Mulhall) *overshot s; chsd ldrs on outer: hung rt over 2f out: sn lost pl* **150/1**
13 *13* **The Tokoloshe**[258] 5-9-7 0............ GregFairley(3) 11 —
(M A Barnes) *s.s: a bhd* **200/1**
6 **14** *2 1/2* **Final Desire**[13] 3561 4-8-12 0............ AndrewHeffernan(7) 12 —
(M Brittain) *s.s and reluctant: a detached in last* **80/1**
1m 28.71s (1.61) **Going Correction** +0.325s/f (Good)
WFA 3 from 4yo+ 7lb **14** Ran SP% **119.7**
Speed ratings (Par 103): **103,98,97,96,95 94,94,93,93,88 81,77,62,59**
CSF £3.98 TOTE £3.10: £1.20, £1.10, £11.50; EX 5.70.
Owner Guy Reed **Bred** G Reed **Trained** Melsonby, N Yorks
FOCUS
An uncompetitive maiden and, although the winner scored in most decisive fashion, the third is rated just 55 and more lowly-rated long-standing maidens were not beaten that far.

3915 THIRSK FAMILY DAY - 3RD AUGUST MEDIAN AUCTION MAIDEN STKS 5f
2:00 (2:07) (Class 4) 2-Y-0 **£5,181** (£1,541; £770; £384) **Stalls** High

Form RPR
300 **1** **Sudden Impact (IRE)**[38] 2737 2-8-12 0............ TPQueally 1 82
(Paul Green) *sn led: rdn wl over 1f out: styd on strly ins fnl f* **9/1**[3]
6 **2** *1 3/4* **Mey Blossom**[23] 3200 2-8-7 0............ MichaelJStainton(5) 2 76
(R M Whitaker) *sn cl up: effrt 2f out and ev ch tl rdn and nt qckn ins fnl f* **20/1**
32 **3** *1 1/4* **Red Alert Day**[14] 3479 2-9-3 0............ SebSanders 13 76
(N A Callaghan) *dwlt: sn chsng ldrs: rdn over 1f out: kpt on same pce* **4/9**[1]
0 **4** *1 1/4* **Tournevr (IRE)**[16] 3417 2-8-12 0............ DaleGibson 5 67
(Jane Chapple-Hyam) *chsd ldrs: rdn over 1f out: kpt on same pce* **50/1**
5 *1 1/2* **Le Toreador** 2-9-3 0............ NCallan 11 66+
(K A Ryan) *trckd ldrs: effrt 2f out: sn rdn and wknd appr fnl f* **5/1**[2]
6 *2* **Swallow Forest** 2-8-12 0............ PaulFessey 9 54
(T D Barron) *chsd ldrs: swtchd lft and rdn 2f out: sn wknd* **33/1**
7 *nk* **Baldemar** 2-9-3 0............ PhillipMakin 8 58
(K R Burke) *in tch: rdn along over 2f out and grad wknd* **16/1**
8 *5* **Red Skipper (IRE)** 2-9-3 0............ PaddyAspell 7 40
(N Wilson) *towards rr: rdn along and hung bdly lft over 2f out: nvr a factor* **66/1**
0U **9** *1/2* **Mill Creek**[18] 3370 2-8-12 0............ RoystonFfrench 14 33
(B Smart) *a in rr* **40/1**
10 *1/2* **County Crystal** 2-9-3 0............ TedDurcan 10 36
(T D Easterby) *s.i.s: a bhd* **28/1**
06 **11** *1 1/4* **Wizzy Izzy (IRE)**[18] 3378 2-8-12 0............ PaulMulrennan 15 27
(N Wilson) *cl up: rdn along 1/2-way: sn wknd* **100/1**
12 *13* **Bagenalstown (IRE)** 2-8-12 0............ NeilBrown(5) 3 —
(M Wellings) *dwlt: a outpcd and bhd* **100/1**
59.77 secs (-0.13) **Going Correction** +0.05s/f (Good) **12** Ran SP% **120.8**
Speed ratings (Par 96): **103,100,98,96,93 90,90,82,81,80 78,57**
CSF £166.11 TOTE £13.20: £2.40, £5.20, £1.02; EX 209.10.
Owner Terry Cummins **Bred** Owen Bourke **Trained** Lydiate, Merseyside
■ A first winner for trainer Paul Green.

FOCUS
With the favourite flopping this was probably just an ordinary maiden event and is best rated through the winner.
NOTEBOOK
Sudden Impact(IRE), who had plenty on her plate on her last two starts, had the worst of the draw. She showed plenty of speed and sticking on in game fashion, was firmly in command at the line. (op 8-1)
Mey Blossom, drawn wide, improved a good deal on her debut effort and there should be even better to come. (op 18-1)
Red Alert Day, dropped back in trip, missed a beat at the start. Driven along, he then ran too freely and never had a lot of room in which to work. This is best overlooked. (tchd 1-2 in places)
Tournevr(IRE), last of 12 on her Polytrack debut, is only small but she showed a lot more here. (op 40-1)
Le Toreador, a rangy, good-bodied half-brother to smart sprinter La Cucaracha, showed a fair level of ability but lack of hard fitness found him out in the end. He should improve a good deal with a little more time and experience. (op 6-1)
Swallow Forest, a well-made newcomer, should improve for the outing.
Baldemar, a strongly-made type, stayed on after getting outpaced and will be suited by six or even seven furlongs. (op 28-1)

3916 EBF ANDY & JUDY FILLERY'S PEARL ANNIVERSARY MAIDEN FILLIES' STKS 7f
2:30 (2:36) (Class 4) 2-Y-0 **£5,181** (£1,541; £770; £384) **Stalls** Low

Form RPR
4 **1** **Rosaleen (IRE)**[23] 3213 2-9-0 0............ TedDurcan 7 85+
(B J Meehan) *hld up in mid-div: hdwy over 3f out: led over 1f out: sn clr: eased towards fin* **11/8**[1]
2 *2 1/2* **Bonjour Allure (IRE)** 2-9-0 0............ RoystonFfrench 12 77+
(Mrs A Duffield) *mid-div: hdwy over 2f out: wnt 2nd over 1f out: no imp* **16/1**
0 **3** *5* **Neve Lieve (IRE)**[23] 3213 2-9-0 0............ MickyFenton 5 64
(M Botti) *led tl over 5f out: chsd ldrs: one pce fnl 2f* **11/1**
6 **4** *1 1/4* **Coffee Cup (IRE)**[30] 2984 2-9-0 0............ AdrianTNicholls 13 61
(G A Swinbank) *in rr: hdwy on outer and pushed wd over 2f out: styd on same pce fnl f* **6/1**[3]
5 *nk* **Irish Pearl (IRE)** 2-9-0 0............ PhillipMakin 11 60
(K R Burke) *in rr: kpt on fnl 2f: nvr nr ldrs* **12/1**
0 **6** *4* **Stateside (CAN)**[34] 2889 2-9-0 0............ TonyHamilton 3 50
(R A Fahey) *chsd ldrs: drvn 3f out: wknd over 1f out* **40/1**
0 **7** *1/2* **Jemima's Art**[14] 3510 2-9-0 0............ DaleGibson 4 49
(M W Easterby) *chsd ldrs: drvn over 3f out: sn outpcd* **40/1**
00 **8** *2* **Limelight (USA)**[51] 2371 2-9-0 0............ SebSanders 6 44
(Sir Mark Prescott) *chsd ldrs: drvn over 3f out: sn outpcd* **20/1**
9 *nk* **Arcetri (IRE)** 2-9-0 0............ NCallan 1 43
(K A Ryan) *t.k.h: sn trcking ldrs: led over 5f out: hung lft over 2f out: hdd & wknd over 1f out* **7/2**[2]
00 **10** *8* **Loose Caboose (IRE)**[25] 3171 2-8-7 0............ RobbieEgan(7) 2 23
(A J McCabe) *dwlt: bhd and detached: hung rt over 1f out* **125/1**
11 *1* **Snickers First** 2-9-0 0............ PaulMulrennan 8 21
(M W Easterby) *s.i.s: sn bhd and detached* **66/1**
12 *4* **Warsaw Waltz** 2-9-0 0............ TPQueally 10 11
(J G Given) *chsd ldrs: hung bdly rt and lost pl over 2f out: bit slipped and heavily eased ins fnl f* **16/1**
1m 28.99s (1.89) **Going Correction** +0.325s/f (Good) **12** Ran SP% **118.3**
Speed ratings (Par 93): **102,99,93,92,91 87,86,84,83,74 73,69**
CSF £26.59 TOTE £2.10: £1.20, £3.30, £3.10; EX 27.90.
Owner F C T Wilson **Bred** Alan Dargan **Trained** Manton, Wilts
FOCUS
No strength in depth and with the second favourite flopping it took little winning, but Rosaleen was value at least double the official margin. The fourth is the best guide to the level.
NOTEBOOK
Rosaleen(IRE), outstanding in the paddock, had to be put about her job but she had this won in a matter of strides, value at least five lengths. She will hold her own in much stronger company than this. (op 6-4)
Bonjour Allure(IRE), an April foal, is still unfurnished. Drawn wide, she went in pursuit of the winner and to her credit stayed on all the way to the line. She can surely go one better.
Neve Lieve(IRE), four lengths behind the winner when they were both making their debut at Kempton, set the pace but was readily brushed aside.
Coffee Cup(IRE), worst drawn, was carried wide when trying to improve. Staying on at the finish, a mile will suit her even better. (op 11-2 tchd 13-2 in a place)
Irish Pearl(IRE), excitable beforehand, stayed on when it was all over and the experience will hopefully have done her a power of good. (op 20-1)
Arcetri(IRE), a daughter of Galileo, is well made but not very big. She pulled her way to the front then hung badly right once in line for home. Entered in the Lowther, she had clearly been showing plenty at home. Official explanation: jockey said filly hung right in home straight (op 4-1 tchd 9-2)
Warsaw Waltz Official explanation: jockey said filly hung badly right and the bit slipped through its mouth

3917 IRISH RACEGOERS CLUB MAIDEN STKS (DIV II) 7f
3:05 (3:15) (Class 5) 3-Y-0+ **£3,238** (£963; £481; £240) **Stalls** Low

Form RPR
1 **Selkirk Sky** 3-8-12 0............ TonyHamilton 8 56+
(R A Fahey) *dwlt and bhd: hdwy over 2f out: swtchd rt and rdn wl over 1f out: styd on strly ins fnl f to ld last 100yds* **9/2**[2]
0-0 **2** *1 1/4* **Rock Diva (IRE)**[108] 998 3-8-12 0............ LeeEnstone 9 53
(P C Haslam) *trckd ldrs: hdwy 3f out: rdn to ld ent fnl f: drvn and hdd last 100yds* **22/1**
-600 **3** *nk* **Slip Star**[58] 2137 4-9-2 36............ GregFairley(3) 12 55
(T J Etherington) *in tch: rdn along and sltly outpcd 1/2-way: swtchd rt and drvn 2f out: styd on ins fnl f* **50/1**
4-4 **4** *nk* **Staked A Claim (IRE)**[20] 3302 3-9-3 0............ PhillipMakin 7 56
(T D Barron) *trckd ldng pair: hdwy to ld 3f out: rdn wl over 1f out: drvn and hdd ent fnl f: one pce* **11/8**[1]
66 **5** *3* **Red Barnet**[23] 3202 3-9-3 0............ DaleGibson 2 48
(M W Easterby) *midfield: hdwy on inner wl over 2f out: sn rdn and styd on appr fnl f: nrst fin* **10/1**[3]
0-0 **6** *hd* **Gizmo**[44] 2581 4-9-10 0............ RoystonFfrench 4 51
(B Smart) *s.i.s and bhd tl styd on fnl 2f: nrst fin* **16/1**
0600 **7** *3/4* **Noravana (IRE)**[41] 2657 3-8-7 45............ ColinHaddon(5) 3 41
(Miss V Haigh) *chsd ldrs on inner: rdn along 3f out: drvn and one pce fnl 2f* **25/1**
0000 **8** *nk* **The Keep**[36] 2806 5-9-5 39............ PaddyAspell 15 43
(R E Barr) *prom: rdn along and ev ch 2f out: sn drvn and wknd over 1f out* **33/1**

0-60 **9** *shd* **Sion Hill (IRE)**[183] 238 6-9-7 38 AndrewElliott(3) 1 48
(John A Harris) *hung rt thrght: rdn to ld and set str pce tl hung bdly rt on home bnd: sn hdd & wknd* **16/1**

04 **10** *½* **Beresford Lady**[36] 2792 3-8-12 0 TedDurcan 14 38
(A D Brown) *in tch: rdn along over 2f out and sn btn* **14/1**

0- **11** *½* **Grey Vision**[254] 6490 4-8-12 0 AndrewHeffernan(7) 10 40
(M Brittain) *s.i.s and bhd tl sme late hdwy* **40/1**

0-00 **12** *5* **Galway Girl (IRE)**[81] 1531 3-8-9 53 DuranFentiman(3) 13 23
(T D Easterby) *a bhd* **10/1**[3]

6-0 **13** *3½* **College Land Boy**[20] 3302 3-9-3 0 MickyFenton 5 19
(J J Quinn) *nvr bttr than midfield* **12/1**

5-60 **14** *3½* **Crosby Millie**[66] 1916 3-8-12 59 PaulMulrennan 11 5
(J R Weymes) *a towards rr* **15/2**

0 **15** *22* **Ronnies Girl**[38] 2740 3-8-12 0 PaulQuinn 6 —
(C J Teague) *a bhd: t.o fnl 3f* **150/1**

1m 29.08s (1.98) **Going Correction** +0.325s/f (Good)
WFA 3 from 4yo+ 7lb **15 Ran SP% 126.7**
Speed ratings (Par 103): **101,99,99,98,95 95,94,94,93,93 92,87,83,79,53**
CSF £112.82 TOTE £5.20: £2.00, £6.30, £14.10; EX 140.20.
Owner Mrs R D Peacock **Bred** Mrs R D Peacock **Trained** Musley Bank, N Yorks

FOCUS
The slowest of the three seven-furlong maiden races and almost certainly very weak form with the third rated just 36.
Sion Hill(IRE) Official explanation: jockey said gelding hung right-handed throughout

3918 HUMBER (S) H'CAP 1m
3:40 (3:49) (Class 6) (0-65,60) 3-Y-O **£2,590** (£770; £385; £192) **Stalls** Low

Form RPR

-001 **1** **Kiss Chase (IRE)**[24] 3175 3-9-3 56 (b) SebSanders 7 65
(J S Goldie) *hld up in rr: hdwy on wd outside over 2f out: styd on to ld jst ins fnl f: drvn out* **4/1**[1]

0030 **2** *2* **Smash N'Grab (IRE)**[11] 3583 3-8-13 52 NCallan 4 56
(K A Ryan) *w ldrs: led over 2f out: edgd rt and hdd jst ins fnl f: no ex* **9/2**[2]

-040 **3** *3* **Myfrenchconnection (IRE)**[67] 1894 3-8-13 52 (p) MickyFenton 3 49
(P T Midgley) *chsd ldrs: one pce fnl 2f* **15/2**

4000 **4** *6* **Sangreal**[10] 3611 3-9-4 60 AndrewElliott(3) 5 43
(K R Burke) *in rr: kpt on fnl 2f: nvr nr ldrs* **14/1**

-500 **5** *1½* **Compton Special**[21] 3281 3-8-9 48 TPQueally 2 28
(J G Given) *hld up in midfield: effrt over 2f out: nvr nr ldrs* **17/2**

-010 **6** *1¾* **Joint Expectations (IRE)**[29] 3040 3-8-12 51 (b) DMylonas 8 27
(Mrs C A Dunnett) *w ldrs: led over 4f out tl over 2f out: wknd over 1f out* **33/1**

5-50 **7** *4* **Meeting Of Minds**[43] 2607 3-8-13 52 TedDurcan 1 19
(W Jarvis) *s.s: sme hdwy over 3f out: wknd over 1f out* **7/1**[3]

0530 **8** *hd* **Denton Hawk**[60] 2091 3-8-11 50 (v[1]) PhillipMakin 6 16
(M Dods) *s.i.s: nvr on terms* **15/2**

00-0 **9** *1¼* **Go Red**[69] 1850 3-8-11 50 PaulMulrennan 10 13
(M W Easterby) *hld up on outer: midfield: effrt over 3f out: nvr a factor* **12/1**

05-0 **10** *7* **Umpa Loompa (IRE)**[130] 711 3-9-1 54 (v) AdrianTNicholls 14 —
(D Nicholls) *led: hung rt and hdd bnd over 4f out: lost pl over 2f out* **20/1**

-205 **11** *¾* **Kyrenia Girl (IRE)**[39] 2713 3-8-11 53 DuranFentiman(3) 9 —
(T D Easterby) *mid-div: lost pl over 4f out: bhd whn hmpd and stmbld ins fnl f* **17/2**

1m 42.82s (3.12) **Going Correction** +0.325s/f (Good) **11 Ran SP% 117.3**
Speed ratings (Par 98): **97,95,92,86,84 82,78,78,77,70 69**
CSF £21.58 CT £130.74 TOTE £4.10: £1.80, £1.90, £2.60; EX 23.80.There was no bid for the winner.
Owner J S Goldie **Bred** Rathasker Stud **Trained** Uplawmoor, E Renfrews

FOCUS
A very moderate event, and the form looks unlikely to prove informative. The winner does not look the easiest of rides and was not sold after the race.
Denton Hawk Official explanation: jockey said gelding missed the break
Umpa Loompa(IRE) Official explanation: jockey said gelding hung right throughout

3919 STANLAND LAUNDRY H'CAP 1m 4f
4:15 (4:15) (Class 4) (0-80,80) 3-Y-O **£5,181** (£1,541; £770; £384) **Stalls** Low

Form RPR

-422 **1** **Cushat Law (IRE)**[32] 2945 3-8-2 61 oh2 PaulFessey 5 67
(W Jarvis) *trckd ldrs: hdwy 3f out: rdn and hung wl over 1f out: sn ev ch: drvn and kpt on to ld wl ins fnl f* **5/1**[3]

51-0 **2** *½* **Fushe Jo**[72] 1773 3-9-4 77 TonyHamilton 7 82
(J Howard Johnson) *led: rdn along over 2f out: drvn over 1f out: hdd and no ex wl ins fnl f* **7/1**

1-04 **3** *½* **Ajaan**[20] 3335 3-9-6 79 TedDurcan 3 84+
(H R A Cecil) *dwlt: sn in tch: hdwy on inner 3f out: effrt and nt clr run over 1f out: swtchd rt and rdn ins fnl f: styd on towards fin* **6/4**[1]

2450 **4** *1¼* **Vanquisher (IRE)**[18] 3367 3-9-0 73 (p) PaulMulrennan 8 75
(W J Haggas) *hld up in rr: hdwy over 2f out: rdn over 1f out: kpt on same pce ins fnl f* **7/2**[2]

5-64 **5** *4* **The Quantum Kid**[48] 2464 3-8-3 62 RoystonFfrench 1 58
(T J Etherington) *chsd ldng pair: rdn along over 2f out: drvn and hld whn n.m.r wl over 1f out: sn wknd* **22/1**

-660 **6** *12* **Prince Golan (IRE)**[14] 3495 3-9-7 80 NCallan 4 57
(K A Ryan) *hld up: rdn along over 3f out and sn btn* **16/1**

3004 **7** *2½* **New World Order (IRE)**[14] 3495 3-8-12 74 AndrewElliott(3) 2 47
(K R Burke) *t.k.h: chsd ldr: rdn along 3f out: drvn over 2f out and sn wknd* **8/1**

2m 38.8s (3.60) **Going Correction** +0.325s/f (Good) **7 Ran SP% 112.7**
Speed ratings (Par 102): **101,100,100,99,96 88,87**
CSF £37.75 CT £75.79 TOTE £5.40: £2.90, £4.00; EX 45.20.
Owner A Reed **Bred** Blush With Love Syndicate **Trained** Newmarket, Suffolk

FOCUS
A fair handicap run at only a modest gallop. The winner was running from out of the handicap but looks progressive and the form is rated through the beaten favourite.
New World Order(IRE) Official explanation: jockey said colt finished distressed

3920 DEEPDALE SOLUTIONS NSPCC FILLIES' H'CAP 6f
4:50 (4:53) (Class 5) (0-70,70) 3-Y-O+ **£2,521** (£2,521; £577; £288) **Stalls** High

Form RPR

4510 **1** **Riquewihr**[7] 3723 7-9-8 65 (p) PaddyAspell 2 75
(J S Wainwright) *trckd ldrs: hdwy 2f out: rdn to ld ins fnl f: jnd on line* **18/1**

-556 **1** *dht* **Gap Princess (IRE)**[20] 3302 3-8-12 60 TonyHamilton 9 69
(R A Fahey) *chsd ldrs: rdn along wl over 1f out: drvn ins fnl f and styd on wl to join ldr on line* **10/1**

/010 **3** *3* **Cadogen Square**[3] 3816 5-8-3 53 (b) DanielleMcCreery(7) 1 54
(D W Chapman) *led: rdn along wl over 1f out: drvn and hdd ins fnl f: kpt on same pce* **25/1**

0220 **4** *1¼* **Monda**[164] 448 5-8-11 54 RoystonFfrench 15 51
(Miss J A Camacho) *chsd ldrs: hdwy 2f out: sn rdn and styd on ins fnl f: nrst fin* **7/1**[3]

0100 **5** *1½* **Petite Mac**[5] 3762 7-8-9 55 AndrewElliott(3) 6 48
(N Bycroft) *cl up on outer: effrt and ev ch 2f out: sn rdn and wknd appr fnl f* **8/1**

0016 **6** *nk* **Word Perfect**[15] 3466 5-9-11 68 (b) DaleGibson 5 60
(M W Easterby) *cl up: rdn along over 2f out: grad wknd* **8/1**

0123 **7** *½* **Rothesay Dancer**[4] 3784 4-8-11 61 KellyHarrison(7) 7 51
(J S Goldie) *hld up: hdwy 2f out: sn rdn and no imp* **11/2**[2]

2201 **8** *4* **Onatopp (IRE)**[23] 3202 3-9-7 69 SebSanders 14 46
(T D Easterby) *hood removed late in stalls: s.i.s and a in rr* **7/2**[1]

0220 **9** *2½* **Rosein**[27] 3108 5-9-12 69 TedDurcan 13 40
(Mrs G S Rees) *s.i.s: a bhd* **7/1**[3]

000 **10** *5* **Jord (IRE)**[33] 2910 3-8-5 60 RobbieEgan(7) 11 14
(A J McCabe) *swvd rt s and rdr briefly lost iron: prom tl rdn along over 2f out and sn wknd* **40/1**

2235 **11** *6* **Diksie Dancer**[58] 2137 3-9-8 70 NCallan 8 7
(K A Ryan) *chsd ldrs: rdn over 2f out and sn wknd* **8/1**

1m 12.21s (-0.29) **Going Correction** +0.05s/f (Good)
WFA 3 from 4yo+ 5lb **11 Ran SP% 116.6**
Speed ratings (Par 100): **103,103,99,97,95 94,94,88,85,78 70**
WIN: Riquewihr £8.90, Gap Princess £6.60; PL: RR £3.70; GP £3.70; EX: RR/GP £82.50, GP/RR £95.70; CSF: RR/GP £92.60, GP/RR £86.92; TR: RR/GP/CS £2,265.88, GP/RR/CS £2,189.61., £7.20.
Owner Dr W D Ashworth **Bred** D Veitch & Musagd Abo Salim **Trained** Musley Bank, N Yorks
Owner S Enwright **Bred** G B Partnership **Trained** Kennythorpe, N Yorks

FOCUS
A modest handicap but a fair race for the grade/sex. Riquewhir is in-foal and landed her second race in three runs. The form looks straightforward, helped by a reasonable time.
Onatopp(IRE) Official explanation: jockey said he had trouble removing blindfold
Rosein Official explanation: jockey said mare missed the break

3921 PERTEMPS PEOPLE DEVELOPMENT "HANDS AND HEELS" APPRENTICE SERIES H'CAP 5f
5:25 (5:29) (Class 5) (0-75,75) 3-Y-O+ **£3,886** (£1,156; £577; £288) **Stalls** High

Form RPR

0064 **1** **Whinhill House**[2] 3836 7-8-6 57 (v) NSLawes(3) 14 66
(D W Barker) *w ldr: kpt on to ld towards fin* **6/1**[2]

0315 **2** *hd* **Dark Champion**[10] 3608 7-8-9 57 (v) WilliamCarson 15 65
(R E Barr) *led tl hdd wl ins fnl f: no ex* **9/2**[1]

5364 **3** *2* **Jilly Why (IRE)**[2] 3853 6-9-7 69 (b) FrankiePickard 11 70
(Paul Green) *towards rr: hdwy 2f out: kpt on same pce ins fnl f* **6/1**[2]

0030 **4** *1½* **Sir Loin**[10] 3608 6-8-5 56 oh2 (b) AdamCarter(3) 3 52
(N Tinkler) *w ldrs: kpt on same pce appr fnl f* **28/1**

6-00 **5** *nk* **Fern House (IRE)**[19] 3345 5-8-3 56 oh11 PaulPickard(5) 9 51
(Garry Moss) *sn chsng ldrs: one pce fnl 2f* **100/1**

0000 **6** *½* **Matsunosuke**[15] 3464 5-9-7 72 ChrisHough(3) 13 65+
(A B Coogan) *hld up in rr: hdwy over 1f out: gng on at fin* **7/1**[3]

0520 **7** *½* **Rare Cross (IRE)**[2] 3836 5-9-5 70 PatrickDonaghy(3) 7 61
(D Shaw) *mid-div: kpt on fnl 2f: nvr trbld ldrs* **12/1**

5204 **8** *hd* **John Keats**[4] 3782 4-9-0 62 (p) GaryBartley 6 52
(J S Goldie) *in rr-div: hdwy over 1f out: kpt on* **6/1**[2]

0065 **9** *1¾* **Paddywack (IRE)**[4] 3791 10-8-12 60 (p) DanielleMcCreery 5 44
(D W Chapman) *towards rr: sme hdwy on outer 2f out: nvr a factor* **10/1**

0000 **10** *shd* **Circuit Dancer (IRE)**[30] 2989 7-9-10 75 AdeleRothery(3) 2 59
(D Nicholls) *racd wd: sn w ldrs: one pce fnl 2f* **16/1**

0000 **11** *nk* **Rosie's Result**[4] 3782 7-8-5 56 oh11 JamesRogers(3) 8 39
(M Todhunter) *chsd ldrs: wknd over 1f out* **66/1**

2326 **12** *1½* **No Time (IRE)**[56] 2202 7-9-1 63 RobbieEgan 10 40
(A J McCabe) *a towards rr* **7/1**[3]

0401 **13** *5* **He's A Rocket (IRE)**[8] 3667 6-8-5 56 6ex oh5 (b) DeclanCannon(3) 1 15
(K R Burke) *swvd lft s: r alone far side: sn chsng ldrs: lost pl over 2f out* **14/1**

59.67 secs (-0.23) **Going Correction** +0.05s/f (Good) **13 Ran SP% 121.3**
Speed ratings (Par 103): **103,102,99,97,96 95,95,94,91,91 91,88,80**
CSF £33.44 CT £151.88 TOTE £9.40: £2.80, £1.70, £2.60; EX 33.60 Place 6 £78.69, Place 5 £68.09..
Owner Destiny Racing Club **Bred** W R And Mrs Arblaster **Trained** Scorton, N Yorks
■ Stewards' Enquiry : Robbie Egan seven-day ban: used whip in hands and heels race (Aug 8-9,13-15,17,24)

FOCUS
A hands and heels event for apprentices dominated by those drawn high. The form is rated around the first two but should be treated with caution.
T/Plt: £56.30 to a £1 stake. Pool: £40,987.40. 530.80 winning tickets. T/Qpdt: £70.00 to a £1 stake. Pool: £2,243.30. 23.70 winning tickets. JR

[3595]WOLVERHAMPTON (A.W) (L-H)
Friday, July 27

OFFICIAL GOING: Standard
Wind: fresh behind

3922 STAY AT THE WOLVERHAMPTON HOLIDAY INN CLAIMING STKS 1m 141y(P)
2:20 (2:21) (Class 6) 3-Y-O+ **£2,730** (£806; £403) **Stalls** Low

Form RPR

0536 **1** **Inside Story (IRE)**[35] 2822 5-9-5 68 (b) WilliamBuick(5) 5 76
(M W Easterby) *trckd ldrs: swtchd rt wl over 1f out: edgd rt u.p: led 1f out straightened up and r.o wl* **7/2**[1]

0312 **2** *2* **Samuel Charles**[10] 3619 9-9-3 70 (p) LiamJones(3) 10 68
(C R Dore) *sn chsd ldrs: ev ch 1f out: nt pce of wnr* **4/1**[2]

0261 **3** *3* **Zelos (IRE)**[6] 3732 3-9-1 63 (b) ChrisCatlin 1 64
(J A Osborne) *mid-div: styd on ins fnl 2f: nvr nrr* **5/1**[3]

5630 **4** *¾* **Kirkhammerton (IRE)**[7] 3714 5-9-2 48 (b) JamesDoyle 4 55
(A J McCabe) *led for 1f: prom: tl rdn and wknd 1f out*

4-00 **5** *½* **Band**[28] 3067 7-9-8 52 J-PGuillambert 13 60
(E S McMahon) *trckd ldr: wnt 2nd over 3f out: rdn and one pce fr over 1f out* **16/1**

036 **6** *2* **Wahoo Sam (USA)**[3] 3814 7-9-10 72 DO'Donohoe 12 58
(K A Ryan) *led after 1f: rdn and hdd 1f out: wknd ins fnl f* **6/1**

3525 **7** *1* **Prince Dayjur (USA)**[125] 770 8-9-10 70 DeanMcKeown 6 56
(J Pearce) *hmpd s: nvr bttr than mid-div* **11/1**

1043 **8** *nk* **Dante's Diamond (IRE)**[11] 3599 5-9-6 60 SamHitchcott 2 51
(R Lee) *nvr bttr than mid-div* **11/2**

553 **9** *5* **Jools**[10] 3615 9-9-6 49 RobertHavlin 3 40
(D K Ivory) *a towards rr* **16/1**

5040 **10** *hd* **Mister Benji**[13] 3534 8-9-4 53 StephenDonohoe 9 38
(B P J Baugh) *mid-div: rdn and wknd 2f out* **33/1**

-360 **11** *nk* **North Walk (IRE)**[11] 3600 4-9-7 62 LiamTreadwell(3) 8 43
(Jennie Candlish) *a bhd* **28/1**

-050 **12** *6* **Sew In Character**[17] 3394 3-8-11 47 FrancisNorton 7 25
(M Blanshard) *stdd s: a bhd* **40/1**

13 *nk* **West End Lad** 4-9-6 0 PaulEddery 11 25
(S R Bowring) *v.s.a: a struggling in rr* **100/1**

1m 49.89s (-1.87) **Going Correction** 0.0s/f (Stan)
WFA 3 from 4yo+ 9lb **13** Ran SP% **121.9**
Speed ratings (Par 101): **108,106,103,102,102 100,99,99,95,94 94,89,89**
CSF £16.94 TOTE £5.00: £1.70, £1.30, £2.00; EX 22.20.The winner was claimed by N Wilson £10,000.
Owner Matthew Green **Bred** Arthur S Phelan **Trained** Sheriff Hutton, N Yorks

FOCUS
A strong wind was blowing them home up the straight and there was a decent tempo to the race. The form is rated fairly positively although the fourth and fifth limit.

3923 SPONSOR A RACE BY CALLING 0870 220 2442 FILLIES' (S) STKS 7f 32y(P)

2:55 (2:56) (Class 6) 2-Y-0 **£2,047** (£604; £302) **Stalls** High

Form RPR

0501 **1** **Marmite (IRE)**[10] 3614 2-9-4 0 (v[1]) LPKeniry 1 60
(E F Vaughan) *s.i.s: sn trckd ldrs: hung lft bef led appr fnl f: drvn out* **4/1**[1]

4400 **2** *1 ½* **Willyn (IRE)**[17] 3398 2-8-12 0 DO'Donohoe 7 50
(J R Weymes) *towards rr whn hmpd 5f out: hdwy on outside: wl over 1f out: rdn r.o to go 2nd nr fin* **6/1**[2]

0 **3** *½* **Ochenvay**[28] 3055 2-8-12 0 RobertHavlin 6 49
(M Quinn) *slowly away: hdwy on ins over 1f out: styd on one pce* **18/1**

00 **4** *1* **Naming Problems**[25] 3171 2-8-12 0 (v[1]) DeanMcKeown 11 47
(K J Burke) *bhd tl hdwy and edgd lft over 2f out: one pce appr fnl f* **40/1**

25 **5** *nk* **Liani (IRE)**[22] 3246 2-8-9 0 LiamJones(3) 2 46
(W M Brisbourne) *mid-div: kpt on one pce fnl f* **4/1**[1]

00 **6** *¾* **Whistful Miss**[15] 3446 2-8-12 0 J-PGuillambert 3 44
(P Howling) *led tl rdn and hdd appr fnl f: nt qckn and fdd fnl f* **40/1**

6505 **7** *2* **Star In The East**[19] 3348 2-8-12 0 FrancisNorton 12 39
(A M Balding) *in tch: rdn 1/2-way: bmpd over 2f out: no hdwy after* **4/1**[1]

000 **8** *3* **Morforwyn**[16] 3423 2-8-9 0 (b[1]) RichardKingscote(3) 9 31
(J A Osborne) *chsd ldrs: rdn 3f out: sn btn* **20/1**

004 **9** *6* **Poppy Perfect**[10] 3614 2-8-12 0 (b[1]) JimmyQuinn 5 16
(J M P Eustace) *prom: wkng whn hmpd over 1f out* **25/1**

04 **10** *5* **Birdsville**[4] 3801 2-8-12 0 SaleemGolam 4 —
(Rae Guest) *t.k.h: prom tl rdn 1/2-way: sn wknd* **13/2**[3]

3334 **11** *12* **Miss Willoughby**[10] 3626 2-9-4 0 ChrisCatlin 8 —
(J Ryan) *s.i.s: a bhd* **16/1**

1m 33.74s (3.34) **Going Correction** 0.0s/f (Stan) **11** Ran SP% **112.3**
Speed ratings (Par 89): **80,78,77,76,76 75,73,69,62,57 43**
CSF £24.27 TOTE £6.20: £2.20, £2.40, £5.20; EX 31.70.The winner was bought in for 6,500gns. Star In The East was claimed by Richard Teatum for £6,000.
Owner Hungerford Park Stud **Bred** Mrs E L Hunter **Trained** Newmarket, Suffolk
■ Just Puddie was withdrawn (14/1, vet's advice). Deduct 5p in the £ under Rule 4.

FOCUS
The way these youngsters weaved around under pressure before the home turn suggests this was a particularly weak seller. However, the winner is rated an average winner for the grade.

NOTEBOOK
Marmite(IRE) added a second win at this level and connections were keen to retain her, as her breeding suggests she will improve as she steps up in trip. A visor was added to try to help her travel through her race, but she is game and fought off challenges early in the straight to be well on top at the line, and confirm she can improve out of this company when getting 1m and more later in the season. She is one to watch for in a staying nursery and easier ground should also suit her. (op 9-2 tchd 7-2)
Willyn(IRE) got mucked around at the back, partly due to her being keen. She stayed on late, enjoying the step up in trip, but is exposed as modest. (tchd 13-2)
Ochenvay did well to finish third, as she was in a hopeless position against the inside rail into the last two furlongs. She kept to the shortest route and came home nicely as others wandered, around and has a seller in her. (op 10-1)
Naming Problems looks one to treat with caution, as she was one of the worst wanderers, despite having a visor added. She made strong headway to look a likely winner going to the final furlong but curled up when faced with the front. The pace she showed around the home bend suggests a drop to 6f might help. (op 33-1)
Liani(IRE), stepping up a furlong, is not making the progress one would have hoped. (op 6-1)
Star In The East, dropping into a seller for the first time, is proving very disappointing for a well-bred sort. (op 7-2)

3924 HORIZONS RESTAURANT MEDIAN AUCTION MAIDEN STKS 5f 216y(P)

3:30 (3:30) (Class 6) 3-4-Y-0 **£2,388** (£705; £352) **Stalls** Low

Form RPR

0-00 **1** **All You Need (IRE)**[62] 2044 3-8-12 70 RussellKennemore(5) 2 76
(R Hollinshead) *chsd ldrs: led jst ins fnl f: r.o wl* **7/2**[2]

540 **2** *1 ¾* **Topflightcoolracer**[17] 3406 3-8-12 70 J-PGuillambert 8 65
(Mrs G S Rees) *led hdd over 4f out: tk narrow ld over 1f out: rdn and hdd jst ins fnl f: kpt on one pce* **4/1**[3]

0-23 **3** *5* **Ella Woodcock (IRE)**[165] 446 3-9-3 65 ChrisCatlin 5 54+
(J A Osborne) *in rr: styd on fr over 1f out to go 3rd wl ins fnl f: no ch w first 2* **10/3**[1]

0 **4** *1 ½* **Lawdy Miss Clawdy**[28] 3046 3-8-12 0 JamesDoyle 6 44
(D W P Arbuthnot) *led over 4f out: rdn and hdd over 1f out: wknd ins fnl f* **16/1**

22-5 **5** *1 ¼* **Darling Belinda**[204] 34 3-8-12 65 RobertHavlin 10 40
(D K Ivory) *sn in rr: hdwy over 2f out: one pce after* **6/1**

0606 **6** *¾* **Avoncreek**[7] 3713 3-9-3 49 PaulEddery 3 43
(B P J Baugh) *a towards rr though sme late hdwy* **22/1**

00 **7** *hd* **Perry's Pride**[17] 3406 3-8-12 0 JimmyQuinn 13 37
(Mrs G S Rees) *trckd ldrs tl rdn and wknd wl over 1f out* **66/1**

-032 **8** *1 ¾* **Siesta (IRE)**[16] 3425 3-8-9 50 (e) LiamJones(3) 9 32
(J R Fanshawe) *in tch whn stmbld 5f out: in rr and nvr on terms after* **9/2**

0020 **9** *2* **Sharpattack**[34] 2895 3-8-12 53 NicolPolli(5) 11 30
(M Botti) *a in rr* **16/1**

0000 **10** *5* **Stoneacre Donny (IRE)**[11] 3583 3-9-3 47 LPKeniry 7 14
(Peter Grayson) *a bhd* **50/1**

0 **11** *2 ½* **Pathway To Glory**[16] 3425 3-9-3 0 FrancisNorton 12 6
(M Quinn) *in tch early: rdn 1/2-way sn wknd* **50/1**

0-0 **12** *1 ¾* **Nellie**[83] 1482 3-8-9 0 StephaneBreux(3) 1 —
(R M Whitaker) *in tch tl lost pl 1/2-way* **66/1**

1m 15.27s (-0.54) **Going Correction** 0.0s/f (Stan) **12** Ran SP% **120.8**
Speed ratings (Par 101): **103,100,94,92,90 89,89,86,84,77 74,71**
CSF £17.79 TOTE £4.10: £2.10, £1.30, £1.30; EX 34.70.
Owner N Chapman **Bred** D J Maher **Trained** Upper Longdon, Staffs

FOCUS
A modest maiden which seems unlikely to have a huge impact on future events and not a race to be with.
Siesta(IRE) Official explanation: jockey said filly suffered interference in running
Stoneacre Donny(IRE) Official explanation: jockey said colt hung right-handed

3925 WOLVERHAMPTON-RACECOURSE.CO.UK NURSERY 5f 216y(P)

4:05 (4:06) (Class 5) 2-Y-0 **£3,562** (£1,059; £529; £264) **Stalls** Low

Form RPR

621 **1** **Cosmic Art**[21] 3283 2-9-7 82 StephenDonohoe 8 90
(E A L Dunlop) *trckd ldr: led 1/2-way: clr over 1f out: kpt up to work* **10/3**[2]

412 **2** *3* **Victorian Bounty**[16] 3426 2-8-13 74 ChrisCatlin 9 73
(E J O'Neill) *led to 1/2-way: no ch w wnr fr over 1f out: jst hld on for 2nd* **3/1**[1]

010 **3** *shd* **Ellemujie**[15] 3462 2-9-4 79 RobertHavlin 13 82+
(D K Ivory) *racd wd towards rr: hdwy over 1f out: r.o fnl f go 3rd nr fin* **8/1**

516 **4** *1* **Fitolini**[27] 3077 2-8-12 73 J-PGuillambert 4 69
(Mrs G S Rees) *slowly away: in tch after 2f: hdwy over 2f out: nvr nr to chal* **8/1**

610 **5** *6* **Weet A Surprise**[14] 3492 2-8-13 74 LPKeniry 11 52
(R Hollinshead) *towards rr: nvr on terms* **50/1**

645 **6** *shd* **Atephobia**[35] 2819 2-8-10 71 FrancisNorton 1 48+
(K R Burke) *towards rr and nvr got into r* **16/1**

0300 **7** *nk* **Seventh Cloud (IRE)**[9] 3642 2-8-7 68 SimonWhitworth 3 45
(A P Jarvis) *chsd ldrs tl rdn and lost pl over 2f out* **66/1**

045 **8** *2 ½* **Lord Of The Wing**[59] 2103 2-8-5 66 JimmyQuinn 10 35
(R M Beckett) *chsd ldrs: rdn over 2f out: sn wknd* **5/1**[3]

3425 **9** *shd* **Demure Princess**[23] 3199 2-8-1 65 LiamJones(3) 2 34
(W G M Turner) *bhd fr 1/2-way* **16/1**

534 **10** *1 ½* **Kinout (IRE)**[45] 2526 2-9-4 79 DO'Donohoe 12 43
(K A Ryan) *hld up: a bhd* **12/1**

1540 **11** *1 ¼* **Ten Down**[16] 3426 2-9-4 82 RichardKingscote(3) 6 42
(J A Osborne) *in tch tl wknd over 2f out* **12/1**

1m 15.39s (-0.42) **Going Correction** 0.0s/f (Stan) **11** Ran SP% **117.6**
Speed ratings (Par 94): **102,98,97,96,88 88,88,84,84,82 80**
CSF £13.75 CT £75.78 TOTE £3.80: £1.40, £1.80, £2.10; EX 12.30.
Owner Byculla Thoroughbreds **Bred** Hellwood Stud Farm **Trained** Newmarket, Suffolk

FOCUS
A decent contest that only really concerned two horses from halfway. The form looks sound and should work out, and the winner could be a nice sprinter in the making. The 'official' ratings shown next to each horse are estimated and for information purposes only.

NOTEBOOK
Cosmic Art ◆ strung out his rivals in the last two furlongs. Connections had feared his rating had suffered for his runaway maiden win, which has not been franked, but he showed he is one to follow, as he again showed good all-round pace that proved too much for those who tried to go with him, while he had stamina to spare to see off the finishers. He faces another rise for this emphatic win but looks the sort to land a big nursery, although connections pointed out that he needs a sound surface on turf, hence his transfer to the All-Weather in the wet weather. (op 11-4 tchd 7-2)
Victorian Bounty had not impressed over this trip on his debut and again tired badly in the dying strides after looking set for a clear-cut second. He harried the winner for over four furlongs and should get back to winning ways returned to 5f. (op 10-3 tchd 7-2 and 11-4)
Ellemujie ran well, as he just missed the break from an outside draw and was forced to race wide throughout, forfeiting ground around the bend into the straight. He stayed on stoutly in the final furlong and can win a nursery when having things more in his favour. (op 12-1)
Fitolini made a strong move around the home bend to get into third place, cornering well. Like the runner-up, she weakened in the final furlong to suggest the minimum trip suits her better. (op 11-2)
Weet A Surprise has not really gone on since landing a very modest maiden at Warwick, but this was a hot contest and she will find easier opportunites. (op 40-1)
Lord Of The Wing did not seem suited by the sixth furlong and, for the time being, will be best suited by the minimum distance. (op 13-2)
Demure Princess Official explanation: jockey said filly suffered interference in running

3926 SPONSOR A RACE BY CALLING 0870 220 2442 H'CAP 1m 141y(P)

4:40 (4:40) (Class 5) (0-75,75) 3-Y-0+ **£1,989** (£1,989; £453) **Stalls** Low

Form RPR

2213 **1** **Hoh Wotanite**[13] 3534 4-9-0 66 (p) RussellKennemore(5) 8 74+
(R Hollinshead) *hld up in rr: hmpd and swtchd lft over 1f out: sustained run to force dead-heat* **6/1**

010 **1** *dht* **Grand Vizier (IRE)**[42] 2633 3-9-0 73 LiamJones(3) 4 80
(C F Wall) *mid-div: hdwy over 2f out: led wl ins fnl f: jnd on line* **20/1**

0-21 **3** *1 ¼* **Muhannak (IRE)**[17] 3406 3-9-5 75 SaleemGolam 6 80
(G A Butler) *in rr: c wd into st: hdwy over 1f out: hung lft but r.o ins fnl f* **4/1**[1]

0-06 **4** *nk* **Empire Dancer (IRE)**[11] 3599 4-9-1 65 MarcHalford(3) 10 70
(C N Allen) *led rdn over 1f out: hdd wl ins fnl f: nt qckn* **25/1**

5234 **5** *nk* **Scamperdale**[16] 3416 5-9-12 73 (p) DeanMcKeown 7 77+
(B P J Baugh) *in rr: rdn over 1f out: r.o wl fnl f: nvr nrr* **11/2**[3]

3002 **6** *shd* **Henry The Seventh**[10] 3622 3-8-13 69 ChrisCatlin 5 72
(J W Hills) *mid-div: rdn over 2f out: hdwy over 1f out: swtchd sharply lft ins fnl f: kpt on* **17/2**

5000 **7** *1 ¼* **Anduril**[26] 2809 6-8-13 60 PaulEddery 9 61
(Miss M E Rowland) *slowly away: in rr tl hdwy over 1f out: styd on* **66/1**

3104 **8** *¾* **Western Roots**[27] 3111 6-9-5 66 (p) JimmyQuinn 12 66
(M Appleby) *chsd ldrs: rdn 2f out: ev ch ent fnl f: fdd* **20/1**

5205 **9** *nk* **Blacktoft (USA)**[18] 3386 4-10-0 75 (e) J-PGuillambert 2 74
(S C Williams) *trckd ldrs: rdn over 1f out: wknd ins fnl f* **13/2**

4402 **10** *1 ½* **Lord Of Dreams (IRE)**[11] 3600 5-9-0 61 JamesDoyle 1 63+
(D W P Arbuthnot) *mid-div: hdwy on ins over 1f out: bdly hmpd ins fnl f: nt rcvr* **9/2**[2]

240 **11** *5* **United Nations**[30] 2986 6-9-7 75 LanceBetts(7) 11 60
(N Wilson) *racd wd in mid-div: bhd fnl 2f* **20/1**

-066 **12** *4* **Latif (USA)**[45] 2527 6-9-1 69 JohnCavanagh(7) 3 45
(Ms Deborah J Evans) *prom tl wknd wl over 1f out* **33/1**

246- **13** 7 **Cursum Perficio**[289] 5908 5-9-12 **73**............................ SamHitchcott 13 34
(R Lee) *prom: rdn over 3f out: wknd over 2f out* **25/1**

1m 50.9s (-0.86) **Going Correction** 0.0s/f (Stan)
WFA 3 from 4yo+ 9lb **13** Ran SP% **118.1**
Speed ratings (Par 103): **103,103,101,101,101 101,100,99,99,97 93,89,83**
WIN: Hoh Wotanite £2.90, Grand Vizier £10.80; PL: HW £1.90, GV £1.90; EX: HW/GV £60.89, GV/HW £62.61; TR: HW/GV/MK £270.38, GV/HW/MK £295.12 CSF £60.89 CT £270.38, £2.20; EX 59.10.
Owner Hintlesham SP Partners **Bred** Yeomanstown Stud **Trained** Newmarket, Suffolk
Owner The Three R'S **Bred** Dunchurch Lodge Stud Co **Trained** Upper Longdon, Staffs
■ Stewards' Enquiry : Chris Catlin four-day ban: careless riding (Aug 7-10)

FOCUS
This was notable for a steadier pace than earlier races, but there were plenty of changes of position in the sprint home to suggest the form is ordinary with dead-heater Hoh Wotanite to form.

3927 RINGSIDE CONFERENCE HALL APPRENTICE H'CAP 2m 119y(P)
5:15 (5:16) (Class 6) (0-65,60) 4-Y-0+ **£2,388** (£705; £352) **Stalls** Low

Form RPR
0-00 **1** **Zonic Boom (FR)**[65] 1406 7-8-13 **49**....................(tp) StephenDonohoe 6 56
(Heather Dalton) *hdwy over 9f out: wnt 2nd 7f out: led 3f out: drvn clr and in command after* **16/1**
420 **2** 2 **Madiba**[15] 3448 8-9-2 **55**.. TravisBlock(3) 11 60
(P Howling) *trckd ldrs: rdn over 2f out: styd on to go 2nd wl ins fnl f* **7/1**[3]
4603 **3** ½ **Squirtle (IRE)**[15] 3473 4-9-3 **53**.. LiamJones 5 57+
(W M Brisbourne) *hld up in rr: hdwy over 1f out: styd on to go 3rd wl ins fnl f* **13/2**[2]
1202 **4** 1 **Diktatorship (IRE)**[11] 3598 4-9-5 **55**.............................. SaleemGolam 4 58
(Jennie Candlish) *trckd ldrs: ev ch over 2f out: chsd wnr tl no ex and lost 2 pls wl ins fnl f* **7/2**[1]
6/66 **5** 1¾ **Rightful Ruler**[8] 3677 5-9-3 **58**......................................(p) LanceBetts(5) 9 59
(N Wilson) *trckd ldr to 7f out: rdn over 2f out: one pce fr over 1f out* **14/1**
6403 **6** 2½ **Lord Nellsson**[12] 2493 11-8-6 **47**...........................(b) ThomasO'Brien(5) 2 45
(Andrew Turnell) *s.i.s: rdn and lost pl 5f out: styd on ins fnl 2f* **12/1**
000/ **7** 3 **Araglin**[17] 3520 8-8-11 **52**... MCGeran(5) 12 47
(J T Stimpson) *in rr early: mid-div whn hmpd over 1f out* **50/1**
0300 **8** 6 **Callitquits (IRE)**[11] 3595 5-8-7 **48**..............................(tp) JackDean(5) 10 35
(Jennie Candlish) *led tl rdn and hdd 3f out: wknd over 1f out* **50/1**
0-46 **9** ½ **Figaro's Quest (IRE)**[20] 3300 5-9-0 **53**............. RussellKennemore(3) 7 40
(C N Kellett) *t.k.h in mid-div: rdn over 4f out: sn btn* **16/1**
6112 **10** 1½ **Silver Mont (IRE)**[52] 2345 4-9-7 **57**..............................(b) MarcHalford 13 42
(S R Bowring) *chsd ldrs: rdn over 3f out: sn wknd* **7/2**[1]
0-65 **11** ¾ **Malibu (IRE)**[11] 3598 6-8-9 **45**.. AndrewMullen 1 29
(S Lycett) *mid-div: rdn over 3f out: wknd qckly* **9/1**
6114 **12** 12 **Comeintothespace (IRE)**[65] 1907 5-8-11 **50**.................. NicolPolli(3) 8 20
(K J Burke) *racd wd in tch: hdwy 6f out: wknd qckly 3f out* **10/1**
-650 **P** **Greyside (USA)**[58] 994 4-9-10 **60**............................(p) DougieCostello 3 —
(C A Mulhall) *mid-div: tl lost action and p.u over 1f out: dismntd* **33/1**

3m 50.61s (7.48) **Going Correction** 0.0s/f (Stan) **13** Ran SP% **122.4**
Speed ratings (Par 101): **82,81,80,80,79 78,76,74,73,73 72,67,—**
CSF £125.93 CT £819.05 TOTE £16.00: £6.40, £3.20, £2.80; EX 147.90 Place 6 £ 45.77, Place 5 £30.21..
Owner C Fletcher & J Tebbutt **Bred** Bloodstock Limited **Trained** Norton, Shropshire

FOCUS
A race to treat with caution as it was run at a crawl, hence the notably slow time, and did not play to the strengths of the stamina-laden runners.
T/Plt: £77.40 to a £1 stake. Pool: £53,169.35. 501.35 winning tickets. T/Qpdt: £26.10 to a £1 stake. Pool: £3,428.40. 96.90 winning tickets. JS

3928 - 3937a (Foreign Racing) - See Raceform Interactive

3894 ASCOT (R-H)
Saturday, July 28

OFFICIAL GOING: Straight course - good (9.9); round course - good to soft (7.9) (overall 8.7)
Wind: virtually nil Weather: overcast , bright spells

3938 KLEENEX WINKFIELD STKS (LISTED RACE) 7f
2:00 (2:02) (Class 1) 2-Y-O
£12,491 (£4,734; £2,369; £1,181; £591; £297) **Stalls** Centre

Form RPR
1 **1** **Raven's Pass (USA)**[11] 3625 2-9-2 0............................ JimmyFortune 5 101+
(J H M Gosden) *gd sort: str: lw: mde all: rdn and qcknd clr over 1f out: impressive* **9/2**[3]
01 **2** 5 **Unnefer (FR)**[35] 2885 2-9-2 0... TedDurcan 4 88
(H R A Cecil) *lw: in tch: lost pl and outpcd 1/2-way: rdn wl over 2f out: styd on to go modest 2nd ins fnl f* **11/2**
110 **3** 1¼ **Mister Hardy**[56] 2232 2-9-2 0.. PaulHanagan 3 85
(R A Fahey) *plld hrd: trckd ldrs: rdn 2f out: chsd wnr vainly wl over 1f out tl ins fnl f* **14/1**
2042 **4** 1 **Aaim To Storm (USA)**[9] 3669 2-9-2 0................................. JHBowman 6 82
(M R Channon) *swtg: hld up in rr: hdwy 2f out: rdn and hanging rt over 1f out: nvr able to chal* **25/1**
1 **5** shd **Firestreak**[43] 2632 2-9-2 0.. RyanMoore 9 82
(R Hannon) *t.k.h: prom: drvn and edgd rt fr 2f out: wknd 1f out* **7/2**[2]
0121 **6** 3½ **Spanish Bounty**[16] 3462 2-9-2 0.. JMurtagh 2 73
(J G Portman) *lw: pressed wnr tl rdn 2f out: fdd over 1f out* **10/1**
1 **7** ¾ **Midships (USA)**[44] 2596 2-9-2 0.................................... RichardHughes 7 71
(Mrs A J Perrett) *lw: settled rr: hdwy wl over 2f out: rdn and hmpd 2f out: no ch after* **10/3**[1]
13 **8** hd **Wigram's Turn (USA)**[14] 3550 2-9-2 0........................ FrancisNorton 10 70
(A M Balding) *trckd ldrs: rdn 2f out: sn wknd* **14/1**
1 **9** 3½ **Montagne D'Or (IRE)**[10] 3635 2-9-2 0................................ JoeFanning 1 61
(M Johnston) *s.i.s: t.k.h and sn cl up: rdn over 2f out: sn struggling* **10/1**
603 **10** 2 **Bellalatino (IRE)**[20] 3348 2-8-11 0.................................... DaleGibson 8 51
(Mrs Norma Pook) *squeezed out sn after s: bhd: struggling bdly 2f out* **100/1**

1m 30.54s (2.44) **Going Correction** +0.30s/f (Good) **10** Ran SP% **115.2**
Speed ratings (Par 102): **98,92,90,89,89 85,84,84,80,78**
CSF £29.13 TOTE £6.20: £2.10, £2.30, £3.40; EX 34.90 Trifecta £944.30 Part won. Pool £1,330.11 - 0.90 winning units..
Owner Stonerside Stable Llc **Bred** Stonerside Stable **Trained** Newmarket, Suffolk

FOCUS
An interesting Listed race in which nine of the ten runners were previous winners and four of those successful in their sole start. The time was less than half a second slower than the later ladies' handicap and although the winner was impressive the form behind is only average for the grade.

NOTEBOOK
Raven's Pass(USA) ◆, who was a surprise winner on his debut at Yarmouth, had clearly benefited from that experience and made all to score in imperious fashion. He looks a really useful prospect and, although quotes of as short as 16/1 for the 2000 Guineas may be premature, he should be up to winning at Group level and will take some beating in his next target, the Champagne Stakes at Doncaster. (op 11-2 tchd 6-1)
Unnefer(FR), who improved from his debut to win his maiden last time, lost a good early pitch before staying on again in the closing stages. He beat the others well enough, but the winner was long gone by the time he arrived on the scene. He is progressing with racing though and may be better suited by some cut in the ground. (op 9-2 tchd 6-1 in places)
Mister Hardy, a dual winner right at the start of the turf season, had been absent since pulling too hard in the Woodcote Stakes at Epsom. He was again very keen early, but showed what he is capable of by sticking to his task all the way to the line. However, he really needs to settle better if he is to fulfill his potential. (op 12-1)
Aaim To Storm(USA), easily the most experienced horse in the line-up, stayed on past tiring rivals but was never really in contention. However, he represents a fair guide to the level of the form. (tchd 28-1)
Firestreak, the winner of a fair Sandown maiden on his debut, was quite keen early but tended to wander under pressure and got involved in the incident that ruined Midships' chance. He can win again before long but probably at a lower level. (op 3-1 tchd 11-4)
Spanish Bounty had been steadily progressive coming into this, but was found out by the step up in both trip and grade. He had given today's fourth 5lb and a three-length beating last time, which entitled him to finish in the frame, so perhaps he was a little below par. He is out of a half-sister to Spanish Ace, so perhaps he may be better kept to sprint trips for the time being. (op 16-1)
Midships(USA), who was backed into favourite, was held up early and was making progress when a couple of his rivals went across his bows and he was squeezed out just as the race began in earnest. That cost him all chance and he can be given another opportunity to show what he is capable of. (op 7-2)
Wigram's Turn(USA), who has stepped up in trip on both his runs since his winning debut, had his chance but appeared not to get home, and a drop back in trip and grade for the moment looks in order. (op 18-1)
Montagne D'Or(IRE) found this step up in class all too much, but did not help himself by missing the break and then racing keenly and making up the ground quickly. (op 9-1 tchd 8-1)

3939 LES AMBASSADEURS CLUB CLASSIFIED STKS 1m 2f
2:35 (2:35) (Class 2) 3-Y-O+ **£12,464** (£3,732; £1,866; £934; £466) **Stalls** High

Form RPR
51-0 **1** **Great Hawk (USA)**[56] 2236 4-9-6 94..............................(v) RyanMoore 1 99
(Sir Michael Stoute) *lw: trckd ldrs: effrt over 3f out: sn drvn: led over 1f out: kpt on wl* **4/1**[2]
0606 **2** 2 **Lundy's Lane (IRE)**[21] 3330 7-9-6 94.............................. FrancisNorton 3 95
(A M Balding) *t.k.h: pressed ldr tl rdn 2f out: sn outpcd: swtchd rt and rallied to go 2nd ins fnl f: no ch w wnr* **5/2**[1]
1315 **3** hd **One Hour**[22] 3272 3-8-10 93... RichardHughes 5 95
(M P Tregoning) *lw: led: rdn 2f out: hdd over 1f out: sn hanging lft: lost 2nd cl home* **5/2**[1]
4003 **4** 7 **Nakheel**[16] 3468 4-9-6 93...(b[1]) RHills 2 81
(M Johnston) *lw: awkward leaving stalls: last most of way: drvn and v brief effrt over 2f out: fnd nthing after* **7/1**
0-01 **5** 1½ **Realism (FR)**[28] 3076 7-9-6 95.. PaulHanagan 6 78
(R A Fahey) *plld hrd: prom: rdn over 3f out: wknd over 2f out* **9/2**[3]

2m 9.88s (1.88) **Going Correction** +0.35s/f (Good)
WFA 3 from 4yo+ 10lb **5** Ran SP% **107.8**
Speed ratings (Par 109): **106,104,104,98,97**
CSF £13.65 TOTE £4.60: £2.20, £1.80; EX 17.90.
Owner Saeed Suhail **Bred** Clover Iv Llc **Trained** Newmarket, Suffolk

FOCUS
A tight little classified event run at a fair gallop but a decisive winner. The form is ordinary, rated around the third to latest form.

NOTEBOOK
Great Hawk(USA), who finished last at Epsom on his previous outing, had the visor, which he wore when successful at Kempton, reapplied. He had to work hard to get the better of the long-time leader, but once in front he ran on strongly enough. The headgear and a right-handed track seem to bring out the best in him, and it will be a surprise if he does not win more good races at around this trip. (op 7-2)
Lundy's Lane(IRE) has contested competitive handicaps in his two outings since returning from three winters in Dubai, but found this more his sort of level and stayed on after getting done for pace when the leaders quickened turning for home. He is now a stone below his highest winning mark and clearly retains a decent level of ability. (op 3-1 tchd 10-3 in places)
One Hour, who made all when winning a handicap at Sandown last month, reverted to those tactics and appeared to have every chance, but once taken on by the winner had nothing more to offer. (tchd 11-4 and 3-1 in places)
Nakheel has never been able to fulfill his juvenile promise due to injury and the application of blinkers made no apparent difference. He also looked reluctant early on and he looks likely to be heading to the sales sooner rather than later. (op 6-1)
Realism(FR), the winner of a decent claimer last time from horses rated much lower, found this a totally different kettle of fish and was well beaten, although he did not help himself by failing to settle. (tchd 4-1)

3940 NATIONAL BANK OF DUBAI CUP (HERITAGE H'CAP) 1m (S)
3:10 (3:10) (Class 2) 3-Y-O
£40,508 (£12,129; £6,064; £3,035; £1,514; £760) **Stalls** Centre

Form RPR
6604 **1** **The Illies (IRE)**[7] 3745 3-7-7 **82** oh5............................. WilliamBuick(5) 3 102
(B W Hills) *lw: wl bhd: rdn and v str run but hanging rt fr 2f out: led jst ins fnl f: in command whn wnt lft cl home* **14/1**
1620 **2** 1½ **Ea (USA)**[15] 3503 3-8-12 **96**.. RyanMoore 18 113
(Sir Michael Stoute) *lw: stdd s: hdwy 3f out: rdn over 2f out: kpt on wl to go 2nd 50yds out: nt rch wnr* **7/2**[1]
5-21 **3** 1¼ **Al Khaleej (IRE)**[7] 3745 3-8-5 **89**... EddieAhern 7 103+
(E A L Dunlop) *lw: in tch: pressed ldr gng wl 3f out: led over 2f out: sn hung rt and rdn: hdd jst ins fnl f: one pce* **4/1**[2]
0120 **4** 2½ **Mr Aviator (USA)**[15] 3503 3-8-1 **85**................................... FrancisNorton 12 93
(R Hannon) *prom: rdn 3f out: outpcd over 1f out: kpt on* **9/1**
5602 **5** 1¾ **Annemasse**[7] 3745 3-8-8 **92**.. JoeFanning 9 96
(M Johnston) *lw: slt ld tl rdn and hdd over 2f out: wknd over 1f out* **9/1**
211 **6** ½ **Gongidas**[16] 3470 3-8-5 **89**..(v[1]) ChrisCatlin 8 92
(Saeed Bin Suroor) *lw: midfield: rdn and outpcd over 3f out: kpt on u.p fnl f* **11/2**[3]
15-3 **7** ½ **Mesbaah (IRE)**[16] 3463 3-8-12 **96**.. RHills 4 98
(M A Jarvis) *midfield: rdn and effrt wl over 2f out: btn wl over 1f out* **10/1**
3000 **8** 1¾ **Habalwatan (IRE)**[16] 3460 3-8-6 **90**..............................(b) DaleGibson 17 88
(C E Brittain) *lw: bmpd s: midfield: rdn 3f out: sn btn* **25/1**
0050 **9** 1¾ **Satulagi (USA)**[38] 2757 3-9-0 **98**..................................... JohnEgan 13 92
(J S Moore) *effrt to press ldrs over 2f out: wknd qckly over 1f out* **25/1**

4100 **10** ½ **Aqmaar**[15] 3503 3-8-8 **92** .... SebSanders 1 85+
(J L Dunlop) *racd alone on stands' rail: w ldrs tl 2f out: sn btn and eased fnl f* **25/1**

30-0 **11** 1 ¾ **Always Fruitful**[15] 3503 3-8-8 **92** .... MichaelHills 11 80
(M Johnston) *wnt lft s: nvr on terms* **33/1**

3352 **12** 1 **Salient**[14] 3553 3-7-12 **82** .... JimmyQuinn 6 68
(J Akehurst) *plld hrd early: rdn wl over 3f out: sn struggling* **14/1**

-153 **13** 1 **Darfour**[15] 3514 3-7-9 **82** oh7 .... DuranFentiman(3) 10 66
(J S Goldie) *a towards rr* **40/1**

3503 **14** 2 ½ **Okikoki**[15] 3491 3-7-12 **82** oh4 .... PaulHanagan 15 60
(W R Muir) *prom 5f: sn rdn and btn* **50/1**

0-00 **15** 7 **El Soprano (IRE)**[17] 3430 3-8-3 **87** .... DO'Donohoe 16 49
(K A Ryan) *wnt rt s: sn prom: rdn 3f out: struggling after: eased and t.o* **40/1**

36-0 **16** 24 **Prince Of Elegance**[21] 3334 3-8-8 **92** ....(p) MJKinane 5 —
(Mrs A J Perrett) *trckd ldrs: drvn 1/2-way and rapidly lost pl: t.o fnl 2f: eased* **33/1**

-610 **17** 41 **Massive (IRE)**[28] 3103 3-9-7 **105** ....(v1) JHBowman 14 —
(M R Channon) *swtg: prom 3f: t.o fr 1/2-way: virtually p.u* **25/1**

1m 41.5s (-0.30) **Going Correction** +0.30s/f (Good) **17** Ran SP% **128.1**
Speed ratings (Par 106): **113,111,110,107,106 105,105,103,101,101 99,98,97,94,87 63,22**
CSF £59.07 CT £255.50 TOTE £17.80: £4.00, £1.70, £1.70, £1.90; EX 106.00 Trifecta £1119.10 Pool £1,891.49 - 1.20 winning units..

Owner John C Grant **Bred** Glashare House Stud **Trained** Lambourn, Berks

FOCUS

A typically competitive three-year-old handicap run at a good gallop and in which the first three came clear. The form looks solid with the runner-up close to his Britannia mark.

NOTEBOOK

The Illies(IRE) had finished behind today's second third and fifth in his two previous outings, although not beaten far, and was racing from out of the handicap, so was not really any better off with those rivals. However, the strong pace playing into his hands and he produced a strong run from off the pace to score, setting a trend that proved successful in the two later handicaps on the straight course. Last season he was able to follow up his initial success by scoring again, so may be capable of doing the same again, but a lot depends on how the Handicapper reacts to this success. (op 16-1)

Ea(USA), who finished runner-up in the Britannia before an apparently below-par effort at Newmarket when today's winner was just behind, was 2lb better off with that rival disregarding the apprentices' allowance. Held up off the pace, he stayed on really well on the opposite side to the winner without ever looking likely to get there. He surely has a good handicap in him, and a stiff mile and a good gallop seem to suit him best. (op 9-2 tchd 5-1)

Al Khaleej(IRE) ◆, who was quite impressive when beaten Annemasse at Newmarket last time with today's winner further behind, looked as if he was going to follow up when cruising to the front passing the intersection with the round course. However, he did not find quite as much as his rider expected and had no answer when the winner swooped. He still looks capable of winning more good handicaps and will be better served by being held up for longer in future. (op 10-3)

Mr Aviator(USA) ◆, who had beaten Al Khaleej at Goodwood over 9f earlier in the season, disappointed when behind today's first two at Newmarket since. This was a better effort, but the way he was running on suggests he needs a return further than this. He seems well suited by a turning track and will be interesting if turned out quickly in a 10f handicap at Goodwood next week. (op 10-1)

Annemasse, runner-up to Al Khaleej at Newmarket last time, was 5lb better off but finished further behind. However, this was a decent effort but perhaps he making the running at such a good pace cost him in the closing stages. It is possible that a turning mile suits him better. (tchd 10-1)

Gongidas, a lightly-raced half-brother to Gonfilia, has looked progressive so far but has shown a marked tendency to hang left and hence the fitting of a visor. However, he was unable to get really involved in this competitive handicap and, although not disgraced, will have to step up again if he is to win one; that is by no means out of the question though. (op 13-2)

Mesbaah(IRE) did not really build on his seasonal return and could do with dropping in the weights. (op 9-1)

Aqmaar was the only one to come stands' side and was well up with the pace until fading in the last quarter mile.

Massive(IRE), in a first-time visor, showed up early but dropped away quickly as if he had a problem Official explanation: trainer had no explanation for the poor form shown

3941 TOTESPORT.COM INTERNATIONAL STKS (HERITAGE H'CAP) 7f

3:45 (3:47) (Class 2) 3-Y-0+

£93,480 (£27,990; £13,995; £7,005; £3,495; £1,755) **Stalls** Centre

Form RPR

0201 **1** **Third Set (IRE)**[17] 3437 4-8-2 **88** 3ex .... JimmyQuinn 4 105+
(R Charlton) *lw: bmpd sn after s: t.k.h: chsd ldrs tl rdn and hdwy 2f out: hung rt and led over 1f out: sn clr: edgd lft cl home* **9/1**[3]

-305 **2** 1 ¼ **Racer Forever (USA)**[15] 3505 4-9-3 **103** ....(b) JimmyFortune 10 113+
(J H M Gosden) *bhd: hdwy and swtchd lft wl over 1f out: sn hrd drvn: fin v strly to go 2nd cl home* **10/1**

6221 **3** 1 ¼ **Binanti**[36] 2817 7-8-6 **92** .... FrancisNorton 22 99
(P R Chamings) *trckd ldrs: led over 2f out: sn rdn and hung lft: hdd over 1f out: one pce ins fnl f* **14/1**

1431 **4** shd **Giganticus (USA)**[15] 3505 4-8-11 **97** 3ex .... RHills 15 104
(B W Hills) *lw: t.k.h in midfield: hdwy 2f out: chsd ldrs and drvn over 1f out: one pce* **11/1**

-060 **5** nk **Burning Incense (IRE)**[28] 3104 4-8-10 **96** .... RichardHughes 8 102+
(R Charlton) *lw: hld up last: swtchd rt and hdwy wl over 1f out: pressed ldrs 1f out: no imp after* **14/1**

5430 **6** 1 ¾ **Mac Love**[28] 3098 6-9-1 **101** .... SebSanders 27 102
(J Noseda) *midfield: drvn 2f out: no imp tl styd on last 50yds* **20/1**

1012 **7** nk **King Of Argos**[15] 3505 4-8-12 **98** .... LDettori 29 98
(E A L Dunlop) *lw: t.k.h: hld up towards rr: hdwy over 2f out: chsd ldrs and rdn over 1f out: wknd fnl 100yds* **15/2**[2]

3030 **8** ¾ **Vortex**[15] 3505 8-9-2 **107** ....(t) NicolPolli(5) 21 105
(Miss Gay Kelleway) *b: b.hind: trckd ldrs: hdwy and ev ch over 1f out: wknd u.p fnl f* **33/1**

3303 **9** hd **Ingleby Arch (USA)**[15] 3500 4-8-4 **90** .... PaulFessey 7 88
(T D Barron) *nvr bttr than midfield: rdn over 2f out: no imp* **50/1**

0015 **10** nk **Game Lad**[14] 3559 5-8-3 **89** .... PaulHanagan 28 86
(T D Easterby) *lw: prom: ev ch and rdn over 2f out: fdd ins fnl f* **50/1**

0150 **11** hd **South Cape**[17] 3437 4-8-2 **88** ow2 .... TPO'Shea 24 84
(M R Channon) *chsd ldrs: hdwy over 2f out: ev ch and rdn wl over 1f out: sn fdd* **12/1**

5200 **12** shd **Trafalgar Bay (IRE)**[14] 3559 4-8-6 **92** ow1 .... FergusSweeney 26 88
(K R Burke) *t.k.h: midfield: n.d* **16/1**

0024 **13** shd **Gallantry**[10] 3650 5-7-10 **85** .... DominicFox(3) 2 81+
(D Shaw) *bmpd sn after s: wl bhd tl styd on u.p fnl f* **40/1**

0060 **14** 1 **Uhoomagoo**[36] 2817 9-8-5 **91** ....(b) DO'Donohoe 25 84
(K A Ryan) *lw: drvn along thrght: nvr plcd to chal* **25/1**

0100 **15** hd **Dingaan (IRE)**[15] 3481 4-7-10 **87** ....(v1) WilliamBuick(5) 18 80
(A M Balding) *awkward leaving stalls: plld hrd in rr: hung rt u.p over 1f out: n.d* **50/1**

1124 **16** nk **Wise Dennis**[36] 2817 5-9-4 **104** .... JMurtagh 12 96
(A P Jarvis) *lw: midfield: rdn and lost pl over 3f out: kpt on but no ch fnl f* **5/1**[1]

1004 **17** ½ **Regal Parade**[21] 3334 3-7-13 **92** .... FrankieMcDonald 13 83
(M Johnston) *hmpd and dropped to rr after 2f: sn drvn along in rr: nvr gng wl after* **25/1**

0500 **18** shd **Malcheek (IRE)**[36] 2817 5-7-12 **87** .... DuranFentiman(3) 17 77
(T D Easterby) *prom tl rdn and ev ch 2f out: wknd qckly 1f out* **66/1**

-440 **19** shd **Partners In Jazz (USA)**[42] 2670 6-8-12 **98** .... MJKinane 14 88
(T D Barron) *sn pushed along and edging rt: no ch fr 1/2-way* **14/1**

0064 **20** ½ **Dhaular Dhar (IRE)**[15] 3505 5-8-11 **97** .... ChrisCatlin 20 86
(J S Goldie) *nvr bttr than midfield* **14/1**

-030 **21** ½ **Dabbers Ridge (IRE)**[15] 3505 5-9-0 **100** .... MichaelHills 5 87
(B W Hills) *prom: rdn 2f out: fdd over 1f out: eased* **11/1**

1066 **22** nk **Phluke**[10] 3650 6-8-4 **90** .... StephenCarson 19 76
(Eve Johnson Houghton) *prom to 1/2-way* **66/1**

4406 **23** nk **Mujood**[23] 3240 4-7-13 **89** ow3 ....(b) ThomasO'Brien(7) 6 78
(Eve Johnson Houghton) *lw: prom to 1/2-way* **80/1**

1000 **24** 1 **Fares (IRE)**[17] 3431 3-8-4 **97** ....(b) JoeFanning 11 80
(C E Brittain) *replated at s: t.k.h in midfield to 1/2-way* **66/1**

5-60 **25** 6 **Steenberg (IRE)**[73] 1770 8-9-2 **102** .... SaleemGolam 1 69
(M H Tompkins) *drvn along in rr: nvr gng wl* **50/1**

3000 **26** shd **King's Caprice**[35] 2858 6-8-11 **102** ....(t) TravisBlock(5) 23 69
(J A Geake) *led tl hdd and lost pl rapidly over 2f out* **50/1**

0005 **27** 5 **Royal Storm (IRE)**[11] 3623 8-8-2 **88** .... DaleGibson 16 41
(Mrs A J Perrett) *prom tl lost pl rapidly over 2f out: t.o and eased* **66/1**

1m 28.31s (0.21) **Going Correction** +0.30s/f (Good)
WFA 3 from 4yo+ 7lb **27** Ran SP% **139.3**
Speed ratings (Par 109): **110,108,107,107,106 104,104,103,103,102 102,102,102,101,101 100,100,100,99,99 98,98,98,96,90**
CSF £92.83 CT £1321.32 TOTE £12.80: £3.60, £3.90, £4.40, £2.80; EX 171.60 Trifecta £2806.00 Pool £24,503.92 - 6.20 winning units..

Owner John Livock **Bred** A Stroud & J Hanly **Trained** Beckhampton, Wilts

FOCUS

A strong renewal of this hot handicap but a comfortable winner who came from off the pace. The form looks sound with the third and fourth setting the standard.

NOTEBOOK

Third Set(IRE) ◆, was well suited by the drying ground, and effectively 6lb well in under just a 3lb penalty, overcame early problems to sweep to the front and score in emphatic fashion. He is clearly improving at a rate of knots and even off his revised mark will take some beating next time. He may possibly reappear at Goodwood next week in the totesport Mile, although he will need a few horses to come out if he is to get a run. (op 10-1 tchd 11-1)

Racer Forever(USA), who ran well in the blinkers in the Bunbury Cup last time, reversed form with three of those that finished narrowly in front of him in that race but was still unlucky. He was held up going really well, but did not get a run when he needed it and, although he finished with a flourish once in the clear, the winner had gone beyond recall. He deserves to win one of these, although off his rating another Listed race is also a possibilty. (op 11-1)

Binanti, winner of the Buckingham Palace Handicap at the Royal meeting, was 5lb higher but ran another fine race. He has been running consistently well of late and helps set the standard. (op 12-1)

Giganticus(USA), winner of the Bunbury Cup last time, could not confirm placings with today's runner-up on 3lb worse terms but ran pretty close to that form. He is another who should continue to perform well in these big handicaps, and another try at a mile is possible. (op 10-1 tchd 12-1 and 14-1 in a place)

Burning Incense(IRE), a stable companion of the winner and trying this trip for the first time, was held up out the back before making good late progress towards the far rail, away from the main action. He looked to get the trip well enough, which opens up further options, but it would be no surprise to see him aimed at the Ayr Gold Cup with the blinkers re-applied. (op 16-1)

Mac Love, who, apart from when racing in Dubai, had not competed in handicap company for over three years but took advantage of a declining handicap mark. He never really figured but this was not a bad effort all the same.

King Of Argos, runner-up in the Bunbury Cup, made late progress having been keen under restraint but never looked likely to get involved and really needs further than this. (op 8-1)

Vortex is a reliable old campaigner and he looked like playing a major part until his effort flattened out in the final furlong.

Trafalgar Bay(IRE) Official explanation: jockey said gelding missed the break

Wise Dennis, who bolted up in the Victoria Cup over course and distance in the spring, probably found the drying ground against him as he ran a rather lacklustre race. He is one to bear in mind if turning up at York's Ebor meeting and the ground is soft. (op 7-1 tchd 8-1 in places)

Dhaular Dhar(IRE), who was fourth in the Bunbury Cup, should have been suited by the way the race was run but never got into it. It is noticeable that his wins have been on sharp, and mostly left-handed tracks, so it would be no surprise if a race around Chester is on his agenda next. (op 12-1)

Dabbers Ridge(IRE), who won this last year, travelled well for a long way, but when the winner went past him he capitulated rather quickly. (op 12-1)

3942 KING GEORGE VI AND QUEEN ELIZABETH STKS (GROUP 1) 1m 4f

4:20 (4:24) (Class 1) 3-Y-0+

£425,850 (£161,400; £80,775; £40,275; £20,175; £10,125) **Stalls** High

Form RPR

1122 **1** **Dylan Thomas (IRE)**[38] 2754 4-9-7 0 .... JMurtagh 5 131
(A P O'Brien, Ire) *lw: travelled strly: hld up in midfield: hdwy 3f out: shkn up to ld over 1f out: sn edgd rt but clr: rdn out: impressive* **5/4**[1]

-335 **2** 4 **Youmzain (IRE)**[34] 2925 4-9-7 118 .... RichardHughes 1 124
(M R Channon) *hld up in last pair: hdwy 3f out: chsd ldr and rdn over 1f out: nt pce of wnr fnl f* **12/1**

1131 **3** 3 ½ **Maraahel (IRE)**[35] 2856 6-9-7 118 ....(v) RHills 3 118
(Sir Michael Stoute) *lw: missed break: sn chsng ldrs: wnt 2nd 8f out: led 2f out: sn rdn: hdd over 1f out: sn outpcd* **6/1**[3]

2502 **4** ½ **Laverock (IRE)**[16] 3461 5-9-7 118 .... LDettori 7 117
(Saeed Bin Suroor) *hld up in midfield: hdwy to trck ldrs 3f out: rdn and outpcd wl over 1f out* **11/1**

-212 **5** 3 **Scorpion (IRE)**[35] 2856 5-9-7 0 .... MJKinane 2 112
(A P O'Brien, Ire) *lw: sn led: rdn and hdd 2f out: wkng whn hmpd over 1f out* **3/1**[2]

-410 **6** 5 **Sergeant Cecil**[37] 2787 8-9-7 115 .... RyanMoore 4 104
(B R Millman) *lw: a bhd: rdn and btn 3f out* **33/1**

-313 **7** 3 ½ **Prince Flori (GER)**[34] 2925 4-9-7 0 .... JimmyFortune 6 99
(S Smrczek, Germany) *w'like: lw: chsd ldr tl 8f out: cl up: n.m.r and effrt 3f out: sn rdn: wknd over 2f out* **10/1**

2m 31.11s (-1.89) **Going Correction** +0.35s/f (Good) **7** Ran SP% **111.8**
Speed ratings (Par 117): **120,117,115,114,112 109,107**
CSF £17.14 TOTE £2.30: £1.40, £5.10; EX 16.30.

Owner Mrs John Magnier & M Tabor **Bred** Tower Bloodstock **Trained** Ballydoyle, Co Tipperary
■ No 'Diamond' in the race title with De Beers having ended their long-term sponsorship.

FOCUS
Not the strongest-ever renewal of this mid-season championship race, especially as no three-year-olds took part, with Authorized and Soldier Of Fortune the most notable absentees, but a contest run at a sound pace and with a worthy and impressive winner. Dylan Thomas achieved an RPR of 130 - a career best by 2lb and very much up to scratch for a King George winner.

NOTEBOOK
Dylan Thomas(IRE) had undeniably the best credentials and the drying ground helped market confidence. This was his first run over 1m4f since winning the Irish Derby, but the good pace set by his stable companion nevertheless suited him and, when asked for his effort, he swept majestically to the front despite shifting towards the inside rail. From that point the result was never in doubt and he kept up the gallop all the way to the line. He was widely quoted for the Arc after the race, but unless Europe has a dry autumn he is unlikely to get his favoured conditions at Longchamp and may be better aimed at the Breeders' Cup Turf and/or the Japan Cup if the ground is against him in France. (op 6-4 tchd 11-10 and 13-8 in a place)
Youmzain(IRE), another who was favoured by the improved ground conditions, ran on from well back and beat the rest comfortably, despite making no impression on the winner. He may meet the winner in the Arc, but a repeat win in the Preis Von Europa could be on the cards first, with trips to the Breeders' Cup and Hong Kong also likely according to his trainer. (op 8-1)
Maraahel(IRE) goes well on this track and confirmed Hardwicke form with Scorpion on worse terms. However, in truth he was well beaten and will probably drop back in trip to try to avenge last year's narrow defeat in the Juddmonte International. (tchd 11-2 and 13-2)
Laverock(IRE), winner of the Group 1 Prix D'Ispahan and Gran Premio del Jockey Club when trained by Carlos Laffon-Parias last year, has not looked quite as good since leaving France and ran about as well as expected. He may be better looking for easier pickings abroad. (op 12-1)
Scorpion(IRE) was weighted to reverse Royal Ascot placings with Maraahel, but a combination of the drying ground and making the running seemed to result in a below-par effort, and he did not look to be moving comfortably under pressure. A return to an easier surface will suit him, and the Irish St Leger and the Arc may provide him with the right conditions. (tchd 7-2)
Sergeant Cecil really needs further than this and had to put behind him a rare poor effort in the Gold Cup. He was always out the back but he picked up £10,125 for beating one home and the 'speed work' may have sharpened him up for an autumn campaign, probably starting with the Lonsdale Cup at York. (op 28-1)
Prince Flori(GER), the best middle-distance horse trained in Germany last season and pretty closely matched with Youmzain on a line through Egerton, was given a positive ride. He tried to go up the inside of Scorpion on the home turn, but could not get by and was the first to crack, dropping right away in the straight. Previous evidence suggests he is a fair bit better than he showed here, and he may be a different proposition on soft ground in the Arc, if taking his chance. (tchd 11-1)

3943 EVELYN HANKINSON MEMORIAL H'CAP STKS (LADIES RACE) 7f
4:55 (5:00) (Class 3) (0-90,90) 3-Y-O+ **£8,744** (£2,711; £1,355; £677) **Stalls** Centre

Form RPR
656 **1** **Middlemarch (IRE)**[35] 2891 7-9-5 **71** oh1..................(v) MrsCBartley 8 81
(J S Goldie) *wl bhd: drvn 3f out: hung rt but styd on remorselessly to ld nr fin* **33/1**
5001 **2** *¾* **Bomber Command (USA)**[14] 3525 4-9-10 **76**............ MissEJJones 14 84
(J W Hills) *lw: chsd ldrs: hdwy to go 2nd over 2f out: sn rdn: led ins fnl f: ct cl home* **10/1**
1300 **3** *hd* **Presumptive (IRE)**[28] 3091 7-10-5 **90**...................... MissFCumani(5) 12 97
(R Charlton) *lw: stdd after s and wl bhd: hdwy over 2f out: chal ins fnl f: kpt on valiantly* **14/1**
-400 **4** *nk* **Macedon**[49] 2469 4-10-0 **80**.. MrsSMoore 6 87
(J S Moore) *lw: wl off pce in midfield: hdwy over 2f out: styd on u.p to chal ins fnl f: hld whn n.m.r nr fin* **10/1**
1065 **5** *1 ¾* **Glenbuck (IRE)**[28] 3091 4-10-0 **85**............................(v) MissJAKidd(5) 13 87
(A Bailey) *led at brisk pce: rdn and hdd over 1f out: wknd last 50yds* **16/1**
-222 **6** *nk* **Blue Java**[23] 3234 6-9-4 **75**...................................(bt[1]) MissVCartmel(5) 17 76
(H Morrison) *chsd ldrs: rdn 2f out: ev ch jst ins fnl f: wknd cl home* **8/1**
4262 **7** *4* **Mezuzah**[8] 3715 7-9-13 **84**.. MissJCoward(5) 20 74
(M W Easterby) *off pce in midfield: drvn and hdwy wl over 2f out: unable to chal* **33/1**
2513 **8** *2* **Indian's Feather (IRE)**[8] 3715 6-9-10 **76**................... MissRDavidson 2 61
(N Tinkler) *chsd ldrs: rdn and hung rt over 2f out: sn btn* **25/1**
5320 **9** *shd* **Gaelic Princess**[17] 3437 7-9-12 **78**.......................... MissCHannaford 16 63
(A G Newcombe) *midfield: sn hanging rt: bmpd along 3f out: nvr on terms* **16/1**
000- **10** *3* **Grand Entrance (IRE)**[325] 5107 4-9-5 **71** oh1......... MissFayeBramley 5 48
(C R Egerton) *taken down early: prom 2f: sn rdn and struggling* **40/1**
0121 **11** *hd* **Starlight Gazer**[9] 3682 4-10-2 **82**............................ MissSBrotherton 15 58
(J A Geake) *lw: nvr on terms* **15/2**[3]
-601 **12** *hd* **Carnivore**[33] 2936 5-10-0 **80**.................................... MissLEllison 9 55
(T D Barron) *lw: last early: a bhd* **13/2**[2]
0040 **13** *shd* **Russian Symphony (USA)**[20] 3350 6-9-8 **74**..............(p) MsKWalsh 11 49
(C R Egerton) *lw: wl off pce in midfield: n.d* **16/1**
0010 **14** *¾* **Bold Marc (IRE)**[21] 3330 5-9-13 **84**........................ MissKellyBurke(5) 19 57
(K R Burke) *chsd ldr tl wknd over 2f out* **16/1**
1105 **15** *2* **Ektimaal**[17] 3437 4-10-8 **88**....................................(t) MissNCarberry 1 56
(E A L Dunlop) *lw: nvr on terms: rdn and btn 2f out* **4/1**[1]
-146 **16** *½* **Grizedale (IRE)**[23] 3234 8-9-6 **75**................................(t) MissARyan(3) 7 41
(J Akehurst) *cl up to 1/2-way* **20/1**
030- **17** *1 ¼* **Thyolo (IRE)**[316] 5346 6-9-10 **81**............................ MissJFerguson(5) 21 44
(C G Cox) *sn outpcd* **22/1**
5525 **18** *shd* **Dr Synn**[17] 3422 6-9-0 **71** oh6...................................... MissZoeLilly(5) 10 34
(J Akehurst) *b: b.hind: sn outpcd and drvn along* **66/1**
1/00 **19** *7* **Top Gear**[82] 1542 5-9-6 **77**...(p) MrsLMongan(5) 3 21
(Mrs L J Mongan) *hanging rt and t.o 2f out* **80/1**
206 **20** *8* **His Master's Voice (IRE)**[15] 3481 4-9-5 **74**.............. MissEFolkes(3) 18 —
(D W P Arbuthnot) *chsd ldrs 4f: t.o* **20/1**
1666 **21** *9* **Arch Of Titus (IRE)**[28] 3078 3-9-0 **76**..........................(t) JennyRiding(3) 4 —
(M L W Bell) *b.hind: a wl bhd: t.o fnl 2f* **33/1**

1m 30.08s (1.98) **Going Correction** +0.30s/f (Good)
WFA 3 from 4yo+ 7lb **21 Ran SP% 136.3**
Speed ratings (Par 107): **100,99,98,98,96 96,91,89,89,85 85,85,85,84,82 81,80,80,72,62 52**
CSF £337.36 CT £4861.33 TOTE £60.30: £11.10, £2.50, £4.30, £2.80; EX 830.90 TRIFECTA Not won..
Owner W M Johnstone **Bred** Swettenham Stud And Hugo Lascelles **Trained** Uplawmoor, E Renfrews
■ Stewards' Enquiry : Jenny Riding caution: used whip when out of contention

FOCUS
One of the top ladies' races of the season, but the pattern followed that of the earlier handicaps on the straight track, with the low-drawn winner coming from off the pace to score. The form appears solid enough with the first three close to their turf marks.

NOTEBOOK
Middlemarch(IRE), who was coaxed back to form last year by his current trainer after a long spell in the wilderness, has often worn some form of headgear but had the visor on for the first time since running in the Champion Stakes back in 2003. He was well behind and appeared to be going nowhere at halfway, but his experienced rider galvanised him into producing a strong run, despite carrying his head awkwardly, to get to the front late on. His wins were gained in the autumn last year so it may be unwise to write off this form. Official explanation: trainer said, regarding apparent improvement in form, that the previous race possibly came too soon.
Bomber Command(USA), who gaind his first win on turf over course and distance last time when fitted with a visor, had the headgear left off this time but still seemed to run his race. However, after rather getting left in front at the quarter-mile pole, he seemed to get tired and was a sitting duck for the winner's late run. To be fair he did respond when that rival went by, which enabled him to hold on to second, but the headgear may just give him the help he needs. (op 12-1)
Presumptive(IRE) was saddled with top weight, although he has won off this mark on Polytrack. He ran on from the back of the field but could not produce the surge of the winner. This was a commendable effort and he is one to bear in mind for if he returns to Sandown, a track that he seems to like. (op 16-1)
Macedon had the ground come in his favour and he produced his best effort since finishing fourth in the Newbury Spring Cup in April. He is 7lb above his last winning mark but is clearly capable of decent form in these big-field handicaps. (op 9-1 tchd 11-1)
Glenbuck(IRE) is well suited by making the running and took the field along for a long way, sticking on quite well once headed. He improved considerably in the late summer last season, recording a four-timer, and is now only 1lb above his last winning mark. He will be of interest if able to get an uncontested lead in the coming weeks. (op 14-1)
Blue Java has had a frustrating series of seconds of late and was tried in a new combination of blinkers for the first time and a tongue tie. He had his chance but faded inside the last and may be suited by waiting tactics; he goes well at Goodwood and that track may help him adopt that style of running. (tchd 9-1 in a place and 17-2 in a place)
Starlight Gazer, who beat Blue Java last time, was 9lb worse off. He never figured and the drying ground does not suit, so he can be expected to do better back on his favoured surface. (op 7-1)
Carnivore, raised 5lb for his last win, was always out the back and only ran on late past beaten rivals. (op 11-1)
Ektimaal was made favourite probably due to his rider, but all his wins have been gained on Polytrack and his best effort on turf was when the ground was soft. Unsurprisingly he did not prove as effective on this sounder surface and never landed a blow. (op 5-1 tchd 7-2 and 6-1 in a place)

3944 CANISBAY BLOODSTOCK H'CAP 6f
5:25 (5:30) (Class 4) (0-85,84) 3-Y-O **£6,477** (£1,927; £963; £481) **Stalls** Centre

Form RPR
1-21 **1** **Edge Closer**[15] 3483 3-9-6 **83**..................................... JimmyFortune 9 96+
(R Hannon) *lw: mde all: rdn over 1f out: hung lft but r.o strly fnl f* **3/1**[1]
1-32 **2** *¾* **Special Day**[64] 1994 3-9-6 **83**.................................... MichaelHills 5 90
(B W Hills) *lw: last early but a in tch: t.k.h: hdwy and squeezed through over 1f out: swtchd lft ins fnl f: r.o wl: carried lft nr fin* **5/1**[2]
1-02 **3** *½* **Fabuleux Millie (IRE)**[38] 2769 3-9-1 **78**..................... SebSanders 12 83
(R M Beckett) *lw: stdd after s: bhd: effrt and hung rt u.p over 1f out: styd on* **11/1**
-265 **4** *½* **Golden Desert (IRE)**[17] 3418 3-9-3 **80**.........................(v[1]) JoeFanning 7 84
(T G Mills) *lw: prom: chsd wnr over 1f out: kpt on same pce fnl f: lost two pls last 50yds* **10/1**
2200 **5** *1* **Captain Jacksparra (IRE)**[15] 3503 3-9-6 **83**.................... JMurtagh 10 84
(K A Ryan) *plld ferociously: stmbld after 2f: hdwy 2f out: no imp u.p fnl f* **8/1**[3]
1-60 **6** *¾* **Bateleur**[17] 3418 3-9-3 **80**.. EdwardCreighton 2 78
(M R Channon) *t.k.h: midfield: drvn and kpt on same pce fnl 2f* **16/1**
0164 **7** *hd* **Lord Theo**[52] 2373 3-9-3 **80**.. JamesDoyle 4 78
(N P Littmoden) *towards rr: drvn wl over 3f out: nt trble ldrs* **20/1**
115- **8** *1* **Abunai**[294] 5809 3-9-5 **82**.. JimmyQuinn 14 76
(R Charlton) *lw: t.k.h: pressed wnr tl over 1f out: wknd fnl f* **14/1**
3140 **9** *1* **Teen Ager (FR)**[15] 3480 3-8-11 **74**.................................. JohnEgan 13 65
(J S Moore) *lw: plld frenetically: bhd: rdn and effrt 2f out: sn no imp* **16/1**
4350 **10** *1* **Count Ceprano (IRE)**[14] 3553 3-9-2 **79**......................... SaleemGolam 8 67
(W R Swinburn) *chsd ldrs: rdn 3f out: wknd over 1f out* **9/1**
-215 **11** *1 ¾* **Farefield Lodge (IRE)**[33] 2942 3-8-10 **76**................ DuranFentiman(3) 6 58
(C G Cox) *lw: prom: rdn over 2f out: edgd lft and sn wknd* **20/1**
1431 **12** *¾* **Baltimore Jack (IRE)**[36] 2821 3-9-7 **84**......................... DaleGibson 1 64
(M W Easterby) *trckd ldrs: rdn 3f out: sn struggling* **14/1**
2505 **13** *½* **Sparkling Eyes**[7] 3746 3-9-2 **79**................................... FrancisNorton 11 57
(C E Brittain) *t.k.h: trckd ldrs tl rdn and wknd 2f out* **10/1**

1m 15.95s (1.05) **Going Correction** +0.30s/f (Good) **13 Ran SP% 123.9**
Speed ratings (Par 102): **105,104,103,102,101 100,100,98,97,96 93,92,92**
CSF £17.41 CT £153.14 TOTE £3.60: £1.90, £2.10, £3.50; EX 10.60 Trifecta £190.30 Pool £957.05 - 3.57 winning units. Place 6 £ 198.32, Place 5 £ 62.54..
Owner Lady Whent And Friends **Bred** Caroline Wilson **Trained** East Everleigh, Wilts

FOCUS
A decent handicap run at a sound gallop and dominated by the market leaders. The form looks solid and the race has been rated positively overall.
Captain Jacksparra(IRE) Official explanation: jockey said colt ran too free early on
T/Jkpt: £15,349.10 to a £1 stake. Pool: £21,618.50. 0.50 winning tickets. T/Plt: £312.90 to a £1 stake. Pool: £194,529.16. 453.75 winning tickets. T/Qpdt: £51.10 to a £1 stake. Pool: £11,685.60. 169.15 winning tickets. SP

3847 LINGFIELD (L-H)
Saturday, July 28

OFFICIAL GOING: All-weather - standard; turf course - good (good to soft in places; 6.9)
Wind: moderate, half behind Weather: Fine becoming cloudy

3945 PLAY GOLF AT LINGFIELD PARK H'CAP 2m (P)
5:55 (5:59) (Class 5) (0-70,70) 3-Y-O+ **£2,817** (£838; £418; £209) **Stalls** Low

Form RPR
0111 **1** **Champagne Shadow (IRE)**[22] 3282 6-9-6 **67**.........(p) TravisBlock(5) 10 77+
(Miss Tor Sturgis) *trckd ldrs: prog to ld over 3f out and sn kicked at least 2l clr: rdn over 1f out: a holding on* **6/1**[3]
-014 **2** *¾* **Strobe**[11] 3624 3-8-5 **64**.. PaulEddery 6 72
(J A Osborne) *chsd ldrs: drvn fr 7f out: prog to chse wnr over 2f out: kpt on u.p but nvr able to mount serious chal* **5/1**[1]
4232 **3** *shd* **Apache Fort**[16] 3457 4-9-5 **61**.................................. PaulDoe 1 70+
(T Keddy) *trckd ldrs: outpcd 3f out: nt clr run sn after: effrt on inner 2f out: styd on fr over 1f out* **7/1**
6040 **4** *1 ¼* **Trifti**[9] 3690 6-9-3 **66**.. JackMitchell(7) 8 72
(C A Cyzer) *hld up in last trio: prog on outer 3f out: rdn 2f out: nt qckn over 1f out: kpt on same pce* **25/1**

2123 **5** *nk* **Bob's Your Uncle**[18] 3397 4-9-5 **61** .... EddieAhern 11 67
(J G Portman) *hld up towards rr: prog 3f out: rdn to chse ldrs 2f out: one pce and no imp after* **11/2**[2]

4262 **6** *1 1/2* **Alnwick**[25] 3189 3-8-2 **61** ow2 .... ChrisCatlin 9 65
(P D Cundell) *settled in rr: snatched up over 9f out: drvn over 4f out and struggling: styd on strly fr over 1f out: no ch* **6/1**[3]

0546 **7** *1* **Coda Agency**[30] 3033 4-8-9 **51** .... DO'Donohoe 2 54+
(D W P Arbuthnot) *dwlt: sn in midfield: outpcd whn n.m.r 3f out: kpt on same pce after* **12/1**

5303 **8** *nk* **Musango**[42] 2667 4-9-12 **68** .... (t) RichardSmith 12 71
(B R Johnson) *dwlt: hld up in last trio: prog on wd outside over 3f out: chsd ldrs 2f out: sn rdn: wknd jst over 1f out* **7/1**

0564 **9** *nk* **Cortesia (IRE)**[28] 3107 4-9-7 **70** .... MCGeran(7) 7 72
(P W Chapple-Hyam) *hld up in last pair: gng wl enough 4f out: rdn 3f out: plugged on fnl 2f on inner: no ch* **20/1**

5063 **10** *3 1/2* **Synonymy**[31] 2996 4-9-8 **64** .... LPKeniry 14 62
(M Blanshard) *hld up in rr: prog to press ldrs 1/2-way: rdn to chal over 3f out: sn btn: wknd over 1f out* **10/1**

3000 **11** *2* **Follow On**[24] 3217 5-9-4 **60** .... (v1) SimonWhitworth 13 56
(A P Jarvis) *hld up in rr: nt clr run over 3f out: no prog over 2f out* **14/1**

00-0 **12** *13* **St Fris**[53] 2332 4-8-9 **51** oh2 .... (v) TPO'Shea 5 31
(J A R Toller) *trckd ldr: rdn to chal 5f out: led 4f out to over 3f out: wknd rapidly* **33/1**

0042 **13** *4* **Into Action**[10] 3653 3-8-3 **69** ow3 .... HaddenFrost(7) 3 44
(R Hannon) *led: thought abt ducking out stable bnd after 6f: hdd & wknd rapidly 4f out* **8/1**

00/0 **14** *2 1/2* **Nesnaas (USA)**[25] 3191 6-9-1 **60** .... EmmettStack(3) 4 32
(M G Rimell) *sn settled in midfield: effrt on outer 6f out: rdn over 4f out: sn wknd* **33/1**

3m 26.57s (-2.22) **Going Correction** -0.05s/f (Stan)
WFA 3 from 4yo+ 17lb — **14** Ran SP% **134.7**
Speed ratings (Par 103): **103,102,102,101,101 101,100,100,100,98 97,91,89,87**
CSF £39.17 CT £228.94 TOTE £5.80: £2.90, £3.10, £3.50; EX 73.40.
Owner Miss Tor Sturgis **Bred** Mrs Kate Watson **Trained** Lambourn, Berks
■ Stewards' Enquiry : T P O'Shea one-day ban: used whip when out of contention (Aug 8)

FOCUS
A modest staying handicap but sound enough with the runner-up, fifth and sixth close to form.

3946 LINGFIELD PARK FOR WEDDINGS H'CAP — 1m 2f (P)
6:30 (6:30) (Class 6) (0-65,63) 3-Y-0+ — **£2,047** (£604; £302) **Stalls** Low

Form — RPR

3044 **1** **Majehar**[22] 3286 5-9-0 **57** .... TravisBlock(5) 14 64
(A G Newcombe) *trckd ldrs on outer: prog over 3f out: rdn to ld over 2f out: drvn and kpt on fr over 1f out* **4/1**[1]

03-0 **2** *1* **Look Of Eagles**[84] 85 5-9-2 **61** ow4 .... KevinTobin(7) 12 66
(C J Mann) *hld up in last trio: prog on outer 3f out: rdn wl over 1f out: styd on to take 2nd ins fnl f: nt rch wnr* **9/1**

0403 **3** *1/2* **And Again (USA)**[11] 3616 4-9-6 **58** .... (p) LPKeniry 6 62
(R A Teal) *prom: led over 3f out to over 2f out: one pce u.p* **5/1**[2]

0000 **4** *nk* **Sir Haydn**[5] 3805 7-9-8 **60** .... (v) EddieAhern 2 63
(J R Jenkins) *t.k.h: hld up in tch: prog to chse ldng pair over 2f out: hrd rdn and kpt on same pce* **7/1**[3]

30-0 **5** *1/2* **Blushing Light (USA)**[164] 461 4-9-8 **60** .... ChrisCatlin 10 62
(M A Magnusson) *hld up in rr: nt clr run over 3f out to over 2f out: drvn and styd on fr over 1f out: nrst fin* **12/1**

-160 **6** *1 1/4* **Stolen Hours (USA)**[24] 3217 7-9-4 **63** .... JackMitchell(7) 7 63
(J Akehurst) *rousted along to go prom: nvr racd w any enthusiasm: rdn 1/2-way: outpcd over 2f out: kpt on fr over 1f out* **8/1**

20-0 **7** *1* **Ground Patrol**[11] 3616 6-8-13 **58** .... JackDean(7) 4 56
(W G M Turner) *hld up towards rr on inner: nt clr run over 3f out to over 2f out: pushed along and no prog wl over 1f out: kpt on* **33/1**

3200 **8** *1 1/4* **Mighty Kitchener (USA)**[8] 3705 4-9-5 **60** .... EmmettStack(3) 3 55
(P Howling) *s.s: hld up in last pair: stl there over 2f out: rdn and sddle slipped over 1f out: kpt on* **12/1**

1050 **9** *hd* **The Bonus King**[12] 3600 7-9-8 **60** .... PaulDoe 1 55
(J Jay) *wl in rr on inner: pushed along 1/2-way: nt clr run over 3f out: off the pce after: no real prog fnl 2f* **12/1**

1430 **10** *1 1/2* **Tabulate**[36] 2831 4-9-8 **60** .... AmirQuinn 13 52
(P Howling) *hld up wl in rr: stdy prog on outer 3f out: trckd ldrs 2f out: rdn and wknd tamely over 1f out* **12/1**

14/0 **11** *1 3/4* **Victory Sign (IRE)**[5] 3795 7-9-3 **58** .... (vt) AlanCreighton(3) 9 47
(P Butler) *rousted along to rch midfield: drvn 1/2-way: steadily lost pl fr 3f out* **33/1**

-100 **12** *6* **King Of Music (USA)**[187] 212 6-9-8 **60** .... RichardSmith 5 37
(G Prodromou) *trckd ldrs on inner: rdn over 3f out: wknd over 2f out* **8/1**

150- **13** *2 1/2* **Granary Girl**[316] 5354 5-8-9 **54** .... JosephineBruning(7) 11 26
(J Pearce) *led to over 3f out: bmpd along and wknd* **20/1**

2m 6.84s (-0.95) **Going Correction** -0.05s/f (Stan) — **13** Ran SP% **122.8**
Speed ratings (Par 101): **101,100,99,99,99 98,97,96,96,95 93,88,86**
CSF £40.43 CT £187.26 TOTE £5.70: £2.20, £4.20, £2.20; EX 66.00.
Owner J R Salter **Bred** Darley **Trained** Yarnscombe, Devon

FOCUS
A moderate but competitive handicap, and although rated through the third to form, is not that solid.
Mighty Kitchener(USA) Official explanation: jockey said saddle slipped

3947 LINGFIELDPARK.CO.UK MAIDEN AUCTION STKS — 5f
7:00 (7:01) (Class 6) 2-Y-0 — **£2,730** (£806; £403) **Stalls** High

Form — RPR

50 **1** **Mac Dalia**[17] 3423 2-8-6 0 .... TPO'Shea 3 72
(M G Quinlan) *settled in 5th: prog on outer 2f out: rdn to chal 1f out: styd on wl to ld last 75yds* **10/1**

006 **2** *1/2* **Lady Vibeeka**[42] 2651 2-8-4 0 .... HayleyTurner 4 69
(Mrs H Sweeting) *pressed ldr: led over 1f out: rdn and edgd lft fnl f: hdd last 75yds* **20/1**

34 **3** *1* **Our Acquaintance**[9] 3687 2-8-11 0 .... PaulDoe 2 72
(W R Muir) *pressed ldng pair: rdn to chal over 1f out: upsides ins fnl f: fdd last 75yds* **11/10**[1]

350 **4** *1 1/4* **Fox's Den**[56] 2241 2-8-9 0 .... EddieAhern 6 66
(R M Beckett) *racd against nr side rail: led to over 1f out: fdd* **7/2**[2]

330 **5** *3/4* **Iamagrey (IRE)**[52] 2349 2-8-1 0 .... TolleyDean(5) 7 60
(J S Moore) *chsd ldng trio: rdn after 2f: nvr pce to make any imp after* **4/1**[3]

6 *1 3/4* **Heaven** 2-8-4 0 .... ChrisCatlin 1 52
(P J Makin) *sn outpcd in last pair: kpt on fr 3f out but nvr rchd ldrs* **14/1**

00 **7** *10* **Days Of Thunder (IRE)**[16] 3471 2-8-4 0 .... MarkCoumbe(7) 5 23
(G F Bridgwater) *sn pushed along and outpcd in last pair: bhd fr 1/2-way* **50/1**

58.67 secs (-0.27) **Going Correction** -0.25s/f (Firm) — **7** Ran SP% **112.3**
Speed ratings (Par 92): **92,91,89,87,86 83,67**
CSF £164.05 TOTE £14.10: £5.30, £5.40; EX 125.90.
Owner Dr Angelo Macchi **Bred** Chippenham Lodge Stud **Trained** Newmarket, Suffolk

FOCUS
A weak juvenile maiden rated around the third and fourth and the time.

NOTEBOOK
Mac Dalia was too keen for her own good on the Polytrack here last time, but she had previously shaped with promise on her debut at Yarmouth and proved good enough to get off the mark at third attempt. This was an ordinary race though, and her connections will no doubt be hoping the Handicapper does not overreact. (op 12-1 tchd 14-1)
Lady Vibeeka clearly stepped up the form she had shown on her three previous starts, but her proximity still suggests this was not much of a race. (op 16-1 tchd 14-1)
Our Acquaintance failed to build on the form of his two previous starts and was a touch disappointing. He now has the option of going for nurseries, but he may just be the type who will often find a few too good. (op 6-4 tchd 13-8 tchd 7-4 in a place)
Fox's Den was well held and the fact he had been declared for a seller earlier in the season suggests he is pretty moderate. (op 4-1)
Iamagrey(IRE) was disappointing at Kempton on her previous start and she again failed to confirm the promise of her first two starts. (op 11-4 tchd 5-2)

3948 DEREK BURRIDGE RACING & GOLF TROPHIES MEDIAN AUCTION MAIDEN STKS — 7f
7:30 (7:38) (Class 6) 3-5-Y-0 — **£2,730** (£806; £403) **Stalls** High

Form — RPR

2522 **1** **Esteem Machine (USA)**[46] 2542 3-9-3 75 .... EddieAhern 4 79+
(R A Teal) *mde all: cruising fr 1/2-way: pushed clr over 1f out: at least 6l clr fnl f: eased* **1/2**[1]

0-0 **2** *3* **Demolition**[28] 3084 3-9-3 0 .... SimonWhitworth 6 58
(C A Cyzer) *chsd clr ldrs: rdn 1/2-way: kpt on to take 2nd ins fnl f: fin wl but no ch w easy wnr* **40/1**

2426 **3** *2 1/2* **Doyles Lodge**[16] 3475 3-9-3 73 .... (v1) DaneO'Neill 7 51
(H Candy) *chsd ldng pair: rdn to chse wnr 3f out: no ch: one pce and lost 2nd ins fnl f* **3/1**[2]

6-6 **4** *9* **Auntie Mame**[19] 3387 3-8-12 0 .... EdwardCreighton 3 22
(D J Coakley) *v reluctant to go to post: chsd ldrs: rdn 1/2-way: no ch and no imp: wknd over 1f out* **14/1**[3]

00 **5** *11* **Dance Steps**[19] 3387 3-8-12 0 .... HayleyTurner 1 —
(Miss K B Boutflower) *lost tch w ldrs by 1/2-way: sn bhd* **50/1**

6 *nk* **Quicklime** 3-8-12 0 .... PaulDoe 5 —
(Jamie Poulton) *s.s: bhd in last pair: nvr a factor* **14/1**[3]

-400 **7** *8* **Caj (IRE)**[143] 636 3-8-9 0 .... EmmettStack(3) 8 —
(Luke Comer, Ire) *chsd wnr to 3f out: hanging lft and wknd: heavily eased fnl f* **20/1**

8 *6* **Wahhaj** 3-9-3 0 .... RichardSmith 2 —
(G Prodromou) *s.s: rn green and sn t.o* **20/1**

1m 25.05s (0.84) **Going Correction** +0.15s/f (Good) — **8** Ran SP% **118.9**
Speed ratings (Par 101): **101,97,94,84,71 71,62,55**
CSF £39.84 TOTE £1.60: £1.10, £6.20, £1.20; EX 21.90.
Owner M Vickers **Bred** Mindy Hodges Powell **Trained** Headley, Surrey

FOCUS
A very weak maiden with the winner value for eight lengths and the field well strung out behind.
Demolition Official explanation: jockey said gelding lost a hind shoe

3949 THE REAL THING LIVE AT LINGFIELDPARK.CO.UK H'CAP — 7f
8:00 (8:02) (Class 5) (0-70,67) 3-Y-0 — **£2,817** (£838; £418; £209) **Stalls** High

Form — RPR

0430 **1** **Cornerstone**[8] 3713 3-8-2 **48** oh3 .... (v1) ChrisCatlin 8 58
(S C Williams) *mde all: shkn up and in command wl over 1f out: edgd lft fnl f: styd on wl* **10/1**

54-0 **2** *2 1/2* **Carlitos Spirit (IRE)**[19] 3384 3-9-0 **60** .... RobertHavlin 1 63
(B R Millman) *hld up in tch: effrt to chse wnr 2f out: sn rdn and no imp* **3/1**[2]

1124 **3** *1 3/4* **Magroom**[25] 3178 3-8-8 **54** .... RichardSmith 5 52
(R J Hodges) *cl up: disp 2nd fr over 3f out to 2f out: one pce* **7/2**[3]

35-0 **4** *3* **Hope Your Safe**[19] 3384 3-8-9 **55** .... DaneO'Neill 7 45
(J R Best) *t.k.h: cl up: rdn over 2f out: fdd over 1f out* **10/1**

025 **5** *1 3/4* **Velocity's Gift**[49] 2477 3-9-5 **65** .... PaulEddery 3 50
(Pat Eddery) *settled in last pair: rdn over 2f out: no rspnse and sn btn* **11/4**[1]

04 **6** *hd* **King Of Tricks**[11] 3611 3-7-9 **48** .... FrankiePickard(7) 2 33
(M D I Usher) *t.k.h early: prom tl wknd 2f out* **14/1**

-500 **7** *1* **Anatolian Prince**[59] 2153 3-8-9 **55** .... HayleyTurner 9 37
(J M P Eustace) *in tch: drvn wl over 2f out: sn struggling and btn* **15/2**

0450 **8** *24* **Doctor Ned**[25] 3175 3-8-3 **49** .... (t) EdwardCreighton 4 —
(Miss Sheena West) *s.i.s: t.k.h early: hld up: rdn and wknd rapidly 3f out: t.o* **16/1**

1m 25.65s (1.44) **Going Correction** +0.15s/f (Good) — **8** Ran SP% **116.4**
Speed ratings (Par 100): **97,94,92,88,86 86,85,57**
CSF £40.94 CT £129.90 TOTE £10.50: £2.90, £1.80, £1.20; EX 88.20.
Owner J W Lovitt & Partners **Bred** Cheveley Park Stud Ltd **Trained** Newmarket, Suffolk

FOCUS
A moderate handicap rated around the runner-up and fourth, but not the most solid.

3950 BRIEFCASE BLUES BROTHERS LIVE AT LINGFIELDPARK.CO.UK H'CAP — 7f 140y
8:30 (8:32) (Class 6) (0-65,60) 3-Y-0+ — **£2,184** (£644; £322) **Stalls** Centre

Form — RPR

0063 **1** **Hansomelle (IRE)**[9] 3690 5-8-13 **49** .... (p) NeilChalmers(3) 18 67
(Miss Sheena West) *in tch in chsng gp: prog 1/2-way: led over 2f out: sn clr: unchal* **9/1**

3144 **2** *9* **Mugeba**[16] 3466 6-9-6 **58** .... (tp) NicolPolli(5) 15 54
(Miss Gay Kelleway) *hld up in rr and off the pce: stdy prog against nr side rail fr 3f out: rdn to chse wnr over 1f out: no imp* **11/2**[1]

0153 **3** *3* **Toms Laughter**[1] 3905 3-9-5 **60** .... DaleGibson 13 46
(B Palling) *prom in chsng gp: outpcd and rdn over 2f out: kpt on fr over 1f out* **7/1**[2]

4004 **4** *hd* **Rubilini**[15] 3490 3-8-9 **50** .... TPO'Shea 8 36
(M R Channon) *wl in rr: rdn bef 1/2-way: styd on u.p fr over 2f out: nrst fin* **12/1**

050 **5** *nk* **Black Sea Pearl**[12] 3591 4-9-8 **60** .... LukeMorris(5) 10 47
(P W D'Arcy) *off the pce in midfield: rdn 3f out: kpt on fnl 2f: n.d* **8/1**[3]

36-0 **6** *5* **Kathleen Kennet**[184] 238 7-8-12 **50** .... TravisBlock(5) 5 | 24
(C Tinkler) *prom in chsng gp: wknd fr over 2f out* **14/1**

6540 **7** *½* **The Tinker Man**[19] 3365 3-8-7 **55** .... FrankiePickard(7) 11 | 26
(M D I Usher) *prom in chsng gp early: lost pl bef 1/2-way: hanging lft and btn over 2f out* **25/1**

4026 **8** *1 ½* **Danawi (IRE)**[20] 3352 4-9-6 **53** .... ChrisCatlin 2 | 22
(M R Hoad) *prom in chsng gp: no prog 1/2-way: struggling wl over 2f out* **11/1**

5051 **9** *2 ½* **Tipsy Lad**[10] 3647 5-8-12 **45** .... (t) DaneO'Neill 9 | 8
(D J S Ffrench Davis) *sn u.p in last trio and wl bhd: plugged on fr over 2f out* **7/1**[2]

0532 **10** *1 ½* **Bens Georgie (IRE)**[7] 3735 5-9-6 **53** .... (v[1]) RobertHavlin 6 | 12
(D K Ivory) *racd freely: led and sn clr: wknd and hdd over 2f out* **7/1**[2]

4400 **11** *¾* **Mr Chocolate Drop (IRE)**[37] 2796 3-8-10 **51** .... PaulEddery 16 | 6
(Miss M E Rowland) *in tch in chsng gp to 1/2-way: sn btn* **40/1**

300- **12** *3 ½* **Contented (IRE)**[394] 3014 5-9-5 **52** .... LPKeniry 14 | —
(Mrs L C Jewell) *prom in chsng gp to 3f out: sn btn* **33/1**

000- **13** *½* **Falcon Flyer**[337] 4774 3-8-3 **47** .... StephaneBreux(3) 17 | —
(J R Best) *nvr bttr than midfield and off the pce: wknd over 2f out* **25/1**

0500 **14** *5* **Royal Guest**[2] 3875 3-9-0 **55** .... EdwardCreighton 4 | —
(M R Channon) *dwlt: nvr bttr than midfield: wknd over 2f out* **11/1**

00-0 **15** *hd* **Ron In Ernest**[16] 3475 3-9-3 **58** .... SimonWhitworth 12 | —
(J A Geake) *stdd s: hld up in last trio and wl off the pce: shkn up and no rspnse 3f out* **20/1**

506- **16** *5* **Gnillah**[301] 5690 4-9-6 **53** .... RichardSmith 1 | —
(B R Johnson) *nvr on terms: wknd 3f out: eased whn no ch over 1f out* **33/1**

0002 **17** *32* **Nightstrike (IRE)**[44] 2592 4-9-7 **57** .... EmmettStack(3) 7 | —
(Luke Comer, Ire) *sn u.p in last trio: t.o fnl 3f* **20/1**

1m 32.39s (0.93) **Going Correction** +0.15s/f (Good)
WFA 3 from 4yo+ 8lb **17** Ran SP% **130.6**
Speed ratings (Par 101): **101,92,89,88,88 83,83,81,79,77 76,73,72,67,67 62,30**
CSF £56.51 CT £297.31 TOTE £13.10: £3.00, £2.30, £1.40, £3.80; EX 55.00 Place 6 £383.18, Place 5 £162.59..
Owner Michael Moriarty **Bred** J Beckett **Trained** Falmer, E Sussex

FOCUS
A moderate handicap run at a strong pace. The high draws dominated and the winner is rated to the best of last season's form.
Bens Georgie(IRE) Official explanation: jockey said mare ran too free
T/Plt: £1,165.10 to a £1 stake. Pool: £57,539.90. 36.05 winning tickets. T/Qpdt: £120.90 to a £1 stake. Pool: £4,038.40. 24.70 winning tickets. JN

3088 NEWCASTLE (L-H)

Saturday, July 28

OFFICIAL GOING: Good (7.2)
Wind: Fresh, half against Weather: Cloudy, fine

3951 123SPORT.COM MAIDEN AUCTION STKS — 7f
2:20 (2:21) (Class 4) 2-Y-0 **£5,181** (£1,541; £770; £384) **Stalls** High

Form | RPR

1 **Jim Martin** 2-8-12 0 .... J-PGuillambert 8 | 78
(J R Weymes) *s.i.s: hld up in tch on far side: effrt 2f out: led wl ins fnl f: r.o wl* **33/1**

4 **2** *1 ¾* **Lady Rochbonne**[18] 3404 2-8-5 0 ow3 .... DeanMcKeown 2 | 67
(Mrs G S Rees) *led far side: clr over 1f out: hdd and no ex wl ins fnl f: 2nd of 7 in gp* **8/1**

3 *2* **Prince Kalamoun (IRE)** 2-8-6 0 .... AndrewElliott(3) 6 | 66
(G A Swinbank) *prom far side: effrt over 2f out: kpt on fnl f: 3rd of 7 in gp* **7/2**[3]

0 **4** *1* **Reel Buddy Blaze**[46] 2532 2-8-8 0 .... PJMcDonald(3) 1 | 65
(T P Tate) *bhd far side tl kpt on fnl 2f: nrst fin: 4th of 7 in gp* **40/1**

3 **5** *7* **Low Flyer (USA)**[30] 3024 2-8-9 0 .... PhillipMakin 5 | 46
(T D Barron) *chsd far side ldrs tl wknd fr 2f out: 5th of 7 in gp* **5/2**[1]

055 **6** *shd* **Invincible Rose (IRE)**[14] 3560 2-7-11 0 ow2 .... AndrewHeffernan(7) 4 | 40
(M Brittain) *rrd s: bhd far side: rdn 3f out: n.d: 6th of 7 in gp* **33/1**

000 **7** *2* **Premier Class (IRE)**[35] 2888 2-8-8 0 .... PaddyAspell 3 | 39
(J S Wainwright) *rrd in stalls: in tch far side tl wknd over 2f out: last of 7 in gp* **28/1**

0 **8** *1 ¼* **Medici Time**[35] 2889 2-8-12 0 .... DavidAllan 15 | 40
(T D Easterby) *chsd stands' side ldrs: led that gp over 1f out: kpt on: no ch w stands' side: 1st of 8 in gp* **22/1**

9 *9* **Roger's Revenge** 2-8-7 0 .... RoystonFfrench 12 | 13
(B Smart) *in tch outside of stands' side gp: effrt and hung lft 1/2-way: no imp fr over 2f out: 2nd of 8 in gp* **8/1**

4 **10** *3 ½* **Tuanku (IRE)**[77] 1680 2-8-12 0 .... TomEaves 17 | 9
(M R Channon) *cl up stands' side tl rdn and outpcd fr 2f out: 3rd of 8 in gp* **10/3**[2]

11 *1 ¼* **Trojan Hero (IRE)** 2-8-9 0 .... SilvestreDeSousa 13 | 3
(A Dickman) *hld up in tch stands' side: effrt over 2f out: sn no imp: 4th of 8 in gp* **20/1**

406 **12** *1 ¼* **Kingstyle (IRE)**[24] 3205 2-8-0 0 .... PatrickDonaghy(7) 9 | —
(M Brittain) *cl up stands' side: ev ch that gp over 1f out: sn btn: 5th of 8 in gp* **66/1**

55 **13** *1 ¾* **Hildegarde (IRE)**[14] 3532 2-8-4 0 .... PaulQuinn 10 | —
(T D Easterby) *hld up in tch stands' side: rdn and hung lft over 2f out: sn outpcd: 6th of 8 in gp* **18/1**

60 **14** *2* **Mujinda**[35] 2888 2-7-12 0 ow3 .... KellyHarrison(7) 16 | —
(M Brittain) *led stands' side to over 1f out: sn btn: 7th of 8 in gp* **100/1**

05 **15** *1 ¾* **Caribbean Cruiser**[20] 3341 2-8-4 0 ow2 .... GaryBartley(7) 14 | —
(Garry Moss) *unruly bef s: in tch stands' side tl wknd over 1f out: last of 8 in gp* **25/1**

1m 32.1s (4.08) **Going Correction** +0.40s/f (Good) **15** Ran SP% **128.6**
Speed ratings (Par 96): **92,90,87,86,78 78,76,74,64,60 59,57,55,53,51**
CSF £274.77 TOTE £35.30: £8.80, £2.30, £1.70; EX 461.90.
Owner Mrs R Morley **Bred** Southill Stud **Trained** Middleham Moor, N Yorks

FOCUS
Not a strong race and one in which the far-side group had a marked advantage over those racing on the near-side rail. The form is rated through time for the moment.

NOTEBOOK
Jim Martin, a half-brother to juvenile sprint winner Quantum Lady and to Polytrack winner Velocitas, was easy to back but created a good impression on this racecourse debut. He should stay 1m and, although life will be tougher from now on, he may be capable of a bit better.
Lady Rochbonne, who showed ability in a race that has thrown up an easy winner on Polytrack, bettered that effort, despite his rider posting 3lb of overweight. She has shown enough to suggest she should find a similar event. (tchd 9-1)
Prince Kalamoun(IRE) ◆, a 10,000 euros half-brother to several winners up to middle distances, attracted plenty of support and showed ability on this racecourse debut. He will be suited by 1m, is in very good hands and is sure to win a race. (op 6-1)
Reel Buddy Blaze left his debut form well behind upped to this trip and on this easier ground. An even stiffer test of stamina will be in his favour and he is the type to win in ordinary handicap company in due course.
Low Flyer(USA), who showed ability over 6f in soft ground at this course on his debut, proved disappointing upped to this trip on this better ground. However, he will be worth another chance in ordinary company. (tchd 3-1)
Invincible Rose(IRE) again had her limitations exposed in this type of event and she will be suited by a drop in grade or the step into ordinary nursery company. (op 28-1)
Medici Time, well beaten on his debut, was again well beaten on the face of it but shaped much better than the bare form as the stands'-side bunch had no chance with the group racing on the far side. He looks more a nursery type and is one to keep an eye on. (op 20-1)
Roger's Revenge Official explanation: jockey said gelding hung left-handed throughout
Tuanku(IRE) Official explanation: trainer's rep had no explanation for the poor form shown

3952 I.T.P.S. CELLULAR SOLUTIONS H'CAP — 6f
2:50 (2:51) (Class 3) (0-90,86) 3-Y-0
£9,348 (£2,799; £1,050; £1,050; £349; £175) **Stalls** High

Form | RPR

2111 **1** **Sundae**[29] 3061 3-9-7 **86** .... DeanMcKeown 2 | 99+
(C F Wall) *trckd ldrs gng wl: rdn to ld over 1f out: kpt on wl: comf* **11/8**[1]

0-44 **2** *1 ½* **Barkass (UAE)**[168] 418 3-8-8 **73** .... TomEaves 8 | 77+
(B Ellison) *hld up: hdwy over 1f out: wnt 2nd ins fnl f: kpt on: bttr for r* **12/1**

5062 **3** *1 ¼* **Top Bid**[19] 3380 3-8-13 **78** .... DavidAllan 4 | 78
(T D Easterby) *pressed ldr: led over 2f out to over 1f out: no ex ins fnl f* **9/2**[2]

5560 **3** *dht* **Sunnyside Tom (IRE)**[35] 2881 3-8-7 **72** .... PaulQuinn 7 | 72
(R A Fahey) *trckd ldrs: effrt over 2f out: edgd lft over 1f out: sn one pce* **7/1**

-113 **5** *3* **Jack Rackham**[59] 2135 3-9-7 **86** .... RoystonFfrench 1 | 76
(B Smart) *towards rr: rdn 1/2-way: short-lived effrt 2f out: no imp fnl f* **6/1**[3]

6-46 **6** *shd* **Ingleby Princess**[14] 3557 3-8-11 **76** .... PhillipMakin 5 | 66+
(T D Barron) *hld up in tch: effrt whn nt clr run over 2f out: hmpd over 1f out: nt rcvr* **8/1**

3255 **7** *3* **Mundo's Magic**[17] 3413 3-8-3 **71** .... AndrewElliott(3) 6 | 51
(G M Moore) *led to over 2f out: wknd over 1f out* **12/1**

1m 16.55s (1.46) **Going Correction** +0.40s/f (Good) **7** Ran SP% **113.6**
Speed ratings (Par 104): **106,104,102,102,98 98,94**
TRICAST: S/B/TB £30.00; S/B/ST £43.63 CSF £19.32 CT £43.63 TOTE £2.20: £1.80, £6.60; EX 23.70.
Owner Peter Gregory **Bred** Jeremy Green And Sons **Trained** Newmarket, Suffolk

FOCUS
Not a strong race for the money but a further step in the right direction from Sundae, who may well be capable of better still.

NOTEBOOK
Sundae ◆ has improved a fair bit with every start this year and he turned in his best effort yet back over this more suitable trip from this 7lb higher mark. The way he travelled before putting the race to bed suggests he may well be able to overcome a further rise and he remains one to keep on the right side on good and easier ground. (op 11-10 tchd 6-4 in a place)
Barkass(UAE) ◆, who showed ability in maidens in winter over 7f and 1m on Polytrack for Marcus Tregoning, caught the eye on this handicap/turf debut and first run over 6f on this first start for new connections. He will be suited by the return to 7f and appeals strongly as the type to win races. (tchd 14-1)
Top Bid had looked in the grip of the Handicapper but, although having the run of the race, again had his limitations exposed, despite attracting plenty of support. He has little room for manoeuvre from his current mark. (op 17-2 tchd 10-1)
Sunnyside Tom(IRE), returned to 6f, ran had the run of the race and ran creditably, He has had his limitations exposed in handicaps so far but he is in very good hands and is not one to be writing off just yet. (op 17-2 tchd 10-1)
Jack Rackham, back in handicap company, may have been suited by an even stronger gallop, but he had his limitations exposed this time. He looks the type that needs things to fall right and he may struggle to win from his current mark of 86. (op 9-2 tchd 4-1)
Ingleby Princess, unsuited by very soft ground at York last time, shaped a fair bit better than the bare form suggests as she was denied room on the inside for much of the last quarter mile. She will be worth another chance in similar company. Official explanation: jockey said filly was denied a clear run (tchd 9-1)

3953 ALLIED IRISH BANK (GB) BEESWING H'CAP — 7f
3:25 (3:26) (Class 3) (0-95,94) 3-Y-0+
£9,971 (£2,985; £1,492; £747; £372; £187) **Stalls** High

Form | RPR

5561 **1** **Balakiref**[13] 3569 8-8-11 **77** .... PhillipMakin 11 | 86
(M Dods) *chsd stands' side ldrs: led appr fnl f: kpt on strly* **11/1**

0-00 **2** *2* **Sir Xaar (IRE)**[96] 1195 4-9-12 **92** .... (t) J-PGuillambert 8 | 96
(B Smart) *bhd and sn pushed along stands' side: hdwy 2f out: chsd wnr ins fnl f: no imp* **14/1**

-615 **3** *2* **Amy Louise (IRE)**[24] 3201 4-9-1 **81** .... TomEaves 10 | 80
(T D Barron) *led stands' side to appr fnl f: kpt on same pce* **8/1**

3320 **4** *¾* **Passion Fruit**[15] 3512 6-9-0 **80** .... DeanMcKeown 9 | 77
(C W Fairhurst) *hld up in tch stands' side: effrt over 2f out: kpt on same pce fnl f* **14/1**

0015 **5** *2* **Inaminute (IRE)**[9] 3670 4-8-9 **78** .... AndrewElliott(3) 4 | 69+
(K R Burke) *led sole far side rival: kpt on same pce fr 2f out* **16/1**

5411 **6** *¾* **Countdown**[14] 3559 5-9-7 **87** .... DavidAllan 5 | 76
(T D Easterby) *in tch: outpcd over 3f out: rallied over 1f out: no imp* **11/4**[1]

6043 **7** *2* **Prince Namid**[6] 3762 5-9-2 **82** .... RoystonFfrench 7 | 66
(Mrs A Duffield) *chsd stands' side ldrs tl wknd over 1f out* **13/2**

2005 **8** *¾* **Yorkshire Blue**[12] 3585 8-8-5 **78** .... GaryBartley(7) 2 | 60
(J S Goldie) *bhd stands' side: rdn 1/2-way: nvr rchd ldrs* **10/1**

0243 **9** *6* **Compton's Eleven**[15] 3488 6-9-4 **84** .... SamHitchcott 1 | 50
(M R Channon) *chsd ldrs on outside of stands' side gp tl wknd wl over 1f out* **11/2**[3]

-600 **10** *2 ½* **Hartshead**[15] 3500 8-9-11 **94** .... PJMcDonald(3) 3 | 53
(G A Swinbank) *chsd ldrs on outside of stands' side gp tl wknd over 2f out* **5/1**[2]

-000 **11** *10* **Inter Vision (USA)**[8] 3720 7-9-7 **87** .... SilvestreDeSousa 6 | 19
(A Dickman) *swtchd to chse far side ldr over 5f out: rdn and wknd fr 2f out* **25/1**

1m 30.01s (1.99) **Going Correction** +0.40s/f (Good) **11** Ran SP% **123.6**
Speed ratings (Par 107): **104,101,99,98,96 95,93,92,85,82 71**
CSF £162.58 CT £907.76 TOTE £10.60: £3.10, £5.90, £2.70; EX 350.70.
Owner Septimus Racing Group **Bred** S R Hope And D Erwin **Trained** Denton, Co Durham
■ Stewards' Enquiry : Dean McKeown one-day ban: careless riding (Aug 8)

FOCUS
A valuable handicap but mainly exposed performers. The larger group raced on the stands' side and the pace was fair. The form is slightly messy but rated through the winner to his best.
NOTEBOOK
Balakiref, 3lb higher than his Haydock success, turned in a career best effort returned to 7f. He has been another fine advert for the skills of Michael Dods this year and he should continue to go well up to this trip on good and easier ground. (op 10-1)
Sir Xaar(IRE) has had some stiff tasks since his last win in August 2005 but, although not looking the most responsive in the early stages, ran his best race of the year tried in the tongue-tie. He has come down the weights but is likely to continue to look vulnerable to the more progressive or well-handicapped types from his current mark. (tchd 16-1)
Amy Louise(IRE), behind Countdown when disappointing at Catterick on her previous start, had the run of the race against the stands' rail and finished ahead of that rival this time. She likes a bit of cut in the ground and should continue to give a good account (tchd 15-2)
Passion Fruit has yet to win this year but ran creditably in this competitive handicap. A strongly-run race over this trip with a bit of give in the ground are her requirements and she should continue to go well in this type of event. (op 12-1)
Inaminute(IRE), who showed a good attitude to beat Passion Fruit at Carlisle last month, failed to confirm placings with that rival but may be a bit better than the bare form as she raced with only one other on the far side. She will need to turn in a career-best effort to win from this mark, though.
Countdown had been in tremendous form on his last two runs with wins at Catterick and in deep ground at York but he was never travelling with much fluency and was beaten some way out this time. More testing ground may suit ideally but he has a bit to prove from this mark. (op 3-1 tchd 10-3 tchd 7-2 in places)
Prince Namid left the impression that the return to sprinting would be in his favour, but the fact that he has not won for over a year means he is not one to take too short a price about in this type of event. (op 7-1 tchd 15-2)

3954 PIMMS SUMMER CLASSIC H'CAP — 5f
4:00 (4:01) (Class 4) (0-85,85) 3-Y-O+
£6,232 (£1,866; £933; £467; £233; £117) **Stalls** High

Form — RPR
0140 1 **Sunrise Safari (IRE)**[15] 3500 4-9-11 **83**.....(v) TomEaves 6 96
(I Semple) *t.k.h: hld up: hdwy over 1f out: kpt on wl to ld nr fin* **8/1**
0216 2 ½ **Elkhorn**[12] 3585 5-9-3 **78**.....(b) PJMcDonald(3) 2 89+
(Miss J A Camacho) *hld up: hdwy over 1f out: led ent fnl f: edgd lft u.p: hdd nr fin* **4/1**[1]
6014 3 hd **Glasshoughton**[8] 3720 4-9-4 **76**..... PhillipMakin 8 86
(M Dods) *t.k.h: in tch: effrt over 1f out: kpt on towards fin* **13/2**
0616 4 ¾ **Garstang**[14] 3536 4-8-5 **68** ow1.....(b) RussellKennemore(5) 12 76+
(Peter Grayson) *unruly bef s: missed break: hld up: effrt whn no room fr over 1f out to wl ins fnl f: kpt on strly towards fin* **14/1**
335 5 hd **Welcome Approach**[11] 3627 4-8-8 **66**..... DeanMcKeown 10 73+
(J R Weymes) *midfield: effrt over 1f out: nt clr run ins fnl f: kpt on towards fin* **9/1**
0314 6 shd **Compton Classic**[2] 3886 5-8-5 **70** 6ex.....(p) GaryBartley(7) 1 77
(J S Goldie) *towards rr on outside: rdn whn hung lft and n.m.r over 1f out: kpt on ins fnl f* **7/1**
020 7 ¾ **Strensall**[3] 3836 10-7-13 **64** oh1..... KellyHarrison(7) 9 68
(R E Barr) *cl up: led appr to ent fnl f: sn no ex* **16/1**
4-45 8 nk **Sea Salt**[19] 3374 4-9-3 **75**..... RoystonFfrench 3 78
(R A Fahey) *prom: effrt and edgd lft over 1f out: sn no ex* **6/1**[3]
1320 9 ¾ **La Vecchia Scuola (IRE)**[6] 3763 3-8-1 **66** oh5 ow2(v) AndrewElliott(3) 11 66
(R Johnson) *cl up tl rdn and one pce fnl f* **33/1**
0060 10 ¾ **Colorus (IRE)**[8] 3720 4-8-8 **73**..... NSLawes(7) 5 70
(M W Easterby) *led to appr fnl f: wknd ins fnl f* **28/1**
1013 11 nk **The Nifty Fox**[15] 3493 3-9-9 **85**..... DavidAllan 7 81
(T D Easterby) *chsd ldrs: rdn over 1f out: wknd ins fnl f* **9/2**[2]
3500 12 1 **Pieter Brueghel (USA)**[70] 1852 8-9-1 **80**..... OliveGaule(7) 4 73
(D Nicholls) *chsd ldrs tl wknd over 1f out* **20/1**

62.57 secs (1.07) **Going Correction** +0.40s/f (Good)
WFA 3 from 4yo+ 4lb **12 Ran SP% 123.1**
Speed ratings (Par 105): **107,106,105,104,104 104,103,102,101,100 99,98**
CSF £40.74 CT £232.43 TOTE £10.00: £3.00, £2.10, £2.60; EX 65.30.
Owner Mrs J Penman **Bred** Mervyn Stewkesbury **Trained** Carluke, S Lanarks
■ Stewards' Enquiry : N S Lawes one-day ban: not riding to draw (Aug 8)
FOCUS
An open handicap but a strong pace played to the strengths of those coming from behind. The form looks sound.
Welcome Approach Official explanation: jockey said gelding was denied a clear run
Compton Classic Official explanation: jockey said gelding was denied a clear run

3955 THOMPKINS GROUP H'CAP — 1m 2f 32y
4:35 (4:37) (Class 4) (0-80,78) 3-Y-O+ **£6,477** (£1,927; £963; £481) **Stalls** Centre

Form — RPR
126 1 **Amanda Carter**[25] 3183 3-7-13 **59**..... SilvestreDeSousa 9 71
(R A Fahey) *in tch: effrt 2f out: led ins fnl f: sn clr* **15/2**
50-4 2 3 **Given A Choice (IRE)**[20] 3346 5-9-9 **73**..... RoystonFfrench 1 79
(M Todhunter) *led to ins fnl f: kpt on same pce* **11/2**[2]
0342 3 hd **Topflight Wildbird**[15] 3502 4-8-7 **60**..... AndrewElliott(3) 6 66
(Mrs G S Rees) *loose in paddock: chsd ldrs: wnt 2nd briefly over 2f out: sn one pce* **12/1**
6343 4 ¾ **Bajan Parkes**[7] 3755 4-9-11 **75**..... DavidAllan 10 79
(E J Alston) *hld up on outside: hdwy 1/2-way: rdn and outpcd over 2f out: rallied over 1f out: no imp* **9/2**[1]
1130 5 ½ **Bijou Dan**[20] 3343 6-9-0 **64**.....(p) DeanMcKeown 4 67
(D W Thompson) *hld up: outpcd and hung lft 3f out: kpt on fnl f: n.d* **16/1**
-430 6 ½ **Parnassian**[19] 3386 7-8-11 **68**.....(v) HarryPoulton(7) 8 70
(J A Geake) *hld up: pushed along over 2f out: sme late hdwy: n.d* **8/1**
0600 7 hd **Nesno (USA)**[24] 3204 4-8-12 **62**..... TomEaves 7 64
(J D Bethell) *in tch: effrt over 2f out: btn fnl f* **33/1**
-064 8 1¼ **Gala Sunday (USA)**[7] 3755 7-8-5 **62**.....(t) NSLawes(7) 3 61
(M W Easterby) *chsd ldrs: rdn over 2f out: sn one pce* **16/1**
1311 9 1¾ **Royal Flynn**[13] 3567 5-10-0 **78**..... PhillipMakin 12 74
(M Dods) *s.i.s: effrt fr rr over 2f out: sn no imp* **9/2**[1]
0-56 10 ¾ **Baan (USA)**[19] 3386 4-10-0 **78**..... J-PGuillambert 2 72
(M Johnston) *cl up: rdn 3f out: btn over 1f out* **6/1**[3]
5526 11 1 **Shy Glance (USA)**[20] 3346 5-9-8 **75**..... PJMcDonald(3) 11 67
(P Monteith) *hld up: pushed along 3f out: sn btn* **9/1**
0006 12 2½ **Magic Sting**[7] 3755 6-8-10 **60**..... PaddyAspell 5 47
(B S Rothwell) *dwlt: sn midfield: rdn over 2f out: sn wknd* **28/1**

2m 13.96s (2.16) **Going Correction** +0.30s/f (Good)
WFA 3 from 4yo+ 10lb **12 Ran SP% 124.8**
Speed ratings (Par 105): **103,100,100,99,99 99,98,97,96,95 95,93**
CSF £51.15 CT £507.79 TOTE £10.50: £2.60, £2.60, £2.90; EX 74.80.
Owner Mrs Janis Macpherson **Bred** James G Thom **Trained** Musley Bank, N Yorks
FOCUS
A run-of-the-mill handicap in which the pace was just fair and the runner-up sets the level.
Royal Flynn Official explanation: trainer said he had no explanation for the poor form shown

3956 SALTWELL SIGNS APPRENTICE H'CAP — 1m 2f 32y
5:10 (5:10) (Class 6) (0-60,60) 3-Y-O+ **£2,266** (£674; £337; £168) **Stalls** Centre

Form — RPR
4004 1 **Dechiper (IRE)**[56] 2254 5-8-12 **51**..... PatrickDonaghy(3) 1 63
(R Johnson) *hld up: hdwy over 4f out: led over 2f out: rdn out fnl f* **6/1**[2]
4613 2 3 **Danalova**[12] 3587 3-8-3 **52**..... JamesRogers(3) 14 58
(R A Fahey) *in tch: effrt over 2f out: chsd wnr ins fnl f: no imp* **6/1**[2]
1334 3 ½ **Desert Hawk**[5] 3805 6-8-11 **54**..... Julie-AnneCumine(7) 4 59
(W M Brisbourne) *hld up in midfield: hdwy over 2f out: chsd wnr wl over 1f out to ins fnl f: one pce* **6/1**[2]
6010 4 2½ **Rotuma (IRE)**[20] 3343 8-9-3 **53**.....(b) PJBenson 3 53
(M Dods) *hld up in midfield: effrt 2f out: kpt on same pce fnl f* **15/2**[3]
00-0 5 2½ **Epicurean**[93] 1258 5-8-13 **54**..... LanceBetts(5) 9 49
(Mrs K Walton) *midfield: hdwy and ev ch over 2f out: wknd over 1f out* **22/1**
2413 6 1½ **Thornaby Green**[5] 3783 6-9-5 **58**..... DeanHeslop(3) 8 50
(T D Barron) *led 2f: chsd ldr: rdn whn n.m.r and outpcd fr 2f out* **3/1**[1]
560 7 2 **Dream On Dreamers (IRE)**[3] 3840 3-7-7 **46** oh1(p) CharlesEddery(7) 11 34
(R C Guest) *chsd ldrs tl rdn and wknd fr 2f out* **22/1**
000/ 8 5 **Thunderclap**[185] 114 8-8-5 **46** oh1.....(p) NSLawes(5) 13 24
(P D Niven) *hld up: rdn over 2f out: nvr rchd ldrs* **40/1**
-000 9 2 **Moonlight Fantasy (IRE)**[65] 1967 4-8-6 **47**..... ChrisHough(5) 5 21
(T D Barron) *t.k.h: led after 2f: clr 1/2-way: hdd & wknd over 2f out* **11/1**
0030 10 1½ **Richtee (IRE)**[11] 3610 6-8-6 **47**.....(p) DeclanCannon(5) 10 18
(I W McInnes) *missed break: rdn in rr over 4f out: nvr on terms* **10/1**
0/0- 11 shd **Troodos Jet**[13] 3137 6-7-7 **46** oh1..... SoniaEaton(7) 6 17
(K W Hogg) *hld up: drvn over 3f out: n.d* **40/1**
2345 12 ½ **The Mighty Ogmore**[5] 3783 3-8-8 **54** ow1.....(p) AlanRutter 12 24
(R C Guest) *bhd: struggling 1/2-way: nvr on terms* **12/1**
0-04 13 1¼ **Noble Edge**[54] 2298 4-8-13 **54**.....(p) AdamCarter(5) 7 21
(Karen McLintock) *chsd ldrs tl wknd fr 2f out* **12/1**

2m 13.96s (2.16) **Going Correction** +0.30s/f (Good)
WFA 3 from 4yo+ 10lb **13 Ran SP% 126.0**
Speed ratings (Par 101): **103,100,100,98,96 95,93,89,87,86 86,86,85**
CSF £42.72 CT £232.98 TOTE £8.90: £3.00, £2.30, £2.10; EX 54.20 Place 6 £ 626.09, Place 5 £ 201.46.
Owner L Armstrong **Bred** Tommy Burns **Trained** Newburn, Tyne & Wear
FOCUS
A moderate handicap in which the pace was soon sound and the form is straightforward rated through the third.
Moonlight Fantasy(IRE) Official explanation: jockey said gelding had no more to give having run too free
Richtee(IRE) Official explanation: jockey said mare missed the break
The Mighty Ogmore Official explanation: jockey said filly never travelled
T/Plt: £1,341.20 to a £1 stake. Pool: £65,594.60. 35.70 winning tickets. T/Qpdt: £129.00 to a £1 stake. Pool: £3,811.05. 21.85 winning tickets. RY

3907
NEWMARKET (JULY) (R-H)
Saturday, July 28
OFFICIAL GOING: Good to firm (firm in places)
Wind: Light, behind Weather: Cloudy with sunny spells

3957 NSPCC E B F MAIDEN STKS (DIV I) — 7f
1:25 (1:27) (Class 4) 2-Y-O **£3,886** (£1,156; £577; £288) **Stalls** High

Form — RPR
2 1 **Fifteen Love (USA)**[17] 3435 2-9-3 0..... SteveDrowne 1 86+
(R Charlton) *trckd ldrs: bmpd over 2f out: led over 1f out: r.o wl* **2/5**[1]
60 2 2½ **Woolfall Treasure**[11] 3625 2-9-3 0..... NCallan 4 76
(G G Margarson) *chsd ldrs: hmpd over 2f out: sn rdn: styd on* **12/1**[3]
3 nk **Dhhamaan (IRE)** 2-9-3 0..... PaulDoe 9 75
(C E Brittain) *chsd ldr: led and hung lft over 2f out: rdn and hdd over 1f out: styd on same pce* **33/1**
4 ½ **Hyde Lea Flyer** 2-9-3 0..... DarryllHolland 3 74
(A King) *hld up: hdwy over 1f out: nt rch ldrs* **22/1**
5 2½ **Aussie Battler (IRE)** 2-9-3 0..... PaulFitzsimons 5 67
(B W Duke) *s.i.s: hld up: hdwy over 1f out: no ex ins fnl f* **33/1**
0 6 hd **Valiant Vicar (USA)**[28] 3095 2-9-3 0..... RobertHavlin 12 67
(B J Meehan) *led: rdn and hdd over 2f out: sn hung lft: styd on same pce appr fnl f* **20/1**
7 1½ **Recoil (IRE)** 2-9-3 0..... PaulEddery 6 63
(Christian Wroe) *hld up: rdn whn nt clr run 2f out: swtchd rt over 1f out: n.d* **40/1**
0 8 nk **Mubher**[17] 3435 2-9-3 0..... IanMongan 10 62
(J L Dunlop) *s.i.s: hdwy over 4f out: wknd over 1f out* **14/1**
9 2½ **Alcimedes** 2-9-3 0..... TPQueally 8 56+
(P W Chapple-Hyam) *chsd ldrs: hung lft over 2f out: wknd over 1f out* **8/1**[2]
10 1 **Criterion** 2-8-10 0..... JamieHamblett(7) 11 53
(Sir Michael Stoute) *mid-div: rdn 1/2-way: wknd 2f out* **12/1**[3]
11 1 **Lord Of Esteem** 2-9-3 0..... MickyFenton 2 51
(J Ryan) *s.s and swvd lft s: a in rr* **66/1**

1m 26.94s (0.16) **Going Correction** -0.275s/f (Firm) **11 Ran SP% 123.5**
Speed ratings (Par 96): **88,85,84,84,81 81,79,79,76,75 73**
CSF £6.21 TOTE £1.50: £1.02, £2.80, £8.00; EX 6.40.
Owner K Abdulla **Bred** Juddmonte Farms Inc **Trained** Beckhampton, Wilts
FOCUS
Fair maiden form but the slower of the two divisions by 1.60sec. The winner did not need to improve on his debut effort.
NOTEBOOK
Fifteen Love(USA), runner-up in what looked a strong maiden here last time out, was made a short price to go one better, and he did it in good style. Likely to stay another furlong, he looks the type who should be able to make his mark at a higher level. (op 4-7 tchd 8-13 in places)
Woolfall Treasure, whose debut effort here gave him a chance of a place if he was able to replicate that effort, ran well despite again not getting the clearest of runs. He looks an interesting type for nurseries over this trip and a mile, but can probably win an ordinary maiden beforehand. (op 14-1)
Dhhamaan(IRE), a half-brother to Haziem, a winner over 1m2f at three, did not cost much but he ran with plenty of promise on his debut and will get a mile later this year.

Hyde Lea Flyer, who cost 35,000gns, is out of a mare who placed over 1m1f and is a half-sister to five winners. His pedigree suggests the best of him will not be seen until he tackles middle distances next year. (op 25-1 tchd 33-1 in places)
Aussie Battler(IRE), a half-brother to Bayreuth, a prolific winner in Japan, holds a Gimcrack entry, but he will have to improve a good deal on this to be worth his place in that line-up.
Valiant Vicar(USA), who is entered in the Group 1 National Stakes, is a half-brother to three winners, including Aches N Pain, a dual sprint winner at in the US. He showed up well for a long way and should come on for the run.

3958 NSPCC E B F MAIDEN STKS (DIV II) 7f
1:55 (1:56) (Class 4) 2-Y-O **£2,521** (£2,521; £577; £288) **Stalls** High

Form RPR
543 **1** **Menadha (USA)**[33] 2949 2-9-3 0 DarrylHolland 8 81+
(M R Channon) *led: rdn and edgd lft ins fnl f: r.o: jnd post* **5/2**[1]
1 *dht* **Autocue** 2-9-3 0 NCallan 7 81+
(Sir Michael Stoute) *a.p: chsd ldr over 2f out: sn rdn: ev ch fr over 1f out: r.o to join wnr post* **5/1**
3 *4* **Pinkindie (USA)** 2-9-3 0 RichardMullen 10 71
(E A L Dunlop) *hld up: plld hrd: edgd lft and outpcd 2f out: styd on ins fnl f: nt trble ldrs* **11/1**
6 **4** *nk* **Taken (IRE)**[11] 3625 2-9-3 0 AdamKirby 2 70
(J R Fanshawe) *hmpd s: hld up: hdwy over 2f out: rdn over 1f out: wknd ins fnl f* **7/2**[3]
5 *hd* **The Riddler (IRE)** 2-9-3 0 TPQueally 5 69
(J A Osborne) *hld up: hdwy over 2f out: rdn and edgd lft over 1f out: wknd ins fnl f* **10/1**
6 *shd* **Fool's Wildcat (USA)** 2-9-3 0 RobertHavlin 4 69
(B J Meehan) *swvd lft s: sn chsng ldrs: rdn 1/2-way: wknd ins fnl f* **3/1**[2]
00 **7** *1* **Isander (USA)**[31] 2991 2-9-3 0 OscarUrbina 3 66
(Mrs A J Perrett) *chsd wnr over 4f: sn rdn: wknd fnl f* **14/1**
1m 25.34s (-1.44) **Going Correction** -0.275s/f (Firm) **7** Ran SP% **116.6**
Speed ratings (Par 96): **97,97,92,92,91 91,90**
Win: A 2.70, M 1.60; Pl A 2.40, M 1.80; Ex: A-M 8.80, M-A 9.10; CSF: A-M 9.28, M-A 8.00.
Owner Sheikh Ahmed Al Maktoum **Bred** Calumet Farm **Trained** West Ilsley, Berks
Owner K Abdulla **Bred** Juddmonte Farms Ltd **Trained** Newmarket, Suffolk

FOCUS
A smaller field lined up for this second division of the maiden, but it was the quicker of the two by 1.60sec. The form seems sound.

NOTEBOOK
Menadha(USA), who had already had three starts, put his experience to good use and attempted to make all. Given a good front-running ride over this longer trip, he was forced to share the spoils on the line, but his previous efforts had suggested he was good enough to win a race such as this, and the pair finished clear of the rest. (op 10-3)
Autocue, a half-brother to Secret Tune, a dual winner over 1m2f and 1m4f at three, was always well placed in a fairly steadily-run race, and he ran on well to join Menadha on the line. He looks the type to improve in a stronger-run race, and easier ground may also be of benefit. (op 10-3)
Pinkindie(USA), whose price rose to 120,000gns when he was sold at the breeze-ups earlier this year, is a half-brother to Big Strike, a dual sprint winner at two in the US, and to a dual winner in Japan. This race was not really run to suit and, as his stable's runners tend to need their debuts, he looks the type to do better in time. (op 8-1)
Taken(IRE) did not seem to improve on his debut perfomance, although this was a slowly-run affair which probably did not suit him. (tchd 4-1)
The Riddler(IRE), whose dam was quite a useful dual winner over sprint trips at two, looks the type to improve with racing. (op 12-1)
Fool's Wildcat(USA), who cost 100,000gns at the breeze-ups, is a half-brother to six winners in the US, mainly at sprint distances. Entered in the Group 1 National Stakes, he should improve for this debut outing. (tchd 7-2)

3959 WOODFORD RESERVE H'CAP 1m 2f
2:25 (2:27) (Class 3) (0-95,89) 3-Y-O+
£8,724 (£2,612; £1,306; £653; £326; £163) **Stalls** Centre

Form RPR
4102 **1** **Sahrati**[21] 3335 3-9-2 **87** PaulDoe 11 95
(C E Brittain) *chsd ldrs: rdn and hung lft fr over 3f out: led 1f out: styd on* **5/1**[3]
-420 **2** *1/2* **King Charles**[16] 3460 3-8-13 **89** PatrickHills(5) 1 96
(E A L Dunlop) *chsd ldrs: led 2f out: rdn and hdd 1f out: styd on* **13/2**
3020 **3** *1 1/2* **Wind Star**[38] 2755 4-10-0 **89** SteveDrowne 12 93
(G A Swinbank) *hld up: hdwy u.p over 1f out: edgd rt ins fnl f: nt rch ldrs* **6/1**
3164 **4** *hd* **Just Observing**[45] 2551 4-9-0 **75** (p) MickyFenton 6 79
(P T Midgley) *prom: rdn over 3f out: styd on* **25/1**
1660 **5** *1* **Hassaad**[14] 3558 4-9-7 **85** LiamJones(3) 10 87
(W J Haggas) *s.s: bhd: rdn over 2f out: hung rt and styd on ins fnl f: nvr nrr* **10/3**[1]
3440 **6** *hd* **Sgt Schultz (IRE)**[31] 2994 4-9-1 **81** TolleyDean(5) 13 82
(J S Moore) *hld up: hdwy 1/2-way: rdn over 1f out: styd on same pce* **33/1**
-600 **7** *1* **Frosty Night (IRE)**[9] 3691 3-8-5 **76** NickyMackay 9 75
(M Johnston) *prom: lost pl 1/2-way: swtchd lft over 1f out: styd on* **33/1**
2340 **8** *3/4* **Active Asset (IRE)**[15] 3509 5-9-10 **85** DarrylHolland 2 83
(M Quinn) *chsd ldrs: rdn over 3f out: wknd fnl f* **16/1**
0-61 **9** *nk* **Kerriemuir Lass (IRE)**[49] 2474 4-9-13 **88** NCallan 8 85
(M A Jarvis) *led: rdn and hdd 2f out: wknd ins fnl f* **9/2**[2]
12-0 **10** *1* **Five A Side**[54] 2305 3-8-11 **85** GregFairley(3) 7 80
(M Johnston) *chsd ldr: rdn over 2f out: wknd fnl f* **14/1**
0064 **11** *6* **Counsel's Opinion (IRE)**[22] 3272 10-9-11 **86** GeorgeBaker 3 69
(C F Wall) *hld up: hdwy u.p over 2f out: wknd and eased fnl f* **9/1**
2m 2.46s (-3.98) **Going Correction** -0.275s/f (Firm)
WFA 3 from 4yo+ 10lb **11** Ran SP% **117.8**
Speed ratings (Par 107): **104,103,102,102,101 101,100,99,99,98 94**
CSF £36.88 CT £198.84 TOTE £6.00: £2.10, £2.70, £2.40; EX 39.00 Trifecta £223.30 Part won. Pool £314.60 - 0.60 winning units..
Owner Saeed Manana **Bred** Darley **Trained** Newmarket, Suffolk

FOCUS
A competitive handicap run at a good pace and straightforward to rate through the third and fourth.

NOTEBOOK
Sahrati, who ran well in defeat at Sandown last time despite not getting a clear run, gained deserved compensation and appreciated the decent pace. He shapes as though he will get further and represents a stable that is in good form at present. (op 9-2)
King Charles, a little below form in a stronger heat over this course and distance at the July meeting, had a 5lb claimer up to help reduce the burden this time. He ran well, but is likely to pay for it with another rise in the weights now. (op 7-1)
Wind Star, back over the trip at which he finished runner-up in the Zetland Gold Cup earlier in the season, looked to be given too much to do and got going all too late. (op 13-2 tchd 7-1)
Just Observing ran a fair race back up in grade but he has looked held off marks in the mid-70s and this performance, although solid, seemed to confirm that view.
Hassaad was suited by the return to running on fast ground, but he lost his race by giving up lengths with a slow start. He also hung right late on so he might not be entirely straightforward. (op 7-2)
Sgt Schultz(IRE), who has still to win a race on turf, remains on a stiff enough mark.
Frosty Night(IRE), who has dropped 11lb in the handicap since the beginning of the season, ran with a bit more promise this time. (op 28-1)
Kerriemuir Lass(IRE) tried to make it a good test down in trip but she was taken on for the lead and failed to run to her best. (tchd 5-1)

3960 WALKER TRANSPORT SERVICES H'CAP 1m
2:55 (2:57) (Class 3) (0-90,90) 3-Y-O
£8,724 (£2,612; £1,306; £653; £326; £163) **Stalls** High

Form RPR
016 **1** **Ragheed (USA)**[51] 2400 3-8-5 **77** LiamJones(3) 6 87
(W J Haggas) *led: hdd over 3f out: led 2f out: sn rdn: styd on gamely* **11/2**[3]
021 **2** *1* **Cactus Rose**[20] 3349 3-9-0 **83** SteveDrowne 1 91
(R Charlton) *hld up in tch: rdn and ev ch fr over 1f out: unable qckn towards fin* **7/2**[1]
231 **3** *1 1/4* **Duchess Royale (IRE)**[19] 3387 3-8-4 **80** (v) JamieHamblett(7) 4 85
(Sir Michael Stoute) *trckd ldrs: rdn and hung rt over 1f out: styd on* **11/2**[3]
16-6 **4** *2* **Manchurian**[63] 2040 3-9-2 **90** LukeMorris(5) 3 91
(M J Wallace) *trckd ldrs: rdn over 1f out: styd on same pce* **6/1**
0-00 **5** *nk* **Millestan (IRE)**[17] 3430 3-9-0 **83** NickyMackay 9 83
(H R A Cecil) *chsd ldrs: rdn over 2f out: no ex fnl f* **11/1**
2112 **6** *1 3/4* **Milla's Rocket (IRE)**[15] 3495 3-8-10 **79** (b) NCallan 10 75
(K A Ryan) *stmbld s: chsd wnr tl led over 3f out: hdd 2f out: sn rdn: wknd fnl f* **5/1**[2]
200 **7** *2 1/2* **Cesc**[57] 2213 3-9-7 **90** DarrylHolland 5 80
(P J Makin) *plld hrd and prom: rdn over 2f out: wknd over 1f out* **14/1**
-100 **8** *hd* **Hannicean**[52] 2354 3-8-9 **78** RobertHavlin 11 68
(M A Jarvis) *hld up: rdn over 2f out: a in rr* **12/1**
3-1U **9** *5* **Fort Amhurst (IRE)**[64] 1987 3-9-2 **85** DaneO'Neill 8 63
(E A L Dunlop) *hmpd sn after s: chsd ldrs: rdn over 2f out: wknd over 1f out* **8/1**
-460 **10** *9* **Teasing**[46] 2534 3-8-4 **73** ow1 (p) RichardMullen 2 31
(J Pearce) *s.s: sn prom: rdn and wknd over 2f out* **33/1**
1m 36.74s (-3.69) **Going Correction** -0.275s/f (Firm) **10** Ran SP% **120.7**
Speed ratings (Par 104): **107,106,104,102,102 100,98,98,93,84**
CSF £26.06 CT £116.52 TOTE £7.80: £2.50, £1.60, £1.80; EX 36.70 Trifecta £161.90 Part won. Pool £228.10 - 0.80 winning units..
Owner Hamdan Al Maktoum **Bred** Swordlestown Stud **Trained** Newmarket, Suffolk
■ Stewards' Enquiry : Liam Jones two-day ban: used whip with excessive frequency (Aug 8-9)

FOCUS
An interesting handicap. The first three are unexposed and are open to improvement, while the fifth is probably the best guide to the level of the form.

NOTEBOOK
Ragheed(USA) ruined his chance by racing too keenly at Sandown, but he settled better this time. Making the early running, he looked likely to be swamped when headed, but he responded well to pressure and ran on well to regain the lead and win a shade cosily in the end. This was only his fourth career start and he looks capable of improving further while the ground remains on top. (old market op 17-2, new market op 9-1)
Cactus Rose, who won a Brighton maiden last time out, looked fairly treated on a mark of 83. Coming clear with the winner, he could not quite get to grips with that rival, but the chances are that he too was well handicapped, and there should be a race to be won with him off this sort of mark. (old market 9-2, new market op 4-1 tchd 9-2 and 10-3)
Duchess Royale(IRE), winner of an ordinary Windsor maiden last time out when fitted with a first-time visor, had the headgear on again and ran a solid race in this more competitive company, although she did hang under pressure. (new market op 15-2 tchd 8-1)
Manchurian, whose juvenile form gave him a chance in this company, left his Haydock reappearance well behind and looks to be returning to form. (new market op 10-1)
Millestan(IRE) has dropped 6lb during the course of this season but she appears to remain held off her current mark. (old market op 16-1, new market op 14-1)
Milla's Rocket(IRE) has been in good form on softer ground of late, and these quicker conditions appeared to find her out. (old market op 7-1,new market op 7-1 tchd 9-2)

3961 THOROUGHBRED BREEDERS' ASSOCIATION GOLF DAY FILLIES' H'CAP 7f
3:30 (3:30) (Class 2) (0-100,96) 3-Y-O+ **£16,192** (£4,817; £2,407; £1,202) **Stalls** High

Form RPR
3223 **1** **Medley**[17] 3430 3-9-9 **93** DaneO'Neill 6 96
(R Hannon) *chsd ldrs: rdn over 2f out: styd on to ld wl ins fnl f* **7/2**[2]
410- **2** *nk* **World's Heroine (IRE)**[301] 5676 3-8-11 **81** NickyMackay 9 83
(G A Butler) *hld up: hdwy and edgd rt over 1f out: r.o wl* **11/1**
11-2 **3** *nk* **Robema**[26] 3158 4-9-2 **79** DarrylHolland 2 83
(J J Quinn) *hld up: hdwy over 2f out: rdn to ld over 1f out: edgd rt and hdd wl ins fnl f* **5/2**[1]
2-44 **4** *3/4* **High 'n Dry (IRE)**[20] 3349 3-8-3 **73** HayleyTurner 4 72
(C A Cyzer) *hld up: rdn whn bmpd over 1f out: r.o wl ins fnl f: nt rch ldrs* **14/1**
125 **5** *nk* **Telltime (IRE)**[17] 3430 3-8-7 **77** ow1 SteveDrowne 1 75
(A M Balding) *led: rdn and hdd over 1f out: styd on same pce ins fnl f* **8/1**
4106 **6** *3/4* **Chantilly Tiffany**[21] 3332 3-9-7 **91** NCallan 8 87
(E A L Dunlop) *chsd ldrs: rdn and hung lft over 1f out: styd on same pce* **8/1**
0-30 **7** *3/4* **Elusive Flash (USA)**[34] 2914 3-9-7 **96** TolleyDean(5) 7 90
(P F I Cole) *chsd ldr tl rdn over 1f out: no ex ins fnl f* **20/1**
0-04 **8** *nk* **Tagula Sunrise (IRE)**[14] 3559 5-9-8 **85** TonyHamilton 3 81
(R A Fahey) *dwlt: hld up: plld hrd: hdwy over 1f out: wknd ins fnl f* **9/2**[3]
33-0 **9** *1 3/4* **Guarantia**[21] 3332 3-9-10 **94** AdamKirby 10 83
(C E Brittain) *chsd ldrs over 5f* **25/1**
0235 **10** *nk* **Damelza (IRE)**[7] 3754 4-8-7 **70** oh1 RichardMullen 5 61
(T D Easterby) *hld up: rdn and wknd over 1f out* **10/1**
1m 24.22s (-2.56) **Going Correction** -0.275s/f (Firm)
WFA 3 from 4yo+ 7lb **10** Ran SP% **123.9**
Speed ratings (Par 96): **103,102,102,101,101 100,99,99,97,96**
CSF £44.89 CT £119.46 TOTE £4.70: £2.00, £3.30, £1.50; EX 67.00 Trifecta £263.80 Pool £371.60 - 1.00 winning units..
Owner The Queen **Bred** The Queen **Trained** East Everleigh, Wilts

FOCUS
Another competitive heat and sound form rated around the fourth and fifth.

NOTEBOOK
Medley, who ran well to finish third in a stronger race at the July meeting, probably did not need to improve too much to win this. Very consistent this season, her trainer suggested that she would not want the ground any quicker than this. (op 4-1)
World's Heroine(IRE), making a belated seasonal reappearance, shaped with distinct promise, but she might just be the type best caught fresh. (op 14-1)

Robema, successful twice on fast ground last season, had shown her versatility by running well on soft ground over 6f on her seasonal reappearance, but these conditions were expected to bring out the best in her and she was well backed. Only caught well inside the last, she ran right up to her best in defeat. (op 7-2)

High 'n Dry(IRE), making her handicap debut, stayed on from last place to get into the mix. She shaped as though finding this trip a touch on the short side, and a mile is likely to suit her. (op 12-1)

Telltime(IRE), two places behind Medley at the July meeting, carried 1lb overweight this time and did not run far off that form. (tchd 9-1)

Chantilly Tiffany won a poor conditions race on the Rowley Mile course in May and her handicap mark has suffered as a consequence. She looks held off this mark in handicap company and has struggled in Listed grade so she is not going to be easy to place. (op 7-1)

Tagula Sunrise(IRE) Official explanation: jockey said mare missed the break

3962 NSPCC MEDIAN AUCTION MAIDEN STKS 6f
4:10 (4:10) (Class 4) 2-Y-O **£3,886** (£1,156; £577; £288) **Stalls** High

Form RPR
045 **1** **Francesca D'Gorgio (USA)**[17] 3432 2-8-12 0 (v) NCallan 7 88+
(J Noseda) *chsd ldr: led over 2f out: hung lft and rdn clr fr over 1f out* **10/11**[1]
4 **2** *3* **Major Willy**[83] 1498 2-9-3 0 TPQueally 3 84
(W Jarvis) *s.i.s: sn chsng ldrs: rdn over 1f out: sn outpcd* **7/1**[3]
2233 **3** *2 1/2* **Aaim For Applause**[15] 3479 2-9-3 0 DarryllHolland 8 76
(M R Channon) *prom: rdn over 2f out: styd on same pce appr fnl f* **7/2**[2]
62 **4** *1/2* **Mudhish (IRE)**[12] 3596 2-8-12 0 AhmedAjtebi(5) 11 75+
(C E Brittain) *chsd ldrs: outpcd 2f out: rdn and hung lft over 1f out: styd on ins fnl f* **16/1**
0 **5** *1/2* **Mr Keppel (IRE)**[15] 3478 2-9-3 0 RobertHavlin 1 73
(J A Osborne) *hld up: hdwy 2f out: no ex fnl f* **40/1**
6 *3/4* **Alls Fair** 2-9-3 0 TonyHamilton 2 71
(R Hannon) *led over 3f: wknd fnl f* **20/1**
7 *1 1/4* **Driven Snow** 2-8-12 0 SteveDrowne 5 62
(R Charlton) *dwlt: sn pushed along in rr: styd on fnl f: nvr nrr* **14/1**
8 *shd* **Shadow Cabinet (IRE)** 2-9-3 0 HayleyTurner 10 67
(M L W Bell) *mid-div: sn drvn along: styd on ins fnl f: n.d* **33/1**
06 **9** *1* **Flying Applause**[19] 3363 2-8-12 0 PatrickHills(5) 6 64
(A King) *trckd ldrs: plld hrd: rdn and wknd over 1f out* **33/1**
0 **10** *hd* **Gipsy Prince**[16] 3465 2-9-3 0 RichardMullen 18 63
(M G Quinlan) *chsd ldrs over 4f* **25/1**
11 *1* **Flashy Photon** 2-9-3 0 DaneO'Neill 4 60
(H Candy) *s.i.s: hld up: sme hdwy over 2f out: sn wknd* **25/1**
12 *nk* **Spic 'n Span** 2-9-3 0 AdamKirby 13 59
(C A Cyzer) *hung lft 4f out: a in rr* **50/1**
0 **13** *nk* **Ile Royale**[31] 2992 2-8-12 0 OscarUrbina 9 53
(C N Allen) *dwlt: sn prom: rdn 1/2-way: wknd over 1f out* **100/1**
0 **14** *9* **Whodouthinkur (IRE)**[11] 3625 2-9-3 0 DMylonas 15 31
(Mrs C A Dunnett) *mid-div: wknd 1/2-way* **100/1**
06 **15** *1/2* **Valentino Sky (USA)**[7] 3747 2-9-3 0 IanMongan 17 30
(N P Littmoden) *hld up: a in rr* **33/1**
16 *2 1/2* **Jimmy Falabella (IRE)** 2-9-3 0 MickyFenton 14 22
(N A Callaghan) *s.s: outpcd* **66/1**
6 **17** *1 1/2* **Bridge Of Fermoy (IRE)**[7] 3733 2-9-0 0 RichardKingscote(3) 16 18
(N A Callaghan) *a in rr* **100/1**

1m 11.59s (-1.76) **Going Correction** -0.275s/f (Firm) **17** Ran SP% **129.8**
Speed ratings (Par 96): **100,96,92,92,91 90,88,88,87,86 85,85,84,72,72 68,66**
CSF £7.37 TOTE £1.90: £1.10, £2.00, £1.40; EX 12.30.
Owner Sir Robert Ogden **Bred** Lavin Bloodstock & Brereton C Jones **Trained** Newmarket, Suffolk

FOCUS
Not a very competitive maiden and an easy-enough task for the smart winner, who was dropping in grade from Group company.

NOTEBOOK
Francesca D'Gorgio(USA), highly tried since her debut, deserved to get off the mark and this proved a fairly straightforward task. Her trainer is now likely to return her to Group company, with the Lowther looking the likely target. Her previous efforts suggest she will demand respect at York. (tchd Evs)

Major Willy, off the track since running a promising race on his debut on the Rowley Mile course in May, had no chance with the Pattern-class winner, but he beat the rest well enough and once again suggested that he will win races in time. (tchd 13-2 tchd 15-2 in places)

Aaim For Applause, who is building up a creditable portfolio of placed efforts, has the ability to win a maiden but keeps bumping into one or two too good. His day will come. (op 9-2)

Mudhish(IRE) ran on well after getting outpaced a quarter mile out. He now has the option of nurseries. (op 25-1)

Mr Keppel(IRE), a half brother to three winners, including Devious Boy, a triple sprint winner at two and later a high-class 1m1f winner at three in the US, and Special Lad, a triple 6f to 7f winner, ran a better race than on his debut and looks to be going the right way. (tchd 33-1)

Alls Fair, who cost 50,000gns, is a half-brother to juvenile sprint winners Even Easier and Grand Place. As his pedigree suggests he showed early speed, and should come on for this debut effort.

Driven Snow, a half-sister to Temperature, a dual winner between 1m and 1m2f, looked in need of the experience but was staying on at the finish and should derive plenty from this.

Valentino Sky(USA) Official explanation: jockey said colt was unsuited by the good to firm (firm in places) ground

Jimmy Falabella(IRE) Official explanation: jockey said gelding ran green

3963 NSPCC H'CAP 1m 6f 175y
4:45 (4:45) (Class 4) (0-85,84) 3-Y-O+ **£5,181** (£1,541; £770; £384) **Stalls** Centre

Form RPR
-142 **1** **Market Forces**[29] 3058 3-8-10 **80** TedDurcan 4 94+
(H R A Cecil) *hld up: hdwy over 2f out: rdn to ld over 1f out: edgd rt and styd on wl* **2/1**[1]
1120 **2** *5* **Noble Minstrel**[35] 2887 4-9-4 **73** (t) NCallan 8 78
(S C Williams) *trckd ldrs: led 2f out: rdn and hdd over 1f out: wknd ins fnl f* **9/2**[3]
-216 **3** *1 1/4* **Latanazul**[31] 2999 3-8-10 **80** RobertHavlin 3 83
(J L Dunlop) *led: rdn and hdd 2f out: wknd over 1f out* **4/1**[2]
0632 **4** *4* **Muntami (IRE)**[29] 2887 6-8-8 **68** LukeMorris(5) 9 66
(John A Harris) *chsd ldrs: rdn over 3f out: wknd over 2f out* **7/1**
-453 **5** *2 1/2* **Boot 'n Toot**[88] 1371 6-8-12 **72** PatrickHills(5) 7 67
(C A Cyzer) *hld up: racd keenly: hdwy over 5f out: rdn and wknd over 2f out* **20/1**
0521 **6** *1* **Nimra (USA)**[16] 3473 4-9-6 **75** (b) TonyHamilton 6 68
(G A Butler) *chsd ldr tl rdn over 3f out: wknd over 2f out* **6/1**
0422 **7** *7* **Dan Buoy (FR)**[23] 3243 4-9-4 **73** DaneO'Neill 2 57
(A King) *plld hrd and sn trcking ldrs: rdn over 3f out: wknd over 2f out: eased fnl f* **8/1**

3m 7.24s (-3.80) **Going Correction** -0.275s/f (Firm)
WFA 3 from 4yo+ 15lb **7** Ran SP% **114.2**
Speed ratings (Par 105): **99,96,95,93,92 91,87**
CSF £11.20 CT £32.06 TOTE £2.90: £1.90, £2.70; EX 13.10.
Owner K Abdulla **Bred** Juddmonte Farms Ltd **Trained** Newmarket, Suffolk

FOCUS
They went a steady pace in this decent handicap but the unexposed Market Forces ran out an impressive winner and looks a stayer to follow. The placed horses set the standard.

3964 NSPCC FAMILY RACE DAY H'CAP 1m 2f
5:20 (5:23) (Class 5) (0-75,75) 3-Y-O **£3,886** (£1,156; £577; £288) **Stalls** Centre

Form RPR
0011 **1** **Ainama (IRE)**[4] 3825 3-8-2 **59** 6ex GregFairley(3) 16 71
(M Wigham) *a.p: led over 2f out: sn rdn and hung lft: styd on* **7/4**[1]
6512 **2** *1/2* **Seeking The Buck (USA)**[18] 3400 3-9-6 **74** (t) TPQueally 4 85
(M A Magnusson) *chsd ldrs: led over 3f out: rdn and hdd over 2f out: unable qckn towards fin* **12/1**
3053 **3** *1* **Alpes Maritimes**[36] 2834 3-9-5 **73** DarryllHolland 6 82
(G Wragg) *hld up: hdwy over 1f out: hung rt and r.o ins fnl f: nt rch ldrs* **8/1**[3]
5044 **4** *nk* **Tifernati**[3] 3848 3-8-8 **65** LiamJones(3) 15 73
(W J Haggas) *hld up: hdwy over 3f out: rdn and ev ch over 1f out: styng on same pce whn hmpd ins fnl f* **8/1**[3]
3256 **5** *3* **Trump Call (IRE)**[16] 3469 3-8-13 **67** TonyHamilton 2 69
(R M Beckett) *hld up: hdwy u.p 3f out: wknd fnl f* **25/1**
3041 **6** *2* **Etain (IRE)**[33] 2940 3-9-5 **73** AdamKirby 1 71
(W R Swinburn) *chsd ldrs: rdn over 3f out: wknd over 1f out* **12/1**
4102 **7** *1* **Mark Of Love (IRE)**[13] 3570 3-8-10 **71** MatthewDavies(7) 18 67
(M R Channon) *hld up: hdwy and hung lft over 1f out: wknd ins fnl f* **14/1**
3206 **8** *2 1/2* **Deadline (UAE)**[61] 2092 3-8-12 **66** MickyFenton 5 57
(P T Midgley) *prom: rdn over 2f out: wknd over 1f out* **40/1**
5333 **9** *1* **King Joshua (IRE)**[52] 2376 3-9-6 **74** AntonyProcter 8 63
(D R C Elsworth) *hld up: hdwy over 2f out: rdn and wknd over 1f out* **16/1**
464 **10** *2 1/2* **Dig Gold (USA)**[9] 3685 3-9-2 **70** NCallan 10 54
(M A Jarvis) *chsd ldrs: rdn over 2f out: sn wknd* **11/2**[2]
6414 **11** *27* **Vallemeldee (IRE)**[17] 3421 3-8-12 **66** TedDurcan 9 —
(P W D'Arcy) *hld up: rdn and wknd 3f out* **16/1**
1100 **12** *10* **Graceful Steps (IRE)**[14] 3555 3-9-6 **74** RichardMullen 13 —
(E J O'Neill) *prom: rdn over 3f out: sn wknd* **25/1**
340 **13** *12* **Djalalabad (FR)**[34] 2909 3-9-0 **68** DMylonas 14 —
(Mrs C A Dunnett) *led over 6f: rdn and wknd 2f out* **50/1**

2m 2.83s (-3.61) **Going Correction** -0.275s/f (Firm) **13** Ran SP% **119.9**
Speed ratings (Par 100): **103,102,101,101,99 97,96,94,93,91 70,62,52**
CSF £22.85 CT £126.12 TOTE £2.60: £1.30, £3.70, £2.90; EX 24.50 Place 6 £ 13.22, Place 5 £ 10.16.
Owner D Morrison **Bred** Roundhill Stud And A Stroud **Trained** Newmarket, Suffolk

FOCUS
They went a decent pace here but the form looks fairly ordinary, with the winner taking advantage of being well in under his penalty. It looks solid rated through the third and fourth.

Vallemeldee(IRE) Official explanation: jockey said filly was unsuited by the good to firm (firm in places) ground; trainer said filly was found to be lame on returning home

T/Plt: £10.80 to a £1 stake. Pool: £76,007.65. 5,115.80 winning tickets. T/Qpdt: £4.80 to a £1 stake. Pool: £3,898.70. 597.40 winning tickets. CR

3549 SALISBURY (R-H)
Saturday, July 28

OFFICIAL GOING: Soft (7.8)
Wind: moderate, half-against.

3965 BUTLER & CO. CARNARVON AMATEUR RIDERS' H'CAP 6f 212y
6:10 (6:12) (Class 5) (0-75,70) 3-Y-O+ **£3,123** (£968; £484; £242) **Stalls** Centre

Form RPR
0010 **1** **Mythical Charm**[17] 3422 8-10-1 55 (t) MrHHaynes(5) 11 64
(J J Bridger) *trckd ldrs: rdn to ld ins fnl f: r.o wl* **14/1**
0500 **2** *1 1/2* **Roman Quest**[15] 3481 4-11-5 68 MrSWalker 12 73
(H Morrison) *slowly away: hld up: hdwy 3f out: led wl over 1f out: hdd ins fnl f: kpt on* **13/2**[3]
0005 **3** *7* **Greenwood**[10] 3644 9-10-8 62 MrFFairchild(5) 1 49
(P G Murphy) *racd stands' side: swtchd lft over 1f out: r.o fnl f: no ch w first 2* **14/1**
1155 **4** *hd* **Mafaheem**[2] 3869 5-11-2 70 RichardEvans(5) 2 56
(P D Evans) *chsd ldrs: rdn over 2f out: one pce after* **5/1**[1]
2164 **5** *hd* **The Grey One (IRE)**[3] 3855 4-10-10 66 (p) MissHDavies(5) 7 52
(J M Bradley) *trckd ldr: led 3f out: hdd wl over 1f out: one pce after* **11/2**[2]
00-3 **6** *1/2* **Miss Porcia**[2] 3868 6-9-12 52 MissLAllan(5) 8 36
(P A Blockley) *prom tl wknd over 1f out* **16/1**
4606 **7** *1 1/4* **Postmaster**[26] 3173 5-9-9 51 oh1 MissSSawyer(7) 13 32
(R Ingram) *in tch on far side tl wknd over 1f out* **16/1**
-443 **8** *1/2* **Mitanni (USA)**[8] 3711 4-11-4 67 (b) MrSDobson 5 47
(Mrs A J Perrett) *bhd: sme hdwy 3f out: nvr on terms* **11/2**[2]
2460 **9** *1* **Moon Forest (IRE)**[18] 3409 5-9-13 53 (p) MissSBradley(5) 6 30
(J M Bradley) *nvr bttr than mid-div* **16/1**
50-0 **10** *4* **Pertemps Green**[10] 3644 4-10-13 62 MrDHDunsdon 3 29
(M S Saunders) *t.k.h: a bhd* **66/1**
0030 **11** *1* **Thomas Lawrence (USA)**[103] 1064 6-10-3 57 MrAshleePrice(5) 9 21
(P A Blockley) *slowly away: a bhd* **12/1**
2050 **12** *2* **Fun In The Sun**[15] 3487 3-9-5 52 (v[1]) MrPCollington(5) 14 11
(P D Evans) *led tl hdd 3f out: sn wknd* **12/1**
4154 **13** *13* **Gee Ceffyl Bach**[19] 3384 3-9-8 56 ow1 MrCAHarris(7) 4 —
(G Woodward) *a bhd: eased fnl f* **8/1**

1m 32.78s (3.72) **Going Correction** +0.60s/f (Yiel)
WFA 3 from 4yo+ 7lb **13** Ran SP% **119.7**
Speed ratings (Par 103): **102,100,92,92,91 91,89,89,88,83 82,80,65**
CSF £102.56 CT £1360.87 TOTE £17.90: £4.30, £2.30, £5.10; EX 169.00.
Owner Tommy Ware **Bred** B J And Mrs Crangle **Trained** Liphook, Hants

FOCUS
A moderate amateurs' event and a routine race of its type. The form is rated around the first two, who were clear.

The Form Book, Raceform Ltd, Compton, RG20 6NL

Mafaheem Official explanation: vet said gelding returned lame

3966 SPIRE HOMECARE LTD CLAIMING STKS 6f 212y

6:40 (6:42) (Class 5) 3-4-Y-O **£3,238** (£963; £481; £240) **Stalls** Centre

Form RPR

000 **1** **Norisan**[16] 3463 3-9-1 92 (b[1]) RyanMoore 4 73
(R Hannon) *in tch: led 2f out: sn clr* **9/4**[2]

5540 **2** *4* **Magic Mountain (IRE)**[43] 2633 3-9-0 82 RichardHughes 3 62
(R Hannon) *trckd ldr: kpt on u.p to hold 2nd ins fnl f* **11/10**[1]

0004 **3** *nk* **Task Complete**[30] 3031 4-8-7 44 StephenCarson 1 50
(Jean-Rene Auvray) *led for 1f: styd prom: r.o u.p fnl f* **9/1**

0350 **4** *hd* **Ruffie (IRE)**[74] 1740 4-8-4 55 ColinHaddon[(5)] 10 51
(Miss Gay Kelleway) *in tch: rdn and kpt on one pce fnl f* **7/1**[3]

4000 **5** *4* **Alloro**[8] 3714 3-8-5 44 (p) AlanDaly 5 41
(D J S Ffrench Davis) *led after 1f: hdd 2f out: wknd fnl f* **25/1**

0 **6** *5* **Camellia's Girl**[12] 3593 4-8-7 0 (t) FrankieMcDonald 9 26
(J J Bridger) *a struggling in rr* **100/1**

50-0 **7** *shd* **Croft (IRE)**[15] 3487 4-8-13 50 TGMcLaughlin 2 32
(M S Saunders) *outpcd thrght* **16/1**

5000 **8** *10* **Hard As Iron**[57] 2224 3-8-8 48 RichardThomas 6 5
(M Blanshard) *outpcd thrght* **20/1**

1m 31.84s (2.78) **Going Correction** +0.60s/f (Yiel)
WFA 3 from 4yo 7lb **8** Ran SP% **116.4**
Speed ratings (Par 103): **108,103,103,102,98 92,92,81**
CSF £5.08 TOTE £3.00: £1.30, £1.10, £2.50; EX 3.50.
Owner The Waney Racing Group Inc **Bred** The National Stud Owner Breeders Club Ltd **Trained** East Everleigh, Wilts

FOCUS
A one-two for trainer Richard Hannon in an uncompetitive race, in which the first two home were superior to the usual claiming-standard contestants. However, the proximity of the rest was disappointing from a form perspective and so the form is limited.

3967 HIGHLAND PARK SINGLE MALT SCOTCH WHISKY MAIDEN STKS 6f

7:10 (7:13) (Class 4) 2-Y-O **£4,210** (£1,252; £625; £312) **Stalls** Centre

Form RPR

0036 **1** **The Name Is Frank**[9] 3687 2-9-3 0 JamesDoyle 10 71
(J W Mullins) *led tl hdd over 1f out: rallied on ins to ld again ins fnl f: all out* **8/1**

2 *hd* **Tadalavil** 2-9-3 0 JHBowman 7 70+
(M R Channon) *chsd ldrs: hrd rdn fnl f to go 2nd cl home* **9/1**

3 *hd* **Monsieur Reynard** 2-8-10 0 KMay[(7)] 4 70
(B J Meehan) *hld up: hdwy on outside over 1f out to press ldrs cl home* **12/1**

02 **4** *1/2* **Kaldoun Kingdom (IRE)**[12] 3592 2-9-3 0 JimmyQuinn 8 68
(E A L Dunlop) *trckd wnr: led over 1f out: hrd rdn and hdd ins fnl f: lost 2nd pls cl home* **9/2**[3]

5 *1/2* **Sahaadi** 2-8-12 0 RichardHughes 6 62
(R Hannon) *mid-div: r.o fnl f: nvr nrr* **8/1**

0 **6** *4* **Spent**[19] 3383 2-9-3 0 GeorgeBaker 5 55
(R M Beckett) *prom on ins tl wknd 1f out* **4/1**[2]

7 *1* **Ike Quebec (FR)** 2-9-3 0 RyanMoore 9 52
(R Hannon) *mid-div: rdn over 2f out: wknd over 1f out* **3/1**[1]

0 **8** *2* **Fervent Prince**[65] 1970 2-9-3 0 PatDobbs 1 46
(H Morrison) *a bhd* **10/1**

9 *2 1/2* **Bahamian Blue (IRE)** 2-9-3 0 FergusSweeney 2 38
(H J L Dunlop) *towards rr: rdn over 2f out: wknd over 1f out* **33/1**

10 *12* **The Hoofer (IRE)** 2-8-12 0 StephenCarson 3 —
(J L Dunlop) *v.s.a and nvr got into r* **14/1**

1m 18.47s (3.49) **Going Correction** +0.60s/f (Yiel) **10** Ran SP% **121.8**
Speed ratings (Par 96): **100,99,99,98,98 92,91,88,85,69**
CSF £81.32 TOTE £9.00: £1.70, £2.50, £3.50; EX 123.50.
Owner Don Hazzard **Bred** Fifehead Farms M C Denning **Trained** Wilsford-Cum-Lake, Wilts
■ A first-ever Flat winner for trainer Seamus Mullins.

FOCUS
Hard to weigh up, especially in the ground, but run at a decent pace and likely to contain a few future winners.

NOTEBOOK
The Name Is Frank had more experience than his rivals, and put it to good use. Better suited by this 6f than 5f, he only just made it in a blanket finish, but his trainer reckons he should stay a furlong farther before long. (op 10-1 tchd 11-1)
Tadalavil, a 16,000gns son of French Guineas winner Clodovil out of an unraced mare with winners in the family, will probably settle down around a mile. However, this was a fine debut which bodes well if he is as effective on faster ground. (op 8-1 tchd 15-2 and 10-1)
Monsieur Reynard, a gelded newcomer, is a 25,000gns son of top-class sprinter Compton Place out of a mare who did well as a juvenile. Making an encouraging debut, he looked capable of following in his dam's footsteps. (op 16-1)
Kaldoun Kingdom(IRE) continues to show promise, and looks versatile as regards ground conditions. He should do well in nurseries if he cannot find a maiden. (op 4-1 tchd 3-1)
Sahaadi, a Dansili filly out of a 1m2f winner in France, shaped well and will be better for the experience. She looks as if 7f would suit, even at this early stage of her career, and should be placed to win soon. (op 4-1)
Spent, a 15,000 euros son of the sprinter Averti, has shown ability in his two races without settling the racing world alight. He looks to be heading for nurseries after one more run and, with his dam having stayed 1m4f, he is likely to be effective over longer trips than his sire as he matures. Official explanation: jockey said colt hung right-handed closing stages (op 8-1)
Ike Quebec(FR), a 55,000 euros son of Dr Fong out of a once-raced mare with winners in the family up to 1m2f, was well-backed to make a winning debut. Though well beaten in the end, he is worth another chance on better ground, and should come into his own at a mile and beyond later in his career. (op 7-2)

3968 BATHWICK TYRES MAIDEN STKS 6f

7:40 (7:43) (Class 4) 3-Y-O+ **£4,857** (£1,445; £722; £360) **Stalls** Centre

Form RPR

0-3 **1** **Raglan Copenhagen**[35] 2878 3-9-3 0 JHBowman 5 67
(B R Millman) *t.k.h: trckd ldr: led 2f out: drvn clr fnl f* **13/8**[1]

60 **2** *3* **Dirty Dancing**[29] 3062 3-8-10 0 AshtonByles[(7)] 1 57
(B W Hills) *hld up in rr: hdwy over 1f out: r.o to go 2nd ins fnl f* **15/2**[2]

0 **3** *1/2* **Vogarth**[28] 3102 3-9-3 0 SaleemGolam 4 56
(B R Millman) *chsd ldrs: styd on to go 2nd over 1f out: one pce and lost 2nd nr fin* **14/1**

4 *3 1/2* **Debdene Bank (IRE)** 4-9-3 0 VinceSlattery 7 41
(Mrs Mary Hambro) *slowly away: rdn over 2f out: nvr rchd ldrs* **20/1**

0-66 **5** *1 3/4* **Madam Patti**[29] 3046 4-9-3 38 SteveDrowne 8 36
(R Ingram) *chsd ldrs tl rdn and wknd over 1f out* **10/1**[3]

5220 **6** *3* **Spiffing (IRE)**[23] 3237 3-9-3 68 GeorgeBaker 2 31
(R M Beckett) *in tch: rdn 2f out: wknd over 1f out* **13/8**[1]

0-6 **7** *3* **Mirko**[18] 3395 3-9-3 0 FergusSweeney 6 22
(B R Millman) *led tl hdd 2f out: sn wknd* **12/1**

- **8** *7* **Cadeaux Cerise (IRE)** 3-8-6 0 ow1 KylieManser[(7)] 3 —
(N I M Rossiter) *v.s.a: racd alone stands' side and a bhd* **33/1**

1m 17.67s (2.69) **Going Correction** +0.60s/f (Yiel)
WFA 3 from 4yo 5lb **8** Ran SP% **119.1**
Speed ratings (Par 105): **106,102,101,96,94 90,86,77**
CSF £16.39 TOTE £3.00: £1.40, £1.30, £3.60; EX 12.80.
Owner W Walsh **Bred** Mrs Maureen Barbara Walsh **Trained** Kentisbeare, Devon

FOCUS
A weakish maiden, but the first three home should win their share of prizemoney at a realistic level.
Spiffing(IRE) Official explanation: trainer said colt was scoped on returning home and was found to have a respiratory infection

3969 TIM OWEN MEMORIAL H'CAP 1m 6f 21y

8:10 (8:13) (Class 5) (0-75,72) 3-Y-0+ **£3,238** (£963; £481; £240)

Form RPR

-521 **1** **Squadron**[43] 2628 3-9-1 **72** RyanMoore 8 79+
(Mrs A J Perrett) *led after 1f: rdn 2f out: kpt up to work and in command fnl f* **11/8**[1]

1-01 **2** *2 1/2* **Rehearsed (IRE)**[14] 3554 4-10-0 **71** SteveDrowne 5 74
(H Morrison) *trckd ldrs: wnt 2nd over 1f out: styd on but nt rch wnr* **5/1**[2]

3200 **3** *1* **Critical Stage (IRE)**[39] 640 8-8-7 **57** HaddenFrost[(7)] 1 59
(J D Frost) *led for 1f: trckd wnr tl over 1f out: nt qckn fnl f* **7/1**

4045 **4** *shd* **Treason Trial**[30] 3033 6-8-12 **55** oh5 JamesDoyle 3 57+
(Stef Liddiard) *hld up: short of room whn hdwy and swtchd lft ent fnl f: styd on* **6/1**[3]

006 **5** *nk* **The Composer**[23] 3243 5-9-1 **58** FergusSweeney 7 59
(M Blanshard) *in tch: rdn 3f out: kpt on fnl f* **9/1**

-000 **6** *2 1/2* **Merchant Bankes**[35] 2890 4-8-12 **55** oh3 SaleemGolam 2 53
(W G M Turner) *in tch: hung lft over 2f out: wknd ins fnl f* **40/1**

4000 **7** *7* **Benny The Bat**[45] 2558 3-8-9 **66** PatDobbs 6 54
(K O Cunningham-Brown) *a bhd: lost tch 4f out* **14/1**

2630 **8** *13* **Adversane**[16] 3473 3-8-12 **69** (v[1]) StephenCarson 4 39
(J L Dunlop) *t.k.h: hld up: wknd wl over 2f out* **8/1**

3m 16.2s (9.20) **Going Correction** +0.60s/f (Yiel)
WFA 3 from 4yo+ 14lb **8** Ran SP% **115.8**
Speed ratings (Par 103): **97,95,95,94,94 93,89,81**
CSF £8.58 CT £35.71 TOTE £2.50: £1.10, £2.10, £2.60; EX 6.60.
Owner Highclere Thoroughbred Racing XXXVI **Bred** B Root **Trained** Pulborough, W Sussex

FOCUS
A modest staying handicap, but the winner looks progressive on soft ground. However, the form is limited, with the fourth and sixth racing from out of the handicap. Hand-timed.

3970 UNITED TAXIS & VALUE CARS FILLIES' H'CAP 6f 212y

8:40 (8:42) (Class 4) (0-85,85) 3-Y-0+ **£6,477** (£1,927; £963; £481) **Stalls** Centre

Form RPR

0-11 **1** **Our Faye**[26] 3154 4-9-12 **79** GeorgeBaker 1 91
(S Kirk) *in tch: wnt 2nd over 2f out: qcknd to ld over 1f out: r.o wl* **5/1**

6-12 **2** *2 1/2* **Ventura (USA)**[12] 3591 3-9-11 **85** RichardHughes 2 87
(Mrs A J Perrett) *led tl rdn and hdd over 1f out: kpt on to hold 2nd but no ch w wnr ins fnl f* **6/4**[1]

1234 **3** *1/2* **Lavenham (IRE)**[15] 3488 4-9-10 **77** RyanMoore 6 81
(R Hannon) *racd in tch thrght: one pce fnl f* **4/1**[3]

4234 **4** *1* **Angel Sprints**[9] 3682 5-9-8 **75** SaleemGolam 4 76
(C J Down) *trckd ldr to over 2f out: wknd fnl f* **11/1**

0116 **5** *3 1/2* **Skyelady**[14] 3525 4-9-6 **78** NeilBrown[(5)] 3 70
(T D Barron) *hld up: rdn 2f out: no hdwy after* **5/2**[2]

1m 34.07s (5.01) **Going Correction** +0.60s/f (Yiel)
WFA 3 from 4yo+ 7lb **5** Ran SP% **113.6**
Speed ratings (Par 102): **95,92,91,90,86**
CSF £13.48 TOTE £4.60: £2.30, £1.40; EX 7.80 Place 6 £188.54, Place 5 £22.81..
Owner J B J Richards **Bred** J B J Richards **Trained** Upper Lambourn, Berks

FOCUS
A decent turnout for the money in terms of quality, but short on numbers. The form looks sound enough, rated around the winner and third.
T/Plt: £227.00 to a £1 stake. Pool: £47,309.10. 152.10 winning tickets. T/Qpdt: £29.40 to a £1 stake. Pool: £4,122.50. 103.60 winning tickets. JS

3884 YORK (L-H)

Saturday, July 28

OFFICIAL GOING: Heavy (soft in places; 5.6)

After two dry days the ground was described as 'testing, very patchy, sticky and very hard work'. The course was narrowed and the safety limit set at 12.
Wind: fresh half-against Weather: fine but blustery

3971 SKYPOKER.COM CLAIMING STKS 1m

1:40 (1:40) (Class 4) 3-Y-0+ **£6,477** (£1,927; £963; £481) **Stalls** Low

Form RPR

0430 **1** **Nevada Desert (IRE)**[4] 3813 7-8-12 78 MichaelJStainton[(5)] 7 78
(R M Whitaker) *led: hdd wl over 2f out and sn rdn along: rallied to ld appr fnl f: drvn out* **11/4**[2]

0062 **2** *1 1/4* **Waterside (IRE)**[14] 3527 8-9-7 88 JimCrowley 5 80
(G L Moore) *trckd ldrs: smooth hdwy 4f out: led wl over 2f out: rdn and hdd appr fnl f: kpt on same pce* **11/4**[2]

0046 **3** *3/4* **Kudbeme**[5] 3793 5-8-6 59 JamieMoriarty[(3)] 2 66
(N Bycroft) *dwlt: sn in tch: hdwy on outer 4f out: rdn to chse ldng pair wl over 1f out: drvn and one pce ins fnl f* **16/1**

5442 **4** *7* **Moonlight Man**[14] 3525 6-9-2 89 PatDobbs 4 58
(R Hannon) *trckd ldrs: hdwy on inner 3f out: rdn 2f out: sn drvn and btn over 1f out* **9/4**[1]

5620 **5** *3/4* **Efidium**[7] 3754 9-8-6 68 DanielleMcCreery[(7)] 1 54
(N Bycroft) *s.i.s: a in rr* **13/2**[3]

-000 **6** *1 1/4* **Just Dust**[9] 3682 3-8-7 74 PaulMulrennan 6 53
(M W Easterby) *in tch: rdn along 1/2-way: sn wknd* **20/1**

0000 **7** *3 1/2* **Drury Lane (IRE)**[13] 3567 7-8-7 45 (b) AnnStokell[(5)] 3 43
(Miss A Stokell) *a towards rr* **100/1**

0345 **8** *4* **Punta Galera (IRE)**[14] 3530 4-8-12 70 RussellKennemore[(5)] 8 39
(Paul Green) *cl up: rdn along 4f out and sn wknd* **14/1**

1m 43.91s (4.41) **Going Correction** +0.675s/f (Yiel)
WFA 3 from 4yo+ 8lb **8** Ran SP% **115.7**
Speed ratings (Par 105): **104,102,102,95,94 93,89,85**
CSF £10.95 TOTE £4.70: £1.20, £1.50, £6.70; EX 14.80.Moonlight Man was claimed by R Harris for £18,000.

Owner J Barry Pemberton **Bred** Bryan Ryan **Trained** Scarcroft, W Yorks

FOCUS
A decent claimer but the form looks unreliable with the third too close and the seventh not that far away.

Punta Galera(IRE) Official explanation: jockey said gelding was unsuited by the heavy (soft in places) ground

3972 SKYBET.COM E B F FILLIES' STKS (H'CAP) 1m 2f 88y
2:10 (2:10) (Class 3) (0-90,80) 3-Y-O+ **£9,715** (£2,890; £1,444; £721) **Stalls** Low

Form RPR

2623 **1** **Gull Wing (IRE)**[32] 2971 3-9-7 **80** JamieSpencer 2 93+
(M L W Bell) *hld up in rr: wd st: gd hdwy 3f out: rdn to ld wl over 1f out and sn clr: easily* **7/2**[2]

5001 **2** 4 **Sell Out**[32] 2971 3-9-6 **79** JimCrowley 3 82
(G Wragg) *hld up in rr: wd st: hdwy 3f out: rdn along 2f out: styd on to chse wnr ins fnl f: no imp* **13/2**

-003 **3** 1 1/4 **Milliegait**[18] 3400 3-9-2 **75** TQuinn 7 76
(T D Easterby) *led: styd far side st: rdn along 3f out: drvn and hdd wl over 1f out: kpt on same pce* **10/1**

-302 **4** 1 1/2 **Sunisa (IRE)**[37] 2794 6-9-13 **76** PaulMulrennan 4 74
(J Mackie) *trckd ldrs: styd far side st: effrt over 3f out: sn rdn and plugged on same pce fnl 2f* **10/1**

4631 **5** 5 **Sister Maria (USA)**[28] 3107 3-9-5 **78** MartinDwyer 8 66
(E A L Dunlop) *trckd ldr: wd st: effrt 3f out and ev ch tl rdn 2f out and sn wknd* **5/1**[3]

3-21 **6** 1/2 **Circle Of Love**[26] 3160 3-9-6 **79** KerrinMcEvoy 5 66
(J L Dunlop) *trckd ldrs: wd st: effrt 3f out: sn rdn and btn 2f out* **15/8**[1]

4314 **7** nk **Musical Beat**[10] 3645 3-9-6 **79** KDarley 6 65
(Miss V Haigh) *chsd ldrs: styd far side st: hdwy 4f out: rdn to chal 3f out and ev ch tl drvn 2f out and sn wknd* **20/1**

5506 **8** 44 **Daring Affair**[65] 1979 6-9-13 **76** PatCosgrave 1 —
(K R Burke) *chsd ldrs: rdn along over 4f out: sn wknd and bhd* **14/1**

2m 16.13s (3.63) **Going Correction** +0.675s/f (Yiel)
WFA 3 from 6yo 10lb **8 Ran SP% 116.6**
Speed ratings (Par 104): **104,100,99,98,94 94,93,58**
CSF £27.03 CT £208.72 TOTE £4.80: £1.70, £2.30, £2.60; EX 29.60 Trifecta £181.40 Part won. Pool £255.05 - 0.50 winning units..

Owner Lady Bamford **Bred** Lady Bamford **Trained** Newmarket, Suffolk

FOCUS
A fair fillies' handicap in which four came to the outside rail in the home straight including the first two. The pace was just ordinary but it turned out to be a true test in the bad ground and the form is given a chance for now.

NOTEBOOK
Gull Wing(IRE), meeting the runner-up on 4lb better terms, was shuffled back early on. She came there with a smooth run and had it won in a matter of strides. Some black type is the target now.

Sell Out, 4lb higher, showed a much better attitude under pressure this time but in the end was no match. (op 6-1)

Milliegait, keen to lead, stuck to her task in willing fashion but in the end the first two, racing wide of her, proved too good. (op 9-1 tchd 17-2)

Sunisa(IRE) looked at her best but is still on the same mark as her last win over a year ago now.

Sister Maria(USA) was running from a 5lb higher mark in a much more competitive event. (op 9-2)

Circle Of Love, wide-margin winner of a weak maiden at Pontefract, found this a different ball game. Official explanation: trainer's rep said he had no explanation for the poor form shown (op 11-4)

3973 SKYBET.COM SILVER CUP STKS (H'CAP) (LISTED RACE) 1m 6f
2:40 (2:40) (Cl 1)(0-110,102) 3-Y-O+ **£19,873** (£7,532; £3,769; £1,879; £941) **Stalls** Low

Form RPR

30-2 **1** **Wing Collar**[7] 3753 6-9-2 92 (p) PaulMulrennan 4 103
(T D Easterby) *in rr: pushed along and outpcd over 5f out: hdwy 3f out: rdn to chse ldr wl over 1f out: drvn and styd on to ld ins fnl f: r.o wl* **7/2**[2]

6662 **2** 3/4 **Macorville (USA)**[28] 3090 4-9-2 92 KDarley 3 102
(G M Moore) *led: qcknd over 4f out: rdn and qcknd 3f out: drvn over 1f out: hdd and kpt on same pce ins fnl f* **8/11**[1]

2220 **3** 8 **Shawhill**[14] 3564 3-8-0 90 DavidKinsella 5 89
(Tom Dascombe) *chsd ldr: hdwy to chal over 4f out and sn rdn: drvn 3f and grad wknd fnl 2f* **10/1**

-654 **4** 1 1/2 **The Whistling Teal**[70] 1833 11-9-10 100 JimCrowley 2 97
(G Wragg) *trckd ldng pair: effrt 4f out: sn rdn along and wknd wl over 2f out* **8/1**[3]

4030 **5** 6 **Akarem**[35] 2856 6-9-12 102 PatCosgrave 7 90
(K R Burke) *trckd ldng pair: effrt 4f out: rdn along over 3f out: sn wknd* **8/1**[3]

3m 8.04s (8.54) **Going Correction** +0.675s/f (Yiel)
WFA 3 from 4yo+ 14lb **5 Ran SP% 111.4**
Speed ratings: **102,101,97,96,92**
CSF £6.62 TOTE £4.30: £2.00, £1.10; EX 7.80.

Owner Mr & Mrs J D Cotton **Bred** B Freiha **Trained** Great Habton, N Yorks
■ This race was transferred from John Smith's Cup day, when it could not be run as parts of the back straight were waterlogged.

FOCUS
Macorville wound it up from the front and gave his all but in the end had to settle for second best, the pair clear although the gap to the third has not been taken too literally in rating the race. The winner confirmed that he has improved again this year.

NOTEBOOK
Wing Collar, the cheekpieces on for this quick return to action, was matched at 60 when detached and struggling on the turn in. He stuck to his guns and master the runner-up late in the day and his penalty should ensure he gets a run in the Ebor. (tchd 4-1)

Macorville(USA), 4lb higher than when runner-up in the Northumberland Plate, wound it up from the front, but after giving his all he had to give best in the closing stages. He looked whacked afterwards and may need time to recover from this. (op 11-10)

Shawhill, 18lb higher than when runner-up in a Windsor handicap, in the end proved no match for the first two. (tchd 8-1)

The Whistling Teal, proven on heavy ground, again ran well below his best and surely retirement beckons sooner rather than later. (op 9-2)

Akarem, with the headgear left off, was warm at the gate and would not drop the bit. He continues off the boil. (tchd 7-1)

3974 SKY BET YORK STKS (GROUP 2) 1m 2f 88y
3:15 (3:15) (Class 1) 3-Y-O+
£56,780 (£21,520; £10,770; £5,370; £2,690; £1,350) **Stalls** Low

Form RPR

-001 **1** **Stage Gift (IRE)**[44] 2617 4-9-2 112 JamieSpencer 7 117+
(Saeed Bin Suroor) *hld up in tch gng wl: smooth hdwy to trck ldrs over 2f out: swtchd lft and rdn to chal over 1f out: wandered and led ins fnl f: styd on* **8/1**[3]

523U **2** 1 1/4 **Eagle Mountain**[14] 3566 3-8-6 0 JAHeffernan 5 114
(A P O'Brien, Ire) *trckd ldrs: hdwy 3f out: effrt to chal 2f out: sn rdn and ev ch tl drvn and nt qckn ins fnl f* **6/5**[1]

-321 **3** hd **Take A Bow**[58] 2182 6-9-2 113 JimCrowley 2 114
(P R Chamings) *a.p: hdwy to ld wl over 2f out and sn rdn: drvn over 1f out: hdd and no ex ins fnl f* **9/1**

12/1 **4** 2 **Winged Cupid (IRE)**[28] 3103 4-9-2 111 KerrinMcEvoy 3 110
(Saeed Bin Suroor) *prom: pushed along 3f out: rdn 2f out: kpt on same pce appr fnl f* **11/4**[2]

5410 **5** 1/2 **Mango Mischief (IRE)**[11] 3628 6-8-13 102 KDarley 4 106
(M R Channon) *led: rdn along 3f out and sn hdd: styd cl up and ev ch tl drvn and wknd appr fnl f* **28/1**

1241 **6** 1 1/2 **Charlie Tokyo (IRE)**[14] 3558 4-9-2 100 (b) JamieMoriarty 6 106
(R A Fahey) *hld up in rr: hdwy 3f out: sn rdn and no imp* **10/1**

-230 **7** 2 1/2 **Mashaahed**[16] 3461 4-9-2 112 MartinDwyer 8 101
(B W Hills) *hld up: effrt and sme hdwy 3f out: rdn over 2f out and sn btn* **20/1**

1253 **8** 23 **Blue Bajan (IRE)**[22] 3271 5-9-2 111 AdrianTNicholls 1 58
(Andrew Turnell) *trckd ldrs: hdwy 4f out: rdn to chal 3f out: sn drvn and wknd over 2f out* **16/1**

2m 13.31s (0.81) **Going Correction** +0.675s/f (Yiel)
WFA 3 from 4yo+ 10lb **8 Ran SP% 116.4**
Speed ratings (Par 115): **115,114,113,112,111 110,108,90**
CSF £18.43 TOTE £10.20: £2.50, £1.20, £2.80; EX 29.20 Trifecta £162.00 Pool £570.60 - 2.50 winning units..

Owner Godolphin **Bred** Ballymacoll Stud Farm Ltd **Trained** Newmarket, Suffolk
■ Stewards' Enquiry : Martin Dwyer two-day ban: careless riding (Aug 8-9)

FOCUS
The field came over to the nearside rail in the straight. Decent form for the grade in only the second running of this event, with Stage Gift up 2lb on his Longchamp effort and Eagle Mountain running to a similar level as the Irish Derby but 7lb off his Epsom form. The overall level is limited by the fifth and sixth.

NOTEBOOK
Stage Gift(IRE) ◆ confirmed the good impression he had made at Longchamp last month. Ridden differently, he travelled best and, pulled out with over a furlong to run, went on to win a shade readily despite hanging and not appearing to be at home in the heavy ground. He is regarded as a Group 1 performer by connections and may be given the chance to prove his worth at that level in the Juddmonte International over this course and distance next month. (op 7-1)

Eagle Mountain, the Derby runner-up and Irish Derby third, was down in trip and tackling older opposition for the first time. Briefly outpaced by the leaders in the straight, he came through to hold every chance but lacked a change of pace in this ground. He will be happier back on a sound surface. (op 6-4 tchd 13-8)

Take A Bow, off the track since a narrow win in the Group 3 Brigadier Gerard Stakes at Sandown two months ago, took a narrow lead with over two to run and battled on willingly once headed. He is a tough and consistent performer. (tchd 10-1)

Winged Cupid(IRE), a shorter-priced stablemate of the winner, was stepping up to this trip for the first time and appeared to stay, but lacked the pace to go with the leaders inside the last quarter mile. This lightly-raced colt has tackled testing ground on his last three runs and remains relatively unexposed on a sound surface. (tchd 3-1)

Mango Mischief(IRE), back against male opponents and up in grade having contested exclusively Listed races this term, set a reasonable pace and stuck on as best she could when headed. (op 33-1)

Charlie Tokyo(IRE) landed the John Smith's Cup over slightly shorter here earlier this month, but faced a stiff task on this big rise in grade and was unable to trouble the principals. (op 12-1 tchd 9-1)

Mashaahed, reverting to hold-up tactics on this drop back in trip, was never able to get into the hunt and gave the impression he was not putting it all in.

Blue Bajan(IRE) Official explanation: jockey said gelding ran flat

3975 SKY BET DASH (HERITAGE H'CAP) 6f
3:50 (3:50) (Class 2) (0-105,103) 3-Y-O+
£31,160 (£9,330; £4,665; £2,335; £1,165; £585) **Stalls** Low

Form RPR

2220 **1** **Zomerlust**[15] 3505 5-9-5 **94** (v[1]) GrahamGibbons 5 103
(J J Quinn) *rrd s: swtchd rt after s: hld up: hdwy on ins over 2f out: qcknd to ld over 1f out: hld on towards fin* **8/1**

2016 **2** 3/4 **Turnkey**[15] 3500 5-8-13 **95** AdeleRothery[(7)] 12 102
(D Nicholls) *hld up in rr: nt clr run over 2f out: gd hdwy on inner over 1f out: styd on wl to chse wnr ins fnl f* **14/1**

3010 **3** 1/2 **Green Park (IRE)**[13] 3573 4-9-4 **93** TQuinn 11 98
(R A Fahey) *hld up: hdwy on ins over 2f out: chsd wnr appr fnl f: no ex ins fnl f* **9/1**

100- **4** 5 **Philharmonic**[289] 5921 6-9-7 **99** JamieMoriarty[(3)] 8 89
(R A Fahey) *trckd ldrs: wknd appr fnl f* **9/1**

0005 **5** 1 1/2 **The Kiddykid (IRE)**[15] 3489 7-9-4 **93** (v) StephenDonohoe 7 79
(P D Evans) *w ldr: wknd appr fnl f* **12/1**

-000 **6** 3/4 **Invincible Force (IRE)**[14] 3529 3-9-4 **98** MartinDwyer 9 82
(Paul Green) *led: hung lft and hdd over 1f out: sn wknd* **33/1**

3050 **7** 1 3/4 **Gift Horse**[15] 3505 7-9-6 **95** KerrinMcEvoy 2 73
(D Nicholls) *in rr: hdwy on outer over 2f out: wknd over 1f out* **8/1**

3131 **8** 1 3/4 **El Bosque (IRE)**[19] 3380 3-9-4 **103** JamesMillman[(5)] 6 76
(B R Millman) *chsd ldrs: lost pl 2f out* **13/2**[3]

3045 **9** nk **Bahamian Pirate (USA)**[15] 3500 12-9-2 **91** AdrianTNicholls 1 63
(D Nicholls) *chsd ldrs on outer: lost pl over 1f out* **12/1**

2046 **10** 1 1/2 **River Falcon**[12] 3586 7-9-6 **95** PatCosgrave 4 63
(J S Goldie) *in tch: sn drvn along: lost pl over 1f out* **10/1**

3401 **11** 15 **Fullandby (IRE)**[12] 3586 5-9-8 **97** KDarley 3 20
(T J Etherington) *hld up in mid-div: stmbld over 2f out: swtchd lft: lost pl over 1f out: eased and sn bhd: struck into* **11/2**[2]

203 **R** **Skhilling Spirit**[14] 3559 4-9-9 **98**...............................(v[1]) JamieSpencer 10 —
(T D Barron) *ref to r: tk no part* **7/2**[1]
1m 14.65s (2.09) **Going Correction** +0.675s/f (Yiel)
WFA 3 from 4yo+ 5lb 12 Ran SP% **127.2**
Speed ratings (Par 109): **113,112,111,104,102 101,99,97,96,94 74,—**
CSF £123.30 CT £1067.67 TOTE £10.70: £2.90, £5.20, £3.00; EX 178.30 Trifecta £714.10 Part won. Pool £1,005.80 - 0.70 winning units..
Owner Dawson And Quinn **Bred** The Lavington Stud **Trained** Settrington, N Yorks

FOCUS
A decent handicap but only the first three, who stayed closest to the nearside rail., showed their form in the ground, finishing clear. The winner and third set the level.

NOTEBOOK
Zomerlust, down in trip after a run over 7f in the Bunbury Cup, returned to winning ways in the first-time visor. After a slow start he made his way over to the near rail and, quickening well when the gap opened in front of him, soon had things under control. Placed in the last two Ayr Silver Cups, he will probably go back to Scotland in September. (op 10-1)
Turnkey adopted the same tactics which brought him a win at Pontefract two starts ago and sat off the pace, travelling comfortably. Running into trouble at about halfway, he was switched back to the rail and had to wait to get a run, by which time the winner had already kicked. He came home strongly once in the clear and was arguably unlucky, but is always going to require luck in running ridden this way. (op 22-1)
Green Park(IRE), thought by his trainer to have been unlucky in Ireland, had ground conditions to suit and ran a solid race, chasing the winner through and only caught for second late on. He is equally effective over this trip as he is over 5f. (op 8-1 tchd 15-2)
Philharmonic, a winner in heavy ground last season, was beaten a fair way by the first three but this was still a satisfcatory return to action after more than nine months off. (op 15-2)
The Kiddykid(IRE), who enjoyed his finest hour in the Group 2 Duke Of York Stakes over course and distance two seasons ago, could be ready for another try at 7f. (op 14-1)
Invincible Force(IRE) set the pace until hanging off the rail under pressure and letting the winner through. There are signs that he is returning to form now for this yard. (op 66-1)
El Bosque(IRE) Official explanation: jockey said gelding never travelled
Fullandby(IRE) was involved in scrimmaging just past halfway and was eventually eased down having been struck into. This running can be written off. Official explanation: vet said gelding had been struck into (op 5-1)
Skhilling Spirit, equipped with a visor for the first time, declined to come out of the stalls. (op 11-2)

3976 SKYBET.COM STKS (H'CAP) 2m 2f
4:30 (4:32) (Class 4) (0-80,80) 3-Y-0+ **£7,772** (£2,312; £1,155; £577) **Stalls** Low

Form RPR
-101 **1** **Gallileo Figaro (USA)**[21] 3300 4-9-1 **70**..................... JerryO'Dwyer[(3)] 9 73
(N B King) *hld up: hdwy over 3f out: led over 1f out: edgd lft: styd on wl* **15/2**
0621 **2** ¾ **Last Flight (IRE)**[22] 3279 3-8-0 **72**.................................... DavidKinsella 4 74
(J L Dunlop) *trckd ldr: drvn over 4f out: chal over 3f out: led over 2f out: hdd over 1f out: no ex wl ins fnl f* **2/1**[1]
0006 **3** 1 ¾ **Establishment**[14] 3533 10-8-10 **65**............................. JamieMoriarty[(3)] 3 66
(John A Harris) *t.k.h in rr: hdwy on outside and sltly hmpd over 3f out: kpt on fnl 2f* **25/1**
3331 **4** ½ **Ronsard (IRE)**[1] 3903 5-9-1 **61** 6ex........................... StephenDonohoe 6 67?
(P D Evans) *hld up in rr: hdwy and swtchd rt over 3f out: kpt on fnl 2f* **16/1**
0324 **5** 3 ½ **Kayf Aramis**[11] 3609 5-9-5 **74**...................................(p) MarcHalford[(3)] 8 70
(J L Spearing) *sn trcking ldrs: jnd ldr over 7f out: n.m.r over 2f out: wknd fnl f* **7/2**[2]
3422 **6** nk **Rocknest Island (IRE)**[21] 3300 4-8-7 **62**...............(p) AndrewMullen[(3)] 7 58
(P D Niven) *hld up: hdwy to chse ldrs over 5f out: lost pl over 2f out* **8/1**
0061 **7** 2 ½ **Winged D'Argent (IRE)**[16] 3467 6-10-0 **80**..............(b) PaulMulrennan 2 73
(B J Llewellyn) *led: qcknd over 6f out: hdd over 2f out: sn wknd* **5/1**[3]
/0-0 **8** 2 ½ **Rosecliff**[18] 3407 5-9-5 **71**...(vt) JimCrowley 5 61
(Heather Dalton) *chsd ldrs: drvn over 5f out: lost pl over 3f out* **33/1**
0242 **9** 19 **Great Quest (IRE)**[30] 3027 5-9-1 **67**....................................... KDarley 1 36
(James Moffatt) *chsd ldrs: drvn over 4f out: lost pl over 1f out: heavily eased* **8/1**
4m 9.04s (10.74) **Going Correction** +0.675s/f (Yiel)
WFA 3 from 4yo+ 20lb 9 Ran SP% **118.9**
Speed ratings (Par 105): **103,102,101,101,100 99,98,97,89**
CSF £23.61 CT £370.28 TOTE £7.30: £1.80, £1.40, £4.80; EX 28.80.
Owner The Not Over Big Partnership **Bred** Finger Rock Farm **Trained** Newmarket, Suffolk
■ Stewards' Enquiry : Stephen Donohoe one-day ban: careless riding (Aug 8)

FOCUS
The pace was very steady and only picked up around six furlongs out, but this was still a test of stamina in the conditions. Again the runners made their way to the near side in the home straight. The form is fairly dubious and it is doubtful if the front pair actually improved.

3977 BET AND WATCH AT SKYBET.COM MAIDEN AUCTION STKS 6f
5:00 (5:04) (Class 4) 2-Y-0 **£6,541** (£1,946; £972; £485) **Stalls** Low

Form RPR
1 **River Ardeche** 2-8-10 0.. KDarley 8 78+
(P C Haslam) *trckd ldrs: led over 2f out: drvn clr fnl f: ducked bdly rt and fell heavily pulling up* **15/2**[3]
0 **2** 6 **Fulford**[72] 1792 2-8-9 0... AdrianTNicholls 10 59
(M Brittain) *chsd ldrs: kpt on to take 2nd ins fnl f: no ch w wnr* **11/1**
05 **3** ½ **Bourbon Highball (IRE)**[8] 3718 2-8-12 0......................... LeeEnstone 11 61
(P C Haslam) *trckd ldrs: kpt on same pce fnl 2f* **6/1**[2]
5 **4** hd **Jonny Lesters Hair (IRE)**[8] 3712 2-8-11 0................. PaulMulrennan 9 59
(T D Easterby) *led tl over 2f out: kpt on same pce* **17/2**
5 3 ½ **Eton Fable (IRE)** 2-8-7 0... AndrewMullen[(3)] 6 47
(W J H Ratcliffe) *s.i.s: outpcd and in rr: kpt on fnl f* **16/1**
04 **6** shd **Pay Pay Pay**[22] 3275 2-8-6 0 ow1.................................... JamieSpencer 4 43
(P D Evans) *in tch: drvn and outpcd over 3f out: no threat after* **7/2**[1]
0 **7** 5 **Saturday Boy**[50] 2432 2-8-10 0.. MartinDwyer 7 32
(Paul Green) *mid-div: outpcd and hrd rdn over 3f out* **14/1**
8 2 ½ **Title Role** 2-9-0 0.. TQuinn 5 29
(P F I Cole) *chsd ldrs: drvn and outpcd over 2f out: lost pl over 1f out* **7/2**[1]
9 1 ½ **Fantastic Lass** 2-8-8 0 ow2.. PatCosgrave 2 18
(R A Fahey) *s.s: a bhd* **11/1**
10 1 ¼ **Gala Casino Star (IRE)** 2-8-10 0............................ JamieMoriarty[(3)] 3 19
(R A Fahey) *s.i.s: outpcd and bhd: hung rt over 1f out* **6/1**[2]
1m 16.61s (4.05) **Going Correction** +0.675s/f (Yiel) 10 Ran SP% **124.5**
Speed ratings (Par 96): **100,92,91,91,86 86,79,76,74,72**
CSF £92.71 TOTE £10.80: £2.70, £4.80, £2.50; EX 136.10.
Owner S A B Dinsmore **Bred** D R Tucker **Trained** Middleham Moor, N Yorks

FOCUS
Only the first four were in this from halfway, the winner eventually drawing well clear. The first four were drawn closest to the nearside rail.

NOTEBOOK
River Ardeche is a brother to 6f Fibresand juvenile winner Bridget's Team and half-brother to winning miler Brace Of Doves, out of a mare who won over 1m2f in Germany. After tracking the pace, he drew steadily clear in the final furlong to score easily, although the margin was probably accentuated by the ground. As he was pulling up he slipped and fell through the rails, but luckily seemed none the worse. (op 8-1)
Fulford, who has some decent sprinters on his dam's side, was not disgraced on his debut at the May meeting and confirmed he has ability on this first run since, getting the best of a three-way tussle for second but no match for the clear winner. (op 10-1)
Bourbon Highball(IRE), having his third run, ran a decent race and confirmed the impression he had left at Pontefract that he is a nursery type. (op 8-1 tchd 9-1)
Jonny Lesters Hair(IRE), sharper for his debut, travelled quite well in front and, while readily left behind by the winner, he stuck on and only just missed out on a place. There should be a race for him. (op 12-1)
Eton Fable(IRE), the first foal of a mare who was placed over 1m in Italy, was quickly outpaced and in rear but was gradually getting the hang of things in the latter stages. (op 20-1)
Pay Pay Pay could not go with the leaders from halfway but is now eligible for nurseries should connections chose that option for her. (op 10-3)
Title Role, whose dam won seven times at up to 1m4f, went with the leaders early but was in trouble before halfway and was steadily left behind. He deserves a chance to show what he can do on better ground and perhaps on sand, as his half-brothers Steely Dan and New Options have both shown a preference for artificial surfaces. Official explanation: jockey said colt lost its action (op 10-3 tchd 4-1)

3978 SKYBETVEGAS.COM STKS (H'CAP) 1m 4f
5:30 (5:30) (Class 4) (0-85,82) 4-Y-0+ **£7,772** (£2,312; £1,155; £577) **Stalls** Centre

Form RPR
2113 **1** **Turn Of Phrase (IRE)**[2] 3888 8-8-10 **71**......................(b) KerrinMcEvoy 3 79
(B Ellison) *trckd ldrs: styd on to ld over 1f out: styd on wl* **7/2**[2]
0430 **2** 2 ½ **Dzesmin (POL)**[15] 3509 5-9-5 **80**..................................(p) MartinDwyer 6 84
(R C Guest) *led: hdd over 1f out: kpt on to regain 2nd nr fin* **5/1**
5512 **3** nk **Great View (IRE)**[13] 3567 8-8-13 **74**.....................................(v) KDarley 7 78
(Mrs A L M King) *trckd ldr: chal 3f out: kpt on same pce fnl f* **9/2**[3]
24-2 **4** 1 **Fringe**[173] 365 4-9-7 **82**.. JimCrowley 5 85
(Jane Chapple-Hyam) *hld up: wnt prom 6f out: nt clr run over 2f out: kpt on same pce* **6/1**
-121 **5** ¾ **Le Soleil (GER)**[36] 2833 6-9-2 **77**.................................... JamieSpencer 2 79
(B J Curley) *hld up in last: effrt over 3f out: rdn and hung lft: nvr able to chal* **6/4**[1]
6106 **6** nk **Torrens (IRE)**[14] 3530 5-9-0 **78**.................................. JamieMoriarty[(3)] 1 79
(R A Fahey) *hld up: effrt over 3f out: nt clr run over 2f out: one pce* **12/1**
2m 39.76s (5.16) **Going Correction** +0.675s/f (Yiel) 6 Ran SP% **119.0**
Speed ratings (Par 105): **102,100,100,99,98 98**
CSF £22.42 TOTE £5.40: £2.20, £2.90; EX 32.60 Place 6 £ 92.87, Place 5 £ 47.19.
Owner Naughty Diesel Ltd **Bred** Moyglare Stud Farm Ltd **Trained** Norton, N Yorks

FOCUS
A fair handicap in which the pace was only ordinary. The principals were always prominent and again the action took place up the near side in the home straight. Turn Of Phrase, below par here two days earlier, bounced back with a career best.
T/Plt: £140.80 to a £1 stake. Pool: £107,839.40. 558.80 winning tickets. T/Qpdt: £35.30 to a £1 stake. Pool: £5,133.60. 107.55 winning tickets. JR

3979 - (Foreign Racing) - See Raceform Interactive

3657 LEOPARDSTOWN (L-H)
Saturday, July 28

OFFICIAL GOING: Yielding (yielding to soft in places)

3980a TYROS STKS (GROUP 3) 7f
6:20 (6:23) 2-Y-0 **£30,790** (£9,033; £4,304; £1,466)

RPR
1 **New Approach (IRE)**[13] 3580 2-9-1 .... KJManning 1 100+
(J S Bolger, Ire) *mde all: strly pressed early st: rdn and styd on wl fr under 2f out: easily* **1/1**[1]
2 2 **Brazilian Star (IRE)**[6] 3774 2-9-1 .... CDHayes 4 95
(Kevin Prendergast, Ire) *sn 2nd: rdn to chal and virtually on terms 2f out: kpt on u.p wout troubling wnr ins fnl f* **6/1**[3]
3 1 ½ **Norman Invader (USA)**[49] 2481 2-9-1 .... DPMcDonogh 2 91
(K J Condon, Ire) *hld up in rr: rdn early st: 3rd and no imp fnl f* **14/1**
4 3 **Minneapolis**[24] 3221 2-9-1 .... KFallon 3 84
(A P O'Brien, Ire) *settled 3rd: rdn and no imp early st: last and no ex fnl f* **13/8**[2]
1m 30.6s (-1.60) **Going Correction** -0.125s/f (Firm) **4** Ran SP% **109.0**
Speed ratings: **104,101,100,96**
CSF £7.16 TOTE £1.60; DF 4.20.
Owner Mrs J S Bolger **Bred** Lodge Park Stud **Trained** Coolcullen, Co Carlow

FOCUS
A newly upgraded Group 3, won in 2006 by Teofilo, and his stable look to have another potential top-notcher in New Approach. He won easily and, while this form looks modest for the grade, is very much one to respect when bidding for the hat-trick as he steps up again in class.

NOTEBOOK
New Approach(IRE), who emulated his stable companion Teofilo when winning the same maiden on debut at Leopardstown last time, is clearly being given an identical campaign by his trainer as that horse and he made it two out of two with a facile display on this step up to Group company. Evidently a horse that likes to race on the pace, he showed a willing attitude when asked to win his race and is value for plenty further than the winning margin. While this may not have been the strongest race for the grade, it now puts him firmly on course for the Futurity Stakes at the Curragh next month - a race also won by Teofilo last term - and it will be fascinating to see whether he can go in again there. (op 5/4)
Brazilian Star(IRE), off the mark at the third attempt at Tipperary six days previously, was unable to dictate over this slightly shorter trip and step up in grade. He did little wrong in defeat, and this must rate another improved effort, but he does look to need all of a 1m now. (op 9/2)
Norman Invader(USA) was never a serious player and left the impression he would prefer a sounder surface. He should have no trouble in finding a maiden.
Minneapolis ran some way below the level of this third in Listed company and must rate a disappointemt. It remains to be seen which way he now goes from here. (op 7/4 tchd 6/4)

3983a MELD STKS (GROUP 3) 1m 2f
7:50 (7:52) 3-Y-0+ **£30,743** (£8,986; £4,256; £1,418)

RPR
1 **Fracas (IRE)**[49] 2483 5-9-7 **111**.. WMLordan 5 112
(David Wachman, Ire) *trckd ldrs in 3rd: impr to chal on outer ent st: led 2f out: edgd lft u.p ins fnl f: kpt on wl* **4/5**[1]

2 1/2 **Red Rock Canyon (IRE)**[29] 3074 3-8-11 88................ CO'Donoghue 2 111
(A P O'Brien, Ire) *chsd ldrs in 4th: rdn 3f out: prog on inner ent st: 2nd and chal ins fnl f: kpt on wl* **14/1**

3 1 **Lord Admiral (USA)**[45] 2586 6-9-10 109.......................... PJSmullen 1 112
(Charles O'Brien, Ire) *hld up in rr: in tch whn rdn ent st: styd on ins fnl f* **10/1**

4 3/4 **Trinity College (USA)**[6] 3772 3-8-11 107.......................... KFallon 4 108
(A P O'Brien, Ire) *chsd ldr in 2nd: rdn 3f out: 3rd whn checked ins fnl f: kpt on* **7/2**[2]

5 1 1/4 **Arch Rebel (USA)**[19] 3391 6-9-7 107..........................(t) NPMadden 6 105
(Noel Meade, Ire) *hld up in 5th: in tch whn rdn ent st: no imp fr over 1f out* **13/2**[3]

6 2 1/2 **You're Beautiful (USA)**[13] 3578 3-8-8 92.......................... DMGrant 3 97
(David Wachman, Ire) *led: rdn and hdd 2f out: no ex fr over 1f out* **16/1**

2m 10.3s (-0.10) **Going Correction** +0.325s/f (Good)
WFA 3 from 5yo+ 10lb **6** Ran SP% **112.8**
Speed ratings: **113,112,111,111,110 108**
CSF £13.93 TOTE £1.70: £1.10, £8.60; DF 25.40.
Owner Joseph Joyce **Bred** Mrs Eileen Purcell **Trained** Goolds Cross, Co Tipperary
■ Stewards' Enquiry : W M Lordan two-day ban: careless riding (Aug 6,7)

NOTEBOOK
Fracas(IRE), who has been in fine form this season, defended his unbeaten record over this course and distance - he won the 2005 Derrinstown Derby Trial here. After settling in third, he came under pressure with 3f to run but found plenty and ran on well to record his first Group race success. He could turn him out again in the Group 2 Royal Whip Stakes at the Curragh next month. (op 4/5 tchd 1/1)
Red Rock Canyon(IRE) was the surprise package of the race. Having shown plenty of ability at two, he had been regressing lately and had come down 12lb in the ratings for his last three runs. He ran on well to challenge for the lead inside the final quarter of a mile but could not match the winner. He has now filled the runner-up spot six times from ten starts.
Lord Admiral(USA), who finished second in this for the last two years, was looking to follow up his victory in the Group 3 Ballycorus Stakes over 7f here last month. He was keeping on over the final furlong and a half but was unable to pick up on the ground - his best form is all on a sound surface. He will continue to pay his way at this level and further Group race success can come his way when he gets conditions to suit. (op 8/1)
Trinity College(USA) was stepping up in grade following his win in a Fairyhouse conditions race six days previously. He had already given best when he was hampered by the winner in the closing stages. He is a useful sort but will need to improve to make his mark at Stakes level.
Arch Rebel(USA) has not been at his best lately and has been unable to build on the form of his third in a Limerick Listed race last month. (op 6/1)

3984 - 3986a (Foreign Racing) - See Raceform Interactive

3779 MAISONS-LAFFITTE (R-H)
Saturday, July 28

OFFICIAL GOING: Good to soft

3987a PRIX EUGENE ADAM (GROUP 2) (STRAIGHT COURSE) 1m 2f (S)
3:20 (3:23) 3-Y-O **£115,541** (£44,595; £21,284; £14,189; £7,095)

RPR

1 **Harland**[22] 3271 3-9-2.......................... PhilipRobinson 7 114
(M A Jarvis) *a cl up on outside: hrd rdn fr over 1f out: drvn to ld on line* **78/10**

2 shd **Regime (IRE)**[56] 2235 3-9-2.......................... TThulliez 3 113
(M L W Bell) *trckd ldr: fnd a gap and qcknd to ld over 1f out: edgd rt ins fnl f: r.o u.p: ct on line* **47/10**

3 2 **Russian Desert (IRE)**[50] 3-9-2.......................... SPasquier 6 109
(A Fabre, France) *hld up on outside: hdwy over 1f out: kpt on u.p fnl f* **23/10**[1]

4 shd **Loup Breton (IRE)**[33] 2952 3-9-2.......................... C-PLemaire 5 109
(E Lellouche, France) *hld up: trying for gap towards outside between wnr and 3rd but nt clr run fr wl over 1f out to ins fnl f: r.o to take 4th on line* **31/10**[2]

5 shd **Asperity (USA)**[20] 3362 3-9-2.......................... IMendizabal 4 109
(J H M Gosden) *led to over 1f out: kpt on u.p fnl f but lost 3rd last strides* **12/1**

6 4 **No Dream (USA)**[33] 2952 3-9-2.......................... OPeslier 1 101
(C Laffon-Parias, France) *racd in 2nd on rails: drvn to chal wl over 1f out: sn one pce* **41/10**[3]

7 3 **Hurricane Fly (IRE)**[33] 2952 3-9-2.......................... JVictoire 2 95
(J-L Pelletan, France) *in tch tl rdn and btn wl over 1f out* **15/1**

2m 1.60s (-7.80) **7** Ran SP% **117.2**
PARI-MUTUEL: WIN 8.80; PL 4.00, 3.00; SF 42.50.
Owner Sheikh Mohammed **Bred** Darley **Trained** Newmarket, Suffolk
■ Stewards' Enquiry : Philip Robinson €200 fine: whip abuse

NOTEBOOK
Harland's connections were really worried before the race that the ground might be a little lively for this talented colt, but he seemed to handle the conditions fine. Waited with in the early part of this straight 1m2f, he came to challenge for the lead at the furlong marker and, although appearing to be a little unbalanced under pressure, he ran on gamely. He did, though, have to survive an objection from the jockey of the runner up.
Regime(IRE), placed just behind the leaders, was short of room one and a half out but quickened well once in the clear. He had a ding dong battle with the winner and was just beaten on the nod. Now he has proved to be up to this level, he could go for similar races and may be aimed at the Guillaume d'Ornano at Deauville.
Russian Desert(IRE), last at halfway, was just beginning his challenge about one a half furlongs out when he made contact with the eventual fourth-placed horse on several occasions.
Loup Breton(IRE) can be considered a little unlucky as, having been towards the tail of the field early on, he had nowhere to go at the two-furlong marker. His jockey decided to go for a gap where he had contact on several occasions with the third past the post and he would have certainly been closer but for the incident. The stewards' decided not to change the order.
Asperity(USA), taken immediately into the lead, was joined by the winner one and a half out and could find only the one pace thereafter. This trip probably tests his stamina to the limit.

3938 ASCOT (R-H)
Sunday, July 29

OFFICIAL GOING: Straight course - good to soft (soft in places); round course - soft
Wind: Light against Weather: Dry

3988 PRINCESS MARGARET INDEPENDENT NEWSPAPER STKS (GROUP 3) (FILLIES) 6f
1:40 (1:43) (Class 1) 2-Y-O
£22,712 (£8,608; £4,308; £2,148; £1,076; £540) **Stalls** Centre

Form RPR

2 1 **Visit**[30] 3055 2-8-12 0.......................... RyanMoore 5 107+
(Sir Michael Stoute) *sltly slowly away: sn mid-div: hdwy 2f out: sn rdn: edgd rt and led ins fnl f: r.o wl* **10/3**[1]

1 2 1 1/2 **Reel Gift**[18] 3417 2-8-12 0.......................... RichardHughes 13 103
(R Hannon) *overall ldr on far side: rdn over 1f out: nt pce of wnr whn hdd ins fnl f* **12/1**

110 3 2 1/2 **Sweepstake (IRE)**[39] 2756 2-8-12 0.......................... PatDobbs 8 95
(R Hannon) *mid-div in centre gp: rdn over 2f out: no imp tl styd on ins fnl f: wnt 3rd nr fin* **11/1**[3]

6104 4 nk **Loch Jipp (USA)**[18] 3432 2-8-12 0.......................... KDarley 1 94
(J S Wainwright) *prom in centre gp: rdn 2f out: wnt 3rd and drifted rt ent fnl f: no ex fnl 75yds* **11/1**[3]

1 5 1/2 **Edge Of Light**[32] 2997 2-8-12 0.......................... JMurtagh 9 93
(B Palling) *s.i.s: hld up in centre gp: rdn and hdwy over 1f out: styng on whn swtchd lft ins fnl f: no ex fnl 75yds* **33/1**

10 6 2 1/2 **Green Oasis (USA)**[18] 3432 2-8-12 0.......................... ChrisCatlin 10 85
(E J O'Neill) *mid-div in centre gp: rdn and hdwy 3f out: one pce fnl f* **22/1**

10 7 shd **Fanatical**[39] 2756 2-8-12 0.......................... RHills 11 85
(E F Vaughan) *chsd ldr on far side: rdn 3f out: one pce fnl f* **8/1**[2]

13 8 1 **Highland Daughter (IRE)**[29] 3096 2-8-12 0............. PhilipRobinson 12 82
(C G Cox) *chsd ldr on far side: rdn over 2f out: wknd fnl f* **8/1**[2]

106 9 2 1/2 **Kylayne**[18] 3432 2-8-12 0.......................... DarryllHolland 4 74
(P W D'Arcy) *chsd ldrs in centre gp: rdn over 2f out: wknd over 1f out* **33/1**

61 10 1 1/4 **Little Knickers**[20] 3363 2-8-12 0.......................... MartinDwyer 3 71
(D K Ivory) *prom in centre gp: rdn over 3f out: wknd over 1f out* **28/1**

51 11 hd **Serena's Storm (IRE)**[25] 3205 2-8-12 0.......................... JHBowman 6 70
(J J Quinn) *a towards rr of centre gp* **25/1**

101 12 1 **Polar Circle (USA)**[29] 3096 2-8-12 0.......................... JimmyFortune 2 67
(P W Chapple-Hyam) *prom in centre gp tl wknd 2f out* **10/3**[1]

631 13 11 **Lady Aquitaine (USA)**[13] 3592 2-8-12 0.......................... JamieSpencer 7 34
(B J Meehan) *s.i.s: a bhd centre gp* **8/1**[2]

1m 16.97s (2.07) **Going Correction** +0.275s/f (Good) **13** Ran SP% **121.4**
Speed ratings (Par 101): **97,95,91,91,90 87,87,85,82,80 80,79,64**
CSF £44.96 TOTE £4.60: £2.10, £3.60, £4.10; EX 29.80 Trifecta £364.80 Pool £967.34 - 1.90 winning units..
Owner K Abdulla **Bred** Juddmonte Farms Ltd **Trained** Newmarket, Suffolk

FOCUS
Three fillies raced on the far side, apart from the remainder. A strong renewal of this event, with Visit's figure bettered only by subsequent 1000 Guineas winner Russian Rhythm in the last eight years. The form looks very strong and Visit looks Guineas material herself. A cracking effort from Reel Gift too with the third and fourth basically confirming their pre-race levels.

NOTEBOOK
Visit ◆, the only filly in the line-up without a previous win to her name, was runner-up on her debut behind Don't Forget Faith in the Newmarket maiden which her stablemates Russian Rhythm and Enthused won en route to victory in this. She took a little time to find her stride before coming with a steady run to lead inside the last, edging over towards the far rail but well on top at the line. Set to tackle races like the Lowther and Cheveley Park later in the season, she looks a very smart prospect and is one of the leading candidates for next year's 1000 Guineas at this stage. (op 7-2 tchd 4-1 and 9-2 in places)
Reel Gift ◆ came here after making a winning debut on Kempton's Polytrack. One of three to race over on the far side, she held the lead overall and travelled strongly. After beginning to edge towards the centre of the track she was carried back towards the rail by the winner, who took her measure inside the last. This was an excellent effort and she can win a Group race. (op 9-1)
Sweepstake(IRE), a stablemate of the runner-up, lost her unbeaten record in the Queen Mary Stakes here but had an excuse that day. On her first try over 6f, she was outpaced at around halfway but was staying on purposefully in the latter stages. The return to this easier ground seemed to suit her. (tchd 10-1)
Loch Jipp(USA), a generally consistent filly, filled the same position in the Group 2 Cherry Hinton Stakes last time. This was a decent effort from a moderate draw, but she hung to her right in the latter stages and this trip looks the limit of her stamina. (tchd 10-1)
Edge Of Light, who made a successful debut over 5f at Salisbury, stepped up on that form on this rise in grade. After a slow start, she improved with over a furlong to run before fading late on as Loch Jipp hung in her path.
Green Oasis(USA) is a very useful filly, but she has now been held twice in Group races since her winning debut on sand. She probably needs 7f now. (op 25-1)
Fanatical, eighth in the Queen Mary after winning over this trip on her debut at Newbury, finished second among the three fillies to race on the far side. (op 12-1)
Highland Daughter(IRE) finished last of the trio to take the far-side route but did turn around Newmarket form with the disappointing Polar Circle. (op 10-1)
Polar Circle(USA), a winner in Listed company at Newmarket, ran here rather than in the Prix de Cabourg at Deauville. She faded tamely with two furlongs to run, andf the ground cannot be put forward as an excuse. (op 4-1)
Lady Aquitaine(USA), who impressed in an ordinary race at Windsor, failed to give her running with the easy ground a likely factor. Official explanation: trainer said filly was unsuited by the good to soft (soft in places) ground (op 15-2)

3989 LONDON CLUBS INTERNATIONAL STKS (HERITAGE H'CAP) 1m 4f
2:15 (2:15) (Class 2) (0-105,103) 3-Y-O+
£37,392 (£11,196; £5,598; £2,802; £1,398; £702) **Stalls** High

Form RPR

3306 1 **Group Captain**[29] 3097 5-9-6 **102**.......................... RichardKingscote(3) 3 116+
(R Charlton) *hld up rr: hdwy & nt clr run over 2f out: cl up whn nt clr run over 1f out: swtchd lft: rdn & styd on strly ins fnl f: led fnl stride* **15/2**

4311 2 hd **Mull Of Dubai**[24] 3242 4-8-8 **87**.......................... JohnEgan 14 98
(J S Moore) *hld up bhd and t.k.h: hdwy and swtchd rt 2f out: rdn and r.o strly to ld over 1f out: ct fnl stride* **12/1**

50-6 3 5 **Before You Go (IRE)**[23] 3272 4-9-5 **98**.......................... MichaelHills 6 101
(T G Mills) *trckd ldrs: rdn over 2f out: ev ch over 1f out: kpt on same pce* **25/1**

The Form Book, Raceform Ltd, Compton, RG20 6NL

/421 **4** ¾ **Misty Dancer**[36] 2861 8-8-9 **88** .... FrancisNorton 1 89
(Miss Venetia Williams) *t.k.h towards rr: hdwy into midfield over 5f out: clsd on ldrs over 2f out: rdn and ev ch over 1f out: kpt on same pce* **11/2**[3]

-262 **5** hd **Solent (IRE)**[36] 2859 5-9-10 **103** .... RichardHughes 5 104
(R Hannon) *shkn up to ld after 2f: rdn and hdd over 1f out: one pce after* **7/2**[1]

3210 **6** ¾ **High Treason (USA)**[16] 3509 5-8-8 **87** .... TPQueally 13 87
(W J Musson) *t.k.h towards rr: nt clr run and swtchd to outer ent st: sn rdn: styd on fr 2f out: nt rch ldrs* **9/1**

-102 **7** 1 ¼ **Dan Dare (USA)**[29] 3105 4-8-8 **87** ....(v) RyanMoore 4 85
(Sir Michael Stoute) *t.k.h in midfield: hdwy and effrt 2f out: fdd ins fnl f* **5/1**[2]

1200 **8** 5 **Halla San**[29] 3090 5-9-1 **94** .... TonyHamilton 7 84
(R A Fahey) *rdn over 4f out: a towards rr* **25/1**

3561 **9** ½ **John Terry (IRE)**[16] 3509 4-8-11 **90** ....(p) JMurtagh 10 79
(Mrs A J Perrett) *led for 2f: trckd ldr: rdn 3f out: wknd over 1f out* **8/1**

0-34 **10** ¾ **Instructor**[59] 1494 6-8-3 **82** .... DaleGibson 12 70
(R A Fahey) *trckd ldrs: rdn over 2f out: wknd over 1f out* **16/1**

50-2 **11** 4 **Masterofthecourt (USA)**[11] 3641 4-8-2 **81** .... ChrisCatlin 11 63
(H Morrison) *mid-div tl 5f out* **6/1**

2m 37.92s (4.92) **Going Correction** +0.625s/f (Yiel) **11** Ran SP% **122.7**
Speed ratings (Par 109): **108,107,104,104,103 103,102,99,98,98 95**
CSF £98.14 CT £2142.70 TOTE £9.10: £2.40, £2.90, £6.30; EX 109.40 TRIFECTA Not won..
Owner Peter Webb **Bred** Hascombe And Valiant Studs **Trained** Beckhampton, Wilts

FOCUS
A competitive handicap run at just an ordinary pace and the form is not all that strong for the grade. The first two finished clear.

NOTEBOOK
Group Captain found himself in handicap company for the first time since winning last year's November Handicap at Windsor. Held up, he had to be switched out before coming with a strong run to catch the runner-up, who had gone clear, winning a shade cosily despite the narrow margin. He could go for the Ebor now, in which he picks up a 4lb penalty to take his weight to 9st 6lb, and soft ground would help his cause there. (op 8-1 tchd 9-1)
Mull Of Dubai was 6lb higher on this bid for the hat-trick, his two previous wins having come over slightly shorter. Held up, in common with the winner, he was pulled out with two furlongs to go and quickened up well to strike the front, going a few lengths clear and looking sure to win. However Group Captain was out after him inside the last and he was claimed almost on the line. He did not do much wrong and finished well clear of the third. (op 11-1)
Before You Go(IRE), back up to this trip on this second run after an absence, had been eased 2lb in the weights. Never far from the pace, he battled on resolutely but was no match for the first two.
Misty Dancer, winner of a 2m3f handicap chase on his last visit to Ascot, was raised 7lb after his recent Ayr win over a furlong further. He had his chance but lacked a change of pace when it mattered. (op 13-2)
Solent(IRE), raised 7lb after getting touched off by Pevensey in the Duke Of Edinburgh over course and distance last time, replicated the front-running tactics he had used that day but was found out off his three-figure mark. (op 6-1)
High Treason(USA), held up as usual and rather keen in the first part of the race, stayed on in the final quarter mile but could not get to the leaders. Twice held from this mark since his win at York, he needs a stronger pace than he got here. (op 17-2 tchd 12-1 in a place)
Dan Dare(USA), the visor retained, was unable to build on his Windsor effort in this stronger company. (op 7-1)
John Terry(IRE), put up 4lb for his win at Newmarket, was equipped with cheekpieces for the first time. Weakening in the straight, he has won in soft ground but is most effective on a sound surface. (op 15-2)
Masterofthecourt(USA) made a promising return to action on the Polytrack recently but was disappointing on this different ground, in trouble not long after halfway. Official explanation: trainer said gelding was unsuited by the soft going (op 5-1)

3990 HONG KONG JOCKEY CLUB SPRINT STKS (HERITAGE H'CAP) 5f
2:50 (2:51) (Class 2) 3-Y-0+

£43,624 (£13,062; £6,531; £3,269; £1,631; £819) **Stalls** Centre

Form RPR

3300 **1** **Stoneacre Lad (IRE)**[13] 3586 4-8-7 **88** ow1........(b) TPQueally 16 104
(Peter Grayson) *chsd ldrs on far side: drvn to ld wl over 1f out: r.o wl and in command fnl f* **66/1**

5132 **2** 2 ½ **Hoh Hoh Hoh**[15] 3526 5-8-5 **86** .... MartinDwyer 2 93
(R J Price) *slowly away: bhd on stands' side: rdn over 2f out: hdwy over 1f out: r.o strly to go 2nd ins fnl f: nt rch wnr* **12/1**

0001 **3** nk **Dig Deep (IRE)**[15] 3528 5-8-4 **88** 5ex........ LiamJones(3) 17 94
(W J Haggas) *rrd stalls: sn chsng ldrs on far side: rdn over 2f out: ev ch wl over 1f out: kpt on but nt pce of wnr* **10/1**[2]

0-52 **4** shd **Tony The Tap**[8] 3749 6-8-0 **81** .... HayleyTurner 20 87
(W R Muir) *sn pushed along in mid-div on far side: hdwy over 1f out: styd on to go 4th ins fnl f* **18/1**

01-4 **5** nk **The Jobber (IRE)**[15] 3526 6-9-4 **99** .... JMurtagh 10 103
(M Blanshard) *hld up on stands' side: hdwy 2f out: sn rdn: r.o ins fnl f* **20/1**

4005 **6** nk **Fantasy Believer**[13] 3586 9-9-1 **96** .... JimmyFortune 5 99
(J J Quinn) *hld up towards rr on stands' side: rdn 2f out: r.o wl ins fnl f: nrst fin* **11/1**[3]

0000 **7** 1 ¼ **Woodcote (IRE)**[17] 3464 5-8-12 **93** ....(be) AdamKirby 26 92
(C G Cox) *racd far side: squeezed out s: towards rr: rdn and hdwy over 1f out: hung lft ins fnl f: kpt on* **25/1**

5045 **8** nk **Cape Royal**[15] 3526 7-8-6 **92** ....(bt) KevinGhunowa(5) 3 90
(J M Bradley) *led stands' side gp but overall prom: rdn over 2f out: kpt on same pce fnl f* **50/1**

-200 **9** hd **Loch Verdi**[17] 3464 4-8-5 **86** .... FrancisNorton 7 83
(A M Balding) *chsd ldrs on stands' side: rdn over 2f out: kpt on same pce fnl f* **25/1**

3014 **10** ½ **Misaro (GER)**[2] 3911 6-8-2 **83** 5ex........(b) AdrianMcCarthy 25 78
(R A Harris) *mid-div on far side: styd on ins fnl f: nt rch ldrs* **14/1**

1100 **11** ½ **King Orchisios (IRE)**[16] 3500 4-9-10 **105** ....(p) JHBowman 28 102+
(K A Ryan) *chsd ldrs on far side: rdn over 2f out: wknd and eased ins fnl f* **50/1**

2615 **12** shd **Mecca's Mate**[16] 3511 6-9-10 **105** 5ex........ TonyHamilton 22 98
(D W Barker) *sn pushed along towards rr on far side: styd on fnl f: nvr trbld ldrs* **20/1**

602 **13** ½ **Tabaret**[9] 3708 4-9-2 **97** .... DeanMcKeown 18 88
(R M Whitaker) *led centre gp of 2: overall ldr 3f out: rdn and hdd wl over 1f out: grad fdd* **18/1**

3120 **14** shd **Golden Dixie (USA)**[15] 3526 8-8-2 **88** .... LukeMorris(5) 23 79
(R A Harris) *a mid-div on far side* **16/1**

3104 **15** nk **Hogmaneigh (IRE)**[14] 3573 4-9-9 **104** .... JamieSpencer 24 94
(S C Williams) *hld up towards rr on far side: sme prog but no threat whn short of room ins fnl f* **9/2**[1]

6-46 **16** ½ **Buachaill Dona (IRE)**[64] 2034 4-9-1 **96** .... AdrianTNicholls 13 84
(D Nicholls) *sn swtchd to far side: a mid-div* **10/1**[2]

-605 **17** nk **Elhamri**[43] 2672 3-9-1 **100** .... RichardHughes 21 89+
(S Kirk) *racd far side: overall ldr for 2f: prom: rdn and hung rt over 1f out: sn wknd* **25/1**

5053 **18** ¾ **Orientor**[13] 3586 9-9-0 **95** .... PhilipRobinson 27 79
(J S Goldie) *a towards rr on far side* **16/1**

1506 **19** shd **Green Manalishi**[28] 3139 6-9-10 **105** .... JohnEgan 1 89
(K A Ryan) *mid-div on stands' side: rdn over 2f out: wknd ent fnl f* **25/1**

4003 **20** nk **Corridor Creeper (FR)**[15] 3526 10-9-1 **96** ....(p) RyanMoore 15 79
(J M Bradley) *racd centre: nvr bttr than mid-div* **25/1**

300 **21** ¾ **Kay Two (IRE)**[29] 3104 5-8-5 **86** .... ChrisCatlin 8 66
(R J Price) *chsd ldrs on stands' side tl wknd over 1f out* **33/1**

2552 **22** 1 ¼ **Blazing Heights**[16] 3515 4-7-12 **82** .... DuranFentiman(3) 9 58
(J S Goldie) *mainly towards rr on stands' side: hung rt ins fnl f* **33/1**

2312 **23** 1 ¼ **Gallery Girl (IRE)**[13] 3586 4-8-4 **85** .... DaleGibson 14 56
(T D Easterby) *chsd ldrs on stands' side tl wknd wl over 1f out* **16/1**

0060 **24** ¾ **Tournedos (IRE)**[30] 3050 5-8-10 **91** .... JoeFanning 11 59
(D Nicholls) *prom on stands' side tl wknd over 1f out* **16/1**

61.36 secs (-0.04) **Going Correction** +0.275s/f (Good)
WFA 3 from 4yo+ 4lb **24** Ran SP% **133.2**
Speed ratings (Par 109): **111,107,106,106,105 105,103,102,102,101 101,100,100,99,99 98,98,96,96,96 95,93,91,89**
CSF £687.63 CT £8481.54 TOTE £97.60: £16.10, £2.60, £4.00, £6.60; EX 3316.30 TRIFECTA Not won..
Owner Richard Teatum **Bred** Mrs Annie Hughes **Trained** Formby, Lancs

FOCUS
A valuable and competitive handicap, and a shock result but the form is rated at face value with the next three home well in on recent form. A group of ten raced on the near side, with a couple down the centre and the rest towards the far side.

NOTEBOOK
Stoneacre Lad(IRE), the outsider of the entire field, sprang a huge surprise in this valuable event, showing ahead inside the two pole and never looking like being caught. Held off similar marks since winning off this mark at Southwell in December, this was only his second win on turf. (tchd 80-1 and 100-1 in places)
Hoh Hoh Hoh had the strong pace he needs and ran a fine race. Recovering from a slow start, he came through to show ahead in the ten-strong group to race on the stands' side but could not trouble the winner who was racing towards the far side. He was already due to be raised 4lb before this.
Dig Deep(IRE) was not inconvenienced by this easier ground and put up a solid effort under the 5lb penalty he picked up for winning over course and distance earlier in the month. (op 9-1 tchd 11-1)
Tony The Tap, having his third run since leaving Bryn Palling, ran a sound race off bottom weight. His last win came exactly three years ago, off a pound lower mark, and creditable though this effort was he has now gone 24 races without a victory. (tchd 16-1 and 20-1)
The Jobber(IRE) was running on determinedly at the end, finishing second in his group but just missing the frame overall. He finished closer to runner-up Hoh Hoh Hoh than he had on his recent reappearance on the same terms. (tchd 25-1)
Fantasy Believer ◆ was doing some sterling late work, again suggesting that a return to 6f will see him regain the winning thread. (op 12-1)
Woodcote(IRE) put in a decent run but again looked less than straightforward.
Cape Royal showed his usual bright pace to lead the larger stands'-side group for much of the way.
King Orchisios(IRE) would have finished a few places closer had he not been eased when his measure had been taken. Official explanation: jockey said gelding hung left
Mecca's Mate, under a 5lb penalty, was outpaced before staying on quite well. (tchd 22-1)
Tabaret, one of just a couple to race down the centre, did noyt have ground conditions in his favour. (tchd 20-1)
Hogmaneigh(IRE) could never get into the hunt but might have finished a bit nearer had he not been briefly short of room late on. Official explanation: jockey said gelding never travelled (op 11-2 tchd 4-1)
Buachaill Dona(IRE), representing last year's winning trainer, was never able to get into the action after his jockey opted to go with the far-side group.

3991 OWEN BROWN EBF CROCKER BULTEEL MAIDEN STKS (C&G) 6f
3:25 (3:26) (Class 4) 2-Y-0 **£6,477** (£1,927; £963; £481) **Stalls** Centre

Form RPR

1 **Atlantic Sport (USA)** 2-9-0 0........ JHBowman 14 93+
(M R Channon) *settled in mid-div: smooth hdwy to join ldrs 2f out: rdn ent fnl f: tk narrow advantage nr fin: drvn out* **5/2**[2]

2 shd **Skadrak (USA)** 2-9-0 0........ JimmyFortune 4 93+
(P W Chapple-Hyam) *trckd ldrs: led narrowly 2f out: rdn and hrd pressed ent fnl f: kpt on but no ex whn hdd nr fin* **2/1**[1]

3 1 **Aqlaam** 2-9-0 0........ RHills 11 90+
(W J Haggas) *hld up: smooth hdwy over 2f out: jnd ldrs over 1f out: rdn and ev ch ent fnl f: no ex* **5/1**[3]

4 4 **Hawaana (IRE)** 2-9-0 0........ MartinDwyer 9 75+
(B W Hills) *hld up: hdwy to chse ldng trio wl over 1f out: sn rdn: kpt on same pce* **12/1**

5 3 **Moral Duty (USA)** 2-9-0 0........ RichardHughes 13 66+
(Pat Eddery) *hld up last: swtchd rt and smooth hdwy over 2f out: rdn to chse ldrs over 1f out: one pce fnl f* **25/1**

6 nk **Arctic Cape** 2-9-0 0........ JoeFanning 3 65
(M Johnston) *led tl 2f out: sn hung lft and one pce* **20/1**

7 2 **Addikt (IRE)** 2-9-0 0........ PatDobbs 8 59
(S Kirk) *mid-div: rdn over 2f out: sn one pce* **40/1**

8 1 ¼ **Mega Watt (IRE)** 2-9-0 0........ DarryllHolland 1 55
(W Jarvis) *s.i.s: a towards rr* **33/1**

9 shd **Richcar (IRE)** 2-9-0 0........ AdamKirby 2 55
(R M Beckett) *a towards rr* **50/1**

10 1 **High Plains (FR)** 2-9-0 0........ RyanMoore 6 52+
(R Hannon) *prom tl wknd wl over 1f out* **12/1**

11 ¾ **Langham House** 2-9-0 0........ JohnEgan 10 50
(J R Jenkins) *a towards rr* **50/1**

12 nk **Yattendon** 2-9-0 0........ JMurtagh 7 49
(S Kirk) *prom tl wknd 2f out* **20/1**

13 1 **Crystal Rock (IRE)** 2-9-0 0........ MichaelHills 5 46+
(B W Hills) *s.i.s: plld hrd in mid-div: effrt and rn green over 2f out: sn wknd* **16/1**

1m 17.1s (2.20) **Going Correction** +0.275s/f (Good) **13** Ran SP% **122.5**
Speed ratings (Par 96): **96,95,94,89,85 84,82,80,80,79 78,77,76**
CSF £7.42 TOTE £3.60: £1.80, £1.50, £2.10; EX 9.90 Trifecta £32.70 Pool £758.45 - 16.46 winning units..
Owner Jaber Abdullah **Bred** Gainsborough Farm Llc **Trained** West Ilsley, Berks

FOCUS
This looked a cracking renewal of this race, which is confined to unraced juveniles. The time was good and this is almost certainly strong form, with the first three, who finished clear, looking nice prospects.

NOTEBOOK
Atlantic Sport(USA) is a half-brother to connections' St James's Palace Stakes winner Zafeen and to high-class juvenile 7f winner Ya Hajar. Arriving here with a good reputation, he travelled up well and showed an admirable attitude to come out on top in a tight finish. He looks a bright prospect and could well be a Group-class colt. (tchd 2-1 and 11-4)

Skadrak(USA) ◆, who was sold for 48,000gns earlier this year, is out of a mare who won over 5f at two. Tracking the pace going nicely before moving to the front, he just missed out after a good head-to-head but was not given a hard time and will soon go one better. He will be hard to beat in a maiden although connections could opt to go for something better with him. (op 15-8 tchd 7-4 and 9-4)

Aqlaam ◆ is the first foal of an unraced sister to the top-class stayer Persian Punch, as well as to smart juvenile Island Magic. He was just outpaced by the leading pair late on but was probably given the most considerate ride of the first three and looks another certain future winner. (op 7-1 tchd 15-2)

Hawaana(IRE) ◆, a 222,000euros yearling, is a half-brother to several winners, including the very useful Royal Intrigue, out of a sister to Haydock Sprint Cup winner Cherokee Rose. Held up early, he improved to get within striking distance of the three leaders entering the last furlong and a half but could not match them for speed late on. A step up to 7f should see him winning.

Moral Duty(USA) ran a promising race on this debut and is another likely future winner from this maiden, with a step up in trip probably going to suit. (op 33-1)

Arctic Cape, a half-brother to the very useful sprinter Andronikos, raced prominently through the first half before getting a little detached at the business end and wandering a little.

3992 SINO GROUP MAIDEN FILLIES' STKS — 1m (S)
4:00 (4:04) (Class 4) 3-Y-O — £6,477 (£1,927; £963; £481) Stalls Centre

Form				RPR
2	1		**Alo Pura**[9] 3710 3-9-0 0 .... PhilipRobinson 3 (M A Jarvis) *chsd ldrs: rdn to chal over 1f out: tk narrow advantage ins fnl f: drifted lft fnl 50yds: jst hld on* **4/1**[2]	82+
54	2	hd	**Safwa (IRE)**[32] 2998 3-9-0 0 .... RHills 4 (Sir Michael Stoute) *trckd ldrs: led over 2f out: rdn and hrd pressed over 1f out: narrowly hdd ins fnl f: rallied: jst hld* **8/1**	81
-406	3	nk	**Fidelia (IRE)**[45] 2597 3-9-0 85 .... RyanMoore 5 (G Wragg) *mid-div: rdn and hdwy 2f out: chal ent fnl f: kpt on but no ex nr fin* **5/1**	80
352	4	hd	**Cassiara**[12] 3607 3-9-0 75 .... (p) JamieSpencer 10 (J Pearce) *wnt rt s: hld up: smooth hdwy fr over 2f out: rdn to chal ent fnl f: kpt on but no ex nr fin* **9/1**	80
42-4	5	4	**Salsa Steps (USA)**[20] 3387 3-9-0 80 .... JimmyFortune 2 (H Morrison) *chsd ldrs: rdn over 2f out: chal over 1f out: wknd fnl f* **9/2**[3]	71
0-2	6	1 3/4	**Josephine Malines**[42] 2693 3-9-0 0 .... AdamKirby 1 (C G Cox) *mid-div: rdn to chse ldrs over 1f out: wknd fnl f* **9/1**	67
2-30	7	nk	**Sues Surprise (IRE)**[58] 2211 3-9-0 102 .... MichaelHills 6 (B W Hills) *hld up: rdn 3f out: no imp* **11/4**[1]	66
	8	5	**With Confidence** 3-9-0 0 .... NeilPollard 11 (D R C Elsworth) *rrd and uns rdr bef s: s.i.s: racd v green and nvr a danger* **50/1**	55
0-42	9	7	**Cow Girl (IRE)**[15] 3561 3-9-0 61 .... JMurtagh 9 (Miss Gay Kelleway) *racd freely: led and sn clr: hdd over 2f out: sn wknd* **20/1**	38
66-	10	27	**Tinted View (USA)**[269] 6309 3-8-7 0 .... KylieManser(7) 8 (Mrs H Sweeting) *racd keenly: trckd clr ldr tl wknd over 3f out* **100/1**	—
0	11	11	**Tagula Song (IRE)**[32] 2998 3-9-0 0 .... RobertHavlin 7 (J A Geake) *mid-div tl wknd 3f out* **100/1**	—

1m 43.63s (1.83) **Going Correction** +0.275s/f (Good) 11 Ran SP% **121.3**
Speed ratings (Par 99): **101,100,100,100,96 94,94,89,82,55 44**
CSF £36.59 TOTE £5.20: £2.10, £3.10, £2.30; EX 37.80 Trifecta £248.90 Pool £1,378.06 - 3.93 winning units.
Owner Sheikh Ahmed Al Maktoum **Bred** T W Bloodstock Ltd **Trained** Newmarket, Suffolk
■ Stewards' Enquiry : Philip Robinson caution: careless riding; one-day ban: used whip with excessive frequency (Aug 9)

FOCUS
Not a strong race, and the pace was only steady through the early stages, the eventual ninth apart, but a good finish with the first four coming clear. The form is rated around the third and fourth.
Cow Girl(IRE) Official explanation: jockey said filly ran too free

3993 CATHAY PACIFIC AIRWAYS H'CAP — 1m 4f
4:35 (4:35) (Class 4) (0-85,85) 3-Y-O — £6,477 (£1,927; £963; £481) Stalls High

Form				RPR
-102	1		**Noojoom (IRE)**[33] 2971 3-8-13 77 .... PatDobbs 12 (M P Tregoning) *led after 2f: styd on strly to assert ent fnl f: pushed out: comf* **8/1**	85
-102	2	1 1/4	**Prince Sabaah (IRE)**[48] 2506 3-9-5 83 .... JimmyFortune 4 (R Hannon) *trckd ldrs: rdn over 2f out: kpt on ins fnl f: snatched 2nd fnl stride* **7/1**[3]	89
0-01	3	hd	**Inchinata (IRE)**[25] 3214 3-8-11 75 .... MichaelHills 7 (B W Hills) *led for 2f: w wnr: rdn and ev ch over 2f out: hld ent fnl f: lost 2nd fnl stride* **20/1**	81
5353	4	3	**Sunley Peace**[24] 3236 3-9-5 83 .... MartinDwyer 6 (D R C Elsworth) *mid-div: rdn wl over 2f out: styd on to go 4th ins fnl f* **9/1**	84
-116	5	nk	**Record Breaker (IRE)**[38] 2790 3-9-7 85 .... JoeFanning 10 (M Johnston) *chsd ldrs: pushed along over 4f out: rdn over 3f out: one pce fnl 2f* **11/4**[1]	85
0310	6	3/4	**Galianna (IRE)**[17] 3458 3-9-2 80 .... JamieSpencer 5 (Pat Eddery) *mid-div: rdn and swtchd lft over 2f out: styd on ins fnl f* **16/1**	79
0-31	7	3/4	**Chord**[23] 3284 3-8-12 76 .... (v) RyanMoore 8 (Sir Michael Stoute) *trckd ldrs: rdn over 2f out: wknd 1f out* **7/1**[3]	74
0000	8	1	**Strikeen (IRE)**[10] 3691 3-8-10 74 .... DarryllHolland 1 (T G Mills) *hld up towards rr: gd hdwy to trck ldrs 4f out: effrt and rn arnd u.p 3f out: one pce fnl 2f* **33/1**	70
5214	9	shd	**Yes One (IRE)**[32] 3003 3-8-10 74 .... JHBowman 13 (J W Hills) *nvr bttr than mid-div* **16/1**	70
6011	10	1 1/4	**Polish Red**[20] 3385 3-9-2 80 .... JohnEgan 3 (G G Margarson) *hld up last: sme hdwy u.p over 2f out: nvr trbld ldrs* **6/1**[2]	74
-6P5	11	2	**Amazing Request**[13] 3590 3-9-4 82 .... RichardHughes 11 (R Charlton) *hld up towards rr: rdn 3f out: no imp* **16/1**	73
5020	12	4	**Mutadarrej (IRE)**[38] 2790 3-9-7 85 .... (b[1]) RHills 9 (J L Dunlop) *hld up towards rr: rdn 3f out: no imp* **14/1**	70
-001	13	6	**Blue Jet (USA)**[18] 3415 3-8-11 75 .... DeanMcKeown 2 (R M Whitaker) *mid-div tl wknd 3f out* **66/1**	50

2m 39.76s (6.76) **Going Correction** +0.625s/f (Yiel) **13** Ran SP% **120.6**
Speed ratings (Par 102): **102,101,101,99,98 98,97,97,97,96 94,92,88**
CSF £62.64 CT £1098.27 TOTE £11.00: £3.00, £2.90, £4.40; EX 70.10 Trifecta £948.40 Part won. Pool £1,335.82 - 0.40 winning units. Place 6 £1,135.62, Place 5 £365.97..
Owner Sheikh Ahmed Al Maktoum **Bred** Darley **Trained** Lambourn, Berks

FOCUS
A decent three-year-old handicap in which the winner made most under a good ride. The principals were always prominent and the form makes sense rated around the runner-up and fourth.
T/Jkpt: Not won. T/Plt: £1,569.30 to a £1 stake. Pool: £158,547.66. 73.75 winning tickets.
T/Qpdt: £76.20 to a £1 stake. Pool: £10,215.80. 99.20 winning tickets. TM

2983 CARLISLE (R-H)
Sunday, July 29
OFFICIAL GOING: Good to firm (good in places; 9.0)
Wind: Fresh, half-behind Weather: Cloudy

3994 CARLISLE UNITED FOOTBALL CLUB MAIDEN STKS (DIV I) — 6f 192y
2:00 (2:00) (Class 5) 3-Y-O+ — £2,169 (£645; £322; £161) Stalls High

Form				RPR
5	1		**Blackat Blackitten (IRE)**[19] 3395 3-9-0 0 .... JamieMoriarty(3) 10 (G A Butler) *in tch: drvn and edgd rt 2f out: led ins fnl f: kpt on strly* **7/1**	78
305	2	1 1/4	**Red Blossom**[17] 3454 3-8-12 71 .... SebSanders 1 (Sir Mark Prescott) *chsd ldrs: effrt and hrd drvn fr over 2f out: sn ev ch: hung rt ins fnl f: kpt on* **9/2**[3]	70
32-2	3	1 1/4	**Cooperstown**[31] 3015 4-9-10 75 .... TomEaves 11 (I Semple) *dwlt: rcvrd and led after 1f: edgd lft and hdd ins fnl f: one pce* **13/8**[1]	75
5-4	4	4	**Denbera Dancer (USA)**[18] 3436 3-9-0 0 .... GregFairley(3) 5 (M Johnston) *t.k.h: led 1f: pressed ldr: ev ch tl wknd ent fnl f* **7/4**[2]	61
2203	5	4	**Mangano**[8] 3752 3-9-3 49 .... StephenDonohoe 2 (A Berry) *s.i.s: sn rdn in rr: no imp fr 2f out* **14/1**	50
0350	6	3/4	**Musette (IRE)**[2] 3914 4-9-0 47 .... MichaelJStainton(5) 7 (R E Barr) *in tch: outpcd 3f out: n.d after* **50/1**	46
4	7	5	**Papa's Princess**[20] 3372 3-8-5 0 .... GaryBartley(7) 9 (J S Goldie) *s.i.s: rdn in rr 1/2-way: nvr on terms* **22/1**	30+
00-0	8	nk	**Mccormack (IRE)**[38] 2795 5-9-10 40 .... DO'Donohoe 6 (Micky Hammond) *bhd: drvn along 1/2-way: sn btn* **150/1**	34
00	9	3 1/2	**Scruffy (IRE)**[11] 3639 3-8-10 0 .... KellyHarrison(7) 8 (C J Teague) *s.i.s: struggling fr 1/2-way* **150/1**	24
00	10	1	**Flying Princess (IRE)**[11] 3639 3-8-5 0 .... AdamCarter(7) 4 (A Berry) *chsd ldrs to 3f out: sn wknd* **200/1**	17

1m 26.1s (-1.00) **Going Correction** -0.10s/f (Good)
WFA 3 from 4yo+ 7lb **10** Ran SP% **119.9**
Speed ratings (Par 103): **101,99,98,93,89 88,82,82,78,76**
CSF £39.12 TOTE £7.50: £1.70, £1.80, £1.30; EX 34.30.
Owner Beetle N Wedge Partnership **Bred** Conor Murphy **Trained** Blewbury, Oxon
■ Stewards' Enquiry : Seb Sanders two-day ban: used whip with excessive frequency (Aug 9-10)

FOCUS
A run-of-the-mill maiden in which the pace was sound and the form looks pretty solid rated around the placed horses.

3995 NORTHERN RACING CLUB MAIDEN AUCTION STKS — 5f
2:30 (2:32) (Class 5) 2-Y-O — £2,817 (£838; £418; £209) Stalls High

Form				RPR
	1		**Lesson In Humility (IRE)** 2-8-7 0 .... PhillipMakin 1 (K R Burke) *chsd ldrs: led over 1f out: sn rdn and flashed tail: hld on wl fnl f* **16/1**	69
063	2	nk	**Stormy Journey**[10] 3673 2-8-9 0 .... TomEaves 8 (Mrs K Walton) *disp ld: rdn over 2f out: kpt on wl u.p: jst hld* **11/1**[3]	70
36	3	nk	**Meydan Dubai (IRE)**[36] 2855 2-9-1 0 .... GeorgeBaker 3 (J R Best) *slt ld to over 1f out: rallied: kpt on fnl f: hld nr fin* **8/15**[1]	75
	4	nk	**Tugalu (IRE)** 2-9-1 0 .... DO'Donohoe 7 (K A Ryan) *chsd ldrs: drvn over 2f out: kpt on wl fnl f* **5/1**[2]	75+
030	5	3/4	**The Magic Blanket (IRE)**[5] 3812 2-8-2 0 .... KristinStubbs(7) 13 (Mrs L Stubbs) *chsd ldrs: effrt and ev ch over 1f out: no ex wl ins fnl f* **33/1**	65
	6	2 1/2	**Admiralcollingwood** 2-8-12 0 .... GrahamGibbons 9 (J J Quinn) *s.i.s: bhd tl styd on fr over 1f out: bttr for r* **25/1**	59
40	7	1/2	**Baby Jack**[32] 2983 2-8-9 0 .... SilvestreDeSousa 5 (D Nicholls) *towards rr: drvn 1/2-way: sme late hdwy: nvr rchd ldrs* **12/1**	54
0	8	1 3/4	**Rewski (IRE)**[13] 3596 2-8-9 0 .... StephenDonohoe 6 (Ms Deborah J Evans) *in tch: outpcd 1/2-way: n.d after* **80/1**	48
00	9	1/2	**Maahe (IRE)**[12] 3606 2-8-7 0 .... JamieMoriarty(3) 4 (R A Fahey) *t.k.h in midfield: outpcd fr 1/2-way* **40/1**	47
00	10	2 1/2	**Paint Stripper**[26] 3192 2-8-5 0 ow1 .... MichaelJStainton(5) 11 (W Storey) *towards rr: drvn 1/2-way: nvr on terms* **100/1**	38
00	11	nk	**Charlie Green (IRE)**[47] 2526 2-8-5 0 .... (t) JohnCavanagh(7) 10 (Paul Green) *s.i.s: nvr on terms* **100/1**	39
	12	8	**Tafira (IRE)** 2-7-11 0 .... DeclanCannon(7) 12 (K R Burke) *s.i.s: a bhd* **50/1**	—

61.27 secs (-0.23) **Going Correction** -0.10s/f (Good) **12** Ran SP% **118.2**
Speed ratings (Par 94): **97,96,96,95,94 90,89,86,85,81 81,68**
CSF £170.69 TOTE £21.90: £4.50, £2.30, £1.10; EX 321.70.
Owner M Nelmes-Crocker **Bred** Kevin Quinn **Trained** Middleham Moor, N Yorks
■ Stewards' Enquiry : John Cavanagh caution: used whip when out of contention.

FOCUS
Little strength in depth but a race in which the pace was sound throughout. The form is pretty average using the runner-up and fifth as guides.

NOTEBOOK
Lesson In Humility(IRE), a 22,000gns half-sister to a 6f juvenile winner, was easy to back but made a winning debut in an ordinary event, despite flashing her tail for pressure. She will stay 6f and, in view of her inexperience here, may well be capable of better. (op 14-1)

Stormy Journey is starting to look exposed but he had the run of the race and turned in his best effort returned to a sound surface. He will be suited by the return to 6f and, although vulnerable to the more progressive types in this grade, looks sure to pick up a minor event in due course. (op 14-1)

Meydan Dubai(IRE), who more than confirmed debut promise when a close sixth in last month's Chesham at Royal Ascot, looked to have sound claims in this uncompetitive event but was found out by the drop back to this trip. The return to 6f and beyond will suit and he remains capable of winning a similar event. (op 4-6 tchd 8-11 tchd 4-5 in places)

Tugalu(IRE) ◆, who cost 29,000gns and is related to winners over 1m and beyond, shaped with promise on this racecourse debut. He will be well suited by 6f and beyond and looks capable of winning in ordinary maiden company. (op 9-2 tchd 4-1 tchd 11-2 in a place)

The Magic Blanket(IRE), who disappointed at Musselburgh from a wide draw on his previous start, is starting to look exposed but he fared better back at this stiffer task. However, he is invariably going to look vulnerable to the more progressive sorts in this type of event. (op 25-1)
Admiralcollingwood ◆, a 14,000gns third foal of a dual 6f-1m winner at three years, showed more than enough after a sluggish start to suggest a modest event or two can be found in due course, especially over further. (op 20-1)

3996 SUPPORT THE EQUINE GRASS SICKNESS FUND CLAIMING STKS 6f 192y
3:00 (3:00) (Class 6) 3-Y-0+ **£2,047** (£604; £302) **Stalls** High

Form RPR
304 **1** **Copper King**[10] 3690 3-9-5 77 StephenDonohoe 2 59
(P D Evans) *chsd ldrs: led 2f out: kpt on wl fnl f* **2/1**[1]
0400 **2** *1 ¾* **Lewis Lloyd (IRE)**[7] 3764 4-8-12 45 (t) MichaelJStainton(5) 9 48
(R E Barr) *s.i.s: bhd tl styd on fnl 2f: nt rch wnr* **18/1**
6600 **3** *shd* **Telepathic (IRE)**[10] 3674 7-8-11 42 KellyHarrison(7) 4 49
(A Berry) *in tch: effrt 2f out: kpt on fnl f: no imp* **40/1**
0060 **4** *¾* **Following Flow (USA)**[5] 3814 5-8-13 47 (p) JamieMoriarty(3) 6 45
(R Allan) *s.i.s: hld up: hdwy over 1f out: no imp* **16/1**[3]
0000 **5** *1 ¾* **Obe One**[34] 2937 7-8-11 42 AdamCarter(7) 3 42
(A Berry) *towards rr: hdwy in centre over 2f out: edgd rt over 1f out: nvr rchd ldrs* **33/1**
1200 **6** *3* **Baylaw Star**[5] 3814 6-9-8 72 PJMcDonald(3) 13 41
(I W McInnes) *w ldr tl outpcd fr 2f out* **5/2**[2]
0060 **7** *1 ¾* **Briery Blaze**[25] 3204 4-8-12 42 PhillipMakin 5 23
(G F Bridgwater) *led tl hung lft and hdd 2f out: sn btn* **33/1**
4222 **8** *1* **Local Poet**[10] 3675 6-9-7 61 (b) TomEaves 1 29
(I Semple) *chsd ldrs tl hung rt and wknd over 2f out* **2/1**[1]
0066 **9** *3* **Coronation Flight**[15] 3538 4-9-0 40 DO'Donohoe 7 14
(F P Murtagh) *missed break: a bhd* **25/1**

1m 26.79s (-0.31) **Going Correction** -0.10s/f (Good)
WFA 3 from 4yo+ 7lb **9** Ran SP% **118.6**
Speed ratings (Par 101): **97,95,94,94,92 88,86,85,82**
CSF £38.82 TOTE £2.90: £1.40, £1.80, £7.20; EX 37.50.Copper King was claimed by J. W. Hills for £15,000.
Owner R Edwards & J Swinnerton **Bred** Miss A V Hill **Trained** Pandy, Monmouths

FOCUS
A poor claimer in which two of the three market leaders disappointed and the form is moderate.

3997 JULIE & DAVID ALLISON DOBIES VAUXHALL H'CAP 7f 200y
3:35 (3:36) (Class 5) (0-70,67) 3-Y-0 **£2,817** (£838; £418; £209) **Stalls** High

Form RPR
0-50 **1** **Alberts Story (USA)**[47] 2530 3-8-2 48 SilvestreDeSousa 14 56
(R A Fahey) *hld up: hdwy 2f out: led ins fnl f: hld on wl* **20/1**
006 **2** *hd* **Caravel (IRE)**[17] 3447 3-9-5 65 SebSanders 8 73+
(Sir Mark Prescott) *bhd: pushed along 1/2-way: hdwy and swtchd rt over 1f out: hrd rdn: kpt on wl fnl f: jst hld* **5/2**[1]
0314 **3** *1* **Palmetto Point**[18] 3429 3-8-7 56 (p) TravisBlock(3) 3 62
(H Morrison) *set decent gallop: led to ins fnl f: kpt on same pce* **4/1**[2]
0-66 **4** *2* **Lilac Moon (GER)**[55] 2312 3-8-9 55 DO'Donohoe 12 56
(Mrs A Duffield) *midfield: effrt over 2f out: kpt on same pce fnl f* **12/1**
0-45 **5** *¾* **Greyfriars Abbey**[15] 3539 3-8-11 60 GregFairley(3) 1 59+
(M Johnston) *bhd: rdn and hdwy over 1f out: kpt on fnl f: nrst fin* **10/1**
332 **6** *½* **Ducal Pip Squeak**[20] 3382 3-9-7 67 PhillipMakin 5 65
(M Dods) *chsd ldrs: rdn over 2f out: sn one pce* **13/2**[3]
-060 **7** *2* **Beck**[144] 636 3-7-10 49 KellyHarrison(7) 13 43
(W M Brisbourne) *midfield: effrt over 2f out: edgd rt: sn no imp* **66/1**
0-00 **8** *1* **Gallows Hill (USA)**[76] 1712 3-7-13 52 ow2 JamesRogers(7) 2 43
(R A Fahey) *chsd ldrs: outpcd over 2f out: n.d after* **33/1**
0500 **9** *nk* **Fun In The Sun**[1] 3965 3-8-7 53 ow1 (v) StephenDonohoe 10 44
(P D Evans) *s.i.s: hld up: effrt centre over 2f out: nvr rchd ldrs* **25/1**
0622 **10** *1 ¼* **Milson's Point (IRE)**[15] 3540 3-9-2 62 TomEaves 6 50
(I Semple) *in tch tl rdn and wknd wl over 1f out* **9/1**
5-00 **11** *2 ½* **Berbatov**[14] 3570 3-7-13 50 ColinHaddon(5) 9 32
(Paul Green) *t.k.h in rr: rdn over 2f out: nvr on terms* **28/1**
0-05 **12** *5* **Buds Dilemma**[40] 2740 3-7-11 48 NataliaGemelova(5) 4 18
(I W McInnes) *chsd ldr tl wknd fr 2f out* **50/1**
000 **13** *3* **Centenary (IRE)**[27] 3161 3-8-11 60 JamieMoriarty(3) 11 24
(J J Quinn) *in tch tl hung lft and wknd 2f out* **10/1**
0030 **14** *1 ½* **Jentris Girl (IRE)**[11] 3639 3-8-9 55 GrahamGibbons 7 15
(T D Easterby) *towards rr: rdn over 3f out: sn btn* **33/1**

1m 38.51s (-1.58) **Going Correction** -0.10s/f (Good) **14** Ran SP% **119.2**
Speed ratings (Par 100): **103,102,101,99,99 98,96,95,95,94 91,86,83,82**
CSF £65.86 CT £261.03 TOTE £23.00: £6.10, £1.60, £1.60; EX 128.90.
Owner Mr & Mrs G Calder **Bred** E G Odette **Trained** Musley Bank, N Yorks

FOCUS
A run-of-the-mill handicap and the pace was again sound. The form looks sound enough rated through the fourth and fifth.
Alberts Story(USA) Official explanation: trainer's rep said, regarding apparent improvement in form, that the gelding previously ran keen but on this occasion settled off a strong pace.

3998 CUMBRIA COMMUNITY FOUNDATION H'CAP 5f 193y
4:10 (4:10) (Class 4) (0-80,79) 4-Y-0+ **£6,477** (£1,927; £963; £481) **Stalls** High

Form RPR
1114 **1** **Whitbarrow (IRE)**[12] 3623 8-9-2 79 (b) JamesMillman(5) 8 92+
(B R Millman) *mde all: rdn and r.o wl fnl 2f* **15/2**
0000 **2** *2* **Steel Blue**[13] 3585 7-8-6 69 MichaelJStainton(5) 3 76
(R M Whitaker) *prom: effrt over 2f out: edgd rt over 1f out: kpt on: nt rch wnr* **14/1**
000 **3** *1* **Choreography**[32] 2985 4-8-5 63 SilvestreDeSousa 13 67
(D Nicholls) *prom: effrt over 2f out: one pce fnl f* **12/1**
355 **4** *1* **Welcome Approach**[1] 3954 4-8-8 66 PhillipMakin 9 67
(J R Weymes) *midfield: effrt over 2f out: kpt on fnl f: no imp* **5/1**[1]
2042 **5** *shd* **Cross Of Lorraine (IRE)**[13] 3585 4-8-6 67 ow1 (b) JamieMoriarty(3) 7 67
(J Wade) *chsd ldrs: drvn over 2f out: one pce over 1f out* **11/2**[2]
1-23 **6** *shd* **Observatory Star (IRE)**[17] 3472 4-8-8 66 (b) GrahamGibbons 5 66
(T D Easterby) *midfield: pushed along whn n.m.r briefly 1/2-way: kpt on fnl f: nrst fin* **7/1**[3]
3600 **7** *2* **Brigadore**[9] 3723 8-8-0 63 ColinHaddon(5) 10 57
(J G Given) *s.i.s: effrt ins over 1f out: n.d* **10/1**
0 **8** *1 ¼* **Titinius (IRE)**[57] 2256 7-8-4 62 DO'Donohoe 11 52
(Micky Hammond) *hld up: pushed along 1/2-way: nvr on terms* **25/1**
33-3 **9** *shd* **Bahamian Duke**[95] 1241 4-7-13 64 DeclanCannon(7) 1 53
(K R Burke) *cl up outside: rdn and wandered fr 2f out: sn outpcd* **10/1**
0604 **10** *¾* **Hit's Only Money (IRE)**[6] 3787 7-7-10 61 oh3 ow1 KellyHarrison(7) 6 48
(J S Goldie) *bhd: pushed along 1/2-way: n.d* **8/1**
3000 **11** *½* **Ellens Academy (IRE)**[14] 3569 12-8-6 67 GregFairley(3) 4 52
(E J Alston) *in tch: pushed along over 2f out: sn btn* **14/1**
-020 **12** *9* **Heureux (USA)**[32] 2985 4-8-13 71 (b) TomEaves 12 27
(J Howard Johnson) *chsd ldrs tl wknd over 2f out* **8/1**

1m 11.7s (-1.91) **Going Correction** -0.10s/f (Good) course record **12** Ran SP% **121.6**
Speed ratings (Par 105): **108,105,104,102,102 102,99,98,97,96 96,84**
CSF £110.72 CT £1282.31 TOTE £8.60: £2.90, £5.60, £4.70; EX 135.40.
Owner Mrs H Brain **Bred** James Burns And A Moynan **Trained** Kentisbeare, Devon

FOCUS
Exposed performers in this ordinary sprint. The pace was sound throughout and the winner raced in the centre but the winner is the best guide with the form behind not that solid.

3999 PROFESSIONAL EVENT STEWARDING H'CAP 6f 192y
4:45 (4:46) (Class 5) (0-70,69) 3-Y-0+ **£2,817** (£838; £418; £209) **Stalls** High

Form RPR
0340 **1** **Pay Time**[20] 3375 8-8-10 56 NeilBrown(5) 2 65
(R E Barr) *chsd ldrs: led over 1f out: edgd lft ins fnl f: kpt on wl* **28/1**
4-53 **2** *1* **Vanilla Delight (IRE)**[36] 2893 4-9-13 68 TomEaves 7 74
(J Howard Johnson) *cl up: effrt and ev ch over 1f out: kpt on ins fnl f* **14/1**
1045 **3** *nk* **Violent Velocity (IRE)**[34] 2936 4-9-9 67 DougieCostello(3) 5 72
(J J Quinn) *hld up in tch: rdn over 2f out: effrt and hdwy over 1f out: kpt on fnl f* **12/1**
2512 **4** *1* **Motafarred (IRE)**[11] 3644 5-9-9 64 SebSanders 12 66
(Micky Hammond) *midfield: pushed along over 3f out: swtchd rt over 1f out: kpt on wl fnl f: nrst fin* **7/2**[1]
6103 **5** *hd* **Eternal Legacy (IRE)**[7] 3765 5-8-6 54 GaryBartley(7) 1 56
(E J Alston) *bhd tl hdwy over 1f out: nrst fin* **16/1**
3020 **6** *shd* **Kabis Amigos**[85] 1481 5-10-0 69 (t) SilvestreDeSousa 14 71
(D Nicholls) *led to over 1f out: sn one pce* **5/1**[2]
221 **7** *hd* **Turn Me On (IRE)**[30] 3067 4-9-8 63 GrahamGibbons 11 64
(T D Walford) *t.k.h early: chsd ldrs: effrt over 2f out: no ex over 1f out* **7/2**[1]
-000 **8** *½* **Brace Of Doves**[41] 2714 5-8-10 54 GregFairley(3) 10 54
(D W Whillans) *prom: effrt and rdn over 2f out: no ex over 1f out* **25/1**
5050 **9** *½* **Franksalot (IRE)**[5] 3816 7-9-11 69 PJMcDonald(3) 13 67
(I W McInnes) *hld up in midfield: rdn over 2f out: no imp* **20/1**
0-6 **10** *shd* **Celtic Spa (IRE)**[2] 3904 5-10-0 69 StephenDonohoe 3 67
(P D Evans) *hld up: effrt outside over 2f out: sn no imp* **20/1**
-300 **11** *2 ½* **Rigat**[26] 3194 4-9-10 65 PhillipMakin 8 56
(T D Barron) *s.i.s: rdn in rr 3f out: n.d* **20/1**
0605 **12** *½* **Ours (IRE)**[18] 3414 4-8-10 54 (p) JamieMoriarty(3) 4 44
(J D Bethell) *s.i.s: nvr on terms* **9/1**[3]
0002 **13** *hd* **Fair Shake (IRE)**[7] 3765 7-9-4 59 (v) FTahir 9 49
(Karen McLintock) *bhd: rdn over 3f out: nvr on terms* **12/1**
445 **14** *3* **Derricks Dotty**[19] 3406 3-9-7 69 DO'Donohoe 6 50
(N J Vaughan) *in tch tl wknd fr 2f out* **9/1**[3]

1m 26.11s (-0.99) **Going Correction** -0.10s/f (Good)
WFA 3 from 4yo+ 7lb **14** Ran SP% **130.6**
Speed ratings (Par 103): **101,99,99,98,98 98,97,97,96,96 93,93,92,89**
CSF £381.93 CT £4937.90 TOTE £43.90: £9.70, £3.30, £5.70; EX 304.10.
Owner Mrs R E Barr **Bred** M Paver & M D M Racing Thoroughbreds Ltd **Trained** Seamer, N Yorks

FOCUS
Another ordinary handicap in which the pace was fair and the form looks sound rated around the placed horses.
Pay Time Official explanation: trainer said, regarding apparent improvement in form, that the mare was suited by the quicker ground.

4000 CARLISLE UNITED FOOTBALL CLUB MAIDEN STKS (DIV II) 6f 192y
5:15 (5:18) (Class 5) 3-Y-0+ **£2,169** (£645; £322; £161) **Stalls** High

Form RPR
3 **1** **One Giant Leap (IRE)**[79] 1633 3-8-9 0 TravisBlock(3) 2 53
(H Morrison) *trckd ldrs: led over 2f out: rdn out* **15/8**[2]
60 **2** *2* **Julian Joachim (USA)**[20] 3382 3-9-3 0 J-PGuillambert 5 53
(G A Swinbank) *in tch: effrt and chsd wnr over 1f out: kpt on ins fnl f* **6/1**[3]
5 **3** *1 ¼* **War Anthem**[17] 3447 3-9-3 0 SebSanders 8 50
(C R Egerton) *s.i.s: effrt fr rr over 2f out: hung rt: kpt on fnl f: nrst fin* **7/4**[1]
4 *¾* **Shevalina (IRE)**[336] 2422 5-9-2 0 JerryO'Dwyer(3) 4 46
(Adrian Sexton, Ire) *cl up tl rdn and no ex over 1f out* **33/1**
0-00 **5** *1* **Bunderos (IRE)**[40] 2740 3-8-9 40 JamieMoriarty(3) 7 40
(R A Fahey) *chsd ldrs tl rdn and no ex over 1f out* **33/1**
5036 **6** *1 ¼* **Musical Chimes**[23] 3277 4-8-12 45 PatrickDonaghy(7) 10 40
(W M Brisbourne) *led to over 2f out: wknd over 1f out* **25/1**
6000 **7** *5* **O'Dwyer (IRE)**[23] 3257 3-9-3 39 SilvestreDeSousa 11 28
(A D Brown) *in tch: drvn 1/2-way: btn over 1f out* **66/1**
8 *5* **Alimacdee** 3-8-12 0 TomEaves 9 10
(I Semple) *s.i.s: nvr on terms* **16/1**
9 *1* **Private Soldier** 4-9-10 0 DO'Donohoe 3 15
(N J Vaughan) *s.i.s: a bhd* **8/1**
10 *8* **Florentino** 3-8-9 0 PJMcDonald(3) 1 —
(C W Thornton) *missed break: nvr on terms* **33/1**

1m 26.9s (-0.20) **Going Correction** -0.10s/f (Good)
WFA 3 from 4yo+ 7lb **10** Ran SP% **116.6**
Speed ratings (Par 103): **97,94,93,92,91 89,84,78,77,68**
CSF £12.87 TOTE £2.50: £1.30, £2.00, £1.20; EX 15.20.
Owner Loddington Bloodstock **Bred** R J Cornelius **Trained** East Ilsley, Berks

FOCUS
An uncompetitive event in which the pace seemed sound but the form is limited by the proximity of the fifth and sixth.
Florentino Official explanation: jockey said filly missed the break

4001 CBS OUTDOOR H'CAP 5f
5:45 (5:47) (Class 5) (0-70,67) 3-Y-0 **£2,817** (£838; £418; £209) **Stalls** High

Form RPR
1334 **1** **Mandurah (IRE)**[51] 2435 3-9-5 65 SilvestreDeSousa 6 74
(D Nicholls) *cl up: effrt over 1f out: led wl ins fnl f: all out* **5/1**[2]
-441 **2** *shd* **Inspainagain (USA)**[34] 2939 3-9-6 66 PhillipMakin 4 75
(T D Barron) *w ldr: led 2f out: sn hrd pressed: hdd wl ins fnl f: rallied: jst failed* **11/4**[2]
315 **3** *4* **Twosheetstothewind**[36] 2867 3-9-6 66 TomEaves 7 61
(M Dods) *led to 2f out: sn rdn and one pce* **10/3**[3]
1164 **4** *1 ¾* **Jojesse**[61] 2120 3-8-10 59 PJMcDonald(3) 2 47
(G A Swinbank) *prom: effrt over 2f out: no imp over 1f out* **9/2**
3416 **5** *hd* **Rue Soleil**[6] 3786 3-8-11 60 JamieMoriarty(3) 5 48
(J R Weymes) *prom tl rdn and outpcd fr 2f out* **12/1**
-430 **6** *7* **Mickleberry (IRE)**[57] 2255 3-8-11 57 SebSanders 1 19
(J D Bethell) *chsd ldrs tl rdn and wknd fr 2f out* **10/1**

065- 7 2 **Bidders Itch**344 4607 3-7-13 48 oh3 .... DominicFox(3) 3 —
(A Berry) *bhd: drvn after 2f: sn wknd* 66/1
-000 8 16 **Winning Spirit (IRE)**11 3637 3-9-0 67 .... OliveGaule(7) 8 —
(D Nicholls) *v s.i.s: t.o thrght* 25/1
60.73 secs (-0.77) **Going Correction** -0.10s/f (Good) 8 Ran SP% **118.6**
Speed ratings (Par 100): **102,101,95,92,92 81,77,52**
CSF £10.12 CT £23.07 TOTE £4.40: £1.50, £1.40, £1.50; EX 13.30 Place 6 £622.41, Place 5 £380.76..
Owner Martin Hignett **Bred** Michael Lyons **Trained** Sessay, N Yorks

FOCUS
Another ordinary handicap and, although the pace was sound, those racing up with the pace again held the edge. The form is modest despite the first two coming clear.
Bidders Itch Official explanation: jockey said filly's bit slipped
T/Plt: £752.50 to a £1 stake. Pool: £59,170.85. 57.40 winning tickets. T/Qpdt: £213.40 to a £1 stake. Pool: £3,143.60. 10.90 winning tickets. RY

3718 PONTEFRACT (L-H)
Sunday, July 29

OFFICIAL GOING: Good to soft (6.1)
10" rain over the previous six weeks but after three dry days the ground was reckoned' mainly soft but patchy'.
Wind: Moderate, half-behind Weather: Fine

4002 TOLENT CONSTRUCTION MAIDEN STKS 5f
2:05 (2:09) (Class 4) 2-Y-0 **£5,181** (£1,541; £770; £384) **Stalls** Low

Form RPR
3 1 **The Real Guru**92 1291 2-9-0 0 .... AndrewMullen(3) 3 74
(Mrs A Duffield) *chsd ldrs: wnt 2nd over 2f out: led appr fnl f: drvn out* 3/12
33 2 2 **Wotashirtfull (IRE)**36 2863 2-9-3 0 .... PaulMulrennan 1 67
(K A Ryan) *led: hdd appr fnl f: fdd last 150yds* 11/41
05 3 ¾ **Glenshee (IRE)**38 2804 2-9-3 0 .... TPO'Shea 2 64
(J J Quinn) *chsd ldrs outpcd 2f out: styd on fnl f* 7/1
0 4 1 ¼ **Lecanvey**73 1792 2-9-3 0 .... PaulHanagan 7 60
(R A Fahey) *chsd ldrs: outpcd over 2f out: hung lft over 1f out: kpt on* 7/23
0 5 ½ **Harlequinn Danseur (IRE)**13 3592 2-9-3 0 ....(t) KimTinkler 6 58
(N Tinkler) *chsd ldrs: outpcd over 2f out: kpt on* 28/1
6 1 ½ **Lamistrelle (IRE)** 2-8-12 0 .... RoystonFfrench 4 47
(Mrs A Duffield) *in rr: sn drvn along: kpt on fnl 2f* 8/1
0 7 shd **Falcon Speed**8 3750 2-8-12 0 .... MickyFenton 9 47
(P T Midgley) *chsd ldrs: outpcd over 2f out: no ch after* 40/1
00 8 2 ½ **Jafra (IRE)**36 2869 2-9-3 0 ....(b1) TedDurcan 10 43
(R M Whitaker) *swvd rt s: chsd ldrs on outer: hung rt thrght: lost pl over 1f out* 22/1
9 13 **Caffrey Kelly** 2-9-3 0 .... PaulFessey 8 —
(J J Quinn) *s.i.s: a outpcd and in rr: bhd fnl 2f* 20/1
000 10 4 **Doubtless**4 3833 2-8-5 0 ....(b) DanielleMcCreery(7) 5 —
(D W Chapman) *s.s: a detached in rr* 125/1
66.55 secs (2.75) **Going Correction** +0.35s/f (Good) 10 Ran SP% **113.3**
Speed ratings (Par 96): **92,88,87,85,84 82,82,78,57,51**
CSF £10.58 TOTE £4.00: £1.70, £1.40, £2.30; EX 12.30.
Owner Adrian & Alison Parry **Bred** And Mrs A Parry **Trained** Constable Burton, N Yorks

FOCUS
Modest but sound form rated around the principals. The winner stepped up on his debut effort, the race rated through the runner-up.

NOTEBOOK
The Real Guru, absent for three months since Leicester due to coughing, won going away and can improve again. He looks ideal nursery material. (op 7-2)
Wotashirtfull(IRE), dropping back in trip, took them along but his stride shortened noticeably in the closing stages. Quicker ground will aid his cause. (op 7-2)
Glenshee(IRE), dropping back a furlong in trip, picked up again late on and 6f in nursery company should be his cup of tea. (op 8-1)
Lecanvey, another dropping back in distance, became outpaced and then showed his inexperience. There ought to be better to come.
Harlequinn Danseur(IRE) showed a lot more than on his debut but will need another outing under his belt before he qualifies for a nursery mark. (op 40-1)
Lamistrelle(IRE), on the leg and narrow, took an age to get going on her debut but was picking up in encouraging fashion late on. This should have opened her eyes. (op 5-1)

4003 YORKSHIRE SOCIETY H'CAP 1m 4f 8y
2:40 (2:40) (Class 5) (0-70,69) 3-Y-0+ **£3,886** (£1,156; £577; £288) **Stalls** Low

Form RPR
0-50 1 **Make Haste (IRE)**72 1812 3-9-4 69 .... SteveDrowne 4 81+
(R Charlton) *sn chsng ldrs: drvn 6f out: wnt 2nd over 2f out: led over 1f out: styd on strly: eased nr fin* 11/101
60-0 2 ½ **Dreams Jewel**20 3365 7-8-12 54 .... NeilChalmers(3) 5 59
(C Roberts) *s.i.s: in rr: hdwy over 2f out: styd on to go 2nd 1f out: no ex* 66/1
3350 3 4 **Patavium (IRE)**22 3300 4-9-0 53 .... PaulFessey 1 52
(E W Tuer) *led: drvn and qcknd 3f out: hdd over 1f out: one pce* 10/32
-501 4 2 ½ **Campbells Lad**11 3638 6-9-7 63 .... PatrickMathers(3) 8 58
(Mrs G S Rees) *hld up in rr: stdy hdwy 5f out: effrt over 2f out: edgd rt and one pce* 14/1
0-01 5 11 **Simply St Lucia**15 3538 5-9-2 55 .... TedDurcan 3 32
(J R Weymes) *trckd ldrs: wknd 2f out* 6/13
2405 6 2 **Ninetyninetreble (IRE)**61 2118 4-10-0 67 .... PaulMulrennan 6 41
(Grant Tuer) *chsd ldrs: lost pl 3f out: sn bhd* 20/1
0-60 7 4 **Caraman (IRE)**158 515 9-9-7 60 .... MickyFenton 7 28
(J J Quinn) *chsd ldrs: lost pl over 1f out* 10/1
1-05 8 50 **Floodlight Fantasy**94 1263 4-9-12 65 ....(p) PaulHanagan 2 —
(Jedd O'Keeffe) *mid-div: drvn 8f out: lost pl over 3f out: sn bhd: t.o* 16/1
2m 43.32s (3.02) **Going Correction** +0.35s/f (Good)
WFA 3 from 4yo+ 12lb 8 Ran SP% **112.9**
Speed ratings (Par 103): **103,102,100,98,91 89,87,53**
CSF £81.89 CT £199.04 TOTE £1.80: £1.20, £6.40, £1.30; EX 84.00.
Owner B E Nielsen **Bred** Epona Bloodstock Ltd **Trained** Beckhampton, Wilts

FOCUS
A moderate handicap in which the placed form is not strong, but the winner is capable of better and the runner-up should be able to find a race.
Ninetyninetreble(IRE) Official explanation: trainer said gelding had had a breathing problem

4004 GRAHAM ROCK MEMORIAL H'CAP 1m 2f 6y
3:15 (3:15) (Class 4) (0-85,84) 3-Y-0 **£6,477** (£1,927; £963; £481) **Stalls** Low

Form RPR
2-63 1 **Sagredo (USA)**16 3495 3-9-7 84 .... PaulHanagan 4 97+
(Sir Mark Prescott) *hld up in last: hdwy on inner over 2f out: led over 1f out: rdn clr: eased towards fin* 5/21
6531 2 4 **John Dillon (IRE)**26 3181 3-8-0 66 ....(v) AndrewElliott(3) 5 69
(P C Haslam) *w ldr: drvn over 3f out: edgd rt then lft over 1f out: styd on to take 2nd last 75yds* 4/1
-314 3 1 ¼ **World Spirit**29 3100 3-8-12 75 .... SteveDrowne 3 76
(Rae Guest) *sn trcking ldrs: effrt over 2f out: wnt 2nd 1f out: kpt on same pce* 6/1
-224 4 6 **Giant Slalom**55 2305 3-8-11 74 .... PaulMulrennan 1 63
(W J Haggas) *tk keen grip: trckd ldrs: led 3f out tl over 1f out: sn wknd* 7/23
1466 5 2 ½ **Woodcraft**22 3335 3-9-2 79 .... TedDurcan 2 63
(B W Hills) *set mod pce: qcknd over 3f out: sn hdd: wknd appr fnl f* 3/12
2m 15.22s (1.14) **Going Correction** +0.35s/f (Good) 5 Ran SP% **110.1**
Speed ratings (Par 102): **109,105,104,100,98**
CSF £12.56 TOTE £2.90: £1.20, £2.40; EX 7.10.
Owner Dr Catherine Wills **Bred** Dr Catherine Wills **Trained** Newmarket, Suffolk

FOCUS
A fair handicap run at a sound gallop and in the end a clear-cut and most decisive winner.
Giant Slalom Official explanation: jockey said gelding had run too freely early on

4005 POMFRET STKS (LISTED RACE) 1m 4y
3:50 (3:50) (Class 1) 3-Y-0+
£17,034 (£6,456; £3,231; £1,611; £807; £405) **Stalls** Low

Form RPR
1-12 1 **Blue Ksar (FR)**57 2233 4-9-5 114 ....(t) TedDurcan 3 104+
(Saeed Bin Suroor) *trckd ldrs: led 2f out: styd on strly* 1/11
2-15 2 2 ½ **Contentious (USA)**22 3332 3-8-2 93 .... RoystonFfrench 5 85
(J L Dunlop) *trckd ldrs: chal over 2f out: styd on same pce* 16/1
2-62 3 ¾ **Tam Lin**23 3271 4-9-1 112 .... SteveDrowne 2 90
(Saeed Bin Suroor) *stdd s: t.k.h: effrt over 2f out: styd on same pce ins fnl f* 15/82
2202 4 1 ½ **Flying Clarets (IRE)**15 3558 4-8-10 92 .... PaulHanagan 4 82
(R A Fahey) *led: shkn up 3f out: hdd 2f out: kpt on same pce* 6/13
006 5 2 ½ **Voliere**18 3437 4-8-10 75 .... SaleemGolam 7 76
(S C Williams) *prom: effrt 3f out: one pce* 66/1
6640 6 1 ¾ **Knapton Hill**2 3897 3-8-2 82 .... PaulQuinn 1 70?
(R Hollinshead) *a in last: kpt on fnl 3f: nvr a factor* 100/1
1m 48.02s (2.32) **Going Correction** +0.35s/f (Good)
WFA 3 from 4yo 8lb 6 Ran SP% **107.4**
Speed ratings (Par 111): **102,99,98,97,94 93**
CSF £16.75 TOTE £1.80: £1.20, £3.30; EX 10.40.
Owner Godolphin **Bred** Meridan Stud And Haras Du Mezeray **Trained** Newmarket, Suffolk
■ The first running of this new Listed race.

FOCUS
A very steady pace and the two rank outsiders were not beaten off that far in the end, so the form cannot be taken too literally although the fifth is the best guide to the level.

NOTEBOOK
Blue Ksar(FR) is straightforward and ultra-reliable and made this look very plain sailing. (op 6-5 tchd 10-11)
Contentious(USA), having just her fifth career start, had 12lb to find with the winner on official ratings and, on paper at least, seemed to turn in an improved effort. (op 11-1)
Tam Lin, 2lb ahead of the winner on official ratings, was dropped in. As usual he took a keen grip but, over a trip short of his best, he stayed on in his own time inside the last. Godolphin are clearly finding their way with him. (op 7-4 tchd 13-8 and 2-1)
Flying Clarets(IRE) had plenty to find but ran her race. (op 13-2 tchd 5-1)
Voliere, whose one previous success was in a Clonmel maiden last year, was tackling an impossible task.
Knapton Hill, making a quick return, had a mountain to climb but picked up a handy £405 for missing her Sunday lunch. She has flattered at this level in the past. (op 66-1)

4006 ST. JOHN AMBULANCE H'CAP 6f
4:25 (4:25) (Class 3) (0-90,88) 3-Y-0+
£8,101 (£2,425; £1,212; £607; £302; £152) **Stalls** Low

Form RPR
3062 1 **Bel Cantor**10 3686 4-8-4 69 ....(p) AndrewMullen(3) 5 83
(W J H Ratcliffe) *mde all: qcknd clr 2f out: styd on strly: unchal* 7/1
-121 2 2 **Genki (IRE)**64 2044 3-9-5 86 .... SteveDrowne 9 93
(R Charlton) *trckd ldrs on outer: edgd lft over 1f out: kpt on wl ins fnl f* 10/31
0032 3 shd **Stonecrabstomorrow (IRE)**14 3569 4-8-11 73 ....(p) PaulHanagan 6 80
(R A Fahey) *trckd ldrs: t.k.h: kpt on same pce appr fnl f* 9/22
1361 4 1 ½ **Bid For Gold**9 3723 3-8-8 75 .... PaulMulrennan 1 76
(Jedd O'Keeffe) *hld up: hdwy on inner over 2f out: kpt on same pce fnl f* 13/2
0006 5 hd **Geojimali**9 3720 5-9-5 81 .... SaleemGolam 2 83
(J S Goldie) *towards rr: hdwy on inner over 2f out: sn chsng ldrs: kpt on same pce* 17/2
0626 6 1 ¾ **Paris Bell**7 3762 5-9-1 77 .... PaulQuinn 8 73
(T D Easterby) *s.i.s: hdwy over 2f out: kpt on same pce: nvr rchd ldrs* 9/1
5024 7 4 **Wheels In Motion (IRE)**17 3470 3-8-11 78 .... MickyFenton 10 60
(T P Tate) *chsd wnr: wknd 1f out* 12/1
3000 8 6 **Campo Bueno (FR)**8 3754 5-8-4 69 oh5 ....(b) PatrickMathers(3) 7 33
(A Berry) *sn in tch: rdn and lost pl over 2f out: sn bhd* 50/1
0320 9 shd **Damika (IRE)**15 3559 4-9-12 88 .... TedDurcan 4 52
(R M Whitaker) *hld up: effrt on outer over 2f out: sn rdn and lost pl* 6/13
00-0 10 7 **Imperial Sword**14 3569 4-9-4 80 .... PaulFessey 3 22
(T D Barron) *chsd ldrs: rdn and lost pl over 2f out: sn bhd* 25/1
1m 17.22s (-0.18) **Going Correction** +0.35s/f (Good)
WFA 3 from 4yo+ 5lb 10 Ran SP% **115.4**
Speed ratings (Par 107): **115,112,112,110,109 107,102,94,94,84**
CSF £30.24 CT £117.56 TOTE £8.40: £2.60, £1.70, £1.70; EX 38.40.
Owner W J H Ratcliffe **Bred** Henry And Mrs Rosemary Moszkowicz **Trained** Wensley, N Yorks

FOCUS
A fair handicap in which the winner always looked in total command and the form looks solid with the placed horses to recent marks.

NOTEBOOK
Bel Cantor, whose last success came from a 2lb higher mark, seemed improved by first-time cheekpieces. He went clear coming off the home turn and was never in any danger. (op 15-2 tchd 8-1 and 13-2)

Genki(IRE), absent for two months and 6lb higher, was on his toes and he continually swished his tail in the paddock. Drawn wide, he kept on strongly in the closing stages and this will not be lost on him. (op 3-1 tchd 7-2 and 4-1 in a place)
Stonecrabstomorrow(IRE), another fitted with first-time cheekpieces, was very keen to get on with it. He might be worth another try over seven and connections will hope for a flat-out gallop. (tchd 4-1)
Bid For Gold found an 8lb hike in the ratings too much. (op 8-1 tchd 6-1)
Geojimali, back on his last winning mark, needs luck in running with his come-from-the-back style and he is happier when able to bounce off the ground. (op 7-1 tchd 9-1)
Paris Bell, warm beforehand, made his usual tardy start and this was not one of his better days. (op 10-1)
Wheels In Motion(IRE) Official explanation: jockey said colt had been keen early on

4007 KEITH HAMMILL MEMORIAL MAIDEN STKS — 1m 4y
4:55 (4:57) (Class 5) 3-4-Y-O — **£4,533** (£1,348; £674; £336) **Stalls** Low

Form				RPR
4	1		**Twilight Star (IRE)**[17] 3447 3-9-3 0 ....(t) TedDurcan 2 (Saeed Bin Suroor) *awkward to load: s.s: hld up: hdwy on ins to ld over 2f out: drvn out* **6/4**[1]	75+
50	2	2	**Meynell**[25] 3214 3-8-12 0 .... SteveDrowne 3 (M A Jarvis) *trckd ldrs: wnt 2nd over 1f out: hung lft and no real imp* **3/1**[3]	65
	3	3	**Parsonagehotelyork (IRE)** 3-8-12 0 .... PaulHanagan 6 (R A Fahey) *reluctant ldr: hdd over 6f out: chal 3f out: fdd fnl f* **5/1**	58+
5-	4	5	**Pearl (IRE)**[257] 6481 3-8-12 0 .... PaulMulrennan 1 (W J Haggas) *trckd ldrs: t.k.h: drvn 3f out: sn outpcd and lost pl* **11/4**[2]	47
	5	9	**Island King (IRE)**[174] 4-9-11 0 .... RoystonFfrench 4 (R Bastiman) *led over 6f out tl over 2f out: lost pl over 1f out* **66/1**	31

1m 50.33s (4.63) **Going Correction** +0.35s/f (Good)
WFA 3 from 4yo 8lb — **5** Ran SP% **109.8**
Speed ratings (Par 103): **90,88,85,80,71**
CSF £6.29 TOTE £2.00: £1.50, £1.40; EX 5.30.
Owner Godolphin **Bred** D G Hardisty Bloodstock **Trained** Newmarket, Suffolk

FOCUS
They ambled round but the winner was right on top at the line. Very modest form rated through the second, but the winner has the raw ability to do better if his temperament does not get the better of him.
Island King(IRE) Official explanation: jockey said gelding had run too freely to post

4008 D & J ELECTRICAL SERVICES LTD H'CAP — 5f
5:25 (5:26) (Class 5) (0-70,65) 3-Y-0+ — **£3,886** (£1,156; £577; £288) **Stalls** Low

Form				RPR
2322	1		**El Potro**[12] 3608 5-9-0 **54** .... SteveDrowne 10 (J R Holt) *mde virtually all: hld on towards fin* **5/2**[1]	65+
0253	2	½	**Joyeaux**[10] 3676 5-9-5 **59** .... PaulMulrennan 4 (J Hetherton) *chsd ldrs: styd on ins fnl f: jst hld* **9/2**[3]	65
6055	3	½	**Miss Daawe**[21] 3342 3-8-3 **47** .... RoystonFfrench 2 (B Ellison) *mid-div: hdwy on ins to chse ldrs over 2f out: kpt on wl ins fnl f* **12/1**	50
0304	4	¾	**Sir Loin**[2] 3921 6-9-0 **54** ....(v) MickyFenton 1 (N Tinkler) *w wnr: fdd towards fin* **5/1**	56
6324	5	¾	**Cleveland**[60] 2149 5-8-9 **54** .... RussellKennemore(5) 12 (R Hollinshead) *w ldrs: wknd last 100yds* **4/1**[2]	53
0000	6	shd	**Greek Secret**[12] 3608 4-8-13 **53** ....(b) PaulHanagan 6 (J O'Reilly) *mid-div: kpt on fr over 1f out: nvr rchd ldrs* **12/1**	51
05-0	7	4	**White Ledger (IRE)**[189] 201 8-8-6 **46** oh1 ....(p) PaulFessey 5 (R E Peacock) *outpcd in rr: styd on fnl 2f: nvr nr ldrs* **40/1**	30
0000	8	2½	**Alexia Rose (IRE)**[6] 3787 5-8-4 **47** oh1 ow1 .... PatrickMathers(3) 11 (A Berry) *a towards rr* **28/1**	22
600	9	1½	**Henry Hall (IRE)**[12] 3627 11-9-4 **58** .... KimTinkler 8 (N Tinkler) *trckd ldrs: lost pl over 1f out* **14/1**	28
-000	10	2½	**Northern Chorus (IRE)**[78] 1669 4-9-8 **65** ....(b[1]) AndrewMullen(3) 9 (J O'Reilly) *chsd ldrs: lost pl over 1f out* **25/1**	26
6200	11	5	**Jellytot (USA)**[11] 3636 4-8-13 **53** .... VHalliday 13 (J O'Reilly) *chsd ldrs on outer: edgd rt and lost pl wl over 1f out* **22/1**	—

64.81 secs (1.01) **Going Correction** +0.35s/f (Good)
WFA 3 from 4yo+ 4lb — **11** Ran SP% **119.6**
Speed ratings (Par 103): **105,104,103,102,101 100,94,90,88,84 76**
CSF £13.23 CT £117.50 TOTE £3.10: £1.40, £1.80, £3.40; EX 12.80 Place 6 £8.20, Place 5 £5.46..
Owner Sovereign Racing **Bred** L A C Ashby **Trained** Peckleton, Leics

FOCUS
A moderate handicap and the winner was not scoring out of turn but at the line the first six were stacked up. Despite that the form looks sound overall.
T/Plt: £11.00 to a £1 stake. Pool: £61,550.40. 4,068.40 winning tickets. T/Qpdt: £4.60 to a £1 stake. Pool: £3,652.30. 580.50 winning tickets. WG

3445 DEAUVILLE (R-H)
Sunday, July 29
OFFICIAL GOING: All-weather - standard; turf course - soft

4009a PRIX DE CABOURG (GROUP 3) — 6f
2:05 (2:04) 2-Y-0 — **£27,027** (£10,811; £8,108; £5,405; £2,703)

			RPR
1		**Alexandros**[15] 3563 2-8-11 .... OPeslier 3 (A Fabre, France) *trckd ldr in 2nd tl led 1f out: r.o strly* **9/4**[2]	106+
2	1½	**Stern Opinion (USA)**[26] 3198 2-8-11 .... SPasquier 2 (P Bary, France) *led to 1f out: one pce* **5/4**[1]	102
3	2	**Wilki (FR)**[28] 3147 2-8-8 .... KFallon 1 (J-M Sauve, France) *racd in 3rd: effrt and hung rt fr 2f out: one pce* **9/2**[3]	93
4	2½	**Rey Davis (IRE)**[7] 3779 2-8-11 .... C-PLemaire 5 (Robert Collet, France) *racd in 4th: nvr a factor* **14/1**	88
5	¾	**Neige Eternel (FR)**[38] 2-8-11 .... J-BHamel 4 (Robert Collet, France) *last thrght* **7/1**	86

1m 13.9s (0.90) — **5** Ran SP% **112.6**
PARI-MUTUEL: WIN 3.40; PL 1.40, 1.30; SF 6.40.
Owner Sheikh Mohammed **Bred** Darley Stud Management Co Ltd **Trained** Chantilly, France

NOTEBOOK
Alexandros ◆ produced a fine performance and looks likely to make it at the highest level. Supplemented into this Group 3 contest, he justified the decision with an authorative success, cruising to the front at the furlong marker having tracked the early leader for much of the way. There was plenty to like about the way he lengthened his stride considering he was hardly put under any pressure at all. He looks a likely candidate for the Prix Morny over the course and distance later in the month.
Stern Opinion(USA) ◆, a drifter in the market, was well held behind the easy winner. He was in trouble at the furlong marker and his connections felt he lacked experience. He may now be aimed at the Prix la Rochette.
Wilki(FR) ran a little free in the early part of this race and never looked like worrying the winner.
Rey Davis(IRE) looked out of his depth in this company.

4010a PRIX D'ASTARTE (GROUP 1) (F&M) (STRAIGHT COURSE) — 1m (R)
3:05 (3:08) 3-Y-0+ — **£96,520** (£38,615; £19,307; £9,645; £4,831)

			RPR
1		**Darjina (FR)**[37] 2814 3-8-7 .... TThulliez 6 (A De Royer-Dupre, France) *racd in 4th: led narrowly 2f out: sn rdn: hld on gamely whn strly pressed ins fnl f* **11/4**[1]	117
2	½	**Missvinski (USA)**[37] 2814 3-8-7 .... C-PLemaire 1 (J-C Rouget, France) *hld up in 10th on ins: swtchd rt and hdwy 2 1/2f out: pressed wnr and ev ch ins fnl f: no ex clsng stages* **20/1**	116
3	½	**Simply Perfect**[18] 3433 3-8-7 .... KFallon 5 (J Noseda) *pressed ldr tl led narrowly 2 1/2f out: hdd 2f out: kpt on gamely u.p fnl 1 1/2f* **11/4**[1]	114
4	1½	**Barshiba (IRE)**[22] 3332 3-8-7 .... TQuinn 12 (D R C Elsworth) *sddle slipped leaving stalls: dropped out in last: hdwy on outside to go 4th over 1f out: kpt on* **25/1**	111
5	½	**Trip To The Moon**[14] 3581 4-9-1 .... TJarnet 10 (M Delzangles, France) *hld up in 11th: rdn 2 1/2f out: hdwy to go 5th 1f out: kpt on* **33/1**	112
6	2½	**Bal De La Rose (IRE)**[30] 3-8-7 .... JVictoire 3 (F Rohaut, France) *racd in 7th: rdn and one pce fnl 1 1/2f* **33/1**	104
7	snk	**Mi Emma (GER)**[37] 2814 3-8-7 .... MJKinane 8 (A Wohler, Germany) *racd in 6th: dropped towards rr over 2f out: swtchd lft over 1f out: kpt on* **7/2**[2]	104
8	6	**Impressionnante**[302] 5701 4-9-1 .... OPeslier 7 (C Laffon-Parias, France) *hld up in 9th: effrt 2f out: edgd rt 1 1/2f out: one pce* **10/1**	92
9	1½	**Utrecht**[28] 3148 3-8-7 .... SPasquier 11 (A Fabre, France) *racd in 8th on outside: effrt 2f out: wknd* **7/1**[3]	86
10	3	**Tianshan (FR)**[29] 3124 4-9-1 .... AlxiBadel 9 (F-X de Chevigny, France) *cl up in 3rd on outside: wknd over 2f out* **66/1**	82
11		**All Is Vanity (FR)**[56] 2290 3-8-7 .... FBlondel 4 (W J S Cargeeg, France) *led to 2 1/2f out: wknd* **86/10**	80
12		**Lokaloka**[42] 2707 3-8-7 .... DVargiu 2 (B Grizzetti, Italy) *trckd ldr in 5th: wknd 2 1/2f out* **73/1**	80

1m 37.1s (-5.20)
WFA 3 from 4yo 8lb — **12** Ran SP% **124.9**
PARI-MUTUEL: WIN 3.30; PL 1.30, 2.80, 1.90; DF 19.10.
Owner Princess Zahra Aga Khan **Bred** Princess Zahra Aga Khan **Trained** Chantilly, France

NOTEBOOK
Darjina(FR), easily the pick of the paddock, this filly completely redeemed her reputation and reversed form with an old rival. Ridden by Thulliez for the first time, she was always well placed and took control a furlong from the finish. As usual she didn't do a great deal once in front, but she was always holding the runner up. She still seems to be progressing and her connections, who will think about the Jacques-Le-Marois, are already talking about the Prix de L'Opera in October.
Missvinski(USA) looked the most likely winner a furlong out, but she could not quite sustain her finishing burst to the line. Held up early on, she arrived on the scene at the furlong marker, but again found Darjina too strong, as she had in the Prix de la Grotte. She is now a possible for the Moulin de Longchamp and is likely to be campaigned in the States later in the year.
Simply Perfect, given every possible chance, she hit the front about a furlong and a half from the finish and battled on gamely to the line. There are no immediate plans, but a campaign in the States is on the cards later in the year.
Barshiba(IRE) ◆ can be considered unlucky as her saddle slipped when leaving the stalls and she lost several lengths. She ran on extremely well in the closing stages and would have certainly been much closer had everything gone as planned. She looks worth following next time.

4012a PRIX JACQUES DE BREMOND (LISTED RACE) (ALL-WEATHER) — 7f 110y
4:05 (4:06) 4-Y-0+ — **£17,568** (£7,027; £5,270; £3,514; £1,757)

			RPR
1		**Bertranicus (FR)**[34] 2953 4-9-2 .... KFallon 10 (L Urbano-Grajales, France) **32/10**[1]	111
2	3	**Chambord (IRE)**[28] 4-8-12 .... SPasquier 7 (A Fabre, France)	100
3	1½	**Sabasha (FR)**[34] 2953 4-8-8 .... FBlondel 11 (F Rohaut, France)	93
4	snk	**Merlerault (USA)**[93] 4-9-2 .... TThulliez 12 (P Demercastel, France) *fin 5th: plcd 4th*	101
5	1	**Farnesina (FR)**[26] 5-8-8 ....(b) JCabre 2 (E Danel, France) *fin 6th: plcd 5th*	90
6	1½	**Indochine (BRZ)**[164] 476 4-8-7 .... C-PLemaire 1 (A De Royer-Dupre, France) *fin 7th: plcd 6th*	86
7	snk	**Alpacco (IRE)**[143] 642 5-8-12 ....(b) DBoeuf 5 (Mario Hofer, Germany) *fin 8th: plcd 7th*	91
8	2½	**Gold Sound (FR)**[36] 5-8-12 ....(b) OPeslier 4 (C Laffon-Parias, France) *fin 9th: plcd 8th*	85
9	shd	**Secret Affair**[215] 5-8-12 .... JVictoire 13 (F Breuss, Germany) *fin 10th: plcd 9th*	85
10		**Suggestive**[52] 2396 9-8-12 ....(b) TQuinn 6 (W J Haggas) *racd in 2nd tl led after 2f: hdd over 1 1/2f out: wknd: fin 11th: plcd 10th: (24/1)*	85
11		**Kavafi (IRE)**[29] 3124 5-9-2 .... MBlancpain 3 (C Laffon-Parias, France) *fin 12th: plcd 11th*	89
D	snk	**Valentino (FR)**[36] 8-8-12 .... FDiFede 9 (A De Royer-Dupre, France) *fin 4th: disqualified: plcd last*	97

1m 28.4s (88.40) — **12** Ran SP% **23.8**
PARI-MUTUEL: WIN 4.20; PL 1.70, 2.50, 2.60; DF 19.90.
Owner J Gispert **Bred** Bernard & Mme Virginie Becquart **Trained** Pau, France

NOTEBOOK
Suggestive was taken into the lead soon after the start and stayed at the head of affairs until the straight, but he dropped out of contention quite quickly once coming under pressure. He was ultimately promoted to tenth position.

2409 MUNICH (L-H)
Sunday, July 29

OFFICIAL GOING: Good
A slow time in the big race coupled with morning showers suggests that the ground was riding a bit softer than the official description.

4013a GROSSER DALLMAYR PREIS-BAYERISCHES ZUCHTRENNEN (GROUP 1) 1m 2f
4:10 (4:18) 3-Y-O+ **£61,486** (£24,324; £12,162; £6,757)

RPR

1 **Soldier Hollow**[42] 2705 7-9-6 .... AStarke 5 121
(P Schiergen, Germany) *hld up in 6th: hdwy to ld 1 1/2f out: r.o strly* **22/10**[1]

2 3 **Formal Decree (GER)**[45] 2617 4-9-6 .... KerrinMcEvoy 3 115
(Saeed Bin Suroor) *chsd clr ldr in 2nd: hdwy to ld jst under 2f out: hdd 1 1/2f out: kpt on at one pce* **39/10**[3]

3 hd **Dominante (GER)**[14] 3-8-4 .... J-PCarvalho 1 109
(A Wohler, Germany) *racd in 3rd: 4th over 1f out: styd on down outside fnl f* **39/10**[3]

4 1 1/2 **Hattan (IRE)**[42] 2706 5-9-6 .... EddieAhern 2 112
(C E Brittain) *racd in 4th: effrt towards ins to go 3rd over 1f out: one pce* **7/2**[2]

5 1/2 **Arcadio (GER)**[35] 2924 5-9-6 .... THellier 7 111
(J Hirschberger, Germany) *hld up in last: styd on fr over 1f out but nvr rchd ldrs* **84/10**

6 1/2 **Waleria (GER)**[35] 2924 4-9-2 .... ASuborics 8 106
(H J Groschel, Germany) *hld up in 8th: rdn over 2f out: styd on at one pce* **144/10**

7 1/2 **Poseidon Adventure (IRE)**[35] 2924 4-9-6 .... EPedroza 9 109
(W Figge, Germany) *racd in 7th: nvr a factor* **74/10**

8 8 **Sommersturm (GER)**[28] 3146 3-8-8 .... FJohansson 6 91
(J Hirschberger, Germany) *racd in 5th: rdn 2f out: sn btn* **114/10**

9 9 **Sommertag (GER)**[32] 3011 4-9-6 ....(b) JiriPalik 4 75
(J Hirschberger, Germany) *led: 8 l clr 4f out: hdd jst under 2f out: eased* **26/1**

2m 9.26s (0.29)
WFA 3 from 4yo+ 10lb **9** Ran SP% **135.1**
(including 10 Euro stake): WIN 32; PL 13, 18, 14; SF 207.
Owner Gestut Park Wiedingen **Bred** Car Colston Hall Stud **Trained** Germany

FOCUS
The two British runners were the first to be put in the stalls - they then had to stand in their boxes for upwards of five minutes while Soldier Hollow was rehoused after breaking through the front of his stall.

NOTEBOOK
Soldier Hollow proved much too strong in the final furlong and a half and may drop back to 1m now, with the Prix du Moulin a possible target.
Formal Decree(GER) ran a solid race, hitting the front with a quarter of a mile to run and, though not having the speed of the winner, he kept on gamely to hold on for second.
Dominante(GER) stayed on well in the closing stages having been a little outpaced early in the straight. She may now be aimed at the Prix de l'Opera.
Hattan(IRE) was possibly upset by the delay before the start and ran a bit flat.

3794 WINDSOR (R-H)
Monday, July 30

OFFICIAL GOING: Good (good to soft in places; 8.0)
Wind: Half-behind, moderate becoming light Weather: Fine

4014 VC CASINO.COM MAIDEN STKS 6f
6:10 (6:12) (Class 4) 2-Y-O **£5,181** (£1,541; £770; £384) **Stalls** High

Form RPR

22 1 **Baronovici (IRE)**[3] 3902 2-9-3 0 .... RyanMoore 5 77+
(R Hannon) *pressed ldrs: rdn to ld over 1f out: in command fnl f: pushed out* **13/8**[1]

0 2 2 **Westwood**[21] 3383 2-9-3 0 .... RobertHavlin 7 71
(D Haydn Jones) *led to over 1f out: hrd rdn and styd on fnl f* **66/1**

5 3 hd **Generous Thought**[65] 2041 2-9-3 0 .... JamieSpencer 6 70
(P Howling) *t.k.h: trckd ldrs: effrt 2f out: tried to cl on wnr 1f out: hung lft and nt qckn* **2/1**[2]

04 4 1/2 **Caradoc Place**[14] 3592 2-9-3 0 .... TedDurcan 3 69
(M P Tregoning) *pressed ldr: rdn and upsides over 1f out: hanging and nt qckn after* **25/1**

5 1 1/4 **Silca Destination** 2-8-12 0 .... TPO'Shea 11 60
(M R Channon) *trckd ldrs: rdn and effrt 2f out: carried lft and no ex fnl f* **5/1**[3]

0 6 1 3/4 **Ambrose Princess (IRE)**[14] 3592 2-8-12 0 .... JohnEgan 14 55
(J S Moore) *towards rr: rdn over 2f out: edgd lft fr over 1f out: styd on fnl f* **33/1**

7 1/2 **American Welcome (IRE)** 2-9-3 0 .... JHBowman 13 58
(B J Meehan) *s.i.s: wl in rr: nudged along 2f out: reminders and styd on fnl f: nrst fin* **20/1**

8 shd **Thunder Gorge (USA)** 2-9-0 0 .... NeilChalmers(3) 2 58
(Mouse Hamilton-Fairley) *free to post: s.v.s: rcvrd and decent spd to chse ldrs: wknd and wandered over 1f out* **100/1**

0 9 1/2 **Queen's Treasure (IRE)**[56] 2316 2-8-12 0 .... MartinDwyer 16 51
(M P Tregoning) *trckd ldrs against nr side rail: no imp over 1f out: fdd* **16/1**

0 10 1/2 **Ski School (IRE)**[13] 3625 2-9-3 0 .... KerrinMcEvoy 4 55
(W J Haggas) *wl in rr: sme prog on wd outside into midfield over 2f out: pushed along and no imp after* **20/1**

0 11 nk **Rich Kid (IRE)**[21] 3363 2-9-3 0 .... RichardSmith 15 54+
(R Hannon) *settled wl in rr: nudged along fr 1/2-way: kpt on steadily but nvr nr ldrs* **40/1**

12 2 **Love Dancer (IRE)** 2-9-3 0 .... HayleyTurner 8 48+
(M L W Bell) *a wl in rr: shkn up and no prog 2f out* **33/1**

00 13 1 1/4 **Mairead's Boy (IRE)**[59] 2193 2-8-12 0 .... TolleyDean(5) 9 44
(J S Moore) *pushed along in midfield: no prog 2f out: wknd* **80/1**

14 4 **Didntcomeback** 2-9-3 0 .... FergusSweeney 12 32
(M S Saunders) *a towards rr: shkn up sn after 1/2-way: wknd 2f out* **66/1**

15 10 **Den's Boy** 2-9-3 0 .... EddieAhern 10 2
(J R Boyle) *rn green and a bhd: t.o* **66/1**

1m 13.83s (0.16) **Going Correction** -0.10s/f (Good) **15** Ran SP% **122.4**
Speed ratings (Par 96): **94,91,91,90,88 86,85,85,84,84 83,81,79,74,60**
CSF £145.00 TOTE £2.70: £1.40, £28.20, £1.20; EX 145.90.
Owner Kemal Kurt **Bred** Ian Bray **Trained** East Everleigh, Wilts

FOCUS
Just a fair juvenile maiden. The winner probably didn't need to improve on the form of his recent Chepstow effort.

NOTEBOOK
Baronovici(IRE), runner-up on both his previous starts, including at Chepstow just three days earlier, made no mistake this time, keeping on best of all having never been too far away. He is clearly quite a tough sort and could make his mark in nurseries. (op 7-4 tchd 15-8)
Westwood improved markedly on the form he showed on his debut over course and distance to take second. He showed good speed to lead up through the early stages and there was plenty to like about the way he kept on once headed. (tchd 50-1)
Generous Thought, who shaped well in a good maiden on his debut at Newmarket over two months previously, again showed ability, but he ruined any chance he had of winning by hanging badly left under pressure, ending up more towards the far side of the track. Official explanation: jockey said colt hung left (op 11-4)
Caradoc Place finished fourth over course and distance on his previous start and his proximity helps give the form a solid look. (op 20-1)
Silca Destination, a daughter of Dubai Destination, first foal of high-class multiple 5f-1m1f winner Golden Silca, made just a respectable debut. She is bred to be pretty decent and could leave this form behind in time. (op 9-2)
Ambrose Princess(IRE) Official explanation: jockey said filly hung left
American Welcome(IRE) Official explanation: jockey said colt ran green
Rich Kid(IRE), a stablemate of the winner, caught the eye and is sure to do better. Official explanation: jockey said colt hung left (op 33-1)
Didntcomeback Official explanation: jockey said gelding suffered interference

4015 PLAY BLACKJACK AT VC CASINO.COM H'CAP 1m 2f 7y
6:40 (6:42) (Class 5) (0-75,74) 3-Y-O+ **£3,238** (£963; £481; £240) **Stalls** Centre

Form RPR

2135 1 **Rustic Gold**[18] 3450 3-8-7 **63** .... EddieAhern 5 71
(J R Best) *trckd ldrs: rdn and effrt over 2f out: led over 1f out: hrd pressed fnl f: jst hld on* **8/1**[3]

3045 2 shd **Norman The Great**[31] 3058 3-9-2 **72** .... JohnEgan 3 80
(Jane Chapple-Hyam) *hld up towards rr: prog fr 3f out: drvn to chal fnl f: jst failed* **9/1**

160- 3 1 1/2 **Golden Sprite**[258] 6474 4-9-3 **63** .... RobertHavlin 10 68
(B R Millman) *t.k.h: hld up: stdy prog fr 3f out: chsd ldrs over 1f out: hrd rdn and nt qckn* **20/1**

1223 4 1 1/2 **Nightspot**[21] 3386 6-10-0 **74** .... StephenCarson 11 76
(Eve Johnson Houghton) *led to over 6f out: w ldr tl led again over 3f out to over 1f out: wknd ins fnl f* **5/1**[2]

1040 5 shd **Double Spectre (IRE)**[53] 2403 5-9-6 **66** .... KerrinMcEvoy 2 68
(Jean-Rene Auvray) *hld up wl in rr: prog into midfield over 2f out: reminders over 1f out: r.o fnl f: nvr nr ldrs* **11/1**

-003 6 hd **Effigy**[11] 3689 3-8-10 **66** .... FergusSweeney 13 67
(H Candy) *cl up: chsd ldng pair over 3f out: drvn 2f out: no ex* **5/2**[1]

-245 7 1 3/4 **Leon Knights**[66] 2010 3-9-3 **73** ....(b[1]) JHBowman 1 71
(G A Butler) *hld up wl in rr: sme prog on outer into midfield over 2f out: rdn and one pce after* **14/1**

00-0 8 1 **Mystic Storm**[19] 3416 4-9-8 **68** ....(t) JamieSpencer 16 64
(Lady Herries) *hld up in last: stl in last pair 2f out: rdn over 1f out: nvr any ch* **8/1**[3]

2156 9 1 1/4 **Uig**[48] 2543 6-9-5 **65** .... TedDurcan 6 58
(H S Howe) *trckd ldng pair early: chsng ldrs over 3f out: sn rdn: fdd fnl 2f* **16/1**

2051 10 2 1/2 **Converti**[14] 3593 3-8-0 **56** ow1 .... HayleyTurner 9 44
(H J Manners) *nvr beyond midfield: no prog over 2f out* **20/1**

5110 11 shd **Birkside**[31] 3048 4-9-11 **71** .... PaulDoe 12 59
(S Dow) *a towards rr: rdn and no prog over 2f out* **20/1**

0620 12 3/4 **Street Life (IRE)**[10] 3705 9-9-2 **69** .... AlanRutter(7) 7 56
(W J Musson) *hld up in last trio: shuffled along and stl in last trio 2f out: nvr nr ldrs* **11/1**

4-00 13 shd **Sagassa**[7] 3794 3-7-10 **55** oh6 .... DominicFox(3) 8 42
(W De Best-Turner) *awkward s: restrained tl plld way through to ld over 6f out: hdd over 3f out: wknd rapidly 2f out* **80/1**

-000 14 3/4 **Apollo Five**[25] 3235 3-9-0 **70** .... TPO'Shea 15 55
(D J Coakley) *in tch in midfield on inner tl wknd 2f out* **33/1**

460 15 13 **Stand In Black (NZ)**[163] 492 3-8-5 **61** ow1 .... MartinDwyer 4 20
(L A Dace) *plld hrd: w ldr for 3f: rdn 4f out: sn wknd: t.o* **50/1**

2m 6.66s (-1.64) **Going Correction** -0.10s/f (Good)
WFA 3 from 4yo+ 10lb **15** Ran SP% **127.1**
Speed ratings (Par 103): **102,101,100,99,99 99,97,97,96,94 94,93,93,92,82**
CSF £75.82 CT £1427.89 TOTE £11.50: £4.10, £2.00, £6.40; EX 86.90.
Owner John Griffin Owen Mullen **Bred** Overbury Partnership **Trained** Hucking, Kent
■ Stewards' Enquiry : John Egan two-day ban: used whip with excessive frequency (Aug 10-11)

FOCUS
A modest handicap and straightforward form, rated through the third.

4016 PLAY AT VC CASINO.COM MAIDEN AUCTION STKS 5f 10y
7:10 (7:11) (Class 4) 2-Y-O **£5,181** (£1,541; £770; £384) **Stalls** High

Form RPR

6 1 **Wise Son**[14] 3589 2-8-13 0 .... KerrinMcEvoy 12 81
(W J Haggas) *mde most: jnd 2f out: edgd lft u.p fnl f: hld on wl* **11/4**[2]

22 2 shd **Foreign Rhythm (IRE)**[16] 3532 2-8-8 0 .... RyanMoore 7 76
(N Tinkler) *pressed wnr: rdn to chal 2f out: upsides after: jst hld nr fin* **15/8**[1]

450 3 2 1/2 **Structura (USA)**[66] 1992 2-8-6 0 .... JohnEgan 3 65
(J S Moore) *t.k.h: hld up in tch: plld out and effrt over 1f out: rn green and hung lft fnl f: kpt on* **12/1**

02 4 hd **Ronsai (USA)**[11] 3668 2-8-5 0 .... RichardSmith 9 63
(R Hannon) *trckd ldng pair: rdn 2f out: outpcd over 1f out: one pce after* **5/1**[3]

5 1 1/4 **Compton Rose** 2-8-6 0 ow1 .... FergusSweeney 8 60
(H Candy) *rn green in rr: shkn up 2f out: styd on ins fnl f: nrst fin* **11/1**

05 6 3/4 **Mistress Cooper**[14] 3589 2-8-7 0 .... TPO'Shea 4 58
(W J Musson) *trckd ldrs: shuffled along fr 2f out: nvr cl enough to chal* **20/1**

650 7 2 **Fabuleux Cherie**[44] 2651 2-8-6 0 ....(b[1]) MartinDwyer 2 50
(W R Muir) *trckd ldng pair: rdn over 1f out: wknd rapidly fnl f* **33/1**

8 1/2 **Wee Buns** 2-8-9 0 .... RobertHavlin 13 51
(S Kirk) *wl in rr: pushed along fr 2f out: kpt on fnl f* **25/1**

0 **9** *1/2* **Mandarinka**[21] 3363 2-9-0 0.. PaulDoe 5 54
(P Winkworth) *dwlt: wl in rr: prog on outer 1/2-way: wknd over 1f out* **11/1**
0 **10** *6* **Eastbourne**[47] 2569 2-8-11 0.. StephenCarson 1 29
(Eve Johnson Houghton) *nvr beyond midfield: wknd over 1f out* **33/1**
4 **11** *shd* **Kinlochard**[11] 3668 2-8-6 0 ow1.. EddieAhern 6 24
(Eve Johnson Houghton) *a in rr and nvr gng the pce: wknd over 1f out* **25/1**
12 *11* **Howe's Jack (IRE)** 2-8-4 0........................ RussellKennemore(5) 11 —
(M C Chapman) *s.v.s: a detached in last: t.o* **66/1**

60.53 secs (-0.57) **Going Correction** -0.10s/f (Good) **12** Ran SP% **122.3**
Speed ratings (Par 96): **100,99,95,95,93 92,89,88,87,77 77,60**
CSF £7.88 TOTE £3.50: £1.50, £1.40, £4.70; EX 11.10.
Owner Wise Move UK Limited **Bred** Southcott Racing Limited **Trained** Newmarket, Suffolk
■ Stewards' Enquiry : John Egan one-day ban: careless riding (Aug 12)

FOCUS
A fair juvenile maiden. Solid form, the winner stepping forward.

NOTEBOOK
Wise Son built on the promise he showed on his debut over course and distance the previous week to run out the narrowest of winners. His rider reported afterwards the colt wanted to edge away from the rail and his connections will look for a different type of track next time. (op 7-2 tchd 9-4)
Foreign Rhythm(IRE), runner-up on both her previous starts, ran another big race in defeat. She was clear of the remainder and really should find a similar race, although she will also now have the option of nurseries. (tchd 9-4)
Structura(USA), a beaten favourite at Haydock on her previous start, raced a little keenly through the early stages and proved no real match for the front two when asked for her effort. (op 14-1 tchd 20-1)
Ronsai(USA) ran a respectable race and will have more options now she is qualified for a nursery mark. (op 9-2 tchd 4-1)
Compton Rose, by Compton Place, a half-sister to dual 6f winner Ben Lomand, out of a dual 5f-1m winner, showed real signs of inexperience and should improve plenty. (op 9-1 tchd 12-1)

4017 VC CASINO.COM FILLIES' H'CAP 6f
7:40 (7:41) (Class 4) (0-80,78) 3-Y-O+ **£6,477** (£1,927; £963; £481) **Stalls High**

Form RPR
340 **1** **Sweet Pickle**[52] 2422 6-9-2 **67**..(e) JamieSpencer 1 74
(J R Boyle) *hld up in last: effrt over 1f out: rdn and r.o fnl f to ld fnl 75yds* **13/2**
3410 **2** *1/2* **Shes Minnie**[9] 3746 4-9-12 **77**.. FergusSweeney 9 82
(P A Blockley) *trckd ldng pair: rdn wl over 1f out: lft in ld ent fnl f: hdd and outpcd fnl 75yds* **5/1**[3]
6050 **3** *1 1/2* **Overwing (IRE)**[13] 3627 4-9-5 **70**.. EddieAhern 7 70
(R M H Cowell) *led: hrd rdn and hdd over 1f out: nt qckn and btn after* **10/1**
102 **4** *shd* **Crystal Gazer (FR)**[7] 3797 3-9-8 **78**.. RyanMoore 4 77
(R Hannon) *hld up in last trio: effrt against nrside rail over 1f out: drvn and kpt on same pce* **2/1**[1]
6042 **5** *nk* **Linda Green**[7] 3784 6-9-7 **72**.. JHBowman 2 71+
(M R Channon) *hld up in last trio: effrt on outer over 1f out: carried bdly lft after and lost all ch: kpt on* **11/4**[2]
0140 **6** *1 1/4* **Kondakova (IRE)**[12] 3649 3-8-12 **73**.. LukeMorris(5) 6 67+
(M L W Bell) *trckd ldng trio: effrt to ld over 1f out: hung bdly lft after: hdd ent fnl f: threw ch away* **12/1**
026 **7** *49* **Pelican Key (IRE)**[11] 3670 3-9-2 **72**.. MartinDwyer 3 —
(D M Simcock) *trckd ldr to jst over 2f out: wknd rapidly and eased: t.o: b.b.v* **10/1**

1m 13.3s (-0.37) **Going Correction** -0.10s/f (Good)
WFA 3 from 4yo+ 5lb **7** Ran SP% **115.9**
Speed ratings (Par 102): **98,97,95,95,94 93,27**
CSF £39.49 CT £324.23 TOTE £7.10: £2.60, £3.60; EX 36.10.
Owner M Khan X2 **Bred** C T Van Hoorn **Trained** Epsom, Surrey

FOCUS
Something of a messy race, and modest form, rated through the runner-up.
Kondakova(IRE) Official explanation: jockey said filly hung badly left
Pelican Key(IRE) Official explanation: jockey said filly bled from the nose

4018 PLAY BLACKJACK AT VC CASINO.COM MAIDEN STKS 1m 67y
8:10 (8:13) (Class 5) 3-4-Y-O **£3,238** (£963; £481; £240) **Stalls High**

Form RPR
0205 **1** **Officer**[11] 3691 3-9-3 73..(v) RyanMoore 8 78
(Sir Michael Stoute) *mde all: shkn up and drew 2 l clr 2f out: drvn out fnl f* **7/4**[2]
-435 **2** *1* **Sonning Star (IRE)**[10] 3710 3-9-3 74.. KerrinMcEvoy 2 76
(D R C Elsworth) *trckd wnr: tried to chal 3f out: nt qckn and looked wl hld 2f out: styd on ins fnl f* **11/10**[1]
3 *7* **Hibiki (IRE)** 3-8-12 0.. TolleyDean(5) 1 60
(J S Moore) *towards rr and wl off the pce: rdn bef 1/2-way: styd on u.p fr 3f out to take 3rd fnl f* **20/1**
40 **4** *3/4* **Marieschi (USA)**[62] 2127 3-9-3 0.. TedDurcan 6 58
(H R A Cecil) *chsd clr ldng pair: clsd over 3f out: sn rdn: outpcd over 2f out* **7/1**[3]
5 *nk* **Ka'u Mauna Kea** 3-8-12 0.. RobertHavlin 7 52
(J A Geake) *off the pce in midfield: nvr on terms: effrt to press for 3rd over 1f out: kpt on* **40/1**
0 **6** *5* **Magic Show**[53] 2402 3-9-3 0.. JohnEgan 5 46
(Jane Chapple-Hyam) *hld up in last trio: wl off the pce but gng wl enough: nudged along and threatened to cl on bunch disputing 3rd over 1f out: eased fnl f* **20/1**
7 *2 1/2* **Forever Bold** 3-9-3 0.. EddieAhern 11 40
(J G Portman) *s.s: detached in last: pushed along fnl 3f: nvr a factor* **33/1**
663 **8** *1* **County Kerry (UAE)**[120] 864 3-8-12 54.. StephenCarson 3 33
(Jean-Rene Auvray) *chsd clr ldng trio: clsd over 3f out: rdn and wknd over 2f out* **25/1**
06 **9** *2* **Screaming Reel**[52] 2433 4-9-11 0.. TPQueally 10 33
(M Wellings) *dwlt: rcvrd into 5th pl after 2f: drvn to cl on ldrs over 3f out: wknd rapidly over 2f out* **66/1**
10 *9* **Lady Pomerol** 3-8-7 0.. LukeMorris(5) 4 8
(Lady Herries) *sn rdn and off the pce in midfield: dropped to last over 2f out: t.o* **22/1**

1m 43.35s (-1.35) **Going Correction** -0.10s/f (Good)
WFA 3 from 4yo 8lb **10** Ran SP% **121.1**
Speed ratings (Par 103): **102,101,94,93,92 87,85,84,82,73**
CSF £3.79 TOTE £2.60: £1.30, £1.10, £3.10; EX 5.00.
Owner Cheveley Park Stud **Bred** Cheveley Park Stud Ltd **Trained** Newmarket, Suffolk

FOCUS
A two-horse race on paper and that is how it turned out. The winner, who dictated the pace, has improved with each run.
Sonning Star(IRE) Official explanation: jockey said gelding hung right

4019 MONDAY NIGHT RACING WITH VC CASINO.COM H'CAP 1m 3f 135y
8:40 (8:41) (Class 5) (0-70,70) 3-Y-O+ **£3,238** (£963; £481; £240) **Stalls Centre**

Form RPR
0353 **1** **Down The Brick (IRE)**[18] 3469 3-8-7 **57**........................(b) FergusSweeney 8 69
(B R Millman) *hld up in midfield: prog 3f out: rdn to ld 2f out: styd on wl* **5/1**[3]
2000 **2** *1* **Imperial Harry**[38] 2833 4-9-11 **66**.. JerryO'Dwyer(3) 2 76
(V Smith) *hld up wl in rr: stdy prog on outer fr 3f out: chsd wnr over 1f out: hrd rdn and styd on: a hld* **14/1**
0605 **3** *3 1/2* **Mr Mischief**[10] 3705 7-9-3 **60**.. RussellKennemore(5) 5 65
(M C Chapman) *trckd ldrs: effrt against nr side rail over 2f out: one pce u.p* **7/1**
0035 **4** *2 1/2* **Recalcitrant**[13] 3617 4-8-9 **54**.. JamieHamblett(7) 4 55
(S Dow) *trckd ldrs: prog to ld over 3f out to 2f out: steadily fdd* **16/1**
2000 **5** *nk* **Up In Arms (IRE)**[21] 3367 3-9-1 **65**.. StephenCarson 9 65
(P Winkworth) *hld up towards rr: effrt 3f out: sme prog over 2f out: drvn and one pce after* **10/1**
0360 **6** *3* **Hatch A Plan (IRE)**[16] 3554 6-9-6 **61**.. TravisBlock(3) 13 57
(Mouse Hamilton-Fairley) *hld up in midfield: cl enough 3f out: nt qckn and no prog fnl 2f* **9/1**
-354 **7** *3 1/2* **Montjeu's Melody (IRE)**[22] 3351 3-9-6 **70**.. EddieAhern 7 60
(J W Hills) *hld up towards rr: effrt over 3f out: sn rdn and no prog* **4/1**[1]
5451 **8** *7* **Elopement (IRE)**[42] 2721 5-9-7 **59**.. JamieSpencer 11 38
(W M Brisbourne) *hld up in last trio: stdy prog against nr side rail fr over 3f out: chsd ldrs wl over 1f out: cajoled along and wknd* **9/2**[2]
0501 **9** *5* **Icannshift (IRE)**[31] 3047 7-9-3 **58**.. NeilChalmers(3) 12 29
(T M Jones) *mde most to over 3f out: wknd over 2f out* **8/1**
200 **10** *6* **Whodunit (UAE)**[28] 3159 3-8-0 **50**.. AdrianMcCarthy 1 11
(P W Hiatt) *t.k.h early: prom tl wknd 3f out* **40/1**
000 **11** *5* **Zen Garden**[30] 3079 6-8-8 **51**.. LukeMorris(5) 10 4
(W M Brisbourne) *nt gng wl in rr early: in tch to 4f out: sn bhd* **33/1**
0600 **12** *22* **Faith And Reason (USA)**[32] 3042 4-9-13 **65**.. TPQueally 3 —
(B J Curley) *mostly pressed ldr to 4f out: sn dropped out w rdr looking down: t.o* **10/1**
6006 **13** *4* **Jamaahir (USA)**[7] 3794 4-9-7 **59**.. TPO'Shea 14 —
(S Lycett) *s.s: rushed up to join ldrs: wknd rapidly 4f out: t.o* **20/1**

2m 27.29s (-2.81) **Going Correction** -0.10s/f (Good)
WFA 3 from 4yo+ 12lb **13** Ran SP% **129.3**
Speed ratings (Par 103): **105,104,102,100,100 98,95,91,87,83 80,65,63**
CSF £78.37 CT £512.83 TOTE £7.30: £2.60, £5.90, £2.20; EX 282.10 Place 6 £ 132.72, Place 5 £ 98.13.
Owner Brick Racing **Bred** David Barry **Trained** Kentisbeare, Devon

FOCUS
A very ordinary handicap run at a sound pace. The race has been rated through the third.
Elopement(IRE) Official explanation: jokey said mare had no more to give
T/Jkpt: Not won. T/Plt: £263.80 to a £1 stake. Pool: £87,744.40. 242.75 winning tickets. T/Qpdt: £35.80 to a £1 stake. Pool: £5,816.10. 120.20 winning tickets. JN

3922 WOLVERHAMPTON (A.W) (L-H)
Monday, July 30

OFFICIAL GOING: Standard
Wind: Moderate across Weather: Sunny

4020 EUROPEAN BREEDERS' FUND MAIDEN STKS 5f 20y(P)
2:15 (2:17) (Class 5) 2-Y-O **£3,238** (£963; £481; £240) **Stalls Low**

Form RPR
32 **1** **Zippi Jazzman (USA)**[14] 3589 2-9-3 0.. SebSanders 3 75+
(R M Beckett) *cl up: led after 1f: rdn wl over 1f out: drvn and kpt on ins fnl f* **8/13**[1]
42 **2** *1* **Know No Fear**[23] 3297 2-9-3 0.. GrahamGibbons 9 71
(J J Quinn) *dwlt: sn trcking ldrs: hdwy to chse wnr wl over 1f out: sn drvn and kpt on same pce* **5/1**[2]
3324 **3** *nk* **Shatter Resistant (IRE)**[21] 3370 2-8-10 0........................ MatthewDavies(7) 4 70
(M R Channon) *in tch: hdwy on outer 2f out: rdn to chse ldng pair whn hung lft ins fnl f: one pce* **11/1**
4 *1* **Miss Bronte** 2-8-7 0.. RussellKennemore(5) 1 61
(R Hollinshead) *chsd ldrs: rdn along 2f out: sn drvn and one pce* **20/1**
6435 **5** *3* **Dalarossie**[16] 3562 2-9-3 0.. DavidAllan 10 56
(E J Alston) *led 1f: cl up: rdn along over 2f out: sn drvn and grad wknd* **14/1**
5 **6** *5* **Monday Morning (IRE)**[80] 1636 2-8-12 0.. EddieAhern 8 33
(M J Wallace) *a towards rr* **8/1**[3]
63 **7** *2 1/2* **Rightcar Ellie (IRE)**[16] 3532 2-8-9 0.. PatrickMathers(3) 5 24
(Peter Grayson) *sn outpcd and a in rr* **14/1**
0 **8** *6* **Nothing To Add**[16] 3560 2-9-3 0.. TomEaves 2 7
(K A Ryan) *sn outpcd and wl bhd fr 1/2-way* **11/1**
0 **9** *3 1/2* **Barbossa**[18] 3465 2-9-3 0.. VHalliday 7 —
(A J McCabe) *chsd ldrs: rdn along 1/2-way: sn wknd* **50/1**
020 **10** *14* **Smileforawhile (IRE)**[47] 2575 2-9-3 0........................(b[1]) DO'Donohoe 6 —
(K A Ryan) *s.i.s: a bhd* **14/1**

62.62 secs (-0.20) **Going Correction** -0.15s/f (Stan) **10** Ran SP% **133.1**
Speed ratings (Par 94): **95,93,92,91,86 78,74,64,59,36**
CSF £5.16 TOTE £1.60: £1.10, £2.10, £2.90; EX 6.30.
Owner Jones, Adams & Williams **Bred** G Watts Humphrey Jnr & Louise I Humphrey **Trained** Whitsbury, Hants

FOCUS
A modest juvenile maiden, run at an average pace. Solid form, set by the exposed third, with the winner not needing to match his Windsor effort.

NOTEBOOK
Zippi Jazzman(USA), having his first run on this surface, deservedly opened his account at the third attempt with a workmanlike display. He has a Gimcrack entry, but that does look ambitious and it is more likely the nursery route which will provide him with further success this term. A sixth furlong should also now suit him. (op 4-6 tchd 8-11)
Know No Fear, a beaten favourite on both his previous two outings, was again not that smart from the gates but still posted another good effort in defeat on this All-Weather bow. He now qualifies for nurseries. (op 9-2)
Shatter Resistant(IRE), another making his All-Weather debut, had his chance and was held before hanging left under pressure. He is fully exposed and helps to set the standard of this form. (op 10-1)

Miss Bronte, a full-sister to her stable's recent three-year-old winner at this venue Metal Guru, was the sole debutante in the line up. She posted a respectable effort and is obviously entitled to come on for the experience.

4021 BOOK TICKETS ON LINE CLAIMING STKS 5f 216y(P)
2:45 (2:51) (Class 6) 3-Y-O+ **£2,047** (£604; £302) **Stalls** Low

Form RPR

5026 **1** **Methaaly (IRE)**[5] 3852 4-9-8 66 JohnEgan 9 77+
(Jane Chapple-Hyam) *mde all: rdn clr wl over 1f out: styd on* **9/4**[1]

3503 **2** 4½ **Mistral Sky**[9] 3735 8-9-4 57 (v) MickyFenton 11 59
(Stef Liddiard) *prom: rdn 2f out: sn drvn, kpt on same pce: fin 3rd, plcd 2nd* **4/1**[2]

000U **3** 1 ½ **Mister Elegant**[117] 920 5-8-7 52 JamieHamblett(7) 5 50
(J L Spearing) *bolted and galloped loose bef s: chsd ldrs: rdn along wl over 2f out and kpt on same pce: fin 4th, 2l, 2½l, 1½l: plcd 3rd* **14/1**

6-4 **4** 1 ½ **Ardennes (IRE)**[37] 2894 3-9-7 0 (t) OscarUrbina 3 56
(M Botti) *chsd ldrs: rdn along 2f out: kpt on u.p ins fnl f: fin 5th, plcd 4th* 16/1

2600 **5** 3 ½ **Black Oval**[16] 3535 6-8-10 48 DominicFox(3) 8 33
(S Parr) *outpcd in rr tl sme late hdwy: fin 6th, plcd 5th* **33/1**

0335 **6** nk **Rann Na Cille (IRE)**[13] 3605 3-9-2 62 (p) DO'Donohoe 4 40
(K A Ryan) *chsd ldrs: rdn along 1/2-way: hdwy to chse wnr 2f out: sn drvn and wknd: fin 7th, plcd 6th* **8/1**

6-00 **7** 3 **Sovereignty (JPN)**[12] 3647 5-9-8 64 FrancisNorton 12 31
(D K Ivory) *a towards rr: fin 8th, plcd 7th* **7/1**

0025 **8** 15 **New Proposal (IRE)**[44] 2665 5-9-8 50 SebSanders 1 —
(A P Jarvis) *midfield on inner: rdn over 2f out and sn wknd: fin 9th, plcd 8th* **8/1**

1000 **9** 15 **Autograph Hunter**[40] 2771 3-9-3 80 (b[1]) GeorgeBaker 10 —
(Peter Grayson) *s.i.s: a bhd: t.o fr 1/2-way: fin 10th, plcd 9th* **6/1**[3]

060- **10** 14 **Lindbergh**[407] 2674 5-9-12 80 EddieAhern 6 —
(A J Lidderdale) *in tch: rdn along 1/2-way: sn wknd: fin 11th, plcd 10th* **15/2**

0503 **D** 2 ½ **Dasheena**[30] 3110 4-8-6 51 (be) RobbieEgan(7) 2 60
(A J McCabe) *fly j. s and bhd: hdwy on outer 2f out: sn rdn and styd on wl fnl f: fin 2nd, 2½l: subs. disq: rider unlicensed* **15/2**

1m 14.2s (-1.61) **Going Correction** -0.15s/f (Stan)
WFA 3 from 4yo+ 5lb **11** Ran SP% **138.8**
Speed ratings (Par 101): **104,98,96,94,89 88,84,64,44,26 100**
CSF £24.63 TOTE £3.60: £2.10, £2.00, £2.50; EX 26.90.The winner was claimed by Michael Mullineaux for £10,000

Owner Franconson Partners **Bred** Scuderia Golden Horse S R L **Trained** Newmarket, Suffolk

FOCUS
A decent race for the grade, and the time was good. The winner won as he was entitled to, but this was still an improved effort.

Autograph Hunter Official explanation: jockey said gelding missed the break

4022 WOLVERHAMPTON-RACECOURSE.CO.UK NURSERY 7f 32y(P)
3:15 (3:18) (Class 5) 2-Y-O **£2,968** (£876; £438) **Stalls** High

Form RPR

043 **1** **Palm Court**[14] 3592 2-8-8 70 ow1 SebSanders 3 81+
(R Charlton) *s.i.s: hdwy into midfield at 1/2-way: chsd ldrs and rdn wl over 1f out: swtchd to outside and drvn ent fnl f: styd on strly to ld nr fin* **9/4**[2]

15 **2** nk **Dixey**[16] 3522 2-9-10 86 PhilipRobinson 2 94+
(M A Jarvis) *trckd ldrs: hdwy to ld wl over 1f out: rdn ent fnl f: hdd and no ex nr fin* **15/8**[1]

006 **3** 5 **Spinning Ridge (IRE)**[14] 3596 2-8-3 68 LiamJones(3) 4 63
(R A Harris) *chsd ldrs: hdwy over 2f out: rdn to chse ldr over 1f out: sn drvn and one pce* **10/1**

250 **4** 1 **Valhillen**[14] 3589 2-8-2 64 FrancisNorton 8 57
(M J Wallace) *led: rdn along and hdd 2f out: sn drvn and kpt on same pce appr fnl f* **10/1**

050 **5** ¾ **Abfabfong (IRE)**[51] 2478 2-7-12 60 oh3 FrankieMcDonald 11 51
(P F I Cole) *t.k.h: prom: rdn along over 2f out: sn drvn and grad wknd appr fnl f* **33/1**

1000 **6** ½ **Feeling Proud (USA)**[18] 3462 2-9-4 80 JohnEgan 10 69
(Jane Chapple-Hyam) *cl up: led 2f out: sn rdn and hdd: drvn and wknd appr fnl f* **10/1**

0003 **7** hd **Hyper Viper (IRE)**[11] 3680 2-7-7 60 (b[1]) LukeMorris(5) 5 49
(J S Moore) *in tch: rdn along and sltly outpcd 1/2-way: styd on u.p fnl f* **10/1**

4305 **8** ½ **Lady Sandicliffe (IRE)**[12] 3642 2-8-7 69 EddieAhern 12 57
(B W Hills) *nvr bttr than in midfield* **7/1**[3]

040 **9** 1 ½ **Blandys Wood**[37] 2876 2-8-3 65 JoeFanning 6 49
(M R Channon) *in tch: rdn along over 2f out and sn wknd* **12/1**

2010 **10** 1 **Ballycroy Boy (IRE)**[70] 1897 2-8-10 72 MickyFenton 1 53
(A Bailey) *outpcd and bhd tl sme late hdwy* **12/1**

400 **11** 9 **Una Auroraborealis**[18] 3465 2-7-12 60 oh3 DavidKinsella 7 19
(J Ryan) *a in rr* **40/1**

410 **12** 6 **Yes Meg**[12] 3642 2-7-9 60 DuranFentiman(3) 9 4
(P F I Cole) *s.i.s: a bhd* **11/1**

1m 30.66s (0.26) **Going Correction** -0.15s/f (Stan) 12 Ran SP% **143.5**
Speed ratings (Par 94): **92,91,85,84,83 83,83,82,80,79 69,62**
CSF £8.73 CT £43.86 TOTE £3.50: £1.10, £1.60, £4.00; EX 7.20.

Owner B E Nielsen **Bred** B E Nielsen **Trained** Beckhampton, Wilts

FOCUS
A modest nursery overall, but cracking efforts from the first two who came clear. The 'official' ratings shown next to each horse are estimated and for information purposes only.

NOTEBOOK
Palm Court, making his nursery and All-Weather bow after the three mandatory runs, did well to overcome a sluggish start and just open his account. A sound surface looks key to him, this extra distance clearly suited, and he remains open to further improvement. It should also be noted his rider put up 1lb overweight. (op 2-1)

Dixey ◆ was always well placed and only narrowly failed to justify market confidence on this return to Polytrack. She has to rate a touch unfortunate as she finished well clear of the remainder and was conceding 16lb to the winner. (op 2-1)

Spinning Ridge(IRE) showed improved form on this nursery debut, yet did not fully convince that he is yet ready for this extra furlong. There are races to be won with him. (op 12-1)

Valhillen was given an aggressive ride for one trying further than 5f for the first time and not that surprisingly failed to last home. This was still a more encouraging effort, however, and a slight drop back in trip should help. (op 14-1)

Abfabfong(IRE), 3lb out of the weights, eventually paid for refusing to settle on this nursery debut. He is another who should appreciate dropping back to 6f.

Feeling Proud(USA) Official explanation: jockey said filly lost a shoe and moved poorly

4023 ENJOY AIR CONDITIONED HORIZONS RESTAURANT H'CAP 1m 141y(P)
3:45 (3:46) (Class 6) (0-65,64) 3-Y-O+ **£2,388** (£705; £352) **Stalls** Low

Form RPR

0324 **1** **Casablanca Minx (IRE)**[6] 3826 4-8-13 50 (v) StephenDonohoe 12 58
(P D Evans) *hld up in rr: stdy hdwy 4f out: rdn to chse ldrs over 1f out: styd on to ld wl ins fnl f* **4/1**[2]

3123 **2** 1 ½ **Golden Spectrum (IRE)**[14] 3600 8-9-8 64 (b) LukeMorris(5) 7 69
(R A Harris) *s.i.s and sn rdn along in rr: hdwy on outer over 2f out: styd on u.p ins fnl f: nrst fin* **4/1**[2]

4400 **3** hd **Wodhill Gold**[19] 3419 6-9-3 54 (b) AdrianMcCarthy 1 59
(D Morris) *led 1f: chsd ldr tl rdn to ld again over 1f out: sn drvn: hdd and nt qckn wl ins fnl f* **11/1**

/306 **4** 1 ¾ **Exotic Venture**[20] 3409 4-9-4 55 SebSanders 4 56
(R M Beckett) *trckd ldrs: hdwy 3f out: rdn 2f out: sn drvn and one pce ent fnl f* **10/1**

0663 **5** shd **Pitbull**[19] 3414 4-9-1 52 (p) GrahamGibbons 2 52
(Mrs G S Rees) *in tch on inner: effrt and rdn whn jinked and hit rail 2f out: sn drvn and kpt on same pce ins fnl f* **6/1**

0-00 **6** 3 **Regal Dream (IRE)**[59] 2225 5-9-4 55 SimonWhitworth 13 49
(J W Unett) *hld up towards rr: hdwy over 3f out: rdn along wl over 1f out: kpt on same pce ent fnl f* **20/1**

00 **7** ½ **Shahadah (IRE)**[44] 2657 5-8-6 50 WilliamCarson(7) 9 43
(R J Price) *hld up towards rr: hdwy 3f out: rdn along 2f out and sn no imp* **33/1**

2012 **8** hd **Holiday Cocktail**[46] 2603 5-9-9 63 DougieCostello(3) 3 55
(J J Quinn) *trckd ldrs: effrt 3f out: rdn 2f out and sn btn* **3/1**[1]

523- **9** nk **Bert's Memory**[221] 6891 3-9-0 60 DO'Donohoe 8 52
(K A Ryan) *prom: rdn along 2f out: sn drvn and wknd wl over 1f out* **14/1**

0000 **10** shd **First Show**[15] 3571 5-9-8 62 (bt) LiamJones(3) 11 53
(R A Harris) *cl up: led after 1f: rdn along over 2f out: drvn and hdd over 1f out: wknd* **11/1**

-054 **11** shd **Greenmeadow**[18] 3451 5-9-7 58 EddieAhern 10 49
(S Kirk) *a towards rr* **5/1**[3]

-050 **12** 5 **Vampyrus**[34] 2965 4-8-13 50 AdamKirby 5 30
(H Candy) *chsd ldrs: rdn along over 4f out and sn wknd* **20/1**

1m 50.9s (-0.86) **Going Correction** -0.15s/f (Stan)
WFA 3 from 4yo+ 9lb **12** Ran SP% **140.8**
Speed ratings (Par 101): **97,95,95,93,93 91,90,90,90,90 90,85**
CSF £24.31 CT £185.79 TOTE £6.20: £2.40, £1.50, £3.90; EX 30.50.

Owner J E Abbey **Bred** Airlie Stud And Widden Stud **Trained** Pandy, Monmouths

FOCUS
A moderate handicap and sound if ordinary form.

Pitbull Official explanation: jockey said gelding became unbalanced after hitting the rail

4024 BOOK YOUR WEDDING HERE H'CAP 5f 216y(P)
4:15 (4:15) (Class 5) (0-75,75) 3-Y-O+ **£2,914** (£867; £433; £216) **Stalls** Low

Form RPR

4001 **1** **Mozakhraf (USA)**[11] 3676 5-8-12 61 DO'Donohoe 6 73+
(K A Ryan) *trckd ldrs: smooth hdwy 2f out: rdn ent fnl f: styd on to ld nr fin* **9/2**[2]

3465 **2** hd **Norcroft**[20] 3396 5-8-4 60 (p) KirstyMilczarek(7) 2 69
(Mrs C A Dunnett) *trckd ldrs: gd hdwy on inner to ld over 1f out: sn rdn: drvn ins fnl f: hdd and no ex nr fin* **8/1**

3064 **3** 1 ½ **Tous Les Deux**[18] 3452 4-9-9 72 GeorgeBaker 4 77
(Peter Grayson) *hld up towards rr: hdwy on inner 1/2-way: swtchd outside and rdn to chse ldrs over 1f out: kpt on u.p ins fnl f* **8/1**

0311 **4** 2 **Quality Street**[5] 3852 5-9-12 75 6ex (p) RichardThomas 13 74
(P Butler) *in tch on outer: effrt and hdwy 2f out: sn rdn and styd on same pce appr fnl f* **15/2**[3]

0023 **5** shd **Dvinsky (USA)**[13] 3623 6-9-10 73 IanMongan 12 71
(P Howling) *cl up: rdn along 2f out: drvn and ev ch over 1f out: wknd ent fnl f* **11/1**

0145 **6** ½ **Winthorpe (IRE)**[11] 3676 7-9-0 63 GrahamGibbons 11 60
(J J Quinn) *chsd ldrs: rdn along 2f out: sn drvn and one pce* **11/1**

0636 **7** nk **Marko Jadeo (IRE)**[13] 3623 9-9-4 72 LukeMorris(5) 7 68
(R A Harris) *s.i.s and bhd: hdwy 2f out: sn rdn and kpt on appr fnl f: nrst fin* **10/1**

155 **8** shd **Gilded Cove**[18] 3472 7-8-13 67 RussellKennemore(5) 8 63
(R Hollinshead) *dwlt: a towards rr* **9/1**

000 **9** ½ **Night Prospector**[44] 2655 7-9-9 75 (p) LiamJones(3) 3 69
(R A Harris) *cl up: led after 2f: drvn and hdd over 1f out: sn wknd* **16/1**

424 **10** 2 ½ **Louphole**[13] 3613 5-9-12 75 SebSanders 5 62
(P J Makin) *dwlt: towards rr: effrt and sme hdwy 1/2-way: rdn along 2f out and sn no imp* **7/2**[1]

6004 **11** ½ **Guildenstern (IRE)**[7] 3802 5-9-6 69 AmirQuinn 1 54
(P Howling) *a in rr* **12/1**

1505 **12** shd **What Do You Know**[13] 3613 4-9-4 70 AndrewElliott(3) 9 55
(A M Hales) *led 2f: cl up tl rdn along wl over 1f out and grad wknd* **9/1**

-005 **13** hd **Hart Of Gold**[47] 2570 3-9-7 75 (p) EddieAhern 10 59
(M J Wallace) *cl up: rdn along 2f out and sn wknd* **10/1**

1m 14.23s (-1.58) **Going Correction** -0.15s/f (Stan)
WFA 3 from 4yo+ 5lb **13** Ran SP% **142.8**
Speed ratings (Par 103): **104,103,101,99,98 98,97,97,97,93 93,92,92**
CSF £49.49 CT £308.55 TOTE £4.10: £1.80, £3.80, £2.20; EX 70.90.

Owner John Coke **Bred** Audley Farm Inc **Trained** Hambleton, N Yorks

FOCUS
A modest sprint. The form has not been rated too positively but the winner was value for a bit extra.

Marko Jadeo(IRE) Official explanation: jockey said gelding missed the break

4025 RINGSIDE - PERFECT FOR PARTY NIGHTS H'CAP 1m 4f 50y(P)
4:45 (4:45) (Class 6) (0-65,59) 3-Y-O+ **£2,388** (£705; £352) **Stalls** Low

Form RPR

1605 **1** **Thorny Mandate**[17] 3496 5-10-0 59 EddieAhern 8 68+
(W M Brisbourne) *hld up towards rr: gd hdwy 3f out: rdn to chse ldrs over 1f out: styd on wl u.p ins fnl f to ld nr fin* **6/1**

4350 **2** nk **Intavac Boy**[84] 1532 6-9-5 55 MichaelJStainton(5) 7 61
(S P Griffiths) *cl up: led wl over 3f out: rdn wl over 1f out: drvn ent fnl f: hdd and no ex nr fin* **7/2**[2]

50-3 **3** ½ **Constant Cheers (IRE)**[13] 3617 4-9-12 57 (v) AdamKirby 6 62
(W R Swinburn) *trckd ldrs: hdwy to chse ldr 2f out: sn rdn and ev ch ins fnl f: drvn and no ex towards fin* **11/2**[3]

0000 **4** *3* **Freddy (ARG)**[14] 3598 8-10-0 **59**.....(bt) FrancisNorton 3 59
(D K Ivory) *dwlt: hld up and bhd: hdwy over 3f out: rdn 2f out: styd on: nrst fin* **9/1**

0254 **5** *2 1/2* **Always Best**[12] 3640 3-9-2 **59**..... JoeFanning 5 55
(M Johnston) *trckd ldrs: rdn along 4f out: plugged on same pce* **6/1**

/003 **6** *5* **Don Jose (USA)**[13] 3610 4-9-8 **53**..... DO'Donohoe 2 41
(N J Vaughan) *led: rdn along and hdd wl over 3f out: drvn 2f out and sn wknd* **14/1**

4021 **7** *4* **Birthday Star (IRE)**[14] 3595 5-9-12 **57**..... SebSanders 12 39
(A G Juckes) *hld up: pushed along 1/2-way: a towards rr* **10/3**[1]

0000 **8** *16* **Li Shih Chen**[13] 3619 4-9-9 **54**..... SimonWhitworth 1 10
(A P Jarvis) *in tch: rdn along 4f out: sn wknd* **20/1**

0500 **9** *8* **Piper General (IRE)**[105] 1069 5-9-13 **58**..... DavidAllan 9 1
(J Balding) *t.k.h: hld up towards rr: effrt over 4f out: sn rdn along and nvr a factor* **16/1**

0630 **10** *15* **A Nod And A Wink (IRE)**[12] 3652 3-8-5 **48**..... BThomas 10 —
(J C Fox) *dwlt: sn in tch: hdwy to chse ldrs on outer 1/2-way: sn rdn along and wknd* **16/1**

0000 **11** *18* **Wellington Hall (GER)**[18] 3457 9-9-7 **52**..... OscarUrbina 4 —
(M Wigham) *chsd ldrs: rdn along over 4f out and sn wknd* **7/1**

2m 40.96s (-1.46) **Going Correction** -0.15s/f (Stan)
WFA 3 from 4yo+ 12lb 11 Ran SP% **135.0**
Speed ratings (Par 101): **98,97,97,95,93 90,87,77,71,61 49**
CSF £31.68 CT £133.47 TOTE £7.90: £3.70, £2.90, £3.30; EX 44.30 Place 6 £ 39.35, Place 5 £ 30.56.
Owner R C Naylor **Bred** Major W R Hern And W H Carson **Trained** Great Ness, Shropshire

FOCUS
A weak handicap which saw the first three come clear. The form is rated through the second.
Freddy(ARG) Official explanation: jockey said horse hung left-handed throughout
Wellington Hall(GER) Official explanation: jockey said gelding lost its action
T/Plt: £40.60 to a £1 stake. Pool: £61,455.55. 1,104.45 winning tickets. T/Qpdt: £23.80 to a £1 stake. Pool: £3,358.50. 104.40 winning tickets. JR

3823 YARMOUTH (L-H)
Monday, July 30

OFFICIAL GOING: Good to firm (8.8)
Wind: fresh behind Weather: bright, partly cloudy

4026 LETHEBY & CHRISTOPHER FILLIES' MAIDEN AUCTION STKS 5f 43y
2:30 (2:30) (Class 6) 2-Y-O **£1,943** (£578; £288; £144) **Stalls** High

Form RPR

6654 **1** **Cocabana**[28] 3162 2-8-8 0..... TPQueally 2 72
(J G Portman) *mde virtually all: pushed along and drew clr over 1f out: readily* **10/3**[2]

62 **2** *2 1/2* **Alabama Spirit (USA)**[26] 3200 2-8-8 0..... DeanMcKeown 1 63
(K R Burke) *chsd ldrs: rdn 2f out: kpt on u.p to go 2nd wl ins fnl f: no ch w wnr* **15/8**[1]

024 **3** *nk* **Jastaanhi**[13] 3606 2-8-0 0..... ColinHaddon(5) 8 59
(J A Pickering) *prom: chsd wnr over 2f out: edgd lft u.p 1f out: kpt on same pce* **15/2**

00 **4** *2* **Victorian Princess (IRE)**[18] 3453 2-8-8 0..... ChrisCatlin 7 55
(E J O'Neill) *pressed wnr tl over 2f out: sonn rdn: wknd fnl f* **12/1**

0260 **5** *1/2* **Hucking Harmony (IRE)**[19] 3426 2-8-4 0..... GregFairley(3) 5 52
(J R Best) *t.k.h: chsd ldrs tl over 2f out: sn rdn and struggling* **11/2**[3]

50 **6** *8* **Day Shift (IRE)**[6] 3823 2-8-7 0..... RichardMullen 6 24
(Rae Guest) *a towards rr: lost tch 1/2-way* **33/1**

7 *3 1/2* **Lady Maya** 2-8-5 0 ow2..... KevinGhunowa(5) 4 15
(Dr J R J Naylor) *s.i.s: a wl outpcd: t.o fr 1/2-way* **33/1**

00 **8** *13* **Queen Be**[11] 3681 2-8-4 0..... RoystonFfrench 9 —
(I W McInnes) *s.i.s: a wl outpcd: t.o fr 1/2-way* **66/1**

40 **9** *3* **Erin Thomas (IRE)**[21] 3378 2-8-6 0 ow1..... JamieSpencer 3 —
(M G Quinlan) *bhd: rdn and lost tch after 2f: virtually p.u fnl f: t.o* **13/2**

60.73 secs (-2.07) **Going Correction** -0.425s/f (Firm) 9 Ran SP% **113.4**
Speed ratings (Par 89): **99,95,94,91,90 77,72,51,46**
CSF £9.65 TOTE £5.20: £1.80, £1.10, £2.50; EX 10.80 Trifecta £40.60 Pool: £600.98, 10.50 winning units.
Owner Hockham Racing **Bred** Catridge Farm Stud Ltd **Trained** Compton, Berks

FOCUS
A weak maiden and guessy form, but a step up from the winner.

NOTEBOOK
Cocabana has been readily held in maidens thus far, latterly when racing alone in heavy ground at Windsor last time, but this was not a strong heat and she seemed to appreciate the return to a faster surface, running out a ready winner. There may be more to come in nurseries, especially if she is turned out under a penalty. (op 3-1 tchd 11-4 and 7-2)
Alabama Spirit(USA) looked set to take all the beating on the form of her recent second at Catterick, but she failed to reproduce the form on this faster surface and was made to look paceless by the winner. She can probably find a maiden before going handicapping and looks ready for an extra furlong now. (tchd 7-4 and 2-1)
Jastaanhi has progressed a little with each start and may be capable of further progress once sent handicapping. (op 10-1 tchd 7-1)
Victorian Princess(IRE) is bred to appreciate much further and it was no surprise to see her struggle to make an impact. She is now qualified for nurseries and should do better in that sphere. (op 20-1)
Hucking Harmony(IRE) continues to fall short and it may take a drop into a lower grade for her to get off the mark. (op 17-2)
Erin Thomas(IRE) Official explanation: jockey said filly moved poorly throughout

4027 GREAT YARMOUTH MERCURY (S) STKS 6f 3y
3:00 (3:01) (Class 6) 2-Y-O **£1,943** (£578; £288; £144) **Stalls** High

Form RPR

4500 **1** **Rough Rock (IRE)**[12] 3642 2-8-11 0.....(b) JamieSpencer 3 70+
(B J Meehan) *mde all: sn clr: in n.d fr 2f out: eased towards fin* **4/6**[1]

405 **2** *6* **Dawn Light (IRE)**[9] 3750 2-8-6 0..... RoystonFfrench 10 44+
(Mrs A Duffield) *bhd: sn rdn: styd on u.p fnl 2f: chsd wnr ins fnl f: no ch* **6/1**[3]

00 **3** *2 1/2* **Little Bones**[25] 3245 2-8-6 0..... ChrisCatlin 2 36
(Rae Guest) *bmpd s: sn bhd and rdn: styd on u.p fnl 2f: wnt 3rd ins fnl f: no ch* **20/1**

0040 **4** *1/2* **Rannoch**[7] 3801 2-8-11 0..... RichardMullen 4 40
(Miss D A McHale) *chsd ldrs: drvn and chsd wnr over 2f out: no imp: lost 2 pls fnl f* **66/1**

5 *2* **Just Mossie** 2-8-4 0..... JackDean(7) 9 34
(W G M Turner) *chsd ldrs: rdn over 3f out: no ch fnl 2f* **28/1**

06 **6** *3/4* **Emily's Dens Joy (IRE)**[7] 3801 2-8-6 0..... SaleemGolam 1 26
(Miss D A McHale) *stdd s: racd in midfield: rdn 1/2-way: sn no ch* **80/1**

3340 **7** *1 1/2* **Miss Willoughby**[3] 3923 2-8-8 0..... MarcHalford(3) 7 27
(J Ryan) *s.i.s: rdn and hdwy to chse ldrs 1/2-way: wknd 2f out* **20/1**

0 **8** *7* **Tomba Maestro**[14] 3589 2-8-11 0..... JimmyQuinn 6 —
(J L Spearing) *chsd wnr tl over 2f out: sn rdn and hung lft: wknd qckly: eased ins fnl f: t.o* **16/1**

431U **9** *26* **Amazing Day**[65] 2028 2-8-11 0..... KevinGhunowa(5) 5 —
(John A Harris) *bhd: rdn over 3f out: sn lost tch: eased and virtually p.u fr over 1f out: t.o* **5/1**[2]

1m 11.98s (-1.72) **Going Correction** -0.425s/f (Firm) 9 Ran SP% **112.5**
Speed ratings (Par 92): **94,86,82,82,79 78,76,67,32**
CSF £4.33 TOTE £1.50: £1.10, £1.70, £4.50; EX 5.30 Trifecta £42.20 Pool: £675.83, 11.37 winning units.The winner was sold to M Foulger for 28,600gns
Owner L P R Partnership **Bred** Mrs B Stroomer **Trained** Manton, Wilts

FOCUS
The facile winner apart, this was a poor race, even by selling standards.

NOTEBOOK
Rough Rock(IRE), dropping into selling company having failed to make an impact in maidens or nurseries, again had the blinkers on and he was made plenty of use of on this drop in trip. Eased down having drawn right away in the final furlong, he fetched a record price for a Yarmouth selling winner and looks worth his place back in a nursery. (op Evens)
Dawn Light(IRE) is another who has been struggling in maidens and she seemed more at home in this company. She was no match for the winner, but can be found a similar race. (op 4-1)
Little Bones is not going to find winning easy, even at this level, but is at least now qualified for low-grade nurseries. (op 22-1 tchd 25-1)
Rannoch is already exposed at this level and his immediate future looks pretty bleak. (tchd 100-1)
Just Mossie, an 800gns son of Ishiguru, made a relatively pleasing and is in the right hands to win a race at this level. (op 25-1)
Amazing Day Official explanation: jockey said colt lost its action on the good to firm ground

4028 SHIRLEY GILL MEMORIAL MAIDEN AUCTION STKS 7f 3y
3:30 (3:36) (Class 6) 2-Y-O **£1,943** (£578; £288; £144) **Stalls** High

Form RPR

06 **1** **Rosy Alexander**[10] 3706 2-8-7 0..... JamieSpencer 10 69+
(N A Callaghan) *wntnr finlft and bmpd s: hld up: hdwy 4f out: led jst over 2f out: sn rdn and hung lft: kpt on* **5/6**[1]

2 *1/2* **Azure Mist** 2-8-7 0..... JimmyQuinn 5 68+
(M H Tompkins) *racd in midfield: hdwy wl over 2f out: ev ch over 1f out: unable qck nr fin* **16/1**

0 **3** *3 1/2* **Hucking Hero (IRE)**[19] 3424 2-8-9 0..... MarcHalford(3) 2 64
(J R Best) *awkward leaving stalls: racd in midfield: hdwy 3f out: hung lft 2f out: chsd ldng pair over 1f out outpcd fnl f* **40/1**

0 **4** *3* **Always Brave**[13] 3625 2-8-9 0..... GregFairley(3) 8 56+
(M Johnston) *w ldrs: led 3f out tl jst over 2f out: sn rdn: wknd 1f out: hung lft ins fnl f* **7/1**[3]

0 **5** *nk* **Ras Laffan**[37] 2889 2-9-1 0..... RichardMullen 14 58
(E S McMahon) *chsd ldrs: rdn and outpcd 3f out: kpt on* **9/1**

0 **6** *2* **Victorian Cape (IRE)**[18] 3471 2-9-1 0..... ChrisCatlin 7 53
(E J O'Neill) *w ldrs: rdn and ev ch over 2f out: wknd over 1f out* **5/1**[2]

7 *5* **Pepper's Ghost** 2-8-9 0..... JerryO'Dwyer(3) 12 37
(Miss J Feilden) *sn bhd: rdn over 4f out: sme late hdwy: n.d* **33/1**

8 *3* **East Coast Girl (IRE)** 2-8-10 0..... PaulEddery 1 27
(J McAuley) *a bhd: no ch last 3f* **50/1**

0 **9** *hd* **Golddigging (IRE)**[12] 3643 2-8-7 0..... TPQueally 9 24
(J G Portman) *bmpd s: nvr gng wl in rr: no ch fr 1/2-way:* **22/1**

10 *nk* **Latimer House (IRE)** 2-8-4 0..... DaleGibson 4 20
(Dr J D Scargill) *s.i.s: a wl bhd:* **66/1**

11 *1* **Rampant Ronnie (USA)** 2-9-1 0..... DarryllHolland 3 28
(P W D'Arcy) *bhd after 2f: no ch fr 1/2-way* **22/1**

0 **12** *1 1/4* **Southwark Newsboy (IRE)**[9] 3733 2-8-9 0..... DMylonas 6 19+
(Mrs C A Dunnett) *led tl 3f out: sn dropped out* **50/1**

1m 24.46s (-2.14) **Going Correction** -0.425s/f (Firm) 12 Ran SP% **119.1**
Speed ratings (Par 92): **95,94,90,87,86 84,78,75,75,74 73,72**
CSF £15.82 TOTE £1.90: £1.30, £3.00, £8.60; EX 16.30 Trifecta £372.90 Part won. Pool: £525.31, 0.84 winning units..
Owner Mrs T A Foreman **Bred** Mrs T A Foreman **Trained** Newmarket, Suffolk

FOCUS
Not a particularly strong maiden, rated through the winner to her previous form.

NOTEBOOK
Rosy Alexander stepped up on her initial effort with a keeping-on sixth at Newmarket recently and had been found a weak race in which to shed her maiden status. Brought through to challenge racing into the final quarter mile, it took her a while to wear down newcomer Azure Mist, but that previous experience came good in the end. She is only ordinary, but remains capable of better in nurseries. (op 10-11 tchd 4-5)
Azure Mist, a 9,000gns daughter of Bahamian Bounty, comes from a stable whose juveniles often need a run, but she clearly knew her job and made the hot favourite work hard for her victory. This was a most satisfactory first run and normal progression should see her winning a similar contest. (tchd 14-1)
Hucking Hero(IRE) stepped up significantly on his debut effort when beating only one home at Lingfield, keeping on for third. He did look a bit awkward under pressure, but this was only his second run and he deserves the benefit of the doubt for the time being. (op 33-1)
Always Brave, whose stable's juveniles have not been performing up to their usual high standards this season, improved on his initial effort over course and distance and will be qualified for nurseries after one more run. (op 9-1 tchd 11-1)
Ras Laffan seemed to improve a little for this faster ground and is another likely to do better once contesting handicaps. (op 10-1 tchd 12-1)
Victorian Cape(IRE) showed little on his debut at Warwick and this was not much better, but he rates as more of a handicap prospect. (op 13-2 tchd 7-1)
Golddigging(IRE) Official explanation: jockey said filly lost her action on the fast, good to firm ground

4029 MARTIN FOULGER MEMORIAL H'CAP 7f 3y
4:00 (4:07) (Class 5) (0-70,70) 3-Y-O+ **£2,914** (£867; £433; £216) **Stalls** High

Form RPR

5-00 **1** **For Life (IRE)**[185] 254 5-8-4 **48** oh3..... NataliaGemelova(5) 3 66
(J E Long) *mde all: pushed clr wl over 1f out: r.o strly* **40/1**

0521 **2** *5* **Riverside Dancer (USA)**[53] 2387 3-9-9 **69**..... JDSmith 13 71
(G A Huffer) *wnt rt s: wl bhd: rdn and hdwy 2f out: edgd lft but styd on fnl f: wnt 2nd nr fin: no ch w wnr* **5/1**[3]

1350 **3** *shd* **Takitwo**[19] 3422 4-9-11 **64**..... JamieSpencer 16 68
(P D Cundell) *hld up wl bhd: rdn and hdwy over 2f out: styd on u.p fnl f: nvr nr wnr* **9/2**[2]

6030 **4** *hd* **Whistleupthewind**[17] 3487 4-8-12 **51**.....(p) DaleGibson 2 55
(J M P Eustace) *stmbld s: sn chsd wnr tl 4f out: rdn over 2f out: chsd wnr and hung lft wl over 2f out: one pce: lost 2 pls nr fin* **14/1**

0006 **5** ½ **Motarjm (USA)**[22] 3349 3-9-4 **67** (t) JerryO'Dwyer[(3)] 9 66+
(H J Collingridge) *in tch: rdn and outpcd 3f out: kpt on fnl f: nvr able to chal* **14/1**

0000 **6** *nk* **Charlottebutterfly**[6] 3826 7-8-9 **48** oh3 RichardMullen 5 50
(P J McBride) *towards rr: rdn wl over 3f out: kpt on fnl f: n.d* **28/1**

4200 **7** *nk* **Arctic Desert**[10] 3711 7-9-11 **64** (t) DarryllHolland 7 65
(Miss Gay Kelleway) *v.s.a: wl bhd: hdwy wl over 1f out: styng on whn hmpd 1f out: kpt on* **14/1**

6603 **8** *1 ½* **Border Artist**[6] 3828 8-9-3 **56** (v) JimmyQuinn 4 53
(J Pearce) *hld up off pce in midfield: hdwy over 2f out: chsd ldrs and rdn 1f out: no imp* **3/1**[1]

2040 **9** ½ **Realy Naughty (IRE)**[12] 3646 3-9-1 **64** RichardKingscote[(3)] 14 56
(B G Powell) *racd in midfield: n.d* **16/1**

0630 **10** ½ **Astorygoeswithit**[35] 2937 4-8-6 **48** oh3 MarcHalford[(3)] 17 42
(Miss K B Boutflower) *chsd ldrs: rdn 1/2-way: wknd over 2f out* **66/1**

0103 **11** ½ **Barataria**[21] 3375 5-9-5 **58** RoystonFfrench 8 51
(R Bastiman) *rrd leaving stalls: a wl bhd* **6/1**

00-0 **12** ¾ **Penny Glitters**[58] 2257 4-8-9 **48** oh1 PaulEddery 12 39
(S Parr) *chsd ldrs: rdn 1/2-way: wknd over 2f out* **66/1**

3463 **13** *hd* **Fantasy Defender (IRE)**[47] 2556 5-8-9 **48** oh1 ChrisCatlin 15 38
(R M H Cowell) *nvr gng wl in rr: nvr on terms* **12/1**

0-00 **14** *1* **Queen's Lodge (IRE)**[11] 3686 7-10-0 **67** TonyHamilton 10 54
(I W McInnes) *chsd ldrs tl 1/2-way: sn wknd* **25/1**

5305 **15** ½ **Inscribed (IRE)**[11] 3667 4-8-11 **50** (b) SaleemGolam 1 36
(G A Huffer) *t.k.h: prom: chsd wnr 4f out tl wl over 1f out: wkng whn hung lft 1f out* **28/1**

0546 **P** **Dowlleh**[38] 2837 3-9-10 **70** SamHitchcott 6 —
(T T Clement) *in tch: pushed along 1/2-way: sn struggling: lost action and p.u ins fnl f* **14/1**

1m 23.13s (-3.47) **Going Correction** -0.425s/f (Firm)
WFA 3 from 4yo+ 7lb **16** Ran SP% **130.5**
Speed ratings (Par 103): **102,96,96,95,95 95,94,92,92,91 91,90,90,89,88** —
CSF £238.35 CT £1166.53 TOTE £66.90: £9.80, £2.00, £1.80, £3.70; EX 715.20 TRIFECTA Not won..
Owner T H Bambridge **Bred** R N Auld **Trained** Caterham, Surrey
■ Stewards' Enquiry : Natalia Gemelova one-day ban: failed to keep straight from stalls (Aug 10)

FOCUS
A moderate handicap. The clear winner returned to his best post-2yo form and the form is sound.
Arctic Desert Official explanation: jockey said gelding was denied a clear run
Barataria Official explanation: jockey said gelding fly-leapt on leaving stalls
Dowlleh Official explanation: vet said gelding bled from the nose

4030 NORFOLK NELSON MUSEUM H'CAP 2m
4:30 (4:36) (Class 6) (0-65,62) 4-Y-0+ **£1,943** (£578; £288; £144) **Stalls** High

Form RPR

5-24 **1** **Sharaab (USA)**[18] 3448 6-8-9 **50** (t) DaleGibson 14 57
(D E Cantillon) *w.w in midfield: hdwy 4f out: chal 2f out: pushed into ld jst ins fnl f: r.o wl* **13/2**[3]

1160 **2** *1 ¼* **Vice Admiral**[37] 2890 4-9-3 **58** PaulMulrennan 15 64
(M W Easterby) *sn led: jnd and rdn 2f out: kpt on wl tl no ex fnl 100yds* **12/1**

2461 **3** *1 ½* **Josh You Are**[20] 3397 4-9-5 **60** PatCosgrave 7 64+
(D E Cantillon) *hld up in rr: hdwy over 3f out: rdn over 2f out: kpt on fnl f: nt pce to rch ldrs* **4/1**[1]

-563 **4** *hd* **Sa Nau**[13] 3630 4-9-1 **56** NeilPollard 16 60
(T Keddy) *hld up in rr: rdn over 5f out: hdwy over 4f out: chsd ldrs and hrd rdn over 2f out: kpt on* **9/1**

-464 **5** *1 ¾* **Rajayoga**[58] 1229 6-8-6 **47** JimmyQuinn 11 49
(M H Tompkins) *hld up in midfield: nt clr run over 3f out: swtchd rt over 2f out: kpt on: nvr able to chal* **9/2**[2]

000 **6** *1 ¾* **Leonardo's Friend**[18] 3448 4-8-12 **56** (t) RichardKingscote[(3)] 12 56
(B G Powell) *hld up in rr: swtchd rt 3f out: rdn over 2f out: no imp* **18/1**

/346 **7** *1* **Festive Chimes (IRE)**[9] 2770 6-9-1 **59** JerryO'Dwyer[(3)] 8 57
(N B King) *w.w towards rr: effrt to chse ldrs over 3f out: wknd over 2f out* **8/1**

1560 **8** *1* **Mahmjra**[11] 3671 5-9-5 **60** EdwardCreighton 13 57
(C N Allen) *t.k.h: chsd ldr after 2f: rdn 4f out: wknd over 2f out* **50/1**

0334 **9** *4* **Blue Hills**[14] 3598 6-8-12 **53** ChrisCatlin 6 45
(P W Hiatt) *in tch: rdn and effrt over 3f out: wknd 2f out* **14/1**

-060 **10** ¾ **Our Monogram**[33] 2996 11-9-7 **62** RoystonFfrench 10 53
(R M Beckett) *chsd ldrs: reminder 7f out: rdn 4f out: sn struggling* **22/1**

0-03 **11** *nk* **Prince Of Medina**[43] 2686 4-8-12 **53** TPQueally 1 44
(J R Best) *chsd ldr for 2f: prom: rdn over 3f out: wknd wl over 2f out* **15/2**

0-01 **12** *1 ¼* **Jayer Gilles**[50] 2493 7-8-11 **57** (v) KevinGhunowa[(5)] 4 47
(Dr J R J Naylor) *t.k.h: hld up in tch: rdn and wknd wl over 2f out* **14/1**

1060 **13** *25* **Himba**[18] 3448 4-8-11 **52** (b[1]) DarryllHolland 9 12
(Mrs A J Perrett) *a last: c wd and brief effrt 4f out: sn no ch: eased fnl f: t.o* **25/1**

3m 27.72s (-3.69) **Going Correction** -0.425s/f (Firm) **13** Ran SP% **120.8**
Speed ratings (Par 101): **92,91,90,90,89 88,88,87,85,85 85,84,72**
CSF £81.53 CT £357.73 TOTE £8.60: £2.80, £4.60, £1.80; EX 99.80 TRIFECTA Not won..
Owner Mrs J Hart, Mrs C Reed & J Baillie **Bred** Shadwell Farm LLC **Trained** Newmarket, Suffolk

FOCUS
A moderate staying handicap, and reasonably sound form with the winner up 4lb for his in-form yard.
Prince Of Medina Official explanation: jockey said gelding was unsuited by the good to firm ground
Himba Official explanation: jockey said gelding would not face the first-time blinkers

4031 ROY & JOAN TANNER MEMORIAL LADY RIDERS' H'CAP 1m 2f 21y
5:00 (5:01) (Class 6) (0-65,65) 3-Y-0+ **£1,873** (£581; £290; £145) **Stalls** Low

Form RPR

0-00 **1** **Regal Sunset (IRE)**[14] 3600 4-9-4 **50** MissMSowerby[(5)] 9 60
(D E Cantillon) *hld up in midfield: stdy hdwy over 4f out: swtchd rt over 2f: chal 1f out: led fnl 100yds: rdn out* **16/1**

4465 **2** *hd* **Ahlawy (IRE)**[30] 3093 4-10-10 **65** MissSBrotherton 14 75
(M W Easterby) *stdd s: hld up wl in rr: c wd and stdy hdwy 3f out: pushed along and r.o wl fnl f: nt quite get up: too much to do* **3/1**[1]

6201 **3** *2* **Danzare**[7] 3805 5-9-11 **52** MissEJJones 4 58
(J L Spearing) *trckd ldrs: wnt 2nd 3f out: led over 1f out: rdn 1f out: hdd and outpcd fnl 100yds* **9/2**[2]

U006 **4** *1 ½* **Billy One Punch**[44] 2665 5-9-13 **61** MissKMargarson[(7)] 7 64
(G G Margarson) *t.k.h: chsd ldrs: n.m.r over 2f out: chsd ldrs over 1f out: nudged along and kpt on same pce fnl f* **10/1**

5504 **5** *6* **Blue Hedges**[64] 2055 5-9-4 **50** MissALHutchinson[(5)] 1 41
(H J Collingridge) *hld up wl bhd: hdwy over 3f out: rdn and kpt on last 2f: nvr able to chal* **7/1**[3]

5-10 **6** *3 ½* **Coronado's Gold (USA)**[31] 3067 6-10-2 **57** MissLEllison 12 41
(B Ellison) *chsd ldrs: wnt 2nd 6f out: led 4f out: rdn 3f out: hdd over 1f out: wknd fnl f* **10/1**

1-30 **7** *nk* **Wind Chime (IRE)**[50] 2492 10-10-0 **55** MissCHannaford 13 38
(A G Newcombe) *t.k.h: hld up wl bhd: rn wd bnd over 4f out: rdn and hdwy 3f out: kpt on but n.d* **14/1**

4340 **8** *1* **Paparaazi (IRE)**[25] 3249 5-10-10 **65** (p) MissFayeBramley 6 46
(I W McInnes) *in tch: hdwy to chse ldrs over 3f out: rdn and stmbld over 2f out: wknd* **14/1**

034 **9** *1* **Moonshine Creek**[13] 3617 5-9-6 **50** MrsMarieKing[(3)] 15 29
(P W Hiatt) *chsd ldrs: effrt and rdn 4f out: wknd 2f out* **15/2**

0300 **10** ½ **Richtee (IRE)**[2] 3956 6-9-6 **47** (p) MissADeniel 5 25
(I W McInnes) *v.s.a: a bhd* **20/1**

6000 **11** *nk* **El Capitan (FR)**[13] 3610 4-9-3 **51** ow2 (b) MissOMaylam[(7)] 11 29
(Miss Gay Kelleway) *t.k.h: chsd ldr tl 6f out: prom after rdn 3f out: wknd over 2f out* **33/1**

6-00 **12** *nk* **Love And Affection**[38] 2831 4-8-13 **47** (t) MissGThorogood[(7)] 8 24
(Miss K B Boutflower) *led tl 4f out: rdn and wknd over 2f out* **50/1**

000- **13** *3 ½* **Ticking**[275] 6225 4-9-8 **52** MissARyan[(3)] 10 22
(T Keddy) *a bhd: c wd and rdn 4f out: no ch fnl 2f* **50/1**

0000 **14** ½ **Love You Always (USA)**[28] 3149 7-9-1 **49** oh1 ow3(t) MissCCasey[(7)] 16 18
(Miss J Feilden) *s.i.s: t.k.h: sn chsng ldrs on outer: wknd 4f out: wl bhd fnl 2f* **33/1**

0023 **15** *1 ¾* **Arabellas Homer**[38] 2843 3-8-11 **48** MrsMMorris 2 14
(Mrs N Macauley) *t.k.h: hld up in midfield: rdn 3f out: sn wknd* **25/1**

2m 7.28s (-0.82) **Going Correction** -0.425s/f (Firm)
WFA 3 from 4yo+ 10lb **15** Ran SP% **123.3**
Speed ratings (Par 101): **86,85,84,83,78 75,75,74,73,73 72,72,69,69,68**
CSF £60.77 CT £265.00 TOTE £26.50: £7.00, £1.80, £1.70; EX 148.90 TRIFECTA Not won.
Place 6 £ 21.08, Place 5 £ 15.00.
Owner Mrs Janet Hart **Bred** Des Swan **Trained** Newmarket, Suffolk

FOCUS
Yet another moderate contest, but sound form for the grade.
T/Plt: £13.30 to a £1 stake. Pool: £68,029.55. 3,711.10 winning tickets. T/Qpdt: £12.00 to a £1 stake. Pool: £3,130.00. 191.70 winning tickets. SP

4032 - 4034a (Foreign Racing) - See Raceform Interactive

GALWAY (R-H)
Monday, July 30
OFFICIAL GOING: Soft to heavy changing to soft after race 3 (6.20)

4035a G.P.T. VAN & TRUCK RENTALS H'CAP 1m 4f
8:15 (8:15) (60-90,82) 3-Y-0 **£8,170** (£1,903; £839; £484)

RPR

1 **Sadler's Kingdom (IRE)**[18] 3469 3-8-7 64 MCHussey 7 83
(R A Fahey) *mid-div: prog 3f out: led u.p bef st: sn clr: styd on wl* **9/2**[1]

2 *2 ½* **Alpine Eagle (IRE)**[52] 2437 3-9-11 82 CO'Donoghue 2 97
(Mrs John Harrington, Ire) *towards rr: rdn to go 4th bef st: sn mod 2nd: no imp and kpt on same pce ins fnl f* **12/1**

3 *4* **Paco Jack (IRE)**[52] 2437 3-8-2 62 SMGorey[(3)] 8 71
(Joseph Crowley, Ire) *mid-div: prog over 3f out: sn almost on terms: no imp u.p and kpt on same pce in 3rd st* **16/1**

4 *2* **Gentleman Jeff (USA)**[77] 1735 3-9-3 74 PJSmullen 12 80
(D K Weld, Ire) *trckd ldrs: impr to dispute ld over 3f out: sn briefly in front: no ex u.p and kpt on same pce st* **6/1**[2]

5 *3 ½* **Winners Toast (IRE)**[23] 3336 3-9-4 75 WMLordan 13 76
(David Wachman, Ire) *led: strly pressed and hdd over 3f out: dropped to 5th and kpt on same pce u.p fr bef st* **20/1**

6 ½ **Dorset Square (IRE)**[12] 3655 3-8-8 72 PTownend[(7)] 6 72
(John Joseph Murphy, Ire) *sn in mid-div: rdn to go 6th bef st: sn no imp: kpt on same pce* **12/1**

7 *1 ¾* **Mullach Na Si**[14] 3601 3-8-6 63 CDHayes 4 61
(W P Mullins, Ire) *towards rr: rdn to go 7th bef st: sn no imp: kpt on same pce* **33/1**

8 *2 ½* **Pretty Demanding (IRE)**[46] 2609 3-8-13 70 MJKinane 1 64+
(M G Quinlan) *towards rr: rdn to go 9th bef st: sn no imp: kpt on same pce* **7/1**[3]

9 *4* **Sagarich (FR)**[30] 3118 3-9-3 74 JMurtagh 9 62
(C F Swan, Ire) *chsd ldrs: 6th over 4f out: lost pl and no imp u.p fr under 3f out* **9/2**[1]

10 *5 ½* **Priory Rock (IRE)**[24] 3293 3-9-5 76 (b[1]) KJManning 11 56
(J S Bolger, Ire) *trckd ldrs in 3rd: clsr in 2nd over 4f out: sn almost on terms: dropped to 8th and no ex u.p fr bef st* **12/1**

11 *nk* **Sonnium (IRE)**[14] 3601 3-8-9 66 DPMcDonogh 10 45
(W P Mullins, Ire) *mid-div: pushed along in 7th over 4f out: lost pl and no imp fr bef st* **7/1**[3]

12 *9* **Miss Fancy Pants**[235] 6737 3-8-7 64 WJSupple 3 30
(Noel Meade, Ire) *chsd ldrs: 5th over 4f out: lost pl and no ex u.p fr under 3f out* **33/1**

13 *19* **Pamper Mee (IRE)**[14] 3601 3-8-1 61 DJMoran[(3)] 5 —
(C F Swan, Ire) *towards rr: no imp u.p fr under 4f out* **50/1**

14 *1 ¾* **Trinidad (USA)**[31] 3069 3-9-5 76 KFallon 14 11
(A P O'Brien, Ire) *trckd ldr in 2nd: niggled along fr early: 3rd over 4f out: lost pl and no ex u.p fr over 3f out* **11/1**

2m 49.04s (5.94) **14** Ran SP% **125.5**
CSF £60.74 CT £822.06 TOTE £6.20: £2.40, £4.50, £5.30; DF 145.70.
Owner J J Staunton **Bred** Tower Bloodstock **Trained** Musley Bank, N Yorks
■ Stewards' Enquiry : M C Hussey three-day ban: used whip with excessive force and frequency (Aug 8-10)

FOCUS
A strong 3yo handicap.

NOTEBOOK
Sadler's Kingdom(IRE), 6lb higher for his win over a shorter trip at Nottingham last time, appreciated the return to this longer trip and scored well. His rider, who was banned for three days for whip abuse, reported the colt was hanging into the straight but once on the rail after straightening for home he knuckled down well under pressure. He is in peak form at present and is entered to run again here later in the week. (op 9/2 tchd 5/1)
Pretty Demanding(IRE) was last passing the six-furlong pole before making some headway on the downhill run to the straight. Her rider accepted the situation close home when her chance was gone. (op 8/1)

The Form Book, Raceform Ltd, Compton, RG20 6NL

[3788] BEVERLEY (R-H)
Tuesday, July 31

OFFICIAL GOING: Good (good to firm in places on bottom bend)
Wind: Light, against Weather: Sunny

4036 NATIONAL FESTIVAL CIRCUS (S) H'CAP 1m 4f 16y
2:05 (2:05) (Class 6) (0-65,60) 3-Y-O **£2,590** (£770; £385; £192) **Stalls** High

Form RPR

3560 **1** **Ellies Faith**[8] 3792 3-8-6 **45**....................(b) PaulFessey 2 44
(N Bycroft) *cl up: led after 1f: rdn along over 2f out: drvn over 1f out: kpt on gamely ins fnl f* **14/1**

0-05 **2** *1* **Namarian (IRE)**[14] 3611 3-8-6 **45**....................(b[1]) DavidAllan 12 43
(T D Easterby) *hld up towards rr: hdwy over 4f out: rdn to chse wnr over 1f out: drvn and ch ins fnl f: no ex towards fin* **10/1**

425 **3** *½* **Bret Maverick (IRE)**[7] 3824 3-9-2 **55**.................... GrahamGibbons 10 52
(J R Weymes) *in tch: hdwy to chse ldrs over 3f out: rdn 2f out and n.m.r: sn chsng wnr: drvn ent fnl f and kpt on same pce* **11/2[3]**

-603 **4** *3* **Lady Pickpocket**[7] 3824 3-8-12 **56**.................... PatrickHills(5) 9 48
(M H Tompkins) *hld up in rr: stdy hdwy 3f out: rdn wl over 1f out: kpt on ins fnl f: nrst fin* **6/1**

-002 **5** *1* **Roxy Singer**[33] 3040 3-8-6 **45**....................(v) PaulMulrennan 1 36
(W J Musson) *hld up in rr: hdwy on outer over 2f out: rdn and hung rt over 1f out: kpt on ins fnl f: nt rch ldrs* **7/1**

-406 **6** *¾* **Watch Out**[8] 3792 3-8-3 **45**....................(b) AndrewMullen(3) 8 34
(M W Easterby) *prom: chsd wnr after 2f: pushed along and edgd lft 3f out: rdn and hung bdly rt 2f out: sn drvn and wknd* **10/3[1]**

0403 **7** *2* **Patavian (IRE)**[17] 3538 3-9-7 **60**....................(p) TomEaves 6 46
(I Semple) *hld up in tch: effrt and hdwy over 3f out: rdn wl over 2f out and sn btn* **4/1[2]**

0046 **8** *nk* **Wingsinmotion (IRE)**[21] 3402 3-8-3 **45**....................(p) MarcHalford(3) 5 31
(Miss Tracy Waggott) *hld up: hdwy to chse ldrs 1/2-way: rdn along 3f out: drvn over 2f out and grad wknd* **16/1**

00-0 **9** *8* **Glenridding**[21] 3399 3-8-6 **45**....................(b[1]) TonyHamilton 4 18
(J G Given) *led 1f: styd prom: rdn along 3f out: drvn and wandered 2f out: sn wknd* **25/1**

0-00 **10** *17* **Glorious View**[28] 3183 3-8-6 **45**....................(b) DaleGibson 7 —
(M W Easterby) *a bhd* **40/1**

0050 **11** *shd* **Hillside Smoki (IRE)**[22] 3377 3-8-3 **45**.................... PatrickMathers(3) 3 —
(A Berry) *dwlt: sn chsng ldrs: pushed along 1/2-way and sn wknd* **100/1**

2m 43.33s (3.12) **Going Correction** +0.10s/f (Good) 11 Ran SP% **114.2**
Speed ratings (Par 98): **93,92,92,90,89 88,87,87,81,70 70**
CSF £140.39 CT £867.35 TOTE £17.70: £3.70, £2.80, £1.90; EX 173.30.The winner was bought in for 5,800gns. Bret Maverick was claimed by B. P. J. Baugh for £6,000.
Owner K Pennington **Bred** K And Mrs Pennington **Trained** Brandsby, N Yorks

FOCUS
A very poor race run to suit the winner. The form is unlikely to work out.
Wingsinmotion(IRE) Official explanation: jockey said filly hung right

4037 EBF GRAHAM AND ROSEN SOLICITORS MAIDEN STKS 7f 100y
2:35 (2:42) (Class 5) 2-Y-O **£3,886** (£1,156; £577; £288) **Stalls** High

Form RPR

4023 **1** **Relinquished**[18] 3508 2-8-12 0.................... AdamKirby 14 73
(J Noseda) *in tch: smooth hdwy and nt clr run 2f out: swtchd lft over 1f out: qcknd to ld ins fnl f: styd on* **2/1[1]**

052 **2** *1¼* **Shannersburg (IRE)**[13] 3635 2-9-3 0.................... ChrisCatlin 8 75
(E J O'Neill) *chsd ldrs: hdwy to ld wl over 1f out: sn rdn: hdd and nt qckn ins fnl f* **6/1[3]**

3 **3** *½* **Doon Haymer (IRE)**[33] 3013 2-9-3 0.................... TomEaves 5 74
(I Semple) *in tch: hdwy over 2f out: rdn to chse ldrs over 1f out: kpt on ins fnl f* **8/1**

43 **4** *½* **Cobo Bay**[25] 3283 2-9-3 0.................... PhillipMakin 13 73
(K A Ryan) *trckd ldrs on inner: effrt 2f out: rdn and ev ch over 1f out: kpt on same pce* **16/1**

0 **5** *nk* **Bavarian Nordic (USA)**[20] 3435 2-9-3 0.................... PaulMulrennan 12 72
(E A L Dunlop) *prom: effrt and n.m.r over 2f out: swtchd lft and rdn wl over 1f out: kpt on ins fnl f* **12/1**

6 *1¼* **Keenes Day (FR)** 2-9-0 0.................... AndrewMullen(3) 3 69
(M Johnston) *dwlt and sn pushed along in rr: rdn along 1/2-way: kpt on u.p fnl 2f: nrst fin* **20/1**

3 **7** *shd* **Tarkheena Prince (USA)**[9] 3760 2-9-3 0.................... GrahamGibbons 1 69
(G A Swinbank) *towards rr: hdwy 3f out: sn pushed along: styd on u.p appr fnl f: nrst fin* **11/4[2]**

00 **8** *6* **Bollin Gull**[38] 2888 2-9-3 0.................... DavidAllan 7 55
(T D Easterby) *sn rdn along: a in rr* **100/1**

0 **9** *½* **China Pink**[69] 1945 2-8-12 0.................... J-PGuillambert 4 49
(Sir Mark Prescott) *cl up: ev ch over 2f out: sn rdn and wknd wl over 1f out* **25/1**

0 **10** *½* **Weetfromthechaff**[28] 3192 2-9-3 0.................... PaulEddery 11 52
(R Hollinshead) *led: rdn along 3f out: drvn and hdd wl over 1f out: wknd* **100/1**

11 *1¾* **Jackday (IRE)** 2-9-3 0.................... PaulFessey 10 48
(T D Easterby) *a towards rr* **66/1**

12 *nk* **Bouggler** 2-9-3 0.................... TonyHamilton 2 48
(Miss J A Camacho) *dwlt: a in rr* **66/1**

13 *9* **Generous Boy** 2-9-3 0.................... DaleGibson 6 26
(T D Easterby) *s.i.s: a bhd* **80/1**

1m 35.35s (1.04) **Going Correction** +0.10s/f (Good) 13 Ran SP% **113.8**
Speed ratings (Par 94): **98,96,96,95,95 93,93,86,86,85 83,83,72**
CSF £12.91 TOTE £2.90: £1.40, £1.90, £2.20; EX 16.30.
Owner Mrs Joya Burns **Bred** Cornerstone Bloodstock Ltd **Trained** Newmarket, Suffolk

FOCUS
A moderate race, with the winner rated 5lb off her best in victory.

NOTEBOOK
Relinquished, the most experienced horse in the race, took advantage of the best draw and opened her account. She is probably a fair sort and can hold her own in better company again. (op 9-4)
Shannersburg(IRE) did everything right but was just outpaced by the winner inside the final furlong. His turn should not be far away and he fully deserves to get his head in front. A mile is unlikely to cause him any problems. (op 7-1 tchd 15-2 and 11-2)
Doon Haymer(IRE) kept on well after being outpaced two furlongs from home, and suggested that he needs at least this far to get involved. The more experience he gains, the better he will become. (op 7-1)
Cobo Bay had a decent draw and appeared to run up to his best. (op 14-1)
Bavarian Nordic(USA) got a bit baulked just over a furlong from home, but kept on well inside the final furlong to close on the leader again. (op 14-1)
Keenes Day(FR) looked very inexperienced and is sure to make progress with time. This was not a bad effort and he should know more next time.
Tarkheena Prince(USA) had the worst of the draw and ran as well as he was entitled to from that stall. (op 9-4 tchd 3-1 in a place)
China Pink did not impress with her head carriage under pressure and is one to treat with caution once her level has been found.
Weetfromthechaff Official explanation: jockey said colt hung left
Jackday(IRE) Official explanation: jockey said colt was hanging up straight
Generous Boy Official explanation: jockey said colt was slowly away from stalls

4038 JAMES BRUIN MEMORIAL H'CAP 5f
3:10 (3:20) (Class 5) (0-75,75) 3-Y-O+ **£3,238** (£963; £481; £240)

Form RPR

2232 **1** **Divine Spirit**[8] 3782 6-8-10 **59**.................... TomEaves 6 73
(M Dods) *trckd ldrs: hdwy wl over 1f out: rdn and styd on ins fnl f: edgd rt and led nr fin* **7/2[1]**

6141 **2** *nk* **Melalchrist**[8] 3791 5-9-12 **75** 6ex....................(b) PaulMulrennan 5 88
(K A Ryan) *qckly away: led: rdn over 1f out: drvn ins fnl f: hdd and no ex nr fin* **6/1[3]**

0142 **3** *nk* **Funfair Wane**[8] 3787 8-8-8 **57**.................... SilvestreDeSousa 7 69
(D Nicholls) *chsd ldr: rdn to chal wl over 1f out and ev ch tl drvn ins fnl f and no ex towards fin* **7/2[1]**

164 **4** *1* **Hotham**[8] 3791 4-9-0 **63**.................... ChrisCatlin 10 71
(N Wilson) *trckd ldrs: effrt and n.m.r wl over 1f out: sn swtchd lft: rdn and ev ch whn n.m.r ins fnl f: kpt on same pce* **11/2[2]**

0402 **5** *1¾* **Kings College Boy**[8] 3791 7-8-13 **62**....................(b) TonyHamilton 4 64
(R A Fahey) *towards rr: hdwy 1/2-way: rdn and kpt on appr fnl f: nrst fin* **6/1[3]**

0303 **6** *2* **Legal Set (IRE)**[5] 3886 11-8-2 **56** oh1....................(b) AnnStokell(5) 9 51
(Miss A Stokell) *dwlt: sn chsng ldrs: rdn along 2f out and grad wknd* **18/1**

5006 **7** *nk* **Ryedale Ovation (IRE)**[8] 3791 4-9-0 **63**.................... DavidAllan 8 57
(T D Easterby) *sn chsng ldrs: rdn along 2f out: drvn and wknd appr fnl f* **13/2**

000- **8** *5* **Mis Chicaf (IRE)**[341] 4729 6-8-0 **56** oh11.................... KellyHarrison(7) 1 32
(D Carroll) *chsd ldrs: rdn over 2f out and sn wknd* **50/1**

-000 **9** *½* **Fairgame Man**[23] 3347 9-8-0 **56** oh11....................(p) DanielleMcCreery(7) 11 30
(J S Wainwright) *a in rr* **50/1**

0300 **10** *3½* **Smokin Beau**[60] 2197 10-9-9 **75**.................... MarcHalford(3) 2 36
(N P Littmoden) *s.i.s: a in rr* **16/1**

0-00 **11** *6* **Sheriff Star**[38] 2893 4-8-4 **56** oh11.................... AndrewMullen(3) 3 —
(G P Kelly) *s.i.s: a bhd* **100/1**

61.68 secs (-2.32) **Going Correction** -0.375s/f (Firm) 11 Ran SP% **117.8**
Speed ratings (Par 103): **103,102,102,100,97 94,93,85,85,79 69**
CSF £24.66 CT £79.34 TOTE £4.00: £1.50, £2.20, £1.60; EX 29.00.
Owner The Newcastle Racing Club **Bred** S R Hope And D Erwin Bloodstock **Trained** Denton, Co Durham

FOCUS
A race to treat with caution due to it being started by flag. It was hand-timed. The second and third got the jump on their rivals, and may have increased their chances as a result. The winner finally took advantage of a reduced mark.

4039 PERSIMMON HOMES STKS (H'CAP) 1m 100y
3:45 (3:45) (Class 4) (0-85,85) 3-Y-O+ **£6,477** (£1,927; £963; £481) **Stalls** High

Form RPR

4301 **1** **Nevada Desert (IRE)**[3] 3971 7-9-7 **84** 6ex.................... MichaelJStainton(5) 3 92
(R M Whitaker) *set stdy pce: qcknd 3f out: rdn and qcknd over 1f out: drvn ins fnl f and hld on gamely* **5/1[3]**

1551 **2** *nk* **Flighty Fellow (IRE)**[11] 3721 7-9-5 **77**....................(b) DavidAllan 6 84+
(T D Easterby) *hld up towards rr: hdwy 3f out: rdn to chse ldrs over 1f out: n.m.r and swtchd rt ent fnl f: sn drvn and kpt on: jst hld* **6/1**

0420 **3** *1¼* **Blue Spinnaker (IRE)**[18] 3513 8-9-13 **85**.................... PaulMulrennan 5 90
(M W Easterby) *trckd ldrs: hdwy over 2f out: rdn and ch over 1f out: sn drvn and kpt on same pce ins fnl f* **11/2**

5320 **4** *2* **Prince Evelith (GER)**[23] 3346 4-9-4 **79**.................... PJMcDonald(3) 7 79
(G A Swinbank) *trckd ldrs: swtchd outside and hdwy over 2f out: rdn and ch over 1f out: sn drvn and one pce ent fnl f* **7/2[1]**

2614 **5** *hd* **Harvest Warrior**[18] 3513 5-9-8 **80**.................... GrahamGibbons 2 80
(T D Easterby) *trckd ldng pair: hdwy to chse wnr 1/2-way: rdn along over 2f out: drvn and hld whn n.m.r ent fnl f: wknd* **9/2[2]**

0-02 **6** *2½* **Riley Boys (IRE)**[25] 3258 6-9-13 **85**.................... TomEaves 1 79
(J G Given) *hld up in rr: hdwy 3f out: rdn wl over 1f out and sn no imp* **10/1**

5500 **7** *hd* **It's A Dream (FR)**[39] 2835 4-9-3 **75**.................... DaleGibson 8 69
(M W Easterby) *t.k.h: chsd wnr to 1/2-way: sn rdn along and wknd over 2f out* **15/2**

3032 **8** *24* **Rodeo**[8] 3790 4-9-2 **74**....................(b) J-PGuillambert 4 15
(C W Thornton) *s.i.s: sn in tch: effrt 3f out: sn rdn and btn 2f out* **16/1**

1m 47.51s (0.11) **Going Correction** +0.10s/f (Good) 8 Ran SP% **113.5**
Speed ratings (Par 105): **103,102,101,99,99 96,96,72**
CSF £34.27 CT £169.28 TOTE £6.30: £2.40, £2.10, £2.30; EX 55.20.
Owner J Barry Pemberton **Bred** Bryan Ryan **Trained** Scarcroft, W Yorks

FOCUS
A decent race in which the winner set a very moderate early gallop. The form is probably unreliable.
Rodeo Official explanation: jockey said gelding hung right leaving stalls

4040 OLD GRAVEL PITS ALLERTHORPE H'CAP 1m 4f 16y
4:20 (4:20) (Class 5) (0-70,69) 3-Y-O+ **£3,238** (£963; £481; £240) **Stalls** High

Form RPR

052 **1** **Don'Tcallmeginger (IRE)**[21] 3403 4-8-6 **52**.................... PatrickHills(5) 6 58
(M H Tompkins) *trckd ldr: effrt 3f out: led over 2f out: rdn over 1f out and styd on wl fnl f* **11/4[1]**

-033 **2** *1½* **Sporting Gesture**[42] 2743 10-9-5 **67**.................... NSLawes(7) 7 71
(M W Easterby) *trckd ldrs: hdwy over 2f out: rdn to chse wnr wl over 1f out: kpt on u.p ins fnl f* **5/1[2]**

2344 **3** *shd* **Augustine**[6] 3854 6-9-12 **67**.................... ChrisCatlin 4 70
(P W Hiatt) *hld up in rr: hdwy over 2f out: effrt and nt clr run wl over 1f out: rdn and styd on strly ins fnl f* **6/1[3]**

54-5 **4** *1½* **Blushing Hilary (IRE)**[11] 3719 4-9-9 **64**....................(p) TomEaves 1 65
(Miss J A Camacho) *chsd ldrs: hdwy 3f out: rdn wl over 1f out: drvn ent fnl f and kpt on same pce* **7/1**

2305 **5** *2* **Ha'Penny Beacon**[62] 2148 4-8-12 **60**.................... KellyHarrison(7) 5 58
(D Carroll) *hld up towards rr: hdwy wl over 2f out: sn rdn and kpt on appr fnl f* **14/1**

56 **6** *1 1/2* **Gloucester**[24] 3301 4-9-11 **69**....................(t) DougieCostello[(3)] 2 64
(J J Quinn) *t.k.h: chsd ldrs on outer: rdn and edgd rt 2f out: wknd over 1f out* **14/1**

-400 **7** *8* **Lucky Find (IRE)**[28] 3193 4-8-3 **51** oh6.................... SophieDoyle[(7)] 3 34
(M Mullineaux) *in tch: rdn along over 3f out and sn wknd* **50/1**

0112 **8** *2* **Red River Rebel**[14] 3610 9-9-0 **55**.................... PaulMulrennan 8 34
(J R Norton) *led: rdn along 3f out: hdd over 2f out: sn drvn and wknd over 1f out* **11/4**[1]

2m 41.19s (0.98) **Going Correction** +0.10s/f (Good) **8** Ran SP% **112.1**
Speed ratings (Par 103): **100,99,98,97,96 95,90,88**
CSF £16.04 CT £73.61 TOTE £2.90: £1.30, £1.80, £1.60; EX 18.70.
Owner Trott Knight Jenkins **Bred** Seamus Murphy **Trained** Newmarket, Suffolk

FOCUS
A competitive handicap for the grade won by an unexposed horse who was back to something like his 2yo form. Ordinary form, but sound.
Red River Rebel Official explanation: jockey said gelding hung left in straight

4041 BOOK ONLINE AT BEVERLEY-RACECOURSE.CO.UK MAIDEN AUCTION FILLIES' STKS 5f
4:50 (4:52) (Class 5) 2-Y-0 **£3,238** (£963; £481; £240)

Form RPR

532 **1** **Revue Princess (IRE)**[10] 3750 2-8-7 0.................... DavidAllan 5 71
(T D Easterby) *qckly away: mde all: rdn wl over 1f out: flashed tail ins fnl f: styd on* **6/4**[1]

2 *2 1/2* **Habbie Heights** 2-7-11 0.................... DanielleMcCreery[(7)] 6 59+
(R Bastiman) *towards rr: hdwy on outer wl over 1f out: str run ent fnl f: fin wl* **25/1**

50 **3** *3/4* **She's Our Dream**[67] 1992 2-8-11 0....................(t) PaulEddery 9 63
(R C Guest) *midfield: rdn along and hdwy 2f out: styd on u.p ins fnl f* **14/1**

02 **4** *3/4* **Best Suited**[22] 3378 2-8-7 0.................... GrahamGibbons 1 57
(J J Quinn) *chsd wnr: rdn over 2f out: drvn wl over 1f out: kpt on same pce ent fnl f* **7/2**[2]

5443 **5** *shd* **Turn And River (IRE)**[14] 3606 2-8-4 0.................... DaleGibson 11 53
(M Brittain) *s.i.s and bhd: rdn along and hdwy 2f out: styd on wl fnl f: nrst fin* **6/1**

6 *hd* **Doric Dream** 2-8-7 0.................... TomEaves 2 56
(B Smart) *chsd ldrs: rdn over 2f out: wandered and wknd wl over 1f out* **9/2**[3]

7 *4* **First Abode** 2-7-13 0 ow2.................... PatrickDonaghy[(7)] 7 40
(M Brittain) *dwlt and bhd tl styd on fnl 2f* **50/1**

8 *1 3/4* **Eternal Optimist (IRE)** 2-8-7 0.................... PaulMulrennan 3 35
(C W Thornton) *nvr bttr than midfield* **33/1**

550 **9** *3 1/2* **Avian Flew**[15] 3596 2-7-13 0.................... ColinHaddon[(5)] 10 19+
(J A Pickering) *chsd ldrs on inner: n.m.r and lost pl after 1 1/2f: sn bhd* **20/1**

000 **10** *8* **Smilodon**[10] 3750 2-8-2 0 ow1.................... PatrickMathers[(3)] 4 —
(A Berry) *a in rr* **100/1**

6 **11** *3/4* **Penny Arcade**[24] 3297 2-8-1 0.................... AndrewMullen[(3)] 8 —
(M E Sowersby) *chsd ldrs to 1/2-way: sn wknd* **66/1**

65.80 secs (1.80) **Going Correction** -0.375s/f (Firm) **11** Ran SP% **117.3**
Speed ratings (Par 91): **70,66,64,63,63 63,56,53,48,35 34**
CSF £51.41 TOTE £2.20: £1.20, £4.50, £2.90; EX 43.80.
Owner S A Heley **Bred** Raymond Shanahan **Trained** Great Habton, N Yorks
■ Stewards' Enquiry : Graham Gibbons one-day ban: anticipated start (Aug 11)

FOCUS
Hand-timed. The second flag start of the day, and as a result the form should be treated with a bit of caution. Just a modest maiden, but it should produce winners at a similar level.

NOTEBOOK
Revue Princess(IRE) had shown a similar level of ability on each of her last two starts and this looked easily her best opportunity yet. Sharply into stride, she led throughout and readily came clear in the final furlong, winning comfortably. Speed is evidently her main asset and she looks capable of further improvement in handicaps. (op 7-4)
Habbie Heights, a 1,500gns daughter of Josr Algarhoud, showed her inexperience early, but really got the hang of things in the final quarter mile and came home strongly to grab second. An extra furlong is going to suit in time and she looks capable of winning a small maiden.
She's Our Dream ran her best race to date in the first-time tongue tie and is now qualified for nurseries, a sphere she should be placed to winning advantage in. (op 11-1)
Best Suited has shown her versatility ground-wise and she ran another sound race. Now qualified for nurseries, she is going to benefit from an extra furlong. (tchd 4-1)
Turn And River(IRE) is already exposed as modest, but she ran a bit better than her finishing position suggests, coming home well having fluffed the start, and is another who would make some appeal on nurseries. (op 9-2 tchd 13-2)
Doric Dream, whose stable have had yet another fine year with their juveniles, could make no impression on this racecourse debut, but she still looked green and can be expected to come on for the outing. (op 6-1 tchd 13-2)

4042 DOROTHY LAIRD MEMORIAL TROPHY (LADIES RACE) (H'CAP) 7f 100y
5:20 (5:21) (Class 6) (0-65,60) 3-Y-0+ **£3,238** (£963; £481; £240)

Form RPR

3321 **1** **Emperor's Well**[10] 3754 8-10-2 **57**.................... MissJCoward[(5)] 7 74
(M W Easterby) *chsd ldr: hdwy 3f out: squeezed through on inner to ld 1 1/2f out: sn rdn clr* **11/4**[1]

0002 **2** *7* **Shotley Mac**[14] 3605 3-9-7 **50**....................(b) DanielleMcCreery 6 47
(N Bycroft) *bhd: gd hdwy 3f out: rdn to chse ldrs wl over 1f out: drvn and kpt on ins fnl f: no ch w wnr* **12/1**

0010 **3** *2* **Drink To Me Only**[18] 3497 4-9-10 **46**.................... KirstyMilczarek 3 41
(J R Weymes) *towards rr: hdwy over 2f out: sn rdn: styd on ins fnl f* **8/1**

6200 **4** *1 3/4* **Favouring (IRE)**[14] 3608 5-9-6 **47**....................(v) MissSEilbeck[(5)] 2 37
(M C Chapman) *chsd ldng pair: rdn along over 2f out: drvn wl over 1f out: sn one pce* **33/1**

3542 **5** *nk* **William John**[23] 3204 4-10-6 **56**....................(tp) MissLEllison 10 45
(B Ellison) *chsd ldrs: rdn along over 2f out: drvn wl over 1f out and sn one pce* **7/2**[2]

5005 **6** *1* **Time To Regret**[11] 3721 7-10-2 **52**....................(p) KellyHarrison 9 39
(I W McInnes) *led: rdn along over 2f out: hdd 1 1/2f out: sn drvn and grad wknd* **12/1**

0540 **7** *1 1/4* **Red Lantern**[57] 2302 6-9-4 **45**.................... MissJoannaMason[(5)] 14 29
(M W Easterby) *chsd ldrs: rdn along over 2f out: sn wknd* **20/1**

5200 **8** *1* **Sands Of Barra (IRE)**[20] 3414 4-10-10 **60**....................(p) NataliaGemelova 5 41
(I W McInnes) *chsd ldrs: rdn over 2f out: drvn: hung rt and wknd wl over 1f out* **11/1**

-000 **9** *5* **Sonar Sound (GER)**[14] 3605 3-9-7 **55**.................... MissKECooper[(5)] 1 21
(T P Tate) *midfield: wd st: nvr a factor* **33/1**

1503 **10** *3/4* **Scotty's Future (IRE)**[8] 3789 9-10-0 **50**.................... MrsCBartley 11 17
(A Berry) *s.i.s: a wl bhd* **11/2**[3]

0-06 **11** *4* **Ten To The Dozen**[14] 3615 4-10-1 **51**.................... MrsMarieKing 13 8
(P W Hiatt) *s.i.s: a bhd* **10/1**

5000 **12** *6* **Vibrato (USA)**[8] 3787 5-9-4 **45**....................(p) MissWGibson[(5)] 8 —
(C J Teague) *a towards rr* **50/1**

0663 **13** *7* **Superjain**[14] 3605 3-9-0 **48**.................... MissNJefferson[(5)] 12 —
(J M Jefferson) *in rr: wd st: nvr a factor* **20/1**

1m 33.3s (-1.01) **Going Correction** +0.10s/f (Good)
WFA 3 from 4yo+ 7lb **13** Ran SP% **125.6**
Speed ratings (Par 101): **109,101,98,96,96 95,93,92,86,86 81,74,66**
CSF £37.19 CT £250.75 TOTE £3.60: £1.50, £2.20, £2.60; EX 37.90 Place 6 £69.57, Place 5 £13.45.
Owner M W Easterby **Bred** M W Easterby & K Hodgson **Trained** Sheriff Hutton, N Yorks

FOCUS
Hand-timed. The third flag start of the day. Emperor's Wells won easily and is clearly in top form at the minute, although he was favoured by the run of the race.
T/Plt: £121.80 to a £1 stake. Pool: £56,030.75. 335.80 winning tickets. T/Qpdt: £16.50 to a £1 stake. Pool: £5,136.90. 229.10 winning tickets. JR

3149 GOODWOOD (R-H)
Tuesday, July 31

OFFICIAL GOING: Good (8.0)
Wind: Light, half against Weather: Glorious

4043 BANK OF SCOTLAND INVESTMENT SERVICE STKS (HERITAGE H'CAP) 1m 1f 192y
2:15 (2:16) (Class 2) 4-Y-0+
£31,160 (£9,330; £4,665; £2,335; £1,165; £585) **Stalls** High

Form RPR

2301 **1** **Championship Point (IRE)**[39] 2815 4-9-10 **109**.................... DarryllHolland 6 118
(M R Channon) *dropped in fr s and hld up in last: stl there 3f out: storming run on outer fr over 2f out: swept past ldr 75yds out: impressive* **8/1**[3]

6110 **2** *3/4* **Lake Poet (IRE)**[39] 2815 4-9-1 **100**.................... SebSanders 3 108
(C E Brittain) *hld up in midfield: prog on outer over 3f out: led jst over 2f out: edgd rt over 1f out: styd on but hdd and outpcd last 75yds* **16/1**

013 **3** *3/4* **Peruvian Prince (USA)**[26] 3242 5-8-0 **85**.................... PaulHanagan 17 91
(R A Fahey) *hld up in midfield: stdy prog through runners fr over 2f out: cl up over 1f out: styd on but nt quite pce to chal* **20/1**

5-54 **4** *2* **Snoqualmie Boy**[90] 1392 4-9-5 **104**.................... TQuinn 10 106
(D R C Elsworth) *lw: hld up in rr: stdy prog on outer fr 3f out: chsd ldr and looked dangerous over 1f out: rdn and no rspnse* **14/1**

6114 **5** *3/4* **Greek Well (IRE)**[17] 3558 4-8-1 **86**.................... DO'Donohoe 9 87
(Sir Michael Stoute) *lw: pushed up to go prom: prog to press ldr wl over 1f out: nt qckn sn after: hld whn n.m.r ins fnl f: fdd* **6/1**[1]

3-15 **6** *1/2* **Emirates Skyline (USA)**[39] 2815 4-9-4 **103**....................(v[1]) KerrinMcEvoy 13 108+
(Saeed Bin Suroor) *trckd ldrs: cl up over 2f out and gng wl: nt clr run 2f out to jst over 1f out: one pce after* **13/2**[2]

5601 **7** *1/2* **Fort Churchill (IRE)**[60] 2218 6-8-4 **89**....................(bt) RoystonFfrench 12 88
(B Ellison) *dwlt: wl in rr: effrt on outer 3f out: hanging and limited prog tl styd on fr over 1f out* **11/1**

-605 **8** *1* **Dansili Dancer**[52] 2446 5-8-12 **97**.................... PhilipRobinson 2 94
(C G Cox) *hld up in rr: tried to cl on ldrs on outer fr 3f out but hanging: nvr on terms* **11/1**

5004 **9** *nk* **Speedy Sam**[4] 3899 4-8-2 **90**.................... AndrewElliott[(3)] 7 86
(K R Burke) *lw: pressed ldr to 1/2-way: styd prom: cl up over 2f out: outpcd and btn wl over 1f out* **16/1**

-420 **10** *2 1/2* **Bandama (IRE)**[38] 2859 4-8-9 **94**.................... SteveDrowne 16 85
(Mrs A J Perrett) *lw: hld up towards rr: effrt on inner whn nt clr run over 2f out: no real prog after* **11/1**

05 **11** *hd* **Nayyir**[52] 2442 9-9-3 **105**....................(b) JamieMoriarty[(3)] 15 96
(G A Butler) *dwlt: hld up wl in rr: shkn up on inner over 2f out: no real rspnse* **25/1**

0533 **12** *1* **Collateral Damage (IRE)**[17] 3558 4-8-2 **87**....................(t) JimmyQuinn 11 76
(T D Easterby) *lw: snatched up in rr after 1f: drvn and effrt 3f out: no real prog whn bmpd arnd wl over 1f out* **16/1**

0045 **13** *nk* **Zero Tolerance (IRE)**[33] 3026 7-8-12 **97**.................... JimmyFortune 18 85
(T D Barron) *hld up in midfield: chsng ldrs over 2f out: wknd over 1f out* **14/1**

4140 **14** *5* **Tabadul (IRE)**[39] 2815 6-8-13 **98**.................... RHills 5 76+
(E A L Dunlop) *lw: prom: led briefly over 2f out: wkng whn n.m.r over 1f out* **18/1**

15 *nk* **Formax (FR)**[101] 5-8-7 **92**.................... MartinDwyer 1 69
(M P Tregoning) *w'like: fast away fr wd draw: led to over 2f out: wkng whn n.m.r over 1f out* **20/1**

3-03 **16** *40* **Night Crescendo (USA)**[86] 1494 4-8-5 **90**.................... JoeFanning 8 —
(Mrs A J Perrett) *chsd ldrs: wknd 3f out: t.o* **8/1**[3]

2m 7.39s (-0.36) **Going Correction** +0.125s/f (Good) **16** Ran SP% **124.5**
Speed ratings (Par 109): **106,105,104,103,102 102,101,101,100,98 98,97,97,93,93 61**
CSF £128.78 CT £2494.24 TOTE £7.90: £2.30, £4.60, £5.10, £4.00; EX 142.70 TRIFECTA Not won..
Owner John Livock **Bred** Mount Coote Stud **Trained** West Ilsley, Berks
■ Stewards' Enquiry : Seb Sanders two-day ban: careless riding (Aug 11-12)

FOCUS
A strong handicap run at a decent pace throughout. A Group-class effort from Championship Point, with improved form from the second and third.

NOTEBOOK
Championship Point(IRE) benefited from the strong early pace and came from last to first to defy a 4lb rise in the weights for his success in the Listed Wolferton Handicap at Royal Ascot. He lost his way after winning the Predominate Stakes here as a three-year-old, but is clearly back to his best now and could be ready for a return to Group company, although he needs a strongly-run race.
Lake Poet(IRE) got much closer to Championship Point than in the Wolferton last time and this was a sound effort in defeat. He is entered in the Ebor, but also has the option of the 1m4f Shergar Cup contest.
Peruvian Prince(USA), on his toes beforehand, ran a fine race off a mark 8lb higher than when winning at Haydock two starts back and did not look to have too many excuses.
Snoqualmie Boy, returned to handicap company for the first time since winning at Salisbury off a mark of 82 in May last year, was produced with every chance and this was a solid effort off the back of a three-month break. (tchd 16-1)
Greek Well(IRE), who ran a good race on unsuitably soft ground in the John Smith's Cup on his previous start, probably paid the price for chasing the strong early pace, but he still fared best of those to race handily. (op 13-2)

The Form Book, Raceform Ltd, Compton, RG20 6NL

Emirates Skyline(USA) ◆, a Melbourne Cup entry who was fitted with a visor for the first time, was continually denied a clear run when trying to stay on and was very unlucky not to finish much closer. Official explanation: jockey said colt ran too free (op 7-1)
Tabadul(IRE) was badly hampered against the rail when just beginning to struggle. (tchd 16-1 and 20-1)
Formax(FR) Official explanation: jockey said gelding ran too free
Night Crescendo(USA) Official explanation: vet said gelding finished distressed

4044 GORDON STKS (GROUP 3) 1m 4f
2:50 (2:57) (Class 1) 3-Y-O

£28,390 (£10,760; £5,385; £2,685; £1,345; £675) **Stalls** Low

Form RPR

2034 **1** **Yellowstone (IRE)**[24] 3331 3-9-0 0 JMurtagh 1 108
(A P O'Brien, Ire) *lw: trckd ldrs: effrt over 2f out: hanging but drvn to ld 1f out: styd on and a holding rival* **5/2**[1]

2-13 **2** *nk* **Aqaleem**[59] 2235 3-9-3 113 RHills 9 110+
(M P Tregoning) *swtg: hld up in last trio: hemmed in over 2f out to over 1f out: got out to press wnr jst ins fnl f: styd on but hld last 100yds* **5/2**[1]

-120 **3** *¾* **Raincoat**[58] 2293 3-9-0 106 RichardHughes 2 106
(J H M Gosden) *lw: t.k.h: hld up in last trio: prog on outer over 2f out: nt qckn over 1f out: styd on ins fnl f: unable to chal* **9/2**[2]

3100 **4** *shd* **Champery (USA)**[24] 3331 3-9-0 107 JoeFanning 7 106+
(M Johnston) *lw: t.k.h: hld up in 6th: nt clr run over 2f out: styd on fr over 1f out: nt rch ldrs* **50/1**

4-14 **5** *1* **Lion Sands**[39] 2813 3-9-0 109 RyanMoore 6 104
(L M Cumani) *lw: sn led and set stdy pce: kicked on 3f out: hdd 1f out: fdd* **6/1**[3]

4031 **6** *nk* **Big Robert**[12] 3683 3-9-0 103 (t) MartinDwyer 8 104
(W R Muir) *hld up in last: rdn over 2f out: no prog tl styd on fnl f: n.d* **33/1**

145 **7** *¾* **Mores Wells**[30] 3142 3-9-3 0 (t) DPMcDonogh 5 109+
(Kevin Prendergast, Ire) *w'like: athletic: trckd ldrs on inner: rdn over 2f out: cl up in 3rd and ev ch of a pl whn hmpd jst ins fnl f: eased* **16/1**

2151 **8** *nk* **Tranquil Tiger**[19] 3458 3-9-0 107 TedDurcan 3 102
(H R A Cecil) *lw: ref to go to post tl dismntd and dragged along: trckd ldr: chal over 3f out: wknd over 1f out* **12/1**

6231 **9** *½* **Heron Bay**[40] 2790 3-9-0 98 SteveDrowne 10 102
(G Wragg) *cl up: rdn over 2f out: lost pl over 1f out: fdd fnl f* **10/1**

2m 40.69s (1.77) **Going Correction** +0.125s/f (Good) **9** Ran SP% **117.2**
Speed ratings (Par 110): **99,98,98,98,97 97,96,96,96**
CSF £8.57 TOTE £3.50: £1.60, £1.40, £1.80; EX 8.60 Trifecta £35.00 Pool: £1,913.10 - 38.70 winning tickets..
Owner M Tabor, D Smith & Mrs John Magnier **Bred** Tullamaine Castle Stud & Partn **Trained** Ballydoyle, Co Tipperary

FOCUS
Traditionally a key St Leger trial. The steady early pace saw a bunched finish, however, and several endured troubled passages. The winner got first run, but deserved his success after running with credit in defeat in some top races previously. However this was 11lb below his Eclipse form. The runner-up still emerges as the best horse at the weights, however, and rates the more credible St Leger candidate.

NOTEBOOK
Yellowstone(IRE), an excellent fourth in the Eclipse last time, was perfectly positioned to strike when the tempo became really serious and ran out a deserved winner. He had only a maiden success to his name coming into this, but has been running creditably in defeat since finishing eighth in the Derby, and while he got first run on a couple of his rivals here, he looked in command of Aqaleem when that rival eventually got in the clear and came with his challenge. Not surprisingly he was immediately cut in the ante-post market for the St Leger, but connections feel this distance may be the limit of his stamina range and he could even drop back in trip now. (op 7-2 tchd 9-4 and 4-1 in places)
Aqaleem, having his first outing since finishing third in the Derby, was undone by the steady early pace and then endured a troubled passage when things started to hot up from the 2f pole. He can rate unfortunate here, but he still had his chance to get on top of the winner when finally in the clear and did seem held by that rival at the line. It could have been a different story with a stronger overall pace, however, and clearly his connections feel he needs all of this distance now, plus it must be remembered that he was giving 3lb to that rival. Out of the pair he rates the more convincing St Leger candidate and, with the likelihood that he will now go straight there, was later cut to as short as 4-1 with some firms for the final Classic in September. (op 9-4 tchd 3-1)
Raincoat, who failed to shine due to the muddling pace in the Prix du Jockey Club last time, proved free due to the lack of early pace and would surely have been seen to better effect in a truly-run race. He is well worthy of another chance over this longer trip and we have yet to see the best of him. (tchd 5-1)
Champery(USA), drafted in as a pacemaker for Authorized in the Eclipse last time out, was held up on this first attempt over the longer distance and ran a deal better than his finishing position suggests. He too proved free early on due to the steady tempo, but was still seemingly full of running prior to finding all sorts of trouble nearing the 2f pole, and would probably have bagged third with a clear passage. This was probably just about his best effort to date in defeat, however, and while his proximity at the finish raises doubts over this form, he is certainly worth another chance to prove it was no fluke.
Lion Sands was responsible for dictating the sedate early tempo and got very much the run of the race out in front. He can have no excuses and this may be as good as he is. Official explanation: jockey said saddle slipped (op 5-1)
Big Robert, up in trip, was doing his best work towards the finish having been given a very patient ride. He is a likeable colt and is yet another who would have been seen in an even better light off a stronger gallop.
Mores Wells ◆, a well-beaten fifth in the Irish Derby last time out, has to rate unlucky not to have been involved in the finish as he was badly hampered on the rails as Lion Sands began to wilt entering the final furlong. He should be rated at least a length better than the bare form and looked much happier on this sounder surface, so deserves to find another opening.
Tranquil Tiger, a gutsy winner of the Listed Bahrain Trophy over an extra furlong last time, rather blotted his copybook on the way to post and that cannot have helped his cause. He still ran creditably enough in the end, and did shape like more of a stayer here, so should certainly not be discounted if turning up for the Ebor next month - for which he has been allotted a weight of 8st 9lb. He also appeals as the type to do better as a four-year-old as he has an abundance of scope and is still evidently somewhat immature.
Heron Bay, up in class, was found out inside the final furlong yet is another who would have surely enjoyed a stronger pace. This good-looking colt remains open to further progression. (tchd 9-1 and 11-1)

4045 BETFAIR CUP (REGISTERED AS THE LENNOX STKS) (GROUP 2) 7f
3:25 (3:30) (Class 1) 3-Y-O+

£85,170 (£32,280; £16,155; £8,055; £4,035; £2,025) **Stalls** High

Form RPR

5011 **1** **Tariq**[41] 2752 3-8-9 114 KerrinMcEvoy 2 118+
(P W Chapple-Hyam) *hld up wl in rr: effrt on wd outside over 2f out: sn rdn: wnt 2nd over 1f out: r.o to ld last 100yds: won gng away* **7/2**[2]

-136 **2** *1 ¼* **Asset (IRE)**[18] 3506 4-9-2 115 RyanMoore 5 115
(R Hannon) *hld up towards rr on outer: effrt over 2f out: sn rdn: wnt 2nd briefly over 1f out: styd on fnl f but outpcd by wnr* **5/2**[1]

0315 **3** *¾* **Dunelight (IRE)**[17] 3523 4-9-2 110 (v) PhilipRobinson 7 113
(C G Cox) *led: drew at least 2 l clr 2f out: stl same advantage ent fnl f: swamped last 100yds* **12/1**

-350 **4** *shd* **Thousand Words**[41] 2752 3-8-9 111 RichardHughes 11 110+
(B W Hills) *hld up in last: stl there over 2f out: swtchd to outer wl over 1f out: r.o fnl f: too much to do* **16/1**

213 **5** *½* **Arabian Gleam**[41] 2752 3-8-9 105 SebSanders 3 113+
(J Noseda) *hld up towards rr: nt clr run over 2f out: trbld passage after tl swtchd rt and r.o fnl f: nt rcvr* **12/1**

5-5 **6** *1 ¼* **Finicius (USA)**[30] 3144 3-8-10 0 ow1 JMurtagh 9 106
(Eoin Griffin, Ire) *w'like: hld up in rr on outer: rdn over 2f out: no prog tl styd on fr over 1f out: nt pce to trble ldrs* **33/1**

10-0 **7** *hd* **Dark Islander (IRE)**[17] 3523 4-9-6 110 EddieAhern 10 111+
(J W Hills) *hld up towards rr on inner: nt clr run over 2f out to jst over 1f out: kpt on same pce whn in the clr fnl f* **33/1**

2012 **8** *nk* **Royal Oath (USA)**[17] 3523 4-9-2 112 (b) JimmyFortune 6 107
(J H M Gosden) *hld up in midfield: effrt whn nt clr run 2f out: kpt on same pce after* **11/2**[3]

10-1 **9** *2 ½* **Dubai's Touch**[122] 839 3-8-9 110 JoeFanning 12 97
(M Johnston) *prom: drvn to dispute 2nd briefly wl over 1f out: sn wknd* **20/1**

5104 **10** *1 ¾* **Assertive**[4] 3894 4-9-2 106 DaneO'Neill 13 95+
(R Hannon) *lw: dwlt: sn in midfield: nt clr run over 2f out: hmpd over 1f out: no ch* **16/1**

0 **11** *¾* **Mutawaajid (AUS)**[18] 3506 4-9-6 110 JHBowman 8 97
(M R Channon) *lw: tk ferocious hold bhd ldrs: drvn to dispute 2nd briefly wl over 1f out: sn wknd* **7/1**

3-64 **12** *2 ½* **Misu Bond (IRE)**[17] 3529 4-9-2 104 RoystonFfrench 4 86
(B Smart) *lw: mostly chsd ldr to wl over 1f out: wknd* **33/1**

5320 **13** *¾* **Levera**[31] 3098 4-9-2 105 TedDurcan 1 84
(A King) *trckd ldrs on outer: wknd over 2f out: no ch whn hmpd jst over 1f out* **50/1**

1m 26.93s (-1.11) **Going Correction** +0.125s/f (Good)
WFA 3 from 4yo 7lb **13** Ran SP% **121.4**
Speed ratings (Par 115): **111,109,108,108,108 106,106,106,103,101 100,97,96**
CSF £12.13 TOTE £4.20: £1.90, £1.60, £3.30; EX 10.00 Trifecta £78.50 Pool: £1,669.88 - 15.10 winning tickets..
Owner Saleh Al Homeizi & Imad Al Sagar **Bred** D R Botterill **Trained** Newmarket, Suffolk

FOCUS
A decent renewal of this Group 2. It was run at a solid pace and the form looks fairly sound, despite some hard-luck stories in behind. The winner did the job nicely and looks capable of making his mark at the top level.

NOTEBOOK
Tariq continued his rise back up the ranks with another ready display to bag the hat-trick. Given his usual patient ride, he again displayed a smart turn of foot to mow down his rivals when asked to win the race and he clearly goes very well on a sound surface. Where he now goes from here is not that clear, as he is still not certain to fully see out 1m in top company, although he was certainly not stopping towards the finish this time. His trainer later indicated he could now head to the Group 1 Haydock Sprint Cup over 6f, before possibly trying the mile in the Queen Elizabeth II Stakes, and then heading out to America for the Breeders' Cup Mile. There is no doubt he has the potential to win in Group 1 company at some stage. (op 5-2)
Asset(IRE), slightly disappointing in the July Cup last time, was ridden to get the extra furlong on this drop back in grade and stayed on towards the finish without threatening the winner. He has now hit a flat spot in both his last two outings and is proving hard to actually win with. Indeed, he has yet to score in Group company. (op 10-3)
Dunelight(IRE) ran his usual solid race from the front at a track he loves. He momentarily looked the winner when quickening up passing the 2f pole, but his early exertions eventually told and he was a sitting duck for the winner at the business end. Faster ground is more to his liking, and he seems at his very best over an extra furlong these days, so he could be interesting in the Celebration Mile back at this venue next month, providing the ground is in his favour there. (op 14-1)
Thousand Words left a disappointing effort in the Jersey well behind him and finished a lot closer to the winner than had been the case there. He would have been seen to better effect had he made his move a little earlier, however, so could be rated a bit better than the bare form and looks right back on track again now. He is now a possible for the Celebration Mile next month, where he could well renew rivalry with Dunelight. Official explanation: jockey said colt suffered interference in running
Arabian Gleam ◆, third behind Tariq in the Jersey last time, endured a troubled passage when attempting to make up his ground and can be rated value for around a length better than the bare form. As the most inexperienced runner in this field he deserves extra credit, and still finished slightly closer to the winner than had been the case at the Royal Meeting, so there is little doubt he can make his mark at this sort of level in due course. (op 10-1)
Finicius(USA) showed his true colours on this step up in grade and no doubt appreciated the sounder surface. He was given a fair bit to do from off the pace, but this was still a clear personal-best effort and he looks well worth trying over 1m again now.
Dark Islander(IRE) got no run when trying to make up his ground from off the pace on the inside rail and shaped a deal better than his finishing position indicates. This was no disgrace under his penalty and he remains one to be interested when reverting to a stiffer test on faster ground.
Royal Oath(USA) was another who did not get a clear run around the 2f marker, but his effort still flattened out when he was in the clear. He is due to go to America before too long in search of further opportunities and can be given another chance when reverting to a more conventional track. Official explanation: jockey said colt suffered interference in running (op 6-1 tchd 13-2)
Assertive must be forgiven this effort as he was still going well enough prior to being hampered. (op 20-1)
Mutawaajid(AUS) has been well hyped since coming over from Australia and shaped as though he needed the extra furlong when running creditably in the July Cup on his British bow last time. However, he gave himself no chance of getting home by refusing to settle and has bit to prove after this. Official explanation: jockey said colt ran too free (op 8-1)

4046 BETFAIR MOLECOMB STKS (GROUP 3) 5f
4:00 (4:03) (Class 1) 2-Y-O

£28,390 (£10,760; £5,385; £2,685; £1,345; £675) **Stalls** Low

Form RPR

1 **1** **Fleeting Spirit (IRE)**[55] 2365 2-8-11 0 JMurtagh 2 106+
(J Noseda) *str: lw: racd against nr side rail: trckd ldrs: effrt 2f out: rdn to dispute ld fnl f: r.o wl and gained upper hand last 75yds* **8/1**

2 **2** *nk* **Kingsgate Native (IRE)**[42] 2737 2-9-0 0 GeorgeBaker 11 108+
(J R Best) *lw: trckd ldrs in centre: wnt prom 2f out: disp ld fnl f: r.o but hld last 50yds* **4/1**[2]

2311 **3** *2 ½* **Captain Gerrard (IRE)**[18] 3492 2-9-0 0 RoystonFfrench 1 99
(B Smart) *led nr side gp: overall ldr fr 2f out but hanging rt: hdd 1f out: outpcd* **11/2**[3]

112 **4** *1¾* **Starlit Sands**[41] 2756 2-8-11 0 .... SebSanders 9 90
(Sir Mark Prescott) *lw: chsd nr side ldrs: rdn 2f out: kpt on but no imp* **5/2**[1]

2261 **5** *¾* **Littlemisssunshine (IRE)**[12] 3668 2-8-11 0 .... (p) JohnEgan 6 87
(J S Moore) *towards rr nr side and outpcd: effrt and swtchd rt 2f out: styd on: nt pce to rch ldrs* **25/1**

1130 **6** *1* **Spirit Of Sharjah (IRE)**[19] 3459 2-9-0 0 .... JimmyFortune 15 86
(Miss J Feilden) *swtg: v s.i.s: last of centre gp and wl off the pce: prog u.p 2f out: one pce fnl f* **7/1**

21 **7** *¾* **Imperial Mint (IRE)**[15] 3589 2-9-0 0 .... DO'Donohoe 8 84
(K A Ryan) *unf: racd on outer of nr side gp: chsd ldrs: outpcd fr 2f out* **20/1**

5010 **8** *1¾* **Major Eazy (IRE)**[9] 3779 2-9-0 0 .... SteveDrowne 7 77
(B J Meehan) *taken down early: chsd nr side ldrs: rdn and struggling 2f out: fdd* **33/1**

252 **9** *1½* **Hobson**[54] 2398 2-9-0 0 .... StephenCarson 4 72
(Eve Johnson Houghton) *racd nr side in midfield: hrd rdn 1/2-way: nt pce to pose a threat* **66/1**

1355 **10** *hd* **Cake (IRE)**[31] 3096 2-8-11 0 .... RichardHughes 12 68
(R Hannon) *w overall ldr in centre to 1/2-way: wknd over 1f out* **12/1**

120 **11** *1¼* **Tia Mia**[41] 2756 2-8-11 0 .... TPQueally 16 64
(J G Given) *overall ldr in centre to 2f out: wknd* **25/1**

402 **12** *1* **Perfect Paula (USA)**[22] 3363 2-8-11 0 .... KerrinMcEvoy 14 60
(B J Meehan) *chsd ldrs in centre: struggling fr 1/2-way* **33/1**

6140 **13** *¾* **Aide Memoir (IRE)**[20] 3432 2-8-11 0 .... MartinDwyer 10 57
(S Kirk) *racd on outer of nr side gp: outpcd bef 1/2-way: struggling after* **20/1**

0144 **14** *2* **Only In Jest**[18] 3492 2-8-11 0 .... (t) TolleyDean 3 50
(W G M Turner) *dwlt: racd nr side: outpcd and sn u.p* **66/1**

0150 **15** *nk* **Enodoc**[42] 2737 2-9-0 0 .... EddieAhern 5 52
(W R Muir) *lw: racd nr side: a outpcd* **66/1**

0160 **16** *hd* **Carleton**[19] 3459 2-9-0 0 .... DarryllHolland 13 51
(M R Channon) *taken down early: racd centre: outpcd and bhd after 2f* **33/1**

57.96 secs (-1.09) **Going Correction** -0.075s/f (Good) **16** Ran SP% **125.8**
Speed ratings (Par 104): **105,104,100,97,96 94,93,90,88,88 86,84,83,80,79 79**
CSF £37.20 TOTE £9.00: £2.80, £2.10, £2.50; EX 50.20 Trifecta £546.20 Pool: £1,769.68 - 2.30 winning tickets..
Owner The Searchers **Bred** Mrs Bernadette Hayden **Trained** Newmarket, Suffolk

FOCUS
A very good renewal of this Group 3 prize and the form is rock-solid and strong for the grade, with the first pair coming clear. Both look very smart sprinting prospects and can rate higher still.

NOTEBOOK
Fleeting Spirit(IRE) ◆, a sprinting type on looks, supplemented her Nottingham maiden win with a gutsy effort on this debut in Group company. She was always near the pace and showed a decent attitude to fend off the runner-up in the final 100 yards, with the aid of the stands' rail no doubt helping her cause. Clearly a smart prospect, she has bundles of pace, and her next port of call could be again over this trip in the Flying Childers. However, a sixth furlong ought to be within her compass and connections did not rule out stepping her up in trip. (op 9-1)
Kingsgate Native(IRE) ◆ confirmed the promise of his debut at Royal Ascot and went down fighting, finishing a clear second best. He too has loads of pace and has to be rated a little unfortunate to have bumped into the winner here, although things may well have been different had he had the benefit of the stands' rail. The Flying Childers could also now be his next target and, while any maiden at this distance would surely be his for the taking, he looks well worth his place in that field in an attempt to break his duck. (op 7-2 tchd 9-2 in places)
Captain Gerrard(IRE), who looks every inch a sprinter, was on his toes in the parade ring. He was soon taking the field along at a strong pace, but started to hang right from halfway on this sounder surface and ultimately looked as though he may be better off over another furlong now. Still he ran very close to his recent level and helps to give this form a solid look. (op 6-1)
Starlit Sands, just touched off in the Queen Mary last time, proved disappointing and failed to improve as could have been expected on this sharper track. If anything her rider would have probably been better off riding her more positively, as she kept on inside the final furlong, and the suspicion remains that she can score in Group company before the season is out, perhaps even over another furlong. (op 9-4 tchd 3-1)
Littlemisssunshine(IRE) was doing her best work late in the day and ran very close to her previous form with Starlit Sands. On this evidence she is worth trying over 6f now and could make her mark in Listed company at some stage.
Spirit Of Sharjah(IRE) was notably sweating before the race and that cannot have helped his cause. However, he really came undone by a very sluggish start and, by the time he found his full stride, the race was effectively over. A sixth furlong now looks best for him, and he no doubt has an engine, but also his fair share of temperament. (op 13-2)
Imperial Mint(IRE), off the mark in a Windsor maiden 15 days previously, probably ran very close to that level on this step up in class and left the impression he may now prefer a stiffer test. (op 33-1)
Cake(IRE) again struggled to see out her race, despite this drop back in trip, and it remains to be seen which way she goes now.

4047 DETICA SUMMER STKS (H'CAP) 1m 6f
4:35 (4:36) (Class 2) (0-105,100) 3-Y-O+
£15,580 (£4,665; £2,332; £1,167; £582; £292) **Stalls** Low

Form RPR

0-16 **1** **Scriptwriter (IRE)**[38] 2859 5-10-0 **100** .... KerrinMcEvoy 8 112+
(Saeed Bin Suroor) *lw: trckd ldrs: plld out 2f out: swept into ld jst over 1f out: sn clr: pushed out* **7/1**[3]

-212 **2** *2½* **Samurai Way**[18] 3509 5-9-5 **91** .... JoeFanning 7 99+
(L M Cumani) *lw: settled in midfield: trckd ldrs over 2f out: waited to chal over 1f out: drvn and r.o to take 2nd but no ch w wnr* **3/1**[1]

0330 **3** *hd* **Tilt**[4] 3898 5-8-11 **86** .... (p) JamieMoriarty(3) 10 94
(B Ellison) *hld up in last trio: rdn on outer over 3f out: styd on fr over 2f out: tk 3rd nr fin* **14/1**

-154 **4** *¾* **Hernando Royal**[18] 3509 4-9-3 **89** .... SteveDrowne 2 96
(H Morrison) *prom: effrt 3f out: rdn to ld briefly over 1f out: outpcd fnl f* **14/1**

4/53 **5** *1* **Night Hour (IRE)**[59] 2236 5-9-2 **88** .... JimmyFortune 14 93
(J H M Gosden) *lw: t.k.h: hld up in rr: prog on inner 3f out: hrd rdn fnl 2f: kpt on one pce* **10/1**

0- **6** *1* **Strategic Mount**[326] 5153 4-9-8 **94** .... TQuinn 1 98
(P F I Cole) *swtg: dwlt: t.k.h and sn prom: stl keen 5f out: effrt over 2f out: chsd ldrs over 1f out: wknd fnl f* **9/1**

2312 **7** *2½* **Swan Queen**[29] 3153 4-9-7 **93** .... PhilipRobinson 3 93
(J L Dunlop) *trckd ldr: led jst over 2f out to over 1f out: wknd rapidly* **12/1**

6410 **8** *4* **Mustajed**[31] 3090 6-9-3 **89** .... JHBowman 11 84
(B R Millman) *settled midfield: effrt 3f out: rdn and chsng ldrs wl over 1f out: sn wknd* **33/1**

6014 **9** *4* **All The Good (IRE)**[31] 3119 4-9-11 **97** .... (b[1]) PatCosgrave 5 86
(G A Butler) *taken down early: t.k.h in midfield: stmbld 1/2-way: rdn over 2f out: no prog: wknd wl over 1f out* **14/1**

-100 **10** *hd* **Cape Secret (IRE)**[31] 3090 4-9-0 **86** .... SebSanders 6 75
(R M Beckett) *led at fair pce: shkn up and hdd jst over 2f out: sn virtually p.u* **10/1**

4-21 **11** *½* **Castle Howard (IRE)**[31] 3105 5-9-11 **97** .... TPQueally 13 85
(W J Musson) *hld up in midfield: sltly hmpd 1/2-way: effrt on outer 3f out: sn wknd tamely* **12/1**

60-5 **12** *3* **Vinando**[38] 2860 6-9-12 **98** .... (bt) PaulHanagan 4 82
(C R Egerton) *dwlt: rousted along and rchd midfield after 2f: rdn 4f out: wknd over 2f out* **50/1**

-110 **13** *5* **Nosferatu (IRE)**[31] 3090 4-9-6 **92** .... RyanMoore 12 69
(Mrs A J Perrett) *hld up in last trio: rdn wl over 3f out and no prog: bhd after* **5/1**[2]

132- **14** *14* **Go Solo**[68] 5367 6-9-4 **90** .... DarryllHolland 9 47
(D E Pipe) *a last: t.o* **33/1**

3m 4.70s (0.73) **Going Correction** +0.125s/f (Good) **14** Ran SP% **125.6**
Speed ratings (Par 109): **102,100,100,100,99 98,97,95,92,92 92,90,87,79**
CSF £29.07 CT £302.78 TOTE £8.50: £2.80, £1.70, £4.80; EX 36.50 Trifecta £604.50 Pool: £1,532.56 - 1.80 winning tickets..
Owner Godolphin **Bred** Newgate Stud Co **Trained** Newmarket, Suffolk

FOCUS
A good, strong handicap and the pace was fair. The third is the best guide for now but the first two could be capable of better.

NOTEBOOK
Scriptwriter(IRE) was disappointing when a beaten favourite in the Duke of Edinburgh Stakes at Royal Ascot on his previous start, but he proved well suited by this step up in trip and ran out a convincing winner. He is flattered a touch by the bare form of his two and a half-length beating of Samurai Way, as that one was denied a clear run at a crucial stage, but this was still a very smart effort considering he was conceding weight all round. He is now around about a 10/1 shot for the Ebor, for which he has picked up a 4lb penalty, but he is also one of a number of Godolphin horses to have been given an entry in the Melbourne Cup. He also holds Shergar Cup entries. (op 8-1)
Samurai Way ◆, racing off a 4lb higher mark than when second to John Terry at Newmarket on his previous start, looked unlucky not to give the winner more to think about. He was continually denied a clear run in the straight and, by the time he finally found an opening, Scriptwriter had bounded clear. One could argue he did not pick up immediately once in the clear, but that is understandable considering how much he had been messed about, and in any case he still secured second. There should be more to come and, like the winner, he holds entries in the Shergar Cup, the Ebor and the Melbourne Cup. (tchd 10-3 and 7-2 in places)
Tilt took well to the fitting of cheekpieces and ran well back in third. He was asked to make his move widest of all in the straight, but he avoided any trouble as a result and kept on to the line. (tchd 16-1 in places)
Hernando Royal, given another try over 1m6f, was produced with every chance and ran a solid race. He has plenty of size and could do better in time.
Night Hour(IRE), trying 1m6f for the first time, ran a respectable race without really building on his third in a good handicap at Epsom on Derby day. Official explanation: jockey said gelding hung both ways (op 9-1)
Strategic Mount ◆, most progressive last season but off the track since going off ridiculously fast on unsuitably easy ground at York last September, had been a non-runner on more than one occasion already this season, so he could have been expected to be relatively straight in the fitness department (and duly looked so in the paddock) for this belated return. However, he was just far too fresh and, having missed the kick, he soon carted his way on to the heels of the leaders and refused to settle for much of the way, still taking a grip on the approach to the straight. He eventually paid for his antics, but lasted longer than one might have expected and this must rate as an encouraging return from this imposing individual, especially considering he is even better on faster ground. He is a 25/1 shot for the Ebor, which looks a very fair price indeed, but he also holds entries in both the Shergar Cup and the Melbourne Cup. Official explanation: jockey said colt reared in stalls and ran too free (tchd 8-1 and 10-1 in places)
Swan Queen Official explanation: jockey said filly hung left in final furlong
Cape Secret(IRE) Official explanation: jockey said gelding lost its action
Nosferatu(IRE) failed to run his race and perhaps his Northumberland Plate run may have taken more out of him than his connections realised. Official explanation: jockey said gelding had no more to give (op 11-2 tchd 6-1)

4048 TATLER SUMMER SEASON EBF MAIDEN STKS (C&G) 6f
5:05 (5:09) (Class 2) 2-Y-O
£9,715 (£2,890; £1,444; £721) **Stalls** Low

Form RPR

3 **1** **Shallal**[10] 3747 2-9-0 0 .... JimmyFortune 9 88+
(P W Chapple-Hyam) *lw: w ldrs: narrow ld 2f out: hrd rdn fnl f: styd on wl and in command towards fin* **4/1**[1]

45 **2** *½* **Eastern Gift**[10] 3733 2-9-0 0 .... RyanMoore 14 86
(R Hannon) *drawn wdst but sn wl there on outer: effrt 2f out: str chal fnl f: jst hld last 75yds* **20/1**

3246 **3** *1¼* **Dream Eater (IRE)**[19] 3459 2-9-0 0 .... FrancisNorton 4 82
(A M Balding) *mde most in narrow ld to 2f out: nt qckn over 1f out: styd on again last 150yds* **4/1**[1]

4 *nk* **Moynahan (USA)** 2-9-0 0 .... TQuinn 1 81
(P F I Cole) *w'like: lw: racd against nr side rail: w ldr to over 2f out: sltly outpcd over 1f out: styd on* **10/1**[2]

5 *1¾* **Royalist (IRE)** 2-9-0 0 .... PhilipRobinson 11 79+
(M A Jarvis) *cmpt: bit bkwd: prom: jnd ldrs 2f out: upsides 1f out: wknd last 150yds* **4/1**[1]

545 **6** *hd* **Paveroc**[42] 2737 2-9-0 0 .... JohnEgan 2 76
(J S Moore) *swtg: chsd ldrs: hrd rdn over 2f out: nt qckn and sn outpcd: kpt on fnl f* **4/1**[1]

7 *shd* **Cigalas** 2-9-0 0 .... MichaelHills 5 78+
(B W Hills) *w'like: scope: s.s: given time to rcvr in last pair: pushed along and prog fr 2f out: styd on ins fnl f: nrst fin* **33/1**

8 *1¼* **Loyal Knight (IRE)** 2-9-0 0 .... KerrinMcEvoy 12 71
(S Kirk) *leggy: scope: sn outpcd in last: reminders over 1f out: styng on ins fnl f* **40/1**

9 *½* **Green Diamond** 2-9-0 0 .... JoeFanning 3 70
(M Johnston) *w'like: bit bkwd: wl in rr and rn green: effrt 2f out: one pce after* **25/1**

10 *nk* **House** 2-9-0 0 .... JHBowman 6 69
(M R Channon) *w'like: chsd ldrs: rdn over 2f out: no imp: fdd over 1f out* **25/1**

0 **11** *¾* **Harry Gee**[22] 3363 2-9-0 0 .... EddieAhern 10 67
(W R Muir) *leggy: chsd ldrs and racd towards outer: rdn 2f out: fdd over 1f out* **100/1**

44 **12** *¾* **Cordell (IRE)**[10] 3747 2-9-0 0 .... RichardHughes 8 65
(R Hannon) *racd on outer in rr: rdn and effrt over 2f out: sn no prog* **20/1**

0 **13** *1¼* **Andaman Sunset**[10] 3747 2-9-0 0 .... DarryllHolland 7 61
(G Wragg) *rn green in rr: effrt over 2f out: no prog wl over 1f out: wknd* **16/1**[3]

14 2 1/2 **Herrbee (IRE)** 2-9-0 0 ..... MartinDwyer 13 53
(M P Tregoning) *w'like: racd on outer in midfield: effrt over 2f out: sn wknd* **20/1**

1m 12.52s (-0.33) **Going Correction** -0.075s/f (Good) **14** Ran SP% **123.3**
Speed ratings (Par 100): **99,98,96,96,93 93,93,91,91,90 89,88,87,83**
CSF £94.57 TOTE £5.00: £2.10, £6.60, £1.80; EX 103.90 Trifecta £591.60 Part won. Pool: £833.30 - 0.40 winning tickets..
Owner Ziad A Galadari **Bred** Galadari Sons Stud Company Limited **Trained** Newmarket, Suffolk

FOCUS
Hard to work out exactly what the bare form is worth, as both Dream Eater and Paveroc were well below form, and few of the newcomers seemed seriously fancied beforehand, but it looked a strong maiden.

NOTEBOOK
Shallal, whose debut third in a Newmarket maiden looked to represent just fair form, had clearly learnt plenty from that and showed improved form to get off the mark. He was soon showing good early speed to race in a handy position and kept on well when asked for his challenge. He may now step up to Listed company, but that would require further improvement and he may be best off at a slightly lower level for the time being. (op 3-1 tchd 9-2 in places)
Eastern Gift did not see out 7f on soft ground at Lingfield on his previous start, but the drop in trip suited and he ran well in second, especially considering he raced rather wide for much of the way having been drawn in the highest stall of all.
Dream Eater(IRE) showed good early speed, but he struggled to sustain his challenge and ran some way below the form he showed in both the Windsor Castle and the July Stakes. This was disappointing, but it is too early to give up on him. (tchd 9-2 in places)
Moynahan(USA), a 150,000gns son of Johannesburg, half-brother to five winners, including European Rose, a triple winner at around 1m1f in the US, out of a 1m winner, shaped nicely on his debut. Having shown up well against the near-side rail for much of the way, he could find only the one pace under pressure and should come a good deal for the experience. A Champagne Stakes entry suggests he is held in high regard.
Royalist(IRE), a 425,000euros King's Best colt, first foal of an unraced half-sister to top-class sprinter Malhub, has been given an entry in the Group 2 Champagne Stakes. He was solid in the market beforehand, but he just looked to race a little too freely and had little left when asked for his effort. This should have taken the freshness out of him and he should improve a fair bit if settling better next time. (op 6-1 tchd 13-2 in places)
Paveroc got warm beforehand and was well below the form he showed when fifth in the Windsor Castle on his previous start. He looked likely to drop away when failing to pick up when initially asked, but he seemed to finally respond to his rider's urgings well inside the final furlong and was noted finishing quite well. This performance posed more questions than it provided answers. (tchd 9-2 in places)
Cigalas, a 75,000gns gelded son of Selkirk, out of a high-class dual sprint winner at two in Australia, has been entered in both the Champagne Stakes and the Royal Lodge. He was never really seen with a chance after missing the break, but was noted doing some good late work and should leave this form behind with the benefit of this experience.
Loyal Knight(IRE), a gelded son of Choisir, half-brother to 6f winner Blues In The Night, out of a 7f juvenile scorer, should have learnt plenty from this. (op 33-1)

4049 TURFTV STKS (H'CAP) 1m
5:40 (5:42) (Class 3) (0-90,90) 3-Y-0+ **£9,715** (£2,890; £1,444; £721) **Stalls** High

Form RPR

0601 **1** **Fremen (USA)**[7] 3813 7-9-8 **84** 6ex ..... AdrianTNicholls 2 95+
(D Nicholls) *dropped in fr wd draw and hld up in last trio: stl there over 2f out: plld wd and rapid prog over 1f out: r.o wl to ld last 75yds* **12/1**

3-41 **2** 1 **Kasumi**[38] 2877 4-8-12 **77** ..... TravisBlock(3) 11 86
(H Morrison) *pressed ldr: led 3f out: drew at least 2 l clr 2f out: stl same ld fnl f: mown down last 75yds* **14/1**

0622 **3** nk **Waterside (IRE)**[3] 3971 8-9-12 **88** ..... RyanMoore 3 96
(G L Moore) *hld up in midfield: dream passage through fr over 2f out: drvn and styd on fnl f: nvr able to chal* **16/1**

0305 **4** 3/4 **Woodcote Place**[18] 3488 4-9-8 **84** ..... JohnEgan 6 93+
(P R Chamings) *hld up in midfield: nt clr run over 2f out to over 1f out: styd on: unable to chal* **25/1**

2002 **5** 1 **Montpellier (IRE)**[13] 3650 4-10-0 **90** ..... JimmyFortune 20 94+
(E A L Dunlop) *lw: hld up wl in rr: effrt on inner and barging match 3f out: nt clr run after tl r.o fnl f: fin w plenty lft* **4/1**[1]

2436 **6** 1 **Full Victory (IRE)**[4] 3900 5-9-7 **83** ..... FergusSweeney 7 85
(R A Farrant) *trckd ldrs: effrt over 2f out: got through to chse ldrs over 1f out: kpt on same pce* **40/1**

6000 **7** nk **The Snatcher (IRE)**[21] 3401 4-9-6 **82** ..... RichardHughes 14 83
(R Hannon) *trckd ldrs: n.m.r over 2f out to wl over 1f out: kpt on: n.d* **20/1**

0055 **8** nk **Yarqus**[41] 2755 4-9-12 **88** ..... (t) KerrinMcEvoy 1 88+
(C E Brittain) *lw: hld up towards rr: bk of main gp and nt clr run over 2f out to over 1f out: shkn up and styd on fnl f: no ch* **25/1**

0033 **9** 2 **Press The Button (GER)**[12] 3672 4-9-3 **79** ..... (p) EddieAhern 15 75
(J R Boyle) *trckd ldrs: cl up in chsng pack over 1f out: fdd* **8/1**[3]

0620 **10** nk **Wavertree Warrior (IRE)**[13] 3650 5-9-11 **87** ..... JamesDoyle 13 82
(N P Littmoden) *pressed ldrs: rdn over 3f out: grad lost pl fr 2f out* **33/1**

5003 **11** 1 1/4 **Marajaa (IRE)**[20] 3437 5-9-8 **84** ..... TedDurcan 12 76+
(W J Musson) *hld up in midfield on inner: nt clr run over 2f out: hmpd over 1f out: no prog whn room fnl f* **9/1**

5244 **12** 1/2 **Cross The Line (IRE)**[17] 3525 5-9-6 **82** ..... SebSanders 8 73
(A P Jarvis) *trckd ldrs: outpcd fr 2f out* **12/1**

-600 **13** 1 **Persian Express (USA)**[80] 1649 4-9-9 **85** ..... MichaelHills 17 74+
(B W Hills) *hld up towards rr on inner: barging match w rival 3f out: nt clr run after: no prog* **20/1**

3113 **14** 3 **Purus (IRE)**[17] 3525 5-9-7 **83** ..... GeorgeBaker 9 65
(R A Teal) *trckd ldrs gng wl: wknd 2f out* **16/1**

0040 **15** shd **Prince Samos (IRE)**[60] 2209 5-9-7 **83** ..... (v) FrancisNorton 4 65
(D Nicholls) *sn in last pair and nvr gng wl: nvr a factor* **33/1**

5031 **16** 3 **Vicious Warrior**[17] 3556 8-9-10 **86** ..... DeanMcKeown 18 61
(R M Whitaker) *led to 3f out: sn btn* **20/1**

1260 **17** 1 **Nawaqees**[20] 3437 4-9-4 **80** ..... RHills 19 52
(J L Dunlop) *dropped out in rr and sn taken towards outer: no prog whn bmpd 2f out* **6/1**[2]

0421 **18** 1 1/4 **Wovoka (IRE)**[4] 3900 4-9-11 **87** 6ex ..... DarryllHolland 16 56
(M R Channon) *hld up and wl in rr: brought v wd over 3f out: no prog* **9/1**

0050 **19** 9 **Prince Of Thebes (IRE)**[24] 3330 6-9-11 **87** ..... PaulDoe 5 36
(J Akehurst) *swtg: bucking to post: prom: rdn over 3f out: wknd over 2f out* **16/1**

0130 **20** 3 1/2 **Royal Dignitary (USA)**[30] 3138 7-9-13 **89** ..... JoeFanning 10 30
(D Nicholls) *pressed ldng pair: sing to lose pl whn squeezed out over 2f out: immediately eased* **40/1**

1m 39.24s (-1.03) **Going Correction** +0.125s/f (Good) **20** Ran SP% **137.8**
Speed ratings (Par 107): **110,109,108,107,106 105,105,105,103,103 101,101,100,97,97 94,93,91,82,79**
CSF £166.05 CT £2797.26 TOTE £17.20: £4.00, £4.00, £2.80, £5.90; EX 385.20 Trifecta £238.40 Pool: £1,847.10 - 5.50 winning tickets. Place 6 £63.67, Place 5 £11.45.

Owner Miss C King Mrs A Seed Ms Finola Devaney **Bred** Flaxman Holdings Ltd **Trained** Sessay, N Yorks
■ Stewards' Enquiry : Adrian T Nicholls three-day ban: careless riding (Aug 11-13)

FOCUS
A decent, competitive handicap. The pace seemed fair. There were the usual hard-luck stories and the bare form has not been rated as highly as it could have been. This was the winner's best figure since his 3yo days.

NOTEBOOK
Fremen(USA) overcame a terrible draw to defy the 6lb penalty he picked up for his recent Musselburgh success. He was dropped in right out the back soon after the start - probably the best thing to do from such a low stall - and still had it all to do at around the two-furlong pole, but he flew home once switched into the clear. He gave a bump to the labouring Nawaqees, but it didn't cost him any momentum and he was able to reel in the positively ridden Kasumi close home. He is in the form of his life and could have more to offer in decent handicap company provided the pace is strong. (tchd 14-1)
Kasumi, raised 3lb for her recent success over an extended 7f at Lingfield, was always well placed by her apprentice and looked all over the winner when kicking a couple of lengths clear around two furlongs out, but she was just pegged back. She has never won over a trip this far and 1m probably just stretches her.
Waterside(IRE) could not take advantage of the drop into claiming company at York just three days earlier, but he showed himself still on a fair mark for handicaps with a game effort in third. He is a remarkable horse.
Woodcote Place was 6lb lower than at the start of the season and he looked unlucky not to finish quite a bit closer, as he had nowhere to go when looking to make his move. (op 28-1 tchd 33-1)
Montpellier(IRE) looked to have the best draw of all in stall 20, but he was never able to get a good position and enjoyed no luck in running in the straight. One would have to think he would have gone very close with a clear run and he could bid for compensation in the Totesport Mile later in the week after creeping at the bottom of the handicap. (op 5-1)
Full Victory(IRE) ran a sound enough race, but he had no easy task off a 13lb higher mark than when last winning. (tchd 50-1)
The Snatcher(IRE) was a little short of room around two furlongs out and he may have been a little unlucky not to finish closer. (op 25-1)
Yarqus had the worst draw of all to overcome and was denied a clear run in the straight. He is better than he was able to show. (op 33-1)
Press The Button(GER), in cheekpieces for the first time and 8lb higher than when second to Illustrious Blue in this race last year, looked to be in the ideal position just off the lead for much of the way, but he found little when asked.
Marajaa(IRE) was continually denied a clear passage and can be considered a lot better than the bare form. (tchd 11-1 in places)
Persian Express(USA) endured a bit of a nightmare passage in the straight and can be forgiven this.
Nawaqees looked one of the best drawn in stall 19 but, like Montpellier from stall 20, he failed to get a good position and ended up making his move very wide in the straight. He was beaten when bumped by the eventual winner around two furlongs out and is better than he was able to show.
Official explanation: vet said colt finished lame (tchd 13-2)
T/Jkpt: Not won. T/Plt: £91.00 to a £1 stake. Pool: £245,076.91. 1,964.40 winning tickets.
T/Qpdt: £15.40 to a £1 stake. Pool: £13,321.50. 638.50 winning tickets. JN

4050 - (Foreign Racing) - See Raceform Interactive

[4032]GALWAY (R-H)
Tuesday, July 31

OFFICIAL GOING: Good to yielding

4051a TOTE GALWAY MILE EUROPEAN BREEDERS FUND H'CAP (PREMIER HANDICAP) 1m 100y
7:00 (7:01) 3-Y-0+
£65,412 (£20,648; £9,837; £3,351; £2,270; £1,189)

RPR

1 **Incline (IRE)**[24] 3338 8-8-2 84 ..... DJMoran(3) 15 93
(R McGlinchey, Ire) *a.p: 2nd fr over 1f out: r.o wl u.p to ld last strides: jst hld on* **25/1**

2 shd **Crooked Throw (IRE)**[9] 3772 8-9-1 94 ..... WJLee 13 103
(C F Swan, Ire) *t.k.h towards rr early: 11th into st: rdn to go 4th 1f out: hung sltly: r.o wl: jst failed* **20/1**

3 hd **Absolute Image (IRE)**[30] 3138 5-8-13 92 ..... (b) PJSmullen 9 100
(D K Weld, Ire) *led early: trckd ldr in 2nd after: led again bef st: sn strly pressed: kpt on same pce and hdd fnl strides* **10/1**

4 1 **Moody Tunes**[24] 3330 4-8-8 87 ..... CO'Donoghue 7 93
(K R Burke) *a.p: 3rd over 1f out: sn no imp u.p: kpt on same pce* **20/1**

5 1/2 **Celtic Dane (IRE)**[31] 3118 3-8-5 92 ..... CDHayes 17 97
(Kevin Prendergast, Ire) *prom early: sn shuffled bk towards rr: r.o wl wout threatening u.p st* **15/2**[2]

6 1 **Tango Foxtrot (IRE)**[13] 3662 5-8-6 85 ..... NGMcCullagh 8 88
(W P Mullins, Ire) *in rr of mid-div: hdwy appr st: kpt on wout threatening u.p* **20/1**

7 1 **Baby Blue Eyes (IRE)**[13] 3662 4-9-1 94 ..... DMGrant 5 95+
(Patrick J Flynn, Ire) *mid-div: 9th fr 1/2-way: 8th whn sltly hmpd appr st: sn no imp u.p: kpt on same pce* **9/1**

8 3/4 **Jumbajukiba**[30] 3138 4-9-9 102 ..... (b) FMBerry 18 101
(Mrs John Harrington, Ire) *prom: t.k.h early: 5th bef st: no ex u.p and kpt on same pce ins fnl f* **8/1**[3]

9 1 **Deauville Vision (IRE)**[16] 3578 4-9-10 103 ..... KFallon 12 100
(M Halford, Ire) *mid-div: dropped towards rr fr 1/2-way: kpt on wout threatening u.p on inner st* **8/1**[3]

10 1/2 **Bolodenka (IRE)**[38] 2891 5-8-12 91 ..... MJKinane 10 87
(R A Fahey) *sn towards rr: kpt on wout threatening u.p st* **4/1**[1]

11 hd **Crossing**[48] 2587 6-9-5 98 ..... WJSupple 14 93
(William J Fitzpatrick, Ire) *sn led: strly pressed and hdd bef st: no ex fr over 1f out* **14/1**

12 1 1/4 **Jalmira (IRE)**[16] 3578 6-8-9 88 ..... WMLordan 6 81
(C F Swan, Ire) *mid-div: 9th appr st: sn no imp u.p* **33/1**

13 1 1/2 **Ridge Boy (IRE)**[13] 3662 6-8-4 86 ..... SMGorey(3) 1 75
(Kevin Prendergast, Ire) *towards rr: no imp u.p fr 1/2-way* **20/1**

14 1 3/4 **Rockazar**[18] 3516 6-7-9 84 ..... (p) MHarley(10) 16 69
(G M Lyons, Ire) *sn towards rr: rdn 1/2-way: sn n.d* **25/1**

15 1 3/4 **Dani's Girl (IRE)**[16] 3578 4-9-1 94 ..... KJManning 3 76
(P A Fahy, Ire) *sn trckd ldrs: 6th appr st: sn no ex u.p* **14/1**

16 1 **Quinmaster (USA)**[23] 2381 5-10-0 107 ..... (tp) PCarberry 11 86
(M Halford, Ire) *sn prom: mainly 3rd: lost pl and no ex u.p fr bef st* **14/1**

17 11 **Saintly Rachel (IRE)**[30] 3138 9-9-2 95 ..... DJCondon 4 50
(C F Swan, Ire) *towards rr: no imp u.p fr 3f out* **66/1**

18 3 1/2 **Kapera (FR)**[37] 2918 4-8-9 88..(b[1]) MCHussey 2 35
(Noel Lawlor, Ire) *sn chsd ldrs: 7th fr 1/2-way: wknd qckly u.p appr st*
33/1

1m 48.8s (-1.40)
WFA 3 from 4yo+ 8lb **18** Ran SP% **127.2**
CSF £442.26 CT £5273.43 TOTE £35.80: £7.10, £4.40, £2.40, £5.50; DF 489.90.
Owner Paul Crossan **Bred** Barronstown Stud & Orpendale **Trained** Inver, Co Donegal

FOCUS
The richest Flat handicap ever run in Ireland, and solid form.

NOTEBOOK
Incline(IRE) avoided any trouble and showed a willing attitude in a tight finish. Official explanation: trainer said, regarding the improved form shown, gelding was not suited by the tacky ground and wide draw last time, adding that its record at this track is good
Moody Tunes bounced back from an undistinguished run at Sandown to run right up to his best, a fine effort on drying ground that might not have been ideal.
Jumbajukiba Official explanation: jockey said gelding met with interference shortly after the start
Bolodenka(IRE), twice a winner in a lower handicap grade at last year's festival, was well backed despite the fact he had not scored since and had never won on ground softer than good. However, he was held up off the pace and never looked likely to get seriously involved. Official explanation: trainer said gelding met trouble in running and did not have a clear run (op 6/1)

4009 DEAUVILLE (R-H)

Tuesday, July 31

OFFICIAL GOING: Turf course - soft; all-weather - standard

4055a PRIX DE PSYCHE (GROUP 3) (FILLIES) 1m 2f

2:20 (2:21) 3-Y-O **£27,027** (£10,811; £8,108; £5,405; £2,703)

RPR

1 **Vadapolina (FR)**[51] 2501 3-9-2 .... SPasquier 6 118+
(A Fabre, France) *hld up: gd hdwy 3f out to ld 2f out: sn 3l clr: easily* **7/5**[1]

2 2 **Believe Me (IRE)**[51] 2501 3-8-12 .... OPeslier 3 108
(J-M Beguigne, France) *hld up: 6th st on ins: swtchd lft over 2f out: tk 2nd over 1f out: kpt on: no ch w wnr* **72/10**[3]

3 3/4 **Diyakalanie (FR)**[51] 2501 3-8-12 .... TThulliez 9 107
(J Boisnard, France) *hld up: 9th st: hdwy whn nt clr run 1 1/2f out: wnt 3rd wl ins fnl f: kpt on* **38/10**[2]

4 1/2 **Hapsburg (FR)**[30] 3148 3-8-12 .... TJarnet 11 106
(E Libaud, France) *in tch: cl 5th on outside: sn rdn: disp 2nd 2f out to over 1f out: kpt on at one pce* **15/1**

5 1 **Neele (IRE)**[32] 3075 3-8-12 .... DBonilla 8 104
(H Steinmetz, Germany) *hld up in rr: last st: styd on fnl 1 1/2f: nvr nr ldrs* **31/1**

6 3/4 **Chill (FR)**[59] 2270 3-8-12 .... C-PLemaire 4 102
(J-C Rouget, France) *hld up: 7th st on ins: n.m.r over 1 1/2f out: styd on fnl f but nvr nr ldrs* **10/1**

7 4 **Turfrose (GER)**[44] 2707 3-8-12 .... KFallon 10 94
(P Giannotti, Italy) *unruly bef s: cl up: led briefly ent st: sn hdd: disputing 2nd 1 1/2f out: wknd* **23/1**

8 2 **Touch My Soul (FR)**[31] 3121 3-9-2 .... AStarke 1 94
(P Schiergen, Germany) *trckd ldr: 4th st: ev ch briefly over 2f out: wknd 1 1/2f out* **13/1**

9 6 **Party (IRE)**[40] 2786 3-8-12 .... DBoeuf 5 78
(R Hannon) *cl up tl lost pl and 8th st: n.d after* **31/1**

10 5 **Posamina (FR)**[91] 1388 3-8-12 .... JVictoire 7 68
(A Fabre, France) *set gd pce to over 2f out: eased* **7/5**[1]

P **Moi Non Plus**[44] 2707 3-8-12 .... DVargiu 2 —
(B Grizzetti, Italy) *in rr whn p.u over 3f out* **16/1**

2m 7.40s (-3.40) **11** Ran SP% **155.1**
PARI-MUTUEL: WIN 2.40 (coupled with Posamina); PL 1.30, 1.70, 1.50;DF 7.00.
Owner H H Aga Khan **Bred** Snc Lagardere Elevage **Trained** Chantilly, France

NOTEBOOK
Vadapolina(FR) was not at all suited by a moderate gallop in the Prix de Diane and completely reversed form with two others on this occasion, posting an impressive victory. Held up early on, she moved smoothly into the lead early in the straight and was eased in the final 50 yards. This was her second Group 3 victory and the filly will now go on to the Prix Vermeille.
Believe Me(IRE) lost nothing in defeat and was given every possible chance. Fourth in the early part of the race, she quickened from one and a half out but had no chance of catching the winner. A longer trip may well be to her advantage and she is another who has been marked down for the Vermeille.
Diyakalanie(FR), based on the Diane form, should have won this race which was run at a true pace. As usual she was held up and she had to be checked a little before making her final run, but she never really looked like catching the runner-up.
Hapsburg(FR) came with the winner at the entrance to the straight up the centre of the track. She could not quicken as well as the others but stayed on well, if one-paced.
Party(IRE), well up until the straight, was a beaten force soon after. She did not run up to her best on this occasion.

4043 GOODWOOD (R-H)

Wednesday, August 1

OFFICIAL GOING: Good (8.2)
Wind: Light, across Weather: Glorious

4056 INVESCO PERPETUAL GOODWOOD STKS (H'CAP) 2m 5f

2:15 (2:16) (Class 2) (0-95,91) 3-Y-0+
£31,160 (£9,330; £4,665; £2,335; £1,165; £585)

Form RPR

164 1 **Secret Ploy**[20] 3467 7-8-6 73.. SteveDrowne 6 80
(H Morrison) *mde most: kicked on 5f out and jnd: narrowly hdd 2f out: sn led again: styd on wl and in command fnl f* **16/1**

0-06 2 1 1/4 **Afrad (FR)**[43] 2736 6-9-9 90.. MichaelHills 4 96
(N J Henderson) *hld up in rr: stdy prog on outer fr 4f out: narrow ld 2f out gng wl: sn hdd: cajoled along and outbattled fnl f* **14/1**

2303 3 hd **Noddies Way**[14] 3653 4-7-7 65 oh4.. LukeMorris(5) 8 71
(J F Panvert) *prom: drvn fr 5f out: kpt pressing ldrs but nvr able to mount a chal: styd on fnl f* **25/1**

121- 4 2 **Esprit De Corps**[43] 6011 5-8-6 73.. JamieSpencer 9 77
(P J Hobbs) *hld up wl in rr: prog on outer fr 3f out: clsd on ldrs jst over 1f out and hanging rt: rdn and immediately downed tools fnl f* **4/1**[1]

6-53 5 hd **Som Tala**[43] 2736 4-9-7 88.. JHBowman 7 92+
(M R Channon) *hld up in last pair: effrt over 3f out: n.m.r briefly wl over 2f out: no real prog tl r.o fr over 1f out: nrst fin* **9/2**[2]

2123 6 1/2 **Great As Gold (IRE)**[15] 3609 8-8-8 78.. PJMcDonald(3) 17 81
(B Ellison) *trckd ldrs: rdn 5f out: lost pl wl over 2f out: kpt on again fr over 1f out* **20/1**

6- 7 1 1/4 **Bauhaus (IRE)**[24] 2653 6-8-2 69 ow1..(b) ChrisCatlin 13 71
(R T Phillips) *hld up in midfield: clsd on ldrs gng wl 4f out: rdn and nt qckn over 2f out: btn after: kpt on* **40/1**

1405 8 2 1/2 **Doctor Scott**[21] 3412 4-8-7 74.. JoeFanning 3 73
(M Johnston) *mostly pressed wnr: chal 6f out to over 3f out: grad wknd over 2f out* **11/1**

302 9 2 1/2 **Pocket Too**[5] 3901 4-7-6 66 oh7 ow1.. KMay(7) 16 63
(M Salaman) *t.k.h: hld up in midfield: tried to cl over 3f out: wknd 2f out* **50/1**

0-11 10 1 1/2 **Full House (IRE)**[43] 2736 8-9-10 91.. JimmyFortune 5 86
(P R Webber) *lw: hld up in last pair: limited prog on outer over 3f out: no ch fnl 2f* **11/2**[3]

-054 11 shd **Screenplay**[13] 3692 6-7-12 65 oh3..(p) PaulHanagan 2 60
(G L Moore) *hld up in midfield: clsd on ldrs on inner 3f out: wknd 2f out* **25/1**

3245 12 1 1/2 **Kayf Aramis**[4] 3976 5-8-7 74.. JimmyQuinn 11 68
(J L Spearing) *prom: hrd rdn 5f out: wknd 3f out: eased over 1f out* **20/1**

1202 13 3 **Noble Minstrel**[4] 3963 4-8-6 73..(t) JimCrowley 10 64
(S C Williams) *lw: hld up towards rr: hrd rdn in midfield over 2f out: sn wknd* **11/1**

-262 14 1 1/2 **Whispering Death**[28] 3216 5-9-1 85..(v) LiamJones(3) 12 74
(W J Haggas) *hld up wl in rr: sme prog over 3f out: hrd rdn over 2f out: wknd wl over 1f out* **15/2**

00/1 15 6 **Commemoration Day (IRE)**[11] 2430 6-8-1 68.......(vt) FrancisNorton 14 51
(M F Harris) *hld up wl in rr: rdn and no prog wl over 3f out* **14/1**

4211 16 36 **Nero West (FR)**[18] 3533 6-8-6 73..(b) TomEaves 1 20
(I Semple) *taken down early: prom: rdn 5f out: wknd rapidly over 3f out: t.o* **20/1**

4m 36.64s (3.54) **Going Correction** +0.025s/f (Good) **16** Ran SP% **127.6**
Speed ratings (Par 109): **94,93,93,92,92 92,91,90,90,89 89,88,87,87,84 71**
CSF £213.79 CT £5527.08 TOTE £20.30: £4.50, £3.50, £4.10, £1.80; EX 269.60 TRIFECTA Not won..
Owner A M Carding **Bred** Coln Valley Stud **Trained** East Ilsley, Berks

FOCUS
Race started by flag. A tactical renewal of this historic staying handicap. The early pace set by the eventual winner was pedestrian, resulting in the market leaders being caught out of their ground when the leaders kicked for home. Probably not form to be posistive about.

NOTEBOOK
Secret Ploy did not get home over a similar marathon trip at Royal Ascot, but that was on soft ground and these conditions were more to his liking. The real key to this success was the very slow early pace that he was allowed to set in the early stages, though. Although off the bridle a fair way out and joined with two furlongs to run, and indeed headed for a short while, he had plenty in reserve and responded well to pressure. While this was clearly a tactical victory, he is still lightly raced on the Flat and open to some more improvement.
Afrad(FR), winner of this two years ago and a decent sixth in the Ascot Stakes last time, was again held up out the back. Given the way the race was run he was badly placed when the leaders quickened off a slow early pace, and finishing well for second was probably a good effort in the circumstances. Clearly a stronger gallop would have suited him.
Noddies Way, who ran well on his last visit here, is still a maiden and was racing from 4lb out of the handicap, but he was always well positioned in a race lacking early pace, and battled on well in the straight for third. He deserves to win a race, but the Handicapper is likely to take the opportunity to bump him up a pound or two for this.
Esprit De Corps has his quirks but he is talented, and having won twice last autumn and over hurdles in June, he came into the race with a progressive profile. He is the type who needs to be delivered late, though, and the steady early pace was all against him. He threatened to throw down a challenge in the straight but it came to nothing and his attitude can be seriously questioned. (op 9-2 tchd 5-1 in places)
Som Tala, third and in front of Afrad at Ascot, was another held up out the back in what turned out to be a very tactical affair. He was never nearer than at the line but he never actually looked like getting there. Yet another who would have appreciated a stronger-run race, he is building up a nice portfolio of solid efforts in these big staying handicaps, but his supporters have yet to see a return on their investment this term. (tchd 5-1 in places)
Great As Gold(IRE), who has done all his winning on turf at Pontefract, was another who was handily placed throughout and for the most part travelled well in that position. He had every chance given the way the race was run and is probably just a bit too high in the handicap at present.
Bauhaus(IRE), fit from hurdling, where he has been successful in two of his last three starts with blinkers applied, had the headgear retained for his return to the Flat. Carrying 1lb overweight, he ran a solid race, and off his current mark a modest little race can surely be found. (op 33-1)
Doctor Scott was well placed in a slowly-run affair, which gave him every chance of seeing out this longer trip. He still failed to see it out, though, and probably needs to drop back to distances around 1m6f. (op 12-1)
Pocket Too, was 7lb wrong at the weights and his rider put up 1lb overweight. He did not run badly in the circumstances but the form is hardly reliable given the way the race was run.
Full House(IRE), another 5lb higher for his Ascot Stakes win - form that had been given numerous boosts by the subsequent successes of those in behind - never got in a blow having been held up at the back of the field in what was a slowly-run affair. Official explanation: jockey said gelding ran too free (tchd 6-1 in places)
Kayf Aramis, who could have done with a bit more give in the ground, was nevertheless well placed throughout in a race lacking pace. He cannot have too many excuses.
Whispering Death was another hold-up performer who was totally unsuited by the way the race was run. (op 8-1)

4057 VEUVE CLICQUOT VINTAGE STKS (GROUP 2) 7f

2:50 (2:51) (Class 1) 2-Y-O
£39,746 (£15,064; £7,539; £3,759; £1,883; £945) **Stalls** High

Form RPR

31 1 **Rio De La Plata (USA)**[21] 3435 2-9-0 0.. LDettori 3 115+
(Saeed Bin Suroor) *lw: hld up in last trio: swtchd lft over 2f out: cruised into ld 2f out and sn clr: nudged along and in n.d fnl f* **8/13**[1]

1 2 2 **Lizard Island (USA)**[31] 3141 2-9-3 0.. JMurtagh 2 110+
(A P O'Brien, Ire) *w'like: hld up in last: effrt over 2f out: prog to go 2nd over 1f out but wnr had flown: styd on stoutly but no ch* **7/1**[3]

21 3 4 **Donegal (USA)**[19] 3510 2-9-0 0.. LPKeniry 5 97
(A M Balding) *trckd ldng pair for 3f: sn rdn: outpcd 2f out: styd on again fnl f* **16/1**

501 4 1 **Scintillo**[26] 3270 2-9-0 0.. RichardHughes 7 94
(R Hannon) *trckd ldr: led briefly jst over 2f out: sn outpcd: wknd ins fnl f* **14/1**

13 5 5 **Ellmau**[19] 3504 2-9-0 0.. ChrisCatlin 4 81+
(E J O'Neill) *lw: led to jst over 2f out: wknd over 1f out* **10/1**

61 **6** *3 1/2* **Il Warrd (IRE)**[18] 3522 2-9-0 0.. MartinDwyer 1 72+
(M P Tregoning) *trckd ldng pair after 3f: chal over 2f out: sn outpcd: wknd and hung lft fnl f* **11/2**[2]

0424 **7** *16* **Aaim To Storm (USA)**[4] 3938 2-9-0 0.............................. JHBowman 6 31+
(M R Channon) *a in last trio: rdn 1/2-way: wknd over 2f out: virtually p.u last 100yds* **80/1**

1m 26.05s (-1.99) **Going Correction** +0.025s/f (Good) **7** Ran SP% **112.7**
Speed ratings (Par 106): **112,109,105,104,98 94,76**
CSF £5.41 TOTE £1.60: £1.10, £2.40; EX 4.60.

Owner Godolphin **Bred** J De Camargo, Robert N Clay Et Al **Trained** Newmarket, Suffolk

FOCUS
Very strong form for the grade with the runner-up posting a solid effort under his penalty. Rio De La Plata looks a top-notcher and, with the potential to rate even higher, could rate the leading juvenile by the end of the season.

NOTEBOOK
Rio De La Plata(USA), very impressive when coming home a clear winner from two subsequent maiden scorers at Newmarket last time, was sent off a short price on this step up in grade, and his supporters never really had a moment's worry. Travelling kindly throughout for Dettori, he quickened up well when sent to the lead two furlongs out, and although he hung right towards the rail while doing so, he kept pulling clear of the rest. The runner-up made some inroads into his superiority late on, but he was beaten comfortably and this son of Rahy has the makings of a top-class performer. Group 1 races beckon, with the National Stakes, Prix Jean-Luc Lagardere and Dewhurst all likely to come into the equation, and the new Breeders' Cup Juvenile Turf also a possibility later in the year. Ladbrokes' quote of 14-1 for the 2000 Guineas did not last long but there is still some 12-1 about, which looks a fair price at present. (op 4-6 tchd 8-11, 4-5 in a place)

Lizard Island(USA), who had to carry a 3lb penalty for his Group 2 success at the Curragh in terrible ground, got warm beforehand. As it happens he probably faced an impossible task giving weight to the Godolphin colt, so he probably ran as well as could be expected. He has a lot of strengthening up to do and will be much more the finished article next year. (op 13-2 tchd 6-1 and 15-2)

Donegal(USA), who bolted up in bad ground at York last time, had a lot more on his plate in this company. He stayed on late after getting outpaced by the impressive winner, and a return to easier ground is likely to suit him. His connections apparently plan on taking in some French races in the autumn, where he should get his ground. (op 20-1)

Scintillo travelled well towards the fore but, when the winner was sent on with two furlongs to run, he was soon left toiling. His performance is probably a fair guide to the form, though, as he had previously run creditably in the Chesham and won at Sandown comfortably enough. (tchd 16-1)

Ellmau, third in the Superlative Stakes on his last start, set a decent pace and probably paid the price. He is better than this run suggests and will be of more interest dropped back to Listed company. (op 12-1)

Il Warrd(IRE), who made a good impression when he won at Ascot, was sent for home too soon and his challenge did not last long. He too will be of more interest at a slightly lower level. (op 9-2 tchd 6-1, 13-2 in a place)

Aaim To Storm(USA), the most exposed runner in the line-up, was having his eighth start of the campaign and was out of his depth. (op 66-1)

4058 BGC SUSSEX STKS (GROUP 1) 1m
3:30 (3:30) (Class 1) 3-Y-O+

£170,340 (£64,560; £32,310; £16,110; £8,070; £4,050) **Stalls** High

Form RPR

3-21 **1** **Ramonti (FR)**[43] 2735 5-9-7 118...(t) LDettori 8 125
(Saeed Bin Suroor) *lw: hld up in 5th: smooth prog on outer 3f out: led 2f out and sn kicked 2 l clr: drvn fnl f: a gng to hold on* **9/2**

1-41 **2** *hd* **Excellent Art**[43] 2734 3-9-0 0.. JamieSpencer 7 124
(A P O'Brien, Ire) *hld up in 6th: pushed along over 3f out: rdn and prog over 2f out: chsd wnr over 1f out: r.o and clsd fnl f: jst hld* **15/8**[1]

-152 **3** *1 3/4* **Jeremy (USA)**[43] 2735 4-9-7 117... RyanMoore 4 121
(Sir Michael Stoute) *swtg: hld up in last: rdn and prog on outer fr over 2f out: disp 2nd over 1f out: kpt on same pce after* **7/2**[3]

1111 **4** *shd* **Asiatic Boy (ARG)**[123] 859 4-9-7 0................................ WCMarwing 2 121+
(M F De Kock, South Africa) *w'like: str: chsd clr ldng pair: clsd and rdn to chal 2f out: sn outpcd: kpt on* **3/1**[2]

100 **5** *5* **Archipenko (USA)**[25] 3331 3-9-0 0................................ DavidMcCabe 6 108
(A P O'Brien, Ire) *swtg: s.i.s: rousted along and eventually led after 3f: hdd 2f out: btn after* **25/1**

-331 **6** *1* **Decado (IRE)**[17] 3579 4-9-7 0... DPMcDonogh 3 107
(Kevin Prendergast, Ire) *w'like: leggy: chsd ldng trio: rdn wl over 3f out: struggling fr over 2f out* **50/1**

1210 **7** *6* **Munaddam (USA)**[32] 3098 5-9-7 110.. RHills 5 93+
(E A L Dunlop) *lw: hld up in 7th: shkn up and no prog wl over 2f out: sn wknd* **14/1**

2044 **8** *1* **Trinity College (USA)**[4] 3983 3-9-0 0................................. JMurtagh 1 90
(A P O'Brien, Ire) *str: led for 3f: w ldr after tl wknd over 2f out: eased over 1f out* **66/1**

1m 37.62s (-2.65) **Going Correction** +0.025s/f (Good)
WFA 3 from 4yo+ 7lb **8** Ran SP% **114.2**
Speed ratings (Par 117): **114,113,112,111,106 105,99,98**
CSF £13.24 TOTE £3.80: £1.20, £1.30, £1.50; EX 12.10 Trifecta £25.50 Pool £4,852.43. - 134.84 winning units..

Owner Godolphin **Bred** S P A Siba **Trained** Newmarket, Suffolk

■ Stewards' Enquiry : Ryan Moore one-day ban: used whip with excessive frequency (Aug 12)

FOCUS
This looked pretty much on a par with most recent renewals, with both the Queen Anne and St James' Palace Stakes winners taking their place in the line up. The addition of UAE 2000 Guineas and Derby winner Asiatic Boy made for a fascinating contest and, with two Ballydoyle pacemakers doing their job, it was run at a proper gallop. In winning Ramonti recorded an RPR just 2lb lower than that of Rock Of Gibraltar's in 2002, and 1lb lower than Giant's Causeway's in 2000, arguably the two best recent winners of the race.

NOTEBOOK
Ramonti(FR), who came into this season with the potential to be one of the world's top milers, made up for his narrow Lockinge defeat with a hard-fought victory in the Queen Anne, but things were going to be tougher here on a less galloping track, especially as Ballydoyle had two pacemakers to scupper this often front-runner. With no choice but to drop in early, he travelled surprisingly well and swept into the lead having made a move towards the outside racing into the final quarter mile. Considering the splendid attitude he showed to win at Royal Ascot, it was always going to take something special to pass him in the final furlong or so, and nothing proved up to the task, as he stuck his neck out willingly to hold the favourite. Becoming the first horse since Rousillon in 1985 to complete the Queen Anne/Sussex Stakes double, a good gallop seems key to him, no matter how he is ridden in a race, and it will take a high-class performance to prevent him completing an unprecedented hat-trick in the Queen Elizabeth II Stakes back at Ascot. (op 3-1 tchd 5-1 in places)

Excellent Art, who was unlucky not to be coming into this off the back of a French Guineas/St James's Palace Stakes double, led home a Ballydoyle 1-2-3 at Royal Ascot and was understandably made favourite in receipt of 7lb from his elders. With two pacemakers employed to ensure a decent gallop, he looked set to have things go his way, but Spencer had him plenty far enough back and surprisingly he lacked the winner's burst of speed. He came to hold every chance in the final quarter mile though and was closing with every stride at they flashed past the post, but just failed. This effort confirmed him as one of the leading three-year-old milers and connections will no doubt be hopeful of reversing the placings with Ramonti should they meet again in the QEII at Ascot. (tchd 7-4 and 2-1, 9-4 in a place)

Jeremy(USA), who may well have beaten Ramonti in the Queen Anne had he not drifted right under pressure, was delievered with his challenge a little later this time, but his old rival had flown by the time he hit top stride and he was unable to get as close on this occasion. The winner was better suited to the stronger pace here and, whilst he looks capable of winning a race at this level, his chance of reversing the form in the QEII look slim. (op 9-2)

Asiatic Boy(ARG) came into this as an unknown quantity, having run away with the UAE 2000 Guineas and Derby, but he was done no favours with the weights as, being bred in the Southern Hemisphere, he is only six months or so older than our three-year-olds, yet is officially classed as being four. Taking this into account, and the fact it was his first run since March, he ran a stormer. Ridden closest to the pace of the principals, he came to have his chance, but lacked Ramonti's pace and looked to get tired late on. A fine physical specimen, 1m2f will be no problem to him and the Juddmonte at York later in the month looks an ideal target for the colt. In the long term he is going to be suited by a return to dirt. (tchd 10-3, 7-2 in places)

Archipenko(USA) looked a fine prospect when taking the Derrinstown Stud Derby Trial earlier in the season, but he failed to make a show in the Derby and was then ridden strangely in the Eclipse. Used as a pacemaker here, he ran as well as could have been expected, but it is a shame to see a one time high-class prospect being sacrificed. (op 33-1)

Decado(IRE), who got warm beforehand, enjoys getting his toe in and the drying ground would not have been in his favour. Placed in last year's Irish Guineas, he is a colt of substantial class and he deserves another chance to show what he can do.

Munaddam(USA), a Listed winner at Haydock back in May, disappointed in a Group 3 at Newmarket last time and it was surprising to see him as short as 14/1 for a race of this nature. As expected he was not good enough to feature. (op 25-1)

Trinity College(USA), the other Ballydoyle pacemaker, is a decent horse in his own right and may sneak a Listed race in his homeland, but it is unlikely this will be the last time he is asked to perform these duties. (tchd 80-1)

4059 BGC STKS (HERITAGE H'CAP) 1m 4f
4:05 (4:09) (Class 2) (0-105,102) 3-Y-O

£52,972 (£15,861; £7,930; £3,969; £1,980; £994) **Stalls** Low

Form RPR

-260 **1** **Regal Flush**[60] 2231 3-8-11 **92**.. RyanMoore 3 105+
(Sir Michael Stoute) *hld up wl in rr: gd prog fr 3f out: swtchd rt 2f out: pressed ldrs 1f out: got through to ld last 100yds: powered away* **14/1**

-131 **2** *3/4* **Camps Bay (USA)**[16] 3590 3-8-6 **87**.............................. JimCrowley 10 98
(Mrs A J Perrett) *lw: settled in rr on outer: rdn and gd prog over 3f out to join ldrs 2f out: led 1f out: hung lft and hdd last 100yds* **16/1**

1102 **3** *1 1/4* **Man Of Vision (USA)**[20] 3460 3-8-10 **91**........................... TPO'Shea 11 100+
(M R Channon) *lw: hld up in rr: prog to midfield 1/2-way: rdn and hdwy 3f out: led 2f out to 1f out: upsides 100yds out: fdd* **6/1**[2]

-211 **4** *2 1/2* **Malt Or Mash (USA)**[13] 3691 3-8-8 **89**............................ PatDobbs 13 94+
(R Hannon) *lw: uns rdr and galloped 6f bef s: w ldrs: led 3f out gng wl: hdd 2f out and sn outpcd: kpt on again ins fnl f* **8/1**

0-31 **5** *nk* **Spanish Hidalgo (IRE)**[11] 3753 3-9-4 **99**.................... KerrinMcEvoy 9 104+
(J L Dunlop) *hld up in rr: stdy prog gng strly over 3f out: rdn to chse ldrs 2f out: n.m.r and nt qckn over 1f out: one pce* **12/1**

3120 **6** *2* **Philatelist (USA)**[41] 2790 3-8-10 **91**............................ PhilipRobinson 6 93
(M A Jarvis) *trckd ldrs: prog to join ldr 2f out: hanging rt after: wknd tamely fnl f* **10/1**

0-11 **7** *1 1/4* **Raffaas**[29] 3189 3-8-4 **85**.. MartinDwyer 2 85
(M P Tregoning) *hld up in last trio: rdn 3f out: styd on fnl 2f: no ch to rch ldrs* **8/1**

-431 **8** *2* **Rosbay (IRE)**[19] 3495 3-8-5 **86**.. DavidAllan 14 83
(T D Easterby) *chsd ldrs: rdn and stl cl up over 2f out: wknd over 1f out* **33/1**

112 **9** *5* **Samira Gold (FR)**[15] 3628 3-9-0 **95**.............................. JamieSpencer 8 84
(L M Cumani) *s.i.s: hld up in last trio: shkn up and no prog over 3f out: plugged on fnl 2f: no threat* **9/2**[1]

2113 **10** *1 1/4* **Secret Tune**[40] 2816 3-9-0 **95**...................................... RichardHughes 12 82
(Pat Eddery) *led: reminders and upped the pce 5f out: hdd 3f out: wknd fnl 2f* **14/1**

3615 **11** *4* **Aureate**[26] 3273 3-8-6 **87**.. TomEaves 1 67
(B Ellison) *hld up in last: nvr a factor* **25/1**

1630 **12** *3/4* **Celestial Halo (IRE)**[41] 2790 3-9-1 **96**........................... MichaelHills 15 75
(B W Hills) *swtg: settled in midfield: chsd ldrs on inner over 4f out: no imp 3f out: sn wknd* **16/1**

3206 **13** *3/4* **Duke Of Tuscany**[20] 3458 3-9-2 **97**.............................. SteveDrowne 5 75
(R Hannon) *lw: chsd ldrs: rdn over 3f out: wknd over 2f out: eased* **33/1**

21-1 **14** *2 1/2* **Mariotto (USA)**[26] 3272 3-9-7 **102**..(t) LDettori 16 76
(Saeed Bin Suroor) *lw: hld up in midifeld: lost pl and shkn up over 4f out: sn btn* **13/2**[3]

2140 **15** *1 3/4* **Eradicate (IRE)**[20] 3461 3-9-4 **99**.................................... JoeFanning 7 70
(M Johnston) *w ldrs tl wknd wl over 2f out* **14/1**

13-3 **16** *34* **Cold Quest (USA)**[12] 3709 3-8-11 **92**............................ JimmyFortune 4 9
(J H M Gosden) *swtg: wl in tch on outer to 3f out: sn wknd: virtually p.u: t.o* **12/1**

2m 35.98s (-2.94) **Going Correction** +0.025s/f (Good) **16** Ran SP% **134.0**
Speed ratings (Par 106): **110,109,108,107,106 105,104,103,99,99 96,95,95,93,92 69**
CSF £238.57 CT £1519.83 TOTE £20.40: £4.60, £4.20, £2.20, £2.40; EX 505.10 Trifecta £1790.20 Pool £2,521.54. - 1 winning unit..

Owner Cheveley Park Stud **Bred** Cheveley Park Stud Ltd **Trained** Newmarket, Suffolk

■ Stewards' Enquiry : Ryan Moore one-day ban: careless riding (Aug 13)

FOCUS
A strong middle-distance handicap, as one would expect at this meeting, and solid form for the grade which should work out well. The winner has more to offer and the next three look progressive too.

NOTEBOOK
Regal Flush had looked a handicapper to follow after finishing second at Newmarket in April, but things had not gone his way subsequently (unlucky in running at Newbury and poorly drawn at Epsom) and he came here with something to prove. Stepping up a couple of furlongs in distance proved just what was required, though, and he found a strong finishing effort to mow his rivals down late on. He looks like fulfilling his potential now and a more galloping track will suit him in future. (op 20-1)

Camps Bay(USA) was 8lb higher than when successful at Windsor but he is proving a very progressive handicapper this season and this was another good effort. He stayed on well from off the pace.

Man Of Vision(USA) had looked likely to appreciate a return to 1m4f when finishing strongly over shorter at Newmarket last time. Strangely, though, he did not quite get home having been brought with what looked a well-timed run. (op 7-1 tchd 8-1 in a place and 15-2 in a place)

Malt Or Mash(USA), another stepping up in trip, was chasing a hat-trick and still looked potentially ahead of the Handicapper on a mark only 5lb higher than when overcoming a troubled passage to dead-heat at Sandown last time. He would not have been done any favours by his antics before the start, though, when he unseated Dobbs and galloped riderless to the 6f start. He travelled well in the race itself, but those earlier exertions possibly took their toll in the closing stages. He deserves another chance.

Spanish Hidalgo(IRE), 9lb higher than at Ripon, showed he can handle good ground as well as a surface with plenty of cut in it, and his performance probably helps set the level of the form. (op 14-1)

Philatelist(USA), who came in for good support, was brought to have every chance two furlongs out, but he did not see the trip out that well. On this evidence he will not mind dropping back to 1m2f. (tchd 11-1)

Raffaas looked to have plenty on his plate off a 10lb higher mark than when winning on Polytrack last time. A confirmed hold-up performer, he stayed on late but never really got competitive. (tchd 15-2, 9-1 in places)

Rosbay(IRE), stepping up to 1m4f for the first time, was taking on a better class of opposition than at York and the ground was quicker this time, too. (op 50-1)

Samira Gold(FR), who did not get the best of runs when runner-up in a fillies' Listed race at Yarmouth last time, looked potentially well treated back in handicap company, but she never got into it from off the pace. A more galloping track is likely to suit her. Official explanation: jockey said filly boiled over before start (op 11-2 tchd 6-1 in a place)

Secret Tune, third in the 2m Queen's Vase last time out, tried to make every yard back in distance, but he was done for toe in the closing stages. (tchd 16-1 in places)

Mariotto(USA) might be the type who runs his best races when allowed his own way in front. Official explanation: jockey said colt lost its action (op 11-2 tchd 7-1 in places)

Cold Quest(USA) Official explanation: jockey said colt was never travelling and hung badly left-handed

4060 WEATHERBYS BANK FILLIES' STKS (H'CAP) 1m 1f

4:40 (4:44) (Class 3) (0-90,90) 3-Y-0+

£10,906 (£3,265; £1,632; £817; £407; £204) **Stalls** High

Form				RPR
5540	**1**		**Fongs Gazelle**[25] 3335 3-8-9 **77** ... RHills 10 (M Johnston) *trckd ldng trio: prog to chal over 1f out: eventually led 1f out: looked in command but jst hld on* **12/1**	86
0203	**2**	*nk*	**Ronaldsay**[18] 3555 3-8-12 **80** ... RichardHughes 13 (R Hannon) *chsd ldng quintet: shkn up 3f out: no prog tl picked up over 1f out: fin strly on outer fnl f: post c too sn* **8/1**	88+
2200	**3**	*1*	**Lady Gloria**[19] 3503 3-9-8 **90** ... TPQueally 8 (J G Given) *trckd ldr: rdn to ld 2f out: hdd 1f out: one pce* **33/1**	96
3523	**4**	*nk*	**Lisathedaddy**[50] 2543 5-9-6 **80** ... GeorgeBaker 7 (B G Powell) *s.i.s: wl in rr tl prog on inner 4f out: chsd ldrs 3f out: rdn and styd on fnl 2f: nvr able to chal* **10/1**	86
51	**5**	*1*	**Fragrancy (IRE)**[16] 3591 3-9-0 **82** ... PhilipRobinson 9 (M A Jarvis) *lw: led to 2f out: nt qckn over 1f out: one pce* **7/1**[3]	86
2-11	**6**	*nk*	**Gold Hush (USA)**[50] 2543 3-9-5 **87** ... KerrinMcEvoy 6 (Sir Michael Stoute) *lw: hld up towards rr and wd: plenty to do 3f out: styd on fr over 1f out: n.d* **3/1**[1]	90+
0-52	**7**	*3*	**Home Sweet Home (IRE)**[34] 3016 4-9-10 **84** ... JoeFanning 17 (L M Cumani) *chsd ldng quintet: lost pl wl over 2f out: hanging and no prog over 1f out: wknd ins fnl f* **14/1**	81
4205	**8**	*1 1/4*	**Cape Velvet (IRE)**[35] 2998 3-8-4 **72** ... MartinDwyer 15 (J W Hills) *t.k.h: trckd ldng pair to 2f out: fdd* **66/1**	66
5113	**9**	*shd*	**Baltic Belle (IRE)**[25] 3334 3-8-8 **81** ... LukeMorris(5) 11 (R Hannon) *drvn in midfield 1/2-way: no prog u.p after* **16/1**	75
4-11	**10**	*nk*	**Rhuepunzel**[20] 3474 3-8-7 **75** ... HayleyTurner 16 (G A Butler) *plld hrd early: hld up in midfield: prog on inner over 2f out: no imp sn after: fdd* **12/1**	68
0-50	**11**	*1 1/2*	**Flor Y Nata (USA)**[15] 3628 4-10-0 **88** ... DavidAllan 12 (Sir Mark Prescott) *missed break and lft 6 l: tacked on to bk of field after 2f: rdn 4f out: sn lft bhd and btn* **25/1**	78
2055	**12**	*2 1/2*	**Spring Goddess (IRE)**[21] 3420 6-8-13 **73** ... JimCrowley 1 (A P Jarvis) *last and labouring 1/2-way on outer: nvr a factor* **50/1**	58
414	**13**	*1 3/4*	**Held Captive (USA)**[19] 3514 3-8-12 **80** ... JimmyFortune 5 (E A L Dunlop) *wl in rr and wd: struggling over 3f out: sn btn* **16/1**	61
1322	**14**	*1/2*	**Gyroscope**[18] 3555 3-9-2 **84** ... RyanMoore 4 (Sir Michael Stoute) *hld up in midfield: rdn and outpcd 3f out: wandering and wknd 2f out* **9/2**[2]	64
-505	**15**	*21*	**Divine Right**[18] 3555 3-9-4 **86** ... LDettori 3 (B J Meehan) *racd wd in rr: nt moving wl 4f out: sn btn: t.o* **20/1**	22

1m 56.34s (-0.52) **Going Correction** +0.025s/f (Good)

WFA 3 from 4yo+ 8lb **15** Ran SP% **124.7**

Speed ratings (Par 104): **103,102,101,101,100 100,97,96,96,96 94,92,91,90,72**

CSF £103.02 CT £3118.89 TOTE £16.50: £4.80, £2.50, £9.10; EX 170.90 Trifecta £869.90 Part won. Pool £1,225.26. - 0.10 winning units..

Owner Around The World Partnership **Bred** Miss S N Ralphs **Trained** Middleham Moor, N Yorks

FOCUS

A competitive enough fillies' handicap likely to produce its share of winners. It was not strongly run but the form seems sound enough through the third and fifth.

NOTEBOOK

Fongs Gazelle, in cracking form back in the spring, reeling off a hat-trick at trips of up to 1m3f, has been struggling off marks in the 80s, but she had been given a few weeks to freshen up and was down 3lb from her last race, so looked one of the more interesting outsiders. Never far away, she edged ahead racing into the final furlong and just did enough to hold off the closing runner-up. She has taken her racing well this season and is a typically progressive three-year-old from the yard.

Ronaldsay, an unfortunate loser when third at Salisbury last time, was always well positioned to strike, but took her time to pick up and the line came too soon. She has been unfortunate on more than one occasion this season and, as she was just touched off over 1m2f at Nottingham earlier in the season, looks well worth another try at that distance. (op 10-1)

Lady Gloria, a highly progressive filly in her first season of racing, started out handicap life off a mark of 75 and would have been a leading fancy here had she not run a shocker at Newmarket last time. Readily dismissed in the market, she came to have every chance racing into the final quarter mile and stuck on well once headed, but was not quite good enough. This effort confirmed her to still be on an upwards curve, but winning is not going to get any easier.

Lisathedaddy has been running well without winning over further and she lacked the speed to quite get there. A more forceful ride over this distance would suit in further and she continues to go the right way. (op 12-1)

Fragrancy(IRE), up 6lb for her recent Windsor victory, was a fortunate winner that day and with the runner-up subsequently getting beaten, she looked vulnerable. Made plenty of use of, she kept plugging away under pressure, but is likely to remain vulnerable off this mark. (op 6-1)

Gold Hush(USA), well on top late on when winning over 1m2f at Salisbury last time, was again ridden with restraint, but in hindsight her rider would have made more use of her stamina, as she got going far too late. She remains capable of better. (tchd 10-3, 7-2 in places)

Home Sweet Home(IRE) was expected to better her recent Hamilton effort back on this faster surface, but she was always going to be vulnerable under her big weight and it was concerning the way in which she hung under pressure.

Rhuepunzel, on a hat-trick following wins in a maiden at Beverley and on her handicap debut at Warwick, had not been put up much for that latest victory and she looked an interesting contender from a good draw. However, she failed to settle and dropped right out in the end. (tchd 11-1)

Flor Y Nata(USA) Official explanation: jockey said filly missed the break

Gyroscope has been struggling to get her head in front since winning her maiden at Windsor and she ran as though something was amiss here. Official explanation: jockey said filly ran flat (op 5-1)

Divine Right Official explanation: jockey said filly moved poorly

4061 LINKS OF LONDON MAIDEN FILLIES' STKS 6f

5:10 (5:15) (Class 2) 2-Y-0 **£10,363** (£3,083; £1,540; £769) **Stalls** Low

Form				RPR
2	**1**		**Fashion Rocks (IRE)**[14] 3648 2-9-0 0 ... JimmyFortune 10 (B J Meehan) *lw: w ldrs: narrow ld wl over 1f out: jnd fnl f: drvn and hld on wl* **4/1**[3]	81
25	**2**	*shd*	**Royal Confidence**[23] 3363 2-9-0 0 ... MichaelHills 15 (B W Hills) *wl in rr on outer: stdy prog fr 1/2-way: rdn to join wnr fnl f: jst hld* **14/1**	81
4	**3**	*1/2*	**Candle Sahara (IRE)**[27] 3233 2-9-0 0 ... JHBowman 8 (M R Channon) *chsd ldrs: pushed along over 2f out: prog over 1f out: chsd ldng pair ins fnl f: styd on but unable to chal* **25/1**	80
	4	*1*	**Fifty (IRE)** 2-9-0 0 ... RichardHughes 14 (R Hannon) *leggy: hld up at rr of main gp and gradually shifted towards nr side: shkn up 2f out: styd on wl fnl f: nrst fin* **22/1**	77+
4	**5**	*3/4*	**Crystany (IRE)**[33] 3055 2-9-0 0 ... TedDurcan 6 (H R A Cecil) *w ldrs: upsides wl over 1f out: fdd fnl f* **7/2**[2]	74
	6	*1 1/4*	**Swanky Lady** 2-9-0 0 ... RyanMoore 7 (R Hannon) *chsd ldrs: pushed along 1/2-way: rdn and kpt on fr over 1f out: n.d* **14/1**	71+
2	**7**	*2*	**Lille Ida**[29] 3187 2-9-0 0 ... MartinDwyer 3 (M P Tregoning) *cl up tl over 1f out: wknd* **4/1**[3]	65
	8	*1 1/4*	**Twiglet (IRE)** 2-9-0 0 ... PhilipRobinson 13 (B W Hills) *w'like: settled at bk of main gp: shuffled along fnl 2f: kpt on steadily: nvr nr ldrs* **50/1**	61+
52	**9**	*2*	**Kashoof**[19] 3507 2-9-0 0 ... RHills 11 (J L Dunlop) *racd on outer: mde most to wl over 1f out: wknd fnl f* **5/2**[1]	55
	10	*1 3/4*	**Contessina (IRE)** 2-9-0 0 ... TQuinn 1 (P F I Cole) *w'like: bit bkwd: spd towards nr side over 3f: wknd wl over 1f out* **25/1**	50
0	**11**	*1/2*	**Smokey Rye**[23] 3383 2-9-0 0 ... FergusSweeney 9 (G L Moore) *chsd ldrs: u.p 1/2-way: wknd 2f out* **66/1**	48
	12	*1 1/2*	**Trinkila (USA)** 2-9-0 0 ... LDettori 5 (P F I Cole) *w'like: leggy: detached fr main gp after 2f: bhd rest of way* **28/1**	44
	13	*4*	**The Jostler** 2-9-0 0 ... ChrisCatlin 4 (B W Hills) *str: bit bkwd: dwlt: in rr of main gp: wknd over 2f out* **66/1**	32
	14	*4*	**Naughty Frida (IRE)** 2-9-0 0 ... KerrinMcEvoy 12 (E A L Dunlop) *w'like: bit bkwd: s.v.s: a t.o* **50/1**	20

1m 11.8s (-1.05) **Going Correction** +0.025s/f (Good) **14** Ran SP% **126.5**

Speed ratings (Par 97): **108,107,107,105,104 103,100,98,96,93 93,91,85,80**

CSF £56.79 TOTE £5.30: £2.10, £4.60, £6.20; EX 79.60 TRIFECTA Not won..

Owner Andrew Rosen **Bred** Swordlestown Stud **Trained** Manton, Wilts

FOCUS

Probably a pretty good fillies' maiden, rated through the principals.

NOTEBOOK

Fashion Rocks(IRE), who ran with plenty of promise on her debut at Lingfield, is well regarded by her trainer, who considers her Group-class material. She did it well enough in the end, and looks likely to benefit from a longer trip in time. (op 5-1 tchd 11-2 in a place)

Royal Confidence came from off the pace to strongly challenge the winner late on. Only narrowly denied, she appreciated the furlong-longer trip and a reproduction of this effort should see her win an average maiden. (op 16-1 tchd 22-1 in a place)

Candle Sahara(IRE), who was too green to do herself true justice on her debut, knew a lot more about what was required this time and ran well in defeat. The quicker ground was very much in her favour, but a more conventional track will suit her in future. (op 28-1)

Fifty(IRE), a half-sister to Audit, a dual middle-distance winner at three, is by Fasliyev, so she should have a bit more speed than him. Held up out the back on her debut, she stayed on well in the latter stages as she got the hang of what was required, and she should be a lot sharper next time. (op 20-1)

Crystany(IRE) looked likely to appreciate this quicker ground but, having raced prominently from the off, she found little at the business end of affairs. This was a little disappointing as she certainly did not build on her promising debut. (op 3-1)

Swanky Lady, who cost 240,000gns, is a half-sister to Selinka, twice a winner in Listed company over 7f and a mile. This was a promising debut and one would imagine that she will derive plenty from it. An ordinary maiden should be within her ability. (op 20-1)

Lille Ida, who showed promise on her debut at Lingfield, had reportedly been going well at home and was well supported on course. In the event, however, she was quite disappointing. (op 5-1)

Twiglet(IRE), a half-sister to Pearl King, a 1m winner at three, was unconsidered in the betting and ran a fair race in the circumstances. She should improve for the run. (op 66-1)

Kashoof, up there from the start, was another who failed to run up to her previous form. Her Newmarket effort suggested that she would be a major player in this company but she proved disappointing. Apparently she lost her action, though. Official explanation: jockey said filly lost its action (op 9-4 tchd 3-1)

Naughty Frida(IRE) Official explanation: jockey said filly missed the break

4062 KENNELS EBF CLASSIFIED STKS 7f

5:45 (5:49) (Class 2) 3-Y-0+

£12,775 (£3,825; £1,912; £957; £477; £239) **Stalls** High

Form				RPR
5100	**1**		**Laa Rayb (USA)**[19] 3503 3-8-12 94 ... JoeFanning 2 (M Johnston) *trckd ldr: led over 2f out: drvn over 1f out: styd on wl* **10/1**	101
5161	**2**	*3/4*	**Diamond Diva**[13] 3670 3-8-9 95 ... EddieAhern 10 (J W Hills) *lw: prom: rdn to chse wnr over 1f out: styd on wl but readily hld ins fnl f* **9/2**[2]	96
0-30	**3**	*nk*	**Minority Report**[42] 2755 7-9-4 92 ... LDettori 12 (L M Cumani) *lw: hld up in rr on inner: nt clr run briefly over 2f out: gd prog over 1f out to chse ldrs fnl f: kpt on same pce last 100yds* **10/3**[1]	103+
2213	**4**	*nk*	**Binanti**[4] 3941 7-9-4 92 ... FrancisNorton 1 (P R Chamings) *lw: trckd ldrs: shkn up and nt qckn 2f out: sn outpcd: styd on fnl f: nvr gng to chal* **9/2**[2]	99
6660	**5**	*1*	**Majuro (IRE)**[41] 2788 3-8-12 95 ... JHBowman 9 (M R Channon) *cl up: outpcd 2f out: kpt on same pce after* **33/1**	94
-000	**6**	*nk*	**Jedburgh**[19] 3505 6-9-4 95 ... (b) TedDurcan 11 (J L Dunlop) *hld up in last trio: nt clr run over 2f out: effrt wl over 1f out: drvn and kpt on: nvr rchd ldrs* **12/1**	95

0162 **7** *shd* **Turnkey**[4] 3975 5-9-4 95 AdeleRothery 13 95
(D Nicholls) *lw: dwlt: hld up in last: taken to wd outside and prog over 2f out: chsd ldrs over 1f out: one pce and no imp after* **15/2**

0200 **8** *2 1/2* **Bonus (IRE)**[39] 2858 7-9-4 93 (bt[1]) JMurtagh 14 88
(G A Butler) *sn settled bhd ldrs: lost pl 2f out: steadily wknd* **16/1**

0050 **9** *3/4* **Royal Storm (IRE)**[4] 3941 8-9-4 86 JimCrowley 4 86
(Mrs A J Perrett) *led to over 2f out: wknd over 1f out* **50/1**

3406 **10** *hd* **Jo'Burg (USA)**[20] 3463 3-8-12 95 RyanMoore 8 84
(Mrs A J Perrett) *settled in midfield: rdn wl over 2f out: no prog: wknd over 1f out* **12/1**

0420 **11** *3/4* **Ceremonial Jade (UAE)**[40] 2817 4-9-4 94 KerrinMcEvoy 5 84
(M Botti) *hld up in last trio: c wd into st: no prog over 2f out: wknd over 1f out* **13/2**[3]

430 **12** *10* **Sand Cat**[25] 3329 4-9-4 95 GeorgeBaker 3 57
(G L Moore) *in tch tl wknd jst over 2f out: sn bhd* **50/1**

1m 27.68s (-0.36) **Going Correction** +0.025s/f (Good)
WFA 3 from 4yo+ 6lb **12** Ran SP% **121.8**
Speed ratings (Par 109): **103,102,101,101,100 99,99,97,96,95 95,83**
CSF £55.67 TOTE £12.30: £3.50, £1.80, £1.70; EX 62.00 Trifecta £120.40 Pool £967.22. - 5.70 winning units. Place 6 £781.80, Place 5 £156.70..
Owner Sheikh Ahmed Al Maktoum **Bred** Darley **Trained** Middleham Moor, N Yorks

FOCUS
A competitive contest with there being little between the whole field at the weights, and it was no surprise to see one of the three-year-olds score. It was steadily run and the time was slower than that recorded by Rio De La Plata in the Vintage Stake earlier on the card. Probably not form to take too literally.

NOTEBOOK
Laa Rayb(USA) looked a top-notch handicapper when winning impressively at Sandown back in June, but disappointing efforts back there and at Newmarket, admittedly off significantly higher marks, led to him being dropped into this classified stakes. Back down in distance, he was made plenty of use of and was always doing enough to hold the latecomers. Still open to plenty of physical improvement, he has the potential to develop into a pattern performer in time. (op 11-1)
Diamond Diva has been progressing nicely, but was up another 5lb and she was unable to quite match the back-to-form winner. This filly remains on an upward curve and connections will no doubt be keen to gain some black type with her at some stage. (op 11-2)
Minority Report, winner of this contest last year, seems to struggle in handicaps these days and he found this a lot easier, looking unfortunate not to get second having been held up in his run. Whilst it is tempting to say he can gain compensation, placing him is not going to be easy. (op 4-1)
Binanti surprised everyone with his Royal Ascot victory, considering he has such a poor win record, but he has since run well off his new mark in the Totesport International at Ascot and this was another fine effort, just lacking a change of gear late on. (tchd 11-2 in a place)
Majuro(IRE), who not for the first time got quite warm, looked one of the more interesting outsiders on the best of his form and he ran well, but could not dominate as he likes to and is likely to remain vulnerable back in handicaps.
Jedburgh looks to be on his way back to something like his best and this slightly unfortunate effort was a further step in the right direction. He can be rated better than the bare form.
Turnkey was interesting on this step back up in trip, having been in good form in sprint handicaps, but he was forced to challenge wide and did not convince with his finishing effort. (op 13-2)
Sand Cat Official explanation: jockey said gelding hung left throughout
T/Jkpt: Not won. T/Plt: £781.80 to a £1 stake. Pool: £236,790.10. 221.10 winning tickets. T/Qpdt: £156.70 to a £1 stake. Pool: £11,504.00. 54.30 winning tickets. JN

3641 KEMPTON (A.W) (R-H)

Wednesday, August 1

OFFICIAL GOING: Standard
Wind: Nil.

4063 WEATHERBYS VAT SERVICES APPRENTICE H'CAP (ROUND 8) 1m (P)
6:20 (6:21) (Class 5) (0-70,66) 4-Y-0+ **£2,817** (£838; £418; £209) **Stalls** High

Form RPR

4313 **1** **Le Chiffre (IRE)**[14] 3644 5-9-9 65 (p) PatrickHills 3 77
(S Curran) *chsd ldrs: led ins fnl 2f: sn rdn: kpt on strly fnl f* **11/2**[3]

-404 **2** *1 3/4* **Chief Exec**[33] 3056 5-9-7 66 HaddenFrost[(3)] 9 74
(B J Llewellyn) *chsd ldrs: rdn to chal ins fnl 2f: kpt on same pce ins fnl f* **15/2**

0032 **3** *1/2* **Bolton Hall (IRE)**[8] 3816 5-9-1 57 JamieMoriarty 13 64+
(R A Fahey) *in rr: rdn 3f out: styd on fr 2f out and gng on cl home but nvr gng pce to press ldrs* **7/2**[1]

3005 **4** *1 1/4* **Wee Charlie Castle (IRE)**[20] 3457 4-8-13 58 (b[1]) AmyBaker[(3)] 2 62
(G C H Chung) *trcking ldrs whn hmpd and lost pl 5f out: sn rcvrd and chsd ldrs over 2f out: wknd ins fnl f* **16/1**

6060 **5** *nk* **October Ben**[14] 3644 4-8-13 60 FrankiePickard[(5)] 5 63
(M D I Usher) *slowly away: in rr and t.k.h: wd into st 3f out: hdwy fr 2f out: fin wl but nvr a threat* **16/1**

6140 **6** *nk* **Colinca's Lad (IRE)**[12] 3711 5-9-3 59 SaleemGolam 6 62
(T T Clement) *led: rdn over 3f out: hdd ins fnl 2f: wknd fnl f* **5/1**[2]

0155 **7** *1 1/2* **Out For A Stroll**[12] 3711 8-8-12 59 FLenclud[(5)] 12 58
(S C Williams) *in rr: hdwy over 2f out: kpt on fnl f but nvr gng pce to trble ldrs* **10/1**

6556 **8** *1 1/2* **Magic Warrior**[14] 3644 7-9-9 65 TravisBlock 14 61
(J C Fox) *in rr: wd into st 3f out: sme prog fnl f: nvr in contention* **8/1**

6206 **9** *1* **Al Rayanah**[8] 3826 4-9-1 60 KirstyMilczarek[(3)] 11 53
(G Prodromou) *slowly away: t.k.h in rr: nvr bttr than mid-div* **33/1**

0505 **10** *nk* **Black Sea Pearl**[4] 3950 4-9-7 63 LiamJones 4 56+
(P W D'Arcy) *in tch: rdn and effrt whn sddle slipped over 2f out: nt rcvr* **11/1**

4000 **11** *1 3/4* **Border Edge**[9] 3799 9-9-2 58 (b) JamesMillman 1 47
(J J Bridger) *a towards rr* **25/1**

12 *1/2* **Raise Again (IRE)**[79] 1733 4-9-0 61 NBazeley[(5)] 10 49
(Mrs P N Dutfield) *mid-div: rdn and effrt over 3f out: nvr in contention* **66/1**

3-00 **13** *nk* **Devonia Plains (IRE)**[87] 1507 5-8-10 55 (b[1]) KMay[(3)] 8 42
(Mrs P N Dutfield) *chsd ldrs: rdn over 3f out: wknd 2f out* **66/1**

1005 **14** *14* **Northern Desert (IRE)**[13] 3675 8-9-7 66 WilliamCarson[(3)] 7 21
(P W Hiatt) *chsd ldrs: rdn 4f out: wknd 3f out* **18/1**

1m 39.94s (-0.86) **Going Correction** -0.075s/f (Stan) **14** Ran SP% **121.4**
Speed ratings (Par 103): **101,99,98,97,97 96,95,93,92,92 90,90,90,76**
CSF £45.84 CT £171.79 TOTE £6.40: £1.50, £3.20, £1.80; EX 45.10.
Owner L M Power **Bred** Agricola Del Parco **Trained** Faringdon, Oxon

FOCUS
A moderate handicap, run at just an average early pace, and it was probably a slight advantage to race prominently. The winner is rated pretty much back to her best.

Black Sea Pearl Official explanation: jockey said saddle slipped

4064 AZURE HOSPITALITY H'CAP 1m (P)
6:50 (6:51) (Class 6) (0-65,65) 3-Y-O **£2,047** (£604; £302) **Stalls** High

Form RPR

4-03 **1** **Good Effect (USA)**[15] 3620 3-9-4 62 SebSanders 1 70
(A P Jarvis) *chsd ldrs: rdn and hdwy fr 2f out: led ins fnl f: drvn out* **9/4**[1]

0600 **2** *3/4* **Shouldntbethere (IRE)**[21] 3429 3-9-5 63 RobertHavlin 9 69
(Mrs P N Dutfield) *in rr: stl plenty to do over 2f out: str run over 1f out and fin wl to take 2nd cl home but a hld by wnr* **33/1**

2301 **3** *1* **Kunte Kinteh**[14] 3639 3-9-7 65 AdrianTNicholls 12 69
(D Nicholls) *led: rdn 2f out: hdd ins fnl f: styd on same pce and ct for 2nd nr fin* **13/2**[3]

-050 **4** *2* **Soldier Field**[42] 2767 3-9-0 61 NeilChalmers[(3)] 7 60
(A M Balding) *mid-div: rdn 3f out: hdwy 2f out: styng on whn n.m.r 1f out: kpt on again cl home* **20/1**

5300 **5** *nk* **Six Of Hearts**[20] 3475 3-9-6 64 TPQueally 5 63
(J A Osborne) *chsd ldrs: rdn to chal ins fnl 2f: sn no imp: wknd wl ins fnl f* **16/1**

030 **6** *3/4* **Mabaahej (USA)**[65] 2083 3-9-7 65 DaneO'Neill 14 62
(B W Hills) *chsd ldr: rdn 3f out: effrt 2f out but never quite gng pce to chal: wknd ins fnl f* **8/1**

4426 **7** *2 1/2* **Inquisitress**[15] 3620 3-8-12 59 LiamJones[(3)] 11 50
(J J Bridger) *chsd ldrs: rdn 3f out: wknd fnl f* **12/1**

0-00 **8** *1 1/4* **Christalini**[48] 2598 3-9-7 65 (b[1]) PatDobbs 13 53
(J C Fox) *t.k.h: chsd ldrs: rdn 3f out: wknd fnl f* **14/1**

2052 **9** *shd* **Astroangel**[8] 3826 3-9-0 63 PatrickHills[(5)] 8 51
(M H Tompkins) *chsd ldrs: rdn along 4f out: effrt over 2f out but nver in contention: wknd fnl f* **7/1**

0002 **10** *6* **Puissant Princess (IRE)**[22] 3393 3-9-6 64 J-PGuillambert 3 38
(J W Hills) *t.k.h: stdd in rr: rdn and effrt over 3f out: nvr in contention* **5/1**[2]

060 **11** *5* **Sea Willow (IRE)**[11] 3743 3-8-13 60 MarcHalford[(3)] 10 23
(D R C Elsworth) *a in rr: no ch whn wd bnd 3f out* **14/1**

000 **12** *1* **Centenary (IRE)**[3] 3997 3-9-2 60 (v[1]) TPO'Shea 4 21
(J J Quinn) *a in rr: no ch whn wd bnd 3f out* **16/1**

00 **13** *2 1/2* **Millenium Sun (IRE)**[15] 3613 3-9-0 65 SCreighton[(7)] 2 20
(E J Creighton) *a in rr* **100/1**

0000 **14** *26* **Not Too Taxing**[91] 1410 3-8-11 62 KMay[(7)] 6 —
(G A Ham) *bhd fr 1/2-way* **40/1**

1m 40.19s (-0.61) **Going Correction** -0.075s/f (Stan) **14** Ran SP% **128.3**
Speed ratings (Par 98): **100,99,98,96,95 95,92,91,91,85 80,79,76,50**
CSF £105.92 CT £473.34 TOTE £3.30: £1.40, £8.20, £1.80; EX 108.10.
Owner Geoffrey Bishop and Ann Jarvis **Bred** Golden Gate Stud **Trained** Twyford, Bucks

FOCUS
A modest three-year-old handicap. Sound form, the winner up 4lb.

4065 DIGIBET CASINO NURSERY 6f (P)
7:20 (7:21) (Class 4) 2-Y-O **£3,886** (£1,156; £577; £288) **Stalls** High

Form RPR

606 **1** **What Katie Did (IRE)**[44] 2724 2-8-7 62 MartinDwyer 7 65
(J A Osborne) *chsd ldrs: hrd rdn over 1f out: styd on wl to ld fnl 50yds: won gng away* **15/2**

224 **2** *1* **Far Gone**[44] 2717 2-9-3 72 HayleyTurner 11 72
(M L W Bell) *trckd ldr: rdn to ld 1f out: hdd and no ex fnl 50yds* **7/1**

3502 **3** *1 1/4* **Bookiebasher Dude**[21] 3423 2-9-7 76 RobertHavlin 12 72
(M Quinn) *led: rdn over 2f out: hdd 1f out: sn one pce* **14/1**

51 **4** *3/4* **Maddy**[21] 3423 2-8-11 66 SebSanders 5 60+
(R M Beckett) *in tch: rdn and outpcd 3f out: rdn and kpt on fr over 1f out: gng on cl home* **6/1**[3]

006 **5** *nk* **Biased Opinion (IRE)**[37] 2949 2-8-9 64 TQuinn 10 57
(H J L Dunlop) *chsd ldrs: rdn over 2f out: styd on same pce fr over 1f out* **11/1**

050 **6** *3/4* **Seeking The Star (CAN)**[35] 2991 2-8-10 70 (b[1]) AhmedAjtebi[(5)] 3 61
(D M Simcock) *s.i.s: bhd: rdn 3f out: styd on u.p fnl 2f: gng on cl home but nvr a danger* **5/1**[2]

3506 **7** *1 1/2* **Evenstorm (USA)**[14] 3648 2-8-12 67 TPQueally 9 53
(B Gubby) *in rr: hdwy on ins fr 2f out: styd on ins fnl f but nvr a danger* **33/1**

064 **8** *3/4* **Our Kally**[18] 3532 2-7-13 61 FrankiePickard[(7)] 8 45
(M D I Usher) *in rr: pushed along fr 1/2-way: mod prog fnl f* **20/1**

0020 **9** *1* **Vigano (IRE)**[19] 3508 2-9-5 74 J-PGuillambert 2 55
(S Kirk) *chsd ldrs: rdn 3f out: wknd 2f out* **16/1**

2032 **10** *1* **Our Sunnie**[8] 3812 2-8-12 67 AdrianTNicholls 4 45
(D Nicholls) *chsd ldrs: rdn: 2f out: continually threw hd up fr over 1f out and sn btn* **12/1**

041 **11** *1 3/4* **Penrice Castle**[41] 2797 2-9-2 71 PatDobbs 6 44
(R Hannon) *in rr but in tch: rdn 1/2-way: nvr in contention after* **9/2**[1]

064 **12** *3/4* **Merchant Navy**[49] 2575 2-9-7 76 DaneO'Neill 1 47
(E A L Dunlop) *outpcd most of way* **7/1**

1m 13.87s (0.17) **Going Correction** -0.075s/f (Stan) **12** Ran SP% **122.2**
Speed ratings (Par 96): **95,93,92,91,90 89,87,86,85,83 81,80**
CSF £61.16 CT £746.96 TOTE £11.00: £3.20, £2.50, £3.10; EX 101.10.
Owner Mountgrange Stud **Bred** Brian Williamson **Trained** Upper Lambourn, Berks

FOCUS
Just a fair nursery, run at a strong early pace. The winner improved on his handicap bow.

NOTEBOOK
What Katie Did(IRE) ◆, making his nursery and All-Weather bow, showed his true colours and broke his duck at the fourth attempt in ready fashion. The strong pace over this extra furlong proved much to his liking and this 80,000gns purchase appeals as the type to progress further in this sphere. (op 8-1)
Far Gone, another stepping into this company for the first time, showed improved form for the step up in trip and return to a sounder surface. She ought to find a race before too long on this evidence. (tchd 11-2)
Bookiebasher Dude again showed decent early speed to lead and stuck to his task when headed nearing the final furlong. He looks high enough in the weights in this sphere, but still reversed form with the fourth and surely similar tactics over 5f now looks to be his best chance of finding a race. (op 10-1 tchd 16-1)
Maddy hit a flat spot before staying on well at the business end and failed to confirm her Lingfield maiden form with the third. She has to prove she is up to this sort of mark now, but another furlong should prove more to her liking on recent evidence. (op 7-2)
Biased Opinion(IRE) ran below his recent level on this switch to a nursery and was another who left the impression he may improve for a stiffer test in this sphere. (op 8-1 tchd 12-1)
Seeking The Star(CAN), popular in the betting ring ahead of this nursery debut, for which he was blinkered first-time, got himself outpaced after a slow start and was never a serious player. He still caught the eye in finishing his race, however, and should be given another chance. (op 8-1 tchd 9-2)

Penrice Castle, off the mark over the minimum trip at Lingfield last time, was never in the hunt from off the pace over this extra furlong. A return to 5f and a more positive ride now looks in order for her. (tchd 4-1)

4066 DIGIBET SPORTS BETTING MAIDEN STKS 6f (P)
7:50 (7:51) (Class 4) 3-Y-0+ **£4,728** (£1,406; £702; £351) **Stalls** High

Form RPR
4045 1 **Even Bolder**[7] 3852 4-9-0 63 (p) SophieDoyle(7) 11 75
(R Simpson) *trckd ldr gng wl appr fnl 2f: shkn up fnl f: hld on wl whn strly chal sn after* **8/1**
0-02 2 hd **Tarkamara (IRE)**[33] 3062 3-8-12 79 TQuinn 5 69
(P F I Cole) *chsd ldrs: wnt 2nd 2f out: sn hrd rdn and styd on to chal ins fnl f but a jst hld by wnr* **11/4**[1]
00 3 4 **Confucius Classic (IRE)**[39] 2878 3-9-3 0 JimCrowley 6 62
(J R Boyle) *chsd ldrs: rdn over 2f out: styd on u.p to go 3rd fnl f but nvr nr ldng pair* **33/1**
0-4 4 2 ½ **Tumbelini**[68] 2012 3-8-12 0 MartinDwyer 9 49+
(C F Wall) *chsd ldrs: rdn over 3f out: kpt on fnl 2f but nvr gng pce to rch ldng trio* **3/1**[2]
2 5 ½ **Oystermouth**[72] 1883 3-8-12 0 PatDobbs 8 47+
(R Charlton) *in rr: rdn 1/2-way: sme prog fr over 1f out but nvr in contention* **7/2**[3]
36 6 1 **Gimme Some Lovin (IRE)**[39] 2878 3-8-12 0 (t) FergusSweeney 1 44+
(D W P Arbuthnot) *s.i.s: in rr: pushed along 3f out: kpt on wl fr over 1f out and gng on cl home but nvr a threat* **7/1**
0- 7 1 ¼ **Vintage (IRE)**[433] 1959 3-8-10 0 JackMitchell(7) 12 45
(P Mitchell) *led tl hdd over 2f out and hung rt: wknd sn after* **25/1**
56 8 4 **Up The Chimney**[50] 2541 3-9-3 0 SebSanders 2 32
(A P Jarvis) *mid-div: rdn 3f out: nvr in contention: wknd 2f out* **12/1**
60 9 1 **Regal Cheer**[22] 3395 3-8-12 0 HayleyTurner 3 24
(C F Wall) *a in rr* **50/1**
\- 10 1 **Danetime Rose (IRE)** 3-8-9 0 AndrewElliott(3) 10 21
(Miss V Haigh) *chsd ldrs: rdn over 3f out: wknd wl over 2f out* **66/1**
11 2 **Ivanasbo** 3-9-3 0 RichardThomas 7 19
(C G Cox) *green and a in rr* **33/1**

1m 12.32s (-1.38) **Going Correction** -0.075s/f (Stan)
WFA 3 from 4yo 4lb 11 Ran SP% **118.4**
Speed ratings (Par 105): **106,105,100,97,96 95,93,88,86,85 82**
CSF £29.45 TOTE £11.60: £2.90, £1.50, £5.40; EX 37.80.
Owner Carnival Quest **Bred** Raffin Bloodstock **Trained** Lambourn, Berks

FOCUS
Essentially a modest maiden, in which the winner was pretty exposed but was still up 6lb. The time was good and a few of these will improve in handicaps.
Ivanasbo Official explanation: jockey said gelding resented the kickback

4067 DIGIBET.COM H'CAP 2m (P)
8:20 (8:21) (Class 5) (0-75,75) 4-Y-0+ **£2,817** (£838; £418; £209) **Stalls** High

Form RPR
1205 1 **Newnham (IRE)**[28] 3216 6-9-0 75 JackMitchell(7) 5 85
(J R Boyle) *hld up in rr: stdy hdwy fr 3f out: swtchd lft 2f out: str run fr over 1f out to ld last half f: comf* **4/1**[1]
0000 2 ¾ **Valance (IRE)**[35] 2994 7-9-5 73 (tp) JHBowman 2 82
(C R Egerton) *chsd ldrs: wnt 2nd 4f out: rdn over 2f out: led 1f out: hdd and outpcd last half f* **10/1**
0/65 3 3 **This Way That Way**[26] 3284 6-8-2 56 oh1 TPO'Shea 7 61
(Ian Williams) *chsd ldr: led 6f out: rdn 3f out: hdd 1f out: sn btn* **20/1**
1111 4 nk **Champagne Shadow (IRE)**[4] 3945 6-9-2 73 6ex (p) TravisBlock(3) 11 78
(Miss Tor Sturgis) *mid-div: rdn over 3f out: styd on fnl 2f: kpt on cl home but nvr a threat* **4/1**[1]
0501 5 ¾ **Mister Completely (IRE)**[14] 3653 6-8-3 64 (v) SophieDoyle(7) 12 68
(Ms J S Doyle) *in rr: racd towards outside and hdwy over 3f out: styd on same pce fnl 2f* **12/1**
0000 6 5 **Follow On**[4] 3945 5-8-6 60 (v) JimCrowley 3 58
(A P Jarvis) *s.i.s: in rr: rdn over 3f out: mod prog fnl 2f* **8/1**[3]
0613 7 2 ½ **Squiffy**[25] 3300 4-8-2 56 oh3 ChrisCatlin 10 51
(P D Cundell) *chsd ldrs: rdn 3f out: wknd 2f out* **11/2**[2]
2420 8 1 **Prince Des Neiges (FR)**[33] 3047 4-8-6 63 AndrewElliott(3) 6 57
(A M Hales) *led after 1f out: hdd 6f out: wknd over 2f out* **14/1**
1261 9 1 ½ **Adage**[16] 3598 4-8-6 60 (t) FergusSweeney 1 52
(David Pinder) *in tch: rdn and sme prog 5f out: wknd 3f out* **4/1**[1]
0/42 10 1 **Voir Dire**[72] 1888 5-8-2 56 oh6 DavidKinsella 9 47
(Mrs P N Dutfield) *a in rr* **14/1**
10/0 11 16 **In Deep**[42] 2770 6-8-2 56 oh6 RichardThomas 4 27
(Mrs P N Dutfield) *sn rdn along: a in rr* **50/1**

3m 28.98s (-2.42) **Going Correction** -0.075s/f (Stan) 11 Ran SP% **123.3**
Speed ratings (Par 103): **103,102,101,100,100 98,96,96,95,95 87**
CSF £48.00 CT £737.01 TOTE £5.60: £2.20, £3.60, £5.00; EX 47.80.
Owner M Khan X2 **Bred** Ballygallon Stud **Trained** Epsom, Surrey

FOCUS
A modest staying handicap and sound form, rated through the third and fourth.

4068 BYRNE GROUP LONDON MILE H'CAP (LONDON MILE QUALIFIER) 1m (P)
8:50 (8:50) (Class 3) (0-90,89) 3-Y-0+
£6,855 (£2,052; £1,026; £513; £256; £128) **Stalls** High

Form RPR
2-20 1 **Evident Pride (USA)**[85] 1568 4-9-4 79 DaneO'Neill 7 89
(B R Johnson) *trckd ldrs: drvn to ld 1f out: hld on wl whn strly chal cl home* **11/2**[2]
0021 2 nk **Electric Warrior (IRE)**[21] 3420 4-9-5 83 AndrewElliott(3) 3 92
(K R Burke) *chsd ldrs: rdn and qcknd to chse wnr jst ins fnl f: r.o wl u.p but a jst hld* **7/1**
1302 3 hd **Mataram (USA)**[129] 777 4-9-5 80 SebSanders 2 89+
(W Jarvis) *t.k.h: hld up in rr: hdwy on outside fr 3f out: str run fr over 1f out and styd on to press ldrs cl home but a jst hld* **5/1**[1]
1324 4 2 **Networker**[21] 3437 4-8-11 72 TQuinn 9 76+
(P J McBride) *plld hrd in rr: hdwy fr 3f out: nt clr run 2f out: kpt on fr over 1f out but nvr gng pce to be competitive* **5/1**[1]
2466 5 ½ **Neardown Beauty (IRE)**[32] 3100 4-9-5 80 JamesDoyle 11 83+
(I A Wood) *hld up in rr: n.m.r 2f out: rapid hdwy fnl f: fin wl but nvr a threat to ldrs* **25/1**
020 6 1 **Cool Box (USA)**[53] 2476 3-9-2 84 JimCrowley 5 85
(Mrs A J Perrett) *chsd ldrs: rdn 3f out: styd on same pce fnl 2f* **16/1**
0016 7 nk **Carmenero (GER)**[32] 3111 4-9-1 76 MartinDwyer 12 76
(W R Muir) *chsd ldrs: rdn over 2f out: wknd fnl f* **25/1**
6640 8 ½ **Robustian**[13] 3672 4-9-5 80 StephenCarson 1 79
(Eve Johnson Houghton) *chsd ldrs on outside: rdn 3f out: wknd fnl f* **16/1**
206 9 nk **Vacation (IRE)**[19] 3513 4-9-8 88 PatrickHills(5) 8 86
(V Smith) *in rr: rdn and effrt whn n.m.r ins fnl 2f: nvr in contention* **10/1**
6505 10 nk **Daniel Thomas (IRE)**[34] 3039 5-9-0 75 AmirQuinn 4 73
(Mrs A L M King) *slowly away: a towards rr* **25/1**
0500 11 1 **Rebellious Spirit**[20] 3470 4-9-5 80 ChrisCatlin 6 75
(P W Hiatt) *w ldr: rdn 3f out: stl upsides u.p over 1f out: wknd qckly* **33/1**
1211 12 ½ **Nan Jan**[14] 3644 5-8-11 72 (t) RobertHavlin 13 66
(R Ingram) *in rr: hdwy whn hmpd over 1f out: nt rcvr* **13/2**
3111 13 ½ **Guilded Warrior**[19] 3488 4-10-0 89 FergusSweeney 10 82
(W S Kittow) *slt ld: rdn over 2f out: wknd qckly over 1f out* **6/1**[3]

1m 40.24s (-0.56) **Going Correction** -0.075s/f (Stan)
WFA 3 from 4yo+ 7lb 13 Ran SP% **124.2**
Speed ratings (Par 107): **99,98,98,96,96 95,94,94,93,93 92,92,91**
CSF £43.74 CT £211.78 TOTE £7.50: £2.70, £2.80, £2.20; EX 81.40.
Owner C Lefevre **Bred** Juddmonte Farms Inc **Trained** Ashtead, Surrey
■ Stewards' Enquiry : Martin Dwyer one-day ban: careless riding (Aug 12)

FOCUS
A decent handicap, but the pace was just modest and the bare form can not be rated too positively. The first three all have good records here.

NOTEBOOK
Evident Pride(USA) appreciated the return to Polytrack and ran out a narrow winner on his return from nearly three months off the track. He did not have much in hand, but remains progressive and can get competitive off higher marks. (op 13-2 tchd 5-1)
Electric Warrior(IRE) ran right up to his best off a 4lb higher mark than when winning over course and distance on his previous start. He is progressing into a useful sort. (op 6-1 tchd 11-2)
Mataram(USA) was asked to come from a long way back off just a modest gallop and ran a cracker to take a close third. (op 13-2 tchd 4-1)
Networker raced keenly early on and did not enjoy the best of runs in the straight, so it is fair to say a stronger pace would have suited better. Official explanation: jockey said gelding ran too free (op 9-2 tchd 13-2)
Neardown Beauty(IRE) found herself well off the pace after starting slowly and was denied a clear run in the straight. Official explanation: jockey said filly was slowly into stride (op 20-1)
Rebellious Spirit Official explanation: jockey said gelding hung right
Nan Jan Official explanation: jockey said mare was denied a clear run
Guilded Warrior has shown improved form on soft turf in recent weeks, but he was unable to defy a career-high mark back on Polytrack. (op 7-1 tchd 8-1)

4069 SHAMROCK H'CAP 1m 3f (P)
9:20 (9:20) (Class 5) (0-70,70) 3-Y-0 **£2,817** (£838; £418; £209) **Stalls** High

Form RPR
-120 1 **Raise The Goblet (IRE)**[30] 3159 3-8-10 62 LiamJones(3) 5 70
(W J Haggas) *trckd ldrs: rdn to ld appr fnl 2f: sn hdd but styd pressing ldr: rallied u.p to ld again last strides* **11/1**
6520 2 hd **Risque Heights**[23] 3372 3-9-4 67 JHBowman 3 75
(G A Butler) *in tch: rdn 3f out: styd on to ld 2f out: kpt on u.p tl ct last strides* **25/1**
04 3 5 **Hill Queen (IRE)**[30] 3166 3-9-6 69 NickyMackay 10 69
(L M Cumani) *chsd ldrs: rdn over 2f out: styd on same pce for wl hld 3rd fr over 1f out* **9/1**
4160 4 ½ **Arctic Wings (IRE)**[48] 2602 3-9-7 70 MartinDwyer 1 69
(W R Muir) *sn led: hdd appr fnl 2f: wknd fnl f* **12/1**
0240 5 ½ **A Mothers Love**[27] 3249 3-8-8 57 TQuinn 7 55
(P J McBride) *t.k.h in rr: hdwy fr 2f out: kpt on ins fnl f but nvr gng pce to rch ldrs* **14/1**
6004 6 1 **Hot Diamond**[12] 3705 3-9-0 66 MarcHalford(3) 4 62
(D R C Elsworth) *in rr: hdwy on outside over 4f out: chsd ldrs 3f out: wknd fnl f* **3/1**[1]
50-0 7 ½ **Nothing Is Forever (IRE)**[72] 1887 3-9-2 65 JimCrowley 14 60
(Mrs A J Perrett) *chsd ldrs: rdn over 3f out: wknd ins fnl 2f* **40/1**
3142 8 nk **Featherlight**[32] 3082 3-8-7 56 RobertHavlin 8 51
(Jamie Poulton) *in rr: rdn and hdwy fr 2f out: nvr gng pce to be competitive* **10/3**[2]
0134 9 ½ **Sweet World**[15] 3622 3-9-0 63 SebSanders 12 57
(A P Jarvis) *in rr: rdn and sme prog fnl 2f: nvr in contention* **14/1**
4401 10 ½ **Personal Column**[20] 3456 3-9-7 70 J-PGuillambert 11 63
(T G Mills) *mid-div: rdn 3f out: n.d after* **6/1**[3]
0-60 11 2 **Bring It On Home**[25] 3335 3-9-5 68 PatDobbs 6 58
(G L Moore) *a towards rr* **20/1**
5350 12 1 ¾ **Force Celebre (IRE)**[48] 2610 3-9-1 69 PatrickHills(5) 9 56
(M H Tompkins) *in rr: sme hdwy 4f out: sn wknd* **25/1**
000- 13 36 **Rikochet**[274] 6285 3-8-10 59 ow1 AmirQuinn 2 —
(Mrs A L M King) *chsd ldrs: rdn 4f out: sn wknd: t.o* **66/1**
-063 P **Penny From Heaven (IRE)**[24] 3351 3-9-5 68 DaneO'Neill 13 —
(E A L Dunlop) *chsd ldrs: rdn and wknd fr 4f out: p.u over 1f out: lame* **14/1**

2m 21.04s (-1.64) **Going Correction** -0.075s/f (Stan) 14 Ran SP% **124.8**
Speed ratings (Par 100): **102,101,98,97,97 96,96,96,95,95 94,92,66,—**
CSF £273.92 CT £2592.47 TOTE £16.00: £4.70, £6.50, £3.50; EX 301.10 Place 6 £198.50, Place 5 £107.09..
Owner J Hanson **Bred** Miss Eileen Grealish **Trained** Newmarket, Suffolk

FOCUS
A modest handicap in which the pace was not strong, and the form has not been rated too positively.
T/Plt: £152.00 to a £1 stake. Pool: £50,484.30. 242.35 winning tickets. T/Qpdt: £32.30 to a £1 stake. Pool: £4,090.30. 93.50 winning tickets. ST

3841 LEICESTER (R-H)
Wednesday, August 1
OFFICIAL GOING: Good to soft (good in places; odd soft patches between 5f and 7f markers; 7.3)
Wind: Nil Weather: Cloudy with sunny spells

4070 E B F POTTERS CARPETS MAIDEN STKS 5f 218y
6:00 (6:00) (Class 4) 2-Y-0 **£4,857** (£1,445; £722; £360) **Stalls** High

Form RPR
3 1 **Oasis Wind**[23] 3383 2-8-12 0 TolleyDean(5) 1 82+
(P F I Cole) *awkward leaving stalls: mde all: pushed clr fr over 1f out* **4/6**[1]
2 4 **Bellomi (IRE)** 2-9-3 0 DarryllHolland 7 70+
(M R Channon) *hld up: hdwy over 2f out: wnt 2nd and hung rt fnl f: no ch w wnr* **9/1**
0 3 2 ½ **Home**[18] 3552 2-9-3 0 StephenDonohoe 6 62+
(E A L Dunlop) *hld up: r.o ins fnl f: nvr trbld ldrs* **14/1**

0 **4** ½ **Jal Music**[13] 3687 2-9-3 0 .... NickyMackay 2 61
(L M Cumani) *prom: chsd wnr over 3f out: rdn over 1f out: wknd ins fnl f* **20/1**
5 1 ¼ **Game Park (USA)** 2-9-3 0 .... JamieSpencer 3 57
(J R Fanshawe) *hld up: hdwy over 2f out: hung rt fr over 1f out: sn wknd* **4/1**[2]
0 **6** ½ **Conquisto**[74] 1832 2-9-3 0 .... AdamKirby 4 55
(C G Cox) *prom: rdn over 2f out: wknd over 1f out* **8/1**[3]
7 3 **Zarees** 2-9-3 0 .... JohnEgan 10 46
(J S Moore) *chsd wnr tl rdn over 3f out: wknd over 2f out* **50/1**
0 **8** 17 **Me Me Me**[8] 3823 2-9-3 0 .... VinceSlattery 5 —
(M J Wallace) *dwlt: outpcd* **66/1**
9 17 **Westwood Dawn** 2-9-3 0 .... JimmyQuinn 8 —
(Mrs N Macauley) *trckd ldrs: racd keenly: wknd over 2f out* **50/1**

1m 12.93s (-0.27) **Going Correction** -0.075s/f (Good) 9 Ran SP% **117.9**
Speed ratings (Par 96): **98,92,89,88,87 86,82,59,37**
CSF £7.85 TOTE £1.50: £1.10, £2.90, £3.80; EX 7.10.
Owner Miss Alfiya Shaykhutdinova **Bred** B Emery **Trained** Whatcombe, Oxon

FOCUS
An ordinary maiden in which the first three all finished with something in the tank. The winner was quite impressive.

NOTEBOOK
Oasis Wind, who shaped with adequate promise on his debut at Windsor, was faced with similar conditions here, but he had clearly improved on that initial effort and led throughout for a smooth success. He is nothing out of the ordinary, but looks capable of better still on a sounder surface and could be interesting in handicaps. (op 5-6 tchd 10-11 in places)
Bellomi(IRE), a 110,000gns son of Lemon Drop Kid, comes from a stable who can ready one to win first time up, but he looked green under pressure and could not mount a challenge to the winner. This was a highly pleasing debut though and he should have little trouble finding a small maiden. (op 15-2 tchd 10-1)
Home, never involved in a 7f maiden at Salisbury on his debut, has clearly learnt from that experience and he shaped much more promisingly. There looks to be a maiden in him, but there is no doubting he will end up contesting handicaps. (tchd 16-1)
Jal Music showed up well early and has clearly learned from his debut effort, but nurseries are where he is likely to excel. (op 14-1)
Game Park(USA) comes from a yard whose juveniles tend to benefit significantly from their debut runs and it is safe to assume he will improve on this next time. (op 10-3)
Conquisto, down the field in a decent Newbury maiden on his debut back in May, had not been seen since, but showed enough to suggest he will be of interest once handicapping. (op 14-1)

4071 LORDS ELECTRICAL CLAIMING STKS 7f 9y
6:35 (6:35) (Class 5) 3-Y-O **£3,238** (£963; £481; £240) **Stalls** Centre

Form RPR
0302 **1** **Smash N'Grab (IRE)**[5] 3918 3-8-13 50 .... AndrewMullen(3) 10 59
(K A Ryan) *mde all: rdn over 1f out: styd on: hung lft towards fin* **15/2**
0605 **2** 1 ¼ **High Five Society**[50] 2538 3-8-13 52 .... (b[1]) PaulEddery 7 53
(S R Bowring) *chsd wnr: rdn and hung rt fr over 1f out: styd on same pce ins fnl f* **10/1**
6020 **3** ¾ **Kassuta**[15] 3605 3-8-2 55 .... (v[1]) JimmyQuinn 11 40
(S C Williams) *chsd ldrs: rdn over 1f out: no ex ins fnl f* **11/2**[3]
2613 **4** nk **Zelos (IRE)**[5] 3922 3-9-3 61 .... (b) JamieSpencer 4 54
(J A Osborne) *wnt lft s: hld up: hdwy over 2f out: sn rdn and hung rt: nt run on* **13/8**[1]
3526 **5** 2 **Fractured Foxy**[61] 2200 3-8-12 67 .... GrahamGibbons 5 43
(J J Quinn) *chsd ldrs: rdn over 2f out: sn edgd rt: no ex ins fnl f* **7/2**[2]
6405 **6** 7 **Totally Free**[6] 3870 3-9-1 58 .... (v) AdamKirby 6 27
(M D I Usher) *prom over 4f* **25/1**
-055 **7** 3 ½ **Inimical**[19] 3490 3-8-8 48 .... LPKeniry 1 11
(W S Kittow) *hmpd s: hld up: effrt over 2f out: sn wknd* **14/1**
0060 **8** 3 **Cherri Fosfate**[64] 2110 3-9-0 63 .... (v) GaryWales(7) 3 16
(D Carroll) *hmpd s: bhd: sme hdwy over 2f out: sn rdn and wknd* **25/1**
0000 **9** 3 ½ **Kings Shillings**[71] 1921 3-8-13 50 .... (v) DanielTudhope 12 —
(D Carroll) *chsd ldrs tl rdn and wknd over 2f out* **66/1**
00-0 **10** 13 **Kerswell**[45] 2696 3-8-8 55 .... DarryllHolland 2 —
(B R Millman) *hmpd s: in rr: rdn and wknd 1/2-way* **20/1**
6 **11** 9 **Correy**[11] 3732 3-8-2 0 .... DaleGibson 9 —
(B Palling) *dwlt: outpcd* **40/1**

1m 25.81s (-0.29) **Going Correction** -0.075s/f (Good) 11 Ran SP% **119.6**
Speed ratings (Par 100): **98,96,95,95,93 85,81,77,73,58 48**
CSF £75.51 TOTE £9.30: £2.80, £4.20, £2.20; EX 54.80.Kassuta was claimed by John A. Harris for £5,000. Zelos was claimed by D. J. Ffrench Davis for £10,000
Owner The Five K Club **Bred** Paul Kavanagh **Trained** Hambleton, N Yorks

FOCUS
A competitive enough claimer and the time was decent for the grade. The form has been rated through the runner-up.
Totally Free Official explanation: jockey said gelding moved poorly throughout
Kerswell Official explanation: jockey said filly hung right

4072 COLOURBANK CARPETS H'CAP 1m 1f 218y
7:05 (7:06) (Class 4) (0-80,78) 3-Y-O **£6,309** (£1,416; £1,416; £472; £235) **Stalls** Centre

Form RPR
03 **1** **Snowed Under**[71] 1922 6-9-9 73 .... DarryllHolland 7 81+
(J D Bethell) *hld up: hdwy over 3f out: rdn to ld over 1f out: edgd rt: styd on* **4/1**[2]
6040 **2** ½ **Fabrian**[6] 3882 9-9-2 71 .... TolleyDean(5) 2 78
(R J Price) *trckd ldr over 8f out: racd keenly: rdn over 2f out: edgd rt: styd on* **10/1**
/2-5 **2** dht **Kintbury Cross**[130] 769 5-9-6 70 .... AdamKirby 8 77
(P D Cundell) *hld up: rdn over 3f out: hdwy appr fnl f: styd on* **25/1**
30-3 **4** nk **Limbo King**[37] 2944 3-9-0 73 .... JamieSpencer 3 79
(J R Fanshawe) *hld up: hdwy over 2f out: rdn over 1f out: chsd wnr ins fnl f: unable qck towards fin* **11/4**[1]
3110 **5** 1 ½ **Royal Flynn**[4] 3955 5-9-11 78 .... RichardKingscote(3) 1 81+
(M Dods) *dwlt: hld up: nt clr run over 2f out: styd on ins fnl f: nvr trbld ldrs* **5/1**
230- **6** 3 **Yeoman Spirit (IRE)**[313] 5511 4-9-9 73 .... LPKeniry 9 70
(A M Balding) *prom: rdn over 3f out: wknd over 1f out* **25/1**
5203 **7** ¾ **Sir Arthur (IRE)**[25] 3301 4-9-8 72 .... JohnEgan 4 68
(B Ellison) *led: rdn and hdd over 1f out: wknd ins fnl f* **7/1**
3-33 **8** nk **Monsoon Wedding**[12] 3722 3-8-8 70 .... GregFairley(3) 6 65
(M Johnston) *chsd ldrs: rdn over 4f out: wknd over 1f out* **9/2**[3]
0500 **9** 12 **Speagle (IRE)**[67] 1819 5-9-8 72 .... DanielTudhope 5 43
(D Carroll) *chsd ldrs: rdn over 2f out: sn wknd* **66/1**

2m 6.37s (-1.93) **Going Correction** -0.075s/f (Good)
WFA 3 from 4yo+ 9lb 9 Ran SP% **112.3**
Speed ratings (Par 105): **104,103,103,103,102 99,99,98,89**
Place: F: £3.80, KC £4.80. Exacta: SU/F £21.50, SU/KC £40.00. CSF: SU/F £20.41, SU/KC £47.43. Tricast: SU/F/KC £433.91, SU/KC/F £461.16 TOTE £5.00: £1.50.
Owner Mrs G Fane **Bred** Mrs G Fane **Trained** Middleham Moor, N Yorks

FOCUS
An ordinary handicap. The winner was value for a little further.
Royal Flynn Official explanation: jockey said gelding was denied a clear run

4073 JULIAN GRAVES FRUIT AND NUT SHOP H'CAP 1m 60y
7:35 (7:36) (Class 5) (0-70,70) 3-Y-O **£4,533** (£1,348; £674; £336) **Stalls** High

Form RPR
0401 **1** **Tina's Ridge (IRE)**[7] 3843 3-8-7 56 6ex .... (p) JamieSpencer 7 63
(R Hollinshead) *hld up: hdwy over 2f out: led ins fnl f: drvn out* **9/2**[1]
3533 **2** 1 ½ **Bidable**[9] 3798 3-8-8 60 .... RichardKingscote(3) 2 64
(B Palling) *led: hdd over 6f out: led over 3f out: sn rdn: hdd and unable qck ins fnl f* **6/1**[3]
-500 **3** nk **Our Ruby**[33] 3056 3-9-1 64 .... (b[1]) AdrianMcCarthy 9 67
(P W Chapple-Hyam) *chsd ldrs: rdn over 2f out: sn ev ch: unable qck ins fnl f* **14/1**
044 **4** ½ **Hot Property (IRE)**[30] 3151 3-8-7 56 .... LPKeniry 8 58+
(W R Muir) *mid-div: rdn over 3f out: outpcd over 2f out: r.o ins fnl f* **16/1**
0020 **5** 1 **Cap St Jean (IRE)**[41] 2796 3-8-8 57 .... PaulEddery 1 57
(R Hollinshead) *hld up: hdwy over 1f out: nt rch ldrs* **20/1**
0340 **6** shd **Heaven's Gates**[18] 3540 3-8-1 53 .... AndrewMullen(3) 11 53
(K A Ryan) *chsd ldrs: rdn over 2f out: styd on same pce appr fnl f* **16/1**
-223 **7** 2 ½ **Pivotalia (IRE)**[20] 3455 3-9-4 67 .... AdamKirby 4 61
(W R Swinburn) *prom: rdn over 2f out: rdn and hung rt over 1f out: sn wknd* **11/2**[2]
-602 **8** 1 **Path To Glory**[20] 3469 3-8-4 58 ow4 .... TolleyDean(5) 5 50
(Miss Z C Davison) *hld up: hmpd 6f out: hdwy over 3f out: rdn and wknd over 1f out* **11/2**[2]
-030 **9** nk **New Light**[9] 3804 3-8-5 54 .... JimmyQuinn 3 45
(Eve Johnson Houghton) *hld up: hung rt fr 1/2-way: n.d* **14/1**
3130 **10** 1 **Lordship (IRE)**[5] 3913 3-8-13 62 .... JohnEgan 10 51
(A W Carroll) *hld up: hmpd 5f out: hdwy over 2f out: sn rdn and wknd* **13/2**
2-00 **11** 2 ½ **Greyt Big Stuff (USA)**[12] 3707 3-9-7 70 .... DarryllHolland 12 53
(Miss Gay Kelleway) *led over 6f out: hdd over 3f out: rdn and wknd over 1f out* **12/1**
060 **12** 19 **Officer Material (IRE)**[65] 2077 3-8-5 54 .... DaleGibson 6 —
(C G Cox) *sn outpcd: lost tch fr 1/2-way* **22/1**

1m 45.1s (-0.20) **Going Correction** -0.075s/f (Good) 12 Ran SP% **118.5**
Speed ratings (Par 100): **98,96,96,95,94 94,92,91,90,89 87,68**
CSF £30.72 CT £359.47 TOTE £5.50: £2.20, £2.50, £4.30; EX 43.70.
Owner John L Marriott **Bred** Mrs Chris Harrington **Trained** Upper Longdon, Staffs
■ Stewards' Enquiry : Adrian McCarthy caution: careless riding

FOCUS
A modest handicap run at a steady pace. The form is rated through the placed horses.
Path To Glory Official explanation: jockey said colt ran too free in early stages
New Light Official explanation: jockey said filly was hampered on bend
Lordship(IRE) Official explanation: jockey said gelding ran too free in early stages
Officer Material(IRE) Official explanation: jockey said gelding slipped on bend

4074 EBF LEICESTER BEARINGS MEDIAN AUCTION MAIDEN FILLIES' STKS 5f 218y
8:05 (8:07) (Class 5) 2-Y-O **£3,562** (£1,059; £529; £264) **Stalls** High

Form RPR
04 **1** **Close To Paradise (IRE)**[12] 3706 2-9-0 0 .... JamieSpencer 6 75+
(E A L Dunlop) *trckd ldrs: led over 2f out: drvn out* **13/8**[1]
2 hd **Our Piccadilly (IRE)** 2-9-0 0 .... LPKeniry 8 74
(W S Kittow) *hmpd s: hld up: hdwy 2f out: rdn to chse wnr over 1f out: ev ch ins fnl f: r.o* **20/1**
04 **3** 4 **Observatory Ridge**[5] 3902 2-9-0 0 .... RichardSmith 9 62
(M D I Usher) *wnt lft s: hld up: hdwy 2f out: rdn over 1f out: no ex fnl f* **16/1**
02 **4** nk **Monte Mayor Birdie (IRE)**[11] 3733 2-9-0 0 .... AdamKirby 7 62
(D Haydn Jones) *led over 3f: sn rdn: wknd ins fnl f* **7/1**[3]
5 1 **Green Earrings (IRE)** 2-8-11 0 .... RichardKingscote(3) 5 59+
(R Charlton) *hld up in tch: outpcd 2f out: styng on whn nt clr run ins fnl f: n.d after* **9/4**[2]
6 ¾ **Maiden Miss (IRE)** 2-9-0 0 .... DarryllHolland 10 56
(M R Channon) *s.i.s: outpcd: r.o ins fnl f: nrst fin* **8/1**
7 5 **Jennifer's Dream (IRE)** 2-8-11 0 .... AndrewMullen(3) 1 41
(K A Ryan) *hld up: hdwy 1/2-way: sn rdn and ev ch: hung rt and wknd over 1f out* **10/1**
0 **8** 2 **April's Quest (IRE)**[14] 3643 2-8-9 0 .... KevinGhunowa(5) 4 35
(David Pinder) *s.i.s: hld up: rdn 1/2-way: wknd 2f out* **66/1**
4 **9** 2 ½ **Silver Deal**[13] 3681 2-8-9 0 .... RussellKennemore(5) 2 28
(J A Pickering) *chsd ldrs 4f* **50/1**
4 **10** ½ **Dark Queen**[21] 3410 2-9-0 0 .... DanielTudhope 3 26
(D Carroll) *chsd ldr tl rdn over 2f out: wknd over 1f out* **50/1**

1m 12.98s (-0.22) **Going Correction** -0.075s/f (Good) 10 Ran SP% **117.6**
Speed ratings (Par 91): **98,97,92,92,90 89,83,80,77,76**
CSF £40.64 TOTE £2.60: £1.10, £6.40, £5.40; EX 50.80.
Owner Mrs G A Rupert **Bred** Sean Gorman **Trained** Newmarket, Suffolk

FOCUS
A fair maiden in which the first two came clear. The winner, third and fourth were all close to their pre-race marks.

NOTEBOOK
Close To Paradise(IRE), fourth in a decent maiden at Newmarket - the sixth Rosy Alexander has won since - got off the mark back down in trip. After quickening into the lead going to the two pole, she had to fend off the runner-up's challenge inside the last. Her immediate future probably lies in nurseries. (tchd 11-8)
Our Piccadilly(IRE), a half-sister to several winners including sprinter Diane's Choice, out of a 6f winner at two, is from a yard not usually noted for its juveniles. She shaped with plenty of promise on this debut, receiving a bump from the third as she left the stalls but coming through to make the favourite work for her victory. A little race should come her way.
Observatory Ridgeagain went left exiting the stalls, this time giving the eventual runner-up a bump. She was bit outpaced by the leaders at halfway but was keeping on at the end, and is now qulaified for nurseries. (op 14-1 tchd 18-1)
Monte Mayor Birdie(IRE), down in trip, again showed plenty of pace but could not sustain it in the latter stages. (op 15-2 tchd 8-1)

Green Earrings(IRE), a 66,000gns daughter of Captain Rio, is a half-sister to Woodboro Kat, a 1m1f winner at three, Countykat, who won at up to 7f, and 6f scorer Hill Of Almhuim. She was not all all knocked about on this debut and this kind introduction should pay dividends. (op 4-1)
Maiden Miss(IRE), a half-sister to four winners including juvenile scorers Tent and Pretty Majestic, could not go the pace for the first two-thirds of the race but was getting the hang of things late on. (op 6-1 tchd 11-2)
Jennifer's Dream(IRE) out of a half-sister to Beyrouth, a high-class performer at around a mile in the US, looked distinctly green on this debut and can be expected to improve. (op 15-2)

4075 CHRISTOPHER SCOTNEY H'CAP — 5f 218y

8:35 (8:35) (Class 5) (0-70,75) 3-Y-0+ **£3,238** (£963; £481; £240) **Stalls** High

Form				RPR
0023	1		**Goodenough Mover**[23] 3368 11-9-2 **63**............(b) RichardKingscote(3) 6	72
			(Andrew Turnell) *a.p: rdn to chse ldr over 1f out: styd on to ld post* **13/2**[3]	
0621	2	*hd*	**Bel Cantor**[3] 4006 4-10-0 **75** 6ex..............................(p) AndrewMullen(3) 2	84
			(W J H Ratcliffe) *led: rdn over 1f out: hdd post* **6/5**[1]	
5033	3	*1 1/4*	**Mistral Sky**[2] 4021 8-8-8 **57**..(v) TolleyDean(5) 7	62
			(Stef Liddiard) *chsd ldrs: rdn over 2f out: no ex towards fin* **9/2**[2]	
3350	4	*hd*	**Xpres Maite**[15] 3608 4-9-2 **60**... PaulEddery 9	64
			(S R Bowring) *hld up: rdn 1/2-way: r.o ins fnl f: nrst fin* **14/1**	
0505	5	*3/4*	**Gavarnie Beau (IRE)**[5] 3906 4-9-6 **64**..........................(b) JimmyQuinn 8	66
			(M Blanshard) *prom: rdn over 2f out: styd on same pce fnl f* **8/1**	
0166	6	*2*	**Word Perfect**[5] 3920 5-9-10 **68**.......................................(b) DaleGibson 1	64
			(M W Easterby) *chsd ldr tl rdn 2f out: wknd ins fnl f* **12/1**	
60-6	7	*4*	**Cerulean Rose**[35] 2982 8-8-10 **54**.. JohnEgan 5	38
			(A W Carroll) *hld up: effrt over 2f out: wknd over 1f out* **11/1**	
30/	8	*7*	**Nok Twice (IRE)**[605] 5480 6-9-7 **65**.............................. DanielTudhope 4	28
			(D Carroll) *dwlt: hld up: rdn over 2f out: sn wknd* **50/1**	

1m 12.17s (-1.03) **Going Correction** -0.075s/f (Good) **8** Ran SP% **112.7**
Speed ratings (Par 103): **103,102,101,100,99 97,91,82**
CSF £14.29 CT £38.53 TOTE £6.20: £1.70, £1.20, £1.70; EX 14.20 Place 6 £100.80, Place 5 £68.80..
Owner D Goodenough Removals & Transport **Bred** G Foster **Trained** Broad Hinton, Wilts

FOCUS
Just a modest handicap, but solid form.
T/Plt: £118.70 to a £1 stake. Pool: £48,063.55. 295.40 winning tickets. T/Qpdt: £15.70 to a £1 stake. Pool: £5,122.90. 240.10 winning tickets. CR

3760 REDCAR (L-H)

Wednesday, August 1

OFFICIAL GOING: Good (9.3)
Wind: Fresh, half-behind Weather: Overcast, breezy

4076 EUROPEAN BREEDERS' FUND MEDIAN AUCTION MAIDEN STKS (DIV I) — 6f

1:35 (1:43) (Class 6) 2-Y-O **£1,808** (£533; £267) **Stalls** Centre

Form				RPR
264	1		**Legendary Guest**[18] 3551 2-9-3 0.................................... DarryllHolland 2	76+
			(M R Channon) *in tch: effrt over 2f out: styd on to ld jst ins fnl f: hld on towards fin* **11/10**[1]	
	2	*3/4*	**Errigal Lad** 2-9-3 0.. DO'Donohoe 9	74+
			(K A Ryan) *sn pushed along in rr: hdwy over 2f out: styd on wl fnl f: nt quite rch wnr* **14/1**	
003	3	*shd*	**Howdigo**[13] 3669 2-9-3 0.. RichardMullen 4	70
			(J R Best) *chsd ldrs: drvn and outpcd over 3f out: swtchd lft over 1f out: kpt on same pce ins fnl f* **10/3**[2]	
P04	4	*hd*	**Everything**[8] 3812 2-8-12 0.. MickyFenton 10	65
			(P T Midgley) *led: hung lft over 1f out: hdd and no ex ins fnl f* **25/1**	
0	5	*1*	**Joinedupwriting**[16] 3582 2-9-3 0.................................. DeanMcKeown 5	67
			(R M Whitaker) *uns rdr and rn loose bef s: s.i.s: hdwy to chse ldrs 3f out: kpt on same pce fnl f* **22/1**	
3	6	*1 1/2*	**Paddy Jack**[24] 3341 2-9-3 0... PhillipMakin 6	62
			(J R Weymes) *w ldr: wknd fnl 150yds* **10/1**[3]	
0	7	*1 3/4*	**Resolute Defender (IRE)**[29] 3192 2-9-3 0.................. PaulMulrennan 3	57
			(J Howard Johnson) *chsd ldrs: wknd appr fnl f* **25/1**	
	8	*3/4*	**Resounding Glory (USA)** 2-9-3 0.......................... RoystonFfrench 7	55
			(Mrs A Duffield) *sn chsng ldrs: fdd appr fnl f* **16/1**	
	9	*1 3/4*	**Arkando (IRE)** 2-8-12 0... LeeEnstone 13	45+
			(K R Burke) *s.s: hdwy 2f out: kpt on: nvr nr ldrs* **20/1**	
406	10	*shd*	**Destinys Dream (IRE)**[15] 3606 2-8-9 0.................. AndrewMullen(3) 11	44
			(Mrs A Duffield) *sn drvn along: chsd ldrs: wknd over 1f out* **22/1**	
	11	*19*	**Dolly No Hair** 2-9-3 0... TonyHamilton 8	—
			(D W Barker) *s.s: sn bhd: t.o 2f out* **33/1**	
	12	*1*	**Fleetway (IRE)** 2-8-12 0... PaulFessey 1	—
			(F Watson) *s.s: bhd: t.o 2f out* **100/1**	
00	13	*1*	**Missabeat (IRE)**[38] 2904 2-8-9 0........................... DuranFentiman(3) 12	—
			(T D Easterby) *sn drvn along: reminders and lost pl 4f out: sn bhd: t.o 2f out* **100/1**	

1m 11.32s (-0.38) **Going Correction** -0.125s/f (Firm) **13** Ran SP% **118.4**
Speed ratings (Par 92): **97,96,95,95,94 92,89,88,86,86 61,59,58**
CSF £16.50 TOTE £1.90: £1.20, £3.90, £1.70; EX 16.60.
Owner John Guest **Bred** J H And J M Wall **Trained** West Ilsley, Berks

FOCUS
A modest juvenile maiden, run at a sound pace. The form can be rated through the third. The winning time was 0.23 seconds slower than the second division.

NOTEBOOK
Legendary Guest, back in trip, returned to near the form that saw him finish second to Winker Watson on his debut back in April and broke his duck at the fourth attempt. He looks best kept to this trip and should make his mark in nurseries. (op 11-8 after early 13-8 in a place)
Errigal Lad ◆, a half-brother to numerous juvenile sprint winners, most notably Phantom Whisper and Maktavish, proved distinctly green through the early parts and clearly needed the experience. He was doing some decent work late on, however, and should go close on his next start. (op 10-1)
Howdigo hit a flat spot before staying on again at the business end and ran close to his recent level, if anything posting just about his best effort to date in defeat. He helps set the level of this form and will now likely switch to a nursery, where this half-brother to his stable's star filly Rising Cross can be expected to enjoy the return to another furlong. (op 4-1)
Everything was given an aggressive ride over this extra furlong and showed much-improved form, despite hanging left under pressure late on. She ought to do better still when switching to a nursery over this trip. (tchd 33-1)
Joinedupwriting, who played up on the way to post, again missed the kick yet still ran with a degree of promise. He is still clearly very much learning his trade, but has a future. (op 20-1 tchd 25-1)

4077 EUROPEAN BREEDERS' FUND MEDIAN AUCTION MAIDEN STKS (DIV II) — 6f

2:05 (2:10) (Class 6) 2-Y-O **£1,808** (£533; £267) **Stalls** Centre

Form				RPR
0	1		**Blue Cross Boy (USA)**[58] 2297 2-9-3 0........................ PaulMulrennan 6	71
			(J Howard Johnson) *cl up: rdn to ld over 1f out: drvn ins fnl f: hld on gamely* **14/1**	
544	2	*hd*	**Carnival Dream**[28] 3205 2-8-9 0.............................. PatrickMathers(3) 4	65
			(A Berry) *led: rdn along 2f out: edgd lft and hdd over 1f out: drvn and rallied wl fnl f: jst hld* **14/1**	
4	3	*3/4*	**Carnival Queen**[33] 3043 2-8-12 0.................................. OscarUrbina 12	63
			(J R Fanshawe) *trckd ldrs: hdwy on outer 1/2-way: rdn to chal 2f out and ev ch: edgd lft and drvn ins fnl f: rdr dropped whip and no ex last 100yds* **9/4**[1]	
	4	*3*	**Hurricane Harriet** 2-8-12 0.. RichardMullen 10	54
			(R M H Cowell) *chsd ldrs: effrt over 2f out: sn rdn and kpt on same pce appr: fnl f* **4/1**[3]	
5306	5	*3 1/2*	**Natural Rhythm (IRE)**[13] 3673 2-9-3 0..................(v[1]) RoystonFfrench 1	49
			(Mrs A Duffield) *prom: effrt to dispute ld 1/2-way: rdn along 2f out and grad wknd* **25/1**	
	6	*1 1/2*	**Desert Lark** 2-9-3 0... PatCosgrave 2	44
			(G A Swinbank) *dwlt and in rr: swtchd rt 1/2-way: styd on fnl 2f: nrst fin* **3/1**[2]	
233	7	*1 1/2*	**Montiboli (IRE)**[32] 3109 2-8-12 0...................................... DO'Donohoe 3	41+
			(K A Ryan) *chsd ldrs: rdn along over 2f out: wknd over 1f out* **5/1**	
60	8	*3*	**Sultan Of The Sand**[12] 3712 2-9-3 0................................ PhillipMakin 8	31
			(C C Bealby) *trckd ldrs: rdn along over 2f out and sn wknd* **50/1**	
6	9	*3/4*	**Fu Wa (USA)**[11] 3750 2-8-5 0.. NSLawes(7) 9	23
			(M W Easterby) *chsd ldrs: rdn along 1/2-way: sn wknd* **40/1**	
0	10	*hd*	**Jimmy Dean**[6] 3866 2-8-12 0.. NeilBrown(5) 11	28
			(M Wellings) *sn outpcd and a bhd* **100/1**	
0	11	*5*	**Night Mystery**[12] 3712 2-9-0 0.................................. DuranFentiman(3) 7	13
			(T D Easterby) *dwlt: a towards rr* **66/1**	
00	12	*4*	**Carlton Mac**[10] 3760 2-8-12 0............................(b) MichaelJStainton(5) 5	—
			(N Bycroft) *sn outpcd and a bhd* **100/1**	

1m 11.09s (-0.61) **Going Correction** -0.125s/f (Firm) **12** Ran SP% **117.5**
Speed ratings (Par 92): **99,98,97,93,89 87,85,81,80,79 73,67**
CSF £181.63 TOTE £15.60: £3.10, £3.60, £1.40; EX 145.00.
Owner Transcend Bloodstock LLP **Bred** Jmj Racing Stables **Trained** Billy Row, Co Durham
■ Stewards' Enquiry : Patrick Mathers five-day ban: used whip with excessive force and frequency (Aug 12-16)
Oscar Urbina one-day ban: used whip down the shoulder in the forehand position (Aug 12)

FOCUS
A modest maiden, although the winning time was 0.23 seconds faster than the first division. The runner-up helps set the standard.

NOTEBOOK
Blue Cross Boy(USA) ran green on his debut over 5f at Carlisle, but he learnt plenty from that and showed improved form to get off the mark. There should be more to come and he can make his mark in nurseries. (op 11-1 tchd 16-1)
Carnival Dream showed good speed on this drop in trip and only just failed to get off the mark. She could find a weak maiden, but also has the option of running in nurseries. (op 12-1 tchd 16-1)
Carnival Queen ran green on her debut over 7f at Folkestone, but she failed to make the expected improvement on this drop in trip and was a touch disappointing. (op 2-1 tchd 15-8)
Hurricane Harriet, a Bertolini half-sister to Cambridgeshire winner Katy Nowaitee, was well backed in the market and showed ability. She finished up well held, but is open to improvement. (tchd 9-2)
Natural Rhythm(IRE) failed to improve for the first-time visor and does not seem to be progressing. (tchd 28-1)
Desert Lark, a 30,000gns son of Sakhee, half-brother to triple sprint winner Alderney Race, out of a smart 6f scorer, was really well backed beforehand, but he looked in need of the experience and could never pose a threat. He should come on a good deal for the experience. (op 13-2)
Montiboli(IRE) could not match the form of her three previous starts and was disappointing. Official explanation: jockey said filly lost its action (op 4-1)

4078 TURFTV BETTING SHOP SERVICE H'CAP — 7f

2:40 (2:43) (Class 5) (0-65,64) 3-Y-O **£2,817** (£838; £418; £209) **Stalls** Centre

Form				RPR
1344	1		**Cheery Cat (USA)**[16] 3583 3-9-2 59..........................(p) TonyHamilton 13	66
			(D W Barker) *trckd ldr: led over 2f out: hld on towards fin* **4/1**[1]	
0156	2	*1/2*	**Distant Sun (USA)**[21] 3413 3-9-7 64.................................. PhillipMakin 8	70
			(I Semple) *trckd ldrs: hung lft over 1f out: no ex towards fin* **7/1**[2]	
6626	3	*hd*	**Aussie Blue (IRE)**[16] 3583 3-8-12 55.........................(b) DeanMcKeown 6	60
			(R M Whitaker) *hld up in mid-div: effrt on outside over 2f out: kpt on wl fnl f* **9/1**[3]	
-230	4	*2*	**Ruthles Philly**[74] 1850 3-8-10 56................................ AndrewMullen(3) 4	56
			(D W Barker) *mid-div: hdwy over 2f out: hung rt and kpt on wl fnl f* **16/1**	
-404	5	*3/4*	**Lady Valentino**[14] 3639 3-8-4 50............................ PatrickMathers(3) 12	48
			(M Dods) *chsd ldrs: kpt on same pce fnl 2f* **10/1**	
-060	6	*hd*	**Jane Of Arc (FR)**[16] 3587 3-9-0 57...................................... PatCosgrave 1	54
			(J S Goldie) *chsd ldrs: one pce fnl 2f* **11/1**	
1546	7	*1 1/2*	**A Big Sky Brewing (USA)**[55] 2389 3-9-1 58..................... PaulFessey 2	51
			(T D Barron) *mid-div: drvn over 3f out: nvr trbld ldrs* **4/1**[1]	
0046	8	*hd*	**La Marmotte (IRE)**[39] 2892 3-8-7 55 ow3........................ NeilBrown(5) 11	47
			(R E Barr) *led tl over 2f out: wknd over 1f out* **12/1**	
000	9	*hd*	**Altos Reales**[37] 2948 3-8-4 50.. DominicFox(3) 5	42
			(D Shaw) *s.i.s: kpt on fnl 2f: nvr on terms* **25/1**	
0-06	10	*1*	**Esteemed Prince**[121] 894 3-8-7 50...........................(e) PaddyAspell 15	39
			(D Shaw) *dwlt: bhd tl kpt on fnl 2f* **33/1**	
3000	11	*shd*	**Soviet Sound (IRE)**[11] 3752 3-8-3 49........................ DuranFentiman(3) 7	38
			(Jedd O'Keeffe) *in rr-div: sn pushed along: kpt on fnl 2f: nvr on terms* **22/1**	
0300	12	*3 1/2*	**Bond Casino**[11] 3752 3-8-10 53.................................. RoystonFfrench 9	32
			(G R Oldroyd) *in rr: sn drvn along: nvr on terms* **22/1**	
000-	13	*5*	**Lady Firecracker (IRE)**[300] 5773 3-9-0 57................ DarryllHolland 10	23
			(J R Best) *in rr: drvn over 3f out: nvr on terms* **16/1**	
0000	14	*6*	**Meridian Grey (USA)**[16] 3583 3-8-7 50.........................(b) DO'Donohoe 3	—
			(K A Ryan) *trckd ldrs: rdn and lost pl over 2f out* **25/1**	
0-00	15	*16*	**Go Red**[5] 3918 3-8-7 50.. PaulMulrennan 14	—
			(M W Easterby) *swvd rt s: reminders sn after s: sn chsng ldrs: lost pl and heavily eased over 2f out: virtually p.u* **25/1**	

1m 24.53s (-0.37) **Going Correction** -0.125s/f (Firm) **15** Ran SP% **122.6**
Speed ratings (Par 100): **97,96,96,93,93 92,91,90,90,89 89,85,79,72,54**
CSF £27.98 CT £250.61 TOTE £3.60: £1.70, £2.30, £2.90; EX 24.60.

Owner Cataractonium Racing Syndicate I **Bred** K L Ramsay & Sarah K Ramsay **Trained** Scorton, N Yorks

FOCUS
A moderate handicap which saw the first three come clear. The form does not look that solid. The winning time was 1.16 slower than the following maiden.
Ruthles Philly Official explanation: jockey said filly hung right throughout
Bond Casino Official explanation: jockey said filly was never travelling

4079 REDCARRACING.CO.UK RATING RELATED MAIDEN STKS 7f
3:15 (3:16) (Class 5) 3-Y-0+ **£2,817** (£838; £418; £209) **Stalls** Centre

Form RPR
6-00 **1** **Queen Noverre (IRE)**[14] 3646 3-8-12 68 JamesDoyle 11 70
(J W Hills) *hld up: hdwy on outer over 2f out: rdn wl over 1f out: styd on wl fnl f to ld last 50yds* **9/1**
2 ½ **Ghafeer (USA)**[27] 3252 3-9-1 69 (b) TonyHamilton 5 72
(B Ellison) *prom: hdwy to ld over 2f out and sn rdn: drvn ins fnl f: hdd and no ex last 50yds* **8/1**
454 **3** ½ **Destour (IRE)**[55] 2393 3-9-1 70 (v[1]) DarryllHolland 13 70
(J Noseda) *trckd ldrs: effrt over 2f out: sn rdn and ev ch tl drvn and no ex wl ins fnl f* **3/1**[2]
0630 **4** 1 ¼ **Jawaab (IRE)**[12] 3707 3-9-1 68 RichardMullen 10 67
(M A Buckley) *in tch: hdwy to chse ldrs 2f out: sn rdn and ch over 1f out: kpt on same pce u.p ins fnl f* **4/1**[3]
0-00 **5** 3 **Samdaniya**[48] 2606 3-8-12 64 SilvestreDeSousa 12 56
(C E Brittain) *s.i.s and bhd tl styd on fnl 2f: nrst fin* **12/1**
4-05 **6** ½ **Golden Topaz (IRE)**[43] 2742 3-8-7 63 NeilBrown(5) 14 54
(J Howard Johnson) *in tch on wd outside: hdwy to chse ldrs 2f out: sn drvn and one pce appr fnl f* **25/1**
-023 **7** *hd* **Zamalik (USA)**[17] 3572 4-9-0 69 GaryBartley(7) 6 57
(E J Alston) *cl up: ev ch over 2f out: sn rdn and wknd* **9/4**[1]
2350 **8** 3 ½ **Diksie Dancer**[5] 3920 3-8-12 70 DO'Donohoe 4 44
(K A Ryan) *led: rdn and hdd over 2f out: wknd ins fnl f* **14/1**
5006 **9** 2 ½ **Contemplation**[21] 3414 4-9-7 50 MickyFenton 2 41
(J Balding) *dwlt: a in rr* **25/1**
0000 **10** 2 **The Keep**[5] 3917 5-9-4 39 PaddyAspell 8 32
(R E Barr) *prom: rdn along 3f out: sn wknd* **66/1**
040 **11** 30 **Tamarack (IRE)**[39] 2878 3-9-1 60 RoystonFfrench 9 —
(W R Muir) *chsd ldrs to 1/2-way: sn wknd* **33/1**
0000 **12** 2 **Maysridge Ofkuwait**[13] 3675 3-8-9 31 PatrickMathers(3) 7 —
(A Berry) *prom: rdn along 1/2-way: sn wknd* **100/1**
1m 23.37s (-1.53) **Going Correction** -0.125s/f (Firm)
WFA 3 from 4yo+ 6lb **12** Ran SP% **124.4**
Speed ratings (Par 103): **103,102,101,100,97 96,96,92,89,87 52,50**
CSF £79.70 TOTE £13.40: £3.80, £3.40, £1.30; EX 111.70.
Owner Jerry Jamgotchian **Bred** W Lazy T Ranch **Trained** Upper Lambourn, Berks

FOCUS
A modest maiden, but the pace was good and the winning time was 1.16 quicker than previous 46-65. Few of thses are progressing.
Tamarack(IRE) Official explanation: jockey said gelding its action

4080 JOHN SMITH'S REDCAR STRAIGHT-MILE CHAMPIONSHIP STKS (H'CAP) (QUALIFIER) 1m
3:55 (3:55) (Class 4) (0-85,82) 3-Y-0 **£4,728** (£1,406; £702; £351) **Stalls** Centre

Form RPR
6040 **1** **Karoo Blue (IRE)**[19] 3503 3-9-5 **80** RichardMullen 4 87
(C E Brittain) *a cl up: led over 2f out: edgd lft and hdd wl over 1f out: sn rdn: styd on u.p to ld last 100yds* **8/1**
2511 **2** ½ **Gleneagles (IRE)**[15] 3605 3-8-8 **76** LanceBetts(7) 2 82
(N Wilson) *hld up: gd hdwy over 2f out: led wl over 1f out: sn rdn: drvn ins fnl f: hdd last 100yds* **14/1**
0465 **3** 3 **Flying Valentino**[30] 3158 3-8-12 **73** DeanMcKeown 5 72
(G A Swinbank) *hld up in rr: stdy hdwy whn nt clr run 2f out: sn swtchd lft and rdn: styd on ins fnl f: nrst fin* **10/1**
0-00 **4** 1 ½ **Atlantic Light**[49] 2578 3-9-7 **82** RoystonFfrench 9 78
(M Johnston) *prom: rdn along over 2f out: drvn over 1f out and kpt on same pce* **33/1**
41 **5** ¾ **Nassau Style**[26] 3276 3-9-3 **78** OscarUrbina 10 72
(J R Fanshawe) *hld up: hdwy on outer 3f out: rdn to chse ldrs whn edgd lft wl over 1f out: sn drvn and btn* **5/2**[1]
-001 **6** 2 ½ **Tommy Tobougg**[23] 3372 3-8-4 **65** PaulFessey 8 53
(I Semple) *hld up in tch: hdwy to chse ldrs whn edgd lft 2f out: sn rdn and kpt on same pce* **9/1**
31-4 **7** 2 **Tarraburn (USA)**[58] 2313 3-8-13 **74** PaulMulrennan 6 57
(J Howard Johnson) *t.k.h: chsd ldrs: rdn along over 3f out: sn wknd* **14/1**
605 **8** ½ **Danum Dancer**[23] 3380 3-9-5 **80** SilvestreDeSousa 3 62
(N Bycroft) *t.k.h: prom tl rdn along wl over 3f out and sn wknd* **11/2**[3]
4106 **9** 1 ¼ **Apache Dawn**[15] 3607 3-9-7 **82** DO'Donohoe 1 61
(K A Ryan) *rrd s: sn trcking ldrs on outer: rdn along 1/2-way and sn wknd* **11/1**
3115 **10** *nk* **Magic Echo**[19] 3495 3-9-2 **77** PhillipMakin 7 56
(M Dods) *led: rdn along and hdd over 2f out: sn wknd* **9/2**[2]
1m 36.51s (-1.29) **Going Correction** -0.125s/f (Firm) **10** Ran SP% **116.9**
Speed ratings (Par 102): **101,100,97,96,95 92,90,90,89,88**
CSF £113.67 CT £1133.80 TOTE £11.00: £3.20, £2.80, £3.30; EX 141.20.
Owner Sheikh Marwan Al Maktoum **Bred** Darley **Trained** Newmarket, Suffolk

FOCUS
A fair three-year-old handicap but the form does not look all that sound. It was the fastest of the three 1m races, 0.78 seconds quicker than the following 46-65, and 1.29 seconds faster than the later claimer.
Nassau Style Official explanation: jockey said gelding was unsuited by the good ground

4081 JOURNEY SOUTH AND ETON ROAD H'CAP 1m
4:30 (4:30) (Class 6) (0-65,66) 3-Y-0+ **£2,817** (£838; £418; £209) **Stalls** Centre

Form RPR
1141 **1** **Sam's Secret**[8] 3816 5-9-10 **66** 6ex NeilBrown(5) 11 75+
(G A Swinbank) *hld up in mid-div: effrt over 2f out: led over 1f out: kpt on wl* **11/10**[1]
2400 **2** 1 ¼ **Tour D'Amour (IRE)**[57] 2338 4-9-6 **57** (b[1]) PaddyAspell 3 63
(R Craggs) *hld up in tch: effrt over 2f out: kpt on wl ins fnl f* **20/1**
5000 **3** *hd* **Waterloo Corner**[12] 3722 5-9-1 **52** PaulMulrennan 13 58
(R Craggs) *w ldrs: led over 2f out tl over 1f out: no ex ins fnl f* **33/1**
2000 **4** 2 **Spinning**[12] 3711 4-9-11 **62** PhillipMakin 15 63
(T D Barron) *sn chsng ldrs: kpt on same pce appr fnl f* **15/2**[2]
4006 **5** 1 ½ **Apsara**[11] 3754 6-9-3 **57** DuranFentiman(3) 9 54
(G M Moore) *led tl over 2f out: fdd fnl f* **16/1**
0463 **6** *nk* **Kudbeme**[4] 3971 5-9-8 **59** PaulFessey 10 56
(N Bycroft) *hld up in rr: hdwy over 3f out: edgd lft and one pce appr fnl f* **10/1**
0000 **7** ½ **It's Unbelievable (USA)**[8] 3816 4-9-6 **57** MickyFenton 7 53
(P T Midgley) *trckd ldrs: t.k.h: wknd 1f out* **20/1**
04 **8** ½ **Moonstreaker**[30] 3161 4-9-1 **57** MichaelJStainton(5) 11 52
(R M Whitaker) *w ldrs: t.k.h: wknd fnl f* **11/1**
4320 **9** ½ **Falimar**[12] 3722 3-9-4 **62** (p) TonyHamilton 14 55
(Miss J A Camacho) *t.k.h: in tch: effrt over 2f out: wknd appr fnl f* **16/1**
6-33 **10** 5 **Howards Rocket**[13] 3675 6-9-2 **53** PatCosgrave 6 35
(J S Goldie) *hld up towards rr: effrt over 2f out: lost pl and eased over 1f out* **9/1**[3]
0-20 **11** 23 **Yo Pedro (IRE)**[38] 2358 5-9-4 **62** KellyHarrison(7) 5 —
(D Carroll) *in rr: drvn 4f out: bhd and eased 2f out: t.o* **16/1**
0060 **12** 2 **Magic Sting**[4] 3955 6-9-9 **60** (v[1]) DO'Donohoe 12 —
(B S Rothwell) *dwlt: t.k.h and sn trcking ldrs: lost pl over 3f out: sn bhd and eased: t.o: b.b.v* **40/1**
1m 37.29s (-0.51) **Going Correction** -0.125s/f (Firm)
WFA 3 from 4yo+ 7lb **12** Ran SP% **117.5**
Speed ratings (Par 101): **97,95,95,93,92 91,91,90,90,85 62,60**
CSF £55.75 CT £830.64 TOTE £1.80: £1.30, £7.50, £10.20; EX 47.80.
Owner Copskam Partnership **Bred** Dandy's Farm **Trained** Melsonby, N Yorks

FOCUS
A very modest handicap and the pace was just ordinary. The winner did not need to improve and the second and third ran to their recent marks. Thewinning time was 0.78 seconds slower than the previous 66-85, but 0.51 seconds quicker than the claimer.
Yo Pedro(IRE) Official explanation: jockey said gelding lost its action
Magic Sting Official explanation: trainer said gelding bled from the nose

4082 REDCAR CONFERENCE CENTRE CLAIMING STKS 1m
5:05 (5:05) (Class 6) 3-Y-0+ **£2,047** (£604; £302) **Stalls** Centre

Form RPR
0134 **1** **Top Jaro (FR)**[19] 3487 4-9-8 68 LiamTreadwell(3) 9 68
(Jennie Candlish) *chsd ldng pair: hdwy 1/2-way: led wl over 2f out: rdn wl over 1f out: kpt on wl u.p fnl f* **9/4**[1]
0060 **2** 2 **Pianoforte (USA)**[29] 3195 5-9-4 53 GaryBartley(7) 6 63
(E J Alston) *hld up in rr: hdwy 3f out: rdn to chse wnr ins fnl f: sn drvn and kpt on* **20/1**
6105 **3** 2 **Bond Diamond**[22] 3405 10-9-2 52 MickyFenton 11 49
(P T Midgley) *in tch: hdwy to chse ldrs over 2f out and sn rdn: drvn over 1f out and kpt on same pce ins fnl f* **17/2**
366 **4** 1 **Wahoo Sam (USA)**[5] 3922 7-9-6 70 (p) DO'Donohoe 15 51
(K A Ryan) *chsd ldr: led after 2f: rdn along and hdd wl over 2f out: drvn wl over 1f out and styd on same pce* **9/2**[2]
220 **5** *nk* **Apache Point (IRE)**[10] 3765 10-9-2 52 KimTinkler 13 46
(N Tinkler) *chsd ldrs: rdn along over 2f out: swtchd lft and drvn over 1f out: no imp* **7/1**[3]
5540 **6** 1 ½ **Jenny Soba**[68] 2008 4-8-6 53 (v[1]) MichaelJStainton(5) 1 38
(R M Whitaker) *wnt lft s and in rr tl styd on fnl 2f* **10/1**
6040 **7** ½ **Primo Way**[24] 3346 6-9-6 70 (b) PhillipMakin 2 46
(I Semple) *chsd ldrs on outer: rdn along over 2f out: grad wknd* **7/1**[3]
1-00 **8** 2 **Roman History (IRE)**[9] 3783 4-9-5 55 (p) SilvestreDeSousa 8 40
(Miss Tracy Waggott) *in tch: rdn along 3f out: sn wknd* **14/1**
0000 **9** 2 ½ **Jaassey**[39] 2893 4-8-12 46 DuranFentiman(3) 4 30
(P T Midgley) *nvr bttr than midfield* **50/1**
6000 **10** 1 ¾ **Harts In Mo Shun (IRE)**[14] 3639 3-8-10 50 PatrickMathers(3) 14 31
(A Berry) *racd wd: in tch: rdn along over 3f out and sn wknd* **66/1**
6040 **11** 8 **Mister Maq**[9] 3789 4-9-2 47 (b) PaulMulrennan 7 9
(A Crook) *bhd fr 1/2-way* **50/1**
005- **12** ½ **Always Esteemed (IRE)**[435] 1923 7-9-2 74 (b) DeanMcKeown 12 8
(J O'Reilly) *led 2f: cl up tl rdn along over 3f out and sn wknd* **12/1**
1m 37.8s **Going Correction** -0.125s/f (Firm)
WFA 3 from 4yo+ 7lb **12** Ran SP% **118.1**
Speed ratings (Par 101): **95,93,91,90,89 88,87,85,83,81 73,72**
CSF £54.83 TOTE £3.00: £1.10, £7.80, £3.70; EX 70.10.Top Jaro was claimed by D. W. Barker for £15,000. Wahoo Sam was claimed by D. W. Barker for £10,000.
Owner Alan Baxter **Bred** Jean Biraben And Robert Labeyrie **Trained** Basford Green, Staffs

FOCUS
A typically moderate claimer. The winner won as he was entitled to at the weights, with the second back to form and the third close to his recent level. The winning time was 1.29 seconds slower than the earlier 66-85, and 0.51 seconds slower than the 46-65.

4083 "GO RACING AT THIRSK THIS FRIDAY" H'CAP 6f
5:40 (5:43) (Class 6) (0-65,65) 3-Y-0+ **£1,943** (£578; £288; £144) **Stalls** Centre

Form RPR
0-00 **1** **Hazelhurst (IRE)**[38] 2905 4-9-4 **63** NeilBrown(5) 15 72
(J Howard Johnson) *s.i.s: hdwy 2f out: led 1f out: drvn out* **22/1**
0132 **2** 1 **Danish Blues (IRE)**[7] 3837 4-9-4 **58** SilvestreDeSousa 1 64
(D Nicholls) *hld up in midfield: hdwy on outside over 2f out: rdr dropped whip and chsd wnr 1f out: no ex wl ins fnl f* **11/2**[2]
1624 **3** 1 ½ **Another Genepi (USA)**[21] 3414 4-9-10 **64** (b) DO'Donohoe 10 65
(K A Ryan) *chsd ldrs: kpt on same pce fnl f* **12/1**
0641 **4** *hd* **Whinhill House**[5] 3921 7-9-3 **57** (v) PatCosgrave 14 58
(D W Barker) *chsd ldrs: lost pl over 3f out: hdwy over 1f out: styd on ins fnl f* **6/1**[3]
0563 **5** *shd* **Compton Plume**[14] 3636 7-9-2 **56** PaulMulrennan 12 56
(M W Easterby) *mid-div: hdwy over 2f out: styd on fnl f* **10/1**
0000 **6** *shd* **Northern Chorus (IRE)**[3] 4008 4-9-11 **65** (v) DeanMcKeown 9 65
(J O'Reilly) *led tl 1f out: fdd ins fnl f* **66/1**
0335 **7** ½ **No Grouse**[18] 3535 7-8-7 **54** KellyHarrison(7) 13 52
(E J Alston) *hld up: hdwy over 2f out: styd on fnl f* **12/1**
0105 **8** 1 **Soto**[12] 3723 4-9-3 **64** NSLawes(7) 6 59
(M W Easterby) *chsd ldrs: drvn over 2f out: wkng whn nt clr run over 1f out* **25/1**
1005 **9** ½ **Petite Mac**[5] 3920 7-8-10 **55** (b) MichaelJStainton(5) 11 49
(N Bycroft) *in rr: hdwy on stands' side 2f out: nvr rchd ldrs* **10/1**
6000 **10** *nk* **Brigadore**[3] 3998 8-9-4 **63** ColinHaddon(5) 5 56
(J G Given) *s.s: sme hdwy 2f out: nvr on terms* **12/1**
221 **11** 1 ¼ **Polar Force**[11] 3735 7-9-8 **62** TGMcLaughlin 2 51
(Mrs C A Dunnett) *chsd ldrs: wknd fnl f* **4/1**[1]
-054 **12** *nk* **Monashee Prince (IRE)**[13] 3667 5-9-5 **59** RichardMullen 3 47
(J R Best) *chsd ldrs: wknd over 1f out* **16/1**
0020 **13** *shd* **Falmassim**[22] 3408 4-9-4 **58** (p) TonyHamilton 8 45
(Miss J A Camacho) *rrd s: sn trcking ldrs: wknd over 1f out* **11/1**
5000 **14** *nk* **Bond Playboy**[7] 3836 7-9-3 **62** (b) SladeO'Hara(5) 7 48
(G R Oldroyd) *s.s: sme hdwy over 2f out: wknd over 1f out* **50/1**

010 **15** ½ **Night In (IRE)**[24] 3345 4-9-8 62..........(t) KimTinkler 4 47
(N Tinkler) *s.i.s: sme hdwy 2f out: sn lost pl* **16/1**

1m 10.8s (-0.90) **Going Correction** -0.125s/f (Firm) **15** Ran SP% **122.7**
Speed ratings (Par 101): **101,99,97,97,97 97,96,95,94,94 92,92,91,91,90**
CSF £137.51 CT £1588.71 TOTE £22.70: £5.90, £2.30, £3.10; EX 142.40 Place 6 £151.88, Place 5 £126.41..
Owner Transcend Bloodstock LLP **Bred** Martin Francis **Trained** Billy Row, Co Durham

FOCUS
A moderate handicap. Ordinary form but solid, the winner back to her 3yo mark.
Petite Mac Official explanation: jockey said mare was unsuited by the good ground
Polar Force Official explanation: jockey said gelding was unsuited by the good ground
Falmassim Official explanation: jockey said gelding reared at start
T/Plt: £97.30 to a £1 stake. Pool: £39,559.70. 296.75 winning tickets. T/Qpdt: £41.30 to a £1 stake. Pool: £2,465.90. 44.15 winning tickets. JR

4084 - 4088a (Foreign Racing) - See Raceform Interactive

[4056]GOODWOOD (R-H)
Thursday, August 2

OFFICIAL GOING: Good (good to firm in places on round course; 8.2)
Wind: Light, across Weather: Rain Race 1, becoming brighter

4089 LILLIE LANGTRY FILLIES' STKS (GROUP 3) 1m 6f
2:15 (2:15) (Class 1) 3-Y-O+

£28,390 (£10,760; £5,385; £2,685; £1,345; £675) **Stalls** Low

Form RPR
-511 **1** **Hi Calypso (IRE)**[36] 2999 3-8-7 86.......... RyanMoore 4 107
(Sir Michael Stoute) *hld up in last: plenty to do whn pce qcknd over 4f out: sustained prog on outer over 3f out: led ins fnl f: drvn out* **3/1**[1]

-123 **2** ½ **Wannabe Posh (IRE)**[46] 2702 4-9-6 99.......... EddieAhern 5 106
(J L Dunlop) *edgy: trckd ldng pair 8f out: wnt 2nd over 3f out: drvn and clsd on ldr after: led over 1f out: hdd ins fnl f: styd on* **3/1**[1]

-100 **3** 1 ½ **Trick Or Treat**[22] 3434 4-9-6 100.......... TPQueally 6 104
(J G Given) *led: kicked on over 4f out: drvn over 2f out: hdd over 1f out: kpt on same pce* **7/1**[3]

2104 **4** ¾ **Brisk Breeze (GER)**[22] 3434 3-8-7 100.......... TedDurcan 8 103
(H R A Cecil) *trckd ldr after 3f to over 3f out: drvn and chsng ldrs after: nvr quite pce to chal* **7/1**[3]

-021 **5** 2 ½ **Pentatonic**[14] 3671 4-9-6 86.......... JamieSpencer 1 99
(L M Cumani) *trckd ldr for 3f: shuffled bk to midfield 5f out: outpcd and rdn 4f out: one pce and no imp after* **5/1**[2]

0-02 **6** 1 ½ **Oh Glory Be (USA)**[36] 3002 4-9-6 90.......... RichardHughes 2 97
(R Hannon) *hld up in last trio: outpcd 4f out: rdn 3f out: no prog* **14/1**

-020 **7** 4 **High Heel Sneakers**[46] 2702 4-9-6 105.......... TQuinn 3 92
(P F I Cole) *settled in midfield: rdn whn pce lifted 4f out: tried to cl briefly over 3f out: sn btn* **12/1**

-225 **8** 1 ½ **Alambic**[20] 3501 4-9-6 97.......... SebSanders 7 90
(Sir Mark Prescott) *lw: hld up in last trio: slipped bnd 5f out: nvr gng wl after: bhd fnl 3f* **9/1**

3m 2.47s (-1.50) **Going Correction** +0.075s/f (Good)
WFA 3 from 4yo 13lb **8** Ran SP% **116.0**
Speed ratings (Par 110): **107,106,105,105,104 103,100,100**
CSF £11.91 TOTE £4.10: £1.60, £1.30, £2.70; EX 9.50 Trifecta £86.20 Pool: £935.72, 7.70 winning units.
Owner Philip Newton **Bred** Philip Newton **Trained** Newmarket, Suffolk

FOCUS
A pretty ordinary contest by Group 3 standards but sound enough rated around the placed horses. The pace was fair from the start and went up another notch when long-time leader Trick Or Treat kicked for home around four furlongs from the finish.

NOTEBOOK
Hi Calypso(IRE) came into this off the back of a couple of wins in just ordinary handicap company, firstly off a mark of just 73 and then off 81, but the step up in trip brought about significant improvement and she proved up to the grade. Having been last away from the stalls, she was held up well off the pace early on and looked to have plenty to do at the top of the straight, but she stayed on very strongly when asked for her challenge towards the outside of the main pack. There was much to like about the way she sustained her finishing burst, albeit the fair gallop played into her hands. She should continue to progress into a smart staying mare and is likely to stay in training next year. (op 4-1)
Wannabe Posh(IRE), third in a Group 3 over 1m4f at Cork on her previous start, was trying this trip for the first time. Never too far away, she was produced with every chance, but was just outstayed late on. She has progressed into a pretty smart filly and should be able to win a black-type race before she is retired to the paddocks. (tchd 7-2)
Trick Or Treat was allowed the run of the race in front, but she probably set a better pace than it looked at the time and she was unable to sustain her challenge after being sent for home quite a way from the finish. She was unable to confirm Haydock form from earlier in the season with Wannabe Posh and was probably not at her very best. Admittedly this was the furthest trip she had tried to date, but she has won over an extended 1m5f on soft ground, so the distance cannot be used as an excuse.
Brisk Breeze(GER) held a good position for much of the way, but she did not really pick up when asked and was below the form she showed when fourth in the Lancashire Oaks (held this year on the Newmarket July course) on her previous start, when Trick Or Treat was back in seventh. (tchd 15-2)
Pentatonic travelled quite well into the straight, but her recent Folkestone success came in a handicap off a mark of just 79 and she struggled to go with a few of these. This was also the furthest trip she has raced over to date and it might have just stretched her in this company. (op 6-1)
Oh Glory Be(USA) had a bit to find with some of these and she offered little on her first try over 1m6f. (op 16-1)

4090 AUDI STKS (REGISTERED AS THE KING GEORGE STAKES) (GROUP 3) 5f
2:50 (2:52) (Class 1) 3-Y-O+

£28,390 (£10,760; £5,385; £2,685; £1,345; £675) **Stalls** Low

Form RPR
2201 **1** **Moorhouse Lad**[21] 3464 4-9-0 99.......... RyanMoore 14 116
(B Smart) *trckd ldr in centre: overall ldr 2f out: clr whn drifted rt fnl f: r.o wl* **10/1**

-154 **2** 2 **Enticing (IRE)**[25] 3344 3-8-8 112.......... JamieSpencer 3 106
(W J Haggas) *b.hind: taken down early: trckd ldrs nr side gng wl: effrt 2f out: drvn and styd on to ld gp nr fin: no ch w wnr* **7/2**[1]

1102 **3** nk **Tax Free (IRE)**[32] 3139 5-9-5 110.......... AdrianTNicholls 5 113
(D Nicholls) *pressed nr side ldr: led gp 1/2-way and drvn: no ch w wnr and edgd rt fnl f* **7/1**

-502 **4** ½ **Wi Dud**[26] 3329 3-8-11 110.......... NCallan 16 106
(K A Ryan) *lw: trckd ldrs in centre: rdn 2f out: styd on same pce and nvr able to chal* **4/1**[2]

0120 **5** nk **Prime Defender**[20] 3506 3-8-11 111.......... MichaelHills 8 105
(B W Hills) *lw: chsd nr side ldrs: rdn 1/2-way: prog over 1f out: nt pce to chal: kpt on* **5/1**[3]

1-45 **6** ½ **The Jobber (IRE)**[4] 3990 6-9-0 99.......... JMurtagh 15 103
(M Blanshard) *chsd ldrs in centre: rdn to dispute 2nd over 1f out: kpt on same pce: n.m.r nr fin* **14/1**

504 **7** 1 ½ **The Tatling (IRE)**[26] 3329 10-9-0 103.......... DarryllHolland 6 98
(J M Bradley) *taken down early: chsd nr side ldrs: rdn bef 1/2-way: kpt on fnl f: n.d* **16/1**

0333 **8** nk **Bond City (IRE)**[19] 3531 5-9-0 103.......... SebSanders 13 97
(G R Oldroyd) *chsd ldrs in centre: rdn over 2f out: sn outpcd* **16/1**

300- **9** nk **Tawaassol (USA)**[293] 5942 4-9-0 104..........(t) RHills 1 96
(Sir Michael Stoute) *sn last of nr side gp: bhd 1/2-way: shkn up over 1f out: styd on ins fnl f* **25/1**

4310 **10** ½ **Terentia**[25] 3344 4-8-11 102.......... RichardMullen 4 91
(E S McMahon) *chsd nr side ldrs: u.p bef 1/2-way: outpcd over 1f out* **20/1**

0-36 **11** hd **Desert Lord**[44] 2733 7-9-10 115..........(b) DO'Donohoe 2 103
(K A Ryan) *b. led nr side gp to 1/2-way: u.p and losing pl after* **16/1**

4100 **12** 3 **Dazed And Amazed**[26] 3329 3-8-11 100.......... RichardHughes 10 82
(R Hannon) *lw: racd centre: nvr on terms w ldrs: struggling fnl 2f* **50/1**

5024 **13** shd **Turn On The Style**[17] 3586 5-9-0 95..........(b) PaulHanagan 7 82
(J Balding) *lw: taken down early: rrd s and slowly away: a in rr on outer of nr side gp* **50/1**

5201 **14** nk **Celtic Mill**[13] 3708 9-9-0 104..........(p) JimmyFortune 12 81
(D W Barker) *prom in centre: u.p 1/2-way: wknd over 1f out: hanging after* **20/1**

0126 **15** 1 **Ajigolo**[105] 1102 4-9-0 97.......... JHBowman 11 77
(M R Channon) *lw: b.hind: racd centre: hld up in last pair of gp: outpcd fr 1/2-way* **66/1**

650 **16** 3 ½ **Classic Encounter (IRE)**[13] 3708 4-9-0 92..........(b[1]) FergusSweeney 17 65
(D M Simcock) *taken down early: led centre gp to 2f out: wknd rapidly* **80/1**

000- **17** 1 **Free Roses (IRE)**[319] 5405 4-8-11 90.......... TPQueally 9 58
(J G Given) *lengthy: lw: rrd s and slowly away: eventually racd w centre gp: a bhd* **66/1**

57.32 secs (-1.73) **Going Correction** -0.025s/f (Good)
WFA 3 from 4yo+ 3lb **17** Ran SP% **126.3**
Speed ratings (Par 113): **112,108,108,107,107 106,103,103,102,102 101,96,96,96,94 89,87**
CSF £43.15 TOTE £12.60: £4.00, £2.00, £2.20; EX 65.60 Trifecta £432.50 Pool: £2,193.14, 3.60 winning units.
Owner Ron Hull **Bred** P Onslow **Trained** Hambleton, N Yorks

FOCUS
An ordinary renewal of this speed test and not rated as positively as it could be. The field split into two groups of similar size, with the winner coming from the group that raced up the middle of the track, and the placed horses coming from the stands'-side group.

NOTEBOOK
Moorhouse Lad, who won a handicap off 93 last time out, successfully stepped up to Group company with another fine display of speed. Although he showed great pace from the off, he had enough in reserve to kick clear approaching the final furlong and win by a cosy two lengths. However, while this track was ideal for him, opportunities to run over a quick five are likely to be few and far between from now on as he is not in the Nunthorpe. (op 12-1)
Enticing(IRE), who got turned over on rain-softened ground at Ayr last time having apparently come into season shortly beforehand, appreciated these quicker conditions and travelled well just off the pace. What positive effect the earplugs she wore had is anyone's guess, but she picked up well when asked, and held off Tax Free in good style to win her race on the stands' side, in the process confirming last year's Molecomb Stakes form with Wi Dud. (tchd 4-1 and 3-1 in a place)
Tax Free(IRE) ran well under his 5lb Group 3 penalty but could not quite edge past his stands'-side companion Enticing in the closing stages. A winner over 6f here last year, it would be good to see him back over that trip, as apart from when he ran on dirt in Dubai he has yet to run a bad race over the distance, recording form figures of 115131 in the process. (tchd 13-2)
Wi Dud, runner-up to Enticing in the Molecomb here as a two-year-old, returned to form at Sandown last time and built on that promise, but the winner was much too strong for him. Second home from the centre group, he again had to settle for finishing behind Enticing. (tchd 9-2 in places)
Prime Defender, dropping back to the minimum trip for the first time since he won his maiden at two, ran well enough, but 5f on a track as sharp as this is probably an insufficient test for him these days. (op 6-1)
The Jobber(IRE), who likes to hear his feet rattling, was running in Group company for the first time having performed with great credit in a couple of top handicaps this season - the latest of which was just four days earlier. He ran well, finished clear of the rest, and might be able to pick up a Listed race over this trip before the season is out. (op 20-1)
The Tatling(IRE) finished out of the first four for the first time in six visits to this track - he won this race in 2003 - and appears to be on a steady downgrade now. (tchd 14-1)
Bond City(IRE) has not always had things go his way this season but he had few excuses on this occasion. (op 20-1)
Tawaassol(USA), a progressive sprinter last season, did not look quite right in his coat for this belated seasonal reappearance. He made some late progress but never got seriously involved, and one would imagine that he will come on quite a bit for the run and appreciate another furlong next time.
Terentia, successful on her only previous visit to this track, was struggling from a fair way out.
Desert Lord had a very tough task under his 10lb Group 1 penalty so he should not be too harshly judged. He showed a lot of pace to halfway.
Free Roses(IRE) reared as the stalls opened and was slowly away, but her chance was not helped either by her rider's indecision as to which group to race with. Official explanation: jockey said filly reared leaving stalls

4091 ABN AMRO GOODWOOD CUP (GROUP 2) 2m
3:25 (3:34) (Class 1) 3-Y-O+

£56,780 (£21,520; £10,770; £5,370; £2,690; £1,350) **Stalls** Low

Form RPR
-510 **1** **Allegretto (IRE)**[42] 2787 4-9-5 107.......... RyanMoore 11 114
(Sir Michael Stoute) *hld up in last quartet: pushed along over 4f out: swtchd to outer and relentless prog fr 3f out: drvn and r.o to ld fnl 100yds* **8/1**[3]

2112 **2** ½ **Veracity**[41] 2816 3-8-5 95 ow1.......... PhilipRobinson 7 114
(M A Jarvis) *hld up in midfield: rdn and prog fr 3f out: narrow ld 1f out: hdd and jst outpcd fnl 100yds* **10/1**

3443 **3** ¾ **Finalmente**[26] 3333 5-9-5 103..........(p) JMurtagh 4 112
(N A Callaghan) *led for 1f: trckd ldr: led 5f out and qcknd: drvn over 3f out: hdd 1f out: kpt on gamely* **16/1**

3211 **4** 5 **Balkan Knight**[26] 3333 7-9-5 107 JohnEgan 5 106
(D R C Elsworth) *b.hind: lw: hld up wl in rr: stdy prog on outer fr over 3f out: chsd ldrs over 1f out: wknd ins fnl f* **8/1**[3]

2522 **5** 1 3/4 **Geordieland (FR)**[42] 2787 6-9-5 114 JamieSpencer 8 104
(J A Osborne) *hld up in last trio: stealthy prog on inner fr 4f out: crusied up to dispute 2nd wl over 1f out: sn rdn and fnd nil* **6/4**[1]

-150 **6** 2 1/2 **Tungsten Strike (USA)**[42] 2787 6-9-5 109 DarryllHolland 9 101
(Mrs A J Perrett) *mostly in 3rd tl chsd ldr over 4f out to over 3f out: fdd fnl 2f* **14/1**

/13- **7** 1/2 **Distinction (IRE)**[406] 2773 8-9-5 115 JimmyFortune 1 100
(Sir Michael Stoute) *trckd ldrs: prog to go 2nd over 3f out to wl over 1f out: wknd* **15/2**[2]

0330 **8** nk **Bulwark (IRE)**[42] 2787 5-9-5 104 (be) JimCrowley 12 100
(Mrs A J Perrett) *hld up in last quartet: hmpd over 4f out: sn rdn: plugged on u.p fnl 3f: nvr a threat* **40/1**

-000 **9** 1 **Land 'n Stars**[65] 2125 7-9-5 106 PaulDoe 13 99
(R A Fahey) *bit bkwd: prom in chsng pack: rdn 4f out: steadily wknd fr over 2f out* **40/1**

6-22 **10** nk **Falpiase (IRE)**[22] 3412 5-9-5 82 EddieAhern 2 98
(J Howard Johnson) *edgy: trckd ldrs: drvn over 3f out: stl chsng u.p over 2f out: wknd over 1f out* **100/1**

5-10 **11** 1/2 **Greenwich Meantime**[33] 3090 7-9-5 99 PaulHanagan 14 98
(R A Fahey) *lw: chsd ldrs: rdn wl over 3f out: no prog over 2f out: wknd wl over 1f out* **20/1**

3356 **12** 2 1/2 **Foxhaven**[21] 3461 5-9-5 109 NCallan 6 95
(P R Chamings) *lw: settled in midfield: rdn wl over 3f out: no prog: wknd wl over 1f out* **33/1**

-202 **13** 6 **Baddam**[40] 2860 5-9-5 106 IanMongan 10 88
(M R Channon) *lw: a in rr: drvn in last over 6f out: nvr gng wl after* **18/1**

50-1 **14** 36 **Rayhani (USA)**[69] 2002 4-9-5 99 MartinDwyer 3 44
(M P Tregoning) *lw: dwlt: t.k.h and sn in midfield: rdn and wknd over 3f out: t.o* **12/1**

3620 **15** 31 **Baizically (IRE)**[61] 2245 4-9-5 89 TPQueally 15 7
(J A Osborne) *swtg: led after 1f: clr after 4f: hdd & wknd rapidly 5f out: t.o* **100/1**

3m 25.61s (-5.18) **Going Correction** +0.075s/f (Good)
WFA 3 from 4yo+ 15lb **15** Ran SP% **123.1**
Speed ratings (Par 115): **115,114,114,111,111 109,109,109,108,108 108,107,104,86,70**
CSF £83.09 TOTE £10.40: £3.00, £3.10, £5.70; EX 128.30 Trifecta £1858.60 Pool: £2,879.65, 1.10 winning units.
Owner Cheveley Park Stud **Bred** Miss K Rausing And Airlie Stud **Trained** Newmarket, Suffolk
■ Allegretto became the first filly to win this race since Gladness in 1958.
■ Stewards' Enquiry : Martin Dwyer five-day ban: improper riding - intentional interference (Aug 13-17)

FOCUS
This looked like a very ordinary renewal of the Goodwood Cup beforehand, with both Yeats and Sergeant Cecil notable absentees, and the race itself did little to change that view. The pace, set by Geordieland's stablemate Baizically, seemed fair for all, and the form is best rated through the third.

NOTEBOOK
Allegretto(IRE) managed to win the Henry II Stakes at Sandown in a first-time visor earlier in the season, but she was too lit up in the Ascot Gold Cup on her previous start and she proved much better without the headgear this time. Held up a long way off the fair gallop, she had to be switched out wide in the straight to get a clear run, but it did not cost her any momentum and she stayed on best of all. This performance is all the more creditable considering a 3lb penalty put her on level weights with all bar one of the colts and geldings. It would be no surprise to see her aimed at something like the Irish St Leger next, as a step up to Group 1 company is the next obvious step having won three Group 2s. Official explanation: trainer's rep said, regarding the improved form shown, filly wore a visor at Ascot and ran too free, but settled better today without a visor
Veracity, the only three-year-old in the line up, showed improved form to run second in the Queen's Vase on his previous start and he looked to step up again with another tremendous effort in defeat. His rider put up 1lb overweight and there will no doubt be some people who feel that made the difference between winning and losing but, whatever the case, this was a huge performance against his elders. Like the winner held up quite a way off the pace, he stayed on most willingly for pressure in the straight and found only one too good. He is entered in the Ebor, but the St Leger is likely to be his next target. One could see him running a big race at Doncaster, such is the rate at which he is improving, but he will have work to do to reverse Ascot form with Mahler, and that one is unlikely to be Ballydoyle's sole representative in the last domestic Classic of the season. (op 12-1)
Finalmente proved a touch disappointing in a four-runner Listed event at Sandown on his previous start but, fitted with cheekpieces for the first time, he returned to the sort of form he showed when fourth in the Ascot Gold Cup. Given a positive ride, he kept on well for pressure in the straight and easily fared best of those to race handily. He can make his mark in Group company. (op 14-1 tchd 18-1 in a place)
Balkan Knight deserved his chance in this grade having won his last two starts in Listed company, the last of which when less than a length in front of Finalmente, but he just came up short of what was required. He was produced with every chance in the straight, and briefly looked dangerous, but the front three ultimately just proved too strong. (tchd 7-1)
Geordieland(FR) was the clear form pick in the absence of Yeats, to whom he ran second in both this race last year and more recently the Ascot Gold Cup, but he came into this winless since he was trained in France back in 2005, and had not always found great deal under pressure. He again failed to deliver when asked for a finishing kick, finding nothing despite being produced beautifully towards the inside rail around two furlongs from the finish, and was no doubt called a few names afterwards. However, one suspects he is not ungenuine, and his lack of will-to-win has more to do with the fact he has broken blood-vessels in the past, as often when a horse bleeds they can be reluctant to ever fully exert themselves again in fear of feeling pain. (op 15-8 tchd 2-1)
Tungsten Strike(USA), who ran like a non-stayer in the Ascot Gold Cup on his previous start, was well enough placed for much of the way, but he did not really pick up in the straight and was below his best.
Distinction(IRE) had not been seen since running third in last year's Ascot Gold Cup and, having travelled quite well for much of the way, he appeared to get tired at the business end, despite looking fit enough in the paddock. He appears to retain plenty of his ability and he should come on a fair bit for the outing, although one will have to be wary of the bounce factor if he is turned out again quickly. (op 7-1)
Bulwark(IRE) has yet to prove himself quite up to this level and he ran about as well as could have been expected. (op 50-1)
Land 'n Stars shaped quite nicely off the back of a two-month break on just his second start for Richard Fahey. (op 33-1)
Falpiase(IRE) was beaten off a mark 82 at Catterick on his previous start and his proximity does not do a great deal for the form, but he is bred to be pretty decent, being a half-brother to Falbrav, and this was clearly his best effort yet. (op 66-1)
Greenwich Meantime will be better off back in handicap company. (op 25-1)
Rayhani(USA), off the track since winning over 1m4f off a mark of 89 over two months previously, had it all to do in this company and was never really going. (op 11-1)

Baizically(IRE) Official explanation: jockey said gelding boiled over in preliminaries

4092 ALPHAMERIC VASE (HERITAGE H'CAP) 1m 1f 192y
4:00 (4:04) (Class 2) 3-Y-O

£62,320 (£18,660; £9,330; £4,670; £2,330; £1,170) **Stalls** High

Form RPR

6114 **1** **Pipedreamer**[21] 3460 3-8-4 93 MartinDwyer 16 108+
(J H M Gosden) *hld up in rr: nt clr run briefly over 2f out: swtchd outside and gd prog over 1f out: led ins fnl f: romped clr* **11/2**[1]

1204 **2** 1 1/2 **Mr Aviator (USA)**[5] 3940 3-7-12 87 oh2 FrancisNorton 8 95
(R Hannon) *mostly in 3rd: drvn over 2f out: r.o over 1f out to chal ent fnl f: brushed aside by wnr fnl 100yds* **9/1**

4141 **3** 1/2 **Six Of Diamonds (IRE)**[14] 3691 3-7-12 87 oh4 DavidKinsella 1 94
(J A Osborne) *led: stl gng strly over 2f out: hrd pressed over 1f out: hdd and outpcd ins fnl f* **20/1**

4005 **4** 1/2 **Players Please (USA)**[15] 3650 3-7-10 88 ow1 LiamJones(3) 10 94
(M Johnston) *prom: rdn on inner to dispute 2nd wl over 1f out: hanging and nt qckn after: kpt on* **17/2**

1450 **5** 1 **Many Volumes (USA)**[21] 3460 3-8-8 97 RichardHughes 6 101
(H R A Cecil) *lw: sn trckd ldr: rdn over 2f out: tried to cl over 1f out: one pce u.p fnl f* **14/1**

5405 **6** hd **Buccellati**[21] 3460 3-7-9 87 oh3 (v1) WilliamBuick(3) 12 91
(A M Balding) *lw: hld up towards rr: rdn wl over 2f out and no rspnse: r.o fnl f: nrst fin* **10/1**

11-5 **7** nk **Proponent (IRE)**[77] 1790 3-8-5 94 SteveDrowne 13 97+
(R Charlton) *lw: pushed up to rch midfield after 1f: effrt on outer gng wl 3f out: chsd ldrs over 1f out: drvn and one pce* **7/1**[2]

-455 **8** hd **Smart Instinct (USA)**[19] 3558 3-8-8 97 PaulHanagan 15 100
(R A Fahey) *hld up in midfield: effrt on inner 3f out: drvn to chse ldrs and cl enough over 1f out: fdd* **14/1**

0-01 **9** 1 1/2 **Smokey Oakey (IRE)**[67] 2057 3-7-12 87 oh1 JimmyQuinn 2 87
(M H Tompkins) *dropped in fr wd draw and hld up in last trio: prog on inner 3f out: rdn and kpt on same pce last 2f: n.d* **20/1**

4211 **10** hd **Emerald Wilderness (IRE)**[14] 3672 3-7-8 90 MCGeran(7) 18 89+
(E A L Dunlop) *mostly in midfield: nt clr run over 2f out: drvn and tried to cl on ldrs over 1f out: one pce fnl f* **14/1**

551 **11** 1 1/2 **Urban Spirit**[22] 3436 3-7-12 87 oh1 DaleGibson 5 83
(B W Hills) *swtg: trckd ldrs: rdn and stl chsng 2f out: wknd over 1f out* **16/1**

0105 **12** 2 1/2 **Halicarnassus (IRE)**[21] 3458 3-9-5 108 JHBowman 4 99
(M R Channon) *hld up wl in rr: rdn 3f out: no real prog* **16/1**

1021 **13** nk **Sahrati**[5] 3959 3-8-4 93 6ex PaulDoe 14 84+
(C E Brittain) *mostly midfield: rdn and no prog whn squeezed for room over 2f out: wknd* **12/1**

-303 **14** nk **Ladies Best**[21] 3460 3-8-3 92 JohnEgan 3 82+
(Sir Michael Stoute) *drvn to try to improve in midfield over 5f out: u.p whn nt clr run over 2f out: wknd* **8/1**[3]

2301 **15** shd **Hearthstead Maison (IRE)**[21] 3460 3-9-4 110 GregFairley(3) 7 100
(M Johnston) *lw: t.k.h early: hld up wl in rr: rdn over 3f out: no prog* **8/1**[3]

200 **16** 5 **Aegean Prince**[28] 3235 3-7-12 87 oh6 AdrianMcCarthy 17 67
(W R Muir) *swtg: hld up in rr: no prog 3f out: sn eased* **66/1**

6-00 **17** 32 **Prince Of Elegance**[5] 3940 3-8-3 92 JoeFanning 9 8
(Mrs A J Perrett) *hld up in last: lost tch 1/2-way: sn t.o* **80/1**

2m 5.87s (-1.88) **Going Correction** +0.075s/f (Good) **17** Ran SP% **131.4**
Speed ratings (Par 106): **110,108,108,108,107 107,106,106,105,105 104,102,101,101,101 97,71**
CSF £55.67 CT £967.68 TOTE £6.60: £1.90, £3.00, £5.40, £3.00; EX 79.50 Trifecta £1538.20 Part won. Pool: £2,166.60, 0.10 winning units..
Owner Cheveley Park Stud **Bred** Cheveley Park Stud Ltd **Trained** Newmarket, Suffolk
■ Stewards' Enquiry : M C Geran three-day: careless riding (Aug 13-15)

FOCUS
A race that is usually one of the most competitive three-year-old handicaps of the season and this year's renewal was no different. They went a sound gallop up front and there were no alarmingly unlucky horses in behind, so the form looks reliable despite the placed horses racing from out of the handicap and the race should produce its share of winners.

NOTEBOOK
Pipedreamer ◆ confirmed the promise of his debut effort with wins at this course and on his handicap debut at Pontefract, but he fell short off this mark at Newmarket last time when only fourth in a similarly hot handicap and needed to pull out more if he was to be successful. Restrained from his good draw, he was forced to come wide with his challenge having met trouble, but really motored in the final furlong and won in the style of a smart performer. On this evidence it is not hard to see him developing into a Listed/Group 3 performer, his trainer knowing what to do with this type, and there is every reason to believe he will stay further in time. (op 13-2)
Mr Aviator(USA) had probably recorded his best effort of the season over this course and distance back in June, when finishing second, and his recent effort at Ascot pointed to a return to the trip suiting. One of many to race from out of the handicap, he was always well positioned and had his chance, but Pipedreamer proved too classy. This distance clearly suits best and he will find another race before long. (op 12-1 tchd 14-1 in a place)
Six Of Diamonds(IRE) ◆, 9lb higher than when dead-heating at Sandown last time, taking into account he was racing from 4lb out of the weights, overcame the worst draw of all to lead and he ran a cracking race, travelling strongly throughout and sticking on dourly once headed. He is clearly a most progressive colt and any further progression will see him winning again sooner rather than later.
Players Please(USA) ◆, unlucky not to get closer that seventh in the Britannia at Royal Ascot, found 1m around Lingfield's tight circuit totally against him last time and he looked a major player on this return to further. Well positioned on the rail just a few back, he held every chance as they raced into the final quarter mile, but could not quicken and did his rider no favours by hanging. It is possible this was not his track and there is a decent race in him at some stage this season. (op 11-1 tchd 12-1 in places)
Many Volumes(USA) fell short at Pattern level earlier in the season, but his recent Newmarket effort behind a couple of these was better and he again ran well. That said, he is currently on a very stiff mark and is going to remain vulnerable to less-exposed horses in handicaps. (op 16-1)
Buccellati has performed well on all bar one of his runs in competitive handicaps this season, most recently when one place behind Pipedreamer at Newmarket, and this was another sound performance in the first-time visor. Often held up in his races, he is usually running on all too late and maybe it is time for connections to consider a change of tactics. (tchd 9-1)
Proponent(IRE) ◆, who lost his unbeaten record when trounced in the Dante, had the faster ground in his favour here, but had been off since May and, having travelled well, his effort fizzled out in the final furlong. It is possible he needed this and he remains capable of better. (op 13-2)
Smart Instinct(USA) has run well in some big handicaps this season, most recently the John Smith's Cup, but having got himself into contention he did not find a great deal and was slightly disappointing in the end. He is likely to remain vulnerable off this mark.
Smokey Oakey(IRE), dropped in from his poor draw, was always going to be doing well to get involved and he could only make limited late headway. He can be rated a bit better than the bare form and remains open to further improvement.
Emerald Wilderness(IRE), on a hat-trick following wins at Windsor and Folkestone, was up a further 4lb and the more competitive nature of this contest was too much for him.

Urban Spirit showed useful form in maidens and lost that tag when upsetting hot-pot Jack Junior at Newmarket last time. However, this was a most competitive contest and, having been close enough with two furlongs to run, he could not get himself into it.
Halicarnassus(IRE) failed to quite get home over 1m5f in the Bahrain Trophy, but this trip proved to be on the sharp side and he struggled to make an impact. He is going to find it hard in handicaps off this sort of mark. (op 20-1 tchd 25-1 in a place)
Sahrati, a tough and progressive son of In The Wings, was shouldering a penalty for his recent Newmarket victory and already looked in trouble when getting slightly impeded. He is better than this and has bounced back from poor runs already this season.
Ladies Best had form tied in with most of these, having finished third in Hearthstead Maison's Newmarket race, but he failed to reproduce that effort and was already beginning to look in trouble when short of room. (op 15-2)
Hearthstead Maison(IRE), whose only two previous handicap ventures had yielded two taking wins, one at each of the Newmarket courses, had looked to fall just short of Group class on several starts in between, but the way in which he defied top weight on the July course suggested otherwise. He had to be respected here depsite being asked to defy a mark of 110, but found himself too far back early on and could never get into it. This was not his running and it would not surprise to see him bounce back in a little Listed/Group 3 contest somewhere. (tchd 17-2 in a place)
Aegean Prince, racing from 6lb out of the weights, flopped in heavy ground at Newbury last time and better should have been expected here looking at his earlier efforts, but he was eased off once beaten and looks to be going the wrong way.
Prince Of Elegance, who looked in need of the outing on his seasonal reappearance at Sandown, has shown absolutely nothing in two subsequent starts and cannot be backed until showing more. The Handicapper will have to relent eventually. (op 66-1 tchd 100-1)

4093 DE BOER STKS (H'CAP) 7f
4:35 (4:36) (Class 2) (0-100,97) 3-Y-O
£24,928 (£7,464; £3,732; £1,400; £1,400; £468) **Stalls** High

Form RPR
1321 **1** **Docofthebay (IRE)**[20] 3480 3-8-13 **89** RyanMoore 12 99
(J A Osborne) *wl in rr: rdn over 2f out: prog but hanging rt over 1f out: drvn to cl fnl f: forced ahd fnl 50yds* **4/1**[2]
2116 **2** ½ **Vitznau (IRE)**[22] 3431 3-8-13 **89** RichardHughes 10 98+
(R Hannon) *lw: hld up in midfield: smooth prog fr 2f out: rdn to ld fnl 150yds: hdd 50yds out* **9/1**
1101 **3** 1 ¼ **Shmookh (USA)**[22] 3431 3-9-7 **97** RHills 19 102+
(J L Dunlop) *lw: trckd ldng trio: smooth prog to ld jst over 2f out: rdn over 1f out: hdd and fdd fnl 150yds* **7/2**[1]
0-12 **4** 1 ¼ **Tombi (USA)**[76] 1825 3-8-9 **85** EddieAhern 5 87+
(J Howard Johnson) *lw: hld up wl in rr on outer: effrt 3f out: drvn and r.o fr over 1f out: nvr pce to chal* **16/1**
1-22 **4** dht **Miss Lucifer (FR)**[68] 2040 3-9-0 **90** MichaelHills 18 92
(B W Hills) *stdd s: hld up wl in rr: stdy prog on inner fr 1/2-way: trckd ldrs gng strly over 1f out: rdn and nt qckn* **8/1**[3]
000 **6** ½ **Cesc**[5] 3960 3-9-0 **90** TQuinn 7 91
(P J Makin) *hld up wl in rr on outer: stl in last pair over 2f out: rdn and r.o fr over 1f out: nrst fin* **33/1**
4100 **7** ½ **Yaroslav (USA)**[20] 3503 3-8-6 **82** (b) SteveDrowne 9 81
(R Charlton) *racd freely: chsd ldr: stl disputing 2nd over 1f out: wknd ins fnl f* **9/1**
0113 **8** nk **Samsons Son**[6] 3913 3-8-8 **84** ow1 DaneO'Neill 8 82
(J R Best) *dwlt: hld up wl in rr on outer: kpt on fnl 2f: n.d* **12/1**
0040 **9** nk **Regal Parade**[5] 3941 3-9-3 **93** JoeFanning 4 91
(M Johnston) *lw: racd wd early: wl in tch: prog over 2f out: rdn to dispute 2nd over 1f out: n.m.r after: wknd fnl f* **12/1**
1433 **10** 1 **Kyle (IRE)**[22] 3418 3-8-9 **85** PatDobbs 17 80
(R Hannon) *trckd ldrs: prog to go 2nd wl over 1f out: sn rdn: wknd ins fnl f* **12/1**
4006 **11** ½ **Voodoo Moon**[9] 3813 3-8-8 **87** GregFairley[(3)] 11 81
(M Johnston) *chsd ldng pair: rdn to try to chal on inner whn hmpd over 2f out: nt rcvr: wknd over 1f out* **22/1**
3100 **12** 1 ½ **Heywood**[24] 3380 3-9-1 **91** JHBowman 16 81
(M R Channon) *edgy: chsd ldrs: rdn wl over 2f out: no prog: fdd* **25/1**
2030 **13** shd **Love On Sight**[20] 3480 3-8-4 **83** WilliamBuick[(3)] 2 72
(A P Jarvis) *swtg: hld up in last: rdn 3f out: no prog and btn after* **33/1**
-054 **14** nk **Teslin (IRE)**[76] 1803 3-9-6 **96** JMurtagh 15 85
(B Ellison) *lw: hld up wl in rr: effrt on inner fr 3f out: no imp wl over 1f out: wknd* **25/1**
0-00 **15** 3 ½ **Rainbow Mirage (IRE)**[22] 3431 3-8-12 **88** RichardMullen 6 67
(E S McMahon) *racd wd in midfield: struggling over 2f out: hanging rt and wknd after* **16/1**
-545 **16** 3 **Soviet Palace (IRE)**[13] 3707 3-8-9 **85** NCallan 14 56
(K A Ryan) *swtg: racd freely: led at str pce to jst over 2f out: wknd rapidly* **22/1**

1m 25.89s (-2.15) **Going Correction** +0.075s/f (Good) **16** Ran SP% **130.4**
Speed ratings (Par 106): **115,114,113,111,111 111,110,110,109,108 108,106,106,105,101 98**
TOTE 4th place: Miss Lucifer £0.80, Tombi £1.80 CSF £39.23 CT £150.83 TOTE £4.20: £1.10, £3.10, £1.70 Trifecta £109.80 Pool: £1,325.86, 8.57 winning units..
Owner Paul J Dixon **Bred** G And Mrs Middlebrook **Trained** Upper Lambourn, Berks
■ This completed a 1,979/1 four-timer for Ryan Moore.

FOCUS
They went a decent gallop in this competitive handicap, and the majority of those involved in the finish came from off the pace. The form has a solid look to it.

NOTEBOOK
Docofthebay(IRE), 4lb higher than when successful at Ascot, just keeps improving, and because he never wins by far he keeps one step ahead of the Handicapper. He needed all of Moore's brilliance to get him up in the closing stages, but while he is undoubtedly a difficult ride, his strike-rate makes it clear that he has plenty of ability. (tchd 9-2)
Vitznau(IRE) travelled well on this return to 7f and looked to have been brought with a well-timed challenge until the winner appeared on the scene. This certainly seems to be his best trip and, while he is likely to edge up the handicap again for this, he remains on the upgrade. (tchd 10-1)
Shmookh(USA), raised 8lb for his Newmarket success, did best of those that raced close to the decent gallop. All around him at the finish were rivals that had been held up further back off the fast pace, so it would be wrong to suggest that he does not get home over this trip. (op 10-3)
Tombi(USA) had a tough task from his draw and his stamina to prove at the trip. However, in the event he saw it out well having challenged out wide. (tchd 17-2 and 9-1 in places)
Miss Lucifer(FR) had been off the track since May so this was a promising return to action. One of the least experienced in the line-up, she stayed on well after travelling quite nicely, and she looks the type who could nick a bit of black type in a fillies-only Listed race somewhere later this season. (tchd 17-2 and 9-1 in places)
Cesc is held off his current mark, but the way the race was run meant that he was able to stay on strongly from the back of the field for a creditable sixth.
Yaroslav(USA) used up too much energy early racing keenly and chasing the strong pace. He was not disgraced in the circumstances. (op 11-1)
Samsons Son was another who stayed on late off the good gallop, but he never threatened for the win. Easier ground seems to suit him. (op 14-1)
Regal Parade, who had an excuse at Ascot last time, had every chance in the straight but was a bit one-paced. He looks held off his current mark.
Voodoo Moon was hampered by the weakening leader on the rail approaching the two-furlong marker, but she was not going anywhere fast at the time. (op 20-1)

4094 EUROPEAN BREEDERS' FUND NEW HAM MAIDEN FILLIES' STKS 7f
5:05 (5:08) (Class 2) 2-Y-O **£10,363** (£3,083; £1,540; £769) **Stalls** High

Form RPR
6 **1** **Celtic Slipper (IRE)**[54] 2457 2-9-0 0 SebSanders 2 78
(R M Beckett) *trckd ldrs: prog on outer 2f out: hanging rt but drvn to ld last 100yds: r.o wl* **33/1**
2 **2** 1 ¼ **Badalona**[13] 3706 2-9-0 0 JamieSpencer 16 75
(M L W Bell) *lw: cl up: effrt to ld over 2f out: drvn over 1f out: hdd and outpcd last 100yds* **5/2**[1]
3 nk **Park Royal (UAE)** 2-9-0 0 JoeFanning 17 74
(M Johnston) *unf: leggy: led after 2f at stdy pce: hdd over 2f out: pressed ldr after: upsides ent fnl f: intimidated & nt qckn last 100yds* **12/1**
4 1 **Dona Alba (IRE)** 2-9-0 0 EddieAhern 7 72
(J L Dunlop) *leggy: scope: dwlt: sn in midfield: prog on inner over 2f out: cl up over 1f out: kpt on but outpcd fnl f* **66/1**
0 **5** 1 ¼ **Top Vision**[20] 3507 2-9-0 0 JHBowman 13 69
(M R Channon) *lw: trckd ldrs: shkn up 2f out: styd on but outspded fr over 1f out* **6/1**
6 **6** 1 ¾ **Lady Zabeen (IRE)**[34] 3055 2-9-0 0 NCallan 8 64
(D M Simcock) *t.k.h: trckd ldrs: rdn 2f out: outpcd fr over 1f out* **16/1**
7 1 **Armure** 2-9-0 0 PhilipRobinson 15 62
(M A Jarvis) *leggy: unf: scope: led at stdy pce for 2f: chsd ldr to over 2f out: outpcd over 1f out* **25/1**
8 nk **Lemon N Sugar (USA)** 2-9-0 0 JMurtagh 10 61+
(J Noseda) *w'like: scope: lw: chsd ldrs: pushed along whn slt bump over 2f out: outpcd fr wl over 1f out* **11/4**[2]
6 **9** nk **Berrynarbor**[59] 2303 2-9-0 0 FergusSweeney 14 60
(A G Newcombe) *chsd ldrs: effrt on inner whn hmpd over 2f out: nt rcvr: one pce after* **50/1**
0 **10** nk **Baraari (USA)**[20] 3507 2-9-0 0 MartinDwyer 4 60
(J L Dunlop) *t.k.h: hld up wl in rr: shuffled along over 2f out: kpt on: no ch* **14/1**
0 **11** nk **Politeia (USA)**[20] 3507 2-9-0 0 RyanMoore 3 59
(R Hannon) *hld up wl in rr: shuffled along and no prog over 2f out* **9/2**[3]
0 **12** ½ **Dream Bee**[22] 3435 2-9-0 0 DaneO'Neill 5 58
(E A L Dunlop) *w'like: bit bkwd: hld up wl in rr: shuffled along and no prog over 2f out* **50/1**
05 **13** hd **Infinite Patience**[10] 3796 2-9-0 0 JohnEgan 11 57
(J S Moore) *hld up towards rr: rdn over 2f out: no prog* **40/1**
14 ½ **Amhooj** 2-9-0 0 WilliamBuick 9 56
(M P Tregoning) *leggy: scope athletic: hld up wl in rr: shkn up 3f out: no prog* **25/1**
15 1 ½ **Zerky (USA)** 2-9-0 0 RHills 6 52
(E A L Dunlop) *w'like: scope: t.k.h: hld up in rr: shuffled along and no prog over 2f out* **20/1**
0 **16** 1 ½ **Kashmina**[13] 3706 2-9-0 0 DarryllHolland 1 48
(M R Channon) *a in last pair: pushed along and struggling 3f out* **25/1**

1m 30.04s (2.00) **Going Correction** +0.075s/f (Good) **16** Ran SP% **135.0**
Speed ratings (Par 97): **91,89,89,88,86 84,83,83,82,82 82,81,81,80,79 77**
CSF £118.56 TOTE £43.50: £9.50, £1.50, £4.90; EX 210.00 TRIFECTA Not won..
Owner P D Savill **Bred** Peter Savill **Trained** Whitsbury, Hants

FOCUS
They did not go a strong pace in this fillies' maiden and the form looks no more than fair. The runner-up is the best guide although the form is somewhat guessy.

NOTEBOOK
Celtic Slipper(IRE) had run with promise on her debut over 6f and this furlong longer trip promised to suit her well. The competition was tougher though, and that was reflected in her SP. She did it well though, finishing well down the outside and running out a clear winner despite hanging right. She looks one for nurseries over a mile in time.
Badalona, runner-up at Newmarket on her debut and well drawn here, looked to have plenty going for her. She did not do a lot wrong in all honesty, just meeting one too good on the day, and a similar race should be within her ability. (old market op 11-4 tchd 3-1 and 10-3 in places)
Park Royal(UAE), who is closely related to a dual six-year-old winner in Saudi Arabia by Green Desert, enjoyed the run of the race and was able to dictate a fairly modest pace for much of the event. She had every chance, but the first two had the benefit of previous experience and she can be expected to come on for this debut. (old market op 14-1 tchd 16-1)
Dona Alba(IRE), a half-sister to Last Flight, a 2m winner at three, was understandably shunned in the betting as she is bred to make a stayer next year. In the circumstances it was highly encouraging that she was able to run so well on her debut.
Top Vision, like on her debut, stayed on well at the finish. She could have done with a stronger pace. (old market op 8-1)
Lady Zabeen(IRE) was not particularly suited by the way the race was run, racing keenly off the steady early gallop and finding herself outpaced as the principals quickened. She is another bred to want a good deal further as a three-year-old. (old market op 20-1)
Armure, whose dam won over 1m2f and is a half-sister to top-class Barathea, is a half-sister herself to four winners at various distances. Unfancied on her debut, she looks another who will improve with time, and middle distances will be her game next season. (old market tchd 33-1)
Lemon N Sugar(USA), bought for $350,000 at the breeze-ups, was well backed from a yard which knows how to get one ready first time up. All did not go to plan on this occasion but she is clearly well regarded and better is likely to be seen of her. (old market op 7-2 tchd 4-1 and 10-3)
Politeia(USA) was another who came in for market support, but in her case it was probably due to people jumping on the Moore bandwagon following his four-timer earlier on the card. (old market op 13-2 and 7-1 in places)

4095 AUDI Q7 CUP STKS (H'CAP) 5f
5:40 (5:41) (Class 3) (0-90,90) 4-Y-O+ **£10,363** (£3,083; £1,540; £769) **Stalls** Low

Form RPR
1500 **1** **Continent**[23] 3401 10-9-2 **85** PaulHanagan 19 95
(D Nicholls) *swtg: t.k.h: hld up in midfield in centre: prog gng strly 2f out: urged along and styd on wl to ld fnl 75yds* **18/1**
3000 **2** ½ **Diane's Choice**[27] 3268 4-8-11 **80** DaneO'Neill 10 88
(J Akehurst) *trckd nr side ldrs: rdn to ld overall over 1f out: collared fnl 75yds* **33/1**
4000 **3** nk **Magic Glade**[21] 3464 8-9-2 **88** RichardKingscote[(3)] 7 95
(Tom Dascombe) *taken down early: chsd nr side ldrs: effrt over 1f out: r.o to chal ins fnl f: jst outpcd* **25/1**
0000 **4** shd **Texas Gold**[19] 3526 9-9-4 **87** MartinDwyer 2 94+
(W R Muir) *towards rr nr side: drvn 1/2-way: r.o wl fnl f: gaining at fin* **14/1**

1405 **5** ½ **Raccoon (IRE)**[12] 3749 7-8-9 **78**.. JohnEgan 20 83
(D W Chapman) *w ldrs in centre: stl upsides whn gps merged 2f out: carried lft 1f out: nt qckn* **14/1**

3161 **6** nk **Safari Mischief**[21] 3452 4-8-7 **79**.................................... LiamJones(3) 22 83
(P Winkworth) *w ldrs in centre: upsides 1f out: one pce fnl f* **16/1**

1502 **7** shd **Rainbow Bay**[8] 3836 4-7-9 **71** oh2.......................(v) MCGeran(7) 16 74
(P D Evans) *wl in rr in centre: prog over 1f out: styd on fnl f: nrst fin* **16/1**

0030 **8** ½ **Indian Trail**[13] 3720 7-9-7 **90**......................................(v) AdrianTNicholls 1 92+
(D Nicholls) *hld up against nr side rail: trapped w nowhere to go fr 1/2-way tl ins fnl f: r.o fnl 100yds: nt rcvr* **15/2**[2]

2240 **9** nk **Bond Boy**[10] 3791 10-8-8 **77**...(b) JamieSpencer 18 77
(G R Oldroyd) *hld up wl in rr in centre: prog fr 2f out: drvn and styd on fnl f: nt rch ldrs* **14/1**

6066 **10** hd **Pic Up Sticks**[46] 2694 8-8-5 **74**.................................... DO'Donohoe 5 74
(B G Powell) *b. dwlt: wl in rr nr side: no prog tl styd on wl fnl f: nrst fin* **12/1**

0140 **11** nk **Misaro (GER)**[4] 3990 6-8-13 **87**.................................(b) LukeMorris(5) 3 86
(R A Harris) *b.hind: lw: dwlt: sn trckd nr side ldrs: one pce fnl f* **10/1**[3]

5-60 **12** shd **Little Edward**[19] 3526 9-9-0 **83**.................................... PaulEddery 17 81
(R J Hodges) *s.i.s: wl in rr in centre: prog fr 2f out: chsng ldrs u.p 1f out: no ex* **33/1**

0053 **13** hd **Mr Wolf**[13] 3720 6-9-3 **86**..(p) JimmyFortune 23 84
(D W Barker) *overall ldr in centre to wl over 1f out: wknd and eased ins fnl f* **7/1**[1]

6250 **14** nk **Talbot Avenue**[27] 3268 9-9-2 **85**... TPQueally 12 81
(M Blanshard) *b. hld up in rr in centre: stdy prog fr 1/2-way to trck ldrs over 1f out: effrt petered out fnl f* **20/1**

-000 **15** nk **Pacific Pride**[28] 3240 4-9-5 **88**.................................(v) GrahamGibbons 11 83
(J J Quinn) *in rr of gp in centre: wl in rr whn gps merged 2f out: hmpd 1f out: styd on nr fin* **14/1**

1223 **16** nk **George The Second**[6] 3906 4-8-2 **71** oh6.......................... DaleGibson 14 65
(Mrs H Sweeting) *off the pce in centre: wl in rr whn gps merged 2f out: n.d* **25/1**

6060 **17** nk **Harry Up**[17] 3586 6-9-3 **86**... NCallan 6 79
(K A Ryan) *lw: led nr side gp to wl over 1f out: wknd fnl f* **25/1**

0100 **18** ¾ **Oranmore Castle (IRE)**[54] 2461 5-8-9 **78**...................(t) SamHitchcott 15 69
(D Nicholls) *taken down early: w ldrs in centre to 1/2-way: sn lost pl and btn* **28/1**

4034 **19** 1½ **Holbeck Ghyll (IRE)**[12] 3749 5-8-6 **78**...................(b[1]) WilliamBuick(3) 9 63
(A M Balding) *s.s: wl in rr nr side: u.p and no prog fr 1/2-way* **7/1**[1]

4240 **20** 1 **Spanish Ace**[54] 2463 6-9-3 **86**.. DarryllHolland 8 68
(J M Bradley) *b. lw: racd centre: nvr on terms: wl in rr whn gps merged 2f out* **33/1**

5353 **21** 1 **Canadian Danehill (IRE)**[12] 3749 5-8-7 **76**...................(p) EddieAhern 4 54
(R M H Cowell) *trckd nrside ldrs: lost pl 2f out: no ch whn hmpd 1f out* **25/1**

6135 **22** 18 **Peopleton Brook**[46] 2694 5-8-11 **80**.............................. JHBowman 21 —
(J M Bradley) *w ldrs in centre: wknd over 1f out: no ch whn hmpd ent fnl f and virtually p.u* **16/1**

57.86 secs (-1.19) **Going Correction** -0.025s/f (Good) **22** Ran SP% **135.5**
Speed ratings (Par 107): **108,107,106,106,105 105,105,104,103,103 103,102,102,102,101 101,100,99,97,95 93,65**
CSF £551.69 CT £14041.04 TOTE £24.00: £5.60, £8.70, £9.00, £4.10; EX 1070.10 TRIFECTA Not won. Place 6 £ 144.61, Place 5 £ 93.36.
Owner Lucayan Stud and G G N Bloodstock **Bred** Juddmonte Farms **Trained** Sessay, N Yorks
■ Stewards' Enquiry : Luke Morris three-day: careless riding (Aug 13-15)

FOCUS
A good, typically competitive sprint handicap and solid enough rated around the third, sixth and seventh. The field split into two groups early on, but they merged into one over two furlongs from the finish, with the field spread out from the stands' rail to the middle of the track. There seemed no great draw bias.

NOTEBOOK
Continent finished last at Pontefract on his previous start, and has always looked best on soft ground, so this was not easy to predict. He also got quite warm beforehand and took a bit of a grip in the race itself, but he had plenty left for the business end and ran out a narrow winner. Although no longer as talented as he used to be, he is still a useful individual and should remain competitive. (op 20-1)
Diane's Choice had not been in much form coming into this and was still 4lb higher than when last winning, but she returned to her best with a blinding effort in defeat. (op 25-1)
Magic Glade has already won four times for his new yard this year and this was another big performance. He is as good as ever.
Texas Gold has not looked the force of old so far this season, but he was 14lb lower than when last winning on turf as a result and returned to some sort of form at a track he often gone well at.
Raccoon(IRE) does not have much in hand of the Handicapper, but this was a solid effort in defeat. (tchd 16-1)
Safari Mischief had a career-high mark to contend with having been raised 5lb for his recent Lingfield success, but he ran with credit.
Rainbow Bay, 2lb out of the handicap, got going too late and looks better over 6f.
Indian Trail, back on more suitable ground, looked unlucky not to be in the shake up as he got no run at all when looking to make his move. He was set to bid for compensation in the Stewards' Sprint Stakes. (tchd 8-1)
Bond Boy was forced to make his move widest of all and is probably a little better than he showed. Official explanation: jockey said gelding hung right-handed (op 16-1 tchd 20-1 in a place)
Mr Wolf promised to be suited by this speed test, but he proved disappointing. Official explanation: jockey said gelding hung left-handed throughout (op 8-1)
Holbeck Ghyll(IRE) never got involved after being slow to find his stride and is proving frustrating. Official explanation: jockey said gelding missed the break (op 6-1)
T/Jkpt: Not won. T/Plt: £104.70 to a £1 stake. Pool: £246,581.55. 1,717.95 winning tickets. T/Qpdt: £45.70 to a £1 stake. Pool: £10,418.30. 168.40 winning tickets. JN

3811 MUSSELBURGH (R-H)

Thursday, August 2

OFFICIAL GOING: Round course - good to firm (good in places); straight course - good (good to firm in places; 8,4)
Wind: Fairly strong, half against Weather: Cloudy

4096 WILKINSONCORR.COM AMATEUR RIDERS' H'CAP 1m 5f
6:10 (6:11) (Class 6) (0-65,65) 4-Y-0+ **£2,498** (£774; £387; £193) **Stalls** High

Form RPR

2554 **1** **Danzatrice**[24] 3371 5-11-1 **59**.. MrSDobson 11 68
(C W Thornton) *hld up: hdwy over 3f out: led and hung lft over 1f out: kpt on strly fnl f* **5/1**[1]

4613 **2** 2 **Kyber**[17] 3584 6-10-10 **54**.. MrsCBartley 14 60
(J S Goldie) *hld up: hdwy to chse ldrs over 3f out: effrt and ev ch over 1f out: one pce fnl f* **5/1**[1]

6051 **3** 1¼ **Thorny Mandate**[3] 4025 5-11-2 **65** 6ex.................. MrBenBrisbourne(5) 3 69
(W M Brisbourne) *bhd tl styd on fr 2f out: nrst fin* **6/1**[2]

2210 **4** 2 **Rudry World (IRE)**[6] 3901 4-10-6 **55**........................ MissMMullineaux(5) 8 56
(M Mullineaux) *hld up: hdwy in centre over 2f out: no imp over 1f out* **12/1**

6451 **5** 4 **Atlantic Gamble (IRE)**[14] 3684 7-11-2 **65**...........(p) MissKellyBurke(5) 5 60
(K R Burke) *mde most to over 1f out: sn no ex* **12/1**

0/46 **6** 1¼ **Oniz Tiptoes (IRE)**[16] 3630 6-10-4 **55**..................(v) MissFRodmell(7) 12 48
(J S Wainwright) *prom: lost pl 1/2-way: sme late hdwy: n.d* **11/1**

4220 **7** 1 **Eijaaz (IRE)**[8] 3840 6-10-9 **56**.. MrSFMagee(3) 7 48
(G A Harker) *midfield: hdwy and prom 3f out: rdn and wknd over 1f out* **14/1**

5-65 **8** 4 **Front Rank (IRE)**[35] 3012 7-10-7 **58**................................ MissNSayer(7) 1 44
(Mrs Dianne Sayer) *bhd: rdn and hung to stands' rail over 2f out: nvr on terms* **33/1**

2-14 **9** 4 **Cumbrian Knight (IRE)**[115] 617 9-9-13 **48**........... MissNJefferson(5) 2 28
(J M Jefferson) *dwlt: effrt fr rr 3f out: n.d* **12/1**

/315 **10** 8 **Grey Samurai**[6] 3901 7-11-2 **60**..(p) MissLEllison 13 28
(B Ellison) *cl up: disp ld over 4f out to over 3f out: wknd over 2f out: eased whn btn over 1f out* **7/1**[3]

-000 **11** 1 **Kyle Of Lochalsh**[9] 3815 7-10-2 **49**...............................(p) MrHHaynes(3) 6 15
(Miss Lucinda V Russell) *chsd ldrs tl wknd over 2f out* **20/1**

-006 **12** 3 **Touch Of Ivory (IRE)**[9] 3815 4-10-10 **57**...................(p) JennyRiding(3) 9 19
(P Monteith) *cl up tl rdn and wknd fr 3f out* **25/1**

6/0- **13** 1¾ **Flying Doctor**[66] 1293 4-10-1 **52**................................ MissJRRichards(7) 4 11
(N G Richards) *bhd: pushed along 4f out: sn btn* **14/1**

0-40 **14** 21 **Brabazon (IRE)**[50] 2567 4-10-9 **60**.......................(b[1]) MrEJO'Connell(7) 10 —
(Barry Potts, Ire) *chsd ldrs tl wknd 3f out: t.o* **12/1**

2m 50.89s (-3.11) **Going Correction** -0.15s/f (Firm) course record **14** Ran SP% **124.1**
Speed ratings (Par 101): **103,101,101,99,97 96,95,93,91,86 85,83,82,69**
CSF £28.81 CT £159.46 TOTE £5.60: £1.70, £2.70, £2.10; EX 37.50.
Owner 980 Racing **Bred** G G A Gregson **Trained** Middleham Moor, N Yorks
■ Stewards' Enquiry : Mr S Dobson two-day ban: careless riding (Aug 16-17)

FOCUS
The ground was mainly good to firm with the round course considered quicker than the straight. Exposed sorts in this moderate handicap but it was run at a decent gallop and the form looks sound rated around the principals.
Grey Samurai Official explanation: jockey said saddle slipped

4097 EUROPEAN BREEDERS' FUND MEDIAN AUCTION MAIDEN FILLIES' STKS 5f
6:40 (6:42) (Class 5) 2-Y-O **£3,886** (£1,156; £577; £288) **Stalls** Low

Form RPR

324 **1** **Cute Ass (IRE)**[27] 3269 2-9-0 0.. PatCosgrave 7 73+
(K R Burke) *mde all: shkn up and edgd lft ent fnl f: sn clr: eased nr fin* **4/9**[1]

40 **2** 2 **Lavande**[36] 2992 2-9-0 0.. TomEaves 2 63
(M J Wallace) *blkd s: in tch: effrt over 1f out: kpt on fnl f: no ch w wnr* **7/1**[3]

6 **3** hd **Easy Wonder (GER)**[37] 2961 2-9-0 0................................. DavidAllan 4 62
(I A Wood) *w ldrs: rdn 2f out: kpt on same pce fnl f* **25/1**

66 **4** 2 **Rio Rocket (IRE)**[17] 3582 2-9-0 0...................................... PaulQuinn 6 55
(G A Swinbank) *prom: effrt on outside over 1f out: edgd rt: sn no ex* **8/1**

442 **5** 2 **Whispering Desert**[16] 3606 2-9-0 0................................. MickyFenton 1 48
(P T Midgley) *w ldrs: drvn and hung bdly rt fr 2f out: sn btn* **6/1**[2]

05 **6** 1¼ **Keep Shining**[43] 2758 2-8-7 0... GaryBartley(7) 3 43
(J S Goldie) *hmpd s: sn rdn in rr: n.d* **50/1**

3060 **7** nk **La Guancha**[9] 3812 2-8-11 0.. PJMcDonald(3) 5 42
(D A Nolan) *chsd ldrs: lost pl 1/2-way: n.d after* **100/1**

61.82 secs (1.32) **Going Correction** +0.05s/f (Good) **7** Ran SP% **113.9**
Speed ratings (Par 91): **91,87,87,84,81 79,78**
CSF £4.22 TOTE £1.30: £1.10, £4.20; EX 4.50.
Owner Bigwigs Bloodstock II **Bred** Ivan And Mrs Eileen Heanen **Trained** Middleham Moor, N Yorks

FOCUS
Not much strength in depth in this juvenile maiden with the winner not needing to be at her best to score.

NOTEBOOK
Cute Ass(IRE), fourth in a Sandown Listed event on her previous start, had by far the best credentials and won as she was entitled to. Making all, she was pushed clear in the final furlong to score eased down, and she now goes for the St Hugh's Stakes at Newbury later this month. (op 1-3 tchd 3-10)
Lavande is better than the bare form as she was squeezed out at the start but was not in the same league as the winner. (op 16-1)
Easy Wonder(GER) improved a little on her debut performance and was only run out of second in the closing stages. (op 20-1)
Rio Rocket(IRE) ran another fair race and is now qualified for a handicap mark. He should prove more effective in that sphere. (op 9-1)
Whispering Desert had her chance but hung badly right from halfway which did not help. Official explanation: jockey said filly hung right-handed throughout (op 15-2 tchd 8-1)

4098 JOHN SMITH'S NO NONSENSE NURSERY 5f
7:15 (7:19) (Class 4) 2-Y-O **£3,886** (£1,156; £577; £288) **Stalls** Low

Form RPR

152 **1** **Rose Siog**[19] 3562 2-9-1 **75**.. TonyHamilton 1 78+
(R A Fahey) *cl up: nt clr run fr 2f out to ent fnl f: qcknd to ld fnl 100yds: comf* **11/4**[1]

0555 **2** 1 **Upstanding**[86] 1553 2-7-13 **66** ow6......................... PatrickDonaghy(7) 11 62
(M Brittain) *mde most to fnl 100yds: kpt on same pce* **66/1**

001 **3** nk **Longoria (IRE)**[63] 2188 2-8-8 **71**.................................. JerryO'Dwyer(3) 7 66
(M G Quinlan) *bhd: hdwy over 1f out: kpt on fnl f* **7/1**

2225 **4** shd **Speedy Senorita (IRE)**[42] 2797 2-8-7 **67**............................. LPKeniry 12 62
(K R Burke) *cl up: ev ch gng wl over 1f out: rdn and no ex ins fnl f* **9/1**

600 **5** 1½ **Orpen's Art (IRE)**[50] 2575 2-7-9 **58** oh3......................... DominicFox(3) 9 48
(N A Callaghan) *prom: effrt over 1f out: edgd lft ins fnl f: kpt on same pce* **6/1**[3]

661 **6** ½ **Glenluji**[61] 2247 2-7-12 **65**.. KellyHarrison(7) 6 53
(J S Goldie) *sn outpcd and struggling: hdwy over 1f out: kpt on fnl f: nrst fin* **16/1**

061 **7** 2½ **Firenza Bond**[19] 3532 2-8-13 **78**................................ SladeO'Hara(5) 4 57
(G R Oldroyd) *blkd s: bhd and outpcd: effrt and hung rt over 1f out: sn no imp* **20/1**

310 **8** 2 **Jennifers Joy (IRE)**[76] 1821 2-9-4 **78**................................ TomEaves 3 50
(M R Channon) *t.k.h: shuffled bk over 3f out: rdn 1/2-way: n.d* **10/3**[2]

6635 **9** 1 1/2 **Cayman Fox**[20] 3492 2-8-12 **75**.................. PJMcDonald(3) 10 41
(James Moffatt) *cl up tl rdn and wknd over 1f out* **12/1**
310 **10** 3 1/2 **Tan Bonita (USA)**[64] 2134 2-9-2 **81**.................. DerekNolan(5) 8 35
(M J Wallace) *in tch: hdwy 1/2-way: wknd over 1f out* **10/1**
6436 **11** 1 **Maracana Boy (IRE)**[14] 3680 2-8-13 **73**..................(b1) PhillipMakin 2 23
(M Dods) *prom tl rdn and wknd fr 2f out* **20/1**
61.87 secs (1.37) **Going Correction** +0.05s/f (Good) **11** Ran SP% **120.2**
Speed ratings (Par 96): **91,89,88,88,86 85,81,78,75,70 68**
CSF £216.42 CT £1210.64 TOTE £3.70: £1.40, £10.10, £1.60; EX 214.60.
Owner The Mick Sweeney Syndicate **Bred** D R Tucker **Trained** Musley Bank, N Yorks

FOCUS
This was quite a competitive nursery, but there was a fair bit of trouble, so the form may not prove entirely reliable and is best assessed through the third.

NOTEBOOK
Rose Siog, a course-and-distance winner on her debut, looked well treated on her form when fifth in the Hilary Needler and, though unable to show that in the testing ground at York on her previous start, she proved it here. Well drawn, she raced prominently but the leaders went across her just after halfway and she was then in a pocket from which she struggled to get out. When she got the gap, she quickened through in good style and is better than the bare form suggests. She could well follow up unless the Handicapper overreacts to this. (op 3-1 tchd 7-2)
Upstanding ran a sound race considering she was carrying 6lb overweight. Making her nursery debut off a mark of 60, she was up there all the way and kept on to hold onto second place. Official explanation: jockey said filly pulled up lame but returned sound (op 40-1)
Longoria(IRE), making her nursery debut, ran on from well back and if she could get a away more quickly will be able to improve on what she has done to date. (op 13-2)
Speedy Senorita(IRE) lived up to her name, but did not quite get home even on this speed-favouring track and may have to be ridden less positively. (op 8-1 tchd 10-1)
Orpen's Art(IRE) attracted support on his nursery debut but, after chasing the leaders, he weakened in the final furlong. (op 5-1 tchd 7-2)
Glenluji was hampered and outpaced early but ran on quite well after being tailed off and shapes as though he needs a stiffer test. (op 18-1)
Firenza Bond, sweating beforehand, was squeezed out at the start but hung right and probably needs easier ground. (op 16-1 tchd 25-1)
Jennifers Joy(IRE), who took a fair hold, was hampered at halfway and her run can be forgotten. (op 4-1)

4099 WILKINSON AND CORR QUALIFIED FINANCIAL RECRUITMENT (S) STKS — 1m
7:45 (7:45) (Class 6) 4-Y-0+ **£2,590** (£770; £385; £192) **Stalls** High

Form RPR
5435 **1** **Kirkby's Treasure**[20] 3497 9-8-12 58.................. PatCosgrave 11 57+
(G A Swinbank) *midfield: hdwy whn nt clr run over 2f out and 1f out: swtchd lft fnl 100yds: r.o to ld nr fin* **5/4**[1]
5-25 **2** 3/4 **Linden's Lady**[24] 3376 7-8-8 46 ow1..................(v) PhillipMakin 3 46
(J R Weymes) *t.k.h: prom: rdn to ld 1f out: kpt on: hdd nr fin* **7/1**[3]
5005 **3** hd **Fairy Monarch (IRE)**[9] 3814 8-8-12 50..................(b) MickyFenton 4 50
(P T Midgley) *hld up: hdwy over 2f out: edgd rt and ev ch 1f out: no ex towards fin* **8/1**
-000 **4** 3/4 **Passionately Royal**[38] 2938 5-8-5 40.................. PatrickDonaghy(7) 7 48
(M Brittain) *chsd ldrs: effrt over 2f out: kpt on same pce fnl f* **100/1**
4005 **5** nk **Beamsley Beacon**[31] 3169 6-8-12 48.................. PaddyAspell 1 47
(S T Mason) *cl up: drvn over 2f out: ev ch 1f out: sn no ex* **25/1**
4404 **6** 1 1/2 **Andorran (GER)**[9] 3814 4-8-12 47..................(tp) DanielTudhope 6 44
(A Dickman) *bhd: hdwy on outside and in tch over 1f out: edgd rt and sn no imp* **4/1**[2]
00-0 **7** 3/4 **Insubordinate**[10] 3783 6-8-5 52.................. KellyHarrison(7) 12 42
(J S Goldie) *s.i.s: hld up: hdwy over 2f out: wknd over 1f out* **16/1**
66 **8** 1 **Knight Of Kintyre (IRE)**[14] 3695 4-8-7 42..................(t) TonyHamilton 8 35
(Barry Potts, Ire) *led to 1f out: sn btn* **25/1**
-000 **9** 3/4 **Height Of Esteem**[33] 3076 4-8-12 40.................. DavidAllan 10 38
(W M Brisbourne) *t.k.h: hld up: effrt over 2f out: n.d* **40/1**
2000 **10** 1 **Slavonic (USA)**[15] 3638 6-8-9 47..................(b) PJMcDonald(3) 5 36
(B Storey) *towards rr: effrt and hung rt over 2f out: btn over 1f out* **33/1**
0053 **11** 3/4 **Pepper Road**[38] 2938 8-8-12 45..................(t) TomEaves 2 34
(R Bastiman) *chsd ldrs tl wknd over 2f out* **12/1**
0606 **12** 3 1/2 **Earthling**[94] 1362 6-8-7 40..................(p) MichaelJStainton(5) 9 26
(D W Chapman) *bhd: pushed along over 3f out: sn btn* **28/1**
1m 41.43s (-1.07) **Going Correction** -0.15s/f (Firm) **12** Ran SP% **118.2**
Speed ratings (Par 101): **99,98,98,97,97 95,94,93,93,92 91,87**
CSF £9.60 TOTE £1.80: £1.10, £1.50, £2.50; EX 9.60.The winner was bought-in for 7,200gns
Owner Kirkby Lonsdale Racing **Bred** Mrs J M Berry **Trained** Melsonby, N Yorks

FOCUS
Exposed and mainly hard-to-win-with sorts in this seller and the winner did not have to be to his recent best to score. The form is limited by the proximity of the fourth.

4100 JOHN SMITH'S EXTRA SMOOTH H'CAP — 7f 30y
8:20 (8:20) (Class 5) (0-75,75) 3-Y-0+ **£3,886** (£1,156; £577; £288) **Stalls** High

Form RPR
1411 **1** **Sam's Secret**[1] 4081 5-9-7 72 12ex.................. PJMcDonald(3) 2 82
(G A Swinbank) *in tch: effrt over 2f out: styd on wl fnl f to ld post* **11/4**[3]
0440 **2** shd **Esoterica (IRE)**[9] 3816 4-8-10 58 ow1..................(b) DanielTudhope 5 68
(J S Goldie) *w ldr: led over 2f out: kpt on wl u.p: hdd post* **14/1**
3050 **3** nk **Champain Sands (IRE)**[15] 3644 8-8-5 60 ow2.................. GaryBartley(7) 4 69+
(E J Alston) *hld up: nt clr run over 2f out over 1f out: kpt on wl fnl f* **14/1**
3663 **4** 1 1/2 **Borodinsky**[8] 3839 6-8-8 56 oh6.................. PaddyAspell 9 61
(R E Barr) *in tch: drvn over 2f out: r.o ins fnl f* **25/1**
000- **5** nk **Sea Storm (IRE)**[451] 1531 9-9-10 72.................. PhillipMakin 3 76
(James Moffatt) *prom tl rdn and nt qckn over 1f out* **50/1**
5401 **6** 1 **Zennerman (IRE)**[17] 3599 4-9-8 75..................(b) NeilBrown(5) 7 76
(K A Ryan) *plld hrd: hld up: hdwy over 1f out: n.d* **5/2**[2]
0064 **7** nk **Coeur Courageux (FR)**[23] 3401 5-9-13 75..................(t) TomEaves 8 76
(D Nicholls) *t.k.h: led to over 2f out: wknd over 1f out* **9/4**[1]
533 **8** 2 1/2 **Wiltshire (IRE)**[15] 3647 5-8-9 57.................. MickyFenton 1 51
(P T Midgley) *hld up in tch: effrt over 2f out: btn over 1f out* **10/1**
00-0 **9** 2 **Ulysees (IRE)**[10] 3787 8-8-13 61.................. TonyHamilton 6 50
(J Barclay) *chsd ldrs tl wknd fr 2f out* **50/1**
1m 29.4s (-0.54) **Going Correction** +0.05s/f (Good) **9** Ran SP% **116.2**
Speed ratings (Par 103): **105,104,104,102,102 101,101,98,95**
CSF £39.80 CT £457.29 TOTE £3.90: £1.50, £4.00, £3.70; EX 46.50.
Owner Copskam Partnership **Bred** Dandy's Farm **Trained** Melsonby, N Yorks

FOCUS
Just an ordinary gallop early on, but they quickened it up from halfway and the overall time was decent. The winner continues on the upgrade but the fourth holds the form down.

Wiltshire(IRE) Official explanation: jockey said gelding hung right-handed in straight

4101 JOHN SMITH'S EXTRA COLD H'CAP — 5f
8:50 (8:51) (Class 5) (0-70,70) 3-Y-0+ **£3,886** (£1,156; £577; £288) **Stalls** Low

Form RPR
200 **1** **Strensall**[5] 3954 10-8-12 **63**.................. NeilBrown(5) 6 76
(R E Barr) *prom: rdn to ld appr fnl f: styd on wl to go clr ins fnl f* **9/2**[2]
3421 **2** 2 1/2 **Malapropism**[17] 3594 7-9-10 **70**.................. TomEaves 9 74
(M R Channon) *t.k.h: led to appr fnl f: kpt on same pce ins fnl f* **2/1**[1]
1200 **3** hd **Maromito (IRE)**[8] 3837 10-8-3 **52**.................. AndrewMullen(3) 5 55
(R Bastiman) *chsd ldrs: effrt and ev ch over 1f out: nt qckn ins fnl f* **20/1**
0403 **4** nk **Toy Top (USA)**[10] 3782 4-8-11 **57**..................(b) PhillipMakin 12 59
(M Dods) *trckd ldrs: effrt whn nt clr run over 2f out to over 1f out: kpt on ins fnl f* **9/2**[2]
-103 **5** 3/4 **Hawaii Prince**[15] 3637 3-9-5 **68**.................. SilvestreDeSousa 10 67
(S T Mason) *prom: rdn whn n.m.r briefly over 1f out: sn one pce* **9/1**[3]
00-0 **6** shd **Bond Becks (IRE)**[55] 2418 7-8-4 **55** ow3.................. MichaelJStainton(5) 4 54+
(G R Oldroyd) *hld up in tch: effrt whn no room over 1f out: kpt on fnl f: nrst fin* **22/1**
0000 **7** 1 3/4 **Vondova**[10] 3787 5-8-8 **57** oh1 ow6.................. PJMcDonald(3) 13 50
(D A Nolan) *w ldrs tl wknd over 1f out* **100/1**
3505 **8** hd **Spirit Of Coniston**[10] 3782 4-8-1 **54**..................(b) KellyHarrison(7) 1 46
(C J Teague) *in tch: drvn over 2f out: one pce over 1f out* **14/1**
0000 **9** 1 1/2 **Melandre**[99] 1241 5-7-13 **52** oh1 ow1.................. PatrickDonaghy(7) 8 39
(M Brittain) *bhd and sn rdn along: effrt centre 1/2-way: btn over 1f out* **40/1**
5045 **10** 1/2 **Egyptian Lord**[21] 3452 4-8-10 **56**..................(b) LPKeniry 3 41
(Peter Grayson) *s.i.s: effrt fr rr over 2f out: sn n.d* **9/1**[3]
5605 **11** 2 1/2 **Jun Fan (USA)**[15] 3636 5-8-6 **52** oh3 ow1.................. TonyHamilton 14 28
(B Ellison) *w ldrs on outside tl wknd fr 2f out* **11/1**
0056 **12** 4 **Lake Hero**[8] 3853 4-9-0 **65**.................. DerekNolan(5) 11 27
(M J Wallace) *towards rr: effrt 1/2-way: btn over 1f out* **18/1**
60.92 secs (0.42) **Going Correction** +0.05s/f (Good)
WFA 3 from 4yo+ 3lb **12** Ran SP% **122.5**
Speed ratings (Par 103): **98,94,93,93,92 91,89,88,86,85 81,75**
CSF £13.86 CT £170.89 TOTE £5.80: £1.10, £1.50, £4.70; EX 20.70 Place 6 £ 23.49, Place 5 £ 13.52.
Owner R E Barr **Bred** M Paver And M D M Racing Thoroughbreds Ltd **Trained** Seamer, N Yorks

FOCUS
A moderate contest full of exposed sprinters but solid-enough form for the grade rated around the first three.
Toy Top(USA) Official explanation: jockey said filly was denied a clear run
Hawaii Prince Official explanation: jockey said gelding hung left throughout
Bond Becks(IRE) Official explanation: jockey said gelding was denied a clear run
Egyptian Lord Official explanation: jockey said gelding missed the break
Lake Hero Official explanation: vet said filly finished lame
T/Plt: £11.70 to a £1 stake. Pool: £52,211.60. 3,251.80 winning tickets. T/Qpdt: £12.60 to a £1 stake. Pool: £4,289.20. 250.40 winning tickets. RY

3712 NOTTINGHAM (L-H)
Thursday, August 2

OFFICIAL GOING: Good (good to soft in places on straight course, good to firm in places on back straight; 8.2)
After 13 dry days the ground was described as 'patchy, mostly on the easy side but no good to firm places anywhere'.
Wind: almost nil Weather: Fine

4102 EUROPEAN BREEDERS' FUND MAIDEN FILLIES' STKS — 6f 15y
2:05 (2:08) (Class 5) 2-Y-0 **£3,562** (£1,059; £529; £264) **Stalls** Low

Form RPR
1 **Mistress Greeley (USA)** 2-9-0 0.................. KerrinMcEvoy 10 74+
(Sir Michael Stoute) *in rr: hdwy 3f out: str run to ld wl ins fnl f: readily* **4/1**[2]
2 3/4 **Divine Power** 2-9-0 0.................. AdamKirby 4 72
(R M Beckett) *hmpd s: sn chsng ldrs: upsides ins fnl f: no ex* **16/1**
3 **3** hd **Pivotal Queen (IRE)**[28] 3245 2-9-0 0.................. NickyMackay 6 71
(L M Cumani) *trckd ldrs: led over 1f out: hdd and no ex fnl 50yds* **2/1**[1]
4 2 **Second Opinion (IRE)** 2-9-0 0.................. HayleyTurner 12 65
(J M P Eustace) *trckd ldrs: led after 2f: hdd over 1f out: wknd fnl 150yds* **33/1**
0 **5** 3/4 **Hasty Lady**[13] 3718 2-9-0 0.................. PaulMulrennan 11 63
(K A Ryan) *chsd ldrs: one pce fnl 2f* **50/1**
6 shd **Falcolnry (IRE)** 2-9-0 0.................. OscarUrbina 3 63
(J R Fanshawe) *wnt rt s: in rr: hdwy 2f out: nvr trbld ldrs* **6/1**
3 **7** hd **Jazz Jam**[10] 3796 2-9-0 0.................. ChrisCatlin 5 62
(P F I Cole) *led 2f: chsd ldrs: rdn over 2f out: one pce* **11/2**[3]
8 1 3/4 **True Time** 2-9-0 0.................. StephenDonohoe 2 57
(E A L Dunlop) *sn outpcd and in rr: sme hdwy 2f out: nvr on terms* **40/1**
04 **9** hd **Cosenza**[36] 2997 2-8-7 0.................. KMay(7) 7 56
(H J L Dunlop) *chsd ldrs: wknd fnl f* **16/1**
10 4 **Fareeha** 2-9-0 0.................. RobertHavlin 8 44
(J H M Gosden) *dwlt: a in rr* **14/1**
0 **11** 1 1/4 **Somarini**[51] 2532 2-9-0 0.................. RoystonFfrench 1 41
(J G Given) *chsd ldrs: rdn and lost pl over 3f out* **100/1**
12 8 **Mistress Rio (IRE)** 2-9-0 0.................. PaulFessey 9 —
(J G Given) *sn outpcd and in rr: bhd fnl 2f* **80/1**
1m 15.86s (0.86) **Going Correction** -0.125s/f (Firm) **12** Ran SP% **111.0**
Speed ratings (Par 91): **89,88,87,85,84 83,83,81,81,75 74,63**
CSF £58.96 TOTE £4.90: £1.40, £4.70, £1.10; EX 91.20.
Owner Mrs R J Jacobs **Bred** L Goichman **Trained** Newmarket, Suffolk

FOCUS
Probably just an average maiden fillies' race and slightly guessy formwise, but the winner will go on to better things and they should be one or two improvers behind her.

NOTEBOOK
Mistress Greeley(USA) ◆, a lengthy March foal, came through strongly and her rider was able to sit up at the line. She will be much better suited by seven and looks useful. (op 7-2)
Divine Power, a likeable May foal, was knocked out of her stride at the start. Upsides well inside the last, at the line the winner very much held the upper hand. She should improve and make her mark. (op 20-1)
Pivotal Queen(IRE), who really took the eye beforehand, struck for home only to miss out in the closing stages. She deserves to find a race. (op 15-8 tchd 7-4)
Second Opinion(IRE), a January foal, is not that big. Soon taking them along, she weakened noticeably in the closing stages.
Hasty Lady stepped up markedly on her debut effort and there may be even better to come especially given a seventh furlong.

Falcolnry(IRE), a medium-sized, quite attractive March foal, took an age to grasp the nettle but she was putting in some pleasing work late on. This will have taught her plenty. (op 10-1)
Jazz Jam, whose dam won the Cherry Hinton, did not improve on her initial effort. (op 9-2)

4103 TURFTV A MATTER OF COURSE H'CAP 5f 13y
2:40 (2:40) (Class 5) (0-75,74) 3-Y-0+ **£3,238** (£963; £481; £240) **Stalls** Low

Form RPR
2321 **1** **Divine Spirit**[2] 4038 6-9-1 **65** 6ex ... RoystonFfrench 7 81
(M Dods) *trckd ldrs: led over 1f out: rdn clr* **3/1**[1]
0604 **2** *3 1/2* **Blessed Place**[8] 3859 7-8-13 **63** ... (t) ChrisCatlin 9 66
(D J S Ffrench Davis) *led: hdd over 1f out: no ch w wnr* **9/1**
6053 **3** *1* **Bobby Rose**[24] 3388 4-8-12 **62** ... (p) RobertHavlin 10 61
(D K Ivory) *hld up in rr: effrt 2f out: kpt on same pce ins fnl f* **13/2**[3]
0-10 **4** *hd* **Controvento**[76] 1806 5-9-8 **72** ... (b) KerrinMcEvoy 11 71
(Eamon Tyrrell, Ire) *chsd ldrs: kpt on same pce fnl f* **14/1**
1562 **5** *1 1/2* **Harrison's Flyer (IRE)**[6] 3906 6-9-1 **70** ... (p) KevinGhunowa(5) 5 63
(J M Bradley) *sn outpcd and in rr: hmpd over 2f out: hung lft and styd on appr fnl f* **7/1**
0632 **6** *shd* **Blue Aura (IRE)**[8] 3859 4-9-8 **72** ... (b) GeorgeBaker 3 65
(R M Beckett) *sn outpcd and in rr: kpt on fnl 2f: nvr nr ldrs* **7/2**[2]
0006 **7** *nk* **Matsunosuke**[6] 3921 5-9-8 **72** ... SaleemGolam 4 64
(A B Coogan) *dwlt: hdwy over 2f out: rdn and wknd 1f out* **10/1**
5016 **8** *1 3/4* **Sands Crooner (IRE)**[16] 3627 4-8-10 **60** ... (v) J-PGuillambert 8 46
(D Shaw) *in rr: sme hdwy on wd outside over 1f out: nvr nr ldrs* **20/1**
3640 **9** *nk* **Puskas (IRE)**[17] 3594 4-9-3 **74** ... (p) BarrySavage(7) 6 58
(J M Bradley) *hld up towards rr: effrt 2f out: nvr nr ldrs* **33/1**
1325 **10** *4* **Monte Major (IRE)**[30] 3184 6-8-10 **60** ... (v) DeanMcKeown 2 30
(D Shaw) *chsd ldrs: lost pl over 1f out* **14/1**
0000 **11** *11* **Danjet (IRE)**[33] 3086 4-8-9 **59** ow1 ... (b[1]) StephenDonohoe 1 —
(J M Bradley) *w ldr racing far side: lost pl 2f out: sn bhd* **50/1**

60.36 secs (-1.44) **Going Correction** -0.125s/f (Firm) **11** Ran SP% **115.1**
Speed ratings (Par 103): **106,100,98,98,96 95,95,92,92,85 68**
CSF £29.26 CT £163.38 TOTE £3.40: £1.30, £2.90, £2.30; EX 31.90.
Owner The Newcastle Racing Club **Bred** S R Hope And D Erwin Bloodstock **Trained** Denton, Co Durham

FOCUS
A modest sprint handicap won in most decisive fashion by the bang in-form Divine Spirit. The time was decent and the form looks solid rated around the first three.
Harrison's Flyer(IRE) Official explanation: jockey said gelding was denied a clear run
Danjet(IRE) Official explanation: vet said filly finished distressed

4104 HAPPY 50TH BIRTHDAY STEVE MILES H'CAP 2m 9y
3:15 (3:16) (Class 6) (0-60,60) 3-Y-0 **£2,388** (£705; £352)

Form RPR
0-53 **1** **Franchoek (IRE)**[7] 3876 3-9-0 **56** ... KerrinMcEvoy 9 63+
(A King) *hld up in rr: hdwy over 3f out: styd on wl to ld nr fin* **13/8**[1]
0211 **2** *3/4* **Toboggan Lady**[15] 3640 3-8-13 **55** ... RoystonFfrench 2 59
(Mrs A Duffield) *in rr: drvn 7f out: hdwy over 3f out: chal over 1f out: no ex wl ins fnl f* **4/1**[2]
4603 **3** *shd* **Serhaaphim**[10] 3792 3-9-0 **56** ... HayleyTurner 7 60
(M L W Bell) *sn trcking ldrs: led over 3f out: hdd and no ex towards fin* **8/1**
0-60 **4** *1* **Susie May**[33] 3082 3-8-11 **53** ... AdamKirby 12 56
(C A Cyzer) *in rr: drvn 10f out: hdwy on ins over 4f out: chsng ldrs over 2f out: edgd lft over 1f out: kpt on same pce ins fnl f* **50/1**
-064 **5** *4* **Dubai Shadow (IRE)**[10] 3803 3-8-13 **60** ... AhmedAjtebi(5) 1 58
(C E Brittain) *dwlt: hdwy to chse ldrs 7f out: edgd lft over 1f out: sn wknd* **20/1**
6365 **6** *4* **Piano Key**[7] 3871 3-8-5 **47** ... RichardSmith 8 40
(M D I Usher) *hld up in rr: sme hdwy 4f out: nvr nr ldrs* **40/1**
7 *2 1/2* **Spinaimanwin (IRE)**[26] 3337 3-8-10 **52** ... StephenDonohoe 3 42
(Ian Williams) *chsd ldrs: wkng whn hmpd over 1f out* **20/1**
0634 **8** *shd* **Lady Traill**[10] 3792 3-8-8 **50** ... ChrisCatlin 5 40
(B W Hills) *chsd ldrs: drvn 9f out: lost pl 7f out: kpt on fnl 3f* **7/1**[3]
2235 **9** *6* **Red Flare (IRE)**[15] 3652 3-8-2 **51** ... MatthewDavies(7) 11 34
(M R Channon) *hld up in mid-div: hdwy to trck ldrs 10f out: wknd 2f out* **11/1**
0063 **10** *2* **Pagan Starprincess**[24] 3379 3-8-13 **55** ... (p) J-PGuillambert 6 35
(G M Moore) *led: rn wd and hdd bnd after 4f: led over 4f out: hdd over 3f out: wknd 2f out: eased* **12/1**
0460 **11** *6* **Galingale (IRE)**[16] 3624 3-8-12 **54** ... PaulFessey 10 27
(Mrs P Sly) *hld up in rr: gd hdwy 6f out: sn chsng ldrs: wknd over 2f out* **33/1**
3-05 **12** *37* **Hemispear**[31] 3166 3-9-2 **58** ... PaulFitzsimons 4 —
(Miss J R Tooth) *trckd ldr: lft in ld on bnd after 4f: hdd over 4f out: sn lost pl and eased: t.o* **80/1**

3m 33.3s (-0.20) **Going Correction** -0.125s/f (Firm) **12** Ran SP% **115.8**
Speed ratings (Par 98): **95,94,94,94,92 90,88,88,85,84 81,63**
CSF £6.74 CT £39.51 TOTE £2.20: £1.40, £1.90, £2.10; EX 12.00.
Owner David Mason **Bred** 6c Stallions Ltd **Trained** Barbury Castle, Wilts
■ Stewards' Enquiry : Ahmed Ajtebi two-day ban: careless riding (Aug 13-14); caution: used whip down filly's shoulder in forehand position

FOCUS
The stalls could not be used. There was a flip start and the race was hand-timed. A low-grade staying handicap run at a very steady pace with little between the first four at the line. The form looks sound enough but limited.

4105 SIMON COX LTD H'CAP 1m 1f 213y
3:50 (3:50) (Class 4) (0-85,90) 3-Y-0+ **£5,181** (£1,541; £770; £384) **Stalls** Low

Form RPR
-631 **1** **Sagredo (USA)**[4] 4004 3-9-12 **90** 6ex ... J-PGuillambert 3 108+
(Sir Mark Prescott) *hld up in last: stdy hdwy over 2f out: drvn and hung lft over 1f out: led fnl 100yds: eased nr fin* **4/6**[1]
0122 **2** *1 1/4* **Top Mark**[8] 3855 5-8-12 **74** ... HarryPoulton(7) 5 86
(J R Boyle) *led: qcknd over 4f out: hdd and no ex ins fnl f* **4/1**[2]
52-2 **3** *6* **Casual Affair**[82] 1673 4-8-9 **64** oh1 ... HayleyTurner 6 64
(J D Bethell) *hld up in rr: drvn 6f out: hdwy over 3f out: tk 3rd over 1f out: eased ins fnl f whn no ch w 1st 2* **14/1**
6005 **4** *2 1/2* **Mighty Moon**[16] 3609 4-9-6 **75** ... RoystonFfrench 8 70
(J O'Reilly) *chsd ldrs: drvn 4f out: one pce* **25/1**
0600 **5** *3* **Boo**[20] 3513 5-9-11 **80** ... LeeEnstone 4 69
(K R Burke) *hld up towards rr: effrt 4f out: nvr nr ldrs* **33/1**
4003 **6** *1 1/4* **Kyoto Summit**[12] 3753 4-10-0 **83** ... PaulMulrennan 9 70
(M W Easterby) *trckd ldr: effrt 4f out: hung rt and wknd over 1f out* **6/1**[3]
260- **7** *hd* **Isidore Bonheur (IRE)**[341] 4805 6-10-0 **83** ... DeanMcKeown 2 69
(G A Swinbank) *trckd ldrs: t.k.h: wknd 2f out* **28/1**
4126 **8** *47* **Yakimov (USA)**[14] 3690 8-9-8 **77** ... VinceSlattery 1 —
(D J Wintle) *chsd ldrs: lost pl over 3f out: sn bhd: t.o* **28/1**

2m 6.23s (-3.47) **Going Correction** -0.125s/f (Firm)
WFA 3 from 4yo+ 9lb **8** Ran SP% **114.6**
Speed ratings (Par 105): **108,107,102,100,97 96,96,59**
CSF £3.33 CT £18.00 TOTE £1.60: £1.10, £1.30, £3.10; EX 4.20.
Owner Dr Catherine Wills **Bred** Dr Catherine Wills **Trained** Newmarket, Suffolk

FOCUS
A decent contest in which the runner-up tried to steal it from the front but in the end the progressive younger horse was much too good. The first two pulled clear but the winner is the only progressive sort.
Kyoto Summit Official explanation: jockey said gelding hung right in straight
Yakimov(USA) Official explanation: jockey said gelding was unsuited by the good (good to soft in places and good to firm in places) ground and that the gelding lost its action

4106 VISITNOTTINGHAM.COM MEDIAN AUCTION MAIDEN STKS 1m 54y
4:20 (4:20) (Class 6) 3-4-Y-0 **£2,388** (£705; £352) **Stalls** Centre

Form RPR
3 **1** **Time Over**[13] 3710 3-8-12 0 ... KerrinMcEvoy 4 68+
(J L Dunlop) *trckd ldrs: led 2f out: shkn up ins fnl f: a in command* **1/3**[1]
0-4 **2** *1 3/4* **Fluffy**[52] 2520 4-9-5 0 ... PaulMulrennan 1 56
(K A Ryan) *trckd ldrs: upsides over 1f out: kpt on same pce* **8/1**[3]
0-0 **3** *1/2* **The Flying Cowboy (IRE)**[13] 3710 3-9-3 0 ... RobertHavlin 5 60
(Jane Chapple-Hyam) *hld up: hdwy over 2f out: kpt on wl fnl f* **33/1**
0- **4** *hd* **Steel Silk (IRE)**[299] 5814 3-9-3 0 ... RoystonFfrench 7 60
(B Smart) *chsd ldrs: reminders over 3f out: sn outpcd: styd on appr fnl f* **25/1**
6-46 **5** *3 1/2* **Saaratt**[33] 3113 3-8-12 72 ... JamesDoyle 8 46
(J W Hills) *t.k.h: led: hdd 2f out: sn lost pl* **13/2**[2]
000 **6** *1/2* **The Graig**[16] 3624 3-9-3 50 ... SaleemGolam 3 50
(C Drew) *trckd ldrs: effrt over 3f out: hung lft and outpcd fnl 2f* **200/1**
7 *2 1/2* **Turban Heights (IRE)** 3-8-12 0 ... ChrisCatlin 6 40
(E J O'Neill) *s.s: in rr and sn pushed along: kpt on fnl 2f: nvr a factor* **20/1**
0633 **8** *3/4* **Flamestone**[19] 3540 3-8-12 46 ... RussellKennemore(5) 2 43
(A E Price) *t.k.h: trckd ldrs: drvn 5f out: outpcd fnl 3f* **80/1**

1m 45.84s (-0.56) **Going Correction** -0.125s/f (Firm)
WFA 3 from 4yo 7lb **8** Ran SP% **112.7**
Speed ratings (Par 101): **97,95,94,94,91 90,88,87**
CSF £3.18 TOTE £1.30: £1.02, £1.40, £4.80; EX 3.60.
Owner R Barnett **Bred** W And R Barnett Ltd **Trained** Arundel, W Sussex

FOCUS
A weak maiden and the long odds-on winner made quite hard work of it. The gallop was very steady and there was not a lot of distance between first and last at the line with the exposed sixth rated just 50 limiting the form, which is best assessed through the placed horses.
The Graig Official explanation: jockey said gelding hung left in straight.
Turban Heights(IRE) Official explanation: jockey said filly ran green

4107 CITY LIFE & COUNTRY LIVING MAGAZINE H'CAP 1m 54y
4:55 (4:56) (Class 5) (0-75,75) 3-Y-0+ **£3,238** (£963; £481; £240) **Stalls** Centre

Form RPR
5100 **1** **Stargazer Jim (FR)**[25] 3346 5-9-12 **73** ... PaulMulrennan 3 83+
(W J Haggas) *hld up in rr: stdy hdwy and nt clr run over 2f out: burst through to ld towards fin* **8/1**
2521 **2** *3/4* **Lap Of Honour (IRE)**[10] 3793 3-9-5 **73** 6ex ... KerrinMcEvoy 2 80
(N A Callaghan) *trckd ldrs: led 2f out: hdd and no ex towards fin* **5/2**[1]
0010 **3** *nk* **Magical Music**[13] 3711 4-8-13 **60** ... J-PGuillambert 12 68
(J Pearce) *hld up in midfield: effrt on outer over 2f out: styd on wl ins fnl f* **20/1**
0-00 **4** *1/2* **Libre**[10] 3799 7-8-10 **57** ... DeanMcKeown 1 63
(F Jordan) *chsd ldrs: styd on same pce appr fnl f* **28/1**
5333 **5** *3/4* **The Osteopath (IRE)**[14] 3682 4-9-12 **73** ... (p) RoystonFfrench 10 78
(M Dods) *chsd ldrs: kpt on same pce fnl 2f* **9/2**[2]
-000 **6** *hd* **King's Majesty (IRE)**[70] 1962 5-9-11 **72** ... VinceSlattery 9 76
(V R A Dartnall) *t.k.h in midfield: hdwy over 3f out: kpt on same pce fnl 2f* **8/1**
00-1 **7** *1* **Mineral Star (IRE)**[35] 3039 5-9-13 **74** ... SaleemGolam 4 76
(M H Tompkins) *hld up in rr: hdwy on ins over 3f out: kpt on same pce fnl 2f* **17/2**
0002 **8** *5* **Rain Stops Play (IRE)**[13] 3711 5-10-0 **75** ... ChrisCatlin 8 65
(M Quinn) *anticipated s and charged gate: led: hdd 2f out: wknd fnl f* **6/1**[3]
0604 **9** *5* **Akram (IRE)**[13] 3715 5-9-9 **70** ... (t) GeorgeBaker 6 49
(Jonjo O'Neill) *trckd ldrs: lost pl 3f out* **25/1**
6060 **10** *3* **Capistrano**[9] 3828 4-9-4 **65** ... (b[1]) PaulFessey 5 37
(Mrs P Sly) *in rr and sn pushed along: bhd fnl 3f* **33/1**
0-60 **U** **Petito (IRE)**[13] 3722 4-8-12 **59** ... StephenDonohoe 11 —
(J L Spearing) *uns rdr leaving stalls* **7/1**

1m 43.51s (-2.89) **Going Correction** -0.125s/f (Firm)
WFA 3 from 4yo+ 7lb **11** Ran SP% **121.3**
Speed ratings (Par 103): **109,108,107,107,106 106,105,100,95,92 —**
CSF £28.01 CT £409.26 TOTE £13.30: £3.30, £1.30, £4.60; EX 50.50 Place 6 £ 5.22, Place 5 £ 3.50.
Owner Nicholas J Hughes **Bred** Sarl Le Lieu Calice And Peter Kavanagh **Trained** Newmarket, Suffolk
■ Stewards' Enquiry : Dean McKeown one-day ban: careless riding (Aug 13)

FOCUS
Modest form rated around the first three, but a sound pace and the winner did well to come from the rear.
T/Plt: £6.40 to a £1 stake. Pool: £51,254.10. 5,798.85 winning tickets. T/Qpdt: £2.40 to a £1 stake. Pool: £3,059.90. 920.30 winning tickets. WG

3878 SANDOWN (R-H)
Thursday, August 2
OFFICIAL GOING: Good (good to firm in places; 8.7)
Wind: Nil

4108 PFA CENTENARY APPRENTICE H'CAP 1m 2f 7y
5:55 (5:56) (Class 5) (0-70,76) 4-Y-0+ **£3,886** (£1,156; £577; £288) **Stalls** High

Form RPR
4502 **1** **Sky Quest (IRE)**[13] 3705 9-9-7 **67** ... JamesMillman 13 76
(J R Boyle) *in rr: hdwy 3f out: drvn to ld appr fnl 2f: hung lft u.p fnl f but a in control* **11/2**[3]
5241 **2** *2* **Lady Friend**[10] 3799 5-10-2 **76** 6ex ... PatrickHills 5 81
(J W Hills) *chsd ldrs: rdn 3f out: drvn to chal ins fnl 2f: no imp on wnr fnl f* **9/2**[1]

0625 **3** 3/4 **Kuster**[20] 3485 11-9-3 **63**....(b) AshleyHamblett 3 67
(L M Cumani) *in rr: stl plenty to do 3f out: hdwy fr 2f out: r.o strly ins fnl f to take 3rd last strides but nvr a danger* **15/2**

-060 **4** 1/2 **Prime Number (IRE)**[22] 3437 5-9-5 **68**.... KirstyMilczarek(3) 2 71
(J Akehurst) *t.k.h and chsng ldrs after 2f: wnt 2nd over 3f out: sn rdn: kpt on same pce ins fnl f and lost 3rd last strides* **14/1**

0050 **5** 1/2 **Wheelavit (IRE)**[23] 592 4-9-2 **67**.... KylieManser(5) 1 69
(B G Powell) *in rr: stl plenty to do 3f out: shkn up and kpt on fnl f: gng on cl home* **14/1**

2231 **6** 1 1/2 **Burgundy**[8] 3854 10-9-9 **72** 6ex....(b) JackMitchell(3) 4 71
(P Mitchell) *in rr: pushed along over 2f out: r.o fnl f but nvr gng pce to be competitive* **15/2**

0653 **7** hd **Star Of Canterbury (IRE)**[22] 3416 4-9-10 **70**.... TravisBlock 9 68
(A P Jarvis) *led: rdn 3f out: hdd appr fnl 2f: wknd fnl f* **5/1**[2]

0110 **8** 1 1/4 **War Of The Roses (IRE)**[99] 1251 4-8-5 **51** oh1.... MarcHalford 6 47
(R Brotherton) *in tch: rdn and sme hdwy fnl 2f: n.d* **20/1**

200- **9** 1 1/2 **Flying Pass**[51] 1400 5-8-12 **58**.... TolleyDean 8 51
(R J Price) *chsd ldrs: rdn 3f out: wknd fnl f* **25/1**

20-0 **10** 3 **Roya**[13] 3705 4-8-12 **61**.... JamieHamblett(3) 12 48
(Miss Gay Kelleway) *in rr: hdwy on ins over 4f out: rdn and nvr quite gng pce to rch ldrs fr 3f out: sn wknd* **33/1**

6240 **11** 1 **Ross Moor**[59] 2321 5-9-3 **66**.... HaddenFrost(3) 11 51
(Mike Murphy) *in tch 7f* **9/2**[1]

000 **12** hd **Lord Laing (USA)**[16] 3630 4-8-0 **51** oh2.... SophieDoyle(5) 7 35
(H J Collingridge) *towards rr most of way* **66/1**

6000 **13** 4 **Play Up Pompey**[15] 3641 5-8-3 **52**.... KMay(3) 10 28
(J J Bridger) *chsd ldr tl over 3f out: wknd ins fnl 2f* **40/1**

2m 11.53s (1.29) **Going Correction** +0.20s/f (Good) **13** Ran SP% **120.8**
Speed ratings (Par 103): **102,100,99,99,99 97,97,96,95,93 92,92,88**
CSF £29.17 CT £191.32 TOTE £5.60: £1.90, £2.00, £2.70; EX 18.40.
Owner M C Cook **Bred** Pendley Farm **Trained** Epsom, Surrey

FOCUS
A modest handicap made up of largely exposed performers. The form is rated through the runner-up but limited by the next three home.
Play Up Pompey Official explanation: trainer said gelding was struck into

4109 PFA CENTENARY CLAIMING STKS 7f 16y
6:25 (6:32) (Class 5) 3-Y-O **£4,533** (£1,348; £674; £336) **Stalls** High

Form RPR

215 **1** **Mick Is Back**[21] 3475 3-9-0 60....(p) RichardHughes 3 63
(J R Boyle) *hld up in rr: stdy hdwy 3f out: led wl over 1f out: pushed out* **9/4**[2]

0562 **2** 1 **Our Herbie**[12] 3732 3-9-3 64....(v) TQuinn 6 63
(J W Hills) *in rr: hdwy 3f out: chsd wnr and rdn fnl f: edgd rt and nt go by* **2/1**[1]

0000 **3** 3 **Meadfoot**[62] 2195 3-8-9 47.... JimCrowley 11 47
(B R Millman) *in tch tl outpcd 3f out: styd on again fr over 1f out: gng on cl home but nvr a danger* **20/1**

6000 **4** shd **Noddledoddle (IRE)**[9] 3824 3-7-9 45....(t) FrankiePickard(7) 5 40
(J Ryan) *chsd ldrs: led 3f out: sn rdn: hdd wl over 1f out: wknd ins fnl f* **33/1**

000 **5** nk **Hamilton House**[44] 2749 3-9-2 63.... JimmyQuinn 8 53
(M H Tompkins) *in rr: hdwy fr 3f out: kpt on same pce fr over 1f out* **17/2**

-005 **6** 1 3/4 **Law Of The Land (IRE)**[20] 3482 3-8-12 57.... RichardMullen 4 44
(W R Muir) *led: rdn and hdd 3f out: wknd fnl f* **8/1**

6-00 **7** hd **Give Evidence**[49] 2601 3-9-0 60....(v) SimonWhitworth 9 46
(A P Jarvis) *chsd ldrs: rdn 3f out: wknd over 1f out* **16/1**

5606 **8** 3/4 **Cantique (IRE)**[10] 3795 3-7-11 46.... SophieDoyle(7) 2 34
(Ms J S Doyle) *chsd ldrs: rdn 3f out: sn btn* **22/1**

0-00 **9** 1 1/2 **Vietnam**[33] 3082 3-8-10 51.... JDSmith 13 36
(S Kirk) *chsd ldrs: rdn over 3f out: wknd fr 2f out* **7/1**[3]

6000 **10** 6 **Noravana (IRE)**[6] 3917 3-8-4 45.... MarcHalford(5) 1 16
(Miss V Haigh) *a towards rr* **40/1**

4000 **11** 1 1/2 **Suntan Lady (IRE)**[10] 3786 3-8-5 48....(v) EdwardCreighton 10 10
(Miss V Haigh) *t.k.h: a towards rr* **50/1**

1m 30.99s (1.65) **Going Correction** +0.20s/f (Good) **11** Ran SP% **120.6**
Speed ratings (Par 100): **98,96,93,93,92 90,90,89,88,81 79**
CSF £6.89 TOTE £2.80: £1.30, £1.30, £6.30; EX 6.30.The winner was claimed by George Margarson for £10,000
Owner M Khan X2 **Bred** J E Abbey **Trained** Epsom, Surrey

FOCUS
Not a strong race and the 'big two' came three lengths clear. The form is pretty sound but limited.

4110 PFA CENTENARY E B F MAIDEN STKS 7f 16y
7:00 (7:03) (Class 4) 2-Y-O **£4,533** (£1,348; £674; £336) **Stalls** High

Form RPR

1 **Campanologist (USA)** 2-9-0 0.... GregFairley(3) 10 81+
(M Johnston) *in rr: gd hdwy fr 2f out: str run and drvn fnl f: qcknd to ld last strides* **15/2**

3 **2** hd **Mut'Ab (USA)**[27] 3270 2-9-3 0.... SebSanders 14 79
(C E Brittain) *led: rdn over 2f out: styd on wl: ct last strides* **11/8**[1]

3 3/4 **Military Power** 2-9-3 0.... TQuinn 3 77+
(J W Hills) *mid-div: str run on outside fr 2f out: fin wl: edgd rt and gng on cl home* **40/1**

02 **4** 3/4 **Mymumsaysimthebest**[19] 3551 2-9-3 0.... PatDobbs 5 75
(R Hannon) *chsd ldrs: rdn over 2f out: styd on same pce ins fnl f* **5/1**[2]

0 **5** shd **Jabal Tariq**[22] 3435 2-9-3 0.... MichaelHills 6 75
(B W Hills) *chsd ldr: rdn over 2f out: wknd fnl half f* **9/1**

6 1 1/2 **Trenchtown (IRE)** 2-9-3 0.... SteveDrowne 11 71
(R Charlton) *in rr: styd on wl fr over 1f out: kpt on cl home but nvr in contention* **16/1**

04 **7** shd **Tayarat (IRE)**[27] 3270 2-8-12 0.... PatrickHills(5) 9 71
(M P Tregoning) *chsd ldrs: shkn up and effrt 2f out: kpt on same pce: hld whn crossed cl home* **13/2**[3]

8 1 1/2 **Tyrrells Wood (IRE)** 2-9-3 0.... TedDurcan 7 67
(T G Mills) *s.i.s: rdn 3f out: mod prog ins fnl f* **20/1**

0 **9** shd **Ride A White Swan**[19] 3551 2-8-12 0.... KevinGhunowa(5) 12 67
(P A Blockley) *chsd ldrs: rdn over 3f out: wknd over 1f out* **50/1**

10 3 **Mganga** 2-9-3 0.... EdwardCreighton 2 59
(M R Channon) *s.i.s: drvn along 4f out: nvr gng pce to get beyond mid-div* **50/1**

06 **11** 1 **Air Chief**[19] 3551 2-9-3 0.... IanMongan 13 57
(H J L Dunlop) *in rr: rdn and effrt into mid-div over 3f out: n.d after* **66/1**

12 3/4 **Cocktail Shaker (USA)** 2-9-3 0.... RichardHughes 8 55
(B J Meehan) *chsd ldrs: rdn 3f out: wknd 2f out* **20/1**

13 1 **Any Given Day (IRE)** 2-9-3 0.... FergusSweeney 4 52
(D M Simcock) *alwasy towards rr* **66/1**

14 nk **Talon (IRE)** 2-9-3 0.... WCMarwing 1 52
(W J Haggas) *a towards rr* **16/1**

1m 31.58s (2.24) **Going Correction** +0.20s/f (Good) **14** Ran SP% **124.5**
Speed ratings (Par 96): **95,94,93,93,92 91,91,89,89,85 84,83,82,82**
CSF £17.81 TOTE £8.80: £2.90, £1.30, £10.30; EX 23.10.
Owner Sheikh Mohammed **Bred** Darley **Trained** Middleham Moor, N Yorks

FOCUS
This could prove to be a good juvenile maiden. It was run at a sound pace and the runner-up gives the form a decent look.

NOTEBOOK
Campanologist(USA) ◆, whose dam is an unraced half-sister to the top-class Singspiel and Rahy amongst others, ran out a somewhat surprising debut winner considering he proved so green in the preliminaries and through the early parts of the race. He clearly has a decent engine, enjoyed the sound surface, and looks sure to come on a bundle for this experience. Considering that his leading stable's juveniles have mostly been disappointing to date this term, and needed their debut outings, this has to bode well for his future and his Group 2 entries look well justified. (op 9-1)
Mut'Ab(USA), the clear form pick on his debut effort over course and distance 27 days previously, posted a solid effort in defeat from the front and was only picked off near the finish. A maiden on one of the smaller tracks would be his for the taking and he does deserve to break his duck after this. He is a solid guide to the form. (op 6-4 tchd 13-8)
Military Power ◆, whose dam was a dual 7-9f winner at 2-3, produced a taking debut effort and was doing some decent late work. His yard is not noted for its juvenile debut winners, so plenty of improvement can now be expected from this son of Dubai Destination, and he looks potentially very useful. (op 33-1)
Mymumsaysimthebest again confirmed he is going the right way with a solid effort in defeat and looked suited by the stiff nature of this track. He was not beaten far and now qualifies for nurseries (op 6-1 tchd 4-1)
Jabal Tariq showed the benefit of his debut in a hot Newmarket maiden (won by Rio De La Plata) 22 days previously and posted a much better effort. He is probably better off switching to a less-demanding test in the short term and should win his maiden in due course. (op 16-1 tchd 20-1)
Trenchtown(IRE), the second foal of an unraced sister to champion US turf mare Fiji, took time to get the hang of things on this racecourse bow and basically stayed on too late in the day. He was not subjected to a hard ride and the kindness should pay off before too long. (op 12-1)
Tayarat(IRE) had his chance yet failed to find an extra gear when it mattered. He already looks in need of further now and becomes eligible for a nursery mark after this. (op 5-1 tchd 7-1)

4111 DRIVERS JONAS H'CAP 1m 14y
7:30 (7:36) (Class 4) (0-80,80) 3-Y-O **£7,772** (£2,312; £1,155; £577) **Stalls** High

Form RPR

-136 **1** **Oceana Gold**[19] 3553 3-9-0 **74**.... WilliamBuick(3) 12 82
(A M Balding) *mde virtually all: drvn and styd on strly over 1f out: edgd rt ins fnl f and hld on wl* **5/1**[3]

3-21 **2** nk **Ballroom Dancer (IRE)**[55] 2428 3-9-9 **80**.... SebSanders 11 87
(J Noseda) *uns rdr bef s: in tch: gd hdwy over 2f out: styd on u.p to chse wnr ins fnl f: kpt on wl but a jst hld* **8/1**

3-53 **3** 2 **Practicallyperfect (IRE)**[50] 2577 3-9-5 **76**.... TedDurcan 14 78
(H R A Cecil) *chsd ldrs: wnt 2nd 2f out: drvn to chal over 1f out: one pce ins fnl f and lost 2nd whn crossed: wknd cl home* **8/1**

0643 **4** 1 1/4 **Rudry Dragon (IRE)**[7] 3877 3-9-2 **78**.... KevinGhunowa(5) 9 78
(P A Blockley) *t.k.h: chsd ldrs: rdn over 2f out: wknd fnl f* **16/1**

2134 **5** 1 **Russian Epic**[31] 3165 3-9-8 **79**.... PhilipRobinson 5 76
(M A Jarvis) *chsd ldrs: rdn 3f out: wknd fnl f* **7/2**[2]

1435 **6** hd **Bold Abbott (USA)**[20] 3480 3-9-9 **80**....(b) JimCrowley 7 77
(Mrs A J Perrett) *in rr: hdwy and nt clr run 2f out: edgd rt sn after: kpt on fnl f but nvr in contention* **20/1**

-020 **7** 3 **Distiller (IRE)**[14] 3691 3-8-13 **70**.... RichardMullen 8 60
(W R Muir) *mid-div: rdn 4f out: styd on same pce fnl 2f* **25/1**

31 **8** 1 **Jamboretta (IRE)**[69] 1988 3-9-9 **80**.... RyanMoore 2 68
(Sir Michael Stoute) *sn w wnr: rdn 3f out: wknd ins fnl 2f* **5/2**[1]

1023 **9** shd **Rule Of Life**[28] 3235 3-9-6 **77**.... RichardHughes 3 64
(B W Hills) *in rr: effrt and nt clr run 2f out: nvr in contention after* **13/2**

4041 **10** 1/2 **Dansil In Distress**[23] 3393 3-8-5 **62** ow1.... JamesDoyle 10 48
(S Kirk) *in rr: sme hdwy 3f out: sn btn* **33/1**

-000 **11** 1/2 **Kilburn**[19] 3553 3-9-9 **80**.... AdamKirby 6 65
(C G Cox) *chsd ldrs: rdn 3f out: wknd appr fnl 2f* **25/1**

4113 **12** 1/2 **Beau Sancy**[8] 3848 3-9-8 **79**.... JoeFanning 13 63
(R A Harris) *in rr: hdwy but stl in rr whn nt clr run 2f out: continually denied clr passage and nt rcvr* **22/1**

1-00 **13** 2 **Putra Laju (IRE)**[64] 2133 3-8-8 **65**.... TQuinn 4 44
(J W Hills) *a towards rr* **66/1**

-314 **14** 2 1/2 **Oscarshall (IRE)**[47] 2662 3-9-0 **71**.... JimmyQuinn 15 45
(M H Tompkins) *hdwy into mid-div over 3f out: sn rdn and btn* **22/1**

1m 43.26s (-0.69) **Going Correction** +0.20s/f (Good) **14** Ran SP% **134.5**
Speed ratings (Par 102): **111,110,108,107,106 106,103,102,102,101 101,100,98,96**
CSF £46.42 CT £267.50 TOTE £7.00: £1.60, £2.70, £2.50; EX 74.40.
Owner The C H F Partnership **Bred** The C H F Partnership **Trained** Kingsclere, Hants
■ Stewards' Enquiry : William Buick one-day ban: used whip with excessive frequency (Aug 13)

FOCUS
A fair handicap that was run at a solid pace and producing a very good time for the grade. The first pair came clear and the form looks sound rated around those in the frame behind the winner.
Rule Of Life Official explanation: jockey said colt was denied a clear run
Putra Laju(IRE) Official explanation: jockey said colt was denied a clear run

4112 WILLIE MCKAY SPORTS MANAGEMENT FILLIES' H'CAP 1m 1f
8:05 (8:07) (Class 5) (0-75,75) 3-Y-O+ **£5,181** (£1,541; £770; £384) **Stalls** High

Form RPR

1560 **1** **Uig**[3] 4015 6-8-12 **65**.... HaddenFrost(7) 8 73
(H S Howe) *chsd ldr after 2f: led over 2f out: rdn over 1f out: hld on all out* **12/1**

6302 **2** nk **Central Force**[21] 3451 3-8-13 **67**.... RyanMoore 12 74+
(E A L Dunlop) *in rr: rdn over 2f out and began to improve: fin strly u.p fnl f: fin wl: nt quite get up* **13/2**

2025 **3** 1/2 **Iolanthe**[12] 3731 3-8-12 **66**.... RichardHughes 1 72
(B J Meehan) *chsd ldrs: rdn to go 2nd fnl f but a jst hld: ct for 2nd cl home* **14/1**

0-13 **4** 1 1/2 **Jill Dawson (IRE)**[52] 2514 4-8-9 **62**.... KirstyMilczarek(7) 4 65
(John Berry) *t.k.h: led after 2f: hdd over 2f out: wknd fnl f* **5/1**[2]

4-00 **5** 1 **Where's Broughton**[22] 3416 4-9-6 **69**.... WilliamBuick(3) 6 69
(W J Musson) *in rr: pushed along and hdwy over 2f out: kpt on fnl f but nvr gng pce to rch ldrs* **20/1**

0211 **6** 1 1/4 **Silca Key**[10] 3785 3-9-7 **75** 6ex.... TedDurcan 5 73
(M R Channon) *chsd ldrs: rdn 3f out: sn one pce: wknd fnl f* **11/2**[3]

-460 **7** *3* **Noora (IRE)**[12] 3731 6-9-13 **73**..............................(v) AdamKirby 10 64
(C G Cox) *in rr: rdn 4f out: mod prog fnl f* **12/1**

1003 **8** *nk* **Lunar River (FR)**[12] 3731 4-9-4 **64**...............................(t) FergusSweeney 2 54
(David Pinder) *s.i.s: a towards rr* **33/1**

333 **9** *3* **Areyaam (USA)**[21] 3454 3-9-5 **73**.................................. NickyMackay 3 57
(L M Cumani) *t.k.h: chsd ldrs: rdn 3f out: sn btn* **4/1**[1]

4-30 **10** *2 1/2* **Feolin**[92] 1407 3-8-13 **67**.. SteveDrowne 7 45
(H Morrison) *led 2f: styd in tch: rdn 4f out: wknd over 2f out* **11/1**

0550 **11** *1 1/4* **Fangorn Forest (IRE)**[9] 3826 4-8-11 **60**......................(b[1]) LiamJones(3) 9 36
(R A Harris) *nvr bttr than mid-div: bhd fr 1/2-way* **25/1**

5052 **12** *1/2* **Smart Cat (IRE)**[14] 3690 4-8-9 **55**...................................(v) SebSanders 11 29
(A P Jarvis) *a towards rr* **6/1**

1m 56.21s (0.10) **Going Correction** +0.20s/f (Good)
WFA 3 from 4yo+ 8lb **12** Ran SP% **121.6**
Speed ratings (Par 100): **107,106,106,104,104 102,100,100,97,95 94,93**
CSF £88.31 CT £1141.22 TOTE £18.30: £4.10, £3.00, £6.00; EX 156.10.
Owner B P Jones **Bred** Mrs Gillian A R Jones And John Balding **Trained** Oakford, Devon

FOCUS
A modest fillies' handicap, but run at a decent pace and rated more positively as a result.

4113 PFA CENTENARY H'CAP 1m 6f
8:35 (8:35) (Class 4) (0-80,78) 3-Y-O **£6,477** (£1,927; £963; £481) **Stalls** Centre

Form RPR

5421 **1** **Duty Free (IRE)**[16] 3624 3-9-5 **74**....................................... SteveDrowne 7 80+
(H Morrison) *trckd ldr: led 2f out: styd on wl whn strly chal ins fnl f* **5/4**[1]

0003 **2** *1/2* **Irish Quest (IRE)**[24] 3367 3-9-0 **69**.............................. PhilipRobinson 5 74
(M A Jarvis) *chsd ldrs: rdn: swtchd rt 1f out and qcknd to chal ins fnl f: outstyd cl home* **3/1**[2]

-226 **3** *1 1/4* **Calzaghe (IRE)**[49] 2602 3-8-9 **67**...............................(v) WilliamBuick(3) 3 70
(A M Balding) *hld up in rr: hdwy on outside fr 2f out: qcknd to chse ldrs over 1f out: hrd rdn and hung rt u.p ins fnl f: sn no imp* **7/1**[3]

5236 **4** *1 1/4* **Sowdrey**[48] 2628 3-9-0 **69**... TedDurcan 8 71
(M R Channon) *in rr but in tch: rdn and hdwy fr 2f out: kpt on fnl f but nvr gng pce to rch ldrs* **16/1**

2626 **5** *shd* **Alnwick**[5] 3945 3-8-4 **59**... JoeFanning 9 60
(P D Cundell) *chsd ldrs: rdn 3f out: edgd rt u.p ins fnl f and styd on same pce* **12/1**

5350 **6** *hd* **Sweetheart**[36] 2999 3-9-3 **72**.. IanMongan 4 73
(Jamie Poulton) *chsd ldrs: rdn 3f out: styd on same pce fr over 1f out* **25/1**

-110 **7** *1/2* **Intiquilla (IRE)**[36] 2999 3-9-9 **78**... JimCrowley 2 78
(Mrs A J Perrett) *in rr: hdwy 4f out: rdn and edgd rt 2f out: styd on same pce* **14/1**

0336 **8** *1* **Dan Tucker**[30] 3189 3-9-5 **74**.. RyanMoore 1 73
(B J Meehan) *hld up in rr: plld lft to outside 3f out: rdn and effrt over 2f out: nvr rchd ldrs and wknd fnl f* **14/1**

3024 **9** *1 1/4* **Guardian Of Truth (IRE)**[27] 3284 3-9-8 **77**............................ PaulDoe 6 74
(W J Knight) *led tl hdd 2f out: sn wknd* **20/1**

3m 7.29s (2.78) **Going Correction** +0.20s/f (Good) **9** Ran SP% **117.5**
Speed ratings (Par 102): **100,99,99,98,98 98,97,97,96**
CSF £5.00 CT £18.30 TOTE £2.00: £1.20, £1.80, £2.10; EX 5.80 Place 6 £ 103.11, Place 5 £ 48.47.
Owner De La Warr Racing **Bred** Mervyn Stewkesbury **Trained** East Ilsley, Berks

FOCUS
A modest three-year-old staying handicap, run at an ordinary pace but the form makes sense.
T/Plt: £69.00 to a £1 stake. Pool: £59,342.50. 627.15 winning tickets. T/Qpdt: £37.40 to a £1 stake. Pool: £4,627.20. 91.40 winning tickets. ST

4084 GALWAY (R-H)
Thursday, August 2

OFFICIAL GOING: Good to yielding

4114a GUINNESS SURGE H'CAP 1m 4f
4:25 (4:26) (50-70,70) 3-Y-O+ **£7,003** (£1,631; £719; £415)

RPR

1 **Eight Up (IRE)**[29] 3225 4-9-13 69.................................. CO'Donoghue 17 81+
(Edward P Harty, Ire) *trckd ldrs on inner: 6th 4f out: smooth hdwy into 2nd over 2f out: led under 1f out: styd on wl* **11/2**[1]

2 *1* **Mine'sasmallone (IRE)**[9] 3831 4-9-2 65.......................... SMLevey(7) 14 75
(D T Hughes, Ire) *trckd ldrs: 6th 1/2-way: hdwy 3f out: led 2 1/2f out: strly pressed appr st: hdd under 1f out: kpt on u.p* **15/2**

3 *6* **The Chip Chopman (IRE)**[6] 2975 5-9-7 70.................(t) PTownend(7) 13 71
(Seamus G O'Donnell, Ire) *trckd ldrs: 4th 4f out: rdn 2 1/2f out: 3rd bef st: kpt on same pce u.p* **7/1**

4 *hd* **Vonne Owen (IRE)**[18] 3576 3-9-1 68.. KFallon 16 69
(John Joseph Murphy, Ire) *trckd ldrs: 5th 1/2-way: lost pl briefly 2 1/2f out: 4th 2f out: kpt on same pce st* **14/1**

5 *2 1/2* **Pretty Demanding (IRE)**[3] 4035 3-9-3 70.......................... MJKinane 5 67
(M G Quinlan) *towards rr: 16th over 2f out: styd on wl st* **13/2**[3]

6 *2 1/2* **Darenjan (IRE)**[39] 2921 4-10-0 70.. RPCleary 11 63
(John Joseph Hanlon, Ire) *hld up: 12th 1/2-way: prog 3f out: kpt on same pce st* **20/1**

7 *shd* **Ask Jack (USA)**[10] 3809 3-9-3 70.. JAHeffernan 9 63
(Joseph G Murphy, Ire) *mid-div: prog on outer over 2f out: 5th into st: no ex fnl f* **16/1**

8 *1 1/4* **Paddy's Day (IRE)**[15] 3663 4-9-9 65...................................... WMLordan 2 56
(T J O'Mara, Ire) *towards rr: kpt on fr over 2f out* **14/1**

9 *4 1/2* **Awash (USA)**[27] 3294 5-9-7 70.. SJGray(7) 10 54
(D Broad, Ire) *towards rr: kpt on wout threatening fr 3f out* **33/1**

10 *4* **Catskill**[9] 6070 5-9-9 65... DPMcDonogh 4 43
(Adrian McGuinness, Ire) *hld up: 11th 1/2-way: no imp fr 2 1/2f out* **8/1**

11 *1 3/4* **Flexible Friend (IRE)**[54] 2484 3-9-1 68..............................(b) PJSmullen 8 44
(D K Weld, Ire) *prom: 2nd 1/2-way: sn drvn along: chal 3f out: no ex and wknd bef st* **6/1**[2]

12 *4* **Bellar (GER)**[37] 2268 4-9-8 67...(p) SMGorey(3) 18 37
(Eoin Doyle, Ire) *cl up: 3rd 1/2-way: wknd fr over 3f out* **20/1**

13 *nk* **Kalamkar (IRE)**[2] 4050 5-9-3 69................................... EJMcNamara(10) 1 38
(S Donohoe, Ire) *hld up towards rr: rdn and no imp fr 3f out* **25/1**

14 *5* **Red Mantilla (UAE)**[668] 5-9-12 68.. FMBerry 15 30
(David Marnane, Ire) *led: hdd 2 1/2f out: wknd and eased appr st* **16/1**

15 *4 1/2* **Dream West (IRE)**[37] 2644 4-9-6 67........................(p) CPGeoghegan(5) 6 22
(Liam Roche, Ire) *nvr a factor* **33/1**

16 *1/2* **Chapel Court (IRE)**[29] 3224 3-9-1 68..............................(b[1]) KJManning 7 22
(T M Walsh, Ire) *s.i.s and a bhd* **20/1**

17 *6* **Compton Court**[22] 3444 5-9-9 65... CDHayes 3 10
(John G Carr, Ire) *mid-div on outer: rdn and sme prog 3f out: no ex and eased appr st* **25/1**

18 *4* **Miracle Card (FR)**[22] 3444 4-9-1 67............................... MHarley(10) 12 6
(R Donohoe, Ire) *mid-div: rdn and wknd fr 3f out* **25/1**

2m 40.47s (-2.63)
WFA 3 from 4yo+ 11lb **18** Ran SP% **135.2**
CSF £44.44 CT £309.95 TOTE £6.00: £1.80, £2.20, £1.70, £3.40; DF 64.30.
Owner Cole Family Syndicate **Bred** Grangemore Stud **Trained** the Curragh, Co Kildare

NOTEBOOK
Eight Up(IRE) was well back heading into the final quarter of a mile and stayed on quite well. A relatively lightly-raced sort, she has gone up 16lb in the weights recently but showed enough to suggest that another handicap might come her way.

4115 - 4116a (Foreign Racing) - See Raceform Interactive

4089 GOODWOOD (R-H)
Friday, August 3

OFFICIAL GOING: Good to firm (good in places; 9.0)
Wind: Virtually nil Weather: Sunny and warm

4117 COUTTS GLORIOUS STKS (LISTED RACE) 1m 4f
2:15 (2:16) (Class 1) 4-Y-O+
£17,034 (£6,456; £3,231; £1,611; £807; £405) **Stalls** Low

Form RPR

34-4 **1** **Purple Moon (IRE)**[42] 2815 4-9-1 97.............................. JamieSpencer 5 113+
(L M Cumani) *lw: stdd s: hld up in rr: pushed along and hdwy on outer over 2f out: led over 1f out: sn edgd rt: rdn out* **11/2**[3]

-103 **2** *2 1/2* **Imperial Star (IRE)**[70] 1985 4-9-4 110............................ JimmyFortune 9 111
(J H M Gosden) *hld up towards rr: gd hdwy on outer 3f out: led 2f out: sn hdd: swtchd lft over 1f out: kpt on same pce* **13/2**

0-20 **3** *nk* **Stotsfold**[63] 2209 4-9-1 104... AdamKirby 10 108+
(W R Swinburn) *taken down early: hld up in rr: hdwy over 2f out: nt clr run over 1f out: r.o wl fnl f: nt rch ldrs* **16/1**

2625 **4** *1* **Hard Top (IRE)**[7] 3912 5-9-1 106.. RyanMoore 8 106
(Sir Michael Stoute) *stdd s: hld up in last pair: hdwy and bmpd wl over 2f out: swtchd rt and bmpd 2f out: styd on fnl f: n.d* **8/1**

/1-1 **5** *nk* **Perfectperformance (USA)**[22] 3468 5-9-1 104........... KerrinMcEvoy 6 105
(Saeed Bin Suroor) *lw: in tch: effrt and short of room 3f out: sn rdn: plugged on fnl f* **7/2**[1]

1032 **6** *3 1/2* **Ballinteni**[28] 3272 5-9-1 89... NCallan 1 100
(D M Simcock) *hld up in midfield: hdwy on inner 5f out: chsd ldrs and rdn over 2f out: wknd fnl f* **33/1**

5340 **7** *1 1/4* **Acropolis (IRE)**[41] 2859 6-9-1 92...................................(v[1]) PaulHanagan 3 98+
(I Semple) *hld up in rr: hdwy on rail over 3f out: nt clr run fr wl over 2f out: no ch* **66/1**

-320 **8** *5* **Camrose**[40] 2907 6-9-1 100...(b) EddieAhern 7 90
(J L Dunlop) *racd in midfield: lost pl 5f out: rdn over 3f out: no ch after* **25/1**

216- **9** *nk* **Hotel Du Cap**[289] 6062 4-9-1 93.. SteveDrowne 4 89
(G Wragg) *chsd ldr tl jst over 2f out: sn wknd* **66/1**

246- **10** *12* **Dragon Dancer**[286] 6103 4-9-1 115.................................... DarryllHolland 11 70
(G Wragg) *pushed along leaving stalls: chsd ldrs: rdn and carried hd awkwardly 3f out: sn btn: eased fnl f: t.o* **11/2**[3]

3613 **11** *4* **Munsef**[34] 3097 5-9-1 110..(b) RHills 12 64
(J L Dunlop) *led tl 2f out: btn whn hmpd over 1f out: eased: t.o* **9/2**[2]

23P0 **12** *18* **The Last Drop (IRE)**[43] 2787 4-9-1 106............................... JMurtagh 2 35
(B W Hills) *chsd ldrs: rdn 4f out: wknd 3f out: eased: t.o* **14/1**

2m 35.08s (-3.84) **Going Correction** -0.075s/f (Good) **12** Ran SP% **117.9**
Speed ratings (Par 111): **109,107,107,106,106 103,103,99,99,91 88,76**
CSF £39.95 TOTE £6.80: £1.90, £2.50, £5.20; EX 43.40 Trifecta £718.10 Pool £1,416.07 - 1.40 winning units..
Owner Craig Bennett **Bred** Gestut Shohrenhof **Trained** Newmarket, Suffolk
■ Stewards' Enquiry : Adam Kirby two-day ban: used whip with excessive force and with his arm above shoulder height (Aug 14-15)

FOCUS
A competitive Listed race run at a decent pace. The principals all came from the rear but the form appears solid with the majority of those immediately behind the first two close to their marks.

NOTEBOOK
Purple Moon(IRE), well at home on fast ground, was back over a more suitable trip on this second run for the yard. He was held up in the rear before making good headway down the outside to lead, going on to score decisively despite edging to his right. He may miss the Ebor, for which a 3lb penalty leaves him looking well treated, and instead run in the Geoffrey Freer at Newbury prior to a crack at the Caulfield and Melbourne Cups. (op 13-2 tchd 7-1 in places)
Imperial Star(IRE), returning from a break since May, relaxed more than he usually does before a race. Tackling a new trip, he improved going well to lead but was immediately tackled by the winner, who went across him as he took the lead and forced him to switch. Unable to counter, his stamina just appeared to be stretched over this trip. (op 11-2)
Stotsfold, patiently ridden once again, finished well after not enjoying a clear passage in the straight and had no problem with the longer trip. Granted his favoured fast ground he is a consistent sort. (op 12-1)
Hard Top(IRE) has not been at his best this term, but was the recipient of a couple of bumps and deserves credit for this performance. (op 9-1 tchd 10-1 in places)
Perfectperformance(USA), back up in trip for what was only his fourth run in the last two years, lacked the pace to seriously trouble the leaders and appeared to be hanging a little in the latter stages. (op 4-1 tchd 9-2 in places)
Ballinteni, back up in trip for this first venture into Listed company, produced a career-best effort. (tchd 40-1 in places)
Acropolis(IRE), tried in a visor, would have finished closer had he not been denied a run against the far rail from the two-furlong pole. He could be on the way back. Official explanation: jockey said gelding was denied a clear run
Dragon Dancer, who suffered a setback in the spring, looked fit for this first run since October. A frustrating maiden last term, beaten a short head by Sir Percy in the Derby, he looked a very awkward customer here and, despite his obvious ability, he is one to avoid. Official explanation: jockey said colt hung right-handed in straight (op 5-1 tchd 6-1 in places)

Munsef, again adopting front-running tactics, set a decent pace for ten furlongs but was headed and on the retreat when getting into trouble. The effect of the blinkers may be wearing off. (tchd 5-1)

4118 OAK TREE STKS (GROUP 3) (F&M) 7f
2:50 (2:56) (Class 1) 3-Y-O+

£28,390 (£10,760; £5,385; £2,685; £1,345; £675) **Stalls** High

Form RPR

2-14 **1** **Wake Up Maggie (IRE)**[30] 3222 4-9-4 104 .... GeorgeBaker 18 112
(C F Wall) *lw: t.k.h: hld up trcking ldrs: hdwy and swtchd off rail 2f out: chal 1f out: pushed into ld last 75yds: pushed out* **11/1**

3413 **2** ½ **Costume**[44] 2757 3-8-9 113 .... RichardHughes 13 106
(J H M Gosden) *trckd ldrs: rdn to ld jst over 1f out: immediately chal: hdd last 75yds: no ex* **10/3**[1]

0-11 **3** 1½ **Redstone Dancer (IRE)**[19] 3575 5-9-4 0 .... PShanahan 15 107
(Miss S Collins, Ire) *str: s.i.s: bhd: hdwy on rail over 2f out: styd on wl fnl f: nt rch ldrs* **8/1**

-021 **4** nk **Selinka**[27] 3332 3-8-9 107 .... RyanMoore 10 101
(R Hannon) *lw: bhd: rdn and hdwy on outer over 2f out: styd on u.p fnl f: nt rch ldrs* **6/1**[2]

-120 **5** ½ **Majestic Roi (USA)**[42] 2814 3-8-12 108 .... JamieSpencer 11 103
(M R Channon) *stdd s: hld up wl bhd: plld to outer and hdwy over 1f out: r.o wl: nt rch ldrs* **15/2**

-106 **6** 1½ **Scarlet Runner**[42] 2814 3-8-12 107 .... KerrinMcEvoy 16 99
(J L Dunlop) *stmbld s: sn in tch: rdn and effrt 2f out: kpt on same pce* **7/1**[3]

-605 **7** hd **Vital Statistics**[44] 2752 3-8-9 102 .... TQuinn 12 95
(D R C Elsworth) *racd in midfield: rdn over 1f out: kpt on same pce* **16/1**

-103 **8** hd **Lady Grace (IRE)**[21] 3511 3-8-9 98 .... MichaelHills 2 95
(W J Haggas) *racd on outer: a towards rr: n.d* **33/1**

-660 **9** ½ **Sesmen**[21] 3511 3-8-9 103 .... NCallan 9 93
(M Botti) *chsd ldrs: rdn 3f out: wknd over 1f out* **50/1**

6250 **10** hd **Leopoldine**[42] 2817 4-9-1 89 .... SteveDrowne 17 95
(H Morrison) *chsd ldr tl over 4f out: styd handy: rdn over 2f out: wknd jst over 1f out* **50/1**

1- **11** ¾ **Rainbow Promises (USA)**[302] 5773 3-8-9 93 .... KDarley 7 91
(B J Meehan) *lw: hld up wl bhd: rdn over 2f out: kpt on but nvr pce to rch ldrs* **16/1**

0000 **12** ¾ **Puggy (IRE)**[42] 2814 3-8-9 100 .... (t) EddieAhern 14 89
(R A Kvisla) *lw: prom: chsd ldr over 4f out: rdn to ld over 2f out: hdd jst over 1f out: sn wknd* **50/1**

5 **13** ¾ **Samya**[82] 1701 3-8-11 0 ow2 .... (t) MMonteriso 1 89
(E Borromeo, Italy) *a towards rr: n.d* **50/1**

0112 **14** 1¼ **Gloved Hand**[21] 3511 5-9-1 99 .... SebSanders 4 85
(R M Beckett) *b: a bhd: nvr on terms* **20/1**

6-11 **15** 6 **Tarteel (USA)**[23] 3430 3-8-9 98 .... RHills 5 67
(J L Dunlop) *lw: t.k.h: hld up bhd: lost tch 2f out: eased fnl f* **12/1**

-200 **16** ¾ **Sander Camillo (USA)**[21] 3506 3-8-9 108 .... JMurtagh 3 65
(J Noseda) *led tl over 2f out: sn btn: eased fnl f* **14/1**

1m 25.48s (-2.56) **Going Correction** -0.075s/f (Good)
WFA 3 from 4yo+ 6lb **16** Ran SP% **122.7**
Speed ratings (Par 113): **111,110,108,108,107 106,105,105,105,104 103,103,102,100,93 93**
CSF £43.50 TOTE £13.70: £3.70, £1.80, £3.00; EX 76.70 Trifecta £362.60 Pool £1,890.03 - 3.70 winning units..
Owner J G Lambton **Bred** Rathmoyle Exports Ltd **Trained** Newmarket, Suffolk
■ Wasseema was withdrawn (14/1, unruly in stalls). Deduct 5p in the £ under Rule 4.

FOCUS
A strong renewal of this event, run at a sound pace and the form looks decent, despite those drawn high dominating.

NOTEBOOK
Wake Up Maggie(IRE) tracked the runner-up through before quickening past her in the last half-furlong to win with a bit to spare. This was a good performance under her penalty and she deserves another go at something better, perhaps the Group 1 Prix de la Foret. (tchd 12-1)
Costume was always well placed and took over going to the furlong pole, but found one too good. Still on the upgrade, she now continues her career in the United States. (op 7-2 tchd 4-1)
Redstone Dancer(IRE), along with the winner, was one of just two penalised runners in the line-up. Running on strongly in the latter stages, she ends her racing career on a high. (op 9-1 tchd 10-1 in places)
Selinka was set plenty to do and despite running on well she could not get to the leaders. The drop to 7f was not ideal and nor was the unconventional track, and she should be kept on the right side when back over a mile on a flatter course. (op 8-1 tchd 11-2)
Majestic Roi(USA), held up going well at the back of the field, ran on well when angled to the outside but was never going to make up the deficit. She is capable of winning again at this level. (op 8-1 tchd 7-1)
Scarlet Runner, down in trip and grade, ran respectably if a little below her recent level. (op 10-1)
Vital Statistics, as in the Jersey Stakes last time, was doing some solid late work. She might need a mile now. (op 14-1)
Rainbow Promises(USA), successful in a Polytrack maiden on her only previous start ten months ago, was fancied for the 1000 Guineas earlier this year but was ruled out after suffering a setback. She shaped encouragingly on this reappearance and there could be improvement in her at a mile.
Puggy(IRE), always up with the pace, moved to the front with over two furlongs to run but could not hold on going to the last.
Sander Camillo(USA), without the blinkers she wore in the July Cup, showed pace on this drop in class but soon dropped away once headed. It is a shame she has not fulfilled the potential she showed last summer. (op 12-1 tchd 16-1 in a place)

4119 TOTESPORT MILE (HERITAGE H'CAP) 1m
3:30 (3:32) (Class 2) 3-Y-O+

£93,480 (£27,990; £13,995; £7,005; £3,495; £1,755) **Stalls** High

Form RPR

2011 **1** **Third Set (IRE)**[6] 3941 4-8-4 90 5ex .... JimmyQuinn 20 112+
(R Charlton) *lw: a gng wl: trckd ldrs tl led 2f out: sn clr: impressive* **5/2**[1]

0210 **2** 3 **Humungous (IRE)**[44] 2755 4-8-13 99 .... (b[1]) RyanMoore 14 111
(C R Egerton) *swtg: awkward s: hld up towards rr: hdwy over 2f out: swtchd rt and bmpd rival wl over 1f out: forced through over 1f out: sn chsng wnr: no imp* **20/1**

0120 **3** 2½ **King Of Argos**[6] 3941 4-8-12 98 .... JMurtagh 13 104
(E A L Dunlop) *lw: racd in midfield: hdwy on outer over 2f out: chsd ldrs over 1f out: kpt on same pce u.p* **6/1**[2]

0-01 **4** ½ **River Tiber**[20] 3527 4-8-12 98 3ex .... JamieSpencer 9 103+
(L M Cumani) *hld up wl bhd: rdn and effrt over 2f out: kpt on u.p fnl f: nt rch ldrs* **10/1**[3]

0025 **5** ¾ **Montpellier (IRE)**[3] 4049 4-8-3 89 .... MartinDwyer 16 92
(E A L Dunlop) *hld up in midfield: hmpd 3f out: swtchd lft and hdwy 2f out: chsd ldrs over 1f out: no ex fnl f* **6/1**[2]

-213 **6** hd **Unshakable (IRE)**[27] 3330 8-8-5 91 .... PaulEddery 2 94+
(Bob Jones) *b.hind: hld up in midfield: hdwy whn bdly hmpd wl over 2f out: no ch after* **20/1**

0556 **7** 1½ **Azarole (IRE)**[161] 540 6-8-11 102 .... TolleyDean[(5)] 6 101
(J S Moore) *w.w in midfield: hdwy 3f out: rdn and hanging rt fr over 2f out: wknd 1f out* **66/1**

0160 **8** 1¼ **Mine (IRE)**[21] 3505 9-9-8 108 .... (v) TQuinn 19 105
(J D Bethell) *hld up wl in rr: n.d* **25/1**

0-14 **9** 7 **Supaseus**[44] 2755 4-8-13 99 .... JohnEgan 8 79
(H Morrison) *led tl 5f out: led again briefly over 2f out: wknd over 1f out* **12/1**

0404 **10** ¾ **Kings Point (IRE)**[36] 3026 6-8-6 92 .... (p) PaulHanagan 5 71
(R A Fahey) *v.s.a: nvr on terms* **33/1**

2650 **11** ½ **My Paris**[21] 3505 6-8-11 97 .... (b) NCallan 10 75+
(K A Ryan) *chsd ldr tl led 5f out: rdn and hdd over 2f out: wknd over 1f out: eased* **33/1**

-124 **12** 1¼ **Pinpoint (IRE)**[64] 2182 5-9-11 111 .... AdamKirby 12 86+
(W R Swinburn) *a bhd: n.d: b.b.v* **10/1**[3]

4130 **13** 16 **Killena Boy (IRE)**[27] 3330 5-8-5 91 .... PaulDoe 11 29+
(W Jarvis) *lw: chsd ldrs: rdn whn bdly hmpd wl over 2f out: no ch after* **33/1**

6032 **14** 23 **Babodana**[34] 3103 7-9-2 102 .... SebSanders 7 —
(M H Tompkins) *lw: in tch: chsng ldrs and rdn whn bdly bmpd 2f out: no ch after: eased* **40/1**

0300 **15** 39 **Vortex**[6] 3941 8-9-7 107 .... (t) JimmyFortune 17 —
(Miss Gay Kelleway) *b.hind: a bhd: no ch whn nrly b.d over 1f out: virtually p.u after* **25/1**

00-1 **16** 5 **Pintle**[57] 2401 7-8-5 91 .... KerrinMcEvoy 1 —
(J L Spearing) *sn prom: rdn and wknd 1/2-way: virtually p.u* **33/1**

0600 **B** **Uhoomagoo**[6] 3941 9-8-7 93 ow2 .... (b) DarryllHolland 15 —
(K A Ryan) *a bhd: no ch whn b.d over 1f out* **33/1**

15-0 **B** **Blades Girl**[13] 3746 4-8-7 93 .... (p) TedDurcan 3 —
(K A Ryan) *a.p: ev ch 3f out: jostled 2f out: 7th and btn whn b.d over 1f out* **100/1**

30-2 **F** **Drumfire (IRE)**[22] 3463 3-8-10 103 .... JoeFanning 4 —
(M Johnston) *chsd ldrs: rdn and bmpd 2f out: 6th whn clipped heels and fell over 1f out* **10/1**[3]

1m 37.48s (-2.79) **Going Correction** -0.075s/f (Good)
WFA 3 from 4yo+ 7lb **19** Ran SP% **129.0**
Speed ratings (Par 109): **110,107,104,104,103 103,101,100,93,92 92,90,74,51,12 7,—,—,—**
CSF £61.54 CT £296.62 TOTE £3.50: £1.50, £3.80, £1.90, £2.90; EX 83.10 Trifecta £720.60 Pool £4,820.99 - 4.75 winning units..
Owner John Livock **Bred** A Stroud & J Hanly **Trained** Beckhampton, Wilts

FOCUS
A typically competitive renewal of this valuable handicap, run at a strong pace with the winner progressive and the runner-up recording a personal best. It was a rough race and there was a nasty pile-up inside the final two furlongs. Those drawn high were again favoured.

NOTEBOOK
Third Set(IRE), well in under the 5lb penalty he picked up for winning the Totesport International the previous weekend, completed the hat-trick in fine style. Well drawn on the inside and racing closer to the pace than at Newmarket or Ascot, he crusied into the lead with a quarter of a mile to run and had no difficulty pulling clear for a comfortable success. He is set to take a further hike in the weights for this, but might be the type for the Cambridgeshire later in the season if the ground is riding fast. (op 3-1)
Humungous(IRE), blinkered for the first time, exited the stalls awkwardly and had to adopt different tactics after making the running on his last two starts. Threading his way through from the rear, he gave Babodana a bump entering the last two furlongs before keeping on well, if never a threat to the easy winner. (tchd 22-1)
King Of Argos, avoiding trouble on the outside, made good progress to go after the leaders but his effort just flattened out inside the last. He had no problem with the return to a mile and finished closer to Third Set than he had at Ascot recently. (op 15-2)
River Tiber ♦, having only his second run since leaving Ireland, ran well under the 3lb penalty incurred at Ascot. He was making good late progress and a slightly longer trip should suit him. (op 9-1)
Montpellier(IRE), again lucky with the draw, repeated his fifth place on the opening day of the meeting. His running style means that things have to drop just right for him. (tchd 13-2 and 7-1 in a place)
Unshakable(IRE), who won this two years ago when 4lb lower, produced a creditable effort from an unfavourable draw, particularly as he was badly impeded with just under three furlongs to run. (op 16-1)
Azarole(IRE), off the track since a spell in Dubai at the beginning of the year, made good progress down the outside from the three-furlong pole but hung right as he did so and was deemed the chief contributor to the pile-up. He faded inside the last as lack of a recent run began to tell.
Supaseus was not the most consistent last year and this effort was below the level he had produced on his two previous outings this season. (op 10-1 tchd 14-1)
My Paris helped set the pace until fading from the two-furlong pole. At least he completed the course, unlike his two stablemates.
Pinpoint(IRE) Official explanation: trainer said gelding bled from the nose
Blades Girl, having her first run over this far, raced up with the pace. Beginning to feel the pinch when getting jostled with a quarter of a mile to run, she managed to keep her feet then but had nowhere to go when Drumfire came down in front of her shortly after. (tchd 9-1 and 11-1)
Drumfire(IRE), on his handicap debut, was under pressure behind the leaders when crashing to the ground with over a furlong to run. Fortunately he seemed none the worse. (tchd 9-1 and 11-1)

4120 RICHMOND STKS (GROUP 2) (C&G) 6f
4:05 (4:06) (Class 1) 2-Y-O

£39,746 (£15,064; £5,649; £5,649; £1,883; £945) **Stalls** Low

Form RPR

153 **1** **Strike The Deal (USA)**[12] 3779 2-9-0 0 .... EddieAhern 7 108
(J Noseda) *lw: hld up towards rr: hdwy over 2f out: rdn to chal 1f out: led ins fnl f: r.o wl* **7/1**

0601 **2** 1¼ **Fat Boy (IRE)**[7] 3910 2-9-0 0 .... RichardHughes 1 104
(R Hannon) *lw: led: rdn wl over 1f out: hdd ins fnl f: kpt on same pce* **8/1**

3 1½ **One Great Cat (USA)**[12] 3767 2-9-0 0 .... JMurtagh 3 100
(A P O'Brien, Ire) *lengthy: w'like: lw: in tch in midfield: rdn and effrt wl over 1f out: ur.p: nt pce to rch ldrs* **3/1**[1]

31 **3** dht **Exhibition (IRE)**[14] 3712 2-9-0 0 .... JamieSpencer 12 100
(N A Callaghan) *hld up in rr: hdwy 2f out: chsd ldrs and rdn jst over 1f out: kpt on same pce last 100yds* **7/1**

11 **5** 1 **Drawnfromthepast (IRE)**[45] 2737 2-9-0 0 .... MartinDwyer 6 97
(J A Osborne) *lw: t.k.h: sn chsng ldrs: rdn 2f out: fdd jst ins fnl f* **7/2**[2]

5331 **6** ¾ **Master Chef (IRE)**[21] 3478 2-9-0 0 .... (b) JimmyFortune 11 94
(J H M Gosden) *s.i.s: hld up: hdwy over 2f out: rdn and briefly short of room 1f out: sn btn* **17/2**

105 **7** 1¾ **Bobs Surprise**[22] 3459 2-9-0 0 .... MichaelHills 2 89
(B W Hills) *swtg: s.i.s: bhd: rdn over 2f out: no hdwy* **13/2**[3]

10 **8** ½ **Roker Park (IRE)**[43] 2785 2-9-0 0 NCallan 4 88
(K R Burke) *swtg: in tch: sddle slipped 1/2-way: rdn 2f out: wknd fnl f* **20/1**

0163 **9** ½ **Cee Bargara**[7] 3910 2-9-0 0 JimCrowley 10 86
(J A Osborne) *pressed ldr: rdn 2f out: wknd over 1f out* **16/1**

1m 11.59s (-1.26) **Going Correction** -0.075s/f (Good) **9** Ran SP% **117.8**
Speed ratings (Par 106): **105,103,101,101,100 99,96,96,95**
3rd place tote: Exhibition £1.30, One Great Cat £0.80; Trifecta: £575.60 (E), £125.10 (OGC). CSF £62.82 TOTE £8.40: £2.40, £1.80; EX 72.10.
Owner The Searchers **Bred** Five-D Thoroughbreds, Llc **Trained** Newmarket, Suffolk

FOCUS
Far from a vintage renewal of the Richmond Stakes, but the form looks solid enough. Most held a chance as the field fanned across the track at the two-furlong marker. The winner and second are progressive but the form, although likely to prove reliable, may not have too much long-term impact.

NOTEBOOK
Strike The Deal(USA) raced too keenly in the Norfolk Stakes and was taught to settle in the Prix Robert Papin next time, leaving him with too much ground to make up. Back over 6f for the first time since his racecourse debut on Polytrack, he came from off the pace to challenge between horses and win decisively. He is going the right way. (tchd 15-2)
Fat Boy(IRE), successful from the front at Ascot, repeated those tactics and bettered his previous form, but could not find a change of gear when headed by the winner inside the last. (op 12-1)
One Great Cat(USA) is out of a sister to Kentucky Derby winner and Coolmore stallion Fusaichi Pegasus. Winner of a 6f maiden in heavy ground at Fairyhouse on his second start, he found things happening too quickly on this sharper track on better ground and could only stay on to secure a share of third place. He looks to need 7f now. (op 11-4 tchd 100-30)
Exhibition(IRE), runner-up to Rio De La Plata before winning at Nottingham, showed improved form on this step up in grade. He looked a threat when looming up on the outside approaching the futlong pole, but did not produce as much as had looked likely. (op 11-4 tchd 100-30)
Drawnfromthepast(IRE), returned to 6f, was below the form he showed when winning the Windsor Castle Stakes last time and could prove best at the minimum trip. (tchd 3-1 and 4-1 in places)
Master Chef(IRE) was allowed to bowl along in front when winning his maiden at Ascot and was not seen to the same effect with these hold-up tactics, although he did run up to form. (op 8-1 tchd 9-1)
Bobs Surprise, unable to recover from a tardy start, has now been found wanting three times at Group 2 level since making a winning debut in a maiden over this course and distance. (op 7-1 tchd 6-1)
Roker Park(IRE), who had gone to post freely, was hampered by a slipping saddle from halfway and deserves another chance. Official explanation: jockey said saddle slipped after 2f (op 25-1)
Cee Bargara, who got warm beforehand, failed to run up to his Ascot form with Fat Boy. He is exposed now.

4121 ROYAL & SUNALLIANCE NURSERY 7f
4:40 (4:40) (Class 2) 2-Y-O **£12,954** (£3,854; £1,926; £962) **Stalls** High

Form RPR

310 **1** **Coasting**[45] 2732 2-9-3 **85** JimCrowley 16 96+
(Mrs A J Perrett) *t.k.h: trckd ldrs: swtchd lft over 1f out: sn led: stormed clr: rdn out* **10/1**

404 **2** *4* **Huzzah (IRE)**[20] 3552 2-8-5 **73** MartinDwyer 3 74
(B W Hills) *stdd s: wl bhd: rdn and weaved through fr over 2f out: r.o wl fnl f: wnt 2nd nr fin: no ch w wnr* **22/1**

10 **3** *nk* **Meeriss (IRE)**[62] 2232 2-9-2 **84** JHBowman 17 84
(M R Channon) *lw: hld up in tch: rdn and effrt 2f out: short of room briefly over 1f out: kpt on same pce* **12/1**

326 **4** *nk* **Miss Firefly**[41] 2869 2-8-3 **71** EdwardCreighton 9 70
(M R Channon) *chsd ldr tl rdn to ld over 2f out: hdd over 1f out: no ch w wnr after: kpt on* **33/1**

51 **5** ½ **The Betchworth Kid**[26] 3348 2-9-0 **82** JimmyFortune 6 80+
(M L W Bell) *sn last and pushed along: hdwy and short of room over 1f out: swtchd lft: r.o strly: nvr nrr* **17/2**

312 **6** *nk* **Shifting Star (IRE)**[20] 3524 2-9-0 **82** AdamKirby 1 79
(W R Swinburn) *lw: chsd ldrs: rdn and effrt 2f out: no imp u.p fnl f* **9/2**[1]

415 **7** *2* **Sofia's Star**[15] 3669 2-9-4 **89** LiamJones[(3)] 7 81
(P Winkworth) *bhd: plld out and rdn wl over 2f out: n.d* **33/1**

511 **8** ½ **Distant Charm (IRE)**[28] 3275 2-9-2 **84** RyanMoore 8 74
(R Hannon) *w.w in midfield: rdn and effrt 2f out: no hdwy over 1f out* **7/1**[2]

4403 **9** *hd* **Kyrie Eleison (IRE)**[9] 3849 2-8-3 **71** FrancisNorton 2 61+
(R Hannon) *lw: racd wd: towards rr: rdn over 2f out: nvr nr ldrs* **33/1**

044 **10** *nk* **Golden Penny**[25] 3383 2-8-9 **77** SteveDrowne 14 66+
(H Morrison) *s.i.s: hdwy on inner over 2f out: rdn and no imp whn n.m.r over 1f out* **15/2**[3]

0231 **11** *nk* **Silver Wind**[15] 3669 2-9-1 **83** (v) StephenDonohoe 4 71
(P D Evans) *t.k.h: in tch: rdn jst over 2f out: wknd over 1f out* **33/1**

5532 **12** *1 ¼* **Farthermost (IRE)**[9] 3850 2-7-12 **66** oh10 DavidKinsella 11 51+
(R Hannon) *hld up in rr: effrt on rail 3f out: nt clr run after: no ch* **9/1**

351 **13** ½ **Hansinger (IRE)**[22] 3465 2-8-11 **79** ChrisCatlin 13 63
(B I Case) *lw: racd in midfield: rdn 2f out: no imp* **16/1**

5353 **14** *hd* **Gulf Coast**[16] 3642 2-8-0 **68** AdrianTNicholls 10 51+
(M Johnston) *chsd ldrs tl 1/2-way: lost pl and rdn 3f out: no ch after* **16/1**

020 **15** ½ **Marning Star**[29] 3238 2-8-7 **75** JohnEgan 5 57
(M R Channon) *a towards rr: n.d* **50/1**

0211 **16** *5* **La Chicaluna**[21] 3494 2-8-10 **78** PaulHanagan 15 47+
(J G Given) *stmbld s: sn led: hdd over 2f out: wkng whn n.m.r over 1f out* **7/1**[2]

0450 **17** *16* **Lady Nova (IRE)**[15] 3680 2-7-12 **66** oh1 (p) AdrianMcCarthy 12 —
(J S Moore) *a towards rr: rdn and btn 3f out: eased fnl f* **40/1**

1m 26.95s (-1.09) **Going Correction** -0.075s/f (Good) **17** Ran SP% **124.5**
Speed ratings (Par 100): **103,98,98,97,97 96,94,93,93,93 93,91,91,90,90 84,66**
CSF £222.81 CT £2766.55 TOTE £11.70: £2.50, £5.80, £3.50, £6.40; EX 271.90 TRIFECTA Not won..
Owner Sir John Ritblat,David & Jennifer Sieff **Bred** Mrs Dare Wigan **Trained** Pulborough, W Sussex
■ Stewards' Enquiry : Jim Crowley one-day ban: careless riding (Aug 14)

FOCUS
A competitive nursery and solid form which should work out. Coasting was impressive and is worth a place in better company.

NOTEBOOK
Coasting ◆, always well placed behind the leaders, struck the front going to the furlong pole and soon came clear to score impressively. He is capable of making an impact at Listed level. (op 9-1)
Huzzah(IRE), closely weighted with Coasting on their Newbury running but not as well drawn as that horse, had to work his way from the back of the field and finished fast for second. (op 20-1)
Meeriss(IRE), found wanting in Listed company at Epsom, ran a sound race upped to this trip for the first time. (op 14-1)
Miss Firefly, unsuited by the heavy ground at Haydock, was tackling 7f for the first time and returned to form, racing up with the pace and only caught for second near the finish. (op 25-1)
The Betchworth Kid ◆, successful over this trip at Brighton, was last entering the home straight and then had to be switched going to the furlong pole, but came home well. Things did not go his way here and he remains unexposed on a conventional track. (op 11-1)
Shifting Star(IRE) failed to find the anticipated improvement for the step up in trip but was not disgraced from his low draw. (op 4-1 tchd 5-1 in a place)
Kyrie Eleison(IRE) was trapped wide from this low draw and this effort should be forgotten.
Golden Penny would have finished a bit closer on this nursery bow but for encountering a bit of trouble in the latter stages. (op 7-1 tchd 8-1 in places)
Farthermost(IRE), who ran a much-improved race on the Lingfield Polytrack recently, was 11lb well in despite racing from 10lb out of the weights but could never get into the action. He did not enjoy a clear passage but it remains to be seen if he can match his sand form on turf. (op 8-1 tchd 10-1 in a place)
La Chicaluna, only a pound higher than when winning on heavy ground at Haydock, adopted the same tactics on this step up in trip but could not hold on in the straight. (op 15-2 tchd 13-2)

4122 TURF CLUB STEWARDS' SPRINT STKS (H'CAP) 6f
5:10 (5:15) (Class 2) 3-Y-O+ **£12,464** (£3,732; £1,866; £934; £466; £234) **Stalls** Low

Form RPR

0103 **1** **Pearly Wey**[7] 3911 4-9-5 **90** PhilipRobinson 9 100
(C G Cox) *hld up bhd on stands' side: hdwy 2f out: styd on wl u.p to ld last 50yds* **8/1**[3]

6-5 **2** *hd* **Joseph Henry**[84] 1619 5-9-0 **85** DavidKinsella 4 94
(D Nicholls) *racd keenly: in tch on stands' side: hdwy to ld overall over 1f out: kpt on u.p tl hdd last 50yds* **16/1**

0300 **3** *1* **Indian Trail**[1] 4095 7-9-5 **90** (v) AdrianTNicholls 19 96+
(D Nicholls) *lw: hld up bhd on far side: nt clr run fr 2f out tl swtchd lft ent fnl f: r.o to go 3rd cl home: nrst fin* **6/1**[1]

0006 **4** ½ **Obe Gold**[11] 3802 5-9-2 **87** (v) JimmyQuinn 16 92
(M R Channon) *racd far side: in tch: hdwy over 2f out: rdn and ev ch 1f out: no ex last 100yds* **33/1**

5000 **5** *1 ¼* **Merlin's Dancer**[13] 3749 7-9-8 **93** JohnEgan 14 94
(S Dow) *chsd ldrs on far side: rdn and ev ch fr over 2f out: no ex last 100yds* **66/1**

4060 **6** *shd* **Mujood**[6] 3941 4-9-4 **89** (b) StephenCarson 28 89
(Eve Johnson Houghton) *chsd ldrs on far side: rdn 2f out: kpt on same pce u.p* **25/1**

4041 **7** *shd* **Border Music**[20] 3526 6-8-13 **84** 3ex (b) FrancisNorton 24 84
(A M Balding) *hld up towards rr on far side: hdwy over 2f out: sn rdn: kpt on steadily but nt pce to rch ldrs* **6/1**[1]

1000 **8** *hd* **Oranmore Castle (IRE)**[1] 4095 5-8-7 **78** (t) SamHitchcott 15 77
(D Nicholls) *led far side: rdn 2f out: kpt on u.p tl no ex ins fnl f* **50/1**

2502 **9** ½ **Namir (IRE)**[14] 3720 5-8-4 **80** ow3 (vt) PatrickHills[(5)] 5 78
(D Shaw) *s.i.s: hld up in rr on stands' side: rdn and effrt over 1f out: no imp fnl f* **33/1**

1522 **10** *hd* **Roman Maze**[7] 3911 7-9-2 **87** RyanMoore 10 84
(W M Brisbourne) *lw: t.k.h: hld up in tch on stands' side: rdn 2f out: kpt on same pce fnl f* **7/1**[2]

0-10 **11** *nk* **Longquan (IRE)**[23] 3431 3-9-8 **97** PatCosgrave 27 93
(P J Makin) *racd in midfield on far side: rdn over 1f out: no imp* **16/1**

0432 **12** *nk* **Idle Power (IRE)**[17] 3623 9-9-0 **85** AmirQuinn 3 80
(J R Boyle) *hld up in rr on stands' side: shkn up and effrt over 2f out: sn no imp* **14/1**

2600 **13** *hd* **The Cayterers**[20] 3549 5-8-1 **77** ow2 (p) KevinGhunowa[(5)] 18 71
(J M Bradley) *chsd ldrs on far side: rdn over 2f out: kpt on same pce* **25/1**

0000 **14** *shd* **Captain Hurricane**[7] 3911 5-9-2 **87** (p) StephenDonohoe 26 81
(B J Meehan) *hld up on far side: nt clr run on far rail over 2f out tl 1f out: kpt on ins fnl f: no ch* **20/1**

-100 **15** *1* **He's A Humbug (IRE)**[13] 3749 3-9-3 **92** NCallan 2 83
(K A Ryan) *led stands' side tl over 1f out: sn wknd* **66/1**

-524 **16** *shd* **Tony The Tap**[5] 3990 6-8-10 **81** MartinDwyer 13 72
(W R Muir) *racd in midfield on far side: rdn over 2f out: wl hld whn hmpd over 1f out* **11/1**

1200 **17** *hd* **Golden Dixie (USA)**[5] 3990 8-9-3 **88** SteveDrowne 6 78
(R A Harris) *b: lw: s.i.s: bhd on stands' side: rdn and hung rt over 1f out: nvr dangerous* **33/1**

0000 **18** ½ **Woodcote (IRE)**[5] 3990 5-9-8 **93** (be) AdamKirby 21 81
(C G Cox) *t.k.h: chsd ldrs on far side: rdn over 2f out: wknd wl over 1f out* **16/1**

0 **19** ¾ **Varadouro (BRZ)**[175] 415 5-8-13 **91** AdeleRothery[(7)] 11 77
(D Nicholls) *chsd ldr on stands' side tl wl over 1f out: sn hung rt and wknd* **80/1**

323 **20** *hd* **Don Pele (IRE)**[9] 3859 5-8-1 **75** (p) LiamJones[(3)] 23 60
(R A Harris) *racd far side: rdn 1/2-way: n.d* **16/1**

3-10 **21** ½ **My Gacho (IRE)**[59] 2339 5-8-13 **84** (b) ChrisCatlin 1 68
(T D Barron) *chsd ldrs on stands' side: drvn wl over 1f out: sn wknd* **33/1**

4005 **22** *1 ¼* **Lady Livius (IRE)**[21] 3481 4-9-5 **90** (b) JimmyFortune 22 70
(R Hannon) *racd on far side in midfield: rdn and btn over 1f out* **33/1**

0300 **23** *nk* **Mine Behind**[7] 3911 7-8-9 **80** RichardThomas 17 59
(J R Best) *a bhd on far side* **50/1**

5325 **24** *3 ½* **Forest Dane**[22] 3464 7-8-12 **83** JimCrowley 12 51
(Mrs N Smith) *hld up in rr on far side: rdn and no hdwy 2f out: eased ins fnl f* **25/1**

0400 **25** *nk* **Fire Up The Band**[62] 2234 8-9-8 **93** PaulHanagan 25 60
(D Nicholls) *a bhd on far side: no ch over 1f out* **22/1**

0000 **26** ¾ **Pacific Pride**[1] 4095 4-9-6 **91** (v) GrahamGibbons 7 55
(J J Quinn) *s.i.s: hld up in tch on stands' side: rdn 2f out: sn btn: eased ins fnl f* **25/1**

4300 **27** *8* **Sand Cat**[2] 4062 4-9-10 **95** JHBowman 8 34
(G L Moore) *prom on stands' side tl 1/2-way: sn wknd: eased ins fnl f* **66/1**

1m 11.35s (-1.50) **Going Correction** -0.075s/f (Good)
WFA 3 from 4yo+ 4lb **27** Ran SP% **139.5**
Speed ratings (Par 109): **107,106,105,104,103 102,102,102,101,101 101,100,100,100,99 98,98,98,97,96 96,94,94,89,88 87,7**
CSF £117.31 CT £867.93 TOTE £10.40: £2.40, £4.20, £2.60, £9.20; EX 202.40 Trifecta £1268.00 Pool £2,143.16 - 1.20 winning units.
Owner Dennis Shaw **Bred** Leydens Farm Stud **Trained** Lambourn, Berks

FOCUS
The consolation race for those that did not make the line-up for the Stewards' Cup and solid-looking form rated through the runner-up. The field split into two groups but the stands'-side group raced a little off the rail and the first two home raced on the outside of the 11 that raced in that group.

NOTEBOOK

Pearly Wey lost his way last year but has been building back to his former heights this term and was already 2lb higher in future for an unlucky-in-running third at Newmarket last time. Settled at the back of the stands'-side group before producing a strong run in the last quarter-mile to land the spoils, he clearly relishes fast ground and in this mood he could yet defy the Handicapper again at this level. (op 12-1)

Joseph Henry, down at 6f for the first time in more than a year, appreciated the drop in trip and nearly pulled it off, but was just denied after racing up with the pace all the way. It is a year since his last win but this fine effort will not earn him any help from the Handicapper. (op 20-1)

Indian Trail, a stablemate of the runner-up, mimicked his unlucky run the previous day over 5f. Drawn in the other group this time, he was buried away last, travelling well, before coming home strongly. He might have won had he not had to be switched past Border Music. (op 7-1)

Obe Gold burst ahead in the far-side group inside the last two furlongs, looking a possible winner, but flattened out late. He has not won for 18 months but has certainly become well handicapped.

Merlin's Dancer, who won this in 2004 when trained by David Nicholls, is getting no relief from the handicapper but showed his usual bright speed.

Mujood, never far away from his high draw, ran a creditable race at a course he obviously likes.

Border Music, who broke his turf duck at Ascot over 5f, was 8lb well-in under his penalty here but could never get into the action despite keeping on nicely. He could well struggle from his revised mark. (tchd 13-2, 7-1 in places)

Oranmore Castle(IRE), who had been restricted to 5f previously this season, including here the day before, ran a good race without quite getting home.

Roman Maze, one place ahead of Pearly Wey last time and due to race off 4lb higher in future, finished quite well but it does look as if the Handicapper is in charge now. (tchd 13-2, 8-1 in a place)

The Cayterers, fitted with cheekpieces, showed more speed in them but still looked to be idling at the finish and has not gone on this season.

Captain Hurricane would have finished a deal closer had he not been short of room from over a quarter of a mile out until getting daylight into the final furlong against the inside rail. He was edging closer at the finish.

4123 TURFTV STKS (H'CAP) 5f

5:45 (5:47) (Class 3) (0-95,94) 3-Y-0

£9,971 (£2,985; £1,492; £747; £372; £187) Stalls Low

Form RPR

2-14 **1** **Marozi (USA)**[11] 3797 3-8-7 **80** PhilipRobinson 10 92+
(M A Jarvis) *lw: awkward leaving stalls: sn chsng ldrs: chal and edgd rt 1f out: led ins fnl f: in command whn edgd lft nr fin* **7/2**[1]

1332 **2** ¾ **Morinqua (IRE)**[21] 3493 3-9-7 **94** JimmyFortune 21 99
(J G Given) *led narrowly: rdn over 1f out: hdd ins fnl f: no ex* **8/1**

-100 **3** hd **Valery Borzov (IRE)**[31] 3197 3-8-7 **80** AdrianTNicholls 18 85
(D Nicholls) *hld up: hdwy 2f out: rdn over 1f out: styd on wl ins fnl f: nt rch ldrs* **8/1**

1134 **4** shd **Rasaman (IRE)**[23] 3418 3-8-10 **83** PaulDoe 20 87
(M A Jarvis) *chsd ldrs: rdn wl over 1f out: unable qckn last 100yds* **20/1**

0260 **5** shd **Southandwest (IRE)**[44] 2752 3-9-0 **87** JohnEgan 15 91
(J S Moore) *t.k.h: hld up: hdwy over 1f out: pushed along and r.o ins fnl f: nt rch ldrs* **33/1**

-221 **6** 1 ¾ **Gentle Guru**[15] 3688 3-8-6 **79** MartinDwyer 17 77
(R T Phillips) *a chsng ldrs: rdn 2f out: kpt on same pce fnl f* **9/1**

2110 **7** ¾ **Mac Gille Eoin**[13] 3749 3-9-3 **90** JimCrowley 6 85
(J Gallagher) *prom: ev ch and rdn wl over 1f out: fdd ins fnl f* **25/1**

5533 **8** ½ **Rocker**[31] 3179 3-8-2 **75** oh1 (v) JimmyQuinn 19 68
(B R Johnson) *chsd ldrs: rdn 2f out: wknd qckly 1f out* **25/1**

2222 **9** ½ **Sohraab**[20] 3528 3-8-13 **86** SteveDrowne 8 77
(H Morrison) *hld up in midfield: rdn and outpcd 2f out: kpt on last 100yds* **13/2**[3]

0126 **10** shd **Northern Fling**[69] 2035 3-8-12 **92** AdeleRothery(7) 1 83
(D Nicholls) *hung rt thrght: nvr bttr than midfield: sme modest late hdwy* **25/1**

0050 **11** nk **Steelcut**[21] 3515 3-8-7 **80** PaulHanagan 14 70
(R A Fahey) *chsd ldrs: rdn 1/2-way: sn struggling* **14/1**

6234 **12** shd **Buckie Massa**[21] 3483 3-8-2 **75** oh2 FrancisNorton 16 65
(S Kirk) *racd in midfield: rdn 1/2-way: no ch after* **33/1**

0000 **13** shd **Bazroy (IRE)**[20] 3553 3-8-9 **82** ow3 StephenDonohoe 11 71
(P D Evans) *a bhd: swtchd rt 1f out: sme late hdwy: nvr on terms* **50/1**

4311 **14** ¾ **Diminuto**[16] 3637 3-7-12 **78** FrankiePickard(7) 7 65
(M D I Usher) *a towards rr* **25/1**

2500 **15** 1 ¼ **Luscivious**[23] 3431 3-9-2 **89** (b) AdamKirby 3 71
(A J McCabe) *pushed along after leaving stalls: rdn 1/2-way: wl hld whn hung rt 1f out* **40/1**

0422 **16** ½ **Mambo Spirit (IRE)**[16] 3637 3-9-2 **89** RyanMoore 12 69
(J G Given) *awkward leaving stalls: sn chsng ldrs: rdn and wknd 2f out* **12/1**

4004 **17** 2 ½ **Frisky Talk (IRE)**[16] 3637 3-8-2 **75** ChrisCatlin 4 46
(B W Hills) *chsd ldrs tl 1/2-way: sn dropped out* **33/1**

0020 **18** 5 **Bookiesindex Boy**[22] 3452 3-8-2 **75** oh3 (b) AdrianMcCarthy 9 28
(J R Jenkins) *chsd ldrs tl 1/2-way: sn wknd: eased ins fnl f* **40/1**

2121 **19** ½ **Obstructive**[21] 3493 3-9-0 **92** PatrickHills(5) 2 43
(D K Ivory) *lw: prom tl 1/2-way: sn wknd: eased ins fnl f* **11/2**[2]

160 **20** 3 **Daddy Cool**[35] 3061 3-8-4 **80** LiamJones(3) 5 21
(W G M Turner) *chsd ldr tl wknd qckly 2f out: eased ins fnl f* **40/1**

57.69 secs (-1.36) **Going Correction** -0.075s/f (Good) **20** Ran SP% **135.8**

Speed ratings (Par 104): **107,105,105,105,105 102,101,100,99,99 98,98,98,97,95 94,90,82,81,77**

CSF £28.94 CT £234.18 TOTE £5.20: £2.00, £2.90, £2.80, £4.70; EX 56.70 Trifecta £1099.40 Part won. Pool £1,548.50 - 0.80 winning units. Place 6 £327.77, Place 5 £67.25..

Owner Sheikh Mohammed **Bred** Gaines-Gentry Thoroughbreds **Trained** Newmarket, Suffolk

FOCUS

A competitive handicap in which the field raced in one group and the place to be was up the centre of the track. The time was good and the form looks solid with the front pair progressive.

NOTEBOOK

Marozi(USA), the least exposed runner in the field, was down at the minimum trip for the first time. Always in the front rank, he got to the filly inside the last and was nicely on top when edging left towards the finish. He is potentially a smart performer on fast ground. (op 4-1)

Morinqua(IRE), one of the fastest sprinters around, was collared by the unexposed favourite inside the last but stuck on for second. She loses nothing in defeat and deserves another chance at Listed level. (tchd 9-1)

Valery Borzov(IRE) soon raced a little way off the pace in the far-side group but came home in good style, showing no repeat of his Thirsk antics. A stiffer track will see him to better advantage. (tchd 15-2)

Rasaman(IRE), racing over the minimum trip for the first time, was always prominent on the outside and kept on for pressure to make the frame. His two wins so far came on Polytrack but he is obviously just as effective on sand. (op 25-1)

Southandwest(IRE), down in trip and tackling much more realistic opposition, showed something of a return to form. Six furlongs is probably his optimum. (op 40-1)

Gentle Gururan creditably under the 4lb penalty for her Sandown win. (op 8-1 tchd 10-1)

Mac Gille Eoin, who raced in the front rank until fading inside the last, does look held by the Handicapper. (op 20-1)

Sohraab did not end a run of six seconsecutive seconds in the way connections would have hoped. (tchd 6-1)

Obstructive, raised 7lb for his defeat of today's runner-up Morinqua at Chester, was disappointing on this different ground from a low draw. (op 13-2)

T/Jkpt: Not won. T/Plt: £544.90 to a £1 stake. Pool: £269,578.66. 361.10 winning tickets. T/Qpdt: £99.40 to a £1 stake. Pool: £12,772.60. 95.00 winning tickets. SP

3567 HAYDOCK (L-H)

Friday, August 3

OFFICIAL GOING: Good to firm (good in places; 9.0)

Wind: Moderate across Weather: Cloudy

4124 LAMBRINI APPRENTICE H'CAP 1m 6f

6:05 (6:05) (Class 5) (0-70,70) 4-Y-0+ £2,968 (£876; £438) Stalls High

Form RPR

430 **1** **Cotton Eyed Joe (IRE)**[13] 3753 6-9-9 **69** PJMcDonald 8 75
(G A Swinbank) *hld up in mid-div: hdwy over 3f out: rdn over 2f out: led ins fnl f: drvn out* **9/2**[1]

0454 **2** nk **Treason Trial**[6] 3969 6-8-2 **51** oh1 KMay(3) 9 55
(Stef Liddiard) *hld up and bhd: rdn over 3f out: hdwy over 2f out: styd on ins fnl f: fin 3rd, 1 ¼l & nk: plcd 2nd* **11/2**[3]

0002 **3** 1 ½ **Red Wine**[8] 3888 8-8-9 **60** RobbieEgan(5) 14 62
(A J McCabe) *hld up in rr: hdwy 2f out: sn rdn: styd on same pce fnl f: fin 4th: plcd 3rd* **7/1**

-224 **4** 1 **Acuzio**[20] 3533 6-8-9 **58** KirstyMilczarek(3) 10 59
(W M Brisbourne) *hld up towards rr: hdwy over 3f out: rdn and edgd lft over 2f out: no ex fnl f: fin 5th: plcd 4th* **13/2**

5121 **5** 1 ¼ **Raffish**[8] 3888 5-9-1 **66** 6ex (p) JackDean(5) 13 65
(M Scudamore) *plld hrd in tch: rdn 3f out: one pce fnl 2f: fin 6th: plcd 5th* **5/1**[2]

246 **6** ½ **Grizebeck (IRE)**[37] 2987 5-9-7 **70** NeilBrown(3) 7 68
(R F Fisher) *led: hdd over 3f out: sn rdn: wknd over 1f out: fin 7th: plcd 6th* **12/1**

000P **7** 3 **Wee Ziggy**[10] 3815 4-8-2 **51** oh6 SCreighton(3) 2 45
(M Mullineaux) *t.k.h: prom tl wknd 3f out: fin 8th: plcd 7th* **80/1**

5040 **8** 2 **Always Baileys (IRE)**[21] 3485 4-8-10 **59** ow3 SladeO'Hara(3) 12 50
(T Wall) *prom: rdn over 4f out: wknd over 2f out: fin 9th: plcd 8th* **33/1**

3524 **9** hd **Sovietta (IRE)**[7] 3901 6-8-7 **53** (t) RussellKennemore 11 44
(A G Newcombe) *stdd s: sn swtchd lft: rdn 4f out: no rspnse: fin 10th: plcd 9th* **12/1**

1226 **10** 7 **Just Waz (USA)**[22] 3467 5-9-0 **60** MichaelJStainton 6 41
(R M Whitaker) *t.k.h: prom tl wknd 4f out: fin 11th: plcd 10th* **10/1**

25-6 **11** 14 **El Dee (IRE)**[164] 503 4-8-0 **51** oh6 HeatherMcGee(5) 1 12
(D Carroll) *bhd fnl 4f: fin 12th: plcd 11th* **50/1**

1215 **D** 1 ¼ **They All Laughed**[15] 3677 4-9-5 **68** JackMitchell(3) 5 73
(P W Hiatt) *hld up and bhd: rapid hdwy over 5f out: led over 3f out: rdn over 2f out: edgd lft and hdd ins fnl f: nt qckn: fin 2nd, 1 ¼,: disq* **9/1**

3m 7.96s (1.67) **Going Correction** -0.25s/f (Firm) **12** Ran SP% **116.7**

Speed ratings (Par 103): **85,84,83,82,81 81,79,78,78,74 66,84**

CSF £28.15 CT £171.87 TOTE £5.50: £2.10, £2.00, £2.30; EX 30.60.

Owner Mrs S Sanbrook **Bred** Tally-Ho Stud **Trained** Melsonby, N Yorks

■ Stewards' Enquiry : Jack Mitchell three-day ban: weighed in light (Aug 14-16)

FOCUS

A modest contest run at a poor gallop, rated through the winner and original runner-up They All Laughed, who was disqualified following an objection by the Clerk of the Scales as his rider weighed in 2lb light. Dubious form.

4125 RIVABINGO.COM MAIDEN AUCTION STKS 6f

6:40 (6:43) (Class 5) 2-Y-0 £2,817 (£838; £418; £209) Stalls High

Form RPR

55 **1** **River Bounty**[9] 3849 2-8-1 0 AndrewElliott(3) 7 70+
(A P Jarvis) *mde all: rdn and edgd lft over 1f out: r.o wl* **15/2**

2 1 ¼ **Bahamian Lad** 2-9-2 0 DeanMcKeown 10 78
(R Hollinshead) *trckd ldrs: nt clr run and swtchd rt over 1f out: kpt on ins fnl f* **18/1**

3 1 ¼ **Jaconet (USA)** 2-8-8 0 PhillipMakin 4 67
(T D Barron) *a.p: rdn over 2f out: ev ch over 1f out: nt qckn ins fnl f* **4/1**[2]

0 **4** 1 ¾ **Scruffy Skip (IRE)**[46] 2710 2-8-11 0 DaleGibson 9 64
(M Dods) *s.i.s: sn mid-div: rdn and hdwy over 1f out: one pce fnl f* **33/1**

6 **5** ½ **Misplaced Fortune**[40] 2904 2-8-4 0 KimTinkler 5 56
(N Tinkler) *chsd ldrs: rdn over 2f out: one pce fnl f* **12/1**

6 ¾ **Next Of Kin (IRE)** 2-8-9 0 TPO'Shea 6 59
(G A Swinbank) *sn outpcd in rr: hdwy over 1f out: nrst fin* **8/1**

7 ¾ **Glenveagh (IRE)** 2-9-2 0 PaulFessey 11 63
(K A Ryan) *s.i.s: sn chsng ldrs: rdn over 2f out: wknd over 1f out* **7/1**[3]

3 **8** 1 ½ **Quick Off The Mark**[24] 3404 2-8-6 0 PaulMulrennan 12 49
(J G Given) *t.k.h: w ldrs: ev ch 2f out: sn rdn: wknd fnl f* **11/4**[1]

9 ¾ **Bond Scissorsister (IRE)** 2-8-1 0 DuranFentiman(3) 8 45
(G R Oldroyd) *rn green: s.i.s: bhd tl sme hdwy over 1f out: no further prog* **50/1**

00 **10** ½ **Saturday Boy**[6] 3977 2-8-5 0 ow1 RussellKennemore(5) 2 49
(Paul Green) *bhd fnl 3f* **50/1**

11 2 **Bowder Stone (IRE)** 2-8-11 0 SaleemGolam 1 44
(M H Tompkins) *s.i.s: a bhd* **10/1**

12 3 **Blindspin** 2-9-2 0 PaddyAspell 3 40
(M Dods) *s.i.s: outpcd* **25/1**

6 **13** 3 **Marlena (IRE)**[14] 3718 2-8-8 0 DavidAllan 14 23
(T D Easterby) *w ldrs: rdn over 2f out: wknd wl over 1f out* **12/1**

1m 14.55s (0.66) **Going Correction** -0.325s/f (Firm) **13** Ran SP% **122.5**

Speed ratings (Par 94): **89,87,85,83,82 81,80,78,77,77 74,70,66**

CSF £133.58 TOTE £10.00: £3.30, £5.90, £1.90; EX 175.50.

Owner Christopher Shankland **Bred** Limestone & Tara Studs **Trained** Twyford, Bucks

■ Stewards' Enquiry : Phillip Makin one-day ban: not riding to draw (Aug 14)

Andrew Elliott one-day ban: not riding to draw (Aug 14)

FOCUS

A moderate-looking maiden in which the winner improved on the bare form of her Kempton run but not by much.

NOTEBOOK

River Bounty, trying turf for the first time, won in good style after making all. One suspects nurseries are on the agenda. (op 8-1 tchd 17-2)

Bahamian Lad looked fairly green on his debut, and did not get the rub of the green either. As long as he makes progression for the effort, an ordinary maiden is within his grasp. (op 25-1 tchd 28-1 in places)

Jaconet(USA), who was taken out of a race at York recently due to the heavy ground, had every chance but never really picked up. She is entitled to have needed this run and can improve from it. (op 6-1)

Scruffy Skip(IRE) seemingly came on for his first run and proved he is going the right way. One suspects he will find his level in handicap company and get another furlong in time. (op 50-1)

Misplaced Fortune still looked in need of the run and will probably benefit from more experience. She was not given a hard time in the last furlong. (op 9-1)

Next Of Kin(IRE) was a huge eyecatcher in the race, as he was well behind 2f from home before picking up the bit and finishing really strongly. He may need some time but obviously possesses ability. (op 20-1)

Quick Off The Mark, who appeared to be sweating quite a bit around the neck, did not look a likely sort to be favourite, as she was beaten on her debut by a horse that cost 800gns and was running for a trainer struggling for form. However, punters saw fit to give her the chance and unsurprisingly she came up short when asked to win her race. Official explanation: jockey said filly ran green (op 5-2)

Bond Scissorsister(IRE) looked very inexperienced throughout and may need more time to mature.

Bowder Stone(IRE), who holds Middle Park and Champagne Stakes entries, did not seem to have a clue during the race and will come on for the run. The penny only seemed to drop late on and he will be better in time. (op 17-2 tchd 8-1)

4126 JEREMY FOX CANCER RESEARCH UK NURSERY 6f

7:10 (7:12) (Class 4) 2-Y-0 £5,505 (£1,637; £818; £408) Stalls High

Form RPR

5121 1 **Lady Rangali (IRE)**[20] 3562 2-8-10 76 RoystonFfrench 5 80
(Mrs A Duffield) *a.p: rdn 3f out: led 1f out: drvn out* **5/2**[1]

1641 2 1 1/4 **Sauze D'Oulx**[15] 3680 2-9-2 87 JamesMillman(5) 9 87
(B R Millman) *hld up: nt clr run on stands' rail jst over 2f out: swtchd lft and hdwy over 1f out: r.o ins fnl f: nt rch wnr* **10/3**[2]

3610 3 1 1/2 **Borasco (USA)**[20] 3524 2-8-4 70 PaulFessey 4 66
(T D Barron) *w ldr: led 3f out: rdn and hdd 1f out: one pce* **5/1**[3]

643 4 4 **Daring Dream (GER)**[20] 3560 2-8-6 72 DavidAllan 3 56
(T D Easterby) *led: hdd 3f out: sn rdn: wknd fnl f* **8/1**

0504 5 1 1/2 **Ridge Wood Dani (IRE)**[20] 3560 2-8-0 66 PaulQuinn 1 45
(E J Alston) *hld up in tch: bmpd over 2f out: sn rdn: wknd fnl f* **18/1**

041 6 2 1/2 **Jane's Delight (IRE)**[13] 3751 2-8-1 70 (v) DuranFentiman(3) 6 42
(G R Oldroyd) *hld up: rdn and short-lived effrt over 1f out* **14/1**

304 7 3/4 **Elusive Deal (USA)**[13] 3750 2-7-12 64 oh1 DaleGibson 2 33
(R A Fahey) *chsd ldrs 3f* **14/1**

436 8 3/4 **Narmeen**[22] 3453 2-8-8 74 TPO'Shea 8 41
(M R Channon) *prom tl wknd over 2f out* **10/1**

5164 9 3 **Fitolini**[7] 3925 2-8-4 73 AndrewElliott(3) 10 31
(Mrs G S Rees) *prom tl rdn and wknd over 1f out* **17/2**

1m 14.48s (0.59) **Going Correction** -0.325s/f (Firm) 9 Ran SP% **117.6**

Speed ratings (Par 96): **89,87,85,80,78 74,73,72,68**

CSF £11.01 CT £38.93 TOTE £3.20: £1.50, £1.40, £2.10; EX 9.90.

Owner Mrs Sarah E Woodhead **Bred** Mrs C Hartery **Trained** Constable Burton, N Yorks

FOCUS

The first two home are on the upgrade and make the form look sound.

NOTEBOOK

Lady Rangali(IRE) has really improved of late and did not mind the step up in trip. She seems to be improving all the time and is ready for a rise in grade. (op 11-4)

Sauze D'Oulx did not have the run of the race and can be counted as slightly unlucky. Much like the winner, he is progressing all the time and may be able to handle himself in a slightly higher grade. (op 7-2 tchd 3-1)

Borasco(USA), a big individual, did not disgrace herself but was getting a lot of weight from the front two and, although running well, will be better suited by 7f in the future. (tchd 9-2)

Daring Dream(GER), back on fast ground for the first time since his debut, ran fairly well but looks ready for a step up in trip again. (tchd 9-1)

Ridge Wood Dani(IRE) got a hefty bump that knocked him off stride at an important point of the race, and did well to recover his position and finish where he did. That said, he would not have won but should have been a bit closer. (op 20-1 tchd 25-1)

Jane's Delight(IRE), so impressive when landing a heavy-ground seller for former connections, seemingly found the step up in grade beyond her.

Narmeen was messed about a couple of times in running and this effort can be excused, although her tendency to hang under pressure is a worry. Official explanation: jockey said filly hung both ways (op 9-1)

Fitolini dropped away rapidly as the race took shape. She has the run of the race and therefore can have no excuses. (op 10-1)

4127 ARENA OPTIONS VULNERABLE TENANTS SUPPORT SCHEME H'CAP 6f

7:45 (7:45) (Class 4) (0-80,80) 3-Y-0 £5,505 (£1,637; £818; £408) Stalls High

Form RPR

3322 1 **Swift Princess (IRE)**[13] 3752 3-8-3 62 (v) DaleGibson 10 75+
(K R Burke) *hld up: swtchd rt and hdwy over 1f out: rdn and r.o under stands' rail to ld post* **6/1**

0131 2 shd **Northern Dare (IRE)**[8] 3885 3-9-7 80 6ex SilvestreDeSousa 9 90
(D Nicholls) *chsd ldrs: rdn over 2f out: ev ch ins fnl f: r.o* **5/2**[1]

-524 3 shd **Gleaming Spirit (IRE)**[49] 2631 3-8-3 65 AndrewElliott(3) 1 75
(A P Jarvis) *w ldr: led 3f out: rdn over 1f out: hdd post* **12/1**

1522 4 1 3/4 **Silca Elegance**[8] 3879 3-8-13 72 TPO'Shea 11 76
(M R Channon) *hld up and bhd: hdwy over 2f out: rdn and ev ch over 1f out: nt qckn ins fnl f* **4/1**[2]

6533 5 1 1/2 **Fish Called Johnny**[8] 3885 3-8-12 71 LPKeniry 5 71
(Peter Grayson) *hld up: rdn over 2f out: nvr able to chal* **14/1**

3433 6 shd **Sunoverregun**[21] 3483 3-8-13 79 HarryPoulton(7) 12 78
(J R Boyle) *chsd ldrs: rdn and ev ch over 1f out: wknd ins fnl f* **5/1**[3]

-120 7 6 **Ken's Girl**[20] 3528 3-9-2 75 RoystonFfrench 2 55
(W S Kittow) *chsd ldrs: rdn over 3f out: wknd over 2f out* **12/1**

1635 8 2 1/2 **Multitude (IRE)**[21] 3491 3-8-8 67 DavidAllan 3 39
(T D Easterby) *stmbld s: a bhd* **12/1**

0033 9 shd **Lemon Silk (IRE)**[17] 3607 3-8-9 68 MickyFenton 4 40
(T P Tate) *led: hdd 3f out: wknd wl over 1f out* **11/1**

1m 13.46s (-0.43) **Going Correction** -0.325s/f (Firm) 9 Ran SP% **117.6**

Speed ratings (Par 102): **96,95,95,93,91 91,83,79,79**

CSF £21.81 CT £178.84 TOTE £5.80: £1.90, £1.40, £3.50; EX 22.20.

Owner T J Naughton **Bred** Mrs S O'Riordan **Trained** Middleham Moor, N Yorks

FOCUS

A solid-looking handicap and the form looks sound for the grade. The first two are on the upgrade.

Ken's Girl Official explanation: jockey said filly stumbled at start

Multitude(IRE) Official explanation: jockey said gelding stumbled at start

4128 BETFRED FILLIES' H'CAP 1m 2f 120y

8:15 (8:16) (Class 5) (0-75,74) 3-Y-0+ £3,238 (£963; £481; £240) Stalls High

Form RPR

2205 1 **Honorable Love**[11] 3785 3-9-0 70 PhillipMakin 7 79
(M Dods) *mde all: rdn over 2f out: drvn out* **9/2**[2]

003 2 1 1/4 **White Moss (IRE)**[11] 3803 3-8-4 60 SaleemGolam 4 67
(M H Tompkins) *hld up in tch: chsd wnr over 2f out: rdn over 1f out: nt qckn ins fnl f* **6/1**[3]

3423 3 2 1/2 **Topflight Wildbird**[6] 3955 4-9-0 60 DeanMcKeown 5 63
(Mrs G S Rees) *hld up and bhd: hdwy on ins over 3f out: sn rdn: kpt on same pce fnl 2f* **9/2**[2]

4145 4 1 1/2 **Vale De Lobo**[20] 3554 5-9-5 74 JamesMillman(5) 9 74
(B R Millman) *hld up: rdn and hdwy on outside 3f out: one pce fnl 2f* **3/1**[1]

4510 5 1/2 **Elopement (IRE)**[4] 4019 5-8-10 59 DuranFentiman(3) 6 58
(W M Brisbourne) *hld up and bhd: rdn over 4f out: styd on fnl 2f: n.d* **9/1**

-005 6 hd **Miss Percy**[12] 3765 3-8-2 58 (p) DaleGibson 8 57
(R A Fahey) *t.k.h in tch: lost pl 6f out: rdn over 4f out: styd on fnl f* **8/1**

536- 7 6 **Bollin Dolly**[291] 6008 4-9-5 65 DavidAllan 3 53
(T D Easterby) *chsd wnr: rdn over 3f out: lost 2nd over 2f out: sn wknd* **7/1**

66-0 8 3 1/2 **Divine River**[55] 2467 4-9-6 69 AndrewElliott(3) 2 50
(A P Jarvis) *t.k.h in rr: rdn 4f out: no rspnse* **16/1**

3004 9 5 **Star Berry**[23] 3428 4-8-10 61 oh8 ow6 SladeO'Hara(5) 1 33
(T Wall) *prom: rdn over 3f out: sn wknd* **33/1**

2m 13.76s (-2.38) **Going Correction** -0.25s/f (Firm)

WFA 3 from 4yo+ 10lb 9 Ran SP% **118.1**

Speed ratings (Par 100): **104,103,101,100,99 99,95,92,89**

CSF £32.45 CT £129.83 TOTE £6.50: £1.90, £2.20, £2.00.

Owner P Taylor **Bred** Gem Sas Di Giulia Montanari Ec **Trained** Denton, Co Durham

FOCUS

Only a modest affair run in a good time. The winner is rated to her initial Ripon effort.

4129 MAGAZINE & SELFRIDGES H'CAP 1m 30y

8:45 (8:46) (Class 5) (0-70,76) 3-Y-0+ £2,817 (£838; £418; £209) Stalls Low

Form RPR

2110 1 **Dudley Docker (IRE)**[99] 1264 5-9-5 66 PJMcDonald(3) 17 70
(C R Dore) *hld up and bhd: smooth hdwy on outside over 2f out: led jst over 1f out: sn rdn and hung lft: r.o* **13/2**[3]

0420 2 1 **Society Music (IRE)**[14] 3721 5-9-7 70 (p) NeilBrown(5) 4 72
(M Dods) *hld up in tch: rdn to ld 2f out: hdd jst over 1f out: hld whn sltly hmpd wl ins fnl f* **3/1**[1]

2131 3 nk **Hoh Wotanite**[7] 3926 4-9-7 72 6ex (p) RussellKennemore(5) 7 75+
(R Hollinshead) *hld up and bhd: hdwy 2f out: rdn 1f out: hld whn n.m.r on ins nr fin* **11/2**[2]

5303 4 shd **Ming Vase**[11] 3793 5-8-8 52 oh2 ow1 MickyFenton 2 53
(P T Midgley) *led: rdn and hdd 2f out: rallied ins fnl f* **12/1**

5503 5 3/4 **Cat Six (USA)**[24] 3393 3-8-10 66 ow6 SladeO'Hara(5) 11 64
(T Wall) *hld up: rdn over 2f out: hdwy over 1f out: kpt on ins fnl f* **20/1**

0404 6 nk **Komreyev Star**[14] 3721 5-8-7 51 oh2 PaulMulrennan 12 50
(R E Peacock) *prom: rdn over 2f out: sn outpcd: styd on ins fnl f* **12/1**

5026 7 1 **Valley Observer (FR)**[17] 3622 3-9-4 69 (b[1]) TPO'Shea 1 64
(W R Swinburn) *a.p: rdn and ev ch whn hung lft on ins rail wl over 1f out: one pce* **7/1**

-060 8 1 3/4 **Ten To The Dozen**[3] 4042 4-8-7 51 DeanMcKeown 9 43
(P W Hiatt) *hld up and bhd: hdwy on ins over 2f out: rdn wl over 1f out: sn no imp* **14/1**

1035 9 3/4 **Eternal Legacy (IRE)**[5] 3999 5-8-10 54 DavidAllan 15 45
(E J Alston) *hld up towards rr: rdn and hdwy over 2f out: wknd fnl f* **11/2**[2]

-404 10 hd **Take To The Skies (IRE)**[16] 3646 3-8-10 64 AndrewElliott(3) 5 53
(A P Jarvis) *hld up and bhd: rdn over 2f out: no rspnse* **12/1**

0-00 11 9 **Bordello**[53] 2521 4-9-8 66 DO'Donohoe 8 35
(K A Ryan) *prom tl rdn and wknd over 2f out* **28/1**

010 12 3/4 **Bahhmirage (IRE)**[37] 2979 4-8-7 51 oh2 LPKeniry 10 19
(C N Kellett) *prom tl rdn and wknd over 2f out* **33/1**

1m 42.77s (-2.74) **Going Correction** -0.25s/f (Firm)

WFA 3 from 4yo+ 7lb 12 Ran SP% **122.5**

Speed ratings (Par 103): **103,102,101,101,100 100,99,97,97,96 87,87**

CSF £26.59 CT £120.67 TOTE £7.90: £2.80, £2.10, £2.00; EX 26.40 Place 6 £48.10, Place 5 £24.45..

Owner Sean J Murphy **Bred** Nuri Fuat Basak **Trained** West Pinchbeck, Lincs

■ Stewards' Enquiry : P J McDonald three-day ban: careless riding (Aug 14-16)

T P O'Shea one-day ban: careless riding (Aug 14)

FOCUS

A moderate handicap and unconvincing form with the fifth out of the weights.

T/Plt: £52.20 to a £1 stake. Pool £49,033.30. 659.30 winning units. T/Qpdt: £5.90 to a £1 stake. Pool £5,367.00. 671.80 winning units. KH

3957 NEWMARKET (JULY) (R-H)

Friday, August 3

OFFICIAL GOING: Good to firm (9.1)

Wind: Fresh across Weather: Sunny

4130 UNICORN ASSET MANAGEMENT JULY COURSE SERIES MEDIAN AUCTION MAIDEN STKS (QUALIFIER) 7f

5:55 (5:57) (Class 4) 2-Y-0 £6,477 (£1,927; £963; £481) Stalls Low

Form RPR

453 1 **Siberian Tiger (IRE)**[20] 3552 2-9-3 0 RichardMullen 7 80
(M R Channon) *chsd ldrs: rdn over 1f out: r.o to ld nr fin* **10/1**

032 2 hd **Always Ready**[17] 3625 2-9-3 0 SebSanders 10 79
(C E Brittain) *chsd ldrs: rdn to ld ins fnl f: hdd nr fin* **10/3**[1]

3 3 hd **Craggy Cat (IRE)**[36] 3037 2-9-3 0 NickyMackay 8 79
(L M Cumani) *led: racd keenly early: rdn and hdd ins fnl f: styd on* **17/2**[3]

50 4 1 **Jack Dawkins (USA)**[17] 3625 2-9-3 0 JMurtagh 3 77+
(H R A Cecil) *hld up in tch: plld hrd: outpcd over 2f out: styd on fr over 1f out* **4/1**[2]

000 5 1 **Asian Power (IRE)**[17] 3625 2-9-0 0 MarcHalford(3) 12 73
(P J O'Gorman) *chsd ldrs: rdn over 2f out: styd on* **66/1**

0 6 3/4 **Noble Citizen (USA)**[34] 3095 2-9-3 0 RichardHughes 5 71
(D M Simcock) *chsd ldrs: reminders over 4f out: outpcd 2f out: styd on fnl f* **4/1**[2]

0 7 2 **Doctor Robert**[37] 2991 2-9-3 0 DaneO'Neill 2 68+
(R Charlton) *hld up: plld hrd: shkn up over 1f out: nvr nr to chal* **25/1**

0060 **8** *1 3/4* **Galley Slave (IRE)**[9] 3841 2-8-10 0 CharlotteKerton(7) 11 62
(M C Chapman) *chsd ldrs: rdn 1/2-way: wknd over 1f out* **80/1**

60 **9** *1 1/4* **Townkab (IRE)**[9] 3850 2-9-3 0 TGMcLaughlin 1 58+
(N P Littmoden) *dwlt: hld up: hdwy u.p over 1f out: eased ins fnl f* **100/1**

10 *7* **Bid To The Beat** 2-9-0 0 JerryO'Dwyer(3) 13 40
(H J Collingridge) *s.i.s: hld up: bhd fr 1/2-way* **25/1**

40 **11** *1* **Mr Fantozzi (IRE)**[42] 2832 2-9-3 0 EddieAhern 6 38
(Miss J Feilden) *prom to 1/2-way* **33/1**

0 **12** *1/2* **Space Pirate**[69] 2041 2-8-12 0 LukeMorris(5) 4 36
(M L W Bell) *hld up: rdn 1/2-way: a in rr* **33/1**

13 *6* **Indy Driver** 2-9-3 0 KerrinMcEvoy 14 21
(J R Fanshawe) *s.i.s: a in rr* **16/1**

14 *hd* **Redford (IRE)** 2-9-3 0 JamieSpencer 15 20+
(M L W Bell) *s.i.s: sn prom: rdn whn rdr dropped reins over 2f out: sn hung lft and wknd* **4/1**[2]

15 *nk* **Lilburn (IRE)** 2-9-3 0 OscarUrbina 9 19
(J R Fanshawe) *s.i.s: hld up: rdn and wknd 1/2-way* **25/1**

1m 26.29s (-0.49) **Going Correction** -0.05s/f (Good) **15** Ran SP% **129.7**
Speed ratings (Par 96): **100,99,99,98,97 96,94,92,90,82 81,80,74,73,73**
CSF £43.88 TOTE £9.50: £2.70, £1.90, £2.00; EX 32.80.
Owner Ridgeway Downs Racing **Bred** Ashley Guest And Mrs John Guest **Trained** West Ilsley, Berks

FOCUS
They went quite a steady gallop in this ordinary maiden for the track and it proved difficult to make up ground from off the pace. The form looks pretty solid.

NOTEBOOK
Siberian Tiger(IRE) had produced two solid efforts in defeat on his previous starts on turf, sandwiched with a lesser performance on the Polytrack, and those performances gave him a chance in this rather modest maiden by Newmarket standards. He stuck no well to get his head in front close home, and certainly has the right attitude. (op 14-1)
Always Ready has improved with every outing and, with Sanders taking over from an apprentice, he looked to be a leading player in this company. He eventually got the better of Craggy Cat on the climb to the line, but was mugged in the dying strides by Siberian Tiger, who got up next to the far rail. (op 4-1)
Craggy Cat(IRE), who shaped as though this seventh furlong would suit him when making his debut at Yarmouth, would have probably preferred to have had a tow from something as he raced plenty keen enough in front. To his credit he battled all the way to the line though, and he can do better held up in a stronger-run race. (op 12-1)
Jack Dawkins(USA), as when sent off favourite at Yarmouth last time, failed to settle. A stronger pace would have suited him as he is bred to get a trip in time, and the way this race developed meant that he was staying on all too late. (tchd 5-1)
Asian Power(IRE) had shown little in three previous starts and his performance does drag down the value of the form. (op 50-1)
Noble Citizen(USA) came in for support as the quicker ground was expected to suit this American-bred colt well. He was another who found the steady early pace against him, though. (op 11-2)
Mr Fantozzi(IRE) Official explanation: jockey said colt was unsuited by the good to firm ground
Redford(IRE), a half-brother to Imperial Valley, a multiple 6f to 1m winner in Italy, had every chance given the way the race panned out, but he weakened tamely and was eased once his chance had gone. He is presumably thought capable of better than this form suggests. (op 11-4)

4131 WINNERSBINGO.CO.UK FILLIES' H'CAP — 1m 4f
6:25 (6:27) (Class 5) (0-70,70) 4-Y-O+ **£3,886** (£1,156; £577; £288) **Stalls** Centre

Form RPR

5-55 **1** **Red Sail**[184] 309 6-8-0 **52** (b) LukeMorris(5) 7 60
(Dr J D Scargill) *hld up in tch: plld hrd: led over 2f out: sn rdn: all out* **11/1**

0-00 **2** *hd* **Ashwell Rose**[11] 3803 5-8-8 **55** oh6 ow4 (v1) EddieAhern 2 63
(J R Jenkins) *s.i.s: hld up: hdwy over 2f out: sn rdn and ev ch: styd on u.p* **100/1**

-320 **3** *2 1/2* **Generous Jem**[41] 2890 4-8-12 **59** SebSanders 6 63
(G G Margarson) *hld up: rdn over 3f out: hdwy over 2f out: no ex ins fnl f* **7/2**[2]

-020 **4** *nk* **Fondness**[46] 1888 4-8-6 **53** (b) JamesDoyle 3 56
(B G Powell) *led: hdd over 10f out: chsd ldr: rdn and ev ch whn hung rt over 2f out: styd on same pce fnl f* **28/1**

60-5 **5** *4* **Spunger**[23] 3427 4-8-12 **59** (v) DaneO'Neill 1 56
(H J L Dunlop) *prom: rdn and ev ch over 1f out: wknd fnl f* **16/1**

4U52 **6** *2 1/2* **Collette's Choice**[10] 3815 4-9-0 **61** (p) TQuinn 4 54
(R A Fahey) *hld up: swtchd rt and hdwy over 3f out: rdn and ev ch over 2f out: wknd over 1f out* **5/2**[1]

6200 **7** *4* **Theatre Royal**[31] 3177 4-8-12 **59** RichardHughes 5 45
(Mouse Hamilton-Fairley) *prom: rdn over 2f out: wknd over 1f out* **16/1**

2022 **8** *1 1/2* **Arsad (IRE)**[65] 2148 4-8-9 **61** AhmedAjtebi(5) 12 45
(C E Brittain) *prom: rdn over 2f out: wknd over 1f out* **5/1**[3]

-010 **9** *8* **Inchmahome**[47] 2692 4-9-4 **65** RichardMullen 10 36
(E F Vaughan) *dwlt: hld up: rdn over 3f out: wknd over 2f out* **10/1**

000- **10** *26* **Unasuming (IRE)**[242] 6705 4-8-4 **51** oh1 NickyMackay 13 —
(J Pearce) *chsd ldrs: rdn 5f out: wknd over 3f out* **40/1**

2244 **11** *20* **Dolce Dovo**[13] 3731 4-9-9 **70** (v1) JamieSpencer 9 —
(W J Haggas) *led over 10f out: rdn: hung rt and hdd over 2f out: n.m.r sn after and wknd: eased* **5/1**[3]

2m 31.9s (-1.01) **Going Correction** -0.05s/f (Good) **11** Ran SP% **120.2**
Speed ratings (Par 100): **101,100,99,99,96 94,92,91,85,68 55**
CSF £819.23 CT £4586.93 TOTE £15.10: £3.90, £10.70, £1.90; EX 1039.50.
Owner Silent Partners **Bred** London Thoroughbred Services Ltd **Trained** Newmarket, Suffolk

FOCUS
A weak fillies' handicap for the track, and pretty dubious form rated through the winner and third.
Dolce Dovo Official explanation: jockey said filly suffered interference in running

4132 UNICORN ASSET MANAGEMENT JULY COURSE SERIES EBF MAIDEN STKS (QUALIFIER) — 6f
7:00 (7:00) (Class 3) 2-Y-O **£6,477** (£1,927; £963; £481) **Stalls** Low

Form RPR

2 **1** **Captain Brilliance (USA)**[22] 3462 2-9-3 0 JMurtagh 5 80+
(J Noseda) *led 1f: chsd ldrs: led over 2f out: r.o wl* **8/11**[1]

2 *2* **Polmaily** 2-9-3 0 RichardHughes 4 74
(B J Meehan) *prom: shkn up over 3f out: r.o ins fnl f* **10/3**[2]

2 **3** *1 1/4* **Papillio (IRE)**[51] 2562 2-9-3 0 NCallan 10 70
(K R Burke) *prom: rdn to chse wnr over 1f out: styd on same pce* **7/1**[3]

4 *shd* **Prevailing Wind** 2-9-3 0 JamieSpencer 2 73+
(J R Fanshawe) *hld up: swtchd rt and hdwy over 1f out: r.o: nrst fin* **9/1**

5 *6* **Kinnego Bay (IRE)** 2-9-3 0 MichaelHills 6 52
(B W Hills) *dwlt: outpcd: hdwy over 2f out: wknd over 1f out* **16/1**

6 *nk* **Ridge Dance** 2-9-3 0 RobertHavlin 1 51
(J H M Gosden) *s.s: outpcd: r.o ins fnl f: nrst fin* **14/1**

7 *1* **Monterrico** 2-9-3 0 SebSanders 3 48
(G Wragg) *chsd ldrs 4f* **33/1**

4 **8** *nk* **Wreningham**[28] 3283 2-9-0 0 JerryO'Dwyer(3) 12 47
(T Keddy) *chsd ldr tl rdn over 1f out: sn wknd* **33/1**

0 **9** *2* **Maccabeus**[10] 3823 2-9-3 0 OscarUrbina 8 41
(P J O'Gorman) *stdd s: plld hrd: led 5f out: rdn: hung lft and hdd over 2f out: wknd over 1f out* **50/1**

0 **10** *6* **Wynberg (IRE)**[8] 3878 2-9-3 0 DaneO'Neill 7 23
(N A Callaghan) *sn pushed along in rr: hung lft thrght: wknd over 2f out* **50/1**

11 *5* **Ocean Legend (IRE)** 2-9-3 0 EddieAhern 11 8
(Miss J Feilden) *dwlt: a in rr: wknd over 2f out* **20/1**

1m 13.2s (-0.15) **Going Correction** -0.05s/f (Good) **11** Ran SP% **130.6**
Speed ratings (Par 98): **99,96,94,94,86 86,84,84,81,73 67**
CSF £3.66 TOTE £1.90: £1.10, £2.10, £1.90; EX 7.50.
Owner Hesmonds Stud **Bred** J R Penn & John Combs **Trained** Newmarket, Suffolk

FOCUS
A steadily-run maiden and the standard is nothing special, but there were one or two noteworthy performances, and the first four finished nicely clear.

NOTEBOOK
Captain Brilliance(USA), who ran with plenty of promise at the July meeting, was well positioned throughout in what was a steadily-run affair, and he picked up in good style when his rider asked him to quicken. He ran out a comfortable winner in the end and deserves a crack at a decent race now - he is entered in all the big juvenile Group races to come. (op 5-6 tchd 11-10, 4-6 in a place)
Polmaily, who has three Group 2 entries, made a promising debut. There was no disgrace in finding the more experienced winner too strong in the closing stages and, given that his stable's juveniles always improve for their first run, he should have little trouble winning his maiden. (tchd 3-1 and 7-2)
Papillio(IRE), who holds Group entries in Britain and Ireland, was always prominent in a race lacking much early pace so he cannot have too many excuses. He lost second place on the climb to the line and, while capable of winning a maiden somewhere, he probably has his limitations. (op 8-1 tchd 11-2)
Prevailing Wind ◆, who cost 320,000gns, is out of a mare who is a half-sister to that top-class filly Fire The Groom, a Grade 1 winner over 1m1f on turf in the US and later dam of the top-class sprinter Stravinsky. Held up in a race lacking early pace, he was poorly placed when the leaders quickened, but he made up plenty of ground late on, running on best of all at the finish, and looks a sure-fire winner of a maiden before being stepped up in grade. Fast ground is likely to be required by this son of Gone West. (op 12-1)
Kinnego Bay(IRE), whose dam was a useful 13-time winning sprinter in the US, won the separate race for fifth and is entitled to come on for his debut. (op 14-1 tchd 11-1)
Ridge Dance, whose dam won over 6f on her juvenile debut and was later placed in the Moyglare Stud Stakes, was much too green to do himself justice and this experience is likely to do him the world of good. Slowly away and struggling out the back for most of the way, he only began to get the hang of things when the race was already over. He will improve a deal for this. (op 11-1)

4133 GL EVENTS H'CAP — 6f
7:30 (7:31) (Class 3) (0-90,90) 3-Y-O+ **£7,772** (£2,312; £1,155; £577) **Stalls** Low

Form RPR

1311 **1** **Bee Eater (IRE)**[13] 3746 3-9-8 **90** SebSanders 2 107
(Sir Mark Prescott) *hld up: swtchd rt and hdwy over 1f out: rdn to ld ins fnl f: flashed tail: r.o wl* **11/10**[1]

-300 **2** *1 1/2* **Come Out Fighting**[28] 3268 4-9-11 **89** JamieSpencer 8 101
(P A Blockley) *wnt rt s: sn chsng ldr: led over 2f out: rdn over 1f out: hdd and unable qckn ins fnl f* **7/1**[3]

-142 **3** *2 1/2* **Trojan Flight**[51] 2566 6-9-3 **81** TQuinn 1 86
(R A Fahey) *hld up: hdwy over 1f out: styd on same pce ins fnl f* **9/2**[2]

020 **4** *nk* **Matuza (IRE)**[17] 3623 4-9-2 **80** RichardMullen 9 84
(W R Muir) *hmpd s: sn chsng ldrs: rdn and hung lft over 1f out: styd on same pce* **14/1**

6110 **5** *1 1/2* **Bertoliver**[41] 2884 3-9-6 **88** KerrinMcEvoy 6 88
(D K Ivory) *led over 3f: rdn over 1f out: wknd fnl f* **12/1**

1640 **6** *1 1/2* **Lord Theo**[6] 3944 3-8-12 **80** JamesDoyle 3 75
(N P Littmoden) *chsd ldrs: rdn over 2f out: wkng whn hmpd over 1f out* **25/1**

0000 **7** *1/2* **Royal Challenge**[57] 2399 6-9-2 **80** NCallan 10 74
(M H Tompkins) *hmpd s: hld up: racd keenly: rdn and wknd over 1f out* **14/1**

5000 **8** *3/4* **Bahiano (IRE)**[42] 2817 6-9-11 **89** RichardHughes 11 80
(C E Brittain) *hld up: wknd over 1f out* **8/1**

0120 **9** *1/2* **Romany Nights (IRE)**[17] 3623 7-8-10 **79** (bt) LukeMorris(5) 7 69
(Miss Gay Kelleway) *chsd ldrs: rdn over 2f out: wknd over 1f out* **12/1**

1m 11.93s (-1.42) **Going Correction** -0.05s/f (Good)
WFA 3 from 4yo+ 4lb **9** Ran SP% **122.0**
Speed ratings (Par 107): **107,105,101,101,99 97,96,95,94**
CSF £10.26 CT £28.70 TOTE £1.90: £1.10, £2.70, £1.60; EX 10.50.
Owner Sir Edmund Loder **Bred** Sir E J Loder **Trained** Newmarket, Suffolk
■ Stewards' Enquiry : Richard Mullen one-day ban: careless riding (Aug 14)

FOCUS
A decent handicap for the grade and a slightly positive view has been taken of the form. The winner is progressive.

NOTEBOOK
Bee Eater(IRE) is not straightforward, but she is talented and continues to improve. Notching her fourth win from five starts, she defied an 8lb higher mark, despite again swishing her tail vigorously in the closing stages. One would imagine that connections will soon be looking to plunder some black type with her. (op 10-11 tchd 6-5 in a place)
Come Out Fighting left behind some below-par efforts on softish ground and bounced back to his best on this quicker terrain. He was back on the mark he won off at Ascot last summer so was entitled to run well, and he was just unlucky to run into a very progressive three-year-old. (op 9-1)
Trojan Flight has been in good form this season and again put up a solid effort. He is on a mark 8lb higher than when last successful though, so the Handicapper looks to have him about right. (op 6-1)
Matuza(IRE) was squeezed out a bit at the start but it was nothing dramatic and he seemed to have every chance in the race itself. He is simply another who looks high enough in the weights for the time being. (op 16-1)
Bertoliver has won over 6f in the past but his improvement this term has come over the minimum trip, and he showed why here, by setting a good gallop in the first half of the race. (op 10-1)
Lord Theo has struggled since winning at Warwick in May. (tchd 28-1)

4134 GPT HALVERTON H'CAP — 7f
8:05 (8:05) (Class 4) (0-85,85) 4-Y-O+ **£5,181** (£1,541; £770; £384) **Stalls** Low

Form RPR

1133 **1** **Ivory Lace**[15] 3670 6-9-7 **83** JamieSpencer 6 90
(S Woodman) *racd stands' side: hld up: hdwy over 1f out: r.o to ld nr fin* **6/1**

3420 **2** *hd* **Orpen Wide (IRE)**[13] 3386 5-9-6 **82**..........................(b) RichardHughes 5 89
(M C Chapman) *racd stands' side: chsd ldr: rdn to ld over 1f out: hdd nr fin: 2nd of 8 in gp* **9/1**

0321 **3** *hd* **Direct Debit (IRE)**[21] 3482 4-9-4 **85**................................ LukeMorris(5) 8 91
(M L W Bell) *racd stands' side: chsd ldrs: rdn over 1f out: r.o: 3rd of 8 in gp* **10/3**[2]

2-40 **4** *1 1/2* **Red Romeo**[21] 3512 6-9-5 **81**.. TQuinn 10 83
(N Wilson) *racd stands' side: chsd ldrs: rdn over 1f out: styd on same pce ins fnl f: 4th of 8 in gp* **12/1**

-000 **5** *hd* **Trimlestown (IRE)**[42] 2835 4-9-2 **78**................................ DaneO'Neill 11 79+
(H Candy) *racd stands' side: s.s: hld up: nt clr run over 1f out: swtchd lft and r.o ins fnl f: nvr able to chal: 5th of 8 in gp* **4/1**[3]

3054 **6** *1 1/4* **Woodcote Place**[3] 4049 4-9-8 **84**.. NCallan 4 82
(P R Chamings) *racd stands' side: chsd ldrs: rdn and edgd lft over 1f out: no ex ins fnl f: 6th of 8 in gp* **3/1**[1]

5400 **7** *1 1/4* **Moayed**[91] 1448 8-8-10 **72**..(b) IanMongan 7 67
(N P Littmoden) *racd stands' side: s.s: hld up: swtchd lft over 1f out: nvr trbld ldrs: 7th of 8 in gp* **20/1**

3020 **8** *nk* **Material Witness (IRE)**[15] 3682 10-8-12 **74**................. RichardMullen 9 68
(W R Muir) *overall ldr stands' side: rdn and hung lft over 2f out: hdd over 1f out: wknd ins fnl f: last of 8 in gp* **20/1**

2060 **9** *3 1/2* **His Master's Voice (IRE)**[6] 3943 4-8-12 **74**.................... SebSanders 2 58
(D W P Arbuthnot) *racd far side: chsd ldr tl led that duo over 2f out: nvr any ch w stands' side* **14/1**

4630 **10** *7* **Irony (IRE)**[16] 3650 8-9-8 **84**... KerrinMcEvoy 3 50
(A M Balding) *led far side over 4f: wknd over 1f out: last of 2 that side* **11/1**

1m 25.33s (-1.45) **Going Correction** -0.05s/f (Good) **10** Ran SP% **124.6**
Speed ratings (Par 105): **106,105,105,103,103 102,100,100,96,88**
CSF £63.21 CT £212.85 TOTE £3.70: £1.80, £3.20, £1.80; EX 35.60.
Owner Sally Woodman J Lenaghan D Mortimer **Bred** D R Tucker **Trained** East Lavant, W Sussex
■ Stewards' Enquiry : Richard Hughes three-day ban: used whip with excessive frequency and without giving gelding time to respond (Aug 14-16)

FOCUS
A fair handicap in which the field split, with the two that elected to race on the far side eventually coming home in the last two positions. The second and third pretty much reproduced their course-and-distance form from race 2835.

4135 NGK SPARK PLUGS H'CAP 1m
8:35 (8:35) (Class 4) (0-80,79) 3-Y-O+ **£5,181** (£1,541; £770; £384) **Stalls** Low

Form RPR

2-06 **1** **Smart Ass (IRE)**[7] 3897 4-9-7 **72**............................... RichardHughes 11 82
(J S Moore) *hld up: plld hrd: hdwy over 1f out: rdn to ld post* **7/1**[3]

0-31 **2** *shd* **Parisian Dream**[52] 2542 3-9-4 **76**.................................... MichaelHills 3 85+
(B W Hills) *chsd ldrs: rdn to ld and edgd rt 1f out: hdd post* **11/4**[1]

0034 **3** *2 1/2* **Sonny Parkin**[14] 3711 5-9-8 **73**...(v) NCallan 8 77
(G A Huffer) *hld up: hdwy over 3f out: rdn and ev ch 1f out: hung rt: styd on same pce* **11/2**[2]

5050 **4** *3/4* **Black Sea Pearl**[2] 4063 4-8-4 **60**.................................... LukeMorris(5) 6 62+
(P W D'Arcy) *chsd ldrs: rdn over 1f out: hmpd ins fnl f: nt rcvr* **20/1**

2000 **5** *shd* **Arctic Desert**[4] 4029 7-8-13 **64**.......................................(t) JamieSpencer 5 66+
(Miss Gay Kelleway) *dwlt: hld up: nt clr run over 1f out: swtchd lft and r.o ins fnl f: nt trble ldrs* **14/1**

30-2 **6** *shd* **Silent Applause**[42] 2831 4-9-5 **70**................................(v[1]) RobertHavlin 2 72
(Dr J D Scargill) *trckd ldrs: rdn over 1f out: styd on* **7/1**[3]

0160 **7** *1 1/4* **Carmenero (GER)**[2] 4068 4-9-11 **76**............................. RichardMullen 9 75
(W R Muir) *plld hrd: hld up: hdwy over 3f out: rdn over 1f out: styd on same pce* **33/1**

0530 **8** *1 1/4* **Old Romney**[14] 3709 3-9-3 **75**... TGMcLaughlin 4 76+
(G A Huffer) *chsd ldrs: led over 2f out: rdn and edgd rt over 1f out: sn hdd: hmpd and wknd ins fnl f* **12/1**

1-00 **9** *1/2* **Trepa (USA)**[83] 1660 3-9-1 **73**... KerrinMcEvoy 10 67
(W Jarvis) *hld up: rdn over 1f out: n.d* **25/1**

0114 **10** *1/2* **Aggravation**[46] 2722 5-9-4 **72**....................................... MarcHalford(3) 13 69+
(D R C Elsworth) *hld up: rdn over 2f out: nt clr run over 1f out: styng on whn hmpd ins fnl f: n.d* **8/1**

0530 **11** *3* **Rubenstar (IRE)**[37] 2986 4-9-12 **77**................................. SebSanders 12 64
(M H Tompkins) *mid-div: rdn and hung lft over 2f out: wknd over 1f out* **7/1**[3]

0000 **12** *1* **Stanley George (IRE)**[7] 3913 3-8-7 **65**.....................(t) MatthewHenry 14 49
(M A Jarvis) *led: rdn and hdd over 2f out: wknd fnl f* **25/1**

6-20 **13** *2* **Ninth House (USA)**[180] 351 5-10-0 **79**.......................(bt) IanMongan 15 59
(N P Littmoden) *hld up: hdwy over 3f out: wknd over 1f out* **20/1**

4450 **14** *nk* **Treasure House (IRE)**[48] 2665 6-8-9 **60**........................... EddieAhern 1 39
(M Blanshard) *prom: rdn over 3f out: wknd over 1f out* **16/1**

1m 39.56s (-0.87) **Going Correction** -0.05s/f (Good)
WFA 3 from 4yo+ 7lb **14** Ran SP% **131.1**
Speed ratings (Par 105): **102,101,99,98,98 98,97,95,95,94 91,90,88,88**
CSF £26.97 CT £126.27 TOTE £5.20: £1.70, £1.90, £2.70; EX 13.10 Place 6 £55.26, Place 5 £18.59..
Owner J Laughton **Bred** M Ervine **Trained** Upper Lambourn, Berks
■ Stewards' Enquiry : T G McLaughlin three-day ban: careless riding (Aug 14-16)

FOCUS
A modest handicap run at a steady early gallop. Ordinary form, the third the best guide.
T/Plt: £49.20 to a £1 stake. Pool £61,292.55. 910.85 winning units. T/Qpdt: £2.60 to a £1 stake. Pool £5,467.40. 1,512.05 winning units. CR

3914 THIRSK (L-H)
Friday, August 3

OFFICIAL GOING: Good to firm (10.4)
After a dry spell the ground was reckoned to be 'just on the quick side of good'.
Wind: Moderate, 1/2 behind Weather: Overcast but dry and warm

4136 PICKERING CASTLE CLAIMING STKS 7f
2:05 (2:06) (Class 5) 2-Y-O **£3,886** (£1,156; £577; £288) **Stalls** Low

Form RPR

4002 **1** **Willyn (IRE)**[7] 3923 2-8-9 0.. PhillipMakin 7 60
(J R Weymes) *mid-div: hdwy over 2f out: led jst ins fnl f: styd on wl* **7/1**

035 **2** *1 3/4* **La Belle Joannie**[13] 3751 2-8-3 0...................................... PaulFessey 12 49
(P T Midgley) *in rr: hdwy 3f out: styd on to take 2nd nr fin* **25/1**

000 **3** *nk* **Lady Bower**[8] 3874 2-8-6 0.. DeanMcKeown 5 52
(M Johnston) *w ldrs: led over 2f out tl jst ins fnl f: no ex* **6/1**[3]

0152 **4** *2* **Alexander Monarchy (IRE)**[51] 2549 2-9-0 0................. TonyHamilton 2 54
(K A Ryan) *mid-div: effrt over 2f out: styd on: nt rch ldrs* **9/2**[2]

00 **5** *nk* **Brilliantsensation (IRE)**[9] 3835 2-8-9 0...................(p) RoystonFfrench 3 49
(J G Given) *w ldrs: led over 4f out tl over 2f out: one pce* **50/1**

0 **6** *shd* **Jazz Stick (IRE)**[18] 3582 2-9-2 0..(p) TomEaves 6 55
(I Semple) *led tl over 4f out: kpt on same pce fnl 2f* **10/1**

1234 **7** *3/4* **Indecision**[9] 3835 2-8-11 0... PaulMulrennan 8 48
(M W Easterby) *hld up in mid-div: effrt over 2f out: keeping on same pce whn n.m.r jst ins fnl f* **8/1**

0131 **8** *hd* **Rio Taffeta**[9] 3835 2-9-2 0.. LPKeniry 1 53
(Peter Grayson) *trckd ldrs: effrt over 2f out: styd on same pce* **2/1**[1]

000 **9** *2* **Llab Nala**[8] 3866 2-9-2 0... TPO'Shea 10 48
(M R Channon) *w ldrs: wknd over 1f out* **33/1**

605 **10** *3/4* **Tenth Night (IRE)**[46] 2723 2-8-12 0................................. MickyFenton 4 44+
(P T Midgley) *chsd ldrs: one pce whn n.m.r jst ins fnl f* **18/1**

000 **11** *2 1/2* **Mimton (IRE)**[17] 3606 2-8-1 0.. LanceBetts(7) 9 31
(N Wilson) *s.i.s: sme hdwy over 2f out: lost pl over 1f out* **100/1**

5 **12** *3 1/2* **Just Mossie**[4] 4027 2-8-5 0.. JackDean(7) 14 26
(W G M Turner) *mid-div: lost pl over 2f out: sn bhd* **50/1**

06 **13** *nk* **Viscount Monty**[13] 3751 2-8-10 0...................................... DavidAllan 11 23
(N Tinkler) *in rr: bhd fnl 2f* **66/1**

000 **14** *13* **King Of Dalyan (IRE)**[9] 3835 2-8-6 0...............................(v) PaulQuinn 13 —
(D Nicholls) *w ldrs: lost pl over 4f out: sn bhd: t.o* **80/1**

1m 27.58s (0.48) **Going Correction** +0.005s/f (Good) **14** Ran SP% **118.2**
Speed ratings (Par 94): **97,95,94,92,92 91,91,90,88,87 84,80,80,65**
CSF £173.10 TOTE £9.80: £2.80, £6.80, £2.80; EX 242.10.La Belle Joannie was claimed by J. M. (Sean) Curran for £4,000. Willyn was claimed by J. S. Goldie for £10,000.
Owner J Wilde **Bred** Stuart McPhee Bloodstock Ltd **Trained** Middleham Moor, N Yorks

FOCUS
Ordinary claiming form but solid enough rated through the fourth.

NOTEBOOK
Willyn(IRE), having her seventh start, swept to the front and won going away. She has at last got her act together but she will be running from Jim Goldie's yard in future. (op 8-1)
La Belle Joannie behaved herself this time and kept on stoutly to snatch second spot. It was enough for her to be claimed cheaply.
Lady Bower, dropped in grade, made the best of her way home against the far-side rail but she is something of a weak finisher. (tchd 7-1)
Alexander Monarchy(IRE), who defeated Rio Taffeta when winning her claimer at Wolverhampton in May, proved suited by the step up in trip and fast ground. (op 5-1 tchd 4-1)
Brilliantsensation(IRE), an exciteable type, ran her best race on her third start fitted with cheekpieces for the first time.
Jazz Stick(IRE), who is not very big, sported cheekpieces rather than blinkers. This is as good as he is.
Indecision, a handful in the paddock, possibly prefers more ease in the ground and was going nowhere when tightened up. (op 17-2)
Rio Taffeta, drawn against the running rail, looked to have a sound chance of making it three wins in four starts but he never threatened to pull it off. Official explanation: jockey said gelding was unsuited by the good to firm ground (op 15-8)
Tenth Night(IRE) Official explanation: jockey said colt was unsuited by the good to firm ground

4137 WEATHERBYS BLOODSTOCK INSURANCE H'CAP 7f
2:40 (2:41) (Class 5) (0-70,71) 3-Y-O+ **£3,886** (£1,156; £577; £288) **Stalls** Low

Form RPR

4402 **1** **Esoterica (IRE)**[1] 4100 4-9-0 **57**..............................(b) DanielTudhope 13 65
(J S Goldie) *w ldrs: led over 4f out: qcknd over 3f out: hld on wl* **4/1**[1]

1332 **2** *1/2* **Million Percent**[9] 3851 8-9-7 **67**................................. PJMcDonald(3) 11 74
(C R Dore) *trckd ldrs: chal over 1f out: no ex towards fin* **9/2**[2]

5101 **3** *1 1/4* **Riquewihr**[7] 3920 7-10-0 **71** 6ex.....................................(p) PaddyAspell 10 75+
(J S Wainwright) *hld up in rr: hdwy over 2f out: styd on fnl f* **8/1**[3]

4106 **4** *nk* **Tough Love**[11] 3790 8-9-13 **70**..(p) DavidAllan 2 73
(T D Easterby) *in rr: hdwy over 2f out: hung lft and swtchd rt over 1f out: kpt on wl* **12/1**

5010 **5** *shd* **Sedge (USA)**[21] 3512 7-9-9 **66**...(b) MickyFenton 5 69
(P T Midgley) *chsd ldrs: styd on same pce fnl f* **14/1**

6100 **6** *hd* **Guadaloup**[25] 3375 5-8-1 **51** oh1.............................. PatrickDonaghy(7) 1 53
(M Brittain) *chsd ldrs: one pce fnl 2f* **40/1**

-344 **7** *2 1/2* **Desert Hunter (IRE)**[16] 3647 4-8-8 **51**.......................... PaulMulrennan 3 46
(Micky Hammond) *t.k.h: w ldrs: wknd appr fnl f* **8/1**[3]

0-00 **8** *hd* **Queen's Composer (IRE)**[12] 3764 4-9-13 **70**............ RoystonFfrench 6 65
(B Smart) *mid-div: hdwy over 2f out: kpt on fnl f* **16/1**

4500 **9** *nk* **Snow Bunting**[42] 2827 9-8-7 **53**.................................... AndrewElliott(3) 8 47
(Jedd O'Keeffe) *rr-div: kpt on fnl 2f: nvr nr ldrs* **14/1**

0005 **10** *1/2* **Hello Nod**[16] 3639 3-8-5 **54**.. PaulFessey 7 47
(Miss J A Camacho) *unruly s: s.i.s: kpt on fnl 2f: nvr on terms* **25/1**

-205 **11** *1 1/2* **Moheebb (IRE)**[11] 3786 3-8-10 **59**...................................... DaleGibson 4 48
(D W Chapman) *in rr: sme hdwy on ins over 2f out: nvr on terms* **16/1**

6040 **12** *3/4* **New Year (IRE)**[25] 3381 3-8-3 **52**.................................... HayleyTurner 15 38
(T P Tate) *led after 1f tl over 4f out: wknd over 1f out* **66/1**

5663 **13** *1/2* **General Feeling (IRE)**[10] 3814 6-8-6 **52**.............. DuranFentiman(3) 12 37
(S T Mason) *a in rr* **12/1**

0062 **14** *1* **Hucking Heat (IRE)**[17] 3620 3-9-1 **64**.......................... J-PGuillambert 9 46
(J R Best) *chsd ldrs: hung rt bnd over 4f out: lost pl 2f out* **14/1**

2001 **15** *1 3/4* **Choysia**[23] 3414 4-9-13 **70**.. TomEaves 14 48
(D W Barker) *led 1f: t.k.h and rn wd bnd over 4f out: sn lost pl* **9/1**

1m 26.08s (-1.02) **Going Correction** +0.005s/f (Good)
WFA 3 from 4yo+ 6lb **15** Ran SP% **125.3**
Speed ratings (Par 103): **105,104,103,102,102 102,99,99,98,98 96,95,95,94,92**
CSF £21.66 CT £144.56 TOTE £4.80: £1.80, £1.70, £3.30; EX 24.20.
Owner Mrs S E Bruce **Bred** A Lyons Bloodstock **Trained** Uplawmoor, E Renfrews

FOCUS
Modest but solid form with the two market leaders to the fore. The winner basically ran to the same level as at Musselburgh the night before.

4138 MCCARTHY AND STONE MAIDEN STKS 1m
3:15 (3:19) (Class 4) 3-Y-O+ **£5,181** (£1,541; £770; £384) **Stalls** Low

Form RPR

462 **1** **Honest Prospector (USA)**[22] 3454 3-9-3 78............. RoystonFfrench 8 81+
(Sir Michael Stoute) *chsd ldrs: outpcd and reminders 4f out: hdwy over 2f out: led over 1f out: rdn clr* **10/11**[1]

2423 **2** *2 1/2* **Arena's Dream (USA)**[36] 3015 3-9-3 71......................... TonyHamilton 11 72
(R A Fahey) *chsd ldr: led over 2f out tl over 1f out: kpt on same pce* **6/4**[2]

56 **3** *7* **March Mate**[16] 3639 3-9-3 0... TomEaves 9 56
(B Ellison) *outpcd and lost pl over 4f out: shkn up and hdwy over 2f out: kpt on to take modest 3rd nr fin* **28/1**

000/ **4** *3/4* **Avontuur (FR)**[727] 4168 5-9-3 45..................(b) DanielleMcCreery(7) 5 55
(D W Chapman) *led tl over 2f out: wknd fnl f: lost 3rd nr line* **100/1**

0 **5** *5* **And Your Point Is (USA)**[28] 3276 3-9-3 0...................... HayleyTurner 6 43
(C R Egerton) *outpcd and lost pl over 4f out: hung bdly lft over 2f out* **25/1**

6 3 **Reddy Ronnie (IRE)** 3-9-3 0 DanielTudhope 12 36
(D Carroll) *in rr: bhd fnl 4f* **50/1**

0 7 6 **Simba's Pride**[15] 3678 3-9-3 0 J-PGuillambert 1 22
(Miss L A Perratt) *s.i.s: nvr a factor* **100/1**

8 5 **Dilmoun (IRE)**[54] 5-9-10 0 (t) PhillipMakin 2 11
(A L T Moore, Ire) *s.v.s: nvr on terms* **9/1**[3]

1m 38.92s (-0.78) **Going Correction** +0.005s/f (Good)
WFA 3 from 4yo+ 7lb 8 Ran SP% **113.6**
Speed ratings (Par 105): **103,100,93,92,87 84,78,73**
CSF £2.37 TOTE £1.80: £1.10, £1.10, £2.80; EX 2.70.
Owner Saeed Suhail **Bred** Charles Nuckols Jr & Sons **Trained** Newmarket, Suffolk
■ Outsiders Missycomelightly, Rita Petite and Shady Bay were all withdrawn after proving unruly before the start. No Rule 4.

FOCUS
£8,000 prize money but a weak maiden lacking any strength in depth behind the first two. The fourth, having his first outing for two years, is rated just 45.
Dilmoun(IRE) Official explanation: jockey said gelding missed the break

4139 ANTHONY FAWCETT MEMORIAL FILLIES' H'CAP 1m 4f
3:50 (3:50) (Class 5) (0-70,68) 3-Y-O **£3,886** (£1,156; £577; £288) **Stalls** Low

Form RPR
0111 1 **Ravenna**[11] 3803 3-8-12 59 6ex HayleyTurner 6 69+
(M P Tregoning) *hld up: stdy hdwy over 5f out: led on bit 2f out: shkn up ins fnl f: easily* **4/7**[1]

0204 2 1 1/4 **Shandelight (IRE)**[18] 3587 3-8-3 50 RoystonFfrench 4 54
(Mrs A Duffield) *led: hung rt bnd over 8f out: hdd over 7f out: led over 3f out tl 2f out: no ch w wnr* **25/1**

0632 3 shd **Dansimar**[17] 3624 3-9-4 65 TPO'Shea 8 69
(M R Channon) *trckd ldrs: effrt over 3f out: kpt on same pce fnl 2f* **11/2**[2]

5232 4 3/4 **Silver Mitzva (IRE)**[23] 3421 3-9-1 62 (p) MickyFenton 9 65
(M Botti) *w ldrs: led over 7f out tl over 3f out: one pce fnl 2f* **15/2**[3]

-235 5 1 3/4 **Freya Tricks**[44] 2760 3-9-6 67 TomEaves 10 67
(I Semple) *hld up in rr: drvn over 4f out: kpt on fnl 2f: nvr rchd ldrs* **14/1**

1400 6 shd **Dee Cee Elle**[18] 3590 3-9-7 68 J-PGuillambert 2 68
(M Johnston) *chsd ldrs: drvn 9f out: outpcd over 3f out: no threat after* **12/1**

0060 7 1 3/4 **Hermanita**[23] 3427 3-8-13 60 TonyHamilton 1 57
(G Wragg) *trckd ldrs: effrt over 3f out: wknd over 1f out* **20/1**

-300 8 1 **Paradise Walk**[55] 2475 3-8-10 60 JamieMoriarty(3) 5 55
(E W Tuer) *t.k.h in midfield: outpcd over 3f out: n.m.r over 2f out: no threat* **50/1**

0050 9 1 1/4 **Foxxy**[25] 3379 3-8-1 51 oh1 ow2 AndrewMullen(3) 3 44
(J R Norton) *in rr: drvn over 3f out: nvr a factor* **50/1**

2m 35.98s (0.78) **Going Correction** +0.005s/f (Good) 9 Ran SP% **117.7**
Speed ratings (Par 97): **97,96,96,95,94 94,93,92,91**
CSF £25.05 CT £49.81 TOTE £1.40: £1.10, £5.80, £1.60; EX 21.10.
Owner Park Walk Racing **Bred** Whitsbury Manor Stud **Trained** Lambourn, Berks

FOCUS
A modest fillies' handicap. Sound form, the well-in winner not needing to improve.

4140 PETER BELL MEMORIAL H'CAP 6f
4:25 (4:25) (Class 4) (0-85,83) 3-Y-O+ **£5,181** (£1,541; £770; £384) **Stalls** High

Form RPR
0002 1 **Steel Blue**[5] 3998 7-8-11 69 HayleyTurner 8 79
(R M Whitaker) *chsd ldrs: effrt over 2f out: styd on to ld last 75yds* **7/1**

02-0 2 nk **Sir Nod**[12] 3762 5-9-6 78 TonyHamilton 5 87
(Miss J A Camacho) *led tl hdd and no ex wl ins fnl f* **33/1**

2260 3 1 **Angaric (IRE)**[24] 3401 4-9-0 72 RoystonFfrench 6 78
(B Smart) *trckd ldrs: effrt 2f out: styd on same pce fnl f* **4/1**[2]

3643 4 hd **Jilly Why (IRE)**[7] 3921 6-8-2 65 (b) NataliaGemelova(5) 10 70+
(Paul Green) *hmpd s: hld up: hdwy and nt clr run 2f out: styd on fnl f* **10/1**

4141 5 1 **Everygrainofsand (IRE)**[11] 3802 4-9-6 78 6ex J-PGuillambert 4 80
(J R Best) *chsd ldrs: hung lft over 1f out: kpt on same pce* **9/2**[3]

0000 6 3/4 **Ellens Academy (IRE)**[5] 3998 12-8-9 67 MickyFenton 7 67+
(E J Alston) *sn outpcd and in rr: kpt on fnl 2f: nvr rchd ldrs* **25/1**

2230 7 nk **Valley Of The Moon (IRE)**[16] 3637 3-8-9 74 JamieMoriarty(3) 1 73
(R A Fahey) *mid-div: kpt on fnl 2f: nvr trbld ldrs* **20/1**

0020 8 nk **First Order**[21] 3500 6-9-11 83 (v) TomEaves 11 81
(I Semple) *hmpd s: in rr: kpt on fnl 2f: nvr a factor* **15/2**

6614 9 2 **River Thames**[12] 3762 4-9-10 82 DO'Donohoe 9 74
(K A Ryan) *swvd rt s: in rr: drvn over 1f out: no rspnse: eased ins fnl f* **7/1**

211 10 3 **Dakota Rain (IRE)**[15] 3686 5-8-7 72 HaddenFrost(7) 2 55
(Jennie Candlish) *chsd ldrs: rdn over 2f out: lost pl over 1f out* **7/2**[1]

1m 11.01s (-1.49) **Going Correction** +0.005s/f (Good)
WFA 3 from 4yo+ 4lb 10 Ran SP% **117.8**
Speed ratings (Par 105): **109,108,107,107,105 104,104,103,101,97**
CSF £218.31 CT £1051.78 TOTE £8.10: £2.50, £6.00, £1.90; EX 156.10.
Owner Country Lane Partnership **Bred** R T And Mrs Watson **Trained** Scarcroft, W Yorks

FOCUS
A fair handicap. The form is fairly sound but the runner-up showed unexpected improvement.
Dakota Rain(IRE) Official explanation: trainer had no explanation for the poor form shown

4141 HELMSLEY APPRENTICE H'CAP 6f
5:00 (5:01) (Class 5) (0-70,69) 3-Y-O+ **£3,886** (£1,156; £577; £288) **Stalls** High

Form RPR
00-6 1 **Zap Attack**[43] 2806 7-8-1 50 oh5 AndrewHeffernan(8) 17 53
(M Brittain) *rrd s: sn chsng ldrs: styd on to ld fnl 50yds* **50/1**

5060 2 nk **Lambency (IRE)**[21] 3497 4-8-9 50 oh5 LanceBetts 13 52
(J S Goldie) *in rr: swtchd stands' side over 1f out: styd on strly ins fnl f: jst hld* **7/1**[3]

-300 3 nk **Frimley's Matterry**[41] 2893 7-8-9 50 oh5 LauraReynolds 18 51+
(R E Barr) *rr-div: hdwy 2f out: styd on fnl f: no ex wl ins fnl f* **16/1**

0103 4 hd **Cadogen Square**[7] 3920 5-8-7 53 (b) PaulPickard(5) 19 53
(D W Chapman) *chsd ldrs: led over 1f out: hdd and no ex wl ins fnl f* **11/2**[1]

1000 5 nk **Sea Land (FR)**[25] 3388 3-9-6 65 NSLawes 1 64
(B Ellison) *racd far side: hld up: effrt 2f out: styd on to ld that side ins fnl f: no ex* **14/1**

-360 6 shd **Joshua's Gold (IRE)**[69] 2033 6-8-11 60 KeithMcDonnell(8) 20 59+
(D Carroll) *mid-div: hdwy on stands' side over 2f out: styd on ins fnl f* **6/1**[2]

-000 7 1 1/4 **The Thrifty Bear**[28] 3259 4-8-9 50 oh5 BradleyRoper 2 45
(C W Fairhurst) *led far side: edgd rt and hdd that side ins fnl f: no ex* **66/1**

2243 8 1 1/2 **Hucking Hope (IRE)**[8] 3872 3-9-0 67 AmeliaHegarty(8) 14 57
(J R Best) *w ldrs: led over 2f out: hdd over 1f out: sn fdd* **7/1**[3]

0600 9 1 **Sir Orpen (IRE)**[26] 3345 4-9-9 67 DeanHeslop(3) 8 54
(T D Barron) *mid-div: hdwy over 1f out: kpt on: nvr nr ldrs* **9/1**

4006 10 1 1/2 **Muara**[51] 2553 5-9-0 55 (p) JamesRogers 7 37
(D W Barker) *chsd ldrs: swtchd far side after 2f: kpt on same pce fnl 2f* **11/1**

00-0 11 1 1/4 **Silidan**[83] 1678 4-9-11 69 PatrickDonaghy(3) 6 47
(M Brittain) *chsd ldrs: wknd over 1f out* **50/1**

6500 12 1 **Maison Dieu**[24] 3409 4-9-1 56 ChrisGlenister 15 31
(E J Alston) *chsd ldrs: wknd over 1f out* **6/1**[2]

6006 13 nk **Black Oval**[4] 4021 6-8-9 50 oh2 MatthewDavies 5 24
(S Parr) *racd far side: trckd ldr that side: lost pl over 1f out* **25/1**

02-0 14 1/2 **Yorke's Folly (USA)**[28] 3259 6-8-9 50 oh5 (v) DeclanCannon 4 22
(C W Fairhurst) *sn towards rr* **28/1**

-060 15 3/4 **Rose Of Inchinor**[66] 2121 4-8-9 50 oh5 SophieDoyle 11 20
(R E Barr) *chsd ldrs: wknd over 1f out* **33/1**

2600 16 hd **Mr Rooney (IRE)**[37] 2989 4-9-8 63 (t) MarkCoumbe 10 32
(D Nicholls) *chsd ldrs: rdn over 2f out: lost pl over 1f out* **14/1**

00-0 17 1/2 **Mis Chicaf (IRE)**[3] 4038 6-8-1 50 oh5 GaryWales(8) 12 18
(D Carroll) *awkward s: chsd ldrs: wknd 2f out* **25/1**

0-00 18 1 1/4 **My Maite Mickey**[11] 3786 3-8-0 50 oh5 (v[1]) CharlesEddery(5) 16 14
(R C Guest) *led tl over 2f out: sn lost pl* **40/1**

1m 12.88s (0.38) **Going Correction** +0.005s/f (Good)
WFA 3 from 4yo+ 4lb 18 Ran SP% **128.4**
Speed ratings (Par 103): **97,96,96,95,95 95,93,91,90,88 86,85,85,84,83 83,82,80**
CSF £371.22 CT £5868.87 TOTE £98.80: £10.10, £2.30, £5.60, £1.50; EX 1988.10 Place 6 £65.86, Place 5 £13.86..
Owner Mel Brittain **Bred** Meon Valley Stud **Trained** Warthill, N Yorks
■ A first riding success for Andrew Heffernan.
■ Stewards' Enquiry : Mark Coumbe one-day ban: used whip with excessive frequency (Aug 14)
Bradley Roper four-day ban: used whip with excessive frequency (Aug 14-17)

FOCUS
A low-grade apprentices' handicap and they raced right across the whole width of the track. High numbers dominated and the form is dubious with the first three all out of the handicap.
T/Plt: £92.90 to a £1 stake. Pool £45,925.10. 363.40 winning units. T/Qpdt: £9.80 to a £1 stake. Pool £3,068.40. 230.50 winning units. WG

4114 GALWAY (R-H)
Friday, August 3

OFFICIAL GOING: Good

4142a ST. JAMES'S GATE RACE 1m 6f
5:40 (5:41) 4-Y-O+ **£9,677** (£2,839; £1,352; £460)

RPR
1 **Rekaab (IRE)**[17] 3632 4-9-6 98 KJManning 6 108+
(Martin Brassil, Ire) *hld up: 7th 5f out: hdwy 3f out: 3rd 2f out: sn chal: led 1f out: sn clr: easily* **10/3**[3]

2 3 **King In Waiting (IRE)**[65] 2161 4-9-2 100 (b) MJKinane 9 100
(John M Oxx, Ire) *trckd ldrs in mod 5th: smooth hdwy 3f out: 2nd and chal 2f out: led ent st: hdd 1f out: sn outpcd: kpt on* **7/4**[1]

3 1 **Glitter Baby (IRE)**[17] 3628 4-8-11 DPMcDonogh 3 94
(M G Quinlan) *trckd ldr in mod 2nd: tk clsr order under 5f out: led 3f out: rdn and strly pressed 2f out: hdd ent st: one pce* **3/1**[2]

4 8 **Young Patriarch**[390] 2688 6-9-2 CO'Donoghue 10 88
(W J Burke, Ire) *hld up in rr: hdwy 3f out: mod 5th and rdn ent st: kpt on* **25/1**

5 3 1/2 **Icklingham (IRE)**[17] 3632 7-9-2 95 (b) WJLee 2 84
(C F Swan, Ire) *trckd ldrs in mod 4th: rdn 3f out: no ex ent st* **5/1**

6 13 **Statute**[27] 3337 5-9-2 42 (bt) CDHayes 1 67
(F J Bowles, Ire) *led: sn clr: rdn and reduced advantage 5f out: hdd 3f out: wknd* **66/1**

7 13 **Carpet Ride**[38] 2974 5-8-13 DJMoran(3) 8 50
(C W J Farrell, Ire) *chsd ldrs in mod 3rd: drvn along under 5f out: sn wknd* **100/1**

8 3 **Olivia Pielak (IRE)**[432] 2058 4-8-11 NGMcCullagh 4 41
(Miss A M Winters, Ire) *chsd ldrs in mod 6th: drvn along over 5f out: sn wknd* **80/1**

9 10 **Tip The Dip (USA)**[303] 4030 7-9-2 50 (t) WMLordan 12 33
(M McDonagh, Ire) *a bhd* **100/1**

10 5 1/2 **Silver Navasha (USA)** 4-8-4 BACurtis(7) 5 21
(John Joseph Murphy, Ire) *a towards rr* **33/1**

3m 8.70s (0.70) 10 Ran SP% **112.6**
CSF £8.99 TOTE £4.30: £1.50, £1.30, £1.40; DF 10.40.
Owner The Monet Partnership **Bred** Shadwell Estate Company Ltd **Trained** Dunmurray, Co Kildare

NOTEBOOK
Glitter Baby(IRE) was left in front when the clear early leader cried enough three furlongs out, and although he appeared to be travelling well, it seems equally clear that being in front such a long way out was not really where she wanted to be. She had no answer to the winner from a furlong out but kept on well to worry the runner-up all the way to the line. (op 3/1 tchd 7/2)

4143 - 4146a (Foreign Racing) - See Raceform Interactive

4117 GOODWOOD (R-H)
Saturday, August 4

OFFICIAL GOING: Good to firm (9.2)
Wind: Light, across Weather: Glorious

4147 BLUESQUARE.COM STKS (H'CAP) 1m 3f
2:10 (2:16) (Class 3) (0-90,90) 3-Y-O
£11,217 (£3,358; £1,679; £840; £419; £210) **Stalls** Low

Form RPR
-344 1 **Sanbuch**[56] 2448 3-9-4 87 (v[1]) JamieSpencer 10 96
(L M Cumani) *lw: s.i.s: reluctant and rousted along in last: drvn 1/2-way: stl last over 2f out: swtchd and str run over 1f out: hung rt but led last 50yds* **7/1**[2]

-143 2 1/2 **Coeur De Lionne (IRE)**[16] 3691 3-9-0 83 DaneO'Neill 8 91
(R Charlton) *lw: trckd ldrs: prog to ld jst over 2f out: 2 l clr over 1f out: styd on but hdd last 50yds* **10/1**

5122 3 3/4 **Seeking The Buck (USA)**[7] 3964 3-8-9 78 (t) ChrisCatlin 12 85
(M A Magnusson) *lw: towards rr: rdn 4f out: struggling 3f out: taken to outer and r.o strly fr over 1f out: nrst fin* **12/1**

5401 4 1/2 **Fongs Gazelle**[3] 4060 3-9-0 83 6ex RHills 16 89
(M Johnston) *hld up in midfield on outer: prog to chse ldr wl over 1f out: hanging bdly rt after: styd on but nvr able to chal* **15/2**[3]

221 **5** 3/4 **Purple Emperor (USA)**[33] 3151 3-9-7 **90**....................(t) KerrinMcEvoy 4 95+
(Saeed Bin Suroor) *lw: trckd ldrs: cl enough and gng strly over 2f out: rdn and kpt on same pce fnl 2f* **5/1**[1]

100- **6** 1 1/2 **Nur Tau (IRE)**[344] 4773 3-8-10 **79**.. MartinDwyer 7 81
(M P Tregoning) *hld up in midfield on inner: effrt over 2f out: nt clr run 1f out: styd on but nvr gng pce to trble ldrs* **66/1**

1141 **7** 1/2 **Guiseppe Verdi (USA)**[45] 2767 3-9-4 **87**..................... JimmyFortune 11 88
(J H M Gosden) *lw: hld up in midfield: gng wl 3f out: shkn up and nt qckn 2f out: btn whn hmpd 1f out* **15/2**[3]

1-30 **8** 1/2 **Zoom One**[38] 2999 3-8-13 **82**... JosedeSouza 2 83
(M P Tregoning) *trckd ldrs on outer: effrt over 2f out: drvn and nt qckn wl over 1f out: fdd* **25/1**

510 **9** 2 **Ascalon**[44] 2789 3-9-4 **87**... JMurtagh 5 84
(Pat Eddery) *lw: towards rr: rdn jst over 3f out and no prog: plugged on* **16/1**

212 **10** 1 1/2 **Fourteenth**[19] 3590 3-8-13 **82**.. RyanMoore 14 77
(Sir Michael Stoute) *hld up wl in rr: rdn and no prog over 2f out: btn whn sltly hmpd over 1f out: hanging rt after* **5/1**[1]

1201 **11** hd **Soft Morning**[28] 3335 3-9-3 **86**.. SebSanders 6 80
(Sir Mark Prescott) *led: rdn and hdd jst over 2f out: pushed along after and steadily fdd* **9/1**

2000 **12** 3/4 **Noticeable (IRE)**[9] 3877 3-8-13 **82**...................................... JHBowman 1 75
(M R Channon) *lw: chsd ldr after 4f: upsides over 2f out: wknd over 1f out* **20/1**

0152 **13** 3 **Happy Go Lily**[52] 2574 3-9-4 **87**... AdamKirby 15 75
(W R Swinburn) *chsd ldr for 4f: rdn over 3f out on inner: wknd fnl 2f* **14/1**

5600 **14** 10 **Fascinatin Rhythm**[9] 3877 3-8-5 **79**................................ LukeMorris(5) 3 50
(V Smith) *nvr bttr than midfield: u.p over 3f out: wknd over 2f out: t.o* **50/1**

2m 23.53s (-3.68) **Going Correction** -0.125s/f (Firm) **14** Ran SP% **120.8**
Speed ratings (Par 104): **108,107,107,106,106 105,104,104,102,101 101,101,98,91**
CSF £73.01 CT £838.98 TOTE £9.30: £3.10, £3.50, £4.00; EX 94.90 Trifecta £972.50 Part won. Pool: £1,369.85 - 0.90 winning tickets..
Owner Scuderia Rencati Srl **Bred** The Lavington Stud **Trained** Newmarket, Suffolk
■ Stewards' Enquiry : Jamie Spencer caution: careless riding

FOCUS
A competitive race, run at a good gallop and the form looks strong and should work out.

NOTEBOOK
Sanbuch, in a first-time visor, looked none to keen to exert himself early on, but they went a good gallop and he stayed on strongly as others began to tire. Even then, he swerved to the right as he came to snatch the race, leaving a clear impression of being talented but quirky so, while undoubtedly capable of even better, he cannot be relied upon too heavily. (op 8-1 tchd 17-2 and 9-1 in a place)
Coeur De Lionne(IRE) has done well in his seven races to date, and was only just run out of it here after looking the likely winner inside the last 2f. He should improve again, so looks capable of winning a similar race, even if he goes up a few pounds. (op 15-2)
Seeking The Buck(USA) not only stayed the longer trip, he ran as if 1m4f should suit. He is still improving, and capable of winning at this level, with fast ground appearing to suit particularly well.
Fongs Gazelle was carrying a 6lb penalty for her victory here three days earlier and it was probably the extra weight, rather than the longer trip, that meant she never quite looked like completing a quick double. However, having been widest of all on the turn, she still put in a creditable effort. (op 13-2 tchd 6-1)
Purple Emperor(USA), carting topweight on his first appearance in a handicap, just about got the trip, though slightly shorter distances probably suit him ideally at present. However, he is not far off winning in this company from 1m1f to 1m3f. (op 7-1)
Nur Tau(IRE), on his toes in the paddock, made an encouraging seasonal debut, and gave the impression that he must have been well below his best when twice running moderately in August last year. He stayed the longer trip well, and is unlikely to start at this sort of price again. (op 50-1)
Guiseppe Verdi(USA), raised 6lb and running in a better race this time, performed respectably. He was done no favours by the winner, but is high enough in the weights now.
Zoom One did his best to overcome a poor draw, and the strong pace helped him settle. However, given a good gallop, he is probably better around 1m2f. (op 20-1)
Fourteenth was a flop, failing to pick up to any degree in the home straight, and may be more effective back on a flatter track. (op 9-2)
Happy Go Lily looked warm in the paddock. (op 18-1)
Fascinatin Rhythm was on her toes in the paddock and failed to get involved during the race.

4148 BLUESQUAREPOKER.COM THOROUGHBRED STKS (LISTED RACE) 1m
2:45 (2:46) (Class 1) 3-Y-O
£17,034 (£6,456; £3,231; £1,611; £807; £405) **Stalls** High

Form RPR

0-10 **1** **Dubai's Touch**[4] 4045 3-9-4 110.................................... RoystonFfrench 7 112
(M Johnston) *sn settled in 3rd: effrt to ld over 2f out: sn pressed: harried on all sides fnl f: hld on gamely* **16/1**

6041 **2** shd **Traffic Guard (USA)**[23] 3463 3-9-0 105...........................(p) JohnEgan 10 108
(J S Moore) *sn settled bhd ldr: pressed wnr fnl 2f: upsides thrght fnl f: jst hld* **9/1**

2015 **3** hd **Tobosa**[27] 3362 3-9-0 114.. MichaelHills 2 108
(W Jarvis) *hld up in last pair: effrt on outer 3f out: stdy prog fr 2f out: r.o fnl f: gaining at fin* **7/2**[1]

31-5 **4** nk **Basaata (USA)**[51] 2599 3-8-9 92... RHills 6 102
(M P Tregoning) *lw: sn restrained bhd ldrs: effrt 3f out: rdn to chal wl over 1f out: nrly upsides fnl f: nt qckn last 75yds* **25/1**

2-30 **5** 3/4 **Rahiyah (USA)**[43] 2814 3-8-9 113.. TedDurcan 4 100
(J Noseda) *lw: sn restrained into midfield: effrt over 2f out: pressed ldrs over 1f out: kpt on but a hld fnl f* **9/2**[2]

4-14 **6** 1 **Italian Girl**[45] 2757 3-8-9 103.. JMurtagh 1 98
(A P Jarvis) *hld up in last trio: shkn up and clsd on ldrs 2f out: nvr quite pce to chal fr over 1f out* **8/1**[3]

2601 **7** shd **Tybalt (USA)**[22] 3503 3-9-0 101.. JimmyFortune 9 103
(J H M Gosden) *hld up in midfield: effrt to cl on ldrs 2f out: cl up whn nt clr run 1f out: swtchd rt and one pce* **7/2**[1]

3342 **8** 13 **Rallying Cry (USA)**[16] 3683 3-9-0 105.........................(t) KerrinMcEvoy 5 73
(Saeed Bin Suroor) *s.i.s: a in last pair: rdn and struggling over 2f out: wknd: t.o* **8/1**[3]

3310 **9** 1 **Eddie Jock (IRE)**[23] 3463 3-9-0 111.............................. JamieSpencer 11 71
(M L W Bell) *won early battle for ld: hdd over 2f out: wknd and eased: t.o* **8/1**[3]

1m 37.2s (-3.07) **Going Correction** -0.125s/f (Firm) **9** Ran SP% **115.7**
Speed ratings (Par 108): **110,109,109,109,108 107,107,94,93**
CSF £151.06 TOTE £15.90: £3.50, £3.00, £1.90; EX 197.90 TRIFECTA Not won..
Owner Salem Suhail **Bred** Miss S N Ralphs **Trained** Middleham Moor, N Yorks

FOCUS
A good Listed race, run at a strong gallop but the first seven finished in a heap and the proximity of the fourth raises doubts about the solidity of the form.

NOTEBOOK
Dubai's Touch showed a lot of guts to hang on in the face of four strong challenges inside the final furlong, especially as he was conceding weight all round. Although things will get even harder from now on, he is tough enough to merit a crack at Group company over 7f or a mile. (op 25-1)
Traffic Guard(USA), very effective on fast ground, has developed into a smart sort at 7f and a mile, and he can hardly go any closer than this without winning. He is good enough to win a Listed contest if his trainer can find the right opportunity, but may go to Turkey next month to contest a Group 2. (op 12-1)
Tobosa acts on ground with give, but is at his best on fast conditions like this. Although not ideally suited by the track, and unable to get his head in front in time, he is well at home at this level, and should stay a bit farther as the season progresses. (op 11-4 tchd 4-1)
Basaata(USA), more lightly-raced than all her rivals, ought to have a bit of improvement in her, and certainly stepped up on earlier efforts to go very close here, being beaten only by three colts. The drop back to a mile suited her, and this well-grown filly looks an interesting sort for the remaining months of the season. (tchd 28-1)
Rahiyah(USA) was never quite finding enough on the outside of the field in the home straight, and looks as if she is going to fall short of earlier expectations. She will not be easy to place, but has the ability to win a decent prize if she can be found the right opening, with a return to all-fillies company looking a realistic move. (op 3-1)
Italian Girl ran a solid race, but again fell just short in Listed company. However, she was not beaten far, so connections are unlikely to be deterred from having another crack at this level.
Tybalt(USA), upped from handicaps, was not quite able to handle the rise in class, but his style of running means there is always the possibility of meeting traffic problems. When everything falls his way, and the gaps appear at the right time, he is lightly-raced enough to do a bit better at this level. (op 5-1 tchd 6-1 in a place)
Rallying Cry(USA) Official explanation: jockey said colt lost its action

4149 BLUE SQUARE NASSAU STKS (GROUP 1) (F&M) 1m 1f 192y
3:20 (3:22) (Class 1) 3-Y-O+
£113,560 (£43,040; £21,540; £10,740; £5,380; £2,700) **Stalls** High

Form RPR

3211 **1** **Peeping Fawn (USA)**[20] 3576 3-8-10 0................................ JMurtagh 8 124+
(A P O'Brien, Ire) *lw: prom: trckd ldr 1/2-way: led over 3f out: drew 3l clr 2f out: shkn up fnl f: unchal* **2/1**[1]

1-12 **2** 1 1/2 **Mandesha (FR)**[41] 2925 4-9-5 0.. CSoumillon 7 121
(A De Royer-Dupre, France) *hld up in last: prog 3f out: rdn to chse clr wnr over 1f out: r.o but nvr remotely nr enough to chal* **7/2**[3]

1112 **3** 3 1/2 **Light Shift (USA)**[20] 3576 3-8-10 118................................. TedDurcan 3 114
(H R A Cecil) *lw: settled in tch: effrt on outer 3f out: sn outpcd: hanging and wandering over 1f out: kpt on to take 3rd nr fin* **3/1**[2]

0205 **4** 1/2 **Sweet Lilly**[24] 3433 3-8-10 105... JHBowman 5 113
(M R Channon) *lw: t.k.h: trckd ldr tl rn wd bnd 1/2-way: rdn to chse wnr over 2f out but outpcd: lost 2nd over 1f out: fdd* **22/1**

000 **5** 2 1/2 **Dont Dili Dali**[18] 3628 4-9-5 100..(p) JohnEgan 4 108
(J S Moore) *chsd ldrs: rdn 3f out: n.m.r and outpcd over 2f out: no ch after* **80/1**

-202 **6** nk **Speciosa (IRE)**[35] 3117 4-9-5 114................................... JamieSpencer 1 107
(Mrs P Sly) *swtg: led to over 3f out: steadily wknd last 2f* **14/1**

1601 **7** 1 1/4 **Yaqeen**[18] 3628 3-8-10 107.. RHills 2 108+
(M A Jarvis) *hld up in last pair: sme prog on outer over 2f out: no imp over 1f out: wknd* **14/1**

-314 **8** 10 **Nannina**[24] 3433 4-9-5 115... JimmyFortune 6 85
(J H M Gosden) *settled in midfield: effrt on inner 3f out: pushed along whn hmpd over 2f out: no ch after: eased* **6/1**

2m 4.53s (-3.22) **Going Correction** -0.125s/f (Firm)
WFA 3 from 4yo 9lb **8** Ran SP% **113.8**
Speed ratings (Par 117): **107,105,103,102,100 100,99,91**
CSF £9.09 TOTE £3.10: £1.30, £1.10, £1.60; EX 10.10 Trifecta £20.90 Pool: £7,067.19 - 239.39 winning tickets..
Owner M Tabor & Mrs John Magnier **Bred** Barnett Enterprises **Trained** Ballydoyle, Co Tipperary

FOCUS
A Group 1 race in every respect, run at a fair gallop, and with the first three favourites filling the frame the form looks sound enough, although the fourth and fifth finished closer than could have been expected given their official ratings.

NOTEBOOK
Peeping Fawn(USA), a strapping sort, goes from strength to strength, and is developing into a very smart filly indeed. Though she had the run of the race, getting a nice lead before kicking on decisively early in the straight, she handled the faster ground really well, and has the words "top class" written all over her. (op 9-4 tchd 5-2 and 15-8)
Mandesha(FR), an athletic sort, allowed the winner first run, and not even a gallant attempt to close in the final 300 yards could get her there in time. However, she looks to be coming back to her best and could well find another Group 1 before the season is out, with a less-undulating track likely to suit. (tchd 4-1)
Light Shift(USA) is probably at her best given a stiffer test of stamina these days, but the main problem was probably the combination of fast ground on this undulating track. She stayed on steadily despite not looking comfortable in the home straight, but never looked remotely dangerous, and has much work to do if she is to close the gap on the winner should they meet again. A trip to the Breeders' Cup is still a possibility. (op 11-4 tchd 10-3 in places)
Sweet Lilly is capable of winning a Group 3, but falls short in Group 1 company. This was a creditable effort, but the first two home were in a different league, and the third not at her best. (op 50-1 tchd 20-1)
Dont Dili Dali has been out of form of late, so this exceeded expectations. However, not even her greatest fan would imagine she is capable of winning a Group 1, especially a hot one like this. (op 100-1)
Speciosa(IRE) is probably most effective on good ground, or with a bit of cut, and her response was not as strong as it can be when at her best.
Yaqeen, who was warm in the paddock, is a high-class filly at her best, and may yet win a Group race, but it is unlikely to be a Group 1. (op 16-1)
Nannina was just beginning to feel the strain when being squeezed up early in the straight. She is a high-class filly at her best, but this was an exceptional line-up, so she would probably have been third at the very best. Official explanation: jockey said he eased the filly after being hampered 2 1/2f out (op 5-1)

4150 BLUESQUARE.COM STEWARDS' CUP (HERITAGE H'CAP) 6f
3:55 (3:58) (Class 2) 3-Y-O+
£62,320 (£18,660; £9,330; £4,670; £2,330; £1,170) **Stalls** Low

Form RPR

-410 **1** **Zidane**[42] 2858 5-9-1 **100**.. JamieSpencer 11 110+
(J R Fanshawe) *racd centre 1st 2f: hld up and wl in rr whn gps merged: drvn and prog wl over 1f out: str run to ld last stride* **6/1**[1]

2200 **2** shd **Borderlescott**[22] 3506 5-9-9 **108**..................................... RoystonFfrench 7 118
(R Bastiman) *w ldr on nr side: overall ldr wl over 2f out: battled on wl fnl f: hdd last stride* **12/1**

-601 **3** ½ **Knot In Wood (IRE)**[22] 3500 5-8-13 **98** 3ex.................. PaulHanagan 25 106+
(R A Fahey) *swtg: racd far side 1st 2f: chsng ldrs whn gps merged: effrt u.p over 1f out: chal fnl f: jst hld* **7/1**[2]

0-22 **4** *hd* **That's Hot (IRE)**[59] 2379 4-9-3 **102**.. TQuinn 13 110
(G M Lyons, Ire) *str: lw: racd centre 1st 2f: towards rr whn gps merged: prog wl over 1f out: r.o u.p fnl f: jst outpcd* **33/1**

5605 **5** ½ **Beaver Patrol (IRE)**[35] 3104 5-8-10 **95**..................................(b[1]) RHills 6 101
(Eve Johnson Houghton) *lw: overall ldr nr side to wl over 2f out: pressed ldr tl ent fnl f: kpt on* **33/1**

5301 **6** *shd* **Balthazaar's Gift (IRE)**[8] 3894 4-9-13 **112** 3ex........... KerrinMcEvoy 26 118+
(L M Cumani) *lw: racd far side 1st 2f: wl in rr whn gps merged: stl wl bhd but gng strly over 1f out: shkn up and fin full of running: hopeless task* **10/1**[3]

6000 **7** 1 ½ **Fayr Jag (IRE)**[8] 3894 8-9-4 **103**... DavidAllan 12 104
(T D Easterby) *lw: racd in centre 1st 2f: chsng ldrs but rdn whn gps merged: prog and tried to chal 1f out: wknd ins fnl f* **50/1**

0056 **8** *shd* **Fantasy Believer**[6] 3990 9-8-11 **96**.............................. JimmyFortune 14 97
(J J Quinn) *lw: racd centre 1st 2f: chsng ldrs whn gps merged: drvn 2f out: kpt on but nvr gng pce to chal* **14/1**

0012 **9** *shd* **Protector (SAF)**[22] 3500 6-9-4 **103**.................................... RyanMoore 4 103
(Miss Gay Kelleway) *swtg: chsd nr side ldrs: rdn 2f out: kpt on but no imp* **14/1**

2220 **10** *nk* **Intrepid Jack**[22] 3505 5-9-5 **104**.. JohnEgan 5 103
(H Morrison) *chsd nr side ldrs but nvr quite on terms: rdn over 2f out: kpt on fnl f* **16/1**

4350 **11** *nk* **Grantley Adams**[22] 3505 4-9-5 **104**................................... JHBowman 10 102
(M R Channon) *dwlt: wl in rr nr side: styd on fr over 1f out: n.d* **20/1**

-343 **12** ½ **Something (IRE)**[22] 3505 5-9-5 **104**.................................... JMurtagh 3 101
(T G Mills) *w nr side ldrs: stl cl up over 1f out: fdd fnl f* **11/1**

0011 **13** *shd* **Machinist (IRE)**[34] 3140 7-8-12 **97** 3ex.................. SilvestreDeSousa 16 94
(D Nicholls) *lw: dwlt: racd centre 1st 2f: wl in rr and u.p 1/2-way: styd on fnl f* **11/1**

0200 **14** *nk* **Bentong (IRE)**[22] 3505 4-8-12 **102**................................(t) TolleyDean[(5)] 8 98
(P F I Cole) *pressed nr side ldrs over 3f: wknd over 1f out* **25/1**

3320 **15** *hd* **Beckermet (IRE)**[42] 2858 5-9-7 **106**................................ MartinDwyer 9 101
(R F Fisher) *lw: chsd nr side ldrs: rdn over 2f out: no imp over 1f out: fdd* **50/1**

32-5 **16** *shd* **Advanced**[105] 1159 4-9-10 **109**... TedDurcan 17 104
(K A Ryan) *lw: racd centre 1st 2f: wl in rr whn gps merged: drvn and no prog over 2f out: plugged on* **33/1**

3520 **17** ½ **Mutamared (USA)**[42] 2858 7-9-2 **101**..................................... NCallan 27 94
(K A Ryan) *taken down early: racd far side 1st 2f: chsng ldrs on wd outside whn gps merged: u.str.p sn after 1/2-way: fdd over 1f out* **16/1**

-401 **18** *nk* **Viking Spirit**[22] 3489 5-8-12 **97** 3ex.................................. AdamKirby 22 89
(W R Swinburn) *racd far side 1st 2f: wl in rr whn gps merged: hanging and no prog over 1f out* **11/1**

040 **19** *shd* **The Tatling (IRE)**[2] 4090 10-9-1 **100**............................ FrancisNorton 21 92
(J M Bradley) *lw: b.hind: racd far side 1st 2f: hld up in rr: rdn and no real prog whn nt clr run briefly 1f out* **40/1**

2606 **20** *nk* **Baron's Pit**[15] 3708 7-9-2 **101**..(b) DaneO'Neill 18 92
(E F Vaughan) *racd far side 1st 2f: a wl in rr* **100/1**

3050 **21** *hd* **Out After Dark**[21] 3526 6-8-5 **95**...............................(p) LukeMorris[(5)] 24 85
(C G Cox) *lw: racd towards far side thrght: hrd drvn in rr over 2f out: no prog* **28/1**

0100 **22** *nk* **Kostar**[61] 2319 6-9-1 **100**... PhilipRobinson 15 89
(C G Cox) *taken down early: racd centre 1st 2f: wl in tch whn gps merged: lost pl fr wl over 1f out* **33/1**

1000 **23** ¾ **King Orchisios (IRE)**[6] 3990 4-9-3 **105**.................(p) JamieMoriarty[(3)] 2 92
(K A Ryan) *prom nr side: hanging bdly and wknd wl over 1f out* **100/1**

4040 **24** *shd* **Mastership (IRE)**[24] 3431 3-8-11 **100**...........................(b) SebSanders 1 86
(C E Brittain) *swtg: racd nr side: nvr on terms w ldrs: struggling over 2f out* **25/1**

2026 **25** *shd* **Qadar (IRE)**[85] 1647 5-8-13 **98**.......................................(b) IanMongan 20 84
(N P Littmoden) *racd far side 1st 2f: a wl in rr: struggling by 1/2-way* **100/1**

1620 **26** *shd* **Ripples Maid**[42] 2858 4-8-12 **100**................................. TravisBlock[(3)] 19 86
(J A Geake) *racd far side 1st 2f: chsng ldrs and wl in tch whn gps merged: wknd rapidly 2f out* **40/1**

3330 **27** 1 ½ **Bond City (IRE)**[2] 4090 5-9-4 **103**...................................... ChrisCatlin 23 84
(G R Oldroyd) *lw: racd far side 1st 2f: prom whn gps merged: sn lost pl: toiling over 2f out* **66/1**

1m 10.5s (-2.35) **Going Correction** -0.125s/f (Firm)
WFA 3 from 4yo+ 4lb **27** Ran SP% **134.6**
Speed ratings (Par 109): **110,109,109,108,108 108,106,106,105,105 105,104,104,103,103 103,102,102,102,101 101,101,100,10**
CSF £67.91 CT £544.26 TOTE £8.30: £3.10, £3.60, £2.60, £5.00; EX 133.30 Trifecta £1629.70 Pool: £59,002.06 - 25.70 winning tickets..
Owner Jan and Peter Hopper **Bred** Mrs J P Hopper And Mrs E M Grundy **Trained** Newmarket, Suffolk

■ Excusez Moi (33/1) was withdrawn at the start on vet's advice. No Rule 4.
■ Stewards' Enquiry : Royston Ffrench one-day ban: used whip with excessive frequency (Aug 15)
T Quinn four-day ban: used whip with excessive frequency and not giving filly time to respond (Aug 15-18)

FOCUS
A typically strong line-up for this ultra-competitive sprint. However, unusually for this race, the runners were all middle to stands' side when the high-drawn runners moved across after two furlongs. The overall form looks solid rated around the runner-up and fifth.

NOTEBOOK
Zidane was given stall 11 - the box nobody else wanted - after his trainer forgot to send a representative when the stalls were allocated. However, in the end it was irrelevant, with no draw bias apparent, and he duly rattled home from 15 lengths off the early pace to get there in the final stride, with the strong tempo being right up his street. (op 7-1)
Borderlescott made a bold bid to win this race for the second year running from a 6lb higher mark, only to be done right on the line. He is a magnificent performer at this trip, and it is surely only a matter of time before he lands his first win in Pattern company. (op 14-1)
Knot In Wood(IRE) has hit a rich vein of form, and is now looking better than any stage of his career. He would be at home in any of the big 6f handicaps for the rest of the season, and should be given due consideration. (op 13-2 tchd 15-2)
That's Hot(IRE), back in handicap company after finishing second at Listed and Group 3 level, ran another fine race, and remains a consistent and talented sprinter. Her mark in Britain looks just about right, despite the rather unflattering starting price.
Beaver Patrol(IRE), who goes well on downhill tracks, ran a corker in the first-time blinkers. However, he has done little wrong in his career, so they may not be necessary.
Balthazaar's Gift(IRE) travelled really well, but began to pick up too late, and might even have won had he got going a fraction earlier. All his four victories have been on yielding ground, but fast ground is not a problem, and this classy sort looks capable of winning more good prizes in any conditions.
Fayr Jag(IRE) appreciated the return to fast ground, running his best race for some time.
Mutamared(USA) was on his toes before the race and never landed a serious blow.
The Tatling(IRE), making a swift reappearance, was on his toes in the paddock before the off. (op 50-1)
Baron's Pit was on his toes before the race and ran very much in accordance with his starting price.

4151 BLUE SQUARE TELEBET EBF MAIDEN STKS (C&G) 7f
4:30 (4:37) (Class 2) 2-Y-O **£10,363** (£3,083; £1,540; £769) **Stalls** High

Form RPR

1 **Latin Lad** 2-9-0 0.. FrancisNorton 19 83
(R Hannon) *w'like: cl cpld: trckd ldrs: effrt over 1f out: got through to ld jst ins fnl f: edgd lft: hld on* **33/1**

2 *nk* **Belgrave Square (USA)**[10] 3861 2-9-0 0........................... JMurtagh 17 82
(A P O'Brien, Ire) *str: lw: hld up in midfield on inner: eased to outer fr over 2f out: shkn up wl over 1f out: r.o wl fnl f: clsng on wnr at fin* **6/1**

3 **3** ¾ **Missioner (USA)**[8] 3896 2-9-0 0................................ RoystonFfrench 15 80
(M Johnston) *lw: chsd ldrs: effrt over 2f out: cl up over 1f out: kpt on but nt quite gng pce to chal* **11/4**[1]

0 **4** *nk* **Talayeb**[24] 3435 2-9-0 0.. RHills 16 79
(M P Tregoning) *lw: prom: rdn to ld over 1f out: hdd jst ins fnl f: hld whn hmpd nr fin* **16/1**

5 1 ¼ **Craigstown** 2-9-0 0.. KerrinMcEvoy 7 76+
(Saeed Bin Suroor) *w'like: neat: wl in rr and racd wd: no prog tl picked up over 1f out: fin wl* **11/1**

3 **6** ¾ **Alan Devonshire**[14] 3733 2-9-0 0... NCallan 14 74
(M H Tompkins) *trckd ldrs: rdn and cl up over 1f out: fdd fnl f* **40/1**

7 ½ **Bouguereau** 2-9-0 0.. MichaelHills 4 73
(P W Chapple-Hyam) *unf: wl in rr and racd wd: shkn up and sme prog on outer fr over 2f out: nvr gng pce to rch ldrs* **5/1**[3]

8 ¾ **Summon Up Theblood** 2-9-0 0....................................... JHBowman 8 71
(M R Channon) *lengthy: tall: bit bkwd: prog fr rr to chse ldrs 3f out: rdn over 2f out: plugged on but n.d* **22/1**

9 ¾ **Dalhaan (USA)** 2-9-0 0.. MartinDwyer 9 69+
(J L Dunlop) *w'like: bit bkwd: s.s: wl in rr: shuffled along and styd on steadily fnl 2f on inner: nvr nrr* **66/1**

6 **10** *shd* **Aye Aye Digby (IRE)**[19] 3592 2-9-0 0............................. DaneO'Neill 10 69
(H Candy) *mostly in midfield: lost pl over 2f out and wl in rr: plugged on again fnl f* **33/1**

3 **11** ½ **Pha Mai Blue**[21] 3551 2-9-0 0... SebSanders 2 68
(W J Knight) *lw: wl in rr and racd wd: prog on outer 3f out: no imp 2f out: wknd over 1f out* **20/1**

12 *nk* **Oli James (USA)** 2-9-0 0.. TQuinn 3 67
(P F I Cole) *w'like: leggy: sn detached in last pair and rn green: no prog tl pushed along and r.o fr over 1f out* **40/1**

13 *nk* **Palmerin** 2-9-0 0... RyanMoore 5 66
(R Hannon) *w'like: a towards rr: shkn up and no real prog over 2f out* **25/1**

3 **14** ¾ **Cool Judgement (IRE)**[35] 3095 2-9-0 0.................... PhilipRobinson 20 64+
(M A Jarvis) *racd freely: led: hdd & wknd rapidly over 1f out* **9/2**[2]

00 **15** ½ **I Certainly May**[23] 3471 2-9-0 0..................................... PaulFitzsimons 11 63
(S Dow) *w'like: scope: bit bkwd: nvr bttr than midfield: u.p and no prog over 2f out: wknd over 1f out* **100/1**

0 **16** *hd* **Upton Grey (IRE)**[24] 3435 2-9-0 0................................ JimmyFortune 13 64+
(J H M Gosden) *cl up tl wknd rapidly wl over 1f out* **13/2**

17 *hd* **Maxwil** 2-9-0 0.. StephenDonohoe 18 62+
(G L Moore) *leggy: s.s: wl in rr: sme prog on inner after 3f: keeping on but no ch whn hmpd 1f out* **100/1**

18 9 **Bravo Bolivar (IRE)** 2-9-0 0.. TedDurcan 1 38+
(J L Dunlop) *w'like: bit bkwd: s.v.s: rn green and a t.o in last* **66/1**

1m 27.19s (-0.85) **Going Correction** -0.125s/f (Firm) **41** Ran SP% **132.0**
Speed ratings (Par 100): **99,98,97,97,96 95,94,93,92,92 92,91,91,90,90 89,89,79**
CSF £222.84 TOTE £45.30: £9.90, £2.60, £1.90; EX 386.50 Trifecta £938.90 Pool: £1,322.40 - 1.00 winning ticket..
Owner Noodles Racing **Bred** Car Colston Hall Stud **Trained** East Everleigh, Wilts

FOCUS
A decent maiden, run at a solid gallop. High draws dominated but the field finished in a heap and the form has not been rated as positively as it might have been, but several will prove better than the bare form.

NOTEBOOK
Latin Lad, a 42,000gns Hernando newcomer, is out of a 7f juvenile winner and should stay farther as he matures, so this was an excellent start to his career. Well drawn, he had enough speed to make this a winning debut, battling well under pressure, and there should be more to come. (op 50-1)
Belgrave Square(USA), a $400,000 son of the top-class juvenile Hennessy, is out of an unraced mare but her family history suggests he should settle down around a mile. Stepping up on his debut over 6f, he did not quite get there in time, but finding a maiden over this trip should be a formality before he goes on to better things. (op 8-1)
Missioner(USA) finished third again, but his first two runs have revealed plenty of ability, and he should be placed to win his maiden. (op 10-3 tchd 7-2)
Talayeb continues on a promising upward curve, and is close to winning in maiden company, though he will also be qualified for nurseries after one more run.
Craigstown ◆, a 130,000gns son of Cape Cross, is a full-brother to Castleton, successful over a mile as a three-year-old. However, he has winners in the family up to 1m4f, so even longer trips may be within his capabilities in due course, and this was an encouraging start to his career from an unhelpful draw. (op 12-1)
Alan Devonshire should have found this race tougher than the one in which he made his debut at Lingfield, but he handled the faster ground well and continues to show promise. (op 50-1)
Bouguereau, a 65,000gns Alhaarth colt, is a half-brother to five winners up to 1m2f. Shortish in the market for this debut, he did not quite live up to that billing from a poor draw, but this Royal Lodge and Derby entry should do better next time. (op 10-3 tchd 6-1)
Summon Up Theblood, a 47,000gns son of the speedy USA juvenile Red Ransom, lacks his natural pace but, being out of a mare who won over 1m2f, that is not surprising. He made a satisfactory debut, and should improve for the experience. (op 20-1)
Dalhaan(USA), a son of Kentucky Derby winner Fusaichi Pegasus, is out of a sister to the top-class Sakhee, so his pedigree is interesting to say the least. Unfancied for this debut, but sure to improve for trips beyond a mile next season, he made a pleasing first appearance here and is one to keep a close eye on.
Cool Judgement(IRE) set off too keenly and ran himself into the ground, but his debut run suggests he can do better. (tchd 4-1)

Upton Grey(IRE) looked fitter than he had done on his debut but still not did play any part in the finish. (op 9-1)

4152 BLUESQUAREPOKER.COM NURSERY STKS (H'CAP) 6f
5:05 (5:09) (Class 3) 2-Y-O £11,658 (£3,468; £1,733; £865) Stalls Low

Form RPR
4231 1 **Fol Hollow (IRE)**[26] 3370 2-8-9 82 AdrianTNicholls 6 88
(D Nicholls) *led after 2f: mde rest: drvn 2f out: hld on gamely fnl f* 20/1
422 2 hd **Atabaas Pride**[19] 3582 2-8-2 75 RoystonFfrench 13 80
(M Johnston) *outpcd in rr and rdn after 2f: prog 2f out: r.o to press wnr nr fin: nt qckn and jst hld* 6/1[2]
3100 3 2 **Waveline (USA)**[24] 3432 2-8-7 87 KMay[(7)] 10 86
(B J Meehan) *squeezed out s: off the pce in last trio: swtchd to nr side and stdy prog fr 2f out: styd on fnl f: nt rch ldng pair* 22/1
61 4 nk **Flawed Genius**[21] 3551 2-8-13 86 RyanMoore 11 87+
(Sir Michael Stoute) *squeezed out s: hld up in last trio and wl off the pce: prog 2f out: trying to cl whn hmpd 1f out: kpt on but nt rcvr* 3/1[1]
405 5 3/4 **Deal Flipper**[38] 2992 2-8-0 73 FrankieMcDonald 15 69
(P Winkworth) *settled in midfield: rdn 2f out: styd on ins fnl f: nt pce to chal* 28/1
41 6 nk **Dark Tara**[21] 3560 2-8-7 80 PaulHanagan 17 75
(R A Fahey) *wl in rr drvn and styd on fr 2f out on wd outside: nvr rchd ldrs* 8/1[3]
22 7 shd **Barraland**[9] 3867 2-7-12 78 ow2 MatthewDavies[(7)] 18 73
(M R Channon) *pressed ldrs tl wknd 1f out* 28/1
3224 8 1 1/4 **Maybe I Wont**[24] 3426 2-7-11 73 WilliamBuick[(3)] 16 64
(S Dow) *chsd ldrs: rdn over 2f out: wl in tch over 1f out: wknd fnl f* 16/1
0323 9 nk **Romany Princess (IRE)**[21] 3524 2-8-4 77 KerrinMcEvoy 5 67
(R Hannon) *trckd ldrs: wknd wl over 1f out* 11/1
5060 10 4 **Evenstorm (USA)**[3] 4065 2-7-7 71 oh4 NataliaGemelova[(5)] 3 49
(B Gubby) *w ldrs over 3f: wknd* 66/1
31 11 1 1/4 **Ten Meropa (USA)**[40] 2949 2-8-12 85 JimmyFortune 7 59
(J A Osborne) *sn wl in rr and nt gng wl: nvr a factor* 6/1[2]
100 12 nk **Monaazalah (IRE)**[22] 3508 2-8-11 84 RHills 14 57
(B W Hills) *swtg: hld up in rr: prog whn nt clr run wl over 1f out: no hdwy after: wknd fnl f* 12/1
1001 13 6 **Vhujon (IRE)**[21] 3550 2-9-7 94 (t) StephenDonohoe 1 49
(P D Evans) *swtg: led for 2f: lost pl sn after 1/2-way: moving sideways and wknd bdly fr over 1f out* 10/1
210 14 1 1/2 **King's Icon (IRE)**[23] 3459 2-8-12 85 MartinDwyer 9 36
(M P Tregoning) *lw: a wl in rr: u.p and no ch whn hmpd over 1f out* 12/1
0321 15 2 **Luscious Lips**[33] 3162 2-8-4 77 FrancisNorton 2 22
(R Hannon) *swtg: w ldrs to 1/2-way: wknd rapidly* 11/1
0012 U **Ocean Transit (IRE)**[21] 3550 2-7-7 71 LukeMorris[(5)] 12 —
(W G M Turner) *chsd ldrs to 1/2-way: no ch whn squeezed out, stmbld and uns rdr over 1f out* 33/1

1m 11.5s (-1.35) **Going Correction** -0.125s/f (Firm) **16** Ran SP% **132.1**
Speed ratings (Par 98): **104,103,101,100,99 99,99,97,97,91 90,89,81,79,77** —
CSF £138.47 CT £2747.72 TOTE £24.30: £3.80, £2.20, £4.40, £1.70; EX 161.10 TRIFECTA Not won..
Owner Dandy Nicholls Racing Club **Bred** Dan O'Brien **Trained** Sessay, N Yorks

FOCUS
A hot nursery, with a strong sprint pace down the hill, run in a good time. The winner has progressed and the form is solid.

NOTEBOOK
Fol Hollow(IRE) ◆, on his toes before the race and from a stable that has done well with its juveniles at this meeting in recent years, is effective at both 5f and 6f and handled the faster ground really well. Though only just scraping home, that should be good news for his handicap mark, since it is likely to keep him very competitive in nurseries for the time being. (op 22-1)
Atabaas Pride finished second for the third race in a row, but there is nothing wrong with his attitude, and a first victory is close at hand. (op 13-2)
Waveline(USA) never fully recovered from being hampered at the start, but she gave it a good shot, and continues to look useful in decent juvenile company. (op 33-1)
Flawed Genius had rotten luck in running, both at the start and entering the last furlong, and would have gone close with a more fluent passage. Though a winner over 7f last time, and lowered in distance here, he looks capable of landing a nice prize at either trip, but the additional furlong probably brings out the best in him. (op 7-2)
Deal Flipper was running in her first nursery, and did herself proud in a well above-average contest. She should stay 7f, and her mark is not far wrong unless the Handicapper over-reacts. (op 25-1)
Dark Tara struggled with the early pace on this faster ground, but cannot be said to have failed to act on it since she picked up pretty well in the final 2f. An extra furlong should suit.
Barraland has been running with credit in lesser company, and kept it up in this hotter race without being quite good enough.
Ten Meropa(USA) was never travelling, suggesting that the track was not ideal. Judged on two earlier efforts, he can do better. (tchd 13-2)
Vhujon(IRE) looked much better than this at Salisbury. Though conceding weight to these smart nursery types was never going to be easy, it was disappointing that he went out so feebly, with the track seeming to unbalance him. (op 9-1)

4153 BLUESQUARECASINO.COM APPRENTICE STKS (H'CAP) 1m 1f
5:40 (5:42) (Class 3) (0-90,90) 4-Y-O+ £9,715 (£2,890; £1,444; £721) Stalls High

Form RPR
0560 1 **Ace Of Hearts**[45] 2755 8-9-2 90 JackMitchell[(5)] 1 98
(C F Wall) *mde all: set stdy pce: kicked clr 3f out: drftd to centre of crse over 1f out: a holding on* 7/1[3]
0206 2 1 1/4 **Pagan Sword**[16] 3672 5-8-9 83 (p) KMay[(5)] 14 89
(Mrs A J Perrett) *dwlt: t.k.h: hld up in midfield: prog to chse wnr wl over 1f out: edgd lft and clsd fnl f: nvr able to chal* 7/1[3]
0133 3 hd **Peruvian Prince (USA)**[4] 4043 5-9-2 85 JamieMoriarty 4 90
(R A Fahey) *hld up in last pair: effrt on outer 3f out but plenty to do: r.o fr over 1f out: clsng on wnr fin but no ch to chal* 11/4[1]
6010 4 shd **Fort Churchill (IRE)**[4] 4043 6-9-6 89 (bt) StephenDonohoe 3 94
(B Ellison) *dwlt: hld up in last trio: prog on inner over 2f out: styd on fr over 1f out: nvr able to chal* 13/2[2]
0400 5 3 1/2 **Prince Samos (IRE)**[4] 4049 5-8-9 83 HarryPoulton[(5)] 13 80
(D Nicholls) *mostly chsd wnr to 3f out: sn outpcd: no imp after* 18/1
-030 6 1/2 **Hue**[20] 3577 6-7-13 75 oh3 ow4 LanceBetts[(7)] 10 71
(B Ellison) *hld up in rr: effrt on inner 3f out: outpcd over 2f out: no imp whn drifted lft 1f out* 33/1
0051 7 1 1/4 **Lucayan Dancer**[21] 3530 7-8-8 84 AdeleRothery[(7)] 6 77
(D Nicholls) *towards rr: bmpd along and no prog 3f out: taken to inner and plugging on one pce whn sltly hmpd 1f out* 8/1
6030 8 3/4 **St Andrews (IRE)**[24] 3437 7-8-12 88 MartinGuest[(7)] 8 80
(M A Jarvis) *lw: hld up towards rr: rdn over 2f out: one pce and no real prog* 14/1
315 9 nk **Final Tune (IRE)**[27] 3346 4-8-5 77 ow2 RussellKennemore[(3)] 5 68
(Miss M E Rowland) *t.k.h: pressed ldrs to over 2f out: wknd* 14/1
0620 10 shd **Langford**[58] 2401 7-8-10 82 PatrickHills[(3)] 9 73
(M H Tompkins) *lw: prom: chsd wnr 3f out to wl over 1f out: wknd u.p* 10/1
0110 11 hd **Logsdail**[38] 2986 7-8-6 75 (p) WilliamBuick 2 65
(G L Moore) *lw: cl up: rdn and no rspnse 3f out: struggling after: wknd over 1f out* 13/2[2]
4040 12 1 1/4 **Invention (USA)**[38] 3002 4-9-1 84 TravisBlock 11 72
(Miss E C Lavelle) *chsd ldrs: rdn over 3f out: sn struggling* 33/1

1m 56.15s (-0.71) **Going Correction** -0.125s/f (Firm) **12** Ran SP% **123.0**
Speed ratings (Par 107): **98,96,96,96,93 93,91,91,91,90 90,89**
CSF £57.63 CT £172.16 TOTE £9.50: £3.10, £2.80, £1.60; EX 70.00 Trifecta £226.50 Pool: £1,276.22 - 4.00 winning tickets. Place 6 £137.37, Place 5 £26.48.
Owner Archangels 1 **Bred** Whitsbury Manor Stud **Trained** Newmarket, Suffolk
■ Stewards' Enquiry : K May one-day ban: used whip with excessive frequency (Aug 15)

FOCUS
An above-average race of its type rated around the winner, third and fourth.

NOTEBOOK
Ace Of Hearts had slipped to a very fair mark, and this switch to apprentice level gave him the chance to outclass his rivals. Though drifting alarmingly left-handed in the final 2f, he found enough to hold on, and is clearly no back-number as long as he is taking on realistic opponents. (op 13-2 tchd 8-1)
Pagan Sword, on his toes before the race, seemed to perk up quite a bit in first-time cheekpieces, so they are worth trying again. He is close to a potentially winning mark if staying near his best. (op 8-1)
Peruvian Prince(USA) had run well when third over 1m2f here four days earlier, and this was another fine effort even though he was never quite arriving in time. He is in good form at present, even off a much higher mark than before his win at Haydock, and may yet defy the Handicapper, particularly over an extra furlong. (tchd 9-4 and 3-1)
Fort Churchill(IRE) is higher in the weights these days, so this was a decent run over a trip which is a bit on the sharp side for him. (op 6-1 tchd 7-1)
Prince Samos(IRE) has been below his best in recent races and, though this was much better than his run over a mile here four days earlier, it was nothing special. He is generally more effective on a flatter track. (op 20-1 tchd 16-1)
Hue has form over much longer trips, so this was not bad effort - which suggests he can be competitive again when stamina is more of an issue. (op 40-1 tchd 50-1)
Lucayan Dancer, raised 5lb for his win at Chester, is now 3lb above his highest winning mark - achieved when winning this race a year ago. (op 7-1)
T/Jkpt: Not won. T/Plt: £143.30 to a £1 stake. Pool: £271,345.66. 1,381.70 winning tickets. T/Qpdt: £9.40 to a £1 stake. Pool: £11,982.90. 939.10 winning tickets. JN

3673 HAMILTON (R-H)
Saturday, August 4

OFFICIAL GOING: Good to firm (good in places; 8.1)
Wind: Light across Weather: fine becoming overcast

4154 FRESH "N" LO AUCTION NURSERY 6f 5y
6:15 (6:16) (Class 4) 2-Y-O £3,886 (£1,156; £577; £288) Stalls Centre

Form RPR
5146 1 **Taurian**[21] 3550 2-9-7 80 TomEaves 5 84
(Mrs L Stubbs) *hld up in tch: rdn over 2f out: hdwy over 1f out: r.o u.p to ld wl ins fnl f* 5/1
4121 2 nk **Lady Benjamin**[22] 3499 2-8-12 71 LeeEnstone 2 74
(P C Haslam) *hmpd s: sn trcking ldrs: led over 1f out: sn rdn: hdd wl ins fnl f: kpt on* 3/1[2]
053 3 2 1/2 **Ezthegezza**[8] 3902 2-8-9 68 DaleGibson 3 64
(J S Moore) *hmpd s: in rr: stl last whn swtchd rt over 2f out: r.o u.p and edgd lft ins fnl f: nrst fin* 9/2[3]
6456 4 1 1/4 **Atephobia**[8] 3925 2-8-7 69 AndrewElliott[(3)] 6 61
(K R Burke) *chsd ldrs: pushed along 1/2-way: rdn and ev ch 2f out: kpt on same pce after* 16/1
004 5 2 **Tintorero**[24] 3424 2-8-2 64 AndrewMullen[(3)] 4 50
(M J Wallace) *slt ld: rdn and edgd lft wl over 1f out: sn hdd: one pce after* 25/1
604 6 1 **Rich James (IRE)**[28] 3297 2-8-7 66 DeanMcKeown 7 49
(J D Bethell) *in tch: pushed along fr 1/2-way: wknd fnl f* 14/1
01 7 3/4 **Bonny's Babe**[53] 2533 2-8-2 61 PaulEddery 8 42
(B Smart) *outpcd in rr: effrt 2f out: no real hdwy: eased fnl 100yds* 12/1
5045 8 nk **Thomas Malory (IRE)**[10] 3841 2-8-1 60 (b[1]) PaulFessey 10 40
(Miss V Haigh) *towards rr: hdwy 1/2-way: ev ch 2f out: sn hung rt and btn* 16/1
0015 9 3/4 **Gin Genereux**[29] 3256 2-8-9 71 GregFairley[(3)] 1 48+
(M Johnston) *wnt rt s: sn w ldr racing keenly: rdn over 2f out: hmpd wl over 1f out: nt rcvr and sn in rr* 5/2[1]

1m 11.91s (-1.19) **Going Correction** -0.25s/f (Firm) **9** Ran SP% **118.4**
Speed ratings (Par 96): **97,96,93,91,88 87,86,86,85**
CSF £20.97 CT £73.48 TOTE £6.90: £2.00, £1.50, £1.60; EX 28.90.
Owner Tyme Partnership **Bred** Angmering Park Stud **Trained** Norton, N. Yorks

FOCUS
An ordinary nursery run at decent pace.

NOTEBOOK
Taurian, on his nursery debut, had no problem with the stiff six furlongs and got up against the rail to collar the filly late on. Yet to race on anything other than fast ground, he has gained both his wins so far here. (op 11-2 tchd 6-1)
Lady Benjamin ran a fine race off a 4lb higher mark than when winning over course and distance last month, only succumbing late on to the winner's challenge.
Ezthegezza, a rare juvenile runner for his trainer here, finished ahead of tonight's winner Taurian at Salisbury two starts back. After being hampered leaving the stalls, he made solid late headway without troubling the first two. Official explanation: jockey said gelding suffered interference at start
Atephobia, dropped 2lb since his nursery debut, was under pressure some way out and did well to plug on for fourth. (op 12-1)
Tintorero showed plenty of pace on this nursery debut but could not get back into it once headed. Official explanation: jockey said colt hung left-handed throughout (op 20-1)

Gin Genereux went right leaving the stalls, hampering the eventual runner-up and third. After racing keenly up with the pace, he was already beginning to struggle when he was impeded shortly after the two pole. Official explanation: trainer said colt ran too free in early stages (op 7-2)

4155 VARIETY CLUB CLAIMING STKS 1m 65y
6:45 (6:47) (Class 6) 3-4-Y-0 **£2,388** (£705; £352) **Stalls** High

Form RPR

0100 **1** **Bold Indian (IRE)**[24] 3411 3-8-11 65 TomEaves 9 57
(I Semple) *hld up towards rr: rdn and hdwy fr 3f out: swtchd lft over 1f out: r.o to ld wl ins fnl f* **5/4**[1]

-060 **2** ½ **Terry Molloy (IRE)**[12] 3804 3-8-11 57 (v[1]) LeeEnstone 4 56
(K R Burke) *led: drvn fr 3f out: hdd and no ex wl ins fnl f* **6/1**[3]

-005 **3** 2 ½ **Bunderos (IRE)**[6] 4000 3-8-2 40 DaleGibson 3 41
(R A Fahey) *in tch: rdn 3f out: chsng ldrs whn n.m.r 2f out: styd on ins fnl f* **20/1**

4-00 **4** ½ **Strife (IRE)**[35] 3076 4-8-11 45 PJMcDonald(3) 6 45
(W M Brisbourne) *trckd ldrs: wnt 2nd 1/2-way: rdn and ev ch whn hung lft over 2f out: no ex fnl f* **25/1**

5100 **5** 2 ½ **Skye But N Ben**[19] 3587 3-8-9 61 (b) NeilBrown(5) 5 46
(T D Barron) *trckd ldr to 1/2-way: remained prom: drvn 3f out: one pce fnl 2f* **5/2**[2]

-050 **6** nk **Blue Madeira**[28] 3335 3-8-13 68 (p) PaulEddery 1 45
(Mrs L Stubbs) *hld up towards rr: rdn 4f out: sn lost tch w ldrs: styd on ins fnl f* **13/2**

7 10 **Roman Fun (IRE)**[62] 2278 3-9-0 0 PaulFessey 8 23
(I Semple) *in tch: rdn and outpcd by ldrs over 3f out: eased whn btn 1f out* **14/1**

0000 **8** 1 **Danehill Warrior (IRE)**[56] 2453 3-7-13 43 (p) CharlesEddery(7) 7 12
(R C Guest) *s.i.s: rdn 1/2-way: a bhd* **66/1**

1m 47.65s (-1.65) **Going Correction** -0.25s/f (Firm)
WFA 3 from 4yo 7lb **8 Ran SP% 117.4**
Speed ratings (Par 101): **98,97,95,94,92 91,81,80**
CSF £9.66 TOTE £2.40: £1.30, £1.80, £3.00; EX 10.30.
Owner R Hyndman **Bred** Dunderry Stud **Trained** Carluke, S Lanarks

FOCUS
This was run at a moderate pace. The runner-up looks the best guide to this ordinary claimer.

4156 MACGREGOR FLOORING COMPANY H'CAP 1m 3f 16y
7:15 (7:17) (Class 6) (0-60,60) 3-Y-0+ **£2,266** (£674; £337; £168) **Stalls** High

Form RPR

0410 **1** **Miss Havisham (IRE)**[19] 3587 3-8-6 **50** DeanMcKeown 3 56
(J R Weymes) *chsd ldrs: rdn to ld 2f out: idled u.p: jst hld on* **28/1**

6030 **2** nk **Intensifier (IRE)**[67] 2105 3-8-6 **50** GrahamGibbons 14 56
(P A Blockley) *chsd ldrs: reminders over 4f out: rdn over 2f out: r.o wl fnl 50yds: jst hld* **11/2**[2]

612 **3** nk **Red Chairman**[15] 3721 5-9-9 **60** (p) DuranFentiman(3) 2 65
(R Johnson) *led: rdn over 2f out: sn wandered and hdd: stl ev ch tl no ex fnl 100yds* **11/2**[2]

003 **4** ½ **Star Of Angels**[16] 3678 3-8-13 **60** GregFairley(3) 10 64
(M Johnston) *trckd ldr: rdn over 3f out: ev ch over 2f out: kpt on same pce ins fnl f* **7/1**

1504 **5** 1 ¾ **The Pen**[16] 3679 5-9-10 **58** PaulMulrennan 12 59
(C W Fairhurst) *in tch: rdn over 3f out: kpt on same pce fnl 2f* **10/3**[1]

6601 **6** nk **English Archer**[16] 3679 4-8-8 **49** DeanHeslop(7) 13 50
(W M Brisbourne) *hld up towards rr: rdn 3f out: styd on ins fnl f: nvr rchd ldrs* **7/1**

0050 **7** 2 **Playtotheaudience**[17] 3647 4-9-8 **56** DaleGibson 9 53
(R A Fahey) *towards rr: rdn 3f out: styd on ins fnl f: nvr nr ldrs* **20/1**

04 **8** 1 ¼ **Quicuyo (GER)**[16] 3678 4-8-11 **48** PJMcDonald(3) 15 43
(P Monteith) *in rr: effrt over 3f out: sme late hdwy* **40/1**

-000 **9** 2 ½ **One And Gone (IRE)**[32] 3181 3-8-6 **50** (p) PaulFessey 4 41
(R A Fahey) *a towards rr* **28/1**

006 **10** ½ **My Causeway Dream (IRE)**[40] 2935 4-8-12 **46** oh1 (v) PaulQuinn 8 36
(J S Wainwright) *in rr: effrt over 3f out: nvr nr ldrs* **66/1**

135 **11** ½ **Zabeel Tower**[11] 3816 4-9-5 **53** PaddyAspell 6 42
(R Allan) *in tch: clsd over 4f out: rdn over 2f out: wknd over 1f out* **17/2**

0-50 **12** ¾ **Forsters Plantin**[18] 3611 3-8-2 **46** oh1 PaulEddery 5 34
(J J Quinn) *in rr of midfield: rdn 4f out: no hdwy* **66/1**

4544 **13** 2 **Volaticus (IRE)**[11] 3815 6-9-6 **54** (b[1]) TomEaves 11 39
(A D Brown) *racd keenly early: trckd ldrs: rdn 3f out: wknd 2f out* **6/1**[3]

5600 **14** 25 **Dream On Dreamers (IRE)**[7] 3956 3-7-9 **46** oh1.(p) CharlesEddery(7) 1 —
(R C Guest) *towards rr: lost tch 3f out: t.o* **66/1**

2m 23.78s (-2.48) **Going Correction** -0.25s/f (Firm)
WFA 3 from 4yo+ 10lb **14 Ran SP% 122.2**
Speed ratings (Par 101): **99,98,98,98,96 96,95,94,92,92 91,91,89,71**
CSF £172.52 CT £997.66 TOTE £32.40: £6.80, £2.70, £2.30; EX 301.50.
Owner High Moor Racing 1 **Bred** Downfield Cottage Stud **Trained** Middleham Moor, N Yorks

FOCUS
A moderate handicap, and sound form for the grade.

4157 RADIO CLYDE MAIDEN STKS 6f 5y
7:45 (7:48) (Class 5) 3-Y-0+ **£2,914** (£867; £433; £216) **Stalls** Centre

Form RPR

20-5 **1** **Luck Will Come (IRE)**[24] 3425 3-8-12 60 PatCosgrave 13 57
(M J Wallace) *trckd ldrs: led appr fnl f: drvn out* **13/2**[3]

5355 **2** hd **Angel Voices (IRE)**[23] 3474 4-9-2 57 PaulMulrennan 14 57
(K R Burke) *cl up: ev ch 2f out: r.o u.p: jst hld* **4/1**[2]

533 **3** nk **Lempicka**[21] 3537 3-8-12 59 GrahamGibbons 11 55
(J J Quinn) *in tch: rdn 2f out: chsd ldrs over 1f out: unable qck wl ins fnl f* **7/2**[1]

0360 **4** nk **Newkeylets**[37] 3017 4-8-11 49 NeilBrown(5) 1 55
(I Semple) *slt ld: hdd appr fnl f: kpt on u.p* **12/1**

2332 **5** ½ **Howards Tipple**[21] 3537 3-9-3 64 (p) TomEaves 9 57+
(I Semple) *hld up bhd ldrs: shkn up 2f out: short of room appr fnl f: unable qck fnl 100yds* **7/2**[1]

6 1 ½ **Tyrannosaurus Rex (IRE)** 3-9-3 0 LeeEnstone 4 53+
(K R Burke) *s.i.s: towards rr: pushed along over 2f out: keeping on towards fin* **28/1**

0 **7** hd **White's Ruby**[28] 3302 3-8-12 0 PaulEddery 8 47
(B Smart) *in tch: rdn over 2f out: sn one pce* **22/1**

602 **8** 3 **Julian Joachim (USA)**[6] 4000 3-9-3 0 DeanMcKeown 6 42
(G A Swinbank) *chsd ldrs: rdn over 2f out: sn wknd* **7/2**[1]

-000 **9** 2 ½ **Compton Lad**[12] 3782 4-9-4 41 PJMcDonald(3) 10 35
(D A Nolan) *hld up towards rr: effrt over 2f out: wknd over 1f out* **150/1**

000/ **10** 22 **Lexicon**[657] 5924 7-8-13 19 GregFairley(3) 5 —
(Mrs J C McGregor) *chsd ldrs: rdn 3f out: sn struggling and lost tch: t.o* **100/1**

11 6 **Newgate Parisien** 4-9-4 0 AndrewMullen(3) 3 —
(Mark Campion) *v.s.a: a bhd: t.o* **100/1**

1m 11.89s (-1.21) **Going Correction** -0.25s/f (Firm)
WFA 3 from 4yo+ 4lb **11 Ran SP% 118.1**
Speed ratings (Par 103): **98,97,97,96,96 94,94,90,86,57 49**
CSF £32.10 TOTE £6.00: £2.30, £1.80, £2.10; EX 30.40.
Owner Greenstead Hall Racing **Bred** Mull Enterprises Ltd **Trained** Newmarket, Suffolk

FOCUS
A modest maiden in which they came stands'-side. The principals finished in a heap and the form has been rated through the fourth.

Howards Tipple Official explanation: jockey said gelding was denied a clear run

Newgate Parisien Official explanation: jockey said gelding missed the break

4158 EUROPEAN BREEDERS' FUND FILLIES' H'CAP 5f 4y
8:15 (8:16) (Class 4) (0-85,75) 3-Y-0+ **£6,477** (£1,927; £963; £481) **Stalls** Centre

Form RPR

1230 **1** **Rothesay Dancer**[8] 3920 4-8-3 **61** KellyHarrison(7) 9 71
(J S Goldie) *midfield: clsd to trck ldrs 1/2-way: swtchd rt ins fnl f: r.o wl to ld nr fin* **9/2**[2]

6265 **2** ½ **Darcy's Pride (IRE)**[17] 3637 3-8-12 **69** AndrewMullen(3) 3 76
(D W Barker) *chsd ldrs: rdn to ld 1f out: hdd and unable qck nr fin* **8/1**

0206 **3** 2 **Ashes (IRE)**[12] 3782 5-8-10 **61** PaulMulrennan 11 62
(K R Burke) *walked to post: narrow ld tl hdd 1f out: kpt on same pce* **6/1**[3]

0363 **4** ½ **Princess Ellis**[13] 3763 3-8-5 **59** DaleGibson 12 57
(E J Alston) *cl up on outside: rdn and ev ch over 1f out: unable qck ins fnl f* **6/1**[3]

0000 **5** ¾ **Vondova**[2] 4101 5-8-8 **62** oh6 ow6 PJMcDonald(3) 4 59
(D A Nolan) *cl up: rdn and sltly outpcd by ldrs 2f out: kpt on ins fnl f* **28/1**

3200 **6** hd **La Vecchia Scuola (IRE)**[7] 3954 3-8-2 **59** (v) DuranFentiman(3) 10 54
(R Johnson) *chsd ldrs: rdn 2f out: kpt on same pce* **12/1**

-104 **7** shd **Controvento (IRE)**[2] 4103 5-9-7 **72** (b) PatCosgrave 2 67
(Eamon Tyrrell, Ire) *chsd ldrs: pushed along 2f out: kpt on same pce* **7/1**

3265 **8** ¾ **Coconut Moon**[15] 3720 5-9-3 **75** GaryBartley(7) 6 70+
(E J Alston) *sn towards rr: effrt over 2f out: no imp on ldrs* **7/2**[1]

3616 **9** 1 ¾ **Feelin Foxy**[22] 3493 3-9-5 **73** (v) DeanMcKeown 7 58
(D Shaw) *s.s: towards rr: n.m.r wl over 1f out: sn shkn up and no imp* **20/1**

4401 **10** ½ **Morristown Music (IRE)**[36] 3054 3-9-0 **68** PaddyAspell 5 52
(J S Wainwright) *a towards rr* **12/1**

2460 **11** hd **Aye Aye Definitely (IRE)**[12] 3784 3-9-3 **71** TonyHamilton 8 54
(R A Fahey) *rdn over 2f out: a towards rr* **12/1**

59.24 secs (-1.96) **Going Correction** -0.25s/f (Firm)
WFA 3 from 4yo+ 3lb **11 Ran SP% 123.9**
Speed ratings (Par 102): **105,104,101,100,99 98,98,97,94,93 93**
CSF £42.95 CT £229.23 TOTE £4.80: £1.90, £4.00, £2.70; EX 63.60.
Owner Highland Racing **Bred** Frank Brady **Trained** Uplawmoor, E Renfrews

FOCUS
Pretty modest form, but sound enough despite the proximity of the fifth.

4159 LA BONNE AUBERGE H'CAP (QUALIFIER FOR THE HAMILTON PARK TOTEPOOL HANDICAP SERIES FINAL) 1m 1f 36y
8:45 (8:45) (Class 5) (0-75,72) 3-Y-0+ **£3,238** (£963; £481; £240) **Stalls** High

Form RPR

-455 **1** **Greyfriars Abbey**[6] 3997 3-8-5 **60** GregFairley(3) 9 76+
(M Johnston) *s.i.s: in rr: last whn rdn over 4f out: gd hdwy on outer fr 3f out: led wl over 1f out: sn rdn clr: eased towards fin* **7/2**[2]

3100 **2** 3 ½ **Regent's Secret (USA)**[11] 3813 7-10-0 **72** (p) DanielTudhope 6 81+
(J S Goldie) *hld up: hdwy over 2f out: wnt 2nd ent fnl f: eased whn no ch w wnr fnl 75yds* **2/1**[1]

4030 **3** 1 ¾ **Hawkit (USA)**[12] 3783 6-9-6 **64** DaleGibson 10 69
(P Monteith) *towards rr: rdn over 2f out: styd on wl ins fnl f: no ch w first two* **20/1**

44-4 **4** ¾ **Sarraaf (IRE)**[21] 3539 11-9-0 **58** TomEaves 8 61
(I Semple) *hld up in rr: shkn up over 2f out: styd on ins fnl f: nvr trbld ldrs* **16/1**

6220 **5** shd **Mandarin Rocket (IRE)**[16] 3675 4-8-9 **53** oh1 PaulMulrennan 2 56
(Miss L A Perratt) *trckd ldrs: rdn and ev ch over 2f out: sn one pce* **25/1**

-426 **6** nk **Barbirolli**[8] 3907 5-9-8 **66** PatCosgrave 5 69
(W M Brisbourne) *in tch: rdn over 3f out: styd on same pce fnl 2f* **9/1**

5254 **7** 1 ¼ **Mystical Ayr (IRE)**[12] 3783 5-8-12 **59** PJMcDonald(3) 11 59
(Miss L A Perratt) *trckd ldrs: rdn to take slt ld over 2f out: hdd wl over 1f out: wknd ins fnl f* **7/1**

0016 **8** ¾ **Best Of The Lot (USA)**[36] 3049 5-9-7 **65** TonyHamilton 4 63
(R A Fahey) *midfield: rdn 3f out: no imp whn n.m.r 1f out* **6/1**[3]

3403 **9** 3 ½ **Anthemion (IRE)**[11] 3816 10-8-8 **55** AndrewMullen(3) 7 46
(Mrs J C McGregor) *led: rdn over 3f out: hdd over 2f out: steadily wknd: eased fnl 100yds* **14/1**

0101 **10** 2 **Ignition**[16] 3675 5-9-2 **60** GrahamGibbons 3 47
(W M Brisbourne) *trckd ldrs: drvn over 3f out: wknd over 1f out* **8/1**

1m 56.67s (-2.99) **Going Correction** -0.25s/f (Firm)
WFA 3 from 4yo+ 8lb **10 Ran SP% 124.6**
Speed ratings (Par 103): **103,99,98,97,97 97,96,95,92,90**
CSF £11.78 CT £129.03 TOTE £5.10: £1.90, £1.60, £3.40; EX 13.50 Place 6 £55.37, Place 5 £30.02.
Owner Greyfriars And White Rose Poultry **Bred** Itchen Valley Stud **Trained** Middleham Moor, N Yorks

FOCUS
Not a strong race but the form seems sound enough. The principals came from the rear. Big improvement from the winner, who is on the upgrade.

Anthemion(IRE) Official explanation: jockey said gelding had a breathing problem

T/Plt: £93.00 to a £1 stake. Pool: £57,029.25. 447.35 winning tickets. T/Qpdt: £26.30 to a £1 stake. Pool: £3,809.30. 107.10 winning tickets. RL

The Form Book, Raceform Ltd, Compton, RG20 6NL

3945 LINGFIELD (L-H)
Saturday, August 4

OFFICIAL GOING: All-weather - standard; turf course - good to firm
Races on turf course hand-timed.
Wind: Modest behind

4160 EUROPEAN BREEDERS' FUND LOGIKA CHARTERED ACCOUNTANTS MAIDEN STKS 5f (P)
5:55 (6:00) (Class 5) 2-Y-O £3,238 (£963; £481; £240) Stalls High

Form RPR
23 1 **Carolina Belle (USA)**[56] 2457 2-8-12 0 JamieSpencer 4 75+
(M J Wallace) *mde all: gng clr whn hung rt wl over 1f out: in n.d fnl f* **4/7**[1]
64 2 4 **Splash The Cash**[35] 3085 2-9-3 0 StephenCarson 6 66
(P Winkworth) *sn pressing wnr: rdn whn sltly hmpd 2f out: sn outpcd by wnr: kpt on* **6/1**[2]
3 nk **Captain Kir (IRE)** 2-9-3 0 AdamKirby 8 65
(B De Haan) *in tch: hdwy to chse ldng pair over 2f out: rdn 2f out: kpt on but no ch w wnr* **14/1**
30 4 3 **Katrina Bee (IRE)**[38] 2997 2-8-12 0 RichardSmith 5 49
(R Hannon) *chsd ldrs tl rdn and outpcd over 2f out: no ch after* **7/1**[3]
5 ¾ **Sir Joey** 2-9-3 0 SamHitchcott 2 51
(J T Stimpson) *in tch: rdn and outpcd over 2f out: kpt on fnl f* **33/1**
6 1 ¼ **Whitcombe Flyer (USA)** 2-9-3 0 (t) JohnEgan 10 47
(Jamie Poulton) *s.i.s: in tch: hdwy to chse ldng trio over 2f out: sn rdn wknd over 1f out* **14/1**
00 7 11 **High Standing (USA)**[11] 3823 2-9-3 0 VinceSlattery 9 7
(N A Callaghan) *sn totally outpcd: t.o fr 1/2-way* **40/1**
8 6 **Newcastle Sam** 2-9-0 0 MarcHalford(3) 3 —
(J J Bridger) *sn hopelessly outpcd: t.o after 2f* **33/1**

59.40 secs (-0.38) **Going Correction** -0.175s/f (Stan) 8 Ran SP% **112.1**
Speed ratings (Par 94): **96,89,89,84,83 81,63,53**
CSF £4.05 TOTE £1.40: £1.02, £1.40, £4.40; EX 3.40.
Owner Plantation Stud **Bred** H Sarkowsky **Trained** Newmarket, Suffolk
■ Joss Stick (14/1) and Klarity (20/1) were withdrawn on vet's advice. Rule 4, deduct 5p in the £.

FOCUS
An ordinary maiden that seemed to be run at a fair tempo. The form is rated through the runner-up and the winner should go on from this.

NOTEBOOK
Carolina Belle(USA) got off the mark with an easy success. The only blemish on the performance was the way she drifted to the middle of the course in the latter stages, but that may have been due to inexperience and she could be capable of better still. (op 8-13 tchd 8-11 in places)
Splash The Cash tried to go with the winner in the early stages but was brushed aside when that rival went for home. However, he has shown more than enough already to suggest he will be winning a race before long. (op 7-1 tchd 11-2)
Captain Kir(IRE), a son of rookie sire Captain Rio, never looked like winning but put up an encouraging performance on his debut. He seemed to know his job well and created a favourable impression, travelling smoothly and keeping on for pressure. Another furlong should prove to be within his reach. (tchd 16-1)
Katrina Bee(IRE) now looks ready for a step up to six furlongs and possibly nursery company. (tchd 8-1)
Sir Joey does not look devoid of ability but was much too green on his debut to make an impact. (op 40-1)
Whitcombe Flyer(USA), wearing a tongue tie for his debut, looked in need of the experience and failed to see out the trip. With the run behind him, he could be capable of better. (op 12-1)

4161 BET NOW AT WBX.COM H'CAP 1m 2f (P)
6:30 (6:31) (Class 6) (0-55,60) 3-Y-O+ £2,047 (£604; £302) Stalls Low

Form RPR
4346 1 **Trevian**[12] 3805 6-9-2 51 AmirQuinn 11 60
(J M Bradley) *hld up in midfield: smooth hdwy over 3f out: chal over 2f out: led over 1f out: rdr dropped whip 1f out: pushed out* **8/1**
0402 2 nk **Ciccone**[12] 3805 4-9-6 55 FergusSweeney 9 63
(G L Moore) *w.w towards rr: rdn and hdwy 3f out: chsd ldng pair over 2f out: styd on: wnt 2nd towards fin: nt quite rch wnr* **11/2**[2]
0631 3 1 **Hansomelle (IRE)**[7] 3950 5-9-8 60 (p) NeilChalmers(3) 13 66
(Miss Sheena West) *chsd ldrs: rdn and hdwy wl over 3f out: led 3f out: hdd over 1f out: unable qckn last 100yds* **13/2**[3]
2000 4 2 ½ **King Of Knight (IRE)**[24] 3419 6-8-10 52 CharlotteKerton(7) 5 53
(G Prodromou) *hld up towards rr: short of room over 2f out: hdwy wl over 1f out: kpt on fnl f: nvr nrr* **20/1**
6034 5 hd **The City Kid (IRE)**[15] 3714 4-9-6 55 (v) JamieSpencer 8 56
(C R Dore) *hld up: hdwy on outer 3f out: drvn to chse ldng trio over 2f out: no imp after* **7/1**
-400 6 2 **Chapter (IRE)**[52] 2582 5-9-2 51 (b) SebSanders 2 48
(Mrs A L M King) *hld up in midfield: rdn over 2f out: kpt on same pce after* **11/1**
3166 7 1 **Oasis Sun (IRE)**[166] 495 4-8-12 47 DaneO'Neill 4 42
(J R Best) *hld up towards rr: hdwy over 3f out: rdn over 2f out: no imp last 2f* **14/1**
0460 8 nk **Hallings Overture (USA)**[31] 3217 8-9-5 54 JohnEgan 7 48+
(C A Horgan) *dropped in after s: hld up in rr: nt clr run over 2f out tl 2f out: weaved through and sme late hdwy: no ch* **10/3**[1]
1005 9 1 ¾ **Don Pasquale**[12] 3805 5-9-6 55 ChrisCatlin 1 46
(J T Stimpson) *stdd s: hld up in last: rdn and effrt 3f out: n.d* **12/1**
2006 10 ¾ **Bowl Of Cherries**[24] 3419 4-9-2 51 (b) AdamKirby 12 40
(I A Wood) *led for 2f: styd prom: rdn over 3f out: wknd over 2f out* **9/1**
4061 11 2 ½ **Orpen Quest (IRE)**[9] 3868 5-9-5 54 AlanDaly 6 38
(M J Attwater) *w.w in midfield: lost pl and rdn over 3f out: no ch after* **14/1**
06-0 12 ¾ **Gnillah**[7] 3950 4-8-8 50 JemmaMarshall(7) 3 33
(B R Johnson) *t.k.h: chsd ldrs tl rdn and wknd wl over 2f out* **50/1**
5000 13 2 **Wally Barge**[10] 3847 4-8-6 48 ChrisHough(7) 14 27
(D K Ivory) *chsd ldrs: wnt 2nd 7f out: led 5f out tl hdd 3f out: sn wknd* **33/1**
0400 14 6 **Valart**[27] 3352 4-9-2 51 (tp) SimonWhitworth 10 18
(A J Lidderdale) *t.k.h: w ldr tl led after 2f: hdd 5f out: wknd 3f out: eased fnl f* **25/1**

2m 6.51s (-1.28) **Going Correction** -0.175s/f (Stan) 14 Ran SP% **129.4**
Speed ratings (Par 101): **98,97,96,94,94 93,92,92,90,90 88,87,85,81**
CSF £53.70 CT £318.49 TOTE £10.30: £3.20, £2.50, £2.50; EX 43.70.
Owner Folly Road Racing Partners (1996) **Bred** L A C Ashby **Trained** Sedbury, Gloucs

FOCUS
A moderate handicap. The form is probably sound for the grade, but most of these rarely win.

4162 BEN MILLS MEDIAN AUCTION MAIDEN STKS 7f 140y
7:00 (7:03) (Class 6) 2-Y-O £2,730 (£806; £403) Stalls Centre

Form RPR
3332 1 **Al Muheer (IRE)**[22] 3508 2-9-3 96 SebSanders 8 94+
(C E Brittain) *mde all on stands' rail: pushed along over 1f out: readily: eased nr fin* **2/5**[1]
0 2 1 ½ **Nezami (IRE)**[9] 3866 2-9-3 0 NCallan 12 88
(B J Meehan) *trckd ldrs: chsd wnr wl over 2f out: rdn and tried to chal over 1f out: no ex last 100yds* **15/2**[2]
3 6 **Princess Lomi (IRE)** 2-8-12 0 ChrisCatlin 11 69+
(E J O'Neill) *sn outpcd in rr: hdwy 2f out: wnt modest 3rd over 1f out: no ch w ldng pair* **12/1**[3]
0 4 5 **Zen Factor**[36] 3043 2-9-3 0 VinceSlattery 9 63
(J G Portman) *wnt rt s: sn chsd wnr tl wl over 2f out: sn wknd* **66/1**
6 5 ¾ **Bozeman Trail**[25] 3404 2-9-3 0 SamHitchcott 5 61
(M R Channon) *racd in midfield: drvn over 3f out: no ch w ldrs after* **12/1**[3]
6 1 **Judgethemoment (USA)** 2-9-3 0 JohnEgan 3 59
(Jane Chapple-Hyam) *in tch in midfield: rdn and hdwy over 2f out: sn hanging lft and no hdwy* **25/1**
7 nk **Okafranca (IRE)** 2-9-3 0 RichardMullen 10 58
(W R Muir) *in tch in midfield: rdn and lost pl over 3f out: no ch after* **33/1**
04 8 ½ **Rosy Dawn**[23] 3446 2-8-12 0 DaneO'Neill 4 52
(H J L Dunlop) *outpcd in rr and rdn 5f out: no ch after* **25/1**
00 9 nk **Danamight (IRE)**[12] 3796 2-8-12 0 NeilPollard 1 51
(G G Margarson) *wnt bdly lft s: hld up and bhd: sme hdwy over 3f out: sn rdn and struggling* **33/1**
6030 10 5 **Bellalatino (IRE)**[7] 3938 2-8-12 59 StephenCarson 6 39
(Mrs Norma Pook) *prom tl rdn and wknd qckly over 2f out* **25/1**
0 11 5 **Aneebee (IRE)**[31] 3213 2-8-12 0 RichardSmith 7 27
(R Hannon) *s.i.s: a bhd: no ch fr 1/2-way: eased fnl f* **25/1**
0 12 17 **Bagenalstown (IRE)**[8] 3915 2-9-3 0 AdamKirby 2 —
(M Wellings) *v.s.a: a wl bhd: t.o fr 1/2-way* **66/1**

1m 28.7s (-2.76) **Going Correction** -0.525s/f (Hard) 2y crse rec 12 Ran SP% **122.8**
Speed ratings (Par 92): **92,90,84,79,78 77,77,76,76,71 66,49**
CSF £3.43 TOTE £1.40: £1.02, £1.90, £3.20; EX 4.60.
Owner Saeed Manana **Bred** Foursome Thoroughbreds **Trained** Newmarket, Suffolk

FOCUS
The winner had already proved himself to be useful and had the advantage of the rail, that proved an asset all night on the straight course. The first four home were closest to the rail throughout and the form may not be as good as it appears. The time was quick, although it should be noted all races on turf were fast.

NOTEBOOK
Al Muheer(IRE) grabbed the favoured rail on the night and was not troubled to win easily. With an important victory now under his belt, the trainer is sure to have grand plans for him, as is often the case, although he has no fancy entries at the moment. (op 4-9 tchd 4-11 and 1-2 in a place)
Nezami(IRE) ran really well and looked a danger to the winner until well inside the two-furlong pole. The way he finished clear of the third suggests he stays 7f, although he should not be inconvenienced if dropped to 6f next time. He ought to be winning soon. (op 13-2 tchd 8-1)
Princess Lomi(IRE) ◆ looked green for much of the race, but really picked up well at the furlong pole to easily win the race for third. She definitely needs 7f at least, and can pick up an ordinary affair next time, especially if kept to races against her own sex. (op 10-1 tchd 9-1)
Zen Factor chased the leaders until about the 2f marker but failed to get home under pressure. He looks a big sort and may need time to strengthen up. (op 100-1)
Bozeman Trail was given a fairly hard ride but never got on terms. He was the first to finish of those who stayed towards the middle of the track, but is another in the field who may need more time. (op 16-1)
Judgethemoment(USA) was readily left behind and did not help his cause by hanging into the middle of the course under pressure. There was a little bit of promise in his effort but he will need to progress to have any chance next time. (op 20-1 tchd 16-1)
Bagenalstown(IRE) Official explanation: jockey said colt had no more to give

4163 LAUREN-JAIE IS 21 TOMORROW H'CAP 7f
7:30 (7:32) (Class 5) (0-75,75) 3-Y-O £2,817 (£838; £418; £209) Stalls High

Form RPR
-100 1 **Nadawat (USA)**[42] 2881 3-9-6 74 SebSanders 4 87+
(J L Dunlop) *hld up and steadily worked way across to stands' rail: hdwy jst over 2f out: led wl over 1f out: sn clr: easily* **7/2**[1]
3-6 2 5 **Ficoma**[77] 1837 3-9-7 75 AdamKirby 6 74
(C G Cox) *hld up in tch: hdwy and nt clr run briefly 2f out: sn swtchd rt and rdn: r.o fnl f to go 2nd last 100yds: no ch w wnr* **5/1**[3]
0-50 3 1 ½ **Bluebelle Dancer (IRE)**[69] 2061 3-8-11 65 RichardMullen 8 60
(W R Muir) *t.k.h: trckd ldrs: hdwy to ld 2f out: sn hdd and hung lft u.p: no ch w wnr after: lost 2nd last 100yds* **9/1**
0020 4 1 **The Skerret**[30] 3237 3-8-5 59 PaulDoe 2 51
(P Winkworth) *awkward leaving stalls: hld up and bhd: hdwy on outer over 2f out: chsd ldrs and drvn 2f out: kpt on same pce* **25/1**
1054 5 2 **Shake On It**[51] 2598 3-9-6 74 (t) StephenCarson 1 61
(Eve Johnson Houghton) *prom: ev ch and rdn over 2f out: sn btn* **7/2**[1]
0-56 6 hd **Swift Cut (IRE)**[57] 2425 3-9-2 70 EddieAhern 3 56
(A P Jarvis) *hld up wl in tch: rdn and wknd jst over 2f out* **4/1**[2]
0066 7 8 **Lordswood (IRE)**[22] 3483 3-7-11 56 oh4 NataliaGemelova(5) 7 21
(J J Bridger) *stdd s: t.k.h: hld up in rr: rdn and struggling 1/2-way: sn no ch* **25/1**
0120 8 1 **Nashharry (IRE)**[33] 3168 3-8-9 63 JohnEgan 5 25
(S Kirk) *w ldr tl 1/2-way: sn rdn and dropped out: no ch last 2f* **16/1**
4236 9 shd **Racing Times**[106] 1117 3-9-2 70 DaneO'Neill 9 32
(W J Knight) *hung lft thrght: led tl 2f out: immediately btn and eased* **7/1**
5-40 10 8 **Pont Wood**[30] 3237 3-8-6 60 ChrisCatlin 10 —
(M Blanshard) *a wl bhd: lost tch 1/2-way: t.o last 2f* **40/1**

1m 21.0s (-3.21) **Going Correction** -0.525s/f (Hard) 10 Ran SP% **119.6**
Speed ratings (Par 100): **97,91,89,88,86 85,76,75,75,66**
CSF £21.42 CT £148.30 TOTE £4.50: £1.60, £2.40, £2.40; EX 26.10.
Owner Hamdan Al Maktoum **Bred** Shadwell Farm LLC **Trained** Arundel, W Sussex

FOCUS
A fair handicap with the winner much improved and the form is best rated through the runner-up.
Racing Times Official explanation: jockey said gelding hung left throughout

4164 WBX.COM WORLD BET EXCHANGE MAIDEN STKS 6f
8:00 (8:02) (Class 5) 3-Y-O+ £2,817 (£838; £418; £209) Stalls High

Form RPR
5-53 1 **Millisecond**[17] 3649 3-8-12 72 NCallan 3 59
(M A Jarvis) *led and sn crossed to stands' rail: hdd 4f out: led again over 2f out: rdn wl over 1f out: jst hld on* **11/8**[2]

40 **2** *shd* **Fleuret**48 2693 3-8-12 0 StephenCarson 7 59+
(Eve Johnson Houghton) *taken down early: stdd s: t.k.h: hld up in rr: rdn and hdwy over 2f out: r.o wl u.p fnl f: wnt 2nd towards fin: jst failed* **14/1**

20-0 **3** *¾* **Laura's Best (IRE)**8 3914 3-8-12 63 EddieAhern 11 57+
(W J Haggas) *hld up wl bhd: swtchd lft and hdwy over 2f out: r.o to dispute 2nd ins fnl f: no ex last 50yds* **15/2**3

0020 **4** *1 ¼* **Batchworth Fleur**26 3388 4-9-2 50 LPKeniry 6 53
(E A Wheeler) *racd in midfield: hdwy over 2f out: kpt on u.p to chse wnr briefly ins fnl f: kpt on* **40/1**

2 **5** *2 ½* **Sweetsformysweet (USA)**25 3395 3-8-12 0 SebSanders 1 46
(J Noseda) *sn pressing ldrs: chsd wnr and rdn 2f out: no imp and hung rt: wknd ins fnl f* **5/4**1

3000 **6** *2* **Early Promise (IRE)**36 3066 3-8-12 57 JimCrowley 8 40
(Mrs A L M King) *stdd s: wl bhd tl modest late hdwy* **20/1**

-000 **7** *hd* **Mostanad**184 320 5-9-7 40 (p) AmirQuinn 9 44
(R A Harris) *chsd ldrs for 2f: lost pl and rdn 1/2-way: hung lft and no prog after* **50/1**

050 **8** *¾* **Canary Girl**33 3163 4-9-2 41 (v) TGMcLaughlin 5 37
(Mrs C A Dunnett) *s.i.s: nvr on terms* **100/1**

-606 **9** *¾* **Master Malarkey**11 3829 4-9-7 43 (b) ChrisCatlin 2 39
(Mrs C A Dunnett) *prom: led 4f out tl over 2f out: sn rdn: wknd over 1f out* **66/1**

0000 **10** *¾* **She's Dunnett**46 2748 4-9-2 40 (t) JohnEgan 4 32
(Mrs C A Dunnett) *nvr trbld ldrs: rdn and no ch fr 1/2-way* **50/1**

-000 **11** *25* **Brief Engagement (IRE)**36 3046 4-9-2 35 EdwardCreighton 10 —
(T D McCarthy) *chsd ldrs for 1f: sn struggling: no ch fr 1/2-way: t.o* **100/1**

69.30 secs (-2.37) **Going Correction** -0.525s/f (Hard)
WFA 3 from 4yo+ 4lb **11** Ran SP% **119.6**
Speed ratings (Par 103): **94,93,92,91,87 85,84,83,82,81 48**
CSF £20.46 TOTE £3.10: £1.10, £3.30, £1.90; EX 19.50.
Owner Helena Springfield Ltd **Bred** Meon Valley Stud **Trained** Newmarket, Suffolk

FOCUS
The stands' rail had it again, but only just. The fourth appeared to run up to her best, so could be the marker for the race.
Sweetsformysweet(USA) Official explanation: jockey said filly hung right

4165 LOGIKA CHARTERED ACCOUNTANTS H'CAP 6f
8:30 (8:31) (Class 6) (0-65,69) 3-Y-0+ **£2,047** (£604; £302) **Stalls** High

Form RPR
044 **1** **Reigning Monarch (USA)**8 3905 4-9-2 **52** SamHitchcott 14 61+
(Miss Z C Davison) *wnt rt s: wl bhd: hdwy and hmpd twice over 2f out: str run on stands' rail over 1f out: led last 100yds: r.o strly* **25/1**

0044 **2** *1 ¼* **Young Bertie**24 3422 4-9-9 **62** (v) TravisBlock(3) 6 67
(H Morrison) *chsd ldrs: rdn and lost pl over 3f out: rallied over 2f out: ev ch over 1f out: nt pce of wnr nr fin* **6/1**2

0022 **3** *shd* **Make My Dream**18 3612 4-9-10 **60** JimCrowley 4 65
(J Gallagher) *in tch: rdn and hdwy over 2f out: ev ch over 1f out: unable to qckn last 100yds* **16/1**

-111 **4** *nk* **Cativo Cavallino**106 1118 4-9-6 **61** NataliaGemelova(5) 2 65
(J E Long) *bhd on outer: pushed along after 2f: hdwy over 2f out: led narrowly over 1f out: hdd last 100yds: no ex and lost 2 pls nr fin* **8/1**

5004 **5** *nk* **Convivial Spirit**54 2518 3-9-8 **62** (t) SebSanders 17 64
(E F Vaughan) *sn wl outpcd in rr: hdwy on stands' rail over 1f out: r.o wl: nt rch ldrs* **11/1**

54 **6** *nk* **Strut The Stage (IRE)**18 3612 3-9-11 **65** PaulFitzsimons 15 66
(B W Duke) *bmpd s: hld up wl in tch: chal 2f out: rdn and edgd lft over 1f out: fdd ins fnl f* **33/1**

000 **7** *1 ¾* **Littledodayno (IRE)**57 2418 4-9-8 **58** NickyMackay 7 55
(M Wigham) *s.i.s: hld up: hdwy jst over 2f out: rdn and no imp over 1f out* **9/4**1

0041 **8** *nk* **Support Fund (IRE)**18 3612 3-9-11 **65** StephenCarson 10 60
(Eve Johnson Houghton) *chsd ldrs for 1f: sn rdn and outpcd: kpt on fnl f: n.d* **25/1**

5430 **9** *1 ¾* **Turkish Sultan (IRE)**8 3906 4-9-2 **57** (p) KevinGhunowa(5) 11 48
(J M Bradley) *sn rdn in rr: n.d* **14/1**

0043 **10** *¾* **Registrar**11 3829 5-9-7 **57** JohnEgan 13 46
(Mrs C A Dunnett) *trckd ldrs: effrt and short of room briefly jst over 2f out: sn wknd* **13/2**3

2021 **11** *½* **Silver Prelude**18 3627 6-9-10 **60** NCallan 9 47
(D K Ivory) *prom: led gng wl 2f out: hdd over 1f out: wknd qckly* **6/1**2

3205 **12** *5* **Beat The Bully**9 3875 3-9-3 **57** LPKeniry 5 28
(I A Wood) *chsd ldrs tl 1/2-way: sn rdn and struggling: no ch last 2f* **50/1**

000- **13** *6* **Clearing Sky (IRE)**242 6713 6-9-6 **56** MatthewHenry 12 10
(J R Boyle) *led tl 2f out: sn dropped out: eased ins fnl f* **33/1**

40U **14** *3* **Trinculo (IRE)**26 3368 10-9-5 **55** (b) AmirQuinn 16 —
(R A Harris) *w ldrs: rdn and wkng whn hung lft and rt over 2f out: eased ins fnl f* **12/1**

69.70 secs (-1.97) **Going Correction** -0.525s/f (Hard)
WFA 3 from 4yo+ 4lb **14** Ran SP% **127.9**
Speed ratings (Par 101): **92,90,90,89,89 89,86,86,83,82 82,75,67,63**
CSF £172.61 CT £2598.03 TOTE £44.10: £9.20, £2.70, £2.90; EX 227.50 Place 6 £62.43, Place 5 £51.30 .
Owner John Belsey **Bred** High Creek Farm **Trained** Hammerwood, E Sussex

FOCUS
A modest event run at a good pace. The form looks reasonably sound for the grade.
Registrar Official explanation: trainer said gelding was unsuited by the fast ground
T/Plt: £112.60 to a £1 stake. Pool: £53,459.35. 346.30 winning tickets. T/Qpdt: £43.10 to a £1 stake. Pool: £3,997.20. 68.50 winning tickets. SP

4130 NEWMARKET (JULY) (R-H)
Saturday, August 4

OFFICIAL GOING: Good to firm (9.4)
Wind: Fresh, across Weather: Sunny

4166 HSS HIRE H'CAP 1m 2f
2:25 (2:26) (Class 3) (0-90,91) 3-Y-0+ **£9,067** (£2,697; £1,348; £673) **Stalls** Centre

Form RPR
142 **1** **Pathos (GER)**15 3709 3-8-9 **83** MarcHalford(3) 5 91+
(D R C Elsworth) *hld up: hdwy 1/2-way: led over 3f out: hung rt over 1f out: drvn out* **7/2**2

21-5 **2** *¾* **Galactic Star**8 3899 4-9-7 **83** J-PGuillambert 2 90+
(Sir Michael Stoute) *trckd ldrs: plld hrd: rdn over 2f out: styd on* **11/2**

1066 **3** *nk* **Torrens (IRE)**7 3978 5-8-9 **78** JamesRogers(7) 4 84
(R A Fahey) *hld up: hdwy over 1f out: styd on* **22/1**

30/5 **4** *1 ¾* **Mutawassel (USA)**38 3002 6-10-0 **90** RichardHughes 9 93
(B W Hills) *hld up in tch: rdn over 2f out: no imp fnl f* **14/1**

6-64 **5** *nk* **Manchurian**7 3960 3-9-3 **88** LPKeniry 1 90
(M J Wallace) *hld up: hdwy over 6f out: rdn and ev ch over 1f out: wknd ins fnl f* **16/1**

21-3 **6** *nk* **Seabow (USA)**9 3882 4-10-0 **90** (t) LDettori 3 91
(Saeed Bin Suroor) *led 8f out: hdd over 3f out: rdn whn nt clr run over 1f out: wknd ins fnl f* **9/4**1

2130 **7** *1* **Cedar Mountain (IRE)**42 2859 4-9-12 **88** RobertHavlin 11 87+
(J H M Gosden) *led: hdd 8f out: rdn over 2f out: wknd fnl f* **4/1**3

0-01 **8** *1 ¼* **Archiestown (USA)**15 3711 4-8-13 **75** KDarley 8 72
(J L Dunlop) *chsd ldrs: rdn over 2f out: wknd fnl f* **12/1**

6000 **9** *nk* **Folio (IRE)**21 3558 7-9-9 **85** TPO'Shea 6 81
(W J Musson) *hld up: rdn over 2f out: wknd fnl f* **40/1**

1123 **10** *½* **Froissee**10 3855 3-8-6 **77** NickyMackay 7 72
(N A Callaghan) *hld up: rdn over 1f out: wknd fnl f* **16/1**

2m 5.72s (-0.72) **Going Correction** -0.15s/f (Firm)
WFA 3 from 4yo+ 9lb **10** Ran SP% **121.3**
Speed ratings (Par 107): **96,95,95,93,93 93,92,91,91,90**
CSF £24.32 CT £378.54 TOTE £4.40: £1.80, £2.00, £4.70; EX 27.00 Trifecta £214.60 Part won. Pool: £302.30 - 0.50 winning tickets..
Owner Richard Green & Matthew Green **Bred** K Nercessian **Trained** Newmarket, Suffolk
■ Stewards' Enquiry : Marc Halford one-day ban: careless riding (Aug 15)

FOCUS
Not a bad handicap, best rated through Torrens, who was back to form on his favoured surface and backed up by the fifth.

NOTEBOOK
Pathos(GER) appreciated the quicker ground and shrugged off a 4lb higher mark for getting beaten here last time to confirm his progressive profile. He won a shade comfortably and this big gelding is the type to keep a step ahead of the Handicapper. (op 4-1 tchd 10-3)
Galactic Star, who had done all his previous racing on soft ground, coped with these quicker conditions well, but he did not help his chance by failing to settle. He ought to get further. Official explanation: jockey said colt ran too free (tchd 13-2)
Torrens(IRE) appreciated the return to a decent surface and lost nothing in defeat to a couple of less-exposed rivals. (op 20-1 tchd 25-1)
Mutawassel(USA), who stays a bit further than this, ran a better race on his favoured quicker ground despite not getting the clearest of runs. (tchd 12-1)
Manchurian did not see the trip out as well as some on his first start over 1m2f. (op 12-1)
Seabow(USA) may have found the ground too fast as he enjoyed the run of the race and can have no excuse on that score. (op 3-1)
Cedar Mountain(IRE) was another to disappoint despite seemingly having conditions in his favour. (op 11-2)
Archiestown(USA) was another found out by the distance. He will appreciate dropping back to a mile. (op 10-1 tchd 9-1)

4167 HSS.COM EBF CONDITIONS STKS 1m
3:00 (3:00) (Class 2) 4-Y-0+ **£12,464** (£3,732; £1,866; £934; £466) **Stalls** Low

Form RPR
3544 **1** **Final Verse**35 3103 4-8-9 102 LPKeniry 3 109
(J S Moore) *hld up: plld hrd: hdwy over 2f out: rdn: hung rt and led 1f out: r.o* **4/1**3

-300 **2** *2* **Metropolitan Man**35 3098 4-8-9 104 RichardHughes 6 104
(D M Simcock) *trckd ldr: racd keenly: rdn 2f out: edgd rt: hmpd and struck over hd by rivals whip 1f out: styd on same pce* **15/8**2

1200 **3** *1 ½* **Count Trevisio (IRE)**45 2755 4-8-9 100 LDettori 2 101
(Saeed Bin Suroor) *led: rdn and hung rt fr over 1f out: hdd 1f out: no ex* **6/4**1

520/ **4** *3 ½* **Troubadour (IRE)**262 6-8-9 95 SteveDrowne 4 93
(W Jarvis) *chsd ldrs: rdn over 2f out: edgd rt and wknd over 1f out* **17/2**

1006 **5** *8* **Kew Green (USA)**59 2368 9-9-4 94 J-PGuillambert 5 84
(P R Webber) *hld up: rdn and wknd over 2f out* **25/1**

1m 37.79s (-2.64) **Going Correction** -0.25s/f (Firm) **5** Ran SP% **109.2**
Speed ratings (Par 109): **103,101,99,96,88**
CSF £11.72 TOTE £4.30: £2.20, £1.40; EX 10.40.
Owner Mrs Fitri Hay **Bred** A Christodoulou **Trained** Upper Lambourn, Berks

FOCUS
A conditions event featuring a number of horses with question marks next to their names. The form is ordinary for the grade, rated around the winner and third.

NOTEBOOK
Final Verse has spent most of his career running on good ground or softer, but his two highest RPRs have been achieved on his only previous two starts on good to firm ground, namely his sixth in last year's 2000 Guineas and third to Manduro in this year's Earl of Sefton Stakes. That sort of form gave him strong claims in this grade and he won cosily enough in the end, despite hanging right over to the stands' rail in the closing stages. (op 10-3 tchd 9-2)
Metropolitan Man only beat one home in a Group 3 race here last time out, but he was not beaten far and this quicker ground looked sure to suit him. He ran well enough but the winner has that bit more class. (tchd 13-8)
Count Trevisio(IRE), who finished down the field in the Hunt Cup last time out, likes to make the running and in this small field it was always possible that he would be able to nick it from the front. In the event he did get the run of the race, but was unable to capitalise on it. Like one or two others in this field, he is a difficult horse to place. Official explanation: jockey said colt hung right (op 2-1)
Troubadour(IRE), who won a Listed race for Aidan O'Brien three years ago, has since paid his way as a successful handicapper in Hong Kong. Making his debut for his new stable and having his first outing since November, he was entitled to need the run. (op 8-1 tchd 9-1)
Kew Green(USA), who has not shown much lately, needs easier ground than this to be seen at his best. Official explanation: jockey said gelding ran too free to post (op 20-1)

4168 UNICORN ASSET MANAGEMENT JULY COURSE SERIES NURSERY (QUALIFIER) 6f
3:35 (3:35) (Class 2) 2-Y-0 **£12,954** (£3,854; £1,444; £1,444) **Stalls** Low

Form RPR
61 **1** **Johar Jamal (IRE)**72 1960 2-8-5 **77** TPO'Shea 9 84+
(M R Channon) *hld up: nt clr run over 1f out: r.o to ld wl ins fnl f* **5/1**2

135 **2** *1 ¼* **Rubirosa (IRE)**25 3398 2-8-10 **82** SteveDrowne 3 85
(M Dods) *dwlt: hld up: hdwy over 1f out: rdn to ld ins fnl f: sn edgd lft: hdd and unable qckn* **8/1**

341 **3** *1* **Bosun Breese**50 2630 2-8-7 **79** LPKeniry 4 79
(P W D'Arcy) *disp ld tl rdn over 1f out: styd on* **10/1**

1150 **3** *dht* **Cracking (IRE)**44 2785 2-9-7 **93** RichardHughes 6 93
(R Hannon) *disp ld tl rdn and hdd over 1f out: edgd rt: styd on* **8/1**

6211 **5** *shd* **Cosmic Art**8 3925 2-9-7 **93** LDettori 5 93
(E A L Dunlop) *trckd ldrs: led over 1f out: rdn and hdd ins fnl f: no ex towards fin* **15/8**1

2614 **6** *1 ½* **Charlotti Carlotti (IRE)**22 3499 2-8-6 **78** KDarley 8 73
(T D Barron) *chsd ldrs: rdn over 2f out: hung rt over 1f out: no ex* **7/1**3

10 **7** *hd* **Just Sort It**[80] 1772 2-8-10 **85** LiamJones(3) 7 80
(W Jarvis) *trckd ldrs: racd keenly: rdn over 1f out: styd on same pce* **25/1**

053 **8** *nk* **Fidelias Dance**[17] 3648 2-8-2 **74** NickyMackay 1 68
(M Johnston) *mid-div: pushed along: hdwy 2f out: sn rdn and ev ch: no ex ins fnl f* **11/1**

2010 **9** *1 1/2* **Presto Levanter**[29] 3269 2-8-1 **73** JimmyQuinn 2 62
(R Hannon) *chsd ldrs: rdn over 2f out: ev ch over 1f out: wknd ins fnl f* **8/1**

1m 12.27s (-1.08) **Going Correction** -0.25s/f (Firm) **9** Ran SP% **118.6**
Speed ratings (Par 100): **97,95,94,94,93 91,91,91,89**WIN: Johar Jamal £6.30. PL: JJ £1.80, Rubirosa £2.20, Cracking £1.40, Bosun Breese £1.70. EX: £52.30. CSF: £45.77. TRIC: JJ/R/C £160.92. JJ/R/BB £196.62. TRIF: JJ/R/C & JJ/R/BB £149.30 - Pool: £420.60 - 0.20 winning tickets. £294.42 c/f to Saturday TOTE £0.0027: £Owner, £Jaber Abdullah, £Bred, £Tally-Ho StudTrained West Ilsley, Berks.

FOCUS
A competitive nursery run at a fair pace. There is more to come from the impressive winner and the form looks pretty sound.

NOTEBOOK
Johar Jamal(IRE), last seen winning her maiden at Goodwood in May, had clearly improved since. She travelled well off the pace and quickened up really well when she hit the rising ground to win quite easily in the end. She can score again in this sphere, but connections have one eye on the upcoming valuable sales races. (op 4-1)
Rubirosa(IRE), whose fifth on his nursery debut was solid form, found the winner much too classy in the end but he beat the rest well enough and his performance is probably a fair guide to how good the race was. The faster ground was certainly no hindrance to him. (op 10-1)
Bosun Breese, who made every yard to win his maiden at Sandown, did not get such an easy time of it up front on this occasion. He got the furlong longer trip well, though. (op 10-1 tchd 11-1)
Cracking(IRE), a creditable fifth in Listed company two starts back before being outclassed at Royal Ascot, appreciated the drop in grade, but 5f probably suits him best. (op 10-1 tchd 11-1)
Cosmic Art is a speedy individual but he had an 11lb higher mark to overcome compared with Wolverhampton last time and both that and the stiff finish at this track were against him. He will be more effective back over a sharper 6f. (op 2-1 tchd 9-4)
Charlotti Carlotti(IRE), racing on fast ground for the first time, was a bit disappointing, once again failing to see out the trip. (op 8-1)

4169 STEVE LAMBERT 40TH BIRTHDAY EBF MAIDEN FILLIES' STKS 7f
4:05 (4:06) (Class 4) 2-Y-0 **£4,533** (£1,348; £674; £336) **Stalls** Low

Form RPR

1 **Sense Of Joy** 2-9-0 0 RichardHughes 2 100+
(J H M Gosden) *wnt rt s: sn trcking ldrs: led over 1f out: edgd rt and rdn clr fnl f* **6/1**[2]

0 **2** *5* **Presbyterian Nun (IRE)**[15] 3706 2-9-0 0 J-PGuillambert 6 85
(J L Dunlop) *chsd ldrs: rdn over 2f out: styd on same pce appr fnl f* **25/1**

3 *1* **Zeu Tin Tin (IRE)** 2-9-0 0 LPKeniry 11 82
(R A Kvisla) *hld up: rdn and hung lft over 2f out: hdwy and hung rt over 1f out: styd on same pce* **50/1**

3 **4** *2 1/2* **Dream Sea**[17] 3643 2-9-0 0 TPO'Shea 1 76
(M R Channon) *chsd ldr: rdn to ld over 2f out: hdd over 1f out: wknd fnl f* **7/1**[3]

0226 **5** *1 3/4* **Pixie's Blue (IRE)**[45] 2768 2-9-0 78 RobertHavlin 5 71
(J H M Gosden) *led over 4f: rdn and wknd over 1f out* **8/1**

6 *3 1/2* **Ruby Light** 2-9-0 0 KDarley 9 62
(Sir Michael Stoute) *hld up: rdn over 2f out: sn wknd* **8/1**

7 *3* **Siyasa (USA)** 2-9-0 0 LDettori 4 54
(Saeed Bin Suroor) *hmpd s: hld up: hdwy over 2f out: sn wknd and eased* **10/11**[1]

0 **8** *nk* **Miss Delila (USA)**[15] 3706 2-9-0 0 JimmyQuinn 7 53
(K A Ryan) *hld up: rdn and wknd 1/2-way* **40/1**

9 *1/2* **Blue Rhapsody** 2-9-0 0 NickyMackay 10 52
(L M Cumani) *hld up: rdn over 2f out: sn wknd* **20/1**

10 *hd* **Tamdiid (USA)** 2-8-9 0 AhmedAjtebi(5) 8 52
(C E Brittain) *chsd ldrs over 4f* **33/1**

1m 24.67s (-2.11) **Going Correction** -0.25s/f (Firm) **10** Ran SP% **117.3**
Speed ratings (Par 93): **102,96,95,92,90 86,82,82,81,81**
CSF £145.07 TOTE £8.20: £1.80, £4.30, £13.50; EX 135.50.
Owner K Abdulla **Bred** Juddmonte Farms Ltd **Trained** Newmarket, Suffolk

FOCUS
A fair maiden on paper and a very impressive performance from the winner backed up by a decent time.

NOTEBOOK
Sense Of Joy, a half-sister to Day Flight, a high-class multiple winner over middle distances, made a highly impressive winning debut. She cruised through the race and picked up well when asked to go and assert, lengthening well when she hit the rising ground. It is open to debate what she beat, but it was a visually taking performance and it comes as no surprise that connections are aiming high with her. She will apparently have one more run and then go to Ascot for the Fillies' Mile. (op 11-2 tchd 5-1)
Presbyterian Nun(IRE), a half-sister to Jedburgh, a multiple 7f winner, In Disguise, a triple middle-distance winner, and Impresonator, a 7f winner at two, won the separate race for second, showing plenty of improvement from her debut. She looks one for nurseries after one more run. (op 20-1)
Zeu Tin Tin(IRE), whose dam was quite a useful 7f winner at two, shaped with promise, staying on quite well despite showing signs of greenness. She should improve.
Dream Sea, who shaped with encouragment on her debut on Polytrack, was towards the fore for much of the race but, like the rest, had no answer when the impressive winner kicked clear. She is another who could make her mark in nursery company after one more run. (tchd 15-2)
Pixie's Blue(IRE), who has an official rating of 78 and was the most experienced in the line-up, again failed to get home. 6f might suit her better at this stage of her career. (tchd 15-2)
Ruby Light, who cost 125,000gns, is a half-sister to Persian Jasmine, a 7f winner at two, and Banjo Patterson, a triple 6f/7f winner at three. She should improve for this debut but might be the type that needs more time. (op 11-1 tchd 15-2)
Siyasa(USA), a sister to top-class multiple middle distance performer Fantastic Light, was sent off a short-priced favourite on her debut, but she proved very disappointing. She was hampered at the start, which could be an excuse though, and is likely to leave this effort behind in time. (op 4-5 tchd Evens)

4170 HALF MOON MONTEGO BAY JAMAICA H'CAP 7f
4:40 (4:40) (Class 4) (0-85,84) 3-Y-0 **£5,181** (£1,541; £770; £384) **Stalls** Low

Form RPR

121 **1** **Big Noise**[35] 3099 3-9-1 **76** RichardHughes 1 89+
(Dr J D Scargill) *hld up: hdwy over 2f out: led over 1f out: shkn up and r.o wl* **7/2**[2]

-322 **2** *2 1/2* **Spriggan**[64] 2196 3-9-2 **77** KDarley 3 81
(C G Cox) *led: rdn and hdd over 1f out: edgd lft: styd on same pce* **14/1**

2-31 **3** *nk* **Flying Goose (IRE)**[23] 3447 3-9-6 **81** NickyMackay 4 84
(L M Cumani) *chsd ldrs: rdn and ev ch over 1f out: hung lft: styd on same pce* **4/1**[3]

4024 **4** *1/2* **Lunces Lad (IRE)**[15] 3707 3-9-6 **81** TPO'Shea 8 82
(M R Channon) *s.i.s: hld up: r.o ins fnl f: nrst fin* **11/1**

2213 **5** *1/2* **Classira (IRE)**[14] 3745 3-9-3 **78** LDettori 5 78
(M A Jarvis) *hld up: hdwy and nt clr run over 1f out: no ex ins fnl f* **5/2**[1]

2-10 **6** *1* **Zonta Zitkala**[21] 3555 3-8-13 **74** J-PGuillambert 11 71
(R M Beckett) *s.i.s: hld up: rdn over 1f out: n.d* **25/1**

32-3 **7** *3/4* **Baylini**[8] 3900 3-9-9 **84** JamesDoyle 9 79
(Ms J S Doyle) *prom: chsd ldr 3f out: rdn and ev ch 2f out: wknd fnl f* **14/1**

-155 **8** *2 1/2* **Keidas (FR)**[12] 3798 3-8-8 **72** LiamJones(3) 2 61
(C F Wall) *chsd ldr 4f: sn rdn: wknd fnl f* **14/1**

031 **9** *3/4* **Satyricon**[53] 2534 3-9-1 **76** (v) JimmyQuinn 7 63
(M Botti) *hld up: rdn over 2f out: wknd over 1f out* **8/1**

4000 **10** *2 1/2* **Leg Sweep**[35] 3099 3-7-13 **67** TobyAtkinson(7) 6 47
(D R C Elsworth) *trckd ldrs: plld hrd: wknd 2f out* **40/1**

1m 25.03s (-1.75) **Going Correction** -0.25s/f (Firm) **10** Ran SP% **116.5**
Speed ratings (Par 102): **100,97,96,96,95 94,93,90,89,87**
CSF £51.63 CT £184.75 TOTE £3.80: £1.50, £3.80, £1.70; EX 51.50.
Owner Theme Tune Partnership **Bred** F B B White **Trained** Newmarket, Suffolk

FOCUS
A fairly open handicap for three-year-olds and pretty solid form rated around the third, fourth and fifth.

4171 MAXJET H'CAP 1m 4f
5:15 (5:15) (Class 4) (0-85,85) 4-Y-0+ **£5,181** (£1,541; £770; £384) **Stalls** Centre

Form RPR

0-06 **1** **Invasian (IRE)**[8] 3899 6-9-7 **83** (e) RobertHavlin 8 92
(P W D'Arcy) *mde all: rdn over 1f out: styd on wl* **20/1**

320- **2** *1 3/4* **Shore Thing (IRE)**[318] 5479 4-8-9 **71** RichardHughes 9 77
(C R Egerton) *chsd ldrs: outpcd over 2f out: rallied over 1f out: r.o* **5/2**[1]

4406 **3** *3/4* **Sgt Schultz (IRE)**[7] 3959 4-9-4 **80** LPKeniry 3 85
(J S Moore) *hld up: hdwy over 2f out: rdn to chse wnr over 1f out: styd on same pce* **12/1**

10-6 **4** *1/2* **Chocolate Caramel (USA)**[10] 3844 5-9-6 **82** JamesDoyle 2 86
(Mrs A J Perrett) *mid-div: lost pl over 4f out: nt clr run over 1f out: r.o ins fnl f* **22/1**

4000 **5** *3/4* **Eva Soneva So Fast (IRE)**[22] 3509 5-9-6 **82** J-PGuillambert 6 86+
(J L Dunlop) *mid-div: effrt and hmpd over 2f out and over 1f out: nt clr run ins fnl f: swtchd lft: r.o: nvr able to chal* **8/1**[3]

0005 **6** *1* **Sienna Storm (IRE)**[35] 3105 4-9-6 **82** JimmyQuinn 12 83
(M H Tompkins) *chsd wnr tl rdn over 1f out: hung rt and wknd ins fnl f* **20/1**

0023 **7** *2 1/2* **Love Always**[16] 3692 5-8-10 **72** KDarley 1 69
(S Dow) *hld up: hdwy over 2f out: sn rdn: wknd fnl f* **10/1**

-630 **8** *2 1/2* **Top Spec (IRE)**[16] 3671 6-8-7 **72** LiamJones(3) 11 65
(J Pearce) *s.i.s: hld up: hdwy over 2f out: wknd over 1f out* **16/1**

6-46 **9** *4* **Solo Flight**[166] 501 10-9-4 **80** SteveDrowne 5 67
(H Morrison) *hld up: rdn over 1f out: n.d* **12/1**

-512 **10** *nk* **Crossbow Creek**[16] 3671 9-9-9 **85** LDettori 7 72
(M G Rimell) *hld up in tch: rdn and hung rt fr over 2f out: wknd over 1f out* **5/2**[1]

0604 **11** *3* **Nelsons Column (IRE)**[14] 3753 4-9-1 **77** NickyMackay 4 59
(G M Moore) *chsd ldrs: rdn over 3f out: wkng whn hmpd over 1f out* **7/1**[2]

2m 29.61s (-3.30) **Going Correction** -0.15s/f (Firm) **11** Ran SP% **125.0**
Speed ratings (Par 105): **105,103,103,103,102 101,100,98,95,95 93**
CSF £72.36 CT £672.07 TOTE £37.00: £8.70, £1.70, £3.40; EX 286.50.
Owner Dr K Sanderson **Bred** Dr Karen Monica Sanderson **Trained** Newmarket, Suffolk

FOCUS
A fairly ordinary handicap dominated from start to finish by Invasian but pretty sound rated around the third and fifth.
Chocolate Caramel(USA) Official explanation: jockey said gelding was denied a clear run
Crossbow Creek Official explanation: jockey said gelding ran too free

4172 HSS HIRE 08457 282828 H'CAP 1m 4f
5:50 (5:51) (Class 5) (0-70,69) 3-Y-0 **£3,886** (£1,156; £577; £288) **Stalls** Centre

Form RPR

0444 **1** **Tifernati**[7] 3964 3-9-3 **66** LiamJones(3) 14 72
(W J Haggas) *hld up: hdwy 2f out: swtchd lft over 1f out: rdn to ld ins fnl f: r.o* **2/1**[1]

064 **2** *1 1/4* **Esclarmonde (IRE)**[26] 3366 3-9-5 **65** NickyMackay 13 69
(L M Cumani) *chsd ldrs: rdn over 2f out: ev ch and edgd rt over 1f out: styd on same pce* **10/1**

5-14 **3** *1/2* **Abounding**[33] 3170 3-9-4 **64** GeorgeBaker 3 67
(R M Beckett) *s.i.s: hld up: hdwy over 3f out: led over 2f out: rdn and hung rt over 1f out: hdd and no ex ins fnl f* **13/2**[2]

2605 **4** *1 1/4* **Mowadeh (IRE)**[10] 3848 3-9-7 **67** TPO'Shea 7 68
(M R Channon) *hld up: outpcd over 3f out: hdwy u.p fr over 1f out: nt rch ldrs* **18/1**

0000 **5** *hd* **Cavalry Twill (IRE)**[51] 2602 3-9-5 **65** (b1) RichardHughes 8 66
(P F I Cole) *chsd ldr: led 3f out: rdn and hdd over 2f out: no ex ins fnl f* **28/1**

0-00 **6** *1 1/4* **Double Banded (IRE)**[17] 3652 3-8-7 **53** LPKeniry 12 55+
(J L Dunlop) *hld up in tch: rdn over 2f out: hmpd 1f out: no ex* **14/1**

4200 **7** *5* **Sonara (IRE)**[11] 3825 3-9-3 **63** JimmyQuinn 10 54
(M H Tompkins) *hld up: nvr nrr* **7/1**[3]

0-40 **8** *nk* **Dangerous Dancer (IRE)**[51] 2597 3-9-5 **65** SteveDrowne 5 56
(R Charlton) *mid-div: hdwy over 4f out: rdn and wknd over 1f out* **9/1**

5204 **9** *1 1/4* **Kindlelight Blue (IRE)**[23] 3456 3-9-9 **69** (e) JamesDoyle 15 58
(N P Littmoden) *chsd ldrs 10f* **16/1**

0500 **10** *9* **Composing (IRE)**[18] 3624 3-9-2 **62** (t) RobertHavlin 6 36
(H Morrison) *chsd ldrs: rdn over 2f out: wknd over 1f out* **22/1**

060 **11** *6* **Present**[24] 3421 3-8-5 **51** oh4 ow1 (v1) JosedeSouza 9 16
(D Morris) *led over 8f: wknd over 2f out* **50/1**

4-40 **12** *7* **Hurricane Thomas (IRE)**[15] 3722 3-9-8 **68** KDarley 1 21
(M Johnston) *hld up: hdwy 1/2-way: wknd wl over 1f out* **9/1**

006 **13** *hd* **Moonfinder (IRE)**[39] 2970 3-8-10 **56** J-PGuillambert 11 9
(J L Dunlop) *chsd ldrs 8f* **22/1**

-404 **14** *nk* **The Wily Woodcock**[50] 2635 3-9-5 **65** EdwardCreighton 2 18
(G Wragg) *hld up: rdn 1/2-way: wknd over 3f out* **10/1**

-000 **15** *3/4* **Best Warning**[51] 2610 3-7-11 **50** oh5 (v1) FrankiePickard(7) 4 1
(J Ryan) *hld up: rdn and wknd 4f out* **80/1**

2m 31.57s (-1.34) **Going Correction** -0.15s/f (Firm) **15** Ran SP% **130.5**
Speed ratings (Par 100): **98,97,96,96,95 95,91,91,90,84 80,76,75,75,75**
CSF £23.74 CT £124.32 TOTE £2.80: £1.40, £4.60, £2.50; EX 33.50 Place 6 £410.30, Place 5 £162.55..
Owner Johnny Townsend **Bred** Miss S N Ralphs **Trained** Newmarket, Suffolk
■ Stewards' Enquiry : George Baker three-day ban: careless riding (Aug 15-17)

FOCUS
Modest handicap form, and not solid enough with the time moderate.
Moonfinder(IRE) Official explanation: jockey said filly was unsuited by the good to firm ground
The Wily Woodcock Official explanation: trainer said colt finished lame
T/Plt: £1,019.10 to a £1 stake. Pool: £98,914.40. 70.85 winning tickets. T/Qpdt: £352.20 to a £1 stake. Pool: £3,998.00. 8.40 winning tickets. CR

4136 THIRSK (L-H)
Saturday, August 4

OFFICIAL GOING: Good to firm (firm in places; 10.8)
The ground had dried out appreciably and was described as 'very firm'.
Wind: Moderate, half-behind Weather: Fine

4173 EUROPEAN BREEDERS' FUND MAIDEN STKS (DIV I) 5f
1:30 (1:31) (Class 4) 2-Y-O **£4,533** (£1,348; £674; £336) **Stalls** High

Form RPR
030 **1** **Hadaf (IRE)**[26] 3363 2-9-3 78 TPQueally 6 80
(M P Tregoning) *cl up: effrt to chal over 2f out: rdn to ld over 1f out: styd on* 11/4[2]
5 **2** ½ **Red Wings (IRE)**[11] 3812 2-8-12 0 PatCosgrave 9 73
(G A Swinbank) *led: rdn along 2f out: drvn and hdd over 1f out: kpt on u.p ins fnl f* 9/1
04 **3** 2 **Piscean (USA)**[19] 3589 2-9-3 0 DaleGibson 2 71
(T Keddy) *dwlt and hmpd s: sn rdn along in rr: hdwy on outer over 2f out: styd on u.p ent fnl f: nrst fin* 5/2[1]
4 ½ **My Kaiser Chief** 2-9-0 0 AndrewMullen(3) 8 69
(W J H Ratcliffe) *wnt rt s and towards rr: gd hdwy on inner 2f out: rdn and kpt on wl appr fnl f* 16/1
5 **5** 1½ **El Tato**[71] 1992 2-9-3 0 PaulMulrennan 3 64
(T D Easterby) *hmpd s: sn prom on outer: rdn along 2f out: drvn and wknd appr fnl f* 8/1
6 2½ **President Elect (IRE)** 2-9-3 0 PhillipMakin 5 55
(T D Barron) *in tch: effrt 2f out: sn rdn and kpt on same pce appr fnl f* 14/1
0 **7** ½ **Scarlet Royal**[13] 3761 2-8-12 0 PaulQuinn 7 48
(Mrs Marjorie Fife) *in midfield: effrt 2f out: sn rdn and hung lft: no imp* 100/1
66 **8** 1¾ **Royal Sovereign (IRE)**[64] 2199 2-9-3 0 TonyHamilton 1 47
(J Howard Johnson) *wnt rt s: prom on outer tl rdn along and wknd 2f out* 28/1
9 ½ **Sweet Hope (USA)** 2-8-12 0 DO'Donohoe 12 43+
(K A Ryan) *dwlt and in rr whn hmpd after 1f: swtchd lft and sme hdwy wl over 1f out: nvr a factor* 7/2[3]
005 **10** 3 **Caprima (IRE)**[40] 2934 2-8-5 57 PatrickDonaghy(7) 4 29
(M Brittain) *rrd and wnt bdly lft s: cl up tl rdn along over 2f out and sn wknd* 100/1
11 ¾ **Son Of Spartacus (IRE)** 2-9-3 0 TomEaves 10 31
(Mrs L Stubbs) *a in rr* 50/1
12 nk **Brough (IRE)** 2-9-3 0 GrahamGibbons 11 30
(J O'Reilly) *chsd ldrs: pushed along and n.m.r over 2f out: sn wknd* 33/1

59.02 secs (-0.88) **Going Correction** -0.45s/f (Firm) **12 Ran SP% 121.5**
Speed ratings (Par 96): **89,88,85,84,81 77,77,74,73,68 67,66**
CSF £27.93 TOTE £3.60: £1.50, £2.80, £1.40; EX 31.80.
Owner Hamdan Al Maktoum **Bred** Shadwell Estate Company Limited **Trained** Lambourn, Berks

FOCUS
Marginally the quicker division but almost certainly the weaker half. Sound, reliable form, the winner and third setting the standard.

NOTEBOOK
Hadaf(IRE), suited by the fast ground, was always doing just enough and nurseries now beckon. (op 5-2)
Red Wings(IRE), a medium-sized filly, stepped up markedly on her debut effort and can surely be placed to go one better.
Piscean(USA), still carrying tons of condition, was flattened at the start. Soon driven along towards the outer, he stuck on but was never going to trouble the first two. He is crying out for six and looks sure to gain compensation. (op 11-4)
My Kaiser Chief, a March foal, is long in the back and a lazy walker. He went sideways at the start but showed ability, keeping on steadily against the stands'-side running rail in the second half of the contest. (op 25-1)
El Tato, absent for over two months since showing ability on his debut, looked some way short of peak fitness. Knocked over at the start, he showed plenty of toe towards the outside. There will surely be better to come. (op 11-1)
President Elect(IRE), quite a big type, is a half-brother to smart sprinter Eastern Purple. He will have learnt plenty and will be suited by a step up to six. (op 12-1)
Scarlet Royal belied her odds, showing a lot more than on her debut and shaping as though she will appreciate a step up in trip. (op 150-1)
Sweet Hope(USA), a $320,000 purchase at the breeze-up sales, holds a Cheveley Park entry. After a slow start and clipping heels after a furlong, she was never in the contest, but is clearly highly regarded. Hopefully she will put this unhappy debut out of her mind. (tchd 10-3)

4174 EUROPEAN BREEDERS' FUND MAIDEN STKS (DIV II) 5f
2:00 (2:03) (Class 4) 2-Y-O **£4,533** (£1,348; £674; £336) **Stalls** High

Form RPR
2322 **1** **Nawaaff**[12] 3781 2-9-3 82 TomEaves 11 80
(M R Channon) *mde all: rdn and edgd lft fnl f: hld on towards fin* 4/5[1]
2 nk **Royal Degree** 2-9-3 0 PaulEddery 4 79+
(B Smart) *sn drvn along to join wnr: rdn appr fnl f: crowded and no ex towards fin* 9/4[2]
0 **3** 5 **Cordon Bleu (IRE)**[21] 3560 2-9-0 0 GregFairley(3) 9 61+
(M Johnston) *sn chsng ldrs: one pce fnl 2f* 9/1[3]
4 3 **Thanxforthat (USA)** 2-9-3 0 GrahamGibbons 7 50
(J J Quinn) *mid-div: kpt on fnl 2f: nvr nr ldrs* 25/1
0 **5** 1 **Tafira (IRE)**[6] 3995 2-8-12 0 LeeEnstone 1 42
(K R Burke) *dwlt: hdwy on outside 2f out: kpt on same pce* 80/1
05 **6** nk **Harlequinn Danseur (IRE)**[6] 4002 2-9-3 0 (t) KimTinkler 10 45
(N Tinkler) *sn outpcd in rr: rdn and hung lft over 1f out: nvr nr ldrs* 33/1
7 nk **Scientific** 2-9-3 0 TonyHamilton 6 44
(R A Fahey) *s.i.s: kpt on fnl 2f: nvr nr ldrs* 25/1
0 **8** hd **First Abode**[4] 4041 2-8-5 0 PatrickDonaghy(7) 3 39
(M Brittain) *mid-div: nvr nr ldrs* 100/1
9 shd **Presidium Star** 2-8-9 0 AndrewElliott(3) 8 38
(G M Moore) *free to post: chsd ldrs: wknd over 1f out* 66/1
30 **10** dist **Seein'Red (IRE)**[68] 2071 2-9-3 0 (p) PaulFessey 5 —
(P T Midgley) *swvd bdly rt s: a t.o last* 50/1

59.31 secs (-0.59) **Going Correction** -0.45s/f (Firm) **45 Ran SP% 112.6**
Speed ratings (Par 96): **86,85,77,72,71 70,70,69,69,—**
CSF £2.30 TOTE £1.60: £1.10, £1.10, £1.80; EX 2.80.
Owner Sheikh Ahmed Al Maktoum **Bred** Whitsbury Manor Stud And Pigeon House Stud **Trained** West Ilsley, Berks
■ Senorita Parkes was withdrawn (10/1; rider D O'Donohoe unseated and injured). R4 applies, deduct 5p in the £.

FOCUS
Marginally the slower division but almost certainly the stronger part. The winner is already rated 82 and the promising runner-up holds big-race entries.

NOTEBOOK
Nawaaff had no Gothenburg in his way this time but he had to dig deep to account for a clearly very well regarded newcomer. He showed plenty of toe and the drop back to 5f was no inconvenience. (op 6-4)
Royal Degree ◆, a 60,000gns March foal, is a robust individual. Soon upsides the winner, he was crowded when he drifted away from the running rail but on the day was only second best. Likely to be much better suited by 6f, he has big-race entries to justify. (op 13-8)
Cordon Bleu(IRE), a useful-looking individual, showed that his debut effort at York on bad ground was all wrong. Though no match in the end for the first two, he will impove again and will be better suited by 6f. (tchd 10-1)
Thanxforthat(USA), noisy in the paddock, stuck on in his own time and this will have taught him plenty.
Tafira(IRE), slowly away and last on her debut just six days earlier, showed a fair bit more this time.
Harlequinn Danseur(IRE) didn't look entirely at home on the very firm ground but is now qualified for a nursery mark. (op 25-1)
Scientific, a good-bodied newcomer, showed ability on her debut and can do better when fitter.

4175 HERTEL NURSERY 5f
2:35 (2:37) (Class 3) 2-Y-O **£7,772** (£2,312; £1,155; £577) **Stalls** High

Form RPR
2331 **1** **Look Busy (IRE)**[11] 3812 2-8-4 75 PatrickMathers(3) 10 87+
(A Berry) *mde all: clr 1/2-way: easily* 7/2[1]
1416 **2** 3½ **Style Award**[22] 3492 2-8-0 71 ow1 AndrewMullen(3) 12 69
(W J H Ratcliffe) *chsd ldrs: rdn along 2f out: kpt on appr fnl f* 5/1
2254 **3** 1¾ **Speedy Senorita (IRE)**[2] 4098 2-7-13 70 ow3 AndrewElliott(3) 5 62
(K R Burke) *wnt lft s: chsd ldrs: rdn along 2f out: kpt on u.p appr fnl f* 9/2[3]
0525 **4** ¾ **Grudge**[26] 3370 2-8-2 70 PaulQuinn 11 59
(D W Barker) *prom: hung bdly lft after 1f and bit slipped: rdn along 1/2-way and sn one pce* 16/1
6105 **5** nk **Weet A Surprise**[8] 3925 2-7-8 69 SophieDoyle(7) 9 57
(R Hollinshead) *in midfield: hdwy and pushed along over 2f out: sn rdn and no imp* 25/1
4355 **6** 1½ **Dalarossie**[5] 4020 2-8-2 70 DaleGibson 7 53
(E J Alston) *chsd ldrs: bunped after 1f: rdn along over 2f out and grad wknd* 16/1
352 **7** 2½ **Elijah Pepper (USA)**[16] 3673 2-8-5 73 PaulFessey 8 47
(T D Barron) *unruly s: in tch: rdn along 1/2-way: n.m.r 2f out and sn eased* 4/1[2]
660 **8** ¾ **Tikinheart (IRE)**[35] 3092 2-7-9 66 oh1 DuranFentiman(3) 2 37
(T D Easterby) *hmpd s: a bhd* 14/1
106 **9** 3 **Lieutenant Pigeon**[37] 3025 2-8-7 75 TomEaves 1 35
(B Smart) *in tch on outer: drvn along 1/2-way: sn wknd* 9/1
3220 **10** 1¼ **Fast Feet**[70] 2024 2-9-2 89 NeilBrown(5) 3 45
(K A Ryan) *hmpd s: a bhd* 6/1

57.59 secs (-2.31) **Going Correction** -0.45s/f (Firm) **10 Ran SP% 123.6**
Speed ratings (Par 98): **100,94,91,90,89 87,83,82,77,75**
CSF £22.64 CT £85.22 TOTE £4.00: £1.70, £2.40, £2.40; EX 30.50.
Owner A Underwood **Bred** Tom And Hazel Russell **Trained** Cockerham, Lancs

FOCUS
A one-horse race and a very fast time compared with the two earlier maiden races. The form should work out.

NOTEBOOK
Look Busy(IRE) ◆, a robust filly, is probably only now fully fit. She hit the traps running and had this won before the halfway mark. She would have lowered the two-year-old record time had she been nudged out and would surely be a banker if turning out under a penalty. Even from her revised mark she will still be of real interest. (op 11-4)
Style Award is clearly going the right away but she proved no match whatsoever for the highly progressive winner. (op 11-2 tchd 6-1)
Speedy Senorita(IRE), having her second outing in under three days, went sideways at the start. She looks all speed. (op 6-1 tchd 15-2)
Grudge hung badly at the intersection with the round course and the bit came through his mouth. In the circumstances he ran with plenty of credit, but he is clearly not straightforward. Official explanation: jockey said bit slipped through the mouth (op 14-1)
Weet A Surprise struggled to go the pace but was staying on in her own time in the closing stages. (op 20-1)
Dalarossie was knocked sideways by the errant Grudge, living up to his name perhaps, at the end of the first furlong.
Elijah Pepper(USA), who gave problems behind the stalls, was going nowhere when tightened up and his rider soon threw in the towel. (op 15-2)

4176 EKOS CONSULTING H'CAP 1m
3:10 (3:10) (Class 3) (0-90,89) 3-Y-O+ **£7,772** (£2,312; £1,155; £577) **Stalls** Low

Form RPR
-214 **1** **Webbow (IRE)**[21] 3556 5-9-4 79 TPQueally 12 88
(T D Easterby) *hld up in rr: smooth hdwy over 2f out: rdn ins fnl f: r.o to ld nr fin* 11/2[2]
3011 **2** nk **Nevada Desert (IRE)**[4] 4039 7-9-4 84 6ex MichaelJStainton(5) 4 92
(R M Whitaker) *chsd ldr: led over 1f out: hdd and no ex towards fin* 8/1
0333 **3** 1¼ **Granston (IRE)**[42] 2891 6-9-11 86 GrahamGibbons 9 91
(J D Bethell) *hld up in mid-div: swtchd lft over 1f out: styd on* 4/1[1]
2005 **4** nk **Goodbye Mr Bond**[22] 3513 7-9-7 89 GaryBartley(7) 8 94
(E J Alston) *hld up in rr: hdwy and nt clr run over 1f out: styd on wl ins fnl f* 14/1
0034 **5** shd **Nanton (USA)**[53] 2536 5-9-11 86 DanielTudhope 6 91
(N Wilson) *chsd ldrs: drvn over 4f out: kpt on wl fnl f* 14/1
1-11 **6** ½ **Atlantic Story (USA)**[181] 351 5-9-1 76 PaulMulrennan 10 79
(M W Easterby) *trckd ldrs: t.k.h: chal over 1f out: no ex* 6/1[3]
3120 **7** 1 **Il Castagno (IRE)**[11] 3813 4-9-7 82 TomEaves 1 83
(B Smart) *led tl over 1f out: kpt on same pce* 8/1
20-5 **8** 1¾ **El Coto**[91] 1480 7-9-8 86 (p) DuranFentiman(3) 5 83
(K A Ryan) *in tch: effrt over 2f out: kpt on same pce* 16/1
2200 **9** nk **Exit Smiling**[21] 3556 5-9-0 75 PaulFessey 11 71
(P T Midgley) *in rr: kpt on fnl 2f: nvr rchd ldrs* 20/1

6205 **10** *hd* **Efidium**[7] 3971 9-8-2 **70** oh3 DanielleMcCreery(7) 7 66
(N Bycroft) *s.i.s: hdwy on wd outside over 2f out: nvr rchd ldrs* **40/1**

3140 **11** *½* **Hula Ballew**[11] 3813 7-9-5 **80** PhillipMakin 15 75
(M Dods) *chsd ldrs: effrt over 2f out: one pce* **16/1**

2400 **12** *nk* **United Nations**[8] 3926 6-8-12 **73** PaddyAspell 3 67
(N Wilson) *s.i.s: hdwy on ins 3f out: wknd fnl f* **50/1**

3441 **13** *shd* **Handsome Falcon**[12] 3790 3-8-8 **76** TonyHamilton 14 70
(R A Fahey) *hld up in midfield: effrt over 2f out: nvr a threat* **8/1**

6420 **14** *2* **Shot Gun**[14] 3745 3-8-11 **79** PatCosgrave 13 68
(M R Channon) *prom: edgd lft and wknd over 1f out* **12/1**

1m 37.41s (-2.29) **Going Correction** -0.10s/f (Good)
WFA 3 from 4yo+ 7lb **14** Ran SP% **125.0**
Speed ratings (Par 107): **107,106,105,105,105 104,103,101,101,101 100,100,100,98**
CSF £50.39 CT £207.27 TOTE £7.00: £2.40, £3.10, £2.20; EX 73.90.
Owner Wentdale Limited **Bred** Joe O'Callaghan **Trained** Great Habton, N Yorks

FOCUS
A strongly-run handicap and rock solid form.

NOTEBOOK
Webbow(IRE) has given problems beforehand in the past but seems a reformed character now. Settled off the pace, he came with a well timed run to put his head in front where it matters most. He now heads for new-look Doncaster's opening meeting. (op 6-1)
Nevada Desert(IRE), under his penalty, is in the form of his life and the very fast ground did not bother him. In the end he was only just picked off. (op 13-2 tchd 6-1)
Granston(IRE), who took this last year from the same mark, had to come wide for a run. Putting in some solid work at the finish, he is clearly as good as ever. (tchd 9-2)
Goodbye Mr Bond, who looked at his very best, put three below-par efforts behind him but this trip is his bare minimum these days. (op 16-1)
Nanton(USA), back after a seven-week break, took plenty of stoking up but was keeping on stoutly at the death. This should have put an edge on him.
Atlantic Story(USA), absent since completing a five-timer on the All-Weather at Kempton in February, saw too much daylight and ran much too freely. He has resumed from his last winning mark and should soon be back in the money. Official explanation: jockey said gelding ran too free (op 13-2 tchd 5-1)
Il Castagno(IRE) is best when able to dominate but he was hustled and hassled in front here. (op 12-1)

4177 TURFTV H'CAP 1m
3:45 (3:45) (Class 5) (0-75,74) 3-Y-0+ **£3,238** (£963; £481; £240) **Stalls** Low

Form RPR

0503 **1** **Champain Sands (IRE)**[2] 4100 8-8-5 **58** GaryBartley(7) 9 69
(E J Alston) *hld up and bhd: gd hdwy 3f out: rdn to chse ldrs ins fnl f: led last 100yds* **4/1**[2]

3211 **2** *1¼* **Emperor's Well**[4] 4042 8-9-3 **63** 6ex PaulMulrennan 11 71
(M W Easterby) *led: clr over 2f out: rdn wl over 1f out: hdd and no ex last 100yds* **2/1**[1]

4010 **3** *2½* **Just Bond (IRE)**[21] 3530 5-9-9 **74** SladeO'Hara(5) 8 76
(G R Oldroyd) *hld up: hdwy on outer over 2f out: sn rdn and styd on ins fnl f: nrst fin* **20/1**

0453 **4** *shd* **Violent Velocity (IRE)**[6] 3999 4-9-7 **67** GrahamGibbons 1 69
(J J Quinn) *hld up: hdwy over 2f out: sn rdn and styd on ins fnl f: nrst fin* **5/1**

00 **5** *shd* **Titinius (IRE)**[6] 3998 7-9-2 **62** PatCosgrave 10 64
(Micky Hammond) *hld up in rr: hdwy over 2f out: rdn wl over 1f out: kpt on ins fnl f* **28/1**

6044 **6** *¾* **Cool Ebony**[11] 3816 4-9-8 **68** PhillipMakin 4 68
(M Dods) *chsd ldrs: rdn along over 2f out: sn drvn and one pce appr fnl f* **9/2**[3]

0200 **7** *¾* **Government (IRE)**[8] 3907 6-8-2 **55** oh9 SophieDoyle(7) 13 53
(M C Chapman) *prom: rdn along 3f out and sn wknd* **100/1**

0-00 **8** *5* **Penny Glitters**[5] 4029 4-8-6 **55** oh8 (b) DominicFox(3) 14 42
(S Parr) *t.k.h: chsd ldrs: hdwy to chse ldr over 3f out: rdn 2f out and sn wknd* **100/1**

06-0 **9** *2½* **Ali D**[15] 3721 9-8-9 **55** oh3 TPQueally 12 36
(G Woodward) *nvr bttr than midfield* **18/1**

-400 **10** *½* **Crosby Vision**[75] 1892 4-9-2 **67** (v[1]) MichaelJStainton(5) 2 47
(J R Weymes) *s.i.s: a in rr* **12/1**

-040 **11** *1¾* **Noble Edge**[7] 3956 4-8-9 **55** oh3 (p) FTahir 5 31
(Karen McLintock) *a bhd* **50/1**

0-03 **12** *¾* **Double Carpet (IRE)**[8] 3914 4-8-10 **56** DanielTudhope 7 30
(G Woodward) *prom: rdn along 3f out: grad wknd* **33/1**

2350 **13** *hd* **Damelza (IRE)**[7] 3961 4-9-4 **67** (t) DuranFentiman(3) 3 40
(T D Easterby) *in tch: effrt 3f out: sn rdn and wknd 2f out* **16/1**

36-0 **14** *31* **Bella Marie**[61] 2315 4-8-9 **55** oh5 TonyHamilton 6 —
(L R James) *a bhd* **66/1**

1m 38.34s (-1.36) **Going Correction** -0.10s/f (Good) **14** Ran SP% **123.6**
Speed ratings (Par 103): **102,100,98,98,98 97,96,91,89,88 86,86,85,54**
CSF £12.16 CT £148.88 TOTE £6.00: £1.90, £1.30, £4.70; EX 15.80.
Owner Geoff & Astrid Long **Bred** Gerrardstown House Stud **Trained** Longton, Lancs

FOCUS
A modest handicap run at a sound pace. The form has a solid look about it but limited by the proximity of the seventh, 9lb 'wrong'.

4178 POLAR FORD MAIDEN FILLIES' STKS 7f
4:20 (4:23) (Class 4) 3-Y-0+ **£5,181** (£1,541; £770; £384) **Stalls** Low

Form RPR

-202 **1** **Apple Blossom (IRE)**[57] 2429 3-9-0 80 TonyHamilton 2 56
(G Wragg) *trckd ldr: led over 1f out: drvn out* **6/4**[2]

4202 **2** *1* **Miss Taboo (IRE)**[17] 3639 3-9-0 53 PatCosgrave 3 53
(P T Midgley) *trckd ldrs: hung lft over 1f out: kpt on same pce* **9/1**

6003 **3** *shd* **Slip Star**[8] 3917 4-9-3 54 PatrickMathers(3) 13 55
(T J Etherington) *chsd ldrs: kpt on same pce appr fnl f* **25/1**

0-0 **4** *1½* **Grey Vision**[8] 3917 4-8-13 0 PatrickDonaghy(7) 4 51
(M Brittain) *unruly s: sn in rr: hdwy on outer over 2f out: edgd lft over 1f out: kpt on* **80/1**

-205 **5** *2* **Crosby Jemma**[8] 3914 3-9-0 50 DanielTudhope 6 43
(J R Weymes) *prom: one pce fnl 2f* **20/1**

0-00 **6** *1¾* **Chicamia**[12] 3786 3-8-7 40 SophieDoyle(7) 8 39
(M Mullineaux) *s.i.s: hdwy 2f out: styd on ins fnl f* **100/1**

4 **7** *nk* **Talk More (USA)**[106] 1128 3-9-0 0 TPQueally 1 38
(J Noseda) *s.i.s: hdwy and wl in tch over 4f out: sn drvn and outpcd: edgd rt and kpt on* **6/5**[1]

-000 **8** *5* **Underthemistletoe (IRE)**[10] 3837 5-9-1 44 (b) MichaelJStainton(5) 11 24
(R E Barr) *t.k.h: led: hdd over 1f out: sn wknd* **100/1**

60- **9** *nk* **Lauder**[233] 6815 3-8-9 0 SladeO'Hara(5) 9 23
(J Balding) *mid-div: rdn 3f out: nvr a threat* **100/1**

0 **10** *2* **Own Gift**[52] 2580 3-8-11 0 DominicFox(3) 5 18
(S Parr) *a in rr* **100/1**

4-4 **11** *6* **Craig Y Nos**[37] 3016 3-8-7 0 AdamCarter(7) 10 2
(A Berry) *uns rdr gng to s: unruly s: virtually ref to r and sn wl bhd* **150/1**

12 *3* **Natco** 3-9-0 0 PhillipMakin 7 —
(M Johnston) *s.i.s: a bhd* **8/1**[3]

05 **13** *32* **Very Wise Kid**[21] 3561 4-8-13 0 GaryBartley(7) 12 —
(P T Midgley) *hung rt thrght: in tch: rn v wd bnd over 3f out: sn bhd: virtually p.u: t.o* **40/1**

1m 27.02s (-0.08) **Going Correction** -0.10s/f (Good)
WFA 3 from 4yo+ 6lb **13** Ran SP% **123.5**
Speed ratings (Par 102): **96,94,94,93,90 88,88,82,82,80 73,69,33**
CSF £15.51 TOTE £2.50: £1.10, £2.20, £6.20; EX 13.60.
Owner Dr Anne J F Gillespie **Bred** Dr A J F Gillespie **Trained** Newmarket, Suffolk

FOCUS
A very modest maiden with the favourite well below par and the runner-up rated a mere 53.
Talk More(USA) Official explanation: trainer's representative said filly was unsuited by the track
Very Wise Kid Official explanation: jockey said filly hung badly right-handed throughout

4179 STEVE AND FI BOUGHTON'S 40TH BIRTHDAY H'CAP 2m
4:55 (4:57) (Class 5) (0-75,75) 4-Y-0+ **£3,886** (£1,156; £577; £288) **Stalls** Low

Form RPR

540/ **1** **Downing Street (IRE)**[71] 5565 6-8-6 **67** ow8 (bt) AdamCarter(7) 3 83
(Jennie Candlish) *bhd: hdwy 6f out: swtchd rt and gd hdwy over 2f out: rdn to ld over 1f out and sn clr* **9/1**

0-10 **2** *13* **Industrial Star (IRE)**[37] 3027 6-9-5 **73** (p) TonyHamilton 9 73
(Micky Hammond) *hld up: hdwy over 5f out: rdn to chse ldr over 2f out: sn drvn and kpt on same pce* **6/1**[3]

2266 **3** *nk* **Karlani (IRE)**[24] 3412 4-8-4 **63** ow1 (b) MichaelJStainton(5) 4 63
(G A Swinbank) *trckd ldr: led over 4f out: rdn clr 3f out: drvn over 1f out: sn hdd and plugged on same pce* **4/1**[2]

3/00 **4** *6* **Top Tenor (IRE)**[10] 3840 7-7-9 **56** oh5 (t) SophieDoyle(7) 6 48
(W Storey) *towards rr: hdwy 3f out: rdn to chse ldrs wl over 1f out: sn hung lft and no imp* **66/1**

0/00 **5** *nk* **Erte**[11] 3815 6-7-13 **56** oh11 (v) DominicFox(3) 1 48
(W Storey) *towards rr: hdwy and in tch 1/2-way: rdn along and outpcd over 4f out: plugged on same pce fnl 2f* **66/1**

2446 **6** *2½* **Qaasi (USA)**[9] 3888 5-7-13 **60** oh1 ow4 PatrickDonaghy(7) 2 49
(M Brittain) *trckd ldrs: effrt over 4f out: rdn along 3f out: drvn and btn 2f out* **16/1**

3314 **7** *nk* **Ronsard (IRE)**[7] 3976 5-8-8 **65** PatrickMathers(3) 5 54
(P D Evans) *hld up: effrt and sme hdwy to chse ldrs over 4f out: sn rdn along and no imp fr wl over 2f out* **8/1**

4233 **8** *1¾* **Boxhall (IRE)**[53] 2250 5-9-0 **68** DanielTudhope 7 55
(N Wilson) *led: rdn along and hdd over 4f out: drvn along 3f out and sn wknd* **4/1**[2]

6-01 **9** *4* **Ostfanni (IRE)**[43] 2825 7-8-11 **65** PatCosgrave 8 47
(M Todhunter) *hld up: effrt 1/2-way: sn rdn along and wknd* **5/2**[1]

5-44 **10** *dist* **White Lightening (IRE)**[22] 3501 4-9-7 **75** TPQueally 10 —
(J Wade) *prom: rdn along over 6f out: sn wknd* **12/1**

3m 25.38s (-5.82) **Going Correction** -0.10s/f (Good) **10** Ran SP% **120.5**
Speed ratings (Par 103): **110,103,103,100,100 98,98,97,95,—**
CSF £64.31 CT £254.95 TOTE £11.80: £3.00, £1.90, £1.80; EX 75.70.
Owner Reuben Fielding **Bred** M Stewkesbury And The Luna Wells Syndic **Trained** Basford Green, Staffs

FOCUS
They went off very fast and the winner came from way off the pace. The fourth and the fifth tie down the overall value of the form.
Ostfanni(IRE) Official explanation: trainer had no explanation for the poor form shown

4180 WHITBY H'CAP (LADIES' RACE) 6f
5:25 (5:27) (Class 6) (0-55,60) 3-Y-0+ **£2,498** (£774; £387; £193) **Stalls** High

Form RPR

0006 **1** **Greek Secret**[6] 4008 4-10-9 **53** (b) MissADeniel 3 64
(J O'Reilly) *racd far side: trckd ldrs: carried lft fnl f: hrd rdn to ld towards fin* **14/1**

5234 **2** *nk* **Conjecture**[11] 3829 5-10-5 **54** MissRBastiman(5) 4 64
(R Bastiman) *overall ldr far side: edgd rt fnl f: hdd nr fin* **12/1**

0064 **3** *2* **Tag Team (IRE)**[10] 3852 6-10-5 **49** MrsMMorris 8 53
(John A Harris) *racd centre: w ldrs: kpt on same pce fnl f* **14/1**

2531 **4** *½* **Orotund**[14] 3752 3-10-1 **52** MissJCoward(3) 19 53
(T D Easterby) *w ldrs stands' side: edgd lft and kpt on same pce fnl f* **6/1**[2]

4630 **5** *1* **Penel (IRE)**[12] 3789 6-9-11 **48** (p) MissWGibson(7) 10 47
(P T Midgley) *mid-div: styd on wl fnl f: nt rch ldrs* **33/1**

3044 **6** *1* **Sir Loin**[6] 4008 6-10-10 **54** (v) MissSBrotherton 17 50
(N Tinkler) *w ldrs: fdd jst ins fnl f* **7/1**[3]

3300 **7** *½* **Tibinta**[16] 3667 3-10-4 **52** MissEFolkes 20 45
(P D Evans) *mid-div stands' side: kpt on fnl 2f: nvr trbld ldrs* **14/1**

0105 **8** *½* **Arfinnit (IRE)**[18] 3618 6-10-4 **48** (v) MissLEllison 15 41
(Mrs A L M King) *mid-div: kpt on fnl 2f: nvr trbld ldrs* **12/1**

0050 **9** *nk* **Petite Mac**[3] 4083 7-10-2 **53** MissERamstrom(7) 9 45
(N Bycroft) *mid-div: kpt on fnl 2f: nvr a threat* **16/1**

0254 **10** *2* **Joy And Pain**[14] 3735 6-10-10 **54** (v) MissFayeBramley 5 39
(M J Attwater) *swvd rt s: racd far side: chsd ldrs: wknd over 1f out* **12/1**

2463 **11** *½* **Wolfman**[43] 2844 5-9-11 **48** (p) MrsJEPugh(7) 11 32
(D W Barker) *mid-div: rdn over 2f out: nvr a threat* **9/1**

45 **12** *hd* **Sparky Vixen**[26] 3372 3-10-7 **55** MrsCBartley 13 37
(G A Swinbank) *in rr: carried lft over 2f out: nvr on terms* **16/1**

3440 **13** *nk* **Butterfly Bud (IRE)**[10] 3839 4-9-13 **50** MissEHickey(7) 2 32
(J O'Reilly) *racd far side: w ldrs: t.k.h: wknd fnl f* **33/1**

3221 **14** *shd* **El Potro**[6] 4008 5-10-9 **60** 6ex MissJessicaHolt(7) 16 42
(J R Holt) *rrd s: sn w ldrs: wknd over 1f out* **5/1**[1]

2000 **15** *nk* **Jellytot (USA)**[6] 4008 4-10-2 **53** (b) MissAColley(7) 14 34
(J O'Reilly) *mid-div: edgd lft over 2f out: sn wknd* **28/1**

3350 **16** *½* **No Grouse**[3] 4083 7-10-7 **54** MissARyan(3) 7 33
(E J Alston) *racd far side: chsd ldrs: swtchd rt after 2f: sn lost pl* **10/1**

0060 **17** *1* **Black Oval**[1] 4141 6-9-13 **48** MrsLHannity(5) 1 24
(S Parr) *racd far side: w ldrs: lost pl and eased over 1f out* **66/1**

0006 **18** *2½* **Polish Emperor (USA)**[12] 3787 7-9-13 **50** MissASmith(7) 18 18
(D W Barker) *s.i.s: a in rr* **16/1**

5055 **19** *hd* **Seesawmilu (IRE)**[10] 3839 4-9-13 **50** (b[1]) MissSESiddall(7) 6 18
(E J Alston) *racd far side: chsd ldrs: lost pl over 1f out* **33/1**

1m 12.21s (-0.29) **Going Correction** -0.45s/f (Firm)
WFA 3 from 4yo+ 4lb **19** Ran SP% **137.0**
Speed ratings (Par 101): **83,82,79,79,77 76,75,75,74,72 71,71,70,70,70 69,68,65,64**
CSF £183.27 CT £2455.63 TOTE £16.30: £3.00, £3.70, £3.30, £2.20; EX 171.50 Place 6 £12.21, Place 5 £7.95..

Owner The Boot & Shoe Ackworth Partnership **Bred** James Clark **Trained** Doncaster, S Yorks
■ Stewards' Enquiry : Mrs L Hannity one-day ban: failed to keep straight from stalls (Aug 16)
FOCUS
They raced all over the track in this low-grade lady riders' handicap. The first two raced towards the far side.
T/Plt: £7.70 to a £1 stake. Pool: £51,599.70. 4,856.65 winning tickets. T/Qpdt: £8.60 to a £1 stake. Pool: £2,539.90. 217.00 winning tickets. JR

4014 WINDSOR (R-H)
Saturday, August 4

OFFICIAL GOING: Good to firm changing to good to firm (firm in places) after race 4 (4.15)
With the ground drying out quickly, a course record was broken and every winning time bettered the standard.
Wind: Light behind Weather: Warm and sunny

4181 NORMA MURRAY'S 50TH BIRTHDAY WEDDING DAY EBF MEDIAN AUCTION MAIDEN STKS 6f
2:30 (2:31) (Class 4) 2-Y-O **£4,857** (£1,445; £722; £360) **Stalls** High

Form RPR
433 **1** **In Honour (IRE)**[15] 3718 2-9-3 80 RichardMullen 5 85
(E S McMahon) *led after 1f: rdn over 1f out: r.o wl* **9/4**[1]
3 **2** 1 ¾ **Rash Judgement**[16] 3687 2-9-3 0 FergusSweeney 2 80
(W S Kittow) *t.k.h: sn prom: chsd wnr over 2f out: rdn over 1f out: nt qckn fnl f* **7/2**[2]
04 **3** 1 ¾ **Gross Prophet**[26] 3363 2-9-0 0 RichardKingscote(3) 4 75
(Tom Dascombe) *hld up towards rr: hdwy over 3f out: rdn 2f out: one pce fnl f* **8/1**
2023 **4** 3 **Magical Speedfit (IRE)**[11] 3823 2-9-3 80 EddieAhern 6 66
(G G Margarson) *a.p: one pce fnl 2f* **9/2**[3]
00 **5** 1 ¼ **El Fuser**[21] 3550 2-9-3 0 AmirQuinn 13 62
(P J Makin) *s.i.s: rdn and hdwy 2f out: no further prog* **33/1**
50 **6** ½ **Bermacha**[17] 3648 2-8-12 0 SaleemGolam 12 55
(W R Muir) *chsd ldrs: no hdwy fnl 2f* **25/1**
7 shd **Sweet Nicole** 2-8-12 0 OscarUrbina 7 55+
(J R Fanshawe) *s.i.s: hdwy 2f out: sn no imp* **11/1**
00 **8** 5 **Riorun (IRE)**[19] 3592 2-9-3 0 JimCrowley 11 45
(J G Portman) *nvr nr ldrs* **66/1**
6 **9** shd **Alls Fair**[7] 3962 2-9-3 0 PatDobbs 9 45
(R Hannon) *towards rr: rdn over 3f out: n.d* **5/1**
50 **10** 4 **Yankee Storm**[18] 3625 2-9-1 0 ow3 DerekNolan(5) 8 36+
(M J Wallace) *hld up in mid-div: nt clr run over 4f out: hdwy over 3f out: rdn and wknd wl over 1f out* **50/1**
00 **11** ½ **Running Buck (USA)**[9] 3878 2-9-3 0 RichardThomas 16 31
(N P Littmoden) *bhd fnl 3f* **80/1**
00 **12** nk **Berties Goodenough**[38] 2977 2-9-3 0 HayleyTurner 10 30
(Andrew Turnell) *chsd ldrs tl wknd over 2f out* **50/1**
0 **13** 1 **Liz Long**[12] 3796 2-8-9 0 EmmettStack(3) 3 22
(P Howling) *s.i.s: t.k.h early: a bhd* **100/1**
56 **14** hd **Xtravaganza (IRE)**[56] 2447 2-8-12 0 MatthewHenry 14 22
(J W Hills) *a bhd* **22/1**
02 **15** 4 **Kaystar Ridge**[29] 3283 2-9-3 0 AdrianMcCarthy 15 15
(D K Ivory) *led 1f: rdn 3f out: wknd over 1f out: eased fnl f* **25/1**

1m 10.92s (-2.75) **Going Correction** -0.475s/f (Firm) 15 Ran SP% **129.9**
Speed ratings (Par 96): **99,96,94,90,88 88,87,81,81,75 75,74,73,73,67**
CSF £9.98 TOTE £3.80: £1.70, £2.00, £3.30; EX 15.00 Trifecta £65.60 Part won. Pool: £92.40 - 0.40 winning tickets..
Owner J C Fretwell **Bred** Sorento Farm **Trained** Lichfield, Staffs
FOCUS
An ordinary contest with several stepping up from the minimum distance and solid form with the time good and the front three marginal improvers.
NOTEBOOK
In Honour(IRE) did not mind being back on fast ground and was nicely on top in the closing stages. He may now step up to conditions class as his trainer thinks he is rated rather high for nurseries. (op 11-4 tchd 3-1 in places)
Rash Judgement ◆ was predictably not inconvenienced by the extra furlong but could not cope with the winner after running freely early on. He should soon take a similar event. (op 3-1)
Gross Prophet, another stepping up from the minimum trip, produced a solid effort on this faster surface.
Magical Speedfit(IRE) may have found the ground plenty quick enough on his first attempt beyond five furlongs. (op 5-1 tchd 4-1)
El Fuser could not sustain his effort after missing the break. (op 40-1)
Bermacha was in much the same position throughout.
Sweet Nicole is a half-sister to Jersey Stakes winner Tariq who landed the Group 2 Betfair Cup at Goodwood earlier in the week. She showed signs of ability after a tardy start and should be better for the experience. (op 12-1 tchd 10-1)
Kaystar Ridge Official explanation: vet said colt moved feelingly post-race, possibly caused by sore shins

4182 OSSIE AND HUTCH MEMORIAL MAIDEN STKS 6f
3:05 (3:06) (Class 5) 3-4-Y-O **£3,238** (£963; £481; £240) **Stalls** High

Form RPR
24 **1** **Jimmy Styles**[42] 2878 3-9-3 0 EddieAhern 10 79
(C G Cox) *a.p: rdn and swtchd lft jst over 1f out: led ins fnl f: r.o wl* **4/5**[1]
-233 **2** ¾ **Wolf River (USA)**[23] 3447 3-9-3 78 FergusSweeney 6 77
(D M Simcock) *led: rdn over 1f out: hdd ins fnl f: nt qckn* **15/8**[2]
4-00 **3** 3 ½ **Swing On A Star (IRE)**[29] 3276 3-8-12 53 SaleemGolam 7 61
(W R Swinburn) *chsd ldr: ev ch 2f out: sn rdn: one pce fnl f* **16/1**
03 **4** 3 ½ **Vogarth**[7] 3968 3-8-13 0 ow1 JamesMillman(5) 4 56
(B R Millman) *hld up in tch: rdn and wknd over 1f out* **8/1**[3]
00 **5** 3 ½ **Half A Tsar (IRE)**[12] 3794 3-8-10 0 JackDean(7) 9 43
(Mark Gillard) *hld up in tch: rdn over 2f out: sn wknd* **66/1**
00 **6** 1 **Withywood (USA)**[25] 3395 3-8-12 0 PatDobbs 1 35
(G L Moore) *nvr nr ldrs* **33/1**
6 **7** ½ **King Roy (IRE)**[35] 3102 3-8-10 0 KylieManser(7) 2 39
(N I M Rossiter) *a bhd* **25/1**
5 **8** 1 **Boleyna (USA)**[104] 1175 3-8-12 0 (e) RichardMullen 3 30
(Rae Guest) *towards rr: rdn over 3f out: sn struggling* **14/1**
-600 **9** 10 **Stars Above**[8] 3904 3-8-12 40 TGMcLaughlin 8 —
(M S Saunders) *a bhd* **66/1**
0006 **U** **Double Valentine**[24] 3425 4-9-2 45 DavidKinsella 5 —
(R Ingram) *uns rdr leaving stalls* **25/1**

1m 10.34s (-3.33) **Going Correction** -0.475s/f (Firm)
WFA 3 from 4yo 4lb 10 Ran SP% **127.6**
Speed ratings (Par 103): **103,102,97,92,88 86,86,84,71,—**
CSF £2.67 TOTE £1.80: £1.10, £1.20, £3.10; EX 2.70 Trifecta £1.60 Pool: £234.56 - 101.50 winning tickets..
Owner Gwyn Powell and Peter Ridgers **Bred** Barry Minty **Trained** Lambourn, Berks
FOCUS
They went 8/1 bar the first two home in this moderate affair. Just an ordinary maiden, but sound form with the first four close to their marks.

4183 READING SPORTING CASINO CONDITIONS STKS 6f
3:40 (3:40) (Class 3) 3-Y-O+
£7,478 (£2,239; £1,119; £560; £279; £140) **Stalls** High

Form RPR
3000 **1** **Presto Shinko (IRE)**[15] 3708 6-8-11 102 (p) HaddenFrost(7) 4 111
(R Hannon) *chsd ldrs: edgd rt and led wl ins fnl f: r.o* **5/2**[2]
200/ **2** ½ **Galeota (IRE)**[700] 4940 5-8-13 110 PatDobbs 7 104
(R Hannon) *led: rdn over 1f out: hdd wl ins fnl f: nt qckn* **9/2**[3]
2205 **3** 1 ½ **Bounty Quest**[15] 3708 5-8-13 103 JimCrowley 1 100
(K A Ryan) *w ldr: rdn 2f out: ev ch over 1f out: nt qckn ins fnl f* **7/1**
-040 **4** nk **Prince Tamino**[162] 547 4-8-13 102 EddieAhern 6 99
(Saeed Bin Suroor) *chsd ldrs: n.m.r briefly over 1f out: rdn and one pce fnl f* **6/4**[1]
2042 **5** ½ **Tony James (IRE)**[22] 3489 5-8-13 96 RichardMullen 5 97
(K O Cunningham-Brown) *s.i.s: hld up: rdn over 2f out: nvr able to chal* **13/2**
-630 **6** 4 **Resplendent Alpha**[108] 1099 3-8-12 95 AmirQuinn 3 87
(P Howling) *s.i.s: hld up: rdn over 2f out: shortlived effrt over 1f out* **25/1**
4006 **7** ½ **Sweet Afton (IRE)**[21] 3526 4-8-8 86 TGMcLaughlin 2 78
(M S Saunders) *hld up: rdn 2f out: no rspnse* **25/1**

1m 10.06s (-3.61) **Going Correction** -0.475s/f (Firm) course record
WFA 3 from 4yo+ 4lb 7 Ran SP% **120.3**
Speed ratings (Par 107): **105,104,102,101,101 95,95**
CSF £15.34 TOTE £4.00: £2.60, £3.00; EX 22.60.
Owner Major A M Everett **Bred** Mrs S O'Riordan **Trained** East Everleigh, Wilts
■ Stewards' Enquiry : Jim Crowley one-day ban: not riding to draw (Aug 15)
FOCUS
An interesting sprint with the course record broken by 0.14 seconds. Only modest form for the grade, the winner rated to this year's best.
NOTEBOOK
Presto Shinko(IRE), back in cheekpieces having tried a visor over five furlongs at Newmarket last time, turned around the form with Bounty Quest. He lowered the course record and is certainly very versatile with regard to ground conditions. (op 4-1)
Galeota(IRE) ◆ was having his first outing for exactly 700 days having been gelded since proving to be infertile at stud. His trainer thought he would need the run and was delighted with this effort against his stablemate. There are more races to be won with him. (tchd 7-2)
Bounty Quest was a pound worse off than when finishing a length and a quarter in front of the winner over the minimum trip at Newmarket last month. The two of them are probably better suited to this trip. (tchd 15-2)
Prince Tamino should not be considered unlucky on his first start since running in Dubai in February.
Tony James(IRE) could never make his presence felt in this company. (op 7-1)
Sweet Afton(IRE) Official explanation: trainer said filly lost a front shoe

4184 ROYAL WINDSOR SUMMER CUP H'CAP 1m 2f 7y
4:15 (4:15) (Class 4) (0-85,87) 3-Y-O+
£12,464 (£3,732; £1,866; £700; £700; £234) **Stalls** Low

Form RPR
-213 **1** **Muhannak (IRE)**[8] 3926 3-8-9 75 StephenCarson 11 84
(G A Butler) *hld up and bhd: rdn and hdwy over 1f out: sn hung lft: r.o to ld cl home* **12/1**
3331 **2** nk **Monte Alto (IRE)**[9] 3877 3-9-7 87 EddieAhern 1 95
(L M Cumani) *t.k.h in tch: swtchd lft over 2f out: rdn over 1f out: led ins fnl f: hdd cl home* **3/1**[1]
0014 **3** 1 ½ **Prize Fighter (IRE)**[30] 3242 5-9-9 80 (b) AdrianMcCarthy 6 85
(H R A Cecil) *s.i.s: sn prom: led over 2f out: rdn and hdd ins fnl f: nt qckn* **12/1**
102/ **4** 1 ¼ **Golden Feather**[17] 3152 5-9-5 79 LiamTreadwell(3) 4 82
(Miss Venetia Williams) *hld up in mid-div: rdn over 3f out: hdwy over 1f out: kpt on same pce* **33/1**
3310 **4** dht **Kavachi (IRE)**[15] 3705 4-8-8 65 RichardMullen 3 68
(G L Moore) *hld up and bhd: rdn and hdwy over 1f out: r.o ins fnl f: nrst fin* **14/1**
1/30 **6** nk **Bull Market (IRE)**[14] 3748 4-9-7 81 RichardKingscote(3) 7 83
(J A Osborne) *chsd ldr: led 6f out: rdn and hdd over 2f out: no ex fnl f* **16/1**
6040 **7** shd **Krugerrand (USA)**[22] 3513 8-9-7 78 FergusSweeney 12 80
(W J Musson) *stdd s: hld up and bhd: rdn and hdwy over 1f out: nvr trbld ldrs* **7/1**[2]
41 **8** 3 **Sun Of The Sea**[24] 3429 3-8-9 75 RichardThomas 5 71
(N P Littmoden) *mid-div: rdn and no hdwy fnl 2f* **3/1**[1]
4106 **9** hd **Del Mar Sunset**[16] 3671 8-9-7 78 PatDobbs 2 73
(W J Haggas) *s.i.s: nvr nr ldrs* **11/1**
0004 **10** 1 ¼ **Red Somerset (USA)**[21] 3527 4-9-3 74 OscarUrbina 9 67
(R J Hodges) *hld up in mid-div: rdn over 3f out: no rspnse* **10/1**[3]
1-50 **11** 3 ½ **Clear Sailing**[9] 3882 4-9-7 78 JimCrowley 13 64
(Mrs A J Perrett) *a bhd* **28/1**
0026 **12** 1 ½ **Brief Goodbye**[9] 3882 7-9-1 79 KirstyMilczarek(7) 8 62
(John Berry) *a bhd* **7/1**[2]
400- **13** 13 **High Bray (GER)**[308] 5677 6-9-3 81 HaddenFrost(7) 14 38
(J D Frost) *led: hdd 6f out: wknd over 2f out* **22/1**

2m 4.95s (-3.35) **Going Correction** -0.475s/f (Firm)
WFA 3 from 4yo+ 9lb 13 Ran SP% **131.1**
Speed ratings (Par 105): **94,93,92,91,91 91,91,88,88,87 84,83,73**
CSF £51.72 CT £476.61 TOTE £13.80: £3.60, £1.70, £3.30; EX 66.30 Trifecta £211.90 Part won. Pool: £298.59 - 0.98 winning tickets..
Owner Fawzi Abdulla Nass **Bred** Mount Coote Stud **Trained** Blewbury, Oxon
FOCUS
A strongly-run, competitive handicap. Sound form, with the first two capable of better.
Brief Goodbye Official explanation: jockey said gelding slipped on the bend; trainer later said gelding was found to have pulled muscles in its hindquarters

The Form Book, Raceform Ltd, Compton, RG20 6NL

High Bray(GER) Official explanation: jockey said gelding lost its action

4185 EXPRESS COLIN BIRCH MEMORIAL FILLIES' H'CAP 1m 3f 135y
4:45 (4:45) (Class 4) (0-85,85) 3-Y-O **£5,181** (£1,541; £770; £384) **Stalls** Low

Form RPR

0143 1 **Maid To Believe**[19] 3590 3-8-9 **73** EddieAhern 6 84
(J L Dunlop) *hld up: hdwy 3f out: rdn to ld over 1f out: r.o wl* **3/1**[3]

-061 2 3 **Tebee**[25] 3400 3-9-0 **78** DavidKinsella 5 84
(J H M Gosden) *led after 2f: rdn 3f out: hdd over 1f out: one pce* **11/2**

0414 3 2 1/2 **Rose Of Petra (IRE)**[16] 3672 3-9-7 **85** JimCrowley 2 87
(Sir Michael Stoute) *led 2f: prom: rdn over 3f out: wknd ins fnl f* **5/2**[1]

4134 4 nk **Fretwork**[19] 3590 3-9-5 **83** PatDobbs 4 84
(R Hannon) *prom: rdn 3f out: wknd over 1f out* **4/1**

0U06 5 4 **Harvest Joy (IRE)**[19] 3590 3-8-12 **76** SaleemGolam 3 70
(B R Millman) *hld up in rr: rdn over 2f out: no rspnse* **20/1**

11 U **Hazy Days**[10] 3848 3-9-0 **78** RichardMullen 1 —
(Sir Mark Prescott) *lost action and uns rdr after 2f: dead* **11/4**[2]

2m 25.51s (-4.59) **Going Correction** -0.475s/f (Firm) **6** Ran SP% **120.4**
Speed ratings (Par 99): **96,94,92,92,89** —
CSF £21.13 TOTE £4.40: £2.10, £3.10; EX 21.50.
Owner Normandie Stud Ltd **Bred** Normandie Stud Ltd **Trained** Arundel, W Sussex

FOCUS
A race marred by the early exit of Hazy Days who suffered a fatal leg injury. The form is rated fairly positively, the fourth the best guide.

4186 COME RACING AGAIN THIS MONDAY EVENING H'CAP 5f 10y
5:20 (5:20) (Class 5) (0-70,70) 3-Y-O **£3,238** (£963; £481; £240) **Stalls** High

Form RPR

2150 1 **Drifting Gold**[16] 3688 3-9-6 **69** (b) EddieAhern 8 74
(C G Cox) *a.p: swtchd lft and rdn over 1f out: r.o to ld last stride* **5/1**

6155 2 hd **Scarlett Heart (IRE)**[17] 3649 3-9-0 **63** JimCrowley 5 67
(J Gallagher) *hld up and bhd: rdn and hdwy over 1f out: led ins fnl f: hdd last stride* **8/1**

-535 3 2 **Galipette**[36] 3046 3-9-5 **68** PatDobbs 3 65
(H R A Cecil) *chsd ldr: rdn 2f out: led jst over 1f out: hdd ins fnl f: nt qckn* **9/2**[3]

-263 4 1/2 **Smirfys Gold (IRE)**[61] 2301 3-8-6 **55** (v) RichardMullen 10 50
(E S McMahon) *led: rdn and hdd jst over 1f out: no ex* **4/1**[2]

1641 5 nk **Mr Forthright**[9] 3870 3-8-4 **58** KevinGhunowa(5) 2 52
(J M Bradley) *bhd: sn rdn along: hdwy on outside over 1f out: one pce fnl f* **9/1**

040 6 1 1/4 **Rhapsilian**[56] 2470 3-8-6 **55** RichardThomas 4 44
(J A Geake) *hld up in mid-div: rdn and no hdwy fnl 2f* **9/1**

0500 7 1/2 **Land Ahoy**[36] 3062 3-8-12 **64** RichardKingscote(3) 7 52
(D W P Arbuthnot) *chsd ldrs: rdn 3f out: wknd over 1f out* **25/1**

4-40 8 1 1/4 **Damhsoir (IRE)**[56] 2444 3-8-2 **51** oh6 AdrianMcCarthy 6 34
(H S Howe) *a towards rr* **40/1**

2045 9 shd **Stoneacre Gareth (IRE)**[11] 3811 3-8-11 **60** (b) HayleyTurner 9 43
(Peter Grayson) *mid-div: rdn over 3f out: sn bhd* **16/1**

2510 10 3 1/2 **Castano**[16] 3688 3-9-2 **70** (v[1]) JamesMillman(5) 1 40
(B R Millman) *dwlt: a bhd* **5/2**[1]

58.69 secs (-2.41) **Going Correction** -0.475s/f (Firm) **10** Ran SP% **126.7**
Speed ratings (Par 100): **100,99,96,95,95 93,92,90,90,84**
CSF £48.98 CT £204.40 TOTE £6.00: £1.90, £2.60, £2.00; EX 56.20 TRIFECTA Not won. Place 6 £101.70, Place 5 £64.93..
Owner Martin C Oliver **Bred** Witney And Warren Enterprises Ltd **Trained** Lambourn, Berks

FOCUS
An open-looking but low-grade sprint handicap. The runner-up is the best guide to the form.
Castano Official explanation: jockey said gelding was never travelling
T/Plt: £146.00 to a £1 stake. Pool: £55,321.05. 276.55 winning tickets. T/Qpdt: £36.40 to a £1 stake. Pool: £2,320.70. 47.10 winning tickets. KH

4187 - 4189a (Foreign Racing) - See Raceform Interactive

4055 DEAUVILLE (R-H)
Saturday, August 4

OFFICIAL GOING: All-weather - standard; turf course - good

4190a PRIX DU CERCLE (LISTED RACE) 5f
2:20 (2:23) 3-Y-O+ **£17,568** (£7,027; £5,270; £3,514; £1,757)

RPR

1 **Only Answer**[23] 3-8-7 OPeslier 10 99
(A Fabre, France) **29/10**[1]

2 hd **The Trader (IRE)**[15] 3708 9-9-0 (b) DBoeuf 13 103
(M Blanshard) *last tl hdwy on outside fr 2 1/2f out: ev ch fnl f: unable qck cl home* **12/1**

3 nk **Ascot Family (IRE)**[28] 3339 3-8-7 YTake 14 97
(A Lyon, France) **16/1**

4 hd **Masta Plasta (IRE)**[15] 3708 4-9-0 C-PLemaire 4 101
(D Nicholls) *a.p on rails: ev ch fnl f: r.o same pce* **66/10**

5 shd **Kocooning (IRE)**[44] 4-8-10 J-BHamel 12 97
(Robert Collet, France) **18/1**

6 3/4 **Sacho (GER)**[24] 3445 9-9-4 AlxiBadel 2 102
(W Kujath, Germany) **11/1**

7 snk **Biniou (IRE)**[44] 2811 4-9-0 TJarnet 3 98
(R M H Cowell) *in tch: nt clr run wl over 1f out: swtchd rt and pushed his way through below dist: r.o: nrest at fin* **22/1**

8 snk **Rakiza (IRE)**[24] 3445 3-8-7 DBonilla 6 92
(F Head, France) **62/10**[3]

9 1/2 **Arc De Triomphe (GER)**[44] 2811 5-9-4 JVictoire 11 99
(D Fechner, Germany) **58/10**[2]

10 2 **Numerieus (FR)**[28] 3339 3-8-7 TThulliez 1 83
(Y De Nicolay, France) **21/1**

11 **Deauville (GER)**[104] 1189 4-9-1 ACrastus 5 89
(Frau E Mader, Germany) **51/1**

12 **Blue Damask (USA)**[303] 5779 4-9-0 SPasquier 7 88
(A Fabre, France) **16/1**

13 **Fulminant (IRE)**[44] 2811 6-9-0 WMongil 8 88
(W Kujath, Germany) **11/1**

14 **Mednaya (IRE)**[24] 3445 4-8-10 FSpanu 9 84
(R Gibson, France) **14/1**

57.10 secs (-1.60)
WFA 3 from 4yo+ 3lb **14** Ran SP% **126.3**
PARI-MUTUEL: WIN 3.90; PL 2.10, 3.70, 4.40; DF 19.60.
Owner Wertheimer Et Frere **Bred** Wertheimer Et Frere **Trained** Chantilly, France

NOTEBOOK
The Trader(IRE), who can be considered a veteran these days, produced a wonderful effort considering he would not have felt totally at home on the firmish ground. He was last early on and came with his run on the outside but was always held throughout the final 100 yards. All being well he could come back for the Prix de Meautry.
Masta Plasta(IRE) always well placed from the start on the rail, kept up the good work to the bitter end and only went down by under a length.
Biniou(IRE) still had plenty to do at the furlong marker, but he ran on really well as the race came to an end. This was a much better performance which augers well for the future.

3529 CHESTER (L-H)
Sunday, August 5

OFFICIAL GOING: Good to firm (good in places; 8.9)
Wind: Light, across Weather: Warm and sunny

4192 EUROPEAN BREEDERS' FUND MAIDEN STKS 7f 2y
2:00 (2:03) (Class 4) 2-Y-O **£5,181** (£1,541; £770; £384) **Stalls** Low

Form RPR

2 1 **Quick Release (IRE)**[53] 2575 2-9-3 0 RichardMullen 5 76
(D M Simcock) *chsd ldrs: rdn to cl over 1f out: styd on wl to ld towards fin* **4/1**[3]

5 2 1/2 **Hold The Gold (IRE)**[23] 3510 2-9-3 0 ChrisCatlin 7 75
(E J O'Neill) *racd keenly: led after 1f: sn clr: rdn over 1f out: ct towards fin* **7/1**

42 3 1/2 **Lady Rochbonne**[8] 3951 2-8-12 0 PaulHanagan 3 68
(Mrs G S Rees) *led for 1f: chsd clr ldr after: rdn to cl over 1f out: lost 2nd ins fnl f but styd on to chal: a hld* **7/2**[2]

5 4 5 **Calistos Quest**[30] 3270 2-9-3 0 J-PGuillambert 10 60+
(M Johnston) *in midfield: sme hdwy over 2f out: chsd ldng trio fnl f: no imp* **10/3**[1]

0 5 5 **Waterloo Dock**[57] 2451 2-9-3 0 FrancisNorton 6 47
(M Quinn) *chsd clr ldrs: sn pushed along: outpcd over 3f out* **20/1**

00 6 3/4 **Prince Desire (IRE)**[36] 3095 2-9-3 0 WCMarwing 9 45
(B W Hills) *rrd sltly s: hld up and bhd: nvr trbld ldrs* **9/2**

255 7 1/2 **Liani (IRE)**[9] 3923 2-8-9 50 LiamJones(3) 8 39
(W M Brisbourne) *in midfield: rdn 3f out: wknd fnl f* **66/1**

5 8 1 1/4 **Intersky Melody (USA)**[20] 3596 2-9-3 0 DeanMcKeown 11 41
(R M Whitaker) *bhd: rdn into midfield over 2f out: wknd fnl f* **22/1**

00 9 nk **Viola Rosa (IRE)**[14] 3760 2-8-9 0 DominicFox(3) 1 35
(D Shaw) *a bhd* **100/1**

10 nk **Mahadee (IRE)** 2-9-3 0 NCallan 2 39
(C E Brittain) *pushed along in rr-div thrght* **12/1**

0 11 1 1/2 **Naked Spark (IRE)**[76] 1896 2-8-5 0 JackDean(7) 4 30
(W G M Turner) *pushed along in midfield: wknd over 3f out* **66/1**

1m 27.87s (-0.60) **Going Correction** -0.125s/f (Firm) **11** Ran SP% **116.8**
Speed ratings (Par 96): **98,97,96,91,85 84,84,82,82,81 80**
CSF £30.34 TOTE £4.10: £1.80, £2.20, £1.80; EX 28.00.
Owner Abdullah Saeed Belhab **Bred** Mrs C Regalado-Gonzalez **Trained** Newmarket, Suffolk

FOCUS
A fair maiden run at a good pace. The first three dominated and finished clear, but the form looks pretty solid nevertheless

NOTEBOOK
Quick Release(IRE) proved very much suited by the step up to 7f and his cause was aided by the fast pace set by the leader. He stayed on well to lead close home and, on this evidence, will benefit from stepping up to a mile. (op 10-3)
Hold The Gold(IRE), who showed plenty of pace on his debut, once again blazed, and around this track being in front is often the place to be. Turning in it looked as though he might hold off his pursuers, but he just got tired towards the end and was caught close home. The fast ground certainly seemed to suit him. (op 9-2)
Lady Rochbonne bounced out well but she was denied the opportunity to make all by Hold The Gold, who went very fast to secure the lead. She kept on well to finish clear of the rest, though, and now has the option of nurseries. (op 9-2)
Calistos Quest, poorly drawn, struggled a little to go the pace around this tight track and will be seen to much better effect on a more galloping course. He will get a mile with few problems. (op 9-2)
Waterloo Dock, a half-brother to Lady le Mans, a 6f winner at two, showed more than on his debut over 5f, which was a little surprising as the step up to 7f did not look sure to suit on pedigree. (op 25-1)
Prince Desire(IRE), another drawn out wide, did not get away well and struggled to get competitive thereafter. Official explanation: jockey said, regarding the running and riding, his orders were to break well and be as handy as possible, but colt fly-leapt as stalls opened and lost ground, which he was unable to make up due to the very fast early pace, adding that having hit the straight he was able to get colt balanced and ran on through tired horses; he also said colt might be better suited by a galloping track and a longer distance (tchd 5-1)

4193 CHESHIRE COUNTY COUNCIL FOSTER NURSERY 6f 18y
2:30 (2:30) (Class 4) 2-Y-O **£4,857** (£1,445; £722; £360) **Stalls** Low

Form RPR

0632 1 **Fathsta (IRE)**[11] 3841 2-7-6 **65** oh1 ow1 KMay(7) 2 72
(S Kirk) *racd keenly: hld up: sn in midfield: hdwy over 2f out: rdn over 1f out: r.o to ld wl ins fnl f: in command towards fin* **4/1**[3]

4122 2 1 1/2 **Victorian Bounty**[9] 3925 2-8-9 **75** ChrisCatlin 1 77
(E J O'Neill) *led: rdn and edgd rt 1f out: hdd wl ins fnl f: hld towards fin* **11/4**[1]

2150 3 2 1/2 **Thunder Bay**[81] 1772 2-9-5 **85** PaulHanagan 5 80
(M R Channon) *chsd ldrs: rdn and ch over 1f out: no ex wl ins fnl f* **6/1**

4250 4 2 1/2 **Demure Princess**[9] 3925 2-7-9 **64** oh4 DuranFentiman(3) 8 51
(W G M Turner) *in rr: rdn over 2f out: hdwy over 1f out: chsd ldrs fnl f: nt pce to chal* **50/1**

3102 5 1 **Russian Reel**[23] 3494 2-9-7 **87** NCallan 6 71
(K A Ryan) *prom: rdn and hung rt ent st over 1f out: wknd fnl f* **3/1**[2]

3001 6 nk **Sudden Impact (IRE)**[9] 3915 2-9-4 **84** EddieAhern 7 67
(Paul Green) *racd keenly in midfield: rdn 2f out: wknd over 1f out* **7/1**

0100 7 1 1/4 **Ballycroy Boy (IRE)**[6] 4022 2-8-6 **72** (b[1]) FrancisNorton 3 51
(A Bailey) *lost pl after 1f: outpcd and bhd over 3f out* **20/1**

041 8 2 1/2 **Mister Christie**[13] 3788 2-8-7 **73** KDarley 9 45
(J G Given) *in rr on outside: rdn over 1f out: nvr on terms* **8/1**

1m 14.71s (-0.94) **Going Correction** -0.125s/f (Firm) **8** Ran SP% **116.3**
Speed ratings (Par 96): **101,99,95,92,91 90,88,85**
CSF £15.75 CT £65.05 TOTE £4.80: £1.60, £1.50, £2.00; EX 14.70.
Owner Speedlith Group **Bred** Brian Miller **Trained** Upper Lambourn, Berks

FOCUS
A competitive nursery, but not particularly strong form.

NOTEBOOK

Fathsta(IRE) raced keenly but he was always well positioned just off the pace and he quickened up well in the closing stages to win a shade comfortably. He was 1lb wrong at the weights and carried 1lb overweight here, but he relished the fast ground and looks on the upgrade.

Victorian Bounty again made the running and, while the winner had a bit too much toe at the finish, he put up a solid effort in defeat. A sharp track suits his style of running. (op 10-3)

Thunder Bay, stepping up to 6f for the first time, had every chance as they swung into the straight, but he did not quite see it out as strongly as the first two. He too appreciated the return to quicker conditions having found the softish ground at York too tiring last time. (op 5-1 tchd 9-2 and 13-2)

Demure Princess, who was 4lb wrong at the weights, stayed on from off the pace but was never a real threat to the first three.

Russian Reel was disappointing, but he did not handle the track that well and it is possible that the ground was quicker than he would care for. Official explanation: jockey said colt hung right-handed in straight (op 10-3 tchd 7-2)

Sudden Impact(IRE), another stepping up to 6f for the first time, also failed to shine on this unique track.

4194 WARWICK INTERNATIONAL H'CAP — 1m 4f 66y

3:05 (3:05) (Class 4) (0-85,83) 3-Y-0+ **£5,829** (£1,734; £866; £432) **Stalls** Low

Form — RPR

6341 **1** **Rhaam**[26] 3402 3-9-0 **80** .... WCMarwing 1 — 84
(B W Hills) *a.p: rdn over 1f out: r.o to ld fnl stride* **10/3**[1]

5010 **2** *hd* **Luna Landing**[43] 2861 4-9-12 **81** .... PaulMulrennan 3 — 85
(Jedd O'Keeffe) *a.p: led wl over 3f out: rdn abt 3 l clr over 1f out: ct fnl stride* **8/1**

1012 **3** *hd* **Prelude**[16] 3719 6-8-6 **64** .... LiamJones(3) 2 — 68
(W M Brisbourne) *handy: rdn and nt qckn over 1f out: r.o towards fin* **7/1**

2245 **4** *1* **Acuzio**[2] 4124 6-8-9 **64** oh6 .... DavidAllan 9 — 66
(W M Brisbourne) *hld up: rdn over 1f out: hdwy ent fnl f: styd on but nt pce of ldrs towards fin* **9/1**

130- **5** *½* **Mr Aitch (IRE)**[219] 4876 5-9-6 **75** .... (t) J-PGuillambert 5 — 76
(R T Phillips) *hld up: nt clr run wl over 1f out: effrt whn n.m.r and hmpd ent fnl f: kpt on towards fin: nt rch ldrs* **12/1**

3400 **6** *½* **Active Asset (IRE)**[8] 3959 5-10-0 **83** .... FrancisNorton 11 — 85+
(M Quinn) *in midfield: rdn over 1f out: nt clr run and snatched up ent fnl f: n.d to ldrs after* **11/1**

-043 **7** *1¾* **Dove Cottage (IRE)**[27] 3385 5-8-13 **68** .... NCallan 10 — 66
(W S Kittow) *led: hdd wl over 3f out: rdn 2f out: fdd ins fnl f* **6/1**[3]

-136 **8** *¾* **Stretton (IRE)**[15] 3753 9-9-4 **80** .... JackMitchell(7) 4 — 76
(J D Bethell) *hld up in rr: hdwy over 2f out: rdn over 1f out: no ex ins fnl f* **4/1**[2]

05-0 **9** *2* **Jack Of Trumps (IRE)**[37] 3060 7-9-7 **76** .... ChrisCatlin 7 — 69
(G Wragg) *in midfield: nt clr run over 1f out: n.m.r and hmpd ent fnl f: sn lost pl: n.d after* **15/2**

2m 38.33s (-2.32) **Going Correction** -0.125s/f (Firm)
WFA 3 from 4yo+ 11lb — **9** Ran SP% **118.8**
Speed ratings (Par 105): **102,101,101,101,100 100,99,98,97**
CSF £31.47 CT £178.90 TOTE £4.70: £1.90, £3.40, £1.90; EX 39.30.

Owner Hamdan Al Maktoum **Bred** Shadwell Estate Company Limited **Trained** Lambourn, Berks

FOCUS

A handicap notable for a fairly steady early pace which counted against those held up off the pace.

4195 HALLIWELL JONES BMW - MILE (HANDICAP STKS) — 7f 122y

3:40 (3:41) (Class 3) (0-95,89) 3-Y-0+ **£10,039** (£2,986; £1,492; £745) **Stalls** Low

Form — RPR

1-23 **1** **Robema**[8] 3961 4-9-4 **79** .... GrahamGibbons 2 — 86
(J J Quinn) *a.p: rdn over 1f out: r.o to ld ins fnl f: jst hld on* **7/2**[1]

0240 **2** *shd* **Gallantry**[8] 3941 5-9-10 **85** .... DeanMcKeown 6 — 92
(D Shaw) *in midfield: hdwy whn nt clr run under 2f out: sn rdn: pressed ldr ins fnl f: r.o* **13/2**[3]

5060 **3** *1¾* **High Curragh**[22] 3557 4-9-10 **85** .... NCallan 8 — 88
(K A Ryan) *prom: led 2f out: sn rdn: hdd ins fnl f: no ex fnl strides* **9/1**

0000 **4** *hd* **Bobski (IRE)**[18] 3650 5-9-5 **80** .... ChrisCatlin 1 — 82
(G A Huffer) *racd keenly: hld up: hdwy over 1f out: r.o ins fnl f: nt pce to rch ldrs* **10/1**

3442 **5** *nk* **Stoic Leader (IRE)**[12] 3813 7-9-2 **77** .... PaulHanagan 4 — 78
(R F Fisher) *led early: in tch: rdn over 2f out: styd on same pce fnl f* **9/2**[2]

4116 **6** *hd* **Countdown**[8] 3953 5-9-12 **87** .... DavidAllan 3 — 88
(T D Easterby) *hld up: rdn and hdwy over 1f out: running on but nt rching ldrs whn n.m.r fnl strides* **8/1**

600 **7** *2½* **Waterline Twenty (IRE)**[17] 3670 4-8-11 **72** .... StephenDonohoe 12 — 67
(P D Evans) *hld up: rdn over 1f out: styd on fnl f: nt rch ldrs* **25/1**

0-56 **8** *2½* **Jubilee Street (IRE)**[75] 1915 8-9-6 **81** .... RoystonFfrench 10 — 69
(Mrs A Duffield) *in midfield: rdn over 4f out: nvr able to chal* **20/1**

3110 **9** *hd* **H Harrison (IRE)**[12] 3813 7-9-3 **81** .... AndrewElliott(3) 7 — 69
(I W McInnes) *sn led: rdn and hdd 2f out: stmbld shortly after: wknd ins fnl f* **10/1**

2006 **10** *¾* **King Harson**[17] 3682 8-8-12 **73** .... PatCosgrave 11 — 59
(J D Bethell) *in tch: rdn over 1f out: sn wknd* **25/1**

0660 **11** *½* **Phluke**[8] 3941 6-10-0 **89** .... StephenCarson 13 — 74
(Eve Johnson Houghton) *hld up: rdn over 1f out: n.d* **14/1**

-634 **12** *3½* **Steady As A Rock (FR)**[23] 3491 3-8-9 **77** .... J-PGuillambert 9 — 53
(M Johnston) *in tch: rdn over 2f out: wknd over 1f out* **7/1**

1m 33.74s (-1.01) **Going Correction** -0.125s/f (Firm)
WFA 3 from 4yo+ 7lb — **12** Ran SP% **124.7**
Speed ratings (Par 107): **100,99,98,97,97 97,94,92,92,91 91,87**
CSF £26.92 CT £196.83 TOTE £4.10: £2.00, £2.70, £3.80; EX 33.20 Trifecta £343.40 Pool £580.50. - 1.20 winning units..

Owner Mrs J O'Connor **Bred** Newsells Park Stud Limited **Trained** Settrington, N Yorks

FOCUS

A fairly competitive handicap on paper but they went only an ordinary gallop and not that many got into it.

NOTEBOOK

Robema, one of the least exposed runners in the line-up, was always well placed just behind the leader and went on to just shade a final half-furlong duel with Gallantry. She is well suited to fast ground and is open to further improvement, and the Handicapper cannot put her up too much for this narrow success. (op 10-3)

Gallantry followed the winner through for much of the race and they both eventually fought out the finish. He likes a sharp, turning course such as this. (op 6-1 tchd 7-1)

High Curragh, who normally tackles sprint distances, did not see the trip out quite as well as the first two. (op 10-1)

Bobski(IRE), who did best of those that were held up further back in the pack, could have done with a stronger pace. (op 16-1)

Stoic Leader(IRE) was being shoved along from some way out but kept on well. A stronger pace would have suited him, too. (op 11-2)

Countdown is now on a mark 4lb higher than when last successful but, more importantly, the ground has turned against him now.

4196 M&S MONEY QUEENSFERRY STKS (LISTED RACE) — 6f 18y

4:10 (4:11) (Class 1) 3-Y-0+

£14,762 (£5,595; £2,800; £1,396; £699; £351) **Stalls** Low

Form — RPR

5060 **1** **Green Manalishi**[7] 3990 6-9-0 105 .... NCallan 4 — 104
(K A Ryan) *broke wl: trckd ldrs: rdn and swtchd lft to chal over 1f out: r.o to ld ins fnl f: hld on wl* **11/2**

4005 **2** *shd* **Baltic King**[9] 3894 7-9-0 107 .... (t) EddieAhern 3 — 104
(H Morrison) *hld up: hdwy 2f out: plld out over 1f out: sltly short of room ins fnl f: fin strly* **11/4**[1]

0006 **3** *1½* **Invincible Force (IRE)**[8] 3975 3-8-10 98 .... FrancisNorton 5 — 99
(Paul Green) *sn led: rdn over 1f out: hdd ins fnl f: no ex towards fin* **22/1**

0640 **4** *hd* **Dhaular Dhar (IRE)**[8] 3941 5-9-0 98 .... DanielTudhope 1 — 99+
(J S Goldie) *hld up bhd: rdn over 1f out: r.o ins fnl f: gaining at fin* **9/2**[3]

0500 **5** *¾* **Drayton (IRE)**[9] 3894 3-8-10 0 .... WCMarwing 10 — 96
(M F De Kock, South Africa) *racd 3 wd: prom: rdn over 1f out: bmpd whn edgd lft and rdr lost whip ins fnl f: kpt on same pce after* **8/1**

-221 **6** *hd* **Final Dynasty**[16] 3720 3-8-5 99 .... PaulHanagan 8 — 90
(Mrs G S Rees) *racd keenly: prom: rdn and pressed ldr 2f out: fdd towards fin* **14/1**

20-3 **7** *shd* **Judd Street**[24] 3464 5-9-0 94 .... StephenCarson 2 — 96
(Eve Johnson Houghton) *broke wl: trckd ldrs: rdn over 1f out: one pce ins fnl f* **4/1**[2]

P403 **8** *3* **Daniella**[15] 3746 5-8-9 76 .... (b) ChrisCatlin 6 — 82
(Rae Guest) *hld up: rdn over 1f out: n.d* **33/1**

3200 **9** *3* **Beckermet (IRE)**[1] 4150 5-9-0 106 .... RoystonFfrench 9 — 78
(R F Fisher) *racd wd: in midfield: outpcd over 2f out: n.d after* **8/1**

00-0 **10** *6* **Free Roses (IRE)**[3] 4090 4-8-9 90 .... TomEaves 7 — 55
(J G Given) *in tch: lost pl over 2f out: sn bhd* **66/1**

1m 13.43s (-2.22) **Going Correction** -0.125s/f (Firm)
WFA 3 from 4yo+ 4lb — **10** Ran SP% **117.9**
Speed ratings (Par 111): **109,108,106,106,105 105,105,101,97,89**
CSF £20.95 TOTE £6.60: £2.40, £1.40, £3.50; EX 17.90.

Owner T Fawcett,S McCarthy,J Brennan&J Smith **Bred** E Aldridge **Trained** Hambleton, N Yorks

FOCUS

A decent enough Listed race and solid enough form for the grade.

NOTEBOOK

Green Manalishi is at his best over 5f but 6f round here takes less getting. He held a clear chance on the ratings back in Listed company and enjoyed a fairly good trip, tracking the pace. He was bit lucky to hold off the fast-finishing favourite, though, as that one had his run momentarily hampered at a crucial stage, and the margin of victory was very slight. (op 6-1 tchd 5-1)

Baltic King has not been at his best this season but he was back in Listed company and held a solid chance on the ratings. He was a bit unlucky not to win in the end as he was slightly hampered by Drayton just as he was switched to challenge, and that slight loss in momentum cost him in the end as he finished strongly to be beaten only a whisker. (op 5-2 tchd 3-1)

Invincible Force(IRE) was well placed throughout and ran a good race at the weights, but he was twice a winner at this track as a juvenile so we already knew that he is suited to the course. (op 20-1)

Dhaular Dhar(IRE) had a bit to find with a few of these but he is very effective around this track and came in for market support, despite the distance being short of ideal. He was running on at the finish as could have been predicted, and will appreciate stepping back up to 7f. (op 6-1)

Drayton(IRE), who was poorly drawn, gave up ground by racing wide throughout. He ran quite well in the circumstances, especially as easier ground suits him ideally. (op 6-1)

Final Dynasty, taking a step up in grade, has done her winning over 5f and is much more comfortable on easier ground. (op 12-1 tchd 10-1)

Judd Street ran well on his reappearance behind subsequent Group 3 winner Moorhouse Lad so it was easy to see why he was popular in the market from a low draw despite having 11lb and more to find on official ratings with the eventual winner and runner-up. (op 6-1)

4197 BETRESCUE ANTEPOSTMAG.COM H'CAP — 1m 2f 75y

4:45 (4:45) (Class 5) (0-75,75) 3-Y-0 **£4,095** (£1,209; £604) **Stalls** High

Form — RPR

3251 **1** **Grand Art (IRE)**[13] 3800 3-9-1 **69** .... NCallan 1 — 81+
(M H Tompkins) *trckd ldrs: hmpd whn n.m.r over 2f out: rdn over 1f out: r.o ins fnl f: led towards fin* **7/2**[1]

5300 **2** *nk* **Old Romney**[2] 4135 3-9-7 **75** .... J-PGuillambert 3 — 83
(G A Huffer) *led: rdn over 1f out: hdd towards fin* **4/1**[2]

0325 **3** *2* **Cheshire Prince**[20] 3587 3-8-7 **61** .... DavidAllan 5 — 65
(W M Brisbourne) *racd keenly: prom: lost pl briefly 6f out: rdn to press ldr over 1f out: no ex towards fin* **9/2**[3]

41 **4** *3½* **Go But Go**[46] 2763 3-9-7 **75** .... ChrisCatlin 6 — 72
(E J O'Neill) *s.i.s: bustled along to sn go into midfield: rdn over 2f out: styd on fr over 1f out: no imp on ldrs* **7/1**

5551 **5** *1¾* **Nota Liberata**[20] 3587 3-8-12 **66** .... (t) NickyMackay 7 — 60
(G M Moore) *in midfield: hdwy on outside to chse ldrs 3f out: wknd 1f out* **7/1**

-000 **6** *5* **Berbatov**[7] 3997 3-7-13 **56** oh6 .... LiamJones(3) 8 — 41
(Paul Green) *hld up: rdn over 2f out: nvr on terms w ldrs* **28/1**

6165 **7** *1½* **Aegis (IRE)**[17] 3689 3-9-5 **73** .... WCMarwing 9 — 55
(B W Hills) *in midfield: hdwy 6f out: lost pl 3f out: n.d after* **6/1**

-020 **8** *5* **Sularno**[27] 3384 3-8-11 **65** .... EddieAhern 10 — 37
(H Morrison) *hld up: pushed along 4f out: nvr on terms* **11/1**

2200 **9** *16* **Stark Contrast (USA)**[11] 3848 3-9-1 **69** .... (b) StephenCarson 2 — 11
(G A Butler) *prom tl rdn and wknd over 2f out: esased whn btn ins fnl f* **16/1**

2m 11.12s (-2.02) **Going Correction** -0.125s/f (Firm) — **9** Ran SP% **117.4**
Speed ratings (Par 100): **103,102,101,98,96 92,91,87,74**
CSF £17.87 CT £64.21 TOTE £4.60: £1.70, £1.90, £1.70; EX 20.70 Place 6 £30.44, Place 5 £12.32. .

Owner Matthew Green **Bred** Mrs Teresa Bergin And Mrs Anne Fitzgerald **Trained** Newmarket, Suffolk

FOCUS

A modest handicap run at a fairly steady early gallop.

T/Plt: £33.50 to a £1 stake. Pool: £88,378.50. 1,925.65 winning tickets. T/Qpdt: £12.40 to a £1 stake. Pool: £3,427.40. 203.30 winning tickets. DO

3232 NEWBURY (L-H)

Sunday, August 5

OFFICIAL GOING: Good to firm (7.4)

Wind: Brisk, across

4198 HOME-START WEST BERKSHIRE EUROPEAN BREEDERS' FUND MAIDEN STKS (DIV I) 6f 8y

1:10 (1:11) (Class 4) 2-Y-O £5,829 (£1,734; £866; £432) Stalls High

Form				RPR
	1		**Tajdeef (USA)** 2-9-3 0 .... RHills 2 (B W Hills) *trckd ldrs: led on bit wl over 1f out: sn clr: impressive* **11/8**[1]	91+
	2	*5*	**Redsensor** 2-9-3 0 .... RyanMoore 7 (R Hannon) *trckd ldr: led over 2f out: hdd wl over 1f out: sn no ch w wnr but styd on wl for 2nd* **9/2**[3]	74
	3	*1 ¼*	**We'Re Delighted** 2-9-3 0 .... JHBowman 9 (M R Channon) *chsd ldrs: rdn over 2f out: styd on fnl f but nvr gng pce to be competitive* **8/1**	70
	4	*2*	**Highland Laddie** 2-9-3 0 .... RobertHavlin 3 (C R Egerton) *chsd ldrs: rdn over 2f out: wknd fnl f* **33/1**	64
	5	*1 ¾*	**Exclamation** 2-9-3 0 .... SteveDrowne 8 (B J Meehan) *s.i.s: bhd: rdn and sme hdwy 2f out: nvr in contention and wknd fnl f* **10/3**[2]	59
00	6	*nk*	**Rich Kid (IRE)**[6] 4014 2-9-3 0 .... PatDobbs 6 (R Hannon) *outpcd tl mod prog fnl f* **12/1**	58+
	7	*½*	**Musashi (IRE)** 2-9-3 0 .... JohnEgan 4 (J S Moore) *s.i.s: rdn and green 1/2-way: a towards rr* **16/1**	57
0	8	*5*	**Golden Dane (IRE)**[48] 2723 2-9-3 0 .... JamesDoyle 10 (I A Wood) *led tl hdd over 2f out: sn wknd* **100/1**	42
	9	*shd*	**Wogan's Sister** 2-8-12 0 .... RichardThomas 5 (I A Wood) *in rr: outpcd 1/2-way: mod hdwy last half f* **50/1**	36
604	10	*2 ½*	**Purple Ransom (IRE)**[40] 2961 2-9-3 59 .... VinceSlattery 1 (I A Wood) *slowly away and in rr: sn rcvrd to chse ldrs: wknd 2f out* **25/1**	34

1m 12.7s (-1.62) **Going Correction** -0.325s/f (Firm) 10 Ran SP% **117.8**

Speed ratings (Par 96): **97,90,88,86,83 83,82,75,75,72**

CSF £7.67 TOTE £2.20: £1.10, £1.70, £2.00; EX 8.80.

Owner Hamdan Al Maktoum **Bred** Shadwell Farm LLC **Trained** Lambourn, Berks

FOCUS

This looked like quite a hot maiden and the winner is a nice prospect. The winning time was 0.40 seconds slower than the second division, although the early pace was just ordinary.

NOTEBOOK

Tajdeef(USA) ◆, a son of Aljabr, half-brother to 7f winner Tawaajud, out of a useful dual 5f-6f winner at two, has been given entries in the Champagne Stakes, the Mill Reef and the Middle Park, and he was extremely well backed. He raced a touch keenly off the modest early gallop, but had plenty left for when it mattered and bounded well clear of his nine rivals to make a very impressive racecourse debut. The winning time was a touch slower than the second division, but the gallop was pretty ordinary through the first couple of furlongs and it would probably be unfair to hold that against him. He won in the style of a potential Group horse and could be aimed at both the Acomb Stakes and the Champagne Stakes over 7f, or stick to 6f for the Mill Reef and Middle Park. (op 7-4 tchd 15-8 in places)

Redsensor, a Redback first foal of a 6f winner at two, who was unplaced but highly tried in two starts over 7f-1m at three, has no Group-race entries. He proved no match for the above average winner, but was a clear second and this must rate as a pleasing debut. (op 4-1)

We'Re Delighted, a 40,000gns son of Tobougg, out of a dual 5f-6f winner at two, is another not entered in any Group races. He never posed a serious threat, but kept on nicely enough in the closing stages and is open to improvement. (op 12-1)

Highland Laddie ◆, a son of Lomitas, is closely related to the quite useful triple middle-distance winner Vinando, who has also been successful over hurdles, out of a multiple 1m winner in Germany, and he has been given an entry in the Royal Lodge. This was a very respectable debut effort and he should be capable of a lot better given the benefit of both time and distance.

Exclamation ◆, a 36,000gns son of Acclamation, half-brother to 1m2f winner Native American, is entered in the Mill Reef, as well as a few sales races. His stable won the second division of this maiden with a well-backed favourite but, although he was not without his supporters in the market either, he was never really seen with a chance after starting slowly. He should know a lot more next time and can improve a fair bit on this. (op 5-2 tchd 7-2)

Rich Kid(IRE) ◆ had shown just moderate form on his two previous starts, but he looked a potential improver at Windsor on his previous start and this was a creditable effort. He can make his mark over further in nursery/handicap company. (op 16-1)

Musashi(IRE), a 30,000gns son of Hawk Wing, half-brother to 1m juvenile winner Aldo L'Argentin, looked in need of the experience and can improve a fair bit on this. (op 18-1)

4199 H.B.L.B. NOVICE STKS 7f (S)

1:40 (1:43) (Class 4) 2-Y-O £5,181 (£1,541; £770; £384) Stalls High

Form				RPR
2	1		**Yahrab (IRE)**[22] 3522 2-8-12 0 .... KerrinMcEvoy 2 (C E Brittain) *trckd ldrs in cl 3rd: wnt 2nd 2f out: shkn up to ld 1f out: sn in control: readily* **11/4**[2]	88+
100	2	*1 ¼*	**Yem Kinn**[22] 3522 2-9-5 91 .... JHBowman 1 (M R Channon) *led and racd alone towards centre of crse: rdn 2f out: hdd 1f out and c rt towards stands' side: kpt on same pce ins fnl f* **11/10**[1]	92
10	3	*4*	**Midships (USA)**[8] 3938 2-9-5 90 .... JimCrowley 3 (Mrs A J Perrett) *chsd ldr: rdn and lost 2nd 2f out: wknd ins fnl f* **10/3**[3]	82
15	4	*6*	**Mutabayen (USA)**[23] 3504 2-9-2 0 .... TedDurcan 6 (B Smart) *trckd ldrs in cl 4th: rdn 3f out: btn 2f out: eased cl home* **11/1**	63
	5	*18*	**Warming Up (IRE)** 2-8-8 0 .... SebSanders 5 (C E Brittain) *slowly away: rdn and rel to r: a wl bhd* **20/1**	8

1m 25.02s (-1.98) **Going Correction** -0.325s/f (Firm) 5 Ran SP% **110.5**

Speed ratings (Par 96): **98,96,92,85,64**

CSF £28.06 TOTE £3.90: £2.00, £3.10; EX 33.10.

Owner Saif Ali **Bred** Swettenham Stud **Trained** Newmarket, Suffolk

FOCUS

This looked like a very good novice event, although the winning time was 0.92 seconds slower than the later nursery won by 87-rated Gothenburg. The runner-up is the best guide to the level for now.

NOTEBOOK

Yahrab(IRE) ◆ confirmed the promise he showed when a very pleasing second in a good race on his debut at Ascot, getting off the mark at the second attempt a shade comfortably. Admittedly the favourite failed to run his race, but this was still a very useful effort and he looks a smart colt in the making. (op 4-1 tchd 9-2)

Yem Kinn ran much better than at Ascot on his previous start, but he was unable to reverse form with the highly-promising Yahrab. (op 14-1)

Midships(USA) proved disappointing in a Listed event at Ascot the previous week and he was again well held. He looked promising when winning over 6f here on his debut, but has not progressed since. (op 3-1 tchd 5-2 and 7-2)

Mutabayen(USA) was below the form he showed when fifth in the Superlative Stakes and was a major disappointment. (op 10-11 tchd 6-5 and 5-4 in places)

Warming Up(IRE), a 20,000gns son of Kalanisi, out of an unraced half-sister to 7f winner Relaxed, was far too green to do himself justice. (op 14-1)

4200 COMMUNITY FURNITURE PROJECT LADIES INVITATION FEGENTRI H'CAP (LADY AMATEUR RIDERS) 1m 2f 6y

2:10 (2:10) (Class 5) (0-70,69) 3-Y-0+ £3,435 (£1,065; £532; £266) Stalls High

Form				RPR
-020	1		**Venir Rouge**[22] 3525 3-10-2 69 .... MissSLangvad 4 (M Salaman) *trckd ldrs: stdd 5f out: hdwy 3f out: rdn 2f out: chsd ldr over 1f out: sddle slipped: styd on to ld fnl half f: readily* **5/2**[1]	80
0325	2	*4*	**Sharmy (IRE)**[38] 3035 11-10-0 58 .... MissSBrotherton 8 (Ian Williams) *chsd ldrs: led 6f out: drvn 5l clr 3f out: wknd and hdd last half f* **4/1**[2]	61
6000	3	*8*	**Zinging**[54] 2540 8-9-5 49 oh4 .... MrsMarieKing 7 (J J Bridger) *t.k.h: chsd ldrs: wnt 2nd briefly over 3f out: sn outpcd: styd on for wl hld 3rd* **20/1**	36
000-	4	*6*	**Larad (IRE)**[242] 6729 6-9-5 49 oh4 .... MsVRodenbusch 9 (J S Moore) *in rr: rdn 3f out: mod prog fnl 2f* **8/1**[3]	24
40	5	*shd*	**Paraguay (USA)**[58] 2423 4-10-10 68 .... MissEJJones 5 (Miss V Haigh) *s.i.s: in rr: rapid hdwy to chse ldr 3f out: sn no imp: wknd 2f out* **5/2**[1]	43
0-00	6	*1 ¼*	**Hill Of Clare (IRE)**[42] 2913 5-9-5 49 oh4 .... MissNWesterlund 3 (G H Jones) *chsd ldr: upsides 6f out: rdn 3f out and sn btn* **20/1**	21
00/0	7	*¾*	**Ren's Magic**[13] 3795 9-9-5 49 oh1 .... (t) MissSZapico 1 (E J Creighton) *t.k.h: a towards rr* **33/1**	20
053-	8	*5*	**Sea Cookie**[245] 6691 3-8-13 52 .... MlleSHusser 6 (W De Best-Turner) *chsd ldrs: chal 6f out: wknd 3f out* **20/1**	13
	9	*30*	**Positano (IRE)**[333] 7-10-5 63 .... (p) MissFayeBramley 2 (M Scudamore) *led tl hdd 6f out: wknd qckly fr 4f out* **8/1**[3]	—

2m 7.73s (-0.98) **Going Correction** -0.325s/f (Firm)

WFA 3 from 4yo+ 9lb 9 Ran SP% **116.6**

Speed ratings (Par 103): **90,86,80,75,75 74,73,69,45**

CSF £12.00 CT £161.78 TOTE £3.90: £1.50, £1.50, £4.20; EX 10.80.

Owner Oaktree Racing **Bred** M A Salaman **Trained** Baydon, Wilts

■ The first winner in Britain for Norwegian rider Sophie Langvad.

FOCUS

A moderate handicap restricted to lady amateur riders and the form is worth little. The pace was strong.

4201 HOME-START WEST BERKSHIRE EUROPEAN BREEDERS' FUND MAIDEN STKS (DIV II) 6f 8y

2:40 (2:41) (Class 4) 2-Y-O £5,829 (£1,734; £866; £432) Stalls High

Form				RPR
	1		**Cat Junior (USA)** 2-9-3 0 .... TedDurcan 6 (B J Meehan) *trckd ldrs: led over 1f out: drvn clr ins fnl f: readily* **1/1**[1]	83+
40	2	*3 ½*	**Harlech Castle**[54] 2526 2-9-3 .... (b[1]) TQuinn 7 (P F I Cole) *led tl hdd over 3f out: slt ld again 2f out: hdd u.p over 1f out: edgd lft and one pce ins fnl f* **9/1**	72
0	3	*1 ½*	**Hustle (IRE)**[23] 3478 2-9-3 0 .... RyanMoore 10 (R Hannon) *chsd ldrs: rdn over 2f out: styd on same pce fr over 1f out* **6/1**[3]	68+
530	4	*1 ½*	**Mansii**[60] 2353 2-9-3 76 .... SebSanders 9 (C E Brittain) *in rr: rdn 1/2-way: kpt on fr 2f out but nvr gng pce to be competitive* **8/1**	63
	5	*1 ½*	**Gaia Prince (USA)** 2-9-3 0 .... JimCrowley 3 (Mrs A J Perrett) *s.i.s: in rr: pushed along 1/2-way: kpt on fnl f but nvr gng pce to be competitive* **16/1**	59
	6	*shd*	**Hit The Roof** 2-9-3 0 .... PatDobbs 2 (R Hannon) *s.i.s: bhd: pushed along 1/2-way: kpt on ins fnl f but nvr in contention* **20/1**	58
0	6	*dht*	**Sheer Bluff (IRE)**[25] 3435 2-9-3 0 .... KerrinMcEvoy 8 (D R C Elsworth) *chsd ldrs: rdn 1/2-way: wknd over 1f out* **9/2**[2]	58
3	8	*1 ½*	**Towy Boy (IRE)**[42] 2911 2-9-3 0 .... JamesDoyle 1 (I A Wood) *w ldr: led over 3f out: hdd 2f out and wknd qckly* **33/1**	54
0	9	*3*	**Randama Bay (IRE)**[43] 2876 2-9-3 0 .... LPKeniry 4 (I A Wood) *a outpcd* **100/1**	45
00	10	*1 ½*	**Holy Storm (IRE)**[10] 3866 2-9-3 0 .... DaneO'Neill 5 (Eve Johnson Houghton) *chsd ldrs over 3f* **66/1**	40

1m 12.3s (-2.02) **Going Correction** -0.325s/f (Firm) 10 Ran SP% **119.6**

Speed ratings (Par 96): **100,95,93,91,89 89,89,87,83,81**

CSF £11.37 TOTE £2.20: £1.20, £2.30, £2.00; EX 16.50.

Owner Roldvale Limited **Bred** March Thoroughbreds **Trained** Manton, Wilts

FOCUS

Another good juvenile maiden with the runner-up the best guide to the level and the winner likely to go on from this. The winning time was 0.40 seconds quicker than the first division.

NOTEBOOK

Cat Junior(USA) ◆, a son of Storm Cat, brother to fairly useful 6f winner The Wild Swan, out of the top-class triple 1m1f-1m2f winner Luna Wells, was not sold at $675,000. An extremely well-backed favourite, he had to be shaken up to see off his rivals, but he was well on top at the finish and recorded a time 0.40 seconds quicker than the winner of the first division. He is entered in the Gimcrack and looks a Pattern horse in the making. (op 11-8)

Harlech Castle was disappointing at Chester when last seen nearly two months previously but, fitted with blinkers for the first time, this was more like it. He probably just ran into a pretty nice type, but an ordinary race should come his way provided he goes the right way, and he also now has the option of going for nurseries. (op 13-2)

Hustle(IRE) ran too bad to be true when a beaten favourite on his debut at Ascot, but this was much better and he seems to be going the right way now. (op 13-2)

Mansii did not run badly but he may be better off in nursery company. (op 17-2)

Gaia Prince(USA) ◆, a $225,000 son of Forestry, first foal of a smart prolific winner in the US at around 1m, has a Derby entry. He showed real signs of inexperience through the early stages, but he gradually got the hang of things and was doing some good late work. He should be able to improve a fair bit on this. (op 14-1)

Sheer Bluff(IRE) failed to improve on the form he showed in a good Newmarket maiden over 7f on his debut and may be more of a nursery/handicap prospect. (op 5-1 and 11-2 in a place)

Hit The Roof, a son of Auction House, out of a mare who was placed over 5f at two, is another who looked in need of the experience and he should improve. (op 5-1 and 11-2 in a place)

4202 LIVING PAINTINGS NURSERY 7f (S)

3:15 (3:15) (Class 4) 2-Y-O £4,663 (£1,387; £693; £346) Stalls High

Form				RPR
21	1		**Gothenburg (UAE)**[13] 3781 2-9-7 87 .... RHills 5 (M Johnston) *trckd ldrs: led over 2f out: c clr fr over 1f out: v easily* **10/11**[1]	103+
0542	2	*7*	**Quick Sands (IRE)**[24] 3446 2-8-7 73 ow1 .... RyanMoore 2 (R Hannon) *chsd ldrs: rdn 3f out: styd on to take 2nd wl ins fnl f but nvr any ch w v easy wnr* **13/2**[2]	71

022 **3** ½ **Non Sucre (USA)**[34] 3171 2-8-8 **74** TedDurcan 1 71
(P A Blockley) *sn prom: drvn to chse wnr over 1f out but nvr any ch: lost 2nd wl ins fnl f* **9/1**[3]
4242 **4** shd **Ruby Delta**[11] 3842 2-8-7 **73** JohnEgan 6 69
(P D Cundell) *in rr: nt clr run 2f out: swtchd sharply lft to outside over 1f out: kpt on cl home but nvr in contention* **9/1**[3]
014 **5** 1 **Eva's Request (IRE)**[18] 3642 2-9-3 **83** JHBowman 4 77
(M R Channon) *in rr: nt clr run 2f out: rdn and squeezed through 1f out: kpt on ins fnl f but nvr in contention* **12/1**
040 **6** 1 **Synge Street**[22] 3550 2-7-12 **64** DavidKinsella 7 55
(R Hannon) *chsd ldrs: rdn fr 3f out: wknd appr fnl f* **9/1**[3]
0464 **7** 1½ **Alfredtheordinary**[28] 3348 2-8-0 **66** oh1 ow2 EdwardCreighton 9 53
(M R Channon) *chsd ldrs: drvn to chal 3f out: wknd over 1f out* **33/1**
6536 **8** ½ **King Bathwick (IRE)**[23] 3508 2-8-0 **66** AdrianMcCarthy 10 52
(B R Millman) *s.i.s: sn in tch: narrow ld 3f out: hdd over 2f out: wknd over 1f out* **14/1**
6004 **9** 8 **Dhaka Dazzle**[27] 3373 2-7-9 **68** oh6 ow4 MatthewDavies(7) 3 33
(M R Channon) *in rr: rdn: hung lft and wknd fr 2f out* **66/1**
6012 **10** 4 **Tamrai Dancer**[30] 3275 2-8-8 **74** SebSanders 8 29
(R M Beckett) *led tl hdd 3f out: wkng whn n.m.r ins fnl 2f* **12/1**

1m 24.1s (-2.90) **Going Correction** -0.325s/f (Firm) **10** Ran SP% **122.2**
Speed ratings (Par 96): **103,95,94,94,93 92,90,89,80,76**
CSF £7.77 CT £37.81 TOTE £1.90: £1.10, £2.20, £2.50; EX 8.50.
Owner Sheikh Mohammed **Bred** Darley **Trained** Middleham Moor, N Yorks

FOCUS
The impressive winner apart, this looked an ordinary nursery although the form is solid enough. The pace was good and the winning time was 0.92 seconds quicker than the earlier novice event.

NOTEBOOK
Gothenburg(UAE) ◆ did not have to be at his best to get off the mark when dropped back to 6f at Ayr on his previous start, but he proved well suited by the step back up in trip on his nursery debut and absolutely hacked up, winning with even more in hand than the official margin suggests. Already entered in a couple of Group 2s, there can be no doubt he is Pattern-class material. He will be almost impossible to beat if turned out in this form under a penalty but, in the longer term, he deserves his chance in something much better. (op 11-10 tchd 6-5)
Quick Sands(IRE), carrying 1lb overweight, shaped as though she could make her mark in nursery company when second at Folkestone on her previous start, but she was just blown away by the hugely impressive Gothenburg. (op 8-1 tchd 9-1)
Non Sucre(USA) had shaped well in maiden company and this was a respectable effort on his nursery debut. (op 8-1)
Ruby Delta, switched to nursery company for the first time, was forced to switch left with his challenge when short of room against the near-side rail and is better than he was able to show. Official explanation: jockey said colt was denied a clear run (op 12-1)
Eva's Request(IRE) lost momentum when stopped in her run against the near-side rail around two furlongs from the finish and she is another better than she was able to show. Official explanation: jockey said filly lost its action 3f out and was denied a clear run (tchd 11-1 and 8-1 in a place)

4203 EUROPEAN BREEDERS' FUND CHALICE STKS (LISTED RACE) (F&M) 1m 4f 5y
3:50 (3:50) (Class 1) 3-Y-O+
£14,762 (£5,595; £2,800; £1,396; £699; £351) **Stalls** High

Form RPR
-322 **1** **Queen's Best**[48] 2720 4-9-2 90 RyanMoore 4 97+
(Sir Michael Stoute) *hld up in rr but in tch: stdy hdwy on outside to ld ins fnl 2f: sn clr: comf* **9/4**[2]
2160 **2** 4 **Wassfa**[25] 3434 4-9-2 73 SebSanders 2 90
(C E Brittain) *in rr but in tch: hrd rdn and hung lft 2f out: styd on u.p fnl f to take 2nd nr fin but nvr any ch w wnr* **33/1**
0-25 **3** ½ **Mont Etoile (IRE)**[25] 3434 4-9-2 104 MichaelHills 5 90
(W J Haggas) *led: rdn and hdd ins fnl 2f: sn outpcd by wnr: lost 2nd nr fin* **6/5**[1]
6156 **4** 1¼ **Marzelline (IRE)**[19] 3628 3-8-5 102 RHills 3 88
(W R Swinburn) *sn in tch: hdwy to chse ldrs fr 5f out: rdn over 3f out: wknd over 1f out* **7/2**[3]
2220 **5** 1 **Lemonette (USA)**[57] 2474 4-9-2 80 TQuinn 6 86
(J W Hills) *chsd ldr: rdn over 4f out: wknd 2f out* **16/1**
4-01 **6** 1¾ **Mirin**[40] 2970 3-8-5 76 KerrinMcEvoy 1 83
(G Wragg) *sn chsng ldrs: rdn over 3f out: wknd over 2f out* **14/1**

2m 30.83s (-5.16) **Going Correction** -0.325s/f (Firm)
WFA 3 from 4yo 11lb **6** Ran SP% **113.9**
Speed ratings (Par 111): **104,101,101,100,99 98**
CSF £57.36 TOTE £2.70: £2.10, £6.20; EX 62.50.
Owner Cheveley Park Stud **Bred** Darley **Trained** Newmarket, Suffolk

FOCUS
An ordinary fillies and mares' Listed contest and, with the pace was just steady early on, the form might want treating with some caution.

NOTEBOOK
Queen's Best did not have things go her way when second in a 1m2f Listed event at Warwick on her previous start, but she proved suited by the step up in trip and ran out a convincing winner, picking up well off the modest gallop. Her two previous wins had both come on soft ground, but this quicker surface posed no problems. Considering the runner-up came into this rated just 73, it would be unwise to get carried away, but she is clearly progressing into a smart sort. (op 3-1)
Wassfa, although finishing last in the Lancashire Oaks on her previous start, had appeared to produce her best effort to date and she confirmed that with another useful performance in this lesser contest. Her effort is all the more creditable considering she appeared to shy away from Michael Hills's whip, who was aboard the labouring Mont Etoile. She looks to be a typical Clive Brittain improver, but is no sure thing to confirm this next time. (op 25-1)
Mont Etoile(IRE) looked to have everything going for her beforehand, for conditions were ideal and she avoided a penalty for her success in last year's Ribblesdale, but she proved disappointing. With no confirmed front runners in the line-up, she was forced to make a lot of her own running at just a steady gallop and she would have been much better served by finishing from off a strong pace. (op 5-4 tchd 11-8 in a place)
Marzelline(IRE) is another who would have benefited from a stonger run race and she also gives the impression she would not mind a bit of give underfoot. (op 3-1 tchd 11-4 and 4-1)
Lemonette(USA), pretty exposed and rated just 80, was basically not good enough. (tchd 18-1)
Mirin found this much tougher than the course-and-distance maiden she won on her previous start and she could make little impression. (op 12-1)

4204 CHUNKY ALLEN RETIREMENT / 60TH BIRTHDAY H'CAP 5f 34y
4:25 (4:25) (Class 4) (0-85,85) 3-Y-O+ **£4,857** (£1,445; £722; £360) **Stalls** High

Form RPR
210- **1** **Maker's Mark (IRE)**[301] 5829 3-9-1 **79** FergusSweeney 8 87
(H Candy) *chsd ldrs: rdn over 1f out: swtchd lft ins fnl f and qcknd to ld fnl 100yds: kpt on strly* **7/1**[3]
000 **2** nk **Peter Island (FR)**[22] 3528 4-9-0 **75** (b) JimCrowley 7 83
(J Gallagher) *led: rdn 2f out: edgd rt ins fnl f: hdd and no ex fnl 100yds* **14/1**
4212 **3** ½ **Malapropism**[3] 4101 7-8-10 **71** ow1 JHBowman 4 77
(M R Channon) *in rr: rdn and hdwy fr 2f out: chsd ldrs ins fnl f: nt qckn fnl 100yds* **10/3**[1]
5625 **4** 1 **Harrison's Flyer (IRE)**[3] 4103 6-8-7 **73** (p) KevinGhunowa(5) 5 75
(J M Bradley) *in rr: swtchd lft to outside and hdwy over 1f out: kpt on ins fnl f but nvr quite gng pce to rch ldrs* **11/1**
2500 **5** nk **Talbot Avenue**[3] 4095 9-9-10 **85** TedDurcan 9 86
(M Blanshard) *chsd ldrs: rdn over 2f out: kpt on same pce tl styd on fnl 100yds* **7/1**[3]
5410 **6** nk **Fromsong (IRE)**[19] 3623 9-9-4 **79** RobertHavlin 6 79
(D K Ivory) *chsd ldrs: rdn 1/2-way: kpt on ins fnl f but nvr quite gng pce to be competitive* **16/1**
0/0- **7** 2 **Avening**[271] 7-9-5 **80** (bt) KerrinMcEvoy 11 73
(Eve Johnson Houghton) *hld up in rr: kpt on ins fnl f but nvr in contention* **8/1**
1350 **8** 3 **Peopleton Brook**[3] 4095 5-9-5 **80** TQuinn 3 62
(J M Bradley) *chsd ldrs: rdn over 2f out: wknd fnl f* **11/1**
4313 **9** nk **Black Moma (IRE)**[17] 3688 3-8-13 **77** RyanMoore 12 57
(R Hannon) *hld up in rr: kpt on fnl f but nvr in contention* **4/1**[2]
5200 **10** 2½ **Bluebok**[7] 2463 6-9-8 **83** (t) SteveDrowne 10 55
(J M Bradley) *outpcd fr 1/2-way* **10/1**
400- **11** 6 **Beau Jazz**[228] 6877 6-8-5 **66** oh21 AdrianMcCarthy 1 17
(W De Best-Turner) *early spd: sn bhd* **100/1**
-050 **12** 1 **Devine Dancer**[11] 3859 4-8-8 **69** (b[1]) DaneO'Neill 2 16
(H Candy) *reluctant to s and wl bhd: nvr in contention* **20/1**

60.16 secs (-2.40) **Going Correction** -0.325s/f (Firm)
WFA 3 from 4yo+ 3lb **12** Ran SP% **123.2**
Speed ratings (Par 105): **106,105,104,103,102 102,98,94,93,89 80,78**
CSF £105.13 CT £393.96 TOTE £9.20: £2.70, £4.20, £1.90; EX 175.70.
Owner First Of Many Partnership **Bred** Chris McHale And Oghill House Stud **Trained** Kingston Warren, Oxon

FOCUS
A fair sprint handicap on paper, but few got into it.
Devine Dancer Official explanation: jockey said filly missed the break

4205 14-21 TIME TO TALK FILLIES' H'CAP 1m 2f 6y
4:55 (4:56) (Class 5) (0-75,75) 3-Y-O **£3,238** (£963; £481; £240) **Stalls** High

Form RPR
-600 **1** **Free Offer**[37] 3058 3-9-5 **73** DaneO'Neill 7 79
(J L Dunlop) *trckd ldrs: rdn to ld 2f out: drvn and hld on wl thrght fnl f* **16/1**
436 **2** hd **Candy Mountain**[41] 2944 3-8-12 **66** RyanMoore 11 71
(L M Cumani) *hld up towards rr: hdwy over 2f out: str run u.p thrght fnl f: gng on cl home but nt quite get up* **5/1**[2]
-443 **3** shd **Rowan River**[51] 2635 3-8-12 **66** TedDurcan 6 71
(M H Tompkins) *chsd ldrs: hrd drvn fr over 2f out: styd on strly thrght fnl f: gng on nr fin but nt quite get up* **6/1**
2502 **4** ½ **Sweet Request**[10] 3871 3-8-7 **61** ow1 SebSanders 10 65+
(R M Beckett) *chsd ldrs tl outpcd over 3f out: hrd rdn and styd on fr over 1f out: fin wl but nt rch ldrs* **8/1**
-056 **5** 1 **Veenwouden**[37] 3056 3-9-4 **72** KerrinMcEvoy 12 74
(E F Vaughan) *in rr and racd towards outside: hdwy fr 2f out: kpt on wl fnl f but nt rch ldrs* **8/1**
4056 **6** nk **Nicomedia (IRE)**[15] 3731 3-8-8 **69** (b) HaddenFrost(7) 16 70
(R Hannon) *in rr: hdwy on outside over 2f out: styd on ins fnl f but nvr quite gng pce to be competitive* **20/1**
-010 **7** shd **Kyloe Belle (USA)**[60] 2362 3-8-5 **59** JamesDoyle 9 60
(Mrs A J Perrett) *chsd ldrs: rdn fr 3f out: one pce fnl f* **16/1**
6-00 **8** nk **Rosie's Glory (USA)**[25] 3421 3-9-2 **70** PaulEddery 3 71
(B J Meehan) *drvn to ld: hdd 2f out: wknd fnl f* **28/1**
41 **9** 2 **Elegant Hawk**[18] 3651 3-9-2 **70** PaulDoe 13 67
(W J Knight) *racd in rr and towards outside: rdn and sme hdwy 3f out: nvr quite gng pce to rch ldrs: wknd over 1f out* **11/2**[3]
0-32 **10** 2 **Abyla**[27] 3365 3-9-1 **69** MartinDwyer 4 62
(M P Tregoning) *in rr: rdn over 3f out: nvr in contention* **9/2**[1]
1620 **11** 1¼ **Cavort (IRE)**[15] 3731 3-9-5 **73** SteveDrowne 2 63
(Pat Eddery) *chsd ldrs: rdn 3f out: sn wknd* **22/1**
3-52 **12** 1 **Scar Tissue**[15] 3730 3-8-8 **62** EdwardCreighton 1 50
(E J Creighton) *chsd ldrs: rdn over 3f out: sn wknd* **25/1**
3120 **13** hd **Passing Hour (USA)**[25] 3421 3-9-7 **75** JHBowman 15 63
(G A Butler) *a towards rr* **12/1**
0000 **14** ½ **Silver Surprise**[34] 3150 3-8-2 **56** oh1 FrankieMcDonald 8 43
(J J Bridger) *a in rr* **66/1**
00-0 **15** 8 **Edgefour (IRE)**[27] 3387 3-8-3 **57** DavidKinsella 5 28
(B I Case) *pressed ldr: rdn over 3f out: sn wknd* **50/1**
062 **P** **Mega Dame (IRE)**[26] 3406 3-8-13 **67** RobertHavlin 14 —
(D Haydn Jones) *in rr whn p.u 5f out* **20/1**

2m 6.21s (-2.50) **Going Correction** -0.325s/f (Firm) **16** Ran SP% **130.8**
Speed ratings (Par 97): **97,96,96,96,95 95,95,95,93,91 90,90,89,89,83** —
CSF £93.71 CT £562.86 TOTE £29.60: £5.00, £1.50, £1.80, £2.80; EX 200.00 Place 6 £40.55, Place 5 £28.33..
Owner The Earl Cadogan **Bred** The Earl Cadogan **Trained** Arundel, W Sussex

FOCUS
A modest but competitive handicap.
Mega Dame(IRE) Official explanation: jockey said filly lost its action
T/Plt: £48.90 to a £1 stake. Pool: £47,012.55. 700.40 winning tickets. T/Qpdt: £12.70 to a £1 stake. Pool: £3,400.50. 196.60 winning tickets. ST

4206 - 4210a (Foreign Racing) - See Raceform Interactive

4187 GALWAY (R-H)
Sunday, August 5

OFFICIAL GOING: Yielding to soft

4211a MICHAEL MCNAMARA & CO. BUILDERS DUBLIN & GALWAY H'CAP (PREMIER HANDICAP) 7f
4:30 (4:32) 3-Y-O+ **£65,979** (£19,358; £9,222; £3,141)

RPR
1 **Hard Rock City (USA)**[11] 3864 7-10-4 106 JAHeffernan 12 112
(M J Grassick, Ire) *trckd ldrs: 5th 1/2-way: 3rd travelling best 2f out: 2nd and chal early st: hmpd and checked briefly cl home: kpt on wl to ld last strides* **8/1**[3]
2 shd **Warriors Key (IRE)**[90] 1547 3-9-0 94 DPMcDonogh 1 98
(Kevin Prendergast, Ire) *in rr of mid-div: 8th 1/2-way: 5th and hdwy 2f out: 3rd and chal early st: led ins fnl f: drifted rt cl home: hdd last strides* **25/1**

3 ¾ **Little White Lie (IRE)**[46] 2779 3-9-4 98 .... CO'Donoghue 15 100
(G M Lyons, Ire) *cl up in 2nd: chal fr over 2f out: led ent st: hdd ins fnl f: kpt on wl* **9/1**
4 6 **Majestic Times (IRE)**[14] 3768 7-9-5 100 .... SFoley(7) 14 88
(Liam McAteer, Ire) *prom: 3rd 1/2-way: cl up and rdn to chal over 2f out: 5th and outpcd ent st: kpt on fnl f* **20/1**
5 3 **King Of Tory (IRE)**[35] 3138 5-9-7 95 .... (b) NGMcCullagh 7 75
(Edward Lynam, Ire) *hld up: 9th 2f out: mod 6th early st: kpt on* **14/1**
6 ½ **Nastrelli (IRE)**[35] 3140 4-9-2 90 .... (p) JMurtagh 13 68
(M Halford, Ire) *mid-div: 7th 1/2-way: 6th 2f out: rdn and no imp: kpt on same pce* **5/2**[1]
7 ¾ **Dani's Girl (IRE)**[5] 4051 4-9-6 94 .... FMBerry 16 70
(P A Fahy, Ire) *led: rdn and strly pressed fr over 2f out: hdd ent st: no ex fnl f* **14/1**
8 ½ **Bolodenka (IRE)**[5] 4051 5-9-0 91 .... JamieMoriarty(3) 2 66
(R A Fahey) *towards rr: kpt on wout threatening fr over 2f out* **13/2**[2]
9 7 **Rockie**[35] 3138 4-9-2 90 .... (tp) WJLee 4 46
(T Hogan, Ire) *nvr a factor* **20/1**
10 2 **Tajneed (IRE)**[21] 3573 4-9-1 89 .... (bt) PJSmullen 5 40
(D K Weld, Ire) *in rr of mid-div: no ex 2f out: eased st* **10/1**
11 2 **Extraterrestrial**[9] 3929 3-8-13 93 .... (b) CDHayes 10 36
(Kevin Prendergast, Ire) *hld up: 9th and effrt over 2f out: no ex bef st* **12/1**
12 2 ½ **Cousteau**[63] 2281 4-9-8 103 .... (t) PTownend(7) 3 42
(John Joseph Hanlon, Ire) *sn chsd ldrs on outer: 6th 1/2-way: sn rdn and wknd* **16/1**
13 ½ **Dynamo Dancer (IRE)**[71] 2052 4-9-10 98 .... WJSupple 9 35
(G M Lyons, Ire) *hld up: no ex fr 2 1/2f out* **9/1**
14 1 **Worldly Wise**[44] 2815 4-9-6 94 .... (b1) DMGrant 11 28
(Patrick J Flynn, Ire) *trckd ldrs: 4th 1/2-way: 7th 2f out: no ex and wknd* **12/1**
15 1 ½ **Excelerate (IRE)**[23] 3516 4-9-9 97 .... MCHussey 6 27
(Edward Lynam, Ire) *hld up: 8th and effrt over 2f out: sn no ex* **10/1**

1m 34.5s (2.90)
WFA 3 from 4yo+ 6lb **16** Ran SP% **139.2**
CSF £219.39 CT £1934.61 TOTE £6.00: £2.20, £9.00, £3.10; DF 286.80.
Owner Mrs E Dolan **Bred** Swettenham Stud **Trained** Pollardstown, Co Kildare

NOTEBOOK
Bolodenka(IRE), last year's winner, found himself short of racing room before the turn in but would not have made an impression anyway. (op 6/1 tchd 7/1)

4212 - (Foreign Racing) - See Raceform Interactive

2502 COLOGNE (R-H)
Sunday, August 5

OFFICIAL GOING: Good

4213a OPPENHEIM PRAMERICA SILBERNE PEITSCHE (GROUP 3) 6f 110y
3:55 (4:05) 3-Y-0+ **£21,622** (£6,757; £3,378; £2,027)

RPR
1 **Lucky Strike**[80] 1800 9-9-5 .... ADeVries 4 108
(A Trybuhl, Germany) *hld up: remained on ins w two others in st: led 1 1/2f out: hld on wl u.p fnl stages* **2/1**[1]
2 ½ **Toylsome**[18] 3666 8-9-5 .... JiriPalik 1 107
(J Hirschberger, Germany) *led: brought main gp wd ent st: hdd 1 1/2f out: kpt on* **13/2**
3 ½ **Key To Pleasure (GER)**[36] 3122 7-9-5 .... ASuborics 8 106
(Mario Hofer, Germany) *hld up: hdwy in centre 2f out: styd on wl fnl f: nrest at fin* **64/10**[3]
4 ¾ **Bahama Mama (IRE)**[28] 3-8-7 .... WPanov 6 98
(W Hickst, Germany) *cl up on outside: styd on at one pce in centre fnl 2f* **2/1**[1]
5 ½ **Smokejumper (GER)**[56] 3-8-11 .... HGrewe 7 100
(Frau E Mader, Germany) *hld up: brought to centre in st: styd on fnl 2f but nvr a factor* **177/10**
6 nk **Santiago Atitlan**[77] 1876 5-9-5 .... EPedroza 3 101
(A Wohler, Germany) *hld up: chsd wnr on ins fr over 2f out: kpt on at one pce* **56/10**[2]
7 3 ½ **Slade (GER)**[36] 3122 5-9-1 .... WMongil 9 87
(M Trybuhl, Germany) *prom: c wd into st: wknd over 1 1/2f out* **26/1**
8 6 **Mood Music**[84] 1698 3-8-11 .... AStarke 5 73
(Mario Hofer, Germany) *4th 1/2-way: c wd into st: sn wknd* **116/10**
9 5 **Lucky It Is (HOL)**[31] 3255 3-8-11 .... ABoschert 2 59
(A Trybuhl, Germany) *prom tl wknd 3f out* **173/10**

1m 16.19s (76.19)
WFA 3 from 5yo+ 4lb **9** Ran SP% **131.1**
(Including 10 Euros stake): WIN 30; PL 13, 20, 20; SF 153.
Owner Stall Lucky Stables International **Bred** Red House Stud **Trained** Germany

4190 DEAUVILLE (R-H)
Sunday, August 5

OFFICIAL GOING: Turf course - good; all-weather - standard

4214a PRIX MAURICE DE GHEEST (GROUP 1) 6f 110y(S)
2:20 (2:24) 3-Y-0+ **£96,520** (£38,615; £19,307; £9,645; £4,831)

RPR
1 **Marchand D'Or (FR)**[23] 3506 4-9-2 .... DBonilla 12 121
(F Head, France) *hld up in last on outside: prog 2f out: pushed along to chal appr fnl f: rdn to ld 100yds out: rdn out* **5/1**[2]
2 1 **Dutch Art**[23] 3506 3-8-12 .... JimmyFortune 10 118
(P W Chapple-Hyam) *hld up on outside: 7th 1/2-way: pushed along to chal 2f out: led appr fnl f: rdn 150yds out: hdd 100yds out: no ex* **6/4**[1]
3 ½ **Silver Touch (IRE)**[36] 3098 4-8-13 .... TPO'Shea 5 114
(M R Channon) *hld up in tch: 6th towards stands' side 1/2-way: r.o wl fnl f to go 3rd: nrst at fin* **20/1**
4 nk **Garnica (FR)**[25] 3445 4-9-2 .... C-PLemaire 2 116
(J-C Rouget, France) *hld up on stands' side: rdn and r.o to go 4th 1f out: no ex cl home* **14/1**
5 1 ½ **Major Cadeaux**[36] 3098 3-8-12 .... RichardHughes 11 112
(R Hannon) *prom in centre: 4th 1/2-way: effrt over 1 1/2f out: styd on steadily fnl f* **8/1**[3]
6 ½ **Satri (IRE)**[14] 3780 5-9-2 .... OPeslier 7 110
(J-M Beguigne, France) *in tch on stands' rail: effrt 1 1/2f out: styd on cl home but n.d* **11/1**
7 ¾ **Bentley Biscuit (AUS)**[23] 3506 6-9-2 .... JamieSpencer 8 108
(Mrs Gai Waterhouse, Australia) *in tch: 5th 1/2-way: effrt to chse ldrs 1 1/2f out: no ex fnl f* **12/1**
8 snk **Moss Vale (IRE)**[47] 2733 6-9-2 .... KFallon 3 108
(D Nicholls) *prom: 3rd half way: rdn and ev ch 2f out: styd on u.p tl wknd 150yds out* **20/1**
9 ½ **New Girlfriend (IRE)**[63] 2291 4-8-13 .... YTake 6 103
(Robert Collet, France) *led on stands' rail: pushed along 1/2-way: hdd 3f out: drvn to hold pl: no ex fr 2f out* **25/1**
10 hd **Tiza (SAF)**[25] 3445 5-9-2 .... CSoumillon 1 106
(A De Royer-Dupre, France) *towards rr: n.d* **11/1**
0 **Tycoon's Hill (IRE)**[25] 3445 8-9-2 .... J-BHamel 4 —
(Robert Collet, France) *hld up towards outside: n.d* **100/1**
0 **Bygone Days**[43] 2857 6-9-2 .... LDettori 13 —
(Saeed Bin Suroor) *mid-div: n.d* **12/1**
0 **Val Jaro (FR)**[25] 3445 4-9-2 .... TJarnet 9 —
(S Morineau, France) *prom: 2nd 1/2-way: led 3f out: drvn 1 1/2f out: hdd appr fnl f: no ex* **66/1**

1m 14.9s (-4.30) **Going Correction** -0.175s/f (Firm)
WFA 3 from 4yo+ 4lb **13** Ran SP% **122.3**
Speed ratings: **117,115,115,114,113 112,111,111,111,110 —,—,—**
PARI-MUTUEL: WIN 4.60; PL 1.60, 1.60, 8.70; DF 5.50.
Owner Mme J-L Giral **Bred** Mme Carla Giral **Trained** France

NOTEBOOK
Marchand D'Or(FR) has emerged as a leading sprinter and is a great credit to his trainer. The four-year-old was winning this event for the second successive year and he only missed the track record by a fifth of a second. Slowly away, he was hampered a little early before being brought with a progressive late run up the centre of the track. He took the advantage running into the final furlong and finally won with something in hand. He will now go back to England for the Betfred Sprint at Haydock Park in September.
Dutch Art ran a brave race considering he was not at all at home on the unusually firm ground. He took a bit of time to really get going and ran on to take a narrow lead at the furlong marker. He did his best to retain it but was run out of things a little later. His rider felt the colt was never going well on the surface and he did win the Morny here last year on very soft ground. He will take up the challenge again at Haydock Park when hopefully conditions will be more suitable.
Silver Touch(IRE), one of the rank outsiders, ran a fantastic race. In mid-division early on, she made her presence felt at the furlong marker and stuck to her guns until the bitter end. Connections were delighted and felt more cut in the ground would have been an advantage. She remains capable of further improvement.
Garnica(FR) was settled in mid-division before starting his run just over a furlong out and only lost third place by a narrow margin. He was slightly interfered with by Dutch Art towards the end of the race.
Major Cadeaux was always well up but finding things a little difficult at the furlong marker. Nevertheless he stayed on, albeit one paced, and this was a good effort from the three-year-old. He is likely to be retired for the season and given a chance to strengthen for his four-year-old campaign.
Moss Vale(IRE) was up at the head of affairs for much of this race, but beaten at the furlong marker. This distance might have been a little extreme for this experienced sprinter who is yet to find his true form this season.
Bygone Days was smartly into stride and he nearly got into the lead half way through the race, but was in trouble at the furlong marker and gradually dropped out of contention.

4215a PRIX DE POMONE (GROUP 2) (F&M) 1m 4f 110y
3:20 (3:22) 3-Y-0+ **£50,068** (£19,324; £9,223; £6,149; £3,074)

RPR
1 **Macleya (GER)**[22] 3565 5-9-4 .... SPasquier 8 104
(A Fabre, France) *in tch: 4th 1/2-way: 5th st: rdn and r.o fnl f: styd on strly cl home to ld on line* **7/2**[3]
2 shd **Pearl Sky (FR)**[98] 1340 4-9-4 .... ACrastus 5 104
(Y De Nicolay, France) *hld up disputing last: 7th on outside st: styd on wl fr 1 1/2f out: chal cl home: ev ch nr fin: unlucky* **14/1**
3 nse **Montare (IRE)**[45] 2787 5-9-4 .... OPeslier 2 104
(J E Pease, France) *prom: 3rd 1/2-way: disputing 2nd on ins st: drvn to ld over 1f out: hrd rdn fnl 100yds: hdd on line* **5/2**[1]
4 nse **Kankakee (USA)**[47] 4-9-4 .... DBonilla 9 104
(J E Pease, France) *led: pushed along 4f out: r.o st: hdd over 1f out: styd on u.p to line: ev ch cl home* **25/1**
5 1 ½ **Kaloura (IRE)**[42] 2926 3-8-7 ow1 .... CSoumillon 7 102
(A Fabre, France) *prom: 2nd 1/2-way: disputing 2nd st: sn drvn: rdn 1 1/2f out: nt pce of ldrs* **3/1**[2]
6 ¾ **Freedonia**[148] 663 5-9-4 .... TGillet 3 100
(J E Hammond, France) *hld up disputing last: effrt 1 1/2f out: styd on but nvr a threat* **5/1**
7 1 ½ **Mary Louhana**[89] 1571 4-9-4 .... TJarnet 1 98
(M Delzangles, France) *mid-div: 6th st: rdn to chse ldrs 2f out: no ex fr 1 1/2f out* **33/1**
8 snk **Princesse Dansante (IRE)**[43] 4-9-4 .... C-PLemaire 4 98
(F Doumen, France) *mid-div: disputing last st: pushed along 2f out: no imp* **33/1**
9 2 ½ **Rising Cross**[25] 3434 4-9-4 .... KFallon 6 94
(J R Best) *hld up: hdwy appr st: 4th and drvn st: sn u.p: one pce fr 1 1/2f out* **12/1**

2m 40.9s (-5.80) **Going Correction** -0.075s/f (Good)
WFA 3 from 4yo+ 11lb **9** Ran SP% **116.5**
Speed ratings: **114,113,113,113,112 112,111,111,109**
PARI-MUTUEL: WIN 5.80; PL 1.80, 2.40, 1.60; DF 22.90.
Owner R C Thompson **Bred** Gestut Schlenderhan **Trained** Chantilly, France

NOTEBOOK
Macleya(GER) is one of the most consistent mares in training and she appears to be getting better with every race. Raced just behind the leaders, she did not have a clear run in the straight but produced some decent acceleration from one and a half out to snatch it in a four-way finish. It was a falsely-run race and she would have won more easily without hindrance. If she comes out of this race well, she could go for the Group 2 Prix Jean Romanet on August 19, but her main autumn targets are the Flower Bowl and the EP Taylor Stakes on the other side of the Atlantic.
Pearl Sky(FR) was the pick of the paddock and ran a fine race. Held up in the early stages, she began her run on the outside from one and a half out and was just caught in the final few strides after battling well throughout the final furlong. She seemed to get this trip well and the filly may now turn out for the Grand Prix de Deauville at the end of the month.
Montare(IRE) was fitted with cheekpieces and was a little fractious in the paddock. Settled on the rail behind her pacemaker, she looked to have won the race with 50 yards to go, but was finally run out of things in the final few strides. Her trainer felt she stopped in front and he was a little disappointed with the effort. The mare now goes for the Prix Vermeille.

Kankakee(USA), put in the race as a pacemaker, very nearly caused a huge surprise, just failing to get back up and was beaten under a neck. She set a steady pace and quickened things up soon after entering the straight. Rather than drop back, she kept staying on and it was a fine performance.
Kaloura(IRE) lacks a change of pace and it would come as no surprise to see the daughter of Sinndar upped to staying distances in the future.
Rising Cross did not appeal in the paddock and was raced on the outside for much of the race. She made some progress rounding the final turn and was close to the leaders at the entrance to the straight. Soon after she was a spent force and dropped right back to finish last.

4216a PRIX DE TOURGEVILLE (LISTED RACE) (C&G) 1m (R)
3:50 (3:53) 3-Y-O **£17,568** (£7,027; £5,270; £3,514; £1,757)

RPR
1 **Vertigineux (FR)**65 3-8-12 ... PSogorb 10 103
(Mme C Dufreche, France)
2 1 1/2 **Grand Vista**28 3362 3-9-2 ... SPasquier 5 104
(A Fabre, France)
3 snk **Lone Wolfe**16 3707 3-8-12 ... JamieSpencer 7 100
(Jane Chapple-Hyam) *prom: 2nd 1/2-way: pushed along to ld st: sn rdn: hdd over 1f out: no ex nr fin* **23/1**1
4 nk **Staraco (FR)**31 3255 3-8-12 ... ASanglard 4 99
(B Goudot, France)
5 1/2 **Makaan (USA)**31 3255 3-8-12 ... (b) DBonilla 8 98
(F Head, France)
6 1/2 **Ilie Nastase (FR)**33 3-8-12 ... TThulliez 2 97
(R Gibson, France)
7 shd **Simbad (FR)**28 3-8-12 ... C-PLemaire 9 97
(P Bary, France)
8 6 **Tumult (GER)**13 3-8-12 ... JVictoire 3 85
(Frau E Mader, Germany)
9 snk **Hando**28 3-8-12 ... OPeslier 1 85
(F Head, France)

1m 41.1s (-1.20) **Going Correction** -0.075s/f (Good) 9 Ran SP% **4.2**
Speed ratings: **103,101,101,101,100 100,99,93,93**
PARI-MUTUEL: WIN 3.90; PL 1.60, 1.70, 3.90; DF 6.70.
Owner Mme C & P Dufreche **Bred** Patrick Dufreche **Trained** France

NOTEBOOK
Lone Wolfe never far from the leaders, he took the advantage early in the straight going well, but was unable to quicken when the winner flashed past him. He stayed on though and was only beaten for second place a few yards before the post. He has now been sold and will continue his career in Hong Kong.

1517 HANOVER (L-H)
Sunday, August 5

OFFICIAL GOING: Good

4217a ICT-ESLAM-CUP (GROUP 2) 1m
4:10 (4:20) 3-Y-O+ **£27,027** (£10,135; £4,054; £2,703)

RPR
1 **Apollo Star (GER)**21 3581 5-9-6 ... AHelfenbein 2 108
(Mario Hofer, Germany) *mde all: remained on ins w 2 chsers ent st: rdn wl over 1f out: r.o wl* **58/10**3
2 1 1/2 **Konig Turf (GER)**21 3581 5-9-6 ... JBojko 8 105
(C Sprengel, Germany) *racd in 3rd: wnt 2nd and kpt to ins ent st: hrd rdn 2f out: nt pce of wnr* **13/2**
3 1/2 **Aspectus (IRE)**21 3581 4-9-6 ... FJohansson 3 104
(H Blume, Germany) *racd in 2nd: 3rd st: kpt on at same pce down ins fr over 2f out* **6/4**1
4 3 1/2 **Aviso (GER)**43 2903 3-8-11 ... THellier 5 95
(J Hirschberger, Germany) *hld up in 6th: 5th and brought wd st: styd on at same pce u.p fnl 2f to take 4th cl home: nvr nr ldrs* **19/10**2
5 shd **Sexy Lady (GER)**19 3628 4-9-2 ... TMundry 4 93
(P Rau, Germany) *racd in 5th: 4th but detached fr front 3 and brought remainder wd ent st: one pce: lost 4th cl home* **61/10**
6 nk **Genios (GER)**28 6-9-6 ... VSchulepov 1 96
(Dr A Bolte, Germany) *racd in 4th: 6th and brought wd st: kpt on at one pce* **42/1**
7 1/2 **Lucidor (GER)**105 4-9-6 ... J-PCarvalho 7 95
(Frau E Mader, Germany) *hld up in last: a in rr* **127/10**
8 shd **Ryono (USA)**43 8-9-6 ... TCastanheira 6 95
(S Smrczek, Germany) *hld up in 7th: a in rr* **37/1**

1m 38.36s (98.36)
WFA 3 from 4yo+ 7lb 8 Ran SP% **128.9**
(Including 10 Euros stake): WIN 68; PL 18, 17, 14; SF 634.
Owner J Spranke **Bred** H Gerwin **Trained** Germany

KLAMPENBORG
Sunday, August 5

OFFICIAL GOING: Good

4218a SCANDINAVIAN OPEN CHAMPIONSHIP (GROUP 3) 1m 4f
3:15 (12:00) 3-Y-O+ **£27,244** (£9,081; £4,541; £2,724; £1,816)

RPR
1 **Equip Hill (SWE)**38 5-9-2 ... (b) P-AGraberg 9 107
(B Bo, Sweden) **72/10**3
2 5 **Caudillo (GER)**59 2409 4-9-2 ... JimmyQuinn 1 99
(Dr A Bolte, Germany) **25/1**
3 1 1/2 **Steelwolf**598 6-9-2 ... LVillarroel 7 97
(B Bo, Sweden) **88/1**
4 1/2 **Django (SWE)**93 4-9-2 ... JohnFortune 14 96
(Caroline Stromberg, Sweden) **105/10**
5 1/2 **Peas And Carrots (DEN)** 4-9-2 ... MSantos 2 95
(L Reuterskiold, Sweden) **9/10**1
6 hd **Alnitak (USA)**38 6-9-2 ... (b) KAndersen 12 95
(B Olsen, Norway) **74/1**
7 1/2 **Lumen (FR)**21 5-8-12 ... DinaDanekilde 11 90
(O Larsen, Sweden) **52/10**2
8 2 **Bongo Bello (DEN)**38 6-9-2 ... JJohansen 15 91
(T Christensen, Denmark) **29/1**
9 2 1/2 **Alpino Chileno (ARG)**38 8-9-2 ... (b) CLopez 10 87
(Rune Haugen, Norway) **32/1**
10 1/2 **Mambo King (DEN)**42 5-9-2 ... FDiaz 4 87
(L Kelp, Sweden) **30/1**
11 2 1/2 **Storm Trooper (GER)**38 7-9-2 ... MLarsen 5 83
(Rune Haugen, Norway) **15/1**
12 1/2 **Road To Mandalay (IRE)**49 4-9-2 ... NCordrey 13 82
(Kjell Ivar Brekstad, Norway) **196/10**
13 3 1/2 **Mick Jerome (IRE)**40 2976 6-9-2 ... ESki 8 77
(Rune Haugen, Norway) **42/1**
14 4 **Zenato (GER)**364 4189 6-9-2 ... GSolis 6 71
(F Reuterskiold, Sweden) **47/1**
15 5 **Highway (IRE)**38 4-9-2 ... (b) MMartinez 3 63
(F Castro, Sweden) **19/1**

2m 31.2s (151.20) **15** Ran SP% **126.1**
TOTE (including 1DKr stake): WIN 8.23; PL 3.36, 8.58, 20.96; SF 37.60.
Owner Katarina Jacobsen & Gunnel Hakansson **Bred** Katarina Jacobsen **Trained** Sweden

3994 CARLISLE (R-H)
Monday, August 6

OFFICIAL GOING: Firm (good to firm in places) (10.3)
The ground had dried right out and was described as 'fast but no jar'. The far rail was the place to be and it was difficult to make ground from off the pace.
Wind: fresh half-against Weather: Fine but breezy and very cool

4219 DOBIES VAUXHALL LADY AMATEUR RIDERS' H'CAP 7f 200y
6:15 (6:15) (Class 5) (0-70,70) 3-Y-O+ **£2,717** (£842; £421; £210) **Stalls** High

Form RPR
0206 1 **Kabis Amigos**8 3999 5-10-6 **69** ... (t) MissARyan(3) 9 76
(D Nicholls) *mde all: sn clr: rdn over 1f out: kpt on wl: unchal* **5/1**2
5260 2 2 1/2 **Shy Glance (USA)**9 3955 5-10-10 **70** ... MissADeniel 8 71+
(P Monteith) *hld up: hdwy over 2f out: styd on to take 2nd nr fin* **4/1**1
1403 3 3/4 **Crafty Fox**20 3619 4-9-7 **58** ... (v) MissKellyBurke(5) 10 58
(A P Jarvis) *chsd ldrs: wnt 2nd over 2f out: kpt on same pce* **14/1**
-000 4 1 1/4 **Uhuru Peak**15 3765 6-9-5 **51** ... (bt) MissSBrotherton 2 48
(M W Easterby) *trckd ldrs: brought wd to r alone stands' side over 4f out: styd on fnl 2f* **11/2**3
0000 5 1 1/2 **Gifted Flame**13 3816 8-10-0 **60** ... MrsCBartley 3 53
(T D Barron) *hld up: hdwy over 3f out: sn chsng ldrs: one pce fnl 2f* **7/1**
25-0 6 1 1/2 **Wee Ellie Coburn**29 3342 3-8-11 **55** ... MissMMullineaux(5) 6 44
(M Mullineaux) *hld up in rr: styd on fnl 2f: nvr nr ldrs* **33/1**
125- 7 shd **Able Mind**296 5972 7-9-7 **58** ... MissHCuthbert(5) 5 48
(D W Thompson) *mid-div: hdwy 3f out: one pce* **7/1**
5030 8 nk **Scotty's Future (IRE)**6 4042 9-8-13 **52** ... MissWGibson(7) 7 41
(A Berry) *sn detached in rr: kpt on fnl 2f: nvr on terms* **25/1**
1010 9 1/2 **Ignition**2 4159 5-10-0 **60** ... MissEJJones 4 48
(W M Brisbourne) *chsd ldrs: drvn over 3f out: lost pl over 1f out* **15/2**
3005 10 hd **Terenzium (IRE)**45 2820 5-9-0 **51** oh3 ... (p) MrsGHogg(5) 11 38
(Micky Hammond) *chsd ldrs: wknd over 1f out* **7/1**
0360 11 10 **Ivana Illyich (IRE)**10 3914 5-9-9 **62** oh6 ow11 ... (p) MissFRodmell(7) 1 26
(J S Wainwright) *s.i.s: sn detached in rr* **80/1**

1m 40.07s (-0.02) **Going Correction** -0.15s/f (Firm)
WFA 3 from 4yo+ 7lb 11 Ran SP% **116.0**
Speed ratings (Par 103): **94,91,90,89,88 86,86,86,85,85 75**
CSF £24.58 CT £222.92 TOTE £6.40: £2.00, £2.20, £2.00; EX 28.20.
Owner GGN Bloodstock Ltd and Ian W Glenton **Bred** Cheveley Park Stud Ltd **Trained** Sessay, N Yorks

FOCUS
A modest lady amateurs' handicap and the winner was given his own way out in front. It is doubtful if he improved as much as the face value of the form suggests.

4220 BEADLE AND HILL CLAIMING STKS 7f 200y
6:45 (6:46) (Class 6) 3-Y-O **£2,047** (£604; £302) **Stalls** High

Form RPR
-664 1 **Lilac Moon (GER)**8 3997 3-8-7 55 ... RoystonFfrench 10 57+
(Mrs A Duffield) *chsd ldrs: drvn over 4f out: wnt 2nd over 2f out: styd on to ld jst ins fnl f: kpt on wl* **11/8**1
0602 2 2 **Terry Molloy (IRE)**2 4155 3-9-0 57 ... (v) PatCosgrave 7 59
(K R Burke) *led tl jst ins fnl f: no ex* **5/2**2
0403 3 1 **Myfrenchconnection (IRE)**10 3918 3-8-10 50 ... PaulMulrennan 6 53
(P T Midgley) *hld up in rr: hdwy over 2f out: kpt on fnl f* **15/2**
00-0 4 5 **Sahara Dawn (IRE)**108 1119 3-8-0 40 ... KellyHarrison(7) 4 38
(D Carroll) *trckd ldrs: t.k.h: one pce fnl 2f* **50/1**
000 5 3 **Grethel (IRE)**20 3611 3-8-4 42 ... PatrickMathers(3) 3 31
(A Berry) *s.i.s: hdwy on outside over 2f out: hung rt over 1f out: nvr nr ldrs* **66/1**
5300 6 1 **Denton Hawk**10 3918 3-8-8 48 ow1 ... (p) PhillipMakin 1 30
(M Dods) *sn chsng ldrs on outer: wknd 2f out* **20/1**
5656 7 7 **Storm Mission (USA)**23 3540 3-8-12 46 ... (t) TomEaves 5 18
(J Mackie) *hld up in rr: effrt 3f out: wknd over 1f out* **5/1**3
-406 8 1 **Reflective Glory (IRE)**43 2905 3-8-7 48 ... (p) TonyHamilton 2 11
(J S Wainwright) *hld up in rr: effrt over 2f out: sn btn* **20/1**
-400 9 1 3/4 **Cadi May**37 3110 3-8-6 51 ow1 ... DavidAllan 9 6
(W M Brisbourne) *trckd ldrs: t.k.h: wknd 2f out* **20/1**
6005 10 19 **Mr Mini Scule**12 3843 3-8-5 45 ... (b) DaleGibson 8 —
(S Wynne) *trckd ldrs: t.k.h: wknd over 2f out: sn bhd and eased* **66/1**

1m 38.53s (-1.56) **Going Correction** -0.15s/f (Firm) **10** Ran SP% **118.3**
Speed ratings (Par 98): **101,99,98,93,90 89,82,81,79,60**
CSF £4.53 TOTE £2.80: £1.20, £1.40, £1.60; EX 6.50.Lilac Moon was claimed by N J Vaughan for £10,000.
Owner Middleham Park Racing Xviii **Bred** Graf Und Grafin Von Stauffenberg **Trained** Constable Burton, N Yorks

FOCUS
A modest claimer and in the end a decisive winner who was claimed. Pretty sound form for the grade.

Mr Mini Scule Official explanation: jockey said gelding ran too freely

4221 WBX.COM WORLD BET EXCHANGE MAIDEN AUCTION STKS 5f

7:15 (7:15) (Class 5) 2-Y-O **£2,817** (£838; £418; £209) **Stalls** High

Form RPR

6322 **1** **Rievaulx Valentino**[28] 3370 2-8-13 75 NCallan 7 80
(K A Ryan) *mde all: kpt on wl fnl f* **6/4**[1]

32 **2** *1 1/2* **Liberty Ship**[40] 2984 2-8-12 0 PatCosgrave 5 74
(J D Bethell) *trckd ldrs: kpt on same pce fnl f: no real imp* **15/8**[2]

4 **3** *hd* **Maid In Bloom**[95] 1422 2-8-4 0 RoystonFfrench 8 65
(B Smart) *s.i.s: sn drvn along: styd on fnl 2f: gng on at fin* **4/1**[3]

0305 **4** *1 3/4* **The Magic Blanket (IRE)**[8] 3995 2-8-3 66 KristinStubbs(7) 2 65
(Mrs L Stubbs) *w wnr: kpt on same pce appr fnl f* **16/1**

3455 **5** *nk* **Varinia (IRE)**[28] 3373 2-7-13 62 PatrickDonaghy(7) 1 60
(M Brittain) *mid-div: hdwy over 2f out: hung rt over 1f out: kpt on* **33/1**

06 **6** *6* **Abbey Express**[14] 3781 2-8-11 0 PhillipMakin 9 43
(M Dods) *prom: drvn over 2f out: wknd over 1f out* **20/1**

00 **7** *1 1/4* **Magnushomestwo (IRE)**[21] 3582 2-8-6 0 PatrickMathers(3) 6 37
(A Berry) *chsd ldrs: rdn over 2f out: lost pl over 1f out* **66/1**

8 *2* **Piccolo Pete** 2-8-10 0 GrahamGibbons 4 31
(J J Quinn) *prom: hung lft: outpcd ands lost pl over 3f out* **25/1**

9 *hd* **Tommytush (IRE)** 2-8-11 0 DavidAllan 3 31
(E J Alston) *s.v.s: a in rr* **25/1**

61.29 secs (-0.21) **Going Correction** -0.15s/f (Firm) **9** Ran SP% **117.6**
Speed ratings (Par 94): **95,92,92,89,89 79,77,74,73**
CSF £4.30 TOTE £2.70: £1.10, £1.10, £1.40; EX 5.70.
Owner Rievaulx Racing Syndicate **Bred** J A Forsyth **Trained** Hambleton, N Yorks

FOCUS
An ordinary maiden and the winner made very hard work of it. Solid form, limited by the proximity of the fifth.

NOTEBOOK
Rievaulx Valentino, with no Fol Hollow in opposition this time, made every yard but he had to be kept right up to his work. (tchd 11-8 and 13-8)
Liberty Ship, who hung on his first two starts, had the rail on his inside to help this time. His rider was in two minds where to deliver his challenge but in the end they were very much second best. He is not straightforward by any means. (op 9-4 tchd 7-4, 5-2 in places)
Maid In Bloom, after a tardy start, was soon flat out. Putting in all her best work at the finish, she is crying out for a sixth furlong. (op 7-2)
The Magic Blanket(IRE) again showed ability but found this company a fraction tougher. (op 12-1)
Varinia(IRE), back in trip, ran better but she is looking fully exposed.
Tommytush(IRE) Official explanation: jockey said colt missed the break

4222 WBX.COM WORLD BET EXCHANGE H'CAP 6f 192y

7:45 (7:45) (Class 4) (0-85,80) 3-Y-O **£4,728** (£1,406; £702; £351) **Stalls** High

Form RPR

4300 **1** **Tencendur (IRE)**[17] 3707 3-8-11 70 AdrianTNicholls 9 78
(D Nicholls) *led over 1f: trckd ldrs: led 2f out: styd on wl* **14/1**

1120 **2** *1 3/4* **Jewelled Dagger (IRE)**[30] 3299 3-9-5 78 (b) TomEaves 2 81
(I Semple) *chsd along on outer: led over 5f out tl 2f out: kpt on fnl f* **6/1**

1605 **3** *1/2* **Gazboolou**[20] 3607 3-9-2 75 PatCosgrave 3 77
(K R Burke) *mid-div: hdwy on outer to chse ldrs over 3f out: styd on fnl f* **6/1**

-400 **4** *1 1/4* **Adaptation**[26] 3437 3-9-6 79 J-PGuillambert 5 78
(M Johnston) *in rr and sn pushed along: hdwy over 2f out: styd on same pce* **5/1**[2]

5603 **5** *hd* **Sunnyside Tom (IRE)**[9] 3952 3-8-12 71 PaulHanagan 6 69
(R A Fahey) *chsd ldrs: kpt on same pce fnl 2f* **11/2**[3]

0025 **6** *1/2* **Osteopathic Remedy (IRE)**[11] 3885 3-9-7 80 PhillipMakin 1 77
(M Dods) *witched rt after s: hld up in rr: effrt on ins over 2f out: nvr trbld ldrs* **7/1**

20-1 **7** *1* **Expensive Detour (IRE)**[86] 1679 3-9-7 80 TonyHamilton 7 74
(Mrs L Stubbs) *chsd ldrs: one pce fnl 2f* **9/1**

4441 **8** *1/2* **Medici Pearl**[20] 3607 3-9-5 78 DavidAllan 4 71
(T D Easterby) *in rr: effrt over 2f out: nvr trbld ldrs* **7/2**[1]

4004 **9** *3 1/2* **Our Blessing (IRE)**[18] 3688 3-9-2 78 AndrewElliott(3) 10 61
(A P Jarvis) *trckd ldrs: lost pl 2f out* **11/1**

1m 25.14s (-1.96) **Going Correction** -0.15s/f (Firm) **9** Ran SP% **120.3**
Speed ratings (Par 102): **105,103,102,101,100 100,99,98,94**
CSF £99.26 CT £576.19 TOTE £14.80: £3.80, £2.30, £2.80; EX 120.60.
Owner Mrs L Scaife, Mrs S Radford **Bred** Michael O'Mahony **Trained** Sessay, N Yorks

FOCUS
A run-of-the-mill handicap and the first pair were one-two throughout. The form makes sense through those two but overall is not that solid.
Medici Pearl Official explanation: jockey said filly was unsuited by the going (firm, good to firm in places)

4223 DOBIES H'CAP 6f 192y

8:15 (8:16) (Class 6) (0-60,60) 3-Y-O+ **£2,047** (£604; £302) **Stalls** High

Form RPR

3601 **1** **Mister Jingles**[13] 3814 4-9-7 53 (v) J-PGuillambert 14 61
(R M Whitaker) *chsd ldrs: styd on wl to ld last 100yds* **11/2**[2]

0400 **2** *1 1/2* **Wisdom's Kiss**[46] 2796 3-9-4 56 (b[1]) PaulFessey 3 58+
(J D Bethell) *t.k.h on outer: trckd ldrs: led over 3f out: hung rt and hdd ins fnl f: no ex* **66/1**

1000 **3** *1* **Falcon's Fire (IRE)**[26] 3411 3-9-5 57 (p) RoystonFfrench 11 56
(Mrs A Duffield) *in tch: effrt over 2f out: styd on fnl f* **13/2**[3]

5024 **4** *1 1/4* **Smart Pick**[12] 3839 4-9-6 52 TomEaves 13 50+
(Mrs L Williamson) *s.i.s: t.k.h in midfield: styd on fnl 2f: nt rch ldrs* **16/1**

3650 **5** *1/2* **Machinate (USA)**[34] 3195 5-9-6 52 DavidAllan 10 48
(W M Brisbourne) *in tch: hdwy over 2f out: kpt on same pce* **13/2**[3]

-006 **6** *1* **Laphonic (USA)**[12] 3839 4-9-3 49 KDarley 12 43+
(T J Etherington) *s.i.s: t.k.h in last: hdwy on ins whn nt clr run over 2f out tl over 1f out: styd on* **12/1**

6050 **7** *1/2* **Ours (IRE)**[8] 3999 4-9-8 54 (b) PatCosgrave 6 46
(J D Bethell) *s.i.s: effrt over 2f out: kpt on: nvr rchd ldrs* **14/1**

6305 **8** *1* **Penel (IRE)**[2] 4180 6-8-13 48 (p) JamieMoriarty(3) 8 38
(P T Midgley) *in rr and sn drvn along: kpt on fnl 2f: nvr a factor* **10/1**

0060 **9** *shd* **Polish Emperor (USA)**[2] 4180 7-9-1 50 AndrewMullen(3) 15 39
(D W Barker) *s.i.s: sn in midfield: wknd over 1f out* **20/1**

1006 **10** *2 1/2* **Guadaloup**[3] 4137 5-8-11 50 PatrickDonaghy(7) 2 33
(M Brittain) *mid-div on outer: kpt on fnl 2f: nvr a threat* **9/1**

2340 **11** *3/4* **Nevinstown (IRE)**[34] 3195 7-9-4 50 (p) TonyHamilton 5 30
(C Grant) *mid-div: hdwy to chse ldrs 3f out: hung rt and fdd over 1f out* **10/1**

3440 **12** *2* **Desert Hunter (IRE)**[3] 4137 4-9-5 51 PaulHanagan 9 26
(Micky Hammond) *t.k.h: sn trcking ldrs on outer: hung lft and rn wd bnd over 4f out: wknd over 1f out* **5/1**[1]

0-00 **13** *2 1/2* **Dumas (IRE)**[55] 2545 3-9-2 57 AndrewElliott(3) 7 25
(A P Jarvis) *led tl over 3f out: lost pl over 1f out* **18/1**

4010 **14** *1 1/4* **Strabinios King**[45] 2829 3-9-8 60 LeeEnstone 1 25
(P C Haslam) *trckd ldrs on outer: t.k.h: lost pl over 1f out* **11/1**

1m 26.69s (-0.41) **Going Correction** -0.15s/f (Firm)
WFA 3 from 4yo+ 6lb **14** Ran SP% **127.0**
Speed ratings (Par 101): **96,94,93,91,91 90,89,88,88,85 84,82,79,77**
CSF £329.75 CT £2523.73 TOTE £4.20: £1.80, £15.60, £1.90; EX 313.70.
Owner James Marshall & Mrs Susan Marshall **Bred** Catridge Farm Stud Ltd **Trained** Scarcroft, W Yorks

FOCUS
A low-grade handicap but the winner is clearly going the right way in a visor. Again it proved hard to make ground from off the pace and the first three were always prominent. Pretty sound form.
Guadaloup Official explanation: trainer later said mare had not been suited by the firm ground
Nevinstown(IRE) Official explanation: jockey said gelding had no more to give.
Desert Hunter(IRE) Official explanation: jockey said gelding hung left-handed.

4224 WBX.COM H'CAP 5f 193y

8:45 (8:48) (Class 6) (0-60,60) 3-Y-O **£2,047** (£604; £302) **Stalls** High

Form RPR

3204 **1** **Missus Molly Brown**[16] 3752 3-8-4 46 PaulHanagan 16 51
(R A Fahey) *trckd ldrs: led over 2f out: hld on towards fin* **9/1**

2035 **2** *3/4* **Mangano**[8] 3994 3-8-4 49 PatrickMathers(3) 12 52
(A Berry) *chsd ldrs: hit over hd by rival rdr's whip and kpt on to take 2nd towards fin* **16/1**

5-03 **3** *1/2* **Mister Always**[197] 202 3-8-8 50 PaulMulrennan 13 51
(B P J Baugh) *chsd ldrs: styd on same pce ins fnl f* **14/1**

0553 **4** *hd* **Miss Daawe**[8] 4008 3-8-7 49 ow2 TomEaves 9 50
(B Ellison) *w ldrs: styd on saqme pce ins fnl f* **7/1**[2]

6003 **5** *1* **Stormburst (IRE)**[29] 3342 3-8-9 51 (v) PhillipMakin 7 49+
(M Dods) *chsd ldrs on outer: kpt on same pce fnl 2f* **12/1**

0000 **6** *nk* **Only A Grand**[14] 3786 3-8-1 46 oh1 (b) AndrewMullen(3) 11 43+
(R Bastiman) *s.i.s: hdwy on ins over 1f out: styng on at fin* **16/1**

5400 **7** *nk* **Nufoudh (IRE)**[11] 3885 3-8-12 57 JamieMoriarty(3) 8 53
(Miss Tracy Waggott) *chsd ldrs: kpt on same pce fnl 2f* **33/1**

6665 **8** *nk* **Alavana (IRE)**[39] 3029 3-8-10 52 TonyHamilton 6 47
(D W Barker) *mid-div: hdwy on outer 2f out: kpt on: nvr rchd ldrs* **16/1**

2100 **9** *1* **Pennyrock (IRE)**[35] 3168 3-9-3 59 GrahamGibbons 4 50+
(J J Quinn) *chsd ldrs on outer: one pce fnl 2f* **12/1**

3-50 **10** *hd* **Amber Isle**[164] 535 3-9-4 60 DanielTudhope 5 51
(D Carroll) *in rr: kpt on fnl 2f: nvr nr ldrs* **33/1**

5005 **11** *nk* **Compton Special**[10] 3918 3-8-4 46 oh1 DaleGibson 1 36
(J G Given) *sn in rr and drvn along: sme hdwy 2f out: nvr a factor* **33/1**

4023 **12** *2 1/2* **Beaumont Boy**[19] 3639 3-9-2 58 PatCosgrave 3 40
(G A Swinbank) *in rr on outer: bhd fnl 2f* **14/1**

024 **13** *2* **Ishibee (IRE)**[14] 3786 3-9-0 56 (p) RoystonFfrench 14 31
(Mrs A Duffield) *led tl over 2f out: wknd over 1f out* **6/1**[1]

042 **14** *4* **Invincible Lad (IRE)**[12] 3846 3-8-13 55 KDarley 10 18
(E J Alston) *s.i.s: a in rr* **8/1**[3]

0015 **15** *1 1/2* **On The Map**[19] 3647 3-8-10 55 AndrewElliott(3) 17 13
(A P Jarvis) *trckd ldrs on inner: lost pl over 2f out* **7/1**[2]

0522 **16** *3/4* **Prince Rossi (IRE)**[17] 3713 3-9-4 60 (p) PaulFessey 2 15
(J D Bethell) *in rr: rdn after 2f: sn bhd: eased* **6/1**[1]

1m 13.15s (-0.46) **Going Correction** -0.15s/f (Firm) **16** Ran SP% **141.0**
Speed ratings (Par 98): **97,96,95,95,93 93,92,92,91,90 90,87,84,79,77 76**
CSF £138.34 CT £971.22 TOTE £10.70: £2.20, £4.80, £6.90, £3.10; EX 134.20 Place 6 £107.38, Plasce 5 £51.15..
Owner J E M Hawkins Ltd **Bred** Bearstone Stud **Trained** Musley Bank, N Yorks
■ Mambomoon (8/1, spread plate at start) was withdrawn. Deduct 10p in the £ under Rule 4.
■ Stewards' Enquiry : Graham Gibbons one-day ban: originally went into stall two (Aug 17)
Tom Eaves two-day ban: careless riding - failed to moderate use of whip (Aug 17-18)

FOCUS
A low-grade sprint handicap and the first three home had double-figure draws. Limited form.
Prince Rossi(IRE) Official explanation: jockey said gelding was never travelling
T/Plt: £177.80 to a £1 stake. Pool: £62,817.25. 257.90 winning tickets. T/Qpdt: £49.30 to a £1 stake. Pool: £3,849.10. 57.70 winning tickets. WG

3750 RIPON (R-H)

Monday, August 6

OFFICIAL GOING: Good to firm

Wind: Light, behind Weather: Cloudy with sunny spells

4225 EBF BBC RADIO YORK 103.7FM & 104.3FM NOVICE STKS 6f

2:20 (2:21) (Class 5) 2-Y-O **£4,210** (£1,252; £625; £312) **Stalls** Low

Form RPR

62 **1** **Calmdownmate (IRE)**[16] 3747 2-8-12 0 PatCosgrave 4 89
(K R Burke) *trckd ldrs: led over 1f out: drvn out* **7/1**

1 **2** *2* **Anosti**[18] 3673 2-8-9 0 NCallan 3 80
(K A Ryan) *sn led: rdn and hung rt fr over 2f out: hdd over 1f out: styd on same pce ins fnl f* **6/1**

21 **3** *1 3/4* **Unilateral (IRE)**[44] 2863 2-9-0 78 PaulEddery 7 80
(B Smart) *hld up in tch: plld hrd: rdn over 1f out: hmpd ins fnl f: wknd nr fin* **9/2**[3]

12 **4** *1/2* **Broken Applause (IRE)**[24] 3492 2-8-11 88 PaulHanagan 5 76
(R A Fahey) *chsd ldr: rdn over 2f out: wknd ins fnl f* **15/8**[1]

10 **5** *3/4* **Dry Speedfit (IRE)**[24] 3504 2-9-2 0 SebSanders 2 78
(G G Margarson) *chsd ldrs: rdn and hung rt over 2f out: wknd ins fnl f* **5/2**[2]

6 *6* **Bunny Hug** 2-8-3 0 RoystonFfrench 1 47
(T D Easterby) *s.i.s: outpcd* **33/1**

1m 13.69s (0.69) **Going Correction** -0.05s/f (Good) **6** Ran SP% **111.3**
Speed ratings (Par 94): **93,90,88,87,86 78**
CSF £45.60 TOTE £8.90: £3.70, £3.00; EX 51.60.
Owner Mrs Maura Gittins **Bred** J Costello **Trained** Middleham Moor, N Yorks

FOCUS
A fair novice event, run at an average pace, featuring five previous winners. The form should prove reliable.

NOTEBOOK
Calmdownmate(IRE) confirmed the promise of his latest improved effort when second at Newmarket and went one better with a dogged display. He settled much better this time, looked happy on the fast ground, and could really have been called the winner nearing the furlong marker. It will be interesting to see where he goes next as he is no doubt progressive. (op 13-2)

Anosti, a debut winner over 5f at Hamilton 18 days previously, did not do a great deal wrong under her penalty but still looked a touch green. She has a future all right, but her Group 1 entry does look very ambitious. (op 4-1)
Unilateral(IRE), off the mark at the second attempt 44 days previously, paid when the race became serious for refusing to settle under restraint through the early stages. She should not be judged too harshly on the back of this effort. (tchd 5-1)
Broken Applause(IRE) got outpaced when the tempo got serious and failed to raise her game on this first attempt on quick ground. She is another who should be given another chance when reverting to easier ground. (op 2-1 tchd 7-4)
Dry Speedfit(IRE), not disgraced in Group 2 company last time, did not prove suited by the drop back to this trip and never looked like justifying market support. He has a little to prove now. (op 7-2)

4226 KGM MOTOR INSURANCE 50TH ANNIVERSARY (S) H'CAP 5f
2:50 (2:50) (Class 6) (0-65,59) 3-Y-O **£2,590** (£770; £385; £192) **Stalls** Low

Form RPR
3350 **1** **Rann Na Cille (IRE)**[7] 4021 3-9-7 **59**........(p) NCallan 6 66
(K A Ryan) *racd stands' side: chsd ldrs: led 1f out: rdn out* **6/1**[2]
2213 **2** ¾ **Silly Gilly (IRE)**[13] 3811 3-9-7 **59**........FrancisNorton 2 63
(K R Burke) *overall ldr stands' side: rdn and hdd 1f out: styd on: 2nd of 13 in gp* **5/1**[1]
1644 **3** 2½ **Jojesse**[8] 4001 3-9-7 **59**........PatCosgrave 11 54
(G A Swinbank) *racd stands' side: mid-div: hdwy u.p over 1f out: r.o: 3rd of 13 in gp* **6/1**[2]
0640 **4** nk **Splendidio**[21] 3588 3-8-10 **48** ow3........PaulMulrennan 5 42+
(Mrs Marjorie Fife) *racd stands' side: hmpd s: hdwy over 1f out: nt clr run ins fnl f: r.o: 4th of 13 in gp* **66/1**
0500 **5** nk **Mandy's Maestro (USA)**[16] 3752 3-8-7 **45**........(b) DeanMcKeown 15 38+
(R M Whitaker) *led far side: rdn and hung rt over 1f out: styd on same pce fnl f: 1st of 7 in gp* **25/1**
00-5 **6** nk **First Valentini**[16] 3752 3-8-11 **49**........PaulFessey 18 41+
(N Bycroft) *racd far side: chsd ldrs: rdn over 1f out: styd on: 2nd of 7 in gp* **25/1**
6204 **7** shd **Eastern Princess**[11] 3869 3-8-8 **49**........(v) WilliamBuick(3) 3 43+
(J W Unett) *chsd ldrs stands's side: rdn over 1f out: nt clr run ins fnl f: styd on: 5th of 13 in gp* **6/1**[2]
3350 **8** 1¾ **Tang**[51] 2652 3-8-5 **50**........JackDean(7) 10 35
(W G M Turner) *racd stands' side: chsd ldrs: rdn 1/2-way: wknd fnl f: 6th of 13 in gp* **33/1**
0-00 **9** hd **Whats Your Game (IRE)**[23] 3537 3-8-7 **45**........TomEaves 4 30
(A Berry) *racd stands' side: chsd ldrs: rdn over 1f out: wknd and hung rt ins fnl f: 7th of 13 in gp* **66/1**
-000 **10** nk **Fly So Free (IRE)**[16] 3752 3-8-12 **50**........AdrianTNicholls 9 34
(D Nicholls) *racd stands' side: chsd ldrs: rdn over 1f out: wknd fnl f: 8th of 13 in gp* **14/1**
0002 **11** shd **Spinning Game**[13] 3811 3-8-2 **47**........(b) DanielleMcCreery(7) 20 30+
(D W Chapman) *racd far side: in rr: nvr nrr: 3rd of 7 in gp* **14/1**
0505 **12** hd **Mandriano (ITY)**[92] 1489 3-8-7 **45**........(p) PaulHanagan 16 28+
(D W Barker) *racd far side: chsd ldrs: rdn over 1f out: sn wknd: 4th of 7 in gp* **33/1**
3006 **13** 1 **The Brat**[13] 3811 3-8-4 **45**........(p) AndrewMullen(3) 17 24
(J S Wainwright) *racd far side: hld up in tch: wknd over 1f out: 5th of 7 in gp* **33/1**
46 **14** 1¼ **King Of Tricks**[9] 3949 3-8-0 **45**........FrankiePickard(7) 13 19
(M D I Usher) *racd stands' side: n.d: 9th of 13 in gp* **25/1**
6456 **15** nk **Mind The Style**[21] 3597 3-9-4 **56**........(b[1]) VinceSlattery 19 29
(W G M Turner) *racd far side: prom 3f: 6th of 7 in gp* **10/1**[3]
0-01 **16** ½ **Savanagh Forest (IRE)**[123] 934 3-8-7 **45**........DavidAllan 7 17
(M Quinn) *racd stands' side: prom: rdn 1/2-way: sn wknd: 10th of 13 in gp* **16/1**
3000 **17** 2 **Banana Belle**[11] 3873 3-8-4 **45**........DominicFox(3) 14 9
(J Ryan) *racd far side: hld up: wknd over 1f out: last of 7 in gp* **16/1**
000 **18** 5 **Afric Star**[21] 3597 3-8-0 **45**........KellyHarrison(7) 8 —
(John A Harris) *racd stands' side: sn outpcd: 11th of 13 in gp* **66/1**
040 **19** 3½ **Northern Candy**[12] 3837 3-8-4 **45**........(p) DuranFentiman(3) 1 —
(A Dickman) *racd stands' side: mid-div: wknd 2f out: 12th of 13 in gp* **66/1**
0-00 **20** 67 **Littlemadgebob**[76] 1912 3-8-0 **45**........MCGeran(7) 12 —
(J R Norton) *racd stands' side: sn outpcd: virtually p.u fnl 2f: last of 13 in gp* **66/1**

59.62 secs (-0.58) **Going Correction** -0.05s/f (Good) **20** Ran SP% **121.5**
Speed ratings (Par 98): **102,100,96,96,95 95,95,92,92,91 91,91,89,87,87 86,83,75,69,—**
CSF £31.34 CT £192.06 TOTE £7.50: £2.20, £1.50, £2.30, £10.30; EX 45.80 Trifecta £211.10 Part won. Pool £297.44 - 0.98 winning units..There was no bid for the winner.
Owner D Mac A'Bhaird **Bred** D Mac A Bhaird **Trained** Hambleton, N Yorks

FOCUS
An ordinary race for the grade, in which the winner is rated to her turf form. Those racing on the stands' side came out on top.
Fly So Free(IRE) Official explanation: jockey said filly hung right-handed throughout.
The Brat Official explanation: jockey said filly hung left.
Littlemadgebob Official explanation: jockey said filly lost her action.

4227 ARMSTRONG MEMORIAL H'CAP 6f
3:20 (3:20) (Class 3) (0-95,95) 3-Y-0+
£10,906 (£3,265; £1,632; £817; £407; £204) **Stalls** Low

Form RPR
5000 **1** **Malcheek (IRE)**[9] 3941 5-9-4 **85**........DavidAllan 4 96
(T D Easterby) *chsd ldr tl led over 3f out: rdn out* **12/1**
0000 **2** 1 **Inter Vision (USA)**[9] 3953 7-9-0 **81** ow1........DanielTudhope 9 89
(A Dickman) *hld up: hdwy over 1f out: sn rdn: r.o* **16/1**
1330 **3** ½ **Caribbean Coral**[21] 3586 8-9-11 **92**........GrahamGibbons 12 98
(J J Quinn) *trckd ldrs: rdn over 1f out: edgd lft ins fnl f: styd on* **11/1**
0050 **4** nk **Yorkshire Blue**[9] 3953 8-8-1 **75**........KellyHarrison(7) 11 80
(J S Goldie) *sn pushed along in rr: hdwy over 1f out: styd on* **12/1**
1141 **5** ¾ **Whitbarrow (IRE)**[8] 3998 8-8-13 **85** 6ex........(b) JamesMillman(5) 3 88
(B R Millman) *led: hdd over 3f out: sn rdn: styd on same pce fnl f* **10/3**[1]
1000 **6** shd **Dingaan (IRE)**[9] 3941 4-9-1 **85**........(v) WilliamBuick(3) 5 87
(A M Balding) *s.i.s: hld up: rdn and swtchd rt over 2f out: hdwy over 1f out: no ex ins fnl f* **8/1**
0021 **7** 1¾ **Steel Blue**[3] 4140 7-8-8 **75** 6ex........HayleyTurner 7 72
(R M Whitaker) *prom: chsd wnr over 2f out: sn rdn: wknd ins fnl f* **11/2**[3]
0100 **8** 3 **Desert Commander (IRE)**[21] 3586 5-9-7 **88**........(b) NCallan 2 75
(K A Ryan) *chsd ldrs: rdn over 2f out: wknd fnl f* **9/2**[2]
2162 **9** 2½ **Elkhorn**[9] 3954 5-8-13 **80**........(b) TomEaves 8 59
(Miss J A Camacho) *hld up: rdn and wknd over 1f out* **11/2**[3]

1m 11.78s (-1.22) **Going Correction** -0.05s/f (Good)
WFA 3 from 4yo+ 4lb **9** Ran SP% **112.7**
Speed ratings (Par 107): **106,104,104,103,102 102,100,96,92**
CSF £179.23 CT £2166.59 TOTE £12.20: £3.10, £5.00, £3.00; EX 279.30 Trifecta £412.90 Part won. Pool £581.63 - 0.10 winning units..
Owner Mrs Susie Dicker **Bred** Carrigbeg Stud **Trained** Great Habton, N Yorks

FOCUS
A good sprint for the class. An improved run from the winner, with the second back to form and the next three close to their marks.

NOTEBOOK
Malcheek(IRE), back in trip, ran out a most game winner under a positive ride and could have been called the winner passing the furlong pole. He had dropped to his last winning mark for this, relished the return to quick ground, and could have a little more to offer over the trip now, despite a likely rise back up in the weights. His trainer later reported he could now return to this course and distance for the competitive Great St Wilfred Handicap later in the month. (op 14-1)
Inter Vision(USA), who won this race from a 4lb higher mark in 2005, was doing all of his best work towards the finish and showed his best form of the current campaign. He can build on this. (op 14-1)
Caribbean Coral has shown all of his previous best form at 5f, so this has to rate a solid effort in defeat under top weight and he continues in good heart. (op 12-1)
Yorkshire Blue, back down in trip, struggled to go the early pace yet was finishing his race with gusto. A return to 7f now looks best for him, but he is not easy predict these days.
Whitbarrow(IRE) had his chance from the front, but simply proved a sitting duck under his penalty. This was no disgrace. (op 7-2 tchd 3-1)
Dingaan(IRE) did not help his cause with a slow start and then looked tricky when asked to make up his ground from off the pace. (op 9-1)
Desert Commander(IRE), back at a track he likes, proved easy to back and looked to down tools when asked for maximum effort. (op 7-2)

4228 WEATHERBYS BLOODSTOCK INSURANCE H'CAP 1m 1f 170y
3:50 (3:50) (Class 4) (0-85,85) 3-Y-0+ **£5,047** (£1,510; £755; £377; £188) **Stalls** High

Form RPR
4652 **1** **Ahlawy (IRE)**[7] 4031 4-8-9 **66** oh1........PaulMulrennan 5 75
(M W Easterby) *hmpd s: hld up: hdwy over 3f out: led over 1f out: sn rdn and edgd rt: r.o* **9/2**[2]
2-00 **2** 1½ **Five A Side**[9] 3959 3-9-0 **80**........J-PGuillambert 3 86
(M Johnston) *chsd ldr tl led over 2f out: rdn and hdd over 1f out: styd on same pce ins fnl f* **11/1**
-560 **3** 1 **Baan (USA)**[9] 3955 4-9-3 **74**........RoystonFfrench 7 78
(M Johnston) *chsd ldrs: rdn over 3f out: styd on u.p* **10/1**
6145 **4** ½ **Harvest Warrior**[6] 4039 5-9-9 **80**........DavidAllan 4 83
(T D Easterby) *s.i.s: hld up: hdwy over 1f out: nt rch ldrs* **10/1**
6650 **5** 1½ **Kildare Sun (IRE)**[37] 3093 5-9-0 **74**........PJMcDonald(3) 10 74
(J Mackie) *hld up: hdwy over 2f out: rdn and edgd rt over 1f out: no ex fnl f* **22/1**
1644 **6** 1½ **Just Observing**[9] 3959 4-9-1 **75**........(p) JamieMoriarty(3) 9 71
(P T Midgley) *prom: rdn over 2f out: wknd over 1f out* **12/1**
3102 **7** nk **Northern Jem**[11] 3877 3-9-5 **85**........SebSanders 11 81+
(G G Margarson) *trckd ldrs: nt clr run fr over 2f out tl wknd ins fnl f* **7/4**[1]
0500 **8** 2½ **Frank Crow**[13] 3813 4-9-0 **71** ow1........DanielTudhope 1 62
(J S Goldie) *prom: rdn over 2f out: wknd over 1f out* **16/1**
2012 **9** 1½ **Little Jimbob**[45] 2828 6-9-3 **74**........PaulHanagan 8 61
(R A Fahey) *led: hdd over 2f out: rdn and wknd over 1f out* **7/1**[3]
6-46 **10** 4 **Kamanda Laugh**[31] 3258 6-10-0 **85**........NCallan 6 64
(K A Ryan) *hld up: edgd rt over 2f out: sn rdn and wknd* **14/1**
60-0 **S** **Isidore Bonheur (IRE)**[4] 4105 6-9-12 **83**........DeanMcKeown 2 —
(G A Swinbank) *hld up: clipped heels and slipped up 2f out* **33/1**

2m 4.14s (-0.86) **Going Correction** -0.05s/f (Good)
WFA 3 from 4yo+ 9lb **11** Ran SP% **121.1**
Speed ratings (Par 105): **101,99,99,98,97 96,95,93,92,89 —**
CSF £55.16 CT £480.90 TOTE £5.40: £1.60, £2.80, £3.70; EX 68.40 Trifecta £248.10 Pool £384.46 - 1.10 winning units..
Owner K Hodgson & Mrs J Hodgson **Bred** Castlemartin Stud And Skymarc Farm **Trained** Sheriff Hutton, N Yorks

FOCUS
A fair handicap, but the slowest of the three races on the round course. The form looks sound and should work out.

4229 BLACK SHEEP BREWERY MAIDEN STKS 1m 4f 10y
4:20 (4:21) (Class 5) 3-Y-0+ **£3,562** (£1,059; £529; £264) **Stalls** High

Form RPR
34-2 **1** **Starry Messenger**[59] 2436 3-8-9 78........WilliamBuick(3) 8 75
(M P Tregoning) *s.i.s: sn chsng ldrs: led over 2f out: rdn and edgd lft wl over 1f out: all out* **6/5**[1]
0-22 **2** shd **Earl Marshal (USA)**[18] 3685 3-9-3 75........(v) SebSanders 9 80
(Sir Michael Stoute) *hld up in tch: chal over 2f out: rdn whn ducked lft wl over 1f out: hung rt ins fnl f: nt run on* **15/8**[2]
0-24 **3** 11 **Crystal Prince**[59] 2436 3-9-3 75........TPQueally 6 62
(T P Tate) *led after 1f: hdd over 6f out: led again over 3f out: rdn and hdd over 2f out: wknd over 1f out* **15/2**
0230 **4** 2 **Ja Myford**[14] 3792 3-9-3 56........(p) PaulMulrennan 7 59
(P T Midgley) *led 1f: chsd ldrs: rdn and ev ch over 2f out: wknd wl over 1f out* **33/1**
45 **5** 11 **Ridge Rose**[18] 3685 3-8-12 0........NickyMackay 2 37
(L M Cumani) *hld up: sme hdwy over 3f out: sn wknd* **7/1**[3]
6 **6** 9 **Rourke Star**[18] 3678 5-9-11 0........PJMcDonald(3) 4 27
(B Storey) *chsd ldr: led over 6f out: hdd over 3f out: sn wknd* **150/1**
0- **7** 12 **La Nuage**[300] 5899 3-8-7 0........RussellKennemore(5) 10 —
(T J Etherington) *sn outpcd* **100/1**
P440 **8** 16 **Ammeyrr**[24] 3502 3-9-3 62........TomEaves 5 —
(A Crook) *sn outpcd* **80/1**
5 **9** 20 **Beauty Shine**[18] 3678 3-8-12 0........KDarley 3 —
(M Johnston) *s.i.s: a bhd* **14/1**
00 **10** 14 **Glad Star (GER)**[76] 1937 4-9-7 0........(b[1]) DanielleMcCreery(7) 1 —
(D W Chapman) *s.s: a bhd* **150/1**

2m 34.93s (-2.07) **Going Correction** -0.05s/f (Good)
WFA 3 from 4yo+ 11lb **10** Ran SP% **117.7**
Speed ratings (Par 103): **104,103,96,95,87 81,73,63,49,40**
CSF £3.63 TOTE £2.50: £1.10, £1.20, £2.40; EX 4.60 Trifecta £21.00 Pool £606.05 - 20.43 winning units..
Owner A E Oppenheimer **Bred** Hascombe & Valiant Studs **Trained** Lambourn, Berks

FOCUS
A modest maiden which saw the market leaders fight out a bobbing finish. They came well clear. The winner did not need to reproduce her previous best but has more to offer.

Glad Star(GER) Official explanation: jockey said gelding was slow away.

4230 BALDFOX INTERNATIONAL LEISURE H'CAP 1m 4f 10y

4:50 (4:50) (Class 5) (0-70,66) 3-Y-0+ £3,238 (£963; £481; £240) Stalls High

Form RPR

4406 **1** **Riguez Dancer**[35] 3155 3-9-2 65 LeeEnstone 9 76+
(P C Haslam) *a.p: chsd ldr 8f out: lft in ld over 4f out: styd on strly* 9/1

-540 **2** 3 1/2 **Admiral Savannah (IRE)**[14] 3792 3-7-9 47 (b[1]) DuranFentiman[(3)] 1 51
(T D Easterby) *trckd ldrs: racd keenly: rdn over 3f out: styd on* 20/1

21-4 **3** nk **Master Nimbus**[47] 2764 7-8-9 47 GrahamGibbons 2 51
(J J Quinn) *chsd ldr 4f: wnt 2nd again 4f out: rdn over 2f out: edgd rt and no ex fnl f* 11/2[3]

2221 **4** 3 1/2 **Light Sentence**[13] 3815 4-10-0 66 NCallan 3 70+
(G A Swinbank) *hld up: hdwy over 2f out: rdn over 1f out: n.m.r and no ex fnl f* 6/5[1]

0000 **5** 4 **Mulaazem**[43] 2906 4-9-11 66 JamieMoriarty[(3)] 8 58
(J Mackie) *hld up: rdn over 2f out: wknd over 1f out* 16/1

044 **6** 14 **Treasure Isle**[10] 3914 3-8-2 51 PaulHanagan 5 20
(R A Fahey) *hld up: effrt over 3f out: wknd over 2f out* 13/2

123 **7** 2 1/2 **Red Chairman**[2] 4156 5-9-8 60 (p) AdrianTNicholls 4 25
(R Johnson) *led: hung lft throughout: hdd over 4f out: wknd and eased wl over 1f out* 9/2[2]

0404 **8** 29 **Tiegs (IRE)**[14] 3795 5-8-6 47 oh2 MarcHalford[(3)] 7 —
(P W Hiatt) *hld up: rdn over 4f out: wknd and eased fnl 3f* 50/1

2m 35.52s (-1.48) **Going Correction** -0.05s/f (Good)
WFA 3 from 4yo+ 11lb 8 Ran SP% **115.0**
Speed ratings (Par 103): **102,99,99,97,94 85,83,64**
CSF £163.42 CT £1081.25 TOTE £10.90: £2.90, £4.60, £2.10; EX 177.80 TRIFECTA Part won. Pool £624.87 - 0.34 winning units. Place 6 £2,127.58, Place 5 £250.25..
Owner Middleham Park Racing Xii **Bred** Plantation Stud **Trained** Middleham Moor, N Yorks

FOCUS
A moderate handicap. The form seems sound enough even though the favourite did not run his race.
Red Chairman Official explanation: jockey said gelding hung left-handed throughout.
T/Jkpt: Not won. T/Plt: £2,130.50 to a £1 stake. Pool: £82,011.20. 28.10 winning tickets. T/Qpdt: £176.50 to a £1 stake. Pool: £5,416.00. 22.70 winning tickets. CR

[4181]WINDSOR (R-H)

Monday, August 6

OFFICIAL GOING: Good to firm (8.3)
Wind: Light, behind Weather: Sunny

4231 BOLLINGER CHAMPAGNE CHALLENGE SERIES H'CAP (FOR GENTLEMAN AMATEUR RIDERS) 1m 3f 135y

6:00 (6:00) (Class 5) (0-75,74) 3-Y-0+ £3,123 (£968; £484; £242) Stalls Low

Form RPR

1453 **1** **Wait For The Will (USA)**[10] 3907 11-11-2 69 (b) MrDHutchison[(3)] 12 77
(G L Moore) *hld up towards rr: smooth prog on inner fr 4f out: rdn to ld jst ins fnl f: hung lft: kpt on* 9/1

0-00 **2** 1/2 **Mystic Storm**[7] 4015 4-11-4 68 (t) MrSWalker 10 75
(Lady Herries) *hld up towards rr: prog 4f out to chse ldr over 2f out: clsd u.p fr 2f out: upsides ent fnl f: carried lft and nt qckn* 15/2[2]

5403 **3** 1 1/2 **Agilete**[39] 3036 5-10-3 56 MrSPearce[(3)] 16 60
(J Pearce) *s.s: hld up wl in rr: prog 3f out: nt clr run over 2f out: clsd on ldrs 1f out: nt qckn last 150yds* 15/2[2]

6031 **4** shd **Regency Red (IRE)**[42] 2946 9-10-0 55 oh3 MrBenBrisbourne[(5)] 1 59
(W M Brisbourne) *dwlt: hld up wl in rr: prog 3f out: squeeze3d through 2f out: styd on to chse ldrs 1f out: one pce* 14/1

6053 **5** 1 1/4 **Mr Mischief**[7] 4019 7-10-5 60 MrAMerriam[(5)] 13 62
(M C Chapman) *hld up in midfield: prog 3f out: rdn whn bmpd 2f out: kpt on fr over 1f out* 11/2[1]

3016 **6** 1 1/2 **Ocean Avenue (IRE)**[23] 3554 8-11-7 74 MrHHaynes[(3)] 6 74
(C A Horgan) *trckd ldr: led 1/2-way: drew 6 l clr over 3f out: hdd & wknd jst ins fnl f* 11/2[1]

3513 **7** 6 **Raquel White**[10] 3901 3-9-8 62 MrRPFlint[(7)] 2 52
(J L Flint) *chsd ldrs: rdn whn bmpd 2f out: wknd over 1f out* 15/2[2]

-001 **8** 1 **Le Corvee (IRE)**[56] 2006 5-11-7 74 MrMJJSmith[(3)] 4 62
(A W Carroll) *prom: chsd clr ldr 4f out to over 2f out: wknd* 15/2[2]

0000 **9** hd **Dancewiththestars (USA)**[10] 3907 3-9-3 55 oh8 (t) MrRBirkett[(5)] 14 43
(Miss J Feilden) *prom tl wknd over 2f out* 50/1

04-0 **10** 12 **Smart John**[24] 3485 7-10-6 63 MrJGoss[(7)] 8 31
(H J Evans) *hld up in midfield: hanging over 4f out: hung lft 3f out: wknd rapidly 2f out* 50/1

-000 **11** 7 **A One (IRE)**[18] 3690 8-9-12 55 oh10 MrDBass[(7)] 9 11
(H J Manners) *led at str pce to 1/2-way: wknd over 3f out: t.o* 66/1

0600 **12** 3/4 **Spinning Dixie (IRE)**[40] 2978 3-9-8 62 oh6 ow7 (t) MrDHannig[(7)] 15 17
(J A Geake) *a bhd: t.o over 3f out* 66/1

653- **13** 1 **King Kasyapa (IRE)**[389] 3431 5-11-0 71 MrDFDevereux[(7)] 3 24
(P Bowen) *prom: wknd and thrashed along 3f out: bmpd 2f out: eased fnl f* 8/1[3]

5460 **14** 2 **Poseidon's Secret (IRE)**[95] 1438 4-11-8 72 (p) MrDHDunsdon 5 22
(Pat Eddery) *prom 7f: sn wknd u.p: t.o* 14/1

01-0 **15** shd **Alekhine (IRE)**[88] 1609 6-10-9 66 MrBAdams[(7)] 11 15
(J R Boyle) *t.k.h: a in rr: t.o* 20/1

1200 **16** 2 **Time For Change (IRE)**[67] 2178 3-9-6 58 MrFFairchild[(5)] 7 4
(P G Murphy) *nvr on terms: t.o* 33/1

2m 28.54s (-1.56) **Going Correction** -0.275s/f (Firm)
WFA 3 from 4yo+ 11lb 16 Ran SP% **126.9**
Speed ratings (Par 103): **94,93,92,92,91 90,86,86,85,77 73,72,72,70,70 69**
CSF £74.81 CT £548.09 TOTE £9.70: £2.40, £3.00, £2.50, £1.30; EX 53.90.
Owner Rdm Racing **Bred** Paul Mellon **Trained** Woodingdean, E Sussex
■ Stewards' Enquiry : Mr D Hutchison two-day ban: careless riding (Aug 17, 26)
Mr Ben Brisbourne ten-day ban: failed to ride out for 3rd place (Aug 17, 22, 26, 31; Sep 1, 3, 5, 7, 10, 25)

FOCUS
A modest amateur riders' handicap run at a strong pace. Solid form.
Dancewiththestars(USA) Official explanation: vet said filly had been struck into.

4232 VC CASINO.COM EBF MAIDEN FILLIES' STKS 6f

6:30 (6:30) (Class 4) 2-Y-O £5,181 (£1,541; £770; £384) Stalls High

Form RPR

1 **Hip** 2-9-0 0 JimmyFortune 16 78
(E A L Dunlop) *chsd ldrs and racd against nr side rail: swtchd lft wl over 1f out: rdn to cl: led last 150yds: styd on wl* 7/1

2 1 1/4 **Street Star (USA)** 2-9-0 0 JamieSpencer 14 74
(J R Fanshawe) *trckd ldrs: rdn to ld over 1f out: hdd and one pce last 150yds* 7/2[1]

0 **3** 1/2 **Superduper**[24] 3507 2-9-0 0 RichardHughes 7 73
(R Hannon) *gd spd to ld and crossed to nr side rail: hdd over 1f out: kpt on* 9/1

4 3 1/2 **No Page (IRE)** 2-9-0 0 MichaelHills 13 62
(B W Hills) *hld up towards rr on inner: stdy prog fr over 2f out: shkn up and edgd lft fnl f: kpt on* 16/1

0 **5** 2 1/2 **Cryptonite Diamond (USA)**[56] 2504 2-9-0 0 AdamKirby 2 55
(W R Swinburn) *trckd across to nr side fr wd draw and hld up in rr: stdy prog over 2f out: pushed along and kpt on: nrst fin* 25/1

5 **6** nk **Silca Destination**[7] 4014 2-9-0 0 TPO'Shea 1 54
(M R Channon) *sn pressing ldrs fr wd draw: rdn over 2f out: outpcd over 1f out* 11/2[3]

7 1 3/4 **Athboy Auction** 2-9-0 0 JimmyQuinn 12 49
(H J Collingridge) *chsd ldrs and racd on wd outside: pushed along and outpcd fr over 1f out* 16/1

8 1/2 **Khandala (IRE)** 2-9-0 0 EddieAhern 6 47
(M L W Bell) *hld up at rr of main gp: a looked to be gng wl but no real prog: do bttr* 40/1

9 nk **Kili Links (IRE)** 2-9-0 0 RyanMoore 11 46
(R Hannon) *s.i.s: sn rdn and struggling in last quartet: nvr a factor: kpt on u.p fnl f* 4/1[2]

10 nk **Hawk Eyed Lady (IRE)** 2-9-0 0 MartinDwyer 10 45
(J A Osborne) *chsd ldrs 4f: sn wknd* 17/2

11 3/4 **Smooth As Silk (IRE)** 2-9-0 0 JimCrowley 5 43
(C R Egerton) *s.s: mostly in last quartet: hanging lft 1/2-way: nvr a factor* 33/1

0 **12** 1 **Medici Gold**[19] 3643 2-9-0 0 SteveDrowne 3 40
(B J Meehan) *towards rr on outer: no prog fnl 2f* 33/1

13 shd **Colmar Magic (IRE)** 2-9-0 0 PatDobbs 8 40
(R Hannon) *chsd ldrs: wknd wl over 1f out* 40/1

14 nk **Then 'n Now** 2-9-0 0 SamHitchcott 4 39
(C A Cyzer) *prom tl wknd rapidly over 2f out* 50/1

15 6 **Mia Haria** 2-9-0 0 JHBowman 9 21
(B R Millman) *a in last trio and sn struggling: wl bhd 1/2-way* 33/1

16 8 **No No Ninette** 2-9-0 0 TQuinn 15 —
(C R Egerton) *sn t.o and rn green* 20/1

1m 11.92s (-1.75) **Going Correction** -0.275s/f (Firm) 16 Ran SP% **126.7**
Speed ratings (Par 93): **100,98,97,93,89 89,86,86,85,85 84,83,83,82,74 63**
CSF £30.22 TOTE £7.70: £2.80, £2.00, £3.20; EX 49.00.
Owner Cheveley Park Stud **Bred** Cheveley Park Stud Ltd **Trained** Newmarket, Suffolk

FOCUS
This looked like quite a good fillies' maiden, although the initial level of the form is a bit guessy.

NOTEBOOK
Hip, a Pivotal half-sister to useful multiple 7f-1m winner Hypnotic, and dual 7f scorer Macedon, out of a useful dual 7f juvenile winner, proved good enough to make a winning debut. She had to be switched with her run, but showed a good attitude once in the clear and was well on top at the finish. She deserves the chance to prove herself in good company. (op 6-1)
Street Star(USA), a daughter of Street Cry who was bought back for 95,000gns, is a half-sister to seven winners, notably useful 1m6f winner Alva Glen, and has been given an entry in the Lowther Stakes. She showed signs of inexperience and ultimately proved no match for the winner, but she is entitled to improve for the experience. (tchd 10-3 and 4-1)
Superduper, down the field on her debut at Newmarket, showed good speed from a far from ideal draw and stuck on when passed. She is going the right way. (op 11-1)
No Page(IRE), a Statue Of Liberty first foal of a dual 5f winner at two, was noted doing some good late work and should improve.
Cryptonite Diamond(USA) was too green to do herself justice on her debut at Pontefract but, although she would have known more this time, her low draw did her few favours and she could never post a serious challenge. She is better than she has shown so far. (op 20-1)
Silca Destination is really well bred, but she showed just modest form on her debut over course and distance the previous week and was again comfortably held. She may be more of a nursery type. (op 4-1)
Athboy Auction, an Auction House half-sister to among others multiple 7f-1m winner Melody Queen, who was later smart in the US, showed ability and can improve on this. (tchd 14-1)
Kili Links(IRE), a 31,000euros daughter of Bahri, half-sister to dual 6f winner Golband, was never really going after starting slowly and failed to justify strong market support. (op 8-1 tchd 10-3)
Hawk Eyed Lady(IRE), an 85,000euros Hawk Wing filly, half-sister to among others very useful prolific sprint winner Whitbarrow, out of a 5f juvenile scorer, has been entered in the Lowther and could be capable of better. (op 8-1 tchd 10-1)
Mia Haria Official explanation: jockey said filly was never travelling.
No No Ninette Official explanation: jockey said filly ran green.

4233 PLAY BLACKJACK AT VC CASINO.COM H'CAP 5f 10y

7:00 (7:02) (Class 5) (0-75,74) 3-Y-0+ £3,238 (£963; £481; £240) Stalls High

Form RPR

6164 **1** **Garstang**[9] 3954 4-9-3 67 (b) LPKeniry 8 79
(Peter Grayson) *s.i.s: pushed up to midfield: effrt towards inner over 1f out: gd prog to ld last 75yds: sn clr* 9/1

3023 **2** 1 1/4 **One Way Ticket**[59] 2411 7-9-3 67 (p) RyanMoore 16 74
(J M Bradley) *led against nr side rail: drvn over 1f out: hdd and outpcd last 75yds* 4/1[1]

2123 **3** 1/2 **Malapropism**[1] 4204 7-9-6 70 JHBowman 15 75
(M R Channon) *hld up bhd ldrs: swtchd lft wl over 1f out: clsd to chal 1f out: fnd little u.p* 9/2[2]

1035 **4** 1/2 **Millfields Dreams**[190] 276 8-8-13 66 JerryO'Dwyer[(3)] 13 69
(M G Quinlan) *wl in rr: rdn and effrt 2f out: swtchd sharply lft over 1f out: styd on: nt rch ldrs* 20/1

203 **5** 1 1/4 **Gwilym (GER)**[21] 3594 4-9-3 72 AshleyHamblett[(5)] 2 71
(D Haydn Jones) *hld up wl in rr on outer: prog fr 1/2-way: chsd ldrs and ch over 1f out: one pce* 9/1

1032 **6** nk **Pretty Miss**[18] 3688 3-9-5 70 JimCrowley 7 70
(H Candy) *mostly chsd ldr to 1f out: wknd ins fnl f* 8/1[3]

6204 **7** hd **Desperate Dan**[25] 3449 6-9-5 69 (b) JamieSpencer 3 66
(J A Osborne) *hld up in rr: stdy prog towards outer fr 1/2-way: clsd on ldrs over 1f out: rdn and nt qckn* 10/1

0060 **8** 1/2 **Matsunosuke**[4] 4103 5-9-6 70 JimmyFortune 1 69+
(A B Coogan) *wl in rr on wd outside: prog hal;fway: rdn and chsng ldrs over 1f out: hld whn nt clr run twice ins fnl f* 8/1[3]

042 **9** shd **Multahab**[20] 3627 8-8-12 62 (t) AdamKirby 10 57
(Miss D A McHale) *hld up bhd ldrs: rdn wl over 1f out: no rspnse* 18/1

5330 **10** 1 3/4 **Rocker**[3] 4123 3-9-7 74 (v) JimmyQuinn 6 63
(B R Johnson) *s.s: mostly in last pair: stl there over 1f out: shkn up and styd on: nvr nr ldrs* 12/1

0000 **11** ¾ **Dancing Mystery**[58] 2479 13-8-12 **62**....(b) TQuinn 12 48
(E A Wheeler) *prom 3f: sn lost pl* **50/1**
6400 **12** 1 **Puskas (IRE)**[4] 4103 4-9-5 **74**....(p) KevinGhunowa(5) 14 56
(J M Bradley) *s.s: a wl in rr: taken towards outer fr 1/2-way: no prog* **25/1**
0555 **13** 8 **Exponential (IRE)**[12] 3859 5-8-10 **60**....(p) SteveDrowne 11 14
(J M Bradley) *trckd ldrs: lost pl 2f out: eased fnl f* **9/1**
6-06 **14** hd **Now Look Out**[69] 2119 3-9-3 **70**....(v[1]) DaneO'Neill 9 23
(E S McMahon) *rousted along to go prom: wknd rapidly wl over 1f out* **33/1**

58.81 secs (-2.29) **Going Correction** -0.275s/f (Firm)
WFA 3 from 4yo+ 3lb **14** Ran SP% **126.0**
Speed ratings (Par 103): **107,105,104,103,101 100,100,99,99,96 95,94,81,80**
CSF £45.30 CT £197.11 TOTE £10.70: £3.70, £2.00, £1.80; EX 60.10.
Owner The Foulrice Twenty **Bred** Mrs S E Barclay **Trained** Formby, Lancs
■ Stewards' Enquiry : J H Bowman one-day ban; careless riding (Aug 17)

FOCUS
Modest but solid sprint form. The fast pace suited the winner's style.
Multahab Official explanation: jockey said gelding hung right from 2 1/2f out.
Rocker Official explanation: jockey said gelding missed the break.

4234 PLAY AT VC CASINO.COM H'CAP — 1m 67y
7:30 (7:30) (Class 4) (0-85,83) 3-Y-0+ **£6,477** (£1,927; £963; £481) **Stalls** High

Form RPR
1630 **1** **Glencalvie (IRE)**[26] 3420 6-9-4 **73**....(p) MartinDwyer 5 82
(J Akehurst) *led: drvn 2f out: narrowly hdd jst over 1f out: led again ins fnl f: kpt on wl* **33/1**
1011 **2** nk **Cnoc Moy (IRE)**[18] 3689 3-9-2 **78**.... GeorgeBaker 1 86+
(C F Wall) *trckd wnr after 3f: gng strly 2f out: shkn up to ld jst over 1f out: hdd and nt qckn ins fnl f* **15/8[1]**
2066 **3** 1 ¼ **Piper's Song (IRE)**[17] 3705 4-8-13 **68**.... DaneO'Neill 9 73
(H Candy) *dwlt: wl in rr: prog fr over 3f out to chse clr ldng pair over 1f out: styd on: nvr able to chal* **9/2[2]**
6005 **4** 1 ¾ **Spanish Don**[18] 3672 9-9-7 **76**.... TQuinn 10 77
(D R C Elsworth) *trckd wnr for 3f: styd cl up: nt qckn and outpcd 2f out: plugged on* **17/2**
0300 **5** nk **Lazy Darren**[16] 3745 3-9-5 **81**....(b[1]) RichardHughes 8 80
(R Hannon) *dwlt: wl in rr: prog over 2f out: chsng ldrs but no imp whn hung bdly lft fnl f* **9/1**
30U- **6** 1 ½ **Celebration Song (IRE)**[322] 5428 4-10-0 **83**.... AdamKirby 2 80
(W R Swinburn) *dwlt: mostly last: drvn over 2f out: kpt on one pce: n.d* **50/1**
5402 **7** 2 ½ **Magic Mountain (IRE)**[9] 3966 3-9-4 **80**.... RyanMoore 7 70
(R Hannon) *wl in rr: drvn 3f out and no prog: no ch after* **14/1**
-003 **8** ½ **Glenmuir (IRE)**[49] 2722 4-9-3 **72**....(b) JHBowman 4 62
(B R Millman) *plld hrd: trckd ldrs tl wknd 2f out* **17/2**
0-50 **9** 1 ¾ **Personify**[10] 3900 5-9-3 **72**....(p) EddieAhern 6 58
(C G Cox) *cl up tl wknd rapidly 2f out: no ch whn n.m.r over 1f out* **15/2[3]**
-000 **10** 2 ½ **Art Market (CAN)**[45] 2835 4-9-6 **75**.... FergusSweeney 11 55
(G L Moore) *hld up in midfield: rdn and no prog 3f out: sn struggling* **66/1**
0304 **11** 28 **Bee Stinger**[40] 2995 5-9-13 **82**.... JamieSpencer 3 —
(I A Wood) *hld up in midfield: rdn 3f out: no prog 2f out: heavily eased: t.o* **11/1**

1m 41.67s (-3.03) **Going Correction** -0.275s/f (Firm)
WFA 3 from 4yo+ 7lb **11** Ran SP% **117.2**
Speed ratings (Par 105): **104,103,102,100,100 98,96,95,94,91 63**
CSF £94.21 CT £360.29 TOTE £32.90: £6.40, £1.10, £2.00; EX 138.90.
Owner Tattenham Corner Racing **Bred** Top Of The Form Syndicate **Trained** Epsom, Surrey

FOCUS
The form looks ordinary for the grade and only the first two ever really got into it. The winner is rated to last year's turf best.
Glencalvie(IRE) Official explanation: trainer said, regarding the improved form shown, he felt the gelding was quirky, and it sulked at Kempton last time but appeared suited by today's good to firm ground
Glenmuir(IRE) Official explanation: jockey said gelding lost its action.
Bee Stinger Official explanation: jockey said gelding moved poorly throughout.

4235 PLAY BLACKJACK AT VC CASINO.COM MAIDEN STKS — 1m 2f 7y
8:00 (8:03) (Class 5) 3-4-Y-0 **£3,886** (£1,156; £577; £288) **Stalls** Low

Form RPR
0-3 **1** **Sugar Ray (IRE)**[26] 3436 3-9-3 0.... RyanMoore 2 84+
(Sir Michael Stoute) *led or disp ld after 2f: def advantage 3f out: punched clr fnl 2f* **2/5[1]**
3 **2** 6 **Hibiki (IRE)**[7] 4018 3-8-12 0.... TolleyDean(5) 3 66
(J S Moore) *hld up in rr: prog over 3f out: chsd wnr over 2f out: lft bhd over 1f out* **8/1[3]**
3 2 ½ **Midsummer Fun (USA)** 3-8-12 0.... KerrinMcEvoy 1 56+
(Saeed Bin Suroor) *cl up: chsd ldng pair over 2f out and rn green: sn outpcd* **4/1[2]**
00 **4** 2 **Lady Dedlock**[98] 1364 3-8-12 0.... EddieAhern 8 52
(C A Cyzer) *hld up in midfield: outpcd over 2f out: pushed along and kpt on one pce* **66/1**
5 4 **Tilly Shilling (IRE)** 3-8-12 0.... JamieSpencer 6 44+
(C R Egerton) *hld up in last: stl last over 2f out: nudged along and styd on in taking style fnl 2f: improve for experience* **33/1**
0 **6** 1 ½ **Airman (IRE)**[37] 3079 4-9-12 0.... GeorgeBaker 10 46
(W M Brisbourne) *led after 1f tl after 2f: w wnr tl hung lft bnd 3f out: sn wknd* **25/1**
7 ½ **Granary** 3-8-12 0.... DaneO'Neill 9 40
(H Candy) *hld up in midfield: outpcd and shkn up 3f out: one pce after* **16/1**
0-0 **8** 1 ¼ **Squirrel Tail**[18] 3685 4-9-12 0.... FergusSweeney 4 43
(E S McMahon) *prom: rdn over 2f out: steadily wknd* **100/1**
0 **9** 7 **Borita (IRE)**[14] 3794 4-9-0 0.... HaddenFrost(7) 5 24
(M Scudamore) *t.k.h: led for 1f: restrained to rr: shkn up over 3f out: sn btn* **100/1**
0 **10** 6 **Sir Jake**[25] 3476 3-9-3 0.... TGMcLaughlin 11 17
(T T Clement) *hld up in midfield: rdn 3f out: wknd over 2f out* **100/1**
00 **11** 10 **Tagula Song (IRE)**[8] 3992 3-8-12 0.... LPKeniry 7 —
(J A Geake) *sn wl in rr: pushed along and struggling 4f out: wknd rapidly over 2f out: t.o* **100/1**

2m 6.11s (-2.19) **Going Correction** -0.275s/f (Firm)
WFA 3 from 4yo 9lb **11** Ran SP% **120.7**
Speed ratings (Par 103): **97,92,90,88,85 84,83,82,77,72 64**
CSF £4.72 TOTE £1.40: £1.02, £1.70, £1.60; EX 5.00.
Owner Philip Newton **Bred** Barronstown Stud And Pacelco S A **Trained** Newmarket, Suffolk

FOCUS
An uncompetitive maiden and weak for this track, the winner apart.
Tilly Shilling(IRE) Official explanation: jockey said filly ran green

4236 MONDAY NIGHT RACING WITH VC CASINO.COM H'CAP — 6f
8:30 (8:30) (Class 5) (0-70,70) 3-Y-0+ **£3,238** (£963; £481; £240) **Stalls** High

Form RPR
-240 **1** **Buy On The Red**[20] 3613 6-9-8 **67**....(p) MartinDwyer 13 74
(W R Muir) *chsd ldr 1f: mostly 3rd after: u.p 2f out: styd on to ld ins fnl f: hld on* **7/2[1]**
0220 **2** nk **The Jay Factor (IRE)**[19] 3646 3-9-3 **66**....(p) DaneO'Neill 12 71
(Pat Eddery) *s.i.s: sn chsd clr ldrs: rdn over 2f out: clsd over 1f out: hanging but pressed wnr last 100yds: a jst hld* **8/1**
0600 **3** 1 **Scarlet Knight**[10] 3906 4-9-7 **66**.... IanMongan 8 69
(P Mitchell) *wl in rr: drvn and prog 2f out: styd on fnl f: nvr quite able to chal* **16/1**
6360 **4** nk **Marko Jadeo (IRE)**[7] 4024 9-9-9 **68**....(p) JamieSpencer 10 70
(R A Harris) *s.s: wl off the pce in last quartet: drvn and prog 2f out: styd on fnl f: nvr quite rchd ldrs* **5/1[2]**
-563 **5** ½ **Drumming Party (USA)**[33] 3212 5-9-1 **60**....(t) LPKeniry 14 60
(A M Balding) *chsd clr ldr after 1f: clsd to ld jst over 1f out: hdd & wknd ins fnl f* **7/1[3]**
3000 **6** 2 ½ **Musical Script (USA)**[20] 3613 4-8-9 **54**....(b[1]) JimmyQuinn 16 46
(Mouse Hamilton-Fairley) *racd freely: led and sn clr: hdd jst over 1f out: hanging and wknd* **16/1**
-300 **7** 2 **Pango's Legacy**[14] 3797 3-9-3 **69**.... TravisBlock(3) 6 55
(H Morrison) *wl in rr and off the pce: effrt on wd outside 1/2-way: no imp over 1f out* **11/1**
2110 **8** ½ **Charlie Delta**[44] 2877 4-9-10 **69**....(b) SteveDrowne 3 53
(J M Bradley) *wl in rr: drvn over 2f out towards outer: no real prog* **9/1**
4-04 **9** shd **Hucking Hill (IRE)**[19] 3649 3-9-5 **68**.... EddieAhern 9 52
(J R Best) *chsd clr ldrs: u.p 1/2-way: no imp: wknd over 1f out* **9/1**
0030 **10** 1 ¾ **Brandywell Boy (IRE)**[12] 3852 4-9-6 **65**.... TQuinn 7 43
(D J S Ffrench Davis) *wl in rr and off the pce: pushed along fnl 2f: nvr on terms* **14/1**
1000 **11** 1 ¼ **Nikki Bea (IRE)**[12] 3851 4-8-10 **55**.... PaulDoe 1 29
(Jamie Poulton) *off the pce towards rr: effrt on outer 1/2-way: no prog over 1f out: wknd* **25/1**
/0-0 **12** 1 ¼ **Sagunt (GER)**[29] 3350 4-9-8 **67**.... AmirQuinn 5 37
(S Curran) *sn lost pl and wl in rr: struggling fr 1/2-way* **33/1**
0000 **13** 2 ½ **Devon Flame**[11] 3869 8-8-4 **56**.... HaddenFrost(7) 11 18
(R J Hodges) *dwlt: a in last quartet: struggling fr 1/2-way* **11/1**

1m 11.76s (-1.91) **Going Correction** -0.275s/f (Firm)
WFA 3 from 4yo+ 4lb **13** Ran SP% **124.4**
Speed ratings (Par 103): **101,100,99,98,98 94,92,91,91,89 87,85,82**
CSF £32.73 CT £413.22 TOTE £5.00: £2.40, £2.50, £5.10; EX 32.20 Place 6 £34.19, Place 5 £8.62..
Owner R Haim **Bred** J Gittins And Capt J H Wilson **Trained** Lambourn, Berks

FOCUS
A modest sprint, but the form is sound.
Musical Script(USA) Official explanation: jockey said gelding was hanging.
Brandywell Boy(IRE) Official explanation: jockey said gelding was never travelling.
Devon Flame Official explanation: jockey said gelding lost a shoe and its action.
T/Plt: £25.90 to a £1 stake. Pool: £98,101.05. 2,757.05 winning tickets. T/Qpdt: £3.30 to a £1 stake. Pool: £6,093.10. 1,339.40 winning tickets. JN

4206 CORK (R-H)
Monday, August 6

OFFICIAL GOING: Soft

4237a PLATINUM STKS (LISTED RACE) — 1m
3:40 (3:40) 3-Y-0+ **£21,993** (£6,452; £3,074; £1,047)

RPR
1 **Jumbajukiba**[6] 4051 4-9-8 101....(b) DJCondon 7 112+
(Mrs John Harrington, Ire) *trckd ldrs in 3rd: 2nd travelling wl fr early st: chal and led under 2f out: rdn and qckly clr: styd on wl: easily* **9/2[2]**
2 4 ½ **She's Our Mark**[22] 3578 3-8-12 105.... DMGrant 8 100
(Patrick J Flynn, Ire) *chsd ldrs: clsr in 3rd over 2f out: sn no imp u.p: wnt 2nd wout troubling wnr ins fnl f* **11/8[1]**
3 2 **Duff (IRE)**[54] 2586 4-9-8 104.... NGMcCullagh 6 99
(Edward Lynam, Ire) *attempted to make all: strly pressed and hdd under 2f out: sn no imp u.p: dropped to 3rd ins fnl f* **8/1**
4 ½ **Navajo Moon (IRE)**[43] 2918 3-8-12 86.... JAHeffernan 10 95
(David Wachman, Ire) *racd mainly in 6th: mod 4th and no imp u.p fr under 2f out: kpt on same pce* **16/1**
5 ½ **Latino Magic (IRE)**[36] 3144 7-9-8 107....(b[1]) PJSmullen 4 97
(D K Weld, Ire) *in rr: 7th and no imp u.p fr 2f out: kpt on same pce* **8/1**
6 4 **Aleagueoftheirown (IRE)**[37] 3116 3-8-12 102.... WJLee 1 86
(David Wachman, Ire) *chsd ldrs: mainly 5th: impr into 4th bef st: no imp u.p and kpt on same pce fr 2f out* **14/1**
7 nk **Dressmaker (USA)**[15] 3772 3-8-12 92.... MJKinane 9 85
(John M Oxx, Ire) *a towards rr: no imp u.p fr over 2f out* **10/1**
8 19 **Quinmaster (USA)**[6] 4051 5-9-11 107....(tp) JMurtagh 2 53
(M Halford, Ire) *trckd ldr in 2nd: rdn bef st: sn lost pl and wknd* **7/1[3]**

1m 40.2s (-4.70)
WFA 3 from 4yo+ 7lb **10** Ran SP% **116.6**
CSF £11.35 TOTE £5.30: £1.60, £1.40, £2.50; DF 17.00.
Owner J P O'Flaherty **Bred** Woodcote Stud Ltd **Trained** Moone, Co Kildare

4238a BOSS CROKER CENTENARY GIVE THANKS STKS (GROUP 3) (F&M) — 1m 4f
4:10 (4:11) 3-Y-0+ **£39,527** (£11,554; £5,472; £1,824)

RPR
1 **Downtown (IRE)**[50] 2702 3-8-10 99.... JAHeffernan 1 101
(David Wachman, Ire) *trckd ldr in 2nd: chal u.p fr 1 1/2f out: styd on wl to ld on line* **8/1**
2 shd **Hasanka (IRE)**[106] 1185 3-8-10 .... MJKinane 3 101
(John M Oxx, Ire) *trckd ldrs: mainly 4th: chal and led over 1 1/2f out: sn strly pressed: hdd on line* **2/1[1]**
3 1 ½ **Nick's Nikita (IRE)**[37] 3119 4-9-10 102.... JMurtagh 6 102+
(M Halford, Ire) *towards rr: niggled along appr st: rdn in mod 5th under 2f out: r.o strly ins fnl f: nt rch 1st 2* **7/2[3]**

4 nk **Uimhir A Haon (IRE)**[22] 3576 3-8-10 100 CO'Donoghue 8 99
(A P O'Brien, Ire) *chsd ldrs: mainly 5th: 4th 1 1/2f out: no imp and kpt on same pce ins fnl f* **3/1**[2]

5 1 1/4 **Dance The Classics (IRE)**[45] 2853 3-8-10 90 (b) NGMcCullagh 7 97
(John M Oxx, Ire) *led: strly pressed and hdd over 1 1/2f out: sn no imp u.p: kpt on same pce* **10/1**

6 13 **Glitter Baby (IRE)**[3] 4142 4-9-7 MCHussey 4 77+
(M G Quinlan) *trckd ldrs in 3rd: 4th over 2f out: sn dropped to 6th and no ex u.p* **12/1**

7 7 **Sina Cova (IRE)**[280] 6267 5-9-7 109 CDHayes 5 67+
(Peter Casey, Ire) *towards rr: 6th over 2f out: sn no ex u.p* **11/1**

8 7 **Impetious**[16] 3744 3-8-10 104 PJSmullen 2 56+
(Eamon Tyrrell, Ire) *towards rr: rdn appr st: bhd fr over 2f out* **20/1**

2m 38.2s (-9.70)
WFA 3 from 4yo+ 11lb **9** Ran SP% **121.5**
CSF £26.10 TOTE £11.60: £2.40, £1.10, £1.60; DF 37.80.
Owner Mrs John Magnier **Bred** Tower Bloodstock **Trained** Goolds Cross, Co Tipperary

FOCUS
The race has been rated through the fourth.

NOTEBOOK
Downtown(IRE) won a Clonmel maiden in May and took a big step forward in a Group 3 over this course and distance in June. She had to deal with much slower ground on this occasion but showed she had made further progress with a gutsy display. This was only her fifth start and she should be open to further progress. (op 7/1)
Hasanka(IRE) looked sure to succeed for much of the final furlong and a half but Downtown, who had previously given the impression that she would stay further, stayed on terms and got back to the front on the line. A promising 1m maiden winner here in September, she was unable to land a blow in the Ballysax Stakes on her seasonal reappearance and was running for the first time since then. This run can be expected to have brought her on and she looks good enough to make her mark at stakes level. (op 2/1 tchd 7/4)
Nick's Nikita(IRE), who was dropping back in trip having finished second in the 1m6f Curragh Cup, has been in good form lately and posted a creditable effort in defeat as she attempted to record her second Group 3 course-and-distance success. She could never get on terms with the front two but was staying on well at the finish. Further stakes race success could well come her way.
Uimhir A Haon(IRE) was looking to build on her sixth in the Irish Oaks last time. She could never quite work her way into a challenging position but was not beaten at all far. She could well prove capable of improving on what she has shown so far. (op 4/1)
Glitter Baby(IRE), who was stakes-placed over 1m3f at Warwick in June, found this a good deal tougher than the conditions event in which she finished third at Galway last week. (op 10/1)

4240a IRISH STALLION FARMS EUROPEAN BREEDERS FUND FILLIES H'CAP 1m 2f
5:10 (5:10) (60-90,90) 3-Y-O+ **£10,996** (£3,226; £1,537; £523)

RPR

1 **Bold Bibi (IRE)**[19] 3654 3-9-1 86 JMurtagh 7 94+
(M Halford, Ire) *trckd ldr in 2nd: led 2 1/2f out: qckly clr: reduced ld fr over 1f out: kpt on wl* **5/2**[1]

2 1 **Chakeera (IRE)**[47] 2783 3-8-4 75 WJSupple 4 80
(Matthieu Palussiere, Ire) *towards rr: prog fr over 4f out: mod 4th under 2f out: rdn to go 2nd and clsd 1 1/2f out: no imp and kpt on same pce ins fnl f* **7/1**

3 1 1/2 **Pretty Demanding (IRE)**[4] 4114 3-8-4 75 MCHussey 10 77
(M G Quinlan) *trckd ldrs: mainly 4th: 3rd over 2f out: no imp u.p and kpt on same pce fr 1 1/2f out* **4/1**[2]

4 1/2 **Miss Maximus (IRE)**[24] 3517 3-8-4 75 NGMcCullagh 6 76+
(C A Murphy, Ire) *mid-div: dropped towards rr fr over 4f out: 7th bef st: kpt on wout threatening u.p fr under 2f out* **7/1**

5 1/2 **Valentina Guest (IRE)**[9] 3984 6-9-5 81 CDHayes 9 81
(Peter Casey, Ire) *trckd ldrs in 3rd: 2nd over 2f out: sn no imp u.p* **6/1**

6 1 **Walk In My Shadow (IRE)**[5] 4087 6-8-4 66 (p) DMGrant 8 64
(Augustine Leahy, Ire) *racd mainly in 6th: no imp u.p fr under 2f out* **11/2**[3]

7 4 1/2 **Flyingit (USA)**[16] 3759 4-8-10 72 PJSmullen 2 62
(Thomas Mullins, Ire) *in rr: no imp u.p st* **16/1**

8 5 **Amonita (GER)**[54] 2587 5-10-0 90 JAHeffernan 1 71
(Annette McMahon, Ire) *led: hdd 2 1/2f out: sn no ex* **16/1**

2m 12.6s (2.60)
WFA 3 from 4yo+ 9lb **10** Ran SP% **115.0**
CSF £20.74 CT £67.63 TOTE £2.20: £1.60, £2.40, £1.30; DF 15.90.
Owner Gerard P Callanan **Bred** Mohammad Al Qatami & Hugo Merr **Trained** the Curragh, Co Kildare

NOTEBOOK
Pretty Demanding(IRE) was having her third start in seven days having been in action twice at Galway. She ran a sound race having held every chance from early in the straight but is some 13lb higher than when last successful. (op 9/2)

4241 - 4245a (Foreign Racing) - See Raceform Interactive

3833
CATTERICK (L-H)
Tuesday, August 7

OFFICIAL GOING: Firm (10.6)
Wind: Light, against Weather: Cloudy with sunny spells

4246 BEST UK RACECOURSES ON TURFTV (S) STKS 1m 7f 177y
2:30 (2:32) (Class 6) 3-5-Y-O **£2,730** (£806; £403) **Stalls** Low

Form RPR

2550 **1** **Mystified (IRE)**[35] 3193 4-9-8 42 (b) PaulHanagan 7 54
(R F Fisher) *stmbld s: sn led: rdn over 3f out: hdd and hmpd ins fnl f: rallied to ld nr fin* **6/1**

4005 **2** *hd* **Mango Masher (IRE)**[14] 3825 3-8-7 60 (p) JamieSpencer 10 54
(C R Egerton) *hld up: hdwy over 3f out: chsd wnr over 1f out: rdn to ld ins fnl f: sn hung lft and hdd: nt run on* **3/1**[1]

0-00 **3** *5* **Emotive**[50] 2714 4-9-8 55 PaulMulrennan 12 48
(F P Murtagh) *hld up: hdwy over 6f out: rdn over 1f out: styd on same pce* **25/1**

-620 **4** *1 1/2* **Attila's Peintre**[15] 3792 3-8-7 62 (b[1]) PhillipMakin 2 46
(P C Haslam) *prom: reminders 1/2-way: styd on same pce fnl 3f* **9/2**[3]

000- **5** *6* **Dimashq**[270] 6423 5-9-3 40 DavidAllan 5 34
(J O'Reilly) *prom: rdn over 3f out: wknd 2f out* **14/1**

0000 **6** *1/2* **Borsch (IRE)**[22] 3584 5-9-8 38 TonyHamilton 1 38
(Miss L A Perratt) *chsd ldrs: rdn and wknd over 2f out* **100/1**

0600 **7** *28* **Silent Street**[45] 2890 4-9-8 40 TomEaves 11 5
(K G Reveley) *chsd ldrs: rdn over 6f out: wknd over 2f out* **8/1**

050- **8** *1 1/4* **Moon Melody (GER)**[86] 2171 4-9-8 58 RoystonFfrench 13 3
(M E Sowersby) *chsd wnr tl rdn over 4f out: wknd over 2f out:* **33/1**

-600 **9** *20* **Cocobean**[13] 3848 3-8-7 37 (tp) AdrianTNicholls 8 —
(M Appleby) *s.s: a in rr* **100/1**

110- **10** *49* **Monash Lad (IRE)**[8] 4393 5-9-8 65 NCallan 14 —
(Mrs K Waldron) *hld up: bhd fnl 6f* **4/1**[2]

64/0 **P** **Jackadandy (USA)**[13] 3840 5-9-5 57 PJMcDonald[(3)] 4 —
(B Storey) *sn pushed along in rr: reminders over 10f out: p.u and dismntd over 8f out* **20/1**

5400 **U** **Gatecrasher**[48] 2770 4-9-8 55 SamHitchcott 3 —
(J W Unett) *stmbld and uns rdr sn after s* **11/1**

0 **P** **The Tokoloshe**[11] 3914 5-9-8 0 GregFairley 9 —
(M A Barnes) *hld up: bhd and rdn over 6f out: t.o whn p.u over 1f out* **150/1**

3m 26.69s (-4.71) **Going Correction** -0.30s/f (Firm)
WFA 3 from 4yo+ 15lb **13** Ran SP% **117.8**
Speed ratings (Par 101): **99,98,96,95,92 92,78,77,67,43 —,—,—**
CSF £22.88 TOTE £7.20: £2.00, £1.60, £6.70; EX 29.80.There was no bid for the winner. Mango Masher was claimed by Philip Sinfield for £6,000.
Owner A D Stoker **Bred** Denis And Mrs Teresa Bergin **Trained** Ulverston, Cumbria
■ Stewards' Enquiry : Phillip Makin three-day ban; weighing in 3lb heavy (Aug 18-20)

FOCUS
A terrible event, won by the 42-rated Mystified who ran to last year's turf form.
Moon Melody(GER) Official explanation: jockey said gelding had no more to give
Cocobean Official explanation: jockey said gelding had no more to give
Monash Lad(IRE) Official explanation: trainer had no explanation for the poor form shown
Jackadandy(USA) Official explanation: vet said gelding was lame right-fore
The Tokoloshe Official explanation: vet said gelding was lame left-fore

4247 GO RACING AT PONTEFRACT TOMORROW MAIDEN STKS 7f
3:00 (3:01) (Class 5) 2-Y-O **£3,238** (£963; £481; £240) **Stalls** Low

Form RPR

0 **1** **Classical World (USA)**[17] 3747 2-9-3 0 TomEaves 7 72+
(Sir Michael Stoute) *led 1f: chsd ldrs: rdn and hung lft over 1f out: led ins fnl f: r.o wl* **9/2**[3]

2 *2 1/2* **Miesko (USA)** 2-9-3 0 GregFairley 3 66+
(M Johnston) *trckd ldrs: plld hrd: led wl over 1f out: sn rdn: hdd and unable qck ins fnl f* **2/1**[1]

3 *1 3/4* **Royal Applord** 2-9-3 0 NCallan 4 61+
(K A Ryan) *hld up: rdn over 2f out: hdwy over 1f out: nrst fin* **10/3**[2]

5 **4** *1/2* **Geezers Colours**[15] 3781 2-9-3 0 PatCosgrave 1 60+
(K R Burke) *stdd s: bhd: rdn and hung lft over 1f out: r.o ins fnl f: nrst fin* **7/1**

060 **5** *3/4* **Straight (IRE)**[13] 3834 2-9-3 57 DaleGibson 9 58
(M Brittain) *chsd ldrs: rdn over 2f out: wknd ins fnl f* **33/1**

6 *2* **Nayarna** 2-8-12 0 RoystonFfrench 6 48
(Mrs A Duffield) *trckd ldrs: rdn over 2f out: wknd over 1f out* **7/1**

6 **7** *1/2* **Moon Spray (USA)**[55] 2562 2-9-3 0 PaulMulrennan 5 52
(K A Ryan) *led 6f out: rdn and hdd wl over 1f out: wknd fnl f* **20/1**

0 **8** *3 1/2* **Kiwi Princess**[56] 2532 2-8-5 0 PatrickDonaghy[(7)] 2 37
(M Brittain) *hld up in tch: rdn 1/2-way: wknd over 2f out* **12/1**

1m 26.31s (-1.05) **Going Correction** -0.30s/f (Firm) **8** Ran SP% **115.0**
Speed ratings (Par 94): **94,91,89,88,87 85,84,80**
CSF £14.02 TOTE £5.60: £1.80, £1.10, £1.50; EX 14.80.
Owner Gainsborough **Bred** Gainsborough Farm Llc **Trained** Newmarket, Suffolk

FOCUS
A modest maiden. The winner improved 12lb from his debut and the next two come from good stables, but the fourth and fifth probably hold down the form.

NOTEBOOK
Classical World(USA), who beat only one home on his debut at Newmarket, comes from a stable whose juveniles often benefit from a run and he showed himself to be a different proposition over this extra furlong. He appeared beaten a furlong out, but got a second wind and was ultimately well on top at the line. He looks likely to stay 1m and remains open to further improvement in nurseries. (op 5-2 tchd 5-1)
Miesko(USA), whose trainer's juveniles have been running better of late, knew his job and was soon in a prominent position. He looked the winner when striking for home, but Classical World proved too strong and he was ultimately well held. There is clearly a maiden in him and he looks likely to come on for the experience. (op 5-2 tchd 15-8)
Royal Applord, a 42,000euros son of Royal Applause, comes from a stable who can ready one to win first time up, but he was not up to the task on this racecourse debut and could only make limited late headway. This was a pleasing debut though and he is another who can find a maiden. (op 11-2)
Geezers Colours, up in trip having shaped reasonably well behind Gothenburg on his debut at Ayr, got going late on to claim fourth and looks more of a nursery type. Official explanation: jockey said, regarding running and riding, his instructions were to take his time with colt as he was keen at home; he added he hung right throughout and failed to come down hill into straight; vet said colt was found to have a nasal discharge (op 10-1 tchd 13-2)
Straight(IRE) continues to find a few too good in maidens and needs a drop in grade. (op 40-1)
Nayarna, a 100,000gns daughter of Nayef, lacked the knowhow to make an impact on this debut and probably needs more time.

4248 BOOK TICKETS ON-LINE AT CATTERICKBRIDGE.CO.UK H'CAP 1m 5f 175y
3:30 (3:30) (Class 4) (0-85,80) 3-Y-O+ **£5,181** (£1,541; £770; £384) **Stalls** Low

Form RPR

3213 **1** **Osolomio (IRE)**[17] 3748 4-10-0 **80** NCallan 1 89+
(G A Swinbank) *mde all: rdn over 1f out: styd on* **4/6**[1]

0332 **2** *1 1/4* **Sporting Gesture**[7] 4040 10-9-1 **67** DaleGibson 2 73
(M W Easterby) *a.p: rdn to chse wnr over 1f out: styd on same pce ins fnl f* **11/2**[3]

0054 **3** *nk* **Mighty Moon**[5] 4105 4-9-9 **75** DavidAllan 3 81
(J O'Reilly) *chsd ldrs: rdn over 3f out: styd on same pce fnl f* **7/1**

6000 **4** *3 1/2* **Frosty Night (IRE)**[10] 3959 3-8-8 **73** GregFairley 5 74
(M Johnston) *chsd wnr tl rdn: hmpd and lost pl wl over 2f out: n.d after* **9/2**[2]

230 **5** *1* **Campli (IRE)**[66] 2253 5-9-3 **69** PaulHanagan 4 68
(Micky Hammond) *dwlt: hld up: hdwy over 3f out: hung lft over 2f out: sn rdn: wkng whn hung lft ins fnl f* **16/1**

2m 59.19s (-5.31) **Going Correction** -0.30s/f (Firm)
WFA 3 from 4yo+ 13lb **5** Ran SP% **111.9**
Speed ratings (Par 105): **103,102,102,100,99**
CSF £4.98 TOTE £1.50: £1.10, £2.10; EX 5.20.
Owner Hokey Cokey Partnership (2) **Bred** Dr T A Ryan **Trained** Melsonby, N Yorks

FOCUS
A fairly competitive heat despite there being only the five runners. The winner keeps improving but was able to dictate here, but the overall form may not prove solid.

Campli(IRE) Official explanation: jockey said gelding stumbled leaving the stalls and hung left in the straight.

4249 TELEPHONE 01748 810165 TO BOOK CORPORATE HOSPITALITY CLAIMING STKS — 1m 3f 214y

4:00 (4:00) (Class 6) 3-Y-O+ — **£2,730** (£806; £403) **Stalls** Low

Form — RPR

3400 **1** **Paparaazi (IRE)**[8] 4031 5-9-6 65 .... DanielTudhope 9 — 64
(I W McInnes) *hld up: hdwy over 4f out: led over 1f out: drvn out* **13/2**[3]

4242 **2** *1/2* **Bridgewater Boys**[20] 3638 6-9-5 63 ....(p) NCallan 4 — 62
(K A Ryan) *stmbld s: sn prom: rdn and ev ch over 1f out: styd on* **5/2**[1]

5014 **3** *2 1/2* **Campbells Lad**[9] 4003 6-9-6 63 .... PatrickMathers(3) 6 — 62
(Mrs G S Rees) *dwlt: hld up: hdwy over 3f out: ev ch over 1f out: sn rdn and fnd nil* **11/2**[2]

00-0 **4** *1 3/4* **Awaken**[30] 3343 6-9-4 55 .... PhillipMakin 8 — 54
(Miss Tracy Waggott) *hld up: hdwy 4f out: rdn over 2f out: styd on same pce appr fnl f* **14/1**

0502 **5** *5* **Mangrove Cay (IRE)**[77] 1934 5-9-9 47 .... TomEaves 3 — 51
(A J Lockwood) *trckd ldrs: rdn over 2f out: wknd over 1f out* **8/1**

000 **6** *nk* **Miss Lovat**[48] 2760 4-8-12 35 .... DavidAllan 12 — 40
(W M Brisbourne) *trckd ldr: racd keenly: rdn over 2f out: sn ev ch: wknd fnl f* **100/1**

5/0- **7** *1 1/2* **Francescas Boy (IRE)**[318] 5082 4-9-4 42 .... AndrewMullen(3) 14 — 46
(P D Niven) *hld up: rdn over 8f out: n.d* **100/1**

0500 **8** *1* **Susiedil (IRE)**[20] 3638 6-9-0 42 ....(v) AdrianTNicholls 1 — 38
(S T Mason) *prom: rdn 8f out: wknd over 2f out* **25/1**

4515 **9** *4* **Atlantic Gamble (IRE)**[5] 4096 7-9-12 65 ....(p) PatCosgrave 13 — 43
(K R Burke) *hld up: plld hrd: hdwy 8f out: rdn and wknd over 1f out* **5/2**[1]

5540 **10** *hd* **Chateau (IRE)**[28] 3405 5-9-2 45 ....(t) RoystonFfrench 7 — 33
(M E Sowersby) *prom: rdn and wknd 4f out* **25/1**

4/10 **11** *nk* **Cadeaux Rouge (IRE)**[20] 3638 6-8-11 46 ....(tp) TonyHamilton 10 — 28
(D W Thompson) *led: rdn over 2f out: wknd and hdd over 1f out* **25/1**

/00- **12** *3* **No Commission (IRE)**[62] 6623 5-9-3 45 .... PaulHanagan 2 — 29
(R F Fisher) *hld up: rdn over 7f out: a bhd* **50/1**

2m 35.92s (-3.08) **Going Correction** -0.30s/f (Firm) — 12 Ran SP% **119.1**
Speed ratings (Par 101): **98,97,96,94,91 91,90,89,86,86 86,84**
CSF £22.13 TOTE £8.90: £2.60, £1.20, £1.60; EX 27.30.
Owner Horses 4 Courses **Bred** A R Nemazee **Trained** Catwick, E Yorks

FOCUS
A modest claimer containing plety of disappointing types. The form is best rated through the third.
Atlantic Gamble(IRE) Official explanation: jockey said gelding was unsuited by the firm ground.

4250 BOOK NOW FOR SATURDAY 22ND SEPTEMBER H'CAP — 7f

4:30 (4:30) (Class 6) (0-65,65) 3-Y-O+ — **£2,730** (£806; £403) **Stalls** Low

Form — RPR

6634 **1** **Borodinsky**[5] 4100 6-8-10 48 .... TomEaves 4 — 57
(R E Barr) *s.i.s: outpcd: hdwy over 1f out: r.o to ld post* **4/1**[2]

5000 **2** *nk* **Maison Dieu**[4] 4141 4-9-4 56 .... NCallan 10 — 64
(E J Alston) *s.i.s: hld up: hdwy over 2f out: rdn to ld ins fnl f: hdd post* **16/1**

3441 **3** *1 3/4* **Cheery Cat (USA)**[6] 4078 3-9-7 65 6ex ....(p) TonyHamilton 6 — 66+
(D W Barker) *disp ld to 1/2-way: chsd ldr: rdn and ev ch ins fnl f: no ex towards fin* **8/1**[3]

6630 **4** *nk* **General Feeling (IRE)**[4] 4137 6-8-11 52 ....(t) DuranFentiman(3) 2 — 55
(S T Mason) *s.i.s: hdwy over 4f out: rdn over 2f out: styd on same pce fnl f* **16/1**

4400 **5** *nk* **Cabourg (IRE)**[27] 3414 4-9-2 54 ....(b) PaulHanagan 8 — 56
(R Bastiman) *prom: rdn over 1f out: styd on same pce* **9/1**

112 **6** *1 1/4* **Bucharest**[20] 3647 4-9-13 65 .... JamieSpencer 5 — 63
(M Wigham) *diputed ld tl def advantage 1/2-way: hrd rdn and hdd ins fnl f: no ex and eased towards fin* **11/8**[1]

2000 **7** *1/2* **Sands Of Barra (IRE)**[7] 4042 4-9-8 60 ....(b[1]) RoystonFfrench 15 — 57
(I W McInnes) *prom: lost pl 5f out: rdn over 2f out: nt trble ldrs* **20/1**

0300 **8** *shd* **Procrastinate (IRE)**[43] 2937 5-8-6 47 .... AndrewMullen(3) 11 — 44
(R F Fisher) *s.s: outpcd: r.o ins fnl f* **40/1**

665 **9** *3 1/2* **Red Barnet**[11] 3917 3-8-11 55 .... PaulMulrennan 14 — 40
(M W Easterby) *sn outpcd* **28/1**

0033 **10** *2 1/2* **Slip Star**[3] 4178 4-9-2 54 .... GregFairley 3 — 35
(T J Etherington) *chsd ldrs 5f* **10/1**

1034 **11** *5* **Cadogen Square**[4] 4141 5-8-8 53 ....(b) DanielleMcCreery(7) 9 — 20
(D W Chapman) *chsd ldrs: wkng whn bmpd 2f out* **16/1**

1m 25.45s (-1.91) **Going Correction** -0.30s/f (Firm)
WFA 3 from 4yo+ 6lb — 11 Ran SP% **120.6**
Speed ratings (Par 101): **98,97,95,95,94 93,92,92,88,86 80**
CSF £66.24 CT £508.58 TOTE £3.50: £1.30, £5.60, £2.60; EX 85.20.
Owner Mrs R E Barr **Bred** R And Mrs Heathcote **Trained** Seamer, N Yorks
■ Stewards' Enquiry : N Callan two-day ban: careless riding (Aug 18-19)

FOCUS
A modest but competitive handicap. Sound form.
Bucharest Official explanation: jockey said gelding hung right throughout.
Sands Of Barra(IRE) Official explanation: jockey said gelding resented the blinkers.

4251 COME RACING AGAIN NEXT FRIDAY NIGHT H'CAP — 5f 212y

5:00 (5:00) (Class 5) (0-75,73) 3-Y-O+ — **£3,238** (£963; £481; £240) **Stalls** Low

Form — RPR

0010 **1** **Choysia**[4] 4137 4-9-8 70 .... TomEaves 11 — 80
(D W Barker) *chsd ldr: rdn to ld ins fnl f: r.o* **12/1**

003 **2** *1* **Choreography**[9] 3998 4-9-1 63 .... AdrianTNicholls 10 — 70
(D Nicholls) *hld up: hdwy over 1f out: r.o* **5/1**[3]

5432 **3** *shd* **Ryedane (IRE)**[13] 3839 5-8-8 59 ....(b) DuranFentiman(3) 1 — 66
(T D Easterby) *hld up: racd keenly: hdwy over 1f out: nt clr run and swtchd lft ins fnl f: r.o* **3/1**[1]

2200 **4** *1/2* **Mulligan's Gold (IRE)**[34] 3203 4-9-1 63 .... DavidAllan 8 — 68
(T D Easterby) *led: rdn over 1f out: hdd and unable qck ins fnl f* **8/1**

1456 **5** *3/4* **Winthorpe (IRE)**[8] 4024 7-9-1 63 ....(v[1]) GrahamGibbons 3 — 66
(J J Quinn) *trckd ldrs: plld hrd: rdn over 1f out: no ex ins fnl f* **16/1**

5020 **6** *1 1/2* **Rainbow Bay**[5] 4095 4-9-11 73 ....(v) NCallan 2 — 71
(P D Evans) *hld up: plld hrd: hdwy over 1f out: sn rdn: nt clr run and no ex ins fnl f* **7/2**[2]

2030 **7** *nk* **High Reach**[16] 3762 7-9-2 71 .... DeanHeslop(7) 9 — 69
(T D Barron) *chsd ldrs: rdn over 1f out: wknd ins fnl f* **12/1**

5411 **8** *3/4* **Charles Parnell (IRE)**[13] 3839 4-9-8 70 .... PhillipMakin 4 — 65+
(M Dods) *hld up: hdwy and nt clr run over 1f out: nvr trbld ldrs* **11/2**

050- **9** *3* **Geordie Dancer (IRE)**[267] 6465 5-8-3 54 oh9 .... PatrickMathers(3) 5 — 40
(A Berry) *a in rr* **100/1**

0-00 **10** *2* **Alugat (IRE)**[50] 2712 4-8-12 60 .... RoystonFfrench 6 — 40
(Mrs A Duffield) *plld hrd and prom: hung rt over 2f out: sn rdn: wknd over 1f out* **20/1**

1m 12.19s (-1.81) **Going Correction** -0.30s/f (Firm) — 10 Ran SP% **117.4**
Speed ratings (Par 103): **100,98,98,97,96 94,94,93,89,86**
CSF £71.52 CT £234.72 TOTE £16.40: £3.90, £2.20, £1.30; EX 55.40.
Owner Mrs J D Trotter **Bred** Mrs John Trotter **Trained** Scorton, N Yorks

FOCUS
A modest handicap. Straightforward form, the winner back to her 3yo best.
Choysia Official explanation: trainer said, regarding the improved form shown, filly was poorly drawn and forced to race wide last time

4252 GORACING.CO.UK H'CAP — 5f

5:30 (5:30) (Class 6) (0-60,60) 3-Y-O+ — **£2,730** (£806; £403) **Stalls** Low

Form — RPR

-005 **1** **Fern House (IRE)**[11] 3921 5-8-13 52 .... PaulHanagan 2 — 60
(Garry Moss) *hld up in tch: rdn over 1f out: r.o to ld post* **20/1**

4034 **2** *hd* **Toy Top (USA)**[5] 4101 4-9-3 56 ....(b) PhillipMakin 9 — 63
(M Dods) *led: rdn over 1f out: hdd post* **7/2**[1]

000 **3** *1 1/4* **Henry Hall (IRE)**[9] 4008 11-9-5 58 .... KimTinkler 8 — 61
(N Tinkler) *prom: chsd ldr 1/2-way: rdn and ev ch ins fnl f: styd on same pce* **14/1**

0056 **4** *1/2* **Blackheath (IRE)**[20] 3636 11-8-13 52 .... SilvestreDeSousa 13 — 53
(D Nicholls) *chsd ldrs: rdn over 1f out: styd on same pce ins fnl f* **11/1**

4004 **5** *2 1/2* **Throw The Dice**[19] 3674 5-8-8 50 .... PatrickMathers(3) 7 — 42
(A Berry) *mid-div: hdwy 1/2-way: no imp fnl f* **5/1**[3]

4206 **6** *1* **Princess Cleo**[43] 2933 4-9-5 58 .... DavidAllan 12 — 46
(T D Easterby) *mid-div: hdwy 1/2-way: sn rdn: styd on same pce appr fnl f* **16/1**

0-06 **7** *nk* **Bond Becks (IRE)**[5] 4101 7-8-13 52 .... JamieSpencer 10 — 39
(G R Oldroyd) *s.i.s: hld up: rdn over 1f out: nvr nrr* **4/1**[2]

3260 **8** *nk* **No Time (IRE)**[11] 3921 7-9-0 60 .... RobbieEgan(7) 4 — 46
(A J McCabe) *mid-div: rdn 1/2-way: n.d* **10/1**

-00 **9** *2 1/2* **That's Blue Chip**[35] 3190 4-9-2 55 .... TomEaves 11 — 32
(P W D'Arcy) *s.i.s: hld up: n.d* **11/1**

001 **10** *1* **Bee Magic**[22] 3597 4-8-12 51 ....(b) SamHitchcott 6 — 24
(C N Kellett) *hld up: rdn 1/2-way: n.d* **25/1**

-066 **11** *nk* **Rudi's Pet (IRE)**[78] 1891 13-8-11 50 .... AdrianTNicholls 1 — 22
(D Nicholls) *chsd ldrs 3f* **12/1**

0000 **12** *1/2* **Melandre**[5] 4101 5-8-4 50 .... PatrickDonaghy(7) 3 — 20
(M Brittain) *chsd ldrs over 3f* **50/1**

0020 **13** *1* **Ballybunion (IRE)**[14] 3829 8-8-11 50 .... PaulMulrennan 15 — 17
(R A Harris) *hld up: rdn and wknd 2f out* **12/1**

050- **14** *shd* **Jadan (IRE)**[395] 3297 6-8-13 52 .... GrahamGibbons 5 — 19
(E J Alston) *chsd ldrs: rdn 1/2-way: sn wknd* **25/1**

59.83 secs (-0.77) **Going Correction** -0.275s/f (Firm)
WFA 3 from 4yo+ 3lb — 14 Ran SP% **127.0**
Speed ratings (Par 101): **95,94,92,91,87 86,85,85,81,79 79,78,76,76**
CSF £90.66 CT £1098.23 TOTE £23.90: £8.80, £1.90, £4.70; EX 160.10 Place 6 £21.27, Place 5 £9.16.
Owner J W Barrett **Bred** Chris McHale & Oghill House Stud **Trained** Bay Horse, Lancs
■ A first winner for trainer Garry Moss.

FOCUS
A moderate sprint and ordinary form. Several of these have slipped to good marks.
Throw The Dice Official explanation: jockey said gelding slipped coming out of the stalls.
That's Blue Chip Official explanation: jockey said gelding was denied a clear run.
Bee Magic Official explanation: jockey said gelding was unsuited by the track.
Rudi's Pet(IRE) Official explanation: jockey said gelding hung right.
T/Plt: £25.20 to a £1 stake. Pool: £69,598.90. 2,008.65 winning tickets. T/Qpdt: £7.00 to a £1 stake. Pool: £4,487.30. 468.70 winning tickets. CR

3901 CHEPSTOW (L-H)

Tuesday, August 7

OFFICIAL GOING: Good to firm (good in places; 8.1)
Wind: Quite strong, against Weather: Dry

4253 BETDIRECT.COM H'CAP — 1m 4f 23y

2:15 (2:16) (Class 6) (0-60,63) 3-Y-O+ — **£2,266** (£674; £337; £168) **Stalls** Low

Form — RPR

3531 **1** **Down The Brick (IRE)**[8] 4019 3-9-3 63 6ex ....(b) FergusSweeney 15 — 73+
(B R Millman) *mid-div: hdwy over 3f out: led over 2f out: styd on wl: comf* **9/4**[1]

6-00 **2** *3* **Sovereign Spirit (IRE)**[197] 215 5-9-10 59 ....(t) AdamKirby 11 — 64
(W R Swinburn) *hld up towards rr: hdwy fr over 5f out: rdn over 2f out: styd on to go 2nd nr fin: no ch w wnr* **10/1**

1240 **3** *hd* **Snake Skin**[15] 3803 4-9-8 60 .... JerryO'Dwyer(3) 9 — 65
(J Gallagher) *in tch: hdwy 4f out: rdn to chse wnr fr 2f out: kpt on but a hld ins fnl f: lost 2nd nr fin* **14/1**

56-2 **4** *hd* **Soviet Sceptre (IRE)**[52] 2656 6-9-5 54 ....(t) DaneO'Neill 17 — 58
(Evan Williams) *mid-div: hdwy 3f out: sn rdn: styd on ins fnl f* **9/2**[2]

0040 **5** *1 1/2* **Orphina (IRE)**[56] 1562 4-8-9 51 ow2 ....(t) KylieManser(7) 4 — 53
(B G Powell) *wnt rt and stdd s: bhd: hdwy 3f out: sn rdn: styd on* **40/1**

4020 **6** *1 1/4* **Rock Haven (IRE)**[11] 3907 5-9-4 56 .... RichardKingscote(3) 14 — 56
(J W Unett) *hld up towards rr: rdn and hdwy over 2f out: kpt on same pce fnl f: b.b.v* **13/2**[3]

0036 **7** *5* **Don Jose (USA)**[8] 4025 4-8-11 53 .... KirstyMilczarek(7) 13 — 45
(N J Vaughan) *led tl over 2f out: grad fdd* **28/1**

0-05 **8** *2 1/2* **Summer Bounty**[15] 3799 11-9-4 53 .... EddieAhern 16 — 41
(F Jordan) *a mid-div* **20/1**

0-02 **9** *nk* **Dreams Jewel**[9] 4003 7-9-2 54 .... NeilChalmers(3) 7 — 41
(C Roberts) *hld up towards rr: rdn over 4f out: sme prog into midfield 3f out: no further imp* **10/1**

00-0 **10** *7* **Jaufrette**[38] 3084 4-9-4 53 .... RichardThomas 12 — 29
(Dr J R J Naylor) *trckd ldrs: rdn over 3f out: sn wknd* **66/1**

06/0 **11** *1 1/4* **Pole Dancer**[67] 2194 4-9-1 50 .... LPKeniry 10 — 24
(W S Kittow) *w ldr: rdn over 3f out: wknd over 2f out* **22/1**

3013 **12** *1 3/4* **General Flumpa**[15] 3805 6-9-3 59 .... LauraReynolds(7) 1 — 30
(Miss Tor Sturgis) *s.i.s: towards rr: sme hdwy u.p over 3f out: sn wknd* **9/1**

0-30 **13** ½ **Harcourt (USA)**[72] [1451] 7-9-3 **55**.................................. MarcHalford(3) 8 26
(M Madgwick) *mid-div tl 3f out* **20/1**

2m 38.16s (-0.56) **Going Correction** -0.15s/f (Firm)
WFA 3 from 4yo+ 11lb **13** Ran SP% **118.4**
Speed ratings (Par 101): **95,93,92,92,91 90,87,85,85,81 80,79,78**
CSF £22.93 CT £263.00 TOTE £3.20: £1.20, £3.60, £5.10; EX 32.20 Trifecta £38.00 Pool: £212.88 - 3.97 winning units..
Owner Brick Racing **Bred** David Barry **Trained** Kentisbeare, Devon

FOCUS
A moderate event run at ordinary gallop early. The form seems sound enough.
Rock Haven(IRE) Official explanation: jockey said gelding bled from the nose.

4254 BETDIRECT.COM GET INVOLVED MEDIAN AUCTION MAIDEN FILLIES' STKS 5f 16y

2:45 (2:51) (Class 5) 2-Y-O **£2,914** (£867; £433; £216) **Stalls** High

Form RPR
12 **1** **Edge Of Gold**[15] [3796] 2-9-0 0.. SteveDrowne 3 73
(B Palling) *mde all: drifted lft 1f out: r.o: pushed out* **4/6**[1]
05 **2** 1 ¼ **Betty Burke**[20] [3648] 2-9-0 0.. EddieAhern 1 68
(H J L Dunlop) *trckd ldrs: rdn over 2f out: wnt 2nd ent fnl f: kpt on but a hld by wnr* **20/1**
320 **3** 1 ½ **Rebel Aclaim (IRE)**[38] [3096] 2-9-0 69.................................. TPO'Shea 6 63
(M G Quinlan) *trckd wnr tl swtchd rt ent fnl f: kpt on same pce* **9/2**[2]
060 **4** 1 ¼ **Don't Tell Anna (IRE)**[19] [3687] 2-9-0 59............................ RyanMoore 4 59
(R Hannon) *in tch: rdn 3f out: swtchd lft 2f out: sn rdn: one pce fnl f* **11/1**
5 ½ **Duty Doctor** 2-9-0 0.. LPKeniry 8 57
(S Kirk) *in tch: rdn 3f out: one pce fnl f* **18/1**
6 1 ¼ **Ava Gee** 2-9-0 0.. AdamKirby 9 52
(B De Haan) *chsd ldrs: rdn wl over 2f out: wknd jst over 1f out* **50/1**
7 1 ¼ **Plaka (FR)** 2-9-0 0.. MartinDwyer 2 48
(J A Osborne) *wnt lft s: hld up: rdn over 2f out: wknd over 1f out* **8/1**[3]
8 20 **Rio L'Oren (IRE)** 2-9-0 0.. SebSanders 7 —
(N J Vaughan) *unsettled stalls: s.i.s: bhd: rdn 3f out: sn wknd* **33/1**

60.60 secs (1.00) **Going Correction** -0.20s/f (Firm) **8** Ran SP% **112.5**
Speed ratings (Par 91): **84,82,79,77,76 74,72,40**
CSF £18.81 TOTE £1.50: £1.02, £4.00, £1.40; EX 16.30 Trifecta £45.10 Pool: £457.98 - 7.20 winning units..
Owner Christopher J Mason **Bred** Christopher J Mason **Trained** Tredodridge, Vale Of Glamorgan

FOCUS
An ordinary maiden dominated by those who had raced. The winner was 7lb off her debut effort, but it is probably a mistake to take this form too literally.

NOTEBOOK
Edge Of Gold, a disqualified winner already, broke her maiden tag with authority but does has a slightly concerning tendency to hang under pressure. She is evidently quite useful and connections should have some fun with her this season at a higher level. (op 5-6 tchd 10-11 in places)
Betty Burke has a bit of size about her and may well be improving with every run. She will be interesting in a low-grade nursery, possibly over further. (op 16-1)
Rebel Aclaim(IRE) has had plenty of chances and helps to set the standard for the race. (op 11-2 tchd 4-1)
Don't Tell Anna(IRE) did not really get home in the final furlong and may well be better suited by further. (op 14-1)
Duty Doctor took a while to get organised but showed just enough to make one think she can find a race in due course. (op 16-1 tchd 20-1)
Ava Gee, a big sort, shaped fairly well on her debut and will definitely be better for the experience.
Plaka(FR) did not look the usual sharp juvenile the stable has run this season and needed the experience. (op 7-1)
Rio L'Oren(IRE) was slowly away and never got into the race as a result. (op 28-1)

4255 BETDIRECTPOKER.COM NURSERY 6f 16y

3:15 (3:18) (Class 5) 2-Y-O **£2,914** (£867; £433; £216) **Stalls** High

Form RPR
6023 **1** **Solent Ridge (IRE)**[13] [3850] 2-8-9 **74**.................................. JohnEgan 9 80
(J S Moore) *chsd leaders: rdn and hdwy 3f out: led over 1f out: r.o wl: rdn out* **15/2**
61 **2** 2 **Maryolini**[22] [3596] 2-8-3 **68**.. MartinDwyer 3 68
(N J Vaughan) *prom: led 2f out: sn rdn and hdd: kpt on but nt pce of wnr* **14/1**
0001 **3** 2 **We Have A Dream**[17] [3734] 2-7-10 **64** oh3 ow1............ LiamJones(3) 12 58
(W R Muir) *prom: rdn over 2f out: kpt on same pce fnl f* **13/2**[3]
2412 **4** shd **Secret Meaning**[19] [3680] 2-7-12 **63**........................(p) AdrianMcCarthy 10 57
(W G M Turner) *chsd ldrs and sn drvn along: styd on fnl f but nvr trbld ldrs* **16/1**
0410 **5** 2 ½ **Ramblin Bob**[25] [3508] 2-8-8 **73** ow2.................................. SebSanders 4 59
(R M Beckett) *led: rdn and hdd 2f out: one pce after* **9/2**[2]
3311 **6** 2 ½ **Brassini**[25] [3486] 2-9-3 **87**.................................. JamesMillman(5) 8 66
(B R Millman) *prom: rdn over 2f out: sn edgd rt and one pce* **7/2**[1]
630 **7** 2 ½ **Night Robe**[11] [3902] 2-7-6 **64** oh3 ow1.................................. KMay(7) 11 35
(P D Evans) *a outpcd towards rr* **33/1**
0450 **8** 1 ½ **Thomas Malory (IRE)**[3] [4154] 2-7-9 **63** oh3...........(b) WilliamBuick(3) 13 30
(Miss V Haigh) *s.i.s: outpcd and bhd: hung lft 3f out: no ch whn sltly hmpd ent fnl f* **25/1**
2151 **9** 19 **Caught In Paradise (IRE)**[21] [3626] 2-8-0 **65** oh1 ow2(b[1]) FrancisNorton 6 —
(A B Haynes) *outpcd and a bhd: t.o* **16/1**
520 **F** **Gasmanfightsback**[49] [2737] 2-9-0 **79**.................................. DaneO'Neill 1 —
(Evan Williams) *prom: rdn over 2f out: 7th and btn whn fell ent fnl f* **16/1**

1m 11.07s (-1.33) **Going Correction** -0.20s/f (Firm) **10** Ran SP% **96.6**
Speed ratings (Par 94): **100,97,94,94,91 87,84,82,57,—**
CSF £71.20 CT £385.33 TOTE £7.40: £2.60, £3.60, £2.80; EX 112.90 Trifecta £194.70 Part won. Pool: £274.28 - 0.30 winning units..
Owner Mrs L Bloxsome,T Wilkinson & J S Moore **Bred** Glending Bloodstock **Trained** Upper Lambourn, Berks
■ Sawpit Sunshine (4/1, unruly in stalls) was withdrawn. Rule 4, deduct 20p in the £.

FOCUS
A fair nursery won by a progressive individual. The form looks sound for the level.

NOTEBOOK
Solent Ridge(IRE), behind Rambling Bob on his debut, has no problem with the drop in trip and the switch to turf, winning cosily when asked to quicken. He seems sure to stay further. (op 17-2)
Maryolini gave the winner a battle for much of the final furlong before being worn down. She is on the upgrade and seems suited by sprint distances for now.
We Have A Dream, running on much faster ground than he won on last time, never really figured off a 9lb higher mark all told and is likely to struggle until coming down the weights. (op 9-1)
Secret Meaning, a winner in selling grade, kept on really well but was never a threat. She looks high in the weights and would appear to need a drop in grade again to be competitive. Official explanation: jockey said filly was unsuited by the good to firm (good in places) ground (tchd 14-1)
Ramblin Bob disappointed once again and he looked a shade keen again in front. Maybe a drop back to 5f is what is required. (op 11-2)
Brassini, trying 6f for the first time, had plenty on giving so much weight away and was below par on this hat-trick bid. (tchd 3-1)
Thomas Malory(IRE) looked a very tricky ride and will be difficult to win with on this evidence. (op 33-1)
Caught In Paradise(IRE) Official explanation: jockey said colt failed to handle the track.

4256 BETDIRECT.COM (S) STKS 1m 14y

3:45 (3:49) (Class 6) 3-Y-O+ **£1,943** (£578; £288; £144) **Stalls** High

Form RPR
0-00 **1** **Croft (IRE)**[10] [3966] 4-9-5 47.......................................(v) TGMcLaughlin 11 54
(M S Saunders) *chsd ldrs: wnt prom 3f out: led 2f out: sn rdn: narrowly hdd ent fnl f: rallied gamely to ld fnl 50yds: drvn out* **40/1**
0005 **2** nk **Goodwood Spirit**[21] [3615] 5-9-5 52.......................................(v) LPKeniry 10 53
(J M Bradley) *bmpd s: sn in tch: rdn to chal over 1f out: tk narrow advantage ent fnl f: hdd fnl 50yds* **5/1**[2]
3 ½ **Check Up (IRE)**[50] 6-9-5 0.. PaulFitzsimons 12 52
(B W Duke) *mid-div: rdn over 2f out: hdwy over 1f out: styd on ins fnl f* **10/1**
0-00 **4** ¾ **Da Bookie (IRE)**[19] [3690] 7-9-5 62.......................... EdwardCreighton 17 50
(E J Creighton) *hld up towards rr: hdwy 3f out: nt clr run briefly wl over 1f: sn rdn: styd on ins fnl f: nrst fin* **12/1**
00-0 **5** hd **What-A-Dancer (IRE)**[53] [2619] 10-9-2 55...................(p) LiamJones(3) 15 50
(R A Harris) *mid-div: stdy prog fr 3f out: rdn to chse ldrs ent fnl f: kpt on same pce* **7/1**[3]
6003 **6** 3 **Homecroft Boy**[13] [3843] 3-8-12 45..........................(b) StephenDonohoe 4 42
(P D Evans) *towards rr: rdn over 2f out: styd on ins fnl f: nvr trbld ldrs* **16/1**
00-3 **7** shd **Travelling Band (IRE)**[18] [3714] 9-9-2 53...............(p) JamieMoriarty(3) 5 42
(J Mackie) *chsd ldrs: rdn over 2f out: wknd fnl f* **4/1**[1]
0005 **8** ½ **Alloro**[10] [3966] 3-8-12 48.. JamesDoyle 7 40
(D J S Ffrench Davis) *prom: rdn over 2f out: wknd over 1f out* **22/1**
0405 **9** 1 **Lizarazu (GER)**[12] [3873] 8-9-5 51...............................(p) AmirQuinn 1 39
(R A Harris) *s.i.s and wnt lft s: towards rr: hdwy 4f out: rdn to chal for 2nd 2f out: wknd ent fnl f* **7/1**[3]
5045 **10** 2 ½ **Saintly Place**[36] [3163] 6-9-10 45.. FrancisNorton 6 38
(A W Carroll) *led: rdn and hdd 2f out: wknd ent fnl f* **11/1**
11 1 ½ **Shanehill (IRE)**[54] 5-9-5 0.. FergusSweeney 8 30
(Evan Williams) *a towards rr* **33/1**
12 nk **Gowna's Hope (IRE)**[63] [6045] 4-9-5 0.................................. DavidKinsella 9 29
(J W Mullins) *s.i.s: a towards rr* **80/1**
003 **13** 3 ½ **Kastan**[35] [3175] 3-8-12 45.. SteveDrowne 3 20
(B Palling) *mid-div tl wknd 2f out* **7/1**[3]
0550 **14** 1 ¼ **Ten Black**[147] [667] 3-8-7 45.. TolleyDean(5) 13 17
(R Brotherton) *mid-div: rdn over 3f out: wknd 2f out* **50/1**
00-0 **15** 8 **Emperor Cat (IRE)**[53] [2619] 6-8-12 45.............................. HaddenFrost(7) 16 —
(Mrs N S Evans) *mid-div: rdn over 2f out: wknd 2f out* **50/1**
60 **16** 57 **Correy**[6] [4071] 3-8-4 0..(b[1]) RichardKingscote(3) 14 —
(B Palling) *a bhd: t.o fnl 3f* **50/1**

1m 34.18s (-1.82) **Going Correction** -0.20s/f (Firm)
WFA 3 from 4yo+ 7lb **16** Ran SP% **122.0**
Speed ratings (Par 101): **101,100,100,99,99 96,96,95,94,92 90,90,86,85,77 20**
CSF £225.73 TOTE £49.20: £9.60, £2.30, £5.20; EX 345.60 TRIFECTA Not won..There was no bid for the winner. Check Up was claimed by R. Flint for £6,000. Da Bookie was claimed by P. A. Blockley for £6,000.
Owner A P Holland **Bred** S Connolly **Trained** Green Ore, Somerset
■ Tom McLaughlin's first winner since a spell out of riding with injury and weight problems.
■ Stewards' Enquiry : T G McLaughlin caution: used whip with excessive frequency

FOCUS
A poor event weakened by the morning withdrawal of the paper favourite. Not form to be with. The time was the slowest, by not a lot, of the three races run at the distance on the day.

4257 BETDIRECT.COM GET INVOLVED FILLIES' H'CAP 1m 14y

4:15 (4:21) (Class 5) (0-75,75) 3-Y-O+ **£3,562** (£1,059; £529; £264) **Stalls** High

Form RPR
5332 **1** **Bidable**[6] [4073] 3-8-3 **60** ow1.................................. RichardKingscote(3) 4 66
(B Palling) *mid-div: hdwy over 2f out: rdn to ld 1f out: sn drifted rt: kpt on: rdn out* **8/1**
60 **2** nk **Celtic Spa (IRE)**[9] [3999] 5-9-6 **67**.............................. StephenDonohoe 11 74
(P D Evans) *mid-div: swtchd rt and rdn 2f out: hdwy sn after: styd on ins fnl f: wnt 2nd nr fin* **16/1**
5500 **3** nk **Fangorn Forest (IRE)**[5] [4112] 4-8-11 **58**.............................. AmirQuinn 5 64
(R A Harris) *wl bhd 5f out: hdwy 3f out: sn rdn: swtchd lft and styd on strly ins fnl f: wnt 3rd cl home: nrst fin* **33/1**
4322 **4** nk **Kashmir Lady (FR)**[15] [3798] 3-9-2 **70**.............................. DaneO'Neill 7 74+
(H Candy) *trckd ldr: rdn to ld wl over 1f out: hdd ent fnl f: no ex: lost 2nd towards fin* **7/2**[1]
2035 **5** 1 ½ **Apply Dapply**[22] [3591] 4-10-0 **75**.................................. SteveDrowne 14 77
(H Morrison) *sn pushed along towards rr: rdn 3f out: no imp tl stayed on fnl f: nvr on terms* **4/1**[2]
302 **6** ½ **Torba (IRE)**[15] [3794] 3-9-0 **71**.................................. TravisBlock(3) 15 71
(Evan Williams) *chsd ldrs: effrt 2f out: one pce fnl f* **12/1**
0-61 **7** 1 ¼ **Dancing Storm**[21] [3615] 4-8-9 **56**.................................. FergusSweeney 6 54
(W S Kittow) *prom: rdn over 2f out: kpt on same pce fnl f* **6/1**[3]
430- **8** ¾ **Palais Polaire**[248] [6674] 5-8-9 **56** oh6...................(p) RichardThomas 8 52
(J A Geake) *wnt rt s: sn chsng ldrs: rdn over 2f out: one pce fnl f* **40/1**
5035 **9** nk **Cat Six (USA)**[4] [4129] 3-8-3 **60**.................................. WilliamBuick(3) 9 54
(T Wall) *s.i.s and carried rt s: sn swtchd lft: bhd: sme late prog: nvr a factor* **15/2**
00-0 **10** 1 ¾ **Maid Of Ale (IRE)**[15] [3798] 3-8-6 **60**.................................. LPKeniry 1 50
(A King) *nvr bttr than mid-div* **33/1**
0-01 **11** 2 **Kims Rose (IRE)**[11] [3904] 4-8-3 **57**.................................. MCGeran(7) 3 44
(R J Price) *led tl 2f out: sn wknd* **14/1**
4-60 **12** 15 **Storm Petrel**[28] [3393] 3-8-8 **62**.................................. SebSanders 10 13
(R M Beckett) *chsd ldrs tl wknd 2f out* **14/1**
0-00 **13** 1 ¾ **Sylvan (IRE)**[15] [3798] 3-9-3 **71**.................................. GeorgeBaker 13 18
(S Kirk) *chsd ldrs tl 3f out* **20/1**
3050 **14** 16 **Divine White**[26] [3451] 4-8-9 **56** oh7.................................. EddieAhern 12 —
(P Bowen) *a towards rr* **50/1**
23-6 **P** **Towy Girl (IRE)**[36] [3154] 3-8-13 **67**.................................. FrancisNorton 2 —
(A W Carroll) *a towards rr: lost tch qckly and p.u 2f out: b.b.v* **12/1**

1m 34.04s (-1.96) **Going Correction** -0.20s/f (Firm)
WFA 3 from 4yo+ 7lb **15** Ran SP% **129.0**
Speed ratings (Par 100): **101,100,100,100,98 98,96,96,95,94 92,77,75,59,—**
CSF £131.42 CT £4127.13 TOTE £9.60: £2.80, £4.90, £8.10; EX 174.10 TRIFECTA Not won..
Owner Flying Eight Partnership **Bred** W D Hodge **Trained** Tredodridge, Vale Of Glamorgan

FOCUS
A modest fillies' handicap and the form does not look that solid, but Bidable deserved this win and is rated up 3lb. The leaders went off a bit quick and the first three all came from off the pace.

Sylvan(IRE) Official explanation: jockey said filly had no more to give.
Towy Girl(IRE) Official explanation: jockey said filly bled from the nose

4258 BETDIRECTPOKER.COM MAIDEN STKS 7f 16y
4:45 (4:52) (Class 5) 3-Y-O+ £2,914 (£867; £433; £216) Stalls High

Form RPR
32 1 **Plucky**[17] 3743 3-8-12 0 RyanMoore 4 78+
(J H M Gosden) *trckd ldr: led over 2f out: r.o wl: pushed out* **4/5**[1]
2 1 1/2 **King Of Dixie (USA)** 3-9-3 0 PaulDoe 8 80
(W J Knight) *mid-div: hdwy 3f out: rdn to chse wnr over 1f out: hung lft ins fnl f: kpt on* **20/1**
023 3 1 1/4 **Own Boss (USA)**[17] 3743 3-9-3 80 PhilipRobinson 11 77
(M A Jarvis) *trckd ldrs: rdn to chse wnr 2f out: kpt on but nt pce of wnr fnl f: lost 2nd nr fin* **9/4**[2]
-6 4 3 1/2 **Schoenberg (USA)**[120] 973 3-9-3 0 SteveDrowne 1 69
(C R Egerton) *mid-div: rdn 3f out: styd on to go 4th ins fnl f: nt pce of ldrs* **12/1**
6-0 5 nk **Timber Treasure (USA)**[17] 3743 3-9-3 0 TPQueally 2 68
(H R A Cecil) *chsd ldrs: rdn over 2f out: 4th and hld whn veered rt 1f out* **10/1**[3]
36 6 3 1/2 **Winning Show**[17] 3743 3-9-0 0 LiamJones(3) 9 60
(R A Harris) *led tl 2f out: sn one pce* **33/1**
06 7 8 **Lithaam (IRE)**[39] 3062 3-8-10 0 BarrySavage(7) 10 42
(J M Bradley) *mid-div tl wknd over 1f out* **20/1**
0 8 5 **Private Soldier**[9] 4000 4-9-9 0 AdamKirby 7 30
(N J Vaughan) *a towards rr* **100/1**
000/ 9 nk **Lady Fas (IRE)**[599] 6591 4-9-4 0 FrancisNorton 6 25
(A W Carroll) *a towards rr* **200/1**
10 1/2 **Shades Of Blue** 4-8-11 0 HaddenFrost(7) 5 23
(C J Down) *s.i.s: a bhd* **200/1**

1m 21.06s (-2.24) **Going Correction** -0.20s/f (Firm)
WFA 3 from 4yo 6lb 10 Ran SP% **113.3**
Speed ratings (Par 103): **104,102,100,96,96 92,83,77,77,76**
CSF £23.44 TOTE £1.80: £1.10, £3.70, £1.20; EX 20.20 Trifecta £28.40 Pool: £1,451.02 - 36.23 winning units..
Owner Cheveley Park Stud **Bred** John Ellis **Trained** Newmarket, Suffolk

FOCUS
The form amongst the principals looks decent for the track, and is pretty sound, but this maiden did lack strength in depth.
Shades Of Blue Official explanation: jockey said filly missed the break.

4259 CHEPSTOW SUNDAY MARKET H'CAP (LADIES RACE) 1m 14y
5:15 (5:19) (Class 5) (0-70,70) 3-Y-O+ £2,935 (£910; £454; £227) Stalls High

Form RPR
3300 1 **Foolish Groom**[21] 3615 6-9-6 53 (p) MissGDGracey-Davison(5) 5 64
(R Hollinshead) *mid-div: smooth hdwy over 2f out: led jst ins fnl f: r.o wl: comf* **8/1**
-004 2 1 3/4 **Libre**[5] 4107 7-9-12 54 MissLEllison 4 61
(F Jordan) *chsd ldr: rdn to ld and hung lft 2f out: hdd jst ins fnl f: no ex* **5/1**[2]
0006 3 1 1/4 **Outer Hebrides**[14] 3828 6-10-4 65 (v) MissSBradley(5) 1 69
(J M Bradley) *led: rdn and hdd 2f out: kpt on same pce* **16/1**
1645 4 nk **The Grey One (IRE)**[10] 3965 4-10-1 64 (p) MissHDavies(7) 13 67
(J M Bradley) *hld up in mid-div: hdwy 2f out: styd on ins fnl f* **8/1**
0005 5 1 3/4 **The Gaikwar (IRE)**[25] 3487 8-10-9 65 (b) MissFayeBramley 2 64
(R A Harris) *mid-div: rdn 4f out: kpt on same pce fnl 2f* **13/2**[3]
0222 6 1 1/4 **Milton's Keen**[11] 3905 4-10-0 56 MissEJJones 11 53
(M Salaman) *chsd ldrs: rdn over 2f out: wknd ent fnl f* **9/2**[1]
004 7 1/2 **Palanoverre (IRE)**[12] 3871 3-9-3 57 (t) MissJFerguson(5) 14 52
(D J S Ffrench Davis) *hld up bhd: styd on fnl f: nvr trbld ldrs* **33/1**
-300 8 1 1/2 **Wind Chime (IRE)**[8] 4031 10-9-13 55 MissCHannaford 6 47
(A G Newcombe) *hld up towards rr: swtchd to standside rails 5f out: effrt 3f out: wknd over 1f out* **9/1**
1063 9 1/2 **Right Option (IRE)**[15] 3795 3-9-4 53 MissSBrotherton 9 44
(J L Flint) *nvr bttr than mid-div* **7/1**
3241 10 nk **Casablanca Minx (IRE)**[8] 4023 4-9-13 55 6ex (v) MissEFolkes 12 45
(P D Evans) *mid-div: effrt 3f out: wknd 2f out* **7/1**
00-4 11 2 **Primeshade Promise**[11] 3904 6-9-5 52 MissAWallace(5) 8 37
(J L Flint) *chsd ldrs: rdn 3f out: wknd 2f out* **25/1**
2000 12 3 1/2 **Raza Cab (IRE)**[45] 2877 5-10-8 64 MrsSMoore 10 41
(Karen George) *chsd ldrs tl 4f out: wkng whn n.m.r over 1f out* **25/1**
0005 13 3 1/2 **Ghaill Force**[55] 2557 5-8-13 46 oh1 (tp) MissZoeLilly(5) 7 15
(P Butler) *v.s.a: a bhd* **100/1**

1m 34.05s (-1.95) **Going Correction** -0.20s/f (Firm)
WFA 3 from 4yo+ 7lb 13 Ran SP% **122.9**
Speed ratings (Par 103): **101,99,98,97,95 94,94,92,92,91 89,86,82**
CSF £47.77 CT £481.49 TOTE £11.50: £3.30, £2.40, £5.90; EX 59.00 TRIFECTA Not won. Place 6 £270.27, Place 5 £132.96.
Owner Dean Wootton **Bred** P J Wightman **Trained** Upper Longdon, Staffs

FOCUS
A moderate amateur riders' handicap but sound form for the grade and an improved effort from the winner.
Casablanca Minx(IRE) Official explanation: jockey said filly had hung left-handed.
T/Jkpt: Not won. T/Plt: £949.40 to a £1 stake. Pool: £85,189.40. 65.50 winning tickets. T/Qpdt: £261.30 to a £1 stake. Pool: £4,555.60. 12.90 winning tickets. TM

4260 - 4264a (Foreign Racing) - See Raceform Interactive

3612 BRIGHTON (L-H)
Wednesday, August 8

OFFICIAL GOING: Firm (9.6)
Wind: Moderate, half behind

4265 TERMINUS AT HAILSHAM EBF MEDIAN AUCTION MAIDEN FILLIES' STKS 6f 209y
2:30 (2:31) (Class 5) 2-Y-O £3,406 (£1,019; £509; £254; £126) Stalls Low

Form RPR
000 1 **Fly Kiss**[49] 2768 2-9-0 50 EddieAhern 6 63
(C E Brittain) *trckd ldrs: led 4f out: rdn over 1f out: hld on wl fnl f* **25/1**
00 2 nk **Smokey Rye**[7] 4061 2-9-0 0 SteveDrowne 4 62
(G L Moore) *a.p: rdn over 2f out: chsd wnr over 1f out: no imp cl home* **5/1**[3]
3 nk **Coral Shores** 2-9-0 0 RyanMoore 2 61+
(P W Chapple-Hyam) *w.w: hdwy over 2f out: hung lft over 1f out: r.o ins fnl f: nvr nrr* **7/2**[2]
030 4 5 **Kintyre Lass (IRE)**[27] 3465 2-9-0 60 StephenCarson 7 48
(B R Millman) *led tl hdd 4f out: rdn over 1f out: wknd ins fnl f* **14/1**
6 5 2 **Maiden Miss (IRE)**[7] 4074 2-9-0 0 DarryllHolland 3 43
(M R Channon) *trckd ldrs early: pushed along fr 1/2-way: hung lft and wknd over 1f out* **13/8**[1]
6 shd **Ten Spot (IRE)** 2-9-0 0 JimCrowley 8 43
(J A Osborne) *slowly away: a in rr* **15/2**
0540 7 1 1/2 **Rubytwosox (IRE)**[21] 3642 2-9-0 64 DaneO'Neill 1 39
(W R Muir) *chsd ldrs tl wknd wl over 1f out* **10/1**
8 21 **Xaarawise** 2-9-0 0 SebSanders 5 —
(M Botti) *s.i.s: racd wd and nvr gng wl: eased fnl f* **14/1**

1m 22.71s (0.01) **Going Correction** -0.15s/f (Firm) 8 Ran SP% **115.0**
Speed ratings (Par 91): **93,92,92,86,84 84,82,58**
CSF £145.40 TOTE £31.20: £6.60, £1.80, £1.50; EX 190.40 TRIFECTA Not won..
Owner Saeed Manana **Bred** L M Cumani **Trained** Newmarket, Suffolk

FOCUS
Very weak maiden form, verging on selling class.

NOTEBOOK
Fly Kiss had shown little on her three previous starts, with 42 being the highest RPR she had achieved prior to this, but she produced an improved effort to get off the mark at the fourth attempt. She clearly appreciated the quick ground, but things are likely to be tougher from now, with her mark of 50 sure to be revised. (op 22-1)
Smokey Rye, like the winner, had shown pretty limited form on her two previous starts and this was a slightly improved performance in defeat. She will have more options now she is qualified for nurseries, but her connections will have to hope the Handicapper does not overreact. She was noted to have swished her tail during the race. (op 7-1)
Coral Shores, a 10,000gns daughter of Carnival Dancer, out of a 7f winner on her juvenile debut, had Ryan Moore booked for her debut, but she proved easy to back. She ran with credit, especially considering she looked green under pressure, but the form looks modest at best. (op 4-1)
Kintyre Lass(IRE) was well held and will probably find her level in moderate handicaps later in her career. (op 10-1)
Maiden Miss(IRE) looked in trouble at about halfway and seemed to become unbalanced when asked to pick up. Both the track and ground may not have been ideal and she can be given another chance to confirm her debut promise. (tchd 11-8 tchd 7-4 in a place)
Ten Spot(IRE), a 45,000euros daughter of Intikhab, first foal of a quite useful 1m juvenile winner, was never seen with a chance after starting slowly and did not look totally at home on the track. (tchd 8-1)

4266 JACK SANDHU PUB CO H'CAP 1m 1f 209y
3:00 (3:03) (Class 5) (0-70,70) 3-Y-O+ £2,839 (£849; £424; £212; £105) Stalls High

Form RPR
0354 1 **Recalcitrant**[9] 4019 4-8-12 54 SebSanders 9 61
(S Dow) *hld up: rdn and hdwy 4f out: led over 2f out: rdn over 1f out all out* **5/1**[2]
160- 2 nk **Cape Diamond (IRE)**[292] 6076 4-9-12 68 EddieAhern 2 74
(W R Swinburn) *trckd ldrs: wnt 2nd wl over 1f out: rdn and ev ch tl no ex nr fin* **12/1**
2-30 3 1/2 **Moon Valley**[13] 3881 4-9-11 67 RyanMoore 4 72
(W J Haggas) *slowly away and hmpd s: in rr tl hdwy over 2f out: r.o wl ins fnl f: nvr nrr* **4/1**[1]
-130 4 3 **Fantasy Crusader**[12] 3907 8-8-10 52 DaneO'Neill 3 51
(R M H Cowell) *swvd rt s: hld up in tch: nt clr run over 1f out: kpt on one pce fnl f* **11/2**[3]
10 5 1 1/2 **Siena Star (IRE)**[20] 3672 9-9-7 68 TolleyDean(5) 8 64+
(Stef Liddiard) *hld up: mde sme late hdwy: nvr nr to chal* **8/1**
4-36 6 nk **Factual Lad**[40] 3048 9-9-4 60 GeorgeBaker 5 56
(B R Millman) *led tl rdn over 1f out: wknd fnl f* **11/2**[3]
3456 7 nk **Katiypour (IRE)**[28] 3420 10-9-7 70 JackMitchell(7) 1 65
(P Mitchell) *t.k.h in rr: effrt on outside 2f out: nvr on terms* **10/1**
6454 8 3/4 **Surdoue**[22] 3616 7-8-9 51 oh6 JimCrowley 6 45
(D Morris) *led tl hdd over 2f out: wknd fnl f* **16/1**
5630 9 3/4 **Picky**[63] 2362 3-8-3 57 WilliamBuick(3) 7 49
(C Tinkler) *trckd ldr to over 3f out: rdn and hld whn short of room over 1f out* **20/1**
1165 10 9 **Drawback (IRE)**[12] 3905 4-9-8 69 (p) LukeMorris(5) 10 43
(R A Harris) *in tch: wnt 2nd 3f out: sn hung lft and wknd over 1f out: sddle slipped* **7/1**

2m 2.95s (0.35) **Going Correction** -0.15s/f (Firm)
WFA 3 from 4yo+ 9lb 10 Ran SP% **118.5**
Speed ratings (Par 103): **92,91,91,88,87 87,87,86,86,78**
CSF £64.45 CT £265.97 TOTE £6.60: £1.90, £4.60, £1.80; EX 109.20 TRIFECTA Not won..
Owner T Staplehurst **Bred** T Staplehurst **Trained** Epsom, Surrey

FOCUS
A moderate handicap run at a pretty ordinary pace. The winner is rated to his mark.
Drawback(IRE) Official explanation: jockey said saddle slipped

4267 STEP CHANGE BARS (S) H'CAP 1m 3f 196y
3:30 (3:34) (Class 6) (0-65,60) 3-Y-O+ £1,943 (£578; £288; £144)

Form RPR
3336 1 **King's Ransom**[27] 3448 4-10-0 60 SebSanders 11 73
(W R Muir) *w.w: smooth hdwy over 2f out: swtchd rt to chal over 1f out: led jst ins fnl f: rdn clr* **11/4**[1]
3146 2 6 **Missie Baileys**[29] 3397 5-9-2 48 (p) IanMongan 15 51
(Mrs L J Mongan) *a.p: ev ch over 2f out: rdn over 1f out: nt pce of wnr fnl f* **7/2**[2]
0-22 3 2 **Princely Ted (IRE)**[22] 3616 6-9-8 54 DaneO'Neill 2 54
(R A Farrant) *trckd ldr: hung lft 5f out: led over 2f out tl hdd jst ins fnl f: wknd* **11/4**[1]
550- 4 3 **Sosueme Now**[284] 6224 3-8-0 50 KMay(7) 3 45
(A B Haynes) *in rr: rdn and hdwy over 2f out: wknd fnl f* **20/1**
0000 5 6 **Yenaled**[13] 3868 10-8-13 45 SteveDrowne 13 31
(J M Bradley) *in tch: effrt over 2f out: one pce after* **12/1**
004 6 5 **Voice Mail**[43] 2963 8-9-3 49 (b) LPKeniry 4 27
(A M Balding) *hld up: rdn 2f out: nvr on terms* **12/1**
0006 7 1 **Bathwick Fancy (IRE)**[21] 3651 3-8-4 47 DavidKinsella 12 23
(J G Portman) *trckd ldr4: led 4f out: hdd over 2f out: wknd over 1f out* **20/1**
000 8 1 **Minstrel Flyer (IRE)**[22] 3616 5-8-13 48 ow3 AlanCreighton(3) 7 22
(E J Creighton) *a towards rr* **40/1**
0-02 9 14 **Littleton Aldor (IRE)**[16] 3795 7-8-11 48 TolleyDean(5) 14 —
(Mark Gillard) *led tl hdd 4f out: rdn and wknd over 2f out* **10/1**[3]
240/ 10 1 **Livia (IRE)**[400] 6541 6-8-13 45 RobertHavlin 8 —
(B J Llewellyn) *hld up in mid-div: wknd 2f out* **20/1**

0/00 **11** *24* **Ren's Magic**[3] 4200 9-9-2 **48**.....................................(t) EdwardCreighton 6 —
(E J Creighton) *a towards rr* **33/1**

2m 30.27s (-1.93) **Going Correction** -0.15s/f (Firm)
WFA 3 from 4yo+ 11lb 11 Ran SP% **119.7**
Speed ratings (Par 101): **100,96,94,92,88 85,84,84,74,74 58**
CSF £11.59 CT £29.09 TOTE £3.70: £1.60, £1.50, £1.60; EX 14.30 Trifecta £23.30 Pool: £406.68 - 12.38 winning units..The winner was sold to S. Gollings for 13,700gns.
Owner Christopher Ransom **Bred** Darley **Trained** Lambourn, Berks
■ Seb Sanders' 100th winner of the season, and he remains locked together with Jamie Spencer at the top of the riders' table.

FOCUS
There was a flag start for this typically weak selling handicap. The top-weighted winner proved in a different league and can be rated value for further, although he did not need to improve on his best form.
Princely Ted(IRE) Official explanation: jockey said gelding hung badly left
Littleton Aldor(IRE) Official explanation: jockey said gelding ran too free and had no more to give
Ren's Magic Official explanation: jockey said gelding lost its action

4268 JOHN SMITH'S BRIGHTON MILE CHALLENGE TROPHY (H'CAP) 7f 214y
4:00 (4:04) (Class 4) (0-80,80) 3-Y-0+
£18,269 (£5,475; £2,740; £1,365; £684; £345) **Stalls** Low

Form RPR
412 **1** **Kasumi**[8] 4049 4-9-4 **77**.. TravisBlock(3) 15 88
(H Morrison) *trckd ldrs: led appr fnl f: r.o gamely* **3/1**[1]

103 **2** *nk* **Tender The Great (IRE)**[23] 3591 4-9-1 **74**.............. RichardKingscote(3) 12 84
(B G Powell) *in tch on outside: hdwy over 1f out to press wnr thrght fnl f* **25/1**

3520 **3** *1 1/2* **Salient**[11] 3940 3-9-3 **80**... PaulDoe 10 86
(J Akehurst) *trckd ldr: ev ch appr fnl f: nt qckn* **14/1**

4400 **4** *3/4* **Councellor (FR)**[51] 2719 5-9-0 **75**.................................(t) TolleyDean(5) 3 80
(Stef Liddiard) *in tch: rdn over 1f out: no ex ins fnl f* **33/1**

2226 **5** *shd* **Blue Java**[11] 3943 6-9-5 **75**..(bt) SteveDrowne 9 80
(H Morrison) *in tch: pushed along over 3f out: kpt on fnl 2f but nt nr to chal* **7/1**

4000 **6** *1 1/4* **Music Note (IRE)**[20] 3682 4-9-7 **77**..................................(t) JohnEgan 6 79
(Miss Gay Kelleway) *led tl rdn and hdd over 1f out: wknd ins fnl f* **20/1**

0143 **7** *1* **Scarlet Flyer (USA)**[31] 3350 4-9-5 **75**.............................(b) RyanMoore 7 75
(G L Moore) *hld up: nt clr run and swtchd lft over 1f out: n.m.r and eased ins fnl f* **6/1**[3]

5-03 **8** *nk* **Don Pietro**[42] 2995 4-9-7 **77**.. EddieAhern 2 76
(D J Coakley) *prom on ins: rdn and ev ch over 1f out: wknd ins fnl f* **14/1**

3244 **9** *shd* **Networker**[7] 4068 4-9-2 **72**... SebSanders 8 71
(P J McBride) *in rr: rdn over 2f out: nvr nr to chal* **5/1**[2]

1035 **10** *nk* **Eager Igor (USA)**[25] 3553 3-9-2 **79**........................(b) StephenCarson 11 76
(Eve Johnson Houghton) *hld up in rr: effrt over 2f out: nvr dan gerous* **16/1**

-003 **11** *hd* **Landucci**[43] 2965 6-8-12 **73**... PatrickHills(5) 4 71
(J W Hills) *in tch: rdn whn hung lft over 1f out: sn btn* **8/1**

3021 **12** *1* **Resplendent Nova**[15] 3828 5-9-6 **76**...................................... AmirQuinn 1 71
(P Howling) *hld up: a bhd* **14/1**

4665 **13** *nk* **Neardown Beauty (IRE)**[7] 4068 4-9-10 **80**.................... JamesDoyle 5 75
(I A Wood) *slowly away: a bhd* **12/1**

1m 32.27s (-2.77) **Going Correction** -0.15s/f (Firm)
WFA 3 from 4yo+ 7lb 13 Ran SP% **124.7**
Speed ratings (Par 105): **107,106,105,104,104 103,102,101,101,101 101,100,99**
CSF £94.52 CT £730.19 TOTE £4.00: £1.50, £8.60, £3.80; EX 140.70 TRIFECTA Not won..
Owner Viscountess Trenchard **Bred** Fonthill Stud **Trained** East Ilsley, Berks

FOCUS
The track's richest race of the season and it produced a competitive line-up. The form looks solid, the winner running to her Goodwood form.
Music Note(IRE) Official explanation: jockey said colt hung right-handed throughout

4269 PULSE BAR SPRINT H'CAP 5f 213y
4:30 (4:30) (Class 4) (0-80,78) 3-Y-0 **£4,731** (£1,416; £708; £354; £176) **Stalls** Low

Form RPR
2340 **1** **Buckie Massa**[5] 4123 3-9-2 **73**... RyanMoore 1 80
(S Kirk) *hld up: rdn over 2f out: hdwy on ins over 1f out: r.o u.str.p to ld ins fnl f* **7/4**[1]

-000 **2** *hd* **Sacre Coeur**[54] 2629 3-9-5 **76**... EddieAhern 2 82
(J L Dunlop) *led: hung rt over 1f out: strly rdn and hdd ins fnl f: kpt on* **14/1**

-606 **3** *2* **Bateleur**[11] 3944 3-9-7 **78**.. EdwardCreighton 4 78
(M R Channon) *bhd: hdwy over 2f olut: chal over 1f out: one pce fnl f* **7/2**[3]

3532 **4** *2* **Dualagi**[34] 3237 3-8-7 **64**.. LPKeniry 6 58
(J S Moore) *plld hrd: trckd ldr tl rdn and wknd appr fnl f: sddle slipped* **8/1**

3-40 **5** *shd* **Fluttering Rose**[20] 3688 3-8-10 **67**..................................... SebSanders 3 61
(R M Beckett) *chsd ldrs: outpcd over 2f out: n.d after* **10/1**

4260 **6** *9* **Inquisitress**[7] 4064 3-7-13 **59**.................................. WilliamBuick(3) 7 26
(J J Bridger) *a bhd* **16/1**

03 **P** **Disco Dan**[41] 3038 3-9-1 **72**.. RobertHavlin 5 —
(D K Ivory) *s.i.s: sn trckd ldrs: lost action over 4f out: sn p.u and dismntd* **3/1**[2]

68.92 secs (-1.18) **Going Correction** -0.15s/f (Firm) 7 Ran SP% **116.3**
Speed ratings (Par 102): **101,100,98,95,95 83,—**
CSF £28.93 TOTE £2.70: £1.50, £6.40; EX 28.90.
Owner M M Matalon **Bred** Exors Of The Late Vernon Matalon **Trained** Upper Lambourn, Berks

FOCUS
Ordinary sprint form for the level, but sound.
Dualagi Official explanation: jockey said filly pulled too hard and saddle slipped

4270 SOUTH EAST LEISURE GROUP H'CAP 7f 214y
5:00 (5:06) (Class 5) (0-70,65) 3-Y-0 **£2,744** (£821; £410; £205; £102) **Stalls** Low

Form RPR
0062 **1** **Caravel (IRE)**[10] 3997 3-9-7 **65**.. SebSanders 7 83+
(Sir Mark Prescott) *trckd ldrs: rdn to ld appr fnl f: sn forged clr* **6/5**[1]

0042 **2** *5* **Awwal Malika (USA)**[12] 3913 3-9-6 **64**.............................. EddieAhern 1 67
(C E Brittain) *a.p on ins: rdn to chse wnr fnl f* **6/1**[2]

5000 **3** *1 1/4* **Royal Guest**[11] 3950 3-8-8 **52**.................................... EdwardCreighton 11 52
(M R Channon) *slowly away: in rr tl rdn and r.o fnl f: nvr nrr* **33/1**

5053 **4** *shd* **Metropolitan Chief**[40] 3057 3-8-9 **58**............................. PatrickHills(5) 4 58
(D M Simcock) *led after 2f: rdn and hdd appr fnl f: one pce after* **14/1**

1243 **5** *hd* **Magroom**[11] 3949 3-8-10 **54**... JimCrowley 5 53
(R J Hodges) *mid-div: rdn over 2f out: kpt on one pce: n.d* **12/1**

0044 **6** *1 1/4* **Rubilini**[11] 3950 3-8-4 **48**.. JohnEgan 2 45
(M R Channon) *chsd ldrs: outpcd over 3f out: hdwy on ins over 1f out: fdd fnl f* **16/1**

0554 **7** *hd* **Fairly Honest**[15] 3824 3-8-12 **59**.................................... MarcHalford(3) 8 55
(P W Hiatt) *led for 2f: chal over 2f out: wknd fnl f* **20/1**

00-5 **8** *3* **Persian Fox (IRE)**[16] 3804 3-9-5 **63**.................................. RobertHavlin 6 52
(G A Huffer) *plld hrd in mid-div: wknd over 2f out* **13/2**[3]

6-55 **9** *hd* **Whaxaar (IRE)**[22] 3620 3-8-13 **57**.. LPKeniry 10 46
(S Kirk) *plld hrd: hld up in mid-div: wknd over 2f out* **16/1**

010 **10** *1 1/2* **Blue Mistral (IRE)**[22] 3615 3-9-5 **63**................................(bt[1]) PaulDoe 3 48
(W J Knight) *slowly away: swtchd rt sn after terms: nvr on terms* **16/1**

0053 **11** *5* **Postsprofit (IRE)**[19] 3705 3-9-4 **65**................................ WilliamBuick(3) 12 39
(N A Callaghan) *s.i.s: plld hrd: hung rt fr over 2f out: nvr on terms* **7/1**

4050 **12** *2* **Kyburg**[36] 3186 3-8-2 **46** oh1.................................(b[1]) FrankieMcDonald 9 15
(P F I Cole) *t.k.h: prom tl wknd wl over 2f out* **66/1**

1m 33.4s (-1.64) **Going Correction** -0.15s/f (Firm) 12 Ran SP% **126.8**
Speed ratings (Par 100): **102,97,95,95,95 94,94,91,90,89 84,82**
CSF £9.08 CT £180.61 TOTE £2.00: £1.30, £2.00, £9.00; EX 7.10 Trifecta £366.20 Pool: £680.64 - 1.32 winning units. Place 6 £39.46, Place 5 £11.89.
Owner Neil Greig - Osborne House **Bred** G A M Grothier **Trained** Newmarket, Suffolk

FOCUS
A modest handicap, but solid form rated through the second and third. There is more to come from Caravel.
T/Jkpt: Not won. T/Plt: £110.10 to a £1 stake. Pool: £70,732.75. 468.70 winning tickets. T/Qpdt: £9.70 to a £1 stake. Pool: £4,830.05. 365.60 winning tickets. JS

4063 KEMPTON (A.W) (R-H)
Wednesday, August 8

OFFICIAL GOING: Standard
Wind: Light, half against Weather: Sunny

4271 WEATHERBYS PRINTING APPRENTICE H'CAP (ROUND 9) 1m 3f (P)
6:20 (6:20) (Class 4) (0-85,80) 4-Y-0+ **£4,728** (£1,406; £702) **Stalls** High

Form RPR
2234 **1** **Nightspot**[9] 4015 6-9-4 **74**.. ThomasO'Brien 2 82
(Eve Johnson Houghton) *mde all: kicked on 4f out: styd on to draw clr fr over 1f out* **5/4**[1]

0545 **2** *4* **Pactolos Way**[12] 3907 4-8-10 **66**... HaddenFrost 1 67
(P R Chamings) *mostly chsd wnr: chal on inner and no room over 2f out: tried again wl over 1f out: sn one pce and btn* **2/1**[2]

1006 **3** *6* **Wild Pitch**[14] 3858 6-9-10 **80**...(b) JackMitchell 4 71
(P Mitchell) *mostly last: effrt 5f out: rdn and nt qckn 3f out: steadily lost tch* **5/2**[3]

2m 23.19s (0.51) **Going Correction** -0.125s/f (Stan) 3 Ran SP% **106.3**
Speed ratings (Par 105): **93,90,85**
CSF £3.85 TOTE £1.90; EX 4.30.
Owner D J Deer **Bred** D J And Mrs Deer **Trained** Blewbury, Oxon

FOCUS
The exposed winner set just a fair pace in this modest apprentice handicap, in which three of the declared runners were absentees.

4272 MICK TURNER 60TH BIRTHDAY H'CAP 1m (P)
6:50 (6:53) (Class 6) (0-65,65) 3-Y-0+ **£2,047** (£604; £302) **Stalls** High

Form RPR
1640 **1** **Im Ova Ere Dad (IRE)**[19] 3711 4-10-0 **65**............................ RyanMoore 3 76
(D E Cantillon) *settled off the pce towards rr: clsd 3f out: plld out and effrt 2f out: rdn and r.o to ld last 100yds: won gng away* **4/1**[2]

6060 **2** *1* **Postmaster**[11] 3965 5-8-8 **52**.....................................(v[1]) JackMitchell(7) 14 61
(R Ingram) *settled in midfield: prog over 3f out: chsd ldr wl over 1f out: clsd to ld ins fnl f: sn hdd and one pce* **11/1**

3131 **3** *2 1/2* **Le Chiffre (IRE)**[7] 4063 5-10-0 **65**...................................(p) GeorgeBaker 6 68
(S Curran) *trckd ldrs: smooth prog to ld over 2f out: rdn and pressed over 1f out: hdd ins fnl f: fin weakly* **6/4**[1]

0030 **4** *2 1/2* **Fateful Attraction**[27] 3455 4-9-13 **64**............................(b) JamesDoyle 12 62
(I A Wood) *cl up on inner: rdn over 2f out: kpt on same pce: no imp on ldrs* **20/1**

1232 **5** *1 3/4* **Golden Spectrum (IRE)**[9] 4023 8-9-6 **64**...................(b) LukeMorris(5) 8 57
(R A Harris) *t.k.h: trckd ldrs: rdn and outpcd 2f out: plugged on* **15/2**[3]

0205 **6** *1 3/4* **High Class Problem (IRE)**[18] 3732 4-9-11 **62**.......................(t) TQuinn 11 51
(P F I Cole) *trckd ldrs: rdn over 2f out: sn outpcd: wknd over 1f out* **14/1**

4053 **7** *nk* **Forced Upon Us**[53] 2668 3-9-1 **59**................................. RichardHughes 2 48
(P J McBride) *a in rr: rdn and struggling over 3f out: plugged on* **8/1**

00P3 **8** *4* **Winds Of Kildare (IRE)**[18] 3732 4-9-0 **51**..................(t) RichardMullen 7 31
(C N Allen) *led to over 2f out: sn wknd* **33/1**

6230 **9** *shd* **Josr's Magic (IRE)**[40] 3056 3-8-9 **60**................................ JCorrigan(7) 1 39
(S W Hall) *mostly chsd ldr to over 2f out: wknd rapidly* **40/1**

0600 **10** *1 1/2* **Capistrano**[6] 4107 4-9-11 **62**...................................... FergusSweeney 13 38
(Mrs P Sly) *s.i.s: sn in midfield: rdn after 3f: struggling and outpcd over 2f out* **25/1**

-540 **11** *nk* **Soul Blazer (USA)**[75] 2004 4-9-11 **65**........................... JerryO'Dwyer(3) 9 40
(Miss Gay Kelleway) *s.i.s: mostly in last pair: rdn and struggling over 3f out: sn bhd* **25/1**

0000 **12** *3/4* **Sofia Royale**[22] 3611 3-9-0 **58**... SteveDrowne 10 31
(B Palling) *s.s: a in last pair: struggling fr 1/2-way* **25/1**

0000 **13** *38* **Not Too Taxing**[7] 4064 3-9-4 **62**.......................................(t) DaneO'Neill 4 —
(G A Ham) *in tch towards rr: wknd rapidly 3f out: t.o* **66/1**

1m 38.95s (-1.85) **Going Correction** -0.125s/f (Stan)
WFA 3 from 4yo+ 7lb 13 Ran SP% **121.0**
Speed ratings (Par 101): **104,103,100,98,96 94,94,90,90,88 88,87,49**
CSF £43.88 CT £98.70 TOTE £6.40: £1.70, £3.50, £1.10; EX 70.60.
Owner Allan Milton **Bred** Golden Vale Stud **Trained** Newmarket, Suffolk
■ Stewards' Enquiry : J Corrigan one-day ban: used whip when out of contention (Aug 19)

FOCUS
A modest handicap, run at a good pace. The form looks solid for the level, although the third was 9lb off his recent course form.

4273 DIGIBET.COM MEDIAN AUCTION MAIDEN STKS 7f (P)
7:20 (7:24) (Class 6) 2-Y-0 **£2,590** (£770; £385; £192) **Stalls** High

Form RPR
1 **Delta Diva (USA)** 2-8-7 0.. TolleyDean(5) 12 70+
(P F I Cole) *w'like: trckd ldrs: effrt whn hmpd over 2f out: prog on inner over 1f out: rdn and styd on wl to ld nr fin* **8/1**[3]

42 **2** hd **Bailey (IRE)**[44] 3949 2-9-3 0 RichardHughes 8 74
(B J Meehan) *w ldr: shkn up to ld jst over 1f out: rdn and kpt on fnl f: hdd nr fin* **4/7**[1]

0 **3** 3/4 **Spic 'n Span**[11] 3962 2-9-3 0 SebSanders 10 72
(C A Cyzer) *lw: trckd ldrs: prog to chal over 1f out: nrly upsides ins fnl f: edgd lft and one pce* **25/1**

42 **4** nk **Freudian Slip**[14] 3835 2-8-12 0 PaulDoe 4 66
(S Curran) *mde most: drvn 2f out: edgd lft and hdd jst over 1f out: one pce* **33/1**

04 **5** 2 **A Dream Come True**[27] 3453 2-8-12 0 RobertHavlin 2 61
(D K Ivory) *trckd ldrs on outer: rdn and cl up 2f out: kpt on same pce* **40/1**

22 **6** 2 **Harbour Blues**[31] 3348 2-9-3 0 RyanMoore 14 61
(C E Brittain) *hld up bhd ldrs: rdn and effrt 2f out: no imp and green over 1f out: wknd fnl f* **7/2**[2]

7 1 1/2 **Havanavich** 2-9-3 0 GeorgeBaker 11 57
(S Kirk) *nvr bttr than midfield: rdn and outpcd fr 2f out: fdd* **25/1**

8 1 1/2 **Duntulm** 2-9-3 0 DaneO'Neill 3 53
(H Candy) *s.s: sn rcvrd to midfield: rdn over 2f out: outpcd and hanging bdly over 1f out: wknd* **18/1**

9 2 1/2 **Graylyn Ruby (FR)** 2-9-3 0 SteveDrowne 13 47
(J Jay) *s.i.s: hld up in rr: effrt on inner over 2f out: nt rch ldrs: wknd over 1f out* **33/1**

0 **10** 1 3/4 **Up The Wycombe**[14] 3849 2-9-3 0 TQuinn 9 42
(S Dow) *s.i.s: a in last trio: struggling 3f out* **100/1**

11 hd **Jolie Fleur** 2-8-12 0 FergusSweeney 7 37
(C Tinkler) *a in rr: struggling wl over 2f out* **80/1**

12 5 **Albany Becky (IRE)** 2-8-9 0 JerryO'Dwyer(3) 6 24
(M G Quinlan) *w'like: racd v wd towards rr: wknd over 2f out* **40/1**

1m 27.56s (0.76) **Going Correction** -0.125s/f (Stan) **12** Ran SP% **122.9**
Speed ratings (Par 92): **90,89,88,88,86 84,82,80,77,75 75,69**
CSF £12.84 TOTE £10.50: £2.80, £1.02, £7.60; EX 19.10.
Owner Christopher Wright **Bred** Stratford Place Stud **Trained** Whatcombe, Oxon

FOCUS
Just a fair maiden and the time was nothing special.

NOTEBOOK
Delta Diva(USA), by Belmont Stakes winner Victory Gallop, out of a winner over 1m4f, was backed in from 16/1 on course and showed a good attitude to make a winning debut. She looked in a bit of trouble when struggling to pick up around two furlongs from the finish, but she gradually got the hang of things and responded well to pressure against the far-side rail, getting up to deny the favourite in the last few strides. The form looks just fair, but she is bred to come into her own over middle-distances as she gets older. (op 16-1)
Bailey(IRE) had shown plenty of ability in a couple of 6f maidens, but he failed to justify a very short price and did not appear to see out this seventh furlong. He still looked a little green when sent to the front soon after the start, flicking his ears, but a lack of stamina looked to be his undoing. (op 8-11 tchd 8-15)
Spic 'n Span improved on the form he showed on his debut on the turf over 6f at Newmarket with a promising effort in third. He hails from a stable that do well with their runners on sand, with 45 of Charlie Cyzer's 55 winners in the last five seasons having come on an artificial surface, and the yard showing a small level-stakes profit on all their runners on either Polytrack or Fibresand over that period. (op 20-1 tchd 28-1)
Freudian Slip, who has changed stables, improved on the form she showed in a couple of runs in turf sellers under a positive ride, but her proximity still suggests the form is limited. (op 25-1)
A Dream Come True again showed ability and she is likely to find her level in handicaps next year. (op 33-1)
Harbour Blues was below the form he had shown when second in a couple of turf maidens and did not look happy on this surface. It's unusual for a horse not to take to Polytrack, but he just never really looked comfortable in the straight and, although he may adapt better as he gets older, he might be better off back on turf for the time being. He will now have the option of running in nurseries. (op 4-1)
Up The Wycombe Official explanation: jockey said colt hung left

4274 DIGIBET CASINO NURSERY 6f (P)
7:50 (7:52) (Class 4) 2-Y-O **£3,886** (£1,156; £577; £288) **Stalls** High

Form RPR
264 **1** **High Days (IRE)**[21] 3648 2-8-8 **71** (t) RyanMoore 4 72
(Sir Michael Stoute) *pressed ldr: rdn over 1f out: drvn ahd nr fin* **11/4**[2]

4655 **2** nk **Replicator**[18] 3734 2-8-3 **69** WilliamBuick(3) 7 69
(Pat Eddery) *t.k.h: led and dictated stdy pce: rdn jst over 1f out: styd on: collared nr fin* **20/1**

5055 **3** hd **Choisky (IRE)**[20] 3680 2-8-4 **67** DavidKinsella 2 67
(J Akehurst) *trckd ldrs: nt qckn 2f out and lost pl: rallied fnl f: gaining on ldng pair fin* **20/1**

2242 **4** 1 1/4 **Far Gone**[7] 4065 2-8-4 **72** LukeMorris(5) 9 68
(M L W Bell) *t.k.h: cl up: rdn and chsng ldng trio fr 2f out: kpt on same pce* **9/4**[1]

51 **5** 1 1/2 **The Game**[14] 3833 2-9-5 **82** LDettori 10 73
(J R Boyle) *t.k.h: cl up: chal on inner 2f out: drvn and nrly upsides 1f out: fdd* **11/2**[3]

2240 **6** 1/2 **Maybe I Wont**[4] 4152 2-8-10 **73** DaneO'Neill 1 63
(S Dow) *dwlt: hld up in rr in steadily run r: effrt over 2f out: outpcd wl over 1f out: no imp after* **8/1**

551 **7** 1 1/4 **Regal Rhythm (IRE)**[84] 1762 2-9-3 **80** SteveDrowne 6 66
(B J Meehan) *plld hrd early: hld up in rr: outpcd over 2f out: n.d after: one pce* **7/1**

610 **8** nk **Little Knickers**[10] 3988 2-9-7 **84** JimCrowley 3 69
(D K Ivory) *awkward s: hld up in rr in steadily run r: outpcd fr 2f out* **12/1**

36 **9** nk **Hold That Call (USA)**[15] 3823 2-8-8 **71** PatDobbs 5 55
(R Hannon) *t.k.h: hld up in rr: outpcd fr 2f out* **20/1**

1m 14.19s (0.49) **Going Correction** -0.125s/f (Stan) **9** Ran SP% **118.4**
Speed ratings (Par 96): **91,90,90,88,86 86,84,83,83**
CSF £59.87 CT £918.07 TOTE £3.90: £1.60, £4.10, £5.30; EX 86.90.
Owner Gainsborough **Bred** Gainsborough Stud Management Ltd **Trained** Newmarket, Suffolk
■ Stewards' Enquiry : Luke Morris one-day ban: used whip above shoulder height (Aug 19)

FOCUS
A fair, competitive nursery, and solid form if nothing special.

NOTEBOOK
High Days(IRE) had not really progressed in three runs in maiden company, but the fitting of a tongue-tie for the first time was clearly a help and she just proved good enough to make a winning nursery debut, keeping on well having taken a bit of a grip early on. The form looks just fair at best but, if her breeding is anything to go by, she is open to more improvement when stepped up in trip, although she would probably have to settle a little better. (op 5-2)
Replicator raced keenly in front, but he still offered plenty under pressure in the straight and was only just worn down. (op 25-1)
Choisky(IRE) hit a bit of a flat spot early in the straight and eventually got going too late, suggesting he might benefit from stronger handling, or possibly the application of headgear to help him concentrate. (op 16-1)

Far Gone was a little keen early on and failed to confirm the promise of her recent course-and-distance second. (op 3-1)
The Game, a recent Catterick maiden winner, was produced with every chance against the far rail, but he found disappointingly little. (op 5-1)

4275 DIGIBET SPORTS BETTING MAIDEN STKS 1m (P)
8:20 (8:23) (Class 5) 3-Y-0+ **£2,817** (£838; £418; £209) **Stalls** High

Form RPR
4 **1** **Amarna (USA)**[13] 3881 3-9-3 0 LDettori 8 81+
(Saeed Bin Suroor) *racd wd early: trckd ldr: shkn up to ld over 1f out and sn in command: pushed out* **7/4**[1]

6 **2** 1/2 **Double Doors**[19] 3710 3-9-3 0 RichardHughes 2 77
(J H M Gosden) *trckd ldrs: shkn up and outpcd over 1f out: r.o to chse wnr ins fnl f: clsd but no real threat* **4/1**[3]

35 **3** 1 1/4 **Andmoreagain (USA)**[15] 3827 3-8-12 0 SebSanders 10 69
(J Noseda) *led: rdn and hdd over 1f out: one pce fnl f* **16/1**

0 **4** 1 3/4 **Nutkin**[19] 3710 3-8-9 0 WilliamBuick(3) 9 65+
(J R Fanshawe) *mounted outside paddock: trckd ldrs: pushed along sn after 1/2-way: outpcd over 2f out: styd on again fr over 1f out* **50/1**

40- **5** 1/2 **Touch Of Style (IRE)**[407] 2960 3-9-3 0 AmirQuinn 12 69
(J R Boyle) *trckd ldrs: shkn up over 2f out: outpcd fr over 1f out* **16/1**

2-6 **6** 1 **Reballo (IRE)**[15] 3827 4-9-10 0 GeorgeBaker 13 68+
(J R Fanshawe) *taken steadily to post: wl plcd bhd ldrs: shuffled along and steadily outpcd fnl 2f: do bttr* **20/1**

7 1/2 **La Lunete** 3-8-12 0 SteveDrowne 14 61
(R Charlton) *unf: lw: wl plcd bhd ldrs: shkn up over 2f out: fdd fr over 1f out* **20/1**

43 **8** 1 1/2 **Axiom**[30] 3382 3-9-3 0 RyanMoore 6 62+
(E A L Dunlop) *hld up wl in rr: nt clr run briefly over 2f out: taken to outer: pushed along and kpt on steadily: nvr nr ldrs* **3/1**[2]

0 **9** 1/2 **Ezdiyaad (IRE)**[18] 3743 3-9-3 0 PatDobbs 3 61
(M P Tregoning) *wl in rr: outpcd fr 3f out: kpt on over 1f out: n.d* **25/1**

06 **10** 1/2 **Magic Show**[9] 4018 3-9-3 0 JohnEgan 1 60
(Jane Chapple-Hyam) *towards rr: effrt but nt on terms w ldng gp wl over 2f out: wknd over 1f out* **66/1**

5 **11** 1 **Elusive Dreams (USA)**[103] 1282 3-9-3 0 RobertHavlin 7 57
(J H M Gosden) *s.s: sn rchd midfield: outpcd over 2f out: grad wknd* **14/1**

5- **12** hd **Rhyming Slang (USA)**[303] 5871 3-9-3 0 TPQueally 5 57
(J Noseda) *hld up wl in rr: taken fr inner to outer over 2f out to over 1f out: reminder ins fnl f: nvr nr ldrs* **14/1**

13 5 **Lady In Blue** 3-8-12 0 EdwardCreighton 4 40
(T D McCarthy) *w'like: dwlt: a wl in rr: outpcd fr 3f out* **100/1**

14 2 1/2 **I'm Agenius** 4-9-5 0 FrankieMcDonald 11 35
(C Roberts) *sn last and nt gng wl: brief effrt to rr of midfield 1/2-way: wknd over 2f out* **100/1**

1m 39.2s (-1.60) **Going Correction** -0.125s/f (Stan)
WFA 3 from 4yo 7lb **14** Ran SP% **125.3**
Speed ratings (Par 103): **103,102,101,99,99 98,97,96,95,95 94,93,88,86**
CSF £8.53 TOTE £2.50: £1.10, £2.20, £5.10; EX 10.90.
Owner Godolphin **Bred** Darley **Trained** Newmarket, Suffolk

FOCUS
An ordinary maiden, run at a solid pace. The first three are all capable of better than the bare form and the race should throw up handicap winners.

4276 TFM NETWORKS LONDON MILE H'CAP (LONDON MILE QUALIFIER) 1m (P)
8:50 (8:53) (Class 4) (0-85,86) 3-Y-0 **£4,728** (£1,406; £702; £351) **Stalls** High

Form RPR
214 **1** **Cape Hawk (IRE)**[25] 3553 3-9-3 **81** RichardHughes 8 89
(R Hannon) *prom on inner: rdn to chal over 1f out: drvn ahd last 100yds: jst hld on* **11/4**[2]

0401 **2** shd **Karoo Blue (IRE)**[7] 4080 3-9-8 **86** 6ex RyanMoore 5 94
(C E Brittain) *hld up in rr: rdn and prog on wd outside fr over 2f out: clsd to chal and upsides last 75yds: jst pipped* **7/1**[3]

-060 **3** 3/4 **Russki (IRE)**[25] 3553 3-8-12 **76** (b) JimCrowley 7 82
(Mrs A J Perrett) *led: drvn and pressed over 1f out: hdd last 100yds: fdd nr fin* **10/1**

-250 **4** 1 **Mafeking (UAE)**[54] 2627 3-8-13 **77** FergusSweeney 12 81
(M R Hoad) *hld up in rr: sme prog on inner 2f out: pushed along and styd on steadily: nvr nrr* **14/1**

-261 **5** nk **Furbeseta**[27] 3455 3-9-0 **78** LDettori 11 81
(L M Cumani) *swtg: hld up in rr: prog on outer 2f out: rdn to chse ldrs 1f out: one pce fnl f and no imp* **5/2**[1]

2310 **6** nk **Transcend**[53] 2671 3-9-2 **80** (b[1]) RobertHavlin 9 82
(J H M Gosden) *trckd ldrs: shkn up 2f out: stl cl enough over 1f out: one pce* **12/1**

313 **7** hd **Vainglory (USA)**[39] 3078 3-9-5 **83** RichardMullen 10 85
(D M Simcock) *t.k.h: hld up in midfield: lost pl and rdn 3f out: effrt again over 1f out: kpt on same pce fnl f* **7/1**[3]

0014 **8** 1 1/4 **Proper (IRE)**[14] 3851 3-8-7 **71** JohnEgan 13 70
(M R Channon) *swtg: hld up and sn towards rr: effrt 2f out: chsd ldrs over 1f out: one pce after: fdd last 100yds* **16/1**

100- **9** nk **Simba Sun (IRE)**[318] 5546 3-9-7 **85** SebSanders 3 83
(R M Beckett) *hld up in last: pushed along and prog to chse ldrs over 1f out and looked threatening: eased briefly ent fnl f: lost pl steadily: bttr for r* **16/1**

1300 **10** 5 **Resplendent Ace (IRE)**[54] 2635 3-8-13 **77** SteveDrowne 2 64
(P Howling) *mostly chsd ldr to over 2f out: wkng whn hmpd over 1f out* **25/1**

3000 **11** 3 **Bed Fellow (IRE)**[25] 3553 3-9-4 **82** (v[1]) TQuinn 1 62
(A P Jarvis) *t.k.h: trckd ldng pair to over 2f out: wkng whn hmpd over 1f out* **25/1**

1m 38.85s (-1.95) **Going Correction** -0.125s/f (Stan) **11** Ran SP% **123.1**
Speed ratings (Par 102): **104,103,103,102,101 101,101,100,99,94 91**
CSF £23.95 CT £172.01 TOTE £3.90: £1.30, £2.50, £4.50; EX 24.00.
Owner Thurloe Thoroughbreds XVII **Bred** John And Leslie Young **Trained** East Everleigh, Wilts

FOCUS
A decent handicap, run at a strong pace. The form is ordinary for the grade, with the field well bunched at the line.

Bed Fellow(IRE) Official explanation: jockey said gelding ran too free

4277 TFM NETWORKS H'CAP 1m 3f (P)
9:20 (9:21) (Class 5) (0-75,73) 3-Y-O **£2,817** (£838; £418; £209) **Stalls** High

Form RPR

0452 **1** **Norman The Great**[9] 4015 3-9-6 **72** JohnEgan 11 78
(Jane Chapple-Hyam) *lw: trckd ldrs: wnt 2nd over 2f out: drvn to ld jst over 1f out: kpt on u.p* **7/2**[1]

044 **2** ½ **Atayeb (USA)**[15] 3827 3-8-13 **65** PatDobbs 7 70
(M P Tregoning) *hld up in midfield: prog over 2f out: drvn and styd on to take 2nd nr fin: nt rch wnr* **11/1**

6260 **3** ½ **Driving Miss Suzie**[28] 3427 3-8-6 **61** (b[1]) WilliamBuick(3) 9 65
(A M Balding) *b: trckd clr ldr: lft in ld 3f out: cajoled along and kpt on reluctantly: hdd jst over 1f out: lost 2nd nr fin* **28/1**

4-24 **4** ½ **Thinking Positive**[35] 3214 3-9-6 **72** RobertHavlin 8 75
(J H M Gosden) *hld up towards rr: prog 4f out: chsd ldrs over 2f out: rdn and kpt on: neve quite able to chal* **9/2**[2]

0300 **5** 1 ¾ **Title Deed (USA)**[102] 1290 3-9-0 **66** JimCrowley 2 66
(A P Jarvis) *trckd ldng pair: lft 2nd 3f out: one pce fnl 2f* **16/1**

5005 **6** 8 **Sir Liam (USA)**[49] 2767 3-9-7 **73** SebSanders 1 60
(P Mitchell) *trckd ldrs: rdn and cl enough over 2f out: sn btn: eased fnl f* **5/1**[3]

0000 **7** 3 **Almahaza (IRE)**[13] 3876 3-7-12 **55** (p) LukeMorris(5) 6 36
(Mrs A J Perrett) *chsd ldrs: drvn and lost pl 4f out: no ch after* **40/1**

6020 **8** 1 **Path To Glory**[7] 4073 3-8-2 **54** DavidKinsella 12 34
(Miss Z C Davison) *led: clr after 3f: hanging lft bnd over 4f out: hung bdly lft bnd 3f out: hdd and lost all ch* **20/1**

0515 **9** 1 ½ **Mandalay Prince**[29] 3400 3-8-8 **60** RichardMullen 3 37
(W J Musson) *a in rr: outpcd fr over 3f out: sn no ch* **15/2**

0026 **10** 4 **Henry The Seventh**[12] 3926 3-9-7 **73** TQuinn 5 43
(J W Hills) *a in last qp: rdn and struggling over 3f out: sn bhd* **11/1**

2450 **11** ½ **Leon Knights**[9] 4015 3-9-7 **73** (b) NickyMackay 4 43
(G A Butler) *hld up: a wl in rr: rdn and struggling over 3f out: sn bhd* **12/1**

1-05 **12** 9 **Mardi**[44] 2945 3-9-6 **72** RyanMoore 10 26
(W J Haggas) *hld up in last trio: wknd 3f out: eased 2f out* **6/1**

2m 20.01s (-2.67) **Going Correction** -0.125s/f (Stan) **12** Ran SP% **124.0**
Speed ratings (Par 100): **104,103,103,102,101 95,93,92,91,88 88,82**
CSF £44.72 CT £964.47 TOTE £4.80: £1.80, £3.50, £4.90; EX 44.80 Place 6 £37.98, Place 5 £17.58.
Owner Ms Jane Chapple-Hyam **Bred** Barton Stud Partnership **Trained** Newmarket, Suffolk

FOCUS
A modest handicap, run at a strong pace. The first four finished in a heap and the form looks sound rated through the fourth. It is doubtful if the winner had to improve.
Path To Glory Official explanation: jockey said colt ran too free and hung badly left
Henry The Seventh Official explanation: jockey said colt was never travelling
Mardi Official explanation: jockey said gelding did not face the kickback
T/Plt: £38.60 to a £1 stake. Pool: £59,542.55. 1,124.05 winning tickets. T/Qpdt: £20.40 to a £1 stake. Pool: £4,126.10. 149.20 winning tickets. JN

3951 NEWCASTLE (L-H)
Wednesday, August 8

OFFICIAL GOING: Good to firm (firm in places; 9.0)
The ground was described as 'very fast but with a good cover of grass so no jar'.
Wind: Light 1/2 behind Weather: Fine and sunny

4278 BARCLAYS BANK NURSERY 7f
2:20 (2:22) (Class 4) 2-Y-O **£4,100** (£1,227; £613; £306; £152) **Stalls** High

Form RPR

0266 **1** **Welcome Return (IRE)**[13] 3884 2-8-7 **63** (b[1]) DavidAllan 8 69
(T D Easterby) *chsd ldrs: drvn and outpcd over 3f out: gd hdwy over 1f out: led 1f out: drvn clr* **20/1**

542 **2** 3 **Madison Heights (IRE)**[35] 3205 2-8-12 **68** PaulMulrennan 6 66
(J Howard Johnson) *w ldr: led over 1f out: sn hdd: hung rt and no ex* **12/1**

642 **3** nk **Dream Express (IRE)**[46] 2889 2-9-2 **72** PhillipMakin 3 69
(M Dods) *w ldrs: hung lft thrght: styd on same pce fnl f* **11/4**[2]

621 **4** nk **Merchant Of Dubai**[23] 3582 2-9-7 **77** NCallan 11 74
(G A Swinbank) *hld up in rr: effrt over 3f out: nt clr run over 1f out and ins fnl f: kpt on* **15/8**[1]

6323 **5** 3 **Transmission (IRE)**[14] 3842 2-9-7 **77** TomEaves 4 66
(B Smart) *sn chsng ldrs: wknd over 1f out* **6/1**[3]

435 **6** 1 ¼ **Casino Night**[27] 3471 2-8-11 **67** GregFairley 2 53
(M Johnston) *swvd lft s: sn chsng ldrs: hung lft over 2f out: lost pl over 1f out* **14/1**

050 **7** ¾ **Marie Camargo**[23] 3582 2-8-0 **56** SilvestreDeSousa 9 40
(R A Fahey) *in rr and drvn along: styd on fnl 2f: nvr nr to chal* **16/1**

000 **8** shd **Aquarian Dancer**[58] 2504 2-7-9 **54** oh7 DominicFox(3) 10 37
(Jedd O'Keeffe) *chsd ldrs: one pce fnl 2f* **100/1**

6001 **9** 1 **Tamara Moon (IRE)**[14] 3838 2-9-2 **72** SamHitchcott 1 53
(M R Channon) *led: swtchd rt after s: hdd & wknd over 1f out* **11/1**

064 **10** 1 ½ **Northgate Lodge (USA)**[110] 1130 2-8-7 **63** DaleGibson 5 40
(M Brittain) *in rr: drvn 3f out: nvr on terms* **66/1**

000 **11** 2 ½ **Tharaya**[48] 2804 2-7-13 **55** PaulQuinn 7 25
(T D Easterby) *in rr: drvn over 3f out: nvr a factor* **33/1**

1m 26.06s (-1.96) **Going Correction** -0.35s/f (Firm) **11** Ran SP% **114.5**
Speed ratings (Par 96): **97,93,93,92,89 88,87,87,85,84 81**
CSF £229.31 CT £883.22 TOTE £22.00: £4.00, £3.40, £1.30; EX 189.30.
Owner Jim McGrath **Bred** J Revs **Trained** Great Habton, N Yorks
■ Stewards' Enquiry : Paul Mulrennan one-day ban: carelss riding (Aug 19)
Sam Hitchcott one-day ban: failed to keep straight from stalls (Aug 19); caution: allowed filly to coast home with no assistance

FOCUS
The form looks fairly sound rated through the runner-up. The winner was back to her best.

NOTEBOOK
Welcome Return(IRE), in first-time blinkers for her handicap debut, seemed to relish the much quicker ground. She had to work hard from off the pace but won going away and a step up to a mile will suit her even better. (tchd 25-1)
Madison Heights(IRE) went much more freely this time but after showing ahead was left for dead by the winner. (op 14-1)
Dream Express(IRE), racing on much quicker ground, tended to hang left throughout. He kept on all the way to the line and will be suited by a step up to a mile. (op 3-1 tchd 10-3 and 5-2)
Merchant Of Dubai, stepping up in trip, was dropped in and met traffic problems. He looked second best on the day but would not want the ground any quicker than he encountered here. (op 11-8)
Transmission(IRE), very warm beforehand, seems to have started life in handicap company from a stiff enough mark. (op 7-1 tchd 11-2)
Casino Night went sideways at the start and proved difficult to keep straight. (op 16-1 tchd 12-1)
Aquarian Dancer Official explanation: jockey said filly lost its action

4279 KPMG MEDIAN AUCTION MAIDEN STKS 6f
2:50 (2:52) (Class 6) 2-Y-O **£2,266** (£674; £337; £168) **Stalls** High

Form RPR

4 **1** **Thompsons Walls (IRE)**[19] 3718 2-9-3 0 LeeEnstone 11 82+
(P C Haslam) *chsd ldr on ins: hung lft and led over 1f out: drvn out* **5/1**[3]

2 2 **Sheekey (IRE)** 2-9-3 0 PatCosgrave 7 76
(G A Swinbank) *sn drvn along: sn chsng ldrs: kpt on wl fnl f* **14/1**

4 **3** nk **Van Bossed (CAN)**[14] 3834 2-9-3 0 AdrianTNicholls 4 75
(D Nicholls) *trckd ldrs: hrd rdn and kpt on same pce fnl f* **11/4**[2]

5 **4** 1 ¼ **Le Toreador**[12] 3915 2-9-3 0 NCallan 3 71
(K A Ryan) *chsd ldrs on outer: kpt on same pce appr fnl f* **13/2**

2 **5** 1 ½ **Kiwi Bay**[19] 3718 2-9-3 0 PhillipMakin 5 67
(M Dods) *t.k.h towards rr: effrt over 2f out: kpt on: nvr trbld ldrs* **2/1**[1]

00 **6** 1 ¼ **Gipsy Prince**[11] 3962 2-8-10 0 MCGeran(7) 2 63
(M G Quinlan) *s.s: styd on fnl 2f: nvr nr ldrs* **14/1**

02 **7** 1 **Fulford**[11] 3977 2-8-10 0 PatrickDonaghy(7) 9 60
(M Brittain) *led: hdd over 1f out: wknd ins fnl f* **25/1**

4060 **8** 5 **Kingstyle (IRE)**[11] 3951 2-9-3 55 DaleGibson 8 45
(M Brittain) *towards rr: wknd over 1f out* **100/1**

550 **9** 1 ¾ **Hildegarde (IRE)**[11] 3951 2-8-12 55 DavidAllan 1 35
(T D Easterby) *sn in rr and drvn along: swtchd rt after s: bhd fnl 2f* **40/1**

54 **10** 2 ½ **Red Delight (IRE)**[20] 3673 2-8-12 0 TonyHamilton 6 27
(R A Fahey) *chsd ldrs: lost pl 2f out* **20/1**

P **Templetuohy Max (IRE)** 2-9-3 0 TomEaves 10 —
(J D Bethell) *p.u after 1f* **33/1**

1m 13.25s (-1.84) **Going Correction** -0.35s/f (Firm) **11** Ran SP% **118.3**
Speed ratings (Par 92): **98,95,94,93,91 89,88,81,79,75** —
CSF £67.28 TOTE £6.40: £2.10, £4.10, £1.70; EX 90.60.
Owner Mr & Mrs Duncan Davidson **Bred** Newlands House Stud **Trained** Middleham Moor, N Yorks

FOCUS
A fair maiden carrying just £2,266 penalty value to the winner. Some likely improvers in the line-up and overall the form looks sound.

NOTEBOOK
Thompsons Walls(IRE), 7lb better off with Kiwi Bay, had the rail to help and in the end ran out a decisive winner. A May foal, he should continue to progress. (op 9-1)
Sheekey(IRE), a tall, rangy March foal, took a while to grasp the nettle. He put in some solid late work and is sure to improve and find a race. (tchd 16-1)
Van Bossed(CAN), encountering much quicker ground, was drawn towards the outer. He improved on his debut effort and can take another step forward. (op 7-2)
Le Toreador, still carrying plenty of condition, looks a slow learner and there should be better to come given a little more time. (op 5-1 tchd 9-2)
Kiwi Bay, a grand type, still looked to be carrying plenty of condition. He was keen in the rear but when asked to improve he looked ill at ease on the very fast ground. He is well worth another chance. Official explanation: jockey said gelding was unsuited by the good to firm (firm in places) ground (op 6-4 tchd 9-4 in a place)
Gipsy Prince, who still looked short of peak fitness, was a springer in the market. He blew his chance at the start but was not beaten that far in the end and appeals as a likely nursery type. Official explanation: jockey said gelding missed the break (op 25-1)
Templetuohy Max(IRE) Official explanation: jockey said colt lost its action

4280 J & G ARCHIBALD BUILDERS MERCHANT H'CAP 2m 19y
3:20 (3:20) (Class 5) (0-70,64) 3-Y-O+ **£3,469** (£1,038; £519; £259; £129) **Stalls** Centre

Form RPR

2663 **1** **Karlani (IRE)**[4] 4179 4-9-12 **62** (b) NCallan 7 71
(G A Swinbank) *in rr: drvn 7f out: hdwy over 3f out: chal 1f out: edgd rt and persuaded to ld nr fin* **7/2**[2]

-014 **2** ½ **Atlantic Coast (IRE)**[13] 3888 3-8-8 **59** (b) GregFairley 4 67
(M Johnston) *trckd ldr: drvn 3f out: led 1f out: hdd and no ex towards fin* **13/2**

1602 **3** 5 **Vice Admiral**[9] 4030 4-9-8 **58** PaulMulrennan 6 60
(M W Easterby) *led: qcknd over 5f out: hdd 1f out: one pce* **11/4**[1]

3-53 **4** 2 **Golden Groom**[20] 3677 4-9-2 **52** PaulEddery 5 52
(C W Fairhurst) *trckd ldrs: t.k.h: effrt 3f out: kpt on same pce* **12/1**

/344 **5** ¾ **Princess Kiotto**[23] 3584 6-10-0 **64** DavidAllan 3 63
(W M Brisbourne) *trckd ldrs: t.k.h: rdn 3f out: one pce* **9/2**[3]

6 **6** 1 ½ **Drumossie (AUS)**[15] 2537 7-9-5 **55** (v) PhillipMakin 2 52
(R C Guest) *hld up in last: drvn 4f out: nvr nr ldrs* **25/1**

603- **7** 2 ½ **Compton Eclaire (IRE)**[7] 5242 7-9-4 **54** (b) DanielTudhope 1 48
(N Wilson) *s.i.s: hld up in mid-div: hrd rdn 3f out: wknd over 1f out* **28/1**

2/00 **8** 10 **Alghaazy (IRE)**[67] 2252 6-8-13 **49** oh4 TonyHamilton 8 31
(Micky Hammond) *mid-div: drvn over 5f out: lost pl 3f out: sn bhd* **66/1**

53-3 **9** 15 **Crathorne (IRE)**[29] 2567 7-9-12 **62** PatCosgrave 9 26
(M Todhunter) *sn trcking ldrs: drvn 5f out: lost pl over 2f out: sn bhd and eased* **9/2**[3]

3m 32.62s (-2.58) **Going Correction** -0.075s/f (Good)
WFA 3 from 4yo+ 15lb **9** Ran SP% **115.1**
Speed ratings (Par 103): **103,102,100,99,98 98,96,91,84**
CSF £25.87 CT £70.55 TOTE £4.60: £2.30, £2.20, £1.30; EX 27.30.
Owner Elliott Brothers **Bred** His Highness The Aga Khan's Studs S C **Trained** Melsonby, N Yorks

FOCUS
A low-grade stayers' handicap run at a steady pace to past halfway. The winner looked a reluctant hero. Ordinary form.
Princess Kiotto Official explanation: jockey said mare ran too free
Crathorne(IRE) Official explanation: trainer had no explanation for the poor form shown

4281 TARMAC H'CAP 7f
3:50 (3:50) (Class 5) (0-75,75) 3-Y-O+ **£4,100** (£1,227; £613; £306; £152) **Stalls** High

Form RPR

1206 **1** **Viva Volta**[26] 3512 4-9-13 **73** (b) DavidAllan 6 84
(T D Easterby) *gifted soft ld: clr over 4f out: drvn out: unchal* **7/2**[2]

4534 **2** 2 ½ **Violent Velocity (IRE)**[4] 4177 4-9-2 **67** JamesMillman(5) 3 71
(J J Quinn) *chsd ldrs on outer: wnt 2nd 2f out: edgd rt: kpt on: no imp* **11/2**

-442 **3** nk **Barkass (UAE)**[11] 3952 3-9-9 **75** TomEaves 5 76
(B Ellison) *hld up in mid-div: effrt over 2f out: styd on wl ins fnl f* **3/1**[1]

3024 **4** ¾ **Sake (IRE)**[16] 3790 5-9-8 **68** KimTinkler 8 69
(N Tinkler) *chsd wnr: drvn 3f out: kpt on same pce* **7/1**

4030 **5** 1 **Neon Blue**[15] 3828 6-9-10 **70** NCallan 4 69
(R M Whitaker) *chsd ldrs: rdn over 2f out: one pce* **4/1**[3]

6040 **6** 1 ¾ **Hit's Only Money (IRE)**[10] 3998 7-8-3 **56** KellyHarrison(7) 7 50
(J S Goldie) *dwlt: hld up in rr: kpt on fnl 2f: nvr a factor* **16/1**

1-44 **7** *1 ½* **Grand Opera (IRE)**[35] 3201 4-9-11 **71**.......................... PaulMulrennan 2 61
(J Howard Johnson) *chsd wnr on outer: drvn 3f out: wknd over 1f out* **10/1**

2043 **8** *1 ¼* **Dispol Isle (IRE)**[16] 3790 5-9-11 **71**.......................... PhillipMakin 1 58
(T D Barron) *dwlt: in rr: sme hdwy over 2f out: nvr on terms* **16/1**

1m 24.91s (-3.11) **Going Correction** -0.35s/f (Firm)
WFA 3 from 4yo+ 6lb **8** Ran SP% **116.0**
Speed ratings (Par 103): **103,100,99,98,97 95,94,92**
CSF £23.45 CT £63.90 TOTE £5.90: £2.00, £2.10, £1.30; EX 24.50.
Owner Mrs Jennifer E Pallister **Bred** T W H And Mrs Dancer **Trained** Great Habton, N Yorks

FOCUS
A most unsatisfactory race in which at first sight the other riders seemed to say after you to David Allan. However the form appears to make sense.

4282 PREMIER TRAFFIC MANAGEMENT RATING RELATED MAIDEN STKS 1m 1f 9y

4:20 (4:20) (Class 5) 3-Y-0+ **£3,469** (£1,038; £519; £259; £129) **Stalls** Centre

Form RPR

2060 **1** **Deadline (UAE)**[11] 3964 3-9-1 **63**.......................... PhillipMakin 4 68
(P T Midgley) *chsd ldr: drvn 3f out: led over 1f out: drew clr* **15/8**[1]

0336 **2** *3 ½* **Ashmal (USA)**[36] 3176 3-8-12 **68**.......................... (b[1]) NCallan 6 58
(J L Dunlop) *trckd ldrs: effrt over 3f out: kpt on to take 2nd ins fnl f: no imp* **9/4**[2]

02-5 **3** *1 ¾* **King Of Rhythm (IRE)**[97] 1440 4-9-9 **70**.......................... DanielTudhope 3 57
(D Carroll) *hld up: hdwy 2f out: styd on to take 3rd nr line* **7/1**

0005 **4** *hd* **Grethel (IRE)**[2] 4220 3-8-5 **42**.......................... AdamCarter(7) 7 54
(A Berry) *led: qcknd over 3f out: hdd over 1f out: one pce* **66/1**

6503 **5** *nk* **Optical Illusion (USA)**[33] 3276 3-9-1 **70**.......................... TomEaves 1 56
(I Semple) *t.k.h in last: kpt on fnl 2f: nvr a threat* **7/2**[3]

0200 **6** *2 ½* **Sir Sandicliffe (IRE)**[26] 3495 3-9-1 **63**.......................... DavidAllan 5 51
(W M Brisbourne) *chsd ldrs: drvn over 3f out: hung lft: fdd fnl f* **10/1**

1m 56.8s (-1.01) **Going Correction** -0.075s/f (Good)
WFA 3 from 4yo 8lb **6** Ran SP% **110.9**
Speed ratings (Par 103): **101,97,96,96,95 93**
CSF £6.20 TOTE £2.30: £1.40, £1.80; EX 6.30.
Owner W B Imison **Bred** Darley **Trained** Westow, N Yorks

FOCUS
A low-grade maiden, which was slowly run. The market told the story and the fourth is rated just 42.

4283 ESH CHARITABLE TRUST APPRENTICE H'CAP 1m 2f 32y

4:50 (4:50) (Class 6) (0-65,62) 3-Y-0 **£2,137** (£635; £317; £158) **Stalls** Centre

Form RPR

3253 **1** **Cheshire Prince**[3] 4197 3-9-4 **61**.......................... DeanHeslop(5) 8 68
(W M Brisbourne) *trckd ldrs: smooth hdwy to ld over 2f out: hld on nr fin* **2/1**[2]

1222 **2** *hd* **Potentiale (IRE)**[15] 3825 3-9-10 **62**.......................... MCGeran 1 69
(J W Hills) *hld up off the pce: stdy hdwy over 2f out: wnt 2nd over 1f out: hung lft ins fnl f: jst hld* **5/4**[1]

0400 **3** *3* **Chip N Pin**[24] 3570 3-8-11 **49**.......................... KellyHarrison 3 50
(T D Easterby) *chsd ldrs: drvn over 3f out: one pce fnl 2f* **13/2**[3]

3000 **4** *3* **Bond Casino**[7] 4078 3-9-1 **53**.......................... SladeO'Hara 5 48
(G R Oldroyd) *hld up in rr: effrt over 2f out: nvr nr to chal* **25/1**

0-00 **5** *2 ½* **Presque Perdre**[22] 3611 3-8-7 **45**.......................... DanielleMcCreery 7 35
(K G Reveley) *led 2f: chsd ldrs: wknd over 1f out* **28/1**

6-06 **6** *12* **Topazleo (IRE)**[30] 3382 3-9-5 **60**.......................... PJBenson(3) 6 26
(J Wade) *s.s: hdwy 6f out: rdn and wknd 2f out: sn bhd* **8/1**

0500 **7** *11* **Hillside Smoki (IRE)**[8] 4036 3-8-2 **45**.......................... (b[1]) AdamCarter(5) 2 —
(A Berry) *s.i.s: sn chsng ldr: led after 2f: sn clr: hdd over 2f out: sn lost pl* **200/1**

2m 11.72s (-0.08) **Going Correction** -0.075s/f (Good) **7** Ran SP% **110.0**
Speed ratings (Par 98): **97,96,94,92,90 80,71**
CSF £4.42 CT £9.80 TOTE £3.40: £1.60, £1.30; EX 5.70 Place 6 £19.29, Place 5 £4.58.
Owner D C Rutter & H Clewlow **Bred** The National Stud **Trained** Great Ness, Shropshire

FOCUS
A steady pace to this low-grade apprentice riders' handicap, the clear leader ignored, and the winner seized the initiative.
T/Plt: £35.70 to a £1 stake. Pool: £59,226.95. 1,210.05 winning tickets. T/Qpdt: £3.50 to a £1 stake. Pool: £3,592.20. 746.00 winning tickets. WG

4002 PONTEFRACT (L-H)

Wednesday, August 8

OFFICIAL GOING: Good to firm (firm in places) changing to firm (good to firm in places) after race 4 (3.40)
Wind: Light, across Weather: Cloudy with sunny spells

4284 BOLLINGER CHAMPAGNE CHALLENGE SERIES H'CAP (FOR GENTLEMAN AMATEUR RIDERS) 1m 2f 6y

2:10 (2:10) (Class 5) (0-75,75) 3-Y-0+ **£4,372** (£1,355; £677; £338) **Stalls** Low

Form RPR

0604 **1** **Snark (IRE)**[12] 3907 4-10-10 **61**.......................... MrSWalker 6 68
(P J Makin) *hld up in tch: chsd ldr over 3f out: rdn to ld over 1f out: edgd lft ins fnl f: styd on* **7/2**[1]

3145 **2** *½* **Bavarica**[39] 3100 5-11-2 **72**.......................... MrRBirkett(5) 4 78
(Miss J Feilden) *trckd ldrs: plld hrd: rdn over 1f out: n.m.r ins fnl f: styd on* **13/2**

-056 **3** *1 ½* **Snowflight**[24] 3570 3-9-9 **60**.......................... MrBMcHugh(5) 7 63+
(R A Fahey) *hld up: hdwy over 1f out: edgd lft: r.o: nt rch ldrs* **10/1**

5414 **4** *½* **Street Warrior (IRE)**[90] 1599 4-11-3 **75**.......................... MrSeanKerr(7) 1 77
(J W Unett) *racd keenly: sn led: rdn and hdd over 1f out: n.m.r ins fnl f: styd on same pce* **6/1**

-300 **5** *¾* **Sol Rojo**[12] 3907 5-10-11 **65**.......................... (v) MrSPearce(3) 8 66
(J Pearce) *s.s: hld up: rdn over 1f out: r.o ins fnl f: nvr nrr* **16/1**

5-33 **6** *nk* **Edas**[20] 3260 5-10-12 **66**.......................... (p) MrMWalford(3) 3 66
(J J Quinn) *chsd ldrs: rdn over 2f out: styd on same pce appr fnl f* **13/2**

3343 **7** *1 ¼* **Desert Hawk**[11] 3956 6-10-0 **56** oh2.......................... MrBenBrisbourne(5) 5 53
(W M Brisbourne) *hld up in tch: dropped to rr over 3f out: n.d after* **11/2**[3]

0010 **8** *2* **Le Corvee (IRE)**[2] 4231 5-11-6 **74**.......................... MrMJJSmith(3) 2 67
(A W Carroll) *plld hrd and prom: rdn and wknd over 1f out* **9/2**[2]

0550 **9** *9* **Royal Sailor (IRE)**[37] 3149 5-9-12 **56** oh11.......................... (p) MrDavidMcMinn(7) 9 31
(J Ryan) *s.s: hld up: hdwy 1/2-way: rdn and wknd over 1f out* **100/1**

2m 15.23s (1.15) **Going Correction** -0.275s/f (Firm)
WFA 3 from 4yo+ 9lb **9** Ran SP% **112.7**
Speed ratings (Par 103): **84,83,82,82,81 81,80,78,71**
CSF £25.72 CT £203.88 TOTE £4.50: £1.30, £2.20, £3.00; EX 22.60.
Owner Keith And Brian Brackpool **Bred** Anthony Rafferty **Trained** Ogbourne Maisey, Wilts

FOCUS
A steadily-run event, and modest handicap form.

4285 PARK HILL MAIDEN STKS (DIV I) 6f

2:40 (2:41) (Class 4) 2-Y-0 **£3,886** (£1,156; £577; £288) **Stalls** Low

Form RPR

640 **1** **American Art (IRE)**[65] 2303 2-9-3 **77**.......................... (t) MichaelHills 6 78
(B W Hills) *chsd ldrs: rdn over 1f out: r.o u.p to ld last strides* **15/8**[1]

04 **2** *nk* **Enactment**[18] 3733 2-9-3 **0**.......................... (t) TedDurcan 7 77
(Sir Michael Stoute) *chsd ldrs: rdn to ld over 1f out: hdd last strides* **3/1**[2]

36 **3** *1 ¾* **Paddy Jack**[7] 4076 2-9-3 **0**.......................... GrahamGibbons 3 72
(J R Weymes) *led: rdn and hdd over 1f out: no ex towards fin* **15/2**

4 *1* **Hammadi (IRE)** 2-9-3 **0**.......................... DO'Donohoe 1 69
(K A Ryan) *s.i.s: hdwy 2f out: sn rdn and ev ch: wknd towards fin* **13/2**

0 **5** *7* **Trip The Light**[19] 3718 2-9-3 **0**.......................... PaulHanagan 5 48
(R A Fahey) *sn pushed along in rr: n.d* **16/1**

00 **6** *hd* **Falcon Speed**[10] 4002 2-8-9 **0**.......................... JamieMoriarty(3) 10 42
(P T Midgley) *chsd ldrs: rdn over 2f out: wknd over 1f out* **50/1**

7 *1 ½* **Southern Mistral** 2-9-3 **0**.......................... TPQueally 8 43
(W J Haggas) *mid-div: rdn 1/2-way: wknd wl over 1f out* **5/1**[3]

0 **8** *½* **Flashy Max**[14] 3833 2-9-0 **0**.......................... AndrewElliott(3) 2 41
(Jedd O'Keeffe) *mid-div: rdn and wknd over 2f out* **66/1**

00 **9** *9* **Wynberg (IRE)**[5] 4132 2-8-10 **0**.......................... BradleyRoper(7) 9 14
(N A Callaghan) *s.i.s: outpcd* **50/1**

1m 16.07s (-1.33) **Going Correction** -0.275s/f (Firm) **9** Ran SP% **112.8**
Speed ratings (Par 96): **97,96,94,92,83 83,81,80,68**
CSF £7.24 TOTE £2.90: £1.20, £1.40, £2.00; EX 5.70.
Owner Matthew Green & T Hyde **Bred** Albert Steigenberger **Trained** Lambourn, Berks

FOCUS
Four pulled clear in what was an ordinary juvenile maiden. The winner confirmed the impression he had made at Newbury and the form seems sound.

NOTEBOOK
American Art(IRE) had shown useful form in two good maidens prior to flopping in soft ground at Leicester last time, but he had been given a break and had a first-time tongue tie applied on this occasion. Again made favourite, he looked a beaten horse with a furlong to run, but really got going in the final half-furlong and got up against the far rail in the final strides. This faster surface is clearly important to the son of Statue Of Liberty and he looks to be crying out for a seventh furlong. (op 13-8 tchd 6-4)
Enactment has not looked one of his stable's better juveniles, failing to improve for the step up to 7f at Lingfield last time, but both his previous runs came in soft ground and, although by Pivotal, perhaps this faster ground helped. Like the winner, he was wearing a first-time tongue tie and there may be more to come from him in nurseries, depending on how the Handicapper treats him. (op 4-1 tchd 5-2)
Paddy Jack has shown a reasonable level of ability on all three starts and looks to be progressing, but he is likely to continue to find himself vulnerable in maidens and may stand more a chance in nurseries. Official explanation: jockey said gelding hung right throughout (op 8-1 tchd 10-1)
Hammadi(IRE), a relatively expensive son of Red Ransom, comes from a stable whose juveniles are hardly flying and he very much shaped as though in need of it. He showed enough to suggest he can win a maiden with normal progression. (op 11-2 tchd 8-1)
Trip The Light stepped up on his initial effort, but does not have the pace to win at this distance, as his breeding also suggests, and he appeals more as a handicap prospect. (op 20-1)
Southern Mistral, a 50,000gns son of Desert Prince, was solid in the market for this debut and a decent showing was clearly anticipated, but he was struggling from past halfway and still looked too inexperienced. Official explanation: jockey said gelding hung right (op 11-2)

4286 PARK HILL MAIDEN STKS (DIV II) 6f

3:10 (3:13) (Class 4) 2-Y-0 **£3,886** (£1,156; £577; £288) **Stalls** Low

Form RPR

2 **1** **Naomh Geileis (USA)**[12] 3895 2-8-12 **0**.......................... J-PGuillambert 1 81
(M Johnston) *mde all: rdn over 1f out: styd on* **8/11**[1]

2 *½* **Sam's Cross (IRE)** 2-9-3 **0**.......................... AdamKirby 2 84+
(W R Swinburn) *s.i.s: hdwy over 4f out: rdn and ev ch ins fnl f: styd on* **11/1**

30 **3** *2 ½* **Honey Monster (IRE)**[15] 3812 2-9-3 **0**.......................... TPQueally 3 77
(Miss V Haigh) *chsd wnr: rdn and ev ch over 1f out: no ex ins fnl f* **50/1**

4 *1 ½* **Rivington Pike (IRE)** 2-9-3 **0**.......................... GrahamGibbons 10 72+
(J J Quinn) *s.i.s: outpcd: r.o ins fnl f: nrst fin* **25/1**

22 **5** *1* **Nickel Silver**[63] 2371 2-9-3 **0**.......................... PhilipRobinson 9 69
(B Smart) *prom: rdn over 1f out: wknd ins fnl f* **4/1**[2]

6 *1 ¼* **Brandane (IRE)** 2-9-3 **0**.......................... RoystonFfrench 8 65
(Mrs A Duffield) *prom: rdn over 2f out: wknd over 1f out* **25/1**

7 *4* **Veronicas Way** 2-8-9 **0**.......................... AndrewElliott(3) 4 48
(G M Moore) *s.i.s: outpcd* **66/1**

2 **8** *10* **Effingham (IRE)**[13] 3878 2-9-3 **0**.......................... MichaelHills 5 23
(B W Hills) *s.i.s: sn pushed along in rr: rdn over 3f out: sn lost tch: eased ins fnl f* **9/2**[3]

9 *3 ½* **Marakai** 2-9-0 **0**.......................... PJMcDonald(3) 6 13
(C Grant) *chsd ldrs over 3f* **100/1**

0 **10** *8* **Sophies Secret**[19] 3706 2-8-7 **0**.......................... RussellKennemore(5) 7 —
(J R Holt) *s.s: outpcd* **200/1**

1m 16.37s (-1.03) **Going Correction** -0.275s/f (Firm) **10** Ran SP% **117.1**
Speed ratings (Par 96): **95,94,91,89,87 86,80,67,62,52**
CSF £10.07 TOTE £1.80: £1.10, £2.80, £6.00; EX 11.50.
Owner Mrs Christine E Budden **Bred** Farfellow Farms Ltd **Trained** Middleham Moor, N Yorks

FOCUS
The stronger of the two divisions. The winner was below her Ascot form in victory but is capable of better.

NOTEBOOK
Naomh Geileis(USA), who went close to making a winning debut at Ascot, was quickly into her stride and was always going to take some stopping from the front. She momentarily looked vulnerable when Sam's Cross drew alongside a furlong out, but found more in a fashion typical of her trainer's horses and was always doing enough. She is evidently useful, but whether or not she will prove up to her Group entries remains to be seen. (op 1-2)
Sam's Cross(IRE), a 95,000euros purchase, comes from a yard who can ready their juveniles first time up and he managed to overcome a sluggish start to hold a good position. Switched to challenge a furlong out, his lack of experience cost him as he looked unsure of what was required when asked for everything, but this was a most pleasing debut and winning an ordinary maiden should prove well within his capabilities. (op 12-1)

Honey Monster(IRE) found the drop to 5f all against him when only ninth at Musselburgh last time, but he had previously shaped well when third on his debut at Lingfield and this was a much better effort back up in trip. He is now qualified for nurseries. (tchd 66-1)

Rivington Pike(IRE), a 40,000euros son of Catcher In The Rye, has already been gelded, but having been slowly into stride he made some good progress through the field and was going on strongly close home. Natural progression should see him winning a small maiden before going handicapping. (op 33-1)

Nickel Silver had finished second on each of his two previous starts and a repeat of those efforts looked certain to see him go well again, but having been up there early on he started to look in trouble and dropped away disappointingly in the final furlong. This was not his true running, but he is at least qualified for handicaps now. (op 7-1)

Effingham(IRE), a promising second over an inadequate 5f on his debut at Sandown, looked to be one of the key players here, but he never recovered from a slow start and ran very flat. He is clearly better than this. (op 5-1)

4287 RBS INVOICE FINANCE H'CAP — 1m 4y

3:40 (3:40) (Class 5) (0-75,72) 3-Y-0 — **£4,533** (£1,348; £674; £336) **Stalls** Low

Form	Pos	Dist	Horse / Details	Jockey	RPR
050	1		**Monkey Glas (IRE)**[20] 3689 3-9-5 **70** (K R Burke) *trckd ldr: rdn to ld over 1f out: styd on* **7/2**[1]	J-PGuillambert 8	76
600	2	¾	**Tri Chara (IRE)**[20] 3685 3-8-9 **60** (R Hollinshead) *trckd ldrs: racd keenly: rdn over 1f out: styd on* **20/1**	GrahamGibbons 4	64
-600	3	2	**Cat De Mille (USA)**[46] 2881 3-9-7 **72** (P W Chapple-Hyam) *s.i.s: hld up: hdwy over 1f out: r.o: nt rch ldrs* **9/2**[2]	MichaelHills 6	72+
1	4	2	**Selkirk Sky**[12] 3917 3-8-9 **60** (R A Fahey) *s.s: plld hrd and sn prom: hung rt over 6f out: rdn over 2f out: no ex ins fnl f* **11/2**[3]	PaulHanagan 7	55
5010	5	2	**Dee Jay Wells**[15] 3816 3-8-9 **63** (B Ellison) *led: rdn and hdd over 1f out: wknd ins fnl f* **15/2**	(t) PJMcDonald(3) 2	53
0004	6	½	**Mix N Match**[48] 2796 3-8-0 **54** (R M Stronge) *hld up: rdn over 2f out: nvr nrr* **16/1**	DuranFentiman(3) 10	43
4631	7	hd	**Chasing Memories (IRE)**[16] 3789 3-8-10 **61** (B Smart) *chsd ldrs: carried wd over 6f out: rdn over 2f out: wknd over 1f out* **8/1**	RoystonFfrench 11	50
4011	8	1	**Tina's Ridge (IRE)**[7] 4073 3-8-4 **60** 6ex (R Hollinshead) *hld up: n.d* **9/2**[2]	(p) RussellKennemore(5) 12	47
6014	9	1	**Distant Pleasure**[24] 3570 3-9-1 **66** (M Dods) *mid-div: rdn over 3f out: wknd over 1f out* **14/1**	PaulFessey 9	50
046	10	13	**Corkscrew Hill (IRE)**[22] 3629 3-8-1 **55** (N A Callaghan) *mid-div: rdn over 3f out: wknd over 2f out* **16/1**	AndrewElliott(3) 1	9

1m 43.5s (-2.20) **Going Correction** -0.275s/f (Firm) — **10** Ran SP% **120.0**

Speed ratings (Par 100): **100,99,97,95,93 92,92,91,90,77**

CSF £79.05 CT £327.92 TOTE £5.10: £2.40, £5.70, £2.60; EX 82.00.

Owner Denis Fehan **Bred** D Bourke And Yuriy Meduedyev **Trained** Middleham Moor, N Yorks

FOCUS

The ground was changed to firm, good to firm in places after this race. An ordinary handicap in which four of the first five were always prominent, but sound-looking form.

Monkey Glas(IRE) Official explanation: trainer said, regarding the improved form shown, yard had been under a cloud prior to colt's last run and pulled hard last time, but it settled better today on better ground

Corkscrew Hill(IRE) Official explanation: trainer said filly was unsuited by the good to firm (firm patches) ground

4288 SUBSCRIBE ONLINE @ RACINGUK.TV H'CAP — 1m 4f 8y

4:10 (4:10) (Class 3) (0-90,90) 3-Y-0+ — **£9,348** (£2,799; £1,399; £700; £349; £175) **Stalls** Low

Form	Pos	Dist	Horse / Details	Jockey	RPR
-043	1		**Ajaan**[12] 3919 3-8-7 80 (H R A Cecil) *s.i.s: hld up: hdwy to ld 2f out: drvn out* **5/1**[3]	(b) TedDurcan 9	91
31-0	2	nk	**Bauer (IRE)**[82] 1822 4-9-13 89 (L M Cumani) *hld up in tch: nt clr run and lost pl over 2f out: hdwy over 1f out: r.o* **9/4**[1]	NickyMackay 5	104+
163	3	1½	**Aajel (USA)**[75] 1987 3-9-0 87 (M P Tregoning) *hld up: hdwy over 3f out: led over 2f out: sn hdd: rdn and edgd lft over 1f out: styd on same pce* **6/1**	RHills 10	96
161	4	4	**Bogside Theatre (IRE)**[26] 3501 3-8-11 87 (G M Moore) *trckd ldrs: rdn and ev ch over 2f out: wknd ins fnl f* **14/1**	AndrewElliott(3) 8	89
0102	5	5	**Luna Landing**[3] 4194 4-9-5 81 (Jedd O'Keeffe) *chsd ldr tl led over 3f out: rdn and hdd over 2f out: wknd over 1f out* **7/2**[2]	PhilipRobinson 4	75
-000	6	½	**Missoula (IRE)**[42] 2987 4-8-10 72 (M H Tompkins) *s.i.s: hld up: rdn over 2f out: n.d* **20/1**	MichaelHills 7	65
1650	7	2	**La Estrella (USA)**[39] 3090 4-9-9 85 (J G Given) *chsd ldrs: rdn over 3f out: wknd 2f out* **8/1**	TPQueally 6	75
-031	8	3	**Corum (IRE)**[39] 3112 4-9-12 88 (Mrs K Waldron) *prom: lost pl over 3f out: sn bhd* **16/1**	(p) GrahamGibbons 2	73
0-P2	9	43	**Fear To Tread (USA)**[14] 3844 4-9-6 82 (Mrs P Sly) *sn led: rdn and hdd over 3f out: wknd over 2f out* **28/1**	PaulHanagan 1	—

2m 33.72s (-6.58) **Going Correction** -0.275s/f (Firm) course record

WFA 3 from 4yo+ 11lb — **9** Ran SP% **115.8**

Speed ratings (Par 107): **110,109,108,106,102 102,101,99,70**

CSF £16.70 CT £68.98 TOTE £5.80: £1.70, £1.70, £2.00; EX 20.20.

Owner Niarchos Family **Bred** Miss K Rausing And Course Investment Limited **Trained** Newmarket, Suffolk

FOCUS

The official going was changed to 'Firm, Good to Firm in places' before this race. A decent handicap run at a good gallop with the progressive first three pulling clear.

NOTEBOOK

Ajaan, a winner in soft ground last autumn, was fitted with blinkers for the first time and a Monty Roberts rug was used for stalls entry. He was slowly away and settled at the back, and his rider appeared to be niggling him along at around the halfway mark. However, he picked up really well to sweep around his field accompanied by the eventual third on the run to the straight and that proved to be a race-winning move. He was inclined to hang as if feeling the ground once in line for home, but kept going well enough to hold off the favourite. He should be able to win again, but may be better suited by easier ground conditions (op 4-1 tchd 7-2)

Bauer(IRE) ◆, having only his second run of the season and first for three months, looked an unlucky loser. He travelled well enough but got caught on the inside when the winner and third made their moves on the outside, and was left with a fair amount of ground to make up in the last quarter mile. He very nearly got up though and can be expected to gain compensation in similar company next time, although the Ebor may be his next outing and that may prove somewhat tougher. (tchd 2-1)

Aajel(USA), who was having just his fourth outing and only his second on turf, was held up at the back and swept around the outside in company with the winner. He could not find an extra gear and tended to hang under pressure on the fast ground, but appeared to get this longer trip and looks to have a future. (op 9-2)

Bogside Theatre(IRE), both of whose wins were on easier ground, had risen 8lb for her last success. She could not cope with the first three in the straight but was well clear of the rest, and with her trainer it would be no surprise to see her over hurdles at some stage.

Luna Landing came into this in good form, having been only narrowly beaten at Chester at the weekend, but he was easily brushed aside by the principals. (op 13-2)

Missoula(IRE), who has been slipping down the ratings, ran on from the rear but in truth was never involved. (tchd 18-1)

Corum(IRE) Official explanation: trainer said colt was unsuited by the firm (good to firm places) ground

Fear To Tread(USA) Official explanation: trainer said colt was unsuited by the firm (good to firm places) ground

4289 CHAPLINS CLUB H'CAP — 5f

4:40 (4:40) (Class 5) (0-75,75) 3-Y-0+ — **£4,533** (£1,348; £674; £336) **Stalls** Low

Form	Pos	Dist	Horse / Details	Jockey	RPR
1315	1		**The History Man (IRE)**[13] 3886 4-8-12 **66** (M Mullineaux) *prom: chsd ldr over 3f out: edgd lft and led ins fnl f: styd on* **12/1**	(b) SCreighton(7) 5	76
554	2	shd	**Welcome Approach**[10] 3998 4-9-2 **66** (J R Weymes) *chsd ldrs: sn pushed along: rdn over 1f out: r.o* **13/2**[3]	AndrewElliott(3) 7	76
4323	3	1½	**Ryedane (IRE)**[1] 4251 5-8-9 **59** (T D Easterby) *trckd ldrs: rdn over 1f out: styd on same pce ins fnl f* **11/4**[1]	(b) DuranFentiman(3) 6	64
0650	4	1¼	**Paddywack (IRE)**[12] 3921 10-8-4 **58** (D W Chapman) *s.i.s: outpcd: nt clr run and swtchd rt over 1f out: r.o wl ins fnl f: nrst fin* **16/1**	(b) AdeleRothery(7) 4	58+
0000	5	hd	**It's Unbelievable (USA)**[7] 4081 4-8-7 **57** ow2 (P T Midgley) *led 4f out: hdd & wknd ins fnl f* **20/1**	(b[1]) JamieMoriarty(3) 1	56
4025	6	½	**Kings College Boy**[8] 4038 7-9-3 **64** (R A Fahey) *sn pushed along in mid-div: rdn 1/2-way: kpt on: nt pce to chal* **4/1**[2]	(b) PaulHanagan 2	62
0600	7	1¼	**Colorus (IRE)**[11] 3954 4-9-7 **71** (M W Easterby) *prom: rdn 1/2-way: styd on same pce appr fnl f* **20/1**	AndrewMullen(3) 11	64
0055	8	2½	**Monashee Brave (IRE)**[14] 3836 4-9-5 **66** (J J Quinn) *sn outpcd: nvr nrr* **8/1**	(p) GrahamGibbons 10	50
3152	9	¾	**Dark Champion**[12] 3921 7-9-1 **62** (R E Barr) *led 1f: chsd ldrs: rdn 1/2-way: wknd over 1f out* **11/1**	(v) PaddyAspell 3	43
00-5	10	4	**Tanforan**[193] 262 5-9-8 **69** (B P J Baugh) *hld up: bhd fr 1/2-way* **20/1**	J-PGuillambert 8	36
2500	11	2	**Jakeini (IRE)**[23] 3594 4-9-9 **70** (E S McMahon) *hld up: bhd fr 1/2-way* **8/1**	(p) TedDurcan 9	30

61.96 secs (-1.84) **Going Correction** -0.275s/f (Firm) — **11** Ran SP% **118.4**

Speed ratings (Par 103): **103,102,100,98,98 97,95,91,90,83 80**

CSF £85.79 CT £276.34 TOTE £13.90: £2.80, £2.20, £2.10; EX 86.00.

Owner D E Simpson & R Farrington-Kirkham **Bred** J Beckett **Trained** Alpraham, Cheshire

■ A first winner in Britain for apprentice Shane Creighton.

FOCUS

A modest handicap run at a sound gallop. Straightforward form for the grade.

Tanforan Official explanation: trainer said gelding was unsuited by the firm (good to firm places) ground

4290 MATTY BOWN MEMORIAL MAIDEN STKS — 1m 4y

5:10 (5:10) (Class 5) 3-Y-0+ — **£3,886** (£1,156; £577; £288) **Stalls** Low

Form	Pos	Dist	Horse / Details	Jockey	RPR
22	1		**Pillar Of Hercules (IRE)**[15] 3827 3-9-3 0 (H R A Cecil) *trckd ldrs: racd keenly: rdn to ld over 1f out: hung rt: r.o* **4/11**[1]	TedDurcan 1	82+
5242	2	3½	**Zifaaf (USA)**[37] 3151 3-8-12 75 (B W Hills) *led: rdn and hdd over 1f out: styd on same pce fnl f* **3/1**[2]	RHills 5	69
0-4	3	6	**Steel Silk (IRE)**[6] 4106 3-9-3 0 (B Smart) *chsd ldr: rdn over 3f out: wknd over 1f out* **20/1**[3]	RoystonFfrench 6	60
	4	1¼	**Johnston's Glory (IRE)** 3-8-5 0 (E J Alston) *chsd ldrs: rdn over 2f out: wknd over 1f out* **66/1**	GaryBartley(7) 3	52
30	5	9	**Benellino**[30] 3366 4-9-7 0 (R M Stronge) *s.i.s: hld up: rdn and wknd over 2f out* **66/1**	DuranFentiman(3) 2	36
	6	29	**Sandarkan (USA)** 3-9-3 0 (G A Swinbank) *hld up: rdn and wknd over 2f out* **20/1**[3]	J-PGuillambert 8	—

1m 43.75s (-1.95) **Going Correction** -0.275s/f (Firm)

WFA 3 from 4yo 7lb — **6** Ran SP% **110.8**

Speed ratings (Par 103): **98,94,88,87,78 49**

CSF £1.56 TOTE £1.60: £1.10, £1.40; EX 1.40.

Owner Plantation Stud **Bred** Eurostrait Ltd **Trained** Newmarket, Suffolk

FOCUS

An uncompetitive maiden in which they bet 20/1 bar two and the principals came well clear. The time was a quarter of a second slower than the earlier handicap.

Sandarkan(USA) Official explanation: jockey said gelding had a breathing problem

4291 AUGUST H'CAP — 6f

5:40 (5:41) (Class 5) (0-75,75) 3-Y-0 — **£3,886** (£1,156; £577; £288) **Stalls** Low

Form	Pos	Dist	Horse / Details	Jockey	RPR
4-00	1		**Woqoodd**[106] 1219 3-8-11 **65** (R A Fahey) *chsd ldrs: led over 1f out: drvn out* **6/1**[3]	PaulHanagan 4	72
4040	2	1¼	**Pickering**[13] 3885 3-8-11 **72** (E J Alston) *s.i.s: hld up: hdwy over 1f out: r.o* **7/1**	GaryBartley(7) 3	75+
003	3	½	**Best One**[15] 3827 3-9-7 **75** (C E Brittain) *hld up in tch: rdn over 1f out: r.o* **16/1**	J-PGuillambert 5	77
2010	4	1¾	**Onatopp (IRE)**[12] 3920 3-9-1 **69** (T D Easterby) *chsd ldr tl rdn over 1f out: no ex ins fnl f* **10/1**	GrahamGibbons 6	65
1061	5	1¼	**Poppy's Rose**[46] 2892 3-8-11 **65** (I W McInnes) *prom: rdn over 2f out: n.m.r ent fnl f: styd on same pce* **5/1**[2]	RoystonFfrench 7	58
2550	6	½	**Mundo's Magic**[11] 3952 3-8-13 **70** (G M Moore) *chsd ldrs: rdn over 1f out: no ex* **8/1**	AndrewElliott(3) 11	61
4653	7	¾	**Flying Valentino**[7] 4080 3-9-5 **73** (G A Swinbank) *hld up: hdwy and nt clr run over 1f out: hmpd ins fnl f: nvr trbld ldrs* **5/2**[1]	TedDurcan 2	62
2304	8	1¼	**Ruthles Philly**[7] 4078 3-7-13 **56** (D W Barker) *led: rdn and hdd over 1f out: sn wknd* **10/1**	AndrewMullen(3) 8	41
-645	9	2	**Tenancy (IRE)**[71] 2120 3-8-10 **67** (A J McCabe) *hld up in tch: plld hrd: effrt over 1f out: sn wknd* **7/1**	JamieMoriarty(3) 1	46
000	10	6	**Cardington Queen**[50] 2740 3-7-9 **56** oh11 (M Mullineaux) *s.i.s: outpcd* **66/1**	SophieDoyle(7) 9	17

1m 15.62s (-1.78) **Going Correction** -0.275s/f (Firm) — **10** Ran SP% **121.2**

Speed ratings (Par 100): **100,98,97,95,93 93,92,90,87,79**

CSF £49.65 CT £652.28 TOTE £8.20: £2.60, £2.60, £2.60; EX 56.70 Place 6 £15.36, Place 5 £6.14.

Owner George Houghton **Bred** Wood Farm Stud (waresley) **Trained** Musley Bank, N Yorks

FOCUS
An ordinary three-year-old sprint featuring some unexposed sorts and run 0.45sec faster than the quicker of the earlier juvenile maidens. The winner was less exposed than most.
Flying Valentino Official explanation: jockey said filly was denied a clear run
Tenancy(IRE) Official explanation: jockey said gelding ran too free
T/Plt: £12.60 to a £1 stake. Pool: £59,708.65. 3,449.15 winning tickets. T/Qpdt: £6.60 to a £1 stake. Pool: £2,973.10. 332.35 winning tickets. CR

4026 YARMOUTH (L-H)
Wednesday, August 8

OFFICIAL GOING: Good to firm (8.6)
Wind: Very breezy Weather: Overcast and cloudy

4292 GEORGE DARLING MEMORIAL CLAIMING STKS — 1m 2f 21y
5:40 (5:41) (Class 6) 3-Y-O — **£1,943** (£578; £288; £144) **Stalls** Low

Form — RPR
1 **Keycavern**[35] 3-9-2 48 ... OscarUrbina 12 — 55
(M Botti) *t.k.h: prom: 4th st: led wl over 2f out: rdn clr over 1f out* **15/2**
6000 2 2½ **Black Mogul**[21] 3652 3-9-3 49 ... (b[1]) HayleyTurner 9 — 51
(W R Muir) *cl up: 3rd st: drvn 4f out: wnt 2nd wl over 1f out: no imp on wnr* **8/1**
0604 3 1½ **Miss Invincible**[18] 3732 3-8-12 49 ... (v[1]) SimonWhitworth 2 — 43
(A P Jarvis) *plld hrd and sn prom: rdn and outpcd 2f out: 5th ent fnl f: plugged on* **12/1**
-002 4 2 **Slavonic Lake**[36] 3186 3-9-1 45 ... (t) JHBowman 14 — 42
(I A Wood) *t.k.h: led after 2f: rdn and hdd wl over 2f out: fdd ins fnl f* **7/2**[3]
4066 5 4 **Camp Counsellor**[18] 3394 3-8-9 52 ... (b) JamieSpencer 13 — 28
(J A Osborne) *hdwy to trck ldrs after 4f: brief effrt 4f out: hrd drvn over 3f out: immediately fnd nil* **10/3**[2]
0 6 ¾ **Wahhaj**[11] 3948 3-8-8 0 ... CharlotteKerton(7) 1 — 33
(G Prodromou) *towards rr: sme prog in midfield 3f out: hanging bdly lft and no ch fr wl over 1f out* **66/1**
0000 7 1 **Bali Belony**[16] 3800 3-8-2 39 ow2 ... (v[1]) KevinGhunowa(5) 8 — 23
(J R Jenkins) *last early: struggling fr 1/2-way* **66/1**
0040 8 4 **Play Straight**[30] 3377 3-8-2 35 ... PatrickMathers(3) 11 — 13
(I W McInnes) *bhd: drvn and fnd nil 5f out* **33/1**
0000 9 3½ **Poyle Ruby**[22] 3622 3-8-9 49 ... MatthewHenry 4 — 10
(M Blanshard) *t.k.h in ld for 2f: kpt hanging rt: lost pl rapidly appr st: t.o* **12/1**
3500 10 23 **Force Celebre (IRE)**[7] 4069 3-9-1 69 ... (b[1]) JimmyQuinn 7 — —
(M H Tompkins) *plld hrd: prom: 2nd st: rdn and lost pl over 3f out: hanging rt and v awkward after: t.o 1f out: eased after* **11/4**[1]
06 11 10 **Holyfield Warrior (IRE)**[27] 3454 3-9-3 0 ... FrancisNorton 6 — —
(I A Wood) *midfield tl 1/2-way: t.o 2f out: eased after* **20/1**

2m 8.07s (-0.03) **Going Correction** -0.05s/f (Good) — **11** Ran SP% **120.9**
Speed ratings (Par 98): **98,96,94,93,90 89,88,85,82,64 56**
CSF £66.10 TOTE £7.90: £1.90, £2.50, £2.80; EX 77.40.Keycavern was claimed by D. Pipe for £16,000. Miss Invincible was claimed by Aiden Murphy for £12,000.
Owner Giuliano Manfredini **Bred** Genesis Green Stud Ltd **Trained** Newmarket, Suffolk

FOCUS
A modest claimer in which many of the field are on the downgrade. The winner is an exception based on her profile in Italy.
Slavonic Lake Official explanation: jockey said gelding ran too free
Poyle Ruby Official explanation: jockey said filly hung right throughout
Holyfield Warrior(IRE) Official explanation: jockey said gelding stumbled

4293 YOUR MORTGAGE SOLUTIONS MAIDEN AUCTION STKS — 7f 3y
6:10 (6:15) (Class 6) 2-Y-O — **£1,943** (£578; £288; £144) **Stalls** High

Form — RPR
0 1 **Imperial Decree**[18] 3747 2-8-5 0 ... FrancisNorton 2 — 72+
(John Berry) *rn green: edging rt early: wd of rest towards far side 1/2-way: clsd to ld over 2f out: sn hung rt: clr ins fnl f: comf* **10/1**
00 2 2½ **Elegant Step**[60] 2468 2-8-7 0 ... AlanDaly 12 — 68
(A P Jarvis) *prom: rdn 1/2-way: wnt 2nd 1f out: one pce and no ch w wnr* **50/1**
5 3 1¼ **River Gleam (IRE)**[28] 3417 2-8-5 0 ... SimonWhitworth 6 — 62
(A P Jarvis) *led: rdn and hdd over 2f out: lost 2nd 1f out: no ex* **7/2**[1]
4 ¾ **Suzi's Decision** 2-8-3 0 ... JimmyQuinn 5 — 58
(P W D'Arcy) *s.s: drvn and effrt over 2f out: hung rt and one pce fnl f* **13/2**
5 1 **Cheque** 2-8-9 0 ... JamieSpencer 10 — 62
(J A Osborne) *bhd: hdwy over 2f out: kpt on steadily wout threatening: will do bttr* **9/2**[3]
0 6 3 **Siryena**[26] 3507 2-8-4 0 ... HayleyTurner 9 — 49
(E A L Dunlop) *dwlt: swtchd towards far side to press ldrs 1/2-way: rdn and wknd 1f out* **14/1**
7 1¼ **Miss Olivia** 2-8-4 0 ... AdrianMcCarthy 4 — 46
(P W Chapple-Hyam) *chsd ldrs: drvn 2f out: sn btn* **8/1**
06 8 4 **Don Picolo**[19] 3712 2-8-4 0 ... KevinGhunowa(5) 7 — 40
(P A Blockley) *chsd ldrs: rdn 1/2-way: btn over 1f out* **28/1**
9 ¾ **City Hustler (USA)** 2-8-10 0 ... MatthewHenry 1 — 39
(J S Moore) *sn drvn in rr: nvr gng wl* **12/1**
10 nk **Sergeant Sharpe** 2-8-5 0 ... AshleyMorgan(7) 13 — 41
(M H Tompkins) *dwlt: a outpcd* **20/1**
11 nk **Halsion Challenge** 2-8-10 0 ... JHBowman 8 — 38
(J R Best) *stdd s: n.d* **4/1**[2]
5 12 3 **Tactical Move**[14] 3833 2-8-5 0 ... PatrickMathers(3) 3 — 28
(Miss V Haigh) *sn pushed along: chsd ldrs tl drvn 1/2-way: sn btn* **66/1**
13 8 **Dorso Rosso (IRE)** 2-8-8 0 ... TGMcLaughlin 15 — 7
(Mrs C A Dunnett) *s.v.s: a struggling: t.o fnl 2f* **50/1**
000 14 8 **Madam Superior**[78] 1919 2-8-1 50 ow1 ... EmmettStack(3) 11 — —
(D J S Ffrench Davis) *struggling 1/2-way: t.o fnl 2f* **100/1**

1m 25.44s (-1.16) **Going Correction** -0.20s/f (Firm) — **14** Ran SP% **122.9**
Speed ratings (Par 92): **98,95,93,92,91 88,86,82,81,81 80,77,68,59**
CSF £459.01 TOTE £11.50: £2.60, £8.60, £2.00; EX 267.40.
Owner The Principes Formation **Bred** Franconson Partners **Trained** Newmarket, Suffolk

FOCUS
A modest juvenile maiden but a reasonable time for the grade.

NOTEBOOK
Imperial Decree, down the field in a decent maiden on her recent Newmarket debut, had been found a lesser contest here and she stepped up from that initial effort to run out a ready winner, relishing the extra furlong. This was a nice performance and, although her trainer is not renowned for his success with juveniles, it would not surprise to see her win again at some stage, probably in nurseries. (op 8-1)
Elegant Step had made little impression in two previous maidens, both fair races, and she was another who found this more realistic, appreciating the extra furlong. There may be more to come in nurseries.
River Gleam(IRE), seemingly the more fancied of the Jarvis pair having made a promising debut at Kempton, ran up to that form over this extra furlong, but it was slightly disappointing she could not get the better of her 50/1 stable companion. She looks more of a nursery type now. (op 10-3 tchd 11-2)
Suzi's Decision did not cost much, but her sire is having a decent season of it so far and she made a promising debut. The step up to 1m is going to suit in future. Official explanation: jockey said filly hung right (op 11-1)
Cheque comes from a yard who can ready one to win first time up, but he looked too inexperienced to do himself justice and could only keep on without threatening. He is one to take from the race. (tchd 10-3)

4294 CONSTITUTION MOTORS HYUNDAI (S) H'CAP — 1m 3y
6:40 (6:44) (Class 6) (0-65,60) 4-Y-O+ — **£1,943** (£578; £288; £144) **Stalls** High

Form — RPR
4065 1 **Viable**[19] 3714 5-9-0 53 ... AlanDaly 1 — 64
(Mrs P Sly) *mde all: drvn over 2f out: clr over 1f out: hld on wl cl home* **10/1**
0540 2 ¾ **Blue Empire (IRE)**[22] 3615 6-9-1 54 ... JamieSpencer 10 — 63
(C R Dore) *taken down early: pressed ldrs: rdn 2f out: wnt 2nd 1f out: kpt on gamely but a hld* **4/1**[1]
300- 3 3 **Marvin Gardens**[310] 5728 4-7-13 45 ... KirstyMilczarek(7) 9 — 47
(John Berry) *prom: rdn 2f out: one pce and n.d fnl f* **20/1**
2024 4 1 **Shunkawakhan (IRE)**[28] 3419 4-8-10 49 ... (p) OscarUrbina 7 — 49
(G C H Chung) *prom: rdn 2f out: last of four who were clr over 1f out: plugged on same pce* **11/2**[2]
0300 5 8 **Jalamid (IRE)**[13] 3873 5-9-7 60 ... JHBowman 3 — 41
(G C Bravery) *bhd: sme prog 1/2-way: nvr anywhere nr ldrs* **9/1**
0100 6 hd **Mamichor**[22] 3616 4-8-7 46 ... (p) RichardSmith 2 — 27
(B R Johnson) *stdd s: sn pressing ldrs: fdd bdly over 1f out* **13/2**[3]
2060 7 1 **Al Rayanah**[7] 4063 4-8-7 53 ... CharlotteKerton(7) 8 — 32
(G Prodromou) *nvr bttr than midfield: struggling fnl 2f* **16/1**
6404 8 1¼ **Fulvio (USA)**[18] 3730 7-8-6 45 ... (v) JimmyQuinn 6 — 21
(P Howling) *stdd s: nvr bttr than midfield: rdn and struggling over 2f out* **25/1**
6-00 9 5 **Pink Bay**[40] 3056 5-8-2 46 ow1 ... (b) KevinGhunowa(5) 4 — 10
(K F Clutterbuck) *sn drvn along in rr: t.o* **50/1**
0366 10 nk **Feelin Irie (IRE)**[29] 3405 4-9-1 54 ... (p) DarrylHolland 5 — 18
(J R Boyle) *chsd wnr 3f out: fdd over 2f out: t.o* **11/2**[2]
5000 11 1½ **Panshir (FR)**[15] 3828 6-8-6 45 ... DMylonas 13 — 5
(Mrs C A Dunnett) *labouring and reluctant after 3f: t.o fnl 2f* **16/1**
00-0 12 ½ **Yorkie**[85] 1739 8-8-6 45 ... (b) AdrianMcCarthy 12 — 4
(J Pearce) *s.s: t.o fnl 2f* **40/1**
0040 13 8 **Cottam Eclipse**[30] 3376 6-8-3 45 ... PatrickMathers(3) 15 — —
(I W McInnes) *taken down early: nvr on terms: drvn 1/2-way: t.o fnl 2f* **22/1**
0006 14 7 **Didnt Tell My Wife**[22] 3616 8-8-1 45 ... NataliaGemelova(5) 14 — —
(Miss K B Boutflower) *a bhd: t.o fnl 2f: eased* **20/1**
0510 15 16 **Tipsy Lad**[11] 3950 5-8-3 45 ... (t) EmmettStack(3) 17 — —
(D J S Ffrench Davis) *s.s: drvn and nvr keen: t.o fnl 3f* **20/1**
6340 16 40 **Veba (USA)**[16] 3805 4-8-6 45 ... HayleyTurner 16 — —
(M D I Usher) *dwlt: nvr gng wl: t.o and eased 3f out: lost action and virtually p.u fnl f* **18/1**

1m 37.96s (-1.94) **Going Correction** -0.20s/f (Firm) — **16** Ran SP% **127.1**
Speed ratings (Par 101): **101,100,97,96,88 88,87,85,80,80 79,78,70,63,47 7**
CSF £47.13 CT £858.00 TOTE £14.20: £3.90, £1.60, £6.30, £2.10; EX 87.90.The winner was bought in for 4,400gns.
Owner Thorney Racing Club **Bred** Mrs H B Raw **Trained** Thorney, Cambs

FOCUS
A fair seller, with the first pair better than this grade last year. The first four were always prominent and finished clear.
Veba(USA) Official explanation: jockey said gelding lost its action

4295 BANHAM POULTRY H'CAP — 7f 3y
7:10 (7:10) (Class 5) (0-75,75) 3-Y-O+ — **£2,914** (£867; £433; £216) **Stalls** High

Form — RPR
-064 1 **Empire Dancer (IRE)**[12] 3926 4-9-1 62 ... FrancisNorton 8 — 68
(C N Allen) *prom: pushed along over 3f out: sustained run fnl f: drvn ahd fnl stride* **18/1**
2465 2 shd **Fiefdom (IRE)**[15] 3813 5-9-11 75 ... (p) PatrickMathers(3) 3 — 81
(I W McInnes) *pressed ldr: rdn to ld 2f out: looked to be holding wnr ins fnl f tl pipped on post* **15/2**
0303 3 1¼ **Chalentina**[57] 2540 4-8-9 56 oh3 ... JimmyQuinn 1 — 59
(P Howling) *led 5f: rdn and stl ev ch 1f out: no ex fnl 100yds* **25/1**
0340 4 ¾ **Mr Cellophane**[22] 3623 4-9-11 72 ... (v[1]) DarrylHolland 6 — 73
(J R Jenkins) *wnt lft s: tk frntic hold in midfield: effrt over 1f out: urged along and nvr going through w effrt* **8/1**
12 5 1 **Expensive Art (IRE)**[13] 3872 3-8-5 65 ... KirstyMilczarek(7) 5 — 63
(N A Callaghan) *stdd s: effrt 1/2-way: chal 1f out and ev ch: wknd fnl 100yds* **11/4**[2]
5002 6 nk **Roman Quest**[11] 3965 4-9-7 68 ... JamieSpencer 4 — 65
(H Morrison) *stdd s: plld hrd in last: brief effrt 2f out: outpcd wl over 1f out: r.o cl home* **2/1**[1]
0201 7 5 **Life's A Whirl**[15] 3826 5-8-13 60 ... (p) DMylonas 7 — 44
(Mrs C A Dunnett) *chsd ldrs tl wknd wl over 1f out* **12/1**
-303 8 3 **Torquemada (IRE)**[60] 2458 6-9-3 64 ... JHBowman 9 — 39
(W Jarvis) *bhd: drvn over 2f out: sn wl btn* **13/2**[3]

1m 25.39s (-1.21) **Going Correction** -0.20s/f (Firm)
WFA 3 from 4yo+ 6lb — **8** Ran SP% **113.0**
Speed ratings (Par 103): **98,97,96,95,94 94,88,84**
CSF £140.94 CT £3380.01 TOTE £24.60: £7.30, £1.40, £8.60; EX 111.80.
Owner Golfers Dream Syndicate **Bred** Golden Vale Stud **Trained** Newmarket, Suffolk

FOCUS
Just a modest handicap and it paid to be close up with the pace, with the first three occupying those positions throughout. The runners came down the centre of the track. The form is sound, rated through the first two.
Expensive Art(IRE) Official explanation: jockey said filly was restless in stalls

Roman Quest Official explanation: jockey said gelding was unsuited by the good to firm ground

4296 EASTERN POWER SYSTEMS H'CAP — 6f 3y
7:40 (7:41) (Class 5) (0-75,69) 3-Y-0+ — £2,914 (£867; £433; £216) Stalls High

Form — RPR

2000 **1** — **Gone'N'Dunnett (IRE)**[15] 3829 8-8-6 **50** oh3..................(v) DMylonas 10 — 58
(Mrs C A Dunnett) *taken down early: bhd and cajoled along and isolated fr rest on stands' side: drvn 1/2-way: styd on over 1f out: led and surged clr cl home* **12/1**

0000 **2** 1 ¼ **Kennington**[15] 3829 7-8-6 **50** oh3.................................... HayleyTurner 7 — 54
(Mrs C A Dunnett) *prom in chsng gp: rdn 1/2-way: chal to ld 100yds out: ct fnl 25yds* **16/1**

4652 **3** *nk* **Norcroft**[9] 4024 5-8-9 **60**..(p) KirstyMilczarek[(7)] 6 — 63
(Mrs C A Dunnett) *chsd ldrs: effrt over 1f out: chal and ev ch wl ins fnl f: no ex cl home* **5/2[1]**

00 **4** *nk* **Nans Lady (IRE)**[15] 3828 4-9-5 **63**................................ FrancisNorton 3 — 65
(E J O'Neill) *midfield: drvn 1/2-way: outpcd over 2f out: rallied and styd on stoutly cl home* **16/1**

6042 **5** ¾ **Blessed Place**[6] 4103 7-9-5 **63**....................................(t) DarryllHolland 1 — 63
(D J S Ffrench Davis) *set fast pce: clr 1/2-way: rdn 2f out: hdd 100yds out: no ex* **11/4[2]**

5046 **6** 1 ¾ **Duke Of Milan (IRE)**[29] 3408 4-8-10 **54**.............................. JamieSpencer 8 — 49
(G C Bravery) *bhd: stdy hdwy over 2f out: rdn and brief effrt over 1f out: btn whn eased cl home* **6/1[3]**

0040 **7** 2 **Guildenstern (IRE)**[9] 4024 5-9-11 **69**................................(p) JimmyQuinn 2 — 58
(P Howling) *midfield: drvn over 2f out: btn over 1f out* **8/1**

50-0 **8** 6 **Riolo (IRE)**[47] 2831 5-8-4 **53**...................................(b) KevinGhunowa[(5)] 5 — 24
(K F Clutterbuck) *missed break: immediately drvn and outpcd* **25/1**

0400 **9** 4 **Must Be Keen**[12] 3906 8-8-1 **50** oh2...................(v) NataliaGemelova[(5)] 4 — 9
(Miss K B Boutflower) *missed break: sn in midfield: drvn 1/2-way: fdd over 2f out* **40/1**

0500 **10** *nk* **Calabaza**[22] 3627 5-8-11 **55** ow2.......................................(b) JHBowman 9 — 13
(W Jarvis) *plld hrd: chsd clr ldr over 3f: sn fdd: eased ins fnl f* **17/2**

1m 12.62s (-1.08) **Going Correction** -0.20s/f (Firm) — **10** Ran SP% **116.9**
Speed ratings (Par 103): **99,97,96,96,95 93,90,82,77,76**
CSF £187.09 CT £637.17 TOTE £12.30: £3.60, £5.00, £1.60; EX 34.20.
Owner Christine Dunnett Racing **Bred** Ocal Bloodstock **Trained** Hingham, Norfolk
■ A triumph for Christine Dunnett, owner and trainer of the first three home.

FOCUS
Most of the action took place up the centre, where Blessed Place set a fast pace, but the winner came up the stands' rail. The Dunnett trio had all slipped to good marks and the form has been rated through the ex-Irish fourth.
Riolo(IRE) Official explanation: jockey said gelding missed the break
Calabaza Official explanation: jockey said gelding ran too free

4297 PKF (UK) LLP H'CAP — 1m 6f 17y
8:10 (8:11) (Class 5) (0-75,73) 3-Y-0+ — £2,914 (£867; £433; £216) Stalls High

Form — RPR

01/1 **1** — **Mickmacmagoole (IRE)**[38] 3145 5-10-0 **73**................. JamieSpencer 1 — 81+
(Seamus G O'Donnell, Ire) *led at slow pce for 2f: 2nd tl led again on bit over 3f out: rdr sn looking rnd: rdn ins fnl f: kpt on wl* **10/11[1]**

6400 **2** 1 ¼ **Domenico (IRE)**[80] 1229 9-8-11 **56** oh6.......................... DarryllHolland 6 — 58
(J R Jenkins) *midfield: swtchd rt 3f out and produced little: kpt on one pce ins fnl f to snatch 2nd: no ch w wnr* **33/1**

0006 **3** *shd* **Follow On**[7] 4067 5-8-11 **56**.. SimonWhitworth 3 — 58
(A P Jarvis) *hld up last for 12f: effrt 2f out: chsd wnr vainly ins fnl f tl lost 2nd nr fin* **16/1**

5634 **4** 1 ¾ **Sa Nau**[9] 4030 4-8-11 **56**... FrancisNorton 9 — 55
(T Keddy) *pressed ldrs: rdn and outpcd over 3f out: plugged on fnl f: n.d* **9/2[3]**

1505 **5** ½ **Sir Duke (IRE)**[22] 3624 3-8-0 **58**...................................... HayleyTurner 5 — 57
(P W D'Arcy) *a towards rr: rdn over 2f out: one pce and nvr looked like chalng ldrs* **15/2**

623- **6** *nk* **El Alamein (IRE)**[340] 5022 4-9-7 **66**................................... JHBowman 7 — 64
(Sir Mark Prescott) *set slow pce after 2f tl hdd over 3f out: sn drvn: racd awkwardly whn fading ins fnl f* **7/2[2]**

0400 **7** 8 **Maria Antonia (IRE)**[108] 1178 4-8-6 **56** oh2............. KevinGhunowa[(5)] 2 — 43
(P A Blockley) *plld hrd and nvr bttr than midfield: wknd over 2f out: eased fnl f* **28/1**

3m 13.19s (7.89) **Going Correction** -0.05s/f (Good)
WFA 3 from 4yo+ 13lb — **7** Ran SP% **116.8**
Speed ratings (Par 103): **75,74,74,73,72 72,68**
CSF £38.43 CT £320.15 TOTE £2.00: £1.40, £6.60; EX 42.30 Place 6 £1,503.76, Place 5 £179.71.
Owner Mrs Edel O'Donnell **Bred** Tower Bloodstock **Trained** Ballinalard, Co Tipperary

FOCUS
The pace was very slow, only really picking up in the home straight. Weakish form, rated through the third.
Maria Antonia(IRE) Official explanation: jockey said filly ran too free
T/Plt: £821.50 to a £1 stake. Pool: £51,204.95. 45.50 winning tickets. T/Qpdt: £112.70 to a £1 stake. Pool: £5,379.80. 35.30 winning tickets. IM

4298 - 4308a (Foreign Racing) - See Raceform Interactive

3866 BATH (L-H)
Thursday, August 9

OFFICIAL GOING: Firm (9.6)
Wind: Almost nil Weather: Fine

4309 BETFAIR APPRENTICE H'CAP (PART OF THE BETFAIR "APPRENTICE TRAINING RACE" SERIES) — 1m 3f 144y
6:00 (6:01) (Class 5) (0-75,73) 3-Y-0 — £2,979 (£886; £442; £221) Stalls Low

Form — RPR

2300 **1** — **Love Brothers**[29] 3416 3-9-3 **71**................................. MatthewDavies[(5)] 6 — 76
(M R Channon) *stdd s: hld up and bhd: hdwy over 3f out: rdn 2f out: led 1f out: edgd lft: r.o* **10/3[2]**

032 **2** ¾ **Aypeeyes (IRE)**[17] 3799 3-9-5 **68**.. KMay 1 — 72
(S Kirk) *a.p: led over 4f out: hrd rdn and hdd 1f out: kpt on* **5/1**

6505 **3** ½ **Plane Painter (IRE)**[14] 3877 3-9-10 **73**....................... WilliamCarson 10 — 76
(M Johnston) *chsd ldr early: lost pl over 7f out: rallied over 2f out: rdn over 1f out: kpt on ins fnl f* **11/4[1]**

3000 **4** 1 ½ **Rumbled**[14] 3875 3-8-11 **60**...(p) KirstyMilczarek 4 — 61
(J A Geake) *s.i.s: hld up and bhd: rdn over 3f out: hdwy 2f out: one pce fnl f* **33/1**

0433 **5** 1 **Arabiyah**[35] 3249 3-8-2 **56**.. HeatherMcGee[(5)] 8 — 55
(L M Cumani) *t.k.h: led: hdd over 4f out: rdn over 2f out: no ex fnl f* **11/2**

6035 **6** 15 **The King And I (IRE)**[31] 3384 3-9-0 **66**........................ AlanRutter[(3)] 9 — 41
(J S Moore) *hld up and bhd: hdwy on outside 3f out: edgd rt and wknd over 1f out* **7/2[3]**

0650 **7** 5 **Leprechaun's Gold (IRE)**[31] 3379 3-7-12 **54** oh3....... DavidProbert[(7)] 2 — 21
(B J Llewellyn) *sn chsng ldr: rdn and wknd over 2f out* **20/1**

5006 **P** — **Zameliana**[28] 3451 3-7-12 **54** oh9.......................... MatthewCosham[(7)] 7 — —
(Dr J R J Naylor) *hld up: sddle sn slipped: bhd whn p.u over 5f out* **100/1**

2m 29.34s (-0.96) **Going Correction** -0.025s/f (Good) — **8** Ran SP% **112.7**
Speed ratings (Par 100): **102,101,101,100,99 89,86,—**
CSF £19.53 CT £50.19 TOTE £4.70: £1.50, £2.00, £1.40; EX 28.30.
Owner Exors Of The Late Graeme Love **Bred** The Kingwood Partnership **Trained** West Ilsley, Berks

FOCUS
The three leaders went off too fast in this very moderate apprentice handicap. The form is rated through the winner with the runner-up to his latest mark but the form may not be that solid.
Zameliana Official explanation: jockey said saddle slipped

4310 123SPORT.COM MAIDEN AUCTION FILLIES' STKS — 5f 161y
6:30 (6:31) (Class 6) 2-Y-0 — £2,266 (£674; £337; £168) Stalls Centre

Form — RPR

0202 **1** — **Meridian Line (IRE)**[14] 3866 2-8-9 72................. RichardKingscote[(3)] 13 — 80
(J G Portman) *a.p: rdn to ld over 1f out: r.o wl* **4/1[2]**

66 **2** 4 **Rathmolyon**[17] 3796 2-8-4 0... FrancisNorton 11 — 58
(D Haydn Jones) *led: rdn and hdd over 1f out: one pce fnl f* **11/1**

00 **3** *nk* **Stand In Flames**[77] 1960 2-8-2 0................................... DavidKinsella 14 — 55
(Pat Eddery) *s.i.s: bhd tl rdn and hdwy on ins over 1f out: r.o ins fnl f* **16/1**

64 **4** ½ **Gower Belle**[17] 3796 2-8-12 0... DaneO'Neill 8 — 64
(W R Muir) *chsd ldrs: rdn over 1f out: one pce fnl f* **8/1**

05 **5** ½ **Too Grand**[14] 3866 2-7-13 0.. WilliamBuick[(3)] 6 — 52
(A M Balding) *bhd: rdn over 2f out: swtchd and carried rt jst over 1f out: late hdwy: nrst fin* **14/1**

0 **6** ½ **Ever Hopeful**[61] 2468 2-8-1 0.. KMay[(7)] 3 — 56
(H J L Dunlop) *a.p: rdn over 2f out: one pce fnl f* **33/1**

7 ¾ **Bathwick Icon (IRE)** 2-8-6 0.. SamHitchcott 2 — 52
(A B Haynes) *s.i.s: rdn and hdwy over 2f out: swtchd rt jst over 1f out: no imp* **11/2[3]**

4503 **8** 5 **Structura (USA)**[10] 4016 2-8-5 66................................. TolleyDean[(5)] 12 — 39
(J S Moore) *t.k.h: chsd ldr tl rdn over 2f out: wknd fnl f* **6/1**

0 **9** *nk* **Imaginemysurprise**[24] 3596 2-7-13 0 ow4............ KirstyMilczarek[(7)] 10 — 34
(J A Geake) *chsd ldrs: rdn over 2f out: wknd wl over 1f out* **66/1**

00 **10** 2 ½ **Agon Eyes (USA)**[30] 3404 2-8-10 0............................... StephenCarson 5 — 29
(D J Coakley) *s.i.s: a bhd* **16/1**

3 **11** 4 **Emef Princess**[16] 3812 2-8-6 0.. SteveDrowne 4 — 12
(K A Ryan) *s.i.s: outpcd* **8/1**

024 **12** 1 ¼ **Ronsai (USA)**[10] 4016 2-8-6 0.. RichardSmith 9 — 7+
(R Hannon) *chsd ldrs tl rdn and wknd over 2f out: fin lame* **7/2[1]**

1m 10.63s (-0.57) **Going Correction** -0.025s/f (Good) — **12** Ran SP% **125.3**
Speed ratings (Par 89): **102,96,96,95,94 94,93,86,86,82 77,75**
CSF £50.97 TOTE £6.60: £2.20, £2.80, £5.60; EX 74.90.
Owner Berkeley Racing **Bred** George Darling **Trained** Compton, Berks

FOCUS
A modest fillies' maiden. High numbers came out on top.

NOTEBOOK
Meridian Line(IRE), runner-up in soft ground over course and distance last time, belied her trainer's concerns over these very different underfoot conditions and skipped away in the latter stages for a comfortable success. She looks the type for nurseries, although she will go up a few pounds for this. (op 7-2 tchd 11-2)
Rathmolyon showed pace to lead on this slight drop back in trip and, though put in her place by the winner, stuck on to secure second. She seems versatile with regard to ground conditions and, now eligible for nurseries, there could be a little race for her. (op 8-1)
Stand In Flames, dropped in at the back following a slightly slow start, stayed on well against the inside rail in the final furlong to snatch third place close home. She is entitled to come on for this first run for 11 weeks and a return to further will suit her. (op 14-1)
Gower Belle, having her third run, and her first on fast turf, ran respectably but could not confirm Windsor form with runner-up Rathmolyon on 8lb worse terms. (op 14-1 tchd 15-2)
Too Grand ◆ was finishing to good effect down the outside when the race was as good as over. She is bred to come into her own over a mile plus and is an interesting prospect for low-grade nurseries over a more suitable trip. (op 16-1)
Imaginemysurprise Official explanation: jockey said filly hung left-handed
Ronsai(USA) dropped back through the field in the last two furlongs and unfortunately returned lame. Official explanation: vet said filly finished lame (op 9-2 tchd 11-2)

4311 GEORGE WIMPEY BRISTOL (S) STKS — 5f 11y
7:00 (7:05) (Class 6) 2-Y-0 — £1,943 (£578; £288; £144) Stalls Centre

Form — RPR

0000 **1** — **Llab Nala**[6] 4136 2-8-9 35.............................. ThomasO'Brien[(7)] 10 — 54
(M R Channon) *bhd: hdwy on outside over 2f out: rdn to ld 1f out: r.o* **14/1**

00 **2** 1 **Ely Une (IRE)**[30] 3404 2-8-6 0.. TolleyDean[(5)] 13 — 46
(J S Moore) *wnt rt s: sn swtchd lft: swtchd rt and hdwy on outside over 1f out: r.o to take 2nd nr fin* **12/1**

0003 **3** ½ **Culzean Bay**[23] 3626 2-8-8 45...................................... NeilChalmers[(3)] 5 — 44
(A Bailey) *w ldr: led over 2f out: rdn and hdd 1f out: nt qckn* **25/1**

6000 **4** 2 **Happy Hacker (IRE)**[21] 3680 2-8-11 53.......................... SteveDrowne 2 — 37
(P D Evans) *prom: rdn over 1f out: wknd ins fnl f* **7/2[1]**

0534 **5** 1 ¼ **Sailing By**[31] 3364 2-8-11 50.. JamesMillman[(5)] 8 — 37
(B R Millman) *chsd ldrs: rdn over 2f out: wknd ins fnl f* **5/1[3]**

0 **6** 1 ½ **Chemise (IRE)**[60] 2488 2-8-11 0.. LPKeniry 1 — 27
(R J Hodges) *hld up towards rr: nt clr run over 1f out: swtchd lft and nt clr run on ins ent fnl f: nvr trbld ldrs* **12/1**

5 **7** ½ **Careenya (IRE)**[31] 3364 2-8-8 0.............................. RichardKingscote[(3)] 4 — 25
(R M Beckett) *chsd ldrs: rdn and wkng whn n.m.r briefly ins fnl f* **14/1**

U535 **8** 1 ¾ **My Sheilas Dream (IRE)**[17] 3788 2-8-9 57...................... JackDean[(7)] 3 — 24
(W G M Turner) *led: rdn and hdd over 2f out: wknd over 1f out* **5/1[3]**

1510 **9** 7 **Caught In Paradise (IRE)**[2] 4255 2-9-7 62...................(b) DaneO'Neill 6 — 4
(A B Haynes) *s.i.s: outpcd* **9/2[2]**

00 **10** 3 ½ **Ruby's Smile**[65] 2333 2-8-11 0... SamHitchcott 7 — —
(R Brotherton) *plld hrd: sn in tch: rdn whn hmpd wl over 1f out: sn wknd* **66/1**

63.19 secs (0.69) **Going Correction** -0.025s/f (Good) — **10** Ran SP% **107.8**
Speed ratings (Par 92): **93,91,90,87,85 83,82,79,68,62**
CSF £142.03 TOTE £13.70: £3.20, £3.80, £3.70; EX 178.30.The winner was bought in for 6,800gns.
Owner Miss F V Cove & Mrs V Beech **Bred** R G Percival **Trained** West Ilsley, Berks
■ Ephesian (9/1, rdr uns & inj at s) and Sonsue (40/1, ref to enter stalls) were withdrawn. R4, deduct 10p in the £.

FOCUS
A very ordinary seller, and something of a messy race.

NOTEBOOK
Llab Nala, tailed off in three maidens and down the field in a claimer on his fourth start, got off the mark on this debut in the bottom grade. Coming from the rear and pushed out once in front, he gave the impression that he is not straightforward and he could struggle to add to this. (op 8-1)

Ely Une(IRE), who showed nothing in two runs for Brendan Duke, was backed down on course on this descent into the bottom grade. She was perhaps unlucky not to reward her supporters, as she was marooned on her own in a separate bank of starting stalls to the others then dived to her right as the gates opened. Impeded early on by the hanging Caught In Paradise, she found herself some way in arrears before keeping on well in the latter stages. The return to 7f will suit her on this evidence. (op 25-1)

Culzean Bay, having her first run on turf away from Yarmouth, has already been beaten at this level but this was a reasonable effort. (op 16-1)

Happy Hacker(IRE), dropped to the lowest level for the first time, had her chance and might have found the ground too firm. (tchd 10-3 and 4-1)

Sailing By, without the blinkers on this first run on fast ground, has now been beaten in four of these. (op 11-2 tchd 6-1)

Chemise(IRE), whose debut running here three months ago caught the attention of the Stewards, although her trainer was exonerated of the charges following an appeal, would have finished closer on this drop in class but for finding her path on the rail blocked. (op 16-1)

Caught In Paradise(IRE), a dual winner in this grade, had run very poorly in first-time blinkers at Chepstow just two days earlier and again did not want to know. (op 7-1 tchd 10-3)

4312 MACFARLANE PACKAGING CLAIMING STKS — 5f 161y
7:30 (7:33) (Class 6) 3-Y-0+ — **£2,072** (£616; £308; £153) **Stalls** Centre

Form / RPR

2566 **1** **Mr Loire**[14] 3879 3-9-5 73 ....(b) DaneO'Neill 6 — 66
(H J L Dunlop) *n.m.r s: in rr: hdwy over 2f out: rdn over 1f out: r.o to ld last strides* **12/1**

-240 **2** *hd* **Danehill Stroller (IRE)**[23] 3618 7-8-11 47 .... LPKeniry 13 — 54
(A M Hales) *a.p: led jst over 2f out: rdn over 1f out: hdd last strides* **5/1**[2]

-503 **3** *nk* **Peruvian Style (IRE)**[14] 3869 6-8-12 52 .... RichardKingscote(3) 8 — 57
(J M Bradley) *hld up: hdwy over 2f out: rdn over 1f out: ev ch fnl f: nt qckn cl home* **3/1**[1]

3000 **4** *1/2* **Tibinta**[5] 4180 3-8-5 52 .... FrancisNorton 1 — 48
(P D Evans) *hld up and bhd: nt clr run on ins 2f out: hdwy fnl f: r.o* **12/1**

0462 **5** *3/4* **Seven No Trumps**[14] 3869 10-8-8 51 .... JakePayne(7) 2 — 53
(J M Bradley) *hld up in tch: rdn wl over 1f out: one pce fnl f* **8/1**

-506 **6** *1/2* **Montemayorprincess (IRE)**[14] 3869 3-8-2 48 ....(p) DavidKinsella 17 — 41
(D Haydn Jones) *hld up and bhd: rdn and hdwy on outside 2f out: one pce fnl f* **16/1**

2360 **7** *2* **Ever Cheerful**[15] 3852 6-9-2 52 ....(v[1]) SteveDrowne 14 — 45
(A B Haynes) *s.i.s: hdwy over 2f out: rdn over 1f out: no ex ins fnl f* **13/2**

0000 **8** *5* **Meikle Barfil**[23] 3618 5-8-11 48 ....(p) TolleyDean(5) 5 — 28
(J M Bradley) *hld up in mid-div: nt clr run wl over 2f out: sn rdn: hdwy over 1f out: wknd ins fnl f* **12/1**

0000 **9** *2 1/2* **Auction Oasis**[14] 3869 3-8-4 45 .... RichardThomas 11 — 11
(B Palling) *broke wl: led 1f: rdn over 2f out: sn wknd* **50/1**

6000 **10** *1 1/4* **Kitchen Sink (IRE)**[29] 3428 5-8-13 48 ....(b) StephenCarson 10 — 12
(Jean-Rene Auvray) *led after 1f: rdn and hdd jst over 2f out: sn wknd* **25/1**

0200 **11** *2 1/2* **Ballybunion (IRE)**[2] 4252 8-8-9 50 .... AlanRutter(7) 4 — 7
(R A Harris) *chsd ldrs: rdn 3f out: sn lost pl* **14/1**

0000 **12** *3* **Night Prospector**[10] 4024 7-9-2 68 ....(b) KylieManser(7) 7 — 4
(R A Harris) *w ldrs on outside: hung rt towards stands' side fr 3f out: sn rdn: wknd wl over 1f out: sn eased* **11/2**[3]

0 **13** *13* **Aaliyah (IRE)**[19] 3732 4-8-1 0 ....(t) SophieDoyle(7) 3 — —
(E J Creighton) *spd for 2f: sn struggling* **66/1**

1m 11.85s (0.65) **Going Correction** -0.025s/f (Good)
WFA 3 from 4yo+ 4lb — **13** Ran SP% **124.4**
Speed ratings (Par 101): **94,93,93,92,91 91,88,81,78,76 73,69,52**
CSF £73.30 TOTE £10.30: £3.50, £2.40, £1.80; EX 89.70.
Owner Mrs Harry Dunlop **Bred** Harts Farm And Stud **Trained** Lambourn, Berks

FOCUS
A modest claimer run in an ordinary time and the form, rated around the placed horses, is moderate.

Night Prospector Official explanation: jockey said gelding hung badly right-handed

4313 REDCIRCLERACING.CO.UK SYNDICATE H'CAP — 1m 5y
8:00 (8:02) (Class 5) (0-75,75) 3-Y-O — **£3,238** (£963; £481; £240) **Stalls** Low

Form / RPR

-006 **1** **Minnis Bay (CAN)**[22] 3646 3-9-5 73 .... LPKeniry 3 — 80
(E F Vaughan) *set mod pce: qcknd 2f out: rdn over 1f out: r.o* **20/1**

4245 **2** *1 1/4* **Nicada (IRE)**[25] 3570 3-8-6 65 ....(p) TolleyDean(5) 4 — 69
(J S Moore) *t.k.h: a.p: hrd rdn and chsd wnr fnl f: nt qckn* **16/1**

0545 **3** *1/2* **Shake On It**[5] 4163 3-9-6 74 ....(t) StephenCarson 1 — 77
(Eve Johnson Houghton) *hld up in mid-div: hdwy over 1f out: rdn and r.o one pce fnl f* **8/1**

4-00 **4** *shd* **Tom Paris**[21] 3689 3-9-2 70 .... FrancisNorton 8 — 73
(W R Muir) *hld up and bhd: hdwy on ins over 1f out: rdn and nt qckn fnl f* **25/1**

4-02 **5** *1/2* **Carlitos Spirit (IRE)**[12] 3949 3-8-5 62 .... WilliamBuick(3) 5 — 63
(B R Millman) *w wnr: lost 2nd over 3f out: rdn over 1f out: one pce* **8/1**

125 **6** *2 1/2* **Last Sovereign**[64] 2354 3-9-7 75 .... SteveDrowne 9 — 71
(R Charlton) *hld up in tch: rdn over 1f out: wknd ins fnl f* **6/4**[1]

0603 **7** *shd* **Alfresco**[29] 3420 3-9-7 75 ....(b) DaneO'Neill 10 — 70
(Pat Eddery) *hld up and bhd: swtchd rt 2f out: short-lived effrt over 1f out* **7/1**[3]

2435 **8** *hd* **Magroom**[1] 4270 3-8-2 56 oh2 .... RichardThomas 7 — 51
(R J Hodges) *hld up in mid-div: bhd fnl 2f* **14/1**

5400 **9** *5* **The Tinker Man**[12] 3950 3-8-2 56 oh3 .... DavidKinsella 2 — 40
(M D I Usher) *prom: chsd wnr over 3f out tl rdn over 2f out: wknd wl over 1f out* **50/1**

2314 **P** **Private Peachey (IRE)**[54] 2668 3-8-11 70 .... JamesMillman(5) 6 — —
(B R Millman) *s.i.s: a bhd: p.u lame over 1f out: dead* **4/1**[2]

1m 40.65s (-0.45) **Going Correction** -0.025s/f (Good) — **10** Ran SP% **117.8**
Speed ratings (Par 100): **101,99,99,99,98 96,96,95,90,—**
CSF £299.93 CT £1814.84 TOTE £22.80: £5.20, £3.30, £2.80; EX 137.70.
Owner John Ferguson Spares Ltd **Bred** D Kenny & Hedgestone Managemen **Trained** Newmarket, Suffolk

FOCUS
An ordinary handicap in which the winner set a very steady pace and this form is pretty dubious.

4314 E.B.F./EXECUTIVE HIRE NEWS FILLIES' H'CAP — 5f 11y
8:30 (8:32) (Class 5) (0-75,72) 3-Y-O+ — **£3,238** (£963; £481; £240) **Stalls** Centre

Form / RPR

1322 **1** **Cosmic Destiny (IRE)**[15] 3853 5-9-1 60 .... LPKeniry 4 — 65
(E F Vaughan) *hld up: hdwy over 1f out: rdn and squeezed through on ins to ld nr fin* **11/2**[3]

05 **2** *hd* **Croeso Bach**[75] 2029 3-7-10 51 oh5 ow1 .... SophieDoyle(7) 7 — 54
(J L Spearing) *led: rdn ins fnl f: hdd nr fin* **40/1**

5456 **3** *hd* **Jucebabe**[15] 3859 4-8-8 53 .... FrancisNorton 6 — 56
(J L Spearing) *t.k.h in tch: rdn 1f out: kpt on* **6/4**[1]

1552 **4** *hd* **Scarlett Heart (IRE)**[5] 4186 3-9-1 63 .... RichardThomas 10 — 65
(J Gallagher) *hld up and bhd: hdwy over 1f out: rdn and kpt on ins fnl f* **3/1**[2]

1000 **5** *1* **Cuppacocoa**[55] 2631 3-9-10 72 .... DaneO'Neill 2 — 72+
(C G Cox) *s.i.s: hld up in rr: nt clr run over 1f out: r.o ins fnl f: nvr able to chal* **7/1**

1-00 **6** *1 3/4* **Minnow**[14] 3886 3-8-6 57 ow2 .... RichardKingscote(3) 1 — 49
(S C Williams) *prom: rdn wl over 1f out: wknd ins fnl f* **16/1**

0035 **7** *4* **Zimbali**[34] 3277 5-8-2 50 oh5 .... WilliamBuick(3) 9 — 28
(J M Bradley) *chsd ldr: rdn over 1f out: wknd fnl f* **10/1**

0542 **8** *2* **Fly Time**[14] 3870 3-8-3 56 ow4 .... TolleyDean(5) 8 — 26
(Mrs L Williamson) *hld up in mid-div: rdn over 2f out: wknd over 1f out* **20/1**

62.46 secs (-0.04) **Going Correction** -0.025s/f (Good)
WFA 3 from 4yo+ 3lb — **8** Ran SP% **115.1**
Speed ratings (Par 100): **99,98,98,98,96 93,87,84**
CSF £174.93 CT £487.08 TOTE £4.00: £1.30, £7.80, £1.50; EX 255.70 Place 6 £2,016.17, Place 5 £1,294.75..
Owner A M Pickering **Bred** The Cruelle People **Trained** Newmarket, Suffolk

FOCUS
They went a relatively steady pace in this fillies' sprint, resulting in a finish of heads. The form is not strong and rather dubious, rated around the winner and third.
T/Plt: £1,485.40 to a £1 stake. Pool: £65,523.70. 32.20 winning tickets. T/Qpdt: £140.50 to a £1 stake. Pool: £4,616.30. 24.30 winning tickets. KH

4265 BRIGHTON (L-H)
Thursday, August 9

OFFICIAL GOING: Firm (9.5)
Wind: Moderate, half-behind.

4315 TOTEPLACEPOT NURSERY — 5f 59y
2:30 (2:31) (Class 5) 2-Y-O — **£2,914** (£867; £433; £216) **Stalls** Low

Form / RPR

633 **1** **Art Sale**[24] 3589 2-9-4 78 .... GeorgeBaker 5 — 83
(G L Moore) *chsd ldrs: hung lft u.p bef led ent fnl f: drvn out* **7/4**[1]

625 **2** *1 1/4* **Natmana**[27] 3478 2-8-7 67 .... TPO'Shea 3 — 70+
(M R Channon) *tk keen hold: hdwy 2f out: hanging lft whn hmpd ins fnl f* **5/1**[2]

5023 **3** *1/2* **Bookiebasher Dude**[8] 4065 2-8-13 73 .... RobertHavlin 6 — 72
(M Quinn) *bhd: rdn and hdwy whn short of room and swtchd rt appr fnl f: r.o ins fnl f* **11/1**

0013 **4** *1/2* **Longoria (IRE)**[7] 4098 2-8-8 71 .... JerryO'Dwyer(3) 2 — 68+
(M G Quinlan) *chsd ldrs: hmpd appr fnl f and nt pce to chal after* **10/1**

01 **5** *nk* **Attribution**[31] 3364 2-8-1 66 ow1 .... KevinGhunowa(5) 10 — 62
(A B Haynes) *racd wd: kpt on fnl f but nvr nr to chal* **16/1**

050 **6** *1 1/2* **Altercation**[31] 3363 2-7-9 58 oh3 .... WilliamBuick(3) 9 — 49
(W Jarvis) *hld up: mde sme hdwy fnl f* **14/1**

505 **7** *nk* **Tina's Best (IRE)**[14] 3874 2-8-6 66 ow1 .... KerrinMcEvoy 12 — 56
(R Hannon) *hld up: rdn 1/2-way: n.d fnl 2f* **13/2**[3]

6005 **8** *nk* **Orpen's Art (IRE)**[7] 4098 2-7-12 58 oh3 ....(b[1]) FrankieMcDonald 1 — 54+
(N A Callaghan) *t.k.h: led tl hdd ent fnl f: bdly hmpd whn wkng ins fnl f* **16/1**

5400 **9** *shd* **Ten Down**[13] 3925 2-9-7 81 .... TPQueally 8 — 72+
(J A Osborne) *prom: wkng whn hmpd ent fnl f* **14/1**

1440 **10** *1/2* **Only In Jest**[9] 4046 2-8-13 80 .... JackDean(7) 4 — 67
(W G M Turner) *chsd ldrs: rdn 2f out: wknd over 1f out* **20/1**

0450 **11** *9* **Lord Of The Wing**[13] 3925 2-8-5 65 ....(b[1]) HayleyTurner 11 — 20
(R M Beckett) *struggling 1/2-way: a bhd* **28/1**

62.25 secs (-0.05) **Going Correction** -0.10s/f (Good) — **11** Ran SP% **117.1**
Speed ratings (Par 94): **96,94,93,92,91 89,88,88,87 73**
CSF £9.80 CT £74.67 TOTE £2.20: £1.60, £1.80, £2.40; EX 10.60 Trifecta £47.20 Pool £334.02. - 5.02 winning units..
Owner R A Green **Bred** Miss R J Dobson **Trained** Woodingdean, E Sussex
■ Stewards' Enquiry : George Baker three-day ban: careless riding (Aug 20, 24-25)

FOCUS
Just an ordinary nursery, but plenty of incident with the winner causing major interference when hanging badly to his left close home.

NOTEBOOK
Art Sale was well backed on his nursery debut having shaped with plenty of promise in three runs in maiden company and he duly justified the market confidence, although things did not go entirely to plan. He hung badly to his left when produced with his effort, causing major interference in behind, not least to the eventual runner-up, and he had to survive a lengthy Stewards' enquiry. He was arguably the best horse in the race, but it looked as though the second past the post, Natmana, would have taken advantage of his waywardness had he not been hampered. He looks capable of progressing in this sphere, although one would not want to see a repeat of these antics, and a more galloping track may suit better. (tchd 6-4)

Natmana ◆ looked an unlucky loser on his nursery debut. Produced with every chance in the straight, he was carried left when trying to stay on and was then badly hampered against the far rail by the eventual winner inside the final furlong. He probably would have won with a clear run and looks capable of making his mark in this sort of company. (op 6-1)

Bookiebasher Dude, dropped in trip, was unable to dominate this time, but that probably helped him see his race out better and he ran well in third. He was another a little short of room in the closing stages, but was not as unlucky as some. (op 16-1)

Longoria(IRE) would have been even closer had she not been badly hampered in all the trouble in the closing stages and this was a fair effort in defeat.

Attribution, bought out of Karl Burke's yard after winning a seller at Bath on his previous start, ran a respectable race in this tougher contest. Official explanation: jockey said colt became unbalanced coming down the hill (op 14-1)

Altercation ran with credit from 3lb out of the weights. (op 12-1)

Orpen's Art(IRE), 3lb out of the handicap and fitted with blinkers for the first time, showed good early speed and may well have been third or fourth had he not been seriously hampered around a furlong from the finish. This was quite encouraging. Official explanation: jockey said colt suffered interference in running (op 20-1)

4316 TOTECOURSE TO COURSE MAIDEN AUCTION STKS 6f 209y

3:00 (3:00) (Class 5) 2-Y-O **£2,839** (£849; £424; £212; £105) **Stalls** Low

Form RPR

624 **1** **Mudhish (IRE)**[12] 3962 2-8-12 77 .... KerrinMcEvoy 9 77
(C E Brittain) *trckd ldrs: rdn to ld jst ins fnl f: hld on u.p* **11/4**[1]

6 **2** *nk* **Barliffey (IRE)**[26] 3552 2-9-1 0 .... TPO'Shea 4 79
(D J Coakley) *slowly away: hdwy on outside over 1f out: r.o strly ins fnl f to go 2nd nr fin* **6/1**[3]

03 **3** *1* **Benhavis**[28] 3471 2-9-2 0 .... EddieAhern 2 78
(J L Dunlop) *a.p: led 2f out: hung lft bef hdd jst ins fnl f: one pce after* **11/4**[1]

2 **4** *1 1/4* **Spiritofthetiger (USA)**[22] 3643 2-8-6 0 .... LPKeniry 1 64+
(R A Teal) *s.i.s: hdwy whn short of room on ins 1f out: one pce after* **4/1**[2]

4425 **5** *shd* **Midnite Blews (IRE)**[35] 3238 2-8-4 68 .... KevinGhunowa[(5)] 7 67
(A B Haynes) *led tl hdd 2f out: wknd appr fnl f* **17/2**

6 *5* **Ten Pole Tudor** 2-8-13 0 .... TPQueally 8 58
(J A Osborne) *hld up on outside: rdn over 2f out: sn btn* **20/1**

0 **7** *11* **Mileaminutemurphy**[31] 3383 2-9-0 0 .... JimCrowley 3 31
(R Hannon) *bhd whn rdn over 2f out: sn wl btn* **14/1**

1m 22.71s (0.01) **Going Correction** -0.10s/f (Good) **7** Ran SP% **109.6**
Speed ratings (Par 94): **95,94,93,92,91 86,73**
CSF £17.93 TOTE £3.50: £2.30, £3.40; EX 21.90 Trifecta £69.10 Pool £461.81. - 4.74 winning units..
Owner Saif Ali **Bred** Darley **Trained** Newmarket, Suffolk

FOCUS
An ordinary juvenile maiden.

NOTEBOOK
Mudhish(IRE) appreciated the step up in trip and narrowly got off the mark at the fourth attempt. He is likely to find things tougher from now on, but the Brittain yard is in great form. (op 5-2)
Barliffey(IRE) confirmed the encouragement of his Salisbury debut and was just held. He struggled to pick up when initially asked, but he relished the climb to the line and was closing fast at the finish. The temptation would be to say he needs 1m already, but there is some speed in his pedigree and he could prove effective over this sort of trip as he gains experience. (op 15-2 tchd 8-1)
Benhavis travelled quite strongly for much of the way, but he failed to find as much as had looked likely and could not build on his recent third at Warwick. (op 5-2)
Spiritofthetiger(USA), the only filly in the field, did not really build on her promising debut effort, but she is probably a little bit better than the bare form suggests and gave the impression she is still learning. (op 3-1)
Midnite Blews(IRE) ran a little better with the cheekpieces left off this time, but this track did not appear to suit. Official explanation: jockey said gelding ran green (op 11-1 tchd 8-1)

4317 CLASSICEVENTMARQUEES.CO.UK FILLIES' H'CAP 6f 209y

3:30 (3:30) (Class 5) (0-70,70) 3-Y-O+ **£2,775** (£830; £415; £207; £103) **Stalls** Low

Form RPR

5-43 **1** **Perfect Treasure (IRE)**[23] 3613 4-9-9 63 .... EddieAhern 8 78
(J A R Toller) *racd wd in tch: wnt 2nd 2f out: rdn and r.o wl to ld fnl 100yds* **10/3**[1]

0500 **2** *1/2* **Ellen's Girl (IRE)**[32] 3352 4-8-8 48 oh2 .... FergusSweeney 4 62
(R Hannon) *led: rdn clr over 2f out: r.o but hdd fnl 100yds* **9/1**

6560 **3** *5* **Flying Encore (IRE)**[15] 3852 3-9-6 66 .... (p) AdamKirby 6 65
(W R Swinburn) *trckd ldr to 2f out: rdn and kpt on to go 3rd ins fnl f* **8/1**

602 **4** *3/4* **Celtic Spa (IRE)**[2] 4257 5-9-13 67 .... StephenDonohoe 5 65+
(P D Evans) *in rr on outside: hdwy over 1f out: nvr on terms* **7/2**[2]

1-6 **5** *1 1/2* **Malaath (IRE)**[89] 1684 3-9-10 70 .... TQuinn 2 62
(E A L Dunlop) *in tch on outside tl wknd ins fnl f* **7/2**[2]

6303 **6** *3/4* **Tilsworth Charlie**[35] 3247 4-9-2 56 .... (v) RobertHavlin 9 48
(J R Jenkins) *mid-div: rdn over 2f out: no hdwy after* **7/1**[3]

4260 **7** *1 1/2* **Lady Edge (IRE)**[23] 3615 5-8-10 55 .... KevinGhunowa[(5)] 1 43
(A W Carroll) *in tch: rdn 1/2-way: sn btn* **14/1**

3500 **8** *2* **Wodhill Be**[16] 3826 7-8-8 48 oh3 .... HayleyTurner 10 31
(D Morris) *slowly away: sme hdwy whn n.m.r over 1f out: dropped out qckly* **33/1**

2600 **9** *8* **My Tiger Lilly**[28] 3455 3-8-4 50 .... SaleemGolam 3 9
(R A Teal) *trckd ldrs tl rdn and wknd over 2f out* **16/1**

1m 21.29s (-1.41) **Going Correction** -0.10s/f (Good)
WFA 3 from 4yo+ 6lb **9** Ran SP% **116.6**
Speed ratings (Par 100): **104,103,97,96,95 94,92,90,81**
CSF £34.14 CT £223.92 TOTE £3.10: £1.20, £3.40, £2.50; EX 33.20 Trifecta £369.80 Part won. Pool £520.34. - 0.34 winning units..
Owner John Drew **Bred** Patrick F Kelly **Trained** Newmarket, Suffolk

FOCUS
A modest fillies' handicap but run at a reasonable gallop and the form looks solid.

4318 TOTESPORT.COM BRIGHTON CHALLENGE CUP (H'CAP) 1m 3f 196y

4:00 (4:03) (Class 4) (0-80,80) 3-Y-O+
£13,934 (£4,176; £2,090; £1,041; £522; £263) **Stalls** High

Form RPR

3133 **1** **Heathyards Pride**[76] 2011 7-9-4 74 .... JimCrowley 7 84
(R Hollinshead) *mid-div: gd hdwy to ld over 2f out: in command fr over 1f out* **13/2**[2]

62 **2** *3 1/2* **Generous Lad (IRE)**[26] 3554 4-8-10 71 .... (p) KevinGhunowa[(5)] 2 75
(A B Haynes) *a in tch: chsd wnr fr wl over 1f out but no imp fnl f* **10/1**

3541 **3** *nk* **Bienheureux**[23] 3617 6-8-4 60 .... (t) HayleyTurner 3 64
(Miss Gay Kelleway) *towards rr: hdwy whn swtchd rt 2f out: styd on to go 3rd 1f out* **8/1**

0216 **4** *4* **Rock Anthem (IRE)**[21] 3691 3-8-10 77 .... KerrinMcEvoy 4 75
(J L Dunlop) *trckd ldrs: rdn over 3f out: one pce fnl 2f* **11/8**[1]

5551 **5** *1 1/4* **Transvestite (IRE)**[22] 3641 5-9-5 80 .... (v) PatrickHills[(5)] 11 76
(J W Hills) *trckd ldr: led over 3f out: hdd over 2f out: wknd over 1f out* **15/2**[3]

1063 **6** *shd* **Blackmail (USA)**[19] 3730 9-8-1 57 .... (b) FrankieMcDonald 1 52
(P Mitchell) *bhd: effrt on outside 2f out: nvr on terms* **25/1**

0005 **7** *1 1/4* **Mostarsil (USA)**[21] 3692 9-8-7 63 .... (p) FergusSweeney 9 56
(G L Moore) *led tl hdd over 3f out: wknd wl over 1f out* **20/1**

4535 **8** *1* **Boot 'n Toot**[12] 3963 6-8-7 70 .... JackMitchell[(7)] 10 62
(C A Cyzer) *a towards rr* **14/1**

0000 **9** *13* **Ariodante**[23] 3617 5-8-2 58 .... EdwardCreighton 6 29
(J M P Eustace) *prom early: bhd fr 1/2-way* **14/1**

0-04 **10** *1/2* **Sualda (IRE)**[21] 3671 8-9-4 74 .... StephenDonohoe 5 44
(P D Evans) *prom: rdn 4f out: sn btn* **14/1**

3100 **11** *dist* **Tromp**[43] 2994 6-9-3 73 .... EddieAhern 8 —
(D J Coakley) *prom tl wknd 3f out: eased whn wl btn over 1f out: t.o* **16/1**

2m 29.95s (-2.25) **Going Correction** -0.10s/f (Good)
WFA 3 from 4yo+ 11lb **11** Ran SP% **121.9**
Speed ratings (Par 105): **103,100,100,97,96 96,96,95,86,86** —
CSF £72.62 CT £538.35 TOTE £8.70: £2.20, £2.70, £2.20; EX 68.90 Trifecta £583.70 Part won. Pool £822.18 - 0.88 winning units..
Owner L A Morgan **Bred** L A Morgan **Trained** Upper Longdon, Staffs

FOCUS
Quality prizemoney, but this was just a fair handicap, although the form looks reasonable rated around the placed horses.
Tromp Official explanation: trainer said gelding was unsuited by the firm ground

4319 TOTESPORT 0800 221 221 H'CAP 7f 214y

4:30 (4:33) (Class 6) (0-60,60) 3-Y-O+ **£1,943** (£578; £288; £144) **Stalls** Low

Form RPR

2052 **1** **Wrighty Almighty (IRE)**[23] 3615 5-9-4 55 .... JimCrowley 6 64
(P R Chamings) *hld up on ins: short of room over 2f out tl squeezed through to ld 1f out: drvn out* **5/1**[2]

6404 **2** *3/4* **Prince Valentine**[23] 3615 6-8-10 47 .... (p) KerrinMcEvoy 1 55
(G L Moore) *a.p: led wl over 1f out: hdd 1f out: rdn and no imp on wnr ins fnl f* **4/1**[1]

0052 **3** *2* **Goodwood Spirit**[2] 4256 5-9-1 52 .... (v) StephenDonohoe 15 55
(J M Bradley) *hld up in rr: hdwy towards outside 3f out: r.o fnl f* **13/2**[3]

0605 **4** *nk* **Moyoko (IRE)**[13] 3904 4-9-1 52 .... TQuinn 12 54
(M Blanshard) *prom: outpcd over 2f out: rallied and r.o fnl f* **16/1**

3000 **5** *1* **Major League (USA)**[34] 3286 5-9-9 60 .... HayleyTurner 5 60
(D Morris) *in tch whn nt clr run over 2f out and again appr fnl f: no ex ins fnl f* **25/1**

1550 **6** *shd* **Out For A Stroll**[8] 4063 8-9-8 59 .... SaleemGolam 10 59
(S C Williams) *hld up: hdwy 3f out: one pce fnl f* **15/2**

4630 **7** *1/2* **Fantasy Defender (IRE)**[10] 4029 5-8-10 47 .... FergusSweeney 4 46
(R M H Cowell) *led after 2f: rdn and hdd wl over 1f out: no ex appr fnl f* **20/1**

00-5 **8** *shd* **Royal Tavira Girl (IRE)**[16] 3826 4-9-1 55 .... JerryO'Dwyer[(3)] 11 53
(M G Quinlan) *racd wd: effrt over 2f out: no ex appr fnl f* **20/1**

00-0 **9** *2* **Hogan's Heroes**[17] 3805 4-9-0 58 .... (p) BradleyRoper[(7)] 3 52
(Eoin Doyle, Ire) *chsd ldr: rdn 3f out: hung lft and wknd over 1f out* **12/1**

1600 **10** *1/2* **Firework**[54] 2665 9-8-9 46 .... AlanDaly 2 39
(E A Wheeler) *mid-div: wknd over 2f out* **33/1**

0345 **11** *3 1/2* **Music Celebre (IRE)**[24] 3600 7-9-0 58 .... (b) JackMitchell[(7)] 9 43
(S Curran) *racd wd: bhd fr over 2f out* **10/1**

5450 **12** *1 3/4* **Murrumbidgee (IRE)**[23] 3615 4-9-2 58 .... (v) PatrickHills[(5)] 14 39
(J W Hills) *slowly away: effrt 3f out: sn bhd* **7/1**

0310 **13** *5* **Danceinthevalley (IRE)**[47] 2875 5-8-11 55 .... ChrisHough[(7)] 7 24
(D K Ivory) *a bhd* **33/1**

00-0 **14** *48* **Julatten (IRE)**[19] 3752 3-8-3 47 .... FrankieMcDonald 13 —
(D J Murphy) *sddle slipped sn after s: led for 2f: out of control after: t.o* **25/1**

1m 35.83s (0.79) **Going Correction** -0.10s/f (Good)
WFA 3 from 4yo+ 7lb **14** Ran SP% **120.0**
Speed ratings (Par 101): **92,91,89,88,87 87,87,87,85,84 81,79,74,26**
CSF £22.55 CT £136.04 TOTE £4.60: £2.10, £1.80, £2.40; EX 18.30 Trifecta £61.20 Pool £312.18 - 3.62 winning units..
Owner The Boccy Hall Evans Tyrrell Partnership **Bred** P Heffernan **Trained** Baughurst, Hants

FOCUS
A moderate but competitive handicap and the form looks modest.
Julatten(IRE) Official explanation: jockey said saddle slipped

4320 TOTEEXACTA BRIGHTON DASH STKS (H'CAP) 5f 213y

5:00 (5:00) (Class 4) (0-80,79) 3-Y-O+ **£4,731** (£1,416; £708; £354; £176) **Stalls** Low

Form RPR

002 **1** **Peter Island (FR)**[4] 4204 4-9-7 75 .... (v) JimCrowley 2 84
(J Gallagher) *trckd ldr: rdn to ld ent fnl f: rdn out* **9/2**[2]

4000 **2** *1/2* **Who's Winning (IRE)**[13] 3911 6-9-8 76 .... TQuinn 1 83
(B G Powell) *chsd ldrs: r.o wl to go 2nd ins fnl f: no imp cl home* **7/1**

0232 **3** *1 1/2* **One Way Ticket**[3] 4233 7-8-13 67 .... (p) StephenDonohoe 8 70
(J M Bradley) *led tl hdd ent fnl f: no ex and lost 2nd ins fnl f* **9/2**[2]

1200 **4** *1 1/4* **Romany Nights (IRE)**[6] 4133 7-9-8 79 .... (bt) JerryO'Dwyer[(3)] 5 78
(Miss Gay Kelleway) *chsd ldrs: rdn over 2f out: r.o ins fnl f* **20/1**

2401 **5** *1 1/4* **Buy On The Red**[3] 4236 6-9-5 73 6ex .... (p) KerrinMcEvoy 3 68
(W R Muir) *trckd ldrs: rdn over 2f out: wknd appr fnl f* **5/2**[1]

2506 **6** *shd* **Chatshow (USA)**[23] 3613 6-8-7 68 .... MarkCoumbe[(7)] 9 63
(A W Carroll) *racd on ins: rdn 2f out: no hdwy after* **11/1**

042 **7** *4* **Summer Recluse (USA)**[23] 3613 8-8-6 65 .... (t) KevinGhunowa[(5)] 6 48
(J M Bradley) *nvr bttr than mid-div* **13/2**[3]

0010 **8** *2 1/2* **Jayanjay**[15] 3859 8-8-13 67 .... EddieAhern 10 42
(P Mitchell) *a bhd* **16/1**

0235 **9** *1* **Dvinsky (USA)**[10] 4024 6-9-5 73 .... AmirQuinn 7 45
(P Howling) *a towards rr* **16/1**

68.51 secs (-1.59) **Going Correction** -0.10s/f (Good) **9** Ran SP% **115.6**
Speed ratings (Par 105): **106,105,103,101,100 99,94,91,89**
CSF £36.00 CT £150.33 TOTE £5.60: £1.90, £1.80, £2.10; EX 31.20 Trifecta £199.60 Pool £433.02 - 1.54 winning units..
Owner C R Marks (banbury) **Bred** E A R L Elevage De La Source **Trained** Moreton-in-Marsh, Gloucs

FOCUS
A fair sprint handicap run at a decent gallop and typically competitive. The front pair are the best guides to the level.
Jayanjay Official explanation: trainer said gelding was unsuited by the firm ground
Dvinsky(USA) Official explanation: jockey said gelding lost its action in the closing stages

4321 TOTESPORTCASINO.COM MAIDEN H'CAP 6f 209y

5:30 (5:31) (Class 6) (0-65,64) 3-Y-O+ **£2,266** (£674; £337; £168) **Stalls** Low

Form RPR

5020 **1** **Razzano (IRE)**[21] 3690 3-8-3 49 .... PatrickHills[(5)] 10 56
(A M Hales) *trckd ldr: chalng whn lft clr over 2f out: kpt on fnl f* **16/1**

-420 **2** *1/2* **Cow Girl (IRE)**[11] 3992 3-9-3 61 .... JerryO'Dwyer[(3)] 3 67+
(Miss Gay Kelleway) *hld up: rdn and hdwy over 1f out: styd on to go 2nd ins fnl f* **14/1**

4300 **3** *1* **Turkish Sultan (IRE)**[5] 4165 4-9-3 57 .... (p) KevinGhunowa[(5)] 9 62
(J M Bradley) *trckd ldrs: rdn over 2f out: r.o fnl f* **13/2**

0400 **4** *1* **Realy Naughty (IRE)**[10] 4029 3-9-9 64 .... TQuinn 8 64
(B G Powell) *mid-div: styd on one pce fr over 1f out* **5/1**[1]

5000 **5** *1¼* **Fun In The Sun**[11] 3997 3-8-7 **48**..........................(v) StephenDonohoe 11 45
(P D Evans) *slowly away: rdn and styd on fr over 1f out: nvr nr to chal* **12/1**

0-24 **6** *½* **Six Of Trumps (IRE)**[30] 3395 3-9-8 **63**.............................. JimCrowley 6 59
(J A Osborne) *trckd ldr: hmpd and lft 2nd over 2f out: hung lft after: nt run on and wknd fnl f* **11/2**[2]

2360 **7** *1¼* **Hessian (IRE)**[16] 3826 3-9-8 **63**.. HayleyTurner 4 55
(M L W Bell) *chsd ldrs: hmpd over 2f out: n.d after* **7/1**

0500 **8** *1* **Salvestro**[23] 3617 4-8-6 **48**... MarkCoumbe(7) 1 39
(A W Carroll) *s.i.s: a in rr* **6/1**[3]

0006 **9** *5* **Spirit Rising**[14] 3872 3-8-4 **45**..(p) JosedeSouza 2 21
(J M Bradley) *in tch tl wknd over 2f out* **33/1**

0400 **10** *1¼* **Sopran Gath (ITY)**[32] 3352 4-9-13 **62**............................. EddieAhern 13 37
(J W Hills) *a bhd* **7/1**

3040 **11** *11* **Lady Duxyana**[23] 3615 4-8-3 **45**..................................... JackMitchell(7) 5 —
(M D I Usher) *bhd whn hmpd over 2f out and again sn after: nt rcvr* **8/1**

00/0 **12** *6* **Danehill Folly (IRE)**[24] 3597 4-8-4 **46** ow1..............(p) BarrySavage(7) 7 —
(J M Bradley) *in tch tl wknd over 2f out* **66/1**

0-04 **U** **Ma Ridge**[56] 2593 3-9-0 **55**.. EdwardCreighton 12 —
(T D McCarthy) *led tl hit rail and uns rdr over 2f out* **33/1**

1m 22.06s (-0.64) **Going Correction** -0.10s/f (Good)
WFA 3 from 4yo 6lb **13** Ran SP% **123.4**
Speed ratings (Par 101): **99,98,97,96,94 94,92,91,85,84 71,65,—**
CSF £227.34 CT £1675.70 TOTE £21.20: £3.90, £4.00, £2.40; EX 146.50 TRIFECTA Not won. Place 6 £75.65, Place 5 £51.60..
Owner Brick Farm Racing **Bred** Brian Killeen **Trained** Preston Capes, Northants

FOCUS
A moderate maiden handicap but the form looks sound rated through the third to recent form.
T/Jkpt: £11,895.50 to a £1 stake. Pool: £25,131.50. 1.50 winning tickets. T/Plt: £63.70 to a £1 stake. Pool: £65,909.35. 755.15 winning tickets. T/Qpdt: £16.50 to a £1 stake. Pool: £3,178.50. 142.40 winning tickets. JS

3872 FOLKESTONE (R-H)
Thursday, August 9

OFFICIAL GOING: Good to firm (8.7)
Wind: Light, half against Weather: Fine

4322 SEAFRANCE.COM H'CAP — 1m 7f 92y
5:40 (5:40) (Class 5) (0-70,67) 3-Y-0+ **£2,817** (£838; £418; £209) **Stalls** Low

Form RPR

0142 **1** **Strobe**[12] 3945 3-8-12 **65**.. TPQueally 8 76+
(J A Osborne) *rn in snatches: lost pl after 3f: pushed along bnd 9f out: stl only 10th 3f out: drvn and r.o fr over 1f out: sustained effrt to ld nr fin* **9/4**[1]

5015 **2** *nk* **Mister Completely (IRE)**[8] 4067 6-9-11 **64**...................(v) JamesDoyle 6 70
(Ms J S Doyle) *hld up in midfield: plenty to do over 2f out: plld out and drvn wl over 1f out: r.o fnl f: jst outpcd* **10/1**

0-55 **3** *nk* **Jack Dawson (IRE)**[22] 3653 10-10-0 **67**........................... GeorgeBaker 9 73
(John Berry) *mistimed s and lost 5l: sn in midfield: effrt over 2f out: barged through wl over 1f out: styd on fnl f but jst outpcd* **9/2**[2]

105- **4** *nk* **Tayman (IRE)**[18] 5691 5-9-11 **64**....................................(b[1]) RobertHavlin 7 69
(Carl Llewellyn) *hld up: quick move to ld after 4f: gng wl 3f out and drew 2l clr 2f out: wknd and overwhelmed nr fin* **20/1**

0601 **5** *6* **President Dan**[14] 3876 3-8-4 **57** ow2.. PaulDoe 5 54
(M R Channon) *hld up in midfield: rapid prog to press ldng pair 5f out: rdn 4f out: wnt 2nd 3f out tl wknd rapidly jst over 1f out* **9/2**[2]

202 **6** *¾* **Madiba**[13] 3927 8-8-12 **51** oh3...................................... SimonWhitworth 2 47
(P Howling) *prom: lost pl 5f out: rdn and effrt again on outer 3f out: fdd fnl 2f* **8/1**

6465 **7** *nk* **Lysander's Quest (IRE)**[136] 792 9-8-9 **51** oh5......... MarcHalford(3) 11 47
(R Ingram) *cl up on inner: disp 2nd 3f out: rdn whn hmpd wl over 1f out: nt rcvr* **14/1**

0420 **8** *7* **Into Action**[12] 3945 3-8-10 **63** ow1.. PatDobbs 12 50
(R Hannon) *led after 2f tl after 4f: chsd ldr to 3f out: wknd u.p* **15/2**[3]

0506 **9** *2* **Arabian Sun**[15] 3848 3-8-11 **64**.. PaulFitzsimons 4 48
(M J Attwater) *chsd ldrs: u.p over 5f out: wknd wl over 2f out* **33/1**

-000 **10** *6* **A Peaceful Man**[41] 2572 3-7-7 **51** oh3.................(p) NataliaGemelova(5) 3 28
(Mrs L C Jewell) *a wl in rr: lost tch over 3f out* **33/1**

225 **11** *½* **Nod's Star**[65] 1032 6-8-12 **51** oh2..(t) AdamKirby 1 27
(Mrs L C Jewell) *led for 2f: restrained into midfield: pushed along over 5f out: wknd over 2f out* **20/1**

0-00 **12** *1¾* **Sadler's Hill (IRE)**[101] 1361 3-7-10 **56** oh4 ow5.............. MCGeran(7) 10 30
(M J McGrath) *a wl in rr: lost tch over 3f out* **50/1**

3m 30.23s (3.03) **Going Correction** -0.05s/f (Good)
WFA 3 from 5yo+ 14lb **12** Ran SP% **123.1**
Speed ratings (Par 103): **89,88,88,88,85 84,84,81,79,76 76,75**
CSF £25.94 CT £99.71 TOTE £3.10: £1.20, £2.60, £1.70; EX 30.20.
Owner Kerr-Dineen Pallett Tullett **Bred** Old Mill Stud **Trained** Upper Lambourn, Berks

FOCUS
A modest staying handicap run at a steady early pace for the first half-mile, resulting in a moderate time. However, the form looks reasonable with the placed horses to their marks.
Nod's Star Official explanation: jockey said mare moved poorly

4323 BACK HERE NEXT THURSDAY EVENING MAIDEN STKS — 6f
6:10 (6:11) (Class 5) 2-Y-0 **£2,817** (£838; £418; £209) **Stalls** Low

Form RPR

4 **1** **Hitchens (IRE)**[14] 3878 2-9-3 0... GeorgeBaker 1 83
(G L Moore) *racd against nr side rail: w ldr: led after 2f: mde most after: rdn jst over 1f out: styd on wl* **13/8**[1]

2333 **2** *½* **Aaim For Applause**[12] 3962 2-9-3 80.................................. TPO'Shea 7 81
(M R Channon) *sn trckd ldrs: pressed wnr fr 2f out: drvn and styd on fr over 1f out: a jst hld* **13/8**[1]

05 **3** *3* **Mr Keppel (IRE)**[12] 3962 2-9-3 0.. TPQueally 3 72
(J A Osborne) *stdd s: t.k.h and hld up in rr: prog over 2f out: chsd ldng pair fnl f: easily outpcd* **7/1**[2]

65 **4** *2½* **Jasmines Hero (USA)**[27] 3479 2-9-3 0.................................. JamesDoyle 2 65
(J S Moore) *trckd ldrs gng wl: rdn and nt qckn 2f out: sn outpcd: plugged on* **7/1**[2]

05 **5** *nk* **Totally Focussed (IRE)**[21] 3687 2-9-3 0...................... PaulFitzsimons 6 64
(S Dow) *led for 2f: w wnr to over 2f out: wknd jst over 1f out* **25/1**

05 **6** *2½* **Dancing Marabout (IRE)**[14] 3878 2-9-3 0........................ RobertHavlin 8 56
(C R Egerton) *trckd ldrs: outpcd fr 2f out: fdd* **20/1**[3]

00 **7** *shd* **Two Imposters (USA)**[55] 2632 2-9-0 0.................... StephaneBreux(3) 5 56
(J R Best) *chsd ldrs: rdn and lost pl over 2f out: wandering and btn after* **66/1**

55 **8** *hd* **Metal Madness (IRE)**[42] 3037 2-9-3 0.................................. PatDobbs 10 55
(M G Quinlan) *dwlt: a in last trio: rdn and no prog over 2f out* **25/1**

06 **9** *¾* **Deckguard**[27] 3478 2-9-0 0.. MarcHalford(3) 4 53
(J S Moore) *settled in last trio: rdn and struggling over 2f out: no ch whn nt clr run briefly over 1f out* **33/1**

0 **10** *3* **Sistos Fascination**[20] 3718 2-9-3 0...................................(t) AdamKirby 11 44+
(M Botti) *hld up in rr: prog on outer over 2f out: sn lost pl again and eased* **40/1**

1m 13.01s (-0.59) **Going Correction** -0.225s/f (Firm) **10** Ran SP% **120.5**
Speed ratings (Par 94): **94,93,89,86,85 82,82,81,80,76**
CSF £3.96 TOTE £2.70: £1.10, £1.10, £1.90; EX 3.50.
Owner R A Green **Bred** Curragh Bloodstock Agency Ltd **Trained** Woodingdean, E Sussex

FOCUS
A fair maiden dominated by those at the head of the market.

NOTEBOOK
Hitchens(IRE), who showed promise on his debut at Sandown, had clearly learnt from that and made the most of his rail draw. He was always up with the pace and settled the race going into the last furlong, winning a shade more comfortably than the official margin. He looks capable of winning in nursery company, although having beaten an 80-rated rival may compromise his chance of getting a good mark. (op 7-4 tchd 5-4)
Aaim For Applause has now been placed in all six of his starts and, after looking well held, was doing his best work at the finish. He is another who should stay further, but his official mark looks on the high side and, although he improved compared with previous encounters with today's third and fourth, it probably means he will have to avoid handicaps until getting off the mark. (op 11-8 tchd 7-4 and 15-8 in places)
Mr Keppel(IRE), who finished a length behind today's runner-up at Newmarket, did not run up to that effort but was quite keen early and had to race wider than the principals. (op 9-1)
Jasmines Hero(USA), who finished five lengths behind today's runner-up at Ascot, was another to run a little below that form, having had every chance. (op 10-1 tchd 12-1)
Totally Focussed(IRE), who ran well enough in a Sandown maiden that is working out, showed up for a fair way but was left behind when the principals joined issue. (op 33-1)

4324 "DREAMS" OF EASTWELL FILLIES' H'CAP — 6f
6:40 (6:44) (Class 5) (0-70,70) 3-Y-0+ **£2,817** (£838; £418; £209) **Stalls** Low

Form RPR

2600 **1** **Jabbara (IRE)**[16] 3829 4-8-1 **51** oh6.............................. AhmedAjtebi(5) 5 61
(C E Brittain) *chsd nr side ldr: rdn to ld over 1f out: styd on wl* **7/1**

0-45 **2** *1¼* **Beautiful Madness (IRE)**[42] 3038 3-9-1 **64**......................... PatDobbs 7 69
(M G Quinlan) *standing sideways as stalls opened: off the pce in midfield nr side: prog 2f out: chsd wnr ins fnl f: kpt on but nvr able to chal* **9/1**

0503 **3** *nk* **Overwing (IRE)**[10] 4017 4-9-11 **70**.................................... RobertHavlin 1 75
(R M H Cowell) *led nr side gp and sn at least 2l clr: rdn and hdd over 1f out: one pce* **5/1**

0165 **4** *1* **Limonia (GER)**[21] 3686 5-8-7 **52** ow1........................... FergusSweeney 8 54+
(Mike Murphy) *led far side pair thrght: on terms 2f out: readily hld fnl f* **9/2**[3]

2430 **5** *¾* **Hucking Hope (IRE)**[6] 4141 3-9-3 **66**................................ GeorgeBaker 2 65
(J R Best) *chsd ldng pair nr side: rdn and no imp 2f out: one pce after* **11/4**[1]

5530 **6** *1* **Piddies Pride (IRE)**[23] 3613 5-8-10 **55**...........................(v) JamesDoyle 6 52
(Miss Gay Kelleway) *dwlt: last pair of nr side gp and sn rdn: nvr gng wl: kpt on fr over 1f out* **7/2**[2]

0660 **7** *5* **Prettilini**[24] 3594 4-8-6 **51** oh3..................................... SimonWhitworth 12 33+
(A W Carroll) *chsd rival far side: no imp 2f out: wknd over 1f out* **12/1**

000 **8** *1¼* **Shortcake**[30] 3395 3-8-4 **53** oh1 ow2................................. SaleemGolam 3 30
(M R Hoad) *dwlt: racd nr side: sn struggling in last pair: nvr a factor* **33/1**

30-0 **9** *2½* **Jessica Wigmo**[34] 3277 4-7-13 **51** oh4................................ MCGeran(7) 9 22
(A W Carroll) *eventually decided to r nr side: a off the pce: brief effrt 2f out: sn wknd* **20/1**

0500 **10** *1* **Kissi Kissi**[135] 801 4-8-6 **51** oh6..............................(v) PaulFitzsimons 11 19
(M J Attwater) *eventually decided to r nr side: a in rr on outer* **22/1**

1m 12.11s (-1.49) **Going Correction** -0.225s/f (Firm)
WFA 3 from 4yo+ 4lb **10** Ran SP% **126.0**
Speed ratings (Par 100): **100,98,97,96,95 94,87,85,82,81**
CSF £71.95 CT £362.53 TOTE £10.90: £3.50, £3.00, £1.60; EX 163.80.
Owner Saeed Manana **Bred** Tower Bloodstock **Trained** Newmarket, Suffolk
■ A first British winner for Dubaian apprentice Ahmed Ajtebi.

FOCUS
A moderate fillies' handicap run 0.90sec faster than the preceding juvenile maiden and best rated through the third. Two runners went to the far side and they were not beaten that far in fourth and seventh.
Piddies Pride(IRE) Official explanation: jockey said mare was never travelling

4325 LOUISE HART MEDIAN AUCTION MAIDEN STKS — 7f (S)
7:10 (7:12) (Class 6) 2-Y-0 **£2,590** (£770; £385; £192) **Stalls** Low

Form RPR

1 **Flight Plan** 2-9-3 0.. SimonWhitworth 5 72
(C A Cyzer) *trckd ldr: rn green but led 2f out: hrd pressed fnl f: hld on wl* **15/2**

0 **2** *hd* **Soggy Dollar**[29] 3435 2-9-3 0... GeorgeBaker 4 71
(M H Tompkins) *hld up bhd ldrs: sltly tapped for toe 2f out: rdn to chse wnr fnl f: clsd and jst failed: too much to do* **9/4**[1]

3 *1* **Stop On** 2-9-3 0.. TPO'Shea 3 68
(M R Channon) *hld up in last: pushed along over 2f out: prog over 1f out: rdn and r.o fnl f: no ch of catching ldrs* **9/4**[1]

4 *nk* **Mcconnell (USA)** 2-9-0 0.. StephaneBreux(3) 9 68
(J R Best) *hld up in rr on outer: prog over 2f out: rdn to chal 1f out: wknd last 100yds* **5/1**[2]

5 *¾* **Totoman** 2-9-3 0.. AdamKirby 6 66+
(G G Margarson) *hld up in rr: prog 2f out: rdn and looked hld whn nt clr run 1f out: kpt on same pce* **6/1**[3]

0 **6** *½* **Bahamian Blue (IRE)**[12] 3967 2-9-3 0.............................. RobertHavlin 10 64
(H J L Dunlop) *mde most to 2f out: cl up 1f out: fdd* **9/1**

0 **7** *9* **Honest Value (IRE)**[15] 3849 2-9-3 0.................................... JamesDoyle 2 40
(Mrs L C Jewell) *racd against nr side rail: trckd ldrs tl wknd 2f out* **20/1**

00 **8** *9* **Safiyeh**[19] 3733 2-8-12 0... PaulFitzsimons 7 11
(M J Attwater) *trckd ldrs tl wknd rapidly 2f out: t.o* **33/1**

1m 28.76s (0.86) **Going Correction** -0.225s/f (Firm) **8** Ran SP% **122.0**
Speed ratings (Par 92): **86,85,84,84,83 82,72,62**
CSF £26.57 TOTE £12.60: £3.30, £1.30, £1.10; EX 55.20.
Owner Mrs Charles Cyzer **Bred** C A Cyzer **Trained** Maplehurst, W Sussex

FOCUS
Probably an ordinary maiden following the withdrawal of the forecast odds-on favourite and run in a slowish time compared with the following handicap, but full of debutants and lightly raced sorts who should improve.

NOTEBOOK

Flight Plan, out of a half-sister to the useful Colonel Cotton, did well to win this considering he ran quite green. This was not a great race but he can be expected to improve for the experience and looks capable of winning more races if doing so. (op 12-1 tchd 14-1)

Soggy Dollar, out of a prolific winner at up to 10f, got a good lead but could not pick up immediately when the winner kicked. He ran on well in the last furlong however, and would have got there in a few more strides. He should be winning a similar contest before too long. (op 4-1)

Stop On ◆, out of a 5f juvenile winner, was held up at the back on this debut and ran on late under considerate handling to finish on the heels of the front two. He should come on a fair amount for the experience and can win his maiden before long. (op 11-4 tchd 3-1)

Mcconnell(USA), out of a half-sister to Motivator, is entered in the Derby. He ran quite well on this debut despite running green and wandering around under pressure. He should have learnt from this but had quite a hard race and his breeding suggests he will not be at his best until next season. (op 5-2)

Totoman, who on the distaff side is bred to be best at 6f, has clearly inherited stamina from his sire Mtoto. He did not get the best of runs from the rear but was not beaten far in the end and is another who should do better in time. (op 4-1)

Bahamian Blue(IRE), who beat only one home on his debut, improved from that and made the running until dropping away in the last furlong. (tchd 8-1 and 10-1)

4326 BOOK ONLINE FOR DISCOUNTED PRICES H'CAP 7f (S)

7:40 (7:43) (Class 5) (0-70,70) 3-Y-O **£2,817** (£838; £418; £209) **Stalls** Low

Form RPR

-446 **1** **Nice To Know (FR)**[38] 3156 3-9-0 **63** AdamKirby 5 74+
(G L Moore) *hld up in midfield: prog to trck ldrs 2f out: drvn to ld 1f out: sn clr: eased last 75yds: uns rdr after fin* **14/1**

-233 **2** *2* **Ella Woodcock (IRE)**[13] 3924 3-9-1 **64** TPQueally 6 68
(J A Osborne) *pressed ldr: led wl over 2f out: drvn and hdd 1f out: kpt on but no ch w wnr* **11/1**

0-31 **3** *2* **Xalted**[185] 360 3-8-3 **52** SaleemGolam 4 51
(S C Williams) *trckd ldrs: rdn and nt qckn 2f out: styd on same pce after* **16/1**

5-04 **4** *nk* **Hope Your Safe**[12] 3949 3-8-1 **53** StephaneBreux(3) 2 51
(J R Best) *pushed along in rr bef 1/2-way: prog 2f out: chsd ldrs over 1f out: sn outpcd: plugged on* **33/1**

0550 **5** *2 ½* **Lindhoven (USA)**[56] 2609 3-8-10 **59** HayleyTurner 3 50
(C E Brittain) *sn wl detached in last and drvn: styd on fnl 2f: no ch* **16/1**

5212 **6** *½* **Riverside Dancer (USA)**[10] 4029 3-8-13 **69** HarryPoulton(7) 7 59
(G A Huffer) *restless stalls and rrd s: trckd ldrs: cl enough over 1f out: sn wknd* **4/1**[2]

0400 **7** *1* **Beckenham's Secret**[23] 3620 3-8-9 **58** (b[1]) FergusSweeney 8 45
(B R Millman) *nvr bttr than midfield: rdn and struggling over 2f out* **22/1**

4-33 **8** *1 ¼* **Titan Triumph**[15] 3851 3-9-7 **70** PaulDoe 1 54
(W J Knight) *mde most against nr side rail tl over 2f out: wknd over 1f out: eased* **11/8**[1]

4042 **9** *4* **Goose Green (IRE)**[14] 3875 3-9-2 **65** GeorgeBaker 9 38
(R J Hodges) *hld up in rr: prog over 2f out: swtchd rt and effrt over 1f out: sn rdn and wknd rapidly* **6/1**[3]

5010 **10** *3* **Kind Of Fizzy**[28] 3474 3-9-2 **65** JimCrowley 10 30
(Rae Guest) *racd on outer of nr side gp: in tch over 4f: sn btn* **25/1**

3533 **11** *3 ½* **Oh So Saucy**[23] 3612 3-8-7 **56** TPO'Shea 12 11
(C F Wall) *racd alone far side: nt on terms over 2f out: eased over 1f out* **10/1**

6-02 **12** *5* **Lay The Cash (USA)**[22] 3649 3-8-9 **58** (b) PatDobbs 11 —
(J S Moore) *prom on outer tl wknd u.p wl over 2f out* **12/1**

1m 26.49s (-1.41) **Going Correction** -0.225s/f (Firm) 12 Ran SP% **131.1**

Speed ratings (Par 100): **99,96,94,94,91 90,89,88,83,80 76,70**

CSF £172.00 CT £2536.05 TOTE £20.20: £5.30, £4.10, £5.90; EX 248.30.

Owner C S C Hancock **Bred** Gainsborough Stud Management Ltd **Trained** Woodingdean, E Sussex

FOCUS

A modest handicap run 2.27secs faster than the preceding maiden. The form is best assessed around the runner-up and fourth.

Titan Triumph Official explanation: trainer said colt was unsuited by the track

Oh So Saucy Official explanation: jockey said filly lost her action

Lay The Cash(USA) Official explanation: jockey said gelding hung right throughout

4327 FOLKESTONE-RACECOURSE.CO.UK FILLIES' H'CAP 1m 1f 149y

8:10 (8:12) (Class 6) (0-65,64) 3-Y-O+ **£2,047** (£604; £302) **Stalls** Low

Form RPR

-005 **1** **Samdaniya**[8] 4079 3-9-11 **64** HayleyTurner 10 71
(C E Brittain) *mde all: pushed along fr 3f out: a holding rivals fnl 2f: rdn out last 75yds* **7/1**

50-0 **2** *1* **Granary Girl**[12] 3946 5-9-8 **52** PaulFitzsimons 12 57
(J Pearce) *hld up in midfield on inner: prog 2f out: drvn and styd on fnl f to take 2nd nr fin: unable to chal* **11/1**

4033 **3** *½* **And Again (USA)**[12] 3946 4-10-0 **58** (p) PatDobbs 8 62
(R A Teal) *trckd wnr: rdn to chal over 2f out: hld u.p 1f out: lost 2nd nr fin* **10/3**[2]

0350 **4** *1 ¼* **She's So Pretty (IRE)**[16] 3826 3-9-10 **63** (p) AdamKirby 5 65+
(W R Swinburn) *hld up in last pair: rdn and struggling over 3f out: taken to wd outside and styd on wl fr over 1f out: nrst fin* **3/1**[1]

-050 **5** *nk* **Barbs Pink Diamond (USA)**[30] 3393 3-9-1 **54** JimCrowley 1 55
(Mrs A J Perrett) *pushed along in midfield 7f out: u.p and no prog 3f out: kpt on fnl f: no ch* **14/1**

00-0 **6** *½* **Falcon Flyer**[12] 3950 3-8-3 **45** StephaneBreux(3) 11 45
(J R Best) *stmbld s: sn trckd ldrs: urged along and no imp 2f out: n.d after* **25/1**

0540 **7** *½* **Greenmeadow**[10] 4023 5-9-9 **53** GeorgeBaker 3 52
(S Kirk) *trckd ldng pair: rdn wl over 2f out: no imp wl over 1f out: wknd sn after* **9/2**[3]

05- **8** *nk* **Antrim Rose**[232] 6879 3-9-7 **60** FergusSweeney 4 58
(E F Vaughan) *hld up in rr: sme prog on outer over 3f out: rdn and no hdwy over 2f out* **14/1**

5-00 **9** *shd* **Baarrij**[16] 3826 3-8-13 **52** SaleemGolam 6 50
(G A Huffer) *mostly wl in rr: u.p and wl btn over 2f out* **25/1**

00- **10** *2* **Lynford Lady**[313] 5690 4-9-5 **49** RobertHavlin 9 43
(P W D'Arcy) *chsd ldrs: rdn over 3f out: no prog over 2f out: fdd* **14/1**

562 **11** *nk* **Split The Wind (USA)**[17] 3800 3-9-9 **62** TPQueally 2 56
(Eve Johnson Houghton) *trckd ldrs: rdn 3f out: no prog over 1f out: sn wknd* **6/1**

0500 **12** *7* **Apolina**[16] 3826 3-7-13 **45** (b) MCGeran(7) 7 25
(Miss K B Boutflower) *heavily restrained sn after s and last after 1f: detached over 3f out: sn bhd* **66/1**

2m 5.08s (-0.15) **Going Correction** -0.05s/f (Good)

WFA 3 from 4yo+ 9lb 12 Ran SP% **130.6**

Speed ratings (Par 98): **98,97,96,95,95 95,94,94,94,92 92,87**

CSF £88.86 CT £315.72 TOTE £8.90: £2.50, £3.10, £1.80; EX 97.60 Place 6 £227.34, Place 5 £150.71..

Owner Saeed Manana **Bred** Darley **Trained** Newmarket, Suffolk

FOCUS

A modest fillies' handicap where it paid to race close to the pace. The form is ordinary rated through the runner-up and backed up by the third.

Split The Wind(USA) Official explanation: jockey said filly had no more to give

T/Plt: £116.90 to a £1 stake. Pool: £49,162.30. 306.75 winning tickets. T/Qpdt: £58.80 to a £1 stake. Pool: £3,921.10. 49.30 winning tickets. JN

4124 HAYDOCK (L-H)

Thursday, August 9

OFFICIAL GOING: Good to firm (firm in places; 9.1)

Wind: Almost nil Weather: Fine

4328 DALKIA MAIDEN AUCTION STKS 6f

2:10 (2:11) (Class 5) 2-Y-O **£2,817** (£838; £418; £209) **Stalls** High

Form RPR

320 **1** **Fitzroy Crossing (USA)**[78] 1938 2-8-11 89 GregFairley 5 82+
(M Johnston) *chsd ldrs: rdn to ld narrowly wl over 1f out: pushed out whn holding on wl towards fin* **2/1**[1]

0 **2** *nk* **Call For Liberty (IRE)**[24] 3582 2-8-13 0 PaulEddery 11 83
(B Smart) *led: bit slipped fr early on: rdn and hdd narrowly wl over 1f out: continued to press wnr ins fnl f: r.o u.p* **16/1**

3 *2* **The Lady Granuaile (USA)** 2-8-11 0 NCallan 12 75
(K A Ryan) *a.p: rdn 2f out: kpt on same pce fnl f* **20/1**

0 **4** *4* **Red Skipper (IRE)**[13] 3915 2-8-9 0 GrahamGibbons 6 61
(N Wilson) *prom: hung lft fr over 3f out: tail flashed u.p: one pce fr over 1f out* **50/1**

53 **5** *¾* **Cracking Nick (IRE)**[24] 3596 2-8-13 0 TedDurcan 2 63
(W R Swinburn) *in midfield: rdn and outpcd over 2f out: kpt on wout troubling ldrs fnl f* **7/1**

0 **6** *½* **Madame Rio (IRE)**[47] 2869 2-8-3 0 AndrewElliott(3) 9 54
(K R Burke) *racd keenly: in midfield: rdn over 2f out: nt pce to chal* **20/1**

7 *2 ½* **Reel Man** 2-8-11 0 RichardHughes 13 52+
(R Hannon) *hld up in rr: pushed along 2f out: nvr trbld ldrs* **6/1**[3]

400 **8** *2* **Personal Choice**[20] 3718 2-8-4 54 DaleGibson 10 39
(M Brittain) *chsd ldrs tl lost pl over 3f out: n.d after* **25/1**

0 **9** *½* **Title Role**[12] 3977 2-8-8 0 TolleyDean(5) 4 46
(P F I Cole) *in tch: losing pl whn stmbld over 3f out: n.d after* **8/1**

3 **10** *3 ½* **Monsieur Reynard**[12] 3967 2-8-11 0 SteveDrowne 1 34
(B J Meehan) *racd keenly: in tch: rdn over 2f out: wknd over 1f out* **3/1**[2]

00 **11** *4* **Peltre**[42] 3025 2-8-0 0 ow3 PatrickDonaghy(7) 3 18
(M Brittain) *sn pushed along: a bhd* **100/1**

050 **12** *1 ½* **Caribbean Cruiser**[12] 3951 2-8-9 60 PaulHanagan 8 15
(Garry Moss) *s.i.s: a bhd* **50/1**

1m 14.0s (0.11) **Going Correction** -0.225s/f (Firm) 12 Ran SP% **120.4**

Speed ratings (Par 94): **97,96,93,88,87 86,83,80,80,75 70,68**

CSF £34.78 TOTE £2.70: £1.60, £4.10, £5.20; EX 36.20.

Owner Favourites Racing XXIII **Bred** Diamond G Ranch, Inc **Trained** Middleham Moor, N Yorks

FOCUS

A fair maiden likely to produce its share of winners.

NOTEBOOK

Fitzroy Crossing(USA), who set a good standard on the evidence of May's Ascot second, when splitting Yem Kinn and subsequent Coventry second Swiss Frank, flopped on his first try at this distance at Ayr last time and is was concerning to see him get so warm beforehand. However, with his stable's juveniles now running better, he was able to get back on track, really digging in under pressure. Connections will no doubt be hoping he can go on again, but he is not going to be the easiest to place with a current rating of 89. (op 5-2 tchd 7-4)

Call For Liberty(IRE), whose stable have had an excellent season with their juveniles, disappointed on his recent Ayr debut, but this faster surface enabled him to show his true colours and he has to go down as an unfortunate loser. It transpired that the bit had slipped through his mouth, explaining why he was hanging slightly under pressure, and it is remarkable he still went so close to winning. He should have little trouble gaining compensation. (op 14-1)

The Lady Granuaile(USA), whose trainer's juveniles are just going through a quiet patch, appeared to know her job and was soon in a prominent position, but that lack of experience counted against her late on and she was left behind by the front two. This was a promising first effort and she should have no trouble winning a fillies' maiden. (op 16-1)

Red Skipper(IRE) was never going the pace over 5f on his Thirsk debut, but he loooks to have learned from that initial experience and seemed more at home over this additional furlong. Being by Captain Rio it is likely that a softer surface will suit, possibly explaining the hanging, and he remains open to further improvement.

Cracking Nick(IRE) has showed up well in a couple of All-Weather maidens, but he proved less effective on this first try on turf and may be more of a nursery type. (op 6-1)

Reel Man, representing connections of former high-class miler Reel Buddy, was unable to make much impression, but it is likely this was needed and he will no doubt benefit from a bit further in time. (op 8-1)

Monsieur Reynard shaped well on his recent Salisbury debut when appearing to handle the soft ground better than most, but he is bred to act on this faster surface and should really have done a lot better. (op 10-3 tchd 7-2 and 4-1 in places)

4329 E B F ZAP 15 YEAR ANNIVERSARY NOVICE FILLIES' STKS 6f

2:40 (2:41) (Class 4) 2-Y-O **£4,857** (£1,445; £722; £360) **Stalls** High

Form RPR

1 **1** **Step Softly**[28] 3446 2-9-0 0 RichardHughes 3 88
(R Hannon) *a.p: rdn to ld narrowly ins fnl f: a jst doing enough* **2/1**[1]

1060 **2** *hd* **Kylayne**[11] 3988 2-9-3 100 TedDurcan 5 91
(P W D'Arcy) *led: rdn over 1f out: hdd narrowly ins fnl f: r.o u.p: a jst hld* **3/1**[3]

1 **3** *3* **Raymi Coya (CAN)**[54] 2663 2-9-0 0 OscarUrbina 6 79
(M Botti) *trckd ldrs: rdn 2f out: nt pce of front pair fnl f* **11/4**[2]

60 **4** *3* **Cosmea**[29] 3423 2-8-10 0 SteveDrowne 4 66?
(A King) *s.i.s: hld up: pushed along over 2f out: nvr trbld ldrs* **33/1**

2224 **5** *½* **Romantic Destiny**[15] 3838 2-8-10 75 NCallan 1 64
(K A Ryan) *racd keenly: prom: rdn 2f out: wknd ent fnl f* **5/1**

05 **6** *9* **Saoodah (IRE)**[37] 3187 2-8-10 0.................... MatthewHenry 2 37
(M A Jarvis) *s.i.s: in rr: pushed along over 2f out: toiling fnl f* **12/1**
1m 14.27s (0.38) **Going Correction** -0.225s/f (Firm) **6** Ran SP% **112.3**
Speed ratings (Par 93): **95,94,90,86,86 74**
CSF £8.32 TOTE £2.70: £1.40, £1.80; EX 8.30.
Owner The Queen **Bred** The Queen **Trained** East Everleigh, Wilts

FOCUS
A competitive enough contest in which the front two came away.

NOTEBOOK
Step Softly, who won in the style of a useful performer on her Folkestone debut, stuck out the 7f extremely well that day and there was a significant doubt as to whether this drop in trip would be in her favour, but having again been ridden prominently, she managed to edge past Kylayne and held on well to score. She has quickly developed into a very useful sort and the daughter of Golan looks well worth her place in a Listed/Group 3 contest, with a return to 7f likely to bring about further improvement. (op 3-1)
Kylayne has solely contested group events since making a winning debut, performing admirably on more than one occasion, and there was no doubting this was easier, but having taken them along, she could not repel the winner and was always just getting run out of it. She is likely to remain a tough horse to place and connections will no doubt be keen to have another go at gaining black type with her. (op 5-2)
Raymi Coya(CAN), a ready winner over 5f on debut at Lingfield, was facing a stiffer test here against better horses and was simply not up to it, lacking the speed of the front pair. This was only her second start and she remains capable of better, but needs to improve to win a race of this nature. (op 5-2 tchd 3-1 in places)
Cosmea has struggled to make an impact in maidens and this was always going to prove beyond her. She will stand more of a chance in low-grade nurseries. (tchd 28-1)
Romantic Destiny, a consistent sort in maidens, ran well off a mark of 75 on her recent handicap debut but could not reproduce the effort and has become disappointing. (tchd 9-2 and 11-2)
Saoodah(IRE) was never going after a slow start, but is another who will stand more of a chance in nurseries.

4330 ZAP FASHION BRANDS H'CAP 6f
3:10 (3:13) (Class 5) (0-70,70) 3-Y-O **£2,817** (£838; £418; £209) **Stalls** High

Form RPR
5241 **1** **Nouveau (GER)**[14] 3872 3-8-9 **63**.................... HaddenFrost(7) 13 78+
(R Hannon) *a.p: led after 2f: rdn over 1f out: r.o wl and in command ins fnl f* **15/8**[1]
6401 **2** *1 3/4* **Rainbow Fox**[17] 3786 3-9-6 **67**.................... PaulHanagan 7 75
(R A Fahey) *chsd ldrs: rdn over 2f out: r.o to take 2nd towards finsh: nt rch wnr* **5/1**[2]
0550 **3** *1* **Zahour Al Yasmeen**[62] 2415 3-9-9 **70**.................... RichardHughes 10 75
(M R Channon) *led for 2f: remained prom: rdn over 1f out: no ex wl ins fnl f: lost 2nd towards fin* **8/1**
0010 **4** *1 1/2* **Mambomoon**[24] 3583 3-8-6 **53**....................(b) DavidAllan 9 53
(T D Easterby) *prom: rdn 2f out: no ex ins fnl f* **16/1**
0352 **5** *3/4* **Mangano**[3] 4224 3-8-1 **51** oh2.................... PatrickMathers(3) 1 49+
(A Berry) *towards rr: rdn over 3f out: hdwy 2f out: kpt on ins fnl f: nt pce of ldrs* **15/2**[3]
6434 **6** *3/4* **Comptonspirit**[38] 3168 3-8-12 **59**.................... SteveDrowne 5 54+
(B P J Baugh) *in midfield: pushed along 3f out: rdn and hdwy 2f out: kpt on same pce ins fnl f* **12/1**
006- **7** *nk* **Botham (USA)**[281] 6295 3-8-5 **52**.................... JohnEgan 8 46
(D J Murphy) *chsd ldrs: rdn over 2f out: one pce fnl f* **20/1**
001 **8** *1* **All You Need (IRE)**[13] 3924 3-9-4 **70**.................... RussellKennemore(5) 3 61+
(R Hollinshead) *cl up on outside: rdn over 2f out: wknd over 1f out* **8/1**
0250 **9** *1 3/4* **Almora Guru**[24] 3583 3-8-7 **59**.................... LukeMorris(5) 12 44
(W M Brisbourne) *hld up: rdn over 2f out: edgd lft over 1f out: no imp fnl f* **14/1**
6066 **10** *2 1/2* **Avoncreek**[13] 3924 3-8-4 **51** oh4.................... PaulEddery 11 28
(B P J Baugh) *rdn over 2f out: a bhd* **66/1**
0-00 **11** *hd* **Russian Silk**[62] 2435 3-9-4 **65**.................... TomEaves 2 42
(Jedd O'Keeffe) *in midfield: rdn 3f out: wknd over 2f out* **40/1**
5060 **12** *3 1/2* **Billy Ruffian**[15] 3837 3-8-8 **55**.................... TedDurcan 4 21
(T D Easterby) *a bhd* **20/1**
1m 13.34s (-0.55) **Going Correction** -0.225s/f (Firm) **12** Ran SP% **119.1**
Speed ratings (Par 100): **101,98,97,95,94 93,92,91,89,85 85,81**
CSF £10.12 CT £63.24 TOTE £2.60: £1.40, £1.90, £2.90; EX 10.20.
Owner Jenny Powell & Sue Jensen **Bred** W Bischoff **Trained** East Everleigh, Wilts

FOCUS
Just a modest sprint handicap rated through the third to her mark and with the fifth and sixth a bit better than the bare form.

4331 ZAP FOOTBALL H'CAP 1m 30y
3:40 (3:43) (Class 3) (0-95,85) 3-Y-O **£11,334** (£3,372; £1,685; £841) **Stalls** Low

Form RPR
1-03 **1** **Sunlight (IRE)**[22] 3645 3-9-7 **83**.................... NCallan 3 90
(M A Jarvis) *towards rr: pushed along briefly 5f out: rdn over 2f out: hdwy ent fnl f: styd on wl to ld towards fin* **7/1**
0-10 **2** *nk* **Snaafy (USA)**[75] 2045 3-9-5 **81**.................... MichaelHills 2 87
(B W Hills) *a.p: led over 2f out: rdn over 1f out: hdd towards fin* **8/1**
0501 **3** *1 1/4* **Monkey Glas (IRE)**[1] 4287 3-8-11 **76** 6ex.................... AndrewElliott(3) 4 79
(K R Burke) *a.p: rdn 2f out: nt qckn ins fnl f* **5/1**[3]
2-10 **4** *1 1/2* **First Buddy**[28] 3463 3-9-6 **82**.................... PaulHanagan 5 82
(W J Haggas) *led: rdn and hdd over 2f out: one pce ins fnl f* **20/1**
2001 **5** *2* **Hunting Tower**[26] 3553 3-9-9 **85**.................... RichardHughes 6 87+
(R Hannon) *hld up: effrt whn nt clr run over 1f out: n.m.r ins fnl f: sn eased* **11/4**[2]
-212 **6** *2* **Ballroom Dancer (IRE)**[7] 4111 3-9-4 **80**.................... JohnEgan 1 71
(J Noseda) *racd keenly: in tch: rdn upsides 3f out tl over 1f out: wknd fnl f* **6/4**[1]
1m 42.66s (-2.85) **Going Correction** -0.20s/f (Firm) **6** Ran SP% **111.7**
Speed ratings (Par 104): **106,105,104,102,100 98**
CSF £57.01 CT £299.87 TOTE £7.90: £2.80, £3.90; EX 50.50.
Owner Lord Harrington **Bred** The Earl Of Harrington **Trained** Newmarket, Suffolk

FOCUS
A good, competitive three-year-old handicap run at a decent gallop and sound form rated around the third and fourth.

NOTEBOOK
Sunlight(IRE), who failed to last home in the Lingfield Oaks Trial on her reappearance, appreciated the drop in grade/trip when third at Kempton last time and held claims in an open event. A change of tactics saw her in rear early, but they worked a treat as she came with a storming run to claim Snaafy in the final strides. There is every chance she will stay a bit further under similar tactics and she looks capable of further improvement. (op 9-1)
Snaafy(USA) could make no impression off a 1lb higher mark on his handicap debut at Newmarket but, with this trip almost certain to suit on breeding, it was no surprise to see him go close. He still looked a bit green in front, this being only his fourth start, and he looks one to keep on-side for a similar event in future. (op 11-1)
Monkey Glas(IRE), back to winning ways the previous day at Pontefract, performed creditably under his 6lb penalty in what was a much better race, but simply bumped into two classier sorts. He has clearly found his best form and there is no reason why he should not continue to go well. (tchd 7-2)
First Buddy, outclassed in a decent race at Newmarket last time, was always likely to prove vulnerable here off a mark of 82, but he kept plugging away once headed and ran well. He needs to improve though if he is to defy this mark. (op 14-1)
Hunting Tower, raised 3lb for his narrow Salisbury victory, never really had a crack at defying the rise as he met a troubled passage throughout the final quarter mile and was eased off once his rider knew it was too late. He deserves another chance. (op 3-1 tchd 10-3)
Ballroom Dancer(IRE) was the disappointment of the race, failing to reproduce her best form and dropping out quickly under pressure having taken a keen grip early on. (op 11-8 tchd 13-8 and 7-4 in places)

4332 ST HELENS H'CAP 1m 3f 200y
4:10 (4:10) (Class 4) (0-85,81) 3-Y-O **£5,505** (£1,637; £818; £408) **Stalls** High

Form RPR
-631 **1** **Mirthful (USA)**[43] 2981 3-9-4 **76**.................... RichardHughes 6 82
(B W Hills) *trckd ldrs: led 7f out: rdn over 1f out: whn pressed: r.o gamely ins fnl f and on top towards fin* **13/2**
1224 **2** *3/4* **Tetouan**[20] 3709 3-9-9 **81**.................... SteveDrowne 3 86
(R Charlton) *s.i.s: sn trckd ldrs: wnt 2nd 4f out: pressed wnr 2f out: sn rdn: nt qckn towards fin* **2/1**[1]
5312 **3** *7* **John Dillon (IRE)**[11] 4004 3-8-5 **66**....................(v) AndrewElliott(3) 4 69
(P C Haslam) *a.p: rdn over 2f out: styd on same pce ins fnl f* **8/1**
4211 **4** *1* **Sadler's Kingdom (IRE)**[10] 4035 3-8-12 **70** 6ex.................... PaulHanagan 5 72
(R A Fahey) *led at slow pce: hdd 7f out: rdn over 3f out: kpt on same pce fr over 1f out* **5/2**[2]
1-40 **5** *1 1/4* **Persian Peril**[59] 2506 3-9-4 **76**.................... NCallan 7 76
(G A Swinbank) *hld up: effrt 2f out: nvr able to chal* **11/1**
3133 **6** *2 1/2* **El Dececy (USA)**[59] 2506 3-9-8 **80**.................... JohnEgan 1 76
(D J Murphy) *hld up: rdn over 2f out: no imp* **5/1**[3]
2m 38.42s (3.43) **Going Correction** -0.20s/f (Firm) **6** Ran SP% **111.3**
Speed ratings (Par 102): **80,79,78,78,77 75**
CSF £19.63 TOTE £5.50: £2.70, £2.00; EX 17.30.
Owner K Abdulla **Bred** Juddmonte Farms Inc **Trained** Lambourn, Berks

FOCUS
A fair handicap but very slowly run and difficult to rate positively despite the placed horses being close to their marks.

4333 ZAP CHARACTER H'CAP 1m 2f 120y
4:40 (4:40) (Class 5) (0-70,70) 3-Y-O+ **£2,817** (£838; £418; £209) **Stalls** High

Form RPR
4550 **1** **Sforzando**[17] 3803 6-9-6 **62**.................... TomEaves 14 72
(Mrs L Stubbs) *in midfield: hdwy over 3f out: rdn and carried hd high whn led ins fnl f: r.o: pushed out towards fin* **6/1**[2]
26-6 **2** *1 1/2* **Mexican Bob**[29] 3416 4-9-8 **64**.................... RichardHughes 1 71
(A King) *in midfield: swtchd rt and hdwy over 2f out: styd on to take 2nd cl home: nt rch wnr* **7/2**[1]
5466 **3** *nk* **Rawdon (IRE)**[17] 3799 6-9-4 **65**....................(v) LukeMorris(5) 7 71
(M L W Bell) *trckd ldrs: rdn to ld 2f out: hdd ins fnl f: kpt on same pce* **7/2**[1]
260- **4** *8* **Neutrino**[16] 5815 5-10-0 **70**....................(b) NCallan 4 62
(P C Haslam) *bmpd s: sn led: rdn and hdd 2f out: wknd fnl f* **7/1**
50-0 **5** *1/2* **Young Scotton**[18] 3765 7-9-1 **57**.................... TedDurcan 12 48
(J D Bethell) *in midfield: rdn 3f out: plugged on at one pce fr over 1f out: no imp on ldrs* **33/1**
0006 **6** *hd* **Newcorp Lad**[20] 3721 7-8-6 **51** oh6.................... AndrewElliott(3) 10 42
(Mrs G S Rees) *in rr: rdn over 2f out: kpt on fnl f: nvr on terms w ldrs* **16/1**
6-20 **7** *4* **Cordier**[67] 1813 5-9-9 **65**.................... PaulHanagan 11 49
(J Mackie) *racd keenly: trckd ldrs: rdn and hung lft whn wkng 2f out* **16/1**
-0P5 **8** *2 1/2* **Everyman**[46] 2915 3-7-13 **51** oh3.................... PaulFessey 6 30
(A W Carroll) *hld up: rdn 3f out: no imp: eased whn n.d fnl f* **33/1**
1305 **9** *3/4* **Bijou Dan**[12] 3955 6-9-6 **62**....................(p) TonyHamilton 3 40
(D W Thompson) *hmpd s: hld up: pushed along 4f out: nvr on terms* **13/2**[3]
5560 **10** *shd* **Boppys Dancer**[16] 3815 4-8-7 **52** oh5 ow1...........(b) JamieMoriarty(3) 13 30
(P T Midgley) *prom tl rdn and wknd over 3f out* **16/1**
060 **11** *1 1/2* **Tavares (IRE)**[14] 3881 4-9-8 **64**.................... GregFairley 2 39
(J Jay) *prom: rdn over 3f out: wknd 2f out* **12/1**
5-00 **12** *3* **Domesday (UAE)**[31] 3376 6-8-5 **52** oh6 ow1...... RussellKennemore(5) 9 21
(W G Harrison) *hld up: rdn 4f out: nvr on terms* **100/1**
2m 15.25s (-0.89) **Going Correction** -0.20s/f (Firm)
WFA 3 from 4yo+ 10lb **12** Ran SP% **116.8**
Speed ratings (Par 103): **101,99,99,93,93 93,90,88,88,88 86,84**
CSF £26.51 CT £85.49 TOTE £6.90: £2.50, £1.60, £1.40; EX 22.10.
Owner Mrs L Stubbs **Bred** M E Wates **Trained** Norton, N. Yorks

FOCUS
Moderate handicap form despite the first three being clear.
Sforzando Official explanation: trainer said, regarding the improved form shown, mare benefited from stronger handling today

4334 JOHN & WYN DUCKWORTH MAIDEN STKS 1m 2f 120y
5:10 (5:11) (Class 5) 3-Y-O+ **£2,817** (£838; £418; £209) **Stalls** High

Form RPR
0324 **1** **Soul Mountain (IRE)**[30] 3399 3-8-9 73.................... MichaelHills 11 83+
(B W Hills) *in midfield: hdwy 4f out: led wl over 1f out: clr fnl f: easily* **1/1**[1]
2 *4* **Russian Invader (IRE)** 3-9-0 0.................... JohnEgan 4 77
(A King) *in midfield: hdwy over 3f out: wnt 2nd over 1f out: no ch w wnr* **7/1**
0-5 **3** *3* **Daweyrr (USA)**[14] 3881 3-9-0 0....................(b) DaleGibson 6 71
(M P Tregoning) *prom: stmbld over 5f out: rdn over 2f out: fnd nil over 1f out* **11/4**[2]
55 **4** *12* **Actilius (IRE)**[31] 3382 3-9-0 0.................... OscarUrbina 5 48+
(M Botti) *led: hdd wl over 1f out: sn wknd* **13/2**[3]
0 **5** *4* **Passing True (IRE)**[36] 3214 3-8-9 0.................... GregFairley 12 35
(M Johnston) *trckd ldrs: pushed along over 3f out: wknd over 1f out* **16/1**
6-6 **6** *1* **Intersky Music (USA)**[70] 4-9-7 0.................... DougieCostello(3) 10 39
(Jonjo O'Neill) *in midfield: toiling fr over 4f out: nvr on terms w ldrs* **20/1**
7 *13* **Hill Cloud**[210] 5-9-10 0.................... DavidAllan 3 14
(W M Brisbourne) *s.s: a bhd* **50/1**
00 **8** *3/4* **Lilymay**[62] 2436 7-8-12 0.................... SoniaEaton(7) 13 7
(B P J Baugh) *in midfield: pushed along 6f out: wknd 5f out* **100/1**
0 **9** *3/4* **Oriental Gift (FR)**[31] 3382 3-9-0 0.................... PaddyAspell 2 11
(J R Norton) *prom tl rdn and wknd qckly over 3f out* **100/1**

The Form Book, Raceform Ltd, Compton, RG20 6NL

0/0 **10** *6* **Satan's Sister**[15] 3847 6-9-5 0........ PaulHanagan 7 —
(Ian Williams) *a bhd* **100/1**
11 *nk* **Mystik Megan**[39] 6-9-5 0........ TomEaves 9 —
(M Mullineaux) *s.s: a bhd* **25/1**

2m 13.65s (-2.49) **Going Correction** -0.20s/f (Firm)
WFA 3 from 4yo+ 10lb **11** Ran SP% **121.9**
Speed ratings (Par 103): **106,103,100,92,89 88,79,78,78,73 73**
CSF £9.14 TOTE £2.10: £1.10, £1.90, £1.70; EX 12.50 Place 6 £134.91, Place 5 £54.09..
Owner Lady Bamford **Bred** Longueville B'Stk & H Lascelles B'Stk **Trained** Lambourn, Berks

FOCUS
An ordinary maiden but run in a good time and rated through the third.
T/Plt: £61.20 to a £1 stake. Pool: £63,766.55. 760.05 winning tickets. T/Qpdt: £15.70 to a £1 stake. Pool: £3,076.70. 144.50 winning tickets. DO

4292 YARMOUTH (L-H)
Thursday, August 9

OFFICIAL GOING: Good to firm (8.7)
Wind: Breezy

4335 EUROPEAN BREEDERS' FUND MAIDEN STKS 6f 3y
2:20 (2:22) (Class 5) 2-Y-O **£3,238** (£963; £481; £240) **Stalls** High

Form RPR
0 **1** **Ernie Owl (USA)**[51] 2732 2-9-3 0........ JamieSpencer 10 81
(B J Meehan) *trckd ldrs: rdn over 2f out: led 1f out: kpt on wl cl home* **15/8**[1]
0620 **2** *hd* **Mister Fips (IRE)**[51] 2737 2-9-3 92........ RyanMoore 4 80
(Jane Chapple-Hyam) *prom: rdn and pressed wnr hrd thrght fnl f: kpt trying but a jst hld* **5/2**[2]
2 **3** *2* **Tadalavil**[12] 3967 2-9-3 0........ JHBowman 3 74
(M R Channon) *led: rdn and hdd over 1f out: no ex fnl 100yds* **11/2**[3]
00 **4** *2* **Ski School (IRE)**[10] 4014 2-9-3 0........ PaulMulrennan 9 68
(W J Haggas) *sn stdd in last: t.k.h early and taken lft after 2f: nvr chal ldrs but kpt on in pleasing style* **33/1**
5 **5** *¾* **Faber Hall Flyer**[16] 3823 2-9-3 0........(t) DMylonas 7 66
(Mrs C A Dunnett) *t.k.h: prom: urged along 2f out: sn btn and hung lft* **40/1**
42 **6** *2½* **Creative (IRE)**[63] 2385 2-9-3 0........ JimmyQuinn 6 58
(M H Tompkins) *pressed ldrs tl rdn and wknd 2f out* **8/1**
7 *5* **Minwir (IRE)** 2-9-3 0........ RHills 8 43
(M A Jarvis) *dwlt: a bhd: n.d fr 1/2-way* **13/2**
0 **8** *3* **Pret A Tout**[19] 3747 2-8-12 0........ NickyMackay 5 29
(P J McBride) *sn drvn along: outpcd after 2f: eased jst ins fnl f* **66/1**

1m 13.04s (-0.66) **Going Correction** -0.30s/f (Firm) **8** Ran SP% **110.1**
Speed ratings (Par 94): **92,91,89,86,85 82,75,71**
CSF £6.09 TOTE £2.40: £1.10, £1.50, £1.90; EX 8.10.
Owner Roldvale Limited **Bred** Stonestreet Mares Llc **Trained** Manton, Wilts

FOCUS
A fair maiden which saw the two market leaders dominate. The winner can rate higher.

NOTEBOOK
Ernie Owl(USA), pitched in at the deep end when running down the field in the Coventry on his debut at Royal Ascot in June, was very well backed to open his account on this drop into maiden company. He duly did the business, but needed all of his leading jockey's strength to prevail and did not look to be in love with the watered ground here. It will be interesting to see where he is pitched in next as he is clearly well regarded, and genuinely fast ground should be much more to his liking in due course. (op 5-2 tchd 3-1 and 7-4)
Mister Fips(IRE), who posted a career-best when ninth in the Windsor Castle last time out, gave his all in defeat and only just lost out to the winner late on. He fully deserves to go one better, but is not going to prove simple to place outside this sphere from an official rating of 92. (op 11-4)
Tadalavil, just held on soft ground at Salisbury on debut 12 days previously, defied market weakness with a sound effort in defeat and had little trouble with the different ground. He is still learning his trade and will be eligible for a nursery mark after his next assignment. (op 7-2)
Ski School(IRE) proved keen under restraint and took time to get going. However, he kept on nicely under a fairly considerate ride in the final furlong and this rates as his best effort to date. His future lies very much with the Handicapper, but he looks to be going the right way now and this Derby entrant will appreciate a stiffer test before too long.
Faber Hall Flyer Official explanation: jockey said gelding hung left
Minwir(IRE), whose dam was a useful 7f winner at two, was never a serious player after a sluggish start and has to rate somewhat disappointing. He is clearly going to need to improve leaps and bounds for this if he is to justify his Group entries, but considering his breeding it may also prove that he leaves this behind when faced with genuinely quick ground. (op 5-1 tchd 9-2)

4336 BET365 BEST ODDS ON EVERY MAIDEN H'CAP 6f 3y
2:50 (2:51) (Class 6) (0-65,65) 3-Y-O+ **£1,943** (£578; £288; £144) **Stalls** High

Form RPR
5243 **1** **Gleaming Spirit (IRE)**[6] 4127 3-9-11 65........ JamieSpencer 7 77
(A P Jarvis) *crossed to far rails to make all on favoured far side: hung rt whn clr w one rival 1f out: a holding her* **3/1**[1]
4533 **2** *nk* **Glencal**[15] 3853 3-8-9 52........ TravisBlock(3) 4 63
(H Morrison) *drvn in 2nd pl thrght: ev ch fnl f and clr of rest: kpt on wl but a hld* **11/2**[3]
-040 **3** *3½* **Willofcourse**[23] 3618 6-8-6 49........ AmyScott(7) 6 51
(H Candy) *pressed ldng pair tl rdn and wknd over 1f out* **9/1**
6-00 **4** *2* **Knead The Dough**[55] 2622 6-8-8 47........ DominicFox(3) 8 43
(A E Price) *a abt same pl: rdn and btn over 1f out* **20/1**
3220 **5** *nk* **Nawayea**[16] 3829 4-8-9 45........ JimmyQuinn 9 40
(C N Allen) *chsd ldrs after 2f: rdn and btn over 1f out* **11/1**
0/00 **6** *1* **Intimate Friend (USA)**[199] 210 6-8-2 45........(t) FrankiePickard(7) 2 40+
(Miss Diana Weeden) *dwlt: hdwy whn hmpd over 1f out: fin w a flourish but no ch* **125/1**
0366 **7** *2* **Musical Chimes**[11] 4000 4-8-6 45........ DuranFentiman(3) 3 31
(W M Brisbourne) *chsd ldrs: sn drvn: btn wl over 1f out* **40/1**
0320 **8** *½* **Siesta (IRE)**[13] 3924 3-8-10 50........(e) IanMongan 17 33
(J R Fanshawe) *kpt hanging lft: nvr bttr than midfield or anywhere nr ldrs* **16/1**
5645 **9** *½* **Nou Camp**[24] 3599 3-8-8 48........ NickyMackay 10 30
(N A Callaghan) *nvr on terms* **10/1**
630 **10** *½* **Detonate**[49] 2798 5-8-9 45........ PaulMulrennan 16 26
(I A Wood) *sn struggling in rr* **20/1**
-000 **11** *½* **Korty**[23] 3620 3-9-1 55........(t) RichardMullen 15 34
(W J Musson) *a bhd* **40/1**
0000 **12** *½* **She's Dunnett**[5] 4164 4-8-9 45........(t) DMylonas 5 23
(Mrs C A Dunnett) *dwlt: sn drvn and nvr gng wl* **40/1**
-000 **13** *nk* **Kindallachan**[23] 3627 4-8-9 45........ J-PGuillambert 11 22
(G C Bravery) *struggling fr 1/2-way* **66/1**
-356 **14** *nk* **Futuristic Dragon (IRE)**[42] 3038 3-9-8 62........(b[1]) PatCosgrave 1 37
(P A Blockley) *chsd ldrs 4f: wkng whn edgd lft over 1f out* **11/1**
3600 **15** *1* **Mannello**[22] 3647 4-8-12 48........(v) AdrianMcCarthy 14 21
(Mrs C A Dunnett) *s.s: nvr gng wl* **14/1**
2455 **16** *1¾* **Welsh Auction**[23] 3612 3-9-9 63........ RyanMoore 13 30
(G A Huffer) *chsd ldrs to 1/2-way: wl btn 2f out* **5/1**[2]
500 **17** *4* **Canary Girl**[5] 4164 4-8-9 45........(v) TGMcLaughlin 12 —
(Mrs C A Dunnett) *rdn and labouring over 3f out* **50/1**

1m 11.49s (-2.21) **Going Correction** -0.30s/f (Firm)
WFA 3 from 4yo+ 4lb **17** Ran SP% **126.4**
Speed ratings (Par 101): **102,101,96,94,93 92,89,89,88,87 87,86,86,85,84 82,76**
CSF £17.67 CT £141.90 TOTE £3.80: £1.40, £2.00, £2.90, £7.90; EX 18.30.
Owner Geoffrey Bishop and Ann Jarvis **Bred** Rathasker Stud **Trained** Twyford, Bucks

FOCUS
A very weak handicap which saw the first pair come clear on the far side. The form is very ordinary with the runner-up the best guide.
Nawayea Official explanation: trainer said filly lost a front shoe

4337 WEATHERBYS PRINTING (S) H'CAP 1m 3y
3:20 (3:21) (Class 6) (0-65,63) 3-Y-O **£1,943** (£578; £288; £144) **Stalls** High

Form RPR
5-05 **1** **Wickedish**[28] 3456 3-8-6 48........(t) RichardMullen 7 55
(C F Wall) *cl up: led over 2f out: rdn and sn bagged far rail to go 3l clr: hld on wl* **15/2**
1-02 **2** *¾* **Gifted Heir (IRE)**[30] 3394 3-9-0 56........ RyanMoore 4 61
(I A Wood) *cl up: chsd wnr over 2f out: sn rdn: kpt on to cl sltly cl home but a hld* **5/2**[1]
0005 **3** *5* **Hamilton House**[7] 4109 3-9-7 63........ JimmyQuinn 5 57
(M H Tompkins) *chsd ldrs: shkn up 1/2-way: effrt wl over 1f out: no ch w ldng pair fnl f* **4/1**[2]
-500 **4** *½* **Meeting Of Minds**[13] 3918 3-8-7 49........ PaulMulrennan 11 41
(W Jarvis) *prom: rdn and racd awkwardly over 2f out: sn btn* **12/1**
0040 **5** *3* **Bubbly Girl**[16] 3824 3-8-6 48........ NickyMackay 13 33
(P J McBride) *chsd ldrs: rdn and btn 2f out* **10/1**
6330 **6** *1½* **Flamestone**[7] 4106 3-8-1 46........ DominicFox(3) 15 28
(A E Price) *nvr bttr than midfield: rdn 3f out: floundering after* **16/1**
0000 **7** *2½* **Millyjean**[30] 3394 3-8-3 45........(b) AdrianMcCarthy 2 21
(John Berry) *t.k.h: led tl rdn and hdd over 2f out: sn lost pl rapidly* **25/1**
0004 **8** *½* **Noddledoddle (IRE)**[7] 4109 3-7-10 45........(t) FrankiePickard(7) 1 20
(J Ryan) *moved bdly to post: struggling over 3f out* **14/1**
000 **9** *9* **Pixie Princess (IRE)**[29] 3425 3-7-10 45........ DanielleMcCreery(7) 8 —
(Miss V Haigh) *struggling after 3f: t.o* **40/1**
0600 **10** *1¼* **All Talk**[16] 3824 3-7-10 45........ LauraReynolds(7) 12 —
(M J Gingell) *virtually bolted to s: rather isolated fr rest in centre: struggling after 3f: t.o* **100/1**
3505 **11** *hd* **Three No Trumps**[42] 3040 3-8-0 45........ DuranFentiman(3) 14 —
(P S Felgate) *struggling over 4f out: t.o* **33/1**
-000 **12** *1¾* **Give Evidence**[7] 4109 3-9-4 60........(v) JamieSpencer 6 7
(A P Jarvis) *hld up in last pl: no ch fr 1/2-way: eased 2f out: t.o* **5/1**[3]
0300 **13** *3½* **Iced Tango**[21] 3686 3-8-1 46 ow1........ EmmettStack(3) 9 —
(F Jordan) *s.s: sn impr to midfield: fdd over 2f out: t.o* **33/1**
0200 **14** *17* **Sharpattack**[13] 3924 3-8-8 50........ NeilPollard 3 —
(M Botti) *s.s: t.o over 2f out: eased fnl f* **16/1**

1m 37.49s (-2.41) **Going Correction** -0.30s/f (Firm) **14** Ran SP% **125.4**
Speed ratings (Par 98): **100,99,94,93,90 89,86,86,77,76 75,74,70,53**
CSF £26.64 CT £91.40 TOTE £8.60: £2.70, £1.50, £2.00; EX 35.90.The winner was bought in for 9,200gns. Gifted Heir was claimed by Mr A. Bailey for £5,000.
Owner Arkland International (uk) Ltd **Bred** Broughton Bloodstock **Trained** Newmarket, Suffolk

FOCUS
A dire event that saw the first pair come clear but the form is pretty limited.
Give Evidence Official explanation: jockey said gelding had no more to give

4338 PARKLANDS LEISURE HOLIDAY CARAVANS FILLIES' H'CAP 1m 3y
3:50 (3:51) (Class 5) (0-75,75) 3-Y-O **£2,914** (£867; £433; £216) **Stalls** High

Form RPR
0-02 **1** **Dancing Jest (IRE)**[22] 3651 3-8-6 60........ NickyMackay 7 63
(Rae Guest) *pressed ldr: drvn over 3f out: led wl over 1f out: hdd 100yds out: lft in ld nr fin* **25/1**
44-3 **2** *nk* **Princess Taylor**[40] 3087 3-9-2 70........(t) JimmyQuinn 8 72
(M Botti) *in midfield: rdn 3f out: effrt whn checked over 1f out: rallied and r.o wl to snatch cl 2nd nr fin* **14/1**
1240 **3** *shd* **Fealeview Lady (USA)**[29] 3430 3-8-12 69........ TravisBlock(3) 3 71
(H Morrison) *cl up: rdn 4f out: chal on outside to ld 100yds out: hung lft and jst ct* **8/1**
524 **4** *2½* **Cassiara**[11] 3992 3-9-7 75........(p) JamieSpencer 5 71
(J Pearce) *stdd in last pl: rdn and btn 2f out: slt late prog* **5/1**[2]
0-24 **5** *1¾* **Comma (USA)**[13] 3913 3-9-2 70........ RyanMoore 1 62
(Sir Michael Stoute) *settled towards rr: hrd drvn over 2f out: unable to chal after* **5/6**[1]
3400 **6** *1¼* **Djalalabad (FR)**[12] 3964 3-8-9 63........ DMylonas 2 52
(Mrs C A Dunnett) *led: hdd wl over 1f out: sn edgd rt: fading whn hung lft fnl f* **66/1**
-444 **7** *1¼* **High 'n Dry (IRE)**[12] 3961 3-9-5 73........ IanMongan 4 59
(C A Cyzer) *chsd ldrs: rdn 2f out: sn racing awkwardly and wl btn* **11/2**[3]
632- **8** *4* **Trickle (USA)**[225] 6951 3-9-0 68........ J-PGuillambert 6 45
(Miss D Mountain) *towards rr: rdn wl over 2f out: sn no ch* **40/1**

1m 37.1s (-2.80) **Going Correction** -0.30s/f (Firm) **8** Ran SP% **112.2**
Speed ratings (Par 97): **102,101,101,99,97 96,94,90**
CSF £310.30 CT £3060.41 TOTE £26.00: £4.20, £2.90, £2.40; EX 157.40.
Owner Mrs J E Lury and O T Lury **Bred** Knocklong House Stud **Trained** Newmarket, Suffolk

FOCUS
A modest fillies' handicap. The first three came clear in a blanket finish but this event did not take much winning.
Princess Taylor Official explanation: jockey said filly was hampered 1f out

4339 "ONE" RAILWAY RIDE THE WHERRY LINES H'CAP 1m 3f 101y
4:20 (4:20) (Class 6) (0-65,65) 3-Y-O **£2,137** (£635; £317; £158) **Stalls** Low

Form RPR
2324 **1** **Silver Mitzva (IRE)**[6] 4139 3-8-13 62........(v) AshleyHamblett(5) 1 75+
(M Botti) *prom: 3rd st: led over 2f out and sn 3l clr on far rail: unchal after: eased fnl 100yds* **13/2**[3]
0-01 **2** *3½* **Smirfy's Silver**[17] 3804 3-9-0 58........ J-PGuillambert 6 64
(E S McMahon) *led: rdn and hdd over 2f out: in vain pursuit of wnr after: styd on one pce* **12/1**

3032 **3** *nk* **Lapina (IRE)**[14] 3876 3-9-4 **62**..........(b) IanMongan 7 67
(Pat Eddery) *bhd early: effrt 3f out: 3rd 2f out: rdn and nvr nr wnr: nt keen to overtake runner up ins fnl f* **9/1**

30-3 **4** *5* **Born West (USA)**[17] 3804 3-9-7 **65**.......... RyanMoore 14 62+
(P W Chapple-Hyam) *8th st: sn rdn and racing awkwardly: plodded past four btn rivals but nvr looked keen or anywhere nr ldrs* **13/2**[3]

04-3 **5** *3* **Tonnante**[16] 3825 3-9-4 **62**.......... PaulMulrennan 8 54
(Sir Mark Prescott) *sn chsng ldr: drvn 4f out: lost pl over 2f out* **5/1**[2]

0-05 **6** *1* **Salto Chico**[68] 2259 3-8-0 **47**.......... DuranFentiman(3) 9 37
(W M Brisbourne) *cl up: 4th and rdn st: no ch fnl 3f* **100/1**

0302 **7** *1* **Intensifier (IRE)**[5] 4156 3-8-8 **52** ow2..........(b) PatCosgrave 4 40
(P A Blockley) *cl up: 5th and drvn st: struggling 3f out* **9/1**

3052 **8** *2* **Mutoon (IRE)**[17] 3804 3-8-11 **55**.......... JamieSpencer 12 40
(S C Williams) *bhd tl v mod prog past struggling rivals in fnl 3f* **7/1**

0000 **9** *8* **Boz**[16] 3825 3-8-4 **48**.......... NickyMackay 13 19
(L M Cumani) *chsd ldrs: 6th and drvn st: sn no rspnse: t.o* **11/1**

400 **10** *nk* **Just Julie (USA)**[15] 3847 3-9-1 **62**.......... TravisBlock(3) 16 33
(N A Callaghan) *last pair much of way: struggling 4f out: t.o fnl 2f* **40/1**

-000 **11** *6* **Barley Moon**[13] 3913 3-8-3 **50**.......... EmmettStack(3) 2 11
(T Keddy) *7th st: sn no ch: t.o* **66/1**

560 **12** *nk* **Ful Of Grace (IRE)**[20] 3710 3-8-8 **57**.......... JamieJones(5) 11 17
(M G Quinlan) *a bhd: t.o fnl 2f* **33/1**

-004 **13** *1 1/2* **Bold Adventure**[17] 3804 3-8-5 **49**.......... RichardMullen 15 7
(W J Musson) *in midfield: shkn up after 3f: nvr gng wl after: t.o fnl 2f* **9/2**[1]

6000 **14** *3 1/2* **Dark Druid (IRE)**[22] 3652 3-8-3 **47**.......... AdrianMcCarthy 5 —
(I A Wood) *nvr bttr than midfield: t.o fnl 2f* **100/1**

0-00 **15** *3/4* **Addictive**[31] 3384 3-8-13 **57**.......... NeilPollard 3 7
(S C Williams) *prom briefly: dropped out bef st: t.o fnl 2f* **28/1**

4-00 **16** *4* **Astral Charmer**[72] 2112 3-9-2 **60**.......... JimmyQuinn 10 4
(M H Tompkins) *last pair: t.o fnl 3f* **33/1**

2m 25.23s (-2.27) **Going Correction** -0.125s/f (Firm) **16** Ran SP% **125.3**
Speed ratings (Par 98): **103,100,100,96,94 93,92,91,85,85 81,80,79,77,76 73**
CSF £81.50 CT £720.74 TOTE £6.70: £1.20, £2.70, £2.20, £2.10; EX 78.20.
Owner A Nencini **Bred** Soc Finanza Locale Consulting Srl **Trained** Newmarket, Suffolk

FOCUS
A poor three-year-old handicap, run at a fair pace. The form is rated through the second and third but does not look that solid.
Intensifier(IRE) Official explanation: jockey said colt hung left

4340 INJURED JOCKEYS FUND H'CAP — 1m 2f 21y
4:50 (4:50) (Class 6) (0-65,61) 3-Y-0+ **£2,137** (£635; £317; £158) **Stalls** Low

Form RPR

00-3 **1** **Darghan (IRE)**[62] 2423 7-9-11 **58**.......... RyanMoore 6 66+
(W J Musson) *settled in rr: stl last st: effrt on outer 3f out: swtchd lft to far rail to go 2nd 1f out: rdn, swtchd rt and led cl home: cleverly* **7/2**[1]

0064 **2** *1/2* **Billy One Punch**[10] 4031 5-10-0 **61**.......... JamieSpencer 13 68+
(G G Margarson) *in midfield: effrt over 3f out: led over 2f out and sn 3 l clr on far rail: drvn 1f out: ct nr fin* **7/2**[1]

0 **3** *3/4* **Mr Napoleon (IRE)**[20] 3705 5-9-2 **56**.......... CharlotteKerton(7) 1 61
(G Prodromou) *towards rr: rdn and effrt 2f out: sn hanging lft: kpt on wl cl home* **16/1**

3502 **4** *1* **Intavac Boy**[10] 4025 6-9-11 **58**.......... TGMcLaughlin 8 61
(S P Griffiths) *led: rdn over 3f out: hdd over 2f out: one pce fnl f* **13/2**[3]

0-34 **5** *4* **Dinner Date**[62] 2423 5-9-3 **53**.......... EmmettStack(3) 2 48
(T Keddy) *towards rr: hdwy over 3f out: rdn to go 2nd briefly 2f out: wknd 1f out* **17/2**

0060 **6** *1 1/4* **Bowl Of Cherries**[5] 4161 4-9-0 **47**..........(v) LeeEnstone 9 40
(I A Wood) *nvr bttr than midfield: drvn 3f out: fnd nil after* **25/1**

0-64 **7** *4* **Memphis Marie**[22] 3651 3-8-7 **49**.......... RichardMullen 12 34
(C N Allen) *cl up: 4th st: rdn 3f out: wknd over 1f out* **20/1**

0-00 **8** *1 1/2* **Showtime Annie**[22] 2823 6-8-12 **45**..........(b) PatCosgrave 4 27
(A Bailey) *bhd: drvn 4f out: sn struggling in last* **66/1**

0-00 **9** *1* **Gyration (IRE)**[104] 1278 3-8-6 **48**.......... PaulMulrennan 5 28
(J G Given) *t.k.h: prom: 3rd st: wknd over 2f out* **20/1**

003 **10** *4* **Dot's Delight**[17] 3800 3-8-11 **60**.......... AshleyMorgan(7) 7 32
(M H Tompkins) *in midfield: rdn and btn 4f out* **20/1**

06-1 **11** *7* **Cheveley Flyer**[23] 3616 4-9-5 **52**.......... JimmyQuinn 10 10
(J Pearce) *bhd: struggling 4f out: t.o and eased* **5/1**[2]

0005 **12** *8* **Royal Amnesty**[15] 3851 4-9-8 **55**.......... IanMongan 14 —
(G C H Chung) *prom: 5th st: rdn 3f out: btn over 2f out: t.o and heavily eased* **12/1**

000 **13** *14* **Panda Power**[31] 3387 3-8-13 **55**.......... J-PGuillambert 15 —
(S C Williams) *last away: sn rushed up into 2nd pl: rdn and fdd rapidly over 4f out: t.o and heavily eased* **40/1**

2m 7.99s (-0.11) **Going Correction** -0.125s/f (Firm)
WFA 3 from 4yo+ 9lb **13** Ran SP% **120.6**
Speed ratings (Par 101): **95,94,94,93,90 89,85,84,83,80 75,68,57**
CSF £13.60 CT £177.23 TOTE £3.40: £2.30, £1.60, £5.70; EX 12.10 Place 6 £116.24, Place 5 £97.20..
Owner S Rudolf **Bred** His Highness The Aga Khan's Studs S C **Trained** Newmarket, Suffolk

FOCUS
A moderate handicap run in a modest time. The form looks fair for the grade and sould enough with those in the frame behind the winner close to their marks.
Royal Amnesty Official explanation: jockey said colt lost its action
T/Plt: £100.30 to a £1 stake. Pool: £55,326.85. 402.30 winning tickets. T/Qpdt: £28.10 to a £1 stake. Pool: £2,317.20. 60.90 winning tickets.

4341 - 4348a (Foreign Racing) - See Raceform Interactive

4328 HAYDOCK (L-H)
Friday, August 10

OFFICIAL GOING: Good to firm (firm in places) (8.9)
Wind: Almost nil Weather: Overcast

4349 COUNTRYWIDE FREIGHT NURSERY — 5f
6:05 (6:05) (Class 4) 2-Y-0 **£4,857** (£1,445; £722; £360) **Stalls** High

Form RPR

545 **1** **Perfect Flight**[55] 2651 2-8-6 **68**.......... PaulHanagan 1 76
(M Blanshard) *chsd ldrs: wnt 2nd over 1f out: r.o to ld wl ins fnl f: rdn out* **18/1**

3311 **2** *1/2* **Look Busy (IRE)**[6] 4175 2-9-2 **81** 6ex.......... PatrickMathers(3) 5 87
(A Berry) *hung lft thrght: led: rdn over 1f out: hdd wl ins fnl f: hld after* **5/4**[1]

5552 **3** *1/2* **Upstanding**[8] 4098 2-7-12 **60**.......... DaleGibson 8 64
(M Brittain) *chsd ldr tl rdn and nt qckn over 1f out: r.o towards fin* **14/1**

31 **4** *3 1/2* **Speed Song**[17] 3823 2-9-4 **83**.......... LiamJones(3) 4 75+
(W J Haggas) *s.i.s: bhd: swtchd lft and hdwy 1f out: styd on ins fnl f: nt pce to trble front trio* **15/8**[2]

3254 **5** *1 1/4* **Carrickmacross (IRE)**[22] 3680 2-8-0 **65**..........(v[1]) AndrewMullen(3) 2 52
(E S McMahon) *s.i.s: bhd: rdn over 2f out: edgd lft over 1f out: wnt rt ins fnl f: r.o: nt pce to chal* **8/1**[3]

0050 **6** *1 1/2* **Caprima (IRE)**[6] 4173 2-7-9 **64** oh3 ow4.......... AndrewHeffernan(7) 9 46
(M Brittain) *midfield: sn pushed along: nvr gng pce to trble ldrs* **100/1**

063 **7** *3* **Linnet Park**[37] 3200 2-8-5 **67**.......... FrancisNorton 7 38
(J G Given) *racd keenly: chsd ldrs: rdn over 2f out: wknd over 1f out* **20/1**

3065 **8** *1 1/4* **Natural Rhythm (IRE)**[9] 4077 2-8-6 **68**..........(b[1]) PaulMulrennan 10 34
(Mrs A Duffield) *a towards rr: sn rdn along and nt keen: nvr on terms* **25/1**

452 **9** *3* **Tanley**[30] 3410 2-7-9 **60** oh2.......... WilliamBuick(3) 3 16
(James Moffatt) *towards rr: sn pushed along: eased whn n.d ins fnl f* **50/1**

60.51 secs (0.39) **Going Correction** -0.35s/f (Firm) **9** Ran SP% **113.8**
Speed ratings (Par 96): **98,97,96,90,88 86,81,79,74**
CSF £39.80 CT £348.38 TOTE £19.10: £2.70, £1.10, £1.90; EX 89.70.
Owner John Drew **Bred** Biddestone Stud **Trained** Upper Lambourn, Berks

FOCUS
A modest nursery, run at a solid pace. The first three came clear and the form looks solid rated around the runner-up.

NOTEBOOK
Perfect Flight got off the mark at the fourth time of asking on this nursery bow. She handled the quick ground without fuss and showed a likeable attitude under pressure when asked to win the race. A sixth furlong will not go amiss again on this evidence and she ought to have more to offer in this sphere. (op 20-1 tchd 25-1)
Look Busy(IRE), bidding for a hat-trick, showed her customary early dash yet rather spoilt her chances by continually wanting to hang left and had got very warm before the start. She was still only just picked off, however, and this was yet another improved effort under the penalty. However, she is now due to race from a 7lb higher mark in the future and life will obviously be tougher. (op Evens tchd 10-11)
Upstanding posted another sound effort in defeat and was not beaten far. She had no trouble with the quicker ground, but did leave the impression she may need a stiffer test now. (tchd 16-1)
Speed Song, making her nursery bow, was taken off her feet through the early parts after making a sluggish start. She was always up against it thereafter and was some way below the level of her maiden success here, but is certainly worthy of another chance to show her true colours in this sphere. Official explanation: jockey said, regarding the running and riding, his orders were to jump out of stalls handy and track the favourite, but filly was slowly away and unable to go the fast pace, so he was unable to be as close to the pace as he had wanted (op 2-1 tchd 7-4 and 9/4)
Carrickmacross(IRE) Official explanation: trainer said colt was unsuited by the good to firm (firm in places) ground
Caprima(IRE) did not fare badly considering her rider was putting up 3lb overweight and she was racing from 4lb out of the handicap. She would probably prefer an easier surface and could be running into some form now.

4350 EBF HAYDOCK PARK PONY CLUB MAIDEN STKS — 6f
6:35 (6:37) (Class 5) 2-Y-0 **£3,238** (£963; £481; £240) **Stalls** High

Form RPR

54 **1** **Chatham Islands (USA)**[44] 2992 2-8-12 0.......... GregFairley 4 72
(M Johnston) *w ldrs: led 1/2-way: rdn over 1f out: r.o ins fnl f and holding on* **5/1**[3]

42 **2** *nk* **Rockfield Lodge (IRE)**[16] 3849 2-9-0 0.......... WilliamBuick(3) 8 76
(J A Osborne) *chsd ldrs: edgd lft wl over 1f out: wnt 2nd 1f out: edgd lft ins fnl f: r.o* **9/4**[1]

3 *1 1/4* **Pintano** 2-9-3 0.......... TomEaves 6 72
(J Howard Johnson) *racd keenly: led: hdd 1/2-way: continued to chse wnr: rdn over 2f out: lost 2nd 1f out: nt qckn ins fnl f* **11/1**

4 *3* **Birkintastic** 2-9-3 0.......... KDarley 5 63
(B J Meehan) *s.i.s: in tch: rdn over 2f out: sn outpcd by ldrs: no imp after* **11/2**

4 **5** *1 1/2* **Diamond Lass (IRE)**[25] 3582 2-8-12 0.......... PaulHanagan 3 54
(R A Fahey) *midfield: rdn and outpcd over 2f out: n.d after* **11/4**[2]

6 *8* **Shaloo Diamond** 2-8-12 0.......... MichaelJStainton(5) 7 35
(R M Whitaker) *s.i.s: towards rr: rdn over 2f out: nvr trbld ldrs* **28/1**

7 *2 1/2* **Barawin (IRE)** 2-8-12 0.......... PhillipMakin 1 22
(K R Burke) *s.i.s: rn green and bhd: outpcd fr 1/2-way* **16/1**

8 *1/2* **Ballochroy (IRE)** 2-9-3 0.......... DaneO'Neill 2 26
(B W Hills) *s.i.s: a outpcd* **12/1**

50 **9** *16* **Quarrymaster (IRE)**[69] 2247 2-9-3 0.......... PaulMulrennan 9 —
(J Howard Johnson) *w ldr tl over 3f out: wknd over 2f out* **33/1**

1m 14.45s (0.56) **Going Correction** -0.35s/f (Firm) **9** Ran SP% **117.8**
Speed ratings (Par 94): **89,88,86,82,80 70,66,66,44**
CSF £17.02 TOTE £6.00: £1.90, £1.20, £3.10; EX 19.80.
Owner Sheikh Mohammed **Bred** Darley **Trained** Middleham Moor, N Yorks

FOCUS
An ordinary juvenile maiden which saw the first pair come clear in a tight finish.

NOTEBOOK
Chatham Islands(USA) proved game to fend off the runner-up near the line and record a first success at the third attempt. She has evidently benefitted for a short break and her yard's juveniles are in much better form now, so it could be that she has more to offer when switching to nurseries. (op 11-2 tchd 9-2, 6-1 in places)
Rockfield Lodge(IRE) did not help his rider by edging left under maximum pressure late on, but he only just gave way to the winner on this turf debut and drop to this shorter trip. He was nicely clear of the remainder, now has the option of nurseries, and should not remain a maiden for too long. (op 11-4 tchd 100-30)
Pintano, a half-brother to his stable's Algol who was a triple 6f winner at two, knew his job as he was smartly away from the gates. However, he eventually paid for refusing to settle and had no more to give at the business end. He has a future and should learn for this debut experience. (op 14-1 tchd 16-1)
Birkintastic, a 60,000gns gelding whose dam scored over hurdles, never figured after a sluggish start and looked in need of the experience. He can be expected to enjoy a step up in trip in due course and should leave this behind as he becomes more streetwise. (tchd 5-1)
Diamond Lass(IRE), fourth on debut at Ayr 25 days previously, failed to find the required change of gear to trouble the principals at any stage and has to rate somewhat disappointing. A return to softer ground could see her back in a better light, however. (tchd 3-1)

4351 LAMBRINI CLAIMING STKS — 6f
7:05 (7:08) (Class 5) 3-Y-0+ **£2,968** (£876; £438) **Stalls** High

Form RPR

0006 **1** **Ellens Academy (IRE)**[7] 4140 12-9-3 67.......... GaryBartley(7) 8 77
(E J Alston) *hld up: hdwy whn nt clr run 2f out: denied run tl appr fnl f: led 1f out: sn clr* **9/1**

020/ **2** *5* **Rydal (USA)**[289] 6-9-11 72.......... WilliamBuick(3) 4 66
(J A Osborne) *midfield: hdwy 2f out: rdn and chalng whn rdr dropped whip 1f out: wnt 2nd ins fnl f but no ch w wnr* **7/1**

3604 **3** *hd* **Marko Jadeo (IRE)**[4] 4236 9-9-5 68............................ LukeMorris(5) 13 61
(R A Harris) *s.i.s: midfield: rdn and hdwy 2f out: ev ch 1f out: nt qckn ins fnl f* **11/4**[1]
0400 **4** *1* **Beverley Beau**[51] 2761 5-8-3 42.............................. KristinStubbs(7) 14 44
(Mrs L Stubbs) *midfield: rdn over 2f out: swtchd lft and hdwy over 1f out: styd on ins fnl f: nt pce of ldrs* **50/1**
40-0 **5** *shd* **Diamond Hurricane (IRE)**[28] 3480 3-8-9 69 ow1.... StephenDonohoe 9 46
(P D Evans) *prom: led 1/2-way: sn rdn: hdd 1f out: no ex ins fnl f* **12/1**
0003 **6** *1/2* **Connect**[18] 3802 10-9-5 75..(b) PatrickHills(5) 12 56
(M H Tompkins) *towards rr: hdwy u.p whn nt clr run 2f out: one pce ins fnl f* **10/3**[2]
0005 **7** *1 1/2* **Stanley Wolfe (IRE)**[16] 3837 4-9-0 45......................... PaulHanagan 10 42
(Garry Moss) *chsd ldrs: rdn over 2f out: wknd ins fnl f* **33/1**
000 **8** *1/2* **Chairman Bobby**[51] 2761 9-8-10 45...............................(p) TonyHamilton 11 36
(D W Barker) *led to 1/2-way: rdn and hdd over 2f out: wknd ins fnl f* **25/1**
230- **9** *6* **Plush**[315] 4123 4-9-11 63..(b[1]) PJMcDonald(3) 5 36
(B P J Baugh) *s.s: a bhd* **20/1**
4100 **10** *3* **Gold Flame**[22] 3686 4-9-2 67... DaneO'Neill 3 15
(H Candy) *prom: rdn and edgd lft 2f out: wknd over 1f out* **5/1**[3]
0000 **11** *1* **Teyaar**[128] 920 11-8-9 43.. NeilChalmers(3) 6 8
(M Wellings) *prom tl rdn and wknd over 2f out* **100/1**

1m 13.59s (-0.30) **Going Correction** -0.35s/f (Firm)
WFA 3 from 4yo+ 4lb **11** Ran SP% **111.1**
Speed ratings (Par 103): **94,87,87,85,85 84,82,82,74,70 68**
CSF £56.71 TOTE £9.20: £2.00, £2.30, £1.50; EX 45.80.
Owner K Lee And I Davies **Bred** Mrs Chris Harrington **Trained** Longton, Lancs
■ Ten Shun was withdrawn (9/1, spread a plate). R4, deduct 10p in the £.
■ Stewards' Enquiry : Dane O'Neill one-day ban: careless riding (Aug 24)

FOCUS
Not a bad claimer. The veteran winner rates value for further than his comfortable winning margin.

4352 MTB GROUP H'CAP 1m 6f
7:35 (7:35) (Class 5) (0-70,69) 4-Y-0+ £2,817 (£838; £418; £209) Stalls High

Form RPR
320- **1** **Hawridge King**[26] 5506 5-9-2 67................................ JamesMillman(5) 6 72
(W S Kittow) *a.p: rdn to ld over 2f out: styd on gamely whn pressed: pushed out towards fin* **7/2**[2]
6033 **2** *1* **Squirtle (IRE)**[14] 3927 4-8-4 53...................................... LiamJones(3) 5 56
(W M Brisbourne) *s.s: in midfield after 2f: hdwy over 3f out: 2nd and str chal fr over 2f out: nt qckn towards fin* **11/2**
2104 **3** *nk* **Rudry World (IRE)**[8] 4096 4-8-0 53............................. SophieDoyle(7) 4 59+
(M Mullineaux) *hld up: hdwy 3f out: nt clr run and hmpd 2f out: swtchd rt over 1f out: r.o ins fnl f: fin strly* **12/1**
4301 **4** *1 1/4* **Cotton Eyed Joe (IRE)**[7] 4124 6-9-6 69..................... PJMcDonald(3) 7 70
(G A Swinbank) *in tch: rdn to chal over 2f out: styd on same pce fr over 1f out* **9/4**[1]
0620 **5** *hd* **My Legal Eagle (IRE)**[14] 3901 13-7-13 50 oh3........... LukeMorris(5) 11 51
(E G Bevan) *hld up: rdn and outpcd over 2f out: styd on ins fnl f: nt rch ldrs* **25/1**
-460 **6** *nk* **Figaro's Quest (IRE)**[14] 3927 5-8-4 50......................... FrancisNorton 1 51
(C N Kellett) *led: hdd over 3f out: one pce fnl f* **50/1**
0630 **7** *nk* **Synonymy**[13] 3945 4-8-6 52..(b) PaulHanagan 8 52
(M Blanshard) *prom: rdn and lost pl over 2f out: kpt on ins fnl f* **4/1**[3]
1300 **8** *1/2* **Fenners (USA)**[15] 3888 4-9-2 62...................................... DaleGibson 2 61
(M W Easterby) *midfield: rdn over 2f out: nvr able to chal* **14/1**
000/ **9** *2* **Borora**[76] 5905 8-9-2 62.. SamHitchcott 10 59
(R Lee) *hld up: pushed along over 3f out: nvr on terms* **18/1**
663- **10** *1 3/4* **Archimboldo (USA)**[17] 3454 4-9-8 68............................(b) DaneO'Neill 3 62
(T Wall) *prom: led over 3f out: rdn and hdd over 2f out: sn wknd* **20/1**

3m 7.97s (1.68) **Going Correction** -0.175s/f (Firm) **10** Ran SP% **118.6**
Speed ratings (Par 103): **88,87,87,86,86 86,86,85,84,83**
CSF £23.09 CT £210.82 TOTE £5.50: £1.90, £1.40, £3.40; EX 42.60.
Owner Eric Gadsden **Bred** Old Mill Stud **Trained** Blackborough, Devon
■ Stewards' Enquiry : P J McDonald one-day ban: careless riding (Aug 24)

FOCUS
A modest staying handicap, run at a steady early pace.

4353 BEN ROBINSON MEMORIAL H'CAP 1m 30y
8:05 (8:05) (Class 5) (0-70,70) 4-Y-0+ £3,238 (£963; £481; £240) Stalls Low

Form RPR
5361 **1** **Inside Story (IRE)**[14] 3922 5-9-4 68.........................(b) WilliamBuick(3) 15 82
(N Wilson) *hld up: swtchd rt and hdwy over 2f out: r.o to ld ins fnl f: won gng away* **8/1**
4202 **2** *3 1/2* **Society Music (IRE)**[7] 4129 5-9-9 70............................(p) PhillipMakin 2 76
(M Dods) *chsd ldrs: rdn to ld 2f out: hdd ins fnl f: nt pce of wnr* **13/2**[3]
3322 **3** *1/2* **Million Percent**[7] 4137 8-9-4 68..................................... LiamJones(3) 16 73
(C R Dore) *hld up: hdwy over 3f out: rdn over 2f out: styd on ins fnl f* **15/2**
5031 **4** *nk* **Champain Sands (IRE)**[6] 4177 8-8-10 64 6ex............. GaryBartley(7) 3 68+
(E J Alston) *s.s: hld up: hdwy whn nt clr run over 2f out: swtchd rt over 1f out: r.o ins fnl f* **4/1**[1]
4021 **5** *shd* **Esoterica (IRE)**[7] 4137 4-9-0 61 6ex...........................(b) DanielTudhope 7 65
(J S Goldie) *midfield: hdwy over 2f out: rdn over 1f out: kpt on ins fnl f* **7/1**
1313 **6** *1* **Hoh Wotanite**[7] 4129 4-9-4 70.........................(p) RussellKennemore(5) 17 72+
(R Hollinshead) *hld up: pushed along over 3f out: hdwy whn nt clr run over 1f out: styd on same pce ins fnl f* **7/1**
4500 **7** *1 1/4* **Treasure House (IRE)**[7] 4135 6-8-13 60......................... FrancisNorton 6 59
(M Blanshard) *midfield: rdn and hdwy to chse ldrs over 2f out: no ex ins fnl f* **16/1**
2112 **8** *6* **Emperor's Well**[6] 4177 8-9-2 63 6ex.................................. DaleGibson 9 48
(M W Easterby) *in tch: rdn over 2f out: wknd over 1f out* **9/2**[2]
-006 **9** *1 1/4* **Regal Dream (IRE)**[11] 4023 5-8-13 60......................... GrahamGibbons 13 42
(J W Unett) *midfield: pushed along and lost pl 4f out: no imp after* **25/1**
664 **10** *6* **Wahoo Sam (USA)**[9] 4082 7-7-9 68............................... TonyHamilton 5 36
(D W Barker) *led: rdn and hdd over 2f out: wknd over 1f out* **25/1**
3450 **11** *1 3/4* **Punta Galera (IRE)**[13] 3971 4-9-7 68..........................(p) J-PGuillambert 10 32
(Paul Green) *chsd ldrs: rdn over 3f out: wknd over 2f out* **33/1**
0-00 **12** *3/4* **Silidan**[7] 4141 4-9-1 69... PatrickDonaghy(7) 12 31
(M Brittain) *prom: rdn over 3f out: wknd 2f out* **66/1**
/0-0 **13** *26* **Ardent Prince**[28] 3487 4-8-10 57...................................... DaneO'Neill 14 —
(Heather Dalton) *s.s: a bhd* **50/1**

1m 42.79s (-2.72) **Going Correction** -0.175s/f (Firm) **13** Ran SP% **119.4**
Speed ratings (Par 103): **106,102,102,101,101 100,99,93,92,86 84,83,57**
CSF £56.54 CT £425.60 TOTE £10.50: £3.40, £2.80, £2.80; EX 82.80.
Owner Mrs N C Wilson **Bred** Arthur S Phelan **Trained** Flaxton, N Yorks

FOCUS
This modest handicap was run at a strong pace. Solid form for the grade.

4354 MAGAZINE AND HARVEY NICHOLS H'CAP 1m 30y
8:35 (8:40) (Class 5) (0-70,71) 3-Y-O £2,817 (£838; £418; £209) Stalls Low

Form RPR
0621 **1** **Caravel (IRE)**[2] 4270 3-9-11 71 6ex............................... PaulMulrennan 8 81+
(Sir Mark Prescott) *midfield: hdwy over 2f out: styd on wl to ld jst over 1f out: in command ins fnl f* **4/6**[1]
2523 **2** *1 3/4* **Just Oscar (GER)**[15] 3875 3-9-2 62.................................... DavidAllan 9 68
(W M Brisbourne) *hld up: hdwy over 2f out: rdn to take 2nd 1f out: edgd lft and kpt on ins fnl f: no imp on wnr* **14/1**
0205 **3** *2* **Cap St Jean (IRE)**[9] 4073 3-8-6 57.................... RussellKennemore(5) 17 58
(R Hollinshead) *racd keenly: hld up: hdwy 3f out: rdn over 2f out: chalng over 1f out: nt qckn ins fnl f* **16/1**
0065 **4** *1 1/4* **Motarjm (USA)**[11] 4029 3-9-4 67...............................(t) JerryO'Dwyer(3) 13 66
(H J Collingridge) *prom: led over 3f out: rdn and hdd jst over 1f out: styd on same pce ins fnl f* **10/1**[3]
6263 **5** *1 1/4* **Aussie Blue (IRE)**[9] 4078 3-8-4 55......................(b) MichaelJStainton(5) 2 51
(R M Whitaker) *led: hdd over 3f out: rdn 2f out: stl chalng over 1f out: no ex ins fnl f* **10/1**[3]
560 **6** *1 1/4* **Prince Noel**[24] 3611 3-7-13 52 ow2.............................(b[1]) LanceBetts(7) 1 45
(N Wilson) *trckd ldrs: rdn over 2f out: edgd rt and lft over 1f out: one pce ins fnl f* **50/1**
0504 **7** *4* **Soldier Field**[9] 4064 3-9-1 61.. FrancisNorton 10 45
(A M Balding) *hld up: rdn over 2f out: sme hdwy over 1f out: nvr rchd ldrs* **18/1**
0565 **8** *5* **Caluba**[37] 3202 3-9-0 60.. PhillipMakin 6 32
(K R Burke) *midfield: hdwy over 4f out: rdn to chal over 2f out: wknd 1f out* **50/1**
0442 **9** *5* **Fistral**[27] 3535 3-8-4 50 oh2... DaleGibson 4 11
(J Hetherton) *a bhd* **33/1**
-501 **10** *1 1/2* **Alberts Story (USA)**[12] 3997 3-8-8 54 6ex...................... PaulHanagan 3 11
(R A Fahey) *midfield: rdn over 3f out: wknd over 2f out* **9/2**[2]
0016 **11** *10* **Leonard Charles**[34] 3299 3-9-5 68...............................(p) LiamJones(3) 15 —
(C R Dore) *trckd ldrs tl rdn and wknd over 2f out* **28/1**

1m 43.95s (-1.56) **Going Correction** -0.175s/f (Firm) **11** Ran SP% **124.5**
Speed ratings (Par 100): **100,98,96,95,93 92,88,83,78,77 67**
CSF £13.34 CT £101.24 TOTE £1.90: £1.20, £2.40, £4.00; EX 16.80 Place 6 £70.21, Place 5 £41.41..
Owner Neil Greig - Osborne House **Bred** G A M Grothier **Trained** Newmarket, Suffolk

FOCUS
A moderate three-year-old handicap won by a progressive sort. Sound enough form.
Alberts Story(USA) Official explanation: jockey said gelding was never travelling
T/Plt: £48.80 to a £1 stake. Pool: £66,943.85. 1,001.00 winning tickets. T/Qpdt: £15.70 to a £1 stake. Pool: £4,562.95. 215.00 winning tickets. DO

4160 LINGFIELD (L-H)
Friday, August 10

OFFICIAL GOING: Turf - good to firm (9.2); aw - standard
Wind: Nil Weather: Sunny, very warm

4355 CHRIS WOTTON CUP H'CAP 1m 2f
2:15 (2:15) (Class 6) (0-65,60) 3-Y-0+ £2,047 (£604; £302) Stalls Low

Form RPR
0000 **1** **Border Edge**[9] 4063 9-9-8 54..(b) NCallan 2 65
(J J Bridger) *mde all: drew 4l clr over 3f out: drvn 2f out: kpt on gamely* **20/1**
6234 **2** *1 1/2* **Chia (IRE)**[31] 3407 4-9-12 58... RobertHavlin 3 66
(D Haydn Jones) *mounted on crse: dwlt: hld up towards rr: prog wl over 2f out: drvn to chse wnr jst over 1f out: hanging lft and nt qckn* **8/1**
3050 **3** *1/2* **Alsadaa (USA)**[39] 3155 4-10-0 60..................................... IanMongan 12 67
(Mrs L J Mongan) *hld up towards rr: rdn and prog over 2f out: kpt on to take 3rd ins fnl f: nvr able to chal* **7/1**[3]
4022 **4** *1 1/4* **Ciccone**[6] 4161 4-9-9 55.. FergusSweeney 4 60
(G L Moore) *sn chsd ldng trio: prog to chse wnr wl over 2f out: sn rdn: no imp and lost 2nd jst over 1f out* **7/2**[1]
1304 **5** *3* **Fantasy Crusader**[2] 4266 8-9-6 52...................................... AdamKirby 13 51
(R M H Cowell) *hld up in midfield: effrt over 2f out: drvn and no imp on ldrs over 1f out* **4/1**[2]
00-0 **6** *2 1/2* **Unasuming (IRE)**[7] 4131 4-9-4 50...............................(p) JimmyQuinn 1 44
(J Pearce) *trckd ldng pair: chsd wnr over 3f out to wl over 2f out: wknd u.p over 1f out* **66/1**
-050 **7** *nk* **Sunburn (IRE)**[29] 3456 3-9-4 59.. JimCrowley 14 52
(Mrs A J Perrett) *dwlt: dropped in fr wd draw and hld up in rr: rdn and no real imp on ldrs over 2f out* **16/1**
4055 **8** *shd* **Paymaster General (IRE)**[29] 3469 3-9-4 59.................. MartinDwyer 9 52
(M D I Usher) *trckd ldrs: rdn and effrt on outer over 2f out: sn no prog: wknd over 1f out* **7/1**[3]
6304 **9** *2* **Kirkhammerton (IRE)**[14] 3922 5-8-9 48......................(b) RobbieEgan(7) 5 37
(A J McCabe) *hld up in rr: stmbld 5f out: rdn and no real prog 3f out* **33/1**
000/ **10** *hd* **Panadin (IRE)**[599] 6612 5-9-1 47..(p) LPKeniry 7 35
(Mrs L C Jewell) *prom: taking t.k.h over 4f out: losing pl whn squeezed out over 2f out: wknd* **66/1**
0001 **11** *3/4* **Takes Tutu (USA)**[20] 3730 8-9-10 56.............................. JamieSpencer 8 43
(C R Dore) *lw: dwlt: hld up in last: detached fr remainder over 4f out: brief effrt 3f out: sn no prog* **8/1**
6300 **12** *hd* **Sixfields Flyer (IRE)**[56] 2635 3-8-9 57..............................(p) KMay(7) 11 43
(Pat Eddery) *a wl in rr: rdn and struggling 3f out* **25/1**
4006 **13** *8* **Chapter (IRE)**[6] 4161 5-9-5 51..(b) TQuinn 6 21
(Mrs A L M King) *chsd wnr over 3f out: wknd rapidly 2f out* **8/1**
0-00 **14** *15* **Soizic (NZ)**[16] 3851 5-10-0 60.. GeorgeBaker 10 —
(L A Dace) *a in rr: rn wd bnd over 3f out: sn btn: eased over 1f out: t.o* **50/1**

2m 8.63s (-1.09) **Going Correction** -0.075s/f (Good)
WFA 3 from 4yo+ 9lb **14** Ran SP% **122.9**
Speed ratings (Par 101): **101,99,99,98,96 94,93,93,92,91 91,91,84,72**
CSF £168.78 CT £1255.45 TOTE £23.70: £7.20, £2.50, £2.90; EX 192.20 TRIFECTA Not won..
Owner Allsorts **Bred** R Hutt **Trained** Liphook, Hants
■ Stewards' Enquiry : K May caution: used whip when out of contention

FOCUS
This moderate handicap was run at a strong pace and few got into it. The form could be slightly better but the winner tends to limit it.
Alsadaa(USA) Official explanation: jockey said gelding suffered interference in running

Soizic(NZ) Official explanation: trainer said mare was unsuited by the track

4356 THE BRIEFCASE BLUES BROTHERS LIVE AT LINGFIELDPARK.CO.UK H'CAP 1m 3f 106y

2:45 (2:45) (Class 5) (0-70,69) 3-Y-O+ **£2,817** (£838; £418; £209) **Stalls** High

Form RPR

0030 **1** **Muraco**[32] 3367 3-9-4 **69**........ MartinDwyer 6 74
(R M Beckett) *prog fr rr to trck ldr after 3f: led over 4f out: rdn and jnd over 3f out: edgd rt 2f out: hld on* **9/4**[1]

-003 **2** *shd* **Cormorant Wharf (IRE)**[62] 2467 7-10-0 **69**........ JimCrowley 4 74
(T E Powell) *lw: s.i.s and pushed along early: prog fr rr 1/2-way: wnt 2nd 4f out and sn jnd wnr: upsides fnl 3f: drvn and fnd little: jst hld* **3/1**[2]

0404 **3** *2 1/2* **Trifti**[13] 3945 6-8-9 **50** oh2........ EddieAhern 8 51
(C A Cyzer) *lw: wl in tch: hrd rdn to chse ldng pair wl over 2f out: cl enough over 1f out: nt qckn* **7/2**[3]

0-05 **4** *1 1/2* **Zirkel (IRE)**[73] 2113 4-9-8 **63**........ NCallan 3 62
(Mrs A L M King) *trckd ldr 3f: styd cl up: rdn 3f out: nt qckn and hld fnl 2f* **7/2**[3]

06-6 **5** *2* **Rashida**[28] 3485 5-8-10 **51**........ TPO'Shea 7 46
(S Lycett) *sn settled in rr: 6th over 4f out: rdn and one pce fr 3f out* **8/1**

000 **6** *7* **Winforjoe (IRE)**[37] 3214 3-7-13 **50** oh5........ FrankieMcDonald 5 34
(J J Bridger) *sn restrained to last: detached over 4f out: n.d after* **50/1**

00-0 **7** *1 3/4* **Liameliss**[66] 1925 5-8-9 **50** oh5........(t) PaulDoe 1 31
(M A Allen) *led to over 4f out: wknd wl over 2f out* **66/1**

2m 32.45s (2.53) **Going Correction** -0.075s/f (Good)
WFA 3 from 4yo+ 10lb **7** Ran SP% **114.8**
Speed ratings (Par 103): **87,86,85,84,82 77,76**
CSF £9.39 CT £22.01 TOTE £2.90: £1.30, £2.20; EX 9.00 Trifecta £28.20 Pool £673.78 - 16.91 winning units..
Owner D & J Newell **Bred** D J And Mrs Newell **Trained** Whitsbury, Hants
■ Stewards' Enquiry : Frankie McDonald caution: used whip when out of contention

FOCUS
Another moderate handicap but poor form rated through the runner-up. The first pair came clear in a bobbing finish.

4357 LINGFIELD PARK GOLF CLUB MAIDEN STKS 1m 6f

3:15 (3:16) (Class 5) 3-Y-O+ **£2,817** (£838; £418; £209) **Stalls** High

Form RPR

4362 **1** **Natural Action**[43] 3041 3-9-0 70........ JamieSpencer 9 70
(W Jarvis) *cl up: wnt 3rd 3f out and trckd ldr over 2f out: looked less than keen to overtake: drvn ahd jst ins fnl f* **11/4**[3]

4640 **2** *1 1/4* **Dig Gold (USA)**[13] 3964 3-9-0 70........ NCallan 13 68
(M A Jarvis) *lw: t.k.h early: trckd ldrs: wnt 2nd over 3f out: led wl over 2f out: sn rdn: plugged on one pce: hdd jst ins fnl f* **5/2**[2]

006 **3** *1 1/2* **Fraternal**[73] 2127 3-9-0 73........ MartinDwyer 12 66
(R Charlton) *mde most: drvn and hdd wl over 2f out: nt qckn and sn in 3rd: kpt on same pce* **5/1**

2234 **4** *6* **Snake's Head**[32] 3367 3-8-9 69........ EddieAhern 15 53
(J L Dunlop) *w ldr for 2f: settled bhd ldrs: rdn 3f out: easily outpcd sn after* **9/4**[1]

64 **5** *5* **Pertemps Power**[24] 3621 3-9-0 0........ JimmyQuinn 11 51
(A D Smith) *t.k.h: hld up: lost tch w ldrs over 4f out but stl gng wl enough: outpcd fr 3f out* **33/1**

0 **6** *5* **Welsh Guard (USA)**[36] 3236 4-9-13 0........ AdamKirby 2 44
(G P Enright) *in tch: str reminders 6f out: lft bhd fr 3f out* **33/1**

00 **7** *11* **Running Rings**[14] 3908 3-8-9 0........ RobertHavlin 10 23
(P W D'Arcy) *s.s: in tch to over 3f out: wknd* **66/1**

8 *1* **Inching West**[105] 5-9-8 0........ PaulEddery 14 22
(C J Down) *dwlt: jnd ldr after 2f: rdn over 5f out: lost 2nd over 3f out: sn wknd* **66/1**

9 *11* **Lagan Legend**[66] 6-9-8 0........(bt) RichardThomas 6 6
(Dr J R J Naylor) *mostly last and sn in trble: t.o over 3f out* **33/1**

3m 10.64s (3.72) **Going Correction** -0.075s/f (Good)
WFA 3 from 4yo+ 13lb **9** Ran SP% **114.5**
Speed ratings (Par 103): **86,85,84,81,78 75,69,68,62**
CSF £9.63 TOTE £4.10: £1.40, £1.30, £1.90; EX 11.60 Trifecta £30.30 Pool £467.37 - 10.95 winning units..
Owner H J W Steckmest And Partners **Bred** Darley **Trained** Newmarket, Suffolk

FOCUS
A modest staying maiden. The form looks straightforward enough but the proximity of the fifth and sixth raises doubts.
Welsh Guard(USA) Official explanation: jockey said gelding was never travelling

4358 BNY MELLON ASSET SERVICING NOVICE STKS 5f (P)

3:45 (3:45) (Class 4) 2-Y-O **£3,886** (£1,156; £577; £288) **Stalls** High

Form RPR

6 **1** **Toolittleyourlate (USA)**[16] 3834 2-8-12 0........ NCallan 3 76
(K A Ryan) *w'like: str: mde all: drvn over 1f out: hld on nr fin* **5/2**[2]

2 *hd* **Safari Time (IRE)** 2-8-4 0........ FrankieMcDonald 4 67
(P Winkworth) *leggy: t.k.h: sn trckd wnr: rdn 2f out: green over 1f out: styd on ins fnl f and gaining at fin* **16/1**

0431 **3** *1/2* **Lord Deevert**[65] 2356 2-8-5 66........ JackDean[(7)] 5 73
(W G M Turner) *chsd ldng pair: rdn over 2f out: outpcd wl over 1f out: styd on again fnl f* **11/1**[3]

1500 **4** *1/2* **Enodoc**[10] 4046 2-9-2 90........ MartinDwyer 2 75
(W R Muir) *trckd ldng pair: rdn 2f out: cl enough on outer over 1f out: nt qckn* **2/1**[1]

2154 **5** *2 1/2* **Diademas (USA)**[27] 3562 2-9-2 81........ JamieSpencer 1 66
(J A Osborne) *hld up in last: brief effrt on inner over 1f out: wknd ins fnl f* **2/1**[1]

60.53 secs (0.75) **Going Correction** -0.025s/f (Stan) **5** Ran SP% **109.5**
Speed ratings (Par 96): **93,92,91,91,87**
CSF £32.59 TOTE £3.10: £1.60, £5.20; EX 50.00.
Owner Mrs T Marnane **Bred** John D Gunther **Trained** Hambleton, N Yorks

FOCUS
A modest novice stakes run in a slow time and form to be cautious about.

NOTEBOOK
Toolittleyourlate(USA), who attracted market support when only sixth on debut at Catterick 16 days previously, showed his true colours on this switch to a sounder surface and proved game in making all. He has an awful long way to go still if he is to justify his Group 1 entry, but he is clearly open to more improvement and will not mind returning to 6f now on this evidence. (op 2-1 tchd 11-4)
Safari Time(IRE) ◆ took time to settle through the early parts and ran green when asked for her effort, but still only just failed to post a winning debut. She looks sure to improve a deal for this experience and no doubt has prizes within her compass this season. (op 25-1)
Lord Deevert, winner of a seller over course and distance 65 days previously, hit a flat spot before staying on again at the business end and ran creditably in this better company. He looks well worth a try in nursery company from his current rating and clearly likes this venue. (op 12-1 tchd 10-1)
Enodoc, markedly down in grade for this All-Weather bow, had every chance yet failed to quicken where it mattered. This was a more encouraging effort in defeat and he has clearly now found his sort of level, with a sixth furlong now likely to suit him better. (op 5-2 tchd 15-8)
Diademas(USA), who only success to date came at Southwell in May, looked ready to mount a big challenge to the leaders when asked for his effort nearing the final furlong pole. However, his effort proved very short lived and indeed something may well have been amiss with him. Official explanation: trainer had no explanation for the poor form shown (tchd 15-8)

4359 THE REAL THING LIVE HERE TOMORROW NIGHT FILLIES' (S) STKS 6f (P)

4:15 (4:28) (Class 6) 2-Y-O **£2,047** (£604; £302) **Stalls** Low

Form RPR

000 **1** **Loose Caboose (IRE)**[14] 3916 2-8-5 42........(p) RobbieEgan[(7)] 11 56
(A J McCabe) *racd v wd thrght: led after 1f: mde most after: urged along and drew clr ins fnl f* **33/1**

2 *2* **Bollywood Style** 2-8-12 0........ JimCrowley 7 50+
(P Winkworth) *w'like: rn green: chsd ldrs: pushed along fr 1/2-way: picked up over 1f out: r.o to go 2nd last 150yds: no imp wnr* **12/1**[3]

004 **3** *2* **Naming Problems**[14] 3923 2-8-12 51........(b[1]) NCallan 4 44
(K J Burke) *trckd ldrs: cl 4th on inner 2f out: sn nt qckn: kpt on same pce fnl f* **12/1**[3]

006 **4** *shd* **Whistful Miss**[14] 3923 2-8-12 47........ IanMongan 10 44
(P Howling) *w ldrs: upsides 2f out: stl chalng 1f out: wknd* **22/1**

3400 **5** *5* **Miss Willoughby**[11] 4027 2-8-10 49........ FrankiePickard[(7)] 6 34
(J Ryan) *rrd s: sn wl bhd in last: plugged on fnl 2f: no ch* **33/1**

026 **6** *1/2* **Tenjack Queen (IRE)**[30] 3417 2-8-12 71........ JamieSpencer 1 34+
(J A Osborne) *lw: racd on inner: led for 1f: w ldrs: upsides 2f out: rdn over 1f out: sn btn: eased* **2/5**[1]

000 **7** *13* **Beyabi**[36] 3245 2-8-12 45........(v[1]) EddieAhern 3 —
(J R Jenkins) *last and bhd fr 1/2-way* **16/1**

002 **P** **Ely Une (IRE)**[1] 4311 2-8-12 0........ MartinDwyer 8 —
(J S Moore) *reluctant to enter stalls: lost action bdly after 100yds and p.u* **6/1**[2]

1m 14.33s (1.52) **Going Correction** -0.025s/f (Stan) **8** Ran SP% **117.2**
Speed ratings (Par 89): **88,85,82,82,75 75,57,—**
CSF £372.19 TOTE £40.00: £11.70, £3.10, £2.40; EX 585.20 TRIFECTA Not won..There was no bid for the winner. Tenjack Queen (no.10) was claimed by Miss Tor Sturgis for £6,000.
Owner Paul J Dixon & Greg McCabe **Bred** Paradime Ltd **Trained** Babworth, Notts
■ Robbie Egan's first winner in Britain. Madam Superior was withdrawn (40/1, refused to go to post). No Rule 4.

FOCUS
A very weak fillies' seller with the third and fourth slightly off recent form. The winner could rate a little higher.

NOTEBOOK
Loose Caboose(IRE), equipped with first-time cheekpieces, came through to score readily enough under her young jockey and got off the mark at the fourth time of asking. The drop into this grade and the application of the headgear clearly worked the oracle. Indeed she could have a little more to offer back in better company when reverting to a more galloping track. (op 40-1 tchd 50-1)
Bollywood Style, nibbled at in the betting ring, proved too green to do herself full justice and left the impression she would come on a deal for this debut experience. She is clearly only of moderate ability, but has one of these within her compass. (op 16-1)
Naming Problems showed a bit more in the first-time blinkers, but lacked any sort of gear change when push came to shove over this shorter trip. (op 14-1)
Whistful Miss failed to raise her game on this drop to 6f and, if anything, a try over the minimum trip now looks warranted. (op 20-1)
Tenjack Queen(IRE), down in grade and the clear form pick, was beaten passing the final furlong marker. This has to rate hugely disappointing and she is obviously going backwards fast. Official explanation: trainer had no explanation for the poor form shown (op 1-2 tchd 8-15 in a place)
Ely Une(IRE), second at Bath 24 hours previously, took time to consent to go forward and then went wrong quickly from the gates. Official explanation: jockey said filly badly lost its action (op 5-1)

4360 LINGFIELDPARK.CO.UK H'CAP 6f (P)

4:45 (4:52) (Class 4) (0-85,85) 3-Y-O **£4,857** (£1,445; £722; £360) **Stalls** Low

Form RPR

2654 **1** **Golden Desert (IRE)**[13] 3944 3-9-2 **80**........(v) AdamKirby 9 86
(T G Mills) *lw: dwlt: rousted along to ld: drvn at least 2l clr 2f out: styd on wl: unchal* **6/1**[3]

1400 **2** *1* **Teen Ager (FR)**[13] 3944 3-8-13 **77**........ LPKeniry 5 80+
(J S Moore) *taken down early: dwlt: hld up in last pair: prog over 1f out: r.o to take 2nd last 75yds: unable to chal* **10/1**

023 **3** *nk* **Fabuleux Millie (IRE)**[13] 3944 3-9-1 **79**........ GeorgeBaker 6 81
(R M Beckett) *lw: hld up in midfield: drvn and nt qckn over 1f out: r.o to go 2nd briefly ins fnl f: no real imp on wnr* **5/1**[2]

2103 **4** *nk* **Buxton**[51] 2769 3-9-2 **80**........ RobertHavlin 8 81
(R Ingram) *hld up bhd ldrs: prog to chse wnr wl over 1f out to ins fnl f: one pce* **16/1**

-146 **5** *nk* **Shustraya**[30] 3418 3-9-4 **82**........ EddieAhern 4 82
(P J Makin) *hld up in last trio: prog over 2f out: clsd on ldrs over 1f out: one pce ins fnl f* **13/2**

4506 **6** *1* **Dubai Magic (USA)**[38] 3188 3-8-13 **77**........ HayleyTurner 2 74
(C E Brittain) *prom on inner: disp 2nd wl over 1f out: wknd ins fnl f* **12/1**

1-42 **7** *hd* **My Love Thomas (IRE)**[65] 2363 3-8-12 **76**........ JamieSpencer 3 73
(E A L Dunlop) *dwlt: hld up in last: prog on inner over 1f out: effrt petered out and eased last 75yds* **11/4**[1]

1136 **8** *hd* **Pusey Street Lady**[20] 3746 3-9-7 **85**........ JimCrowley 10 81
(J Gallagher) *racd wd in midfield: lost pl over 2f out and sn outpcd in last trio: kpt on fnl f* **10/1**

6-64 **9** *3 1/2* **Minaash (USA)**[200] 216 3-8-5 **74**........ AhmedAjtebi[(5)] 1 60
(D M Simcock) *nvr bttr than midfield on inner: wknd over 1f out* **33/1**

343- **10** *nk* **Onenightinlisbon (IRE)**[237] 6846 3-9-0 **78**........ NCallan 7 63
(K R Burke) *bit bkwd: trckd ldrs on outer: lost pl 2f out: sn btn* **11/1**

0535 **11** *7* **Tudor Prince (IRE)**[16] 3857 3-9-3 **81**........(b[1]) MartinDwyer 11 45
(B J Meehan) *mostly chsd wnr to wl over 1f out: wknd rapidly* **16/1**

1m 12.02s (-0.79) **Going Correction** -0.025s/f (Stan) **11** Ran SP% **119.9**
Speed ratings (Par 102): **104,102,102,101,101 100,99,99,94,94 85**
CSF £66.07 CT £327.15 TOTE £8.30: £2.30, £3.50, £2.30; EX 113.40 Trifecta £282.30 Part won. Pool £397.64 - 0.34 winning units..
Owner S Parker **Bred** Mervyn Stewkesbury **Trained** Headley, Surrey

FOCUS
A fair three-year-old handicap, run at a sound-enough pace with the form rated around the winner and third, and backed up by the fourth.

My Love Thomas(IRE) Official explanation: jockey said filly hung left

4361 BOOK ONLINE FOR DISCOUNTED PRICES FILLIES' H'CAP 7f (P)

5:15 (5:18) (Class 6) (0-65,65) 3-Y-0+ £2,047 (£604; £302) Stalls Low

Form RPR

0600 **1** **Meditation**[16] 3851 5-9-9 **61** JamesDoyle 14 72
(I A Wood) *off the pce in midfield early: prog over 2f out: rdn and r.o over 1f out: led last 75yds* **20/1**

4440 **2** 1 1/4 **Baby Dordan (IRE)**[38] 3178 3-9-2 **60** LPKeniry 7 66
(H J L Dunlop) *prom: drvn and effrt over 2f out: led jst over 1f out: hdd & wknd last 75yds* **9/1**

0000 **3** 1 1/2 **Nikki Bea (IRE)**[4] 4236 4-9-8 **60** PaulDoe 4 64
(Jamie Poulton) *ldng trio: rdn over 2f out: nt qckn over 1f out: styd on ins fnl f* **7/1**[3]

2203 **4** 1/2 **Lii Najma**[17] 3826 4-9-8 **65** AhmedAjtebi(5) 10 68
(C E Brittain) *chsd ldrs: rdn over 2f out: kpt on fr over 1f out: nt pce to rch ldrs* **3/1**[1]

5032 **5** 1 **Dasheena**[11] 4021 4-8-6 **51** (be) RobbieEgan(7) 3 51
(A J McCabe) *stmbld s: bdly hmpd in last trio over 5f out: wl bhd after: r.o fnl 2f: fin wl* **6/1**[2]

0-00 **6** 3/4 **Julatten (IRE)**[1] 4319 3-8-3 **47** RichardThomas 12 43
(D J Murphy) *mostly chsd ldr: drvn to ld briefly over 1f out: wknd ins fnl f* **16/1**

2053 **7** 1 **Scarlet Oak**[32] 3369 3-9-5 **63** AdamKirby 2 56
(D J S Ffrench Davis) *s.v.s: wl off the pce in last trio: sme prog into midfield 3f out but nvr on terms* **10/1**

0602 **8** 3 **Day By Day**[23] 3646 3-9-2 **60** (b) MartinDwyer 6 45
(B J Meehan) *led at str pce: hdd over 1f out: wknd rapidly* **7/1**[3]

-000 **9** nk **Tokyo Jo (IRE)**[17] 3826 3-9-0 **58** TGMcLaughlin 5 42
(T T Clement) *pushed along towards rr over 4f out and struggling: nvr a factor: no ch whn nt clr run briefly 2f out* **50/1**

-005 **10** 1/2 **Sunny Afternoon**[29] 3451 7-8-1 **46** RichardRowe(7) 13 31
(R Rowe) *a off the pce towards rr: no ch whn carried v wd bnd 2f out* **40/1**

0006 **11** hd **Early Promise (IRE)**[6] 4164 3-8-6 **57** HaddenFrost(7) 9 39
(Mrs A L M King) *hld up: sn outpcd and wl bhd: nvr threatened after* **33/1**

5053 **12** 6 **Imperial Lucky (IRE)**[93] 1588 4-9-13 **65** JimCrowley 8 33
(D K Ivory) *chsd ldrs: u.p fr 3f out: wknd rapidly on inner 2f out* **7/1**[3]

4300 **13** 8 **Tabulate**[13] 3946 4-9-8 **60** IanMongan 1 7
(P Howling) *hmpd in last trio over 5f out: wl bhd after: c v wd bnd 2f out: t.o* **12/1**

1m 24.84s (-1.05) **Going Correction** -0.025s/f (Stan)
WFA 3 from 4yo+ 6lb **13** Ran SP% **121.6**
Speed ratings (Par 98): **105,103,101,101,100 99,98,94,94,93 93,86,77**
CSF £188.50 CT £1455.70 TOTE £30.20: £6.50, £3.60, £3.20; EX 241.50 TRIFECTA Not won. Place 6 £495.76, Place 5 £124.66..
Owner Paddy Barrett **Bred** P E Barrett **Trained** Upper Lambourn, Berks

FOCUS
A modest fillies' handicap, run at a fair pace, and solid form rated around the placed horses.
Meditation Official explanation: trainer's rep said, regarding the improved form shown, today was a drop in class for mare
Scarlet Oak Official explanation: jockey said filly missed the break
Tabulate Official explanation: jockey said filly didn't face the kickback and hung right
T/Plt: £666.70 to a £1 stake. Pool: £66,586.90. 72.90 winning tickets. T/Qpdt: £46.50 to a £1 stake. Pool: £4,636.10. 73.70 winning tickets. JN

4166
NEWMARKET (JULY) (R-H)
Friday, August 10

OFFICIAL GOING: Good to firm (8.7)
Wind: Almost nil Weather: Fine and sunny

4362 WILSON BROWNE MAIDEN STKS 7f

5:45 (5:48) (Class 4) 2-Y-0 £4,533 (£1,348; £674; £336) Stalls Low

Form RPR

1 **Tanweer (USA)** 2-9-3 0 RHills 16 83+
(Sir Michael Stoute) *hld up: hdwy over 1f out: hung lft ins fnl f: r.o to ld nr fin* **4/1**[2]

2 nk **The Which Doctor** 2-9-3 0 TPQueally 12 76
(J Noseda) *hld up in tch: rdn to ld 1f out: hdd nr fin* **33/1**

3 shd **Swift Gift** 2-9-3 0 NickyMackay 8 76
(B J Meehan) *chsd ldrs: led over 1f out: sn rdn and hdd: styd on* **50/1**

4 1 **Lodi (IRE)** 2-9-3 0 SteveDrowne 1 73
(B J Meehan) *chsd ldrs: rdn and ev ch over 1f out: styd on same pce ins fnl f* **40/1**

5 3/4 **Dusk** 2-9-3 0 KerrinMcEvoy 4 71+
(J L Dunlop) *s.i.s: hld up: hdwy over 2f out: rdn over 1f out: styd on* **18/1**

6 hd **Hadron Collider (FR)** 2-9-3 0 RichardHughes 11 71
(R Hannon) *chsd ldrs: rdn over 1f out: styd on same pce* **16/1**

7 nk **Conduit (IRE)** 2-9-3 0 RyanMoore 2 70+
(Sir Michael Stoute) *prom: rdn over 1f out: styd on* **7/1**[3]

8 shd **It's A Date** 2-9-0 0 RichardKingscote(3) 20 70
(A King) *hld up: hdwy over 1f out: nt rch ldrs* **50/1**

9 hd **Bigalo's Magic (UAE)** 2-9-3 0 TPO'Shea 13 69
(E J O'Neill) *chsd ldrs: rdn over 2f out: styd on same pce fnl f* **33/1**

10 3/4 **Silver Rime (FR)** 2-9-3 0 PatDobbs 19 67
(R Hannon) *hld up: hdwy over 1f out: nt trble ldrs* **33/1**

11 1/2 **Sinbad The Sailor** 2-9-3 0 TQuinn 17 66
(J W Hills) *hld up: hdwy over 1f out: no ex ins fnl f* **66/1**

12 1 1/2 **Enroller (IRE)** 2-9-3 0 RichardMullen 3 62
(W R Muir) *chsd ldr: led 5f out: hdd over 3f out: wknd fnl f* **50/1**

13 hd **Vineyard** 2-9-3 0 MichaelHills 6 61
(W J Haggas) *led: hdd 5f out: led again over 3f out: hdd over 1f out: wknd fnl f* **20/1**

14 hd **Yaddree** 2-9-3 0 PhilipRobinson 14 61
(M A Jarvis) *chsd ldrs: rdn over 2f out: edgd lft and wknd over 1f out* **9/1**

15 1 1/4 **Dream Green (IRE)** 2-9-3 0 JHBowman 15 57
(M R Channon) *prom: rdn over 2f out: wknd over 1f out* **25/1**

16 1/2 **Sun** 2-9-3 0 OscarUrbina 18 56
(P W Chapple-Hyam) *s.i.s: hld up: rdn over 2f out: a in rr* **14/1**

17 2 **Woodcutter (IRE)** 2-9-3 0 JimmyFortune 7 51
(J H M Gosden) *prom over 5f* **7/2**[1]

18 1 3/4 **Swaziland** 2-9-3 0 TedDurcan 10 46
(J Noseda) *s.i.s: hld up: wknd over 1f out* **12/1**

19 3 1/2 **Memphis City (USA)** 2-9-3 0 LDettori 5 36
(J Noseda) *s.s: hld up: sme hdwy 1/2-way: wknd over 2f out* **10/1**

20 3 1/2 **Port Quin** 2-9-3 0 MickyFenton 9 27
(G Wragg) *s.i.s: hdwy 4f out: hung lft and wknd 2f out* **50/1**

1m 26.59s (-0.19) **Going Correction** -0.075s/f (Good) **20** Ran SP% **128.5**
Speed ratings (Par 96): **98,97,97,96,95 95,94,94,94,93 93,91,91,91,89 89,86,84,80,76**
CSF £145.71 TOTE £5.70: £2.00, £10.90, £15.80; EX 287.00.
Owner Hamdan Al Maktoum **Bred** Betty L Mabee And Larry Mabee **Trained** Newmarket, Suffolk

FOCUS
A maiden for unraced juveniles, contested by colts and geldings and, although the time was much slower than the fast-run nursery, it was faster than the seller and about right for the grade and is ratred as average for now. The runners were spread across the track in the latter stages.

NOTEBOOK
Tanweer(USA) ◆, a $320,000 half-brother to a couple of prolific winners in the USA, made a taking winning debut. He came from off the pace and picked up well up the hill to catch the runner-up. He has a Derby and Dewhurst entry, so is clearly well thought-of, and should go on to better things. (op 11-2)
The Which Doctor ◆, whose dam won at this trip as a juvenile, is a half-brother to a 12f winner. His stable's juveniles have been going well, but this one was clearly unfancied and ran a fine race, only losing out close home. He should be capable of winning his maiden at least. (op 40-1)
Swift Gift, a half-brother to a couple of decent sorts in Piano Player and Morning Farewell, is from a yard whose juveniles have appeared more forward for their first outings than in previous seasons but even so he was unconsidered in the betting. He showed up throughout and stuck on well up the climb to the line, and is another who should not be long in getting off the mark.
Lodi(IRE), another from the Meehan yard and a half-brother to winners at six and 12f, is by a sprinter and ran quite well to finish on the heels of the placed horses. He looked as if he would come on a fair amount for the experience. (op 50-1)
Dusk, from the family of Crystal Gazing, missed the break by finished quite well under a considerate ride and looks the sort who will make up into a decent three-year-old, although that does not preclude him being able to win this season. (op 25-1)
Hadron Collider(FR), a 90,000euros half-brother to a couple of winners at 1m-10f in France, showed up for a long way and will be suited by another couple of furlongs in time (op 20-1)
Conduit(IRE), related to the stable's Hard Top and from the family of Spectrum, has a Royal Lodge and Derby entry. He ran reasonably but looks another who will come into his own next season. (tchd 11-2)
It's A Date is by a sprinter but related to a number of middle-distance performers and so this was not a bad effort.
Bigalo's Magic(UAE), from the family of top US mare Flawlessly, was making his debut for a trainer who does well with his juveniles. However, they usually do not go unbacked when scoring and this one was not 'expected', so connections will have been pleased with this debut.
Woodcutter(IRE), a 170,000 euros half-brother to Chelsea Rose, was backed in to favourite but performed well below expectations. He has clearly shown something at home and can be expected to leave this effort behind in time. Official explanation: jockey said colt was unsuited by the good to firm ground (op 11-4)

4363 HEADLAND INTERNATIONAL (S) STKS 7f

6:15 (6:16) (Class 4) 2-Y-0 £3,886 (£1,156; £577; £288) Stalls Low

Form RPR

40 **1** **Tuanku (IRE)**[13] 3951 2-8-13 0 JHBowman 9 64
(M R Channon) *hld up in tch: rdn to ld over 1f out: r.o* **4/1**[2]

60 **2** 1 1/2 **Bridge Of Fermoy (IRE)**[13] 3962 2-8-13 0 LDettori 10 60
(N A Callaghan) *stdd s: bhd: hdwy over 1f out: sn rdn: styd on same pce ins fnl f* **20/1**

663 **3** 3/4 **What's For Tea**[16] 3835 2-8-5 55 RichardKingscote(3) 4 53
(Tom Dascombe) *hld up: swtchd lft and hdwy over 2f out: rdn and ev ch over 1f out: sn hung rt: styd on same pce* **7/1**

0 **4** 1 1/4 **Grimes Hope (IRE)**[27] 3552 2-8-13 0 RichardHughes 1 55
(R Hannon) *prom: lost pl over 4f out: bmpd over 2f out: rallied over 1f out: no ex ins fnl f* **11/2**

06 **5** shd **Victorian Cape (IRE)**[11] 4028 2-8-13 0 RyanMoore 11 54
(E J O'Neill) *sn outpcd: hdwy u.p over 1f out: no ex ins fnl f* **11/4**[1]

004 **6** 2 1/2 **Friction**[34] 3296 2-8-8 46 TPO'Shea 8 43
(J G Portman) *sn pushed along in rr: sme hdwy over 2f out: wknd over 1f out* **25/1**

003 **7** 2 1/2 **Little Bones**[11] 4027 2-8-8 0 TedDurcan 5 36
(Rae Guest) *hld up: effrt over 2f out: wknd over 1f out* **20/1**

500 **8** 1 3/4 **Amwell House**[28] 3479 2-8-13 45 StephenCarson 12 36
(J R Jenkins) *sn led: hdd 2f out: sn rdn and wknd* **66/1**

6050 **9** hd **Tenth Night (IRE)**[7] 4136 2-8-13 59 (p) MickyFenton 6 36
(P T Midgley) *chsd ldrs over 5f* **25/1**

000 **10** 1/2 **Mairead's Boy (IRE)**[11] 4014 2-8-13 0 (p) SimonWhitworth 7 34
(J S Moore) *chsd ldrs: led 2f out: rdn and hdd over 1f out: wknd fnl f* **40/1**

06 **11** 2 **Ambrose Princess (IRE)**[11] 4014 2-8-3 0 TolleyDean(5) 3 24
(J S Moore) *hld up in tch: rdn whn hmpd over 2f out: sn wknd* **9/2**[3]

0200 **12** 10 **Distant Noble**[23] 3642 2-8-10 55 TravisBlock(3) 2 —
(R Brotherton) *chsd ldrs: rdn whn hmpd over 2f out: sn wknd: eased fnl f* **20/1**

1m 26.96s (0.18) **Going Correction** -0.075s/f (Good) **12** Ran SP% **118.6**
Speed ratings (Par 96): **95,93,92,91,90 88,85,83,82,82 80,68**
CSF £84.12 TOTE £4.40: £2.00, £2.70, £2.00; EX 39.20.The winner was bought in for £10,500.
Owner Box 41 **Bred** Stone Ridge Farm **Trained** West Ilsley, Berks
■ Stewards' Enquiry : Richard Kingscote three-day ban: careless riding (Aug 24-26)

FOCUS
This seller was the slowest of the three juvenile races over the trip, although the form is slightly above average for the grade and the winner may be able to score in better company.

NOTEBOOK
Tuanku(IRE), who made his debut in a Warwick maiden that has now produced seven subsequent winners, had been giving problems at the stalls and, gelded between his first two outings, disappointed last time. However, encountering fast ground for the first time and dropped in grade, he came from off the pace and powered up the hill to win decisively. He was retained by connections and looks capable of winning a nursery on this evidence, especially as with a 55-rated filly in third he should get a reasonable mark. (op 3-1)
Bridge Of Fermoy(IRE) had been well beaten on both his starts, but this drop in grade helped him produce a decent effort, coming through on the coat-tails of the winner but never looking like closing the gap. He now qualifies for a handicap mark and may be able to make his mark in that sphere. (op 16-1 tchd 14-1)
What's For Tea, who has already been beaten in this grade, was having her first run away from Catterick and first on fast ground. She stayed on from the rear despite hanging, and her proximity tends to set the standard but also limit the form. (op 9-1 tchd 10-1)
Grimes Hope(IRE), who showed some ability in a reasonable-looking Salisbury maiden on his debut, recovered after losing his pitch and being hampered to finish well up the hill. He looks as if he can step up on this effort in time. (op 8-1)
Victorian Cape(IRE), who was backed in a maiden aution last time, was well supported on this drop in grade. He appeared to be struggling before halfway, but picked up to have a chance in the dip before his effort flattened out. He now qualifies for a handicap mark, but has something to prove before he can be backed with confidence. (op 4-1 tchd 5-2)

Ambrose Princess(IRE), another dropping in grade, had shown a measure of ability in 6f Windsor maidens, but faded after getting a bump at around the quarter-mile pole. (op 100-30 tchd 5-1)

4364 UNICORN ASSET MANAGEMENT JULY COURSE SERIES NURSERY (QUALIFIER) 7f

6:45 (6:46) (Class 3) 2-Y-O **£6,477** (£1,927; £963; £481) **Stalls** Low

Form RPR
323 **1** **Red Alert Day**[14] 3915 2-9-6 **82**.................................. LDettori 12 93+
(N A Callaghan) *hld up: plld hrd: hdwy 2f out: rdn to ld 1f out: edgd lft: r.o* **7/2**[2]
0103 **2** *1 3/4* **Ellemujie**[14] 3925 2-9-4 **80**.................................. JHBowman 15 86
(D K Ivory) *hld up: hdwy over 1f out: edgd lft: sn rdn: styd on same pce ins fnl f* **25/1**
5602 **3** *3/4* **Talk Of Saafend (IRE)**[14] 3909 2-8-5 **67**.................. DavidKinsella 2 71
(R Hannon) *prom: led wl over 1f out: sn rdn and hdd: no ex ins fnl f* **16/1**
0431 **4** *1 1/4* **Palm Court**[11] 4022 2-8-13 **75** 6ex.......................... SteveDrowne 11 78+
(R Charlton) *hld up: nt clr run over 2f out: hdwy over 1f out: nt trble ldrs* **5/1**[3]
053 **5** *3* **Duke Of Touraine (IRE)**[16] 3834 2-9-0 **76**.................. TQuinn 10 69
(P C Haslam) *hld up: rdn over 1f out: styd on ins fnl f: nvr nrr* **16/1**
3211 **6** *hd* **Elna Bright**[14] 3909 2-9-7 **83**.................................. RyanMoore 1 75
(R Hannon) *hld up: hdwy over 2f out: rdn over 1f out: wknd ins fnl f* **10/3**[1]
0600 **7** *1* **Galley Slave (IRE)**[7] 4130 2-7-5 **60** oh8.................. CharlotteKerton(7) 8 49
(M C Chapman) *trckd ldr: racd keenly: led 3f out: rdn and hdd wl over 1f out: sn edgd lft and wknd* **100/1**
545 **8** *1* **Timewatch**[65] 2371 2-8-8 **70**.................................. RoystonFfrench 5 57
(M Johnston) *led 4f: wknd over 1f out* **25/1**
3264 **9** *1 1/2* **Miss Firefly**[7] 4121 2-8-9 **71**.................................. TPO'Shea 3 54
(M R Channon) *hld up: hdwy over 2f out: wknd over 1f out* **14/1**
1212 **10** *1 1/4* **Lady Benjamin**[6] 4154 2-8-6 **71**.................................. AndrewElliott(3) 7 50+
(P C Haslam) *trckd ldrs: racd keenly: rdn over 2f out: hmpd and wknd over 1f out* **9/1**
051 **11** *nk* **Night Skier (IRE)**[15] 3874 2-9-6 **82**.................................. RichardHughes 9 60
(J L Dunlop) *hld up in tch: rdn whn hmpd over 1f out: sn wknd* **10/1**
054 **12** *1/2* **Tobogganist**[16] 3850 2-8-11 **73**.................................. TedDurcan 6 50+
(W Jarvis) *s.i.s: sn chsng ldrs: wkng whn hmpd over 1f out* **14/1**
026 **13** *1* **Latin Scholar (IRE)**[32] 3383 2-9-0 **76**.................................. JimmyFortune 14 50
(A King) *chsd ldrs: rdn over 2f out: hung lft and wknd over 1f out* **20/1**

1m 25.03s (-1.75) **Going Correction** -0.075s/f (Good) 13 Ran SP% **119.6**
Speed ratings (Par 98): **107,105,104,102,99 99,97,96,95,93 93,92,91**
CSF £96.30 CT £1296.65 TOTE £3.90: £1.80, £8.10, £5.70; EX 100.30.
Owner Gallagher Equine Ltd **Bred** Darley **Trained** Newmarket, Suffolk

FOCUS
A decent nursery run in a very good time for a race of its type, much the fastest of the three juvenile races over the trip at the meeting. The placed horses are rated as slight improvers and the form could rate higher.

NOTEBOOK
Red Alert Day ◆, who had been beaten at odds-on on his previous two starts, was a different proposition stepped up to 7f. Held up at the back of a sound gallop, he cruised through to lead and found enough to settle the issue up the hill. The time was very good and now he has got off the mark he could well go on to better things. (op 5-1 tchd 11-2)
Ellemujie, whose best previous efforts had been on Polytrack, was held up at the back just ahead of the winner. He came through at the same time but could not match that rival's pace up the hill. He seemed to stay the longer trip and his ability to act on the fast ground gives connections more alternatives, so there could be a decent race in him before the end of the season. (op 20-1)
Talk Of Saafend(IRE), who was runner-up in one of these races over course and distance last month, did best of those to race close to the pace. She seems to be improving with racing and there should be a similar event in her off this sort of mark. (op 20-1)
Palm Court has been progressing with racing and got off the mark on his handicap debut on Polytrack last time. This was another step forward under a 6lb penalty and he should be able to find easier opportunities off this sort of mark. (op 9-2 tchd 4-1)
Duke Of Touraine(IRE), another who has improved with racing, was stepping up in trip for this nursery debut and encountering fast ground for the first time. He never really got into contention but was noted staying on late and will find easier opportunities to get off the mark. (tchd 18-1)
Elna Bright, who beat today's third when winning one of these qualifiers over course and distance last month, was 1lb worse off with that rival. He could not confirm that form after appearing to have every chance and it is difficult to find an obvious excuse for a below-par effort. (op 4-1)
Latin Scholar(IRE) Official explanation: jockey said colt was unsuited by the good to firm ground

4365 MYKAL INDUSTRIES H'CAP 1m 2f

7:15 (7:15) (Class 5) (0-75,75) 3-Y-O+ **£3,886** (£1,156; £577; £288) **Stalls** Centre

Form RPR
3022 **1** **Central Force**[8] 4112 3-8-11 **67**.................................. RyanMoore 12 80
(E A L Dunlop) *hld up: hdwy over 1f out: led ins fnl f: r.o* **7/2**[1]
2152 **2** *1 1/2* **Veiled Applause**[16] 3854 4-9-13 **74**.................................. GeorgeBaker 11 84
(R M Beckett) *hld up: hdwy over 2f out: rdn to ld over 1f out: hung lft and hdd ins fnl f: styd on same pce* **4/1**[2]
0343 **3** *1 1/2* **Sonny Parkin**[7] 4135 5-9-12 **73**..................................(v) LDettori 8 80
(G A Huffer) *hld up: hdwy and n.m.r over 1f out: no ex ins fnl f* **9/2**[3]
6446 **4** *2 1/2* **Just Observing**[4] 4228 4-10-0 **75**..................................(p) MickyFenton 9 77
(P T Midgley) *chsd ldr: led over 3f out: rdn and hdd over 1f out: hung lft and wknd ins fnl f* **12/1**
5021 **5** *2* **Sky Quest (IRE)**[8] 4108 9-8-13 **67**.................................. HarryPoulton(7) 3 65
(J R Boyle) *hld up: hdwy over 2f out: rdn over 1f out: wknd fnl f* **7/2**[1]
663 **6** *1 3/4* **Haasem (USA)**[63] 2433 4-9-11 **72**.................................. EddieAhern 7 67
(J R Jenkins) *chsd ldrs: rdn over 2f out: wknd over 1f out* **16/1**
00-0 **7** *3 1/2* **Foodbroker Founder**[26] 2512 7-9-9 **70**..................................(b[1]) TQuinn 10 58
(D R C Elsworth) *led: racd keenly: hdd over 3f out: wknd fnl f* **20/1**
50-0 **8** *3 1/2* **Astrobella**[77] 2011 4-9-9 **70**.................................. JimmyQuinn 2 51
(M H Tompkins) *hld up: rdn over 2f out: sn wknd* **20/1**
000- **9** *nk* **Terminate (GER)**[341] 5047 5-8-11 **58**.................................. JamieSpencer 1 38
(N A Callaghan) *hld up: plld hrd: effrt over 2f out: sn wknd* **20/1**
6110 **10** *7* **Royal Premier (IRE)**[67] 2321 4-9-7 **68**..................................(v) RichardHughes 6 34
(H J Collingridge) *chsd ldrs: rdn over 2f out: wknd over 1f out: eased* **8/1**
-010 **11** *3* **Iceman George**[21] 3709 3-9-5 **75**.................................. RichardMullen 5 35
(D Morris) *mid-div: rdn over 3f out: wknd over 2f out* **50/1**

2m 5.15s (-1.29) **Going Correction** -0.075s/f (Good)
WFA 3 from 4yo+ 9lb 11 Ran SP% **123.6**
Speed ratings (Par 103): **102,100,99,97,96 94,91,89,88,83 80**
CSF £17.58 CT £66.80 TOTE £3.50: £1.80, £1.90, £1.50; EX 25.10.
Owner Mohammed Jaber **Bred** Zubieta Ltd **Trained** Newmarket, Suffolk

FOCUS
A fair handicap run at a sound gallop in which the principals came from off the pace and the form looks solid enough.
Foodbroker Founder Official explanation: jockey said gelding ran too free

Royal Premier(IRE) Official explanation: jockey said gelding had no more to give

4366 FIRESTONE BUILDING PRODUCTS CONDITIONS STKS 1m 2f

7:45 (7:45) (Class 3) 3-Y-O+

£8,724 (£2,612; £1,306; £653; £326; £163) **Stalls** Centre

Form RPR
4505 **1** **Many Volumes (USA)**[8] 4092 3-8-7 97.................................. RichardHughes 5 99+
(H R A Cecil) *hld up: hdwy over 1f out: edgd lft and led ins fnl f: r.o wl* **15/8**[2]
-544 **2** *2 1/2* **Snoqualmie Boy**[10] 4043 4-8-13 104.................................. TQuinn 2 91
(D R C Elsworth) *a.p: led over 1f out: sn rdn: edgd lft and hdd ins fnl f: unable qckn* **1/1**[1]
-000 **3** *3* **Heroes**[50] 2788 3-8-4 86.................................. TPO'Shea 1 85
(G A Huffer) *hld up: hdwy over 2f out: rdn over 1f out: wknd ins fnl f* **16/1**
4006 **4** *1* **Active Asset (IRE)**[5] 4194 5-9-7 83.................................. TedDurcan 4 91?
(M Quinn) *chsd ldrs: hrd rdn fr over 2f out tl rdr dropped whip over 1f out: no ex* **33/1**
5 *1 1/4* **Champus (GER)**[33] 3-8-10 0.................................. RyanMoore 3 87
(C Von Der Recke, Germany) *chsd ldr tl led over 6f out: rdn over 2f out: sn hung lft: hdd & wknd over 1f out* **14/1**
632 **6** *11* **Candy Critic (ARG)**[155] 648 5-8-13 0..................................(bt) JamieSpencer 8 59+
(M F De Kock, South Africa) *led: hdd over 6f out: wknd over 1f out: eased* **8/1**[3]
3003 **7** *4* **Ranavalona**[25] 3593 3-7-13 51..................................(t) DavidKinsella 7 46?
(C Smith) *s.s: a bhd* **100/1**

2m 4.22s (-2.22) **Going Correction** -0.075s/f (Good)
WFA 3 from 4yo+ 9lb 7 Ran SP% **112.4**
Speed ratings (Par 107): **105,103,100,99,98 90,86**
CSF £3.90 TOTE £2.80: £1.50, £1.60; EX 4.70.
Owner K Abdulla **Bred** Juddmonte Farms Inc **Trained** Newmarket, Suffolk

FOCUS
An interesting conditions race featuring two overseas challengers.

NOTEBOOK
Many Volumes(USA) ◆, who ran well in a hot handicap at Goodwood last time, had 10lb to find with the favourite judged on official ratings but settled well and produced late, had two much pace for that rival. This comfortable success should boost his confidence and, if ridden the same way in the future, he could progress into a Listed performer. (op 11-4)
Snoqualmie Boy, a Listed winner last season, has eased in the ratings but still looked to have plenty in hand of his rivals on official figures. He travelled well enough but was unable to match the pace of the winner in the final furlong. He may be worth another try at a mile and a half. (op 5-6 tchd 11-10 and 4-5)
Heroes has shown the ability to handle fast ground but his win came on soft and, being by Diktat, could do with a return to that sort of going. He had a stiff task on official ratings so this was not a bad effort. (op 20-1 tchd 12-1)
Active Asset(IRE), another with a lot to find on official ratings, did his best but could not find the extra pace, especially with his jockey losing his whip. He needs a return to handicaps and a longer trip, and possibly a switch back to the All-Weather will help him. (op 20-1)
Champus(GER), a German-trained colt who has already won in France and Holland this season, likes to front run and disputed the lead for much of the way. However, when the challengers came he got tired and hung badly left on the fast ground under pressure. Official explanation: jockey said colt hung left (op 12-1 tchd 10-1)
Candy Critic(ARG), who won the South African Oaks last year, was having her first outing since running in Dubai in March. She made the running but folded very quickly, and a combination of needing the outing and the fast ground may have produced what was a disappointing performance. She can do better with some cut in the ground. (op 7-1 tchd 11-2)

4367 MINERAL STAR H'CAP 6f

8:15 (8:15) (Class 4) (0-85,83) 3-Y-O+ **£5,181** (£1,541; £770; £384) **Stalls** Low

Form RPR
20-1 **1** **Tamagin (USA)**[19] 3762 4-9-8 **80**.................................. PatCosgrave 1 91
(K A Ryan) *mde all: racd alone far side tl rdn and hung rt fr over 2f out: styd on gamely* **6/1**
0064 **2** *1/2* **Obe Gold**[7] 4122 5-9-11 **83**..................................(v) JHBowman 4 93
(M R Channon) *hld up: racd centre: hdwy over 1f out: edgd rt: rdn and ev ch ins fnl f: kpt on* **15/8**[1]
104 **3** *1 3/4* **Abwaab**[53] 2725 4-9-7 **79**..................................(b) MickyFenton 2 83
(Eve Johnson Houghton) *racd centre: chsd wnr: rdn and hung rt over 1f out: styd on same pce fnl f* **14/1**
0430 **4** *nk* **Prince Namid**[13] 3953 5-9-9 **81**..................................(p) RoystonFfrench 6 84
(Mrs A Duffield) *racd centre: chsd ldrs: rdn over 1f out: hung rt and no ex ins fnl f* **8/1**
4202 **5** *1* **Orpen Wide (IRE)**[7] 4134 5-9-10 **82**..................................(v[1]) RichardHughes 7 82
(M C Chapman) *racd centre: hld up: effrt and edgd rt over 1f out: no imp fnl f* **10/3**[2]
1106 **6** *3 1/2* **Brunelleschi**[48] 2882 4-9-6 **78**..................................(b) RyanMoore 3 68
(M G Quinlan) *racd centre: hld up: rdn and hung rt over 1f out: sn wknd* **5/1**[3]
4050 **7** *12* **Figaro Flyer (IRE)**[18] 3802 4-9-0 **72**.................................. AmirQuinn 8 26
(P Howling) *swtchd to r alone stands' side: prom over 3f* **16/1**

1m 12.24s (-1.11) **Going Correction** -0.075s/f (Good) 7 Ran SP% **112.5**
Speed ratings (Par 105): **104,103,101,100,99 94,78**
CSF £17.12 CT £148.50 TOTE £5.50: £2.60, £1.70; EX 10.80 Place 6 £171.99, Place 5 £34.08..
Owner Tariq Al Nisf **Bred** Stonehaven Farm LLC **Trained** Hambleton, N Yorks

FOCUS
A decent sprint handicap in which the field all went separate ways early but ended up near the stands' rail.
Figaro Flyer(IRE) Official explanation: jockey said gelding hung right
T/Jkpt: £7,100.00 to a £1 stake. Pool: £10,000.00. 1 winning ticket. T/Plt: £276.30 to a £1 stake. Pool: £75,420.90. 199.20 winning tickets. T/Qpdt: £20.40 to a £1 stake. Pool: £5,234.60. 189.00 winning tickets. CR

4368 - 4370a (Foreign Racing) - See Raceform Interactive

3935 WEXFORD (R-H)

Friday, August 10

OFFICIAL GOING: Good

4371a BROMPTON RECRUITMENT IRELAND (QR) RACE 2m

7:55 (7:55) 4-Y-O+ **£5,135** (£1,196; £527; £304) **Stalls** Far side

RPR
1 **Farmer Brown (IRE)**[8] 3224 6-10-10 .... MissNCarberry 71
(P Hughes, Ire) *hld up: 6th 6f out: 4th 4f out: 2nd and smooth hdwy 3f out: led over 2f out: rdn st: strly pressed ins fnl f: all out* **4/7**[1]

The Form Book, Raceform Ltd, Compton, RG20 6NL

2 shd **Tomorrow's Dream (IRE)**[129] 9-10-3 .... MissLBoswell(7) 73+
(M Halford, Ire) *led: clr early: hdd 4f out: 3rd 3f out: r.o wl under tender handling st: jst failed* **25/1**
3 1 1/4 **Laetitia (IRE)**[9] 4086 7-10-0 .... MrJJDoyle(5) 65
(C Byrnes, Ire) *hld up: 7th 6f out: 6th 4f out: 4th and hdwy st: 3rd and pushed out fnl f: kpt on wl* **6/1**[3]
4 2 1/2 **Artless (USA)**[25] 3584 4-11-5 .... MrJTMcNamara 76
(Sir Mark Prescott) *trckd ldrs in 3rd: 2nd 6f out: led 4f out: rdn and hdd over 2f out: 4th and no ex fnl f* **7/2**[2]
5 2 1/2 **Ballyhoctor (IRE)**[7] 4978 9-10-3 42.......................... MrMJByrne(7) 65
(James Vincent Slevin, Ire) *trckd ldrs: 5th 6f out: rdn 4f out: kpt on same pce fr over 2f out* **50/1**
5 dht **Roman Villa (USA)**[35] 3292 5-10-7 72.......................... MrMFahey(7) 69
(Mrs John Harrington, Ire) *chsd ldrs: 6th 1/2-way: 8th 6f out: kpt on one pce fr 3f out* **20/1**
7 3/4 **Pearly Jack**[10] 4050 9-10-11 74.......................... MrMJO'Connor(3) 68
(D E Fitzgerald, Ire) *prom: 2nd 1/2-way: 3rd and pushed along 6f out: wknd fr 3f out* **16/1**
8 13 **Borouj (IRE)**[9] 4084 5-10-9 70.......................... MrBTO'Connell(5) 53
(Philip Fenton, Ire) *hld up: no imp fr over 3f out* **66/1**
9 11 **Busaco**[3] 4264 5-10-7 61.......................... MissPaulineRyan(7) 41
(K J Condon, Ire) *mid-div: 7th over 6f out: sn lost pl: no ex fr 4f out* **66/1**
10 4 **Taraba (IRE)**[287] 4-10-13 .... JPO'Farrell(3) 39
(Miss S Collins, Ire) *in rr: reminders 1/2-way: no ex fr 4f out* **25/1**
11 16 **Medieval Mercy (IRE)**[65] 2383 8-10-2 ow2.......................... MrJPMcKeown(5) 12
(P E I Newell, Ire) *trckd ldrs in 4th: wknd fr over 4f out* **100/1**

3m 43.2s (3.20) **11** Ran SP% **124.4**
CSF £27.74 TOTE £1.80: £1.10, £4.10, £1.60; DF 33.00.
Owner Plantation Stud **Bred** T F Cusack **Trained** Bagenalstown, Co Carlow

3988 ASCOT (R-H)

Saturday, August 11

OFFICIAL GOING: Good to firm

A change in format to the Shergar Cup, with two teams becoming four namely Great Britain, Ireland, Europe and the Rest of the World.
Wind: Virtually nil Weather: cloudy but warm

4372 BARCLAYS SHERGAR CUP JUVENILE (NURSERY) 7f

1:10 (1:11) (Class 2) 2-Y-0

£17,234 (£6,034; £2,758; £2,152; £1,897; £1,379) **Stalls** Low

Form RPR
064 **1** **Relative Order**[23] 3669 2-7-12 **74**.......................... HayleyTurner 10 80
(J R Best) *hld up towards rr: hdwy on outer 3f out: rdn and chsd ldr over 2f out: led jst over 1f out: edgd lft but r.o wl fnl f* **33/1**
2210 **2** 3/4 **Gypsy Baby (IRE)**[16] 3880 2-8-7 **83**.......................... FJohansson 4 87
(R Hannon) *hld up in rr: nt clr run over 2f out: swtchd lft 2f out: gd hdwy to chal ins fnl f: unable qckn last 50yds* **10/1**
2463 **3** nk **Dream Eater (IRE)**[11] 4048 2-9-7 **97**.......................... JimmyFortune 3 100
(A M Balding) *rrd leaving stalls and bmpd s: hld up in last: rdn and gd hdwy 2f out: chal jst ins fnl f: no ex last 50yds* **8/1**
4236 **4** 1 3/4 **Ordinance (USA)**[15] 3896 2-8-11 **87**.......................... LDettori 6 85
(T G Mills) *t.k.h: hld up in rr: hdwy over 2f out: rdn and short of room jst 2f out: kpt on one pce* **13/2**[2]
214 **5** 1 **Archived (IRE)**[28] 3524 2-8-9 **85**.......................... DPMcDonogh 8 81
(M G Quinlan) *trckd ldrs tl led centre gp 3f out: led overall 2f out: hdd and sltly hmpd 1f out: one pce after* **7/1**[3]
5013 **6** 1/2 **Dan Tucket**[15] 3909 2-8-6 **82**.......................... KDarley 9 76
(M R Channon) *wnt rt s: hld up towards rr: rdn and effrt 2f out: nvr pce to rch ldrs* **10/1**
110 **7** hd **Burnwynd Boy**[53] 2732 2-9-4 **94**.......................... JHBowman 5 88
(I Semple) *prom tl rdn and lost pl 1/2-way: kpt on same pce last 2f* **7/1**[3]
6160 **8** 1 **Stage Acclaim (IRE)**[32] 3398 2-8-4 **80**.......................... YTake 7 71
(B R Millman) *led centre gp tl 3f out: rdn and wknd wl over 1f out* **16/1**
1640 **9** 2 1/2 **Dalkey Girl (IRE)**[16] 3880 2-8-3 **79**.......................... MartinDwyer 1 63
(V Smith) *racd alone on stands' rail: led overall and clr: rdn and hdd 2f out: sn wknd* **25/1**
3101 **10** 3/4 **Coasting**[8] 4121 2-9-1 **91** 6ex.......................... ASuborics 2 73
(Mrs A J Perrett) *racd keenly: prom: rdn over 2f out: sn struggling: no ch over 1f out* **7/4**[1]

1m 26.76s (-1.34) **Going Correction** -0.175s/f (Firm) 2y crse rec **10** Ran SP% **116.7**
Speed ratings (Par 100): **100,99,98,96,95 95,94,93,90,90**
CSF £331.00 CT £2970.55 TOTE £55.40: £10.70, £2.00, £2.50; EX 485.30 TRIFECTA Not won..
Owner Heading For The Rocks Partnership **Bred** John And Mrs Caroline Penny **Trained** Hucking, Kent
■ Relative Order broke the 'new' juvenile course record by more than a second.

FOCUS

The first running of this race as a nursery and with the time good the form looks solid despite the surprise winner.

NOTEBOOK

Relative Order, who failed to build on a promising debut effort in two subsequent starts, was up in trip for this handicap debut and he showed dramatically improved form, coming through to take it up over a furlong out and really sticking it out under pressure to cause a minor shock. There is no reason to believe this was a fluke and he deserves a chance to confirm this promise. Official explanation: trainer said, regarding the improved form shown, colt was unsuited by racing on the far side at Folkestone last time and was also suited by today's step up in trip

Gypsy Baby(IRE), a soft-ground winning maiden at Folkestone, found the rise to Listed level too much at Sandown last time, but this was more realistic and she ran an improved race, looking a little unlucky not to finish closer having been forced to switch with her run. She just managed to take second and this progressive filly remains capable of better still. (op 8-1)

Dream Eater(IRE) has shown a decent level of form on every start, but remains a maiden after yet another good effort in defeat. Not beaten far in Listed and Group 3 company earlier in the season, this represented a drop in grade and he ran a fine race under his big weight, being done no favours by rearing coming out of the stalls. He could be the type who just keeps finding one or two too good, but the ability is clearly there. (op 11-1)

Ordinance(USA) looked a leading player on the evidence of his third behind Il Warrd and Yahrab in a novice stakes over this course and distance last month, but he proved somewhat disappointing, although hampered, back in maiden company last time and had a bit to prove. In rear early, he made gradual progress through the field, but was never really in a threatening position and was beaten fair and square. (op 8-1)

Archived(IRE), held off this mark on his recent handicap debut, had his hopes pinned on improving for the extra distance and struck for home plenty soon enough, but was beaten when interfered with a furlong out. (op 8-1 tchd 9-1)

Coasting, who found the rise into Group 2 company too much when down the field in the Coventry, made light of a mark of 85 on his recent nursery debut at Goodwood and was understandably made favourite off a 6lb penalty. However, having taken a good grip early on, he really began to struggle and dropped out tamely. This was clearly not his form and it may be no coincidence his two poor runs have both come at this course. Official explanation: trainer later said that colt scoped dirty (op 5-4 tchd 2-1 in a place)

4373 TITANIC QUARTER SHERGAR CUP DISTAFF (H'CAP) (F&M) 6f

1:45 (1:45) (Class 2) (0-100,100) 4-Y-0+

£17,234 (£6,034; £2,758; £2,152; £1,897; £1,379) **Stalls** Low

Form RPR
-111 **1** **Our Faye**[14] 3970 4-8-10 **82** 3ex.......................... JimmyFortune 8 95
(S Kirk) *bdly hmpd s: hld up in rr: hdwy on outer over 1f out: sn rdn: r.o wl to ld last 75yds* **9/2**[1]
-410 **2** 3/4 **Dark Missile**[29] 3511 4-10-0 **100**.......................... HayleyTurner 4 111+
(A M Balding) *trckd ldrs: led gng wl over 1f out: rdn 1f out: hdd last 75yds: kpt on* **9/2**[1]
-040 **3** 3/4 **Tagula Sunrise (IRE)**[14] 3961 5-8-13 **85**.......................... DBeadman 1 94
(R A Fahey) *bhd: rdn wl over 1f out: styd on u.p: wnt 3rd ins fnl f: nt rch ldrs* **10/1**
2000 **4** 1 1/4 **Loch Verdi**[13] 3990 4-8-13 **85**.......................... JHBowman 3 90
(A M Balding) *led tl over 3f out: styd handy: rdn wl over 1f out: kpt on same pce fnl f* **13/2**
4122 **5** 1 1/2 **China Cherub**[21] 3746 4-9-1 **87**..........................(b) KDarley 2 87
(R Hannon) *chsd ldrs: rdn over 2f out: wknd over 1f out* **6/1**[3]
2500 **6** nk **Leopoldine**[8] 4118 4-9-3 **89**.......................... DPMcDonogh 5 88
(H Morrison) *stmbld and wnt bdly rt s: sn chsng ldr: led over 3f out tl rdn and hdd over 1f out: wknd ins fnl f* **13/2**
2104 **7** 7 **Keyaki (IRE)**[23] 3670 6-9-0 **86**.......................... LDettori 9 64
(C F Wall) *hmpd s: sn in midfield: rdn and hdwy over 2f out: wknd qckly jst over 1f out* **11/2**[2]
0060 **8** nk **Sweet Afton (IRE)**[7] 4183 4-9-0 **86**.......................... MartinDwyer 6 63
(M S Saunders) *bdly hmpd s: chsd ldrs tl rdn and wknd 2f out* **25/1**
2000 **9** 1 **Perfect Story (IRE)**[29] 3511 5-8-13 **85**.......................... ASuborics 10 59
(J A R Toller) *a bhd: no ch last 2f* **16/1**
0-00 **10** 1 1/4 **Free Roses (IRE)**[6] 4196 4-9-4 **90**..........................(b1) KJManning 7 61
(J G Given) *bdly hmpd s: a wl bhd* **40/1**

1m 13.08s (-1.82) **Going Correction** -0.175s/f (Firm) **10** Ran SP% **114.0**
Speed ratings (Par 109): **105,104,103,101,99 98,89,89,87,86**
CSF £23.68 CT £194.36 TOTE £4.40: £2.20, £2.00, £2.20; EX 12.80 Trifecta £326.60 Pool: £1,035.29 - 2.25 winning units..
Owner J B J Richards **Bred** J B J Richards **Trained** Upper Lambourn, Berks

FOCUS

A good renewal of the Distaff, with Wokingham winner Dark Missile only finding the highly-progressive Our Faye too strong. The form looks sound enough through the runner-up to Wokingham form, backed up by the third.

NOTEBOOK

Our Faye has improved out of all recognition this season, winning off a mark of 69 at Salisbury in June and completing the hat-trick back there off a 10lb higher mark last time. A winner on fast and soft ground, the underfoot conditions were not going to prove a problem and she managed to overcome the drop in trip to defy a 3lb penalty. This was a smart effort considering she got interfered with coming out of the gates and connections are now likely to go in search of some black type with her. (op 7-2 tchd 5-1 in a place)

Dark Missile, gallant winner of the Wokingham off a 4lb lower mark, flopped in a Group 3 at York last time, but the return to a quicker surface enabled her to show her true form and she ran a fine race in concession of so much weight. She can make her mark at Pattern level, but still needs to make that leap. (op 7-2)

Tagula Sunrise(IRE), back down in trip, has not been getting home in softer ground and she seemed better suited to these conditions. She got going too late, but is going to benefit from a more positive ride in future and can find a race off this sort of mark. (op 8-1)

Loch Verdi, still 9lb higher than when last winning, tends to do most of her racing at 5f and she blazed the early trail. Passed at halfway, she stuck on well for pressure without being able to get back at the leaders and looks worth persevering with at this distance. (op 10-1 tchd 6-1)

China Cherub has been enjoying a decent run of form and the improvement has definitely coincided with her wearing blinkers. However, she was racing here off an 11lb higher mark than when last winning and it proved too much in this competitive contest, dropping out having held every chance with two to run. (op 9-2)

Leopoldine ran well considering she stumbled leaving the stalls and gave Sweet Afton a hefty bump, showing bright speed, but she could not sustain and probably deserves another chance. Official explanation: jockey said filly stumbled at start (op 8-1 tchd 17-2)

Free Roses(IRE) Official explanation: jockey said filly jumped right leaving stalls

4374 PORTHAULT SHERGAR CUP SPRINT (H'CAP) 6f

2:20 (2:25) (Class 2) (0-100,100) 3-Y-0

£17,234 (£6,034; £2,758; £2,152; £1,897; £1,379) **Stalls** Low

Form RPR
1212 **1** **Genki (IRE)**[13] 4006 3-8-12 **86**.......................... KJManning 5 97
(R Charlton) *t.k.h: hld up towards rr: hdwy 2f out: rdn to chal jst over 1f out: led ins fnl f: r.o strly* **6/4**[1]
-120 **2** 2 **Lipocco**[31] 3431 3-9-12 **100**.......................... DPMcDonogh 2 105
(R M Beckett) *led and sn clr: rdn over 1f out: hdd ins fnl f: nt pce of wnr last 100yds* **15/2**[3]
2011 **3** 3/4 **King's Apostle (IRE)**[31] 3418 3-8-13 **87**.......................... JHBowman 7 90
(W J Haggas) *racd in midfield: hdwy over 3f out: chsd ldr and hung rt over 1f out: one pce fnl f* **5/1**[2]
2605 **4** nk **Southandwest (IRE)**[8] 4123 3-8-13 **87**.......................... FJohansson 6 89
(J S Moore) *t.k.h: hld up in rr: rdn 2f out: plugged on fnl f: nt trble ldrs* **15/2**[3]
1000 **5** 1 1/2 **Dazed And Amazed**[9] 4090 3-9-12 **100**.......................... JimmyFortune 3 98
(R Hannon) *wnt rt s: bhd: swtchd lft and hdwy wl over 1f out: no imp fnl f* **12/1**
1000 **6** 1 1/4 **Heywood**[9] 4093 3-9-3 **91**.......................... YTake 8 85
(M R Channon) *chsd ldr tl over 2f out: sn rdn and struggling* **16/1**
0063 **7** shd **Invincible Force (IRE)**[6] 4196 3-9-10 **98**.......................... MartinDwyer 10 91
(Paul Green) *t.k.h: in tch: chsd ldr over 2f out tl over 1f out: sn wknd* **9/1**
6306 **8** 1 1/4 **Resplendent Alpha**[7] 4183 3-9-7 **95**..........................(t) DBeadman 9 85
(P Howling) *s.i.s: bhd: effrt u.p over 2f out: sn no imp* **33/1**
0540 **9** nk **Everymanforhimself (IRE)**[42] 3078 3-8-13 **87**..........................(b) HayleyTurner 1 76
(J G Given) *in tch tl rdn 1/2-way: sn struggling* **16/1**

1m 13.34s (-1.56) **Going Correction** -0.175s/f (Firm) **10** Ran SP% **112.6**
Speed ratings (Par 106): **103,100,99,98,96 95,95,93,93**
CSF £12.00 CT £36.02 TOTE £2.30: £1.30, £2.80, £2.00; EX 15.00 Trifecta £45.40 Pool: £897.06 - 14.01 winning units..
Owner Ms Gillian Khosla **Bred** Rathbarry Stud **Trained** Beckhampton, Wilts
■ Siren's Gift (A. Suborics, 8/1) was withdrawn after refusing to enter the stalls. R4, deduct 10p in the £.

FOCUS
A decent three-year-old sprint and sound form with the placed horses to their marks.

NOTEBOOK
Genki(IRE) ◆ has developed into a really progressive sprint handicapper, winning a decent race at Newmarket back in May before finding only the one too good against older horses at Pontefract last time. Off the same mark here, he appreciated returning to race against his own age group and powered home to win readily, confirming earlier form with the runner-up. A further rise will follow, but there is no reason why he cannot continue to progress. (op 11-4 tchd 11-8)

Lipocco has progressed into a smart sprinter this season and on earlier Newmarket form there was very little between him and Genki, but having set a decent gallop he was gradually reeled in and left trailing in the final half a furlong. This showed his recent July course running to be all wrong, but he is going to continue to find it tough going off this sort of mark. (op 7-1)

King's Apostle(IRE), on a hat-trick following wins at Redcar and Kempton, was up a further 5lb and it all proved too much in this better contest, being unable to race on with the winner in the final furlong. He is a winner over 7f and could have more to offer at that distance now. (tchd 9-2 and 11-2)

Southandwest(IRE), who found things happening a little too quickly when dropped back to 5f at Goodwood last time, gave the impression he wanted to go a little faster early on, and in hindsight his rider may have been better to let him as he was never nearer than at the finish. He could still do with some further assistance from the Handicapper, but he is beginning to find some form again. (op 8-1)

Dazed And Amazed has been struggling to make and impression in Group events, but equally this mark was always going to prove beyond him on this return to handicaps and he is likely to remain hard to place. (op 14-1 tchd 11-1)

Heywood has lost his form and this effort further confirmed him to be poorly handicapped at present. (op 20-1)

Invincible Force(IRE), who has been giving a good account of himself against older horses, was unable to lead on this occasion and he failed to reproduce his best form. (tchd 10-1)

4375 CARVILL SHERGAR CUP STAYERS (H'CAP) 2m
2:55 (2:57) (Class 2) (0-100,99) 4-Y-0+

£17,234 (£6,034; £2,758; £2,152; £1,897; £1,379) **Stalls** High

Form				RPR
1/40	1		**Leg Spinner (IRE)**[10] 3090 6-8-13 **86** ... YTake 3 *(A J Martin, Ire) stdd s: hld up in last: shkn up and gd hdwy over 1f out: led jst ins fnl f: readily* **5/2**[1]	99+
/0-3	2	1 1/4	**Caracciola (GER)**[21] 3153 10-9-0 **87** ... JHBowman 2 (N J Henderson) *w.w in tch: hdwy over 2f out: led jst over 1f out: sn hdd: no ch w wnr* **20/1**	94
-010	3	1 1/4	**Colloquial**[42] 3090 6-9-4 **91** ... (v) HayleyTurner 5 (H Candy) *chsd ldrs: hdwy to press ldr over 2f out: sn rdn: one pce fnl f* **8/1**	97
6-33	4	3/4	**Golden Quest**[49] 2860 6-9-9 **96** ... KJManning 9 (M Johnston) *chsd ldr for 2f: chsd ldrs after: rdn and nt clr run over 1f out: rdn and effrt on rail 1f out: rdr dropped whip ins fnl f: one pce* **9/2**[2]	101
0501	5	1 1/4	**Odiham**[15] 3898 6-9-5 **92** 3ex ... (v) DBeadman 10 (H Morrison) *led: hrd pressed and rdn over 2f out: hdd jst over 1f out: no ex* **11/2**[3]	95
6360	6	3/4	**Lets Roll**[21] 3753 6-8-13 **86** ... LDettori 4 (C W Thornton) *w.w in tch: hdwy to press ldrs over 2f out: wknd over 1f out* **14/1**	88
-100	7	hd	**Greenwich Meantime**[9] 4091 7-9-12 **99** ... FJohansson 7 (R A Fahey) *hld up towards rr: rdn and effrt 2f out: n.m.r over 1f out: kpt on same pce* **8/1**	101+
00-3	8	3/4	**Mirjan (IRE)**[15] 3898 11-9-3 **90** ... (b) JimmyFortune 1 (L Lungo) *stdd s: hld up in last pair: nvr trbld ldrs* **16/1**	91
0-01	9	1 1/2	**Nobelix (IRE)**[21] 3748 5-9-1 **88** ... KDarley 8 (J R Fanshawe) *hld up in midfield: hdwy on outer over 2f out: wknd over 1f out* **8/1**	87
0-50	10	58	**Vinando**[11] 4047 6-9-11 **98** ... (tp) ASuborics 6 (C R Egerton) *reminder after 1f: chsd ldr after 2f tl 4f out: sn rdn and wknd: virtually p.u fnl f* **33/1**	28

3m 31.93s (1.77) **Going Correction** +0.10s/f (Good) **10** Ran SP% **115.7**
Speed ratings (Par 109): **99,98,97,97,96 96,96,95,95,66**
CSF £57.67 CT £354.23 TOTE £3.30: £1.60, £5.30, £3.00; EX 48.20 Trifecta £247.10 Pool: £1,176.38 - 3.38 winning units..

Owner W A Moffett **Bred** Steven Nolan **Trained** Summerhill, Co. Meath

FOCUS
A good staying handicap likely to produce its share of winners, although the time was moderate and it is hard to rate too positively.

NOTEBOOK
Leg Spinner(IRE), a tailed-off last in the Northumberland Plate, has since shown his wellbeing with a win back over hurdles at Galway and, off the same mark as when fourth in the Ascot Stakes earlier in the year, he ran out a ready winner. Brought with a perfectly-timed run, he swept into the lead racing into the final furlong and won comfortably, suggesting there are more decent prizes in this lightly-raced six-year-old. (tchd 2-1 and 11-4 in places)

Caracciola(GER), who did not give much of a show over hurdles at Market Rasen the other day, had previously run well at Goodwood over an inadequate 1m6f and this first try at 2m on a fast surface looked ideal for the ageing gelding. Ridden confidently, he was delivered with a well-timed challenge, but could not repel Leg Spinner who swept past him no sooner than he had come to lead. These are his ideal conditions and there looks to be a decent race in him off this sort of mark. (op 12-1)

Colloquial has never been the most consistent, but his Northumberland Plate effort could be forgiven on account of the testing ground and this was a much better showing, sticking on gallantly once headed. He is not brilliantly handicapped though and is likely to remain vulnerable off this mark.

Golden Quest, renewing an old rivalry with Leg Spinner having been beaten a short head by him in the 2005 Ascot Stakes, has returned from injury with a couple of solid efforts in defeat and this was another fine run considering he would not have enjoyed the ground and did not get the clearest of runs. He is a classy stayer on his day and could be one for a big staying handicap later in the season, maybe something like the Cesarewitch. (op 11-2)

Odiham, shouldering a 3lb penalty for his recent course and distance success, was soon bowling along in front and ran his race, but could not repel the challengers and was simply found out by this better class of opposition. (op 7-1 tchd 5-1)

Greenwich Meantime, this year's Chester Cup winner, was another to flop in the Northumberland Plate and he could be forgiven only finishing 11th in the Goodwood Cup, but better could have been expected of him here, especially back on faster ground, and in the end he could only plod on at the one pace. (tchd 9-1)

Nobelix(IRE) was unable to build on his recent Newmarket victory and ran too badly for it to be put down to the 5lb rise. (op 7-1)

4376 MICHAEL PAGE INTERNATIONAL SHERGAR CUP CHALLENGE (H'CAP) 1m 4f
3:30 (3:32) (Class 2) (0-100,98) 4-Y-0+

£17,234 (£6,034; £2,758; £2,152; £1,897; £1,379) **Stalls** High

Form				RPR
0-6	1		**Strategic Mount**[11] 4047 4-9-8 **94** ... LDettori 5 (P F I Cole) *hld up in rr: hdwy on outer over 2f out: rdn to chal over 1f out: led narrowly ins fnl f: r.o wl* **11/8**[1]	102
5610	2	hd	**John Terry (IRE)**[13] 3989 4-9-4 **90** ... YTake 6 (Mrs A J Perrett) *w.w in midfield: hdwy over 2f out: pressed wnr over 1f out: kpt on but a jst hld* **8/1**	98
3400	3	2	**Acropolis (IRE)**[8] 4117 6-9-6 **92** ... (v) DBeadman 9 (I Semple) *hld up in rr: swtchd lft and hdwy on outer over 1f out: styd on to go 3rd last 100yds: nt trble ldng pair* **12/1**	97
4100	4	1	**Mustajed**[11] 4047 6-9-3 **89** ... MartinDwyer 10 (B R Millman) *hld up towards rr: n.m.r over 2f out tl jst over 1f out: styd on fnl f: nt trble ldrs* **8/1**	92
0-50	5	nk	**Gavroche (IRE)**[70] 2236 6-9-6 **92** ... KJManning 7 (J R Boyle) *hld up in rr: nt clr run over 2f out tl swtchd lft over 1f out: styd on fnl f: nt pce to rch ldrs* **14/1**	95
5000	6	nk	**Corriolanus (GER)**[30] 3461 7-9-9 **95** ... FJohansson 8 (A M Balding) *chsd ldrs: wnt 2nd 4f out: led over 2f out: sn rdn: hdd ins fnl f: wknd last 100yds* **25/1**	97
-610	7	1/2	**Kerriemuir Lass (IRE)**[14] 3959 4-9-2 **88** ... DPMcDonogh 2 (M A Jarvis) *chsd ldr after 2f tl 4f out: rdn over 2f out: wknd over 1f out* **7/1**[3]	89
0613	8	hd	**Dunaskin (IRE)**[15] 3899 7-9-7 **93** ... JimmyFortune 3 (Karen McLintock) *led tl hdd over 2f out: wknd over 1f out* **7/1**[3]	94
4200	9	2	**Bandama (IRE)**[11] 4043 4-9-8 **94** ... HayleyTurner 4 (Mrs A J Perrett) *chsd ldr for 2f: styd handy tl lost pl and nt clr run over 2f out: no ch after* **13/2**[2]	92

2m 34.09s (1.09) **Going Correction** +0.10s/f (Good) **9** Ran SP% **120.9**
Speed ratings (Par 109): **100,99,98,97,97 97,97,97,95**
CSF £14.08 CT £101.32 TOTE £2.50: £1.30, £1.90, £2.80; EX 15.30 Trifecta £162.90 Pool: £1,370.06 - 5.97 winning units..

Owner Ben & Sir Martyn Arbib **Bred** Arbib Bloodstock Partnership **Trained** Whatcombe, Oxon

FOCUS
A pretty ordinary handicap for the grade, full of exposed performers, but Strategic Mount was the exception and he was probably not at his best to win here. The form makes sense through the horses in the frame behind the winner to their marks.

NOTEBOOK
Strategic Mount ◆, a highly-progressive handicapper at three who ran well for a long way having pulled hard on his seasonal reappearance at Glorious Goodwood, was making a relatively quick return to the track, but he looked a standout on the best of his form and this faster surface was expected to suit. Usually a front-runner, he was ridden with more restraint on this occasion, but still travelled strongly into contention off the home bend and just managed to do enough once getting to the lead. Not at his best to win here, there looks to be more to come from this fine, big son of Montjeu and the 10/1 generally on offer for the Totesport Ebor makes plenty of appeal, with his penalty for this win making him certain of a run. He will land a valuable prize at some stage, and would also make a smashing hurdler. (op 2-1 tchd 9-4)

John Terry(IRE) finally got the fast ground he needs when winning at Newmarket two starts back, and he was always going to struggle when returned to a slower surface over this course and distance last time. Going without the cheekpieces on this occasion, he showed himself in his true light back on this quicker ground and only narrowly failed to get to the winner. He has never gone beyond 1m4f, but shapes as though he may improve for the step up and is in the right hands to progress further. (op 15-2)

Acropolis(IRE) has somewhat fallen from grace, having finished fourth in the Arc a few years back, but he continues to slip in the weights and this was a more promising effort. He has yet to make much of an impact over further, but shapes as though well worth another try at it. (op 11-1)

Mustajed, a ready winner at Salisbury back in June, has been struggling off this new mark and, although this was a shade better back on faster ground, he does not make much appeal off his current rating. (tchd 7-1)

Gavroche(IRE) has been contesting some hot handicaps, but he got no luck on this slight drop in grade, getting blocked at a vital stage before running on too late. He may well have challenged for third had he got a clear run through and could be interesting next time.

Corriolanus(GER) struggled to make an impact off a stiff mark in handicaps at Nad Al Sheba earlier in the year, and he was always going to struggle against the likes of Papal Bull on his reppearance in the Princess Of Wales's Stakes at Newmarket. The Handicapper gave him a chance here though and he ran well for a long way, suggesting a bit more leniency will enable him to win again.

Kerriemuir Lass(IRE) has proved a bit hit-and-miss this season and she dropped away tamely in the final furlong. (op 11-2 tchd 15-2)

Dunaskin(IRE) was responsible for the early pace, but he could not sustain it and was readily left trailing. (op 13-2)

Bandama(IRE) was eased right off having had nowhere to go and can safely have the run ignored. Official explanation: jockey said colt was denied a clear run (op 7-1 tchd 15-2)

4377 SODEXHO PRESTIGE SHERGAR CUP MILE (H'CAP) 1m (R)
4:05 (4:07) (Class 2) (0-100,95) 4-Y-0+

£17,234 (£6,034; £2,758; £2,152; £1,897; £1,379) **Stalls** High

Form				RPR
3033	1		**Benandonner (USA)**[18] 3813 4-9-2 **85** ... JHBowman 10 (R A Fahey) *trckd ldrs on inner: hdwy to chal 1f out: led wl ins fnl f: r.o wl* **5/1**[2]	96+
5601	2	1/2	**Ace Of Hearts**[7] 4153 8-9-7 **90** ... MartinDwyer 3 (C F Wall) *led: rdn 2f out: hdd wl ins fnl f: no ex towards fin* **5/2**[1]	100
6003	3	2 1/2	**Pentecost**[28] 3527 8-9-10 **93** ... (p) DBeadman 7 (A M Balding) *t.k.h: hld up in rr: rdn and effrt wl over 1f out: kpt on fnl f: wnt 3rd last 75yds: nt trble ldrs* **8/1**	97
1500	4	shd	**South Cape**[14] 3941 4-9-2 **85** ... KJManning 9 (M R Channon) *racd in midfield: rdn 2f out: kpt on same pce u.p fnl f* **11/2**[3]	89
6223	5	1/2	**Waterside (IRE)**[11] 4049 8-9-5 **88** ... ASuborics 5 (G L Moore) *t.k.h: pressed ldr: rdn 2f out: wknd ins fnl f* **8/1**	91
4210	6	1 3/4	**Wovoka (IRE)**[11] 4049 4-9-1 **84** 3ex ... LDettori 1 (M R Channon) *dropped in after s: hld up in last: effrt and nt clr run on rail over 2f out tl over 1f out: rdn and no hdwy after* **13/2**	83
0-26	7	hd	**Cape Of Luck (IRE)**[28] 3527 4-9-7 **90** ... FJohansson 8 (P Mitchell) *hld up in rr: nt clr run over 2f out tl over 1f out: no imp fnl f* **16/1**	88
0500	8	3/4	**Prince Of Thebes (IRE)**[11] 4049 6-9-4 **87** ... DPMcDonogh 2 (J Akehurst) *trckd ldrs: rdn wl over 2f out: wknd over 1f out* **15/2**	84

The Form Book, Raceform Ltd, Compton, RG20 6NL

2030 **9** 3 1/2 **Bustan (IRE)**[50] 2817 8-9-9 **92**.. YTake 4 81
(G C Bravery) *in tch on outer: rdn over 2f out: wknd wl over 1f out* **14/1**
1m 40.99s (-1.11) **Going Correction** +0.10s/f (Good) **10** Ran SP% **120.5**
Speed ratings (Par 109): **109,108,106,105,105 103,103,102,99**
CSF £18.78 CT £102.07 TOTE £9.30: £2.90, £1.70, £2.10; EX 30.40 Trifecta £232.10 Pool: £29,276.13 - 89.53 winning units. Place 6 £96.99, Place 5 £9.34.
Owner J C Parsons & Sinead Parsons **Bred** Gainsborough Farm Llc **Trained** Musley Bank, N Yorks
■ This win for Hugh Bowman secured the Shergar Cup for the Rest of the World team. Musadif (K. Darley, 25/1) w/d, bolted bef s
■ Stewards' Enquiry : D Beadman seven-day ban: used whip with excessive frequency (Aug 22-28)

FOCUS
A race made up of largely exposed handicappers although the winner is generally progressive and rated as up 3lb.

NOTEBOOK
Benandonner(USA) has been creeping up the handicap without winning, racing here off an 11lb higher mark than when last successful, but this was not a particularly strong event and he came through late under a well-judged ride by Bowman to score readily. The problem however is a further rise is going to follow and he may not be up to defying it unless improving again. (op 13-2)
Ace Of Hearts, back to form with a bang when making all in an apprentices' handicap at Goodwood, went unpenalised for that victory and was rightly made favourite, but he had no answer to the winner's late burst and was forced to settle for second. He should continue to pay his way, but a rise will not make winning any easier for him. (op 3-1 tchd 9-4)
Pentecost, winner of this in 2003 and 2004, could only manage sixth last year, but he bettered that with a fine performance, just edging out South Cape, and the cheekpieces definitely appear to have helped. (op 6-1)
South Cape has struggled to make much of an impact in hot handicaps the last twice, but the Handicapper has eased him a few pounds and the less-fierce nature of this race appeared to suit him well. (op 13-2 tchd 15-2)
Waterside(IRE) is a grand old performer and it was asking a lot for him to take a race such as this, but he gave it his all and it was only in the final furlong he cried enough. It has been roughly a year since his last turf win and he is likely to remain vulnerable to less-exposed animals. (op 7-1 tchd 9-1)
Wovoka(IRE), a course and distance winner in July, came too wide when disappointing at Goodwood last time and he got little luck in running here, being trapped with nowhere to go for the best part of a furlong. The run is safely ignored. (op 7-1)
Prince Of Thebes(IRE), successful in this contest a year ago, was able to race off a 6lb lower mark here, but that is because he has lost his form this season and this was yet another disappointing performance. (op 8-1 tchd 7-1)
T/Plt: £140.30 to a £1 stake. Pool: £118,294.65. 615.25 winning tickets. T/Qpdt: £5.10 to a £1 stake. Pool: £7,759.50. 1,124.95 winning tickets. SP

3781 AYR (L-H)
Saturday, August 11

OFFICIAL GOING: Good to soft changing to soft after race 5 (7.50)
A miserably wet evening with the ground deteriorating.
Wind: Light, across Weather: Raining

4378 WATERAID EBF MAIDEN STKS 6f
5:50 (5:51) (Class 5) 2-Y-O **£3,886** (£1,156; £577; £288) **Stalls** Centre

Form RPR
6 **1** **Arctic Cape**[13] 3991 2-9-3 0.. J-PGuillambert 7 85+
(M Johnston) *led: hdd jst over 2f out: sn rdn and hung lft: led 1f out: drvn out* **7/2**[2]
33 **2** 3/4 **Quest For Success (IRE)**[19] 3781 2-9-3 0.................... PaulHanagan 5 83
(R A Fahey) *trckd ldrs: rdn over 1f out: kpt on ins fnl f* **9/4**[1]
4 **3** 3 1/2 **Chivola (IRE)**[45] 2983 2-9-3 0.. PaulEddery 11 73+
(B Smart) *w wnr: led jst over 2f out: rdn and hdd 1f out: no ex ins fnl f* **6/1**
4 **4** 4 **Another Decree**[19] 3781 2-9-3 0...................................... PhillipMakin 3 61
(M Dods) *hld up and bhd: rdn and hdwy over 2f out: wknd over 1f out* **5/1**[3]
5 **5** 1 1/4 **Howards Hope**[26] 3582 2-9-3 0.. TomEaves 8 57
(I Semple) *chsd ldrs tl wknd wl over 1f out* **10/1**
6 1/2 **Oasis Davis** 2-9-0 0.. JamieMoriarty(3) 6 55
(K A Ryan) *s.i.s: sn swtchd rt to stands' rail: rdn 2f out: a bhd* **9/1**
4 **7** 14 **Novestar (IRE)**[17] 3833 2-9-3 0.. TPQueally 4 13
(Mrs A Duffield) *w ldrs: rdn 3f out: sn wknd* **33/1**
8 nk **Swift Acclaim (IRE)** 2-8-12 0.. PatCosgrave 1 7
(K R Burke) *bhd fnl 3f* **18/1**
2 **9** nk **Habbie Heights**[11] 4041 2-8-12 0................................. PaulMulrennan 2 —
(R Bastiman) *in tch tl wknd qckly over 2f out: sn eased* **14/1**
1m 15.73s (2.06) **Going Correction** +0.325s/f (Good) **9** Ran SP% **117.9**
Speed ratings (Par 94): **99,98,93,88,86 85,67,66,66**
CSF £12.09 TOTE £3.60: £1.60, £1.30, £2.60; EX 9.80.
Owner Mrs Christine Brown **Bred** Mrs R D Peacock **Trained** Middleham Moor, N Yorks

FOCUS
The rain-softened ground took its toll on most of these juveniles after the runners soon tacked towards the stands' rail. The first three were clear and the form looks fair for the track.

NOTEBOOK
Arctic Cape, whose stable had won this race four times in the last six years, had made his debut in similar ground at Ascot. He again showed a tendency to hang left when headed but still managed to come back and make his jockey's journey from Redcar for one ride pay off. (op 5-2 tchd 9-4)
Quest For Success(IRE) ◆ continues to knock on the door and his turn is near. (op 3-1)
Chivola(IRE) had the advantage of the stands' rail to race against and may do better on decent ground. (tchd 7-1)
Another Decree is another who probably wants a sounder surface. (op 7-1 tchd 8-1)
Howards Hope was beaten further than when making his debut on similar ground over course and distance last month. (op 14-1 tchd 16-1)
Oasis Davis is out of a sister to a dual ten-furlong Group 1 winner. (op 8-1 tchd 10-1)
Novestar(IRE) Official explanation: jockey said colt was unsuited by the good to soft ground
Habbie Heights Official explanation: jockey said filly hung left

4379 WATERAID LADIES NIGHT CLAIMING STKS 5f
6:20 (6:21) (Class 5) 3-Y-O+ **£3,238** (£963; £481; £240) **Stalls** Centre

Form RPR
0630 **1** **Lake Chini (IRE)**[17] 3837 5-8-13 60................................(b) DaleGibson 2 53
(M W Easterby) *racd keenly: w ldrs: led jst over 1f out: drvn out* **10/3**[3]
4055 **2** 1 1/2 **Raccoon (IRE)**[9] 4095 7-9-6 77.. TomEaves 8 55
(D W Chapman) *led: rdn and hdd jst over 1f out: kpt on same pce* **15/8**[1]
4600 **3** hd **Aye Aye Definitely (IRE)**[7] 4158 3-8-9 67..................... PaulHanagan 7 46
(R A Fahey) *s.i.s: hld up in rr on stands' rail: plld out and hdwy over 1f out: rdn and nt qckn ins fnl f* **3/1**[2]
0-00 **4** 1 1/2 **Indian Spark**[19] 3787 13-8-8 60...................................... GaryBartley(7) 4 43
(J S Goldie) *hld up in rr: rdn over 1f out: late hdwy: nrst fin* **11/2**
0000 **5** 1/2 **Alfie Lee (IRE)**[29] 3498 10-8-3 30...............................(t) PaulPickard(7) 3 37
(D A Nolan) *t.k.h in tch: swtchd lft wl over 1f out: sn ev ch: wknd wl ins fnl f* **100/1**
0-66 **6** nk **Valiant Romeo**[23] 3667 7-9-6 45.................................... PaulMulrennan 6 46
(R Bastiman) *w ldr: rdn and ev ch over 1f out: wknd fnl f* **14/1**
-000 **7** 11 **Orpenlina (IRE)**[26] 3597 4-7-12 38............................... KellyHarrison(7) 1 —
(Peter Grayson) *hld up: rdn 2f out: sn struggling* **16/1**
61.97 secs (1.53) **Going Correction** +0.325s/f (Good)
WFA 3 from 4yo+ 3lb **7** Ran SP% **111.8**
Speed ratings (Par 103): **100,97,97,94,94 93,76**
CSF £9.53 TOTE £4.40: £2.00, £1.50; EX 12.00.
Owner Mrs Jean Turpin **Bred** Paul McEnery **Trained** Sheriff Hutton, N Yorks

FOCUS
The runners again came over to the stands' side in this modest claimer. The form is limited by the lowly-rated fifth and sixth.

4380 SPLISH SPLASH FLUSH H'CAP 1m 7f
6:50 (6:50) (Class 6) (0-65,65) 4-Y-O+ **£3,238** (£963; £481; £240) **Stalls** Low

Form RPR
0000 **1** **City Miss**[26] 3584 4-7-11 **46** oh1 ow2............................ KellyHarrison(7) 8 51
(Miss L A Perratt) *sn chsng ldr: rdn over 1f out: styd on to ld nr fin* **25/1**
/00- **2** 1/2 **Mcqueen (IRE)**[27] 3454 7-8-13 **57**.................................... PatCosgrave 7 60
(J T Stimpson) *led: rdn wl over 1f out: ct nr fin* **12/1**
2 **3** 1 1/2 **Balakar (IRE)**[7] 4188 11-8-11 **55**..............................(p) PaulMulrennan 5 56
(J J Lambe, Ire) *hld up towards rr: rdn over 3f out: swtchd rt ins fnl f: styd on wl towards fin: nvr nrr* **10/3**[1]
00/6 **4** nk **Named At Dinner**[11] 2391 6-8-3 **47** oh1 ow1...................... PaulEddery 9 48
(Miss Lucinda V Russell) *hld up in tch: rdn over 3f out: edgd lft 1f out: one pce* **8/1**[3]
56 **5** nk **Sinatas (GER)**[26] 3584 4-8-8 **52** ow1.............................. PhillipMakin 1 52
(P Monteith) *chsd ldr early: prom: rdn over 3f out: one pce fnl f* **9/2**[2]
5541 **6** 3/4 **Danzatrice**[9] 4096 5-9-6 **64**.. TomEaves 10 63
(C W Thornton) *hld up and bhd: rdn over 3f out: hdwy on ins over 2f out: one pce fnl f* **10/3**[1]
040 **7** 1 **Quicuyo (GER)**[7] 4156 4-8-3 **47** oh1 ow4.................. PatrickMathers(3) 3 48
(P Monteith) *hld up in tch: rdn over 3f out: wknd wl ins fnl f* **9/1**
0/3- **8** 1 3/4 **Haiban**[7] 4188 5-9-4 **65**.. JamieMoriarty(3) 11 61
(J J Lambe, Ire) *a in rr* **17/2**
/14- **9** 46 **Elaala (USA)**[12] 6957 5-8-5 **49**.. DaleGibson 2 —
(J T Stimpson) *hld up in mid-div: rdn and struggling over 3f out: eased whn no ch fnl 2f* **10/1**
3m 29.27s (6.80) **Going Correction** +0.20s/f (Good) **9** Ran SP% **116.6**
Speed ratings (Par 101): **89,88,87,87,87 87,86,85,61**
CSF £293.68 CT £1269.56 TOTE £22.70: £4.60, £2.50, £1.60; EX 773.40.
Owner The Hon Miss Heather Galbraith **Bred** Miss Heather Galbraith **Trained** Ayr, S Ayrshire

FOCUS
A poor stayers' handicap with a surprise winner and the form nowhere near solid.
Elaala(USA) Official explanation: jockey said mare finished distressed

4381 MOUCHEL PARKMAN H'CAP 6f
7:20 (7:22) (Class 5) (0-75,77) 3-Y-O+ **£3,886** (£1,156; £577; £288) **Stalls** Centre

Form RPR
3146 **1** **Compton Classic**[14] 3954 5-8-13 **70**.............................. GaryBartley(7) 10 82
(J S Goldie) *racd stands' side: hld up gng wl: hdwy over 1f out: led gp jst ins fnl f: r.o wl to take overall ld nr fin* **8/1**
1666 **2** 1 **Word Perfect**[10] 4075 5-9-2 **66**....................................(b) DaleGibson 7 75
(M W Easterby) *w ldr far side: overall ld over 1f out: rdn and hdd nr fin* **14/1**
4012 **3** 1 1/2 **Rainbow Fox**[2] 4330 3-8-10 **67**.................................. JamieMoriarty(3) 3 70
(R A Fahey) *racd far side: hld up: hdwy over 1f out: chsd ldr fnl f: nt qckn: fin 2nd of 6 in gp* **5/1**[2]
4110 **4** 2 **Charles Parnell (IRE)**[4] 4251 4-9-6 **70**.......................... PhillipMakin 14 68
(M Dods) *racd stands' side: hld up: hdwy over 2f out: led gp wl over 1f out tl ins fnl f: one pce: fin 2nd of 7 in gp* **6/1**[3]
4051 **5** 1 1/2 **Dorn Dancer (IRE)**[19] 3784 5-8-13 **63**............................. PatCosgrave 5 56
(D W Barker) *hld up far side: rdn and hdwy over 1f out: one pce fnl f: fin 3rd of 6 in gp* **9/1**
6212 **6** 1/2 **Bel Cantor**[10] 4075 4-9-6 **77**....................................(p) DeanHeslop(7) 2 68
(W J H Ratcliffe) *racd far side: led: rdn and hdd over 1f out: wknd ins fnl f: fin 4th of 6 in gp* **9/2**[1]
0005 **7** 1/2 **Obe One**[13] 3996 7-8-3 **56** oh11.............................(b) PatrickMathers(3) 8 46
(A Berry) *racd stands' side: hld up: rdn 2f out: kpt on same pce fnl f: fin 3rd of 7 in gp* **50/1**
1050 **8** 1 3/4 **Soto**[10] 4083 4-8-5 **62**.. NSLawes(7) 13 46
(M W Easterby) *racd stands' side: prom: rdn over 2f out: wknd over 1f out: fin 4th of 7 in gp* **12/1**
0005 **9** hd **Vondova**[7] 4158 5-7-13 **56** oh2...................................... PaulPickard(7) 11 39
(D A Nolan) *led stands' side: hdd over 1f out: sn wknd: fin 5th of 7 in gp* **28/1**
0011 **10** 2 **Mozakhraf (USA)**[12] 4024 5-9-1 **65**................................. PaulHanagan 4 42
(K A Ryan) *racd far side: chsd ldrs: rdn and wknd wl over 1f out: fin 5th of 6 in gp* **9/2**[1]
2220 **11** 1 1/4 **Local Poet**[13] 3996 6-8-10 **60**...(b) TomEaves 1 33
(I Semple) *racd far side: chsd ldrs: rdn and wknd over 2f out: fin last of 6 in gp* **18/1**
00/4 **12** 13 **Avontuur (FR)**[8] 4138 5-7-13 **56** oh8................(b) DanielleMcCreery(7) 12 —
(D W Chapman) *racd stands' side: prom tl rdn and wknd wl over 1f out: fin 6th of 7 in gp* **33/1**
6220 **13** 13 **Milson's Point (IRE)**[13] 3997 3-8-8 **62** ow2................... PaulMulrennan 9 —
(I Semple) *racd stands' side: prom: rdn over 2f out: sn wknd: fin last of 7 in gp* **12/1**
1m 14.67s (1.00) **Going Correction** +0.325s/f (Good)
WFA 3 from 4yo+ 4lb **13** Ran SP% **124.1**
Speed ratings (Par 103): **106,104,102,100,98 97,96,94,94,91 89,72,55**
CSF £117.74 CT £647.11 TOTE £9.10: £2.80, £4.20, £2.80; EX 76.40.
Owner Jim Goldie Racing Club **Bred** James Thom And Sons And Peter Orr **Trained** Uplawmoor, E Renfrews

FOCUS
The field split into two groups in this modest handicap but the time was decent in the conditions and the form looks solid.
Mozakhraf(USA) Official explanation: jockey said gelding was unsuited by the good to soft ground

Milson's Point(IRE) Official explanation: trainer had no explanation for the poor form shown

4382 END WATER POVERTY H'CAP — 1m 1f 20y

7:50 (7:51) (Class 5) (0-75,74) 3-Y-0+ **£3,886** (£1,156; £577; £288) **Stalls** Low

Form — RPR

0303 **1** **Hawkit (USA)**[7] 4159 6-9-4 **64** DaleGibson 8 76
(P Monteith) *hld up in tch: rdn to ld 1f out: rdn out* **5/1**[3]

3434 **2** 1 1/2 **Bajan Parkes**[14] 3955 4-9-7 **74** GaryBartley(7) 5 83
(E J Alston) *hld up in rr: swtchd lft and hdwy over 2f out: sn rdn: r.o to take 2nd post* **4/1**[1]

0446 **3** *shd* **Cool Ebony**[7] 4177 4-9-6 **66** PaulMulrennan 2 75
(M Dods) *led: rdn over 2f out: hdd 1f out: no ex wl ins fnl f: lost 2nd post* **6/1**

3256 **4** *4* **King Of The Moors (USA)**[20] 3764 4-9-12 **72** PhillipMakin 1 72
(T D Barron) *prom: rdn over 2f out: wknd fnl f* **7/1**

0121 **5** 1 1/4 **Neil's Legacy (IRE)**[19] 3783 5-9-7 **67** PatCosgrave 6 65
(Miss L A Perratt) *chsd ldr: ev ch over 2f out: sn rdn and carried hd high: wknd fnl f* **4/1**[1]

0011 **6** *7* **Kiss Chase (IRE)**[15] 3918 3-7-13 **60** (b) KellyHarrison(7) 7 43
(J S Goldie) *hld up in tch: rdn over 2f out: sn wknd* **7/1**

261 **7** *8* **Amanda Carter**[14] 3955 3-8-12 **66** PaulHanagan 4 32
(R A Fahey) *hld up: no ch fnl 3f* **9/2**[2]

2m 0.94s (0.94) **Going Correction** +0.20s/f (Good)
WFA 3 from 4yo+ 8lb — **7** Ran SP% **114.1**
Speed ratings (Par 103): **103,101,101,98,96 90,83**
CSF £25.06 CT £121.67 TOTE £6.60: £3.40, £2.80; EX 30.40.
Owner A McLuckie **Bred** Hargus Sexton And Sandra Sexton **Trained** Rosewell, Midlothian

FOCUS
A moderate event that should prove sound with the first three close to their marks.
Kiss Chase(IRE) Official explanation: jockey said gelding was unsuited by the good to soft ground
Amanda Carter Official explanation: jockey said filly was unsuited by the good to soft ground

4383 WATER FOR LIFE H'CAP — 1m 1f 20y

8:20 (8:20) (Class 6) (0-60,60) 3-Y-0+ **£2,730** (£806; £403) **Stalls** Low

Form — RPR

2540 **1** **Mystical Ayr (IRE)**[7] 4159 5-9-8 **58** PhillipMakin 1 69
(Miss L A Perratt) *hld up and bhd: hdwy on outside over 2f out: rdn whn edgd lft and led over 1f out: r.o wl* **11/2**[2]

4136 **2** 2 1/2 **Thornaby Green**[14] 3956 6-9-1 **58** DeanHeslop(7) 7 63
(T D Barron) *prom: wnt 2nd over 6f out: led over 2f out: rdn and hdd over 1f out: one pce* **9/1**

0246 **3** *1* **Royal Citadel (IRE)**[18] 3816 4-8-9 **52** KellyHarrison(7) 5 55
(Mrs L B Normile) *led over 1f: a.p: rdn over 2f out: one pce fnl f* **16/1**

0060 **4** *3/4* **Touch Of Ivory (IRE)**[9] 4096 4-8-13 **52** (p) PatrickMathers(3) 4 53
(P Monteith) *s.i.s: hld up in rr: rdn and hdwy on ins 2f out: one pce fnl f* **33/1**

3-11 **5** *3* **Whittinghamvillage**[29] 3497 6-8-13 **52** AndrewElliott(3) 3 47
(D W Whillans) *hld up towards rr: rdn and hdwy on outside over 1f out: sn edgd lft: no further prog* **5/2**[1]

0160 **6** *1* **Mayadeen (IRE)**[18] 3816 5-9-4 **54** (b) TomEaves 9 46
(I Semple) *s.i.s: sn prom: rdn 2f out: wknd fnl f* **10/1**

0000 **7** *1* **Anduril**[6] 3926 6-9-10 **60** (v[1]) PaulEddery 11 50
(Miss M E Rowland) *hld up in mid-div: rdn over 2f out: sme hdwy over 1f out: wknd ins fnl f* **16/1**

0500 **8** *5* **Playtotheaudience**[7] 4156 4-9-4 **54** PaulHanagan 6 33
(R A Fahey) *prom: rdn over 3f out: wknd 2f out* **11/1**

2205 **9** *3/4* **Mandarin Rocket (IRE)**[7] 4159 4-8-13 **52** JamieMoriarty(3) 10 30
(Miss L A Perratt) *a bhd* **9/1**

-400 **10** *hd* **Haifa (IRE)**[54] 2714 4-9-8 **58** (p) DaleGibson 12 35
(Mrs A Duffield) *hdwy to ld over 7f out: rdn and hdd over 2f out: wknd over 1f out* **11/1**

0640 **11** 3 1/2 **Gala Sunday (USA)**[14] 3955 7-9-7 **57** (t) PaulMulrennan 2 26
(M W Easterby) *hld up towards rr: rdn 3f out: eased whn btn fnl 2f* **7/1**[3]

0520 **12** *4* **Key Partners (IRE)**[37] 3243 6-9-8 **58** PatCosgrave 8 19
(J T Stimpson) *hld up in mid-div: rdn and wknd 2f out: eased whn no ch ins fnl f* **20/1**

2m 1.39s (1.39) **Going Correction** +0.20s/f (Good) — **12** Ran SP% **121.7**
Speed ratings (Par 101): **101,98,97,97,94 93,92,88,87,87 84,80**
CSF £56.01 CT £761.29 TOTE £5.30: £1.60, £3.50, £5.40; EX 58.90.
Owner Ayrshire Racing **Bred** Miss Rosemary McManus **Trained** Ayr, S Ayrshire

FOCUS
A very modest affair but sound enough rated around the first two.
Gala Sunday(USA) Official explanation: jockey said gelding was never travelling

4384 WATERAID H'CAP — 5f

8:50 (8:50) (Class 6) (0-65,64) 3-Y-0 **£2,590** (£770; £385; £192) **Stalls** Centre

Form — RPR

3325 **1** **Howards Tipple**[7] 4157 3-9-5 **62** (p) TomEaves 10 66
(I Semple) *a.p: rdn over 1f out: r.o u.p to ld last stride* **6/4**[1]

0020 **2** *hd* **Spinning Game**[5] 4226 3-7-11 **47** (b) DanielleMcCreery(7) 1 50
(D W Chapman) *racd along centre: hdwy to ld over 2f out: rdn ins fnl f: ct last stride* **12/1**

2236 **3** 1 1/4 **Moonlight Applause**[26] 3588 3-8-11 **54** PaulMulrennan 4 53
(T D Easterby) *led: hdd over 2f out: rdn over 1f out: r.o one pce fnl f* **9/2**[2]

3064 **4** *2* **Beechside (IRE)**[47] 2939 3-8-4 **47** DaleGibson 11 39
(W A Murphy, Ire) *hld up and bhd: hdwy 1f out: rdn and kpt on same pce ins fnl f* **9/1**

5050 **5** 1 1/2 **Mandriano (ITY)**[5] 4226 3-8-2 **45** (p) PaulHanagan 3 31
(D W Barker) *chsd ldr: rdn wl over 1f out: one pce* **14/1**

0030 **6** *3/4* **Kilvickeon (IRE)**[36] 3281 3-8-3 **47** ow2 PatrickMathers(3) 5 32
(Peter Grayson) *hld up in mid-div: rdn over 1f out: no hdwy* **6/1**[3]

0000 **7** 1 1/4 **Senora Lenorah**[18] 3811 3-7-11 **45** ow2 PaulPickard(7) 9 26
(D A Nolan) *prom: rdn 2f out: sn wknd* **33/1**

-000 **8** 1 1/4 **Whats Your Game (IRE)**[5] 4226 3-8-1 **45** ow2 AndrewElliott(3) 2 21
(A Berry) *hld up and bhd: short-lived effrt 2f out* **20/1**

0420 **9** 1 1/4 **Invincible Lad (IRE)**[5] 4224 3-8-5 **55** (p) GaryBartley(7) 6 25
(E J Alston) *a bhd* **6/1**[3]

62.90 secs (2.46) **Going Correction** +0.325s/f (Good) — **9** Ran SP% **118.8**
Speed ratings (Par 98): **93,92,90,87,85 83,81,79,77**
CSF £22.84 CT £71.42 TOTE £2.40: £1.30, £3.50, £1.40; EX 32.70 Place 6 £193.21, Place 5 £131.03.
Owner Gordon McDowall **Bred** New Hall Stud **Trained** Carluke, S Lanarks

FOCUS
A mediocre handicap and modest form, although reasonable enough with the third and fifth to their marks.
T/Plt: £727.90 to a £1 stake. Pool: £52,854.25. 53.00 winning tickets. T/Qpdt: £133.00 to a £1 stake. Pool: £3,165.30. 17.60 winning tickets. KH

4349 HAYDOCK (L-H)

Saturday, August 11

OFFICIAL GOING: Good to firm (firm in places)
Wind: Light, across Weather: Sunny

4385 COMMHOIST H'CAP — 1m 30y

1:25 (1:26) (Class 2) (0-100,100) 3-Y-0+ **£14,573** (£4,335; £2,166; £1,082) **Stalls** Low

Form — RPR

6025 **1** **Annemasse**[14] 3940 3-8-13 **92** GregFairley 9 103
(M Johnston) *trckd ldrs: rdn to ld over 2f out: r.o wl and in command towards fin* **4/1**[1]

0212 **2** 2 1/2 **Electric Warrior (IRE)**[10] 4068 4-9-0 **86** PatCosgrave 1 92
(K R Burke) *trckd ldrs: rdn to take 2nd over 1f out: pressed wnr ent fnl f: nt qckn fnl 100yds* **15/2**

1120 **3** *hd* **Flipando (IRE)**[28] 3558 6-10-0 **100** PhillipMakin 7 106
(T D Barron) *hld up: rdn over 2f out: hdwy over 1f out: styd on wl and gng on towards fin* **9/2**[2]

0112 **4** *2* **Nevada Desert (IRE)**[7] 4176 7-8-10 **87** MichaelJStainton(5) 5 88
(R M Whitaker) *prom: rdn and pressed wnr 2f out: lost 2nd over 1f out: kpt on same pce ins fnl f* **6/1**

0054 **5** 1 3/4 **Goodbye Mr Bond**[7] 4176 7-9-3 **89** EddieAhern 3 86
(E J Alston) *hld up: rdn and hdwy to chse ldrs over 2f out: one pce fnl f* **5/1**[3]

0000 **6** *5* **Valdan (IRE)**[51] 2788 3-8-8 **87** ow2 StephenDonohoe 8 71
(P D Evans) *hld up: rdn over 2f out: no imp* **25/1**

4040 **7** 1 1/2 **Kings Point (IRE)**[8] 4119 6-9-4 **90** (p) PaulHanagan 2 72
(R A Fahey) *led: rdn and hdd over 2f out: wknd over 1f out* **5/1**[3]

-002 **8** 1 1/4 **Sir Xaar (IRE)**[14] 3953 4-9-7 **93** (t) TomEaves 4 72
(B Smart) *s.i.s: in rr: pushed along briefly after s: rdn over 4f out: nvr on terms* **8/1**

0200 **9** *3* **Sendalam (FR)**[50] 2817 5-9-11 **97** NCallan 6 69
(J S Moore) *midfield: rdn over 2f out: wknd over 1f out* **33/1**

1m 41.42s (-4.09) **Going Correction** -0.20s/f (Firm)
WFA 3 from 4yo+ 7lb — **9** Ran SP% **115.5**
Speed ratings (Par 109): **112,109,109,107,105 100,99,97,94**
CSF £34.29 CT £140.65 TOTE £5.00: £2.20, £2.50, £1.90; EX 39.00 Trifecta £82.30 Part won. Pool: £116.00 - 0.50 winning units..
Owner Brian Yeardley Continental Ltd **Bred** Newsells Park Stud Limited **Trained** Middleham Moor, N Yorks

FOCUS
A decent handicap, run at a sound pace. The form looks solid rated through the third.

NOTEBOOK
Annemasse ◆, well backed, was ridden with a bit more restraint this time and came home to score with a deal left up his sleeve. He deserved this success as he has run some gallant races in defeat from this mark in better company of late and should be high on confidence now. The type his trainer does so well with, he should be given plenty of respect if turning out under a penalty. (op 11-2)
Electric Warrior(IRE), 3lb higher, looked a brief threat to the winner, but it was clear that rival had his measure inside the final furlong. This was still a solid effort in defeat, and his best on turf for some time, but the likelihood is he will go up a few pounds again now. (op 8-1 tchd 7-1)
Flipando(IRE) was doing his best work towards the finish and posted a perfectly respectable effort under top weight. He gives the form a decent look. (tchd 5-1)
Nevada Desert(IRE) proved one paced when push came to shove but did not lose a great deal in defeat from a 2lb higher mark. (op 11-2)
Goodbye Mr Bond was another who looked one paced at the business end and a return to easier ground should prove more to his liking in due course. (tchd 9-2)
Valdan(IRE) Official explanation: jockey said gelding hung right throughout
Sir Xaar(IRE) Official explanation: jockey said colt was never travelling; vet said colt lost both front shoes

4386 CORAL.CO.UK H'CAP — 5f

2:00 (2:00) (Class 2) (0-100,98) 3-Y-0+ **£16,192** (£4,817; £2,407; £1,202) **Stalls** High

Form — RPR

0-30 **1** **Judd Street**[6] 4196 5-9-7 **94** PhillipMakin 12 106
(Eve Johnson Houghton) *chsd ldrs: prog on stands' rail to ld jst ins fnl f: r.o* **8/1**

0450 **2** 1 1/4 **Cape Royal**[13] 3990 7-8-12 **90** (bt) KevinGhunowa(5) 13 98
(J M Bradley) *led: rdn appr fnl f: edgd lft 1f out: sn hdd: hld towards fin* **14/1**

0600 **3** 3 1/2 **Harry Up**[9] 4095 6-8-11 **84** NCallan 8 79
(K A Ryan) *chsd ldrs: rdn over 1f out: nt pce of front pair ins fnl f* **18/1**

020 **4** *hd* **Tabaret**[13] 3990 4-9-5 **97** MichaelJStainton(5) 2 91
(R M Whitaker) *hld up: rdn and hdwy on outside over 2f out: kpt on ins fnl f: nt pce of ldrs* **14/1**

3601 **5** *3/4* **Ishi Adiva**[21] 3749 3-8-12 **91** RichardKingscote(3) 11 82
(Tom Dascombe) *in tch: rdn over 1f out: swtchd lft ent fnl f: nt pce to chal* **11/1**

0005 **6** *hd* **Merlin's Dancer**[8] 4122 7-9-4 **91** JimCrowley 10 82
(S Dow) *prom: rdn over 1f out: wknd ins fnl f* **14/1**

0460 **7** *shd* **River Falcon**[14] 3975 7-9-7 **94** (p) PaulHanagan 6 84
(J S Goldie) *in rr: rdn over 1f out: styd on fnl f: nvr nrr* **14/1**

1322 **8** *shd* **Hoh Hoh Hoh**[13] 3990 5-9-3 **90** KerrinMcEvoy 5 80+
(R J Price) *s.s: towards rr: hdwy 2f out: rdn over 1f out: one pce ins fnl f* **4/1**[1]

1260 **9** *1/2* **Ajigolo**[9] 4090 4-9-9 **96** TPO'Shea 14 87+
(M R Channon) *hld up in midfield: rdn over 1f out: nt clr run ent fnl f: no real prog after* **25/1**

1301 **10** *3/4* **Aegean Dancer**[63] 2463 5-9-1 **88** TomEaves 7 74
(B Smart) *in tch: rdn over 1f out: one pce fnl f* **5/1**[2]

0004 **11** 1 3/4 **Texas Gold**[9] 4095 9-9-1 **88** EddieAhern 4 67
(W R Muir) *midfield: rdn over 1f out: sn outpcd* **7/1**[3]

0013 **12** *2* **Dig Deep (IRE)**[13] 3990 5-9-3 **90** PaulMulrennan 3 62
(W J Haggas) *midfield tl rdn and wknd over 1f out* **7/1**[3]

21-0 **13** 2 1/2 **Yungaburra (IRE)**[92] 1616 3-9-8 **98** (t) FrancisNorton 1 61
(D J Murphy) *a bhd* **40/1**

58.94 secs (-1.18) **Going Correction** -0.425s/f (Firm)
WFA 3 from 4yo+ 3lb — **13** Ran SP% **119.3**
Speed ratings (Par 109): **108,106,100,100,98 98,98,98,97,96 93,90,86**
CSF £114.94 CT £1960.91 TOTE £9.40: £2.90, £5.40, £6.30; EX 155.70 TRIFECTA Not won..
Owner R F Johnson Houghton **Bred** R F Johnson Houghton **Trained** Blewbury, Oxon

FOCUS
A competitive sprint run at a good pace which saw those drawn high at an advantage and the form cannot be taken literally.

NOTEBOOK
Judd Street, back in trip, ran out a ready winner from his decent draw and opened his account for the current season at the third attempt. He was far from disgraced in Listed company last time, but this is really his level and the fast ground was much to his liking. However, he is not going to prove easy to place successfully from a higher mark again now.
Cape Royal showed up well from the front and ran his usual game race in defeat. He has always been at least placed to date from a mark of 90, but no doubt the Handicapper will put him up a pound or two again after this.
Harry Up was unable to dictate as he prefers, but still ran a gallant race in defeat on ground he enjoys. He is simply in the Handicapper's grip. (op 16-1 tchd 20-1)
Tabaret finished his race well and fared the best of those drawn low. He seemingly goes on any ground and really deserves a change of fortune, but is another who looks in the Handicapper's grip.
Ishi Adiva Official explanation: trainer said filly was unsuited by the good to firm (firm in places) ground
River Falcon would have found this ground plenty fast enough and got going too late in the day. (op 12-1)
Hoh Hoh Hoh was always going to struggle after missing the kick and is capable of better on his day. Official explanation: jockey said gelding missed the break (op 11-2)
Dig Deep(IRE) Official explanation: jockey said gelding was never travelling

4387 TOTEPOOL ROSE OF LANCASTER STKS (GROUP 3) 1m 2f 120y
2:35 (2:35) (Class 1) 3-Y-0+
£36,907 (£13,988; £7,000; £3,490; £1,748; £877) **Stalls** High

Form RPR
1050 **1** **Halicarnassus (IRE)**[9] 4092 3-8-7 108 TPO'Shea 4 111
(M R Channon) *hld up in rr: swtchd rt and hdwy over 1f out: edgd lft and r.o to ld wl ins fnl f: pushed out fnl strides* **9/1**
20S2 **2** 1 ¼ **Formal Decree (GER)**[13] 4013 4-9-7 112 KerrinMcEvoy 3 113
(Saeed Bin Suroor) *hld up bhd ldrs: rdn to ld over 1f out: edgd sltly rt ins fnl f: sn hdd: hld fnl strides* **9/4**[2]
3111 **3** hd **Zaham (USA)**[51] 2789 3-8-7 105 RHills 2 109
(M Johnston) *led at stdy pce: rdn 2f out: hdd over 1f out: stl ev ch and pressing for ld whn n.m.r wl ins fnl f: kpt on* **11/8**[1]
3010 **4** nk **Hearthstead Maison (IRE)**[9] 4092 3-8-7 110 GregFairley 1 108
(M Johnston) *a.p: rdn and ev ch fr 2f out: abt a nk down in 4th whn n.m.r and hmpd wl ins fnl f: hld after* **5/1**[3]
6356 **5** 3 **Kandidate**[35] 3331 5-9-7 112 (t) EddieAhern 7 106
(C E Brittain) *racd keenly: stdd bhd ldrs after 2f: rdn 2f out: no imp* **8/1**
6434 **6** 7 **Rudry Dragon (IRE)**[9] 4111 3-8-7 77 KevinGhunowa 5 89?
(P A Blockley) *hld up: pushed along 3f out: lft bhd fnl 1f* **80/1**
2m 15.76s (-0.38) **Going Correction** -0.20s/f (Firm)
WFA 3 from 4yo+ 10lb **6** Ran SP% **111.9**
Speed ratings (Par 113): **99,98,97,97,95 90**
CSF £29.40 TOTE £11.60: £4.00, £1.60; EX 33.10.
Owner Box 41 **Bred** Yeomanstown Lodge Stud **Trained** West Ilsley, Berks

FOCUS
Not the strongest Group 3. It was run at just a steady early pace and the form should be treated with a degree of caution.

NOTEBOOK
Halicarnassus(IRE) showed a turn of foot when asked for his effort and registered his first success in Group company since his juvenile season with a little left up his sleeve at the finish. He seems best when racing in small fields, clearly relishes fast ground and is the type his trainer tends to excel with. (op 12-1 tchd 8-1)
Formal Decree(GER) proved keen early on due to the lack of real pace on and would not have found this race run to suit him. He still held every chance. (op 5-2 tchd 2-1)
Zaham(USA), making his debut in Group company, would have probably been better off going faster through the early stages. He looked held when he got tightened for room by the eventual winner late on. (tchd 7-4)
Hearthstead Maison(IRE) was another done no favours by the winner inside the final furlong and should be rated a little better than the bare form. He may appreciate stepping back up in trip again before long and has the talent to score at this level. (op 11-2 tchd 6-1 and 9-2)

4388 TOTESPORT.COM OLD NEWTON CUP (HERITAGE H'CAP) 1m 3f 200y
3:10 (3:11) (Class 2) 3-Y-0+
£52,972 (£15,861; £7,930; £3,969; £1,980; £994) **Stalls** High

Form RPR
6050 **1** **Dansili Dancer**[11] 4043 5-9-3 95 PaulMulrennan 8 106
(C G Cox) *midfield: rdn and hdwy over 2f out: nosed ahd ins fnl f: r.o* **15/2**
0055 **2** ½ **Futun**[49] 2859 4-9-2 94 EddieAhern 7 104+
(L M Cumani) *hld up and ref to settle: hdwy 3f out: rdn and hung rt over 1f out: r.o wl and gaining towards fin* **7/2**[1]
4214 **3** shd **Misty Dancer**[13] 3989 8-8-9 87 KerrinMcEvoy 2 97
(Miss Venetia Williams) *trckd ldrs: rdn to ld over 2f out: hdd ins fnl f: nt qckn towards fin* **11/2**[3]
6062 **4** ¾ **Lundy's Lane (IRE)**[14] 3939 7-9-1 93 FrancisNorton 11 105+
(A M Balding) *midfield: nt clr run over 2f out: swtchd lft whn rdn and hdwy over 1f out: sn snatched up whn nt clr run: str run towards fin: n.m.r fnl stride* **7/1**
0140 **5** 1 **All The Good (IRE)**[11] 4047 4-9-4 96 NickyMackay 10 103
(G A Butler) *hld up: rdn and hdwy over 2f out: chsng ldrs whn carried rt ins fnl f: kpt on* **9/1**
5330 **6** 2 **Collateral Damage (IRE)**[11] 4043 4-8-7 85 (t) DavidAllan 5 89
(T D Easterby) *midfield: rdn over 2f out: kpt on u.p ins fnl f: nt pce to trble ldrs* **12/1**
3-21 **7** nk **Tears Of A Clown (IRE)**[15] 3899 4-8-12 90 TPQueally 13 94
(J A Osborne) *hld up in rr: rdn over 2f out: hdwy over 1f out: kpt on same pce ins fnl f: nvr able to chal* **9/2**[2]
0203 **8** ½ **Wind Star**[14] 3959 4-8-11 89 PatCosgrave 9 92
(G A Swinbank) *hld up: rdn whn n.m.r and hmpd 2f out: no imp on ldrs* **8/1**
-015 **9** 1 **Realism (FR)**[14] 3939 7-8-12 90 (p) PaulHanagan 6 91
(R A Fahey) *racd keenly w ldr: rdn and lost pl over 2f out: n.d after* **20/1**
1000 **10** 4 **Luberon**[28] 3558 4-9-10 102 GregFairley 4 97
(M Johnston) *led: rdn 3f out: hdd over 2f out: wknd 1f out* **28/1**
1040 **11** 1 ¾ **My Arch**[29] 3509 5-8-9 87 (p) NCallan 1 79
(K A Ryan) *prom: rdn and ev ch over 2f out: wkng whn n.m.r 1f out* **22/1**
2m 30.99s (-4.00) **Going Correction** -0.20s/f (Firm) **11** Ran SP% **121.4**
Speed ratings (Par 109): **105,104,104,104,103 102,101,101,100,98 97**
CSF £34.20 CT £161.59 TOTE £9.40: £2.90, £2.00, £2.00; EX 45.50 Trifecta £211.40 Pool: £714.70 - 2.40 winning units..
Owner The Troupers **Bred** The Magic Slipper Partnership **Trained** Lambourn, Berks
■ This long-established handicap was re-scheduled after the abandonment of the July meeting.

FOCUS
No more than a fair renewal of this traditonally strong handicap. It was run at just a modest early pace and the form is worth treating with some caution.

NOTEBOOK
Dansili Dancer, having his first run over this far, was given a peach of a ride and proved game where it mattered to score. He has run consistently at this level all season and clearly got the longer trip without fuss, although the modest early pace would have helped him in that respect. While things will be tougher for him from a higher mark, he is open to further improvement over the trip. (op 7-1 tchd 8-1)
Futun, very well backed, was respresenting a trainer who had won this race three times in the last ten years. He ultimately spoilt his chances by refusing to settle however, and was staying on all too late towards the finish. No doubt he is tricky, but this is his ground and he does have a decent prize within his compass when consenting to settle better. (op 10-3)
Misty Dancer did not go down without a fight once headed inside the final furlong and ran with credit in defeat. This versatile eight-year-old does not look weighted out of winning again just yet. (op 7-1 tchd 15-2)
Lundy's Lane(IRE) ◆, back up in trip, endured a luckless passage from off the pace and has to rate unlucky. He would have enjoyed a stronger early pace and, on this evidence, his turn may not be too far off again. (op 14-1)
Tears Of A Clown(IRE), a market drifter, was another who would have been seen to better advantage off a stronger pace. We have yet to see the best of him. (op 7-2)
Wind Star, who looked to have been laid out for this, should be rated better than his finishing position as he met trouble when trying to make up his ground nearing the 2f pole.
Luberon Official explanation: jockey said colt ran too freely

4389 COMMHOIST LOGISTICS H'CAP 6f
3:45 (3:46) (Class 3) (0-90,92) 3-Y-0+ **£9,715** (£2,890; £1,444; £721) **Stalls** High

Form RPR
0603 **1** **High Curragh**[6] 4195 4-9-6 85 NCallan 13 93
(K A Ryan) *chsd ldrs: rdn and edgd lft whn led 1f out: r.o u.p* **4/1**[1]
0340 **2** nk **Holbeck Ghyll (IRE)**[9] 4095 5-8-11 76 FrancisNorton 3 83
(A M Balding) *chsd ldrs: led briefly over 1f out: sn carried lft: continued to press wnr ins fnl f: hld fnl strides* **10/1**
0000 **3** ½ **Bazroy (IRE)**[8] 4123 3-8-9 78 (v) StephenDonohoe 14 83
(P D Evans) *hld up: hdwy 1/2-way: rdn and swtchd lft over 1f out: r.o ins fnl f: gng on at fin* **14/1**
6110 **4** ½ **Stamford Blue**[27] 3569 6-9-1 85 (b) LukeMorris[(5)] 6 89
(R A Harris) *in rr: outpcd over 3f out: hdwy over 1f out: edgd lft ins fnl f: r.o and gaining nr fin* **8/1**
302 **5** 2 **Bo McGinty (IRE)**[16] 3886 6-8-12 77 (b) PaulHanagan 11 75
(R A Fahey) *prom: rdn over 2f out: no ex ins fnl f* **13/2**[2]
0065 **6** shd **Geojimali**[13] 4006 5-9-1 80 DanielTudhope 7 85+
(J S Goldie) *s.i.s: bhd: hdwy whn nt clr run and snatched up ent fnl f: r.o: nrst fin* **10/1**
-100 **7** nk **My Gacho (IRE)**[8] 4122 5-9-4 83 (b) PhillipMakin 8 80
(T D Barron) *led: edgd lft over 1f out: sn bmpd and hdd: fdd ins fnl f* **16/1**
0000 **8** ½ **Captain Hurricane**[8] 4122 5-9-5 84 (p) EddieAhern 10 79
(B J Meehan) *midfield: rdn 2f out: one pce ins fnl f* **7/1**[3]
230 **9** hd **Don Pele (IRE)**[8] 4122 5-8-11 76 (p) JimCrowley 9 71
(R A Harris) *midfield: rdn over 2f out: nvr able to chal* **14/1**
0606 **10** hd **Mujood**[8] 4122 4-9-8 87 (b) NelsonDeSouza 5 81
(Eve Johnson Houghton) *midfield: rdn over 2f out: sme hdwy over 1f out: one pce ins fnl f* **25/1**
4-3 **11** 1 **Coseadrom (IRE)**[17] 3836 5-8-12 77 TPQueally 12 68
(M F Harris) *midfield: n.m.r over 4f out: nt clr run over 2f out: sn rdn: no imp* **9/1**
0-60 **12** 2 **Pretty Majestic (IRE)**[31] 3431 3-9-5 88 TPO'Shea 4 72
(M R Channon) *towards rr: rdn over 2f out: nvr on terms* **16/1**
3002 **13** 1 **Come Out Fighting**[8] 4133 4-9-13 92 KerrinMcEvoy 2 74
(P A Blockley) *midfield: rdn over 2f out: wknd over 1f out* **7/1**[3]
-000 **14** 1 **Swing The Ring (IRE)**[15] 3911 4-9-6 85 (b) PaulMulrennan 1 64
(A Berry) *chsd ldrs: rdn 1/2-way: sn wknd* **66/1**
1m 12.73s (-1.16) **Going Correction** -0.425s/f (Firm)
WFA 3 from 4yo+ 4lb **14** Ran SP% **128.1**
Speed ratings (Par 107): **97,96,95,95,92 92,92,91,91,90 89,86,85,84**
CSF £47.48 CT £549.20 TOTE £5.90: £2.00, £3.90, £4.80; EX 63.40.
Owner Mrs D Davenport,T&R Fawcett,J Nattrass **Bred** Wheelersland Stud **Trained** Hambleton, N Yorks

FOCUS
A fair sprint handicap in which once more it paid to be drawn high. The form is rated around the first three.

NOTEBOOK
High Curragh just did enough to justify favouritism and get up under a typically strong ride from Callan. He is no doubt best over this trip on a sound surface and it was his first success since his juvenile campaign, but he would not be one to go overboard about when bidding to follow up from a higher mark. (op 5-1 tchd 6-1)
Holbeck Ghyll(IRE), with the blinkers abandoned on this step up in trip, deserves extra credit as he was drawn unfavourably low and was not done many favours by the winner late in the day. That said, he has never been easy to predict. (tchd 9-1)
Bazroy(IRE) showed improved form for the re-application of a visor and step back up to the extra furlong. His turn may not be far off again, but he is no doubt best kept to this trip.
Stamford Blue hit a flat spot at a crucial stage before staying on again all too late. He would have found this ground plenty fast enough. (op 12-1 tchd 15-2)
Geojimali ◆ was always playing catch up after a slow start, but he was still full of running when being hampered and must be rated a deal better than the bare form. He is currently 1lb lower than his last winning mark and looks ready to strike in the coming weeks when things go more his way.
My Gacho(IRE) Official explanation: jockey said gelding hung left in final 2f

4390 SPORTS360.CO.UK H'CAP 6f
4:20 (4:20) (Class 5) (0-70,70) 4-Y-0+ **£3,886** (£1,156; £577; £288) **Stalls** High

Form RPR
344 **1** **Katie Boo (IRE)**[19] 3784 5-9-3 64 FrancisNorton 2 76
(A Berry) *midfield: swtchd lft and hdwy over 1f out: r.o to ld ins fnl f: in command towards fin* **6/1**[2]
2040 **2** ½ **John Keats**[15] 3921 4-8-13 60 DanielTudhope 5 70
(J S Goldie) *in tch: rdn to ld 1f out: hdd ins fnl f: nt qckn towards fin* **13/2**[3]
0130 **3** 2 **Talcen Gwyn (IRE)**[26] 3594 5-8-8 60 KevinGhunowa[(5)] 6 64
(M F Harris) *a.p: rdn to ld over 1f out: sn hdd: styd on same pce ins fnl f* **20/1**
0602 **4** ½ **Lambency (IRE)**[8] 4141 4-8-4 51 NickyMackay 11 54
(J S Goldie) *hld up: rdn and hdwy over 2f out: styd on ins fnl f: nvr nrr* **15/2**
0312 **5** 1 ¼ **Roman Quintet (IRE)**[28] 3549 7-9-6 67 EddieAhern 12 66
(R J Price) *led: rdn and hdd over 1f out: no ex ins fnl f* **2/1**[1]
0000 **6** ¾ **Brigadore**[10] 4083 8-8-13 60 KerrinMcEvoy 13 57
(J G Given) *chsd ldrs: rdn over 1f out: one pce ins fnl f* **7/1**
210 **7** hd **Turn Me On (IRE)**[13] 3999 4-9-2 63 JimCrowley 4 59
(T D Walford) *prom: rdn over 1f out: fdd ins fnl f* **7/1**

0660 **8** *nk* **Enjoy The Buzz**[30] 3449 8-7-11 **51** oh3................................(p) KMay(7) 10 46
(J M Bradley) *midfield: rdn 2f out: nt pce to chal* **33/1**
5364 **9** *3* **Nautical**[23] 3686 9-9-4 **65**.. JamesDoyle 8 51
(A W Carroll) *hld up: rdn 2f out: nvr on terms* **9/1**
46-0 **10** *hd* **Cursum Perficio**[15] 3926 5-9-9 **70**.............................. NelsonDeSouza 14 55
(R Lee) *in tch: rdn 2f out: wknd over 1f out* **33/1**
306 **11** *97* **Steeley Fox**[65] 2393 4-8-11 **58**... NCallan 1 —
(J M Bradley) *bhd: eased fr 1/2-way: virtually p.u fnl f* **20/1**

1m 12.92s (-0.97) **Going Correction** -0.425s/f (Firm) **11** Ran SP% **123.1**
Speed ratings (Par 103): **96,95,92,92,90 89,89,88,84,84** —
CSF £44.75 CT £745.75 TOTE £5.20: £1.90, £2.50, £5.40; EX 40.50.
Owner The Early Doors Partnership **Bred** Michael McGlynn **Trained** Cockerham, Lancs

FOCUS
A moderate sprint handicap but solid enough form. Most of the runners elected to come up the middle of the track.
Steeley Fox Official explanation: jockey said gelding lost its action

4391 ACADEMY LEASING H'CAP — 1m 6f
4:50 (4:50) (Class 5) (0-70,65) 3-Y-O **£3,886** (£1,156; £577; £288) **Stalls** High

Form RPR
-020 **1** **Alleviate (IRE)**[25] 3624 3-9-1 **57**.. NCallan 5 68+
(Sir Mark Prescott) *sn led: mde rest: clr whn wandered over 1f out: kpt on wl and a doing enough towards fin* **7/1**[3]
0652 **2** *½* **Shine And Rise (IRE)**[30] 3450 3-9-9 **65**.......................... EddieAhern 1 72
(C G Cox) *ref to settle: trckd ldrs: swtchd rt 2f out: chsd wnr over 1f out: r.o and clsd ins fnl f: hld fnl strides* **11/2**[2]
-531 **3** *1 ½* **Franchoek (IRE)**[9] 4104 3-9-3 **59**............................... KerrinMcEvoy 15 64+
(A King) *hld up: stdy hdwy 3f out: n.m.r and hmpd 2f out: styd on ins fnl f: nt rch ldrs* **7/4**[1]
6015 **4** *½* **President Dan**[2] 4322 3-8-13 **55**.. TPO'Shea 14 59
(M R Channon) *hld up: rdn over 2f out: hdwy over 1f out: edgd lft ins fnl f: styd on on wl* **8/1**
-334 **5** *3* **Hatton Flight**[18] 3825 3-9-4 **60**..................................(b[1]) FrancisNorton 8 60
(A M Balding) *racd keenly: trckd ldrs: rdn over 3f out: one pce ins fnl f: eased whn hld towards fin* **8/1**
6550 **6** *1 ½* **Sendali (FR)**[19] 3792 3-8-11 **53**... DavidAllan 12 51
(J D Bethell) *midfield: rdn over 2f out: nvr able to chal* **33/1**
0030 **7** *1* **Lightning Queen (USA)**[24] 3640 3-7-13 **48**........................ KMay(7) 10 45
(B W Hills) *chsd ldrs: rdn over 3f out: no ex over 1f out* **16/1**
-004 **8** *½* **Cornell Precedent**[28] 3540 3-7-13 **46**......................... LukeMorris(5) 13 42
(J J Quinn) *midfield: rdn over 3f out: one pce fr over 1f out* **40/1**
0-00 **9** *¾* **Nothing Is Forever (IRE)**[10] 4069 3-9-4 **60**.................. JimCrowley 16 55
(Mrs A J Perrett) *prom: rdn 4f out: edgd lft 2f out: wknd ins fnl f* **25/1**
000 **10** *shd* **Victory Mile (USA)**[42] 3084 3-9-3 **59**....................... StephenDonohoe 17 54
(B J Meehan) *hld up: rdn over 1f out: kpt on fnl f: nvr able to chal* **33/1**
0-64 **11** *½* **Tivers Song (USA)**[39] 3189 3-9-9 **65**.............................. JamesDoyle 7 59
(Mrs A J Perrett) *midfield: rdn over 2f out: no imp whn n.m.r and hmpd over 1f out* **22/1**
404 **12** *1 ½* **Starr Flyer**[48] 2909 3-8-3 **50**..................................... KevinGhunowa(5) 3 42
(A Bailey) *midfield: rdn over 2f out: wknd over 1f out* **33/1**
2545 **13** *nk* **Always Best**[12] 4025 3-9-1 **57**.. GregFairley 4 48
(M Johnston) *led early: remained prom: rdn over 2f out: wknd fnl f* **8/1**
0330 **14** *3 ½* **Still Dreaming**[24] 3640 3-9-9 **65**................................. DanielTudhope 9 51
(M Dods) *midfield: pushed along over 4f out: wknd 2f out* **33/1**
-052 **15** *26* **Namarian (IRE)**[11] 4036 3-8-4 **46**................................(b) NelsonDeSouza 6 —
(T D Easterby) *racd keenly: bhd after 2f* **40/1**

3m 3.31s (-2.98) **Going Correction** -0.20s/f (Firm) **15** Ran SP% **128.3**
Speed ratings (Par 100): **100,99,98,98,96 96,95,95,94,94 94,93,93,91,76**
CSF £44.18 CT £100.23 TOTE £9.10: £2.90, £2.60, £1.40; EX 66.70 Place 6 £527.85, Place 5 £255.66.
Owner Mrs Sonia Rogers **Bred** Miss K Rausing & Airlie Stud **Trained** Newmarket, Suffolk

FOCUS
A moderate staying handicap but the form looks sound enough for the grade.
Hatton Flight Official explanation: jockey said gelding ran too freely
Namarian(IRE) Official explanation: jockey said filly ran too freely
T/Jkpt: Not won. T/Plt: £1,263.60 to a £1 stake. Pool: £100,662.80. 58.15 winning tickets. T/Qpdt: £85.40 to a £1 stake. Pool: £4,616.70. 40.00 winning tickets. DO

4355 LINGFIELD (L-H)
Saturday, August 11

OFFICIAL GOING: All-weather - standard; turf course - good to firm
Wind: Light behind Weather: Sunny, very warm

4392 WBX.COM £25 BET FOR NEW ACCOUNTS MEDIAN AUCTION MAIDEN STKS — 1m 2f (P)
5:40 (5:43) (Class 6) 3-4-Y-O **£2,730** (£806; £403) **Stalls** Low

Form RPR
5202 **1** **Risque Heights**[10] 4069 3-9-3 71.................................... GeorgeBaker 12 78+
(G A Butler) *hld up towards rr: smooth prog over 3f out to trck ldr over 2f out: led over 1f out: sn clr: easily* **5/2**[1]
4 **2** *2 ½* **Tropical Strait (IRE)**[19] 3794 4-9-12 0...................... FergusSweeney 9 73+
(D W P Arbuthnot) *rn in snatches: drvn in midfield 1/2-way: prog and nt clr run over 2f out: r.o to take 2nd last 100yds: no ch w wnr* **4/1**[2]
5-0 **3** *1 ¼* **Verbatim**[113] 1127 3-8-9 0... WilliamBuick(3) 8 62
(A M Balding) *hld up in midfield: rdn and prog over 4f out to go 3rd over 2f out: outpcd over 1f out: kpt on same pce and 2nd briefly ins fnl f* **16/1**
03 **4** *1 ½* **Blue Space**[24] 3651 3-8-12 0... AmirQuinn 5 59
(P J Makin) *trckd ldr 3f: styd prom: drvn and outpcd over 2f out: styd on again fnl f* **8/1**
3330 **5** *2* **Orama's Ghost**[45] 2981 3-8-12 72.................................. JimmyFortune 3 55
(Sir Michael Stoute) *pushed up to ld: rdn and hdd over 1f out: wknd rapidly fnl f* **9/2**[3]
6630 **6** *2 ½* **County Kerry (UAE)**[12] 4018 3-8-5 54........................(t) SophieDoyle(7) 4 50+
(Jean-Rene Auvray) *hld up in midfield: gng strly whn nt clr run over 2f out: sn outpcd: no ch whn rdn fnl f: do bttr* **66/1**
4 **7** *3 ½* **Meon Mix**[89] 1725 3-8-12 0.. MickyFenton 7 43
(J R Fanshawe) *dwlt: hld up towards rr: gng wl enough over 3f out: rdn and outpcd sn after: n.d fnl 2f* **7/1**
8 *2 ½* **How's Business** 3-8-12 0....................................... SimonWhitworth 10 38
(C A Cyzer) *racd wd towards rr: lft bhd fr 4f out and drvn: plugged on fr over 1f out* **50/1**
0 **9** *5* **Lady Pomerol**[12] 4018 3-8-5 0.................................... JackMitchell(7) 6 28
(Lady Herries) *a towards rr: rdn and struggling wl over 3f out* **80/1**
63 **10** *hd* **Eastwell Smiles**[42] 3084 3-9-0 0.................................(t) TravisBlock(3) 1 33
(R T Phillips) *prom: drvn over 3f out: lost pl and btn over 2f out* **7/1**
2 **11** *hd* **Neboisha**[58] 2593 3-8-12 0.. IanMongan 2 27
(P Howling) *trckd ldrs: drvn and lost pl rapidly over 2f out* **20/1**
12 *½* **Stroppi Poppi** 3-8-12 0.. FrankieMcDonald 13 26
(Jean-Rene Auvray) *s.s: mostly last and a bhd* **66/1**
0-00 **13** *nk* **Iceni Princess**[19] 3800 3-8-12 40... PaulDoe 11 26
(P Howling) *w ldr after 3f to over 2f out: wknd rapidly* **100/1**

2m 6.36s (-1.43) **Going Correction** -0.075s/f (Stan)
WFA 3 from 4yo 9lb **13** Ran SP% **120.7**
Speed ratings (Par 101): **102,100,99,97,96 94,91,89,85,85 85,84,84**
CSF £11.95 TOTE £4.20: £1.10, £2.30, £3.90; EX 13.00.
Owner Serendipity Syndicate 2006 **Bred** R Charles **Trained** Blewbury, Oxon

FOCUS
A routine older-horse maiden, but run at a good good pace, and the winner looks progressive. The placed horses, backed up by the sixth, set the level for the form.
Meon Mix Official explanation: jockey said filly hung left and was distressed
Stroppi Poppi Official explanation: jockey said filly missed the break

4393 EUROPEAN BREEDERS' FUND MAIDEN STKS — 1m (P)
6:10 (6:11) (Class 5) 2-Y-O **£3,141** (£934; £467; £233) **Stalls** High

Form RPR
2 **1** **Pegasus Again (USA)**[49] 2855 2-9-3 0................................... LDettori 12 84+
(T G Mills) *racd wd in midfield: prog to trck ldng pair over 2f out: drvn over 1f out and hung fire: led jst ins fnl f and swished tail: styd on* **8/11**[1]
3 **2** *1 ¼* **Dhhamaan (IRE)**[14] 3957 2-9-3 0... PaulDoe 5 81
(C E Brittain) *pressed ldng pair: narrow ld 3f out: drvn over 1f out: hdd jst ins fnl f: styd on same pce* **16/1**
3 *2 ½* **Aboriginie (USA)** 2-9-3 0.. JimmyFortune 1 78+
(J H M Gosden) *s.i.s: sn trckd ldrs: outpcd in 4th over 2f out: shkn up over 1f out: hanging lft but kpt on wl* **5/1**[3]
5 **4** *1 ¼* **Tomorrow's World (IRE)**[22] 3706 2-8-9 0.................. WilliamBuick(3) 3 72+
(Sir Michael Stoute) *s.s: in tch in rr: pushed along fr 1/2-way: wl outpcd 3f out: styd on wl fnl f* **9/2**[2]
5 *2* **Shadows Fall (USA)** 2-8-12 0.. TolleyDean(5) 8 68
(P F I Cole) *t.k.h in midfield: outpcd over 2f out: pushed along and kpt on one pce after* **50/1**
6 *1* **Art Currency (USA)** 2-9-3 0... IanMongan 2 65
(M J Wallace) *w ldr: led 5f out to 3f out: stl upsides wl over 1f out: wknd rapidly fnl f* **33/1**
0 **7** *1* **Cool The Heels (IRE)**[28] 3552 2-9-3 0.......................... SimonWhitworth 6 63
(J S Moore) *t.k.h: trckd ldrs: outpcd over 2f out and pushed along: n.d after* **100/1**
005 **8** *3* **Ostinata (IRE)**[71] 2193 2-8-12 52................................ PaulFitzsimons 4 51
(B W Duke) *led for 3f: styd prom tl wknd over 2f out* **100/1**
9 *¾* **Wikaala (USA)** 2-9-3 0... MartinDwyer 7 54
(M P Tregoning) *sn lost pl and in rr: outpcd fr 3f out: n.d after* **12/1**
10 *3* **All Lit Up** 2-9-3 0.. FergusSweeney 9 47
(A King) *sn pushed along and rn green: a wl in rr* **50/1**
0 **11** *nk* **Paul The Carpet (UAE)**[30] 3471 2-9-3 0....................... SamHitchcott 11 47
(P F I Cole) *struggling in rr after 2f: nvr a factor* **100/1**

1m 39.24s (-0.19) **Going Correction** -0.075s/f (Stan) **11** Ran SP% **116.2**
Speed ratings (Par 94): **97,95,93,92,90 89,88,85,84,81 80**
CSF £14.90 TOTE £1.60: £1.10, £4.00, £2.10; EX 10.30.
Owner T G Mills **Bred** Stonestreet Mares Llc **Trained** Headley, Surrey

FOCUS
A decent maiden of its type, but run at an ordinary gallop, but the form is sound rated through the fourth and eighth.

NOTEBOOK
Pegasus Again(USA) duly got off the mark at the second time of asking, but he was not over-impressive, and the tail-swishing does not inspire confidence. That said, he did land the odds and can be given the benefit of the doubt, with his next outing likely to reveal more about his long-term prospects. (op 4-5 tchd 4-7)
Dhhamaan(IRE) gave the odds-on winner a decent race. He has run well on turf and sand, and is capable of finding a maiden on either surface. (op 14-1 tchd 18-1)
Aboriginie(USA) ◆, a half-brother to Breeders' Cup Juvenile winner Wilko, is by the Dubai World Cup winner Street Cry and from a good family in the USA. He is, therefore, bred to do the job, and this first attempt offered plenty of promise. Official explanation: jockey said colt ran very green (op 7-2 tchd 13-2)
Tomorrow's World(IRE) has come home well in both outings to date, this time having missed the break. She should have no problem finding some suitable opprtunities. (op 5-1 tchd 11-2)
Shadows Fall(USA), a $70,000 son of Dynaformer, a high-class winner up to 1m2f in the USA, and his dam is a half-sister to several winning sprinters, so it is not yet clear what his best trip will be, though starting him off over a mile suggests he is not the speediest. However, he travelled enthusiastically for a long way, and should improve.
Art Currency(USA) is a son of Dubai World Cup winner Street Cry, and his dam Lady In Silver won the French Oaks. Though not getting home on this debut, after finding himself in front very early, he should be suited by even longer trips in due course.

4394 JOIN WBX.COM FOR FREE FOOTBALL SHIRT H'CAP — 7f (P)
6:40 (6:41) (Class 5) (0-70,70) 3-Y-O+ **£2,817** (£838; £418; £209) **Stalls** Low

Form RPR
1334 **1** **Divertimenti (IRE)**[36] 3285 3-9-8 **70**............................... GeorgeBaker 11 80
(C R Dore) *t.k.h: trckd ldrs: smooth prog to go 2nd 2f out: shkn up to ld jst over 1f out: r.o wl* **11/2**[3]
4042 **2** *1 ½* **Chief Exec**[10] 4063 5-9-5 **68**... HaddenFrost(7) 8 76
(B J Llewellyn) *hld up at rr of main gp: gd run through fr 2f out to chse ldng pair over 1f out: wnt 2nd last 150yds: no imp on wnr* **15/2**
6412 **3** *hd* **Ebraam (USA)**[17] 3852 4-9-6 **65**................................... DominicFox(3) 9 78+
(D Shaw) *t.k.h: hld up towards rr: prog whn nt clr run and snatched up on outer 2f out: r.o wl fnl f: nrly snatched 2nd* **11/2**[3]
4040 **4** *1 ¼* **King After**[56] 2665 5-8-9 **54**..................................(v) StephaneBreux(3) 4 58
(J R Best) *pressed ldr: led 3f out: rdn and hdd jst over 1f out: wknd* **14/1**
0326 **5** *2 ½* **Scuba (IRE)**[39] 3191 5-9-1 **57**..(b) SteveDrowne 6 54
(H Morrison) *wl in rr: drvn and struggling 3f out: styd on fr over 1f out: n.d* **5/1**[2]
5221 **6** *1* **Napoleon Dynamite (IRE)**[58] 2593 3-9-3 **70**................ PatrickHills(5) 3 63
(J W Hills) *hld up in tch: smooth hdwy 2f out to chse ldng pair briefly wl over 1f out: sn rdn and wknd* **7/1**
3500 **7** *1 ½* **Quantum Leap**[34] 3350 10-8-12 **61**..........................(p) ThomasBubb(7) 12 52
(S Dow) *hld up and sn detached in last: stl there whn nt clr run over 1f out: bmpd along and styd on* **25/1**
4421 **8** *shd* **Reeling N' Rocking (IRE)**[17] 3851 4-9-9 **68**.................... WilliamBuick(3) 1 58
(B W Hills) *trckd ldrs on inner: pushed along and lost pl over 2f out: effrt over 1f out: sn btn* **9/2**[1]

410 **9** *1 ¾* **Charming Ballet (IRE)**[49] 2879 4-9-5 **61**....................(b) IanMongan 10 47
(N P Littmoden) *prom towards outer: upsides 3f out tl jst over 2f out: wknd over 1f out* **25/1**

0306 **10** *¾* **Royal Orissa**[21] 3735 5-9-0 **56**.................................. LPKeniry 5 40
(D Haydn Jones) *a wl in rr: rdn at bk of main gp over 2f out: no prog* **16/1**

0560 **11** *2* **Rogers Lodger**[103] 1346 3-8-4 **52**.......................... MartinDwyer 13 28
(J Akehurst) *racd v wd thrght: prom: upsides 3f out tl wnt v wd bnd 2f out: wknd* **33/1**

6353 **12** *7* **Ask Yer Dad**[24] 3646 3-9-3 **65**...........................(b[1]) MickyFenton 2 22
(Mrs P Sly) *led to 3f out: wknd rapidly 2f out* **12/1**

1m 24.79s (-1.10) **Going Correction** -0.075s/f (Stan)
WFA 3 from 4yo+ 6lb 12 Ran SP% **120.8**
Speed ratings (Par 103): **103,101,101,99,96 95,93,93,91,90 88,80**
CSF £46.41 CT £242.69 TOTE £8.10: £2.50, £3.30, £2.00; EX 62.10.
Owner Page, Ward, Marsh **Bred** Airlie Stud **Trained** West Pinchbeck, Lincs

FOCUS
A moderate but competitive handicap that looks solid rated around the placed horses.
Rogers Lodger Official explanation: jockey said gelding lost its action on final bend

4395 SPECIALIST LIABILITY SERVICES H'CAP 7f 140y

7:10 (7:12) (Class 6) (0-65,65) 3-Y-0+ **£2,047** (£604; £302) **Stalls** Centre

Form RPR

-020 **1** **The Fifth Member (IRE)**[33] 3384 3-9-6 **65**.................. MartinDwyer 14 78
(J R Boyle) *a ldng trio: rdn and def advantage over 1f out: styd on wl* **8/1**[3]

-001 **2** *2* **For Life (IRE)**[12] 4029 5-9-1 **58**.......................... NataliaGemelova(5) 3 67
(J E Long) *racd awkwardly early: mde most to jst over 1f out: one pce fnl f* **12/1**

6313 **3** *1* **Hansomelle (IRE)**[7] 4161 5-9-6 **61**........................(p) NeilChalmers(3) 10 74+
(Miss Sheena West) *hld up in rr: trapped on inner bhd rivals 3f out to wl over 1f out: str run fnl f: gaining fast at fin* **4/1**[2]

0602 **4** *2 ½* **Postmaster**[3] 4272 5-8-7 **48**........................(v) WilliamBuick(3) 9 48
(R Ingram) *sn detached in last pair and nt gng wl: scrubbed along fr 5f out: prog over 2f out: kpt on to snatch 4th nr fin* **7/2**[1]

0000 **5** *nk* **Titus Lumpus (IRE)**[43] 3048 4-9-1 **53**........................(b[1]) IanMongan 18 53
(R M Flower) *cl up: rdn 3f out: tried to cl on ldrs over 1f out: hanging bdly lft fnl f and kpt on* **33/1**

5003 **6** *¾* **Our Ruby**[10] 4073 3-9-6 **65**........................(b) AdrianMcCarthy 8 62
(P W Chapple-Hyam) *w ldng pair: stl upsides 2f out: wknd ins fnl f* **12/1**

0130 **7** *1 ¾* **Pearl Farm**[58] 2592 6-9-4 **56**.......................... FergusSweeney 12 49
(C A Horgan) *nvr bttr than midfield: outpcd fr 2f out: no imp after* **10/1**

0204 **8** *3* **The Skerret**[7] 4163 3-8-12 **57**.................................. PaulDoe 2 42
(P Winkworth) *chsd ldrs on outer: effrt over 2f out: 4th briefly wl over 1f out: sn wknd* **25/1**

0001 **9** *2* **Poppets Sweetlove**[44] 3032 3-9-2 **61**.......................... SteveDrowne 5 41
(A B Haynes) *dwlt: towards rr on outer: nvr rchd ldrs: wl btn over 1f out* **16/1**

0053 **10** *hd* **Greenwood**[14] 3965 9-9-8 **60**.......................... RobertHavlin 13 40
(P G Murphy) *settled in midfield: rdn over 2f out: wknd wl over 1f out* **10/1**

1015 **11** *2* **Wodhill Schnaps**[18] 3828 6-8-13 **51**........................(v) MickyFenton 11 26
(D Morris) *wl in rr: no prog over 2f out: n.d after* **25/1**

020 **12** *½* **Sahara Prince (IRE)**[95] 500 7-8-9 **47**.......................... RichardThomas 15 21
(K A Morgan) *chsd ldrs towards nr side: no imp over 2f out: sn wknd* **16/1**

0300 **13** *½* **Thomas Lawrence (USA)**[14] 3965 6-9-1 **53**......... FrankieMcDonald 17 26
(P A Blockley) *trckd ldrs: rdn over 2f out: hanging and wknd wl over 1f out* **25/1**

4505 **14** *1 ¾* **Capricho (IRE)**[23] 3682 10-9-4 **63**........................(b) KirstyMilczarek(7) 1 31
(J Akehurst) *trckd ldrs: rdn 3f out: steadily wknd fnl 2f* **16/1**

0-00 **15** *9* **Pertemps Green**[14] 3965 4-9-6 **58**.......................... TGMcLaughlin 16 —
(M S Saunders) *chsd ldrs: u.p over 3f out: wknd over 2f out* **25/1**

0000 **16** *1 ¾* **Imperial Gain (USA)**[18] 3828 4-9-12 **64**........................(v) LPKeniry 7 6
(J M Bradley) *t.k.h: cl up tl wknd rapidly u.p over 2f out: eased* **16/1**

0-05 **17** *3* **Hey Presto**[51] 2802 7-8-0 **45**.......................... RichardRowe(7) 6 —
(R Rowe) *dwlt: trckd across to nr side and wl detached in last: a bhd* **33/1**

2366 **18** *9* **Marmooq**[67] 2336 4-9-3 **55**.......................... PaulFitzsimons 4 —
(M J Attwater) *prom early: u.p 5f out: wknd over 3f out: t.o: b.b.v* **16/1**

1m 29.14s (-2.32) **Going Correction** -0.275s/f (Firm)
WFA 3 from 4yo+ 7lb 18 Ran SP% **137.6**
Speed ratings (Par 101): **100,98,97,94,94 93,91,88,86,86 84,84,83,81,72 71,68,59**
CSF £104.05 CT £474.31 TOTE £10.50: £2.90, £5.10, £1.60, £1.90; EX 210.50.
Owner Chris Simpson, Miss Elizabeth Ross **Bred** Ms Amy Mulligan **Trained** Epsom, Surrey

FOCUS
A modest sprint, but run at a decent pace, and with the form solid several of these should win more races at this level.
Hansomelle(IRE) ◆ Official explanation: jockey said mare was denied a clear run
Imperial Gain(USA) Official explanation: jockey said gelding had no more to give
Marmooq Official explanation: vet said gelding had bled from the nose

4396 MARY HEPBURN BIRTHDAY H'CAP 6f

7:40 (7:41) (Class 5) (0-75,74) 3-Y-0+ **£2,817** (£838; £418; £209) **Stalls** High

Form RPR

2344 **1** **Angel Sprints**[14] 3970 5-9-7 **73**.......................... WilliamBuick(3) 6 83
(C J Down) *pressed ldrs: urged along and led over 1f out: rdn out and in command last 150yds* **11/2**[2]

2035 **2** *1 ¼* **Gwilym (GER)**[5] 4233 4-9-4 **72**.......................... AshleyHamblett(5) 5 78
(D Haydn Jones) *led main gp and racd against nr side rail: drvn over 2f out: hdd over 1f out: edgd lft but styd on* **11/2**[2]

1434 **3** *½* **Caustic Wit (IRE)**[15] 3906 9-9-4 **67**.......................... TGMcLaughlin 8 72
(M S Saunders) *pressed ldr: rdn and upsides 2f out: nt qckn over 1f out: kpt on same pce* **11/2**[2]

0425 **4** *2* **Linda Green**[12] 4017 6-9-4 **74**.......................... ThomasO'Brien(7) 12 73+
(M R Channon) *hld up in tch and racd against nr side rail: rdn over 2f out: nt qckn and sn outpcd: edgd lft but styd on fnl f* **8/1**

5030 **5** *½* **Plateau**[24] 3644 8-9-0 **63**.......................... IanMongan 14 60
(C R Dore) *hld up towards rr: rdn over 2f out: kpt on fnl f: nt pce to rch ldrs* **17/2**

5635 **6** *½* **Drumming Party (USA)**[5] 4236 5-8-11 **60**........................(t) LPKeniry 1 56
(A M Balding) *hld up but sn trckd ldrs: rdn over 2f out: fdd over 1f out* **6/1**[3]

546 **7** *1* **Strut The Stage (IRE)**[7] 4165 3-8-11 **64**.......................... PaulFitzsimons 4 57
(B W Duke) *hld up towards rr: shkn up 2f out: n.d after: kpt on* **25/1**

0-60 **8** *¾* **Cerulean Rose**[10] 4075 8-8-6 **55** oh4.......................... RichardThomas 11 45
(A W Carroll) *trckd ldrs: rdn over 2f out: wknd over 1f out* **20/1**

0354 **9** *hd* **Millfields Dreams**[5] 4233 8-9-0 **66**.......................... JerryO'Dwyer(3) 13 56
(M G Quinlan) *s.i.s: hld up in rr: rdn over 2f out: sn outpcd: n.d after* **7/2**[1]

0520 **10** *nk* **Smile For Us**[59] 2576 4-8-13 **62**........................(b) RobertHavlin 2 51
(C Drew) *racd freely and alone in centre: led: wnt across to far side 1/2-way: sn lost ld and btn* **33/1**

1306 **11** *2 ½* **Blue Knight (IRE)**[56] 2664 8-8-6 **55** oh10........................(p) PaulDoe 3 36
(P Howling) *hld up: a in rr: rdn and struggling over 2f out* **50/1**

0040 **12** *½* **Frisky Talk (IRE)**[8] 4123 3-9-3 **70**.......................... MartinDwyer 10 50
(B W Hills) *free to post: t.k.h and hld up: effrt whn nt clr run and snatched up 2f out: wknd* **12/1**

69.49 secs (-2.18) **Going Correction** -0.275s/f (Firm)
WFA 3 from 4yo+ 4lb 12 Ran SP% **125.5**
Speed ratings (Par 103): **103,101,100,98,97 96,95,94,94,93 90,89**
CSF £36.72 CT £181.75 TOTE £6.90: £2.40, £2.90, £2.10; EX 70.80.
Owner Exors Of The Late Mrs L M Halloran **Bred** Bishopswood Bloodstock And Trickledown Stud **Trained** Mutterton, Devon

FOCUS
A moderate sprint, but containing many useful sorts at this level, and sound enough rated around the placed horses to their marks.
Smile For Us Official explanation: jockey said gelding hung left

4397 THE BRIEFCASE BLUES BROTHERS LIVE AT LINGFIELDPARK.CO.UK H'CAP 6f

8:10 (8:13) (Class 6) (0-60,60) 3-Y-0+ **£2,047** (£604; £302) **Stalls** High

Form RPR

0-05 **1** **Inka Dancer (IRE)**[71] 2217 5-9-2 **57**.......................... WilliamBuick(3) 17 65
(B Palling) *racd against nr side rail: trckd ldrs: drvn over 1f out: r.o fnl f to ld nr fin* **13/2**[3]

0223 **2** *nk* **Make My Dream**[7] 4165 4-9-8 **60**.......................... MartinDwyer 12 67
(J Gallagher) *w ldrs: drvn to ld jst over 1f out: kpt on: hdd nr fin* **6/1**[2]

0002 **3** *¾* **Kennington**[3] 4296 7-8-9 **47**.......................... TGMcLaughlin 6 52
(Mrs C A Dunnett) *hld up in midfield: rdn and prog 2f out: styd on fnl f: nrst fin* **6/1**[2]

2420 **4** *½* **Digital**[19] 3787 10-8-13 **58**.......................... ThomasO'Brien(7) 14 62
(M R Channon) *s.i.s: hld up towards rr: nt clr run briefly 2f out: hanging lft but r.o fnl f: gaining at fin* **6/1**[2]

0001 **5** *shd* **Gone'N'Dunnett (IRE)**[3] 4296 8-9-1 **53** 6ex....................(v) DMylonas 13 56
(Mrs C A Dunnett) *w ldrs: rdn to ld 2f out to jst over 1f out: wknd last 150yds* **10/1**

00-0 **6** *nk* **Contented (IRE)**[14] 3950 5-8-12 **50**........................(p) LPKeniry 4 52
(Mrs L C Jewell) *hld up wl in rr: hmpd 2f out and in last pair: swtchd to nr side: r.o fnl f: nrst fin* **50/1**

-400 **7** *hd* **Damhsoir (IRE)**[7] 4186 3-8-4 **46** oh1.......................... AdrianMcCarthy 7 47
(H S Howe) *racd on outer: wl in tch: effrt u.p and cl up 1f out: fdd* **50/1**

0600 **8** *shd* **Balerno**[28] 3549 8-9-2 **54**.......................... IanMongan 10 55
(Mrs L J Mongan) *hld up towards rr: rdn 2f out: prog over 1f out: styd on: nvr rchd ldrs* **16/1**

0441 **9** *1* **Reigning Monarch (USA)**[7] 4165 4-9-5 **57**.......................... SamHitchcott 1 55
(Miss Z C Davison) *racd on wd outside in mdfield: rdn and prog 2f out: kpt on u.p but nvr pce to rch ldrs* **10/1**

441 **10** *shd* **Piccostar**[25] 3618 4-9-2 **54**........................(v) SteveDrowne 18 52
(A B Haynes) *hld up in midfield: prog to chse ldrs and cl enough over 1f out: fdd ins fnl f* **10/1**

0450 **11** *1 ½* **Saintly Place**[4] 4256 6-8-8 **46** oh1.......................... SimonWhitworth 15 40
(A W Carroll) *dwlt: rcvrd to chse ldrs after 1f: no imp over 1f out: fdd* **20/1**

3100 **12** *hd* **Mambazo**[23] 3667 5-8-5 **50**........................(e) WilliamCarson(7) 16 43
(S C Williams) *racd against nr side rail: led: drifted lft and hdd 2f out: wknd over 1f out* **9/1**

2300 **13** *1 ½* **Josr's Magic (IRE)**[3] 4272 3-8-11 **60**.......................... JCorrigan(7) 2 48
(S W Hall) *racd on outer: hld up in rr: urged along vigorously and no prog over 2f out* **50/1**

0006 **14** *shd* **Flower Of Cork (IRE)**[50] 2844 3-8-3 **52**....................(p) SophieDoyle(7) 3 39
(Ms J S Doyle) *dwlt and squeezed out s: racd on outer and a in rr* **50/1**

402 **15** *nk* **Briery Lane (IRE)**[18] 3829 6-9-4 **56**.......................... AmirQuinn 11 43
(J M Bradley) *hld up in midfield: rdn over 2f out: n.m.r sn after: wknd jst over 1f out* **11/2**[1]

4000 **16** *1 ½* **Only If I Laugh**[31] 3422 6-8-9 **47**.......................... PaulFitzsimons 9 30
(M J Attwater) *a in rr: rdn and struggling over 2f out* **33/1**

5000 **17** *4* **Sparkwell**[17] 3859 5-9-3 **58**.......................... DominicFox(3) 5 29
(D Shaw) *taken down early: stdd s: t.k.h and hld up in last: stl there whn hmpd on inner over 1f out* **25/1**

1m 10.31s (-1.36) **Going Correction** -0.275s/f (Firm)
WFA 3 from 4yo+ 4lb 17 Ran SP% **134.1**
Speed ratings (Par 101): **98,97,96,95,95 95,95,95,93,93 91,91,89,89,88 86,81**
CSF £47.14 CT £266.02 TOTE £9.70: £1.80, £1.70, £2.30, £2.30; EX 35.30 Place 6 £44.51, Place 5 £24.75..
Owner Mrs Anita Quinn **Bred** Humphrey Okeke **Trained** Tredodridge, Vale Of Glamorgan

FOCUS
An ultra-competitive if low-grade sprint, run at a furious gallop, and sound but limited form.
Sparkwell Official explanation: vet said gelding had bled from the nose
T/Plt: £54.40 to a £1 stake. Pool: £54,035.60. 723.90 winning tickets. T/Qpdt: £32.90 to a £1 stake. Pool: £3,653.50. 82.00 winning tickets. JN

4362 NEWMARKET (JULY) (R-H)

Saturday, August 11

OFFICIAL GOING: Firm
Wind: Light, behind Weather: Cloudy

4398 SKYBET.COM FOR ALL YOUR FOOTBALL BETTING H'CAP 2m 24y

2:15 (2:15) (Class 3) (0-90,85) 3-Y-0+ **£9,067** (£2,697; £1,348; £673) **Stalls** High

Form RPR

3534 **1** **Sunley Peace**[13] 3993 3-8-10 **82**.......................... TQuinn 7 94
(D R C Elsworth) *a.p: chsd ldr over 3f out: rdn to ld over 1f out: styd on wl* **10/3**[3]

1000 **2** *6* **Cape Secret (IRE)**[11] 4047 4-10-0 **85**.......................... GeorgeBaker 2 91
(R M Beckett) *led: rdn and hdd over 1f out: styd on same pce* **5/2**[1]

0431 **3** *6* **Trance (IRE)**[72] 2170 7-9-11 **82**.......................... PaulFessey 4 80
(T D Barron) *hld up: hdwy u.p over 2f out: no imp fr over 1f out* **8/1**

4050 **4** *7* **Doctor Scott**[10] 4056 4-9-1 **72**.......................... MichaelHills 1 61
(M Johnston) *hld up: hdwy 1/2-way: rdn over 3f out: wknd wl over 1f out* **3/1**[2]

06-0 **5** *20* **Michabo (IRE)**[17] 3858 6-9-8 **82**.......................... TravisBlock(3) 9 47
(P Bowen) *chsd ldr over 9f: sn rdn: wknd over 2f out: eased* **20/1**

00-0 **6** *23* **Mr Ed (IRE)**[26] 2449 9-9-2 **73**........................(p) JimmyQuinn 8 11
(P Bowen) *rdn 1/2-way: a bhd: lost tch fnl 4f* **16/1**

-100 **7** *2* **Tribe**[21] 3748 5-9-5 **76**.. RichardHughes 6 11
(P R Webber) *stmbld s: prom: chsd ldr over 6f out tl rdn and wknd over 3f out* **11/2**

3m 21.1s (-5.89) **Going Correction** -0.025s/f (Good)
WFA 3 from 4yo+ 15lb **7** Ran SP% **113.8**
Speed ratings (Par 107): **113,110,107,103,93 82,81**
CSF £11.99 CT £59.42 TOTE £4.70: £2.10, £2.40; EX 15.90 Trifecta £29.40 Pool: £215.40 - 5.20 winning units..
Owner Davies, Sunley, Coombs & Cox **Bred** Milton Park Stud Partnership **Trained** Newmarket, Suffolk

FOCUS
A decent staying handicap in which they went a good gallop and ultimately finished well strung out.

NOTEBOOK
Sunley Peace ◆, whose best effort this season was in the Queen's Vase on his only previous attempt at this trip, got off the mark at the 11th attempt with a comfortable succes. He travelled well throughout and, although the runner-up looked to be holding him at the quarter-mile pole, he picked up really well on meeting thr rising ground and came right away. He will go up a fair amount for this, but looks a progressive stayer in the making. (op 5-2 tchd 7-2)
Cape Secret(IRE) set off in front as usual and got an uncontested lead. He had most of his rivals in trouble by the three-furlong pole, but began to feel the pinch himself on meeting the rising ground and the winner swept by. This was another decent effort, but all his wins have been at 1m6f and this trip appears to be beyond the limit of his stamina. (op 7-2)
Trance(IRE), who had trip and ground to suit, was held up at the back and, although close enough half a mile out, could only stay on at one pace and never reached those at the head of affairs. (op 7-1)
Doctor Scott, who ran well until his stamina gave out in the Goodwood Stakes last time, again travelled well until weakening in the last quarter mile. (op 7-2 tchd 11-4)
Tribe showed up early but dropped away as if something was amiss. Official explanation: jockey said gelding hung left (op 6-1)

4399 PREMIERSHIP KICK OFF WITH SKYBET.COM H'CAP 1m 2f
2:50 (2:50) (Class 2) (0-100,93) 3-Y-0+ **£11,658** (£3,468; £1,733; £865) **Stalls** High

Form RPR
4600 **1** **Star Of Light**[15] 3899 6-10-0 **93**.. RichardHughes 1 100
(B J Meehan) *mde all: rdn over 1f out: styd on gamely* **5/2**[2]
0160 **2** *1* **Zaif (IRE)**[16] 3882 4-9-3 **82**.. TQuinn 5 87
(D R C Elsworth) *hld up: hdwy over 1f out: sn rdn: styd on* **4/1**[3]
3-36 **3** *hd* **Resonate (IRE)**[28] 3558 9-9-6 **85**.. DaneO'Neill 2 90
(A G Newcombe) *chsd ldrs: rdn over 1f out: styd on same pce ins fnl f* **11/2**
0326 **4** *nk* **Ballinteni**[8] 4117 5-9-11 **90**.. RyanMoore 6 94
(D M Simcock) *a.p: chsd wnr over 2f out: rdn over 1f out: edgd rt and no ex ins fnl f* **15/8**[1]
0-00 **5** *2 1/2* **Always Fruitful**[14] 3940 3-9-0 **88**.. MichaelHills 7 87
(M Johnston) *hld up: rdn over 1f out: nt trble ldrs* **8/1**
0 **6** *27* **Florista Gg (URU)**[28] 3527 4-9-3 **87**.. TolleyDean(5) 3 32
(J S Moore) *chsd wnr tl rdn over 2f out: wknd wl over 1f out* **28/1**

2m 4.29s (-2.15) **Going Correction** -0.025s/f (Good)
WFA 3 from 4yo+ 9lb **6** Ran SP% **113.3**
Speed ratings (Par 109): **107,106,106,105,103 82**
CSF £13.08 CT £48.59 TOTE £2.90: £1.80, £2.10; EX 10.60 Trifecta £59.40 Pool: £209.44 - 2.50 winning units..
Owner J H Widdows **Bred** J H Widdows **Trained** Manton, Wilts

FOCUS
A decent handicap run at a fair gallop and producing a close finish. The form is best rated around the first two.

NOTEBOOK
Star Of Light, who is often held up in his races, adopted totally different tactics and they paid off. Given a good ride from the front, Hughes kept something up his sleeve and his mount responded well for pressure to resist several challenges on the climb to the line. These tactics are unlikely to be adopted in the big-field handicaps he usually contests, but at least he can be ridden closer to the pace in future and a trip to York followed by another crack at the John Smith's Handicap at Newbury look likely after this. (op 11-4 tchd 2-1)
Zaif(IRE), who won his maiden over course and distance last season, was held up at the back and was the last to deliver his challenge. However, he could not get past the winner and may need to drop a further pound or two before winning again, that said the yard is in good form at present. (op 9-2)
Resonate(IRE), who has been lightly raced this season, had every chance but could not find the extra required in the last half-furlong. He would have preferred some cut in the ground but, as his favourite track Epsom is closed until next year, connections may opt for an autumn campaign on Polytrack, as he is much better handicapped on that surface. (op 5-1 tchd 6-1)
Ballinteni, who an so well at Goodwood last time, was another to have every chance but his effort flattened out up the hill. He may have found this ground faster than ideal and can be given another chance on a more forgiving surface and possibly a flat track. (tchd 5-2)
Always Fruitful never got involved from off the pace. (op 10-1)
Florista Gg(URU), who won a Uruguayan Guineas, is struggling since coming to this country and dropped away quickly after keeping the winner company form the best part of a mile. (op 16-1)

4400 SKYBET.COM SWEET SOLERA STKS (GROUP 3) (FILLIES) 7f
3:25 (3:26) (Class 1) 2-Y-0
£22,712 (£8,608; £4,308; £2,148; £1,076; £540) **Stalls** High

Form RPR
41 **1** **Albabilia (IRE)**[15] 3895 2-8-12 0.. RyanMoore 2 102
(C E Brittain) *chsd ldrs: led over 1f out: sn hung rt: rdn out* **7/2**[3]
1 **2** *1/2* **Don't Forget Faith (USA)**[43] 3055 2-8-12 0................ PhilipRobinson 7 100+
(C G Cox) *hld up: edgd lft and hdwy over 1f out: sn rdn: n.m.r ins fnl f: r.o* **5/2**[2]
415 **3** *3/4* **Kay Es Jay (FR)**[16] 3880 2-8-12 90.. MichaelHills 1 98
(B W Hills) *led: rdn and hdd over 1f out: edgd rt: styd on same pce ins fnl f: n.m.r towards fin* **16/1**
1 **4** *2* **Queen Scarlet (IRE)**[22] 3706 2-8-12 0.. SteveDrowne 8 93
(B J Meehan) *prom: rdn and edgd rt over 1f out: styd on same pce fnl f* **7/1**
0602 **5** *3* **Kylayne**[2] 4329 2-8-12 100.. TQuinn 5 85
(P W D'Arcy) *prom: chsd ldr 1/2-way tl rdn and wknd over 1f out* **25/1**
21 **6** *1 1/4* **Gone Fast (USA)**[19] 3796 2-8-12 0.. JamieSpencer 4 82
(J R Fanshawe) *hld up: hdwy over 2f out: rdn over 1f out: wknd and eased fnl f* **2/1**[1]
136 **7** *shd* **Baffled (USA)**[28] 3522 2-8-12 97.. TedDurcan 3 81
(J Noseda) *chsd ldr tl rdn 1/2-way: wknd 2f out* **14/1**

1m 25.67s (-1.11) **Going Correction** -0.025s/f (Good) **7** Ran SP% **113.0**
Speed ratings (Par 101): **105,104,103,101,97 96,96**
CSF £12.38 TOTE £4.80: £2.30, £1.60; EX 14.00 Trifecta £152.10 Pool: £299.92 - 1.40 winning units..
Owner Saif Ali **Bred** Paul And Eilidh Hyland **Trained** Newmarket, Suffolk
■ Sweepstake (8/1, uns rdr & ran loose at s) was withdrawn. Rule 4, deduct 10p in the £ from board prices. New market formed.

FOCUS
A fair renewal of this Group 3 and the fastest of the three races over the trip on the day, beating even the following Class 2 handicap but the form is rated no more than average for now. The field raced stands' side.

NOTEBOOK
Albabilia(IRE) ◆, who finished fourth on her debut here before beating a subsequent winner at Ascot, is clearly progressing with racing and she put up a professional performance on this step up in trip to win this decent contest. She is in all the big fillies' races and a trip to Ireland for the Moyglare Stud Stakes followed by the Meon Valley Stud Fillies' Mile could be the favoured route. (old market op 9-2, new market op 4-1)
Don't Forget Faith(USA) ◆, who beat the subsequent Princess Margaret Stakes winner Visit on their respective debuts in a contest that has otherwise not worked out that well, was held up at the back and delivered her challenge nearest to the rail. However, she showed signs of greenness when asked for her effort and the more experienced winner was always holding her. Hopefully this will have taught her something and she looks more than capable of winning a Group race, although she is qualified for a couple of the big sales races and, having already earned black type, connections may bid for the big rewards in one of those events. (old market op 9-4 tchd 5-2, new market tchd 11-4 and 3-1 in a place)
Kay Es Jay(FR), who won her maiden on Polytrack, adopted different tactics to those employed at Sandown last time and they proved more successful. She ran with plenty of credit and looks capable of winning at Listed level on this evidence. (old market op 20-1, new market thcd 14-1)
Queen Scarlet(IRE), a half-sister to Nannina who won her maiden over course and distance, seemed to have her chance but got caught out on the run down into the dip before staying on again. (old market tchd 15-2, new market op 6-1 tchd 11-2)
Kylayne, who had been narrowly beaten in a lower-grade contest just two days previously, had run her best race when sixth in the Cherry Hinton on this track. However, despite doing her best again, that effort flatters her and she is likely to continue to struggle in this grade. (old market op 20-1, new market op 16-1)
Gone Fast(USA) well backed here following her clear-cut maiden win at Windsor, was settled out the back but did not look nearly as effective on this much faster going and her effort was somewhat short-lived. Official explanation: trainer had no explanation for the poor form shown (old market op 5-2, new market op op 2-1 tchd 6-4)
Baffled(USA), a winner on her debut on Polytrack, also finished third in a Group 3 at Royal Ascot. However, that was on easy ground and her two subsequent efforts on fast going have been well below that level. A return to an easier surface or Polytrack may see her in a different light. (old market op 20-1 tchd 16-1)

4401 INTERACTIVE FOOTBALL BETTING WITH SKYBET LIVE STKS (H'CAP) 7f
4:00 (4:00) (Class 2) (0-105,100) 3-Y-0+
£18,696 (£5,598; £2,799; £1,401; £699; £351) **Stalls** High

Form RPR
4314 **1** **Giganticus (USA)**[14] 3941 4-9-11 **98**.. MichaelHills 12 109
(B W Hills) *chsd ldrs: rdn to ld 1f out: edgd lft: r.o* **7/2**[2]
4200 **2** *1 1/4* **Ceremonial Jade (UAE)**[10] 4062 4-9-3 **90**....................(t) OscarUrbina 1 98
(M Botti) *chsd ldrs: rdn to ld over 1f out: sn edgd rt and hdd: styd on same pce* **11/1**
4400 **3** *shd* **Partners In Jazz (USA)**[14] 3941 6-9-10 **97**........................ DaneO'Neill 7 105
(T D Barron) *hld up: hdwy over 1f out: styd on* **16/1**
4142 **4** *shd* **Artimino**[29] 3503 3-9-5 **98**..(t) JamieSpencer 8 103
(J R Fanshawe) *hld up in tch: rdn over 1f out: edgd lft: styd on* **7/4**[1]
0060 **5** *1 1/4* **Voodoo Moon**[9] 4093 3-8-6 **85**.. JimmyQuinn 4 87
(M Johnston) *led: rdn and hdd over 1f out: nt clr run sn after: styd on same pce* **16/1**
4306 **6** *1/2* **Mac Love**[14] 3941 6-9-13 **100**.. RyanMoore 10 103
(J Noseda) *hld up: hdwy over 1f out: nt trble ldrs* **5/1**[3]
6060 **7** *hd* **Baron's Pit**[7] 4150 7-9-10 **97**.. ChrisCatlin 11 99
(E F Vaughan) *chsd ldrs: hung lft over 2f out: sn rdn: no ex fnl f* **22/1**
6300 **8** *1/2* **Irony (IRE)**[8] 4134 8-8-9 **82**..(p) LPKeniry 9 83
(A M Balding) *chsd ldr: rdn over 2f out: wknd fnl f* **50/1**
0000 **9** *2* **Bahiano (IRE)**[8] 4133 6-8-12 **85**.. PhilipRobinson 3 80
(C E Brittain) *chsd ldrs over 5f* **16/1**
1166 **10** *hd* **Countdown**[6] 4195 5-9-0 **87**.. TedDurcan 2 82
(T D Easterby) *hld up in tch: rdn over 2f out: wknd over 1f out* **28/1**
3030 **11** *3* **Ingleby Arch (USA)**[14] 3941 4-9-1 **88**............................(b) PaulFessey 6 75
(T D Barron) *hld up: rdn over 2f out: a in rr* **14/1**

1m 26.44s (-0.34) **Going Correction** -0.025s/f (Good)
WFA 3 from 4yo+ 6lb **11** Ran SP% **117.7**
Speed ratings (Par 109): **100,98,98,98,96 96,96,95,93,93 89**
CSF £41.01 CT £561.65 TOTE £3.90: £1.50, £2.60, £4.90; EX 43.30 Trifecta £454.60 Part won. Pool: £640.40 - 0.50 winning units..
Owner DM James,Cavendish Inv Ltd,Matthew Green **Bred** Gaines-Gentry Thoroughbreds Et Al **Trained** Lambourn, Berks

FOCUS
A good handicap but run at a steady early gallop, resulting in a three-furlong sprint and a time slower than both the juvenile fillies' races over the trip so not a race to take too literally. The field split into two in the early stages but converged towards the stands' side at about the two pole

NOTEBOOK
Giganticus(USA), who won the Bunbury Cup here last month, had run well in another big handicap since. He was always close to the pace and once getting to the front never looked like conceding his advantage. He is a progressive sort who is ideally suited by a straight 7f and fast ground. There may be a suitable race for him at Doncaster, and in the longer term connections are thinking of taking him to Dubai early next year. (op 11-4 tchd 5-2)
Ceremonial Jade(UAE) ◆, another who is something of a specialist at this trip, although he does stay a mile, had been dropped to his last winning mark and put up a fine effort, sticking on well once the winner too his measure. He looks capable of picking up a decent race with his stable in pretty good heart at present. (op 14-1)
Partners In Jazz(USA), who finished well behind the winner at Ascot, ran his best race since his seasonal debut and can be given extra credit as he was held up off the steady gallop.
Artimino has been running consistently well since scoring on the Rowley Mile in the spring, but he is now running off a stone higher mark than when taking that race and the Handicapper looks to have his measure at present. (op 2-1 tchd 9-4)
Voodoo Moon who has been held since beating today's fourth at Beverley on her seasonal debut, has dropped back to that winning mark though and ran up arguably her best race since. The faster the ground the better for her. (op 20-1)
Mac Love, who has slipped to a mark that allows him to contest handicaps now, was another to run on having been held up in a slowly-run race. He has gone nearly three years without winning a race, but his shrewd trainer may now have a chance to coax that elusive victory out of him. (op 11-2)

Baron's Pit, having one of his rare attempts at this trip, had the headgear he has worn recently left off. He had every chance before his effort flattened out up the hill. (op 25-1)

4402 WYCK HALL STUD MAIDEN FILLIES' STKS 7f
4:30 (4:31) (Class 4) 2-Y-O £4,533 (£1,348; £674; £336) Stalls High

Form RPR

1 **Cape Amber (IRE)** 2-9-0 0 JamieSpencer 10 91+
(P W Chapple-Hyam) *s.i.s: sn chsng ldrs: led over 1f out: rdn out* 10/3[2]

4 2 3 **Fifty (IRE)**[10] 4061 2-9-0 0 RichardHughes 4 83
(R Hannon) *led over 5f: no ex ins fnl f* 7/2[3]

0 3 1 ½ **Redeemed**[43] 3055 2-9-0 0 PhilipRobinson 15 79
(B J Meehan) *hld up: hdwy over 2f out: hung lft fnl f: nt rch ldrs* 12/1

420 4 1 **Miss Emma May (IRE)**[50] 2812 2-9-0 85 TQuinn 1 76
(D R C Elsworth) *dwlt: sn prom: nt clr run over 2f out: rdn and edgd lft over 1f out: no ex* 3/1[1]

5 1 **Burn The Breeze (IRE)** 2-9-0 0 TedDurcan 3 73+
(H R A Cecil) *chsd ldrs: rdn over 1f out: wknd ins fnl f* 14/1

6 ¾ **Sovereign's Honour (USA)** 2-9-0 0 RyanMoore 7 71+
(Sir Michael Stoute) *wnt rt s: mid-div: pushed along 1/2-way: nvr trbld ldrs* 11/2

0 7 1 ¼ **Fareeha**[9] 4102 2-9-0 0 DavidKinsella 2 68+
(J H M Gosden) *hld up: nt clr run over 2f out: nvr trbld ldrs* 33/1

8 ½ **Frivolous (IRE)** 2-9-0 0 RobertHavlin 16 67
(J H M Gosden) *chsd ldrs: hung lft and wknd over 1f out* 16/1

9 1 **Ever Dreaming (USA)** 2-9-0 0 LPKeniry 11 64
(A M Balding) *chsd ldrs over 5f* 80/1

10 ½ **Fleur De Montjeu (IRE)** 2-9-0 0 AdamKirby 5 63
(W R Swinburn) *hld up in tch: effrt over 2f out: wknd over 1f out* 33/1

11 ½ **Magical Fantasy (USA)** 2-9-0 0 OscarUrbina 13 61
(J Nicol) *hld up in tch: rdn and hung lft 2f out: sn wknd* 66/1

12 1 **Calypso Charms** 2-9-0 0 PaulFessey 19 58
(M L W Bell) *hld up: rdn over 2f out: n.d* 80/1

13 ¾ **Sparkling Montjeu (IRE)** 2-9-0 0 MatthewHenry 8 56
(J W Hills) *s.i.s and hmpd s: outpcd* 80/1

14 2 **Stormy View (USA)** 2-9-0 0 DaneO'Neill 14 51
(J H M Gosden) *hld up: rdn 1/2-way: a in rr* 25/1

15 nk **Lavender And Lace** 2-8-7 0 JamieHamblett(7) 9 50
(Sir Michael Stoute) *s.s: outpcd* 50/1

00 16 2 ½ **Ile Royale**[14] 3962 2-9-0 0 JimmyQuinn 6 43
(C N Allen) *unruly in stalls: prom over 5f* 100/1

0 17 1 ½ **Rhode Island Red (USA)**[24] 3643 2-9-0 0 ChrisCatlin 18 39
(B J Meehan) *s.i.s: sn prom: wknd 2f out* 50/1

0 18 3 ½ **Angel Pie**[24] 3643 2-9-0 0 SteveDrowne 17 30
(R Charlton) *s.i.s: outpcd* 50/1

1m 26.42s (-0.36) **Going Correction** -0.025s/f (Good) 18 Ran SP% **127.7**
Speed ratings (Par 93): **101,97,95,94,93 92,91,90,89,89 88,87,86,84,83 80,79,75**
CSF £15.08 TOTE £5.60: £2.10, £1.90, £4.10; EX 21.70.
Owner Five Horses Ltd **Bred** Five Horses Ltd **Trained** Newmarket, Suffolk

FOCUS
A decent-looking fillies' maiden run 0.75 sec slower than the earlier Group 3 but faster than the preceding older-horse handicap and rated around the fourth and fifth. The field raced centre to far side this time.

NOTEBOOK
Cape Amber(IRE) ◆, a half-sister to the smart Nyramba and from the family of Oh So Sharp, made a fine winning debut. She overcame a ponderous start to take the lead over a furlong out and drew away up the hill in good style from a more experienced rival. She is entered in the Cheveley Park and Fillies' Mile, with the latter the more likely target if she goes the right way. She looks to have some maturing to do and could develop into a very good filly next season. (tchd 4-1)
Fifty(IRE), who ran well on her debut at Goodwood the previous week, set the pace and had all the others cooked bar the winner at the quarter-mile pole. She kept going once headed and should have no trouble winning a maiden, but possibly came up against a high-class performer in the making here. (op 3-1 tchd 9-4)
Redeemed had finished well behind Don't Forget Faith and Visit on her debut and built on that effort. She came from off the pace and stayed on without ever looking likely to trouble the winner. (op 8-1)
Miss Emma May(IRE), the most experienced in the line-up, had the ground and draw against her in a Group 3 last time. She seemed to have her chance although a little short of room at one point, but could make no impression in the closing stages. She is possibly the guide to the level of the form. Official explanation: jockey said filly was slowly away (op 5-1)
Burn The Breeze(IRE), related to juvenile winners and middle-distance winners at three plus, put up a promising performance on this debut, getting a tow from the leaders for a long way before fading. She should come on for the outing. (op 16-1)
Sovereign's Honour(USA), a $550,000 first foal of a winner at 7f-1m, showed ability without ever getting seriously involved. She is another who is likely to have learnt a lot from the experience. (op 9-1)
Fareeha, out of a half-sister to Malhoob, ran on late from the rear and should do better in time. (op 50-1)
Frivolous(IRE), the first foal of a 10f winner, raced prominently before hanging on the ground and weakening in the closing stages. She clearly has ability and will be better suited by slightly easier conditions.
Ever Dreaming(USA), a $60,000 half-sister to seven winners in the USA, ran a nice race on this debut and was not knocked about when her chance had gone. She can be expected to improve a fair amount for the run.

4403 LLOYDS TSB COMMERCIAL BANKING MAIDEN STKS 1m 4f
5:05 (5:06) (Class 4) 3-Y-O+ £5,181 (£1,541; £770; £384) Stalls High

Form RPR

4632 1 **Ancient Culture**[15] 3908 3-9-1 78 (bt[1]) RyanMoore 8 85
(Sir Michael Stoute) *chsd ldrs: rdn over 2f out: nt clr run over 1f out: sn led: drvn out* 5/2[2]

3 2 ¾ **Longspur**[23] 3685 3-9-1 0 TedDurcan 1 84
(Saeed Bin Suroor) *s.s: hung lft and hdwy over 1f out: rdn: hung rt and ev ch ins fnl f: unable qckn* 5/2[2]

3320 3 3 ½ **Coyote Creek**[16] 3883 3-9-1 78 JamieSpencer 7 78
(E F Vaughan) *hld up: hdwy over 2f out: rdn and ev ch whn hung rt over 1f out: no ex* 7/4[1]

003 4 4 **Two Timer (IRE)**[17] 3847 3-9-1 82 TQuinn 2 72
(D R C Elsworth) *led: hung lft fr over 3f out: hdd over 1f out: sn wknd* 16/1

02 5 hd **Precept**[17] 3847 3-8-10 0 DaneO'Neill 10 66+
(H Candy) *chsd ldr tl rdn over 2f out: looking hld whn bdly hmpd and wknd over 1f out* 8/1[3]

0 6 15 **Blush On Cue (USA)**[38] 3214 3-8-10 0 RobertHavlin 5 42
(J H M Gosden) *chsd ldrs tl wknd over 2f out* 28/1

2m 30.73s (-2.18) **Going Correction** -0.025s/f (Good)
WFA 3 from 4yo+ 11lb 6 Ran SP% **113.9**
Speed ratings (Par 105): **106,105,103,100,100 90**
CSF £9.43 TOTE £3.20: £1.70, £2.00; EX 7.30.
Owner K Abdulla **Bred** Juddmonte Farms Ltd **Trained** Newmarket, Suffolk

FOCUS
An ordinary maiden for the track with the four outsiders absentees. The pace was decent for the grade but, although it could ne rated higher, not a race to be with.
Two Timer(IRE) Official explanation: jockey said colt hung left

4404 EUROPEAN BREEDERS' FUND FILLIES' H'CAP 1m
5:35 (5:35) (Class 4) (0-80,80) 3-Y-O+ £5,829 (£1,734; £866; £432) Stalls High

Form RPR

6-05 1 **Guacamole**[24] 3645 3-9-6 79 MichaelHills 2 84
(B W Hills) *chsd ldrs: rdn and edgd lft 1f out: sn led: r.o u.p* 15/2

-061 2 ½ **Smart Ass (IRE)**[8] 4135 4-9-12 78 RichardHughes 1 83+
(J S Moore) *stdd s: hld up: swtchd lft over 2f out: hdwy over 1f out: sn rdn and hung rt: styd on* 13/8[1]

0065 3 1 **Voliere**[13] 4005 4-9-9 75 SaleemGolam 3 78
(S C Williams) *chsd ldr tl led over 3f out: rdn over 1f out: hdd and unable qckn ins fnl f* 9/1

30-0 4 1 **Sling Back (IRE)**[29] 3516 6-9-11 80 JerryO'Dwyer(3) 4 81
(Eamon Tyrrell, Ire) *chsd ldrs: rdn over 1f out: styd on same pce* 16/1

2-10 5 shd **Royal Fantasy (IRE)**[101] 1395 4-9-7 73 JamieSpencer 5 73
(J R Fanshawe) *hld up: hdwy over 2f out: rdn whn hmpd ins fnl f: no ex* 11/4[2]

5155 6 shd **Emily's Place (IRE)**[19] 3793 4-9-1 67 JimmyQuinn 7 67
(J Pearce) *chsd ldrs: rdn over 2f out: no ex fnl f* 12/1

1560 7 8 **Symbol Of Peace (IRE)**[82] 1905 4-9-10 76 RyanMoore 6 58
(J W Unett) *led over 4f: wknd over 1f out* 13/2[3]

1m 40.77s (0.34) **Going Correction** -0.025s/f (Good)
WFA 3 from 4yo+ 7lb 7 Ran SP% **113.4**
Speed ratings (Par 102): **97,96,95,94,94 94,86**
CSF £19.86 TOTE £8.00: £3.10, £1.50; EX 21.90 Place 6 £55.55, Place 5 £34.61.
Owner Jeremy Gompertz & Patrick Milmo **Bred** Jeremy Gompertz **Trained** Lambourn, Berks

FOCUS
A fair fillies' handicap run at a moderate gallop and rated around the winner and third.
Sling Back(IRE) Official explanation: jockey said mare was denied a clear run
T/Plt: £72.50 to a £1 stake. Pool: £91,397.15. 919.30 winning tickets. T/Qpdt: £12.10 to a £1 stake. Pool: £3,620.50. 219.90 winning tickets. CR

4076 REDCAR (L-H)
Saturday, August 11

OFFICIAL GOING: Firm (good to firm in places; 10.7)
28mm water had been put down over the previous six days resulting in ground 'good to firm at worst'.
Wind: Moderate, half behind Weather: Overcast but fine and dry

4405 TURFTV BETTING SHOP SERVICE (S) STKS 6f
1:55 (1:57) (Class 6) 2-Y-O £2,047 (£604; £302) Stalls Centre

Form RPR

1 **Steal My Fire (IRE)** 2-8-11 0 RichardMullen 2 61+
(E J O'Neill) *mde all: clr over 1f out: eased towards fin* 11/10[1]

456 2 2½ **Elusive Lady (IRE)**[18] 3812 2-8-3 48 AndrewMullen(3) 10 44
(J R Weymes) *mid-div: hmpd after 1f: hdwy over 2f out: carried lft ins fnl f: kpt on: fin 3rd, 2½l & shd: plcd 2nd* 11/1

0001 3 shd **Llab Nala**[2] 4311 2-8-10 49 ThomasO'Brien(7) 11 55
(M R Channon) *chsd ldrs: rdn over 2f out: edgd lft and kpt on fnl f: no ch w wnr: fin 2nd, 2½l: plcd 3rd* 7/1[3]

0U0 4 8 **Mill Creek**[15] 3915 2-8-7 0 ow1 TonyHamilton 12 19
(B Smart) *mid-div: hdwy over 2f out: kpt on fnl f* 20/1

0450 5 ¾ **Little Finch (IRE)**[32] 3398 2-8-7 47 (b) NeilBrown(5) 4 22
(R C Guest) *chsd ldrs: hung lft and wknd over 1f out* 33/1

000 6 shd **Carlton Mac**[10] 4077 2-8-11 34 SilvestreDeSousa 5 20
(N Bycroft) *in rr: kpt on fnl 2f: nvr nr ldrs* 100/1

0000 7 ½ **Mimton (IRE)**[8] 4136 2-7-13 39 LanceBetts(7) 1 14
(N Wilson) *swtchd rt after s: chsd ldrs: wknd over 1f out* 50/1

00 8 nk **Lady See (IRE)**[24] 3635 2-8-3 0 DuranFentiman(3) 13 13
(T D Easterby) *mid-div: outpcd over 2f out: kpt on fnl f* 40/1

4052 9 3 ½ **Dawn Light (IRE)**[12] 4027 2-8-6 55 RoystonFfrench 3 2
(Mrs A Duffield) *stmbld s: sn chsng ldrs: wknd 2f out* 7/2[2]

10 2 **Its Sensational** 2-8-3 0 AndrewElliott(3) 14 —
(K R Burke) *s.s: sn wl bhd: sme hdwy fnl 2f* 16/1

6505 11 nk **Fraamington**[32] 3392 2-8-4 41 MatthewDavies(7) 8 —
(M R Channon) *hmpd after 1f: sn outpcd and in rr* 25/1

00 12 1 ¼ **Social Height (IRE)**[21] 3751 2-8-8 0 PJMcDonald(3) 6 —
(A Berry) *sn outpcd and towards rr* 100/1

005 13 1 ½ **Brilliantsensation (IRE)**[8] 4136 2-8-11 55 (p) J-PGuillambert 9 —
(J G Given) *w ldrs: edgd rt and lost pl 2f out* 9/1

000 14 2 ½ **Lay Down Darling**[21] 3751 2-8-6 35 KimTinkler 7 —
(N Tinkler) *hmpd after 1f: prom: lost pl over 2f out* 100/1

1m 12.18s (0.48) **Going Correction** -0.075s/f (Good) 14 Ran SP% **125.5**
Speed ratings (Par 92): **93,89,89,78,77 77,77,76,72,69 68,67,65,61**
CSF £15.32 TOTE £1.90: £1.20, £2.80, £2.70; EX 15.50.The winner was bought in for 16,000gns.
Owner J C Fretwell **Bred** R Honniball **Trained** Averham Park, Notts
■ Stewards' Enquiry : Lance Betts five-day ban: careless riding (Aug 22-26)
Thomas O'Brien two-day ban: careless riding (Aug 25-26)

FOCUS
A poor contest in which the heavily-backed winner was never in any danger, the first three well clear.

NOTEBOOK
Steal My Fire(IRE) stood out like a beacon in the fog in the paddock. Backed as if defeat was out of the question he certainly knew his job and always looked in total control. Connections were quite happy to dig deep to retain him and he is clearly a cut or two above selling-race class. (op 5-4 tchd 11-8 in places)
Elusive Lady(IRE), dropped in grade, looked very fit. Knocked out of her stride at the end of the first furlong, she was then carried halfway across the track by the runner-up. She deserves to find a similar event. Official explanation: jockey said filly suffered interference
Llab Nala, making a quick return, was on his toes and swishing his tail in the paddock. His rider persisted in using his whip in the wrong hand, carrying Elusive Lady across the track. The placings were reversed and the boy given a two-day ban. (op 5-1)

Mill Creek, in a seller for the first time, continually swished her tail beforehand. She runs as though she really needs a seventh furlong. (op 25-1)
Little Finch(IRE), who gave problems going down, has achieved little since he took an identical event in first-time blinkers at Catterick in May.
Carlton Mac Official explanation: jockey said gelding had no more to give
Dawn Light(IRE), who is only small, almost came down leaving the stalls. Official explanation: jockey said filly stumbled at start (op 4-1 tchd 10-3 and 9-2 in a place)
Lay Down Darling Official explanation: jockey said filly suffered interference

4406 DESTINY RACING CLUB NURSERY 6f
2:30 (2:31) (Class 3) 2-Y-O **£9,715** (£2,890; £1,444; £721) **Stalls** Centre

Form RPR
435 **1** **Cat Whistle**[21] 3747 2-8-11 **73**........................ TonyHamilton 4 80
(R A Fahey) *hld up: effrt 2f out: hung rt and led 1f out: r.o strly* **6/1**[3]
61 **2** *2 1/2* **Wise Son**[12] 4016 2-9-4 **83**........................ LiamJones(3) 8 82
(W J Haggas) *chsd ldrs: fly-jmpd over 1f out: kpt on wl: no ch w wnr* **4/1**[1]
461 **3** *1/2* **Bohobe (IRE)**[38] 3200 2-8-12 **74**........................ SilvestreDeSousa 9 71
(J G Given) *chsd ldrs stands' side: rdn and outpcd over 2f out: styd on fnl f* **12/1**
1430 **4** *shd* **Bahama Baileys**[32] 3398 2-9-2 **78**........................ J-PGuillambert 2 75
(M Johnston) *stmbld s: chsd ldrs: led over 2f out: hdd and edgd rt 1f out: no ex* **4/1**[1]
211 **5** *hd* **Lady Rangali (IRE)**[8] 4126 2-9-6 **82**........................ RoystonFfrench 3 78
(Mrs A Duffield) *chsd ldrs: edgd rt after 1f: nt clr run and swtchd lft ins fnl f: kpt on wl* **4/1**[1]
3400 **6** *1/2* **Cristal Clear (IRE)**[42] 3096 2-9-6 **82**........................ RichardMullen 5 77
(T D Easterby) *chsd ldrs: bmpd after 1f: kpt on same pce fnl f* **9/2**[2]
4564 **7** *hd* **Atephobia**[7] 4154 2-8-0 **65**........................ AndrewElliott(3) 7 59
(K R Burke) *led tl over 2f out: kpt on same pce appr fnl f* **14/1**
024 **8** *1* **Best Suited**[11] 4041 2-7-10 **61**........................ DuranFentiman(3) 1 52
(J J Quinn) *chsd ldrs on outer: one pce fnl 2f* **16/1**
503 **9** *12* **She's Our Dream**[11] 4041 2-8-1 **66**........................(t) AndrewMullen(3) 10 19
(R C Guest) *chsd ldrs: rdn over 2f out: sn lost pl and bhd* **25/1**
1m 11.27s (-0.43) **Going Correction** -0.075s/f (Good) **9** Ran SP% **116.6**
Speed ratings (Par 98): **99,95,95,94,94 93,93,92,76**
CSF £30.54 CT £283.12 TOTE £8.30: £1.90, £2.10, £2.90; EX 48.30 TRIFECTA Not won..
Owner R A Fahey **Bred** Genesis Green Stud Ltd **Trained** Musley Bank, N Yorks

FOCUS
A tight nursery that was won in most convincing fashion and the form looks solid although there were traffic problems and Lady Rangali looked second best.

NOTEBOOK
Cat Whistle, who looked a picture of health, has inclined to be too keen and her rider was at pains to settle her off the pace. Despite tending to hang she came there strongly and scored in most convincing fashion. Hopefully she is still learning and will go on from here. (op 11-2)
Wise Son, who is only small, was stepping up to six on his handicap bow. He seemed to strike into himself coming to the final furlong but kept on gamely to finish second best. (op 9-2)
Bohobe(IRE), back over six and encountering much quicker ground, was sticking on strongly at the finish and will be suited by a slightly stiffer test.
Bahama Baileys, who has plenty of size and scope, lost his footing exiting the traps. He edged right under pressure closing the door in Lady Rangali's face. Official explanation: jockey said colt stumbled at start (op 5-1)
Lady Rangali(IRE), 6lb higher, was involved in some scrimmaging early on. She was left short of room and forced to switch inside the last and was probably second best on the day. Official explanation: jockey said filly was denied a clear run (op 3-1)
Cristal Clear(IRE), again running without any headgear, was tightened up early on. She stuck on in her own time in the closing stages and this might be as good as she is. (op 11-2 tchd 4-1)

4407 TRANSMORE VAN HIRE LTD H'CAP 7f
3:05 (3:05) (Class 4) (0-80,79) 3-Y-O+ **£4,728** (£1,406; £702; £351) **Stalls** Centre

Form RPR
3204 **1** **Passion Fruit**[14] 3953 6-9-10 **79**........................ AndrewElliott(3) 1 89
(C W Fairhurst) *hld up detached in last: gd hdwy on wd outside over 1f out: led ins fnl f: hld on towards fin* **14/1**
236 **2** *nk* **Observatory Star (IRE)**[13] 3998 4-8-13 **65**........................(b) RichardMullen 6 74
(T D Easterby) *hld up: hdwy 2f out: swtchd lft over 1f out: hung lft and styd on wl fnl f: jst hld* **11/2**[2]
5561 **3** *3/4* **Gap Princess (IRE)**[15] 3920 3-8-6 **64**........................ TonyHamilton 3 69
(R A Fahey) *chsd ldrs: led 1f out: sn hdd and no ex* **7/1**
0305 **4** *2 1/2* **Neon Blue**[3] 4281 6-8-11 **70**........................(b[1]) SCreighton(7) 9 70
(R M Whitaker) *chsd ldrs: kpt on same pce fnl 2f* **11/1**
4000 **5** *shd* **Crosby Vision**[7] 4177 4-8-13 **65**........................ J-PGuillambert 4 65
(J R Weymes) *sn drvn along: led after 2f: hdd 1f out: one pce* **20/1**
4111 **6** *2 1/2* **Sam's Secret**[9] 4100 5-9-8 **77**........................ PJMcDonald(3) 10 70
(G A Swinbank) *trckd ldrs: effrt 2f out: kpt on same pce* **9/2**[1]
0105 **7** *2 1/2* **Sedge (USA)**[8] 4137 7-8-13 **65**........................(b) LeeEnstone 13 52
(P T Midgley) *chsd ldrs: pushed along 3f out: one pce* **25/1**
4425 **8** *nk* **Stoic Leader (IRE)**[6] 4195 7-9-8 **77**........................ AndrewMullen(3) 11 63
(R F Fisher) *led 2f: lost pl and hmpd over 1f out: no ch after* **6/1**[3]
3401 **9** *3/4* **Pay Time**[13] 3999 8-8-8 **60**........................ RoystonFfrench 12 44
(R E Barr) *chsd ldrs: rdn 3f out: wknd 2f out* **11/1**
6000 **10** *3/4* **Sir Orpen (IRE)**[8] 4141 4-8-8 **65**........................(p) NeilBrown(5) 8 47
(T D Barron) *in rr: rdn over 3f out: nvr a factor* **14/1**
1064 **11** *1 1/4* **Tough Love**[8] 4137 8-9-0 **69**........................(p) DuranFentiman(3) 5 47
(T D Easterby) *hld up in mid-div: effrt over 2f out: edgd lft and sn btn* **12/1**
5000 **12** *1/2* **Lincolneurocruiser**[18] 3828 5-8-6 **63**........................ RussellKennemore(5) 7 40
(Mrs N Macauley) *sn chsng ldrs: lost pl 3f out* **22/1**
1013 **13** *1 1/2* **Riquewihr**[8] 4137 7-9-5 **71**........................(p) PaddyAspell 14 44
(J S Wainwright) *hld up in rr: effrt over 2f out: no imp* **10/1**
1m 22.96s (-1.94) **Going Correction** -0.075s/f (Good)
WFA 3 from 4yo+ 6lb **13** Ran SP% **120.1**
Speed ratings (Par 105): **108,107,106,103,103 100,98,97,96,96 94,94,92**
CSF £87.31 CT £453.33 TOTE £17.40: £3.50, £2.50, £3.20; EX 112.50 Trifecta £162.60 Part won. Pool: £229.10 - 0.10 winning units..
Owner G H & S Leggott **Bred** G H And Simon Leggott **Trained** Middleham Moor, N Yorks
■ Stewards' Enquiry : Richard Mullen one-day ban: careless riding (Aug 24)

FOCUS
An ordinary contest but solid form with a best-ever performance from the winner and the placed horses running to their pre-race marks.

4408 JOHN SMITH'S REDCAR STRAIGHT-MILE CHAMPIONSHIP H'CAP (QUALIFIER) 1m
3:40 (3:41) (Class 3) (0-90,90) 3-Y-O+ **£10,363** (£3,083; £1,540; £769) **Stalls** Centre

Form RPR
0161 **1** **Ragheed (USA)**[14] 3960 3-8-8 **82**........................ LiamJones(3) 4 95+
(W J Haggas) *mde all: qcknd over 2f out: r.o strly: v readily* **4/6**[1]
6000 **2** *3* **Hartshead**[14] 3953 8-9-9 **90**........................ PJMcDonald(3) 2 94
(G A Swinbank) *hld up wl in tch: effrt and chsd wnr over 1f out: no imp* **4/1**[2]
1341 **3** *3* **Top Jaro (FR)**[10] 4082 4-8-4 **71** oh3........................ AndrewMullen(3) 3 68
(D W Barker) *sn w ldrs: rdn over 2f out: one pce* **5/1**[3]
2050 **4** *1 1/4* **Efidium**[7] 4176 9-8-4 **71** oh4........................ AndrewElliott(3) 1 65
(N Bycroft) *sn trcking ldrs: effrt over 2f out: one pce* **14/1**
40-0 **5** *5* **Go Tech**[123] 993 7-8-13 **80**........................ DuranFentiman(3) 6 63
(T D Easterby) *w wnr: t.k.h: rdn over 2f out: wknd over 1f out* **11/1**
1m 37.07s (-0.73) **Going Correction** -0.075s/f (Good)
WFA 3 from 4yo+ 7lb **5** Ran SP% **111.7**
Speed ratings (Par 107): **100,97,94,92,87**
CSF £3.77 TOTE £1.60: £1.10, £1.70; EX 3.90.
Owner Hamdan Al Maktoum **Bred** Swordlestown Stud **Trained** Newmarket, Suffolk

FOCUS
A decent contest but a weak turnout and a very straightforward task for the progressive three-year-old. The third sets the standard.

NOTEBOOK
Ragheed(USA), 5lb higher, enjoyed himself in front and picking up the pace in his own time accounted for older horses with a fair bit in hand. (op 10-11 tchd evens in a place)
Hartshead, 3lb below his last winning mark, showed a return to form but was no match for the highly progressive younger horse. (tchd 7-2)
Top Jaro(FR), having his first outing for his new connections, was running from 3lb out of the handicap. (op 6-1)
Efidium, 4lb 'wrong', likes it here but was biting off more than he could chew. (tchd 12-1 and 16-1)
Go Tech, having just his second start this time and his first since April, was full of himself but ran as if the outing was very much needed. (op 6-1)

4409 MARY REVELEY RACING CLUB H'CAP 1m 6f 19y
4:10 (4:11) (Class 6) (0-65,65) 3-Y-O+ **£1,943** (£578; £288; £144) **Stalls** Low

Form RPR
4-05 **1** **Abstract Folly (IRE)**[18] 3815 5-9-11 **62**........................ PJMcDonald(3) 9 70
(J D Bethell) *swtchd lft after s: hld up: hdwy over 4f out: wnt 2nd over 2f out: shkn up to ld 1f out: styd on wl* **8/1**
6323 **2** *1 1/2* **Dansimar**[8] 4139 3-8-11 **65**........................ MatthewDavies(7) 10 70
(M R Channon) *sn trcking ldrs: wnt 2nd over 6f out: led over 3f out tl 1f out: no ex* **10/3**[2]
0616 **3** *1 3/4* **Mr Crystal (FR)**[40] 3159 3-8-10 **57**........................ TonyHamilton 1 60
(Micky Hammond) *hld up in midfield: effrt 4f out: kpt on same pce fnl 2f* **15/2**
6353 **4** *3 1/2* **Let It Be**[49] 2890 6-9-1 **54**........................ NeilBrown(5) 5 52
(K G Reveley) *hld up in midfield: hdwy over 3f out: one pce fnl 2f* **5/2**[1]
650 **5** *1 3/4* **Square Dealer**[24] 3638 6-9-2 **50**........................(b) PaddyAspell 8 46
(J R Norton) *led after 2f: hdd over 3f out: one pce* **33/1**
066- **6** *3 1/2* **Rajam**[226] 5960 9-8-11 **45**........................(p) LeeEnstone 6 36
(P C Haslam) *hld up in midfield: effrt 4f out: wknd over 1f out* **15/2**
2112 **7** *1/2* **Toboggan Lady**[9] 4104 3-8-8 **55**........................(p) RoystonFfrench 7 45
(Mrs A Duffield) *chsd ldrs: effrt over 4f out: edgd lft and lost pl over 1f out: eased* **7/2**[3]
-005 **8** *3 1/2* **Zaville**[158] 628 5-8-13 **50**........................(b) AndrewMullen(3) 2 35
(J O'Reilly) *swvd lft s: hld up in rr: effrt 3f out: nvr on terms* **18/1**
0060 **9** *31* **My Causeway Dream (IRE)**[7] 4156 4-8-11 **45**....(v) SilvestreDeSousa 4 —
(J S Wainwright) *led 2f: chsd ldrs: lost pl 3f out: sn bhd and eased: virtually p.u* **50/1**
6440 **10** *4* **Piccolomini**[49] 2890 5-8-8 **45**........................(p) LiamJones(3) 3 —
(E W Tuer) *hld up in rr: lost pl and eased over 2f out: virtually p.u* **25/1**
0000 **11** *35* **College Rebel**[136] 808 6-8-8 **45**........................ DuranFentiman(3) 11 —
(J F Coupland) *sn chsng ldrs: wd bnd after 2f: drvn over 6f out: lost pl over 4f out: sn bhd and eased: hopeleslly t.o: virtually p.u* **66/1**
3m 0.95s (-4.07) **Going Correction** -0.075s/f (Good)
WFA 3 from 4yo+ 13lb **11** Ran SP% **124.0**
Speed ratings (Par 101): **108,107,106,104,103 101,100,98,81,78 58**
CSF £36.13 CT £218.41 TOTE £9.80: £2.80, £1.90, £2.30; EX 46.90.
Owner Clarendon Thoroughbred Racing **Bred** John Neary **Trained** Middleham Moor, N Yorks

FOCUS
A low-grade handicap won in ready fashion by the top-weight. The form looks solid at this level rated through the placed horses.
Toboggan Lady Official explanation: jockey said filly was unsuited by the firm (good to firm in places) ground
Piccolomini Official explanation: jockey said gelding was never travelling

4410 RACING UK CHANNEL 432 CLAIMING STKS 1m 1f
4:40 (4:40) (Class 6) 4-Y-O+ **£2,047** (£604; £302) **Stalls** Low

Form RPR
0-04 **1** **Awaken**[4] 4249 6-9-0 55........................ RoystonFrench 9 56
(Miss Tracy Waggott) *hld up: hdwy on outer over 3f out: styd on to ld towards fin* **4/1**[2]
-000 **2** *1/2* **Roman History (IRE)**[10] 4082 4-8-13 50........................(p) SilvestreDeSousa 1 54
(Miss Tracy Waggott) *trckd ldrs: chal over 3f out: led 1f out: hdd and no ex towards fin* **9/1**
0055 **3** *1* **Beamsley Beacon**[9] 4099 6-8-11 48........................ PaddyAspell 2 50
(S T Mason) *led tl 1f out: no ex* **8/1**
205 **4** *1* **Apache Point (IRE)**[10] 4082 10-8-7 50........................ KimTinkler 3 44
(N Tinkler) *chsd ldrs: chal over 2f out: one pce fnl f* **6/4**[1]
4002 **5** *3* **Lewis Lloyd (IRE)**[13] 3996 4-9-0 44........................(t) NeilBrown(5) 8 49
(R E Barr) *hld up in rr: hdwy on ins over 3f out: one pce fnl 2f* **7/1**[3]
-660 **6** *10* **Phoenix Nights (IRE)**[23] 2843 7-8-11 40........................ LeeEnstone 7 19
(A Berry) *hld up in rr: hdwy 4f out: wknd 2f out* **25/1**
00-0 **7** *2* **Lord Conyers (IRE)**[22] 3723 8-7-13 40........................ LiamJones(3) 4 6
(G Woodward) *w ldrs: lost pl over 2f out* **25/1**
4-60 **8** *27* **Splodger Mac (IRE)**[77] 2027 8-8-4 47........................ DuranFentiman(3) 5 —
(N Bycroft) *trckd ldrs: drvn over 4f out: lost pl over 2f out: eased and sn bhd* **9/1**
00-0 **9** *21* **Salisbury World (IRE)**[51] 2795 4-8-11 36........................ TonyHamilton 6 —
(J F Coupland) *s.s: t.k.h: jnd ldrs after 2f: lost pl over 3f out: sn bhd and eased fnl 2f* **50/1**
1m 52.73s (-0.67) **Going Correction** -0.075s/f (Good) **9** Ran SP% **113.3**
Speed ratings (Par 101): **99,98,97,96,94 85,83,59,40**
CSF £37.68 TOTE £4.40: £1.90, £2.60, £2.60; EX 31.60.
Owner Miss T Waggott **Bred** Juddmonte Farms **Trained** Spennymoor, Co Durham

FOCUS
A poor claimer but the form looks pretty sound rated round the first three home.

4411 COME RACING HERE TOMORROW MEDIAN AUCTION MAIDEN STKS — 1m 1f
5:15 (5:15) (Class 5) 3-4-Y-0 — £2,817 (£838; £418; £209) Stalls Low

Form | | | | RPR
2324 **1** **Jibajaba (USA)**[16] 3889 3-9-3 74 .... TonyHamilton 2 — 50
(R A Fahey) *trckd ldrs: chal on bit over 2f out: rdn to ld over 1f out: hld on towards fin* **2/5**[1]

6-50 **2** *nk* **Musical Land (IRE)**[89] 1708 3-9-0 66 .... AndrewMullen(3) 6 — 49
(J R Weymes) *trckd ldrs: drvn: outpcd and hung lft over 4f out: styd on strly fnl f: jst hld* **10/1**

0022 **3** *1/2* **Shotley Mac**[11] 4042 3-8-12 50 .... (b) NeilBrown(5) 3 — 48
(N Bycroft) *led tl over 1f out: kpt on same pce ins fnl f* **11/2**[2]

-400 **4** *shd* **Cranworth Blaze**[47] 2951 3-8-9 43 .... (be[1]) PJMcDonald(3) 5 — 43
(T J Etherington) *w ldr: effrt 4f out: styd on ins fnl f* **66/1**

20- **5** *14* **Starbougg**[330] 5332 3-8-12 0 .... RoystonFfrench 1 — 12
(K G Reveley) *hld up in last: drvn over 5f out: lost pl over 3f out: sn bhd* **7/1**[3]

000 **6** *8* **Scruffy (IRE)**[13] 3994 3-9-3 39 .... PaddyAspell 4 — —
(C J Teague) *hld up wl in tch: rdn and lost pl over 3f out: sn bhd* **80/1**

1m 54.14s (0.74) **Going Correction** -0.075s/f (Good) **6** Ran SP% **111.1**
Speed ratings (Par 103): **93,92,92,92,79 72**
CSF £5.41 TOTE £1.40: £1.10, £3.50; EX 4.10 Place 6 £90.13, Place 5 £60.27.
Owner J H Tattersall **Bred** K West **Trained** Musley Bank, N Yorks

FOCUS
A very poor median auction race run at a steady gallop and just a length between the first four at the line. The form is severely limited by the proximity of the 43-rated fourth.
T/Plt: £106.70 to a £1 stake. Pool: £53,185.85. 363.55 winning tickets. T/Qpdt: £40.70 to a £1 stake. Pool: £2,384.80. 43.30 winning tickets. WG

ARLINGTON (L-H)
Saturday, August 11

OFFICIAL GOING: Good

4412a SECRETARIAT STKS (GRADE 1) — 1m 2f
9:10 (9:17) 3-Y-0
£122,449 (£40,816; £20,408; £10,204; £6,122; £4,082)

| | | | RPR
1 **Shamdinan (FR)**[41] 3142 3-8-7 .... JRLeparoux 8 — 115
(Doug O'Neill, U.S.A) *held up in 8th, closed up over 3f out, 6th on outside straight, soon chasing leader, driven to lead close home* **48/10**[3]

2 *1/2* **Red Giant (USA)**[21] 3-8-11 .... GKGomez 5 — 118
(T Pletcher, U.S.A) *always in touch, racing in 5th, 3rd straight, led 1 1/2f out, soon 1 1/2 lengths up, ridden & caught close home* **28/10**[2]

3 *5 1/2* **Going Ballistic (USA)**[21] 3-8-9 .... CMBerry 1 — 106
(D Von Hemel, U.S.A) *raced in 6th, 7th straight, edged to outside, reached 3rd 1f out, ran on same pace* **103/10**

4 *1 3/4* **Admiralofthefleet (USA)**[35] 3331 3-8-9 .... (b) MJKinane 2 — 103
(A P O'Brien, Ire) *close up on inside, 5th & not clear run entering straight, switched out over 1f out, stayed on same pace* **9/5**[1]

5 *1 1/4* **Love Dubai (USA)**[21] 3-8-7 .... (b) CLanerie 6 — 99
(Michael J Maker, U.S.A) *towards rear, last & ridden straight, no real headway* **55/1**

6 *2* **Mostacolli Mort (USA)**[41] 3-8-7 .... (b) VEspinoza 7 — 95
(J Canani, U.S.A) *last to 4f out, 8th straight, never a factor* **275/10**

7 *1 3/4* **Lattice (USA)**[21] 3-8-11 .... RAlbarado 4 — 96
(W Mott, U.S.A) *prominent, went 2nd on outside entering straight, soon one pace* **48/10**[3]

8 *nse* **Pleasant Strike (USA)**[21] 3-8-9 .... RRDouglas 9 — 94
(T Pletcher, U.S.A) *led to 1 1/2f out* **128/10**

9 *6 3/4* **Fleeting Shadow (IRE)**[20] 3772 3-8-7 .... (b) PJSmullen 3 — 80
(D K Weld, Ire) *pressed leader, 4th straight, beaten when squeezed back over 1f out* **237/10**

2m 4.02s (2.38) **9** Ran SP% **122.0**
PARI-MUTUEL (including $2 stakes): WIN 11.60; PL (1-2) 6.00, 4.00; SHOW (1-2-3) 4.80, 3.20, 4.60; SF 47.20.
Owner Triple B Farms **Bred** H H The Aga Khan's Studs S C **Trained** USA

NOTEBOOK
Admiralofthefleet(USA), who should have been suited by the trip and ground, was wearing blinkers for the first time and had every chance, but they did not bring about the required improvement.

4413a BEVERLY D STKS (GRADE 1) (F&M) — 1m 1f 110y(T)
9:45 (9:50) 3-Y-0+
£229,592 (£76,531; £38,265; £19,133; £11,480; £7,653)

| | | | RPR
1 **Royal Highness (GER)**[28] 5-8-11 .... RRDouglas 7 — 116
(Christophe Clement, U.S.A) *raced in 6th, ridden to challenge inside final f, led well inside final f, driven out & ran on well* **92/10**

2 *hd* **Irridescence (SAF)**[31] 3433 6-8-11 .... JMurtagh 3 — 116
(M F De Kock, South Africa) *tracked leader, 2nd straight, led over 1f out, headed well inside final f, ran on* **9/2**

3 *2 1/2* **Lady Of Venice (FR)**[36] 4-8-11 .... JRLeparoux 4 — 112
(P L Biancone, U.S.A) *raced in 5th, 6th straight, headway on outside from over 1f out, kept on same pace final f* **3/1**[3]

4 *4 1/2* **Citronnade (USA)**[41] 4-8-11 .... DFlores 1 — 103
(R J Frankel, U.S.A) *raced in 4th, 5th straight on outside, soon one pace* **11/5**[1]

5 *1/2* **Jennie R. (USA)**[21] 6-8-11 .... (b) EBaird 5 — 103
(Michele Boyce, U.S.A) *led to over 1f out* **302/10**

6 *1* **Honey Ryder (USA)**[35] 6-8-11 .... GKGomez 6 — 101
(T Pletcher, U.S.A) *last most of way, ridden entering straight, no progress* **23/10**[2]

7 *3/4* **Lahudood**[27] 4-8-11 .... RAlbarado 2 — 99
(K McLaughlin, U.S.A) *raced in 3rd, 4th straight, soon beaten* **214/10**

1m 56.68s (1.21) **7** Ran SP% **122.2**
PARI-MUTUEL: WIN 20.40; PL (1-2) 9.40, 6.60; SHOW (1-2-3) 5.60, 4.40, 3.40; SF 128.00.
Owner Monceaux Stable **Bred** Gestut Etzean **Trained** USA

4414a ARLINGTON MILLION XXV (GRADE 1) — 1m 2f
10:40 (10:44) 3-Y-0+
£306,122 (£102,041; £51,020; £20,408; £20,408; £10,204)

| | | | RPR
1 **Jambalaya (CAN)**[20] 5-9-0 .... RAlbarado 1 — 116
(Catherine Day Phillips, Canada) *always close up, 3rd straight on inside, driven to lead well inside final f, ran on well* **76/10**

2 *3/4* **The Tin Man (USA)**[42] 9-9-0 .... VEspinoza 4 — 115
(Richard E Mandella, U.S.A) *tracked leader, challenged approaching straight, led over 1f out, soon driven, headed well inside final f, ran on* **2/1**[1]

3 *nse* **Doctor Dino (FR)**[83] 1877 5-9-0 .... JMurtagh 3 — 115
(R Gibson, France) *always close up, 5th straight, ran on under pressure final f, just missed 2nd* **49/10**

4 *nk* **Stream Cat (USA)**[38] 4-9-0 .... (b) JRLeparoux 6 — 114
(P L Biancone, U.S.A) *held up in 6th to straight, headway on outside 1f out, stayed on to dead- heat for 4th on line* **149/10**

4 *dht* **Sunriver (USA)**[27] 4-9-0 .... GKGomez 2 — 114
(T Pletcher, U.S.A) *led to over 1f out, one pace* **27/10**[2]

6 *1/2* **Danak (IRE)**[76] 2064 4-9-0 .... MJKinane 7 — 113
(John M Oxx, Ire) *held up in rear but always in touch, last on inside straight, ran on under pressure final f, nearest at finish* **41/10**[3]

7 *2* **Pressing (IRE)**[52] 2754 4-9-0 .... DFlores 5 — 110
(M A Jarvis) *close up disputing 3rd, 4th on outside straight, ridden & one paced 5th when hit by 3rd's whip 1f out, no chance after* **144/10**

2m 4.76s (3.12) **7** Ran SP% **121.3**
PARI-MUTUEL: WIN 17.20; PL (1-2) 6.60, 3.80; SHOW (1-2-3) 3.80, 2.60, 3.60; SF 62.60.
Owner Kingfield Farms **Bred** Gustav Schickedanz **Trained** Canada

NOTEBOOK
Danak(IRE), who lost his unbeaten record behind Notnowcato, Dylan Thomas and Youmzain on his first try in group 1 company in the Tattersalls Gold Cup, never really figured on this return from a break, although he was not beaten far in the end.
Pressing(IRE), a Group 3 winner and placed at this level in Italy, was making his debut for a trainer who did so well for the owner with Rakti. He was close enough turning in but was on the retreat when getting hit by another rider's whip.

SARATOGA (R-H)
Saturday, August 11

OFFICIAL GOING: Firm

4415a SWORD DANCER INVITATIONAL (GRADE 1) — 1m 4f
10:20 (10:22) 3-Y-0
£153,061 (£51,020; £25,510; £12,755; £7,653; £1,276)

| | | | RPR
1 **Grand Couturier**[28] 4-8-4 .... CHBorel 6 — 120
(R Ribaudo, U.S.A) **156/10**

2 *3* **English Channel (USA)**[35] 5-8-11 .... JRVelazquez 4 — 122
(T Pletcher, U.S.A) **3/5**[1]

3 *2 3/4* **Trippi's Storm (USA)**[27] 4-8-4 .... (b) JCastellano 2 — 111
(S Hough, U.S.A) **49/10**[3]

4 *1* **Crown Point (USA)**[273] 5-8-4 .... (b) RBejarano 5 — 109
(D Donk, U.S.A) **45/1**

5 *1 3/4* **Always First**[38] 6-8-4 .... (b) CVelasquez 8 — 107
(T Voss, U.S.A) **42/10**[2]

6 *4* **Embossed (IRE)**[35] 5-8-4 .... (b) ECoa 3 — 101
(Niall M O'Callaghan, U.S.A) **29/1**

7 *27* **Fri Guy (USA)**[35] 4-8-4 .... EPrado 1 — 60
(Dale Romans, U.S.A) **217/10**

8 *26* **Ramazutti (USA)**[38] 5-8-6 .... (b) KDesormeaux 7 — 23
(T Pletcher, U.S.A) **24/1**

2m 26.59s (146.59) **8** Ran SP% **118.6**
PARI-MUTUEL (Including $2 stake): WIN 33.20; PL (1-2) 7.50, 2.70; SHOW (1-2-3) 4.30, 2.10, 3.00; SF 84.50.
Owner Marc Keller **Bred** Tom Wilson **Trained** USA

4070 LEICESTER (R-H)
Sunday, August 12

OFFICIAL GOING: Firm (good to firm in places) (9.6)
Wind: Light, behind Weather: Cloudy with sunny spells

4416 RUTLAND (S) STKS — 7f 9y
2:20 (2:21) (Class 6) 3-4-Y-0 — £2,590 (£770; £385; £192) Stalls Low

Form | | | | RPR
0405 **1** **Finsbury**[44] 3056 4-8-9 69 .... AmyBaker(7) 14 — 56
(Miss J Feilden) *mid-div: hdwy over 2f out: rdn to ld over 1f out: sn hung lft: styd on* **3/1**[1]

-004 **2** *1 3/4* **Strife (IRE)**[8] 4155 4-8-13 47 .... PJMcDonald(3) 3 — 52
(W M Brisbourne) *wnt rt s: chsd ldrs: rdn and hung rt over 1f out: styd on* **28/1**

0022 **3** *1 1/4* **Calloff The Search**[17] 3873 3-8-10 53 .... (v) SaleemGolam 12 — 47
(W G M Turner) *chsd ldrs: rdn and ev ch over 1f out: styd on same pce* **7/1**[2]

00-0 **4** *3/4* **Buckle And Hyde**[102] 1400 4-8-11 45 .... TedDurcan 10 — 42
(Mrs A L M King) *hld up: hdwy over 1f out: styd on* **80/1**

0000 **5** *shd* **Halfwaytoparadise**[25] 3636 4-8-6 47 .... (p) TolleyDean(5) 8 — 42
(W G M Turner) *led: rdn and hdd over 1f out: styd on same pce* **50/1**

0210 **6** *1* **Strike Force**[18] 3839 3-9-1 62 .... (p) JamieSpencer 5 — 47
(R A Harris) *hmpd s: hld up: styd on ins fnl f: nrst fin* **3/1**[1]

0600 **7** *1/2* **Al Rayanah**[4] 4294 4-8-4 53 .... CharlotteKerton(7) 18 — 38
(G Prodromou) *chsd ldrs: rdn over 2f out: wknd over 1f out* **14/1**

5 **8** *1/2* **Fine Art World (IRE)**[44] 3044 3-8-7 0 .... WilliamBuick(3) 13 — 39
(N A Callaghan) *chsd ldrs: rdn over 2f out: wknd over 1f out* **16/1**

0203 **9** *1 3/4* **Kassuta**[11] 4071 3-8-0 50 .... (v) LukeMorris(5) 2 — 30
(John A Harris) *chsd ldrs over 5f* **10/1**[3]

0350 **10** *shd* **Mine The Balance (IRE)**[17] 3869 4-8-9 48.........(b) ThomasO'Brien(7) 15 36
(H J Manners) *mid-div: hdwy and edgd rt over 2f out: wknd over 1f out* **33/1**
0056 **11** *½* **Law Of The Land (IRE)**[10] 4109 3-8-10 55............................ TQuinn 17 33
(W R Muir) *chsd ldrs over 5f* **7/1**[2]
4000 **12** *2½* **Cadi May**[6] 4220 3-8-5 50.. PaulQuinn 7 21
(W M Brisbourne) *hmpd s: chsd ldrs: wkng whn hmpd over 2f out* **100/1**
6-00 **13** *3½* **Ancient Site (USA)**[20] 3786 3-8-10 42............................. AdamKirby 11 17
(B P J Baugh) *a in rr* **100/1**
0000 **14** *1½* **Kings Shillings**[11] 4071 3-9-1 45.................................(b) HayleyTurner 9 18
(D Carroll) *mid-div: rdn 1/2-way: wknd over 2f out* **50/1**
0005 **15** *1* **Fun In The Sun**[3] 4321 3-8-3 48.................................(v) MCGeran(7) 16 10
(P D Evans) *s.s: outpcd: hdwy 3f out: sn rdn and wknd* **12/1**
00-0 **16** *1¾* **Endless Night**[186] 379 4-8-13 55............................... JerryO'Dwyer(3) 6 7
(A M Hales) *s.i.s and hmpd s: a in rr* **20/1**
000- **17** *2* **Night Rainbow (IRE)**[346] 4970 4-8-11 52........................ SteveDrowne 1 —
(P G Murphy) *hld up: wknd over 2f out* **40/1**

1m 24.7s (-1.40) **Going Correction** -0.20s/f (Firm)
WFA 3 from 4yo 6lb 17 Ran SP% **125.1**
Speed ratings (Par 101): **100,98,96,95,95 94,93,93,91,91 90,87,83,82,80 78,76**
CSF £106.80 TOTE £4.00: £2.60, £7.60, £1.90; EX 86.70 TRIFECTA Not won..The winner was sold to Milton Bradley for 9,500gns. Strike Force was claimed by Hugh Collingridge for £6,000.
Owner Mrs R P Aggio **Bred** O Pointing **Trained** Exning, Suffolk
■ Stewards' Enquiry : P J McDonald two-day ban: careless riding (Aug 25-26)

FOCUS
Moderate form best rated through the third.
Strike Force Official explanation: jockey said gelding was too keen to post and was hampered at start
Cadi May Official explanation: jockey said filly lost a shoe
Fun In The Sun Official explanation: jockey said gelding missed the break

4417 E B F ROBINS AND DAY PEUGEOT 4007 MAIDEN STKS 7f 9y
2:50 (2:53) (Class 4) 2-Y-O **£4,731** (£1,416; £708; £354; £176) **Stalls** Low

Form RPR
4 **1** **Hawaana (IRE)**[14] 3991 2-9-3 0.. RHills 12 79+
(B W Hills) *trckd ldrs: led over 2f out: shkn up fnl f: r.o wl* **6/5**[1]
2 *2* **Doctor Fremantle** 2-9-3 0... JamieSpencer 10 74+
(Sir Michael Stoute) *hld up: racd keenly: hdwy over 2f out: chsd wnr over 1f out: styd on same pce ins fnl f* **13/8**[2]
3 *1¼* **Strategic Mover (USA)** 2-9-3 0...(t) TQuinn 9 71+
(P F I Cole) *prom: outpcd 2f out: styd on ins fnl f* **16/1**
63 **4** *hd* **Parliamentary (JPN)**[39] 3205 2-9-3 0.............................. MichaelHills 3 70
(M Johnston) *led: hdd over 4f out: rdn over 2f out: styd on same pce appr fnl f* **15/2**[3]
00 **5** *3½* **Weetfromthechaff**[12] 4037 2-9-3 0....................................... PaulQuinn 6 61
(R Hollinshead) *hld up: plld hrd: hdwy over 2f out: wknd over 1f out* **100/1**
40 **6** *6* **Janet's Delight**[17] 3874 2-8-9 0.................................. WilliamBuick(3) 11 39
(S Curran) *chsd ldrs: led 1/2-way: rdn and hdd over 2f out: wknd wl over 1f out* **66/1**
7 *3* **Potemkin (USA)** 2-9-3 0.. TedDurcan 4 36
(A King) *hld up: sme hdwy over 2f out: sn wknd* **40/1**
0 **8** *1½* **Love Dancer (IRE)**[13] 4014 2-9-3 0...................................... HayleyTurner 1 32
(M L W Bell) *s.i.s: sn prom: wknd over 2f out* **50/1**
00 **9** *3* **Just Jimmy (IRE)**[21] 3760 2-9-3 0.................................... SaleemGolam 8 24
(P D Evans) *w ldr: plld hrd: led over 4f out: hdd 1/2-way: wknd over 2f out* **40/1**
050 **10** *1½* **Titfer (IRE)**[34] 3363 2-8-10 68.. MarkCoumbe(7) 5 20
(A W Carroll) *hld up in tch: plld hrd: wknd 3f out* **66/1**
00 **11** *29* **Jimmy Dean**[11] 4077 2-9-3 0.. AdamKirby 2 —
(M Wellings) *chsd ldrs: hung lft over 4f out: sn wknd* **100/1**

1m 24.83s (-1.27) **Going Correction** -0.20s/f (Firm) 11 Ran SP% **113.0**
Speed ratings (Par 96): **99,96,95,95,91 84,80,79,75,73 40**
CSF £3.00 TOTE £2.00: £1.50, £1.10, £2.30; EX 3.70 Trifecta £18.60 Pool: £128.30 - 4.89 winning units..
Owner Hamdan Al Maktoum **Bred** Norelands Bloodstock, J Hanly & H Lascelles **Trained** Lambourn, Berks

FOCUS
A fair maiden, and the first four probably all have races in them.

NOTEBOOK
Hawaana(IRE), fourth in a hot maiden at Ascot on his debut, made a good impression in building on that effort and won in fine style. He looks likely to cope with a step up in class and will no doubt be soon contesting Pattern races. (op 11-10 tchd 5-4)
Doctor Fremantle, a brother to Summer Shower, a dual 1m4f winner in France, was the only other one in the race that the market gave any credit to, and he duly followed the favourite home. His pedigree suggests that the best of him will not be seen until he tackles middle distances next year, but he should win at least a maiden this term. (op 6-4 tchd 15-8)
Strategic Mover(USA), whose dam was a smart, multiple-winning miler on turf in the US, wore a tongue tie on his debut. He shaped with encouragement, staying on again after getting outpaced two furlongs out, and looks the type that will be suited by a mile.
Parliamentary(JPN) is now eligible to run in nurseries and could do well in that sphere. Being by Diktat one would imagine that softer ground will suit him, too. (op 10-1 tchd 7-1)
Weetfromthechaff ran by far his best race to date despite pulling for his head in the early stages. He looks the type who will pay his way on the All-Weather. Official explanation: jockey said colt hung left-handed

4418 COALVILLE GLASS & GLAZING H'CAP 1m 60y
3:20 (3:21) (Class 5) (0-75,73) 3-Y-O+ **£4,533** (£1,348; £674; £336) **Stalls** High

Form RPR
5124 **1** **Motafarred (IRE)**[14] 3999 5-9-5 **64**................................ JamieSpencer 7 76
(Micky Hammond) *hld up: hdwy over 3f out: chsd ldr over 1f out: rdn to ld ins fnl f: r.o* **11/4**[1]
0541 **2** *¾* **Optimus (USA)**[24] 3690 5-9-11 **70**.. TQuinn 4 80
(B G Powell) *hld up: hdwy over 3f out: rdn over 1f out: r.o* **5/1**[2]
-050 **3** *½* **Red Rudy**[41] 3149 5-9-1 **60**... AdamKirby 12 69
(A W Carroll) *led: clr 1/2-way: rdn over 1f out: hdd and unable qckn ins fnl f* **12/1**
5000 **4** *¾* **Speagle (IRE)**[11] 4072 5-9-8 **67**.. HayleyTurner 3 74
(D Carroll) *chsd ldrs: rdn over 2f out: styd on* **40/1**
2345 **5** *½* **Scamperdale**[16] 3926 5-9-12 **71**.................................(p) SteveDrowne 11 78+
(B P J Baugh) *prom: rdn over 2f out: nt clr run and outpcd over 1f out: hung rt and r.o ins fnl f* **17/2**
000 **6** *4* **Waterline Twenty (IRE)**[7] 4195 4-9-13 **72**................. SaleemGolam 10 69
(P D Evans) *hld up: rdn over 2f out: nt trble ldrs* **16/1**
5000 **7** *1* **Rebellious Spirit**[11] 4068 4-9-11 **73**.............................. TravisBlock(3) 8 67
(P W Hiatt) *chsd ldrs: rdn over 2f out: wknd fnl f* **20/1**
0624 **8** *1* **Coup D'Etat**[19] 3828 5-9-9 **68**...(b) TedDurcan 1 60
(R A Harris) *s.i.s: hld up: rdn over 2f out: n.d* **7/1**[3]
2205 **9** *3½* **Barons Spy (IRE)**[38] 3239 6-9-8 **72**.............................. TolleyDean(5) 5 56
(R J Price) *hld up: hdwy over 2f out: sn rdn: wknd fnl f* **8/1**
0000 **10** *1½* **A One (IRE)**[6] 4231 8-8-2 **54** oh9.. MCGeran(7) 9 35
(H J Manners) *chsd ldr tl rdn over 2f out: wknd over 1f out* **80/1**
0055 **11** *4* **The Gaikwar (IRE)**[5] 4259 8-9-1 **65**...........................(b) LukeMorris(5) 6 36
(R A Harris) *s.s: hld up: rdn over 2f out: a in rr* **8/1**
1406 **12** *6* **Colinca's Lad (IRE)**[11] 4063 5-9-3 **65**......................... PJMcDonald(3) 2 23
(T T Clement) *hld up: rdn over 3f out: wknd over 2f out* **12/1**

1m 43.89s (-1.41) **Going Correction** -0.20s/f (Firm) 12 Ran SP% **118.3**
Speed ratings (Par 103): **99,98,97,97,96 92,91,90,87,85 81,75**
CSF £15.34 CT £145.79 TOTE £3.30: £2.20, £2.20, £3.60; EX 15.10 Trifecta £114.60 Pool: £256.79 - 1.59 winning units..
Owner R D Bickenson **Bred** Shadwell Estate Company Limited **Trained** Middleham Moor, N Yorks

FOCUS
Modest handicap form but solid enough for the grade.
Rebellious Spirit Official explanation: jockey said gelding hung right-handed

4419 CHRISTINE RODWELL 30TH ANNIVERSARY H'CAP 1m 1f 218y
3:50 (3:50) (Class 4) (0-85,84) 3-Y-O+ **£5,047** (£1,510; £755; £377; £188) **Stalls** High

Form RPR
-201 **1** **Ideally (IRE)**[34] 3366 3-9-0 **79**.. MichaelHills 6 88+
(B W Hills) *mde all: rdn over 1f out: r.o* **9/1**
2062 **2** *2* **Pagan Sword**[8] 4153 5-9-7 **84**...(p) KMay(7) 7 89
(Mrs A J Perrett) *hld up: hdwy over 2f out: rdn over 1f out: styd on* **11/2**
2-35 **3** *½* **Princess Cocoa (IRE)**[36] 3301 4-8-13 **69**........................ AdamKirby 3 73
(R A Fahey) *a.p: rdn to chse wnr over 2f out: styd on same pce fnl f* **9/1**
-606 **4** *¾* **Rationale (IRE)**[22] 3748 4-9-11 **81**.................................. SteveDrowne 2 84
(S C Williams) *stdd s: hld up and bhd: r.o ins fnl f: nvr nr to chal* **9/2**[3]
0210 **5** *¾* **Gold Prospect**[23] 3709 3-9-1 **80**.. JamieSpencer 8 81
(M L W Bell) *hld up: hdwy and hung rt over 1f out: styd on same pce fnl f* **3/1**[1]
402 **6** *½* **Fabrian**[11] 4072 9-8-11 **72**.. TolleyDean(5) 4 72
(R J Price) *trckd wnr tl rdn over 2f out: styd on same pce appr fnl f* **10/1**
31 **7** *4* **Snowed Under**[11] 4072 6-9-6 **76**.. TQuinn 1 68
(J D Bethell) *chsd ldrs: rdn over 2f out: wknd over 1f out: eased* **4/1**[2]
024 **8** *1¼* **Can Can Star**[18] 3844 4-9-4 **74**.. TedDurcan 5 64
(A W Carroll) *hld up: hdwy over 2f out: wknd over 1f out* **8/1**

2m 5.25s (-3.05) **Going Correction** -0.20s/f (Firm)
WFA 3 from 4yo+ 9lb 8 Ran SP% **118.8**
Speed ratings (Par 105): **104,102,102,101,100 100,97,96**
CSF £59.72 CT £467.13 TOTE £10.30: £2.90, £2.10, £1.80; EX 51.20 Trifecta £176.40 Part won. Pool: £248.55 - 0.80 winning units..
Owner Gainsborough **Bred** Gainsborough Stud Ltd **Trained** Lambourn, Berks

FOCUS
A fair handicap won by one of the two three-year-olds in the line-up.
Rationale(IRE) Official explanation: trainer said gelding lost a hind shoe and slipped on bend
Snowed Under Official explanation: jockey said gelding ran flat

4420 LEICESTER MERCURY FAMILY FUN DAY H'CAP 7f 9y
4:20 (4:22) (Class 2) (0-100,95) 3-Y-O
£9,971 (£2,985; £1,492; £747; £372; £187) **Stalls** Low

Form RPR
-531 **1** **Lovelace**[78] 2040 3-8-11 **85**.. JamieSpencer 2 97
(M Johnston) *racd centre: mde all: rdn clr fnl f* **7/2**[2]
-224 **2** *3½* **Miss Lucifer (FR)**[10] 4093 3-9-2 **90**.............................. MichaelHills 3 93
(B W Hills) *racd centre: hld up in tch: rdn to chse wnr over 1f out: sn outpcd* **13/2**[3]
0000 **3** *4* **Fares (IRE)**[15] 3941 3-9-4 **92**... TedDurcan 1 84
(C E Brittain) *led stands' side duo tl hung rt and jnd centre gp 1/2-way: chsd ldrs: rdn over 2f out: wknd over 1f out* **25/1**
-115 **4** *¾* **Mutanaseb (USA)**[36] 3330 3-9-7 **95**...................................... RHills 4 85
(M A Jarvis) *racd centre: chsd ldrs: rdn over 2f out: wknd over 1f out* **8/13**[1]
1255 **5** *1¾* **Telltime (IRE)**[15] 3961 3-7-13 **76**.................................. WilliamBuick(3) 5 61
(A M Balding) *racd centre: chsd ldrs tl rdn and wknd over 1f out* **18/1**
4060 **6** *nk* **Jo'Burg (USA)**[11] 4062 3-9-2 **90**.................................... SteveDrowne 6 74
(Mrs A J Perrett) *chsd ldr stands' side tl edgd rt and jnd centre 3f out: sn bhd* **20/1**

1m 23.34s (-2.76) **Going Correction** -0.20s/f (Firm) 6 Ran SP% **111.3**
Speed ratings (Par 106): **107,103,98,97,95 95**
CSF £25.02 TOTE £3.60: £1.50, £2.40; EX 20.50.
Owner Hamad Suhail **Bred** Mrs Mary Taylor **Trained** Middleham Moor, N Yorks

FOCUS
Despite the small field they split into two groups until halfway. The form looks solid for the grade.

NOTEBOOK
Lovelace, given a break since winning at Haydock in May, has clearly thrived in the meantime and won this with authority. He is likely to score again while in this form and looks a three-year-old to have on-side for a big handicap this late summer/autumn. (op 4-1 tchd 10-3)
Miss Lucifer(FR), who was narrowly beaten by Lovelace at Haydock earlier in the campaign, had the benefit of a recent outing at Goodwood, but she was unable to reverse placings with the Johnston colt. She finished clear of the rest, though. (op 9-2)
Fares(IRE), who was without the usual blinkers, made the running on the stands' side to halfway. He remains too high in the weights owing to his Listed success on Polytrack in April. (op 16-1)
Mutanaseb(USA) did not get home over a mile at Sandown last time and the drop back to 7f looked sure to suit. However, he had never before raced on ground quicker than good to soft, so it was a little surprising that he was so very well backed. He deserves another chance to show his true worth on an easier surface. Official explanation: jockey said colt ran flat (op Evens)
Telltime(IRE) is another who probably found the ground too fast. (op 10-1)
Jo'Burg(USA) has been dropped 5lb by the Handicapper since his last outing but remains out of form. (op 12-1)

4421 LEICESTERSHIRE AND RUTLAND LIFE H'CAP 1m 3f 183y
4:50 (4:50) (Class 5) (0-75,75) 4-Y-O+ **£5,047** (£1,510; £755; £377; £188) **Stalls** High

Form RPR
2-23 **1** **Fisher Bridge (IRE)**[18] 3854 4-9-7 **75**................................. AdamKirby 2 83+
(W R Swinburn) *chsd ldrs: rdn to ld and hung rt fr over 2f out: styd on* **5/4**[1]
41-0 **2** *¾* **Is It Me (USA)**[122] 354 4-9-4 **72**.. TedDurcan 8 79
(A W Carroll) *stmbld s: sn led: rdn and hdd over 2f out: ev ch and n.m.r fr over 1f out: no ex nr fin* **11/2**
0200 **3** *3½* **Fossgate**[32] 3412 6-9-6 **74**... TQuinn 9 75
(J D Bethell) *hld up: hdwy 1/2-way: rdn and hung rt over 1f out: styd on same pce* **5/2**[2]

5123 **4** *7* **Great View (IRE)**[15] 3978 8-9-6 **74**......(v) JamieSpencer 4 64
(Mrs A L M King) *hld up: hdwy over 4f out: rdn and hung rt over 2f out: wknd over 1f out* **4/1**[3]

/0-5 **5** *12* **Hunting Lodge (IRE)**[16] 3903 6-7-11 **58** oh1 ow2...... MCGeran(7) 7 29
(H J Manners) *chsd ldrs: lost pl over 9f out: n.d after* **25/1**

6 *11* **Cearan (CZE)**[17] 4-8-3 **60**...... WilliamBuick(3) 3 13
(F Jordan) *chsd ldrs: rdn 9f out: wknd over 3f out* **25/1**

22-6 **7** *17* **Vehari**[25] 2113 4-8-5 **66**...... MarkCoumbe(7) 10 —
(G F Bridgwater) *hld up: bhd fr 1/2-way* **40/1**

2m 32.37s (-2.13) **Going Correction** -0.20s/f (Firm) **7** Ran SP% **118.5**
Speed ratings (Par 103): **99,98,96,91,83 76,64**
CSF £9.27 CT £15.84 TOTE £2.00: £1.10, £2.70; EX 12.10 Trifecta £43.70 Pool: £307.17 - 4.98 winning units. Place 6 £110.13, Place 5 £48.37.
Owner Mrs P W Harris **Bred** Pendley Farm **Trained** Aldbury, Herts

FOCUS
Modest handicap form but pleasing efforts from the first two.
Fossgate Official explanation: jockey said gelding hung right
T/Plt: £42.90 to a £1 stake. Pool: £64,341.65. 1,094.65 winning tickets. T/Qpdt: £10.00 to a £1 stake. Pool: £3,135.10. 230.50 winning tickets. CR

4405 REDCAR (L-H)
Sunday, August 12

OFFICIAL GOING: Firm (good to firm in places) changing to good to firm (firm in places) after 3.10 (race 3)
After a heavy storm immediately before the first race the ground was 'good to firm, loose on top and easing slightly after more heavy showers'.
Wind: Light, half behind Weather: Changeable with heavy thundery showers

4422 EBF MACMILLAN CANCER SUPPORT CHARITY DAY MAIDEN FILLIES' STKS 7f
2:10 (2:11) (Class 5) 2-Y-O **£3,465** (£1,030; £515; £257) **Stalls** Centre

Form RPR

2 **1** **Winter Bloom (USA)**[17] 3874 2-9-0 0...... RichardHughes 7 79+
(H R A Cecil) *hld up in midfield: effrt over 2f out: led on bit jst ins fnl f: smoothly* **7/4**[2]

00 **2** *1* **Coachhouse Lady (USA)**[48] 2949 2-9-0 0...... TonyHamilton 3 69
(K A Ryan) *trckd ldrs: kpt on wl ins fnl f: no ch w wnr* **22/1**

5442 **3** *3/4* **Carnival Dream**[11] 4077 2-9-0 66...... TomEaves 10 67
(A Berry) *led tl hdd jst ins fnl f: no ex* **10/1**[3]

43 **4** *1* **Candle Sahara (IRE)**[11] 4061 2-9-0 0...... JHBowman 8 64
(M R Channon) *trckd ldrs: rdn over 2f out: kpt on same pce* **6/5**[1]

60 **5** *3* **Marlena (IRE)**[9] 4125 2-9-0 0...... DavidAllan 11 56+
(T D Easterby) *hld up in rr: hdwy over 2f out: nvr trbld ldrs* **50/1**

00 **6** *5* **Noplace For A Lady**[65] 2432 2-9-0 0...... KDarley 13 43
(N Tinkler) *hld up in mid-div: hdwy over 3f out: wknd over 1f out* **100/1**

0 **7** *2 1/2* **Miss Skycat (USA)**[46] 2983 2-9-0 0...... PhillipMakin 5 36
(T D Barron) *swvd rt s: chsd ldrs: lost pl 2f out* **25/1**

8 *hd* **Mchepple** 2-8-11 0...... DominicFox(3) 12 35
(W Storey) *dwlt: bhd tl sme late hdwy* **100/1**

00 **9** *hd* **China Pink**[12] 4037 2-9-0 0...... PaulMulrennan 2 35
(Sir Mark Prescott) *t.k.h: sn trcking ldrs on outer: wknd over 1f out* **33/1**

10 *nk* **Silken Spell** 2-9-0 0...... RoystonFfrench 4 34
(Mrs A Duffield) *hld up: a in rr* **50/1**

11 *3* **Marramed** 2-9-0 0...... ChrisCatlin 1 26
(E J O'Neill) *swvd lft s: a in rr* **20/1**

00 **12** *1 1/4* **Jemima's Art**[16] 3916 2-8-7 0...... NSLawes(7) 6 23
(M W Easterby) *bmpd s: sn chsng ldrs: drvn over 3f out: sn lost pl* **66/1**

13 *1 1/2* **Midnight Mystique (IRE)** 2-9-0 0...... PaulFessey 9 19
(T D Barron) *chsd ldrs: rdn and lost pl over 2f out* **50/1**

1m 25.75s (0.85) **Going Correction** +0.05s/f (Good) **13** Ran SP% **116.2**
Speed ratings (Par 91): **97,95,95,93,90 84,81,81,81,81 77,76,74**
CSF £43.62 TOTE £2.60: £1.50, £3.30, £1.70; EX 43.10.
Owner K Abdulla **Bred** Juddmonte Farms Inc **Trained** Newmarket, Suffolk

FOCUS
Probably just an average event with the exposed third rated just 66.

NOTEBOOK
Winter Bloom(USA), a tall, lean type, showed plenty of knee action going to post. She had to be nudged along to make progress but was hard on the steel when striking the front. This level track suited her ideally and she should improve again. (op 13-8)
Coachhouse Lady(USA), who had quite a reputation when making her debut, ran much better if in the end very much second best. (op 40-1)
Carnival Dream, very warm at the start, took them along but the winner was simply waiting to put the knife in. (op 12-1)
Candle Sahara(IRE), who looked very fit indeed, showed a very moderate action going to post and the ground may have been too quick for her. (op 11-10 tchd 10-11 tchd 5-4 in a place)
Marlena(IRE), dropped in at the start, kept on steadily in her own time and she will be of interest in a nursery.
Noplace For A Lady showed a lot more than on her first two starts. Back after a two-month break, she looks a likely nursery type.

4423 MICHAEL POOLE ESTATE AGENTS SUPPORTING MACMILLAN H'CAP 6f
2:40 (2:41) (Class 6) (0-60,60) 3-Y-O+ **£2,047** (£604; £302) **Stalls** Centre

Form RPR

1026 **1** **Inca Soldier (FR)**[23] 3723 4-9-4 **56**...... PaulEddery 3 69
(R C Guest) *hld up in rr: hdwy over 2f out: hrd rdn and styd on to ld nr fin* **8/1**

0200 **2** *nk* **Never Without Me**[52] 2805 7-9-6 **58**...... ChrisCatlin 7 70
(J F Coupland) *trckd ldrs: led appr fnl f: edgd lft and hdd nr fin* **25/1**

2006 **3** *1 1/4* **La Vecchia Scuola (IRE)**[8] 4158 3-8-10 **59**......(v) KellyHarrison(7) 8 66
(R Johnson) *w ldrs: styd on same pce ins fnl f* **14/1**

000 **4** *1/2* **Littledodayno (IRE)**[8] 4165 4-9-4 **56**...... RichardHughes 4 63
(M Wigham) *hld up in tch: effrt over 2f out: kpt on same pce fnl f* **9/2**[2]

4000 **5** *hd* **Nufoudh (IRE)**[6] 4224 3-8-12 **57**...... JamieMoriarty(3) 10 62
(Miss Tracy Waggott) *broke smartly: led: edgd rt and hdd appr fnl f: kpt on same pce* **50/1**

5635 **6** *1/2* **Compton Plume**[11] 4083 7-9-2 **54**......(b) DaleGibson 5 59
(M W Easterby) *chsd ldrs: kpt on same pce appr fnl f* **10/1**

0-02 **7** *nk* **Royal Composer (IRE)**[75] 2121 4-9-8 **60**...... DavidAllan 14 64
(T D Easterby) *sn chsng ldrs: reminders after 2f: kpt on same pce appr fnl f* **16/1**

0061 **8** *1 1/2* **Greek Secret**[8] 4180 4-9-4 **56**......(b) TomEaves 2 55
(J O'Reilly) *hld up: hdwy over 2f out: kpt on same pce fnl f* **7/1**[3]

330 **9** *hd* **Wiltshire (IRE)**[10] 4100 5-9-4 **56**...... MickyFenton 6 55
(P T Midgley) *in rr: sn drvn along: kpt on fnl 2f: nvr a threat* **12/1**

0060 **10** *1 1/2* **Muara**[9] 4141 5-9-0 **52**......(p) TonyHamilton 12 46
(D W Barker) *s.i.s: sn drvn along in rr: nvr a factor* **25/1**

0-61 **11** *nk* **Zap Attack**[9] 4141 7-8-7 **52**...... AndrewHeffernan(7) 1 45
(M Brittain) *chsd ldrs: hung lft and fdd 1f out* **28/1**

0002 **12** *nk* **Maison Dieu**[5] 4250 4-9-2 **54**...... KDarley 9 46
(E J Alston) *s.i.s: sn drvn along in mid-div: wknd over 1f out* **3/1**[1]

5050 **13** *3/4* **Spirit Of Coniston**[10] 4101 4-9-0 **52**......(b) RoystonFfrench 13 42
(C J Teague) *mid-div: sn drvn along: wknd over 1f out* **25/1**

5160 **14** *3 1/2* **Bold Haze**[20] 3787 5-9-0 **57**......(v) MichaelJStainton(5) 15 37
(Miss S E Hall) *s.i.s: sn drvn along: a in rr* **9/1**

56 **15** *15* **Goldan Jess (IRE)**[89] 1749 3-9-4 **60**......(v[1]) PaulFessey 11 —
(D Carroll) *sn bhd: virtually p.u 2f out* **66/1**

1m 10.87s (-0.83) **Going Correction** +0.05s/f (Good)
WFA 3 from 4yo+ 4lb **15** Ran SP% **124.6**
Speed ratings (Par 101): **107,106,104,104,104 103,102,100,100,98 98,97,96,92,72**
CSF £207.60 CT £2772.89 TOTE £15.80: £4.60, £5.20, £4.30; EX 157.70.
Owner Keith Middleton **Bred** Sheikh Sultan B K B Z Al Nahyan **Trained** Carburton, Notts
■ Stewards' Enquiry : Andrew Heffernan caution: used whip down the shoulder in the forehand position

FOCUS
A low grade sprint handicap with not a lot to choose between the first six home at the line.

4424 UNIVERSITY OF TEESSIDE SUPPORTING MACMILLAN MAIDEN H'CAP 1m 2f
3:10 (3:10) (Class 5) (0-75,71) 3-Y-O+ **£2,817** (£838; £418; £209) **Stalls** Low

Form RPR

0200 **1** **Distiller (IRE)**[10] 4111 3-9-11 **68**...... RichardMullen 2 72
(W R Muir) *trckd ldrs: effrt over 2f out: led 1f out: hld on towards fin* **4/1**[1]

4003 **2** *3/4* **Chip N Pin**[4] 4283 3-8-6 **49**...... DavidAllan 5 51
(T D Easterby) *chsd ldrs: rdn to ld over 2f out: hdd 1f out: no ex* **4/1**[1]

0003 **3** *hd* **Waterloo Corner**[11] 4081 5-9-6 **54**...... PaulMulrennan 3 56
(R Craggs) *chsd ldrs: rdn and outpcd over 2f out: styd on fnl f* **8/1**

0035 **4** *shd* **Moment Of Clarity**[23] 3722 5-8-13 **47**...... PaulEddery 1 49
(R C Guest) *hld up in rr: stdy hdwy 3f out: plld wd and styd on wl fnl f* **11/2**[3]

4232 **5** *1 1/4* **Arena's Dream (USA)**[9] 4138 3-10-0 **71**......(p) TonyHamilton 7 70
(R A Fahey) *sn chsng ldrs: effrt over 3f out: kpt on same pce fnl 2f* **9/2**[2]

052- **6** *6* **Divine Love (IRE)**[296] 6073 3-10-0 **71**...... ChrisCatlin 8 58
(E J O'Neill) *sn trcking ldrs: chal over 2f out: wknd over 1f out* **8/1**

0000 **7** *1 3/4* **Danehill Warrior (IRE)**[8] 4155 3-8-2 **45**......(p) DaleGibson 9 29
(R C Guest) *led: t.k.h: shkn up over 3f out: hdd over 2f out: sn lost pl* **50/1**

6406 **8** *1 1/4* **Caviar Heights (IRE)**[27] 3587 3-8-7 **50**......(b) PaulFessey 4 31
(Miss L A Perratt) *s.i.s: effrt over 3f out: lost pl over 1f out* **16/1**

0-00 **9** *4* **Mccormack (IRE)**[14] 3994 5-8-11 **45**...... MickyFenton 6 18
(Micky Hammond) *hld up in rr: effrt over 3f out: nvr a factor* **40/1**

543- **10** *17* **Robbie Scott**[322] 5552 3-9-6 **63**...... GregFairley 10 2
(M Johnston) *mid-div: drvn and lost pl over 5f out: hung lft: bhd fnl 2f* **7/1**

2m 7.49s (0.69) **Going Correction** +0.05s/f (Good)
WFA 3 from 5yo 9lb **10** Ran SP% **118.6**
Speed ratings (Par 103): **99,98,98,98,97 92,90,89,86,73**
CSF £20.30 CT £123.90 TOTE £5.70: £2.40, £1.50, £2.50; EX 28.60.
Owner D G Clarke & C L A Edginton **Bred** Mount Coote Stud **Trained** Lambourn, Berks

FOCUS
A maiden handicap run at just a steady pace.

4425 HAWKINS ROSS SOLICITORS SUPPORTING MACMILLAN H'CAP 6f
3:40 (3:40) (Class 4) (0-85,84) 3-Y-O **£4,728** (£1,406; £702; £351) **Stalls** Centre

Form RPR

0504 **1** **Lady Lily (IRE)**[50] 2884 3-9-5 **82**...... RichardHughes 8 86
(H R A Cecil) *racd alone stands' side: w ldrs: hung lft and led over 1f out: kpt on wl ins fnl f* **5/2**[2]

0414 **2** *3/4* **Charlie Tipple**[17] 3885 3-8-10 **73**...... MickyFenton 1 75
(T D Easterby) *racd towards far side: chsd ldrs: no ex ins fnl f* **9/2**[3]

6063 **3** *3/4* **Bateleur**[4] 4269 3-9-1 **78**...... JHBowman 4 78
(M R Channon) *led tl over 1f out: kpt on same pce ins fnl f* **9/4**[1]

2300 **4** *1 1/4* **Valley Of The Moon (IRE)**[9] 4140 3-8-6 **72**...... JamieMoriarty(3) 3 68
(R A Fahey) *chsd ldrs: effrt over 2f out: kepping on same pce whn n.m.r and swtchd rt ins fnl f* **7/1**

3166 **5** *2 1/2* **Baybshambles (IRE)**[21] 3763 3-7-13 **65** oh11...... DuranFentiman(3) 7 53
(R E Barr) *w ldrs: t.k.h: fdd appr fnl f* **28/1**

4310 **6** *2 1/2* **Baltimore Jack (IRE)**[15] 3944 3-9-6 **83**...... DaleGibson 6 63
(M W Easterby) *chsd ldrs: drvn over 2f out: wknd over 1f out* **8/1**

5506 **7** *1* **Mundo's Magic**[4] 4291 3-8-7 **70**......(p) KDarley 5 46
(G M Moore) *s.i.s: drvn over 2f out: nvr a factor* **9/1**

1m 11.78s (0.08) **Going Correction** +0.05s/f (Good) **7** Ran SP% **114.6**
Speed ratings (Par 102): **101,100,99,97,94 90,89**
CSF £14.27 CT £27.80 TOTE £2.50: £1.90, £2.20; EX 11.70.
Owner Diamond Racing Ltd **Bred** Owen Bourke **Trained** Newmarket, Suffolk

FOCUS
Initially the winner raced towards the stands' side and the runner-up towards the far side but they finished in a heap.

4426 REDCAR CRICKET CLUB (S) STKS 1m 2f
4:10 (4:12) (Class 6) 3-5-Y-O **£2,047** (£604; £302) **Stalls** Low

Form RPR

5406 **1** **Jenny Soba**[11] 4082 4-8-10 50......(v) MichaelJStainton(5) 6 55
(R M Whitaker) *trckd ldrs: led jst ins fnl f: styd on* **5/1**[3]

0000 **2** *2 1/2* **Moonlight Fantasy (IRE)**[15] 3956 4-9-1 46...... NeilBrown(5) 15 55
(T D Barron) *hld up in rr: smooth hdwy to ld over 2f out: edgd rt and hdd jst ins fnl f: fnd little* **11/2**

0040 **3** *2 1/2* **Fantastic Delight**[27] 3584 4-9-1 43...... KDarley 12 45
(G M Moore) *in tch: drvn 6f out: chsng ldrs over 3f out: kpt on same pce* **9/2**[2]

5601 **4** *6* **Ellies Faith**[12] 4036 3-8-12 48......(b) PaulFessey 2 39
(N Bycroft) *stl had hood on whn stalls opened: hld up in rr: stdy hdwy over 3f out: edgd lft over 1f out: nvr nr ldrs* **8/1**

5400 **5** *shd* **Chateau (IRE)**[5] 4249 5-9-6 45......(tp) PaulMulrennan 11 38
(M E Sowersby) *mde most tl hdd over 2f out: wknd over 1f out* **25/1**

006 **6** *2 1/2* **Miss Lovat**[5] 4249 4-9-1 35...... DavidAllan 7 28
(W M Brisbourne) *chsd ldrs: one pce fnl 2f* **22/1**

00-4 **7** *3 1/2* **Alice Howe**[18] 3843 3-8-6 40...... RichardMullen 3 21
(W R Muir) *mid-div: kpt on fnl 2f: nvr nr ldrs* **25/1**

0230 **8** *2 1/2* **Arabellas Homer**[13] 4031 3-8-3 48...... DuranFentiman(3) 13 16
(Mrs N Macauley) *t.k.h: trckd ldrs: lost pl over 1f out* **20/1**

0-00 9 7 **Soylent Green**[18] 3843 3-8-6 25 PaulEddery 8 —
(S Parr) *a towards rr* **100/1**
3506 10 1¾ **Musette (IRE)**[14] 3994 4-9-1 45 TomEaves 4 —
(R E Barr) *t.k.h in rr: nvr on terms* **16/1**
0000 11 4 **One And Gone (IRE)**[8] 4156 3-8-11 45 (p) TonyHamilton 9 —
(R A Fahey) *w ldrs: wknd over 2f out: heavily eased ins fnl f* **15/2**
0000 12 ½ **Night Reveller (IRE)**[24] 3593 4-8-10 26 RussellKennemore(5) 1 —
(M C Chapman) *sn in tch: lost pl over 3f out* **100/1**
6335 13 nk **Desert Lightning (IRE)**[17] 3868 5-9-6 52 RoystonFfrench 14 —
(I W McInnes) *mid-div: effrt over 3f out: hung rt and sn lost pl* **7/2**[1]
54 14 ½ **Raguany (IRE)**[12] 3538 5-9-1 39 GregFairley 10 —
(B Mactaggart) *chsd ldrs: rdn over 4f out: edgd lft and lost pl over 2f out* **40/1**
0- 15 15 **Out Of Town**[253] 6675 3-8-11 0 ChrisCatlin 5 —
(R C Guest) *w ldrs: lost pl over 3f out: sn bhd: t.o* **16/1**

2m 7.00s (0.20) **Going Correction** +0.05s/f (Good)
WFA 3 from 4yo+ 9lb **15** Ran SP% **128.3**
Speed ratings (Par 101): **101,99,97,92,92 90,87,85,79,78 75,74,74,74,62**
CSF £32.52 TOTE £7.70: £2.40, £2.70, £2.30; EX 66.00.There was no bid for the winner. Fantastic Delight was claimed by Brendan Powell for £6,000.
Owner A T Bell **Bred** Theakston Stud **Trained** Scarcroft, W Yorks
■ Stewards' Enquiry : Neil Brown caution: careless riding

FOCUS
A rock-bottom seller.
Ellies Faith Official explanation: jockey said he had difficulty removing the blinds as stalls opened and so was slowly away
Desert Lightning(IRE) Official explanation: jockey said gelding hung right throughout

4427 JOURNEY SOUTH / ETON ROAD PLAY 25TH AUGUST H'CAP 1m
4:40 (4:42) (Class 6) (0-60,62) 3-Y-O+ **£2,047** (£604; £302) **Stalls** Centre

Form RPR
4351 1 **Kirkby's Treasure**[10] 4099 9-9-8 58 PaulMulrennan 3 66
(G A Swinbank) *hld up towards rr: stdy hdwy over 2f out: hrd rdn: edgd lft and styd on to ld towards fin* **10/3**[1]
6341 2 nk **Borodinsky**[5] 4250 6-9-12 62 6ex TomEaves 6 69
(R E Barr) *w ldrs: led over 3f out: hdd and no ex towards fin* **9/1**
4630 3 1¼ **Wolfman**[8] 4180 5-8-11 47 TonyHamilton 4 51
(D W Barker) *w ldrs: chal over 3f out: styd on same pce fnl f* **7/1**[3]
2000 4 shd **Government (IRE)**[8] 4177 6-8-8 49 RussellKennemore(5) 11 53
(M C Chapman) *led tl over 3f out: hrd rdn and kpt on wl fnl f* **16/1**
0600 5 1 **Beck**[14] 3997 3-7-11 47 KellyHarrison(7) 1 49
(W M Brisbourne) *trckd ldrs on outside: chal over 3f out: one pce fnl f* **12/1**
0602 6 1 **Pianoforte (USA)**[11] 4082 5-9-1 58 GaryBartley(7) 15 57
(E J Alston) *hld up in rr: effrt over 2f out: styd on: nvr trbld ldrs* **4/1**[2]
0210 7 1¾ **Shaftesbury Avenue (USA)**[74] 2149 4-9-9 59 (bt) DavidAllan 9 54
(J O'Reilly) *dwlt: hrd rdn and hdwy over 3f out: nvr rchd ldrs* **12/1**
6000 8 1½ **Musicmaestroplease (IRE)**[48] 2947 4-9-5 58 DominicFox(3) 2 50
(S Parr) *hld up: hdwy to chse ldrs 3f out: wknd over 1f out* **28/1**
0-04 9 ¾ **Grey Vision**[8] 4178 4-8-8 51 PatrickDonaghy(7) 7 41
(M Brittain) *chsd ldrs: wknd 2f out* **33/1**
0 10 ¾ **Anything Once (USA)**[113] 1167 4-9-4 54 (v[1]) ChrisCatlin 14 42
(D Carroll) *chsd ldrs: wknd 2f out* **66/1**
4002 11 hd **Tour D'Amour (IRE)**[11] 4081 4-9-4 59 (b) NeilBrown(5) 8 47
(R Craggs) *chsd ldrs: wknd over 2f out* **15/2**
6-00 12 1¾ **Ali D**[8] 4177 9-9-2 52 TGMcLaughlin 13 36
(G Woodward) *dwlt: reminders after s: racd stands' side: hdwy to chse ldrs 4f out: lost pl over 1f out* **22/1**
1053 13 1¼ **Bond Diamond**[11] 4082 10-9-0 50 MickyFenton 12 31
(P T Midgley) *hld up: hdwy 3f out: sn chsng ldrs: lost pl over 1f out* **9/1**
000 14 ½ **Newsround**[20] 3787 5-8-9 45 (b) DaleGibson 10 25
(D W Chapman) *w ldrs: wknd over 2f out* **14/1**

1m 39.0s (1.20) **Going Correction** +0.05s/f (Good)
WFA 3 from 4yo+ 7lb **14** Ran SP% **127.5**
Speed ratings (Par 101): **96,95,94,94,93 92,90,89,88,87 87,85,84,83**
CSF £34.93 CT £180.39 TOTE £3.40: £1.80, £3.20, £3.00; EX 24.30 Place 6 £208.67, Place 5 £113.14.
Owner Kirkby Lonsdale Racing **Bred** Mrs J M Berry **Trained** Melsonby, N Yorks
■ Stewards' Enquiry : Paul Mulrennan two-day ban: used whip with excessive frequency (Aug 24-25)

FOCUS
A low-grade handicap with little between the first four at the line.
T/Jkpt: Not won. T/Plt: £423.40 to a £1 stake. Pool: £65,691.00. 113.25 winning tickets. T/Qpdt: £23.90 to a £1 stake. Pool: £3,800.40. 117.40 winning tickets. WG

4020 WOLVERHAMPTON (A.W) (L-H)
Sunday, August 12

OFFICIAL GOING: Standard
Wind: Moderate, half behind Weather: Fine

4428 RINGSIDE CONFERENCE SUITE MAIDEN AUCTION FILLIES' STKS 7f 32y(P)
2:30 (2:31) (Class 6) 2-Y-O **£2,730** (£806; £403) **Stalls** High

Form RPR
1 **Fits Of Giggles (IRE)** 2-8-10 0 TPQueally 8 66
(J G Given) *chsd ldr: rdn to ld wl over 1f out: drvn out* **20/1**
3 2 hd **Suzi Spends (IRE)**[62] 2504 2-8-8 0 J-PGuillambert 7 63
(M Johnston) *hld up in mid-div: rdn over 2f out: hdwy over 1f out: ev ch wl ins fnl f: r.o* **9/4**[1]
3 1¾ **Lady Of The Park (IRE)** 2-8-10 0 GrahamGibbons 12 60
(P A Blockley) *s.i.s: hld up in mid-div: rdn and hdwy on outside over 1f out: kpt on ins fnl f* **22/1**
2550 4 ¾ **Liani (IRE)**[7] 4192 2-8-1 50 LiamJones(3) 10 52
(W M Brisbourne) *hld up in tch: rdn and swtchd lft wl over 1f out: no ex ins fnl f* **40/1**
423 5 nk **Lady Rochbonne**[7] 4192 2-8-1 0 AndrewElliott(3) 11 51
(Mrs G S Rees) *t.k.h: a.p: rdn wl over 1f out: one pce fnl f* **5/2**[2]
005 6 1 **Frammenti**[43] 3109 2-8-1 55 RobbieEgan(7) 9 53
(A J McCabe) *hld up and bhd: rdn 3f out: styd on ins fnl f: n.d* **40/1**
0340 7 1¼ **Pretty Bonnie**[32] 3424 2-8-6 60 JimCrowley 2 49
(J G Portman) *led: rdn and hdd wl over 1f out: wknd ins fnl f* **16/1**[3]
06 8 nk **Bookiebasher Babe (IRE)**[54] 2746 2-8-8 0 ow2 SamHitchcott 1 49
(M Quinn) *hld up towards rr: rdn and short-lived effrt on ins over 1f out* **33/1**
03 9 ½ **Ochenvay**[16] 3923 2-8-8 0 ow2 RobertHavlin 5 47
(M Quinn) *s.i.s: a bhd* **25/1**
00 10 2 **April's Quest (IRE)**[11] 4074 2-8-8 0 FergusSweeney 6 42
(David Pinder) *a bhd* **100/1**
0 11 1½ **Latimer House (IRE)**[13] 4028 2-8-4 0 JimmyQuinn 4 34
(Dr J D Scargill) *hld up in tch: rdn over 3f out: wknd over 1f out* **66/1**

1m 32.03s (1.63) **Going Correction** -0.025s/f (Stan) **11** Ran SP% **88.5**
Speed ratings (Par 89): **89,88,86,85,85 84,83,82,82,79 78**
CSF £32.99 TOTE £11.30: £2.90, £1.20, £5.10; EX 35.90.
Owner David Eiffe **Bred** P Monagnan And J Collins And G Dillon **Trained** Willoughton, Lincs
■ Izzibizzi was withdrawn (2/1F, unruly in stalls.) R4 applies, deduct 30p in the £.

FOCUS
A moderate affair. The proximity of Liani, who has been beaten in a seller, does nothing for the form.

NOTEBOOK
Fits Of Giggles(IRE), a 22,000euros half-sister to two winning sprinters, won this in game fashion and, as she hails from a stable whose two-year-olds almost invariably come on for the run, she can be expected to improve for this experience. (op 14-1)
Suzi Spends(IRE), third on her debut over 6f at Pontefract two months ago, probably ran to a same mark here and, while she is obviously nothing special, she does not need to improve much to pick up a race of this calibre. (op 5-2)
Lady Of The Park(IRE), a 20,000euros half-sister to five winners including Gipsy Rose Lee, gave a bit of ground away at the start and, in the circumstances, did well to come through for third. (op 20-1)
Liani(IRE) appeared to run with credit on this return to Polytrack considering her price, but she is exposed and has already been beaten in selling company. (op 50-1)
Lady Rochbonne had finished a long way ahead of Liani at Chester last time so this was a step backwards. (op 11-4 tchd 3-1)

4429 SUNDAY MERCURY GREAT FOR MIDLANDS SPORT H'CAP 1m 141y(P)
3:00 (3:00) (Class 4) (0-80,80) 3-Y-O **£4,857** (£1,445; £722; £360) **Stalls** Low

Form RPR
553 1 **Dream Lodge (IRE)**[20] 3785 3-9-4 77 TPQueally 3 84
(J G Given) *chsd ldr: led over 3f out: rdn and hung rt fr over 1f out: drvn out* **10/3**[2]
0401 2 1¾ **Mr Grand Lodge (FR)**[27] 3600 3-8-12 71 NickyMackay 1 74
(L M Cumani) *hld up in tch: chsd wnr 3f out: rdn whn rdr dropped whip and carried rt over 1f out: nt qckn* **5/2**[1]
2244 3 ½ **Giant Slalom**[14] 4004 3-8-12 74 LiamJones(3) 5 76
(W J Haggas) *t.k.h in mid-div: hdwy over 2f out: swtchd lft wl over 1f out: rdn and nt qckn fnl f* **4/1**[3]
333 4 ¾ **Marquee (IRE)**[28] 3183 3-8-1 65 oh5 ow4 KevinGhunowa(5) 7 65
(P A Blockley) *hld up and bhd: hdwy on ins over 2f out: rdn wl over 1f out: r.o one pce fnl f* **7/1**
-001 5 2½ **Queen Noverre (IRE)**[11] 4079 3-8-12 71 JamesDoyle 4 65
(J W Hills) *hld up towards rr: rdn 3f out: c wd and sme hdwy over 1f out: no imp fnl f* **12/1**
2160 6 1¾ **Ella Y Rossa**[106] 1310 3-8-4 63 JimmyQuinn 9 53
(P D Evans) *hld up and bhd: carried rt after 1f: sme hdwy on ins wl over 1f out: sn rdn: no further prog* **25/1**
0600 7 6 **Cherri Fosfate**[11] 4071 3-8-9 68 (v) GrahamGibbons 6 45
(D Carroll) *bhd: carried sltly rt after 1f: hdwy 6f out: rdn and wknd over 2f out* **20/1**
420 8 3½ **Zach's Harmoney (USA)**[50] 2886 3-9-2 75 RobertHavlin 8 43
(B J Meehan) *prom: rdn over 3f out: wknd over 2f out* **12/1**
2 9 91 **Dress To Impress (IRE)**[196] 280 3-9-7 80 FergusSweeney 10 —
(J R Boyle) *led: hdd over 3f out: wknd qckly over 2f out: sn eased and virtually p.u* **10/1**

1m 51.23s (-0.53) **Going Correction** -0.025s/f (Stan) **9** Ran SP% **117.2**
Speed ratings (Par 102): **101,99,99,98,96 94,89,86,5**
CSF £12.32 CT £34.07 TOTE £6.40: £1.90, £1.90, £1.70; EX 16.10.
Owner The G-Guck Group **Bred** C H Wacker Iii **Trained** Willoughton, Lincs

FOCUS
An average affair, but a triumph for Grand Lodge, sire of the first two home.

4430 COE CANTER MAIDEN FILLIES' STKS 1m 1f 103y(P)
3:30 (3:30) (Class 5) 3-Y-O+ **£3,071** (£906; £453) **Stalls** Low

Form RPR
23 1 **Salsa Verdi (USA)**[39] 3214 3-8-12 0 JimmyFortune 2 70
(Saeed Bin Suroor) *chsd ldr: rdn over 2f out: led 1f out: r.o* **6/4**[1]
-300 2 1 **Sues Surprise (IRE)**[14] 3992 3-8-12 102 DaneO'Neill 3 68
(B W Hills) *led: rdn over 2f out: hdd 1f out: nt qckn* **7/4**[2]
3 nk **Look Far** 3-8-12 0 SamHitchcott 10 67
(N J Vaughan) *hld up and bhd: hdwy 3f out: sn rdn: edgd lft wl over 1f out: styd on towards fin* **50/1**
25 4 4 **Take The Gold (IRE)**[16] 3908 3-8-7 0 PatrickHills(5) 8 59
(M A Jarvis) *hld up and bhd: rdn and hdwy over 2f out: no imp fr over 1f out* **9/2**[3]
0 5 1 **Susanna's Dance**[83] 1901 3-8-12 0 (t) NickyMackay 5 57
(M Botti) *mid-div: hdwy over 5f out: rdn over 3f out: wknd wl over 1f out* **16/1**
00 6 5 **Princess Aimee**[34] 3365 7-8-13 0 HaddenFrost(7) 7 47
(D Burchell) *nvr nr ldrs* **66/1**
0 7 3½ **Sierra Rose**[51] 2836 3-8-12 0 JamesDoyle 1 40
(P J McBride) *hld up in tch: rdn over 3f out: wknd over 2f out* **40/1**
4 8 13 **Shevalina (IRE)**[14] 4000 5-9-6 0 TPQueally 11 14
(Adrian Sexton, Ire) *t.k.h early: prom: rdn over 3f out: wknd wl over 2f out* **25/1**
062P 9 9 **Mega Dame (IRE)**[7] 4205 3-8-12 67 RobertHavlin 4 —
(D Haydn Jones) *prom tl rdn and wknd 4f out* **16/1**
10 nk **Crescentia** 4-9-6 0 JimCrowley 6 —
(Jane Chapple-Hyam) *mid-div: pushed along over 6f out: bhd fnl 5f* **33/1**
11 3 **Llizaam** 3-8-12 0 FergusSweeney 9 —
(J T Stimpson) *a bhd* **80/1**

2m 3.18s (0.56) **Going Correction** -0.025s/f (Stan)
WFA 3 from 4yo+ 8lb **11** Ran SP% **120.2**
Speed ratings (Par 100): **96,95,94,91,90 85,82,71,63,63 60**
CSF £4.22 TOTE £3.00: £1.20, £1.40, £5.50; EX 5.50.
Owner Godolphin **Bred** Gainsborough Farm Llc **Trained** Newmarket, Suffolk

The Form Book, Raceform Ltd, Compton, RG20 6NL

FOCUS
A fair maiden for the track with a Godolphin inmate beating a filly rated 102.

4431 HORIZONS AIR CONDITIONED RESTAURANT CONDITIONS STKS 5f 216y(P)
4:00 (4:00) (Class 4) 2-Y-O **£4,533** (£1,348; £674; £336) **Stalls** Low

Form RPR
2115 **1** **Cosmic Art**[8] 4168 2-8-10 93 DaneO'Neill 1 84
(E A L Dunlop) *led over 1f: chsd ldr: rdn 2f out: r.o to ld cl home* **8/11**[1]
52 **2** *nk* **Hold The Gold (IRE)**[7] 4192 2-8-10 0 GrahamGibbons 5 84
(E J O'Neill) *chsd ldr: led over 4f out: rdn over 1f out: hdd cl home* **10/3**[2]
1 **3** *½* **Soopacal (IRE)**[36] 3297 2-8-12 0 JimmyFortune 6 84
(B Smart) *s.i.s: rdn and hdwy wl over 1f out: kpt on ins fnl f* **8/1**
110 **4** *4* **Spitfire**[31] 3459 2-8-12 90 StephenCarson 7 72
(J R Jenkins) *t.k.h in tch: rdn and wknd 2f out* **5/1**[3]
1m 15.2s (-0.61) **Going Correction** -0.025s/f (Stan) **4** Ran SP% **108.8**
Speed ratings (Par 96): **103,102,101,96**
CSF £3.45 TOTE £1.70; EX 2.80.
Owner Byculla Thoroughbreds **Bred** Hellwood Stud Farm **Trained** Newmarket, Suffolk

FOCUS
Despite the three non-runners this was still a decent little heat and the winning time was very respectable.

NOTEBOOK
Cosmic Art had his limitations exposed off top-weight in a Newmarket nursery last week, but was by no means disgraced in fifth. A reproduction of that form was probably good enough to take this, though he needed some strong driving in the final furlong to wear down Hold The Gold. This was his third course win, but there is no reason why he cannot prove equally effective on turf. (op 11-10)
Hold The Gold(IRE), who had raced keenly in front and been caught close home in a 7f Chester maiden last time, stepped up again on that effort here and his turn should not be far off. (tchd 3-1 and 4-1)
Soopacal(IRE), a heavy-ground winner on his Beverley debut, struggled with the pace here but was doing some good work in the closing stages. (op 5-1)
Spitfire raced keenly on this All-Weather debut and struggled to negotiate the home bend. He is likely to do better back in turf nurseries, but it remains to be seen whether he can justify his current mark of 90. (op 4-1)

4432 SUNDAY MERCURY MIDLANDS BORN AND READ H'CAP 5f 20y(P)
4:30 (4:31) (Class 5) (0-75,72) 3-Y-O **£3,238** (£963; £481; £240) **Stalls** Low

Form RPR
5402 **1** **Topflightcoolracer**[16] 3924 3-8-13 67 AndrewElliott(3) 5 79
(Mrs G S Rees) *hld up: hdwy on ins 2f out: led wl over 1f out: rdn and flashed tail jst ins fnl f: sn clr* **15/2**
6160 **2** *4* **Feelin Foxy**[8] 4158 3-9-7 72 (v) DaneO'Neill 2 70
(D Shaw) *a.p: rdn over 1f out: wnt 2nd ins fnl f: no ch w wnr* **13/2**[3]
2132 **3** *½* **Silly Gilly (IRE)**[6] 4226 3-8-8 59 FergusSweeney 6 55
(K R Burke) *chsd ldrs: rdn and carried wd ent st: kpt on towards fin* **9/2**[2]
0630 **4** *1 ½* **New York Oscar (IRE)**[44] 3054 3-9-0 72 (b) RobbieEgan(7) 3 62
(A J McCabe) *chsd ldr: led 2f out: rdn and hdd wl over 1f out: wknd ins fnl f* **12/1**
0005 **5** *2 ½* **Grange Lili (IRE)**[28] 3568 3-9-2 67 LPKeniry 7 48
(Peter Grayson) *s.i.s: outpcd* **16/1**
0263 **6** *1 ½* **Charlotte Grey**[17] 3879 3-8-10 66 PatrickHills(5) 1 42
(C N Allen) *led: rdn and hdd 2f out: wknd fnl f* **3/1**[1]
61.99 secs (-0.83) **Going Correction** -0.025s/f (Stan) **6** Ran SP% **81.9**
Speed ratings (Par 100): **105,98,97,95,91 89**
CSF £27.06 TOTE £7.40: £3.20, £1.80; EX 36.10.
Owner P Bamford **Bred** Dandy's Farm **Trained** Sollom, Lancs
■ Contentious was withdrawn at the start on vet's advice (9/4F). R4 applies, deduct 30p in the £.

FOCUS
A modest affair won convincingly by the only unexposed member of the field.

4433 FAMILY FUN AT WOLVERHAMPTON RACECOURSE H'CAP 1m 141y(P)
5:00 (5:00) (Class 5) (0-70,69) 3-Y-O+ **£3,238** (£963; £481; £240) **Stalls** Low

Form RPR
5101 **1** **Mountain Cat (IRE)**[26] 3620 3-9-5 69 JimmyFortune 3 78+
(W J Musson) *chsd ldr: rdn to ld jst ins fnl f: drvn out* **6/4**[1]
3- **2** *1 ¼* **Carlowsantana (IRE)**[12] 4053 4-9-8 67 JerryO'Dwyer(3) 1 73
(Adrian Sexton, Ire) *led: rdn over 2f out: hdd jst ins fnl f: nt qckn cl home* **25/1**
566 **3** *hd* **Willow Dancer (IRE)**[17] 3881 3-9-5 69 SaleemGolam 4 75
(W R Swinburn) *a.p: rdn over 2f out: kpt on towards fin* **16/1**
4020 **4** *nk* **Lord Of Dreams (IRE)**[16] 3926 5-9-8 64 JamesDoyle 11 69
(D W P Arbuthnot) *hld up in mid-div: hdwy over 3f out: rdn over 2f out: kpt on towards fin* **11/1**
3224 **5** *½* **Hits Only Cash**[54] 2748 5-9-3 59 J-PGuillambert 10 63
(J Pearce) *hld up in mid-div: rdn over 2f out: hdwy over 1f out: kpt on ins fnl f* **9/1**[3]
2410 **6** *nk* **Casablanca Minx (IRE)**[5] 4259 4-8-10 55 (v) AndrewElliott(3) 5 58
(P D Evans) *hld up in mid-div: hdwy on ins wl over 1f out: rdn and one pce fnl f* **10/1**
0506 **7** *1* **Merrymadcap (IRE)**[18] 3855 5-9-13 69 DaneO'Neill 9 70
(M Blanshard) *hld up and bhd: c wd st: rdn and hdwy on outside fnl f: nvr nrr* **9/1**[3]
060 **8** *¾* **Arithmatix (USA)**[49] 2913 3-8-12 62 NickyMackay 8 61
(G A Butler) *hld up in mid-div: rdn over 2f out: no hdwy* **16/1**
4432 **9** *1 ½* **Green Pirate**[33] 3409 5-8-13 58 (p) LiamJones(3) 7 54
(W M Brisbourne) *a towards rr* **6/1**[2]
-500 **10** *1 ½* **She's Our Lass (IRE)**[90] 1720 6-9-11 67 DanielTudhope 13 59
(D Carroll) *a towards rr* **33/1**
100- **11** *nk* **Zendaro**[73] 5775 5-9-2 58 JimmyQuinn 6 50
(C C Bealby) *t.k.h early: prom: rdn over 3f out: wknd over 2f out* **40/1**
2325 **12** *1 ¼* **Golden Spectrum (IRE)**[4] 4272 8-9-4 65 (b) LukeMorris(5) 12 54
(R A Harris) *s.i.s: a bhd* **14/1**
1040 **13** *10* **Western Roots**[16] 3926 6-9-8 64 (p) JimCrowley 2 30
(M Appleby) *a in rr* **14/1**
1m 51.37s (-0.39) **Going Correction** -0.025s/f (Stan)
WFA 3 from 4yo+ 8lb **13** Ran SP% **126.0**
Speed ratings (Par 103): **100,98,98,98,98 97,96,96,94,93 93,92,83**
CSF £53.86 CT £442.55 TOTE £2.10: £1.40, £8.70, £3.40; EX 105.70 Place 6 £28.38, Place 5 £14.68.
Owner S Rudolf **Bred** Mrs Mary Gallagher **Trained** Newmarket, Suffolk

FOCUS
A routine handicap dominated by those that raced handily.
Casablanca Minx(IRE) Official explanation: jockey said filly suffered interference in running
Green Pirate Official explanation: jockey said gelding suffered interference in running
Zendaro Official explanation: jockey said gelding hung left

T/Plt: £136.70 to a £1 stake. Pool: £56,833.70. 303.35 winning tickets. T/Qpdt: £62.70 to a £1 stake. Pool: £2,970.00. 35.00 winning tickets. KH

4434 - (Foreign Racing) - See Raceform Interactive

3573 **CURRAGH** (R-H)
Sunday, August 12

OFFICIAL GOING: Soft to heavy

4435a UNITED ARAB EMIRATES ROYAL WHIP STKS (GROUP 2) 1m 2f
2:45 (2:46) 3-Y-O+ **£54,898** (£16,047; £7,601; £2,533)

RPR
1 **Eagle Mountain**[15] 3974 3-9-3 117 KFallon 5 117
(A P O'Brien, Ire) *settled 3rd: tk clsr order after 1/2-way: led over 2f out: strly pressed fr 1 1/2f out: styd on wl to assert cl home* **4/5**[1]
2 *2 ½* **Alexander Tango (IRE)**[28] 3578 3-8-11 108 WMLordan 3 106
(T Stack, Ire) *hld up in tch: hdwy early st: 2nd and chal fr 1 1/2f out: ev ch: no ex cl home* **8/1**
3 *6* **Decado (IRE)**[11] 4058 4-9-9 110 DPMcDonogh 4 98
(Kevin Prendergast, Ire) *led: strly pressed fr 4f out: hdd over 2f out: sn no ex* **10/3**[2]
4 *9* **Championship Point (IRE)**[12] 4043 4-9-9 TPO'Shea 1 82
(M R Channon) *sn 2nd: cl up and rdn to chal ent st: wknd 2f out* **4/1**[3]
2m 15.5s (6.20) **Going Correction** +0.90s/f (Soft)
WFA 3 from 4yo 9lb **5** Ran SP% **109.7**
Speed ratings: **111,109,104,97**
CSF £7.51 TOTE £1.50; DF 5.60.
Owner Derrick Smith **Bred** London Thoroughbred Services L **Trained** Ballydoyle, Co Tipperary
■ Stewards' Enquiry : K Fallon caution: careless riding

FOCUS
The winner did not have to reproduce his Derby figure to win this Group 2 event. The race has been rated through the runner-up.

NOTEBOOK
Eagle Mountain, the Derby runner-up and Irish Derby third, recorded his first win of the season in workmanlike style. In front from over two furlongs out - he edged right as he took the lead in a move which led to a severe careless riding caution for Kieren Fallon - he stuck to his task although it was only well inside the final furlong that he shook off the attentions of the runner-up. His two previous successes, including the Group 2 Beresford Stakes, were achieved here on testing ground last year, but connections are convinced that he is better on less testing ground. Plans are fluid, although the Irish Champion Stakes got a mention in the immediate aftermath and, while he has yet to win over 1m4f, Fallon believes the colt is capable of winning a top-level race over the trip, given better ground and being held up for a late run. (op 11/10)
Alexander Tango(IRE), a Group 3 winner over 1m and successful here at Listed level over 1m1f on her previous start, was trying this trip for the first time. Held up in rear before arriving with her challenge, she put it up to the winner from over a furlong out and had every chance before wilting somewhat in the last half-furlong. The impression left was that she did not quite get the distance in the very testing ground. (op 11/2)
Decado(IRE), whose three wins, including the Group 3 International Stakes over 1m1f here last month, were all achieved on a testing surface, found the ground, and possibly the opposition, a bit quick for him in the Sussex Stakes. He made the running, but appeared beaten when headed and squeezed for room by the winner two furlongs out. (op 4/1 tchd 9/2)
Championship Point(IRE), back at this level after handicap wins at Royal Ascot and Goodwood on his previous two starts, raced in second place until the final bend and was the first beaten, dropping away quickly early in the straight. He had never previously encountered ground anywhere near as testing as this. (op 11/4)

4437a INDEPENDENT WATER'FORD WEDGWOOD PHOENIX STKS (GROUP 1) (ENTIRE COLTS & FILLIES) 6f
3:45 (3:45) 2-Y-O
£122,027 (£38,918; £18,648; £6,486; £4,459; £2,432)

RPR
1 **Saoirse Abu (USA)**[25] 3659 2-8-12 (b[1]) KJManning 1 110
(J S Bolger, Ire) *cl up on stands' rail: led under 2f out: hdd 1f out: rallied u.p: regained ld cl home: styd on* **25/1**
2 *1* **Henrythenavigator (USA)**[54] 2732 2-9-1 KFallon 7 110+
(A P O'Brien, Ire) *trckd ldrs in 4th: impr to chal 2f out: led 1f out: kpt on u.p: hdd cl home* **1/2**[1]
3 *1 ¾* **Elletelle (IRE)**[32] 3432 2-8-12 JMurtagh 6 102
(G M Lyons, Ire) *rrd up leaving stalls and s.i.s: hld up in tch: prog into 4th 1 1/2f out: 3rd ins fnl f: no ex cl home* **9/2**[2]
4 *2 ½* **The Loan Express (IRE)**[53] 2756 2-8-12 WMLordan 4 95
(T Stack, Ire) *hld up in 5th: prog into 3rd under 2f out: chal and virtually on terms 1f out: no ex ins fnl f* **16/1**
5 *3* **Warsaw (IRE)**[52] 2785 2-9-1 JAHeffernan 2 89
(A P O'Brien, Ire) *led: rdn 1/2-way: hdd under 2f out: sn no ex* **8/1**[3]
6 *hd* **Captain Royale (IRE)**[52] 2803 2-9-1 MJKinane 3 88
(J Noseda) *chsd ldrs in 3rd: rdn and lost pl 2f out: sn no ex* **10/1**
1m 18.8s (4.30) **Going Correction** +0.80s/f (Soft) **7** Ran SP% **114.8**
Speed ratings: **103,101,99,96,92 91**
CSF £40.24 TOTE £22.20: £8.20, £1.10; DF 42.50.
Owner Ennistown Stud **Bred** White Cloud B'Sk,Omar Trevino&N&PP **Trained** Coolcullen, Co Carlow

FOCUS
The first Group 1 race of the year for juveniles and it drew together a small but interesting field featuring the unbeaten Coventry Stakes hero Henrythenavigator taking on the Queen Mary Stakes winner Elletelle.

NOTEBOOK
Saoirse Abu(USA) improved markedly on her recent efforts to spring a surprise. She had looked a smart prospect when winning a maiden here in May and went on to chase home You'resothrilling in a Group 3 at Naas the following month. Her third in last month's Silver Flash Stakes appeared to leave her with plenty to do at this level, but she rose to the challenge in admirable style and posted a career-best effort. Wearing first-time blinkers, she raced in second until taking over two furlongs out. She was then headed by Henrythenavigator a furlong out but rallied tenaciously under pressure to regain the advantage close home. This display was well in advance of her previous form, but this daughter of Mr Greeley was probably well suited by the prevailing conditions and trainer Jim Bolger felt that there might not have been enough use made of her in the Silver Flash last time. He added that the blinkers probably did not make a huge difference to the winner but that they might have helped her concentration. The Moyglare Stakes, where she will step back up to 7f, is now on the agenda and this display indicates that she is a formidable opponent on this ground. Cashmans' 33-1 for next year's 1000 Guineas looks a realistic offer. (op 33/1)

Henrythenavigator(USA) lost his unbeaten record and was eased in the betting for next year's 2000 Guineas, but it would be churlish to hold this defeat on testing ground against him. He had looked a top-notch juvenile on his previous two starts, but both of those victories had come on good to firm ground. He looked to be in trouble some way out, improved under pressure to move to the front a furlong out, but was unable to raise his effort on the ground as the winner launched a renewed challenge on his outer. Trainer Aidan O'Brien and jockey Kieren Fallon reported that he was not at all suited by this ground and he should be able to leave this form behind back on a sound surface. He remains an exciting prospect and this was not a true reflection of his abilities. (op 4/7)

Elletelle(IRE) was again slowly away from the stalls, but that made little difference to the result and she too was another that struggled to produce her best on this ground following fine performances in the Queen Mary and when an unlucky third under a Group 2 penalty in the Cherry Hinton at Newmarket. She tracked the runner-up for much of the race, but could not pick up when it mattered. She can do better and remains a leading contender for the Cheveley Park Stakes. (op 7/2)

The Loan Express(IRE) did not seem to see out this trip on the ground, having given the impression when third in the Queen Mary that she would do better stepping up to this distance. She moved into the front rank a furlong out, but had no more to give shortly afterwards. This was not a bad effort and she remains capable of landing a good prize.

Warsaw(IRE) set the pace but was struggling once headed by the winner. He too was unproven on this ground, but does not seem to have progressed since winning a 5f Listed event from The Loan Express here in May.

Captain Royale(IRE) was taking a big step up in class from the Ripon maiden he won in June and was struggling to make an impression from some way out. It is significant that his trainer decided to let him take his chance at this level and it could be unwise to read too much into this effort. (op 9/1)

4438a PATRICK P. O'LEARY MEMORIAL PHOENIX SPRINT STKS (GROUP 3) — 6f

4:15 (4:16) 3-Y-0+ **£32,939** (£9,628; £4,560; £1,520)

			RPR
1		**Al Qasi (IRE)**[16] 3894 4-9-5 ... KerrinMcEvoy 3 (P W Chapple-Hyam) *trckd ldrs: 5th 1/2-way: 3rd and hdwy 1 1/2f out: 2nd and chal fnl f: led 100yds out: styd on wl* **9/4**[2]	118
2	1 1/4	**Evening Time (IRE)**[15] 3982 3-8-12 110 ... DPMcDonogh 8 (Kevin Prendergast, Ire) *a.p: 3rd 1/2-way: led 1 1/2f out: rdn and strly pressed fnl f: hdd 100yds out: no ex cl home* **6/4**[1]	110
3	3 1/2	**Grecian Dancer**[15] 3982 4-9-2 99 ... JMurtagh 6 (Charles O'Brien, Ire) *bhd: last and outpcd 1/2-way: rdn over 2f out: mod 4th 1f out: kpt on u.p* **25/1**	101
4	nk	**Aahayson**[43] 3104 3-9-1 ... PatCosgrave 1 (K R Burke) *led: rdn and strly pressed 2f out: hdd 1 1/2f out: 3rd 1f out: no ex* **10/1**	102
5	3 1/2	**Assertive**[12] 4045 4-9-5 ... (b) KJManning 4 (R Hannon) *cl up: 4th 1/2-way: 3rd and rdn 2f out: sn no ex* **8/1**[3]	92
6	2	**Fonthill Road (IRE)**[16] 3894 7-9-5 ... PaulHanagan 9 (R A Fahey) *dwlt: sn chsd ldrs on outer: 5th bef 1/2-way: wknd fr 2f out* **8/1**[3]	86
7	5	**Advanced**[8] 4150 4-9-5 ... NCallan 5 (K A Ryan) *cl up: 2nd 1/2-way: wknd fr 2f out: eased ins fnl f* **11/1**	71

1m 17.3s (2.80) **Going Correction** +0.80s/f (Soft)
WFA 3 from 4yo+ 4lb **9** Ran SP% **114.3**
Speed ratings: **113,111,106,106,101 98,92**
CSF £6.00 TOTE £3.30: £2.10, £1.50; DF 7.30.
Owner Ziad A Galadari **Bred** T C Butler **Trained** Newmarket, Suffolk

FOCUS
A decent sprint that attracted a powerful English challenge. It has been rated through the third.

NOTEBOOK

Al Qasi(IRE), who progressed very well in handicaps last term, had shown enough when sixth in the Duke of York Stakes and in chasing home Balthazaar's Gift at Ascot last time to suggest that he could land a decent prize. Already proven in soft ground, he started to make good headway under pressure over a furlong out and stayed on well under the stands'-side rail to overhaul Evening Time 100 yards from home. A relatively lightly raced sort, he could yet make further progress, and there are more good prizes to be won with him. (op 5/2 tchd 11/4)

Evening Time(IRE) came here off a highly impressive victory in a fillies' Listed race at Leopardstown last month. She travelled well in a good position for most of the race and appeared to have taken command when going to the front over a furlong out. However, she was unable to shake off the winner and had no more to give late on. This was still a creditable display and she should be able to make her mark at this level. (op 6/4 tchd 11/8)

Grecian Dancer was never in a position to mount a telling challenge but stayed on quite well from over a furlong out. This was the second time that she has reached the frame at Stakes level and she has been a real credit to connections, having progressed significantly since winning a handicap over this course and distance off 70 in April. She could yet be good enough to win a Listed race. (op 33/1)

Aahayson made much of the running, but had no more to give nearing the final furlong. He has already done well this season, winning three times, and appeals as the type to do well next year. His last victory came on soft ground, but all his previous successes were achieved on good ground or quicker. (op 8/1)

Assertive held a good position from the outset but was struggling to make an impression inside the final two furlongs. He is a smart sort and can probably make his mark at this level at some stage, but he needs quicker ground. (op 7/1)

4440a BALLYGALLON STUD DEBUTANTE STKS (GROUP 2) (FILLIES) — 7f

5:15 (5:16) 2-Y-0 **£54,898** (£16,047; £7,601; £2,533)

			RPR
1		**Campfire Glow (IRE)**[12] 4052 2-8-12 ... PJSmullen 1 (D K Weld, Ire) *trckd ldrs in 5th: 4th and prog on stands' rail 2f out: led ins fnl f: kpt on wl u.p: jst hld on* **12/1**	101+
2	nk	**Listen (IRE)**[44] 3071 2-8-12 ... KFallon 2 (A P O'Brien, Ire) *hld up: last 2f out: hdwy on stands' rail over 1f out: r.o strly ins fnl f: nrst at fin* **9/10**[1]	105+
3	1 1/4	**Tuscan Evening (IRE)**[28] 3574 2-8-12 ... DMGrant 9 (John Joseph Murphy, Ire) *hld up in tch: hdwy on outer 1/2-way: 2nd 2f out: led over 1f out: hdd ins fnl f: no ex cl home* **25/1**	97
4	1	**Ariege (USA)**[27] 3603 2-8-12 ... WJLee 5 (T Stack, Ire) *led and disp: strly pressed fr 2f out: hdd over 1f out: no ex* **12/1**	94
5	2 1/2	**Prima Luce (IRE)**[25] 3660 2-8-12 ... DJMoran 7 (J S Bolger, Ire) *prom: 2nd early: lost pl over 2f out: kpt on same pce fr 1 1/2f out* **50/1**	88
6	1 1/2	**Sharleez (IRE)**[21] 3766 2-8-12 ... MJKinane 8 (John M Oxx, Ire) *hld up in tch: 5th 2f out: sn rdn: no imp fr over 1f out* **4/1**[2]	84
7	1 3/4	**Solas Na Greine (IRE)**[60] 2583 2-8-12 ... KJManning 3 (J S Bolger, Ire) *hld up in tch: rdn and no imp fr under 2f out* **14/1**	79
8	1 1/4	**Triskel**[25] 3659 2-8-12 ... WMLordan 4 (T Stack, Ire) *trckd ldrs: 6th early: no ex fr under 2f out* **5/1**[3]	76
9	nk	**Rainbow Crossing**[25] 3659 2-8-12 ... DPMcDonogh 6 (Kevin Prendergast, Ire) *cl up and disp ld: 3rd 2f out: sn wknd* **16/1**	75

1m 33.1s (5.60) **Going Correction** +0.90s/f (Soft) **9** Ran SP% **123.0**
Speed ratings: **104,103,102,101,98 96,94,93,92**
CSF £24.85 TOTE £14.40: £4.40, £1.10, £6.00; DF 34.40.
Owner Dr R Lambe **Bred** Ski Lodge Partnership **Trained** The Curragh, Co Kildare

FOCUS
This traditional stepping stone to the Moyglare Stakes brought together a useful-looking field.

NOTEBOOK

Campfire Glow(IRE) made a victorious return to action just 12 days after winning a Galway maiden. The winner was always well placed in a race run at quite a steady pace, and improved into the front rank over a furlong out. She led inside the distance and ran on well to hold off Listen. Dermot Weld holds her in some regard and sees her as a 1000 Guineas filly for next year, adding that she is also quite versatile in terms of ground preference. The Moyglare Stakes or the Parknasilla Hotel Goffs Fillies Million are under consideration for what will be her only other run this season. She is clearly a talented filly and did well to win this race, which came very quickly after Galway. It could be that we have yet to see the best of her. (op 10/1)

Listen(IRE) lost nothing in defeat and confirmed herself a high-class filly as she attempted to follow up her debut Listed victory here in June. She trailed the field under two furlongs out, but came home strongly and would have got up in another stride or two. On this evidence she could take some beating if returning for the Moyglare and she can be rated a very good prospect for next year. (op 5/4)

Tuscan Evening(IRE), who was no match for Myboycharlie in the Anglesey Stakes, ran another good race in defeat and finished the same distance behind the runner-up as when they met in that aforementioned Listed event. She got to the front a furlong out, but could do no more when the winner took over. This was the fourth time that she has reached the frame at Stakes level and she will have no trouble winning a maiden when pointed in that direction.

Ariege(USA) was taking a big step up in class from the Killarney maiden that she won last month and acquitted herself well after helping to force the pace. She stuck to her task well once coming under pressure and looks quite capable of picking up black type. This was only her second start. (op 10/1)

Prima Luce(IRE) ran respectably on her debut in a Leopardstown maiden and was not at all disgraced as she moved up to this grade for her next start, looking as though she would be well suited by stepping back up to a mile. It will not be long before she picks up a maiden.

Sharleez(IRE) was unable to mount a telling challenge and appeared to find this assignment beyond her, having won a Fairyhouse maiden on her only other start last month. (op 7/2)

Solas Na Greine(IRE) ran with considerable promise when second to Mad About You in a Leopardstown maiden in June, but struggled to make an impression on much softer ground. She is capable of better.

Triskel looked to have every chance on her Silver Flash Stakes win and was going well after halfway, but she was struggling once coming under pressure. This was not her true form. (op 5/1 tchd 9/2)

Rainbow Crossing has been unable to build on last month's Gowran maiden win where she accounted for Triskel.

4439 - 4441a (Foreign Racing) - See Raceform Interactive

4213 COLOGNE (R-H)

Sunday, August 12

OFFICIAL GOING: Soft

4442a RHEINLAND-POKAL DER SPARKASSE KOLNBONN (GROUP 1) — 1m 4f

4:15 (4:21) 3-Y-0+ **£67,568** (£22,297; £10,135; £4,730)

			RPR
1		**Saddex**[70] 2292 4-9-6 ... TMundry 1 (P Rau, Germany) *led 1f: pressed ldr on rails: led 5f out: r.o wl* **13/10**[2]	118
2	1 1/4	**First Stream (GER)**[21] 3778 3-8-7 ... ASuborics 4 (Mario Hofer, Germany) *a cl up: cl 4th on ins st: trying for run on rails fr over 2f out: swtchd out jst ins fnl f: r.o* **15/2**	114
3	1/2	**Bussoni (GER)**[29] 3565 6-9-6 ... AHelfenbein 6 (H Blume, Germany) *a cl up: wnt 2nd after 5f: outpcd 4f out: last st: rallied on outside fnl f to take 3rd last strides* **4/1**[3]	115
4	3/4	**Laverock (IRE)**[15] 3942 5-9-6 ... LDettori 2 (Saeed Bin Suroor) *led after 1f: hdd 5f out: 2nd st: rdn over 2f out: lost 3rd last strides* **6/5**[1]	114
5	1 1/2	**Egerton (GER)**[21] 3778 6-9-6 ... EPedroza 3 (P Rau, Germany) *a cl up: 3rd st: rdn and cl 3rd whn sltly hmpd by 3rd ins fnl f: no ch after* **74/10**	112

2m 30.7s (-2.20)
WFA 3 from 4yo+ 11lb **5** Ran SP% **132.6**
(Including 10 Euros stake): WIN 23; PL 14, 21; SF 111.
Owner Stall Avena **Bred** The Niarchos Family **Trained** Germany

NOTEBOOK

Saddex gained his third win from three starts this season and his first Group 1. He will now be aimed at the Arc and could take in the Grosser Preis von Baden on the way.

Laverock(IRE), who was fourth in the King George last time, was made favourite and set an ordinary gallop. However, he was headed before the end of the back straight and was struggling soon after turning in.

4443 - 4444a (Foreign Racing) - See Raceform Interactive

4214 DEAUVILLE (R-H)

Sunday, August 12

OFFICIAL GOING: Turf - good; aw - standard

4445a PRIX DU HARAS DE FRESNAY-LE-BUFFARD-JACQUES LE MAROIS (GROUP 1) — 1m (R)

3:20 (3:23) 3-Y-0+ **£231,649** (£92,676; £46,338; £23,149; £11,595)

			RPR
1		**Manduro (GER)**[53] 2754 5-9-4 ... SPasquier 1 (A Fabre, France) *racd in 2nd: pushed along to chal 2f out: drvn to ld appr fnl f: wnt clr fnl f: drvn out* **4/5**[1]	124+
2	3	**Holocene (USA)**[95] 1593 3-8-11 ... C-PLemaire 4 (P Bary, France) *hld up in last: pushed along and r.o 2f out: wnt 4th 1 1/2f out: rdn and styd on wl fnl f: tk 2nd fnl strides* **26/1**	114
3	1/2	**Turtle Bowl (IRE)**[54] 2735 5-9-4 ... CSoumillon 3 (F Rohaut, France) *racd in 4th: pushed along to chse ldrs 1 1/2f out: rdn and wnt 2nd fnl f: nt pce of wnr fnl 100yds: lost 2nd fnl strides* **17/2**	113
4	4	**Toylsome**[7] 4213 8-9-4 ... JVictoire 2 (J Hirschberger, Germany) *led: pushed along 3f out: hdd appr fnl f: styd on tl no ex fnl 100yds* **4/5**[1]	105

5 ½ **Stormy River (FR)**[21] 3780 4-9-4 .... TThulliez 6 104
(N Clement, France) *hld up in 5th: shkn up 2f out: no imp* **62/10**[3]

6 5 **Lawman (FR)**[35] 3362 3-8-11 .... OPeslier 5 93
(J-M Beguigne, France) *racd in cl 3rd: disputing 2nd 1/2-way: pushed along 2 1/2f out: outpcd 2f out: btn and dropped to last 1 1/2f out* **18/10**[2]

1m 37.4s (-4.90) **Going Correction** -0.475s/f (Firm)
WFA 3 from 4yo+ 7lb 6 Ran SP% **174.9**
Speed ratings: **105,102,101,97,97 92**
PARI-MUTUEL: WIN 1.80 (coupled with Toylsome); PL 1.20, 4.60; SF 34.20.
Owner Baron G Von Ullmann **Bred** Rolf Brunner **Trained** Chantilly, France

FOCUS
The pace was steady and the time of this Group 1 was slower than the Listed handicap earlier in the card.

NOTEBOOK
Manduro(GER), who has developed into an outstanding individual, he added this Group 1 mile to his laurels in style. He looked magnificent in the paddock and was taken quietly to post before the other five runners. He settled behind his lead horse before taking over at the head of affairs a furlong and a half out. He appeared to accelerate on two occasions and eventually passed the post on his own. Unbeaten in four races this season, he is already the best middle-distance horse in the world and now his connections have decided to target the Arc de Triomphe via the Prix Foy. As there is a stamina doubt about his staying one and a half miles, the Breeders' Cup Classic is also being talked about as a possible target. It will take an exceptional horse that will topple him from his pedestal this season.
Holocene(USA) ran above expectations but he would not have been put in this race just because his owner's stud were the sponsors. He was certainly ridden for a place and was outpaced a little when things warmed up before finishing well to grab second place in the last 50 yards. He has always been highly rated and his connections will keep him at this level and distance as he is now to be aimed at the Prix du Moulin de Longchamp.
Turtle Bowl(IRE) ran a fair race, finishing slightly closer to the winner than he had in the Prix d'Ispahan, and started to pursue the winner from one and a half out. He never looked likely to trouble his old rival and was finally run out of second place in the dying stages. His trainer reported that the horse has recently had problems with his feet and that he was certainly feeling the ground during the final 100m. He is now to be prepared for the Topkapi Trophy in Turkey on September 9.
Toylsome, the winner's pacemaker, did an excellent job and credit must go to his young jockey who set a sensible pace from the start. It must have been very satisfying for the connections of the winner to also pick up €34,260 for fourth as he stayed on stayed until the end and finished ahead of a pair of Group 1 winners.
Stormy River(FR), fourth in this race last season, gained a confidence-boosting win in a Group 3 last time but was well held, although actually finishing closer to the winner than he did in the Prix d'Ispahan.
Lawman(FR) came into this off the back of wins in the Prix du Jockey-Club and Prix Jean Prat, but put up a disappointing show. He should have been able to handle the ground but perhaps he was was unsuited by being held up, as he has made the running in his three recent wins. He is certainly better than this.

4173 THIRSK (L-H)
Monday, August 13

OFFICIAL GOING: Good (good to firm in places)
Wind: moderate behind Weather: Fine

4447 E B F BEATRICE STEPHENSON MEMORIAL MEDIAN AUCTION MAIDEN STKS 5f
5:55 (5:58) (Class 5) 2-Y-O £3,886 (£1,156; £577; £288) **Stalls** High

Form RPR

420 **1** **Sophie's Girl**[52] 2812 2-8-12 76 .... KDarley 11 74
(P W Chapple-Hyam) *chsd ldng pair: effrt 2f out: sn rdn: styd on ent fnl f to ld fnl 100yds* **11/10**[1]

332 **2** nk **Wotashirtfull (IRE)**[15] 4002 2-9-3 71 .... NCallan 4 78
(K A Ryan) *cl up: rdn to ld over 1f out: drvn ent fnl f: hdd and nt qckn fnl 100yds* **11/2**[3]

222 **3** 2 ½ **Foreign Rhythm (IRE)**[14] 4016 2-8-12 77 .... JohnEgan 6 64
(N Tinkler) *chsd ldrs: hdwy 2f out: sn rdn and kpt on same pce fnl f* **5/2**[2]

4 **4** ½ **My Kaiser Chief**[9] 4173 2-9-3 0 .... PaulMulrennan 7 67
(W J H Ratcliffe) *led: rdn along 2f out: hdd over 1f out: sn drvn and kpt on same pce* **9/1**

04 **5** 1 ½ **Lecanvey**[15] 4002 2-9-3 0 .... PaulHanagan 10 62
(R A Fahey) *sn pushed along towards rr: hdwy 1/2-way: rdn and edgd lft wl over 1f out: kpt on ins fnl f* **14/1**

0630 **6** 1 ¾ **Discanti (IRE)**[27] 3606 2-9-3 66 .... (t) DavidAllan 5 55
(T D Easterby) *s.i.s and bhd: hdwy 1/2-way: sn rdn and hung lft wl over 1f out: nvr a factor* **22/1**

6 **7** ¾ **Swallow Forest**[17] 3915 2-8-12 0 .... PaulFessey 1 48
(T D Barron) *wnt lft s: in rr and swtchd to stands' rail after 1f: hdwy over 2f out: sn rdn and wknd* **40/1**

40 **8** 5 **Dark Queen**[12] 4074 2-8-12 0 .... DanielTudhope 3 30
(D Carroll) *outpcd and bhd fr 1/2-way* **100/1**

59.05 secs (-0.85) **Going Correction** -0.325s/f (Firm) 8 Ran SP% **116.0**
Speed ratings (Par 94): **93,92,88,87,85 82,81,73**
CSF £7.89 TOTE £2.20: £1.10, £1.80, £1.10; EX 7.30.
Owner Iraj Parvizi **Bred** Jeremy Green And Sons **Trained** Newmarket, Suffolk

FOCUS
A fair maiden in which the first two came clear. The third has been rated as running a stone below his previous three runs.

NOTEBOOK
Sophie's Girl found an ideal opportunity to open her winning account having been unplaced and probably outclassed in Group 3 company at Royal Ascot on her latest start. She found this affair more in keeping with her ability, and, doing her best work inside the final furlong, got on top towards the finish. (op 5-4 tchd 10-11 and 11-8 in places)
Wotashirtfull(IRE) confirmed his previous promise and, although he has now failed in three attempts to break his maiden, he remains a decent prospect, not least because he finished clear of the rest. (op 13-2 tchd 7-1)
Foreign Rhythm(IRE), with three creditable efforts under her belt, never looked likely to build on that promise. Looking to hang to her left for much of the race, she may not have found this track to her liking, particularly as this was probably the liveliest ground she has raced on so far. (tchd 11-4)
My Kaiser Chief showed the benefit of his first run with an improved effort, but was found wanting late in the race. (op 8-1 tchd 11-1)
Lecanvey was far from disgraced on the quickest ground he has experienced to date. He may be more of a nursery type. (op 16-1 tchd 20-1)
Discanti(IRE) Official explanation: jockey said colt hung left-handed throughout

4448 FINN'S MAIDEN AUCTION STKS 7f
6:25 (6:26) (Class 5) 2-Y-O £3,886 (£1,156; £577; £288) **Stalls** Low

Form RPR

0 **1** **Casa Catalina (IRE)**[19] 3850 2-8-10 0 .... J-PGuillambert 4 81+
(M Johnston) *chsd ldrs: hdwy to ld wl over 1f out: sn rdn and clr ent fnl f: styd on wl* **16/1**

2 **2** 2 ½ **Graceful Descent (FR)**[18] 3884 2-8-7 0 .... PaulHanagan 5 71
(R A Fahey) *in tch: pushed along 3f out: hdwy 2f out: rdn to chse wnr over 1f out: sn drvn and kpt on same pce* **7/4**[1]

0 **3** 4 **Mega Watt (IRE)**[15] 3991 2-8-12 0 .... PaulMulrennan 8 65
(W Jarvis) *prom: effrt to ld over 2f out: sn rdn: hdd wl over 1f out and kpt on samepce appr fnl f* **7/2**[3]

33 **4** 1 ¾ **Red Cauldron**[22] 3761 2-9-1 0 .... ChrisCatlin 3 63
(E J O'Neill) *midfield and rdn along 1/2-way: hdwy wl over 2f out: chsd ldrs and drvn wl over 1f out: sn no imp* **2/1**[2]

00 **5** 1 ½ **Medici Time**[16] 3951 2-8-12 0 .... DavidAllan 12 56+
(T D Easterby) *towards rr: hdwy 3f out: rdn 2f out: styd on appr fnl f: nrst fin* **12/1**

0 **6** ¾ **Jackday (IRE)**[13] 4037 2-8-12 0 .... KDarley 2 54+
(T D Easterby) *s.i.s and bhd: rdn along 3f out: styd on wl u.p fnl 2f: nrst fin* **40/1**

0 **7** nk **Buju**[46] 3024 2-8-9 0 .... JohnEgan 9 51
(N Tinkler) *hld up in rr: hdwy 3f out: rdn and chsd ldrs on outer 2f out: sn no imp* **80/1**

0 **8** shd **Sand Maiden (IRE)**[24] 3718 2-8-1 0 .... DuranFentiman(3) 1 45
(T D Easterby) *s.i.s and bhd: hdwy 3f out: rdn over 2f out: styng on whn nt clr run and swtchd rt 1 1/2f out: sn drvn and no imp* **66/1**

9 4 **Jetta Joy (IRE)** 2-8-7 0 .... RoystonFfrench 10 38
(Mrs A Duffield) *dwlt: a in rr* **50/1**

50 **10** ¾ **Intersky Melody (USA)**[8] 4192 2-8-4 0 .... MichaelJStainton(5) 11 37
(R M Whitaker) *in tch whn n.m.r and bmpd bnd after 2 1/2f: bhd fr 1/2-way* **22/1**

0 **11** 1 ½ **Honeycott (IRE)**[24] 3718 2-8-10 0 .... PaulFessey 14 43+
(J D Bethell) *prom: rdn along wl over 2f out: wkng whn bdly hmpd 1 1/2f out* **100/1**

12 1 **Just Sam (IRE)** 2-8-4 0 .... PaulQuinn 7 26
(D Carroll) *chsd ldrs whn n.m.r bnd after 2 1/2f: rdn along 3f out and sn wknd* **40/1**

0 **13** nk **Flaxton (UAE)**[31] 3510 2-8-9 0 .... DaleGibson 6 30
(M Brittain) *led: rdn along 3f out: sn hdd & wknd* **100/1**

1m 27.61s (0.51) **Going Correction** +0.075s/f (Good) 13 Ran SP% **121.4**
Speed ratings (Par 94): **100,97,92,90,88 88,87,87,82,82 80,79,78**
CSF £44.12 TOTE £22.80: £4.10, £1.50, £1.50; EX 60.70.
Owner Christopher Wright **Bred** Miss J Murphy **Trained** Middleham Moor, N Yorks
■ Stewards' Enquiry : Duran Fentiman three-day ban: careless riding (Aug 24-26)

FOCUS
An ordinary maiden in which the first two came clear. There were too many improvers at big prices down the field to rate this race positively.

NOTEBOOK
Casa Catalina(IRE), who had made no show first time out on Polytrack at Lingfield, looked a wholly different filly here, powering into the lead and winning in the style of a decent prospect. Ground conditions here seemed ideal for her and she will stay further in time on this evidence.
Graceful Descent(FR), who had shaped well on desperate ground on her debut at York, had different conditions to contend with here and ran a sound race, albeit without being able to reach the winner. (op 13-8 tchd 2-1 and 9-4 in a place)
Mega Watt(IRE), who missed the break and never figured on his debut, made a bold bid but failed to see out his race anything like as well as the first two. (op 4-1 tchd 9-2)
Red Cauldron, running on quickish ground for the first time, was unable to make his presence felt. (op 5-2 tchd 11-4 in places)
Medici Time, not well drawn, ran respectably, and, having had three runs, now qualifies for a handicap mark. He may prove more competitive in nurseries. (op 14-1)
Jackday(IRE), again slowly away, ran on quite well in the closing stages and looks the sort to be suited by longer trips and handicap company. (op 33-1)
Honeycott(IRE) Official explanation: jockey said filly suffered interference in running

4449 THE BUCK INN AT MAUNBY (S) H'CAP 1m
6:55 (6:55) (Class 6) (0-65,64) 3-Y-O+ £2,590 (£770; £385; £192) **Stalls** Low

Form RPR

5402 **1** **Blue Empire (IRE)**[5] 4294 6-9-4 54 .... (p) JohnEgan 14 65+
(C R Dore) *trckd ldrs: hdwy 3f out: led wl over 1f out: rdn clr ent fnl f: styd on* **3/1**[1]

0004 **2** 3 **Passionately Royal**[11] 4099 5-8-9 45 .... KDarley 3 49
(M Brittain) *sn led: rdn along over 2f out: drvn and hdd wl over 1f out: kpt on u.p* **12/1**

0553 **3** ½ **Beamsley Beacon**[2] 4410 6-8-12 48 .... PaddyAspell 12 51
(S T Mason) *cl up: rdn and ev ch over 2f out: drvn and one pce fr over 1f out* **9/1**

4046 **4** ½ **Andorran (GER)**[11] 4099 4-8-12 47 ow1 .... (b[1]) DanielTudhope 5 50+
(A Dickman) *dwlt and towards rr: hdwy 3f out: rdn 2f out: styd on appr fnl f: nrst fin* **8/1**

3000 **5** 3 ½ **Baby Barry**[68] 2370 10-8-11 50 .... DominicFox(3) 9 44
(S Parr) *chsd ldrs: rdn along over 2f out: sn one pce* **20/1**

6003 **6** hd **Crush On You**[34] 3405 4-8-9 45 .... NCallan 6 38
(R Hollinshead) *in tch: rdn along over 2f out: sn rdn and kpt on same pce* **6/1**[2]

0053 **7** 1 ½ **Fairy Monarch (IRE)**[11] 4099 8-9-0 50 .... (b) MickyFenton 2 40
(P T Midgley) *in rr: hdwy 3f out: rdn along 2f out: kpt on same pce u.p appr fnl f* **13/2**[3]

0600 **8** ¾ **Black Oval**[9] 4180 6-8-12 48 .... PaulEddery 13 36
(S Parr) *hld up and bhd: gd hdwy over 2f out: swtchd rt and rdn over 1f out: no imp ins fnl f* **33/1**

2-64 **9** nk **Lilac Star**[111] 1227 4-10-0 64 .... IPoullis 1 51
(Pat Eddery) *in tch on inner: hdwy over 2f out: sn rdn and wknd* **13/2**[3]

005 **10** 3 **Cecina Marina**[53] 2792 4-8-8 47 .... PJMcDonald(3) 11 27
(C W Thornton) *a towards rr* **33/1**

0000 **11** 3 **Soviet Sound (IRE)**[12] 4078 3-8-2 45 .... DaleGibson 15 19
(Jedd O'Keeffe) *a in rr* **22/1**

4060 **12** 1 ¼ **Reflective Glory (IRE)**[7] 4220 3-8-5 48 .... (p) RoystonFfrench 18 19
(J S Wainwright) *chsd ldrs: rdn along wl over 2f out: sn wknd* **50/1**

3600 **13** ¾ **Ivana Illyich (IRE)**[7] 4219 5-8-9 45 .... (p) TonyHamilton 17 14
(J S Wainwright) *a in rr* **40/1**

0505 **14** 2 ½ **Filey Buoy**[38] 3257 5-8-4 45 .... (v) MichaelJStainton(5) 10 8
(R M Whitaker) *a in rr* **14/1**

-600 **15** *20* **Splodger Mac (IRE)**[2] 4410 8-8-8 **47**........................ DuranFentiman(3) 8 —
(N Bycroft) *prom: rdn along over 3f out: sn wknd* **33/1**

1m 39.86s (0.16) **Going Correction** +0.075s/f (Good)
WFA 3 from 4yo+ 7lb **15** Ran SP% **123.8**
Speed ratings (Par 101): **102,99,98,98,94 94,92,92,91,88 85,84,83,81,61**
CSF £38.97 CT £310.45 TOTE £4.10: £1.90, £4.00, £3.70; EX 52.30.There was no bid for the winner. Andorran was claimed by A. Bailey for £6,000. Lilac Star was claimed by T Clement for £6,000
Owner Mrs Jennifer Marsh **Bred** Yeomanstown Stud **Trained** West Pinchbeck, Lincs

FOCUS
A typically moderate seller but the winner, who did not need to improve on his Yarmouth second, scored decisively.
Crush On You Official explanation: jockey said filly was denied a clear run

4450 HARES OF SNAPE H'CAP — 1m
7:25 (7:25) (Class 5) (0-75,76) 3-Y-0 **£3,886** (£1,156; £577; £288) **Stalls** Low

Form RPR
6036 **1** **Spume (IRE)**[39] 3235 3-9-7 **75**..(t) JohnEgan 8 80
(D J Murphy) *hld up in rr: hdwy on outer over 2f out: rdn to chal and hung lft over 1f out: drvn to ld ins fnl f: edgd lft and kpt on* **8/1**
3001 **2** *2* **Tencendur (IRE)**[7] 4222 3-9-3 **76** 6ex.................... MichaelJStainton(5) 7 76
(D Nicholls) *led: rdn along over 2f out: drvn over 1f out: hdd and no ex ins fnl f* **2/1**[1]
1000 **3** *shd* **Pennyrock (IRE)**[7] 4224 3-8-5 **59**............................. SilvestreDeSousa 1 59
(J J Quinn) *in tch: effrt on inner 3f out: sn rdn and outpcd wl over 1f out: styd on u.p ins fnl f* **13/2**
0646 **4** *shd* **Kalasam**[17] 3913 3-9-2 **70**.. NCallan 6 71+
(W R Muir) *trckd ldrs: hdwy over 2f out: effrt and ev ch whn bdly hmpd over 1f out: rallied ins fnl f: styng on wl towards fin* **3/1**[2]
0606 **5** *1* **Jane Of Arc (FR)**[12] 4078 3-7-13 **56** oh1.................. DuranFentiman(3) 4 53
(J S Goldie) *chsd ldr: rdn along to chal 2f out: ev ch whn n.m.r over 1f out: kpt on same pce* **12/1**
621 **6** *2* **Dressed To Dance (IRE)**[18] 3875 3-9-1 **69**..........................(v) KDarley 2 62
(N Tinkler) *dwlt: t.k.h and in tch: effrt to chse ldrs 2f out: rdn over 1f out and sn one pce* **11/2**[3]
206 **7** *2 1/2* **Run Free**[21] 3785 3-8-13 **67**... DanielTudhope 9 54
(N Wilson) *a in rr* **12/1**
1600 **8** *1* **Coconut Queen (IRE)**[27] 3607 3-9-4 **72**...................(p) RoystonFfrench 3 57
(Mrs A Duffield) *t.k.h: chsd ldr: rdn along over 2f out and grad wknd* **20/1**

1m 40.32s (0.62) **Going Correction** +0.075s/f (Good) **8** Ran SP% **118.3**
Speed ratings (Par 100): **99,97,96,96,95 93,91,90**
CSF £25.36 CT £115.36 TOTE £9.70: £2.60, £1.20, £2.90; EX 35.60.
Owner Willie McKay **Bred** Ballymacoll Stud Farm Ltd **Trained** Bawtry, S Yorks
■ A first British winner for trainer Danny Murphy, who recently took over from Tim Pitt.
■ Stewards' Enquiry : John Egan caution: careless riding; three-day ban: careless riding (Aug 24-26)

FOCUS
A fair handicap but several suffered interference in the closing stages. The form loks modest for the grade.

4451 BLACK SHEEP BREWERY H'CAP — 2m
7:55 (7:55) (Class 6) (0-65,57) 4-Y-0+ **£2,590** (£770; £385; £192) **Stalls** Low

Form RPR
/005 **1** **Erte**[9] 4179 6-8-10 **49**..(v) DominicFox(3) 7 51
(W Storey) *hld up: hdwy over 4f out: chsd ldrs 3f out: rdn to chal over 1f out: slt ld ent fnl f: sn drvn and jst hld on* **28/1**
-241 **2** *shd* **Sharaab (USA)**[14] 4030 6-9-4 **54**..(t) DaleGibson 8 56
(D E Cantillon) *hld up: hdwy over 4f out: led wl over 2f out: rdn wl over 1f out: hdd ent fnl f: drvn and rallied towards fin: jst hld* **10/11**[1]
0-06 **3** *3 1/2* **Sweet Lavinia**[41] 3193 4-8-9 **45**.. PaulFessey 3 43
(J D Bethell) *led 2f: prom tl rdn along and kpt on same pce fr 3f out* **14/1**
1120 **4** *nk* **Silver Mont (IRE)**[17] 3927 4-9-7 **57**..................................(b) PaulEddery 4 54
(S R Bowring) *trckd ldrs: hdwy over 4f out: chsd ldrs over 2f out: sn rdn and one pce* **8/1**
/05- **5** *6* **Kerry's Blade (IRE)**[13] 256 5-9-0 **50**.................................... PaulMulrennan 5 40
(Micky Hammond) *hld up in rr: effrt and sme hdwy 3f out: sn rdn along and nvr nr ldrs* **25/1**
0530 **6** *1/2* **Compton Commander**[41] 3193 9-8-2 **45**........(p) DanielleMcCreery(7) 10 35
(E W Tuer) *hld up in tch: hdwy 4f out: rdn along over 3f out and sn outpcd* **33/1**
06-4 **7** *9* **Next Flight (IRE)**[97] 1556 8-8-11 **47**.. DavidAllan 2 26
(R E Barr) *hld up in tch: effrt over 3f out: sn rdn along and n.d* **15/2**[3]
0006 **8** *3* **Leonardo's Friend**[14] 4030 4-9-4 **54**..(t) NCallan 9 29
(B G Powell) *led after 2f: rdn along 3f out: sn hdd & wknd* **9/2**[2]
03-0 **9** *7* **Compton Eclaire (IRE)**[5] 4280 7-9-4 **54**.....................(b) TonyHamilton 6 21
(N Wilson) *trckd ldr: rdn along over 4f out: wkng whn n.m.r bnd over 3f out: sn bhd* **12/1**

3m 33.42s (2.22) **Going Correction** +0.075s/f (Good) **9** Ran SP% **118.0**
Speed ratings (Par 101): **97,96,95,95,92 91,87,85,82**
CSF £54.71 CT £424.37 TOTE £45.40: £7.40, £1.10, £3.90; EX 97.00.
Owner V Thompson **Bred** Biddestone Stud **Trained** Muggleswick, Co Durham
■ Stewards' Enquiry : Dale Gibson caution: used whip down the shoulder in forehand position

FOCUS
A low-grade staying handicap that developed into a duel in the last furlong or so. The form is poor.
Erte Official explanation: trainer had no explanation for the apparent improvement in form
Leonardo's Friend Official explanation: jockey said gelding had no more to give

4452 TURFTV H'CAP — 5f
8:25 (8:25) (Class 4) (0-85,84) 3-Y-0 **£5,181** (£1,541; £770; £384) **Stalls** High

Form RPR
1402 **1** **Ishetoo**[18] 3885 3-8-9 **77**.. MichaelJStainton(5) 9 87
(A Dickman) *trckd ldrs: effrt whn nt clr run and swtchd lft over 1f out: qcknd to ld jst ins fnl f: sn clr* **10/3**[2]
0224 **2** *2 1/2* **Windjammer**[29] 3568 3-8-11 **74**... DavidAllan 10 75
(T D Easterby) *trckd ldrs: hdwy on stands' rail wl over 1f out: rdn and ev ch ent fnl f: kpt on: no ch w wnr* **11/4**[1]
0540 **3** *nk* **Durova (IRE)**[49] 2950 3-8-1 **67**.................................. DuranFentiman(3) 11 67
(T D Easterby) *towards rr: hdwy 2f out: swtchd lft and rdn over 1f out: kpt on ins fnl f* **25/1**
1035 **4** *1 1/4* **Hawaii Prince**[11] 4101 3-8-4 **67**.................................. SilvestreDeSousa 2 62
(S T Mason) *cl up: rdn to ld briefly 1f out: sn hdd and kpt on same pce* **20/1**
1034 **5** *1 3/4* **Baileys Outshine**[45] 3061 3-9-0 **77**.. TPQueally 5 66
(J G Given) *led: rdn along 2f out: drvn and hdd 1f out: wknd* **16/1**
0130 **6** *nk* **The Nifty Fox**[16] 3954 3-9-7 **84**.. TomEaves 8 72
(T D Easterby) *hld up in tch: effrt wl over 1f out: sn rdn and no imp ins fnl f* **15/2**
0500 **7** *1/2* **Steelcut**[10] 4123 3-9-0 **77**.. TonyHamilton 6 63
(R A Fahey) *chsd ldrs: rdn along wl over 1f out and sn btn* **7/1**
4412 **8** *3/4* **Inspainagain (USA)**[15] 4001 3-8-9 **72**................................. PhillipMakin 7 56
(T D Barron) *dwlt: a in rr* **6/1**[3]
3041 **9** *3* **Foxy Music**[29] 3568 3-9-5 **82**.. KDarley 4 55
(E J Alston) *a in rr* **10/1**
634 **10** *1* **Pegasus Dancer (FR)**[33] 3413 3-8-9 **72**.................................... NCallan 1 41
(K A Ryan) *prom on outer: rdn along 2f out and sn wknd* **14/1**

58.01 secs (-1.89) **Going Correction** -0.325s/f (Firm) **10** Ran SP% **118.5**
Speed ratings (Par 102): **102,98,97,95,92 92,91,90,85,83**
CSF £13.19 CT £185.96 TOTE £4.80: £1.90, £1.50, £6.70; EX 11.00 Place 6 £ 11.46, Place 5 £ 10.24.
Owner John H Sissons **Bred** Longdon Stud Ltd **Trained** Sandhutton, N Yorks

FOCUS
A fair handicap with plenty of in-form sprinters and sound enough form.
T/Plt: £8.90 to a £1 stake. Pool: £64,004.25. 5,241.50 winning tickets. T/Qpdt: £8.00 to a £1 stake. Pool: £3,572.20. 330.40 winning tickets. JR

4231 WINDSOR (R-H)
Monday, August 13

OFFICIAL GOING: Good to firm (good in places; 8.1)
Wind: Moderate behind

4453 SANTA RACE ROSA TRACK (TRINIDAD & TOBAGO) FILLIES' AUCTION NURSERY — 6f
5:45 (5:46) (Class 5) 2-Y-0 **£3,886** (£1,156; £577; £288) **Stalls** High

Form RPR
012U **1** **Ocean Transit (IRE)**[9] 4152 2-8-10 **71**.............................. JackDean(7) 10 76
(W G M Turner) *chsd ldrs: rdn to ld appr fnl f: kpt on wl* **16/1**
0410 **2** *3/4* **Penrice Castle**[12] 4065 2-9-0 **68**.................................... RichardHughes 2 70
(R Hannon) *stdd in rr: t.k.h: hld up: stdy hdwy over 2f out: rdn to chse wnr fnl f but a hld* **14/1**
4055 **3** *1* **Deal Flipper**[9] 4152 2-9-3 **71**.. JimCrowley 4 70
(P Winkworth) *chsd ldrs: carried hd awkwardly whn rdn to chal fr 3f out: styd on fnl f but nvr gng pce of ldng pair* **13/2**[3]
622 **4** *shd* **Alabama Spirit (USA)**[14] 4026 2-8-12 **69**.................. AndrewElliott(3) 13 68
(K R Burke) *chsd ldrs: drvn to chal 2f out and ld sn after: hdd appr fnl f and styd on same pce* **9/2**[1]
2265 **5** *1 1/2* **Pixie's Blue (IRE)**[9] 4169 2-9-7 **75**................................ JimmyFortune 16 70
(J H M Gosden) *trckd ldrs: drvn and nt clr run fr ins fnl 2f: styd on fnl f but n.d* **6/1**[2]
020 **6** *1* **Bettys Touch**[52] 2832 2-8-2 **56**.. NickyMackay 3 48
(W J Musson) *in rr: hdwy and rdn fr 3f out: chsd ldrs ins fnl 2f: wknd ins fnl f* **8/1**
514 **7** *hd* **Maddy**[12] 4065 2-8-12 **66**... SebSanders 15 57+
(R M Beckett) *in rr on ins but in tch: n.m.r fr 2f out and sn pushed along kpt on ins fnl f but nvr in contention* **9/2**[1]
51 **8** *1* **Farsighted**[18] 3884 2-9-7 **75**... HayleyTurner 9 63
(J M P Eustace) *in tch: rdn and hdwy over 2f out: nvr quite gng pce to rch ldrs: wknd fnl f* **10/1**
3000 **9** *1* **Seventh Cloud (IRE)**[17] 3925 2-8-6 **60**......................... SimonWhitworth 12 45
(A P Jarvis) *led tl hdd ins fnl 2f: wknd fnl f* **66/1**
665 **10** *shd* **Leading Edge (IRE)**[19] 3834 2-9-0 **68**.. TPO'Shea 8 53
(M R Channon) *outpcd most of way tl mod late prog* **25/1**
300 **11** *2* **Carry On Cleo**[28] 3596 2-7-9 **56**... KMay(7) 14 35
(P D Evans) *pressed ldrs over 3f: wknd 2f out* **25/1**
0604 **12** *nk* **Don't Tell Anna (IRE)**[6] 4254 2-8-8 **62**............................ SteveDrowne 5 40
(R Hannon) *rdn 3f out: a towards rr* **16/1**
004 **13** *2 1/2* **Victorian Princess (IRE)**[14] 4026 2-8-3 **57**.................. FrancisNorton 6 27
(E J O'Neill) *t.k.h: pressed ldrs: ev ch 2f out: sn btn* **14/1**
0040 **14** *6* **Bold Diva**[41] 3174 2-7-12 **52** oh7................................... AdrianMcCarthy 1 4
(A W Carroll) *in rr: rdn and sme hdwy over 2f out: sn btn* **66/1**

1m 13.05s (-0.62) **Going Correction** -0.125s/f (Firm) **14** Ran SP% **120.0**
Speed ratings (Par 91): **99,98,96,96,94 93,92,91,90,90 87,87,83,75**
CSF £216.75 CT £1650.78 TOTE £27.20: £6.20, £4.10, £3.10; EX 723.10.
Owner Pride of the West Racing Club **Bred** Mike Channon Bloodstock Ltd **Trained** Sigwells, Somerset

FOCUS
A commendable winning time for a race of its type and solid enough form rated around the runner-up and fourth.

NOTEBOOK
Ocean Transit(IRE), who unseated at Chepstow when behind Deal Flipper last time, responded most gamely to her rider's urgings passing two out and eventually came home to score her first success outside of plating company. The quick surface was much to her liking and she is clearly a fair sort on her day, but whether she will build on this from a higher mark remains to be seen. (op 20-1)
Penrice Castle proved keen under restraint after making a sluggish start, but still came through to run a solid race in defeat from her unfavourably low draw. This was just her second outing on turf and we have yet to quite see the best of her just yet. (op 16-1)
Deal Flipper, 2lb lower, was given every chance and did not do a great deal wrong in defeat, despite showing a somewhat awkward head carriage travelling into the home straight. She probably needs a stiffer track over this distance, however. (op 6-1 tchd 7-1)
Alabama Spirit(USA), a runner-up in maiden company the last twice, can have no excuses on this nursery bow and was not disgraced from her decent draw. She seemed to get the extra furlong well enough. (op 11-2 tchd 4-1)
Pixie's Blue(IRE), back in trip, was denied a clear passage in the final two furlongs and looked to finish full of running. She really deserves a change of fortune and is capable of defying this mark when getting the breaks. (op 7-2 tchd 10-3)
Maddy was another who endured a troublesome passage from the two-furlong pole and can be rated better than the bare form. A more prominent ride over this distance in the future should help. Official explanation: jockey said filly was denied a clear run (op 5-1 tchd 7-1)
Victorian Princess(IRE) Official explanation: jockey said filly ran too free

4454 VC CASINO.COM MAIDEN STKS — 6f
6:15 (6:16) (Class 4) 2-Y-0 **£5,181** (£1,541; £770; £384) **Stalls** High

Form RPR
1 **Lytton** 2-9-3 0.. AdamKirby 11 78+
(W R Swinburn) *trckd ldrs: chal inside fnl f: qcknd to ld fnl 50yds: readily* **11/2**[3]

0 **2** 1 **Crystal Rock (IRE)**[15] 3991 2-9-3 0 ... MichaelHills 13 75
(B W Hills) *trckd ldrs: chal 1f out: led jst ins fnl f: hdd and outpcd fnl 50yds* **12/1**

02 **3** ½ **Westwood**[14] 4014 2-9-3 0 ... RobertHavlin 4 74
(D Haydn Jones) *led: rdn over 2f out: kpt slt advantage tl hdd jst ins fnl f* **25/1**

0 **4** 1½ **Thunder Gorge (USA)**[14] 4014 2-9-3 0 ... FergusSweeney 12 69+
(Mouse Hamilton-Fairley) *s.i.s: in rr: hdwy over 2f out: styd on fnl f but nvr quite gng pce to be competitive* **100/1**

03 **5** shd **Superduper**[7] 4232 2-8-12 0 ... JimmyFortune 15 64
(R Hannon) *chsd ldrs: chal 2f out: sn hrd rdn: wknd wl ins fnl f* **10/3**[2]

5 **6** 5 **Moral Duty (USA)**[15] 3991 2-9-3 0 ... RichardHughes 3 66+
(Pat Eddery) *trckd ldrs: rdn and effrt over 2f out: nvr quite gng pce to chal: wknd and eased whn lost action ins fnl f* **7/4**[1]

6 **7** ½ **Maximus Aurelius (IRE)**[80] 1990 2-9-3 0 ... DaneO'Neill 16 52
(J Jay) *chsd ldrs: rdn over 2f out: wknd over 1f out* **6/1**

0 **8** ½ **American Welcome (IRE)**[14] 4014 2-9-3 0 ... SteveDrowne 1 51+
(B J Meehan) *in rr tl styd on fr over 1f out: nvr in contention* **40/1**

9 ¾ **Miss Jolyon (USA)** 2-8-12 0 ... PhilipRobinson 9 43+
(M A Jarvis) *nvr gng pce to be competitive* **33/1**

10 3 **Peas In A Pod** 2-9-3 0 ... JamieSpencer 2 39+
(J R Fanshawe) *s.i.s: in rr: mod prog 2f out: nvr in contention* **12/1**

20 **11** 2½ **Vixens Daughter**[84] 1896 2-8-12 0 ... JimCrowley 6 27
(R T Phillips) *chsd ldrs: rdn 3f out: wknd fr 2f out* **100/1**

66 **12** 1 **Champagne Dancer**[39] 3238 2-9-3 0 ... TQuinn 10 29
(D J S Ffrench Davis) *sn outpcd* **66/1**

0 **13** 2½ **No No Ninette**[7] 4232 2-8-12 0 ... (b[1]) SebSanders 14 16
(C R Egerton) *early spd: sn outpcd* **66/1**

00 **14** 6 **Jay Gee Wigmo**[63] 2510 2-9-3 0 ... FrancisNorton 8 3
(A W Carroll) *s.i.s: a bhd* **100/1**

15 1¾ **Theonebox (USA)** 2-9-3 0 ... VinceSlattery 5 —
(M J Wallace) *a in rr* **100/1**

0 **16** 3½ **Howe's Jack (IRE)**[14] 4016 2-9-3 0 ow5 ... AdrianScholes(5) 7 —
(M C Chapman) *slowly away: effrt into mid-div 1/2-way: sn wknd* **100/1**

1m 12.86s (-0.81) **Going Correction** -0.125s/f (Firm) **16** Ran SP% **121.7**
Speed ratings (Par 96): **100,98,98,96,95 89,88,87,86,82 79,78,74,66,64 59**
CSF £67.03 TOTE £7.70: £3.00, £4.20, £4.50; EX 139.60.
Owner Mrs P W Harris **Bred** Pendley Farm **Trained** Aldbury, Herts

FOCUS
A fair winning time for the type of race and, although there is little solid to go on, the form should be fine.

NOTEBOOK
Lytton ◆, the third foal of high-class juvenile sprinter Dora Carrington, emulated his dam by getting off the mark at the first time of asking and did the job in good fashion. He broke smartly, but ran green from halfway and his rider needed to get serious nearing the two-furlong marker. The response was pleasing and, once switched to the outside for his challenge, there was only going to be one outcome. He clearly enjoyed the quick surface and looks sure to improve for the experience, so should be given plenty of respect wherever he turns up next. (op 5-1 tchd 6-1)
Crystal Rock(IRE) ◆, last of 13 on his debut at Ascot last month, showed the clear benefit of that experience and put in a greatly-improved effort. In contrast to the winner, he is bred to come into his own over a longer trip and, on this evidence, should not remain a maiden for too much longer. (op 8-1)
Westwood ◆ showed his latest improved effort to be no fluke and used plenty of early speed to track across from his low draw. He was still going sweetly passing the two-furlong pole and, while he got this trip well enough, it may be that a drop back to the minimum will pay dividends. He now also has the option of nurseries. (tchd 33-1)
Thunder Gorge(USA) was always playing catch-up after missing the break, but he fared by far the best of those to come from off the pace and was noted finishing his race in pleasing fashion. He is still clearly learning his trade, but looks on an upward curve and is one to keep an eye on with a view to nurseries after his next assignment.
Superduper, third over course and distance a week previously, had every chance from her decent draw and can have no excuses. She is going to enjoy another furlong before the season's end and it may be that she finds a little more improvement when switching to nurseries. (op 11-4 tchd 5-2)
Moral Duty(USA), fifth in a decent heat at Ascot on his debut 15 days previously, got no cover from his low draw and proved too keen for his own good as a result. Not surprisingly, he paid the price when push came to shove and is better than he showed here, with a return to slightly easier ground in due course likely to suit him better. Official explanation: jockey said colt pulled bit through its mouth (op 15-8 tchd 2-1 and 13-8)
Maximus Aurelius(IRE), well backed, was found out nearing the final furlong and failed to build on the level of his Goodwood debut. He still looks in need of more time. (op 10-1)

4455 PLAY BLACKJACK AT VC CASINO.COM H'CAP — 1m 67y
6:45 (6:45) (Class 4) (0-85,83) 3-Y-0+ **£6,477** (£1,927; £963; £481) **Stalls** High

Form RPR

6000 **1** **Persian Express (USA)**[13] 4049 4-9-11 **80** ... MichaelHills 6 89
(B W Hills) *trckd ldrs in 3rd: drvn to chal 1f out: styd on to ld fnl 100yds* **6/1**[3]

0204 **2** ¾ **Highland Harvest**[49] 2943 3-8-12 **74** ... TQuinn 1 81
(D R C Elsworth) *led: rdn and styd on fr over 2f out: kpt slt advantage tl hdd fnl 100yds: kpt on* **6/1**[3]

-111 **3** nk **Super Frank (IRE)**[187] 384 4-9-2 **71** ... SebSanders 8 77
(J Akehurst) *trckd ldr: drvn to chal over 1f out: stl upsides ins fnl f: rdr dropped reins last half f: sn rcvrd but a hld* **5/1**[2]

-201 **4** shd **Evident Pride (USA)**[12] 4068 4-10-0 **83** ... DaneO'Neill 5 89
(B R Johnson) *mid-div but in tch: rdn and hdwy to chse ldrs over 1f out: nvr quite gng pce to chal and one pce ins fnl f* **4/1**[1]

1140 **5** 2 **Aggravation**[10] 4135 5-8-13 **71** ... MarcHalford(3) 2 72
(D R C Elsworth) *in rr: rdn and hdwy 2f out: nvr gng pce to be competitive* **4/1**[1]

6024 **6** 3 **Celtic Spa (IRE)**[4] 4317 5-8-12 **67** ... StephenDonohoe 7 62
(P D Evans) *towards rr most of way* **12/1**

3255 **7** 1¼ **Harare**[17] 3900 6-9-7 **76** ... (v) JamieSpencer 4 68
(R J Price) *a in rr* **5/1**[2]

5050 **8** shd **Daniel Thomas (IRE)**[12] 4068 5-9-3 **72** ... EddieAhern 3 63
(Mrs A L M King) *slowly away: sn rcvrd and in tch 5f out: rdn over 3f out: wknd fr 2f out* **22/1**

1m 43.92s (-0.78) **Going Correction** 0.0s/f (Good)
WFA 3 from 4yo+ 7lb **8** Ran SP% **113.9**
Speed ratings (Par 105): **103,102,101,101,99 96,95,95**
CSF £41.23 CT £194.30 TOTE £7.20: £2.40, £2.00, £2.20; EX 41.10.
Owner D M James **Bred** Kingswood Farm **Trained** Lambourn, Berks

FOCUS
A fair handicap run at a strong pace. The first four were closely covered at the finish and the form looks reliable.

4456 PLAY AT VC CASINO.COM H'CAP — 6f
7:15 (7:15) (Class 3) (0-95,95) 3-Y-0+ **£10,094** (£3,020; £1,510; £755; £376) **Stalls** High

Form RPR

2230 **1** **Phantom Whisper**[17] 3911 4-9-4 **88** ... JimCrowley 9 98
(B R Millman) *mde all: hrd drvn and styd on gamely fr over 1f out* **8/1**

6055 **2** 1¼ **Beaver Patrol (IRE)**[9] 4150 5-9-11 **95** ... KerrinMcEvoy 2 101
(Eve Johnson Houghton) *trckd ldrs in 3rd: rdn to chse wnr appr fnl f but a hld* **7/4**[1]

2000 **3** 1 **Golden Dixie (USA)**[10] 4122 8-9-4 **88** ... JamieSpencer 1 91
(R A Harris) *in rr: swtchd rt to stands' side 2f out: styd on u.p fnl f to take 3rd last strides but nvr gng pce to rch ldrs* **18/1**

0410 **4** hd **Border Music**[10] 4122 6-9-8 **92** ... (b) FrancisNorton 4 95
(A M Balding) *trckd ldrs: travelling comf 2f out: rdn over 1f out: fnd little off bit: lost 3rd fnl strides* **7/1**[3]

0055 **5** ¾ **The Kiddykid (IRE)**[16] 3975 7-9-6 **90** ... (v) StephenDonohoe 7 90
(P D Evans) *chsd wnr: rdn over 3f out: lost 2nd: edgd lft over 1f out and sn wknd* **7/1**[3]

0642 **6** 1¼ **Obe Gold**[3] 4367 5-9-3 **87** ... (v) TPO'Shea 3 84
(M R Channon) *sn pushed along and in tch: nvr gng pce to be competitive fr 1/2-way* **7/2**[2]

3000 **7** 1¼ **One More Round (USA)**[78] 2058 9-9-9 **93** ... (b) JamesDoyle 8 86
(N P Littmoden) *outpcd fr 1/2-way* **16/1**

1005 **8** ½ **Adantino**[21] 3802 8-8-4 **79** ... (b) TolleyDean(5) 5 70
(B R Millman) *sn outpcd* **20/1**

0060 **9** 40 **Lucayos**[31] 3481 4-8-9 **82** ... RichardKingscote(3) 6 —
(Mrs H Sweeting) *slowly away: nvr travelling: virtually p.u fnl 2f* **22/1**

1m 11.79s (-1.88) **Going Correction** -0.125s/f (Firm) **9** Ran SP% **115.0**
Speed ratings (Par 107): **107,105,104,103,102 101,99,98,45**
CSF £22.28 CT £250.19 TOTE £8.30: £2.40, £1.50, £4.50; EX 28.30.
Owner Mrs Tina Ann Dormer **Bred** R Lawson **Trained** Kentisbeare, Devon

FOCUS
A fair handicap for the grade, run at a good pace. The form looks solid enough rated through the runner-up.

NOTEBOOK
Phantom Whisper deservedly got off the mark for the year at the ninth attempt by bravely making all at a track he enjoys. He was drawn best of all and the change to front-running tactis was a wise decision. This has to rate just about his best ever effort. (op 7-1 tchd 13-2)
Beaver Patrol(IRE), fifth in the Stewards' Cup last time, did not fare too well with the draw, but he emerged to post a solid effort in defeat under the burden of top weight. He holds few secrets from the Handicapper, but clearly remains in good heart and gives the form a decent look. (op 9-4 tchd 5-2 in a place)
Golden Dixie(USA) finished his race with purpose but never looked like seriously threatening the pacesetters. He is worth riding more positively over this trip in the future. (op 14-1 tchd 20-1)
Border Music looked a threat to all passing the two-furlong pole, but his response when push came to shove was minimal and he was eventually well held. (op 15-2 tchd 8-1)
The Kiddykid(IRE) is coming down in the handicap but seems to be struggling to find his optimum trip at present. Perhaps he is now worth a try over the minimum trip once more. (op 15-2)
Obe Gold struggled to go the early pace and ran below par. He may well have found this coming too soon, however. (op 4-1)
Lucayos Official explanation: jockey said gelding never travelled

4457 PLAY BLACKJACK AT VC CASINO.COM MAIDEN STKS — 1m 67y
7:45 (7:47) (Class 5) 3-Y-0+ **£3,238** (£963; £481; £240) **Stalls** High

Form RPR

46- **1** **Noisy Silence (IRE)**[289] 6220 3-9-3 0 ... TPO'Shea 4 83
(E F Vaughan) *trckd ldr after 1f: slt ld fr 3f out: hrd drvn whn strly chal thrght fnl f: kpt on gamely fnl strides* **12/1**

3 **2** shd **King's Event (USA)**[116] 1100 3-9-3 0 ... SebSanders 1 83+
(Sir Michael Stoute) *in tch: hdwy 3f out: drvn to chal 1f out and upsides u.p thrght fnl f: no ex fnl strides* **10/3**[2]

3 1½ **Abydos** 3-9-3 0 ... KerrinMcEvoy 11 79+
(Saeed Bin Suroor) *trckd ldrs: pushed along and one pce 2f out: kpt on again ins fnl f but nvr gng pce of ldng pair* **9/1**

0232 **4** 1¾ **Know The Law**[18] 3881 3-9-3 76 ... TQuinn 9 75
(D R C Elsworth) *chsd ldrs: rdn and effrt over 2f out: one pce ins fnl f* **5/1**[3]

-200 **5** 3 **Waymark (IRE)**[25] 3689 3-9-3 75 ... PhilipRobinson 8 68
(M A Jarvis) *led tl narrowly hdd 3f out: kpt on fnl 2f but nvr in contention after* **14/1**

06- **6** ½ **Indigo Rose (IRE)**[297] 6071 3-8-12 0 ... JimmyFortune 6 62
(J H M Gosden) *s.i.s: in rr tl hdwy over 3f out: rdn sn after: wknd fr 2f out* **33/1**

7 hd **Out Of Court** 3-9-3 0 ... SimonWhitworth 13 67
(C A Cyzer) *in rr and green: hung lft fr 3f out but kpt on wl fnl 2f: nvr in contention* **100/1**

05 **8** 3½ **And Your Point Is (USA)**[10] 4138 3-9-3 0 ... SteveDrowne 10 58
(C R Egerton) *chsd ldrs: rdn 3f out: wknd over 2f out* **100/1**

0 **9** 1¾ **Quaglino Way (GR)**[59] 2625 3-9-3 0 ... FrancisNorton 2 54
(P R Chamings) *in rr: mod prog fnl 2f* **66/1**

10 3½ **Al Naahadth (USA)** 3-9-3 0 ... LDettori 12 46
(Saeed Bin Suroor) *in rr: rdn over 4f out: no rspnse* **2/1**[1]

0 **11** 1¾ **Amichi**[24] 3710 3-8-12 0 ... FergusSweeney 5 37
(G L Moore) *a in rr* **100/1**

43 **12** ½ **Hazytoo**[103] 1398 3-9-3 0 ... JamieSpencer 14 41
(N A Callaghan) *t.k.h and stdd in mid-div early: bhd fnl 3f* **13/2**

1m 44.06s (-0.64) **Going Correction** 0.0s/f (Good)
WFA 3 from 5yo 7lb **12** Ran SP% **118.2**
Speed ratings (Par 103): **103,102,101,99,96 96,95,92,90,87 85,84**
CSF £51.58 TOTE £15.60: £3.60, £1.80, £3.40; EX 65.80.
Owner W J Gredley **Bred** Newsells Park Stud **Trained** Newmarket, Suffolk

FOCUS
This could prove to be a good maiden as the season progresses. It was run at a solid pace and the form is rated through the 76-rated fourth.
Indigo Rose(IRE) Official explanation: jockey said filly stumbled on leaving stalls
Al Naahadth(USA) Official explanation: jockey said colt stumbled on leaving stalls
Hazytoo Official explanation: jockey said colt hung badly left on bend

4458 VC CASINO.COM H'CAP — 1m 3f 135y
8:15 (8:15) (Class 5) (0-70,70) 3-Y-0+ **£3,238** (£963; £481; £240) **Stalls** Low

Form RPR

0-33 **1** **Constant Cheers (IRE)**[14] 4025 4-9-3 **59** ... (p) AdamKirby 7 67
(W R Swinburn) *trckd ldrs: rdn to ld and hung rt over 2f out: hung bdly lft over 1f out: styd on wl u.p thrght fnl f* **15/2**[2]

00-5 **2** *nk* **Colinette**[66] 2431 4-9-4 **60** .... SteveDrowne 1 67
(R T Phillips) *hld up in rr: stdy hdwy fr 3f out styng on whn n.m.r over 1f out: str chal u.p thrght fnl f: no ex last strides* **40/1**
3304 **3** *2* **Turner's Touch**[26] 3641 5-9-6 **62** .... (b) GeorgeBaker 5 66
(G L Moore) *in rr: hdwy fr 3f out: styd on to chse ldrs over 1f out and n.m.r: hung lft ins fnl f and nt run on* **11/1**
5311 **4** *shd* **Down The Brick (IRE)**[6] 4253 3-9-2 **69** 6ex .... (b) FergusSweeney 9 75+
(B R Millman) *in tch: hdwy whn hmpd on rail 2f out: kpt on ins fnl f but nvr gng pce to rch ldrs* **13/8**[1]
0405 **5** *¾* **Double Spectre (IRE)**[14] 4015 5-9-9 **65** .... DaneO'Neill 8 68
(Jean-Rene Auvray) *in tch: hdwy 3f out: drvn to press ldrs 2f out: no ex ins fnl f* **12/1**
1606 **6** *4* **Stolen Hours (USA)**[16] 3946 7-9-5 **61** .... SebSanders 6 57
(J Akehurst) *mid-div: hdwy over 3f out to chse ldrs 2f out: wknd fnl f* **9/1**[3]
-251 **7** *¾* **Pothos Way (GR)**[61] 2572 4-9-6 **62** .... JimCrowley 10 57+
(P R Chamings) *chsd ldrs: rdn and one pce whn hmpd over 1f out: sn wknd* **10/1**
0005 **8** *3* **Up In Arms (IRE)**[14] 4019 3-8-10 **63** .... (b[1]) StephenCarson 12 53
(P Winkworth) *pressed ldrs: led 6f out: rdn 3f out: hdd over 2f out and sn n.m.r on rails: wknd qckly* **16/1**
5-43 **9** *¾* **Niqaab**[42] 3160 3-9-2 **69** .... RichardMullen 4 58
(W J Musson) *in rr: sme hdwy fr 4f out: in tch 3f out: wknd over 1f out* **16/1**
3606 **10** *½* **Hatch A Plan (IRE)**[14] 4019 6-8-13 **58** .... TravisBlock(3) 3 46
(Mouse Hamilton-Fairley) *sn slt ld: hdd after 2f: styd chsng ldrs tl wknd and hmpd over 1f out* **14/1**
5600 **11** *13* **Mahmjra**[14] 4030 5-8-13 **55** .... NickyMackay 2 22
(C N Allen) *in tch: rdn over 3f out: sn wknd* **20/1**
4-62 **12** *2½* **Tafiya**[21] 3803 4-9-10 **66** .... EddieAhern 11 29
(J W Hills) *led after 2f: hdd 6f out: wknd over 2f out* **9/1**[3]
P00/ **13** *25* **Present Oriented (USA)**[289] 3209 6-9-9 **70** ..... RussellKennemore(5) 13 —
(M C Chapman) *a in rr* **40/1**

2m 29.02s (-1.08) **Going Correction** 0.0s/f (Good)
WFA 3 from 4yo+ 11lb 13 Ran SP% **123.0**
Speed ratings (Par 103): **103,102,101,101,100 98,97,95,95,94 86,84,67**
CSF £289.64 CT £3276.12 TOTE £9.40: £3.20, £8.80, £3.20; EX 312.70 Place 6 £2,039.87, Place 5 £ 349.71.
Owner Mr & Mrs W R Swinburn **Bred** Pendley Farm **Trained** Aldbury, Herts

FOCUS
A modest handicap, run at a decent pace. The first pair came clear but there are doubts over the strength of the form.
Mahmjra Official explanation: jockey said gelding never travelled
Tafiya Official explanation: trainer said filly lost a shoe during the race
T/Jkpt: Not won. T/Plt: £2,674.80 to a £1 stake. Pool: £87,573.35. 23.90 winning tickets. T/Qpdt: £58.40 to a £1 stake. Pool: £7,375.40. 93.30 winning tickets. ST

[4428] WOLVERHAMPTON (A.W) (L-H)

Monday, August 13

OFFICIAL GOING: Standard
Wind: Fresh behind Weather: Overcast

4459 EUROPEAN BREEDERS' FUND MEDIAN AUCTION MAIDEN STKS 5f 216y(P)
2:30 (2:30) (Class 5) 2-Y-O £3,886 (£1,156; £577; £288) Stalls Low

Form RPR
043 **1** **Gross Prophet**[9] 4181 2-9-0 74 .... RichardKingscote(3) 2 81
(Tom Dascombe) *chsd ldrs: led over 2f out: rdn and hung rt fr over 1f out: r.o* **4/1**[2]
4 **2** *1½* **Tugalu (IRE)**[15] 3995 2-9-3 0 .... NCallan 6 78+
(K A Ryan) *a.p: rdn to chse wnr over 1f out: edgd rt: styd on same pce ins fnl f* **3/1**[1]
0 **3** *5* **Highland Love**[24] 3718 2-9-0 0 .... TravisBlock(3) 8 60
(Jedd O'Keeffe) *sn outpcd: hdwy over 1f out: hung lft ins fnl f: nrst fin* **40/1**
4 *4* **One Called Alice** 2-8-12 0 .... JamesDoyle 4 42+
(J R Holt) *s.s: outpcd: r.o ins fnl f: nvr nrr* **66/1**
0 **5** *nk* **Wee Buns**[14] 4016 2-9-3 0 .... LPKeniry 9 46
(S Kirk) *sn outpcd: nt clr run over 1f out: r.o ins fnl f: nvr nrr* **33/1**
3532 **6** *1¾* **Ben**[25] 3687 2-9-3 76 .... RobertHavlin 5 40
(P G Murphy) *hld up in tch: rdn over 1f out: wknd fnl f* **9/2**[3]
240 **7** *nk* **Nothing Likea Dame**[31] 3507 2-8-12 72 .... TPQueally 11 34
(D J Coakley) *mid-div: rdn 1/2-way: hdwy over 2f out: wknd over 1f out* **10/1**
060 **8** *nk* **Frizzini**[20] 3812 2-9-3 55 .... TomEaves 12 38
(N Tinkler) *led over 3f: rdn and wknd over 1f out* **66/1**
54 **9** *1* **Musical Charm (IRE)**[86] 1848 2-8-12 0 .... SebSanders 7 30
(T D Easterby) *mid-div: sn drvn along: wknd over 2f out* **5/1**
4 **10** *5* **Gaitskell**[123] 1007 2-9-3 0 .... GrahamGibbons 10 19
(R Hollinshead) *mid-div: hdwy 1/2-way: rdn and wknd over 1f out* **11/1**
5 **11** *5* **Sir Joey**[9] 4160 2-9-3 0 .... SamHitchcott 1 3
(J T Stimpson) *sn pushed along in rr: wknd over 2f out* **40/1**
03 **12** *1½* **Keeparryappy (IRE)**[91] 1706 2-9-3 0 .... PatCosgrave 3 —
(K R Burke) *chsd ldrs over 3f* **12/1**

1m 15.79s (-0.02) **Going Correction** -0.15s/f (Stan) 12 Ran SP% **115.8**
Speed ratings (Par 94): **94,92,85,80,79 77,76,76,75,68 61,59**
CSF £15.49 TOTE £5.30: £1.50, £2.00, £16.70; EX 17.80 TRIFECTA Not won..
Owner Alan Solomon **Bred** A D Solomon **Trained** Lambourn, Berks

FOCUS
An ordinary event in which very few ever got competitive and they finished well strung out.

NOTEBOOK
Gross Prophet, who had shown enough in his three previous outings to suggest he could win like this, made full use of the inviting gap that opened up for him on the inside turning in. Despite hanging right in the home straight, he was always doing enough to hold off the favourite and nurseries now beckon. (op 9-2 tchd 3-1)
Tugalu(IRE), up a furlong from his turf debut, was always in a great position and had every chance, but could never quite summon the pace to get to the winner. He is nothing special, but will benefit from going up in trip again. (op 9-4)
Highland Love, well beaten in soft ground on his Pontefract debut, was never in the race and it is debatable how much he achieved in running on for a very remote third. He is bred to need further in any case and may be capable of a bit more once handicapped. (op 66-1)
One Called Alice, the only newcomer in the field, cost just 1,500gns as a yearling but her dam was a dual winner whose family achieved plenty of success on the continent. However, she completely ruined her chance at the start by walking out of the stalls and soon found herself in a detached last. She did run on past beaten horses to finish a remote fourth, but the margin between her and the front three at the line means it would be wrong to get too carried away. Still, she can be rated a few lengths better than this and her pedigree suggests a mile will eventually be her trip. Official explanation: jockey said filly missed the break
Wee Buns did not step up much from his debut over this extra furlong. Official explanation: jockey said gelding was unlucky in runing
Ben, by far the most experienced in the field - this was his ninth start - was close enough on the inside turning for home, but could make no impression from then on. This was a step backwards and he now looks well and truly exposed.

4460 LADBROKES IN WOLVERHAMPTON (S) STKS 1m 4f 50y(P)
3:00 (3:00) (Class 6) 3-Y-O+ £2,047 (£604; £302) Stalls Low

Form RPR
412 **1** **Annambo**[44] 3112 7-9-12 80 .... CColombi 6 71+
(S C Williams) *hld up: hdwy over 5f out: chsd ldr over 2f out: led over 1f out: rdn clr* **8/15**[1]
-000 **2** *10* **Showtime Annie**[4] 4340 6-8-13 35 .... (b) NeilChalmers(3) 7 45
(A Bailey) *hld up: hdwy over 4f out: led over 2f out: rdn and hdd over 1f out: wknd fnl f* **100/1**
0345 **3** *hd* **The City Kid (IRE)**[9] 4161 4-9-4 53 .... LiamJones(3) 9 50
(C R Dore) *hld up: hdwy over 3f out: rdn over 1f out: sn wknd* **12/1**[3]
2422 **4** *2* **Bridgewater Boys**[6] 4249 6-9-12 56 .... (p) PatCosgrave 2 52
(K A Ryan) *chsd ldrs tl rdn and wknd over 2f out* **4/1**[2]
0000 **5** *12* **Cool Isle**[28] 3593 4-9-2 42 .... (b) IanMongan 10 23
(P Howling) *hld up in tch: led over 3f out: rdn and hdd over 2f out: sn wknd* **33/1**
-020 **6** *7* **Littleton Aldor (IRE)**[5] 4267 7-9-7 48 .... SebSanders 4 16
(Mark Gillard) *led: hdd whn hmpd over 3f out: sn wknd* **25/1**
0645 **7** *12* **Ceol Eile (IRE)**[21] 3795 4-9-2 44 .... (b[1]) RobertHavlin 3 —
(D Haydn Jones) *chsd ldr: rdn over 4f out: hmpd and wknd over 3f out* **40/1**
0030 **8** *10* **Snake Hips**[46] 3035 3-8-7 54 .... (b) RichardKingscote(3) 5 —
(B Palling) *chsd ldrs over 7f* **16/1**
5 **9** *46* **Mustang Du Gueslan (FR)**[25] 3684 7-9-7 0 .... TomEaves 1 —
(D W Thompson) *chsd ldrs: rdn and lost pl over 6f out: sn bhd* **66/1**

2m 40.69s (-1.73) **Going Correction** -0.15s/f (Stan)
WFA 3 from 4yo+ 11lb 9 Ran SP% **110.5**
Speed ratings (Par 101): **99,92,92,90,82 78,70,63,32**
CSF £107.23 TOTE £1.40: £1.10, £8.30, £2.50; EX 75.40 Trifecta £225.50 Pool: £460.68, 1.45 winning units.The winner was sold to R A Harris for 14,000gns. The City Kid was claimed by Luke McGarrigle £6,000
Owner Stuart C Williams **Bred** Sheikh Mohammed Bin Rashid Al Maktoum **Trained** Newmarket, Suffolk
■ A winner on his first ride in Britain for Italian jockey Claudio Colombi.
■ Stewards' Enquiry : Neil Chalmers three-day ban: careless riding (Aug 24-26)

FOCUS
A one-horse race and, apart from the winner, this was an awful seller. The beaten horses will find it hard to find many winning opportunities, even at this sort of level.

4461 LADBROKES, HOME OF FOOTBALL BETTING NURSERY 7f 32y(P)
3:30 (3:30) (Class 5) 2-Y-O £3,238 (£963; £481; £240) Stalls High

Form RPR
434 **1** **Cobo Bay**[13] 4037 2-9-4 **72** .... PatCosgrave 11 83
(K A Ryan) *mde all: clr over 2f out: rdn out* **11/1**
6061 **2** *3* **What Katie Did (IRE)**[12] 4065 2-9-1 **69** .... TPQueally 3 72+
(J A Osborne) *prom: nt clr run over 2f out: chsd wnr over 1f out: sn rdn: styd on* **7/2**[2]
0231 **3** *2* **Relinquished**[13] 4037 2-9-5 **73** .... SebSanders 9 71
(J Noseda) *hld up: hdwy over 2f out: rdn over 1f out: styd on* **5/2**[1]
060 **4** *1¼* **Valentino Sky (USA)**[16] 3962 2-9-2 **70** .... IanMongan 4 64
(N P Littmoden) *prom: rdn to chse wnr over 2f out: wknd fnl f* **10/1**
3530 **5** *1¼* **Gulf Coast**[10] 4121 2-8-12 **66** .... (b[1]) GregFairley 10 57
(M Johnston) *hld up: hdwy 3f out: rdn and wknd over 1f out* **9/2**[3]
0640 **6** *shd* **Nathan Dee**[26] 3642 2-7-12 **55** .... LiamJones(3) 6 45
(Mrs H Sweeting) *sn pushed along in rr: styd on ins fnl f: nvr nrr* **16/1**
31 **7** *4* **Geoffdaw**[122] 1021 2-9-7 **75** .... TomEaves 8 55
(M J Wallace) *dwlt: hld up: rdn over 3f out: a in rr* **9/1**
053 **8** *½* **Glenshee (IRE)**[15] 4002 2-9-1 **69** .... GrahamGibbons 5 47
(J J Quinn) *mid-div: rdn 1/2-way: sn wknd* **12/1**
504 **9** *1½* **Lavemill (IRE)**[62] 2533 2-7-12 **52** oh7 .... DavidKinsella 2 26
(R F Fisher) *mid-div: rdn 1/2-way: wknd over 2f out* **100/1**
1034 **10** *13* **Nestor Protector (IRE)**[23] 3734 2-8-5 **64** .... KevinGhunowa(5) 1 —
(A B Haynes) *chsd wnr tl rdn and wknd over 2f out* **25/1**

1m 30.3s (-0.10) **Going Correction** -0.15s/f (Stan) 10 Ran SP% **114.8**
Speed ratings (Par 94): **94,90,88,86,85 85,80,80,78,63**
CSF £48.64 CT £131.14 TOTE £10.80: £2.20, £1.70, £1.20; EX 54.80 Trifecta £163.90 Pool: £399.54, 1.73 winning units.
Owner The C H F Partnership **Bred** The C H F Partnership **Trained** Hambleton, N Yorks

FOCUS
Not many got into this and it developed into a rather uncompetitive nursery. It has been rated fairly positively, though.

NOTEBOOK
Cobo Bay, making his nursery debut after showing ability in three maidens, was 6lb better off with Relinquished for a beating of just over two lengths at Beverley last time. The key to the form turnaround, however, was being given a positive ride from the start and, once kicked clear on the crown of the home bend, he never looked like getting caught. He still has a bit of scope and should be able to find another opportunity or two. (op 14-1)
What Katie Did(IRE), raised 7lb for his Kempton victory, was trying this trip for the first time. He held a good position just behind the leaders for much of the way but, just as the winner was scampering away out in front turning for home, he was meeting traffic problems. Once he was finally out in the clear, he had far too much ground to make up. (tchd 10-3 and 4-1)
Relinquished, making her sand debut, was close enough on the outside rounding the home bend, but did not find as much off the bridle as had looked likely and comprehensively failed to confirm Beverley form with the winner on 6lb worse terms. (op 9-4 tchd 2-1 and 3-1)
Valentino Sky(USA), unplaced in three turf maidens, had every chance but did not appear to see out the extra furlong on this sand debut. (op 15-2)
Gulf Coast tried to get into the race starting the home bend, but never got anywhere near. The first-time blinkers made no difference and he does not seem to be progressing. (op 5-1 tchd 11-2)
Geoffdaw, trying further than the minimum trip for the first time in only his third outing, did not help his chances by missing the break, but he was entitled to need this first run in four months. (tchd 11-1)
Lavemill(IRE) Official explanation: jockey said filly hung right throughout

4462 LADBROKES SERIOUS ABOUT SERVICE H'CAP 7f 32y(P)
4:00 (4:00) (Class 5) (0-75,75) 3-Y-O+ £3,071 (£906; £453) Stalls High

Form RPR
0640 **1** **Coeur Courageux (FR)**[11] 4100 5-9-10 **73** .... (t) GrahamGibbons 4 86+
(D Nicholls) *hld up: hdwy over 2f out: led ins fnl f: rdn out* **9/2**[2]

0643 **2** 2 1/2 **Tous Les Deux**[14] 4024 4-9-9 **72** .... LPKeniry 10 78
(Peter Grayson) *stdd s: hld up: hdwy over 2f out: rdn over 1f out: styd on* **13/2**
6243 **3** 2 1/2 **Another Genepi (USA)**[12] 4083 4-9-3 **66** ....(b) PatCosgrave 11 66
(K A Ryan) *led 6f out: clr over 2f out: rdn over 1f out: hdd and no ex ins fnl f* **6/1**[3]
0620 **4** 1/2 **Ochre Bay**[28] 3599 4-9-5 **73** .... RussellKennemore(5) 2 71
(R Hollinshead) *hld up: hdwy 2f out: nt rch ldrs* **8/1**
4250 **5** 1 1/2 **Stoic Leader (IRE)**[2] 4407 7-9-2 **65** .... TomEaves 3 59+
(R F Fisher) *chsd ldrs: rdn over 2f out: styd on same pce* **7/2**[1]
041 **6** 6 **Copper King**[15] 3996 3-9-5 **74** .... JamesDoyle 1 50
(J W Hills) *chsd ldrs: hmpd over 2f out: sn wknd* **10/1**
000- **7** 3 **Grand Jour (IRE)**[236] 6888 4-9-7 **70** ....(b[1]) PaulDoe 5 40
(B P J Baugh) *mid-div: rdn 1/2-way: sn wknd* **25/1**
3650 **8** 4 **Ionian**[24] 3711 4-9-9 **72** .... JimmyQuinn 9 31
(Pat Eddery) *s.i.s: outpcd* **9/1**
-000 **9** 3/4 **Red Contact (USA)**[41] 3195 6-9-7 **70** ....(p) TPQueally 6 27
(A Dickman) *chsd ldrs 4f* **40/1**
200- **10** 6 **Lord Of The East**[352] 4790 8-9-12 **75** .... LeeEnstone 7 16
(I W McInnes) *led 1f: chsd ldrs tl wknd 3f out* **40/1**
6-00 **11** 1 1/4 **Miss Jenny (IRE)**[33] 3430 3-9-2 **74** ....(b[1]) LiamJones(3) 8 9
(B J Meehan) *prom over 4f* **20/1**
2106 **12** 1/2 **Looks Could Kill (USA)**[19] 3851 5-9-2 **65** .... DavidKinsella 12 1
(A B Haynes) *sn pushed along: in rr fr 1/2-way* **16/1**

1m 29.12s (-1.28) **Going Correction** -0.15s/f (Stan)
WFA 3 from 4yo+ 6lb **12** Ran SP% **117.6**
Speed ratings (Par 103): **101,98,95,94,93 86,82,78,77,70 69,68**
CSF £32.13 CT £178.16 TOTE £5.90: £2.00, £1.80, £2.30; EX 35.30 Trifecta £143.30 Pool: £318.95, 1.58 winning units.
Owner William Wallace Partnership **Bred** Star Pastures Management Et Al **Trained** Sessay, N Yorks

FOCUS
They went a decent pace in this and the front five came a very long way clear of the others. The form looks solid for the grade.
Looks Could Kill(USA) Official explanation: jockey said gelding hung right throughout

4463 LADBROKES IN THE COMMUNITY CHARITABLE TRUST H'CAP 2m 119y(P)
4:30 (4:30) (Class 6) (0-65,64) 4-Y-0+ **£2,388** (£705; £352) **Stalls** Low

Form RPR
0152 **1** **Mister Completely (IRE)**[4] 4322 6-9-6 **63** ....(v) JamesDoyle 13 76
(Ms J S Doyle) *hld up: hdwy over 2f out: chsd ldr over 1f out: rdn to ld ins fnl f: styd on wl* **11/2**[3]
4613 **2** 5 **Josh You Are**[14] 4030 4-9-7 **64** .... PatCosgrave 5 71
(D E Cantillon) *hld up: hdwy over 4f out: led over 2f out: rdn and hdd ins fnl f: styd on same pce* **9/2**[2]
6300 **3** 9 **Synonymy**[3] 4352 4-9-5 **62** ....(b) JimmyQuinn 3 58
(M Blanshard) *prom: rdn and ev ch over 2f out: wknd over 1f out* **11/2**[3]
-020 **4** 4 **Dreams Jewel**[6] 4253 7-8-10 **56** .... NeilChalmers(3) 7 47
(C Roberts) *hld up: rdn 1/2-way: hdwy over 4f out: rdn and wknd over 2f out* **33/1**
026 **5** nk **Madiba**[4] 4322 8-8-12 **55** .... TPQueally 6 46
(P Howling) *prom: rdn over 3f out: wknd over 2f out* **12/1**
3055 **6** 1 3/4 **Ha'Penny Beacon**[13] 4040 4-8-9 **59** .... KellyHarrison(7) 4 48
(D Carroll) *mid-div: rdn over 4f out: wknd over 2f out* **25/1**
1223 **7** 1 1/4 **Rare Coincidence**[19] 3840 6-9-6 **63** ....(p) TomEaves 8 50
(R F Fisher) *led: hdd 4f out: rdn and wknd over 2f out* **8/1**
0610 **8** shd **Orpen Quest (IRE)**[9] 4161 5-8-11 **54** .... AlanDaly 12 41
(M J Attwater) *hld up: effrt over 2f out: sn wknd* **40/1**
22 **9** 5 **Power Again (GER)**[32] 3448 6-8-12 **55** .... PaulDoe 11 36
(P R Chamings) *hld up: hdwy 10f out: led 4f out: rdn and hdd over 2f out: sn wknd* **3/1**[1]
4/00 **10** 8 **Victory Sign (IRE)**[16] 3946 7-8-9 **55** ow3 ....(tp) AlanCreighton(3) 9 27
(P Butler) *s.i.s: hld up: rdn 1/2-way: wknd 6f out* **80/1**
0-04 **11** 1/2 **Pukka Tique**[36] 443 4-8-11 **54** .... GrahamGibbons 2 25
(Miss J S Davis) *chsd ldr over 4f: rdn 5f out: wknd over 3f out* **33/1**
2024 **12** 3 **Diktatorship (IRE)**[17] 3927 4-8-13 **56** .... SamHitchcott 1 24
(Jennie Candlish) *prom: chsd ldr 12f out: rdn over 3f out: wkng whn n.m.r over 2f out* **11/1**

3m 40.35s (-2.78) **Going Correction** -0.15s/f (Stan) **12** Ran SP% **114.5**
Speed ratings (Par 101): **100,97,93,91,91 90,89,89,87,83 83,82**
CSF £28.00 CT £142.11 TOTE £6.20: £2.20, £1.70, £1.50; EX 40.50 Trifecta £161.40 Pool: £340.99, 1.50 winning units.
Owner Ms J S Doyle **Bred** Eamonn Griffin **Trained** Upper Lambourn, Berks

FOCUS
A moderate handicap, but at least the pace was solid and this became a true test of stamina, hence the decent margins separating the principals at the line. The form looks sound for the grade.
Power Again(GER) Official explanation: trainer had no explanation for the poor form shown

4464 LADBROKES YOUR BEST BET APPRENTICE H'CAP 1m 1f 103y(P)
5:00 (5:00) (Class 6) (0-60,60) 4-Y-0+ **£2,388** (£705; £352) **Stalls** Low

Form RPR
5203 **1** **Pelham Crescent (IRE)**[46] 3034 4-8-8 **54** .... LanceBetts(5) 13 65
(B Palling) *chsd ldr: rdn to ld ins fnl f: r.o* **7/1**
4060 **2** 1 1/2 **My Michelle**[63] 2521 6-9-5 **60** .... AlanRutter 11 68
(B Palling) *led: clr 6f out: rdn over 1f out: hdd and unable qck ins fnl f* **7/1**
3430 **3** 3 **Desert Hawk**[5] 4284 6-8-10 **54** ....(b) DeanHeslop(3) 9 56+
(W M Brisbourne) *mid-div: hdwy over 1f out: nt trble ldrs* **5/1**[2]
0-36 **4** 1 3/4 **Miss Porcia**[16] 3965 6-8-1 **49** .... BrydieKilloran(7) 5 48
(P A Blockley) *chsd ldrs: rdn over 2f out: wknd fnl f* **20/1**
-000 **5** 2 **Sea Frolic (IRE)**[56] 2716 6-8-2 **46** oh1 .... SoniaEaton(3) 6 41
(Jennie Candlish) *hld up in tch: rdn over 2f out: wknd over 1f out* **33/1**
35-4 **6** 1 1/2 **Abbeygate**[185] 402 6-8-1 **47** .... BradleyRoper(5) 12 39
(T Keddy) *s.s: hld up: hdwy over 2f out: sn rdn and wknd* **10/1**
40 **7** 1/2 **Shevalina (IRE)**[1] 4430 5-8-5 **46** .... JemmaMarshall 7 37
(Adrian Sexton, Ire) *s.s: hld up: plld hrd: rdn over 2f out: sn wknd* **33/1**
0314 **8** 1 3/4 **Regency Red (IRE)**[7] 4231 9-8-4 **52** .... Julie-AnneCumine(7) 1 39
(W M Brisbourne) *hld up: effrt over 2f out: n.d* **13/2**[3]
0-05 **9** nk **Blushing Light (USA)**[16] 3946 4-9-2 **60** ....(t) SophieDoyle(3) 4 46
(M A Magnusson) *hld up: hdwy over 2f out: sn wknd* **15/2**
/65- **10** shd **Kings Topic (USA)**[472] 1276 7-8-13 **59** .... RyanBird(5) 2 45
(A B Haynes) *chsd ldrs: hmpd and lost pl over 6f out: sn bhd* **9/2**[1]
0-00 **11** 7 **Roya**[11] 4108 4-9-2 **57** .... HarryPoulton 10 29
(Miss Gay Kelleway) *hld up: rdn over 3f out: sn wknd* **15/2**

2m 1.26s (-1.36) **Going Correction** -0.15s/f (Stan) **11** Ran SP% **116.4**
Speed ratings (Par 101): **100,98,96,94,92 91,90,89,89,88 82**
Place 6 £ 29.72, Place 5 £ 16.65 CSF £53.53 CT £266.19 TOTE £9.00: £2.80, £2.10, £2.30; EX 64.60 Trifecta £134.50 Pool: £358.14, 1.89 winning units.

Owner Bryn Palling **Bred** Cathal M Ryan **Trained** Tredodridge, Vale Of Glamorgan
■ Stewards' Enquiry : Dean Heslop four-day ban: careless riding (Aug 24-27)

FOCUS
Another run-of-the-mill apprentice handicap in which the pace was quite decent. Not many got into it, though, and the first two home were up there from the off. The form looks ordinary.
T/Plt: £30.00 to a £1 stake. Pool: £65,128.50. 1,583.75 winning tickets. T/Qpdt: £11.60 to a £1 stake. Pool: £3,779.40. 240.80 winning tickets. CR

4315 BRIGHTON (L-H)
Tuesday, August 14

OFFICIAL GOING: Good to firm
Even though the ground was officially good to firm, the rain encouraged many riders to come wide, though there did not appear to be a huge advantage.
Wind: Strong, half against Weather: Rain

4469 JIMMY HEAL MEMORIAL APPRENTICE H'CAP 7f 214y
2:00 (2:01) (Class 6) (0-65,64) 4-Y-0+ **£2,072** (£616; £308; £153) **Stalls** Low

Form RPR
0040 **1** **Parthenope**[43] 3149 4-8-2 **47** ow2 .... JackDean(5) 1 54
(J A Geake) *bhd: gd hdwy 2f out: slt ld 1f out: re-jnd fnl 50yds: jst prevailed* **40/1**
5610 **2** shd **Legal Lover (IRE)**[48] 2979 5-9-10 **64** .... RussellKennemore 4 71
(R Hollinshead) *in tch: led over 2f out: narrowly hdd 1f out: drvn bk level fnl 50yds: jst pipped* **4/1**[2]
4042 **3** 1 3/4 **Prince Valentine**[5] 4319 6-8-2 **47** ....(p) JemmaMarshall(5) 2 50
(G L Moore) *hld up in midfield: hdwy 2f out: drvn to chse ldrs over 1f out: nt qckn fnl f* **7/2**[1]
0400 **4** shd **Lady Duxyana**[5] 4321 4-8-0 **45** ....(v) FrankiePickard(5) 12 48
(M D I Usher) *dwlt: sn in midfield: effrt whn nt clr run and swtchd rt over 1f out: carried hd high: styd on* **25/1**
4500 **5** 1 1/4 **Bollywood (IRE)**[22] 3799 4-8-5 **45** .... NicolPolli 3 45
(J J Bridger) *sn rdn along and bhd: hdwy over 1f out: nt pce to rch ldrs* **12/1**
0600 **6** 3/4 **Ten To The Dozen**[11] 4129 4-8-6 **49** .... KMay(3) 8 47
(P W Hiatt) *chsd ldrs: drvn along over 2f out: 4th and hld whn squeezed for room over 1f out* **14/1**
1006 **7** 5 **Mamichor**[6] 4294 4-8-4 **47** ow1 ....(b) JamieHamblett(3) 5 34
(B R Johnson) *chsd ldr: led 5f out tl over 2f out: wknd wl over 1f out* **7/1**
0-50 **8** 3 **Royal Tavira Girl (IRE)**[5] 4319 4-8-12 **55** .... ThomasO'Brien(3) 9 35
(M G Quinlan) *outpcd and nvr gng wl: a bhd* **9/1**
-252 **9** 12 **Linden's Lady**[12] 4099 7-8-6 **46** ....(v) PatrickHills 7 —
(J R Weymes) *t.k.h: prom tl wknd and eased over 2f out* **6/1**[3]
0260 **10** 2 1/2 **Danawi (IRE)**[17] 3950 4-8-11 **51** .... AshleyHamblett 6 —
(M R Hoad) *led 3f: hung rt and wnt wd st: wknd and eased 3f out* **7/1**

1m 39.36s (4.32) **Going Correction** +0.55s/f (Yiel) **10** Ran SP% **112.2**
Speed ratings (Par 101): **100,99,98,98,96 96,91,88,76,73**
CSF £187.70 CT £620.71 TOTE £53.40: £12.00, £1.80, £1.30; EX 221.40 TRIFECTA Not won..
Owner Dr and Mrs John Merrington **Bred** Theakston Stud **Trained** Kimpton, Hants
■ Stewards' Enquiry : Jemma Marshall three-day ban: used whip with excessive frequency (Aug 25-27)

FOCUS
A low-grade race, but competitive enough, and the pace was solid, with the field coming up the middle. The race is best rated around the runner-up, who goes well here.
Prince Valentine Official explanation: trainer said gelding was unsuited by the good to firm going
Lady Duxyana Official explanation: jockey said filly suffered interference in running
Linden's Lady Official explanation: jockey said mare felt lame in running; trainer's rep said mare lost a hind shoe
Danawi(IRE) Official explanation: jockey said gelding hung right

4470 DAVID BARWICK SEVENTIETH BIRTHDAY MEDIAN AUCTION MAIDEN STKS 7f 214y
2:30 (2:30) (Class 5) 3-5-Y-0 **£2,775** (£830; £415; £207) **Stalls** Low

Form RPR
232 **1** **Commandment (IRE)**[49] 2962 3-9-3 **75** .... JimmyFortune 3 59+
(E A L Dunlop) *trckd ldr: led over 1f out: pushed clr: readily* **2/9**[1]
5000 **2** 2 1/2 **Elmasong**[37] 3349 3-8-7 **41** .... TolleyDean(5) 1 48
(J J Bridger) *led: rdn and qcknd over 2f out: hdd over 1f out: nt pce of wnr* **50/1**
-465 **3** 1 **Saaratt**[12] 4106 3-8-12 **69** .... EddieAhern 2 46
(J W Hills) *plld hrd: trckd ldng pair: rdn over 1f out: one pce* **5/1**[2]
0- **4** 12 **Artistic Liason**[398] 3402 3-8-12 **0** .... OscarUrbina 4 18
(G C H Chung) *a last: rdn and lost tch 2f out* **16/1**[3]

1m 39.52s (4.48) **Going Correction** +0.55s/f (Yiel) **4** Ran SP% **106.3**
Speed ratings (Par 103): **99,96,95,83**
CSF £12.29 TOTE £1.20; EX 13.40.
Owner Highclere Thoroughbred Racing XXXVII **Bred** South House Stud **Trained** Newmarket, Suffolk

FOCUS
A weakly-contested race, with the winner looking different class. The runners came towards the stands' side.
Commandment(IRE) Official explanation: vet said gelding had bled from the nose
Artistic Liason Official explanation: jockey said filly was unsuited by the track

4471 IAN CARNABY (S) STKS 5f 213y
3:00 (3:00) (Class 6) 3-Y-0+ **£1,943** (£578; £288; £144) **Stalls** Low

Form RPR
240 **1** **Ishibee (IRE)**[8] 4224 3-8-10 **56** ....(p) SebSanders 16 54
(Mrs A Duffield) *chsd ldrs: c to stands' rail st: led 1f out: rdn out* **5/1**[1]
460 **2** 1 1/2 **King Of Tricks**[8] 4226 3-8-3 **45** .... FrankiePickard(7) 15 50
(M D I Usher) *towards rr: rdn and r.o fnl 2f: edgd lft fnl f: tk 2nd fnl 50yds* **40/1**
3060 **3** 1/2 **Blue Knight (IRE)**[3] 4396 8-9-5 **41** ....(p) AmirQuinn 2 53
(P Howling) *prom: styd alone on far rail ent st: nt qckn fnl f* **14/1**
0060 **4** nk **Flower Of Cork (IRE)**[3] 4397 3-8-6 **53** ow1 ....(p) JamesDoyle 9 43
(Ms J S Doyle) *w ldr: led over 2f out tl 1f out: one pce* **14/1**
0600 **5** 1 1/4 **She Whispers (IRE)**[20] 3837 4-8-9 **41** .... FergusSweeney 7 38
(R Hollinshead) *hld up in rr: promising hdwy 2f out: rdn to chse ldrs over 1f out: no ex* **20/1**
0300 **6** nk **Sham Ruby**[19] 3873 5-8-9 **43** ....(t) OscarUrbina 10 37
(M R Bosley) *hld up in midfield: rdn over 2f out: in tch whn hmpd over 1f out: styd on same pce* **16/1**
2050 **7** 1/2 **Princely Vale (IRE)**[27] 3636 5-8-7 **48** ....(p) JackDean(7) 3 41
(W G M Turner) *w ldrs: hung bdly lft towards far rail wl over 1f out: wknd fnl f* **8/1**[3]

0-06 **8** 3/4 **Von Wessex**[19] 3873 5-8-9 45 TolleyDean(5) 14 39
(W G M Turner) *prom tl wknd over 1f out* **33/1**

006U **9** 1/2 **Double Valentine**[10] 4182 4-8-9 45 DavidKinsella 5 32
(R Ingram) *bhd: mod effrt in centre 2f out: nt pce to chal* **16/1**

5304 **10** 1/2 **Tuscan Flyer**[54] 2791 9-9-0 45 (b) TPQueally 13 36
(R Bastiman) *sn led: hdd over 2f out: wkng and btn whn n.m.r 1f out* **6/1**[2]

2205 **11** nk **Nawayea**[5] 4336 4-8-9 45 JimmyQuinn 11 30
(C N Allen) *rrd s and missed break: sn chsng ldrs: wknd over 1f out* **6/1**[2]

-000 **12** shd **Alfie Tupper (IRE)**[20] 3851 4-9-0 65 SimonWhitworth 6 35
(S Kirk) *bhd: rdn over 3f out: n.d* **5/1**[1]

066- **13** 8 **Noble Mount**[244] 6805 6-8-9 42 (p) KevinGhunowa(5) 8 11
(A B Haynes) *mid-div: rdn over 3f out: sn outpcd* **25/1**

0330 **14** shd **Valeesha**[50] 2948 3-8-5 45 SaleemGolam 12 5
(W G M Turner) *in tch: rdn 4f out: wknd 2f out* **33/1**

1m 12.54s (2.44) **Going Correction** +0.55s/f (Yiel)
WFA 3 from 4yo+ 4lb **14** Ran SP% **115.0**
Speed ratings (Par 101): **105,103,102,101,100 99,99,98,97,96 96,96,85,85**
CSF £218.58 TOTE £3.80: £1.90, £14.10, £5.60; EX 161.90 TRIFECTA Not won..The winner was sold to John Bridger for 5,400gns.
Owner D K Barker & Lee Bolingbroke **Bred** Ambersham Stud **Trained** Constable Burton, N Yorks

FOCUS
A competitive seller, run at a decent gallop, though the form is barely banded class. All bar one runner headed for the stands' side in the straight, with one other edging back across later on.
Nawayea Official explanation: jockey said filly missed the break

4472 MALSAR KEST FILLIES' H'CAP — 1m 1f 209y
3:30 (3:31) (Class 5) (0-70,65) 3-Y-O+ **£2,839** (£849; £424; £212; £105) **Stalls** High

Form RPR

021U **1** **Chant De Guerre (USA)**[19] 3876 3-9-0 58 JimmyQuinn 1 61
(P Mitchell) *chsd ldrs: led 4f out and claimed stands' rail: hdd over 2f out: led again over 1f out: all out* **4/1**[2]

0-00 **2** shd **Little Carmela**[19] 3881 3-8-6 50 SaleemGolam 8 53+
(S C Williams) *in tch: wnt for stands' rail and hmpd over 3f out: rallied and hung lft over 1f out: styd on wl fnl f: nrly jnd wnr on line* **17/2**

5000 **3** 1 **Little Miss Tara (IRE)**[21] 3826 3-9-2 65 (v) KevinGhunowa(5) 4 66
(A B Haynes) *wnt lft s: hld up in rr: hdwy 2f out: drvn to chal over 1f out: nt qckn fnl f* **16/1**

0100 **4** 4 **Kyloe Belle (USA)**[9] 4205 3-9-1 59 SebSanders 6 52
(Mrs A J Perrett) *chsd ldrs tl no ex over 1f out* **9/4**[1]

0030 **5** 1 **Lunar River (FR)**[12] 4112 4-10-0 63 (t) FergusSweeney 7 54
(David Pinder) *in tch: led over 2f out tl over 1f out: sn wknd* **5/1**[3]

-001 **6** 7 **Mayireneyrbel**[105] 1368 3-8-11 55 EddieAhern 3 32
(J Akehurst) *led 3f: lost pl 4f out: rallied and hrd rdn 2f out: sn wknd* **5/1**[3]

-000 **7** 15 **Elounda (IRE)**[18] 3913 3-9-4 62 TPQueally 5 9
(H R A Cecil) *led after 3f tl 4f out: wknd qckly over 2f out: eased whn no ch fnl f: sddle slipped* **6/1**

2m 6.93s (4.33) **Going Correction** +0.55s/f (Yiel)
WFA 3 from 4yo 9lb **7** Ran SP% **114.8**
Speed ratings (Par 100): **104,103,103,99,99 93,81**
CSF £37.03 CT £488.56 TOTE £3.80: £2.30, £5.20; EX 41.30 Trifecta £346.70 Pool: £639.81 - 1.31 winning units..
Owner Mrs Patricia Mitchell **Bred** Shadwell Farm LLC **Trained** Epsom, Surrey

FOCUS
Visibility was deteriorating by now, but much of this modest handicap could be seen via TV cameras. The runners came stands' side in the straight. The form is weak, no better than plating class.
Elounda(IRE) Official explanation: jockey said saddle slipped

4473 HAPPY BIRTHDAY JOHN PEDERSON CLAIMING STKS — 1m 3f 196y
4:00 (4:01) (Class 5) 3-4-Y-O **£2,775** (£830; £415; £207; £103) **Stalls** High

Form RPR

-604 **1** **Susie May**[12] 4104 3-8-9 52 ow1 SebSanders 8 65
(C A Cyzer) *4th and in tch 9f out: in ld by 1 1/2 l 1f out: drvn clr* **15/8**[2]

4200 **2** 7 **Prince Des Neiges (FR)**[13] 4067 4-9-5 61 EddieAhern 6 55+
(A M Hales) *cl 2nd 9f out: 2nd and hld by wnr 1f out: one pce* **11/10**[1]

0056 **3** 17 **Marbaa (IRE)**[19] 3868 4-9-1 46 (p) TPQueally 7 22
(S Dow) *3rd and in tch 9f out: 8 l 3rd and wl btn 1f out* **6/1**[3]

005 **4** 6 **Roymar**[33] 3476 3-8-4 46 ow1 NeilChalmers(3) 4 15
(M Appleby) *fair 5th 9f out: 4th and no ch 1f out* **20/1**

0030 **5** 22 **Coffin Dodger**[28] 3629 4-8-10 36 JimmyQuinn 5 —
(C N Allen) *missed break by 20 l: modest 6th 9f out: a bhd* **20/1**

-000 **6** 6 **Sadler's Hill (IRE)**[5] 4322 3-9-1 47 (b[1]) LPKeniry 3 —
(M J McGrath) *in ld 9f out: wl bhd 1f out* **40/1**

5500 **7** 110 **Shaika**[40] 3250 4-8-4 49 CharlotteKerton(7) 1 —
(G Prodromou) *ref to leave stalls and lft 1f: effectively tk no part* **20/1**

2m 35.99s (3.79) **Going Correction** +0.55s/f (Yiel)
WFA 3 from 4yo 11lb **7** Ran SP% **113.4**
Speed ratings (Par 103): **109,104,93,89,74 70,—**
CSF £4.05 TOTE £2.70: £1.70, £1.20; EX 5.10 Trifecta £15.20 Pool: £620.26 - 28.87 winning units..Susie May was subject to a friendly claim.
Owner Mrs Charles Cyzer **Bred** Bottisham Heath Stud **Trained** Maplehurst, W Sussex

FOCUS
A decent winning time for a claimer but, with a sea-fret keeping visibility down to just over a furlong, it is hard to say much more. The runners all came to the stands' rail in the straight.
Coffin Dodger Official explanation: jockey said filly missed the break

4474 BET365 CALL 08000 322365 H'CAP — 6f 209y
4:30 (4:30) (Class 5) (0-70,69) 3-Y-O+ **£2,775** (£830; £415; £207; £103) **Stalls** Low

Form RPR

4066 **1** **Millfield (IRE)**[62] 2556 4-9-5 55 GeorgeBaker 5 63
(P R Chamings) *cl 3rd 4f out: claimed stands' rail st: slt ld over 1f out: drvn out* **13/8**[1]

2600 **2** 1 **Lady Edge (IRE)**[5] 4317 5-9-0 55 KevinGhunowa(5) 3 60
(A W Carroll) *disp ld tl over 2f out: styd alone far side: cl 3rd over 1f out: kpt on wl* **12/1**

2606 **3** 1 3/4 **Inquisitress**[6] 4269 3-8-10 57 TolleyDean(5) 2 55
(J J Bridger) *cl 4th 4f out: slt ld over 2f out tl over 1f out: no ex ins fnl f* **12/1**

5141 **4** 2 1/2 **Majestical (IRE)**[21] 3829 5-9-4 54 (p) EddieAhern 6 48
(V Smith) *mod 5th 4f out and over 1f out: styd on same pce* **7/2**[3]

5506 **5** 1/2 **Out For A Stroll**[5] 4319 8-9-7 57 SebSanders 7 49
(S C Williams) *disp ld tl over 2f out: 3rd and hld over 1f out: wknd fnl f* **7/4**[2]

1m 26.6s (3.90) **Going Correction** +0.55s/f (Yiel)
WFA 3 from 4yo+ 6lb **5** Ran SP% **112.1**
Speed ratings (Par 103): **99,97,95,93,92**
CSF £19.64 TOTE £2.60: £1.30, £4.00; EX 20.40 Place 6 £49.80, Place 5 £26.48.
Owner Patrick Chamings Sprint Club **Bred** Limestone Stud **Trained** Baughurst, Hants

FOCUS
Obscured by a sea fret, which restricted visibility of this modest handicap to just over a furlong. All bar the runner-up came towards the stands' rail in the straight. Neither the second nor third represents solid form and the race looks weak.
Majestical(IRE) Official explanation: trainer said gelding lost a shoe
T/Plt: £45.50 to a £1 stake. Pool: £59,270.25. 950.50 winning tickets. T/Qpdt: £22.40 to a £1 stake. Pool: £3,114.30. 102.50 winning tickets. LM

4096 MUSSELBURGH (R-H)
Tuesday, August 14

OFFICIAL GOING: Good changing to soft after 7.00 (race 3)
Wind: Moderate, half behind Weather: Raining

4475 CMYK APPRENTICE H'CAP — 1m 6f
6:00 (6:02) (Class 6) (0-65,62) 4-Y-O+ **£2,590** (£770; £385; £192) **Stalls** High

Form RPR

6132 **1** **Kyber**[12] 4096 6-8-12 55 GaryBartley(5) 11 59
(J S Goldie) *trckd ldng pair: smooth hdwy to ld 3f out: rdn clr appr fnl f: styd on* **2/1**[1]

060- **2** 2 1/2 **Living On A Prayer**[460] 1616 4-8-12 50 MarkLawson 4 50
(Michael McElhone, Ire) *hld up towards rr: hdwy on outer 3f out: rdn to chse ldrs over 1f out: edgd rt and one pce fnl f* **33/1**

4-54 **3** 1/2 **Blushing Hilary (IRE)**[14] 4040 4-9-8 60 DougieCostello 1 60
(Miss J A Camacho) *hld up towards rr: stdy hdwy 3f out: effrt and ch wl over 1f out: sn rdn and kpt on same pce* **13/2**

4202 **4** 2 **York Cliff**[31] 3533 9-9-10 62 LiamJones 2 59
(W M Brisbourne) *towards rr: pushed along 4f out: rdn 3f out: styd on fnl 2f: nt rch ldrs* **3/1**[2]

0006 **5** 1/2 **Borsch (IRE)**[7] 4246 5-8-2 45 KellyHarrison(5) 10 41
(Miss L A Perratt) *trckd ldrs: hdwy 3f out: rdn to chal over 2f out and ev ch tl drvn appr fnl f and wknd* **50/1**

/020 **6** 7 **Dance Sauvage**[67] 2434 4-8-13 51 AndrewMullen 3 37
(C W Thornton) *hld up towards rr: hdwy over 5f out: rdn to chse ldrs over 2f out: sn drvn and wknd* **6/1**[3]

5-00 **7** 1 1/2 **Scurra**[47] 3012 8-8-0 45 LanceBetts(7) 8 29
(A C Whillans) *cl up: effrt to ld briefly over 3f out: sn rdn and hdd: grad wknd fnl 2f* **25/1**

-030 **8** 1 1/4 **High Frequency (IRE)**[42] 3193 6-8-0 45 (v) DeanHeslop(7) 9 27
(A Crook) *chsd ldrs: rdn along 3f out: wknd fnl 2f* **33/1**

0000 **9** 1 1/4 **The Dunion**[53] 2825 4-8-1 46 ow1 AdamCarter(7) 5 27
(Miss L A Perratt) *a towards rr* **20/1**

300/ **10** 23 **Forever My Lord**[351] 5998 9-8-8 46 DuranFentiman 7 —
(W A Murphy, Ire) *led: rdn along 4f out: hdd over 3f out and sn wknd* **25/1**

R **Danticat (USA)**[18] 3937 6-8-12 50 (bt) JamieMoriarty 6 —
(John J Coleman, Ire) *ref to r* **13/2**

3m 9.56s (3.86) **Going Correction** +0.25s/f (Good) **11** Ran SP% **119.6**
Speed ratings (Par 101): **98,96,96,95,94 90,90,89,88,75 —**
CSF £85.92 CT £383.87 TOTE £3.20: £1.20, £8.20, £2.40; EX 77.90.
Owner Great Northern Partnership **Bred** P B Holmes **Trained** Uplawmoor, E Renfrews

FOCUS
A moderate-looking contest run in soft-looking ground up the home straight. The form looks weak as the winner put up the only remotely solid performance.

4476 MAPEI UK AND SCOTMAT CARPETS NURSERY — 5f
6:30 (6:30) (Class 5) 2-Y-O **£3,886** (£1,156; £577; £288) **Stalls** Low

Form RPR

454 **1** **Choisette**[41] 3200 2-7-12 58 oh5 PaulFessey 6 64
(B Smart) *mde all: rdn wl over 1f out: styd on strly* **4/1**

4162 **2** 2 1/2 **Style Award**[10] 4175 2-8-9 72 AndrewMullen(3) 1 69
(W J H Ratcliffe) *trckd ldrs: hdwy 2f out: rdn and ch ent fnl f: sn drvn and nt qckn* **11/4**[2]

2330 **3** 1 **Next Best**[22] 3788 2-7-5 58 oh9 DanielleMcCreery(7) 8 51
(A Berry) *chsd ldrs on outer: hdwy wl over 1f out: sn rdn and kpt on same pce fnl f* **50/1**

31 **4** 8 **The Real Guru**[16] 4002 2-9-7 81 RoystonFfrench 2 46
(Mrs A Duffield) *sn rdn along to chse ldrs: hdwy 2f out: drvn over 1f out and kpt on same pce* **7/2**[3]

6146 **5** shd **Charlotti Carlotti (IRE)**[10] 4168 2-9-2 76 KDarley 5 40
(T D Barron) *cl up: rdn along 1/2-way: sn wknd* **9/4**[1]

0610 **6** 4 **Firenza Bond**[12] 4098 2-9-1 75 TomEaves 7 25
(G R Oldroyd) *s.i.s: rdn and sme hdwy on outer 2f out: sn drvn and btn* **10/1**

62.13 secs (1.63) **Going Correction** +0.25s/f (Good) **6** Ran SP% **110.7**
Speed ratings (Par 94): **96,92,90,77,77 71**
CSF £14.92 CT £437.16 TOTE £3.70: £1.50, £1.80; EX 15.10.
Owner Pinnacle Choisir Partnership **Bred** M R M Bloodstock **Trained** Hambleton, N Yorks

FOCUS
A very moderate event and questionable form with the first two in the market failing to run their races.

NOTEBOOK
Choisette made full use of a low weight and good draw to win nicely. However, with the rank outsider finishing third, the form looks very questionable and she would be no good thing to follow this success up. (op 5-2)
Style Award ran a cracker trying to give so much weight away and probably emerges as the best horse from the race. She looks a great horse to own as she seems to go on any ground and tries her very best every time. (op 10-3 tchd 4-1)
Next Best has been beaten in sellers and claimers so does not do too much to boost the level of the form. (op 66-1)
The Real Guru ran no sort of race so is either too high in the weights already or just did not handle the easy ground. Official explanation: trainer said colt scoped dirty after the race (op 3-1 tchd 11-4)
Charlotti Carlotti(IRE) did not enjoy the best of runs but hardly threatened to take a hand. She would have finished just in front of The Real Guru with a clearer run. (op 7-2)
Firenza Bond was heavily restrained leaving the stalls, possibly due to interference, and unsurprisingly never got into race. It is best to forget this run. Official explanation: jockey said gelding hung right-handed and moved poorly throughout (op 9-1)

4477 PINKIE MAINS FARM H'CAP — 1m
7:00 (7:01) (Class 6) (0-65,65) 4-Y-O+ **£2,590** (£770; £385; £192) **Stalls** High

Form RPR

6640 **1** **Wahoo Sam (USA)**[4] 4353 7-9-7 65 (p) TonyHamilton 8 72
(D W Barker) *mde all: qcknd clr over 2f out: rdn over 1f out: drvn ins fnl f: jst hld on* **7/1**[3]

5401 **2** *hd* **Mystical Ayr (IRE)**[3] 4383 5-8-13 **64** 6ex........................ GaryBartley[(7)] 7 70
(Miss L A Perratt) *towards rr: pushed along 3f out: hdwy 2f out: rdn to chse ldrs over 1f out: sn drvn and styd on strly ins fnl f: jst failed* **3/1**[1]
5 **3** *1 3/4* **Camolin (IRE)**[55] 2764 4-8-3 **47** oh1 ow1................(b) AdrianTNicholls 14 49
(Michael McElhone, Ire) *sltly hmpd s and bhd tl hdwy over 2f out: sn rdn and styd on ins fnl f: nrst fin* **18/1**
-106 **4** *1* **Coronado's Gold (USA)**[15] 4031 6-8-8 **55**............... JamieMoriarty[(3)] 5 55
(B Ellison) *chsd ldrs on outer: hdwy over 2f out: rdn wl over 1f out: drvn and kpt on same pce fnl f* **10/1**
1500 **5** *1 1/2* **Lobengula (IRE)**[23] 3765 5-9-4 **62**..................................... LeeEnstone 9 59
(I W McInnes) *chsd wnr: rdn along over 2f out: drvn wl over 1f out: sn one pce* **20/1**
0-06 **6** *nk* **Redwood Rocks (IRE)**[85] 1892 6-9-4 **62**................. RoystonFfrench 13 58
(B Smart) *chsd ldrs on inner: hdwy to chse wnr over 2f out: drvn over 1f out: wknd ent fnl f* **13/2**[2]
4-44 **7** *hd* **Sarraaf (IRE)**[10] 4159 11-8-13 **57**....................................... TomEaves 11 52
(I Semple) *trckd ldrs: effrt 3f out: sn rdn and wknd fnl 2f* **7/1**[3]
0000 **8** *3* **Brace Of Doves**[16] 3999 5-8-6 **53**........................... AndrewMullen[(3)] 10 42
(D W Whillans) *nvr nr ldrs* **14/1**
6600 **9** *3* **First Rhapsody (IRE)**[24] 3754 5-7-13 **46** oh1............... DominicFox[(3)] 1 28
(T J Etherington) *midfield: rdn along 1/2-way: nvr a factor* **25/1**
0103 **10** *12* **Drink To Me Only**[14] 4042 4-8-2 **46**.................................... DaleGibson 4 —
(J R Weymes) *a towards rr* **3/1**[1]
00-0 **11** *18* **George's Flyer (IRE)**[221] 42 4-8-2 **46** oh1..................(v) PaulFessey 3 —
(R A Fahey) *a bhd* **16/1**

1m 44.21s (1.71) **Going Correction** +0.25s/f (Good) 11 Ran SP% **123.8**
Speed ratings (Par 101): **101,100,99,98,96 96,96,93,90,78 60**
CSF £29.85 CT £387.45 TOTE £9.90: £2.50, £1.60, £5.40; EX 31.00.
Owner Jason Holland **Bred** Stonereath Farms Inc **Trained** Scorton, N Yorks

FOCUS
A modest handicap run at a decent tempo. There are doubts over the form with the runner-up apparently posting a personal best under her apprentice rider.
Drink To Me Only Official explanation: jockey said gelding hung both ways throughout
George's Flyer(IRE) Official explanation: jockey said gelding was unsuited by the soft ground

4478 WALKER LOVE & CO (S) STKS 5f
7:30 (7:30) (Class 6) 3-Y-O+ **£2,590** (£770; £385; £192) **Stalls** Low

Form RPR
1322 **1** **Danish Blues (IRE)**[13] 4083 4-9-5 59........................ AdrianTNicholls 9 59
(D Nicholls) *squeezed out s: pushed along in rr after 2f: gd hdwy 2f out: swtchd lft and rdn to chal over 1f out: styd on to ld last 100yds* **10/11**[1]
-030 **2** *hd* **Radiator Rooney (IRE)**[107] 1327 4-8-11 57...........(b) JamieMoriarty[(3)] 2 53
(Patrick Morris, Ire) *cl up: rdn to ld 1f out: sn drvn: hdd and nt qckn last 100yds* **4/1**[2]
0400 **3** *1 1/2* **Four Kings**[92] 1711 6-9-0 44.. FTahir 7 48
(Karen McLintock) *hld up in rr: hdwy on outer wl over 1f out: sn rdn and styd on ins fnl f: nrst fin* **40/1**
4400 **4** *1/2* **Sharp Hat**[22] 3782 13-9-0 48.. DaleGibson 4 46
(D W Chapman) *a.p: rdn along wl over 1f out: kpt on same pce ins fnl f* **7/1**[3]
6050 **5** *1/2* **Jun Fan (USA)**[12] 4101 5-9-0 48.. PatCosgrave 8 44
(B Ellison) *dwlt and bhd: hdwy over 2f out: rdn to chse ldrs over 1f out: sn drvn and kpt on same pce* **11/1**
0600 **6** *1 1/2* **Signor Whippee**[37] 3347 4-8-7 45.....................(b) AdamCarter[(7)] 5 39
(A Berry) *chsd ldrs: hdwy on inner over 1f out: sn rdn and no imp* **25/1**
00 **7** *3 1/2* **Seafield Towers**[22] 3782 7-9-0 49.......................(p) RoystonFfrench 6 26
(Miss L A Perratt) *chsd ldrs: rdn along wl over 1f out: drvn and wknd ent fnl f* **10/1**
0005 **8** *1* **Alfie Lee (IRE)**[3] 4379 10-8-7 30.................................(t) PaulPickard[(7)] 11 22
(D A Nolan) *chsd ldrs: rdn along 2f out: sn wknd* **66/1**
6404 **9** *2* **Splendidio**[8] 4226 3-8-7 43 ow1............................... TonyHamilton 14 11
(Mrs Marjorie Fife) *led: rdn along wl over 1f out: hdd 1f out: sn edgd rt and wknd* **25/1**
5005 **10** *12* **Mandy's Maestro (USA)**[8] 4226 3-8-6 45.........(b) MichaelJStainton[(5)] 1 —
(R M Whitaker) *sn outpcd and a towards rr* **12/1**

64.24 secs (3.74) **Going Correction** +0.775s/f (Yiel)
WFA 3 from 4yo+ 3lb 10 Ran SP% **121.6**
Speed ratings (Par 101): **101,100,98,97,96 94,88,87,83,64**
CSF £4.72 TOTE £1.80: £1.10, £1.60, £10.90; EX 5.90.There was no bid for the winner.
Owner Ian Bishop **Bred** Tally-Ho Stud **Trained** Sessay, N Yorks

FOCUS
A routine seller run on deteriorating ground in which the pair best in at the weights by some way finished first and second, though in reverse order.
Signor Whippee Official explanation: jockey said gelding was denied a clear run
Seafield Towers Official explanation: jockey said gelding was unsuited by the soft ground
Splendidio Official explanation: jockey said filly hung right-handed

4479 BANK OF SCOTLAND REAL ESTATE H'CAP 7f 30y
8:00 (8:00) (Class 5) (0-75,75) 3-Y-O+ **£3,886** (£1,156; £577; £288) **Stalls** High

Form RPR
5000 **1** **Frank Crow**[8] 4228 4-9-1 **70**.. GaryBartley[(7)] 4 78
(J S Goldie) *towards rr: hdwy wl over 2f out: rdn wl over 1f out: styd on strly u.p ins fnl f to ld nr line* **11/2**
1-10 **2** *nk* **La Matanza**[66] 2466 4-9-13 **75**... PaulFessey 9 82
(T D Barron) *trckd ldrs: hdwy 3f out: rdn to ld over 1f out: drvn ins fnl f: hdd nr line* **7/2**[1]
6011 **3** *1/2* **Mister Jingles**[8] 4223 4-8-6 **59** 6ex......................(v) MichaelJStainton[(5)] 2 65
(R M Whitaker) *chsd ldrs: hdwy on outer 2f out: sn rdn and styd on ent fnl f: ev ch tl drvn and nt qckn towards fin* **5/1**
1562 **4** *2 1/2* **Distant Sun (USA)**[13] 4078 3-8-11 **65**............................ TomEaves 8 62
(I Semple) *in tch: hdwy 3f out: rdn to chse ldrs 2f out: drvn over 1f out: kpt on same pce* **5/1**
2006 **5** *2 1/2* **Baylaw Star**[16] 3996 6-9-4 **66**................................. RoystonFfrench 7 58
(I W McInnes) *led: rdn along 3f out: hdd 2f out: sn drvn and wknd appr fnl f* **14/1**
2061 **6** *6* **Kabis Amigos**[8] 4219 5-9-13 **75** 6ex............................(t) AdrianTNicholls 3 51
(D Nicholls) *cl up: rdn to ld 2f out: drvn and hdd appr fnl f: wknd* **4/1**[2]
0/40 **7** *27* **Avontuur (FR)**[3] 4381 5-8-1 **56** oh8.....................(b) DanielleMcCreery[(7)] 5 —
(D W Chapman) *stdd s: t.k.h: hld up in rr: sddle slipped 3f out* **40/1**
2 **8** *13* **Ghafeer (USA)**[13] 4079 3-9-0 **71**............................(b) JamieMoriarty[(3)] 6 —
(B Ellison) *sn outpcd and a towards rr: wl bhd fr 1/2-way* **9/2**[3]

1m 34.37s (4.43) **Going Correction** +0.775s/f (Yiel)
WFA 3 from 4yo+ 6lb 8 Ran SP% **118.2**
Speed ratings (Par 103): **105,104,104,101,98 91,60,45**
CSF £26.02 CT £104.57 TOTE £8.30: £2.20, £1.40, £2.20; EX 58.40.
Owner Mrs Janis Macpherson **Bred** Southill Stud **Trained** Uplawmoor, E Renfrews

FOCUS
With two confirmed front-runners in Baylaw Star and Kabis Amigos taking each other on this was always likely to be run at a decent clip, but the ever more testing ground took its toll and they merely set it up for the closers.
Kabis Amigos Official explanation: jockey said gelding was unsuited by the soft ground
Avontuur(FR) Official explanation: jockey said gelding stumbled and she lost her irons

4480 PHILIP'S 40TH BETTING, BURGUNDY AND BRIE H'CAP 7f 30y
8:30 (8:33) (Class 6) (0-65,65) 3-Y-O **£2,590** (£770; £385; £192) **Stalls** High

Form RPR
3525 **1** **Mangano**[5] 4330 3-8-1 **52**... DanielleMcCreery[(7)] 4 55
(A Berry) *towards rr: effrt and pushed along 3f out: rdn and hdwy 2f out: styd on u.p ins fnl f to ld nr line* **12/1**
2050 **2** *hd* **Moheebb (IRE)**[11] 4137 3-8-8 **55**...................................... LiamJones[(3)] 6 57
(D W Chapman) *bhd: hdwy over 2f out: rdn wl over 1f out: str run ent fnl f: led last 50yds: hdd nr line* **7/1**
0005 **3** *1/2* **Nufoudh (IRE)**[2] 4423 3-8-10 **57**................................ JamieMoriarty[(3)] 8 58
(Miss Tracy Waggott) *chsd ldrs: hdwy over 2f out: sn rdn: drvn and ev ch ins fnl f: no ex last 50yds* **16/1**
3013 **4** *3/4* **Kunte Kinteh**[13] 4064 3-9-7 **65**.................................... AdrianTNicholls 5 64+
(D Nicholls) *cl up: led wl over 2f out and sn clr: rdn and edgd lft over 1f out: drvn ent fnl f: hdd and no ex last 100yds* **5/1**[2]
0-16 **5** *1 1/2* **Vesuvio**[19] 3885 3-9-4 **62**... KDarley 1 57
(C W Thornton) *towards rr: pushed along 1/2-way: rdn and hdwy over 2f out: styd on u.p ent fnl f: nrst fin* **13/2**[3]
3040 **6** *5* **Ruthles Philly**[6] 4291 3-8-11 **55**................................ TonyHamilton 2 36
(D W Barker) *led: rdn along and hdd wl over 2f out: sn drvn and grad wknd* **20/1**
-045 **7** *3 1/2* **Davaye**[29] 3583 3-9-6 **64**.. LeeEnstone 3 36
(K R Burke) *chsd ldng pair: rdn wl over 2f out: drvn wl over 1f out: sn wknd* **14/1**
5232 **8** *2* **Just Oscar (GER)**[4] 4354 3-9-4 **62**.................................. DavidAllan 11 28
(W M Brisbourne) *in tch: rdn along over 2f out: grad wknd* **3/1**[1]
23-0 **9** *2 1/2* **Bert's Memory**[15] 4023 3-9-5 **63**............................(p) PatCosgrave 13 22
(K A Ryan) *chsd ldrs: rdn along wl over 2f out and sn wknd* **20/1**
-000 **10** *3 1/2* **Gallows Hill (USA)**[16] 3997 3-8-6 **50**............................ DaleGibson 12 —
(R A Fahey) *a towards rr* **14/1**
-050 **11** *5* **Buds Dilemma**[16] 3997 3-8-4 **48**............................... RoystonFfrench 10 —
(I W McInnes) *midfield: rdn along 3f out: no hdwy* **40/1**
3222 **12** *1* **Five Wishes**[53] 2829 3-9-2 **60**.. PaulFessey 14 —
(M Dods) *a bhd* **3/1**[1]

1m 36.19s (6.25) **Going Correction** +0.775s/f (Yiel) 12 Ran SP% **131.4**
Speed ratings (Par 98): **95,94,94,93,91 85,81,79,76,72 67,65**
CSF £101.60 CT £1398.27 TOTE £15.00: £3.80, £2.70, £3.70; EX 121.60 Place 6 £216.68, Place 5 £98.81.
Owner Anthony White **Bred** Wood Farm Stud **Trained** Cockerham, Lancs
■ Stewards' Enquiry : Liam Jones two-day ban: used whip with excessive frequency (Aug 25-26)

FOCUS
A moderate handicap in which the riders decided to steer clear of the inside rail in the home straight and come middle to stands' side. The pace was decent given the conditions.
T/Plt: £218.30 to a £1 stake. Pool: £64,509.65. 215.65 winning tickets. T/Qpdt: £65.50 to a £1 stake. Pool: £4,386.60. 49.50 winning tickets. JR

4102 NOTTINGHAM (L-H)
Tuesday, August 14

OFFICIAL GOING: Good (good to soft in places) (7.7)
Wind: Light, half against Weather: Early rain clearing to leave sunny spells

4481 JOHN SMITH'S CISWO APPRENTICE H'CAP 1m 1f 213y
5:45 (5:45) (Class 5) (0-75,75) 4-Y-0+ **£2,914** (£867; £433; £216) **Stalls** Low

Form RPR
1222 **1** **Top Mark**[12] 4105 5-9-7 **75**.. HarryPoulton[(3)] 2 84
(J R Boyle) *mde all: rdn over 1f out: r.o* **9/4**[1]
5653 **2** *1 1/4* **Gallego**[33] 3457 5-8-5 **56** oh1..................................... KirstyMilczarek 8 63
(R J Price) *s.s: hld up: hdwy over 3f out: rdn to chse wnr fnl f: styd on same pce* **9/2**[3]
2310 **3** *3/4* **Ermine Grey**[18] 3907 6-8-1 **57**....................................... SophieDoyle[(5)] 4 62
(A W Carroll) *s.i.s: hld up: hdwy 6f out: outpcd over 1f out: styd on ins fnl f* **11/1**
5603 **4** *3/4* **Baan (USA)**[8] 4228 4-9-9 **74**.. WilliamCarson 3 78
(M Johnston) *chsd wnr over 4f: rdn over 3f out: edgd lft and styd on same pce appr fnl f* **7/2**[2]
4306 **5** *nk* **Parnassian**[17] 3955 7-8-10 **66**...............................(v) MatthewDavies[(5)] 6 69
(J A Geake) *prom: racd keenly: chsd wnr over 5f out: rdn over 2f out: no ex fnl f* **7/2**[2]
0004 **6** *1 1/2* **Spinning**[13] 4081 4-8-9 **60**... NeilBrown 7 60
(T D Barron) *chsd ldrs: rdn over 2f out: wknd ins fnl f* **9/1**

2m 13.71s (4.01) **Going Correction** +0.20s/f (Good) 6 Ran SP% **111.7**
Speed ratings (Par 103): **91,90,89,88,88 87**
CSF £12.53 CT £86.68 TOTE £2.40: £1.30, £2.60; EX 11.80.
Owner M Khan X2 **Bred** Ewar Stud Farms **Trained** Epsom, Surrey

FOCUS
A modest handicap, confined to apprentice riders, run at an uneven pace. The winner enjoyed the run of the race.

4482 E.B.F./JOHN SMITH'S PLEASLEY MINERS WELFARE NOVICE STKS 1m 54y
6:15 (6:15) (Class 5) 2-Y-O **£4,533** (£1,348; £674; £336) **Stalls** Centre

Form RPR
0522 **1** **Shannersburg (IRE)**[14] 4037 2-8-12 76............................ ChrisCatlin 3 81
(E J O'Neill) *chsd ldr: led over 2f out: edgd lft ins fnl f: rdn out* **8/1**[3]
012 **2** *2* **Unnefer (FR)**[17] 3938 2-9-4 90.. TedDurcan 5 82
(H R A Cecil) *hld up in tch: rdn over 2f out: edgd rt over 1f out: styd on same pce* **8/15**[1]
1 **3** *1* **Semah Harold**[35] 3404 2-9-2 0.................................... GrahamGibbons 2 78
(E S McMahon) *sn led: hdd over 2f out: rdn over 1f out: no ex ins fnl f* **14/1**
1 **4** *3 1/2* **Jim Martin**[17] 3951 2-9-4 0.. J-PGuillambert 1 72
(J R Weymes) *trckd ldrs: racd keenly: rdn over 2f out: wknd over 1f out* **7/1**[2]
5 *nk* **Piermarini** 2-8-12 0... GregFairley 6 65
(M Johnston) *prom: rdn over 2f out: hung lft and wknd over 1f out* **7/1**[2]

1m 47.06s (0.66) **Going Correction** +0.20s/f (Good) 5 Ran SP% **108.0**
Speed ratings (Par 94): **104,102,101,97,97**
CSF £12.57 TOTE £8.20: £3.40, £1.10; EX 14.00.

Owner Mrs S J Brookhouse **Bred** Dermot Cantillon & Fiona Craig **Trained** Averham Park, Notts

FOCUS

An interesting novice event for the grade. It produced a very decent winning time for a race like this, especially considering that the early pace was just average.

NOTEBOOK

Shannersburg(IRE) relished the easing ground and opened his account at the fifth time of asking in ready fashion. He took the bull by the horns nearing the two-furlong pole and never really looked in trouble therafter, scoring with a little in hand. Although he probably handled the ground best of all, the step up to this trip no doubt worked the oracle and he rates as progressive. (op 15-2)

Unnefer(FR) was not seen at his best on this softening ground, despite having previously won his maiden on an easy surface at Ascot. He would have also benefitted from a more positive ride as the race panned out, so is certainly not one to judge too harshly on the back of this effort. However, he does still have to really prove that he is worthy of his official mark of 90. (tchd 4-9, 4-7 and 4-6 in a place)

Semah Harold, who defied odds of 20-1 when winning on his debut at Wolverhampton 35 days previously, was given a positive ride on this switch to turf over the extra furlong. He was found out nearing the final furlong, but was still not at all disgraced and should prove a little happier when reverting to a sounder surface in due course. (op 11-1 tchd 16-1)

Jim Martin did not help his cause by running too freely and got bogged down shortly after passing the two-furlong marker. He may be better off reverting to 7f in the short term. (op 13-2 tchd 8-1)

Piermarini, a 52,000gns brother to the decent stayer Cruzspiel, hung fire when asked for maximum effort and was well beaten off in the end. He is entitled to improve a deal for this debut experience, however, and may well prefer better ground. (op 8-1 tchd 10-1)

4483 POINTON'S DEFECT-FREE HANDOVER H'CAP — 1m 6f 15y

6:45 (6:46) (Class 3) (0-90,85) 3-Y-O+ **£7,124** (£2,119; £1,059; £529) **Stalls** Low

Form				RPR
230	**1**		**Sphinx (FR)**[18] [3898] 9-10-0 **83**........(b) JohnEgan 1 (Jamie Poulton) *hld up: hdwy over 5f out: rdn to ld over 1f out: styd on wl* **6/1**[3]	93+
2111	**2**	*3*	**Olimpo (FR)**[26] [3692] 6-9-9 **83**........ JamesMillman(5) 3 (B R Millman) *led: hung rt thrght: rdn and hdd over 1f out: no ex fnl f* **5/1**[2]	88
0544	**3**	*hd*	**Salute (IRE)**[24] [3748] 8-9-13 **82**........ RobertHavlin 4 (P G Murphy) *chsd ldrs: rdn over 2f out: no ex fnl f* **14/1**	87
1022	**4**	*3 1/2*	**Prince Sabaah (IRE)**[16] [3993] 3-9-3 **85**........ RyanMoore 7 (R Hannon) *trckd ldr: rdn over 4f out: wknd fnl f* **5/4**[1]	85
-012	**5**	*15*	**Rehearsed (IRE)**[17] [3969] 4-9-3 **72**........ SteveDrowne 6 (H Morrison) *stmbld s: hld up: pushed along 10f out: wknd over 3f out* **6/1**[3]	51
1621	**6**	*82*	**Takafu (USA)**[20] [3858] 5-10-0 **83**........ IanMongan 8 (W S Kittow) *s.i.s: sn chsng ldrs: wknd over 3f out* **6/1**[3]	—

3m 7.22s (0.12) **Going Correction** +0.20s/f (Good)
WFA 3 from 4yo+ 13lb **6** Ran SP% **110.6**
Speed ratings (Par 107): **107,105,105,103,94 47**
CSF £33.91 CT £380.35 TOTE £7.30: £4.40, £3.60; EX 31.20.

Owner R W Huggins **Bred** M Arbib **Trained** Whitcombe, Dorset

FOCUS

A good staying handicap, run at a strong pace. The winner is value for a bit further and is unbeaten now in three outings over this course and distance. The first two have been rated as both posting personal bests.

NOTEBOOK

Sphinx(FR) bounced right back to form on this more suitable surface and did the job comfortably. The decent early pace played right into his hands, he rates value for a bit further than the winning margin and he has now been successful on all of his three outings over this course and distance. It would not be the biggest surprise to see him follow up granted similar underfoot conditions, although this was his highest winning mark to date.

Olimpo(FR), bidding fo a four-timer off a 4lb higher mark, was given his usual positive ride, but he tended to hang to his right throughout and was not at his very best. He still has to truly prove his stamina over this trip. Official explanation: jockey said gelding hung right (op 4-1 tchd 11-2)

Salute(IRE) continues to run well in defeat and helps to set the level of this form. He is going need some respite in the weights to win again, however, and that is not going to happen with efforts such as this. (tchd 20-1)

Prince Sabaah(IRE), the sole three-year-old in the field and well backed, simply failed to get home on this further step up in trip on the softening ground. A drop back to 1m4f now looks in order. (op 7-4)

Rehearsed(IRE) has shown all of her best form on much quicker ground and could never get into this. (op 5-1 tchd 9-2)

Takafu(USA), 2lb higher, ran a dismal race and clearly something was amiss with him. Official explanation: vet said gelding was found to have a sore pharynx (op 11-2)

4484 JOHN SMITH'S CHURCH WARSOP MINERS WELFARE NURSERY — 6f 15y

7:15 (7:17) (Class 5) 2-Y-O **£2,914** (£867; £433; £216) **Stalls** High

Form				RPR
2220	**1**		**Irving Place**[32] [3508] 2-9-4 **75**........ HayleyTurner 8 (M L W Bell) *hld up: plld hrd: nt clr run over 2f out: hdwy over 1f out: rdn to ld wl ins fnl f* **10/1**	78
0013	**2**	*hd*	**We Have A Dream**[7] [4255] 2-8-3 **60**........ FrancisNorton 6 (W R Muir) *led: rdn over 1f out: hdd wl ins fnl f* **9/2**[2]	62
01	**3**	*1 1/4*	**Ginger Pickle**[28] [3606] 2-9-7 **78**........ J-PGuillambert 7 (J R Weymes) *s.i.s: hld up: swtchd lft and hdwy over 1f out: r.o* **10/1**	76
024	**4**	*1*	**Kaldoun Kingdom (IRE)**[17] [3967] 2-9-1 **72**........ TedDurcan 2 (E A L Dunlop) *hld up: hdwy 2f out: rdn over 1f out: no ex wl ins fnl f* **6/1**	67
5316	**5**	*shd*	**Barbarossa**[31] [3524] 2-9-7 **78**........ RyanMoore 3 (R Hannon) *s.i.s: hld up: hdwy over 2f out: rdn and ev ch over 1f out: edgd lft and no ex ins fnl f* **3/1**[1]	73
056	**6**	*1 1/2*	**Mistress Cooper**[15] [4016] 2-8-5 **62**........ NickyMackay 9 (W J Musson) *chsd ldrs: rdn over 2f out: no ex fnl f* **13/2**	52
010	**7**	*1 1/4*	**Bonny's Babe**[10] [4154] 2-8-1 **58** ow1........ ChrisCatlin 4 (B Smart) *s.i.s: hld up: pushed along 1/2-way: rdn and hung lft over 1f out: n.d* **25/1**	44
0321	**8**	*3 1/2*	**Brixworth Scribe**[48] [2984] 2-9-3 **74**........ PaulEddery 5 (B Smart) *chsd ldr: rdn and ev ch whn hung lft wl over 1f out: sn wknd* **5/1**[3]	49
1524	**9**	*shd*	**Alexander Monarchy (IRE)**[11] [4136] 2-8-8 **65**........ NCallan 1 (K A Ryan) *chsd ldrs: rdn over 2f out: wknd over 1f out* **20/1**	39

1m 16.52s (1.52) **Going Correction** +0.05s/f (Good) **9** Ran SP% **114.3**
Speed ratings (Par 94): **91,90,89,87,87 85,83,79,79**
CSF £53.98 CT £465.49 TOTE £12.30: £2.80, £1.70, £3.00; EX 69.10.

Owner M Hawtin Mrs A Scotney & D Asplin **Bred** Whitsbury Manor Stud **Trained** Newmarket, Suffolk

FOCUS

A modest nursery run at a fair pace. The first pair came clear and the form looks sound.

NOTEBOOK

Irving Place, back in trip, once again refused to settle under restraint in the early stages but still had enough in the tank to get up at the business end. This would have been the easiest ground he has raced on to date and he is best kept to this trip for the short term, but he must consent to relax through his races if he is to progress further. (op 14-1)

We Have A Dream, dropped 4lb, gave his all from the front and only just got reeled in. He was nicely clear of the remainder, but will no doubt now go back up in the weights for this. (op 8-1)

Ginger Pickle, off the mark over 5f last time, was always struggling after missing the break and never seriously figured. He still finished his race well, however, and this was no disgrace under top weight on his nursery bow. (op 7-1)

Kaldoun Kingdom(IRE) failed to raise his game on this switch to a nursery, but ideally he wants quicker ground and is not one to give up on just yet. Another furlong may also be to his liking now. (op 5-1 tchd 9-2)

Barbarossa, popular in the betting ring, emerged to have every chance despite his slow start and can have no excuses. (op 7-2)

Brixworth Scribe, back up in trip on this nursery debut, hung fire when asked for his maximum effort and is one to have reservations about on this evidence. (op 4-1)

4485 JOHN SMITH'S GREASELY MINERS WELFARE CONDITIONS STKS — 5f 13y

7:45 (7:45) (Class 4) 3-Y-O+ **£6,232** (£1,866; £933; £467) **Stalls** High

Form				RPR
00/2	**1**		**Galeota (IRE)**[10] [4183] 5-8-11 107........ RyanMoore 3 (R Hannon) *w ldr tl led over 3f out: rdn out* **1/1**[1]	107+
0000	**2**	*1 1/4*	**Biniou (IRE)**[10] [4190] 4-8-11 100........ RobertHavlin 7 (R M H Cowell) *hld up in tch: plld hrd: trckd wnr 1/2-way: rdn and ev ch 1f out: styd on same pce* **4/1**[3]	103
0434	**3**	*1/2*	**Masta Plasta (IRE)**[10] [4190] 4-8-11 98........ TedDurcan 8 (D Nicholls) *chsd ldrs: rdn over 1f out: styd on same pce ins fnl f* **15/8**[2]	101
0500	**4**	*9*	**Axis Shield (IRE)**[25] [3708] 4-8-6 45........ HayleyTurner 4 (M C Chapman) *led: hdd over 3f out: rdn: edgd lft and wknd over 1f out* **100/1**	64?

60.78 secs (-1.02) **Going Correction** +0.05s/f (Good)
WFA 3 from 4yo+ 3lb **4** Ran SP% **105.8**
Speed ratings (Par 105): **110,108,107,92**
CSF £5.07 TOTE £2.20; EX 4.40.

Owner Robin Blunt **Bred** W Maxwell Ervine **Trained** East Everleigh, Wilts

FOCUS

A decent little conditions sprint but dubious form, with none of the first three particularly solid.

4486 JOHN SMITH'S NOTTS LADIES SECTION H'CAP — 5f 13y

8:15 (8:17) (Class 5) (0-70,70) 3-Y-O+ **£2,914** (£867; £433; £216) **Stalls** High

Form				RPR
	1		**Haajes**[53] [2849] 3-9-6 **69**........ JohnEgan 2 (D J Murphy) *sn outpcd: hdwy u.p over 1f out: led ins fnl f: r.o* **9/1**	78
0200	**2**	*1 3/4*	**Bookiesindex Boy**[11] [4123] 3-9-7 **70**........ TedDurcan 1 (J R Jenkins) *hld up: hdwy 2f out: rdn over 1f out: styd on same pce ins fnl f* **20/1**	73
3-30	**3**	*hd*	**Bahamian Duke**[16] [3998] 4-9-3 **63**........ J-PGuillambert 8 (K R Burke) *s.i.s: outpcd: r.o ins fnl f: nrst fin* **8/1**[3]	65
-063	**4**	*1*	**After The Show**[22] [3791] 6-9-10 **70**........ ChrisCatlin 6 (Rae Guest) *s.i.s: sn chsng ldrs: rdn over 2f out: styd on same pce fnl f* **7/2**[1]	68
0210	**5**	*nk*	**Silver Prelude**[10] [4165] 6-9-0 **60**........ NCallan 3 (D K Ivory) *led: rdn over 1f out: edgd lft and hdd ins fnl f: no ex* **8/1**[3]	57
0533	**6**	*2*	**Bobby Rose**[12] [4103] 4-9-2 **62**........(b1) RobertHavlin 4 (D K Ivory) *chsd ldrs: rdn over 2f out: wknd ins fnl f* **9/2**[2]	52
3000	**7**	*3/4*	**Smokin Beau**[14] [4038] 10-9-5 **70**........ HaddenFrost(5) 7 (N P Littmoden) *w ldr tl rdn 1/2-way: wknd fnl f* **14/1**	57
5-10	**8**	*3 1/2*	**Steel City Boy (IRE)**[81] [1999] 4-9-9 **69**........ DanielTudhope 5 (D Carroll) *chsd ldrs over 3f* **9/1**	44
660-	**9**	*shd*	**Niteowl Lad (IRE)**[375] [4110] 5-9-10 **70**........ PaulMulrennan 12 (J Balding) *hld up in tch: rdn and wknd over 1f out* **33/1**	44
0021	**10**	*4*	**Our Fugitive (IRE)**[18] [3906] 5-9-7 **67**........(b) FrancisNorton 11 (A W Carroll) *chsd ldrs: rdn 1/2-way: wknd over 1f out* **7/2**[1]	27

61.58 secs (-0.22) **Going Correction** +0.05s/f (Good)
WFA 3 from 4yo+ 3lb **10** Ran SP% **119.2**
Speed ratings (Par 103): **103,100,99,98,97 94,93,87,87,81**
CSF £175.10 CT £1543.52 TOTE £15.00: £4.10, £1.90, £3.30; EX 190.50 Place 6 £386.20, Place 5 £175.24.

Owner Willie McKay **Bred** Irish National Stud **Trained** Bawtry, S Yorks

FOCUS

A modest sprint handicap run at a good pace. The form can be rated through the third.

Bahamian Duke Official explanation: jockey said gelding suffered interference at start

Our Fugitive(IRE) Official explanation: jockey said gelding never travelled

T/Plt: £922.10 to a £1 stake. Pool: £62,340.35. 49.35 winning tickets. T/Qpdt: £184.90 to a £1 stake. Pool: £4,049.20. 16.20 winning tickets. CR

4036 BEVERLEY (R-H)

Wednesday, August 15

OFFICIAL GOING: Good to firm (good in places) (9.7) changing to good after race 3 (3.10)

The ground was reckoned to be riding 'on the easy side of good'.

Wind: light 1/2 behind Weather: overcast, light showers

4487 EBF SPORTHULL.CO.UK MAIDEN STKS — 7f 100y

2:10 (2:12) (Class 4) 2-Y-O **£5,829** (£1,734; £866; £432) **Stalls** High

Form				RPR
2	**1**		**Bonjour Allure (IRE)**[19] [3916] 2-8-12 0........ SebSanders 15 (Mrs A Duffield) *chsd ldrs: styd on wl fnl f: n.m.r but led post* **5/2**[2]	81
	2	*shd*	**Dubai Time** 2-9-3 0........ NCallan 13 (K A Ryan) *w ldr: led over 3f out: kpt on wl: edgd rt and hdd post* **5/1**[3]	85+
0	**3**	*2 1/2*	**Floristry**[41] [3245] 2-8-12 0........ KDarley 5 (Sir Michael Stoute) *trckd ldrs: chal over 3f out: edgd lft over 1f out: kpt on same pce* **7/1**	74
6	**4**	*1 1/4*	**Hampstead Heath (IRE)**[61] [2632] 2-9-3 0........ J-PGuillambert 14 (M Johnston) *t.k.h: sn trcking ldrs: checked 6f out: effrt 3f out: styd on same pce* **9/4**[1]	76
05	**5**	*2*	**Bavarian Nordic (USA)**[15] [4037] 2-9-3 0........ StephenDonohoe 7 (E A L Dunlop) *hld up in midfield: effrt 3f out: nvr nr ldrs* **9/1**	71
56	**6**	*6*	**The Last Bottle (IRE)**[70] [2371] 2-9-3 0........ MickyFenton 6 (T P Tate) *hld up towards rr: pushed wd 6f out: kpt on fnl 2f: nvr nr ldrs* **12/1**	56

The Form Book, Raceform Ltd, Compton, RG20 6NL

0 **7** *4* **Talon (IRE)**[13] 4110 2-9-3 0 .... PaulMulrennan 1 46
(W J Haggas) *swtchd rt after s: bhd tl kpt on fnl 3f* **40/1**
06 **8** *shd* **Stateside (CAN)**[19] 3916 2-8-12 0 .... PaulHanagan 9 41
(R A Fahey) *s.i.s: kpt on fnl 2f: nvr a factor* **40/1**
5 **9** *3/4* **Eton Fable (IRE)**[18] 3977 2-9-3 0 .... TPQueally 11 44
(W J H Ratcliffe) *promint: carried wd over 3f out: hung rt and wknd over 1f out* **25/1**
0 **10** *4* **Mahadee (IRE)**[10] 4192 2-9-0 0 .... WilliamBuick(3) 4 34
(C E Brittain) *sn bhd and drvn along: nvr on terms* **33/1**
00 **11** *7* **Cottam Breeze**[24] 3760 2-8-12 0 .... PaddyAspell 3 11
(M W Easterby) *chsd ldrs: c wd and lost pl over 3f out* **100/1**
0 **12** *2 1/2* **Brough (IRE)**[11] 4173 2-8-10 0 .... JamesO'Reilly(7) 10 10
(J O'Reilly) *led: hung lft: c wd and hdd over 3f out: sn lost pl* **100/1**
13 *6* **Miss Holderness** 2-8-12 0 .... DavidAllan 8 —
(J O'Reilly) *s.i.s: a bhd* **100/1**
14 *1 3/4* **Halton Castle** 2-9-3 0 .... GrahamGibbons 12 —
(E J Alston) *chsd ldrs: lost pl over 2f out: sn bhd and eased* **50/1**

1m 33.46s (-0.85) **Going Correction** -0.25s/f (Firm) **14** Ran SP% **122.8**
Speed ratings (Par 96): **94,93,91,89,87 80,75,75,74,70 62,59,52,50**
CSF £15.19 TOTE £4.00: £1.60, £2.10, £2.70; EX 19.60.
Owner Middleham Park Racing XLVIII **Bred** Mount Coote Partnership **Trained** Constable Burton, N Yorks
■ Stewards' Enquiry : N Callan caution: careless riding

FOCUS
A fair two-year-old maiden for this track in which stamina was at a premium but the form looks pretty solid.

NOTEBOOK
Bonjour Allure(IRE) knew her job this time and, staying on in most determined fashion, put her head in front on the line despite being tightened up by the runner-up. She looks a fair long-term prospect. (tchd 3-1)
Dubai Time, a medium-sized, most likeable March foal, knew his job. After being matched at 1.01 on the exchanges, he tired slightly and rolled towards the running rail well inside the last. Had he dead-heated he would have been stood down. He can surely go one better soon. (op 8-1)
Floristry, quite a big filly who stands over plenty of ground, again showed ability but she is still not the finished article and, after challenging the runner-up, she drifted towards the centre of the track. (op 11-2)
Hampstead Heath(IRE), a short-backed, robust type, took a fierce grip and had to be checked at the crossing leaving the back straight. He was very slow to pick up, but stayed on all the way to the line. This should have completed his education. Official explanation: jockey said colt ran too free (op 5-2 tchd 15-8)
Bavarian Nordic(USA) again showed ability and a mile nursery will suit him ideally. (tchd 8-1 and 10-1)
The Last Bottle(IRE), absent for ten weeks after being gelded, was knocked back in traffic at the crossing leaving the back straight. He kept on in his own time and this will have hopefully helped settle him down. The nursery route is now open.
Brough(IRE) Official explanation: jockey said colt hung left-handed
Halton Castle Official explanation: jockey said gelding was struck into

4488 JOURNAL CLAIMING STKS 1m 100y
2:40 (2:43) (Class 5) 3-Y-0+ **£2,914** (£867; £433; £216) **Stalls** High

Form RPR
4000 **1** **United Nations**[11] 4176 6-9-13 70 .... SebSanders 11 76
(N Wilson) *trckd ldrs: led over 1f out: sn drvn clr* **1/1**[1]
5000 **2** *8* **Credential**[32] 3530 5-9-11 56 .... StephenDonohoe 6 56
(John A Harris) *s.i.s: hdwy 3f out: styd on to take 2nd ins fnl f: no ch w wnr* **9/2**[2]
-600 **3** *2 1/2* **Sion Hill (IRE)**[19] 3917 6-9-5 45 ....(p) TPQueally 2 44
(John A Harris) *chsd ldr: led 3f out tl over 1f out: one pce* **25/1**
1600 **4** *8* **Weet Yer Tern (IRE)**[62] 1210 5-9-6 44 .... KDarley 1 27
(W M Brisbourne) *hld up in rr: hdwy over 2f out: kpt on fnl f: nvr on terms* **14/1**
0000 **5** *nk* **Height Of Esteem**[13] 4099 4-9-5 38 .... DavidAllan 12 25
(W M Brisbourne) *t.k.h in rr: hdwy 3f out: nvr a factor* **33/1**
0400 **6** *hd* **Cottam Eclipse**[7] 4294 6-9-0 44 .... MarkLawson(3) 8 22
(I W McInnes) *led tl 3f out: lost pl over 1f out* **20/1**
0000 **7** *8* **Pixie Princess (IRE)**[6] 4337 3-8-11 40 .... MickyFenton 7 5
(Miss V Haigh) *chsd ldrs: effrt centre over 2f out: sn wknd* **50/1**
5050 **8** *1/2* **Filey Buoy**[2] 4449 5-8-12 43 ....(v) MichaelJStainton(5) 9 3
(R M Whitaker) *prom: effrt centre over 2f out: sn wknd* **8/1**
000 **9** *3* **Afric Star**[9] 4226 3-8-3 38 ow3 .... AndrewElliott(3) 4 —
(John A Harris) *sn bhd and drvn along: nvr a factor* **50/1**
0056 **10** *1* **Time To Regret**[15] 4042 7-9-5 50 .... DanielTudhope 5 —
(I W McInnes) *in tch: c stands' side 3f out: sn lost pl* **11/2**[3]
260/ **11** *hd* **Forest Viking (IRE)**[740] 3185 5-9-5 43 ....(p) PaddyAspell 13 —
(J S Wainwright) *hld up in rr: sme hdwy over 4f out: wknd fnl 2f* **16/1**
6000 **12** *1* **Splodger Mac (IRE)**[2] 4449 8-9-2 47 .... DuranFentiman(3) 10 —
(N Bycroft) *mid-div: drvn and lost pl 6f out: sn bhd* **18/1**
00-0 **13** *3/4* **Marryl**[26] 3714 3-8-7 33 ....(b) AndrewMullen(3) 3 —
(M W Easterby) *sn bhd and drvn along* **66/1**

1m 46.28s (-1.12) **Going Correction** -0.25s/f (Firm)
WFA 3 from 4yo+ 7lb **13** Ran SP% **129.5**
Speed ratings (Par 103): **95,87,84,76,76 76,68,67,64,63 63,62,61**
CSF £5.71 TOTE £2.10: £1.30, £1.70, £6.40; EX 7.90.The winner was claimed by M W Easterby for £10,000.
Owner Mrs Karan Ridley **Bred** Cyril Humphris **Trained** Flaxton, N Yorks

FOCUS
A typical claimer and a runaway success for the winner who was clear top on official ratings, but not that solid in behind.

4489 CORPORATE SPORT YOU WEAR IT WELL H'CAP 5f
3:10 (3:10) (Class 4) (0-85,83) 3-Y-0+ **£6,477** (£1,927; £963; £481) **Stalls** High

Form RPR
1412 **1** **Melalchrist**[15] 4038 5-9-6 79 ....(b) NCallan 7 91
(K A Ryan) *mde all: kpt on u.p fnl f: hld on towards fin* **11/4**[2]
3140 **2** *1/2* **Efistorm**[39] 3298 6-9-10 83 .... TPQueally 5 93
(C R Dore) *chsd ldrs: wnt 2nd over 1f out: kpt on wl towards fin* **14/1**
5542 **3** *2* **Welcome Approach**[7] 4289 4-8-3 65 .... AndrewElliott(3) 3 68
(J R Weymes) *chsd ldrs on outer: outpcd over 2f out: styd on wl fnl f* **11/2**[3]
1641 **4** *1/2* **Garstang**[9] 4233 4-9-0 73 6ex ....(b) LPKeniry 2 74
(Peter Grayson) *s.s: swtchd rt after s: hdwy and hung rt over 1f out: nt rch ldrs* **12/1**
3151 **5** *hd* **The History Man (IRE)**[7] 4289 4-8-6 72 6ex ....(b) SCreighton(7) 8 72
(M Mullineaux) *chsd wnr: wknd fnl f* **12/1**
5020 **6** *3 1/2* **Namir (IRE)**[12] 4122 5-9-1 77 ....(vt) DuranFentiman(3) 9 65
(D Shaw) *in rr: kpt on fnl 2f: nvr on terms* **8/1**
025 **7** *3/4* **Bo McGinty (IRE)**[4] 4389 6-9-4 77 ....(b) PaulHanagan 1 62
(R A Fahey) *in tch on outer: lost pl over 2f out* **13/2**
5050 **8** *1 1/4* **Sparkling Eyes**[18] 3944 3-9-1 77 .... J-PGuillambert 4 57
(C E Brittain) *a towards rr* **25/1**
3211 **9** *3 1/2* **Divine Spirit**[13] 4103 6-9-1 74 .... SebSanders 10 42
(M Dods) *chsd ldrs: wknd over 1f out: bhd whn eased ins fnl f* **5/2**[1]

62.18 secs (-1.82) **Going Correction** -0.25s/f (Firm)
WFA 3 from 4yo+ 3lb **9** Ran SP% **121.0**
Speed ratings (Par 105): **104,103,100,99,98 93,92,90,84**
CSF £43.06 CT £206.33 TOTE £3.70: £1.40, £4.40, £2.40; EX 74.10.
Owner T G S Wood **Bred** A C M Spalding **Trained** Hambleton, N Yorks

FOCUS
A competitive sprint handicap dominated by the all-the-way winner, helped by racing close to the far rail. The form looks solid with the runner-up to form.
Divine Spirit Official explanation: jockey said gelding lost its action 2f out

4490 WBX.COM H'CAP 2m 35y
3:40 (3:40) (Class 4) (0-85,81) 3-Y-0+ **£5,181** (£1,541; £770; £384) **Stalls** High

Form RPR
2-06 **1** **Sivota (IRE)**[55] 2808 3-7-11 62 .... WilliamBuick(3) 6 70
(T P Tate) *trckd ldrs: wnt 2nd 4f out: led over 1f out: kpt on wl* **13/2**
2042 **2** *2* **Serpentaria**[29] 3609 3-9-5 81 .... SebSanders 4 86
(Sir Mark Prescott) *hld up in tch: stdy hdwy over 3f out: styd on fnl f: snatched 2nd nr fin* **1/1**[1]
1200 **3** *hd* **Mister Arjay (USA)**[35] 3412 7-9-13 74 .... PaulHanagan 1 79
(B Ellison) *led: qcknd 6f out: hdd over 1f out: kpt on same pce* **9/1**
6324 **4** *8* **Muntami (IRE)**[18] 3963 6-9-6 67 .... StephenDonohoe 5 62
(John A Harris) *hld up in rr: hdwy 7f out: wknd over 1f out* **6/1**[3]
-102 **5** *1* **Industrial Star (IRE)**[11] 4179 6-9-11 72 ....(p) KDarley 3 66
(Micky Hammond) *chsd ldrs: drvn 5f out: outpcd over 3f out: wknd 2f out* **5/1**[2]
00-5 **6** *55* **Double Deputy (IRE)**[10] 3027 6-10-0 75 ....(p) GrahamGibbons 2 3
(J J Quinn) *chsd ldrs: drvn 6f out: lost pl over 3f out: sn bhd: t.o* **7/1**

3m 38.06s (-1.44) **Going Correction** -0.075s/f (Good)
WFA 3 from 6yo+ 15lb **6** Ran SP% **116.8**
Speed ratings (Par 105): **100,99,98,94,94 66**
CSF £14.27 TOTE £6.70: £3.10, £1.30; EX 16.30.
Owner S M Racing **Bred** M Duffy **Trained** Tadcaster, N Yorks

FOCUS
A tactical affair in which the two three-year-olds finished first and second. The well-handled winner stole a march on the runner-up and the form is not entirely solid.

4491 EAST RIDING MAIL H'CAP 1m 1f 207y
4:10 (4:11) (Class 5) (0-70,80) 3-Y-0 **£3,562** (£1,059; £529; £264) **Stalls** High

Form RPR
3000 **1** **Paradise Walk**[12] 4139 3-8-7 56 .... PaulHanagan 7 71
(E W Tuer) *hld up in mid-div: gd hdwy over 2f out: led jst ins fnl f: styd on strly: readily* **12/1**
0223 **2** *3* **Shotley Mac**[4] 4411 3-8-2 51 oh1 ....(b) PaulFessey 11 60
(N Bycroft) *led: qcknd over 3f out: clr over 2f out: hdd and no ex jst ins fnl f* **13/2**[3]
06-0 **3** *6* **Golden Folly**[23] 3804 3-8-1 53 .... WilliamBuick(3) 12 50
(Lady Herries) *sn trcking ldrs: kpt on same pce fnl 2f* **9/1**
-640 **4** *1* **Green Day Packer (IRE)**[5] 893 3-8-6 58 .... AndrewElliott(3) 6 53
(P C Haslam) *trckd ldrs: t.k.h: one pce fnl 3f* **4/1**[2]
4033 **5** *2 1/2* **Myfrenchconnection (IRE)**[9] 4220 3-7-13 51 oh1. DuranFentiman(3) 1 41
(P T Midgley) *in rr: kpt on fnl 3f: nvr nr ldrs* **12/1**
0-16 **6** *4* **Surprise Pension (IRE)**[43] 3181 3-8-6 55 .... GrahamGibbons 5 37
(J J Quinn) *chsd ldrs: hung lft and wknd over 2f out* **9/4**[1]
5540 **7** *1 3/4* **Fairly Honest**[7] 4270 3-8-3 59 .... WilliamCarson(7) 10 38
(P W Hiatt) *t.k.h in rr: brought wd and racd alone stands' side over 3f out: nvr a factor* **9/1**
0000 **8** *9* **Cardington Queen**[7] 4291 3-7-9 51 oh6 .... DanielleMcCreery(7) 4 12
(M Mullineaux) *s.i.s: a in rr: bhd fnl 3f* **66/1**
1560 **9** *13* **Tutor (IRE)**[27] 3691 3-9-7 70 ....(tp) NCallan 9 —
(W J Haggas) *trckd ldrs: t.k.h: rdn and wknd over 2f out* **8/1**
0-00 **10** *6* **Remark (IRE)**[44] 3159 3-7-13 51 oh1 ....(t) AndrewMullen(3) 3 —
(M W Easterby) *a in rr: bhd fnl 3f* **8/1**
06-0 **11** *26* **Little Rutland**[23] 3804 3-8-7 56 ow1 .... MickyFenton 8 —
(E J O'Neill) *sn trcking ldrs: t.k.h: drvn over 4f out: sn lost pl and bhd: t.o* **40/1**

2m 5.53s (-1.77) **Going Correction** -0.075s/f (Good) **11** Ran SP% **125.6**
Speed ratings (Par 100): **104,101,96,96,94 90,89,82,71,67 46**
CSF £94.05 CT £759.39 TOTE £17.30: £4.80, £2.30, £2.70; EX 114.30.
Owner E Tuer **Bred** Coln Valley Stud **Trained** Great Smeaton, N Yorks

FOCUS
A modest handicap run at a steady pace before the runner-up started to wind it up from the front. The form looks sound enough.
Surprise Pension(IRE) Official explanation: jockey said gelding was unsuited by the loose ground
Fairly Honest Official explanation: jockey said gelding hung left throughout

4492 MAIL NEWS AND MEDIA MAIDEN STKS 1m 1f 207y
4:40 (4:41) (Class 5) 3-Y-0+ **£3,562** (£1,059; £529; £264) **Stalls** High

Form RPR
1 **Milne Graden** 3-9-3 0 .... TPQueally 4 78
(J Noseda) *trckd ldrs: t.k.h: shkn up over 5f out: reminders over 3f out: wnt 2nd 2f out: hung rt: led jst ins fnl f: styd on* **11/4**[2]
03 **2** *2* **Muqadam (IRE)**[37] 3365 3-9-3 0 .... KDarley 6 74
(Sir Michael Stoute) *trckd ldrs: chal 5f out: led 3f out: edgd lft and hdd jst ins fnl f: no ex* **4/7**[1]
0 **3** *12* **Final Overture (FR)**[38] 3349 3-8-12 0 .... PaulHanagan 2 45
(H R A Cecil) *hld up in tch: drvn over 4f out: outpcd fnl 2f* **9/1**[3]
00 **4** *8* **Private Soldier**[8] 4258 4-9-12 0 .... SamHitchcott 7 34
(N J Vaughan) *t.k.h: sn trcking ldrs: led 5f out tl 3f out: wknd over 1f out* **50/1**
24 **5** *13* **Lan Kwai Fong**[32] 3561 3-8-12 0 .... DavidAllan 3 —
(T D Easterby) *led early: lost pl over 5f out: sn bhd* **12/1**
05-0 **6** *15* **Rythm N Rhyme (IRE)**[27] 3684 8-9-9 32 .... AndrewElliott(3) 5 —
(John A Harris) *sn led: hdd 5f out: lost pl over 3f out: sn bhd* **50/1**

2m 6.14s (-1.16) **Going Correction** -0.075s/f (Good)
WFA 3 from 4yo+ 9lb **6** Ran SP% **111.9**
Speed ratings (Par 103): **101,99,89,83,73 61**
CSF £4.62 TOTE £3.90: £1.90, £1.10; EX 5.70.
Owner Mrs Susan Roy **Bred** Newsells Park Stud Limited **Trained** Newmarket, Suffolk

FOCUS
An uncompetitive maiden with the first two a long way clear and the runner-up setting a modest standard. The expensively-bred winner has the potential to go on to better things.

4493 MAILHOMES.CO.UK H'CAP — 1m 4f 16y
5:10 (5:10) (Class 6) (0-65,65) 3-Y-0+ — £2,914 (£867; £433; £216) Stalls High

Form — RPR

3424 **1** **Music Review**[26] 3719 3-9-2 **64** .... PaulHanagan 9 — 77
(R A Fahey) *trckd ldrs: chal on ins over 2f out: led over 1f out: styd on wl* **9/2**[2]

21 **2** *1 1/4* **Don'Tcallmeginger (IRE)**[15] 4040 4-8-11 **53** .... PatrickHills(5) 12 — 64
(M H Tompkins) *led: hdd over 1f out: kpt on same pce ins fnl f* **15/8**[1]

0513 **3** *5* **Thorny Mandate**[13] 4096 5-10-0 **65** .... KDarley 10 — 68
(W M Brisbourne) *hld up in rr: hdwy and nt clr run over 2f out: swtchd outside and styd on* **12/1**

2-23 **4** *1/2* **Casual Affair**[13] 4105 4-9-12 **63** .... NCallan 3 — 65
(J D Bethell) *chsd ldrs: one pce fnl 2f* **11/2**[3]

5045 **5** *nk* **The Pen**[11] 4156 5-9-3 **57** .... AndrewElliott(3) 4 — 59
(C W Fairhurst) *in rr: hdwy on outer over 2f out: styd on fnl f* **8/1**

0-65 **6** *1* **Parchment (IRE)**[29] 3610 5-9-6 **57** ....(b) PaddyAspell 7 — 57
(A J Lockwood) *hld up in rr: hdwy 3f out: kpt on one pce* **11/1**

00-6 **7** *2* **Rocket Force (USA)**[28] 3638 7-9-12 **63** .... DanielTudhope 6 — 60
(N Wilson) *trckd ldrs: wknd over 1f out* **25/1**

6440 **8** *1 1/4* **Garibaldi (GER)**[82] 2007 5-9-3 **54** ....(b) DavidAllan 8 — 49
(J O'Reilly) *hld up in rr: hdwy 7f out: wknd 2f out* **20/1**

3503 **9** *6* **Patavium (IRE)**[17] 4003 4-8-13 **50** .... PaulFessey 5 — 35
(E W Tuer) *in tch on outer: wknd over 2f out* **9/1**

0-00 **10** *8* **Rosecliff**[18] 3976 5-10-0 **65** ....(tp) StephenDonohoe 1 — 38
(Heather Dalton) *swtchd rt after s: in rr: drvn 6f out: bhd fnl 3f* **16/1**

0/05 **11** *9* **Adjami (IRE)**[21] 3844 6-9-10 **61** .... TPQueally 2 — 19
(John A Harris) *trckd ldrs: wknd 4f out: sn bhd* **25/1**

2m 38.54s (-1.67) **Going Correction** -0.075s/f (Good)
WFA 3 from 4yo+ 11lb — **11** Ran SP% **123.8**
Speed ratings (Par 101): **102,101,97,97,97 96,95,94,90,85 79**
CSF £13.72 CT £97.39 TOTE £5.90: £1.80, £1.50, £2.70; EX 18.00 Place 6 £38.82, Place 5 £20.51.
Owner R A Fahey **Bred** Darley **Trained** Musley Bank, N Yorks

FOCUS
A modest handicap run at just a steady pace but a progressive winner and the form could be rated a little higher.
The Pen Official explanation: jockey said mare suffered interference going into 1st bend
Rosecliff Official explanation: jockey said gelding was unsuited by the loose ground
T/Plt: £26.60 to a £1 stake. Pool: £45,804.80. 1,254.00 winning tickets. T/Qpdt: £11.80 to a £1 stake. Pool: £2,066.90. 128.60 winning tickets. WG

4154 HAMILTON (R-H)
Wednesday, August 15

OFFICIAL GOING: Good to soft (6.5)
Wind: Slight across Weather: fine and showery

4494 PERTEMPS PEOPLE DEVELOPMENT "HANDS AND HEELS" APPRENTICE H'CAP (ROUND 4 OF APPRENTICE SERIES) — 6f 5y
5:50 (5:53) (Class 6) (0-65,64) 3-Y-0+ — £2,266 (£674; £337; £168) Stalls Low

Form — RPR

0603 **1** **The Salwick Flyer (IRE)**[27] 3674 4-8-9 **50** .... NSLawes(5) 12 — 57
(I Semple) *a.p: led 1/2-way: rdn and kpt on gamely fnl f* **6/1**[3]

-000 **2** *3/4* **Cumberland Road**[19] 3914 4-8-4 **45** ....(v) SophieDoyle(5) 4 — 50
(C A Mulhall) *sn prom: rdn along 2f out: kpt on ins fnl f* **125/1**

3604 **3** *shd* **Newkeylets**[11] 4157 4-8-8 **49** .... JamesRogers(5) 5 — 53
(I Semple) *a.p: rdn along 2f out: kpt on ins fnl f* **25/1**

0413 **4** *shd* **Rondo**[23] 3787 4-8-10 **51** .... DeanHeslop(5) 10 — 55+
(T D Barron) *slty hmpd s and bhd: gd hdwy 2f out: rdn and styd on same pce ins fnl f* **3/1**[1]

0000 **5** *1 3/4* **Bond Playboy**[14] 4083 7-9-4 **57** ....(p) PJBenson(3) 6 — 56
(G R Oldroyd) *wnt rt s: midfield tl hdwy 2f out: sn rdn and kpt on ins fnl f: nrst fin* **33/1**

032 **6** *hd* **Choreography**[8] 4251 4-9-7 **62** .... AdeleRothery(5) 7 — 60
(D Nicholls) *trckd ldrs: hdwy over 2f out: rdn wl over 1f out: drvn and no imp ent fnl f* **7/2**[2]

6450 **7** *3/4* **Oeuf A La Neige**[23] 3787 7-8-7 **48** .... LanceBetts(5) 2 — 44
(Miss L A Perratt) *dwlt and bhd tl styd on fnl 2f: nrst fin* **14/1**

442 **8** *1/2* **Mugeba**[18] 3950 6-9-5 **58** ....(vt) HarryPoulton(3) 11 — 53
(Miss Gay Kelleway) *trckd ldrs on outer: hdwy to chse wnr wl over 1f out: drvn ent fnl f and sn wknd* **6/1**[3]

6003 **9** *2* **Telepathic (IRE)**[17] 3996 7-8-5 **46** ow1 .... AdamCarter(5) 8 — 35
(A Berry) *sltly hmpd s: a towards rr* **25/1**

0302 **10** *nk* **Radiator Rooney (IRE)**[1] 4478 4-9-2 **57** ....(b) PatrickDonaghy(5) 3 — 45
(Patrick Morris, Ire) *cl up: rdn along over 2f out: sn wknd* **11/1**

4554 **11** *5* **Breaking Shadow (IRE)**[26] 3723 5-9-11 **64** .... WJCafferty(3) 1 — 37
(M A Peill) *led: rdn along and hdd 1/2-way: sn wknd* **15/2**

1m 15.54s (2.44) **Going Correction** +0.25s/f (Good) — **11** Ran SP% **114.0**
Speed ratings (Par 101): **93,92,91,91,89 89,88,87,84,84 77**
CSF £611.97 CT £16354.40 TOTE £8.50: £2.60, £38.40, £4.10; EX 695.70.
Owner The Irish Mafia **Bred** Piercetown Stud **Trained** Carluke, S Lanarks

FOCUS
A competitive low-grade handicap rated around the winner and third to recent form.
Mugeba Official explanation: jockey said mare hung right-handed throughout

4495 TARMAC LTD EBF NOVICE STKS — 1m 65y
6:20 (6:20) (Class 4) 2-Y-0 — £4,533 (£1,348; £674; £336) Stalls High

Form — RPR

3 **1** **McCartney (GER)**[21] 3856 2-8-12 **0** .... GregFairley 1 — 95+
(M Johnston) *trckd ldng pair gng wl: smooth hdwy to ld 2f out: sn clr* **6/4**[1]

33 **2** *7* **Doon Haymer (IRE)**[15] 4037 2-8-12 **0** .... TomEaves 5 — 74
(I Semple) *trckd ldrs: chsd along over 3f out and sn rdn: styd on ins fnl f: no ch w wnr* **9/2**[3]

412 **3** *1/2* **Nine Stories (IRE)**[21] 3838 2-9-5 **85** .... PaulMulrennan 7 — 80
(J Howard Johnson) *led 3f: cl up: rdn along 3f out: drvn wl over 1f out and sn one pce* **7/2**[2]

5221 **4** *1 1/4* **Shannersburg (IRE)**[1] 4482 2-9-5 **76** .... PatCosgrave 6 — 74
(E J O'Neill) *clsd up: led after 3f: rdn along 3f out: hdd 2f out: one pce* **7/2**[2]

5 *2* **World Tour** 2-8-8 **0** .... PhillipMakin 8 — 61
(I Semple) *s.i.s and towards rr: hdwy over 3f out: rdn and in tch 2f out: sn no imp* **66/1**

0 **6** *10* **Livvy Inn (USA)**[76] 2166 2-8-12 **0** .... LeeEnstone 2 — 42
(Miss Lucinda V Russell) *s.i.s: a in rr* **200/1**

7 *18* **Rio Novo** 2-8-8 **0** .... TonyHamilton 4 — —
(J Howard Johnson) *s.i.s: a bhd* **28/1**

1m 50.83s (1.53) **Going Correction** +0.40s/f (Good) — **7** Ran SP% **108.1**
Speed ratings (Par 96): **108,101,100,99,97 87,69**
CSF £7.63 TOTE £2.20: £1.30, £2.50; EX 5.10.
Owner Sheikh Mohammed **Bred** Gestut Brummerhof **Trained** Middleham Moor, N Yorks

FOCUS
A fair contest and a very smart winning time for the type of race, 3.33 seconds faster than the following older-horse claimer. The form is not easy to assess with the fourth tending to limit.

NOTEBOOK
McCartney(GER) ◆ built on the promise of his debut in a good maiden at Sandown where he apparently disappointed his trainer having been well regarded beforehand. He could hardly have been more impressive despite having been coughing a little on the lead up to this race and looks very useful. (op 5-6 tchd 4-5)
Doon Haymer(IRE) did not mind the longer trip and came through to secure the runner-up spot but it was a case of the winner first and the rest nowhere. (op 7-1 tchd 15-2)
Nine Stories(IRE), stepping up from seven, had a tough task in trying to concede 7lb to the winner and just got run out of second. (op 9-2 tchd 5-1)
Shannersburg(IRE) had more to do under his penalty than when scoring at Nottingham the previous evening. (tchd 5-1)
World Tour, a half-brother to five and nine furlong winner Connotation, had a pretty stiff task on his debut. (op 50-1)

4496 "ONE FIR RICK" RICKY MARTIN MEMORIAL CLAIMING STKS — 1m 65y
6:55 (6:56) (Class 6) 3-Y-0+ — £2,388 (£705; £352) Stalls High

Form — RPR

0400 **1** **Primo Way**[14] 4082 6-8-13 **67** .... TomEaves 1 — 50
(I Semple) *hld up in rr: gd hdwy on inner over 2f out: swtchd lft and rdn ins fnl f: styd on strly to ld nr line* **11/2**[3]

5260 **2** *nk* **Dark Charm (FR)**[36] 3403 8-9-0 **65** ....(p) JamieMoriarty(3) 7 — 54
(R A Fahey) *hld up in tch: hdwy over 2f out: rdn and n.m.r ins fnl f: styd on wl towards fin* **4/1**[2]

4460 **3** *hd* **Boundless Prospect (USA)**[21] 3855 8-9-8 **72** .... NicolPolli(5) 3 — 63
(Miss Gay Kelleway) *trckd ldrs: hdwy over 2f out: led wl over 1f out: sn rdn and edgd rt: hdd and no ex nr fin* **8/1**

-330 **4** *1/2* **Howards Rocket**[14] 4081 6-8-12 **50** .... KellyHarrison(5) 12 — 52
(J S Goldie) *hld up in tch: hdwy 3f out: rdn to chse ldrs over 1f out: kpt on u.p ins fnl f* **11/1**

2010 **5** *nk* **Surwaki (USA)**[26] 3711 5-9-13 **72** .... PaulMulrennan 13 — 61
(R M H Cowell) *set stdy pce: qcknd 3f out: rdn 2f out: sn hdd: drvn and grad wknd ins fnl f* **3/1**[1]

4005 **6** *shd* **Prince Samos (IRE)**[11] 4153 5-9-13 **80** .... AdrianTNicholls 2 — 61
(D Nicholls) *trckd ldr: effrt and swtchd lft 2f out: sn rdn and ev ch tl drvn and nt qckn ins fnl f* **3/1**[1]

0 **7** *1 3/4* **Sierras Future**[27] 3678 3-8-10 **0** ....(b) PhillipMakin 5 — 47
(I Semple) *in rr tl styd on fnl 2f* **50/1**

66 **8** *1/2* **Rourke Star**[9] 4229 5-8-10 **0** .... PatCosgrave 6 — 39
(B Storey) *s.i.s and bhd: hdwy on outer and in tch over 3f out: rdn along over 2f out: sn one pce* **66/1**

0-00 **9** *2 1/2* **Ulysees (IRE)**[13] 4100 8-9-3 **55** .... TonyHamilton 10 — 40
(J Barclay) *chsd ldrs: rdn along 3f out: sn wknd* **16/1**

10 *20* **Biarritz**[31] 6-9-1 **0** .... NSLawes(7) 11 — —
(Mrs J C McGregor) *s.i.s: a bhd* **100/1**

1m 54.16s (4.86) **Going Correction** +0.40s/f (Good)
WFA 3 from 5yo+ 7lb — **10** Ran SP% **115.2**
Speed ratings (Par 101): **91,90,90,90,89 89,87,87,84,64**
CSF £27.36 TOTE £7.30: £1.80, £1.80, £2.50; EX 27.80.The winner was subject to a friendly claim.
Owner Gordon McDowall **Bred** Mrs P A Reditt And M J Reditt **Trained** Carluke, S Lanarks
■ Stewards' Enquiry : Nicol Polli one-day ban: careless riding (Aug 26)

FOCUS
A bunch finish to this modest claimer which turned into a sprint in the final three furlongs. The form is limited by the proximity of the fourth.

4497 CAPTAIN J. C. STEWART H'CAP — 1m 1f 36y
7:25 (7:25) (Class 4) (0-80,80) 3-Y-0+ — £6,477 (£1,927; £963; £481) Stalls High

Form — RPR

3031 **1** **Hawkit (USA)**[4] 4382 6-9-3 **70** 6ex .... PaulMulrennan 3 — 78
(P Monteith) *trckd ldrs: hdwy on bit 3f out: cl up 2f out: shkn up to ld over 1f out: pushed out* **4/1**[3]

4211 **2** *1 3/4* **Montrachet**[23] 3798 3-8-13 **77** .... JamieMoriarty(3) 1 — 81
(M L W Bell) *hld up in rr: hdwy on outer 3f out: rdn to chse wnr and hung rt ins fnl f: kpt on same pce* **13/8**[1]

-010 **3** *3/4* **Tsaroxy (IRE)**[49] 2987 5-9-3 **75** .... NeilBrown(5) 4 — 78
(J Howard Johnson) *in tch: pushed along over 3f out: rdn over 2f out: styd on u.p appr fnl f* **7/2**[2]

3400 **4** *3/4* **Emerald Bay (IRE)**[22] 3813 5-9-13 **80** .... TomEaves 5 — 81
(I Semple) *led and sn clr: rdn along 3f out: jnd 2f out: sn hdd & wknd appr fnl f* **6/1**

-004 **5** *17* **Atlantic Light**[14] 4080 3-9-5 **80** .... GregFairley 2 — 43
(M Johnston) *chsd ldr: rdn along 4f out: wknd 3f out* **5/1**

2m 3.06s (3.40) **Going Correction** +0.40s/f (Good)
WFA 3 from 5yo+ 8lb — **5** Ran SP% **111.3**
Speed ratings (Par 105): **100,98,97,97,82**
CSF £11.11 TOTE £5.20: £1.30, £1.40; EX 10.20.
Owner A McLuckie **Bred** Hargus Sexton And Sandra Sexton **Trained** Rosewell, Midlothian

FOCUS
Quite an interesting little handicap rated around the winner and third.

4498 NESSCO TELECOMS H'CAP — 5f 4y
8:00 (8:00) (Class 5) (0-70,70) 3-Y-0+ — £3,238 (£963; £481; £240) Stalls Low

Form — RPR

1423 **1** **Funfair Wane**[15] 4038 8-9-0 **60** .... AdrianTNicholls 8 — 72
(D Nicholls) *mde all: rdn wl over 1f out: drvn and edgd rt ins fnl f: hld on wl* **5/2**[1]

441 **2** *1/2* **Katie Boo (IRE)**[4] 4390 5-9-10 **70** 6ex .... TomEaves 3 — 81
(A Berry) *trckd ldrs: effrt and nt clr wl over 1f out: swtchd rt and rdn ent fnl f: styd on wl* **7/2**[2]

2532 **3** *1 1/4* **Joyeaux**[17] 4008 5-9-0 **60** .... PaulMulrennan 4 — 66
(J Hetherton) *hld up: swtchd lft and gd hdwy on inner over 1f out: sn rdn and kpt on* **4/1**[3]

The Form Book, Raceform Ltd, Compton, RG20 6NL

644 **4** *nk* **Hotham**[15] 4038 4-9-3 **63** TonyHamilton 7 68
(N Wilson) *in tch: hdwy to chse ldrs 1/2-way: effrt and ev ch ent fnl f: sn rdn and kpt on same pce* **13/2**

0324 **5** *½* **Ptarmigan Ridge**[32] 3536 11-9-5 **70** NeilBrown(5) 9 73
(Miss L A Perratt) *trckd ldrs on outer: effrt 2f out and sn ev ch: rdn ent fnl f and one pce* **7/1**

-000 **6** *3* **Mutayam**[23] 3782 7-8-4 **57** oh6 ow6 (t) LanceBetts(7) 2 49
(D A Nolan) *chsd ldrs on outer: rdn along 2f out: sn wknd* **150/1**

3300 **7** *1* **Miacarla**[29] 3608 4-8-5 **51** oh1 GregFairley 1 40
(A Berry) *trckd ldrs: effrt and n.m.r wl over 1f out: sn rdn and btn* **14/1**

1040 **8** *1½* **Controvento (IRE)**[11] 4158 5-9-10 **70** PatCosgrave 5 53
(Eamon Tyrrell, Ire) *chsd ldrs: rdn along 2f out: sn wknd* **12/1**

0050 **9** *¾* **Vondova**[4] 4381 5-8-1 **54** PaulPickard(7) 6 35
(D A Nolan) *a in rr* **40/1**

61.19 secs (-0.01) **Going Correction** +0.25s/f (Good) **9** Ran SP% **114.1**
Speed ratings (Par 103): **110,109,107,106,105 101,99,97,95**
CSF £11.08 CT £32.91 TOTE £3.90: £1.30, £1.40, £1.70; EX 11.90.
Owner The Wayward Lads **Bred** J K Keegan **Trained** Sessay, N Yorks

FOCUS
A modest handicap but a decent winning time for the grade and, with several coming into this modest affair in good form, the form looks solid.

4499 MECCA BINGO H'CAP — 1m 4f 17y
8:30 (8:31) (Class 5) (0-70,71) 3-Y-0+ **£3,238** (£963; £481; £240) **Stalls** High

Form RPR

1043 **1** **Rudry World (IRE)**[5] 4352 4-9-0 **53** SophieDoyle(7) 5 69+
(M Mullineaux) *midfield: smooth hdwy 4f out: chal on bit over 2f out: shkn up to ld wl over 1f out: sn clr: styd on* **7/2**[1]

5413 **2** *2½* **Bienheureux**[6] 4318 6-9-9 **60** (t) NicolPolli(5) 11 69
(Miss Gay Kelleway) *hld up in rr: stdy hdwy on inner over 3f out: swtchd lft to chse wnr wl over 1f out: drvn ent fnl f and no imp* **13/2**

0034 **3** *8* **Star Of Angels**[11] 4156 3-9-4 **61** GregFairley 4 57
(M Johnston) *prom: effrt 3f out: sn rdn and one pce fr wl over 1f out* **4/1**[2]

4233 **4** *2½* **Topflight Wildbird**[12] 4128 4-10-0 **60** PatCosgrave 13 52
(Mrs G S Rees) *hld up in rr: stdy hdwy 4f out: rdn along over 2f out: drvn and kpt on same pce appr fnl f* **8/1**

2236 **5** *¾* **News Of The Day (IRE)**[25] 3501 3-9-9 **66** PhillipMakin 9 57
(P Monteith) *trckd ldrs: hdwy to ld 3f out: rdn over 2f out: hdd wl over 1f out: sn drvn and wknd ent fnl f* **8/1**

6444 **6** *7* **Grey Outlook**[51] 2935 4-9-5 **51** TomEaves 6 31
(Miss L A Perratt) *chsd ldrs: effrt on outer 3f out: sn rdn and wknd wl over 1f out* **6/1**

00-0 **7** *11* **Silent Beauty (IRE)**[96] 1635 3-8-4 **47** ow2 AdrianTNicholls 2 9
(S C Williams) *in rr: pushed along and sme hdwy over 3f out: sn rdn and btn 2f out* **5/1**[3]

00P0 **8** *26* **Wee Ziggy**[12] 4124 4-8-6 **45** LanceBetts(7) 8 —
(M Mullineaux) *prom: rdn along over 3f out and sn wknd* **33/1**

52-0 **9** *1* **Macaroni Gin (IRE)**[95] 1659 3-9-7 **64** PaulMulrennan 7 —
(J Howard Johnson) *led: rdn along and hdd 3f out: sn wknd* **20/1**

00-0 **10** *13* **Wolf Pack**[109] 1311 5-8-6 **45** PaulPickard(7) 3 —
(D A Nolan) *in tch: rdn along over 4f out and sn wknd* **100/1**

2m 41.77s (2.59) **Going Correction** +0.40s/f (Good)
WFA 3 from 4yo+ 11lb **10** Ran SP% **117.4**
Speed ratings (Par 103): **107,105,100,98,97 93,85,68,67,59**
CSF £26.38 CT £95.36 TOTE £4.70: £1.60, £2.20, £1.80; EX 27.40 Place 6 376.59, Place 5 £9.79.
Owner The Bellflower Rudry World Partnership **Bred** Richard Leonard **Trained** Alpraham, Cheshire

FOCUS
This modest event did not turn out to be as competitive as expected, with the good pace meaning the field finished strung out on the ground. The form is rated fairly positively through the runner-up.
Silent Beauty(IRE) Official explanation: jockey said filly hung right
Macaroni Gin(IRE) Official explanation: jockey said gelding hung left
T/Plt: £62.70 to a £1 stake. Pool: £53,465.70. 621.60 winning tickets. T/Qpdt: £5.40 to a £1 stake. Pool: £4,906.90. 671.60 winning tickets. JR

3965 SALISBURY (R-H)
Wednesday, August 15

OFFICIAL GOING: Good to soft (soft in places) (8.6)
Wind: brisk ahead

4500 SOVEREIGN WINDOWS UK EBF MAIDEN STKS — 6f
2:30 (2:32) (Class 4) 2-Y-O **£4,533** (£1,348; £674; £336) **Stalls** Centre

Form RPR

5456 **1** **Paveroc**[15] 4048 2-9-3 **96** JohnEgan 10 78
(J S Moore) *trckd ldrs: led ins fnl 2f: drvn and styd on wl fnl f* **2/1**[1]

2 **2** *1¼* **Redsensor**[10] 4198 2-9-3 0 RyanMoore 5 74
(R Hannon) *chsd ldrs: drvn to chal 2f out: kpt on fnl f but nt pce of wnr* **9/4**[2]

0 **3** *1½* **Ike Quebec (FR)**[18] 3967 2-9-3 0 KerrinMcEvoy 14 69
(R Hannon) *lw: led: rdn and hdd ins fnl 2f: wknd fnl half f* **13/2**[3]

06 **4** *hd* **Spent**[18] 3967 2-9-3 0 DaneO'Neill 3 69
(R M Beckett) *in rr: hdwy on outside appr fnl f: fin strly* **16/1**

00 **5** *nk* **Fervent Prince**[18] 3967 2-9-3 0 SteveDrowne 13 68
(H Morrison) *chsd ldrs: rdn 2f out: one pce fr over 1f out* **33/1**

0 **6** *nk* **Musashi (IRE)**[10] 4198 2-9-3 0 JamesDoyle 4 67
(J S Moore) *s.i.s: in rr: pushed along and hdwy fr 2f out: kpt on ins fnl f but nvr gng pce to rch ldrs* **50/1**

03 **7** *1½* **Home**[14] 4070 2-9-3 0 DavidKinsella 2 62
(E A L Dunlop) *edgy: in rr: shkn up and hung lft ins fnl 2f: edgd rt and kpt on 1f out but nvr in contention* **10/1**

8 *shd* **Prime Aspiration (USA)** 2-9-3 0 PaulEddery 8 62+
(Christian Wroe) *w'like: b.hind: s.i.s: rr: pushed along over 2f ouyt: hdwy fnl f but nvr in contention* **20/1**

9 *¾* **Red Rumour (IRE)** 2-9-3 0 TedDurcan 1 59+
(R M Beckett) *strong: scope: s.i.s: green and sn nudged along in rr: stl bhd whn nt clr run ins fnl 2f: mod prog ins fnl f* **14/1**

0 **10** *nk* **Lady Maya**[16] 4026 2-8-12 0 FergusSweeney 9 53
(Dr J R J Naylor) *s.i.s: sn rcvrd into mid-div: rdn 3f out: wknd over 1f out* **150/1**

0 **11** *1½* **Herrbee (IRE)**[15] 4048 2-9-3 0 JosedeSouza 11 53
(M P Tregoning) *chsd ldrs: rdn over 2f out: wknd over 1f out* **12/1**

00 **12** *½* **Queen's Treasure (IRE)**[16] 4014 2-8-12 0 PatDobbs 7 47
(M P Tregoning) *chsd ldrs: rdn and ev ch 2f out: sn wknd* **25/1**

0 **13** *32* **Newcastle Sam**[11] 4160 2-8-12 0 TolleyDean(5) 12 —
(J J Bridger) *hmpd in rr after 1f: sn bhd: virtually p.u fr over 1f out* **125/1**

1m 16.87s (1.89) **Going Correction** +0.30s/f (Good) **13** Ran SP% **121.7**
Speed ratings (Par 96): **99,97,95,95,94 94,92,92,91,90 88,88,45**
CSF £6.30 TOTE £2.70: £1.30, £1.20, £2.50; EX 7.40.
Owner Uplands Acquisitions Limited **Bred** Brundeanlaws Stud **Trained** Upper Lambourn, Berks
■ Stewards' Enquiry : Fergus Sweeney two-day ban: careless riding (Aug 26-27)

FOCUS
There was a blustery wind blowing into the faces of the runners. A fair maiden in which they bet 10-1 bar three and those three filled the placings. The form makes sense assessed through the runner-up.

NOTEBOOK
Paveroc has been competing in some good company, including when a close fifth in the Windsor Castle, and put that experience to good use to get off the mark. Connections may well let him take his chance in the Gimcrack, but whatever his fate there he looks capable of winning his share as he has some physical scope. (op 9-4 tchd 13-8 and 5-2 in a place)
Redsensor went off favourite to build on his second in a Newbury maiden and had every chance, but the winner proved too strong in the final furlong. He should not be too long in getting off the mark. (op 13-8 tchd 5-2)
Ike Quebec(FR), a stable companion of the runner-up, was supported in the ring and reversed previous form with Spent. (op 10-1)
Spent was doing his best work late and only narrowly missed a place. (op 25-1)
Fervent Prince had finished behind Ike Quebec and Spent last time and pretty much confirmed that form, helping to set the standard. (op 28-1)
Musashi(IRE), a stablemate of the winner, ran reasonably and may need more time. (op 33-1)
Home, who whipped round and lost his rider leaving the paddock, tended to hang in the race. He is now qualified for handicaps. (op 9-1)

4501 IRISH THOROUGHBRED MARKETING NURSERY — 6f 212y
3:00 (3:03) (Class 5) 2-Y-O **£3,238** (£963; £481; £240) **Stalls** Centre

Form RPR

553 **1** **Mizooka**[20] 3866 2-8-4 **66** NelsonDeSouza 4 74
(R M Beckett) *trckd ldrs: rdn to ld over 1f out: styd on gamely u.p fnl f* **13/2**[3]

51 **2** *¾* **Safari Sunup (IRE)**[25] 3733 2-9-2 **78** StephenCarson 13 83
(P Winkworth) *chsd ldr: led over 2f out: rdn and hdd over 1f out: styd on but a hld by wnr* **14/1**

0210 **3** *1½* **Dubai Dynamo**[57] 2732 2-8-13 **75** JohnEgan 6 76
(J S Moore) *in rr: rdn and hdwy fr 3f out: styd on to chse ldrs over 1f out: nt qckn ins fnl f* **7/1**

030 **4** *1½* **Kristal Glory (IRE)**[32] 3551 2-7-12 **60** DavidKinsella 8 57
(J L Dunlop) *in tch: drvn and hdwy over 2f out: styd on same pce ins fnl f* **25/1**

020 **5** *1* **Albaqaa**[29] 3625 2-9-2 **78** SteveDrowne 5 72
(E A L Dunlop) *lw: in rr: hdwy over 2f out: nvr gng pce to trble ldrs and one pce ins fnl f* **13/2**[3]

035 **6** *1¼* **Determind Stand (USA)**[29] 3625 2-8-13 **75** (v[1]) RyanMoore 11 66
(Sir Michael Stoute) *s.i.s: in rr: rdn over 2f out: sn edgd rt: nvr gng pce to be competitive* **11/2**[1]

5422 **7** *1¾* **Quick Sands (IRE)**[10] 4202 2-8-10 **72** TedDurcan 7 58
(R Hannon) *in tch: rdn 3f out: wknd over 1f out* **7/1**

5110 **8** *1* **Distant Charm (IRE)**[12] 4121 2-9-1 **82** HaddenFrost(5) 9 65
(R Hannon) *chsd ldrs: rdn 3f out: wknd ins fnl 2f* **6/1**[2]

043 **9** *1¼* **Observatory Ridge**[14] 4074 2-8-4 **66** RichardSmith 12 46
(M D I Usher) *rrd and slowly away: hdwy 2f out: sme prog over 1f out but nvr in contention* **33/1**

5431 **10** *10* **Menadha (USA)**[18] 3958 2-9-7 **83** TPO'Shea 14 36
(M R Channon) *lw: led: 4 l clr 4f out: hdd over 2f out: sn wknd* **8/1**

000 **11** *nk* **Aberavon**[25] 3747 2-8-5 **67** KerrinMcEvoy 1 19
(D R C Elsworth) *chsd ldrs tl wknd qckly 2f out* **16/1**

005 **12** *¾* **Lisselan Prospect (USA)**[61] 2624 2-8-4 **66** PaulEddery 3 16
(Mrs A J Perrett) *a towards rr* **50/1**

0361 **13** *¾* **The Name Is Frank**[18] 3967 2-8-11 **73** JamesDoyle 10 21
(J W Mullins) *chsd ldrs to 1/2-way* **14/1**

1m 30.06s (1.00) **Going Correction** +0.30s/f (Good) **13** Ran SP% **120.4**
Speed ratings (Par 94): **106,105,103,101,100 99,97,96,94,83 82,81,81**
CSF £93.40 CT £687.01 TOTE £6.70: £2.20, £4.70, £3.00; EX 63.10.
Owner M S T Partnership **Bred** Catridge Farm Stud Ltd **Trained** Whitsbury, Hants
■ A belated first winner of the year for injury-hit Nelson De Souza.

FOCUS
An interesting nursery in which the top weight Menadha went off at a rate of knots resulting in a fair time. The form is rated positively around the fairly solid third and fourth.

NOTEBOOK
Mizooka, who was stepping up in trip for this handicap debut, proved well suited by the strong gallop. She should stay even further in time and will keep to nurseries for the time being. (op 15-2 tchd 6-1)
Safari Sunup(IRE), who had trip and ground to suit, appeared to step up on that effort and did well considering he took over when the leader faded and set sail for home.
Dubai Dynamo, who was having his first run since finishing unplaced in the Coventry, performed well and was keeping on steadily at the finish, suggesting the break had done him good. (op 15-2 tchd 8-1)
Kristal Glory(IRE), who was well beaten in a course-and-distance maiden last time, ran better on this handicap debut and may be able to win a nursery off this mark. (op 20-1)
Albaqaa is still a maiden and this was not a bad effort on his handicap debut, although he is another who had the ground coming in his favour. (tchd 7-1)
Determind Stand(USA) was equipped with a visor for the first time and was held up at the back. He ran on but never looked likely to figure. (op 6-1 tchd 5-1)
Aberavon, one of the more interesting one's for this handicap debut, was a bit free to post and she failed to see her race out. (op 12-1)
The Name Is Frank Official explanation: jockey said colt hung right-handed

4502 GOLDRING SECURITY SERVICES PEMBROKE CUP (H'CAP) — 1m
3:30 (3:34) (Class 4) (0-85,84) 3-Y-O **£5,181** (£1,541; £770; £384) **Stalls** High

Form RPR

115 **1** **Padlocked (IRE)**[68] 2426 3-9-1 **83** AhmedAjtebi(5) 10 91
(D M Simcock) *t.k.h: chsd ldr: slt ld appr fnl 2f: hung lft over 1f out: edgd rt jst ins fnl f: kpt on wl* **9/2**[2]

0511 **2** *1½* **Bajan Pride**[19] 3913 3-9-3 **80** RyanMoore 9 85
(R Hannon) *lw: hld up in tch: hdwy 3f out: pressed wnr over 1f out tl ins ffnl f: sn one pce* **5/1**[3]

1002 **3** *1* **Leptis Magna**[19] 3900 3-9-0 **77** TedDurcan 5 79
(D R C Elsworth) *s.i.s: in rr: hdwy over 1f out: styd on wl to chse ldrs ins fnl f but nvr gng pce to chal* **6/1**

5030 **4** *hd* **Okikoki**[18] 3940 3-9-0 **77** SteveDrowne 7 79
(W R Muir) *lw: led tl hdd appr fnl 2f: styd on same pce fr over 1f out* **12/1**

0522 **5** ¾ **Princess Zada**[19] 3904 3-8-6 **69** ow1 FergusSweeney 8 69
(B R Millman) *lw: chsd ldrs: rdn and effrt 2f out: nvr quite gng pce to chal: wknd ins fnl f* **9/1**
1020 **6** 1 **Mark Of Love (IRE)**[18] 3964 3-8-1 **71** MatthewDavies(7) 1 69
(M R Channon) *hld up in rr: hdwy on outside over 2f out: nvr quite gng pce to rch ldrs and no further prog* **6/1**
0050 **7** 1 ¾ **Mubaashir (IRE)**[54] 2835 3-9-7 **84** DaneO'Neill 6 78
(E A L Dunlop) *in rr: rdn and swtchd rt wl over 1f out: nvr in contention* **25/1**
1221 **8** 4 **Blue Monkey (IRE)**[21] 3855 3-9-1 **81** TravisBlock(3) 3 66
(M L W Bell) *chsd ldrs: rdn over 2f out: wknd wl over 1f out* **4/1**[1]
6-62 **9** 9 **Regal Quest (IRE)**[21] 3845 3-9-2 **79** JohnEgan 2 43
(S Kirk) *lw: t.k.h early: in tch: rdn 3f out: wknd ins fnl 2f* **12/1**
630- **10** 13 **Moorlander (USA)**[302] 6023 3-8-7 **70** KerrinMcEvoy 11 4
(Mrs A J Perrett) *in rr: sme hdwy 3f out: sn wknd* **16/1**

1m 44.63s (1.54) **Going Correction** +0.30s/f (Good) **10** Ran SP% **118.5**
Speed ratings (Par 102): **104,102,101,101,100 99,97,93,84,71**
CSF £27.84 CT £140.47 TOTE £6.30: £2.20, £1.80, £2.60; EX 37.10.
Owner Saif Misfer **Bred** Patrick F Kelly **Trained** Newmarket, Suffolk

FOCUS
A fair handicap with the majority of the field closely matched on official figures and the form looks sound rated around the third and fourth.
Okikoki Official explanation: jockey said gelding hung left-handed

4503 EUROPEAN BREEDERS' FUND UPAVON FILLIES' STKS (LISTED RACE) 1m 1f 198y
4:00 (4:03) (Class 1) 3-Y-O+
£21,576 (£8,177; £4,092; £2,040; £1,022; £513) **Stalls** High

Form RPR
124 **1** **Promising Lead**[48] 3028 3-8-7 98 ow2 RyanMoore 8 102+
(Sir Michael Stoute) *lw: trckd ldrs in 3rd: rdn to ld over 2f out: drvn out* **5/2**[2]
0012 **2** 2 ½ **Sell Out**[18] 3972 3-8-7 83 ow2 SteveDrowne 10 97
(G Wragg) *hld up in rr: rdn and hdwy fr 2f out: styd on to take 2nd last strides but no ch w wnr* **16/1**
0420 **3** shd **Russian Rosie (IRE)**[39] 3332 3-8-5 97 JamesDoyle 3 95
(J G Portman) *chsd ldr: rdn over 2f out: chsd wnr ins fnl f but no ch: ct for 2nd last strides* **25/1**
4-40 **4** nk **Shorthand**[55] 2786 3-8-5 101 KerrinMcEvoy 7 94
(Sir Michael Stoute) *swtg: led: rdn 3f out: hdd over 2f out: one pce fnl f* **4/1**[3]
4402 **5** 2 **Fann (USA)**[19] 3897 4-9-0 102 JohnEgan 4 90
(C E Brittain) *in rr but in tch: hdwy 4f out: rdn 3f out: outpcd fr over 1f out* **12/1**
2-60 **6** ½ **Hollow Ridge**[56] 2757 3-8-5 90 StephenCarson 1 89
(B W Hills) *plld hrd in rr: rdn and styd on fnl 2f but nvr in contention* **22/1**
0124 **7** ½ **Barshiba (IRE)**[17] 4010 3-8-9 110 TedDurcan 6 92
(D R C Elsworth) *lw: hld up in rr: sme prog but hung lft to r wd and alone fr 3f out: nvr in contention* **11/8**[1]
55-0 **8** 11 **Tiana**[19] 3897 4-9-0 92 FrancisNorton 5 66
(Mrs A J Perrett) *chsd ldrs: rdn 3f out: sn btn* **20/1**

2m 11.24s (2.78) **Going Correction** +0.30s/f (Good)
WFA 3 from 4yo 9lb **8** Ran SP% **117.2**
Speed ratings (Par 108): **100,98,97,97,96 95,95,86**
CSF £39.60 TOTE £3.60: £1.50, £2.50, £3.90; EX 45.30.
Owner K Abdulla **Bred** Juddmonte Farms Ltd **Trained** Newmarket, Suffolk

FOCUS
A valuable fillies' Listed race and a decisive winner, but the winning time was only 0.14 seconds faster than the following 51-68 handicap suggesting the form is not the most solid.

NOTEBOOK
Promising Lead ◆ had been found out by the soft ground at Newcastle last time, but on this less-testing surface was a different proposition. After settling in behind the keen Shorthand, she came through to take the lead inside the last quarter-mile and drew away for a decisive victory. She should continue to hold her own at this level and may be up to winning a Group race. (op 10-3)
Sell Out was dropping in trip and finished well, having been held up at the back on her first try at this level, and with black type secured looks the sort for a race like the Galtres Stakes at York. (op 25-1)
Russian Rosie(IRE) continues to run well at this level, finishing placed for the third time in this grade, and helps set the level of the form. (op 20-1)
Shorthand was quite keen in front early on and could not respond when the winner went by. (op 11-2)
Fann(USA) was a big market drifter and never got into the race having been held up. (op 7-1)
Barshiba(IRE) was a big disappointment. She had finished fourth in the Group 1 Prix d'Astarte last time on soft ground and was a well-backed favourite. She was always out the back and never got into the race having come wide in the straight. Connections reported she did not handle the track and they will probably revert to flatter tracks in the future, with the Matron Stakes at the Curragh mentioned as a possible target. Her jockey reported that the filly had hung left. Official explanation: jockey said filly hung left-handed (op 5-4 tchd 6-4)

4504 STELLA ARTOIS H'CAP 1m 1f 198y
4:30 (4:32) (Class 5) (0-70,70) 3-Y-O+ **£3,238** (£963; £481; £240) **Stalls** High

Form RPR
0046 **1** **Hot Diamond**[14] 4069 3-9-1 **66** ow1 AntonyProcter 6 81
(D R C Elsworth) *lw: s.i.s: in rr: hdwy fr 2f out: wnt to far aise and racd alone over 1f out: led ins fnl f: readily* **5/1**[2]
640 **2** 5 **Art Professor (IRE)**[22] 3827 3-9-0 **65** RyanMoore 3 70
(J W Hills) *s.i.s: in rr: hdwy fr 3f out: styd on u.p fnl f to take 2nd last strides but no ch w ready wnr* **7/1**
2565 **3** shd **Trump Call (IRE)**[18] 3964 3-9-0 **65** JohnEgan 5 70
(R M Beckett) *chsd ldr 6f out: rdn to ld ins fnl 3f: hdd ins fnl f: sn outpcd by ready wnr: lost 2nd last strides* **9/2**[1]
4564 **4** 1 ½ **Mae Cigan (FR)**[31] 3567 4-9-1 **57** SteveDrowne 1 59
(M Blanshard) *in rr: rdn and hdwy fr 3f out: styd on fnl f but nvr in contention w ldng trio* **13/2**
5452 **5** 4 **Pactolos Way**[7] 4271 4-9-8 **64** PaulDoe 14 58
(P R Chamings) *led: rdn and hdd ins fnl 3f: wknd over 1f out* **8/1**
5003 **6** shd **Fangorn Forest (IRE)**[8] 4257 4-9-2 **58** AmirQuinn 2 52
(R A Harris) *b. in rr: mod prog fr 2f out: kpt on nr fin* **16/1**
620 **7** 1 ½ **Split The Wind (USA)**[6] 4327 3-8-11 **62** StephenCarson 13 53
(Eve Johnson Houghton) *chsd ldrs: rdn 3f out: wknd ins fnl 2f* **25/1**
60-3 **8** 3 ½ **Golden Sprite**[16] 4015 4-9-8 **64** DaneO'Neill 11 48
(B R Millman) *chsd ldrs: rdn over 3f out: wknd appr fnl 2f* **11/2**[3]
322 **9** 1 ½ **Aypeeyes (IRE)**[6] 4309 3-9-3 **68** SimonWhitworth 7 49
(S Kirk) *prom: chsd ldrs 4f out: wknd fr 3f out* **5/1**[2]
6306 **10** 13 **County Kerry (UAE)**[4] 4392 3-8-0 **51** oh1 FrankieMcDonald 12 6
(Jean-Rene Auvray) *t.k.h chsd ldrs to 3f oit: sn wknd* **25/1**

3600 **11** 15 **Brean Dot Com (IRE)**[29] 3622 3-8-2 **53** oh1 ow2 RichardThomas 9 —
(Mrs P N Dutfield) *lw: a in rr* **40/1**
/60- **12** 17 **Highband**[235] 5567 4-8-4 **51** oh6 TolleyDean(5) 10 —
(M Madgwick) *a in rr* **100/1**

2m 11.36s (2.90) **Going Correction** +0.30s/f (Good)
WFA 3 from 4yo+ 9lb **12** Ran SP% **120.8**
Speed ratings (Par 103): **100,96,95,94,91 91,90,87,86,75 63,50**
CSF £39.60 CT £172.55 TOTE £7.00: £2.20, £2.20, £2.30; EX 47.00.
Owner J C Smith **Bred** The Earl Of Halifax **Trained** Newmarket, Suffolk

FOCUS
A modest handicap run fractionally slower than the preceding Listed race. The main body of the field came up the centre of the track in the straight, but the winner stuck to the far rail. The form looks reliable through the third.

4505 AXMINSTER CARPETS APPRENTICE H'CAP 6f 212y
5:00 (5:03) (Class 5) (0-70,68) 3-Y-O+ **£3,238** (£963; £481; £240) **Stalls** Centre

Form RPR
0063 **1** **Outer Hebrides**[8] 4259 6-9-11 **65** (v) HaddenFrost 1 77
(J M Bradley) *mde all: drvn out fnl 2f and styd on wl* **9/1**
5250 **2** 2 ½ **Dr Synn**[18] 3943 6-9-11 **65** KirstyMilczarek 12 70
(J Akehurst) *chsd wnr fr over 4f out: styd on but a hld fnl 2f* **8/1**[3]
5622 **3** ¾ **Our Herbie**[13] 4109 3-9-3 **63** (v) RussellKennemore 6 64
(J W Hills) *in rr: stmbld over 4f out: swtchd lft to outside 3f out: kpt on fr over 1f out and gng on cl home but nvr a threat* **7/1**[2]
2536 **4** 1 **Gracie's Gift (IRE)**[31] 3571 5-9-4 **61** (p) JamieHamblett(3) 9 61
(A G Newcombe) *towards rr whan hmpd over 4f out: swtchd lft to outside over 2f out and kpt on fr over 1f out but nvr in contention* **9/2**[1]
4204 **5** shd **Digital**[4] 4397 10-8-10 **58** MatthewDavies(8) 14 58
(M R Channon) *in rr whn edgd rt to ins over 4f out: hdwy fr 3f out: chsd ldrs ins fnl 2f but nvr gng pce to be competitive* **9/2**[1]
3065 **6** 2 ½ **Run For Ede'S**[36] 3393 3-8-13 **62** (p) AlanRutter(3) 4 53
(P M Phelan) *chsd ldrs: rdn 3f out: wknd over 1f out* **14/1**
20-4 **7** 2 **Seaflower Reef (IRE)**[23] 3798 3-8-12 **66** DavidProbert(8) 7 52
(A M Balding) *broke wl: sn towards rr: nvr gng pce to trble ldrs after* **20/1**
0-00 **8** hd **Marker**[33] 3487 7-8-9 **52** (b) JemmaMarshall(3) 5 39
(J D Frost) *chsd ldrs: rdn 3f out: wknd fr 2f out* **12/1**
-000 **9** 1 ¾ **Devonia Plains (IRE)**[14] 4063 5-8-6 **54** ow2 NBazeley(8) 13 37
(Mrs P N Dutfield) *chsd ldrs: rdn 3f out: wknd 2f out* **33/1**
2056 **10** 2 ½ **High Class Problem (IRE)**[7] 4272 4-9-8 **62** (t) TolleyDean 10 38
(P F I Cole) *chsd ldrs over 4f* **20/1**
0000 **11** 2 **Leg Sweep**[11] 4170 3-8-10 **64** TobyAtkinson(8) 2 32
(D R C Elsworth) *hmpd s: slowly away: sme prog 1/2-way: sn wknd* **28/1**
0060 **12** ½ **Alfredian Park**[41] 3235 3-9-5 **65** ThomasO'Brien 11 32
(S Kirk) *chsd ldrs to 1/2-way* **25/1**
0026 **13** 1 ¼ **Roman Quest**[7] 4295 4-9-6 **68** RyanBird(8) 8 34
(H Morrison) *lw: v.s.a: rcvrd into mid-div whn hit rails repeatedly over 4f out: wknd ins fnl 3f* **9/2**[1]

1m 31.19s (2.13) **Going Correction** +0.30s/f (Good)
WFA 3 from 4yo+ 6lb **13** Ran SP% **122.3**
Speed ratings (Par 103): **99,96,95,94,94 91,88,88,86,83 81,80,79**
CSF £75.07 CT £564.71 TOTE £12.30: £3.60, £2.90, £1.60; EX 104.50 Place 6 £174.03, Place 5 £147.30.
Owner Asterix Partnership **Bred** St Clare Hall Stud **Trained** Sedbury, Gloucs

FOCUS
An ordinary apprentice handicap run 1.13sec slower than the earlier nursery and rated around the first two.
T/Jkpt: £7,100.00 to a £1 stake. Pool: £10,000.00. 0.50 winning tickets. T/Plt: £294.50 to a £1 stake. Pool: £67,269.10. 166.70 winning tickets. T/Qpdt: £47.10 to a £1 stake. Pool: £3,818.80. 59.90 winning tickets. ST

4108 SANDOWN (R-H)
Wednesday, August 15
OFFICIAL GOING: Good changing to good (good to soft in places) after race 3
Wind: Moderate, across Weather: Overcast, raining between races 2-3

4506 BIG NIGHT DOWN UNDER MAIDEN STKS 5f 6y
5:30 (5:31) (Class 5) 2-Y-O **£3,886** (£1,156; £577; £288) **Stalls** High

Form RPR
252 **1** **Royal Confidence**[14] 4061 2-8-12 85 MichaelHills 5 77+
(B W Hills) *trckd ldrs: stdy prog to ld 1f out: sn in command: comf* **4/9**[1]
2 2 **Dubai Power** 2-8-12 0 PhilipRobinson 6 69+
(C E Brittain) *in tch in midfield: outpcd and reminder over 1f out: pushed along and styd on fnl f to take 2nd last stride* **14/1**
440 **3** shd **Cordell (IRE)**[15] 4048 2-9-3 80 PatDobbs 1 74
(R Hannon) *trckd ldr: rdn to chal over 1f out: outpcd jst ins fnl f: kpt on* **6/1**[2]
0 **4** shd **Wild Bill Tracey**[37] 3370 2-9-3 0 JimmyFortune 2 74
(M J Wallace) *led: rdn and hdd 1f out: lost 2 pls nr fin* **16/1**
60 **5** 1 **Dome Rock (IRE)**[70] 2349 2-9-3 0 NickyMackay 4 70+
(L M Cumani) *dwlt: hld up in last pair: outpcd wl over 1f out: kpt on* **7/1**[3]
6 hd **Wavertree Princess (IRE)** 2-8-9 0 RichardKingscote(3) 7 64+
(N P Littmoden) *s.s: hld up in last pair: outpcd on outer 2f out: kpt on fnl f* **25/1**
6 **7** shd **Ava Gee**[8] 4254 2-8-12 0 DavidKinsella 3 65+
(B De Haan) *trckd ldng pair: rdn 2f out: keeping on but hld whn nt clr run last 75yds: eased* **66/1**

63.17 secs (0.96) **Going Correction** +0.025s/f (Good) **7** Ran SP% **113.9**
Speed ratings (Par 94): **93,89,89,89,87 87,87**
CSF £8.56 TOTE £1.40: £1.10, £3.70; EX 5.90.
Owner D M James **Bred** D M James **Trained** Lambourn, Berks

FOCUS
A modest and uncompetitive maiden where the form makes sense rated around the third and fifth to their marks, but the proximity of the fourth raises doubts.

NOTEBOOK
Royal Confidence, who had shown more than enough to suggest she could take this in three previous attempts, twice finishing second, did not necessarily look certain to be suited by the drop in trip, but her class saw her through and she got well on top late on to win readily. She seems to be progressing and remains capable of better still in nurseries. (tchd 2-5 and 1-2 in places)
Dubai Power, a 150,000gns daughter of Cadeaux Genereux, comes from a yard whose juveniles tend to need their first run and as a result this has to go down as a pretty pleasing effort. The step up to 6f is going to suit in time and he looks a ready-made maiden winner.
Cordell(IRE) has not really progressed and he will stand more of a chance in nurseries. (op 7-1)
Wild Bill Tracey improved on his initial effort at Musselburgh and is another likely type for nurseries.

Dome Rock(IRE), who needed this to qualify for a handicap mark, continues to find 5f on the sharp side and he may well do better once upped in trip for nurseries. Official explanation: jockey said colt hung left (op 8-1 tchd 9-1)
Wavertree Princess(IRE) Official explanation: jockey said filly stumbled on leaving stalls
Ava Gee Official explanation: jockey said filly was denied a clear run

4507 WILLIAMHILLCASINO.COM - THE FIRST ONLINE SUPERCASINO H'CAP 5f 6y

6:00 (6:02) (Class 4) (0-80,80) 4-Y-0+ **£5,181** (£1,541; £770; £384) **Stalls** High

Form RPR
0600 **1** **Matsunosuke**[9] 4233 5-8-12 **69** ... JimmyFortune 13 82
(A B Coogan) *settled in 5th: prog to trck ldng pair over 1f out: rdn to ld ins fnl f: r.o wl* **10/3**[1]
4102 **2** *1* **Shes Minnie**[16] 4017 4-9-7 **78** ... FergusSweeney 7 88
(P A Blockley) *hld up in last pair: prog over 1f out: got through and r.o fnl f: tk 2nd nr fin: n.d to wnr* **11/1**
646- **3** *1/2* **Grand Show**[257] 6660 5-9-7 **78** ... TedDurcan 5 86
(W R Swinburn) *hld up in midfield and racd on outer: effrt over 1f out: styd on fnl f: nt pce to chal* **15/2**
-600 **4** *hd* **Little Edward**[13] 4095 9-9-8 **79** ... PaulEddery 2 86+
(R J Hodges) *t.k.h: hld up in last: prog over 1f out: nt clr run ins fnl f: r.o: nt rch ldrs* **9/1**
1233 **5** *hd* **Malapropism**[9] 4233 7-8-13 **70** ... TPO'Shea 10 76
(M R Channon) *chsd ldr: rdn 2f out: kpt on to ld jst ins fnl f: sn hdd and nt qckn* **4/1**[2]
0000 **6** *nk* **Royal Challenge**[12] 4133 6-9-6 **77** ... MichaelHills 9 82+
(M H Tompkins) *t.k.h: hld up towards rr: nt clr run on inner over 1f out and jst ins fnl f: styd on nr fin* **5/1**[3]
0425 **7** *nk* **Blessed Place**[7] 4296 7-8-3 **63** ... (t) StephaneBreux(3) 12 67
(D J S Ffrench Davis) *led: gng strly 2f out: hdd ins fnl f: fdd* **11/2**
6254 **8** *2* **Harrison's Flyer (IRE)**[10] 4204 6-8-12 **72** ... (p) TravisBlock(3) 3 69
(J M Bradley) *chsd ldng pair: rdn and edgd lft over 1f out: wknd fnl f* **12/1**
60-0 **9** *nk* **Lindbergh**[16] 4021 5-9-4 **75** ... JamesDoyle 14 71
(A J Lidderdale) *chsd ldng pair: rdn wl over 1f out: wknd ins fnl f* **33/1**

61.66 secs (-0.55) **Going Correction** +0.025s/f (Good) **9** Ran SP% **115.9**
Speed ratings (Par 105): **105,103,102,102,101 101,101,97,97**
CSF £41.00 CT £259.47 TOTE £4.10: £1.80, £2.20, £2.70; EX 32.70.
Owner A B Coogan **Bred** R Coogan **Trained** Soham, Cambs
■ Stewards' Enquiry : Fergus Sweeney one-day ban: careless riding (Aug 28)

FOCUS
A fair sprint handicap and solid form rated through the runner-up.
Royal Challenge Official explanation: jockey said gelding was denied a clear run

4508 WOODFORD RESERVE BOURBON MEDIAN AUCTION MAIDEN STKS 7f 16y

6:35 (6:40) (Class 4) 2-Y-0 **£4,533** (£1,348; £674; £336) **Stalls** High

Form RPR
2 **1** **Redolent (IRE)**[32] 3552 2-9-3 0 ... RyanMoore 14 84
(R Hannon) *mde all: rdn over 1f out: forged clr fnl f* **6/5**[1]
2 *2 1/2* **Rattan (USA)** 2-9-3 0 ... TedDurcan 3 78
(H R A Cecil) *trckd ldrs: prog to go 2nd over 1f out and looked threatening: outpcd by wnr fnl f* **11/2**[3]
0 **3** *1* **Loyal Knight (IRE)**[15] 4048 2-9-3 0 ... KerrinMcEvoy 7 75
(S Kirk) *chsd ldng pair to 2f out: sn outpcd: kpt on again fnl f* **9/2**[2]
4 *1 1/4* **Blue Sky Basin** 2-9-3 0 ... FrancisNorton 4 72
(A M Balding) *dwlt: settled in midfield: prog to chse ldrs 2f out: sn outpcd: kpt on fnl f* **20/1**
0 **5** *hd* **Red Merlin (IRE)**[19] 3896 2-9-3 0 ... PhilipRobinson 6 71
(C G Cox) *trckd ldrs: lost pl on outer over 2f out: pushed along and styd on again last 150yds* **12/1**
04 **6** *nk* **Resplendent Light**[21] 3849 2-9-3 0 ... JimmyFortune 11 70
(W R Muir) *chsd wnr to over 1f out: wknd fnl f* **10/1**
5 **7** *3* **Warming Up (IRE)**[10] 4199 2-9-3 0 ... PatDobbs 8 62
(C E Brittain) *rel to r early: wl in rr: sme prog 2f out: kpt on: n.d* **33/1**
0 **8** *1 1/4* **Cocktail Shaker (USA)**[13] 4110 2-9-3 0 ... DaneO'Neill 5 59
(B J Meehan) *prom: pushed along over 2f out: steadily fdd* **33/1**
9 *shd* **Sabre Light** 2-9-3 0 ... FergusSweeney 13 59
(G L Moore) *dwlt: nvr beyond midfield: no real prog fnl 2f* **50/1**
10 *1 1/4* **Dr Livingstone (IRE)** 2-9-3 0 ... SteveDrowne 12 55
(C R Egerton) *dwlt: rn green in last pair: shkn up 3f out: modest late prog* **20/1**
11 *nk* **Downhiller (IRE)** 2-9-3 0 ... EddieAhern 9 54
(J L Dunlop) *hld up in midfield: effrt on inner to chse ldrs over 2f out: wknd over 1f out* **20/1**
12 *1* **Ray Diamond** 2-9-3 0 ... JamesDoyle 2 52
(N P Littmoden) *dwlt: a in rr: shkn up and no prog over 2f out* **50/1**
13 *3 1/2* **Aston Boy** 2-9-3 0 ... NickyMackay 1 42
(M Blanshard) *dwlt: mostly in last pair: shkn up over 2f out: no prog* **66/1**
14 *6* **Ryan's Rock** 2-9-0 0 ... RichardKingscote(3) 10 26
(T D McCarthy) *dwlt: rn green and a wl in rr: wknd over 2f out* **66/1**

1m 31.7s (2.36) **Going Correction** +0.225s/f (Good) **14** Ran SP% **122.9**
Speed ratings (Par 96): **95,92,91,89,89 89,85,84,84,82 82,81,77,70**
CSF £6.91 TOTE £2.00: £1.20, £2.00, £2.10; EX 8.00.
Owner De La Warr Racing **Bred** R O'Callaghan And D Veitch **Trained** East Everleigh, Wilts

FOCUS
A decent maiden likely to produce winners and the winner was quite impressive with the third setting a resonable level of form.

NOTEBOOK
Redolent(IRE), a promising second at Salisbury on debut, was always going to take the beating from a handy draw and Moore wasted little time hanging around, sending the son of Redback straight to the front. He readily came clear under pressure and won in the style of a useful colt. He has no big entries, but his owner's were keen to have a crack at the Goffs Million with him. (op 11-8 tchd 11-10 and 6-4 in places)
Rattan(USA), whose trainer enjoyed much success with this ones sire, appeared to know his job and was soon in a good position, but the winner always seemed to have his measure and he had to settle for second best. This was a promising debut though and winning an ordinary maiden should not prove overly difficult. (op 5-1 tchd 9-2)
Loyal Knight(IRE), whose promising debut effort pointed to this step up in trip suiting, was again done for toe, but there is definitely a decent level of ability there and he will be qualified for nurseries after one more run. (tchd 5-1)
Blue Sky Basin, whose stable's juveniles have been needing a run or two this season, shaped promisingly considering and natural progression should see him winning an ordinary maiden, possibly over 1m. (tchd 25-1)
Red Merlin(IRE) stepped up on his initial effort at Ascot and will be qualified for a handicap mark after one more run. He is one to keep an eye on. (op 14-1 tchd 16-1)
Resplendent Light again shaped well and the son of Fantastic Light will become more of a betting proposition once tackling 1m in nurseries. (tchd 12-1)

4509 XL INSURANCE H'CAP 7f 16y

7:05 (7:12) (Class 3) (0-90,87) 3-Y-0 **£7,772** (£2,312; £1,155; £577) **Stalls** High

Form RPR
3211 **1** **Shevchenko (IRE)**[21] 3857 3-9-9 **87** ... SebSanders 6 99+
(J Noseda) *hld up in 4th: smooth prog fr 2f out: led 1f out: drvn to assert: in command last 100yds* **5/6**[1]
-512 **2** *1 1/2* **Perfect Star**[21] 3857 3-9-6 **84** ... PhilipRobinson 4 89
(C G Cox) *trckd ldr: rdn to ld wl over 1f out: hdd 1f out: kpt on same pce* **10/3**[2]
-005 **3** *1/2* **Millestan (IRE)**[18] 3960 3-9-3 **81** ... TedDurcan 3 85
(H R A Cecil) *hld up in last pair: rdn over 2f out: prog u.p over 1f out: styd on ins fnl f* **8/1**
0033 **4** *1 1/2* **Princess Valerina**[33] 3480 3-9-6 **84** ... MichaelHills 5 84
(B W Hills) *racd freely: ldr: rdn to ld wl over 1f out: fdd* **15/2**[3]
001 **5** *1 1/2* **Norisan**[18] 3966 3-9-9 **87** ... (b) RyanMoore 8 83
(R Hannon) *chsd ldng pair: rdn wl over 2f out: grad fdd over 1f out* **14/1**
1-0 **6** *5* **Benllech**[23] 3797 3-9-2 **80** ... KerrinMcEvoy 7 62
(S Kirk) *hld up in last pair: rdn over 2f out: sn wknd* **33/1**

1m 29.69s (0.35) **Going Correction** +0.225s/f (Good) **6** Ran SP% **110.1**
Speed ratings (Par 104): **107,105,104,103,101 95**
CSF £3.62 CT £10.11 TOTE £1.70: £1.20, £1.80; EX 3.20.
Owner M Tabor, Mrs J Magnier & D Smith **Bred** Jim Fleming **Trained** Newmarket, Suffolk

FOCUS
A decent handicap for the grade, run at a strong pace. Solid form through the third backed up by a decent time.

NOTEBOOK
Shevchenko(IRE) ◆ continued his progression with a most ready display to land the hat-trick, despite having been raised 8lb for his previous course-and-distance success. The generous early pace was right up his street, and he looked to idle when in front, so should be rated value for further than the bare margin. He has been in the form of his life since being gelded in June and deserves a crack at a decent handicap over this trip now, with the totesport.com stakes at Ascot mext month looking a realistic target. (op 8-11 tchd 4-6)
Perfect Star remains in good form and did nothing wrong in defeat, yet failed to reverse previous course-and-distance form with the winner despite racing on 6lb better terms with that rival. She can be found another race. (op 4-1)
Millestan(IRE) was doing her best work towards the finish and posted just about her best effort of the current campaign. She needs to be ridden more promiently over this trip, however. (op 12-1)
Princess Valerina paid the price for refusing to settle on the early pace and was done with before the final furlong marker. She is better than this on her day, but still probably ran close to her official mark in defeat all the same. (op 6-1)
Norisan, dropped 5lb despite winning in claiming company last time, put up an improved effort on this step back up in grade yet was found out passing the 2f marker. (op 12-1)

4510 YOU DON'T NEED A DABBER @ WILLIAMHILLBINGO.COM H'CAP 1m 2f 7y

7:40 (7:42) (Class 4) (0-80,80) 3-Y-0 **£5,181** (£1,541; £770; £384) **Stalls** High

Form RPR
-031 **1** **Good Effect (USA)**[14] 4064 3-8-9 66 ... SebSanders 4 75
(A P Jarvis) *trckd ldrs: prog over 2f out: drvn to ld wl over 1f out: hrd pressed fnl f: jst prevailed* **14/1**
0-02 **2** *shd* **Demolition**[18] 3948 3-8-4 61 oh1 ... SimonWhitworth 6 70
(C A Cyzer) *tk fierce hold early: hld up in midfield: rdn and prog over 2f out: pressed wnr fnl f: upsides nr fin: jst pipped* **33/1**
2204 **3** *2* **Oakley Heffert (IRE)**[37] 3385 3-9-5 76 ... (b) RyanMoore 9 81
(R Hannon) *sn trckd ldr: rdn to ld over 2f out: hdd wl over 1f out: stl cl up ent fnl f: one pce* **5/1**[2]
2131 **4** *1* **Muhannak (IRE)**[11] 4184 3-9-9 80 ... NickyMackay 11 83
(G A Butler) *dwlt: sn in midfield: reminder after 3f: rdn and prog over 2f out: chsd ldrs 1f out: one pce fnl f* **5/1**[2]
521 **5** *3/4* **Dar Es Salaam**[36] 3399 3-9-7 78 ... JimmyFortune 8 80
(E A L Dunlop) *s.s: rchd midfield after 2f: drvn over 2f out: nt qckn and hld after: plugged on* **15/8**[1]
216 **6** *shd* **Wise Little Girl**[20] 3877 3-9-4 75 ... PhilipRobinson 1 76
(M A Jarvis) *prom: rdn and nt qckn over 2f out: one pce and no imp after* **14/1**
1650 **7** *2 1/2* **Aegis (IRE)**[10] 4197 3-9-2 73 ... MichaelHills 10 69
(B W Hills) *prom: rdn on inner over 2f out: fdd over 1f out* **18/1**
0056 **8** *shd* **Sir Liam (USA)**[7] 4277 3-9-2 73 ... (p) IanMongan 3 69
(P Mitchell) *settled in last trio: rdn wl over 2f out: no real prog* **50/1**
0350 **9** *1* **Eager Igor (USA)**[7] 4268 3-9-8 79 ... StephenCarson 7 73
(Eve Johnson Houghton) *settled in last pair: nt clr run briefly over 2f out: pushed along and nvr nr ldrs after* **10/1**
040 **10** *19* **Madam Vouvray**[42] 3214 3-8-9 66 ... TedDurcan 2 22
(B J Meehan) *rdn in detached last over 6f out: t.o* **40/1**
31 **11** *3* **Time Over**[13] 4106 3-9-1 72 ... KerrinMcEvoy 5 22
(J L Dunlop) *led: drvn and hdd over 2f out: wknd rapidly and eased: t.o* **6/1**[3]

2m 11.62s (1.38) **Going Correction** +0.225s/f (Good) **11** Ran SP% **117.4**
Speed ratings (Par 102): **103,102,101,100,99 99,97,97,96,81 79**
CSF £398.65 CT £2618.50 TOTE £18.20: £4.00, £6.30, £2.00; EX 284.80.
Owner Geoffrey Bishop and Ann Jarvis **Bred** Golden Gate Stud **Trained** Twyford, Bucks

FOCUS
A fair three-year-old handicap run at a solid pace. The first two came clear in a bobbing finish and solid form with the third close to his mark.

4511 PLAY IN THE CARIBBEAN @ WILLIAMHILLPOKER.COM H'CAP 1m 6f

8:10 (8:13) (Class 4) (0-80,78) 3-Y-0 **£5,829** (£1,734; £866; £432) **Stalls** Centre

Form RPR
0201 **1** **Alleviate (IRE)**[4] 4391 3-8-8 63 6ex ... SebSanders 2 76
(Sir Mark Prescott) *trckd ldr: led after 5f: mde rest: rdn over 2f out: styd on strly* **11/4**[2]
4211 **2** *2 1/2* **Duty Free (IRE)**[13] 4113 3-9-7 76 ... SteveDrowne 9 85
(H Morrison) *prom: lost pl 6f out: stdy prog to chse wnr over 2f out: drvn wl over 1f out: styd on but no imp* **9/4**[1]
6122 **3** *1 1/4* **Jawaaneb (USA)**[21] 3848 3-9-8 77 ... TedDurcan 10 85
(J L Dunlop) *mostly in midfield: rdn and prog over 2f out: chsd ldng pair wl over 1f out: kpt on same pce and no imp* **11/1**
4 *5* **Kavaloti (IRE)**[62] 3-9-8 77 ... (b) FergusSweeney 6 78
(G L Moore) *dwlt and rousted along in last: stl last and u.p over 3f out: styd on fnl 2f: nrst fin* **25/1**
3360 **5** *1* **Dan Tucker**[13] 4113 3-9-2 71 ... JimmyFortune 5 70
(B J Meehan) *hld up towards rr: stdy prog on outer 3f out to dispute 3rd 2f out: sn rdn and wknd* **16/1**

352 **6** 1 1/2 **I Predict A Riot (IRE)**34 3473 3-9-4 73 EddieAhern 7 70
(J W Hills) *dwlt: prog fr rr to chse wnr 1/2-way: hrd rdn and lost 2nd over 2f out: wknd* **10/1**

3005 **7** 1 1/4 **Title Deed (USA)**7 4277 3-8-11 66 PatDobbs 3 61
(A P Jarvis) *led for 5f: drvn 3f out: wknd over 2f out* **50/1**

0261 **8** 3/4 **Its Moon (IRE)**26 3719 3-9-6 75 KerrinMcEvoy 1 69
(T D Walford) *cl up: rdn 3f out: wknd fr over 2f out* **8/1**

3106 **9** 1 1/2 **Galianna (IRE)**17 3993 3-9-9 78 DaneO'Neill 8 70
(Pat Eddery) *squeezed out after 1f: trckd ldrs: lost pl after 5f: wl in rr 5f out: rdn and struggling 3f out* **11/1**

5211 **10** 6 **Squadron**18 3969 3-9-9 78 RyanMoore 4 62
(Mrs A J Perrett) *hld up: prog to trck ldrs after 4f and racd wd: rdn 3f out: wknd over 2f out* **7/1**3

3m 7.15s (2.64) **Going Correction** +0.225s/f (Good) **10** Ran SP% **118.5**
Speed ratings (Par 102): **101,99,98,96,95 94,93,93,92,89**
CSF £9.54 CT £58.39 TOTE £3.90: £1.80, £1.40, £2.80; EX 8.90 Place 6 £17.68, Place 5 £13.66.
Owner Mrs Sonia Rogers **Bred** Miss K Rausing & Airlie Stud **Trained** Newmarket, Suffolk
■ Stewards' Enquiry : Pat Dobbs three-day ban: careless riding (Aug 26-28)

FOCUS
A fair three-year-old staying handicap, run at a sound pace. The first three all rate progressive.
T/Plt: £39.00 to a £1 stake. Pool: £59,788.35. 1,117.30 winning tickets. T/Qpdt: £15.70 to a £1 stake. Pool: £4,511.50. 211.70 winning tickets. JN

4335YARMOUTH (L-H)

Wednesday, August 15

OFFICIAL GOING: Good to firm (good in straight)
Wind: breezy Weather: cloudy and warm

4512 WBX.COM £25 FREE BET FOR NEW ACCOUNTS (S) STKS 5f 43y
2:20 (2:21) (Class 6) 2-Y-O **£1,943** (£578; £288; £144) **Stalls** High

Form RPR

0 **1** **Smokeyourpipe (IRE)**100 1540 2-8-9 0 LiamJones(3) 6 55
(J L Spearing) *sn rdn along: effrt under driving 2f out: sustained run fnl f to ld fnl 100yds: all out* **4/1**2

0033 **2** nk **Culzean Bay**6 4311 2-8-4 45 NeilChalmers(3) 9 49
(A Bailey) *taken down early: led: rdn 2f out: hdd fnl 100yds: kpt on* **9/1**

045 **3** 1 **Tintorero**11 4154 2-8-12 59 (v1) JamieSpencer 2 50
(M J Wallace) *settled in rr: effrt 2f out: rdn and ev ch fr over 1f out: kpt hanging lft and nt run on* **8/11**1

5 **4** 9 **Tiara Princess (IRE)**27 3681 2-8-7 0 (b1) RichardMullen 3 13
(Rae Guest) *nvr gng wl: cl up tl drvn over 2f out: hung lft and nt keen after* **6/1**3

000 **5** nk **Lightning Lad**22 3823 2-8-12 40 EddieAhern 5 17
(J R Jenkins) *stdd s: racd in last pl: struggling 1/2-way* **22/1**

00 **6** 5 **Tomba Maestro**16 4027 2-8-12 0 ChrisCatlin 4 —
(J L Spearing) *pressed ldr tl lost pl v rapidly over 1f out* **40/1**

64.72 secs (1.92) **Going Correction** +0.20s/f (Good) **6** Ran SP% **109.0**
Speed ratings (Par 92): **92,91,89,75,75 67**
CSF £34.85 TOTE £4.20: £2.10, £2.20; EX 42.90 TRIFECTA Pool £383.35 - 2.02 winning units..The winner was sold to M Quinn for 4,600gns. Culzean Bay was claimed by G Newton for £5,000.
Owner J Spearing **Bred** A B Mulholland **Trained** Kinnersley, Worcs

FOCUS
A weak contest in which the front three drew nine lengths clear of the remainder and the form looks sound enough.

NOTEBOOK
Smokeyourpipe(IRE), too inexperienced to make an impact in a fair maiden on his debut at Windsor in May, had been off since but this drop in grade was always going to see him in a better light and he just did enough to score, rallying strongly under pressure. A step up to 6f is going to suit in time and he looks capable of winning more races. (op 7-1)
Culzean Bay has improved with racing and her two most recent efforts pointed to a big run here. Soon in front, she really pressed on in the final furlong, but could not repel the winner's late charge and was narrowly denied. This is her level and she deserves to win one of these eventually. (op 7-1)
Tintorero made no impact off a mark of 64 on his recent handicap debut, but this was easier and better was expected in the first-time visor. Made a very short price, he was ridden with plenty of confidence by Spencer but, having reached a challenging position, he found very little and threw his chance away by hanging. Official explanation: jockey said colt hung left (op 4-5 tchd 4-6)
Tiara Princess(IRE), who cost just 2,500gns, did not show a lot on her recent debut in this grade at Leicester, and the application of blinkers made little difference. (op 9-2 tchd 13-2)

4513 WBX.COM 0% COMMISSION ON BIG RACES MAIDEN FILLIES' STKS 6f 3y
2:50 (2:53) (Class 5) 3-Y-O **£2,849** (£847; £423; £211) **Stalls** High

Form RPR

-452 **1** **Beautiful Madness (IRE)**6 4324 3-9-0 64 EddieAhern 2 71
(M G Quinlan) *settled in rr: effrt 2f out: rdn over 1f out: led fnl 100yds: sn in command* **3/1**2

-022 **2** 3 **Tarkamara (IRE)**14 4066 3-9-0 75 JamieSpencer 3 61
(P F I Cole) *prom: led 2f out: drvn 1f out: hdd 100yds out: immediately outpcd* **8/15**1

3 1/2 **O Fourlunda** 3-9-0 0 HayleyTurner 8 60
(C E Brittain) *t.k.h early: cl up: drvn over 2f out: racd awkwardly and hung lft: btn 1f out* **18/1**

4332 **4** 1 **Candyland (IRE)**128 974 3-9-0 60 ChrisCatlin 1 57
(M Quinn) *led 4f: sn drvn: outpcd by ldng pair over 1f out* **12/1**3

04- **5** 7 **Mariaverdi**253 6710 3-9-0 0 RobertHavlin 5 34
(B J Meehan) *chsd ldrs tl rdn and lost tch tamely 2f out* **20/1**

6 shd **Southwarknewsflash** 3-8-9 0 (t) KevinGhunowa(5) 7 34
(Mrs C A Dunnett) *dwlt: rdn and extremely green: a wl bhd but showed valiant attitude and nt disgracd* **66/1**

50 **7** 10 **Boleyna (USA)**11 4182 3-9-0 0 (e) RichardMullen 6 2
(Rae Guest) *plld hrd: prom briefly: drvn 3f out: struggling bdly after: t.o* **50/1**

1m 15.96s (2.26) **Going Correction** +0.20s/f (Good) **7** Ran SP% **111.4**
Speed ratings (Par 97): **92,88,87,86,76 76,63**
CSF £4.65 TOTE £4.10: £1.70, £1.10; EX 5.90 Trifecta £24.40 Pool £512.09 - 14.87 winning units..
Owner P Bohan **Bred** Patrick Bohan **Trained** Newmarket, Suffolk

FOCUS
A weak maiden and dubious form with the winner rated to his best handicap effort.

Southwarknewsflash Official explanation: jockey said filly missed the break

4514 JOIN WBX.COM FOR FREE FOOTBALL SHIRT FILLIES' H'CAP 6f 3y
3:20 (3:21) (Class 5) (0-70,63) 3-Y-O **£2,914** (£867; £433; £216) **Stalls** High

Form RPR

6020 **1** **Day By Day**5 4361 3-9-4 60 (b) RobertHavlin 5 67
(B J Meehan) *sn pressing ldr: rdn to ld over 1f out: kpt on wl fnl 100yds* **13/2**

0-03 **2** 1 1/4 **Laura's Best (IRE)**11 4164 3-9-7 63 EddieAhern 6 66
(W J Haggas) *towards rr: effrt 2f out: rdn to go 2nd cl home: nt rch wnr* **5/1**3

0150 **3** hd **On The Map**9 4224 3-8-13 55 (v) RichardMullen 7 57
(A P Jarvis) *drvn to ld: hdd over 1f out: one pce ins fnl f* **16/1**

0-51 **4** nk **Luck Will Come (IRE)**11 4157 3-9-4 60 JamieSpencer 2 61
(M J Wallace) *dropped out in last pl: rdn and hdwy 2f out: wnt 2nd v briefly wl ins fnl f: nvr looked like winning* **7/4**1

50 **5** 1 1/2 **Time Share (IRE)**24 3763 3-9-1 57 (be) HayleyTurner 8 54
(J Ryan) *chsd ldrs: hrd rdn and outpcd 2f out: sme prog ins fnl f* **9/1**

-010 **6** 4 **Savanagh Forest (IRE)**9 4226 3-8-0 45 LiamJones(3) 4 29
(M Quinn) *chsd ldrs: drvn 2f out: sn btn* **28/1**

-313 **7** 2 1/2 **Xalted**6 4326 3-8-10 52 SaleemGolam 1 28
(S C Williams) *swtchd lft and racd alone far side: btn wl over 1f out* **7/2**2

0404 **8** 5 **Retaliate**21 3845 3-8-8 50 ChrisCatlin 3 10
(M Quinn) *s.s: struggling fr 1/2-way: eased fnl f* **16/1**

1m 14.46s (0.76) **Going Correction** +0.20s/f (Good) **8** Ran SP% **113.8**
Speed ratings (Par 97): **102,100,100,99,97 92,89,82**
CSF £38.42 CT £496.36 TOTE £9.90: £2.80, £2.20, £5.70; EX 33.60 Trifecta £419.30 Part won. Pool £590.69 - 0.78 winning units..
Owner T G & Mrs M E Holdcroft **Bred** Bearstone Stud & T Herbert Jackson **Trained** Manton, Wilts

FOCUS
A moderate handicap run at a steady tempo and not a race to be with.

4515 WBX.COM 0% COMMISSION ON WIGAN V MIDDLESBOROUGH H'CAP 7f 3y
3:50 (3:52) (Class 5) (0-75,75) 3-Y-O+ **£2,914** (£867; £433; £216) **Stalls** High

Form RPR

5065 **1** **Out For A Stroll**1 4474 8-8-9 57 SaleemGolam 2 63
(S C Williams) *chsd ldrs on outside: drvn 3f out: sustained run to ld fnl 75yds: gamely* **8/1**

1104 **2** hd **Golden Prospect**19 3900 3-9-2 70 EddieAhern 1 73
(J W Hills) *bhd: drvn 2f out: gd prog after: drvn ahd briefly 100yds out: no ex fnl strides* **4/1**2

-60U **3** 1/2 **Petito (IRE)**13 4107 4-8-8 59 LiamJones(3) 8 63
(J L Spearing) *towards rr: effrt whn checked briefly 2f out: rallied ins fnl f: kpt on cl home* **6/1**3

6000 **4** 1 1/4 **The Cayterers**12 4122 5-9-6 73 (p) KevinGhunowa(5) 4 74
(J M Bradley) *t.k.h: prom: rdn 1/2-way: led over 1f out: hdd 100yds out: nt qckn* **10/1**

-566 **5** 3/4 **Swift Cut (IRE)**11 4163 3-8-13 67 RichardMullen 11 64
(A P Jarvis) *cl up: drvn and one pce over 1f out: kpt on fnl 100yds* **18/1**

4652 **6** nk **Fiefdom (IRE)**7 4295 5-9-10 75 (p) JerryO'Dwyer(3) 10 73
(I W McInnes) *pressed ldr tl drvn and edgd lft 2f out: no ex fnl f* **6/1**3

0304 **7** hd **Whistleupthewind**16 4029 4-8-8 56 oh5 (p) DaleGibson 7 53
(J M P Eustace) *kpt hanging lft: led tl drvn and hdd over 1f out: nt qckn* **14/1**

4000 **8** hd **Moayed**12 4134 8-9-7 69 (b) IanMongan 3 66
(N P Littmoden) *s.s: drvn and nvr gng wl in rr* **20/1**

0502 **9** 2 1/2 **Kaveri (USA)**22 3828 4-9-8 70 JamieSpencer 6 60
(C E Brittain) *t.k.h in midfield: swtchd lft to chal over 1f out: sn btn* **5/2**1

0/0- **10** 16 **Knickyknackienoo**441 2141 6-8-8 56 oh7 ChrisCatlin 5 3
(T T Clement) *struggling over 2f out: eased fnl f* **66/1**

1m 27.44s (0.84) **Going Correction** +0.20s/f (Good)
WFA 3 from 4yo+ 6lb **10** Ran SP% **115.5**
Speed ratings (Par 103): **103,102,102,100,99 99,99,99,96,77**
CSF £39.66 CT £213.11 TOTE £10.00: £2.30, £1.70, £2.10; EX 51.50 TRIFECTA Not won..
Owner The Nomads **Bred** Exors Of The Late Mrs F G Allen **Trained** Newmarket, Suffolk
■ Stewards' Enquiry : Eddie Ahern caution: careless riding

FOCUS
A modest handicap rated around the placed horses and the form makes sense.
Out For A Stroll Official explanation: trainer could offer no explanation for the apparent improvement in form
Fiefdom(IRE) Official explanation: jockey said gelding hung left from 3f out
Whistleupthewind Official explanation: jockey said filly hung left throughout
Moayed Official explanation: jockey said gelding was slowly away

4516 WBX.COM £25 FREE BET FOR NEW ACCOUNTS CLAIMING STKS 1m 2f 21y
4:20 (4:22) (Class 6) 3-Y-O **£1,943** (£578; £288; £144) **Stalls** Low

Form RPR

-255 **1** **Jocheski (IRE)**188 392 3-9-5 64 JamieSpencer 4 63+
(M J Wallace) *led 1f: settled in trcking ldrs and gng wl: led wl over 2f out: rdn 1f out: comf* **11/8**1

5000 **2** 1 1/2 **Anatolian Prince**18 3949 3-8-5 50 (t) DaleGibson 6 46
(J M P Eustace) *dropped out in last pl: prog 3f out: chsd wnr over 2f out: drvn and no imp* **9/2**3

6300 **3** shd **Picky**7 4266 3-8-7 57 (v1) ChrisCatlin 1 48
(C Tinkler) *sn stdd towards rr: effrt 3f out: rdn 2f out: duelled for 2nd fnl f: one pce and no ch w wnr* **4/1**2

0000 **4** 9 **Dancewiththestars (USA)**9 4231 3-8-3 47 (t) AmyBaker(7) 7 33
(Miss J Feilden) *cl up: disp 2nd briefly 3f out: wknd tamely 2f out* **8/1**

-000 **5** 2 1/2 **Baarrij**6 4327 3-8-4 52 SaleemGolam 2 22
(G A Huffer) *nvr bttr than midfield: rdn 3f out: nt keen and sn labouring* **5/1**

0000 **6** 8 **Panda Power**6 4340 3-8-2 55 (v1) JimmyQuinn 3 4
(S C Williams) *led after 1f and sn pulling hrd: rdn and hdd wl over 2f out: reluctant and dropped out qckly: t.o* **18/1**

06 **7** 12 **Wahhaj**7 4292 3-8-12 0 CharlotteKerton(7) 5 —
(G Prodromou) *sn chsng ldr: lost pl over 3f out and hung lft: t.o over 1f out* **66/1**

2m 8.88s (0.78) **Going Correction** +0.05s/f (Good) **7** Ran SP% **114.8**
Speed ratings (Par 98): **98,96,96,89,87 81,71**
CSF £8.03 TOTE £1.90: £1.20, £2.20; EX 7.50.
Owner Mrs Ruby Williams **Bred** E O'Leary **Trained** Newmarket, Suffolk

FOCUS
A typically moderate claimer rated through the third and the form should be treated with a degree of caution.

4517 WBX.COM 0% COMMISSION ON BIG RACES H'CAP 1m 2f 21y
4:50 (4:50) (Class 6) (0-65,65) 3-Y-O+ **£1,943** (£578; £288; £144) **Stalls** Low

Form RPR

1043 **1** **Princess Lavinia**[34] 3451 4-9-11 **62** .... RobertHavlin 1 72
(G Wragg) *led 2f: cl up tl led again wl over 2f out: rdn and hung lft over 1f out: hld on gamely* **10/1**

0642 **2** *nk* **Billy One Punch**[6] 4340 5-9-10 **61** .... JamieSpencer 2 70
(G G Margarson) *stdd in midfield: effrt and rdn 2f out: wnt 2nd fnl 100yds: drvn and r.o: jst hld cl home* **13/8**[1]

4663 **3** *2 1/2* **Rawdon (IRE)**[6] 4333 6-10-0 **65** .... (v) HayleyTurner 8 69
(M L W Bell) *cl up: led 3f out tl wl over 2f out: v one pce fnl f: lost 2nd 100yds out* **4/1**[2]

0054 **4** *1 1/4* **Wee Charlie Castle (IRE)**[14] 4063 4-8-13 **50** .... (b) OscarUrbina 3 52
(G C H Chung) *on his toes and taken down early: s.i.s: bhd: swtchd rt and effrt wd over 2f out: nvr able to chal* **11/1**

5044 **5** *5* **Magic Amigo**[41] 3249 6-9-0 **51** .... (v) JimmyQuinn 5 43
(J R Jenkins) *hdstr to post: led at gd pce after 2f tl rdn and hdd 3f out: btn wl over 1f out* **11/1**

-001 **6** *shd* **Regal Sunset (IRE)**[16] 4031 4-9-4 **55** .... DaleGibson 9 46
(D E Cantillon) *bhd: rdn over 3f out: sn no imp* **13/2**[3]

0050 **7** *4* **Don Pasquale**[11] 4161 5-9-4 **55** .... ChrisCatlin 6 38
(J T Stimpson) *last tl 1/2-way: brief effrt 4f out: rdn and sn btn* **16/1**

050- **8** *shd* **Pleasing Gift**[264] 6584 4-8-8 **48** .... LiamJones(3) 4 31
(J M P Eustace) *pressed ldrs: rdn over 3f out: wknd over 2f out* **50/1**

3461 **9** *1 3/4* **Trevian**[11] 4161 6-9-0 **56** .... KevinGhunowa(5) 12 36
(J M Bradley) *plld hrd and chsd ldrs: drvn 4f out: wknd 3f out: eased fnl f* **16/1**

03 **10** *11* **Mr Napoleon (IRE)**[6] 4340 5-8-12 **56** .... CharlotteKerton(7) 11 14
(G Prodromou) *racd on outside: wl plcd tl 1/2-way: wknd 4f out: struggling bdly fnl 2f: t.o* **14/1**

2m 9.31s (1.21) **Going Correction** +0.05s/f (Good)
WFA 3 from 4yo+ 9lb **10** Ran SP% **117.6**
Speed ratings (Par 101): **97,96,94,93,89 89,86,86,85,76**
CSF £26.82 CT £79.74 TOTE £11.30: £3.40, £1.30, £1.80; EX 38.60 Trifecta £124.00 Pool £324.89 - 1.86 winning units..
Owner D R Hunnisett **Bred** Mrs E Y Hunnisett **Trained** Newmarket, Suffolk

FOCUS
A moderate handicap run at an ordinary pace. The first two pulled clear but the modest time tends to limit confidence.

4518 JOIN WBX.COM FOR FREE FOOTBALL SHIRT H'CAP 1m 3f 101y
5:20 (5:22) (Class 5) (0-70,68) 3-Y-O **£2,914** (£867; £433; £216) **Stalls** Low

Form RPR

0425 **1** **Western Point (IRE)**[20] 3876 3-8-5 **52** .... JimmyQuinn 4 66
(Sir Mark Prescott) *prom: rdn 4f out: led 2f out: hung lft whn in control 120yds out: styd on dourly* **11/4**[1]

1201 **2** *1 1/2* **Raise The Goblet (IRE)**[14] 4069 3-9-3 **67** .... LiamJones(3) 10 78
(W J Haggas) *led: drvn and hdd 2f out: one pce and hld whn crossed 120yds out: hanging rt after* **3/1**[2]

000 **3** *1/2* **Spanish Diva**[25] 3743 3-9-7 **68** .... OscarUrbina 2 78
(S C Williams) *last away: sn in midfield: rdn 4f out: 3rd and hanging lft fnl 2f: kpt on wout threatening* **11/1**

520 **4** *6* **Blockley (USA)**[23] 3804 3-8-9 **56** .... (v) JamieSpencer 7 56
(Ian Williams) *pressed ldr: drvn over 4f out: lost 2nd 3f out: fdd wl over 1f out* **13/2**

0645 **5** *1* **Dubai Shadow (IRE)**[13] 4104 3-8-11 **58** .... HayleyTurner 8 56
(C E Brittain) *midfield: rdn 5f out: struggling fnl 3f* **10/1**

5055 **6** *nk* **Sir Duke (IRE)**[7] 4297 3-8-11 **58** .... (v1) RobertHavlin 3 56
(P W D'Arcy) *in rr-div: lost tch over 3f out* **9/2**[3]

1340 **7** *4* **Sweet World**[14] 4069 3-9-1 **62** .... RichardMullen 1 53
(A P Jarvis) *last pair much of way: lost tch 4f out* **12/1**

-640 **8** *1 3/4* **Memphis Marie**[6] 4340 3-8-2 **49** .... ChrisCatlin 5 37
(C N Allen) *midfield: lost tch tamely 4f out* **25/1**

5-60 **9** *nk* **Mystical Moon**[66] 2490 3-9-3 **64** .... DaleGibson 9 51
(Lady Herries) *cl up tl rdn and lost pl over 5f out* **20/1**

0660 **10** *9* **Wightgar**[23] 3792 3-7-9 **49** oh3 .... (tp) AmyBaker(7) 6 21
(R A Kvisla) *last pair: struggling 1/2-way: t.o* **66/1**

2m 26.61s (-0.89) **Going Correction** +0.05s/f (Good) **10** Ran SP% **118.4**
Speed ratings (Par 100): **105,103,103,99,98 98,95,94,93,87**
CSF £11.09 CT £78.58 TOTE £3.60: £1.80, £1.40, £3.80; EX 12.20 Trifecta £111.80 Pool £349.87 - 2.22 winning units. Place 6 £55.29, Place 5 £15.69.
Owner Charles C Walker-Osborne House III **Bred** Mount Coote Stud **Trained** Newmarket, Suffolk

FOCUS
Another moderate handicap, but it was run at a strong pace and the form looks fair and is rated positively through the runner-up.
T/Plt: £132.70 to a £1 stake. Pool: £58,301.85. 320.70 winning tickets. T/Qpdt: £32.50 to a £1 stake. Pool: £3,728.10. 84.70 winning tickets. IM

4443 DEAUVILLE (R-H)
Wednesday, August 15

OFFICIAL GOING: Turf - good; aw - standard

4520a PRIX GONTAUT-BIRON - BEACHCOMBER HOTELS ROYAL PALM (GROUP 3) 1m 2f
2:55 (2:57) 4-Y-O+ **£27,027** (£10,811; £8,108; £5,405; £2,703)

RPR

1 **Echo Of Light**[32] 3523 5-8-9 .... (p) LDettori 13 110
(Saeed Bin Suroor) *mde all: pushed along 1 1/2f out and r.o: rdn fnl f: jst hld on gamely* **16/10**[1]

2 *shd* **Atlantic Air (FR)**[28] 3665 5-9-1 .... TThulliez 8 115
(Y De Nicolay, France) *mid-div: disputing 6th st: r.o fr 1 1/2f out: drvn and wnt 2nd 1f out: chal fnl 100yds: jst failed* **87/10**

3 *snk* **Kocab**[28] 3665 5-8-9 .... SPasquier 10 109
(A Fabre, France) *mid-div: cl 8th st: r.o wl fr 1 1/2f out: disputing 2nd fnl f: styd on wl to line: nrest at fin* **9/1**

4 *2* **Major Grace (FR)**[46] 3124 4-8-9 .... ACrastus 11 105
(Y De Nicolay, France) *hld up: 10th st: pushed along and hdwy in centre fr over 1 1/2f out: styd on steadily and tk 4th 100yds out* **44/1**

5 *3/4* **Elasos (FR)**[28] 3665 5-8-11 .... DBonilla 4 106
(D Sepulchre, France) *mid-div: disputing 6th st: rdn 1 1/2f out: styd on but n.d* **27/1**

6 *hd* **Echoes Rock (GER)**[24] 3780 4-8-9 .... JVictoire 3 103
(A Fabre, France) *prom: 3rd st: rdn and wnt 2nd 2f out: wknd fnl f* **10/1**

7 *snk* **Dickens (GER)**[24] 3778 4-8-9 .... CSoumillon 2 103
(H Blume, Germany) *hld up: sme late hdwy but n.d* **56/10**[2]

8 *2* **Musketier (GER)**[20] 5-8-9 .... OPeslier 5 99
(P Bary, France) *racd in 2nd: pushed along st: sn lost pl: one pce fr 1 1/2f out* **16/1**

9 *3/4* **Merlerault (USA)**[17] 4012 4-8-9 .... RonanThomas 6 97
(P Demercastel, France) *in tch: 5th st: pushed along 1 1/2f out: styd on tl no ex fr over 1f out* **51/1**

10 *3* **Numide (FR)**[62] 2617 4-8-9 .... C-PLemaire 7 91
(J-C Rouget, France) *hld up: last st: nvr in contention* **7/1**[3]

0 **Cocodrail (IRE)**[122] 6-8-9 .... DBoeuf 12 —
(F Brogi, Italy) *towards rr: wkng ent st* **40/1**

0 **Monachesi (IRE)**[287] 4-8-9 .... TJarnet 9 —
(F & L Camici, Italy) *in tch: 4th st: wknd 1 1/2f out* **57/1**

0 **Willywell (FR)**[28] 3665 5-8-11 .... IMendizabal 1 —
(J-P Gauvin, France) *missed break and racd towards rr: 12th st: nvr a factor* **32/1**

2m 5.40s (-5.40) **13** Ran SP% **116.3**
PARI-MUTUEL: WIN 2.60; PL 1.50, 2.60, 2.40; DF 11.80.
Owner Godolphin **Bred** Kilcarn Stud **Trained** Newmarket, Suffolk

NOTEBOOK
Echo Of Light was refitted with cheekpieces, which certainly helped him to settle down during the race and keep a straight line. He was asked to go from pillar to post and fairly flew down the back straight and around the turn. With two furlongs left to run he looked likely to win by several lengths, but his stride began to shorten inside the final furlong and in the end he only just held on under considerable pressure. This was his first win in nearly 11 months and, all being well, he will go on to try and land the Daniel Wildenstein for the second consecutive year at Longchamp in October.
Atlantic Air(FR), considering he was giving weight to the others, put up a fine performance having lifted this event a year ago. In mid-division early, he was extracated to challenge halfway up the straight and was cutting down the winner with every stride, but the post came a metre too early. He was slightly unlucky rounding the final turn, which could have been the difference between success and defeat, and his next likely race is the Prix Dollar at Longchamp on October 6th.
Kocab was given every possible chance and made his challenge together with the winner. He was putting in his best work at the finish and this was another solid performance.
Major Grace(FR), who had plenty to do coming into the straight, made steady progress from two out up the centre of the track and was running on at the finish, but never looked likely to catch the first three.

4487 BEVERLEY (R-H)
Thursday, August 16

OFFICIAL GOING: Good (9.7)
After just 3mm rain overnight the ground was described as 'mainly good but loose on top'.
Wind: Fresh, half-against Weather: fine but blustery

4521 WAITROSE WILLERBY (S) H'CAP 1m 4f 16y
2:10 (2:11) (Class 6) (0-60,58) 3-Y-O+ **£2,914** (£867; £433; £216) **Stalls** High

Form RPR

3140 **1** **Regency Red (IRE)**[3] 4464 9-9-6 **52** .... NCallan 7 58+
(W M Brisbourne) *hld up in mid-div: smooth hdwy over 4f out: shkn up to ld 1f out: wnt clr: v comf* **3/1**[1]

4040 **2** *4* **Tiegs (IRE)**[10] 4230 5-8-13 **45** .... DavidAllan 2 41
(P W Hiatt) *chsd ldr: chal over 3f out: led over 1f out: sn hdd and no ex* **20/1**

0050 **3** *shd* **Cecina Marina**[3] 4449 4-9-1 **47** .... PaulMulrennan 8 43
(C W Thornton) *mid-div: hdwy over 2f out: kpt on wl fnl f* **25/1**

-654 **4** *1 1/2* **Red Sun**[15] 3840 10-9-8 **54** .... (tp) PhillipMakin 5 48
(R C Guest) *hdwy to chse ldrs 9f out: drvn over 5f out: one pce fnl 2f* **10/1**

0-1 **5** *3 1/2* **Revolving World (IRE)**[71] 2372 4-9-7 **53** .... (t) KDarley 12 41
(L R James) *s.s: hdwy on outer over 2f out: hung rt over 1f out: nvr nr to chal* **13/2**

000- **6** *1 1/4* **Perfect Punch**[48] 2871 8-9-9 **55** .... TomEaves 6 41
(K G Reveley) *s.i.s: outpcd and sn bhd: kpt on fnl 2f: nvr on terms* **12/1**

6014 **7** *hd* **Ellies Faith**[4] 4426 3-8-6 **48** .... (b) PaulFessey 11 34
(N Bycroft) *led: hdd & wknd over 1f out* **9/2**[3]

000- **8** *1/2* **Arch Folly**[269] 6540 5-9-5 **54** .... LiamJones(3) 4 39
(R J Price) *in rr-div: effrt over 4f out: hmpd over 2f out: nvr a factor* **16/1**

50-0 **9** *4* **Moon Melody (GER)**[9] 4246 4-9-12 **58** .... RoystonFfrench 3 36
(M E Sowersby) *trckd ldrs: reminders over 4f out: wknd over 2f out* **66/1**

5025 **10** *6* **Mangrove Cay (IRE)**[9] 4249 5-9-1 **47** .... PatCosgrave 9 16
(A J Lockwood) *chsd ldrs: hung lft and lost pl over 2f out: bhd and eased ins fnl f: lame* **7/2**[2]

2m 41.85s (1.64) **Going Correction** +0.075s/f (Good)
WFA 3 from 4yo+ 10lb **10** Ran SP% **111.5**
Speed ratings (Par 101): **97,94,94,93,90 90,89,89,86,82**
CSF £60.32 CT £1081.52 TOTE £4.60: £1.60, £5.40, £8.20; EX 67.70.There was no bid for the winner.
Owner Hamerton, Twidle **Bred** Patrick J Burke **Trained** Great Ness, Shropshire
■ Halland was withdrawn (11/1, refused to enter stalls). R4 applies, deduct 5p in the £.

FOCUS
Moderate form but the winner once again showed himself a handy performer in this sort of company.
Arch Folly Official explanation: jockey said gelding was denied a clear run
Mangrove Cay(IRE) Official explanation: jockey said gelding hung left; vet said gelding returned lame

4522 EBF PRESTIGE RECRUITMENT SPECIALISTS MAIDEN FILLIES' STKS 5f
2:40 (2:40) (Class 4) 2-Y-O **£5,181** (£1,541; £770; £384) **Stalls** High

Form RPR

62 **1** **Mey Blossom**[20] 3915 2-8-9 0 .... MichaelJStainton(5) 9 79+
(R M Whitaker) *mde virtually all: rdn clr over 1f out: readily* **11/8**[1]

2 *5* **Princess Rhianna (IRE)** 2-9-0 0 .... LeeEnstone 1 61
(K R Burke) *in rr-div: hdwy on outer 2f out: styd on wl ins fnl f* **40/1**

6 **3** *3/4* **On Instinct (IRE)**[69] 2416 2-9-0 0 .... RoystonFfrench 10 63+
(B Smart) *hld up towards rr: hdwy 2f out: kpt on wl fnl f* **20/1**

52 **4** 3/4 **Red Wings (IRE)**[12] 4173 2-9-0 0 .... PatCosgrave 3 56
(G A Swinbank) *jnd wnr after 1f: wknd fnl 150yds* **11/4**[2]
5 2 1/2 **Midnight Oasis** 2-9-0 0 .... SebSanders 5 47
(Rae Guest) *trckd ldrs: effrt 2f out: kpt on same pce* **12/1**
0000 **6** 1/2 **Eboracum Dream**[37] 3398 2-9-0 52 .... (b) DavidAllan 2 45
(T D Easterby) *swvd lft s: in rr: kpt on fnl 2f: nvr nr ldrs* **66/1**
0 **7** 2 **Joint Agency (IRE)**[26] 3750 2-9-0 0 .... DanielTudhope 8 38
(N Wilson) *chsd ldrs: effrt and edgd rt over 1f out: sn wknd* **66/1**
00 **8** shd **Scarlet Royal**[12] 4173 2-9-0 0 .... PaulQuinn 4 37
(Mrs Marjorie Fife) *sn outpcd and in rr: hdwy and edgd rt over 1f out: nvr nr ldrs* **100/1**
0 **9** 2 **Eternal Optimist (IRE)**[16] 4041 2-9-0 0 .... PaulMulrennan 13 30
(C W Thornton) *chsd ldrs: wknd over 1f out* **40/1**
4 **10** 1 1/2 **Miss Bronte**[17] 4020 2-8-9 0 .... RussellKennemore(5) 6 25
(R Hollinshead) *chsd ldrs: wknd appr fnl f* **8/1**
11 3/4 **James's Lass (IRE)** 2-9-0 0 .... PaulHanagan 11 22
(R A Fahey) *dwlt: reminders after 1f: hdwy over 2f out: wkng whn hmpd over 1f out* **14/1**
12 7 **Kiowa Princess** 2-9-0 0 .... PhillipMakin 12 —
(M Dods) *dwlt: sn prom: wkng whn hmpd over 1f out* **6/1**[3]
0 **13** shd **Lady From Westow**[56] 2803 2-8-11 0 .... JamieMoriarty(3) 7 —
(P T Midgley) *hld up in mid-div: hung rt and lost pl over 1f out* **100/1**

65.36 secs (1.36) **Going Correction** +0.175s/f (Good) **13** Ran SP% **123.1**
Speed ratings (Par 93): **96,88,86,85,81 80,77,77,74,71 70,59,59**
CSF £82.79 TOTE £2.60: £1.10, £5.90, £4.80; EX 118.40.
Owner Waz Developments Ltd **Bred** Hellwood Stud Farm **Trained** Scarcroft, W Yorks
■ Stewards' Enquiry : Daniel Tudhope one-day ban: careless riding (Aug 27)

FOCUS
Probably a useful performance from the winner in this otherwise modest maiden. The fourth was below form and there is not much strength in depth in this.

NOTEBOOK
Mey Blossom, whose second at Thirsk had been given a boost when the third won a nursery next time off 82, looked to hold strong claims and she duly made every yard for a clear-cut win. Highly regarded by her trainer, she is likely to be chasing black type sooner rather than later. (op 15-8 tchd 2-1 in a place)
Princess Rhianna(IRE), a half-sister to four winners including Mr Picchio, a multiple sprint winner in Italy, Come What July, a multiple 1m to 1m6f winner, and Jimmy Byrne, a multiple 7f to 1m2f winner, had no chance with the useful winner, but this was still an encouraging debut effort, especially from her poor draw. She should improve. (op 33-1)
On Instinct(IRE), who was too keen on her debut two months ago, settled better this time and stayed on well from off the pace. She is likely to be suited by further in time as she is out of a mare who won over middle distances at three. (op 14-1)
Red Wings(IRE) had to work hard to join the eventual winner from her low draw and probably paid for that effort in the closing stages. She is now eligible to run in nurseries. (op 7-2)
Midnight Oasis, a half-sister to Group 3 5f winner Miss Anabaa, and to useful prolific winning sprint handicappers Move It and Out After Dark, hails from a stable not really known for sending out juvenile debutante winners. This was a satisfactory start and she should do better in time. (tchd 14-1)
Eboracum Dream found this trip on the short side. She has a mark of 52 and would be better running in selling company. (op 50-1)
Kiowa Princess Official explanation: jockey said filly ran green

4523 SPORTHULL.CO.UK H'CAP 1m 1f 207y
3:15 (3:15) (Class 3) (0-90,90) 3-Y-O+ £7,124 (£2,119; £1,059; £529) Stalls High

Form RPR
2231 **1** **Ravarino (USA)**[26] 3731 3-8-11 79 .... SebSanders 7 91+
(Sir Michael Stoute) *chsd ldrs: led over 1f out: edgd rt: hld on gamely* **7/2**[2]
634- **2** 1 **Zonergem**[104] 5776 9-10-0 88 .... NCallan 4 94
(Lady Herries) *swtchd rt after 1f: hld up in rr: effrt on inner over 3f out: chal appr fnl f: no ex ins fnl f* **18/1**
0000 **3** 2 **Habalwatan (IRE)**[19] 3940 3-9-0 87 .... AhmedAjtebi(5) 1 89
(C E Brittain) *trckd ldrs: stdd and taken to rr after 2f: effrt over 3f out: styd on fnl f* **9/1**
1454 **4** nk **Harvest Warrior**[10] 4228 5-9-5 79 .... DavidAllan 2 80
(T D Easterby) *swtchd rt after s: last and pushed along: hdwy 3f out: styd on same pce appr fnl f* **6/1**[3]
2341 **5** 3/4 **Nightspot**[8] 4271 6-8-6 73 .... ThomasO'Brien(7) 10 73
(Eve Johnson Houghton) *mde most: hrd rdn and hdd over 1f out: wknd fnl f* **11/4**[1]
4410 **6** 2 **Domino Dancer (IRE)**[26] 3753 3-9-4 86 .... PaulMulrennan 8 82
(J Wade) *t.k.h in rr: hdwy and hung lft over 2f out: racd wd: styd on fnl f* **20/1**
0060 **7** 7 **Best Prospect (IRE)**[34] 3509 5-9-13 87 .... (t) PhillipMakin 6 69
(M Dods) *w ldr: wknd over 1f out* **6/1**[3]
16 **8** 7 **Idle No More (USA)**[61] 2669 3-9-8 90 .... KDarley 3 58
(J H M Gosden) *trckd ldrs: drvn over 4f out: wkng whn sltly hmpd over 2f out: sn bhd* **6/1**[3]
-026 **9** 2 1/2 **Riley Boys (IRE)**[16] 4039 6-9-10 84 .... PaulHanagan 9 47
(J G Given) *chsd ldrs: effrt 3f out: wknd over 1f out* **12/1**

2m 5.21s (-2.09) **Going Correction** +0.075s/f (Good)
WFA 3 from 5yo+ 8lb **9** Ran SP% **119.5**
Speed ratings (Par 107): **111,110,108,108,107 106,100,94,92**
CSF £65.76 CT £534.66 TOTE £3.80: £1.50, £3.50, £2.60; EX 51.90.
Owner Gainsborough **Bred** Gainsborough Farm Llc **Trained** Newmarket, Suffolk
■ Stewards' Enquiry : Thomas O'Brien one-day ban: used whip with excessive frequency (Aug 27)

FOCUS
Not a bad handicap, and the decent pace led to a fair winning time for the grade. Those in the frame behind the winner all came from off the pace and the form could be rated a little higher.

NOTEBOOK
Ravarino(USA), who got off the mark on Polytrack last time, had an 8lb higher mark to overcome here, but she showed herself to be a progressive filly with a success that was gained a shade cosily despite having raced fairly close to the decent early pace. She looks likely to improve again and a hat-trick is clearly on the cards. (op 10-3 tchd 4-1 in a place)
Zonergem, off the track since May and last seen running on turf on the Flat back in July 2005, has gone well fresh in the past, and the race was certainly run to suit him as they went quite quick early. He has never been an easy horse to win with, though. (tchd 16-1)
Habalwatan(IRE), missing the usual blinkers, was contesting a lower grade of contest than he usually takes part in and ran a better race. He was, however, another beneficiary of the good gallop set up front and was able to stay on well from off the pace. (op 14-1)
Harvest Warrior, who needs softer ground to be seen at his best, struggled to go the early pace, but in the end that good gallop helped him get into contention for a place late on. (op 17-2 tchd 9-1)
Nightspot, who won an apprentices' race on Polytrack last time, got to race off a 1lb lower mark here so had a clear chance at the weights. However, he is a horse who likes to be up there and on this occasion he helped set a pace which was too hot. He eventually paid the price and dropped out of contention with a furlong to run. (op 10-3)
Domino Dancer(IRE) did not help his rider much as he was keen in the early stages and hung over to the stands' side in the straight. Official explanation: jockey said gelding hung left (op 25-1)

4524 NAPOLEONS CASINO & RESTAURANT NURSERY 7f 100y
3:50 (3:51) (Class 5) 2-Y-O £3,238 (£963; £481; £240) Stalls High

Form RPR
0001 **1** **Fly Kiss**[8] 4265 2-8-0 56 6ex .... AhmedAjtebi(5) 10 63
(C E Brittain) *hmpd s: sn chsng ldrs: led over 1f out: styd on wl* **6/1**[2]
4060 **2** 1 **Destinys Dream (IRE)**[15] 4076 2-8-7 58 .... RoystonFfrench 2 62+
(Mrs A Duffield) *sn in rr: hdwy on outer over 1f out: fin strly but too late to rch wnr* **50/1**
260 **3** 1 1/4 **Boomtown**[36] 3435 2-9-1 69 .... AndrewMullen(3) 9 70
(M Johnston) *swtchd rt s: chsd ldrs: kpt on same pce appr fnl f* **7/2**[1]
600 **4** 1 1/2 **Townkab (IRE)**[13] 4130 2-8-10 61 .... NCallan 11 58
(N P Littmoden) *mid-div: effrt over 2f out: styd on: nt rch ldrs* **9/1**
5500 **5** 1 **Hildegarde (IRE)**[8] 4279 2-8-6 57 ow2 .... (b[1]) DavidAllan 15 52
(T D Easterby) *led tl over 1f out: one pce* **25/1**
4050 **6** 1 **Hurstpierpoint (IRE)**[22] 3838 2-8-8 59 .... PaulHanagan 12 51
(R A Fahey) *mid-div: hmpd over 2f out: styd on appr fnl f* **22/1**
0546 **7** 1/2 **Insomnitas**[29] 3642 2-8-9 60 .... PaulMulrennan 6 51
(M G Quinlan) *mid-div: effrt and checked over 2f out: kpt on: nvr rchd ldrs* **25/1**
005 **8** 3/4 **Moonlight Gambler (IRE)**[54] 2869 2-8-1 55 .... DuranFentiman(3) 14 44
(T D Easterby) *chsd ldrs: drvn along over 4f out: outpcd fnl 2f* **33/1**
4640 **9** shd **Alfredtheordinary**[11] 4202 2-8-12 63 .... SamHitchcott 3 52
(M R Channon) *in rr: rn wd bnd over 3f out: nvr a factor* **25/1**
053 **10** 1/2 **Bourbon Highball (IRE)**[19] 3977 2-9-2 67 .... LeeEnstone 4 55
(P C Haslam) *mid-div: effrt on outer over 2f out: nvr nr ldrs* **14/1**
000 **11** nk **Saturday Boy**[13] 4125 2-8-1 55 .... LiamJones(3) 13 42
(Paul Green) *s.i.s: hung lft bnd over 3f out: kpt on fnl 2f: nvr on terms* **50/1**
0013 **12** 3/4 **Pequeno Dinero (IRE)**[22] 3838 2-8-6 62 .... KellyHarrison(5) 16 47
(C W Fairhurst) *w ldrs: wknd over 1f out* **8/1**[3]
0302 **13** 2 1/2 **Suite Francaise**[38] 3373 2-8-9 60 .... SebSanders 7 39
(Sir Mark Prescott) *s.i.s: bhd and drvn along: kpt on fnl 2f* **7/2**[1]
0005 **14** 4 **Asian Power (IRE)**[13] 4130 2-9-7 72 .... KDarley 5 41
(P J O'Gorman) *in rr: wd bnd over 3f out: nvr on terms* **8/1**[3]
1340 **15** 10 **Allahor**[20] 3909 2-9-5 70 .... TomEaves 8 14
(A Berry) *sn in rr: t.o 3f out* **50/1**

1m 35.05s (0.74) **Going Correction** +0.075s/f (Good) **15** Ran SP% **122.3**
Speed ratings (Par 94): **98,96,95,93,92 91,90,90,89,89 88,88,85,80,69**
CSF £292.46 CT £1244.23 TOTE £7.50: £2.60, £10.40, £2.00; EX 270.60.
Owner Saeed Manana **Bred** L M Cumani **Trained** Newmarket, Suffolk
■ Stewards' Enquiry : Andrew Mullen one-day ban: careless riding (Aug 27)

FOCUS
Modest nursery form but largely sound with the third and fourth close to maiden form.

NOTEBOOK
Fly Kiss, who showed improved form to get off the mark at Brighton last time out, followed up in good style under a 6lb penalty on this very different track. She travelled well and won in the manner of a progressive filly, and on this evidence a mile should pose few problems in time. (op 9-2)
Destinys Dream(IRE), who had looked to be crying out for this trip, certainly showed improved form for it, staying on strongly to be nearest at the finish on this handicap debut.
Boomtown, another debuting in handicap company, was not taking on anything of Rio De La Plata's class this time, and he ran a promising race having been near the pace throughout. He should be able to win a similar race and quicker ground will suit him. (op 5-1 tchd 11-2)
Townkab(IRE) ran his best race to date on his handicap debut but he already looks to need a mile. (op 12-1 tchd 17-2)
Hildegarde(IRE), blinkered for her nursery debut, showed a lot more early speed this time and made full use of her high draw. She did not run badly considering that she carried 2lb overweight.
Hurstpierpoint(IRE) ran poorly at Catterick last time on his handicap debut but this was more encouraging. (tchd 20-1)
Saturday Boy Official explanation: jockey said colt failed to handle bend
Suite Francaise should have been suited by this stiffer track but she failed to build on her promising Musselburgh run. (op 4-1 tchd 9-2 in a place)

4525 MARKS AND SPENCER HULL FILLIES' H'CAP 5f
4:25 (4:25) (Class 5) (0-70,68) 3-Y-O+ £3,238 (£963; £481; £240) Stalls High

Form RPR
6001 **1** **Jabbara (IRE)**[7] 4324 4-8-1 51 6ex .... AhmedAjtebi(5) 12 59+
(C E Brittain) *mid-div: hdwy over 2f out: led jst ins fnl f: styd on wl* **10/3**[1]
6434 **2** 1 1/2 **Jilly Why (IRE)**[13] 4140 6-9-6 68 .... (b) SebSanders 10 71
(Paul Green) *bmpd s: hdwy to chse ldrs over 2f out: kpt on same pce ins fnl f* **5/1**[2]
5534 **3** 1/2 **Miss Daawe**[10] 4224 3-8-2 49 oh2 .... RoystonFfrench 4 50+
(B Ellison) *chsd ldrs: edgd rt and kpt on same pce ins fnl f* **12/1**
0202 **4** shd **Spinning Game**[5] 4384 3-7-9 49 oh2 .... (b) DanielleMcCreery(7) 15 50
(D W Chapman) *in rr-div: hdwy over 2f out: styd on wl fnl f* **16/1**
2-00 **5** 1 1/4 **Yorke's Folly (USA)**[13] 4141 6-8-4 49 oh4 .... (b) PaulFessey 13 44
(C W Fairhurst) *hld up towards rr: gd hdwy over 1f out: edgd rt and kpt on wl ins fnl f* **28/1**
0342 **6** nk **Toy Top (USA)**[9] 4252 4-8-11 56 .... (b) PhillipMakin 7 50
(M Dods) *mid-div: hdwy to chse ldrs over 2f out: edgd rt and nt qckn fnl f* **11/2**[3]
-251 **7** shd **Metal Guru**[45] 3168 3-9-2 68 .... RussellKennemore(5) 6 62
(R Hollinshead) *mid-div: kpt on fnl 2f: nt rch ldrs* **14/1**
1046 **8** 1/2 **Mystery Pips**[45] 3169 7-8-4 49 oh1 .... (v) KimTinkler 8 41
(N Tinkler) *led tl hdd & wknd jst ins fnl f* **33/1**
6005 **9** nk **Violet's Pride**[55] 2844 3-8-2 52 .... (v) DominicFox(3) 9 43
(S Parr) *bmpd s: hdwy over 3f out: sn chsng ldrs: kpt on same pce appr fnl f* **50/1**
0000 **10** 1/2 **Alexia Rose (IRE)**[18] 4008 5-8-1 49 oh4 .... (t) AndrewMullen(3) 2 41+
(A Berry) *dwlt: swtchd rt after s: bhd: hdwy 2f out: styng on whn nt clr run ins fnl f* **40/1**
0-00 **11** nk **Mis Chicaf (IRE)**[13] 4141 6-7-13 49 oh4 .... KellyHarrison(5) 16 37
(D Carroll) *mid-div: hdwy on inner over 1f out: styng on whn nt clr run ins fnl f* **25/1**
2063 **12** nk **Ashes (IRE)**[12] 4158 5-8-12 60 .... AndrewElliott(3) 11 47
(K R Burke) *swvd bdly lft s: hdwy to chse ldrs over 3f out: wknd over 1f out* **6/1**
3501 **13** 1 1/4 **Rann Na Cille (IRE)**[10] 4226 3-9-3 64 6ex .... (p) NCallan 5 56+
(K A Ryan) *chsd ldrs: wkng whn hmpd twice and eased ins fnl f* **12/1**
0000 **14** nk **Boppys Dream**[54] 2894 5-8-4 49 oh4 .... (p) PaulHanagan 1 31
(P T Midgley) *swtchd rt to r far side after 1f: nvr bttr than mid-div* **66/1**
2066 **15** 3 **Princess Cleo**[9] 4252 4-8-13 58 .... (p) PaulMulrennan 3 29
(T D Easterby) *racd alone stands' side: chsd ldrs: lost pl over 1f out* **20/1**
4010 **16** 1 1/4 **Morristown Music (IRE)**[12] 4158 3-9-6 67 .... PaddyAspell 14 32
(J S Wainwright) *chsd ldrs: lost pl over 1f out* **20/1**

The Form Book, Raceform Ltd, Compton, RG20 6NL

0300 **17** *5* **Musical Parkes**[33] 3537 3-8-2 **52**........................(b[1]) DuranFentiman(3) 17 —
(W J H Ratcliffe) *stmbld s: bhd fnl 2f* **20/1**

64.58 secs (0.58) **Going Correction** +0.175s/f (Good)
WFA 3 from 4yo+ 2lb **17** Ran SP% **127.8**
Speed ratings (Par 100): **102,99,98,98,96 95,95,94,94,93 93,92,90,90,85 82,74**
CSF £17.22 CT £197.20 TOTE £4.40: £1.80, £2.00, £2.60, £3.50; EX 26.90.
Owner Saeed Manana **Bred** Tower Bloodstock **Trained** Newmarket, Suffolk

FOCUS
Moderate sprint handicap form with a third of the field racing from out of the handicap,and the winner not having to improve to score.
Ashes(IRE) Official explanation: jockey said mare jumped left at start and collided
Rann Na Cille(IRE) Official explanation: jockey said filly suffered interference in running
Musical Parkes Official explanation: jockey said filly stumbled at start

4526 ANDREW M JACKSON SOLICITORS H'CAP (FOR AMATEUR RIDERS) 1m 100y
5:00 (5:00) (Class 6) (0-65,65) 3-Y-0+ **£3,123** (£968; £484; £242) **Stalls** High

Form RPR
323 **1** **Bolton Hall (IRE)**[15] 4063 5-10-11 **60**.......... MrBMcHugh(5) 14 69
(R A Fahey) *hmpd s: mid-div: hdwy over 2f out: styd on to ld jst ins fnl f: drvn out* **6/4**[1]
3005 **2** *1 1/4* **Sol Rojo**[8] 4284 5-11-4 **65**..........(b) MrSPearce(3) 13 71
(J Pearce) *hmpd s: hld up in rr: hdwy on inner over 2f out: styd on to take 2nd ins fnl f* **9/1**
0006 **3** *1* **Berbatov**[11] 4197 3-9-4 **47**.......... MrBAdams(7) 16 50
(Paul Green) *hld up towards rr: hdwy on outer over 2f out: edgd rt and styd on fnl f* **28/1**
6022 **4** *hd* **Terry Molloy (IRE)**[10] 4220 3-10-2 **57**..........(v) MissKellyBurke(5) 5 59
(K R Burke) *led tl hdd jst ins fnl f: wknd towards fin* **17/2**
0-00 **5** *nk* **Alasil (USA)**[20] 3907 7-10-3 **54**.......... MrMPrice(7) 10 57
(R J Price) *chsd ldrs: kpt on same pce fnl 2f* **16/1**
0206 **6** *3/4* **Rock Haven (IRE)**[9] 4253 5-10-5 **56**.......... MrSeanKerr(7) 4 57
(J W Unett) *in rr: hdwy 3f out: edgd rt and styd on fnl f* **5/1**[2]
1560 **7** *1/2* **Malinsa Blue (IRE)**[34] 3502 5-11-6 **64**.......... MissLEllison 9 64
(B Ellison) *chsd ldrs: edgd rt and kpt on same pce fnl f* **8/1**[3]
5-00 **8** *3/4* **Mycenean Prince (USA)**[15] 468 4-9-9 **46** oh1.......(b) MrCAHarris(7) 12 44
(R C Guest) *in rr: hdwy on ins over 2f out: n.m.r: styd on towards fin* **25/1**
-400 **9** *1/2* **Monsieur Dumas (IRE)**[29] 3640 3-10-3 **58**.......... MissRBastiman(5) 15 54
(R Bastiman) *swvd lft s: in rr: hdwy on outer over 2f out: hung rt over 1f out: nvr a factor* **20/1**
5-06 **10** *hd* **Wee Ellie Coburn**[10] 4219 3-10-0 **55**.......... MissMMullineaux(5) 11 51
(M Mullineaux) *sn chsng ldrs: one pce fnl 2f* **25/1**
-000 **11** *1 3/4* **Fadansil**[28] 3675 4-9-13 **46** oh1.......... MrHHaynes(3) 8 38
(J Wade) *trckd ldr: hrd rdn over 2f out: wknd over 1f out* **66/1**
6003 **12** *1 3/4* **Sion Hill (IRE)**[1] 4488 6-10-2 **46** oh1..........(p) MrSWalker 6 34
(John A Harris) *trckd ldrs: wknd over 1f out* **25/1**
0300 **13** *1/2* **Scotty's Future (IRE)**[10] 4219 9-10-8 **52**.......... MrsCBartley 2 39
(A Berry) *s.i.s: bhd: hdwy in centre over 2f out: nvr a factor* **20/1**
0004 **14** *3 1/2* **Sangreal**[20] 3918 3-9-13 **56**.......... MissLEBurke(7) 1 34
(K R Burke) *a in rr* **50/1**
0-00 **15** *12* **Katie Kingfisher**[79] 2110 3-9-3 **46** oh1.......... MrJPearce(7) 17 —
(M Wigham) *in rr: bhd whn hang bdly lft over 1f out* **25/1**

1m 49.09s (1.69) **Going Correction** +0.075s/f (Good)
WFA 3 from 4yo+ 6lb **15** Ran SP% **126.0**
Speed ratings (Par 101): **94,92,91,91,91 90,90,89,88,88 86,85,84,81,69**
CSF £13.79 CT £278.61 TOTE £2.40: £1.30, £2.80, £7.60; EX 22.40 Place 6 £107.93, Place 5 £38.68.
Owner J J Staunton **Bred** M Duffy **Trained** Musley Bank, N Yorks

FOCUS
A moderate handicap run at a steady early pace, and as usual a high draw proved a benefit. The form looks sound rated around the first two.
T/Plt: £101.20 to a £1 stake. Pool: £51,116.75. 368.60 winning tickets. T/Qpdt: £22.80 to a £1 stake. Pool: £3,035.40. 98.50 winning tickets. WG

4253 CHEPSTOW (L-H)
Thursday, August 16

OFFICIAL GOING: Good
Wind: Almost nil Weather: Fine but chilly

4527 DIGIBET MEDIAN AUCTION MAIDEN STKS 6f 16y
5:50 (5:50) (Class 6) 2-Y-0 **£2,072** (£616; £308; £153) **Stalls** High

Form RPR
0223 **1** **Non Sucre (USA)**[11] 4202 2-9-3 74..........(b[1]) StephenDonohoe 1 73
(P A Blockley) *led over 4f out: clr over 2f out: rdn over 1f out: edgd rt ins fnl f: r.o* **4/1**[2]
0 **2** *nk* **Our Chairman (IRE)**[38] 3383 2-9-3 0.......... RyanMoore 13 72
(R Hannon) *hld up in mid-div on stands' rail: hdwy over 2f out: chsd wnr jst over 1f out: kpt on* **1/1**[1]
0 **3** *1 1/2* **Clifton Dancer**[71] 2365 2-8-12 0.......... RichardThomas 3 63
(Tom Dascombe) *a.p: rdn to chse wnr over 2f out tl jst over 1f out: nt qckn ins fnl f* **20/1**
40 **4** *2* **Wreningham**[13] 4132 2-9-0 0.......... JerryO'Dwyer(3) 2 62
(T Keddy) *t.k.h in mid-div: hdwy 3f out: sn rdn: one pce fnl f* **40/1**
006 **5** *2 1/2* **Amber Ridge**[21] 3866 2-9-3 49.......... DaleGibson 11 54
(B P J Baugh) *bhd: hdwy over 3f out: rdn over 2f out: nvr able to chal* **125/1**
6063 **6** *2* **Myriola**[55] 2818 2-8-12 64.......... DavidKinsella 5 43
(B Palling) *led over 1f: chsd wnr tl rdn over 2f out: wknd wl over 1f out* **16/1**
64 **7** *1 1/2* **Greystoke Prince**[35] 3465 2-9-3 0.......... AdamKirby 6 44
(W R Swinburn) *towards rr: hdwy and swtchd lft jst over 2f out: no further prog* **8/1**[3]
8 *1 1/4* **Shakespeare's Son** 2-8-12 0.......... TolleyDean(5) 7 40
(H J Evans) *s.i.s and sltly hmpd: hdwy on outside over 2f out: no imp fnl f* **66/1**
5 **9** *3/4* **Lady Jinks**[20] 3902 2-8-5 0.......... FrankiePickard(7) 8 33
(M D I Usher) *a bhd* **33/1**
10 *nk* **Ochoa (IRE)** 2-8-12 0.......... PhilipRobinson 12 32
(C G Cox) *s.i.s: a bhd* **4/1**[2]
0 **11** *5* **Millennium Storm (GER)**[35] 3471 2-9-3 0.......... AdrianMcCarthy 9 22
(M F Harris) *prom: rdn 4f out: sn wknd* **100/1**
0 **12** *6* **Defnikov**[131] 942 2-8-10 0.......... MatthewDavies(7) 4 —
(A B Haynes) *a bhd* **80/1**

4500 **13** *nk* **Lord Of The Wing**[7] 4315 2-9-3 65.......... JimmyQuinn 10 —
(R M Beckett) *prom tl rdn and wknd over 2f out* **40/1**

1m 13.85s (1.45) **Going Correction** +0.125s/f (Good) **13** Ran SP% **124.1**
Speed ratings (Par 92): **95,94,92,89,86 83,81,80,79,78 72,64,63**
CSF £8.35 TOTE £6.80: £2.40, £1.10, £6.60; EX 15.60.
Owner O Murphy **Bred** C Grosso **Trained** Lambourn, Berks

FOCUS
A very ordinary maiden and sound enough although limited by the proximity of the fifth.

NOTEBOOK
Non Sucre(USA) managed to hold on after being lit up by the blinkers which were fitted to help him concentrate on this drop back to six furlongs. (op 11-2 tchd 13-2)
Our Chairman(IRE) ◆, a heavily-backed favourite, could not quite overhaul the winner. He should appreciate an extra furlong and can soon get off the mark. (op 5-4 tchd 10-11)
Clifton Dancer, a half-sister to three juvenile winners at up to six furlongs, stepped up considerably on her debut. She can continue to progress at a modest level. (tchd 25-1)
Wreningham was not disgraced after running freely on this return to the bottom grade. (op 33-1 tchd 50-1)
Amber Ridge seemed to put up an improved performance but that is not saying a lot. (op 100-1)
Myriola was back up in distance for her first start since leaving James Given. (tchd 18-1)
Greystoke Prince Official explanation: jockey said colt was never travelling.
Ochoa(IRE) Official explanation: jockey said filly hung left

4528 JOHN SMITH'S (S) STKS 1m 4f 23y
6:20 (6:21) (Class 6) 3-Y-0 **£1,943** (£578; £288; £144) **Stalls** Low

Form RPR
600 **1** **Correy**[9] 4256 3-8-7 0.......... DavidKinsella 7 45
(B Palling) *w ldr: led over 5f out: rdn 3f out: clr 2f out: r.o* **66/1**
0630 **2** *2 1/2* **Right Option (IRE)**[9] 4259 3-8-12 53.......... KevinGhunowa(5) 1 51
(J L Flint) *t.k.h: a.p: nt clr run on ins over 5f out: swtchd rt over 4f out: rdn over 3f out: kpt on same pce fnl f* **2/1**[1]
00 **3** *2 1/2* **Hook Money (IRE)**[22] 3847 3-8-12 0.......... AdamKirby 4 42
(D W P Arbuthnot) *led: hdd over 5f out: rdn to chse wnr over 2f out: no ex ins fnl f* **16/1**
6500 **4** *1 1/2* **Leprechaun's Gold (IRE)**[7] 4309 3-8-12 51.......... StephenDonohoe 5 40
(B J Llewellyn) *hld up in rr: rdn over 3f out: styd on fnl f* **8/1**[3]
50-4 **5** *1/2* **Sosueme Now**[8] 4267 3-8-8 50 ow1.......... RyanMoore 3 35
(A B Haynes) *hld up and bhd: rdn 4f out: nvr nr ldrs* **3/1**[2]
6034 **6** *4* **Lady Pickpocket**[16] 4036 3-8-7 52.......... JimmyQuinn 6 27
(M H Tompkins) *prom: chsd wnr over 5f out tl rdn and wknd over 2f out* **2/1**[1]
006 **7** *15* **Glentimon (IRE)**[30] 3621 3-8-12 45.......... SimonWhitworth 2 8
(S Kirk) *hld up towards rr: rdn over 4f out: lost tch over 2f out* **33/1**

2m 47.96s (9.24) **Going Correction** +0.575s/f (Yiel) **7** Ran SP% **113.1**
Speed ratings (Par 98): **92,90,88,87,87 84,74**
CSF £191.96 TOTE £18.00: £4.50, £1.80; EX 130.30.The winner was sold to Pete Pointing for 4,600gns. Hook Money was claimed by Mike Thomas for £6,000.
Owner Five To Follow **Bred** Mrs D J Hughes **Trained** Tredodridge, Vale Of Glamorgan

FOCUS
A modest time for a dreadful seller and best rated through the runner-up to recent form in the grade.
Correy Official explanation: trainer said, regarding the apparent improvement in form, filly had been better suited by today's step up in trip
Right Option(IRE) Official explanation: jockey said gelding felt wrong on pulling up; vet said gelding had been struck into

4529 PLAY 123SPORT.COM TO WIN REAL MONEY MAIDEN H'CAP 6f 16y
6:50 (6:52) (Class 6) (0-65,65) 3-Y-0 **£2,266** (£674; £337; £168) **Stalls** High

Form RPR
5332 **1** **Glencal**[7] 4336 3-8-8 **52**.......... RyanMoore 14 64
(H Morrison) *a.p: rdn and hung lft over 1f out: led ent fnl f: r.o wl* **4/6**[1]
0003 **2** *3* **Royal Guest**[8] 4270 3-8-1 **52**.......... MatthewDavies(7) 10 55
(M R Channon) *hld up: hdwy 3f out: rdn to ld over 1f out: hdd ent fnl f: one pce* **6/1**[2]
5460 **3** *1 1/4* **Strut The Stage (IRE)**[5] 4396 3-9-6 **64**.......... PaulFitzsimons 8 63
(B W Duke) *hld up in mid-div: rdn and hdwy over 2f out: r.o ins fnl f* **16/1**
5000 **4** *1/2* **Minnie Mill**[105] 1437 3-8-11 **55**.......... PaulEddery 4 53
(B P J Baugh) *hld up and bhd: rdn over 2f out: hdwy over 1f out: one pce fnl f* **80/1**
2460 **5** *1 1/4* **Wadnagin (IRE)**[24] 3786 3-8-10 **54**.......... RichardThomas 17 48
(I A Wood) *hld up and bhd: hdwy over 1f out: nt rch ldrs* **11/1**[3]
542- **6** *hd* **Murrisk**[73] 2326 3-8-13 **60**.......... JerryO'Dwyer(3) 6 53
(Eamon Tyrrell, Ire) *led: rdn and hdd over 1f out: wknd ins fnl f* **33/1**
4602 **7** *hd* **King Of Tricks**[2] 4471 3-7-9 **46** oh1.......... FrankiePickard(7) 5 39
(M D I Usher) *hld up and bhd: hdwy over 3f out: rdn over 2f out: one pce whn nt clr run briefly ins fnl f* **14/1**
-500 **8** *2* **Danehill Kikin (IRE)**[21] 3875 3-9-1 **59**..........(t) PhilipRobinson 11 46
(B W Hills) *s.i.s: nvr trbld ldrs* **33/1**
45R **9** *shd* **Sherjawy (IRE)**[21] 3879 3-8-5 **49**..........(b) AdrianMcCarthy 7 36
(Miss Z C Davison) *prom: rdn over 2f out: wknd fnl f* **100/1**
5600 **10** *3/4* **Fervent**[62] 2622 3-8-8 **57**.......... KevinGhunowa(5) 1 41
(J M Bradley) *prom: rdn over 2f out: sn wknd* **20/1**
5000 **11** *1* **Land Ahoy**[12] 4186 3-9-2 **60**.......... JimmyQuinn 13 41
(D W P Arbuthnot) *prom: swtchd lft over 3f out: wknd over 1f out* **33/1**
5420 **12** *4* **Fly Time**[7] 4314 3-8-3 **52**.......... TolleyDean(5) 15 21
(Mrs L Williamson) *bhd fnl 2f* **50/1**
0000 **13** *shd* **Capping (IRE)**[48] 3066 3-9-0 **58**..........(vt) AdamKirby 16 27
(W R Swinburn) *a bhd* **20/1**
6-00 **14** *6* **Silver Flame**[80] 2080 3-8-6 **50**.......... DavidKinsella 9 1
(A W Carroll) *a bhd* **100/1**

1m 12.97s (0.57) **Going Correction** +0.125s/f (Good) **14** Ran SP% **118.7**
Speed ratings (Par 98): **101,97,95,94,93 92,92,89,89,88 87,82,81,73**
CSF £3.82 CT £35.86 TOTE £1.60: £1.10, £2.50, £5.00; EX 6.30.
Owner The Caledonian Racing Society **Bred** Fonthill Stud **Trained** East Ilsley, Berks

FOCUS
A poor handicap and sound enough form rated around the third and fourth.
Danehill Kikin(IRE) Official explanation: jockey said filly would not face the kickback.

4530 WEATHERBYS PRINTING MAIDEN STKS 7f 16y
7:20 (7:26) (Class 5) 3-Y-0+ **£2,914** (£867; £433; £216) **Stalls** High

Form RPR
3-00 **1** **Guarantia**[19] 3961 3-8-12 90.......... RyanMoore 9 58
(C E Brittain) *wnt rt s: sn led: rdn jst over 1f out: edgd rt ins fnl f: drvn out* **4/5**[1]
3003 **2** *2* **Turkish Sultan (IRE)**[7] 4321 4-9-3 55..........(v[1]) KevinGhunowa(5) 15 60
(J M Bradley) *a.p: chsd wnr over 3f out: rdn over 2f out: kpt on same pce fnl f* **9/1**

3/- **3** *3* **Call Me Punch**[747] 3929 6-9-8 0 StephenDonohoe 7 52
(E S McMahon) *a.p: rdn and one pce fnl 2f* **7/1**[3]
0-60 **4** *4* **Mirko**[19] 3968 3-9-3 56 (t) PaulFitzsimons 4 40
(B R Millman) *hld up in tch: rdn over 2f out: wknd over 1f out* **50/1**
20-0 **5** *hd* **Dragon Flower (USA)**[50] 2998 3-8-12 72 PhilipRobinson 13 34
(B W Hills) *prom: rdn over 3f out: wknd over 2f out* **5/1**[2]
0-00 **6** *½* **Danjoe**[37] 3406 3-8-12 43 TolleyDean(5) 6 38
(R Brotherton) *led early: prom: rdn over 2f out: wknd wl over 1f out* **100/1**
0 **7** *½* **Ivanasbo**[15] 4066 3-9-3 0 AdamKirby 16 37
(C G Cox) *bhd tl hung lft and styd on fnl 2f: n.d* **66/1**
0 **8** *shd* **Takaamul**[32] 3572 4-9-3 63 AdrianScholes(5) 12 38
(K A Morgan) *mid-div: hung lft and btn over 1f out* **25/1**
00-0 **9** *4* **Bright**[192] 240 4-9-5 32 JerryO'Dwyer(3) 14 28
(W K Goldsworthy) *prom 4f* **100/1**
10 *1 ½* **Lady Lorins** 3-8-12 0 HayleyTurner 10 17
(Andrew Turnell) *hmpd s: sn wl bhd* **50/1**
11 *¾* **Kaateb (IRE)** 4-9-8 0 DaleGibson 8 22
(W J Haggas) *s.i.s: a bhd* **11/1**
0-0 **12** *shd* **King's Attitude**[29] 3639 3-9-3 0 RichardThomas 3 20
(R A Harris) *a bhd* **100/1**
-000 **13** *8* **For Eileen**[21] 3873 3-8-12 42 (p) AdrianMcCarthy 2 —
(Miss K B Boutflower) *prom tl rdn and wknd over 3f out* **100/1**
60 **14** *5* **King Roy (IRE)**[12] 4182 3-9-3 0 PaulEddery 5 —
(N I M Rossiter) *a in rr* **100/1**
15 *39* **Bit Of A Monkey** 3-9-3 0 SimonWhitworth 11 —
(L P Grassick) *s.s: sn t.o* **100/1**

1m 25.01s (1.71) **Going Correction** +0.125s/f (Good)
WFA 3 from 4yo+ 5lb **15** Ran SP% **118.3**
Speed ratings (Par 103): **95,92,89,84,84 83,83,83,78,76 76,75,66,61,16**
CSF £8.38 TOTE £1.90: £1.10, £2.30, £2.00; EX 9.70.
Owner Saeed Manana **Bred** Darley **Trained** Newmarket, Suffolk

FOCUS
A weak maiden with the level set and limited by the runner-up.
For Eileen Official explanation: jockey said filly hung left-handed
King Roy(IRE) Official explanation: jockey said filly hung left-handed.

4531 DRAGON TRUCK AND VAN MAIDEN STKS (H'CAP) 2m 2f
7:50 (7:54) (Class 6) (0-65,65) 3-Y-0+ £2,266 (£674; £337; £168) Stalls Low

Form RPR
4645 **1** **Rajayoga**[17] 4030 6-9-0 49 oh2 JimmyQuinn 5 54
(M H Tompkins) *hld up in mid-div: hdwy over 6f out: rdn into ld over 2f out: drvn out* **9/2**[3]
2503 **2** *1* **Conny Nobel (IRE)**[20] 3903 3-8-1 52 ow2 RichardThomas 11 56
(C Roberts) *hld up and bhd: hdwy on outside over 2f out: rdn and chsd wnr fnl f: styd on* **33/1**
3232 **3** *1 ¼* **Dansimar**[5] 4409 3-8-7 65 MatthewDavies(7) 2 68
(M R Channon) *hld up and bhd: hdwy over 5f out: rdn over 2f out: nt qckn fnl f* **10/3**[2]
0204 **4** *2* **Fondness**[13] 4131 4-9-4 53 HayleyTurner 12 53
(B G Powell) *hld up towards rr: hdwy 5f out: one pce fnl 2f* **25/1**
0-50 **5** *1 ½* **Openide**[125] 291 6-9-4 53 PaulFitzsimons 6 52
(B W Duke) *prom: lost pl over 4f out: styd on fnl f* **20/1**
0300 **6** *1 ¼* **Lightning Queen (USA)**[5] 4391 3-7-5 49 oh1 KMay(7) 3 46
(B W Hills) *hld up and bhd: rdn and effrt over 4f out: sme late hdwy* **10/1**
0052 **7** *nk* **Tobougg Welcome (IRE)**[24] 3792 3-7-12 49 oh3 DaleGibson 4 46
(S C Williams) *prom: led over 6f out: rdn and hdd over 2f out: wknd over 1f out* **11/4**[1]
6/ **8** *nk* **Menelaus**[96] 1655 6-9-10 59 (p) JamesDoyle 9 56
(K A Morgan) *mid-div: rdn 10f out: lost pl over 4f out: n.d after* **33/1**
4200 **9** *1 ¼* **Into Action**[7] 4322 3-8-11 62 (b[1]) RyanMoore 13 57
(R Hannon) *prom: rdn over 3f out: wknd over 2f out* **10/1**
/000 **10** *1 ¼* **Silver Dreamer (IRE)**[37] 3397 5-9-0 49 oh4 AdrianMcCarthy 8 43
(H S Howe) *prom: rdn 3f out: wknd 2f out* **50/1**
5460 **11** *10* **Coda Agency**[19] 3945 4-9-0 49 oh3 PhilipRobinson 10 32
(D W P Arbuthnot) *led: hdd over 6f out: wknd over 2f out* **15/2**
0/0- **12** *1 ¼* **Methodical**[111] 230 5-9-0 49 oh3 AdamKirby 7 31
(B G Powell) *hld up in mid-div: hdwy over 4f out: rdn 3f out: sn wknd* **25/1**

4m 10.11s (9.49) **Going Correction** +0.575s/f (Yiel)
WFA 3 from 4yo+ 16lb **12** Ran SP% **118.2**
Speed ratings (Par 101): **101,100,100,99,98 97,97,97,97,96 92,91**
CSF £154.27 CT £561.92 TOTE £7.60: £2.70, £4.10, £2.10; EX 306.20.
Owner Mystic Meg Limited **Bred** Mystic Meg Limited **Trained** Newmarket, Suffolk

FOCUS
A modest staying handicap rated through the winner to his best in the past year and backed up by the third.

4532 JOHN SMITH'S EXTRA SMOOTH H'CAP 1m 14y
8:20 (8:26) (Class 6) (0-55,59) 3-Y-0+ £2,266 (£674; £337; £168) Stalls High

Form RPR
5002 **1** **Ellen's Girl (IRE)**[7] 4317 4-8-10 46 RyanMoore 8 63
(R Hannon) *a.p: led over 4f out: shkn up and clr over 1f out: r.o wl* **10/3**[1]
0602 **2** *4* **My Michelle**[3] 4464 6-9-5 55 DaleGibson 9 63
(B Palling) *a.p: chsd wnr 3f out: sn rdn: no imp fnl 2f* **4/1**[2]
0200 **3** *2 ½* **Sahara Prince (IRE)**[5] 4395 7-8-11 47 (p) JamesDoyle 2 49
(K A Morgan) *led over 3f: rdn and one pce fnl 2f* **28/1**
6054 **4** *shd* **Moyoko (IRE)**[7] 4319 4-9-2 52 JimmyQuinn 1 54
(M Blanshard) *hld up towards rr: rdn and hdwy over 2f out: kpt on same pce fnl f* **11/1**
3001 **5** *6* **Foolish Groom**[9] 4259 6-9-4 59 6ex (p) HaddenFrost(5) 5 47
(R Hollinshead) *hld up towards rr: stdy hdwy over 2f out: nvr nr to chal* **4/1**[2]
5000 **6** *nk* **Salvestro**[7] 4321 4-8-5 48 MarkCoumbe(7) 14 36
(A W Carroll) *hld up in tch: rdn over 3f out: wknd 2f out* **25/1**
-005 **7** *2 ½* **Band**[20] 3922 7-9-2 52 StephenDonohoe 17 34
(E S McMahon) *sn prom: rdn 3f out: sn wknd* **10/1**[3]
0-05 **8** *½* **What-A-Dancer (IRE)**[9] 4256 10-9-0 55 (b) KevinGhunowa(5) 15 36
(R A Harris) *n.d* **25/1**
525- **9** *1 ¾* **Ai Hawa (IRE)**[22] 3865 4-8-11 50 JerryO'Dwyer(3) 4 27
(Eamon Tyrrell, Ire) *hld up in mid-div: rdn 3f out: wknd wl over 1f out* **25/1**
000 **10** *½* **Shahadah (IRE)**[17] 4023 5-8-9 50 TolleyDean(5) 7 25
(R J Price) *dwlt: nvr nr ldrs* **50/1**
4000 **11** *nk* **Valart**[12] 4161 4-9-2 52 (tp) RichardThomas 11 27
(A J Lidderdale) *s.v.s: nvr nr ldrs* **33/1**
0523 **12** *nk* **Goodwood Spirit**[7] 4319 5-9-2 52 (v) AdrianMcCarthy 6 26
(J M Bradley) *stdd s: plld hrd: sn mid-div: wknd 2f out* **11/1**
-001 **13** *3 ½* **Croft (IRE)**[9] 4256 4-9-3 53 6ex (v) AdamKirby 12 19
(M S Saunders) *hld up in tch: rdn over 3f out: wknd over 2f out* **20/1**
-000 **14** *3 ½* **Gary's Indian (IRE)**[48] 3067 4-9-0 50 PaulEddery 3 8
(B P J Baugh) *a bhd* **80/1**
0300 **15** *2 ½* **New Light**[15] 4073 3-8-10 52 StephenCarson 13 —
(Eve Johnson Houghton) *a towards rr* **25/1**
0660 **16** *3* **Fly By Jove (IRE)**[10] 2077 4-8-10 46 (bt[1]) HayleyTurner 16 —
(Jane Southcombe) *hld up in tch: wknd over 3f out* **40/1**
0046 **17** *1* **Mix N Match**[8] 4287 3-8-12 54 NelsonDeSouza 10 —
(R M Stronge) *plld hrd: chsd ldr: wknd over 3f out* **16/1**

1m 36.66s (0.66) **Going Correction** +0.125s/f (Good)
WFA 3 from 4yo+ 6lb **17** Ran SP% **126.9**
Speed ratings (Par 101): **101,97,94,94,88 88,85,85,83,82 82,82,78,75,72 69,68**
CSF £14.67 CT £350.97 TOTE £4.30: £1.80, £1.90, £3.30, £2.60; EX 13.70 Place 6 £11.31, Place 5 £7.98.
Owner Con Harrington **Bred** Mrs Chris Harrington **Trained** East Everleigh, Wilts

FOCUS
A convincing victory by the well-handicapped Ellen's Girl in this moderate affair and sound enough form rated around the runner-up and fourth.
Shahadah(IRE) Official explanation: jockey said mare ran too freely
Valart Official explanation: jockey said filly missed the break.
T/Plt: £23.30 to a £1 stake. Pool: £60,085.50. 1,877.05 winning tickets. T/Qpdt: £4.10 to a £1 stake. Pool: £4,091.10. 723.40 winning tickets. KH

4322 FOLKESTONE (R-H)
Thursday, August 16

OFFICIAL GOING: Good to soft
Wind: Light, across Weather: Heavy rain for an hour before racing; becoming bright

4533 FOLKESTONE-RACECOURSE.CO.UK H'CAP 1m 1f 149y
5:30 (5:31) (Class 6) (0-50,53) 3-Y-0+ £2,184 (£644; £322) Stalls Low

Form RPR
3442 **1** **Bethanys Boy (IRE)**[31] 3595 6-8-12 50 VinceSlattery 5 56+
(D J Daly) *t.k.h: trckd ldrs: clsd 3f out: led 2f out and sn in command: eased last 75yds* **5/1**[1]
-000 **2** *2* **Kings Art (IRE)**[65] 2530 3-8-4 50 TPO'Shea 14 50
(W M Brisbourne) *stmbld s: a in ldng trio: rdn and sltly outpcd 2f out: wnt 2nd 1f out: kpt on but no ch w wnr* **14/1**
0000 **3** *1 ¼* **Boz**[7] 4339 3-8-2 48 (b[1]) NickyMackay 11 45
(L M Cumani) *settled in midfield: prog to chse ldng trio but outpcd over 2f out: styd on: nrst fin* **8/1**
6-06 **4** *¾* **Kathleen Kennet**[19] 3950 7-8-10 48 RobertHavlin 2 44+
(C Tinkler) *hld up in last trio: effrt on wd outside over 2f out: drvn and styd on: no ch of rching ldrs* **12/1**
0-60 **5** *hd* **Noah Jameel**[200] 274 5-8-10 48 FergusSweeney 9 43
(A G Newcombe) *hld up wl in rr: sme prog but outpcd whn nt clr run over 2f out: shuffled along and kpt on steadily: nvr nr ldrs* **12/1**
6600 **6** *1 ¾* **Reveur**[45] 3173 4-8-11 49 ow1 IanMongan 1 41
(K R Burke) *sn pressed ldr: led 3f out to 2f out: wknd* **13/2**[2]
0004 **7** *2* **King Of Knight (IRE)**[12] 4161 6-8-1 46 CharlotteKerton(7) 8 34
(G Prodromou) *s.i.s: hld up towards rr: prog over 2f out but already outpcd: rdn and kpt on one pce* **10/1**
0602 **8** *¾* **Grand Sefton**[21] 3868 4-8-12 50 (t) MickyFenton 13 36
(Stef Liddiard) *s.i.s: t.k.h: hld up in midfield: outpcd whn effrt and nt clr run over 2f out: rdn and no prog after* **11/1**
1660 **9** *10* **Oasis Sun (IRE)**[12] 4161 4-8-6 47 (v) StephaneBreux(3) 4 12
(J R Best) *wl in tch: rdn and outpcd over 2f out: sn wknd* **20/1**
2004 **10** *2* **Bertrada (IRE)**[142] 794 3-8-0 53 ow3 JemmaMarshall(7) 10 14
(G P Enright) *hld up in last pair: last and pushed along over 3f out: sn bhd* **14/1**
0500 **11** *nk* **The Bonus King**[19] 3946 7-8-12 50 SaleemGolam 12 10
(J Jay) *chsd ldrs tl wknd wl over 2f out: wl bhd over 1f out* **7/1**[3]
0500 **12** *3* **Break Out**[24] 3804 3-8-1 47 ow1 FrankieMcDonald 7 1
(J M Bradley) *nvr beyond midfield: rdn 4f out: wknd over 2f out: sn bhd* **66/1**
0-06 **13** *nk* **Unasuming (IRE)**[6] 4355 4-8-10 48 (b[1]) OscarUrbina 3 1
(J Pearce) *hld up in last trio: pushed along and no prog 3f out: bhd fnl 2f* **12/1**
3650 **14** *14* **Red Raptor**[175] 524 6-8-6 47 (t) TravisBlock(3) 6 —
(J A Geake) *t.k.h: led to 3f out: wknd rapidly: t.o* **7/1**[3]

2m 7.82s (2.59) **Going Correction** +0.35s/f (Good)
WFA 3 from 4yo+ 8lb **14** Ran SP% **126.2**
Speed ratings (Par 101): **103,101,100,99,99 98,96,96,88,86 86,83,83,72**
CSF £80.54 CT £571.54 TOTE £5.80: £2.00, £5.40, £5.00; EX 39.40.
Owner Ms S Hamilton **Bred** K And Mrs Cullen **Trained** Newmarket, Suffolk
■ Declan Daly's first winner since resuming training this summer.

FOCUS
Not much better than a selling handicap and the form is weak.
Grand Sefton Official explanation: jockey said gelding was denied a clear run.
The Bonus King Official explanation: jockey said gelding was denied a clear run.

4534 FOLKESTONE RACECOURSE FOR EXHIBITIONS H'CAP 1m 4f
6:00 (6:01) (Class 6) (0-55,57) 3-Y-0+ £2,184 (£644; £322) Stalls Low

Form RPR
0405 **1** **Orphina (IRE)**[9] 4253 4-8-6 49 (t) KylieManser(7) 4 56+
(B G Powell) *hld up wl in rr: prog on wd outside over 2f out: shuffled along and r.o to ld last 150yds: nt fully extended* **10/1**
6016 **2** *½* **English Archer**[12] 4156 4-8-12 48 DaneO'Neill 9 54
(W M Brisbourne) *hld up in midfield: prog 3f out: rdn over 2f out: styd on to chal and upsides 1f out: one pce* **7/2**[2]
0505 **3** *hd* **Barbs Pink Diamond (USA)**[7] 4327 3-8-8 54 OscarUrbina 7 60
(Mrs A J Perrett) *trckd ldrs: rdn and effrt over 2f out: led over 1f out: hdd and one pce last 150yds* **8/1**
2000 **4** *5* **Mighty Kitchener (USA)**[19] 3946 4-9-4 54 IanMongan 1 52
(P Howling) *racd wd: wl in tch: effrt 3f out: drvn and outpcd over 1f out: n.d after* **8/1**
60/6 **5** *nk* **Neckar Valley (IRE)**[52] 2946 8-9-3 53 NickyMackay 3 50
(J G Portman) *prom: rdn 3f out: wl outpcd 2f out: plugged on* **16/1**
-030 **6** *1 ¼* **Prince Of Medina**[17] 4030 4-9-1 51 TPO'Shea 11 46+
(J R Best) *hld up in last pair: rdn and struggling over 4f out: sn bhd: styd on fnl 2f* **10/3**[1]
0-01 **7** *1 ½* **Alqaayid**[19] 6-9-4 57 ow5 SColas(3) 8 50
(P W Hiatt) *hld up towards rr: rdn 3f out: nt pce to trble ldrs fnl 2f* **10/1**

00-0 **8** 1/2 **Lynford Lady**[7] 4327 4-8-13 **49**.......... RobertHavlin 5 41
(P W D'Arcy) *led: wd bnd after 2f and hdd: trckd ldr tl led wl over 3f out: hdd & wknd over 1f out* **16/1**

0-05 **9** 4 **Amnesty**[21] 3280 8-9-5 **55**..........(be) FergusSweeney 12 41
(G L Moore) *hld up towards rr on inner: prog over 2f out: chsng ldrs wl over 1f out: sn wknd* **7/1**[3]

-300 **10** 2 **Harcourt (USA)**[9] 4253 7-9-5 **55**..........(p) SaleemGolam 6 37
(M Madgwick) *prom: rdn over 3f out: sn pressed ldr: wknd rapidly 2f out* **20/1**

0-00 **11** 15 **Hocinail (FR)**[71] 2362 3-8-4 **50**.......... FrankieMcDonald 13 8
(P Winkworth) *t.k.h: led after 2f to wl over 3f out: wknd rapidly: t.o* **25/1**

0000 **12** 4 **Royal Tender (IRE)**[30] 3624 3-8-1 **50**..........(b) EmmettStack(3) 2 2
(B G Powell) *rel to r: rcvrd to chse ldrs 7f out: wknd rapidly over 4f out: wl t.o* **33/1**

00U- **13** dist **Commander Wish**[283] 6378 4-9-2 **52**.......... MickyFenton 10 —
(Lucinda Featherstone) *awkward s: a last: u.p 1/2-way: wl t.o* **50/1**

2m 44.21s (3.71) **Going Correction** +0.35s/f (Good)
WFA 3 from 4yo+ 10lb **13** Ran SP% **123.5**
Speed ratings (Par 101): **101,100,100,97,97 96,95,94,92,90 80,78,—**
CSF £44.79 CT £307.66 TOTE £12.10: £2.80, £1.80, £2.30; EX 68.80.
Owner Jeff Mould & Shaun Tilley **Bred** Sweetmans Bloodstock **Trained** Lambourn, Berks

FOCUS
As was the case with the opener, this was little better than a selling handicap but the form looks sound enough rated around the placed horses.

4535 IRISH NIGHT AUGUST 22ND CLASSIFIED STKS — 1m 7f 92y
6:30 (6:31) (Class 7) 3-Y-0+ **£2,047** (£604; £302) **Stalls** Low

Form RPR

00/4 **1** **Montgomery**[67] 2493 6-9-11 42.......... DaneO'Neill 10 47
(A G Newcombe) *settled in midfield: rdn and prog over 3f out: effrt on outer to ld jst over 1f out: styd on* **3/1**[1]

50-0 **2** 1 1/2 **Kimpton Carer**[22] 3847 3-8-9 43..........(t) TravisBlock(3) 11 45
(J A Geake) *sn settled bhd ldrs: effrt 3f out: rdn to chal and upsides over 1f out: fnd nil* **25/1**

6000 **3** 1/2 **Bluecrop Boy**[32] 2140 3-8-12 39..........(p) OscarUrbina 3 44
(D J S Ffrench Davis) *mde most: forced to qckn over 7f out: kpt on wl whn pressed: hdd and one pce jst over 1f out* **33/1**

30/- **4** nk **Sonoma (IRE)**[31] 3743 7-9-4 42.......... KylieManser(7) 8 44+
(B G Powell) *rel to r: wl in rr: outpcd over 3f out: shuffled along on outer fr 2f out: styd on strly fnl f* **7/1**

0025 **5** 9 **Roxy Singer**[16] 4036 3-8-12 44..........(v) FergusSweeney 14 32
(W J Musson) *hld up in midfield: effrt over 3f out: drvn to chse ldrs over 2f out: wknd over 1f out* **10/3**[2]

0/00 **6** 1/2 **Cambo (FR)**[50] 2996 6-9-8 44..........(bt) NeilChalmers(3) 2 32
(Miss Sheena West) *prom: rdn to chse ldr over 2f out: wknd rapidly over 1f out* **16/1**

100/ **7** 2 1/2 **Courant D'Air (IRE)**[508] 6344 6-9-8 38.......... LiamTreadwell(3) 7 28
(Lucinda Featherstone) *nvr bttr than midfield: u.p and wl outpcd fr 3f out* **16/1**

-000 **8** 2 1/2 **Classic Hall (IRE)**[24] 3805 4-9-11 37.......... MickyFenton 6 25
(T Keddy) *t.k.h: hld up in tch: prog to join ldr over 7f out and pce increased: wknd over 2f out* **33/1**

0-04 **9** 1 1/2 **Lady Korrianda**[54] 2874 6-9-11 43.......... VinceSlattery 4 23
(R Curtis) *t.k.h: trckd ldrs: wl outpcd fr 3f out: no ch after* **25/1**

003 **10** 11 **War Feather**[77] 2176 5-9-11 45.......... RobertHavlin 1 9
(T D McCarthy) *dwlt: a wl in rr: lost tch over 3f out* **11/1**

3030 **11** dist **Cragganmore Creek**[72] 2345 4-9-11 39..........(v) IanMongan 12 —
(D Morris) *in tch tl wknd rapidly 4f out: t.o and virtually p.u fnl 2f* **8/1**

/000 **P** **Captain Marryat**[37] 3397 6-9-11 43.......... PaulDoe 9 —
(J Akehurst) *dwlt: a bhd: t.o 4f out: p.u 2f out* **6/1**[3]

3m 37.3s (10.10) **Going Correction** +0.35s/f (Good)
WFA 3 from 4yo+ 13lb **12** Ran SP% **119.6**
Speed ratings (Par 97): **87,86,85,85,80 80,79,78,77,71 —,—**
CSF £87.03 TOTE £4.20: £2.70, £4.40, £9.20; EX 101.70.
Owner A G Newcombe **Bred** Barton Stud Partnership **Trained** Yarnscombe, Devon

FOCUS
The front four came clear in what was a truly terrible event. Unsurprisingly the time was moderate, even for a race like this and, although the winner is to form the placed horses are not solid.
Classic Hall(IRE) Official explanation: jockey said filly ran too freely.
Cragganmore Creek Official explanation: jockey said gelding lost its action.
Captain Marryat Official explanation: jockey said gelding lost its action.

4536 FOLKESTONE RACECOURSE FOR CONFERENCES H'CAP — 5f
7:00 (7:00) (Class 6) (0-65,70) 3-Y-0 **£2,184** (£644; £322) **Stalls** Low

Form RPR

6200 **1** **Stir Crazy (IRE)**[24] 3786 3-8-11 **54**.......... TPO'Shea 2 64
(M R Channon) *racd against nr side rail: trckd ldrs: wnt 2nd over 1f out: got through fnl f to ld last 100yds: rdn out* **10/1**

3610 **2** 1 **Rosie Cross (IRE)**[29] 3649 3-8-10 **58**.......... PatrickHills(5) 3 64
(Eve Johnson Houghton) *racd towards nr side rail: led: rdn over 1f out: hdd and one pce last 100yds* **5/1**[3]

0306 **3** 1 **Kilvickeon (IRE)**[5] 4384 3-7-13 **47**.......... LukeMorris(5) 1 49
(Peter Grayson) *s.i.s: outpcd in last quartet 1/2-way: styd on fr over 1f out: drvn to take 3rd nr fin* **13/2**

4521 **4** nk **Beautiful Madness (IRE)**[1] 4513 3-9-10 **70** 6ex.......... NeilChalmers(3) 4 71
(M G Quinlan) *trckd ldrs: effrt to dispute 2nd over 1f out: nt qckn fnl f* **7/4**[1]

0660 **5** 2 **Chingford (IRE)**[36] 3425 3-8-2 **45**..........(b) NickyMackay 5 39
(J G Portman) *lost pl over 3f out and pushed along: one pce u.p fnl 2f* **20/1**

6415 **6** 2 **Mr Forthright**[12] 4186 3-9-1 **58**.......... DaneO'Neill 10 45
(J M Bradley) *racd on outer: struggling in rr bef 1/2-way: no ch fnl 2f* **9/2**[2]

-006 **7** 3/4 **She Wont Wait**[64] 2560 3-8-2 **45**..........(b) FrankieMcDonald 6 29
(T M Jones) *a struggling in rr: detached in last 2f out* **33/1**

2-55 **8** 1 **Darling Belinda**[20] 3924 3-9-3 **60**..........(p) RobertHavlin 9 41
(D K Ivory) *dwlt: racd on outer: a struggling in rr* **20/1**

000 **9** 1 1/2 **Millenium Sun (IRE)**[15] 4064 3-9-0 **60**.......... AlanCreighton(3) 7 35
(E J Creighton) *mostly chsd ldr to over 1f out: urged along vigorously and wknd* **66/1**

-006 **10** 1 1/4 **Minnow**[7] 4314 3-8-12 **55**..........(b[1]) SaleemGolam 8 26
(S C Williams) *prog on outer to press ldrs after 2f: wknd wl over 1f out* **11/1**

60.02 secs (-0.78) **Going Correction** -0.175s/f (Firm) **10** Ran SP% **115.9**
Speed ratings (Par 98): **99,97,95,95,92 88,87,86,83,81**
CSF £56.49 CT £287.66 TOTE £7.20: £2.60, £2.90, £2.30; EX 29.50.
Owner Miss F V Cove & Mrs V Beech **Bred** Paddy Kennedy **Trained** West Ilsley, Berks
■ Stewards' Enquiry : Frankie McDonald one-day ban: used whip when out of contention (Aug 27)

FOCUS
A poor sprint handicap rated around those in the frame behind the winner.

4537 FOLKESTONE-RACECOURSE.CO.UK MAIDEN AUCTION STKS — 6f
7:30 (7:31) (Class 5) 2-Y-0 **£2,849** (£847; £423; £211) **Stalls** Low

Form RPR

0 **1** **Flashy Photon**[19] 3962 2-8-9 0.......... DaneO'Neill 8 75
(H Candy) *sn trckd ldr and racd against nr side rail: got through to ld jst ins fnl f: rdn out* **6/1**[3]

343 **2** 1 1/4 **Our Acquaintance**[19] 3947 2-8-13 74.......... RichardMullen 7 75
(W R Muir) *racd towards nr side rail: led: rdn over 1f out: hdd jst ins fnl f: kpt on* **11/4**[2]

5 **3** hd **Good Gorsoon (USA)**[63] 2600 2-9-1 0.......... OscarUrbina 1 76+
(B W Hills) *hld up in midfield: taken off rail 1/2-way: effrt 2f out: plld out over 1f out: rdn and nt qckn fnl f* **7/4**[1]

4 4 **The Willowy Wigeon** 2-8-4 0.......... FrankieMcDonald 12 53+
(P Winkworth) *racd towards outer: pressed ldrs tl fdd over 1f out* **66/1**

65 **5** 1/2 **Maiden Miss (IRE)**[8] 4265 2-8-8 0.......... TPO'Shea 4 55
(M R Channon) *chsd ldrs: rdn whn slt stumble over 1f out: outpcd after* **7/1**

0 **6** 1 **The Hoofer (IRE)**[19] 3967 2-8-6 0.......... RobertHavlin 11 50
(J L Dunlop) *prom: shkn up 2f out: fdd over 1f out* **33/1**

2406 **7** nk **Maybe I Wont**[8] 4274 2-9-3 73.......... IanMongan 13 60
(S Dow) *settled in midfield towards outer: effrt over 2f out: wknd over 1f out* **8/1**

0 **8** 1/2 **Zarees**[15] 4070 2-8-9 0.......... FergusSweeney 6 50
(J S Moore) *s.i.s: wl in rr and rn green: kpt on fr over 1f out: n.d* **66/1**

9 5 **Racey Rachel (IRE)** 2-8-8 0.......... LPKeniry 5 33
(E F Vaughan) *chsd ldrs tl wknd wl over 1f out* **16/1**

10 1 3/4 **Lady Cobra** 2-8-4 0.......... PaulDoe 3 24
(C E Brittain) *s.s: detached in last and rn green: nvr a factor* **20/1**

11 1 1/4 **Grand Cuvee** 2-8-10 0.......... PatrickHills(5) 10 31
(D M Simcock) *s.v.s: drvn up on wd outside 1/2-way: sn wknd* **25/1**

12 2 **Sweet Dane (IRE)** 2-8-3 0.......... LukeMorris(5) 2 17
(V Smith) *racd on outer: in tch: wkng whn slt stumble 2f out: sddle slipped* **33/1**

13 15 **Landed Gent (IRE)** 2-8-11 0.......... MickyFenton 14 —
(Miss V Haigh) *restless stalls: in tch on outer over 3f out: wknd rapidly: t.o* **66/1**

1m 13.96s (0.36) **Going Correction** -0.175s/f (Firm) **13** Ran SP% **125.8**
Speed ratings (Par 94): **90,88,88,82,82 80,80,79,73,70 69,66,46**
CSF £22.94 TOTE £8.00: £3.30, £1.80, £1.70; EX 34.20.
Owner Trolley Action **Bred** London Thoroughbred Services Ltd **Trained** Kingston Warren, Oxon

FOCUS
A modest maiden, but still it was easily the most interesting race on the card. The form looks straightforward rated around the runner-up and the fifth.

NOTEBOOK
Flashy Photon, unable to make an impact following a sluggish start on his debut at Newmarket, was faced with significantly weaker opposition and he managed to get himself a good position on the stands' rail from his poor draw. He had to wait for the gap, but it came and he proved good enough to go through and score, suggesting there might be more to come in nurseries. (op 7-1)

Our Acquaintance has run to a similar level on each of his four starts, but has not yet proved good enough to win one and was done for speed late on here. He will no doubt find a race eventually, but is going to remain vulnerable to improvers. (op 10-3 tchd 7-2)

Good Gorsoon(USA), effectively down in grade having made his debut behind the smart River Proud at Newbury, allowed the front pair a bit too much of a head start and had to come with his challenge away from the favoured stands' rail. He can be rated a bit better than the bare form. (op 13-8 tchd 9-4)

The Willowy Wigeon, who cost just £500, comes from a stable who can get the odd decent juvenile, but that was always going to be unlikely with this considering her price tag and, although she showed good speed, winning a maiden is not going to prove easy for her. (op 100-1)

Maiden Miss(IRE) needed this to qualify for a handicap mark and she looks the type to fare better in low-grade nurseries. (op 9-1 tchd 10-1)

Sweet Dane(IRE) Official explanation: jockey said filly lost its action and saddle slipped

4538 FOLKESTONE RACECOURSE FOR WEDDINGS H'CAP — 7f (S)
8:00 (8:00) (Class 5) (0-75,74) 3-Y-0 **£3,238** (£963; £481; £240) **Stalls** Low

Form RPR

2332 **1** **Ella Woodcock (IRE)**[7] 4326 3-8-11 **64**.......... DaneO'Neill 4 74
(J A Osborne) *a in ldng trio: chal 2f out: rdn to ld 1f out: styd on wl* **9/4**[1]

0422 **2** 1 1/4 **Awwal Malika (USA)**[8] 4270 3-8-11 **64**.......... PaulDoe 5 71
(C E Brittain) *led at stdy pce for 2f: pressed ldr: led again wl over 1f out to 1f out: nt qckn* **3/1**[2]

1300 **3** 3/4 **Lordship (IRE)**[15] 4073 3-8-2 **60**.......... LukeMorris(5) 10 65+
(A W Carroll) *hld up in last pair: prog on outer over 2f out: pressed ldng pair 1f out: one pce after* **7/1**

6500 **4** 1 1/2 **Ede's Dot Com (IRE)**[29] 3644 3-8-11 **64**.......... IanMongan 2 65
(P M Phelan) *t.k.h: led after 2f to wl over 1f out: fdd* **22/1**

0534 **5** 2 1/2 **Metropolitan Chief**[8] 4270 3-8-5 **58**.......... TPO'Shea 7 52
(D M Simcock) *hld up bhd ldrs: lost pl 1/2-way: swtchd to outer 2f out: no imp* **13/2**

5610 **6** 1 3/4 **Tipsy Prince**[29] 3646 3-9-6 **73**.......... FergusSweeney 6 62
(David Pinder) *t.k.h: hld up bhd ldrs: rdn over 2f out: outpcd and btn over 1f out* **8/1**

5044 **7** 1 **Perlachy**[114] 1219 3-8-7 **60**.......... LPKeniry 8 47
(Mrs N Macauley) *hld up bhd ldrs: rdn over 2f out: sn btn* **25/1**

1024 **8** 13 **Jack Oliver**[42] 3237 3-9-6 **73**.......... RobertHavlin 9 25
(B J Meehan) *t.k.h: hld up on outer: wknd rapidly over 2f out: t.o* **11/2**[3]

1m 27.11s (-0.79) **Going Correction** -0.175s/f (Firm) **8** Ran SP% **116.3**
Speed ratings (Par 100): **97,95,94,93,90 88,87,72**
CSF £9.28 CT £40.04 TOTE £4.20: £1.50, £1.40, £1.50; EX 7.90 Place 6 £111.98, Place 5 £39.41.
Owner Cavendish Star Racing **Bred** Pippa Hackett **Trained** Upper Lambourn, Berks

FOCUS
A modest handicap and the form is ordinary if sound enough rated around the first two.

T/Plt: £69.60 to a £1 stake. Pool: £46,590.65. 488.65 winning tickets. T/Qpdt: £19.30 to a £1 stake. Pool: £4,059.60. 155.20 winning tickets. JN

4500 SALISBURY (R-H)

Thursday, August 16

OFFICIAL GOING: Good to soft (8.2)

Wind: Mild, against Weather: dry

4539 CHAMPAGNE JOSEPH PERRIER MAIDEN AUCTION STKS (DIV I) 6f 212y

2:00 (2:06) (Class 5) 2-Y-O £2,590 (£770; £385; £192) **Stalls** Centre

Form					RPR
	1		**Goodwood Starlight (IRE)** 2-8-13 0	EddieAhern 2	75
			(J L Dunlop) *w'like: hld up in mid-div: swtchd rt and hdwy over 2f out: shkn up to ld ins fnl f: drifted lft and r.o wl*	**12/1**	
4	**2**	*2 ½*	**Blues Minor (IRE)**[62] 2630 2-9-2 0	RyanMoore 8	71
			(R Hannon) *lw: led: rdn over 2f out: drifted lft and hdd ins fnl f: no ex*	**2/1**[1]	
05	**3**	*shd*	**Stubbs Art (IRE)**[68] 2478 2-8-10 0	MarcHalford[(3)] 4	68
			(D R C Elsworth) *lw: s.i.s: towards rr: stdy prog fr over 2f out: rdn over 1f out: r.o: jst failed to snatch 2nd: nrst fin*	**11/2**[3]	
0	**4**	*1 ¾*	**City Hustler (USA)**[8] 4293 2-8-4 0	TolleyDean[(5)] 6	59
			(J S Moore) *trckd ldrs: rdn over 2f out: kpt on same pce fnl f*	**12/1**	
30	**5**	*½*	**Pha Mai Blue**[12] 4151 2-9-2 0	JamieSpencer 7	65
			(W J Knight) *lw: chsd ldrs: rdn over 2f out: ev ch over 1f out: kpt on same pce fnl f*	**9/4**[2]	
	6	*7*	**Gunnadoit (USA)** 2-9-2 0	AdamKirby 1	46
			(C G Cox) *unf: bit bkwd: chsd ldrs: rdn over 2f out: wknd over 1f out*	**9/1**	
0	**7**	*1 ¼*	**Any Given Day (IRE)**[14] 4110 2-8-13 0	J-PGuillambert 9	40
			(D M Simcock) *w'like: nvr bttr than mid-div*	**33/1**	
00	**8**	*1 ½*	**Jemiliah**[63] 2590 2-8-11 0	SteveDrowne 11	34
			(B J Meehan) *towards rr: sme late prog: nvr a factor*	**33/1**	
	9	*2 ½*	**Bathwick Man** 2-8-13 0	JimCrowley 13	29
			(B R Millman) *w'like: trckd ldrs: rdn 3f out: sn wknd*	**20/1**	
	10	*1 ¾*	**Holden Caulfield (IRE)** 2-8-6 0	NeilChalmers[(3)] 14	20
			(Mouse Hamilton-Fairley) *w'like: bit bkwd: nvr bttr than mid-div*	**50/1**	
06	**11**	*½*	**Help (IRE)**[28] 3681 2-8-7 0 ow10	(b) NBazeley[(7)] 5	24
			(Mrs P N Dutfield) *chsd ldrs: hung lft and rdn 3f out: sn wknd*	**100/1**	
	12	*11*	**Red Army Commander (IRE)** 2-9-2 0	PaulEddery 3	—
			(Christian Wroe) *w'like: s.i.s: a towards rr*	**50/1**	

1m 32.87s (3.81) **Going Correction** +0.40s/f (Good) **12 Ran SP% 120.4**

Speed ratings (Par 94): **94,91,91,89,88 80,79,77,74,72 71,59**

CSF £35.43 TOTE £14.60: £2.70, £1.40, £2.20; EX 46.60.

Owner Goodwood Racehorse Owners Group Fourteen **Bred** Lynn Lodge Stud **Trained** Arundel, W Sussex

FOCUS

The ground rode much slower than it had done on the previous day; Ryan Moore described it as dead. This was the first division of a maiden that has thrown up the odd decent performer. Caldra, Dark Islander and Joint Aspiration have taken the race in the last three years; the first five came clear. The form is mixed with the placed horses the best guide.

NOTEBOOK

Goodwood Starlight(IRE), a 32,000gns half-brother to Spinning, deserves plenty of credit for winning this as he was the only one that really came from off the pace. He stretched clear once hitting the front and was not stopping passing the line, so a mile looks well within his scope this season. His connections look like they have a decent sort on their hands. (op 16-1)

Blues Minor(IRE) ran satisfactorily on his debut at Sandown, and did not go off unfancied. He set a very moderate gallop in front and would have always been at an advantage. Battling on well despite looking tired, he will win something similar. (op 9-4 tchd 5-2)

Stubbs Art(IRE), taking another step up in trip, this Derby entrant ran another race full of promise and looks like a horse with a future. He has plenty of size about him and he will improve again. (op 9-2 tchd 6-1)

City Hustler(USA), backed at long prices, was always harassing Blues Minor at the head of affairs but did not pick up when asked. It was a big improvement on his debut effort and he is clearly thought capable of winning judging on the market support. (op 50-1)

Pha Mai Blue shaped fairly well on his debut before finding a maiden at Glorious Goodwood much too hot for him. He has been given plenty of nice entries, including Group 1s, and is obviously thought capable of good things, but he pulled much too hard in the gluey conditions and failed to see out the trip. (op 2-1 tchd 5-2 in a place)

Gunnadoit(USA) was chased up to be with the leaders early but weakened to finish well adrift of the first five. (op 8-1)

Any Given Day(IRE) stayed on when the race was all but over and appears to need more time.

4540 CHAMPAGNE JOSEPH PERRIER MAIDEN AUCTION STKS (DIV II) 6f 212y

2:30 (2:37) (Class 5) 2-Y-O £2,590 (£770; £385; £192) **Stalls** Centre

Form					RPR
60	**1**		**Aye Aye Digby (IRE)**[12] 4151 2-8-11 0	JimmyFortune 2	81
			(H Candy) *trckd ldrs: rdn to ld 2f out: rn green and veered lft 1f out: in command whn hung rt fnl 45yds: rdn out*	**10/3**[2]	
0	**2**	*¾*	**Dauberval (IRE)**[42] 3233 2-8-13 0	DPMcDonogh 13	81
			(S Kirk) *mid-div: rdn and hdwy 2f out: wnt 2nd over 1f out: ev ch ins fnl f: hld nr fin*	**11/1**	
04	**3**	*2*	**Dubai Samurai**[20] 3896 2-9-2 0	LDettori 4	78
			(J W Hills) *mid-div: rdn and stdy prog fr over 2f out: wnt 3rd ent fnl f: no further imp*	**6/4**[1]	
0	**4**	*1 ¼*	**Palmerin**[12] 4151 2-9-2 0	RyanMoore 11	75
			(R Hannon) *chsd ldr: rdn over 2f out: ev ch over 1f out: kpt on same pce*	**6/1**[3]	
	5	*2 ½*	**Charmel's Lad** 2-8-13 0	AdamKirby 6	65+
			(W R Swinburn) *strong: lw: s.i.s: towards rr: rdn and hdwy fr over 2f out: styd on fnl f: nt rch ldrs*	**25/1**	
0	**6**	*½*	**Oronsay**[35] 3465 2-8-4 0	ChrisCatlin 12	55
			(B R Millman) *w'like: led: rdn and hdd 2f out: wknd fnl f*	**66/1**	
	7	*3*	**Looter (FR)** 2-8-11 0	EddieAhern 3	54+
			(J L Dunlop) *w'like: leggy: hld up and bhd: rdn over 2f out: styd on fnl f: nvr trbld ldrs*	**12/1**	
	8	*2*	**Wabbraan (USA)** 2-9-2 0	J-PGuillambert 8	53
			(D M Simcock) *w'like: s.i.s: bhd: sme late prog: n.d*	**20/1**	
	9	*3*	**Mio Fiore** 2-8-7 0 ow1	SteveDrowne 7	36
			(M Blanshard) *leggy: mid-div: rdn 3f out: grad fdd*	**66/1**	
00	**10**	*¾*	**Belle Bellino (FR)**[24] 3796 2-8-11 0	JimCrowley 10	38
			(B R Millman) *mid-div: rdn over 3f out: wknd 2f out*	**14/1**	
	11	*1*	**Stellar Rose (USA)** 2-8-4 0	NelsonDeSouza 1	29
			(B J Meehan) *mid-div: effrt 3f out: wknd 2f out*	**16/1**	
0	**12**	*7*	**Agglestone Rock**[37] 3404 2-8-2 0	JackDean[(7)] 9	15
			(W G M Turner) *chsd ldrs: rdn 3f out: sn btn*	**66/1**	
0	**13**	*5*	**Banjo Bandit (IRE)**[33] 3551 2-8-8 0	TolleyDean[(5)] 5	5
			(J S Moore) *a towards rr*	**50/1**	

1m 32.45s (3.39) **Going Correction** +0.40s/f (Good) **13 Ran SP% 121.0**

Speed ratings (Par 94): **96,95,92,91,88 88,84,82,78,78 76,68,63**

CSF £38.11 TOTE £5.20: £1.60, £3.60, £1.20; EX 59.90.

Owner Trolley Action **Bred** G J King **Trained** Kingston Warren, Oxon

FOCUS

They went a decent pace thanks to Oronsay in what was probably the stronger of the two divisions, although again the form is somewhat muddling.

NOTEBOOK

Aye Aye Digby(IRE), a son of Captain Rio who has been finding himself struggling for speed on faster surfaces, was always likely to be suited by the slight ease in the ground and he travelled much more kindly throughout the race. Driven into the lead two furlongs out, he still looked green and wandered badly left under pressure, but was always just doing enough and won with a bit to spare. His stable has been going through a bit of a dry spell, but are just starting to hit form and this colt looks the type to flourish in handicaps in the autumn, when he should have easy ground at his disposal. (op 4-1 tchd 9-2)

Dauberval(IRE), whose trainer took a division of this maiden last year with the smart Caldra, appreciated the less-taxing conditions than on his debut in heavy ground at Newbury and ran a hugely-improved race. Niggled from an early stage, he stuck to it well, but the winner was always pulling out too much. Genuinely quick ground may enable him to improve again and he is going to benefit from 1m in time. (op 15-2)

Dubai Samurai, down the field behind subsequent Vintage Stakes winner Rio De La Plata on debut at Newmarket, stepped up significantly on that when a close-up fourth in a fair-looking maiden at Ascot last month, and he set a strong standard in what was nothing more than an average maiden. Well supported in the market beforehand, Dettori looked a significant booking, but he was being ridden fully two furlongs out and was simply unable to quicken up. There is a maiden in him, but connections may opt to go down the nursery route now. (op 15-8 tchd 11-8)

Palmerin, although by Champion Sprinter Oasis Dream, has stamina on his dam's side and improved on his initial effort, but is very much a nursery type and is unlikely to be winning a maiden. (op 5-1)

Charmel's Lad, a 30,000gns son of Compton Place, comes from a stable that can ready one to win first time up, but he was soon on the back foot following a slow start. However, he made some decent late progress to claim a never-nearer fifth and there will be easier opportunities. (tchd 20-1)

Oronsay showed a lot more than she had done on her debut at Nottingham and appeals as the type to do better in ordinary nurseries. (op 50-1)

Looter(FR), whose yard took the first division with a newcomer, was nibbled at in the market, but found it tough going early on, getting outpaced and having to be ridden along. Things finally clicked though and it was pleasing to see him going on at the end of his race, and it will be no surprise to see him rise his game next time, possibly over 1m. (op 14-1)

4541 MARY WORT MEMORIAL MAIDEN STKS 6f 212y

3:05 (3:09) (Class 4) 3-4-Y-O £4,857 (£1,445; £722; £360) **Stalls** Centre

Form					RPR
50	**1**		**Elusive Dreams (USA)**[8] 4275 3-9-3 0	JimmyFortune 11	68
			(J H M Gosden) *hld up in mid-div: swtchd lft and hdwy 2f out: chal ent fnl f: sn edgd rt: led fnl 100yds: r.o wl*	**6/1**[2]	
53	**2**	*1 ½*	**War Anthem**[18] 4000 3-9-3 0	(b[1]) SteveDrowne 10	64
			(C R Egerton) *a.p: rdn 2f out: ev ch ins fnl f: nt pce of wnr fnl 75yds*	**6/1**[2]	
3-	**3**	*¾*	**Namibian Pink (IRE)**[239] 6879 3-8-12 0	TPQueally 5	57
			(R M Beckett) *in tch: hdwy over 2f out: rdn to ld over 1f out: hdd fnl 100yds: no ex*	**8/1**	
0	**4**	*1*	**With Confidence**[18] 3992 3-8-9 0	MarcHalford[(3)] 4	54
			(D R C Elsworth) *a.p: rdn over 2f out: ev ch ins fnl f: no ex fnl 100yds*	**12/1**	
	5	*½*	**Highest Esteem** 3-9-3 0	EddieAhern 2	58
			(G L Moore) *w'like: strong: s.i.s: sn mid-div: rdn over 2f out: no imp tl styd on ins fnl f*	**16/1**	
	6	*nk*	**Iguacu** 3-9-3 0	ChrisCatlin 12	57
			(J L Spearing) *w'like: s.i.s: towards rr: hdwy over 2f out: rdn to chse ldrs over 1f out: kpt on same pce*	**20/1**	
4220	**7**	*2 ½*	**Castara Bay**[28] 3689 3-9-3 75	RyanMoore 14	50
			(R Hannon) *mid-div: rdn and hdwy 2f out: chsd ldrs ent fnl f: fdd fnl 100yds*	**2/1**[1]	
00	**8**	*3 ½*	**Katie Coniston**[36] 3425 3-8-7 0	KevinGhunowa[(5)] 3	36
			(Dr J R J Naylor) *led: rdn and hdd over 1f out: wknd*	**66/1**	
	9	*1*	**Hawridge Miss** 3-8-12 0	JimCrowley 6	33
			(B R Millman) *w'like: mainly towards rr*	**20/1**	
-603	**10**	*nk*	**Shavoulin (USA)**[168] 595 3-9-3 85	(e[1]) PaulEddery 13	37
			(Christian Wroe) *swtg: trckd ldrs: rdn wl over 2f out: wknd over 1f out*	**13/2**[3]	
	11	*½*	**Tiger Trail (GER)** 3-9-3 0	JamesDoyle 9	36
			(Mrs N Smith) *lengthy: dwlt bdly: bhd: rdn and hdwy over 2f out: sn hung lft: wknd over 1f out*	**40/1**	
	12	*4*	**Trigger's Friend** 3-8-12 0	MichaelHills 8	20
			(Jamie Poulton) *w'like: bit bkwd: s.i.s: racd green and a bhd*	**33/1**	
0-0	**13**	*2*	**Vintage (IRE)**[15] 4066 3-9-3 0	JamieSpencer 7	20
			(P Mitchell) *t.k.h in mid-div: rdn over 2f out: sn wknd*	**12/1**	

1m 32.64s (3.58) **Going Correction** +0.40s/f (Good)

WFA 3 from 4yo 5lb **13 Ran SP% 124.0**

Speed ratings (Par 105): **95,93,92,91,90 90,87,83,82,82 81,76,74**

CSF £41.19 TOTE £6.10: £1.80, £2.10, £3.00; EX 44.90.

Owner H R H Princess Haya Of Jordan **Bred** Summerwind Farm **Trained** Newmarket, Suffolk

FOCUS

An ordinary maiden run slower than the preceding juvenile maiden and a race that probably did not take a lot of winning. It is debatable as to whether the form, rated around those in the frame behind the winner, will be worth following in the short-term.

Vintage(IRE) Official explanation: jockey said gelding ran too free

4542 EUROPEAN BREEDERS' FUND FILLIES' H'CAP 1m 4f

3:40 (3:40) (Class 4) (0-80,73) 3-Y-O+ £6,477 (£1,927; £963; £481) **Stalls** High

Form					RPR
0565	**1**		**Veenwouden**[11] 4205 3-9-5 72	RyanMoore 6	84
			(E F Vaughan) *hld up in last: smooth prog fr 3f out: led wl over 1f out: forged clr ent fnl f: readily*	**3/1**[2]	
4221	**2**	*4*	**Cushat Law (IRE)**[20] 3919 3-8-12 65	HayleyTurner 7	71
			(W Jarvis) *trckd ldrs: rdn to chal over 2f out: ev ch over 1f out: nt pce of wnr ent fnl f*	**9/2**[3]	
31-1	**3**	*3 ½*	**Hazelnut**[27] 3705 4-9-7 64	JamieSpencer 1	64
			(J R Fanshawe) *lw: mid-div: hdwy 3f out: led briefly 2f out: sn rdn: fdd ins fnl f*	**11/8**[1]	
0230	**4**	*½*	**Love Always**[12] 4171 5-9-7 71	JamieHamblett[(7)] 10	70
			(S Dow) *trckd ldrs: rdn 2f out: one pce after*	**12/1**	
3-10	**5**	*shd*	**Starparty (USA)**[36] 3421 3-9-5 72	JimCrowley 4	71
			(Mrs A J Perrett) *w ldr: led 4f out: rdn 3f out: hdd wl over 1f out: one pce ent fnl f*	**14/1**	

00-2 **6** 1 1/2 **Lindy Lou**[114] 1217 3-9-2 **69** SimonWhitworth 8 66
(C A Cyzer) *hw: hld up towards rr: hdwy 3f out to trck ldrs: effrt 2f out: one pce sn after* **16/1**
200 **7** 13 **Mercury Blue**[50] 2981 3-9-0 **67** DPMcDonogh 2 43
(S Kirk) *a towards rr* **16/1**
2300 **8** 6 **Letham Island (IRE)**[50] 2985 3-9-6 **73** ChrisCatlin 5 39
(R M Stronge) *led tl 4f out: sn wknd* **33/1**
0000 **9** 1/2 **Silver Surprise**[11] 4205 3-7-9 **55** KMay[(7)] 3 20
(J J Bridger) *mid-div: nudged along over 4f out: wknd over 1f out* **100/1**

2m 40.67s (4.31) **Going Correction** +0.40s/f (Good)
WFA 3 from 4yo+ 10lb **9** Ran SP% **115.3**
Speed ratings (Par 102): **101,98,96,95,95 94,85,81,81**
CSF £16.98 CT £25.60 TOTE £4.10: £1.50, £1.70, £1.10; EX 19.70.
Owner Wood Hall Stud Limited **Bred** Wood Hall Stud **Trained** Newmarket, Suffolk

FOCUS
A modest fillies' handicap in which the pace was ordinary but the form looks solid and could be a few pounds better.
Lindy Lou Official explanation: trainer's rep said filly lost an off-fore shoe

4543 TOTESPORT.COM SOVEREIGN STKS (GROUP 3) 1m
4:15 (4:15) (Class 1) 3-Y-O+
£36,907 (£13,988; £7,000; £3,490; £1,748; £877) **Stalls** High

Form RPR
3641 **1** **Pride Of Nation (IRE)**[21] 3887 5-9-0 107 JamieSpencer 3 116
(L M Cumani) *hw: trckd ldrs: rdn to chal over 1f out: hung rt and led ins fnl f: kpt on wl: rdn out* **5/2**[1]
311 **2** 1 1/4 **Ordnance Row**[40] 3330 4-9-0 105 RyanMoore 10 113
(R Hannon) *trckd ldr: rdn over 2f out: led over 1f out: short of room on rails whn hdd ins fnl f: no ex* **11/4**[2]
4-45 **3** 3/4 **Olympian Odyssey**[168] 600 4-9-0 116 LDettori 7 111
(Saeed Bin Suroor) *hw: hld up: swtchd lft and hdwy 2f out: sn rdn: wnt 3rd ent fnl f: kpt on but a hld by ldng pair* **10/3**[3]
111- **4** 1 1/2 **Caldra (IRE)**[313] 5805 3-8-8 109 DPMcDonogh 11 107
(S Kirk) *bit bkwd: b. trckd ldrs: rdn over 2f out: kpt on same pce fnl f* **10/1**
3504 **5** 3/4 **Thousand Words**[16] 4045 3-8-8 111 MichaelHills 1 105
(B W Hills) *hw: led: qcknd 4l clr over 3f out: rdn and hdd over 1f out: one pce fnl f* **9/2**
5441 **6** 1 1/2 **Final Verse**[12] 4167 4-9-0 106 JohnEgan 12 103
(J S Moore) *restrained s: swtchd lft and effrt 2f out: one pce fnl f* **20/1**
-046 **7** 4 **Secret World (IRE)**[21] 3887 4-9-0 111 TPQueally 4 93
(J Noseda) *hw: t.k.h: hld up: effrt 2f out: wknd ent fnl f* **16/1**

1m 43.9s (0.81) **Going Correction** +0.40s/f (Good)
WFA 3 from 4yo+ 6lb **7** Ran SP% **116.2**
Speed ratings: **111,109,109,107,106 105,101**
CSF £10.03 TOTE £4.00: £2.30, £2.40; EX 11.20.
Owner Equibreed S.R.L. **Bred** Deni S R L **Trained** Newmarket, Suffolk
■ Stewards' Enquiry : Spencer three-day ban: careless riding (Aug 27-29); interf. to Ordnance Row

FOCUS
This is always a well-supported Group race and this renewal was no exception despite the withdrawals during the day. The form is not the most solid.

NOTEBOOK
Pride Of Nation(IRE), who was wearing earplugs again, handles easy ground well but he started to hang once coming under pressure and edged right in on the runner-up in the closing stages and definitely caused interference. Spencer had the whip in his left hand, which did not help, and resulted in him being banned for three days, but his mount was almost certainly the best horse on the day and deserved to keep the race, his first Group success. (op 4-1)
Ordnance Row finished in front of Pride Of Nation at Sandown in July and was not disgraced in the slightest in defeat. An improver all season, something similar can come his way before the end of the year. (tchd 5-2 and 3-1)
Olympian Odyssey ◆ was having his first run since being beaten under two lengths in a Group 2 race in Dubai at the beginning of March. The form of that race has worked out really nicely since and helps to give this race plenty of substance. He had handled soft ground in the past and stayed on really well, and whilst looking relatively fit and very well, he can improve for the run. (op 3-1 tchd 4-1)
Caldra(IRE) ◆ was faced with an exceptionally tough task on his seasonal debut. His last three wins of 2006 came in races that have produced many, many decent winners and it was just a matter of seeing whether he had trained on. He showed more than enough to suggest he has and will be interesting next time. (tchd 8-1)
Thousand Words took them along early and should have really quickened away after having the run of the race. However, he weakened disappointingly under pressure but could be the sort of horse to follow next season, if kept in training, as he is a tall horse and may still be growing. (tchd 4-1)
Final Verse, a recent conditions race winner at Newmarket, never got on terms after being settled in the rear.
Secret World(IRE) ran poorly again on less than ideal ground. One cannot forget the way he ran in the Locking earlier in the year and he will surely prove better on quicker going. (op 12-1)

4544 UKW - KNIGHTS & CO H'CAP 1m 6f 21y
4:50 (4:51) (Class 5) (0-70,67) 3-Y-O+ **£3,238** (£963; £481; £240) Flip start

Form RPR
311 **1** **Colwyn Bay (IRE)**[35] 3448 5-9-9 **62** (p) JamieSpencer 12 70+
(Jane Chapple-Hyam) *hld up towards rr: drvn along and hdwy 3f out: led over 1f out: hrd rdn ins fnl f: all out* **6/4**[1]
216 **2** 1/2 **Raffish**[13] 4124 5-9-7 **67** (p) JackDean[(7)] 11 74
(M Scudamore) *racd keenly in mid-div: hdwy 5f out: led wl over 2f out: sn rdn: hdd over 1f out: rallied u.p: hld fnl 50yds* **15/2**[3]
314- **3** shd **Aphorism**[238] 6893 4-9-12 **65** J-PGuillambert 13 72+
(J R Fanshawe) *hw: mid-div: hdwy and nt clr run 2f out: sn swtchd lft and rdn: 6l 6th ent fnl f: hung rt and fin strly fnl 75yds: wnt cl 3rd fnl stride* **7/1**[2]
4 shd **Kerayasi (FR)**[107] 5-9-11 **64** JimmyFortune 6 71
(G L Moore) *mid-div: rdn to chal 3f out: ev ch ins fnl f: no ex: lost 3rd fnl stride* **9/1**
5560 **5** 2 1/2 **Most Definitely (IRE)**[54] 2887 7-9-12 **65** JimCrowley 7 68
(R M Stronge) *hld up and bhd: hdwy 3f out: rdn to chal for 3rd ent fnl f: kpt on same pce* **12/1**
0065 **6** 1 1/4 **The Composer**[19] 3969 5-9-5 **58** SteveDrowne 1 59
(M Blanshard) *trckd ldrs: rdn to chal 3f out: ev ch over 1f out: wknd ent fnl f* **8/1**
00-6 **7** 1 3/4 **Dovedale**[20] 3901 7-8-6 **52** MCGeran[(7)] 3 51
(Mrs S D Williams) *hld up towards rr: rdn 3f out: sme late hdwy and hung rt fr over 1f out: nvr a danger* **20/1**
0000 **8** 4 **Benny The Bat**[19] 3969 3-8-13 **64** JamesDoyle 8 57
(K O Cunningham-Brown) *mid-div: hdwy over 4f out: rdn over 3f out: wknd over 1f out* **33/1**
364- **9** 3/4 **Take A Mile (IRE)**[82] 5422 5-9-5 **58** DPMcDonogh 4 50
(B G Powell) *trckd ldrs: rdn and ev ch 3f out: wknd 2f out* **16/1**
050/ **10** 3/4 **Rabbit**[17] 504 6-9-2 **55** JohnEgan 14 46
(M Sheppard) *trckd ldr: rdn over 3f out: sn wknd* **11/1**
0060 **11** 13 **Jamaahir (USA)**[17] 4019 4-9-3 **56** ChrisCatlin 5 29
(S Lycett) *racd freely: led tl over 2f out: sn wknd* **50/1**

3m 11.0s (4.00) **Going Correction** +0.40s/f (Good)
WFA 3 from 4yo+ 12lb **11** Ran SP% **116.9**
Speed ratings (Par 103): **104,103,103,103,102 101,100,98,97,97 89**
CSF £12.50 CT £62.33 TOTE £2.10: £1.20, £2.60, £1.90; EX 13.40.
Owner Philip M Hickey **Bred** Tower Bloodstock **Trained** Newmarket, Suffolk

FOCUS
Just a fair gallop for this staying handicap and a good number had chances in the last two furlongs. The form is sound with the runner-up to his mark and the sixth to his latest course and distance form. This race was started using a flip start and was thereford hand-timed.

4545 CARMEN WINES FILLIES' H'CAP 6f
5:20 (5:21) (Class 5) (0-70,70) 3-Y-O+ **£3,238** (£963; £481; £240) **Stalls** Centre

Form RPR
015 **1** **Pragmatist**[26] 3735 3-8-9 **58** JimCrowley 7 67+
(P Winkworth) *edgy: hld up: rdn over 2f out: hdwy and nt clr run briefly over 1f out: str run ins fnl f: led fnl 75yds: rdn out* **10/1**
-051 **2** 1/2 **Inka Dancer (IRE)**[5] 4397 5-9-0 **63** 6ex WilliamBuick[(3)] 4 70+
(B Palling) *s.i.s: bhd: swtchd lft and hdwy over 2f out: bhd ldrs whn nt clr run over 1f out: swtchd further lft: r.o strly but hung rt ins fnl f: nt quite catch wnr* **7/2**[1]
004 **3** 3/4 **Nans Lady (IRE)**[8] 4296 4-9-3 **63** ChrisCatlin 10 68
(E J O'Neill) *hw: mid-div: rdn over 2f out: hdwy over 1f out: wnt 3rd ent fnl f: kpt on* **10/1**
1654 **4** 3/4 **Limonia (GER)**[7] 4324 5-8-5 **51** JamesDoyle 12 53
(Mike Murphy) *led: rdn over 2f out: hdd over 1f out: rallied to ld again ins fnl f: no ex whn hdd fnl 75yds* **6/1**[2]
3036 **5** hd **Tilsworth Charlie**[7] 4317 4-8-10 **56** (b[1]) JohnEgan 11 58
(J R Jenkins) *chsd ldrs: rdn over 2f out: led over 1f out: hung rt and hdd ins fnl f: no ex* **9/1**
2215 **6** 1 **Excessive**[27] 3713 3-9-0 **63** JamieSpencer 2 61
(W Jarvis) *hld up: swtchd lft and hdwy 2f out: sn rdn: styng on whn hmpd ins fnl f: no further imp* **7/2**[1]
4563 **7** 3 **Jucebabe**[7] 4314 4-8-4 **53** MarcHalford[(3)] 6 42
(J L Spearing) *mid-div: effrt 2f out: wknd ent fnl f* **7/1**[3]
0406 **8** 1/2 **Rhapsilian**[12] 4186 3-8-4 **53** NelsonDeSouza 14 40
(J A Geake) *b.hind: chsd ldrs: rdn over 2f out: wknd fnl f* **14/1**
5-03 **9** shd **Serene Dancer**[34] 3482 4-8-7 **53** ow1 SteveDrowne 8 40
(Mrs P N Dutfield) *chsd ldrs: rdn over 2f out: wknd ent fnl f* **25/1**
600 **10** nk **Cerulean Rose**[5] 4396 8-8-2 **55** ow4 JamieHamblett[(7)] 1 41
(A W Carroll) *hw: edgy: mid-div: effrt 2f out: wknd over 1f out* **14/1**
0-00 **11** nk **Jessica Wigmo**[7] 4324 4-7-12 **51** oh4 KMay[(7)] 3 36
(A W Carroll) *hld up: swtchd lft and shortlived effrt 2f out* **50/1**
-010 **12** 2 1/2 **Kims Rose (IRE)**[9] 4257 4-8-4 **57** MCGeran[(7)] 9 34
(R J Price) *prom: rdn over 2f out: wknd over 1f out* **16/1**

1m 16.79s (1.81) **Going Correction** +0.40s/f (Good)
WFA 3 from 4yo+ 3lb **12** Ran SP% **124.4**
Speed ratings (Par 100): **103,102,101,100,100 98,94,94,93,93 93,89**
CSF £47.19 CT £381.35 TOTE £14.40: £3.70, £2.00, £3.50; EX 70.30 Place 6 £8.22, Place 5 £4.64.
Owner Mrs Jenny Willment **Bred** Mrs J A M Willment **Trained** Chiddingfold, Surrey

FOCUS
A fairly low-grade handicap for fillies but virtually everything had a chance inside the final two furlongs.
T/Jkpt: Not won. T/Plt: £14.60 to a £1 stake. Pool: £55,434.95. 2,755.55 winning tickets. T/Qpdt: £6.90 to a £1 stake. Pool: £2,992.00. 316.40 winning tickets. TM

4506 SANDOWN (R-H)
Thursday, August 16

OFFICIAL GOING: Good to soft (soft in places on round course) (sprint 6.9, round 6.8)
Wind: Virtually nil

4546 GENTLEMAN'S DAY ON 10TH NOVEMBER H'CAP 5f 6y
2:20 (2:21) (Class 5) (0-75,73) 3-Y-O **£4,533** (£1,348; £674; £336) **Stalls** High

Form RPR
5324 **1** **Dualagi**[8] 4269 3-9-0 **64** LPKeniry 6 71
(J S Moore) *hld up in rr but in tch: smooth hdwy over 1f out: carried lft 1f out: qcknd to ld fnl 100yds: pushed out* **6/1**
3153 **2** 1/2 **Twosheetstothewind**[18] 4001 3-9-1 **65** KerrinMcEvoy 9 70
(M Dods) *chsd ldrs: rdn and qcknd to ld jst ins fnl f: hdd and outpcd fnl 100yds* **7/2**[2]
3300 **3** 2 1/2 **Rocker**[10] 4233 3-9-4 **73** (v) PatrickHills[(5)] 8 69
(B R Johnson) *chsd ldr: led over 1f out: edgd lft and hdd jst ins fnl f: wknd nr fin* **9/2**[3]
-200 **4** 1 1/2 **Russian Gift (IRE)**[38] 3369 3-9-3 **67** MickyFenton 1 58
(C G Cox) *in rr: rdn 1/2-way: styd on fr over 1f out but nvr gng pce to rch ldrs* **14/1**
1406 **5** 3/4 **Kondakova (IRE)**[17] 4017 3-9-8 **72** (v[1]) TedDurcan 2 60
(M L W Bell) *slowly away: sn rcvrd: hdwy to chse ldrs 2f out: kpt on same pce fnl f* **20/1**
5224 **6** 2 1/2 **Silca Elegance**[13] 4127 3-9-9 **73** TPO'Shea 7 52
(M R Channon) *trckd ldrs: rdn 2f out: wknd fnl f* **11/4**[1]
4641 **7** 1 1/4 **Billy Red**[21] 3879 3-9-2 **66** (b) PatDobbs 4 41
(J R Jenkins) *sn led: hdd over 1f out: sn hung rt and hit rail: sn btn* **10/1**
3P-4 **8** 9 **Fast Freddie**[117] 1161 3-9-6 **70** JohnEgan 3 12
(D J Murphy) *chsd ldrs: rdn 3f out: wknd 2f out: eased whn no ch fnl f* **11/2**

62.92 secs (0.71) **Going Correction** +0.15s/f (Good) **8** Ran SP% **117.3**
Speed ratings (Par 100): **100,99,95,92,91 87,85,71**
CSF £28.06 CT £104.74 TOTE £7.90: £2.20, £1.80, £2.20; EX 35.00.
Owner Uplands Acquisitions Limited **Bred** B Burrough **Trained** Upper Lambourn, Berks
■ Stewards' Enquiry : L P Keniry two-day ban: careless riding (Aug 27-28)

FOCUS
Despite the rain since the previous day the winning time still suggested the sprint track was riding a bit quicker than the round course. This was an ordinary sprint in which the leaders may have gone off a bit too quick and set it up for the closers and the form looks modest.
Silca Elegance Official explanation: jockey said colt had no more to give

Fast Freddie Official explanation: jockey said gelding lost its action

4547 EBF VARIETY CLUB DAY MAIDEN STKS 1m 14y

2:50 (2:52) (Class 5) 2-Y-O **£4,533** (£1,348; £674; £336) **Stalls** High

Form				RPR
52	**1**		**Jedediah**[22] 3856 2-9-3 0 FrancisNorton 5	91+
			(A M Balding) *in tch: pushed along and hdwy over 3f out: led ins fnl 2f: in control fnl f: comf* **5/6**[1]	
	2	*1*	**Kandahar Run** 2-9-3 0 TedDurcan 12	87
			(H R A Cecil) *hld up in rr: hdwy 3f out: edgd lft and green over 1f out: styd on to chse wnr fnl f and kpt on wl cl home but no ch w wnr* **7/1**[3]	
0	**3**	*4*	**La Columbina**[20] 3895 2-8-12 0 PatDobbs 4	72
			(R Hannon) *chsd ldrs: shkn up: v green and lost pl over 2f out: kpt on again over 1f out: gng on cl home but nvr a threat* **33/1**	
0	**4**	*1*	**Tyrrells Wood (IRE)**[14] 4110 2-9-3 0 KerrinMcEvoy 13	75+
			(T G Mills) *s.i.s: t.k.h and stdd in rr: hdwy fr 2f out: kpt on fnl f but nvr in contention* **10/1**	
6	**5**	*2 1/2*	**Al Azy (IRE)**[22] 3856 2-9-3 0 RHills 3	69
			(J L Dunlop) *chsd ldr 5f out: led 3f out: hdd ins fnl 2f: wknd fnl f* **20/1**	
0	**6**	*1 3/4*	**Maxwil**[12] 4151 2-9-3 0 RichardMullen 1	65
			(G L Moore) *s.i.s: in rr: pushed along and hdwy fr over 1f out: kpt on ins fnl f but nvr in contention* **40/1**	
06	**7**	*1 1/4*	**Ovthenight (IRE)**[22] 3842 2-9-3 0 MickyFenton 2	62
			(Mrs P Sly) *in tch: rdn 4f out: wknd fr 2f out* **66/1**	
	8	*3/4*	**Tarbolton (IRE)** 2-9-3 0 GregFairley 8	61
			(M Johnston) *chsd ldrs: rdn 4f out: wknd 2f out* **8/1**	
4	**9**	*nk*	**Hyde Lea Flyer**[19] 3957 2-9-3 0 DaneO'Neill 6	60
			(A King) *t.k.h: chsd ldrs: rdn over 3f out: wknd fr 2f out* **5/1**[2]	
00	**10**	*5*	**Miss Cruisecontrol**[21] 3874 2-8-12 0 LPKeniry 10	43
			(J R Best) *in tch: rdn 4f out: wknd fr 3f out* **100/1**	
034	**11**	*3/4*	**Softly Killing Me**[22] 3842 2-8-12 61 FergusSweeney 7	42
			(J Gallagher) *led tl hdd 3f out: wknd appr fnl 2f* **25/1**	
000	**12**	*48*	**Jermajesty (IRE)**[22] 3850 2-9-3 50 (p) TPO'Shea 11	—
			(J R Boyle) *sn bhd: t.o fnl 3f* **100/1**	

1m 45.56s (1.61) **Going Correction** +0.325s/f (Good) 12 Ran SP% **121.4**
Speed ratings (Par 94): **104,103,99,98,95 93,92,91,91,86 85,37**
CSF £7.01 TOTE £1.90: £1.20, £2.40, £7.20; EX 9.10.
Owner Mr & Mrs P McMahon Mr & Mrs Peter Pausewang **Bred** Dunchurch Lodge Stud Company **Trained** Kingsclere, Hants

FOCUS
Not the strongest of maidens in terms of depth, but a few of these did show varying degrees of promise with the runner close to Chesham form. The runners came stands' side in the home straight, as they usually do on easier ground, and the winning time was faster than the fillies' maiden and the claimer, both for older horses over the same trip, later on the card.

NOTEBOOK
Jedediah ◆ confirmed the promise of his first two outings and relished this step up to a mile. The further they went, the better he was going and his rider could even afford to take things easy in the closing stages. Stamina appears to be his forte and he now looks ready for something better. (op Evens tchd 11-10, 4-5 and 5-4 in places)
Kandahar Run ◆, a 50,000gns half-brother to three winners including the top-class Grey Lilas, showed plenty of ability on this debut. Forced to make his effort much further away from the hedge than the favourite, he is probably a little flattered to have finished so close to the eased-down winner, but he pulled a long way clear of the others and he looks one to follow. (op 8-1)
La Columbina ◆, who found 6f totally inadequate on her debut, still looked in need of the experience but the longer trip suited her and she was noted doing some decent late work up the stands' rail without being able to go with the front pair. She looks the type that will improve with experience and there are races to be won with her.
Tyrrells Wood(IRE) ◆, up a furlong from his debut here a fortnight earlier, was another doing his best work late. He is bred to appreciate middle-distances and there should be better to come from him in time. (op 14-1)
Al Azy(IRE), given a much more positive ride than when a long way behind Jedediah here on his debut last month, had every chance but did not get home. He did narrow the gap with his old rival a little, but still the best of him may not be seen until next year. (op 11-1)
Maxwil, who only beaten one home when 100-1 on his Goodwood debut, showed a bit more this time. He is bred to stay and looks one for handicaps in time. (tchd 50-1)
Hyde Lea Flyer failed to confirm the promise of his debut in a slowly-run Newmarket maiden and it remains to be seen how strong that race was. (op 9-2 tchd 6-1)

4548 WOODFORD RESERVE BOURBON H'CAP 7f 16y

3:25 (3:26) (Class 3) (0-90,90) 3-Y-O+ **£8,420** (£2,505; £1,251; £625) **Stalls** High

Form				RPR
-000	**1**		**Jamieson Gold (IRE)**[33] 3525 4-9-4 **82** RHills 10	89
			(B W Hills) *in tch: hdwy 3f out: led ins fnl 2f: rdn and styd on strly thrght fnl f* **13/2**	
0005	**2**	*nk*	**Trimlestown (IRE)**[13] 4134 4-8-13 **77** DaneO'Neill 1	83+
			(H Candy) *in rr but in tch: shkn up and n.m.r ins fnl 2f: swtchd rt and r.o strly fnl f: nt quite get up* **11/4**[1]	
3046	**3**	*nk*	**Bonnie Prince Blue**[34] 3488 4-8-7 **76** PatrickHills[(5)] 5	81
			(B W Hills) *in tch: pushed along over 2f out: styd on wl fnl f and gng on nr fin but a jst hld* **14/1**	
6200	**4**	*1/2*	**Wavertree Warrior (IRE)**[16] 4049 5-9-7 **85** (b[1]) IanMongan 4	89
			(N P Littmoden) *chsd ldr tl led over 3f out: hdd ins fnl 2f: styd on same pce ins fnl f* **14/1**	
0030	**5**	*1/2*	**Marajaa (IRE)**[16] 4049 5-9-6 **84** TedDurcan 3	87+
			(W J Musson) *in rr: n.m.r 2f out: swtchd rt and hdwy fnl f: kpt on but nvr gng pce to rch ldrs* **5/1**[2]	
1042	**6**	*1*	**Sailor King (IRE)**[28] 3682 5-9-1 **79** KerrinMcEvoy 12	79
			(D K Ivory) *chsd ldrs: drvn and ev ch over 1f out: wknd ins fnl f* **5/1**[2]	
0006	**7**	*1*	**Music Note (IRE)**[8] 4268 4-8-8 **77** (t) NicolPolli[(5)] 7	74
			(Miss Gay Kelleway) *led: racd alone far side and up w main gp tl one pce fnl f* **16/1**	
0006	**8**	*2*	**Dingaan (IRE)**[10] 4227 4-9-7 **85** (v) LPKeniry 11	77
			(A M Balding) *slowly away: rdn 3f out: a towards rr and nvr in contention* **14/1**	
0546	**9**	*nk*	**Woodcote Place**[13] 4134 4-9-6 **84** FrancisNorton 8	75
			(P R Chamings) *rrd stalls: slowly away: rdn and hung rt 2f out: no prog and hung bdly lft fnl f* **6/1**[3]	
1460	**10**	*2*	**Grizedale (IRE)**[19] 3943 8-8-10 **74** (t) PaulDoe 9	60
			(J Akehurst) *chsd ldrs: rdn 3f out: wknd fr 2f out* **25/1**	

1m 31.94s (2.60) **Going Correction** +0.325s/f (Good) 10 Ran SP% **117.3**
Speed ratings (Par 107): **98,97,97,96,96 95,93,91,91,88**
CSF £24.87 CT £251.48 TOTE £7.50: £2.20, £1.50, £5.00; EX 27.90 Trifecta £333.70 Part won. Pool: £470.10 - 0.90 winning tickets..
Owner John C Grant & D M James **Bred** Yeomanstown Stud **Trained** Lambourn, Berks
■ Stewards' Enquiry : Ian Mongan caution: used whip down shoulder in forehand position

FOCUS
The best race on the card, but they did not go a great pace and they finished in a bit of a heap, so the form is not the most solid. Apart from Music Note, the whole field came over to the stands' side in the straight.

NOTEBOOK
Jamieson Gold(IRE) had been disappointing in three outings so far this season, but he seems to come into his own at this time of year and he was down to a mark 6lb lower than for his last win. The ground had come right for him too and the way he battled on to hold off his rivals over the last couple of furlongs was very commendable. (tchd 7-1)
Trimlestown(IRE) ◆, well backed, is attractively handicapped these days and the softening ground was in his favour too, but he had to rather weave his way through the field to put in an effort and his late run was always going to fall a few strides short. With her stable coming into a bit of form just now, she should be able to make amends before too long. (op 7-2)
Bonnie Prince Blue, down to a career-low mark, kept battling away and was still going forward at the line. This was his best effort on turf for some time and there should be a similar race in him off this sort of mark. (tchd 16-1)
Wavertree Warrior(IRE), blinkered for the first time, would probably have preferred a stronger early pace and was eventually forced to be positive himself. He could not hold off the leading trio in the run to the line, but to his credit he did not drop away completely. He has dropped to a more feasible mark now and should be capable of winning off it when the race is run more to suit. (op 10-1)
Marajaa(IRE), not for the first time, met traffic problems when trying to get closer and once in the clear he was never quite doing enough. He would probably have preferred the rain to have stayed away, but even so he is the type that needs everything to fall just right, as one solitary career victory will testify. (op 9-2)
Sailor King(IRE), raised 2lb for finishing second at Leicester, did not see his race out after holding every chance and although he has won on turf in France, his very best form since arriving here has been on Polytrack. (op 13-2)
Music Note(IRE) would have found this trip sharp enough, especially in a race run at such an ordinary gallop. His rider decided to stay on the far side in isolation after turning for home and, although he seemed to be in touch with the main group on the stands' side entering the last furlong, he ended up comfortable held. How much the tactic affected his chance is impossible to say.
Dingaan(IRE) Official explanation: jockey said gelding missed break and was slowly away
Woodcote Place Official explanation: jockey said colt hung right

4549 ONE BIG SATURDAY CONCERT 18TH AUGUST MAIDEN FILLIES' STKS 1m 14y

4:00 (4:03) (Class 5) 3-Y-O+ **£4,533** (£1,348; £674; £336) **Stalls** High

Form				RPR
542	**1**		**Safwa (IRE)**[18] 3992 3-8-12 79 RHills 1	81+
			(Sir Michael Stoute) *sn led: mde rest: shkn up 2f out: c clr fnl f: eased cl home* **5/4**[1]	
4063	**2**	*3*	**Fidelia (IRE)**[18] 3992 3-8-12 79 TedDurcan 6	73+
			(G Wragg) *chsd wnr fr 6f out: rdn and effrt over 2f out: nvr gng pce to trble wnr: eased whn wl hld ins fnl f* **13/8**[2]	
	3	*2 1/2*	**Evening Affair** 3-8-12 0 KerrinMcEvoy 4	64
			(Saeed Bin Suroor) *hld up in tch: rdn and hdwy over 2f out: nvr gng pce to trble ldng pair and sn outpcd* **4/1**[3]	
	4	*1/2*	**Miss Habershon** 3-8-9 0 RichardKingscote[(3)] 2	63?
			(A King) *in rr but in tch: rdn and styd on same pce fnl 2f* **33/1**	
04-0	**5**	*hd*	**Regal Curtsy**[108] 1345 3-8-12 65 PaulDoe 3	63?
			(P R Chamings) *chsd ldrs: rdn 3f out: one pce fnl 2f* **33/1**	
00	**6**	*13*	**Southside Star**[28] 3685 3-8-12 0 DaneO'Neill 5	33
			(H J L Dunlop) *in rr but in tch: rdn and effrt fr 3f out: nvr in contention: wknd fr 2f out* **50/1**	

1m 50.11s (6.16) **Going Correction** +0.325s/f (Good) 6 Ran SP% **110.4**
Speed ratings (Par 100): **82,79,76,76,75 62**
CSF £3.40 TOTE £2.20: £1.30, £1.20; EX 3.80.
Owner Hamdan Al Maktoum **Bred** Shadwell Estate Company Limited **Trained** Newmarket, Suffolk

FOCUS
A moderate maiden, run at a dawdle, and the winning time was by far the slowest of the three over the trip on the day. Only half the field had a realistic chance according to the betting and the market got it spot-on, but the form may not add up to a great deal. Again all six came stands' side in the home straight

4550 SANDOWN SWINGING 60'S CHRISTMAS PARTIES CLAIMING STKS 1m 14y

4:35 (4:37) (Class 5) 3-Y-O **£3,886** (£1,156; £577; £288) **Stalls** High

Form				RPR
000	**1**		**Vietnam**[14] 4109 3-8-4 46 (b[1]) FrancisNorton 2	54
			(S Kirk) *in rr: hdwy over 2f out: styd on to ld jst ins fnl f: hung rt but a in command* **16/1**	
6520	**2**	*1 1/4*	**Fizzy Bella**[24] 3804 3-7-13 52 LukeMorris[(5)] 7	51
			(M G Quinlan) *in rr: hdwy over 2f out: sn chalng: led appr fnl f: hdd jst ins fnl f: sn outpcd* **4/1**[3]	
4020	**3**	*3*	**Magic Mountain (IRE)**[10] 4234 3-9-5 80 PatDobbs 4	59
			(R Hannon) *chsd ldrs: chal 3f out: slt ld over 2f out and hrd drvn: hdd appr fnl f: wknd ins fnl f* **6/5**[1]	
0210	**4**	*1 1/2*	**Winged Farasi**[30] 3620 3-9-0 63 (p) AmirQuinn 3	51
			(R A Harris) *chsd ldrs: rdn and ev ch 2f out: wknd fnl f* **5/2**[2]	
4-00	**5**	*1/2*	**Doonigan (IRE)**[75] 2262 3-8-7 53 LPKeniry 1	43
			(A M Balding) *chsd ldr: rdn and effrt 2f out: wknd over 1f out* **12/1**	
0006	**6**	*1 3/4*	**Espejo (IRE)**[22] 3843 3-8-6 60 RichardMullen 5	37
			(W J Musson) *led tl hdd over 2f out: wknd over 1f out* **16/1**	

1m 46.09s (2.14) **Going Correction** +0.325s/f (Good) 6 Ran SP% **113.5**
Speed ratings (Par 100): **102,100,97,96,95 94**
CSF £78.37 TOTE £21.60: £6.10, £2.60; EX 109.50.The winner was claimed by G. A. Huffer for £5,000.
Owner John Breslin **Bred** D R Tucker **Trained** Upper Lambourn, Berks

FOCUS
A modest claimer and the result was not the one that adjusted official ratings would have suggested, making the form far from solid, but the pace was fair enough and the front pair pulled clear.
Winged Farasi Official explanation: jockey said colt was unsuited by the good to soft (soft in places) ground

4551 OLBG.CO.UK SPONSORS GREATWOOD OPEN DAY H'CAP 1m 1f

5:10 (5:10) (Class 4) (0-85,82) 3-Y-O+ **£6,477** (£1,927; £963; £481) **Stalls** High

Form				RPR
0230	**1**		**Rule Of Life**[14] 4111 3-9-2 77 RHills 9	87
			(B W Hills) *mde all: rdn 2f out: styd on wl thrght fnl f* **3/1**[1]	
5601	**2**	*2 1/2*	**Uig**[14] 4112 6-8-10 **69** HaddenFrost[(5)] 10	73
			(H S Howe) *chsd wnr thrght: ev ch u.p 2f out: outpcd ins fnl f* **15/2**	
00	**3**	*3/4*	**Aegean Prince**[14] 4092 3-9-6 **81** (p) RichardMullen 7	83
			(W R Muir) *in rr: hdwy over 2f out: chsd ldrs fnl f but no imp* **14/1**	

0640 **4** ½ **Counsel's Opinion (IRE)**[19] 3959 10-9-13 81 TedDurcan 4 82
(C F Wall) *in tch: pushed along 2f out: kpt on ins fnl f but nvr gng pce to rch ldrs* **8/1**

0000 **5** ½ **Folio (IRE)**[12] 4166 7-9-7 82 AlanRutter(7) 2 82
(W J Musson) *in rr: hdwy 4f out: shkn up to chse ldrs fr 2f out: one pce whn rdr dropped reins fnl 100yds: sn rcvrd and one pce* **14/1**

2245 **6** 1¼ **Cinematic (IRE)**[29] 3641 4-9-4 72 AmirQuinn 11 69
(J R Boyle) *plld hrd: in tch: rdn and styd on same pce fnl 2f* **9/1**

200- **7** shd **Willhego**[551] 377 6-9-12 80 FrancisNorton 6 77
(J R Best) *chsd ldrs: rdn over 2f out: wknd fnl f* **25/1**

00 **8** ¾ **Kervriou (FR)**[66] 2512 4-9-3 71 LPKeniry 3 67
(A M Balding) *s.i.s: rdn over 2f out: no rspnse* **16/1**

5234 **9** nk **Lisathedaddy**[15] 4060 5-9-10 81 RichardKingscote(3) 1 76
(B G Powell) *chsd ldrs: rdn over 2f out: wknd fnl f* **7/2**[2]

4000 **10** 7 **Art Modern (IRE)**[41] 3272 5-9-11 79 (b) PatDobbs 5 58
(G L Moore) *a towards rr* **20/1**

3200 **11** ¾ **Gaelic Princess**[19] 3943 7-9-9 77 KerrinMcEvoy 8 55
(A G Newcombe) *s.i.s: sme prog 3f out: sn wknd* **11/2**[3]

1m 58.2s (2.09) **Going Correction** +0.325s/f (Good)
WFA 3 from 4yo+ 7lb **11** Ran SP% **123.3**
Speed ratings (Par 105): **103,100,100,99,99 98,98,97,97,90 90**
CSF £27.52 CT £285.04 TOTE £4.20: £1.60, £2.50, £4.20; EX 22.00 Place 6 £108.66, Place 5 £43.15.
Owner K Abdulla **Bred** Juddmonte Farms Ltd **Trained** Lambourn, Berks

FOCUS
Quite a competitive handicap, but one dominated by the pace-setters with the front pair basically holding those positions throughout. The form is rated at face value for now with the second and fifth to their latest marks.
T/Plt: £121.50 to a £1 stake. Pool: £56,209.65. 337.50 winning tickets. T/Qpdt: £93.00 to a £1 stake. Pool: £3,019.10. 24.00 winning tickets. ST

4552 - 4556a (Foreign Racing) - See Raceform Interactive

4519 DEAUVILLE (R-H)
Thursday, August 16

OFFICIAL GOING: Turf - good; aw - standard

4557a PRIX MINERVE SHADWELL (GROUP 3) (FILLIES) 1m 4f 110y
3:05 (3:07) 3-Y-O **£27,027** (£10,811; £8,108; £5,405; £2,703)

RPR

1 **Synopsis (IRE)**[33] 3564 3-8-9 SPasquier 10 110
(A Fabre, France) *hld up: hdwy and 6th into st on outside: drvn to ld jst ins fnl f: r.o* **119/10**[3]

2 1½ **Darsha (FR)**[18] 3-8-9 CSoumillon 4 108
(A De Royer-Dupre, France) *mid-div tl dropped bk over 4f out: hdwy and 7th st: rdn over 1f out: styd on one pce u.p*

3 hd **Dancing Lady (FR)**[75] 2270 3-8-10 ow1 OPeslier 5 108
(J-M Beguigne, France) *trckd ldr after 2f: 2nd st: rdn and ev ch 1f out: sn one pce* **31/1**

4 shd **Van Gosh**[33] 3564 3-8-9 JVictoire 11 107
(A Fabre, France) *a.p: 3rd st: sn u.p: styd on same pce* **13/1**

5 ¾ **Baroness Richter (IRE)**[56] 2786 3-8-9 C-PLemaire 9 106
(J-C Rouget, France) *mid-div: hdwy and 6th st: rdn and looking for gap towards outside whn n.m.r 1 1/2f out: kpt on one pce* **6/1**[2]

6 1½ **Mrs Lindsay (USA)**[67] 2501 3-8-13 JMurtagh 2 108
(F Rohaut, France) *led: 4 l clr over 4f out: rdn 2f out: hdd jst ins fnl f: one pce* **27/10**[1]

7 3 **Topka (FR)**[53] 2926 3-8-9 TJarnet 1 99
(F Doumen, France) *trckd ldr early: 5th and pushed along st: btn over 1f out* **35/1**

8 10 **Athlone (IRE)**[46] 3-8-9 DBoeuf 6 83
(A & G Botti, Italy) *prom: rdn wl over 3f out: 8th and btn st* **25/1**

9 2 **Orion Girl (GER)**[65] 2547 3-8-9 TThulliez 8 80
(H-A Pantall, France) *a bhd: 11th and btn st* **52/1**

10 ½ **Artistica (IRE)**[75] 2270 3-8-9 AlxiBadel 13 79
(A Fabre, France) *mid-div to 4f out: 10th and btn st*

11 **La Hernanda (IRE)**[53] 2926 3-8-9 IMendizabal 7 79
(H-A Pantall, France) *mid-div: 9th st: sn btn* **25/1**

12 **Zillione (FR)**[48] 3-8-9 MGuyon 12 79
(H Billot, France) *last thrght* **85/1**

2m 41.4s (-5.30) **12** Ran SP% **72.9**
PARI-MUTUEL: WIN 12.90; PL 3.10, 1.70, 5.80; DF 13.30.
Owner Sheikh Mohammed **Bred** Darley **Trained** Chantilly, France

NOTEBOOK
Synopsis(IRE), who has always been highly rated, won her first group race in style. She was dropped out early on and was not really seen until the straight when brought with a run up the centre of the track, but she quickened impressively and dominated the final half-furlong. A progressive sort, she will now be aimed at the Prix Vermeille at Longchamp next month.
Darsha(FR) never really seemed happy in the race. Towards the tail of the field early on, she was always close to the rail and still had plenty to do entering the straight. She did lengthen her stride from a furlong and a half out but never looked like pegging back the winner, and her trainer felt that she was not at home on the false ground. She will probably next be seen out in the Prix du Luctece.
Dancing Lady(FR) was in second position for much of the race. She made a forward move early in the straight and took a slight lead before being overwhelmed by the winner and runner-up. She only lost second place at the end of this race and is a very consistent individual.
Van Gosh was always well up and given every possible chance. Third into the straight, she battled all the way to the line and this outing will certainly be useful experience for the future, when she should make it at Group 3 level.

4246 CATTERICK (L-H)
Friday, August 17

OFFICIAL GOING: Good (good to firm in places)
Wind: Virtually nil Weather: Fine

4558 CHRISTMAS PARTY RACEDAY - TUESDAY 18TH DECEMBER AMATEUR RIDERS' H'CAP 1m 3f 214y
5:35 (5:35) (Class 5) (0-75,71) 3-Y-0+ **£3,123** (£968; £484; £242) **Stalls** Low

Form RPR

0036 **1** **Hugs Destiny (IRE)**[23] 3840 6-10-1 55 (t) MissAngelaBarnes(5) 6 64
(M A Barnes) *set stdy pce: qcknd 4f out: rdn wl over 1f out: kpt on wl* **11/1**

3322 **2** ½ **Sporting Gesture**[10] 4248 10-11-2 65 MissSBrotherton 7 73
(M W Easterby) *hld up and bhd: hdwy over 3f out: str run on inner wl over 1f out: rdn to chse wnr ins fnl f: kpt on* **7/2**[1]

2454 **3** 2½ **Acuzio**[12] 4194 6-10-8 57 MissEJJones 2 61
(W M Brisbourne) *hld up: hdwy to chse ldrs over 2f out and sn rdn: drvn over 1f out and kpt on same pce* **9/2**[3]

0-02 **4** nk **Granary Girl**[8] 4327 5-10-0 52 MrSPearce(3) 3 56
(J Pearce) *hld up and bhd: gd hdwy on outer over 2f out: rdn to chse ldrs and ch over 1f out: sn drvn and one pce* **7/1**

U526 **5** ½ **Collette's Choice**[14] 4131 4-10-8 62 (p) MrBMcHugh(5) 4 65
(R A Fahey) *hld up: hdwy 4f out: chsd ldrs 2f out: sn rdn and one pce* **11/2**

1432 **6** 1¾ **Court Of Appeal**[35] 3496 10-11-7 70 (tp) MissLEllison 1 70
(B Ellison) *chsd ldr: rdn along 3f out: wknd fnl 2f* **5/1**

3001 **7** 1 **Love Brothers**[8] 4309 3-10-7 71 MissMichelleSaunders(5) 8 70
(M R Channon) *trckd ldng pair: hdwy to chse wnr over 3f out: rdn over 2f out: drvn wl over 1f out and sn wknd* **4/1**[2]

2m 40.1s (1.10) **Going Correction** +0.05s/f (Good)
WFA 3 from 4yo+ 10lb **7** Ran SP% **113.3**
Speed ratings (Par 103): **98,97,96,95,95 94,93**
CSF £48.20 CT £200.81 TOTE £12.30: £4.00, £1.70.
Owner J G White **Bred** Matt Gleeson **Trained** Farlam, Cumbria
■ Rudry World (2/1) was withdrawn on vet's advice. R4 applies, deduct 30p in the £.

FOCUS
A modest amateurs' handicap but straightforward form with the first two and the fourth to their marks.

4559 ENTERTAIN CLIENTS AT CATTERICK RACECOURSE (S) STKS 7f
6:05 (6:07) (Class 6) 2-Y-O **£2,730** (£806; £403) **Stalls** Low

Form RPR

0650 **1** **Natural Rhythm (IRE)**[7] 4349 2-8-11 65 RoystonFfrench 7 55+
(Mrs A Duffield) *hld up: gd hdwy over 2f out: rdn to chal on outer over 1f out: kpt on u.p ins fnl f to ld last 75yds* **2/1**[1]

2633 **2** nk **Shipboard Romance (IRE)**[25] 3801 2-8-3 46 AndrewElliott(3) 3 49
(P D Evans) *cl up: rdn to ld wl over 1f out: drvn ins fnl f: hdd and no ex fnl 75yds* **9/2**[3]

204 **3** ½ **Giggling Monkey**[45] 3174 2-8-6 53 ChrisCatlin 1 48
(P D Evans) *trckd ldng pair: hdwy 2f out: rdn to chal over 1f out and ev ch tl drvn and nt qckn wl ins fnl f* **9/4**[2]

0456 **4** 3½ **Amy Lionheart**[23] 3835 2-8-6 38 KimTinkler 5 39
(N Tinkler) *t.k.h: chsd ldrs: hdwy 2f out: sn rdn and ch tl wknd appr fnl f* **33/1**

5 2½ **Jendas Jem** 2-8-6 0 PaulFessey 6 32+
(Mrs A Duffield) *s.i.s and bhd tl styd on fnl 2f* **16/1**

60 **6** 5 **Penny Arcade**[17] 4041 2-7-13 0 DeclanCannon(7) 2 19
(M E Sowersby) *led: rdn along 2f out: sn drvn and hdd over 1f out: wknd* **40/1**

4505 **7** 21 **Little Finch (IRE)**[6] 4405 2-8-2 47 ow1 (b) KevinGhunowa(5) 11 —
(R C Guest) *dwlt: a in rr: hmpd on bnd over 2 1/2f out and no ch after* **14/1**

0000 **8** 1¾ **Doubtless**[19] 4002 2-7-13 23 DanielleMcCreery(7) 4 —
(D W Chapman) *in tch tl rn v wd bnd over 2f out and sn bhd* **125/1**

000 **9** 3 **Social Height (IRE)**[6] 4405 2-8-8 0 PatrickMathers(3) 9 —
(A Berry) *in tch tl bdly hmpd on bnd over 2f out and virtually p.u after* **100/1**

1m 29.76s (2.40) **Going Correction** +0.05s/f (Good) **9** Ran SP% **102.0**
Speed ratings (Par 92): **88,87,87,83,80 74,50,48,45**
CSF £8.68 TOTE £2.60: £1.10, £1.70, £1.30; EX 11.20.The winner was sold to D W Chapman for 6,000gns
Owner I Farrington **Bred** Mark Commins **Trained** Constable Burton, N Yorks
■ Limestone was withdrawn (13/2, vet's advice). R4 applies, deduct 10p in the £.

FOCUS
This was a very moderate affair and the form is weak, with the runner-up and fourth setting the standard.

NOTEBOOK
Natural Rhythm(IRE), best in on official figures, had a good chance of opening his account and he did so but only just. He is reported to have "an engine" but had not seemed entirely keen to put his best foot forward. (op 15-8 tchd 5-2)
Shipboard Romance(IRE) has been running well enough in similar company and this was probably her best effort with the trip suiting. She had had plenty to find with the winner on official figures. (tchd 4-1)
Giggling Monkey was well-backed and had every chance and there did not appear to be any excuses, although she ran as well compared with the winner as her official rating entitled her to. (op 3-1 tchd 15-8)
Amy Lionheart, another with plenty to find, was keen and having had every chance may have found this trip a furlong too far.
Jendas Jem, making her racecourse bow and a stable companion of the winner, lost any chance she might have had with a slow start. However, she kept on to finish a deal closer than it seemed she could and with this experience behind her she could win a similar sort of race. (op 20-1)
Doubtless wanted to go straight on coming out of the bend and badly hampered Social Height, who was nearly brought down. (op 100-1)

4560 DURHAM CHESHIRE HOME NURSERY 5f 212y
6:40 (6:40) (Class 4) 2-Y-O **£5,181** (£1,541; £770; £384) **Stalls** Low

Form RPR

1222 **1** **Victorian Bounty**[12] 4193 2-9-6 75 ChrisCatlin 6 81
(E J O'Neill) *mde all: rdn clr over 1f out: styd on wl* **3/1**[1]

5446 **2** 2 **Angle Of Attack (IRE)**[23] 3841 2-8-12 67 PaulHanagan 3 70+
(R A Fahey) *in tch whn hmpd on bnd after 2f: gd hdwy on inner 2f out: rdn over 1f out: kpt on ins fnl f* **10/1**[3]

2252 **3** nk **Ramatni**[23] 3833 2-9-2 71 JimmyQuinn 7 70+
(M Johnston) *towards rr and rn wd home turn: gd hdwy on outer 2f out: rdn to chse wnr ins fnl f: drvn and no ex towards fin* **12/1**

4541 **4** 1 **Choisette**[3] 4476 2-8-4 59 6ex PaulFessey 11 55
(B Smart) *cl up: rdn along 2f out: ev ch tl drvn and one pce appr fnl f* **3/1**[1]

4423 **5** nk **Carnival Dream**[5] 4422 2-8-11 66 RoystonFfrench 8 61+
(A Berry) *prom whn n.m.r on bnd after 2f: chsd ldrs tl rdn and one pce appr fnl f* **7/1**[2]

0134 **6** shd **Longoria (IRE)**[8] 4315 2-8-13 71 JerryO'Dwyer(3) 2 66+
(M G Quinlan) *trckd ldrs on inner whn n.m.r and sltly hmpd on bnd after 2f: hdwy to chse wnr 2f out: sn rdn and one pce appr fnl f* **14/1**

6600 **7** 1 **Tikinheart (IRE)**[13] 4175 2-8-2 60 AndrewMullen(3) 4 52
(T D Easterby) *s.i.s and bhd tl styd on fnl 2f: nrst fin* **20/1**

00 **8** ½ **Geordie Girl**[35] 3507 2-8-7 65 PJMcDonald(3) 1 55
(R C Guest) *towards rr tl rdn and kpt on fnl 2f: nvr a factor* **14/1**

220 **9** *2* **Barraland**[13] 4152 2-9-7 **76** .... TPO'Shea 9 60
(M R Channon) *chsd ldrs: rdn along over 2f out and sn wknd* **7/1**[2]
222 **10** *½* **Prignsov Dancer (IRE)**[25] 3788 2-8-10 **65** .... (p) LeeEnstone 5 48
(P C Haslam) *hld up: effrt and sme hdwy over 2f out: sn rdn and btn* **25/1**
003 **11** *1 ¾* **Rope Bridge (IRE)**[25] 3788 2-8-1 **59** .... (b[1]) AndrewElliott(3) 12 37
(T D Easterby) *racd wd: a in rr* **80/1**
3230 **12** *½* **Select Committee**[31] 3606 2-9-0 **69** .... PatCosgrave 10 45
(J J Quinn) *hld up: effrt and sme hdwy over 2f out: sn rdn and btn* **16/1**
1m 13.98s (-0.02) **Going Correction** +0.05s/f (Good) **12** Ran SP% **120.8**
Speed ratings (Par 96): **102,99,98,97,97 97,95,95,92,91 89,88**
CSF £35.38 CT £325.26 TOTE £4.10: £1.60, £4.50, £2.80; EX 57.50.
Owner Victory Racing **Bred** Mrs P D Gray And Mr H Farr **Trained** Averham Park, Notts

FOCUS
A competitive little nursery at its level although they were well bunched behind the winner. The form looks pretty solid backed up by the time.

NOTEBOOK
Victorian Bounty, who made all and saw the trip out well to win decisively. However, there had been trouble in behind on the home turn (op 5-1 tchd 11-4)
Angle Of Attack(IRE) appeared to be badly hampered and his rider had to take drastic action. It is to his credit that he fought back and stayed on gamely to take the runner-up spot. It would have been very interesting if he had had a clear passage. Official explanation: jockey said gelding failed to negotiate first bend (op 11-1)
Ramatni apparently stumbled early on and did not appear to handle the bend at all well, so she had plenty to do turning in. She kept on under pressure and may be suited by another furlong. Official explanation: jockey said filly stumbled at start (op 10-1)
Choisette, a winner three days earlier at Musselburgh and shouldering a penalty, showed good speed again and was far from disgraced but five furlongs may be her trip at present. (op 2-1 tchd 7-2)
Carnival Dream was another seemingly hampered on the bend, not to the degree of the runner-up, but it could not have done her a lot of good and she ran a decent race in the circumstances. (op 8-1 tchd 13-2)
Longoria(IRE) was another sufferer but came to have every chance before weakening in the closing stages. On this evidence it may well be that she is still best suited by the minimum trip. (tchd 12-1)

4561 BOOK ON-LINE AT CATTERICKBRIDGE.CO.UK CLAIMING STKS 5f
7:10 (7:10) (Class 6) 3-Y-O+ **£2,730** (£806; £403) **Stalls** Low

Form RPR
0552 **1** **Raccoon (IRE)**[6] 4379 7-9-4 77 .... PJMcDonald(3) 1 71
(D W Chapman) *mde all: qcknd over 1f out: pushed out* **5/6**[1]
0564 **2** *¾* **Blackheath (IRE)**[10] 4252 11-8-10 52 .... SilvestreDeSousa 2 57
(D Nicholls) *cl up: rdn along 2f out: drvn and kpt on ins fnl f* **8/1**[3]
0006 **3** *1* **Northern Chorus (IRE)**[16] 4083 4-8-8 63 .... (v) JamesO'Reilly(7) 9 58
(J O'Reilly) *chsd ldrs: rdn along 2f out: drvn and kpt on same pce fnl f* **16/1**
3-00 **4** *½* **Larky's Lob**[94] 1755 8-8-13 47 .... VHalliday 5 55
(J O'Reilly) *in tch: hdwy 2f out: sn rdn and kpt on ins fnl f* **40/1**
0000 **5** *12* **Meikle Barfil**[8] 4312 5-8-8 48 .... (tp) KevinGhunowa(5) 10 11
(J M Bradley) *in tch: swtchd rt and hdwy wl over 1f out: sn rdn and kpt on same pce* **40/1**
0005 **6** *nk* **It's Unbelievable (USA)**[9] 4289 4-8-13 55 .... (b) MickyFenton 13 10
(P T Midgley) *dwlt and towards rr: hdwy on wd outside wl over 1f out: sn rdn and kpt on ins fnl f: nrst fin* **16/1**
4625 **7** *shd* **Seven No Trumps**[8] 4312 10-8-4 51 .... JakePayne(7) 6 8
(J M Bradley) *towards rr tl styd on appr fnl f* **20/1**
0600 **8** *hd* **Pat Will (IRE)**[62] 2652 3-8-4 45 .... PaulHanagan 8 —
(P D Evans) *hld up towards rr: hdwy 2f out: sn rdn and no imp appr fnl f* **66/1**
0460 **9** *1* **Mystery Pips**[1] 4525 7-8-6 48 .... (v) KimTinkler 12 —
(N Tinkler) *s.i.s and bhd tl styd on appr fnl f* **33/1**
60 **10** *shd* **Ten Shun**[25] 3802 4-8-8 69 .... AndrewElliott(3) 14 —
(P D Evans) *a towards rr* **11/1**
6032 **11** *¾* **Ruby's Dream**[29] 3667 5-8-7 46 .... (p) ChrisCatlin 4 —
(J M Bradley) *chsd ldrs: rdn along over 2f out and sn wknd* **12/1**
6443 **12** *1* **Jojesse**[11] 4226 3-9-3 56 .... PatCosgrave 3 5+
(G A Swinbank) *sltly hmpd s: a towards rr* **7/1**[2]
6-40 **13** *1* **Trombone Tom**[57] 2791 4-9-1 45 .... PaddyAspell 7 —
(J R Norton) *prom: rdn along 2f out: sn wknd* **100/1**
-650 **14** *hd* **Twinned (IRE)**[55] 2875 4-8-8 50 ow1 .... JerryO'Dwyer(3) 11 —
(M J Wilkinson) *a towards rr* **100/1**
0460 **15** *4* **La Marmotte (IRE)**[16] 4078 3-7-13 52 .... DuranFentiman(3) 15 —
(R E Barr) *racd wd: a in rr* **40/1**
59.34 secs (-1.26) **Going Correction** -0.225s/f (Firm)
WFA 3 from 4yo+ 2lb **15** Ran SP% **124.4**
Speed ratings (Par 101): **101,99,98,97,78 77,77,77,75,75 74,72,71,70,64**
CSF £7.53 TOTE £1.70: £1.10, £2.00, £6.10; EX 9.30.
Owner P D Savill **Bred** P D Savill **Trained** Stillington, N Yorks

FOCUS
A modest claimer with the usual mix of abilitites and dominated by the pair drawn closest to the far rail. The form is rated around the runner-up and fourth.
It's Unbelievable(USA) Official explanation: jockey said gelding missed the break
Mystery Pips Official explanation: jockey said mare slipped at start

4562 COME RACING AGAIN ON 29TH AUGUST H'CAP 7f
7:45 (7:45) (Class 6) (0-60,62) 3-Y-O+ **£2,730** (£806; £403) **Stalls** Low

Form RPR
3606 **1** **Joshua's Gold (IRE)**[14] 4141 6-9-9 **60** .... (v) DanielTudhope 2 70
(D Carroll) *trckd ldrs: smooth hdwy to ld wl over 1f out: rdn ins fnl f: edgd lft towards fin* **9/2**[1]
3500 **2** *¾* **No Grouse**[13] 4180 7-9-1 **52** .... DavidAllan 13 60+
(E J Alston) *hld up in rr: gd hdwy on outer 2f out: rdn and styd on strly ins fnl f* **18/1**
0053 **3** *nk* **Nufoudh (IRE)**[3] 4480 3-8-12 **57** .... AndrewElliott(3) 6 63+
(Miss Tracy Waggott) *led: rdn along 2f out: sn hdd: drvn and ev ch ins fnl f: n.m.r on inner and lost 2nd nr fin* **9/1**[3]
4010 **4** *½* **Pay Time**[6] 4407 8-9-4 **60** .... NeilBrown(5) 1 66
(R E Barr) *dwlt: sn in midfield: hdwy to chse ldrs 2f out: sn rdn and kpt on same pce ins fnl f* **16/1**
0261 **5** *nk* **Inca Soldier (FR)**[5] 4423 4-9-8 **62** 6ex .... PJMcDonald(3) 5 67
(R C Guest) *hld up in tch: effrt and sltly outpcd over 2f out: swtchd outside and rdn over 1f out: styd on ins fnl f: nrst fin* **9/2**[1]
6030 **6** *1* **Border Artist**[18] 4029 8-9-4 **55** .... JimmyQuinn 10 62+
(J Pearce) *hld up in midfield: hdwy 2f out: styng on whn n.m.r over 1f out: kpt on ins fnl f* **11/1**
6635 **7** *shd* **Pitbull**[18] 4023 4-9-1 **52** .... (p) PaulHanagan 15 54+
(Mrs G S Rees) *hld up and bhd: effrt and nt clr run over 1f out: swtchd outside and kpt on ins fnl f: nrst fin* **8/1**[2]
0102 **8** *shd* **Attacca**[32] 3599 6-9-3 **54** .... TPO'Shea 8 56
(J R Weymes) *cl up: rdn along over 2f out: sn drvn and grad wknd* **10/1**
0100 **9** *1* **Night In (IRE)**[16] 4083 4-9-9 **60** .... KimTinkler 4 59
(N Tinkler) *hld up in midfield: hdwy on inner 2f out: rdn to chse ldrs wl over 1f out: wknd ins fnl f* **28/1**
0000 **10** *nk* **Sands Of Barra (IRE)**[10] 4250 4-9-7 **58** .... (p) RoystonFfrench 12 56
(I W McInnes) *chsd ldrs: rdn along over 2f out: grad wknd* **28/1**
4600 **11** *hd* **Moon Forest (IRE)**[20] 3965 5-8-8 **50** .... (p) KevinGhunowa(5) 11 48
(J M Bradley) *midfield: hdwy to chse ldrs 3f out: sn rdn and wknd wl over 1f out* **25/1**
1030 **12** *¾* **Barataria**[18] 4029 5-9-4 **58** .... JamieMoriarty(3) 7 54
(R Bastiman) *a towards rr* **9/1**[3]
4400 **13** *hd* **Desert Hunter (IRE)**[11] 4223 4-8-13 **50** .... PatCosgrave 14 45
(Micky Hammond) *plld hrd: hld up: a in rr* **25/1**
0540 **14** *hd* **Zhitomir**[37] 3414 9-9-0 **51** .... PhillipMakin 3 45
(M Dods) *chsd ldrs: rdn along over 2f out and sn wknd* **14/1**
4636 **15** *1 ¼* **Kudbeme**[16] 4081 5-9-7 **58** .... PaulFessey 9 49
(N Bycroft) *s.i.s: a bhd* **12/1**
1m 27.12s (-0.24) **Going Correction** +0.05s/f (Good)
WFA 3 from 4yo+ 5lb **15** Ran SP% **125.0**
Speed ratings (Par 101): **103,102,101,101,100 99,99,99,98,98 97,96,96,96,95**
CSF £91.48 CT £729.94 TOTE £5.50: £1.80, £4.80, £3.30; EX 139.60.
Owner Andy Helm, Simon Bean, David Jones **Bred** M G Masterson **Trained** Sledmere, E Yorks
■ Stewards' Enquiry : David Allan two-day ban; careless riding (Aug 28-29)
Daniel Tudhope two-day ban: careless riding (Aug 28-29)

FOCUS
A moderate handicap but run at a fair gallop and the form appears sound with the first five close to their marks.
Border Artist Official explanation: jockey said gelding was denied a clear run
Pitbull Official explanation: jockey said gelding hung left
Desert Hunter(IRE) Official explanation: jockey said gelding ran too free

4563 GO RACING AT RIPON TOMORROW MAIDEN STKS 1m 3f 214y
8:15 (8:15) (Class 5) 3-Y-O+ **£3,238** (£963; £481; £240) **Stalls** Low

Form RPR
6224 **1** **Yossi (IRE)**[23] 3847 3-9-2 80 .... JimmyQuinn 3 64+
(M H Tompkins) *trckd ldrs: hdwy to chse ldr over 2f out: rdn to ld over 1f out: drvn and kpt on towards fin* **1/4**[1]
4-2 **2** *½* **Inasus (GER)**[103] 1491 3-9-2 0 .... GregFairley 1 63+
(M Johnston) *led: rdn along over 2f out: drvn and hdd over 1f out: kpt on u.p fnl f* **7/2**[2]
0-00 **3** *12* **Matinee Idol**[45] 3193 4-9-7 39 .... PaulHanagan 5 39
(Mrs S Lamyman) *chsd ldrs: rdn along 3f out: sn drvn and plugged on one pce* **50/1**
4400 **4** *1 ¼* **Ammeyrr**[11] 4229 3-8-11 59 .... KellyHarrison(5) 2 42
(A Crook) *in tch: effrt and sme hdwy wl over 2f out: sn rdn and outpcd* **50/1**
0 **5** *1 ¼* **Hill Cloud**[8] 4334 5-9-9 0 .... LiamTreadwell(3) 6 40
(W M Brisbourne) *wnt rt s: a in rr* **50/1**
6 *1 ¼* **Resaass (USA)** 4-9-12 0 .... DavidAllan 4 38
(J O'Reilly) *prom: hdwy to chse ldr after 3f: rdn along 3f out: wknd fnl 2f* **25/1**[3]
2m 37.82s (-1.18) **Going Correction** +0.05s/f (Good)
WFA 3 from 4yo+ 10lb **6** Ran SP% **112.0**
Speed ratings (Par 103): **105,104,96,95,95 94**
CSF £1.38 TOTE £1.30: £1.10, £1.20; EX 1.90 Place 6 £ 14.96, Place 5 £ 5.06.
Owner Russell Trew **Bred** Knockainey Stud **Trained** Newmarket, Suffolk

FOCUS
An uncompetptpve maiden with the two favourites pulling well clear with the winner not needing to be at his best to score.
T/Plt: £36.90. Pool £48,942.55, 967.45 winning tickets T/Qpdt: £15.70. Pool £4,748.20, 222.90 winning tickets JR

DONCASTER (L-H)
Friday, August 17

OFFICIAL GOING: Good to firm (9.2)
Doncaster's first meeting since a jumps fixture on December 19, 2005, the course having closed for redevelopment.
Wind: virtually nil Weather: overcast

4564 SYKES LAWN TURF EBF MAIDEN FILLIES' STKS (DIV I) 7f
2:00 (2:04) (Class 4) 2-Y-O **£5,829** (£1,734; £866; £432) **Stalls** High

Form RPR
1 **Lady Jane Digby** 2-9-0 0 .... GregFairley 13 82
(M Johnston) *settled wl in tch: hdwy 2f out: nt clr run over 1f out: shkn up and qcknd to ld fnl 100yds: sn clr* **20/1**
2 *2 ½* **Quotation** 2-9-0 0 .... RyanMoore 9 75
(Sir Michael Stoute) *pushed along early: midfield: swtchd lft wl over 1f out: 5th ent fnl f: r.o wl to snatch 2nd* **6/1**[3]
3 **3** *½* **Zeu Tin Tin (IRE)**[13] 4169 2-9-0 0 .... KerrinMcEvoy 8 74
(R A Kvisla) *chsd ldr: drvn to ld 1f out: hdd fnl 100yds: nt qckn* **9/2**[2]
3 **4** *nk* **Marwah**[28] 3706 2-9-0 0 .... PaulHanagan 6 73
(E A L Dunlop) *t.k.h: chsd ldrs: rdn and effrt over 1f out: kpt on same pce* **4/1**[1]
5 *1* **Ceka Dancer (IRE)** 2-9-0 0 .... ChrisCatlin 2 71
(E J O'Neill) *t.k.h: prom: rdn and ev ch wl over 1f out: fdd jst ins fnl f* **10/1**
6 *1 ½* **Deira Dubai** 2-9-0 0 .... MichaelHills 11 67
(B W Hills) *stdd in rr: weaved through and hdwy over 1f out: r.o wl ins fnl f* **9/1**
7 *nk* **Mollyatti** 2-9-0 0 .... MickyFenton 4 66
(Miss V Haigh) *led at stdy pce: rdn wl over 1f out: hdd 1f out: hmpd sn after: wknd fnl 100yds* **100/1**
0 **8** *½* **Chrystal Venture (IRE)**[28] 3706 2-9-0 0 .... PaulMulrennan 10 65
(A J McCabe) *chsd ldrs: rdn wl over 1f out: sn btn* **100/1**
9 *½* **L'Etincelle (IRE)** 2-9-0 0 .... TedDurcan 3 63
(H R A Cecil) *a bhd* **33/1**
5 **10** *nk* **Double On Red**[21] 3895 2-9-0 0 .... HayleyTurner 5 63
(J M P Eustace) *midfield on outer: rdn over 2f out: sn struggling* **7/1**
0 **11** *½* **Beat The Rain**[28] 3706 2-9-0 0 .... RobertHavlin 14 61
(J H M Gosden) *hld up in rr on rail: nvr looked dangerous* **10/1**

05 **12** *hd* **Top Vision**[15] 4094 2-9-0 0 .... TPO'Shea 12 61+
(M R Channon) *towards rr: nt clr run over 2f out tl ins fnl f: nvr on terms* **7/1**

6 **13** *3/4* **Lamistrelle (IRE)**[19] 4002 2-9-0 0 .... RoystonFfrench 1 59
(Mrs A Duffield) *midfield: rdn and struggling 1/2-way* **100/1**

14 *shd* **Red Lily (IRE)** 2-9-0 0 .... JamieSpencer 7 59
(J R Fanshawe) *stdd s: last and no ch over 2f out* **20/1**

1m 27.26s (-0.51) **Going Correction** -0.10s/f (Good) **14** Ran SP% **121.1**
Speed ratings (Par 93): **98,95,94,94,93 91,91,90,89,89 88,88,87,87**
CSF £132.10 TOTE £20.70: £4.60, £2.90, £2.20; EX 153.80.
Owner Miss K Rausing **Bred** Miss K Rausing **Trained** Middleham Moor, N Yorks
■ Stewards' Enquiry : Michael Hills one-day ban; careless riding (Aug 28)

FOCUS
A fair fillies' maiden on paper and, although the early pace was not strong, the final time was 0.44sec quicker than the second division.

NOTEBOOK
Lady Jane Digby, a half-sister to several winners, notably high-class older miler Gateman, and Suprise Encounter, a smart performer at 7f and 1m, ran out a clear winner on her debut and looks a filly with a future. Always well placed near the stands'-side rail, she quickened up in good style when asked to go and win her race, and on this evidence it will not be long before she tackles Pattern company. (op 25-1)
Quotation is a sister to Commentary, who won over 6f at two, but she looks to need further herself. Pushed along at halfway, she stayed on really well to take second, and she can probably win over this trip off a better pace, but a mile is going to suit her before the season is out. (op 8-1)
Zeu Tin Tin(IRE) did the form of her third behind Sense Of Joy no harm with a solid effort in defeat. She had the benefit of experience over the first two but could not make it pay. (op 6-1)
Marwah, like Zeu Tin Tin, finished third in a Newmarket maiden last time. Not ideally drawn here, she failed to build on that effort, but this was probably a decent maiden and there will be easier opportunities for her. (op 10-3)
Ceka Dancer(IRE), a half-sister to a number of winners, many as juveniles, was also poorly drawn. She showed good speed early on but raced too keenly for her own good in the process, and in the circumstances she did well to finish fifth. She can only improve for this. (op 8-1 tchd 14-1)
Deira Dubai, a half-sister to Agenda, quite a useful 1m2f winner at three, has a Cheveley Park entry and was held up out the back. She made some late progress through the pack but was never going to trouble the principals. A stronger pace would have suited her and she can do better. (op 11-1)
Mollyatti crossed over from her low draw to make the running on the stands'-side rail. Able to dictate a steady pace, she is probably flattered by her finishing position.
Red Lily(IRE) Official explanation: jockey said filly suffered interference in running

4565 SYKES LAWN TURF EBF MAIDEN FILLIES' STKS (DIV II) 7f
2:30 (2:37) (Class 4) 2-Y-O **£5,829** (£1,734; £866; £432) **Stalls** High

Form RPR

6 **1** **Falcolnry (IRE)**[15] 4102 2-9-0 0 .... JamieSpencer 9 80
(J R Fanshawe) *dropped out in last pl: stdy prog wl over 2f out: chal ent fnl f: led fnl 100yds: kpt on* **10/3**[2]

2 *1* **Sugar Mint (IRE)** 2-9-0 0 .... MichaelHills 4 77
(B W Hills) *towards rr on outer but gng wl: hdwy 3f out: led over 1f out: drvn and hdd and hit on nose 100yds out: no ex* **13/8**[1]

3 *2 1/2* **Black Dahlia** 2-9-0 0 .... NCallan 13 71+
(A J McCabe) *hld up in rr: hmpd after 1f: hdwy over 2f out: nt clr run over 1f out tl ins fnl f: r.o to go 3rd fnl 75yds* **40/1**

4 *3/4* **Heritage Coast (USA)** 2-9-0 0 .... RyanMoore 3 69
(Sir Michael Stoute) *prom: rdn and lost pl 2f out: plugged on fnl f* **4/1**[3]

0 **5** *nk* **Step This Way (USA)**[26] 3760 2-9-0 0 .... GregFairley 12 68
(M Johnston) *led at stdy pce: rdn and hdd over 1f out: sn outpcd by ldng pair but kpt on* **10/1**

6 *1 3/4* **Darley Star** 2-9-0 0 .... JohnEgan 10 63
(C E Brittain) *midfield: rdn 3f out: nvr trbld ldrs after* **25/1**

0 **7** *1/2* **Zerky (USA)**[15] 4094 2-9-0 0 .... KerrinMcEvoy 7 62
(E A L Dunlop) *towards rr: rdn and brief effrt 2f out: nvr on terms* **9/1**

8 *3 1/2* **Futune (IRE)** 2-9-0 0 .... RobertHavlin 6 53
(B J Meehan) *s.i.s: sme prog over 2f out: sn wl btn* **33/1**

9 *1 1/4* **Madam Carwell** 2-9-0 0 .... TPQueally 2 50
(J G Given) *prom: chsd ldr 3f out tl wl over 1f out: sn wknd* **25/1**

6 **10** *1* **Bunny Hug**[11] 4225 2-9-0 0 .... DavidAllan 8 47
(T D Easterby) *sn pushed along in rr: no ch last 2f* **50/1**

0 **11** *5* **Fantastic Lass**[20] 3977 2-9-0 0 .... PaulHanagan 11 34
(R A Fahey) *drvn after 2f: nvr gng wl* **33/1**

00 **12** *10* **Eighty Twenty**[79] 2147 2-9-0 0 .... PaulMulrennan 5 —
(M W Easterby) *chsd ldr 4f: rdn and cumbersme and stopped to nthing: t.o* **66/1**

1m 27.7s (-0.07) **Going Correction** -0.10s/f (Good) **12** Ran SP% **119.7**
Speed ratings (Par 93): **96,94,92,91,90 88,88,84,82,81 75,64**
CSF £8.65 TOTE £4.40: £1.60, £1.50, £6.60; EX 10.40.
Owner Mr & Mrs Duncan Davidson **Bred** Michael Begley **Trained** Newmarket, Suffolk

FOCUS
Again there was a steady early pace and the race developed into something of a sprint. It was the slower of the two divisions by 0.44sec.

NOTEBOOK
Falcolnry(IRE), who is a half-sister to Live In Fear, a 5f winner at three, was too green to do herself justice on her debut, but she did show ability and on this occasion she settled well out the back and found the best turn of foot off the fairly steady early pace. Entries in the Lowther and Cheveley Park Stakes indicate the regard in which she is held and she can only improve. (op 7-2)
Sugar Mint(IRE), whose dam is an unraced half-sister to Breeders' Cup Classic winner Arcangues, is a half-sister to Anna's Rock, a 7f winner at two. Entered in the Fillies' Mile and Moyglare Stud Stakes, she is evidently well regarded and she was sent off a short price to make a winning debut. She travelled well off the pace, but the steady early gallop probably did not suit her ideally and in the end she was just seen off by a speedier filly. She should have little trouble winning her maiden before going on to better things. (op 6-4 tchd 7-4 in places)
Black Dahlia, who cost just 5,000gns, is a half-sister to prolific 1m2f to 2m winner Cold Turkey. The betting suggested that she would not be playing too much of a part in this race but in the event she ran a blinder, overcoming trouble in running to take third. She looks to have been a shrewd purchase, even at this stage. (op 50-1)
Heritage Coast(USA), whose dam won twice at Listed level over middle distances and is a half-sister to Dante Stakes winner Tenby, could have done with a stronger gallop as she is bred to come into her own over a lot further next year. (op 9-2)
Step This Way(USA), a half-sister to Kid Grindstone, a very useful multiple winner at 1m plus on turf in the US, did not show a lot on her debut after being hampered early, but she cost a bit and is Group 1 entered so improvement was expected. She was well drawn this time and got to make the running at a steady pace so in the circumstances it was a little disappointing that she did not do a little better. (tchd 12-1)
Darley Star, a half-sister to Amerigo Vespucci, a 1m2f winner at three, is another who is unlikely to be seen at her best until her three-year-old season.
Zerky(USA), who cost $300,000 and is a sister to Penny's Gold, a multiple winning miler in France and the US, did not show a great deal on her debut and, although this was a bit more encouraging, she has a long way to go to justify her Fillies' Mile entry. (tchd 10-1)

4566 ISG H'CAP 1m (R)
3:05 (3:13) (Class 3) (0-95,95) 3-Y-0+ **£12,285** (£3,627; £1,814) **Stalls** Low

Form RPR

2141 **1** **Webbow (IRE)**[13] 4176 5-8-13 **83** .... DavidAllan 10 95+
(T D Easterby) *taken down early: wl bhd: rdn over 2f out: swtchd outside and str run to ld ins fnl f: bit cosily* **5/1**[2]

-550 **2** *nk* **Ekhtiaar**[36] 3460 3-9-1 **91** .... RyanMoore 1 101+
(J H M Gosden) *chsd ldrs: hdwy over 2f out: ev ch over 1f out: pressed wnr hrd ins fnl f: hld fnl 50yds* **7/2**[1]

5-30 **3** *3/4* **Mesbaah (IRE)**[20] 3940 3-9-4 **94** .... PhilipRobinson 18 102
(M A Jarvis) *taken down early: prom: rdn to ld jst over 1f out tl ins fnl f: nt qckn fnl 100yds* **12/1**

1361 **4** *1 3/4* **Oceana Gold**[15] 4111 3-8-0 **79** .... WilliamBuick(3) 11 83
(A M Balding) *t.k.h in ld: rdn wl over 1f out: hdd over 1f out: one pce* **10/1**

3333 **5** *shd* **Granston (IRE)**[13] 4176 6-9-2 **86** .... KerrinMcEvoy 13 91
(J D Bethell) *chsd ldrs: rdn to chal over 1f out: outpcd fnl 100yds* **8/1**[3]

004 **6** *hd* **Macedon**[20] 3943 4-8-11 **81** .... JohnEgan 15 85
(J S Moore) *t.k.h: hdwy on outer 3f out: ev ch over 1f out: no ex* **10/1**

6400 **7** *nk* **Robustian**[16] 4068 4-8-9 **82** ....(b[1]) JerryO'Dwyer(3) 6 86
(Eve Johnson Houghton) *t.k.h trcking ldrs: rdn to chal over 1f out: fnd little* **16/1**

20/4 **8** *3/4* **Troubadour (IRE)**[13] 4167 6-9-11 **95** .... TedDurcan 17 97+
(W Jarvis) *stdd s: t.k.h in rr: hdwy over 2f out: rdn and no imp over 1f out* **33/1**

3136 **9** *nk* **Hoh Wotanite**[7] 4353 4-8-6 **76** oh3 ....(p) RoystonFfrench 3 77
(R Hollinshead) *sn pushed along in midfield: rdn and swtchd rt over 2f out: nvr able to chal* **33/1**

0310 **10** *nk* **Vicious Warrior**[17] 4049 8-9-2 **86** .... PaulMulrennan 20 87
(R M Whitaker) *plld hrd in rr: swtchd outside 2f out: kpt on but n.d* **33/1**

0002 **11** *nk* **Hartshead**[6] 4408 8-9-3 **90** .... PJMcDonald(3) 9 90
(G A Swinbank) *chsd ldrs: rdn 2f out: one pce* **14/1**

-460 **12** *nk* **Kamanda Laugh**[11] 4228 6-9-1 **85** .... NCallan 12 84
(K A Ryan) *nvr bttr than midfield: eased ins fnl f* **33/1**

203 **13** *1 1/4* **Blue Spinnaker (IRE)**[17] 4039 8-8-8 **85** .... NSLawes(7) 8 81
(M W Easterby) *bhd: rdn 2f out: nvr on terms* **16/1**

1126 **14** *hd* **Zaahid (IRE)**[35] 3503 3-8-10 **86** .... MichaelHills 7 81
(B W Hills) *chsd ldrs: ev ch over 1f out: sn btn and eased* **10/1**

2110 **15** *1 1/4* **Slate (IRE)**[57] 2788 3-9-2 **92** .... MickyFenton 4 84
(Miss V Haigh) *chsd ldrs: rdn over 3f out: sn struggling* **25/1**

00-0 **16** *1/2* **Musadif (USA)**[90] 1836 9-9-11 **95** ....(t) FergusSweeney 5 87
(R A Kvisla) *taken down early: plld hrd in rr: n.d* **100/1**

2110 **17** *hd* **Fortunate Isle (USA)**[34] 3558 5-9-7 **91** .... PaulHanagan 19 82
(R A Fahey) *bhd on outer: nvr on terms* **20/1**

3140 **18** *6* **Musical Beat**[20] 3972 3-8-3 **79** .... ChrisCatlin 2 56
(Miss V Haigh) *pressed ldrs tl fdd qckly jst over 2f out* **50/1**

034R **19** *7* **Quai Du Roi (IRE)**[125] 1040 5-8-0 **77** .... AdeleRothery(7) 14 39
(D Nicholls) *lost 100yds at s and a maintaining disadvantage* **100/1**

1m 37.57s (-3.04) **Going Correction** -0.20s/f (Firm)
WFA 3 from 4yo+ 6lb **19** Ran SP% **127.7**
Speed ratings (Par 107): **107,106,105,104,104 103,103,102,102,102 101,101,100,100,98 98,98,92,85**
CSF £21.30 CT £216.26 TOTE £6.00: £1.80, £1.90, £4.40, £2.60; EX 24.80.
Owner Wentdale Limited **Bred** Joe O'Callaghan **Trained** Great Habton, N Yorks

FOCUS
Perhaps not as competitive a handicap as the numbers suggested, but sound enough form nevertheless.

NOTEBOOK
Webbow(IRE) continues to progress up the handicapping ladder, this time defying a 4lb higher mark than when last successful and recording his third win from five starts this season. He is the type who likes to challenge from off the pace, and the assessor is finding it difficult to get a handle on him, so another success - he is apparently being aimed at a valuable race at Ayr next - could well fall his way before his progress is halted. (op 9-2)
Ekhtiaar, back to his ideal trip, was again made favourite and returned to his best. He was unlucky to run into a highly progressive rival in Webbow as he did nothing wrong, hitting the front at what appeared to be the ideal time. (tchd 4-1)
Mesbaah(IRE), the Hamdan third string according to jockey hats, was given every chance and simply found a couple too strong. His current mark looks a shade high and, while he should continue to give a good account, he is likely to remain vulnerable to something a bit better off at the weights. (op 11-1)
Oceana Gold, 5lb higher for his Sandown success, again tried to make all, but he raced a bit too keenly for his own good out in front and that cost him in the latter stages. He remains capable of better.
Granston(IRE) was 4lb better off with Webbow for a length and a half beating at Thirsk last time, but the turnaround in the weights proved insufficient to reverse the form.
Macedon had looked set for a good campaign when finishing fourth in the Newbury Spring Cup back in April, but things have just not gone his way for one reason or another. He may be the type that needs plenty of time between his races as he seems to run his best races when fresh. (tchd 11-1)
Robustian, who was back on the mark he last won off, had blinkers on for the first time, but he did not find a great deal when brought to challenge inside the final two furlongs. (op 20-1)
Troubadour(IRE) ran alright but he is likely to require a little help from the Handicapper before he begins winning again.
Kamanda Laugh Official explanation: jockey said gelding was denied a clear run
Musadif(USA) Official explanation: jockey said gelding ran too free

4567 A1 MEDICAL & GENERAL LTD H'CAP 5f 140y
3:40 (3:44) (Class 3) (0-95,95) 3-Y-0+ **£11,658** (£3,468; £1,733; £865) **Stalls** High

Form RPR

0003 **1** **Golden Dixie (USA)**[4] 4456 8-9-3 **88** .... KerrinMcEvoy 13 97
(R A Harris) *bhd on stands' side: rdn and gd hdwy over 1f out: styd on wl to ld fnl stride* **8/1**[3]

0656 **2** *shd* **Geojimali**[6] 4389 5-8-9 **80** .... SaleemGolam 7 89+
(J S Goldie) *s.i.s: wl bhd on far side: gd prog over 1f out: led overall ins fnl f: pipped post* **13/2**[2]

1135 **3** *shd* **Jack Rackham**[20] 3952 3-8-11 **85** .... RoystonFfrench 12 93
(B Smart) *chsd ldrs stands' side: drvn 1/2-way: ev ch ins fnl f: r.o cl home* **20/1**

0004 **4** *1 1/2* **Loch Verdi**[6] 4373 4-8-10 **84** .... WilliamBuick(3) 15 87
(A M Balding) *led stands' side: rdn over 1f out: hdd ins fnl f: fdd cl home* **13/2**[2]

0500 **5** *shd* **Gift Horse**[20] 3975 7-9-8 **93**........................(v[1]) JamieSpencer 10 96+
(D Nicholls) *dropped out in last pl on stands' side: stl plenty to do but on bridle over 1f out: shkn up and r.o cl home* **11/2**[1]

0260 **6** *½* **Qadar (IRE)**[13] 4150 5-9-10 **95**........................(b) RyanMoore 6 96
(N P Littmoden) *s.i.s: bhd on far side: effrt u.p 2f out: no imp fnl f* **25/1**

3000 **7** *¾* **Distinctly Game**[21] 3911 5-8-13 **84**........................ NCallan 3 83
(K A Ryan) *midfield on far side: hdwy 2f out: ch 1f out: wknd fnl 100yds* **25/1**

3120 **8** *1 ¼* **Gallery Girl (IRE)**[19] 3990 4-9-1 **86**........................ DavidAllan 17 81
(T D Easterby) *chsd ldrs stands' side: wnt 2nd over 1f out tl 1f out: wknd* **12/1**

3303 **9** *¾* **Caribbean Coral**[11] 4227 8-9-4 **92**........................ PJMcDonald(3) 16 84
(J J Quinn) *s.s: bhd on stands' side: no ch* **10/1**

00 **10** *½* **Varadouro (BRZ)**[14] 4122 5-9-2 **87**........................ PaulHanagan 11 77
(D Nicholls) *sn rdn in rr on stands' side: nvr on terms* **66/1**

-535 **11** *1 ½* **Avertuoso**[83] 2022 3-8-9 **86**........................(v[1]) MarkLawson(3) 18 71
(B Smart) *chsd ldrs stands' side tl over 1f out: sn wknd* **20/1**

2400 **12** *nk* **Spanish Ace**[15] 4095 6-8-8 **84**........................ KevinGhunowa(5) 5 68
(J M Bradley) *sn rdn: chsd ldrs far side tl wknd 2f out* **33/1**

1400 **13** *1* **Misaro (GER)**[15] 4095 6-8-10 **84**........................(b) LiamJones(3) 2 65
(R A Harris) *racd on far rail: prom tl fdd 2f out* **33/1**

0000 **14** *shd* **Woodcote (IRE)**[14] 4122 5-9-5 **90**........................(be) PhilipRobinson 4 71
(C G Cox) *taken down early: led far side tl rdn and hdd jst ins fnl f: lost pl rapidly* **11/1**

0130 **15** *hd* **Dig Deep (IRE)**[6] 4386 5-9-5 **90**........................ PaulMulrennan 20 70
(W J Haggas) *taken down early: chsd ldrs stands' side: drvn wl over 1f out: sn btn* **12/1**

5135 **16** *½* **Mimi Mouse**[35] 3515 5-8-9 **80**........................ TedDurcan 8 58
(T D Easterby) *in tch far side: rdn and hung rt 2f out: sn btn* **25/1**

0030 **17** *1 ¼* **Corridor Creeper (FR)**[19] 3990 10-9-1 **93**........................(p) BarrySavage(7) 14 67
(J M Bradley) *chsd ldrs stands' side: rdn 1/2-way: sn lost pl* **20/1**

0021 **18** *1 ¾* **Peter Island (FR)**[8] 4320 4-8-10 **81** 6ex........................(v) ChrisCatlin 1 49
(J Gallagher) *w ldr far side over 2f: sn lost pl v bdly to be labouring in rr* **20/1**

67.50 secs (-0.50) **Going Correction** -0.10s/f (Good)
WFA 3 from 4yo+ 3lb **18** Ran SP% **123.9**
Speed ratings (Par 107): **99,98,98,96,96 95,94,93,92,91 89,89,87,87,87 86,85,82**
CSF £50.64 CT £1030.83 TOTE £10.40: £2.60, £2.20, £4.80, £2.10; EX 88.00.
Owner Mrs Vicki Davies **Bred** G Strawbridge Jr **Trained** Earlswood, Monmouths

FOCUS
The field split into two groups early on but finished wide across the track and there appeared no bias.

NOTEBOOK
Golden Dixie(USA) usually finishes with a rare rattle and on this occasion it took him to the front in the final stride. He appreciates a decent pace in his races and, having now won over this course and distance, the Portland Handicap next month will surely be uppermost in his connections' thoughts. (op 7-1)
Geojimali, who ran better than his fnishing position suggests at Haydock last time, was slowly away as usual but came through from the back of the pack on the far side to win his race, only to be gubbed on the line. He is not enjoying the best of luck at present. (tchd 7-1 in a place)
Jack Rackham, one of only two three-year-olds in the race, was ridden closer to the pace this time and returned to form. He has scope for further improvement and, as he appreciates fast ground, connections will no doubt be hoping for a dry autumn.
Loch Verdi, who made the running on the stands' side, ran well again, especially considering that most of those involved at the finish came from off the pace, but she appears to have few secrets from the Handicapper now. (op 6-1)
Gift Horse, who ran quite well the last time Spencer was on board, wore a visor for the first time and his supporters sent him off favourite. He travelled well out the back but did not get the best of runs through and was never going to get there. He has dropped a fair way in the handicap over the past year and there is a decent prize still in him. Perhaps it will be the Portland, back over this course and distance, or the Ayr Gold Cup. Official explanation: jockey said gelding was denied a clear run (op 6-1)
Qadar(IRE) has still to win a race on turf and remains a difficult horse with which to win any type of race.
Distinctly Game ran a fair race but he is another who appears to have little in hand off his current mark. (op 33-1)
Gallery Girl(IRE), who made all in a class 4 race at Ayr in June, has found things a bit tougher back in better company since.

4568 FIRST TRANSPENNINE EXPRESS MAIDEN STKS 1m 2f 60y
4:10 (4:14) (Class 4) 3-Y-O £6,477 (£1,927; £963; £481) Stalls Low

Form RPR

2-4 **1** **Broomielaw**[121] 1093 3-9-3 0........................ RyanMoore 6 97+
(E A L Dunlop) *chsd ldng pair: led on bit 3f out: pushed clr over 1f out: readily* **8/13**[1]

2 *3* **Bright Mind** 3-9-3 0........................ RobertHavlin 11 86+
(J H M Gosden) *v.s.a hld up in rr: hdwy to chse ldng pair 3f out: chsd wnr 1f out: no ch but kpt on* **16/1**

0533 **3** *3 ½* **Alpes Maritimes**[20] 3964 3-9-3 76........................ NCallan 10 79
(G Wragg) *t.k.h: hdwy over 3f out: chsd wnr over 2f out: sn rdn and hung rt: wknd 1f out* **9/2**[2]

0- **4** *3 ½* **Theta**[276] 6481 3-8-12 0........................ TedDurcan 5 67
(H R A Cecil) *w.w: rdn and effrt 3f out: no ch last 2f* **50/1**

6-24 **5** *4* **Inchlaggan (IRE)**[97] 1659 3-9-3 76........................ MichaelHills 8 64
(B W Hills) *mostly 2nd tl over 2f out: sn lost pl* **14/1**

6 *3 ½* **Bukit Tinggi (IRE)** 3-9-3 0........................ PhilipRobinson 7 57+
(M A Jarvis) *s.i.s: wl bhd kpt on steadily last 2f: no ch but nt disgracd* **14/1**

0 **7** *¾* **Penang (IRE)**[146] 764 3-8-12 0........................ JohnEgan 9 51
(C E Brittain) *bhd: rdn and btn over 3f out* **66/1**

4352 **8** *shd* **Sonning Star (IRE)**[18] 4018 3-9-3 74........................ KerrinMcEvoy 2 55
(D R C Elsworth) *t.k.h: led and clr tl hdd 3f out: sn dropped out* **8/1**[3]

0030 **9** *6* **Ranavalona**[7] 4366 3-8-12 51........................(t) MickyFenton 3 38
(C Smith) *bhd and rdn over 3f out: sn t.o* **100/1**

10 *2* **Mounafes** 3-9-3 0........................ PaulMulrennan 4 39
(G A Butler) *chsd ldrs tl rdn and lost pl 1/2-way: racd awkwardly after: t.o over 2f out* **50/1**

2m 6.89s (-4.94) **Going Correction** -0.20s/f (Firm) **10** Ran SP% **116.8**
Speed ratings (Par 102): **111,108,105,103,99 97,96,96,91,89**
CSF £13.28 TOTE £1.60: £1.10, £3.40, £1.40; EX 12.70.
Owner Lady Ferguson **Bred** Biddestone Stud **Trained** Newmarket, Suffolk

FOCUS
An ordinary maiden but the first two will win more races.
Sonning Star(IRE) Official explanation: jockey said gelding hung right-handed
Ranavalona Official explanation: jockey said filly had a breathing problem

4569 MERRYWEATHERS CELEBRATING 175 YEARS STKS (HERITAGE H'CAP) 2m 2f
4:45 (4:46) (Class 2) (0-105,97) 3-Y-0+
£31,160 (£9,330; £4,665; £2,335; £1,165; £585) Stalls Low

Form RPR

0420 **1** **Desert Sea (IRE)**[21] 3898 4-8-8 **81**........................ FergusSweeney 16 89+
(D W P Arbuthnot) *midfield: swtchd rt and qcknd off slow pce to ld 2f out: dashed clr and hung lft: drvn out* **20/1**

2620 **2** *½* **Whispering Death**[16] 4056 5-8-11 **84**........................(v) KerrinMcEvoy 10 91+
(W J Haggas) *awkward stalls and v.s.a: sn in tch: stl last over 2f out: styd on reluctantly fnl f* **7/1**[3]

-001 **3** *1 ¼* **Inchnadamph**[37] 3412 7-8-10 **83**........................(t) PaulMulrennan 5 89
(T J Fitzgerald) *hld up in rr: drvn and hdwy over 2f out: chsd wnr 1f out tl fnl 100yds: plugged on* **7/1**[3]

3010 **4** *1 ¼* **Enjoy The Moment**[21] 3898 4-9-10 **97**........................ JamieSpencer 4 103+
(J A Osborne) *hld up in rr: nt clr run and swtchd lft over 2f out: nt clr run after tl swtchd grad rt over 1f out: clr run fnl 100yds: kpt on* **7/2**[2]

1236 **5** *1* **Great As Gold (IRE)**[16] 4056 8-8-5 **78**........................ SaleemGolam 11 81
(B Ellison) *t.k.h: chsd ldrs tl 3f out: rdn and outpcd 3f out: kpt on again fnl f* **40/1**

-060 **6** *hd* **Kasthari (IRE)**[59] 2736 8-9-5 **92**........................ NCallan 15 95
(J D Bethell) *t.k.h: chsd ldr tl 3f out: one pce* **25/1**

-535 **7** *shd* **Som Tala**[16] 4056 4-9-1 **88**........................ TPO'Shea 1 91
(M R Channon) *in tch in midfield: rdn and effrt 3f out: no imp* **3/1**[1]

1312 **8** *shd* **Thewhirlingdervish (IRE)**[21] 3898 9-8-6 **79**........................ DavidAllan 7 82
(T D Easterby) *bhd: rdn and no hdwy 3f out: kpt on fnl f* **12/1**

-334 **9** *¾* **Golden Quest**[6] 4375 6-9-9 **96**........................ GregFairley 9 98
(M Johnston) *reluctant to go to s: led at slow pce tl 3f out: plodded on* **7/1**[3]

2020 **10** *nk* **Noble Minstrel**[16] 4056 4-7-12 **74**........................(t) WilliamBuick(3) 3 76
(S C Williams) *chsd ldrs: rdn 3f out: wknd over 1f out* **25/1**

40/1 **11** *3 ½* **Downing Street (IRE)**[13] 4179 6-8-7 **80**........................(bt) RobertHavlin 2 78
(Jennie Candlish) *hld up in rr: smooth hdwy on outer 4f out: led 3f out tl 2f out: sn btn* **16/1**

-220 **12** *15* **Falpiase (IRE)**[15] 4091 5-9-3 **90**........................ RyanMoore 8 71
(J Howard Johnson) *in tch: hdwy to chse ldrs and rdn over 3f out: wknd 2f out: eased ins fnl f* **14/1**

4m 1.00s (3.07) **Going Correction** -0.20s/f (Firm) **12** Ran SP% **119.9**
Speed ratings (Par 109): **85,84,84,83,83 83,83,83,82,82 81,74**
CSF £150.25 CT £1099.26 TOTE £27.20: £6.00, £2.90, £2.90; EX 205.30.
Owner Bonusprint **Bred** Peter McGlynn **Trained** Compton, Berks
■ Stewards' Enquiry : Jamie Spencer one-day ban: careless riding (Aug 30)

FOCUS
A steadily-run staying contest which did not suit a number of the runners.

NOTEBOOK
Desert Sea(IRE) quickened up well off the steady pace and was always holding the late finish of Whispering Death. The step up in trip had promised to suit him, but given the way the race was run it was not a true test. He was the one who found the best turn of foot, though, and that will stand him in good stead in future. (op 18-1)
Whispering Death was very slowly away and lost a number of lengths at the start. Fortunately for him, the early pace was pedestrian and he was able to latch on to the back of the bunch quite quickly. It was still quite something to see him emerge as the only real challenger to the eventual winner, though, and he deserves plenty of credit. Official explanation: jockey said gelding missed the break
Inchnadamph, although a winner at Catterick last time, was expected to be more at home back on this more galloping track. He would not have been suited by the lack of pace, though, and while he was brought from the back of the field to have his chance, he lacked the pace of the first two. This performance showed us that he remains in good form, however.
Enjoy The Moment again found himself involved in a slowly-run affair and was denied a clear run on a number of occasions. He will be better suited by a stronger-run race. Official explanation: jockey said gelding was denied a clear run
Great As Gold(IRE), just as at Goodwood, overachieved due to being handily placed throughout in a steadily-run race.
Kasthari(IRE) was another flattered by the way the race was run as he was close to the front end throughout in a race lacking true pace.
Som Tala again let his band of followers down and it really is strange how connections have not reverted to front-running tactics with him as he is clearly vulnerable in races not run at a true gallop. (op 10-3 tchd 7-2)
Golden Quest was able to dictate a steady gallop in front but could not take advantage of it. (op 8-1)

4570 SOVEREIGN HEALTH CARE HEARTBEAT APPEAL H'CAP 1m 6f 132y
5:15 (5:20) (Class 3) (0-90,83) 3-Y-O £11,658 (£3,468; £1,733; £865) Stalls Low

Form RPR

0310 **1** **Phreeze**[22] 3883 3-9-4 **78**........................ NCallan 2 84
(G A Swinbank) *disp 3rd pl: rdn 3f out: outpcd 2f out: 4th ent fnl f: styd on doggedly to ld fnl strides* **15/2**

5053 **2** *hd* **Plane Painter (IRE)**[8] 4309 3-8-13 **73**........................ GregFairley 6 78
(M Johnston) *led: rdn over 3f out: hdd over 1f out: sn led again: wobbled rt u.p: jst ct* **7/1**

1311 **3** *½* **Bollin Felix**[39] 3379 3-9-4 **78**........................(b) DavidAllan 3 82
(T D Easterby) *disp 3rd pl: wnt 2nd briefly 3f out: outpcd 2f out: rallied 1f out: fnd little and no ex fnl 75yds* **11/4**[2]

-110 **4** *2 ½* **Raffaas**[16] 4059 3-9-9 **83**........................ TPQueally 4 84+
(M P Tregoning) *hld up last: effrt 3f out but kpt hanging lft after: drvn ahd briefly over 1f out: wkng qckly cl home* **5/2**[1]

263 **5** *6* **Calzaghe (IRE)**[15] 4113 3-8-3 **66**........................(v) WilliamBuick(3) 1 59
(A M Balding) *last pair: rdn 3f out: reluctant and racing awkwardly after: btn 2f out* **4/1**[3]

2163 **6** *22* **Latanazul**[20] 3963 3-9-6 **80**........................ RyanMoore 5 45
(J L Dunlop) *pressed ldr: rdn 4f out: hrd rdn and lost pl bdly 3f out: eased over 2f out: t.o* **5/1**

3m 6.67s (-3.07) **Going Correction** -0.20s/f (Firm) **6** Ran SP% **116.2**
Speed ratings (Par 104): **100,99,99,98,95 83**
CSF £57.88 TOTE £10.70: £3.50, £3.10; EX 71.10 Place 6 £ 71.13, Place 5 £ 28.83.
Owner W J Gredley **Bred** Belgrave Bloodstock & Ocean Bstock **Trained** Melsonby, N Yorks
■ Stewards' Enquiry : William Buick one-day ban; careless riding (Aug 28)

FOCUS
A fairly competitive handicap which produced a tight finish.

NOTEBOOK
Phreeze disappointed last time at Sandown on a much softer surface, but his previous win at Newmarket had suggested he had the right attitude, and he won this in good style, responding to pressure to get up in the final strides. A decent pace is what he seems to need, he stays well and looks the type to improve again. (op 7-1 tchd 8-1)

Plane Painter(IRE), stepping up another three furlongs in distance, was given a good front-running ride by Fairley and found more when headed approaching the final furlong so that he looked like getting home until mugged in the final moments. He clearly stays well and this opens up new opportunities for him. (op 13-2)
Bollin Felix, running off an 11lb higher mark than when an easy winner at Ripon last time, had much quicker ground to deal with and ran well in the circumstances. Back on a softer surface he may well be able to defy his new mark.
Raffaas came there to win his race inside the final two furlongs but seemed to not quite get home. (op 11-4)
Calzaghe(IRE) again looked far from co-operative. (op 6-1)
T/Jkpt: Not won. T/Plt: £109.20 to a £1 stake. Pool: £81,803.25. 546.85 winning tickets. T/Qpdt: £25.40 to a £1 stake. Pool: £5,036.40. 146.70 winning tickets. SP

4198 NEWBURY (L-H)
Friday, August 17

OFFICIAL GOING: Good (6.8)
Wind: Brisk against

4571 TERENCE O'ROURKE EBF MAIDEN STKS (C&G) 6f 8y
1:40 (1:41) (Class 4) 2-Y-O **£6,477** (£1,927; £963; £481) **Stalls** High

Form RPR
1 **Newly Elected (IRE)** 2-9-0 0 RichardMullen 15 83+
(E S McMahon) *w'like: scope: lw: strong: mid-div: hdwy 2f out: n.m.r over 1f out: squeezed through ins fnl f and qckrd to ld fnl 75yds: readily* **25/1**
452 2 1 **Eastern Gift**[17] 4048 2-9-0 88 PatDobbs 7 80
(R Hannon) *lw: trckd ldrs: drvn to chal fr ins fnl 2f: led jst ins fnl f: hdd and outpcd fnl 75yds* **9/4**[1]
6 3 ¾ **Fool's Wildcat (USA)**[20] 3958 2-9-0 0 StephenDonohoe 8 78
(B J Meehan) *pressed ldrs: rdn over 2f out: sn chalng: kpt on ins fnl f but nvr quite gng pce to catch ldng pair* **15/2**
4 shd **Almoutaz (USA)** 2-9-0 0 RHills 4 77
(B W Hills) *strong: gd sort: lengthy: t.k.h early: drvn to take slt ld ins fnl 2f: hdd jst ins fnl f: styd on same pce* **10/1**
5 nk **Striking Spirit** 2-9-0 0 RichardHughes 2 77
(B W Hills) *w'like: s.i.s: sn in tch: hdwy to trck ldrs over 1f out: n.m.r ins fnl f: kpt on same pce* **9/1**
2 6 1¼ **Miesko (USA)**[10] 4247 2-9-0 0 J-PGuillambert 11 73+
(M Johnston) *unf: lw: rrd stalls and slowly away: rcvrd into mid-div 1/2-way: hdwy and swtchd lft over 1f out: kpt on but nt rch ldrs* **7/2**[2]
6 7 nk **Ridge Dance**[14] 4132 2-9-0 0 JimmyFortune 13 72
(J H M Gosden) *lw: in tch: hdwy over 2f out: sn pushed along: n.m.r 1f out and styd on same pce* **7/1**[3]
8 1¼ **Silver Regent (USA)** 2-9-0 0 JimCrowley 9 68
(Mrs A J Perrett) *unf: bit bkwd: s.i.s: in rr: hdwy 3f out: kpt on same pce fnl f* **25/1**
9 ¾ **Choiseau (IRE)** 2-9-0 0 DaneO'Neill 5 66
(Pat Eddery) *w'like: strong: s.i.s: bhd: kpt on fr over 1f out and gng on cl home: nvr in contention* **50/1**
0 10 1 **Follow The Band**[67] 2510 2-9-0 0 RichardSmith 6 63
(R Hannon) *lw: chsd ldrs: rdn over 2f out: wknd fnl f* **33/1**
06 11 1¼ **Classical Rhythm (IRE)**[65] 2569 2-9-0 0 AmirQuinn 10 59
(J R Boyle) *chsd ldrs: drvn to chal over 2f out: wknd over 1f out* **33/1**
12 shd **Papuan Prince (IRE)** 2-9-0 0 LPKeniry 1 59
(S Kirk) *w'like: edgy: outpcd tl mod late prog* **100/1**
13 ¾ **Mwindaji** 2-9-0 0 SamHitchcott 14 57
(M R Channon) *w'like: outpcd* **66/1**
0 14 1½ **Mystic Art (IRE)**[32] 3592 2-9-0 0 SebSanders 16 52
(C R Egerton) *led tl hdd ins fnl 2f: wknd over 1f out* **33/1**
15 1 **Yes Eighteen (IRE)** 2-9-0 0 EddieAhern 3 49
(J W Hills) *leggy: sn reminders: a in rr* **100/1**

1m 16.26s (1.94) **Going Correction** +0.075s/f (Good) **15 Ran SP% 118.3**
Speed ratings (Par 96): **90,88,87,87,87 85,85,83,82,81 79,79,78,76,74**
CSF £75.98 TOTE £45.30: £8.80, £1.30, £3.00; EX 206.00.
Owner J C Fretwell **Bred** R Ernst And Castletown Stud **Trained** Lichfield, Staffs

FOCUS
A good juvenile maiden likely to produce its share of winners, but the time was nothing special and the runner-up has been rated below previous form.

NOTEBOOK
Newly Elected(IRE), whose stable can ready the odd newcomer, was dismissed in the market, but being by current leading first-season sire Acclamation he could not be totally discounted and actually ran out a quite impressive winner. Having to wait for his run, he quickened up well once in the clear and was nicely on top at the line. He holds no notable entries, but looks well worth a rise in grade following this. (op 22-1)
Eastern Gift set a strong standard having shown decent form on two of his three previous outings, but he once again came up short and was simply unable to match the winner's late change of pace. His turn will come eventually and, although disappointing on his one previous try at 7f, he is bred to stay it and looks well worth another try. (op 2-1 tchd 5-2 in places and 15-8 in a place)
Fool's Wildcat(USA), who did not quite last home in a fair 7f maiden here on debut, showed more second time up and finished his race off well having been up there throughout. He is clearly up to winning an ordinary maiden, but looks unlikely to be at his best until contesting nurseries. (op 12-1)
Almoutaz(USA) ◆ comes from a classy American family, dam a half-sister to Breeders' Cup Turf winner Johar, and herself a top-class mare, so it was no surprise to see him show up well on this racecourse debut. He still looked green once getting to the front, but this should bring him on mentally and a rise in distance is likely to see him winning a standard maiden. (op 8-1)
Striking Spirit ◆, a speedily-bred son of Oasis Dream who holds several Group-race entries, was sluggish out of the gate, but quickly found a position and looked a danger with two to run, but he found himself a bit squeezed for racing room at a vital stage and was then not knocked about. This was a pleasing debut and he looks another ready-made maiden winner. (op 12-1)
Miesko(USA), caught close home on his debut over 7f at Catterick, was expected to be suited by the drop in trip, but he effectively lost his race coming out of the stalls, rearing and costing himself ground when it would no doubt have been the plan to ride him prominently. He ran pretty well considering and should not be ignored in a similar contest. (op 9-2 tchd 5-1 in a place)
Ridge Dance, who shaped as though in need of 7f when sixth on his recent debut at Newmarket, was kept to this distance and once again he lacked the speed to challenge. It could be that connections see him as more of a handicap type and he will be qualified for a mark after one more run. (op 13-2 tchd 6-1)
Silver Regent(USA), whose stable's newcomers often benefit from a run, was always going to struggle following a slow start, but he was at least going on towards the end of his race and he looks another likely to benefit from an extra furlong next time.

4572 TFM NETWORKS H'CAP 1m 5f 61y
2:10 (2:12) (Class 3) (0-90,90) 3-Y-O+ **£7,124** (£2,119; £1,059; £529) **Stalls** Centre

Form RPR
0320 1 **Magicalmysterytour (IRE)**[35] 3509 4-9-9 85 EddieAhern 3 97+
(W J Musson) *lw: broke wl: stdd towards rr 6f out: stdy hdwy over 3f out to ld jst ins fnl 2f: shkn up and styd on strly thrght fnl f* **8/1**
0551 2 1¾ **Silver Suitor (IRE)**[21] 3908 3-8-12 85 JimmyFortune 5 94+
(D R C Elsworth) *lw: in tch: hdwy 5f out: drvn to chal 2f out: kpt on wl fnl f to secure 2nd but a readily hld by wnr* **11/4**[1]
0-33 3 ¾ **Candle**[23] 3844 4-9-5 81 DaneO'Neill 8 89
(H Candy) *in rr but in tch: hdwy over 3f out: drvn to chal over 2f out: kpt on same pce u.p fr over 1f out* **12/1**
621/ 4 2½ **Cutting Crew (USA)**[1115] 4229 6-10-0 90 AdamKirby 4 94
(W R Swinburn) *led: rdn and kpt on fr 3f out: hdd jst ins fnl 2f: wknd ins fnl f* **16/1**
500- 5 2½ **Katies Tuitor**[62] 5109 4-8-11 73 PaulFitzsimons 9 74
(B W Duke) *lw: prom: chsd ldr 5f out: chal fr over 3f out tl over 2f out: wknd fnl f* **66/1**
1415 6 ½ **Madaarek (USA)**[34] 3533 3-8-11 84 RHills 6 84
(E A L Dunlop) *in rr: hdwy fr 3f out: sn rdn and nvr gng pce to rch ldrs: wknd over 1f out* **7/1**[3]
0005 7 nk **Eva Soneva So Fast (IRE)**[13] 4171 5-9-5 81 SebSanders 1 80
(J L Dunlop) *chsd ldrs: rdn over 2f out: sn btn* **8/1**
1021 8 17 **Noojoom (IRE)**[19] 3993 3-8-12 85 PatDobbs 11 59
(M P Tregoning) *chsd ldrs: rdn over 3f out: wknd over 2f out* **7/1**[3]
6P50 9 5 **Amazing Request**[19] 3993 3-8-8 81 ow1 RichardHughes 2 47
(R Charlton) *chsd ldrs: rdn 4f out: wknd fr 3f out* **14/1**
2442 10 2½ **Prince Nureyev (IRE)**[39] 3385 7-9-4 80 StephenCarson 10 43
(B R Millman) *a towards rr* **14/1**
20-2 11 18 **Shore Thing (IRE)**[13] 4171 4-8-10 72 JimCrowley 7 8
(C R Egerton) *chsd ldrs: rdn over 3f out: sn wknd* **5/1**[2]

2m 50.31s (-0.68) **Going Correction** +0.125s/f (Good)
WFA 3 from 4yo+ 11lb **11 Ran SP% 119.0**
Speed ratings (Par 107): **107,105,105,103,102 102,101,91,88,86 75**
CSF £30.57 CT £271.18 TOTE £10.60: £3.10, £1.80, £3.40; EX 44.10.
Owner M Dunne **Bred** Premier Bloodstock **Trained** Newmarket, Suffolk

FOCUS
A good, competitive handicap run in a decent time and rated positively through the third.

NOTEBOOK
Magicalmysterytour(IRE) has shown improved form this season and his most recent outing, a slightly unlucky seventh at Newmarket, again pointed to this rise in distance suiting. A strong traveller throughout, he quickened best from over a furlong out and won a shade comfortably. There may well be more to come from him at this sort of distance and next week's Ebor would seem an ideal race, but even with the penalty he is unlikely to get in. (tchd 9-1 in places)
Silver Suitor(IRE) ◆, a fine, big son of Swain who relished the step up to 1m4f when winning at Newmarket last time, looked potentially well treated for this handicap debut and, with the further rise in distance expected to bring about improvement, he was rightly made favourite. Plenty far enough back early on, he made good headway around runners to hold every chance, but his rider failed to maximise his ability to gallop relentlessly and he was done for speed by the winner. He gives every indication that he will get 2m in time, but he can prove fully effective at this distance if ridden more positively. There is almost certainly more to come. (tchd 3-1)
Candle has been keeping on well at the end of hers races over 1m4f and she looked well worth another try at this distance. She came to have every chance but, like the runner-up, could not match the winner for speed and perhaps she will benefit from returning to a slower surface. (op 11-1 tchd 14-1)
Cutting Crew(USA), recently withdrawn because of a vet's certificate, has been off the track since July 2004, but looked fit enough considering. Dropped just 2lb by the Handicapper despite the lengthy absence, he attempted to make all and ran well for a long way, so definitely showed he retains plenty of ability. How he gets on in future totally depends on how he comes out of this.
Katies Tuitor, last seen finishing a respectable third over hurdles, was trying this distance for the first time on the Flat, but despite her breeding, sire Kayf Tara a dual Gold Cup winner, she appeared not to last homet. It was still a fair effort in what was a good handicap though and there may yet be more to come from her.
Noojoom(IRE) has been progressive and the way she won when dominating at Ascot last time pointed to another big run. However, up a further 8lb and trying a new distance she failed to run to form and the way she dropped away late on was slightly disconcerting. (op 6-1)
Amazing Request Official explanation: jockey said colt stopped quickly
Shore Thing(IRE) is usually most consistent, but it is possible this came too soon after his promising reappearance second at Newmarket and may explain why he dropped away so tamely. Official explanation: vet said gelding was found to have an irregular heart beat on return (op 11-2 tchd 9-2)

4573 BATHWICK TYRES ST HUGH'S STKS (LISTED RACE) (FILLIES) 5f 34y
2:40 (2:43) (Class 1) 2-Y-O
£12,207 (£4,626; £2,315; £1,154; £578; £290) **Stalls** High

Form RPR
3550 1 **Cake (IRE)**[17] 4046 2-8-12 98 PatDobbs 5 98
(R Hannon) *lw: trckd ldr in centre crse: rdn 2f out: styd on strly to ld fnl 75yds: hld on wl whn chal cl home* **9/1**
3241 2 nk **Cute Ass (IRE)**[15] 4097 2-8-12 83 RichardMullen 2 97
(K R Burke) *chsd ldrs in centre crse: rdn 2f out: qckrd u.p wl ins fnl f: fin fast: nt quite get up* **16/1**
4020 3 nk **Perfect Paula (USA)**[17] 4046 2-8-12 82 RHills 6 96
(B J Meehan) *led in centre crse and overall ldr: rdn over 1f out: hdd fnl 75yds: kpt on same pce* **20/1**
15 4 1 **Edge Of Light**[19] 3988 2-8-12 0 FrancisNorton 1 92
(B Palling) *racd centre crse: outpcd but in tch: hdwy fnl f: fin strly but nt rch ldrs* **9/1**
100 5 nk **Fanatical**[19] 3988 2-8-12 96 JimmyFortune 4 91
(E F Vaughan) *b.hind: chsd ldrs in centre crse: outpcd over 1f out: kpt on again cl home* **8/1**[3]
1124 6 1¾ **Starlit Sands**[17] 4046 2-8-12 103 SebSanders 11 85
(Sir Mark Prescott) *lw: racd stands' side and led that gp but a hld by those in centre: rdn 2f out: styd on same pce* **10/11**[1]
2615 7 4 **Littlemisssunshine (IRE)**[17] 4046 2-8-12 98 (p) LPKeniry 8 71
(J S Moore) *chsd ldr stands' side: rdn over 2f out: outpcd fnl f* **6/1**[2]
2100 8 2½ **Eileen's Violet (IRE)**[37] 3432 2-9-1 90 StephenDonohoe 9 65
(P D Evans) *racd stands' side: a outpcd* **33/1**
413 9 1¾ **Rocking**[29] 3668 2-8-12 81 EddieAhern 10 55
(W J Haggas) *racd stands' side: a outpcd* **16/1**

6541 **10** 1 1/4 **Cocabana**[18] 4026 2-8-12 70 JimCrowley 7 51
(J G Portman) *racd stands' side: chsd ldrs to 1/2-way* **33/1**
62.32 secs (-0.24) **Going Correction** +0.075s/f (Good) 10 Ran SP% **120.2**
Speed ratings (Par 99): **104,103,103,101,100 98,91,87,84,82**
CSF £141.45 TOTE £12.10: £2.70, £2.90, £4.50; EX 168.70.
Owner Simon Leech & Des Anderson **Bred** Carpet Lady Partnership **Trained** East Everleigh, Wilts

FOCUS
Not a strong renewal of this Listed race as it turned out, and there was a definite bias with the group that raced towards the centre of the track having the first five home. The form is rated slightly below average for the grade.

NOTEBOOK
Cake(IRE) has generally found it tough going since stepping into Pattern company and her most recent effort, when well behind Starlit Sands, pointed to her again struggling here. However, with that one appearing to be in the wrong group she was left to beat a couple of inferior rivals and really showed a good attitude in doing so. This is as good as it is going to get for her and she is likely to struggle once stepped back up to group company. Official explanation: trainer's rep said, regarding apparent improvement in form, that the filly was better suited by the drop in class and waiting tactics compared to running more prominently from a less favourable draw at Goodwood. (op 12-1)
Cute Ass(IRE), who readily shed her maiden tag at Musselburgh last time, had previously run well in a weak Listed contest at Sandown and she very nearly caused a minor shock. Speed is what she is all about, but this was again not the strongest of Listed races and it would be unwise to get carried away with this effort. (op 14-1)
Perfect Paula(USA), still a maiden, has twice been highly tried when well behind Starlit Sands, but she showed plenty of early pace and really stuck on gamely when pressed, losing out by two necks. Connections should really concentrate of winning a maiden with her now. (op 33-1)
Edge Of Light, a course and distance winner on debut, got going a bit too late over 6f at Ascot last time and it was a case of the same here. She was not beaten far at the line and is probably the one to take from the race, with a return to 6f likely to suit. (op 8-1)
Fanatical, another course winner on debut, was not far behind Edge Of Light at Ascot and she again ran well, without quite suggesting she is up to this grade.
Starlit Sands had the beating of most of these judged on her last two races, but having led those towards the stands' side she found herself readily outpaced by those towards the centre and proved most disappointing. She looks worth another chance though and may be ready for 6f now. (op 11-10 tchd 6-5 in places)
Littlemisssunshine(IRE), although already beaten three times by Starlit Sands, looked one of the more likely dangers, but as it turned out she was with the wrong group and once again came off worse with the favourite. (op 13-2 tchd 7-1 in a place)

4574 CHRISTOPHER SMITH ASSOCIATES H'CAP — 6f 8y
3:15 (3:16) (Class 4) (0-80,80) 3-Y-O **£4,857** (£1,445; £722; £360) **Stalls** High

Form RPR
241 **1** **Jimmy Styles**[13] 4182 3-9-5 **78** EddieAhern 15 97+
(C G Cox) *lw: trckd ldrs gng wl: qcknd to ld 1f out: sn clr: easily* **9/1**
5221 **2** 3 **Esteem Machine (USA)**[20] 3948 3-9-4 **77** DaneO'Neill 5 84
(R A Teal) *trckd ldrs: led ins fnl 3f: rdn 2f out: hdd 1f out: kpt on wl for 2nd but no ch w wnr* **4/1**[1]
51 **3** 3/4 **Blackat Blackitten (IRE)**[19] 3994 3-9-5 **78** RichardHughes 11 83+
(G A Butler) *lw: in rr: hdwy and rdn 2f out: r.o fnl f and fin wl but nvr gng pce to be competitive* **17/2**
2150 **4** nk **Farefield Lodge (IRE)**[20] 3944 3-8-13 **72** AdamKirby 12 76+
(C G Cox) *in rr: pushed along 1/2-way: kpt on wl fr over 1f out and gng on cl home but nvr gng pce to rch ldrs* **33/1**
5230 **5** 1 1/2 **King's Bastion (IRE)**[25] 3797 3-9-2 **80** LukeMorris(5) 14 79
(M L W Bell) *in rr: pushed along 1/2-way: styd on fnl f but nvr gng pce to rch ldrs* **12/1**
2411 **6** 1/2 **Nouveau (GER)**[8] 4330 3-8-5 **69** 6ex HaddenFrost(5) 9 67
(R Hannon) *lw: pressed ldrs to 1/2-way: stl ev ch 2f out: wknd ins fnl f* **5/1**[2]
-440 **7** 1 **Roodolph**[76] 2243 3-9-3 **76** (t) StephenCarson 10 71
(Eve Johnson Houghton) *hld up in rr: rdn over 2f out: r.o ins fnl f but nvr in contention* **20/1**
0-31 **8** 1/2 **Raglan Copenhagen**[20] 3968 3-8-8 **67** JimCrowley 13 60
(B R Millman) *led 2f: rdn 1/2-way: wknd fnl f* **7/1**[3]
0233 **9** nk **Fabuleux Millie (IRE)**[7] 4360 3-9-6 **79** SebSanders 4 71
(R M Beckett) *in rr: pushed along and hdwy into mid-div 1/2-way: sn rdn and no prog fnl 2f* **7/1**[3]
3401 **10** 1 **Buckie Massa**[9] 4269 3-9-5 **78** 6ex LPKeniry 1 67
(S Kirk) *lw: in rr: pushed along 1/2-way: sme prog fnl 2f but nvr in contention* **20/1**
-010 **11** 8 **Equuleus Pictor**[22] 3885 3-8-10 **69** FrancisNorton 16 34
(J L Spearing) *chsd ldrs: rdn 1/2-way: sn wknd: eased whn no ch ins fnl f* **12/1**
0 **12** 3 1/2 **Double Bill (USA)**[37] 3418 3-9-2 **75** (b[1]) JimmyFortune 2 30
(P F I Cole) *slowly itno stride: in rr: hdwy and in tch 1/2-way: wknd 2f out* **11/1**
6220 **13** 2 **Miss Ippolita**[29] 3688 3-9-4 **77** RichardMullen 8 26
(J R Jenkins) *chsd ldrs 4f* **50/1**
3000 **14** nk **Fairfield Princess**[34] 3528 3-9-4 **77** TGMcLaughlin 6 25
(M S Saunders) *w ldr: led 4f out: hdd ins fnl 3f: wknd 2f out* **50/1**
1m 12.75s (-1.57) **Going Correction** +0.075s/f (Good) 14 Ran SP% **122.3**
Speed ratings (Par 102): **113,109,108,107,105 104,103,102,102,101 90,85,83,82**
CSF £43.12 CT £334.64 TOTE £7.80: £2.30, £2.20, £2.70; EX 60.70.
Owner Gwyn Powell and Peter Ridgers **Bred** Barry Minty **Trained** Lambourn, Berks

FOCUS
A competitive three-year-old sprint run in a very good time for the class and the form looks solid rated through the runner-up.
Double Bill(USA) Official explanation: jockey said colt stopped quickly

4575 STUART MICHAEL ASSOCIATES MAIDEN FILLIES' STKS — 7f (S)
3:50 (3:51) (Class 5) 3-Y-O+ **£3,562** (£1,059; £529; £264) **Stalls** High

Form RPR
353 **1** **Andmoreagain (USA)**[9] 4275 3-8-12 0 RHills 8 72
(J Noseda) *in tch: hdwy to ld over 1f out: drvn out* **9/2**[3]
0 **2** 1/2 **Mini Mosa**[22] 3881 3-8-12 0 JimmyFortune 9 71
(J H M Gosden) *lw: stdd s: in rr: hdwy over 2f out: hrd drvn and styd on to chse wnr ins fnl f but a hld* **14/1**
35 **3** 1 **Paradise Dancer (IRE)**[42] 3276 3-8-12 0 RichardHughes 6 68
(Pat Eddery) *in tch: hdwy over 1f out: styd on ins fnl f but nt pce to rch ldrs* **7/1**
3052 **4** nk **Red Blossom**[19] 3994 3-8-12 70 SebSanders 4 67
(Sir Mark Prescott) *lw: led 1f: led again over 3f out: rdn: 2f out: carried hd high and hdd over 1f out: wandered and wknd ins fnl f* **7/2**[1]
4440 **5** 1 1/4 **High 'n Dry (IRE)**[8] 4338 3-8-12 73 RichardMullen 7 64
(C A Cyzer) *rrd stalls: bhd: hdwy fr 2f out: kpt on ins fnl f but nvr in contention* **4/1**[2]

30 **6** 7 **Rolexa**[39] 3387 3-8-7 0 LukeMorris(5) 1 45
(C G Cox) *reminders over 4f out: sn rdn and effrt over 2f out: nvr gng pce to be competitive: sn wknd* **4/1**[2]
5-00 **7** 7 **Rangali Belle**[30] 3651 3-8-12 55 SimonWhitworth 5 26
(C A Horgan) *led after 1f: t.k.h: hdd over 3f out: wknd qckly 2f out* **66/1**
-0 **8** 1 **Cadeaux Cerise (IRE)**[20] 3968 3-8-12 0 StephenDonohoe 2 23
(N I M Rossiter) *s.i.s: bhd fr 1/2-way* **100/1**
0- **9** 2 1/2 **Orange**[370] 4373 3-8-12 0 EddieAhern 10 16
(W J Haggas) *a in rr* **7/1**
5 **10** hd **Ka'u Mauna Kea**[18] 4018 3-8-12 0 StephenCarson 3 16
(J A Geake) *a in rr* **66/1**
1m 27.28s (0.28) **Going Correction** +0.075s/f (Good) 10 Ran SP% **116.0**
Speed ratings (Par 100): **101,100,99,98,97 89,81,80,77,77**
CSF £64.39 TOTE £5.40: £1.70, £3.20, £2.20; EX 54.40.
Owner Ms Gillian Khosla **Bred** WinStar Farm Llc **Trained** Newmarket, Suffolk

FOCUS
This was a modest maiden for the course, but competitive at the same time. With the fourth disappointing the winner is assessed as making slight improvement.

4576 PETER BRETT ASSOCIATES H'CAP — 2m
4:20 (4:20) (Class 5) (0-70,69) 3-Y-O+ **£3,238** (£963; £481; £240) **Stalls** High

Form RPR
0142 **1** **Atlantic Coast (IRE)**[9] 4280 3-8-4 **59** (v[1]) FrancisNorton 12 70
(M Johnston) *chsd ldrs: rdn fr 3f out: rallied to ld jst ins fnl f: hrd drvn and hung rt cl home: all out* **10/3**[1]
5050 **2** 1 1/4 **High Point (IRE)**[44] 3216 9-9-11 **66** SimonWhitworth 8 76
(G P Enright) *in tch: hdwy 4f out: pressed ldrs 3f out: kpt on fnl 2f and styd on to take 2nd cl home but no imp on wnr* **16/1**
0/01 **3** nk **Fourth Dimension (IRE)**[31] 3630 8-9-7 **67** JamesMillman(5) 9 76
(Miss T Spearing) *hld up in rr: stdy hdwy fr 4f out to ld ins fnl 3f: rdn 2f out: hdd jst ins fnl f: styd on same pce and ct for 2nd cl home* **12/1**
-010 **4** 7 **Jayer Gilles**[18] 4030 7-9-1 **56** (v) AlanDaly 3 57
(Dr J R J Naylor) *in rr: hdwy fr 4f out: sn hrd drvn: styd on u.p fr 2f out and hung lft over 1f out: kpt on but nvr in contention* **33/1**
1235 **5** 1 1/2 **Bob's Your Uncle**[20] 3945 4-9-6 **61** SebSanders 13 60
(J G Portman) *in rr: hdwy 7f out: chsd ldrs and rdn 3f out: wknd fr 2f out* **9/1**
1521 **6** 4 **Mister Completely (IRE)**[4] 4463 6-9-7 **69** 6ex (v) SophieDoyle(7) 11 63
(Ms J S Doyle) *in rr: rdn and mod prog fr 3f out: nvr in contention* **9/1**
3445 **7** 3/4 **Princess Kiotto**[9] 4280 6-9-4 **64** LukeMorris(5) 15 57
(W M Brisbourne) *plld hrd: led after 3f: hdd ins fnl 3f: sn btn* **12/1**
0002 **8** 1/2 **Valance (IRE)**[16] 4067 7-10-0 **69** (tp) NelsonDeSouza 7 62
(C R Egerton) *in tch: chsd ldrs 5f out: wknd over 2f out* **9/1**
2323 **9** 1/2 **Apache Fort**[20] 3945 4-9-4 **62** EmmettStack(3) 14 54
(T Keddy) *chsd ldrs: drvn to chal 3f out: sn wknd* **8/1**[3]
0-06 **10** 7 **Liberman (IRE)**[30] 3653 9-8-12 **60** ThomasO'Brien(7) 4 44
(R Curtis) *b.hind: in rr: rdn along 10f out: nvr in contention* **40/1**
3140 **11** 4 **Ronsard (IRE)**[13] 4179 5-9-9 **64** StephenDonohoe 5 43
(P D Evans) *a towards rr* **25/1**
0600 **12** 3 **Himba**[18] 4030 4-8-12 **53** oh3 JimCrowley 10 28
(Mrs A J Perrett) *lw: led 3f: styd prom tl wknd 4f out* **50/1**
5640 **13** shd **Cortesia (IRE)**[20] 3945 4-9-13 **68** RichardMullen 2 43
(P W Chapple-Hyam) *chsd ldrs to 4f out* **16/1**
000- **14** 2 1/2 **Hills Of Aran**[147] 6108 5-9-7 **62** PatDobbs 16 34
(W K Goldsworthy) *in tch to 1/2-way* **14/1**
6-0 **15** 40 **Bauhaus (IRE)**[16] 4056 6-9-9 **67** (b) TravisBlock(3) 6 —
(R T Phillips) *chsd ldrs 10f: t.o* **9/2**[2]
3m 32.61s (-2.25) **Going Correction** +0.125s/f (Good)
WFA 3 from 4yo+ 14lb 15 Ran SP% **127.4**
Speed ratings (Par 103): **110,109,109,105,104 102,102,102,102,98 96,95,95,93,73**
CSF £61.36 CT £604.21 TOTE £3.70: £2.00, £7.60, £4.30; EX 94.90.
Owner Atlantic Racing Limited **Bred** Gigginstown House **Trained** Middleham Moor, N Yorks

FOCUS
A moderate staying handicap won by the sole three-year-old in the field. The form is rated through the runner-up to this year's turf form.
Princess Kiotto Official explanation: jockey said mare ran too free
Hills Of Aran Official explanation: trainer said gelding was unsuited by the good ground

4577 JACK COLLING POLAR JEST APPRENTICE H'CAP — 1m 1f
4:55 (4:56) (Class 5) (0-70,74) 4-Y-O+ **£3,238** (£963; £481; £240) **Stalls** Centre

Form RPR
350 **1** **Corrib (IRE)**[35] 3487 4-8-9 **58** AlanRutter(5) 3 68+
(B Palling) *lw: in rr: hdwy over 2f out: nt clr run and swtchd lft over 1f out: styd on wl fnl f to ld nr fin* **20/1**
0-06 **2** nk **Mister Benedictine**[33] 314 4-9-4 **67** JackDean(5) 6 73
(B W Duke) *lw: in tch: hdwy on outside 3f out: slt ld over 2f out: hdd wl over 1f out: led again last half f: hdd and no ex nr fin* **9/1**[3]
0605 **3** 1 1/4 **October Ben**[16] 4063 4-8-7 **56** FrankiePickard(5) 14 59
(M D I Usher) *in rr: hdwy on outside fr 3f out: chal over 2f out tl slt ld wl over 1f out: hdd and one pce last half f* **14/1**
3611 **4** 1 **Inside Story (IRE)**[7] 4353 5-10-2 **74** 6ex (b) LukeMorris 7 75
(N Wilson) *lw: sn in mid-div: pushed along and no hdwy 3f out: styd on fr 2f out: kpt on ins fnl f but nvr gng pce to press ldrs* **9/4**[1]
045 **5** 1 **Silver Blue (IRE)**[29] 3690 4-8-13 **60** HaddenFrost(3) 11 59
(R Hannon) *lw: in rr: hdwy 4f out: chsd ldrs fr 2f out: one pce ins fnl f* **8/1**[2]
6460 **6** 1/2 **Royal Indulgence**[34] 3530 7-7-8 **54** JackMitchell(3) 1 52
(W M Brisbourne) *in rr: hdwy over 2f out: nt clr run ins fnl 2f and wnt rt: swtchd lft 1f out: kpt on ins fnl f but nvr in contention* **9/1**[3]
0101 **7** 1 **Mythical Charm**[20] 3965 8-9-0 **58** (t) NicolPolli 2 54
(J J Bridger) *chsd ldrs: rdn to chal over 2f out: wknd fnl f* **14/1**
1250 **8** 1/2 **Linda's Colin (IRE)**[146] 770 5-9-2 **65** MatthewDavies(5) 4 60
(R A Harris) *b. in tch 1/2-way: hdwy over 3f out: one pce fnl 2f* **25/1**
405 **9** 1 3/4 **Paraguay (USA)**[12] 4200 4-9-7 **68** SCreighton(3) 12 59
(Miss V Haigh) *in rr: pushed along 3f out: mod prog fr over 1f out* **20/1**
3400 **10** 1 1/2 **Veba (USA)**[9] 4294 4-8-2 **49** oh4 ThomasO'Brien(3) 13 36
(M D I Usher) *in rr: mod prog fnl f* **66/1**
0001 **11** 3/4 **Border Edge**[7] 4355 9-9-2 **60** 6ex (b) JamesMillman 15 46
(J J Bridger) *led: sn clr: hdd over 2f out: sn btn* **10/1**
2106 **12** 3 1/2 **Seneschal**[80] 2107 6-9-4 **65** KMay(3) 10 43
(A B Haynes) *chsd ldrs: ev ch over 2f out: sn wknd* **33/1**
-000 **13** 1 3/4 **Soizic (NZ)**[7] 4355 5-8-11 **60** HarryPoulton(5) 9 34
(L A Dace) *chsd ldrs tl wknd over 2f out* **100/1**

2046 **14** *½* **Justcallmehandsome**[50] 4035 5-8-0 **49** oh4............ LauraReynolds(5) 8 22
(D J S Ffrench Davis) *chsd ldrs over 6f* **25/1**

1m 56.38s (1.79) **Going Correction** +0.125s/f (Good) **14** Ran SP% **106.9**
Speed ratings (Par 103): **97,96,95,94,93 93,92,92,90,89 88,85,83,83**
CSF £134.58 CT £1681.04 TOTE £28.40: £7.70, £3.40, £4.70; EX 253.40 Place 6 £1,257.47, Place 5 £ 595.73.
Owner Derek And Jean Clee **Bred** Dr John Waldron **Trained** Tredodridge, Vale Of Glamorgan
■ Jill Dawson was withdrawn (11/2, refused to enter stalls.) R4 applies, deduct 15p in the £.

FOCUS
A moderate apprentices' handicap rated through the winner at face value.
T/Plt: £2,101.10 to a £1 stake. Pool: £69,653.30. 24.20 winning tickets. T/Qpdt: £207.10 to a £1 stake. Pool: £3,330.90. 11.90 winning tickets. ST

4278 NEWCASTLE (L-H)
Friday, August 17

OFFICIAL GOING: Good (7.9)
40mm rain over the previous four days but in drying conditions the ground was 'perfect, fresh on the far side from the mile to the junction with the round track'
Wind: fresh 1/2 against Weather: fine but overcast at times and quite blustery

4578 PAUL BENTLEY IS 40 /EBF MEDIAN AUCTION MAIDEN STKS 7f
2:20 (2:22) (Class 6) 2-Y-O **£2,839** (£849; £424; £212; £105) **Stalls** Low

Form RPR

36 **1** **Alan Devonshire**[13] 4151 2-9-3 0.................................. JimmyQuinn 14 80+
(M H Tompkins) *trckd ldrs: led over 2f out: drew clr fnl f* **2/1**[1]

3 **2** *3* **Prince Kalamoun (IRE)**[20] 3951 2-9-3 0........................ PatCosgrave 6 73
(G A Swinbank) *hld up in midfield: hdwy over 2f out: n.m.r over 1f out: styd on to take 2nd ins fnl f: no ch w wnr* **7/2**[3]

3 *3* **Society Venue** 2-9-0 0.. AndrewElliott(3) 12 65
(Jedd O'Keeffe) *in tch: effrt over 2f out: kpt on to take 3rd ins fnl f* **100/1**

0 **4** *½* **Grecian Slave**[26] 3760 2-9-3 0.. PaulEddery 9 64
(B Smart) *chsd ldrs: kpt on same pce appr fnl f* **28/1**

5 *nk* **Boy Blue** 2-9-3 0... SilvestreDeSousa 10 63
(D Nicholls) *s.i.s: hld up: hdwy over 2f out: kpt on same pce fnl f* **40/1**

66 **6** *1* **Rapidity**[26] 3760 2-8-10 0.. MCGeran(7) 1 61
(E J O'Neill) *hld up in mid-div: effrt and nt clr run over 2f out: kpt on same pce* **16/1**

7 *1 ½* **Social Spirit (IRE)** 2-8-12 0... PhillipMakin 7 52
(J R Weymes) *mid-div: lost pl over 3f out: kpt on fnl f* **25/1**

8 *nk* **Safari Dancer (IRE)** 2-9-3 0... TonyHamilton 2 59+
(I Semple) *chsd ldrs: wkng whn hmpd over 1f out* **14/1**

9 *3* **Shot Through (USA)** 2-9-3 0.. LeeEnstone 11 49
(P C Haslam) *in rr: sn drvn along: sme hdwy over 2f out: sn wknd* **33/1**

00 **10** *nk* **Flower Appeal**[26] 3761 2-8-12 0...................................... DaleGibson 13 43
(M W Easterby) *s.i.s: a in rr* **100/1**

43 **11** *1 ¾* **Van Bossed (CAN)**[9] 4279 2-9-3 0............................ AdrianTNicholls 8 43
(D Nicholls) *chsd ldrs: hrd rdn and wknd appr fnl f* **9/4**[2]

006 **12** *9* **Astrol**[34] 3560 2-8-9 40..(b1) DuranFentiman(3) 5 16
(T D Easterby) *led tl over 2f out: lost pl over 1f out* **100/1**

0 **13** *1 ½* **Scientific**[13] 4174 2-9-0 0.. JamieMoriarty(3) 3 17
(R A Fahey) *mid-div: sn drvn along: lost pl over 2f out: sn bhd* **40/1**

0 **F** **Laterly (IRE)**[70] 2432 2-8-12 0.............................. MichaelJStainton(5) 4 —
(T P Tate) *rrd up s and fell* **25/1**

1m 29.42s (1.40) **Going Correction** +0.10s/f (Good) **14** Ran SP% **120.8**
Speed ratings (Par 92): **95,91,88,87,87 86,84,84,80,80 78,67,66,—**
CSF £8.53 TOTE £2.70: £1.20, £2.30, £12.00; EX 9.20 Trifecta £141.40 Part won. Pool: £199.22, 0.34 winning units..
Owner Russell Trew Ltd **Bred** The Lavington Stud **Trained** Newmarket, Suffolk

FOCUS
Probably just an ordinary maiden race rated through the winner to his debut form, although not very solid down the field.

NOTEBOOK
Alan Devonshire, who lacks scope, travelled strongly and made this look relatively simple. (op 13-8)
Prince Kalamoun(IRE) met traffic problems but was only second best anyway. (op 11-4)
Society Venue, an April foal, stands over a fair amount of ground. Noisy in the paddock, he stuck on in good style and this will have taught him plenty. (tchd 80-1)
Grecian Slave is not very big but showed a fair bit more than he had done on his debut a month earlier. (op 33-1)
Boy Blue, a February foal, lacks size and scope but made a satisfactory bow. (op 50-1 tchd 66-1 and 33-1)
Rapidity, a tall type, was having his third start and would have finished closer with a better run. He is now qualified for a nursery mark. (op 20-1)
Van Bossed(CAN) was in the thick of things from the off but he weakened badly in the final furlong. Six furlongs looks his maximum at least for the time being. (op 4-1)

4579 LUMSDEN AND CARROLL FILLIES' H'CAP 1m 3y(S)
2:50 (2:52) (Class 5) (0-75,75) 3-Y-O **£3,785** (£1,132; £566; £283; £141) **Stalls** Low

Form RPR

0063 **1** **La Vecchia Scuola (IRE)**[5] 4423 3-8-0 **59**...............(v) KellyHarrison(5) 1 66
(R Johnson) *led: qcknd over 2f out: hld on wl* **8/1**

4-32 **2** *1* **Princess Taylor**[8] 4338 3-8-11 **70**.........................(t) AshleyHamblett(5) 3 75
(M Botti) *chsd wnr: rdn and hung lft over 1f out: kpt on same pce ins fnl f* **10/3**[1]

0054 **3** *1 ½* **Grethel (IRE)**[9] 4282 3-7-9 **56** oh11........................ DanielleMcCreery(7) 4 58
(A Berry) *sn chsng ldrs: drvn over 2f out: kpt on same pce* **66/1**

0520 **4** *½* **Astroangel**[16] 4064 3-8-8 **62**...(v1) JimmyQuinn 2 62
(M H Tompkins) *dwlt: hdwy over 3f out: nt clr run over 2f out: styd on same pce appr fnl f* **14/1**

6310 **5** *3 ½* **Chasing Memories (IRE)**[9] 4287 3-8-7 **61**................... TonyHamilton 5 53
(B Smart) *sn chsng ldrs: hrd rdn over 2f out: fdd fnl f* **7/1**

0033 **6** *3* **Milliegait**[20] 3972 3-9-4 **75**... DuranFentiman(3) 8 60
(T D Easterby) *hld up in rr: effrt over 2f out: nvr nr ldrs* **9/2**[3]

6065 **7** *shd* **Jane Of Arc (FR)**[4] 4450 3-8-3 **57** oh1 ow1................ AdrianTNicholls 6 42
(J S Goldie) *hld up in rr: rdn over 2f out: nvr on terms* **5/1**

0340 **8** *2 ½* **House Maiden (IRE)**[69] 2475 3-8-5 **59**.............................(p) DaleGibson 7 38
(D M Simcock) *s.i.s: in rr: drvn over 3f out: nvr a factor* **14/1**

641 **9** *3* **Sweet Clover**[34] 3561 3-8-9 **66**...................................... AndrewElliott(3) 9 39
(K R Burke) *trckd ldrs on outer: effrt over 2f out: sn rdn and wknd* **4/1**[2]

1m 43.12s (1.22) **Going Correction** +0.10s/f (Good) **9** Ran SP% **116.4**
Speed ratings (Par 97): **97,96,94,94,90 87,87,84,81**
CSF £35.15 CT £1657.92 TOTE £12.20: £3.60, £1.30, £14.00; EX 54.50 TRIFECTA Not won..
Owner Graham D Brown **Bred** Maurice Craig **Trained** Newburn, Tyne & Wear

FOCUS
A modest fillies' handicap inn which the winner was given her own way in front and her young rider deserves full marks. The form is rated around the first two to their recent marks.
Sweet Clover Official explanation: jockey said filly was unsuited by the slow pace

4580 NALCO (S) STKS 1m 2f 32y
3:25 (3:27) (Class 6) 3-Y-O+ **£1,943** (£578; £288; £144) **Stalls** Centre

Form RPR

3302 **1** **Ruby Legend**[28] 3714 9-9-5 55......................................(b) PhillipMakin 5 59
(K G Reveley) *trckd ldrs: smooth hdwy to ld appr fnl f: drvn out* **9/2**[3]

054 **2** *2 ½* **Apache Point (IRE)**[6] 4410 10-9-5 50................................. KimTinkler 3 54
(N Tinkler) *hld up in midfield: hdwy over 2f out: wnt 3rd over 1f out: kpt on to take 2nd nr fin: no imp on wnr* **12/1**

0002 **3** *nk* **Moonlight Fantasy (IRE)**[5] 4426 4-9-0 46..................... NeilBrown(5) 8 54
(T D Barron) *t.k.h: led after 2f: hdd appr fnl f: wknd towards fin* **7/2**[1]

6500 **4** *3* **Blushing Prince (IRE)**[4] 3907 9-9-5 48.........................(tp) PaulEddery 7 48
(R C Guest) *hld up in rr: hdwy on outer over 2f out: kpt on: nvr rchd ldrs* **22/1**

1606 **5** *1* **Mayadeen (IRE)**[6] 4383 5-9-10 54...................................... PaulFessey 9 51
(I Semple) *hld up in rr: hdwy on ins over 2f out: nt clr run over 1f out: kpt on same pce* **6/1**

-560 **6** *shd* **Fiddlers Creek (IRE)**[33] 2810 8-9-2 45....................(p) AndrewElliott(3) 4 46
(R Allan) *trckd ldrs: one pce fnl 2f* **25/1**

-000 **7** *shd* **Domesday (UAE)**[8] 4333 6-9-2 40.............................. DominicFox(3) 11 46
(W G Harrison) *chsd ldrs: pushed wd bnd after 2f: drvn over 3f out: kpt on one pce* **100/1**

0104 **8** *nk* **Rotuma (IRE)**[20] 3956 8-9-7 52................................(b) JamieMoriarty(3) 6 50
(M Dods) *led 2f: chsd ldrs: one pce fnl 2f* **7/1**

0053 **9** *shd* **Hamilton House**[8] 4337 3-8-11 60.................................... JimmyQuinn 1 45
(M H Tompkins) *chsd ldrs: drvn over 3f out: one pce* **4/1**[2]

0 **10** *6* **Nortelco (IRE)**[99] 1301 4-9-5 0...................................... PatCosgrave 12 34
(Micky Hammond) *pushed wd and lost pl bnd after 2f: sn in rr: drvn over 3f out: sn btn* **66/1**

3005 **11** *5* **Jalamid (IRE)**[9] 4294 5-9-5 60...................................... TonyHamilton 10 24
(G C Bravery) *mid-div: lost pl over 2f out* **10/1**

0-03 **12** *hd* **Explode**[30] 3638 10-9-5 44...(b) CO'Donoghue 13 24
(Miss L C Siddall) *pushed wd bnd and lost pl after 2f: in rr: nvr a factor* **40/1**

6000 **13** *4* **Ivana Illyich (IRE)**[4] 4449 5-9-0 43...............................(b) PaddyAspell 2 11
(J S Wainwright) *s.i.s: hdwy into midfield 7f out: lost pl over 2f out: sn bhd* **40/1**

2m 10.52s (-1.28) **Going Correction** -0.10s/f (Good)
WFA 3 from 4yo+ 8lb **13** Ran SP% **119.5**
Speed ratings (Par 101): **101,99,98,96,95 95,95,95,95,90 86,86,82**
CSF £53.76 TOTE £5.20: £1.70, £2.90, £2.10; EX 34.40 Trifecta £200.50 Pool: £285.27, 1.01 winning units.There was no bid for the winner. Jalmaid was claimed by D. Maloney for £6,000
Owner Mrs J M Grimston **Bred** Huttons Ambo Stud **Trained** Lingdale, Redcar & Cleveland

FOCUS
A rock-bottom selling race rated through the third to the balance of his form.

4581 NORTHUMBRIAN WATER H'CAP 7f
4:00 (4:00) (Class 4) (0-85,85) 3-Y-O+ **£5,047** (£1,510; £755; £377; £188) **Stalls** Low

Form RPR

561 **1** **Middlemarch (IRE)**[20] 3943 7-8-10 **75**........................(v) GaryBartley(7) 5 86
(J S Goldie) *racd far side: hld up in midfield: hdwy over 2f out: str run to ld jst ins fnl f: styd on wl* **7/1**[2]

0100 **2** *1 ½* **Kenmore**[25] 3791 5-9-2 **74**.. SilvestreDeSousa 16 81
(J G Given) *racd stands' side: trckd ldrs: led and edgd lft over 1f out: kpt on wl: 1st of 6 that gp* **16/1**

3614 **3** *1 ½* **Bid For Gold**[19] 4006 3-8-8 **74**.................................. JamieMoriarty(3) 17 75
(Jedd O'Keeffe) *racd stands' side: sn in last and drvn along: hdwy over 2f out: hmpd over 1f out styd on wl: 2nd of 6 that gp* **12/1**

3603 **4** *½* **Hiccups**[43] 3239 7-9-9 **81**... JimmyQuinn 2 84+
(M Dods) *racd far side: hld up in tch: effrt and n.m.r over 1f out: styd on wl ins fnl f* **14/1**

0504 **5** *hd* **Yorkshire Blue**[11] 4227 8-9-3 **75**.................................. DanielTudhope 6 76
(J S Goldie) *racd far side: hld up in midfield: effrt 2f out: kpt on wl fnl f* **11/1**

3644 **6** *½* **Musca (IRE)**[31] 3607 3-9-3 **80**... PaulEddery 3 78
(J Wade) *racd far side: chsd ldrs: led that gp over 1f out: hdd jst ins fnl f: no ex* **20/1**

2050 **7** *1 ½* **Crocodile Bay (IRE)**[37] 3416 4-8-11 **69**..................... AdrianTNicholls 4 65
(D Nicholls) *racd far side: mid-div: edgd rt over 1f out: kpt on steadily fnl 2f* **14/1**

2041 **8** *hd* **Passion Fruit**[6] 4407 6-9-10 **85** 6ex............................ AndrewElliott(3) 9 80
(C W Fairhurst) *racd far side: hld up: hdwy on outer over 3f out: kpt on same pce fnl 2f* **7/1**[2]

0002 **9** *nk* **Inter Vision (USA)**[11] 4227 7-9-5 **80**....................... DuranFentiman(3) 12 74
(A Dickman) *racd stands' side: hld up: effrt over 2f out: nvr rchd ldrs: 3rd of 6 that gp* **9/1**[3]

0-50 **10** *hd* **El Coto**[13] 4176 7-9-12 **84**...(p) PatCosgrave 10 78
(K A Ryan) *racd far side: w ldr: edgd rt over 1f out: one pce* **10/1**

5000 **11** *¾* **It's A Dream (FR)**[17] 4039 4-8-11 **72**........................ AndrewMullen(3) 1 64
(M W Easterby) *s.i.s: racd far side: sn in mid-div: nvr a threat* **16/1**

0-00 **12** *½* **Imperial Sword**[19] 4006 4-9-3 **75**.. PaulFessey 8 65
(T D Barron) *racd far side: in rr: sltly hmpd over 1f out: nvr a factor* **40/1**

1400 **13** *¾* **Hula Ballew**[13] 4176 7-9-6 **78**.. PaddyAspell 7 66
(M Dods) *led far side: hdd & wknd over 1f out* **33/1**

5611 **14** *½* **Balakiref**[20] 3953 8-9-6 **83**.. NeilBrown(5) 14 70
(M Dods) *s.i.s: swtchd lft after s and racd far side: hld up: hdwy over 2f out: wknd over 1f out* **5/1**[1]

0006 **15** *¾* **Just Dust**[20] 3971 3-8-6 **69**... DaleGibson 15 52
(M W Easterby) *racd stands' side: led that gp tl hdd & wknd over 2f out: 4th of 6 that gp* **25/1**

6153 **16** *2 ½* **Amy Louise (IRE)**[20] 3953 4-9-8 **80**.............................. PhillipMakin 13 58
(T D Barron) *racd stands' side: trckd ldr: led that gp over 2f out: hdd & wknd over 1f out: 5th of 6 that gp* **9/1**[3]

110- **17** *2 ½* **Elusive Warrior (USA)**[238] 6919 4-8-7 **65** oh1.........(p) TonyHamilton 11 37
(R A Fahey) *racd stands' side: trckd ldrs: wkng whn hmpd over 1f out: last of 6 that gp* **25/1**

1m 28.28s (0.26) **Going Correction** +0.10s/f (Good)
WFA 3 from 4yo+ 5lb **17** Ran SP% **129.7**
Speed ratings (Par 105): **102,100,98,98,97 97,95,95,94,94 93,93,92,91,90 88,85**
CSF £113.55 CT £1401.91 TOTE £9.60: £2.40, £4.70, £3.70, £3.20; EX 194.10 TRIFECTA Not won..
Owner W M Johnstone **Bred** Swettenham Stud And Hugo Lascelles **Trained** Uplawmoor, E Renfrews

■ Stewards' Enquiry : Silvestre De Sousa one-day ban; careless riding (Aug 28); caution; careless riding
Adrian T Nicholls two-day ban; careless riding (Aug 28-29)

FOCUS
A fair handicap in which they split into two unequal groups but there was not that much between both sides at the finish. The form could rate higher but is best rated through recent form.
Crocodile Bay(IRE) Official explanation: jockey said gelding was denied a clear run

4582 CONNOR LIAM SADLER H'CAP 1m 2f 32y
4:30 (4:32) (Class 5) (0-70,67) 3-Y-0+ **£3,785** (£1,132; £566; £283; £141) **Stalls** Centre

Form RPR
1362 **1** **Thornaby Green**[6] 4383 6-8-12 **58**.............................. DeanHeslop(7) 10 67
(T D Barron) *mde all: kpt on wl fnl 2f: hld on towards fin* **10/1**
6140 **2** *nk* **Sudden Impulse**[28] 3719 6-10-0 **67**.......................... SilvestreDeSousa 4 78+
(A D Brown) *in tch: hdwy and nt clr run over 1f out: wnt 2nd ins fnl f: r.o wl: jst hld* **12/1**
566 **3** *1 1/2* **Gloucester**[17] 4040 4-9-9 **65**.. DougieCostello(3) 2 73+
(J J Quinn) *prom gng wl: effrt and nt clr run over 1f out: styd on ins fnl f* **12/1**
5154 **4** *hd* **Keisha Kayleigh (IRE)**[35] 3497 4-9-0 **56**................(v) JamieMoriarty(3) 8 61
(B Ellison) *s.i.s: hdwy on outer 3f out: styd on wl fnl f* **14/1**
0041 **5** *1 1/4* **Dechiper (IRE)**[20] 3956 5-8-11 **57**.......................... PatrickDonaghy(7) 12 60
(R Johnson) *chsd ldrs: kpt on same pce appr fnl f* **7/1**[3]
5000 **6** *hd* **Trouble Mountain (USA)**[33] 3567 10-9-12 **65**................(t) DaleGibson 3 67
(M W Easterby) *in rr: drvn over 3f out: styd on fnl 2f* **16/1**
0160 **7** *3/4* **Best Of The Lot (USA)**[13] 4159 5-9-11 **64**.................... TonyHamilton 6 65
(R A Fahey) *trckd ldrs: effrt over 2f out: kpt on same pce appr fnl f* **17/2**
032 **8** *shd* **White Moss (IRE)**[14] 4128 3-9-0 **61**.............................. JimmyQuinn 5 62
(M H Tompkins) *trckd ldrs: one pce fnl 2f* **6/1**[2]
0002 **8** *dht* **Roman History (IRE)**[6] 4410 4-8-11 **50**......................(p) PhillipMakin 11 51
(Miss Tracy Waggott) *chsd wnr: one pce fnl 2f* **18/1**
400- **10** *hd* **Farne Island**[368] 4426 4-9-7 **60**................................... DanielTudhope 16 60
(Micky Hammond) *in rr-div: hdwy on outer 2f out: nvr nr ldrs* **80/1**
2200 **11** *3/4* **Eijaaz (IRE)**[15] 4096 6-8-8 **54**.................................. GaryBartley(7) 13 53
(G A Harker) *hld up in rr: hdwy on ins over 2f out: styng on same pce whn hmpd jst ins fnl f* **20/1**
4101 **12** *1 1/2* **Miss Havisham (IRE)**[13] 4156 3-8-4 **54**.................. AndrewMullen(3) 15 50
(J R Weymes) *in rr: sme hdwy and hrd rdn 3f out: nvr on terms* **20/1**
206 **13** *2* **Sedgwick**[25] 3783 5-9-9 **67**... NeilBrown(5) 1 59
(J G Given) *chsd ldrs: wkng whn n.m.r on ins jst ins fnl f* **8/1**
4266 **14** *2* **Barbirolli**[13] 4159 5-9-9 **65**....................................... DuranFentiman(3) 17 54
(W M Brisbourne) *in rr: effrt 3f out: nvr on terms* **20/1**
3450 **15** *hd* **The Mighty Ogmore**[20] 3956 3-8-4 **51**..........................(v[1]) PaulEddery 7 39
(R C Guest) *in rr-div: effrt 3f out: nvr on terms* **33/1**
0/ **16** *2 1/2* **Estate**[33] 2903 5-9-1 **61**.. MCGeran(7) 14 44
(E J O'Neill) *hld up in rr: nvr on terms* **18/1**
17 *1* **Katalak (IRE)**[30] 3663 4-9-6 **59**.. CO'Donoghue 9 41
(J P Broderick, Ire) *in tch: rdn over 3f out: sn btn* **4/1**[1]

2m 9.99s (-1.81) **Going Correction** -0.10s/f (Good)
WFA 3 from 4yo+ 8lb **17 Ran SP% 134.4**
Speed ratings (Par 103): **103,102,101,101,100 100,99,99,99,99 98,97,96,94,94 92,91**
CSF £128.64 CT £1504.35 TOTE £13.20: £2.30, £3.60, £2.80, £3.80; EX 187.60 TRIFECTA Not won..
Owner K J Alderson **Bred** Mrs S Broadhurst **Trained** Maunby, N Yorks
■ Stewards' Enquiry : C O'Donoghue one-day ban; used whip when out of contention (Aug 28)

FOCUS
A modest handicap with the all-the-way winner given his own way but the pace was decent and the form appears sound.

4583 EC HARRIS H'CAP 6f
5:05 (5:07) (Class 6) (0-65,70) 3-Y-0+ **£2,266** (£674; £337; £168) **Stalls** Low

Form RPR
0402 **1** **John Keats**[6] 4390 4-9-6 **60**...................................... DanielTudhope 9 76+
(J S Goldie) *in tch: hdwy to ld over 1f out: drvn clr* **5/2**[1]
2204 **2** *3* **Monda**[21] 3920 5-8-12 **52**.. TonyHamilton 3 58
(Miss J A Camacho) *chsd ldrs: wnt 2nd 1f out: no ch w wnr* **10/1**
00-0 **3** *nk* **Toberogan (IRE)**[11] 4241 6-8-6 **46**................................. DaleGibson 11 51
(W A Murphy, Ire) *in tch: drvn over 2f out: kpt on wl fnl f* **16/1**
0061 **4** *1* **Ellens Academy (IRE)**[7] 4351 12-9-9 **70** 6ex............. GaryBartley(7) 12 72
(E J Alston) *hld up in rr: edgd lft and hdwy over 1f out: styd on* **8/1**[3]
4005 **5** *2* **Cabourg (IRE)**[10] 4250 4-8-11 **54**...................(b) JamieMoriarty(3) 13 49
(R Bastiman) *t.k.h in rr: styd on fnl 2f: nvr rchd ldrs* **20/1**
5653 **6** *1/2* **Dunn Deal (IRE)**[23] 3837 7-8-5 **45**...................................... PaulQuinn 4 39
(J Balding) *in tch: effrt over 2f out: kpt on fnl f* **8/1**[3]
3000 **7** *1/2* **Rigat**[19] 3999 4-9-8 **62**... PhillipMakin 7 54
(T D Barron) *mid-div: drvn over 4f out: nvr rchd ldrs* **20/1**
6024 **8** *1 3/4* **Lambency (IRE)**[6] 4390 4-8-6 **51**.............................. KellyHarrison(5) 6 38
(J S Goldie) *s.i.s: in tch whn stmbld over 4f out: one pce fnl 2f* **10/1**
-004 **9** *1 1/4* **Knead The Dough**[8] 4336 6-8-4 **47**......................... DominicFox(3) 14 30+
(A E Price) *racd alone stands' side: outpcd fnl 2f* **33/1**
5000 **10** *hd* **Champagne Cracker**[25] 3782 6-8-9 **54**........................ NeilBrown(5) 8 36
(M Dods) *chsd ldrs: wknd appr fnl f* **25/1**
5314 **11** *1* **Orotund**[13] 4180 3-8-6 **52**....................................... DuranFentiman(3) 2 31
(T D Easterby) *w ldr: led over 2f out tl over 1f out: wknd* **8/1**[3]
0600 **12** *2 1/2* **Polish Emperor (USA)**[11] 4223 7-8-4 **48**........................ PaddyAspell 5 19
(D W Barker) *s.i.s: in rr: rdn over 2f out: sn bhd* **33/1**
0000 **13** *5* **The Thrifty Bear**[14] 4141 4-8-6 **46**................................ PaulEddery 10 —
(C W Fairhurst) *led tl over 2f out: sn lost pl* **33/1**
0000 **14** *1/2* **Fairgame Man**[17] 4038 9-7-12 **45**........................(p) JamesRogers(7) 15 —
(J S Wainwright) *hld up in rr: bhd fnl 3f* **50/1**
4134 **L** **Rondo**[2] 4494 4-8-4 **51**.. DeanHeslop(7) 1 —
(T D Barron) *ref to r: lft at s* **4/1**[2]

1m 14.59s (-0.50) **Going Correction** +0.10s/f (Good)
WFA 3 from 4yo+ 3lb **15 Ran SP% 130.1**
Speed ratings (Par 101): **107,103,102,101,98 97,97,94,93,93 91,88,81,81,—**
CSF £28.59 CT £369.88 TOTE £3.30: £1.50, £4.10, £5.60; EX 41.50 Trifecta £262.50 Part won. Pool: £369.85, 0.44 winning units. Place 6 £ 294.54, Place 5 £ 173.03.
Owner Tough Construction Ltd **Bred** R Preece **Trained** Uplawmoor, E Renfrews

FOCUS
A moderate contest in which the time was good and the form looks sound rated around the principals.
T/Plt: £264.10 to a £1 stake. Pool: £58,666.25. 162.10 winning tickets. T/Qpdt: £77.00 to a £1 stake. Pool: £3,270.40. 31.40 winning tickets. WG

4398 NEWMARKET (JULY) (R-H)
Friday, August 17
OFFICIAL GOING: Good, changing to good to firm after race 2 (5.55)
Wind: Light across Weather: Overcast

4584 TURFTV MEDIAN AUCTION MAIDEN STKS 7f
5:25 (5:31) (Class 4) 2-Y-0 **£3,886** (£1,156; £577; £288) **Stalls** Low

Form RPR
0 **1** **Redesignation (IRE)**[90] 1832 2-9-3 0.................................. LDettori 11 82
(R Hannon) *a.p: rdn to ld and edgd lft 1f out: r.o* **4/1**[3]
2 *nk* **Timetable** 2-9-3 0.. RichardHughes 6 81
(H R A Cecil) *s.i.s: hdwy over 5f out: rdn and ev ch fnl f: r.o* **3/1**[2]
3 *3* **Mon Plaisir (USA)** 2-9-3 0....................................... J-PGuillambert 5 74
(J L Dunlop) *s.i.s: hld up: hdwy over 1f out: nt rch ldrs* **20/1**
02 **4** *nk* **Nezami (IRE)**[13] 4162 2-9-3 0.. KDarley 2 73
(B J Meehan) *chsd ldr: led 2f out: rdn and hdd 1f out: wknd towards fin* **6/4**[1]
0 **5** *3* **Shadow Cabinet (IRE)**[20] 3962 2-9-3 0............................ HayleyTurner 8 66
(M L W Bell) *chsd ldrs tl rdn and wknd over 1f out* **10/1**
00 **6** *2* **Space Pirate**[14] 4130 2-9-3 0.. IanMongan 4 61
(M L W Bell) *hld up: hdwy over 2f out: wknd over 1f out* **66/1**
7 *hd* **Long Distance (FR)** 2-9-3 0...................................... OscarUrbina 12 60
(J R Fanshawe) *hld up: swtchd lft and hdwy over 1f out: nvr trbld ldrs* **20/1**
0 **8** *nk* **Alcimedes**[20] 3957 2-9-3 0... JimmyFortune 3 59
(P W Chapple-Hyam) *chsd ldrs over 5f* **14/1**
6000 **9** *1* **Galley Slave (IRE)**[7] 4364 2-8-12 58.................. RussellKennemore(5) 7 57
(M C Chapman) *led 5f: sn rdn: wknd fnl f* **66/1**
0 **10** *1 3/4* **Graylyn Ruby (FR)**[9] 4273 2-9-3 0.............................. MatthewHenry 9 52
(J Jay) *hld up: rdn 1/2-way: wknd 2f out* **66/1**
11 *1/2* **Ablaan (USA)** 2-9-3 0.. EddieAhern 10 51
(M F De Kock, South Africa) *hld up: rdn 1/2-way: wknd 2f out* **20/1**
0006 **12** *9* **Race The Moon (IRE)**[21] 3909 2-9-3 62.................(p) AntonyProcter 14 29
(V Smith) *hld up in tch: rdn: hung lft and wknd over 2f out* **50/1**
13 *6* **Kabuku** 2-9-3 0... PaulDoe 13 14
(M H Tompkins) *dwlt: outpcd* **66/1**

1m 26.28s (-0.50) **Going Correction** -0.025s/f (Good) **13 Ran SP% 123.0**
Speed ratings (Par 96): **101,100,97,96,93 91,90,90,89,87 86,76,69**
CSF £15.71 TOTE £5.50: £1.70, £1.60, £5.70; EX 19.70.
Owner Fergus Jones **Bred** D G Iceton **Trained** East Everleigh, Wilts

FOCUS
A fair maiden and nice performances from the first three with the time decent and those with previous experience setting the standard.

NOTEBOOK
Redesignation(IRE), who finished in mid-division on his debut at Newbury in a race that has thrown up several winners, had less to beat here and appreciated the extra furlong and quicker ground. He could develop into a useful performer in nursery company. (op 9-2 tchd 7-2)
Timetable, a half-brother to Passage Of Time, a top-class two-year-old and this year's Musidora winner, holds entries in all the major Group races to come and shaped with plenty of promise on his debut. He should improve plenty for this experience. (tchd 7-2)
Mon Plaisir(USA), a half-brother to The Penny Drops, a multiple winner on turf in the US, and Western Swing, a dirt sprint winner, was another newcomer to shape with promise, especially as he hails from a stable whose two-year-olds invariably improve a good deal for their debuts. (op 25-1)
Nezami(IRE), who chased home a very useful performer in Al Muheer at Lingfield last time, looked to hold strong claims on that effort, but he failed to repeat it, being unable to stay with the first two in the closing stages. On the plus side, he does have the option of nurseries now. (tchd 7-4)
Shadow Cabinet(IRE), a brother to Undertone, a 6f winner on her only start at two, ran a bit better than on his debut here 20 days earlier. He looks one for nurseries after one more run. (tchd 9-1)
Space Pirate, half-sister to Polar Kingdom, a multiple winner over 6f and 7f, ran a lot better than on his first two starts, and will be suited by a drop back to sprinting in handicap company.

4585 NEWMARKETRACECOURSES.CO.UK H'CAP 6f
5:55 (5:58) (Class 4) (0-85,84) 3-Y-0+ **£5,181** (£1,541; £770; £384) **Stalls** Low

Form RPR
5120 **1** **Barney McGrew (IRE)**[48] 3104 4-9-10 **84**......................... OscarUrbina 4 92+
(J A R Toller) *hld up in tch: rdn to ld over 1f out: jst hld on* **6/1**[3]
4640 **2** *nk* **Curtail (IRE)**[32] 3586 4-9-10 **84**.. IanMongan 8 91
(I Semple) *hld up: rdn over 2f out: hdwy over 1f out: edgd lft ins fnl f: r.o* **17/2**
0040 **3** *1/2* **Our Blessing (IRE)**[11] 4222 3-9-1 **78**.......................... RichardHughes 6 84
(A P Jarvis) *a.p: rdn and swtchd rt over 1f out: r.o u.p* **33/1**
2025 **4** *1 1/2* **Orpen Wide (IRE)**[7] 4367 5-9-5 **84**..................(b) RussellKennemore(5) 1 85
(M C Chapman) *led: rdn: hung rt and hdd over 1f out: styd on same pce* **16/1**
026- **5** *nk* **Lipizza (IRE)**[364] 4577 4-9-1 **75**.. LDettori 5 75
(N A Callaghan) *hld up: rdn over 2f out: hdwy over 1f out: n.m.r and no ex wl ins fnl f* **7/1**
0012 **6** *nk* **Bomber Command (USA)**[20] 3943 4-8-13 **78**............(v) PatrickHills(5) 2 77
(J W Hills) *chsd ldrs: rdn and ev ch over 1f out: no ex ins fnl f* **7/2**[1]
0210 **7** *shd* **Steel Blue**[11] 4227 7-8-12 **72**.. HayleyTurner 7 71
(R M Whitaker) *hld up: rdn over 2f out: r.o ins fnl f: nvr nrr* **12/1**
043 **8** *shd* **Abwaab**[7] 4367 4-9-5 **79**...(b) JimmyFortune 15 78
(Eve Johnson Houghton) *racd wd: in rr: hdwy over 1f out: nt trble ldrs* **7/1**
6001 **9** *1/2* **Matsunosuke**[2] 4507 5-9-1 **75** 6ex.. EddieAhern 10 72
(A B Coogan) *hld up: hdwy 1/2-way: rdn over 1f out: styd on same pce* **11/2**[2]
1015 **10** *nk* **Nobilissima (IRE)**[25] 3797 3-9-0 **80**.............................. MarcHalford(3) 3 76
(J L Spearing) *chsd ldr: rdn 1/2-way: wknd ins fnl f* **16/1**
30 **11** *nk* **Coseadrom (IRE)**[6] 4389 5-9-3 **77**............................... J-PGuillambert 11 72
(M F Harris) *hld up: rdn over 2f out: styd on ins fnl f: nvr trbld ldrs* **16/1**
-404 **12** *3 1/2* **Red Romeo**[14] 4134 6-8-13 **80**.. LanceBetts(7) 14 65
(N Wilson) *racd wd: rdn and hung lft over 1f out: a in rr* **16/1**
0005 **13** *1 1/4* **Kingscross**[33] 3569 9-8-7 **67**... KDarley 9 48
(M Blanshard) *sn pushed along in rr: n.d* **16/1**
0036 **14** *nk* **Connect**[7] 4351 10-8-8 **75**....................................(b) AshleyMorgan(7) 13 55
(M H Tompkins) *mid-div: rdn over 2f out: wknd wl over 1f out* **40/1**

1m 12.09s (-1.26) **Going Correction** -0.025s/f (Good)
WFA 3 from 4yo+ 3lb **14 Ran SP% 129.9**
Speed ratings (Par 105): **107,106,105,103,103 103,103,102,102,101 101,96,95,94**
CSF £61.20 CT £1614.56 TOTE £5.90: £2.10, £4.00, £9.40; EX 64.10.
Owner M A Whelton **Bred** Mrs H B Raw **Trained** Newmarket, Suffolk

The Form Book, Raceform Ltd, Compton, RG20 6NL

FOCUS
A competitive sprint handicap run at a fair pace and best rated through the runner-up to this year's form.
Barney McGrew(IRE) Official explanation: trainer said, regarding apparent improvement in form, that the gelding was better suited by the quicker ground
Orpen Wide(IRE) Official explanation: jockey said gelding hung right
Matsunosuke Official explanation: jockey said gelding ran flat

4586 STABLECARE EBF MAIDEN STKS 1m
6:25 (6:26) (Class 4) 2-Y-O £4,533 (£1,348; £674; £336) Stalls High

Form RPR
3 **1** **Centennial (IRE)**[31] 3625 2-9-3 0 JimmyFortune 2 83+
(J H M Gosden) *chsd ldr: led over 6f out: drvn out* 4/6[1]
0 **2** 1 3/4 **Moville (IRE)**[21] 3896 2-9-3 0 MichaelHills 4 79
(B W Hills) *hld up in tch: nt clr run over 1f out: sn chsng wnr: r.o* 7/1[3]
3 1 **Tomintoul Flyer** 2-9-3 0 TedDurcan 8 77
(H R A Cecil) *wnt lft s: hld up: hdwy over 1f out: edgd lft and styd on same pce ins fnl f* 12/1
0 **4** 1 3/4 **City Of The Kings (IRE)**[36] 3462 2-9-3 0 RichardHughes 3 73+
(R Hannon) *chsd ldrs: rdn whn nt clr run and outpcd over 1f out: styd on ins fnl f* 6/1[2]
6 **5** hd **Keenes Day (FR)**[17] 4037 2-9-3 0 J-PGuillambert 5 72
(M Johnston) *led: hdd over 6f out: rdn over 2f out: wknd ins fnl f* 8/1
06 **6** 2 1/2 **Sheer Bluff (IRE)**[12] 4201 2-9-3 0 AntonyProcter 9 66
(D R C Elsworth) *chsd ldrs: rdn over 1f out: sn wknd* 20/1
7 4 **Vilna (USA)** 2-9-3 0 JamieSpencer 6 57
(N A Callaghan) *s.i.s and hmpd s: rdn over 2f out: wknd over 1f out* 16/1
00 **8** 22 **Howe's Jack (IRE)**[4] 4454 2-8-12 0 RussellKennemore(5) 7 —
(M C Chapman) *hmpd s: hld up: hdwy over 3f out: rdn over 2f out: sn wknd* 100/1

1m 41.87s (1.44) **Going Correction** -0.025s/f (Good) 8 Ran SP% **117.2**
Speed ratings (Par 96): **91,89,88,86,86 83,79,57**
CSF £6.32 TOTE £1.70: £1.10, £2.10, £2.50; EX 5.50.
Owner Exors of the Late Mrs Shirley H Taylor **Bred** W Lazy T Ltd **Trained** Newmarket, Suffolk

FOCUS
Probably just a fair maiden but the winner did it nicely enough, building on his debut promise, although the time limits to some extent.

NOTEBOOK
Centennial(IRE) was a big price on his debut at Yarmouth but ran with a deal of promise, staying on well behind his stablemate and subsequent Listed winner Raven's Pass despite running green, and he had clearly learnt plenty from that. He stretched clear in the closing stages to win in good fashion and, while this was probably not a strong race, he looks a nice type and could make up into a very useful middle-distance horse next year. (op 4-5 tchd 8-13)
Moville(IRE), who caught the eye when not knocked about on his debut, stepped up on that and again shaped with promise. He will be eligible for nurseries after one more run and could be interesting in that company. (op 9-1)
Tomintoul Flyer, a half-brother to six winners, including useful German 1m2f performer Metaxas and fairly useful 7f to 1m winner Top Dirham, shaped with promise. He holds a Royal Lodge entry, but he will have to improve for this debut to be considered for that Group 2 contest. (op 9-1)
City Of The Kings(IRE), a half-brother to Bouncing Bowdler, a very useful multiple winner between 5f and 1m, and winning miler One Putra, made his debut in a decent event here at the July meeting. He was done for toe in a steadily-run contest that day and the same thing happened again here. He will be seen to better effect off a stronger gallop. (op 9-2 tchd 13-2)
Keenes Day(FR), a half-brother to Adaptation, a dual 6f winner at two, and Razed, a 1m winner as a juvenile, set an ordinary gallop. He looks more of a longer-term prospect. (op 7-1)
Sheer Bluff(IRE) is now eligible for a handicap mark, and he should be more effective in that sphere. (tchd 25-1)
Vilna(USA), who cost 220,000euros, is a half-brother to two sprint winners in the US and has plenty of speed in his pedigree, so he will be of more interest when dropped back in distance. (op 12-1 tchd 11-1)

4587 PORTLAND PLACE PROPERTIES H'CAP 1m
7:00 (7:00) (Class 5) (0-75,75) 3-Y-O+ £3,886 (£1,156; £577; £288) Stalls Low

Form RPR
3433 **1** **Sonny Parkin**[7] 4365 5-9-11 **73** (v) LDettori 2 83
(G A Huffer) *hld up and bhd: swtchd lft and hdwy over 1f out: led ins fnl f: r.o* 9/2[2]
026 **2** nk **Fabrian**[5] 4419 9-9-7 **72** LiamJones(3) 8 81
(R J Price) *trckd ldr: rdn to ld over 1f out: hdd ins fnl f: r.o* 9/1
0-26 **3** 1 **Silent Applause**[14] 4135 4-9-7 **69** TedDurcan 9 76
(Dr J D Scargill) *chsd ldrs: rdn over 3f out: hung lft and ev ch over 1f out: styd on same pce ins fnl f* 8/1
005 **4** nk **Arctic Desert**[14] 4135 7-9-1 **63** (t) RichardHughes 4 69
(Miss Gay Kelleway) *hld up: hdwy over 1f out: sn rdn: styd on* 8/1
0440 **5** 5 **Eastern Emperor**[37] 3416 3-9-4 **72** AdamKirby 5 66
(W R Swinburn) *hld up: racd keenly: hdwy over 2f out: rdn over 1f out: wknd ins fnl f* 12/1
0020 **6** 1 **Rain Stops Play (IRE)**[15] 4107 5-9-13 **75** JamieSpencer 11 67
(M Quinn) *led: rdn and hdd over 1f out: wknd ins fnl f* 5/1[3]
0663 **7** 3 **Piper's Song (IRE)**[11] 4234 4-9-6 **68** DaneO'Neill 12 53
(H Candy) *chsd ldrs: rdn over 1f out: wknd fnl f* 7/2[1]
-200 **8** 1 **Ninth House (USA)**[14] 4135 5-9-13 **75** (bt) IanMongan 6 58
(N P Littmoden) *hld up: nt clr run fr over 2f out: n.d* 40/1
0000 **9** 3 1/2 **Lincolneurocruiser**[6] 4407 5-8-10 **63** RussellKennemore(5) 7 38
(Mrs N Macauley) *chsd ldrs: rdn over 2f out: wknd over 1f out* 50/1
031 **10** hd **Trivia (IRE)**[65] 2554 3-9-4 **72** JimmyFortune 10 46
(N A Callaghan) *rrd s: hld up: hdwy over 2f out: rdn and wknd over 1f out* 6/1
1500 **11** 1 **Genari**[44] 3215 4-9-8 **75** (t) TolleyDean(5) 13 47
(P F I Cole) *hld up: rdn over 2f out: wknd over 1f out* 14/1

1m 39.05s (-1.38) **Going Correction** -0.025s/f (Good)
WFA 3 from 4yo+ 6lb 11 Ran SP% **122.3**
Speed ratings (Par 103): **105,104,103,103,98 97,94,93,89,89 88**
CSF £46.86 CT £328.48 TOTE £4.10: £1.40, £4.20, £3.30; EX 58.40.
Owner Fran O'Brien **Bred** Blenheim Bloodstock **Trained** Newmarket, Suffolk
■ Stewards' Enquiry : Eddie Ahern £600 fine: doubly declared

FOCUS
An ordinary handicap but run at a good pace and solid enough with the first four clear and the third and fourth setting the level.

4588 NGK SPARK PLUGS CONDITIONS STKS 1m 4f
7:30 (7:32) (Class 2) 3-Y-O+ £11,217 (£3,358; £1,679; £840) Stalls High

Form RPR
0-63 **1** **Before You Go (IRE)**[19] 3989 4-9-0 98 MichaelHills 2 106
(T G Mills) *led: hdd over 2f out: rallied to ld and edgd rt over 1f out: r.o* 7/2[2]
3200 **2** 4 **Camrose**[14] 4117 6-9-0 99 (b) JimmyFortune 4 100
(J L Dunlop) *chsd ldrs: outpcd over 2f out: styd on ins fnl f* 5/1[3]
3-12 **3** 2 1/2 **Familiar Territory**[21] 3899 4-9-0 105 LDettori 1 96+
(Saeed Bin Suroor) *hld up: hdwy over 5f out: led over 2f out: rdn: edgd rt and hdd over 1f out: wknd ins fnl f* 4/9[1]
03 **4** 58 **Little Darlin**[29] 3683 3-8-4 0 ow5 MarcHalford 3 3
(G J Smith) *chsd wnr: rdn over 4f out: wknd over 3f out* 80/1

2m 33.23s (0.32) **Going Correction** -0.025s/f (Good)
WFA 3 from 4yo+ 10lb 4 Ran SP% **109.4**
Speed ratings (Par 109): **97,94,92,54**
CSF £18.40 TOTE £4.90; EX 21.40.
Owner Mrs Tina Smith **Bred** The Niarchos Family **Trained** Headley, Surrey

FOCUS
This is probably not strong form for the grade of race with the winner the best guide.

NOTEBOOK
Before You Go(IRE) is a difficult horse to place off his current mark and so this represented a good opportunity to regain the winning thread. Having looked booked for second when headed by the Godolphin colt, he rallied under pressure to regain the lead and ran on well to win quite easily in the end. The form is probably not that strong for the grade of race, but that will not bother his connections. He coped well with the ground, which looked fast enough for him beforehand, and the way he finished his race suggested that he will stay a bit further. (op 3-1)
Camrose has not quite managed to win a Listed race despite numerous attempts, and his last two efforts had been very disappointing. This was a drop in grade and a potential confidence-booster, but he never really looked like troubling Before You Go or Familiar Territory until running on to deny the latter, who weakened badly late on, second place. (op 11-2 tchd 6-1)
Familiar Territory was the pick at the weights and took it up apparently going well approaching the two-furlong marker, but he weakened surprisingly quickly and lost not only first place but second as well in the closing stages. He was unproven at this distance, but it did not look like it was just a lack of stamina that was to blame. Official explanation: jockey said colt lost its action (tchd 2-5, 1-2 in places)
Little Darlin was totally out of her depth. (op 100-1)

4589 NEWMARKET NIGHTS FILLIES' H'CAP 7f
8:05 (8:05) (Class 3) (0-95,95) 3-Y-O+ £7,772 (£2,312; £1,155; £577) Stalls Low

Form RPR
2261 **1** **Medicea Sidera**[27] 3743 3-8-12 **81** JimmyFortune 4 87
(E F Vaughan) *racd centre: mde virtually all: rdn out* 9/2[2]
-212 **2** 3/4 **Yandina (IRE)**[29] 3670 4-9-2 **80** MichaelHills 11 86
(B W Hills) *racd centre: hld up in tch: rdn and hung lft fr over 1f out: styd on* 9/2[2]
0614 **3** 3/4 **Steam Cuisine**[37] 3430 3-9-4 **87** TedDurcan 1 89+
(M G Quinlan) *racd centre: hld up: hdwy and hung lft over 1f out: styd on same pce towards fin* 2/1[1]
1001 **4** nk **Nadawat (USA)**[13] 4163 3-8-13 **82** RHills 12 83
(J L Dunlop) *racd centre: chsd ldrs: rdn and ev ch whn hung lft over 1f out: styd on same pce* 7/1[3]
4500 **5** 3/4 **Tara Too (IRE)**[31] 3623 4-8-8 **72** (b) FrankieMcDonald 9 73
(J G Portman) *racd centre: hmpd s: hld up: racd keenly: rdn over 1f out: r.o ins fnl f: nt trble ldrs* 33/1
10-2 **6** 2 1/2 **World's Heroine (IRE)**[20] 3961 3-8-13 **82** NickyMackay 7 74
(G A Butler) *racd centre: hmpd s: sn chsng ldrs: rdn over 2f out: wkng whn hmpd 1f out* 8/1
4351 **7** 3/4 **Jacaranda Ridge**[24] 3827 3-8-11 **80** KDarley 6 70
(M A Jarvis) *racd centre: chsd wnr tl rdn and wknd over 1f out* 10/1
0155 **8** 1 1/2 **Inaminute (IRE)**[20] 3953 4-8-13 **77** JamieSpencer 2 65
(K R Burke) *racd alone far side: prom: rdn over 2f out: wknd fnl f* 16/1
2343 **9** 3 **Lavenham (IRE)**[20] 3970 4-8-12 **76** RichardHughes 3 56
(R Hannon) *racd centre: hld up: rdn and wknd over 1f out: eased* 8/1

1m 25.72s (-1.06) **Going Correction** -0.025s/f (Good)
WFA 3 from 4yo 5lb 9 Ran SP% **122.3**
Speed ratings (Par 104): **105,104,103,102,102 99,98,96,93**
CSF £26.78 CT £54.55 TOTE £5.90: £2.10, £2.40, £1.30; EX 33.00 Place 6 £ 201.10, Place 5 £ 103.99.
Owner M A Whelton **Bred** Broughton Bloodstock **Trained** Newmarket, Suffolk

FOCUS
A competitive fillies' handicap featuring a number of in-form performers and rated around the placed horses.

NOTEBOOK
Medicea Sidera, a winner of a maiden over this course and distance last time out, was only raised 2lb for that success and took advantage by bravely making almost every yard. She is clearly progressive and, while she will need to continue on an upward curve to defy another rise in the handicap, that is entirely possible. (op 4-1 tchd 5-1)
Yandina(IRE) had seen her Folkestone form given a boost by the subsequent performances of the winner and third and held every chance off a 2lb higher mark. She ran well in what was probably a strong race of its type and should soon go one better. (op 6-1)
Steam Cuisine, fourth in a handicap at the July meeting in which Medicea Sidera finished sixth, ran well again but failed to confirm the form despite being 1lb better off at the weights. (op 11-4 tchd 15-8)
Nadawat(USA), who was flattered by racing on the best ground at Lingfield last time, had an 8lb higher mark to contend with here and ran a very fair race in the circumstances. (op 9-2)
Tara Too(IRE), who has dropped a stone in the handicap this term, ran a better race and could be a filly to be interested in now that she seems to be returning to form.
World's Heroine(IRE) did not quite build on the promise of her reappearance outing here last month, but she did not enjoy the best of luck in running. (op 13-2)
T/Plt: £242.50, Pool £58,353.05 175.60 winning tickets T/Qpdt: £34.50. Pool £5,466.40, 117.10 winning tickets CR

4392 LINGFIELD (L-H)
Saturday, August 18

OFFICIAL GOING: Aw: standard; turf: good changing to good to soft after race 4 (7.00pm)
Weather: Rain

4591 BET NOW AT WBX.COM CLAIMING STKS 1m (P)
5:30 (5:33) (Class 6) 3-Y-O £2,047 (£604; £302) Stalls High

Form RPR
3600 **1** **Hessian (IRE)**[9] 4321 3-8-12 67 HayleyTurner 6 65
(M L W Bell) *in tch: hdwy to ld jst over 2f out: rdn clr over 1f out: styd on wl* 5/2[2]
-064 **2** 2 **Split Briefs (IRE)**[39] 3406 3-9-2 65 NickyMackay 9 64
(D J Daly) *hld up in rr: hdwy on outer over 2f out: rdn to chse wnr wl over 1f out: no imp fnl f* 11/2[3]

3005 **3** 3 1/2 **Six Of Hearts**[17] 4064 3-9-3 62 MickyFenton 8 57
(J A Osborne) *in tch: hdwy 3f out: chsd wnr briefly 2f out: no imp u.p after* **9/1**

0003 **4** 1/2 **Meadfoot**[16] 4109 3-8-10 47 FergusSweeney 3 49
(B R Millman) *racd in midfield: rdn 1/2-way: kpt on fnl f: nt pce to trble ldrs* **25/1**

0304 **5** 1 1/4 **Amazing King (IRE)**[32] 3619 3-8-10 58 JackDean(7) 2 53
(W G M Turner) *in tch in midfield: effrt and drvn over 2f out: no real imp* **40/1**

4200 **6** 1 1/4 **Zach's Harmoney (USA)**[6] 4429 3-8-11 75 (p) IanMongan 1 44
(B J Meehan) *t.k.h: chsd ldrs: n.m.r over 2f out: rdn and wknd wl over 1f out* **6/1**

0300 **7** 2 **Brave Jack (IRE)**[31] 3652 3-9-0 53 (v[1]) StephaneBreux(3) 10 46
(J R Best) *chsd ldr tl 2f out: sn wknd* **25/1**

6223 **8** 1 3/4 **Our Herbie**[3] 4505 3-9-2 63 (v) PatrickHills(5) 11 46
(J W Hills) *hld up in rr: drvn and reluctant 1/2-way: n.d* **2/1**[1]

0210 **9** 4 **Red Current**[28] 3731 3-9-2 58 AmirQuinn 4 31
(R A Harris) *s.i.s: hmpd after 1f: nvr on terms* **25/1**

0000 **10** 3/4 **Dark Druid (IRE)**[9] 4339 3-8-0 48 SophieDoyle(7) 5 21
(I A Wood) *s.i.s: a bhd* **66/1**

030 **11** 8 **Kastan**[11] 4256 3-8-5 45 ow1 RichardKingscote(3) 12 3
(B Palling) *dismntd and led to s: led tl 3f out: sn wknd: eased fnl f: t.o* **25/1**

-000 **12** 7 **Dumas (IRE)**[12] 4223 3-8-13 50 (v[1]) SimonWhitworth 7 —
(A P Jarvis) *s.i.s: a bhd: t.o and eased fnl f* **33/1**

1m 37.63s (-1.80) **Going Correction** -0.225s/f (Stan) 12 Ran SP% **123.8**
Speed ratings (Par 98): **100,98,94,94,92 91,89,87,83,83 75,68**
CSF £16.26 TOTE £4.20: £1.80, £1.90, £4.10; EX 27.60.Hessian was claimed by Paul Howling for £10,000. Zach's Harmoney was claimed by Michael Appleby for £7,000
Owner Deal,Lea,Scotney,Asplin & Chellingworth **Bred** Rathbarry Stud **Trained** Newmarket, Suffolk
■ Stewards' Enquiry : Sophie Doyle one-day ban: excessive use of the whip (Aug 29)
Ian Mongan two-day ban: careless riding (Aug 29-30)

FOCUS
A routine claimer and tempo to match. The form looks fairly solid with the runner-up, fourth and fifth all to their marks.
Red Current Official explanation: jockey said filly was hampered after a furlong

4592 LINGFIELD PARK FOR WEDDINGS H'CAP — 1m 2f (P)
6:00 (6:01) (Class 6) (0-62,60) 3-Y-O+ **£2,047** (£604; £302) **Stalls** Low

Form RPR

2040 **1** **Kindlelight Blue (IRE)**[14] 4172 3-8-11 **60** PatrickHills(5) 11 69
(N P Littmoden) *dwlt: gd hdwy to chse ldrs 8f out: led and pushed clr over 3f out: rdr dropped reins ent fnl f: all out* **8/1**

0010 **2** 3/4 **Takes Tutu (USA)**[8] 4355 8-9-1 **54** (p) LiamJones(3) 13 62+
(C R Dore) *hld up in last trio: stl plenty to do wl over 1f out: str run fnl f: wnt 2nd towards fin: jst hld* **10/1**

65-0 **3** 3/4 **Kings Topic (USA)**[5] 4464 7-9-9 **59** SamHitchcott 7 65
(A B Haynes) *racd in midfield: hdwy over 3f out: rdn to chse wnr over 2f out: kpt on u.p: lost 2nd nr fin* **20/1**

2031 **4** 3 1/2 **Pelham Crescent (IRE)**[5] 4464 4-8-11 **54** LanceBetts(7) 4 53+
(B Palling) *chsd ldrs: shuffled bk and lost pl over 3f out: bhd and swtchd rt over 1f out: r.o wl fnl f: nvr able to chal* **15/8**[1]

0004 **5** 1/2 **Sir Haydn**[21] 3946 7-9-10 **60** (v) FergusSweeney 2 58
(J R Jenkins) *hmpd after 1f: hld up in midfield: rdn and effrt over 3f out: kpt on fnl f but nvr gng pce to rch ldrs* **7/1**[3]

0005 **6** 1 1/4 **Titus Lumpus (IRE)**[7] 4395 4-9-0 **50** (p) TGMcLaughlin 3 46
(R M Flower) *led for 1f: mostly 2nd after tl over 2f out: wknd over 1f out* **20/1**

4060 **7** 2 1/2 **Ganache (IRE)**[26] 3799 5-9-1 **56** HaddenFrost(5) 1 47
(P R Chamings) *t.k.h: led after 1f tl over 3f out: wknd 2f out: sddle slipped* **12/1**

4360 **8** 1 1/4 **Port 'n Starboard**[50] 3063 6-9-10 **60** SimonWhitworth 6 48
(C A Cyzer) *racd in midfield: hdwy over 3f out: rdn to chse ldrs 2f out: wknd over 1f out* **16/1**

2-00 **9** 1/2 **Regal Ovation**[86] 1972 3-8-12 **56** SaleemGolam 8 43
(W R Muir) *chsd ldrs: rdn over 4f out: wknd over 2f out* **33/1**

4600 **10** 1 1/4 **Hallings Overture (USA)**[14] 4161 8-9-3 **53** PaulEddery 14 38
(C A Horgan) *hld up in rr: rdn wl over 2f out: no hdwy* **8/1**

3000 **11** 1 3/4 **Tabulate**[8] 4361 4-9-8 **58** AmirQuinn 12 39
(P Howling) *t.k.h: hld up in rr: n.d* **66/1**

3132 **12** shd **Windy Prospect**[95] 1739 5-9-8 **58** IanMongan 5 39
(Mrs L J Mongan) *bhd: rdn over 4f out: no ch last 2f* **6/1**[2]

2m 5.85s (-1.94) **Going Correction** -0.225s/f (Stan)
WFA 3 from 4yo+ 8lb 12 Ran SP% **120.4**
Speed ratings (Par 101): **98,97,96,94,93 92,90,89,89,88 86,86**
CSF £83.01 CT £1558.86 TOTE £8.80: £1.80, £3.20, £7.40; EX 128.10.
Owner Kindlelight Ltd **Bred** Benedikt Fassbender **Trained** Newmarket, Suffolk

FOCUS
A very modest handicap, but run at a strong early pace, but the overall time was ordinary and the form looks slightly suspect.
Sir Haydn Official explanation: jockey said gelding hung left
Ganache(IRE) Official explanation: jockey said saddle slipped
Tabulate Official explanation: jockey said filly moved poorly throughout
Windy Prospect Official explanation: jockey said gelding did not face the kickback

4593 KARA & WAYNE WEDDING DAY MAIDEN STKS — 6f
6:30 (6:32) (Class 5) 2-Y-O **£2,817** (£838; £418; £209) **Stalls** High

Form RPR

6 **1** **Vive Les Rouges**[51] 3037 2-8-12 0 IanMongan 3 79
(C F Wall) *pressed ldrs: wnt 2nd 4f out: shkn up to ld 1f out: pushed along and hld on wl cl home* **20/1**

2 **2** hd **Bellomi (IRE)**[17] 4070 2-9-3 0 TPO'Shea 6 83
(M R Channon) *chsd ldng trio: wnt 3rd 2f out: sn rdn: styd on u.p fnl f: hld cl home* **7/2**[2]

42 **3** nk **Major Willy**[21] 3962 2-9-3 0 SebSanders 10 83
(W Jarvis) *led tl rdn and hdd 1f out: unable qckn fnl f* **1/2**[1]

4 3 **Austintatious (USA)** 2-9-3 0 ChrisCatlin 4 74
(B J Meehan) *off pce in midfield: rdn 1/2-way: kpt on fnl f: nvr able to chal* **14/1**[3]

00 **5** 3/4 **Jelly Mo**[22] 3895 2-8-7 0 PatrickHills(5) 12 66
(J W Hills) *bhd: rdn wl over 2f out: styd on steadily fnl f: nvr nr ldrs* **28/1**

00 **6** 5 **Mandarinka**[19] 4016 2-9-3 0 StephenCarson 5 56
(P Winkworth) *chsd ldr for 2f: prom tl wknd qckly 2f out* **40/1**

00 **7** 3 1/2 **New Minerton (IRE)**[53] 2969 2-8-12 0 FergusSweeney 1 41
(B R Millman) *a bhd: no ch fr 1/2-way* **100/1**

00 **8** 3 **Love Dancer (IRE)**[6] 4417 2-9-3 0 HayleyTurner 9 37
(M L W Bell) *sn pushed along in rr: no ch fr 1/2-way* **33/1**

9 10 **Hawk And I (IRE)** 2-9-3 0 NickyMackay 8 7
(R A Kvisla) *s.i.s: a wl bhd: t.o last 2f* **20/1**

10 4 **Jevington Star (IRE)** 2-9-3 0 MickyFenton 2 —
(R M Flower) *sn pushed along and outpcd in rr: t.o fr 1/2-way* **100/1**

000 **11** 3 1/2 **Starfinch**[24] 3856 2-8-12 48 FrankieMcDonald 11 —
(J J Bridger) *in tch for 2f: sn dropped out: t.o last 2f* **100/1**

1m 11.55s (-0.12) **Going Correction** -0.15s/f (Firm) 11 Ran SP% **116.9**
Speed ratings (Par 94): **94,93,93,89,88 81,77,73,59,54 49**
CSF £84.59 TOTE £25.90: £5.10, £1.40, £1.02; EX 145.30.
Owner John E Sims **Bred** Farmers Hill Stud **Trained** Newmarket, Suffolk

FOCUS
A fair maiden, run at a good pace, with several future winners likely to be in the line-up and the form looks pretty solid.

NOTEBOOK
Vive Les Rouges landed a surprise victory, beating several rivals - colts included - who had shown previous promise. This was a big step up on her debut, but she was only dossing in the last 200 yards and gave the impression that there is more to come as she gains experience. (op 25-1 tchd 16-1 in places)
Bellomi(IRE) finished runner-up for the second time in two attempts, but looks capable of going one better. (op 4-1 tchd 9-2)
Major Willy, though unable to justify favouritism, was only just touched off, and is good enough to find a maiden. (tchd 4-7 in a place)
Austintatious(USA), a son of the high-class American miler Distorted Humour, has winners in the family up to 1m2f, and changed hands for $150,000 earlier this year. He was getting the hang of things late on, and this Racing Post Trophy entry should improve enough to win over 7f or a mile. (tchd 11-1)
Jelly Mo ran her best race to date, and is one to note in nurseries now she is qualified. (op 33-1)
Mandarinka has not been getting home in his races to date, but 5f nurseries should suit him better than this. (op 33-1)
Hawk And I(IRE) Official explanation: jockey said colt never travelled

4594 HEAR THE NEWS @ TNAUK.ORG.UK H'CAP — 6f
7:00 (7:00) (Class 5) (0-70,70) 4-Y-O+ **£2,817** (£838; £418; £209) **Stalls** High

Form RPR

1114 **1** **Cativo Cavallino**[14] 4165 4-8-7 **61** NataliaGemelova(5) 7 76
(J E Long) *chsd ldrs: pushed along: led wl over 1f out: sn edgd lft but drew clr: in command and edgd rt ins fnl f: easily* **11/2**[3]

0-00 **2** 5 **Proud Killer**[40] 3388 4-8-13 **62** FergusSweeney 11 61
(J R Jenkins) *chsd ldr: rdn 2f out: chsd wnr jst ins fnl f: no imp* **16/1**

0231 **3** 1/2 **Goodenough Mover**[17] 4075 11-9-3 **66** (b) HayleyTurner 12 63
(Andrew Turnell) *led on stands' rail: hdd wl over 1f out: kpt on same pce after: lost 2nd jst ins fnl f* **7/2**[1]

0100 **4** 3/4 **Jayanjay**[9] 4320 8-9-3 **66** SebSanders 13 61
(P Mitchell) *in tch: rdn and effrt wl over 1f out: kpt on same pce u.p* **8/1**

6523 **5** hd **Norcroft**[10] 4296 5-8-4 **60** (p) KirstyMilczarek(7) 6 54
(Mrs C A Dunnett) *bhd: rdn and hdwy over 2f out: kpt on u.p but nvr nr wnr* **5/1**[2]

40 **6** 3 1/2 **King Egbert (FR)**[23] 3869 6-8-2 **51** oh1 NickyMackay 14 34
(R J Price) *chsd ldrs: sltly hmpd after 1f: sn pushed along: no ch last 2f* **13/2**

6600 **7** 3 **Enjoy The Buzz**[7] 4390 8-7-13 **51** oh4 (p) LiamJones(3) 2 25
(J M Bradley) *racd on outer: effrt u.p 2f out: n.d: wknd ins fnl f* **20/1**

2230 **8** 2 1/2 **George The Second**[16] 4095 4-9-1 **67** RichardKingscote(3) 3 33
(Mrs H Sweeting) *chsd ldrs: rdn and wknd 2f out: eased ins fnl f* **7/2**[1]

0660 **9** shd **Hollow Jo**[39] 3396 7-9-3 **66** MickyFenton 5 31
(J R Jenkins) *chsd ldrs for 2f: sn rdn and lost pl* **14/1**

000- **10** 1 1/4 **Chateau Nicol**[242] 6868 8-9-0 **70** (v) KylieManser(7) 8 31
(B G Powell) *a bhd* **25/1**

3060 **11** 7 **Steeley Fox**[7] 4390 4-8-3 **59** ow1 (t) BarrySavage(7) 4 —
(J M Bradley) *a struggling: wl bhd fr 1/2-way* **40/1**

1m 11.68s (0.01) **Going Correction** +0.05s/f (Good) 11 Ran SP% **124.5**
Speed ratings (Par 103): **101,94,93,92,92 87,83,80,80,78 69**
CSF £92.52 CT £360.87 TOTE £6.90: £2.70, £4.60, £1.90; EX 162.10.
Owner P Saxon **Bred** Miss A M Rees **Trained** Caterham, Surrey

FOCUS
A modest sprint, but a predictably good pace. It looked competitive on paper, only to be turned into a procession by the much-improved winner and the form is taken at face value despite there not being many with solid form behind.

4595 LINGFIELDPARK.CO.UK (S) STKS — 7f 140y
7:30 (7:32) (Class 6) 3-Y-O+ **£2,047** (£604; £302) **Stalls** Centre

Form RPR

6-00 **1** **Tequila Sheila (IRE)**[61] 2714 5-8-10 45 FergusSweeney 2 58+
(K R Burke) *mde all in centre: clr over 2f out: in n.d after: eased cl home* **7/1**[3]

5005 **2** 5 **Bollywood (IRE)**[4] 4469 4-9-1 44 (p) FrankieMcDonald 8 47
(J J Bridger) *chsd ldng pair: rdn over 2f out: sn no ch w wnr after: wnt modest 2nd over 1f out: plugged on* **12/1**

0005 **3** 3 **Halfwaytoparadise**[6] 4416 4-8-10 47 (p) SaleemGolam 12 35
(W G M Turner) *taken down early: chsd wnr: rdn over 2f out: sn no ch w wnr: lost 2nd over 1f out* **10/1**

40 **4** 2 **Stagnite**[43] 3285 7-8-12 47 JerryO'Dwyer(3) 11 35
(Karen George) *hld up in midfield: rdn wl over 2f out: hrd drvn wl over 1f out: nvr on terms* **20/1**

0000 **5** 3/4 **Give Evidence**[9] 4337 3-8-9 51 SimonWhitworth 4 33
(A P Jarvis) *nvr bttr than midfield: kpt on u.p fnl f: nvr nr wnr* **33/1**

-066 **6** 3/4 **Acosta**[37] 3450 3-8-2 47 (v[1]) MatthewCosham(7) 1 31
(Dr J R J Naylor) *racd on outer: wl bhd tl modest late hdwy: nvr on terms* **66/1**

0563 **7** 2 **Marbaa (IRE)**[4] 4473 4-9-1 46 (p) IanMongan 9 26
(S Dow) *nvr bttr than midfield: drvn and no ch fr 1/2-way* **6/1**[2]

5600 **8** 3 1/2 **Rogers Lodger**[7] 4394 3-8-9 48 PaulDoe 10 17
(J Akehurst) *chsd ldrs: rdn 1/2-way: sn wl btn* **16/1**

-050 **9** 1 **What-A-Dancer (IRE)**[2] 4532 10-8-12 50 (b) LiamJones(3) 7 15
(R A Harris) *a wl bhd: no ch fr 1/2-way* **10/1**

5250 **10** 2 **Prince Dayjur (USA)**[22] 3922 8-9-1 68 SebSanders 5 10
(J Pearce) *a bhd* **11/8**[1]

30-0 **11** 1/2 **Start Of Authority**[95] 1739 6-9-1 47 ChrisCatlin 6 8
(J Gallagher) *nvr bttr than midfield: rdn and wknd 3f out* **8/1**

6000 **12** 10 **Black Oval**[5] 4449 6-8-10 48 PaulEddery 3 —
(S Parr) *a wl bhd: t.o* **25/1**

1m 34.27s (2.81) **Going Correction** +0.25s/f (Good)
WFA 3 from 4yo+ 6lb 12 Ran SP% **124.8**
Speed ratings (Par 101): **95,90,87,85,84 83,81,78,77,75 74,64**
CSF £89.06 TOTE £5.30: £1.60, £3.90, £3.20; EX 64.80.There was no bid for the winner.

Owner Lee Westwood **Bred** Martyn J McEnery **Trained** Middleham Moor, N Yorks
FOCUS
A routine seller, run at a fair pace, in which the favourite ran poorly. The runner-up is the best guide to the level.
What-A-Dancer(IRE) Official explanation: jockey said gelding never travelled
Prince Dayjur(USA) Official explanation: jockey said gelding never travelled

4596 WBX.COM WORLD BET EXCHANGE FILLIES' H'CAP 7f 140y
8:00 (8:03) (Class 6) (0-65,61) 3-Y-0+ **£2,047** (£604; £302) **Stalls** Centre

Form RPR
3133 **1** **Hansomelle (IRE)**[7] 4395 5-9-10 **61**........................(p) NeilChalmers(3) 14 75+
(Miss Sheena West) *cl up and travelling wl: led over 2f out: clr wl over 1f out: v easily* **10/11**[1]
0446 **2** *6* **Rubilini**[10] 4270 3-8-6 **46**........................ TPO'Shea 11 45
(M R Channon) *prom: rdn and ev ch 2f out: wl hld whn hung lft 1f out* **9/2**[2]
3656 **3** *1 1/2* **Piano Key**[16] 4104 3-7-12 **45**........................ MCGeran(7) 12 40
(M D I Usher) *racd in midfield: rdn wl over 2f out: kpt on to go modest 3rd 1f out: nvr nr wnr* **14/1**
/006 **4** *2 1/2* **Intimate Friend (USA)**[9] 4336 6-8-4 **45**................(t) FrankiePickard(7) 13 34
(Miss Diana Weeden) *led tl over 2f out: no ch w wnr over 1f out: fdd ins fnl f* **33/1**
0006 **5** *1 1/2* **Charlottebutterfly**[19] 4029 7-8-12 **46**........................ IanMongan 10 31
(P J McBride) *cl up: rdn 1/2-way: wknd 2f out* **12/1**
4004 **6** *nk* **Lady Duxyana**[4] 4469 4-8-11 **45**........................(v) HayleyTurner 3 30
(M D I Usher) *v.s.a: wl bhd: kpt on past btn horses fnl f: no ch* **7/1**[3]
0000 **7** *3/4* **Tokyo Jo (IRE)**[8] 4361 3-9-0 **54**........................ TGMcLaughlin 5 37
(T T Clement) *racd in midfield: rdn 1/2-way: hrd drvn and wknd over 2f out* **20/1**
0000 **8** *3 1/2* **Noravana (IRE)**[16] 4109 3-8-5 **45**........................ NelsonDeSouza 7 19
(Miss V Haigh) *stdd after s: t.k.h and hld up bhd: rdn 1/2-way: sn no ch* **40/1**
-044 **9** *3 1/2* **Hope Your Safe**[9] 4326 3-8-8 **51**........................ StephaneBreux(3) 8 16
(J R Best) *chsd ldr: rdn over 2f out: sn wknd: eased ins fnl f:* **7/1**[3]
66-0 **10** *9* **Tinted View (USA)**[20] 3992 3-9-1 **55**........................ MickyFenton 4 —
(Mrs H Sweeting) *bhd: rdn and struggling 1/2-way: no ch last 3f: t.o* **33/1**
-000 **11** *11* **Demi Sec**[75] 2304 4-8-8 **45**........................(b[1]) JerryO'Dwyer(3) 1 —
(Dr J D Scargill) *a bhd: lost tch 1/2-way: eased wl over 1f out: t.o* **33/1**

1m 34.82s (3.36) **Going Correction** +0.45s/f (Yiel)
WFA 3 from 4yo+ 6lb **11** Ran SP% **125.9**
Speed ratings (Par 98): **101,95,93,91,89 89,88,84,81,72 61**
CSF £5.28 CT £40.45 TOTE £2.00: £1.10, £2.00, £4.70; EX 8.50 Place 6 £182.84, Place 5 £87.38..
Owner Michael Moriarty **Bred** J Beckett **Trained** Falmer, E Sussex
FOCUS
A moderate fillies' race, run at an ordinary tempo, but the winner, who was a class above the rest, is in fine form and improving.
Lady Duxyana Official explanation: jockey said filly missed the break
Tokyo Jo(IRE) Official explanation: jockey said filly was unsuited by the good to soft ground
Demi Sec Official explanation: jockey said filly never travelled
T/Plt: £205.20 to a £1 stake. Pool: £51,697.70. 183.90 winning tickets. T/Qpdt: £8.00 to a £1 stake. Pool: £4,476.40. 411.00 winning tickets. SP

4571 NEWBURY (L-H)
Saturday, August 18
OFFICIAL GOING: Good (6.8) changing to good to soft after race 3 (2.45pm)
Wind: Brisk, across Weather: Raining

4597 BATHWICK TYRES LADIES DERBY H'CAP (FOR LADY AMATEUR RIDERS) 1m 4f 5y
1:40 (1:41) (Class 4) (0-80,80) 3-Y-0+ **£12,492** (£3,874; £1,936; £968) **Stalls** Centre

Form RPR
4441 **1** **Tifernati**[14] 4172 3-9-6 **72**........................ MrsCBartley 3 85+
(W J Haggas) *trckd ldrs: wnt 2nd ins fnl 3f: str run fr over 1f out to ld ins fnl f: r.o strly* **5/1**[2]
1223 **2** *5* **Seeking The Buck (USA)**[14] 4147 3-9-13 **79**........(bt[1]) MissNCarberry 7 84+
(M A Magnusson) *chsd ldrs: chal 4f out: sn led: drvn 4l clr ins fnl 3f: styd on same pce and hdd ins fnl f: kpt on wl for 2nd* **9/4**[1]
414 **3** *1* **Go But Go**[13] 4197 3-9-8 **74**........................ MsKWalsh 10 77
(E J O'Neill) *in rr: stl plenty to do 3f out: hdwy fr 2f out: styd on wl fr over 1f out and gng on cl home but nt rch ldng duo* **20/1**
-002 **4** *nk* **Mystic Storm**[12] 4231 4-9-10 **69**........................ MissMSowerby(3) 8 72
(Lady Herries) *in rr: stl plenty to do over 2f out: r.o strly fr over 1f out: gng on cl home* **14/1**
1111 **5** *1/2* **Ravenna**[15] 4139 3-9-7 **73**........................ MissEJJones 13 75
(M P Tregoning) *chsd ldrs: rdn over 2f out: sn no imp and one pce fnl f* **7/1**[3]
4531 **6** *1* **Wait For The Will (USA)**[12] 4231 11-9-11 **72**..(b) MissHayleyMoore(5) 4 72
(G L Moore) *mid-div: hdwy over 2f out: kpt on fnl f but nt rch ldrs* **12/1**
2-52 **7** *hd* **Kintbury Cross**[17] 4072 5-10-1 **71**........................ MissSBrotherton 2 71
(P D Cundell) *in tch: lost position over 4f out: drvn over 2f out: kpt on ins fnl f but nvr in contention* **9/1**
1146 **8** *3/4* **Penang Cinta**[49] 3112 4-10-1 **71**........................ MissEFolkes 14 70
(P D Evans) *t.k.h in rr: c wd into home st and hdwy fr 2f out: nvr gng pce to rch ldrs* **33/1**
0032 **9** *3/4* **Cormorant Wharf (IRE)**[8] 4356 7-9-11 **70**................ MrsMarieKing(3) 5 68
(T E Powell) *chsd ldrs: rdn 3f out: one pce fnl 2f* **25/1**
4063 **10** *3* **Sgt Schultz (IRE)**[14] 4171 4-10-7 **80**........... MissGDGracey-Davison(3) 9 73
(J S Moore) *in rr: wd into st and stl plenty to do over 2f out: styd on fr over 1f out: nvr in contention* **25/1**
0663 **11** *1/2* **Torrens (IRE)**[14] 4166 5-10-9 **79**........................ MissADeniel 11 71
(R A Fahey) *mid-div: rdn 3f out: wknd fr 2f out* **16/1**
4455 **12** *2* **Polish Power (GER)**[23] 3882 7-10-6 **76**........................ MrsSMoore 1 65
(J S Moore) *in rr: mod prog fr over 1f out* **16/1**
1234 **13** *3/4* **Great View (IRE)**[6] 4421 8-10-4 **74**........................(p) MissLEllison 6 62
(Mrs A L M King) *w ldr 7f out tl slt ld 4f out: sn hdd: wknd fr 2f out* **12/1**
-460 **14** *7* **Solo Flight**[14] 4171 10-10-1 **76**........................ MissVCartmel(5) 16 52
(H Morrison) *slowly away: hdwy and wd into st 5f out: wknd fr 3f out* **20/1**
30-0 **15** *3/4* **Thyolo (IRE)**[21] 3943 6-10-5 **80**........................ MissJFerguson(5) 15 55
(C G Cox) *bhd most of way* **20/1**
/306 **16** *3 1/2* **Bull Market (IRE)**[14] 4184 4-10-10 **80**........................ MissFayeBramley 12 50
(J A Osborne) *t.k.h: slt ld tl hdd 4f out: sn btn* **25/1**

2m 39.39s (3.40) **Going Correction** +0.425s/f (Yiel)
WFA 3 from 4yo+ 10lb **16** Ran SP% **132.5**
Speed ratings (Par 105): **105,101,101,100,100 99,99,99,98,96 96,95,94,89,89 87**
CSF £16.24 CT £229.64 TOTE £7.70: £2.00, £1.10, £5.60, £4.10; EX 25.80.
Owner Johnny Townsend **Bred** Miss S N Ralphs **Trained** Newmarket, Suffolk
FOCUS
A fair amateur riders' handicap run at a decent pace. The winner is progressive and the form is rated through the third.

4598 USK VALLEY STUD STKS (REGISTERED AS THE WASHINGTON SINGER STAKES) (LISTED RACE) 7f (S)
2:10 (2:15) (Class 1) 2-Y-0
£12,207 (£4,626; £2,315; £1,154; £578; £290) **Stalls** Centre

Form RPR
1 **1** **Sharp Nephew**[40] 3383 2-9-0 0........................ LDettori 7 100+
(B J Meehan) *in tch: pushed along 3f out: drvn to chal 1f out: led last half f: hld on wl* **7/2**[1]
1 **2** *hd* **Latin Lad**[14] 4151 2-9-0 0........................ RyanMoore 10 100+
(R Hannon) *towards rr but in tch: drvn and hdwy over 1f out: str run fnl f and fin wl: nt quite get up* **5/1**[3]
5014 **3** *1/2* **Scintillo**[17] 4057 2-9-0 94........................ JamieSpencer 3 98
(R Hannon) *chsd ldrs: rdn to take slt ld over 1f out and hung rt u.p: hdd last half f: kpt on wl* **13/2**
4 *1/2* **Melodramatic (IRE)** 2-8-6 0........................ SteveDrowne 5 89
(R Charlton) *s.i.s: bhd: gd hdwy 2f out: chsd ldrs 1f out: kpt on wl but nt quite pce to chal thrght fnl f: should improve* **7/1**
5 *hd* **Slam** 2-8-11 0........................ RichardHughes 11 94
(B W Hills) *s.i.s: bhd: hdwy fr 2f out and pushed along: styd on to chse ldrs ins fnl f and nvr quite gng pce to chal: should improve* **16/1**
24 **6** *hd* **Ramona Chase**[56] 2855 2-9-0 0........................ DPMcDonogh 6 96
(S Kirk) *t.k.h early and stdd in rr: rdn and hdwy 2f out: chal over 1f out: sltly hmpd sn after: kpt on same pce ins fnl f* **9/2**[2]
1 **7** *5* **Flight Plan**[9] 4325 2-9-0 0........................ SimonWhitworth 8 84
(C A Cyzer) *t.k.h: chsd ldr: rdn over 2f out: one pce whn hmpd appr fnl f: sn wknd* **50/1**
21 **8** *1 3/4* **Better Hand (IRE)**[24] 3856 2-9-0 0........................ TPO'Shea 1 79
(M R Channon) *led: rdn over 2f out: hdd over 1f out and hmpd: sn wknd* **7/2**[1]
9 *16* **Tharawaat (IRE)** 2-8-11 0........................ RHills 4 36
(B W Hills) *s.i.s: in rr and sn pushed along: wknd fr 1/2-way* **25/1**
10 *1* **Shishio** 2-8-11 0........................ MickyFenton 9 34
(W De Best-Turner) *s.i.s: plld hrd: sn bhd* **100/1**

1m 26.53s (-0.47) **Going Correction** 0.0s/f (Good) **10** Ran SP% **117.8**
Speed ratings (Par 102): **102,101,101,100,100 100,94,92,74,73**
CSF £21.23 TOTE £4.20: £1.70, £2.10, £2.60; EX 20.00 Trifecta £59.60 Pool £411.82 - 4.90 winning units.
Owner Saleh Al Homeizi & Imad Al Sagar **Bred** Keith Wills **Trained** Manton, Wilts
■ Stewards' Enquiry : Jamie Spencer three-day ban: careless riding (Aug 31- Sep 2)
FOCUS
The pace was strong from the outset, but the first six home finished in a heap and the bare form looks just ordinary for the grade.
NOTEBOOK
Sharp Nephew built on the promise he showed when winning on his debut at Windsor to follow up in this Listed contest, but he was made to work hard. Having had to be niggled along to keep tabs on the leaders, he stayed on strongly for pressure, clearly appreciating the strong pace, and just managed to hold off the fast-finishing Latin Lad. He has a host of big-race entries and could be aimed at the Champagne Stakes. (op 9-2)
Latin Lad was an unconsidered 33/1 shot when winning on his debut at Goodwood, but there was clearly no fluke about that success and he ran a terrific race in defeat stepped up in class. He took a while to pick up, but was flying at the finish and would probably have got up in a few more strides. (op 7-1)
Scintillo, fourth in the Vintage Stakes on his previous start, ran a game race in this lesser contest, but he did not help his chance by hanging right under pressure. (op 8-1)
Melodramatic(IRE) ◆, a daughter of Sadler's Wells, who is closely related to top-class sprinter Tante Rose, out of a smart multiple 5f-7f winner, holds entries in the Moyglare, the Fillies' Mile and the Cheveley Park Stakes. She made a most eye-catching racecourse debut, keeping on very nicely in the closing stages despite showing signs of inexperience and this must rates a terrific effort against a bunch of colts with some useful form to their name. She looks a smart filly in the making. (op 9-2)
Slam ◆, a Beat Hollow colt, out of an unraced half-sister to 1m3f winner Ballet Suite, was another debutant to run with real credit. Slowly away from the stalls, he took a while to pick up when asked, but kept on very nicely in the closing stages. There should be plenty of improvement to come and he looks capable of developing into a useful sort. (op 25-1)
Ramona Chase looked slightly unlucky in the Chesham Stakes on his previous start but, although slightly hampered again this time, he never really looked like winning. He again took a bit of a grip and will need to learn to settle better in future. (op 7-2)
Flight Plan ◆, who landed a bit of a gamble when winning on his debut at Folkestone, would have been a few lengths closer had he not been hampered around a furlong from the finish. He is clearly useful. (op 66-1)
Better Hand(IRE) probably went off a bit too quick. (op 4-1)

4599 CGA GEOFFREY FREER STKS (GROUP 3) 1m 5f 61y
2:45 (2:47) (Class 1) 3-Y-0+ **£26,686** (£10,114; £5,061; £2,523; £1,264) **Stalls** Centre

Form RPR
-451 **1** **Papal Bull**[37] 3461 4-9-7 118........................ RyanMoore 6 120
(Sir Michael Stoute) *hld up in rr: nudged along 4f out: hdwy 3f out: trckd ldr over 2f out: led appr fnl f: sn in command: comf* **6/4**[1]
-242 **2** *4* **Shahin (USA)**[37] 3461 4-9-3 113........................(v) RHills 3 110
(M P Tregoning) *led after 3f: hdd over 7f out: led over 4f out: pushed along over 2f out: hdd appr fnl f and sn outpcd* **3/1**[3]
0000 **3** *4* **Land 'n Stars**[16] 4091 7-9-3 102........................ PaulDoe 4 104
(R A Fahey) *trckd ldrs: upsides 6f out to 5f out: rdn 3f out: styd on same pce* **20/1**
6544 **4** *10* **The Whistling Teal**[21] 3973 11-9-3 98........................ SteveDrowne 2 89
(G Wragg) *led 3f: led again over 7f out: hdd over 4f out: wknd fr 3f out* **25/1**
0-11 **5** *18* **Classic Punch (IRE)**[22] 3912 4-9-3 110........................ LDettori 1 62
(D R C Elsworth) *t.k.h: hld up in rr: pushed along and c towards stands' side over 4f out: no rspnse and sn wknd* **7/4**[2]

2m 53.89s (2.90) **Going Correction** +0.55s/f (Yiel) **5** Ran SP% **110.0**
Speed ratings (Par 113): **113,110,108,101,90**
CSF £6.37 TOTE £2.20: £1.40, £1.80; EX 6.60.
Owner Mrs J Magnier, D Smith & M Tabor **Bred** B H And C F D Simpson **Trained** Newmarket, Suffolk

FOCUS
An uncompetitive renewal of the Geoffrey Freer Stakes, which was downgraded to a Group 3 last year. The pace was good, despite the small field. An improved run from Papal Bull at face value, but the form looks less than solid.

NOTEBOOK
Papal Bull is a very quirky individual, but Ryan Moore got a good tune out of him in the Princess of Wales's Stakes on the July course last time and, with the champion back aboard, he was able to follow up in this lesser contest, with a 4lb penalty not nearly enough to stop him. The good pace played into his hands and he proved far too good for this lot, hardly displaying any signs of waywardness in the process. This was the furthest trip he has raced over to date, but he saw his race out very well and gives the impression he will stay even further. It would be unwise to get carried away, especially with his main market rival running a stinker, but he probably deserves another chance in a big race. (tchd 11-8)

Shahin(USA), who dead-heated for second behind Papal Bull at Newmarket on his previous start, ran another good race in defeat, but he never really looked like doing enough to reverse form with the Stoute runner. (op 7-2 tchd 4-1)

Land 'n Stars probably ran about as well as could have been expected and could do even better when returned to further. (tchd 22-1)

The Whistling Teal has been a wonderful horse over the years, but he has not shown much on his last three starts. (tchd 22-1)

Classic Punch(IRE) had created a good impression when landing a Listed race and a conditions contest on the July course recently, but he ran no sort of race returned to Group company for the first time since contesting last year's Gordon Stakes. Official explanation: jockey said gelding lost its action (op 13-8)

4600 CGA HUNGERFORD STKS (GROUP 2) 7f (S)

3:20 (3:22) (Class 1) 3-Y-O+

£48,263 (£18,292; £9,154; £4,564; £2,286; £1,147) **Stalls** Centre

Form				RPR
-100	1		**Red Evie (IRE)**[38] 3433 4-9-4 115 ... JamieSpencer 3 (M L W Bell) *hld up in rr: n.m.r over 1f out and stl plenty to do: swtchd rt and rapid hdwy ins fnl f to ld on line* **5/1**[3]	117+
-034	2	shd	**Welsh Emperor (IRE)**[49] 3098 8-9-3 109 ... MickyFenton 10 (T P Tate) *stmbld stalls: sn rcvrd and led over 5f out: rdn fr 2f out: repelled all chals ins fnl f tl hdd on line* **10/1**	116
410-	3	1	**Stronghold**[308] 5962 5-9-3 114 ... RichardHughes 2 (J H M Gosden) *trckd ldrs: rdn and styd on fr 2f out: pressed ldr ins fnl f but nvr quite on terms: outpcd nr fin* **7/1**	113
-141	4	nk	**Wake Up Maggie (IRE)**[15] 4118 4-9-0 104 ... GeorgeBaker 8 (C F Wall) *hld up in rr: smooth hdwy over 1f out: edgd sltly lft ins fnl f and r.o to press ldr: run flattened out fnl 100yds* **9/2**[2]	109
-013	5	1 1/4	**Silver Touch (IRE)**[13] 4214 4-9-0 107 ... TPO'Shea 6 (M R Channon) *trckd ldrs: stl travelling wl 2f out: rdn over 1f out and styd on same pce* **11/4**[1]	106
1	6	3	**Per Incanto (USA)**[90] 1876 3-8-12 0 ... RHills 7 (J L Dunlop) *led tl hdd over 5f out: drvn to press ldr fr 2f out: wknd fnl f* **10/1**	101
2000	7	1 1/4	**Beckermet (IRE)**[13] 4196 5-9-3 106 ... SteveDrowne 9 (R F Fisher) *trckd ldrs: rdn 2f out and sn wknd* **50/1**	97
-101	8	1	**Dubai's Touch**[14] 4148 3-8-12 110 ... GregFairley 4 (M Johnston) *chsd ldrs: drvn to chal ins fnl 3f tl over 2f out: wknd over 1f out* **16/1**	94
0-00	9	1 1/2	**Dark Islander (IRE)**[18] 4045 4-9-5 110 ... MichaelHills 5 (J W Hills) *s.i.s: in tch 1/2-way: rdn 3f out: no imp: wknd 2f out* **20/1**	92
113-	10	hd	**Caradak (IRE)**[308] 5982 6-9-7 115 ... LDettori 11 (Saeed Bin Suroor) *in rr but in tch: rdn 3f out: wknd 2f out* **6/1**	94

1m 26.09s (-0.91) **Going Correction** +0.225s/f (Good)
WFA 3 from 4yo+ 5lb 10 Ran SP% **119.1**
Speed ratings (Par 115): **114,113,112,112,110 107,106,104,103,103**
CSF £55.38 TOTE £5.20: £1.90, £2.60, £3.00; EX 56.20 Trifecta £613.00 Pool £1,381.50 - 1.60 winning units..
Owner Terry Neill **Bred** Dermot Cantillon & Forenaghts **Trained** Newmarket, Suffolk

FOCUS
A cracking renewal of the Hungerford Stakes, really competitive. The pace was sound throughout and the form looks solid.

NOTEBOOK
Red Evie(IRE) came into this with a bit to prove, having run below-par in both the Queen Anne and the Falmouth Stakes since winning the Lockinge here earlier in the year, and she had a 4lb penalty to contend with for that success, but she bounced back to her best in dramatic fashion. Holding her up well off the pace early on, her rider took an age to get after her, and she was then short of room around a furlong and a half from the finish, but she picked up in great style once in the clear to grab long-time leader Welsh Emperor in the final strides. She could now bid to follow up last year's success in the Matron Stakes at Leopardstown, and the Prix de la Foret is another option. (op 9-2 tchd 4-1)

Welsh Emperor(IRE) had been running well this season without finding his very best form, but he built on his recent fourth at Newmarket and only just failed to follow up last year's success in this race. He stumbled slightly on leaving the stalls, but it didn't cost him any ground and he ran a fine race from the front, seeing off all bar the fast-finishing Red Evie. He is entered in the Haydock Sprint Cup and that race looks a suitable target. (tchd 9-1)

Stronghold had not been seen since running well down the field in the Challenge Stakes ten months previously, but he returned to action not far off his best. This will no doubt have delighted his connections and he should be able to go on from this. (op 15-2 tchd 9-1)

Wake Up Maggie(IRE), successful in a Group 3 against her own sex at Goodwood on her previous start, looked threatening at one point, but her effort flattened out a touch late on and this ground was probably a little softer than she would have liked. (tchd 11-2)

Silver Touch(IRE) ◆, third in the Group 1 Prix Maurice de Gheest on her previous start, always just looked to be doing a little too much in the hands of O'Shea and she could find only the one pace when it mattered. All three of her career wins have come this trip, and she obviously stays, but not for the first time she gave the impression she can prove fully effective over sprint distances. She is entered in the Haydock Sprint Cup and that could the race for her. (op 7-2)

Per Incanto(USA), purchased by Hamdan Al Maktoum and transferred to John Dunlop's yard after impressively landing a 6f Group 3 when trained in Italy back in May, made a very respectable British debut. He showed plenty of early speed, but just raced a little too freely and failed to sustain his challenge late on against mainly match-fit rivals. He should see this sort of trip out better in future with the benefit of this outing, and a faster surface should also help him, but it may just be that sprinting is his game. (op 8-1)

Beckermet(IRE) ran about as well as could have been expected in this company. (op 66-1 tchd 33-1)

Dubai's Touch found this much tougher than the Listed contest he landed at Goodwood on his previous start. (op 14-1)

Caradak(IRE) had not run since October, his reappearance having been delayed by surgery to a fetlock. He has always looked at his best on quick ground and he would not have appreciated the easing conditions. (op 8-1)

4601 CGA LADIES DAY H'CAP 7f (S)

3:55 (3:57) (Class 2) (0-100,100) 3-Y-O+

£12,464 (£3,732; £1,866; £934; £466; £234) **Stalls** Centre

Form				RPR
5311	1		**Lovelace**[6] 4420 3-8-13 91 6ex ... JamieSpencer 13 (M Johnston) *chsd ldrs: led 2f out: hrd drvn and styd on wl fnl f* **5/2**[1]	102
-106	2	1	**Folly Lodge**[28] 3745 3-8-7 85 ... MichaelHills 14 (B W Hills) *s.i.s: in rr: hdwy over 2f out: styd on wl to chse wnr ins fnl f but a hld* **17/2**	93
4003	3	3/4	**Partners In Jazz (USA)**[7] 4401 6-9-10 97 ... RyanMoore 12 (T D Barron) *in rr: hdwy over 2f out: styd on wl to chse wnr ins fnl f but a hld: ct for 2nd nr fin* **9/2**[3]	105
0001	4	3/4	**Jamieson Gold (IRE)**[2] 4548 4-9-1 88 6ex ... RHills 7 (B W Hills) *chsd ldrs: rdn over 2f out: styd same pce fnl f* **6/1**	94
6605	5	3/4	**Majuro (IRE)**[17] 4062 3-9-1 93 ... ChrisCatlin 4 (M R Channon) *chsd ldrs: rdn over 2f out: styd on same pce fnl f* **33/1**	95
-260	6	1 1/4	**Cape Of Luck (IRE)**[7] 4377 4-9-1 88 ... LDettori 10 (P Mitchell) *hld up off pce in rr: pushed along 2f out: hdwy fnl f and gng on cl home: nvr in contention* **14/1**	89
6600	7	nk	**Phluke**[13] 4195 6-9-0 87 ... StephenCarson 2 (Eve Johnson Houghton) *chsd ldrs: rdn over 2f out: wknd fnl f* **50/1**	87
0	8	3	**Formax (FR)**[18] 4043 5-9-2 89 ... SteveDrowne 8 (M P Tregoning) *in tch: rdn over 2f out: wknd over 1f out* **33/1**	81
0605	9	nk	**Burning Incense (IRE)**[21] 3941 4-9-9 96 ... RichardHughes 5 (R Charlton) *in rr: rdn over 2f out: nvr in contention* **7/2**[2]	87
0020	10	1 1/2	**Go On Be A Tiger (USA)**[37] 3463 3-8-12 90 ... TPO'Shea 1 (M R Channon) *in rr: rdn over 2f out: nvr in contention* **33/1**	75
0500	11	3/4	**Royal Storm (IRE)**[17] 4062 8-8-9 82 ... JimCrowley 11 (Mrs A J Perrett) *chsd ldrs: rdn 3f out: wknd 2f out* **50/1**	67
0555	12	nk	**The Kiddykid (IRE)**[5] 4456 7-9-3 90 ... StephenDonohoe 9 (P D Evans) *led: hdd over 3f out: sn led again: hdd u.p 2f out: sn wknd* **25/1**	74
0000	13	4	**King's Caprice**[21] 3941 6-9-6 99 ... (t) TravisBlock(3) 3 (J A Geake) *trckd ldr: slt ld over 3f out: sn hdd: wknd over 2f out* **16/1**	72
0-10	14	1/2	**Seal Point (USA)**[140] 859 3-9-8 100 ... PaulEddery 6 (Christian Wroe) *s.i.s: a in rr* **66/1**	70

1m 26.92s (-0.08) **Going Correction** +0.225s/f (Good)
WFA 3 from 4yo+ 5lb 14 Ran SP% **124.4**
Speed ratings (Par 109): **109,107,107,106,105 103,103,100,99,98 97,96,92,91**
CSF £24.48 CT £94.00 TOTE £3.20: £1.60, £3.30, £2.10; EX 32.80 Trifecta £179.70 Pool £835.50 - 3.30 winning units..
Owner Hamad Suhail **Bred** Mrs Mary Taylor **Trained** Middleham Moor, N Yorks

FOCUS
A decent handicap and the time was good, just 0.83 seconds slower than the Group 2 Hungerford Stakes. The form looks very solid, with the progressive winner up another 5lb.

NOTEBOOK
Lovelace ◆ looked well-in under the penalty he picked up for his recent emphatic success at Leicester, but both that win and his victory at Haydock the time before came on quick ground and, being by Royal Applause, there had to be doubts about him handling the easy ground, even though he won his maiden on ground with soft in the description. As it turned out, the conditions did not pose him any problems whatsoever and he completed the hat-trick in decisive fashion, recording a decent time in the process. He has a most progressive profile and is a smart prospect for the remainder of this season and beyond. (op 3-1)

Folly Lodge, representing last year's winning stable, would not have minded the easy ground and ran well off bottom weight. (op 8-1 tchd 15-2)

Partners In Jazz(USA) is a very useful handicapper who usually runs well in these types of races, but the two who finished in front of him were less exposed. (op 5-1)

Jamieson Gold(IRE), whose 6lb penalty for his recent Sandown win put him on the same mark as when landing this race last year, ran a creditable race in defeat. (op 13-2)

Majuro(IRE) has been highly tried this season and is clearly well regarded. This looks to be his sort of level and he ran well, especially considering he was a touch short of room around a furlong out.

Cape Of Luck(IRE) was well off the pace for much of the way and it was a surprise to see him finish so close. He has never won beyond 7f, but on this evidence he is surely worth another try over 1m. (op 12-1)

Burning Incense(IRE) never got involved and was a little disappointing. (op 4-1)

4602 BBC RADIO BERKSHIRE EUROPEAN BREEDERS' FUND MAIDEN FILLIES' STKS 6f 8y

4:25 (4:29) (Class 4) 2-Y-O

£6,477 (£1,927; £963; £481) **Stalls** Centre

Form				RPR
4	1		**Rinterval (IRE)**[22] 3895 2-9-0 0 ... RichardHughes 5 (R Hannon) *trckd ldrs: led 1f out: pushed out fnl f* **7/4**[1]	85
30	2	2	**Amylee (IRE)**[22] 3895 2-9-0 0 ... JamieSpencer 12 (C G Cox) *chsd ldrs: rdn 2f out: kpt on to chse wnr ins fnl f but no imp* **11/1**	79
	3	shd	**Applauded (IRE)** 2-9-0 0 ... SteveDrowne 7 (B J Meehan) *s.i.s: in rr: hdwy over 2f out: kpt on wl fnl f but nvr gng pce to trble wnr* **5/1**[3]	79
0	4	1/2	**Frivolous (IRE)**[7] 4402 2-9-0 0 ... RobertHavlin 8 (J H M Gosden) *led: rdn 2f out: hdd 1f out: one pce* **16/1**	77
	5	1 1/2	**Au Pair (IRE)** 2-9-0 0 ... KDarley 16 (P W Chapple-Hyam) *s.i.s: swished tail thrght: sn chsng ldrs: rdn over 1f out: styd on same pce* **10/1**	73
	6	3/4	**Clifton Four (USA)** 2-9-0 0 ... RyanMoore 3 (R Hannon) *chsd ldrs: rdn over 2f out: kpt on but nvr gng pce to be competitive* **25/1**	70
0	7	1 1/2	**The Jostler**[17] 4061 2-9-0 0 ... ChrisCatlin 4 (B W Hills) *in rr: pushed along over 2f out: r.o ins fnl f but nvr in contention* **40/1**	66
00	8	1/2	**Polish Priory (IRE)**[110] 1354 2-9-0 0 ... StephenDonohoe 1 (P D Evans) *pressed ldrs: rdn over 2f out: wknd appr* **100/1**	64
	9	nk	**Albaraari** 2-9-0 0 ... RHills 10 (Sir Michael Stoute) *slowly away: bhd tl kpt on fr over 1f out* **9/1**	64
6	10	1 1/2	**Acquifer**[22] 3895 2-9-0 0 ... LDettori 14 (J L Dunlop) *in rr tl styd on fr over 1f out: nvr in contention* **9/2**[2]	59
0	11	3/4	**Colmar Magic (IRE)**[12] 4232 2-9-0 0 ... RichardSmith 6 (R Hannon) *chsd ldrs: rdn over 3f out: wknd ins fnl 2f* **66/1**	57
	12	1/2	**Dellini (IRE)** 2-9-0 0 ... TPO'Shea 2 (M R Channon) *slowly away: a towards rr* **20/1**	55
	13	1 3/4	**Cheviot Red** 2-9-0 0 ... NelsonDeSouza 13 (B J Meehan) *a towards rr* **20/1**	50

00 **14** *11* **Victoria Valentine**[29] 3706 2-9-0 0 MichaelHills 15 17
(B W Hills) *early spd* **16/1**

50 **15** *6* **Talamahana**[53] 2968 2-9-0 0 DPMcDonogh 11 —
(S Kirk) *chsd ldrs over 3f* **40/1**

1m 15.86s (1.54) **Going Correction** +0.225s/f (Good) **15** Ran SP% **131.1**
Speed ratings (Par 93): **98,95,95,94,92 91,89,88,88,86 85,84,82,67,59**
CSF £23.97 TOTE £2.50: £1.40, £3.70, £2.50; EX 28.70.
Owner Fergus Jones **Bred** Irish National Stud **Trained** East Everleigh, Wilts

FOCUS
A fair fillies' maiden rated around the runner-up to the level of her debut.

NOTEBOOK
Rinterval(IRE) built on the promise she showed when fourth in a good maiden at Ascot on her debut to get off the mark at the second attempt. She does not hold any Group-race entries, but took this in good style and her connections may be tempted to let her take her chance in the Goffs Fillies Million in September. (op 2-1 tchd 13-8 and 9-4 in place)
Amylee(IRE) failed to confirm the promise of her Salisbury debut effort when well behind today's winner at Ascot on her previous start, but this was much better. Also a Goffs Fillies Million entrant, she looks capable of winning a maiden, but also now has the option of going down the nursery route. (op 12-1)
Applauded(IRE), a Royal Applause half-sister to high-class 1m4f winner Thakafaat, who was also a 7f winner at two, out of a 6f juvenile scorer, fared best of the newcomers in third. She was left with a fair bit to do after starting slowly, but there was a lot to like about the way she stuck to her task late on and she should be able to improve. (op 7-2)
Frivolous(IRE) showed good pace on this drop in trip and looked to improve on the form she showed on her debut at Newmarket. (op 14-1)
Au Pair(IRE), a Domedriver half-sister to multiple 1m4f-2m winner Let It Be, out of a 1m juvenile winner, showed plenty of ability on her racecourse debut, although it was a little bit concerning that she continually swished her tail. She should be suited by a step up in trip. (op 12-1)
Clifton Four(USA), an 80,000gns daughter of Forest Wildcat, half-sister to dual 1m2f winner Blacktoft, out of a winner over 1m2f, offered some promise on her debut and should improve with time and distance.
Albaraari, a 200,000gns daughter of Green Desert, closely related to Moondreamer, who was placed over 1m4f, out of a dual 1m-1m2f winner in France, was never seen with a chance but should improve a fair bit for the experience. (op 12-1)
Acquifer failed to build on the form she showed behind today's winner on her debut. (op 8-1)

4603 MIRAGE SIGNS H'CAP — 1m 2f 6y
5:00 (5:00) (Class 4) (0-85,84) 3-Y-O **£5,181** (£1,541; £770; £384) **Stalls** Centre

Form RPR

1 **1** **Pippa Greene**[147] 764 3-9-5 **82** JamieSpencer 9 94+
(P F I Cole) *hld up in rr: hdwy over 2f out: led over 1f out: hung rt u.p ins fnl f and kpt on strly* **9/2**[2]

1260 **2** *2* **Gulf Express (USA)**[58] 2788 3-9-7 **84** RyanMoore 13 92+
(Sir Michael Stoute) *hld up in rr: hdwy fr 3f out: rdn to chse wnr ins fnl f but no imp* **7/2**[1]

1000 **3** *2 1/2* **Hannicean**[21] 3960 3-8-12 **75** KDarley 8 78
(M A Jarvis) *w ldr tl led over 3f out: sn rdn: hdd over 1f out and styd on same pce* **20/1**

2021 **4** *nk* **Risque Heights**[7] 4392 3-9-0 **77** GeorgeBaker 3 79
(G A Butler) *in tch: rdn and hdwy 2f out: pressed ldrs over 1f out: wknd ins fnl f* **10/1**

5312 **5** *2* **Novikov**[36] 3514 3-9-7 **84** RobertHavlin 4 82
(J H M Gosden) *chsd ldrs: drvn to chal 2f out: wknd over 1f out* **13/2**[3]

431 **6** *7* **Viva La Flag (USA)**[23] 3881 3-9-2 **79** LDettori 12 63
(J L Dunlop) *chsd ldrs: rdn 3f out: wknd 2f out* **7/2**[1]

6060 **7** *3/4* **Opera Crown (IRE)**[46] 3189 3-8-2 **65** NelsonDeSouza 6 48
(P F I Cole) *t.k.h: chsd ldrs to 3f out: sn wknd* **33/1**

0146 **8** *11* **Radical Views**[36] 3495 3-8-12 **75** MichaelHills 7 36
(B W Hills) *bhd most of way* **16/1**

3130 **9** *9* **Surrey Spinner**[85] 1987 3-9-6 **83** JimCrowley 5 26
(Mrs A J Perrett) *slt ld tl hdd over 3f out and wknd rapidly* **12/1**

0305 **10** *2 1/2* **Eau Good**[29] 3709 3-9-6 **83** RichardHughes 2 21
(B G Powell) *a towards rr* **7/1**

2m 12.23s (3.52) **Going Correction** +0.55s/f (Yiel) **10** Ran SP% **118.8**
Speed ratings (Par 102): **107,105,103,103,101 95,95,86,79,77**
CSF £21.10 CT £290.23 TOTE £4.70: £1.50, £1.90, £6.50; EX 27.90 Place 6 £35.78, Place 5 £18.22..
Owner R A H Evans **Bred** D And Mrs V Fleet **Trained** Whatcombe, Oxon

FOCUS
A decent handicap on paper, but the early pace was not that strong and the form probably wants treating with some caution.
Eau Good Official explanation: jockey said gelding lost its action
T/Jkpt: £2,958.00 to a £1 stake. Pool: £18,748.50. 4.50 winning tickets. T/Plt: £80.90 to a £1 stake. Pool: £130,111.45. 1,172.90 winning tickets. T/Qpdt: £16.60 to a £1 stake. Pool: £5,532.00. 246.15 winning tickets. ST

4584
NEWMARKET (JULY) (R-H)
Saturday, August 18

OFFICIAL GOING: Good (8.5)
Wind: Fresh across Weather: Overcast

4604 UNICORN ASSET MANAGEMENT JULY COURSE SERIES EBF MAIDEN STKS (QUALIFIER) — 6f
1:55 (1:55) (Class 3) 2-Y-O **£6,477** (£1,927; £963; £481) **Stalls** Low

Form RPR

1 **Young Pretender (FR)** 2-9-3 0 MartinDwyer 3 91+
(J H M Gosden) *s.i.s: hld up: hdwy to ld over 1f out: sn hung rt: r.o wl* **7/2**[2]

0 **2** *3* **House**[18] 4048 2-9-3 0 TedDurcan 1 82
(M R Channon) *hld up in tch: rdn to chse wnr fnl f: no imp* **7/2**[2]

3 *2 1/2* **Manassas (IRE)** 2-9-3 0 JohnEgan 2 75
(B J Meehan) *prom: rdn over 2f out: styd on same pce appr fnl f* **6/1**[3]

200 **4** *nk* **Atheer Dubai (IRE)**[37] 3459 2-9-3 91 EddieAhern 4 74
(C E Brittain) *chsd clr ldr: rdn over 1f out: wknd ins fnl f* **6/4**[1]

0 **5** *3 1/2* **Memphis City (USA)**[8] 4362 2-9-3 0 SebSanders 6 63
(J Noseda) *s.i.s: hld up: hdwy u.p over 1f out: wknd fnl f* **14/1**

00 **6** *2 1/2* **Maccabeus**[15] 4132 2-9-0 0 JerryO'Dwyer(3) 7 56
(P J O'Gorman) *led and sn clr: hdd and wknd over 1f out* **40/1**

00 **7** *shd* **Battlecruiser (IRE)**[49] 3092 2-9-3 0 DaneO'Neill 5 55
(M Johnston) *chsd ldrs: rdn 1/2-way: wknd 2f out* **10/1**

1m 13.94s (0.59) **Going Correction** +0.15s/f (Good) **7** Ran SP% **116.9**
Speed ratings (Par 98): **102,98,94,94,89 86,86**
CSF £16.81 TOTE £4.20: £2.20, £2.40; EX 18.90.
Owner H R H Princess Haya Of Jordan **Bred** Carl Holt **Trained** Newmarket, Suffolk

FOCUS
A decent maiden won in taking style by debutant Young Pretender and the form looks sound.

NOTEBOOK
Young Pretender(FR), a 175,000gns son of Oasis Dream, is bred to be effective at up to 1m2f on his dam's side, but he showed here that his sire has injected a fair amount of speed and, judging by the way he pulled clear, it is not going to be long before he is contesting Group events. Slowly away, he impressed with the way in which he travelled into contention and still looked quite green under pressure, suggesting there is improvement to come. He is in both the Dewhurst and Racing Post Trophy, but connections may opt to go for something a little smaller first. (tchd 4-1)
House, who looked as though the run would do him good on his recent Goodwood debut, came with his challenge from over a furlong out, but found himself readily outpaced by the winner and could make no real impression. He came away from the third and should have no trouble finding a standard maiden. (op 9-2 tchd 10-3)
Manassas(IRE), a Mill Reef entrant, comes from a stable who can get one ready first time and he shaped nicely back in third, just getting the better of favourite Atheer Dubai. It is reasonable to expect improvement and he looks another capable of landing a maiden. (op 13-2)
Atheer Dubai(IRE) had shown a decent level of ability in each of his three previous starts, twice in Group 2s, and this drop in grade was exactly what he needed, but it looks as though he has failed to make any further progression and he proved to be no match for the smart-looking winner. This was obviously disappointing and he looks one to have reservations over now. (op 7-4 tchd 15-8)
Memphis City(USA), who beat only one home on his recent course debut, was down in trip and ran a little better, but looks like more a nursery type. (op 11-1)
Maccabeus cut out the early running at a decent clip, but was never going to stay there and he is another likely sort for nurseries.
Battlecruiser(IRE) has thus far been a bit disappointing and he again failed to offer much. However, his trainer's juveniles are beginning to hit top form now and this fellow could not be ignored in handicaps. (tchd 8-1)

4605 LLOYDS TSB INSURANCE NURSERY — 5f
2:25 (2:25) (Class 3) 2-Y-O **£6,477** (£1,927; £963; £481) **Stalls** Low

Form RPR

12 **1** **Little Big Boy (IRE)**[36] 3486 2-9-0 **77** EddieAhern 6 80
(R Hannon) *s.i.s: hld up: hdwy over 1f out: rdn to ld ins fnl f: r.o* **5/1**[3]

520 **2** *1/2* **Kashoof**[17] 4061 2-9-7 **84** MartinDwyer 8 85
(J L Dunlop) *mid-div: sn pushed along: hdwy 1/2-way: led over 1f out: rdn and hdd ins fnl f: r.o* **5/1**[3]

3116 **3** *nk* **Brassini**[11] 4255 2-9-7 **84** DaneO'Neill 5 84
(B R Millman) *chsd ldrs: rdn over 1f out: r.o* **6/1**

3230 **4** *3/4* **Rio Princess (IRE)**[38] 3417 2-8-11 **74** JohnEgan 4 71
(T G Mills) *prom: outpcd 1/2-way: r.o ins fnl f* **8/1**

1503 **5** *2 1/2* **Thunder Bay**[13] 4193 2-9-5 **82** SamHitchcott 3 70
(M R Channon) *prom: outpcd over 3f out: rallied over 1f out: styd on same pce ins fnl f* **4/1**[2]

3211 **6** *hd* **Concertmaster**[38] 3426 2-9-5 **82** SebSanders 2 54
(R M Beckett) *chsd ldrs: rdn over 1f out: wknd ins fnl f* **3/1**[1]

6260 **7** *3* **Baytown Blaze**[77] 2232 2-9-0 **77** HayleyTurner 1 65
(J Ryan) *chsd ldr: rdn whn bmpd over 1f out: wknd ins fnl f* **25/1**

0050 **8** *1 1/4* **Orpen's Art (IRE)**[9] 4315 2-7-9 **61** oh6 (b) WilliamBuick(3) 7 38
(N A Callaghan) *sn led: rdn: hung lft and hdd over 1f out: wknd ins fnl f* **16/1**

61.08 secs (1.52) **Going Correction** +0.15s/f (Good) **8** Ran SP% **113.5**
Speed ratings (Par 98): **93,92,91,90,86 86,81,79**
CSF £29.60 CT £151.75 TOTE £3.90: £1.60, £2.20, £2.20; EX 13.70 Trifecta £34.00 Pool £258.60 - 5.40 winning units..
Owner Kemal Kurt **Bred** Tally-Ho Stud **Trained** East Everleigh, Wilts

FOCUS
A competitive nursery and solid enough with those in behind the winner near their marks.

NOTEBOOK
Little Big Boy(IRE), unable to build on his winning debut when second in soft ground at Chepstow, appreciated the return to a sounder surface and ran on well under pressure to make a winning handicap debut. He will need to progress again to defy a rise, but this son of Danetime, who is all about speed, is in good hands to do so. (op 13-2)
Kashoof had the form to win this having finished second to the smart Laureldean Gale at the course last month, but she flopped at Goodwood last time and looked vulnerable to an improver here, with there being a question mark over whether she had the speed to cope with 5f. She got a little outpaced after a couple of furlongs, but really got going in the final quarter mile and looked the winner when going on a furlong out, but Little Big Boy soon had her move covered and she was done for speed in the end. Winning a handicap is not going to prove easy off this sort of mark, but at a return to 6f should suit. (op 10-3)
Brassini, who failed to stay the 6f trip when bidding for a hat-trick at Chepstow last time, seemed more comfortable over this distance and he ran well off a 3lb lower mark. (op 13-2)
Rio Princess(IRE) had shown some fair form in maidens, but she needed to have progressed to defy this mark on her handicap debut and she was not up to it over what proved an inadequate trip. (op 10-1)
Thunder Bay did well back in the spring, but his two handicap efforts have both suggested he is too high in the weights at present.
Concertmaster, on a hat-trick following wins on the Polytrack at Kempton and Lingfield, did not run his race back on turf and dropped out tamely in the final furlong. This was clearly not his form. (op 7-2)

4606 SKYBET.COM GREY HORSE H'CAP — 6f
3:00 (3:00) (Class 4) (0-85,83) 3-Y-O+
£12,464 (£3,732; £1,866; £934; £466; £234) **Stalls** Low

Form RPR

2430 **1** **Compton's Eleven**[21] 3953 6-9-10 **83** TedDurcan 15 89
(M R Channon) *chsd ldrs: rdn to ld 1f out: r.o* **5/1**[2]

2540 **2** *shd* **Certain Justice (USA)**[179] 509 9-8-11 **70** HayleyTurner 17 76
(Stef Liddiard) *hld up: rdn over 2f out: hdwy over 1f out: chsd wnr fnl f: r.o* **12/1**

2000 **3** *1 1/4* **Grey Boy (GER)**[64] 2626 6-8-3 **69** MarkCoumbe(7) 9 71
(A W Carroll) *chsd ldrs: led 2f out: rdn and hdd 1f out: styd on same pce* **20/1**

-060 **4** *3/4* **Bridge It Jo**[50] 3061 3-9-1 **80** JerryO'Dwyer(3) 8 79
(G G Margarson) *hld up: swtchd rt over 1f out: r.o ins fnl f: nt rch ldrs* **50/1**

3606 **5** *hd* **Star Strider**[30] 3688 3-8-8 **70** (p) MartinDwyer 13 69
(A M Balding) *hld up: plld hrd: hdwy over 2f out: rdn over 1f out: styd on same pce ins fnl f* **20/1**

3640 **6** *1* **Nautical**[7] 4390 9-8-2 **64** LiamJones(3) 18 60
(A W Carroll) *s.i.s: hld up: hdwy over 1f out: sn rdn: styd on same pce* **9/1**

660 **7** *shd* **Pic Up Sticks**[16] 4095 8-8-8 **70** RichardKingscote(3) 1 65
(B G Powell) *chsd ldrs: rdn and ev ch over 1f out: no ex ins fnl f* **7/2**[1]

40-6 **8** *hd* **Middleton Grey**[34] 3572 9-8-9 **68** (b) FergusSweeney 6 63
(A G Newcombe) *s.i.s and hld up: hdwy 2f out: sn rdn: no ex ins fnl f* **8/1**[3]

2226 **9** *1* **Milton's Keen**[11] 4259 4-7-9 **57** oh1 WilliamBuick(3) 5 49
(M Salaman) *led: hdd over 4f out: rdn whn nt clr run and outpcd over 1f out: r.o ins fnl f* **11/1**

420 **10** ¾ **Summer Recluse (USA)**[9] 4320 8-8-7 **66** ow2..................(t) JohnEgan 7 55
(J M Bradley) *hld up: rdn over 2f out: no imp fnl f* **12/1**

00-0 **11** *hd* **Clearing Sky (IRE)**[14] 4165 6-8-2 **61** oh7 ow4........... MatthewHenry 12 50
(J R Boyle) *chsd ldrs: led over 2f out: sn hdd: wknd ins fnl f* **20/1**

3036 **12** ¾ **Legal Set (IRE)**[18] 4038 11-8-2 **66** oh2 ow9................(b) AnnStokell(5) 11 52
(Miss A Stokell) *chsd ldrs: wkng whn n.m.r over 1f out* **66/1**

6266 **13** *1* **Paris Bell**[20] 4006 5-9-3 **76**.. PaulQuinn 14 59
(T D Easterby) *dwlt: hld up: plld hrd: rdn whn hmpd 1f out: n.d* **8/1**[3]

5050 **14** *shd* **Capricho (IRE)**[7] 4395 10-8-1 **60**..................................(b) DaleGibson 4 43
(J Akehurst) *chsd ldrs: lost pl over 3f out: in rr whn hmpd over 1f out* **16/1**

136 **15** *1* **Calypso King**[30] 3676 4-8-6 **65**... LPKeniry 3 44
(Peter Grayson) *prom: rdn 2f out: wknd 1f out* **25/1**

00-6 **16** 1½ **Silver Appraisal**[88] 1923 3-7-6 **61** oh1 ow1........................... KMay(7) 10 36
(Pat Eddery) *chsd ldrs: wkng whn hmpd over 1f out* **33/1**

262- **17** *4* **Centreboard (USA)**[358] 4754 3-8-10 **72**........................... SebSanders 2 34
(M W Easterby) *led over 4f out: hdd over 2f out: wknd over 1f out* **12/1**

1m 13.72s (0.37) **Going Correction** +0.15s/f (Good)
WFA 3 from 4yo+ 3lb **17** Ran SP% **132.9**
Speed ratings (Par 105): **103,102,101,100,99 98,98,98,96,95 95,94,93,93,91 89,84**
CSF £64.17 CT £1193.81 TOTE £6.10: £2.00, £3.80, £5.80, £7.40; EX 85.00 Trifecta £651.50 Part won. Pool £917.70 - 0.10 winning units..
Owner PCM Racing **Bred** Lady Cobham **Trained** West Ilsley, Berks

FOCUS
A competitive sprint handicap for greys likely to produce winners with the form straightforward through the runner-up.
Compton's Eleven Official explanation: trainer's rep had no explanation for the apparent improvement in form
Paris Bell Official explanation: jockey said gelding suffered interference in running

4607 LLOYDS TSB COMMERCIAL BANKING H'CAP 6f
3:35 (3:35) (Class 2) (0-105,102) 3-Y-O
£18,696 (£5,598; £2,799; £1,401; £699; £351) **Stalls** Low

Form RPR

0113 **1** **King's Apostle (IRE)**[7] 4374 3-8-3 **87**............................. LiamJones(3) 1 96
(W J Haggas) *trckd ldrs: rdn to ld ins fnl f: r.o* **16/1**

1120 **2** ½ **Off The Record**[29] 3720 3-9-0 **95**.. OscarUrbina 8 102
(J G Given) *chsd ldr: shkn up over 2f out: rdn to ld over 1f out: hdd ins fnl f: r.o* **9/2**[2]

1312 **3** *nk* **Northern Dare (IRE)**[15] 4127 3-8-2 **83** oh1............. SilvestreDeSousa 2 89
(D Nicholls) *led: rdn and hdd over 1f out: ev ch ins fnl f: r.o* **9/1**

4330 **4** 1¼ **Kyle (IRE)**[16] 4093 3-8-4 **85**.. MartinDwyer 4 87
(R Hannon) *hld up: hdwy over 1f out: nt rch ldrs* **16/1**

-322 **5** *hd* **Special Day**[21] 3944 3-8-8 **89** ow3..................................... SebSanders 5 90
(B W Hills) *hld up: swtchd rt and hdwy over 1f out: rdn and hung lft ins fnl f: styd on* **11/2**[3]

1211 **6** ¾ **Royal Rock**[26] 3797 3-9-0 **95**... TedDurcan 7 94
(C F Wall) *hld up in tch: rdn over 1f out: styd on same pce fnl f* **7/4**[1]

15-0 **7** *nk* **Abunai**[21] 3944 3-7-13 **83** oh3... WilliamBuick(3) 6 81
(R Charlton) *trckd ldrs: rdn over 1f out: no ex ins fnl f* **8/1**

0400 **8** 1¾ **Mastership (IRE)**[14] 4150 3-9-3 **98**..................................(b) EddieAhern 9 90
(C E Brittain) *hld up: effrt over 2f out: wknd fnl f* **7/1**

1310 **9** *1* **El Bosque (IRE)**[21] 3975 3-9-2 **102**........................... JamesMillman(5) 3 91
(B R Millman) *mid-div: pushed along 1/2-way: wknd fnl f* **25/1**

1m 12.71s (-0.64) **Going Correction** +0.15s/f (Good) **9** Ran SP% **119.2**
Speed ratings (Par 106): **110,109,108,107,107 106,105,103,101**
CSF £89.25 CT £711.05 TOTE £16.20: £2.80, £2.20, £3.20; EX 85.50 TRIFECTA Not won..
Owner Wentworth Racing (pty) Ltd **Bred** Wentworth Racing **Trained** Newmarket, Suffolk

FOCUS
A good three-year-old sprint handicap and solid form rated around the placed horses.

NOTEBOOK
King's Apostle(IRE) fell short off this mark when bidding for a hat-trick at Ascot last time, but he was still not beaten far and it was a surprise to see him so readily dismissed in the market at 16/1. Always well positioned, he quickened to lead over a furlong out and was always just doing enough to hold the persistent Off The Record, who was challenging more towards the centre track. He is evidently still on the up should not be put up too much for this, so can continue to give a good account.
Off The Record, a multiple All-Weather winner, ran the first poor race of his career when faced with soft ground over 5f at Pontefract last time, but he bounced right back to his best and the way he was finishing suggested he would have benefited from being made more use of. He still seems to be progressing. (op 5-1)
Northern Dare(IRE) has been most progressive of late, shooting up 20lb in the last five weeks, and this was another fine effort from 1lb out of the handicap. There are few people better with sprinters than his trainer and there should be more to come. (op 8-1 tchd 10-1)
Kyle(IRE) has been running well off marks in the 80s without suggesting he is quite up to winning a good handicap and that was again the case here. (op 20-1)
Special Day, whose rider was putting up 3lb overweight, has been edging up the weights without winning and she is unlikely to be eased much for this. (op 15-2)
Royal Rock, another really progressive handicap sprinter, was a harsh-looking 11lb higher than when winning at Windsor last time and having travelled well he was unable to pick up in his customary fashion. It is probable this mark proved beyond him, but there is still time for him to improve again. Official explanation: jockey said gelding was unsuited by the good ground (op 15-8 tchd 2-1)
Abunai has yet to recapture her best form and may still be in need of more time. (op 15-2)
Mastership(IRE), who caught the eye of many when 'winning' the far-side race in a hugely competitive handicap at the July meeting, was never involved from a poor draw in the Stewards' Cup latest, but much better could have been expected here and the way in which he folded under pressure was particularly disappointing. He has tons of ability, but it is proving quite difficult to get him to win. (op 8-1 tchd 13-2)

4608 LLOYDS TSB CARDNET H'CAP 1m
4:10 (4:10) (Class 4) (0-85,88) 3-Y-O **£5,181** (£1,541; £770; £384) **Stalls** Low

Form RPR

5212 **1** **Lap Of Honour (IRE)**[16] 4107 3-8-8 **75**..................... WilliamBuick(3) 11 82
(N A Callaghan) *mde virtually all: rdn over 1f out: jst hld on* **15/2**

6221 **2** *nk* **Celtic Change (IRE)**[27] 3764 3-8-12 **76**............................ TedDurcan 6 82+
(M Dods) *hld up in tch: rdn over 1f out: r.o* **7/2**[2]

432 **3** *hd* **Fondled**[52] 2998 3-9-0 **78**.. OscarUrbina 7 84+
(J R Fanshawe) *s.i.s: hld up: hdwy and nt clr run over 1f out: sn rdn: r.o* **11/2**[3]

-051 **4** *nk* **Guacamole**[7] 4404 3-9-5 **83**.. SebSanders 3 88
(B W Hills) *hld up in tch: nt clr run and lost pl over 1f out: r.o ins fnl f* **9/1**

565- **5** ½ **Balnagore**[310] 5916 3-8-8 **72**.. LPKeniry 5 76
(J L Dunlop) *s.i.s: hld up: rdn over 1f out: r.o: nrst fin* **25/1**

-361 **6** 1½ **Mia's Boy**[60] 2740 3-8-9 **73**.. MartinDwyer 1 74
(P W Chapple-Hyam) *w wnr tl rdn over 1f out: edgd rt: styd on same pce* **11/4**[1]

4012 **7** ¾ **Karoo Blue (IRE)**[10] 4276 3-9-5 **88**................................ AhmedAjtebi(5) 9 87
(C E Brittain) *chsd ldrs: rdn over 2f out: no ex fnl f* **7/1**

0623 **8** *shd* **Top Bid**[21] 3952 3-8-13 **77**.. JohnEgan 8 76
(T D Easterby) *hld up: rdn over 2f out: nvr trbld ldrs* **20/1**

0000 **9** *hd* **Bed Fellow (IRE)**[10] 4276 3-8-11 **75**................................ DaneO'Neill 2 73
(A P Jarvis) *chsd ldrs: rdn and edgd lft over 1f out: wknd ins fnl f* **40/1**

0603 **10** *10* **Russki (IRE)**[10] 4276 3-8-12 **76**...(b) PatDobbs 4 51
(Mrs A J Perrett) *chsd ldrs: rdn over 2f out: wknd fnl f* **25/1**

3005 **11** *8* **Lazy Darren**[12] 4234 3-9-1 **79**..(v[1]) EddieAhern 10 36
(R Hannon) *hld up: rdn over 2f out: wknd over 1f out* **10/1**

1m 40.63s (0.20) **Going Correction** +0.15s/f (Good) **11** Ran SP% **122.5**
Speed ratings (Par 102): **105,104,104,104,103 102,101,101,101,91 83**
CSF £33.96 CT £165.28 TOTE £8.00: £2.10, £2.00, £2.20; EX 39.60.
Owner Michael Tabor **Bred** Ben Sangster **Trained** Newmarket, Suffolk
■ Stewards' Enquiry : Ted Durcan one-day ban: used whip with excessive frequency and without allowing time to respond (Aug 29)

FOCUS
A fair handicap and another race where the form looks solid rated around the placed horses and likely to produce future winners.
Mia's Boy Official explanation: jockey said colt was unsuited by the good ground
Lazy Darren Official explanation: jockey said gelding was unsuited by the good ground

4609 LLOYDS TSB FINANCIAL MARKETS DIVISION H'CAP 1m 4f
4:45 (4:45) (Class 4) (0-85,84) 3-Y-O+ **£5,181** (£1,541; £770; £384) **Stalls** High

Form RPR

610 **1** **Horseford Hill**[23] 3883 3-8-13 **78**... TedDurcan 1 86
(D R C Elsworth) *hld up: hdwy u.p and hung rt over 1f out: hung lft wl ins fnl f: led post* **4/1**[3]

2400 **2** *shd* **Ross Moor**[16] 4108 5-8-6 **64**... WilliamBuick(3) 5 72
(Mike Murphy) *hld up: hdwy over 5f out: led over 2f out: sn rdn: edgd rt over 1f out: hdd post* **12/1**

0151 **3** 2½ **Kingscape (IRE)**[44] 3249 4-9-4 **73**.................................... OscarUrbina 8 77
(J R Fanshawe) *hld up: hdwy over 2f out: rdn to chse wnr and edgd rt over 1f out: styd on same pce ins fnl f* **10/3**[2]

0064 **4** *2* **Active Asset (IRE)**[8] 4366 5-10-0 **83**...................................... JohnEgan 4 84
(M Quinn) *hld up in tch: racd keenly: lost pl over 3f out: styd on ins fnl f* **8/1**

2221 **5** *1* **Dawn Sky**[24] 3847 3-9-5 **84**..(p) SebSanders 7 83
(M A Jarvis) *led: rdn and hdd over 2f out: wknd fnl f* **3/1**[1]

0-64 **6** ¾ **Chocolate Caramel (USA)**[14] 4171 5-9-12 **81**..................... PatDobbs 6 79
(Mrs A J Perrett) *chsd ldrs: rdn over 2f out: wknd over 1f out* **8/1**

0056 **7** 1½ **Sienna Storm (IRE)**[14] 4171 4-9-10 **79**...........................(b) EddieAhern 2 75
(M H Tompkins) *chsd ldrs: rdn over 2f out: wknd over 1f out* **12/1**

0200 **8** *16* **Mutadarrej (IRE)**[20] 3993 3-9-5 **84**...........................(b) MartinDwyer 3 54
(J L Dunlop) *chsd ldr: rdn whn hung rt and lft over 2f out: wknd over 1f out* **7/1**

2m 35.52s (2.61) **Going Correction** +0.15s/f (Good)
WFA 3 from 4yo+ 10lb **8** Ran SP% **118.2**
Speed ratings (Par 105): **97,96,95,93,93 92,91,81**
CSF £51.76 CT £179.06 TOTE £6.40: £2.10, £3.40, £1.60; EX 66.60.
Owner Raymond Tooth **Bred** Darley **Trained** Newmarket, Suffolk

FOCUS
A fair handicap in which Horseford Hill and Ross Moor fought out a cracking finish. The pace was steady however, and the form is probably modest.

4610 LLOYDS TSB AGRICULTURE H'CAP 1m 2f
5:20 (5:20) (Class 5) (0-70,74) 3-Y-O+ **£3,886** (£1,156; £577; £288) **Stalls** High

Form RPR

4433 **1** **Rowan River**[13] 4205 3-9-5 **69**.. MartinDwyer 7 77+
(M H Tompkins) *chsd ldrs: rdn to ld over 1f out: swvd rt ins fnl f: jst hld on* **7/2**[2]

0201 **2** *nk* **Venir Rouge**[13] 4200 3-9-7 **74**.................................... WilliamBuick(3) 10 80
(M Salaman) *hld up: hdwy u.p and hung lft over 1f out: nt clr run ins fnl f: rdr dropped whip sn after: styd on* **11/4**[1]

6400 **3** *4* **Gala Sunday (USA)**[7] 4383 7-8-13 **55**..........................(bt) DaleGibson 8 53
(M W Easterby) *chsd ldr tl led over 2f out: rdn and hdd over 1f out: no ex* **7/1**[3]

0000 **4** 1¾ **Fantasy Ride**[57] 2833 5-9-10 **66**... OscarUrbina 2 61
(J Pearce) *chsd ldrs: rdn whn nt clr run and lost pl over 2f out: styd on ins fnl f* **16/1**

3100 **5** 1½ **Jackie Kiely**[81] 2106 6-9-9 **70**..(t) TolleyDean(5) 6 62
(R Brotherton) *hld up: hdwy over 3f out: rdn over 1f out: wknd fnl f* **14/1**

26-0 **6** *shd* **Bay Of Light**[22] 3913 3-9-6 **70**...................................... AdrianMcCarthy 9 61
(P W Chapple-Hyam) *chsd ldrs: rdn over 2f out: wknd over 1f out* **33/1**

-000 **7** 2½ **Colton**[44] 3249 4-9-10 **66**.. PatDobbs 12 52
(J M P Eustace) *hld up: rdn over 3f out: n.d* **12/1**

4020 **8** *5* **Art Investor**[57] 2833 4-9-3 **59**..(b) TedDurcan 4 35
(D R C Elsworth) *hld up: rdn over 3f out: a in rr* **7/1**[3]

6200 **9** 1¼ **Street Life (IRE)**[19] 4015 9-9-5 **68**................................ AlanRutter(7) 1 42
(W J Musson) *a bhd* **9/1**

6000 **10** *3* **Faith And Reason (USA)**[19] 4019 4-9-3 **62**..........(t) JerryO'Dwyer(3) 11 30
(B J Curley) *led: clr 7f out: hdd over 2f out: wknd over 1f out* **20/1**

4263 **11** 3½ **Doyles Lodge**[21] 3948 3-9-6 **70**... DaneO'Neill 5 31
(H Candy) *bhd: rdn and wknd over 3f out* **7/1**[3]

0000 **12** *27* **Drury Lane (IRE)**[21] 3971 7-8-4 **51** oh6.......................... AnnStokell(5) 3 —
(Miss A Stokell) *sn bhd: t.o fnl 4f* **66/1**

2m 8.11s (1.67) **Going Correction** +0.15s/f (Good)
WFA 3 from 4yo+ 8lb **12** Ran SP% **125.8**
Speed ratings (Par 103): **99,98,95,94,92 92,90,86,85,83 80,59**
CSF £14.26 CT £67.95 TOTE £4.80: £1.80, £1.70, £2.80; EX 13.50 Place 6 £236.18, Place 5 £120.78..
Owner Rowan Farm and River Racing Partnership **Bred** Rowan Farm Stud **Trained** Newmarket, Suffolk

FOCUS
Not a strong race, but two in-form handicappers came clear and the form is given a chance, although the less-than-solid fourth and sixth limit confidence.
T/Plt: £444.70 to a £1 stake. Pool: £89,502.95. 146.90 winning tickets. T/Qpdt: £79.30 to a £1 stake. Pool: £4,309.50. 40.20 winning tickets. CR

[4225]RIPON (R-H)

Saturday, August 18

OFFICIAL GOING: Good

Wind: Moderate, half behind Weather: Overcast and raining

4611 ARK DE TRIUMPH MAIDEN AUCTION STKS (DIV I) 6f

2:05 (2:06) (Class 4) 2-Y-O **£3,886** (£1,156; £577; £288) **Stalls** Low

Form RPR

23 **1** **Tadalavil**[9] 4335 2-8-13 0 FrancisNorton 3 79
(M R Channon) *cl up: effrt to ld 1f out: rdn ins fnl f and kpt on wl* **11/4**[1]

53 **2** 1 3/4 **River Gleam (IRE)**[10] 4293 2-8-4 0 RichardMullen 1 65
(A P Jarvis) *led: bit slipped through mouth after 1f and a edging rt: rdn along 2f out: hdd 1f out: kpt on wl u.p ins fnl f* **6/1**

05 **3** 2 1/2 **Hasty Lady**[16] 4102 2-8-12 0 PaulMulrennan 5 65
(K A Ryan) *chsd ldrs: rdn 2f out: drvn and kpt on same pce fnl f* **14/1**

2 **4** nk **Harrison George (IRE)**[49] 3092 2-9-3 0 PaulHanagan 8 69
(R A Fahey) *dwlt and sn rdn along: in tch 1/2-way: swtchd rt and drvn to chse ldrs 2f out: kpt on same pce* **3/1**[2]

3 **5** 3/4 **Jaconet (USA)**[15] 4125 2-8-10 0 PaulFessey 2 60
(T D Barron) *trckd ldrs on inner: hdwy over 2f out: sn rdn and no imp appr fnl f* **11/2**[3]

6 2 1/2 **Ivestar (IRE)** 2-9-3 0 AdrianTNicholls 9 60
(D Nicholls) *s.i.s and bhd: hdwy over 2f out: styd on ins fnl f: nrst fin* **33/1**

55 **7** 2 1/2 **El Tato**[14] 4173 2-9-1 0 DavidAllan 6 50
(T D Easterby) *chsd ldrs: rdn along over 2f out: grad wknd* **20/1**

0 **8** shd **Bahamian Ballad**[45] 3200 2-8-5 0 AndrewElliott(3) 12 43
(J D Bethell) *chsd ldrs: rdn along over 2f out: sn wknd* **50/1**

0632 **9** 1 1/2 **Stormy Journey**[20] 3995 2-8-8 70 PJMcDonald(3) 10 41
(Mrs K Walton) *a towards rr* **14/1**

6 **10** 4 **Next Of Kin (IRE)**[15] 4125 2-8-9 0 PatCosgrave 4 27
(G A Swinbank) *a in rr* **8/1**

0 **11** 1 3/4 **Mistress Rio (IRE)**[16] 4102 2-8-4 0 RoystonFfrench 11 17
(J G Given) *outpcd and bhd fr 1/2-way* **66/1**

0 **12** 2 1/2 **Shot Through (USA)**[1] 4578 2-8-9 0 LeeEnstone 13 15
(P C Haslam) *wnt rt s: a bhd* **66/1**

1m 12.88s (-0.12) **Going Correction** 0.0s/f (Good) **12** Ran SP% **118.4**
Speed ratings (Par 96): **100,97,94,93,92 89,86,86,84,78 76,73**
CSF £18.82 TOTE £4.10: £1.60, £2.20, £3.50; EX 27.50 Trifecta £92.40 Part won. Pool £130.21 - 0.30 winning units..
Owner A R Parrish **Bred** Theakston Stud **Trained** West Ilsley, Berks

FOCUS
An ordinary maiden in which a low draw proved a handy advantage. It was the quicker of the two divisions by 0.79sec.

NOTEBOOK
Tadalavil, well drawn and never far off the pace on the stands' side, went on with a furlong to run and did it nicely enough. The Handicapper is unlikely to go overboard and so he should be able to pay his way in nursery company. (op 7-2)
River Gleam(IRE) had the best draw and made the most of it, setting the pace next to the stands' rail. She had every chance, although was not helped by having the bit slip through her mouth, and she was certainly suited by the drop back to 6f. The nursery option is now open to her. (op 15-2)
Hasty Lady is another now eligible to run in nurseries. She shapes as though she will get another furlong. (op 12-1 tchd 10-1)
Harrison George(IRE), second in heavy ground on his debut, had quicker conditions to deal with this time. He still shapes as though another furlong is going to suit him. (op 11-4 tchd 10-3)
Jaconet(USA), another who was well drawn, failed to improve on her debut effort at Haydock, although that was a weaker affair. (tchd 5-1 and 6-1)
Ivestar(IRE) was not drawn well and lacked the previous experience of the main contenders. He ran green but stayed on quite nicely to be closest at the finish, and he should do better in time.

4612 ARK DE TRIUMPH MAIDEN AUCTION STKS (DIV II) 6f

2:35 (2:38) (Class 4) 2-Y-O **£3,886** (£1,156; £577; £288) **Stalls** Low

Form RPR

0 **1** **Baldemar**[22] 3915 2-9-1 0 FrancisNorton 7 74
(K R Burke) *trckd ldr: smooth hdwy to ld over 1f out: rdn and hung rt ins fnl f: kpt on* **15/2**

05 **2** nk **Joinedupwriting**[17] 4076 2-8-11 0 PaulMulrennan 9 69
(R M Whitaker) *chsd ldrs: hdwy over 2f out and sn rdn: styd on wl u.p ins fnl f: jst hld* **9/2**[3]

020 **3** 1 3/4 **Fulford**[10] 4279 2-8-9 65 AdrianTNicholls 10 62
(M Brittain) *sn led: rdn 2f out: edgd rt and hdd over 1f out: kpt on same pce* **14/1**

0 **4** 1 1/4 **Veronicas Way**[10] 4286 2-8-1 0 AndrewElliott(3) 1 53
(G M Moore) *chsd ldrs: rdn along over 2f out: sn one pce* **25/1**

0 **5** 3 **Gala Casino Star (IRE)**[21] 3977 2-8-12 0 JamieMoriarty(3) 3 55
(R A Fahey) *in tch: pushed along to chse ldrs over 2f out: sn rdn and no imp appr fnl f* **25/1**

6 **6** 1 **When Yer Ready (IRE)**[49] 3092 2-8-13 0 DavidAllan 2 50
(T D Easterby) *towards rr tl sme late hdwy* **6/1**

54 **7** 3/4 **Zabougg**[27] 3761 2-8-11 0 PatCosgrave 11 46
(G A Swinbank) *dwlt: sltly hmpd after 1f: in tch on outer: rdn along over 2f out and sn no imp* **7/2**[2]

00 **8** 3 **Flashy Max**[10] 4285 2-8-9 0 TonyHamilton 4 35
(Jedd O'Keeffe) *wnt rt s: a in rr* **80/1**

4 **9** nk **Thanxforthat (USA)**[14] 4174 2-8-11 0 GrahamGibbons 6 36
(J J Quinn) *a in rr* **11/1**

35 **10** 1 1/4 **Low Flyer (USA)**[21] 3951 2-8-11 0 PaulFessey 8 32
(T D Barron) *sltly hmpd after 1f and a in rr* **10/3**[1]

11 1/2 **Blazing Mask (IRE)** 2-8-8 0 RoystonFfrench 5 28
(Mrs A Duffield) *bmpd s: a in rr* **25/1**

1m 13.67s (0.67) **Going Correction** 0.0s/f (Good) **11** Ran SP% **117.3**
Speed ratings (Par 96): **95,94,92,90,86 85,84,80,79,78 77**
CSF £39.63 TOTE £10.80: £2.40, £2.20, £4.50; EX 61.50 TRIFECTA Not won..
Owner A Rhodes Haulage And P Timmins **Bred** Hellwood Stud Farm **Trained** Middleham Moor, N Yorks
■ Stewards' Enquiry : Francis Norton one-day ban: careless riding (Aug 29)

FOCUS
The slower of the two divisions by 0.79sec, and fairly modest form judged by the performance of the 65-rated third.

NOTEBOOK
Baldemar found 5f too short on his debut at Thirsk but that was a fair event and he showed the necessary improvement to get off the mark here. A son of Namid, softer ground is unlikely to cause him any problems. (op 7-1 tchd 13-2)
Joinedupwriting probably did not have to improve much from his fifth at Redcar last time to run the winner close. He is progressing along the right lines, and handicaps are now an option for him. (op 6-1)
Fulford, who has an official rating of 65, showed good speed to lead the field, but he paid for his efforts in the closing stages. His performance is probably a fair guide to the level of the form. (op 20-1)
Veronicas Way, a half-sister to Mormeatmic, a multiple 5f winner, and Wellcome Inn, a dual winner over middle distances, had the best draw and improved on her debut effort. She needs one more run to be eligible for nurseries.
Gala Casino Star(IRE), who did not go unsupported on his debut when last of ten in heavy ground, showed a bit more this time, but he probably needs another furlong. (op 16-1)
When Yer Ready(IRE) is another who failed to improve on his debut effort, despite having his supporters in the ring. (op 8-1)
Zabougg, who was not well drawn, was hampered early as his rider tried to get a decent position but he also hung under pressure and might not be entirely straightforward. Official explanation: jockey said colt hung left throughout (op 3-1 tchd 4-1)
Flashy Max Official explanation: jockey said colt became unbalanced on the undulations
Low Flyer(USA), a beaten favourite for a second race in succession, never got in a blow. (op 5-1)

4613 A. RHODES HAULAGE RIPON HORN BLOWER CONDITIONS STKS 6f

3:10 (3:11) (Class 3) 2-Y-O **£6,309** (£1,888; £944; £472; £235) **Stalls** Low

Form RPR

1 **1** **Sporting Art (USA)**[36] 3479 2-9-5 0 PaulHanagan 2 95
(G L Moore) *trckd ldrs: hdwy on inner 2f out: rdn to chal ent fnl f: drvn and styd on to ld nr fin* **5/2**[1]

1 **2** nk **Lesson In Humility (IRE)**[20] 3995 2-8-9 0 AndrewElliott(3) 6 87
(K R Burke) *led after 1f: rdn over 1f out: drvn: flashed tail and edgd rt ins fnl f: hdd and no ex nr fin* **20/1**

1 **3** 2 1/2 **Choose Your Moment**[52] 2983 2-9-5 0 LeeEnstone 3 87
(P C Haslam) *s.i.s and bhd tl styd on fnl 2f: nrst fin* **5/2**[1]

1200 **4** 3 1/2 **Tia Mia**[18] 4046 2-8-12 95 TPQueally 1 69
(J G Given) *led 1f: trckd ldrs: effrt over 2f out: sn rdn and wknd* **11/4**[2]

1600 **5** 1 **Carleton**[18] 4046 2-9-3 96 MatthewDavies(7) 5 78
(M R Channon) *chsd ldrs on outer: rdn along 2f out and btn over 1f out* **14/1**

1033 **6** 1/2 **Golan Knight (IRE)**[24] 3841 2-9-5 80 PaulMulrennan 4 72
(K A Ryan) *chsd ldrs: rdn along over 2f out: sn drvn and wknd* **17/2**[3]

01 **7** 19 **Kalhan Sands (IRE)**[24] 3834 2-9-5 83 PatCosgrave 7 15
(G A Swinbank) *wnt rt s: in tch tl outpcd and bhd fr 1/2-way* **14/1**

1m 12.64s (-0.36) **Going Correction** 0.0s/f (Good) **7** Ran SP% **112.4**
Speed ratings (Par 98): **102,101,98,93,92 91,66**
CSF £47.78 TOTE £3.40: £2.00, £4.20; EX 32.10.
Owner R A Green **Bred** Frank Penn & John R Penn **Trained** Woodingdean, E Sussex

FOCUS
A decent little race featuring four last-time-out winners.

NOTEBOOK
Sporting Art(USA), a shock winner at Ascot on his debut, showed himself to be a progressive colt by beating this useful field. Brought with a well-timed challenge, he won a shade cosily and now deserves to take his chance in Pattern company. (op 9-4)
Lesson In Humility(IRE) again flashed her tail under pressure, which is disconcerting, but she ran well from the front and was only caught close home. She finished clear of the rest and will be of interest when racing in fillies-only company. (op 16-1)
Choose Your Moment was slowly away and struggled in the early part of the race, but he stayed on well in the closing stages, again suggesting that a seventh furlong is very much required now. (op 11-4, tchd 3-1 in places)
Tia Mia, dropping back in grade having found Group company too tough on her last two starts, was not sure to be suited by the step up to 6f, and she certainly did not see it out as well as some of her rivals. Official explanation: trainer said filly was in season (op 3-1 tchd 10-3)
Carleton, the most experienced runner in the line-up, was another dropping in grade having failed to make much of a mark in Group company on his last three starts. He was beaten a fair way out. (op 16-1)
Golan Knight(IRE) came in for some support in the market but he had to be rushed up to hold a prominent position early and was easily beaten off in the end. Official ratings gave him plenty to do in this company, and he will be of more interest back in nurseries. (op 12-1 tchd 14-1)
Kalhan Sands(IRE) Official explanation: jockey said colt was unsuited by the undulations; trainer said colt was found to have a misplaced vertebrae

4614 WILLIAM HILL GREAT ST WILFRID STKS (HERITAGE H'CAP) 6f

3:45 (3:45) (Class 2) (0-105,102) 3-Y-O+
£37,392 (£11,196; £5,598; £2,802; £1,398; £351) **Stalls** Low

Form RPR

1000 **1** **Kostar**[14] 4150 6-9-6 **98** PhilipRobinson 22 107
(C G Cox) *mde all far side: rdn wl over 1f out: drvn ins fnl f and hld on gamely* **10/1**

-100 **2** shd **Obe Brave**[184] 472 4-9-8 **100** RichardMullen 20 109
(M R Channon) *cl up far side: rdn wl over 1f out: drvn and ev ch ins fnl f tl no ex nr fin* **14/1**

3003 **3** 1/2 **Indian Trail**[15] 4122 7-9-0 **92** (v) AdrianTNicholls 9 100+
(D Nicholls) *swtchd to far rail after s: in tch: effrt and swtchd lft wl over 1f out: sn rdn and hdwy ent fnl f: styd on* **9/1**

0001 **4** 1 **Malcheek (IRE)**[12] 4227 5-8-11 **89** DavidAllan 21 94
(T D Easterby) *cl up far side: rdn 2f out and ev ch tl drvn and one pce ent fnl f* **8/1**[2]

400 **5** shd **The Tatling (IRE)**[14] 4150 10-9-3 **100** KevinGhunowa(5) 19 104
(J M Bradley) *chsd ldrs stands' side: effrt 2f out: sn rdn and kpt on same pce ins fnl f* **33/1**

2201 **6** 2 **Zomerlust**[21] 3975 5-9-7 **99** (v) GrahamGibbons 23 97
(J J Quinn) *chsd ldrs far side: rdn along 2f out: drvn and kpt on same pce fnl f* **13/2**[1]

2600 **6** dht **Ajigolo**[7] 4386 4-9-2 **94** TPQueally 15 92
(M R Channon) *chsd ldrs far side: rdn 2f out: drvn and kpt on same pce fnl f* **33/1**

0560 **8** 1/2 **Fantasy Believer**[14] 4150 9-9-3 **95** JimmyQuinn 18 92
(J J Quinn) *in tch far side: effrt 2f out: sn rdn and kpt on same pce appr fnl f* **17/2**[3]

111 **9** 1 1/4 **Orpsie Boy (IRE)**[36] 3481 4-8-11 **94** LukeMorris(5) 11 91+
(N P Littmoden) *hld up far side: hdwy 2f out: sn rdn and no imp appr fnl f* **10/1**

4010 **10** nk **Fullandby (IRE)**[21] 3975 5-9-2 **97** PJMcDonald(3) 4 89+
(T J Etherington) *hld up stands' side: hdwy 2f out: sn rdn and kpt on: no ch w far side* **20/1**

6404 **11** 1/2 **Dhaular Dhar (IRE)**[13] 4196 5-9-6 **98** DanielTudhope 1 89+
(J S Goldie) *trckd ldr stands' side: effrt 2f out: sn rdn and kpt on: no ch w far side gp* **20/1**

6144 **12** *hd* **Ice Planet**[36] 3500 6-8-10 **91** .... AndrewMullen(3) 3 81+
(D Nicholls) *led stands' side: rdn along wl over 1f out: kpt on: no ch w wnr* **16/1**

0000 **13** *nk* **Fayr Jag (IRE)**[14] 4150 8-9-8 **100** .... PaulMulrennan 13 89
(T D Easterby) *rrd s: in tch far side: effrt over 2f out: sn rdn and no hdwy* **22/1**

0450 **14** *nk* **Bahamian Pirate (USA)**[21] 3975 12-8-11 **89** .... FrancisNorton 17 77
(D Nicholls) *racd far side: a in midfield* **25/1**

0000 **15** *nk* **One More Round (USA)**[5] 4456 9-9-1 **93** .... (b) RoystonFfrench 8 80
(N P Littmoden) *a towards rr far side* **66/1**

00-4 **16** *hd* **Philharmonic**[21] 3975 6-9-6 **98** .... PaulHanagan 6 85
(R A Fahey) *cl up stands' side: effrt 2f out: sn rdn and kpt on: no ch w far side gp* **14/1**

3500 **17** *nk* **Grantley Adams**[14] 4150 4-9-3 **102** .... MatthewDavies(7) 2 88
(M R Channon) *trckd ldrs stands' side: effrt 2f out: sn rdn and btn* **22/1**

1620 **18** *3/4* **Turnkey**[17] 4062 5-8-13 **98** .... AdeleRothery(7) 14 82
(D Nicholls) *hld up: a in rr far side* **20/1**

1600 **19** *2 1/2* **Wyatt Earp (IRE)**[36] 3500 6-8-10 **91** .... JamieMoriarty(3) 7 67
(R A Fahey) *in tch stands' side: rdn along 2f out: sn btn* **25/1**

5220 **20** *nk* **Roman Maze**[15] 4122 7-8-12 **90** .... JamesDoyle 5 65
(W M Brisbourne) *hld up stands' side: nvr a factor* **40/1**

0-60 **21** *14* **Chookie Heiton (IRE)**[33] 3586 9-8-12 **90** .... TonyHamilton 12 23
(I Semple) *racd far side: in rr fr 1/2-way* **66/1**

03R **22** *32* **Skhilling Spirit**[21] 3975 4-9-6 **98** .... PaulFessey 16 —
(T D Barron) *lft 100yds and virtually ref to r: a t.o* **12/1**

1m 11.61s (-1.39) **Going Correction** 0.0s/f (Good) **22** Ran SP% **132.0**
Speed ratings (Par 109): **109,108,108,106,106 104,104,103,101,101 100,100,100,99,99 98,98,97,94,93 75,32**
CSF £125.30 CT £1357.81 TOTE £13.20: £3.40, £4.10, £2.90, £2.70; EX 108.20 Trifecta £5343.10 Pool £14,298.70 - 1.90 winning units..
Owner Mrs P Scott-Dunn And Mrs F J Ryan **Bred** Mrs P Scott-Dunn **Trained** Lambourn, Berks

FOCUS
A competitive renewal and, as has tended to be the case more often than not in this race, the high-drawn horses held an advantage over those drawn low.

NOTEBOOK
Kostar, who apparently would not let himself down on the fast ground at Goodwood last time, was well drawn in the second highest stall and bravely made every yard. He deserves plenty of credit for fighting off the strong challenge of Obe Brave close home, but he was certainly helped a great deal by being drawn where he was, and that must be borne in mind when assessing his chance of defying a higher mark. (op 14-1)

Obe Brave had been off the track since running at the Dubai carnival back in February, but he has gone well fresh in the past and the drop back to 6f promised to suit. Well drawn in stall 20, he was never far off the pace and pushed the eventual winner all the way to the line.

Indian Trail has had more than his share of bad luck this season and on this occasion his draw did him few favours. Switched to race with the far-side group from his single-figure stall, he did well to finish where he did given the way that those who raced prominently next to the far-side rail held such a big advantage, and there is surely a big pot to be won with him somewhere before the season is out. The Portland or Ayr Gold Cup immediately spring to mind. (tchd 8-1)

Malcheek(IRE), who was raised 4lb for a tidy win over this course and distance earlier in the month, could have done without the rain easing the ground to good, as he is best when it is rattling - his form figures on good to firm or firm ground when ridden by David Allan read 11331300311. He was, however, well drawn in stall 21 and ran a sound race. Official explanation: jockey said saddle slipped (op 9-1)

The Tatling(IRE) has always been at his best over 5f, and he did not quite see this trip out as strongly as some, but like so many others he benefited from being drawn high.

Zomerlust, who bounced back to winning form in a first-time visor last time, had the headgear on again. He had the best of the draw but not the speed to take best advantage of it on a track which tends to favour pace horses, and softer ground would undoubtedly have helped him. (op 28-1)

Ajigolo appreciated the return to 6f and posted a sound effort from what was a fair draw. He has yet to return to his smart two-year-old form, but there are handicaps to be won with him in the future, and he showed a liking for Polytrack last winter so he will have that option again later this year. (op 28-1)

Fantasy Believer, who ran a solid race in the Stewards' Cup last time out, was fairly drawn in 18, but he proved a little disappointing. He has run with credit without winning on a number of occasions this year and remains capable of popping up at some point. (op 11-1 tchd 12-1 and 15-2)

Orpsie Boy(IRE), like Indian Trail, had an awkward middle draw and chose to race with the far-side group. He has been in great form this summer, improving from a 77-rated performer at the beginning of the season to a mark of 94 now, and it would be precipitant to assume that his improvement has come to an end based on this performance. (op 11-1 tchd 9-1)

Fullandby(IRE), who was runner-up in this race last year off an 11lb lower mark, brought home the stands'-side group. He had no chance with those that raced on the far side as things turned out. (op 16-1)

Dhaular Dhar(IRE), who would have been suited by the easier ground than he encountered when running well in Listed company at Chester last time, ran a sound race to finish second on the unfavoured stands' side.

Ice Planet, third in this race last year off a 1lb lower mark, finished third this time on the unfavoured stands' side. (op 18-1 tchd 20-1)

4615 EUROPEAN BREEDERS' FUND FILLIES' H'CAP — 1m 1f 170y
4:20 (4:20) (Class 4) (0-80,79) 3-Y-O **£7,255** (£2,171; £1,085; £542; £270) **Stalls** High

Form RPR

-160 **1** **Malyana**[73] 2369 3-9-6 **77** .... PhilipRobinson 1 84
(M A Jarvis) *hld up in rr: hdwy on outer 3f out: pushed along 2f out: rdn over 1f out: styd on ins fnl f to ld on post* **9/2**[2]

-353 **2** *nk* **Princess Cocoa (IRE)**[6] 4419 4-9-6 **69** .... PaulHanagan 10 76
(R A Fahey) *trckd ldrs: effrt on inner 2f out: rdn and squeezed through to ld ent fnl f: sn drvn hdd on post* **5/1**[3]

6315 **3** *1/2* **Sister Maria (USA)**[21] 3972 3-9-5 **76** .... RoystonFfrench 7 82
(E A L Dunlop) *cl up: led 2f out: sn rdn: drvn and hdd ent fnl f: kpt on u.p* **11/4**[1]

3241 **4** *nk* **Soul Mountain (IRE)**[9] 4334 3-9-8 **79** .... FrancisNorton 3 84
(B W Hills) *trckd ldrs: hdwy 3f out: rdn to chal 2f out and ev ch tl drvn and one pce ins fnl f* **11/4**[1]

36-0 **5** *3/4* **Bollin Dolly**[15] 4128 4-9-1 **64** .... DavidAllan 2 68
(T D Easterby) *hld up: hdwy 3f out: rdn to chse ldrs over 1f out: kpt on same pce ins fnl f* **16/1**

1502 **6** *4* **Jeu D'Esprit (IRE)**[28] 3754 4-9-4 **67** .... TPQueally 5 63
(J G Given) *chsd ldrs: rdn along 3f out: sn one pce* **14/1**

2116 **7** *1 3/4* **Silca Key**[16] 4112 3-9-5 **76** .... RichardMullen 9 68
(M R Channon) *led: rdn along 3f out: hdd 2f out: drvn and wknd over 1f out* **17/2**

4061 **8** *nk* **Jenny Soba**[6] 4426 4-8-6 **58** 6ex oh2 .... (v) AndrewElliott(3) 8 49
(R M Whitaker) *hld up: effrt and sme hdwy 3f out: sn rdn along and wknd* **16/1**

2m 4.95s (-0.05) **Going Correction** 0.0s/f (Good)
WFA 3 from 4yo 8lb **8** Ran SP% **117.1**
Speed ratings (Par 102): **100,99,99,99,98 95,93,93**
CSF £27.95 CT £73.43 TOTE £6.10: £2.00, £1.60, £1.50; EX 29.50 Trifecta £87.10 Pool £507.93 - 4.14 winning units..
Owner Sheikh Ahmed Al Maktoum **Bred** Darley **Trained** Newmarket, Suffolk
■ Stewards' Enquiry : Philip Robinson caution: used whip with excessive frequency

FOCUS
An ordinary fillies' handicap in which the pace was fair.

4616 E-TECH GROUP GEOFF JEWSON MEMORIAL MAIDEN STKS — 5f
4:50 (4:51) (Class 5) 3-Y-O+ **£3,886** (£1,156; £577; £288) **Stalls** Low

Form RPR

2363 **1** **Moonlight Applause**[7] 4384 3-8-12 53 .... DavidAllan 8 58
(T D Easterby) *chsd ldrs: hdwy 2f out: rdn and styd on to ld ins fnl f* **3/1**[1]

4224 **2** *1/2* **By The Edge (IRE)**[25] 3811 3-8-7 50 .... NeilBrown(5) 3 56+
(T D Barron) *hld up and swtchd to r alone far side after 1 1/2f: hdwy 2f out: rdn and ev ch ins fnl f: no ex towards fin* **4/1**[3]

6450 **3** *3/4* **Tenancy (IRE)**[10] 4291 3-8-10 65 .... (p) RobbieEgan(7) 2 58
(A J McCabe) *led: rdn along wl over 1f out: drvn and hdd ins fnl f: no ex* **4/1**[3]

25 **4** *3* **Sweetsformysweet (USA)**[14] 4164 3-8-12 0 .... TPQueally 5 43
(J Noseda) *trckd ldrs: swtchd rt and hdwy wl over 1f out: sn rdn and one pce* **10/3**[2]

0050 **5** *2 1/2* **Violet's Pride**[2] 4525 3-8-12 52 .... (v) PaulHanagan 12 34
(S Parr) *chsd ldr: rdn along 2f out: grad wknd* **14/1**

0-56 **6** *3* **First Valentini**[12] 4226 3-8-12 48 .... PaulFessey 10 23
(N Bycroft) *chsd ldrs: rdn along 2f out: sn outpcd* **33/1**

7 *2* **Chicken George (IRE)** 3-9-3 0 .... AdrianTNicholls 15 21
(D Nicholls) *towards rr: pushed along on outer 1/2-way: n.d* **9/1**

6-3 **8** *4* **Midnight Sky**[24] 3846 3-8-12 0 .... RichardMullen 9 —
(Rae Guest) *a towards rr* **14/1**

60- **9** *2* **Piccolo Diamante (USA)**[282] 6414 3-8-10 0 .... (t) JamesO'Reilly(7) 7 —
(D J Murphy) *a in rr* **16/1**

000- **10** *2 1/2* **Tatillius (IRE)**[309] 5951 4-9-0 25 .... (t) KevinGhunowa(5) 1 —
(J M Bradley) *chsd ldrs: rdn along 2f out: sn wknd* **80/1**

11 *3/4* **Champagne Sue** 3-8-12 0 .... TonyHamilton 11 —
(D W Barker) *a in rr* **20/1**

12 *dist* **Florentine Lady** 4-8-11 0 .... DominicFox(3) 14 —
(D Shaw) *s.i.s: virtually ref to r and a t.o* **50/1**

59.86 secs (-0.34) **Going Correction** 0.0s/f (Good)
WFA 3 from 4yo 2lb **12** Ran SP% **128.2**
Speed ratings (Par 103): **102,101,100,95,91 86,83,76,73,69 68,—**
CSF £16.20 TOTE £4.70: £1.70, £2.00, £2.00; EX 21.70 Trifecta £158.80 Pool £226.03 - 1.01 winning units.
Owner Solwind Racing Partnership **Bred** Slatch Farm Stud **Trained** Great Habton, N Yorks
■ Stewards' Enquiry : David Allan one-day ban: used whip with excessive frequency (Aug 29)

FOCUS
A poor maiden, no better than selling grade.

4617 RIPON CATHEDRAL H'CAP — 1m 4f 10y
5:25 (5:25) (Class 3) (0-90,86) 3-Y-O
£7,790 (£2,332; £1,166; £583; £291; £146) **Stalls** High

Form RPR

3310 **1** **Black Rock (IRE)**[37] 3460 3-9-5 **84** .... PhilipRobinson 9 91
(M A Jarvis) *set stdy pce: qcknd 3f out: rdn over 1f out: edgd lft ent fnl f: sn drvn and styd on wl* **2/1**[1]

4310 **2** *1 1/2* **Rosbay (IRE)**[17] 4059 3-9-7 **86** .... DavidAllan 2 90
(T D Easterby) *hld up: stdy hdwy 3f out: swtchd rt and rdn over 1f out: styd on ins fnl f* **10/1**

-005 **3** *hd* **Always Fruitful**[7] 4399 3-9-7 **86** .... RoystonFfrench 3 90
(M Johnston) *trckd ldrs: hdwy 3f out: swtchd lft and rdn wl over 1f out: drvn to chse wnr ent fnl f: sn drvn and nt qckn* **10/1**

1222 **4** *4* **Smugglers Bay (IRE)**[23] 3889 3-8-7 **72** .... (b) PaulMulrennan 6 70
(T D Easterby) *plld hrd: chsd ldrs: hdwy to chal over 2f out: sn rdn and ev ch tl drvn and wknd ent fnl f* **17/2**

-013 **5** *1/2* **Inchinata (IRE)**[20] 3993 3-8-12 **77** .... FrancisNorton 7 74
(B W Hills) *prom: effrt 3f out: rdn 2f out and ev ch tl drvn and one pce appr fnl f* **6/1**[3]

00-1 **6** *hd* **Sumner (IRE)**[86] 1972 3-8-7 **72** .... JimmyQuinn 1 68
(M H Tompkins) *hld up in tch: hdwy on outer 3f out: rdn and hung rt wl over 1f out: sn btn* **10/1**

0-1 **7** *1 1/4* **Alaghiraar (IRE)**[30] 3685 3-9-2 **81** .... TPQueally 4 75
(J L Dunlop) *hld up in rr: effrt 3f out and sn rdn along: drvn and hung rt over 1f out: nvr a factor* **4/1**[2]

-433 **8** *30* **Moonwalking**[92] 1827 3-8-10 **75** .... PaulHanagan 5 21
(Jedd O'Keeffe) *cl up: rdn along over 2f out: sn wknd* **16/1**

-405 **9** *3 1/2* **Persian Peril**[9] 4332 3-8-10 **75** .... PatCosgrave 8 16
(G A Swinbank) *hld up: a towards rr* **18/1**

2m 38.04s (1.04) **Going Correction** 0.0s/f (Good) **9** Ran SP% **116.6**
Speed ratings (Par 104): **96,95,94,92,91 91,90,70,68**
CSF £23.72 CT £164.77 TOTE £2.70: £1.20, £3.30, £2.90; EX 25.80 TRIFECTA Pool £350.37 - 3.52 winning units. Place 6 £117.90, Place 5 £51.85..
Owner A D Spence **Bred** Rockhart Trading Ltd **Trained** Newmarket, Suffolk
■ Stewards' Enquiry : Francis Norton one-day ban: careless riding (Aug 30)

FOCUS
A fair handicap but the steady pace was against a number of the runners.

NOTEBOOK
Black Rock(IRE) was disappointing on his handicap debut at Newmarket, but this represented an easier task and the combination of a step up in trip and being allowed to dictate a steady gallop allowed him to bounce back to winning ways. He completed a treble on the card for Philip Robinson. (op 9-4)

Rosbay(IRE), like the winner taking on slightly weaker opposition than on his previous start, stayed on well to take second, but the way the race was run he had no chance of catching Black Rock. A stronger pace would have probably suited him. (op 11-1 tchd 9-1)

Always Fruitful, another stepping up to 1m4f for the first time, was always well placed behind the leader on the inner, and came to have his chance when switched, but he could never cut back the well-ridden winner and lost second place close home. (op 8-1)

Smugglers Bay(IRE), who was also stepping up in trip, did not help his chance of getting home by failing to settle. (op 11-1 tchd 8-1)

Inchinata(IRE), well placed in a race lacking pace, had her chance and was a little disappointing. (op 8-1 tchd 5-1)

Sumner(IRE), who was raised 8lb for his win in a class 6 Salisbury handicap back in May, had more on his plate in this company on his return from a break. He threatened to challenge down the outside two furlongs out but it came to nothing. (op 8-1)
Alaghiraar(IRE) promised to be suited by this longer trip, but having been held up out the back off a steady pace, he was left trailing early in the straight and made only a little headway. A stronger pace would have suited him and he is the sort to improve with racing. (op 7-2)
T/Plt: £161.90 to a £1 stake. Pool: £84,725.90. 382.00 winning tickets. T/Qpdt: £37.00 to a £1 stake. Pool: £4,602.20. 91.80 winning tickets. JR

4618 - 4624a (Foreign Racing) - See Raceform Interactive

4556 DEAUVILLE (R-H)

Saturday, August 18

OFFICIAL GOING: Aw: standard; turf: good

4625a CRITERIUM DU FONDS EUROPEEN DE L'ELEVAGE (LISTED RACE) (ROUND) 1m (R)

2:20 (2:21) 2-Y-0 **£41,216** (£16,486; £12,365; £8,243; £4,122)

			RPR
1		**Gipson Dessert (USA)**19 2-8-8 ... C-PLemaire 3 (J-C Rouget, France) **52/10**1	99
2	1 ½	**Blue Chagall (FR)**31 2-8-11 ... JVictoire 2 (H-A Pantall, France)	99
3	1 ½	**Americain (USA)**23 2-8-11 ... OPeslier 7 (A Fabre, France)	95
4	½	**Bouguereau**14 4151 2-8-11 ... JimmyFortune 6 (P W Chapple-Hyam) *trckd ldrs: 3rd 1/2-way: rdn 1f out: nt threaten ldrs* **11/1**2	94
5	1 ½	**Salut L'Africain (FR)**6 4444 2-9-2 ... CSoumillon 8 (Robert Collet, France)	96
6	½	**Rey Davis (IRE)**6 4444 2-8-11 ... J-BHamel 4 (Robert Collet, France)	90
7	nse	**Rava (IRE)**16 2-8-8 ... TThulliez 5 (J-C Rouget, France)	87
8	1 ½	**Woolfall Treasure**21 3957 2-8-11 ... SPasquier 1 (G G Margarson) *cl up: led 1/2-way: drvn 2 1/2f out: hdd 1 1/2f out: wknd* **15/1**3	86
9	3	**Neige Eternel (FR)**6 4444 2-8-11 ... DBoeuf 9 (Robert Collet, France)	80

1m 43.8s (1.50) **9** Ran SP% **30.7**
PARI-MUTUEL: WIN 6.20; PL 1.80, 1.80, 1.40; DF 10.40.
Owner Ecurie I M Fares **Bred** Fares Farm Inc **Trained** Pau, France

NOTEBOOK
Bouguereau, supplemented into this Listed event, was well placed rounding the final turn and then one paced in the straight. He lost third position inside the final furlong.
Woolfall Treasure was one of the co-leaders in this slowly run race but was a beaten force from one and a half out. He gradually fell away on the rail.

4626a PRIX DU CALVADOS - HARAS DES CAPUCINES (GROUP 3) (FILLIES) (STRAIGHT) 7f

2:50 (2:55) 2-Y-0 **£27,027** (£10,811; £8,108; £5,405; £2,703)

			RPR
1		**Proviso**38 2-8-9 ... SPasquier 5 (A Fabre, France) *hld up in tch: 8th 1/2-way: pushed along and qcknd 2 1/2f out: led over 1 1/2f out: rdn and fnd more whn chal fnl f* **9/10**1	111
2	½	**Laureldean Gale (USA)**36 3507 2-8-9 ... JimmyFortune 2 (P W Chapple-Hyam) *hld up towards stands' side: 7th and pushed along 1/2-way: rdn and wnt 2nd 1 1/2f out: chal fnl f: r.o but a jst hld* **7/2**2	110
3	6	**Lady Deauville (FR)**23 3880 2-8-9 ... OPeslier 1 (P A Blockley) *led to 2 1/2f out: rdn and styd on fr over 1f out* **13/1**	95
4	2 ½	**Naomh Geileis (USA)**10 4286 2-8-9 ... J-PGuillambert 4 (M Johnston) *prom: 2nd 1/2-way: pushed along over 2f out: rdn 1 1/2f out: styd on at one pce* **31/1**	89
5	3	**Evergrey (FR)**28 2-8-9 ... TThulliez 8 (P Khozian, France) *hld up in last: styd on fnl f but n.d* **24/1**	81
6	nk	**Without Precedent (FR)**58 2-8-9 ... ACrastus 3 (Y De Nicolay, France) *in tch: cl 6th 1/2-way: rdn and outpcd 2f out* **30/1**	80
7	3	**Luna Royale (IRE)**17 2-8-9 ... JVictoire 9 (H-A Pantall, France) *hld up: 5th on outside 1/2-way: pushed along 2 1/2f out: n.d* **66/10**3	73
8	2	**Kay Es Jay (FR)**7 4400 2-8-9 ... CSoumillon 6 (B W Hills) **10/1**	68
9	1	**Kirkinola**23 2-8-9 ... MBlancpain 7 (C Laffon-Parias, France) *prom: disputing 2nd 1/2-way: rdn 2f out: unable qck* **36/1**	65

1m 21.1s (-4.20) **9** Ran SP% **117.3**
PARI-MUTUEL: WIN 1.90; PL 1.10, 1.90, 2.10; DF 3.20.
Owner K Abdulla **Bred** Juddmonte Farms Ltd **Trained** Chantilly, France

NOTEBOOK
Proviso, who came into this race with a big reputation, having dominated a field first time out, made a challenge on the outside two furlongs out and then battled with the runner-up throughout the final stages. She had to pull out all the stops and she will have gained a lot of experience from this outing. She will now either go for the Fillies' Mile at Ascot or the Marcel Boussac.
Laureldean Gale(USA), held up in the early stages, joined battle with the winner at the furlong marker and only failed in her quest after her heroic effort. She will also have gained valuable experience from this outing and my clash again with the winner in the Fillies' Mile.
Lady Deauville(FR) was soon at the head of affairs at a sensible pace. When the race got serious, she could not go with the front pair and just stayed on at the same pace. It was a genuine effort and she was not extended to hold third place.
Naomh Geileis(USA) was soon well placed after the start, but could not race on with the front three from over a furlong out. She remains capable of better back down in grade.
Kay Es Jay(FR) was up with the leaders until early in the straight and then gradually dropped back to finish second last

4627a PRIX GUILLAUME D'ORNANO - HARAS D'ETREHAM (GROUP 2) 1m 2f

3:20 (3:27) 3-Y-0 **£52,183** (£20,141; £9,613; £6,408; £3,204)

			RPR
1		**Literato (FR)**76 2293 3-8-12 ... C-PLemaire 7 (J-C Rouget, France) *towards rr: last 1/2-way: 9th st: drvn and r.o 1 1/2f out: r.o strly fnl f to ld cl home* **6/5**1	114
2	½	**Spirit One (FR)**76 2293 3-8-12 ... DBoeuf 1 (P Demercastel, France) *first to show: led after 4 1/2f: qcknd up wl 2f out: wnt clr 1 1/2f out: rdn fnl f: hdd cl home* **12/1**	113
3	2 ½	**Loup Breton (IRE)**21 3987 3-8-12 ... OPeslier 9 (E Lellouche, France) *mid-div: disputing 5th st: rdn over 1 1/2f out: styd on steadily and tk 3rd 100yds out* **11/1**	109
4	¾	**El Comodin (IRE)**41 3361 3-8-12 ... SPasquier 11 (A Fabre, France) *led 3f: in tch 1/2-way: 3rd st: drvn and wnt 2nd 1 1/2f out: no ex* **49/10**2	107
5	hd	**Regime (IRE)**21 3987 3-8-12 ... TThulliez 4 (M L W Bell) *hld up: rdn and disputing 5th st: styd on wl fr over 1f out: nrest at fin* **79/10**3	107
6	2	**Hello My Lord (FR)**20 4011 3-8-12 ... TGillet 3 (Mme C Head-Maarek, France) *racd in rr: last st: styd on wl fr over 1f out: nrest at fin* **27/1**	103
7	3	**Champery (USA)**18 4044 3-8-12 ... J-PGuillambert 5 (M Johnston) *mid-div: more prom by 1/2-way: drvn 3f out: 2nd st: rdn 2f out: styd on tl no ex fnl f* **28/1**	98
8	4	**Russian Desert (IRE)**21 3987 3-8-12 ... JVictoire 10 (A Fabre, France) *mid-div: disputing 5th on outside st: sn pushed along: rdn 1 1/2f out: unable qck* **17/1**	91
9	5	**Striving Storm (USA)**48 3142 3-8-12 ... JimmyFortune 8 (P W Chapple-Hyam) *prom: led 3f to 4 1/2f: bk into mid-div fr 1/2-way: disputing 5th st: drvn over 2f out: sn one pce* **25/1**	82
F		**Quest For Honor**76 2293 3-9-2 ... CSoumillon 2 (A Fabre, France) *towards rr early: hdwy 4f out: 4th st: short of room on rails bhd Champery 2f out and fell* **84/10**	—

2m 3.90s (-6.90) **10** Ran SP% **116.7**
PARI-MUTUEL: WIN 2.20; PL 1.30, 2.80, 2.60; DF 16.00.
Owner H Morin **Bred** Bsh Of Administrativa **Trained** Pau, France

NOTEBOOK
Literato(FR) was a spectacular victor. Dropped out last from the start, he was still in the same position at the entrance to the straight, but flew home to mow down his rivals to take the lead close home. The colt must have made up something like six-lengths inside the final furlong and has certainly done well since his second in the Jockey-Club. He is being specially prepared for the Champion Stakes in October and will be prepared for the Group 1 Newmarket event with a run in the Prix du Prince d'Orange over this distance at Longchamp on September 22.
Spirit One(FR) was returning to something like his best and he should pick up another group race by the end of the season. He was a little bit fresh on this occasion and ran free early on when in the lead. He quickened well in the straight and looked to have the race at his mercy one out but was just caught in the final 25 yards. It would be no surprise if he also turns out for the Prince d'Orange where he would be two kilos better off with the winner.
Loup Breton(IRE), given plenty to do on this occasion, ran his usual honest race. Putting in his best work at the finish he took third place running into the final furlong. A very consistent individual who has not always been lucky. At least a Group 3 race should come to him one day.
El Comodin(IRE), dropped in at this level for the first time, ran a fair race and could have probably done with more cut in the ground. He was outpaced early in the straight and was then one paced to the line. A nice colt who is still on the upgrade.
Regime(IRE) did not have the same zip as he did last time at Maisons-Laffitte. Held up early on, he tried to get on terms with the leaders half way up the straight but did not go through with his challenge. His jockey felt he did not run up to his best and suggested blinkers could help in the future.
Champery(USA), never far from the leaders, was raced on the rail throughout. He came under strong pressure early in the straight before dropping away.

4415 SARATOGA (R-H)

Saturday, August 18

OFFICIAL GOING: Fast

4628a ALABAMA STKS (GRADE 1) (FILLIES) (DIRT) 1m 2f (D)

10:20 (10:26) 3-Y-0

£183,673 (£61,224; £30,612; £15,306; £9,184; £3,061)

			RPR
1		**Lady Joanne (USA)**19 3-8-9 ... CHBorel 7 (C Nafzger, U.S.A) **9/2**3	115
2	nk	**Lear's Princess (USA)**28 3810 3-8-9 ... ECoa 6 (K McLaughlin, U.S.A) **48/10**	114
3	1 ½	**Octave (USA)**28 3810 3-8-9 ... JRVelazquez 4 (T Pletcher, U.S.A) **51/20**2	111
4	4 ½	**Moon Catcher (USA)**35 3-8-9 ...(b) KDesormeaux 1 (T F Ritchey, U.S.A) **109/10**	103
5	hd	**Panty Raid (USA)**42 3340 3-8-9 ... EPrado 2 (T Pletcher, U.S.A) **47/20**1	103
6	1 ¼	**Tough Tiz's Sis (USA)**69 3-8-9 ...(b) RBejarano 3 (B Baffert, U.S.A) **155/10**	101
7	29	**Folk (USA)**28 3810 3-8-9 ... GKGomez 5 (Saeed Bin Suroor) **83/10**	48

2m 3.62s (123.62) **7** Ran SP% **118.7**
PARI-MUTUEL (Including $2 stake): WIN 11.00; PL (1-2) 5.30, 5.30; SHOW (1-2-3) 3.20, 3.00, 2.60; SF 57.00.
Owner Bentley L Smith **Bred** Bentley L Smith **Trained** USA

4309 BATH (L-H)

Sunday, August 19

OFFICIAL GOING: Good (good to soft in places; 7.4) changing to good to soft after race 5 (4.30)

There were 17 non-runners on the card due to the change in the going.
Wind: Fresh, half-against

4629 ALLEN FORD MAIDEN AUCTION STKS 5f 11y

2:30 (2:34) (Class 6) 2-Y-0 **£2,072** (£616; £308; £153) **Stalls** Centre

Form				RPR
2520	1		**Hobson**19 4046 2-8-9 80 ... StephenCarson 4 (Eve Johnson Houghton) *a.p: rdn to ld ins fnl f: r.o wl* **6/4**1	67+
06	2	½	**Blue Zenith (IRE)**71 2443 2-8-6 0 ow2 ... JohnEgan 2 (J S Moore) *w ldr: led 1/2-way: rdn and hdd ins fnl f: kpt on* **8/1**	62
06	3	1 ¼	**Ever Hopeful**10 4310 2-8-8 0 ... MartinDwyer 6 (H J L Dunlop) *led to 1/2-way: styd prom: rdn and kpt on one pce fnl f* **33/1**	60
05	4	½	**Wee Buns**6 4459 2-8-9 0 ... LPKeniry 8 (S Kirk) *towards rr: hdwy and swtchd rt over 1f out: styd on fnl f* **25/1**	59

30 **5** 1/2 **Towy Boy (IRE)**[14] 4201 2-9-1 0 JamesDoyle 5 63
(I A Wood) *towards rr: rdn and hdwy over 1f out: styd on* **50/1**

00 **6** 1/2 **Golden Dane (IRE)**[14] 4198 2-8-4 0 SophieDoyle(7) 15 57
(I A Wood) *nvr bttr than mid-div though kpt on fnl f* **100/1**

54 **7** *hd* **Polar Annie**[24] 3866 2-8-0 0 ow2 MickyFenton 3 54
(M S Saunders) *prom tl one pce ent fnl f* **7/1**[3]

8 *nk* **Willit (IRE)** 2-8-3 0 ThomasO'Brien(7) 11 55
(M R Channon) *bhd: styd on fr over 1f out: nvr nrr* **25/1**

3243 **9** 1 1/4 **Shatter Resistant (IRE)**[20] 4020 2-9-1 72 RichardHughes 10 55
(M R Channon) *in tch tl rdn and wknd fnl f* **4/1**[2]

06 **10** 1 **Chemise (IRE)**[10] 4311 2-8-8 0 SteveDrowne 7 44
(R J Hodges) *a towards rr* **100/1**

0062 **11** 3/4 **Lady Vibeeka**[22] 3947 2-8-4 70 HayleyTurner 13 38
(Mrs H Sweeting) *prom tl rdn and wknd over 1f out* **7/1**[3]

000 **12** 4 **Treacle Noir (IRE)**[24] 3866 2-8-7 0 RichardKingscote(3) 14 29
(Tom Dascombe) *a bhd* **66/1**

3 **13** 1 1/4 **Captain Kir (IRE)**[15] 4160 2-9-1 0 AdamKirby 1 30
(B De Haan) *chsd ldrs tl rdn and wknd qckly appr fnl f* **14/1**

0 **14** 4 **Joss Stick**[34] 3589 2-8-9 0 AmirQuinn 12 9
(P J Makin) *a bhd* **11/1**

65.12 secs (2.62) **Going Correction** +0.325s/f (Good) **14** Ran SP% **127.2**
Speed ratings (Par 92): **92,91,89,88,87 86,86,86,84,82 81,74,72,66**
CSF £14.89 TOTE £2.90: £1.50, £3.60, £4.80; EX 25.80 TRIFECTA Not won..
Owner Anthony Pye-Jeary And Mel Smith **Bred** Hunscote House Farm Stud **Trained** Blewbury, Oxon

FOCUS
A moderate juvenile maiden in which the winner did not have to reproduce her best. The time was slow.

NOTEBOOK
Hobson, outclassed in the Molecomb last time, relished the drop in class and lost his maiden tag at the fifth time of asking. This would have just about have been the easiest ground he has raced on to date, and he should prove happier on a faster surface in the future, but whether he is really up to an official mark of 80 still remains to be seen. (op 11-4)
Blue Zenith(IRE) showed her best form to date on this drop back to the minimum and was a clear second best. She did leave the impression another furlong should really suit her again before too long and now has the option of nurseries. It should also be noted that her rider put up 2lb overweight. (op 12-1)
Ever Hopeful, having her first outing over this trip, posted an improved effort and showed good early dash. She ought to find life a fair bit easier now she is eligible for nurseries. (op 25-1)
Wee Buns, back down in trip, has now been outpaced through the early stages on each of his three runs to date. He did finish his race well though and, while his pedigree suggests speed, it may be that he really wants a stiffer test. He is another who now qualifies for nurseries. (op 40-1)
Towy Boy(IRE) put in an encouraging effort and was noted staying on with some promise inside the final furlong. He is yet another who should find life easier now he is eligible for nurseries. Official explanation: jockey said colt hung left-handed (op 40-1)
Golden Dane(IRE) lacked the pace required for this shorter trip, but he was keeping on once the race was effectively over and turned in an improved effort in defeat. He now has the option of nurseries.
Shatter Resistant(IRE) ran below his recent level on this return to the turf and is in danger of going the wrong way. (op 9-2 tchd 5-1)
Joss Stick Official explanation: jockey said colt never travelled

4630 ROBINS & DAY PEUGEOT MAIDEN STKS 1m 3f 144y
3:00 (3:05) (Class 5) 3-Y-O+ **£2,849** (£847; £423; £211) **Stalls** Low

Form RPR

1 **Dustoori** 3-9-3 0 RHills 9 79+
(Saeed Bin Suroor) *trckd ldr: led wl over 1f out: in command fnl f* **11/2**[2]

04 **2** 1 1/2 **Adorabella (IRE)**[41] 3365 4-9-8 0 DaneO'Neill 11 73+
(A King) *towards rr: stdy hdwy fr 1/2-way: swtchd rt over 1f out: styd on to go 2nd ins fnl f* **20/1**

0002 **3** 1/2 **Imperial Harry**[20] 4019 4-9-10 69 JerryO'Dwyer(3) 6 75
(V Smith) *in tch: rdn to chse wnr over 1f out tl ins fnl f* **7/1**

323 **4** 1 1/2 **Louviere**[38] 3476 3-8-12 75 RichardHughes 5 68
(Pat Eddery) *trckd ldrs: rdn fr 4f out: one pce fnl 2f* **7/4**[1]

0420 **5** 5 **Anthea**[39] 3429 3-8-12 60 FergusSweeney 10 60
(B R Millman) *led tl hdd wl over 1f out: sn btn* **9/1**

0 **6** 1 3/4 **How's Business**[8] 4392 3-8-12 0 SimonWhitworth 8 57
(C A Cyzer) *mid-div: rdn 3f out: one pce after* **66/1**

533- **7** 3/4 **Altenburg (FR)**[216] 5429 5-9-13 78 JamesDoyle 7 61
(Mrs N Smith) *mid-div tl rdn and wknd 2f out* **15/2**

3 **8** 1/2 **Midsummer Fun (USA)**[13] 4235 3-8-12 0 KerrinMcEvoy 15 55
(Saeed Bin Suroor) *trckd ldrs: rdn over 2f out: wknd over 1f out* **6/1**[3]

5 **9** 2 **Tilly Shilling (IRE)**[13] 4235 3-8-12 0 SteveDrowne 1 52
(C R Egerton) *mid-div: rdn and wknd over 1f out* **20/1**

00 **10** 5 **Borita (IRE)**[13] 4235 4-9-1 0 JackDean(7) 2 44
(M Scudamore) *a towards rr* **100/1**

0 **11** 6 **Beths Choice**[38] 3476 6-9-6 0 PietroRomeo(7) 16 39
(J M Bradley) *prom tl wknd 2f out* **100/1**

0 **12** 6 **Kitebrook**[25] 3847 6-9-8 0 VinceSlattery 17 25
(Mrs Mary Hambro) *in tch tl rdn 1/2-way: sn bhd* **100/1**

0- **13** 2 1/2 **Kurumda**[281] 6434 3-9-3 0 (p) NelsonDeSouza 4 26
(C R Egerton) *a bhd* **25/1**

0-0 **14** 32 **Pink Notes**[27] 3794 3-8-12 0 HaddenFrost(5) 14 —
(R J Hodges) *a bhd: t.o* **100/1**

15 22 **Double Rainbow (IRE)** 4-9-13 0 JohnEgan 12 —
(Jamie Poulton) *a bhd: t.o* **33/1**

2m 32.57s (2.27) **Going Correction** +0.275s/f (Good)
WFA 3 from 4yo+ 10lb **15** Ran SP% **122.1**
Speed ratings (Par 103): **103,102,101,100,97 96,95,95,94,90 86,82,81,59,45**
CSF £116.75 TOTE £7.60: £2.70, £4.60, £2.80; EX 226.10 TRIFECTA Not won..
Owner Godolphin **Bred** Shadwell Estate Company Limited **Trained** Newmarket, Suffolk

FOCUS
A modest maiden, run at a sound enough pace. Sound form rated through the third anf fifth.
Double Rainbow(IRE) Official explanation: jockey said colt had a breathing problem

4631 MRG VOLVO FOR LIFE H'CAP 1m 2f 46y
3:30 (3:30) (Class 4) (0-80,80) 3-Y-O+ **£4,792** (£1,425; £712; £355) **Stalls** Low

Form RPR

0330 **1** **Press The Button (GER)**[19] 4049 4-9-12 78 KerrinMcEvoy 7 88+
(J R Boyle) *sn trckd ldr: rdn to ld over 1f out: sn clr* **7/2**[2]

-030 **2** 3 **Don Pietro**[11] 4268 4-9-9 75 DaneO'Neill 1 78
(D J Coakley) *mid-div: rdn and styd on to chse wnr fnl f* **7/1**

5003 **3** 3/4 **Stravara**[36] 3530 4-8-6 61 oh1 WilliamBuick(3) 4 63
(R Hollinshead) *hld up: racd wd into strt: styd on fr over 1f out: nvr nrr* **17/2**

4521 **4** 3/4 **Norman The Great**[11] 4277 3-9-4 78 JohnEgan 3 78
(Jane Chapple-Hyam) *hld up: hdwy on outside over 2f out: one pce after* **15/8**[1]

0510 **5** *nk* **Mystery River (USA)**[30] 3705 3-9-1 75 RichardHughes 9 74
(B J Meehan) *led tl rdn and hdd over 1f out: wknd* **16/1**

0-20 **6** 4 **Masterofthecourt (USA)**[21] 3989 4-10-0 80 SteveDrowne 10 71
(H Morrison) *trckd ldrs: rdn and wknd over 1f out* **4/1**[3]

4144 **7** 1 **Street Warrior (IRE)**[11] 4284 4-9-9 75 KDarley 2 64
(J W Unett) *slowly away: a struggling in rr* **10/1**

2m 14.58s (3.58) **Going Correction** +0.50s/f (Yiel)
WFA 3 from 4yo+ 8lb **7** Ran SP% **115.0**
Speed ratings (Par 105): **105,102,102,101,101 97,97**
CSF £28.03 CT £192.48 TOTE £5.30: £2.30, £3.50; EX 39.30 Trifecta £182.80 Part won. Pool £257.57 - 0.68 winning units..
Owner Brian McAtavey **Bred** Gestut Sommerberg **Trained** Epsom, Surrey

FOCUS
A fair handicap, run at a moderate pace. The winner is value for a bit further, but the form, rated through the runner-up, is held down by the proximity of the third.

4632 PLATINUM MOTOR GROUP & WELLSWAY LTD FILLIES' H'CAP 1m 5y
4:00 (4:00) (Class 5) (0-70,69) 3-Y-O+ **£3,076** (£915; £457; £228) **Stalls** Low

Form RPR

0021 **1** **Ellen's Girl (IRE)**[3] 4532 4-9-2 58 6ex RichardHughes 5 65+
(R Hannon) *mde all: shkn up appr fnl f: r.o wl* **1/1**[1]

0246 **2** 1 **Celtic Spa (IRE)**[6] 4455 5-9-13 69 StephenDonohoe 3 74
(P D Evans) *trckd ldrs: wnt 2nd 2f out: kpt on but no imp ins fnl f* **9/1**

0103 **3** *nk* **Magical Music**[17] 4107 4-9-5 61 FrancisNorton 10 65+
(J Pearce) *hld up: rdn and hdwy on ins over 1f out: r.o ins fnl f: nvr nrr* **9/2**[2]

2400 **4** 1 3/4 **Lady Aspen (IRE)**[44] 3277 4-9-4 60 FergusSweeney 4 60
(Ian Williams) *mid-div: rdn wl over 1f out: one pce fnl f* **20/1**

3000 **5** 1 **It's No Problem (IRE)**[16] 3904 3-7-13 50 WilliamBuick(3) 8 48
(M Salaman) *hld up in rr: hdwy on outside over 2f out: sn rdn and no further prog* **20/1**

0000 **6** 2 1/2 **Altos Reales**[18] 4078 3-7-13 50 oh3 DominicFox(3) 6 42
(D Shaw) *a towards rr* **50/1**

0036 **7** 6 **Fangorn Forest (IRE)**[4] 4504 4-9-3 59 AmirQuinn 7 37
(R A Harris) *a towards rr* **10/1**

0350 **8** 3/4 **Cat Six (USA)**[12] 4257 3-9-2 64 DaneO'Neill 2 41
(T Wall) *slowly away: t.k.h and sn in tch: rdn whn wknd 2f out* **20/1**

0253 **9** *nk* **Iolanthe**[17] 4112 3-9-6 68 KDarley 1 44
(B J Meehan) *trckd wnr to 2f out: sn wknd* **5/1**[3]

1m 44.24s (3.14) **Going Correction** +0.50s/f (Yiel)
WFA 3 from 4yo+ 6lb **9** Ran SP% **120.2**
Speed ratings (Par 100): **104,103,102,100,99 97,91,90,90**
CSF £11.09 CT £32.41 TOTE £1.70: £1.10, £2.90, £1.50; EX 17.30 Trifecta £49.70 Pool £272.46 - 3.89 winning units..
Owner Con Harrington **Bred** Mrs Chris Harrington **Trained** East Everleigh, Wilts

FOCUS
A moderate fillies' handicap. The winner, who remains progressive, set an ordinary pace and few got into this.

4633 EUROPEAN BREEDERS' FUND DICK HERN FILLIES' STKS (LISTED RACE) 1m 5y
4:30 (4:33) (Class 1) 3-Y-O+
£14,762 (£5,595; £2,800; £1,396; £699; £351) **Stalls** Low

Form RPR

0-10 **1** **Pintle**[16] 4119 7-9-0 90 KerrinMcEvoy 10 98
(J L Spearing) *trckd ldr: rdn to ld ins fnl f: r.o* **22/1**

6600 **2** 3/4 **Sesmen**[16] 4118 3-8-8 101 (t) MickyFenton 1 96
(M Botti) *led: clr 3f out: rdn and hdd ins fnl f* **12/1**

01-4 **3** 2 **Wagtail**[23] 3897 4-9-5 95 SteveDrowne 6 97
(E A L Dunlop) *trckd ldrs thrght: kpt on one pce fnl f* **11/2**

-225 **4** 3/4 **Sudoor**[23] 3897 3-8-8 102 MartinDwyer 12 90
(J L Dunlop) *hld up in rr: rdn 2f out: r.o fnl f: nvr nrr* **7/1**

1111 **5** *nk* **Our Faye**[8] 4373 4-9-0 85 GeorgeBaker 9 89
(S Kirk) *hld up in rr: hdwy over 2f out: one pce fnl f* **5/1**[3]

612 **6** *nk* **Smart Ass (IRE)**[8] 4404 4-9-0 78 JohnEgan 5 89
(J S Moore) *towards rr: c wd into st: nvr on terms* **16/1**

1-54 **7** 5 **Basaata (USA)**[15] 4148 3-8-8 99 RHills 3 77
(M P Tregoning) *in tch: rdn over 2f out: wknd over 1f out* **5/2**[1]

1-0 **8** 7 **Rainbow Promises (USA)**[16] 4118 3-8-8 94 KDarley 4 61
(B J Meehan) *in mid-div: rdn 3f out: sn btn* **11/4**[2]

1m 42.96s (1.86) **Going Correction** +0.50s/f (Yiel)
WFA 3 from 4yo+ 6lb **8** Ran SP% **117.7**
Speed ratings (Par 108): **110,109,107,106,106 105,100,93**
CSF £259.63 TOTE £32.90: £5.30, £3.90, £2.30; EX 292.50 TRIFECTA Not won..
Owner Robert Heathcote **Bred** R And Mrs Heathcote **Trained** Kinnersley, Worcs

FOCUS
Just an average fillies' Listed event, run at an ordinary pace with the principals always prominent. The ground had eased before this and the form is not easy to assess.

NOTEBOOK
Pintle, unplaced in four previous outings at this level, showed her true colours and bounced back to her best to score. This obviously has to rate her best effort to date, she showed battling qualities when it mattered, and her paddock value will now have been nicely enhanced. Official explanation: trainer said, regarding the improved form shown, mare had been better suited by racing handily here (op 20-1)
Sesmen was given an aggressive ride on this drop back in grade and only gave way to the winner late on. She was allowed very much the run of the race, but it was still her most encouraging effort as a three-year-old and she has clearly now found her level again. (op 10-1)
Wagtail was only found out by her penalty and did nothing wrong in defeat. She has resumed in great heart this term. (op 13-2 tchd 7-1)
Sudoor failed to raise her game for the drop back in trip, yet still ran her race and ideally wants faster ground. (op 10-1)
Our Faye, unbeaten in four previous outings this term, never threatened from off the pace yet was not really disgraced at the weights on this first try in Listed company. This may also have come just a little too soon for her. (op 4-1)
Basaata(USA), easy to back, ran well below her best and did not prove suited by the easier ground. She is not one to write off just yet. Official explanation: jockey said filly was unsuited by the good to soft ground (op 15-8)

The Form Book, Raceform Ltd, Compton, RG20 6NL

Rainbow Promises(USA) was in trouble a long way from home and has seemingly not trained on from two-to-three. However, given her breeding surely a sounder surface is what she needs. (op 6-1 tchd 5-2)

4634 HARTWELL BEST PRICE CAR H'CAP 5f 161y
5:00 (5:01) (Class 5) (0-75,75) 3-Y-0+ **£3,076** (£915; £457; £228) **Stalls** Centre

Form RPR
513 **1** **Impromptu**[27] 3797 3-9-10 **75**.............................. GeorgeBaker 2 86
(R M Beckett) *a in tch: hdwy to ld appr fnl f: rdn out* **10/3**[1]
2-14 **2** ½ **Dixieland Boy (IRE)**[199] 323 4-9-5 **67**.............................. SteveDrowne 1 76
(P J Makin) *trckd ldrs: ev ch ent fnl f: kpt on ins fnl f* **7/1**
4343 **3** 2 **Caustic Wit (IRE)**[8] 4396 9-9-4 **66**.............................. TGMcLaughlin 9 68
(M S Saunders) *towards rr: hdwy over 1f out: r.o: nt rch first 2* **7/2**[2]
2212 **4** 3 **Currency**[64] 2664 10-8-7 **62**.............................. BarrySavage(7) 3 54
(J M Bradley) *trckd ldr: fdd ins fnl f* **10/1**
4200 **5** ½ **Summer Recluse (USA)**[1] 4606 8-9-2 **64**..............(t) StephenDonohoe 7 54
(J M Bradley) *slowly away: in rr: hdwy on ins appr fnl f: kpt on* **6/1**[3]
4250 **6** nk **Blessed Place**[4] 4507 7-9-1 **63**..............................(t) TQuinn 8 52
(D J S Ffrench Davis) *led tl hdd appr fnl f: wknd ins fnl f* **6/1**[3]
00-0 **7** ¾ **Grand Jour (IRE)**[6] 4462 4-9-0 **65**.............................. WilliamBuick(3) 6 52
(B P J Baugh) *a towards rr* **33/1**
2540 **8** 6 **Harrison's Flyer (IRE)**[4] 4507 6-9-5 **72**..............(p) KevinGhunowa(5) 11 38
(J M Bradley) *in rr: c wd into st: nvr on terms* **6/1**[3]
5661 **9** hd **Mr Loire**[10] 4312 3-9-7 **72**..............................(b) DaneO'Neill 5 38
(H J L Dunlop) *slowly away: a bhd* **20/1**

1m 14.15s (2.95) **Going Correction** +0.55s/f (Yiel)
WFA 3 from 4yo+ 3lb 9 Ran SP% **117.5**
Speed ratings (Par 103): **102,101,98,94,94 93,92,84,84**
CSF £27.60 CT £87.65 TOTE £3.10: £1.60, £2.40, £1.20; EX 32.50 Trifecta £94.10 Pool £507.86 - 3.83 winning units..
Owner C F Colquhoun **Bred** Mrs S Joint **Trained** Whitsbury, Hants

FOCUS
A modest sprint handicap. The form looks sound enough rated through the second.

4635 MERCEDES-BENZ OF BATH AT PEASEDOWN H'CAP 5f 11y
5:30 (5:30) (Class 6) (0-60,60) 3-Y-0+ **£2,266** (£674; £337; £168) **Stalls** Centre

Form RPR
020 **1** **Briery Lane (IRE)**[8] 4397 6-9-1 **55**.............................. StephenDonohoe 5 64
(J M Bradley) *towards rr: hdwy whn swtchd lft 2f out: rdn to ld appr fnl f: r.o* **11/2**[3]
005 **2** ½ **Endless Summer**[34] 3594 10-9-1 **55**.............................. FrancisNorton 8 63
(A W Carroll) *in tch: hrd rdn to chse wnr ins fnl f: no imp* **11/4**[1]
0000 **3** 1 ¼ **Rare Breed**[26] 3829 4-9-0 **54**.............................. TGMcLaughlin 3 57
(Mrs L Stubbs) *towards rr: rdn 2f out: r.o to snatch 3rd cl home* **16/1**
5630 **4** nk **Jucebabe**[3] 4545 4-8-12 **55**..............................(p) LiamJones(3) 13 57
(J L Spearing) *s.i.s: sn in tch: wl there 1f out: lost 3rd cl home* **4/1**[2]
-140 **5** 3 **Elvina**[90] 1902 6-8-7 **47**.............................. RichardThomas 10 38
(A G Newcombe) *chsd ldr: rdn 2f out: wknd fnl f* **20/1**
0006 **6** shd **Decider (USA)**[47] 3190 4-9-1 **55**.............................. LPKeniry 6 46
(J M Bradley) *mid-div: rdn 1/2-way: wknd fnl f* **11/1**
0006 **7** ½ **Whistler**[23] 3906 10-8-9 **49**..............................(p) PaulFitzsimons 17 38
(Miss J R Tooth) *in mid-div: one pce fnl f* **16/1**
-000 **8** 1 **Smart Cassie**[67] 2553 4-8-8 **48** oh1 ow2..............(b[1]) MickyFenton 11 33
(H J Evans) *led tl rdn and hdd over 1f out: wknd qckly* **50/1**
0604 **9** shd **Flower Of Cork (IRE)**[5] 4471 3-8-7 **49**..............(p) JamesDoyle 4 34
(Ms J S Doyle) *nvr bttr than mid-div* **20/1**
0160 **10** ¾ **Sands Crooner (IRE)**[17] 4103 4-9-5 **59**..............(v) DaneO'Neill 15 41
(D Shaw) *a bhd* **7/1**
0000 **11** 5 **Millenium Sun (IRE)**[3] 4536 3-9-1 **60**.............................. AlanCreighton(3) 2 24
(E J Creighton) *a struggling in rr* **33/1**
000 **12** 8 **That's Blue Chip**[12] 4252 4-8-12 **52**.............................. JohnEgan 7 —
(P W D'Arcy) *chsd ldrs to 1/2-way: sn bhd* **17/2**

64.95 secs (2.45) **Going Correction** +0.55s/f (Yiel)
WFA 3 from 4yo+ 2lb 12 Ran SP% **119.6**
Speed ratings (Par 101): **102,101,99,98,93 93,92,91,91,90 82,69**
CSF £20.20 CT £237.49 TOTE £7.00: £2.40, £1.80, £5.20; EX 36.70 TRIFECTA Not won. Place 6 £286.82, Place 5 £151.56..
Owner Delamere Cottage Racing Partners (1996) **Bred** Simon And Helen Plumbly **Trained** Sedbury, Gloucs

FOCUS
A weak sprint handicap run on the worst ground on the card. The pace was strong and the first three came from the rear. Fairly sound form.
T/Plt: £726.00 to a £1 stake. Pool: £64,353.90. 64.70 winning tickets. T/Qpdt: £80.60 to a £1 stake. Pool: £4,022.40. 36.90 winning tickets. JS

4284 PONTEFRACT (L-H)
Sunday, August 19

OFFICIAL GOING: Good (7.3) changing to good to soft after race 2 (2.40)
Wind: Virtually nil Weather: Overcast and rain

4636 EUROPEAN BREEDERS' FUND EVELYN WILKS 95TH BIRTHDAY MAIDEN STKS 5f
2:10 (2:13) (Class 4) 2-Y-0 **£5,181** (£1,541; £770; £384) **Stalls** Low

Form RPR
02 **1** **Mister Fips (IRE)**[10] 4335 2-9-3 86.............................. JamieSpencer 1 83
(Jane Chapple-Hyam) *qckly away: mde all: rdn over 1f out: edgd rt wl ins fnl f: kpt on* **1/1**[1]
3332 **2** ½ **Aaim For Applause**[10] 4323 2-9-3 80.............................. TPO'Shea 6 81
(M R Channon) *trckd wnr: hdwy 2f out: rdn to chal over 1f out and ev ch tl drvn and nt qckn wl ins fnl f* **15/8**[2]
0 **3** 10 **Glenveagh (IRE)**[16] 4125 2-9-3 0.............................. PatCosgrave 4 45+
(K A Ryan) *chsd ldrs: rdn along 2f out: sn one pce* **16/1**
36 **4** 1 ½ **Lekin Sedona (IRE)**[25] 3833 2-9-3 0.............................. PaulHanagan 9 40
(J M Saville) *wnt rt s: towards rr: hdwy 2f out: sn rdn and kpt on same pce* **33/1**
5 ½ **Rio Sands** 2-8-12 0.............................. NataliaGemelova(5) 7 38
(R M Whitaker) *s.i.s and bhd: hdwy 2f out: styd on appr fnl f: nrst fin* **22/1**
6 1 ¼ **Captain Macarry (IRE)** 2-9-3 0.............................. RoystonFfrench 3 33
(B Smart) *bhd: rdn along over 2f out: nvr a factor* **7/1**[3]
05 **7** 3 ½ **Tafira (IRE)**[15] 4174 2-8-12 0.............................. LeeEnstone 2 16
(K R Burke) *dwlt: a towards rr* **40/1**
8 3 **Captain Turbot (IRE)** 2-9-3 0.............................. TonyHamilton 8 10
(D W Barker) *prom: rdn along over 2f out and sn wknd* **33/1**
0 **9** 3 **Presidium Star**[15] 4174 2-8-9 0.............................. AndrewElliott(3) 5 —
(G M Moore) *outpcd and bhd fr 1/2-way* **100/1**

64.64 secs (0.84) **Going Correction** +0.15s/f (Good) 9 Ran SP% **116.8**
Speed ratings (Par 96): **99,98,82,79,79 77,71,66,61**
CSF £2.89 TOTE £1.90: £1.02, £1.20, £3.50; EX 3.40.
Owner Mark & Sue Harniman **Bred** Tally-Ho Stud **Trained** Newmarket, Suffolk

FOCUS
Only two got into this, finishing well clear. The form is rated through the runner-up.

NOTEBOOK
Mister Fips(IRE) got off the mark at the sixth attempt, confirming the promise he'd shown on a couple of previous occasions. The drop back in trip proved no problem and, making all following a good break from his low draw, he appeared to show more resolution than the runner-up to score driven out. He's rated 86, and probably ran close to that mark, but he might find a few less exposed sorts too good in nurseries. (op 5-4)
Aaim For Applause had a series of placed efforts to his name, and although he was ten lengths clear of the remainder, he left the impression he was keeping a bit back for himself, for he didn't appear that keen to go past the winner. He's capable of winning a race, probably over further. (op 9-4)
Glenveagh(IRE) chased the leaders but never got to them. He appears to be taking a little time to come to himself, but it would be no surprise if he progressed and he could be interesting in nurseries after another run. (op 10-1)
Lekin Sedona(IRE) never got on terms, but small nurseries will beckon now. (op 28-1)
Rio Sands missed the break, but ran on steadily to finish a well-beaten fifth. He'll improve on this.

4637 SUNDAY PLATE H'CAP 1m 4f 8y
2:40 (2:40) (Class 3) (0-95,93) 3-Y-0+ **£9,348** (£2,799; £1,399; £700; £349; £175) **Stalls** Low

Form RPR
1165 **1** **Record Breaker (IRE)**[21] 3993 3-8-9 **84**.............................. GregFairley 10 97
(M Johnston) *trckd ldr: hdwy to ld wl over 2f out: rdn clr wl over 1f out: styd on wl fnl f* **3/1**[2]
/535 **2** 3 **Night Hour (IRE)**[19] 4047 5-9-9 **88**.............................. LDettori 4 96
(J H M Gosden) *hld up in tch: hdwy over 3f out: chsd wnr wl over 1f out: drvn: edgd lft and no imp ins fnl f* **11/4**[1]
115 **3** 7 **Just Lille (IRE)**[29] 3755 4-9-3 **82**..............................(p) RoystonFfrench 7 79
(Mrs A Duffield) *chsd ldrs: rdn along 3f out: kpt on same pce u.p fnl 2f* **20/1**
-300 **4** nk **Galient (IRE)**[92] 1844 4-10-0 **93**.............................. PhilipRobinson 1 89
(M A Jarvis) *in tch: effrt 3f out: sn rdn along and kpt on same pce fnl 2f* **10/1**
302 **5** 2 ½ **Dzesmin (POL)**[22] 3978 5-9-1 **80**..............................(p) JamieSpencer 8 72
(R C Guest) *hld up in rr: hdwy over 4f out: rdn along on outer wl over 2f out and no further prog* **5/1**
013- **6** ½ **St Savarin (FR)**[260] 6677 6-9-11 **90**.............................. PaulHanagan 3 82
(R A Fahey) *in rr: pushed along over 4f out: sn outpcd* **18/1**
13-0 **7** 2 **Leslingtaylor (IRE)**[78] 2236 5-8-12 **77**.............................. GrahamGibbons 6 65
(J J Quinn) *hld up: a in rr* **9/2**[3]
6500 **8** ½ **La Estrella (USA)**[11] 4288 4-9-5 **84**..............................(b[1]) TPQueally 9 72
(J G Given) *led: rdn along and hdd wl over 2f out: sn wknd* **20/1**
1331 **9** 13 **Heathyards Pride**[10] 4318 7-9-1 **80**.............................. TedDurcan 5 47
(R Hollinshead) *chsd ldng pair: rdn along over 3f out: sn wknd* **11/1**

2m 40.85s (0.55) **Going Correction** +0.15s/f (Good)
WFA 3 from 4yo+ 10lb 9 Ran SP% **118.7**
Speed ratings (Par 107): **104,102,97,97,95 95,93,93,84**
CSF £12.11 CT £134.37 TOTE £3.90: £1.40, £1.70, £3.30; EX 19.40.
Owner Leung Kai Fai & Vincent Leung **Bred** Sir E J Loder **Trained** Middleham Moor, N Yorks

FOCUS
This was a competitive handicap in which the winner was always well placed. The first two were clear.

NOTEBOOK
Record Breaker(IRE) had run creditably in two decent handicaps since his two wins in the spring and, dropped in grade, ran out a decisive winner. Racing in second, he was sent on before the straight and ran on in good style. He'll go up again in the weights, but with his stable in good form, he could well defy a further rise. (op 10-3 tchd 7-2)
Night Hour(IRE) ran a sound enough race in second, coming from off the pace and keeping on. On the positive side was the fact that he drew clear of the remainder, but the negative is that not for the first time he hung under pressure and looked less than straightforward. Official explanation: jockey said gelding hung left-handed. (op 3-1 tchd 7-2)
Just Lille(IRE) is high in the weights after her four-timer earlier in the season but, though well back in third, wasn't disgraced. She shapes as though she will stay 1m4f, but better ground would be in her favour. (op 25-1)
Galient(IRE) hasn't been in the best of form this term but shaped a little better here without the cheekpieces, although he will need to improve again before he's winning. (tchd 9-1)
Dzesmin(POL) continues in the grip of the handicapper. (op 9-2 tchd 11-2)
St Savarin(FR) was keen on his belated seasonal reappearance. (op 20-1 tchd 16-1)
La Estrella(USA) was keen in first-time blinkers and did not see it out.

4638 FRONTLINE COMPLETE BATHROOM H'CAP 2m 1f 22y
3:10 (3:13) (Class 5) (0-70,66) 3-Y-0+ **£3,886** (£1,156; £577; £288) **Stalls** Low

Form RPR
-321 **1** **Kentucky Boy (IRE)**[27] 3792 3-8-0 **55**.............................. AndrewElliott(3) 2 67
(Jedd O'Keeffe) *prom: rdn along over 3f out: led wl over 2f out and sn clr: drvn ins fnl f and styd on wl* **9/4**[1]
6344 **2** 2 ½ **Sa Nau**[11] 4297 4-9-3 **55**.............................. NickyMackay 10 64
(T Keddy) *trckd ldrs: effrt 3f out: rdn to chse wnr wl over 1f out: sn drvn and no imp ins fnl f* **11/2**
0535 **3** 5 **Mr Mischief**[13] 4231 7-9-1 **58**.............................. RussellKennemore(5) 9 62
(M C Chapman) *hld up in rr: gd hdwy on outer over 2f out: sn rdn and styd on ins fnl f* **6/1**
6023 **4** 3 ½ **Vice Admiral**[11] 4280 4-9-0 **59**.............................. NSLawes(7) 12 59
(M W Easterby) *sn led: rdn along over 3f out: hdd wl over 2f out: sn drvn and one pce* **8/1**
4226 **5** nk **Rocknest Island (IRE)**[22] 3976 4-9-6 **61**..............(p) AndrewMullen(3) 6 60
(P D Niven) *hld up in rr: stdy hdwy over 6f out: rdn to chse ldrs over 3f out: sn drvn and kpt on same pce fnl 2f* **5/1**[3]
00-0 **6** 1 **Magnum Opus (IRE)**[23] 3901 5-9-3 **62**.............................. JamesO'Reilly(7) 13 60
(D J Murphy) *hld up in rr: hdwy on outer over 4f out: rdn and ch over 2f out: sn drvn and wknd* **33/1**
05-5 **7** 12 **Kerry's Blade (IRE)**[6] 4451 5-8-12 **50**.............................. PaulHanagan 1 35
(Micky Hammond) *chsd ldrs: rdn along 4f out and sn wknd* **22/1**
00/0 **8** 5 **Araglin**[23] 3927 8-8-12 **50**.............................. TPO'Shea 5 30
(J T Stimpson) *a towards rr* **40/1**
23-6 **9** 22 **El Alamein (IRE)**[11] 4297 4-9-13 **65**.............................. SebSanders 3 20
(Sir Mark Prescott) *prom: effrt 6f out: rdn along 4f out: wknd over 3f out* **7/2**[2]

0000 **10** *17* **College Rebel**[8] 4409 6-8-9 **47** oh2 ChrisCatlin 11 —
(J F Coupland) *a towards rr* **80/1**

4m 3.30s (12.80) **Going Correction** +0.15s/f (Good)
WFA 3 from 4yo+ 14lb **10** Ran SP% **121.4**
Speed ratings (Par 103): **75,73,71,69,69 69,63,61,50,42**
CSF £15.44 CT £68.41 TOTE £3.10: £1.40, £2.20, £2.60; EX 18.30.
Owner A Walker **Bred** Eclipse Thoroughbreds Inc **Trained** Middleham Moor, N Yorks

FOCUS
Just an ordinary gallop to this and those who raced close to the pace were at an advantage. The winner is progressive.

4639 EBF SLATCH FARM STUD FLYING FILLIES' STKS (LISTED RACE) 6f
3:40 (3:41) (Class 1) 3-Y-O+
£25,551 (£9,684; £4,846; £2,416; £1,210; £607) **Stalls** Low

Form RPR

6200 **1** **Ripples Maid**[15] 4150 4-9-4 98 RoystonFfrench 11 105
(J A Geake) *a.p on outer: hdwy 2f out: rdn to ld ins fnl f: styd on wl* **12/1**

1612 **2** *1 1/4* **Diamond Diva**[18] 4062 3-8-11 94 EddieAhern 2 97
(J W Hills) *hld up in tch: gd hdwy over 2f out: led wl over 1f out: rdn and hdd ins fnl f: snd drvn and kpt on* **13/2**[3]

3111 **3** *1 1/2* **Bee Eater (IRE)**[16] 4133 3-8-11 99 SebSanders 10 92
(Sir Mark Prescott) *chsd ldrs: rdn along wl over 1f out: styd on u.p ins fnl f* **6/4**[1]

1360 **4** *2 1/2* **Pusey Street Lady**[9] 4360 3-8-11 85 ChrisCatlin 3 84
(J Gallagher) *prom: lost pl and towards rr 1/2-way: hdwy 2f out: rdn and styd on appr fnl f* **40/1**

0000 **5** *3* **Puggy (IRE)**[16] 4118 3-8-11 93 (t) NickyMackay 9 75
(R A Kvisla) *hld up in tch: hdwy to chse ldrs 2f out: sn rdn and no imp appr fnl f* **16/1**

2216 **6** *1* **Final Dynasty**[14] 4196 3-8-11 99 PaulHanagan 1 71
(Mrs G S Rees) *led: rdn along 2f out: sn hdd: drvn and one pce appr fnl f* **14/1**

0130 **7** *shd* **Riquewihr**[8] 4407 7-9-0 71 (p) PaddyAspell 7 71
(J S Wainwright) *hld up in rr: hdwy 2f out: sn rdn and no imp* **80/1**

0101 **8** *1/2* **Choysia**[12] 4251 4-9-0 70 TomEaves 8 69
(D W Barker) *cl up: rdn along 2f out: sn wknd* **50/1**

5414 **9** *5* **Thunderousapplause**[25] 3857 3-8-11 85 PatCosgrave 5 53
(K A Ryan) *prom: rdn along 1/2-way: sn wknd* **50/1**

31P1 **10** *10* **Song Of Passion (IRE)**[36] 3529 4-9-0 101 JamieSpencer 4 21
(R Hannon) *cl up: ev ch over 2f out: sn rdn and wknd* **9/4**[2]

46-2 **11** *7* **Moone Cross (IRE)**[22] 3982 4-9-0 0 TPO'Shea 6 —
(Mrs John Harrington, Ire) *in tch: rdn along 1/2-way: sn lost pl and bhd* **14/1**

1m 16.0s (-1.40) **Going Correction** +0.15s/f (Good)
WFA 3 from 4yo+ 3lb **11** Ran SP% **118.6**
Speed ratings (Par 108): **115,113,111,108,104 102,102,101,95,81 72**
CSF £87.47 TOTE £16.00: £3.60, £2.00, £1.10; EX 111.80.
Owner Rex Mead & David Mead **Bred** Compton Down Stud **Trained** Kimpton, Hants
■ Stewards' Enquiry : T P O'Shea two-day ban: careless riding (Aug 30-31)

FOCUS
A competitive fillies' Listed event and fair form for the grade. The first three all raced middle to stands' side in the straight.

NOTEBOOK
Ripples Maid was third in this race a year ago. Down the field in the Stewards' Cup and the Wokingham on her last two starts, she bounced back to form, challenging wide and running on well in the straight. She's exposed and this is her level, but she's clearly in good form. (op 14-1)
Diamond Diva, up in grade and down in trip, ran a sound race, showing plenty of pace and keeping on well. On this evidence she can win in this company. (op 9-1)
Bee Eater(IRE), who had been in good form in handicaps, wasn't quite up to winning in this grade, but wasn't disgraced either, keeping on without getting to the leaders. Interestingly the first three all raced middle to stands' side in the straight. (op 11-8 tchd 13-8)
Pusey Street Ladyfaced a very stiff task at the weights, and ran creditably though won't have done her handicap mark any favours.
Final Dynasty showed plenty of speed, but was beaten early in the straight. (op 12-1)
Song Of Passion(IRE) dropped right away after showing good speed until well into the straight. Official explanation: trainer had no explanation for the poor form shown (op 11-4)
Moone Cross(IRE) Official explanation: jockey said filly was never travelling.

4640 UNISON PROTECTING PUBLIC SERVICES H'CAP 1m 4y
4:10 (4:10) (Class 3) (0-90,90) 3-Y-O
£9,348 (£2,799; £1,399; £700; £349; £175) **Stalls** Low

Form RPR

-312 **1** **Parisian Dream**[16] 4135 3-8-12 **81** JamieSpencer 6 90
(B W Hills) *a.p: effrt to ld wl over 1f out and sn rdn: drvn ins fnl f and hld on gamely* **3/1**[1]

2110 **2** *nk* **Emerald Wilderness (IRE)**[17] 4092 3-9-7 **90** LDettori 10 98
(E A L Dunlop) *prom tl lost pl and bhd after 3f: hdwy over 2f out: rdn to chal over 1f out: sn drvn and kpt on fnl f: jst hld* **7/2**[2]

1116 **3** *1 1/4* **The Grey Berry**[36] 3556 3-9-3 **86** GrahamGibbons 8 91
(T D Walford) *hld up in tch: pushed along and outpcd wl over 2f out: styd on appr fnl f: nrst fin* **13/2**

0601 **4** *2* **Deadline (UAE)**[11] 4282 3-8-1 **73** AndrewMullen(3) 1 74
(P T Midgley) *in midfield: hdwy on inner 3f out: rdn to chse ldrs wl over 1f out: sn drvn and one pce* **25/1**

1126 **5** *1/2* **Milla's Rocket (IRE)**[22] 3960 3-8-10 **79** (b) PatCosgrave 4 78
(K A Ryan) *prom: led 3f out: rdn and hdd wl over 1f out: drvn and wknd ent fnl f* **12/1**

4621 **6** *3* **Honest Prospector (USA)**[16] 4138 3-8-9 **78** RoystonFfrench 9 70
(Sir Michael Stoute) *chsd ldrs: pushed along 1/2-way: rdn 3f out and sn btn* **13/2**

4410 **7** *3/4* **Medici Pearl**[13] 4222 3-8-9 **78** DavidAllan 2 69
(T D Easterby) *a towards rr* **11/1**

-211 **8** *2* **Danehillsundance (IRE)**[43] 3334 3-9-5 **88** SebSanders 7 74
(R Hannon) *prom: rdn along over 3f out and sn wknd* **6/1**[3]

3000 **9** *shd* **Billy Dane (IRE)**[36] 3559 3-9-4 **87** PaulHanagan 5 73
(R A Fahey) *sn led: rdn along and hdd 3f out: sn wknd* **12/1**

1m 45.78s (0.08) **Going Correction** +0.15s/f (Good) **9** Ran SP% **115.7**
Speed ratings (Par 104): **105,104,103,101,100 97,97,95,95**
CSF £13.53 CT £63.08 TOTE £3.40: £1.10, £1.70, £2.30; EX 12.40.
Owner J Hanson **Bred** Mrs A D Bourne **Trained** Lambourn, Berks

FOCUS
Quite an interesting handicap. Solid form, the front pair progressing a bit further.

NOTEBOOK
Parisian Dream maintained his improvement. A Salisbury maiden winner who was runner-up in a Newmarket handicap on his previous start, he looked to face a stiff task off a 5lb higher mark here, but went on over a furlong out and showed plenty of resolution to get home in a driving finish. He should continue on the upgrade. (tchd 11-4 and 10-3)
Emerald Wilderness(IRE), who had raced keenly for an apprentice rider on his previous start, settled and ran much better this time, throwing down a determined challenge in the last furlong but just held. He's gone up 15lb for his three wins this time, but this trip would have been plenty sharp enough for him, and he could well find another race when stepped back up to 1m2f. (op 11-2)
The Grey Berry, who has progressed well this season, took time to pick up but stayed on well and left the impression he may get further. (op 9-2)
Deadline(UAE) did really well considering he was put up 10lb for winning an ordinary maiden on his previous start, and like several in this field he left the impression he's still on the upgrade. (op 22-1)
Honest Prospector(USA) Official explanation: jockey said colt was unsuited by ground (good to soft).
Danehillsundance(IRE), 3lb higher, dropped right out in the straight after racing prominently. (tchd 13-2)

4641 UNISON DIANE SHEPPARD MEMORIAL MAIDEN STKS 1m 4y
4:40 (4:41) (Class 4) 3-Y-O+ **£6,477** (£1,927; £963; £481) **Stalls** Low

Form RPR

2422 **1** **Zifaaf (USA)**[11] 4290 3-8-10 75 JamieSpencer 10 67
(B W Hills) *hld up in tch: hdwy on outer 3f out: led wl over 1f out: sn rdn clr: styd on* **2/1**[2]

0-60 **2** *2 1/2* **Zain (IRE)**[73] 2389 3-9-1 43 (t) TPQueally 2 66
(J G Given) *trckd ldrs: hdwy over 2f out: sn rdn and styd on ins fnl f: nrst fin* **33/1**

62 **3** *hd* **Double Doors**[11] 4275 3-9-1 0 RobertHavlin 3 66
(J H M Gosden) *trckd ldrs: hdwy over 2f out: sn rdn and styd on ins fnl f* **15/8**[1]

0033 **4** *2 1/2* **Best One**[11] 4291 3-9-1 75 SebSanders 1 60
(C E Brittain) *trckd ldrs: hdwy to ld wl over 2f out: sn rdn and hdd wl over 1f out: wknd ins fnl f* **11/2**

040 **5** *3 1/2* **Beresford Lady**[23] 3917 3-8-10 50 SilvestreDeSousa 6 47
(A D Brown) *prom: rdn along over 3f out: drvn over 2f out and sn wknd* **66/1**

0 **6** *nk* **Natco**[15] 4178 3-8-10 0 GregFairley 9 46
(M Johnston) *prom: rdn along over 3f out: wknd over 2f out* **33/1**

6 **7** *2 1/2* **Reddy Ronnie (IRE)**[16] 4138 3-9-1 0 DanielTudhope 7 45
(D Carroll) *set stdy pce: rdn along and hdd wl over 2f out: sn wknd* **100/1**

8 *1* **Mysterious World (IRE)** 3-8-12 0 PJMcDonald(3) 8 43
(Mrs K Walton) *a in rr* **100/1**

5 **9** *3/4* **Island King (IRE)**[21] 4007 4-9-7 0 RoystonFfrench 11 41
(R Bastiman) *a in rr* **100/1**

0 **10** *2 1/2* **Florentino**[21] 4000 3-8-10 0 DavidAllan 5 31
(C W Thornton) *a in rr* **100/1**

U **11** *dist* **Colourful Score (USA)**[38] 3454 3-9-1 0 (t) LDettori 4 —
(Saeed Bin Suroor) *virtually ref to r* **7/2**[3]

1m 47.27s (1.57) **Going Correction** +0.15s/f (Good)
WFA 3 from 4yo 6lb **11** Ran SP% **117.1**
Speed ratings (Par 105): **98,95,95,92,89 89,86,85,84,82** —
CSF £68.38 TOTE £3.20: £1.02, £7.50, £1.60; EX 80.50.
Owner Hamdan Al Maktoum **Bred** Shadwell Farm LLC **Trained** Lambourn, Berks

FOCUS
Not much strength in depth in this maiden, which was run at a steady pace. The form horses were not at their best and the form is dubious.

4642 TREVOR WOODS MEMORIAL H'CAP 5f
5:10 (5:10) (Class 5) (0-70,70) 3-Y-O+ **£3,886** (£1,156; £577; £144; £144) **Stalls** Low

Form RPR

2002 **1** **Never Without Me**[7] 4423 7-8-11 **58** ChrisCatlin 13 72
(J F Coupland) *trckd ldrs: hdwy 2f out: rdn over 1f out: drvn and kpt on to ld wl ins fnl f* **9/2**[2]

6504 **2** *1* **Paddywack (IRE)**[11] 4289 10-8-3 **57** (b) DanielleMcCreery(7) 14 67
(D W Chapman) *s.i.s: hdwy 2f out: sn chsng ldr: rdn to ld 1f out: hdd and nt qckn wl ins fnl f* **13/2**

3405 **3** *1 1/2* **Viewforth**[26] 3829 9-8-4 **51** oh3 (b) RoystonFfrench 11 56
(M A Buckley) *chsd ldrs: rdn along 2f out: styd on fnl f* **9/1**

0000 **4** *3/4* **Making Music**[33] 3608 4-8-1 **51** oh5 (b) DuranFentiman(3) 9 53
(T D Easterby) *prom: hdwy to ld over 2f out: rdn and hdd wl over 1f out: grad wknd* **14/1**

2004 **4** *dht* **Mulligan's Gold (IRE)**[12] 4251 4-9-1 **62** (p) DavidAllan 4 64
(T D Easterby) *prom: hdwy on inner to ld wl over 1f out: sn rdn and hdd 1f out: kpt on same pce* **6/1**[3]

-303 **6** *shd* **Triple Shadow**[34] 3583 3-9-1 **64** JamieSpencer 1 66
(T D Barron) *trckd ldrs: effrt over 2f out: sn rdn and no imp* **5/2**[1]

0615 **7** *3/4* **Poppy's Rose**[11] 4291 3-9-2 **65** DanielTudhope 3 64
(I W McInnes) *a towards rr* **13/2**

6-00 **8** *1/2* **College Land Boy**[23] 3917 3-8-9 **58** GrahamGibbons 6 55
(J J Quinn) *bhd fr 1/2-way* **28/1**

0003 **9** *5* **Henry Hall (IRE)**[12] 4252 11-8-8 **55** KimTinkler 5 34
(N Tinkler) *led: rdn along and hdd over 2f out: sn wknd* **10/1**

-500 **10** *2* **Stepaside (IRE)**[87] 1965 3-8-11 **60** SilvestreDeSousa 10 32
(A D Brown) *rdn along and bhd fr 1/2-way* **40/1**

63.75 secs (-0.05) **Going Correction** +0.15s/f (Good)
WFA 3 from 4yo+ 2lb **10** Ran SP% **119.4**
Speed ratings (Par 103): **106,104,102,100,100 100,99,98,90,87**
CSF £34.82 CT £214.31 TOTE £5.70: £2.20, £2.10, £2.70; EX 38.50 Place 6 £5.89, Place 5 £5.10..
Owner J F Coupland **Bred** Miss Nathalie Lismonde **Trained** Grimsby, Lincs

FOCUS
Plenty of exposed and hard-to-win-with sorts in this sprint. Solid form despite the first two racing on opposite sides of the track.

T/Jkpt: Not won. T/Plt: £8.60 to a £1 stake. Pool: £75,752.40. 6,400.40 winning tickets. T/Qpdt: £3.60 to a £1 stake. Pool: £2,989.50. 598.10 winning tickets. JR

4643 - 4646a (Foreign Racing) - See Raceform Interactive

3979 LEOPARDSTOWN (L-H)

Sunday, August 19

OFFICIAL GOING: Yielding

4647a BALLYROAN STKS (GROUP 3) 1m 4f
4:15 (4:15) 3-Y-0+ £30,743 (£8,986; £4,256; £1,418)

RPR

1 **Mores Wells**[19] 4044 3-9-0 109 (t) DPMcDonogh 2 115
(Kevin Prendergast, Ire) *a.p: 3rd 1/2-way: cl 4th 4f out: chal ent st: led 1 1/2f out: drifted lft u.p ins fnl f: kpt on wl* **5/2**[1]

2 ½ **Fracas (IRE)**[22] 3983 5-9-10 111 WMLordan 6 114
(David Wachman, Ire) *trckd ldrs in 4th: 3rd and prog 3f out: 2nd and chal early st: ev ch fr over 1f out: kpt on u.p* **5/2**[1]

3 hd **Arch Rebel (USA)**[22] 3983 6-9-7 107 (p) FMBerry 3 111
(Noel Meade, Ire) *hld up towards rr: 5th and hdwy appr st: 3rd and swtchd to inner over 1f out: nt clr run: kpt on u.p* **12/1**

4 6 **Nick's Nikita (IRE)**[13] 4238 4-9-7 103 JMurtagh 1 102
(M Halford, Ire) *trckd ldrs in 5th: 6th and effrt appr st: mod 4th and kpt on same pce fnl f* **4/1**[2]

5 2 **Temlett (IRE)**[32] 3664 3-8-11 104 JAHeffernan 5 99
(W P Mullins, Ire) *led: strly pressed st: hdd 1 1/2f out: wknd fnl f* **12/1**

6 ¾ **Prince Erik**[49] 3142 3-8-11 106 PJSmullen 4 98
(D K Weld, Ire) *prom: 2nd bef 1/2-way: rdn appr st: sn wknd* **11/2**[3]

7 4 ½ **King In Waiting (IRE)**[16] 4142 4-9-7 98 (b) MJKinane 7 91
(John M Oxx, Ire) *hld up in rr: no imp fr 3f out* **12/1**

2m 36.5s (-3.40) **Going Correction** +0.05s/f (Good)
WFA 3 from 4yo+ 10lb 7 Ran SP% **115.6**
Speed ratings: **113,112,112,108,107 106,103**
CSF £8.97 TOTE £3.90: £1.80, £1.90; DF 8.40.
Owner Iona Equine Syndicate **Bred** Cliveden Stud Ltd & Ocean Bloo **Trained** Friarstown, Co Kildare

FOCUS
The runner-up and third are pretty consistent at this level and the form looks solid for the grade.

NOTEBOOK
Mores Wells, chasing his first win since the Ballysax Stakes here in April, returned to form. He had no luck in running in the Gordon Stakes at Goodwood last time and before that he had run quite respectably when fifth in the Irish Derby. Improving to challenge for the lead two furlongs from home, he soon made his way to the front and, despite drifting left under pressure in the closing stages, kept on well. A talented sort at his best, he should have a good future and his trainer intends aiming him at the Irish St Leger. On pedigree the trip should not be a problem and Prendergast feels that he is at his best on good ground and is improving. (op 3/1)
Fracas(IRE) ran right up to his best to finish an honourable second. A reliable sort, he has done his winning over 1m2f but saw out this trip well. He remained a constant threat to Mores Wells over the final two furlongs but just could not quite find a way past. He showed there are more races to be won with him at Listed and Group 3 level. (op 7/4)
Arch Rebel(USA) kept on quite well over the final furlong and a half and looked a big threat to the winner at one stage, but he could do no more late on. A multiple Listed winner, he has not been at his best this season, but this was encouraging.
Nick's Nikita(IRE) has been running well at this level lately but was not at her best on this occasion and was struggling to make an impression from early in the straight. (op 9/2)
Temlett(IRE) probably ran a bit better than his final position suggests. He made the running and was still in front two furlongs from home but could do no more when headed by the winner. He made excellent progress in handicaps earlier this season but has found life tougher since moving into stakes company.
Prince Erik was just a couple of lengths off the winner in the Irish Derby but failed to reproduce that effort and was a spent force turning in. He has shown much better form and it would be unwise to read too much into this performance. (op 5/1)

4648a DESMOND STKS (GROUP 3) 1m
4:45 (4:45) 3-Y-0+ £30,743 (£8,986; £4,256; £1,418)

RPR

1 **She's Our Mark**[13] 4237 3-8-12 105 DMGrant 4 106
(Patrick J Flynn, Ire) *hld up towards rr: 6th 3f out: hdwy on inner ent st: led under 1f out: r.o wl* **5/1**[2]

2 ½ **Eastern Appeal (IRE)**[67] 2586 4-9-7 105 JMurtagh 8 109
(M Halford, Ire) *trckd ldrs in 3rd: prog ent st: cl 2nd and chal 1f out: kpt on u.p* **8/1**

3 1 **Haatef (USA)**[28] 3768 3-9-1 116 (t) DPMcDonogh 3 105
(Kevin Prendergast, Ire) *trckd ldrs in 4th: rdn st: no imp ins fnl f: kpt on cl home* **13/8**[1]

4 1 **Lord Admiral (USA)**[22] 3983 6-9-10 109 MJKinane 6 107
(Charles O'Brien, Ire) *trckd ldr in 2nd: rdn to ld early st: hdd under 1f out: no ex cl home* **11/2**[3]

5 2 ½ **Danehill Music (IRE)**[35] 3579 4-9-4 104 WMLordan 5 95
(David Wachman, Ire) *towards rr: last and rdn 3f out: prog into 6th early st: kpt on same pce fr over 1f out* **7/1**

6 hd **Deauville Vision (IRE)**[19] 4051 4-9-4 102 RPCleary 7 95
(M Halford, Ire) *hld up in tch: 6th 1/2-way: no imp st* **10/1**

7 3 ½ **Anna Karenina (IRE)**[85] 2053 4-9-4 102 JAHeffernan 2 87
(David Wachman, Ire) *chsd ldrs in 5th: wknd st* **12/1**

8 4 **Zafonical Storm (USA)**[106] 1471 3-9-1 DJMoran 1 80
(B W Duke) *led: rdn and hdd early st: sn wknd* **20/1**

1m 42.6s (-1.80) **Going Correction** +0.05s/f (Good)
WFA 3 from 4yo+ 6lb 8 Ran SP% **115.3**
Speed ratings: **111,110,109,108,106 105,102,98**
CSF £44.47 TOTE £5.90: £1.50, £2.50, £1.30; DF 52.60.
Owner B & M Syndicate **Bred** M Barrett & Redmyre Bloodstock **Trained** Carrick-On-Suir, Co Waterford

FOCUS
The race has been rated around the runner-up to her previous best and the third to his recent level.

NOTEBOOK
She's Our Mark produced the performance of her life to lift this Group 3 prize. Her latest victory came off a mark of 82 in a Curragh handicap in May, but she had since reached the frame in several stakes races, including when chasing home the talented fillies Alexander Tango and Redstone Dancer. Her latest second to Jumbajukiba appeared to leave her with something to find, but she stepped up markedly on that performance. After settling towards the rear, she started to make progress on the inside turning in and ran on well to lead with a furlong to run. She will run in the Group 1 Matron Stakes over course and distance next month, and will have to improve markedly to make her presence felt against the likes of Arch Swing and Red Evie, but she has been a thorough credit to her connections and has established herself as a smart stakes performer this season. She can win more good races. (op 5/1 tchd 6/1)
Eastern Appeal(IRE), the Athasi Stakes winner, ran well on her first start for two months. She held every chance from early in the straight and kept on well over the final furlong. There could be better to come from her after this outing and she can continue to hold her own at this level.
Haatef(USA), a 6f Listed winner at Fairyhouse last time, looked to have every chance of winning his first race at this level and had plenty to spare over his rivals on official ratings. However, he was somewhat disappointing. He travelled well into the straight but struggled to quicken when the leaders picked up inside the final two furlongs. He was keeping on again in the closing stages and seemed to see out the trip well enough. There were no obvious excuses for him but he is surely capable of better. (op 11/8 tchd 7/4)
Lord Admiral(USA) took over in front early in the straight but had no more to give when headed by the winner. He is very consistent at this level and the good pace would have helped him, but he needs quicker ground to be seen at his best. (op 5/1)
Danehill Music(IRE) needs softer ground to be seen at her best.
Deauville Vision(IRE) was unable to make her presence felt. Her career-best effort in the Irish Lincoln was achieved on considerably slower ground than she encountered here. (op 8/1)

4649a IRISH STALLION FARMS EUROPEAN BREEDERS FUND HURRY HARRIET STKS (LISTED RACE) (F&M) 1m 1f 100y
5:15 (5:15) 3-Y-0+ £21,993 (£6,452; £3,074; £1,047)

RPR

1 **Baby Blue Eyes (IRE)**[19] 4051 4-9-6 94 DMGrant 1 109+
(Patrick J Flynn, Ire) *hld up in tch: 6th and smooth hdwy on inner appr st: led under 2f out: qcknd clr: eased 100yds out* **12/1**

2 4 **Magic Carpet (IRE)**[105] 1509 3-8-12 91 JMurtagh 2 99
(David Wachman, Ire) *hld up: 7th 1/2-way: prog 2f out: mod 2nd and kpt on fnl f* **10/1**[3]

3 2 ½ **Arkadina (IRE)**[42] 3358 3-8-12 91 WMLordan 7 95
(David Wachman, Ire) *chsd ldrs: 5th 1/2-way: 4th and rdn early st: kpt on same pce* **10/1**[3]

4 nk **Crossing**[19] 4051 6-9-6 98 DPMcDonogh 3 95
(William J Fitzpatrick, Ire) *trckd ldrs: 6th 1/2-way: prog under 3f out: mod 2nd 1 1/2f out: no ex fnl f* **20/1**

5 shd **Bon Nuit (IRE)**[85] 2053 5-9-6 99 NGMcCullagh 9 95
(Mrs John Harrington, Ire) *trckd ldrs: 4th 1/2-way: 5th and rdn early st: kpt on same pce* **16/1**

6 3 ½ **Offbeat Fashion (IRE)**[84] 2065 3-8-12 97 PJSmullen 8 87
(D K Weld, Ire) *hld up: 8th appr st: kpt on same pce* **12/1**

7 3 ½ **You're Beautiful (USA)**[22] 3983 3-8-12 92 CO'Donoghue 4 81
(David Wachman, Ire) *cl 2nd: led over 3f out: rdn and hdd 2f out: sn wknd* **16/1**

8 3 **Mount Eliza (IRE)**[63] 2702 5-9-9 96 PShanahan 6 80
(Charles O'Brien, Ire) *a bhd: no imp fr 3f out: eased fnl f* **33/1**

9 1 **Timarwa (IRE)**[35] 3576 3-8-12 109 MJKinane 5 74
(John M Oxx, Ire) *led: hdd over 3f out: rdn and wknd ent st: eased fnl f* **8/13**[1]

10 20 **Uimhir A Haon (IRE)**[13] 4238 3-8-12 100 JAHeffernan 10 38
(A P O'Brien, Ire) *chsd ldrs in 3rd: rdn and wknd over 3f out: virtually p.u st* **5/1**[2]

1m 57.0s (-0.60) **Going Correction** +0.05s/f (Good)
WFA 3 from 4yo+ 7lb 10 Ran SP% **131.6**
Speed ratings: **104,100,98,97,97 94,91,88,88,70**
CSF £141.46 TOTE £17.70: £4.20, £2.70, £2.90; DF 82.90.
Owner Sammaya Syndicate **Bred** Gainsborough Stud Management L **Trained** Carrick-On-Suir, Co Waterford
■ Race switched from the recent abandoned fixture at Gowran Park.

FOCUS
With the favourite disappointing this took less winning than had looked likely, but the winner was still impressive. The race has been rated through the fifth.

NOTEBOOK
Baby Blue Eyes(IRE), who won a Tralee handicap off a mark of 50 just under a year ago, produced a devastating display to run out an emphatic winner of this rescheduled Listed event. She failed to make an impact in a valuable Galway handicap last time but had previously confirmed herself a progressive sort with handicap successes at Gowran and over 1m1f at this track. She scythed through the field to lead just inside the final two furlongs, soon opened up an unassailable lead and was eased down in the closing stages. She will go next for the Dance Design Stakes at the Curragh in two weeks and on this evidence she will play a leading role. (op 10/1)
Magic Carpet(IRE), having her first start since she won a Gowran maiden on her debut in early May, was keeping on quite well in the closing stages without being able to land a blow at the winner. There should be better to come from her and she could prove capable of making her mark at Listed level. (op 7/1)
Arkadina(IRE) was an impressive winner of an extended 1m1f handicap at Gowran early last month and vindicated her connections' decision to pitch her in at this level. She was under pressure before the straight but was keeping on over the final furlong and looks as though she might improve over further. This was only the fifth start of her career and she can improve again.
Crossing improved to go second with well over a furlong to run but was unable to sustain the effort. A decent handicapper, she probably wants faster ground to be seen at her best and will be worth another try at this level. (op 14/1)
Bon Nuit(IRE) should improve on her first start since May, but she was unable to build on the promise of her second to Anna Pavlova in a 1m2f Listed event at Navan in April. (op 14/1)
Offbeat Fashion(IRE) was unable to make her presence felt. (op 8/1)
You're Beautiful(USA) moved to the front before the straight but folded once headed by the winner. (op 12/1)
Timarwa(IRE) was disappointing and dropped out of contention early in the straight. This was way below the form she showed to finish fourth in the Pretty Polly Stakes and Irish Oaks, and she can show the run to be all wrong. She was later reported to be sore behind by the vet. Official explanation: vet said filly was sore behind post-race (op 4/6)
Uimhir A Haon(IRE) was reported by her rider to have hung throughout and was reported to be injured behind by the vet. Official explanation: jockey said filly hung badly throughout; vet said filly was injured behind post-race (op 11/2)

4650 - (Foreign Racing) - See Raceform Interactive

BREMEN

Sunday, August 19

OFFICIAL GOING: Good

4651a WALTHER J JACOBS-STUTENPREIS (GROUP 3) (F&M) 1m 3f
4:15 (4:19) 3-Y-0+ £21,622 (£6,757; £3,378; £2,027)

RPR

1 **Majounes Song**[29] 3744 3-8-8 J-PGuillambert 2 105
(M Johnston) *racd in 5th to st: hdwy on ins: led appr fnl f: drvn out* **179/10**

2 hd **Ioannina**[42] 4-9-5 THellier 8 107
(J Hirschberger, Germany) *trckd ldr tl led wl over 2f out: hdd 2f out: ev ch ins fnl f: no ex clsng stages* **57/10**

3 1 ½ **Red Diva**[36] 3564 3-8-8 ASuborics 6 103
(Mario Hofer, Germany) *hld up in 6th to st: hdwy over 1f out: kpt on same pce fnl f* **98/10**

4 3/4 **Scatina (IRE)**[39] [3434] 3-8-8 .... ASchikora 7 101
(Mario Hofer, Germany) *led to wl over 2f out: 2nd st: led again 2f out to appr fnl f: one pce* **103/10**

5 *hd* **Neele (IRE)**[19] [4055] 3-8-8 .... EPedroza 1 101
(H Steinmetz, Germany) *hld up in rr: last st: effrt on outside 2f out: kpt on but nvr able to chal* **9/2**[3]

6 1 3/4 **Avanti Polonia (GER)**[51] [3075] 3-8-8 .... AStarke 5 98
(P Schiergen, Germany) *racd in 4th: wnt 3rd appr st: btn over 1f out* **5/2**[2]

7 5 **La Dancia (IRE)**[81] [2165] 4-9-5 .... TMundry 4 92
(P Rau, Germany) *racd in 3rd: 4th st: btn wl over 1f out* **9/5**[1]

2m 22.9s (142.90)
WFA 3 from 4yo 9lb **7** Ran SP% **120.8**
(including ten euro stakes): WIN 189; PL 43, 21, 26; SF 967.
Owner Mrs R J Jacobs **Bred** Newsells Park Stud Limited **Trained** Middleham Moor, N Yorks

NOTEBOOK
Majounes Song has struggled in Pattern company at home but she found the competition a bit easier here, and recording a success in this Group 3 event will have done her paddocks value no harm at all.

[4625]DEAUVILLE (R-H)

Sunday, August 19

OFFICIAL GOING: Turf course - soft; all-weather - standard

4652a DARLEY PRIX JEAN ROMANET (GROUP 2) (F&M) 1m 2f

2:20 (2:28) 4-Y-O+ **£50,068** (£19,324; £9,223; £6,149; £3,074)

RPR

1 **Satwa Queen (FR)**[60] [2753] 5-8-11 .... TThulliez 10 109
(J De Roualle, France) *mid-div: 5th st: hdwy wl over 1f out: chal 1f out: r.o to ld last stride* **13/8**[1]

2 *shd* **Bahia Breeze**[39] [3433] 5-8-11 .... JimmyFortune 2 109
(Rae Guest) *disp 3rd: cl 4th st: led over 1 1/2f out: sn hrd rdn: hung lft u.p 150yds out: r.o: ct last stride* **12/1**

3 2 **Dynaforce (USA)**[33] 4-8-11 .... SPasquier 11 105
(A Fabre, France) *disp 3rd: 3rd st: r.o same pce fnl 1 1/2f* **11/2**[3]

4 *snk* **Musical Way (FR)**[50] [3117] 5-8-11 .... RonanThomas 4 105
(P Van De Poele, France) *mid-div: 6th st: hdwy to dispute 3rd 1f out: kpt on one pce* **10/1**

5 1 1/2 **Green Girl (FR)**[86] 5-8-11 .... DBonilla 1 102
(J E Hammond, France) *reluctant to load and uns rdr: hld up in rr: 10th st: styd on wl fnl f: nrest at fin* **33/1**

6 *shd* **Heaven Sent**[36] [3523] 4-8-11 .... RyanMoore 7 102
(Sir Michael Stoute) *mid-div: 7th st: brought towards outside: kpt on but nvr able to chal* **3/1**[2]

7 *hd* **Daaly Babet (FR)**[42] 4-8-11 .... DBoeuf 5 102
(C Scandella, France) *led to over 1 1/2f out* **25/1**

8 *nse* **Mango Mischief (IRE)**[22] [3974] 6-8-11 .... KFallon 9 102
(M R Channon) *trckd ldr: 2nd st: rdn wl over 1f out: ev ch 1 1/2f out: sn wknd* **12/1**

9 1 1/2 **Gwenseb (FR)**[34] 4-8-11 ....(b) OPeslier 8 99
(C Laffon-Parias, France) *hld up: rdn 3f out: last st: brought wdst: hdwy wl over 1f out: no ex fr dist* **10/1**

10 5 **Histoire De Moeurs (FR)**[34] 4-8-11 .... CSoumillon 6 90
(Y De Nicolay, France) *hld up in rr: last over 3f out: 8th st: effrt on outside wl over 1f out: btn over 1f out* **16/1**

11 **Joshua's Princess (SAF)**[22] 6-8-11 .... JAuge 3 90
(J E Hammond, France) *mid-div to 3f out: 9th st: sn bhd* **33/1**

2m 11.1s (0.30) **Going Correction** +0.325s/f (Good) **11** Ran SP% **127.7**
Speed ratings: **111,110,109,109,108 107,107,107,106,102 102**
PARI-MUTUEL: WIN 2.00; PL 1.20, 2.80, 1.70; DF 13.20 (British CSF 25.98).
Owner S Lamprell **Bred** Ste Sogir **Trained** France

NOTEBOOK
Satwa Queen(FR), thoroughly deserved to win this race for the second year in succession, had to force her way through early in the straight before taking on the lead at the furlong marker. The mare was then hampered a bit by the runner-up and she fought back bravely to literally get up on the line. She has kept her form amazingly well over the years and was well suited by the cut in the ground. Her target is again the Prix de L'Opera and she does deserve a success at Group 1 level. Thoroughly game and genuine.
Bahia Breeze was always well placed on the rail before taking the advantage one and a half out. She then had a battle royal with the winner and hung left a little when under pressure. Her jockey was fined €300 and she might have been disqualified if she had won. A very game mare.
Dynaforce(USA) stayed on, but never got a blow in at the front pair.
Musical Way(FR) made her effort on the far side at the start of the straight. She stayed on at the same pace throughout the final stages and was fitted with cheekpieces.
Heaven Sent flattered a little in the straight but was never really a danger. She was undoubtedly unsuited by the very testing ground and this performance is best forgotten.
Mango Mischief(IRE), well up from the start, was always well there until the straight where she made no further progress before gradually dropping out of contention.

4653a DARLEY PRIX MORNY (GROUP 1) (C&F) 6f

2:50 (3:00) 2-Y-O **£135,128** (£54,061; £27,030; £13,503; £6,764)

RPR

1 **Myboycharlie (IRE)**[35] [3574] 2-8-13 .... KFallon 6 118
(T Stack, Ire) *hld up disputing last: 5th 1/2-way: smooth hdwy to chal 1 1/2f out: pushed along to ld 1f out: drifted rt fnl f: drvn out* **6/4**[1]

2 2 **Natagora (FR)**[28] [3779] 2-8-10 .... C-PLemaire 3 109
(P Bary, France) *led after 1f: pushed along 1 1/2f out: hdd 1f out: styd on* **7/4**[2]

3 1/2 **Alexandros**[21] [4009] 2-8-13 .... SPasquier 7 111
(A Fabre, France) *hld up in rr: last 1/2-way: pushed along and r.o over 2f out: wnt 3rd appr fnl f: rdn and styd on: nrest at fin* **11/4**[3]

4 6 **Etenia (USA)**[29] 2-8-10 .... YBarberot 5 90
(S Wattel, France) *settled in 4th: pushed along over 1 1/2f out: nvr in chalng position* **50/1**

5 1 **Flying Blue (FR)**[14] 2-8-13 .... TThulliez 4 90
(R Martin-Sanchez, Spain) *led 1f: 2nd 1/2-way: pushed along 2f out: u.p 1 1/2f out: no ex* **50/1**

6 *nk* **Ensis (SPA)**[56] 2-8-10 .... JEJarcovsky 1 86
(O Rodriguez, Spain) *prom in 3rd on rail: pushed along 2f out: rdn and one pce fr 1 1/2f out* **50/1**

1m 13.1s (0.10) **Going Correction** +0.225s/f (Good) **6** Ran SP% **108.9**
Speed ratings: **108,105,104,96,95 94**
PARI-MUTUEL: WIN 2.50; PL 1.50, 1.40; SF 7.80 (British CSF 4.13).
Owner Mrs John Magnier **Bred** Denis Noonan **Trained** Golden, Co Tipperary

NOTEBOOK
Myboycharlie(IRE) is surely a Classic colt in the making. On this occasion he made some other pretty smart juveniles look pretty ordinary and he totally dominated the final furlong. The colt has already been talked about as a possible for the Newmarket 2000 Guineas next year. Settled behind the leaders early on, he made his challenge up the centre of the track and quickened well in the testing ground. The race was over in just a few strides and he looks like an individual who will stay a little further. Connections are not sure about his next target, but it could well be the Middle Park Stakes at Newmarket.
Natagora(FR) was not really suited by the soft ground which blunted her speed. The filly set out to make all at a sensible pace and everything appeared to be going well at the halfway stage. When tackled one out, she had nothing in reserve and stayed on gamely to hold second place. She was beaten by a better on the day but nevertheless went down fighting. It would be no surprise if she was in the line up for the Cheveley Park Stakes in October.
Alexandros had every chance but was not quite good enough and probably another who was not suited by the sudden change in the ground. He attempted to make a forward move when things quickened up and then just stayed on one paced. He never quite made it into second place.
Etenia(USA) was never seen with a real chance and was behind early on. She took fourth place inside the final furlong and was not up to this level.

4654a DARLEY PRIX DE LA NONETTE (GROUP 3) (FILLIES) 1m 2f

3:20 (3:30) 3-Y-O **£27,027** (£10,811; £8,108; £5,405; £2,703)

RPR

1 **Tashelka (FR)**[35] 3-9-0 .... SPasquier 5 114
(A Fabre, France) *disp 4th: rdn 1 1/2f out: r.o to ld 150yds out: r.o wl cl home* **9/2**[3]

2 2 1/2 **Diyakalanie (FR)**[19] [4055] 3-9-0 .... TThulliez 3 109
(J Boisnard, France) *racd in 3rd: disputing cl 2nd st: rdn to ld over 1f out to 150yds out: styd on* **5/1**

3 1 1/2 **Beatrix Kiddo (FR)**[70] [2501] 3-9-0 .... CSoumillon 2 106
(Robert Collet, France) *hld up in 6th: disputing 4th st: drvn and r.o 1 1/2f out: wnt 3rd fnl f: kpt on* **14/1**

4 1 **Mystic Lips (GER)**[77] [2294] 3-9-0 .... AHelfenbein 7 105
(Andreas Lowe, Germany) *led: pushed along 2f out: hdd over 1f out: sn rdn and one pce* **5/2**[2]

5 1 1/2 **Chill (FR)**[19] [4055] 3-9-0 .... C-PLemaire 4 102
(J-C Rouget, France) *hld up in last: 6th st: n.d* **25/1**

6 3 **Sweet Lilly**[15] [4149] 3-9-0 .... RyanMoore 1 96
(M R Channon) *disp 4th: last but in tch on ins st: rdn 1 1/2f out: unable qck* **10/1**

7 1 **Legerete (USA)**[56] [2926] 3-9-0 .... OPeslier 6 95
(A Fabre, France) *racd in 2nd: disputing 2nd st: pushed along 2f out: sn rdn and one pce* **2/1**[1]

2m 10.2s (-0.60) **Going Correction** +0.325s/f (Good) **7** Ran SP% **116.4**
Speed ratings: **115,113,111,111,109 107,106**
PARI-MUTUEL: WIN 3.50; PL 1.90, 2.60; SF 16.30 (British CSF 27.86).
Owner Sheikh Mohammed **Bred** H H The Aga Khan's Studs S C **Trained** Chantilly, France

NOTEBOOK
Tashelka(FR), who seems to be improving with every outing, was a bargain buy at a mixed sale last February. She was then sold on to her current owner and this filly has now added a Group 3 to a Listed victory and she could even go on to better things. Always going well in fourth position, she came with her run up the centre of the track and dominated the final furlong. She acted very well on the testing ground and is now being marked down for the Prix Vermeille next month.
Diyakalanie(FR) was given every possible chance, but could not go with the winner in the final stages. She took the lead one out and just stayed on but it was nevertheless a decent performance.
Beatrix Kiddo(FR), held up for much of this race, was putting in her best work as the race came to a close and took third place inside the final furlong. This filly is not quite up to this class.
Mystic Lips(GER) tried to make all the running and took quite a strong hold. She was swamped by other runners early in the straight and then stayed on one paced to the line.
Sweet Lilly was never seen with a chance and finished a well-beaten sixth, failing to give her running.

4655a DARLEY PRIX KERGORLAY (GROUP 2) 1m 7f

3:50 (4:02) 3-Y-O+ **£50,068** (£19,324; £9,223; £6,149; £3,074)

RPR

1 **Getaway (GER)**[323] [5700] 4-9-4 .... SPasquier 2 114
(A Fabre, France) *mid-div: 5th st on ins: sn clsd up: led over 1f out: pushed out and r.o wl* **4/1**[2]

2 1/2 **Lord Du Sud (FR)**[59] [2787] 6-9-6 .... C-PLemaire 6 115
(J-C Rouget, France) *led to over 1f out: rdn and r.o same pce fnl f* **7/4**[1]

3 *nk* **Ponte Tresa (FR)**[36] [3565] 4-9-1 .... OPeslier 9 110
(Y De Nicolay, France) *mid-div: 4th st: effrt on outside: r.o u.p fnl f to take 3rd last strides* **5/1**[3]

4 *nse* **Le Miracle (GER)**[36] [3565] 6-9-4 .... DBoeuf 7 113
(W Baltromei, Germany) *hld up: 7th st: hdwy on outside fr over 1f out: tk 4th last strides* **5/1**[3]

5 *hd* **Varevees**[24] [3893] 4-9-1 .... TJarnet 1 109
(J Boisnard, France) *trckd ldr to 6f out: 3rd st: chal between 1st and 2nd appr fnl f: one pce in 3rd and lost two pls last strides* **8/1**

6 3 **Walk In The Park (IRE)**[41] 5-9-4 .... KFallon 8 109
(J E Hammond, France) *racd in 3rd tl wnt 2nd 6f out: chal 1 1/2f out: rdn and btn 1f out* **9/1**

7 1 1/2 **Latin Mood (FR)**[24] [3893] 4-9-4 .... CSoumillon 5 107
(P Demercastel, France) *racd in 8th: last st: a bhd* **20/1**

8 *snk* **Blushing King (FR)**[32] [3665] 5-9-4 .... YGourraud 4 107?
(J-L Guillochon, France) *uns rdr twice on way to s: s.i.s: last tl 8th st: sme hdwy wl over 1f out: btn over 1f out* **46/1**

9 1 1/2 **Meshugah (IRE)**[31] 3-8-6 ow1.. TThulliez 3 107?
(R Gibson, France) *racd in 4th: 5th st: wknd 1 1/2f out* **33/1**

3m 22.1s (2.10) **Going Correction** +0.325s/f (Good)
WFA 3 from 4yo+ 13lb **9** Ran SP% **120.6**
Speed ratings: **107,106,106,106,106 104,104,103,103**
PARI-MUTUEL: WIN 7.00; PL 1.50, 1.10, 1.40; DF 5.10 (British CSF 11.74).
Owner Baron G Von Ullmann **Bred** Baron G Von Ullmann **Trained** Chantilly, France

NOTEBOOK
Getaway(GER), off the track for 11 months coming into this, put up an excellent display and one that augers well for the future. Raced on the rail in mid division for much of this event, he came up the centre of the track and took control of the race early in the final furlong. The colt stayed on really well and certainly likes a bit of cut in the ground. He has now been marked down for the Prix du Cadran and is a very promising Cup horse in the making.

Lord Du Sud(FR) was made the odds-on favourite following the downpour and he looked likely to win the race for the second year running as the field entered the straight. He had made all the running to this point but could not pull out that little bit extra when challenged at the furlong marker. He was performing for the first time since the Ascot Gold Cup and he will only be raced when there is cut in the ground.
Ponte Tresa(FR) had plenty of support in this race and was given every chance. Fourth early on and round the final turn, she made a forward move from two out and took third place close home. The filly was putting in her best work at the finish.
Le Miracle(GER) was held up for a late run and he came on the stands' side and made up plenty of late ground. He was only beaten by inches for third place and under a length by the winner. He normally shows better form on faster ground and could now go for back-to-back wins in the Gladiateur.

[4416]LEICESTER (R-H)

Monday, August 20

OFFICIAL GOING: Good to soft (soft in places; 7.0)
There were 22 non-runners on account of the ease in ground conditions.
Wind: Light behind Weather: Cloudy with sunny spells

4656 EUROPEAN BREEDERS' FUND MAIDEN STKS 7f 9y
2:30 (2:33) (Class 4) 2-Y-O **£4,533** (£1,348; £674; £336) **Stalls** Low

Form				RPR
	1		**Spacious** 2-8-12 0 ... JamieSpencer 3 (J R Fanshawe) *stdd s: hld up: hdwy 3f out: led over 1f out: r.o wl* **10/1**	89+
5	2	4	**Dr Faustus (IRE)**[26] 3856 2-9-3 0 ... RyanMoore 8 (Sir Michael Stoute) *chsd ldr: led over 2f out: rdn: hung lft and hdd over 1f out: styd on same pce* **8/15**[1]	84
	3	nk	**Alfathaa** 2-9-3 0 ... RHills 12 (W J Haggas) *chsd ldrs: rdn over 1f out: styd on same pce* **8/1**[2]	83
0	4	½	**Redford (IRE)**[17] 4130 2-9-3 0 ... TQuinn 10 (M L W Bell) *hld up in tch: rdn and edgd lft over 1f out: styd on same pce* **8/1**[2]	82
	5	8	**Gardes (IRE)** 2-9-3 0 ... JohnEgan 13 (Jane Chapple-Hyam) *led over 4f: wknd over 1f out* **33/1**	62
	6	1 ½	**Metaphorical** 2-9-3 0 ... J-PGuillambert 2 (M Johnston) *s.i.s: sn chsng ldrs: wknd over 1f out* **17/2**[3]	58
0	7	1	**Mganga**[18] 4110 2-8-10 0 ... ThomasO'Brien(7) 14 (M R Channon) *s.i.s: hdwy over 5f out: rdn 1/2-way: wknd over 2f out* **40/1**	56
	8	1	**Balais Folly (FR)** 2-9-3 0 ... SteveDrowne 1 (B Palling) *s.i.s: in rr: bhd fr 1/2-way* **66/1**	53
	9	½	**Lacala (IRE)** 2-8-12 0 ... JamesDoyle 9 (Jane Chapple-Hyam) *s.i.s: sn prom: wknd 3f out* **150/1**	47
	10	13	**Aim** 2-9-3 0 ... PaulDoe 4 (J R Jenkins) *dwlt: outpcd* **150/1**	20

1m 27.91s (1.81) **Going Correction** +0.20s/f (Good) **10 Ran SP% 115.3**
Speed ratings (Par 96): **97,92,92,91,82 80,79,78,77,62**
CSF £15.64 TOTE £10.30: £2.40, £1.02, £1.90; EX 22.00 Trifecta £55.50 Pool £329.14 - 4.21 winning units..
Owner Cheveley Park Stud **Bred** Cheveley Park Stud Ltd **Trained** Newmarket, Suffolk

FOCUS
A good maiden likely to produce winners. The first four finished clear and the winner looks a potential Group filly.

NOTEBOOK
Spacious, a half-sister to the stable's useful handicapper Artimino, comes from a stable who can ready the odd first time out winner and she won in the style of a smart performer, travelling strongly throughout before pulling right away in the final furlong. Providing Nayef with his first winner as a sire, she holds no notable entries, but is very much viewed as a three-year-old and will not be asked to do much more this year. (op 8-1)
Dr Faustus(IRE), who is from an extremely good family, shaped promisingly on his recent Sandown debut and the softer ground here looked in the son of Sadler's Wells' favour. However, he once again fell short through a lack of pace and was forced to make do with second. The step up to 1m should see him winning an ordinary maiden. (op 4-7 tchd 1-2)
Alfathaa, another son of Nayef, comes from a yard whose debutant's often need a run and as a result this has to go down as a highly promising effort. He will stay 1m in time, but looks capable of winning at this distance. (op 9-1)
Redford(IRE), a fine, big son of Bahri, showed little on his Newmarket debut, but the softer ground here seemed to show him in a better light and he finished on the heels of the placed horses. He looks to be crying out for 1m and connections now have the choice of trying to win a maiden or giving him one more run for a handicap mark. Either way he looks one to keep on side. (op 7-1 tchd 9-1)
Gardes(IRE), a 50,000euros son of Xaar, struggled to make an impact in what was a decent maiden and will find easier opportunities. (op 28-1)
Metaphorical, whose stable's juveniles have started to hit form, showed some good early speed, but dropped away disappointingly and will need to step up. (op 8-1 tchd 10-1)

4657 GEORGE ROGERS "LIFETIME IN RACING" H'CAP 7f 9y
3:00 (3:02) (Class 4) (0-80,79) 4-Y-0+ **£4,857** (£1,445; £722; £360) **Stalls** Low

Form				RPR
6240	1		**Coup D'Etat**[8] 4418 5-8-10 **68** ... (b) JohnEgan 14 (R A Harris) *stdd s: hld up: hdwy over 2f out: rdn to ld nr fin* **8/1**[3]	79
2050	2	nk	**Barons Spy (IRE)**[8] 4418 6-8-9 **72** ... RussellKennemore(5) 12 (R J Price) *hld up in tch: led over 2f out: rdn over 1f out: hdd nr fin* **12/1**	82
2265	3	3 ½	**Blue Java**[12] 4268 6-9-2 **74** ... (t) SteveDrowne 10 (H Morrison) *hld up in tch: rdn over 2f out: styd on same pce fnl f* **3/1**[1]	75
00-0	4	¾	**Namid Reprobate (IRE)**[61] 2771 4-9-6 **78** ... TQuinn 4 (P F I Cole) *s.i.s: hld up: rdn 1/2-way: hdwy over 1f out: nt rch ldrs* **16/1**	77
0503	5	1	**Red Rudy**[8] 4418 5-7-13 **60** ... DuranFentiman(3) 11 (A W Carroll) *chsd ldrs: ev ch over 2f out: sn rdn: styd on same pce appr fnl f* **8/1**[3]	56
3404	6	3	**Mr Cellophane**[12] 4295 4-8-13 **71** ... PaulDoe 2 (J R Jenkins) *trckd ldrs: racd keenly: rdn over 2f out: wknd over 1f out* **14/1**	59
4221	7	¾	**Indian Edge**[38] 3487 6-8-9 **72** ... TolleyDean(5) 1 (B Palling) *led: hdd over 4f out: rdn and wknd 2f out* **7/1**	58
0426	8	hd	**Sailor King (IRE)**[4] 4548 5-9-2 **79** ... JamesMillman(5) 6 (D K Ivory) *chsd ldr tl led over 4f out: rdn and hdd over 2f out: sn wknd* **7/2**[2]	64

1m 28.24s (2.14) **Going Correction** +0.20s/f (Good) **8 Ran SP% 114.7**
Speed ratings (Par 105): **95,94,90,89,88 85,84,84**
CSF £96.84 CT £352.92 TOTE £8.60: £2.10, £4.90, £1.10; EX 70.70 Trifecta £59.60 Pool £369.92 - 4.40 winning units..
Owner Mrs Ruth M Serrell **Bred** Bishop Wilton Stud **Trained** Earlswood, Monmouths

FOCUS
A modest handicap in which high draws came out on top. The winner was up a length on this year's form.
Indian Edge Official explanation: jockey said gelding had been unsuited by being taken on early in the race
Sailor King(IRE) Official explanation: trainer said gelding ran too freely early on, adding that the race had come too quickly after its previous races four days ago

4658 JACKIE WOOLMAN BIRTHDAY H'CAP 5f 218y
3:30 (3:30) (Class 5) (0-70,67) 3-Y-O **£3,238** (£963; £481; £240) **Stalls** Low

Form				RPR
3221	1		**Swift Princess (IRE)**[17] 4127 3-9-5 **65** ... (v) JamieSpencer 7 (K R Burke) *trckd ldrs: led on bit ins fnl f: easily* **4/6**[1]	81+
6052	2	2 ½	**High Five Society**[19] 4071 3-8-4 **50** ... (b) PaulEddery 10 (S R Bowring) *led: rdn over 1f out: hdd and unable qck ins fnl f* **9/2**[2]	50
-403	3	3	**Cassie's Choice (IRE)**[40] 3413 3-9-7 **67** ... PaulMulrennan 4 (B Smart) *chsd ldrs: rdn over 2f out: styd on same pce* **13/2**[3]	57
5-00	4	½	**Umpa Loompa (IRE)**[24] 3918 3-8-3 **52** ... (v) AndrewMullen(3) 1 (D Nicholls) *prom: racd keenly: jnd ldr 4f out tl rdn over 2f out: hung lft over 1f out: no ex* **28/1**	41
60-0	5	2	**Lauder**[16] 4178 3-7-13 **48** oh3 ... DuranFentiman(3) 11 (J Balding) *in rr: rdn over 2f out: n.d* **40/1**	30
2024	6	shd	**Spinning Game**[4] 4525 3-7-11 **50** ... (b) DanielleMcCreery(7) 6 (D W Chapman) *s.i.s: outpcd* **9/1**	32
0550	7	2 ½	**Bentley**[29] 3763 3-8-13 **59** ... (v) SteveDrowne 3 (D Shaw) *hld up in tch: racd keenly: rdn over 2f out: sn wknd* **14/1**	33
420-	8	122	**Straw Boy**[322] 5730 3-8-5 **56** ... TolleyDean(5) 2 (R Brotherton) *in tch: rdn over 3f out: wknd over 2f out* **25/1**	—

1m 14.39s (1.19) **Going Correction** +0.20s/f (Good) **8 Ran SP% 117.9**
Speed ratings (Par 100): **100,96,92,92,89 89,85,—**
CSF £4.08 CT £11.38 TOTE £1.70: £1.10, £1.80, £1.10; EX 6.00 Trifecta £17.60 Pool £416.60 - 16.79 winning units..
Owner T J Naughton **Bred** Mrs S O'Riordan **Trained** Middleham Moor, N Yorks

FOCUS
Not a strong race, but the progressive Swift Princess won readily. Just modest form.
Umpa Loompa(IRE) Official explanation: jockey said gelding hung right-handed throughout

4659 KIRBY MUXLOE MEDIAN AUCTION MAIDEN STKS 1m 60y
4:00 (4:01) (Class 5) 3-4-Y-O **£3,238** (£963; £481; £240) **Stalls** Low

Form				RPR
0	1		**Turban Heights (IRE)**[18] 4106 3-8-12 0 ... JamesDoyle 8 (E J O'Neill) *chsd ldrs: led over 2f out: rdn and hung lft over 1f out: styd on wl* **12/1**	73
-562	2	4	**Handset (USA)**[68] 2581 3-8-12 68 ... RichardHughes 5 (H R A Cecil) *chsd ldrs: rdn and ev ch over 1f out: styd on same pce* **1/1**[1]	64
50-	3	hd	**Alecia (IRE)**[359] 4824 3-8-9 0 ... NeilChalmers(3) 6 (A M Balding) *hld up: hdwy over 2f out: sn rdn: styd on* **3/1**[2]	64
33-6	4	7	**Beech Games**[63] 184 3-9-3 77 ... JamieSpencer 10 (F Jordan) *hld up in tch: rdn and wknd over 1f out* **7/2**[3]	52
0	5	1 ¾	**West End Lad**[24] 3922 4-9-6 0 ... DuranFentiman(3) 11 (S R Bowring) *hld up: hdwy over 2f out: rdn and ev ch over 1f out: sn wknd* **100/1**	48
0	6	1 ½	**I'm Agenius**[12] 4275 4-9-4 0 ... TGMcLaughlin 7 (C Roberts) *s.i.s: hld up: hdwy over 2f out: rdn over 1f out: wknd fnl f* **100/1**	40
	7	3	**Fifth Zak** 3-9-3 0 ... PaulEddery 9 (S R Bowring) *s.s: outpcd* **33/1**	38
0	8	1 ¾	**Newgate Parisien**[16] 4157 4-9-6 0 ... AndrewMullen(3) 2 (Mark Campion) *led 1f: chsd ldr tl rdn over 2f out: sn wknd* **150/1**	34
	9	6	**Duetto (IRE)**[21] 4-8-11 0 ... JackDean(7) 3 (M Scudamore) *s.i.s: rcvrd to ld 7f out: rdn and hdd over 2f out: sn wknd* **80/1**	15
	10	14	**Rita Petite** 3-8-5 0 ... DanielleMcCreery(7) 4 (D W Chapman) *s.s: outpcd* **200/1**	—

1m 48.96s (3.66) **Going Correction** +0.50s/f (Yiel)
WFA 3 from 4yo 6lb **10 Ran SP% 112.2**
Speed ratings (Par 103): **101,97,96,89,88 86,83,81,75,61**
CSF £24.09 TOTE £10.70: £1.80, £1.10, £1.30; EX 28.70 Trifecta £71.60 Pool £645.22 - 6.39 winning units..
Owner Raymond N R Auld **Bred** R N Auld **Trained** Averham Park, Notts

FOCUS
A very weak maiden in which the winner showed big improvement from her debut. The winner looks far from solid.
Newgate Parisien Official explanation: jockey said gelding hung throughout

4660 LEICESTER RACECOURSE CONFERENCE CENTRE H'CAP 1m 1f 218y
4:30 (4:31) (Class 6) (0-60,60) 3-Y-0+ **£2,590** (£770; £385; £192) **Stalls** High

Form				RPR
0-03	1		**The Flying Cowboy (IRE)**[18] 4106 3-9-0 **60** ... TGMcLaughlin 12 (Jane Chapple-Hyam) *chsd ldrs: led over 1f out: rdn and hung lft ins fnl f: styd on* **9/2**[2]	69+
6532	2	½	**Gallego**[6] 4481 5-8-10 **55** ... KirstyMilczarek(7) 13 (R J Price) *s.s: hld up: hdwy over 3f out: rdn over 1f out: r.o* **11/4**[1]	60+
46-0	3	1	**Captain Oats (IRE)**[220] 110 4-8-6 **51** ... KylieManser(7) 3 (Mrs P Ford) *hld up in tch: plld hrd: chsd ldr 1/2-way: rdn over 2f out: styd on* **80/1**	54
0-55	4	¾	**Spunger**[17] 4131 4-9-5 **57** ... (v) RHills 1 (H J L Dunlop) *mid-div: hdwy over 2f out: sn rdn: styd on* **10/1**	59
4606	5	¾	**Royal Indulgence**[3] 4577 7-8-9 **54** ... JackMitchell(7) 4 (W M Brisbourne) *s.v.s: bhd: styd on fnl 2f: nt rch ldrs* **13/2**[3]	54+
0400	6	shd	**Western Roots**[8] 4433 6-9-0 **52** ... JohnEgan 16 (M Appleby) *led: rdn and hdd over 1f out: no ex ins fnl f* **25/1**	52
0433	7	¾	**Brastar Jelois (FR)**[35] 3595 4-9-1 **58** ... RussellKennemore(5) 11 (R Hollinshead) *hld up: hdwy over 3f out: sn rdn: no ex fnl f* **7/1**	56
500-	8	shd	**You Live And Learn**[335] 5451 4-9-6 **58** ... SteveDrowne 6 (H Morrison) *chsd ldrs: rdn over 2f out: no ex fnl f* **12/1**	56
1100	9	2	**War Of The Roses (IRE)**[18] 4108 4-8-9 **50** ... AndrewMullen(3) 10 (R Brotherton) *prom: rdn over 2f out: styd on same pce appr fnl f* **12/1**	44
0500	10	2	**Don Pasquale**[5] 4517 5-8-10 **55** ... JamesO'Reilly(7) 5 (J T Stimpson) *hld up: hdwy over 2f out: sn rdn: wknd ins fnl f* **14/1**	45
0600	11	3 ½	**Tavares (IRE)**[11] 4333 4-9-8 **60** ... JamesDoyle 17 (J Jay) *chsd ldrs over 7f* **12/1**	43
0	12	nk	**Raise Again (IRE)**[19] 4063 4-9-6 **58** ... PaulEddery 9 (Mrs P N Dutfield) *hld up: sme hdwy over 2f out: sn wknd* **66/1**	41
0060	13	4	**Contemplation**[19] 4079 4-8-12 **50** ... DavidAllan 7 (J Balding) *hld up: hdwy over 2f out: sn wknd* **25/1**	25

0004 **14** 1 3/4 **Freddy (ARG)**21 4025 8-9-6 **58**.............................(bt) AdrianMcCarthy 14 29
(D K Ivory) *sn pushed along and prom: rdn 1/2-way: wknd 3f out* **20/1**

2m 12.59s (4.29) **Going Correction** +0.50s/f (Yiel)
WFA 3 from 4yo+ 8lb **14** Ran SP% **124.7**
Speed ratings (Par 101): **102,101,100,100,99 99,98,98,97,95 92,92,89,88**
CSF £16.99 CT £910.52 TOTE £6.00: £2.30, £1.50, £20.30; EX 22.10 TRIFECTA Not won..
Owner Mark & Sue Harniman **Bred** Gerard Phelan And Liam Phelan **Trained** Newmarket, Suffolk

FOCUS
A moderate handicap in which they went no real pace. The winner, up 6lb on the bare form, was value for a bit extra.
You Live And Learn Official explanation: jockey said filly stumbled several times

4661 WOODHOUSE EAVES SPRINT H'CAP 5f 2y
5:00 (5:01) (Class 6) (0-60,60) 3-Y-O **£2,590** (£770; £385; £192) **Stalls** Low

Form RPR
45 **1** **Back In The Red (IRE)**109 1437 3-9-2 **58**........................ JohnEgan 13 67
(R A Harris) *hld up: pushed along 1/2-way: hdwy over 1f out: rdn to ld wl ins fnl f* **13/2**
4346 **2** *nk* **Comptonspirit**11 4330 3-9-2 **58**...................................(p) SteveDrowne 11 66
(B P J Baugh) *led: rdn over 1f out: hdd wl ins fnl f* **8/1**
2242 **3** 1 1/2 **By The Edge (IRE)**2 4616 3-8-8 **50**........................... PaulMulrennan 14 53
(T D Barron) *chsd ldrs: rdn over 1f out: styd on same pce ins fnl f* **4/1**2
45R0 **4** 1 1/2 **Sherjawy (IRE)**4 4529 3-8-7 **49**...............................(b) AdrianMcCarthy 15 46
(Miss Z C Davison) *chsd ldrs: rdn over 1f out: no ex ins fnl f* **66/1**
0301 **5** *nk* **Lord Of The Reins (IRE)**26 3846 3-8-10 **55**.............. DominicFox(3) 10 51
(D Shaw) *hld up in tch: outpcd 2f out: r.o ins fnl f* **12/1**
0040 **6** 2 **Noddledoddle (IRE)**11 4337 3-8-4 **46** oh1.......................(b1) PaulDoe 2 35
(J Ryan) *hmpd s: sn prom: rdn and hung rt over 1f out: no ex* **50/1**
2634 **7** *hd* **Smirfys Gold (IRE)**16 4186 3-8-12 **54**..(vt) TQuinn 8 42
(E S McMahon) *chsd ldrs: rdn over 1f out: wknd ins fnl f* **7/2**1
4100 **8** 3 **Mujart**34 3608 3-8-5 **52**.. RussellKennemore(5) 1 29
(J A Pickering) *chsd ldrs: rdn over 1f out: sn wknd* **16/1**
2001 **9** 3 **Stir Crazy (IRE)**4 4536 3-8-11 **60** 6ex.................... MatthewDavies(7) 12 27
(M R Channon) *hld up: sme hdwy over 1f out: sn wknd* **11/2**3
3000 **10** 2 1/2 **Musical Parkes**4 4525 3-8-7 **52**................................ AndrewMullen(3) 6 10
(W J H Ratcliffe) *wnt lft s: outpcd* **40/1**
0535 **11** 1 1/2 **The Geester**45 3281 3-8-7 **49**..(b) PaulEddery 7 —
(S R Bowring) *chsd ldrs: hung rt and wknd over 1f out* **16/1**
0604 **12** 1/2 **The Cube**29 3763 3-8-1 **46** oh1............................(b) DuranFentiman(3) 16 —
(J Balding) *chsd ldrs over 3f* **17/2**

62.18 secs (1.28) **Going Correction** +0.20s/f (Good) **12** Ran SP% **117.9**
Speed ratings (Par 98): **97,96,94,91,91 88,87,82,78,74 71,70**
CSF £57.00 CT £237.09 TOTE £7.70: £2.10, £2.70, £2.00; EX 46.00 Trifecta £86.40 Pool £316.46 - 2.60 winning units. Place 6 £12.53, Place 5 £10.26.
Owner Mrs Ruth M Serrell **Bred** Mrs Rachanee Butler **Trained** Earlswood, Monmouths

FOCUS
A moderate handicap. Sound but limited form.
T/Jkpt: Not won. T/Plt: £16.10 to a £1 stake. Pool: £72,592.95. 3,276.00 winning tickets. T/Qpdt: £6.60 to a £1 stake. Pool: £3,363.40. 372.70 winning tickets. CR

4453 WINDSOR (R-H)
Monday, August 20
OFFICIAL GOING: Soft (good to soft in places; 6.4)
Wind: Almost nil Weather: Overcast becoming bright

4662 EUROPEAN BREEDERS' FUND MAIDEN FILLIES' STKS 6f
5:30 (5:30) (Class 5) 2-Y-O **£4,533** (£1,348; £674; £336) **Stalls** High

Form RPR
5 **1** **Irish Pearl (IRE)**24 3916 2-9-0 0.............................. FergusSweeney 10 82
(K R Burke) *pressed ldrs: decisive move to ld jst over 2f out and sn 2 l clr: rdn out and styd on wl* **16/1**
2 **2** 2 1/2 **Our Piccadilly (IRE)**19 4074 2-9-0 0.................................. LPKeniry 2 74
(W S Kittow) *hld up in rr: prog and hanging lft 1/2-way: rdn to chse wnr wl over 1f out: styd on but no imp* **7/1**3
2 **3** 3/4 **Divine Power**18 4102 2-9-0 0.. SebSanders 11 72
(R M Beckett) *pressed ldrs gng wl: effrt but outpcd by wnr 2f out: styd on: nvr able to chal* **15/8**2
0 **4** 2 1/2 **Then 'n Now**14 4232 2-9-0 0..................................... SimonWhitworth 12 64
(C A Cyzer) *settled in midfield: outpcd 2f out: shkn up and styd on fnl f* **66/1**
0 **5** 1 1/2 **Hawk Eyed Lady (IRE)**14 4232 2-9-0 0........................ MartinDwyer 1 60
(J A Osborne) *s.i.s: wl in rr but in tch: outpcd 2f out: shkn up over 1f out: kpt on steadily* **33/1**
00 **6** *nk* **Princess India (IRE)**33 3648 2-9-0 0............................ JimCrowley 7 59
(P Winkworth) *trckd ldrs: lost pl and rdn 2f out: plugged on fnl f* **66/1**
6 **7** 3/4 **Swanky Lady**19 4061 2-9-0 0...................................... RichardHughes 4 57
(R Hannon) *led: shkn up and hdd jst over 2f out: sn btn: wknd over 1f out* **11/10**1
0 **8** 3/4 **Lenouska (IRE)**49 3152 2-9-0 0... PatDobbs 14 54
(B De Haan) *hld up towards rr but in tch: outpcd 2f out: shkn up and kpt on* **66/1**
0 **9** 2 **True Time**18 4102 2-9-0 0... RyanMoore 5 48
(E A L Dunlop) *trckd ldrs: lost pl over 2f out: no ch whn hmpd over 1f out* **20/1**
0 **10** 1 1/2 **Blue Rhapsody**16 4169 2-9-0 0....................................... NickyMackay 3 44
(L M Cumani) *taken down early: trckd ldrs to 1/2-way: pushed along and steadily wknd* **33/1**
11 2 **Fairy Wood (IRE)** 2-9-0 0.. DaneO'Neill 9 38
(J L Dunlop) *s.s: in tch in rr: shkn up and no prog over 2f out: wknd* **33/1**
12 5 **Miss Mozart** 2-8-11 0... TravisBlock(3) 6 23
(H Morrison) *pressed ldr to wl over 2f out: hanging bdly lft and wknd rapidly* **50/1**
13 9 **Veras Joy** 2-9-0 0... J-PGuillambert 8 —
(T D McCarthy) *s.s: rn green and a last: t.o* **100/1**

1m 14.8s (1.13) **Going Correction** +0.25s/f (Good) **13** Ran SP% **121.8**
Speed ratings (Par 91): **102,98,97,94,92 91,90,89,87,85 82,75,63**
CSF £116.63 TOTE £14.30: £2.30, £2.00, £1.40; EX 83.40.
Owner M J Halligan **Bred** Jim Halligan **Trained** Middleham Moor, N Yorks

FOCUS
This looked a reasonable fillies' maiden and the winning time was decent for a race like this. They all raced far side in the straight. The form seems sound enough.

NOTEBOOK
Irish Pearl(IRE) ◆ improved significantly on the form she showed on her debut over 7f at Thirsk, displaying plenty of speed on this drop in trip and running out a convincing winner. It remains to be seen what the form is worth, but she looks a pretty useful filly. (op 14-1)
Our Piccadilly(IRE) confirmed the promise she showed when a close second on her debut at Leicester, but the winner was just too good. (op 6-1)
Divine Power, although not running badly, did not exactly build on the form she showed when second on her debut at Nottingham. (op 2-1 tchd 9-4)
Then 'n Now improved quite a bit on the form she showed on her debut over course and distance and looks to be coming along nicely.
Hawk Eyed Lady(IRE) ◆ was never seen with a serious chance after starting slowly, but she was keeping on quite nicely late on and improved on the form she showed on her debut. She held an entry in the Lowther Stakes earlier in the year and could be one to keep an eye on. (tchd 40-1)
Princess India(IRE) was not given too hard a time once her chance had gone and she could be one to watch now she is qualified for nurseries/handicaps.
Swanky Lady always looked to be doing a bit too much in the hands of Richard Hughes and she had little to offer once let down. She had shown plenty of ability on her debut at Goodwood and can be given another chance. (op 13-8)
True Time Official explanation: jockey said filly suffered interference in running

4663 VC CASINO.COM (S) STKS 1m 3f 135y
6:00 (6:00) (Class 5) 3-Y-O+ **£3,886** (£1,156; £577; £288) **Stalls** Low

Form RPR
4224 **1** **Bridgewater Boys**7 4460 6-9-10 62.....................................(p) NCallan 4 57
(K A Ryan) *mde all: hanging lft fr 3f out: hung lft to far rail 2f out: drvn and plugged on: all out* **8/11**1
0346 **2** 1/2 **Lady Pickpocket**4 4528 3-8-4 52.................................. SaleemGolam 3 46
(M H Tompkins) *chsd ldrs: drvn to go 2nd over 1f out: plugged on but nvr quite rchd wnr* **4/1**2
0006 **3** 1/2 **Winforjoe (IRE)**10 4356 3-7-11 38... KMay(7) 7 45
(J J Bridger) *trckd ldrs: shkn up and hanging 3f out: plugged on same pce* **40/1**
-364 **4** *shd* **Miss Porcia**7 4464 6-9-0 49....................................... FrankieMcDonald 1 46+
(P A Blockley) *t.k.h: mostly pressed wnr: trying to chal whn hmpd wl over 1f out: kpt on one pce after: nt rcvr* **5/1**3
0002 **5** 2 1/2 **Showtime Annie**7 4460 6-8-11 35............................(b) NeilChalmers(3) 2 43+
(A Bailey) *hld up in last pair: effrt 4f out: chsng ldrs but rdn whn hmpd wl over 1f out: no ch after* **8/1**
0-00 **6** 26 **Bright**4 4530 4-9-5 32.. DaneO'Neill 5 —
(W K Goldsworthy) *a in last pair: pushed along 4f out: wknd over 2f out: t.o* **33/1**

2m 38.58s (8.48) **Going Correction** +0.55s/f (Yiel)
WFA 3 from 4yo+ 10lb **6** Ran SP% **111.1**
Speed ratings (Par 103): **93,92,92,92,90 73**
CSF £3.86 TOTE £1.70: £1.20, £2.10; EX 3.50.The winner was sold to G L Moore for £6,000.
Owner Bishopthorpe Racing **Bred** Southill Stud **Trained** Hambleton, N Yorks
■ Stewards' Enquiry : N Callan four-day ban: careless riding (Aug 31, Sep 1-3)

FOCUS
A terrible race and the winning time was modest, even by selling standards. The form is practically worthless.

4664 VC CASINO.COM H'CAP 5f 10y
6:30 (6:30) (Class 4) (0-85,84) 3-Y-O+ **£6,309** (£1,888; £944; £472; £235) **Stalls** High

Form RPR
1022 **1** **Shes Minnie**5 4507 4-9-3 **78**.................................. FergusSweeney 11 88
(P A Blockley) *chsd ldrs: rdn and prog to ld wl over 1f out: hanging lft sn after: drvn out* **4/1**2
2300 **2** *nk* **Don Pele (IRE)**9 4389 5-8-11 **75**...................................(p) LiamJones(3) 8 84
(R A Harris) *pressed ldrs: rdn over 2f out: kpt on u.p to go 2nd ins fnl f: clsng grad on wnr at fin* **10/1**
4106 **3** 1 1/4 **Fromsong (IRE)**15 4204 9-9-1 **76**................................ SaleemGolam 9 81
(D K Ivory) *mde most to wl over 1f out: chsd wnr tl ins fnl f: kpt on* **11/1**
0311 **4** *hd* **Bahamian Ballet**26 3836 5-9-9 **84**.............................. J-PGuillambert 4 88
(E S McMahon) *trckd ldrs gng wl: effrt to try to chal over 1f out: nt qckn* **9/2**3
0002 **5** 1/2 **Diane's Choice**18 4095 4-9-7 **82**.................................. DaneO'Neill 14 84
(J Akehurst) *racd on outer: wl on terms: rdn 2f out: kpt on same pce fnl f: nvr able to chal* **8/1**
6326 **6** *nk* **Blue Aura (IRE)**18 4103 4-8-12 **73**.............................(b) SebSanders 10 78+
(R M Beckett) *dwlt: hld up in tch: effrt whn nt clr run twice over 1f out: kpt on fnl f: no ch* **13/2**
0211 **7** *hd* **Makabul**42 3388 4-8-13 **74**.. KerrinMcEvoy 13 74
(B R Millman) *trckd ldrs: rdn and nt qckn wl over 1f out: kpt on* **10/3**1
3130 **8** 1 3/4 **Black Moma (IRE)**15 4204 3-8-13 **76**........................ RichardHughes 3 70
(R Hannon) *w ldrs: upsides 2f out: wknd rapidly 1f out* **12/1**
/0-0 **9** 3/4 **Avening**15 4204 7-9-0 **75**..(bt) StephenCarson 7 66
(Eve Johnson Houghton) *dwlt: in tch: effrt against far side rail over 2f out: hld whn nt clr run over 1f out: fdd* **12/1**
0-00 **10** 7 **Lindbergh**5 4507 5-9-0 **75**... DavidKinsella 16 41
(A J Lidderdale) *racd on outer: wl there to wl over 1f out: wknd rapidly* **66/1**

61.67 secs (0.57) **Going Correction** +0.25s/f (Good)
WFA 3 from 4yo+ 2lb **10** Ran SP% **120.0**
Speed ratings (Par 105): **105,104,102,102,101 100,100,97,96,85**
CSF £45.19 CT £415.96 TOTE £5.30: £1.90, £3.80, £2.30; EX 128.00.
Owner S G Martin **Bred** Stewart Martin And Alan Purvis **Trained** Lambourn, Berks

FOCUS
A fair sprint handicap, and sound but ordinary form. They raced middle to far side in the straight.
Bahamian Ballet Official explanation: jockey said gelding met trouble in running in the closing stages
Lindbergh Official explanation: jockey said gelding had no more to give

4665 PLAY AT VC CASINO.COM FILLIES' H'CAP 1m 67y
7:00 (7:00) (Class 4) (0-85,80) 3-Y-O+ **£6,309** (£1,888; £944; £472; £235) **Stalls** High

Form RPR
-110 **1** **Rhuepunzel**19 4060 3-9-5 **76**... NickyMackay 7 82
(G A Butler) *t.k.h early: cl up: wnt 2nd 1/2-way: led gp on far side over 3f out: drvn and styd on wl fr over 1f out* **9/2**3
2313 **2** 1 **Duchess Royale (IRE)**23 3960 3-9-9 **80**........................(v) RyanMoore 1 84
(Sir Michael Stoute) *trckd ldrs: chsd wnr on far side 2f out: nt qckn over 1f out: kpt on u.p* **13/8**1
1130 **3** 3/4 **Baltic Belle (IRE)**19 4060 3-9-9 **80**............................... RichardHughes 3 82
(R Hannon) *trckd ldr to 1/2-way: chsd wnr on far side to 2f out: one pce after* **13/2**
0530 **4** 1 3/4 **Imperial Lucky (IRE)**10 4361 4-8-8 **59** oh3.................... RobertHavlin 5 57
(D K Ivory) *stdd s: t.k.h and hld up in last pair: rdn 3f out: one pce and no imp fnl 2f* **25/1**
0653 **5** 5 **Voliere**9 4404 4-9-10 **75**.. SaleemGolam 4 61+
(S C Williams) *led: gng wl whn styd alone nr side in st: no ch fr over 1f out* **7/1**

The Form Book, Raceform Ltd, Compton, RG20 6NL

5130 **6** *12* **Indian's Feather (IRE)**[23] 3943 6-9-10 **75**.............................. LDettori 2 34
(N Tinkler) *a last: pushed along 1/2-way: t.o fnl 2f* **11/4**[2]

1m 48.39s (3.69) **Going Correction** +0.55s/f (Yiel)
WFA 3 from 4yo+ 6lb **6** Ran SP% **112.6**
Speed ratings (Par 102): **103,102,101,99,94 82**
CSF £12.38 TOTE £6.20: £2.40, £1.70; EX 15.80.
Owner The Fairy Story Partnership **Bred** Deepwood Farm Stud **Trained** Blewbury, Oxon

FOCUS
A fair fillies' handicap. Voliere stayed stands' side in the straight and Imperial Lucky raced up the middle, but the far side looked the place to be, albeit there wasn't that much in it. The winner is progressing.

4666 PLAY BLACKJACK AT VC CASINO.COM MAIDEN STKS 1m 67y
7:30 (7:30) (Class 5) 3-4-Y-0 **£3,238** (£963; £481; £240) **Stalls** High

Form RPR

32 **1** **King's Event (USA)**[7] 4457 3-9-3 0.............................. RyanMoore 11 88+
(Sir Michael Stoute) *trckd ldr: led jst over 2f out and kicked on: styd on strly: readily* **4/5**[1]

5-0 **2** *2 1/2* **Rhyming Slang (USA)**[12] 4275 3-9-3 0.............................. TPQueally 8 76
(J Noseda) *hld up in last pair: gd prog on outer fr 3f out: chsd wnr wl over 1f out: no imp but styd on wl* **28/1**

623 **3** *2* **Shela House**[25] 3881 3-9-3 76.............................. JamieSpencer 5 72
(J R Fanshawe) *hld up towards rr: prog over 2f out: chsd ldng pair over 1f out: kpt on but no imp on ldng pair* **3/1**[2]

4 *2* **Dear Maurice** 3-9-3 0.............................. DaneO'Neill 7 67+
(E A L Dunlop) *dwlt: hld up wl in rr: last pair and pushed along over 2f out: prog wl over 1f out: styd on but no ch w ldrs* **33/1**

00 **5** *1 3/4* **Quaglino Way (GR)**[7] 4457 3-9-3 0.............................. JimCrowley 14 63
(P R Chamings) *dwlt: sn trckd ldrs: disp 2nd 2f out: easily outpcd after* **66/1**

6 *3* **Fixation** 3-9-3 0.............................. RichardHughes 3 56+
(Mrs A J Perrett) *trckd ldrs: hanging bdly lft and outpcd fr 2f out* **20/1**

0- **7** *1/2* **Juzilla (IRE)**[336] 5424 3-8-12 0.............................. AdamKirby 9 50
(W R Swinburn) *dwlt: hld up towards rr: gng wl enough 3f out: sn outpcd and pushed along: fdd* **33/1**

8 *shd* **Storm Lily (USA)** 3-8-12 0.............................. KerrinMcEvoy 10 50
(Saeed Bin Suroor) *towards rr: prog to trck ldrs over 2f out: wknd over 1f out* **12/1**

9 *nk* **Smash Hit (IRE)** 4-9-9 0.............................. FergusSweeney 4 54
(David Pinder) *hld up in last pair: wl outpcd fr over 2f out: kpt on fr over 1f out* **66/1**

0 **10** *5* **Forever Bold**[21] 4018 3-9-3 0.............................. VinceSlattery 1 43
(J G Portman) *hld up in rr: last and outpcd over 2f out: n.d after* **100/1**

11 *1/2* **Impenetrable (USA)** 3-9-3 0.............................. LDettori 12 41
(Saeed Bin Suroor) *trckd ldrs: pushed along over 3f out: wknd over 2f out: bhd over 1f out* **6/1**[3]

0 **12** *1/2* **Lady In Blue**[12] 4275 3-8-12 0.............................. RobertHavlin 6 35
(T D McCarthy) *led to jst over 2f out: wkng rapidly whn hmpd over 1f out* **100/1**

R **Audley** 3-8-12 0.............................. (t) MartinDwyer 13 —
(M P Tregoning) *ref to r* **33/1**

1m 48.09s (3.39) **Going Correction** +0.55s/f (Yiel)
WFA 3 from 4yo 6lb **13** Ran SP% **124.5**
Speed ratings (Par 103): **105,102,100,98,96 93,93,93,92,87 87,86,—**
CSF £39.85 TOTE £1.90: £1.10, £4.30, £1.30; EX 35.60.
Owner Saeed Suhail **Bred** R McDonald **Trained** Newmarket, Suffolk

FOCUS
A fair maiden contest in which the winner was value for extra and the runner-up was up 10lb on his previous best. They raced far side in the straight.
Fixation Official explanation: jockey said colt ducked sharply left approaching furlong mark
Juzilla(IRE) Official explanation: jockey said filly ran too freely early
Impenetrable(USA) Official explanation: jockey said colt never travelled
Audley Official explanation: jockey said filly refused to race

4667 MONDAY NIGHT RACING WITH VC CASINO.COM H'CAP 1m 2f 7y
8:00 (8:00) (Class 5) (0-75,74) 3-Y-0+ **£3,238** (£963; £481; £240) **Stalls** Low

Form RPR

0053 **1** **Prime Powered (IRE)**[28] 3799 6-9-11 **69**.............................. SebSanders 3 78
(R M Beckett) *trckd ldr to 1/2-way: styd cl up: rdn to ld over 1f out: wl in command fnl f* **6/1**

005- **2** *1 1/2* **Perfect Reward**[299] 6173 3-8-10 **62**.............................. JimCrowley 9 68
(Mrs A J Perrett) *hld up in rr: rdn over 3f out: prog over 2f out: chsd wnr and drifted lft fnl f: no imp* **11/1**

60-2 **3** *1 3/4* **Cape Diamond (IRE)**[12] 4266 4-9-13 **71**.............................. AdamKirby 4 74
(W R Swinburn) *hld up in tch: gng wl over 2f out: hanging and nt qckn over 1f out: kpt on to take 3rd ins fnl f* **7/1**

446 **4** *1* **Vincenzio (IRE)**[42] 3366 3-9-6 **72**.............................. LDettori 2 73
(C R Egerton) *led at stdy pce: kicked on wl over 3f out: hdd over 1f out: nt qckn: eased nr fin* **4/1**[3]

00-0 **5** *shd* **Terminate (GER)**[10] 4365 5-8-12 **56**.............................. SimonWhitworth 10 56
(N A Callaghan) *s.v.s: sn in tch: last and outpcd over 2f out: styd on fr over 1f out* **20/1**

3104 **6** *1/2* **Kavachi (IRE)**[16] 4184 4-9-6 **64**.............................. RyanMoore 7 63
(G L Moore) *hld up tl t.k.h and pressed ldr 1/2-way: stl chalng 2f out: sn btn* **3/1**[1]

-200 **7** *1 1/4* **Mister Right (IRE)**[70] 1959 6-10-0 **72**.............................. DaneO'Neill 5 69
(D J S Ffrench Davis) *dwlt: hld up in tch: effrt against far rail over 2f out: wl hld whn n.m.r ent fnl f* **20/1**

0205 **8** *2* **Dispol Veleta**[28] 3789 6-9-0 **58**.............................. J-PGuillambert 8 51
(Miss T Spearing) *hld up in tch: drvn wl over 2f out: wknd wl over 1f out* **16/1**

0-34 **9** *2* **Limbo King**[19] 4072 3-9-8 **74**.............................. (v[1]) JamieSpencer 11 63
(J R Fanshawe) *hld up in tch: rdn over 3f out: no prog: wknd 2f out* **10/3**[2]

2m 15.79s (7.49) **Going Correction** +0.55s/f (Yiel)
WFA 3 from 4yo+ 8lb **9** Ran SP% **118.6**
Speed ratings (Par 103): **92,90,89,88,88 88,87,85,83**
CSF £71.28 CT £470.03 TOTE £7.30: £2.30, £2.60, £1.70; EX 78.50 Place 6 £62.78, Place 5 £32.73..
Owner I J & C G Heseltine **Bred** Caribbean Quest Partnership **Trained** Whitsbury, Hants

FOCUS
A modest handicap and, with the pace very steady for much of the way, the form probably wants treating with some caution. Unsurprisingly the winning time was moderate for the grade. They raced far side in the straight.
Dispol Veleta Official explanation: jockey said mare hung badly right-handed throughout
Limbo King Official explanation: jockey said he had no explanation for the colt's poor performance
T/Plt: £41.60 to a £1 stake. Pool: £79,251.70. 1,387.95 winning tickets. T/Qpdt: £16.20 to a £1 stake. Pool: £7,125.50. 324.90 winning tickets. JN

4459 WOLVERHAMPTON (A.W) (L-H)
Monday, August 20

OFFICIAL GOING: Standard
Wind: Moderate, against

4668 BET NOW AT WBX.COM H'CAP 5f 216y(P)
2:15 (2:19) (Class 6) (0-50,50) 3-Y-0+ **£2,559** (£755; £378) **Stalls** Low

Form RPR

1050 **1** **Arfinnit (IRE)**[16] 4180 6-8-7 **48**.............................. (v) LiamJones(3) 11 58
(Mrs A L M King) *hld up towards rr: rdn and hdwy over 1f out: str run to ld post* **20/1**

0403 **2** *shd* **Willofcourse**[11] 4336 6-8-3 **48**.............................. AmyScott(7) 1 58
(H Candy) *mid-div: hdwy over 2f out: n.m.r over 1f out: rallied to ld ins fnl f: hdd post* **6/1**[2]

5642 **3** *1 1/2* **Blackheath (IRE)**[3] 4561 11-8-12 **50**.............................. SilvestreDeSousa 13 55
(D Nicholls) *trckd ldrs: led 2f out: rdn and hdd ins fnl f: kpt on but no ex* **6/1**[2]

6000 **4** *hd* **Moon Forest (IRE)**[3] 4562 5-8-12 **50**.............................. (p) StephenDonohoe 6 55+
(J M Bradley) *in rr: hdwy on ins over 1f out: r.o fnl f: nvr nrr* **7/1**[3]

4342 **5** *1/2* **Jilly Why (IRE)**[4] 4525 6-8-12 **50**.............................. (b) FrancisNorton 12 53
(Paul Green) *mid-div: hdwy on outside 1/2-way: one pce fr over 1f out* **5/1**[1]

6031 **6** *nk* **The Salwick Flyer (IRE)**[5] 4494 4-8-12 **50**.............................. TomEaves 10 52
(I Semple) *prom: rdn over 2f out: one pce appr fnl f* **6/1**[2]

5600 **7** *1/2* **Muktasb (USA)**[27] 3829 6-8-9 **47**.............................. (v) AdamKirby 8 47+
(D Shaw) *s.i.s: hld up: hmpd whn hdwy on ins over 1f out: n.d after* **16/1**

010 **8** *1* **Bee Magic**[13] 4252 4-8-12 **50**.............................. (b) ChrisCatlin 3 47
(C N Kellett) *t.k.h: in tch: rdn 2f out: wkng whn hmpd over 1f out* **25/1**

0004 **9** *2* **Government (IRE)**[8] 4427 6-8-6 **49**.............................. NicolPolli(5) 9 40
(M C Chapman) *trckd ldrs: rdn over 2f out: wkng whn hmpd over 1f out* **16/1**

0106 **10** *nk* **Coalite (IRE)**[48] 3195 4-8-12 **50**.............................. (p) RoystonFfrench 7 40
(A D Brown) *towards rr: rdn 1/2-way: one pce fnl 2f* **8/1**

0200 **11** *2* **North Fleet**[51] 3106 4-8-5 **48**.............................. (p) KevinGhunowa(5) 5 31
(J M Bradley) *in tch: rdn 1/2-way: wknd 2f out* **20/1**

2000 **12** *shd* **Ballybunion (IRE)**[11] 4312 8-8-7 **50**.............................. LukeMorris(5) 2 33
(R A Harris) *in tch: rdn 1/2-way: wknd wl over 1f out* **33/1**

-000 **13** *5* **Creme Brulee**[157] 690 4-8-11 **49**.............................. PaulHanagan 4 16
(P T Dalton) *led tl hdd 2f out: wknd rapidly* **25/1**

1m 15.38s (-0.43) **Going Correction** -0.075s/f (Stan) **13** Ran SP% **115.1**
Speed ratings (Par 101): **99,98,96,96,95 95,94,93,90,90 87,87,81**
CSF £123.50 CT £847.94 TOTE £26.80: £5.90, £2.70, £2.40; EX 180.30.
Owner All The Kings Horses **Bred** Robert De Vere Hunt **Trained** Wilmcote, Warwicks

FOCUS
A very moderate sprint handicap, but competitive nonetheless and they were spread right across the track on the crown of the home bend. The winner was back to his best form in the past couple of years.
Muktasb(USA) Official explanation: jockey said gelding was denied a clear run
Government(IRE) Official explanation: trainer said gelding bled from the nose

4669 WOLVERHAMPTON-RACECOURSE.CO.UK NURSERY 5f 216y(P)
2:45 (2:46) (Class 4) 2-Y-0 **£4,533** (£1,348; £674; £336) **Stalls** Low

Form RPR

0612 **1** **What Katie Did (IRE)**[7] 4461 2-8-10 **69**.............................. MartinDwyer 3 73+
(J A Osborne) *mid-div: rdn over 3f out: hdwy 2f out: led ins fnl f: rdn out* **5/4**[1]

660 **2** *1/2* **Bencorr (USA)**[37] 3560 2-8-7 **66**.............................. TPQueally 2 68
(M J Wallace) *s.i.s: making hdwy whn swtchd rt over 1f out: r.o to go 2nd ins fnl f* **11/1**

6103 **3** *1 1/2* **Borasco (USA)**[17] 4126 2-8-10 **69**.............................. TomEaves 9 67
(T D Barron) *trckd ldr: rdn over 2f out: ev ch appr fnl f: lost 2nd ins fnl f* **8/1**

0416 **4** *1/2* **Jane's Delight (IRE)**[17] 4126 2-8-5 **67**.............................. (v) AndrewElliott(3) 6 63
(G R Oldroyd) *sn led: rdn 1/2-way: wkng whn hdd ins fnl f* **50/1**

612 **5** *1 1/2* **Maryolini**[13] 4255 2-8-11 **70**.............................. ChrisCatlin 1 62
(N J Vaughan) *towards rr: effrt over 1f out: nvr nr to chal* **5/1**[2]

0065 **6** *1 1/4* **Biased Opinion (IRE)**[19] 4065 2-8-4 **63**.............................. FrancisNorton 4 51
(H J L Dunlop) *trckd ldrs: rdn 1/2-way: wknd ins fnl f* **8/1**

0003 **7** *2 1/2* **Lady Bower**[17] 4136 2-7-13 **58**.............................. RoystonFfrench 10 38
(M Johnston) *mid-div: bhd fnl 2f* **20/1**

3221 **8** *1 1/4* **Rievaulx Valentino**[14] 4221 2-9-7 **80**.............................. PatCosgrave 7 57
(K A Ryan) *trckd ldrs: rdn 1/2-way: wknd 2f out* **13/2**[3]

0536 **9** *2* **Bazguy**[39] 3465 2-9-2 **75**.............................. StephenDonohoe 8 46
(P D Evans) *outpcd: a in rr* **16/1**

0000 **10** *16* **Doubtless**[3] 4559 2-7-12 **57** oh12.............................. DavidKinsella 5 —
(D W Chapman) *slowly away and outpcd: virtually t.o* **100/1**

1m 15.46s (-0.35) **Going Correction** -0.075s/f (Stan) **10** Ran SP% **118.6**
Speed ratings (Par 96): **99,98,96,95,93 92,88,87,84,63**
CSF £17.06 CT £85.80 TOTE £1.90: £1.50, £3.70, £3.60; EX 19.40.
Owner Mountgrange Stud **Bred** Brian Williamson **Trained** Upper Lambourn, Berks

FOCUS
A fair nursery and they went a very decent pace which had several of these struggling from an early stage. The winner is progressing well and the form looks solid enough.

NOTEBOOK
What Katie Did(IRE) ◆, possibly unlucky over an extra furlong here last time, went off a well-backed favourite. He had to be nudged along to stay in touch thanks to the frantic early pace, but his stamina came into play and once he went to the front there was only going to be one winner. There is probably more to come from him back up in trip. (op 7-4)
Bencorr(USA), making his nursery debut after showing a little ability in three maidens, was taken off his feet early but made relentless progress in the second half of the contest and was still going forward at the line. He was a very expensive purchase and this performance suggests that at least he has the ability to start repaying some of it. (op 8-1)
Borasco(USA), making her sand debut, was always up there and had every chance but lacked pace where it mattered. She was successful in her only previous try over 7f and looks to need a return to that trip. (tchd 9-1)
Jane's Delight(IRE), who has looked basically plating-class up to now, ran a fine race from the front and considering the pace she set she lasted a lot longer than might have been expected.
Maryolini, a course-and-distance winner on her only previous try on sand, was totally unable to go the early pace and her finishing position was as close as she got. She is very much sprint bred so would not obviously be suited by going up in trip. (op 4-1)
Biased Opinion(IRE) did not go unbacked despite having not yet made the frame, but after holding every chance on the inside turning in he then faded out of it and finished further behind the winner than he did at Kempton last time despite being 8lb better off. (op 11-1)

Rievaulx Valentino, making his sand and nursery debuts and up a furlong for the first time, was under severe pressure on the turn for home and ended up well beaten. Official explanation: jockey said colt hung right-handed throughout (op 7-1 tchd 8-1)

4670 BOOK EARLY FOR CHRISTMAS H'CAP 1m 5f 194y(P)
3:15 (3:15) (Class 6) (0-65,62) 3-Y-0+ £2,559 (£755; £378) Stalls Low

Form RPR
0004 **1** **Mighty Kitchener (USA)**[4] 4534 4-9-8 **59** IanMongan 6 67+
(P Howling) *hld up: hdwy 3f out: edging lft u.p whn led 1f out: drvn out* **7/1**
0-00 **2** 1 1/2 **Ardent Prince**[10] 4353 4-9-2 **53** GrahamGibbons 4 59
(Heather Dalton) *t.k.h: led after 1f: hdd after 4f: styd prom: swtchd rt over 1f out: carried lft by wnr ent fnl f: styd on one pce* **33/1**
44-5 **3** 2 **Candarli (IRE)**[15] 39 11-9-8 **59** FrancisNorton 8 62
(D R Gandolfo) *mid-div: gd hdwy to ld over 6f out: hdd 1f out and wkng whn hmpd sn after* **25/1**
0361 **4** 1 **Hugs Destiny (IRE)**[3] 4558 6-9-4 **60** 6ex (t) NeilBrown(5) 1 62
(M A Barnes) *led for 1f: styd in tch: outpcd 4f out: kpt on one pce fnl 2f* **6/1**[3]
0143 **5** 1 1/2 **Campbells Lad**[13] 4249 6-9-9 **60** PaulHanagan 10 60
(Mrs G S Rees) *slowly away: in rr: hdwy whn rdn over 2f out but nvr rchd ldrs* **16/1**
4466 **6** 1 1/4 **Qaasi (USA)**[16] 4179 5-9-2 **53** DanielTudhope 13 51
(M Brittain) *towards rr: hdwy on ins wl over 1f out but nvr nr to chal* **8/1**
2024 **7** 2 **York Cliff**[6] 4475 9-9-8 **62** LiamJones(3) 3 57
(W M Brisbourne) *bhd: hdwy over 4f out: rdn over 2f out: one pce ent fnl f* **8/1**
0240 **8** 4 **Diktatorship (IRE)**[7] 4463 4-9-5 **56** SamHitchcott 12 45
(Jennie Candlish) *hld up: hdwy over 4f out: wknd over 1f out* **12/1**
0-00 **9** 2 **Lynford Lady**[4] 4534 4-9-3 **54** (p) RobertHavlin 11 41
(P W D'Arcy) *in tch: rdn 3f out: wknd wl over 1f out* **33/1**
3340 **10** 7 **Blue Hills**[21] 4030 6-9-9 **60** (v) ChrisCatlin 9 37
(P W Hiatt) *trckd ldrs: rdn 4f out: sn wknd* **11/2**[2]
0332 **11** 1/2 **Squirtle (IRE)**[10] 4352 4-8-11 **53** LukeMorris(5) 2 29
(W M Brisbourne) *v.s.a: a bhd* **9/2**[1]
400U **12** 1/2 **Gatecrasher**[13] 4246 4-9-2 **58** AdrianScholes(5) 7 33
(J W Unett) *hld up in mid-div: wknd over 3f out* **66/1**
-001 **13** 11 **Zonic Boom (FR)**[24] 3927 7-9-4 **55** (b[1]) StephenDonohoe 5 15
(Heather Dalton) *slowly away: t.k.h and led after 4f: hdd over 6f out: wknd 5f out* **8/1**

3m 5.91s (-1.46) **Going Correction** -0.075s/f (Stan) 13 Ran SP% **118.5**
Speed ratings (Par 101): **101,100,99,98,97 96,95,93,92,88 88,87,81**
CSF £226.65 CT £5355.33 TOTE £7.00: £2.30, £10.10, £6.70; EX 308.00.
Owner S J Hammond **Bred** D Considine **Trained** Newmarket, Suffolk
■ Stewards' Enquiry : Graham Gibbons one-day ban: careless riding (Aug 31)

FOCUS
A modest staying handicap run at just a fair pace. Fairly sound form.

4671 RINGSIDE SUITE MEDIAN AUCTION MAIDEN STKS 7f 32y(P)
3:45 (3:45) (Class 5) 3-4-Y-0 £3,071 (£906; £453) Stalls High

Form RPR
3222 **1** **Spriggan**[16] 4170 3-9-3 78 AdamKirby 4 70
(C G Cox) *mde all: rdn over 1f out: in command after* **4/6**[1]
-520 **2** 3 1/2 **Orchestrator (IRE)**[33] 3646 3-9-3 71 RobertHavlin 5 60
(T G Mills) *stdd s: rdn 3f out: t.k.h: r.o to go 2nd ins fnl f* **4/1**[2]
6 **3** 3/4 **Tyrannosaurus Rex (IRE)**[16] 4157 3-9-3 0 LeeEnstone 1 58
(K R Burke) *s.i.s: rdn over 2f out: hung lft but styd on fr over 1f out* **4/1**[2]
3- **4** nk **Agitator**[296] 6222 3-9-3 0 GrahamGibbons 6 58
(Mrs G S Rees) *trckd ldr: rdn over 1f out: wknd ins fnl f* **20/1**[3]
30-0 **5** 5 **Boucheen**[111] 1380 4-9-8 43 SamHitchcott 7 46
(J W Unett) *bhd: rdn 1/2-way: nvr on terms* **33/1**
00-0 **6** 1/2 **Axis Mundi (IRE)**[52] 3051 3-8-9 40 AndrewElliott(3) 8 38
(T J Etherington) *mid-div: wknd 3f out* **100/1**
000- **7** 20 **Lady Toyah (IRE)**[293] 6278 3-8-9 32 LiamJones(3) 3 —
(Mrs L Williamson) *trckd ldrs: rdn 1/2-way: sn btn* **100/1**

1m 29.65s (-0.75) **Going Correction** -0.075s/f (Stan)
WFA 3 from 4yo 5lb 7 Ran SP% **109.7**
Speed ratings (Par 103): **101,97,96,95,90 89,66**
CSF £3.22 TOTE £1.50: £1.10, £2.50; EX 3.30.
Owner C V Cruden **Bred** Ambersham Stud **Trained** Lambourn, Berks

FOCUS
A very uncompetitive maiden with only three holding realistic chances and they finished very much as the market suggested they should. The winner was 11lb off his best in getting off the mark.

4672 WBX.COM WORLD BET EXCHANGE H'CAP 1m 141y(P)
4:15 (4:15) (Class 4) (0-80,83) 3-Y-0+ £6,477 (£1,927; £963; £481) Stalls Low

Form RPR
0103 **1** **Just Bond (IRE)**[16] 4177 5-9-5 **80** SladeO'Hara(5) 3 89
(G R Oldroyd) *mid-div: hdwy on ins over 1f out: led ins fnl f: all out* **12/1**
5531 **2** nk **Dream Lodge (IRE)**[8] 4429 3-9-6 **83** 6ex TPQueally 9 91
(J G Given) *trckd ldrs: wnt 2nd 6f out: rdn 3f out: led 2f out: hdd ins fnl f: no ex cl home* **4/1**[2]
0000 **3** 1 **Red Contact (USA)**[7] 4462 6-9-0 **70** (p) DanielTudhope 4 76
(A Dickman) *trckd ldr: rdn 3f out: kpt on one pce fnl f* **66/1**
5060 **4** hd **Merrymadcap (IRE)**[8] 4433 5-8-13 **69** FrancisNorton 13 75
(M Blanshard) *hld up in rr: rdn over 2f out: hdwy over 1f out: r.o fnl f* **16/1**
1360 **5** 1/2 **Hoh Wotanite**[3] 4566 4-9-3 **73** (p) RoystonFfrench 11 77
(R Hollinshead) *in rr: hdwy on outside over 1f out: r.o fnl f: nvr nrr* **6/1**[3]
6401 **6** 1/2 **Coeur Courageux (FR)**[7] 4462 5-9-9 **79** 6ex (t) GrahamGibbons 12 82
(D Nicholls) *stdd s: bhd tl hdwy on outside over 2f out: one pce fnl f* **3/1**[1]
6106 **7** hd **Bold Diktator**[7] 2469 5-9-5 **78** RichardKingscote(3) 7 81
(Tom Dascombe) *s.i.s: bhd tl hdwy on ins over 1f out: nvr nr to chal* **8/1**
4016 **8** nk **Zennerman (IRE)**[18] 4100 4-9-5 **75** (p) PatCosgrave 5 77
(K A Ryan) *bhd: making hdwy whn edgd lft 1f out: one pce after* **14/1**
2110 **9** 3 **Nan Jan**[19] 4068 5-9-2 **72** (t) RobertHavlin 10 67
(R Ingram) *mid-div: rdn 3f out: hld whn hmpd 1f out* **10/1**
1044 **10** 1/2 **Desert Leader (IRE)**[175] 564 6-9-3 **73** AdamKirby 6 67
(R W Price) *in tch: rdn 2f out: edgd lft and wknd fnl f* **33/1**
1202 **11** 2 **Jewelled Dagger (IRE)**[14] 4222 3-8-11 **74** (b) TomEaves 1 63
(I Semple) *led tl hdd 2f out: wknd qckly* **8/1**
2564 **12** 3 **King Of The Moors (USA)**[9] 4382 4-8-9 **70** NeilBrown(5) 8 53
(T D Barron) *prom: rdn 3f out: wknd 2f out* **20/1**

1m 49.74s (-2.02) **Going Correction** -0.075s/f (Stan)
WFA 3 from 4yo+ 7lb 12 Ran SP% **120.0**
Speed ratings (Par 105): **105,104,103,103,103 102,102,102,99,99 97,94**
CSF £59.39 CT £3132.45 TOTE £16.40: £5.40, £2.10, £14.60; EX 64.70.
Owner R C Bond **Bred** Schwindibode Ag **Trained** Brawby, N Yorks

FOCUS
A decent handicap and one run at a solid pace thanks to Jewelled Dagger. The form looks pretty sound, with a career best from Just Bond.
Bold Diktator Official explanation: jockey said gelding reared up leaving stalls

4673 HOTEL & CONFERENCING AT WOLVERHAMPTON RACECOURSE CLASSIFIED STKS 1m 141y(P)
4:45 (4:45) (Class 7) 3-Y-0+ £1,706 (£503; £252) Stalls Low

Form RPR
/0-0 **1** **Faraday (IRE)**[141] 242 4-9-5 45 TPQueally 1 59+
(B J Curley) *hld up in mid-div and rdn confidently: hdwy and edgd rt over 1f out: shkn up to ld ins fnl f* **5/4**[1]
0000 **2** 3/4 **Fancy (IRE)**[76] 2336 4-8-12 45 SophieDoyle(7) 7 53
(R A Farrant) *trckd ldrs: rdn and led briefly ins fnl f: kpt on* **16/1**
5400 **3** 2 1/2 **Dexileos (IRE)**[30] 3730 8-9-3 45 ow5 ChrisCavanagh(7) 4 52
(David Pinder) *led after 1f: rdn 3f out: hdd ins fnl f: no ex* **14/1**
-640 **4** 2 **La Cuvee**[43] 3351 3-8-12 45 (b[1]) PaulHanagan 13 43
(B G Powell) *in rr: hdwy on outside over 2f out: edgd lft over 1f out and no imp after* **8/1**[3]
0-00 **5** 1/2 **Silent Beauty (IRE)**[5] 4499 3-8-12 45 GrahamGibbons 9 41
(S C Williams) *in rr: sme hdwy on ins over 1f out but nvr on terms* **12/1**
3000 **6** 1 **Thomas Lawrence (USA)**[9] 4395 6-9-5 45 PatCosgrave 10 39
(P A Blockley) *trckd ldrs: rdn over 2f out: wknd over 1f out* **8/1**[3]
0050 **7** 1/2 **Betteras Bertie**[29] 3765 4-9-5 45 DanielTudhope 2 38
(M Brittain) *in rr: rdn over 3f out: c wd into st: kpt on fnl f but n.d* **14/1**
0600 **8** 3/4 **The Diamond Bond**[28] 3789 3-8-12 45 ChrisCatlin 12 36
(G R Oldroyd) *mid-div: rdn over 2f out: nvr bttr than mid-div* **25/1**
000/ **9** nk **Dashing Dane**[958] 29 7-9-5 45 RoystonFfrench 5 36
(Mrs Marjorie Fife) *led for 1f: prom tl wknd qckly oveR 1f out* **50/1**
4040 **10** nk **Fulvio (USA)**[12] 4294 7-9-5 45 (v) IanMongan 11 35
(P Howling) *a bhd* **9/2**[2]
0036 **11** 1 1/2 **Homecroft Boy**[13] 4256 3-8-12 45 (v) StephenDonohoe 3 31
(P D Evans) *a struggling in rr* **12/1**
0-04 **12** dist **Buckle And Hyde**[8] 4416 4-9-5 45 AdamKirby 6 —
(Mrs A L M King) *in tch early: wknd over 2f out: t.o* **14/1**

1m 51.43s (-0.33) **Going Correction** -0.075s/f (Stan)
WFA 3 from 4yo+ 7lb 12 Ran SP% **131.9**
Speed ratings (Par 97): **98,97,95,93,92 92,91,90,90,90 89,—**
CSF £29.83 TOTE £2.30: £1.40, £6.60, £4.20; EX 49.60 Place 6 £341.17, Place 5 £123.48.
Owner Curley Leisure **Bred** K Nercessian **Trained** Newmarket, Suffolk

FOCUS
Until December 31 this would have been called a banded stakes, but however you dress it up this was a dire contest and the only interest was over the Curley-trained favourite, who can rate higher. Sound form for the grade, however.
Buckle And Hyde Official explanation: jockey said filly lost its action
T/Plt: £866.90 to a £1 stake. Pool: £73,101.00. 61.55 winning tickets. T/Qpdt: £90.50 to a £1 stake. Pool: £3,952.50. 32.30 winning tickets. JS

4512 YARMOUTH (L-H)
Monday, August 20 (eve)
4674 Meeting Abandoned - Waterlogged

4469 BRIGHTON (L-H)
Tuesday, August 21
OFFICIAL GOING: Good to soft
Wind: Fresh, half behind Weather: Cloudy

4683 EBF 3663 FIRST FOR FOOD SERVICE MAIDEN STKS 6f 209y
2:20 (2:20) (Class 5) 2-Y-0 £3,497 (£1,040; £520; £259) Stalls Low

Form RPR
053 **1** **Mr Keppel (IRE)**[12] 4323 2-9-3 73 MartinDwyer 2 71
(J A Osborne) *prom: led wl over 1f out: hrd rdn and hld on wl fnl f* **15/8**[1]
6 **2** shd **Art Currency (USA)**[10] 4393 2-9-3 0 ChrisCatlin 6 71
(M J Wallace) *prom: slt ld over 2f out tl wl over 1f out: rallied and str chal ins fnl f: r.o* **6/1**[3]
3 1 1/2 **Pragmatism** 2-9-3 0 J-PGuillambert 8 67
(M Johnston) *led 2f: rdn and bdly lost pl 4f out: hdwy and hrd rdn over 1f out: styd on* **5/2**[2]
00 **4** 1 1/4 **Dream Bee**[19] 4094 2-8-12 0 JimmyQuinn 9 59
(E A L Dunlop) *s.i.s: towards rr: rdn and hdwy on outside over 3f out: one pce appr fnl f* **16/1**
0553 **5** 3 1/2 **Choisky (IRE)**[13] 4274 2-9-3 62 NickyMackay 7 54
(J Akehurst) *in tch: hrd rdn over 2f out: sn outpcd* **8/1**
00 **6** 1/2 **Medici Gold**[15] 4232 2-8-12 0 NelsonDeSouza 5 48
(B J Meehan) *bhd: rdn and sme hdwy 2f out: nvr rchd ldrs* **40/1**
7 3/4 **Desert Life (IRE)** 2-9-3 0 VinceSlattery 4 51
(R A Harris) *s.s: hld up in rr: swtchd wd and sme hdwy 3f out: styd on steadily fnl f* **100/1**
000 **8** nk **Mister Cafnex (IRE)**[96] 1781 2-8-10 40 JackDean(7) 1 50
(B W Duke) *on and off the bridle in rr: nvr a factor* **100/1**
0 **9** 1 **Enchanted Lady**[49] 3187 2-8-12 0 RobertHavlin 3 43
(H J L Dunlop) *towards rr: rdn over 4f out: n.d* **66/1**
0063 **10** 1/2 **Spinning Ridge (IRE)**[22] 4022 2-9-3 65 JimCrowley 10 47
(R A Harris) *w ldrs: led after 2f tl over 2f out: wknd over 1f out* **10/1**
0 **11** 7 **Bravo Bolivar (IRE)**[17] 4151 2-9-3 0 TQuinn 11 28
(J L Dunlop) *s.i.s and needed early rousting: sn drvn up to chse ldrs: wknd over 2f out* **22/1**

1m 25.67s (2.97) **Going Correction** +0.30s/f (Good) 11 Ran SP% **114.0**
Speed ratings (Par 94): **95,94,93,91,87 87,86,85,84,84 76**
CSF £12.78 TOTE £2.70: £1.10, £2.00, £1.60; EX 11.40 Trifecta £32.70 Pool £380.96. - 8.26 winning units..
Owner Mountgrange Stud **Bred** Mrs C F Van Straubenzee And Miss A Gibson Flemi **Trained** Upper Lambourn, Berks

FOCUS
An ordinary juvenile maiden. The first two fought out a battling finish and the form looks straightforward, although the proximity of the eighth raises doubts.

NOTEBOOK
Mr Keppel(IRE), officially rated 73 after three previous outings in maidens, dug deep inside the final furlong to just get off the mark in a bobbing finish. He proved a little free early on, and did not look totally at home on this very different track, so he can be rated a little better than the bare margin. The step up to this trip evidently helped. (tchd 7-4 and 2-1)

Art Currency(USA) ◆, sixth on his debut over 1m at Lingfield ten days previously, gave his all in defeat on this switch to turf and only lost out by the smallest margin. He shaped as though he needs an extra furlong now and can be placed to gain compensation in the coming weeks. (op 5-1 tchd 9-2)
Pragmatism, bred to make a two-year-old, knew his job as he was well away from the gates, but ultimately lost the race when becoming badly outpaced on the turn into the home straight. He finished well, however, when meeting the rising finish and this still rates a pleasing enough start to his career. No doubt he will prove sharper next time, and he has a future. (op 11-4)
Dream Bee, down in grade, overcame a sluggish start and posted her most encouraging effort to date. She looks in need of a stiffer test, is going the right way, and now has the option of nurseries. (op 12-1)
Choisky(IRE) ran his race yet simply failed to see out the extra furlong anywhere near as well as the principals and was well held. He helps to set the level of this form. (op 9-1 tchd 10-1)

4684 WILLIAM HILL COURTWICK SHOP - STAFF DAY OUT FILLIES' H'CAP 7f 214y
2:55 (2:55) (Class 6) (0-65,65) 3-Y-O **£1,943** (£578; £288; £144) **Stalls** Low

Form RPR
-300 1 **Feolin**[19] 4112 3-9-4 65 TravisBlock(3) 14 75+
(H Morrison) *mde all at gd pce: travelling best fr 1/2-way: rdn and in control fnl 2f: a holding on* **16/1**
503 2 1 3/4 **Bluebelle Dancer (IRE)**[17] 4163 3-9-6 64 MartinDwyer 2 67
(W R Muir) *mid-div: rdn over 3f out: hdwy on rail 2f out: styd on to chse wnr fnl 100yds* **9/2**[1]
000- 3 hd **Slo Mo Shun**[273] 6558 3-8-5 49 JimmyQuinn 6 52
(H J L Dunlop) *in tch: rdn over 3f out: styd on to chse wnr 1f out: kpt on same pce: lost 2nd fnl 100yds* **33/1**
5004 4 1 1/4 **Meeting Of Minds**[12] 4337 3-7-13 46 WilliamBuick(3) 5 46
(W Jarvis) *t.k.h in midfield: rdn over 3f out: hdwy and wandered over 1f out: styd on* **12/1**
4202 5 nk **Cow Girl (IRE)**[12] 4321 3-9-1 62 JerryO'Dwyer(3) 4 61
(Miss Gay Kelleway) *s.s: wl bhd tl hdwy on outside 2f out: rdn along and nt pce to chal* **13/2**[3]
-021 6 3/4 **Dancing Jest (IRE)**[12] 4338 3-9-4 62 NickyMackay 10 59
(Rae Guest) *prom: rdn and outpcd 3f out: 6th and hld whn nt clr run and swtchd lft over 1f out: one pce* **9/2**[1]
4462 7 3 **Rubilini**[3] 4596 3-8-3 47 ow1 TPO'Shea 12 37
(M R Channon) *chsd wnr: hung bdly lft ins fnl 2f: lost 2nd and wknd 1f out* **11/2**[2]
0002 8 1 1/4 **Elmasong**[7] 4470 3-8-2 46 oh1 FrankieMcDonald 7 33
(J J Bridger) *in tch: rdn over 3f out: n.m.r and checked over 2f out: no imp* **33/1**
6063 9 1 1/2 **Inquisitress**[7] 4474 3-8-9 53 J-PGuillambert 13 37
(J J Bridger) *prom and gng bttr than all except wnr tl wknd wl over 1f out* **12/1**
0020 10 2 **Puissant Princess (IRE)**[20] 4064 3-9-6 64 TQuinn 3 43
(J W Hills) *t.k.h towards rr: rdn over 3f out: n.d* **12/1**
0-00 11 nk **Edgefour (IRE)**[16] 4205 3-8-5 52 RichardKingscote(3) 1 31
(B I Case) *bhd: rdn over 3f out: nvr a factor* **33/1**
410 12 nk **Dansil In Distress**[19] 4111 3-9-0 58 LPKeniry 8 36
(S Kirk) *mid-div: hrd rdn 3f out: n.d fnl 2f* **7/1**
0000 13 12 **Poyle Ruby**[13] 4292 3-8-2 46 oh1 ChrisCatlin 9 —
(M Blanshard) *a towards rr: wl bhd fnl 3f* **66/1**
000 14 2 1/2 **Silver Flame**[5] 4529 3-8-6 50 HayleyTurner 11 —
(A W Carroll) *chsd ldrs tl hrd rdn and wknd qckly over 2f out* **50/1**
1m 37.23s (2.19) **Going Correction** +0.30s/f (Good) **14** Ran SP% **118.8**
Speed ratings (Par 95): **101,99,99,97,97 96,93,92,91,89 88,88,76,73**
CSF £82.90 CT £2436.93 TOTE £22.20: £4.70, £2.00, £6.30; EX 121.20 TRIFECTA Not won..
Owner Mrs C R Philipson & Mrs H G Lascelles **Bred** Exors Of The Late Major C R Philipson And Mrs Ph **Trained** East Ilsley, Berks

FOCUS
A weak fillies' handicap, run at a solid pace. The first two are rated back to their 2yo form.
Puissant Princess(IRE) Official explanation: jockey said filly never travelled

4685 BET ONLINE @ WILLIAMHILL.CO.UK (S) STKS 6f 209y
3:30 (3:31) (Class 6) 3-Y-O+ **£1,943** (£578; £288; £144) **Stalls** Low

Form RPR
6006 1 **Ten To The Dozen**[7] 4469 4-9-1 49 ChrisCatlin 1 59
(P W Hiatt) *chsd ldrs: led over 1f out: rdn clr fnl f* **9/2**[1]
0053 2 2 **Halfwaytoparadise**[3] 4595 4-8-10 47 (p) SaleemGolam 15 49
(W G M Turner) *led tl over 1f out: nt qckn fnl f* **15/2**
6300 3 3 **Fantasy Defender (IRE)**[12] 4319 5-9-1 44 JimmyQuinn 8 46
(R M H Cowell) *in tch: effrt over 2f out: kpt on to take 3rd ins fnl f* **7/1**
500 4 1/2 **Fire At Will**[26] 3868 5-8-8 40 (v) MarkCoumbe(7) 12 44
(A W Carroll) *s.s: hld up and bhd: rdn over 2f out: styd on strly fnl f* **16/1**
00-0 5 1/2 **Baytown Valentina**[78] 2304 4-8-8 38 ow1 (p) JerryO'Dwyer(3) 2 39
(R Brotherton) *prom: rdn and rdr dropped whip 2f out: no ex 1f out* **66/1**
-000 6 1 1/4 **Huxley (IRE)**[119] 1206 8-9-1 42 (t) VinceSlattery 11 40+
(D J Wintle) *missed break and lost 10l: wl bhd tl rdn and styd on wl fnl 2f: nvr nrr* **25/1**
6020 7 1 **King Of Tricks**[5] 4529 3-8-3 44 FrankiePickard(7) 14 37
(M D I Usher) *mid-div: outpcd and hrd rdn 3f out: n.d* **9/1**
0556 8 3/4 **Rowan Pursuit**[69] 2559 6-8-10 33 (b) AdamKirby 4 30
(E A Wheeler) *mid-div tl dropped to rr after 2f: drvn along most of way after: sme late hdwy* **66/1**
0603 9 shd **Blue Knight (IRE)**[7] 4471 8-9-6 41 (p) AmirQuinn 3 40
(P Howling) *mid-div: modest effrt over 2f out: no imp* **8/1**
6450 10 2 **Nou Camp**[12] 4336 3-8-3 47 KirstyMilczarek(7) 5 29
(N A Callaghan) *plld hrd: prom tl wknd over 1f out* **11/2**[2]
3006 11 1/2 **Sham Ruby**[7] 4471 5-8-10 43 (t) JimCrowley 16 23
(M R Bosley) *bhd: rdn 3f out: nvr a factor* **16/1**
530 12 1 1/2 **Jools**[25] 3922 9-9-6 52 RobertHavlin 6 29
(D K Ivory) *hld up in tch and gng wl: shkn up 2f out: jockey nt happy: eased over 1f out* **13/2**[3]
0000 13 1/2 **Iced Diamond (IRE)**[38] 3534 8-9-1 45 LPKeniry 7 22
(S Wynne) *s.s: sn rdn along: a in rr gp* **18/1**
000- 14 1/2 **Lord Blue Boy**[325] 5687 3-8-3 54 JackDean(7) 10 21
(W G M Turner) *dwlt: sn in midfield: hrd rdn and wknd 3f out* **40/1**
1m 24.95s (2.25) **Going Correction** +0.30s/f (Good)
WFA 3 from 4yo+ 5lb **14** Ran SP% **118.6**
Speed ratings (Par 101): **99,96,93,92,92 90,89,88,88,86 85,84,83,82**
CSF £36.26 TOTE £6.40: £2.90, £3.00, £2.20; EX 55.90 Trifecta £250.60 Part won. Pool £353.00. - 0.44 winning units..There was no bid for the winner.
Owner Clive Roberts Vince Walsh **Bred** S J Mear **Trained** Hook Norton, Oxon

FOCUS
An ordinary seller which few got into from off the pace. The form seems sound.
Jools Official explanation: trainer said gelding was unsuited by the good to soft ground

4686 DITCH THE DABBER @ WILLIAMHILLBINGO.COM H'CAP 1m 1f 209y
4:05 (4:05) (Class 5) (0-70,70) 3-Y-O+ **£2,775** (£830; £415; £207; £103) **Stalls** High

Form RPR
1650 1 **Drawback (IRE)**[13] 4266 4-9-8 69 (p) HaddenFrost(5) 9 77
(R A Harris) *stdd s: t.k.h: hld up: smooth effrt 2f out: rdn to ld fnl 100yds: pushed out nr fin* **12/1**
-303 2 1/2 **Moon Valley**[13] 4266 4-9-13 69 (b[1]) J-PGuillambert 5 76
(W J Haggas) *chsd ldrs: led over 4f out: hrd rdn and hdd fnl 100yds: hld nr fin* **9/2**[2]
6464 3 3 **Kalasam**[8] 4450 3-9-6 70 MartinDwyer 6 71
(W R Muir) *led tl over 4f out: styd w ldrs: no ex fnl f* **4/1**[1]
0200 4 6 **View From The Top**[42] 3406 3-9-1 65 JimmyQuinn 11 54
(Sir Mark Prescott) *wnt rt s: hld up in rr: hdwy into midfield 5f out: rdn 3f out: nt pce to chal* **12/1**
3541 5 shd **Recalcitrant**[13] 4266 4-8-9 58 JamieHamblett(7) 3 47
(S Dow) *plld hrd: in tch: jnd ldrs 4f out: outpcd and swtchd lft over 2f out: sn btn* **9/2**[2]
0003 6 2 1/2 **Little Miss Tara (IRE)**[7] 4472 3-9-1 65 (v) SamHitchcott 7 49
(A B Haynes) *hld up towards rr: hdwy on outside to join ldrs 4f out: rdn and btn over 2f out* **7/1**
-000 7 5 **Pink Bay**[13] 4294 5-8-2 51 oh6 MCGeran(7) 1 25
(K F Clutterbuck) *chsd ldrs: lost pl 5f out and sn towards rr: rdn and n.d fnl 4f* **66/1**
600- 8 hd **Grand Silence (IRE)**[328] 5612 4-10-0 70 AdamKirby 2 43
(W R Swinburn) *towards rr: rdn 4f out: n.d* **7/1**
046 9 3/4 **Voice Mail**[13] 4267 8-8-2 51 oh4 (b) DavidProbert(7) 4 23
(A M Balding) *hld up towards rr: hdwy 5f out: wknd over 2f out* **28/1**
0006 10 2 1/2 **Dora Explora**[18] 2942 3-9-6 70 ChrisCatlin 10 37
(D J Wintle) *in tch tl wknd 4f out* **22/1**
4205 11 hd **Under Fire (IRE)**[192] 426 4-9-0 56 HayleyTurner 8 23
(A W Carroll) *prom: chalng whn squeezed out 3f out: nt rcvr* **6/1**[3]
2m 6.84s (4.24) **Going Correction** +0.30s/f (Good)
WFA 3 from 4yo+ 8lb **11** Ran SP% **120.3**
Speed ratings (Par 103): **95,94,92,87,87 85,81,81,80,78 78**
CSF £65.86 CT £262.43 TOTE £19.90: £4.50, £2.30, £1.90; EX 96.30 Trifecta £180.10 Part won. Pool £253.70 - 0.50 winning units..
Owner B & T Hicks Transport Limited **Bred** Mrs H B Raw **Trained** Earlswood, Monmouths
■ Stewards' Enquiry : Martin Dwyer two-day ban: careless riding (Sep 1-2)

FOCUS
A modest handicap, run at a steady pace. The first pair came clear and the form is rated through the third.

4687 HEADS-UP @ WILLIAMHILLPOKER.COM H'CAP 1m 3f 196y
4:40 (4:41) (Class 5) (0-70,69) 3-Y-O **£2,775** (£830; £415; £207; £103) **Stalls** High

Form RPR
4251 1 **Western Point (IRE)**[6] 4518 3-8-10 **58** 6ex JimmyQuinn 3 69
(Sir Mark Prescott) *hld up in tch: rdn to ld over 2f out: strly chal and edgd lft fnl f: all out* **6/4**[1]
-002 2 hd **Little Carmela**[7] 4472 3-8-3 **51** ow1 SaleemGolam 6 62
(S C Williams) *trckd ldrs: hld in bhd rivals 3f out: drvn to chal whn carried lft fnl f: r.o* **9/1**
0002 3 11 **Black Mogul**[13] 4292 3-8-5 **53** (b) MartinDwyer 5 46
(W R Muir) *trckd ldr: led 5f out and sn increased tempo: hdd over 2f out: wknd qckly over 1f out* **16/1**
0154 4 2 **President Dan**[10] 4391 3-8-7 **55** TPO'Shea 1 45
(M R Channon) *towards rr: rdn 5f out: kpt on past btn horses fnl 2f* **9/2**[3]
3220 5 4 **Aypeeyes (IRE)**[6] 4504 3-9-7 **69** LPKeniry 2 52
(S Kirk) *hld up in rr: hdwy to chse ldrs 4f out: hrd rdn and wknd over 2f out* **8/1**
005 6 8 **Kings Story (IRE)**[43] 3366 3-9-4 **66** AdamKirby 4 37
(W R Swinburn) *settled in 6th: rdn over 4f out: sn bhd* **7/2**[2]
0-00 7 7 **Peppermint Green**[28] 3826 3-9-6 **68** NickyMackay 8 27
(L M Cumani) *chsd ldrs: lost pl 5f out: sn bhd* **12/1**
0020 8 8 **Desert Soul**[80] 2248 3-8-13 **61** SamHitchcott 7 8
(R H York) *led and set modest pce tl 5f out: wknd 3f out* **33/1**
2m 34.93s (2.73) **Going Correction** +0.30s/f (Good) **8** Ran SP% **118.0**
Speed ratings (Par 100): **102,101,94,93,90 85,80,75**
CSF £17.20 CT £161.86 TOTE £2.40: £1.10, £2.10, £3.30; EX 15.70 Trifecta £122.20 Pool £607.78 - 3.53 winning units..
Owner Charles C Walker-Osborne House III **Bred** Mount Coote Stud **Trained** Newmarket, Suffolk

FOCUS
A moderate three-year-old handicap, run at an ordinary early pace. Good efforts from the front pair to finish well clear.
Kings Story(IRE) Official explanation: jockey said colt never travelled
Desert Soul Official explanation: trainer said colt failed to stay the trip

4688 WILLIAM HILL LITTLEHAMPTON SHOP - STAFF DAY OUT H'CAP 6f 209y
5:10 (5:10) (Class 5) (0-70,70) 3-Y-O+ **£2,775** (£830; £415; £207; £103) **Stalls** Low

Form RPR
31 1 **Perfect Treasure (IRE)**[12] 4317 4-9-12 70 RobertHavlin 7 82
(J A R Toller) *led after 2f: hrd rdn over 1f out: drvn clr ins fnl f* **15/8**[2]
0521 2 2 1/2 **Wrighty Almighty (IRE)**[12] 4319 5-9-3 61 JimCrowley 2 66
(P R Chamings) *stdd s: hld up in rr: hdwy to chal over 1f out: nt qckn fnl f* **6/4**[1]
5000 3 2 **Quantum Leap**[10] 4394 10-8-9 60 (p) ThomasBubb(7) 1 60
(S Dow) *hld up in tch: rdn to press ldrs 2f out: no ex 1f out* **12/1**
0010 4 nk **Croft (IRE)**[5] 4532 4-8-10 54 (v) TGMcLaughlin 4 53
(M S Saunders) *cl up: outpcd over 2f out: sn btn* **16/1**
00 5 3 1/2 **Riolo (IRE)**[13] 4296 5-8-7 54 oh1 ow3 (b) JerryO'Dwyer(3) 8 43
(K F Clutterbuck) *cl up tl hrd rdn and wknd over 2f out* **12/1**
6002 6 1/2 **Lady Edge (IRE)**[7] 4474 5-8-8 52 HayleyTurner 6 40
(A W Carroll) *led 2f: styd alone far side st: wknd over 1f out* **7/1**[3]
1m 26.36s (3.66) **Going Correction** +0.30s/f (Good) **6** Ran SP% **108.5**
Speed ratings (Par 103): **91,88,85,85,81 80**
CSF £4.68 CT £17.98 TOTE £2.60: £1.50, £1.30; EX 4.60 Trifecta £11.70 Pool £484.09 - 29.25 winning units..
Owner John Drew **Bred** Patrick F Kelly **Trained** Newmarket, Suffolk

FOCUS
A modest handicap, run at a steady early pace. All bar one of the runners came stands' side. Improved form from the winner.

4689 CHIPS @ WILLIAMHILLCASINO.COM H'CAP — 5f 59y
5:40 (5:40) (Class 6) (0-65,65) 3-Y-O+ **£2,137** (£635; £317; £158) **Stalls** Low

Form — RPR

3221 **1** **Cosmic Destiny (IRE)**[12] 4314 5-9-9 65 LPKeniry 9 — 73
(E F Vaughan) *hld up in midfield: hdwy and swtchd rt over 1f out: drvn to ld fnl 50yds* **7/1**[3]

6060 **2** ½ **Master Malarkey**[17] 4164 4-8-4 46 oh1 (b) ChrisCatlin 15 — 52
(Mrs C A Dunnett) *disp ld: led over 2f out: edgd lft ins fnl f: kpt on: hdd fnl 50yds* **33/1**

6000 **3** ¾ **Hello Roberto**[27] 3853 6-8-6 53 (p) HaddenFrost(5) 1 — 56
(R A Harris) *mid-div: hdwy to press ldrs over 1f out: kpt on fnl f* **10/1**

000 **4** hd **Night Prospector**[12] 4312 7-9-7 63 (p) JimCrowley 7 — 65
(R A Harris) *outpcd towards rr: rdn and r.o fnl 2f: nrst fin* **10/1**

0060 **5** 1 ¾ **Whistler**[2] 4635 10-8-7 49 (p) PaulFitzsimons 4 — 45
(Miss J R Tooth) *outpcd and bhd: hdwy over 1f out: nt rch ldrs* **9/1**

0000 **6** ¾ **Dancing Mystery**[15] 4233 13-9-2 58 (b) TQuinn 5 — 51
(E A Wheeler) *in tch: effrt 2f out: styd on same pce* **16/1**

303 **7** ½ **Talcen Gwyn (IRE)**[10] 4390 5-9-4 60 FergusSweeney 11 — 51
(M F Harris) *chsd ldrs: outpcd fnl 2f* **3/1**[1]

5336 **8** nk **Bobby Rose**[7] 4486 4-9-6 62 RobertHavlin 10 — 52
(D K Ivory) *mid-div: effrt and swtchd rt to stands' rail over 1f out: no imp* **7/1**[3]

0000 **9** ½ **Kindallachan**[12] 4336 4-8-1 46 oh1 WilliamBuick(3) 3 — 35
(G C Bravery) *hmpd s: outpcd and bhd: sme late hdwy* **33/1**

420 **10** hd **Multahab**[15] 4233 8-9-5 61 (t) AdamKirby 2 — 49
(M Wigham) *prom tl wknd over 1f out* **11/2**[2]

3600 **11** hd **Ever Cheerful**[12] 4312 6-8-8 50 ow1 (v) SamHitchcott 14 — 37
(A B Haynes) *wd: a towards rr* **16/1**

0015 **12** hd **Gone'N'Dunnett (IRE)**[10] 4397 8-8-11 53 (v) DMylonas 8 — 39
(Mrs C A Dunnett) *mid-div: effrt and hung lft over 1f out: nvr able to chal* **11/1**

0000 **13** hd **Banana Belle**[15] 4226 3-7-9 46 oh1 FrankiePickard(7) 12 — 32
(J Ryan) *dwlt: outpcd: a bhd* **66/1**

0000 **14** 1 ½ **Spinetail Rufous (IRE)**[48] 3212 9-8-4 46 oh1 (b) AdrianMcCarthy 6 — 26
(Miss Z C Davison) *chsd ldrs tl wknd ins fnl 2f* **50/1**

0066 **15** 2 ½ **Sofinella (IRE)**[180] 523 4-8-4 46 oh1 HayleyTurner 16 — 17
(A W Carroll) *disp ld tl over 2f out: hung lft: chsng ldrs but btn whn bmpd 1f out* **28/1**

63.09 secs (0.79) **Going Correction** +0.30s/f (Good)
WFA 3 from 4yo+ 2lb — **15** Ran SP% **126.4**
Speed ratings (Par 101): **105,104,103,102,99 98,97,97,96,96 95,95,95,92,88**
CSF £238.57 CT £2386.74 TOTE £6.40: £3.20, £5.10, £3.10; EX 311.00 TRIFECTA Not won. Place 6 £22.61, Place 5 £19.09..
Owner A M Pickering **Bred** The Cruelle People **Trained** Newmarket, Suffolk

FOCUS
A moderate sprint and the form should be treated with some caution. A career best from the in-form winner.
Ever Cheerful Official explanation: jockey said gelding failed to come down the hill
Spinetail Rufous(IRE) Official explanation: trainer said gelding was unsuited by the good to soft ground
T/Plt: £24.00 to a £1 stake. Pool: £57,967.45. 1,762.40 winning tickets. T/Qpdt: £5.10 to a £1 stake. Pool: £4,347.00. 628.40 winning tickets. LM

3971 YORK (L-H)
Tuesday, August 21
OFFICIAL GOING: Good (good to soft in places; 7.2)
Wind: Slight, against Weather: Overcast

4690 SYMPHONY GROUP STKS (H'CAP) — 1m 4f
1:30 (1:33) (Class 2) (0-100,100) 3-Y-O+ **£19,431** (£5,781; £2,889; £1,443) **Stalls** Centre

Form — RPR

1-52 **1** **Galactic Star**[17] 4166 4-8-13 85 RyanMoore 16 — 104+
(Sir Michael Stoute) *lw: hld up in rr: gd hdwy over 3f out: rdn over 1f out: styd on to ld last 150yds* **6/1**[1]

6130 **2** 1 **Dunaskin (IRE)**[10] 4376 7-9-10 96 JMurtagh 6 — 106
(Karen McLintock) *cl up: effrt to ld over 3f out: rdn 2f out: drvn ent fnl f: hdd and no ex last 150yds* **33/1**

3 3 **Rajeh (IRE)**[75] 5699 4-8-9 84 LiamJones(3) 8 — 89
(J L Spearing) *chsd ldrs: hdwy 3f out: rdn along 2f out: drvn over 1f out and kpt on wl u.p ins fnl f* **66/1**

3112 **4** ½ **Mull Of Dubai**[23] 3989 4-9-6 92 JohnEgan 4 — 96
(J S Moore) *lw: hld up in rr: gd hdwy 4f out: rdn to chse ldrs 2f out: drvn and kpt on same pce ent fnl f* **8/1**[3]

3303 **5** nk **Nawamees (IRE)**[30] 3509 9-8-12 84 (p) JimmyFortune 1 — 88
(G L Moore) *trckd ldrs: hdwy 3f out: chal 2f out and ev ch tl drvn and one pce ent fnl f* **16/1**

2030 **6** nk **Wind Star**[10] 4388 4-9-3 89 NCallan 10 — 92
(G A Swinbank) *in midfield on inner: hdwy over 2f out: sn edgd rt and rdn: chsd ldrs 2f out: sn drvn and kpt on same pce ent fnl f* **20/1**

-061 **7** ¾ **Invasian (IRE)**[17] 4171 6-9-2 88 (e) TPQueally 7 — 90
(P W D'Arcy) *led: rdn along and hdd over 3f out: drvn 2f out and grad wknd* **20/1**

4003 **8** hd **Acropolis (IRE)**[10] 4376 6-9-6 92 (v) TomEaves 20 — 94
(I Semple) *in midfield: hdwy over 3f out: rdn over 2f out: kpt on same pce* **25/1**

0150 **9** ½ **Realism (FR)**[10] 4388 7-9-2 88 PaulHanagan 9 — 89
(R A Fahey) *hld up: hdwy 3f out: rdn along 2f out: kpt on appr fnl f: nt rch ldrs* **40/1**

1544 **10** hd **Hernando Royal**[21] 4047 4-9-3 89 SteveDrowne 5 — 90
(H Morrison) *lw: chsd ldrs: rdn along 3f out: drvn over 2f out and sn one pce* **7/1**[2]

0036 **11** shd **Kyoto Summit**[19] 4105 4-8-11 83 PaulMulrennan 17 — 84
(M W Easterby) *hld up in rr: hdwy 3f out: sn rdn along and styd on ins fnl f: nt rch ldrs* **33/1**

2106 **12** 1 ¼ **High Treason (USA)**[23] 3989 5-9-0 86 TedDurcan 11 — 85
(W J Musson) *hld up: a towards rr* **6/1**[1]

0552 **13** 1 ¾ **Futun**[10] 4388 4-9-12 98 JamieSpencer 19 — 94
(L M Cumani) *lw: hld up and bhd: hdwy 3f out: rdn along over 2f out and sn no imp* **7/1**[2]

0305 **14** ½ **Akarem**[24] 3973 6-10-0 100 PhillipMakin 13 — 95
(K R Burke) *in tch: rdn along 3f out: sn wknd* **33/1**

0510 **15** 24 **Lucayan Dancer**[17] 4153 7-8-12 84 AdrianTNicholls 18 — 41
(D Nicholls) *hld up: a towards rr* **50/1**

1400 **16** 1 ½ **Eradicate (IRE)**[20] 4059 3-9-2 98 KDarley 14 — 52
(M Johnston) *in tch: rdn along over 3f out and sn wknd* **12/1**

40-0 **17** 3 ½ **Diktatorial**[75] 2397 5-8-9 81 SebSanders 2 — 30
(J Howard Johnson) *trckd ldr: rdn along over 5f out: drvn and wkng whn n.m.r 3f out: sn bhd* **33/1**

0-12 **18** 2 ½ **Greek Envoy**[39] 3513 3-9-0 96 MickyFenton 15 — 41
(T P Tate) *lw: in midfield: rdn along 1/2-way: sn lost pl and bhd fnl 3f* **7/1**[2]

10- **19** 4 **Trezene (USA)**[47] 5-9-8 94 EddieAhern 12 — 32
(G L Moore) *chsd ldrs on outer: rdn along over 4f out: sn wknd* **25/1**

2m 33.95s (-0.65) **Going Correction** +0.225s/f (Good)
WFA 3 from 4yo+ 10lb — **19** Ran SP% **125.6**
Speed ratings (Par 109): **111,110,108,108,107 107,107,106,106,106 106,105,104,104,88 87,84,83,80**
CSF £211.55 CT £11448.50 TOTE £5.50: £1.70, £9.00, £14.70, £2.00; EX 254.70 TRIFECTA Not won..
Owner Saeed Suhail **Bred** Hascombe And Valiant Studs **Trained** Newmarket, Suffolk

FOCUS
A competitive handicap run at a good pace and the form looks solid, rated through the runner-up and third.

NOTEBOOK
Galactic Star ◆, who ran well at Newmarket last time despite pulling in the early stages, promised to be happier back on this easier surface and the extra distance was only going to help him. In a race in which the pace was decent, he settled out the back, picked up well in the closing stages as the leaders tired, and in the end ran out quite a comfortable winner. Given the way this track tends to favour pace horses rather than those that are held up, it was a great effort, and there should be even better to come this autumn. (tchd 13-2)
Dunaskin(IRE), who seems to need a little cut in the ground these days to show his best, had conditions to suit and arguably put up a career-best effort. This track tends to suit those who race handily, so he could be flattered, but at least he showed he is just as effective over 1m4f as he is over 1m2f.
Rajeh(IRE), who was in winning form over hurdles earlier in the year, was having his first outing on the Flat for his current stable. He looked to have plenty on his plate, a view reflected in his SP, but he was another who was shrewdly ridden near the pace on a track that tends to favour pace horses. (op 50-1)
Mull Of Dubai is now on a mark 11lb higher than when last successful, so things were not going to be easy for him, but he ran well, staying on from the back of the field, like the winner, on a track that usually favours horses ridden more prominently. It is difficult to escape the conclusion, however, that the Handicapper just about has his measure now. (op 15-2)
Nawamees(IRE), another who was handy throughout, quite often runs well in these big handicaps but he just does not win. (tchd 20-1)
Wind Star seemed to get the trip alright but he has looked held off marks in the mid-to-high 80s for a year now and this performance did not alter that view.
Invasian(IRE) had to go a step quicker than he would have liked in front this time but this track favours his style of running and he was far from disgraced off a mark 5lb higher than when dominating throughout at Newmarket 17 days earlier.
Acropolis(IRE) has not won for a long time but he could well pop up one day in one of these races. He is a hold-up performer who needs a strong pace and this track would not have been ideal for him.
Kyoto Summit was staying on late but never really got involved. He is normally ridden closer to the pace but his draw made that difficult on this occasion.
High Treason(USA), who ran well on consecutive days here at the Dante meeting, proved very disappointing. This was not his true form. (op 8-1)
Futun, who is not the easiest of rides, is probably at his best on quicker ground.
Lucayan Dancer Official explanation: jockey said gelding had no more to give.
Greek Envoy, whose recent progress has been made in soft ground, did not find conditions as testing this time, and his stamina for this longer trip has yet to be proven. Official explanation: jockey said gelding ran flat (op 6-1)

4691 WEATHERBYS INSURANCE LONSDALE CUP (GROUP 2) — 2m 88y
2:00 (2:01) (Class 1) 3-Y-O+
£70,975 (£26,900; £13,462; £6,712; £3,362; £1,687) **Stalls** Low

Form — RPR

0-12 **1** **Septimus (IRE)**[81] 2210 4-9-1 0 JMurtagh 2 — 115+
(A P O'Brien, Ire) *trckd ldng pair: smooth hdwy 3f out: swtchd rt and led over 1f out: rdn ins fnl f and styd on wl* **6/5**[1]

2114 **2** 1 **Balkan Knight**[19] 4091 7-9-1 106 JimmyFortune 8 — 114
(D R C Elsworth) *lw: hld up towards rr: gd hdwy 3f out: swtchd lft and rdn over 1f out: styd on to chal ent fnl f: sn drvn and ev ch: no ex towards fin* **12/1**

2-12 **3** 1 **Anna Pavlova**[96] 1789 4-8-12 110 PaulHanagan 4 — 110
(R A Fahey) *hld up in rr: gd hdwy over 3f out: swtchd lft and rdn over 1f out: ev ch ins fnl f: hung lft and one pce towards fin* **11/1**

13-0 **4** 5 **Distinction (IRE)**[19] 4091 8-9-1 114 RyanMoore 6 — 107
(Sir Michael Stoute) *lw: trckd ldr: led 1/2-way: rdn along over 2f out: hdd over 1f out: sn drvn and one pce* **4/1**[2]

4106 **5** 3 **Sergeant Cecil**[24] 3942 8-9-6 115 LDettori 7 — 108
(B R Millman) *hld up and bhd: hdwy 4f out: sn rdn along and nvr rchd ldrs* **6/1**[3]

10-4 **6** nk **Percussionist (IRE)**[95] 1823 6-9-1 114 DarryllHolland 3 — 103
(J Howard Johnson) *led to 1/2-way: rdn along over 4f out: drvn wl over 2f out and sn btn* **12/1**

-021 **7** 3 ½ **Juniper Girl (IRE)**[52] 3090 4-8-12 97 LukeMorris 9 — 96
(M L W Bell) *in tch: effrt over 3f out: sn rdn along and wknd over 2f out* **14/1**

-110 **8** 2 **Souvenance**[56] 2976 4-8-12 98 SebSanders 1 — 93
(Sir Mark Prescott) *chsd ldrs: rdn along 3f out: drvn 2f out and sn wknd* **33/1**

1/11 **9** 47 **Mickmacmagoole (IRE)**[13] 4297 5-9-1 0 JamieSpencer 5 — 40
(Seamus G O'Donnell, Ire) *in tch: rdn along over 4f out: sn wknd* **66/1**

3m 38.82s (218.82) — **9** Ran SP% **114.6**
CSF £17.62 TOTE £2.10: £1.40, £2.30, £2.70; EX 19.80 Trifecta £92.90 Pool £3,639.57. - 27.80 winning units..
Owner D Smith, Mrs J Magnier, M Tabor **Bred** Barronstown Stud & Orpendale **Trained** Ballydoyle, Co Tipperary

FOCUS
A fascinating renewal with high-class middle-distance runner Septimus trying his hand in the staying division for the first time. It was not a proper test at the distance as a result of just a steady early gallop, and the form looks worth treating with caution.

NOTEBOOK

Septimus(IRE) ◆ has a similar profile to the yard's dual Gold Cup winner Yeats, in that he fell just short of the very top performers over middle-distances but is a resolute galloper, so it had always looked likely that he would stay this sort of trip. Off since his credible effort in the Coronation Cup, this looked the ideal race to start him off in, with the ground riding perfectly. Never far from the lead, he readily took it up from Distinction over a furlong out and was never doing any more than he had to once in front. This was a most satisfactory performance and, although he may not quite have the same turn of foot Yeats does, it looks as though his trainer has found a ready-made replacement. Races such as the Irish St Leger, Doncaster Cup and Melbourne Cup are now likely to come under consideration. (op 11-8 tchd 11-10 and 6-4)

Balkan Knight is a smart stayer when granted his favoured slow conditions and he came into this in fine form having finished fourth in the Goodwood Cup. In rear early, he travelled strongly into contention, but could not quite get to the winner having been switched and was always being held. This was a career-best from the seven-year-old and he too will have to be considered for races such as the Irish St Leger and Doncaster Cup. (tchd 14-1)

Anna Pavlova, a smart filly over shorter, had finished second over 1m6f in the Park Hill Stakes here last September, but that looked about as far as she wanted to go that day and there was a significant doubt as to whether she would stay this trip. In fine form earlier in the season, she was returning from a three-month break and travelled very strongly, but started to hang and looked to be running out of steam as they passed the line. She clearly stays this trip, but not as strongly as some and there will be easier opportunites for her in the autumn, given her love of soft ground. (op 10-1 tchd 16-1 in a place)

Distinction(IRE) has been one of the leading stayers for the past couple of seasons and he ran well for a long way on his belated reappearance before eventually finishing seventh in the Goodwood Cup. A horse with a fine record at this course, he looked one of the leading dangers to the favourite with a run under his belt and upped the pace when going on down the far side. However, it became clear from three furlongs out that he was a sitting duck and in the end he was left trailing by the front trio. It is possible he still needed this, but there is also the chance his best days are behind him now at the age of eight. (tchd 9-2)

Sergeant Cecil, heroic winner of this last year, has not been at his best of late, although in fairness he had no realistic chance in the King George last time. Back up in trip, he was always going to be vulnerable under his Group 1 penalty and could only make laboured late headway, having been well in rear early on. All the evidence suggests he is past his best now, but his next target is likely to be for a repeat bid in the Doncaster Cup - staged here last season. (op 11-2)

Percussionist(IRE) showed a spell over hurdles had not affected him when proving as good as ever in last season's Yorkshire Cup, and he was not beaten far in this year's renewal, this time after a chasing campaign. In front is where he likes to be, but Distinction took over at past halfway and he was under pressure fully half a mile from home. This effort was a good bit below his best. (op 11-1)

Juniper Girl(IRE), a remarkable winner of the Northumberland Plate on her most recent outing, faced a completely different test here against some good stayers and she was simply not good enough. Perhaps a drop back into good handicaps/Listed company is what is required.

Souvenance was out of her depth and fell away late on.

Mickmacmagoole(IRE), a fair handicapper, only stayed in touch as long as he did due to the steady pace and was then dropped like a stone once things heated up.

4692 LADBROKES GREAT VOLTIGEUR STKS (GROUP 2) (C&G) 1m 4f

2:35 (2:36) (Class 1) 3-Y-O

£76,653 (£29,052; £14,539; £7,249; £3,631; £1,822) **Stalls** Centre

Form				RPR
1424	**1**		**Lucarno (USA)**[40] 3461 3-8-12 113 ... JimmyFortune 7 (J H M Gosden) *lw: racd wd: a.p: hdwy on bit 3f out and sn cl up: led over 1f out: rdn ent fnl f and styd on strly* **7/2**[2]	120+
0341	**2**	*1*	**Yellowstone (IRE)**[21] 4044 3-8-12 0 ... JMurtagh 9 (A P O'Brien, Ire) *lw: hld up towards rr: smooth hdwy 3f out: effrt & nt clr run over 1f out: swtchd lft & rdn ent fnl f: drvn & no imp towards fin* **9/4**[1]	117+
33	**3**	*½*	**Macarthur**[100] 1693 3-8-12 0 ... RyanMoore 8 (A P O'Brien, Ire) *w'like: str: hld up in rr: hdwy on outer 3f out: rdn to chse ldrs and edgd rt over1f out: sn drvn and ch ins fnl f: kpt on same pce* **12/1**	114
20	**4**	*1 ¼*	**Acapulco (IRE)**[80] 2235 3-8-12 0 ... JAHeffernan 6 (A P O'Brien, Ire) *prom: rdn along wl over 2f out: drvn and one pce appr fnl f* **15/2**	112
01	**5**	*shd*	**Mahler**[60] 2816 3-8-12 0 ... MJKinane 3 (A P O'Brien, Ire) *mde most tl rdn along 2f out: hdd over 1f: drvn ent fnl f and wknd* **6/1**	112
1154	**6**	*1 ½*	**Spice Route**[40] 3458 3-8-12 108 ... EddieAhern 5 (M L W Bell) *hld up in rr: gd hdwy 3f out: rdn to chse ldrs over 1f out: wknd appr fnl f* **20/1**	110
0104	**7**	*8*	**Hearthstead Maison (IRE)**[10] 4387 3-8-12 110 ... GregFairley 4 (M Johnston) *in tch: hdwy to chse ldrs over 4f out: sn rdn along and grad wknd fnl 2f* **20/1**	97
2310	**8**	*18*	**Heron Bay**[21] 4044 3-8-12 98 ... SteveDrowne 1 (G Wragg) *prom on inner: effrt 4f out: sn rdn along and wknd fnl 2f* **18/1**	68
2114	**9**	*20*	**Boscobel**[51] 3142 3-9-1 115 ... LDettori 2 (M Johnston) *prom: rdn along 1/2-way: sn wknd and eased fnl 3f* **9/2**[3]	39

2m 33.07s (-1.53) **Going Correction** +0.225s/f (Good) 9 Ran SP% **119.7**
Speed ratings (Par 112): **114,113,113,112,112 111,105,93,80**
CSF £12.31 TOTE £4.90: £1.40, £1.50, £3.80; EX 15.10 Trifecta £153.80 Pool £5,522.40. - 25.48 winning units..

Owner George Strawbridge **Bred** Augustin Stable **Trained** Newmarket, Suffolk

FOCUS

A decent renewal featuring, among others, the Gordon Stakes winner, King Edward VII winner and Derby fourth. The front two both shaped as if they are a bit better than the bare form, which looks solid enough.

NOTEBOOK

Lucarno(USA) was a bit disappointing when beaten at the Newmarket July meeting, but that was his sixth start in 12 weeks, and he had been given a six-week break since then. Freshened up by the absence, he travelled strongly close to the pace and always looked the most likely winner. He did not pull clear as he had threatened to do, but won cosily enough, and the bookmaker reaction was to cut him to a best price 7-1 for the St Leger. There will be question marks about him getting that longer trip, but his rider was confident on that score and this is traditionally the best trial for the final Classic. (op 9-2)

Yellowstone(IRE), who has been kept very busy this term but takes his racing well, did not enjoy such a clear run as the winner, having to be switched to challenge a furlong out, but it is doubtful he would have beaten him even if he had seen daylight a bit earlier. It was a solid effort, but this was the third time this season that he has finished behind Lucarno, and a top price of 11-1 for the St Leger makes little appeal. (tchd 2-1 and 11-4 in a place)

Macarthur, who was up there in the betting for the Derby prior to disappointing in the Derrinstown Stud Derby Trial back in May, had been absent since and his weakness in the market suggested he would need this outing. In the circumstances he ran well, staying on steadily from off the pace. He shapes as though he will improve for another step up in distance, and any softening of the ground will also play to his strengths, so he might well develop into a leading candidate for the final Classic, especially if his stablemate Soldier Of Fortune misses the race. (op 10-1)

Acapulco(IRE), having his first outing since the Derby, had a lot to prove on form and got a little warm beforehand, but he was heavily backed from big prices in the morning. This slightly easier ground promised to suit him and, being lightly raced and having had a nice break since Epsom, he had the potential to show improvement. He ran well enough, but will need to progress again to be a serious player in the Leger. (op 12-1)

Mahler, having won the Queen's Vase over 2m last time, had plenty of use made of him back in distance. He was unable to shake off his speedier rivals, though, and came in last of the O'Brien quartet in the end. It is quite possible that he needed this run more than had been expected, having been off since Ascot, and while he has drifted to as big as 10-1 for the St Leger with Coral, he remains a 4-1 shot with Ladbrokes. (op 9-2 tchd 13-2 and 7-1)

Spice Route has struggled since moving into Pattern company, but he did not run at all badly here and it would not be a surprise to see him pick up a Listed race on his favoured easy ground.

Hearthstead Maison(IRE), who has run his best races on fast ground, is not up to this class. Official explanation: trainer said colt was unsuited by ground (good, good to soft in places)

Heron Bay, who finished last behind Yellowstone in the Gordon Stakes, is another who might need a fast surface to be seen at his best. (op 16-1)

Boscobel, who had a stiff task giving 3lb all round, ran too badly to be true and presumably something was amiss. Official explanation: trainer said colt was unsuited by ground (good, good to soft in places); jockey said colt lost its action. (op 6-1)

4693 JUDDMONTE INTERNATIONAL STKS (GROUP 1) 1m 2f 88y

3:10 (3:10) (Class 1) 3-Y-O+

£298,095 (£112,980; £56,542; £28,192; £14,122; £7,087) **Stalls** Low

Form				RPR
-112	**1**		**Authorized (IRE)**[45] 3331 3-8-11 126 ... LDettori 1 (P W Chapple-Hyam) *hld up towards rr: gd hdwy 3f out: cl up 2f out qcknd to ld over 1f out: rdn ins fnl f and styd on wl* **6/4**[1]	131+
1221	**2**	*1*	**Dylan Thomas (IRE)**[24] 3942 4-9-5 0 ... JMurtagh 7 (A P O'Brien, Ire) *lw: hld up in rr: hdwy 3f out: nt clr run wl over 1f out: swtchd lft and rdn to chse wnr ins fnl f: sn drvn and nt qckn* **2/1**[2]	128
4131	**3**	*3*	**Notnowcato**[45] 3331 5-9-5 123 ... RyanMoore 4 (Sir Michael Stoute) *trckd ldr: hdwy to ld wl over 2f out: rdn wl over 1f out: hdd appr fnl f and kpt on same pce* **7/2**[3]	122
-442	**4**	*nk*	**Duke Of Marmalade (IRE)**[63] 2734 3-8-11 0 ... MJKinane 2 (A P O'Brien, Ire) *lw: trckd ldrs: hdwy over 3f out and sn cl up: rdn: n.m.r and outpcd 2f out: kpt on u.p ins fnl f* **12/1**	121+
1114	**5**	*3*	**Asiatic Boy (ARG)**[20] 4058 4-9-4 0 ... JamieSpencer 6 (M F De Kock, South Africa) *trckd ldrs: effrt over 2f out: sn rdn and kpt on same pce fr over 1f out* **12/1**	115
4524	**6**	*1 ½*	**Hattan (IRE)**[23] 4013 5-9-5 110 ... SebSanders 5 (C E Brittain) *hld up in rr: hdwy 3f out: rdn to chse ldrs 2f out: sn drvn and btn* **100/1**	113
	7	*1 ¾*	**Song Of Hiawatha**[59] 2899 3-8-11 0 ... JAHeffernan 3 (A P O'Brien, Ire) *w'like: led: rdn along 4f out: hdd wl over 2f out and grad wknd* **200/1**	110

2m 11.82s (-0.68) **Going Correction** +0.225s/f (Good)
WFA 3 from 4yo+ 8lb 7 Ran SP% **112.4**
Speed ratings (Par 117): **111,110,107,107,105 103,102**
CSF £4.56 TOTE £2.50: £1.60, £1.60; EX 6.10.

Owner Saleh Al Homeizi & Imad Al Sagar **Bred** Marengo Investments And Knighton House Ltd And M **Trained** Newmarket, Suffolk

■ Authorized is the first Derby winner since High Chaparral to win another race after Epsom.

FOCUS

A top-notch renewal of the International Stakes. Authorized confirmed his position as the season's leading three-year-old and is entitled to rate alongside Manduro among the top turf horses. Dylan Thomas ran to his 1m2f form, but Notnowcato was a bit below his best. Song Of Hiawatha set a reasonable pace and stayed in the centre of the track in the home straight, with the other six tacking over to the stands' side.

NOTEBOOK

Authorized(IRE), whose reputation took a slight knock with his defeat by Notnowcato in a tactical Eclipse, returned to his best with a fine performance. Having got slightly warm in the pre-parade ring, he raced a little keenly off the pace, but improved on the outer of the bunch in the home straight before quickening to the front with over a furlong to go. Staying on strongly for pressure, he was always holding Dylan Thomas on whom he slightly took first run. Set to go for the Arc now, where he will clash with Manduro and perhaps Peeping Fawn, he will be suited by the return to 1m4f at Longchamp. (op 15-8, tchd 2-1)

Dylan Thomas(IRE), back down in trip after his comfortable win in the King George, ran a fine race but just found the Derby winner too good. Held up, he was hemmed in near the rail in the home straight with Authorized on his outer, and when that rival quickened to the front he took a stride or two to get out after him. He stayed on well inside the last, but was always being held. The ground was slower than he would have preferred and he loses nothing in defeat. (tchd 15-8 and 9-4)

Notnowcato, who short-headed his stablemate Maraahel in last year's renewal, could not repeat his Sandown superiority over Authorized but ran another sound race, if a little below his best. After tracking the pacesetter, he showed in front not long after the three pole but could not resist the challenges going to the last. (op 11-4)

Duke Of Marmalade(IRE), in the frame in the English and Irish Guineas and the St James's Palace Stakes, ran well on this first try over this trip and against older opposition. He lost a prominent pitch when slightly short of room with two furlongs to run, dropping to the back of the field, but was staying on well again inside the last and nearly got up for third. There is more to come from him at around this trip. (tchd 14-1)

Asiatic Boy(ARG) was partnered by Spencer for the first time, his regular rider Marwing having returned to South Africa. He travelled well in mid-division, but could only keep on at the same pace when the race began in earnest. This trip seemed to stretch his stamina a little, and he does not seem quite as effective on turf as he is on dirt. (tchd 14-1)

Hattan(IRE) ran his race with no excuses, but has now been found wanting no fewer than 18 times in Group company since taking the Chester Vase in May 2005.

Song Of Hiawatha, runner-up in the Ulster Derby, a handicap, at Down Royal last time, performed pacemaking duties. Racing alone in the centre of the track in the home straight, he did edge over towards the stands' rail under pressure and was still right there with around a quarter of a mile to run before being eased. He was not beaten that far and is obviously a smart performer. (op 150-1)

4694 TATTERSALLS MILLIONS ACOMB STKS (GROUP 3) 7f

3:50 (3:51) (Class 1) 2-Y-O **£23,708** (£8,964; £4,480; £2,240) **Stalls** Low

Form				RPR
1	**1**		**Fast Company (IRE)**[38] 3552 2-9-0 0 ... RyanMoore 9 (B J Meehan) *athletic: lw: hld up: gd hdwy over 2f out: qcknd to ld wl over 1f out: sn clr* **11/4**[2]	107+
	2	*3 ½*	**Lucifer Sam (USA)**[22] 4032 2-9-0 0 ... JMurtagh 4 (A P O'Brien, Ire) *w'like: athletic: trckd ldrs: hdwy over 2f out: sn rdn and kpt on u.p fnl f* **2/1**[1]	97
21	**3**	*hd*	**Without A Prayer (IRE)**[27] 3849 2-9-0 88 ... SebSanders 8 (R M Beckett) *hld up in rr: hdwy over 2f out: swtchd rt and rdn wl over 1f out: kpt on ins fnl f* **14/1**	96
1	**4**	*2*	**Campanologist (USA)**[19] 4110 2-9-0 0 ... GregFairley 2 (M Johnston) *w'like: scope: lw: t.k.h: trckd ldrs: hdwy on outer 3f out: led briefly 2f out: sn rdn and wknd over 1f out* **6/1**	91

621 **5** ¾ **Calmdownmate (IRE)**[15] 4225 2-9-0 91 PatCosgrave 7 89
(K R Burke) *trckd ldrs: hdwy over 2f out: sn rdn and ch tl drvn and wknd over 1f out* **25/1**

1 **6** 1 ¾ **Legislation**[31] 3747 2-9-0 0 JimmyFortune 3 85
(J H M Gosden) *lw: t.k.h: led: hdd over 3f out: ch and rdn whn n.m.r 2f out: sn wknd* **4/1**[3]

32 **7** ½ **Mut'Ab (USA)**[19] 4110 2-9-0 0 KerrinMcEvoy 6 84
(C E Brittain) *lw: cl up: led over 3f out: rdn and hdd 2f out: sn wknd* **10/1**

1m 26.66s (1.26) **Going Correction** +0.225s/f (Good) **7** Ran SP% **113.9**
Speed ratings (Par 104): **101,97,96,94,93 91,91**
CSF £8.61 TOTE £3.90: £2.40, £1.80; EX 11.30 Trifecta £65.90 Pool £1,126.36. - 12.12 winning units..
Owner Earle I Mack **Bred** Limetree Stud Ltd And Aerial Bloodstock **Trained** Manton, Wilts

FOCUS
A race with a mixed history, some of the better winners including Classic heroes King's Best and Rule Of Law, but the way in which Fast Company quickened up suggests he could go on to taste success at the highest level. The fifth helps set a reasonable standard for the form.

NOTEBOOK
Fast Company(IRE) ◆, an impressive winner on his debut at Salisbury (both placed horses won next time), had softer ground to contend with and was deposed as market leader by the strongly-supported Lucifer Sam. However, this multiple Group-entrant came there travelling best of all racing into the final quarter mile and the change of pace he showed to scoot clear was most impressive. There have been equally impressive winners of this in the past who have not gone on, but this fine-looking son of Danehill Dancer is clearly held in the highest of regard and he is entitled to go close in whatever his next chosen target may be, with something like the Champagne Stakes at Doncaster next month appealing as the ideal target. (op 2-1, tchd 3-1)
Lucifer Sam(USA) has got better with each run on softer going in Ireland and he could have done with the ease in the ground here, but he was strongly supported nonetheless. Soon well positioned, he found himself outpaced at a critical stage of the race and the winner had flown by the time he hit top gear. Evidently in need of 1m, he is clearly a smart juvenile without being one of the Ballydoyle stars. (op 3-1, tchd 100-30)
Without A Prayer(IRE) stepped up enormously on his easy Lingfield maiden win, coming through with Lucifer Sam and just missing out on second. The winner was in a different league, but he is clearly very useful and will find easier opportunities, with the step up to 1m likely to help coax further improvement. (op 10-1)
Campanologist(USA), a narrow winner at Sandown on his debut, comes from a stable that has a fine record in this race and he looked a big danger when looming up towards the outside over two furlongs out, but was blown away by the Fast Company and in the end dropped away quite disappointingly. He may need his sights lowering a little. (tchd 5-1)
Calmdownmate(IRE), up in trip and grade following his win in a 6f novice stakes at Ripon, briefly threatened to make a bid for the placings, but he was beaten fully a furlong out and is clearly not up to this level. (op 20-1)
Legislation did it well on his recent Newmarket debut, but the combination of a rise in both trip and grade proved too much for the son of Oasis Dream and he was already beaten when tightened for room two furlongs out. (tchd 9-2)
Mut'Ab(USA), narrowly edged out by Campanologist at Sandown and the only non-winner in the race, showed up well to a point, but he was found wanting in the class department when it came down to it. (op 20-1, tchd 25-1)

4695 IRWIN MITCHELL SOLICITORS STKS (NURSERY) 6f
4:25 (4:27) (Class 2) 2-Y-O £16,192 (£4,817; £2,407; £1,202) **Stalls** High

Form RPR

4006 **1** **Cristal Clear (IRE)**[10] 4406 2-8-13 80 DavidAllan 10 90+
(T D Easterby) *bhd: hdwy 2f out: swtchd lft and rdn over 1f out: styd on u.p: led towards fin* **33/1**

31 **2** *nk* **Oasis Wind**[20] 4070 2-8-12 84 TolleyDean(5) 6 95+
(P F I Cole) *lw: prom centre: overall ldr wl over 1f out: rdn ins fnl f: hdd and nt qckn towards fin* **4/1**[1]

41 **3** ¾ **Hitchens (IRE)**[12] 4323 2-9-1 82 JamieSpencer 14 91+
(G L Moore) *lw: hld up in rr: swtchd to stands' rail and hdwy whn nt clr run 2f out and again over 1f out: swtchd lft ent fnl f and styd on: nrst fin* **9/1**

5221 **4** *shd* **Guertino (IRE)**[64] 2710 2-9-6 87 PaulEddery 3 94
(B Smart) *hmpd s and bhd: gd hdwy centre over 2f out: rdn to chse ldrs over 1f out: kpt on ins fnl f* **20/1**

2103 **5** 1 **Dubai Dynamo**[6] 4501 2-8-8 75 JohnEgan 17 79
(J S Moore) *in tch stands' rail: rdn along and swtchd lft wl over 1f out: kpt on ins fnl f* **11/1**

2311 **6** 1 ¼ **Fol Hollow (IRE)**[17] 4152 2-9-7 88 AdrianTNicholls 11 88
(D Nicholls) *sn led and swtchd to stands' rail: rdn over 2f out: hdd wl over 1f out: wandered and wknd ins fnl f* **12/1**

3623 **7** ¾ **Kersaint (IRE)**[39] 3492 2-9-5 86 NCallan 19 84
(K A Ryan) *chsd ldr stands' rail: rdn along 2f out: drvn and one pce ent fnl f* **16/1**

1352 **8** 1 **Rubirosa (IRE)**[17] 4168 2-9-4 85 PhillipMakin 20 80
(M Dods) *in tch stands' rail: swtchd lft and hdwy 2f out: sn rdn and kpt on same pce ins fnl f* **33/1**

614 **9** 2 **Flawed Genius**[17] 4152 2-9-7 88 (t) RyanMoore 4 77
(Sir Michael Stoute) *lw: hmpd s and towards rr: stdy hdwy over 2f out: rdn wl over 1f out: no imp* **15/2**

4331 **10** *hd* **In Honour (IRE)**[17] 4181 2-9-2 83 RichardMullen 1 71
(E S McMahon) *prom centre: rdn along 2f out: sn drvn and kpt on same pce* **10/1**

31 **11** 1 ¼ **Legal Eagle (IRE)**[47] 3233 2-9-7 88 JimmyFortune 5 72
(J H M Gosden) *prom centre: rdn along over 2f out: grad wknd* **7/1**[3]

3126 **12** ½ **Shifting Star (IRE)**[18] 4121 2-9-1 82 KerrinMcEvoy 8 65
(W R Swinburn) *lw: prom: rdn along 2f out and grad wknd* **5/1**[2]

2641 **13** *hd* **Legendary Guest**[20] 4076 2-8-13 80 DarryllHolland 7 62
(M R Channon) *in midfield: hdwy over 2f out: rdn to chse ldrs wl over 1f out: sn btn* **20/1**

416 **14** 1 **Dark Tara**[17] 4152 2-8-10 77 PaulHanagan 9 56
(R A Fahey) *lw: a in rr* **14/1**

2310 **15** ½ **Silver Wind**[18] 4121 2-9-1 82 (v) StephenDonohoe 12 60
(P D Evans) *towards rr fr 1/2-way* **66/1**

4304 **16** 4 **Bahama Baileys**[10] 4406 2-8-10 77 (b[1]) GregFairley 18 43
(M Johnston) *chsd ldr stands' rail: rdn along wl over 2f out and sn wknd* **33/1**

413 **17** 1 ½ **Bosun Breese**[17] 4168 2-8-12 79 TedDurcan 15 40
(P W D'Arcy) *in tch: rdn along 1/2-way: sn wknd* **40/1**

1m 13.65s (1.09) **Going Correction** +0.225s/f (Good) **17** Ran SP% **130.9**
Speed ratings (Par 100): **101,100,99,99,98 96,95,94,91,91 89,88,88,87,86 81,79**
CSF £163.07 CT £1402.72 TOTE £49.20: £6.60, £1.80, £2.50, £4.50; EX 268.60 TRIFECTA Not won..
Owner Mrs Jennifer E Pallister **Bred** Castlefarm Stud **Trained** Great Habton, N Yorks

FOCUS
Cracking nursery form and a race sure to produce winners. Cristal Clear was back to her best and both the second and the unlucky-in-running third can be rated higher than the bare form.

NOTEBOOK
Cristal Clear(IRE), eased 2lb since her nursery debut, returned to her best form. Held up at the back of the field, and taken over to race on the stands' side, she was in last place at halfway and still had a good deal on approaching the final furlong but, weaving through under a fine ride, she produced a strong run to catch the favourite close home. She is not the most consistent but this type of event suits her more than small-field conditions races.
Oasis Wind ◆, comfortable winner of a Leicester maiden on easy ground, was well supported for this nursery debut. Showing bright pace down the centre of the track, he established a clear advantage going into the final furlong only to be collared near the line as Cristal Clear finished fast. The moral winner in many ways, he should be able to atone for this and is a smart prospect with pretensions to winning in Listed company. (op 7-2)
Hitchens(IRE) ◆, making his nursery debut after a maiden success at Folkestone, was probably an unlucky loser. Held up in rear, he travelled well but Spencer had to sit and suffer from the two pole as he found his path repeatedly blocked. Eventually in the clear entering the final furlong, he ran on strongly but the damage had been done. Although he might well have won with a clear passage, it should be pointed out that the winner actually started her run from behind him. (op 12-1)
Guertino(IRE), returning to action after nine weeks off, ran a solid race after receiving a bump at the start and was only run out of second place inside the last. (op 16-1)
Dubai Dynamo, whose yard won this race with Dubai Builder a year ago, ran a decent race on this drop back in trip but might not mind a return to 7f. Official explanation: jockey said colt hung left-handed. (op 14-1)
Fol Hollow(IRE), who went up 6lb for his win at Glorious Goodwood despite only scoring by a head, ran well from the front and only faded out of the frame inside the final furlong. (tchd 14-1)
Kersaint(IRE) ran respectably back over 6f and on a sound surface after a couple of runs over the minimum trip in soft ground at Chester. (op 20-1)
Legal Eagle(IRE) Official explanation: jockey said colt ran too freely.
Shifting Star(IRE), back down in trip, had also been found wanting off this mark at Goodwood. (op 17-2 tchd 9-1)
Bosun Breese Official explanation: jockey said colt was upset in stalls.

4696 PATRINGTON HAVEN LEISURE PARK STKS (H'CAP) 5f
5:00 (5:01) (Class 2) (0-100,100) 4-Y-O+£16,192 (£4,817; £2,407; £1,202) **Stalls** High

Form RPR

4600 **1** **River Falcon**[10] 4386 7-8-13 92 DanielTudhope 2 104
(J S Goldie) *hmpd s and bhd: gd hdwy on wd outside wl over 1f out: sn rdn and str run ins fnl f to ld last 75yds* **11/1**

3220 **2** 1 **Hoh Hoh Hoh**[10] 4386 5-8-9 88 SebSanders 10 96+
(R J Price) *lw: dwlt and bhd: smooth hdwy 1/2-way: trckd ldrs and nt clr run over 1f out and ent fnl f: sn rdn and styd on wl towards fin* **6/1**[1]

460 **3** ¾ **Buachaill Dona (IRE)**[23] 3990 4-9-1 94 AdrianTNicholls 13 99
(D Nicholls) *lw: trckd ldrs: swtchd rt to stands' rails over 1f out: rdn and qcknd to ld ins fnl f: hdd and no ex last 75yds* **7/1**[3]

4-00 **4** ½ **Northern Empire (IRE)**[96] 1788 4-8-11 90 NCallan 8 94+
(K A Ryan) *lw: chsd ldrs centre: hdwy 2f out: sn rdn and kpt on u.p ins fnl f* **20/1**

4000 **5** 1 ½ **Fire Up The Band**[18] 4122 8-8-3 89 OliveGaule(7) 9 87
(D Nicholls) *trckd ldrs centre: gd hdwy to ld over 1f out: sn rdn: edgd rt and hdd ins fnl f: one pce* **33/1**

-301 **6** *nk* **Judd Street**[10] 4386 5-9-7 100 StephenCarson 6 97
(Eve Johnson Houghton) *lw: trckd ldrs: effrt 2f out and ch tl rdn and nt qckn ent fnl f* **9/1**

4502 **7** *shd* **Cape Royal**[10] 4386 7-8-8 92 (bt) KevinGhunowa(5) 17 89
(J M Bradley) *cl up stands' rail: led after 2f: rdn along wl over 1f out: sn hdd and kpt on same pce ins fnl f* **14/1**

005 **8** *hd* **Talbot Avenue**[16] 4204 9-8-3 82 RoystonFfrench 4 78
(M Blanshard) *chsd ldrs centre: effrt 2f out: sn rdn and one pce ent fnl f* **20/1**

1402 **9** *nk* **Efistorm**[6] 4489 6-8-1 83 LiamJones(3) 15 78
(C R Dore) *in tch: effrt 2f out: sn rdn and kpt on same pce appr fnl f* **15/2**

0300 **10** ½ **Corridor Creeper (FR)**[4] 4567 10-9-0 93 (p) RyanMoore 16 86
(J M Bradley) *chsd ldrs stands' side: rdn along 2f out: drvn and one pce appr fnl f* **20/1**

0103 **11** *nk* **Green Park (IRE)**[24] 3975 4-9-2 95 PaulHanagan 3 87
(R A Fahey) *wnt lft s: hdwy 2f out: sn rdn and no imp* **8/1**

0020 **12** ½ **Inter Vision (USA)**[4] 4581 7-8-3 82 DaleGibson 12 72
(A Dickman) *in tch: rdn along 2f out: grad wknd* **33/1**

5001 **13** *hd* **Continent**[19] 4095 10-8-10 89 SilvestreDeSousa 18 78
(D Nicholls) *a in midfield* **20/1**

204 **14** 2 ½ **Tabaret**[10] 4386 4-9-2 95 JimmyFortune 14 75
(R M Whitaker) *cl up stands' rail: rdn along 2f out: grad wknd* **13/2**[2]

-000 **15** ½ **Guto**[80] 2237 4-8-8 87 PatCosgrave 5 66
(K A Ryan) *prom centre: rdn along 2f out: grad wknd* **40/1**

0056 **16** *shd* **Merlin's Dancer**[10] 4386 7-8-10 89 JohnEgan 20 67
(S Dow) *overall ldr stands' rail for 2f: prom tl rdn 2f out and sn wknd* **25/1**

1200 **17** *hd* **Gallery Girl (IRE)**[4] 4567 4-8-7 86 DavidAllan 19 64
(T D Easterby) *chsd ldrs stands' rail: rdn along 2f out and sn wknd* **16/1**

-000 **18** *nk* **Overstayed (IRE)**[53] 3050 4-8-7 86 ow2 TomEaves 1 63
(I Semple) *wnt rt s: in tch on wd outside: pushed along 1/2-way: sn rdn and wknd* **66/1**

59.35 secs (0.03) **Going Correction** +0.225s/f (Good) **18** Ran SP% **126.6**
Speed ratings (Par 109): **108,106,105,104,102 101,101,101,100,99 99,98,98,94,93 93,92,92**
CSF £67.50 CT £528.91 TOTE £16.20: £3.00, £1.60, £2.30, £5.30; EX 98.00 Trifecta £2497.20 Pool £3,868.98. - 1.10 winning units. Place 6 £26.08, Place 5 £7.05..
Owner F Brady, E Bruce & S Bruce **Bred** Manor Farm Packers Ltd **Trained** Uplawmoor, E Renfrews

FOCUS
A strongly-run handicap that played into the hands of those held up off the pace. The winner and third set the level and the three just outside the frame raced up with the pace early and deserve extra credit.

NOTEBOOK
River Falcon has always run well over the minimum trip at this track - his record now reads 7111 - but a losing run stretching back to May 2005 was enough to put most people off backing him here. The race was very much run to suit him, though, and he came through from off the pace to lead well inside the last. He will remain feasibly weighted after reassessment, but whether things will drop as kindly next time is open to question. (op 14-1 tchd 10-1)
Hoh Hoh Hoh left behind a modest effort at Haydock last time and bounced back to his best despite not enjoying the clearest of runs. He was another very much suited by the strong gallop and, as he remains progressive, there could yet be a big handicap in him. (op 7-1 tchd 11-2 and 13-2)
Buachaill Dona(IRE) has not lived up to the promise he showed last term but he was back at the scene of his biggest win at three and this was far more encouraging. Switched to join those racing on the stands' side, he weaved his way through from the back of the field to come with what looked like a winning run, only to find the pair who finished more towards the centre getting the better of him close home. (op 6-1)
Northern Empire(IRE) ◆, running for the first time since May and debuting for his new trainer Kevin Ryan, ran a lot better than he has for some time. With this run under his belt he looks one to keep in mind for a similar event, as he is very well handicapped on his best form. (op 18-1)

Fire Up The Band did best of those who raced up with the strong gallop. While pace horses are generally favoured at this track, the leaders went a bit too quick on this occasion and it is to his credit that he kept on to hold fifth place. He was rated 105 following his win in a conditions race back in April so is another on a good mark if able to build on this effort.
Judd Street had easier ground to deal with compared with Haydock and not such an obvious draw bias in his favour, but he still ran well off a 6lb higher mark. (op 8-1)
Cape Royal, who finished second to Judd Street at Haydock, again followed him home here having shown lots of pace throughout. He is running consistently at present. (op 12-1)
Talbot Avenue remains a difficult horse to win with.
Efistorm usually contests lower grade races than this so it was a bit surprising to see him quite well backed. (op 10-1 and 11-1)
Green Park(IRE), who is now on a mark 7lb higher than when successful at Newcastle in June, needs softer ground than he had here to be seen at his best. (op 10-1 tchd 11-1)
Tabaret never seems to run two races alike. (op 7-1)
Overstayed(IRE) Official explanation: jockey said gelding hung right-handed.
T/Jkpt: £26,408.80 to a £1 stake. Pool: £37,195.50. 1.00 winning ticket. T/Plt: £32.70 to a £1 stake. Pool: £230,252.75. 5,134.60 winning tickets. T/Qpdt: £6.50 to a £1 stake. Pool: £10,279.60. 1,160.60 winning tickets. JR

4697 - 4700a (Foreign Racing) - See Raceform Interactive

[4219] CARLISLE (R-H)
Wednesday, August 22

OFFICIAL GOING: Good (8.6)
Wind: Breezy, half against Weather: Fine

4701 CBS OUTDOOR H'CAP — 6f 192y
2:15 (2:16) (Class 6) (0-65,63) 3-Y-O+ — **£1,943** (£578; £288; £144) Stalls High

Form — RPR
6350 **1** **Pitbull**[5] 4562 4-8-12 **52** ... (p) LiamJones(3) 9 — 61
(Mrs G S Rees) *hld up: hdwy 2f out: led wl ins fnl f: kpt on wl* — 4/1[1]
6304 **2** *nk* **General Feeling (IRE)**[15] 4250 6-8-10 **50** ... (t) MichaelJStainton(3) 11 — 58
(S T Mason) *hld up ins: hdwy to ld 2f out: sn rdn and edgd rt: hdd wl ins fnl f: kpt on* — 10/1
6303 **3** *3* **Wolfman**[10] 4427 5-8-10 **47** ... RoystonFfrench 10 — 47
(D W Barker) *led to 2f out: sn drvn along: kpt on same pce fnl f* — 9/2[2]
3040 **4** *nk* **Megalo Maniac**[38] 3572 4-9-6 **57** ... TonyHamilton 2 — 56
(R A Fahey) *prom: effrt and ev ch 2f out: one pce fnl f* — 10/1
0134 **5** *hd* **Top Dirham**[32] 3754 9-9-4 **55** ... DaleGibson 13 — 54
(M W Easterby) *t.k.h: prom: effrt over 2f out: one pce over 1f out* — 6/1[3]
5000 **6** *hd* **Snow Bunting**[19] 4137 9-8-10 **50** ... AndrewElliott(3) 4 — 48+
(Jedd O'Keeffe) *hld up: hdwy towards stands' side over 1f out: no imp fnl f* — 12/1
0330 **7** *1* **Grand Diamond (IRE)**[29] 3816 3-8-11 **60** ... (p) GaryBartley(7) 8 — 55
(J S Goldie) *in tch: effrt and ev ch 2f out: sn rdn and one pce* — 12/1
2520 **8** *1/2* **Linden's Lady**[8] 4469 7-8-9 **46** ... (v) StephenDonohoe 7 — 40
(J R Weymes) *midfield: drvn and edgd rt 2f out: sn outpcd* — 16/1
0000 **9** *hd* **Musicmaestroplease (IRE)**[10] 4427 4-9-4 **58** ... DominicFox(3) 3 — 51
(S Parr) *racd wd in midfield: effrt and ev ch 2f out: sn no ex* — 50/1
0016 **10** *3/4* **Tommy Tobougg**[21] 4080 3-9-1 **62** ... NeilBrown(5) 15 — 53
(I Semple) *t.k.h: chsd ldrs tl wknd 2f out* — 8/1
-610 **11** *2 1/2* **Zap Attack**[10] 4423 7-8-8 **52** ... AndrewHeffernan(7) 12 — 37
(M Brittain) *plld hrd in midfield: wknd 2f out: eased whn btn ins fnl f* — 40/1
-000 **12** *nk* **Bordello**[19] 4129 4-9-9 **63** ... AndrewMullen(3) 6 — 47
(K A Ryan) *cl up tl rdn and wknd fr 2f out* — 40/1
0005 **13** *1* **Gifted Flame**[16] 4219 8-9-7 **58** ... PhillipMakin 1 — 39
(T D Barron) *dwlt: effrt fr rr over 2f out: n.d* — 9/1
0-20 **14** *3 1/2* **Cadwell**[144] 849 3-8-13 **55** ... (bt[1]) SaleemGolam 14 — 27
(D J Murphy) *plld hrd: chsd ldrs tl wknd over 2f out* — 16/1
4000 **15** *1 1/2* **Desert Hunter (IRE)**[5] 4562 4-8-12 **49** ... RichardMullen 5 — 17
(Micky Hammond) *stdd s: t.k.h in rr: rdn over 2f out: sn btn* — 33/1

1m 27.63s (0.53) **Going Correction** +0.125s/f (Good)
WFA 3 from 4yo+ 5lb — 15 Ran SP% **128.7**
Speed ratings (Par 101): **101,100,97,96,96 96,95,94,94,93 90,90,89,85,83**
CSF £46.38 CT £197.57 TOTE £4.30: £2.00, £3.10, £2.10; EX 49.30.
Owner Mrs G S Rees **Bred** J Gittins And Capt J H Wilson **Trained** Sollom, Lancs

FOCUS
A modest handicap in which the pace was sound throughout. The field fanned across the course in the straight. Sound form among the principals.
Gifted Flame Official explanation: jockey said gelding missed the break
Desert Hunter(IRE) Official explanation: jockey said gelding finished distressed

4702 FELIXTHEFASTTRACTOR.CO.UK EUROPEAN BREEDERS' FUND MEDIAN AUCTION MAIDEN STKS — 5f
2:50 (2:52) (Class 6) 2-Y-O — **£2,730** (£806; £403) Stalls High

Form — RPR
4425 **1** **Whispering Desert**[20] 4097 2-8-12 58 ... FrankieMcDonald 7 — 63
(P T Midgley) *prom: effrt 2f out: kpt on wl fnl f: led cl home* — 20/1
422 **2** *shd* **Know No Fear**[23] 4020 2-9-3 73 ... TonyHamilton 9 — 68
(J J Quinn) *led: rdn 2f out: kpt on fnl f: hdd cl home* — 5/2[2]
363 **3** *hd* **Paddy Jack**[14] 4285 2-9-3 72 ... PhillipMakin 5 — 67
(J R Weymes) *w ldr: drvn 1/2-way: kpt on u.p fnl f: jst hld* — 3/1[3]
4 *1* **C'Mon You Irons (IRE)** 2-9-3 0 ... RoystonFfrench 2 — 64
(B Smart) *bhd and sn pushed along: hdwy 1/2-way: edgd rt over 1f out: kpt on fnl f: nrst fin* — 7/1
5 *2* **Blitzen (IRE)** 2-9-3 0 ... RichardMullen 1 — 56
(E S McMahon) *s.i.s: rn green in rr: hdwy appr fnl f: nrst fin* — 6/4[1]
3430 **6** *3/4* **Rocheport**[28] 3834 2-9-3 65 ... PaddyAspell 10 — 54
(J Howard Johnson) *prom tl rdn and outpcd fr 2f out* — 14/1
30 **7** *3 1/2* **Emef Princess**[13] 4310 2-8-9 0 ... AndrewMullen(3) 3 — 36
(K A Ryan) *chsd ldrs tl wknd fr 2f out* — 40/1

61.73 secs (0.23) **Going Correction** -0.125s/f (Firm) — 7 Ran SP% **119.9**
Speed ratings (Par 92): **93,92,92,90,87 86,80**
CSF £74.14 TOTE £40.10: £8.20, £1.30; EX 113.40.
Owner J F Wright **Bred** Juddmonte Farms Ltd **Trained** Westow, N Yorks

FOCUS
An ordinary event in which the pace was sound and the action unfolded against the inside rail. Slight improvement from the winner.

NOTEBOOK
Whispering Desert, who looked to find the ground too quick on her previous start, looked exposed as ordinary but she turned in an improved effort to get off the mark at the fifth attempt. She left the impression that the step up to 6f would suit but she is going to find life tougher in nursery company after reassessment. (op 14-1)
Know No Fear jumped off on terms this time and ran as well as he ever has done. He has had a few chances now but, although he had the run of the race against the inside rail this time, he looks capable of picking up a similarly ordinary event. (op 3-1)
Paddy Jack, like the runner-up, had shown a fair level of form in three starts and he seemed to give it his best shot dropped to the minimum trip for the first time. He looks a good guide to the worth of this form, and should continue to give a good account at an ordinary level. (op 5-2 tchd 7-2)
C'Mon You Irons(IRE), a 21,000euro first foal of a half-sister to a couple of winners up to 1m, was relatively easy to back on this racecourse debut but showed ability. He will be suited by the step up to 6f and is open to improvement. (op 6-1 tchd 9-1)
Blitzen(IRE), a 15,000euro half-brother to a fair Irish juvenile 7f winner, looked fit enough on this racecourse debut but he was far too green to do himself justice. He will be suited by a stiffer test of stamina and is likely to fare better in due course. (op 2-1 tchd 11-8 and 9-4 in places)
Rocheport, well beaten on his first run on easy ground at Catterick on his previous start, fared better back on this sound surface but left the impression that the step into modest nursery company and a much stiffer test of stamina would be more to his liking.

4703 WEATHERBYS BANK H'CAP — 5f
3:25 (3:25) (Class 4) (0-80,80) 3-Y-O+ — **£5,181** (£1,541; £770; £384) Stalls High

Form — RPR
0143 **1** **Glasshoughton**[25] 3954 4-9-7 **78** ... PhillipMakin 3 — 89
(M Dods) *mde all: rdn and kpt on strly fnl f* — 7/1[2]
2-02 **2** *1 1/2* **Sir Nod**[19] 4140 5-9-9 **80** ... PaddyAspell 12 — 86
(Miss J A Camacho) *w wnr: ev ch tl no ex ins fnl f* — 12/1
6000 **3** *nk* **Colorus (IRE)**[14] 4289 4-8-11 **68** ... DaleGibson 6 — 73
(M W Easterby) *in tch: effrt and hdwy over 1f out: kpt on fnl f* — 33/1
2110 **4** *nk* **Divine Spirit**[7] 4489 6-9-3 **74** ... RoystonFfrench 11 — 78
(M Dods) *prom: drvn 1/2-way: kpt on u.p fnl f* — 10/1
1423 **5** *3/4* **Trojan Flight**[19] 4133 6-9-2 **80** ... JamesRogers(7) 10 — 84+
(R A Fahey) *dwlt: bhd tl hdwy over 1f out: kpt on fnl f: nrst fin* — 7/1[2]
0006 **6** *hd* **Royal Challenge**[7] 4507 6-9-6 **77** ... SaleemGolam 1 — 77
(M H Tompkins) *chsd ldrs: rdn and hung rt 2f out: one pce fnl f* — 8/1[3]
3245 **7** *nk* **Ptarmigan Ridge**[7] 4498 11-8-8 **70** ... KellyHarrison(5) 2 — 69
(Miss L A Perratt) *in tch on outside: effrt 2f out: no ex fnl f* — 20/1
0256 **8** *nk* **Kings College Boy**[14] 4289 7-8-6 **63** ... (b) TonyHamilton 5 — 61
(R A Fahey) *bhd tl sme late hdwy: nrst fin* — 12/1
2652 **9** *1/2* **Darcy's Pride (IRE)**[18] 4158 3-8-12 **74** ... AndrewMullen(3) 7 — 70
(D W Barker) *chsd ldrs tl rdn and no ex over 1f out* — 25/1
412 **10** *1/2* **Katie Boo (IRE)**[7] 4498 5-8-11 **68** ... StephenDonohoe 8 — 65+
(A Berry) *in tch tl edgd rt and outpcd fr 2f out* — 2/1[1]
00-0 **11** *1/2* **Kerry's Dream**[27] 3885 3-9-4 **77** ... RichardMullen 4 — 70
(T D Easterby) *bhd: drvn 1/2-way: nvr rchd ldrs* — 66/1
1461 **12** *hd* **Compton Classic**[11] 4381 5-8-13 **77** ... GaryBartley(7) 9 — 69
(J S Goldie) *midfield: rdn and edgd rt 2f out: n.d* — 8/1[3]
-303 **13** *1 1/4* **Bahamian Duke**[8] 4486 4-8-3 **63** ... AndrewElliott(3) 14 — 51
(K R Burke) *bhd and sn drvn along: nvr on terms* — 12/1
001 **14** *1 1/4* **Strensall**[20] 4101 10-8-8 **70** ... NeilBrown(5) 13 — 53
(R E Barr) *hld up ins: rdn 1/2-way: nvr on terms* — 16/1
0206 **15** *1 1/2* **Rainbow Bay**[15] 4251 4-8-12 **72** ... MichaelJStainton(3) 15 — 50
(P D Evans) *bhd: wknd fr 2f out* — 20/1

60.24 secs (-1.26) **Going Correction** -0.125s/f (Firm)
WFA 3 from 4yo+ 2lb — 15 Ran SP% **136.4**
Speed ratings (Par 105): **105,102,102,101,100 100,99,99,98,97 96,96,94,92,90**
CSF £94.34 CT £2754.42 TOTE £11.00: £3.30, £4.60, £8.00; EX 157.20.
Owner J N Blackburn **Bred** Theakston Stud **Trained** Denton, Co Durham
■ Stewards' Enquiry : James Rogers four-day ban: careless riding (Sep 2-5)

FOCUS
A fair sprint in which the pace was sound throughout but, as so often at this course, those racing prominently held the edge. The form seems sound.

4704 LLOYD JAGUAR AND LAND ROVER H'CAP — 7f 200y
4:00 (4:02) (Class 5) (0-75,81) 3-Y-O+ — **£2,817** (£838; £418; £209) Stalls High

Form — RPR
0502 **1** **Moheebb (IRE)**[8] 4480 3-7-13 **56** oh1 ... LiamJones(3) 3 — 63
(D W Chapman) *chsd ldrs: hung rt and led 2f out: rdn and kpt on wl fnl f* — 6/1
5342 **2** *1 1/2* **Violent Velocity (IRE)**[14] 4281 4-9-0 **67** ... NeilBrown(5) 14 — 71
(J J Quinn) *prom: effrt and chsd wnr wl over 1f out: kpt on ins fnl f* — 3/1[2]
05 **3** *3/4* **Titinius (IRE)**[18] 4177 7-9-0 **62** ... TonyHamilton 8 — 64
(Micky Hammond) *in tch: effrt over 2f out: kpt on fnl f: nrst fin* — 16/1
0001 **4** *1/2* **Frank Crow**[8] 4479 4-9-3 **72** 6ex ... GaryBartley(7) 4 — 73
(J S Goldie) *bhd tl styd on fr 2f out: nrst fin* — 9/2[3]
3000 **5** *1/2* **Scotty's Future (IRE)**[6] 4526 9-8-1 **56** oh6 ... DanielleMcCreery(7) 15 — 56
(A Berry) *sn wl bhd: gd hdwy fnl 2f: nvr rchd ldrs* — 20/1
0033 **6** *3/4* **Waterloo Corner**[10] 4424 5-8-5 **56** oh2 ... AndrewElliott(3) 12 — 54
(R Craggs) *hld up: rdn over 2f out: effrt ins over 1f out: no imp* — 9/1
0005 **7** *1/2* **Crosby Vision**[11] 4407 4-9-1 **63** ... PhillipMakin 1 — 60
(J R Weymes) *chsd ldrs tl wknd over 1f out* — 8/1
0230 **8** *hd* **Zamalik (USA)**[21] 4079 4-9-5 **67** ... StephenDonohoe 10 — 64
(E J Alston) *hld up: rdn over 2f out: n.d* — 11/1
3304 **9** *1/2* **Howards Rocket**[7] 4496 6-8-3 **56** oh6 ... KellyHarrison(5) 2 — 51
(J S Goldie) *midfield: effrt and edgd rt 2f out: sn btn* — 12/1
4030 **10** *3/4* **Anthemion (IRE)**[18] 4159 10-8-5 **56** oh1 ... AndrewMullen(3) 6 — 50
(Mrs J C McGregor) *led to 2f out: sn rdn and btn* — 22/1
0361 **11** *1 3/4* **Spume (IRE)**[9] 4450 3-9-6 **81** 6ex ... (t) JamesO'Reilly(7) 5 — 71
(D J Murphy) *in tch tl rdn and wknd wl over 1f out* — 11/4[1]
-560 **12** *hd* **Moving Story**[33] 3721 4-8-8 **56** oh10 ... FrankieMcDonald 7 — 45
(P T Midgley) *cl up: ev ch over 2f out: wknd over 1f out* — 66/1

1m 40.18s (0.09) **Going Correction** +0.125s/f (Good)
WFA 3 from 4yo+ 6lb — 12 Ran SP% **137.8**
Speed ratings (Par 103): **104,102,101,101,100 100,99,99,98,98 96,96**
CSF £28.12 CT £307.64 TOTE £8.00: £2.30, £1.70, £4.80; EX 34.40.
Owner Michael Hill **Bred** Hascombe & Valiant Studs **Trained** Stillington, N Yorks
■ Stewards' Enquiry : Liam Jones caution: careless riding

FOCUS
A run-of-the-mill event in which the pace was soon sound. Sound form, limited by the fifth.

4705 CBS OUTDOOR FILLIES' H'CAP — 6f 192y
4:35 (4:36) (Class 5) (0-70,70) 3-Y-O+ — **£2,817** (£838; £418; £209) Stalls High

Form — RPR
0104 **1** **Pay Time**[5] 4562 8-8-13 **60** ... MichaelJStainton(3) 3 — 67
(R E Barr) *mde most: rdn over 2f out: hld on wl towards fin* — 7/1
0350 **2** *shd* **Eternal Legacy (IRE)**[19] 4129 5-8-8 **52** ... StephenDonohoe 11 — 59
(E J Alston) *hld up: hdwy wl over 1f out: kpt on fnl f: jst hld* — 15/2
0104 **3** *1/2* **Onatopp (IRE)**[14] 4291 3-9-4 **67** ... RichardMullen 4 — 70
(T D Easterby) *prom: rdn and outpcd over 2f out: rallied fnl f: nt rch first two* — 10/1
0-02 **4** *3/4* **Rock Diva (IRE)**[26] 3917 3-8-3 **55** ... LiamJones(3) 5 — 56
(P C Haslam) *chsd ldrs: drvn over 2f out: one pce fnl f* — 9/1

6650 **5** 1 **Alavana (IRE)**[16] 4224 3-8-2 **51** oh1 .... RoystonFfrench 12 50
(D W Barker) *chsd ldrs: rdn over 2f out: one pce fnl f* **16/1**

5650 **6** hd **Caluba**[12] 4354 3-8-4 **56** .... AndrewElliott(3) 8 54
(K R Burke) *bhd: hdwy centre over 2f out: no imrpession fnl f* **33/1**

0430 **7** nk **Dispol Isle (IRE)**[14] 4281 5-9-7 **70** .... NeilBrown(5) 10 69
(T D Barron) *midfield: outpcd over 2f out: kpt on fnl f: no imp* **13/2[3]**

3500 **8** 3/4 **Diksie Dancer**[21] 4079 3-8-13 **62** .... PhillipMakin 1 57
(K A Ryan) *early ldr: pressed wnr: rdn over 2f out: no ex over 1f out* **25/1**

0060 **9** nk **Guadaloup**[16] 4223 5-8-0 **51** oh1 .... PatrickDonaghy(7) 15 47
(M Brittain) *in tch tl rdn and no ex fr 2f out* **16/1**

-040 **10** nk **Grey Vision**[10] 4427 4-8-0 **51** .... AndrewHeffernan(7) 13 47
(M Brittain) *midfield: rdn 3f out: btn over 1f out* **28/1**

14 **11** hd **Selkirk Sky**[14] 4287 3-8-11 **60** .... TonyHamilton 7 53
(R A Fahey) *hld up: rdn 3f out: nvr rchd ldrs* **5/1[2]**

-115 **12** 1 1/2 **Whittinghamvillage**[11] 4383 6-8-5 **52** .... AndrewMullen(3) 6 43
(D W Whillans) *racd wd in midfield: shortlived effrt over 2f out: edgd rt and sn btn* **13/2[3]**

-532 **13** 1/2 **Vanilla Delight (IRE)**[24] 3999 4-9-11 **69** .... PaddyAspell 14 59
(J Howard Johnson) *s.i.s: rdn 3f out: btn over 1f out* **7/2[1]**

1m 27.83s (0.73) **Going Correction** +0.125s/f (Good)
WFA 3 from 4yo+ 5lb **13** Ran SP% **130.9**
Speed ratings (Par 100): **100,99,99,98,97 97,96,95,95,95 94,93,92**
CSF £63.59 CT £566.18 TOTE £11.60: £3.10, £3.00, £3.20; EX 83.80.
Owner Mrs R E Barr **Bred** M Paver & M D M Racing Thoroughbreds Ltd **Trained** Seamer, N Yorks

FOCUS
An ordinary gallop to this run-of-the-mill handicap. Just modest form.
Vanilla Delight(IRE) Official explanation: jockey said filly missed the break

4706 CBS OUTDOOR AMATEUR RIDERS' H'CAP 5f 193y
5:10 (5:10) (Class 6) (0-60,60) 3-Y-0+ **£1,977** (£608; £304) **Stalls** High

Form RPR

6301 **1** **Lake Chini (IRE)**[11] 4379 5-11-0 **60** ....(b) MissJoannaMason(7) 5 73
(M W Easterby) *w ldr: led 1/2-way: rdn and edgd rt ins fnl f: hld on wl* **12/1**

0500 **2** 1/2 **Soto**[11] 4381 4-11-0 **60** .... MrCCollins(7) 9 71
(M W Easterby) *chsd ldrs: effrt 2f out: ev ch ins fnl f: kpt on: hld nr fin* **12/1**

2342 **3** 3 **Conjecture**[18] 4180 5-10-11 **55** .... MissRBastiman(5) 3 56
(R Bastiman) *prom: rdn 2f out: kpt on fnl f: nt rch first two* **5/1[2]**

-004 **4** 3/4 **Larky's Lob**[5] 4561 8-10-1 **47** .... MissAColley(7) 10 46
(J O'Reilly) *towards rr: effrt and hdwy 2f out: kpt on: nrst fin* **10/1**

0310 **5** 1 **Quicks The Word**[30] 3787 7-10-9 **53** .... MissHCuthbert(5) 11 49
(T A K Cuthbert) *prom: effrt 2f out: no ex appr fnl f* **16/1**

0406 **6** 1 1/4 **Hit's Only Money (IRE)**[14] 4281 7-11-0 **53** .... MrsCBartley 2 45
(J S Goldie) *sn bhd: shkn up and hdwy over 1f out: nrst fin* **8/1**

0304 **7** 1/2 **George The Best (IRE)**[34] 3676 6-10-11 **55** .... MrsGHogg(5) 17 45
(Micky Hammond) *s.i.s: hdwy: sme late hdwy: nvr a factor* **10/1**

0005 **8** nk **Bond Playboy**[7] 4494 7-11-4 **57** ....(v) MrSWalker 13 46
(G R Oldroyd) *missed break: bhd tl sme late hdwy: nvr on terms* **11/1**

0650 **9** nk **Memphis Man**[34] 3686 4-10-6 **50** .... RichardEvans(5) 1 38
(P D Evans) *sn bhd on outside: drvn 1/2-way: nvr on terms* **12/1**

2041 **10** shd **Missus Molly Brown**[16] 4224 3-10-3 **50** .... MrBMcHugh(5) 12 38
(R A Fahey) *midfield: effrt over 2f out: btn over 1f out* **7/2[1]**

0610 **11** nk **Greek Secret**[10] 4423 4-11-3 **56** ....(b) MissADeniel 15 43
(J O'Reilly) *hld up: pushed along over 2f out: sn btn* **11/1**

000- **12** 1 1/4 **Angelofthenorth**[314] 5928 5-10-2 **48** .... MrMHunter(7) 14 31
(C J Teague) *midfield: pushed along over 2f out: btn over 1f out* **50/1**

50-0 **13** 3/4 **Jadan (IRE)**[15] 4252 6-10-4 **50** .... MissSESiddall(7) 8 31
(E J Alston) *chsd ldrs tl rdn and wknd over 1f out* **50/1**

0020 **14** 1 3/4 **River Club**[45] 3342 3-11-1 **57** .... MissSBrotherton 4 32
(G A Swinbank) *bhd: pushed along 1/2-way: nvr on terms* **15/2[3]**

3003 **15** 2 1/2 **Frimley's Matterry**[19] 4141 7-10-8 **50** .... JennyRiding(3) 16 17
(R E Barr) *towards rr: hmpd bnd over 3f out: sn btn* **20/1**

000- **16** 3 1/2 **Diamond Josh**[235] 6990 5-10-3 **47** .... MissMMullineaux(5) 6 3
(M Mullineaux) *t.k.h: led to 1/2-way: wknd 2f out* **40/1**

0-20 **17** 5 **Hiats**[31] 3764 5-10-5 **47** ....(p) MrHHaynes(3) 7 —
(R Craggs) *chsd ldrs to over 2f out: sn btn* **33/1**

1m 13.69s (0.08) **Going Correction** -0.125s/f (Firm)
WFA 3 from 4yo+ 3lb **17** Ran SP% **139.6**
Speed ratings (Par 101): **94,93,89,88,87 85,84,84,83,83 83,81,80,78,75 70,63**
CSF £163.04 CT £846.56 TOTE £15.60: £2.20, £6.10, £1.80, £3.40; EX 246.60 Place 6 £1,318.45, Place 5 £663.70..
Owner Mrs Jean Turpin **Bred** Paul McEnery **Trained** Sheriff Hutton, N Yorks
■ The first winner for Joanna Mason, granddaughter of winning trainer Mick Easterby.

FOCUS
A modest handicap and, although the pace was sound, those held up were again at a disadvantage. Ordinary form, rated at face value in the light of a fast time.
Frimley's Matterry Official explanation: rider said gelding suffered interference in running
T/Plt: £563.70 to a £1 stake. Pool: £42,124.70. 54.55 winning tickets. T/Qpdt: £85.60 to a £1 stake. Pool: £2,985.80. 25.80 winning tickets. RY

4533 FOLKESTONE (R-H)
Wednesday, August 22

OFFICIAL GOING: Heavy (soft in places)
Wind: Gusty, half against Weather: Miserable, raining

4707 ARENA LEISURE PLC MAIDEN STKS 1m 1f 149y
5:20 (5:21) (Class 5) 3-Y-0+ **£2,817** (£838; £418; £209) **Stalls** Low

Form RPR

04 **1** **Nutkin**[14] 4275 3-8-12 0 .... OscarUrbina 1 68+
(J R Fanshawe) *trckd ldrs: wnt 2nd over 2f out: shuffled into ld 1f out: sn in command* **2/1[1]**

2330 **2** 3 1/2 **Maslak (IRE)**[77] 2354 3-9-3 75 .... ChrisCatlin 13 68
(P W Hiatt) *led after 2f: kicked on over 2f out: hdd 1f out: hld whn heavily eased fnl 75yds* **5/2[2]**

60-0 **3** 9 **Ernmoor**[50] 3186 5-9-11 41 .... StephenCarson 8 48
(J R Jenkins) *t.k.h: led 2f: chsd ldr to over 2f out: sn outpcd and btn* **50/1**

6636 **4** 7 **Haasem (USA)**[12] 4365 4-9-11 70 .... TedDurcan 12 34
(J R Jenkins) *s.i.s: in tch: drvn into 4th over 2f out but already wl outpcd: no ch after* **10/3[3]**

00 **5** 2 **Hugo Quick**[27] 3881 3-9-0 0 .... NeilChalmers(3) 10 30
(T M Jones) *hld up in last pair: outpcd fr 3f out: no ch after* **25/1**

000- **6** nk **Ceris Star (IRE)**[349] 5125 3-9-3 52 .... RobertHavlin 11 29
(B R Millman) *in tch: outpcd 3f out: drvn and no imp over 2f out: wl btn after* **20/1**

0 **7** 4 **Adore Moi**[84] 2153 5-9-6 0 .... SamHitchcott 3 16
(R W Price) *awkward in stalls and v.s.a: mostly last: lost tch 3f out* **40/1**

8 13 **Royal Rainbow** 3-9-3 0 .... AdamKirby 5 —
(T G Mills) *cl up but rn v green: wknd rapidly over 2f out: t.o* **6/1**

2m 14.39s (9.16) **Going Correction** +1.00s/f (Soft)
WFA 3 from 4yo+ 8lb **8** Ran SP% **112.3**
Speed ratings (Par 103): **103,100,93,87,85 85,82,71**
CSF £6.75 TOTE £2.00: £1.10, £1.60, £6.30; EX 8.90.
Owner Lord Vestey **Bred** Stowell Park Stud **Trained** Newmarket, Suffolk

FOCUS
A weak maiden, run at a fair pace, and the field finished strung out. Dubious form, but the winner can rate higher, particulalry if the handicapper rates this race through the third and not the second.

4708 FOLKESTONE-RACECOURSE.CO.UK H'CAP 1m 4f
5:50 (5:50) (Class 5) (0-70,70) 3-Y-0+ **£2,817** (£838; £418; £209) **Stalls** Low

Form RPR

5010 **1** **Icannshift (IRE)**[23] 4019 7-8-12 **57** .... NeilChalmers(3) 5 64
(T M Jones) *mde virtually all: drew clr fr 4f out: 5 l up 2f out: drvn over 1f out: jst hld on* **15/2**

4132 **2** shd **Bienheureux**[7] 4499 6-8-13 **60** ....(t) NicolPolli(5) 7 67+
(Miss Gay Kelleway) *hld up: nt clr run wl over 3f out: prog to chse clr wnr wl over 1f out: styd on and grad clsd: jst failed* **5/2[2]**

/66- **3** 11 **Qualify**[271] 1867 4-10-0 **70** .... DaneO'Neill 3 60
(Miss Sheena West) *dwlt: hld up in last pair: effrt on wd outside 4f out: chsd clr wnr over 2f out to wl over 1f out: btn after* **25/1**

212 **4** 3 **Don'Tcallmeginger (IRE)**[7] 4493 4-8-11 **53** .... TedDurcan 6 39
(M H Tompkins) *in tch: outpcd 4f out: wnt 2nd jst over 3f out to over 2f out: wknd* **2/1[1]**

0004 **5** 4 **Rumbled**[13] 4309 3-8-0 **59** ....(p) KirstyMilczarek(7) 4 39
(J A Geake) *s.s: nvr looked keen and mostly last: lost tch 4f out* **22/1**

1000 **6** 27 **Montchara (IRE)**[33] 3705 4-9-8 **64** .... SteveDrowne 8 3
(G Wragg) *cl up: chsd wnr briefly over 3f out: sn shkn up and wknd rapidly: eased: t.o* **9/2[3]**

2144 **7** 3 **Sand Repeal (IRE)**[36] 3630 5-9-10 **66** ....(v) ChrisCatlin 9 1
(Miss J Feilden) *mostly chsd wnr to over 3f out: wknd rapidly: t.o* **15/2**

2m 51.62s (11.12) **Going Correction** +1.00s/f (Soft)
WFA 3 from 4yo+ 10lb **7** Ran SP% **111.8**
Speed ratings (Par 103): **102,101,94,92,89 71,69**
CSF £25.41 CT £439.53 TOTE £10.10: £3.00, £1.90; EX 25.40.
Owner T M Jones **Bred** Piercetown Stud **Trained** Albury Heath, Surrey

FOCUS
A moderate handicap which saw the first two come well clear. The winner got the run of things and the form has been rated through the second.
Icannshift(IRE) Official explanation: trainer said, concerning the apparently improved form, that gelding was unable to dominate last time, was able to today
Sand Repeal(IRE) Official explanation: jockey said gelding tired on the ground

4709 NEXT MEETING SUNDAY SEPTEMBER 2ND MAIDEN AUCTION STKS 7f (S)
6:20 (6:22) (Class 5) 2-Y-0 **£2,817** (£838; £418; £209) **Stalls** Low

Form RPR

1 **Mistress Eva** 2-8-11 0 .... StephenCarson 10 67
(P Winkworth) *racd against nr side rail: chsd ldrs and rn green: effrt 2f out: rdn and styd on to ld post 75yds* **40/1**

02 **2** nk **Soggy Dollar**[13] 4325 2-9-2 0 .... TedDurcan 11 71
(M H Tompkins) *racd against nr side rail: led: drvn over 1f out: hdd and no ex last 75yds* **9/1**

4 **3** 1 1/2 **Suzi's Decision**[14] 4293 2-8-4 0 .... ChrisCatlin 13 55
(P W D'Arcy) *dwlt and bmpd s: sn pressed ldr: chal over 2f out: hanging and nt qckn over 1f out: one pce fnl f* **3/1[2]**

4 2 1/2 **Moment's Notice** 2-8-13 0 .... SimonWhitworth 3 58
(S Kirk) *dwlt: settled in last pair: pushed along and prog to chse ldrs over 1f out: one pce fnl f* **40/1**

0 **5** 2 1/2 **Brave Mave**[40] 3507 2-8-11 0 .... PaulDoe 6 50
(W Jarvis) *wl in rr: rdn and outpcd over 2f out: plugged on fnl f* **11/2[3]**

2424 **6** nk **Ruby Delta**[17] 4202 2-8-9 73 .... DaneO'Neill 14 47
(P D Cundell) *dwlt and wnt lft s: sn pressed ldng pair: rdn over 2f out: btn over 1f out: fdd* **11/10[1]**

7 3 **Priceless Speedfit** 2-8-4 0 .... MartinDwyer 5 35
(G G Margarson) *dwlt: sn racd on wd outside: wl in tch: rdn over 2f out: wknd over 1f out* **22/1**

0 **8** 1/2 **Halsion Challenge**[14] 4293 2-8-11 0 .... RobertHavlin 4 40
(J R Best) *t.k.h early: trckd ldrs: rdn over 2f out: wknd wl over 1f out* **16/1**

9 11 **Teadancer (IRE)** 2-8-1 0 .... EmmettStack(3) 12 6
(J G Portman) *dwlt and bmpd s: in tch on outer: wknd over 2f out: t.o* **66/1**

1m 32.8s (4.90) **Going Correction** +0.60s/f (Yiel) **9** Ran SP% **114.6**
Speed ratings (Par 94): **96,95,93,91,88 87,84,83,71**
CSF £348.64 TOTE £42.50: £5.10, £1.70, £1.20; EX 138.00.
Owner Mrs F A Veasey **Bred** Mrs F A Veasey **Trained** Chiddingfold, Surrey

FOCUS
An ordinary juvenile maiden which has been rated conservatively. The first pair raced against the stands' rail.

NOTEBOOK
Mistress Eva, a 20,000gns half-sister to winners at up to 1m4f, defied market weakness to get her career off to a perfect start. She had the notable advantage of racing against the stands' rail, but she handled the deep surface without much fuss and knuckled down well at the business end. Her connections feel she will prove better on a sounder surface in due course and, considering she ran distinctly green at times, further improvement looks assured. (op 25-1)
Soggy Dollar, runner-up over course and distance 13 days previously, also raced against the stands'-side rail and was only picked off in the dying strides. He evidently goes on any ground, now has the option of nurseries, and deserves to find a race now. (op 9-2)
Suzi's Decision, fourth at Yarmouth on her debut a fortnight previously, overcame trouble at the start to adopt a handy position but eventually hung when put under maximum pressure from two out and did not look to handle this softer ground that well. This was still another sound enough effort in defeat, she will be eligible for nurseries after her next outing, and she should appreciate going over another furlong before the season's end. (op 7-2 tchd 11-4)
Moment's Notice, the first foal of an unraced half-sister to this year's Champion Hurdle winner Sublimity, looked clueless through the early parts and was doing his best work inside the final two furlongs. This gelding should benefit a deal for the debut experience. (op 20-1)

Brave Mave failed to step up on the level of her Newmarket debut 40 days previously and took an age to pick up on this much deeper surface. Official explanation: jockey said, regarding the running and riding, filly ran green last time and he wanted to give her a positive ride but having suffered interference early on he had chased her along and was pushing from 3f out; vet said filly was lame on the right foreleg (op 9-1)

Ruby Delta, well backed, ran well below his recent level on this return to easier ground and has to rate as very disappointing. He has it to prove now. (op 7-4 tchd 15-8)

4710 FOLKESTONE RACECOURSE FOR WEDDINGS H'CAP — 7f (S)

6:50 (6:51) (Class 4) (0-80,80) 3-Y-O **£4,605** (£1,378; £689; £344; £171) **Stalls** Low

Form — RPR

3003 **1** **Lordship (IRE)**[6] 4538 3-7-11 **61** oh1 LukeMorris(5) 2 — 69
(A W Carroll) *dwlt: hld up in last pair tl prog against nr side rail to trck ldrs 4f out: rdn to ld wl over 1f out: sn clr* **11/2**

-025 **2** 3 1/2 **Carlitos Spirit (IRE)**[13] 4313 3-8-3 **62** ChrisCatlin 5 — 61
(B R Millman) *w ldr: led 3f out: hanging 2f out: sn hdd: no ch w wnr fnl f* **6/1**

2163 **3** 1 3/4 **Summer Dancer (IRE)**[39] 3553 3-9-0 **76** MarcHalford(3) 8 — 70
(D R C Elsworth) *hld up in last: stl there 2f out: rdn and styd on to take 3rd ins fnl f: hopeless task* **11/4[1]**

2135 **4** 2 1/2 **Classira (IRE)**[18] 4170 3-9-5 **78** TedDurcan 6 — 66
(M A Jarvis) *chsd ldrs tl wknd u.p over 1f out* **5/1[3]**

5066 **5** 5 **Dubai Magic (USA)**[12] 4360 3-8-11 **75** (t) AhmedAjtebi(5) 4 — 50
(C E Brittain) *awkward s: disp ld to 3f out: sn struggling* **8/1**

000 **6** 1 1/2 **Cheap Street**[46] 3334 3-9-7 **80** (b) DaneO'Neill 10 — 51
(J G Portman) *racd on wd outside: chsd ldrs: rdn over 2f out: wknd over 1f out* **12/1**

0304 **7** 6 **Okikoki**[7] 4502 3-9-4 **77** (b) MartinDwyer 9 — 32
(W R Muir) *racd on outer: w ldr to 3f out: wknd 2f out* **9/2[2]**

6154 **8** 14 **Yerevan**[58] 2942 3-9-6 **79** SteveDrowne 3 — —
(R T Phillips) *chsd ldrs tl wknd rapidly 2f out: eased fnl f: t.o* **18/1**

1m 31.03s (3.13) **Going Correction** +0.60s/f (Yiel) **8** Ran SP% **115.3**
Speed ratings (Par 102): **106,102,100,97,91 89,82,66**
CSF £38.52 CT £110.59 TOTE £5.10: £2.10, £2.80, £1.90; EX 37.20.
Owner Group 1 Racing (1994) Ltd **Bred** John Costello **Trained** Cropthorne, Worcs

FOCUS

Just a modest handicap, run at a fair pace in the heavy ground.

4711 FOLKESTONE RACECOURSE FOR CONFERENCES H'CAP — 6f

7:20 (7:20) (Class 6) (0-65,70) 3-Y-O **£2,047** (£604; £302) **Stalls** Low

Form — RPR

4222 **1** **Awwal Malika (USA)**[6] 4538 3-9-2 **64** AhmedAjtebi(5) 1 — 71
(C E Brittain) *trckd ldrs: squeezed through to ld over 2f out: edgd lft ins fnl f: rdn out* **4/7[1]**

0-62 **2** 1 1/4 **Having A Ball**[79] 2304 3-8-6 **49** ChrisCatlin 8 — 52
(P D Cundell) *led to 3f out: sn pushed along on inner: chsd wnr over 1f out: no imp ins fnl f* **4/1[2]**

2040 **3** 3 1/2 **The Skerret**[11] 4395 3-8-11 **54** PaulDoe 9 — 47
(P Winkworth) *dwlt: hld up in tch: prog on outer to chal over 2f out: btn over 1f out: fdd* **11/2[3]**

505 **4** 8 **Time Share (IRE)**[7] 4514 3-8-9 **57** (p) LukeMorris(5) 2 — 26
(J Ryan) *awkward s: sn pressed ldr: led 3f out to over 2f out: wknd v tamely* **10/1**

1m 17.8s (4.20) **Going Correction** +0.60s/f (Yiel) **4** Ran SP% **108.1**
Speed ratings (Par 98): **96,94,89,79**
CSF £3.15 TOTE £1.50; EX 2.70.
Owner Saif Ali **Bred** Swettenham Stud **Trained** Newmarket, Suffolk
■ Stewards' Enquiry : Ahmed Ajtebi one-day ban: careless riding (Sep 2)

FOCUS

A poor handicap, decimated by the non-runners, and the form should be treated with a little caution.

4712 FOLKESTONE-RACECOURSE.CO.UK FILLIES' H'CAP — 5f

7:50 (7:50) (Class 5) (0-75,68) 3-Y-O+ **£2,817** (£838; £418; £209) **Stalls** Low

Form — RPR

6544 **1** **Limonia (GER)**[6] 4545 5-8-2 **50** KevinGhunowa(5) 2 — 55
(Mike Murphy) *racd on inner: led 1f: styd cl up: hrd rdn to ld again jst ins fnl f: kpt on* **11/8[1]**

3354 **2** 1 **Hythe Bay**[27] 3879 3-9-8 **67** SteveDrowne 1 — 69
(J R Best) *reluctant to post: pressed ldrs on outer: led over 1f out: hdd and one pce jst ins fnl f* **4/1[3]**

5033 **3** 2 1/2 **Overwing (IRE)**[13] 4324 4-9-11 **68** RobertHavlin 3 — 62
(R M H Cowell) *led after 1f tl over 1f out: nt qckn* **2/1[2]**

0055 **4** 7 **Grange Lili (IRE)**[10] 4432 3-9-8 **67** AdamKirby 4 — 37
(Peter Grayson) *v.s.a: a detached and struggling* **20/1**

4464 **5** 31 **Lady Hopeful (IRE)**[51] 3169 5-8-6 **49** oh4 (b) AdrianMcCarthy 5 — —
(Peter Grayson) *racd v wd: prog to press ldrs 1/2-way: wknd rapidly and eased wl over 1f out: t.o* **10/1**

64.13 secs (3.33) **Going Correction** +0.60s/f (Yiel)
WFA 3 from 4yo+ 2lb **5** Ran SP% **109.3**
Speed ratings (Par 100): **97,95,91,80,30**
CSF £7.13 TOTE £2.40: £1.20, £2.20; EX 6.00 Place 6 £56.12, Place 5 £35.78..
Owner M Murphy **Bred** D Furstin Zu Oettingen-Wallerstein **Trained** Westoning, Beds

FOCUS

A moderate little sprint handicap run in bad ground. The form can be rated through the first two.

Lady Hopeful(IRE) Official explanation: jockey said mare lost its action

T/Plt: £35.80 to a £1 stake. Pool: £48,008.45. 977.70 winning tickets. T/Qpdt: £10.90 to a £1 stake. Pool: £4,546.20. 307.30 winning tickets. JN

4494 HAMILTON (R-H)

Wednesday, August 22

OFFICIAL GOING: Good to soft (good in places; 6.8)

The ground had dried right out and was described as 'just on the easy side of good'.

Wind: Almost nil Weather: Fine, sunny and very warm

4713 PHILIPS CLAIMING STKS — 1m 1f 36y

2:25 (2:25) (Class 6) 3-Y-O+ **£2,388** (£705; £352) **Stalls** High

Form — RPR

-500 **1** **El Coto**[5] 4581 7-9-10 84 (p) JamieMoriarty(3) 8 — 64
(K A Ryan) *trckd ldrs: hung lft and led over 1f out: hld on towards fin* **13/8[1]**

0056 **2** 1/2 **Prince Samos (IRE)**[7] 4496 5-9-10 80 (v) SilvestreDeSousa 14 — 60
(D Nicholls) *sn chsng ldrs: sn drvn along: edgd lft and mde effrt on outer over 3f out: upsides over 1f out: no ex towards fin* **2/1[2]**

00 **3** 1 1/2 **Sierras Future**[7] 4496 3-8-12 0 (b) PaulFessey 10 — 52
(I Semple) *s.i.s: bhd: hdwy over 3f out: edgd rt and styd on wl fnl 2f* **40/1**

40 **4** 1 1/4 **Papa's Princess**[24] 3994 3-8-11 0 LeeEnstone 13 — 49
(J S Goldie) *mid-div: effrt over 3f out: kpt on fnl f* **33/1**

3040 **5** 1 1/2 **Kirkhammerton (IRE)**[9] 4355 5-8-8 48 (b) RobbieEgan(7) 12 — 43
(A J McCabe) *sn chsng ldrs: one pce fnl 2f* **50/1**

0025 **6** 4 **Showtime Annie**[2] 4663 6-8-10 35 (b) HayleyTurner 3 — 30
(A Bailey) *hld up in rr: styd on fnl 2f: nvr nr ldrs* **22/1**

3034 **7** 3 **Ming Vase**[19] 4129 5-9-2 52 MickyFenton 2 — 30
(P T Midgley) *w ldr: wknd jst ins fnl f* **14/1**

000/ **8** 4 **Stravonian**[608] 1377 7-8-12 37 DuranFentiman(3) 9 — 21
(D A Nolan) *mid-div: effrt 3f out: sn btn* **500/1**

0200 **9** hd **Defi (IRE)**[40] 3502 5-9-3 66 (b) TomEaves 11 — 22
(I Semple) *led tl over 1f out: sn wknd* **10/1**

00 **10** shd **Simba's Pride**[19] 4138 3-9-3 0 GregFairley 6 — 29
(Miss L A Perratt) *chsd ldrs: wknd over 2f out* **200/1**

0000 **11** 3 1/2 **Drury Lane (IRE)**[4] 4610 7-8-12 45 (b) AnnStokell(5) 7 — 15
(Miss A Stokell) *a in rr* **200/1**

5606 **12** nk **Fiddlers Creek (IRE)**[5] 4580 8-8-11 45 (v) PJMcDonald(3) 1 — 11
(R Allan) *mid-div: lost pl 3f out* **40/1**

-215 **13** 18 **Soldiers Quest**[116] 1293 3-9-6 86 LPKeniry 4 — —
(Peter Grayson) *in rr: rdn 4f out: sn bhd: t.o* **5/1[3]**

0000 **14** 9 **Harts In Mo Shun (IRE)**[21] 4082 3-8-5 45 ow1 (b) PatrickMathers(3) 5 — —
(A Berry) *t.k.h: sn trcking ldrs: lost pl over 5f out: sn bhd: t.o* **200/1**

2m 0.23s (0.57) **Going Correction** +0.025s/f (Good)
WFA 3 from 5yo+ 7lb **14** Ran SP% **119.7**
Speed ratings (Par 101): **98,97,96,95,93 90,87,84,83,83 80,80,64,56**
CSF £4.69 TOTE £2.70: £1.10, £1.30, £15.40; EX 6.60.
Owner R J H Ltd & J P Hames **Bred** J H Widdows **Trained** Hambleton, N Yorks

FOCUS

The first two were closely matched on official ratings but the proximity of the fifth, who had 20lb to find, holds down the overall value of the form.

Soldiers Quest Official explanation: vet said colt was lame left hind and right fore

4714 ST ANDREW'S FIRST AID H'CAP — 6f 5y

3:00 (3:00) (Class 6) (0-65,65) 3-Y-O **£2,388** (£705; £352) **Stalls** Low

Form — RPR

5624 **1** **Distant Sun (USA)**[8] 4479 3-9-7 **65** TomEaves 6 — 76
(I Semple) *sn chsng ldrs: hdwy to ld 1f out: sn drew clr: v readily* **3/1[1]**

3140 **2** 4 **Orotund**[5] 4583 3-8-5 **52** DuranFentiman(3) 7 — 51
(T D Easterby) *chsd ldrs: led over 2f out: hdd 1f out: no ch w wnr* **3/1[1]**

4420 **3** nk **Fistral**[12] 4354 3-8-4 **48** (b[1]) SilvestreDeSousa 3 — 46
(J Hetherton) *sn outpcd and in rr: hdwy over 1f out: styd on wl ins fnl f* **11/2[2]**

1323 **4** 3/4 **Silly Gilly (IRE)**[10] 4432 3-9-4 **62** LeeEnstone 5 — 58
(K R Burke) *chsd ldrs: kpt on same pce appr fnl f* **6/1[3]**

5251 **5** nk **Mangano**[8] 4480 3-8-9 **56** 6ex PatrickMathers(3) 11 — 51
(A Berry) *sn chsng ldrs on outer: sn drvn along: kpt on same pce appr fnl f* **6/1[3]**

5010 **6** 5 **Rann Na Cille (IRE)**[6] 4525 3-9-4 **65** (p) JamieMoriarty(3) 1 — 45
(K A Ryan) *chsd ldrs: wknd appr fnl f* **8/1**

03-6 **7** 3/4 **Vanatina (IRE)**[40] 3490 3-8-9 **53** GregFairley 8 — 31
(Heather Dalton) *chsd ldrs: wknd over 1f out* **16/1**

0505 **8** 5 **Mandriano (ITY)**[11] 4384 3-8-2 **46** oh1 (v) PaulFessey 10 — 9
(D W Barker) *led: edgd lft: hdd over 2f out: sn wknd* **16/1**

65-0 **9** 3 1/2 **Bidders Itch**[24] 4001 3-7-9 **46** oh1 SophieDoyle(7) 4 — —
(A Berry) *dwlt: hdwy 2f out: edgd rt: hrd rdn and wknd over 1f out* **100/1**

0000 **10** 2 **Senora Lenorah**[11] 4384 3-7-11 **48** oh1 ow2 PaulPickard(7) 9 — —
(D A Nolan) *dwlt: sme hdwy on wd outside 2f out: sn lost pl* **100/1**

1m 13.01s (-0.09) **Going Correction** +0.025s/f (Good) **10** Ran SP% **118.8**
Speed ratings (Par 98): **101,95,95,94,93 87,86,79,74,72**
CSF £11.67 CT £47.16 TOTE £3.30: £1.70, £1.90, £2.00; EX 15.30.
Owner Gordon McDowall **Bred** Forging Oaks Llc **Trained** Carluke, S Lanarks
■ Stewards' Enquiry : Sophie Doyle two-day ban: used whip with excessive force when filly was showing no response (Sep 2-3)

FOCUS

A modest handicap run at a good pace. The form has been rated a bit negatively.

4715 EARNOCK MAIDEN CLAIMING STKS — 5f 4y

3:35 (3:35) (Class 6) 2-Y-O **£2,388** (£705; £352) **Stalls** Low

Form — RPR

2543 **1** **Speedy Senorita (IRE)**[18] 4175 2-9-0 66 LeeEnstone 10 — 65
(K R Burke) *mde all: shkn up over 1f out: r.o strly* **7/4[1]**

4520 **2** 2 **Tanley**[12] 4349 2-8-8 54 (p) PJMcDonald(3) 1 — 55
(James Moffatt) *in tch: hdwy and edgd rt over 1f out: styd on wl to take 2nd ins fnl f* **25/1**

06 **3** 1 1/2 **Jazz Stick (IRE)**[19] 4136 2-8-12 0 (v[1]) TomEaves 9 — 50
(I Semple) *chsd ldrs on outside: kpt on same pce fnl f* **9/1**

0030 **4** nk **Rope Bridge (IRE)**[5] 4560 2-8-13 59 (b) DuranFentiman(3) 3 — 53
(T D Easterby) *chsd ldrs: rdn and hung rt over 2f out: kpt on fnl f* **20/1**

400 **5** 1 3/4 **Baby Jack**[24] 3995 2-9-5 61 SilvestreDeSousa 5 — 50
(D Nicholls) *chsd ldrs: effrt over 2f out: fdd fnl f* **8/1**

664 **6** 1/2 **Rio Rocket (IRE)**[20] 4097 2-8-9 64 PaulQuinn 7 — 38
(G A Swinbank) *chsd ldrs: one pce fnl 2f* **11/4[2]**

5050 **7** 1 3/4 **Star In The East**[26] 3923 2-8-6 58 LPKeniry 4 — 29
(Peter Grayson) *chsd ldrs: fdd fnl f* **7/1[3]**

0600 **8** 1 3/4 **La Guancha**[20] 4097 2-8-4 53 (tp) GregFairley 2 — 21
(D A Nolan) *dwlt: sn chsng ldrs: wknd 2f out* **50/1**

006 **9** 1 3/4 **Falcon Speed**[14] 4285 2-8-7 50 MickyFenton 6 — 17
(P T Midgley) *chsd ldrs: outpcd and lost pl after 2f* **20/1**

6 **10** 24 **Robslastcall**[76] 2385 2-8-5 0 PatrickMathers(3) 8 — —
(A Berry) *dwlt: swtchd lft after s: sn outpcd and wl bhd: t.o* **80/1**

61.51 secs (0.31) **Going Correction** +0.025s/f (Good) **10** Ran SP% **113.2**
Speed ratings (Par 92): **98,94,92,91,89 88,85,82,79,41**
CSF £54.87 TOTE £2.60: £1.10, £4.90, £2.50; EX 48.00.Tanley was claimed by J. F. Coupland for £7,000.
Owner F D C Racing Club **Bred** R McEnery And Vincent Millett **Trained** Middleham Moor, N Yorks

FOCUS

A very modest event. The winner was entitled to break her duck, and a seemingly improved effort from the runner-up who was claimed.

NOTEBOOK

Speedy Senorita(IRE), one of those with a good chance on official figures, sat on the bridle in front and, when shaken up, had this won in a matter of strides. She was not winning out of turn. (tchd 13-8 and 15-8)

Tanley, who had 9lb to find with the winner, sported first-time cheekpieces. He snatched second spot near the line and was claimed. (op 16-1)
Jazz Stick(IRE), who is not very big, wore a visor this time. He kept on his own time down the outside and will be suited by a return to seven. (op 8-1)
Rope Bridge(IRE), with the blinkers on again, had plenty to find and looked unenthusiastic. (op 16-1)
Baby Jack had plenty to find and was on his toes and swishing his tail beforehand. (op 13-2)
Rio Rocket(IRE), 3lb ahead of the winner on official figures, continually swished her tail in the paddock. Dropped in grade, she looked to have no valid excuse. (op 4-1)
Falcon Speed Official explanation: jockey said filly hung left-handed throughout

4716 RBS SCOTTISH TROPHY H'CAP — 1m 65y
4:10 (4:10) (Class 4) (0-85,80) 3-Y-O+ **£7,772** (£2,312; £1,155; £577) **Stalls** High

Form — RPR
2602 **1** **Dark Charm (FR)**[7] 4496 8-8-9 **65**.........................(p) JamieMoriarty(3) 11 — 75
(R A Fahey) *hld up in midfield: edgd lft and hdwy over 2f out: styd on down outer to ld last 75yds* **7/1**[3]
4012 **2** ½ **Mystical Ayr (IRE)**[8] 4477 5-8-7 **63**........................ DuranFentiman(3) 12 — 72
(Miss L A Perratt) *chsd ldrs: styd on to chal ins fnl f: no ex* **5/1**[1]
5512 **3** 1¼ **Flighty Fellow (IRE)**[22] 4039 7-9-12 **79**...................(b) MickyFenton 5 — 85
(T D Easterby) *sn chsng ldrs: kpt on same pce fnl f* **7/1**[3]
2602 **4** nk **Shy Glance (USA)**[16] 4219 5-9-0 **70**............................ MarkLawson(3) 8 — 75
(P Monteith) *chsd ldr: led 3f out: wknd and hdd wl ins fnl f* **9/1**
0-0S **5** 1¼ **Isidore Bonheur (IRE)**[16] 4228 6-9-10 **80**................... PJMcDonald(3) 3 — 83+
(G A Swinbank) *hld up in rr: styd on fnl 2f: nvr rchd ldrs* **25/1**
5412 **6** 1¾ **Tizzy May (FR)**[30] 3793 7-9-5 **72**....................................... HayleyTurner 9 — 71
(B Ellison) *chsd ldrs: drvn over 3f out: one pce fnl 2f* **15/2**
3010 **7** 1¾ **Stolen Glance**[31] 3764 4-9-3 **77**... NSLawes(7) 6 — 72
(M W Easterby) *s.i.s: hdwy on outside over 3f out: nvr nr ldrs* **18/1**
3413 **8** hd **Top Jaro (FR)**[11] 4408 4-9-1 **68**.. PaulFessey 2 — 62
(D W Barker) *led at mod pce: qcknd over 3f out: sn hdd: wknd fnl f* **9/1**
1002 **9** 1½ **Regent's Secret (USA)**[18] 4159 7-9-8 **75**..................(p) LeeEnstone 1 — 66
(J S Goldie) *hld up in rr: hdwy on ins over 3f out: nvr nr ldrs* **6/1**[2]
2-23 **10** 6 **Cooperstown**[24] 3994 4-9-8 **75**.. TomEaves 7 — 52
(I Semple) *chsd ldrs on outer: outpcd over 4f out: sn lost pl* **12/1**
2134 **11** 5 **Silent Storm**[50] 3188 7-9-1 **68**.. LPKeniry 4 — 33
(Peter Grayson) *hld up in rr: bhd fnl 3f* **20/1**
21- **12** 1¼ **Dollar Chick (IRE)**[399] 3633 3-9-6 **79**............................... GregFairley 10 — 41
(M Johnston) *s.i.s: t.k.h and sn trcking ldrs: lost pl 3f out* **6/1**[2]

1m 49.61s (0.31) **Going Correction** +0.025s/f (Good)
WFA 3 from 4yo+ 6lb — **12** Ran SP% **123.6**
Speed ratings (Par 105): **99,98,97,96,95 93,92,92,90,84 79,78**
CSF £43.81 CT £266.58 TOTE £11.30: £2.20, £2.10, £2.10; EX 58.40.
Owner R A Fahey **Bred** Cyril Humphris **Trained** Musley Bank, N Yorks

FOCUS
An ordinary but competitive handicap run at a very steady pace to halfway. The form should prove sound at this level.
Regent's Secret(USA) Official explanation: jockey said gelding was unsuited by the slow early pace

4717 FIELD AND LAWN MARQUEES H'CAP — 1m 4f 17y
4:45 (4:45) (Class 5) (0-70,70) 3-Y-O+ **£3,238** (£963; £481; £240) **Stalls** High

Form — RPR
0431 **1** **Rudry World (IRE)**[7] 4499 4-8-13 **60** 6ex..................... SophieDoyle(7) 1 — 76+
(M Mullineaux) *upset in stalls: dwlt: hld up in rr: smooth hdwy 4f out: led 2f out: edgd rt and sn clr: readily* **9/4**[1]
0024 **2** 2 **Red Wine**[19] 4124 8-8-13 **60**.. RobbieEgan(7) 12 — 69
(A J McCabe) *hld up in rr: stdy hdwy on outer 3f out: hung rt and styd on to take 2nd ins fnl f: no ch w wnr* **7/1**[3]
-534 **3** 1½ **Golden Groom**[14] 4280 4-8-10 **50**...................................... PaulFessey 10 — 57
(C W Fairhurst) *chsd ldrs: led 3f out: hdd 2f out: one pce* **8/1**
4241 **4** shd **Music Review**[7] 4493 3-9-3 **70** 6ex.............................. JamieMoriarty(3) 7 — 77
(R A Fahey) *dwlt: sn chsng ldrs: effrt over 3f out: kpt on same pce fnl 2f* **5/2**[2]
0306 **5** 5 **Hue**[18] 4153 6-10-0 **68**... TomEaves 2 — 67
(B Ellison) *chsd ldrs: pushed along 7f: one pce fnl 3f* **7/1**[3]
2420 **6** 3 **Great Quest (IRE)**[25] 3976 5-9-11 **65**.................................... MickyFenton 8 — 59
(James Moffatt) *hld up in rr: drvn over 4f out: nvr nr ldrs* **14/1**
0066 **7** 1 **Newcorp Lad**[13] 4333 7-8-9 **49** oh4.................................. HayleyTurner 9 — 41
(Mrs G S Rees) *hld up in rr: hdwy 3f out: wknd over 1f out* **40/1**
2334 **8** 2½ **Topflight Wildbird**[7] 4499 4-9-6 **60**... LPKeniry 3 — 48
(Mrs G S Rees) *hmpd s: sn chsng ldrs: wknd 2f out* **10/1**
4446 **9** 3 **Grey Outlook**[7] 4499 4-8-8 **51**.. MarkLawson(3) 5 — 35
(Miss L A Perratt) *trckd ldrs: lost pl over 1f out* **14/1**
10 14 **Breiz Dream's (FR)**[122] 5-8-13 **53**.................................... GregFairley 11 — 14
(Heather Dalton) *led: drvn over 5f out: hdd 3f out: sn lost pl and bhd* **20/1**
-050 **11** 1¾ **Floodlight Fantasy**[24] 4003 4-9-5 **62**....................(b) DuranFentiman(3) 4 — 20
(Jedd O'Keeffe) *wnt lft s: mid-div: rdn 4f out: sn lost pl and bhd* **50/1**

2m 37.85s (-1.33) **Going Correction** +0.025s/f (Good)
WFA 3 from 4yo+ 10lb — **11** Ran SP% **127.0**
Speed ratings (Par 103): **105,103,102,102,99 97,96,94,92,83 82**
CSF £20.34 CT £116.88 TOTE £2.80: £1.40, £2.70, £3.10; EX 24.90.
Owner The Bellflower Rudry World Partnership **Bred** Richard Leonard **Trained** Alpraham, Cheshire

FOCUS
A modest handicap run at a sound pace and a most convincing and fast-improving winner, rated value for 4l. Solid form for the grade.

4718 ROSS RATING RELATED MAIDEN STKS — 1m 3f 16y
5:15 (5:15) (Class 6) 3-4-Y-O **£2,388** (£705; £352) **Stalls** High

Form — RPR
2534 **1** **Spritza (IRE)**[41] 3450 3-8-12 60.. HayleyTurner 8 — 61+
(M L W Bell) *trckd ldrs gng wl: led on bit over 2f out: shkn up and wnt clr over 1f out: heavily eased ins fnal f* **1/1**[1]
0464 **2** 4 **Andorran (GER)**[9] 4449 4-9-10 47.................................(b) MickyFenton 3 — 54
(A Bailey) *s.s: t.k.h: hdwy to trck ldrs 7f out: nt clr run over 3f out: kpt on to take 2nd over 1f out: no ch w wnr* **18/1**
0032 **3** 1¼ **Chip N Pin**[10] 4424 3-8-9 49.. DuranFentiman(3) 6 — 49
(T D Easterby) *chsd ldrs: kpt on same pce fnl 2f* **10/1**
-060 **4** nk **Forrest Flyer (IRE)**[37] 3587 3-8-12 52........................ PJMcDonald(3) 10 — 51
(Miss L A Perratt) *in tch: outpcd over 5f out: swtchd lft and styd on ins fnl f* **14/1**
0563 **5** 4 **Snowflight**[14] 4284 3-8-12 60..................................... JamieMoriarty(3) 1 — 45
(R A Fahey) *hld up in rr: hdwy on outside over 3f out: sn chsng ldrs: wknd fnl f* **2/1**[2]
0-00 **6** 10 **Glenridding**[22] 4036 3-9-1 42.................................(b) PaulFessey 5 — 28
(J G Given) *led: hdd over 2f out: wknd qckly over 1f out* **66/1**
050- **7** 6 **Crystal Annie**[318] 5844 4-9-7 55.. GregFairley 9 — 14
(Heather Dalton) *in rr: hdwy 4f out: lost pl over 2f out* **50/1**
0 **8** 5 **Roman Fun (IRE)**[18] 4155 3-8-12 50...............................(p) TomEaves 11 — 6
(I Semple) *chsd ldrs: lost pl over 2f out: sn bhd* **40/1**
006- **9** 8 **Butlers Best**[272] 6570 3-9-1 58... LPKeniry 4 — —
(E J O'Neill) *tk fierce hold in rr: hdwy 4f out: sn lost pl and bhd* **8/1**[3]
0000 **10** 4 **Pixie Princess (IRE)**[7] 4488 3-8-9 40................... PatrickMathers(3) 2 — —
(Miss V Haigh) *mid-div: lost pl over 3f out: sn bhd* **100/1**

2m 27.88s (1.62) **Going Correction** +0.025s/f (Good)
WFA 3 from 4yo 9lb — **10** Ran SP% **122.3**
Speed ratings (Par 101): **95,92,91,90,88 80,76,72,66,64**
CSF £24.85 TOTE £2.00: £1.10, £3.60, £1.90; EX 18.90.
Owner The Royal Ascot Racing Club **Bred** Pat Garvey **Trained** Newmarket, Suffolk

FOCUS
A weak 0-60 maiden race and a very easy winner with the runner-up rated just 47.

4719 NEILSLAND H'CAP — 6f 5y
5:45 (5:46) (Class 5) (0-70,69) 3-Y-O+ **£3,238** (£963; £481; £240) **Stalls** Low

Form — RPR
6662 **1** **Word Perfect**[11] 4381 5-9-10 **69**.......................................(b) DaleGibson 1 — 77
(M W Easterby) *mde all: edgd rt over 2f out: drvn rt out* **5/2**[1]
5323 **2** 1 **Joyeaux**[7] 4498 5-8-12 **60**.. DuranFentiman(3) 10 — 65
(J Hetherton) *hld up: stdy hdwy 2f out: chal 1f out: no ex ins fnl f* **10/3**[2]
3251 **3** 1¼ **Howards Tipple**[11] 4384 3-9-4 **66**..................................(p) TomEaves 7 — 67
(I Semple) *chsd wnr: kpt on same pce fnl f* **5/1**
0020 **4** 2 **Regal Raider (IRE)**[29] 3814 4-9-1 **60**.................................. PaulFessey 8 — 55
(I Semple) *hld up: edgd lft over 3f out: kpt on fnl 2f: nvr threatened ldrs* **11/1**
0-50 **5** ½ **Tanforan**[14] 4289 5-9-4 **66**...(p) JamieMoriarty(3) 2 — 60
(B P J Baugh) *chsd ldrs: effrt 2f out: styd on fnl f* **20/1**
4500 **6** nk **Oeuf A La Neige**[7] 4494 7-8-5 **50** oh2................................ GregFairley 5 — 43
(Miss L A Perratt) *hld up in tch: effrt 2f out: nvr trbld ldrs* **8/1**
0050 **7** ¾ **Obe One**[11] 4381 7-8-4 **52** oh5 ow2......................(b) PatrickMathers(3) 3 — 43
(A Berry) *sn chsng ldrs: wknd over 1f out* **33/1**
0360 **8** ¾ **Legal Set (IRE)**[4] 4606 11-8-5 **55**...................................(b) AnnStokell(5) 9 — 43
(Miss A Stokell) *chsd ldrs on outside: hung rt and lost pl over 1f out* **14/1**
134L **9** 2½ **Rondo**[5] 4583 4-7-13 **51**... DeanHeslop(7) 6 — 32
(T D Barron) *virtually ref to r: detached in rr: passed one rival* **7/2**[3]
0006 **10** 2 **Mutayam**[7] 4498 7-8-7 **52** oh5 ow2..(t) MickyFenton 4 — 27
(D A Nolan) *hld up: effrt over 2f out: nvr a factor* **50/1**

1m 12.28s (-0.82) **Going Correction** +0.025s/f (Good)
WFA 3 from 4yo+ 3lb — **10** Ran SP% **126.3**
Speed ratings (Par 103): **106,104,103,100,99 99,98,97,93,91**
CSF £11.81 CT £42.56 TOTE £3.10: £1.90, £1.80, £2.10; EX 18.00 Place 6 £14.72, Place 5 £10.74..
Owner Mrs Jean Turpin **Bred** Mrs Jean Turpin **Trained** Sheriff Hutton, N Yorks

FOCUS
A modest sprint handicap but a game and worthy winner who is in foal. Solid form.
Legal Set(IRE) Official explanation: jockey said gelding hung right-handed in the final 2f
Rondo Official explanation: jockey said gelding missed the break
T/Plt: £10.40 to a £1 stake. Pool: £34,126.90. 2,375.45 winning tickets. T/Qpdt: £4.40 to a £1 stake. Pool: £2,234.80. 375.30 winning tickets. WG

4690 YORK (L-H)
Wednesday, August 22

OFFICIAL GOING: Good (good to soft in places; 7.0)
Wind: Moderate against Weather: Sunny and blustery

4720 ROYAL & SUNALLIANCE AND MOTABILITY STKS (H'CAP) — 1m 2f 88y
1:30 (1:31) (Class 2) (0-105,99) 3-Y-O+ **£19,431** (£5,781; £2,889; £1,443) **Stalls** Low

Form — RPR
1145 **1** **Greek Well (IRE)**[22] 4043 4-9-0 **86**...........................(v[1]) KerrinMcEvoy 14 — 96
(Sir Michael Stoute) *lw: hld up: hdwy over 2f out: rdn to ld wl ins fnl f* **8/1**[3]
1333 **2** hd **Peruvian Prince (USA)**[18] 4153 5-9-2 **88**..................... PaulHanagan 20 — 97
(R A Fahey) *hld up: hdwy and n.m.r over 1f out: sn rdn: r.o* **16/1**
-321 **3** ½ **Font**[41] 3476 4-9-1 **87**... JMurtagh 17 — 95
(J R Fanshawe) *lw: hld up: hdwy 4f out: led over 1f out: rdn and hdd wl ins fnl f* **10/1**
0550 **4** 1 **Yarqus**[22] 4049 4-9-1 **87**...(t) SebSanders 16 — 93
(C E Brittain) *hld up: edgd rt 3f out: hdwy u.p over 1f out: nt rch ldrs* **20/1**
0345 **5** hd **Nanton (USA)**[18] 4176 5-8-13 **85**.................................... DanielTudhope 3 — 91
(N Wilson) *chsd ldrs: rdn to ld over 2f out: hdd over 1f out: styd on same pce ins fnl f* **25/1**
-010 **6** shd **Smokey Oakey (IRE)**[20] 4092 3-8-6 **86**............................ JimmyQuinn 8 — 92
(M H Tompkins) *hld up in tch: rdn and edgd lft over 1f out: styd on* **10/1**
1-01 **7** 1¼ **Great Hawk (USA)**[25] 3939 4-9-13 **99**...........................(v) RyanMoore 19 — 102
(Sir Michael Stoute) *lw: hld up: hdwy u.p over 1f out: no ex ins fnl f* **12/1**
6001 **8** ½ **Star Of Light**[11] 4399 6-9-10 **96**.. MichaelHills 2 — 98
(B J Meehan) *chsd ldr: led over 7f out: rdn and hdd over 2f out: no ex fnl f* **14/1**
0054 **9** shd **Players Please (USA)**[20] 4092 3-8-10 **90**.............................. NCallan 12 — 92
(M Johnston) *lw: chsd ldrs: rdn over 2f out: no ex fnl f* **9/1**
0500 **10** ½ **Impeller (IRE)**[26] 3899 8-9-9 **95**.. JohnEgan 11 — 96
(J S Moore) *hld up: effrt whn hmpd over 1f out: n.d* **28/1**
121- **11** 1¾ **Heaven Knows**[362] 4763 4-9-7 **93**.. RHills 6 — 91
(W J Haggas) *hld up: hdwy over 3f out: sn rdn: wknd ins fnl f* **7/2**[1]
3306 **12** hd **Collateral Damage (IRE)**[11] 4388 4-8-12 **84**..................(t) DavidAllan 9 — 82
(T D Easterby) *mid-div: rdn over 2f out: nt clr run over 1f out: nvr trbld ldrs* **18/1**
1152 **13** 2 **Hurlingham**[120] 1230 3-8-7 **87**..................................... PaulMulrennan 13 — 81
(M W Easterby) *hld up: rdn over 2f out: n.d* **50/1**
-014 **14** 5 **River Tiber**[19] 4119 4-9-12 **98**... JamieSpencer 1 — 82
(L M Cumani) *lw: hld up in tch: rdn over 2f out: wknd over 1f out: eased* **15/2**[2]
0104 **15** 2 **Fort Churchill (IRE)**[18] 4153 6-9-4 **90**.....................(bt) JimmyFortune 5 — 71
(B Ellison) *led: hdd over 7f out: chsd ldrs: rdn over 2f out: wknd over 1f out* **25/1**
1000 **16** 5 **Plum Pudding (IRE)**[46] 3330 4-9-10 **96**................................. PatDobbs 4 — 67
(R Hannon) *chsd ldrs: rdn over 2f out: wknd over 1f out* **33/1**
0000 **17** 21 **Luberon**[11] 4388 4-9-12 **98**... KDarley 10 — 29
(M Johnston) *chsd ldrs: rdn whn hmpd and wknd 3f out* **40/1**

23-6 **18** *35* **Ofaraby**[110] 1449 7-9-13 **99**.. PhilipRobinson 7 —
(M A Jarvis) *hld up: rdn over 2f out: a in rr: eased ins fnl f* **25/1**

2m 13.06s (0.56) **Going Correction** +0.275s/f (Good)
WFA 3 from 4yo+ 8lb **18** Ran SP% **125.9**
Speed ratings (Par 109): **108,107,107,106,106 106,105,105,104,104 103,102,101,97,95 91,74,46**
CSF £119.01 CT £1318.55 TOTE £9.50: £2.70, £3.80, £2.60, £4.60; EX 151.70 Trifecta £1309.80 Part won. Pool £1,844.80 - 0.10 winning units..
Owner Ballymacoll Stud **Bred** Ballymacoll Stud Farm Ltd **Trained** Newmarket, Suffolk
■ Stewards' Enquiry : Jimmy Quinn two-day ban: careless riding (Sep 2-3)

FOCUS
A very competitive handicap, run at no more than a modest early pace. The first three came clear and the form looks solid.

NOTEBOOK
Greek Well(IRE), visored for the first time, was given a very patient ride and, once brought over to the stands' side in the home straight, found the gaps opening at the right time. He showed a good attitude when it mattered to get on top in the closing stages and no doubt the headgear had the desired effect. This has to rate as his best effort to date, he deserves extra credit for coming from behind off the modest gallop, and there is little doubt he is happiest on good ground. It is likely that we have still to see the best of him, but one will have to take it on trust that the visor holds the same effect next time. (op 9-1)
Peruvian Prince(USA), drawn widest of all, emerged from off the pace to throw down a strong challenge towards the middle of the track and only just failed to get up. His 3lb weight reverse for finishing in front of the winner at Goodwood last time was enough to make the difference, but he is now back to his best and compensation is richly deserved. (op 18-1)
Font, belatedly off the mark in maiden company last time, was still travelling sweetly nearing the final furlong and momentarily looked the winner when hitting the front. He may have just got there a little too soon, however, as he could not sustain his effort where it mattered and was always going to be pegged back in the closing stages. This was still a greatly-improved effort, indeed a career-best display, and he is clearly progressing now. (op 12-1)
Yarqus was ridden to get the longer trip and, while coming through from off the pace to post a perfectly respectable effort in defeat, he never looked a serious threat. He rates a sound benchmark for this form, but holds no secrets from the Handicapper and has not won since April 2006.
Nanton(USA), up in trip, fared best of those to race handily and stuck gamely to his task under maximum pressure. He is holding his form well at present and could be nearing another success. (tchd 33-1 in a place)
Smokey Oakey(IRE), unlucky in running at Goodwood last time, was representing the stable that won this last year with Topatoo. He again failed to get the breaks when it mattered and can once more be rated a little better than his finishing position would indicate. (op 12-1)
Great Hawk(USA), 5lb higher, was far from disgraced under top weight in this very competitive handicap and is not one to abandon just yet. (op 9-1)
Impeller(IRE) was just starting to wind up prior to being hampered and has to be rated better than the bare form. Official explanation: jockey said gelding suffered interference (tchd 33-1)
Heaven Knows, who looked fit enough for his belated seasonal return, was not surprisingly very popular in the betting as he has been given an entry in the Group 1 Champion Stakes and had been privately purchased by Hamdam Al Maktoum during the off-season. He showed the ability remains with a fair effort, and he should come on a deal for the outing, but on this evidence he will not be taking up his Group 1 entry. It may also transpire that he needs a stiffer test now. (op 100-30 tchd 4-1 in places)
Ofaraby Official explanation: jockey said gelding lost its action

4721 IRELAND GIMCRACK STKS (GROUP 2) (C&G) 6f
2:00 (2:00) (Class 1) 2-Y-O
£76,653 (£29,052; £14,539; £7,249; £3,631; £1,822) **Stalls** High

Form RPR
14 **1** **Sir Gerry (USA)**[26] 3910 2-8-12 0................................... JamieSpencer 5 112+
(J R Fanshawe) *lw: hld up in rr: swtchd rnd field and gd hdwy on outer 2f out: qcknd to ld over 1f out: rdn ent fnl f and kpt on* **4/1**[2]
2 *3/4* **Great Barrier Reef (USA)** 2-8-12 0................................... JMurtagh 2 109+
(A P O'Brien, Ire) *w'like: scope: lw: trckd ldrs: hdwy on outer over 2f out: effrt and ev ch over 1f out: sn rdn and kpt on same pce ins fnl f* **8/1**
1223 **3** *3* **Swiss Franc**[41] 3459 2-8-12 108.. RyanMoore 4 100
(D R C Elsworth) *lw: t.k.h: chsd ldrs: effrt and ch 2f out: sn rdn: edgd rt and one pce appr fnl f* **5/4**[1]
210 **4** *1/2* **Imperial Mint (IRE)**[22] 4046 2-8-12 81.. NCallan 6 99+
(K A Ryan) *chsd ldrs: rdn along over 2f out: grad wknd* **25/1**
612 **5** *1 1/4* **Nacho Libre**[51] 3157 2-8-12 95.. MichaelHills 3 95
(B W Hills) *cl up: led 2f out and sn rdn: hdd over 1f out and wknd ent fnl f* **10/1**
4561 **6** *1 1/2* **Paveroc**[7] 4500 2-8-12 96.. JohnEgan 7 90
(J S Moore) *chsd ldrs: rdn along over 2f out: sn wknd* **40/1**
2125 **7** *2 1/2* **Art Advisor (IRE)**[31] 3779 2-8-12 103................................ SebSanders 8 83
(J Howard Johnson) *led: rdn along and hdd 2f out: grad wknd* **6/1**[3]
11 **8** *1 1/2* **Easy Target (FR)**[51] 3157 2-8-12 0................................... PaulEddery 1 78
(B Smart) *lw: s.i.s: swtchd to stands' rail and sn trcking ldrs: effrt and nt clr run 2f out: sn rdn and hung rt: lost action and eased ent fnl f* **11/1**

1m 14.16s (1.60) **Going Correction** +0.275s/f (Good) **8** Ran SP% **113.6**
Speed ratings (Par 106): **100,99,95,94,92 90,87,85**
CSF £35.07 TOTE £5.30: £1.80, £1.70, £1.10; EX 41.30 Trifecta £37.30 Pool £1,250.66 - 23.80 winning units..
Owner Mrs Gerry Galligan **Bred** Dr Catherine Wills **Trained** Newmarket, Suffolk

FOCUS
A fair renewal of this Group 2 juvenile prize, although not that much strength in depth. It was run at a modest early pace and the first pair came clear. The winner put in a taking display and looks well worth his place in top company now, while the debutant runner-up clearly has a very bright future.

NOTEBOOK
Sir Gerry(USA), who came unstuck on fast ground in a falsely-run affair at Newmarket last time, showed his true colours with a taking display on this big step up in grade. Having been settled at the back of the pack, it was clear passing halfway that he was not going to find the gaps on the stands' rail, so his rider wisely took the decision to go wide of his rivals and make his challenge. The response when he was asked to win his race was impressive, as he quickened smartly, and this easier ground was evidently much more to his liking. While this looks just a fair renewal of this Group 2, he is unquestionably worth a shot at the top level now and, while he has a host of fancy entries, not surprisingly the Middle Park was later put up by his connections as a likely next port of call, and he should get the strong pace he requires in that event. In the longer term, with regards to a possible crack at the 2000 Guineas, the way he raced here would suggest another furlong is within his compass, but he is by a speedy sire who is best known for producing sprinters - although his dam did win over 1m at three. (op 7-2 tchd 9-2)
Great Barrier Reef(USA) ◆, a $550,000 Mr Greeley colt, was pitched in very much at the deep end for this racecourse bow yet was representing top connections who nearly won this with a debutant in 2000. He ultimately ran a blinder in defeat, coming through to edge to the front nearing the final furlong, and only failing to match the more experienced winner's speed late on. A colt with plenty of scope, he should really now win his maiden before going onto better things, with the likelihood of another furlong sure to suit before long. (op 6-1 tchd 9-1)
Swiss Franc, the clear form pick on his placed efforts in the Coventry and July Stakes, failed to improve as could have been expected for the return to an easier surface and proved too keen through the early parts to do himself full justice. He may be better off when reverting to a more patient tactics, and a faster pace should again prove more up his street. However, he is in danger of becoming a little exposed now and winning opportunities are not going to be that simple to find. (op 6-4)
Imperial Mint(IRE), second to the winner at Thirsk on their respective debuts in July, ran his best race to date on this step up to the extra furlong, but again hit a flat spot at a crucial stage. He will now shoot up in the ratings, yet he still has more to offer this season and looks worth keeping to this distance. (tchd 22-1)
Nacho Libre was always up with the modest early tempo and did little wrong in defeat, reversing Pontefract form with Easy Target. He evidently needs to drop in grade again, however.
Paveroc, off the mark at the fifth attempt in a Salisbury maiden last time, was put in his place passing the 2f pole on this marked step back up in grade. He looks high in the ratings, but can find easier opportunities all the same. (op 33-1)
Art Advisor(IRE) failed to get home under front-running tactics on this first attempt at the longer trip. He deserves to be ridden more patiently over this trip in the future. (op 8-1)
Easy Target(FR), unbeaten in two previous outings, including when just edging out Nacho Libre in a conditions event at Pontefract 51 days previously, did not help his cause by missing the kick and then found trouble nearing 2f out when trying to make up his ground. He hung fire thereafter and lost his action late on, so is clearly better than he was able to show on this debut in Group company. That said however, he is evidently a headstrong character. Official explanation: jockey said colt hung right (op 10-1 tchd 9-1)

4722 TOTESPORT EBOR STKS (HERITAGE H'CAP) 1m 6f
2:35 (2:37) (Class 2) 3-Y-0+
£124,640 (£37,320; £18,660; £9,340; £4,660; £2,340) **Stalls** Low

Form RPR
4-41 **1** **Purple Moon (IRE)**[19] 4117 4-9-4 **101** 4ex................... JamieSpencer 14 112+
(L M Cumani) *hld up towards rr: gd hdwy 3f out: n.m.r and swtchd lft 2f out: rdn to ld wl over 1f out: drvn ins fnl f: edgd rt and styd on gamely* **7/2**[1]
1 **2** *3/4* **Honolulu (IRE)**[61] 2851 3-9-2 **111**.. JMurtagh 19 121+
(A P O'Brien, Ire) *w'like: lengthy: lw: hld up towards rr: gd hdwy 3f out: effrt and n.m.r 2f out: sn swtchd lft and rdn: swtchd rt and styd on u.p to chse wnr ins fnl f* **7/1**[3]
-161 **3** *2 1/2* **Scriptwriter (IRE)**[22] 4047 5-9-7 **104** 4ex.................... KerrinMcEvoy 6 110
(Saeed Bin Suroor) *lw: hld up in midfield: smooth hdwy 3f out: led briefly 2f out: sn hdd and rdn: edgd lft and kpt on same pce ins fnl f* **11/2**[2]
4 *3/4* **Minkowski**[27] 4-8-10 **93**..(t) SebSanders 3 98
(J E Hammond, France) *w'like: swtg: hld up towards rr: hdwy on outer 3f out: rdn to chse ldrs over 1f out: kpt on u.p ins fnl f* **8/1**
0-21 **5** *shd* **Wing Collar**[25] 3973 6-8-13 **96** 4ex.................................(p) DavidAllan 13 101
(T D Easterby) *hld up in rr: smooth hdwy over 3f out: rdn to chse ldrs wl over 1f out: drvn and kpt on same pce ins fnl f* **14/1**
-561 **6** *1 3/4* **El Tango (GER)**[57] 2976 5-9-5 **102**... AStarke 5 105
(P Schiergen, Germany) *hld up in rr: hdwy on outer 3f out: rdn to chse ldrs wl over 1f out: sn drvn and kpt on same pce* **100/1**
-210 **7** *3 1/2* **Castle Howard (IRE)**[22] 4047 5-9-0 **97**.............................. TPQueally 16 95+
(W J Musson) *lw: in tch tl pushed along and outpcd over 2f out: swtchd lft and n.m.r wl over 1f out and again appr fnl f: styd on wl fnl f* **50/1**
1102 **8** *1 3/4* **Lake Poet (IRE)**[22] 4043 4-9-3 **100**................................ PhilipRobinson 9 95
(C E Brittain) *in tch: pushed along to trck ldrs whn hmpd wl over 2f out: sn rdn and kpt on same pce fr over 1f out* **22/1**
1100 **9** *nk* **Nosferatu (IRE)**[22] 4047 4-8-9 **92**....................................... JimCrowley 10 87
(Mrs A J Perrett) *in tch: rdn along 3f out: sn drvn and wknd* **50/1**
3061 **10** *nk* **Group Captain**[24] 3989 5-9-6 **106** 4ex.................. RichardKingscote[(3)] 2 100
(R Charlton) *trckd ldrs on inner: effrt and ch over 2f out: sn rdn: wknd wl over 1f out* **16/1**
/30 **11** *1* **Hitchcock (USA)**[39] 3558 4-9-6 **103**..................................... MJKinane 18 96
(A P O'Brien, Ire) *swtg: racd wd: in tch: rdn along 4f out: wknd 3f out* **16/1**
0635 **12** *1* **Mudawin (IRE)**[26] 3898 6-8-12 **95**.. JohnEgan 1 87
(Jane Chapple-Hyam) *s.i.s and rr: sme hdwy 3f out: sn rdn and nvr a factor* **20/1**
2625 **13** *3/4* **Solent (IRE)**[24] 3989 5-9-6 **103**...................................... JimmyFortune 7 94
(R Hannon) *swtg: hld up: a towards rr* **33/1**
1405 **14** *1/2* **All The Good (IRE)**[11] 4388 4-9-0 **97**................................. EddieAhern 8 87
(G A Butler) *prom: hdwy to ld over 3f out: sn rdn and hung rt over 2f out: sn hdd and grad wknd* **25/1**
4414 **15** *2* **Ogee**[26] 3898 4-8-11 **94**..(v[1]) RyanMoore 11 81
(Sir Michael Stoute) *lw: sn led: rdn along and hdd over 3f out: drvn over 2f out and sn wknd* **12/1**
1510 **16** *1/2* **Tranquil Tiger**[22] 4044 3-8-12 **107**.............................. RichardHughes 15 93
(H R A Cecil) *lw: trckd ldrs: effrt 3f out: sn rdn and wknd 2f out* **10/1**
4-32 **17** *3 1/2* **Mutawaffer**[96] 1822 6-8-9 **92**.. PaulHanagan 12 73
(R A Fahey) *cl up: rdn along over 5f out: sn wknd* **33/1**
61 **18** *2* **Strategic Mount**[11] 4376 4-9-1 **98** 4ex...................................... TQuinn 4 77
(P F I Cole) *prom: effrt and ch 3f out: sn rdn and hmpd: wknd* **18/1**
-010 **19** *1/2* **Pevensey (IRE)**[39] 3558 5-9-1 **98**................................ GrahamGibbons 20 76
(J J Quinn) *a in rr* **20/1**

2m 59.26s (-0.24) **Going Correction** +0.275s/f (Good)
WFA 3 from 4yo+ 12lb **20** Ran SP% **130.2**
Speed ratings (Par 109): **111,110,109,108,108 107,105,104,104,104 103,103,102,102,101 101,99,97,97**
CSF £24.83 CT £142.23 TOTE £4.50: £1.80, £2.20, £2.30, £2.50; EX 31.30 Trifecta £230.80 Pool £5,137.04 - 15.80 winning units..
Owner Craig Bennett **Bred** Gestut Shohrenhof **Trained** Newmarket, Suffolk
■ Stewards' Enquiry : Eddie Ahern three-day ban: careless riding (Sep 2-4)

FOCUS
A typically competitive Ebor with plenty of depth, and solid form, rated around the third, fourth and fifth. The pace looked solid without being anything like breakneck, but it was still too much for those that helped set it as those that figured at the finish all came from the back. The field came centre to stands' side on reaching the home straight.

NOTEBOOK
Purple Moon(IRE) ◆, on his toes beforehand, was trying this sort of trip for the first time on the level and although he was carrying a 4lb penalty for his victory at Glorious Goodwood, he was still 8lb well in compared with his revised mark. He was all the rage in the market leading up to the race and justified the support in great style. Patiently ridden, the only question was whether he would find a clear route through. He did have to change course a couple of times, but still arrived there in plenty of time and the race was his as soon as he hit the front, even though he appeared to idle once there. He still does not have that many miles on the clock so he could well go on to even greater heights. He will be aimed now at the Melbourne Cup. (tchd 4-1 in places)

Honolulu(IRE) ◆, winner of a Limerick Listed event last time, faced a stiff task for a three-year-old off a mark of 111 in only his fourth outing. Weaving his way through from off the pace up the home straight, he finally found a route through against the stands' rail and was closing in on the idling winner all the way to the line. This was a cracking effort for a colt still learning the game, for he emerges much the best horse in the race when w.f.a is applied. He is still in both the English and Irish St Legers and would not be out of place in either. (op 11-1)

Scriptwriter(IRE), proven over the trip and, like the winner, carrying a 4lb penalty for a win at Glorious Goodwood, was nonetheless 4lb well in compared with his future mark. Travelling very well when looming up to the leaders down the middle of the track, he could not match the finishing pace of the front pair in the latter stages but lost very little in defeat. He will not find too many more opportunities in handicaps and it seems likely he will be back in Listed or even Group company before too long. (op 13-2 tchd 7-1)

Minkowski, a three-time winner in France trying this trip for the first time, put in some decent late work down the centre of the track without ever being able to land an effective blow. His profile suggests that he would have preferred softer ground than this. (tchd 13-2, 9-1 in a place)

Wing Collar, carrying a 4lb penalty for his course-and-distance victory last month, was produced to hold every chance and was just found wanting for a decisive turn of foot. He absolutely loves it here and has returned from his long layoff looking better than ever. (op 16-1)

El Tango(GER), winner of four Listed races and a Group 3 in his native Germany, stayed on really well down the centre of the track and ran a blinder considering his monster price, especially as he relishes genuinely soft ground.

Castle Howard(IRE) ◆, beaten a long way behind Scriptwriter at Glorious Goodwood, got into all sorts of bother in the home straight and by the time he got out into the clear it was far too late. He can be rated quite a bit closer than his finishing position.

Lake Poet(IRE) was starting to come under pressure, but was not completely out of it, when suffering in the chain reaction started by the errant All The Good over a quarter of a mile from home. Official explanation: jockey said colt suffered interference (op 25-1)

Hitchcock(USA) was kept noticeably wide of the field racing down the far straight, but it did him little good and this looked a case of lack of stamina. (op 14-1)

Mudawin(IRE), 7lb higher than when causing a shock in this last year, gave his rivals a start after getting restless in the stalls and never really looked like getting involved.

All The Good(IRE) moved smoothly to the front down the centre of the track entering the last half-mile, but almost immediately started to hang right as he came under pressure and stopped as if shot. (op 33-1)

Ogee almost certainly did too much too soon in the first-time visor. (op 14-1)

Strategic Mount, carrying a 4lb penalty for his Goodwood victory, has gained all four of his victories on faster ground. Edgy beforehand, he was up with the pace from the start and looked to have run his race when slightly hampered by the hanging All The Good under half a mile from home. Official explanation: jockey said colt suffered interference (op 16-1)

4723 DARLEY YORKSHIRE OAKS (GROUP 1) (F&M) 1m 4f

3:10 (3:13) (Class 1) 3-Y-O+

£164,662 (£62,408; £31,233; £15,573; £7,801; £3,915) **Stalls** Centre

Form RPR

2111 **1** **Peeping Fawn (USA)**[18] [4149] 3-8-11 0 JMurtagh 8 123+
(A P O'Brien, Ire) *lw: hld up: hdwy over 3f out: led over 2f out: pushed clr fr over 1f out: eased towards fin* **4/9**[1]

5101 **2** *4* **Allegretto (IRE)**[20] [4091] 4-9-7 107 (v) RyanMoore 7 113
(Sir Michael Stoute) *prom: chsd ldr 7f out: rdn and ev ch over 2f out: outpcd fr over 1f out* **9/1**[3]

1003 **3** *5* **Trick Or Treat**[20] [4089] 4-9-7 100 TPQueally 2 105
(J G Given) *led: rdn and hdd over 2f out: wknd fnl f* **66/1**

6423 **4** *1 1/4* **Under The Rainbow**[32] [3744] 4-9-7 100 NCallan 6 103
(B W Hills) *chsd ldrs: rdn over 2f out: wknd fnl f* **100/1**

-103 **5** *1/2* **Dalvina**[62] [2786] 3-8-11 109 JamieSpencer 3 102
(E A L Dunlop) *chsd ldr 5f: rdn over 3f out: wknd over 1f out* **25/1**

0001 **6** *1/2* **Darrfonah (IRE)**[69] [2599] 3-8-11 99 (t) KerrinMcEvoy 4 101
(C E Brittain) *hld up: rdn over 2f out: a in rr* **80/1**

1211 **7** *1/2* **Silkwood**[62] [2786] 3-8-11 114 PhilipRobinson 1 101
(M A Jarvis) *hld up in tch: rdn over 2f out: hung lft and wknd over 1f out* **10/3**[2]

2m 32.7s (-1.90) **Going Correction** +0.275s/f (Good)
WFA 3 from 4yo 10lb **7** Ran SP% **109.9**
Speed ratings (Par 117): **117,114,111,110,109 109,109**
CSF £4.80 TOTE £1.40: £1.10, £3.90; EX 4.70 Trifecta £63.30 Pool £4,709.99 - 52.80 winning units..

Owner M Tabor & Mrs John Magnier **Bred** Barnett Enterprises **Trained** Ballydoyle, Co Tipperary

■ Stewards' Enquiry : Jamie Spencer one-day ban: entered incorrect stall (Sep 3)

FOCUS

A race lacking strength in depth, with only two looking to have a serious chance, and it was high-rolling filly Peeping Fawn who made it four consecutive Group 1 victories being value for more than the official margin, with the runner-up and third setting the standard. The winner's stablemate Alexandrova was declared to make her belated seasonal debut but was ruled out by a setback.

NOTEBOOK

Peeping Fawn(USA) has become quite a story, for the filly who needed four attempts at losing her maiden status back in the spring was winning her fourth consecutive Group 1 contest, and once again doing it with ease. Placed behind Finsceal Beo in the Irish 1000 Guineas, she appeared a shade unlucky when second in the Epsom Oaks, but has not looked back since, winning both the Pretty Polly and Irish Oaks at the Curragh, before taking the Nassau Stakes at Glorious Goodwood, and now this. She is perhaps the hottest horse around at the minute and, with Mandesha set to go down the Arc route, the Prix De L'Opera on Arc day would be hers for the taking. There has been talk of her going for the Paris showpiece herself, which is not the most ludicrous of suggestions, but the L'Opera followed by a trip to America for the Filly & Mare Turf is surely the preferred route. (op 1-2 after early 4-7 in places, tchd 2-5)

Allegretto(IRE), third behind Alexandrova in this a year ago, has since shown herself to be a high-class stayer and she showed a fine, battling attitude to win the Goodwood Cup last time. This drop in trip was never going to be in her favour and she faced an almost impossible task trying to concede 10lb to Peeping Fawn, but the re-application of the visor saw her race a lot more sweetly and she readily drew clear of the remainder. Stamina is her strong suit and she is likely to be a player in races such as the Irish St Leger and Doncaster Cup. (tchd 10-1)

Trick Or Treat has progressed through the ranks and gained her first win at Pattern level when taking a Listed event at Haydock back in May. She has struggled the last twice in Group contests, but had the run of things here and was able to hang on for a flattering third. This will go down as a valuable addition to her c.v, but she is probably no better than Group 3 level and will find easier opportunities. (op 100-1)

Under The Rainbow returned to something like her best when second behind Turbo Linn at Newmarket last time and this was another fine effort in a race she had no realistic chance of winning. Placed in the Chester Cup earlier in the year, she is probably best at trips in excess of this, but remains winless since the 2005 Pretty Polly.

Dalvina, rampant winner of this year's Pretty Polly, beat a weak field that day and she has since had her limitations exposed in the Oaks, and more recently the Ribblesdale at Royal Ascot. This is probably as good as she is.

Darrfonah(IRE) appreciated the drop in grade when winning a Listed race at Newbury last time, but she found this all too hot to handle and never really got going. (op 66-1)

Silkwood announced herself as one of the better middle-distance fillies around when impressively winning the Ribblesdale, and her trainer has made no secret of the regard in which she is held. Whilst she would have preferred the ground genuinely quick, she was expected to handle this, so it was most disappointing the way in which she dropped out, looking awkward and hanging under pressure. There was evidently something amiss and she deserves another chance to show her worth. Official explanation: trainer was unable to explain the poor form shown (op 3-1 tchd 7-2, 4-1 in places)

4724 JULIA GRAVES ROSES STKS (LISTED RACE) 5f

3:50 (3:51) (Class 1) 2-Y-O **£17,781** (£6,723; £3,360; £1,680) **Stalls** High

Form RPR

3113 **1** **Captain Gerrard (IRE)**[22] [4046] 2-9-0 104 RyanMoore 6 107+
(B Smart) *lw: mde most: rdn wl over 1f out: styd on strly ins fnl f* **6/4**[1]

5501 **2** *2* **Cake (IRE)**[5] [4573] 2-8-12 98 PatDobbs 2 98
(R Hannon) *lw: hmpd s and towards rr: hdwy 2f out: sn rdn: styd on to chse wnr ent fnl f: drvn and no imp* **8/1**

1310 **3** *1 1/2* **Fred's Lad**[64] [2737] 2-9-0 94 PaulMulrennan 7 94
(M W Easterby) *chsd ldrs: rdn along 2f out: drvn over 1f out: kpt on u.p fnl f* **11/1**

4 *hd* **Proud Linus (USA)** 2-9-0 0 DanielTudhope 5 94
(D Carroll) *w'like: athletic: towards rr: pushed along and hdwy wl over 1f out: sn rdn and kpt on ins fnl f: nrest at fin* **100/1**

61 **5** *hd* **Toolittleyourlate (USA)**[12] [4358] 2-9-0 77 NCallan 4 93
(K A Ryan) *chsd ldrs: rdn along wl over 1f out: no ex ins fnl f* **33/1**

611 **6** *1* **Sailor At Sea (USA)**[27] [3867] 2-9-0 86 RichardHughes 9 89
(R Charlton) *lw: stdd s: sn trcking ldrs: effrt and n.m.r 2f out: sn one pce* **7/2**[2]

6005 **7** *3/4* **Carleton**[4] [4613] 2-9-0 96 DarryllHolland 10 87
(M R Channon) *a towards rr* **28/1**

100 **8** *3/4* **Roker Park (IRE)**[19] [4120] 2-9-0 94 PatCosgrave 1 84
(K R Burke) *in tch on wd outside: rdn along 2f out: sn wknd* **12/1**

231 **9** *1 1/4* **Carolina Belle (USA)**[18] [4160] 2-8-9 78 JamieSpencer 3 74
(M J Wallace) *chsd ldrs to 1/2-way: sn wknd* **20/1**

120 **10** *1* **Bespoke Boy**[62] [2785] 2-9-0 96 JimmyFortune 8 76
(P C Haslam) *cl up: rdn 2f out and sn wknd* **5/1**[3]

60.30 secs (0.98) **Going Correction** +0.275s/f (Good) **10** Ran SP% **118.2**
Speed ratings (Par 102): **103,99,97,97,96 95,93,92,90,89**
CSF £14.28 TOTE £2.40: £1.10, £2.20, £2.40; EX 13.90 Trifecta £53.30 Pool £1,832.78 - 24.40 winning units..

Owner R C Bond **Bred** Alan Dargan **Trained** Hambleton, N Yorks

FOCUS

A solid race for the grade with the time about right for the level and it went to the form horse Captain Gerrard.

NOTEBOOK

Captain Gerrard(IRE) ◆ set a strong standard on the form of his recent Molecomb third and was soon at the head of affairs. In what was a pretty ordinary contest for the level, it soon became clear there was little coming from behind and he ran on strongly to win with a bit to spare. This speedy son of Oasis Dream is now Flying Childers-bound and he heads there with every chance of following up. (op 13-8 tchd 7-4)

Cake(IRE), right back to form when winning the St Hugh's Stakes at Newbury the previous weekend, was faced with a better class of opposition here and she ran mightily well, especially as she carried a penalty and seemed to get interfered with coming out of the stalls. She did best of those coming from behind and looks at home in this grade. (op 7-1)

Fred's Lad, who edged out Captain Gerrard at Beverley earlier in the season, ran well for a long way in the Windsor Castle at Royal Ascot and this was another fine effort. He has yet to try 6f, but looks worth a go at it now he seems to settle a bit better in his races. (op 12-1)

Proud Linus(USA) ◆, whose first-season sire Proud Citizen has made a promising start, was thrown in at the deep end for this racecourse debut and ran surprisingly well, really getting going in the final quarter mile having been outpaced and running green in rear early on. He would appear to be a ready-made maiden winner.

Toolittleyourlate(USA) improved on his debut effort to score narrowly over 5f at Lingfield last time and he ran a lot better than he was entitled to in what was a significantly stronger contest. He will find easier opportunities, but the Handicapper is likely to nudge him up for a few pounds following this.

Sailor At Sea(USA), winner of a couple of average events at Sandown and Bath, was surprisingly short in the betting considering he has been officially rated some 18lb lower than Captain Gerrard and he did not prove good enough, already looking held when squeezed for room. He may not be the easiest to place. (tchd 11-4)

Bespoke Boy, one of the better early-season juveniles who finished second in the Woodcote Stakes at Epsom, did not meet expectations at Royal Ascot and he was the main disappointment of the race on his first appearance since. He seems to be going the wrong way. Official explanation: jockey said colt had no more to give (op 7-1)

4725 NEWITTS.COM CONVIVIAL MAIDEN STKS 6f

4:25 (4:25) (Class 2) 2-Y-O **£16,192** (£4,817; £2,407; £1,202) **Stalls** High

Form RPR

4 **1** **Moynahan (USA)**[22] [4048] 2-9-3 0 TQuinn 6 94+
(P F I Cole) *a.p: chsd ldr over 1f out: rdn to ld ins fnl f: r.o* **5/1**[2]

2 *2 1/2* **Iguazu Falls (USA)** 2-9-3 0 KerrinMcEvoy 4 90+
(Saeed Bin Suroor) *w'like: scope: lw: hld up: hdwy over 1f out: sn rdn: r.o wl* **10/1**

4 **3** *1* **Hammadi (IRE)**[14] [4285] 2-9-3 0 NCallan 1 84
(K A Ryan) *unf: lw: led: racd keenly: rdn and edgd lft over 1f out: hdd and no ex ins fnl f* **33/1**

4 *1/2* **Glorious Gift (IRE)** 2-9-3 0 JimmyFortune 9 82
(P W Chapple-Hyam) *lengthy: unf: s.i.s: hld up: nt clr run over 2f out: shkn up over 1f out: nt trble ldrs* **9/1**

5 *nk* **Silvanus (IRE)** 2-9-3 0 MichaelHills 3 81
(W J Haggas) *leggy: unf: hld up: nt clr run over 2f out: r.o ins fnl f: nrst at fin* **33/1**

6 *shd* **Otaared** 2-9-3 0 PhilipRobinson 7 81
(M A Jarvis) *str: bit bkwd: mid-div: hdwy over 2f out: styd on same pce ins fnl f* **8/1**

7 *1 1/4* **Greatwallofchina (USA)** 2-9-3 0 JMurtagh 2 77
(A P O'Brien, Ire) *str: bit bkwdL gd bodied: sn pushed along in rr: nvr nrr* **15/8**[1]

22 **8** *1/2* **Redsensor**[7] [4500] 2-9-3 0 RyanMoore 10 76
(R Hannon) *lw: chsd ldr tl rdn over 1f out: wknd ins fnl f* **10/1**

9 *shd* **Giant Love (USA)** 2-9-3 0 SebSanders 8 75
(M Johnston) *w'like: scope: tall: lengthy: s.s: hdwy over 2f out: wknd fnl f* **33/1**

10 *4* **Eseej (USA)** 2-9-3 0 RHills 11 63
(B W Hills) *w'like: scope: bit bkwd: s.i.s: hld up: plld hrd: hdwy over 3f out: shkn up over 1f out: sn wknd* **8/1**

11 *3 1/2* **Patthepainter (GER)** 2-9-3 0 PatCosgrave 5 53
(K R Burke) *leggy: bit bkwd: chsd ldrs over 3f* **66/1**

12 1 1/4 **Pure Scandal** 2-9-3 0 .... PaulMulrennan 12 49
(M W Easterby) *w'like: mid-div: n.m.r and lost pl 1/2-way: sn bhd* **100/1**

3 13 1 3/4 **Park Royal (UAE)**[20] 4094 2-8-12 0 .... JamieSpencer 13 39
(M Johnston) *chsd ldrs over 3f* **15/2**[3]

1m 14.43s (1.87) **Going Correction** +0.275s/f (Good) **13** Ran SP% **124.9**
Speed ratings (Par 100): **98,94,93,92,92 92,90,89,89,84 79,78,75**
CSF £55.26 TOTE £5.80: £2.30, £3.70, £8.60; EX 77.80 Trifecta £807.40 Pool £1,137.30 - 1.00 winning unit..
Owner D S Lee **Bred** Stonestreet Mares Llc **Trained** Whatcombe, Oxon

FOCUS
A very valuable maiden, but one with a chequered recent history. Only Stravinsky and Court Masterpiece in the last ten years have gone on to success at the highest level whilst most of the other recent winners have hardly made names for themselves. The winning time was only 0.27 seconds slower than the Gimcrack but, although it remains to be seen how strong the form is, a few of these did put in eye-catching performances and there should be a number of winners come from the race. They looked a very nice bunch in the paddock.

NOTEBOOK
Moynahan(USA) ◆ was edgy beforehand, but he was still able to confirm the promise of his Goodwood debut, producing a tidy turn of foot to cut down the leader and win going away. He should get a bit further on breeding and looks a nice prospect. (op 7-2)
Iguazu Falls(USA) ◆, a half-brother to two winners including the useful Advice, looked quite a nice type and is a very good walker. He stayed on very nicely down the middle of the track without being by any means beaten up and this was a pleasing debut. He should come on a lot for this and his breeding suggests he will come into his own when stepped up to 1m. (op 11-1 tchd 12-1)
Hammadi(IRE), quite an attractive sort, had shown ability on his debut in what was no more than an ordinary Pontefract maiden and was almost certainly up against much stiffer rivals here. Nonetheless he carted himself to the front early from the widest stall and, rather than fight him, his rider gave him his head and allowed him to stride on. It looked at one stage as though he might not get caught, but his earlier exertions took their toll inside the last furlong and he was swamped by the front pair. Winning an ordinary maiden should be a formality for him now. (op 40-1)
Glorious Gift(IRE) ◆, out of a half-sister to three winners including the top-class Germany and a smart performer in the US, looked a nice type beforehand. He did not have much room to play with on the nearside at one stage, but still showed enough to suggest he has a future. Although by a top-class sprinter, there is plenty of stamina on the dam's side of his pedigree. (op 15-2)
Silvanus(IRE) ◆, a 140,000gns brother to the useful Contest, looked quite a nice type in the paddock. Held up early, he enjoyed no luck at all when attempting to get closer mid-race and was noted finishing to some purpose at the line. This was a most eye-catching debut and he is one to note. (op 25-1)
Otaared ◆, a brother to the useful Laa Rayb and a half-brother to five winners including the high-class Bint Allayl and Kheleyf, showed some ability on this debut and plenty of improvement can be expected. (op 10-1)
Greatwallofchina(USA), a half-brother to Beauty Bright, was all the rage in the market to make a winning debut, but he just looked in need of the run beforehand and never looked like getting involved, appearing to need the experience more than was expected. The betting suggested he is thought capable of much better than this. (op 3-1 tchd 100-30 in places)
Redsensor was the most experienced in the line-up, but after showing up for a long way was firmly put in his place. He may need his sights lowering a little if he is to get off the mark. (op 8-1)
Giant Love(USA) shaped nicely on his racecourse debut, but he still looks on the weak side.
Eseej(USA), whose dam is from the family of Bint Salsabil, looked a nice type in the paddock and attracted market support, but he ultimately proved too green to do himself justice. (op 14-1)
Park Royal(UAE) Official explanation: jockey said filly became upset in stalls

4726 EVENTMASTERS STKS (H'CAP) 5f
5:00 (5:01) (Class 2) (0-100,98) 3-Y-O **£16,192** (£4,817; £2,407; £1,202) **Stalls** High

Form RPR

1260 1 **Northern Fling**[19] 4123 3-8-13 **90** .... GrahamGibbons 20 100+
(D Nicholls) *trckd ldrs stands' side: hdwy 2f out: rdn to ld ins fnl f: drvn and edgd lft last 50yds: hld on wl* **25/1**

3225 2 *nk* **Special Day**[4] 4607 3-8-9 **86** .... MichaelHills 11 95
(B W Hills) *hld up centre: gd hdwy wl over 1f out: rdn to chal ent fnl f and ev ch tl drvn: edgd rt and nt qckn towards fin* **9/1**

3 *nk* **Peak District (IRE)**[80] 2283 3-8-13 **90** .... JamieSpencer 4 98+
(David Wachman, Ire) *lw: hld up and bhd centre: hdwy 1/2-way: trckd ldrs wl over 1f out: rdn to chal ent fnl f: sn drvn and ev ch: edgd rt and no ex nr fin* **10/3**[1]

3322 4 3 **Morinqua (IRE)**[19] 4123 3-9-5 **96** .... TPQueally 8 93
(J G Given) *lw: overall ldr centre: rdn along wl over 2f out: drvn and hdd ins fnl f: kpt on same pce* **9/1**

-304 5 *nk* **Blue Echo**[40] 3511 3-9-2 **93** .... PhilipRobinson 18 89
(M A Jarvis) *led stands' side gp: rdn along 2f out: hdd over 1f out: sn drvn and kpt on same pce* **8/1**

0-10 6 *shd* **Makshoof (IRE)**[60] 2884 3-8-7 **84** .... NCallan 13 80
(K A Ryan) *in tch centre: rdn along 2f out: styd on same pce u.p ent fnl f* **33/1**

1003 7 *shd* **Valery Borzov (IRE)**[19] 4123 3-8-4 **81** .... AdrianTNicholls 15 76+
(D Nicholls) *lw: in tch centre: hdwy 2f out: sn rdn and kpt on same pce ent fnl f* **4/1**[2]

5000 8 1/2 **Luscivious**[19] 4123 3-8-9 **86** .... TQuinn 9 79
(A J McCabe) *chsd ldrs centre: rdn along 2f out: kpt on same pce appr fnl f* **40/1**

6050 9 1 **Elhamri**[24] 3990 3-9-6 **97** .... RichardHughes 7 87
(S Kirk) *chsd ldrs centre: rdn along 2f out and grad wknd appr fnl f* **16/1**

1306 10 *shd* **The Nifty Fox**[9] 4452 3-8-7 **84** .... DavidAllan 10 73
(T D Easterby) *bhd centre and rdn along 1/2-way: styd on appr last: nvr a factor* **33/1**

10-1 11 *hd* **Maker's Mark (IRE)**[17] 4204 3-8-7 **84** .... FergusSweeney 17 73
(H Candy) *cl up stands' rail: rdn along 2f out: grad wknd* **12/1**

0-00 12 1/2 **Zanida (IRE)**[42] 3430 3-8-7 **84** ....(b[1]) PatCosgrave 12 71
(K R Burke) *a towards rr centre* **33/1**

1112 13 *shd* **Fathom Five (IRE)**[39] 3531 3-9-7 **98** .... RyanMoore 3 85
(B Smart) *cl up: rdn along 2f out: drvn and wknd over 1f out* **13/2**[3]

1344 14 1 1/4 **Rasaman (IRE)**[19] 4123 3-8-4 **84** .... WilliamBuick[(3)] 2 66
(M A Jarvis) *chsd ldrs centre: rdn along 2f out and sn wknd* **10/1**

0005 15 3/4 **Dazed And Amazed**[11] 4374 3-9-6 **97** ....(b[1]) JimmyFortune 16 76
(R Hannon) *chsd ldrs stands' side: rdn along 2f out and sn wknd* **33/1**

1-00 16 1 3/4 **Yungaburra (IRE)**[11] 4386 3-9-4 **95** .... JohnEgan 19 68
(D J Murphy) *chsd ldrs stands' side: rdn along over 2f out: sn wknd* **66/1**

0630 17 2 1/2 **Invincible Force (IRE)**[11] 4374 3-9-7 **98** .... SebSanders 1 62+
(Paul Green) *racd alone far side: cl up: rdn 2f out: sddle sn slipped and wknd* **50/1**

1000 18 *nk* **He's A Humbug (IRE)**[19] 4122 3-8-11 **88** ....(p) PaulMulrennan 5 51
(K A Ryan) *chsd ldrs centre: rdn along over 2f out: sn wknd* **50/1**

0410 19 1/2 **Foxy Music**[9] 4452 3-8-7 **84** ow2 .... KDarley 6 45
(E J Alston) *chsd ldrs centre: rdn along over 2f out and sn wknd* **66/1**

006 20 7 **Just Joey**[35] 3637 3-8-2 **79** oh1 .... PaulHanagan 14 15
(J R Weymes) *a bhd* **66/1**

60.03 secs (0.71) **Going Correction** +0.275s/f (Good) **20** Ran SP% **136.6**
Speed ratings (Par 106): **105,104,104,99,98 98,98,97,96,95 95,94,94,92,91 88,84,84,83,72**
CSF £244.54 CT £992.40 TOTE £51.90: £7.40, £2.50, £1.90, £2.10; EX 476.90 Trifecta £1626.10 Part won. Pool £2,290.30 - 0.20 winning units. Place 6 £67.00, Place 5 £14.68..
Owner Jim Dale/Jason Berry **Bred** Lady Juliet Tadgell **Trained** Sessay, N Yorks

FOCUS
A typically hot York sprint handicap in which most of the runners raced centre to stands' side, though one raced alone against the far rail. The front three managed to pull a fair way clear of the others and the form looks solid rated through the third.

NOTEBOOK
Northern Fling, who was done no favours by the draw at Goodwood last time, was in a good berth on this occasion judged on the evidence of this meeting so far. His last two wins had come over 6f, but this strongly-run race over the minimum trip proved no problem for him and, after being produced with his effort towards the stands' side, battled on well to score. He is in the right hands to find other opportunities in races like this. (tchd 28-1)
Special Day ◆, able to race off her correct mark this time, was over the minimum trip for the first time since winning on her sole start at two. Produced with her effort down the centre of the track, she only just lost out and is still relatively unexposed. (op 10-1)
Peak District(IRE), an Irish challenger, was very well backed to win this but he was not well away at all and, given how close he came to winning, that may have been vital. He did not see the racecourse until March of this year and there will be other days. (op 4-1 tchd 3-1, 5-1 in places)
Morinqua(IRE) had Northern Fling well behind her when runner-up at Goodwood last time, but she was much more favoured by the draw on that occasion. She showed her usual dazzling speed down the centre of the track and, although she could not hold off the front trio in the latter stages, managed to cling on to fourth. She is very consistent, but is on a career-high mark now and the Handicapper looks to have her.
Blue Echo, making her handicap debut after fours runs in Pattern company, showed her customary early dash down the stands' rail, but was always just behind Morinqua down the middle and probably achieved as much as could be expected. (op 10-1)
Makshoof(IRE), still 5lb higher than for his last win, was far from disgraced but could really do with another furlong. (tchd 40-1 in places)
Valery Borzov(IRE), closely matched with Morinqua on Goodwood running when both finished ahead of Northern Fling, seemed to have every chance and on a line through the filly probably ran close to his mark. He still has not had that much racing. (tchd 9-2)
Fathom Five(IRE), with so much early pace in the field, could not dominate on this occasion and that was probably as much of a problem as being 6lb higher than for his last win. (op 15-2 tchd 8-1)
Invincible Force(IRE) took the solo route against the far rail from his low draw and still looked to be in touch with the main bulk of the field when appearing to jink slightly at a piece of paper blowing across the track. It was not long before his saddle started to go and his rider spent the second half of the contest with his feet out of the stirrups. This effort can be ignored. Official explanation: jockey said saddle slipped (op 40-1)
T/Jkpt: £2,460.80 to a £1 stake. Pool: £15,597.00. 4.50 winning tickets. T/Plt: £41.90 to a £1 stake. Pool: £195,812.55. 3,408.15 winning tickets. T/Qpdt: £5.80 to a £1 stake. Pool: £9,813.10. 1,248.35 winning tickets. JR

4727 - 4730a (Foreign Racing) - See Raceform Interactive

4192 CHESTER (L-H)
Thursday, August 23

OFFICIAL GOING: Good to firm (8.3)
The ground was described as 'just on the quick side of good, a lovely racing surface'. Rail moved out 3m from home turn and 5m from the 6f start.
Wind: mod 1/2 against Weather: overcast, cool and breezy

4731 ALMOND RESORTS H'CAP 7f 122y
5:40 (5:41) (Class 6) (0-65,65) 3-Y-0+ **£2,730** (£806; £403) **Stalls** Low

Form RPR

0000 1 **Sands Of Barra (IRE)**[6] 4562 4-9-4 **58** .... DanielTudhope 2 67
(I W McInnes) *chsd ldrs: led 1f out: kpt on wl* **10/1**

0060 2 1 1/2 **Regal Dream (IRE)**[13] 4353 5-9-4 **58** .... GrahamGibbons 4 63
(J W Unett) *in rr-div: hdwy over 2f out: styd on ins to take 2nd ins fnl f* **16/1**

0641 3 1/2 **Empire Dancer (IRE)**[15] 4295 4-9-11 **65** .... FrancisNorton 11 69
(C N Allen) *swtchd lft after s: led tl 1f out: no ex* **8/1**

0020 4 1 **Maison Dieu**[11] 4423 4-8-12 **59** .... GaryBartley[(7)] 3 60+
(E J Alston) *hld up in rr: hdwy over 1f out: styd on wl ins fnl f* **10/1**

2320 5 2 1/2 **Just Oscar (GER)**[9] 4480 3-9-4 **64** .... DavidAllan 1 59
(W M Brisbourne) *mid-div: pushed along over 4f out: swtchd rt 2f out: one pce fnl 2f* **7/1**[3]

2560 6 1 3/4 **Supercast (IRE)**[146] 831 4-9-6 **63** .... LiamJones[(3)] 10 54
(W M Brisbourne) *chsd ldrs: sltly hmpd 2f out: kpt on same pce over 1f out* **33/1**

0032 7 1 **Turkish Sultan (IRE)**[7] 4530 4-8-11 **56** ....(v) HaddenFrost[(5)] 8 44
(J M Bradley) *chsd ldrs: hmpd 2f out: sn fdd* **11/2**[2]

6040 8 1/2 **Akram (IRE)**[21] 4107 5-9-8 **65** .... JamieMoriarty[(3)] 14 52
(Jonjo O'Neill) *mid-div: sn pushed along: lost pl over 1f out: lame* **25/1**

0631 9 1/2 **Outer Hebrides**[8] 4505 6-9-11 **65** ....(v) StephenDonohoe 5 51
(J M Bradley) *chsd ldr: lost pl over 1f out* **9/4**[1]

2500 10 5 **Linda's Colin (IRE)**[6] 4577 5-9-6 **65** .... LukeMorris[(5)] 6 38
(R A Harris) *mid-div: drvn over 4f out: lost pl 2f out* **7/1**[3]

0005 11 1 1/4 **Major League (USA)**[14] 4319 5-9-5 **59** .... RichardMullen 7 29
(D Morris) *a in rr* **14/1**

1m 34.61s (-0.14) **Going Correction** +0.10s/f (Good)
WFA 3 from 4yo+ 6lb **11** Ran SP% **119.8**
Speed ratings (Par 101): **104,102,102,101,98 96,95,95,94,89 88**
CSF £161.39 CT £1380.51 TOTE £11.90: £4.00, £5.60, £2.50; EX 147.50.
Owner Wold Construction Company **Bred** Sunderland Holdings Inc **Trained** Catwick, E Yorks
■ Stewards' Enquiry : David Allan three-day ban: careless riding (Sep 3-5)

FOCUS
A low-grade handicap run at a strong pace. The third is the best guide to this modest form.
Supercast(IRE) Official explanation: jockey said gelding was denied a clear run
Akram(IRE) Official explanation: vet said gelding was lame
Linda's Colin(IRE) Official explanation: vet said gelding finished distressed

4732 ADOS H'CAP 1m 4f 66y
6:10 (6:10) (Class 4) (0-85,84) 3-Y-0+ **£5,505** (£1,637; £818; £408) **Stalls** Low

Form RPR

0123 1 **Prelude**[18] 4194 6-8-7 **66** .... LiamJones[(3)] 2 70
(W M Brisbourne) *chsd ldrs: drvn over 4f out: styd on to ld ins fnl f* **8/1**

0532 2 1 **Plane Painter (IRE)**[6] 4570 3-8-7 **73** .... GregFairley 11 75
(M Johnston) *chsd ldrs: led over 4f out: hdd and no ex ins fnl f* **3/1**[1]

4543 **3** *hd* **Acuzio**[6] 4558 6-8-9 **65** oh1 .... DavidAllan 6 67
(W M Brisbourne) *t.k.h towards rr: stdy hdwy over 1f out: styd on same pce ins fnl f* **14/1**

5133 **4** *¾* **Thorny Mandate**[8] 4493 5-8-9 **65** .... RichardMullen 1 65
(W M Brisbourne) *dwlt: hld up in rr: hdwy and nt clr run over 1f out: styd on: nt rch ldrs* **8/1**

3222 **5** *½* **Sporting Gesture**[6] 4558 10-8-9 **65** .... DaleGibson 4 65
(M W Easterby) *trckd ldrs: kpt on same pce appr fnl f* **6/1**[2]

3361 **6** *1* **King's Ransom**[15] 4267 4-9-5 **75** .... FrancisNorton 10 73
(S Gollings) *s.i.s: in rr: hdwy and hung lft over 1f out: nvr rchd ldrs* **16/1**

1360 **7** *¾* **Stretton (IRE)**[18] 4194 9-9-6 **79** .... PJMcDonald(3) 7 76
(J D Bethell) *hld up in rr: hdwy over 3f out: kpt on same pce: nvr rchd ldrs* **8/1**

30-5 **8** *2* **Mr Aitch (IRE)**[18] 4194 5-8-12 **75** .... (t) EJMcNamara(7) 5 69
(R T Phillips) *chsd ldrs: chal 4f out: sn hrd drvn: wknd over 1f out* **8/1**

0625 **9** *2* **Advancement**[28] 3888 4-8-9 **65** .... TonyHamilton 3 55
(R A Fahey) *hld up in mid-div: hdwy over 1f out: nvr nr ldrs* **25/1**

1025 **10** *8* **Luna Landing**[15] 4288 4-10-0 **84** .... PaulMulrennan 9 62
(Jedd O'Keeffe) *led tl over 4f out: lost pl over 2f out: eased ins fnl f* **12/1**

5626 **11** *1 ¼* **Red Lancer**[53] 3143 6-9-11 **81** .... AdrianTNicholls 8 57
(D Nicholls) *hld up in mid-div: hdwy to chse ldrs 7f out: lost pl and eased over 1f out* **15/2**[3]

2m 40.19s (-0.46) **Going Correction** +0.10s/f (Good)
WFA 3 from 4yo+ 10lb **11** Ran SP% **119.6**
Speed ratings (Par 105): **105,104,104,103,103 102,102,100,99,94 93**
CSF £32.75 CT £341.46 TOTE £6.80: £2.90, £1.60, £5.00; EX 41.50.
Owner A P Burgoyne **Bred** Cheveley Park Stud Ltd **Trained** Great Ness, Shropshire

FOCUS
Just a fair pace and the first two were in the thick of the action from flag fall. The runner-up looks the safest guide to what might prove dubious form.
Red Lancer Official explanation: jockey said gelding lost its action

4733 HIC-CUP WINES LTD MEDIAN AUCTION MAIDEN STKS 6f 18y
6:40 (6:42) (Class 5) 2-Y-O **£3,238** (£963; £481; £240) **Stalls** Low

Form RPR

00 **1** **Harry Gee**[23] 4048 2-9-3 0 .... RichardMullen 2 76
(W R Muir) *chsd ldrs: styd on ins to ld ins fnl f: drvn out* **11/2**[2]

2424 **2** *1* **Far Gone**[15] 4274 2-8-12 74 .... HayleyTurner 1 68
(M L W Bell) *led: rdn and hung rt over 1f out: hdd and no ex ins fnl f* **4/5**[1]

0 **3** *2 ½* **East Coast Girl (IRE)**[24] 4028 2-8-12 0 .... TGMcLaughlin 5 61
(J McAuley) *chsd ldrs: chal 2f out: kpt on same pce fnl f* **80/1**

4 *1 ¾* **Excitement (IRE)** 2-8-9 0 .... JamieMoriarty(3) 12 55
(R A Fahey) *t.k.h on wd outside: lost pl over 1f out: styd on wl ins fnl f* **28/1**

5 *nk* **All In The Red (IRE)** 2-9-0 0 .... JerryO'Dwyer(3) 6 59
(Miss Gay Kelleway) *chsd ldrs: kpt on same pce over 1f out* **14/1**

6 *½* **Afton View (IRE)** 2-9-3 0 .... GrahamGibbons 8 58
(D J Murphy) *s.s: hdwy over 2f out: nvr nr to chal* **22/1**

7 *1* **Cealtra Star (IRE)** 2-8-9 0 .... AndrewMullen(3) 9 50
(K A Ryan) *sn drvn along: hdwy over 2f out: kpt on: nvr nr ldrs* **25/1**

8 *nk* **Misterisland (IRE)** 2-9-3 0 .... StephenDonohoe 4 54
(J A Osborne) *sn outpcd and bhd: styd on fnl 2f: nvr nr ldrs* **11/1**[3]

9 *4* **Melwood Dreams** 2-9-3 0 .... FrancisNorton 11 42
(Paul Green) *upset in stalls: sn chsng ldrs: lost pl over 1f out* **66/1**

10 *2* **Master Of Arts (USA)** 2-9-3 0 .... PaulMulrennan 10 36
(Sir Mark Prescott) *s.s: a outpcd and in rr* **14/1**

11 *1 ¾* **Stagecoach Topaz (USA)** 2-9-3 0 .... GregFairley 7 31
(M Johnston) *prom: lost pl over 2f out* **11/2**[2]

1m 17.18s (1.53) **Going Correction** +0.10s/f (Good) **11** Ran SP% **122.4**
Speed ratings (Par 94): **93,91,88,86,85 84,83,83,77,75 72**
CSF £10.27 TOTE £7.70: £2.10, £1.10, £7.70; EX 12.40.
Owner Martin P Graham **Bred** Mrs M L Parry **Trained** Lambourn, Berks

FOCUS
Just an ordinary maiden with the exposed runner-up rated 74. Low numbers prevailed.

NOTEBOOK
Harry Gee, having his third start, stuck to the rail and gained the upper hand inside the last. Nurseries now presumably beckon. (op 8-1)
Far Gone, easily the most experienced in the line-up, had the plum draw. She hung off the fence once in line for home leaving the door ajar for the winner. (op 5-4)
East Coast Girl(IRE) improved a good deal on her debut effort three weeks earlier. (op 100-1 tchd 66-1)
Excitement(IRE), a leggy, rather immature April foal, had the worst of the draw and, taking a tug, her rider had difficulty tucking her in. She made good ground late in the day and this will have taught her plenty. (op 25-1 tchd 22-1)
All In The Red(IRE), a March foal, is a sturdy, well-made type. He showed plenty of toe and should improve for the outing. (tchd 16-1)
Afton View(IRE), an April foal, was coltish and noisy in the paddock. After missing the break he stuck on in the short home straight. He has a lot to learn and will be much better suited by 7f or a mile. (op 16-1)
Cealtra Star(IRE), a May foal, has plenty of size and scope and showed ability on her debut from her outside draw. There should be better to come. (op 20-1 tchd 16-1)
Misterisland(IRE), a late May foal, is on the leg and narrow. He put in some pleasing late work and should be capable of better given a little more time. (op 8-1)

4734 SARTORI MENSWEAR H'CAP 5f 16y
7:10 (7:11) (Class 6) (0-65,66) 3-Y-O+ **£2,730** (£806; £403) **Stalls** Low

Form RPR

2506 **1** **Blessed Place**[4] 4634 7-9-2 **63** .... (t) AshleyHamblett(5) 2 71
(D J S Ffrench Davis) *mde all: kpt on fnl f: jst hld on* **9/2**[2]

261 **2** *shd* **Methaaly (IRE)**[24] 4021 4-9-5 **64** .... LiamJones(3) 1 72
(M Mullineaux) *stmbld sltly s: sn chsng wnr: styd on fnl f: jst hld* **9/4**[1]

0466 **3** *2 ½* **Nusoor (IRE)**[29] 3836 4-9-8 **64** .... (b) GrahamGibbons 12 63
(Peter Grayson) *s.i.s: swtchd lft after s: effrt and n.m.r 2f out: kpt on same pce fnl f* **33/1**

0003 **4** *½* **Hello Roberto**[2] 4689 6-8-6 **53** .... (p) LukeMorris(5) 7 50
(R A Harris) *hmpd s: detached in last: hdwy over 1f out: edgd lft and styd on fnl f* **9/2**[2]

3234 **5** *2 ½* **Silly Gilly (IRE)**[1] 4714 3-9-4 **62** .... FrancisNorton 8 50
(K R Burke) *chsd ldrs: wknd over 1f out* **10/1**[3]

4231 **6** *1 ¼* **Funfair Wane**[8] 4498 8-9-10 **66** 6ex .... AdrianTNicholls 6 49
(D Nicholls) *hmpd s: mid-div: sme hdwy over 1f out: sn wknd* **9/2**[2]

0066 **7** *1 ¼* **Decider (USA)**[4] 4635 4-8-13 **55** .... StephenDonohoe 10 34
(J M Bradley) *in rr: effrt on wd outside over 1f out: hung lft: nvr on terms* **14/1**

5550 **8** *3 ½* **Exponential (IRE)**[17] 4233 5-8-10 **57** .... (b) KevinGhunowa(5) 5 23
(J M Bradley) *wnt rt s: sn chsng ldrs: lost pl over 1f out* **16/1**

0450 **9** *3 ½* **Egyptian Lord**[21] 4101 4-8-12 **54** .... (b) TonyHamilton 3 8+
(Peter Grayson) *in rr: hmpd on inner over 1f out* **12/1**

62.25 secs (0.20) **Going Correction** +0.10s/f (Good)
WFA 3 from 4yo+ 2lb **9** Ran SP% **117.6**
Speed ratings (Par 101): **102,101,97,97,93 91,89,83,77**
CSF £15.34 CT £301.41 TOTE £6.00: £2.00, £1.50, £5.50; EX 19.10.
Owner S J Edwards **Bred** Mrs W H Gibson Fleming **Trained** Lambourn, Berks

FOCUS
The pair drawn one and two dominated and had the finish to themselves. The winner is rated to this year's form.
Decider(USA) Official explanation: jockey said colt hung left

4735 MERCEDES-BENZ OF CHESTER H'CAP 1m 2f 75y
7:40 (7:40) (Class 5) (0-75,75) 3-Y-O **£3,400** (£1,011; £505; £252) **Stalls** High

Form RPR

2531 **1** **Cheshire Prince**[15] 4283 3-8-8 **65** .... LiamJones(3) 6 73+
(W M Brisbourne) *trckd ldrs: wnt 2nd over 3f out: led over 1f out: rdn clr* **4/1**[2]

6003 **2** *5* **Cat De Mille (USA)**[15] 4287 3-9-4 **72** .... AdrianMcCarthy 5 68+
(P W Chapple-Hyam) *hld up in rr: hdwy over 3f out: styd on same pce fnl f* **9/2**[3]

4253 **3** *hd* **Bret Maverick (IRE)**[23] 4036 3-8-2 **56** oh1 .... (p) FrancisNorton 1 52
(B P J Baugh) *reminders after s: led after 1f: hdd 4f out: one pce fnl 2f* **20/1**

0056 **4** *3* **Miss Percy**[20] 4128 3-8-3 **57** .... DaleGibson 10 47
(R A Fahey) *t.k.h in rr: hdwy 4f out: one pce over 1f out* **16/1**

1-25 **5** *½* **Algarade**[57] 2999 3-9-7 **75** .... PaulMulrennan 2 64
(Sir Mark Prescott) *t.k.h: led 1f: trckd ldr: led 4f out: hdd over 1f out: hung rt and sn wknd* **11/10**[1]

0100 **6** *½* **Iceman George**[13] 4365 3-9-1 **69** .... (v[1]) RichardMullen 9 57
(D Morris) *in rr: drvn 6f out: lost pl 3f out: kpt on fnl f* **16/1**

0004 **7** *¾* **Frosty Night (IRE)**[16] 4248 3-9-4 **72** .... GregFairley 7 59
(M Johnston) *chsd ldrs: pushed along 6f out: lost pl over 2f out* **8/1**

-022 **8** *1 ½* **Gifted Heir (IRE)**[14] 4337 3-8-3 **60** .... NeilChalmers(3) 8 44
(A Bailey) *sn trcking ldrs on outer: lost pl over 1f out* **20/1**

2m 14.65s (1.51) **Going Correction** +0.10s/f (Good) **8** Ran SP% **118.2**
Speed ratings (Par 100): **97,93,92,90,90 89,89,87**
CSF £23.22 CT £315.22 TOTE £4.40: £1.40, £1.90, £3.30; EX 26.20.
Owner D C Rutter & H Clewlow **Bred** The National Stud **Trained** Great Ness, Shropshire

FOCUS
No great pace but a ready winner who runs this unique track exceptionally well. Modest form with the favourite flopping.

4736 HARVEY NICHOLS MAIDEN FILLIES' STKS 7f 122y
8:10 (8:11) (Class 5) 3-Y-O+ **£3,071** (£906; £453) **Stalls** Low

Form RPR

5- **1** **Red Blooded Woman (USA)**[344] 5296 3-8-12 0 .... EddieAhern 7 57+
(J Noseda) *led after 1f: shkn up over 1f out: styd on strly: readily* **11/10**[1]

0600 **2** *2* **Briery Blaze**[25] 3996 4-9-4 35 .... GrahamGibbons 4 52
(J W Unett) *in rr: hdwy 3f out: hung lft and wnt 2nd over 1f out: no imp* **50/1**

-006 **3** *3 ½* **Chicamia**[19] 4178 3-8-5 44 .... SophieDoyle(7) 5 43
(M Mullineaux) *s.i.s: hdwy over 3f out: kpt on to take 3rd ins fnl f* **25/1**

0330 **4** *1 ¼* **Slip Star**[16] 4250 4-9-4 53 .... GregFairley 2 40
(T J Etherington) *t.k.h: led 1f: chsd ldrs: one pce fnl 2f* **7/1**[3]

600 **5** *½* **Littlemissdynamite**[31] 3800 4-9-4 45 .... TGMcLaughlin 10 39
(J McAuley) *s.i.s: drvn over 4f out: kpt on: nvr a threat* **33/1**

6 *¾* **Little Red Roaster (USA)**[361] 4856 3-8-12 0 .... StephenDonohoe 1 37
(P D Evans) *in rr: hdwy on wd outside over 1f out: nvr nr ldrs* **14/1**

4 **7** *5* **Johnston's Glory (IRE)**[15] 4290 3-8-5 0 .... GaryBartley(7) 11 24
(E J Alston) *hld up: hdwy over 3f out: wknd fnl f* **8/1**

00 **8** *3* **Lady Johanna (USA)**[27] 3914 3-8-12 0 .... PatCosgrave 8 17
(K R Burke) *sn chsng ldrs: lost pl 3f out* **33/1**

0245 **9** *2 ½* **Wells Of Badr (IRE)**[28] 3872 3-8-12 67 .... AdrianMcCarthy 9 11
(P W Chapple-Hyam) *chsd ldrs: sn drvn along: hung rt and wknd over 1f out* **3/1**[2]

3660 **10** *5* **Musical Chimes**[14] 4336 4-9-1 44 .... LiamJones(3) 6 —
(W M Brisbourne) *chsd ldrs: drvn 4f out: hung rt and lost pl over 1f out* **14/1**

1m 35.6s (0.85) **Going Correction** +0.10s/f (Good)
WFA 3 from 4yo+ 6lb **10** Ran SP% **121.3**
Speed ratings (Par 100): **99,97,93,92,91 91,86,83,80,75**
CSF £91.36 TOTE £2.00: £1.10, £10.70, £5.90; EX 98.70 Place 6 £201.55, Place 5 £20.03.
Owner Nicholas Cooper **Bred** D Brosnan **Trained** Newmarket, Suffolk

FOCUS
A very weak maiden with the runner-up rated just 35, but the unexposed winner has plenty of potential. It has been rated through the third.
Wells Of Badr(IRE) Official explanation: jockey said filly was never travelling and hung right
Musical Chimes Official explanation: jockey said filly hung throughout
T/Plt: £268.90 to a £1 stake. Pool: £58,400.65. 158.50 winning tickets. T/Qpdt: £13.20 to a £1 stake. Pool: £5,916.10. 330.70 winning tickets. WG

4591 LINGFIELD (L-H)
Thursday, August 23

OFFICIAL GOING: Standard
Wind: Light, against Weather: Overcast

4737 LINGFIELDPARK.CO.UK NURSERY 5f (P)
2:25 (2:25) (Class 6) 2-Y-O **£2,184** (£644; £322) **Stalls** High

Form RPR

0203 **1** **Perfect Paula (USA)**[6] 4573 2-9-7 **82** .... DaneO'Neill 6 84
(B J Meehan) *mde all and sn 2l clr: looked wl in command 1f out: tired and jst hld on* **1/1**[1]

015 **2** *hd* **Attribution**[14] 4315 2-8-4 **65** .... DavidKinsella 7 66
(A B Haynes) *racd on outer in rr: prog over 2f out: drvn and no imp tl r.o to take 2nd last 75yds: clsng fast at fin* **25/1**

0600 **3** *hd* **Evenstorm (USA)**[19] 4152 2-8-1 **62** .... FrankieMcDonald 10 62
(B Gubby) *prom: rdn and no imp on ldng pair over 2f out: styd on wl fnl f: jst hld* **40/1**

321 **4** *1* **Zippi Jazzman (USA)**[24] 4020 2-9-3 **78** .... (b[1]) SebSanders 3 75
(R M Beckett) *chsd wnr: clr of rest after 2f: drvn and no imp 2f out: hanging bdly lft and lost 2nd last 75yds* **2/1**[2]

3100 **5** ½ **Jennifers Joy (IRE)**[21] 4098 2-9-3 78 SamHitchcott 2 73
(M R Channon) *sn rdn and struggling to go the pce: no prog tl styd on fnl f: n.d* **14/1**
4060 **6** nk **Maybe I Wont**[7] 4537 2-8-10 71 NickyMackay 8 65
(S Dow) *chsd ldng pair: drvn and no imp fr 1/2-way: kpt on fnl f* **14/1**
206 **7** hd **Flying Indian**[43] 3426 2-8-4 65 MartinDwyer 5 58
(A M Balding) *sn outpcd in rr: kpt on fr over 1f out: n.d* **10/1**[3]
4313 **8** 2 **Lord Deevert**[13] 4358 2-8-6 74 JackDean(7) 1 60
(W G M Turner) *dwlt: rdn in midfield on inner 1/2-way: no prog* **25/1**
642 **9** hd **Splash The Cash**[19] 4160 2-8-10 71 StephenCarson 4 56
(P Winkworth) *dwlt: a in rr: rdn and struggling fr 1/2-way* **14/1**
5030 **10** 11 **Structura (USA)**[14] 4310 2-8-2 68 TolleyDean(5) 9 14
(J S Moore) *lft abt 15 l s: a t.o* **25/1**

59.11 secs (-0.67) **Going Correction** -0.225s/f (Stan) **10** Ran SP% **126.4**
Speed ratings (Par 92): **96,95,95,93,92 92,92,88,88,71**
CSF £40.61 CT £737.79 TOTE £1.80: £1.40, £8.30, £8.40; EX 43.90 Trifecta £266.50 Part won. Pool: £375.48 - 0.30 winning tickets..
Owner Gold Group International Ltd **Bred** Marablue Farm Llc **Trained** Manton, Wilts

FOCUS
This looked an uncompetitive nursery beforehand, with two of the ten-strong field totally dominating the market and the favourite officially 17lb well-in, but that's not how it turned out. Solid, if modest form.

NOTEBOOK
Perfect Paula(USA) won with very little in hand and did little to justify the 17lb rise in the handicap that awaits following her recent third in a Listed contest at Newbury. Sent to the front soon after leaving the stalls, she set a good clip from the outset and had most of these in trouble on the home bend, but she began to tire inside the final furlong and was being closed down all the way to the line. That said, one felt Dane O'Neill was confident the line would come in time. On the bare form of this success, she is going to struggle off her mark but, as her connections pointed out afterwards, she was entitled to need this experience having never previous raced on Polytrack. She is likely to be returned to Listed company in search of some more black type. (op 13-8)
Attribution, picked up out of Karl Burke's yard after winning a seller, was reported to have become unbalanced when fifth on his nursery debut at Brighton last time and this was a better performance. He is not very big, but should remain competitive off light weights in nursery company. (op 20-1)
Evenstorm(USA) has shown bits and pieces of reasonable form and this was a decent effort in defeat. She could find a small race before the season is out.
Zippi Jazzman(USA), fitted with blinkers for the first time, looked the one most likely to give the favourite a race beforehand, but he ruined his chance by hanging badly left under pressure in the straight. He had not been at his best despite winning at Wolverhampton on his previous start and looks best watched for the time being. Official explanation: jockey said colt hung left (op 7-4)
Jennifers Joy(IRE) had not progressed in a couple of runs since winning her maiden at Warwick earlier in the season, but this was a respectable effort. (op 12-1)
Maybe I Wont did not run badly, but does not seem to be progressing.
Structura(USA) Official explanation: jockey said filly missed the break

4738 PHOENIX GLOBAL MARKETING MAIDEN FILLIES' STKS 1m 4f (P)
3:00 (3:00) (Class 5) 3-Y-0+ **£2,849** (£847; £423; £211) **Stalls** Low

Form RPR
0442 **1** **Atayeb (USA)**[15] 4277 3-8-12 69 MartinDwyer 8 57
(M P Tregoning) *hld up in tch: pushed along over 3f out: rdn to chse ldr over 2f out: no imp tl styd on to ld last 50yds* **2/1**[2]
-244 **2** ½ **Thinking Positive**[15] 4277 3-8-12 74 RobertHavlin 4 57
(J H M Gosden) *trckd ldng pair: led gng easily over 3f out: rdn over 1f out: worn down last 50yds* **4/6**[1]
025 **3** 8 **Sadler's Leap (IRE)**[49] 3236 4-9-8 65 DaneO'Neill 5 44
(Pat Eddery) *hld up in tch: rdn over 3f out: outpcd over 2f out: plugged on to take modest 3rd last 150yds* **12/1**
-620 **4** 2½ **Tafiya**[10] 4458 4-9-8 66 JamesDoyle 1 40
(J W Hills) *led for 1f: led again briefly wl over 3f out: chsd ldr to over 2f out: easily outpcd after* **8/1**[3]
0000 **5** 1¾ **Sterling Moll**[75] 2471 4-9-5 40 DominicFox(3) 3 37
(W De Best-Turner) *s.s: detached in last: rdn over 4f out: sn outpcd* **80/1**
00 **6** 11 **Kitebrook**[4] 4630 6-9-8 0 VinceSlattery 7 19
(Mrs Mary Hambro) *led after 1f to wl over 3f out: sn wknd and bhd* **66/1**
0 **7** 32 **Elegans**[136] 977 3-8-12 0 DMylonas 2 —
(Mrs C A Dunnett) *t.k.h early: in tch tl wknd over 4f out: t.o* **66/1**

2m 30.78s (-3.61) **Going Correction** -0.225s/f (Stan)
WFA 3 from 4yo+ 10lb **7** Ran SP% **116.3**
Speed ratings (Par 100): **103,102,97,95,94 87,65**
CSF £3.79 TOTE £3.10: £1.30, £1.30; EX 5.00 Trifecta £13.50 Pool: £594.39 - 31.17 winning tickets..
Owner Hamdan Al Maktoum **Bred** Shadwell Farm LLC **Trained** Lambourn, Berks

FOCUS
Only four of these could have been seriously considered beforehand and this was a weak fillies' maiden. The winning time was nearly five seconds quicker than the following 46-60 handicap, but they crawled in that race and it would be unwise to compare the two times. The fifth holds down the form.

4739 DIGITAL LOOK H'CAP 1m 4f (P)
3:35 (3:35) (Class 6) (0-60,60) 3-Y-0+ **£1,414** (£1,414; £322) **Stalls** Low

Form RPR
0102 **1** **Takes Tutu (USA)**[5] 4592 8-9-4 54 (p) AdamKirby 8 59
(C R Dore) *cl up: effrt over 2f out: jnd ldr 1f out: styd on wl* **4/1**[3]
0441 **1** dht **Majehar**[26] 3946 5-9-7 60 TravisBlock(3) 9 65
(A G Newcombe) *trckd ldrs on outer: effrt to chal 2f out: narrow ld over 1f out: sn jnd: styd on wl* **9/4**[1]
0610 **3** shd **Zalkani (IRE)**[152] 767 7-9-9 59 GeorgeBaker 2 64
(J Pearce) *hld up in midfield: nt clr run on inner briefly over 2f out: prog over 1f out: chal fnl f: jst failed* **7/2**[2]
0636 **4** ¾ **Blackmail (USA)**[14] 4318 9-9-5 55 (b) SebSanders 5 59
(P Mitchell) *trckd ldr after 2f: led 3f out and sed dash for home: narrowly hdd over 1f out: nt qckn fnl f* **5/1**
4000 **5** nk **Sopran Gath (ITY)**[14] 4321 4-9-9 59 JamesDoyle 7 62
(J W Hills) *hld up in last trio in slowly run r: prog 2f out to chse ldrs over 1f out: hanging and nt qckn: styd on ins fnl f* **14/1**
0-00 **6** 1½ **Ground Patrol**[26] 3946 6-8-13 56 JackDean(7) 10 57
(W G M Turner) *dwlt: plld hrd: hld up in midfield: effrt to chse ldrs over 1f out: no imp: fading nr fin* **12/1**
6600 **7** 6 **Oasis Sun (IRE)**[7] 4533 4-8-11 47 (v) DaneO'Neill 4 38
(J R Best) *dwlt: hld up in rr in slowly run r: prog on outer over 2f out: outpcd off bnd sn after: no ch over 1f out* **16/1**
0600 **8** ½ **Mid Valley**[48] 3286 4-8-11 47 PaulDoe 11 37
(J R Jenkins) *t.k.h: hld up in last in slowly run r: prog on wd outside 3f out: lost grnd bnd 2f out: no ch after* **25/1**
0550 **9** hd **Fuel Cell (IRE)**[13] 2027 6-9-0 50 VHalliday 3 40
(J O'Reilly) *towards rr: outpcd in last 3f out: n.d after* **16/1**
5064 **10** nk **Kilmeena Magic**[28] 3868 5-8-10 46 oh1 MartinDwyer 6 36
(J C Fox) *led at slow pce to 3f out: losing pl whn hmpd on inner over 2f out* **16/1**
0000 **11** nk **Royal Tender (IRE)**[7] 4534 3-8-1 50 EmmettStack(3) 1 39
(B G Powell) *rel to r: sn in ldng trio: lost pl qckly over 2f out* **33/1**

2m 35.16s (0.77) **Going Correction** -0.225s/f (Stan)
WFA 3 from 4yo+ 10lb **11** Ran SP% **128.5**
Speed ratings (Par 101): **88,88,87,87,87 86,82,81,81,81 81**WIN: Majehar £1.70, Takes Tutu £2.50. PL: M £1.80, TT £1.30, Zalkani £2.30. EX: M/TT £10.00, TT/M £8.20. CSF: M/TT £6.23, TT/M £7.40. TRIC: M/TT/Z £16.81, TT/M/Z £18.67. TRIF: M/TT/Z £17.70 - 5.98 w/u, TT/M/Z £24.70 - 4.30 w/u. Pool: £229.67. 27 Trifecta £0Owner J R Salter Bred.
Owner Page, Ward, Marsh **Bred** Harbor View Farm **Trained** West Pinchbeck, Lincs
■ Stewards' Enquiry : Emmett Stack one-day ban: used whip when out of contention (Sep 3)

FOCUS
They went a very steady pace for much of the way in what was a modest middle-distance handicap, resulting in a dead-heat and a bunch finish, and the form wants treating with real caution. The winning time was almost five seconds slower than the earlier fillies' maiden run over the same trip.
Kilmeena Magic Official explanation: jockey said mare hung right on final bend

4740 ANN CADLE MEMORIAL H'CAP 6f (P)
4:10 (4:11) (Class 5) (0-70,73) 3-Y-0 **£3,238** (£963; £481; £240) **Stalls** Low

Form RPR
0201 **1** **Day By Day**[8] 4514 3-9-2 65 6ex (b) RobertHavlin 7 70
(B J Meehan) *w ldrs: led 1/2-way: kicked 2 l clr wl over 1f out: drvn and hld on* **10/1**
4100 **2** ½ **Chattan Clan**[43] 3420 3-9-7 70 (t) FergusSweeney 10 73
(R A Kvisla) *wl plcd: rdn to chse wnr 2f out: clsd grad fnl f: a hld* **50/1**
0-10 **3** nk **Maysarah (IRE)**[45] 3369 3-9-3 66 NickyMackay 11 68+
(G A Butler) *dwlt: hld up in last: prog over 2f out: chsd ldrs over 1f out: styd on fnl f: nrst fin* **14/1**
-040 **4** nk **Hucking Hill (IRE)**[17] 4236 3-9-7 70 (b) GeorgeBaker 8 71
(J R Best) *hld up in midfield: prog over 2f out: chsd ldrs over 1f out: kpt on same pce: nvr able to chal* **9/1**
4021 **5** ¾ **Topflightcoolracer**[11] 4432 3-9-10 73 6ex SebSanders 4 72
(Mrs G S Rees) *dwlt: in tch: trckd ldrs over 2f out: swtchd to inner wl over 1f out: one pce and no imp on ldrs last 150yds* **11/4**[1]
0010 **6** ½ **All You Need (IRE)**[14] 4330 3-9-0 68 RussellKennemore(5) 9 65+
(R Hollinshead) *hld up in rr: gng strly 1/2-way: nt clr run briefly over 2f out: prog over 1f out: kpt on: nvr rchd ldrs* **4/1**[2]
2126 **7** ½ **Riverside Dancer (USA)**[14] 4326 3-8-13 69 HarryPoulton(7) 2 64
(G A Huffer) *rrd bdly s: in tch in rr: effrt on inner 2f out: chsd ldrs over 1f out: nt qckn after* **8/1**
-020 **8** nk **Lay The Cash (USA)**[14] 4326 3-8-13 62 (b) LPKeniry 3 57
(J S Moore) *led: drvn over 3f out: sn hdd: styd chsng ldrs u.p: fdd fnl f* **14/1**
-405 **9** 4 **Fluttering Rose**[15] 4269 3-9-1 64 MartinDwyer 6 46
(R M Beckett) *trckd ldrs: rdn over 2f out: sn lost pl: n.d over 1f out* **11/1**
2202 **10** 2 **The Jay Factor (IRE)**[17] 4236 3-9-4 67 (p) DaneO'Neill 12 42
(Pat Eddery) *a in rr on outer: rdn 1/2-way: struggling and reluctant fnl 2f* **6/1**[3]
31-0 **11** 2 **Juncea**[42] 3466 3-9-4 70 TravisBlock(3) 5 39
(H Morrison) *w ldrs: rdn over 2f out: sn lost pl: wknd rapidly over 1f out* **12/1**
1200 **12** 1¾ **Nashharry (IRE)**[19] 4163 3-8-13 62 JamesDoyle 1 25
(S Kirk) *chsd ldrs 2f: drvn and lost pl rapidly 1/2-way* **25/1**

1m 11.32s (-1.49) **Going Correction** -0.225s/f (Stan) **12** Ran SP% **126.3**
Speed ratings (Par 100): **100,99,98,98,97 96,96,95,90,87 85,82**
CSF £434.83 CT £6860.67 TOTE £13.00: £3.80, £13.80, £5.70; EX 651.00 TRIFECTA Not won..
Owner T G & Mrs M E Holdcroft **Bred** Bearstone Stud & T Herbert Jackson **Trained** Manton, Wilts

FOCUS
Just a modest three-year-old sprint handicap, but competitive enough for the level, with all bar one of the 12 runners coming into this with at least one win to their name. The first two were always up with the pace. The winning time was 1.08 seconds quicker than the following 0-45 contest.
Hucking Hill(IRE) Official explanation: jockey said gelding hung left

4741 BOOK ONLINE FOR DISCOUNTED PRICES CLASSIFIED STKS 6f (P)
4:45 (4:45) (Class 7) 3-Y-0+ **£2,047** (£604; £302) **Stalls** Low

Form RPR
06U0 **1** **Double Valentine**[9] 4471 4-8-8 45 HarryPoulton(7) 6 51
(R Ingram) *dwlt: last tl over 2f out: rdn and prog after: styd on wl u.p to ld last 100yds* **8/1**
0000 **2** ½ **Miss Mujahid Times**[30] 3814 4-9-1 45 (p) AdamKirby 4 50
(A D Brown) *pressed ldr: led 1/2-way: drvn and edgd rt over 1f out: hdd last 100yds: kpt on* **10/1**
5403 **3** ½ **A Teen**[52] 3163 9-9-1 45 IanMongan 7 48
(P Howling) *in tch: prog and rdn over 2f out: chsng ldrs but nt qckn over 1f out: styd on ins fnl f* **7/1**
4004 **4** 1¼ **Beverley Beau**[13] 4351 5-8-8 45 KristinStubbs(7) 5 44
(Mrs L Stubbs) *chsd ldrs: shovelled along fr 1/2-way: stl in tch over 1f out: one pce* **6/1**[3]
0050 **5** nk **Compton Special**[17] 4224 3-8-12 45 TPQueally 8 43
(J G Given) *awkward s: sn prom: pressed ldr wl over 2f out: rdn to chal over 1f out: fnd nil* **7/2**[2]
600 **6** 1 **Simpleton**[84] 2173 4-9-1 45 DaneO'Neill 2 40
(J R Best) *chsd ldrs: lost pl and rdn 1/2-way: nt clr run over 2f out: one pce after* **12/1**
000 **7** 1¼ **Perry's Pride**[27] 3924 3-8-12 45 SebSanders 9 36
(Mrs G S Rees) *racd wd: prog and cl up 1/2-way: lost grnd bnd 2f out: n.d after* **12/1**
-060 **8** ¾ **Von Wessex**[9] 4471 5-8-8 45 JackDean(7) 10 33
(W G M Turner) *rdn after 2f: a struggling in rr* **16/1**
006 **9** 5 **Julatten (IRE)**[13] 4361 3-8-12 45 MartinDwyer 3 17
(D J Murphy) *led to 1/2-way: lost pl rapidly* **2/1**[1]

1m 12.4s (-0.41) **Going Correction** -0.225s/f (Stan)
WFA 3 from 4yo+ 3lb **9** Ran SP% **123.8**
Speed ratings (Par 97): **93,92,91,90,89 88,86,85,78**
CSF £90.46 TOTE £11.20: £2.30, £3.40, £2.30; EX 95.10 Trifecta £201.00 Pool: £379.39 - 1.34 winning tickets..
Owner Ellangowan Racing Partners **Bred** Ellangowan Racing Partners **Trained** Epsom, Surrey

FOCUS
A classified event restricted to horses rated 45 or lower, so the form is obviously pretty moderate. The winning time was 1.08 seconds slower than the previous handicap.
Miss Mujahid Times Official explanation: jockey said filly hung right

Julatten(IRE) Official explanation: jockey was unable to offer any explanation for the poor form shown

4742 LINGFIELD PARK FOR WEDDINGS H'CAP — 1m 2f (P)
5:20 (5:21) (Class 6) (0-60,66) 3-Y-O — £2,184 (£644; £322) Stalls Low

Form — RPR

034 **1** **Blue Space**[12] 4392 3-9-4 60 .... SebSanders 10 67+
(P J Makin) *prom: led over 2f out and rdn clr: drvn fnl f: unchal* **15/8**[1]

0401 **2** *1 1/4* **Kindlelight Blue (IRE)**[5] 4592 3-9-5 66 6ex .... PatrickHills[(5)] 3 68
(N P Littmoden) *dwlt: t.k.h and midfield after 4f: prog 3f out: rdn and nt qckn over 2f out: kpt on fnl f to take 2nd last stride* **15/8**[1]

5-0 **3** *shd* **Antrim Rose**[14] 4327 3-9-3 59 .... LPKeniry 2 61
(E F Vaughan) *hld up in midfield: prog over 3f out: drvn to chse wnr over 1f out: no real imp: lost 2nd last stride* **14/1**[3]

1060 **4** *3* **Polyquest (IRE)**[41] 3502 3-9-0 56 .... NickyMackay 13 52+
(G A Butler) *hld up in last trio: sme prog over 3f out but sn drvn: r.o to take 4th fnl f: no ch* **8/1**[2]

3003 **5** *hd* **Picky**[8] 4516 3-8-11 53 .... (v) FergusSweeney 11 49
(C Tinkler) *led for 2f: rdn to ld again over 3f out to over 2f out: wknd fnl f* **16/1**

0-60 **6** *1 3/4* **Danehill Silver**[52] 3159 3-9-4 60 .... DaneO'Neill 4 52
(R Hollinshead) *settled in midfield: outpcd over 2f out: rdn and no prog after* **33/1**

0000 **7** *1/2* **Heights Of Golan**[37] 3620 3-9-0 56 .... (p) JamesDoyle 7 47
(I A Wood) *awkward to post: hld up bhd ldrs: cl enough 3f out: nt qckn over 2f out: fdd* **16/1**

2000 **8** *3* **Time For Change (IRE)**[17] 4231 3-9-2 58 .... RobertHavlin 14 43
(P G Murphy) *hld up: last tl over 3f out: nudged along and nvr nr ldrs* **40/1**

3000 **9** *2 1/2* **Josr's Magic (IRE)**[12] 4397 3-8-8 57 .... JCorrigan[(7)] 12 37
(S W Hall) *led after 2f and set gd pce: hdd over 3f out: wknd 2f out* **50/1**

-520 **10** *1* **Scar Tissue**[18] 4205 3-8-9 51 .... MartinDwyer 6 29
(E J Creighton) *sn restrained bhd ldrs: rdn 3f out: sn outpcd and btn* **8/1**[2]

-033 **11** *1* **Mister Always**[17] 4224 3-8-9 51 ow1 .... AdamKirby 9 27
(B P J Baugh) *hld up in last trio: sme prog over 3f out but sn rdn: outpcd over 2f out: no ch after* **20/1**

6000 **12** *5* **Brean Dot Com (IRE)**[8] 4504 3-8-8 50 .... SamHitchcott 1 16
(Mrs P N Dutfield) *pushed along towards rr 6f out: struggling fr 4f out* **33/1**

000 **13** *nk* **My Spring Rose**[45] 3387 3-9-1 57 .... StephenCarson 5 23
(J R Jenkins) *a towards rr: struggling over 3f out: sn no ch* **40/1**

0040 **14** *18* **Bertrada (IRE)**[7] 4533 3-8-1 50 .... JemmaMarshall[(7)] 8 —
(G P Enright) *racd wd in midfield: dropped to last over 3f out: t.o* **66/1**

2m 4.69s (-3.10) **Going Correction** -0.225s/f (Stan) **14** Ran SP% **129.2**
Speed ratings (Par 98): **103,102,101,99,99 97,97,95,93,92 91,87,87,72**
CSF £4.81 CT £41.81 TOTE £2.40: £1.70, £1.30, £4.30; EX 7.50 Trifecta £11.70 Pool: £192.95 - 11.69 winning tickets. Place 6 £206.51, Place 5 £97.53.
Owner Dr John Wilson and Partners **Bred** Ashley House Stud **Trained** Ogbourne Maisey, Wilts

FOCUS
Just a moderate middle-distance handicap for three-year-olds, but the pace was fair and the proximity of recent course-and-distance winner Kindlelight Blue helps give the form a solid look.
Kindlelight Blue(IRE) Official explanation: jockey said gelding hung left
Danehill Silver Official explanation: jockey said gelding hung left
Josr's Magic(IRE) Official explanation: vet said gelding was lame
Mister Always Official explanation: jockey said gelding did not stay
Brean Dot Com(IRE) Official explanation: jockey said gelding was never travelling
T/Plt: £100.50 to a £1 stake. Pool: £39,692.50. 288.30 winning tickets. T/Qpdt: £44.10 to a £1 stake. Pool: £2,260.20. 37.90 winning tickets. JN

4720 YORK (L-H)
Thursday, August 23

OFFICIAL GOING: Good (good to firm in places in home straight, good to soft in places in back straight; 7.7)
Wind: Slight, against Weather: Sunny

4743 £300000 ST LEGER YEARLING STKS — 6f
1:35 (1:36) (Class 2) 2-Y-O
£187,691 (£75,076; £37,538; £18,750; £9,375; £9,375) Stalls High

Form — RPR

2104 **1** **Dark Angel (IRE)**[42] 3459 2-8-11 91 .... MichaelHills 2 99+
(B W Hills) *trckd ldrs in centre: hdwy to ld 2f out: rdn over 1f out: styd on* **3/1**[1]

2102 **2** *1* **Gypsy Baby (IRE)**[12] 4372 2-8-7 83 ow1 .... RichardHughes 11 92
(R Hannon) *lw: hld up in midfield: hdwy 2f out: swtchd rt and rdn ent fnl f: styd on wl towards fin* **11/1**

1151 **3** *1/2* **Cosmic Art**[11] 4431 2-8-11 0 .... KerrinMcEvoy 6 95
(E A L Dunlop) *a.p in centre: rdn 2f out: drvn and kpt on ins fnl f* **14/1**

341 **4** *1/2* **Berbice (IRE)**[69] 2624 2-8-11 90 .... RyanMoore 7 93
(R Hannon) *lw: chsd ldrs: rdn along 2f out: drvn over 1f out: kpt on u.p ins fnl f* **8/1**[3]

1103 **5** *shd* **Mister Hardy**[26] 3938 2-8-11 88 .... TonyHamilton 1 93
(R A Fahey) *in tch in centre: hdwy to chse ldrs 2f out: sn rdn and kpt on same pce ent fnl f* **28/1**

024 **6** *1/2* **Mymumsaysimthebest**[21] 4110 2-8-11 0 .... JimmyFortune 3 91
(R Hannon) *a.p in centre: effrt 2f out: sn rdn and ev ch tl drvn and wknd ent fnl f* **66/1**

611 **7** *hd* **Johar Jamal (IRE)**[19] 4168 2-8-6 77 .... TPO'Shea 5 86
(M R Channon) *lw: in tch in centre: hdwy to chse ldrs wl over 1f out: sn rdn and kpt on same pce ent fnl f* **6/1**[2]

7 *dht* **Dedo (IRE)**[18] 4207 2-8-11 0 .... DPMcDonogh 15 91
(Kevin Prendergast, Ire) *w'like: chsd ldrs in centre: rdn along 2f out: drvn over 1f out and kpt on same pce* **9/1**

4216 **9** *3/4* **Mazzanti**[27] 3910 2-8-11 84 .... FrancisNorton 12 89+
(K A Ryan) *towards rr: stmbld and bhd after 1f: hdwy wl over 1f out: sn rdn and styd on ins fnl f: nrst fin* **100/1**

2131 **10** *nk* **Pelican Prince**[40] 3524 2-8-11 79 .... PatCosgrave 17 87
(K R Burke) *in tch towards stands' rail: rdn along and hdwy 2f out: styd on same pce u.p fnl f* **66/1**

1025 **11** *nk* **Russian Reel**[18] 4193 2-8-11 85 .... DarryllHolland 20 87
(K A Ryan) *towards rr: hdwy nr stands' rail 2f out: sn rdn and edgd rt: kpt on same pce u.p ins fnl f* **100/1**

12 **12** *1/2* **Philario (IRE)**[27] 3910 2-8-11 0 .... PhillipMakin 19 85
(K R Burke) *lw: chsd ldrs towards stands' rail: rdn along 2f out: grad wknd* **11/1**

332 **13** *1* **Quest For Success (IRE)**[12] 4378 2-8-11 0 .... PaulHanagan 13 82
(R A Fahey) *towards rr: hdwy 2f out: sn rdn and no imp appr fnl f* **25/1**

115 **14** *nk* **Drawnfromthepast (IRE)**[20] 4120 2-9-2 99 .... JamieSpencer 18 86
(J A Osborne) *wnt lft s: hld up and bhd: sme hdwy nr stands' rail whn nt clr run over 1f out: nvr a factor* **9/1**

1426 **15** *hd* **New Jersey (IRE)**[32] 3779 2-8-11 90 .... NCallan 4 81
(K A Ryan) *chsd ldrs in centre: rdn along 2f out and sn wknd* **18/1**

4123 **16** *3/4* **Nine Stories (IRE)**[8] 4495 2-8-11 82 .... PaulMulrennan 10 78
(J Howard Johnson) *dwlt: a in rr* **100/1**

014 **17** *3/4* **Grylls (USA)**[54] 3077 2-8-11 83 .... PatDobbs 16 76
(R Hannon) *t.k.h: hld up in rr towards stands' rail: pushed along wl over 2f out and nvr a factor* **50/1**

411 **18** *1* **Apollo Shark (IRE)**[45] 3373 2-8-11 75 .... TomEaves 14 73
(J Howard Johnson) *chsd ldrs: rdn along over 2f out: grad wknd* **50/1**

1630 **19** *4* **Cee Bargara**[20] 4120 2-8-11 102 .... (b[1]) JimCrowley 9 61
(J A Osborne) *led centre gp and sn clr: rdn along and hdd 2f out: hung rt and wknd qckly* **14/1**

2200 **20** *5* **Fast Feet**[19] 4175 2-8-11 89 .... TedDurcan 8 46
(K A Ryan) *chsd ldrs in centre: rdn along 2f out and sn wknd* **80/1**

1m 12.37s (-0.19) **Going Correction** +0.05s/f (Good) **20** Ran SP% **124.1**
Speed ratings (Par 100): **103,101,101,100,100 99,99,99,98,97 97,96,95,95,94 93,92,91,86,79**
CSF £34.43 TOTE £3.60: £1.80, £4.20, £5.10; EX 48.40 Trifecta £693.20 Pool: £1,366.90 - 1.40 winning tickets..
Owner The Hon Mrs J M Corbett & C Wright **Bred** Yeomanstown Stud **Trained** Lambourn, Berks
■ This was the most valuable two-year-old race in Britain this season.

FOCUS
A very competitive contest, though a fair range of abilities, with 23lb covering the 20 runners on official ratings. The field raced centre to stands' side, which is where the stalls were, but those that came down the middle had the edge. There was never going to be any hanging around in this and the winning time was 0.25 seconds faster than the Lowther. The winner was 6lb off his best but otherwise the form looks pretty solid.

NOTEBOOK
Dark Angel(IRE), on his toes beforehand, had upwards of 5lb in hand of his rivals on adjusted official ratings mainly thanks to his fourth behind Winker Watson in the July Stakes, but he still had some ground to make up on Drawnfromthepast on Windsor Castle running on 5lb better terms. The extra furlong was very much to his advantage, however, and after getting a lovely tow from Cee Bargara down the middle track the race was his as soon as that one faded and he was asked to go and win his race. This was a wonderful prize to win, but a victory in Pattern company would be even better and he looks capable of that. (op 11-4 tchd 7-2)
Gypsy Baby(IRE), carrying 1lb overweight but nonetheless well supported in the market, was dropping back in trip after four runs over 7f and there was always the danger that she would find herself with too much to do. That is how it turned out, and despite a withering late run which saw her carve her way through several rivals, she was never a threat to the favourite. She has already been found out in Listed company and been beaten in a nursery, but on this evidence she is surely capable of winning a nice prize or two back over further. (op 16-1)
Cosmic Art, a three-time winner on Polytrack but unplaced in both previous tries on turf, was never far away in the middle of the course and kept going all the way to the line to net his connections a nice prize for finishing third. This shows that he can go on grass when the going is not too quick. (op 16-1)
Berbice(IRE), long odds-on when winning a weak Goodwood maiden last time that has not really worked out, had shown that he possessed a touch of class prior to that when fourth in the Woodcote. Never too far off the pace, he kept on going right to the line to show that there are more races to be won with him.
Mister Hardy was suited by the rapid pace, as it gave him less of a reason to pull, and he emerged from this with a lot of credit. He has not had that much racing since winning the Brocklesby and with this ability to handle soft ground proven, should be able to find another opportunity during the autumn.
Mymumsaysimthebest was worst in at the weights on official ratings, but he dispelled that with a cracking effort and was right on the shoulder of the winner until the last furlong. He surely cannot remain a maiden for much longer, but the Handicapper would be entitled to raise him for this so he could be interesting if turned out fairly quickly in a nursery off his current mark of 82.
Dedo(IRE), an Irish challenger bidding for a hat-trick, ran with credit but may have been better suited by softer ground. (tchd 5-1, 13-2 in a place)
Johar Jamal(IRE), another bidding for a hat-trick, could never land a blow but probably ran up to her best. (tchd 5-1, 13-2 in a place)
Drawnfromthepast(IRE), conceding weight to all his rivals due to his 5lb penalty for winning the Windsor Castle, was held up towards the stands' side from his high draw whilst the main action was taking place down the centre. Trying to stay on when switched to the stands' rail, he soon found his path blocked by the hanging Russian Reel and the position was accepted. It would be pushing things to say he would have got into the frame, but he would have finished much closer than this. (op 8-1)
New Jersey(IRE) was very much on his toes beforehand. (op 25-1)
Cee Bargara basically bolted in the first-time blinkers and merely succeeded in running himself into the ground.

4744 JAGUAR CARS LOWTHER STKS (GROUP 2) (FILLIES) — 6f
2:05 (2:06) (Class 1) 2-Y-O — £50,379 (£19,048; £9,520; £4,760) Stalls High

Form — RPR

03 **1** **Nahoodh (IRE)**[27] 3895 2-8-12 0 .... JamieSpencer 4 106
(M R Channon) *lw: scope: hld up in rr: swtchd wd and gd hdwy 2f out: rdn to ld 1f out: hung lft ins fnl f: kpt on* **15/2**

21 **2** *1/2* **Visit**[25] 3988 2-8-12 0 .... RyanMoore 5 105
(Sir Michael Stoute) *lw: trckd ldrs: effrt and n.m.r 2f out: rdn over 1f out: kpt on ins fnl f* **6/4**[1]

11 **3** *3/4* **Fleeting Spirit (IRE)**[23] 4046 2-8-12 0 .... JMurtagh 6 102
(J Noseda) *cl: led over 2f out: rdn and hdd 1f out: sn drvn and kpt on same pce* **11/4**[2]

213 **4** *shd* **Unilateral (IRE)**[17] 4225 2-8-12 78 .... PaulEddery 9 102
(B Smart) *hld up in rr: swtchd lft over 2f out: rdn wl over 1f out: styd on ins fnl f* **100/1**

102 **5** *nk* **Festoso (IRE)**[43] 3432 2-8-12 103 .... PhilipRobinson 3 101
(H J L Dunlop) *trckd ldrs: hdwy on outer 2f out and sn ev ch: rdn over 1f out and one pce ins fnl f* **20/1**

21 **6** *1 1/4* **Fashion Rocks (IRE)**[22] 4061 2-8-12 0 .... JimmyFortune 7 97
(B J Meehan) *lw: cl up: rdn along whn n.m.r and hmpd 2f out: one pce after* **16/1**

2245 **7** *nk* **Romantic Destiny**[14] 4329 2-8-12 75 .... (b[1]) FrancisNorton 1 96
(K A Ryan) *lw: led: rdn along and hdd over 2f out: sn edgd lft: drvn and wknd over 1f out* **150/1**

020 **8** *1/2* **Thought Is Free**[43] 3432 2-8-12 92 .... JohnEgan 10 95
(J S Moore) *hld up: hdwy 2f out: sn rdn and no imp* **100/1**

2121 **9** *4* **You'resothrilling (USA)**[43] 3432 2-9-1 0 .... MJKinane 8 86
(A P O'Brien, Ire) *lw: prom on inner: rdn along and hld whn hmpd 2f out: bhd after* **7/2**[3]

35 **10** *1 1/4* **Honky Tonk Sally**[41] 3507 2-8-12 0 NCallan 2 79
(M L W Bell) *t.k.h: chsd ldrs: rdn along over 2f out and sn wknd* **50/1**

1m 12.62s (0.06) **Going Correction** +0.05s/f (Good) **10** Ran SP% **115.9**

Speed ratings (Par 103): **101,100,99,99,98 97,96,96,90,89**

CSF £18.91 TOTE £9.70: £2.20, £1.30, £1.40; EX 25.50 Trifecta £57.80 Pool: £1,515.68 - 18.59 winning tickets..

Owner Jaber Abdullah **Bred** Petra Bloodstock Agency Ltd **Trained** West Ilsley, Berks

FOCUS

A decent renewal of what is always one of the major juvenile fillies' races, although the time was unexceptional, being a quarter of a second slower than the preceding sales race. Improvement from Nahoodh, but Visit and Fleeting Spirit were a little off their best and You'resothrilling was well below her Newmarket form. N.B: Visit subs. tested positive for ACP and may be disqualified.

NOTEBOOK

Nahoodh(IRE) ◆ came into this a maiden having made her debut in the Cherry Hinton and then looked unlucky when a close third behind subsequent Sweet Solera winner Albabilia in a maiden at Ascot. That race has worked out well though and she boosted the form even further with a decisive victory. She is likely to go for the Cheveley Park, as her owner also has Nijoom Dubai and that filly is being aimed at the Moyglare Stud Stakes. Her breeding suggests she will get a mile plus next season and, a filly with a fair amount of scope, she could be the one to give her trainer that elusive 1000 Guineas winner; she is 14/1 for that race after this success.

Visit ◆, whose form tied in quite closely with the winner through Don't Forget Faith and Albabilia, was well backed having won the Group 3 Princess Margaret Stakes since. She seemed well enough placed but, although she did not get the opening quite when she needed it, she took time to pick up before staying on well late. She is likely to renew rivalry with the winner in the Cheveley Park, and the stiffer track there should be in her favour. (op 13-8 tchd 7-4 in places)

Fleeting Spirit(IRE) won the Molecomb last time, beating Kingsgate Native, who went on to win the Nunthorpe later on this card. However, she was quite keen early on this step up in trip and her effort seemed to flatten out in the last furlong. She looks a real speed-ball and a drop back to the minimum trip for the Flying Childers looks a suitable option next. (op 5-2)

Unilateral(IRE), who failed to settle when beaten in novice company at Ripon last time, was more amenable this time and ran really well, only just missing out on earning black type. She had quite a hard race in the process but, given time to recover, the Firth Of Clyde Stakes at Ayr's Western meeting next month could provide a suitable opportunity for her.

Festoso(IRE), who had the winner behind when finishing runner-up in the Cherry Hinton, had her chance but faded out of the placings in the last furlong. She helps set the level of the form. (op 25-1)

Fashion Rocks(IRE), who got off the mark in a maiden at Goodwood, was on the heels of the leaders when suffering in the general bunching that took place in the last quarter mile and could not pick up from that point. She may be capable of better. (op 14-1)

Romantic Destiny, blinkered for the first time, was out of her depth but helped ensure a decent gallop and did well to finish as close as she did. (tchd 200-1)

Thought Is Free, who finished four and a half lengths behind Festoso in the Cherry Hinton with today's winner behind, did not run badly. She is still a maiden and should have no difficulty picking up a race at that level before stepping back up to Listed class.

You'resothrilling(USA), who beat today's winner, fifth and eighth when taking the Cherry Hinton on the back of some really solid efforts, showed up on the rail but appeared to be struggling when knocked against the rail as the field bunched at around the two pole. That ended whatever chance she had, but she has looked in need of a longer trip in her previous outings and, although she is in the Moyglare Stud Stakes, that is only ten days away, so it may be worth aiming her at the Meon Valley Stud Fillies' Mile at Ascot. (op 4-1 tchd 9-2)

Honky Tonk Sally, who was not far behind Visit on their respective debuts and ran well in a hot Newmarket maiden subsequently, pulled too hard early and unsurprisingly failed to last home. She is another who should have no trouble winning her maiden, providing she settles better. (op 66-1)

4745 ADDLESHAW GODDARD STKS (H'CAP) 1m

2:35 (2:39) (Class 2) (0-105,104) 3-Y-O+ **£25,908** (£7,708; £3,852; £1,924) **Stalls** Low

Form RPR

6041 **1** **The Illies (IRE)**[26] 3940 3-8-3 **89** WilliamBuick(3) 11 101+
(B W Hills) *lw: hld up towards rr: gd hdwy over 2f out: rdn to ld jst ins fnl f: kpt on wl* **5/1**[1]

3211 **2** *1 1/2* **Docofthebay (IRE)**[21] 4093 3-8-13 **96** RyanMoore 12 105+
(J A Osborne) *s.i.s and bhd: gd hdwy over 2f out: rdn and n.m.r over 1f out: styd on strly ins fnl f* **7/1**[3]

2133 **3** *nk* **We'll Come**[34] 3707 3-8-7 **90** PhilipRobinson 5 98
(M A Jarvis) *lw: hld up: gd hdwy 3f out: trckd ldrs 2f out: chal over 1f out and ev ch tl rdn and nt qckn ins fnl f* **13/2**[2]

1300 **4** *1/2* **Royal Dignitary (USA)**[23] 4049 7-8-12 **89** SilvestreDeSousa 4 97+
(D Nicholls) *led: rdn along 2f out: drvn over 1f out: hdd jst ins fnl f and kpt on same pce* **40/1**

6011 **5** *1/2* **Fremen (USA)**[23] 4049 7-8-12 **89** AdrianTNicholls 7 96
(D Nicholls) *lw: hld up towards rr: gd hdwy over 2f out: rdn to chal over 1f out and ev ch tl drvn and one pce ins fnl f* **15/2**

0331 **6** *1* **Benandonner (USA)**[12] 4377 4-9-0 **91** PaulHanagan 3 96
(R A Fahey) *trckd ldrs: hdwy and cl up over 2f out: sn rdn and kpt on same pce* **11/1**

1203 **7** *1/2* **Flipando (IRE)**[12] 4385 6-9-9 **100** JamieSpencer 20 103
(T D Barron) *swtg: hld up in rr: hdwy wl over 2f out: rdn over 1f out: sn wandered and no imp ent fnl f* **14/1**

1124 **8** *nk* **Nevada Desert (IRE)**[12] 4385 7-8-7 **87** MichaelJStainton(3) 19 90+
(R M Whitaker) *in tch on outer: effrt and nt muich room over 2f out: sn rdn and kpt on same pce appr fnl f* **40/1**

6500 **9** *1 3/4* **My Paris**[20] 4119 6-9-4 **95** NCallan 10 94
(K A Ryan) *cl up: rdn along over 2f out: drvn wl over 1f out and grad wknd* **25/1**

0320 **10** *nk* **Babodana**[20] 4119 7-9-9 **100** TedDurcan 8 98
(M H Tompkins) *lw: a in midfield* **33/1**

102 **11** *1* **Humungous (IRE)**[20] 4119 4-9-13 **104** (b) JMurtagh 1 100
(C R Egerton) *chsd ldrs: hdwy 2f out: sn rdn and hung rt: drvn and wknd appr fnl f* **10/1**

0400 **12** *1 1/2* **Kings Point (IRE)**[12] 4385 6-8-9 **86** (p) RichardHughes 6 78
(R A Fahey) *hld up in rr: sme hdwy over 2f out: sn rdn and n.d* **25/1**

0251 **13** *hd* **Annemasse**[12] 4385 3-9-1 **98** GregFairley 14 89
(M Johnston) *lw: chsd ldrs: rdn along 3f out: grad wknd appr fnl f* **10/1**

2620 **14** *1 1/2* **Mezuzah**[26] 3943 7-8-8 **85** oh2 PaulMulrennan 18 73
(M W Easterby) *lw: a in rr* **80/1**

2106 **15** *1/2* **Wovoka (IRE)**[12] 4377 4-8-8 **85** oh1 DarryllHolland 13 72
(M R Channon) *a in rr* **40/1**

0020 **16** *3* **Sir Xaar (IRE)**[12] 4385 4-9-2 **93** (t) RoystonFfrench 9 73
(B Smart) *chsd ldrs: rdn along 3f out: sn wknd* **28/1**

115- **17** *22* **Smart Enough**[327] 5675 4-9-12 **103** KerrinMcEvoy 16 33
(M A Magnusson) *bit bkwd: cl up: rdn along wl over 2f out and grad wknd* **7/1**[3]

P216 **18** *5* **Very Wise**[98] 1791 5-9-6 **97** RHills 15 15
(W J Haggas) *cl up: rdn along over 3f out and sn wknd* **12/1**

1m 37.11s (-2.39) **Going Correction** +0.05s/f (Good)

WFA 3 from 4yo+ 6lb **18** Ran SP% **130.3**

Speed ratings (Par 109): **113,111,111,110,110 109,108,108,106,106 105,103,103,102,101 98,76,71**

CSF £37.83 CT £249.74 TOTE £5.60: £2.00, £1.70, £2.40, £11.40; EX 37.60 Trifecta £148.60 Pool: £2,303.60 - 11.00 winning tickets..

Owner John C Grant **Bred** Glashare House Stud **Trained** Lambourn, Berks

FOCUS

A typically competitive renewal of this handicap and the placings were filled by a trio of consistent and progressive three-year-olds. The form has a solid look. The early pace was decent, which appeared to help those held up, and the bulk of the field came down the centre of the track in the home straight.

NOTEBOOK

The Illies(IRE) ◆, raised 7lb for his Ascot victory, got the strong pace he needs and was delivered with precision timing to win going away. Even a slipping saddle near the finish proved no problem to him and even though the Handicapper will continue to hike him up, in his current mood it is very possible he could go in again. He may go for the Cambridgeshire and that race looks tailor-made for him. (tchd 11-2)

Docofthebay(IRE), up another 7lb in his hat-trick bid, was ridden with plenty of confidence but he never saw much daylight when he needed a gap. He eventually followed the winner through, but his rival had got first run on him and he was making no impression on him in the closing stages, even though he stayed on to grab second. The authority with which the favourite scored makes it hard to argue that he was unlucky, but this was still another fine effort from this incredibly consistent colt. (op 15-2 tchd 8-1)

We'll Come ◆, back over arguably his best trip off a 5lb higher mark, got himself into a state in the stalls and had to be taken out and trotted around to make sure he could take part. To his great credit, not only did he take part but he was brought through to hold every chance and went down fighting. His problems beforehand would not have done him any good, so he can be given extra credit for this and the best of him is probably still to be seen. (op 8-1)

Royal Dignitary(USA) ◆, who would have been helped by the drying ground, would probably have preferred it even quicker, but he still ran with plenty of credit and emerged best of those that helped force the pace in a race otherwise dominated by closers. This was a big improvement on his last two starts and it would be no surprise to see him find an opportunity before too long.

Fremen(USA), up another 5lb in his hat-trick bid, was brought through to hold every chance but was never quite doing enough. The Handicapper looks to have him for the time being. (op 8-1)

Benandonner(USA), raised 6lb for his Shergar Cup Mile victory, could never dominate in a competitive race like this and probably ran up to his best in the circumstances. He is on a career-high mark now, so will need to find improvement from somewhere in order to defy it. (op 10-1)

Flipando(IRE) was switched right off out the back in a race run to suit, but although he stayed on past a few rivals he never looked like getting near the leaders. He still looks handicapped to the hilt at present.

Kings Point(IRE) got quite warm beforehand and was edgy.

Smart Enough, winner of this race last year but absent for 11 months since finishing fifth in last season's Cambridgeshire, was on his toes beforehand. After showing up for a long way, this looked a classic case of a horse blowing up. (op 9-1)

Very Wise was soon rushed up to take a handy position, but weakened very tamely soon after starting up the home straight. He was entitled to just need this after three months off, but he has won following a much longer layoff in the past so he does have a small question mark hanging over him after this.

4746 COOLMORE NUNTHORPE STKS (GROUP 1) 5f

3:10 (3:15) (Class 1) 2-Y-O+

£136,158 (£51,604; £25,826; £12,877; £6,450; £3,237) **Stalls** High

Form RPR

22 **1** **Kingsgate Native (IRE)**[23] 4046 2-8-1 0 JimmyQuinn 13 115
(J R Best) *lw: t.k.h early: chsd ldrs: led centre over 1f out: edgd lft u.p ins fnl f: kpt on strly* **12/1**

-360 **2** *1 3/4* **Desert Lord**[21] 4090 7-9-11 115 (b) DarryllHolland 7 117
(K A Ryan) *racd towards far side: disp ld to over 1f out: edgd rt u.p: kpt on ins fnl f: nt rch wnr* **20/1**

1225 **3** *hd* **Dandy Man (IRE)**[41] 3506 4-9-11 0 PShanahan 16 116
(Tracey Collins, Ire) *lw: cl up stands' side: led 1/2-way to over 1f out: kpt on same pce ins fnl f* **9/4**[1]

2043 **4** *3/4* **Red Clubs (IRE)**[41] 3506 4-9-11 114 MichaelHills 2 114+
(B W Hills) *lw: outpcd towards far side: hdwy over 1f out: edgd lft: kpt on ins fnl f: nrst fin* **7/1**[3]

5024 **5** *nk* **Wi Dud**[21] 4090 3-9-9 110 TedDurcan 12 113+
(K A Ryan) *sn outpcd towards stands' side: hdwy over 1f out: nrst fin* **25/1**

2101 **6** *shd* **Hoh Mike (IRE)**[47] 3329 3-9-9 110 JamieSpencer 8 112+
(M L W Bell) *sn outpcd and bhd centre: gd hdwy over 1f out: nrst fin* **10/1**

-100 **7** *shd* **Amadeus Wolf**[41] 3506 4-9-11 114 NCallan 5 112
(K A Ryan) *lw: chsd ldrs centre: rdn over 2f out: no ex over 1f out* **10/1**

1150 **8** *1/2* **Sierra Vista**[47] 3329 7-9-8 109 PaulHanagan 10 107
(D W Barker) *slt ld centre to 1/2-way: sn drvn along: no ex appr fnl f* **40/1**

30 **9** *hd* **Magnus (AUS)**[61] 2857 5-9-11 0 (b) KerrinMcEvoy 15 109
(P Moody, Australia) *swtg: in tch stands' side: drvn over 2f out: no imp over 1f out* **6/1**[2]

3210 **10** *1* **Beauty Is Truth (IRE)**[65] 2733 3-9-6 0 (b) TThulliez 14 103
(Robert Collet, France) *in tch towards stands' side: pushed along 2f out: edgd both ways and sn outpcd* **16/1**

2011 **11** *1/2* **Moorhouse Lad**[21] 4090 4-9-11 0 RyanMoore 4 104
(B Smart) *prom towards far side: drvn 2f out: hung lft: sn no ex* **7/1**[3]

2010 **12** *3/4* **Celtic Mill**[21] 4090 9-9-11 104 PatCosgrave 3 101
(D W Barker) *prom towards far side: drvn 1/2-way: wknd wl over 1f out* **100/1**

0601 **13** *1 1/2* **Green Manalishi**[18] 4196 6-9-11 105 RichardHughes 1 96
(K A Ryan) *hld up bhd ldrs towards far side: pushed along 2f out: sn outpcd* **100/1**

6150 **14** *3 1/2* **Mecca's Mate**[25] 3990 6-9-8 100 TonyHamilton 6 80
(D W Barker) *uns rdr and loose bef s: sn rdn along in midfield in centre: wknd fr 2f out* **100/1**

4005 **15** *1 3/4* **The Tatling (IRE)**[5] 4614 10-9-11 103 KevinGhunowa 17 77
(J M Bradley) *s.i.s: bhd and outpcd towards stands' side: nvr on terms* **80/1**

2-56 **16** *1 3/4* **Reverence**[27] 3894 6-9-11 116 KDarley 9 71
(E J Alston) *midfield centre: drvn over 2f out: sn btn: b.b.v* **14/1**

58.14 secs (-1.18) **Going Correction** +0.05s/f (Good)

WFA 2 from 3yo 24lb 3 from 4yo+ 2lb **16** Ran SP% **123.7**

Speed ratings: **111,108,107,106,106 106,105,105,104,103 102,101,98,93,90 87**

CSF £240.37 TOTE £16.70: £4.90, £8.60, £1.70; EX 551.50 Trifecta £4445.80 Part won. Pool £6,261.72 - 0.40 winning tickets..

Owner John Mayne **Bred** Peter McCutcheon **Trained** Hucking, Kent

■ Kingsgate Native was the first 2yo to win this since Lyric Fantasy in 1992. John Best's and Jimmy Quinn's first Group 1 winner.

FOCUS

A modest time for a Group 1, but a remarkable one for a two-year-old. There are slight reservations over the form, with Dandy Man not at his best and the Racing Post's weight-for-age scale allowing juveniles 8lb less than the official scale does. The race is best rated around the runner-up and fifth, and Kingsgate Native's figure fits with the best of his previous form.

NOTEBOOK

Kingsgate Native(IRE) ◆ came into this race a maiden, having been narrowly beaten on his debut in the Windsor Castle and then suffered a similar fate in the Molecomb. However, despite taking on older rivals, he never looked like getting beaten once he hit the front below the distance, and ran out a pretty decisive winner. He could well aim for the Flying Childers, but will have a penalty for that now, and may be better off going for the Prix de l'Abbaye, as most of his likely main rivals were behind him here. (op 11-1 tchd 10-1)

Desert Lord, who won the Prix de l'Abbaye last season, has had a light campaign and ran his best race since. He ran really well, but had no answer when challenged by the winner, who enjoyed a massive weight for age allowance. If the winner turns up at Longchamp he will struggle to reverse the placings, but otherwise he should go very close to repeating his 2006 success in that race.

Dandy Man(IRE) has been mainly hitting the bar in top 5f races since taking the Palace House last season, having not had the best of luck with the draw. He did not have that problem this time, but still found himself racing apart from the principals and was a little below his best. He deserves to pick up a big one and presumably connections will be thinking in terms of Longchamp, although he will not want the ground too soft. (op 5-2 tchd 11-4 in places)

Red Clubs(IRE) ◆ continues to acquit himself well in the top sprints but again showed that 5f is too short for him, doing his best work late on. He is likely to go for the Betfred Sprint Cup next with a major chance, with the Diadem, a race he won last season, another possible. (op 8-1)

Wi Dud, whose two previous successes were over this course and distance, was doing his best work late on. He finished runner-up in the Middle Park on one of his only two attempts over 6f, and looks worth another try at that trip, possibly in the Betfred Sprint Cup. (op 33-1)

Hoh Mike(IRE), like the two immediately in front of him, was doing his best work at the finish. He has looked well suited by a stiff five this season and has won over six, and although he is in the Flying Five at the Curragh next weekend, he may be best aiming for the Diadem over a track at which he has a good record. Official explanation: jockey said colt was never travelling (op 9-1 tchd 8-1)

Amadeus Wolf, who has won twice at this course, including the Duke Of York in the spring, was dropping back to this trip for the first time this season and did his best. He is another who is likely to have the Betfred Sprint at Haydock on the agenda. (op 12-1)

Sierra Vista who has been held in Group races since winning the Temple Stakes when completing a hat-trick in the spring, ran really well on her first attempt at this level. (op 33-1)

Magnus(AUS), an Australian challenger who has not been seen since being unplaced in the Golden Jubilee four days after finishing half a length behind Dandy Man in the King's Stand, got very warm and was also on his toes beforehand. He showed up for a fair way but was in trouble soon after halfway and just kept on at the one pace. (tchd 13-2)

Moorhouse Lad, who showed blistering pace when winning the Audi (King George) Stakes at Goodwood, had been supplemented for this race but either could not lie up or was settled and then failed to pick up when asked. He has done well but may not be quite up to this level and so the Listed Scarbrough Stakes at Doncaster and the Rous Stakes at Newmarket may offer suitable opportunities providing the ground does not go against him. (op 8-1)

Green Manalishi Official explanation: jockey said gelding was never travelling

Reverence, who won this last year, has had his problems this season and found the drying ground going against him. He faded out of contention in the second half of the race and was subsequently found to have bled, something he has never done before. Official explanation: vet said gelding bled from the nose

4747 SKF CITY OF YORK STKS (LISTED RACE) 7f

3:50 (3:50) (Class 1) 3-Y-O+ **£20,744** (£7,843; £3,920; £1,960) **Stalls** Low

Form RPR

3-43 **1** **Duff (IRE)**[17] [4237] 4-9-0 0 .... DPMcDonogh 3 110
(Edward Lynam, Ire) *w'like: mde all: qcknd clr 2f out: rdn over 1f out: drvn ins fnl f and hld on gamely* **14/1**

-500 **2** *nk* **Advanced**[11] [4438] 4-9-0 107 .... NCallan 1 109
(K A Ryan) *trckd wnr: effrt 2f out: rdn to chal over 1f out: sn drvn and ev ch tl no ex last 50yds* **18/1**

3052 **3** *½* **Racer Forever (USA)**[26] [3941] 4-9-0 107 .... (b) JimmyFortune 8 108
(J H M Gosden) *lw: hld up: smooth hdwy over 2f out: chsd ldng pair over 1f out: rdn to chal and ev ch ins fnl f: sn drvn and fnd little last 50yds* **13/8**[1]

1600 **4** *3 ½* **Mine (IRE)**[20] [4119] 9-9-5 106 .... (v) TQuinn 12 103
(J D Bethell) *bhd: hdwy over 2f out: sn rdn and styd on ent fnl f: nrst fin* **16/1**

5560 **5** *½* **Azarole (IRE)**[20] [4119] 6-9-0 100 .... JohnEgan 13 97+
(J S Moore) *hld up in rr: hdwy over 2f out: swtchd lft and rdn over 1f out: sn drvn: edgd rt and kpt on same pce ent fnl f* **20/1**

3206 **6** *shd* **Fonthill Road (IRE)**[11] [4438] 7-9-0 104 .... PaulHanagan 4 97
(R A Fahey) *lw: dwlt: sn in tch: rdn along 2f out: drvn over 1f out and no imp* **14/1**

13-2 **7** *nk* **Jack Sullivan (USA)**[166] [656] 6-9-0 112 .... EddieAhern 14 96+
(G A Butler) *hld up in rr: hdwy over 2f out: sn rdn along and no imp whn drvn and edgd lft ent fnl f* **15/2**[3]

0030 **8** *nk* **Royal Power (IRE)**[117] [1305] 4-9-0 103 .... DarryllHolland 6 95
(M R Channon) *chsd ldrs: rdn along 2f out: grad wknd* **20/1**

44-6 **9** *1 ½* **Somnus**[40] [3529] 7-9-0 110 .... MJKinane 7 91
(T D Easterby) *chsd ldrs: rdn along over 2f out: drvn and no imp whn edgd lft ent fnl f: wknd* **7/1**[2]

1500 **10** *¾* **Areyoutalkingtome**[117] [1305] 4-9-0 111 .... SimonWhitworth 9 89
(C A Cyzer) *lw: hld up in tch: rdn along wl over 2f out: drvn and styng on same pce whn squeezed out 1f out* **25/1**

0110 **11** *½* **Machinist (IRE)**[19] [4150] 7-9-0 102 .... SilvestreDeSousa 11 88
(D Nicholls) *midfield: hdwy on outer 3f out: rdn along 2f out and sn wknd* **12/1**

1300 **12** *½* **Riquewihr**[4] [4639] 7-8-9 70 .... (p) PaddyAspell 16 81?
(J S Wainwright) *a in rr* **125/1**

0300 **13** *3* **Dabbers Ridge (IRE)**[26] [3941] 5-9-0 99 .... MichaelHills 5 78
(B W Hills) *in tch on outer: rdn along 2f out: sn wknd* **8/1**

-150 **14** *3* **New Seeker**[77] [2396] 7-9-5 109 .... (b) TomEaves 2 75
(P F I Cole) *cl up: rdn along 3f out: sn wknd* **20/1**

1m 23.5s (-1.90) **Going Correction** +0.05s/f (Good)
WFA 3 from 4yo+ 5lb **14** Ran SP% **124.6**
Speed ratings (Par 111): **112,111,111,107,106 106,106,105,104,103 102,102,98,95**
CSF £234.07 TOTE £14.90: £3.50, £6.50, £1.50; EX 189.80 TRIFECTA Not won..
Owner Kilboy Estate **Bred** Kilboy Estate **Trained** Dunshaughlin, Co Meath

FOCUS

Not a strong race for the grade, run at just a fair gallop. The form is not that rock solid as several were returning from breaks and many of the field came here out of form.

NOTEBOOK

Duff(IRE), a front-runner who has been pretty consistent without winning at this level in Ireland, won the early battle for the lead and then showed a commendably game attitude to hold off the challengers on either side in the last furlong. He looks a progressive sort and could have more to offer, but needs decent ground. (op 16-1)

Advanced ◆, who has not had that much racing in the year or so since joining Kevin Ryan, has nevertheless been placed in the Ayr Gold Cup and at Group 3 level. He ran really well on this step back up in trip, but could not peg back the winner. He could well be aimed at the big Ayr sprint again, and if he can repeat this should be a major player. (op 14-1)

Racer Forever(USA), returning to this grade after being campaigned in big handicaps so far this season, moved up after being settled early and had every chance inside the last, but could not get past the game winner and flattened out late on. He is a talented gelding but not most resolute, so may not prove easy to place successfully. (op 2-1 tchd 9-4 in places)

Mine(IRE), whose sole win this season was over this trip in this grade, was held up as usual and ran on late, but by the time he arrived on the scene the first three were beyond recall. Nevertheless, he was giving weight away all round and ran pretty close to his mark on a line through the placed horses. Official explanation: jockey said horse hung left (op 14-1)

Azarole(IRE) ◆, who raced in Dubai in the winter, did not quite run up to his effort at Goodwood on his return from a break, but he will not mind a softening in the ground and could well be one to keep an eye on in the next few weeks. (tchd 22-1)

Fonthill Road(IRE), who has not won since taking the Ayr Gold Cup last season, looked to have the race run to suit but could not pick up on the ground. He will be aiming for the big sprint again, but he is rated 7lb higher than last year. (op 10-1)

Jack Sullivan(USA) was having his first outing since March and only his second in 18 months and showed promise, keeping on late. He clearly retains some ability and will be of interest back on an artificial surface. (op 17-2 tchd 7-1)

Royal Power(IRE), another returning from a break having raced in Dubai, showed up early before fading and was entitled to need the outing. (op 28-1 tchd 33-1)

Somnus, who only recently made his seasonal debut, found the drying ground going against him and he was too keen early, so it was no surprise he faded in the closing stages. (op 8-1 tchd 10-1 in places)

Areyoutalkingtome Official explanation: jockey said colt suffered interference inside final furlong

4748 EUROPEAN BREEDERS' FUND GALTRES STKS (LISTED RACE) 1m 4f

4:25 (4:27) (Class 1) 3-Y-O+ **£20,744** (£7,843; £3,920; £1,960) **Stalls** Centre

Form RPR

1232 **1** **Wannabe Posh (IRE)**[21] [4089] 4-9-4 103 .... EddieAhern 5 106
(J L Dunlop) *prom: effrt and chsd wnr over 2f out: led and edgd lft ins fnl f: pushed out* **5/2**[2]

1044 **2** *1 ¾* **Brisk Breeze (GER)**[21] [4089] 3-8-8 100 .... TedDurcan 3 103
(H R A Cecil) *lw: set modest pce: rdn over 2f out: hdd ins fnl f: kpt on same pce* **9/1**

40-0 **3** *½* **Mussoorie (FR)**[113] [1421] 4-9-4 103 .... JimmyFortune 10 102
(J H M Gosden) *w'like: lengthy: hld up in midfield: effrt over 2f out: kpt on fnl f: nrst fin* **20/1**

6231 **4** *1* **Gull Wing (IRE)**[26] [3972] 3-8-8 89 .... JamieSpencer 12 101
(M L W Bell) *stdd and swtchd lft s: hld up in last on ins: stdy hdwy 3f out: rdn 2f out: kpt on u.p fnl f* **5/1**[3]

11 **5** *shd* **Winter Sunrise**[34] [3709] 3-8-8 94 .... RyanMoore 2 100
(Sir Michael Stoute) *hld up on ins: pushed along fr over 3f out: outpcd and edgd lft 2f out: kpt on fnl f: no imp* **7/4**[1]

0200 **6** *hd* **High Heel Sneakers**[21] [4089] 4-9-10 103 .... (b1) TQuinn 9 106
(P F I Cole) *t.k.h: cl up: chsd ldr 1/2-way to over 2f out: hung lft and sn outpcd: no imp fnl f* **25/1**

605- **7** *1 ¼* **Guilia**[301] [6191] 4-9-4 98 .... ChrisCatlin 6 98
(Rae Guest) *bit bkwd: hld up: effrt and drvn 3f out: no imp over 1f out* **25/1**

504P **8** *4* **Restless Soul**[28] [3876] 3-8-8 51 .... SimonWhitworth 4 92?
(C A Cyzer) *t.k.h: chsd ldr to 1/2-way: rdn and wknd fr 2f out* **150/1**

-103 **9** *3 ½* **Dance Of Light (USA)**[37] [3628] 3-8-8 94 .... KerrinMcEvoy 1 86
(Sir Michael Stoute) *prom tl rdn and wknd fr 2f out* **7/1**

2m 33.06s (-1.54) **Going Correction** +0.05s/f (Good)
WFA 3 from 4yo 10lb **9** Ran SP% **117.2**
Speed ratings (Par 111): **107,105,105,104,104 104,103,101,98**
CSF £24.20 TOTE £3.20: £1.30, £2.40, £3.90; EX 22.40 Trifecta £655.70 Pool: £1,200.64 - 1.30 winning tickets..
Owner Nicholas Cooper **Bred** Vizcaya Ag **Trained** Arundel, W Sussex

■ Stewards' Enquiry : Simon Whitworth one-day ban: use whip down the shoulder in the forehand position (Sep 2)

FOCUS

An average renewal of this fillies' Listed contest run at a reasonable gallop and, although somewhat dubious behind, the form makes sense rated around the front pair.

NOTEBOOK

Wannabe Posh(IRE) is a thoroughly likeable and consistent filly, and gained a a deserved first success at this level with a typically resolute display. Always in a good position, she proved just too strong for the long-time leader in the last furlong and was drawing away at the line. She could go next for the Park Hill at Doncaster, but she is arguably best suited by this distance and so connections may opt for the Princess Royal and/or the St Simon Stakes, with the Prix de Royallieu another possibility, although a sound surface is another requirement. (op 11-4 tchd 3-1 in places)

Brisk Breeze(GER) was 3lb worse off with the winner having finished two and quarter lengths behind her at Goodwood last time. She was ridden more positively over this trip and, although closing the gap a little, could not pick up when challenged. She looks worth a try back over 1m6f in the Park Hill, and ridden the same way she may be able to run the finish out of her rivals. (op 11-1)

Mussoorie(FR) ◆, Listed placed at 1m1f in France last season when trained by Richard Gibson, was having her first start for her current trainer and first run since May. She put up a decent performance, finishing as if she would not be inconvenienced by a longer trip. It will be no surprise if she takes her chance in the Park Hill and cut in the ground would help her chance. (op 16-1)

Gull Wing(IRE), having just her second try at this level, adopted similar tactics to when scoring over 1m2f here at the end of last month. She made progress but could not get close enough to deliver a challenge, and it may be that a softer surface suits her best. (tchd 4-1)

Winter Sunrise, a half-sister to Shortest Day, had won her two previous starts and went off favourite, but she looked dull in her coat. She appeared to be found out by a combination of the step up in both trip and class, and although she kept on to the line, never looked likely to deliver a telling blow. (op 13-8 tchd 15-8, 2-1 in places)

High Heel Sneakers, equipped with blinkers for the first time, was on her toes beforehand and was quite free in the race itself, but she stuck on well enough and performed better than of late. Her only success since her juvenile days was a Listed race over 1m5f on Polytrack last October, her only try on that surface, and it will be no surprise if connections have that race in mind again this season. (op 50-1 tchd 22-1)

Dance Of Light(USA), who was well beaten in the Oaks, ran much better when placed in this grade over 1m2f last time. She seemed to travel well enough, but lost her place as the tempo quickened and was allowed to come home in her own time. She is surely capable of better than this, and a more positive ride back at 1m2f may suit best (op 8-1 tchd 9-1)

4749 STEWART FORSYTH MEMORIAL MELROSE STKS (H'CAP) 1m 6f

5:00 (5:01) (Class 2) (0-100,99) 3-Y-O **£16,192** (£4,817; £2,407; £1,202) **Stalls** Low

Form RPR

15 **1** **Speed Gifted**[33] [3753] 3-8-11 89 .... JamieSpencer 13 109+
(L M Cumani) *w'like: scope: lw: hld up: smooth hdwy 3f out: rdn to ld over 1f out: kpt on strly: readily* **4/1**[1]

6300 **2** *2* **Celestial Halo (IRE)**[22] 4059 3-8-13 **94**........................ WilliamBuick(3) 5 106
(B W Hills) *lw: hld up in midfield on outside: hdwy to press wnr over 1f out: kpt on fnl f: no imp* **16/1**

1464 **3** *1 1/4* **Metaphoric (IRE)**[28] 3883 3-9-2 **94**....................................(t) KDarley 14 104
(M L W Bell) *hld up: rdn 4f out: kpt on wl fnl 2f: nt rch first two* **20/1**

5341 **4** *nk* **Sunley Peace**[12] 4398 3-8-11 **89**.. TQuinn 2 99
(D R C Elsworth) *in tch: niggled over 4f out: effrt and ev ch over 1f out: nt qckn* **7/1**[2]

2302 **5** *1 1/4* **Dansant**[28] 3883 3-8-13 **91**.. EddieAhern 4 99
(G A Butler) *hld up in tch: hdwy and ev ch over 1f out: sn one pce* **25/1**

-315 **6** *shd* **Spanish Hidalgo (IRE)**[22] 4059 3-9-7 **99**..................... KerrinMcEvoy 11 107
(J L Dunlop) *lw: hld up: stdy hdwy over 3f out: rdn 2f out: one pce* **11/1**

2114 **7** *1 3/4* **Malt Or Mash (USA)**[22] 4059 3-8-11 **89**............................. PatDobbs 19 94+
(R Hannon) *lw: hld up: rdn over 3f out: kpt on fnl f: n.d* **15/2**[3]

0422 **8** *3/4* **Serpentaria**[8] 4490 3-8-3 **81**... PaulHanagan 12 85
(Sir Mark Prescott) *chsd ldrs: led 4f out to over 1f out: no ex* **14/1**

1312 **9** *1 1/2* **Camps Bay (USA)**[22] 4059 3-9-1 **93**.................................. JimCrowley 6 95
(Mrs A J Perrett) *lw: hld up: effrt and rdn 3f out: no imp fnl 2f* **10/1**

0210 **10** *shd* **Sahrati**[21] 4092 3-8-13 **91**... JimmyFortune 7 93
(C E Brittain) *led 2f: prom tl rdn and outpcd fr over 2f out* **33/1**

6321 **11** *nk* **Ancient Culture**[12] 4403 3-8-6 **84**.................................(bt) RyanMoore 17 86
(Sir Michael Stoute) *bhd: rdn along 4f out: sme late hdwy: nvr on terms* **12/1**

1614 **12** *nk* **Bogside Theatre (IRE)**[15] 4288 3-8-5 **86**................. AndrewElliott(3) 15 87
(G M Moore) *prom: effrt over 3f out: wknd over 1f out* **33/1**

1432 **13** *1 1/2* **Coeur De Lionne (IRE)**[19] 4147 3-8-8 **86**...................... SteveDrowne 1 85
(R Charlton) *lw: in tch: effrt over 3f out: btn over 1f out* **16/1**

3411 **14** *5* **Rhaam**[18] 4194 3-8-6 **84**... RHills 8 76
(B W Hills) *lw: hld up: rdn 4f out: nvr able to chal* **15/2**[3]

3113 **15** *3 1/2* **Bollin Felix**[6] 4570 3-8-2 **80** oh2..(b) TPO'Shea 16 67
(T D Easterby) *hld up in tch: hdwy to press ldr 7f out: wknd fr 3f out* **14/1**

0411 **16** *1* **Tempelstern (GER)**[28] 3883 3-9-4 **96**.............................(b) TedDurcan 9 82
(H R A Cecil) *led after 2f to 4f out: wknd 3f out: eased whn no ch over 1f out* **12/1**

0-03 **17** *2 1/2* **Philanthropy**[54] 3105 3-8-8 **86**.. NCallan 10 68
(K A Ryan) *prom tl rdn and wknd over 2f out: eased whn btn over 1f out* **66/1**

1-02 **18** *7* **Fushe Jo**[27] 3919 3-8-2 **80** oh1.................................... RoystonFfrench 18 53
(J Howard Johnson) *cl up tl wknd fr 3f out* **50/1**

4106 **19** *3/4* **Domino Dancer (IRE)**[7] 4523 3-8-8 **86**.................................. TomEaves 3 58
(J Wade) *plld hrd: hld up in last: rdn and struggling fr 4f out* **100/1**

2m 57.11s (-2.39) **Going Correction** +0.05s/f (Good) **19** Ran SP% **132.9**
Speed ratings (Par 106): **108,106,106,105,105 105,104,103,102,102 102,102,101,98,96 96,94,90,90**
CSF £72.73 CT £1213.37 TOTE £4.90: £2.00, £5.00, £7.50, £2.40; EX 111.50 Trifecta £1212.20 Part won. Pool: £1,707.46 - 0.10 winning tickets. Place 6 £68.10, Place 5 £28.84.
Owner JMC Breed & Race Limited **Bred** B W Hills & R A N Bonnycastle **Trained** Newmarket, Suffolk

■ Stewards' Enquiry : Eddie Ahern five-day ban: used whip with excessive frequency, down the shoulder in the forehand position, and without allowing colt time to respond (Sep 5-9)

FOCUS
A much bigger field for this race than in recent years and ultra-competitive as a result. The pace was decent too and this became a true test of stamina. The form has been rated positively and the winner looks capable of better.

NOTEBOOK
Speed Gifted ◆, representing the same trainer/jockey combination as were successful in the previous day's Ebor, is a horse with loads of scope. He was 9lb better off with Spanish Hidalgo for a near ten-length beating at Ripon last time, but the heavy ground was probably against him there and these drying conditions saw him reverse the form in no uncertain terms. He demonstrated a decent turn of foot to prevail in some style and he looks likely to go on to much better things. (op 5-1 tchd 11-2 in places)
Celestial Halo(IRE) ◆, disappointing in both starts since finishing third of four behind Soldier Of Fortune in the Chester Vase, came with a decent late effort down the outside of the track but could not match the finishing pace of the progressive winner. This was much more like it though and the longer trip obviously suited him.
Metaphoric(IRE) ◆, over nine lengths behind Tempelstern at Sandown last time, was a stone better off with him here but this better ground, stronger pace and the application of a tongue-tie saw an improved effort. Even this looked an inadequate test though, as he was doing his best work late but was never getting there in time. A return to further should see him winning again.
Sunley Peace, raised 7lb for his Newmarket win, was never far away and still looked to be travelling well halfway up the home straight but when this became a test of finishing pace he was just found wanting. This was a fair effort, but he looks to need every bit of 2m. (op 8-1)
Dansant, closely matched with Metaphoric and Tempelstern on Sandown running, was brought to hold every chance but lacked the pace to land an effective blow. (op 28-1)
Spanish Hidalgo(IRE), up in trip, had Speed Gifted well behind him at Ripon two starts ago, but could not confirm the form on 9lb worse terms on this less-testing surface. He was still not disgraced in trying to concede weight all round in such a hot handicap. (op 12-1)
Malt Or Mash(USA), who got rid of his jockey and galloped loose before finishing decent fourth at Goodwood last time, got loose in the paddock again here and was very much on his toes. Under the circumstances, he ran another blinder over this longer trip and if he can be sorted out there is a decent handicap to be won with him. (op 6-1 tchd 8-1, 9-1 in places)
Serpentaria was given every chance, but she lacked finishing pace and looks an out-and-out stayer.
Tempelstern(GER), who had a couple of these behind him when bolting up at Sandown last time, was put up a stone in his bid for a hat-trick and after showing at the sharp end for over a mile, eventually dropped right out. The ground may have dried up a bit too much for him, but even so this suggests the Handicapper has overreacted. (op 9-1)
Domino Dancer(IRE) Official explanation: jockey said gelding hung left throughout
T/Jkpt: Not won. T/Plt: £27.90 to a £1 stake. Pool: £245,922.50. 6,417.45 winning tickets. T/Qpdt: £11.60 to a £1 stake. Pool: £8,954.50. 568.40 winning tickets. JR

4750 - 4754a (Foreign Racing) - See Raceform Interactive

4629 BATH (L-H)

Friday, August 24

OFFICIAL GOING: Good to firm (firm in places; 9.6)
Conditions rode pretty quick.
Wind: virtually nil Weather: warm and sunny

4755 BATH ALES HOP POLE MAIDEN AUCTION STKS 5f 161y
5:25 (5:27) (Class 5) 2-Y-O £2,849 (£847; £423; £211) Stalls Centre

Form RPR

53 **1** **Good Gorsoon (USA)**[8] 4537 2-9-0 0.............................. JamieSpencer 1 83+
(B W Hills) *mid-div: smooth hdwy 3f out: nt clr run and swtchd rt enteing fnl f: sn led: easily* **13/8**[1]

0233 **2** *3* **Bookiebasher Dude**[15] 4315 2-8-13 73........................... MartinDwyer 8 72
(M Quinn) *led: rdn over 2f out: hdd jst ins fnl f: nt pce of easy wnr* **9/1**

6 **3** *nk* **Heaven**[27] 3947 2-8-3 0... ChrisCatlin 7 61
(P J Makin) *chsd ldrs: rdn and ev ch whn hung lft ent fnl f: kpt on same pce* **25/1**

00 **4** *1 3/4* **Imaginemysurprise**[15] 4310 2-8-3 0.............................. DavidKinsella 10 55
(J A Geake) *mid-div: rdn 3f out: styd on ins fnl f: nrst fin* **100/1**

2640 **5** *shd* **Miss Firefly**[14] 4364 2-8-11 71... TPO'Shea 3 63
(M R Channon) *prom: rdn over 3f out: ev ch 2f out: one pce fnl f* **6/1**[3]

6 **6** *hd* **Wavertree Princess (IRE)**[9] 4506 2-8-9 0....................... JamesDoyle 4 60
(N P Littmoden) *chsd ldrs: rdn over 2f out: hld whn n.m.r ent fnl f* **10/1**

7 *3/4* **Sparkler** 2-8-7 0... JimCrowley 9 56
(P Winkworth) *s.i.s: bhd: styng on whn nt clr run ins fnl f: nvr trbld ldrs* **14/1**

023 **8** *shd* **Westwood**[11] 4454 2-8-11 0.. RobertHavlin 6 60
(D Haydn Jones) *prom: rdn and ev ch over 2f out: wknd fnl f* **7/2**[2]

9 *3/4* **Drumhallagh (IRE)** 2-9-0 0... SebSanders 13 60
(Tom Dascombe) *a towards rr* **33/1**

10 *1 1/2* **No To Trident** 2-8-9 0 ow1... AlanDaly 2 51
(P D Evans) *s.i.s: a bhd* **66/1**

11 *2 1/2* **Our Tallulah (IRE)** 2-8-7 0.. FergusSweeney 12 41
(C G Cox) *v.s.a: a bhd* **14/1**

60 **12** *4* **Diamond Soles (IRE)**[78] 2398 2-8-12 0............................ IanMongan 11 33
(B J Meehan) *mid-div: rdn over 3f out: wknd 2f out* **33/1**

06 **13** *8* **Captain Jack Black**[36] 3669 2-8-9 0.................................(t) LPKeniry 5 4
(M R Bosley) *s.i.s: sn pushed along in mid-div: wknd over 2f out* **100/1**

1m 11.06s (-0.14) **Going Correction** -0.225s/f (Firm) **13** Ran SP% **120.2**
Speed ratings (Par 94): **91,87,86,84,84 83,82,82,81,79 76,71,60**
CSF £16.95 TOTE £2.60: £1.10, £2.10, £5.60; EX 18.10.
Owner Triermore Stud & Partner **Bred** Jayeff 'B' Stables **Trained** Lambourn, Berks

FOCUS
An ordinary event in which the winner stepped forward and the second helps with the standard.

NOTEBOOK
Good Gorsoon(USA) had shown enough on soft ground last time to suggest he would play a major hand in the outcome, and he did not let his supporters down. It was not the greatest of races, but he could do no more than win the way he did. He will be suited by another furlong because he was certainly not stopping once in the clear, and his future now lies in nursery company. The handicapper will have a pretty good handle on the form as the runner-up is rated 73. (op 7-4 tchd 15-8)
Bookiebasher Dude is beginning to look quite exposed but there must be one of these ordinary races in him. (op 12-1)
Heaven was stepping up the best part of a furlong and it seemed to suit her. She needs one more outing to get a mark for nurseries. (op 16-1)
Imaginemysurprise stayed on to some effect and is now eligible for a rating after three runs. On this evidence she will want further.
Miss Firefly seemed unsuited by this drop in trip. (op 7-1)
Sparkler caught the eye doing some good work late on on this debut. She fell out of the stalls and ran green until the penny dropped, after which she stayed on without being knocked about. She is one to consider in the future. (op 10-1 tchd 9-1)
Diamond Soles(IRE) Official explanation: jockey said filly hung right-handed

4756 E.B.F./BATH ALES SALAMANDER MAIDEN FILLIES' STKS 5f 11y
5:55 (5:58) (Class 5) 2-Y-O £3,238 (£963; £481; £240) Stalls Centre

Form RPR

020 **1** **Dresden Doll (USA)**[37] 3648 2-9-0 79............................ JamieSpencer 1 77
(M L W Bell) *a.p: rdn to ld jst ins fnl f: kpt on wl: rdn out* **3/1**[1]

662 **2** *3/4* **Rathmolyon**[15] 4310 2-9-0 68.. RobertHavlin 8 74
(D Haydn Jones) *led: rdn 2f out: hdd jst ins fnl f: kpt on but a hld* **11/1**

052 **3** *3* **Betty Burke**[17] 4254 2-9-0 74.. DaneO'Neill 7 63
(H J L Dunlop) *chsd ldrs: rdn over 2f out: kpt on same pce fnl f* **11/2**

2 **4** *1 1/4* **Safari Time (IRE)**[14] 4358 2-9-0 0...................................... JimCrowley 14 59
(P Winkworth) *chsd ldrs: rdn over 2f out: kpt on same pce fnl f* **5/1**[3]

5 *nk* **Showtime Ice** 2-8-11 0.. WilliamBuick(3) 5 58
(M J Wallace) *s.i.s: sn in tch: effrt and hung rt over 1f out: fdd* **40/1**

56 **6** *1 3/4* **Silca Destination**[18] 4232 2-9-0 0... TPO'Shea 2 51
(M R Channon) *in tch: rdn over 2f out: wknd fnl f* **16/1**

4 **7** *1 3/4* **Second Opinion (IRE)**[22] 4102 2-9-0 0.................. StephenDonohoe 11 45
(J M P Eustace) *mid-div: short lived effrt over 2f out* **9/2**[2]

8 *1 3/4* **Tense (IRE)** 2-9-0 0.. MartinDwyer 12 39
(J A Osborne) *slowly away and carried rt s: bhd: sme late prog but nvr on terms* **22/1**

5 **9** *nk* **Midnight Oasis**[8] 4522 2-9-0 0... SebSanders 13 38
(Rae Guest) *in tch: effrt over 2f out: wknd fnl f* **8/1**

10 *3 1/2* **Little Evie** 2-9-0 0... FrancisNorton 3 25
(R J Hodges) *s.i.s: a towards rr* **66/1**

11 *1 3/4* **Autumn Star (IRE)** 2-8-7 0... MatthewDavies(7) 9 19
(M R Channon) *wnt bdly rt s: a bhd* **14/1**

12 *shd* **April Reigns** 2-9-0 0... AlanDaly 16 18
(D Burchell) *mid-div tl wknd 2f out* **100/1**

000 **13** *3/4* **Ballyhealy Lady**[36] 3687 2-8-9 57.................................. PatrickHills(5) 15 16
(D K Ivory) *s.i.s: sn mid-div: rdn over 3f out: wknd over 2f out* **66/1**

00 **14** *8* **Rhode Island Red (USA)**[13] 4402 2-9-0 0.......................(t) IanMongan 6 —
(B J Meehan) *unsettled stalls: s.i.s: a bhd* **28/1**

62.02 secs (-0.48) **Going Correction** -0.225s/f (Firm) **14** Ran SP% **121.4**
Speed ratings (Par 91): **94,92,88,86,85 82,79,77,76,71 68,68,66,54**
CSF £36.60 TOTE £4.60: £1.70, £3.70, £2.30; EX 47.60.
Owner Sheikh Marwan Al Maktoum **Bred** Darley **Trained** Newmarket, Suffolk

FOCUS
A modest event which could have been rated up to 6lb better. The first two came clear.

NOTEBOOK
Dresden Doll(USA) came into the race as the highest rated of those with marks and did not have to improve too much to win because the runner-up is officially a good few pounds lower. She had run poorly on sand last time, but it was a different story back on turf and down in trip. However, whether she can progress further has to be open to debate. (op 2-1 tchd 7-2)
Rathmolyon appeared to run above herself on official ratings on this step back to the minimum trip. Both she and the winner drew clear, but it is probably folly to get too carried away about the bare form. (op 12-1 tchd 10-1)
Betty Burke should have been second according to the ratings, so she did not build on her recent Chepstow second. (op 8-1)
Safari Time(IRE) had every chance on what was her first run on turf. She may need further. (op 7-1)

Showtime Ice did best of those without previous experience and she should come on for this effort.

4757 BATH ALES WILD HARE ORGANIC ALE (S) STKS — 1m 3f 144y
6:25 (6:27) (Class 6) 3-4-Y-0 — £1,943 (£578; £288; £144) Stalls Low

Form — RPR

0000 **1** — **Victory Mile (USA)**[13] 4391 3-8-11 56 ...... StephenDonohoe 6 — 51
(B J Meehan) *mid-div: rdn and hdwy 3f out: edgd lft and led over 2f out: hrd pressed thrght fnl f: hld on gamely* — **10/3**[2]

2551 **2** *hd* **Jocheski (IRE)**[9] 4516 3-9-2 64 ...... JamieSpencer 2 — 55
(M J Wallace) *hld up towards rr: swtchd rt and hdwy over 2f out: sn rdn: chal wnr thrght fnl f: hld cl home* — **11/10**[1]

000 **3** *1 1/2* **Investment Pearl (IRE)**[28] 3901 4-9-2 46 ...... FrancisNorton 7 — 43
(D R Gandolfo) *prom: led over 5f out: rdn and narrowly hdd over 2f out: rallied gamely: no ex fnl 75yds* — **25/1**

650- **4** *2 1/2* **Forever Autumn**[10] 2712 4-9-7 60 ...... DaneO'Neill 10 — 44
(D G Bridgwater) *led tl over 5f out: styd pressing ldrs: rdn over 2f out: one pce fr over 1f out* — **25/1**

0-45 **5** *4* **Sosueme Now**[8] 4528 3-8-1 48 ...... KevinGhunowa(5) 8 — 33
(A B Haynes) *mid-div: pushed along and hdwy 4f out: rdn over 2f out: wknd 1f out* — **16/1**

505 **6** *3 1/2* **Tumble Jill (IRE)**[52] 3186 3-8-6 44 ......(p) FrankieMcDonald 9 — 27
(J J Bridger) *trckd ldrs: rdn over 3f out: sltly hmpd over 2f out: wknd 1f out* — **25/1**

0300 **7** *2* **Snake Hips**[11] 4460 3-8-8 54 ......(b) WilliamBuick(3) 1 — 29
(B Palling) *chsd ldrs: rdn over 2f out: wknd over 1f out* — **7/1**[3]

0-00 **8** *shd* **King's Attitude**[8] 4530 3-8-11 0 ...... SebSanders 5 — 29
(R A Harris) *a towards rr* — **9/1**

0054 **9** *12* **Roymar**[10] 4473 3-8-6 46 ...... ChrisCatlin 4 — 4
(M Appleby) *a bhd: lost tch 3f out* — **25/1**

2m 31.52s (1.22) **Going Correction** -0.225s/f (Firm)
WFA 3 from 4yo 10lb — **9** Ran SP% **114.5**
Speed ratings (Par 101): **86,85,84,83,80 78,76,76,68**
CSF £6.90 TOTE £4.80: £1.40, £1.10, £6.60; EX 9.20.The winner was bought by Milton Harris for 11,200gns. Jocheski was claimed by W Bloomfield for £6,000.
Owner Joe L Allbritton **Bred** Harrison Stables, Inc **Trained** Manton, Wilts

FOCUS
A weak seller which was slowly run.

4758 BATH ALES SPA H'CAP — 1m 5f 22y
6:55 (6:55) (Class 5) (0-70,71) 3-Y-O — £3,238 (£963; £481; £240) Stalls Low

Form — RPR

3345 **1** — **Hatton Flight**[13] 4391 3-8-9 58 ......(b) FrancisNorton 11 — 66
(A M Balding) *mid-div: hdwy and swtchd rt 3f out: sn rdn: led jst ins fnl f: styd on wl* — **7/1**[3]

2364 **2** *1 3/4* **Sowdrey**[22] 4113 3-9-3 66 ...... TPO'Shea 8 — 71
(M R Channon) *hld up towards rr: shkn up and hdwy over 4f out: hrd rdn to chse ldrs over 2f out: hung lft over 1f out: styd on to go 2nd fnl strides* — **8/1**

2011 **3** *hd* **Alleviate (IRE)**[9] 4511 3-9-8 71 6ex ...... SebSanders 1 — 76
(Sir Mark Prescott) *led: rdn over 2f out: hdd jst ins fnl f: no ex and lost 2nd fnl strides* — **11/10**[1]

3255 **4** *1 3/4* **Daylami Dreams**[105] 1637 3-9-7 70 ...... LPKeniry 3 — 72
(J S Moore) *trckd ldrs: rdn 3f out: kpt on same pce fnl 2f* — **20/1**

4010 **5** *12* **Bathwick Breeze**[31] 3825 3-8-10 59 ......(b[1]) DavidKinsella 10 — 43
(A B Haynes) *w ldr: short of room over 2f out: sn rdn: wknd over 1f out* — **25/1**

0642 **6** *2 1/2* **Esclarmonde (IRE)**[20] 4172 3-9-5 68 ...... JamieSpencer 7 — 71+
(L M Cumani) *trckd ldrs: rousted along after 3f: rdn to chse ldr over 2f out: cl 4th but hld whn lost action and eased ent fnl f* — **11/4**[2]

6502 **7** *5* **Rainbow Flame**[31] 3824 3-8-13 62 ...... JimCrowley 6 — 35
(Tom Dascombe) *mid-div: rdn over 3f out: wknd 2f out* — **20/1**

0062 **8** *3 1/2* **Kyllachy Storm**[58] 2978 3-8-2 51 ...... ChrisCatlin 2 — 19
(R J Hodges) *a towards rr* — **25/1**

0-00 **9** *12* **Ron In Ernest**[27] 3950 3-8-6 55 ...... StephenCarson 4 — 5
(J A Geake) *in tch: stmbld on bnd after 3f: bhd fnl 5f* — **66/1**

2m 48.73s (-2.77) **Going Correction** -0.225s/f (Firm) — **9** Ran SP% **116.6**
Speed ratings (Par 100): **99,97,97,96,89 87,84,82,75**
CSF £54.87 CT £107.63 TOTE £8.10: £2.10, £2.10, £1.10; EX 49.20.
Owner David Brownlow **Bred** Fittocks Stud Ltd **Trained** Kingsclere, Hants

FOCUS
They went a very good pace, resulting in the time being inside standard. The market leaders were a bit disappointing in this modest handicap, in which the second is the best guide.
Bathwick Breeze Official explanation: jockey said gelding had no more to give
Esclarmonde(IRE) Official explanation: jockey said filly hung left-handed

4759 BATH ALES GEM H'CAP — 5f 11y
7:25 (7:28) (Class 5) (0-70,70) 3-Y-O — £3,238 (£963; £481; £240) Stalls Centre

Form — RPR

51 **1** — **Back In The Red (IRE)**[4] 4661 3-9-1 64 6ex ...... SebSanders 1 — 79
(R A Harris) *mde all: r.o strly to assert ent fnl f: rdn out: readily* — **4/1**[1]

52 **2** *5* **Croeso Bach**[15] 4314 3-7-12 54 ...... SophieDoyle(7) 9 — 51
(J L Spearing) *w wnr: rdn 2f out: rdr lost whip sn after: nt pce of wnr ent fnl f* — **14/1**

6102 **3** *1/2* **Rosie Cross (IRE)**[8] 4536 3-8-4 58 ...... PatrickHills(5) 6 — 53
(Eve Johnson Houghton) *chsd ldrs: sltly outpcd 2f out: kpt on fnl f* — **11/2**[3]

1602 **4** *1* **Feelin Foxy**[12] 4432 3-9-7 70 ......(v) DaneO'Neill 2 — 61
(D Shaw) *chsd ldrs: rdn wl over 2f out: kpt on same pce fr over 1f out* — **16/1**

524 **5** *3/4* **Scarlett Heart (IRE)**[15] 4314 3-9-5 68 ...... JimCrowley 5 — 57
(J Gallagher) *chsd ldrs: rdn 2f out: one pce after* — **8/1**

4156 **6** *nk* **Mr Forthright**[8] 4536 3-8-4 58 ...... KevinGhunowa(5) 14 — 46
(J M Bradley) *chsd ldrs tl outpcd 3f out: styd on again ins fnl f* — **15/2**

366 **7** *hd* **Gimme Some Lovin (IRE)**[23] 4066 3-8-11 60 ......(t) FergusSweeney 3 — 47
(D W P Arbuthnot) *s.i.s: sn mid-div: rdn 3f out: one pce fnl 2f* — **9/1**

2510 **8** *nk* **Metal Guru**[8] 4525 3-9-0 68 ...... RussellKennemore(5) 12 — 54
(R Hollinshead) *towards rr: clsng whn clipped heels over 2f out: sn hung lft: no furhter imp* — **13/2**

035 **9** *2* **Loves Bidding**[29] 3879 3-9-2 65 ......(v) ChrisCatlin 10 — 44
(R Ingram) *mainly towards rr* — **33/1**

5066 **10** *hd* **Montemayorprincess (IRE)**[15] 4312 3-8-2 51 oh4....(p) DavidKinsella 8 — 29
(D Haydn Jones) *hmpd s: bhd: sme late prog into 7th whn nt clr run ins fnl f: no imp after* — **28/1**

0000 **11** *7* **Land Ahoy**[8] 4529 3-8-11 60 ...... MartinDwyer 7 — 13
(D W P Arbuthnot) *wnt rt s: early spd: bhd fnl 3f* — **20/1**

0032 **12** *2* **Royal Guest**[8] 4529 3-8-3 52 ...... TPO'Shea 11 — —
(M R Channon) *s.i.s: sn mid-div: rdn 3f out: sn btn* — **5/1**[2]

60.50 secs (-2.00) **Going Correction** -0.225s/f (Firm) — **12** Ran SP% **122.0**
Speed ratings (Par 100): **107,99,98,96,95 94,94,94,90,90 79,76**
CSF £62.48 CT £321.69 TOTE £4.80: £2.20, £3.40, £2.40; EX 59.70.
Owner Mrs Ruth M Serrell **Bred** Mrs Rachanee Butler **Trained** Earlswood, Monmouths

FOCUS
A big step up from the winner, but it seems no fluke with the second running her race.
Metal Guru Official explanation: jockey said filly hung badly left-handed
Montemayorprincess(IRE) Official explanation: jockey said filly hung left-handed throughout

4760 BATH ALES BARNSTORMER H'CAP — 1m 5y
7:55 (7:57) (Class 6) (0-65,64) 3-Y-O — £2,072 (£616; £308; £153) Stalls Low

Form — RPR

3143 **1** — **Palmetto Point**[26] 3997 3-8-12 58 ......(p) TravisBlock(3) 12 — 68
(H Morrison) *in tch: hdwy 2f out: sn rdn: hung lft and chal ent fnl f: led cl home* — **5/2**[1]

6134 **2** *shd* **Zelos (IRE)**[23] 4071 3-9-2 59 ......(b) JimCrowley 1 — 69
(D J S Ffrench Davis) *mid-div: swtchd rt and hdwy 2f out: sn rdn: led ent fnl f: hdd cl home* — **11/1**

0000 **3** *5* **Apollo Five**[25] 4015 3-9-7 64 ...... TPO'Shea 16 — 62
(D J Coakley) *trckd ldr: led wl over 2f out: sn rdn: hdd ent fnl f: kpt on same pce* — **12/1**

3321 **4** *3/4* **Bidable**[17] 4257 3-9-6 63 ...... SebSanders 10 — 60
(B Palling) *t.k.h in mid-div: rdn 3f out: sn swtchd rt: styd on fnl f* — **10/3**[2]

0100 **5** *shd* **Blue Mistral (IRE)**[16] 4270 3-9-2 62 ......(vt) WilliamBuick(3) 9 — 58
(W J Knight) *s.i.s: bhd: rdn and stdy prog fr 3f out: styd on fnl f* — **20/1**

5-40 **6** *2* **Balliasta (IRE)**[68] 2693 3-9-7 64 ...... MartinDwyer 13 — 56
(B W Hills) *towards rr: rdn over 3f out: styd on fnl f: nvr a danger* — **7/1**[3]

0050 **7** *1 1/2* **Fun In The Sun**[12] 4416 3-8-4 47 ......(v) FrancisNorton 4 — 35
(P D Evans) *towards rr: rdn 3f out: styd on fr over 1f out: nvr a danger* — **25/1**

-050 **8** *1 1/4* **Woodins Way**[29] 3881 3-9-3 60 ...... AdamKirby 5 — 45
(P J Makin) *trckd ldrs: rdn over 3f out: grad fdd* — **9/1**

0660 **9** *1 1/4* **Lordswood (IRE)**[20] 4163 3-8-8 51 ...... FrankieMcDonald 6 — 34
(J J Bridger) *mid-div tl wknd 2f out* — **100/1**

4000 **10** *nk* **Beckenham's Secret**[15] 4326 3-8-12 55 ......(b) FergusSweeney 8 — 37
(B R Millman) *led: rdn and hdd wl over 2f out: grad wknd* — **25/1**

0-60 **11** *5* **Wishing On A Star**[44] 3421 3-9-6 63 ......(b[1]) ChrisCatlin 11 — 33
(E J O'Neill) *trckd ldrs: hung rt on bnd 5f out: rdn over 3f out: wknd 2f out* — **25/1**

1604 **12** *4* **Dance Of Dreams**[29] 3875 3-9-0 57 ...... IanMongan 15 — 18
(N P Littmoden) *mid-div tl wknd over 2f out* — **20/1**

1m 39.1s (-2.00) **Going Correction** -0.225s/f (Firm) — **12** Ran SP% **112.2**
Speed ratings (Par 98): **101,100,95,95,95 93,91,90,89,88 83,79**
CSF £24.53 CT £243.75 TOTE £3.00: £1.30, £2.50, £4.20; EX 27.10 Place 6 £18.25, Place 5 £9.24.
Owner M T Bevan & H Scott-Barrett **Bred** Wyck Hall Stud Ltd **Trained** East Ilsley, Berks
■ April Fool (10/1) was withdrawn on vet's advice. R4 applies, deduct 5p in the £.

FOCUS
An ordinary handicap but the front two were clear so the form is likely to prove solid for the grade.
T/Plt: £10.90 to a £1 stake. Pool: £56,251.60. 3,760.90 winning tickets. T/Qpdt: £5.00 to a £1 stake. Pool: £4,501.40. 663.60 winning tickets. TM

4597 NEWBURY (L-H)
Friday, August 24

OFFICIAL GOING: Good (7.0)
The best ground looked to be towards the far rail in the first three races, but there was no apparent bias in the final four contests.
Wind: virtually nil

4761 DESIGNER WAY VACATION CLUB MEDIAN AUCTION MAIDEN STKS (DIV I) — 7f (S)
12:50 (12:56) (Class 5) 2-Y-O — £3,562 (£1,059; £529; £264) Stalls Centre

Form — RPR

0 **1** — **Marchpane**[29] 3866 2-8-12 0 ...... MartinDwyer 4 — 75
(R M Beckett) *leggy: scope: chsd ldrs: led over 1f out: rdn and hdd last half f: styd on gamely to re-assert cl home* — **40/1**

2 *nk* **Copperwood** 2-9-3 0 ...... PaulDoe 2 — 79+
(M Blanshard) *lengthy: bit bkwd: in rr: hdwy 3f 3f out: rdn and styd on to ld last half f: hdd and no ex cl home* — **66/1**

0 **3** *4* **Little Toto**[29] 3866 2-9-3 0 ...... FergusSweeney 13 — 69
(C G Cox) *w'like: leggy: led tl hdd over 1f out: sn outpcd by ldng duo but styd on to hold 3rd ins fnl f* — **33/1**

0 **4** *nk* **Ballochroy (IRE)**[14] 4350 2-9-3 0 ...... DaneO'Neill 1 — 68
(B W Hills) *w'like: towards rr early: hdwy 3f out: chsd ldrs 2f out and sn pushed along kpt on ins fnl f but nvr gng pce to trble ldng duo* — **33/1**

3 **5** *1 3/4* **We'Re Delighted**[19] 4198 2-9-3 0 ...... TPO'Shea 14 — 63
(M R Channon) *chsd ldrs: rdn 2f out: wknd fnl f* — **9/4**[1]

0 **6** *3* **Distant Diamond (IRE)**[30] 3850 2-9-3 0 ...... AdamKirby 10 — 55
(W R Swinburn) *in tch: rdn 3f out: no imp on ldrs fnl 2f* — **25/1**

6 **7** *1/2* **Hit The Roof**[19] 4201 2-9-3 0 ...... PatDobbs 7 — 54
(R Hannon) *chsd ldrs: rdn over 2f out: wknd over 1f out* — **13/2**

8 *3* **Oxbridge** 2-9-3 0 ...... SebSanders 6 — 46
(B J Meehan) *unf: in rr: sn pushed along in rr: mod prog fnl f* — **6/1**[3]

9 *1* **Summer Winds** 2-9-3 0 ...... JimCrowley 15 — 44
(T G Mills) *unf: slowly away: sn in tch: rdn 3f out: wknd fr 2f out* — **9/1**

50 **10** *3/4* **Lady Jinks**[8] 4527 2-8-12 0 ...... RichardSmith 8 — 37
(M D I Usher) *neat: chsd ldrs: rdn 3f out: sn btn* — **66/1**

11 *nk* **River N' Blues (IRE)** 2-8-7 0 ...... KevinGhunowa(5) 12 — 36
(Dr J R J Naylor) *unf: chsd ldrs: rdn 3f out: wknd 2f out* — **80/1**

12 *3/4* **Reel Star** 2-9-3 0 ...... LPKeniry 3 — 39
(S Kirk) *w'like: str: bit bkwd: mid-div: rdn 3f out: wknd over 2f out* — **20/1**

0 **13** *3 1/2* **In A Pickle**[29] 3874 2-8-12 0 ...... RobertHavlin 5 — 25
(H J L Dunlop) *w'like: pressed ldrs 4f* — **16/1**

0 **14** *shd* **Morestead (IRE)**[28] 3896 2-9-3 0 ...... GeorgeBaker 11 — 30
(B G Powell) *chsd ldrs 4f* — **4/1**[2]

15 *3* **Tobago Bay** 2-9-3 0 ...... ChrisCatlin 9 — 22
(M R Channon) *w'like: bhd fr 1/2-way* — **16/1**

1m 27.37s (0.37) **Going Correction** -0.10s/f (Good) — **15** Ran SP% **121.3**
Speed ratings (Par 94): **93,92,88,87,85 82,81,78,77,76 75,75,71,71,67**
CSF £1577.52 TOTE £80.60: £15.80, £16.50, £9.20; EX 1096.80.
Owner A D G Oldrey **Bred** A D G Oldrey **Trained** Whitsbury, Hants

FOCUS
The first four home returned at 33/1 or bigger and this looked a weak maiden for the track. The first two finished clear. The winning time was almost a full second slower than the second division, and this certainly looked the lesser of the two races. The pace looked just ordinary through the early stages, but they finished surprisingly well strung out. They raced down the middle of the track for much of the way, but the first two home ended up racing towards the far-side rail and that looked the place to be.

NOTEBOOK
Marchpane was beaten a long way over an extended 5f on her debut at Bath, but that run clearly brought her on significantly and she was a different filly over this longer trip. She battled on well when challenged by the newcomer Copperwood, putting her experience to good use, and there was a nice gap back to the third. However, both she and the runner-up may have been racing on the best ground towards the far side of the track, and it remains to be seen what the form is worth. (op 33-1)

Copperwood, a Bahamian Bounty colt, half-brother to 1m winner Sophie's Dream, out of a 7f scorer, made a very pleasing racecourse debut. He looked the most likely winner when throwing down a strong challenge inside the final furlong - he was matched at 1.01 on the exchanges - but he was just found out by his inexperience. He should be capable of progressing, but it has to be noted that along with the eventual winner, he was possibly on the best ground towards the far rail, and only time will tell what this form is worth. (op 50-1)

Little Toto actually finished seven lengths in front of Marchpane when down the field on his debut at Bath but, although unable to confirm form, this was still a much-improved performance, especially considering he raced more towards the middle of the track than the front pair. (op 40-1)

Ballochroy(IRE) ran better than when beaten a long way over 6f on his debut at Haydock and seems to be going the right way. He should find his level once handicapped. (op 20-1)

We'Re Delighted ran nowhere near the form he showed when third in what looked a hot race over 6f here on his debut and was disappointing. (op 5-2 tchd 11-4)

Distant Diamond(IRE), down the field on the Polytrack at Lingfield on his debut, was not given too hard a time once his chance had gone and is another who should come into his own when handicapped. (op 33-1 tchd 22-1)

Oxbridge, a Tomba colt, brother to triple 7f-1m1f winner Midnight Lace, out of a winner over 2m3f, was not without support on his racecourse debut. He never landed a blow, but hinted at ability and should be capable of better in time. (op 11-2 tchd 13-2)

Morestead(IRE) showed plenty of ability on his debut at Ascot, but this was a disappointing effort. (op 7-2)

4762 INCENTIVE LEISURE GROUP NURSERY — 6f 8y

1:20 (1:25) (Class 4) 2-Y-O — **£3,886** (£1,156; £577; £288) **Stalls** Centre

Form — RPR

402 **1** **Harlech Castle**[19] 4201 2-8-13 **81** .... TolleyDean(5) 2 — 89
(P F I Cole) *chsd ldrs: pushed along after 2f: heavy reminders over 3f out: stdy on u.p to ld last half f: rdn out* **10/1**

541 **2** 1 ½ **Chatham Islands (USA)**[14] 4350 2-8-11 **74** .... GregFairley 10 — 78
(M Johnston) *lw: chsd ldrs: led ins fnl 3f: kpt on u.p fr over 1f out: hdd and no ex last half f* **11/1**

5510 **3** nk **Regal Rhythm (IRE)**[16] 4274 2-9-3 **80** .... MartinDwyer 14 — 83
(B J Meehan) *in tch: t.k.h: hdwy 3f out: drvn to press ldr jst ins fnl f: kpt on same pce* **33/1**

551 **4** 1 **River Bounty**[21] 4125 2-8-6 **72** .... AndrewElliott(3) 11 — 72
(A P Jarvis) *pressed ldrs: led after 1f: hdd ins fnl 3f: styd wl there tl outpcd ins fnl f* **16/1**

036 **5** ¾ **Richardthesecond (IRE)**[41] 3532 2-8-2 **65** ow2 .... NelsonDeSouza 3 — 62
(R M Beckett) *lw: led 1f: styd pressing ldrs: rdn over 2f out: one pce ins fnl f* **25/1**

6321 **6** shd **Fathsta (IRE)**[19] 4193 2-8-9 **72** .... LPKeniry 7 — 69
(S Kirk) *chsd ldrs: rdn over 2f out: sn one pce* **11/2**[2]

060 **7** 1 ½ **Flying Applause**[27] 3962 2-8-5 **68** .... ChrisCatlin 6 — 61
(A King) *lw: s.i.s: in rr: rdn and sme hdwy fr 3f out: nvr gng pce to be competitive* **14/1**

0132 **8** 2 **We Have A Dream**[10] 4484 2-8-0 **63** ow2 .... FrancisNorton 13 — 50
(W R Muir) *chsd ldrs: rdn 3f out: wknd fnl f* **8/1**[3]

531 **9** ½ **Nylla**[34] 3750 2-8-12 **75** .... TPO'Shea 5 — 60
(M R Channon) *mid-div: rdn 1/2-way: sn wknd* **8/1**[3]

4124 **10** hd **Secret Meaning**[17] 4255 2-8-0 **63** .... (p) AdrianMcCarthy 8 — 47
(W G M Turner) *chsd ldrs 4f* **50/1**

3221 **11** shd **Sinead Of Aglish (IRE)**[67] 2717 2-8-11 **79** .... KevinGhunowa(5) 12 — 63
(A B Haynes) *s.i.s: outpcd thrght* **14/1**

616 **12** nk **Captain Royale (IRE)**[12] 4437 2-9-7 **84** .... SebSanders 9 — 67
(J Noseda) *lw: chsd ldrs: rdn over 2f out: wknd over 1f out* **5/2**[1]

3230 **13** 2 ½ **Party In The Park**[66] 2737 2-9-0 **77** .... PatDobbs 4 — 53
(R Hannon) *outpcd most of way* **8/1**[3]

2504 **14** 2 ½ **Demure Princess**[19] 4193 2-7-9 **61** oh3 .... WilliamBuick(3) 1 — 29
(W G M Turner) *chsd ldrs over 3f* **25/1**

1m 13.18s (-1.14) **Going Correction** -0.10s/f (Good) — **14** Ran SP% **126.5**
Speed ratings (Par 96): **103,101,100,99,98 98,96,93,92,92 92,92,88,85**
CSF £117.49 CT £3623.63 TOTE £11.70: £3.10, £3.10, £6.50; EX 114.20.
Owner Elite Racing Club **Bred** Elite Racing Club **Trained** Whatcombe, Oxon

FOCUS
A fair nursery and the form looks solid. The majority of these raced up the middle of the track, but the winner was the only runner to race far side, with the rail again looking advantageous.

NOTEBOOK
Harlech Castle built on the promise of his recent second in a good maiden over course and distance, despite having the blinkers left off this time. If anything, he may have been seen to even better effect with the headgear left on, for he seemed to hit a bit of a flat spot before finally responding well to strong pressure. This was a useful effort, but the bare result may just want treating with a little caution as he was the only runner to race against the far rail; the same route taken by the winner of the previous race. (op 17-2 tchd 11-1)

Chatham Islands(USA), off the mark over this trip in a Haydock maiden on her previous start, ran right up to form under a positive ride towards the middle of the track, but she was eventually worn down by a rival racing against the far-side rail. (op 15-2)

Regal Rhythm(IRE) ran much better than on his nursery debut at Kempton last time, keeping on well for pressure despite having taken a little bit of a grip through the early stages.

River Bounty found this tougher than the Haydock maiden she won on her previous start, but she ran well and is quietly progressive. (op 14-1)

Richardthesecond(IRE), having his first run since leaving Mark Brisbourne's yard, offered some promise on his nursery debut with his rider putting up 2lb overweight. He could find a small race off his current sort of mark.

Fathsta(IRE) lacked a change of pace when it mattered and could not defy a 7lb rise in the weights for his recent Chester success, with Newbury providing a rather different test. (tchd 9-2)

Captain Royale(IRE) failed to beat a rival in the Phoenix Stakes on his previous start, but his stable are not known for over-facing their horses and it was no surprise to see him made favourite dropped significantly in class, especially as he was able to race off a mark 6lb lower than in future. However, he ran disappointingly and, being by Captain Rio, this ground probably wasn't soft enough for him. (op 11-4 tchd 9-4)

4763 MARSHALL'S PEUGEOT CLAIMING STKS — 1m 2f 6y

1:50 (1:53) (Class 4) 3-4-Y-O — **£4,857** (£1,445; £722; £360) **Stalls** Centre

Form — RPR

0050 **1** **Up In Arms (IRE)**[11] 4458 3-8-7 63 .... JimCrowley 6 — 65
(P Winkworth) *trckd ldrs in 3rd but 7 l off clr ldr 5f out: styd on to go 2nd over 1f out: kpt on wl to ld last stride* **7/2**[1]

4406 **2** shd **Tufton**[42] 3482 4-9-5 85 .... (t) AshleyHamblett(5) 4 — 74
(M Botti) *led: sn clr and 6 l ahd 5f out: stl clr 2f out: rdn and edgd rt 1f out: kpt on but ct last stride* **7/2**[1]

0560 **3** 3 ½ **Law Of The Land (IRE)**[12] 4416 3-8-3 55 .... ChrisCatlin 5 — 54
(W R Muir) *stdd s: in rr: rdn over 3f out: styd on u.p fnl 2f: kpt on ins fnl f but nvr gng pce to rch ldng duo* **33/1**

0203 **4** 2 **Magic Mountain (IRE)**[8] 4550 3-9-1 77 .... SebSanders 8 — 62
(R Hannon) *racd in 4th and 12 l off clr ldr 5f out: rdn over 3f out: sme hdwy 2f but but nvr in contention: wknd ins fnl f* **7/2**[1]

1100 **5** shd **Birkside**[25] 4015 4-8-13 70 .... PaulDoe 7 — 52
(S Dow) *stdd s: in rr: rdn over 3f out: styd on fnl 2f but nvr in contention* **6/1**[2]

0-26 **6** 1 ½ **Lindy Lou**[8] 4542 3-8-10 69 .... SimonWhitworth 3 — 54
(C A Cyzer) *chsd clr ldr: rdn and no imp fr 3f out: wknd appr fnl f* **7/2**[1]

0000 **7** 26 **Hard As Iron**[10] 3966 3-8-4 46 .... FrancisNorton 1 — —
(M Blanshard) *a in rr* **40/1**

0002 **8** 5 **Anatolian Prince**[9] 4516 3-8-3 50 .... (t) MartinDwyer 2 — —
(J M P Eustace) *a in rr: lost tch fnl 3f* **14/1**[3]

2m 9.19s (0.48) **Going Correction** -0.10s/f (Good)
WFA 3 from 4yo 8lb — **8** Ran SP% **115.2**
Speed ratings (Par 105): **94,93,91,89,89 88,67,63**
CSF £15.85 TOTE £4.90: £1.70, £1.90, £4.90; EX 19.30.
Owner Sundae Best **Bred** John O'Dwyer And J Ryan **Trained** Chiddingfold, Surrey

FOCUS
A reasonable claimer on paper, but the form probably wants treating with some caution. The pace was steady through the first couple of furlongs, but Tufton soon increased the gallop when pulling his way into a clear lead and, ignored by his seven rivals, he very nearly held on. Up In Arms was the only horse to make up any ground from off the pace and he had the benefit of the far rail to run against late on, just like the winners of the two previous races.
Anatolian Prince Official explanation: trainer said colt has a breathing problem

4764 DESIGNER WAY VACATION CLUB MEDIAN AUCTION MAIDEN STKS (DIV II) — 7f (S)

2:20 (2:23) (Class 5) 2-Y-O — **£3,562** (£1,059; £529; £264) **Stalls** Centre

Form — RPR

1 **Perfect Act** 2-8-12 0 .... AdamKirby 13 — 80+
(C G Cox) *w'like: athletic: lw: in rr: rdn along 1/2-way: gd hdwy ins fnl 2f and str run to ld last half f: sn in command: won gng away* **4/1**[2]

00 **2** 2 ½ **Doctor Robert**[21] 4130 2-9-3 0 .... ChrisCatlin 9 — 79
(R Charlton) *lw: chsd ldrs: rdn and ev ch fr 2f out: one pce jst ins fnl f: styd on again to take 2nd cl home* **10/1**

4 **3** nk **Lodi (IRE)**[14] 4362 2-9-3 0 .... RobertHavlin 4 — 78
(B J Meehan) *trckd ldrs: led over 2f out: hrd drvn over 1f out: hdd and outpcd last half f: lost 2nd cl home* **7/2**[1]

5320 **4** nk **Farthermost (IRE)**[21] 4121 2-9-3 68 .... PatDobbs 1 — 77
(R Hannon) *led tl hdd over 2f out: outpcd ins fnl f* **9/1**

5 3 ½ **Chief Eric** 2-9-0 0 .... WilliamBuick(3) 12 — 69
(B I Case) *w'like: str: bit bkwd: in rr and pushed along 1/2-way: styd on wl appr fnl f and kpt on cl home but nvr in contention* **66/1**

5 **6** shd **Challow Hills (USA)**[37] 3643 2-8-12 0 .... DaneO'Neill 7 — 63
(B W Hills) *towards rr tl hdwy 3f out: nvr rchd ldrs and one pce fnl f* **17/2**

7 1 ½ **Flight To Quality** 2-9-3 0 .... GregFairley 11 — 65
(M Johnston) *w'like: in tch: rdn and hdwy 3f out: chsd ldrs u.p 2f out: wknd appr fnl f* **20/1**

8 ¾ **Samurai Warrior** 2-9-3 0 .... FergusSweeney 8 — 63
(P J Makin) *w'like: bit bkwd: in tch: pushed along 1/2-way: nvr gng pce to be competitive* **50/1**

0 **9** 2 **Richcar (IRE)**[26] 3991 2-9-3 0 .... SebSanders 3 — 58
(R M Beckett) *str: pressed ldrs: rdn and ev ch over 2f out: sn wknd* **13/2**[3]

10 nk **Dubai Land** 2-9-3 0 .... TPO'Shea 6 — 57
(M R Channon) *leggy: swtg: green and pushed along in rr: mod late prog* **25/1**

00 **11** ½ **Ride A White Swan**[22] 4110 2-8-12 0 .... KevinGhunowa(5) 5 — 56
(P A Blockley) *nvr bttr than mid-div* **50/1**

4 **12** nk **Rivington Pike (IRE)**[16] 4286 2-9-3 0 .... LPKeniry 2 — 55
(J J Quinn) *unf: scope: chsd ldrs over 4f: kpt on again wl ins fnl f* **13/2**[3]

13 shd **Harting Hill** 2-9-3 0 .... MartinDwyer 15 — 55
(M P Tregoning) *unf: slowly away: mod prog fr over 1f out* **20/1**

0 **14** 5 **Okafranca (IRE)**[20] 4162 2-9-3 0 .... FrancisNorton 10 — 42
(W R Muir) *a outpcd* **40/1**

1m 26.38s (-0.62) **Going Correction** -0.10s/f (Good) — **14** Ran SP% **119.7**
Speed ratings (Par 94): **99,96,95,95,91 91,89,88,86,86 85,85,85,79**
CSF £40.18 TOTE £5.60: £2.40, £3.10, £1.70; EX 52.80.
Owner Dr Bridget Drew & E E Dedman **Bred** Howard Barton Stud **Trained** Lambourn, Berks

FOCUS
Again probably just an ordinary maiden by Newbury's standards, but the winning time was virtually a second quicker than the first division and this looked the better of the two races. They all tended to race up the middle of the track, surprisingly shunning the far rail.

NOTEBOOK
Perfect Act ◆, a 26,000gns daughter of Act One, out of a mare who was placed over 6f at two, was well backed in the morning before drifting out a little on course. She came under pressure a fair way from the finish, but gradually got the hang of things and stayed on in taking fashion to ultimately win decisively. This did not look a great race, but she created a favourable impression and deserves her chance in a good race. She could take her chance in the £300000 St Leger sales race at Doncaster. (op 5-2)

Doctor Robert confirmed the promise of his recent Newmarket effort, but he was no match for the winner. He seems to be going the right way and is now qualified for a handicap mark. (op 8-1)

Lodi(IRE) ran a respectable race in third without really improving on the form he showed when fourth in a maiden for unraced juveniles on his debut at Newmarket. (op 3-1 tchd 11-4)

Farthermost(IRE) was not at his best when well weighted in a nursery at Goodwood on his previous start, but he ran his race this time and this looks about as good as he is. (op 14-1)

Chief Eric, a Slickly colt, half-brother to a winner in Sweden, out of a mare who was placed in France, was noted keeping on from a fair way back and this was a pleasing introduction. His stable have had a juvenile winner already this season and this one looks to possess plenty of ability. (op 50-1)

Challow Hills(USA) did not really build on the form she showed on her debut at Kempton and she may not be seen at her best until tackling further next year. (op 8-1 tchd 9-1)
Ride A White Swan Official explanation: jockey said colt was never travelling
Rivington Pike(IRE) came all the way down from North Yorkshire, the only representative from the John Quinn yard at the meeting, but he failed to confirm the promise he showed when a running-on fourth on his debut over 6f at Pontefract. (op 8-1)
Okafranca(IRE) Official explanation: jockey said colt hung right

4765 TIMELINX.COM MAIDEN FILLIES' STKS — 1m 2f 6y
2:50 (2:53) (Class 5) 3-Y-O+ — **£3,886** (£1,156; £577; £288) **Stalls** Centre

Form — RPR
63- **1** **Kahara**[310] 6049 3-8-12 0 ... SebSanders 7 — 81+
(L M Cumani) *lw: hld up in rr: hdwy over 3f out: trckd wnr 2f out: drvn to ld wl over 1f out: styd on strly* **15/8**[2]
4-24 **2** 2 **Fringe**[27] 3978 4-9-6 80 ... JimCrowley 3 — 75
(Jane Chapple-Hyam) *lw: chsd ldrs: rdn and effrt over 2f out: outpcd over 1f out: styd on again ins fnl f and tk 2nd on line but no ch w wnr* **7/4**[1]
4-3 **3** shd **Teodora Adivina**[116] 1364 3-8-12 0 ... MartinDwyer 1 — 75
(H R A Cecil) *w'like: led: rdn over 2f out: hdd wl over 1f out: one pce ins fnl f: ct for 2nd last stride* **4/1**[3]
0 **4** 5 **Granary**[18] 4235 3-8-12 0 ... DaneO'Neill 5 — 65
(H Candy) *w'like: chsd ldr: rdn 3f out: lost 2nd 2f out: wknd over 1f out* **33/1**
06-6 **5** nk **Indigo Rose (IRE)**[11] 4457 3-8-12 0 ... RobertHavlin 4 — 64
(J H M Gosden) *in tch: rdn and effrt over 2f out: nvr gng pce to be competitive: sn btn* **12/1**
0 **6** 9 **Thermidora**[65] 2766 3-8-12 0 ... OscarUrbina 8 — 46
(J R Fanshawe) *rdn 4f out: a towards rr* **14/1**
00 **7** 2 1/2 **Slip Silver**[55] 3084 3-8-12 0 ... PatDobbs 6 — 41
(P J Makin) *s.i.s: a in rr: no ch fnl 4f* **50/1**
05 **8** 22 **Susanna's Dance**[12] 4430 3-8-12 0 ... (vt[1]) GregFairley 2 — —
(M Botti) *w'like: chsd ldrs: rdn over 4f out and wknd qckly* **25/1**

2m 7.44s (-1.27) **Going Correction** -0.10s/f (Good)
WFA 3 from 4yo 8lb — **8** Ran SP% **114.3**
Speed ratings (Par 100): **101,99,99,95,95 87,85,68**
CSF £5.44 TOTE £2.70: £1.20, £1.10, £1.40; EX 6.20.
Owner Fittocks Stud & Mrs John Magnier **Bred** Fittocks Stud **Trained** Newmarket, Suffolk

FOCUS
The bare form of this fillies' maiden looks just ordinary, with the runner-up probably not running up to her official mark of 80, but a couple of these appeal as quite interesting types. The early pace was only steady.

4766 TURFSURF EQUINE SURFACING FILLIES' H'CAP — 1m 4f 5y
3:25 (3:25) (Class 5) (0-70,69) 3-Y-O+ — **£3,238** (£963; £481; £240) **Stalls** Centre

Form — RPR
3203 **1** **Generous Jem**[21] 4131 4-9-6 59 ... GeorgeBaker 8 — 70
(G G Margarson) *hld up in rr: stdy hdwy fr 3f out: styd on strly u.p to ld last half f: readily* **10/1**[3]
410 **2** 1 1/4 **Elegant Hawk**[19] 4205 3-9-6 69 ... PaulDoe 10 — 78
(W J Knight) *lw: in rr: hdwy over 3f out: drvn to ld over 1f out: hdd and one pce last half f* **10/1**[3]
143 **3** 2 **Abounding**[20] 4172 3-9-3 66 ... SebSanders 3 — 72
(R M Beckett) *lw: in rr: hdwy fr 3f out: drvn to chse ldrs over 1f out: kpt on same pce ins fnl f* **4/1**[2]
2212 **4** 1 3/4 **Cushat Law (IRE)**[8] 4542 3-9-2 65 ... MartinDwyer 6 — 68
(W Jarvis) *chsd ldrs: rdn and effrt over 2f out: nvr quite gng pce to chal: wknd ins fnl f* **4/1**[2]
2403 **5** 2 **Snake Skin**[17] 4253 4-9-4 60 ... JerryO'Dwyer[(3)] 1 — 60
(J Gallagher) *chsd ldr: led 3f out: sn hrd drvn: hdd over 1f out: wknd ins fnl f* **20/1**
0040 **6** 3/4 **Palanoverre (IRE)**[17] 4259 3-8-6 55 ... (t) FrancisNorton 2 — 54
(D J S Ffrench Davis) *mid-div: rdn and effrt over 3f out: wknd over 1f out* **33/1**
4051 **7** 3 1/2 **Orphina (IRE)**[8] 4534 4-8-9 55 6ex ... (t) KylieManser[(7)] 4 — 48
(B G Powell) *in rr tl mod prog fnl f* **20/1**
-005 **8** 1/2 **Where's Broughton**[22] 4112 4-10-0 67 ... TPO'Shea 14 — 59
(W J Musson) *lw: stdd towards rr: sme prog towards outside over 2f out: nvr rchd ldrs and sn wknd* **12/1**
-002 **9** 1 1/4 **Ashwell Rose**[21] 4131 5-9-6 59 ... (v) AdamKirby 9 — 49
(J R Jenkins) *chsd ldrs: rdn 3f out: sn btn* **33/1**
0005 **10** shd **It's No Problem (IRE)**[2] 4632 3-8-1 50 ... DavidKinsella 5 — 40
(M Salaman) *in tch: shkn up over 2f out: sn dropped away* **33/1**
2603 **11** 2 1/2 **Driving Miss Suzie**[16] 4277 3-8-12 64 ... (v[1]) WilliamBuick[(3)] 13 — 50
(A M Balding) *b.hind: sn led: hdd 3f out: wknd over 2f out* **20/1**
4362 **12** 4 **Candy Mountain**[19] 4205 3-9-6 69 ... RobertHavlin 12 — 49
(L M Cumani) *in tch: hdwy towards outside 5f out: chsd ldrs over 3f out: wknd over 2f out* **3/1**[1]
0203 **13** 5 **Pentasilea**[39] 3598 4-9-9 62 ... (v[1]) DaneO'Neill 11 — 34
(H J L Dunlop) *chsd ldrs tl wknd qckly 3f out* **12/1**
1004 **14** 5 **Kyloe Belle (USA)**[10] 4472 3-8-10 59 ... OscarUrbina 7 — 23
(Mrs A J Perrett) *chsd ldrs: rdn and wknd 3f out* **50/1**

2m 35.67s (-0.32) **Going Correction** -0.10s/f (Good)
WFA 3 from 4yo+ 10lb — **14** Ran SP% **123.6**
Speed ratings (Par 100): **97,96,94,93,92 91,89,89,88,88 86,83,80,77**
CSF £99.71 CT £477.11 TOTE £11.50: £3.80, £4.70, £2.40; EX 118.00.
Owner Norcroft Park Stud **Bred** Norcroft Park Stud **Trained** Newmarket, Suffolk

FOCUS
This looked like quite a good fillies' handicap for the grade, with the proximity of the both third and fourth-placed horses helping to give the form a very solid look. The first three all came from off the good pace.
Candy Mountain Official explanation: trainer's representative said filly may have failed to stay 12f

4767 T SQUARED GROUP APPRENTICE H'CAP — 6f 8y
4:00 (4:00) (Class 5) (0-75,74) 3-Y-O+ — **£3,238** (£963; £481; £240) **Stalls** Centre

Form — RPR
4310 **1** **Tamino (IRE)**[31] 3828 4-8-11 64 ow2 ... (t) RyanBird[(5)] 8 — 77
(H Morrison) *in tch: hdwy 2f out to ld 1f out: drvn out* **7/2**[1]
0300 **2** 1 **Brandywell Boy (IRE)**[18] 4236 4-8-9 62 ... KylieManser[(3)] 9 — 70
(D J S Ffrench Davis) *lw: led over 4f out: shkn up and hdd 1f out: styd on same pce* **10/1**
0006 **3** 1 3/4 **Musical Script (USA)**[18] 4236 4-8-5 55 oh3 ... (b) JamieHamblett 3 — 58
(Mouse Hamilton-Fairley) *t.k.h: hld up in rr but in tch: hdwy over 1f out: kpt on ins fnl f but nvr quite gng pce to chal* **16/1**
0400 **4** shd **High Ridge**[32] 3802 8-8-10 65 ... (p) PietroRomeo[(5)] 4 — 67
(J M Bradley) *b: in rr: vigorously drvn and hdwy over 1f out: styd on ins fnl f but nvr gng pce to chal* **25/1**
056 **5** hd **Sun Catcher (IRE)**[28] 3905 4-9-10 74 ... (b) HaddenFrost 6 — 76
(R Hannon) *chsd ldrs: rdn to chal fr 2f out: no ex ins fnl f* **7/1**
0004 **6** hd **The Cayterers**[9] 4515 5-9-6 73 ... (p) PJBenson[(3)] 2 — 74
(J M Bradley) *chsd ldrs: ev ch over 1f out: sn one pce* **5/1**[3]
3433 **7** hd **Caustic Wit (IRE)**[5] 4634 9-9-2 66 ... JackDean 1 — 67
(M S Saunders) *chsd ldrs: ev ch over 1f out: one pce* **4/1**[2]
-002 **8** nk **Proud Killer**[6] 4594 4-8-12 62 ... JamieJones 7 — 62
(J R Jenkins) *led tl over 4f out: styd chsng ldrs: wknd ins fnl f* **11/1**
401 **9** 3 1/2 **Sweet Pickle**[25] 4017 6-9-3 70 ... (e) HarryPoulton[(3)] 5 — 59
(J R Boyle) *s.i.s: a outpcd* **13/2**
1100 **10** 1 3/4 **Charlie Delta**[18] 4236 4-9-0 67 ... (b) AlanRutter[(3)] 10 — 51
(J M Bradley) *chsd ldrs 4f* **12/1**

1m 13.24s (-1.08) **Going Correction** -0.10s/f (Good) — **10** Ran SP% **119.6**
Speed ratings (Par 103): **103,101,99,99,98 98,98,98,93,91**
CSF £40.39 CT £515.92 TOTE £5.20: £1.90, £2.80, £5.60; EX 50.10 Place 6 ££3194.48, Place 5 £93.96.
Owner H Scott-Barrett & Lord Margadale **Bred** Century Bloodstock **Trained** East Ilsley, Berks

FOCUS
A modest sprint handicap restricted to apprentices who had not ridden more than 25 winners. They were spread out all over the track in the closing stages. The winner is progressing but most of the others are going the opposite way.
T/Plt: £37,034.20 to a £1 stake. Pool: £50,731.80. 0.30 winning tickets. T/Qpdt: £18.80 to a £1 stake. Pool: £4,462.30. 175.40 winning tickets. ST

4578 NEWCASTLE (L-H)
Friday, August 24

OFFICIAL GOING: Good (good to firm in places; 8.0)
Wind: Breezy, half against Weather: Fine

4768 EARL BEAZER OF DUNSTON APPRENTICE H'CAP — 6f
5:35 (5:35) (Class 6) (0-65,65) 3-Y-O+ — **£2,266** (£674; £337; £168) **Stalls** Low

Form — RPR
0240 **1** **Lambency (IRE)**[7] 4583 4-8-7 51 ... GaryBartley[(3)] 15 — 61
(J S Goldie) *bhd: stdy hdwy 1/2-way: rdn to ld ins fnl f: r.o wl* **5/1**[2]
0500 **2** 2 **Petite Mac**[20] 4180 7-8-9 53 ow1 ... JamesO'Reilly[(3)] 13 — 57
(N Bycroft) *midfield: rdn over 3f out: rallied to ld 2f out to ins fnl f: kpt on same pce* **7/1**
0500 **3** nk **Obe One**[2] 4719 7-8-0 46 oh1 ... PatrickDonaghy[(5)] 17 — 49
(A Berry) *towards rr: hdwy and prom over 1f out: kpt on ins fnl f* **8/1**
0500 **4** 1 **Dazzler Mac**[33] 3765 6-8-3 49 ow2 ... MarkCoumbe[(5)] 7 — 48
(N Bycroft) *bhd tl kpt on fr 2f out: nrst fin* **7/1**
1414 **5** 1 1/2 **Majestical (IRE)**[10] 4474 5-8-13 54 ... (p) LukeMorris 1 — 49
(V Smith) *dwlt: bhd tl hdwy over 1f out: kpt on but no further imp last 100yds* **4/1**[1]
/400 **6** 3 **Avontuur (FR)**[10] 4479 5-8-2 48 ... (b) AdeleRothery[(5)] 14 — 33
(D W Chapman) *led after 2f to 2f out: rdn and no ex fnl f* **20/1**
0000 **7** 1 **Foreign Edition (IRE)**[74] 2508 5-9-6 64 ... MCGeran[(3)] 4 — 46
(Miss J A Camacho) *led 2f: cl up tl wknd appr fnl f* **6/1**[3]
0050 **8** 1 1/4 **Stanley Wolfe (IRE)**[14] 4351 4-8-3 49 oh1 ow3 ... AdamCarter[(5)] 2 — 27
(Garry Moss) *prom tl rdn and wknd appr fnl f* **12/1**
0000 **9** 1 1/4 **Rosie's Result**[28] 3921 7-8-2 46 oh1 ... AmyBaker[(3)] 5 — 20
(M Todhunter) *chsd ldrs tl wknd over 1f out* **25/1**
0-00 **10** 2 1/2 **Woodwee**[88] 2091 4-8-0 46 oh1 ... LauraReynolds[(5)] 8 — 12
(R E Barr) *chsd ldrs tl wknd over 2f out* **14/1**
6100 **11** 3/4 **Grand View**[114] 1400 11-8-1 47 ... (p) JemmaMarshall[(5)] 6 — 10
(J R Weymes) *towards rr: struggling 1/2-way: n.d* **25/1**
-000 **12** 2 **Mint**[114] 1404 4-8-9 55 ... NSLawes[(5)] 3 — 12
(D W Barker) *w ldrs tl wknd wl over 1f out* **12/1**
4500 **13** 17 **Bandos**[46] 3376 7-7-12 46 oh1 ... TimothyMeadows[(7)] 10 — —
(M Smith) *s.i.s and rdr lost irons: bhd: lost tch fr over 2f out* **25/1**

1m 14.91s (-0.18) **Going Correction** -0.025s/f (Good) — **13** Ran SP% **125.4**
Speed ratings (Par 101): **100,97,96,95,93 89,88,86,84,81 80,77,55**
CSF £40.01 CT £225.90 TOTE £7.60: £2.60, £2.00, £2.10; EX 48.60.
Owner The Reluctant Suitor's **Bred** Mount Coote Stud, Richard Pegum & M Bell Racing **Trained** Uplawmoor, E Renfrews

FOCUS
A modest handicap run at a decent gallop and one in which the field raced centre-to-far side. The winner is rated back to her best.
Lambency(IRE) Official explanation: trainer's rep had no explanation for the apparent improvement in form

4769 WOR SYLVIES GREAT NORTH AIR AMBULANCE NOVICE AUCTION STKS — 6f
6:05 (6:05) (Class 5) 2-Y-O — **£3,785** (£1,132; £566; £283; £141) **Stalls** Low

Form — RPR
1461 **1** **Taurian**[20] 4154 2-9-7 84 ... TomEaves 4 — 87
(Mrs L Stubbs) *hld up in tch: effrt 2f out: led ins fnl f: rdn out* **4/1**[3]
2145 **2** 2 **Archived (IRE)**[13] 4372 2-9-2 84 ... JamieMoriarty[(3)] 3 — 79
(M G Quinlan) *trckd ldrs: drvn over 2f out: chsd wnr ins fnl f: r.o* **7/4**[1]
6400 **3** 1 1/4 **Dalkey Girl (IRE)**[13] 4372 2-8-3 79 ... LukeMorris[(5)] 5 — 64
(V Smith) *trckd ldrs: rdn over 2f out: kpt on same pce fnl f* **11/4**[2]
4 3/4 **Monadreen Flyer (IRE)**[19] 4207 2-9-8 0 ... PaulHanagan 7 — 76
(Daniel Mark Loughnane, Ire) *led: rdn and edgd lft over 1f out: hdd and no ex ins fnl f* **14/1**
04 **5** nk **Scruffy Skip (IRE)**[21] 4125 2-8-11 0 ... DaleGibson 8 — 64
(M Dods) *hld up: shkn up and hdwy over 1f out: kpt on fnl f: no imp* **33/1**
5 **6** 1 **Grand Value (USA)**[29] 3884 2-8-4 0 ... PaulFessey 2 — 54
(T D Barron) *in tch: effrt over 2f out: no imp fnl f* **20/1**
32 **7** 4 **Suzi Spends (IRE)**[12] 4428 2-8-3 0 ... AndrewMullen[(3)] 9 — 44
(M Johnston) *sn chsng ldr: rdn over 2f out: wknd over 1f out* **5/1**

1m 16.11s (1.02) **Going Correction** -0.025s/f (Good) — **7** Ran SP% **114.1**
Speed ratings (Par 94): **92,89,87,86,86 84,79**
CSF £11.39 TOTE £5.00: £2.10, £1.80; EX 16.40.
Owner Tyme Partnership **Bred** Angmering Park Stud **Trained** Norton, N. Yorks

FOCUS
An ordinary event in which the pace was just fair and the field raced far side. The winner is progressive.

NOTEBOOK
Taurian, who has only raced on a sound surface, is a steadily progressive performer who turned in his best effort. He won with a bit more in hand than the official margin suggests and, although life will be tougher after reassessment, he may be capable of a bit better still. (op 10-3 tchd 5-1)
Archived(IRE), down in distance, is a consistent sort who looks a fair guide to the worth of this form. He will be suited by the return to 7f, is in good hands and may be capable of a bit better. (op 2-1 tchd 5-2)

Dalkey Girl(IRE), down a furlong in trip, was again below her best despite claiming third. (tchd 2-1 and 3-1)

Monadreen Flyer(IRE), a winner at Cork in June, was not disgraced dropped in distance but left the impression that the return to 7f would be more to his liking. He looks capable of winning away from progressive sorts in ordinary nursery company. (tchd 12-1)

Scruffy Skip(IRE) ◆, who showed improved form on his previous start, confirmed that promise and left the strong impression that the step up to 7f and the step into modest handicap company would be to his liking. He is one to keep an eye on. (op 25-1)

Grand Value(USA), soundly beaten over 7f in heavy ground at York on her debut, fared better this time but left the impression that the return to that trip and beyond and the step into modest handicaps would be in her favour. (tchd 25-1)

4770 INTERCEIL.CO.UK 25TH ANNIVERSARY CLAIMING STKS 7f

6:35 (6:35) (Class 6) 2-Y-O **£2,266** (£674; £337; £168) **Stalls** Low

Form RPR

4356 **1** **Casino Night**[16] 4278 2-8-8 63 ... KDarley 13 63+
(M Johnston) *mde all stands' side: overall ldr over 2f out: r.o strly* **2/1**[1]

2 *6* **Reel Buddy Star** 2-8-9 0 ... MickyFenton 5 49
(T P Tate) *missed break: racd far side: hdwy to ld that gp ins fnl f: no ch w stands' side wnr: 1st of 10 in gp* **16/1**

00 **3** *1 1/4* **Buju**[11] 4448 2-8-13 0 ... TomEaves 2 50
(N Tinkler) *hld up far side: hdwy over 2f out: kpt on fnl f: no imp: 2nd of 10 in gp* **33/1**

0520 **4** *shd* **Dawn Light (IRE)**[13] 4405 2-8-4 53 ...(p) RoystonFfrench 12 41
(Mrs A Duffield) *chsd stands' side wnr: rdn over 2f out: sn one pce: 2nd of 4 in gp* **14/1**

2220 **5** *1/2* **Prigsnov Dancer (IRE)**[7] 4560 2-8-13 65 ... LeeEnstone 7 48
(P C Haslam) *prom far side: effrt over 2f out: one pce over 1f out: 3rd of 10 in gp* **5/1**[3]

4563 **6** *1/2* **Elusive Lady (IRE)**[13] 4405 2-9-2 48 ... PhillipMakin 9 50
(J R Weymes) *in tch far side: led that gp over 2f out to ins fnl f: no ex: 4th of 10 in gp* **12/1**

0021 **7** *nk* **Willyn (IRE)**[21] 4136 2-9-2 65 ... DanielTudhope 1 49
(J S Goldie) *chsd far side ldrs: effrt over 2f out: one pce over 1f out: 5th of 10 in gp* **7/2**[2]

0040 **8** *1/2* **Dhaka Dazzle**[19] 4202 2-8-13 56 ... SamHitchcott 15 45
(M R Channon) *chsd stands' side ldrs: drvn over 2f out: sn no ex: 3rd of 4 in gp* **14/1**

0 **9** *1 1/2* **Green's Delight**[30] 3834 2-8-8 0 ... DaleGibson 16 36
(M W Easterby) *hld up stand's side: rdn 3f out: sn btn: last of 4 in gp* **28/1**

00 **10** *hd* **Somarini**[22] 4102 2-8-4 0 ... PaulHanagan 8 32
(J G Given) *chsd far side ldrs tl wknd fr 2f out: 6th of 10 in gp* **12/1**

0 **11** *10* **Piccolo Pete**[18] 4221 2-9-7 0 ... GrahamGibbons 11 24
(J J Quinn) *in tch far side tl wknd over 2f out: 7th of 10 in gp* **33/1**

4564 **12** *5* **Amy Lionheart**[7] 4559 2-8-4 38 ... KimTinkler 4 —
(N Tinkler) *led far side to over 2f out: sn btn: 8th of 10 in gp* **33/1**

0006 **13** *2* **Carlton Mac**[13] 4405 2-8-13 34 ... PaulFessey 10 —
(N Bycroft) *towards rr far side: struggling 3f out: sn btn: 9th of 10 in gp* **100/1**

0000 **14** *36* **Social Height (IRE)**[7] 4559 2-8-11 34 ... AdrianTNicholls 3 —
(A Berry) *bhd far side: lost tch fr 1/2-way: last of 10 in gp: lame* **100/1**

1m 29.18s (1.16) **Going Correction** -0.025s/f (Good) **14** Ran SP% **121.1**
Speed ratings (Par 92): **92,85,83,83,83 82,82,81,79,79 68,62,60,19**
CSF £36.69 TOTE £3.10: £1.80, £5.10, £12.00; EX 90.50.The winner was claimed by J Weymes for £8,000. Reel Buddy Star was claimed by J W Armstrong for £6,000.

Owner J Shack **Bred** Kingsmead Breeders **Trained** Middleham Moor, N Yorks

FOCUS
Not the most competitive of events but a fair pace and one in which the stands'-side winner scored with plenty in hand. She did not need to run to her previous best to score.

NOTEBOOK
Casino Night, dropped in grade, had a good chance at the weights but turned in her best effort to win by a wide margin and was claimed by John Weymes for £8,000. While clearly a fair sort in this grade, life is going to be tougher back in nursery company after reassessment. (op 7-4 tchd 9-4)

Reel Buddy Star, who cost only 6,000gns and is out of an unraced half-sister to a bumper and a hurdles winner, fared the best of the larger group to race on the far side. He may be capable of a bit better, especially over 1m and beyond and he is up to winning a similar event. (op 20-1)

Buju, who bettered her debut form on his previous outing, ran to a similar level here. Although this form is only moderate, he is worth a try over 1m and may do better in ordinary nursery company. (tchd 28-1)

Dawn Light(IRE), upped to 7f and tried in cheekpieces for the first time, bettered the form of her previous run over 6f and seemed to have no problems with this trip. She looks capable of winning a modest event.

Prigsnov Dancer(IRE) looked to have fair claims at the weights but he proved a bit of a disappointment on his first run over this trip. He may do better in nursery company but may have to come down in the weights before he is able to get off the mark. (op 9-2 tchd 11-2)

Elusive Lady(IRE), who turned in an improved effort on her previous start, ran creditably in the face of a stiff task but she may have to step into modest handicap company if she is to get off the mark. (tchd 11-1)

Social Height(IRE) Official explanation: vet said gelding finished lame

4771 PPER&D POWER CHILL MAIDEN STKS 1m 2f 32y

7:05 (7:07) (Class 5) 3-4-Y-O **£3,154** (£944; £472; £236; £117) **Stalls** Centre

Form RPR

5-00 **1** **Spell Casting (USA)**[91] 2002 4-9-11 77 ... RoystonFfrench 5 74
(M H Tompkins) *hld up: hdwy to ld over 1f out: edgd lft ins fnl f: kpt on wl* **13/8**[2]

2 *2* **Royal Jasra** 3-9-3 0 ... PaulHanagan 4 70
(E A L Dunlop) *hld up in tch: effrt and ev ch over 1f out: kpt on ins fnl f* **6/1**[3]

4 **3** *9* **Exclusionist**[67] 2726 3-9-3 0 ... KDarley 2 52
(J Noseda) *chsd ldr: sn pushed along: hrd drvn and outpcd over 2f out: n.d after* **10/11**[1]

00-6 **4** *1 1/4* **Flaming Cat (IRE)**[36] 3675 4-9-11 45 ...(p) PaddyAspell 9 49
(F Watson) *bhd: rdn over 3f out: kpt on fnl f: n.d* **66/1**

5 *2 1/2* **Drama Kid (IRE)**[25] 1983 4-9-3 0 ... JamieMoriarty[(3)] 7 39
(Daniel Mark Loughnane, Ire) *hld up: rdn over 3f out: nvr rchd ldrs* **33/1**

4004 **6** *3/4* **Ammeyrr**[7] 4563 3-8-12 56 ...(v[1]) KellyHarrison[(5)] 8 43
(A Crook) *t.k.h: led to over 1f out: sn btn* **50/1**

20-5 **7** *1 1/4* **Starbougg**[13] 4411 3-8-12 68 ... PhillipMakin 1 35
(K G Reveley) *in tch: rdn over 3f out: wknd over 2f out* **20/1**

05-3 **8** *1/2* **Soubriquet (IRE)**[125] 956 4-9-11 55 ...(t) DavidAllan 10 39
(M A Barnes) *chsd ldrs tl rdn and wknd over 2f out* **14/1**

00 **9** *32* **Florentino**[5] 4641 3-8-12 0 ... TomEaves 6 —
(C W Thornton) *hld up: rdn 3f out: sn btn* **80/1**

2m 10.02s (-1.78) **Going Correction** -0.15s/f (Firm)
WFA 3 from 4yo 8lb **9** Ran SP% **123.8**
Speed ratings (Par 103): **101,99,92,91,89 88,87,87,61**
CSF £12.48 TOTE £2.90: £1.10, £1.50, £1.20; EX 14.10.

Owner Mrs M H Tompkins **Bred** Airlie Stud **Trained** Newmarket, Suffolk

FOCUS
An uncompetitive event but one in which the pace was soon fair. Weak form overall, held down by the fourth, and the winner was a stone off his best figure.

4772 ROFLOW.COM ENVIRONMENTAL ENGINEERING H'CAP 1m 2f 32y

7:35 (7:37) (Class 5) (0-75,68) 3-Y-O+ **£3,469** (£1,038; £519; £259; £129) **Stalls** Centre

Form RPR

0415 **1** **Dechiper (IRE)**[7] 4582 5-8-10 57 ... PatrickDonaghy[(7)] 4 65
(R Johnson) *hld up: hdwy over 2f out: led wl ins fnl f: kpt on wl* **4/1**[2]

230 **2** *3/4* **Red Chairman**[18] 4230 5-9-3 62 ...(p) KellyHarrison[(5)] 10 68
(R Johnson) *t.k.h: led and clr: hdd and no ex wl ins fnl f* **10/1**

1215 **3** *1/2* **Neil's Legacy (IRE)**[13] 4382 5-9-7 66 ... NeilBrown[(5)] 8 71
(Miss L A Perratt) *hld up in tch: effrt over 2f out: edgd lft over 1f out: ch wl ins fnl f: hld nr fin* **7/1**

0006 **4** *nk* **Trouble Mountain (USA)**[7] 4582 10-9-11 65 ...(t) DaleGibson 6 69
(M W Easterby) *hld up: pushed along over 2f out: kpt on fnl f: no imp* **8/1**

5663 **5** *1* **Gloucester**[7] 4582 4-9-11 65 ... GrahamGibbons 5 67
(J J Quinn) *t.k.h: prom: effrt over 2f out: no ex fnl f* **5/2**[1]

5501 **6** *1 3/4* **Sforzando**[15] 4333 6-10-0 68 ... TomEaves 7 67
(Mrs L Stubbs) *in tch: effrt over 2f out: sn one pce* **15/2**

23-0 **7** *5* **Boppys Pride**[226] 89 4-9-3 57 ... PaulHanagan 1 46
(R A Fahey) *chsd clr ldr: drvn 3f out: btn over 1f out* **9/2**[3]

-000 **8** *10* **Missouri (USA)**[31] 3815 4-8-9 49 oh4 ...(t) DavidAllan 2 18
(M A Barnes) *chsd ldrs: drvn 1/2-way: rallied: wknd fr 3f out* **33/1**

030- **9** *14* **Malech (IRE)**[237] 5568 4-9-10 64 ... PhillipMakin 3 5
(K G Reveley) *slolwly into stride: bhd: rdn over 3f out: sn struggling* **33/1**

2m 8.85s (-2.95) **Going Correction** -0.15s/f (Firm) **9** Ran SP% **117.1**
Speed ratings (Par 103): **105,104,104,103,102 101,97,89,78**
CSF £44.09 CT £270.17 TOTE £6.30: £2.00, £3.30, £2.10; EX 35.00.

Owner L Armstrong **Bred** Tommy Burns **Trained** Newburn, Tyne & Wear

FOCUS
A run-of-the-mill handicap in which the pace was soon sound. The form makes sense.

Sforzando Official explanation: trainer said mare was in season

Malech(IRE) Official explanation: jockey said gelding had a breathing problem

4773 HD FINANCIAL SOLUTIONS H'CAP 5f

8:05 (8:05) (Class 6) (0-60,66) 3-Y-O+ **£2,590** (£770; £385; £192) **Stalls** Low

Form RPR

0004 **1** **Making Music**[5] 4642 4-8-6 46 ...(b) DavidAllan 8 56
(T D Easterby) *mde all far side: rdn 2f out: hld on wl fnl f* **7/1**[3]

3011 **2** *1/2* **Lake Chini (IRE)**[2] 4706 5-9-12 66 6ex ...(b) DaleGibson 9 74
(M W Easterby) *chsd wnr far side: drvn over 2f out: kpt on u.p fnl f: 2nd of 9 in gp* **7/2**[1]

5343 **3** *1* **Miss Daawe**[8] 4525 3-8-7 49 ... RoystonFfrench 3 53
(B Ellison) *chsd far side ldrs: effrt 2f out: kpt on u.p fnl f: 3rd of 9 in gp* **6/1**[2]

0030 **4** *1/2* **Henry Hall (IRE)**[5] 4642 11-9-1 55 ... KimTinkler 11 58
(N Tinkler) *t.k.h: chsd far side ldrs tl rdn and nt qckn fnl f: 4th of 9 in gp* **14/1**

-060 **5** *nk* **Bond Becks (IRE)**[17] 4252 7-8-9 54 ow4 ... SladeO'Hara[(5)] 10 56
(G R Oldroyd) *t.k.h: in tch far side: effrt over 2f out: one pce fnl f: 5th of 9 in gp* **20/1**

0003 **6** *hd* **Rare Breed**[5] 4635 4-9-0 54 ... TGMcLaughlin 2 55
(Mrs L Stubbs) *bhd far side tl hdwy over 1f out: nrst fin: 6th of 9 in gp* **7/1**[3]

0051 **7** *1/2* **Fern House (IRE)**[17] 4252 5-9-1 55 ... PaulHanagan 1 54
(Garry Moss) *bhd far side tl kpt on fnl f: no imp: 7th of 9 in gp* **9/1**

0505 **8** *1 1/4* **Jun Fan (USA)**[10] 4478 5-8-8 48 ...(tp) PhillipMakin 15 43
(B Ellison) *s.i.s and swtchd to r far side: hld up: rdn over 2f out: no imp fnl f: 8th of 9 in gp* **33/1**

2003 **9** *shd* **Maromito (IRE)**[22] 4101 10-8-9 52 ... AndrewMullen[(3)] 14 46
(R Bastiman) *led stands' side: rdn and hung lft over 2f out: kpt on: no ch w far side: 1st of 5 in gp* **14/1**

0200 **10** *1 1/2* **Falmassim**[23] 4083 4-9-2 56 ... TomEaves 17 45
(Miss J A Camacho) *sn cl up stands' side: rdn over 2f out: sn one pce: 2nd of 8 in gp* **11/1**

000 **11** *hd* **Seafield Towers**[10] 4478 7-8-6 49 ...(p) MarkLawson[(3)] 16 37
(Miss L A Perratt) *prom stands' side: drvn 1/2-way: sn one pce: 3rd of 5 in gp* **33/1**

4004 **12** *hd* **Sharp Hat**[10] 4478 13-8-8 48 ... AdrianTNicholls 5 35
(D W Chapman) *towards rr far side: drvn over 2f out: wknd over 1f out: last of 9 in gp* **20/1**

5500 **13** *3* **Strawberry Patch (IRE)**[41] 3535 8-8-3 48 ... KellyHarrison[(5)] 13 25
(J S Goldie) *bhd: drvn 1/2-way: nvr rchd ldrs: 4th of 5 in gp* **7/1**[3]

000 **14** *2 1/2* **Russian Silk**[15] 4330 3-9-1 60 ...(b[1]) JamieMoriarty[(3)] 12 28
(Jedd O'Keeffe) *in tch on outside of stands' side gp: rdn 1/2-way: sn btn: last of 5 in gp* **40/1**

60.93 secs (-0.57) **Going Correction** -0.025s/f (Good)
WFA 3 from 4yo+ 2lb **14** Ran SP% **123.5**
Speed ratings (Par 101): **103,102,100,99,99 99,98,96,96,93 93,93,88,84**
CSF £30.46 CT £162.73 TOTE £8.90: £2.40, £2.20, £2.50; EX 36.60 Place 6 £61.18, Place 5 £14.91.

Owner Jonathan Gill **Bred** Redmyre Bloodstock And Stuart McPhee **Trained** Great Habton, N Yorks

■ Stewards' Enquiry : Andrew Mullen one-day ban: failed to ride to draw (Sep 4)

FOCUS
An ordinary event but one in which the pace was sound. The smaller stands side group were at a disadvantage compared to those that raced far side. Modest but sound form.

Rare Breed Official explanation: jockey said gelding lost a front shoe

Maromito(IRE) Official explanation: jockey said gelding hung left-handed

T/Plt: £90.00 to a £1 stake. Pool: £51,224.25. 415.40 winning tickets. T/Qpdt: £37.60 to a £1 stake. Pool: £4,427.10. 87.00 winning tickets. RY

4604 **NEWMARKET (JULY)** (R-H)

Friday, August 24

OFFICIAL GOING: Soft (5.9)

Wind: light across Weather: Overcast

4774 EUROPEAN BREEDERS' FUND MAIDEN FILLIES' STKS — 7f

2:10 (2:11) (Class 4) 2-Y-O — **£4,533** (£1,348; £674; £336) **Stalls** Low

Form — RPR

1 **Kotsi (IRE)** 2-9-0 0 .... JimmyFortune 5 78+
(E F Vaughan) *chsd ldrs: led over 1f out: rdn out* **5/1[2]**

2 ½ **Annie Skates (USA)** 2-8-11 0 .... LiamJones(3) 4 77
(Jane Chapple-Hyam) *chsd ldrs: rdn over 1f out: r.o* **11/2[3]**

3 1 **Basque Beauty** 2-9-0 0 .... RHills 15 74
(W J Haggas) *wnt rt s: sn prom: rdn over 1f out: styd on* **33/1**

4204 4 shd **Miss Emma May (IRE)**[13] 4402 2-9-0 83 .... TQuinn 11 74
(D R C Elsworth) *hld up: swtchd rt and hdwy over 1f out: r.o* **10/3[1]**

5 5 ¾ **Sahaadi**[27] 3967 2-9-0 0 .... RichardHughes 3 72
(R Hannon) *led to 1/2-way: rdn over 1f out: styd on same pce* **7/1**

6 nk **Trumpet Lily** 2-9-0 0 .... PatCosgrave 9 71
(J G Portman) *chsd ldrs: rdn over 1f out: no ex ins fnl f* **50/1**

7 1 ¾ **Star Of Gibraltar** 2-9-0 0 .... EddieAhern 6 67
(J L Dunlop) *hld up: rdn over 1f out: r.o: nt rch ldrs* **12/1**

0 8 1 **Manhattan Dream (USA)**[28] 3895 2-9-0 0 .... MichaelHills 13 64
(B W Hills) *chsd ldrs: rdn and ev ch over 1f out: wknd ins fnl f* **6/1**

9 ½ **Broken Moon** 2-9-0 0 .... JamieSpencer 10 63
(J R Fanshawe) *hld up: styd on ins fnl f: nvr nrr* **16/1**

00 10 ½ **Kashmina**[22] 4094 2-9-0 0 .... DarryllHolland 8 62
(M R Channon) *chsd ldr tl led 1/2-way: rdn and hdd over 1f out: sn wknd* **28/1**

11 1 ½ **Miss Rochester (IRE)** 2-9-0 0 .... RyanMoore 17 58+
(Sir Michael Stoute) *hld up: n.d* **7/1**

12 1 ½ **Gingham** 2-9-0 0 .... NickyMackay 2 54+
(L M Cumani) *s.i.s: sn chsng ldrs: rdn over 4f out: wknd over 2f out* **33/1**

13 5 **Crazy About You (IRE)** 2-9-0 0 .... SteveDrowne 7 42+
(B W Hills) *hld up: a in rr* **33/1**

14 2 **Striving (IRE)** 2-9-0 0 .... JDSmith 16 37
(Sir Michael Stoute) *dwlt and hmpd s: a in rr* **25/1**

00 15 14 **L'Orage**[53] 3152 2-9-0 0 .... HayleyTurner 14 —
(J Ryan) *prom: wkng whn nt mcuh room over 2f out* **100/1**

0 16 5 **Kili Links (IRE)**[18] 4232 2-9-0 0 .... TedDurcan 1 —
(R Hannon) *chsd ldrs over 4f* **33/1**

17 6 **Zarene** 2-9-0 0 .... SaleemGolam 12 —
(P W D'Arcy) *sn pushed along in rr: bhd fr 1/2-way* **100/1**

1m 30.75s (3.97) **Going Correction** +0.475s/f (Yiel) 17 Ran SP% **131.0**
Speed ratings (Par 93): **96,95,94,94,93 92,90,89,89,88 86,85,79,77,61 55,48**
CSF £32.51 TOTE £9.60: £3.30, £2.60, £6.60; EX 108.00.
Owner A E Oppenheimer **Bred** Hascombe And Valiant Studs **Trained** Newmarket, Suffolk

FOCUS
The field threatened to split into two early with the larger group of nine going to the far rail, but the group of eight that started off down the middle soon shifted over to join them. Not much form to go on, but this did not look the strongest of Newmarket maidens, although the front three were all newcomers and there should be a few future winners amongst this bunch.

NOTEBOOK
Kotsi(IRE) ♦, a half-sister to four winners including Sir George Turner and Tissifer, represented an in-form stable and she certainly knew her job at the first time of asking. She showed a decent attitude up the hill to hold off the late challenge of the runner-up and there should be more to come from her. (op 10-1 tchd 12-1)
Annie Skates(USA) ♦, a 70,000gns two-year-old, is a half-sister to four winners in the US. Produced with her effort on meeting the rising ground, she kept trying but the winner was too determined. With her pedigree suggesting she would not get much further than this, she should not take long in going one better and would be especially interesting if tried on sand. (op 7-2)
Basque Beauty ♦, a 60,000 half-sister to three winners, was a little errant at the start but ultimately finished well down the centre of the track and probably did well considering she was drawn wider than the front pair. She is bred to stay much further than this so should improve as she goes up in trip.
Miss Emma May(IRE) stayed on well down the middle of the track and was nearest at the line, but she was by far the most experienced in the field and was beaten by three newcomers. The fact that she could not take advantage of this return to maiden company suggests she could be hard to place from now on. (op 4-1 tchd 3-1)
Sahaadi, up a furlong from her debut, was given a positive ride but was made to look one paced over the last couple of furlongs. She did not really progress for the longer trip as might have been expected and although one winner has come out of her debut contest, that form looks ordinary. (op 8-1)
Trumpet Lily, a half-sister to three winners on the Flat and one over hurdles, did show some ability on this debut and although she is by a sprinter, her winning siblings all stayed middle distances and this effort suggests she has inherited a bit of stamina herself.
Broken Moon Official explanation: jockey said filly hung right under pressure

4775 DBS ST LEGER YEARLING STKS — 6f

2:40 (2:44) (Class 2) 2-Y-O

£24,625 (£9,850; £4,925; £2,460; £1,230; £1,230) **Stalls** Low

Form — RPR

121 1 **Edge Of Gold**[17] 4254 2-8-6 0 .... SteveDrowne 1 80
(B Palling) *chsd ldrs: edgd rt and led over 1f out: rdn out* **5/1[3]**

410 2 ½ **Artsu**[41] 3524 2-8-11 77 .... JamieSpencer 15 84
(M L W Bell) *plld hrd: hld up and bhd: rapid hdwy over 1f out: sn hrd rdn: hung lft and ev ch: styd on* **12/1**

1521 3 ½ **Rose Siog**[22] 4098 2-8-6 75 .... TonyHamilton 2 77
(R A Fahey) *hld up: hdwy over 2f out: rdn and ev ch fr over 1f out: unable qck towards fin* **5/1[3]**

52 4 1 ¾ **Geestring (IRE)**[59] 2968 2-8-7 0 ow1 .... RichardHughes 6 73
(R Hannon) *prom: outpcd 1/2-way: styd on ins fnl f* **10/3[1]**

03 5 hd **Clifton Dancer**[8] 4527 2-8-6 0 .... RichardThomas 18 71
(Tom Dascombe) *mid-div: hdwy u.p over 1f out: styd on* **33/1**

5001 6 1 ¼ **Rough Rock (IRE)**[25] 4027 2-8-11 71 .... (bt) DarryllHolland 8 72
(Miss Gay Kelleway) *led: rdn: edgd rt and hdd over 1f out: no ex* **33/1**

221 7 1 **Baronovici (IRE)**[25] 4014 2-8-11 0 .... RyanMoore 3 69
(R Hannon) *hld up: hdwy 2f out: sn rdn: wknd ins fnl f* **4/1[2]**

1640 8 hd **Fitolini**[21] 4126 2-8-7 73 ow1 .... TQuinn 17 65
(Mrs G S Rees) *s.i.s: hdwy over 1f out: no ex ins fnl f* **50/1**

30 9 1 ½ **Monsieur Reynard**[15] 4328 2-8-11 0 .... JimmyFortune 13 64+
(B J Meehan) *chsd ldrs: rdn and hung rt over 1f out: sn wknd and eased* **25/1**

4 10 nk **Birkintastic**[14] 4350 2-8-11 0 .... RHills 20 63
(B J Meehan) *chsd ldrs over 4f* **14/1**

3432 11 ¾ **Our Acquaintance**[8] 4537 2-8-11 0 .... NickyMackay 19 61
(W R Muir) *chsd ldrs: rdn and ev ch over 1f out: sn wknd* **16/1**

3510 12 ½ **Hansinger (IRE)**[21] 4121 2-8-11 0 .... TedDurcan 12 60
(B I Case) *sn pushed along in rr: rdn over 1f out: n.d* **16/1**

01 13 1 ¼ **Baldemar**[6] 4612 2-8-11 0 .... PatCosgrave 7 56
(K R Burke) *plld hrd and prom: wknd over 2f out* **25/1**

2330 14 10 **Montiboli (IRE)**[23] 4077 2-8-6 68 .... (p) MatthewHenry 5 21
(K A Ryan) *s.i.s: rdn 1/2-way: a in rr* **100/1**

5360 15 2 ½ **Bazguy**[4] 4669 2-8-11 74 .... (t) LiamJones 10 18
(P D Evans) *mid-div: rdn 1/2-way: wknd over 2f out* **66/1**

6000 16 3 **Tikinheart (IRE)**[7] 4560 2-8-11 65 .... EddieAhern 14 9
(T D Easterby) *s.i.s: hdwy over 2f out: sn wknd* **66/1**

00 17 1 ¾ **Resolute Defender (IRE)**[23] 4076 2-8-11 0 .... SaleemGolam 4 4
(J Howard Johnson) *chsd ldrs over 3f* **100/1**

1m 15.73s (2.38) **Going Correction** +0.475s/f (Yiel) 17 Ran SP% **123.0**
Speed ratings (Par 100): **103,102,101,99,99 97,96,95,93,93 92,91,90,76,73 69,67**
CSF £59.62 TOTE £6.90: £2.50, £3.10, £2.40; EX 84.70.
Owner Christopher J Mason **Bred** Christopher J Mason **Trained** Tredodridge, Vale Of Glamorgan
■ This race was for those eliminated at the 48-hour stage of the previous day's £300000 St Leger Yearling Stakes at York.

FOCUS
A wide spectrum of abilities as is often the case in races like this, but there were some fair sorts amongst them and the pace was decent resulting in a good time. The form looks sound enough. The runners mainly came down the centre of the track.

NOTEBOOK
Edge Of Gold, disqualified in favour of Geestring when first past the post on her Newbury debut, has not done much wrong since then and the soft ground was never going to be a problem. Never far away, she did hang slightly to her left after hitting the front a furlong out, but nothing like to the same degree as in the past and she ran out a worthy winner. She is doing the yard proud. (tchd 11-2)
Artsu, given a patient ride on ground he likes, was forced to make his effort closest to the stands' rail whilst the pace was down the middle. Despite the determination of his rider, he could never quite get to the winner but this was still a decent effort considering he would have been 10lb better off with the winner and 12lb better off with the third in a nursery. Official explanation: jockey said gelding hung badly left under pressure (op 16-1)
Rose Siog, best in on adjusted official ratings, was trying this trip for the first time and had every chance but was outbattled. The trip did not seem to be a problem. (op 9-2 tchd 11-2)
Geestring(IRE), who was awarded the race after getting hampered by Edge In Gold at Newbury last time, was rather surprisingly made favourite to beat her on merit here even though she had the advantage of previous experience on the first occasion and was also 3lb worse off including her rider's overweight. She was always struggling to go the pace though, and her final position was as close as she got. Despite her speedy pedigree, the evidence of this suggests she needs another furlong now. (op 3-1 tchd 11-4)
Clifton Dancer was taking a big step up in class, but emerged with a great deal of credit. Much will depend on how the Handicapper interprets this with nurseries in mind, but an ordinary maiden should be within her compass.
Rough Rock(IRE), fitted with a tongue-tie alongside the blinkers, attempted the same tactics as proved successful in a seller at Yarmouth last time, but he was on much softer ground here and he failed to see his race out.
Baronovici(IRE) never managed to get involved and, given that he has proven form on both fast and soft ground, it is difficult to find too many excuses. Official explanation: jockey said colt was unsuited by the soft ground (op 9-2)
Monsieur Reynard Official explanation: jockey said gelding ran too free
Tikinheart(IRE) Official explanation: jockey said colt was unsuited by the soft ground

4776 RENAULT VANS NURSERY — 1m

3:15 (3:16) (Class 4) 2-Y-O — **£5,181** (£1,541; £770; £384) **Stalls** Low

Form — RPR

4341 1 **Cobo Bay**[11] 4461 2-8-13 78 6ex .... PatCosgrave 15 85
(K A Ryan) *chsd ldr tl led over 2f out: rdn and hung rt ins fnl f: r.o* **11/1**

6004 2 1 ¾ **Townkab (IRE)**[8] 4524 2-7-12 63 oh2 .... NickyMackay 3 66
(N P Littmoden) *hld up: hdwy over 1f out: r.o* **20/1**

515 3 hd **The Betchworth Kid**[21] 4121 2-9-3 82 .... HayleyTurner 7 85
(M L W Bell) *hld up: pushed along over 3f out: r.o wl ins fnl f: nrst fin* **4/1[2]**

0322 4 nk **Always Ready**[21] 4130 2-8-7 77 .... AhmedAjtebi(5) 12 79
(C E Brittain) *chsd ldrs: rdn over 1f out: styd on same pce ins fnl f* **5/1**

422 5 ½ **Bailey (IRE)**[16] 4273 2-9-0 79 .... JimmyFortune 11 80
(B J Meehan) *led: racd keenly: hdd over 2f out: rdn over 1f out: no ex ins fnl f* **12/1**

006 6 nk **Prince Desire (IRE)**[19] 4192 2-8-6 71 .... RHills 2 71
(B W Hills) *hld up in tch: nt clr run and lost pl over 1f out: r.o ins fnl f* **9/2[3]**

004 7 2 **Indian Days**[35] 3712 2-8-7 72 .... EddieAhern 13 68+
(J G Given) *s.i.s: hld up: r.o ins fnl f: nvr nr to chal* **20/1**

602 8 hd **Bridge Of Fermoy (IRE)**[14] 4363 2-7-7 63 .... (t) NicolPolli(5) 8 58
(Miss Gay Kelleway) *chsd ldrs: rdn and hung rt over 1f out: wknd fnl f* **50/1**

103 9 1 ½ **Meeriss (IRE)**[21] 4121 2-9-7 86 .... DarryllHolland 14 78
(M R Channon) *hld up: rdn over 1f out: n.d* **12/1**

10 10 1 ¾ **Rescue Me**[29] 3880 2-8-8 73 .... RichardHughes 4 61
(R Hannon) *hld up: hdwy over 1f out: wknd ins fnl f* **16/1**

0050 11 nk **Asian Power (IRE)**[8] 4524 2-8-7 72 .... TedDurcan 1 60
(P J O'Gorman) *chsd ldrs: rdn 2f out: wknd fnl f* **40/1**

4000 12 hd **Una Auroraborealis**[25] 4022 2-7-12 63 oh11 .... SilvestreDeSousa 10 50
(J Ryan) *hld up: racd keenly: hdwy over 2f out: rdn and wknd over 1f out* **100/1**

01 13 nk **Classical World (USA)**[17] 4247 2-8-10 75 .... RyanMoore 9 62
(Sir Michael Stoute) *hld up: effrt over 2f out: sn wknd* **7/2[1]**

1m 45.23s (4.80) **Going Correction** +0.475s/f (Yiel) 13 Ran SP% **121.6**
Speed ratings (Par 96): **95,93,93,92,92 91,89,89,88,86 86,86,85**
CSF £220.19 CT £1074.14 TOTE £12.00: £3.10, £6.80, £1.70; EX 264.20 TRIFECTA Not won..
Owner The C H F Partnership **Bred** The C H F Partnership **Trained** Hambleton, N Yorks

FOCUS
A fair nursery run at an even gallop, but not many got into it. The field stayed against the far rail this time.

NOTEBOOK
Cobo Bay ♦, carrying a 6lb penalty for his Wolverhampton victory, was again ridden to the fore and, despite wandering a little after hitting the front, was always in control. He relished the soft ground and is beginning to look a progressive sort, so may not have finished winning yet. (op 10-1 tchd 9-1)
Townkab(IRE) ♦, 2lb wrong, finished well from off the pace but the winner was already home and dry. He looks to have his fair share of stamina as even this trip in testing ground seemed barely far enough.
The Betchworth Kid, as at Goodwood, gave himself plenty to do and even over this longer trip in the testing conditions he did not get going until the race was over. He looks to need even further already. (tchd 7-2 and 9-2)

Always Ready, making his nursery debut, was always in a good position and kept on trying but again found one or two too good. He handles this ground and his stamina seemed to hold up, but on balance he may prefer it faster. (op 13-2)
Bailey(IRE), who had questions to answer over the trip on this nursery debut especially in this ground, did not help himself by taking a grip out in front. He did try his best to keep tabs on the winner once he had gone past, but the final climb to the line saw him empty. (op 10-1)
Prince Desire(IRE) ◆, aother making his nursery debut, met all sorts of trouble when trying to get closer and can be rated a fair bit better than this. He is one to watch for a similar event. Official explanation: jockey said colt was unsuited by the soft ground (op 4-1 tchd 11-2)
Indian Days Official explanation: jockey said, regarding running and riding, his orders were, on colt's first run over a mile, to settle and relax it, and to do his best, adding that he was able to settle it and being anxious to race on what he felt was the best ground on the fair rail, moved across, having been content to track the favourite early on; however, he was briefly unable to gain a clear run as he asked to quicken approaching final furlong, further adding that it appeared well suiited by the trip, staying on well when meeting the rising ground final furlong
Classical World(USA) was never in the race, but this ground was the complete opposite to that he scored on at Catterick so there is a possible excuse there. (op 4-1 tchd 10-3)

4777 RENAULT MASTER E B F MAIDEN STKS (C&G) 7f
3:50 (3:51) (Class 4) 2-Y-O **£4,533** (£1,348; £674; £336) **Stalls** Low

Form RPR
1 **Yankadi (USA)** 2-9-0 0 RichardHughes 3 86+
(B W Hills) *led 6f out: hdd over 2f out: rdn to ld 1f out: r.o* **8/1**
2 *2* **Rochefort (IRE)** 2-9-0 0 JimmyFortune 13 81+
(J H M Gosden) *s.i.s: hdwy over 1f out: sn hung lft: r.o* **4/1**[1]
3 *½* **Mountain Pride (IRE)** 2-9-0 0 TedDurcan 1 80+
(J L Dunlop) *hld up: hdwy over 1f out: r.o* **7/1**[3]
0 **4** *nk* **Silver Rime (FR)**[14] 4362 2-9-0 0 MichaelHills 12 79
(R Hannon) *chsd ldr: led over 2f out: rdn and hdd 1f out: no ex ins fnl f* **11/2**[2]
5 *1 ½* **Lord Peter Flint (IRE)** 2-9-0 0 RHills 6 75
(B J Meehan) *hld up in tch: shkn up over 1f out: styd on same pce fnl f* **17/2**
6 *2 ½* **Sky Dive** 2-9-0 0 NickyMackay 16 69+
(L M Cumani) *chsd ldrs tl hung lft and wknd over 1f out* **12/1**
7 *2* **Bazergan (IRE)** 2-8-9 0 AhmedAjtebi(5) 8 64
(C E Brittain) *hld up in tch: rdn and lost pl 1/2-way: n.d* **16/1**
0 **8** *nk* **Perks (IRE)**[28] 3896 2-9-0 0 TQuinn 14 63
(J L Dunlop) *s.i.s: hld up: styd on ins fnl f: nvr nrr* **8/1**
9 *3* **Confidence Trick (USA)** 2-9-0 0 RyanMoore 4 56
(Sir Michael Stoute) *chsd ldrs: rdn over 2f out: edgd lft and wknd over 1f out* **10/1**
05 **10** *5* **Lunar Limelight**[55] 3085 2-9-0 0 AmirQuinn 5 43
(P J Makin) *chsd ldrs over 5f* **28/1**
0 **11** *3* **Vilna (USA)**[7] 4586 2-9-0 0 RichardThomas 10 36
(N A Callaghan) *dwlt: sn prom: wknd over 2f out* **33/1**
30 **12** *2 ½* **King Supreme (IRE)**[41] 3522 2-9-0 0 HayleyTurner 15 30
(R Hannon) *hld up: wknd over 2f out* **14/1**
0 **13** *1* **Dream Green (IRE)**[14] 4362 2-9-0 0 DarryllHolland 7 27
(M R Channon) *hld up: plld hrd: rdn and wknd over 2f out* **20/1**

1m 30.73s (3.95) **Going Correction** +0.475s/f (Yiel) **13** Ran SP% **121.1**
Speed ratings (Par 96): **96,93,93,92,91 88,85,85,82,76 73,70,69**
CSF £39.62 TOTE £7.40: £2.50, £1.70, £2.60; EX 31.30.
Owner K Abdulla **Bred** Juddmonte Farms Inc **Trained** Lambourn, Berks

FOCUS
A fair maiden with the first three home all debutants and open to further improvement, though the time was only fractionally faster than the earlier fillies' equivalent. Plenty of these should progress. The runners were more inclined to come down the middle this time, but again not that many got into it.

NOTEBOOK
Yankadi(USA) ◆, a half-brother to Short Dance, was weak in the market but was very soon at the head of affairs. He did look cooked when Silver Rime headed him entering the last couple of furlongs, but to his great credit he battled his way back to the front and was ultimately well on top at the line. The way he drifted in the betting suggests he was thought unlikely to make a winning debut by someone, so even though he does not hold any fancy entries this was a very encouraging start. (op 5-1)
Rochefort(IRE) ◆, who fetched 105,000gns as a foal, is a half-brother to a top-class colt in Germany and a half-brother to three other winners. He stayed on very nicely towards the end in the testing conditions and it should not be long before he goes one better. (op 11-2)
Mountain Pride(IRE) ◆, a half-brother to Wilford Maverick, caught the eye with the way he was finishing. The stable's juveniles usually improve with racing and this Derby and Racing Post Trophy entry should win races. (op 15-2 tchd 9-1)
Silver Rime(FR), who had the benefit of a previous outing, was racing on very different ground. Ridden much more prominently this time, he looked the one to beat when moving ahead of the eventual winner entering the last quarter-mile, but he could never press home his advantage and failed to see his race out. (op 13-2 tchd 5-1)
Lord Peter Flint(IRE), a 90,000euros half-brother to three-time winner Bold Bibi, made an encouraging debut. His sire was a top-class sprinter, but this effort suggests he possesses a bit more stamina and he is likely to improve for this experience. (op 8-1 tchd 10-1)
Sky Dive, a 21,000gns yearling out of a half-sister to Shamshir and Fern, ran well for a long way and looks the type that will come into his own over a bit further next season. (op 10-1)
Perks(IRE) Official explanation: jockey said colt became upset in stalls
Dream Green(IRE) Official explanation: jockey said colt ran too keen

4778 RENAULT TRAFIC CLAIMING STKS 7f
4:25 (4:25) (Class 5) 3-Y-O **£3,886** (£1,156; £577; £288) **Stalls** Low

Form RPR
0015 **1** **Norisan**[9] 4509 3-9-9 87 (b) RyanMoore 3 77
(R Hannon) *chsd ldrs: rdn to ld ins fnl f: styd on* **6/5**[1]
222 **2** *½* **Chjimes (IRE)**[33] 3762 3-9-9 77 PatCosgrave 1 75
(K R Burke) *chsd ldr: led over 1f out: rdn and hdd ins fnl f: styd on* **5/2**[2]
11-3 **3** *½* **Bussel (USA)**[227] 76 3-9-1 75 LiamJones(3) 6 69
(W J Haggas) *hld up: hdwy over 2f out: rdn and ev ch ins fnl f: unable qck nr fin* **8/1**[3]
6304 **4** *nk* **Jawaab (IRE)**[23] 4079 3-9-9 67 TQuinn 9 73
(M A Buckley) *hld up: hdwy over 2f out: rdn and ev ch over 1f out: styd on same pce ins fnl f* **12/1**
3530 **5** *5* **Ask Yer Dad**[13] 4394 3-8-11 64 (p) SteveDrowne 8 48
(Mrs P Sly) *prom over 5f* **12/1**
50 **6** *4* **Fine Art World (IRE)**[12] 4416 3-8-9 0 RichardThomas 7 35
(N A Callaghan) *chsd ldrs: rdn over 2f out: sn wknd* **50/1**
0000 **7** *2* **Millyjean**[15] 4337 3-8-2 41 (b) HayleyTurner 2 22
(John Berry) *led: racd keenly: hdd & wknd over 1f out* **100/1**
0240 **8** *5* **Jack Oliver**[8] 4538 3-9-5 73 RichardHughes 4 26
(B J Meehan) *stdd s: hld up: rdn over 2f out: sn wknd* **12/1**
00-0 **9** *37* **Yearning (IRE)**[157] 713 3-8-1 47 EmmettStack(3) 5 —
(J G Portman) *hld up: rdn and wknd 1/2-way* **100/1**

1m 29.81s (3.03) **Going Correction** +0.475s/f (Yiel) **9** Ran SP% **112.2**
Speed ratings (Par 100): **101,100,99,99,93 89,86,81,38**
CSF £3.97 TOTE £2.20: £1.10, £1.30, £1.80; EX 4.70.
Owner The Waney Racing Group Inc **Bred** The National Stud Owner Breeders Club Ltd **Trained** East Everleigh, Wilts

FOCUS
A fair claimer that developed into something of a war of attrition over the last couple of furlongs. The runners came down the centre of the track and the front trio were the three most favoured by the weights.
Millyjean Official explanation: jockey said filly ran too free
Yearning(IRE) Official explanation: jockey said filly was never travelling

4779 BREHENY H'CAP 1m 6f 175y
5:00 (5:00) (Class 3) (0-95,93) 3-Y-0+ **£9,067** (£2,697; £1,348; £673) **Stalls** High

Form RPR
0431 **1** **Ajaan**[16] 4288 3-8-8 86 (b) TedDurcan 4 94+
(H R A Cecil) *chsd ldders: rdn to ld over 2f out: sn hung rt: styd on u.p* **11/10**[1]
051 **2** *¾* **Newnham (IRE)**[23] 4067 6-8-8 80 JackMitchell(7) 2 87
(J R Boyle) *hld up: rdn and swtchd lft over 2f out: hdwy to chse wnr over 1f out: hung rt ins fnl f: styd on* **7/1**
6311 **3** *5* **Mirthful (USA)**[15] 4332 3-8-4 82 HayleyTurner 3 83
(B W Hills) *chsd ldr tl rdn over 2f out: styd on same pce appr fnl f* **7/2**[3]
-042 **4** *nk* **Velvet Heights (IRE)**[34] 3748 5-9-7 86 EddieAhern 1 86
(J L Dunlop) *sn led: rdn and hdd over 2f out: styd on same pce appr fnl f* **9/4**[2]

3m 21.03s (9.99) **Going Correction** +0.475s/f (Yiel)
WFA 3 from 4yo+ 13lb **4** Ran SP% **113.1**
Speed ratings (Par 107): **92,91,88,88**
CSF £9.10 TOTE £2.00; EX 10.40.
Owner Niarchos Family **Bred** Miss K Rausing And Course Investment Limited **Trained** Newmarket, Suffolk

FOCUS
A race weakened by the two non-runners and in such a small field this was always going to be tactical. The quartet were almost in a line coming to the last two furlongs, but despite the modest pace and the moderate time, the contest was still dominated by the pair that were held up. The form does not look the most solid.

NOTEBOOK
Ajaan, upped in trip and with the blinkers retained, was held up until being set alight approaching the last quarter-mile and, once switched to the stands' rail, needed to be put under maximum pressure to hold off the runner-up. Whilst the modest pace meant this was not the test of stamina it might have been, it still took some getting in the ground so it may be best to take a positive view of this performance. (op 10-11 tchd 5-4 and 11-8 in places)
Newnham(IRE), raised 5lb for his Kempton victory, has to come from off the pace so it was no surprise to see him dropped out last. However, this performance was even better than it looked as he hardly had a strong pace to run at, was the first off the bridle, and was forced to make his effort very wide which saw him rather isolated in no man's land down the centre of the track. The fact that he made the favourite fight so hard does him credit and whilst this seven-time Polytrack winner is yet to score on turf, it is surely only a matter of time. (op 9-1)
Mirthful(USA), bidding for a hat-trick off a 6lb higher mark, was always in the slipstream of the leader but once asked for more effort she was made to look woefully one-paced. The combination of the longer trip and soft ground did not appear to suit her at all. (op 10-3 tchd 4-1)
Velvet Heights(IRE) was allowed to dictate at his own pace, but once put under pressure by his rivals he had little left in reserve. He has won on a slowish surface before, but was not at his best here. (op 10-3 tchd 2-1)

4780 RENAULT KANGOO H'CAP 5f
5:30 (5:30) (Class 4) (0-85,84) 3-Y-0+ **£5,181** (£1,541; £770; £384) **Stalls** Low

Form RPR
4020 **1** **Efistorm**[3] 4696 6-9-5 83 LiamJones(3) 9 94
(C R Dore) *racd centre: in rr: hdwy 1/2-way: rdn to ld ins fnl f: r.o* **2/1**[1]
2650 **2** *½* **Coconut Moon**[20] 4158 5-8-11 72 EddieAhern 5 81
(E J Alston) *racd far side: s.i.s: rcvrd to ld 4f out: rdn and hung rt fr over 1f out: hdd ins fnl f: styd on* **8/1**[3]
3530 **3** *nk* **Canadian Danehill (IRE)**[22] 4095 5-9-0 75 (p) RyanMoore 6 83
(R M H Cowell) *racd towards far side: led 1f: chsd ldrs: rdn over 1f out: styd on* **9/1**
6402 **4** *5* **Curtail (IRE)**[7] 4585 4-9-9 84 TonyHamilton 7 74
(I Semple) *racd far side: chsd ldrs: rdn over 1f out: wknd ins fnl f* **3/1**[2]
2400 **5** *1* **Bond Boy**[22] 4095 10-8-12 73 (b) JimmyFortune 4 59
(G R Oldroyd) *racd far side: chsd ldrs: rdn over 1f out: wknd ins fnl f* **3/1**[2]
0210 **6** *2* **Bold Minstrel (IRE)**[78] 2399 5-9-4 79 TedDurcan 8 58
(M Quinn) *racd centre: chsd ldrs 3f* **25/1**
0500 **7** *1 ½* **Figaro Flyer (IRE)**[14] 4367 4-8-9 70 ow1 AmirQuinn 10 44
(P Howling) *s.i.s: swtchd to r alone stands' side 4f out: outpcd* **16/1**

61.27 secs (1.71) **Going Correction** +0.475s/f (Yiel) **7** Ran SP% **114.2**
Speed ratings (Par 105): **105,104,103,95,94 90,88**
CSF £18.88 CT £116.71 TOTE £2.90: £1.80, £2.80; EX 18.90 Place 6 £82.38, Place 5 £33.84..
Owner Sean J Murphy **Bred** E Duggan And D Churchman **Trained** West Pinchbeck, Lincs

FOCUS
A fair little sprint handicap, but a complete mess of a contest as despite the small field the runners were spread the full width of the track in dribs and drabs. As things turned out, the centre of the track looked the place to be and those that raced on either flank seemed to face an impossible task. The form among the first three still seems sound enough.
Bond Boy Official explanation: jockey said gelding moved poorly
Figaro Flyer(IRE) Official explanation: jockey said gelding hung right
T/Jkpt: Not won. T/Plt: £172.10 to a £1 stake. Pool: £86,364.60. 366.30 winning tickets. T/Qpdt: £6.10 to a £1 stake. Pool: £5,101.85. 614.30 winning tickets. CR

4447 THIRSK (L-H)
Friday, August 24
OFFICIAL GOING: Good to firm (good in places)
Wind: virtually nil Weather: Fine and sunny

4781 EUROPEAN BREEDERS' FUND MAIDEN STKS (DIV I) 6f
1:30 (1:31) (Class 4) 2-Y-O **£4,533** (£1,348; £674; £336) **Stalls** High

Form RPR
600 **1** **Fyodorovich (USA)**[38] 3625 2-9-3 61 (v[1]) MickyFenton 10 79
(J S Wainwright) *chsd ldrs: hdwy 2f out: rdn over 1f out: styd on wl to ld ins fnl f* **33/1**

02 **2** *3* **Call For Liberty (IRE)**[15] 4328 2-9-3 0 .... PaulEddery 13 73+
(B Smart) *trckd ldrs: pushed along and hdwy 2f out: rdn to chal ent fnl f and ev ch tl hung lft: no ex towards fin* **4/5**[1]

05 **3** *1* **Strictly Elsie (IRE)**[33] 3761 2-8-12 0 .... PaddyAspell 8 62
(J R Norton) *prom: rdn along and sltly outpcd 2f out: swtchd rt and styd on u.p ins fnl f* **50/1**

54 **4** *1* **Le Toreador**[16] 4279 2-9-3 0 .... NCallan 2 64
(K A Ryan) *led: rdn along 2f out: drvn over 1f out: edgd lft and hdd ins fnl f: one pce* **13/2**[3]

0 **5** *1* **Just Sam (IRE)**[11] 4448 2-8-12 0 .... DanielTudhope 1 56
(D Carroll) *prom: rdn along 2f out: wknd appr fnl f* **100/1**

6 *nk* **Smarterthanuthink (USA)** 2-9-3 0 .... PaulHanagan 5 60
(R A Fahey) *dwlt: sn pushed along in rr: stdy hdwy on inner 2f out: styd on ins fnl f: nrst fin* **20/1**

056 **7** *¾* **Harlequinn Danseur (IRE)**[20] 4174 2-9-3 62 .... KimTinkler 12 58
(N Tinkler) *towards rr tl sme late hdwy* **80/1**

8 *nk* **Glittering Prize (UAE)** 2-8-12 0 .... RoystonFfrench 4 52
(M Johnston) *in tch: hdwy over 2f out: sn rdn and no imp* **12/1**

00 **9** *1 ½* **American Welcome (IRE)**[11] 4454 2-9-3 0 .... PhilipRobinson 7 53
(B J Meehan) *in tch: rdn along 1/2-way: sn wknd* **14/1**

0 **10** *2 ½* **Visconti**[44] 3435 2-9-3 0 .... KDarley 3 45
(P W Chapple-Hyam) *chsd ldrs on outer: rdn along over 2f out and sn wknd* **7/2**[2]

0 **11** *1 ½* **Dolly No Hair**[23] 4076 2-9-3 0 .... TomEaves 6 41
(D W Barker) *a in rr* **100/1**

0 **12** *2 ½* **Trojan Hero (IRE)**[27] 3951 2-9-3 0 .... DaleGibson 9 33
(A Dickman) *a in rr* **50/1**

1m 14.25s (1.75) **Going Correction** +0.175s/f (Good) 12 Ran SP% **120.3**
Speed ratings (Par 96): **95,91,89,88,87 86,85,85,83,79 77,74**
CSF £60.45 TOTE £58.40: £10.10, £1.10, £7.60; EX 91.60.
Owner Charles Wentworth **Bred** Liberation Farm And Brandywine Farm Llc **Trained** Kennythorpe, N Yorks
■ Stewards' Enquiry : N Callan one-day ban: failed to ride to draw (Sep 4)

FOCUS
A modest maiden that looks solid enough form-wise behind the surprise winner.

NOTEBOOK
Fyodorovich(USA), who had plenty to find on previous form, clearly improved for the first-time visor. Racing towards the stands' side from his high draw, he was keen early but came through in the last 2f after tracking the leaders and drew away in the final furlong. He does not look easy, as he was sweating up beforehand and was led down to the post, but he will look well-in if he goes for a quick follow-up in a nursery, as he came into the race with a mark of 61.
Call For Liberty(IRE) was the form pick following his Haydock second, but he never seemed happy here, hanging off the rail and being pushed along at an early stage. Though he had a chance inside the last furlong, he was left behind by the winner. (op 5-6 tchd 10-11 and evens in places)
Strictly Elsie(IRE) got outpaced a quarter-mile out but ran on again and shaped as though she may stay further. This was a step up on previous efforts on her first try on fast ground. (op 66-1)
Le Toreador was drawn out wide and did plenty of running early on to get across towards the stands'-side rail, so it is not that surprising he did not get home. (op 8-1)
Just Sam(IRE), related to several speedy juveniles, seemed to step up on her debut effort.
Smarterthanuthink(USA), a $72,000 North American-bred colt, was not disgraced on this debut.

4782 EUROPEAN BREEDERS' FUND MAIDEN STKS (DIV II) 6f
2:00 (2:01) (Class 4) 2-Y-O **£4,533** (£1,348; £674; £336) **Stalls** High

Form RPR

1 **Cape Vale (IRE)** 2-9-3 0 .... AdrianTNicholls 5 80+
(D Nicholls) *in tch: smooth hdwy over 2f out: rdn over 1f out: styd on ins fnl f to ld last 50yds* **28/1**

42 **2** *1* **Tugalu (IRE)**[11] 4459 2-9-3 0 .... NCallan 11 77
(K A Ryan) *led: rdn along wl over 1f out: drvn and hung lft ins fnl f: hdd and no ex last 50yds* **5/4**[1]

3 *nk* **Recent Times** 2-8-12 0 .... DavidAllan 6 71+
(T D Easterby) *towards rr: pushed along 1/2-way: hdwy 2f out: rdn and kpt on ins fnl f: nrst fin* **33/1**

4 *hd* **Kal Barg** 2-9-3 0 .... PhilipRobinson 3 77+
(M A Jarvis) *in tch on outer: hdwy to chse ldrs over 2f out: rdn and styng on whn hmpd ins fnl f* **7/2**[2]

43 **5** *hd* **Chivola (IRE)**[13] 4378 2-9-3 0 .... PaulEddery 4 75
(B Smart) *chsd ldrs: hdwy 2f out: sn rdn and ev ch tl drvn and one pce ent fnl f* **6/1**[3]

6 *5* **Silent Master (USA)** 2-9-3 0 .... KerrinMcEvoy 2 60
(M Johnston) *bhd tl sme hdwy wl over 1f out: nvr nr to chal* **11/1**

3 **7** *½* **Society Venue**[7] 4578 2-9-0 0 .... JamieMoriarty[(3)] 9 59
(Jedd O'Keeffe) *bhd tl sme late hdwy* **28/1**

0 **8** *nk* **Zabeel Tiger**[71] 2596 2-9-3 0 .... TomEaves 7 58
(M R Channon) *prom: rdn along over 2f out and grad wknd* **8/1**

0 **9** *2 ½* **Midnight Mystique (IRE)**[12] 4422 2-8-12 0 .... PaulFessey 8 45
(T D Barron) *a in rr* **100/1**

6 **10** *2 ½* **Brandane (IRE)**[16] 4286 2-9-3 0 ....(v[1]) RoystonFfrench 10 43
(Mrs A Duffield) *t.k.h: chsd ldrs to 1/2-way: sn wknd* **14/1**

00 **11** *5* **Flaxton (UAE)**[11] 4448 2-9-3 0 .... MickyFenton 1 28
(M Brittain) *in tch on outer tl lost pl and bhd fr 1/2-way* **150/1**

12 *18* **Flemish Art (IRE)** 2-9-3 0 .... PaulHanagan 12 —
(M J Wallace) *chsd ldrs on inner: rdn along over 2f out: sn edgd lft and wknd: eased fnl f* **25/1**

1m 14.17s (1.67) **Going Correction** +0.20s/f (Good) 12 Ran SP% **122.4**
Speed ratings (Par 96): **96,94,94,94,93 87,86,86,82,79 72,48**
CSF £63.88 TOTE £26.30: £7.30, £1.10, £6.80; EX 135.70.
Owner Lady O'Reilly **Bred** Derek Veitch **Trained** Sessay, N Yorks
■ Stewards' Enquiry : Adrian T Nicholls one-day ban; careless riding (Sep 4)

FOCUS
This looks likely to turn out to be the stronger of the two divisions, and a pretty good race for the track with the first five clear and the runner-up and fifth setting the standard.

NOTEBOOK
Cape Vale(IRE) ◆, a debutant half-brother to top sprinter Moss Vale, travelled well just off the pace and was driven out to go on in the last furlong. He is the sort who should progress. (op 25-1 tchd 22-1 and 33-1)
Tugalu(IRE) had shown promise on his two previous starts, the latest on the All-Weather. He led but was tending to edge off the rails from halfway and went further left in the final furlong, so perhaps easier ground will suit him. (op 5-2)
Recent Times, the first foal of a half-sister to Welsh Emperor among others, was another to make a promising debut. She ran on really well in the last furlong and should come on for the experience.
Kal Barg, a half-brother to Turnkey, was not ideally drawn on this debut and raced towards the middle but, although not given a hard race, he kept on well and would have finished even closer but for being hampered inside the last furlong. (op 5-2)
Chivola(IRE) chased up the leaders and finished a fair fifth, the five coming clear of the rest. He now qualifies for a handicap mark. (op 5-1)

Brandane(IRE) Official explanation: trainer said colt scoped dirty post race
Flemish Art(IRE) Official explanation: jockey said colt lost its action halfway

4783 BLACK SWAN HELMSLEY (S) STKS 7f
2:30 (2:30) (Class 5) 2-Y-O **£3,886** (£1,156; £577; £288) **Stalls** Low

Form RPR

64 **1** **Coffee Cup (IRE)**[28] 3916 2-8-6 0 .... KerrinMcEvoy 6 63+
(G A Swinbank) *led 2f: cl up: led again wl over 2f out: rdn clr over 1f out: comf* **6/4**[1]

3050 **2** *2 ½* **Lady Sandicliffe (IRE)**[25] 4022 2-8-6 66 .... KDarley 11 57
(B W Hills) *prom: pushed along 3f out: hdwy to chse wnr 2f out: sn rdn and hung lft over 1f out: one pce* **10/3**[2]

6501 **3** *2 ½* **Natural Rhythm (IRE)**[7] 4559 2-9-3 62 .... TomEaves 2 61
(D W Chapman) *bhd: hdwy over 2f out: rdn and n.m.r wl over 1f out: styd on ins fnl f: nrst fin* **14/1**

5240 **4** *1* **Alexander Monarchy (IRE)**[10] 4484 2-8-12 65 .... NCallan 8 53
(K A Ryan) *chsd ldrs: rdn along over 2f out and sn one pce* **14/1**

6400 **5** *1* **Alfredtheordinary**[8] 4524 2-8-11 61 .... SamHitchcott 7 50
(M R Channon) *chsd ldrs: rdn along wl over 2f out: swtchd rt wl over 1f out: sn drvn and no imp* **7/1**

2340 **6** *½* **Indecision**[21] 4136 2-8-10 61 ....(p) NSLawes[(7)] 5 55
(M W Easterby) *prom: led after 2f: rdn along and hdd wl over 2f out: sn wknd* **20/1**

0530 **7** *nk* **Glenshee (IRE)**[11] 4461 2-8-11 69 .... GrahamGibbons 3 48
(J J Quinn) *chsd ldrs on inner: rdn along wl over 2f out and sn wknd* **11/2**[3]

0366 **8** *3 ½* **Handsinthemist (IRE)**[32] 3788 2-8-8 54 ow2 .... MickyFenton 14 36
(P T Midgley) *t.k.h: in tch on outer: effrt over 2f out: sn rdn and no imp* **40/1**

0 **9** *shd* **Tagula King (IRE)**[128] 1087 2-8-11 0 ....(v[1]) DanielTudhope 4 38
(D Carroll) *s.i.s: a bhd* **40/1**

0 **10** *2 ½* **Mchepple**[12] 4422 2-8-3 0 .... DominicFox[(3)] 9 27
(W Storey) *a in rr* **66/1**

0000 **11** *8* **Bantham Bay**[43] 3446 2-8-6 53 .... RoystonFfrench 1 —
(B J Meehan) *a towards rr* **16/1**

1m 29.01s (1.91) **Going Correction** +0.20s/f (Good) 11 Ran SP% **121.3**
Speed ratings (Par 94): **97,94,91,90,89 88,88,84,83,81 71**
CSF £6.33 TOTE £2.60: £1.30, £2.40, £3.00; EX 8.30.The winner was bought in for 16,500 gns. Lady Sandicliffe was claimed by Mrs L Nelson for £10,000.
Owner Mr & Mrs William Barker 2 **Bred** T J Pabst **Trained** Melsonby, N Yorks

FOCUS
Mainly exposed sorts in this seller and the form is average for the grade. The winner is capable of better.

NOTEBOOK
Coffee Cup(IRE), who had run creditably in a couple of maidens prior to this, was always travelling well up with the pace and never looked like being beaten. She is not very big, but may be able to make her mark in nurseries. (tchd 15-8)
Lady Sandicliffe(IRE) is more exposed than the winner, and she had every chance, but was never finding enough. (op 7-2 tchd 3-1)
Natural Rhythm(IRE), who was carrying a penalty, stayed on well from off the pace but was well held by the first two.
Alexander Monarchy(IRE) is fairly exposed now, and she did not run to anything near her previous performance, finishing well held.
Alfredtheordinary, who has had plenty of runs, seems suited by the trip and ground and helps to set the level of the form. (op 8-1 tchd 13-2)
Indecision, in first-time cheekpieces, showed up for some way but probably prefers easier ground. (op 22-1 tchd 16-1)
Glenshee(IRE), another whose best efforts have been on softer ground, was in trouble entering the last quarter mile. (op 13-2 tchd 7-1 and 5-1)

4784 TURFTV MAIDEN AUCTION STKS 7f
3:00 (3:01) (Class 5) 2-Y-O **£3,886** (£1,156; £577; £288) **Stalls** Low

Form RPR

1 **Rosa Grace** 2-8-8 0 .... PhilipRobinson 9 75+
(Rae Guest) *sn outpcd and bhd 1/2-way: hdwy 3f out: swtchd outside and rdn along 2f out: styd on wl appr fnl f: led last 100yds: swvd bdly lft nr line* **16/1**

0 **2** *1 ¼* **Green Diamond**[24] 4048 2-9-2 0 .... RoystonFfrench 3 80
(M Johnston) *prom: effrt to ld 2f out: sn rdn and edgd lft ent fnl f: drvn and hdd last 100yds: hld whn hmpd nr line* **11/4**[2]

54 **3** *¾* **Jonny Lesters Hair (IRE)**[27] 3977 2-8-11 0 .... DavidAllan 6 73
(T D Easterby) *led: rdn 3f out: hdd 2f out: drvn and one pce ent fnl f* **10/1**[3]

3 **4** *4* **Swift Gift**[14] 4362 2-8-13 0 .... KDarley 14 65+
(B J Meehan) *in tch: hdwy to chse ldrs 2f out: sn rdn and kpt on same pce* **11/4**[2]

00 **5** *¾* **Sand Maiden (IRE)**[11] 4448 2-8-4 0 .... PaulHanagan 2 54
(T D Easterby) *in tch on inner: hdwy to chse ldrs 2f out: sn rdn and kpt on same pce appr fnl f* **50/1**

05 **6** *1 ½* **Ras Laffan**[25] 4028 2-8-11 0 .... GrahamGibbons 13 57
(E S McMahon) *prom: rdn along over 2f out: sn one pce* **25/1**

7 *1 ¾* **Beetuna (IRE)** 2-9-2 0 .... PaulEddery 7 57
(B Smart) *towards rr: rdn along over 2f out: nvr nr ldrs* **28/1**

00 **8** *shd* **Kiwi Princess**[17] 4247 2-8-4 0 .... AdrianTNicholls 8 45
(M Brittain) *a towards rr* **100/1**

32 **9** *1 ½* **Dhhamaan (IRE)**[13] 4393 2-8-9 0 .... KerrinMcEvoy 10 46
(C E Brittain) *chsd ldrs: rdn along wl over 2f out and grad wknd* **9/4**[1]

0 **10** *3 ½* **Son Of Spartacus (IRE)**[20] 4173 2-8-11 0 .... TomEaves 4 39
(Mrs L Stubbs) *in tch: rdn along 3f out and sn wknd* **100/1**

0 **11** *12* **Mollyatti**[7] 4564 2-8-8 0 .... MickyFenton 1 —
(Miss V Haigh) *prom on inner: rdn along 3f out: drvn and wknd wl over 1f out* **16/1**

0 **12** *2 ½* **Dareios (GER)**[47] 3341 2-8-11 0 .... NCallan 5 —
(G A Swinbank) *sn outpcd and a wl bhd* **33/1**

13 *12* **Call Of Ktulu (IRE)** 2-9-2 0 .... PaddyAspell 12 —
(J S Wainwright) *sn outpcd and t.o fr 1/2-way* **50/1**

0 **R** **Fellrunner (IRE)**[33] 3761 2-8-2 0 .... DanielleMcCreery[(7)] 11 —
(A Berry) *v.s.a and sn ref to r* **200/1**

1m 28.91s (1.81) **Going Correction** +0.20s/f (Good) 14 Ran SP% **121.6**
Speed ratings (Par 94): **97,95,94,90,89 87,85,85,83,79 66,63,49,—**
CSF £58.68 TOTE £20.70: £3.50, £1.60, £2.70; EX 103.70.
Owner E P Duggan **Bred** Worksop Manor Stud **Trained** Newmarket, Suffolk
■ Stewards' Enquiry : N Callan one-day ban; not riding to draw (Sep 4)

FOCUS
Probably no more than a fair juvenile auction race, though it was won in decent style by the winner.

The Form Book, Raceform Ltd, Compton, RG20 6NL

NOTEBOOK
Rosa Grace ◆, a 30,000gns half-sister to Secret Night out of a triple winning sprinter, picked up well wide from off the pace to get in front inside the last furlong and win going away. She is the sort who should improve with racing.
Green Diamond confirmed the promise of his debut run at Goodwood and, after racing close to the pace, battled away only to be worn down close home. There should be races in him. (op 7-2)
Jonny Lesters Hair(IRE), whose two previous runs had been on testing ground, improved on this quicker going, racing up with the pace and keeping on to pull well clear of the rest. Official explanation: jockey said colt hung right (op 28-1)
Swift Gift, who had no easy task from his wide draw, did not really improve from his debut run but he kept on. (op 15-8 tchd 3-1 in places)
Sand Maiden(IRE) was another to improve on previous efforts and is now qualified for a handicap mark. (op 40-1 tchd 66-1)
Ras Laffan did not improve on previous efforts, but also now qualifies for a mark.
Dhhamaan(IRE), who had shown promise on his two previous starts, was a little disappointing this time. (op 11-4)
Mollyatti Official explanation: jockey said filly lost its action
Dareios(GER) Official explanation: jockey said colt missed the break

4785 NATTRASS CONSTRUCTION H'CAP — 1m
3:35 (3:35) (Class 3) (0-90,89) 3-Y-O — **£7,772** (£2,312; £1,155; £577) **Stalls** Low

Form — RPR
116 **1** **Gongidas**[27] 3940 3-9-9 **89**.....(v) KerrinMcEvoy 4 — 97+
(Saeed Bin Suroor) *trckd ldrs: hdwy over 2f out: rdn and hung lft over 1f out: drvn and hung lft ins fnl f: styd on to ld last stride* **6/4**[1]
0256 **2** *shd* **Osteopathic Remedy (IRE)**[18] 4222 3-8-12 **78**..... TomEaves 5 — 83
(M Dods) *trckd ldrs: hdwy over 2f out: rdn to ld wl over 1f out: drvn ins fnl f: hdd on line* **20/1**
5244 **3** *1 1/4* **Cassiara**[15] 4338 3-8-12 **78**.....(p) NCallan 7 — 80
(J Pearce) *hld up in rr: hdwy over 2f out: nt clr run and swtchd outside over 1f out: rdn and styd on ins fnl f: nrst fin* **20/1**
15 **4** *shd* **Fragrancy (IRE)**[23] 4060 3-9-2 **82**..... PhilipRobinson 6 — 84
(M A Jarvis) *t.k.h: prom: rdn along and sltly outpcd over 2f out: styng on whn bmpd over 1f out: kpt on same pce u.p ins fnl f* **10/3**[2]
0605 **5** *1* **Voodoo Moon**[13] 4401 3-9-4 **84**..... RoystonFfrench 8 — 83
(M Johnston) *trckd ldr: hdwy to chal 2f out: ev ch tl drvn and one pce ins fnl f* **6/1**[3]
6053 **6** *6* **Gazboolou**[18] 4222 3-8-9 **75**..... PhillipMakin 1 — 61
(K R Burke) *chsd ldrs: rdn along over 2f out: sn drvn and wknd over 1f out* **11/1**
1423 **7** *3 1/2* **Hazzard County (USA)**[37] 3650 3-9-7 **87**..... PaulHanagan 3 — 65
(D M Simcock) *t.k.h: hld up in rr: effrt and sme hdwy 2f out: sn rdn and btn wl over 1f out* **7/1**
0012 **8** *11* **Tencendur (IRE)**[11] 4450 3-8-9 **75**..... AdrianTNicholls 2 — 27
(D Nicholls) *led: rdn along over 2f out: hdd wl over 1f out: sn wknd and eased ins fnl f* **12/1**

1m 40.99s (1.29) **Going Correction** +0.20s/f (Good) — **8** Ran SP% **115.4**
Speed ratings (Par 104): **101,100,99,99,98 92,89,78**
CSF £36.09 CT £440.35 TOTE £2.10: £1.10, £3.50, £3.00; EX 30.00.
Owner Godolphin **Bred** Karl-Dieter Ellerbracke **Trained** Newmarket, Suffolk

FOCUS
Just a fair gallop to this decent mile handicap for three-year-olds. The winner, another boost for The Illies' Ascot race, has more ability than he cares to show.

NOTEBOOK
Gongidas made it three wins from five starts but, despite that record, he looks a horror as he sports a visor, hangs both left and right, and appears to be trying to get out of putting his best foot forward. However, McEvoy seems to get on well with him and, with a mixture of strength and guile, he got him up bang on the line. The colt leaves the impression he has a fair bit more ability than he cares to show but, though he is never going to look easy, he would be interesting if he were to be gelded. (op 15-8 tchd 2-1)
Osteopathic Remedy(IRE) handled this faster ground well and came back to form with a sound run in second, going on over a furlong out but being caught right on the line. He looks a more straightforward sort than the winner, but his record is just one win from ten starts. (op 25-1)
Cassiara has not won in 16 starts, and though she ran on well after meeting trouble, she was never going to be a real threat. (op 18-1 tchd 16-1)
Fragrancy(IRE) raced keenly close to the pace before getting outpaced, but ran on again despite meeting a bit of trouble. (op 3-1 tchd 7-2)
Voodoo Moon had every chance and was clear of the rest. (tchd 5-1)
Hazzard County(USA) was keen, but his rider reported that he stumbled on the top bend and was never travelling afterwards. Official explanation: jockey said colt stumbled on top bend and was never travelling (op 11-2 tchd 9-1)
Tencendur(IRE) Official explanation: jockey said gelding hung right-handed in home straight

4786 RACING UK H'CAP — 2m
4:10 (4:10) (Class 4) (0-85,85) 4-Y-0+ — **£5,181** (£1,541; £770; £384) **Stalls** Low

Form — RPR
2000 **1** **Billich**[55] 3112 4-8-13 **75**..... NCallan 7 — 84+
(D E Cantillon) *hld up in rr: pushed along and hdwy on wd outside 3f out: rdn 2f out: styd on wl to ld ins fnl f* **5/1**
2340 **2** *1* **Indonesia**[34] 3748 5-8-12 **74**..... DanielTudhope 4 — 81
(T D Walford) *hld up: gd hdwy 4f out: rdn to ld wl over 1f out: drvn and hdd ins fnl f: kpt on* **3/1**[2]
-051 **3** *shd* **Abstract Folly (IRE)**[13] 4409 5-8-5 **67**..... KerrinMcEvoy 5 — 74
(J D Bethell) *hld up: stdy hdwy 3f out: rdn and ev ch over 1f out: drvn and one pce ins fnl f* **4/1**[3]
4313 **4** *3 1/2* **Trance (IRE)**[13] 4398 7-9-5 **81**..... PhillipMakin 2 — 84
(T D Barron) *trckd ldr: hdwy to chal 3f out: sn rdn: wknd over 1f out* **4/1**[3]
0504 **5** *4* **Doctor Scott**[13] 4398 4-8-8 **70**..... RoystonFfrench 6 — 68
(M Johnston) *led: rdn along 3f out: drvn and hdd wl over 1f out: sn wknd* **11/4**[1]
0310 **6** *5* **Corum (IRE)**[16] 4288 4-9-6 **85**.....(p) DominicFox[(3)] 1 — 77
(Mrs K Waldron) *in tch: rdn along over 4f out: sn wknd* **16/1**

3m 34.16s (2.96) **Going Correction** +0.20s/f (Good) — **6** Ran SP% **114.2**
Speed ratings (Par 105): **100,99,99,97,95 93**
CSF £20.77 CT £65.09 TOTE £6.50: £2.70, £2.10; EX 23.10.
Owner Mrs Julie Mitchell **Bred** Mascalls Stud **Trained** Newmarket, Suffolk

FOCUS
A slightly muddling gallop to this fair staying handicap. The form is rated through the runner-up.

4787 COME RACING ON SEPTEMBER 8TH APPRENTICE STKS (FILLIES' H'CAP) — 5f
4:45 (4:45) (Class 5) (0-70,68) 3-Y-0+ — **£3,886** (£1,156; £577; £288) **Stalls** High

Form — RPR
3426 **1** **Toy Top (USA)**[8] 4525 4-8-12 **57**.....(b) NeilBrown[(3)] 4 — 68
(M Dods) *qckly away: mde all: rdn over 1f out: styd on strly u.p ins fnl f* **9/2**[1]
3000 **2** *1 1/2* **Miacarla**[9] 4498 4-8-3 **50**..... DeclanCannon[(5)] 11 — 56
(A Berry) *trckd ldrs: hdwy 2f out: rdn to chse wnr ins fnl f: nt qckn* **8/1**
0660 **3** *2 1/2* **Princess Cleo**[8] 4525 4-8-10 **55**.....(p) SladeO'Hara[(3)] 10 — 52
(T D Easterby) *a.p: effrt to chse wnr 2f out: sn rdn and one pce ins fnl f* **11/2**[2]
4600 **4** *nk* **Mystery Pips**[7] 4561 7-8-2 **49** oh1.....(v) FrankiePickard[(5)] 7 — 45
(N Tinkler) *prom: rdn along 2f out: kpt on same pce appr fnl f* **10/1**
2301 **5** *2* **Rothesay Dancer**[20] 4158 4-9-9 **68**..... KellyHarrison[(3)] 3 — 63+
(J S Goldie) *hld up in rr: hdwy 2f out: swtchd lft and rdn ent fnl f: no imp* **6/1**[3]
0500 **6** *1* **Vondova**[9] 4498 5-8-3 **52**..... PaulPickard[(7)] 6 — 37
(D A Nolan) *midfield: rdn along 2f out: n.d* **40/1**
0333 **7** *1/2* **Overwing (IRE)**[2] 4712 4-9-12 **68**..... JamesMillman 5 — 51
(R M H Cowell) *chsd ldrs: rdn along 2f out: sn no imp* **9/2**[1]
0000 **8** *nk* **Smiddy Hill**[43] 3449 5-8-7 **52**..... SCreighton[(3)] 12 — 34
(R Bastiman) *chsd ldrs: rdn along over 2f out: sn wknd* **8/1**
-005 **9** *1/2* **Yorke's Folly (USA)**[8] 4525 6-8-2 **49** oh4.....(b) BradleyRoper[(5)] 13 — 29
(C W Fairhurst) *a towards rr* **8/1**
0-30 **10** *1 1/2* **Heidi Hi**[37] 3639 3-8-3 **52**..... JamesRogers[(5)] 9 — 27
(J R Turner) *a in rr* **33/1**
0406 **11** *2 1/2* **Ruthies Philly**[10] 4480 3-8-3 **54**..... AshleyMorgan[(7)] 2 — 20
(D W Barker) *prom on wd outside: rdn along 2f out and sn wknd* **28/1**
0246 **12** *3 1/2* **Spinning Game**[4] 4658 3-8-3 **50**.....(b) DanielleMcCreery[(3)] 8 — 3
(D W Chapman) *s.i.s: a bhd* **16/1**

59.49 secs (-0.41) **Going Correction** -0.075s/f (Good)
WFA 3 from 4yo+ 2lb — **12** Ran SP% **123.2**
Speed ratings (Par 100): **100,97,93,93,89 88,87,87,86,83 79,74**
CSF £41.81 CT £210.86 TOTE £6.00: £2.00, £3.10, £2.30; EX 55.90 Place 6 £74.78, Place 5 £46.65.
Owner D Vic Roper **Bred** L Kengye **Trained** Denton, Co Durham
■ Stewards' Enquiry : Neil Brown one-day ban; not riding to draw (Sep 4)

FOCUS
Just a run-of-the-mill sprint for fillies. The form seems sound, rated through the runner-up.
T/Plt: £126.60 to a £1 stake. Pool: £42,924.25. 247.45 winning tickets. T/Qpdt: £71.40 to a £1 stake. Pool: £2,423.50. 25.10 winning tickets. JR

4788 - 4794a (Foreign Racing) - See Raceform Interactive

4521 BEVERLEY (R-H)
Saturday, August 25

OFFICIAL GOING: Good to firm (9.3)
Wind: Virtually nil Weather: Fine and sunny

4795 TOTESPORTCASINO.COM MAIDEN STKS (DIV I) — 5f
1:30 (1:34) (Class 5) 3-Y-0+ — **£2,590** (£770; £385; £192) **Stalls** High

Form — RPR
6-30 **1** **Midnight Sky**[7] 4616 3-8-12 45..... NCallan 2 — 54
(Rae Guest) *prom: hdwy to ld over 1f out: rdn ins fnl f and styd on* **11/1**
2 *1 1/4* **Alto Vertigo**[252] 4-9-5 0..... LeeEnstone 4 — 55
(P C Haslam) *chsd ldrs: hdwy 2f out: rdn and ch ent fnl f: sn drvn and kpt on same pce* **20/1**
4503 **3** *4* **Tenancy (IRE)**[7] 4616 3-8-10 60.....(p) RobbieEgan[(7)] 1 — 40
(A J McCabe) *wnt lft s: cl up on wd outside: ev ch 2f out: sn rdn: edgd rt and wknd over 1f out* **7/4**[1]
4-44 **4** *shd* **Staked A Claim (IRE)**[29] 3917 3-9-3 59.....(b[1]) PhillipMakin 9 — 40
(T D Barron) *midfield and sn pushed along: effrt and swtchd lft 2f out: sn rdn and kpt on ins fnl f* **15/8**[2]
/-00 **5** *nk* **Princess Charlmane (IRE)**[49] 3302 4-9-0 37..... PaddyAspell 8 — 34
(C J Teague) *chsd ldrs: rdn along 2f out: sn wandered and wknd* **50/1**
0505 **6** *1 3/4* **Violet's Pride**[7] 4616 3-8-12 50.....(v) HayleyTurner 6 — 28
(S Parr) *chsd ldrs: rdn and n.m.r wl over 1f out: sn wknd* **7/1**[3]
-056 **7** *3* **Village Storm (IRE)**[65] 2792 4-9-5 32..... TomEaves 7 — 22
(C J Teague) *sn outpcd and bhd fr 1/2-way* **50/1**
8 *1 3/4* **Josama** 3-8-12 0..... RoystonFfrench 3 — 11
(R Bastiman) *sn rn green: outpcd and bhd fr 1/2-way* **16/1**
066- **9** *4* **Wotavadun (IRE)**[255] 6806 4-9-5 40.....(be) FrancisNorton 5 — 1
(B P J Baugh) *sn led: rdn along 2f out: hdd over 1f out and sn wknd* **28/1**
10 *16* **Monasheemini (IRE)** 4-9-0 0..... DavidAllan 11 — —
(Mrs N Macauley) *s.i.s: a wl bhd* **16/1**

64.08 secs (0.08) **Going Correction** -0.15s/f (Firm)
WFA 3 from 4yo 2lb — **10** Ran SP% **115.9**
Speed ratings (Par 103): **93,91,84,84,83 81,76,73,67,41**
CSF £203.99 TOTE £11.20: £2.90, £3.70, £1.20; EX 155.30.
Owner C J Mills **Bred** C J Mills **Trained** Newmarket, Suffolk
■ Stewards' Enquiry : David Allan one-day ban: used whip in the forehand position down the shoulder (Sep 6)

FOCUS
This looked a very poor maiden with the winner rated just 45. The favourite was again below form.
Midnight Sky Official explanation: trainer said, regarding apparent improvement in form, that the filly was better suited by the faster ground

4796 EUROPEAN BREEDERS' FUND SPECIOSA MAIDEN FILLIES' STKS — 7f 100y
2:00 (2:02) (Class 4) 2-Y-O — **£4,533** (£1,348; £674; £336) **Stalls** High

Form — RPR
1 **Jadaara** 2-9-0 0..... GregFairley 7 — 83+
(M Johnston) *chsd ldng pair: hdwy over 2f out: led appr fnl f: sn rdn and styd on wl* **14/1**
22 **2** *1 1/2* **Badalona**[23] 4094 2-9-0 0..... HayleyTurner 10 — 79
(M L W Bell) *in tch: hdwy over 2f out: swtchd lft and rdn over 1f out: sn drvn and kpt on ins fnl f* **11/8**[1]
00 **3** *3/4* **Starfala**[30] 3874 2-9-0 0..... NelsonDeSouza 13 — 77
(P F I Cole) *in tch: hdwy over 2f out: rdn wl over 1f out: styd on strly ins fnl f* **33/1**
0 **4** *nk* **Armure**[23] 4094 2-9-0 0..... PhilipRobinson 4 — 77
(M A Jarvis) *chsd ldrs: hdwy on outer over 2f out: rdn and rn green over 1f out: kpt on same pce fnl f* **5/1**[2]
002 **5** *2* **Coachhouse Lady (USA)**[13] 4422 2-9-0 71..... NCallan 12 — 72
(K A Ryan) *chsd ldr: hdwy to ld 2f out: sn rdn and edgd rt: drvn and hdd appr fnl f: wknd* **11/2**[3]
6 *1/2* **Lanterns Of Gold** 2-9-0 0..... RoystonFfrench 6 — 71
(Mrs A Duffield) *in rr and pushed along 1/2-way: hdwy 2f out: styd on ins fnl f: nrst fin* **66/1**
0 **7** *1 1/4* **Free Fallin**[36] 3706 2-9-0 0..... TedDurcan 11 — 68+
(P W Chapple-Hyam) *sn led: rdn along and hdd 2f out: sn n.m.r and wknd* **11/2**[3]

35 **8** *3 ½* **Threestoneburn (USA)**[62] 3-9-0 2-9-0 0 LeeEnstone 2 60
(P C Haslam) *hld up: a in rr* **14/1**

0 **9** *2 ½* **Fernlawn Hope (IRE)**[52] 3213 2-8-7 0 RobbieEgan(7) 8 54
(J A Osborne) *a in rr* **40/1**

03 **10** *1* **Neve Lieve (IRE)**[29] 3916 2-9-0 0 MickyFenton 5 51
(M Botti) *midfield: rdn along 3f out: sn wknd* **14/1**

0 **11** *8* **Khibraat**[30] 3874 2-9-0 0 TomEaves 1 33
(E A L Dunlop) *stdd and swtchd rt s: hld up: a in rr* **33/1**

0 **12** *2 ½* **Kalanda Kurl (IRE)**[34] 3761 2-9-0 0 TonyHamilton 3 27
(J J Quinn) *a towards rr* **100/1**

000 **13** *3* **Cottam Breeze**[10] 4487 2-8-7 35 NSLawes(7) 9 20
(M W Easterby) *s.i.s: a in rr* **150/1**

1m 31.61s (-2.70) **Going Correction** -0.35s/f (Firm) **13** Ran SP% **121.0**
Speed ratings (Par 93): **101,99,98,98,95 95,93,89,86,85 76,73,70**
CSF £33.50 TOTE £15.20: £5.40, £1.10, £15.60; EX 40.70.
Owner Sheikh Ahmed Al Maktoum **Bred** Darley **Trained** Middleham Moor, N Yorks
■ Stewards' Enquiry : Royston Ffrench one-day ban: entered wrong stall (Sep 5)
Tony Hamilton one-day ban: careless riding (Sep 5)

FOCUS
Not as strong a maiden as the numbers might suggest, but some big stables were represented and thanks to a solid pace the winning time was very decent for a race like this, 0.8 seconds quicker than the three-year-old handicap that followed. The second and fifth help set the level of the form.

NOTEBOOK
Jadaara ♦, a half-sister to two winners including a three-time winner in the US, certainly knew her job and picked up really when when asked. She should get a bit further than this and looks a filly with a future.
Badalona was always handy, but once pulled out for her effort could not produce quite enough to register that elusive first victory. She probably ran into a decent newcomer here and she will get it right one day, but after finishing runner-up in all three of her starts she is unlikely to be a big price when she does. (op 11-10 tchd 6-4 in a place)
Starfala was finishing in good style and this was a big improvement on her two previous efforts. As her pedigree is all stamina, this stiffer track was probably the reason and it is worth noting that her half-sister Under The Rainbow scored over 1m 2f as a two-year-old. (op 40-1)
Armure was brought to hold every chance on the outside, but tended to run about a bit and still looked in need of the experience. Middle-distances will be the making of her and the best of her is likely to be seen next year. (op 9-2 tchd 4-1)
Coachhouse Lady(USA) one of the most experienced fillies in the field, tried to make it count and was in front halfway up the home straight, but failed to see her race out. She lacks the scope of those that finished ahead of her and it may be worth switching her to nurseries now. (op 13-2)
Lanterns Of Gold, a 47,000gns half-sister to three winners including the smart juvenile Diktatorial, was noted staying on nicely at the end and should come on for this. Her pedigree suggests she will appreciate further.
Free Fallin, as on his debut, had the run of the race out in front and there seemed few excuses. (op 15-2 tchd 8-1)

4797 TOTEEXACTA H'CAP — 7f 100y
2:30 (2:33) (Class 5) (0-75,75) 3-Y-0+ **£3,886** (£1,156; £577; £288) **Stalls** High

Form RPR

0113 **1** **Mister Jingles**[11] 4479 4-8-11 **60** (v) HayleyTurner 10 67
(R M Whitaker) *mde all: pushed clr 2f out: rdn over 1f out: drvn ins fnl f: hld on gamely* **13/2**[3]

231 **2** *hd* **Bolton Hall (IRE)**[9] 4526 5-9-0 **63** PaulHanagan 12 69
(R A Fahey) *hld up towards rr: gd hdwy on inner over 2f out: swtchd outside and effrt wl over 1f out: ev ch whn rdn and hung bdly rt ins fnl f and again nr fin* **10/3**[1]

0160 **3** *½* **Zennerman (IRE)**[5] 4672 4-9-12 **75** (b) NCallan 6 80
(K A Ryan) *hld up in rr: gd hdwy on inner wl over 1f out: rdn and ch ins fnl f: kpt on* **5/1**[2]

5000 **4** *½* **Treasure House (IRE)**[15] 4353 6-8-7 **56** DaleGibson 8 61+
(M Blanshard) *hld up: hdwy over 2f out: rdn over 1f out: ev ch ins fnl f tl bdly hmpd and snatched up nr fin* **8/1**

4423 **5** *nk* **Barkass (UAE)**[17] 4281 3-9-7 **75** TomEaves 3 76
(B Ellison) *chsd ldrs: rdn along and outpcd over 2f out: styd on u.p ins fnl f* **10/3**[1]

0500 **6** *1 ¼* **Franksalot (IRE)**[27] 3999 7-9-4 **67** RoystonFfrench 2 67
(I W McInnes) *hld up: hdwy 2f out: sn rdn and kpt on ins fnl f: nrst fin* **16/1**

3023 **7** *1 ¼* **Mataram (USA)**[24] 4068 4-9-12 **75** TedDurcan 7 72
(W Jarvis) *hld up in rr: effrt on outer over 2f out: sn rdn and kpt on insiude fnl f: nt rch ldrs* **5/1**[2]

0530 **8** *¾* **Fairy Monarch (IRE)**[12] 4449 8-8-8 **57** oh8 ow1 (b) MickyFenton 11 52+
(P T Midgley) *trckd ldrs: hdwy 3f out: rdn wl over 1f out: ev ch whn hmpd ins fnl f and nt rcvr* **66/1**

1050 **9** *2 ½* **Sedge (USA)**[14] 4407 7-9-0 **63** PaulFessey 1 51+
(P T Midgley) *prom: effrt 2f out: rdn and ev ch whn hmpd ins fnl f: nt rcvr* **20/1**

3500 **10** *3 ½* **Damelza (IRE)**[21] 4177 4-9-2 **65** DavidAllan 9 45
(T D Easterby) *a in rr* **20/1**

0036 **11** *15* **Pawn In Life (IRE)**[44] 3470 9-8-7 **56** oh11 (b) NickyMackay 4 —
(D W Chapman) *prom: rdn along 3f out and sn wknd* **100/1**

1m 32.41s (-1.90) **Going Correction** -0.35s/f (Firm)
WFA 3 from 4yo+ 5lb **11** Ran SP% **121.8**
Speed ratings (Par 103): **96,95,95,94,94 92,91,90,87,83 66**
CSF £28.67 CT £124.03 TOTE £7.70: £1.90, £1.80, £2.30; EX 19.50.
Owner James Marshall & Mrs Susan Marshall **Bred** Catridge Farm Stud Ltd **Trained** Scarcroft, W Yorks

FOCUS
A very messy race and as often happens at this track plenty of trouble in the latter stages. A moderate pace was a major factor in that and the resulting time was modest, 0.8 seconds slower than the preceding juvenile fillies' maiden. The form looks somewhat dubious.
Bolton Hall(IRE) Official explanation: jockey said gelding hung both ways inside final furlong

4798 TOTEPOOL BEVERLEY BULLET SPRINT STKS (LISTED RACE) — 5f
3:00 (3:03) (Class 1) 3-Y-0+ **£17,781** (£6,723; £3,360; £1,680) **Stalls** High

Form RPR

24-0 **1** **Hellvelyn**[43] 3506 3-8-12 112 TedDurcan 6 117
(B Smart) *hld up: gd hdwy on wd outside 2f out: rdn ent fnl f: styd on to ld nr line* **4/1**[2]

2002 **2** *shd* **Borderlescott**[21] 4150 5-9-0 112 RoystonFfrench 8 117
(R Bastiman) *trckd ldrs: cl up 2f out: rdn to ld ent fnl f: edgd lft drvn and hdd nr line* **7/4**[1]

1244 **3** *3* **Peace Offering (IRE)**[42] 3531 7-9-7 108 AdrianTNicholls 7 113
(D Nicholls) *led: rdn along 2f out: hdd ent fnl f: sn drvn and kpt on same pce* **20/1**

-456 **4** *1* **The Jobber (IRE)**[23] 4090 6-9-0 100 PaulHanagan 5 102+
(M Blanshard) *plld hrd: trckd ldrs: edgd rt after 2f: rdn wl over 1f out and kpt on ins fnl f* **12/1**

0000 **5** *shd* **Fayr Jag (IRE)**[7] 4614 8-9-0 100 DavidAllan 12 102+
(T D Easterby) *chsd ldrs whn hmpd and lost pl after 2f: hdwy 2f out: styd on u.p ins fnl f: nrst fin* **12/1**

2053 **6** *½* **Bounty Quest**[21] 4183 5-9-0 100 NCallan 11 100
(K A Ryan) *prom: rdn along 2f out: drvn and one pce appr fnl f* **40/1**

00-0 **7** *1 ¼* **Tawaassol (USA)**[23] 4090 4-9-0 101 (t) TomEaves 14 96
(Sir Michael Stoute) *hld up in rr tl sme late hdwy* **15/2**[3]

-116 **8** *shd* **Pivotal's Princess (IRE)**[48] 3344 5-8-9 102 PhilipRobinson 3 90
(E S McMahon) *trckd ldrs: effrt 2f out: sn rdn and btn* **9/1**

2040 **9** *nk* **Tabaret**[4] 4696 4-9-0 95 HayleyTurner 13 94
(R M Whitaker) *chsd ldrs on inner: rdn along and n.m.r 2f out: grad wknd appr fnl f* **20/1**

0052 **10** *½* **Baltic King**[20] 4196 7-9-0 105 (t) MickyFenton 1 93
(H Morrison) *hmpd s: a in rr* **8/1**

2000 **11** *3* **Folga**[35] 3746 5-8-9 90 TonyHamilton 10 77
(J G Given) *a in rr* **66/1**

0003 **12** *1* **Strike Up The Band**[154] 762 4-9-4 106 SilvestreDeSousa 2 82
(D Nicholls) *wnt lft s: chsd ldrs: rdn along over 2f out and sn wknd* **20/1**

61.83 secs (-2.17) **Going Correction** -0.15s/f (Firm)
WFA 3 from 4yo+ 2lb **12** Ran SP% **122.8**
Speed ratings (Par 111): **111,110,106,104,104 103,101,101,100,100 95,93**
CSF £11.02 TOTE £5.30: £2.10, £1.40, £5.50; EX 15.20.
Owner H E Sheikh Rashid Bin Mohammed **Bred** N E and Mrs Poole and Trickledown Stud **Trained** Hambleton, N Yorks

FOCUS
A decent field for this Listed contest and the pace was solid. Decent form, and it was also the 'right' result in so far as the finish was dominated by the pair most favoured by the weights.

NOTEBOOK
Hellvelyn, who has been racing at Group 1 level since winning last season's Coventry Stakes, had obviously been given enough time to recover from his belated reappearance in the July Cup, in which he was far from disgraced. Despite seeing plenty of daylight on the outside from his low draw, he showed a splendid attitude to cut down a very tough rival and just win with nothing to spare. There are still enough opportunities for him to continue to make up for lost time this term, and he may take on Sakhee's Secret again in the Betfred Sprint Cup, but the Diadem back at his beloved Ascot later next month would appear a more suitable target. (tchd 7-2)
Borderlescott was always up there and looked the one to beat when sent for home a furlong out, but despite doing nothing wrong he had the prize cruelly snatched from him yet again and has been incredibly unlucky this season. In fact he has been beaten a length or less in six of his last nine outings, yet his official mark has continually crept up throughout that period. (op 9-4)
Peace Offering(IRE), back on a faster surface, soon bagged the inside rail and tried to make every yard, but a combination of his Group 3 penalty and this stiff track found him out. Considering he was 11lb badly in with the front pair compared to a handicap, he still emerged with credit. (tchd 18-1)
The Jobber(IRE) loves this ground, but he took a fierce hold despite the decent pace and that was always likely to count against him later on on a stiff track like this. Under the circumstances, he did well to hang on to fourth but he is still to show that he is quite up to this level and he will certainly need to settle better if he is to make an impact. (op 14-1)
Fayr Jag(IRE), nothing like as good has he was, is very hard to win with these days, but he is still capable of running a creditable race when he can hear his feet rattle and that was again the case here. (op 14-1)
Bounty Quest, taking a step back up in class on his third outing for the yard, was always in a handy position and had every chance, but he does not look the easiest to place at present.
Baltic King took a left hook from Strike Up The Band on leaving the stalls and never managed to get into the race after that. (op 7-1)
Strike Up The Band swerved violently to his left on leaving the stalls, hampering Balting King in the process, but although he managed to get back in touch with the leaders he had nothing left over the last couple of furlongs. (op 33-1)

4799 TOTESPORT.COM STKS (HERITAGE H'CAP) — 1m 1f 207y
3:35 (3:36) (Class 2) (0-105,97) 3-Y-0 **£32,385** (£9,635; £4,815; £2,405) **Stalls** High

Form RPR

540 **1** **Teslin (IRE)**[23] 4093 3-9-3 **93** DavidAllan 17 106
(B Ellison) *hld up: hdwy over 2f out: swtchd outside and rdn over 1f out: str run to chal and wandered ins fnl f: led nr fin* **33/1**

3312 **2** *¾* **Monte Alto (IRE)**[21] 4184 3-9-0 **90** NickyMackay 9 101
(L M Cumani) *hld up in midfield: hdwy over 3f out: chsd ldrs 2f out: rdn to ld ins fnl f: drvn and hdd towards fin* **7/1**[3]

0003 **3** *1 ½* **Habalwatan (IRE)**[9] 4523 3-8-11 **87** HayleyTurner 4 95
(C E Brittain) *hld up towards rr: hdwy 2f out: rdn and styd on ins fnl f: nrst fin* **25/1**

-461 **4** *nk* **Cabinet (IRE)**[30] 3882 3-8-13 **89** TomEaves 13 96+
(Sir Michael Stoute) *trckd ldrs on inner: effrt and n.m.r 2f out: rdn and hmpd over 1f out: squeezed through and styd on wl fnl f* **8/1**

1206 **5** *1 ¼* **Philatelist (USA)**[24] 4059 3-9-0 **90** (b[1]) PhilipRobinson 2 95
(M A Jarvis) *trckd ldrs: hdwy to ld 2f out: rdn and hdd ins fnl f: wknd* **9/1**

-116 **6** *nk* **Gold Hush (USA)**[24] 4060 3-8-11 **87** TedDurcan 16 91+
(Sir Michael Stoute) *hld up in tch on inner: hdwy over 2f out: rdn and n.m.r 1f out: kpt on u.p ins fnl f* **6/1**[2]

1324 **7** *nk* **Warm Embraces (IRE)**[37] 3691 3-8-3 **79** SilvestreDeSousa 6 83
(D R C Elsworth) *chsd ldrs on outer: rdn along over 2f out: drvn over 1f out and kpt on same pce* **8/1**

1651 **8** *nk* **Record Breaker (IRE)**[6] 4637 3-9-0 **90** 6ex GregFairley 15 93
(M Johnston) *cl up: rdn along wl over 2f out: drvn and edgd rt over 1f out: grad wknd* **5/2**[1]

4550 **9** *½* **Smart Instinct (USA)**[23] 4092 3-9-7 **97** PaulHanagan 10 99
(R A Fahey) *trckd ldrs: rdn along 3f out: drvn wl over 1f out and kpt on same pce* **20/1**

1314 **10** *½* **Muhannak (IRE)**[10] 4510 3-8-4 **80** DaleGibson 12 81
(G A Butler) *dwlt and towards rr: hdwy over 2f out: sn rdn and no imp* **16/1**

2300 **11** *2* **Dubai Twilight**[44] 3460 3-9-0 **90** FrancisNorton 3 87
(B W Hills) *in tch: effrt over 2f out: sn rdn and no imp* **22/1**

1413 **12** *1* **Six Of Diamonds (IRE)**[23] 4092 3-9-0 **90** NCallan 7 85
(J A Osborne) *sn led: rdn along 3f out: hdd 2f out and grad wknd* **8/1**

-645 **13** *½* **Manchurian**[21] 4166 3-8-10 **86** PhillipMakin 5 80
(M J Wallace) *midfield: hdwy and in tch 4f out: rdn along wl over 2f out and grad wknd* **25/1**

6-50 **14** *6* **Vorteeva (USA)**[44] 3460 3-9-3 **93** LeeEnstone 14 75
(K R Burke) *dwlt: a in rr* **100/1**

2m 2.24s (-5.06) **Going Correction** -0.35s/f (Firm) **14** Ran SP% **125.3**
Speed ratings (Par 106): **106,105,104,103,102 102,102,102,101,101 99,99,98,93**
CSF £245.39 CT £5866.69 TOTE £41.90: £8.80, £2.30, £5.80; EX 660.90 Trifecta £7773.10 Pool: £54,740.67 - 5.00 winning units..
Owner Mr & Mrs D A Gamble **Bred** Saud Bin Saad **Trained** Norton, N Yorks

The Form Book, Raceform Ltd, Compton, RG20 6NL

FOCUS
A very competitive handicap run at a good pace, but still with the usual hard-luck stories. The form still seems sound enough. It was also a race of changing fortunes with three different horses looking sure to win at various stages in the last couple of furlongs.

NOTEBOOK
Teslin(IRE) ◆ managed to beat Aqaleem and Authorized in the Haynes, Hanson & Clark Stakes just under a year ago, but a lot of water has flowed under the bridge since then as have his reproductive glands. Having his second start since the operation and for his new yard after leaving Mark Johnston, he was settled off the pace before being pulled out for his effort a furlong from home. He did look as though he might throw it away by hanging momentarily under pressure, but gathered himself together in time to swoop past the leader near the line. Although unlikely to reach the heights that seemed possible a year ago, his new yard have obviously done a great job with him and he should continue to make his mark in decent handicap company. The Cambridgeshire is a possibility and that race could well suit him.
Monte Alto(IRE) ◆, up another 3lb, looked to have been delivered with precision timing and seemed sure to collect, but then the winner engaged the afterburner and he had the race snatched from him. He is yet to finish out of the first three in nine attempts and there should be more to come from this consistent colt. (tchd 15-2)
Habalwatan(IRE), a three-time winner on Polytrack but yet to collect on turf, finished in fine style if a little too late. He holds his form well despite being kept very busy and is surely capable of picking up a race on grass off this sort of mark. (tchd 20-1)
Cabinet(IRE) ◆, up 7lb for his Sandown win, had questions to answer on this quick ground, but he looked sure to play a part in the finish as he was travelling extremely well just behind the leaders on the rail throughout. However, he was repeatedly thwarted in his attempts to find a gap between the leading pair and by the time he managed to get out the race was over. He would have gone very close with a clear run and should not take long in gaining compensation. (op 7-1)
Philatelist(USA), dropping in trip after four runs over 1m 4f and blinkered for the first time, came through to lead halfway up the home straight and it looked as though he would take some beating, but he failed to stamp his authority on the race and rather surprisingly folded like a non-stayer. (op 10-1)
Gold Hush(USA) ◆, switched off against the inside rail, enjoyed no luck at all when trying to get closer halfway up the home straight and can be rated a lot closer than her finishing position.
Official explanation: jockey said filly was denied a clear run (tchd 11-2)
Warm Embraces(IRE) was not disgraced, but still shaped as though he needs a greater test of stamina. Official explanation: jockey said colt hung right-handed in final 3f (op 10-1)
Record Breaker(IRE), carrying a 6lb penalty for his Pontefract victory over further, was ridden close to the pace to make use of his stamina, but he did not find much off the bridle and eventually dropped away. (op 3-1 tchd 9-4)
Vorteeva(USA) Official explanation: trainer's representative said gelding finished distressed

4800 TOTESPORT 0800 221 221 H'CAP 5f
4:05 (4:08) (Class 5) (0-75,75) 3-Y-0+ £4,533 (£1,348; £674; £336) Stalls High

Form RPR
2560 **1** **Kings College Boy**[3] 4703 7-8-11 **63**.........................(b) PaulHanagan 8 71
(R A Fahey) *trckd ldrs: hdwy over 1f out: rdn ent fnl f: kpt on to ld last 50yds* **8/1**[3]
5423 **2** *nk* **Welcome Approach**[10] 4489 4-9-3 **69**.......................... PhillipMakin 6 76
(J R Weymes) *chsd ldrs: hdwy 2f out: rdn to ld 1f out: drvn: hdd and nt qckn last 50yds* **10/1**
444 **3** *nk* **Hotham**[10] 4498 4-8-10 **62**.......................... SilvestreDeSousa 7 68
(N Wilson) *chsd ldrs: rdn along wl over 1f out: kpt on u.p ins fnl f* **6/1**[2]
0021 **4** *1/2* **Never Without Me**[6] 4642 7-8-12 **69** 6ex.......................... NeilBrown(5) 11 73
(J F Coupland) *chsd ldrs: effrt and nt clr run 2f out and over 1f out: rdn and styd on ins fnl f: nrst fin* **8/1**[3]
0003 **5** *3/4* **Colorus (IRE)**[3] 4703 4-9-2 **68**.......................... DaleGibson 10 70
(M W Easterby) *a.p: effrt and ev ch over 1f out: rdn and unable qck ins fnl f* **8/1**[3]
5042 **6** *shd* **Paddywack (IRE)**[6] 4642 10-7-12 **57**..............(b) DanielleMcCreery(7) 14 58+
(D W Chapman) *s.i.s and bhd: hdwy 2f out: rdn and nt clr run over 1f out: kpt on ins fnl f: nrst fin* **5/1**[1]
1341 **7** *1/2* **Desert Opal**[31] 3859 7-9-9 **75**.......................... (p) PhilipRobinson 4 74
(C R Dore) *towards rr: hdwy on outer 2f out: sn rdn and kpt on ins fnl f: nrst fin* **5/1**[1]
0300 **8** *shd* **Cornus**[34] 3762 5-8-9 **68**..........................(be) RobbieEgan(7) 5 67+
(A J McCabe) *dwlt and bhd: gd hdwy on outer over 1f out: styd on ins fnl f: nrst fin* **28/1**
0044 **9** *1* **Mulligan's Gold (IRE)**[6] 4642 4-8-10 **62**..........................(p) TedDurcan 2 57+
(T D Easterby) *hld up in rr: hdwy 2f out: sn rdn and kpt on appr fnl fur;png* **12/1**
00 **10** *hd* **Coseadrom (IRE)**[8] 4585 5-9-7 **73**.......................... FrancisNorton 3 68
(M F Harris) *dwlt and bhd tl sme late hdwy* **25/1**
0300 **11** *2 1/2* **High Reach**[18] 4251 7-9-3 **69**.......................... PaulFessey 9 55
(T D Barron) *chsd ldr: rdn along wl over 1f out: sn wknd* **16/1**
60-0 **12** *1 3/4* **Niteowl Lad (IRE)**[11] 4486 5-8-13 **65**.......................... DavidAllan 1 44
(J Balding) *nvr nr ldrs* **66/1**
0550 **13** *1 1/2* **Monashee Brave (IRE)**[17] 4289 4-8-11 **63**..........(v[1]) NelsonDeSouza 12 37
(J J Quinn) *prom: rdn along 2f out: grad wknd* **12/1**
0056 **14** *hd* **It's Unbelievable (USA)**[8] 4561 4-8-4 **56** oh3..........(b) HayleyTurner 13 29
(P T Midgley) *led: rdn along 2f out: hdd & wknd 1f out* **20/1**

63.16 secs (-0.84) **Going Correction** -0.15s/f (Firm) **14** Ran SP% **124.9**
Speed ratings (Par 103): **100,99,99,98,97 96,96,95,94,94 90,87,84,84**
CSF £85.62 CT £527.92 TOTE £10.50: £2.80, £2.80, £2.20; EX 110.10.
Owner The Cosmic Cases **Bred** Lady Jennifer Green **Trained** Musley Bank, N Yorks

FOCUS
An ordinary sprint handicap contested by the usual suspects. Several had every chance and the principals all finished in a heap.
Paddywack(IRE) Official explanation: jockey said gelding missed the break

4801 TOTESPORTCASINO.COM MAIDEN STKS (DIV II) 5f
4:40 (4:41) (Class 5) 3-Y-0+ £2,590 (£770; £385; £192) Stalls High

Form RPR
020 **1** **Royal Composer (IRE)**[13] 4423 4-9-5 59..........................(b[1]) DavidAllan 6 59
(T D Easterby) *cl up: led after 1f: rdn wl over 1f out: styd on* **9/2**[3]
6040 **2** *1 3/4* **The Cube**[5] 4661 3-8-10 45.......................... RobbieEgan(7) 8 53
(J Balding) *sn rdn along towards rr: hdwy 2f out: styd on wl fnl f* **16/1**
0440 **3** *3/4* **Perlachy**[9] 4538 3-9-3 58.......................... HayleyTurner 2 50
(Mrs N Macauley) *towards rr: hdwy wl over 1f out: sn rdn and styd on wl fnl f* **14/1**
4 *3/4* **Tumbleweed Di** 3-8-8 0 ow1.......................... SladeO'Hara(5) 11 43
(G R Oldroyd) *chsd ldrs on inner: nt clr run and swtchd lft over 1f out: kpt on u.p ins fnl f* **33/1**
0222 **5** *nk* **Tarkamara (IRE)**[10] 4513 3-8-12 70.......................... NelsonDeSouza 9 41
(P F I Cole) *trckd ldrs: effrt 2f out and sn rdn: drvn appr fnl f and sn btn* **10/11**[1]
000 **6** *1 1/4* **Ducal Regancy Red**[52] 3202 3-8-5 37.......................... NSLawes(7) 7 37
(C J Teague) *led early: cl up tl rdn: edgd rt and wknd over 1f out* **66/1**
0000 **7** *nk* **Boppys Dream**[9] 4525 5-9-0 42..........................(p) PaulFessey 5 36
(P T Midgley) *in rr: hdwy wl over 1f out: sn rdn and no imp ins fnl f* **33/1**
00 **8** *2* **Takaamul**[9] 4530 4-9-0 55..........................(p) NeilBrown(5) 1 33
(K A Morgan) *chsd ldrs: rdn 2f out and sn wknd* **7/2**[2]
04 **9** *1* **Lawdy Miss Clawdy**[29] 3924 3-8-12 0.......................... TedDurcan 3 25
(D W P Arbuthnot) *chsd ldrs: rdn 2f out: sn drvn and wknd* **8/1**

64.08 secs (0.08) **Going Correction** -0.15s/f (Firm)
WFA 3 from 4yo+ 2lb **9** Ran SP% **123.8**
Speed ratings (Par 103): **93,90,89,87,87 85,84,81,80**
CSF £75.44 TOTE £6.40: £1.70, £4.10, £3.50; EX 90.90.
Owner Mrs B Oughtred **Bred** N P Hearson **Trained** Great Habton, N Yorks

FOCUS
The winning time was identical to the first division. The similarities do not end there - this was just as dire.
Tarkamara(IRE) Official explanation: trainer had no explanation for the poor form shown

4802 PERTEMPS PEOPLE DEVELOPMENT "HANDS AND HEELS" APPRENTICE MAIDEN H'CAP 1m 1f 207y
5:10 (5:11) (Class 6) (0-65,59) 4-Y-0+ £3,238 (£963; £481; £240) Stalls High

Form RPR
2522 **1** **Selkirk Grace**[46] 3397 7-9-8 **59**..........................(p) AmyBaker 4 66
(K A Morgan) *in tch: wd st and hdwy towards stands' rail over 2f out: led wl over 1f out: kpt on wl towards fin* **11/4**[1]
0354 **2** *hd* **Moment Of Clarity**[13] 4424 5-8-12 **49**.......................... DanielleMcCreery 7 56
(R C Guest) *hld up towards rr: gd hdwy 2f out: rdn and styd on ins fnl f: jst hld* **4/1**[2]
0000 **3** *1* **Fadansil**[9] 4526 4-8-5 **45**.......................... JamesRogers(3) 6 50
(J Wade) *towards rr: hdwy 2f out: styd on wl fnl f: nrst fin* **33/1**
0-06 **4** *hd* **Miss Sure Bond (IRE)**[35] 3752 4-9-1 **52**.......................... AlanRutter 11 56
(G R Oldroyd) *bhd: hdwy 2f out: styd on wl appr fnl f: nrst fin* **11/1**
050 **5** *1 1/4* **Mandarin Rocket (IRE)**[14] 4383 4-9-0 **51**.......................... RobbieEgan 5 53
(Miss L A Perratt) *chsd ldrs: hdwy 3f out: rdn and ch 2f out: one pce appr fnl f* **11/1**
02-0 **6** *1 3/4* **Royal Master**[12] 1579 5-9-1 **55**.......................... DeclanCannon(3) 10 53
(P C Haslam) *chsd ldrs: hdwy over 2f out and ev ch tl wknd ent fnl f* **5/1**
0000 **7** *3/4* **Rose Muwasim**[35] 3730 4-8-5 **45**.......................... MatthewDavies(3) 1 42
(S Parr) *chsd ldrs: rdn along over 2f out: grad wknd* **40/1**
0000 **8** *3/4* **Valart**[9] 4532 4-8-10 **47**..........................(tp) MCGeran 2 42
(A J Lidderdale) *a towards rr* **14/1**
340 **9** *3/4* **Moonshine Creek**[26] 4031 5-8-11 **48**.......................... WilliamCarson 3 42
(P W Hiatt) *led 4f: led again 5f out: rdn and hdd wl over 1f out: sn wknd* **9/2**[3]
4006 **10** *9* **Cottam Eclipse**[10] 4488 6-8-5 **45**.......................... PatrickDonaghy(3) 9 21
(I W McInnes) *chsd ldrs: hdwy to ld after 4f: hdd 1/2-way: rdn along over 2f out and sn wknd* **28/1**
5400 **11** *5* **Red Lantern**[25] 4042 6-8-5 **45**.......................... NSLawes(3) 8 11
(M W Easterby) *midfield: effrt and hdwy on inner 3f out: sn rdn and wknd* **12/1**

2m 5.48s (-1.82) **Going Correction** -0.35s/f (Firm) **11** Ran SP% **121.4**
Speed ratings (Par 101): **93,92,92,91,90 89,88,88,87,80 76**
CSF £13.76 CT £305.83 TOTE £3.10: £1.20, £2.00, £9.40; EX 17.70 Place 6 £220.22, Place 5 £107.59.
Owner D S Cooper **Bred** Raffin Stud **Trained** Little Marcle, H'fords
■ Stewards' Enquiry : Alan Rutter caution: careless riding

FOCUS
A weak handicap in which Moonshine Creek and Cottam Eclipse lit each other up and ran themselves into the ground, but even so the final time was modest which suggests they went off far too quick. The runners hung all over the track once in line for home and the winner was certainly not inconvenienced by coming right over to the stands' rail.
T/Plt: £191.00 to a £1 stake. Pool: £59,378.90. 226.85 winning tickets. T/Qpdt: £41.00 to a £1 stake. Pool: £3,244.30. 58.50 winning tickets. JR

4147 GOODWOOD (R-H)
Saturday, August 25

OFFICIAL GOING: Good (7.8)
Wind: Nil

4803 WINDFLOWER MARCH STKS (LISTED RACE) 1m 6f
2:05 (2:05) (Class 1) 3-Y-0+
£17,034 (£6,456; £3,231; £1,611; £807; £405) Stalls High

Form RPR
1506 **1** **Tungsten Strike (USA)**[23] 4091 6-9-12 108.......................... DarryllHolland 1 118
(Mrs A J Perrett) *mde all: drvn and styd on strly fr 3f out: unchal* **9/1**
-323 **2** *6* **Samuel**[44] 3458 3-8-7 105.......................... EddieAhern 2 103
(J L Dunlop) *chsd ldrs: rdn and styd on fr 3f out: tk 2nd jst ins fnl f but no ch w wnr* **4/1**[2]
0003 **3** *1 1/2* **Land 'n Stars**[7] 4599 7-9-7 102.......................... PaulDoe 3 103
(R A Fahey) *chsd wnr: rdn fr 4f out and no imp fr 3f out: wknd and lost 2nd jst ins fnl f and hld on all out for 3rd* **16/1**
3115 **4** *shd* **Ivy Creek (USA)**[44] 3461 4-9-10 113.......................... SteveDrowne 9 105
(G Wragg) *mid-div: rdn over 3f out: styd on fnl 2f to press for 3rd cl home but nvr any ch w unchal wnr* **5/2**[1]
0-10 **5** *7* **Rayhani (USA)**[23] 4091 4-9-7 99.......................... LDettori 8 93
(M P Tregoning) *clsd on ldng duo over 5f out: rdn over 3f out and sme prog: nvr gng pce to be competitive after and wknd over 1f out* **7/1**
1100 **6** *3/4* **Souvenance**[4] 4691 4-9-2 98.......................... SebSanders 5 87
(Sir Mark Prescott) *rdn along over 3f out: a towards rr* **10/1**
6254 **7** *shd* **Hard Top (IRE)**[22] 4117 5-9-7 106.......................... RyanMoore 6 91
(Sir Michael Stoute) *hld up in rr: rdn over 3f out: minimal rspnse tl mod prog cl home* **5/1**[3]
1130 **8** *1 1/4* **Secret Tune**[24] 4059 3-8-7 94.......................... RichardHughes 4 88
(Pat Eddery) *chsd ldrs: rdn 4f out: wknd ins fnl 3f* **16/1**
0316 **9** *3/4* **Big Robert**[25] 4044 3-8-7 107..........................(t) JimCrowley 7 87
(W R Muir) *chsd ldrs tl wknd over 3f out* **8/1**

3m 4.47s (0.50) **Going Correction** +0.275s/f (Good)
WFA 3 from 4yo+ 12lb **9** Ran SP% **119.7**
Speed ratings (Par 111): **109,105,104,104,100 100,100,99,99**
CSF £46.64 TOTE £13.80: £3.00, £1.90, £4.10; EX 67.10 Trifecta £273.40 Pool: £462.20 - 1.20 winning units..
Owner John Connolly **Bred** Minster Stud **Trained** Pulborough, W Sussex

FOCUS
A good staying event, but Tungsten Strike dictated it at a perfect tempo for him, so it gave the impression of being rather tactical. Improved form from the winner on the face of it, but not entirely convincing.

NOTEBOOK

Tungsten Strike(USA) had given the impression that this trip was a minimum for him these days, but Holland judged the pace to perfection. He is a smart stayer on his day, but the rider can take much of the credit for this success. (op 12-1)

Samuel is improving for a test of stamina, and ought to stay 2m on this evidence. With the staying division a relatively weak department, he should not remain a maiden for much longer. (op 10-3 tchd 9-2)

Land 'n Stars seems to be rediscovering his old form, having taken time to acclimatise to his new surroundings, but he should be more competitive again from now on.

Ivy Creek(USA) gave the impression that he stayed the longer trip, but this tactical affair did not bring out the best in him. Though he is worth another crack at a longer distance like this, a return to 1m4f would not be a problem. (op 9-4 tchd 11-4)

Rayhani(USA) excels at 1m4f, and attempts at longer trips have not been successful, so a drop back in trip looks inevitable. (op 8-1)

Souvenance ought to have been suited by the drop back in trip, but trying to come from behind in a race run this way was not ideal. She is capable of a better show. (op 16-1)

Hard Top(IRE) retains a fair amount of ability, but is not an easy horse to win with these days, and the step back up in trip did not produce dividends. (op 6-1 tchd 9-2)

Big Robert did not run his race, but it transpired there was an excuse. Official explanation: vet said colt was distressed (tchd 15-2)

4804 TOTESCOOP6 PRESTIGE STKS (GROUP 3) (FILLIES) 7f

2:35 (2:38) (Class 1) 2-Y-O

£21,576 (£8,177; £4,092; £2,040; £1,022; £513) **Stalls** High

Form RPR

1 **1** **Sense Of Joy**[21] 4169 2-9-0 0 RichardHughes 6 96+
(J H M Gosden) *hld up in tch: pushed along over 2f out: qcknd appr fnl f and styd on wl to ld fnl 75yds: readily* **4/7**[1]

61 **2** ½ **Celtic Slipper (IRE)**[23] 4094 2-9-0 86 SebSanders 4 93
(R M Beckett) *trckd ldr 4f out: drvn to ld wl over 1f out: hdd fnl 75yds: nt pce of wnr but kpt on wl for clr 2nd* **17/2**

145 **3** 2 **Eva's Request (IRE)**[20] 4202 2-9-0 83 DarryllHolland 5 88
(M R Channon) *hld up in rr: rdn over 2f out and one pce tl qcknd ins fnl f and fin strly* **40/1**

41 **4** ½ **Rosaleen (IRE)**[29] 3916 2-9-0 86 LDettori 2 87
(B J Meehan) *sn led and set mod pce first 3f: rdn 3f out: hdd wl over 1f out: one pce ins fnl f* **5/1**[2]

0011 **5** 1 ¾ **Fly Kiss**[9] 4524 2-9-0 65 AhmedAjtebi 7 82
(C E Brittain) *chsd ldr 3f: styd cl up: n.m.r on rail over 2f out: sn rdn: wknd fnl f* **33/1**

1 **6** hd **Mistress Greeley (USA)**[23] 4102 2-9-0 0 RyanMoore 8 82
(Sir Michael Stoute) *t.k.h: chsd ldrs: rdn 3f out: wknd fnl f* **11/2**[3]

1 **7** 3 ½ **Dusty Moon**[44] 3453 2-9-0 0 EddieAhern 3 73+
(W J Knight) *rdn 3f out: a towards rr* **14/1**

1m 29.57s (1.53) **Going Correction** +0.275s/f (Good) **7** Ran SP% **118.3**

Speed ratings (Par 101): **102,101,99,98,96 96,92**

CSF £7.15 TOTE £1.60: £1.20, £3.00; EX 7.10 Trifecta £60.00 Pool: £490.28 - 5.80 winning units..

Owner K Abdulla **Bred** Juddmonte Farms Ltd **Trained** Newmarket, Suffolk

FOCUS

A slow early pace saw them finish in a heap, and it would be impossible to rate the form highly. The race has been rated well below its usual standard and the winner failed to reproduce her impressive debut level, but she was always going to win despite getting up only late on, and she remains a decent prospect.

NOTEBOOK

Sense Of Joy ◆ did not win by far, but continues to give the impression that she is a filly with a future, scoring a shade more comfortably than the margin would suggest. A better pace is likely to play to her strengths even more, and the Fillies' Mile at Ascot, which the stable has won recently with Playful Act and Nannina, is likely to be on the agenda provided the ground does not come up soft. (op 1-2 tchd 4-9)

Celtic Slipper(IRE) did well to get so close to the progressive winner, giving her a good race in the process. She looks a tough sort and should continue to give a good account of herself at this level, but she is probably slightly flattered by the margin. (op 16-1)

Eva's Request(IRE) ran remarkably well for a filly who had been beaten in nurseries, but the slow pace did not bring out the best in some of those who finished behind her. She deserves every credit, but life in handicaps will be even tougher after this. (op 50-1 tchd 66-1)

Rosaleen(IRE) had the run of the race, and is therefore slightly flattered by the result. She is a useful filly, but apparently short of the best. (op 8-1)

Fly Kiss had won a nursery off mark of 56 last time, and her proximity helps to hold down the form. Like the third, she probably benefited from the lack of a good early gallop, which failed to sort out the stars from the handicappers. (op 40-1)

Mistress Greeley(USA) was treading water in the final furlong, despite the lack of early pace, and should benefit from a return to 6f. (tchd 6-1)

4805 TOTESPORT.COM CELEBRATION MILE (GROUP 2) 1m

3:10 (3:11) (Class 1) 3-Y-O+

£62,117 (£23,542; £11,782; £4,408; £4,408; £1,476) **Stalls** High

Form RPR

1156 **1** **Echelon**[56] 3117 5-8-12 109 RyanMoore 3 116
(Sir Michael Stoute) *stdd towards rr but wl in tch: drvn and hdwy over 2f out: led 1f out: drvn out ins fnl f* **7/1**

-151 **2** 1 ¼ **Cesare**[42] 3523 6-9-4 115 JamieSpencer 1 119
(J R Fanshawe) *hld up towards rr but in tch w ldrs: rdn and gd hdwy fr 2f out: chsd wnr jst ins fnl f: kpt on but a repelled* **11/10**[1]

-121 **3** 1 ½ **Blue Ksar (FR)**[27] 4005 4-9-1 114 (t) LDettori 6 113
(Saeed Bin Suroor) *chsd ldrs: wnt 2nd 2f out: drvn and nvr quite gng pce to chal: outpcd ins fnl f and eased whn hld dying strides* **4/1**[2]

153 **4** 2 **Dunelight (IRE)**[25] 4045 4-9-1 110 (v) DaneO'Neill 8 108
(C G Cox) *led: rdn over 2f out: hdd 1f out: wknd ins fnl f* **9/2**[3]

0214 **4** dht **Selinka**[22] 4118 3-8-6 107 EddieAhern 7 104
(R Hannon) *hld up towards rr: rdn 3f out: swtchd lft 2f out: styd on u.p fnl f but nvr in contention* **20/1**

4130 **6** 1 ½ **Charlie Cool**[42] 3523 4-9-1 106 (v) DarryllHolland 2 105
(W J Haggas) *chsd ldr to 2f out: wknd over 1f out* **25/1**

0311 **7** 2 **Blythe Knight (IRE)**[84] 2233 7-9-1 112 GrahamGibbons 4 100
(J J Quinn) *towards rr but in tch: rdn 3f out: no imp on ldrs and sn btn* **14/1**

5-56 **8** 7 **Finicius (USA)**[25] 4045 3-8-9 0 RichardHughes 5 83
(Eoin Griffin, Ire) *chsd ldrs tl over 2f out* **20/1**

1m 38.97s (-1.30) **Going Correction** +0.275s/f (Good)

WFA 3 from 4yo+ 6lb **8** Ran SP% **118.3**

Speed ratings (Par 115): **117,115,114,112,112 110,108,101**

CSF £15.37 TOTE £7.90: £1.90, £1.20, £1.60; EX 14.10 Trifecta £29.00 Pool: £1,300.25 - 31.74 winning units..

Owner Cheveley Park Stud **Bred** Cheveley Park Stud Ltd **Trained** Newmarket, Suffolk

■ Sir Michael Stoute's seventh win in the race, and his fifth since 2000.

FOCUS

A routine pace, particularly for a race of this quality, but a solid winning time for a Group 2. Ordinary form for the grade, although the winner has been raised 4lb.

NOTEBOOK

Echelon appreciated the return to a mile, and this four-time Group 3 winner battled on heroically to win at Group 2 level for the first time. Her half-sister Chic won this in 2004 and 2005, and the Cheveley Park Stud, who also own the runner-up here, have a fine record in the race in recent years. (op 11-2)

Cesare did his best to get past his owners' apparent second string, but she was in no mood to be passed and he had to settle for second. However, he remains a very useful performer at Group 2 level, and would not be out of place back in Group 1 company either, though whether he is quite good enough to win one is a matter for debate. (op 6-5 tchd Evens, 11-8 in a place and 5-4 in places)

Blue Ksar(FR) is a straightforward sort who can be relied upon to run his race, and put in a sterling effort in this higher grade. He is certainly up to winning a Group 3, and could not be ruled out if having another crack at this level. (op 11-2 tchd 6-1 in a place)

Dunelight(IRE) made the running as usual, but he did not overdo it and so can be considered to have just about run his race. Though he has never won a Pattern contest, a Group 3 is well within his reach, particularly if he is allowed his own way up front. (tchd 5-1)

Selinka was running on at the finish and ran a sound race against the colts here, with the return to the longer trip predictably proving to be in her favour. Back in Group 3 company, she could be a serious contender. (tchd 5-1)

Charlie Cool ran as well as could have been expected, but was essentially outclassed in the end by some very smart rivals. (op 66-1 tchd 20-1)

Blythe Knight(IRE)'s recent improvement has been a revelation, but he was returning from a near three-month break and was below his best, Blue Ksar comfortably reversing the Epsom Group 3 placings. The Prix Dollar at Longchamp is on the agenda before he returns to hurdling. (tchd 12-1)

Finicius(USA) Official explanation: jockey said colt was unsuited by the good ground

4806 SOUTH COAST STKS (H'CAP) 6f

3:45 (3:46) (Class 3) (0-95,95) 3-Y-O+ **£7,772** (£2,312; £1,155; £577) **Stalls** Low

Form RPR

0031 **1** **Golden Dixie (USA)**[8] 4567 8-9-6 91 RyanMoore 4 101
(R A Harris) *hld up in rr: rdn: swtchd rt and hdwy ins fnl 2f: str run to ld 1f out: drvn out* **6/1**[1]

1100 **2** 1 ½ **Mac Gille Eoin**[22] 4123 3-9-1 89 JimCrowley 12 94
(J Gallagher) *chsd ldrs: led ins fnl 3f: hdd and rdn 1f out: styd on wl to hold 2nd but nt pce of wnr* **12/1**

0554 **3** nk **Greenslades**[43] 3489 8-9-7 92 EddieAhern 6 96
(P J Makin) *hld up in tch: hdwy appr fnl f: drvn and r.o wl cl home to press for 2nd but nvr gng pce to trble wnr* **8/1**

6000 **4** ½ **Wyatt Earp (IRE)**[7] 4614 6-9-4 89 PaulDoe 3 91
(R A Fahey) *towards rr: rdn over 2f out: hdwy over 1f out and chsd ldrs ins fnl f: one pce cl home* **9/1**

1104 **5** 1 ¼ **Stamford Blue**[14] 4389 6-8-9 85 (b) LukeMorris[(5)] 7 83
(R A Harris) *towards rr: drvn along 1/2-way: hdwy fnl f: kpt on cl home but nvr gng pce to rch ldrs* **7/1**[3]

0425 **6** 1 ¾ **Tony James (IRE)**[21] 4183 5-9-10 95 DaneO'Neill 10 88
(K O Cunningham-Brown) *chsd ldrs: rdn 3f out: wknd ins fnl f* **14/1**

1225 **7** nk **China Cherub**[14] 4373 4-9-2 87 (b) RichardHughes 2 79
(R Hannon) *chsd ldrs: rdn over 2f out: wknd ins fnl f* **15/2**

5000 **8** hd **Royal Storm (IRE)**[7] 4601 8-8-6 77 SimonWhitworth 9 68
(Mrs A J Perrett) *in tch: rdn and outpcd 2f out: nvr in contention after* **25/1**

6060 **9** ¾ **Mujood**[14] 4389 4-9-0 85 (v) StephenCarson 11 74
(Eve Johnson Houghton) *chsd ldrs: drvn to chal over 2f out: wknd fnl f* **8/1**

20-0 **10** hd **Oi Vay Joe (IRE)**[84] 2243 3-8-10 84 AdamKirby 8 72
(W Jarvis) *towards rr early: drvn and hdwy to cl on ldrs 2f out: wknd ins fnl f* **33/1**

6015 **11** ½ **Ishi Adiva**[14] 4386 3-9-2 90 SteveDrowne 1 77
(Tom Dascombe) *outpcd thrght tl modest prog nr fin* **20/1**

0040 **12** 1 ¾ **Texas Gold**[14] 4386 9-8-9 87 JackMitchell[(7)] 14 68
(W R Muir) *towards rr: hdwy on far side to press ldrs ins fnl 2f: wknd fnl f* **7/1**[3]

6006 **13** 3 ½ **Ajigolo**[7] 4614 4-9-7 92 DarryllHolland 5 62
(M R Channon) *chsd ldrs over 3f* **13/2**[2]

0000 **14** 2 **Pacific Pride**[22] 4122 4-9-0 85 (b) GrahamGibbons 13 48
(J J Quinn) *led tl hdd ins fnl 3f: sn btn* **16/1**

1m 12.83s (-0.02) **Going Correction** +0.175s/f (Good)

WFA 3 from 4yo+ 3lb **14** Ran SP% **128.4**

Speed ratings (Par 107): **107,105,104,103,102 99,99,99,98,98 97,95,90,87**

CSF £81.16 CT £615.22 TOTE £5.80: £2.30, £4.80, £4.20; EX 109.30 Trifecta £758.60 Part won. Pool: £1,068.50 - 0.10 winning units..

Owner Mrs Vicki Davies **Bred** G Strawbridge Jr **Trained** Earlswood, Monmouths

FOCUS

Solid sprint handicap form, with the third to this year's course and distance level and personal bests from the first two. The form could be rated even higher.

NOTEBOOK

Golden Dixie(USA) retains his enthusiasm remarkably well, and has hit a particularly rich vein of form of late. He takes a while to get going, but when he starts to power home it seems very hard for others to live with him in this mood and, like all sprinters on a roll, he must be on the short-list until he shows signs of flagging. The Portland is his target now. (tchd 11-2)

Mac Gille Eoin is more than a stone higher in the weights these days, but put in a brave attempt to defy the Handicapper. The return to 6f was in his favour, but any further rise - even at this trip - would make things difficult for him. (tchd 14-1)

Greenslades ◆ is on a fair mark at present, and gives the impression that he is about to hit peak form. Though finishing well here, he did not get home over 7f last time, and a strongly-run 6f probably suits him best. (op 10-1 tchd 11-1)

Wyatt Earp(IRE) bounced back to form after a lean spell, though he was still 1 lb above his highest winning mark. However, this was much more like it, and he should be given particular consideration if returning to York, where he has won three times in the past. (op 8-1 tchd 10-1)

Stamford Blue put in another sound effort despite his recent hike up the weights, but on this occasion he was never travelling well enough to suggest he would make it in time. He deserves full marks, but the Handicapper appears to have got him at long last. (op 8-1)

Tony James(IRE), carrying topweight despite not having won since 2004, is nonethess running quite well at present, and a drop of a few pounds might yet get him back into the winner's enclosure. (op 12-1)

China Cherub has had a great season, but the Handicapper has caught up with him now and his form is starting to flatten out. (op 8-1 tchd 7-1)

Royal Storm(IRE) is much lower in the weights these days, having effectively lost his form altogether, but there was just a glimmer of his old ability here. (op 33-1)

Texas Gold often runs well here, but he is best at 5f.

Ajigolo Official explanation: jockey said colt hung right

Pacific Pride had headgear back on and didn't last long after racing freely in front.

4807 NJS STKS (H'CAP) 7f
4:15 (4:19) (Class 5) (0-70,72) 3-Y-0+ £3,238 (£963; £481; £240) Stalls High

Form RPR
-330 1 **Titan Triumph**[16] 4326 3-9-7 **70**..............(t) RichardHughes 5 79+
(W J Knight) *hld up towards rr and patiently rdn tl shkn up to cl ins fnl 2f: str run appr fnl f to ld last half f: comf* **10/1**
0201 2 ¾ **The Fifth Member (IRE)**[14] 4395 3-9-6 **69**.............. DarryllHolland 10 76
(J R Boyle) *led 1f: styd chsng ldrs: rdn 3f out: styd on to chal last half f: sn outpcd by wnr but kpt on wl to hold 2nd* **3/1**[1]
4051 3 ½ **Finsbury**[13] 4416 4-9-11 **69**.............. SteveDrowne 2 76
(J M Bradley) *s.i.s: bhd: hdwy and n.m.r over 2f out: styd on wl fr over 1f out and kpt on cl home but nvr quite gng pce to rch ldng duo* **16/1**
2034 4 nk **Lii Najma**[15] 4361 4-9-1 **64**.............. AhmedAjtebi(5) 14 70
(C E Brittain) *led after 1f: rdn 2f out: hdd and outpcd last half f* **12/1**
0004 5 1 ¼ **Moon Forest (IRE)**[5] 4668 5-8-2 **51** oh3..............(p) LukeMorris(5) 13 54
(J M Bradley) *towards rr: hdwy and n.m.r 3f out: styd on fr over 1f out and gng on cl home but nvr gng pce to be competitive* **16/1**
0200 6 nk **Material Witness (IRE)**[22] 4134 10-9-5 **70**.............. JackMitchell(7) 8 72
(W R Muir) *chsd ldrs: rdn over 2f out: wknd ins fnl f* **12/1**
0320 7 1 ¾ **Turkish Sultan (IRE)**[2] 4731 4-8-7 **56**..............(v) KevinGhunowa(5) 6 53
(J M Bradley) *chsd ldrs: rdn 3f out: wknd ins fnl f* **25/1**
3503 8 2 ½ **Takitwo**[26] 4029 4-9-6 **64**.............. DaneO'Neill 11 55
(P D Cundell) *in tch: pushed along and no prog fnl 3f* **8/1**[3]
6003 9 nk **Scarlet Knight**[19] 4236 4-9-7 **65**.............. JimCrowley 4 55
(P Mitchell) *mid-div: towards outside and in rr bnd over 3f out: nvr gng pce to be competitive* **16/1**
1042 10 nk **Golden Prospect**[10] 4515 3-9-8 **71**.............. EddieAhern 3 58
(J W Hills) *towards rr: nvr gng pce to get into contention* **8/1**[3]
-000 11 2 **Simplify**[70] 2664 5-8-8 **52** oh6 ow1..............(b) SamHitchcott 7 36
(T M Jones) *towards outside bnd into st over 3f out: nvr in contention* **66/1**
2502 12 1 ½ **Dr Synn**[10] 4505 6-9-0 **65**.............. KirstyMilczarek(7) 1 45
(J Akehurst) *towards outside bnd over 3f out: a in rr: b.b.v* **14/1**
2401 13 3 ½ **Coup D'Etat**[5] 4657 5-10-0 **72** 6ex..............(b) RyanMoore 15 42
(R A Harris) *chsd ldrs: rdn 3f out: btn over 2f out* **4/1**[2]
0045 14 2 **Convivial Spirit**[21] 4165 3-8-13 **62**..............(t) PaulDoe 12 25
(E F Vaughan) *chsd ldrs over 4f* **9/1**

1m 28.81s (0.77) **Going Correction** +0.275s/f (Good)
WFA 3 from 4yo+ 5lb 14 Ran SP% **131.4**
Speed ratings (Par 103): **106,105,104,104,102 102,100,97,97,96 94,92,88,86**
CSF £43.63 CT £526.54 TOTE £13.70: £4.60, £1.80, £4.40; EX 81.20.
Owner Hesmonds Stud **Bred** Hesmonds Stud Ltd **Trained** Patching, W Sussex

FOCUS
A competitive race, run at a fair gallop, and the form looks sound. The winner did particularly well, as the race was not really run to suit horses held up.
Dr Synn Official explanation: trainer said gelding bled from the nose
Coup D'Etat Official explanation: jockey said gelding ran too free

4808 DICK CAREY "LIFETIME IN RACING" MEDIAN AUCTION MAIDEN STKS 6f
4:50 (4:52) (Class 5) 3-4-Y-0 £3,238 (£963; £481; £240) Stalls Low

Form RPR
402 1 **Fleuret**[21] 4164 3-8-12 **65**.............. StephenCarson 4 73
(Eve Johnson Houghton) *trckd ldrs: drvn and qcknd to ld last half f: kpt on wl u.p* **6/1**
2 ½ **Distant Drama (USA)** 3-8-12 **0**.............. RyanMoore 1 71
(J Noseda) *towards rr: sn drvn along and 5 l off pce over 3f out: hdwy over 1f out and edgd rt: str run to press ldrs wl ins fnl f but a jst hld by wnr* **7/2**[2]
05-2 3 1 **Gilded Youth**[95] 1923 3-9-3 **77**.............. DaneO'Neill 8 73
(H Candy) *trckd ldrs: rdn to ld over 1f out: hdd and no ex last half f* **2/1**[1]
2232 4 1 **Make My Dream**[14] 4397 4-9-1 **63**.............. LukeMorris(5) 6 70
(J Gallagher) *disp ld tl def advantage over 2f out: hdd over 1f out: wknd fnl 100yds* **5/1**[3]
6- 5 4 **Edge End**[294] 6330 3-9-3 **0**.............. PaulDoe 3 57
(R A Farrant) *chsd ldrs: rdn 1/2-way: wknd appr fnl f* **20/1**
6 3 ½ **Mexilhoeira** 3-8-12 **0**.............. AdamKirby 2 41
(C G Cox) *slowly away: a rdn in rr and wl off the pce* **16/1**
63 7 ¾ **Tyrannosaurus Rex (IRE)**[5] 4671 3-9-3 **0**.............. EddieAhern 7 43
(K R Burke) *disp ld over 3f: wknd fr 2f out* **10/1**

1m 13.39s (0.54) **Going Correction** +0.175s/f (Good)
WFA 3 from 4yo 3lb 7 Ran SP% **106.2**
Speed ratings (Par 103): **103,102,101,99,94 89,88**
CSF £23.16 TOTE £6.10: £3.00, £2.30; EX 20.50.
Owner Wyck Hall Stud **Bred** Wyck Hall Stud Ltd **Trained** Blewbury, Oxon
■ Oystermouth was withdrawn (15/2, rider S. Drowne inj at start). R4, deduct 10p in the £.

FOCUS
Not a great-looking race on paper, but this may prove a little better than expected.
Tyrannosaurus Rex(IRE) Official explanation: jockey said colt resented being taken on for the lead

4809 TURFTV IS FOR BETTING SHOPS MAIDEN STKS (H'CAP) 2m
5:25 (5:26) (Class 5) (0-70,70) 3-Y-0 £3,238 (£963; £481; £240) Stalls Low

Form RPR
0032 1 **Irish Quest (IRE)**[23] 4113 3-9-9 **70**.............. RyanMoore 5 78+
(M A Jarvis) *trckd ldr: led jst ins fnl 3f: drvn and r.o gamely whn strly chal thrght fnl f* **6/4**[1]
004 2 hd **Lady Dedlock**[19] 4235 3-8-4 **51** oh1.............. SimonWhitworth 4 56
(C A Cyzer) *towards rr but in tch: hdwy 3f out: drvn to chse wnr 2f out: str chal throughtout fnl f and gaining on wnr last strides: nt quite get up* **25/1**
6265 3 2 ½ **Alnwick**[23] 4113 3-8-9 **56**.............. DaneO'Neill 7 58
(P D Cundell) *chsd ldrs: rdn over 3f out: outpcd by ldng duo fnl f* **13/2**[2]
5000 4 2 **Composing (IRE)**[21] 4172 3-8-11 **58**..............(t) StephenCarson 3 58
(H Morrison) *towards rr: rdn and hdwy on outside fr 3f out: nvr gng pce to be competitive and one pce fnl 2f* **16/1**
00-2 5 ¾ **Dansilver**[29] 3903 3-8-8 **55** ow2.............. SamHitchcott 2 54
(D J Wintle) *led: hdd ins fnl 3f: wknd over 1f out* **14/1**
253 6 nk **Pugnacious Lady**[59] 2981 3-9-7 **68**.............. EddieAhern 1 66
(J W Hills) *chsd ldrs: rdn and n.m.r over 2f out: sn btn* **10/1**
0 7 4 **Spinaimanwin (IRE)**[23] 4104 3-8-2 **54** oh1 ow3.... KevinGhunowa(5) 10 48
(Ian Williams) *towards rr: effrt 3f out: nvr in contention and sn wknd* **33/1**
2000 8 1 ¼ **Into Action**[9] 4531 3-8-7 **59**.............. HaddenFrost(5) 6 51
(R Hannon) *towards rr: effrt on over 3f out: sn wknd* **25/1**
6054 9 4 **Mowadeh (IRE)**[21] 4172 3-9-6 **67**.............. RichardHughes 12 54
(M R Channon) *hld up in rr: rdn over 3f out: no rspnse* **15/2**[3]
0000 10 7 **Almahaza (IRE)**[17] 4277 3-8-0 **52**..............(p) LukeMorris(5) 9 31
(Mrs A J Perrett) *t.k.h: chsd ldrs: rdn and wknd over 3f out* **40/1**

3m 39.21s (8.42) **Going Correction** +0.275s/f (Good) 10 Ran SP% **99.8**
Speed ratings (Par 100): **89,88,87,86,86 86,84,83,81,78**
CSF £32.37 CT £89.20 TOTE £1.90: £1.10, £6.60, £2.10; EX 47.60 Place 6 £143.04, Place 5 £30.01.
Owner A D Spence **Bred** Epona Bloodstock Ltd **Trained** Newmarket, Suffolk
■ Shine And Rise was withdrawn (5/2, lame at start). R4, deduct 25p in the £.

FOCUS
A modest race, and run at a steady pace, producing a very moderate winning time for the class. The form is not up to that much, but the winner looks capable of better again granted a proper test of stamina.
T/Plt: £123.70 to a £1 stake. Pool: £110,801.60. 653.75 winning tickets. T/Qpdt: £25.00 to a £1 stake. Pool: £4,688.60. 138.25 winning tickets. ST

4774 **# NEWMARKET (JULY) (R-H)**
Saturday, August 25
OFFICIAL GOING: Soft (good to soft in places)
The card included the historic Newmarket Town Plate, won by Lease ridden by Derek Jackson for Champion Hurdle-winning trainer John Carr.
Wind: Light, across Weather: Fine and sunny

4810 EUROPEAN BREEDERS' FUND MAIDEN STKS 6f
1:50 (1:53) (Class 4) 2-Y-0 £4,533 (£1,348; £674; £336) Stalls High

Form RPR
00 1 **Upton Grey (IRE)**[21] 4151 2-9-3 **0**.............. JimmyFortune 10 82+
(J H M Gosden) *hld up: hdwy 1/2-way: led 2f out: r.o wl: eased nr fin* **11/4**[2]
2 1 ¾ **Maimoona (IRE)** 2-8-12 **0**.............. RHills 4 72
(W J Haggas) *hld up: hdwy over 2f out: chsd wnr over 1f out: styd on same pce* **7/2**[3]
05 3 5 **Memphis City (USA)**[7] 4604 2-9-3 **0**.............. MartinDwyer 1 62
(J Noseda) *chsd ldr: rdn and ev ch 2f out: edgd rt and wknd fnl f* **8/1**
4 1 ¼ **Kalligal** 2-8-12 **0**.............. RobertHavlin 5 53
(R Ingram) *s.i.s: hld up: hdwy over 1f out: wknd fnl f* **33/1**
42 5 3 ½ **Blues Minor (IRE)**[9] 4539 2-9-3 **0**.............. PatDobbs 8 48+
(R Hannon) *led: rdn and hdd 2f out: sn wknd* **9/4**[1]
55 6 2 ½ **Sharps Gold**[33] 3801 2-8-10 **0** ow1..............(t) JerryO'Dwyer(3) 6 36
(P J McBride) *chsd ldrs over 4f* **100/1**
0000 7 hd **Aberavon**[10] 4501 2-8-12 **65**..............(b[1]) TQuinn 7 34
(D R C Elsworth) *hld up: plld hrd: rdn: hung rt and wknd over 1f out* **16/1**
8 1 ¼ **Educated Risk** 2-9-3 **0**.............. MichaelHills 3 36
(W J Haggas) *s.i.s: outpcd* **8/1**
00 9 shd **Miss Deeds (IRE)**[52] 3200 2-8-12 **0**.............. TGMcLaughlin 9 30
(N P Littmoden) *prom: racd keenly: wknd wl over 1f out* **33/1**

1m 15.16s (1.81) **Going Correction** +0.175s/f (Good) 9 Ran SP% **114.6**
Speed ratings (Par 96): **94,91,85,83,78 75,75,73,73**
CSF £12.61 TOTE £4.10: £1.40, £1.40, £2.50; EX 14.50.
Owner H R H Princess Haya Of Jordan **Bred** Hascombe & Valiant Studs **Trained** Newmarket, Suffolk

FOCUS
This maiden lacked strength in depth and the bare form is just ordinary by Newmarket's standards and not the most solid. They raced up the middle of the track.

NOTEBOOK
Upton Grey(IRE) did not offer much at Goodwood last time, but he had previously shown plenty of ability in a good maiden here on his debut and he was able to confirm that promise to get off the mark at the third attempt. He was dropping a furlong in trip, but showed good mid-race speed to move into a challenging position and was always holding the newcomer, Maimoona, in the closing stages, appearing to relish the soft ground. He is likely to find things tougher from now on, but is at least on the right track and there should be plenty more to come. (op 3-1)
Maimoona(IRE), a Pivotal half-sister to Emaara, who was placed over 5f-6f, out of a 6f juvenile winner, does not hold any Group-race entries, but this was a respectable debut. She was always being held by the eventual winner in the closing stages, but there was a nice gap back to the remainder and she should be able to build on this. (op 4-1 tchd 9-2)
Memphis City(USA) did not really pick up when asked and proved no match for the front two. He has shown only modest form so far, but is now qualified for a handicap mark and could do better. (op 13-2)
Kalligal, a 10,000gns daughter of Kyllachy, half-sister to among others quite useful 6f juvenile winner Online Investor, out of a 5f winner, shaped quite nicely on her debut back in fourth. She is open to plenty of improvement.
Blues Minor(IRE) dropped out of contention very quickly and was well below the form he had shown on his two previous starts. (tchd 5-2 in places and 2-1 in a place)
Aberavon Official explanation: jockey said filly would not face the blinkers

4811 CHRIS BLACKWELL MEMORIAL H'CAP 7f
2:20 (2:22) (Class 3) (0-90,89) 3-Y-0 £9,067 (£2,697; £1,348; £673) Stalls High

Form RPR
2121 1 **Lap Of Honour (IRE)**[7] 4608 3-8-7 **78**.............. WilliamBuick(3) 1 90
(N A Callaghan) *racd far side: chsd ldr: led that gp and overall ldr over 2f out: rdn out* **4/1**[1]
3106 2 1 ½ **Transcend**[17] 4276 3-8-11 **79**..............(p) JimmyFortune 8 87
(J H M Gosden) *racd centre: chsd ldrs: led that gp 3f out: rdn over 1f out: styd on: 1st of 12 in gp* **10/1**
2443 3 ¾ **Giant Slalom**[13] 4429 3-8-4 **72**.............. MartinDwyer 12 78
(W J Haggas) *swtchd to r stands' side over 5f out: led that pair tl overall ldr 3f out: rdn and hdd over 2f out: sn hung lft: kpt on: 2nd of 12 in gp* **8/1**[3]
0-25 4 1 ½ **Jaasoos (IRE)**[91] 2040 3-9-2 **84**.............. MatthewHenry 16 86
(M A Jarvis) *racd centre: chsd ldrs: rdn over 2f out: no ex fnl f: 3rd of 12 in gp* **14/1**
-313 5 1 **Flying Goose (IRE)**[21] 4170 3-8-13 **81**.............. KerrinMcEvoy 10 80
(L M Cumani) *racd centre: hld up: hdwy over 2f out: rdn over 1f out: hung lft and wknd ins fnl f: 4th of 12 in gp* **4/1**[1]
406 6 ½ **Lord Theo**[22] 4133 3-8-10 **78**.............. IanMongan 3 76
(N P Littmoden) *racd far side: overall ldr 4f: rdn over 1f out: styd on same pce: 2nd of 3 in gp* **66/1**
6230 7 2 ½ **Top Bid**[7] 4608 3-8-9 **77** ow1.............. MichaelHills 2 68
(T D Easterby) *racd far side: prom: rdn over 2f out: wknd fnl f: last of 3 in gp* **16/1**
2-10 8 3 **Thabaat**[107] 1603 3-9-1 **83**.............. RHills 4 66
(B W Hills) *racd centre: chsd ldrs: rdn and wknd over 1f out: 5th of 12 in gp* **13/2**[2]

0066 **9** *4* **College Scholar (GER)**[47] 3380 3-9-5 **87** OscarUrbina 6 59
(E A L Dunlop) *racd centre: hld up in tch: wknd 2f out: 6th of 12 in gp* **14/1**

0244 **10** *nk* **Lunces Lad (IRE)**[21] 4170 3-8-13 **81** TPO'Shea 7 52
(M R Channon) *racd centre: dwlt: sn prom: rdn over 2f out: wknd over 1f out: 7th of 12 in gp* **11/1**

006 **11** *nk* **Cesc**[23] 4093 3-9-7 **89** TQuinn 5 60
(P J Makin) *racd centre: hld up: hdwy over 2f out: wknd over 1f out: 8th of 12 in gp* **20/1**

4312 **12** *1 ½* **Masai Moon**[79] 2400 3-9-3 **85** RobertHavlin 9 52
(B R Millman) *led centre 4f: wknd 2f out: 9th of 12 in gp* **16/1**

1000 **13** *1 ½* **Yaroslav (USA)**[23] 4093 3-8-13 **81** (b) ChrisCatlin 11 44
(R Charlton) *racd centre: hld up: rdn and wknd over 2f out: 10th of 12 in gp* **9/1**

1530 **14** *7* **Darfour**[28] 3940 3-8-4 **75** AndrewElliott[(3)] 13 19
(J S Goldie) *carried stands' side over 5f out: chsd ldr tl edgd lft and wknd 2f out: 11th of 12 in gp* **25/1**

40-5 **15** *5* **Touch Of Style (IRE)**[17] 4275 3-9-3 **85** AmirQuinn 14 15
(J R Boyle) *racd centre: hld up: plld hrd: wknd 3f out: last of 12 in gp* **50/1**

1m 26.91s (0.13) **Going Correction** +0.175s/f (Good) **15** Ran SP% **129.0**
Speed ratings (Par 104): **106,104,103,101,100 100,97,93,89,88 88,86,85,77,71**
CSF £46.50 CT £330.31 TOTE £4.60: £2.00, £3.80, £3.40; EX 47.00 Trifecta £559.20 Part won. Pool: £787.64 - 0.10 winning units..
Owner Michael Tabor **Bred** Ben Sangster **Trained** Newmarket, Suffolk

FOCUS
Quite a good handicap and rated at face value but possibly not entirely solid. The field split into three groups and the winner raced towards the far side of the track.

NOTEBOOK
Lap Of Honour(IRE) raced in a group of just three on the far side of the track, well away from the main group up the middle, but he got a good lead and picked up well to defy a 3lb rise in the weights for his recent course success. His two previous wins had both come over 1m, but he had sufficient speed to cope with the drop in trip and is clearly improving. (op 9-2 tchd 7-2 and 5-1 in places)
Transcend, dropped in trip and returned to turf, ran right up to form with the cheekpieces replacing blinkers.
Giant Slalom was given a really positive ride towards stands' side of the track and ran a solid race in third. (tchd 7-1)
Jaasoos(IRE) had never previously raced on ground this soft, but he seemed to handle the conditions well enough and this was a creditable performance. (op 16-1)
Flying Goose(IRE) did not really build on his recent course-and-distance third and this ground was probably softer than he would have liked. (op 5-1)
Lord Theo raced with the eventual winner towards the far side of the track and this was a reasonable effort. (op 50-1)
Yaroslav(USA) Official explanation: trainer said colt was unsuited by the soft (good to soft in places) ground
Touch Of Style(IRE) Official explanation: jockey said gelding clipped heels early on and was never travelling thereafter

4812 UNICORN ASSET MANAGEMENT JULY COURSE SERIES FINAL STKS (NURSERY H'CAP) 7f
2:50 (2:52) (Class 2) 2-Y-O **£32,385** (£9,635; £4,815; £2,405) **Stalls** High

Form RPR

0136 **1** **Dan Tucket**[14] 4372 2-8-7 **81** TPO'Shea 5 84
(M R Channon) *racd far side: chsd ldr: rdn over 2f out: overall ldr 1f out: styd on u.p* **8/1**[3]

6023 **2** *½* **Talk Of Saafend (IRE)**[15] 4364 2-7-12 **72** oh3 DavidKinsella 6 74+
(R Hannon) *racd far side: hld up: hdwy and bmpd 2f out: nt clr run over 1f out: sn rdn: r.o: fin 3rd, ½l & hd: plcd 2nd* **14/1**

3231 **3** *hd* **Red Alert Day**[15] 4364 2-9-2 **93** WilliamBuick[(3)] 1 95
(N A Callaghan) *racd far side: hld up in tch: outpcd 1/2-way: swtchd rt and hdwy 2f out: sn rdn and edgd rt: r.o: fin 2nd, ½l: plcd 3rd* **9/4**[1]

4003 **4** *hd* **Dalkey Girl (IRE)**[1] 4769 2-7-13 **80** ow1 AshleyMorgan[(7)] 11 80
(V Smith) *racd centre: chsd ldrs: rdn and hung lft 2f out: rdr dropped reins over 1f out: r.o* **20/1**

3316 **5** *½* **Master Chef (IRE)**[22] 4120 2-9-7 **95** (b) JimmyFortune 10 94
(J H M Gosden) *led centre: overall ldr over 5f out: rdn and hung lft over 1f out: sn hdd: no ex ins fnl f* **8/1**[3]

1032 **6** *2* **Ellemujie**[15] 4364 2-8-10 **84** RobertHavlin 12 78
(D K Ivory) *racd centre: hld up: rdn over 1f out: nvr trbld ldrs* **11/1**

3114 **7** *nk* **Runswick Bay**[29] 3909 2-8-8 **85** JamieMoriarty[(3)] 3 78
(G M Moore) *racd far side: led overall tl hdd over 5f out: continued to ld that gp tl rdn over 1f out: no ex fnl f* **10/1**

2116 **8** *4* **Elna Bright**[15] 4364 2-8-9 **83** PatDobbs 2 66
(R Hannon) *racd far side: chsd ldrs: rdn over 1f out: wknd fnl f* **10/1**

043 **9** *5* **Piscean (USA)**[21] 4173 2-7-7 **72** oh1 NicolPolli[(5)] 9 43
(T Keddy) *racd centre: dwlt: hld up: plld hrd: wknd over 1f out* **10/1**

1503 **10** *shd* **Cracking (IRE)**[21] 4168 2-9-5 **93** RichardMullen 7 64
(R Hannon) *racd far side: chsd ldrs over 5f* **20/1**

100 **11** *nk* **Just Sort It**[21] 4168 2-8-7 **81** MartinDwyer 8 51
(W Jarvis) *racd centre: chsd ldr: hung lft fr 1/2-way: wknd 2f out* **33/1**

4314 **12** *3* **Palm Court**[15] 4364 2-8-1 **75** (b[1]) ChrisCatlin 4 37
(R Charlton) *dwlt: racd far side: hdwy 4f out: rdn over 2f out: sn wknd* **9/2**[2]

1m 28.04s (1.26) **Going Correction** +0.175s/f (Good) **12** Ran SP% **125.9**
Speed ratings (Par 100): **99,98,98,97,97 95,94,90,84,84 84,80**
CSF £118.52 CT £346.52 TOTE £10.10: £2.80, £5.10, £1.80; EX 161.80 TRIFECTA Not won..
Owner Box 41 **Bred** Grasshopper 2000 Ltd **Trained** West Ilsley, Berks
■ Stewards' Enquiry : William Buick four-day ban: careless riding (Sep 5-7, 9)

FOCUS
A very valuable nursery and understandably competitive. The first five home finished in a bit of a bunch, but the form looks solid enough. The field split into two groups through the early stages, with a few of these racing far side and another bunch sticking to the middle of the track, but there was not much between them at the line.

NOTEBOOK
Dan Tucket had never previously raced on ground this soft, but he handled it well and, always in a handy position towards the far side of the track, he battled on gamely to come out on top in a bunch finish. This was his third success of the year and he should continue to run well in similar company.
Talk Of Saafend(IRE), who from 3lb out of the handicap was effectively 5lb higher than when third behind Red Alert Day over course and distance on her previous start, managed to reverse form with that rival, albeit with a little help from the Stewards'. She probably would have been second past the post had Red Alert Day not taken her ground when switching out with his effort, and she is clearly progressive. She could continue to run well off low weights in this type of event, or shoulder a bigger weight in a lesser contest.
Red Alert Day had to wait longer than was ideal for a gap and took Talk Of Saafend's ground when switched out with his effort. He stuck on for pressure to narrowly take second, but was subsequently placed third behind Talk Of Saafend, and it would be hard to argue with the decision. All that aside, this was a good effort off a mark 11lb higher than when winning over course and distance on his previous start. (op 11-4, tchd 3-1 in places)
Dalkey Girl(IRE), third over 6f at Newcastle the previous day, may well have been second had her rider not dropped his reins around a furlong from the finish. She is clearly very tough. (op 16-1)
Master Chef(IRE) raced too freely out in front on his first try over the trip. (tchd 15-2)
Palm Court ran no sort of race in first-time blinkers and may not have appreciated the soft ground. Official explanation: trainer said colt was unsuited by the soft (good to soft in places) ground (op 5-1)

4813 COUNTRYWIDE STEEL AND TUBES HOPEFUL STKS (LISTED RACE) 6f
3:25 (3:25) (Class 1) 3-Y-O+
£15,330 (£5,810; £2,907; £1,449; £726; £364) **Stalls** High

Form RPR

0000 **1** **Beckermet (IRE)**[7] 4600 5-9-0 **100** ChrisCatlin 1 114
(R F Fisher) *swtchd to r far side: mde all: sn clr of that gp: rdn and hung rt fr over 1f out: r.o* **25/1**

3016 **2** *5* **Balthazaar's Gift (IRE)**[21] 4150 4-9-7 **113** JimmyFortune 2 106
(L M Cumani) *racd far side: hld up: hdwy u.p over 1f out: sn chsng wnr: no imp* **8/11**[1]

0002 **3** *¾* **Biniou (IRE)**[11] 4485 4-9-0 **100** RobertHavlin 7 97
(R M H Cowell) *racd far side: hld up: hdwy over 1f out: nt trble ldrs* **50/1**

0001 **4** *½* **Presto Shinko (IRE)**[21] 4183 6-9-0 **108** (p) PatDobbs 5 95
(R Hannon) *racd far side: chsd wnr tl rdn over 1f out: no ex* **7/1**[3]

-050 **5** *hd* **Conquest (IRE)**[67] 2733 3-8-11 **109** MichaelHills 6 95
(W J Haggas) *racd alone stands' side: up w wnr over 4f: wknd fnl f* **14/1**

4040 **6** *1 ¼* **Rising Shadow (IRE)**[43] 3506 6-9-4 **107** KerrinMcEvoy 3 95
(T D Barron) *racd far side: chsd ldrs over 4f* **15/2**

1306 **7** *nk* **Firenze**[43] 3511 6-8-13 **103** OscarUrbina 9 89
(J R Fanshawe) *racd far side: sn pushed along in rr: n.d* **9/2**[2]

1m 12.53s (-0.82) **Going Correction** +0.175s/f (Good)
WFA 3 from 4yo+ 3lb **7** Ran SP% **112.8**
Speed ratings (Par 111): **112,105,104,103,103 101,101**
CSF £43.22 TOTE £29.50: £7.40, £1.20; EX 69.40 TRIFECTA Not won..
Owner Great Head House Taylor Nash Edwards **Bred** Fritz Von Ball Moss **Trained** Ulverston, Cumbria

FOCUS
Beckermet was allowed an uncontested lead and the bare form of this Listed contest looks suspect. They all raced far side, with the exception of Conquest, who raced alone against the stands' rail.

NOTEBOOK
Beckermet(IRE) could make little impression in the Group 2 Hungerford Stakes over 7f at Newbury the previous weekend, but he was suited by both the drop in class and trip and, allowed a very soft lead, he routed his six rivals. He was inclined to edge to his right in the closing stages, with Conquest on the stands' side a possible distraction, but he never looked like being caught. He is obviously very smart on his day and this was a terrific effort, but it would be unwise to get carried away with the bare form considering everything fell into place. (op 20-1 tchd 16-1)
Balthazaar's Gift(IRE), the winner of a Group 3 at Ascot before looking a shade unlucky under a big weight in the Stewards' Cup, was not at his best under his 7lb penalty. The leader had basically been given too much rope out in front and he never looked like making up the lost ground. (op 5-6 tchd Evens ,4-6 and 11-10 in a place)
Biniou(IRE) shaped as though returning to form when second at Nottingham on his previous start and there was plenty of encouragement in this effort as well. The way he travelled suggested he will be suited by a return to 5f and it would be no surprise to see him try and improve on last year's fourth in the Prix de l'Abbaye back at Longchamp later in the season, although that will obviously be much tougher than his recent assignments. (tchd 40-1)
Presto Shinko(IRE) could not repeat the form he showed when winning a conditions event at Windsor on his previous outing. (tchd 8-1)
Conquest(IRE), gelded since he was last seen over two months previously, raced alone against the stands'-side rail and, although appearing to be on terms with those on the far side for much of the way, he finished up well held. (op 12-1 tchd 8-1)
Rising Shadow(IRE) is at his best finishing from well off a strong pace and he did not have the race run to suit. Official explanation: jockey said gelding did not move well (op 7-1)
Firenze does not mind a bit of give in the ground, but she seemed to find these conditions too testing, just as she had at York on her previous start. (op 4-1 tchd 7-2)

4814 ROYAL BRITISH LEGION H'CAP 1m 2f
4:00 (4:00) (Class 3) (0-95,94) 3-Y-O+ **£9,067** (£2,697; £1,348; £673) **Stalls** High

Form RPR

1214 **1** **Night Cru**[30] 3882 4-9-9 **89** GeorgeBaker 8 103
(C F Wall) *chsd ldr: wnt far side ent st: led over 4f out: rdn over 1f out: styd on gamely* **10/3**[1]

0355 **2** *shd* **Apply Dapply**[18] 4257 4-8-6 **75** TravisBlock[(3)] 2 89
(H Morrison) *a.p: wnt far side ent st: chsd wnr 2f out: rdn and ev ch ins fnl f: styd on: 2nd of 10 in gp* **8/1**

4202 **3** *6* **King Charles**[28] 3959 3-8-12 **91** PatrickHills[(5)] 4 93+
(E A L Dunlop) *hld up: wnt far side ent st: hdwy u.p 3f out: styd on same pce fnl f: 3rd of 10 in gp* **9/2**[2]

3301 **4** *1 ½* **Press The Button (GER)**[6] 4631 4-9-4 **84** 6ex KerrinMcEvoy 12 83
(J R Boyle) *led: wnt far side: ent st: hdd over 4f out: rdn over 2f out: wknd fnl f: 4th of 10 in gp* **6/1**[3]

0143 **5** *8* **Prize Fighter (IRE)**[21] 4184 5-9-0 **80** (b) JimmyFortune 3 63
(H R A Cecil) *s.i.s: sn chsng ldrs: wnt far side ent st: rdn and wknd over 1f out: 5th of 10 in gp* **7/1**

1602 **6** *shd* **Zaif (IRE)**[14] 4399 4-9-2 **82** AntonyProcter 13 65
(D R C Elsworth) *hld up: wnt far side ent st: rdn and wknd over 2f out: 6th of 10 in gp* **12/1**

-010 **7** *1 ¼* **Archiestown (USA)**[21] 4166 4-8-9 **75** RichardMullen 1 55
(J L Dunlop) *hld up: wnt far side ent st: rdn and wknd over 2f out: 7th of 10 in gp* **25/1**

1350 **8** *¾* **Dragon Slayer (IRE)**[188] 493 5-9-0 **80** RobertHavlin 6 59
(Ian Williams) *prom: wnt far side ent st: rdn and wknd over 2f out: 8th of 10 in gp* **33/1**

6002 **9** *2* **Weightless**[30] 3882 7-9-12 **92** IanMongan 11 67
(N P Littmoden) *chsd ldrs: styd stands' side ent st and led that pair: up w ldrs far side tl wknd over 2f out: 1st of 2 in gp* **14/1**

51-0 **10** *1 ¾* **Tommy Toogood (IRE)**[45] 3437 4-9-2 **82** MichaelHills 5 53
(B W Hills) *hld up: wnt far side ent st: hdwy over 3f out: sn rdn: wknd wl over 1f out: 9th of 10 in gp* **8/1**

1100 **11** *nk* **Fortunate Isle (USA)**[8] 4566 5-9-7 **90** JamieMoriarty[(3)] 9 61
(R A Fahey) *mid-div tl styd stands' side ent st: chsd ldr tl rdn and wknd over 2f out: last of 2 that side* **20/1**

-500 **12** *7* **Flor Y Nata (USA)**[24] 4060 4-9-2 **82**.................... MartinDwyer 7 39
(Sir Mark Prescott) *s.s: bhd: wnt far side ent st: wknd wl over 2f out: last of 10 in gp* **20/1**

2m 7.49s (1.05) **Going Correction** +0.175s/f (Good)
WFA 3 from 4yo+ 8lb 12 Ran SP% **120.9**
Speed ratings (Par 107): **102,101,97,95,89 89,88,87,86,84 84,79**
CSF £29.28 CT £124.45 TOTE £3.90: £1.70, £3.10, £2.30; EX 37.30.
Owner Archangels 2 **Bred** Jeremy Green And Sons **Trained** Newmarket, Suffolk

FOCUS
A good handicap, but despite an ordinary gallop this proved to be quite a test and they finished well strung out. Both Weightless and Fortunate Isle stayed stands' side in the straight, but they had little chance with those on the far side of the track.

NOTEBOOK
Night Cru just managed to defy an 8lb higher mark than when winning over course and distance two starts previously, battling on well to hold off the improved Apply Dapply. There was a long gap back to the remainder and he is progressing into a very useful handicapper. He is entered in the Cambridgeshire. (op 7-2 tchd 4-1 in places)
Apply Dapply ◆ had never previously raced over a trip this far, but she improved for the extra distance and was just denied. She was well clear of the remainder and could progress into a very useful sort over this sort of trip.
King Charles had never previously raced on ground this soft, but he seemed to handle the conditions and ran well off a mark 3lb higher than when second over course and distance on his previous start. (op 6-1 tchd 7-1)
Press The Button(GER) bolted up on his first try over this trip at Bath last time, but this was tougher and he could not defy his 6lb penalty. The ground was probably a little softer than he would have liked. Official explanation: jockey said gelding hung right (tchd 5-1)
Prize Fighter(IRE) had conditions to suit and could have been expected to fare better. (op 6-1)
Flor Y Nata(USA) Official explanation: jockey said filly missed the break

4815 9TH/12TH ROYAL LANCERS MAIDEN STKS 1m
4:35 (4:38) (Class 5) 3-Y-O+ **£4,533** (£1,348; £674; £336) **Stalls** High

Form RPR
00 **1** **Ezdiyaad (IRE)**[17] 4275 3-9-3 0.................... RHills 9 85
(M P Tregoning) *chsd ldrs: rdn to ld 2f out: styd on wl* **20/1**
2324 **2** *2 ½* **Know The Law**[12] 4457 3-9-0 76.................... MarcHalford(3) 1 79
(D R C Elsworth) *hld up: hdwy over 2f out: rdn over 1f out: styd on* **5/1**[2]
3 *shd* **Viva Vettori** 3-9-3 0.................... AntonyProcter 2 79+
(D R C Elsworth) *s.s: outpcd: nt clr run fr over 2f out tl r.o ins fnl f* **40/1**
0 **4** *hd* **La Lunete**[17] 4275 3-8-12 0.................... OscarUrbina 11 74+
(R Charlton) *hld up: hdwy over 1f out: edgd lft: styd on* **16/1**
3 **5** *1 ¼* **Abydos**[12] 4457 3-9-3 0.................... KerrinMcEvoy 3 76
(Saeed Bin Suroor) *chsd ldrs: rdn over 2f out: no ex fnl f* **7/4**[1]
6 *½* **Zero Cool (USA)** 3-9-3 0.................... JimmyFortune 12 75
(J H M Gosden) *prom: rdn over 1f out: styd on same pce* **5/1**[2]
0 **7** *½* **Kaateb (IRE)**[9] 4530 4-9-9 0.................... MartinDwyer 4 73
(W J Haggas) *chsd ldr: led over 2f out: sn hdd: wknd ins fnl f* **50/1**
8 *¾* **Bankable (IRE)** 3-9-3 0.................... GeorgeBaker 15 72+
(L M Cumani) *s.s: hld up: hdwy whn hmpd 1f out: nvr trbld ldrs* **12/1**
0 **9** *½* **Give Me A Break**[126] 1143 3-9-3 0.................... AdrianMcCarthy 6 71
(P W Chapple-Hyam) *plld hrd and prom: rdn over 2f out: wknd fnl f* **12/1**
4003 **10** *5* **Hope Road**[41] 3567 3-9-3 72.................... PatDobbs 14 59
(J R Fanshawe) *hld up: effrt over 2f out: wknd over 1f out* **6/1**[3]
55-0 **11** *1* **Ardmaddy (IRE)**[117] 1343 3-9-3 55.................... TPO'Shea 5 57
(J A R Toller) *led over 5f: wknd over 1f out* **66/1**
0 **12** *2 ½* **King Zeal (IRE)**[63] 2880 3-9-3 0.................... TGMcLaughlin 7 51
(M Wigham) *hld up: rdn 3f out: wknd wl over 1f out* **50/1**
00 **13** *10* **Sierra Rose**[13] 4430 3-8-9 0.................... JerryO'Dwyer(3) 8 23
(P J McBride) *prom 5f* **100/1**
2005 **14** *17* **Waymark (IRE)**[12] 4457 3-9-3 73.................... MatthewHenry 16 —
(M A Jarvis) *stmbld s: hdwy over 5f out: rdn and wknd over 2f out* **14/1**
6-3 **R** **Moral Code (IRE)**[222] 141 3-9-3 0.................... RichardMullen 13 —
(E J O'Neill) *unruly in stalls: swvd rt leaving stalls and ref to r* **14/1**

1m 41.64s (1.21) **Going Correction** +0.175s/f (Good)
WFA 3 from 4yo 6lb 15 Ran SP% **132.2**
Speed ratings (Par 103): **100,97,97,97,95 95,94,94,93,88 87,85,75,58,—**
CSF £124.57 TOTE £32.10: £6.90, £2.10, £7.50; EX 247.30.
Owner Hamdan Al Maktoum **Bred** Shadwell Estate Co Ltd **Trained** Lambourn, Berks

FOCUS
An ordinary maiden and not a great deal to go on, so the runner-up is the best key to the form for now.

4816 DAVID COSGROVE MEMORIAL H'CAP 6f
5:05 (5:07) (Class 4) (0-85,84) 3-Y-O+ **£5,181** (£1,541; £770; £384) **Stalls** High

Form RPR
2212 **1** **Esteem Machine (USA)**[8] 4574 3-9-1 **78**.................... KerrinMcEvoy 12 93
(R A Teal) *mde all: rdn out* **4/1**[2]
0150 **2** *2 ½* **Nobilissima (IRE)**[8] 4585 3-8-13 **79**.................... MarcHalford(3) 8 86
(J L Spearing) *w wnr tl rdn over 1f out: styd on same pce ins fnl f* **25/1**
5640 **3** *1* **Swinbrook (USA)**[29] 3911 6-9-6 **80**....................(v) RobertHavlin 9 84
(J A R Toller) *mid-div: hdwy over 2f out: rdn over 1f out: no ex ins fnl f* **6/1**
0323 **4** *½* **Stonecrabstomorrow (IRE)**[27] 4006 4-8-11 **74**..(p) JamieMoriarty(3) 11 76
(R A Fahey) *chsd ldrs: rdn over 2f out: styd on same pce ins fnl f* **11/2**[3]
4320 **5** *nk* **Idle Power (IRE)**[22] 4122 9-9-10 **84**.................... AmirQuinn 1 85
(J R Boyle) *racd alone far side: w ldrs tl rdn and edgd rt over 1f out: styd on same pce* **10/1**
6562 **6** *nk* **Geojimali**[8] 4567 5-9-1 **82**.................... GaryBartley(7) 6 82+
(J S Goldie) *hld up and bhd: r.o ins fnl f: nrst fin* **11/4**[1]
0634 **7** *shd* **After The Show**[11] 4486 6-8-9 **69**.................... OscarUrbina 5 69
(Rae Guest) *hld up: hdwy u.p over 1f out: no imp ins fnl f* **16/1**
2505 **8** *1 ¼* **Stoic Leader (IRE)**[12] 4462 7-9-3 **77**.................... ChrisCatlin 3 73
(R F Fisher) *mid-div: rdn 1/2-way: nt trble ldrs* **25/1**
1066 **9** *½* **Brunelleschi**[15] 4367 4-8-13 **76**....................(b) JerryO'Dwyer(3) 7 71
(M G Quinlan) *hld up: rdn over 1f out: n.d* **20/1**
4254 **10** *2 ½* **Linda Green**[14] 4396 6-8-13 **73**.................... TPO'Shea 10 60
(M R Channon) *mid-div: rdn 1/2-way: wknd 2f out* **16/1**
3441 **11** *10* **Angel Sprints**[14] 4396 5-9-0 **77**.................... TravisBlock(3) 2 34
(C J Down) *chsd ldrs over 4f: eased ins fnl f* **7/1**
430 **12** *1 ¾* **Abwaab**[8] 4585 4-8-13 **78**....................(b) PatrickHills(5) 13 30
(Eve Johnson Houghton) *chsd ldrs: rdn 1/2-way: edgd rt and wknd over 1f out: eased* **12/1**

1m 13.27s (-0.08) **Going Correction** +0.175s/f (Good)
WFA 3 from 4yo+ 3lb 12 Ran SP% **129.8**
Speed ratings (Par 105): **107,103,102,101,101 100,100,99,98,95 81,79**
CSF £112.57 CT £618.97 TOTE £5.10: £1.90, £7.40, £2.60; EX 134.50 Place 6 £120.66, Place 5 £45.71.
Owner M Vickers **Bred** Mindy Hodges Powell **Trained** Headley, Surrey
■ Stewards' Enquiry : Amir Quinn one-day ban: failed to ride to draw (Sep 5)

FOCUS
A fair sprint handicap that favoured those racing prominently. The form is rated around those in the frame behind the winner.
Angel Sprints Official explanation: jockey said mare did not handle the soft (good to soft in places) ground
T/Jkpt: Not won. T/Plt: £233.50 to a £1 stake. Pool: £192,190.34. 600.60 winning tickets. T/Qpdt: £22.40 to a £1 stake. Pool: £4,191.40. 137.95 winning tickets. CR

4422 REDCAR (L-H)
Saturday, August 25

OFFICIAL GOING: Good to firm (9.4)
Wind: Fresh, half behind Weather: Cloudy

4817 COME DANCING WITH THE LADY JOCKEYS H'CAP (FOR LADY RIDERS) 1m 2f
5:30 (5:30) (Class 5) (0-75,72) 3-Y-O+ **£2,717** (£842; £421; £210) **Stalls** Low

Form RPR
6521 **1** **Ahlawy (IRE)**[19] 4228 4-10-4 **72**.................... MissJoannaMason(7) 3 86
(M W Easterby) *hld up in tch: hdwy 3f out: led over 1f out: pushed out: readily* **7/4**[1]
5425 **2** *5* **William John**[25] 4042 4-9-8 **55**....................(tp) MissLEllison 9 59
(B Ellison) *prom: effrt and ev ch over 2f out: sn chsng wnr: edgd lft over 1f out: sn one pce* **4/1**[2]
030/ **3** *5* **Skiddaw Jones**[15] 4885 7-9-1 **53** oh8....................(t) MissAngelaBarnes(5) 4 47
(M A Barnes) *pressed ldr: chal 1/2-way: led 3f to over 1f out: sn outpcd* **25/1**
0343 **4** *1 ½* **Star Of Angels**[10] 4499 3-9-1 **59**....................(b[1]) MissARyan(3) 7 50
(M Johnston) *hld up: struggling 1/2-way: kpt on fr 2f out: nrst fin* **8/1**
2003 **5** *shd* **Fossgate**[13] 4421 6-10-4 **72**.................... MissJMBethell(7) 8 63
(J D Bethell) *hld up: outpcd over 4f out: kpt on fnl f: n.d* **5/1**[3]
1120 **6** *hd* **Emperor's Well**[15] 4353 8-10-7 **68**.................... MissSBrotherton 6 58
(M W Easterby) *led to 3f out: rdn and wknd 2f out* **6/1**
2232 **7** *1 ½* **Shotley Mac**[10] 4491 3-8-7 **55**....................(b) MissERamstrom(7) 2 42
(N Bycroft) *t.k.h and sddle sn slipped: chsd ldrs: effrt 3f out: btn over 1f out* **8/1**
000 **R** **Glad Star (GER)**[19] 4229 4-9-6 **53** oh8....................(p) MissADeniel 1 —
(D W Chapman) *ref to r* **200/1**

2m 6.88s (0.08) **Going Correction** 0.0s/f (Good)
WFA 3 from 4yo+ 8lb 8 Ran SP% **113.9**
Speed ratings (Par 103): **99,95,91,89,89 89,88,—**
CSF £8.74 CT £122.87 TOTE £2.40: £1.20, £2.20, £4.20; EX 12.20.
Owner K Hodgson & Mrs J Hodgson **Bred** Castlemartin Stud And Skymarc Farm **Trained** Sheriff Hutton, N Yorks

FOCUS
A modest event and one in which the pace took until halfway to increase. The winner is a progressive type capable of better but the form is not the most solid.

4818 MARKET CROSS JEWELLERS MEDIAN AUCTION MAIDEN STKS 6f
6:00 (6:01) (Class 5) 2-Y-O **£2,817** (£838; £418; £209) **Stalls** Centre

Form RPR
33 **1** **Craggy Cat (IRE)**[22] 4130 2-9-3 0.................... NickyMackay 13 79+
(L M Cumani) *trckd ldrs: led over 2f out: sn hrd pressed: hld on wl fnl f* **11/8**[1]
2 *nk* **Bonny Rose** 2-8-12 0.................... GregFairley 11 73
(M Johnston) *trckd ldrs: chal over 2f out: rdn and edgd lft over 1f out: kpt on fnl f: hld nr fin* **11/1**
3 *1 ¼* **Accused (IRE)** 2-9-3 0.................... SebSanders 10 74+
(J Noseda) *hld up bhd ldrs: stdy hdwy over 2f out: shkn up over 1f out: rn green: kpt on fnl f* **11/4**[2]
65 **4** *nk* **Misplaced Fortune**[22] 4125 2-8-12 0.................... KimTinkler 5 68
(N Tinkler) *trckd ldrs: rdn 2f out: kpt on u.p fnl f* **20/1**
3 **5** *½* **Pintano**[15] 4350 2-9-3 0.................... TomEaves 2 72
(J Howard Johnson) *cl up on outside: effrt and ev ch over 1f out: outpcd fnl f* **7/2**[3]
6 **6** *1* **Ivestar (IRE)**[7] 4611 2-9-3 0.................... AdrianTNicholls 1 69
(D Nicholls) *midfield: pushed along over 2f out: kpt on fnl f: no imp* **16/1**
7 *½* **Island Music (IRE)** 2-8-12 0.................... PaddyAspell 9 62
(J J Quinn) *bhd tl hdwy over 1f out: nrst fin* **66/1**
0 **8** *1 ½* **Tommytush (IRE)**[19] 4221 2-9-3 0.................... MickyFenton 8 63
(E J Alston) *slt ld to over 2f out: wknd over 1f out* **100/1**
04 **9** *¾* **Red Skipper (IRE)**[16] 4328 2-9-3 0.................... DanielTudhope 4 61
(N Wilson) *w ldr to over 2f out: wknd over 1f out* **40/1**
60 **10** *8* **Moon Spray (USA)**[18] 4247 2-9-3 0.................... NCallan 3 37
(K A Ryan) *dwlt: hld up: outpcd over 2f out: sn btn* **50/1**
40 **11** *2 ½* **Novestar (IRE)**[14] 4378 2-9-3 0.................... RoystonFfrench 12 29
(Mrs A Duffield) *t.k.h: in tch to 1/2-way: sn wknd* **66/1**
12 *5* **Kyzer Chief** 2-9-0 0.................... MarkLawson(3) 7 14
(R E Barr) *dwlt and wnt lft s: hung lft thrght: sn struggling* **100/1**

1m 11.94s (0.24) **Going Correction** -0.15s/f (Firm) 12 Ran SP% **119.3**
Speed ratings (Par 94): **92,91,89,89,88 87,86,84,83,73 69,63**
CSF £18.71 TOTE £2.20: £1.10, £3.80, £1.50; EX 22.20.
Owner JMC Breed & Race Limited **Bred** Ian Fair **Trained** Newmarket, Suffolk

FOCUS
Little strength in depth and, although the winner was basically to form, the proximity of the fourth confirms this bare form is ordinary at best.

NOTEBOOK
Craggy Cat(IRE), dropped in distance, did not have to improve too much to get off the mark but he did show a willing attitude for pressure in the closing stages. He will be suited by the return to 7f and is the type to win in ordinary nursery company. (op 6-5 tchd 6-4 in places)
Bonny Rose, who has several winners from sprint to middle distances in her pedigree, was relatively easy to back but showed more than enough on this racecourse debut to suggest she is capable of winning a similar event with this experience behind her. She should have no problems with 7f and is one to keep an eye on. (op 12-1)
Accused(IRE) ◆, who cost 360,000euros and is a half-brother to a 6f juvenile winner, is not a bad sort who shaped pleasingly without being at all knocked about on this racecourse debut. He is the type to improve with this run behind him and is more than capable of winning a similar event. (op 9-4)
Misplaced Fortune, who has shown ability at a modest level on her two previous starts, ran to a similar level this time and looks a fair guide as to the worth of this form. However, she leaves the impression that she will be capable of better once stepped into nursery company and upped to 7f. (op 33-1)
Pintano, who shaped well, despite racing keenly and hanging, on his debut at Haydock, failed to build on that form but was far from disgraced and looks capable of picking up a modest event at some point. (op 6-1)

Ivestar(IRE), who hinted at ability on his debut at Ripon, fared a bit better this time and once again left the impression that a much stiffer overall test of stamina would have been in his favour. He is one to look out for in nursery company. (op 25-1)
Kyzer Chief Official explanation: jockey said gelding was slow away

4819 RACING UK NOVICE MEDIAN AUCTION STKS — 7f
6:30 (6:32) (Class 5) 2-Y-O — **£2,817** (£838; £418; £209) **Stalls** Centre

Form — RPR

1 — **Screen Star (IRE)** 2-8-8 0 ... RoystonFfrench 3 — 102+
(M Johnston) *cl up: led after 2f: pushed clr fr 2f out: eased wl ins fnl f* — **7/2**[2]

41 **2** 11 **Thompsons Walls (IRE)**[17] 4279 2-9-3 83 ... LeeEnstone 4 — 82
(P C Haslam) *t.k.h: chsd ldrs: effrt and chsd wnr over 2f out: edgd lft over 1f out: no imp* — **3/1**[1]

6 **3** 2 ½ **Shaloo Diamond**[15] 4350 2-8-10 0 ... MichaelJStainton(3) 1 — 72
(R M Whitaker) *in tch: drvn and outpcd over 2f out: kpt on fnl f: no imp* — **100/1**

1 **4** ¾ **Salingers Star (IRE)**[62] 2904 2-9-2 0 ... SebSanders 6 — 73
(G A Swinbank) *chsd ldrs: drvn over 2f out: sn one pce* — **3/1**[1]

143 **5** 1 **Miss Bootylishes**[35] 3734 2-9-0 72 ... PaulHanagan 5 — 68
(A B Haynes) *bhd and sn outpcd: sme late hdwy: nvr on terms* — **8/1**

44 **6** 1 ¼ **Celtic Strand (IRE)**[67] 2739 2-8-13 0 ... MickyFenton 2 — 64
(T P Tate) *chsd ldrs tl rdn and wknd over 2f out* — **11/1**

7 5 **Love Cat (USA)** 2-8-13 0 ... NCallan 9 — 51
(K A Ryan) *dwlt: sn prom: rdn and wknd over 2f out* — **11/1**

01 **8** ¾ **Blue Cross Boy (USA)**[24] 4077 2-9-3 75 ... TomEaves 8 — 53
(J Howard Johnson) *led 2f: cl up tl wknd over 2f out* — **7/1**[3]

1m 22.41s (-2.49) **Going Correction** -0.15s/f (Firm) — 8 Ran SP% **113.5**
Speed ratings (Par 94): **108,95,92,91,90 89,83,82**
CSF £14.21 TOTE £4.80: £1.40, £1.80, £13.40; EX 18.90.
Owner Sheikh Mohammed **Bred** Darley **Trained** Middleham Moor, N Yorks

FOCUS
Four previous winners but an impressive performance from newcomer Screen Star, who turned in an outstanding winning time for a race of this type and who appeals strongly as the type to hold her own in much better company.

NOTEBOOK
Screen Star(IRE) ◆, a half-sister to a bumper winner and to a 7f three-year-old scorer, turned in a most impressive display (in a very quick time) on this racecourse debut. The filly, who has plenty of physical scope, is the sort to hold her own at a much higher level and her next outing is eagerly awaited. (op 4-1 tchd 5-1)
Thompsons Walls(IRE), a 6f maiden winner at Newcastle on his previous start, probably ran to a similar level over this longer trip but had little chance with the impressive winner. He does not look entirely straightforward as he tends to race keenly and tends to edge left but he is a fair sort who should continue to give a good account. (op 7-2)
Shaloo Diamond, well beaten on his debut, turned in a much better effort over this longer trip to divide a couple of previous winners. He should have no problems with 1m and is entitled to improve again for this experience.
Salingers Star(IRE), who won an ordinary fillies event over 6f on easy ground on her debut, failed to build on that and left the impression that this ground may have been plenty quick enough. However she was far from disgraced, is in good hands and may do better in nursery company back on an easy surface. (op 15-8)
Miss Bootylishes has had her limitations exposed in this type of event and once again showed a tendency to hang to her left. She may be suited by a bit more cut in the ground and should be suited by the return to ordinary nursery company. Official explanation: jockey said filly hung left-handed in early stages (op 10-1)
Celtic Strand(IRE), who had shown ability at a modest level on his first two starts, was found out in this stronger event but he is now qualified for a handicap mark and may be capable of a bit better in run-of-the-mill nurseries over this trip and beyond. Official explanation: jockey said colt hung right-handed (op 14-1 tchd 16-1)

4820 JOHN SMITH'S REDCAR STRAIGHT-MILE CHAMPIONSHIP STKS (H'CAP) (QUALIFIER) — 1m
7:00 (7:00) (Class 4) (0-80,75) 3-Y-O+ — **£5,181** (£1,541; £770; £384) **Stalls** Centre

Form — RPR

362 **1** **Observatory Star (IRE)**[14] 4407 4-9-6 68 ... (p) DavidAllan 7 — 77
(T D Easterby) *in tch: effrt over 2f out: led ins fnl f: hld on wl* — **5/1**[2]

1241 **2** ½ **Motafarred (IRE)**[13] 4418 5-9-5 67 ... SebSanders 9 — 75
(Micky Hammond) *led main centre gp: overall ldr over 2f out: hdd ins fnl f: r.o* — **9/2**[1]

0504 **3** 1 **Efidium**[14] 4408 9-9-0 67 ... NeilBrown(5) 13 — 73
(N Bycroft) *hld up: hdwy stands' side over 2f out: kpt on ins fnl f* — **18/1**

0001 **4** nk **United Nations**[10] 4488 6-9-8 70 ... DanielTudhope 6 — 75
(M W Easterby) *dwlt: bhd tl styd on fr 2f out: nrst fin* — **11/2**[3]

2000 **5** hd **Exit Smiling**[21] 4176 5-9-11 73 ... MickyFenton 2 — 78
(P T Midgley) *chsd far side ldr: effrt over 2f out: one pce ins fnl f* — **10/1**

0314 **6** 1 ½ **Champain Sands (IRE)**[15] 4353 8-8-13 66 ... KellyHarrison(5) 11 — 67
(E J Alston) *dwlt: hld up: hdwy over 3f out: no imp over 1f out* — **11/1**

0616 **7** hd **Kabis Amigos**[11] 4479 5-9-12 74 ... (t) AdrianTNicholls 14 — 75
(D Nicholls) *chsd ldrs tl rdn and no ex appr fnl f* — **14/1**

4000 **8** ½ **Hula Ballew**[8] 4581 7-9-13 75 ... PhillipMakin 8 — 75
(M Dods) *midfield: drvn and outpcd 3f out: kpt on fnl f* — **16/1**

0-10 **9** shd **Mineral Star (IRE)**[23] 4107 5-9-12 74 ... NCallan 12 — 74
(M H Tompkins) *trckd ldrs gng wl: rdn and edgd lft 2f out: sn no ex* — **8/1**

6026 **10** 3 **Pianoforte (USA)**[13] 4427 5-8-9 57 ... PaulHanagan 3 — 50
(E J Alston) *prom: drvn 3f out: edgd lft and wknd wl over 1f out* — **16/1**

6401 **11** 5 **Wahoo Sam (USA)**[11] 4477 7-9-6 68 ... (p) PaddyAspell 1 — 49
(D W Barker) *racd w one other far side: overall ldr to over 2f out: sn rdn and btn* — **20/1**

440- **12** 4 **Kaymich Perfecto**[345] 5320 7-9-7 72 ... MichaelJStainton(3) 10 — 44
(R M Whitaker) *bhd: rdn 3f out: n.d* — **33/1**

3412 **13** ¾ **Borodinsky**[13] 4427 6-9-2 64 ... TomEaves 15 — 34
(R E Barr) *prom to 1/2-way: sn rdn and wknd* — **16/1**

0244 **14** 1 **Sake (IRE)**[17] 4281 5-9-5 67 ... KimTinkler 4 — 35
(N Tinkler) *cl up tl wknd 3f out* — **22/1**

1064 **15** 5 **Coronado's Gold (USA)**[11] 4477 6-8-8 56 oh2 ... RoystonFfrench 5 — 12
(B Ellison) *prom 3f: sn rdn and struggling* — **11/1**

1m 36.57s (-1.23) **Going Correction** -0.15s/f (Firm) — 15 Ran SP% **128.7**
Speed ratings (Par 105): **100,99,98,98,98 96,96,95,95,92 87,83,82,81,76**
CSF £28.85 CT £406.37 TOTE £6.80: £2.70, £2.60, £5.30; EX 23.30.
Owner Mr & Mrs J D Cotton **Bred** C J Foy **Trained** Great Habton, N Yorks

FOCUS
A modest event run at a decent gallop and one in which the majority of the field raced in the centre. The form looks sound rated around the third and fourth.

Coronado's Gold(USA) Official explanation: jockey said gelding was never travelling

4821 BBC TEES MARK TURNBULL IN THE MORNING H'CAP — 1m 6f 19y
7:30 (7:31) (Class 6) (0-65,64) 3-Y-O — **£1,943** (£578; £288; £144) **Stalls** Low

Form — RPR

2000 **1** **Sonara (IRE)**[21] 4172 3-9-4 61 ... NCallan 7 — 71+
(M H Tompkins) *t.k.h: hld up: stdy hdwy over 3f out: rdn to ld 1f out: hld on wl* — **5/1**[3]

-400 **2** ½ **Hurricane Thomas (IRE)**[21] 4172 3-9-7 64 ... GregFairley 2 — 72+
(M Johnston) *towards rr: effrt and swtchd over 2f out: hdwy to press wnr ins fnl f: r.o* — **16/1**

6163 **3** 4 **Mr Crystal (FR)**[14] 4409 3-8-11 57 ... MichaelJStainton(3) 8 — 59
(Micky Hammond) *chsd ldrs: outpcd over 2f out: kpt on fnl f: no ch w first two* — **9/2**[2]

5402 **4** nk **Admiral Savannah (IRE)**[19] 4230 3-8-5 48 ow1 ... (b) DavidAllan 10 — 50
(T D Easterby) *midfield: hdwy and ev ch over 2f out: no ex over 1f out* — **7/1**

0-40 **5** nk **Sangfroid**[33] 3792 3-8-3 46 ... PaulHanagan 9 — 47
(Sir Mark Prescott) *plld hrd: led after 6f to over 2f out: rallied: no ex over 1f out* — **10/3**[1]

0006 **6** nk **Chunky's Choice (IRE)**[61] 2945 3-9-3 60 ... SebSanders 3 — 61
(J Noseda) *t.k.h: prom: hdwy to ld over 2f out: hdd 1f out: sn btn* — **15/2**

4335 **7** 2 ½ **Arabiyah**[16] 4309 3-8-12 55 ... NickyMackay 4 — 52
(L M Cumani) *hld up in midfield: hdwy to press ldrs over 2f out: rdn and wknd wl over 1f out* — **5/1**[3]

0040 **8** ½ **Firestorm (IRE)**[33] 3792 3-7-11 45 ... KellyHarrison(5) 6 — 42
(C W Fairhurst) *bhd: rdn 4f out: sme late hdwy: nvr on terms* — **50/1**

5506 **9** 8 **Sendali (FR)**[14] 4391 3-8-7 50 ... (p) PhillipMakin 12 — 35
(J D Bethell) *hld up: hdwy and prom 1/2-way: rdn and wknd fr 3f out* — **12/1**

5600 **10** 10 **Ful Of Grace (IRE)**[16] 4339 3-8-10 53 ... TomEaves 1 — 24
(M G Quinlan) *hld up: drvn 4f out: sn btn* — **50/1**

00-0 **11** ¾ **Kyrhena**[38] 3640 3-8-2 45 ... RoystonFfrench 5 — 15
(C W Thornton) *t.k.h: led 6f: cl up tl wknd fr 3f out* — **100/1**

0000 **12** 3 **Ingleby Hill (IRE)**[54] 3159 3-8-3 46 ... PaulFessey 11 — 12
(T D Barron) *midfield: hdwy and cl up 1/2-way: rdn and wknd fr over 2f out* — **25/1**

3m 4.26s (-0.76) **Going Correction** 0.0s/f (Good) — 12 Ran SP% **121.2**
Speed ratings (Par 98): **102,101,99,99,99 98,97,97,92,86 86,84**
CSF £81.79 CT £393.20 TOTE £6.50: £2.40, £3.30, £2.30; EX 103.30.
Owner Mrs Beryl Lockey **Bred** Kevin Gaffney **Trained** Newmarket, Suffolk

FOCUS
A modest handicap in which the steady pace means this is not a reliable form guide and in any case the form is pretty modest rated around the third, fourth and fifth.

4822 CELEBRATING MO MOWLAM H'CAP — 6f
8:00 (8:03) (Class 6) (0-65,63) 3-Y-O+ — **£2,047** (£604; £302) **Stalls** Centre

Form — RPR

0305 **1** **Plateau**[14] 4396 8-9-8 61 ... NCallan 11 — 72
(C R Dore) *in tch: rdn over 2f out: edgd lft and styd on to ld ins fnl f: kpt on wl* — **8/1**

3233 **2** nk **Ryedane (IRE)**[17] 4289 5-9-6 59 ... (b) DavidAllan 12 — 69
(T D Easterby) *chsd ldrs: effrt and ev ch fr over 1f out: kpt on: hld cl home* — **4/1**[2]

326 **3** 1 ½ **Choreography**[10] 4494 4-9-10 63 ... (v[1]) AdrianTNicholls 7 — 69
(D Nicholls) *midfield: drvn over 2f out: kpt on fnl f: nt rch first two* — **7/2**[1]

0533 **4** hd **Nufoudh (IRE)**[8] 4562 3-9-2 58 ... RoystonFfrench 10 — 63
(Miss Tracy Waggott) *pressed ldr: led over 1f out to ins fnl f: no ex* — **12/1**

0046 **5** nk **Spinning**[11] 4481 4-9-5 58 ... (b) PhillipMakin 5 — 62
(T D Barron) *towards rr: drvn 1/2-way: kpt on fr over 1f out: nrst fin* — **12/1**

0515 **6** nk **Dorn Dancer (IRE)**[14] 4381 5-9-10 63 ... PaddyAspell 4 — 66+
(D W Barker) *bhd tl styd on fr 2f out: nrst fin* — **18/1**

5002 **7** 1 ¼ **Soto**[3] 4706 4-9-7 60 ... DaleGibson 15 — 59
(M W Easterby) *in tch: drvn over 2f out: sn no imp* — **11/2**[3]

0063 **8** hd **Northern Chorus (IRE)**[8] 4561 4-9-0 60 ... (v) JamesO'Reilly(7) 8 — 58
(J O'Reilly) *led to over 1f out: sn btn* — **16/1**

6504 **9** hd **Ocean Gift**[30] 3873 5-9-9 62 ... KimTinkler 3 — 60
(N Tinkler) *bhd: pushed along 1/2-way: nvr rchd ldrs* — **14/1**

0000 **10** 1 ½ **Rigat**[8] 4583 4-9-1 59 ... NeilBrown(5) 14 — 52
(T D Barron) *dwlt: pushed along in rr 1/2-way: nvr on terms* — **11/1**

0030 **11** shd **Frimley's Matterry**[3] 4706 7-8-8 50 ... MichaelJStainton(3) 2 — 43
(R E Barr) *towards rr: drvn 1/2-way: sn btn* — **20/1**

6100 **12** shd **Greek Secret**[3] 4706 4-9-3 56 ... PaulHanagan 1 — 48
(J O'Reilly) *t.k.h: hld up: rdn over 2f out: sn btn* — **12/1**

4400 **13** 1 ½ **Butterfly Bud (IRE)**[21] 4180 4-8-9 48 ... TomEaves 9 — 35
(J O'Reilly) *dwlt: sn prom: rdn and wknd over 2f out* — **33/1**

4003 **14** shd **Four Kings**[11] 4478 6-8-10 49 ... FTahir 6 — 36
(Karen McLintock) *chsd ldrs tl wknd fr over 2f out* — **66/1**

0340 **15** ¾ **Cadogen Square**[18] 4250 5-8-7 53 ... DanielleMcCreery(7) 13 — 38
(D W Chapman) *towards rr: drvn 1/2-way: sn btn* — **50/1**

1m 10.61s (-1.09) **Going Correction** -0.15s/f (Firm)
WFA 3 from 4yo+ 3lb — 15 Ran SP% **129.1**
Speed ratings (Par 101): **101,100,98,98,97 97,95,95,95,93 93,93,91,90,89**
CSF £41.52 CT £140.40 TOTE £13.10: £3.60, £2.10, £2.50; EX 46.90 Place 6 £26.90, Place 5 £16.53.
Owner Page, Ward, Marsh **Bred** Juddmonte Farms **Trained** West Pinchbeck, Lincs

FOCUS
A run-of-the-mill handicap but, although the pace was sound, those attempting to come from off the pace were at a disadvantage. Despite that the form looks solid enough judged around the first three.

T/Plt: £58.30 to a £1 stake. Pool: £42,428.45. 531.05 winning tickets. T/Qpdt: £36.20 to a £1 stake. Pool: £3,532.50. 72.05 winning tickets. RY

4662 WINDSOR (R-H)
Saturday, August 25

OFFICIAL GOING: Good (7.6)
Wind: Virtually nil Weather: Sunny

4823 TOTEPLACEPOT E B F NOVICE MEDIAN AUCTION STKS — 6f
5:15 (5:15) (Class 5) 2-Y-O — **£4,533** (£1,348; £674; £336) **Stalls** High

Form — RPR

32 **1** **Rash Judgement**[21] 4181 2-8-12 0 ... FergusSweeney 1 — 80
(W S Kittow) *t.k.h: a.p: led over 1f out: r.o wl* — **2/1**[2]

363 **2** 2 **Meydan Dubai (IRE)**[27] 3995 2-8-12 93 ... JamieSpencer 9 — 74
(J R Best) *led tl rdn and hdd over 1f out: nt pce of wnr* — **1/1**[1]

6410 **3** 1 1/2 **Legendary Guest**[4] 4695 2-8-11 80 .... AshleyHamblett(5) 4 74
(M R Channon) *trckd ldrs: outpcd 1/2-way: styd on fnl f* **7/1**[3]
50 **4** 1 1/2 **Elizabeth's Quest**[31] 3850 2-8-0 0 .... SophieDoyle(7) 8 60
(R Simpson) *towards rr: hdwy whn hung lft over 1f out: nvr nr to chal* **50/1**
3210 **5** 1/2 **Luscious Lips**[21] 4152 2-8-13 77 .... RichardSmith 7 65
(R Hannon) *chsd ldrs: rdn 2f out: sn wknd* **10/1**
0210 **6** 1 **Supermassive Muse (IRE)**[42] 3550 2-9-2 81 .... (t) TQuinn 3 65
(E S McMahon) *trckd ldrs: rdn and wknd 2f out* **16/1**
00 **7** 1 1/2 **Honest Value (IRE)**[16] 4325 2-8-12 0 .... RichardThomas 5 56
(Mrs L C Jewell) *in tch tl rdn 1/2-way: sn wknd* **150/1**
00 **8** 1 3/4 **Border Defence (IRE)**[136] 999 2-8-12 0 .... FrankieMcDonald 2 51
(P A Blockley) *rrd up leaving stalls: a bhd* **100/1**

1m 13.2s (-0.47) **Going Correction** -0.15s/f (Firm) 8 Ran SP% **114.4**
Speed ratings (Par 94): **97,94,92,90,89 88,86,84**
CSF £4.32 TOTE £3.60: £1.30, £1.10, £2.20; EX 6.00.
Owner Reg Gifford **Bred** D R Tucker **Trained** Blackborough, Devon

FOCUS
A decent race for the grade and solid enough form rated around the winner and third.

NOTEBOOK
Rash Judgement, who had shown plenty of promise when placed on his two previous outings against a couple of decent sorts, got off the mark despite again racing freely. He looks a useful type but will have to continue on the upgrade, as he is unlikely to be that well treated in handicaps having beaten a 93-rated colt here. (op 7-2)
Meydan Dubai(IRE), who was found out by the drop back to 5f last time, was more at home at this trip and set off in front. However, the winner proved too strong in the last furlong and he may need to return to 7f in order to get off the mark, although he should find easier opportunities than this. (op 8-11)
Legendary Guest, who struggled in a nursery at the Ebor meeting earlier in the week, found this level more to his liking but was unable to lie up before running on, which suggests another try at 7f will be in his favour. (op 15-2)
Elizabeth's Quest, who looked to need 7f on her debut but failed to get home when tried over it last time, was making her debut on turf. She again looked as if this trip is too short for her, although her breeding suggests she should be effective at it and maybe better will be seen of her once she is handicapped.
Luscious Lips had won and finished second over 5f here earlier in the season, but both those efforts were on much softer ground and she does not look as effective on this surface. (op 11-1 tchd 12-1)
Supermassive Muse(IRE), another who gained his success on easy ground, has form on fast so could have been expected to run better. However, he was fitted with a tongue tie for the first time and was unfancied in the market, and his performance here suggests his official rating is on the high side. (op 10-1)

4824 TOTESPORT 0800 221 221 (S) STKS 5f 10y
5:45 (5:45) (Class 5) 2-Y-O **£3,238** (£963; £481; £240) **Stalls** High

Form RPR
6500 **1** **Fabuleux Cherie**[26] 4016 2-8-6 55 .... MartinDwyer 6 57
(W R Muir) *a.p: led over 1f out: edgd rt: drvn out* **3/1**[2]
04 **2** 1 1/2 **Grimes Hope (IRE)**[15] 4363 2-8-11 0 .... JimmyFortune 1 57
(R Hannon) *mid-div: outpcd 1/2-way: rdn and styd on to go 2nd ins fnl f* **11/4**[1]
0000 **3** 1 1/2 **Seventh Cloud (IRE)**[12] 4453 2-8-3 55 .... AndrewElliott(3) 3 46
(A P Jarvis) *trckd ldr: led 2f out: hdd and edgd rt over 1f out: lost 2nd ins fnl f* **6/1**
154 **4** 1 **No Point (IRE)**[97] 1857 2-8-11 46 .... FrankieMcDonald 10 48
(P A Blockley) *chsd ldrs: rdn and one pce fnl f* **14/1**
5350 **5** 1/2 **My Sheilas Dream (IRE)**[16] 4311 2-8-11 54 .... (p) AlanDaly 4 46
(W G M Turner) *led tl rdn and hdd 2f out: sn wknd* **12/1**
453 **6** nk **Tintorero**[10] 4512 2-8-11 55 .... (v) GrahamGibbons 9 45
(M J Wallace) *chsd ldrs: hld whn n.m.r over 1f out: wknd* **4/1**[3]
0000 **7** 3 **Mairead's Boy (IRE)**[15] 4363 2-8-11 48 .... (p) NeilPollard 7 34
(J S Moore) *slowly away: a bhd* **16/1**
0000 **8** 2 1/2 **Beyabi**[15] 4359 2-8-7 45 ow1 .... FergusSweeney 2 21
(J R Jenkins) *unruly in stalls: a bhd* **40/1**
5100 **9** 4 **Caught In Paradise (IRE)**[16] 4311 2-8-13 60 .... EmmettStack(3) 8 16
(A B Haynes) *a outpcd in rr* **12/1**
0064 **10** 1/2 **Whistful Miss**[15] 4359 2-8-6 48 .... RichardThomas 5 4
(P Howling) *outpcd: a in rr* **20/1**

61.42 secs (0.32) **Going Correction** -0.15s/f (Firm) **10** Ran SP% **121.1**
Speed ratings (Par 94): **91,88,86,84,83 83,78,74,68,67**
CSF £12.25 TOTE £4.20: £1.80, £1.80, £2.70; EX 9.90.The winner was bought in for £7,400. Grimes Hope was claimed by Claes Bjorling for £6,000.
Owner David & Gwyn Joseph **Bred** J K Beckitt And Son **Trained** Lambourn, Berks

FOCUS
A run-of-the-mill juvenile seller and average form for the grade, rated around the first two and the fourth.

NOTEBOOK
Fabuleux Cherie had the blinkers she wore last time left off on this drop in grade and did not appear to need them as she found enough under pressure once taking the lead on the outside of her field to hold off the favourite. Connections went to 7,400gns to retain her at the subsequent auction. (op 11-4)
Grimes Hope(IRE), who ran well in a better seller over 7f at Newmarket last time, followed the winner through without ever looking likely to get to her. The drop in trip on this easier track was not in his favour, but he has been claimed and may find opportunities for his new Scandinavian connections. (tchd 7-2)
Seventh Cloud(IRE), a free-running filly who was also dropping in grade, made a bold bid and was only run out of it in the closing stages. She looks capable of scoring at this level, and may be worth another try on Polytrack. (op 8-1)
No Point(IRE) won on her debut but has been exposed since in this grade under a penalty. She is clearly very moderate but being by Point Given she may be worth a try on sand. (op 16-1)
My Sheilas Dream(IRE), another who won on her debut, has run reasonably in sellers and claimers since and showed plenty of pace before fading in the first-time cheekpieces. (op 11-1)
Tintorero, with the visor on again, did not get the clearest of runs late on but looked held at the time and connections are struggling to find the key to him. Possibly a gelding operation may produce some improvement. Official explanation: jockey said colt hung left in the final furlong (op 5-1)
Caught In Paradise(IRE) Official explanation: jockey said colt was never travelling

4825 TOTEPOOL AUGUST STKS (LISTED RACE) 1m 3f 135y
6:15 (6:15) (Class 1) 3-Y-O+
£14,762 (£5,595; £2,800; £1,396; £699; £351) **Stalls** High

Form RPR
46-0 **1** **Dragon Dancer**[22] 4117 4-9-2 106 .... DarryllHolland 2 111
(G Wragg) *trckd ldr: chal over 2f out: rdn to ld wl ins fnl f* **7/1**[3]
-115 **2** 1 **Classic Punch (IRE)**[7] 4599 4-9-7 110 .... TQuinn 4 114
(D R C Elsworth) *led at stdy pce: qcknd 3f out: rdn and hdd wl ins fnl f* **7/1**[3]
1032 **3** 1/2 **Imperial Star (IRE)**[22] 4117 4-9-7 110 .... JimmyFortune 5 113
(J H M Gosden) *chsd ldrs: rdn over 3f out: nt qckn fnl f* **11/8**[1]
1-44 **4** 5 **Hawridge Prince**[115] 1393 7-9-2 110 .... JimCrowley 3 100
(B R Millman) *racd in tch: hdwy 6f out: rdn and wknd over 1f out* **8/1**
-623 **5** 1/2 **Tam Lin**[27] 4005 4-9-2 112 .... LDettori 6 99
(Saeed Bin Suroor) *t.k.h: hld up in last pl: hdwy over 3f out: hung rt u.p and wknd over 1f out* **7/4**[2]
0224 **6** 7 **Ciccone**[15] 4355 4-8-11 57 .... (p) FergusSweeney 1 82?
(G L Moore) *t.k.h: hld up: rdn over 2f out: sn btn* **100/1**

2m 31.21s (1.11) **Going Correction** +0.225s/f (Good) **6** Ran SP% **115.6**
Speed ratings (Par 111): **105,104,104,100,100 95**
CSF £53.92 TOTE £8.70: £3.20, £3.10; EX 73.70.
Owner J L C Pearce **Bred** Miss K Rausing And Abbey Bloodstock **Trained** Newmarket, Suffolk

FOCUS
A decent Listed contest run at an ordinary pace that did not pick up until the last half-mile. Dragon Dancer finally got off the mark but the lack of pace lends caution to the form.

NOTEBOOK
Dragon Dancer, who was touched off in last year's Derby, had failed to build on that in five subsequent runs and was well beaten at Goodwood on his belated return to action. However, that outing had clearly brought him on and, always close up, his determined challenge finally wore down the resolute runner-up. He may be able to build on this, but Group 3s are likely to be his grade rather than tilting at the top level. (op 8-1 tchd 13-2)
Classic Punch(IRE) is an admirable sort in this grade but was well beaten when held up in the Geoffrey Freer the previous weekend. However, he seemed much happier making the running and stuck on tenaciously, although unable to resist the persistent challenge of the winner. Like his half-brother, he is the sort who may continue to improve with age. (op 4-1 tchd 8-1)
Imperial Star(IRE), runner-up to the subsequent Ebor winner when giving weight in a Listed race at Goodwood, was made favourite largely on the strength of that and the fact he had won on his two previous visits to this track. He appeared to have every chance but the first two pulled out more in the closing stages. He is not going to be easy to place but may be worth aiming for the Churchill Stakes later in the year, as he won on his only previous try on Polytrack, and it would be no surprise if he was campaigned in Dubai over the winter. (op 13-8 tchd 7-4 and 11-10, 2-1 in a place)
Hawridge Prince, who stays much further than this, ran as well as could be expected on this return from nearly four months off. He is likely to be aimed at the Fenwolf Stakes at Ascot and the Jockey Club Cup, both of which he won last season. (op 15-2 tchd 12-1)
Tam Lin, who won the Winter Hill Stakes on this card last year, has had cut in the ground on his three previous outings this season. He showed his usual tendency to pull for his head on this step back up in trip and came to deliver his challenge at about the two pole, but then hung and dropped away tamely as though he had some sort of problem. (op 5-2)

4826 TOTESPORT.COM WINTER HILL STKS (GROUP 3) 1m 2f 7y
6:45 (6:47) (Class 1) 3-Y-O+
£28,390 (£10,760; £5,385; £2,685; £1,345; £675) **Stalls** Low

Form RPR
3221 **1** **Queen's Best**[20] 4203 4-8-11 94 .... RyanMoore 1 110
(Sir Michael Stoute) *hld up: swtchd lft wl over 2f out: sn mde hdwy: rdn to ld ins fnl f* **8/1**
2/14 **2** 1/2 **Winged Cupid (IRE)**[28] 3974 4-9-0 110 .... LDettori 3 112
(Saeed Bin Suroor) *trckd ldr: led over 2f out: rdn and hdd ins fnl f: no ex nr fin* **15/8**[1]
2-32 **3** 3/4 **Cougar Bay (IRE)**[41] 3579 4-9-0 0 .... JamieSpencer 8 110
(David Wachman, Ire) *trckd ldrs: rdn and kpt on fnl f* **8/1**
-230 **4** 1 **Sunshine Kid (USA)**[83] 2293 3-8-6 101 .... MartinDwyer 2 108
(J H M Gosden) *in tch: rdn 3f out: ev ch over 1f out: nt qckn ins fnl f* **17/2**
112 **5** 1 1/4 **Ordnance Row**[9] 4543 4-9-0 105 .... RichardHughes 9 106
(R Hannon) *mid-div: rdn 3f out: one pce ins fnl 2f* **7/1**[3]
0114 **6** shd **Championship Point (IRE)**[13] 4435 4-9-0 115 .... DarryllHolland 4 105
(M R Channon) *t.k.h in rr: hmpd wl over 2f out: kpt on but nt pce to chal after* **5/1**[2]
16-0 **7** 1 **Hotel Du Cap**[22] 4117 4-9-0 89 .... JimmyFortune 6 103
(G Wragg) *mid-div: rdn 3f out: sn outpcd* **40/1**
-214 **8** 3 **Topatoo**[50] 3271 5-9-1 105 .... MichaelHills 7 98
(M H Tompkins) *a bhd: no hdwy ins fnl 3f* **25/1**
3213 **P** **Take A Bow**[28] 3974 6-9-4 113 .... JimCrowley 5 —
(P R Chamings) *trckd ldrs: tl wknd rapidly over 3f out: sn p.u and dismntd: broke leg: dead* **5/1**[2]

2m 7.98s (-0.32) **Going Correction** +0.225s/f (Good)
WFA 3 from 4yo+ 8lb **9** Ran SP% **119.6**
Speed ratings (Par 113): **110,109,109,108,107 107,106,103,—**
CSF £24.29 TOTE £7.80: £2.20, £1.40, £2.20; EX 31.30.
Owner Cheveley Park Stud **Bred** Darley **Trained** Newmarket, Suffolk
■ Stewards' Enquiry : Ryan Moore one-day ban; careless riding (Sep 5)

FOCUS
A fair renewal of this Group 3 run at just a fair gallop. The form makes sense rated around the third and fourth.

NOTEBOOK
Queen's Best ◆, who tends to come to herself in the second half of the year, followed up her recent Listed win against fillies by beating the colts to take her first Group race. She was still last at the intersection, but she picked up well from that point, although it took a fair while to wear down the favourite. She is on a roll at present and, although she is entered in the Blandford Stakes over this trip at the Curragh next month, she also looks the ideal sort for races such as the Princess Royal or Prix de Royallieu and the St Simon Stakes, with possible soft ground holding no fears for her. (op 6-1)
Winged Cupid(IRE), a Listed winner over a mile around here on his reappearance after a long absence in June, had been well held on his first attempt at this trip on heavy ground last time. He was ridden positively again and looked the likely winner when going on at a the quarter-mile pole. However, he could produce nothing extra under pressure and the filly wore him down close home. He has a couple of big-race entries, but this is his level at present and it would not be the biggest surprise if he dropped back to a mile next time. (op 5-2 tchd 11-4)
Cougar Bay(IRE) is a pretty consistent sort who appeared to run his race, racing on the heels of the leaders and having every chance before failing to pick up sufficiently late in the day. He is a fair guide to the level of the form but may need the blinkers re-applied to enable him to produce that little extra needed to get his head in front. Official explanation: jockey said gelding hung left under pressure (tchd 9-1)
Sunshine Kid(USA), who has been placed in Group 2 company, has not quite lived up to initial promise but has not had that much racing and was making his first appearance since the Prix du Jockey Club in June. He ran reasonably before fading late on as if the outing was needed. He looks capable of scoring at this level, but he is in the valuable John Smith's Handicap at Newbury next month and would be very interesting if taking his chance there. (op 12-1 tchd 14-1)
Ordnance Row has been progressing nicely this summer, but his recent good efforts have all been on easy ground and the faster ground and step up in distance appeared to find him out. He would be of considerable interest if aimed at the Cambridgeshire in a month's time. (op 8-1)
Championship Point(IRE), another who has been in good form of late, did not really settle at the back and was hampered when Take A Bow stopped quickly just after the intersection. He does seem best on a right-handed track and a return to Goodwood or Ascot is likely to see him in the best light, with the Cumberland Lodge a possible target. (op 10-3 tchd 11-2 in a place)

Hotel Du Cap was ridden positively on this drop in trip but was done for speed late on. It may be worth running him in the September Stakes at Kempton, as he won his only race on Polytrack at that course. (op 50-1)
Topatoo is a useful mare but much better at York than anywhere else and, returning from a short break, she was allowed to come home in her own time once beaten. This should have set her up nicely for a tilt at the Strensall Stakes at the Knavesmire next month, which looks her most likely target. (op 33-1)
Take A Bow, a tough and genuine individual, sadly broke a leg and had to be put down. He won five times for connections, including the Group 3 Brigadier Gerard Stakes, and was also beaten a neck in the Cambridgeshire in 2004; his earnings exceeded £164,000. (op 11-2 tchd 6-1)

4827 READING EVENING POST H'CAP — 1m 67y
7:15 (7:17) (Class 4) (0-85,85) 3-Y-O+ **£6,309** (£1,888; £944; £472; £235) **Stalls** High

Form — RPR
0300 **1** **St Andrews (IRE)**[21] 4153 7-9-13 **85** ... JimmyFortune 12 — 93
(M A Jarvis) *hld up: hdwy whn hmpd 2f out: strly rdn to ld cl home* **12/1**
0003 **2** *nk* **Heroes**[15] 4366 3-9-6 **84** ... TPO'Shea 6 — 91
(G A Huffer) *s.i.s: hdwy to ld wl over 1f out: rdn and hdd cl home* **6/1**[2]
032 **3** *3/4* **Tender The Great (IRE)**[17] 4268 4-9-5 **77** ... TQuinn 8 — 83
(B G Powell) *mid-div: hdwy whn swtchd rt 2f out: kpt on fnl f* **12/1**
3220 **4** *1* **Gyroscope**[24] 4060 3-9-6 **84** ... RyanMoore 10 — 87+
(Sir Michael Stoute) *in rr: rdn and hdwy 2f out: kpt on fnl f: nvr nr to chal* **4/1**[1]
2004 **5** *nk* **Wavertree Warrior (IRE)**[9] 4548 5-9-13 **85** ...(b) IanMongan 11 — 88
(N P Littmoden) *a in tch: rdn over 1f out: kpt on one pce* **8/1**
00-0 **6** *1* **Simba Sun (IRE)**[17] 4276 3-9-5 **83** ... JimCrowley 1 — 83
(R M Beckett) *hld up: sme hdwy 2f out: kpt on one pce* **25/1**
0100 **7** *nk* **Bold Marc (IRE)**[28] 3943 5-9-8 **83** ... AndrewElliott(3) 9 — 83
(K R Burke) *prom: led 6f out: hdd wl over 1f out: no ex fnl f* **15/2**[3]
5112 **8** *3* **Bajan Pride**[10] 4502 3-9-4 **82** ... RichardHughes 7 — 75
(R Hannon) *led tl hdd 6f out: wknd over 1f out* **4/1**[1]
204 **9** *1 1/2* **Matuza (IRE)**[22] 4133 4-9-7 **79** ... MartinDwyer 5 — 69
(W R Muir) *a towards rr* **16/1**
6250 **10** *2 1/2* **Master Pegasus**[29] 3900 4-9-10 **82** ... GeorgeBaker 4 — 66
(C F Wall) *prom tl rdn and wknd 2f out* **9/1**
0104 **11** *shd* **Wigwam Willie (IRE)**[32] 3813 5-9-5 **82** ...(p) NataliaGemelova(5) 13 — 66
(K A Ryan) *chsd ldrs tl wknd 2f out* **11/1**
0000 **12** *6* **Lopinot (IRE)**[42] 3525 4-9-2 **74** ... PatDobbs 14 — 44
(P J Makin) *s.i.s: sn in tch: wknd over 2f out* **50/1**
6200 **13** *nk* **Langford**[21] 4153 7-9-6 **78** ... MichaelHills 3 — 47
(M H Tompkins) *in rr: rdn 4f out: nvr on terms* **16/1**

1m 44.14s (-0.56) **Going Correction** +0.225s/f (Good)
WFA 3 from 4yo+ 6lb — **13** Ran SP% **128.5**
Speed ratings (Par 105): **111,110,109,108,108 107,107,104,102,100 100,94,93**
CSF £88.63 CT £947.62 TOTE £17.80: £4.40, £2.70, £3.10; EX 146.60.
Owner M A Jarvis **Bred** P D Savill **Trained** Newmarket, Suffolk
■ Stewards' Enquiry : T Quinn one-day ban: careless riding (Sep 5)

FOCUS
A decent handicap run at a strong gallop and the time was very good for the grade, 1.36sec faster than the concluding event. Ordinary form for the type of race.
Master Pegasus Official explanation: jockey said gelding ran too free
Lopinot(IRE) Official explanation: trainer said gelding scoped dirty after the race

4828 COME RACING AGAIN MONDAY 1ST OCTOBER FILLIES' H'CAP — 1m 67y
7:45 (7:45) (Class 5) (0-75,75) 3-Y-O+ **£3,238** (£963; £481; £240) **Stalls** High

Form — RPR
0211 **1** **Ellen's Girl (IRE)**[6] 4632 4-9-4 **60** 6ex ... RichardHughes 7 — 67+
(R Hannon) *trckd ldrs: led jst ins fnl f: nudged out cleverly* **11/8**[1]
3143 **2** *nk* **World Spirit**[27] 4004 3-9-13 **75** ... ChrisCatlin 3 — 80
(Rae Guest) *a in tch: led briefly 1f out: edgd lft but kpt on to line* **4/1**[2]
050 **3** *1 1/2* **Cape Velvet (IRE)**[24] 4060 3-9-5 **67** ... MartinDwyer 9 — 69
(J W Hills) *t.k.h: led tl hdd ent fnl f: kpt on one pce* **6/1**
0-50 **4** *1/2* **Pirouetting**[36] 3711 4-9-13 **69** ... MichaelHills 11 — 70
(B W Hills) *in tch tl rdn 3f out: rdn and swtchd lft wl over 1f out: styd on fnl f* **11/2**[3]
53-0 **5** *2* **Sea Cookie**[20] 4200 3-8-2 **50** ... FrankieMcDonald 8 — 46
(W De Best-Turner) *bhd: rdn over 2f out: passed btn horses ins fnl f* **66/1**
5304 **6** *1 3/4* **Imperial Lucky (IRE)**[5] 4665 4-9-0 **56** ... RobertHavlin 1 — 49
(D K Ivory) *s.i.s: hdwy over 3f out: wknd over 1f out* **10/1**
-000 **7** *1 1/4* **Sagassa**[26] 4015 3-7-13 **50** oh1 ... DominicFox(3) 4 — 39
(W De Best-Turner) *s.i.s: t.k.h: hld up and nvr on terms* **100/1**
6200 **8** *1/2* **Cavort (IRE)**[20] 4205 3-9-9 **71** ... JimmyFortune 10 — 59
(Pat Eddery) *trckd ldrs: rdn over 3f out: wknd over 1f out* **9/1**
/0-0 **9** *17* **Mother's Day**[135] 1016 4-9-1 **64** ... HarryPoulton(7) 6 — 14
(L A Dace) *trckd ldr: tl wknd qckly 2f out: t.o* **40/1**

1m 45.5s (0.80) **Going Correction** +0.225s/f (Good)
WFA 3 from 4yo 6lb — **9** Ran SP% **115.8**
Speed ratings (Par 100): **105,104,103,102,100 98,97,97,80**
CSF £6.93 CT £24.69 TOTE £2.60: £1.10, £1.70, £2.40; EX 5.70 Place 6 £104.86, Place 5 £95.84.
Owner Con Harrington **Bred** Mrs Chris Harrington **Trained** East Everleigh, Wilts

FOCUS
A modest fillies' handicap run 1.36sec slower than the preceding contest. The winner is progressive but this form is not strong.
T/Plt: £106.20 to a £1 stake. Pool: £52,027.00. 357.60 winning tickets. T/Qpdt: £49.10 to a £1 stake. Pool: £4,447.70. 66.90 winning tickets. JS

4829 - (Foreign Racing) - See Raceform Interactive

4434 CURRAGH (R-H)
Saturday, August 25

OFFICIAL GOING: Soft

4830a CILL DARA SECURITIES BALLYCULLEN STKS (LISTED RACE) — 1m 6f
2:25 (2:25) 3-Y-O+ **£24,192** (£7,097; £3,381; £1,152)

RPR
1 **Red Moloney (USA)**[45] 3442 3-8-11 99 ... DPMcDonogh 8 — 109
(Kevin Prendergast, Ire) *trckd ldrs in 5th: 4th travelling wl ent st: led 2f out: rdn and styd on wl: comf* **6/1**
2 *3* **Hasanka (IRE)**[19] 4238 3-8-8 102 ... MJKinane 6 — 102
(John M Oxx, Ire) *trckd ldrs: 4th 1/2-way: 3rd travelling wl ent st: impr into 2nd under 2f out: rdn and kpt on wl wout troubling wnr* **4/1**[2]
3 *2 1/2* **Vision Of Grandeur (IRE)**[76] 2498 3-8-11 101 ...(b) PJSmullen 4 — 102
(D K Weld, Ire) *hld up towards rr: 6th and prog early st: 3rd 1 1/2f out: kpt on same pce* **5/1**[3]
4 *3 1/2* **Attercliffe (IRE)**[64] 2851 4-9-9 99 ... JMurtagh 5 — 97
(Noel Meade, Ire) *settled 2nd: drvn along over 4f out: chal early st: no ex fr over 1f out* **10/1**
5 *3 1/2* **Alpine Eagle (IRE)**[12] 4468 3-8-11 90 ... CO'Donoghue 1 — 93
(Mrs John Harrington, Ire) *trckd ldrs in 6th: rdn ent st: 5th and no imp fr 1 1/2f out* **10/1**
6 *3* **Peppertree Lane (IRE)**[56] 3119 4-9-12 ... KDarley 3 — 92
(M Johnston) *led: strly pressed early st: hdd 2f out: wknd qckly* **6/4**[1]
7 *nk* **Virginia Woolf**[55] 3143 5-9-6 93 ... KFallon 9 — 85
(D T Hughes, Ire) *prom: 3rd 1/2-way: drvn along over 4f out: wknd early st* **25/1**
8 *dist* **Olivia Pielak (IRE)**[22] 4142 4-9-6 ... FMBerry 7 — —
(Miss A M Winters, Ire) *a bhd: wknd appr st: t.o* **200/1**

3m 8.50s (6.20) **Going Correction** +0.50s/f (Yiel)
WFA 3 from 4yo+ 12lb — **9** Ran SP% **113.5**
Speed ratings: **102,100,98,96,94 93,92,—**
CSF £29.70 TOTE £6.80: £1.70, £1.60, £2.10; DF 40.20.
Owner Norman Ormiston **Bred** Linda Clough **Trained** Friarstown, Co Kildare

FOCUS
There were plenty of progressive types in this Listed event and it has been rated through the runner-up.

NOTEBOOK
Red Moloney(USA) put his rivals to the sword in good style and looks a horse with a fine future. He came into this race chasing a hat-trick, but was facing a significantly tougher assignment than the one presented to him when he landed a 1m2f Naas handicap off a mark of 87 last month. Taking a major step up in trip, he was content to look on from midfield for much of the race, but eased into the reckoning rounding the final turn and was still going well when hitting the front two furlongs from home. He picked up well to soon go clear and saw out this trip well. His trainer feels that he will be a better horse next year and indicated that he might only have one more run this season. He seems quite versatile in terms of ground preference, is definitely open to further progress and can be expected to hold his own at a higher level than this.
Hasanka(IRE) was looking to build on her close second to Downtown in a 1m4f Group 3 at Cork earlier in the month. She emerged to chase the winner from over a furlong out, but never looked like getting on terms with that rival. This was a respectable effort and she should be able to make her mark in a Listed race at some stage. (op 7/2)
Vision Of Grandeur(IRE) had not run since June, when he completed a hat-trick of victories with an impressive display in a Roscommon handicap. He acquitted himself well in this higher grade and could well improve off this run. He would probably prefer better ground, too.
Attercliffe(IRE) showed more than on his reappearance at Limerick in June, but he will have to improve to make his mark at this level. He was under pressure before the straight and kept on without being able to land a telling blow. (op 8/1)
Alpine Eagle(IRE) faced a far more demanding challenge than when running out a wide-margin winner of a 1m4f conditions event at Ballinrobe last time. He found this test beyond him, but could still be of interest in a handicap off his current mark. (op 11/1)
Peppertree Lane(IRE) looked to have an excellent chance of following up his Curragh Cup success. He once again set out to make all, but was a spent force from early in the straight and something was surely amiss with him. He was reported to be sore behind. Official explanation: vet said colt finished sore behind

4832a TATTERSALLS IRELAND SALE STKS — 6f
3:30 (3:31) 2-Y-O
£99,324 (£38,513; £23,310; £13,175; £4,054; £2,027)

RPR
1 **Sudden Impact (IRE)**[20] 4193 2-8-11 ... FMBerry 10 — 97+
(Paul Green) *mde all: rdn clr over 1f out: r.o strly: v easily* **11/1**
2 *6* **Invincible Ash (IRE)**[19] 4242 2-8-11 ... JMurtagh 11 — 79
(M Halford, Ire) *chsd ldrs: prog under 2f out: 3rd over 1f out: kpt on same pce u.p* **14/1**
3 *1/2* **Houston Dynimo (IRE)**[6] 4645 2-9-2 ... DPMcDonogh 1 — 82
(Kevin Prendergast, Ire) *dwlt: sn mid-div: prog 2f out: 5th over 1f out: kpt on same pce u.p* **11/4**[1]
4 *2 1/2* **Nikindi (IRE)**[129] 1094 2-9-2 ... LPKeniry 8 — 75
(J S Moore) *trckd ldrs: 5th 1/2-way: rdn 2f out: kpt on same pce fr over 1f out* **13/2**[3]
5 *1/2* **Yali (IRE)**[28] 3979 2-8-11 ... WJSupple 3 — 73+
(Francis Ennis, Ire) *mid-div: prog whn nt clr run 2f out: 7th 1f out: sn swtchd and nt clr run: kpt on* **10/1**
6 *1/2* **Dohasa (IRE)**[59] 3005 2-9-2 ...(b[1]) CO'Donoghue 5 — 72
(G M Lyons, Ire) *prom on stands' rail: 3rd 1/2-way: 2nd and chal under 2f out: no ex fnl f* **66/1**
7 *2 1/2* **Ceol Loch Aoidh (IRE)**[13] 4434 2-8-11 ...(p) KJManning 9 — 59
(J S Bolger, Ire) *prom: 2nd 1/2-way: 3rd u.p over 1 1/2f out: no ex fnl f* **25/1**
8 *4 1/2* **Amarama (IRE)**[25] 4052 2-8-11 ... PBBeggy 21 — 46
(David P Myerscough, Ire) *towards rr: kpt on fr 2f out* **16/1**
9 *3/4* **Imperial Decree**[17] 4293 2-8-11 ... WMLordan 4 — 43
(John Berry) *mid-div: kpt on same pce fr under 2f out* **11/1**
10 *1/2* **Wooden King (IRE)**[50] 3270 2-9-2 ... PShanahan 6 — 47
(P D Evans) *nvr bttr than mid-div* **100/1**
11 *1/2* **Southwest Star (IRE)**[45] 3423 2-9-2 ... TolleyDean 17 — 45
(J S Moore) *towards rr: kpt on wout threatening fr under 2f out* **66/1**
12 *1 3/4* **Sir George (IRE)**[72] 2604 2-9-2 ... KFallon 7 — 40
(P W Chapple-Hyam) *mid-div: no imp fr 2f out* **5/1**[2]
13 *1* **Rochester Falls (IRE)**[30] 3890 2-8-11 ... CDHayes 14 — 32
(Kevin Prendergast, Ire) *towards rr: no imp fr 2f out* **33/1**
14 *shd* **She Floats (IRE)**[30] 3890 2-8-11 ... NGMcCullagh 13 — 32
(Enda Kelly, Ire) *in rr of mid-div: no ex fr over 2f out* **100/1**
15 *2 1/2* **Five Satins (IRE)**[59] 3005 2-8-11 ... JAHeffernan 2 — 24
(M J Grassick, Ire) *prom on stands' rail tl 1/2-way: sn wknd* **66/1**
16 *7* **Creative (IRE)**[16] 4335 2-9-2 ... SaleemGolam 18 — 8
(M H Tompkins) *chsd ldrs in centre: 6th u.p over 2f out: sn wknd* **25/1**
17 *1* **Polish Priory (IRE)**[7] 4602 2-8-11 ... DJMoran 22 — —
(P D Evans) *chsd ldrs in centre to 1/2-way: rdn and wknd* **100/1**
18 *1* **Vhujon (IRE)**[21] 4152 2-9-2 ...(t) StephenDonohoe 12 — 2
(P D Evans) *a towards rr* **12/1**
19 *shd* **Au Pair (IRE)**[7] 4602 2-8-11 ... KDarley 20 — —
(P W Chapple-Hyam) *dwlt: chsd ldrs in mid-div: swished tail: wknd 2f out* **12/1**
20 *3* **Papillio (IRE)**[22] 4132 2-9-2 ... PatCosgrave 15 — —
(K R Burke) *chsd ldrs in centre: 6th after 1/2-way: effrt 2f out: sn wknd* **12/1**
21 *3* **Ezthegezza**[21] 4154 2-9-2 ... PJSmullen 16 — —
(J S Moore) *a towards rr: eased fnl f* **16/1**

22 7 **Crafty George (IRE)**[34] 3767 2-9-2 .... MCHussey 19 —
(J G Coogan, Ire) *a bhd: trailing fr over 2f out* **66/1**

1m 15.8s (1.30) **Going Correction** +0.35s/f (Good) 22 Ran SP% **143.5**
Speed ratings: **105,97,96,93,92 91,88,82,81,80 80,77,76,76,72 63,62,60,60,56 52,43**
CSF £171.82 TOTE £14.00: £3.70, £2.70, £2.20, £2.60; DF 137.20.
Owner Terry Cummins **Bred** Owen Bourke **Trained** Lydiate, Merseyside

FOCUS
The level of the form behind the easy winner is nothing special, but she looks Listed class at least.

NOTEBOOK
Sudden Impact(IRE) produced an impressive display from the front to run out a clear-cut winner. One of just four previous winners in the line-up, she was not at her best at Chester last time, but had previously produced a useful effort to win a Thirsk maiden. She came away smartly to show up well in the front rank from the outset and nothing was going better heading towards the final furlong. She was starting to draw clear at this point and came well clear in the closing stages to record an emphatic victory. Her trainer felt that she would be well suited by the soft ground and is hopeful that she will eventually make up into a Group-class performer. On this evidence she can hold her own in better company and will be well worth her place at stakes level.
Invincible Ash(IRE) made an encouraging debut at Naas earlier in the month when running fourth to Domingues in an auction race and showed that she had made good progress from that run. She was unable to match the winner in the closing stages, but will not have any trouble landing a maiden.
Houston Dynimo(IRE) had shown some good form in maidens and looked to have a leading chance on some of those efforts, but he was dropping back from 7f. He could never quite work his way into a challenging position having been a little slower away than some of his rivals and can do better moving back up in trip. (op 7/2)
Nikindi(IRE) had not run since April, when he showed a useful level of form in two outings, and he acquitted himself well on his first try at this trip. He will improve from this run and can win more races this season. (op 9/1)
Yali(IRE) did not enjoy the clearest of runs through from over two furlongs out and this was the difference between her finishing in the frame and filling fifth. She ran creditably on her debut at Leopardstown last month and is good enough to win a maiden. (op 9/1)
Dohasa(IRE) was upsides the winner with over a furlong to run, but he could do no more inside the distance. He looks like he will be well suited by dropping back to 5f.
Ceol Loch Aoidh(IRE) was not disgraced after racing prominently for much of the race and fared much better than when finishing down the field in a maiden over this course and distance 13 days ago.
Imperial Decree was never in a position to challenge and possibly found the drop back from 7f too much.
Sir George(IRE) was never able to get involved. (op 9/2)

4833a GALILEO EUROPEAN BREEDERS FUND FUTURITY STKS (GROUP 2) 7f
4:00 (4:00) 2-Y-O **£52,364** (£16,047; £7,601; £2,533; £1,689)

RPR
1 **New Approach (IRE)**[28] 3980 2-9-1 .... KJManning 3 116+
(J S Bolger, Ire) *mde virtually all: rdn and edgd clr 2f out: kpt on wl fnl f* **8/11**[1]
2 3 **Curtain Call (FR)**[38] 3660 2-9-1 .... FMBerry 5 108
(Mrs John Harrington, Ire) *mod 4th: rdn over 2f out: 3rd 1f out: styd on to go 2nd nr fin* **40/1**
3 nk **Henrythenavigator (USA)**[13] 4437 2-9-4 .... KFallon 4 110
(A P O'Brien, Ire) *chsd ldrs: mod 3rd and drvn along 1/2-way: tk clsr order over 2f out: 2nd over 1f out: no imp: no ex cl home* **11/10**[2]
4 11 **Warsaw (IRE)**[13] 4437 2-9-1 .... JAHeffernan 2 80
(A P O'Brien, Ire) *cl 2nd to over 2f out: sn no ex and wknd* **25/1**[3]
5 30 **Pretty Ballerina (USA)**[69] 2699 2-8-12 .... JMurtagh 1 —
(John Joseph Murphy, Ire) *a bhd: trailing thrght: eased fnl f* **66/1**

1m 29.0s (1.50) **Going Correction** +0.35s/f (Good) 5 Ran SP% **113.3**
Speed ratings: **105,101,101,88,54**
CSF £25.68 TOTE £1.60: £1.10, £12.70; DF 18.00.
Owner Mrs J S Bolger **Bred** Lodge Park Stud **Trained** Coolcullen, Co Carlow

FOCUS
A race that has been won by some top-class horses in recent years, most recently last season's outstanding juvenile Teofilo. The winner was impressive but there is a slight question mark over the value of the form.

NOTEBOOK
New Approach(IRE) emerged victorious with an authoritative display. His trainer has made no secret of the regard in which he holds the Galileo colt and it was perhaps quite significant that his path to this race was identical to the one followed by Teofilo. This promised to be the winner's toughest assignment to date and he passed the examination with flying colours. He and Warsaw helped to set a searching early pace that carried them some way clear of Henrythenavigator. Warsaw gave best with two furlongs to run, and it was at this point that Henrythenavigator threatened to get involved. However, hard as he tried, he could never bridge the gap to New Approach, who kept on strongly in the closing stages to cement his position as one of the most exciting juveniles around. Bolger now has the option of sending his charge for either the Parknasilla Hotel Goffs Million or the Irish National Stakes. The colt looks ready to make a successful transition to the highest level and he will take some beating wherever he goes for the remainder of this season. In the longer term he has firmly established himself as one of the forerunners for next year's Classics.
Curtain Call(FR) came through to take second late on. He was struggling to go the early pace but, to his credit, stuck to his task under pressure and came home quite well. He should be well suited by stepping up to 1m, and a maiden victory looks a mere formality on this effort. (op 25/1)
Henrythenavigator(USA) was returning to action 13 days after losing his unbeaten record in the Phoenix Stakes. He steadily closed down the front pair after halfway, having found himself some way back in third early on. However, he could never get on terms with New Approach and had no more to give inside the final furlong, eventually losing second close home. The Kingmambo colt looked a top-drawer juvenile when winning the Coventry, but he has twice met with defeat on soft ground since then. He has questions to answer now, but it would be unfair to draw any firm conclusions about him until he gets back on his favoured good ground. (op 5/4)
Warsaw(IRE) has been unable to build on his early-season promise.
Pretty Ballerina(USA) was in trouble a long way from home.

4836a NEWMARKETRACECOURSES.CO.UK H'CAP 7f
5:35 (5:36) (50-80,79) 3-Y-0+ **£6,303** (£1,468; £647; £373)

RPR
1 **Jilly Why (IRE)**[5] 4668 6-9-3 68 ....(b) JAHeffernan 11 81+
(Paul Green) *trckd ldrs: 8th after 1/2-way: 6th 1 1/2f out: sn led: kpt on wl fr over 1f out* **12/1**
2 1 1/4 **Prince Livius (IRE)**[6] 4650 4-8-1 62 ....(t) EJMcNamara[(10)] 13 70+
(T Hogan, Ire) *mid-div on stands' rail: rdn 2 1/2f out: 5th over 1f out: kpt on wl* **11/1**
3 1 1/2 **Fields Of Green**[18] 4260 4-7-11 55 ....(p) SFoley[(7)] 15 59
(M Halford, Ire) *mid-div: hdwy over 2f out: led briefly 1 1/2f out: 3rd and no ex wl ins fnl f* **7/1**[2]
4 1 **Liffey Bank (IRE)**[13] 4439 3-8-13 69 ....(b) KJManning 10 70
(J T Gorman, Ire) *prom: 2nd 1/2-way: chal over 1 1/2f out: no ex fnl f* **12/1**
5 shd **Distant Times**[20] 4210 6-8-12 63 ....(b) PShanahan 2 64
(Liam McAteer, Ire) *hld up: hdwy on outer 2f out: 4th 1f out: kpt on same pce* **20/1**
6 3 1/2 **Chapelizod (IRE)**[45] 3439 4-8-9 60 ....(p) NGMcCullagh 3 52
(T G McCourt, Ire) *cl up on stands' rail: led 2f out: rdn and hdd under 1 1/2f out: kpt on same pce* **12/1**
7 nk **Twin Sun's (IRE)**[18] 4262 4-9-3 68 .... WJLee 7 59
(Timothy Doyle, Ire) *in rr of mid-div: rdn and kpt on fr 2f out* **33/1**
8 nk **Desert Rat (IRE)**[12] 4466 3-8-7 63 ....(p) PJSmullen 16 53
(J T Gorman, Ire) *cl up: disp ld 1/2-way: rdn and hdd 2f out: kpt on same pce* **8/1**[3]
9 shd **Hazelwood Ridge (IRE)**[17] 4308 4-8-9 60 .... DavidMcCabe 4 50
(Joseph Fox, Ire) *hld up in rr: kpt on one pce fr 2f out* **14/1**
10 nk **Tar (IRE)**[38] 3661 3-9-2 75 .... CPGeoghegan[(3)] 5 64
(Kevin Prendergast, Ire) *hld up towards rr: kpt on same pce fr over 1 1/2f out* **12/1**
11 1 3/4 **Over The Tylery (IRE)**[29] 3930 3-8-5 64 ....(b) PBBeggy[(3)] 17 48
(Eamon Tyrrell, Ire) *trckd ldrs: 5th 1/2-way: rdn over 2f out: sn no ex* **12/1**
12 1 3/4 **Miss Una (IRE)**[20] 4210 5-9-6 71 .... DPMcDonogh 12 50
(Patrick Martin, Ire) *chsd ldrs: 6th 1/2-way: no ex fr 2f out* **6/1**[1]
13 5 **Miss Latina (IRE)**[23] 4115 4-9-6 71 .... CO'Donoghue 19 37
(P J Prendergast, Ire) *in rr of mid-div: no ex fr over 2f out* **16/1**
14 1/2 **Ludwigshafen (IRE)**[19] 4244 3-9-2 72 .... FMBerry 9 37
(John Geoghegan, Ire) *chsd ldrs to 1/2-way: sn no ex* **10/1**
15 shd **Famous Seamus (IRE)**[25] 4053 4-9-4 69 ....(b) MCHussey 18 33
(T J O'Mara, Ire) *nvr a factor* **12/1**
16 3 **Sherafey (IRE)**[5] 4681 3-8-1 60 ....(b[1]) SMGorey[(3)] 6 16
(Edgar Byrne, Ire) *sn led: jnd 1/2-way: hdd & wknd 2f out* **25/1**
17 3 1/2 **Regaleya (IRE)**[140] 951 4-9-4 79 ....(t) SMMcGuinness[(10)] 8 26
(H Rogers, Ire) *a bhd* **20/1**
18 3 1/2 **Inwood (IRE)**[25] 4053 4-9-11 76 ....(t) JMurtagh 14 13
(Paul Magnier, Ire) *bhd: no ex fr 2f out: eased fnl f* **7/1**[2]
L **Tyreless Endeavour (IRE)**[50] 3289 3-8-13 74 .... OCasey[(5)] 1 —
(Peter Casey, Ire) *ltt at s* **25/1**

1m 29.0s (1.50) **Going Correction** +0.35s/f (Good)
WFA 3 from 4yo+ 5lb **20** Ran SP% **146.7**
Speed ratings: **105,103,101,100,100 96,96,95,95,95 93,91,85,85,85 81,77,73,—**
CSF £152.75 CT £1046.84 TOTE £11.10: £2.20, £4.10, £1.60, £4.20; DF 570.30.
Owner Paul Green (Oaklea) **Bred** K & Mrs Cullen **Trained** Lydiate, Merseyside

NOTEBOOK
Jilly Why(IRE), who came over as a travelling companion for Sudden Impact, obliged to win her first race since September 2005. The six-year-old had been holding her form well in a busy campaign and was having her fourth start of the month here. After settling just in behind the leaders, she improved to strike the front with over a furlong to run and soon came clear. This was not the strongest of races, but she won with something to spare and could be able to strike again before the end of the season.
Inwood(IRE) Official explanation: jockey said colt choked from halfway
T/Jkpt: @662.30. Pool of @13,246.50 - 15 winning units. T/Plt: @193.40. Pool of @9,661.50.
II

4834 - 4836a (Foreign Racing) - See Raceform Interactive

1872 BADEN-BADEN (L-H)
Saturday, August 25

OFFICIAL GOING: Good

4837a PREIS DER SCHMUCKWELTEN PFORZHEIM (BBAG SALES RACE) (FILLIES) 6f
2:45 (2:52) 2-Y-O
£33,784 (£13,514; £8,446; £6,757; £3,378; £1,689)

RPR
1 **Manipura (GER)**[20] 2-9-2 .... EPedroza 4 89
(A Wohler, Germany) **18/10**[1]
2 7 **Sina (GER)** 2-9-2 .... AStarke 1 68
(W Hickst, Germany) **106/10**
3 1/2 **My Summer Of Love (FR)** 2-9-2 .... ADeVries 7 66
(K Woodburn) **111/10**
4 nse **Easy Wonder (GER)**[23] 4097 2-9-2 .... JamesDoyle 5 66
(I A Wood) *racd in 2nd: 4th and rdn along ent st: kpt on at one pce* **34/10**[3]
5 1/2 **Trendy (GER)** 2-9-2 .... J-PCarvalho 6 65
(H J Groschel, Germany) **11/1**
6 nk **De La Vista (GER)** 2-9-2 .... WPanov 8 64
(W Hickst, Germany) **122/10**
7 1/2 **Lips Arrow (GER)** 2-9-2 ....(b) AHelfenbein 3 62
(Andreas Lowe, Germany) **22/1**
8 1 1/2 **Sacota** 2-9-2 .... TMundry 9 58
(E Kurdu, Germany) **26/1**
9 18 **Fly My Dream (GER)** 2-9-2 .... ASuborics 2 4
(Mario Hofer, Germany) **28/10**[2]
10 1 1/4 **Auenlove (GER)** 2-9-2 .... JiriPalik 10 —
(M Weber, Germany) **21/1**

69.72 secs (-0.57) **10** Ran SP% **130.1**
(including 10 Europ stake): WIN 28; PL 17, 27, 29; SF 382.
Owner Stall Dagobert **Bred** Stiftung Gestut Fahrhof **Trained** Germany

NOTEBOOK
Easy Wonder(GER) is progressing with racing and connections were taking advantage of her qualification for this valuable race. They were rewarded with a good prize for finishing fourth, just missing out on the placings, and she looks capable of winning before too long.

4838a PREIS DER SPARKASSEN-FINANZGRUPPE (GROUP 3) 1m 2f
4:00 (4:11) 4-Y-0+ **£22,297** (£9,459; £3,378; £2,027)

RPR
1 **Wiesenpfad (FR)**[21] 4-9-0 .... ADeVries 4 115
(W Hickst, Germany) *in tch in 5th or 6th: hdwy to ld 1f out: r.o strly* **29/10**[1]
2 2 1/2 **Kiton (GER)**[21] 4191 6-8-12 .... TMundry 6 108
(P Rau, Germany) *hld up in 7th or 8th: styd on down outside fr over 1f out: fin wl* **103/10**
3 1 1/2 **Simple Exchange (IRE)**[21] 6-8-13 ow3 .... THellier 3 106
(A Savujev, Czech Republic) *prom in 3rd or 4th: hrd rdn and ev ch over 1 1/2f out: one pce* **30/1**

4 nk **Fair Breeze (GER)**[57] 3075 4-8-7 .... ASuborics 7 100
(Mario Hofer, Germany) *cl up on ins: kpt on steadily on ins rail fnl 2f* **117/10**

5 hd **Waleria (GER)**[27] 4013 4-8-10 .... JBojko 13 102
(H J Groschel, Germany) *cl up: hdwy to ld 1 1/2f out: hdd 1f out: one pce* **42/10**[2]

6 1 1/2 **Soterio (GER)**[49] 7-8-10 .... WMongil 9 100
(W Baltromei, Germany) *hld up: styd on steadily fnl 2f* **28/1**

7 shd **Simonas (IRE)**[308] 6109 8-9-0 .... EPedroza 11 104
(A Wohler, Germany) *hld up in rr: sme late hdwy* **5/1**[3]

8 3 **Chiron (GER)**[279] 6529 6-8-10 .... ABoschert 2 94
(Dr A Bolte, Germany) *set str pce: led to 1 1/2f out: wknd* **23/1**

9 1 **Sexy Lady (GER)**[20] 4217 4-8-5 .... ABest 12 87
(P Rau, Germany) *a towards rr* **163/10**

10 1 1/2 **One Little David (GER)**[20] 7-8-10 .... J-PCarvalho 5 90
(P Vovcenko, Germany) *nvr bttr than midfield* **153/10**

11 5 **Poseidon Adventure (IRE)**[27] 4013 4-8-12 .... AHelfenbein 8 83
(W Figge, Germany) *nvr a factor* **5/1**[3]

12 2 **Dream Of Gold (GER)**[48] 4-8-10 ....(b) APietsch 1 77
(D K Richardson, Germany) *racd in 2nd: wknd over 2f out* **47/1**

13 1 **Nordtanzerin (GER)**[57] 3075 4-8-12 .... AStarke 10 77
(P Schiergen, Germany) *nvr a factor* **84/10**

2m 0.83s (-4.16) 13 Ran SP% **130.4**
WIN 39; PL 20, 29, 53; SF 577.
Owner Frau Heide Harzheim **Bred** Gestut Ravensberg **Trained** Germany

[4795] BEVERLEY (R-H)
Sunday, August 26

OFFICIAL GOING: Good to firm (9.4)
After 5mm water had been put on the straight course and the home turn overnight the verdict was 'much better, quick ground but safe'.
Wind: moderate 1/2 against Weather: fine

4841 EUROPEAN BREEDERS' FUND MAIDEN STKS 1m 100y
2:00 (2:00) (Class 5) 2-Y-O £3,562 (£1,059; £529; £264) Stalls High

Form RPR
65 1 **Keenes Day (FR)**[9] 4586 2-9-3 0 .... GregFairley 2 75
(M Johnston) *hld up: n.m.r over 3f out: swtchd ins 2f out: led ins fnl f: jst hld on* **2/1**[1]

5 2 shd **The Riddler (IRE)**[29] 3958 2-9-3 0 .... KDarley 8 75
(J A Osborne) *set mod pce: qcknd 4f out: hdd ins fnl f: rallied and jst hld* **2/1**[1]

3 3 2 **Stop On**[17] 4325 2-9-3 0 .... DarrylHolland 5 71
(M R Channon) *sn trcking ldrs: rdn and edgd lft over 2f out: edgd rt and styd on same pce ins fnl f* **5/2**[2]

6 4 1 **Elk Trail (IRE)**[64] 2889 2-9-3 0 .... MickyFenton 3 69
(T P Tate) *stmbld s: sn trcking ldrs: one pce fnl 2f* **16/1**

0602 5 1 1/4 **Destinys Dream (IRE)**[10] 4524 2-8-12 62 .... RoystonFfrench 1 61
(Mrs A Duffield) *hld up: effrt on outer over 3f out: edgd lft: kpt on same pce fnl 2f* **7/1**[3]

1m 48.81s (1.41) **Going Correction** -0.075s/f (Good) 5 Ran SP% **113.6**
Speed ratings (Par 94): **89,88,86,85,84**
CSF £6.58 TOTE £3.00: £1.10, £2.10; EX 6.10.
Owner Mrs R J Jacobs **Bred** Newsells Park Stud Ltd **Trained** Middleham Moor, N Yorks

FOCUS
A modest maiden run at a steady pace. The principals did not step forward on their previous form.

NOTEBOOK
Keenes Day(FR), who had a little more expereince than his main rivals, was held up and then got the gap up the rail when the runner-up drifted. He got to the front and did enough to hold of the renewed effort of that rival. He should not get too high a handicap mark after this. (tchd 9-4)
The Riddler(IRE) ◆, whose dam won over sprint trips as a juvenile, has clearly inherited stamina from his sire. He made the running but drifted off the rail in the straight letting the winner through, which arguably cost him the race. He should be able to pick up a similar contest before long. (op 7-2)
Stop On, another out of a sprint juvenile winner, caught the eye on his debut but appeared to have every chance here and was not good enough. He is likely to be seen in a better light once he is qualified for handicaps. (op 9-4 tchd 2-1)
Elk Trail(IRE), whose debut was on totally different ground two months previously, is bred to be speedy but races as if he needs time and distance. (op 14-1)
Destinys Dream(IRE), the most experienced in the field, put up her best effort on this course last time, when runner-up in an extended 7f nursery off a mark of 58. She was unable to land a blow having been held up, and may have preferred a stronger gallop. She is still a reasonable guide to the level of this contest. (op 11-2)

4842 JOHN JENKINS MEMORIAL CLAIMING STKS 7f 100y
2:35 (2:35) (Class 5) 3-Y-O £3,238 (£963; £481; £240) Stalls High

Form RPR
0335 1 **Myfrenchconnection (IRE)**[11] 4491 3-8-12 51 .... MickyFenton 16 57
(P T Midgley) *trckd ldrs: styd on to ld wl ins fnl f* **7/1**

4045 2 nk **Lady Valentino**[25] 4078 3-8-9 49 .... TomEaves 15 53
(M Dods) *led: stuck on fnl 2f: hdd nr fin* **14/1**

0003 3 3 **Pennyrock (IRE)**[13] 4450 3-9-0 59 .... GrahamGibbons 1 51+
(J J Quinn) *towards rr: hdwy over 3f out: nt clr run over 2f out: edgd lft over 1f out: swtchd ins and styd on last 150yds* **4/1**[2]

0450 4 hd **Davaye**[12] 4480 3-8-11 62 .... PaulMulrennan 12 47
(K R Burke) *trckd ldrs: effrt over 3f out: kpt on same pce fnl 2f* **13/2**[3]

6000 5 2 1/2 **Cherri Fosfate**[14] 4429 3-9-0 54 ....(b) DanielTudhope 2 44+
(D Carroll) *s.i.s: hdwy on outside over 3f out: hung bdly rt over 1f out: nvr rchd ldrs* **20/1**

-566 6 3/4 **First Valentini**[8] 4616 3-8-7 45 .... PaulFessey 14 35
(N Bycroft) *in rr: styd on fnl 2f: nt rch ldrs* **33/1**

0330 7 1 **Mister Always**[3] 4742 3-8-12 50 .... GaryBartley[(7)] 9 45
(B P J Baugh) *in rr: hdwy over 2f out: nvr nr ldrs* **20/1**

5300 8 nk **Tenterhooks (IRE)**[69] 2718 3-7-10 43 ....(be) DanielleMcCreery[(7)] 4 28
(A J McCabe) *chsd ldrs: edgd rt over 2f out: one pce* **40/1**

0-04 9 2 **Sahara Dawn (IRE)**[20] 4220 3-8-4 40 .... KellyHarrison[(5)] 13 29
(D Carroll) *mid-div: kpt on fnl 2f: nvr on terms* **40/1**

0050 10 shd **Mandy's Maestro (USA)**[12] 4478 3-8-10 43 .... TonyHamilton 5 30
(R M Whitaker) *chsd ldrs: wknd over 1f out* **40/1**

0053 11 4 **Bunderos (IRE)**[22] 4155 3-8-4 44 .... DaleGibson 8 14
(R A Fahey) *mid-div: drvn over 4f out: lost pl over 2f out* **14/1**

3021 12 2 1/2 **Smash N'Grab (IRE)**[25] 4071 3-8-11 56 .... NCallan 11 14
(K A Ryan) *chsd ldrs: effrt 3f out: wkng whn hmpd over 1f out: sn eased* **2/1**[1]

03-0 13 4 **Captain Nemo (USA)**[46] 3411 3-9-0 65 ....(b[1]) PhillipMakin 10 7
(T D Barron) *in rr: drvn over 3f out: nvr on terms* **17/2**

0004 14 6 **Flushed**[40] 3605 3-8-1 47 ....(be) RobbieEgan[(7)] 3 —
(A J McCabe) *chsd ldrs on outer: lost pl over 2f out* **50/1**

1m 32.96s (-1.35) **Going Correction** -0.075s/f (Good) 14 Ran SP% **124.8**
Speed ratings (Par 100): **104,103,100,100,97 96,95,94,92,92 87,84,80,73**
CSF £96.85 TOTE £9.80: £2.70, £3.90, £2.20; EX 130.20.Pennyrock was claimed by Alan Edward Jones for £10,000.
Owner J F Wright **Bred** Mrs Stephanie Winters **Trained** Westow, N Yorks

FOCUS
A moderate contest but run at a good gallop, although it was not easy to come from off the pace. The form has been rated around the first two.
Smash N'Grab(IRE) Official explanation: jockey said filly was unsuited by the ground

4843 CHARLES ELSEY MEMORIAL H'CAP 1m 4f 16y
3:05 (3:05) (Class 5) (0-75,75) 3-Y-O+ £3,886 (£1,156; £577; £288) Stalls High

Form RPR
-501 1 **Make Haste (IRE)**[28] 4003 3-9-3 74 .... NCallan 5 82+
(R Charlton) *chsd ldrs: pushed along 6f out: n.m.r over 2f out: swtchd outside over 1f out: str run to ld nr fin* **7/4**[1]

1053 2 nk **Pretty Demanding (IRE)**[20] 4240 3-9-2 73 .... DarrylHolland 8 81
(M G Quinlan) *hld up in rr: hdwy over 3f out: led 1f out: jst ct* **11/1**

-336 3 1 3/4 **Edas**[8] 4284 5-9-3 64 .... GrahamGibbons 11 69
(J J Quinn) *led early: trckd ldrs: chal 1f out: styd on same pce* **9/1**

6040 4 1 **Nelsons Column (IRE)**[22] 4171 4-10-0 75 .... TomEaves 10 78
(G M Moore) *sn led: hdd 1f out: kpt on same pce* **16/1**

2610 5 3/4 **Its Moon (IRE)**[11] 4511 3-9-3 74 .... DanielTudhope 2 76
(T D Walford) *hld up: smooth hdwy over 4f out: styd on same pce fnl 2f* **8/1**[3]

4006 6 3/4 **Dee Cee Elle**[23] 4139 3-8-7 64 .... GregFairley 7 65
(M Johnston) *chsd ldrs: edgd rt over 1f out: one pce* **11/2**[2]

6034 7 2 1/2 **Baan (USA)**[12] 4481 4-9-13 74 .... RoystonFfrench 1 71
(M Johnston) *drvn along to chse ldrs 9f out: wknd over 1f out* **10/1**

1-00 8 shd **Zefooha (FR)**[73] 2598 3-8-8 70 .... KellyHarrison[(5)] 6 67
(T D Walford) *hld up in midfield: effrt over 2f out: nvr trbld ldrs* **33/1**

5-00 9 2 1/2 **Jack Of Trumps (IRE)**[21] 4194 7-9-12 73 .... TonyHamilton 3 66
(G Wragg) *hld up in mid-div: effrt and edgd rt over 2f out: btn whn hmpd over 1f out* **8/1**[3]

5600 10 8 **Boppys Dancer**[17] 4333 4-8-9 56 oh10 ....(p) MickyFenton 9 36
(P T Midgley) *in rr: hung bdly lft over 3f out and racd alone stands' side: sn bhd* **66/1**

-000 11 6 **Rosie's Glory (USA)**[21] 4205 3-8-12 69 .... KDarley 12 39
(B J Meehan) *chsd ldrs: drvn over 4f out: wkng whn hmpd over 1f out: lost pl and eased* **14/1**

2m 38.04s (-2.17) **Going Correction** -0.075s/f (Good)
WFA 3 from 4yo+ 10lb 11 Ran SP% **118.4**
Speed ratings (Par 103): **104,103,102,101,101 100,99,99,97,92 88**
CSF £22.88 CT £142.24 TOTE £2.70: £1.30, £2.30, £3.00; EX 22.70.
Owner B E Nielsen **Bred** Epona Bloodstock Ltd **Trained** Beckhampton, Wilts
■ Stewards' Enquiry : N Callan 14-day ban (takes into account previous offences; 3 days deferred): careless riding (Sep 14-24)

FOCUS
A fair handicap in which the favourite made hard work of scoring. The front pair are progressive and the form has been rated at face value.
Boppys Dancer Official explanation: jockey said gelding hung left

4844 BRITANNIA RESCUE NURSERY 5f
3:40 (3:40) (Class 3) 2-Y-O £6,477 (£1,927; £963; £481) Stalls High

Form RPR
031 1 **Secret Asset (IRE)**[78] 2451 2-9-7 88 .... DavidAllan 5 94
(W M Brisbourne) *mde all: stmbld sn after s: kpt on wl fnl f* **4/1**[3]

6252 2 1 **Natmana**[17] 4315 2-8-3 70 .... RoystonFfrench 3 72
(M R Channon) *chsd ldng pair: wnt 2nd over 1f out: kpt on same pce* **11/4**[1]

013 3 1 3/4 **Ginger Pickle**[12] 4484 2-8-12 79 .... PhillipMakin 4 75
(J R Weymes) *chsd ldrs: sn drvn along: styd on fnl f* **15/2**

1622 4 1/2 **Style Award**[12] 4476 2-8-2 72 .... AndrewMullen[(3)] 2 66
(W J H Ratcliffe) *trckd ldrs: kpt on same pce appr fnl f* **6/1**

322 5 3 **Liberty Ship**[20] 4221 2-8-8 75 .... DarrylHolland 1 58
(J D Bethell) *sn drvn along on outer: nvr gng pce* **11/2**

633 6 shd **Woodford Regen**[32] 3833 2-7-5 65 .... AdeleRothery[(7)] 6 48
(M W Easterby) *outpcd and lost pl over 3f out: edgd lft over 1f out: kpt on ins fnl f* **28/1**

2021 7 2 **Meridian Line (IRE)**[17] 4310 2-9-2 83 .... NCallan 8 59
(J G Portman) *chsd wnr: wknd over 1f out* **3/1**[2]

63.09 secs (-0.91) **Going Correction** -0.225s/f (Firm) 7 Ran SP% **116.5**
Speed ratings (Par 98): **98,96,93,92,88 87,84**
CSF £15.99 CT £79.14 TOTE £4.40: £2.00, £2.50; EX 16.10.
Owner Kinsale Racing **Bred** Mrs C Hartery **Trained** Great Ness, Shropshire

FOCUS
A fair nursery and the form should work out.

NOTEBOOK
Secret Asset(IRE), who had subsequent Listed winner Captain Gerrard among his victims when scoring at Haydock in June, had not run since (he refused to go in the stalls at Bath a month ago) and was giving a fair amount of weight away all round. However, he broke well and made all the running, never looking likely to be reeled in. He is a progressive sort and may be worth a try in better company this autumn, although he is untried on any ground other than fast. (op 3-1)
Natmana has now been runner-up in three of his five starts, but appeared to do nothing wrong although he could make no impression on the winner from halfway. He will find easier tasks though and a stiff track seems to suit. (op 4-1)
Ginger Pickle, dropping back in trip and racing on fast ground for the first time, stayed on late again and gives the impression that he needs soft ground to be seen at his best. (op 8-1)
Style Award is a fair guide to the level of the form, having run similar races in nurseries this month. She needs some help from the Handicapper if she is going to win again this year though. (op 5-1 tchd 13-2)
Liberty Ship, making his handicap debut, never really got into contention. (op 5-1 tchd 9-2 and 6-1)
Woodford Regen was unable to go the pace on her first try on fast ground. (op 16-1)

Meridian Line(IRE) tried to match strides with the winner early on and paid the penalty in the closing stages. Official explanation: trainer had no explanation for the poor form shown; jockey said filly had no more to give (op 4-1 tchd 9-2)

4845 BEVERLEY LIONS MAIDEN STKS — 1m 1f 207y

4:15 (4:16) (Class 5) 3-Y-0+ — £3,238 (£963; £481; £240) Stalls High

Form				RPR
3	1		**Evening Affair**[10] 4549 3-8-12 0 DarryllHolland 4	53
			(Saeed Bin Suroor) *sn w ldrs: chal over 5f out: led over 1f out: hung lft: hld on towards fin* **3/1**[2]	
032	2	hd	**Muqadam (IRE)**[11] 4492 3-9-3 71 KDarley 3	58
			(Sir Michael Stoute) *trckd ldrs: effrt over 3f out: rdn over 2f out: upsides jst ins fnl f: edgd rt and jst hld* **2/5**[1]	
0-00	3	½	**Hits Only Vic (USA)**[192] 469 3-9-3 44 DanielTudhope 2	57
			(D Carroll) *hld up wl in tch: effrt over 3f out: upsides jst ins fnl f: no ex* **33/1**	
-502	4	4	**Musical Land (IRE)**[15] 4411 3-9-3 63 PhillipMakin 7	49
			(J R Weymes) *trckd ldr: reminders over 3f out: upsides jst ins fnl f: sn wknd* **10/1**[3]	
000	5	3	**Whodunit (UAE)**[27] 4019 3-9-3 48 DavidAllan 6	43
			(P W Hiatt) *led: hdd over 1f out: wknd fnl 150yds* **28/1**	

2m 6.40s (-0.90) **Going Correction** -0.075s/f (Good)
WFA 3 from 4yo 8lb — **5** Ran SP% **111.9**
Speed ratings (Par 103): **100,99,99,96,93**
CSF £4.69 TOTE £3.50: £1.40, £1.10; EX 5.00.
Owner Godolphin **Bred** Darley **Trained** Newmarket, Suffolk
■ Stewards' Enquiry : K Darley caution: careless riding

FOCUS
A weak and uncompetitive maiden that was steadily run and produced a surprisingly close finish. The third and fifth hold down the form.

4846 RACING AGAIN ON 11TH SEPTEMBER FILLIES' H'CAP — 1m 1f 207y

4:50 (4:50) (Class 6) (0-65,65) 3-Y-0+ — £3,238 (£963; £481; £240) Stalls High

Form				RPR
0001	1		**Paradise Walk**[11] 4491 3-9-7 65 PaulMulrennan 6	72+
			(E W Tuer) *trckd ldrs: led over 1f out: styd on wl ins fnl f* **7/2**[2]	
-006	2	1 ½	**Kimono My House**[33] 3825 3-8-8 52 TonyHamilton 14	56
			(J G Given) *in tch: effrt over 3f out: styd on and upsides jst ins fnl f: kpt on same pce* **16/1**	
4330	3	nk	**Brastar Jelois (FR)**[6] 4660 4-9-3 58 (p) RussellKennemore(5) 8	61
			(R Hollinshead) *hld up in rr: hdwy on outside over 4f out: almost upsides jst ins fnl f: kpt on same pce* **10/1**	
6-05	4	½	**Bollin Dolly**[8] 4615 4-9-13 63 DavidAllan 4	65+
			(T D Easterby) *hld up wl in tch: nt clr run over 2f out: styd on and upsides jst ins fnl f: no ex* **3/1**[1]	
-041	5	4	**Awaken**[15] 4410 6-9-5 55 RoystonFfrench 12	49
			(Miss Tracy Waggott) *hld up in rr: hdwy 3f out: nvr rchd ldrs* **7/1**	
0256	6	½	**Showtime Annie**[4] 4713 6-8-12 48 (b) MickyFenton 16	41
			(A Bailey) *trckd ldrs: effrt 3f out: upsides 1f out: sn wknd* **16/1**	
0006	7	½	**Altos Reales**[7] 4632 3-8-0 47 DominicFox(3) 10	39
			(D Shaw) *s.i.s: reminders after s: in rr tl styd on fnl 2f: nvr nr ldrs* **25/1**	
2463	8	nk	**Royal Citadel (IRE)**[15] 4383 4-8-9 50 KellyHarrison(5) 13	42
			(Mrs L B Normile) *chsd ldrs: one pce fnl 2f* **6/1**[3]	
3200	9	1 ¼	**Falimar**[25] 4081 3-9-2 60 TomEaves 5	49
			(Miss J A Camacho) *trckd ldrs: wkng whn n.m.r over 1f out* **14/1**	
0500	10	3 ½	**Buds Dilemma**[12] 4480 3-8-1 45 PaulQuinn 9	27
			(I W McInnes) *led: hung lft and hdd over 2f out: wknd and eased over 1f out* **50/1**	
6360	11	hd	**Kudbeme**[9] 4562 5-9-3 56 JamieMoriarty(3) 7	38
			(N Bycroft) *s.v.s: hdwy on ins over 4f out: chsng ldrs over 1f out: hung rt and wknd* **15/2**	
00	12	2 ½	**Summer Gift**[64] 2894 4-9-5 55 GregFairley 15	32
			(J O'Reilly) *trckd ldr: led on ins over 2f out: hdd over 1f out: wknd qckly* **25/1**	

2m 5.67s (-1.63) **Going Correction** -0.075s/f (Good)
WFA 3 from 4yo+ 8lb — **12** Ran SP% **122.9**
Speed ratings (Par 98): **103,101,101,101,97 97,97,96,95,93 92,90**
CSF £59.89 CT £530.60 TOTE £3.50: £1.80, £4.30, £3.40; EX 121.20 Place 6 £43.40, Place 5 £30.16 .
Owner E Tuer **Bred** Coln Valley Stud **Trained** Great Smeaton, N Yorks

FOCUS
A moderate fillies' handicap in which the principals came from off the pace and the first four were clear. The winner is progressive but this was not a strong race.
Bollin Dolly Official explanation: jockey said filly was denied a clear run
Buds Dilemma Official explanation: jockey said filly hung left
T/Plt: £86.60 to a £1 stake. Pool: £50,639.40. 426.85 winning tickets. T/Qpdt: £7.00 to a £1 stake. Pool: £2,821.20. 295.90 winning tickets. WG

4803 GOODWOOD (R-H)

Sunday, August 26

OFFICIAL GOING: Good
Wind: light, acorss Weather: Sunny, warm

4847 BBC SOUTHERN COUNTIES RADIO STKS (H'CAP) — 1m 1f

2:10 (2:12) (Class 4) (0-85,85) 3-Y-0 — £6,477 (£1,927; £963; £481) Stalls High

Form				RPR
211	1		**Caravel (IRE)**[16] 4354 3-9-2 78 SebSanders 8	98+
			(Sir Mark Prescott) *trckd ldrs: prog over 2f out: led over 1f out and sn rdn clr: in n.d after* **2/1**[1]	
310	2	2	**Jamboretta (IRE)**[24] 4111 3-9-2 78 RyanMoore 1	90
			(Sir Michael Stoute) *dropped in fr wd draw and hld up in last pair: stl in last trio whn nt clr run 2f out: r.o wl to take 2nd fnl 100yds: no ch w wnr* **6/1**[3]	
2301	3	1 ¾	**Rule Of Life**[10] 4551 3-9-6 82 RichardHughes 12	90
			(B W Hills) *trckd ldrs: rdn wl over 2f out and nt qckn: styd on fr over 1f out: tk 3rd nr fin: no threat to ldng pair* **5/1**[2]	
0311	4	nk	**Good Effect (USA)**[11] 4510 3-8-6 71 AndrewElliott(3) 7	78
			(A P Jarvis) *chsd ldr to wl over 1f out: wnt 2nd again jst over 1f out: no ch w wnr: edgd rt after: wknd fnl 100yds* **16/1**	
1130	5	shd	**Samsons Son**[24] 4093 3-9-7 83 DaneO'Neill 5	90
			(J R Best) *hld up towards rr: rdn and prog over 2f out: nt on terms w ldrs wl over 1f out: styd on same pce* **12/1**	
-533	6	2 ½	**Practicallyperfect (IRE)**[24] 4111 3-9-0 76 JimmyFortune 4	78
			(P D Evans) *hld up in midfield: prog over 2f out to press ldrs wl over 1f out: hanging rt after: wknd fnl f* **12/1**	
0015	7	1	**Hunting Tower**[17] 4331 3-9-9 85 LDettori 3	85
			(R Hannon) *hld up in last: rdn on outer 3f out: modest prog 2f out: wl btn over 1f out* **17/2**	
-300	8	nk	**Zoom One**[22] 4147 3-9-5 81 JosedeSouza 11	80
			(M P Tregoning) *settled in midfield: shkn up and no prog 2f out: no imp on ldrs after* **13/2**	
1130	9	½	**Beau Sancy**[24] 4111 3-8-12 79 LukeMorris(5) 10	77
			(R A Harris) *sn in midfield: u.p and struggling over 3f out: brief effrt 2f out: sn no prog* **20/1**	
1336	10	3 ½	**El Dececy (USA)**[17] 4332 3-9-5 81 TPO'Shea 15	72
			(D J Murphy) *led: kicked on over 3f out: hrd rdn over 2f out: hdd & wknd over 1f out* **40/1**	
3610	11	3	**Spume (IRE)**[4] 4704 3-9-3 79 (t) LPKeniry 9	63
			(D J Murphy) *a towards rr: last and wl btn jst over 2f out* **33/1**	
3050	12	½	**Eau Good**[8] 4603 3-9-7 83 MichaelHills 13	66
			(B G Powell) *hld up in rr on inner: shkn up over 2f out: no prog: wknd wl over 1f out* **25/1**	
-000	13	11	**Prince Of Elegance**[24] 4092 3-9-7 83 JimCrowley 6	43
			(Mrs A J Perrett) *prom: hrd rdn over 3f out: sn wknd: t.o* **66/1**	

1m 55.52s (-1.34) **Going Correction** +0.05s/f (Good) — **13** Ran SP% **124.9**
Speed ratings (Par 102): **107,105,103,103,103 101,100,99,99,96 93,93,83**
CSF £13.66 CT £59.11 TOTE £2.80: £1.50, £2.30, £2.20; EX 14.30.
Owner Neil Greig - Osborne House **Bred** G A M Grothier **Trained** Newmarket, Suffolk

FOCUS
A decent three-year-old handicap run at a good pace and with the time decent and the first three progressive the form looks solid.

4848 CHICHESTER OBSERVER FILLIES' STKS (H'CAP) — 7f

2:45 (2:45) (Class 4) (0-85,85) 3-Y-0 — £6,477 (£1,927; £963; £481) Stalls High

Form				RPR
4461	1		**Nice To Know (FR)**[17] 4326 3-8-9 71 RyanMoore 6	78
			(G L Moore) *settled wl in rr: rdn and prog wl over 1f out: led last 100yds: a holding rivals after* **9/2**[1]	
321	2	½	**Plucky**[19] 4258 3-9-6 82 JimmyFortune 4	88
			(J H M Gosden) *hld up wl in rr: prog on outer wl over 1f out: led ins fnl f: sn hdd: styd on* **5/1**[2]	
0053	3	shd	**Millestan (IRE)**[11] 4509 3-9-6 82 RichardHughes 3	88
			(H R A Cecil) *hld up in last trio: stl last wl over 1f out: rdn and r.o wl fnl f: too much to do* **8/1**	
5613	4	1	**Gap Princess (IRE)**[15] 4407 3-8-4 66 oh1 PaulHanagan 1	69
			(R A Fahey) *sn trckd ldrs on outer: rdn 2f out: drifted to inner over 1f out: styd on: nt pce to chal* **20/1**	
2615	5	shd	**Furbeseta**[18] 4276 3-9-2 78 LDettori 11	81
			(L M Cumani) *trckd ldrs: swtchd to inner ins 2f out: rdn to ld jst over 1f out: hdd and outpcd ins fnl f* **6/1**[3]	
1465	6	1 ¼	**Shustraya**[16] 4360 3-9-5 81 GeorgeBaker 13	80
			(P J Makin) *hld up wl in rr on inner: stl in last pair wl over 1f out: rdn and styd on: nt pce to chal* **20/1**	
2216	7	¾	**Gentle Guru**[23] 4123 3-9-3 79 JimCrowley 10	76+
			(R T Phillips) *hld up in midfield: n.m.r over 2f out to over 1f out: styd on same pce: n.d* **14/1**	
-106	8	½	**Zonta Zitkala**[22] 4170 3-8-10 72 SebSanders 8	68
			(R M Beckett) *swtchd to r on inner sn after s: hld up and t.k.h: effrt 2f out: hanging and nt qckn over 1f out: kpt on* **20/1**	
3224	9	nk	**Kashmir Lady (FR)**[19] 4257 3-8-9 71 ow1 DaneO'Neill 5	66
			(H Candy) *dwlt: hld up in rr on outer: rdn over 2f out: plugged on same pce* **16/1**	
-620	10	hd	**Regal Quest (IRE)**[11] 4502 3-9-2 78 LPKeniry 15	73
			(S Kirk) *hld up in midfield on inner: cl up over 1f out: fdd fnl f* **40/1**	
032	11	nk	**Bluebelle Dancer (IRE)**[5] 4684 3-8-4 66 oh2 PaulDoe 7	60
			(W R Muir) *pressed ldr: upsides over 1f out: sn wknd* **33/1**	
3-62	12	1 ¾	**Ficoma**[22] 4163 3-8-13 75 AdamKirby 14	64
			(C G Cox) *led at mod pce: rdn 2f out: hdd & wknd jst over 1f out* **8/1**	
-600	13	1 ½	**Pretty Majestic (IRE)**[15] 4389 3-9-9 85 (v[1]) TPO'Shea 2	70
			(M R Channon) *awkward s: t.k.h and sn pressed ldng pair: wknd over 1f out* **20/1**	
2021	14	nk	**Apple Blossom (IRE)**[22] 4178 3-8-12 77 AndrewElliott(3) 12	61
			(G Wragg) *cl up on inner tl wknd jst over 1f out* **14/1**	
0334	15	2 ½	**Princess Valerina**[11] 4509 3-9-7 83 MichaelHills 9	60
			(B W Hills) *trckd ldrs: rdn and wknd wl over 1f out* **11/1**	

1m 28.17s (0.13) **Going Correction** +0.05s/f (Good) — **15** Ran SP% **123.3**
Speed ratings (Par 99): **101,100,100,99,99 97,96,96,95,95 95,93,91,91,88**
CSF £23.75 CT £181.54 TOTE £5.00: £1.90, £2.00, £3.50; EX 12.20.
Owner C S C Hancock **Bred** Gainsborough Stud Management Ltd **Trained** Woodingdean, E Sussex

FOCUS
A good fillies' handicap on paper, but the pace was steady for much of the way, resulting in a few of these being short of room as the field bunched up early in the straight, and the form probably wants treating with some caution.

4849 E B F ALICE KEPPEL STKS (FILLIES' H'CAP) (LISTED RACE) — 1m 1f 192y

3:20 (3:23) (Class 1) (0-110,98) 3-Y-0+
£15,898 (£6,025; £3,015; £1,503; £753; £378) Stalls High

Form				RPR
1120	1		**Samira Gold (FR)**[25] 4059 3-9-5 94 SebSanders 6	103
			(L M Cumani) *hld up in wl in rr: rdn over 2f out: prog on outer wl over 1f out: r.o wl fnl f to ld nr fin* **4/1**[2]	
-104	2	½	**Cliche (IRE)**[50] 3332 3-9-7 96 RyanMoore 5	104
			(Sir Michael Stoute) *trckd ldrs: prog to ld over 2f out: drvn over 1f out: styd on: hdd nr fin* **4/1**[2]	
4203	3	1	**Russian Rosie (IRE)**[11] 4503 3-9-6 95 JamesDoyle 9	101
			(J G Portman) *prom: rdn to chse ldr 2f out to ins fnl f: kpt on same pce* **25/1**	
2032	4	hd	**Ronaldsay**[25] 4060 3-8-9 84 RichardHughes 3	90
			(R Hannon) *hld up in last pair: effrt over 2f out: rdn and nt qckn wl over 1f out: styd on wl fnl f: unable to chal* **6/1**[3]	
5450	5	shd	**Summer's Eve**[30] 3897 4-9-10 91 DaneO'Neill 4	96
			(H Candy) *hld up wl in rr: prog on outer gng wl 3f out: rdn and nt qckn 2f out: styd on fnl f: nvr able to chal* **12/1**	
2024	6	¾	**Flying Clarets (IRE)**[28] 4005 4-9-11 92 PaulHanagan 2	96
			(R A Fahey) *trckd ldrs: prog to ld over 6f out and injected pce: styd on inner and hdd over 2f out: one pce* **8/1**	

/0-5 **7** *4* **Chatila (USA)**[113] 1466 4-9-9 **90** JimmyFortune 1 86
(J H M Gosden) *dwlt: wl in rr: prog on inner over 3f out: chsng ldrs 2f out: hanging and no imp over 1f out: wknd* **25/1**

1-10 **8** *3/4* **Measured Tempo**[86] 2211 3-9-9 **98** LDettori 12 97+
(Saeed Bin Suroor) *settled in midfield: hanging fr over 4f out: effrt to chse ldrs 2f out: sn wknd and eased* **3/1**[1]

1355 **9** *nk* **La Spezia (IRE)**[36] 3744 3-9-3 **92** JimCrowley 7 86
(M L W Bell) *dwlt: pushed up to chse ldrs: wknd 2f out* **25/1**

1/0- **10** *2 1/2* **High Reef (FR)**[23] 4143 9-9-5 **86** LPKeniry 11 75
(C F Swan, Ire) *a towards rr: shkn up and no prog over 2f out* **16/1**

1050 **11** *3* **Fusili (IRE)**[162] 701 4-9-9 **90** GeorgeBaker 10 73
(N P Littmoden) *led to over 6f out: chsd ldr to wl over 2f out: wknd wl over 1f out: heavily eased last 150yds* **40/1**

0-50 **12** *11* **Cumin (USA)**[30] 3897 3-9-6 **95** MichaelHills 8 56
(B W Hills) *nvr beyond midfield: wknd wl over 2f out: t.o* **16/1**

2m 7.48s (-0.27) **Going Correction** +0.05s/f (Good)
WFA 3 from 4yo+ 8lb **12** Ran SP% **123.8**
Speed ratings (Par 108): **103,102,101,101,101 100,97,97,96,94 92,83**
CSF £20.55 CT £368.42 TOTE £5.70: £2.10, £1.90, £4.60; EX 26.10.
Owner Jaber Abdullah **Bred** L L C Woodside Farms **Trained** Newmarket, Suffolk

FOCUS
A reasonable fillies' and mares' Listed handicap, although none of these were rated in the 100s. The first three all improved and the form looks solid. The pace was good.

NOTEBOOK
Samira Gold(FR) ◆ boiled over when below form in a 1m4f handicap at the Glorious meeting last time, but she had previously shown herself a smart prospect and, seemingly much calmer this time around, she was able to confirm that earlier promise. She was given plenty to do, especially considering she is not the type to find an immediate burst of speed when first coming under pressure, but she kept responding and gradually reeled in Cliche. She should do even better over further when ridden a little closer to the pace and looks a Group-class filly in the making. (op 7-2)
Cliche(IRE) was trying her furthest trip to date and, although eventually pegged back by the smart Samira Gold, she saw this trip out well. She could be capable of even better when there is some give underfoot. (op 6-1)
Russian Rosie(IRE), making her handicap debut, kept on well in the straight having been in a good position throughout and picked up some more black type. She deserves to pick up a similar race and could find opportunities abroad. (op 20-1)
Ronaldsay ran a solid race off a mark 4lb higher than when second over 1m1f here on her previous start and just missed out on some black type. (op 8-1)
Summer's Eve did not run badly, but she probably wants slightly easier ground. (op 14-1)
Flying Clarets(IRE) had plenty to do off top weight and she did not run too badly under a positive ride. (tchd 7-1)
Measured Tempo, having her first run since disappointing in the Oaks at Epsom, compromised her chance by hanging badly and was reported to have lost her action. There were high expectations for her at the start of the season, but she has yet to go on as one might have hoped. Official explanation: jockey said filly lost its action (tchd 7-2 and 4-1 in a place)
Fusili(IRE) Official explanation: jockey said filly had no more to give

4850 FEGENTRI WORLD CUP OF NATIONS STKS (AMATEUR RIDERS' H'CAP) (FOR THE RICHMOND BRISSAC TROPHY) 1m 1f

3:55 (3:57) (Class 5) (0-75,72) 3-Y-0+ **£6,246** (£1,937; £968; £484) **Stalls** High

Form RPR

6041 **1** **Snark (IRE)**[18] 4284 4-11-5 **65** MllePProd'homme 12 73
(P J Makin) *pressed ldr: clr of rest 1/2-way: led and reminder 3f out: shuffled along and hld on fnl 2f* **9/2**[2]

5412 **2** *3/4* **Optimus (USA)**[14] 4418 5-11-11 **71** MrHHaynes 10 77
(B G Powell) *chsd clr ldrs: hrd rdn to cl 2f out: nt qckn 1f out: kpt on to take 2nd last stride* **5/2**[1]

0550 **3** *shd* **The Gaikwar (IRE)**[14] 4418 8-11-3 **63** (b) MrEMontford 1 69
(R A Harris) *chsd clr ldrs: u.str.p fr 3f out: clsd and ch 1f out: kpt on same pce* **20/1**

0105 **4** *1/2* **Surwaki (USA)**[11] 4496 5-11-7 **67** (p) MissKSchmitt 2 72
(R M H Cowell) *led to 3f out: nudged along and pressed wnr after nt qckn fnl f* **11/1**

3045 **5** *1* **Fantasy Crusader**[16] 4355 8-10-7 **53** oh3 MissLLammers 7 56
(R M H Cowell) *off the pce in midfield: urged along and kpt on fr over 2f out: nrst fin* **8/1**

-432 **6** *2* **Blu Manruna**[202] 363 4-10-10 **56** (b) MrCFais 8 54
(J Akehurst) *chsd clr ldng pair: clsd and rdn 2f out: hanging and fnd nil over 1f out* **12/1**

1005 **7** *3/4* **Jackie Kiely**[8] 4610 6-11-7 **67** (t) MissEMarcialis 3 64
(R Brotherton) *stdd s: hld up in rr: rdn and off the pce over 2f out: plugged on* **20/1**

4500 **8** *hd* **Murrumbidgee (IRE)**[17] 4319 4-10-10 **56** ow1 (t) MrLoekVanDerHam 6 52
(J W Hills) *wl in rr: brought to wd outside 3f out: plugged on: nvr on terms* **15/2**[3]

050 **9** *hd* **Paraguay (USA)**[9] 4577 4-11-6 **66** MissDGillam 9 62
(Miss V Haigh) *nvr bttr than midfield: no imp on ldrs over 2f out: n.d after* **14/1**

2523 **10** *8* **Height Of Spirits**[55] 3149 5-10-7 **53** oh8 MrGWood 5 32
(T D McCarthy) *dwlt: a bhd* **14/1**

1010 **11** *nk* **Mythical Charm**[9] 4577 8-10-12 **58** (t) MrsCBartley 4 37
(J J Bridger) *nvr on terms w ldrs: wknd 2f out* **17/2**

4/2- **12** *15* **Turtle Soup (IRE)**[165] 866 11-11-12 **72** MissNadineForde 11 19
(J J Bridger) *prom 4f: sn lost pl: t.o* **25/1**

1m 58.9s (2.04) **Going Correction** +0.05s/f (Good) **12** Ran SP% **122.9**
Speed ratings (Par 103): **92,91,91,90,89 88,87,87,87,80 79,66**
CSF £16.25 CT £215.89 TOTE £5.80: £2.30, £1.50, £6.70; EX 12.50.
Owner Keith And Brian Brackpool **Bred** Anthony Rafferty **Trained** Ogbourne Maisey, Wilts
■ The first winner in Britain for French rider Pauline Prod'homme.

FOCUS
Modest form and probably a race to treat with caution as they went only a steady pace under these amateurs.

4851 TURFTV.CO.UK STKS (H'CAP) 7f

4:30 (4:30) (Class 2) (0-105,100) 3-Y-0+
£12,464 (£3,732; £1,866; £934; £466; £234) **Stalls** High

Form RPR

1203 **1** **King Of Argos**[23] 4119 4-9-12 **100** RyanMoore 5 110
(E A L Dunlop) *hld up in last pair: gd prog wl over 1f out: drvn on outer and r.o to ld last 50yds* **4/1**[2]

6120 **2** *1/2* **White Deer (USA)**[43] 3559 3-9-1 **94** SebSanders 10 101
(M Johnston) *trckd clr ldng pair: clsd 2f out: rdn to ld jst ins fnl f: kpt on wl: hdd last 50yds* **12/1**

2235 **3** *nk* **Waterside (IRE)**[15] 4377 8-9-0 **88** GeorgeBaker 7 96
(G L Moore) *hld up in midfield: clsd 2f out: rdn to chal 1f out: jst outpcd last 100yds* **12/1**

1162 **4** *shd* **Vitznau (IRE)**[24] 4093 3-9-1 **94** RichardHughes 6 100+
(R Hannon) *hld up in midfield gng wl: clsd on ldrs 2f out: chal 1f out: nt qckn and hld after* **9/2**[3]

0610 **5** *shd* **Commando Scott (IRE)**[85] 2237 6-8-13 **87** PaulHanagan 9 94
(I W McInnes) *t.k.h early: hld up bhd clr ldrs: clsd 2f out: chal and upsides 1f out: sn nt qckn: kpt on nr fin* **50/1**

1-33 **6** *nk* **Escape Route (USA)**[96] 1930 3-8-12 **91** JimmyFortune 1 96+
(J H M Gosden) *hld up in last: stl there wl over 1f out: prog on outer sn after: r.o: nt rch ldrs* **7/1**

-303 **7** *shd* **Minority Report**[25] 4062 7-9-7 **95** LDettori 3 101
(L M Cumani) *hld up in last trio: rdn over 2f out: prog on outer over 1f out: styd on but nt pce to chal* **7/2**[1]

0006 **8** *nk* **Jedburgh**[25] 4062 6-9-5 **93** (b) DaneO'Neill 2 99
(J L Dunlop) *hld up in rr on inner: prog 2f out: clsd and looked dangerous 1f out: nt qckn* **11/1**

0060 **9** *1/2* **Dingaan (IRE)**[10] 4548 4-8-8 **82** LPKeniry 12 86+
(A M Balding) *stdd s: hld up: trcking ldrs whn nt clr run 2f out: rdn and nt qckn 1f out* **33/1**

2134 **10** *1/2* **Binanti**[25] 4062 7-9-6 **94** JimCrowley 13 97
(P R Chamings) *trckd clr ldrs: clsd 2f out: led on inner jst over 1f out: immediately hung lft: hdd jst ins fnl f: gave up* **17/2**

1331 **11** *1 1/2* **Ivory Lace**[23] 4134 6-8-12 **86** JamesDoyle 8 85
(S Woodman) *towards rr: rdn over 2f out: struggling wl over 1f out: swtchd to inner 1f out: one pce after* **12/1**

5000 **12** *3* **Prince Of Thebes (IRE)**[15] 4377 6-8-10 **84** PaulDoe 11 75
(J Akehurst) *rousted to ld and mde most at blistering pce: hdd jst over 1f out: wkng whn squeezed out sn after* **25/1**

1100 **13** *2* **H Harrison (IRE)**[21] 4195 7-8-4 **81** oh1 AndrewElliott(3) 4 66
(I W McInnes) *w ldr at str pce and sn clr of rest: wknd 2f out* **50/1**

1m 26.52s (-1.52) **Going Correction** +0.05s/f (Good)
WFA 3 from 4yo+ 5lb **13** Ran SP% **125.5**
Speed ratings (Par 109): **110,109,109,108,108 108,108,108,107,106 105,101,99**
CSF £53.01 CT £548.23 TOTE £5.90: £2.30, £3.80, £3.90; EX 65.20.
Owner P G Goulandris **Bred** Chippenham Lodge Stud Ltd **Trained** Newmarket, Suffolk

FOCUS
This looked a good handicap beforehand, but the two leaders went off too fast, setting the race up for the closers, and the principals finished in a heap. The form wants treating with some caution, with the third perhaps the best guide.

NOTEBOOK
King Of Argos came into this in great form having run third in the big 1m handicap at the Glorious meeting and, with the race very much run to suit, he picked up smartly from off the pace to gain his third win of the year. This was a good effort off top weight and he is clearly very decent over 7f-1m when the pace is strong. (op 5-1)
White Deer(USA) ◆, gelded since he was last seen, ran a huge race in defeat considering he was asked to chase down the furious gallop and this must rate as a career best. He very much appeals as one to follow. (op 10-1)
Waterside(IRE) continues in tremendous form and this was a terrific effort in defeat, especially considering he is often at his best when helping force the pace, which was obviously not possible this time with the leaders going off too fast. It has been said plenty of times in the past, but he really is a credit to his connections. (op 16-1)
Vitznau(IRE) ran a respectable race but he was probably just found out by a 5lb rise in the weights for his recent course-and-distance second. (op 5-1 tchd 4-1)
Commando Scott(IRE) ran close to his best off the back of a near three-month break. (op 66-1)
Escape Route(USA) probably just lacked the race sharpness of some of these having been off the track for over three months, and he ought to be able to improve on this. (tchd 13-2)
Minority Report had been raised 3lb for his recent third in a classified contest over course and distance and he just lacked the pace of some of these. (op 4-1 tchd 10-3)
Dingaan(IRE) would have been closer with a clearer run. Official explanation: jockey said gelding was denied a clear run

4852 GG CLUB MAIDEN AUCTION STKS 1m

5:05 (5:06) (Class 5) 2-Y-0 **£3,238** (£963; £481; £240) **Stalls** High

Form RPR

02 **1** **Dauberval (IRE)**[10] 4540 2-9-0 0 RichardHughes 7 85+
(S Kirk) *trckd ldrs gng wl: effrt 2f out: w ldr fnl f: r.o and led last strides* **4/1**[2]

6 **2** *hd* **Trenchtown (IRE)**[24] 4110 2-8-12 0 LDettori 3 83+
(R Charlton) *hld up in rr: pushed along and prog over 2f out: swtchd to inner and rdn to ld narrowly jst over 1f out: r.o: hdd last strides* **2/1**[1]

22 **3** *5* **Graceful Descent (FR)**[13] 4448 2-8-6 0 PaulHanagan 10 66
(R A Fahey) *hld up in tch: nt clr run briefly 3f out: sn pushed along: outpcd wl over 1f out: kpt on to take 3rd nr fin* **4/1**[2]

04 **4** *hd* **Always Brave**[27] 4028 2-8-10 0 SebSanders 4 69
(M Johnston) *led 3f: w ldr: led wl over 2f out: drvn and hdd jst over 1f out: sn wl outpcd: lost 3rd nr fin* **16/1**

033 **5** *1* **Benhavis**[17] 4316 2-9-1 83 RyanMoore 8 72
(J L Dunlop) *chsd ldrs: rdn over 2f out: cl enough over 1f out: hanging rt and sn btn* **4/1**[2]

002 **6** *nk* **Elegant Step**[18] 4293 2-8-3 70 AndrewElliott(3) 5 62
(A P Jarvis) *chsd ldrs: pushed along 3f out: outpcd fr 2f out* **20/1**

5 **7** *3 1/2* **Shadows Fall (USA)**[15] 4393 2-8-13 0 JimmyFortune 11 62
(P F I Cole) *hld up in rr: prog on inner 3f out: outpcd fr 2f out* **14/1**

8 *nk* **Flying Time** 2-8-4 0 TPO'Shea 9 52
(M R Channon) *dwlt: wl in rr: rdn 3f out: no real prog* **33/1**

0 **9** *3/4* **Ever Dreaming (USA)**[15] 4402 2-8-10 0 LPKeniry 6 56
(A M Balding) *w ldr: led after 3f to wl over 2f out: wknd wl over 1f out* **25/1**

10 *9* **Pay The Grey** 2-8-8 0 DaneO'Neill 2 34
(R Hannon) *s.s: a in last trio: nvr a factor* **9/1**[3]

0 **11** *9* **Landed Gent (IRE)**[10] 4537 2-8-10 0 JamesDoyle 1 17
(Miss V Haigh) *chsd ldrs 3f: struggling in rr fr 3f out: t.o* **100/1**

1m 40.26s (-0.01) **Going Correction** +0.05s/f (Good) **11** Ran SP% **128.4**
Speed ratings (Par 94): **102,101,96,96,95 95,91,91,90,81 72**
CSF £13.29 TOTE £5.10: £1.70, £1.50, £2.10; EX 13.30.
Owner Norman Ormiston **Bred** B Kennedy **Trained** Upper Lambourn, Berks

FOCUS
A reasonable maiden and the front two pulled well clear. The winning time was very decent for a race like this and the form ought to work out.

NOTEBOOK
Dauberval(IRE) ◆ confirmed the improved form he showed when second at second at Salisbury on his previous start to get off the mark at the third attempt. He showed a good attitude to come out on top in a thrilling battle with Trenchtown and, with a nice gap back to the remainder, this looks like useful form. (op 5-1 tchd 10-3)
Trenchtown(IRE) ◆ stepped up on the form he showed when sixth in a hot maiden on his debut at Sandown and was just denied. He will have learnt plenty from this and is likely to prove hard to beat in similar company next time. (op 9-4 tchd 11-4)

Graceful Descent(FR) took an age to get organised in the straight and did not look at home on this track. She can do better and will have more options now she is handicapped. (op 7-2 tchd 10-3, 9-2 and 5-1 in places)
Always Brave ran his race and did not look to have any excuses. He is another now qualified for a handicap mark and he should find his level.
Benhavis was not at his best at Brighton on his previous start and this was another slightly disappointing effort. He looks flattered by his official mark of 83, but perhaps a return to a flatter track will help. Official explanation: trainer said colt had a breathing problem (op 5-1)

4853 TURFTV FOR BETTING SHOPS APPRENTICE STKS (H'CAP) 6f
5:40 (5:41) (Class 6) (0-65,63) 3-Y-0+ £3,238 (£963; £481; £240) Stalls Low

Form RPR
0-06 **1** **Contented (IRE)**[15] 4397 5-8-8 **49**..............................(p) SCreighton(5) 17 63
(Mrs L C Jewell) *racd on outer: w ldrs: overall ldr 1/2-way: wl in command over 1f out: rdn out* **16/1**
3360 **2** *1 1/2* **Bobby Rose**[5] 4689 4-9-5 **60**.......................... JamesO'Reilly(5) 15 69
(D K Ivory) *cl up on outer: chsd wnr fr 2f out: no imp: styd on* **14/1**
0442 **3** *1* **Young Bertie**[22] 4165 4-9-12 **62**..........................(v) TravisBlock 19 68
(H Morrison) *trckd ldrs on outer: rdn 2f out: styd on same pce fr over 1f out* **10/3**[1]
4032 **4** *shd* **Willofcourse**[6] 4668 6-8-5 **48**.......................... AmyScott(7) 2 53
(H Candy) *racd towards nr side: chsd ldrs: prog 2f out: pushed along and kpt on same pce fr over 1f out* **6/1**[2]
00U4 **5** *1 1/4* **Mister Elegant**[27] 4021 5-8-8 **49**.......................... SophieDoyle(5) 11 50
(J L Spearing) *towards rr: outpcd fr 2f out and no ch: styd on wl fnl f* **16/1**
100 **6** *shd* **Charming Ballet (IRE)**[15] 4394 4-9-5 **60**..................(b) HaddenFrost(5) 3 61
(N P Littmoden) *racd towards nr side: overall ldr to 1/2-way: hld whn hung rt over 1f out: fdd* **12/1**
204 **7** *1/2* **Batchworth Fleur**[22] 4164 4-9-0 **50**.......................... StephaneBreux 8 50
(E A Wheeler) *racd towards nr side: nvr on terms w ldrs: kpt on fr over 1f out* **20/1**
1503 **8** *1/2* **On The Map**[11] 4514 3-9-2 **55**..........................(v) AndrewElliott 5 53
(A P Jarvis) *pressed ldrs to 2f out: nt qckn and lost pl: one pce fnl f* **25/1**
5033 **9** *hd* **Peruvian Style (IRE)**[17] 4312 6-8-13 **52**.......................... TolleyDean(3) 14 49
(J M Bradley) *chsd ldrs: u.p bef 1/2-way: no imp fr 2f out* **12/1**
2124 **10** *nk* **Currency**[7] 4634 10-9-12 **62**.......................... LiamTreadwell 13 58
(J M Bradley) *sn rdn and struggling in rr: nvr on terms: kpt on fnl f* **7/1**[3]
0500 **11** *1/2* **Capricho (IRE)**[8] 4606 10-9-4 **57**..........................(b) JamesMillman(3) 12 52
(J Akehurst) *chsd ldrs on outer: rdn over 2f out: no imp: fdd fnl f* **16/1**
2045 **12** *nk* **Digital**[11] 4505 10-9-1 **58**.......................... MatthewDavies(7) 1 52
(M R Channon) *restless in stalls: sn bhd: last and virtually t.o 1/2-way: modest late prog* **12/1**
004 **13** *nk* **Night Prospector**[5] 4689 7-9-10 **63**..........................(p) LukeMorris(3) 10 56
(R A Harris) *chsd ldrs: rdn and lost pl fr 2f out: no ch whn hmpd twice jst ins fnl f* **7/1**[3]
5500 **14** *1 1/2* **Exponential (IRE)**[3] 4734 5-9-0 **57**..........................(p) PietroRomeo(7) 4 45
(J M Bradley) *chsd ldrs to 1/2-way: urged along and grad wknd* **20/1**
0200 **15** *1/2* **King Of Tricks**[5] 4685 3-8-5 **49**.......................... FrankiePickard(5) 7 35
(M D I Usher) *sn outpcd: a struggling* **66/1**
4000 **16** *1/2* **Veba (USA)**[9] 4577 4-8-4 **45**.......................... ThomasO'Brien(5) 18 30
(M D I Usher) *nvr looked keen: a in rr* **66/1**
2401 **17** *3/4* **Ishibee (IRE)**[12] 4471 3-8-10 **54**..........................(p) KMay(5) 9 36
(J J Bridger) *a towards rr: no ch fnl 2f* **14/1**
0660 **18** *4* **Parkside Pursuit**[38] 3667 9-8-7 **48**.......................... JackMitchell(5) 6 18
(J M Bradley) *dwlt: a struggling in last pair* **20/1**

1m 12.35s (-0.50) **Going Correction** -0.05s/f (Good)
WFA 3 from 4yo+ 3lb 18 Ran SP% **137.5**
Speed ratings (Par 101): **101,99,97,97,95 95,95,94,94,93 93,92,92,90,89 88,87,82**
CSF £231.41 CT £708.33 TOTE £28.00: £4.60, £4.50, £1.50, £2.30; EX 827.80 Place 6 £46.97, Place 5 £32.88.
Owner O J C Shannon Mrs Linda Beasley **Bred** Barry Noonan And Denis Noonan **Trained** Sutton Valence, Kent
■ Stewards' Enquiry : Andrew Elliott three-day ban: careless riding (Sep 6,7,9)

FOCUS
A modest but competitive sprint handicap restricted to apprentices who had not ridden more than 50 winners. The form seems sound. They raced down the middle of the track.
T/Jkpt: £21,315.00 to a £1 stake. Pool: £45,031.70. 1.50 winning tickets. T/Plt: £37.20 to a £1 stake. Pool: £96,880.25. 1,897.25 winning tickets. T/Qpdt: £14.50 to a £1 stake. Pool: £4,670.10. 237.60 winning tickets. JN

4512 YARMOUTH (L-H)
Sunday, August 26

OFFICIAL GOING: Good to soft (good in places; 7.4) changing to good (good to soft in places) after race 5 (4.05)
Wind: fresh half-behind Weather: Fine and sunny

4854 E B F EASTERN DAILY PRESS "MAKES NORFOLK LIFE COMPLETE" MAIDEN STKS 6f 3y
1:50 (1:55) (Class 5) 2-Y-0 £3,562 (£1,059; £529; £264) Stalls High

Form RPR
1 **Ancien Regime (IRE)** 2-9-3 0.......................... PhilipRobinson 8 84+
(M A Jarvis) *led: hdd over 4f out: led again over 2f out: rdn out* **9/2**[3]
2 **2** *1 3/4* **Street Star (USA)**[20] 4232 2-8-12 0.......................... JamieSpencer 5 74
(J R Fanshawe) *hld up in tch: plld hrd: chsd wnr and edgd lft over 1f out: no ex towards fin* **5/6**[1]
55 **3** *1* **Faber Hall Flyer**[17] 4335 2-9-3 0..........................(t) DMylonas 12 76
(Mrs C A Dunnett) *racd alone towards stands' side: led over 4f out to over 2f out: rdn and hung lft over 1f out: styd on same pce ins fnl f* **40/1**
4 *hd* **Ibn Khaldun (USA)** 2-9-3 0.......................... TedDurcan 3 75
(Saeed Bin Suroor) *s.s: hdwy over 1f out: nt trble ldrs* **10/3**[2]
5 *6* **Fairmont (IRE)** 2-8-12 0.......................... NickyMackay 4 52+
(M Johnston) *mid-div: rdn over 2f out: sn wknd* **16/1**
0 **6** *shd* **Minwir (IRE)**[17] 4335 2-9-3 0.......................... MatthewHenry 11 57
(M A Jarvis) *s.i.s: sn chsng ldrs: rdn over 1f out: wknd fnl f* **40/1**
04 **7** *1/2* **Bury Treasure (IRE)**[33] 3823 2-9-3 0.......................... ChrisCatlin 6 55
(Miss Gay Kelleway) *prom: rdn 1/2-way: wknd wl over 1f out* **33/1**
8 *nk* **Baunagain (IRE)** 2-9-3 0.......................... RichardMullen 1 54
(M J Wallace) *dwlt and wnt lft s: n.d* **66/1**
9 *3* **Payne Relief (IRE)** 2-8-12 0.......................... HayleyTurner 7 40
(M L W Bell) *mid-div: lost pl 1/2-way: sn bhd* **25/1**
10 *1/2* **Regal Veil** 2-8-12 0.......................... SaleemGolam 2 39
(S C Williams) *sn pushed along: a in rr* **100/1**
0 **11** *2 1/2* **Peas In A Pod**[13] 4454 2-9-3 0.......................... OscarUrbina 9 36
(J R Fanshawe) *hld up: bhd fr 1/2-way* **25/1**
00 **12** *4* **Moss Way**[74] 2569 2-9-3 0.......................... NeilPollard 10 24
(W J Musson) *prom to 1/2-way* **100/1**

1m 13.34s (-0.36) **Going Correction** -0.20s/f (Firm) 12 Ran SP% **120.7**
Speed ratings (Par 94): **94,91,90,90,82 81,81,80,76,76 72,67**
CSF £8.35 TOTE £7.20: £1.60, £1.10, £5.00; EX 10.60 TRIFECTA Not won..
Owner Sheikh Mohammed **Bred** Deerforest Stud **Trained** Newmarket, Suffolk

FOCUS
A decent maiden in which four drew clear, although the fact 40/1 shot Faber Hall Flyer was one of them is slightly unsettling. The second is probably the best guide.

NOTEBOOK
Ancien Regime(IRE), a 60,000gns son of King's Best, knew his job well enough to lead through the early stages and really knuckled down under pressure, always doing too much for the favourite. This was a promising start to his career and the Dewhurst entrant looks capable of better, with a step up to 7f looking likely to suit. (op 13-2 tchd 7-1)
Street Star(USA), who looked the one to beat on the evidence of her debut second at Windsor, was restrained in rear early, but gave the impression she was wanting to go faster and as a result did not settle. She came to have every chance, but having got there was unable to find any more and was always being held by the winner. (op Evens tchd 4-5)
Faber Hall Flyer had shaped quite well in a couple of course maidens and this was easily his best effort to date, racing alone towards the stands' side and sticking on well despite not quite being on terms with the winner. He is now qualified for a nursery mark. (tchd 50-1)
Ibn Khaldun(USA), a non-runner because of the soft ground the previous day, is regally bred, being by Dubai Destination out of Irish 1000 Guineas winner Gossamer, but he was always on the back foot following a sluggish start and, though making some late headway, it was all too late. Clear of the rest, this was a promising start and he should have no trouble winning an ordinary maiden, with the step up to 7f going to suit. (op 11-4)
Fairmont(IRE), whose stable's juveniles have really hit form now, is bred to be effective at this sort of distance, but she was struggling to stick with the principals from past halfway and looked in need of the experience. (op 12-1)
Minwir(IRE) improved a little on his initial effort, but was still well held and appeals as more of a nursery type.
Peas In A Pod Official explanation: jockey said gelding was unsuited by the good to soft (good in places) ground

4855 NORWICH EVENING NEWS COMMUNITY FILLIES' H'CAP 7f 3y
2:20 (2:23) (Class 5) (0-75,74) 3-Y-0+ £3,238 (£963; £481; £240) Stalls High

Form RPR
5005 **1** **Tara Too (IRE)**[9] 4589 4-9-12 **70**..........................(b) FrankieMcDonald 3 81
(J G Portman) *a.p: rdn to ld over 1f out: edgd lft ins fnl f: styd on* **8/1**[3]
0365 **2** *1/2* **Tilsworth Charlie**[10] 4545 4-8-10 **54**..........................(b) TedDurcan 6 64
(J R Jenkins) *hld up in tch: rdn and ev ch whn edgd lft ins fnl f: nt qckn nr fin* **8/1**[3]
3040 **3** *3 1/2* **Whistleupthewind**[11] 4515 4-8-7 **51**.......................... HayleyTurner 11 52
(J M P Eustace) *chsd ldrs: rdn: hung lft and outpcd over 1f out: styd on nr fin* **10/1**
3552 **4** *hd* **Angel Voices (IRE)**[22] 4157 4-8-13 **57**.......................... RichardMullen 10 57
(K R Burke) *chsd ldrs: rdn and ev ch over 1f out: no ex ins fnl f* **5/1**[2]
004 **5** *nk* **Littledodayno (IRE)**[14] 4423 4-8-12 **56**..........................(p) PhilipRobinson 12 55
(M Wigham) *s.i.s: hld up: styd on ins fnl f: nvr nrr* **8/1**[3]
4-60 **6** *3/4* **Joyful Tears (IRE)**[83] 2317 3-9-3 **66**.......................... TGMcLaughlin 1 63
(M G Quinlan) *dwlt: hld up: hdwy over 1f out: nt trble ldrs* **33/1**
6001 **7** *hd* **Meditation**[16] 4361 5-9-9 **67**.......................... IanMongan 13 64
(I A Wood) *chsd ldr tl rdn over 2f out: wknd ins fnl f* **8/1**[3]
2065 **8** *1* **Ensign's Trick**[41] 3588 3-8-6 **60**.......................... AshleyHamblett(5) 7 54
(W M Brisbourne) *unruly in stalls: led: rdn and hdd over 1f out: wknd ins fnl f* **33/1**
621 **9** *5* **What A Treasure (IRE)**[32] 3845 3-9-11 **74**.......................... NickyMackay 9 54
(L M Cumani) *hld up in tch: rdn over 2f out: wknd over 1f out* **3/1**[1]
32-0 **10** *hd* **Trickle (USA)**[17] 4338 3-9-2 **65**.......................... PaulEddery 5 45
(Miss D Mountain) *s.i.s: hld up: rdn over 2f out: sn wknd* **40/1**
5000 **11** *7* **Wodhill Be**[17] 4317 7-8-7 **51** oh6.......................... AdrianMcCarthy 8 12
(D Morris) *hld up: wknd 2f out* **66/1**
1-65 **12** *2 1/2* **Malaath (IRE)**[17] 4317 3-9-5 **68**.......................... JamieSpencer 4 22
(E A L Dunlop) *s.i.s: hld up: wknd over 2f out* **5/1**[2]

1m 24.95s (-1.65) **Going Correction** -0.20s/f (Firm)
WFA 3 from 4yo+ 5lb 12 Ran SP% **121.7**
Speed ratings (Par 100): **101,100,96,96,95 95,94,93,87,87 79,76**
CSF £70.84 CT £668.54 TOTE £10.90: £3.20, £2.90, £3.00; EX 93.70 TRIFECTA Not won..
Owner Prof C D Green **Bred** Tally-Ho Stud **Trained** Compton, Berks

FOCUS
A moderate fillies' handicap. The first two finished clear and the form is rated through them.
Whistleupthewind Official explanation: jockey said filly hung left throughout
What A Treasure(IRE) Official explanation: jockey said filly was unsuited by the good to soft (good in places) ground
Malaath(IRE) Official explanation: jockey said filly was unsuited by the good to soft (good in places) ground

4856 GREAT YARMOUTH MERCURY H'CAP 1m 3y
2:55 (2:56) (Class 6) (0-60,60) 3-Y-0+ £2,137 (£635; £317; £158) Stalls High

Form RPR
2245 **1** **Hits Only Cash**[14] 4433 5-9-8 **58**.......................... JamieSpencer 9 70
(J Pearce) *hld up: hdwy over 2f out: rdn to ld 1f out: r.o* **3/1**[1]
0042 **2** *1 1/2* **Libre**[19] 4259 7-9-7 **57**.......................... TGMcLaughlin 5 66
(F Jordan) *a.p: led over 1f out: sn rdn: edgd lft and hdd: styd on same pce* **8/1**
-005 **3** *2* **Alasil (USA)**[10] 4526 7-9-3 **53**.......................... PhilipRobinson 10 57
(R J Price) *chsd ldrs: rdn and ev ch over 1f out: no ex ins fnl f* **4/1**[2]
0600 **4** *2 1/2* **Sea Willow (IRE)**[25] 4064 3-9-1 **60**.......................... MarcHalford(3) 2 58
(D R C Elsworth) *chsd ldr tl rdn over 2f out: styd on same pce appr fnl f* **33/1**
0 **5** *1/2* **Our Kes (IRE)**[32] 3851 5-9-8 **58**.......................... AmirQuinn 3 56
(P Howling) *s.s: hld up: swtchd rt and r.o ins fnl f: nrst fin* **16/1**
4006 **6** *1/2* **Djalalabad (FR)**[17] 4338 3-9-4 **60**.......................... DMylonas 6 55
(Mrs C A Dunnett) *led: racd keenly: rdn and hdd over 1f out: wknd ins fnl f* **28/1**
0530 **7** *1 1/4* **Forced Upon Us**[18] 4272 3-9-1 **57**.......................... RichardMullen 12 49
(P J McBride) *hld up: hdwy u.p over 2f out: no ex fnl f* **14/1**
420 **8** *shd* **Mugeba**[11] 4494 6-9-6 **56**..........................(t) HayleyTurner 7 49
(Miss Gay Kelleway) *chsd ldrs: rdn over 1f out: wknd ins fnl f* **7/1**[3]
0304 **9** *1 1/2* **Fateful Attraction**[18] 4272 4-8-12 **48**..........................(b) IanMongan 14 38
(I A Wood) *s.i.s: hdwy u.p over 2f out: bmpd ins fnl f: n.d* **11/1**
0005 **10** *1* **Brouhaha**[30] 3913 3-8-11 **53**..........................(t) OscarUrbina 4 39
(Miss Diana Weeden) *chsd ldrs: rdn and wknd over 1f out* **20/1**
4033 **11** *1 1/4* **Crafty Fox**[20] 4219 4-9-6 **56**.......................... TedDurcan 17 41
(John A Harris) *hld up: rdn over 2f out: a in rr* **8/1**

6006 **12** *1* **Dictatrix**[83] 2309 4-9-7 **60**..........(p) JerryO'Dwyer(3) 16 42
(C R Dore) *dwlt: hld up: a in rr* **25/1**

2503 **13** *6* **Show Me The Lolly (FR)**[186] 517 7-8-6 **47** ow1.......... PatrickHills(5) 8 16
(J McAuley) *mid-div: rdn over 2f out: sn wknd* **14/1**

0001 **14** *6* **Vietnam**[10] 4550 3-8-13 **55**.......... DavidKinsella 15 9
(G A Huffer) *free to post: chsd ldrs to 1/2-way: b.b.v* **14/1**

060 **15** *21* **Screaming Reel**[27] 4018 4-9-0 **50**.......... AdrianMcCarthy 1 —
(M Wellings) *mid-dvision: rdn and lost pl 1/2-way: sn bhd* **66/1**

1m 38.85s (-1.05) **Going Correction** -0.20s/f (Firm)
WFA 3 from 4yo+ 6lb **15** Ran SP% **130.4**
Speed ratings (Par 101): **97,95,93,91,90 90,88,88,87,86 84,83,77,71,50**
CSF £27.94 CT £105.17 TOTE £4.10: £1.90, £2.60, £2.60; EX 34.60 Trifecta £129.30 Part won. Pool £182.20 - 0.50 winning units..
Owner Clive Whiting **Bred** G S Shropshire **Trained** Newmarket, Suffolk

FOCUS
Not much of race, but it did see a well overdue first handicap win for Hits Only Cash. The form seems solid enough.
Vietnam Official explanation: trainer said gelding bled from the nose
Screaming Reel Official explanation: trainer said gelding lost two shoes

4857 MERCURY ONLINE: YARMOUTHMERCURY.CO.UK H'CAP 5f 43y
3:30 (3:30) (Class 5) (0-70,66) 3-Y-0+ **£3,238** (£963; £481; £240) **Stalls** High

Form RPR

06 **1** **King Egbert (FR)**[8] 4594 6-8-6 **49**.......... NickyMackay 4 60
(R J Price) *in rr: hdwy to chse ldr over 1f out: r.o u.p to ld post* **10/3**[3]

0602 **2** *shd* **Master Malarkey**[5] 4689 4-8-4 **47** oh2..........(b) ChrisCatlin 3 58
(Mrs C A Dunnett) *chsd ldrs: led 2f out: rdn fnl f: hdd post* **11/4**[2]

4053 **3** *3* **Viewforth**[7] 4642 9-8-5 **48**..........(b) HayleyTurner 5 48
(M A Buckley) *chsd ldrs: outpcd over 1f out: styd on ins fnl f* **5/2**[1]

5000 **4** *1/2* **Jakeini (IRE)**[18] 4289 4-9-9 **66**..........(p) RichardMullen 1 64
(E S McMahon) *s.i.s: sn prom: rdn over 1f out: no ex fnl f* **4/1**

-666 **5** *3 1/2* **Valiant Romeo**[15] 4379 7-8-4 **47** oh2..........(v) SaleemGolam 7 32
(R Bastiman) *sn outpcd* **8/1**

-050 **6** *3 1/2* **Prime Recreation**[185] 523 10-8-4 **47** oh2.......... DavidKinsella 8 20
(P S Felgate) *led 3f: wknd over 1f out* **25/1**

61.76 secs (-1.04) **Going Correction** -0.20s/f (Firm) **6** Ran SP% **113.3**
Speed ratings (Par 103): **100,99,95,94,88 83**
CSF £13.13 CT £25.40 TOTE £5.70: £2.50, £1.90; EX 17.50 Trifecta £35.20 Pool £149.15 - 3.00 winning units..
Owner Bob Dean **Bred** Eric Puerari **Trained** Ullingswick, H'fords

FOCUS
A very poor contest, but it was strongly run and the form makes sense.

4858 EDP24.CO.UK H'CAP 1m 2f 21y
4:05 (4:05) (Class 6) (0-65,74) 3-Y-0 **£2,137** (£635; £317; £158) **Stalls** Low

Form RPR

424 **1** **Magdalene**[34] 3789 3-9-4 **62**.......... ChrisCatlin 6 73
(Rae Guest) *mid-div: hdwy over 3f out: swtchd rt over 1f out: r.o u.p to ld post* **11/2**

060 **2** *hd* **Magic Show**[18] 4275 3-9-2 **60**.......... TedDurcan 11 70
(Jane Chapple-Hyam) *a.p: chsd ldr over 2f out: rdn to ld ins fnl f: edgd rt: hdd post* **5/1**[3]

-012 **3** *2* **Smirfy's Silver**[17] 4339 3-9-0 **58**.......... RichardMullen 1 64
(E S McMahon) *led: rdn over 1f out: hdd and no ex ins fnl f* **7/2**[2]

0461 **4** *shd* **Hot Diamond**[11] 4504 3-10-2 **74**.......... AntonyProcter 4 80
(D R C Elsworth) *dwlt: hld up: hdwy over 2f out: rdn over 1f out: nt rch ldrs* **10/3**[1]

0654 **5** *1* **Motarjm (USA)**[16] 4354 3-9-4 **65**..........(t) JerryO'Dwyer(3) 5 69
(H J Collingridge) *chsd ldrs: rdn over 1f out: styd on same pce* **12/1**

4-50 **6** *9* **Ommadawn (IRE)**[69] 2726 3-9-6 **64**.......... JamieSpencer 9 50
(J R Fanshawe) *hld up: hdwy over 1f out: nvr nrr* **11/1**

25-P **7** *3 1/2* **Go Dude**[73] 2609 3-9-4 **62**..........(p) TGMcLaughlin 3 41
(J Ryan) *s.i.s: sn chsng ldrs: rdn and wknd over 2f out* **33/1**

0530 **8** *nk* **Postsprofit (IRE)**[18] 4270 3-9-6 **64**.......... OscarUrbina 10 42
(N A Callaghan) *dwlt: hld up: rdn over 3f out: a in rr* **14/1**

0260 **9** *3 1/2* **Henry The Seventh**[18] 4277 3-8-11 **60**.......... PatrickHills(5) 8 31
(J W Hills) *mid-div: effrt over 3f out: sn wknd* **20/1**

151 **10** *5* **Mick Is Back**[24] 4109 3-9-3 **61**..........(v[1]) NeilPollard 12 22
(G G Margarson) *hld up: racd keenly: a in rr* **12/1**

0002 **11** *5* **Kings Art (IRE)**[10] 4533 3-8-9 **53**.......... DavidKinsella 2 4
(W M Brisbourne) *chsd ldr tl rdn and wknd over 2f out* **25/1**

0-46 **12** *16* **El Dottore**[46] 3415 3-9-7 **65**.......... HayleyTurner 7 —
(M L W Bell) *mid-div: rdn over 3f out: sn wknd* **20/1**

2m 7.65s (-0.45) **Going Correction** +0.125s/f (Good) **12** Ran SP% **124.0**
Speed ratings (Par 98): **106,105,104,104,103 96,93,93,90,86 82,69**
CSF £33.07 CT £113.97 TOTE £9.10: £2.10, £1.90, £2.10; EX 54.90 Trifecta £234.40 Part won. Pool £330.18 - 0.20 winning units..
Owner Mrs Paula Smith **Bred** Mrs James Wigan **Trained** Newmarket, Suffolk

FOCUS
A smart winning time for the grade, 2.71 seconds quicker than the later apprentice handicap for older horses. The first two were unexposed at the trip and the form has been rated positively.

4859 EDP SHOP LOCAL CAMPAIGN H'CAP 1m 6f 17y
4:40 (4:41) (Class 6) (0-65,62) 3-Y-0+ **£2,137** (£635; £317; £158) **Stalls** Low

Form RPR

4543 **1** **Treason Trial**[23] 4124 6-9-5 **53**.......... HayleyTurner 8 62
(Stef Liddiard) *hld up: hdwy over 3f out: led 2f out: sn hdd: styd on u.p to ld wl ins fnl f* **3/1**[2]

0323 **2** *nk* **Lapina (IRE)**[17] 4339 3-9-2 **62**..........(b) IanMongan 13 70
(Pat Eddery) *hld up: hdwy over 3f out: led over 1f out: sn rdn: hdd wl ins fnl f* **7/2**[3]

6334 **3** *nk* **Pairumani Princess (IRE)**[31] 3876 3-9-2 **62**.......... JamieSpencer 11 70
(E A L Dunlop) *hld up: swtchd lft and hdwy over 2f out: rdn over 1f out: r.o: nt rch ldrs* **2/1**[1]

0004 **4** *7* **Wavertree One Off**[21] 3250 5-8-11 **45**..........(b) TGMcLaughlin 3 43
(J Ryan) *chsd ldrs: rdn over 2f out: wknd over 1f out* **33/1**

0-06 **5** *shd* **Magnum Opus (IRE)**[7] 4638 5-9-11 **62**..........(t) JerryO'Dwyer(3) 12 60
(D J Murphy) *hld up: hdwy u.p over 1f out: nt trble ldrs* **16/1**

4002 **6** *2* **Domenico (IRE)**[18] 4297 9-9-6 **54**.......... TedDurcan 9 49
(J R Jenkins) *mid-div: hdwy over 3f out: sn rdn: nt clr run over 2f out: wknd over 1f out* **10/1**

4606 **7** *3* **Figaro's Quest (IRE)**[16] 4352 5-9-0 **48**..........(b) ChrisCatlin 5 39
(C N Kellett) *led after 1f: rdn and hdd 2f out: wknd fnl f* **11/1**

0665 **8** *hd* **Camp Counsellor**[18] 4292 3-7-11 **50**..........(p) LauraReynolds(7) 4 41
(M J Gingell) *hld up in tch: rdn over 3f out: wknd over 2f out* **50/1**

0000 **9** *3 1/2* **Zen Garden**[27] 4019 6-9-0 **48**.......... RichardMullen 1 34
(W M Brisbourne) *led 1f: chsd ldrs tl wknd over 3f out* **28/1**

0-00 **10** *nk* **St Fris**[29] 3945 4-8-10 **47**..........(v) MarcHalford(3) 6 32
(J A R Toller) *hld up: rdn over 4f out: wknd over 3f out* **20/1**

0-00 **11** *shd* **Keagles (ITY)**[96] 1926 4-8-8 **47**.......... NataliaGemelova(5) 10 32
(J E Long) *plld hrd: sn trcking ldr: rdn over 2f out: wknd over 1f out* **40/1**

004 **12** *67* **Long Gone**[38] 3684 4-8-11 **45**..........(p) AdrianMcCarthy 7 —
(John A Harris) *chsd ldrs: rn wd bnd over 12f out: wknd 6f out* **50/1**

3m 6.43s (1.13) **Going Correction** +0.125s/f (Good)
WFA 3 from 4yo+ 12lb **12** Ran SP% **121.4**
Speed ratings (Par 101): **101,100,100,96,96 95,93,93,91,91 91,53**
CSF £13.37 CT £25.81 TOTE £3.90: £1.50, £1.70, £1.40; EX 14.60 Trifecta £44.40 Pool £725.79 - 11.60 winning units..
Owner Mrs Stef Liddiard **Bred** A Pereira, Arnstein Stud **Trained** Great Shefford, Berks

FOCUS
A cracking finish to what was a moderate handicap. The first three all came from the rear and finished clear.

4860 BETFAIR APPRENTICE TRAINING SERIES H'CAP 1m 2f 21y
5:15 (5:16) (Class 6) (0-65,62) 4-Y-0+ **£2,137** (£635; £317; £158) **Stalls** Low

Form RPR

4303 **1** **Desert Hawk**[13] 4464 6-9-1 **53**.......... PatrickHills 8 57
(W M Brisbourne) *hld up in tch: rdn and hung lft over 1f out: sn led: styd on* **11/4**[1]

0-00 **2** *1/2* **Dream Master (IRE)**[88] 2154 4-8-2 **45**.......... BradleyRoper(5) 9 48
(J Ryan) *hld up: hdwy over 1f out: r.o: nt rch wnr* **66/1**

0002 **3** *nk* **Credential**[11] 4488 5-9-4 **56**.......... MCGeran 3 58
(John A Harris) *hld up: hdwy over 2f out: rdn over 1f out: r.o* **15/2**

342 **4** *shd* **Rowan Lodge (IRE)**[52] 3241 5-9-4 **59**.......... HarryPoulton(3) 7 61
(J R Boyle) *chsd ldr: led over 3f out: rdn and hdd 1f out: no ex nr fin* **11/4**[1]

054 **5** *2* **Arctic Desert**[9] 4587 7-9-7 **62**..........(t) AlanRutter(3) 2 60
(Miss Gay Kelleway) *hld up: racd keenly: hdwy over 3f out: ev ch over 1f out: wknd wl ins fnl f* **13/2**[3]

4642 **6** *3/4* **Andorran (GER)**[4] 4718 4-8-2 **47**.......... NatashaEaton(7) 5 43
(A Bailey) *s.i.s: hld up: r.o ins fnl f: nvr nrr* **15/2**

5-43 **7** *3* **Desert Island Miss**[60] 2990 4-9-8 **60**..........(p) KirstyMilczarek 10 50
(W R Swinburn) *trckd ldrs: plld hrd: ev ch over 2f out: sn rdn: wknd over 1f out* **11/2**[2]

0000 **8** *hd* **Sheriff's Deputy**[83] 2307 7-8-0 **45**.......... PaulPickard(7) 4 35
(C N Kellett) *chsd ldrs: led 4f out: sn hdd: wknd over 2f out* **66/1**

-050 **9** *nk* **Summer Bounty**[19] 4253 11-8-12 **50**.......... WilliamCarson 6 39
(F Jordan) *s.i.s: sn prom: ev ch over 2f out: rdn and wknd over 1f out* **20/1**

5400 **10** *38* **Soul Blazer (USA)**[18] 4272 4-8-10 **55**.......... MJMurphy(7) 1 —
(Miss Gay Kelleway) *led 6f: sn rdn and wknd* **33/1**

2m 10.36s (2.26) **Going Correction** +0.125s/f (Good) **10** Ran SP% **116.3**
Speed ratings (Par 101): **95,94,94,94,92 92,89,89,89,58**
CSF £232.55 CT £1231.52 TOTE £2.60: £1.40, £8.90, £2.40; EX 196.70 Place 6 £47.18, Place 5 £34.01.
Owner J Jones Racing Ltd **Bred** C J Mills **Trained** Great Ness, Shropshire

FOCUS
A weak race, rated through the fourth, and a modest winning time for the class.
T/Plt: £67.90 to a £1 stake. Pool: £64,274.20. 690.25 winning tickets. T/Qpdt: £6.70 to a £1 stake. Pool: £3,911.50. 430.70 winning tickets. CR

4861 - 4863a (Foreign Racing) - See Raceform Interactive

DUNDALK (A.W) (L-H)
Sunday, August 26

OFFICIAL GOING: Standard
This was the first meeting to be held on an artificial surface, in this case Polytrack, in Ireland. It was also the first meeting at Dundalk for five years.

4864a MCR ENVIRONMENTAL MOURNE H'CAP (PREMIER HANDICAP) 6f
4:00 (4:01) 3-Y-0+ **£26,391** (£7,743; £3,689; £1,256)

RPR

1 **Rainbow Rising (IRE)**[42] 3573 5-9-5 93.......... PJSmullen 3 98
(Adrian McGuinness, Ire) *hld up: prog on inner early st: 5th whn swtchd rt 1f out: sn chal: kpt on wl to ld on line* **11/2**[1]

2 *shd* **Benwilt Breeze (IRE)**[17] 4346 5-9-10 98..........(t) WJSupple 13 103
(G M Lyons, Ire) *hld up in tch: 5th and hdwy ent st: led 1 1/2f out: strly pressed fnl f: hdd on line* **11/1**

3 *1/2* **Senor Benny (USA)**[17] 4346 8-10-0 102.......... KFallon 9 106
(M McDonagh, Ire) *hld up towards rr: hdwy on outer early st: 4th 1f out: kpt on wl* **8/1**

4 *1 3/4* **Majestic Times (IRE)**[21] 4211 7-9-12 100.......... JAHeffernan 12 98
(Liam McAteer, Ire) *prom on outer: 3rd and chal ent st: led under 2f out: hdd 1 1/2f out: kpt on* **14/1**

5 *hd* **Ireland's Call (IRE)**[56] 3140 6-8-12 91.......... OCasey(5) 4 53
(Peter Casey, Ire) *cl 2nd: chal ent st: 3rd over 1f out: kpt on* **25/1**

6 *3/4* **Bonus (IRE)**[25] 4062 7-9-12 100.......... EddieAhern 10 98
(G A Butler) *mid-div: 7th into st: styng on whn hmpd ovr 1f out: nt rcvr* **15/2**

7 *hd* **An Tadh (IRE)**[92] 2050 4-10-5 107..........(p) JMurtagh 2 102
(G M Lyons, Ire) *trckd ldrs: 4th into st: rdn to chal whn hmpd and checked ins fnl f: no ex* **11/2**[1]

8 *hd* **Namaya (IRE)**[83] 2323 4-10-8 110.......... KJManning 1 105
(J S Bolger, Ire) *towards rr: kpt on wout threatening st* **15/2**

9 *3/4* **Warriors Key (IRE)**[21] 4211 3-9-8 99.......... DPMcDonogh 7 93
(Kevin Prendergast, Ire) *hld up: sme prog whn nt clr run 1f out: no ex* **6/1**[2]

10 *1 1/4* **Murfreesboro**[332] 5642 4-9-7 95.......... RPCleary 5 87
(M Halford, Ire) *hld up: no imp st* **25/1**

11 *3 1/2* **That's Hot (IRE)**[22] 4150 4-10-2 104.......... CO'Donoghue 14 92
(G M Lyons, Ire) *hld up: 6th and prog whn sltly hmpd early st: no ex* **7/1**[3]

12 *1/2* **Saint Andrew (IRE)**[49] 3356 3-8-11 88.......... CDHayes 6 66
(Peter Casey, Ire) *nvr a factor* **12/1**

13 *1 3/4* **Osterhase (IRE)**[83] 2324 8-10-8 110..........(b) FMBerry 8 86
(J E Mulhern, Ire) *sn led: rdn and hdd early st: no ex whn eased fnl f* **8/1**

14 *3* **Flash McGahon (IRE)**[56] 3139 3-9-8 99..........(b) MJKinane 11 70
(John M Oxx, Ire) *chsd ldrs early: no ex ent st* **14/1**

1m 13.45s (73.45)
WFA 3 from 4yo+ 3lb **14** Ran SP% **140.4**
CSF £77.84 CT £525.19 TOTE £4.70: £2.30, £8.20, £3.50; DF 148.10.
Owner Goose Syndicate **Bred** John Osbourne & Edgeridge Ltd **Trained** Lusk, Co Dublin

NOTEBOOK
Bonus(IRE), a dual Polytrack winner in Britain and narrowly beaten in a Lingfield Listed event on his last appearance on the surface back in March, travelled well just behind the leader and was in the process of putting in an effort when the gap closed in front of him over a furlong out and there was no way back. He can be rated better than his finishing position. (op 8/1)

4865a MCR CIVIL ENGINEERING H'CAP (DIV I) 1m
4:30 (4:30) (50-70,70) 3-Y-0+ **£5,602** (£1,305; £575; £332)

RPR

1 **Roy's Delight (IRE)**[84] 2278 3-9-5 67 CO'Donoghue 4 73
(Edward P Harty, Ire) *trckd ldrs in 4th: impr to chal ent st: led 2f out: strly pressed fnl f: kpt on wl: all out* **8/1**

2 *shd* **Zaharath Al Bustan**[74] 2588 4-9-13 69 KFallon 2 75
(E D Delany, Ire) *trckd ldrs on inner: 6th 1/2-way: 5th and hdwy early st: 3rd whn briefly short of room over 1f out: 2nd and chal ins fnl f: ev ch: jst failed* **1/1**[1]

3 *1 3/4* **Mo Cheoil Thu (IRE)**[39] 3663 3-9-0 69 MHarley(7) 14 72
(Desmond McDonogh, Ire) *mid-div on outer: 7th 1/2-way: 5th early st: kpt on* **20/1**

4 *nk* **Happy Moments (IRE)**[78] 2484 5-9-9 68 (t) SMGorey(3) 5 70
(Reginald Roberts, Ire) *hld up: 11th 1/2-way: prog ent st: 6th over 1f out: kpt on* **20/1**

5 *nk* **Leap The Liffey (IRE)**[100] 1830 4-9-9 65 PJSmullen 13 66
(Mrs Valerie Keatley, Ire) *hld up towards rr: hdwy on outer early st: 6th under 1 1/2f out: kpt on* **25/1**

6 *nk* **Marino Lil (IRE)**[58] 3072 3-9-5 67 KJManning 6 68
(J S Bolger, Ire) *trckd ldrs in 5th: prog ent st: 2nd and chal under 2f out: no ex fnl f* **7/1**

7 *hd* **Man Of Aran**[20] 4245 7-10-0 70 (p) JMurtagh 12 70
(M Halford, Ire) *cl up: disp ld 1/2-way: led appr st: hdd 2f out: no ex ins fnl f* **14/1**

8 *3/4* **Spanish Parade (IRE)**[10] 4085 3-9-2 67 (t) DJMoran(3) 9 66
(Eoin Griffin, Ire) *in rr of mid-div: 9th after 1/2-way: one pce st* **10/1**

9 *1/2* **Santa Gertrudis (IRE)**[48] 3390 3-9-3 65 DPMcDonogh 7 63
(Kevin Prendergast, Ire) *settled towards rr: one pce st* **14/1**

10 *1/2* **Shaykhan (IRE)**[20] 4245 9-9-6 69 MJLane(7) 1 66
(James Leavy, Ire) *prom: 3rd 1/2-way: effrt on inner ent st: no ex fr 1 1/2f out* **13/2**[3]

11 *1/2* **Leon Knights**[18] 4277 3-9-7 69 EddieAhern 10 65
(G A Butler) *hld up: 10th 1/2-way: no ex st* **7/1**

12 *hd* **Actuality**[128] 1140 5-9-6 65 CPGeoghegan(3) 8 60
(Patrick Martin, Ire) *a towards rr* **20/1**

13 *6* **Survival Story (IRE)**[308] 6111 3-9-4 66 MJKinane 11 49
(Noel Meade, Ire) *mid-div: 8th 1/2-way: wknd appr st* **5/1**[2]

14 *dist* **Please The King (IRE)**[300] 6264 3-9-5 67 (tp) FMBerry 3 —
(T Hogan, Ire) *led: jnd 1/2-way: rdn and hdd appr st: wknd qckly: eased 1 1/2f out: t.o* **14/1**

1m 41.08s (101.08)
WFA 3 from 4yo+ 6lb **14** Ran SP% **163.3**
CSF £21.33 CT £224.05 TOTE £10.60: £2.60, £1.50, £16.20; DF 30.30.
Owner Magnificent Ten Syndicate **Bred** Mrs J Naughton **Trained** the Curragh, Co Kildare

NOTEBOOK
Leon Knights, down in trip and without the blinkers, could never get into the argument.

4867a MCR GROUP EUROPEAN BREEDERS FUND AUGUST H'CAP (PREMIER HANDICAP) 1m 2f 150y
5:30 (5:38) 3-Y-0+ **£32,989** (£9,679; £4,611; £1,570)

RPR

1 **Emmpat (IRE)**[24] 5697 9-9-4 92 WJLee 7 100
(C F Swan, Ire) *mid-div: 7th 1/2-way: 6th and hdwy appr st: 2nd ins fnl f: styd on wl to ld last strides* **12/1**

2 *hd* **All The Good (IRE)**[4] 4722 4-9-8 96 EddieAhern 6 104
(G A Butler) *trckd ldrs in 4th: smooth hdwy to ld early st: strly pressed wl ins fnl f: hdd last strides* **7/1**[3]

3 *1 1/4* **Ezima (IRE)**[91] 2066 3-8-9 91 KJManning 1 98
(J S Bolger, Ire) *chsd ldrs in 6th: rdn to go 3rd 1 1/2f out: kpt on ins fnl f* **7/1**[3]

4 *2 1/2* **Vincenzio Galilei (USA)**[46] 3442 3-9-1 97 (b[1]) JMurtagh 14 99
(G M Lyons, Ire) *in rr of mid-div: prog ent st: 5th over 1f out: kpt on* **3/1**[2]

5 *1 1/2* **Worldly Wise**[21] 4211 4-9-5 93 DMGrant 8 92
(Patrick J Flynn, Ire) *trckd ldrs in 5th: prog early st: 3rd over 1f out: no ex ins fnl f* **14/1**

6 *2 1/2* **Definate Spectacle (IRE)**[24] 3772 7-9-6 94 (t) MJKinane 9 86
(Noel Meade, Ire) *hld up towards rr: kpt on fr 1 1/2f out* **10/1**

7 *3/4* **Boo**[24] 4105 5-9-7 95 (b[1]) CO'Donoghue 12 86
(K R Burke) *towards rr: 11th bef 1/2-way: kpt on st* **20/1**

8 *2* **Lazio (GER)**[45] 783 6-10-2 104 WMLordan 11 91
(S J Mahon, Ire) *mid-div: 8th 1/2-way: kpt on same pce st* **20/1**

9 *2* **Celtic Dane (IRE)**[26] 4051 3-8-11 93 DPMcDonogh 4 78
(Kevin Prendergast, Ire) *trckd ldrs in 3rd: rdn appr st: sn no ex and wknd* **6/4**[1]

10 *3* **Cousteau**[4] 4728 4-9-8 103 5ex (t) SFoley(7) 10 81
(John Joseph Hanlon, Ire) *sn led: hdd early st: wknd fr 1 1/2f out* **10/1**

11 *1 1/2* **Film Festival (USA)**[56] 3138 4-9-6 94 RPCleary 5 70
(M Halford, Ire) *settled 2nd: rdn and wknd ent st* **16/1**

12 *1 1/2* **Saintly Rachel (IRE)**[26] 4051 9-9-4 92 JAHeffernan 2 65
(C F Swan, Ire) *in rr of mid-div: no ex fr 3f out* **25/1**

13 *4* **King Rama (USA)**[23] 4143 6-9-6 94 KFallon 13 60
(John E Kiely, Ire) *a towards rr* **7/1**[3]

14 *1* **Merveilles**[64] 2899 4-9-0 88 FMBerry 3 52
(Mrs John Harrington, Ire) *slowly away and a bhd* **12/1**

WFA 3 from 4yo+ 9lb **14** Ran SP% **162.0**
CSF £122.99 CT £690.61 TOTE £12.60: £3.40, £2.10, £3.70; DF 171.20.
Owner Michael D Mee **Bred** Michael Phelan **Trained** Cloughjordan, Co Tipperary

NOTEBOOK
Emmpat(IRE), a useful dual-purpose horse, was having his first run on the Flat for 11 months.

All The Good(IRE), making a quick reappearance after finishing tired in the Ebor four days earlier, has gained his last three wins over half a mile further than this and although successful over this trip on Polytrack in Britain, that was when he was a two-year-old. Sensibly ridden close to the pace and always travelling well, he was sent for home soon after turning in and quickly had most of his rivals in trouble. He looked likely to score, but there was always the danger that something would emerge from the pack and do him for finishing pace and he was cruelly cut down near the line. However, this effort still fully vindicated his connections' decision to bring him here. (op 8/1 tchd 9/1)

Boo, winner of his first three starts on Polytrack in Britain but mainly disappointing since, was still 6lb higher than for his last win in December 2005. Given a patient ride, he had to be switched very wide after straightening up for home, but although he stayed on he was never anywhere near the leaders. The first-time blinkers did not appear to have much of an effect.

4868 - (Foreign Racing) - See Raceform Interactive

4837 BADEN-BADEN (L-H)
Sunday, August 26

OFFICIAL GOING: Good

4869a BESTWETTEN.DE - 137 GOLDEN PEITSCHE (GROUP 2) 6f
4:00 (4:08) 3-Y-0+ **£28,378** (£11,486; £4,730; £2,703)

RPR

1 **Electric Beat**[44] 3506 4-9-2 TMundry 5 105
(C Sprengel, Germany) *in tch on ins: 4th st: led 1 1/2f out: r.o wl* **66/10**

2 *3/4* **Santiago Atitlan**[21] 4213 5-9-2 EPedroza 1 103
(A Wohler, Germany) *prom: led 1/2-way: hdd 1 1/2f out: styd on but hld by wnr* **21/1**

3 *hd* **Bahama Mama (IRE)**[21] 4213 3-8-7 AStarke 7 97
(W Hickst, Germany) *settled in tch: 3rd st: kpt on steadily fnl stages* **15/2**

4 *1* **Sonny Red (IRE)**[30] 3894 3-8-11 FrancisNorton 9 98
(R Hannon) *in tch in centre: styd on fr over 1f out: nrst at fin* **22/10**[1]

5 *1/2* **Adamantinos**[116] 1420 3-8-11 J-PCarvalho 8 96
(Frau E Mader, Germany) *mid-div in centre: nvr threatened ldrs* **24/1**

6 *hd* **Lucky Strike**[21] 4213 9-9-2 ADeVries 12 97
(A Trybuhl, Germany) *settled on ins: effrt 1 1/2f out: no imp on ldrs* **23/10**[2]

7 *nk* **Shinko's Best (IRE)**[39] 3666 6-9-2 NRichter 2 97
(A Kleinkorres, Germany) *led on rail to 1/2-way: 2nd st: rdn and no ex fr 1 1/2f out* **27/1**

8 *1 1/4* **Arc De Triomphe (GER)**[22] 4190 5-9-2 THellier 6 93
(D Fechner, Germany) *prom on wd outside: pushed along st: styd on tl no ex fnl 150yds* **30/1**

9 *3/4* **Mood Music**[21] 4213 3-8-11 AHelfenbein 3 89
(Mario Hofer, Germany) *in tch on rail: no imp st* **42/1**

10 *2* **New Girlfriend (IRE)**[21] 4213 4-8-11 SMaillot 11 80
(Robert Collet, France) *hld up: n.d* **49/10**[3]

11 *1 1/4* **Matrix (GER)**[46] 3445 6-9-2 WMongil 10 81
(W Baltromei, Germany) *towards rr: pushed along 2f out: no imp* **30/1**

12 *2* **Key To Pleasure (GER)**[21] 4213 7-9-2 ASuborics 4 75
(Mario Hofer, Germany) *prom on rail to 1/2-way: one pce st* **151/10**

69.04 secs (-1.25)
WFA 3 from 4yo+ 3lb **12** Ran SP% **130.5**
(Including 10 Euros stake): WIN 76; PL 24, 49, 22; SF 1,071.
Owner Rennstall Directa **Bred** T E Pocock **Trained** Germany

NOTEBOOK
Sonny Red(IRE), placed in a Group 3 at Ascot on his drop back to this trip last time, went off the marginal favourite but was doing his best work late as if a return to seven would be in his favour on this ground. He may need a softer surface to be effective at this trip.

4652 DEAUVILLE (R-H)
Sunday, August 26

OFFICIAL GOING: Turf course - soft; all-weather - standard

4871a PRIX DE MEAUTRY LUCIEN BARRIERE (GROUP 3) 6f
2:20 (2:19) 3-Y-0+ **£27,027** (£10,811; £8,108; £5,405; £2,703)

RPR

1 **Garnica (FR)**[21] 4214 4-9-5 C-PLemaire 8 118
(J-C Rouget, France) *prom: disputing 2nd 1/2-way: chal 1 1/2f out: led 1f out: r.o wl fnl f* **6/4**[1]

2 *1 1/2* **Le Cadre Noir (IRE)**[42] 3-8-11 MDemuro 3 108
(A Renzoni, Italy) *trckd ldrs: 7th 1/2-way: hdwy on outside over 1 1/2f out: wnt 2nd fnl f: kpt on* **4/1**[2]

3 *3/4* **Tiza (SAF)**[21] 4214 5-9-5 CSoumillon 5 111
(A De Royer-Dupre, France) *in tch: disputing 4th 1/2-way: styd on fnl f to take 3rd on line* **9/2**[3]

4 *nse* **Eisteddfod**[44] 3500 6-9-1 SPasquier 9 107
(P F I Cole) *cl up: disputing 2nd 1/2-way: disputing ld appr fnl f: rdn 1f out: no ex and lost 3rd on line* **9/2**[3]

5 *3/4* **The Trader (IRE)**[22] 4190 9-9-1 (b) DBoeuf 2 104
(M Blanshard) *hld up: 8th 1/2-way: pushed along 2f out: swtchd stands' side 1 1/2f out: rdn and styd on fnl f: nrest at fin* **10/1**

6 *snk* **Sabasha (FR)**[28] 4012 4-8-11 FBlondel 4 100
(F Rohaut, France) *in tch: disputing 4th 1/2-way: rdn 1 1/2f out: one pce* **25/1**

7 *shd* **Val Jaro (FR)**[21] 4214 4-9-1 THuet 7 104
(S Morineau, France) *led to 1f out: wknd fnl 100yds* **33/1**

8 *3* **Iron Lips**[50] 3339 3-8-8 OPeslier 10 91
(C Laffon-Parias, France) *in tch: disputing 4th 1/2-way: rdn 1 1/2f out: unable qckn* **20/1**

9 *1 1/2* **Ascot Family (IRE)**[22] 4190 3-8-8 0 YBarberot 1 86
(A Lyon, France) *hld up: last 1/2-way: nvr in contention* **20/1**

1m 12.2s (-0.80) **Going Correction** +0.30s/f (Good)
WFA 3 from 4yo+ 3lb **9** Ran SP% **121.8**
Speed ratings: **117,115,114,113,112 112,112,108,106**
PARI-MUTUEL: WIN 2.00; PL 1.10, 1.50, 1.30; DF 6.50.
Owner E A Gann **Bred** Jean Pierre Dubois **Trained** Pau, France

NOTEBOOK
Garnica(FR), a really consistent and genuine performer, never looked like tasting defeat in this sprint. Always in the leading group, he quickened from one and a half out and finally outclassed his rivals. He acted well on the soft ground and will now be aimed at the Prix de la Foret.

Le Cadre Noir(IRE), a very good-looking individual, was not suited by the soft ground but nevertheless put up a decent performance. In mid-division early on, he was brought with a run up the centre of the track but never threatened the winner. He will now go back to Italy and will be aimed at the Premio Omenoni in mid-October.
Tiza(SAF), in mid-division for much of this sprint, was putting in his best work at the finish. He was well backed but did not appear too happy on the soft ground. This ex-South African gelding is now likely to turn out for the Prix du Petit Couvert at Longchamp.
Eisteddfod, smartly away, was only beaten a nose for third place. He hung a little left at the two-furlong marker but stuck to the task until the bitter end.
The Trader(IRE) as usual was dropped out last and was putting in his best work at the finish. He quickened from one and a half out and came with a run up the stands' rails.

4872a GRAND PRIX DE DEAUVILLE LUCIEN BARRIERE (GROUP 2) 1m 4f 110y
2:50 (2:52) 3-Y-0+ **£67,568** (£30,986; £14,789; £9,859; £4,930)

RPR
1 **Irish Wells (FR)**63 2925 4-9-3 DBoeuf 7 117
(F Rohaut, France) *led after 3f: pushed along and r.o 2f out: rdn and styd on wl fnl f* **9/2**3
2 *1* **Poet Laureate**22 4191 3-8-6 KerrinMcEvoy 3 115
(A Fabre, France) *in tch: 3rd on ins st: wnt 2nd 1 1/2f out: nt pce of wnr* **2/1**1
3 *2* **Champs Elysees**43 3565 4-9-3 SPasquier 1 112
(A Fabre, France) *prom: 2nd and pushed along st: pressing ldr 2f out: lost 2nd 1 1/2f out: styd on at one pce* **11/2**
4 *3* **Pearl Sky (FR)**21 4215 4-9-0 ACrastus 5 105
(Y De Nicolay, France) *hld up: disputing last on rail st: sn pushed along: rdn and wnt 4th 2f out: nvr in chalng position* **8/1**
5 *5* **Sagara (USA)**43 3566 3-8-6 C-PLemaire 8 100
(J E Pease, France) *hld up: disputing last st: styd on down outside fnl 1 1/2f but n.d* **10/3**2
6 *4* **Anton Chekhov**56 3146 3-8-9 ABoschert 2 97
(U Ostmann, Germany) *led 3f: 2nd 1/2-way: lost pl 3f out: 5th and wkng st* **12/1**
7 *6* **Princesse Dansante (IRE)**21 4215 4-9-0 TThulliez 6 82
(F Doumen, France) *in tch: 4th and pushed along on outside st: sn rdn and one pce* **40/1**

2m 45.5s (-1.20) **Going Correction** +0.30s/f (Good)
WFA 3 from 4yo+ 10lb 7 Ran SP% **111.2**
Speed ratings: **115,114,113,111,108 105,102**
PARI-MUTUEL: WIN 6.20; PL 2.40, 1.80; DF 6.50.
Owner B Van Dalfsen **Bred** Eight International Racing Ltd **Trained** Sauvagnon, France

NOTEBOOK
Irish Wells(FR), a very game and consistent individual, looked superb in the paddock and did nothing wrong during the race. After the field passed the stands, his jockey felt there was not enough pace so the pair took up the running with a full ten furlongs left to run. He accelerated well early in the straight and finally won with something in hand. His trainer feels he might not be up to the quality of the Arc so a likely target is the big Group 1 race in Milan on October 14.
Poet Laureate, a fine, outstanding grey who is still learning the business, raced on the rail in fifth position for much of the race, and was extracted to challenge one and a half out. At that point the colt looked dangerous but he could not quicken when asked and was finally well held by the winner. He has a lot of scope for improvement and will surely win a Group race in the not too distance future. The colt will also turn into a fine four-year-old.
Champs Elysees, given every possible chance, was not quite good enough. Always well placed, he was asked to quicken early in the straight but could only stay on at the same pace. He is a Group 3 performer and ran up to his level.
Pearl Sky(FR) nearly fell rounding the first turn while being held up. The filly was putting in her best work at the finish but was never really dangerous.

4873a PRIX QUINCEY LUCIEN BARRIERE (GROUP 3) (STRAIGHT COURSE) 1m (R)
3:20 (3:26) 3-Y-0+ **£27,027** (£10,811; £8,108; £5,405; £2,703)

RPR
1 **Kavafi (IRE)**28 4012 5-9-0 MBlancpain 3 107
(C Laffon-Parias, France) *hld up in rr on rails: last 2f out: str run fr over 1f out to ld last strides* **12/1**
2 *nk* **Ricine (IRE)**24 5-8-13 F-XBertras 13 105
(F Rohaut, France) *a in tch on outside: rdn over 1f out: narrow ldr ins fnl 100yds tl hdd last strides* **10/1**
3 *nse* **Spirito Del Vento (FR)**77 2500 4-9-7 OPeslier 6 113
(J-M Beguigne, France) *trckd ldrs: hrd rdn appr fnl f: ev ch ins fnl 100yds: unable qckn cl home* **7/4**1
4 *nk* **Kilometre Neuf (FR)**39 3665 4-9-0 DBonilla 9 105
(F Doumen, France) *hld up towards rr: hdwy over 1f out: styng on whn nt clr run 150yds out: nrest at fin* **25/1**
5 *nk* **Air Bag (FR)**14 4443 3-8-5 TJarnet 8 102
(Mme C Barande-Barbe, France) *a.p: racing keenly: led over 2f out tl ins fnl 100yds: one pce* **33/1**
6 *½* **Whazzis**30 3897 3-8-5 (v) KerrinMcEvoy 10 101
(W J Haggas) *cl up on outside: ev ch over 1f out: one pce* **9/2**3
7 *¾* **Major Grace (FR)**11 4520 4-9-0 TThulliez 7 102
(Y De Nicolay, France) *pressed ldr to over 2f out: kpt on one pce* **14/1**
8 *snk* **Chinandega (FR)**10 4556 3-8-12 ACrastus 4 106
(P Demercastel, France) *pressed ldr early: settled in mid-div: kpt on but nvr a factor* **16/1**
9 *snk* **Stop Making Sense**29 5-9-0 SPasquier 2 102
(A Fabre, France) *led to over 2f out: rdn and no ex fr over 1f out* **4/1**2
10 *nse* **Highest Height (FR)**10 4556 3-8-5 (b) DBoeuf 5 99
(D Smaga, France) *a in rr: styd on fr dist* **33/1**
11 **Ryono (USA)**21 4217 8-9-2 (b) TCastanheira 12 —
(S Smrczek, Germany) *a towards rr* **40/1**
12 **Staraco (FR)**21 4216 3-8-8 CSoumillon 1 —
(B Goudot, France) *trckd ldr on rails tl wkng over 1 1/2f out: eased* **11/1**

1m 42.5s (0.20) **Going Correction** +0.30s/f (Good)
WFA 3 from 4yo+ 6lb 12 Ran SP% **124.4**
Speed ratings: **111,110,110,110,110 109,108,108,108,108 108,108**
PARI-MUTUEL: WIN 10.00; PL 2.70, 4.80, 1.50; DF 135.40.
Owner L Marinopoulos **Bred** Stilvi Compania Financiera S A **Trained** Chantilly, France

NOTEBOOK
Kavafi(IRE) still had a lot to do at the furlong marker having been held up for a late challenge. Brought with a beautifully-timed run on the rail, he got up in the final few strides. This consistent horse will probably go on to the Prix Daniel Wildenstein next month.
Ricine(IRE), well backed in the morning, put in one of her best performances this season. She was also held up for a late run, which was made up the centre of the track. Wearing cheekpieces here, she barely gets a mile and did not quite go through with her challenge, and has now been marked down for the Premio Chiusura at Milan in November.
Spirito Del Vento(FR), never far from the leading group, was outpaced when things quickened up at the two-furlong marker. He stayed on one-paced and is now being aimed at the Prix de la Foret.
Kilometre Neuf(FR) did not get much luck inside the final furlong, but he finished best of all and would certainly have finished closer to the winner but for interference.
Whazzis was always well up but could not be covered up. She challenged for the lead one and a half out and just stayed on as the race came to an end. She was only beaten just over a length in a race that was run at a slow pace early on.

OVREVOLL (R-H)
Sunday, August 26

OFFICIAL GOING: Good

4874a MARIT SVEAAS MINNELOP (GROUP 3) 1m 1f
2:20 (12:00) 3-Y-0+ **£82,034** (£21,329; £9,844; £5,906; £3,938)

RPR
1 **Funny Legend (NOR)**38 6-8-13 FJohansson 7 98
(Wido Neuroth, Norway) *a wl in tch: chal 1 1/2f out: led 1f out: comf* **19/10**1
2 *2½* **Maybach**33 6-9-4 P-AGraberg 1 98
(B Bo, Sweden) *hld up in rr to st: str run on outside fr over 1f out: fin wl* **17/1**
3 *1½* **The Pirate (DEN)**17 4-9-4 YvonneDurant 3 95
(Niels Petersen, Norway) *towards rr to st: styd on fnl 2f* **127/10**
4 *hd* **Angel De Madrid (CHI)**63 6-9-4 JohnFortune 6 95
(Rune Haugen, Norway) *hld up towards rr: hdwy fnl 2f: nrest at fin* **22/1**
5 *hd* **Salt Track (ARG)**24 7-9-4 ESki 2 94
(Niels Petersen, Norway) *s.s: hdwy on ins fr over 1f out: nrest at fin* **68/10**3
6 *1½* **Crimson And Gold**21 5-9-4 (b) FDiaz 5 92
(L Reuterskiold, Sweden) *a in tch: effrt wl over 1f out: no ex fnl f* **29/1**
7 *1* **Wazir (USA)**24 5-9-4 (b) MSantos 8 90
(L Reuterskiold, Sweden) *prom: 4th st: ev ch wl over 1f out: one pce* **47/1**
8 *½* **Art Attack (GER)**17 4-9-4 JJohansen 13 89
(Rune Haugen, Norway) *racd in 4th: 3rd st: sn wknd* **78/10**
9 *2½* **Firello (NOR)**59 7-9-4 TJorgensen 14 84
(W Togersen, Norway) *trckd ldr to 1/2-way: lft 2nd over 3f out: btn 2f out* **31/1**
10 *½* **Jubilation**33 8-9-4 MMartinez 4 83
(F Reuterskiold, Sweden) *trckd ldr: lft in ld over 3f out: hdd 1f out: wknd qckly* **28/1**
11 *1* **Snoqualmie Boy**16 4366 4-9-4 TQuinn 9 81
(D R C Elsworth) *nvr nrr than mid-div: btn over 1f out* **31/10**2
12 *8* **Forthe Millionkiss (GER)**49 3-8-11 DMoffatt 10 66
(U Ostmann, Germany) *a towards rr* **132/10**
13 *4* **Fly Society (DEN)**21 6-9-4 KAndersen 15 58
(S Jensen, Denmark) *a towards rr* **50/1**
U **Hovman (DEN)**24 8-9-6 LSantos 12 —
(Ms C Erichsen, Norway) *led: stl clr whn uns rdr over 3f out* **21/1**

1m 48.8s (-1.10)
WFA 3 from 4yo+ 7lb 14 Ran SP% **125.8**
(including one krone stakes): WIN 2.91; PL 1.53, 2.86, 3.35; DF 12.64.
Owner Stall E & F **Bred** Stall E & F **Trained** Norway

NOTEBOOK
Snoqualmie Boy went off favourite for this valuable Group 3 having been in decent form in Britain but never figured and this was a disappointing effort.

4527 CHEPSTOW (L-H)
Monday, August 27

OFFICIAL GOING: Good to firm (9.0)
Wind: Moderate, behind

4875 EUROPEAN BREEDERS' FUND FILLIES' MEDIAN AUCTION MAIDEN STKS 1m 14y
2:30 (2:32) (Class 5) 2-Y-0 **£3,562** (£1,059; £529; £264) **Stalls** High

Form RPR
1 **Spell Caster** 2-9-0 0 SebSanders 8 84+
(R M Beckett) *in tch: hdwy 3f out: led ins fnl 2f: qcknd over 1f out: styd on wl fnl f: readily* **14/1**
0 2 *1½* **Ballora (FR)**31 3895 2-9-0 0 SimonWhitworth 2 81+
(S Kirk) *chsd ldrs: drvn to go 2nd over 1f out: styd on wl for clr 2nd but no ch w ready wnr* **9/2**2
03 3 *3* **La Columbina**11 4547 2-9-0 0 RyanMoore 13 74
(R Hannon) *trckd ldr: led 3f out: hdd ins fnl 2f: sn hrd drvn: lost 2nd over 1f out: wknd ins fnl f* **15/8**1
0 4 *7* **Trinkila (USA)**26 4061 2-9-0 0 TQuinn 6 59
(P F I Cole) *chsd ldrs: rdn over 3f out: wknd over 1f out* **16/1**
5 5 *2½* **Green Earrings (IRE)**26 4074 2-9-0 0 SteveDrowne 14 53
(R Charlton) *in tch: hdwy to chse ldrs 3f out: sn rdn: wknd over 1f out* **9/2**2
6 *1* **Shaama Rose (FR)** 2-9-0 0 DarryllHolland 7 51
(M R Channon) *s.i.s: bhd: sme hdwy 3f out: nvr in contention* **7/1**3
2043 7 *1* **Giggling Monkey**10 4559 2-9-0 50 StephenDonohoe 9 49
(P D Evans) *chsd ldrs: rdn over 3f out: wknd qckly fr 2f out* **18/1**
0 8 *1½* **Mia Haria**21 4232 2-9-0 0 PaulFitzsimons 12 46
(B R Millman) *chsd ldrs: rdn 4f out: wknd over 2f out* **80/1**
9 *nk* **Les Allues (IRE)** 2-8-11 0 NeilChalmers(3) 1 45
(H S Howe) *s.i.s and wnt lft s: rr: hung lft and no ch fnl 3f* **100/1**
00 10 *1* **Aneebee (IRE)**23 4162 2-8-9 0 HaddenFrost(5) 16 43
(R Hannon) *a towards rr* **40/1**
0400 11 *½* **Bold Diva**14 4453 2-8-9 40 (b1) LukeMorris(5) 10 42
(A W Carroll) *t.k.h: led tl hdd 3f out: sn wknd* **66/1**
0 12 *2* **Jolie Fleur**19 4273 2-8-11 0 RichardKingscote(3) 3 37
(C Tinkler) *wnt rt s: pressed ldrs to 1/2-way* **100/1**
13 *2½* **Anamarka** 2-9-0 0 DaneO'Neill 11 32
(H Candy) *s.i.s: a towards rr* **8/1**
14 *1¾* **Fortunella** 2-9-0 0 IanMongan 15 28
(P Howling) *a in rr* **50/1**
00 15 *23* **Sophies Secret**19 4286 2-9-0 0 SamHitchcott 5 —
(J R Holt) *hmpd s and slowly away: a wl bhd* **100/1**

16 *102* **Ice Choice (IRE)** 2-9-0 0 SaleemGolam 4 —
(Mark Gillard) *hmpd s: sn t.o* **100/1**

1m 33.19s (-2.81) **Going Correction** -0.30s/f (Firm) **16** Ran SP% **123.7**
Speed ratings (Par 91): **102,100,97,90,88 87,86,84,84,83 82,80,78,76,53** —
CSF £76.72 TOTE £15.60: £4.20, £2.20, £1.50; EX 127.20.
Owner D P Barrie & M J Rees **Bred** P E Clinton **Trained** Whitsbury, Hants

FOCUS
A good juvenile fillies' maiden. The form looks solid and it was a very decent time for a race like this and 0.2 seconds faster than the boys' equivalent.

NOTEBOOK
Spell Caster ◆, a 38,000gns purchase whose pedigree suggests a mix of speed and stamina, picked up readily when asked to win her race and got the job done at the first time of asking. Considering she proved so easy to back ahead of this racecourse bow it is fair to assume that she will improve a deal for the experience and she looks to have a bright future, as she clearly stays well. (op 9-1)
Ballora(FR) ◆, not disgraced when down the field on her debut at Ascot in a hot 6f fillies' maiden a month ago, showed the benefit of that experience and put in an improved effort over this longer trip. She was put in her place by the winner, but finished a clear second best and no doubt has a similar race within her compass. It should also be noted that nurseries will be an option after her next assignment and her Group 1 entry is clearly flying too high. (op 11-2)
La Columbina, third over this trip at Sandown last time, had her chance under a positive ride and ran very close to her recent level. She now has the option of nurseries and, on this evidence, could be better off dropping back to 7f for the short term. (tchd 7-4, 2-1, 9-4 in places and 5-2 in a place)
Trinkila(USA) showed improved form on this step up in trip, but still did not get home anywhere near as well as the principals. She appeals as more of a nursery type, for which she will be eligible after her next outing, and a drop back to 7f now looks in order. (op 20-1)
Green Earrings(IRE) ran below her debut form and failed to stay the longer trip. She probably also wants easier ground. (op 4-1 tchd 5-1)
Shaama Rose(FR), a 75,000euros purchase bred to be effective over this trip at two, was always playing catch-up after a slow start and never figured. She was nibbled at in the betting, however, and should learn plenty for the experience so should prove sharper next time. (op 14-1)
Bold Diva Official explanation: jockey said saddle slipped
Sophies Secret Official explanation: jockey said filly was never travelling
Ice Choice(IRE) Official explanation: jockey said filly felt wrong in running

4876 EUROPEAN BREEDERS' FUND MAIDEN STKS 1m 14y
3:05 (3:06) (Class 5) 2-Y-O **£3,562** (£1,059; £529; £264) **Stalls** High

Form RPR
5 **1** **Bencoolen (IRE)**[31] 3896 2-9-0 0 SteveDrowne 5 82+
(R Charlton) *a.p: led wl over 1f out: r.o wl: pushed out* **2/1**[1]
0 **2** *1 1/2* **Meer Kat (IRE)**[44] 3551 2-8-11 0 RichardKingscote(3) 12 80+
(R Charlton) *s.i.s: sn mid-div: rdn and hdwy over 1f out: styd on fnl f* **20/1**
4 **3** *shd* **Sainglend**[33] 3856 2-9-0 0 DaneO'Neill 1 78
(H Candy) *prom: rdn and ev ch 2f out: kpt on but nt pce of wnr fnl f* **5/1**[3]
0 **4** *2* **Summon Up Theblood**[23] 4151 2-9-0 0 DarryllHolland 9 74
(M R Channon) *led: rdn and hdd wl over 1f out: kpt on same pce* **5/1**[3]
0 **5** *1/2* **Black Jacari (IRE)**[44] 3552 2-9-0 0 SimonWhitworth 8 73
(A King) *s.i.s: towards rr: hdwy 4f out: rdn over 2f out: one pce fnl f* **25/1**
0 **6** *2* **Nikolaievich (IRE)**[44] 3551 2-9-0 0 TQuinn 7 69
(P F I Cole) *bhd: rdn 3f out: styd on ins fnl f: nvr trbld ldrs* **33/1**
6 **7** *3/4* **Hadron Collider (FR)**[17] 4362 2-9-0 0 RyanMoore 4 67
(R Hannon) *prom: rdn 2f out: sn outpcd* **7/1**
0 **8** *nk* **Desert Life (IRE)**[6] 4683 2-8-9 0 LukeMorris(5) 10 66
(R A Harris) *chsd ldrs: rdn and hung lft over 2f out: wknd over 1f out* **66/1**
54 **9** *1 3/4* **Calistos Quest**[22] 4192 2-9-0 0 SebSanders 11 62
(M Johnston) *chsd ldrs: rdn over 3f out: wknd over 1f out* **3/1**[2]
10 *2* **Festival Dreams** 2-8-7 0 SCreighton(7) 2 58
(Miss J S Davis) *chsd ldrs: rdn over 2f out: wknd fnl f* **66/1**
11 *5* **Follow Your Spirit** 2-8-9 0 KevinGhunowa(5) 6 47
(B Palling) *bhd fnl 3f* **25/1**
05 **12** *hd* **Paddy Rielly (IRE)**[33] 3842 2-9-0 0 StephenDonohoe 3 47
(P D Evans) *a towards rr* **50/1**

1m 33.39s (-2.61) **Going Correction** -0.30s/f (Firm) **12** Ran SP% **124.5**
Speed ratings (Par 94): **101,99,99,97,96 94,94,93,92,90 85,84**
CSF £50.78 TOTE £3.00: £1.40, £3.90, £2.20; EX 28.20.
Owner De La Warr Racing **Bred** Darley **Trained** Beckhampton, Wilts

FOCUS
Despite being 0.2 seconds slower than the preceding fillies' equivalent, the time was still decent for a race of its type and 0.58 seconds faster than the later handicap for older horses. Solid maiden form.

NOTEBOOK
Bencoolen(IRE), a decent fifth on his debut at Ascot last time, appreciated the extra furlong and did not have to be fully extended to lose his maiden tag. This proves his versatility as regards underfoot conditions and further improvement looks assured, so it will be interesting to see where he is pitched in next. (op 9-4 tchd 7-4 and 5-2 in a place)
Meer Kat(IRE) ◆, slow to break, stepped up markedly on his debut form over this longer distance and was doing his best work towards the finish under a somewhat considerate ride. He is clearly going in the right direction and should not remain a maiden for long. (tchd 14-1)
Sainglend posted a slight improvement on his debut at Sandown in July and got the extra furlong well enough, helping to set the level of this form. He has a maiden within his compass and will also be qualified for a nursery mark after his next assignment. (op 4-1 tchd 7-2)
Summon Up Theblood had his chance from the front and got the extra furlong well, but lacked the pace of the principals. He ran right up to his debut form here, rating a sound benchmark for the form, and already looks in need of a stiffer test. He is another who will be qualified for nurseries after his next start. (tchd 7-1)
Nikolaievich(IRE) enjoyed this longer trip and showed improved form, but still looks to be very much learning his trade. He should do better when entering nurseries, however, looks more of a three-year-old in the making and should stay up to 1m4f next season. (op 25-1)
Calistos Quest, once again well backed, failed to improve as could have been expected for the extra furlong yet was beaten too early for stamina to have been a real excuse. This was still a slight improvement on his Chester form and it may be that he fares better now he is eligible for nurseries. (op 5-1)
Paddy Rielly(IRE) Official explanation: jockey said gelding was unsuited by the good to firm ground

4877 JOIN WBX.COM FOR FREE FOOTBALL SHIRT H'CAP 2m 49y
3:40 (3:41) (Class 6) (0-65,62) 3-Y-O **£2,590** (£770; £385; £192) **Stalls** Low

Form RPR
5313 **1** **Franchoek (IRE)**[16] 4391 3-9-6 61 RyanMoore 2 71+
(A King) *in tch: hdwy 4f out: led appr fnl 2f: sn in command: comf* **4/7**[1]
6302 **2** *2* **Right Option (IRE)**[11] 4528 3-8-7 53 KevinGhunowa(5) 4 60
(J L Flint) *in rr: hdwy fr 5f out: rdn 3f out: styd on to chse wnr fnl f and kpt on wl but a comf hld* **25/1**
-350 **3** *1 1/2* **Apache Chant (USA)**[56] 3150 3-8-4 50 LukeMorris(5) 5 55
(A W Carroll) *in rr: hdwy over 4f out: chsd ldrs over 2f out: styd on to go 3rd over 1f out and kpt on ins fnl f but a hld by ldng duo* **33/1**
0520 **4** *3/4* **Tobougg Welcome (IRE)**[11] 4531 3-8-5 46 SaleemGolam 6 51
(S C Williams) *chsd ldrs: wnt 2nd and rdn 3f out: no imp on wnr 2f out: wknd fnl f* **7/1**[2]
5032 **5** *1 1/4* **Conny Nobel (IRE)**[11] 4531 3-8-12 53 RichardThomas 9 56
(C Roberts) *hld up in rr: pushed along and hdwy over 3f out: kpt on fnl 2f but nvr in contention* **12/1**
-000 **6** *3* **Regal Ovation**[9] 4592 3-8-11 52 DarryllHolland 7 51
(W R Muir) *led 1f: styd trcking ldr tl led over 4f out: hdd appr fnl 2f: wknd over 1f out* **20/1**
-056 **7** *6* **Salto Chico**[18] 4339 3-8-4 48 ow3 MarcHalford(3) 8 40
(W M Brisbourne) *in rr: pushed along over 3f out: sme prog fnl 2f: nvr in contention* **28/1**
402 **8** *3* **Red**[56] 3166 3-9-7 62 SebSanders 10 51
(R M Beckett) *in rr: n.m.r in rr after 2f: mod prog on outside over 3f out: sn pushed along and no futher prog* **15/2**[3]
645 **9** *3 1/2* **Pertemps Power**[17] 4357 3-8-9 55 HaddenFrost(5) 11 39
(A D Smith) *in rr: hdwy and pushed along 4f out: wknd 3f out* **25/1**
-000 **10** *5* **On Watch**[32] 3876 3-8-9 50 (v[1]) DaneO'Neill 1 28
(H Candy) *chsd ldrs: rdn 3f out: sn btn* **33/1**
6340 **11** *3/4* **Lady Traill**[25] 4104 3-8-7 48 (b[1]) TQuinn 3 26
(B W Hills) *led after 1f: hdd over 4f out: wknd 3f out* **16/1**
0400 **12** *3 1/2* **Madam Vouvray**[12] 4510 3-9-6 61 SteveDrowne 13 34
(B J Meehan) *chsd ldrs tl wknd 4f out* **25/1**

3m 37.46s (-1.94) **Going Correction** -0.15s/f (Firm) **12** Ran SP% **127.1**
Speed ratings (Par 98): **98,97,96,95,95 93,90,89,87,85 84,82**
CSF £27.61 CT £308.89 TOTE £1.70: £1.10, £4.10, £13.30; EX 23.60.
Owner David Mason **Bred** 6c Stallions Ltd **Trained** Barbury Castle, Wilts

FOCUS
A moderate three-year-old staying handicap, run at an average gallop. The progressive winner is value for a bit further than the bare margin.

4878 WBX.COM £25 BET FOR NEW ACCOUNTS H'CAP 1m 2f 36y
4:15 (4:24) (Class 6) (0-65,65) 3-Y-0+ **£2,720** (£809; £404; £202) **Stalls** Low

Form RPR
6065 **1** **Royal Indulgence**[7] 4660 7-8-13 53 MarcHalford(3) 4 62
(W M Brisbourne) *chsd ldrs: rdn to ld 2f out: in command fnl f: comf* **12/1**
5024 **2** *1* **Sweet Request**[22] 4205 3-9-5 64 SebSanders 13 71
(R M Beckett) *mid-div: hdwy over 2f out: edgd lft but r.o ins fnl f* **6/1**[2]
-554 **3** *1 1/4* **Spunger**[7] 4660 4-9-6 57 (v) DaneO'Neill 16 62
(H J L Dunlop) *mid-div: hdwy over 2f out: sn rdn: hung lft but styd on ins fnl f* **12/1**
4610 **4** *1/2* **Trevian**[12] 4517 6-8-13 55 KevinGhunowa(5) 6 59
(J M Bradley) *chsd ldrs: rdn over 3f out: kpt on u.p but a hld fnl 2f* **25/1**
0004 **5** *1* **Speagle (IRE)**[15] 4418 5-10-0 65 DarryllHolland 10 67
(D Carroll) *chsd ldrs: led jst ins 3f out: rdn and hdd 2f out: kpt on same pce* **8/1**[3]
4055 **6** *1/2* **Double Spectre (IRE)**[14] 4458 5-9-13 64 IanMongan 9 65
(Jean-Rene Auvray) *hld up towards rr: rdn and sme hdwy over 2f out: kpt on same pce* **11/1**
2424 **7** *hd* **Hazarayna**[35] 3800 3-9-6 65 (v[1]) StephenDonohoe 14 65
(P D Evans) *chsd ldrs: rdn 3f out: one pce fnl 2f* **20/1**
2222 **8** *2 1/2* **Potentiale (IRE)**[19] 4283 3-9-6 65 RyanMoore 11 60
(J W Hills) *mid-div: rdn 3f out: sme hdwy and edgd lft over 1f out: no further imp* **15/8**[1]
105- **9** *3/4* **Play Master (IRE)**[359] 905 6-9-11 62 RichardThomas 15 56
(C Roberts) *a towards rr* **40/1**
-366 **10** *3 1/2* **Factual Lad**[19] 4266 9-9-7 58 SteveDrowne 8 45
(B R Millman) *led and set gd pce: rdn and hdd wl over 2f out: remained cl up tl wknd over 1f out* **20/1**
3103 **11** *nk* **Ermine Grey**[13] 4481 6-9-5 56 SaleemGolam 5 42
(A W Carroll) *mid-div tl 4f out* **14/1**
0360 **12** *21* **Fangorn Forest (IRE)**[8] 4632 4-9-2 58 LukeMorris(5) 7 2
(R A Harris) *s.i.s: a bhd* **16/1**

2m 8.74s (-1.16) **Going Correction** -0.15s/f (Firm)
WFA 3 from 4yo+ 8lb **12** Ran SP% **112.3**
Speed ratings (Par 101): **98,97,96,95,95 94,94,92,91,89 88,72**
CSF £66.71 CT £664.28 TOTE £15.70: £3.40, £2.20, £2.90; EX 50.90.
Owner P G Evans **Bred** P V And Mrs J P Jackson **Trained** Great Ness, Shropshire
■ Pelham Crescent (15/2) and Golden Sprite (20/1) were withdrawn after proving unruly in the stalls. R4, deduct 10p in the £.

FOCUS
Another ordinary handicap where they went very fast up front and all barring the winner paid the penalty. The form looks sound.
Factual Lad Official explanation: jockey said gelding lost its action
Ermine Grey Official explanation: jockey said gelding was never travelling

4879 HAGUE PRINT MANAGEMENT 0161 876 8787 H'CAP 7f 16y
4:50 (4:55) (Class 6) (0-65,64) 3-Y-0+ **£2,720** (£809; £404; £202) **Stalls** High

Form RPR
5035 **1** **Red Rudy**[7] 4657 5-9-8 60 SebSanders 10 73
(A W Carroll) *chsd ldrs: rdn to ld fnl 110yds: sn in command and pushed out* **9/2**[2]
0422 **2** *1 1/4* **Chief Exec**[16] 4394 5-8-13 56 HaddenFrost(5) 3 65
(B J Llewellyn) *pressed ldrs: slt advantage 3f out: rdn over 1f out: hdd and no ex fnl 110yds* **9/2**[2]
2260 **3** *2* **Milton's Keen**[9] 4606 4-8-12 55 LukeMorris(5) 2 59
(M Salaman) *in tch: hdwy 3f out: drvn to chse ldrs ins fnl 2f: one pce ins fnl f* **8/1**
0600 **4** *1/2* **Isphahan**[34] 3828 4-9-8 60 (p) SteveDrowne 9 63
(A M Balding) *sn slt ld: hdd 3f out: rdn over 2f out: wknd ins fnl f* **20/1**
0504 **5** *1/2* **Three Counties (IRE)**[72] 2665 6-9-4 56 RichardThomas 14 57
(N I M Rossiter) *in tch: rdn and outpcd 1/2-way: kpt on again ins fnl f: nt pce to rch ldrs* **25/1**
0000 **6** *shd* **Alfie Tupper (IRE)**[13] 4471 4-9-6 58 SimonWhitworth 16 59
(S Kirk) *in rr: rdn along 3f out: hdwy appr fnl f: kpt on cl home but nvr in contention* **25/1**
60U3 **7** *1/2* **Petito (IRE)**[12] 4515 4-9-7 59 RyanMoore 5 62+
(J L Spearing) *in rr: sn rdn along: mod prog u.p fr over 1f out: nvr in contention* **7/2**[1]
0306 **8** *hd* **Border Artist**[10] 4562 8-9-2 54 TQuinn 4 53
(J Pearce) *chsd ldrs: rdn and outpcd over 2f out: nvr in contention after* **8/1**

1060 **9** *nk* **Seneschal**[10] 4577 6-9-11 **63** SamHitchcott 1 61
(A B Haynes) *chsd ldrs: rdn and effrt over 2f out: nvr quite on terms and wknd appr fnl f* **25/1**

0-03 **10** *1* **The Crooked Ring**[32] 3873 5-9-4 **56** DaneO'Neill 13 52
(A G Newcombe) *sn towards rr and rdn: sme prog over 2f out: n.d* **14/1**

6005 **11** *¾* **Small Stakes (IRE)**[80] 2427 5-9-12 **64** (vt) DarryllHolland 8 58
(P J Makin) *sn rdn in rr and outpcd thrght* **7/1**[3]

0052 **12** *shd* **Mango Masher (IRE)**[20] 4246 3-8-12 **60** (p) KevinGhunowa[(5)] 11 51
(J M Bradley) *sn outpcd* **16/1**

0460 **13** *½* **Slipasearcher (IRE)**[44] 3549 3-9-1 **58** (v) StephenDonohoe 12 48
(P D Evans) *chsd ldrs: outpcd fr 1/2-way* **33/1**

1m 22.49s (-0.81) **Going Correction** -0.30s/f (Firm)
WFA 3 from 4yo+ 5lb **13** Ran SP% **125.1**
Speed ratings (Par 101): **92,90,88,87,87 87,86,86,85,84 83,83,83**
CSF £24.48 CT £170.29 TOTE £5.90: £2.10, £2.30, £3.00; EX 33.10.
Owner Winding Wheel Partnership **Bred** Mrs C J Tribe **Trained** Cropthorne, Worcs

FOCUS
Once again they wanted to be away from the stands' side rail and all the action was down the centre in a modest handicap where the top and bottom weights were separated by only 11lb. The winning time was moderate for the grade. The winner was back to something like last year's course-and-distance form.
The Crooked Ring Official explanation: jockey said gelding's stride shortened 1f out
Small Stakes(IRE) Official explanation: trainer said gelding did not face the tongue-tie

4880 WBX.COM 0% COMMISSION ON BIG RACES H'CAP 1m 14y
5:25 (5:27) (Class 5) (0-70,72) 3-Y-0+ **£3,886** (£1,156; £577; £288) **Stalls** High

Form RPR

6401 **1** **Im Ova Ere Dad (IRE)**[19] 4272 4-9-6 **65** RyanMoore 8 77+
(D E Cantillon) *hld up towards rr: hdwy 2f out: led over 1f out: edgd lft but r.o wl: rdn out* **10/3**[1]

6454 **2** *¾* **The Grey One (IRE)**[20] 4259 4-8-13 **63** (p) KevinGhunowa[(5)] 16 70
(J M Bradley) *mid-div: hdwy 2f out: sn rdn: str run ins fnl f but nvr able to catch wnr* **11/1**

-500 **3** *1* **Personify**[21] 4234 5-9-10 **69** (p) DaneO'Neill 2 74
(C G Cox) *chsd ldrs: rdn over 2f out: ev ch over 1f out: kpt on but a hld ins fnl f* **8/1**

1556 **4** *shd* **Emily's Place (IRE)**[16] 4404 4-9-6 **65** PaulFitzsimons 14 69
(J Pearce) *mid-div: rdn and hdwy over 1f out: styd on* **16/1**

2462 **5** *1¼* **Celtic Spa (IRE)**[8] 4632 5-9-10 **69** StephenDonohoe 3 71
(P D Evans) *chsd ldrs: rdn over 2f out: ch over 1f out: kpt on same pce* **8/1**

5000 **6** *hd* **She's Our Lass (IRE)**[15] 4433 6-9-11 **70** (v[1]) DarryllHolland 6 71
(D Carroll) *s.i.s: towards rr: hdwy 2f out: sn swtchd rt: styd on same pce fnl f* **14/1**

0651 **7** *½* **Out For A Stroll**[12] 4515 8-9-0 **59** SaleemGolam 1 59
(S C Williams) *mid-div: rdn and hdwy over 1f out: kpt on same pce fnl f* **12/1**

0000 **8** *1* **Golden Square**[4] 3600 5-7-13 **51** oh6 (b) KirstyMilczarek[(7)] 5 49
(A W Carroll) *led tl wl over 3f out: rdn over 2f out: one pce fnl f* **80/1**

3250 **9** *1* **Golden Spectrum (IRE)**[15] 4433 8-8-13 **63** (b) LukeMorris[(5)] 13 58
(R A Harris) *chsd ldrs: led wl over 3f out: rdn and hdd over 1f out: fdd* **25/1**

0015 **10** *4* **Foolish Groom**[11] 4532 6-8-7 **59** (p) AmyBaker[(7)] 12 45
(R Hollinshead) *a towards rr* **9/1**

416 **11** *2½* **Copper King**[14] 4462 3-9-5 **70** TQuinn 11 50
(J W Hills) *mid-div: rdn over 2f out: styng on whn nt clr run over 1f out: no ch and eased after* **12/1**

0003 **12** *½* **Grey Boy (GER)**[9] 4606 6-9-10 **69** SebSanders 17 48
(A W Carroll) *prom: rdn over 2f out: sn btn* **11/2**[2]

0104 **13** *1¾* **Croft (IRE)**[6] 4688 4-8-8 **53** (v) RichardThomas 7 28
(M S Saunders) *in tch: struggling 4f out: nt a danger after* **33/1**

31 **14** *3* **One Giant Leap (IRE)**[29] 4000 3-9-2 **67** SteveDrowne 9 35
(H Morrison) *a towards rr* **6/1**[3]

0000 **15** *shd* **Pachello (IRE)**[45] 3497 5-7-13 **51** oh6 (v[1]) PietroRomeo[(7)] 4 19
(J M Bradley) *mid-div: hdwy to chse ldrs 4f out: wknd over 1f out* **66/1**

0/0- **16** *7* **New Diamond**[395] 3894 8-8-4 **52** oh4 ow1 MarcHalford[(3)] 10 4
(Mrs P Ford) *prom for 3f* **66/1**

1m 33.97s (-2.03) **Going Correction** -0.30s/f (Firm)
WFA 3 from 4yo+ 6lb **16** Ran SP% **132.2**
Speed ratings (Par 103): **98,97,96,96,94 94,94,93,92,88 85,85,83,80,80 73**
CSF £44.19 CT £305.69 TOTE £4.20: £1.40, £3.40, £3.30, £5.50; EX 59.00.
Owner Allan Milton **Bred** Golden Vale Stud **Trained** Newmarket, Suffolk

FOCUS
A steadily-run affair but fairly reliable form rated through the runner-up. The winner shaped better than the bare form.

4881 WBX.COM 0% COMMISSION ON BIG FOOTBALL MATCHES H'CAP 5f 16y
5:55 (6:03) (Class 6) (0-60,59) 3-Y-0+ **£2,590** (£770; £385; £192) **Stalls** High

Form RPR

6304 **1** **Jucebabe**[8] 4635 4-8-11 **55** (p) HaddenFrost[(5)] 14 64
(J L Spearing) *t.k.h: pressed ldrs: led wl ins fnl f: hld on all out* **10/1**

0450 **2** *shd* **Digital**[1] 4853 10-8-12 **58** (v[1]) MatthewDavies[(7)] 11 67
(M R Channon) *s.i.s: bhd: rapid hdwy appr fnl f: fin fast: jst failed* **10/1**

052 **3** *¾* **Endless Summer**[8] 4635 10-9-2 **55** SebSanders 7 61
(A W Carroll) *in rr: hdwy 1f out: str run ins fnl f: nt quite pce to chal* **5/2**[1]

1210 **4** *shd* **Dematraf (IRE)**[49] 3368 5-9-6 **59** StephenDonohoe 5 65
(P D Evans) *sn pressing ldrs: styd on u.p ins fnl f: no ex cl home* **9/1**

0034 **5** *hd* **Hello Roberto**[4] 4734 6-8-9 **53** (p) LukeMorris[(5)] 13 58
(R A Harris) *disp ld tl slt but def advantage 2f out: styd on u.p tl hdd and no ex wl ins fnl f* **13/2**[3]

2210 **6** *hd* **El Potro**[23] 4180 5-9-4 **57** SteveDrowne 16 61
(J R Holt) *disp ld tl over 3f out: styd pressing ldrs: kpt on same pce ins fnl f* **7/1**

0660 **7** *shd* **Decider (USA)**[4] 4734 4-9-2 **55** DaneO'Neill 12 59
(J M Bradley) *pressed ldrs: rdn and kpt on same pce ins fnl f* **28/1**

0605 **8** *1* **Whistler**[6] 4689 10-8-10 **49** (b) PaulFitzsimons 2 49
(Miss J R Tooth) *in rr: hdwy over 1f out: kpt on ins fnl f but nvr quite gng pce to chal* **20/1**

0330 **9** *½* **Peruvian Style (IRE)**[1] 4853 6-8-13 **52** RyanMoore 1 51
(J M Bradley) *pressed ldrs: wkng whn n.m.r ins fnl f* **4/1**[2]

0005 **10** *1* **Meikle Barfil**[10] 4561 5-8-4 **48** (tp) KevinGhunowa[(5)] 15 43
(J M Bradley) *in tch: rdn and one pce fnl 2f* **25/1**

6250 **11** *nk* **Seven No Trumps**[10] 4561 10-8-10 **49** TQuinn 3 43
(J M Bradley) *chsd ldrs: wkng whn hmpd ins fnl f* **16/1**

000 **12** *2* **Jessica Wigmo**[11] 4545 4-8-6 **45** RichardThomas 8 32
(A W Carroll) *in tch: outpcd fr over 1f out* **66/1**

10 **13** *nk* **Piccostar**[16] 4397 4-9-1 **54** (v) SamHitchcott 9 40
(A B Haynes) *chsd ldrs 3f* **25/1**

0040 **14** *1¾* **Knead The Dough**[10] 4583 6-8-4 **46** ow1 MarcHalford[(3)] 6 25
(A E Price) *chsd ldrs to 1/2-way* **25/1**

58.77 secs (-0.83) **Going Correction** -0.30s/f (Firm) **14** Ran SP% **129.7**
Speed ratings (Par 101): **94,93,92,92,92 91,91,90,89,87 87,84,83,80**
CSF £105.42 CT £346.67 TOTE £10.10: £2.30, £4.40, £1.80; EX 120.30 Place 6 £64.17, Place 5 £44.79.
Owner G M Eales **Bred** G M Eales **Trained** Kinnersley, Worcs

FOCUS
They went a good pace in this handicap and the form looks solid, despite the fact that the winning time was modest for the class of contest.
T/Jkpt: Not won. T/Plt: £114.50 to a £1 stake. Pool: £60,798.50. 387.60 winning tickets. T/Qpdt: £45.10 to a £1 stake. Pool: £2,279.60. 37.40 winning tickets. ST

4271 KEMPTON (A.W) (R-H)
Monday, August 27

OFFICIAL GOING: Standard
Wind: Moderate, half against Weather: Sunny

4882 E B F NO BETTER WAY TO OWN RACEHORSES MEDIAN AUCTION MAIDEN STKS (DIV I) 7f (P)
1:45 (1:47) (Class 5) 2-Y-0 **£2,590** (£770; £385; £192) **Stalls** High

Form RPR

4 **1** **Blue Sky Basin**[12] 4508 2-9-3 0 FrancisNorton 8 76
(A M Balding) *chsd ldr: rdn 2f out: led jst over 1f out: drvn out and hld on* **2/1**[1]

06 **2** *nk* **Noble Citizen (USA)**[24] 4130 2-9-3 0 MichaelHills 11 76
(D M Simcock) *cl up: trckd ldng pair over 1f out: effrt and rdn ent fnl f: clsd on wnr nr fin* **7/2**[2]

3 *1* **Tenjack King** 2-9-3 0 JimmyFortune 2 73+
(J A Osborne) *settled in rr fr wd draw: pushed along 3f out: gd prog fr 2f out: styd on wl fnl f: nrst fin* **14/1**

424 **4** *¾* **Freudian Slip**[19] 4273 2-8-12 70 PaulDoe 9 66
(S Curran) *led: rdn over 2f out: hdd jst over 1f out: fdd fnl 100yds* **14/1**

00 **5** *shd* **Title Role**[18] 4328 2-8-12 0 TolleyDean[(5)] 5 71
(P F I Cole) *prom: pushed along fr over 2f out: styd on but nvr quite able to chal* **50/1**

6 *1* **La Rosa Nostra** 2-8-12 0 AdamKirby 3 63+
(W R Swinburn) *dwlt: wl in rr and rn green early: shkn up and prog fr 2f out: kpt on* **4/1**[3]

7 *½* **Pediment** 2-8-12 0 OscarUrbina 1 62+
(J R Fanshawe) *dwlt: wl in rr early: prog fr over 2f out: shkn up and keeping on whn n.m.r 1f out* **15/2**

6 **8** *3½* **Irish Artist (FR)**[73] 2624 2-9-3 0 RichardSmith 10 58
(R Hannon) *mostly midfield: rdn on inner and nt look keen over 2f out: sn btn* **20/1**

0 **9** *9* **Jevington Star (IRE)**[9] 4593 2-9-3 0 NelsonDeSouza 7 34
(R M Flower) *chsd ldrs: rdn over 2f out: sn wknd* **66/1**

10 *2* **Daggerman** 2-9-3 0 HayleyTurner 12 29
(P A Blockley) *s.i.s: a in last trio and struggling: wl bhd fnl 2f* **50/1**

11 *4* **Lady Amy** 2-8-5 0 AmyBaker[(7)] 4 14
(Miss J Feilden) *racd wd towards rr: v wd bnd 3f out: sn bhd* **66/1**

06 **12** *10* **Valiant Vicar (USA)**[30] 3957 2-9-3 0 LDettori 6 —
(B J Meehan) *rdn to go prom: wknd 1/2-way: t.o* **8/1**

1m 26.19s (-0.61) **Going Correction** -0.10s/f (Stan) **12** Ran SP% **123.4**
Speed ratings (Par 94): **99,98,97,96,96 95,94,90,80,78 73,62**
CSF £8.96 TOTE £2.90: £1.10, £1.90, £3.70; EX 10.60.
Owner George Strawbridge **Bred** George Strawbridge **Trained** Kingsclere, Hants

FOCUS
A fair maiden and a couple of these showed promise for the future. The first two showed slight improvement. The winning time was 0.44 seconds faster than the second division.

NOTEBOOK
Blue Sky Basin duly stepped up from his Sandown debut, but the way he needed plenty of assistance to force his way to the front suggests he will improve over further, just as his breeding would suggest. (op 7-4)
Noble Citizen(USA), switched to sand for the first time after two outings on turf, has a pedigree which suggested he would handle the surface and he stayed on right to the line to record his best effort yet. He should be able to win an ordinary maiden on sand and now also has the option of nurseries. (op 4-1 tchd 10-3)
Tenjack King ◆, a 54,000gns half-brother to three winners including one in the US, ran a most eye-catching debut, finishing strongly down the outside from well off the pace, and it would not be the biggest surprise if he were to emerge the best of these in time. He will get 1m and his pedigree suggests that will be his trip. (op 20-1)
Freudian Slip, the most experienced in the line-up, tried to make that count by quickly bagging the rail from her high draw and she attempted to make every yard. Sticking to the inside all the way up the home straight, she was gradually worn down. She may be a former plater, but she has already run well at this track before so her proximity does not drag the form down and her official mark of 70 provides a benchmark.
Title Role, well beaten in two turf maidens, has a pedigree which suggested he would be suited by the switch to sand and longer trip and duly did so. He had every chance down the middle of the track, but lacked a decisive turn of foot and will probably be suited by going up in trip again. Nurseries are an option for him now.
La Rosa Nostra, an 85,000euros filly out of a sister to the high-class Summerland, looked to need this initial experience, but was far from disgraced and the stable's youngsters often need time. (tchd 11-2)
Pediment, a half-sister to Ice Palace, Palatial and Portal who was a runner later on at this meeting, looked to have run her race when getting squeezed between Tenjack King and La Rosa Nostra a furlong out. Better can now be expected from her. (op 8-1)
Valiant Vicar(USA) Official explanation: jockey said colt was never travelling

4883 E B F NO BETTER WAY TO OWN RACEHORSES MEDIAN AUCTION MAIDEN STKS (DIV II) 7f (P)
2:15 (2:17) (Class 5) 2-Y-0 **£2,590** (£770; £385; £192) **Stalls** High

Form RPR

45 **1** **Copywriter**[33] 3850 2-9-3 0 JimmyFortune 8 81+
(J H M Gosden) *trckd ldrs: plld out and effrt over 2f out: led over 1f out: pushed clr: comf* **4/6**[1]

2 *3* **Tension Mounts (IRE)** 2-9-3 0 FrancisNorton 11 73
(J A Osborne) *trckd ldng pair to 3f out: styd cl up: shkn up and effrt to go 2nd jst ins fnl f: kpt on but no ch w wnr* **16/1**

0 **3** *2* **Ocean Legend (IRE)**[24] 4132 2-9-3 0 .... NickyMackay 7 68
(Miss J Feilden) *led 1f: chsd ldr: led over 2f out to over 1f out: tired ins fnl f* **50/1**

0 **4** *3/4* **Havanavich**[19] 4273 2-9-3 0 .... RHills 9 66
(S Kirk) *towards rr: prog on inner over 2f out: rdn and kpt on: n.d* **14/1**

05 **5** *3/4* **Shadow Cabinet (IRE)**[10] 4584 2-9-3 0 .... HayleyTurner 2 64
(M L W Bell) *rn in snatches and sn urged along in rr: styd on fr over 1f out: n.d* **4/1[2]**

00 **6** *3/4* **Exodia**[38] 3706 2-8-12 0 .... MichaelHills 4 57
(Jane Chapple-Hyam) *s.i.s: rousted along to ld after 1f: hdd over 2f out: wknd over 1f out* **9/1[3]**

0352 **7** *1 1/4* **La Belle Joannie**[24] 4136 2-8-12 55 .... PaulDoe 10 54
(S Curran) *prog fr rr to press ldrs 3f out: rdn over 2f out: wknd over 1f out* **20/1**

0 **8** *hd* **Sabre Light**[12] 4508 2-9-3 0 .... AdamKirby 5 58
(G L Moore) *nvr bttr than midfield: u.p and no prog 3f out* **16/1**

9 *1 1/4* **Mujahope** 2-8-12 0 .... NicolPolli(5) 6 55
(M Botti) *prom tl wknd wl over 1f out* **25/1**

0 **10** *2* **Futune (IRE)**[10] 4565 2-8-12 0 .... LDettori 3 45
(B J Meehan) *hld up fr wd draw: a in rr: brought wd in st: rn green and no prog* **11/1**

1m 26.63s (-0.17) **Going Correction** -0.10s/f (Stan) **10** Ran SP% **127.3**
Speed ratings (Par 94): **96,92,90,89,88 87,86,86,84,82**
CSF £16.59 TOTE £1.70: £1.20, £3.50, £12.20; EX 14.70.

Owner H R H Princess Haya Of Jordan **Bred** Whitsbury Manor Stud & Pigeon House Stud **Trained** Newmarket, Suffolk

FOCUS
Not a competitive race on paper, but this looked just about the stronger of the two divisions, although the time was 0.44 seconds slower. The fifth and seventh help with the standard.

NOTEBOOK
Copywriter made up for his Lingfield blip with a straightforward success and the longer straight here was probably much more to his liking. The form does not look anything special though, and his future may now depend on how the Handicapper interprets this. (op 11-10 tchd 6-5 tchd 9-4 in places)

Tension Mounts(IRE), a 60,000euros half-brother to five winners, had every chance and kept on to finish a clear second best. He should improve and his pedigree suggests that he would not get much further than this. (tchd 14-1)

Ocean Legend(IRE) was tailed-off last on his Newmarket debut, but his pedigree suggested he might appreciate the switch to sand - his half-brother is a winner at this track - and he duly posted a much-improved effort. The form may not be anything special, but he is obviously not without ability and he may be one for handicaps on this surface in the longer term. (op 40-1)

Havanavich was unplaced on his debut over course and distance earlier this month and the form of that race has not really worked out - a horse that finished over five lengths in front of him there finished fourth in the first division of this race. He did not really fare much better here and his best hope is that he will get a favourable handicap mark after one more run.

Shadow Cabinet(IRE), switched to sand after showing a little ability in two turf maidens, never really looked like getting in a blow but now qualifies for a mark which will open up a few more opportunities. (op 9-2 tchd 5-1)

Exodia, another switching to sand after showing little in two Newmarket maidens, was vigorously ridden to bag the lead but was comfortably picked off in the home straight. She now qualifies for a mark and she should stay quite a bit further than this on breeding. (op 8-1 tchd 10-1)

Sabre Light Official explanation: jockey said colt was never travelling

4884 WALTERSWINBURNRACING.CO.UK H'CAP 7f (P)
2:50 (2:50) (Class 5) (0-75,75) 3-Y-0+ **£3,238** (£963; £481; £240) **Stalls** High

Form RPR

0030 **1** **Landucci**[19] 4268 6-9-5 70 .... (p) PatrickHills(5) 6 83
(J W Hills) *trckd ldrs: clsd over 1f out: shkn up to ld jst ins fnl f: r.o wl* **9/1**

2-66 **2** *1 1/2* **Reballo (IRE)**[19] 4275 4-9-6 66 .... OscarUrbina 12 81+
(J R Fanshawe) *hld up in midfield on inner: nt clr run 2f out to 1f out: rdn and r.o to take 2nd last stride: hopeless task* **9/2[2]**

4123 **3** *shd* **Ebraam (USA)**[16] 4394 4-9-3 66 .... DominicFox(3) 13 75
(D Shaw) *trckd ldrs on inner: prog 2f out: led over 1f out: hdd and outpcd jst ins fnl f: lost 2nd last stride* **9/2[2]**

3341 **4** *1 1/2* **Divertimenti (IRE)**[16] 4394 3-9-10 75 .... LDettori 5 78
(C R Dore) *hld up wl in rr on outer: prog 2f out: clsd on ldrs 1f out: one pce fnl f* **7/2[1]**

5603 **5** *1/2* **Flying Encore (IRE)**[18] 4317 3-9-0 65 .... (p) AdamKirby 11 66
(W R Swinburn) *prom: rdn over 2f out: kpt on same pce: nvr able to chal* **11/1**

0140 **6** *nk* **Proper (IRE)**[19] 4276 3-9-5 70 .... JimmyFortune 14 70
(M R Channon) *mde most to over 1f out: fdd* **11/2[3]**

5402 **7** *nk* **Certain Justice (USA)**[9] 4606 9-9-12 72 .... HayleyTurner 4 74
(Stef Liddiard) *towards rr on outer: effrt over 2f out: limited prog over 1f out: kpt on same pce* **10/1**

5055 **8** *3/4* **Gavarnie Beau (IRE)**[26] 4075 4-9-2 62 .... FrancisNorton 10 62
(M Blanshard) *mostly in midfield: lost pl u.p 2f out: no ch after* **16/1**

4040 **9** *nk* **Take To The Skies (IRE)**[24] 4129 3-8-11 62 .... NelsonDeSouza 1 59
(A P Jarvis) *restrained s fr wd draw: hld up in rr: gd prog on inner 2f out: wknd jst over 1f out* **40/1**

4015 **10** *1* **Middle Eastern**[89] 2145 5-8-5 58 .... SophieDoyle(7) 9 54
(P A Blockley) *w ldr: led briefly 1/2-way: wknd u.p wl over 1f out* **16/1**

0620 **11** *1 1/2* **Hucking Heat (IRE)**[24] 4137 3-8-12 66 .... StephaneBreux(3) 8 56
(J R Best) *a in rr: rdn and no prog over 2f out* **20/1**

0003 **12** *1 1/4* **Quantum Leap**[6] 4688 10-9-0 60 .... (p) NickyMackay 7 49
(S Dow) *racd wd and a wl in rr* **20/1**

0-00 **13** *5* **Sagunt (GER)**[21] 4236 4-9-3 63 .... PaulDoe 3 38
(S Curran) *prom tl wknd u.p 2f out* **50/1**

00-0 **14** *5* **Chateau Nicol**[9] 4594 8-9-9 69 .... (v) MichaelHills 2 31
(B G Powell) *chsd ldrs: wl in tch over 2f out: sn wknd rapidly* **33/1**

1m 26.19s (-0.61) **Going Correction** -0.10s/f (Stan)
WFA 3 from 4yo+ 5lb **14** Ran SP% **130.0**
Speed ratings (Par 103): **99,97,97,95,94 94,94,93,93,91 90,88,83,77**
CSF £50.60 CT £223.15 TOTE £11.90: £3.40, £2.20, £2.10; EX 79.80.

Owner R J Tufft **Bred** D J And Mrs Deer **Trained** Upper Lambourn, Berks

■ Stewards' Enquiry : L Dettori one-day ban: entered the wrong stall (Sep 7)

FOCUS
A competitive handicap, but a modest one and the time was ordinary. Several still had a chance coming to the last furlong. The form seems sound enough and has been rated at face value.

Reballo(IRE) ◆ Official explanation: jockey said gelding was denied a clear run

4885 OWN A SHARE WITH WALTER SWINBURN H'CAP 6f (P)
3:25 (3:26) (Class 5) (0-75,76) 3-Y-0 **£3,238** (£963; £481; £240) **Stalls** High

Form RPR

-640 **1** **Minaash (USA)**[17] 4360 3-8-13 70 .... AhmedAjtebi(5) 8 79
(D M Simcock) *chsd ldng pair: prog on inner 2f out: led over 1f out: sn hrd pressed: edgd lft but styd on wl* **10/1**

0404 **2** *1/2* **Hucking Hill (IRE)**[4] 4740 3-9-1 70 .... StephaneBreux(3) 4 77
(J R Best) *in tch towards rr: rdn and prog on outer over 2f out: clsd to chal 1f out: nt qckn and hld last 100yds* **11/2[3]**

4116 **3** *1* **Nouveau (GER)**[10] 4574 3-9-4 70 .... JimmyFortune 5 74
(R Hannon) *chsd ldrs: rdn to cl 2f out: upsides 1f out: one pce fnl f* **11/4[1]**

0000 **4** *2* **Jord (IRE)**[31] 3920 3-9-2 73 .... TolleyDean(5) 3 71
(A J McCabe) *chsd clr ldr: rdn to cl over 2f out: upsides jst over 1f out: wknd ins fnl f* **50/1**

131 **5** *1 3/4* **Impromptu**[8] 4634 3-9-10 76 6ex .... AdamKirby 9 69
(R M Beckett) *chsd ldrs: hrd rdn to try to cl 2f out: hld over 1f out: eased last 75yds* **10/3[2]**

0060 **6** *4* **Minnow**[11] 4536 3-8-3 62 .... WilliamCarson(7) 7 43
(S C Williams) *in tch in midfield: rdn over 2f out: no prog* **25/1**

-003 **7** *hd* **Swing On A Star (IRE)**[23] 4182 3-8-8 60 .... NickyMackay 10 40
(W R Swinburn) *led at scorching pce and sn clr: wknd and hdd over 1f out* **9/1**

5500 **8** *2* **Bentley**[7] 4658 3-8-4 59 .... (v) DominicFox(3) 2 33
(D Shaw) *outpcd and a struggling* **50/1**

500 **9** *nk* **Tahdeed**[32] 3881 3-9-1 67 .... (bt[1]) RHills 1 40
(Sir Michael Stoute) *rel to r: t.o tl laboured late prog* **11/2[3]**

0200 **10** *1 1/4* **Lay The Cash (USA)**[4] 4740 3-8-10 62 .... (b) FrancisNorton 6 32
(J S Moore) *a in rr: lost tch bef 1/2-way* **8/1**

1m 12.67s (-1.03) **Going Correction** -0.10s/f (Stan) **10** Ran SP% **118.5**
Speed ratings (Par 100): **102,101,100,97,95 89,89,86,86,84**
CSF £64.38 CT £195.16 TOTE £17.90: £4.80, £2.20, £1.40; EX 111.50.

Owner Sultan Ali **Bred** G Watts Humphrey Jr **Trained** Newmarket, Suffolk

FOCUS
An ordinary little sprint handicap, but with Swing On A Star going off at a rate of knots there was certainly no hanging about. A fairly positive view has been taken of the form.

Impromptu Official explanation: jockey said gelding finished distressed

Tahdeed Official explanation: jockey said colt was extremely colty

4886 LIVE THE DREAM WITH WALTER SWINBURN H'CAP 6f (P)
4:00 (4:00) (Class 2) (0-105,103) 3-Y-0+
£9,971 (£2,985; £1,492; £747; £372; £187) **Stalls** High

Form RPR

0025 **1** **Diane's Choice**[7] 4664 4-8-5 84 oh2 .... NickyMackay 3 92
(J Akehurst) *led 1f: chsd clr ldr: clsd to ld again jst over 1f out: 2 l clr 100yds out: jst lasted* **14/1**

4010 **2** *nk* **Viking Spirit**[23] 4150 5-9-7 100 .... AdamKirby 2 107
(W R Swinburn) *chsd clr ldng pair: rdn over 2f out: clsd fr over 1f out: chsd wnr ins fnl f: gaining at fin* **3/1[1]**

0000 **3** *hd* **Woodcote (IRE)**[10] 4567 5-8-8 87 .... (be) OscarUrbina 5 93
(C G Cox) *chsd clr ldrs: rdn over 2f out: styd on fr over 1f out: nvr quite able to chal* **8/1**

0600 **4** *3/4* **Dingaan (IRE)**[1] 4851 4-8-9 88 .... FrancisNorton 4 92
(A M Balding) *hld up in rr and off the pce: cajoled along fr 2f out: styd on fnl f: nt rch ldrs* **12/1**

0126 **5** *1 1/4* **Bomber Command (USA)**[10] 4585 4-8-11 95 .... PatrickHills(5) 6 95
(J W Hills) *wl in rr: rdn bef 1/2-way: reluctant 2f out: styd on ins fnl f* **7/1**

4424 **6** *3/4* **Moonlight Man**[30] 3971 6-8-8 87 .... HayleyTurner 9 85
(C R Dore) *rdn on inner in midfield: 1/2-way: a struggling to go the pce* **12/1**

5200 **7** *1/2* **Mutamared (USA)**[23] 4150 7-9-10 103 .... MichaelHills 7 99
(K A Ryan) *nvr beyond midfield: rdn over 2f out: nt pce to make any inroads* **7/2[2]**

0404 **8** *hd* **Prince Tamino**[23] 4183 4-9-7 100 .... (v[1]) LDettori 1 95
(Saeed Bin Suroor) *led after 1f and sn clr at str pce: hdd & wknd rapidly jst over 1f out* **9/2[3]**

3002 **9** *2* **Wessex (USA)**[127] 1179 7-8-10 89 .... RHills 8 78
(P A Blockley) *a in rr: rdn on inner over 2f out: no prog* **14/1**

1m 12.25s (-1.45) **Going Correction** -0.10s/f (Stan) **9** Ran SP% **117.7**
Speed ratings (Par 109): **105,104,104,103,101 100,100,99,97**
CSF £57.07 CT £371.88 TOTE £18.80: £3.50, £1.50, £2.90; EX 91.80.

Owner The Grass Is Greener Partnership Ii **Bred** Green Pastures Farm **Trained** Epsom, Surrey

FOCUS
A decent little sprint handicap and furious early pace thanks to Prince Tamino, though that must have taken its toll as the final time was ordinary. Very few ever got into this. The form is rated through the third.

NOTEBOOK
Diane's Choice, who has shown plenty of ability on sand though she was racing on the surface for the first time in ten months, broke very well but was more than happy to take a lead from the trailblazing Prince Tamino. She pounced on that rival coming to the last furlong and that proved a race-winning move, as she only just managed to hang on but never looked like getting caught. (op 16-1)

Viking Spirit found himself off a 6lb higher mark than when placed three times on Polytrack last autumn. Having his first run on sand since, he was content to sit just off the rapid pace but took a little too long to hit top stride when coming under pressure, and although he was cutting the winner down at the line he never looked like getting there. (op 7-2)

Woodcote(IRE), having his first try on sand in his 27th race, did not come into this in the greatest of form on turf but this was a much better effort and he was closing in on the front pair all the way to the line. He is now 7lb lower than for his last win and if he can build on this there should be a race in him on this surface. (op 11-1)

Dingaan(IRE), a three-time winner on Polytrack in the first half of 2006 and off the same mark as for the last of those, was having his first try on this surface since May of that year and was turning out quickly after finishing unplaced at Goodwood the previous day. He was staying on well at the line and it may be that he needs the extra furlong on this surface these days.

Bomber Command(USA) has a good record here, but he found everything happening too quickly for him over this trip and his finishing position was as close as he got. (op 6-1 tchd 15-2)

Moonlight Man, trying this trip for the first time in over two years, was completely taken off his feet.

Mutamared(USA) could never get into the race and looks handicapped to the hilt. (op 10-3 tchd 4-1)

Prince Tamino circled the field from his outside draw and went off at a rate of knots in the first-time visor. Not surprisingly he eventually fell in a heap. (op 4-1)

Wessex(USA), returning from four months off, was a springer in the market but never looked like justifying the support. (op 25-1)

4887 E B F BE A PART OF WALTER SWINBURN CONDITIONS STKS 1m 3f (P)

4:35 (4:35) (Class 3) 3-Y-0+ **£6,855** (£2,052; £1,026; £513) **Stalls** High

Form RPR

-510 **1** **Al Tharib (USA)**[66] 2813 3-8-8 101 RHills 2 109+
(Sir Michael Stoute) *mde all: shkn up and drew clr over 1f out: unchal* **5/4**[1]

1564 **2** *4* **Marzelline (IRE)**[22] 4203 3-8-3 102 NickyMackay 3 94
(W R Swinburn) *settled in 3rd: pushed along 3f out: rdn to take 2nd ins fnl f: no ch w wnr* **7/2**[3]

2060 **3** *hd* **Duke Of Tuscany**[26] 4059 3-8-8 96 FrancisNorton 1 99
(R Hannon) *chsd wnr: pushed along fr 4f out: no imp 2f out: lost 2nd ins fnl f* **5/1**

3P34 **4** *nk* **Portal**[37] 3744 4-8-12 101 OscarUrbina 4 93
(J R Fanshawe) *hld up in last: pushed along 3f out: effrt to dispute 2nd over 1f out: one pce* **5/2**[2]

2m 18.15s (-4.53) **Going Correction** -0.10s/f (Stan)
WFA 3 from 4yo 9lb **4** Ran SP% **111.9**
Speed ratings (Par 107): **112,109,108,108**
CSF £6.10 TOTE £2.00; EX 4.80.

Owner Hamdan Al Maktoum **Bred** Phillips Racing Partnership **Trained** Newmarket, Suffolk

FOCUS
A tight little contest and despite the small field, they still took 0.93 seconds off the course record for this still relatively new trip. Al Tharib impressed, showing smart form.

NOTEBOOK
Al Tharib(USA), racing for the first time since finishing last in the King Edward VII Stakes at Royal Ascot, was allowed to set the pace and there are few better than Hills at judging the pace correctly on a front-runner. He found plenty when asked to put the race to bed and the Group 3 September Stakes back here next month would seem a tempting target. Whether he will be allowed to dominate like he did here is questionable, though that contest does not normally attract a big field so he may get his way again. (op 7-4 tchd 15-8 in places)

Marzelline(IRE) could never get on terms with the winner, but battled on well to just win the separate race for second. She would have been 6lb better off with the favourite in a handicap and is likely to continue to be difficult to place off her current mark. (op 3-1 tchd 11-4)

Duke Of Tuscany would have been upwards of 5lb better off with his rivals in a handicap and is yet to really prove he wants this far, so he probably achieved as much as could be expected. (op 6-1 tchd 13-2)

Portal, given a patient ride, could never land a telling blow from off the pace. She should have done better at the weights and as she likes to hear her feet rattle on turf, perhaps this surface did not suit her. (op 2-1 tchd 11-4 tchd 3-1 in a place)

4888 BE A WINNER WITH WALTER SWINBURN H'CAP 1m 3f (P)

5:10 (5:11) (Class 3) (0-90,89) 3-Y-0+ **£6,855** (£2,052; £1,026; £513; £256; £128) **Stalls** High

Form RPR

1004 **1** **Mustajed**[16] 4376 6-9-2 77 LDettori 9 86
(B R Millman) *trckd ldr: narrow ld over 2f out: sn hrd rdn: hld on* **7/2**[1]

0525 **2** *hd* **I Have Dreamed (IRE)**[45] 3509 5-9-13 88 (b) AdamKirby 1 96+
(T G Mills) *t.k.h: hld up in last pair: prog on inner wl over 1f out: drvn and r.o to cl on wnr nr fin: too much to do* **5/1**[2]

-363 **3** *3/4* **Resonate (IRE)**[16] 4399 9-8-12 73 OscarUrbina 2 80
(A G Newcombe) *hld up in 5th: clsd on ldrs over 2f out: gng strly over 1f out: rdn ent fnl f: styd on but nvr chal* **7/2**[1]

6100 **4** *nk* **Kerriemuir Lass (IRE)**[16] 4376 4-9-12 87 JimmyFortune 6 93
(M A Jarvis) *led: stdd pce after 4f: narrowly hdd over 2f out: pressed wnr tl no ex ins fnl f* **6/1**[3]

0622 **5** *1/2* **Pagan Sword**[15] 4419 5-9-3 85 (p) KMay[(7)] 7 91
(Mrs A J Perrett) *t.k.h: trckd ldng pair: cl up and seemingly gng strly over 1f out: shkn up and fnd nil* **7/1**

0/54 **6** *1* **Mutawassel (USA)**[23] 4166 6-10-0 89 MichaelHills 8 93
(B W Hills) *trckd ldng trio: shkn up and nt qckn over 2f out: kpt on same pce fr over 1f out* **8/1**

2060 **7** *4* **Vacation (IRE)**[26] 4068 4-9-6 86 TolleyDean[(5)] 3 83
(V Smith) *hld up in last pair: c wd bnd 3f out: wknd 2f out* **12/1**

1003 **8** *3/4* **William's Way**[59] 3060 5-9-11 86 FrancisNorton 4 82
(I A Wood) *plld hrd: hld up in 6th: wknd 2f out* **7/1**

2m 22.58s (-0.10) **Going Correction** -0.10s/f (Stan)
WFA 3 from 4yo+ 9lb **8** Ran SP% **119.2**
Speed ratings (Par 107): **96,95,95,95,94 94,91,90**
CSF £22.16 CT £66.59 TOTE £4.40: £1.70, £1.80, £1.70; EX 26.60.

Owner Double P Partnership **Bred** Shadwell Estate Company Limited **Trained** Kentisbeare, Devon

■ Stewards' Enquiry : Adam Kirby one-day ban: used whip with excessive force without giving gelding time to respond (Sep 7)

FOCUS
A fair handicap on paper, but the pace was uneven and the winning time was 4.43 seonds slower than the preceding conditions event. The form could have been rated a bit higher.

NOTEBOOK
Mustajed, 6lb lower than for his last run on sand, was also 12lb lower than for his last outing on turf. He was always in a good position in a steadily-run race and, after hitting the front, showed plenty of guts to hang on to win with nothing to spare. (tchd 5-1)

I Have Dreamed(IRE), 4lb higher than when touched off here in June and 7lb higher than for his last win, needs to be delivered late but he needed a stronger pace to run at over this trip and did not get it. His late effort was always going to fall a stride or two short, despite his rider giving it everything, and he is the sort for whom everything has to fall just right. (op 6-1)

Resonate(IRE), like the winner able to run off a 12lb lower mark than for his last outing on turf, was another not suited by the way the race was run and he was never quite getting there in time. He is still a relatively fresh horse this year and it would be no surprise to see him try and go one better in the November Handicap at the end of the season, where the ground should be ideal and the race should be run to suit. (op 9-2 tchd 11-2)

Kerriemuir Lass(IRE), just over a length behind Mustajed at Ascot last time, found herself 11lb worse off with that rival on this sand debut. She was allowed to set her own pace as she likes to do and did her best to hold on, but was done for foot late on. (op 8-1 tchd 11-2)

Pagan Sword, 3lb lower than when last on sand, looked sure to play a part in the finish as he was travelling really well behind the leaders up the home straight but, not for the first time, flattered to deceive. (op 11-2)

Mutawassel(USA), down another 1lb and trying sand for the first time, failed to pick up when asked and would have preferred a stronger gallop. (op 15-2 tchd 7-1)

William's Way Official explanation: jockey said gelding ran too keen throughout

4889 GO RACING WITH WALTER SWINBURN RACING H'CAP 1m (P)

5:40 (5:42) (Class 4) (0-80,80) 3-Y-0+ **£5,181** (£1,541; £770; £384) **Stalls** High

Form RPR

41 **1** **Amarna (USA)**[19] 4275 3-9-6 78 LDettori 4 88+
(Saeed Bin Suroor) *prom on outer: wnt 2nd jst over 2f out: drvn to chal over 1f out: led ins fnl f: won gng away* **10/11**[1]

0061 **2** *1 1/4* **Minnis Bay (CAN)**[18] 4313 3-9-5 77 RHills 14 84
(E F Vaughan) *led: gng strly over 2f out: pressed over 1f out: hdd ins fnl f: outpcd nr fin* **7/1**[2]

2504 **3** *1* **Mafeking (UAE)**[19] 4276 3-9-5 77 PaulDoe 9 81
(M R Hoad) *chsd ldrs: rdn over 2f out: styd on fr over 1f out: nvr able to chal* **14/1**

6001 **4** *hd* **Hessian (IRE)**[9] 4591 3-8-9 67 HayleyTurner 11 71
(P Howling) *prom: rdn over 2f out: kpt on same pce fr over 1f out* **14/1**

2230 **5** *1 1/4* **Pivotalia (IRE)**[26] 4073 3-8-1 66 KMay[(7)] 10 67
(W R Swinburn) *mostly chsd ldr to jst over 2f out: one pce fr over 1f out* **20/1**

5300 **6** *shd* **Rubenstar (IRE)**[24] 4135 4-9-4 75 PatrickHills[(5)] 3 77
(M H Tompkins) *hld up in rr and racd on outer: rdn and prog 2f out: hanging over 1f out: kpt on: nvr rchd ldrs* **12/1**

6030 **7** *1/2* **Alfresco**[18] 4313 3-9-6 78 (b) JimmyFortune 2 78+
(Pat Eddery) *stdd s: hld up in last trio: prog on inner wl over 1f out: rdn ins fnl f: no imp* **16/1**

2456 **8** *1/2* **Cinematic (IRE)**[11] 4551 4-9-4 70 AmirQuinn 7 70
(J R Boyle) *stdd s: hld up in rr: prog on inner 2f out: sn drvn: no imp after* **14/1**

2000 **9** *1* **Ninth House (USA)**[10] 4587 5-9-9 80 (bt) TolleyDean[(5)] 12 77
(N P Littmoden) *t.k.h: hld up in midfield: rdn and no prog over 2f out* **33/1**

0604 **10** *1 3/4* **Merrymadcap (IRE)**[7] 4672 5-9-1 67 FrancisNorton 1 60
(M Blanshard) *hld up in last trio and racd wd: rdn and no prog over 2f out* **11/1**

415 **11** *hd* **Nassau Style**[26] 4080 3-9-6 78 OscarUrbina 13 70
(J R Fanshawe) *hld up in midfield: tried to angle out for effrt 2f out: shkn up and no imp over 1f out: fdd ins fnl f* **12/1**

560 **12** *hd* **Up The Chimney**[26] 4066 3-8-4 62 NelsonDeSouza 6 53
(A P Jarvis) *stdd s: hld up wl in rr: nvr a factor* **33/1**

0-40 **13** *19* **Tempsford Flyer (IRE)**[79] 2469 4-9-10 76 MichaelHills 8 25
(J W Hills) *in tch to 1/2-way: sn bhd: dismntd after fin: sddle slipped* **8/1**[3]

1m 39.24s (-1.56) **Going Correction** -0.10s/f (Stan)
WFA 3 from 4yo+ 6lb **13** Ran SP% **136.2**
Speed ratings (Par 105): **103,101,100,100,99 99,98,98,97,95 95,95,76**
CSF £9.03 CT £73.31 TOTE £1.90: £1.30, £3.00, £3.30; EX 7.70 Place 6 £40.88, Place 5 £25.17.

Owner Godolphin **Bred** Darley **Trained** Newmarket, Suffolk

FOCUS
Quite a competitive handicap, but the pace was not strong and the principals were always prominent. The form is not rated too positively but it was probably won by a horse that is a bit better than this class.

Tempsford Flyer(IRE) Official explanation: jockey said saddle slipped

T/Plt: £78.50 to a £1 stake. Pool: £43,840.55. 407.45 winning tickets. T/Qpdt: £58.20 to a £1 stake. Pool: £1,695.15. 21.55 winning tickets. JN

4768 NEWCASTLE (L-H)

Monday, August 27

OFFICIAL GOING: Good (good to firm in places)

Wind: Breezy, half against Weather: Cloudy, bright

4890 EUROPEAN BREEDERS' FUND MAIDEN STKS 7f

2:10 (2:10) (Class 4) 2-Y-0 **£4,100** (£1,227; £613; £306; £152) **Stalls** High

Form RPR

1 **Alexander Castle (USA)** 2-9-3 0 NCallan 4 87+
(K A Ryan) *hld up in tch: n.m.r 3f out: smooth hdwy to ld over 1f out: pushed clr: readily* **5/1**[2]

4 **2** *3 1/2* **Inspector Clouseau (IRE)**[45] 3510 2-9-3 0 MickyFenton 5 73
(T P Tate) *led to over 1f out: kpt on u.p: no ch w wnr* **25/1**

4360 **3** *4* **Narmeen**[24] 4126 2-8-12 72 TPO'Shea 7 58
(M R Channon) *cl up: ev ch and hung lft 2f out: sn outpcd* **25/1**

5 **4** *1/2* **Craigstown**[23] 4151 2-9-3 0 KerrinMcEvoy 3 62
(Saeed Bin Suroor) *sn chsng ldrs: effrt over 2f out: sn outpcd: n.d after* **2/5**[1]

0 **5** *2 1/2* **Safari Dancer (IRE)**[10] 4578 2-9-3 0 TomEaves 10 59+
(I Semple) *hld up: sme hdwy over 2f out: nvr rchd ldrs* **33/1**

0 **6** *2* **Blazing Mask (IRE)**[9] 4612 2-8-12 0 PaulHanagan 6 46
(Mrs A Duffield) *towards rr: drvn 1/2-way: nvr able to chal* **100/1**

7 *1 1/4* **Sonny Sam (IRE)** 2-9-3 0 PaulFessey 8 47
(M H Tompkins) *dwlt: bhd: struggling after 2f: nvr on terms* **28/1**

8 *1/2* **Actabou** 2-9-3 0 PhillipMakin 9 46
(M Dods) *sn pushed along towards rr: struggling fr 1/2-way* **66/1**

0 **9** *8* **Tarbolton (IRE)**[11] 4547 2-9-3 0 RoystonFfrench 2 26
(M Johnston) *cl up tl wknd over 2f out* **8/1**[3]

1m 28.22s (0.20) **Going Correction** +0.075s/f (Good) **9** Ran SP% **115.8**
Speed ratings (Par 96): **101,97,92,91,89 86,85,84,75**
CSF £104.63 TOTE £5.50: £1.90, £4.20, £6.40; EX 101.70 Trifecta £207.90 Part won. Pool: £292.88 - 0.34 winning tickets..

Owner Noel O'Callaghan **Bred** Helen K Groves Revokable Trust **Trained** Hambleton, N Yorks

FOCUS
Little strength in depth and the market leader was a big disappointment but this was a fair winning time for a race of its type and the winner is the type to progress again.

NOTEBOOK
Alexander Castle(USA) ◆, a 90,000gns half-brother to a winner in the States, is a bit on the leg at present but he clearly knew his job on this racecourse debut and he turned in a fluent performance. His task was simplified with the disappointing run of the market leader but he could do no more than win with plenty in hand and he is the sort to hold his own in stronger company. (op 4-1 tchd 11-2 in places)

Inspector Clouseau(IRE), well beaten in soft ground on his debut at York, still looks on the immature side but had the run of the race and showed much-improved form. He should have no problems with 1m but is the sort to do best once handicapped. (tchd 28-1)

Narmeen, a leggy, unfurnished sort who was on her toes in the paddock, was not disgraced but she has had a few chances now and she is likely to continue to look vulnerable in this type of event.

Craigstown, who shaped with promise on his debut at Goodwood, looked to have solid claims in this company but proved a big disappointment and found little once pressure was applied. While it is too soon to write him off, a watching brief may be the best advice for his next start. (op 1-2)

Safari Dancer(IRE) ran to a similar level of form as on his debut and his future is going to lie in run-of-the-mill handicaps over further in due course.
Blazing Mask(IRE), well beaten on her debut at Ripon earlier in the month, fared little better over this longer trip and she is going to continue to look vulnerable in this type of event.

4891 ST JAMES SECURITY CLAIMING STKS 1m 3y(S)

2:45 (2:45) (Class 6) 3-Y-O+ **£1,943** (£578; £288; £144) **Stalls** High

Form				RPR
3050	1		**Penel (IRE)**[21] 4223 6-9-3 46.....(p) MickyFenton 3 (P T Midgley) *hld up: hdwy 2f out: led ins fnl f: rdn out* **8/1**[3]	55
-200	2	½	**Yo Pedro (IRE)**[26] 4081 5-9-5 60.....(b[1]) NCallan 7 (D Carroll) *hld up: smooth hdwy over 2f out: effrt and ch ins fnl f: sn rdn: hld last 50yds* **6/1**[2]	56
0000	3	2	**Domesday (UAE)**[10] 4580 6-9-2 43..... DuranFentiman[(3)] 14 (W G Harrison) *cl up: led over 1f out to ins fnl f: nt qckn* **20/1**	51
5202	4	1 ½	**Fizzy Bella**[11] 4550 3-8-11 52..... NeilBrown[(5)] 12 (M G Quinlan) *chsd ldrs: effrt and ev ch over 1f out: no ex ins fnl f* **7/2**[1]	51
0604	5	1	**Following Flow (USA)**[29] 3996 5-9-2 43..... AndrewElliott[(3)] 11 (R Allan) *bhd: rdn over 3f out: hdwy and swtchd lft over 1f out: no imp ins fnl f* **18/1**	45
0065	6	4	**Baylaw Star**[13] 4479 6-9-13 64..... LeeEnstone 4 (I W McInnes) *led to over 1f out: sn rdn and btn* **17/2**	44
1655	7	nk	**Nuit Sombre (IRE)**[46] 3470 7-9-13 72.....(p) KDarley 2 (G A Harker) *racd alone far side: showed up tl outpcd fr 2f out* **7/2**[1]	43
0-20	8	1 ¼	**Judge Neptune**[35] 3785 3-9-0 61.....(v[1]) GaryBartley[(7)] 8 (J S Goldie) *dwlt: bhd: rdn over 3f out: n.d* **10/1**	40
600/	9	3	**Monroe Gold**[381] 6152 7-9-5 31.....(v) TPO'Shea 6 (Jennie Candlish) *chsd ldrs tl wknd over 2f out* **100/1**	26
0042	10	2	**Passionately Royal**[14] 4449 5-9-2 46..... PatrickDonaghy[(7)] 10 (M Brittain) *chsd ldrs tl wknd fr 3f out* **11/1**	25
5000	11	7	**Hillside Smoki (IRE)**[19] 4283 3-8-8 8.....(b) RoystonFfrench 5 (A Berry) *towards rr: drvn 1/2-way: nvr on terms* **200/1**	—
00-0	12	1 ¼	**Just Intersky (USA)**[24] 67 4-9-13 70..... PaulHanagan 9 (R M Whitaker) *chsd ldrs tl wknd over 2f out* **9/1**	10
0	13	5	**Biarritz**[12] 4496 6-9-8 0..... TomEaves 13 (Mrs J C McGregor) *a bhd* **200/1**	—

1m 44.14s (2.24) **Going Correction** +0.075s/f (Good)
WFA 3 from 4yo+ 6lb **13** Ran SP% **119.8**
Speed ratings (Par 101): **91,90,88,87,86 82,81,80,77,75 68,67,62**
CSF £55.16 TOTE £12.40: £3.50, £2.40, £10.90; EX 74.90 TRIFECTA Not won..
Owner Mrs K L Midgley **Bred** M Ervine **Trained** Westow, N Yorks
■ Stewards' Enquiry : Lee Enstone one-day ban: failed to keep straight from stalls (Sep 7)

FOCUS
Not a strong race of its type and a moderate winning time, even for a claimer. The form is rated through the fourth and the fifth.
Passionately Royal Official explanation: jockey said gelding finished distressed

4892 CHISHOLM BOOKMAKERS BLAYDON NURSERY 1m 3y(S)

3:20 (3:21) (Class 3) 2-Y-O
£12,152 (£3,638; £1,819; £910; £454; £228) **Stalls** High

Form				RPR
401	1		**Tuanku (IRE)**[17] 4363 2-8-13 67..... TPO'Shea 1 (M R Channon) *hld up: nt clr run over 2f out: sn swtchd lft: led ins fnl f: kpt on wl* **25/1**	69
2661	2	nk	**Welcome Return (IRE)**[19] 4278 2-9-4 72.....(b) KDarley 4 (T D Easterby) *hld up in tch: smooth hdwy to ld wl over 1f out: edgd rt: hdd ins fnl f: kpt on u.p towards fin* **8/1**	73
0200	3	shd	**Marning Star**[24] 4121 2-9-4 72..... PatCosgrave 6 (M R Channon) *hld up: effrt 2f out: ev ch ins fnl f: kpt on: hld nr fin* **50/1**	73
2313	4	3	**Relinquished**[14] 4461 2-9-7 75..... KerrinMcEvoy 7 (J Noseda) *midfield: effrt whn nt clr run over 2f out: effrt over 1f out: no imp fnl f* **7/2**[1]	70
2603	5	½	**Boomtown**[11] 4524 2-9-3 71..... RoystonFfrench 8 (M Johnston) *chsd ldrs: rdn whn n.m.r and outpcd wl over 1f out: kpt on fnl f: no imp* **9/2**[2]	64
5013	6	5	**Natural Rhythm (IRE)**[3] 4783 2-8-6 60..... PaulFessey 11 (D W Chapman) *in tch on ins: nt clr run over 2f out to over 1f out: sn n.d* **12/1**	42
062	7	hd	**Twilight Belle (IRE)**[83] 2344 2-8-11 65..... DaleGibson 3 (K R Burke) *towards rr: drvn over 2f out: n.d* **25/1**	47
005	8	¾	**Medici Time**[14] 4448 2-8-3 60..... DuranFentiman[(3)] 2 (T D Easterby) *s.i.s and wnt lft s: bhd on ins: hdwy over 1f out: n.d* **16/1**	40
5422	9	2 ½	**Madison Heights (IRE)**[19] 4278 2-9-2 70..... TomEaves 9 (J Howard Johnson) *cl up: led briefly 2f out: wknd appr fnl f* **12/1**	45
6602	10	2 ½	**Bencorr (USA)**[7] 4669 2-8-12 66..... PaulHanagan 5 (M J Wallace) *prom: effrt and ch over 2f out: rdn and wknd over 1f out* **11/2**[3]	35
0535	11	¾	**Duke Of Touraine (IRE)**[17] 4364 2-9-4 75..... AndrewElliott[(3)] 12 (P C Haslam) *led to 2f out: wkng whn hmpd wl over 1f out* **11/1**	43
6423	12	26	**Dream Express (IRE)**[19] 4278 2-9-5 73.....(p) PhillipMakin 10 (M Dods) *sn cl up: drvn 1/2-way: wknd over 2f out: sn lost tch* **11/2**[3]	—

1m 42.71s (0.81) **Going Correction** +0.075s/f (Good) **12** Ran SP% **121.5**
Speed ratings (Par 98): **98,97,97,94,94 89,88,88,85,83 82,56**
CSF £215.69 CT £9779.37 TOTE £24.30: £4.20, £2.50, £10.20; EX 129.70 TRIFECTA Not won..
Owner Box 41 **Bred** Stone Ridge Farm **Trained** West Ilsley, Berks

FOCUS
Not the race it used to be but still a competitive event for a fairly valuable prize. The pace was sound and the first three pulled clear of the remainder, with the fourth helping set the level.

NOTEBOOK
Tuanku(IRE), a 7f selling winner on his previous start, turned in an improved display on this handicap debut and first run over this longer trip. He should get further still, seems to have a good attitude and, as he has only had four runs, may be capable of better still.
Welcome Return(IRE), who showed improved form to win a 7f nursery in first-time blinkers at this course on her previous start, bettered that form after travelling much better from this 9lb higher mark. She kept galloping all the way to the line and, although she will be up in the weights again, appeals as the sort to win again around this trip. (op 5-1)
Marning Star, soundly beaten on his nursery debut at Goodwood on his previous start, proved well suited by the stiffer test of stamina that this race had to offer and he turned in a career-best effort. He finished clear of the remainder, handles a bit of cut in the ground and looks sure to win a race.
Relinquished, who had been running creditably in races that have thrown up winners, looks a bit better than the bare form as he was short of room at a crucial stage. Whether his troubled run cost him a winning chance is debatable but he is a fair sort around this trip and he should continue to give a good account. (op 9-2)
Boomtown, who turned in an improved effort on his handicap debut last time, bettered that form in this stronger race and left the impression that an even stiffer test of stamina would have been in his favour. He is sure to win a race for his current handler. (tchd 5-1)
Natural Rhythm(IRE) was more exposed than the majority but had been running creditably and was another to shape a bit better than the bare form suggested. There will be easier opportunities in the coming weeks than this one and he is capable of winning in modest company from his current mark. (tchd 11-1)
Duke Of Touraine(IRE) looked worth a try over this trip judging on the form he showed on his nursery debut and ran a bit better than the bare form suggested. He is not one to write off just yet. (tchd 9-1)
Dream Express(IRE), closely matched with the runner-up on a recent course run, ran a stinker in the first-time cheekpieces and presumably the headgear will be dispensed with next time. Official explanation: trainer had no explanation for the poor form shown (op 8-1)

4893 INTERSKY 50 CLUB H'CAP 2m 19y

3:55 (3:55) (Class 3) (0-95,92) 3-Y-O+
£7,790 (£2,332; £1,166; £583; £291; £146) **Stalls** Centre

Form				RPR
0-30	1		**Mirjan (IRE)**[16] 4375 11-9-10 88.....(b) PaulHanagan 1 (L Lungo) *prom: rdn 4f out: outpcd over 2f out: kpt on wl fnl f to ld nr fin* **7/1**	96
0606	2	shd	**Kasthari (IRE)**[10] 4569 8-10-0 92..... NCallan 4 (J D Bethell) *cl up: led and edgd lft 3f out: sn drvn: kpt on fnl f: hdd nr fin* **9/1**	100
5350	3	1	**Som Tala**[10] 4569 4-9-10 88..... TPO'Shea 6 (M R Channon) *cl up: led after 6f to 3f out: rallied: kpt on same pce ins fnl f* **5/4**[1]	95
0/10	4	5	**Downing Street (IRE)**[10] 4569 6-8-11 78.....(bt) AndrewElliott[(3)] 3 (Jennie Candlish) *bhd: struggling over 6f out: kpt on wl fnl 2f: nrst fin* **11/2**[3]	79
3120	5	nk	**Thewhirlingdervish (IRE)**[10] 4569 9-9-1 79..... KDarley 5 (T D Easterby) *hld up in tch: pushed along fr 1/2-way: outpcd 4f out: rallied over 2f out: no ex over 1f out* **5/1**[2]	80+
2003	6	5	**Mister Arjay (USA)**[12] 4490 7-8-12 76 oh1..... TomEaves 7 (B Ellison) *led 6f: w ldr: rdn and wknd over 2f out* **8/1**	70
2550	7	40	**Kames Park (IRE)**[65] 2861 5-9-5 83..... RoystonFfrench 2 (Mrs H O Graham) *stdd s: hld up: rdn over 6f out: sn struggling* **20/1**	29

3m 33.17s (-2.03) **Going Correction** -0.025s/f (Good) **7** Ran SP% **114.9**
Speed ratings (Par 107): **104,103,103,100,100 98,78**
CSF £66.10 TOTE £8.80: £4.00, £4.50; EX 53.10.
Owner Len Lungo Racing Limited **Bred** His Highness The Aga Khan's Studs S C **Trained** Carrutherstown, D'fries & G'way
■ Stewards' Enquiry : K Darley three-day ban: failed to ride out for fourth place (Sep 7, 9-10)

FOCUS
A fair handicap but mainly exposed performers and the gallop was fair at best. It is hard to rate the form too positively in the circumstances.

NOTEBOOK
Mirjan(IRE) would have been suited by a stronger pace but he showed a good attitude to notch his third win over this course and distance and his second win in this particular event. He has been a fine servant to connections but he may find things tougher in more competitive company after reassessment. (op 13-2)
Kasthari(IRE) has slipped in the weights in the last 12 months but turned in his best effort of the year on this fourth start for his current yard. Although showing a tendency to edge left, he did very little wrong otherwise but, although capable of winning a similar event away from progressive or well handicapped sorts, is not one to be lumping on at short odds. (op 7-1 tchd 10-1)
Som Tala, who had been running creditably in stronger handicaps than this one on his last couple of starts, had the run of the race and turned in another creditable effort to finish clear of the remainder. He has little margin for error from this mark, though. (op 7-4)
Downing Street(IRE) was not disgraced in terms of the bare form but looked a tricky ride, dropping himself right out before consenting to run on in the straight. A stronger overall gallop may have suited but he will have to improve to win from his current mark. (op 8-1)
Thewhirlingdervish(IRE), in good form this year, was never travelling with much fluency and, although his rider was found guilty of taking it easy in the closing stages, he was a fair way below his very best. Easier ground may suit ideally and he is worth another chance. (op 9-2 tchd 4-1)
Mister Arjay(USA), whose form has been patchy since his last win at Redcar in May, stays this trip and had the run of the race but proved disappointing and he is not one to be placing too much faith in. (tchd 13-2)
Kames Park(IRE), whose form has been patchy since his two Polytrack wins in March, was soundly beaten on this first run for new connections. (op 14-1)

4894 INTERSKYGROUP.COM H'CAP 1m 4f 93y

4:30 (4:30) (Class 6) (0-65,63) 3-Y-O **£3,238** (£963; £481; £240) **Stalls** Centre

Form				RPR
-006	1		**Double Banded (IRE)**[23] 4172 3-8-10 52..... KerrinMcEvoy 5 (J L Dunlop) *hld up in tch: effrt over 2f out: hung lft: chsd wnr appr fnl f: styd on to ld towards fin* **3/1**[1]	61+
0631	2	nk	**La Vecchia Scuola (IRE)**[10] 4579 3-9-2 63.....(v) KellyHarrison[(5)] 6 (R Johnson) *set stdy pce: led: rdn over 1f out: kpt on: hdd towards fin* **11/1**	69
0003	3	1 ½	**Boz**[11] 4533 3-8-7 49.....(b) KDarley 8 (L M Cumani) *t.k.h: prom: effrt and pressed wnr over 2f out to appr fnl f: one pce* **4/1**[2]	53
0003	4	½	**Falcon's Fire (IRE)**[9] 4223 3-9-0 56..... RoystonFfrench 4 (Mrs A Duffield) *t.k.h: chsd ldrs: effrt over 2f out: edgd rt and one pce fnl f* **7/1**	59
5450	5	3	**Always Best**[16] 4391 3-8-8 53..... AndrewElliott[(3)] 9 (M Johnston) *pressed ldr: rdn and hung lft fr 3f out: outpcd fnl 2f* **11/2**	51
1544	6	1 ¼	**President Dan**[6] 4687 3-8-13 55..... TPO'Shea 3 (M R Channon) *hld up: drvn 3f out: no imp fr 2f out* **9/2**[3]	51
-006	7	1 ¼	**Etoile D'Or (IRE)**[35] 3804 3-9-1 57..... NCallan 1 (M H Tompkins) *hld up: rdn 3f out: nvr on terms* **12/1**	51
0040	8	¾	**Cornell Precedent**[16] 4391 3-8-3 45..... PaulHanagan 7 (J J Quinn) *hld up in tch: drvn 3f out: sn btn* **12/1**	38

2m 43.24s (-0.31) **Going Correction** -0.025s/f (Good) **8** Ran SP% **114.8**
Speed ratings (Par 98): **100,99,98,98,96 95,94,94**
CSF £37.01 CT £133.16 TOTE £2.80: £1.50, £2.50, £1.40; EX 35.40 Trifecta £255.70 Part won. Pool: £360.20 - 0.34 winning tickets..
Owner Sir Thomas Pilkington **Bred** Sir Thomas Pilkington **Trained** Arundel, W Sussex
■ Stewards' Enquiry : Kelly Harrison one-day ban: careless riding (Sep 7)

FOCUS
A run-of-the-mill handicap in which the pace was only fair. The form may not prove too sound, but the winner looks to be getting his act together.

4895 CHISHOLM BOOKMAKERS NOW OPEN AT NEWCASTLE AIRPORT H'CAP 6f
5:05 (5:05) (Class 4) (0-80,78) 3-Y-0+
£7,478 (£2,239; £1,119; £560; £279; £140) Stalls High

Form RPR
2110 1 **Dakota Rain (IRE)**[24] 4140 5-9-4 72 TPO'Shea 10 87+
(Jennie Candlish) *mde all: rdn over 2f out: kpt on wl fnl f* 8/1
0123 2 2 ½ **Rainbow Fox**[16] 4381 3-8-11 68 PaulHanagan 8 75
(R A Fahey) *chsd ldrs: effrt and wnt 2nd appr fnl f: kpt on: nt rch wnr* 11/2[3]
4030 3 1 ½ **Guest Connections**[31] 3911 4-9-5 73 (v) AdrianTNicholls 7 76
(D Nicholls) *prom: effrt 2f out: edgd lft: kpt on same pce fnl f* 7/1
1104 4 1 **Charles Parnell (IRE)**[16] 4381 4-9-2 70 PhillipMakin 5 70
(M Dods) *sn in tch: effrt over 2f out: kpt on fnl f: nrst fin* 7/1
2061 5 1 **Viva Volta**[19] 4281 4-9-10 78 (b) KDarley 4 75
(T D Easterby) *pressed wnr tl rdn and no ex over 1f out* 3/1[1]
5045 6 1 **Yorkshire Blue**[10] 4581 8-8-13 74 GaryBartley[(7)] 1 68
(J S Goldie) *bhd: drvn 1/2-way: kpt on fnl f: n.d* 7/2[2]
0360 7 2 **Connect**[10] 4585 10-9-2 70 (b) NCallan 6 58
(M H Tompkins) *in tch: drvn 1/2-way: btn over 1f out* 16/1
-000 8 5 **Imperial Sword**[10] 4581 4-9-2 70 PaulFessey 2 43
(T D Barron) *bhd: rdn 1/2-way: nvr on terms* 14/1
00-0 9 14 **Lord Of The East**[14] 4462 8-9-9 77 LeeEnstone 9 8
(I W McInnes) *towards rr: drvn 1/2-way: sn struggling: t.o* 25/1

1m 12.65s (-2.44) **Going Correction** -0.225s/f (Firm)
WFA 3 from 4yo+ 3lb 9 Ran SP% **115.1**
Speed ratings (Par 105): **107,103,101,100,99 97,95,88,69**
CSF £51.30 CT £325.10 TOTE £10.10: £2.20, £1.70, £2.20; EX 40.40 Trifecta £260.40 Part won. Pool: £366.80 - 0.34 winning tickets..
Owner P and Mrs G A Clarke **Bred** Islanmore Stud **Trained** Basford Green, Staffs

FOCUS
A run-of-the-mill sprint in which the pace seemed sound but those attempting to come from off the pace were at a disadvantage. The form is rated through the second.

4896 RACECOURSE VIDEO SERVICES H'CAP 5f
5:35 (5:35) (Class 5) (0-75,72) 3-Y-0 £3,469 (£1,038; £519; £259; £129) Stalls High

Form RPR
4221 1 **Nomoreblondes**[34] 3811 3-8-12 63 (p) MickyFenton 7 70
(P T Midgley) *mde all: rdn 2f out: hld on wl fnl f* 11/1
3341 2 1 ½ **Mandurah (IRE)**[29] 4001 3-9-7 72 AdrianTNicholls 8 74
(D Nicholls) *pressed wnr: effrt 2f out: kpt on same pce ins fnl f* 13/2[3]
6340 3 ½ **Pegasus Dancer (FR)**[14] 4452 3-9-5 70 (p) NCallan 3 70
(K A Ryan) *chsd ldrs: drvn over 2f out: one pce fnl f* 12/1
1665 4 hd **Bayshambles (IRE)**[15] 4425 3-8-3 54 RoystonFfrench 6 56+
(R E Barr) *bhd tl gd hdwy over 1f out: kpt on: nrst fin* 25/1
3036 5 shd **Triple Shadow**[8] 4642 3-8-12 63 PhillipMakin 10 62
(T D Barron) *hld up: hdwy over 1f out: kpt on fnl f: no imp* 5/1[2]
3241 6 hd **Dualagi**[11] 4546 3-9-5 70 KDarley 9 68
(J S Moore) *sn bhd: effrt on outside over 2f out: no imp ins fnl f* 5/1[2]
0-60 7 1 ¾ **Nabra**[61] 3000 3-8-4 55 DaleGibson 12 47
(M Brittain) *midfield: outpcd over 2f out: sn no imp* 33/1
1500 8 1 ¾ **Sunley Sovereign**[97] 1932 3-8-8 59 ow1 TomEaves 5 45
(D W Chapman) *in tch: outpcd 2f out: sn no ex* 40/1
-001 9 shd **Woqoodd**[19] 4291 3-9-5 70 PaulHanagan 4 55
(R A Fahey) *prom to 1/2-way: sn rdn and lost pl: n.d after* 5/2[1]
-004 10 1 **Umpa Loompa (IRE)**[7] 4658 3-8-2 53 oh1 (v) PaulFessey 1 35
(D Nicholls) *chsd ldrs tl rdn and wknd over 1f out* 20/1
0010 11 1 ½ **Stir Crazy (IRE)**[7] 4661 3-8-8 59 TPO'Shea 11 35
(M R Channon) *towards rr: outpcd 1/2-way: n.d after* 9/1
5403 12 1 ¾ **Durova (IRE)**[14] 4452 3-8-12 66 DuranFentiman[(3)] 2 36
(T D Easterby) *prom: drvn 1/2-way: wknd over 1f out* 17/2

60.68 secs (-0.82) **Going Correction** -0.225s/f (Firm) 12 Ran SP% **125.8**
Speed ratings (Par 100): **97,94,93,93,93 93,90,87,87,85 83,80**
CSF £82.61 CT £909.76 TOTE £8.50: £2.50, £2.90, £5.50; EX 79.10 TRIFECTA Not won. Place 6 £10,579.72, Place 5 £1,883.31..
Owner Anthony D Copley **Bred** P John And Redmyre Bloodstock **Trained** Westow, N Yorks

FOCUS
Another run-of-the-mill sprint in which the field raced centre to stands side. Modest form.
Umpa Loompa(IRE) Official explanation: jockey said gelding hung right-handed throughout
T/Plt: £6,512.60 to a £1 stake. Pool: £53,528.65. 6.00 winning tickets. T/Qpdt: £100.00 to a £1 stake. Pool: £3,541.85. 26.20 winning tickets. RY

4611 RIPON (R-H)
Monday, August 27

OFFICIAL GOING: Good to firm (9.1)
Wind: Moderate, across Weather: Fine and sunny

4897 SOLBERGE HALL IS A THOROUGHBRED HOTEL (S) STKS 6f
2:25 (2:26) (Class 6) 2-Y-0 £2,730 (£806; £403) Stalls Low

Form RPR
060 1 **Ambrose Princess (IRE)**[17] 4363 2-8-11 56 RichardHughes 2 58
(J S Moore) *chsd ldrs: hdwy over 2f out: rdn to ld over 1f out: drvn ins fnl f and hld on wl* 4/1[3]
0030 2 nk **Little Bones**[17] 4363 2-8-11 45 (t) TedDurcan 12 57
(Rae Guest) *sn outpcd in rr: hdwy 1/2-way: rdn wl over 1f out: styd on to chse wnr ins fnl f: drvn and one pce towards fin* 8/1
0U04 3 8 **Mill Creek**[16] 4405 2-8-8 42 (v[1]) MarkLawson[(3)] 11 33
(B Smart) *prom on outer: rdn along and hung bdly rt over 2f out: kpt on same pce* 20/1
00 4 ½ **First Abode**[23] 4174 2-8-11 0 PaulMulrennan 5 32
(M Brittain) *chsd ldrs: rdn along and outpcd over 2f out: plugged on u.p appr fnl f* 22/1
0240 5 1 ¾ **Best Suited**[16] 4406 2-8-11 59 GrahamGibbons 7 26
(J J Quinn) *prom: effrt to chal over 2f out: sn rdn and ev ch tl drvn appr fnl f and sn wknd* 2/1[1]
5005 6 1 ¾ **Hildegarde (IRE)**[11] 4524 2-8-11 54 (b) DavidAllan 1 21
(T D Easterby) *led: rdn along 2f out: drvn and hdd over 1f out: wknd qckly* 11/4[2]
0050 7 ½ **Brilliantsensation (IRE)**[16] 4405 2-9-2 53 (b[1]) TPQueally 9 25
(J G Given) *prom: rdn along over 2f out and sn wknd* 25/1
0000 8 5 **Smilodon**[27] 4041 2-8-4 40 AdamCarter[(7)] 10 5
(A Berry) *dwlt: a in rr* 66/1
0004 9 ½ **Happy Hacker (IRE)**[18] 4311 2-8-8 48 (v[1]) JamieMoriarty[(3)] 4 —
(P D Evans) *sn outpcd and a bhd* 17/2
0 10 1 **Caffrey Kelly**[29] 4002 2-9-2 0 TonyHamilton 6 5
(J J Quinn) *chsd ldrs on outer: rdn along 1/2-way: sn wknd* 25/1
0000 11 4 **Lay Down Darling**[16] 4405 2-8-11 30 (v[1]) KimTinkler 3 —
(N Tinkler) *prom: rdn along bef 1/2-way and sn wknd* 66/1

1m 15.01s (2.01) **Going Correction** +0.05s/f (Good) 11 Ran SP% **121.4**
Speed ratings (Par 92): **88,87,76,76,73 71,70,64,63,62 56**
CSF £33.59 TOTE £6.30: £1.80, £2.50, £3.30; EX 39.90.The winner was bought in for 7,400gns. Little Bones was claimed by J. F. Coupland for £6,000.
Owner R S S Ambrose, H Wilson & J Wells **Bred** Tally-Ho Stud **Trained** Upper Lambourn, Berks

FOCUS
A dire affair. The first pair came well clear and it might be that they can rate higher.

NOTEBOOK
Ambrose Princess(IRE), back in trip, had been hampered over 7f last time and was clearly better than that run suggested. She appreciated being ridden positively over this sharper test and showed a resilient attitude towards the finish. This is her sort of level, but her pedigree indicates she ought to enjoy the return to another furlong or so before the season is out. (op 5-1)
Little Bones, in front of the winner at Newmarket last time, did not prove anywhere near as suited by the drop back in trip as that rival and was doing all of her best work at the finish. She only just failed to get up, however, and finished well clear of the remainder so a similar race is clearly within her compass. The return to 7f should see her go one better in this class. (op 9-1 tchd 7-1)
Mill Creek, equipped with a first-time visor, showed early dash yet hung markedly right on the outside of the pace from the 2f pole. She is clearly not straightforward, but should prove happier when racing with more cover in the future. (op 18-1)
First Abode, down in class, proved very one-paced over this extra furlong and if anything shaped as though she would appreciate 7f. (op 20-1)
Best Suited dropped out tamely after looking to have every chance nearing the final furlong and ran well below her recent level on this drop in class. (tchd 15-8 and 9-4)
Hildegarde(IRE) again tried to dictate, but the shorter trip was not in her favour and the blinkers evidently failed to have a positive effect this time. Official explanation: jockey said filly hung right (op 3-1 tchd 7-2)

4898 BILLY NEVETT MEMORIAL H'CAP 6f
3:00 (3:02) (Class 4) (0-85,85) 3-Y-0 £5,362 (£1,604; £802; £401; £199) Stalls Low

Form RPR
-124 1 **Tombi (USA)**[25] 4093 3-9-7 85 EddieAhern 12 95+
(J Howard Johnson) *trckd ldrs far side: hdwy to ld over 1f out: sn rdn and r.o wl* 5/2[1]
5350 2 2 ½ **Avertuoso**[10] 4567 3-9-6 84 RichardHughes 11 86
(B Smart) *trckd ldrs far side: hdwy and ev ch wl over 1f out: sn rdn and kpt on same pce ins fnl f* 16/1
5400 3 1 **Everymanforhimself (IRE)**[16] 4374 3-9-6 84 TPQueally 1 83
(J G Given) *prom stands' side: swtchd rt and rdn 2f out: styd on u.p to ld stands' side gp ent fnl f: no ch w first two on far side* 20/1
3106 4 1 **Baltimore Jack (IRE)**[15] 4425 3-9-4 82 PaulMulrennan 2 78
(M W Easterby) *led stands' side gp: rdn along 2f out: drvn and one pce fr over 1f out* 16/1
4142 5 shd **Charlie Tipple**[15] 4425 3-8-10 74 DavidAllan 3 69+
(T D Easterby) *towards rr stands' side: hdwy over 2f out: rdn and styd on ins fnl f: nrst fin* 11/2[2]
0060 6 1 **Just Joey**[5] 4726 3-9-0 78 (b[1]) GrahamGibbons 10 70
(J R Weymes) *prom far side: rdn along and ev ch 2f out: sn drvn and kpt on same pce* 40/1
6035 7 nk **Sunnyside Tom (IRE)**[21] 4222 3-8-6 70 TonyHamilton 8 61
(R A Fahey) *overall ldr far side: rdn along over 2f out: hdd over 1f out and grad wknd* 12/1
0604 8 1 ½ **Bridge It Jo**[9] 4606 3-8-12 79 JerryO'Dwyer[(3)] 14 65
(G G Margarson) *in tch far side: effrt over 2f out: sn rdn and wknd wl over 1f out* 16/1
5450 9 ½ **Soviet Palace (IRE)**[25] 4093 3-9-2 83 JamieMoriarty[(3)] 5 68
(K A Ryan) *a towards rr stands' side* 14/1
-000 10 hd **Fantasy Parkes**[93] 2044 3-9-7 85 TedDurcan 15 69
(K A Ryan) *a towards rr far side* 25/1
0402 11 3 **Pickering**[19] 4291 3-8-9 73 GregFairley 7 47
(E J Alston) *cl up stands' side: rdn along 2f out and sn wknd* 10/1[3]
6350 12 3 **Multitude (IRE)**[24] 4127 3-8-2 66 (b[1]) PaulQuinn 6 31
(T D Easterby) *a towards rr stands' side* 40/1
50 13 1 ¼ **Danum Dancer**[26] 4080 3-9-0 78 (b) SilvestreDeSousa 9 39
(N Bycroft) *chsd ldrs far side: rdn along 1/2-way: sn wknd* 12/1
0006 14 1 **Valdan (IRE)**[16] 4385 3-9-2 83 PJMcDonald[(3)] 4 41
(P D Evans) *chsd ldrs stands' side: rdn along over 2f out and sn wknd* 22/1

1m 12.98s (-0.02) **Going Correction** +0.05s/f (Good) 14 Ran SP% **110.6**
Speed ratings (Par 102): **102,98,97,96,95 94,94,92,91,91 87,83,81,80**
CSF £33.00 CT £428.20 TOTE £3.10: £1.40, £4.80, £6.80; EX 40.60.
Owner Transcend Bloodstock LLP **Bred** Sun Valley Farm **Trained** Billy Row, Co Durham
■ Ishetoo was withdrawn (9/2, unruly in stalls). R4, deduct 15p in the £.

FOCUS
A decent sprint handicap which saw seven runners go far side and seven on the stands' side. The first two home were on the far side and those on the stands' side seemed at a disadvantage.
Baltimore Jack(IRE) Official explanation: jockey said gelding hung right-handed throughout
Multitude(IRE) Official explanation: jockey said gelding was never travelling
Danum Dancer Official explanation: jockey said saddle slipped
Valdan(IRE) Official explanation: jockey said gelding hung right-handed throughout

4899 RIPON CHAMPION TWO YRS OLD TROPHY, 2007 (LISTED RACE) 6f
3:35 (3:35) (Class 1) 2-Y-0
£17,034 (£6,456; £3,231; £1,611; £807; £405) Stalls Low

Form RPR
6012 1 **Fat Boy (IRE)**[24] 4120 2-9-2 104 RichardHughes 6 104+
(R Hannon) *mde all: qcknd clr over 1f out: comf* 4/7[1]
12 2 3 **Anosti**[21] 4225 2-8-11 82 TedDurcan 5 90
(K A Ryan) *towards rr: hdwy 1/2-way: sn rdn and hung rt 2f out: drvn and kpt on ins fnl f* 22/1
0061 3 2 ½ **Cristal Clear (IRE)**[6] 4695 2-8-11 80 DavidAllan 3 83
(T D Easterby) *dwlt and sn outpcd in rr: hdwy 2f out: kpt on appr fnl f: n.d* 7/2[2]
12 4 ½ **Lesson In Humility (IRE)**[9] 4613 2-8-11 84 TonyHamilton 7 81
(K R Burke) *chsd wnr: rdn along 2f out: sn drvn and wknd over 1f out* 17/2[3]

The Form Book, Raceform Ltd, Compton, RG20 6NL

13 **5** 3 1/2 **Soopacal (IRE)**[15] 4431 2-9-2 87 PaulMulrennan 4 76
(B Smart) *chsd ldrs: rdn along over 2f out: sn drvn and wknd* **20/1**
1 **6** *shd* **Fits Of Giggles (IRE)**[15] 4428 2-8-11 0 TPQueally 1 70
(J G Given) *a in rr* **28/1**
1216 **7** 2 **Spanish Bounty**[30] 3938 2-9-2 95 EddieAhern 2 69
(J G Portman) *trckd ldrs: effrt 2f out: sn rdn and btn* **12/1**
1m 12.56s (-0.44) **Going Correction** +0.05s/f (Good) **7** Ran SP% **116.7**
Speed ratings (Par 102): **104,100,96,96,91 91,88**
CSF £19.98 TOTE £1.50: £1.10, £5.50; EX 16.90.
Owner M Sines **Bred** Peter Mooney **Trained** East Everleigh, Wilts

FOCUS
An average renewal of this juvenile Listed event. The form looks straightforward enough and the winner posted a slight career best.

NOTEBOOK
Fat Boy(IRE), who just failed to last home in the Group 2 Richmond Stakes last time, got his own way out in front again and produced a career-best effort to go one better and resume winning ways. He is clearly a difficult juvenile to catch over this trip now and must rate value for further than his winning margin as he looked to have plenty left up his sleeve at the finish. While this may not have been a string renewal of this Listed prize, he is well worth his chance in Group company again and something like the Mill Reef at Newbury next month looks tailor-made for him - providing the ground has not turned soft. (op 8-11 tchd 4-5 in places)
Anosti, up in class, again hung to her right when put under pressure and rates a little flattered by her proximity to the comfortable winner. However, this was still her best effort to date and she does look a deal better than her official mark of 82. If she can learn to keep a straight line then she could well find a race of this standard before the year is out, but really her Group 1 entry is aiming too high. (op 16-1)
Cristal Clear(IRE), a last-gasp winner of a York nursery six days previously, again got herself outpaced through the early stages and was always getting there too late. This was still another improved display, however, and she now looks to be crying out for a stiffer test. (op 4-1 tchd 9-2)
Lesson In Humility(IRE) ran a little below her recent level on this step up in class and now looks as though she will benefit from a drop back to 5f. (op 7-1)
Soopacal(IRE) was never a serious player in this better company and really wants easier ground. (tchd 16-1)
Spanish Bounty, back in trip, has now failed to run up to the level of his Newmarket success in two outings at this level and it could be that something went amiss. Official explanation: trainer said colt was not suited by the good to firm ground (op 14-1 tchd 11-1)

4900 RIPON ROWELS H'CAP 1m
4:10 (4:11) (Class 2) (0-100,94) 3-Y-0+
£12,464 (£3,732; £1,866; £934; £466; £234) **Stalls** High

Form RPR
0500 **1** **Bolodenka (IRE)**[22] 4211 5-9-7 **88** TonyHamilton 8 98
(R A Fahey) *trckd ldrs on inner: swtchd lft and hdwy 2f out: rdn to chal over 1f out: drvn ins fnl f: styd on u.p to ld nr fin* **13/2**[3]
1611 **2** *hd* **Ragheed (USA)**[16] 4408 3-9-1 **91** LiamJones(3) 9 101
(W J Haggas) *led: qcknd 3f out: rdn along and edgd lft wl over 1f out: jnd: drvn and edgd rt ins fnl f: hdd and no ex nr fin* **5/2**[1]
6012 **3** 1 1/4 **Ace Of Hearts**[16] 4377 8-9-13 **94** RichardHughes 2 102+
(C F Wall) *trckd ldrs: effrt: nt clr run and swtchd rt over 1f out: nt clr run on inner and swtchd lft ins fnl f: rdn and styd on wl nr fin* **11/4**[2]
5123 **4** 3 1/2 **Flighty Fellow (IRE)**[5] 4716 7-8-12 **79** (b) DavidAllan 5 78+
(T D Easterby) *hld up in rr: rdn along 3f out: hdwy 2f out: styd on u.p appr fnl f: nt rch ldrs* **8/1**
1240 **5** 3/4 **Nevada Desert (IRE)**[4] 4745 7-9-3 **87** MichaelJStainton(3) 1 84
(R M Whitaker) *cl up: rdn along over 2f out: drvn wl over 1f out and kpt on same pce* **8/1**
0400 **6** 1 **Regal Parade**[25] 4093 3-9-4 **91** GregFairley 4 86
(M Johnston) *chsd ldrs on outer: rdn along over 2f out: sn drvn: edgd rt and wknd wl over 1f out* **17/2**
030 **7** 1 3/4 **Blue Spinnaker (IRE)**[10] 4566 8-8-10 **84** NSLawes(7) 6 75
(M W Easterby) *hld up: effrt and sme hdwy 3f out: sn rdn and n.d* **18/1**
0/40 **8** 1 3/4 **Troubadour (IRE)**[10] 4566 6-9-12 **93** TedDurcan 7 80
(W Jarvis) *chsd ldrs: rdn along over 2f out: sn drvn and wknd wl over 1f out* **12/1**
0260 **9** 3/4 **Riley Boys (IRE)**[11] 4523 6-9-1 **82** TPQueally 3 67
(J G Given) *hld up in rr: effrt and sme hdwy 3f out: sn rdn and btn 2f out* **50/1**
1m 39.74s (-1.36) **Going Correction** +0.15s/f (Good)
WFA 3 from 5yo+ 6lb **9** Ran SP% **116.2**
Speed ratings (Par 109): **112,111,110,107,106 105,103,101,101**
CSF £23.28 CT £55.95 TOTE £7.70: £2.00, £1.60, £1.60; EX 28.60.
Owner Enda Hunston **Bred** Kildaragh Stud **Trained** Musley Bank, N Yorks

FOCUS
A good handicap for the grade. Sound form, best rated through the third.

NOTEBOOK
Bolodenka(IRE), who was very well backed when running twice without placing at the Galway festival, once again met plenty of support in the betting ring and this time obliged with a narrow success. He relished the return to a suitably faster surface and this was his highest winning mark to date, so it will be interesting to see how he copes now with a likely rise back up in the weights. (op 10-1)
Ragheed(USA), bidding for a hat-trick from a 9lb higher mark, gained his favoured position in the lead and so nearly made all. He has been transformed since switching to front-running tactics and is certainly still progressing. (op 15-8)
Ace Of Hearts, another 4lb higher, has to rate unfortunate as he was denied a clear run on more than one occasion inside the final furlong. He is right at the top of his game at present and, on this evidence, may not be weighted out of winning again just yet. (op 7-2)
Flighty Fellow(IRE) is high enough in the weights now, but he really needs a stiffer test over this trip nowadays and was not disgraced. (tchd 17-2)
Nevada Desert(IRE) ran his race and has held his form well since winning back-to-back races in July, thus helping to give this form a decent look. (op 15-2 tchd 9-1)

4901 SOLBERGE SILKS BRASSERIE MAIDEN STKS 1m
4:45 (4:45) (Class 5) 3-4-Y-0 **£3,238** (£963; £481; £240) **Stalls** High

Form RPR
0632 **1** **Fidelia (IRE)**[11] 4549 3-8-12 78 TedDurcan 4 62+
(G Wragg) *trckd ldr: smooth hdwy to ld 2f out: sn clr: easily* **2/5**[1]
6-05 **2** 5 **Timber Treasure (USA)**[20] 4258 3-9-3 74 (v[1]) TPQueally 2 53
(H R A Cecil) *t.k.h: trckd ldng pair: hdwy 3f out: rdn to chse wnr wl over 1f out: sn drvn and no imp* **11/4**[2]
-000 **3** 3 **Gyration (IRE)**[18] 4340 3-9-3 44 (p) DavidAllan 6 46
(J G Given) *led: rdn along 3f out: drvn and hdd 2f out: sn wknd* **28/1**
06 **4** 8 **Natco**[8] 4641 3-8-12 0 GregFairley 5 22
(M Johnston) *in tch: sn chsd along: rdn to chse ldrs over 3f out: drvn wl over 2f out and sn btn* **10/1**[3]
0 **5** 1 **Betterlatethanever (IRE)**[40] 3639 3-9-3 0 PaulQuinn 3 25
(C J Teague) *a in rr* **80/1**
00 **6** 1 **Oriental Gift (FR)**[18] 4334 3-9-3 0 PaulMulrennan 1 23
(J R Norton) *t.k.h: chsd ldrs: rdn along 3f out: sn wknd* **80/1**
1m 42.28s (1.18) **Going Correction** +0.15s/f (Good) **6** Ran SP% **113.1**
Speed ratings (Par 103): **100,95,92,84,83 82**
CSF £1.82 TOTE £1.40: £1.10, £2.00; EX 1.70.
Owner A E Oppenheimer **Bred** Hascombe And Valiant Studs **Trained** Newmarket, Suffolk

FOCUS
A weak maiden. The winner had little to beat and did not have to run near to her previous best.

4902 PATELEY BRIDGE H'CAP 1m 1f 170y
5:20 (5:20) (Class 5) (0-70,70) 3-Y-0 **£3,238** (£963; £481; £240) **Stalls** High

Form RPR
4551 **1** **Greyfriars Abbey**[23] 4159 3-9-7 **70** GregFairley 1 73+
(M Johnston) *dwlt and sn pushed along in rr: rdn along to chse ldrs over 3f out: drvn to ld ent fnl f: styd on wl* **11/10**[1]
0000 **2** 1 1/4 **Centenary (IRE)**[17] 4064 3-8-6 **55** (p) GrahamGibbons 3 55
(J J Quinn) *t.k.h: trckd ldrs: hdwy over 2f out: rdn to chse ldrs over 1f out: styd on u.p ins fnl f* **28/1**
0543 **3** *shd* **Grethel (IRE)**[10] 4579 3-7-13 **55** DanielleMcCreery(7) 5 55
(A Berry) *trckd ldrs: hdwy to ld 1/2-way: rdn over 2f out: drvn and hdd ent fnl f: one pce* **33/1**
532 **4** 1/2 **War Anthem**[11] 4541 3-9-4 **67** (b) RichardHughes 2 66
(C R Egerton) *sn led: stdd and hdd 1/2-way: trckd ldrs tl hdwy on bit 3f out and sn ev ch: rdn wl over 1f out: drvn and wknd ent fnl f* **5/2**[2]
0360 **5** 3/4 **Bollin Fergus**[9] 3029 3-8-6 **55** DavidAllan 8 52
(T D Easterby) *hld up in rr: gd hdwy on outer over 2f out: rdn to chse ldrs wl over 1f out: sn drvn and one pce* **17/2**[3]
3406 **6** 3 1/2 **Heaven's Gates**[26] 4073 3-7-12 **52** NataliaGemelova(5) 6 42
(K A Ryan) *chsd ldrs on inner: rdn along over 2f out: sn rdn and kpt on same pce appr fnl f* **10/1**
0-43 **7** 5 **Steel Silk (IRE)**[19] 4290 3-9-2 **68** (v[1]) MarkLawson(3) 7 48
(B Smart) *hld up: effrt 4f out: sn rdn along and btn* **14/1**
645 **8** 7 **The Quantum Kid**[31] 3919 3-8-8 **60** (b[1]) PJMcDonald(3) 4 25
(T J Etherington) *t.k.h: cl up tl rdn along 3f out and sn wknd* **14/1**
2m 6.41s (1.41) **Going Correction** +0.15s/f (Good) **8** Ran SP% **115.5**
Speed ratings (Par 100): **100,99,98,98,97 95,91,85**
CSF £38.41 CT £677.72 TOTE £1.90: £1.10, £7.20, £4.80; EX 56.30 Place 6 £20.06, Place 5 £4.35.
Owner Greyfriars And White Rose Poultry **Bred** Itchen Valley Stud **Trained** Middleham Moor, N Yorks

FOCUS
A moderate handicap and the form looks worth treating with some caution, although the winner remains progressive.
T/Plt: £28.50 to a £1 stake. Pool: £56,273.35. 1,441.25 winning tickets. T/Qpdt: £1.60 to a £1 stake. Pool: £3,439.10. 1,505.25 winning tickets. JR

3471 WARWICK (L-H)
Monday, August 27

OFFICIAL GOING: Good to firm
Wind: Light across Weather: Cloudy with sunny spells

4903 TURFTV NURSERY 5f 110y
2:00 (2:02) (Class 5) (0-75,73) 2-Y-0 **£3,238** (£963; £481; £120; £120) **Stalls** Centre

Form RPR
5045 **1** **Ridge Wood Dani (IRE)**[24] 4126 2-8-8 **60** MatthewHenry 13 66
(E J Alston) *outpcd: hdwy over 1f out: led ins fnl f: r.o wl* **20/1**
0566 **2** 1 1/4 **Mistress Cooper**[13] 4484 2-8-8 **60** JohnEgan 14 62
(W J Musson) *chsd ldr: led over 1f out: hdd and unable qck ins fnl f* **10/1**
005 **3** 1 1/4 **Fervent Prince**[12] 4500 2-9-4 **73** TravisBlock(3) 6 71+
(H Morrison) *s.i.s: outpcd: edgd lft over 1f out: r.o ins fnl f: nvr nrr* **7/1**[3]
6650 **4** *hd* **Leading Edge (IRE)**[14] 4453 2-8-12 **64** ChrisCatlin 7 61
(M R Channon) *s.i.s: hdwy and nt clr run over 1f out: swtchd rt and r.o ins fnl f* **20/1**
0152 **4** *dht* **Attribution**[4] 4737 2-8-13 **65** DavidKinsella 11 62
(A B Haynes) *mid-div: rdn 1/2-way: edgd lft and styd on ins fnl f* **11/2**[1]
0244 **6** 1/2 **Kaldoun Kingdom (IRE)**[13] 4484 2-9-4 **70** TGMcLaughlin 12 66
(E A L Dunlop) *mid-div: rdn 1/2-way: hdwy and hung lft over 1f out: no ex ins fnl f* **15/2**
450 **7** 2 **Andrasta**[103] 1762 2-9-3 **69** PaulEddery 4 58
(B J Meehan) *chsd ldrs: rdn over 1f out: wknd ins fnl f* **22/1**
5410 **8** 3/4 **Cocabana**[10] 4573 2-9-4 **70** JamesDoyle 1 56
(J G Portman) *prom: rdn over 1f out: wknd ins fnl f* **7/1**[3]
330 **9** 1 **Sandy Par**[39] 3687 2-9-2 **68** JimCrowley 8 51
(P Winkworth) *prom: n.m.r over 2f out: wknd ins fnl f* **9/1**
0330 **10** 5 **A Wish For You**[47] 3426 2-9-2 **68** RobertHavlin 9 35
(D K Ivory) *chsd ldrs: n.m.r over 2f out: wknd over 1f out* **20/1**
0300 **11** 1 **Bellalatino (IRE)**[23] 4162 2-8-2 **57** EmmettStack(3) 2 20
(Mrs Norma Pook) *s.i.s: outpcd* **50/1**
3260 **12** *nk* **Advertisement**[49] 3363 2-9-5 **71** PhilipRobinson 16 33
(C G Cox) *chsd ldrs: rdn: hung lft and wknd over 1f out* **13/2**[2]
000 **13** 3/4 **Running Buck (USA)**[23] 4181 2-7-12 **57** MCGeran(7) 10 17
(N P Littmoden) *dwlt: outpcd* **14/1**
1545 **14** *shd* **Diademas (USA)**[17] 4358 2-9-7 **73** (b[1]) MartinDwyer 5 33
(J A Osborne) *led: rdn and hdd appr fnl f: hmpd and wknd 1f out* **9/1**
66.98 secs (1.09) **Going Correction** +0.05s/f (Good) **14** Ran SP% **121.8**
Speed ratings (Par 94): **94,92,90,90,90 89,87,86,84,78 76,76,75,75**
CSF £197.86 CT £1598.43 TOTE £26.70: £7.90, £4.80, £2.60; EX 232.30.
Owner Con Harrington **Bred** C Harrington **Trained** Longton, Lancs
■ Stewards' Enquiry : Chris Catlin two-day ban: careless riding (Sep 7,9)
Philip Robinson one-day ban: entered the wrong stall (Sep 7)

FOCUS
A decent nursery likely to produce its share of winners. The winner and second ran to their mark, with a promising effort from the third.

NOTEBOOK
Ridge Wood Dani(IRE), unable to make any real impression on his recent handicap debut at Haydock, had been dropped 6lb, but again looked to be struggling early on here as he found himself outpaced in rear. However, he really got motoring in the final quarter mile and came through to win well, suggesting he may be a sprinter to follow at the right level. (op 16-1)
Mistress Cooper improved on her initial effort in handicaps and seemed to appreciate this faster surface, just finding one too good on the day. She should find a race before long off this sort of mark. (op 11-1 tchd 12-1)
Fervent Prince improved a little with each start in maidens, all at Salisbury, and he took a further step forward to finish third on this handicap debut. He was a costly purchase and has clearly not turned out to be as good as connections would have liked, but there are clearly races in him if this run is anything to go by. (op 10-1)

Attribution has twice run well off similar marks in nurseries since winning a seller at Bath earlier in the season and this was another reasonable effort, without quite doing enough to suggest he can win at the moment. (op 6-1 tchd 7-1)
Leading Edge(IRE) ◆ is bred to appreciate trips of 1m-plus, so having been outpaced throughout on her recent nursery debut over 6f at Windsor it was something of a surprise to see her dropped in trip. She coped remarkably well though, looking a bit unlucky not to reach the placings, but there can be no question she is going benefit from a return to further and it is surely a matter of time before the daughter of Clodovil is winning. (op 6-1 tchd 7-1)
Andrasta Official explanation: jockey said filly hung right
Cocabana Official explanation: jockey said filly was never travelling
Advertisement Official explanation: jockey said gelding slipped on bend
Diademas(USA) Official explanation: jockey said colt ran too freely

4904 RACING UK MAIDEN AUCTION STKS 7f 26y
2:35 (2:37) (Class 5) 2-Y-O £3,238 (£963; £481; £240) **Stalls** Low

Form RPR
00 **1** **Dancer's Legacy**[46] 3471 2-8-11 0..............................(t) TGMcLaughlin 4 70
(E A L Dunlop) *a.p: racd keenly: rdn to ld ins fnl f: r.o* **33/1**
62 **2** *hd* **Barliffey (IRE)**[18] 4316 2-9-1 0.. JohnEgan 2 74
(D J Coakley) *s.i.s: hld up: swtchd rt over 2f out: hdwy over 1f out: rdn and ev ch ins fnl f: r.o* **5/2**[1]
3 *1 1/2* **Boot Strap Bill** 2-8-9 0.. JamesDoyle 5 64
(Miss J R Tooth) *s.i.s: hld up: hdwy over 1f out: rdn whn n.m.r ins fnl f: edgd lft: unable qck towards fin* **33/1**
5 **4** *1* **Cheque**[19] 4293 2-8-9 0.. MartinDwyer 11 61+
(J A Osborne) *hld up in tch: rdn and nt clr run ins fnl f: styd on same pce* **3/1**[2]
4 **5** *1/2* **Weet By Far**[46] 3471 2-8-4 0.. PaulEddery 14 55
(R Hollinshead) *led: rdn and hdd ins fnl f: no ex* **8/1**
0 **6** *3/4* **Khana Ras (IRE)**[107] 1680 2-9-0 0................................ RichardMullen 6 63
(E J O'Neill) *chsd ldr: rdn over 2f out: no ex ins fnl f* **14/1**
4 **7** *shd* **The Willowy Wigeon**[11] 4537 2-8-6 0 ow2.................. StephenCarson 1 55
(P Winkworth) *prom: rdn over 2f out: no ex ins fnl f* **14/1**
0 **8** *3/4* **Bathwick Icon (IRE)**[18] 4310 2-8-6 0............................ DavidKinsella 7 53
(A B Haynes) *chsd ldrs: rdn over 2f out: no ex fnl f* **14/1**
00 **9** *3/4* **Mganga**[7] 4656 2-8-6 0.. AshleyHamblett(5) 10 56
(M R Channon) *s.i.s: hld up: rdn over 2f out: n.d* **20/1**
0 **10** *6* **Potemkin (USA)**[15] 4417 2-9-1 0.. ChrisCatlin 3 45
(A King) *hld up: hmpd 6f out: n.d* **25/1**
3 **11** *1/2* **Coral Shores**[19] 4265 2-8-6 0...................................... AdrianMcCarthy 9 35
(P W Chapple-Hyam) *plld hrd and prom: hung rt 1/2-way: rdn over 1f out: sn wknd* **9/2**[3]
6 **12** *1/2* **Ten Pole Tudor**[18] 4316 2-8-7 0...................................... RyanRaftery(7) 8 42
(J A Osborne) *in rr: hung rt 1/2-way: n.d* **28/1**
0 **13** *2 1/2* **Lancaster Lad (IRE)**[44] 3552 2-8-9 0.............................. RobertHavlin 12 30
(A B Haynes) *s.i.s: hld up: rdn 1/2-way: n.d* **50/1**

1m 24.44s (0.24) **Going Correction** -0.075s/f (Good) 13 Ran SP% **122.8**
Speed ratings (Par 94): **95,94,93,91,91 90,90,89,88,81 81,80,77**
CSF £111.84 TOTE £40.20: £7.00, £1.40, £7.90; EX 167.40.
Owner Miltil Consortium **Bred** Floors Farming **Trained** Newmarket, Suffolk

FOCUS
A modest maiden, but it should produce the odd winner. An improved effort from Dancer's Legacy.

NOTEBOOK
Dancer's Legacy, green and clueless on each of his two previous starts, did not cost much and needed this to qualify for a handicap mark, but it was interesting he was equipped with a first-time tongue tie and it made all the difference. Never far from the lead, he looked likely to be swamped just over half a furlong out, but kept finding and was a willing winner. There may well be more to come from the son of Nayef and he remains capable of better in nurseries, with the step up to 1m almost certain to suit. Official explanation: trainer said, regarding apparent improvement in form, that the colt benefited from the application of a tongue strap. (op 40-1)
Barliffey(IRE), who played up in the preliminaries, has improved a little with each run and kept on strongly having had to be switched. Just losing out in the end, his turn will come eventually and perhaps a more galloping track will see him in a better light. (tchd 2-1)
Boot Strap Bill, who cost just 4,500gns, ran surprisingly well on this racecourse debut and is likely to find easier opportunities. By Timeless Times, he may well prove best at sprint trips. (op 66-1)
Cheque, a promising fifth on his debut at Yarmouth, did not get the clearest of runs late on, but he would have been playing for places at best and connections may now decide to go down the handicap route with him. (op 5-1)
Weet By Far was unable to build on her initial effort over course and distance, but she was again not beaten far and considering she cost just 800gns, she has done well so far. (op 12-1)
Coral Shores, not beaten far on her recent Brighton debut, failed by some way to build on it and does not look one of her yard's better juveniles. Official explanation: jockey said the bit slipped through the filly's mouth (op 9-4)
Ten Pole Tudor Official explanation: jockey said, regarding running and riding, his orders were to jump off and settle behind the leaders, and make his effort in the home straight, adding that he was unable to carry them out when the gelding jumped slowly from the stalls, further adding that having been shuffled back through the field and ran wide on bend, they were adrift, asked for an effort approaching final furlong but, owing to the fact this was his first ride in public he was not able to be very vigorous

4905 WARWICKRACECOURSE.CO.UK MAIDEN STKS (DIV I) 7f 26y
3:10 (3:14) (Class 5) 3-Y-O+ £2,590 (£770; £385; £192) **Stalls** Low

Form RPR
0233 **1** **Own Boss (USA)**[20] 4258 3-9-3 80.............................. PhilipRobinson 9 80+
(M A Jarvis) *chsd ldrs: led over 2f out: rdn clr fr over 1f out* **4/7**[1]
430 **2** *5* **Hazytoo**[14] 4457 3-9-0 77.. WilliamBuick(3) 7 66
(N A Callaghan) *chsd ldrs: rdn over 2f out: styd on same pce appr fnl f* **11/2**[2]
0- **3** *1 1/2* **Capania (IRE)**[289] 6433 3-8-12 0.................................. RichardMullen 2 57
(Pat Eddery) *chsd ldrs: hung lft 2f out: styd on same pce appr fnl f* **20/1**
00 **4** *1/2* **Word Of Warning**[64] 2913 3-9-3 0.................................. RobertHavlin 8 61+
(G Wragg) *hld up: styd on appr fnl f: nvr trbld ldrs* **25/1**
33 **5** *nk* **Affrettando (IRE)**[47] 3425 3-9-3 0.................................. JohnEgan 10 60
(J A R Toller) *hld up: hdwy 1/2-way: sn rdn: hung lft over 1f out: no ex* **10/1**[3]
0000 **6** *1 1/2* **Blue Bird's Dream**[38] 3721 4-9-8 53............................ MatthewHenry 6 58
(E J Alston) *sn led: hdd over 2f out: wknd fnl f* **40/1**
0- **7** *1 1/2* **Balanchine Moon**[299] 6290 3-8-12 0.............................. MartinDwyer 11 47
(M P Tregoning) *dwlt: hld up: plld hrd: nvr nr to chal* **14/1**
0000 **8** *1 1/4* **Mostanad**[23] 4164 5-9-8 44.. JimCrowley 5 51
(R A Harris) *hld up: rdn and wknd over 1f out* **66/1**
9 *3/4* **Lily La Belle** 3-8-12 0.. JamesDoyle 3 42
(A W Carroll) *hld up: rdn over 1f out: n.d* **25/1**
3/-3 **10** *4* **Call Me Punch**[11] 4530 6-9-8 0...................................... ChrisCatlin 12 38
(E S McMahon) *chsd ldrs over 4f* **11/1**
11 *1 3/4* **Ring Of Charm** 5-9-0 0.. TravisBlock(3) 4 28
(C J Down) *s.s: outpcd* **40/1**

1m 22.81s (-1.39) **Going Correction** -0.075s/f (Good)
WFA 3 from 4yo+ 5lb 11 Ran SP% **122.0**
Speed ratings (Par 103): **104,98,96,96,95 93,92,90,89,85 83**
CSF £3.71 TOTE £1.50: £1.02, £2.30, £6.00; EX 5.40.
Owner Sheikh Ahmed Al Maktoum **Bred** Darley **Trained** Newmarket, Suffolk

FOCUS
A modest maiden, but the winning time was just under a second faster than the second division. The winner did not need to be at his best and the form seems to make sense.
Ring Of Charm Official explanation: jockey said mare missed the break

4906 SYD MERCER MEMORIAL H'CAP 2m 39y
3:45 (3:45) (Class 5) (0-70,68) 3-Y-O+ £2,914 (£867; £433; £216) **Stalls** Low

Form RPR
4450 **1** **Princess Kiotto**[10] 4576 6-9-11 **60**............................ RichardMullen 2 66
(W M Brisbourne) *chsd ldr tl led 9f out: rdn over 1f out: hdd ins fnl f: rallied to ld towards fin* **8/1**[3]
1421 **2** *hd* **Strobe**[18] 4322 3-9-5 **68**.. MartinDwyer 5 74
(J A Osborne) *a.p: shkn up 10f out: chsd wnr over 8f out: rdn over 3f out: led ins fnl f: hdd towards fin* **9/4**[1]
5216 **3** *1* **Mister Completely (IRE)**[10] 4576 6-10-0 **63**..................(v) JamesDoyle 1 68
(Ms J S Doyle) *hld up: hdwy 1/2-way: rdn and ev ch ins fnl f: no ex nr fin* **6/1**[2]
3442 **4** *3/4* **Sa Nau**[8] 4638 4-9-6 **55**.. PhilipRobinson 3 59
(T Keddy) *a.p: rdn and ev ch over 1f out: styd on same pce* **9/4**[1]
00-2 **5** *hd* **Mcqueen (IRE)**[16] 4380 7-9-5 **59**.......................... RussellKennemore(5) 4 63
(J T Stimpson) *led: hdd 9f out: chsd ldrs: rdn over 3f out: ev ch over 1f out: no ex ins fnl f* **16/1**
3320 **6** *nk* **Squirtle (IRE)**[7] 4670 4-9-5 **54**.. JohnEgan 6 58
(W M Brisbourne) *s.s: hld up: rdn over 2f out: styd on: nt trble ldrs* **8/1**[3]
6205 **7** *2 1/2* **My Legal Eagle (IRE)**[17] 4352 13-8-6 **48**...................... JackMitchell(7) 8 49
(E G Bevan) *s.s: hld up: rdn over 2f out: n.d* **20/1**
0010 **8** *42* **Zonic Boom (FR)**[7] 4670 7-9-3 **55**..............................(tp) WilliamBuick(3) 7 5
(Heather Dalton) *s.s: hld up: rdn 1/2-way: wknd over 3f out* **11/1**

3m 34.03s (1.33) **Going Correction** -0.075s/f (Good)
WFA 3 from 4yo+ 14lb 8 Ran SP% **117.0**
Speed ratings (Par 103): **93,92,92,92,91 91,90,69**
CSF £27.09 CT £118.95 TOTE £11.30: £2.40, £1.30, £2.20; EX 37.80.
Owner Roy Matthews **Bred** R Matthews **Trained** Great Ness, Shropshire

FOCUS
A trappy and steadily-run handicap in which the front six were covered by around two lengths. The winning time was just modest.

4907 BETFAIR CONDITIONS STKS 7f 26y
4:20 (4:20) (Class 4) 3-Y-O+ £5,181 (£1,541; £770; £384) **Stalls** Low

Form RPR
3-20 **1** **Jack Sullivan (USA)**[4] 4747 6-8-11 112..................(p) StephenCarson 2 91
(G A Butler) *chsd ldr: rdn to ld over 1f out: edgd lft: r.o* **11/10**[1]
051- **2** *3/4* **Candidato Roy (ARG)**[246] 6-8-11 0.............................. MartinDwyer 4 89
(W J Haggas) *trckd ldrs: rdn over 1f out: r.o* **13/2**[3]
0/21 **3** *3/4* **Galeota (IRE)**[13] 4485 5-9-4 107...................................... JimCrowley 1 94
(R Hannon) *led: rdn and hdd over 1f out: no ex wl ins fnl f* **6/4**[2]
003 **4** *3* **Confucius Classic (IRE)**[26] 4066 3-8-6 56................ RichardMullen 5 77
(J G Boyle) *hld up: rdn 1/2-way: nt trble ldrs* **33/1**
6406 **5** *1 3/4* **Knapton Hill**[29] 4005 3-7-12 79.................................... WilliamBuick(3) 3 67
(R Hollinshead) *sn pushed along in rr: effrt over 2f out: wknd over 1f out* **14/1**
446 **6** *14* **Safranine (IRE)**[35] 3784 10-8-1 54................................ AnnStokell(5) 6 31
(Miss A Stokell) *s.i.s: hdwy over 5f out: wknd 3f out* **50/1**

1m 21.96s (-2.24) **Going Correction** -0.075s/f (Good)
WFA 3 from 5yo+ 5lb 6 Ran SP% **112.5**
Speed ratings (Par 105): **109,108,107,103,101 85**
CSF £9.14 TOTE £2.30: £1.40, £3.20; EX 12.10.
Owner The International Carnival Partnership **Bred** Hermitage Farm L L C **Trained** Blewbury, Oxon

FOCUS
A race lacking strength in depth and the close proximity of the 56-rated fourth does little for the form. The form looks unreliable but could have been rated 18lb+ higher through the first three.
Safranine(IRE) Official explanation: jockey said saddle slipped

4908 WARWICKRACECOURSE.CO.UK MAIDEN STKS (DIV II) 7f 26y
4:55 (5:00) (Class 5) 3-Y-O+ £2,590 (£770; £385; £192) **Stalls** Low

Form RPR
1 **Musaalem (USA)** 3-9-3 0.. MartinDwyer 5 58+
(W J Haggas) *trckd ldrs: plld hrd: led over 1f out: rdn out* **11/10**[1]
0000 **2** *1 3/4* **Batchworth Blaise**[72] 2664 4-9-3 41.................... RussellKennemore(5) 7 56
(E A Wheeler) *s.i.s: hld up: hdwy over 1f out: r.o* **80/1**
0-05 **3** *3/4* **Dragon Flower (USA)**[11] 4530 3-8-12 65........................ PaulEddery 10 47
(B W Hills) *chsd ldrs: rdn 1/2-way: styd on same pce fnl f* **8/1**
R **4** *3/4* **Audley**[7] 4666 3-8-9 0.. WilliamBuick(3) 11 45
(M P Tregoning) *s.i.s: hld up: hdwy and nt clr run over 1f out: edgd lft ins fnl f: r.o* **14/1**
5 *1/2* **Thea Di Bisanzio (IRE)** 3-8-12 0...................................... JimCrowley 8 43
(G A Butler) *hld up: hdwy over 1f out: r.o: nt rch ldrs* **7/1**[3]
06 **6** *1/2* **Airman (IRE)**[21] 4235 4-9-8 0......................................(p) RichardMullen 3 49
(W M Brisbourne) *hld up in tch: rdn over 1f out: styd on same pce* **14/1**
6 **7** *1* **Iguacu**[11] 4541 3-9-3 0.. ChrisCatlin 9 44
(J L Spearing) *led: rdn and hdd over 1f out: wknd ins fnl f* **11/2**[2]
8 *2* **Frigid** 3-8-7 0.. AshleyHamblett(5) 12 34
(L M Cumani) *s.i.s: sn prom: chsd ldr 1/2-way: rdn and ev ch over 1f out: sn wknd* **14/1**
9 *shd* **Barbar** 4-9-8 0.. StephenCarson 6 41
(Eve Johnson Houghton) *hld up: hdwy over 2f out: wknd over 1f out* **20/1**
50-0 **10** *10* **Dhurwah (IRE)**[88] 2174 4-9-0 42...................................... EmmettStack(3) 4 9
(T Keddy) *plld hrd and prom: nt clr run 1/2-way: rdn and wknd over 1f out* **100/1**
0 **11** *5* **Shades Of Blue**[20] 4258 4-9-0 0.. TravisBlock(3) 1 —
(C J Down) *a in rr* **66/1**
12 *4* **Beau Bramble** 3-9-3 0.. GeorgeBaker 2 —
(C F Wall) *s.i.s: outpcd* **14/1**

1m 23.77s (-0.43) **Going Correction** -0.075s/f (Good)
WFA 3 from 4yo 5lb 12 Ran SP% **121.8**
Speed ratings (Par 103): **99,97,96,95,94 94,93,90,90,79 73,68**
CSF £162.49 TOTE £1.70: £1.20, £15.50, £2.20; EX 108.80.
Owner Hamdan Al Maktoum **Bred** Shadwell Farm LLC **Trained** Newmarket, Suffolk

FOCUS
The winning time was just under a second slower than the first division, and this was definitely the weaker of the two. With the second rated just 41 this is really dubious form.
Beau Bramble Official explanation: jockey said gelding ran green

4909 ENTERTAIN CLIENTS AT WARWICK RACECOURSE H'CAP 1m 2f 188y
5:30 (5:30) (Class 4) (0-80,80) 3-Y-O+ £5,181 (£1,541; £770; £384) Stalls Low

Form RPR
205 1 **Lemonette (USA)**[22] 4203 4-9-11 **80** .... WilliamBuick(3) 1 89
(J W Hills) *chsd ldrs: led over 1f out: rdn out* **9/1**
4000 2 1 1/2 **Robustian**[10] 4566 4-10-0 **80** ....(b) StephenCarson 2 86
(Eve Johnson Houghton) *hld up: rdn over 2f out: hdwy over 1f out: r.o* **8/1**[3]
4342 3 3/4 **Bajan Parkes**[16] 4382 4-9-10 **76** .... PhilipRobinson 4 81
(E J Alston) *led: hdd 9f out: rdn and ev ch over 1f out: styd on same pce ins fnl f* **5/1**[2]
6404 4 1/2 **Counsel's Opinion (IRE)**[11] 4551 10-10-0 **80** .... GeorgeBaker 7 84
(C F Wall) *hld up: hdwy 5f out: rdn over 1f out: r.o* **8/1**[3]
0430 5 nk **Dove Cottage (IRE)**[22] 4194 5-9-1 **67** .... ChrisCatlin 11 71
(W S Kittow) *w ldr tl led 9f out: rdn and hdd over 1f out: no ex ins fnl f* **14/1**
40/1 6 1/2 **Jacaranda (IRE)**[31] 3907 7-8-13 **65** .... JimCrowley 8 68
(P J Hobbs) *s.i.s: hld up: hdwy u.p over 1f out: nt rch ldrs* **3/1**[1]
2304 7 hd **Love Always**[11] 4542 5-9-4 **70** .... JamesDoyle 5 72
(S Dow) *chsd ldrs: rdn over 2f out: no ex fnl f* **12/1**
1060 8 1/2 **Del Mar Sunset**[23] 4184 8-9-11 **77** .... MartinDwyer 6 79
(W J Haggas) *hld up: plld hrd: effrt and nt clr run 1f out: n.d* **14/1**
0400 9 1/2 **Krugerrand (USA)**[23] 4184 8-9-11 **77** .... RichardMullen 3 78
(W J Musson) *hld up: effrt and nt clr run ins fnl f: nvr trbld ldrs* **11/1**
6501 10 1 1/2 **Drawback (IRE)**[6] 4686 4-9-4 **75** 6ex ....(p) JamesMillman(5) 12 73
(R A Harris) *s.i.s: hld up: rdn over 1f out: n.d* **12/1**
5214 11 1/2 **Norman The Great**[8] 4631 3-9-3 **78** .... JohnEgan 9 75
(Jane Chapple-Hyam) *chsd ldrs: rdn over 2f out: wknd fnl f* **11/1**
3665 12 4 **Urban Warrior**[51] 3335 3-8-7 **71** .... EmmettStack(3) 10 62
(Mrs Norma Pook) *hld up: hdwy 1/2-way: rdn and wknd over 2f out* **25/1**

2m 17.88s (-1.52) **Going Correction** -0.075s/f (Good)
WFA 3 from 4yo+ 9lb **12** Ran SP% **123.1**
Speed ratings (Par 105): **102,100,100,100,99 99,99,98,98,97 97,94**
CSF £82.37 CT £410.35 TOTE £10.80: £3.30, £3.50, £2.20; EX 76.30.
Owner Jerry Jamgotchian **Bred** Castleton Lyons **Trained** Upper Lambourn, Berks
FOCUS
A fair handicap run at only a steady pace, and nothing got into it from the rear. The form makes sense among the principals.
Krugerrand(USA) Official explanation: jockey said gelding was denied a clear run
Drawback(IRE) Official explanation: jockey said gelding finished sore

4910 WARWICK RACECOURSE FOR CONFERENCES H'CAP 1m 4f 134y
6:00 (6:00) (Class 5) (0-75,75) 3-Y-O+ £2,914 (£867; £433; £216) Stalls Low

Form RPR
6402 1 **Dig Gold (USA)**[17] 4357 3-8-12 **70** .... PhilipRobinson 7 83
(M A Jarvis) *chsd ldr tl led 5f out: drvn out* **10/3**[1]
20-1 2 3/4 **Hawridge King**[17] 4352 5-9-5 **71** .... JamesMillman(5) 6 83
(W S Kittow) *hld up: hdwy to chse wnr over 1f out: sn rdn: r.o* **7/2**[2]
0505 3 3 1/2 **Wheelavit (IRE)**[14] 4108 4-9-4 **65** .... GeorgeBaker 1 72
(B G Powell) *hld up: hdwy 3f out: nt clr run 2f out: swtchd rt: styd on: nvr able to chal* **8/1**
1604 4 2 **Arctic Wings (IRE)**[26] 4069 3-8-12 **70** .... MartinDwyer 2 74
(W R Muir) *trckd ldrs: racd keenly: rdn over 2f out: wknd ins fnl f* **14/1**
0301 5 1 1/4 **Muraco**[17] 4356 3-8-13 **71** .... JohnEgan 4 73
(R M Beckett) *chsd ldrs: rdn over 3f out: wknd over 1f out* **8/1**
1-02 6 hd **Is It Me (USA)**[15] 4421 4-10-0 **75** .... JamesDoyle 5 77
(A W Carroll) *led over 7f: rdn over 2f out: wknd fnl f* **8/1**
0-00 7 2 **Thyolo (IRE)**[9] 4597 6-9-11 **72** .... JimCrowley 9 71
(C G Cox) *hld up: rdn over 3f out: n.d* **10/1**
1334 8 5 **Thorny Mandate**[4] 4732 5-9-3 **64** .... RichardMullen 3 55
(W M Brisbourne) *hld up in tch: rdn over 2f out: wkng whn nt clr run over 1f out: sn hung lft* **9/2**[3]
4-00 9 2 1/2 **Smart John**[21] 4231 7-8-13 **60** .... ChrisCatlin 8 48
(H J Evans) *mid-div: wknd 3f out* **25/1**

2m 40.25s (-3.35) **Going Correction** -0.075s/f (Good)
WFA 3 from 4yo+ 11lb **9** Ran SP% **116.4**
Speed ratings (Par 103): **107,106,104,103,102 102,101,97,96**
CSF £15.33 CT £85.94 TOTE £3.50: £1.60, £1.70, £2.90; EX 14.50 Place 6 £62.29, Place 5 £9.39.
Owner Sheikh Ahmed Al Maktoum **Bred** Darley **Trained** Newmarket, Suffolk
FOCUS
Just a modest handicap, but the form seems sound.
T/Plt: £94.00 to a £1 stake. Pool: £38,559.30. 299.20 winning tickets. T/Qpdt: £6.50 to a £1 stake. Pool: £2,056.10. 233.80 winning tickets. CR

4737 LINGFIELD (L-H)
Tuesday, August 28

OFFICIAL GOING: Standard
Wind: Light, against becoming nil by race 4 Weather: Fine but cloudy

4914 ALNO KITCHENS CLASSIFIED STKS 1m 4f (P)
2:15 (2:15) (Class 7) 3-Y-O+ £1,365 (£403; £201) Stalls Low

Form RPR
000- 1 **Me Fein**[320] 5915 3-8-12 45 .... TPQueally 7 63+
(B J Curley) *settled in 4th: wnt 2nd over 3f out: led over 1f out: canter* **5/4**[1]
0300 2 1 1/2 **Cragganmore Creek**[12] 4535 4-9-3 44 ....(v) LukeMorris(5) 8 48
(D Morris) *wl in rr and pushed along 8f out: prog u.p fr 4f out to go 3rd 2f out: chsd wnr fnl f: no ch* **20/1**
3 2 1/2 **Bernabeu (IRE)**[306] 6194 5-9-8 42 .... PaulDoe 4 44
(S Curran) *led: kicked clr 4f out: hdd over 1f out: no ch w wnr: tired fnl f* **10/1**[3]
0402 4 1/2 **Tiegs (IRE)**[12] 4521 5-9-8 42 .... ChrisCatlin 14 43
(P W Hiatt) *mostly chsd ldr to over 3f out: sn drvn: one pce* **12/1**
030 5 2 1/2 **War Feather**[12] 4535 5-9-8 44 ....(p) RobertHavlin 6 39
(T D McCarthy) *hld up towards rr: prog but wl outpcd over 3f out: kpt on same pce after* **12/1**
563 6 3/4 **Piano Key**[10] 4596 3-8-12 42 .... HayleyTurner 10 38
(M D I Usher) *chsd ldrs: outpcd over 3f out and rdn: n.d after: plugged on* **20/1**
0400 7 6 **Fulvio (USA)**[8] 4673 7-9-8 45 .... IanMongan 16 28
(P Howling) *t.k.h: hld up wl in rr: bdly outpcd fr 4f out: no ch after* **33/1**
-003 8 nk **Go Amwell**[184] 558 4-9-8 45 .... RyanMoore 5 28
(J R Jenkins) *dwlt: hld up wl in rr: bdly outpcd fr 4f out and u.str.p: bhd after* **9/2**[2]
0-06 9 3/4 **Falcon Flyer**[19] 4327 3-8-9 42 .... StephaneBreux(3) 9 27
(J R Best) *chsd ldrs: outpcd 4f out: no ch after* **16/1**
0255 10 3 1/2 **Roxy Singer**[12] 4535 3-8-12 43 .... TPO'Shea 11 21
(W J Musson) *dwlt: racd wd towards rr: outpcd 4f out: no ch after* **11/1**
000 11 7 **Shahadah (IRE)**[12] 4532 5-9-3 45 .... TolleyDean(5) 1 10
(R J Price) *mostly in 3rd: rdn to dispute 2nd 4f out: wknd rapidly 3f out* **40/1**
-003 12 1 1/2 **Royal Axminster**[56] 3186 12-9-1 45 .... NBazeley(7) 15 8
(Mrs P N Dutfield) *hld up wl in rr: bdly outpcd fr 4f out: bhd after* **28/1**
6/00 13 1/2 **Pole Dancer**[21] 4253 4-9-8 45 ....(b[1]) DaneO'Neill 3 7
(W S Kittow) *dwlt and reminders: sn in midfield: rdn and wknd over 4f out* **33/1**
5553 14 11 **Gertie (IRE)**[14] 3274 3-8-9 45 .... AlanCreighton(3) 12 —
(E J Creighton) *u.p on outer over 5f out: sn wknd and bhd* **33/1**
/000 15 22 **Ren's Magic**[20] 4267 9-9-1 44 ....(v) SCreighton(7) 2 —
(E J Creighton) *chsd ldrs tl wknd rapidly 5f out: t.o* **100/1**
00/0 P **Panadin (IRE)**[18] 4355 5-9-8 43 ....(p) AdamKirby 13 —
(Mrs L C Jewell) *in tch tl lost action and p.u over 5f out* **100/1**

2m 32.94s (-1.45) **Going Correction** -0.20s/f (Stan)
WFA 3 from 4yo+ 10lb **16** Ran SP% **127.5**
Speed ratings (Par 97): **96,95,93,93,91 90,86,86,86,83 79,78,77,70,55** —
CSF £37.19 TOTE £2.50: £1.60, £5.50, £3.90; EX 40.80.
Owner Curley Leisure **Bred** Irish National Stud **Trained** Newmarket, Suffolk
FOCUS
A classified contest restricted to horses rated 45 or lower, so obviously a moderate contest and the form looks weak rated around the third and fourth. The early pace was just steady and the winning time was 1.60 seconds slower than the following claimer.
Ren's Magic Official explanation: jockey said gelding lost its action

4915 ALNO.CO.UK CLAIMING STKS 1m 4f (P)
2:45 (2:48) (Class 6) 3-Y-O+ £2,047 (£604; £302) Stalls Low

Form RPR
3030 1 **Musango**[31] 3945 4-9-10 67 ....(t) RichardSmith 8 71
(B R Johnson) *trckd ldrs: prog over 3f out: led jst over 2f out: hrd pressed fnl f: jst hld on* **15/2**[3]
0-66 2 hd **Looks The Business (IRE)**[22] 3407 6-9-1 64 .... JackDean(7) 3 69
(W G M Turner) *settled in midfield: rdn over 4f out: prog over 3f out: wnt 2nd wl over 1f out: clsd grad ins fnl f: jst failed* **25/1**
600 3 nk **Noora (IRE)**[26] 4112 6-9-0 70 ....(v) AdamKirby 1 61
(C G Cox) *reluctant early: sn midfield: prog over 3f out: drvn on inner over 1f out: chal fnl f: fnd nil* **10/1**
3043 4 1/2 **Turner's Touch**[15] 4458 5-9-12 70 ....(b) RyanMoore 12 72
(G L Moore) *hld up wl in rr: stdy prog over 3f out: drvn to cl on ldrs 1f out: ref to overtake* **9/4**[2]
1114 5 3 **Champagne Shadow (IRE)**[27] 4067 6-9-5 72 ....(p) TravisBlock(3) 9 63
(Miss Tor Sturgis) *chsd ldrs: u.p after 3f: effrt to go 2nd over 3f out: losing pl whn twice hmpd over 2f out: one pce after* **2/1**[1]
4043 6 8 **Trifti**[18] 4356 6-9-0 66 .... JackMitchell(7) 6 49
(C A Cyzer) *sn prom: led 7f out: clr over 4f out: hdd & wknd jst over 2f out* **14/1**
5032 7 2 1/2 **Stagehand (IRE)**[41] 3652 3-8-10 64 .... ChrisCatlin 2 44
(B R Millman) *chsd ldrs: easily outpcd fr over 4f out* **8/1**
0-00 8 1 1/2 **Endless Night**[16] 4416 4-8-10 50 .... PatrickHills(5) 5 37
(A M Hales) *hld up wl in rr: bdly outpcd fr 4f out: no ch after* **66/1**
5020 9 3 **Rainbow Flame**[4] 4758 3-8-12 62 ....(b) RichardKingscote(3) 7 42
(Tom Dascombe) *prom: rdn to chse ldr over 5f out to over 3f out: wknd rapidly* **20/1**
-010 10 2 1/2 **Alqaayid**[12] 4534 6-9-7 45 ow2 .... SColas(3) 13 37
(P W Hiatt) *dwlt: hld up in rr: outpcd fr 4f out: sn rdn and no ch* **66/1**
3600 11 11 **Port 'n Starboard**[10] 4592 6-9-3 58 .... SimonWhitworth 4 12
(C A Cyzer) *rel to r: a in last trio: wl bhd 4f out* **33/1**
-000 12 7 **Haneen (USA)**[43] 3600 4-8-11 50 .... SamHitchcott 10 —
(R W Price) *led to 7f out: wknd rapidly over 5f out: t.o* **100/1**
0000 13 16 **Ariodante**[19] 4318 5-9-4 61 ....(b[1]) HayleyTurner 11 —
(J M P Eustace) *s.v.s: sn rcvrd and prom: wknd rapidly over 4f out: t.o* **25/1**

2m 31.34s (-3.05) **Going Correction** -0.20s/f (Stan)
WFA 3 from 4yo+ 10lb **13** Ran SP% **122.1**
Speed ratings (Par 101): **102,101,101,101,99 94,92,91,89,87 80,75,65**
CSF £185.48 TOTE £9.00: £3.30, £4.40, £2.60; EX 249.20.Turner's Touch was the subject of a friendly claaim.
Owner Tann Racing **Bred** Juddmonte Farms Ltd **Trained** Ashtead, Surrey
■ Stewards' Enquiry : Richard Smith one-day ban: careless riding (Sep 9)
FOCUS
A reasonable claimer and, with the pace good, the winning time was 1.60 seconds quicker than the previous 0-45 classified contest. The form looks sound enough rated through the runner-up.
Rainbow Flame Official explanation: jockey said gelding hung left

4916 ALNO SOUTHERN CONTRACTS NOVICE AUCTION STKS 7f (P)
3:15 (3:16) (Class 6) 2-Y-O £2,388 (£705; £352) Stalls Low

Form RPR
0231 1 **Solent Ridge (IRE)**[21] 4255 2-9-3 81 .... JohnEgan 4 83
(J S Moore) *trckd ldng pair: effrt over 2f out: drvn to ld on outer 1f out: hung lft: styd on* **5/2**[1]
02 2 1 **Izzibizzi**[33] 3874 2-8-7 0 ow1 .... StephenDonohoe 6 70
(E A L Dunlop) *hld up in last pair: prog over 2f out: got through on inner to chal 1f out: nt qckn* **11/4**[2]
0431 3 3/4 **Gross Prophet**[15] 4459 2-8-12 78 .... RichardKingscote(3) 3 76
(Tom Dascombe) *led: drvn and hdd 1f out: hld whn sltly hmpd 100yds out* **10/3**[3]
0 4 5 **Bigalo's Magic (UAE)**[18] 4362 2-8-9 0 .... ChrisCatlin 2 57
(E J O'Neill) *pressed ldr on inner to over 1f out: wknd fnl f* **9/2**
5 4 **Heart Of Dubai (USA)** 2-8-11 0 .... RyanMoore 1 49
(C E Brittain) *s.i.s: sn trckd ldng pair: rdn over 2f out: sn wknd* **8/1**

0 **6** *19* **Dorso Rosso (IRE)**[20] 4293 2-8-10 0 ow1 .... AdamKirby 5 —
(Mrs C A Dunnett) *sn pushed along: in tch in last pair to 3f out: sn t.o*
100/1

1m 25.27s (-0.62) **Going Correction** -0.20s/f (Stan) **6** Ran SP% **108.6**
Speed ratings (Par 92): **95,93,93,87,82 61**
CSF £9.00 TOTE £3.60: £2.10, £1.50; EX 11.10.
Owner Mrs L Bloxsome,T Wilkinson & J S Moore **Bred** Glending Bloodstock **Trained** Upper Lambourn, Berks

FOCUS
Just an ordinary novice contest with the form solid enough rated around those in the frame behind the winner.

NOTEBOOK
Solent Ridge(IRE) had appeared suited by a return to 6f when winning his maiden at Chepstow on his previous start, but he had no problems at all with this longer trip and ran out a decisive winner, although he did hang to his left under pressure close home. He has plenty of size about him and should make a lovely three-year-old, but he may not be finished with for the season just yet, with his connections considering running him in a stakes race in Canada at the end of September. (op 9-2)
Izzibizzi did not look entirely straightforward when dead-heating for second in a 7f Folkestone maiden last time, edging right under pressure and appearing to carry her head at a slight angle, but she had previously shaped encouragingly in a good race on her debut over 6f on the July course. She did not appear to do much wrong this time but, having been produced with her challenge towards the inside, she just found the winner too strong. She might be able to pick up a modest maiden, but will also now have the option of going for nurseries. (op 9-4)
Gross Prophet created a good impression when off the mark in a 6f maiden at Wolverhampton on his previous start, but this extra furlong just looked to stretch him. Given a positive ride, it looked as though he might take a bit of passing when travelling well into the home straight, but his stamina probably just gave out. (op 5-2 tchd 9-4)
Bigalo's Magic(UAE) shaped nicely when mid-division on his debut in a 7f maiden on the Newmarket July course, but that race had not been working out and he was well held switched to a winners' race. He should have learnt plenty from this, though, as he was given a proper ride by Catlin, and it would be no surprise to see an improved effort next time. (tchd 4-1 and 11-2)
Heart Of Dubai(USA), by Outofthebox, a Grade 1 winner on the dirt in the US and half-brother to a very smart prolific winning sprinter at two and three in the US, out of a multiple sprint scorer, had a stiff enough task on his debut and was well held. (tchd 9-1)

4917 ALNO..... THE WORLD OF KITCHENS H'CAP — 1m 5f (P)
3:45 (3:46) (Class 4) (0-85,85) 3-Y-O+ £4,728 (£1,406; £702; £351) Stalls Low

Form RPR
5350 **1** **Boot 'n Toot**[19] 4318 6-8-9 **71** .... PatrickHills(5) 10 81
(C A Cyzer) *hld up in 7th: prog on outer wl over 2f out: rdn to ld jst over 1f out: styd on wl* **20/1**
/24- **2** *2* **Land Of Light**[341] 4931 4-8-10 **67** .... RyanMoore 8 74
(G L Moore) *settled in midfield: effrt over 2f out: rdn to chal over 1f out: hanging and nt qckn: kpt on fnl f* **13/2**
-646 **3** *hd* **Chocolate Caramel (USA)**[10] 4609 5-10-0 **85** .... JimCrowley 4 92
(Mrs A J Perrett) *trckd ldng trio: effrt on inner 2f out: drvn to chal over 1f out: nt qckn fnl f* **10/1**
1-50 **4** *2* **Captain General**[97] 1949 5-8-12 **69** .... MartinDwyer 6 73
(J A R Toller) *settled in midfield: lost pl and n.m.r briefly wl over 2f out: nt qckn 2f out: styd on fnl f* **4/1**[2]
2131 **5** *1 1/4* **Osolomio (IRE)**[21] 4248 4-9-12 **83** .... KerrinMcEvoy 7 85
(G A Swinbank) *led to over 1f out: sn btn* **6/4**[1]
4143 **6** *1 1/4* **Go But Go**[10] 4597 3-8-6 **74** .... ChrisCatlin 9 74
(E J O'Neill) *trckd ldr: drvn to chal and upsides over 1f out: wknd fnl f* **9/2**[3]
0644 **7** *4* **Active Asset (IRE)**[10] 4609 5-9-10 **81** .... FrancisNorton 2 75
(M Quinn) *trckd ldng pair tl wknd wl over 2f out* **12/1**
8 *15* **Chockdee (FR)**[407] 7-9-9 **80** ....(tp) JohnEgan 3 52
(M J McGrath) *s.v.s: a last: lost tch over 3f out: t.o* **50/1**

2m 45.17s (-3.13) **Going Correction** -0.20s/f (Stan)
WFA 3 from 4yo+ 11lb **8** Ran SP% **115.0**
Speed ratings (Par 105): **101,99,99,98,97 96,94,85**
CSF £143.45 CT £1390.95 TOTE £10.70: £2.00, £3.10, £3.00; EX 132.20.
Owner Mrs Charles Cyzer **Bred** C A Cyzer **Trained** Maplehurst, W Sussex

FOCUS
This looked like an ordinary handicap for the grade but makes sense rated around the winner and third.

4918 ALNOCONTRACTS.CO.UK H'CAP — 1m (P)
4:15 (4:16) (Class 6) (0-60,64) 3-Y-O £2,047 (£604; £302) Stalls High

Form RPR
1431 **1** **Palmetto Point**[4] 4760 3-9-5 **64** 6ex ....(p) TravisBlock(3) 10 71+
(H Morrison) *racd wd: cl up: jnd ldrs over 3f out: led wl over 1f out and kicked 2 l clr: pressed last 100yds: jst hld on* **5/6**[1]
0656 **2** *shd* **Run For Ede'S**[13] 4505 3-9-3 **59** ....(p) IanMongan 11 63
(P M Phelan) *chsd ldrs: effrt over 2f out: drvn to go 2nd over 1f out: chal last 100yds: jst failed* **13/2**[2]
1606 **3** *1 1/4* **Ella Y Rossa**[16] 4429 3-9-4 **60** .... StephenDonohoe 9 61
(P D Evans) *hld up: last and rdn over 4f out: sn outpcd: prog wl over 1f out: styd on to take 3rd 1f out: clsng at fin* **15/2**[3]
006 **4** *3* **Withywood (USA)**[24] 4182 3-8-6 **48** .... RichardMullen 12 42
(G L Moore) *t.k.h early and racd awkwardly: hld up in last pair: rdn over 2f out: styd on to take 4th ins fnl f: n.d* **20/1**
04-5 **5** *nk* **Mariaverdi**[13] 4513 3-8-8 **50** .... ChrisCatlin 6 44
(B J Meehan) *pressed ldrs: rdn over 3f out: outpcd over 1f out: plugged on* **16/1**
44-6 **6** *3/4* **Ponte Vecchio (IRE)**[230] 93 3-8-7 **49** .... JimCrowley 8 41
(J R Boyle) *w ldr: stl upsides 2f out: fdd over 1f out* **25/1**
660 **7** *3/4* **Hannahbecc**[33] 3881 3-9-4 **60** .... SaleemGolam 2 50+
(S C Williams) *hld up: hmpd over 2f out: effrt and nt clr run over 1f out: styng on but no ch whn hmpd jst ins fnl f* **25/1**
3324 **8** *1 1/4* **Candyland (IRE)**[13] 4513 3-8-10 **52** .... FrancisNorton 4 39
(M Quinn) *led at str pce but a pressed: hdd wl over 1f out: sn wknd* **10/1**
000 **9** *2* **Straight Face (IRE)**[67] 2837 3-8-13 **55** ....(v) NickyMackay 5 38
(M Wigham) *chsd ldrs: u.p over 3f out: wknd over 1f out* **13/2**[2]
-000 **10** *11* **Rangali Belle**[11] 4575 3-8-11 **53** .... SimonWhitworth 1 10
(C A Horgan) *lost pl after 2f: hmpd on inner sn after: dropped out fr 1/2-way: t.o* **66/1**

1m 38.19s (-1.24) **Going Correction** -0.20s/f (Stan) **10** Ran SP% **121.9**
Speed ratings (Par 98): **98,97,96,93,93 92,91,90,88,77**
CSF £6.79 CT £28.62 TOTE £1.60: £1.20, £2.10, £1.70; EX 8.40.
Owner M T Bevan & H Scott-Barrett **Bred** Wyck Hall Stud Ltd **Trained** East Ilsley, Berks

FOCUS
A moderate but competitive three-year-old handicap and sound form rated around the placed horses with the winner value for a little more.

Hannahbecc ◆ Official explanation: jockey said filly was denied a clear run

4919 ALNO KITCHENS@SEVENOAKS H'CAP — 6f (P)
4:45 (4:45) (Class 6) (0-60,70) 3-Y-O £2,047 (£604; £302) Stalls Low

Form RPR
3015 **1** **Lord Of The Reins (IRE)**[8] 4661 3-8-13 **55** .... DaneO'Neill 7 67+
(D Shaw) *dwlt: wl in rr: prog and plld out over 1f out: styd on strly to ld last 150yds: sn clr* **12/1**
0-41 **2** *1 1/2* **Shaded Edge**[48] 3425 3-9-0 **56** .... JamesDoyle 3 63
(D W P Arbuthnot) *pressed ldr: rdn to ld over 2f out: hdd and outpcd last 150yds: kpt on* **4/1**[2]
-514 **3** *2* **Luck Will Come (IRE)**[13] 4514 3-9-4 **60** .... RyanMoore 1 61
(M J Wallace) *hld up in midfield on inner: effrt 2f out: styd on fr over 1f out: nt pce to chal* **4/1**[2]
11 **4** *shd* **Back In The Red (IRE)**[4] 4759 3-10-0 **70** 12ex .... JohnEgan 11 71
(R A Harris) *racd wd: pressed ldrs: effrt over 2f out: rdn to chal over 1f out: one pce fnl f* **7/4**[1]
0020 **5** *3/4* **Emma Jean Lad (IRE)**[38] 3752 3-9-1 **57** .... SimonWhitworth 12 55
(J S Moore) *stdd s and swtchd to inner fr wd draw: last to 2f out: taken to outer and then inner over 1f out: styd on: n.d* **10/1**[3]
4300 **6** *3/4* **Golden Brown (IRE)**[42] 3622 3-9-4 **60** .... JimCrowley 8 56
(David Pinder) *hld up in midfield: rdn and no prog whn slt bump over 1f out: styd on same pce* **40/1**
000 **7** *shd* **Polish Prize**[35] 3827 3-8-13 **55** .... AdamKirby 10 51
(W R Swinburn) *racd wd in rr: no real prog whn slt bump over 1f out: kpt on fnl f* **16/1**
-550 **8** *1/2* **Darling Belinda**[12] 4536 3-9-2 **58** ....(p) RobertHavlin 4 52
(D K Ivory) *chsd ldrs: rdn over 2f out: no prog over 1f out: fdd* **25/1**
000 **9** *1 1/2* **Victory Spirit**[33] 3872 3-9-4 **60** ....(b[1]) MartinDwyer 5 50
(H J L Dunlop) *hld up wl in rr: effrt over 2f out: no real prog over 1f out* **22/1**
3560 **10** *2 1/2* **Futuristic Dragon (IRE)**[19] 4336 3-8-12 **59** .... KevinGhunowa(5) 9 41
(P A Blockley) *prom: pressed ldr over 2f out to over 1f out: wknd rapidly* **16/1**
445- **11** *37* **Ten For Tosca (IRE)**[343] 5448 3-8-8 **55** .... LukeMorris(5) 6 —
(R A Harris) *led to over 2f out: wknd rapidly: t.o* **25/1**

1m 12.9s (0.09) **Going Correction** -0.20s/f (Stan) **11** Ran SP% **119.4**
Speed ratings (Par 98): **91,89,86,86,85 84,84,83,81,78 28**
CSF £58.10 CT £236.29 TOTE £16.40: £3.10, £1.70, £1.40; EX 67.90 Place 6 £199.02, Place 5 £122.41.
Owner Danethorpe Racing Partnership **Bred** C Farrell **Trained** Danethorpe, Notts
■ Stewards' Enquiry : Dane O'Neill two-day ban: careless riding (Sep 9,10)

FOCUS
A moderate three-year-old sprint handicap and the time was ordinary. However, the form makes sense rated around the placed horses.
Darling Belinda Official explanation: jockey said filly hung right
Ten For Tosca(IRE) Official explanation: jockey said gelding stopped quickly
T/Plt: £689.70 to a £1 stake. Pool: £69,167.75. 73.20 winning tickets. T/Qpdt: £25.70 to a £1 stake. Pool: £5,192.10. 149.20 winning tickets. JN

4897 RIPON (R-H)
Tuesday, August 28

OFFICIAL GOING: Good to firm (9.4)
Wind: Virtually nil Weather: Overcast

4920 CLARO (S) STKS — 1m 1f 170y
2:30 (2:31) (Class 5) 3-4-Y-O £3,238 (£963; £481; £240) Stalls High

Form RPR
0023 **1** **Moonlight Fantasy (IRE)**[11] 4580 4-9-1 50 .... NeilBrown(5) 2 52+
(T D Barron) *in tch: smooth hdwy to trck ldrs over 2f out: shkn up to ld ent fnl f: sn rdn and rdr dropped whip: kpt on* **11/4**[1]
606 **2** *1 1/2* **Prince Noel**[18] 4354 3-8-12 50 .... SebSanders 15 49+
(N Wilson) *trckd ldrs on inner tl hmpd and lost pl bnd over 5f out: swtchd lft and hdwy 3f out: rdn to chse wnr ent fnl f: kpt on* **9/2**[3]
0300 **3** *3/4* **Ranavalona**[11] 4568 3-8-7 47 ....(t) PaulHanagan 9 42
(C Smith) *a.p: rdn 2f out and sn ev ch tl drvn and one pce ins fnl f* **20/1**
5004 **4** *2* **Leprechaun's Gold (IRE)**[12] 4528 3-8-7 48 .... HaddenFrost(5) 7 43
(B J Llewellyn) *hld up: stdy hdwy on inner 3f out: nt clr run and swtchd lft over 1f out: sn rdn and styd on ins fnl f: nrst fin* **14/1**
066 **5** *1/2* **Miss Lovat**[16] 4426 4-9-7 39 .... DavidAllan 8 43
(W M Brisbourne) *t.k.h: led after 2f: rdn along over 2f out: drvn over 1f out: hdd and edgd rt entering fnl f: wknd* **40/1**
0610 **6** *1/2* **Jenny Soba**[10] 4615 4-8-12 50 ....(v) MichaelJStainton(3) 14 36
(R M Whitaker) *trckd ldrs: hdwy on inner 2f out: nt clr run and swtchd lft jst ins fnl f: sn rdn and one pce* **3/1**[2]
0-00 **7** *4* **Hogan's Heroes**[19] 4319 4-9-3 0 ....(p) JerryO'Dwyer(3) 5 33
(Eoin Doyle, Ire) *hld up in rr: swtchd outside and hdwy 3f out: rdn to chse ldrs wl over 1f out: sn drvn and one pce* **13/2**
00 **8** *1/2* **Anything Once (USA)**[16] 4427 4-9-6 51 ....(b[1]) DarryllHolland 6 32
(D Carroll) *hld up in midfield: hdwy to trck ldrs 3f out: rdn along and styng on whn stmbld and lost action over 1f out: eased* **25/1**
0-05 **9** *2 1/2* **Boucheen**[8] 4671 4-9-6 43 .... GrahamGibbons 1 26
(J W Unett) *hld up towards rr: hdwy 3f out: sn rdn along and no imp fnl 2f* **22/1**
00 **10** *shd* **Nortelco (IRE)**[11] 4580 4-9-6 0 ....(t) PatCosgrave 3 26
(Micky Hammond) *chsd ldrs: rdn along over 2f out: drvn and wknd wl over 1f out* **100/1**
-000 **11** *1 3/4* **Remark (IRE)**[13] 4491 3-8-12 45 .... PaulMulrennan 12 22
(M W Easterby) *t.k.h: hld up: a in rr* **20/1**
2300 **12** *shd* **Arabellas Homer**[16] 4426 3-8-4 45 .... DuranFentiman(3) 11 17
(Mrs N Macauley) *towards rr: hdwy 3f out: rdn along over 2f out and sn wknd* **50/1**
0025 **13** *1/2* **Lewis Lloyd (IRE)**[17] 4410 4-9-9 46 ....(t) MarkLawson(3) 16 27
(R E Barr) *hld up: a in rr* **16/1**
0000 **14** *3* **Night Reveller (IRE)**[10] 4426 4-8-10 24 .... RussellKennemore(5) 10 10
(M C Chapman) *prom: rdn along over 3f out and sn wknd* **100/1**
060 **15** *1/2* **Musette (IRE)**[16] 4426 4-9-1 45 .... TomEaves 13 9
(R E Barr) *led 2f: cl up tl rdn along 3f out and sn wknd* **50/1**

0000 **U** **Danehill Warrior (IRE)**[16] 4424 3-8-5 40..............(b[1]) CharlesEddery(7) 4 —
(R C Guest) *stdd and swtchd rt s: towards rr whn slipped and uns rdr bnd over 5f out* **66/1**

2m 5.57s (0.57) **Going Correction** -0.15s/f (Firm)
WFA 3 from 4yo 8lb **16** Ran SP% **124.4**
Speed ratings (Par 103): **91,89,89,87,87 86,83,83,81,81 79,79,79,76,76** —
CSF £14.27 TOTE £3.30: £1.50, £2.20, £4.20; EX 23.10 Trifecta £147.00 Part won. Pool: £207.10 - 0.20 winning units..The winner was sold to Mr J. Roundtree for 8,800gns. Jenny Soba was claimed by Lucinda Featherstone for £6,000.

Owner Mount Pleasant Farm Racing Partnership **Bred** Rockhart Trading Ltd **Trained** Maunby, N Yorks

FOCUS
A typically weak seller and the form is somewhat messy. It was a moderate time, even for a race of this standard.

Anything Once(USA) Official explanation: jockey said he lost stirrup iron and gelding lost its action

4921 SAPPER CONDITIONS STKS 5f
3:00 (3:01) (Class 3) 2-Y-O

£6,232 (£1,866; £933; £467; £233; £117) **Stalls** Low

Form RPR
3116 **1** **Fol Hollow (IRE)**[7] 4695 2-8-11 88.............................. AndrewMullen(3) 4 92
(D Nicholls) *cl up: rdn to ld wl over 1f out: edgd rt ins fnl f and drvn out* **2/1**[1]

112 **2** ½ **Look Busy (IRE)**[18] 4349 2-8-9 88.................................. PaulHanagan 7 85
(A Berry) *wnt rt s and bhd: gd hdwy on outer over 2f out: sn rdn and styd on strly ins fnl f* **3/1**[2]

331 **3** ¾ **Art Sale**[19] 4315 2-9-0 85.. SebSanders 6 87
(G L Moore) *outpcd in rr: hdwy 2f out: sn rdn and styd on ins fnl f: nrst fin* **10/3**[3]

621 **4** 1 ¼ **Mey Blossom**[12] 4522 2-8-10 85............................ MichaelJStainton(3) 5 82
(R M Whitaker) *chsd ldng pair: effrt 2f out: sn rdn and kpt on same pce appr fnl f* **10/1**

231 **5** 2 **Tadalavil**[10] 4611 2-9-4 86... DarryllHolland 8 79
(M R Channon) *chsd ldng pair: rdn along 2f out and sn wknd* **8/1**

6 **6** 1 ½ **Oasis Davis**[17] 4378 2-9-0 0.. NCallan 3 70
(K A Ryan) *s.i.s: sn chsng ldrs: rdn along 1/2-way and sn wknd* **20/1**

1 **7** 1 ¼ **Cheshire Rose**[50] 3378 2-8-11 0.. PaulFessey 1 62
(T D Barron) *led: rdn along over 2f out: hdd wl over 1f out and sn wknd* **12/1**

59.09 secs (-1.11) **Going Correction** -0.15s/f (Firm) **7** Ran SP% **114.1**
Speed ratings (Par 98): **102,101,100,98,94 92,90**
CSF £8.13 TOTE £3.00: £1.80, £2.40; EX 9.80 Trifecta £21.80 Pool: £422.49 - 13.74 winning units..

Owner Dandy Nicholls Racing Club **Bred** Dan O'Brien **Trained** Sessay, N Yorks

FOCUS
A tight conditions event, run at a solid pace. The form looks straightforward enough and solid rated through the winner.

NOTEBOOK
Fol Hollow(IRE) relished this drop back to the minimum trip and has now been successful on three of his last four outings. He is a headstrong sprinter, but is evidently still progressing and his versatility as regards underfoot conditions is a notable advantage. (op 9-4 tchd 5-2)

Look Busy(IRE) was unable to get near the front through the early parts this time and was doing all of her best work towards the finish. She had an obvious chance at the weights and is developing into a very consistent juvenile. (op 11-4 tchd 9-4)

Art Sale, raised 7lb for getting off the mark at Brighton last time, was another who struggled to go the early pace and can be rated a little better than the bare form as he was a little tight for room when making his challenge inside the final furlong. He remains on an upward curve and a step up to 6f may now prove more to his liking. (op 5-1)

Mey Blossom was made to look one paced when push came to shove on this step up in grade. She was still not disgraced at the weights and is another who may now appreciate a stiffer test. (op 7-1)

Tadalavil, having his first run over this shorter trip, had a stiff enough task at these weights and should prove better off in nurseries. He still has a bit to do to prove he is worthy of an official mark of 86, however. (op 11-1)

4922 CITY OF RIPON H'CAP 1m 1f 170y
3:30 (3:30) (Class 3) (0-90,90) 3-Y-O+

£9,348 (£2,799; £1,399; £700; £349; £175) **Stalls** High

Form RPR
2631 **1** **Suits Me**[38] 3755 4-8-8 71 oh1.. MickyFenton 6 81
(T P Tate) *chsd ldr: hdwy to ld over 2f out: rdn over 1f out: drvn ins fnl f and kpt on wl* **7/1**[3]

0-05 **2** ½ **Go Tech**[17] 4408 7-8-13 76... DavidAllan 8 85+
(T D Easterby) *hld up in rr: gd hdwy on outer over 2f out: rdn and str run ent fnl f: kpt on* **14/1**

1102 **3** nk **Emerald Wilderness (IRE)**[9] 4640 3-9-5 90.................. SebSanders 11 98
(E A L Dunlop) *in tch: hdwy 3f out: rdn to chal over 1f out and ev ch tl drvn: wandered and one pce wl ins fnl f* **11/8**[1]

10 **4** 3 **Snowed Under**[16] 4419 6-8-13 76................................ DarryllHolland 10 78
(J D Bethell) *chsd ldrs: hdwy 3f out: rdn and ch 2f out: sn drvn and wknd appr fnl f* **16/1**

0545 **5** ¾ **Goodbye Mr Bond**[17] 4385 7-9-11 88.. KDarley 2 88
(E J Alston) *hld up in rr: hdwy wl over 2f out: rdn to chse ldrs over 1f out: kpt on same pce ins fnl f* **6/1**[2]

0120 **6** 1 **Little Jimbob**[22] 4228 6-8-9 72... PaulHanagan 5 70
(R A Fahey) *prom: rdn along over 2f out: drvn over 1f out and sn one pce* **16/1**

0 **7** nk **Southern Regent (IND)**[201] 398 6-9-13 90.......................... NCallan 1 88
(G A Swinbank) *hld up in rr: effrt and sme hdwy on outer wl over 2f out: sn rdn and no imp* **16/1**

3100 **8** shd **Vicious Warrior**[11] 4566 8-9-8 85.................................. PaulMulrennan 3 83
(R M Whitaker) *hld up: effrt and sme hdwy wl over 2f out: rdn wl over 1f out and sn wknd* **20/1**

0254 **9** 2 ½ **Orpen Wide (IRE)**[11] 4585 5-9-1 83...............(b) RussellKennemore(5) 12 75
(M C Chapman) *led: pushed clr 1/2-way: rdn 3f out: hdd over 2f out and sn wknd* **16/1**

0020 **10** 3 **Hartshead**[11] 4566 8-9-9 89... PJMcDonald(3) 9 75
(G A Swinbank) *hld up towards rr: effrt 4f out: sn rdn and no hdwy* **20/1**

5600 **11** 6 **Symbol Of Peace (IRE)**[17] 4404 4-8-11 74.............. GrahamGibbons 4 47
(J W Unett) *in tch: rdn along 3f out: sn wknd* **33/1**

4544 **12** hd **Harvest Warrior**[12] 4523 5-8-13 79............................ DuranFentiman(3) 7 52
(T D Easterby) *dwlt: a in rr* **12/1**

2m 2.67s (-2.33) **Going Correction** -0.15s/f (Firm)
WFA 3 from 4yo+ 8lb **12** Ran SP% **119.2**
Speed ratings (Par 107): **103,102,102,99,99 98,98,98,96,93 89,88**
CSF £98.49 CT £213.98 TOTE £7.90: £2.20, £4.30, £1.10; EX 117.20 Trifecta £342.50 Part won. Pool: £482.45 - 0.20 winning units..

Owner D E Cook **Bred** R S A Urquhart **Trained** Tadcaster, N Yorks

FOCUS
A fair handicap and although the time was nearly three seconds quicker than the earlier seller, it was still ordinary for the grade. It still paid to race handily though, and not that many got into it. The form is rated at face value through the third.

NOTEBOOK
Suits Me, raised 3lb for his victory on totally different ground over course and distance last month and with another 1lb of overweight, is very versatile with regard to going requirements. Content to let the clear leader get on with it whilst leading the main bulk of the field, he was sent for home halfway up the home straight as the pace-setter folded and showed a decent attitude to keep a couple of challengers at bay and win all-out. (op 8-1)

Go Tech was given a patient ride before finishing well and he only just failed to get up. This was a decent effort considering this is a track that suits front runners and, as he is now 7lb lower than for his last win, is one to watch out for on similarly quick ground. (op 10-1)

Emerald Wilderness(IRE), back over his best trip, was produced with his effort between horses in plenty of time but found less than had looked likely under pressure and perhaps this undulating track was not entirely to his liking. (op 6-4 tchd 13-8 and 5-4)

Snowed Under, very much a Leicester specialist, had every chance but could do nothing to stop the front three from running away from him. He was running in this race for the third consecutive year and this was his best placing. (tchd 18-1)

Goodbye Mr Bond made up a fair amount of late ground and deserves some credit as it is not easy to come from well off the pace here. (op 7-1 tchd 15-2 and 11-2)

Little Jimbob, whose best recent form has been in claimers, ran with credit on a track that would have suited his style of running, but with Orpen Wide in the field he had no chance of being able to dominate on his own. (tchd 20-1)

Orpen Wide(IRE), who has been sprinting lately, went off like a sprinter but even on a front-runners' track like this he had no chance of lasting out. (op 14-1)

4923 RIPON LAND ROVER NURSERY 6f
4:00 (4:01) (Class 4) 2-Y-O **£5,181** (£1,541; £770; £384) **Stalls** Low

Form RPR
4201 **1** **Sophie's Girl**[15] 4447 2-9-1 76... KDarley 10 82
(P W Chapple-Hyam) *prom: rdn over 1f out: styd on to ld ins fnl f: kpt on* **6/1**

5304 **2** 1 ¼ **Mansii**[23] 4201 2-8-12 73.. SebSanders 1 75
(C E Brittain) *trckd ldrs: effrt and nt clr run over 1f out: swtchd rt and rdn ent fnl f: sn chsng wnr: kpt on* **8/1**

P044 **3** 1 **Everything**[27] 4076 2-8-10 71... MickyFenton 5 70
(P T Midgley) *cl up: rdn to ld appr 1f out: drvn and hdd ins fnl f: kpt on same pce* **33/1**

0530 **4** hd **Fidelias Dance**[24] 4168 2-8-11 72.. GregFairley 9 70
(M Johnston) *chsd ldrs: rdn along over 1f out: kpt on same pce* **14/1**

3322 **5** ½ **Aaim For Applause**[9] 4636 2-9-5 80..........................(v[1]) DarryllHolland 7 77
(M R Channon) *in tch: effrt over 2f out: sn rdn and kpt on same pce fnl f* **11/4**[1]

265 **6** nk **Eager Diva (USA)**[97] 1945 2-9-0 75.. NCallan 12 71
(K A Ryan) *racd alone far side: prom: rdn along 2f out: kpt on same pce* **14/1**

314 **7** 1 ¼ **Speed Song**[18] 4349 2-9-4 82.. LiamJones(3) 6 74
(W J Haggas) *towards rr: rdn along 1/2-way: swtchd rt and drvn wl over 1f out: sn no imp* **7/2**[2]

4462 **8** ¾ **Angle Of Attack (IRE)**[11] 4560 2-8-7 68............................ PaulHanagan 3 58
(R A Fahey) *led: rdn along 2f out: hdd over 1f out and sn wknd* **4/1**[3]

000 **9** 2 ½ **Transcendent (IRE)**[40] 3687 2-7-13 60 oh2 ow1............. JimmyQuinn 4 43
(J D Bethell) *a in rr* **100/1**

005 **10** 1 ¾ **Weetfromthechaff**[16] 4417 2-8-4 65....................................... PaulQuinn 8 42
(R Hollinshead) *a in rr* **33/1**

0203 **11** hd **Fulford**[10] 4612 2-7-13 67 ow1................................. PatrickDonaghy(7) 11 44
(M Brittain) *in tch: rdn along over 2f out and sn wknd* **25/1**

0000 **12** 38 **Doubtless**[8] 4669 2-7-5 59 oh14................................ DanielleMcCreery(7) 2 —
(D W Chapman) *sn outpcd and bhd fr 1/2-way* **200/1**

1m 12.55s (-0.45) **Going Correction** -0.15s/f (Firm) **12** Ran SP% **118.8**
Speed ratings (Par 96): **97,95,94,93,93 92,91,90,86,84 84,33**
CSF £51.69 CT £1495.59 TOTE £7.60: £2.40, £2.40, £6.50; EX 49.60 Trifecta £436.10 Part won. Pool: £614.28 - 0.84 winning units..

Owner Iraj Parvizi **Bred** Jeremy Green And Sons **Trained** Newmarket, Suffolk

FOCUS
A reasonable nursery in which all bar one of the runners raced stands' side. The form looks solid.

NOTEBOOK
Sophie's Girl, making her nursery debut, was always up with the pace and came away to win with some authority. The only time she had tried this trip before was when out of her depth in the Albany Stakes at Royal Ascot, but this showed that she gets it well and there may be more to come from her. (op 11-2)

Mansii, another making his nursery debut, did not have a great deal of room to play with when trying to get closer a furlong from home and, by the time he saw daylight, the winner was away. He would never have beaten her, but would have been closer. (op 7-1)

Everything ran another decent race on this nursery debut and was helped by racing handily on a track which suits that style of running. There should be a small race in her.

Fidelias Dance, 2lb lower than when beating just one home on her nursery debut, ran better here having been prominent from the start. Her breeding suggests she needs a bit further. (op 12-1 tchd 16-1)

Aaim For Applause, a well-backed favourite in the first-time visor, had every chance but could never land a blow and this was the first time in eight outings he has not finished second or third. (op 7-2)

Eager Diva(USA) was taken over to race alone from the highest stall, but although she seemed to be in touch with the stands'-side group coming to the last furlong, she was then left behind. She is still to prove she stays this trip. (op 12-1)

Speed Song, trying this trip for the first time, could never land a blow and having already been soundly beaten off 1lb higher, it appears that she was given too stiff a mark for her Yarmouth victory. (tchd 10-3)

Angle Of Attack(IRE) was given a positive ride, but did not get home and it appears he needs a sharper track in order to see out this trip. (op 11-2)

4924 SMILER AND BRENDA "LIFETIME IN RACING" FILLIES' MAIDEN AUCTION STKS 5f
4:30 (4:31) (Class 5) 2-Y-O **£3,238** (£963; £481; £240) **Stalls** Low

Form RPR
0 **1** **Jennifer's Dream (IRE)**[27] 4074 2-8-11 0 NCallan 2 79+
(K A Ryan) *dwlt: sn trcking ldrs: hdwy to ld 1 1/2f out: rdn ins fnl f and styd on wl* **14/1**
2 1 **Love Of Dubai (USA)** 2-8-2 0 AhmedAjtebi(5) 12 72+
(C E Brittain) *midfield: gd hdwy on outer over 2f out: rdn and edgd lft ent fnl f: kpt on u.p* **14/1**
3 nk **Tobar Suil Lady (IRE)** 2-8-1 0 AndrewMullen(3) 6 68+
(K A Ryan) *midfield: hdwy over 2f out: swtchd lft to stands' rails and rdn over 1f out: styd on strly ins fnl f* **33/1**
5523 **4** 1 **Upstanding**[18] 4349 2-8-4 66 DaleGibson 8 64
(M Brittain) *cl up: rdn to ld briefly 2f out: sn hdd and kpt on same pce u.p fnl f* **7/2**[1]
0523 **5** 1 1/4 **Betty Burke**[4] 4756 2-8-7 72 EddieAhern 5 63
(H J L Dunlop) *prom: rdn and hung rt wl over 1f out: sn drvn and one pce* **7/2**[1]
43 **6** 1 3/4 **Maid In Bloom**[22] 4221 2-8-4 0 RoystonFfrench 13 53
(B Smart) *chsd ldrs: rdn along and keeping on whn n.m.r wl over 1f out: one pce after* **9/2**[2]
42 **7** 2 1/2 **Lambrini Lace (IRE)**[61] 3030 2-8-8 0 LiamJones(3) 3 51
(Mrs L Williamson) *chsd ldrs: rdn along 2f out: grad wknd* **11/1**
2 **8** 3 1/2 **Princess Rhianna (IRE)**[12] 4522 2-8-11 0 LeeEnstone 7 39
(K R Burke) *chsd ldrs: rdn along over 2f out: sn btn* **13/2**[3]
0 **9** 1 3/4 **Miss Olivia**[20] 4293 2-8-4 0 AdrianMcCarthy 10 25
(P W Chapple-Hyam) *a towards rr* **33/1**
0 **10** 1/2 **Willit (IRE)**[9] 4629 2-8-11 0 DarryllHolland 11 31
(M R Channon) *a towards rr* **7/1**
060 **11** 1/2 **Wizzy Izzy (IRE)**[32] 3915 2-8-11 35 (b[1]) GrahamGibbons 4 29
(N Wilson) *led: rdn along over 2f out: sn hdd & wknd* **100/1**
00 **12** 5 **Eternal Optimist (IRE)**[12] 4522 2-8-4 0 PaulHanagan 1 4
(C W Thornton) *sn outpcd: a towards rr* **66/1**
4 **13** 6 **Bellas Chicas (IRE)**[122] 1302 2-8-4 0 PaulFessey 9 —
(P T Midgley) *a towards rr* **28/1**

59.69 secs (-0.51) **Going Correction** -0.15s/f (Firm) **13 Ran SP% 121.9**
Speed ratings (Par 91): **98,96,95,94,92 89,85,79,77,76 75,67,57**
CSF £192.17 TOTE £18.50: £3.70, £3.60, £9.70; EX 137.30 Trifecta £347.70 Part won. Pool: £489.84 - 0.34 winning units..
Owner M G White **Bred** Mountain View Stud **Trained** Hambleton, N Yorks

FOCUS
A modest fillies' maiden that looks solid enough rated through the fourth.

NOTEBOOK
Jennifer's Dream(IRE) appreciated the drop back to the minimum trip and showed good early speed. This was not a great maiden but she did it well enough and will surely not be given too stiff a mark for the switch to nurseries. (op 12-1)
Love Of Dubai(USA), a half-sister to a US sprint winner, was not well drawn and ran a highly promising race in the circumstances as she was stuck on the outside throughout. She hails from a stable whose juveniles do not tend to win first time up and so she is entitled to improve a fair bit for this. (op 12-1)
Tobar Suil Lady(IRE), whose dam was placed over 7f at in France, is, like her stablemate who won the race, by Statue Of Liberty. The way she was staying on at the finish suggests that she will be suited by stepping up to 6f. (op 40-1)
Upstanding, who has an official rating of 66 and was the most experienced filly in this field, is beginning to look exposed. She had every chance. (op 9-2)
Betty Burke was a bit below her best at Bath last time and again disappointed, failing to run to her current mark of 72. (op 3-1 tchd 11-4 and 4-1)
Maid In Bloom, poorly drawn, got chopped for room inside the last two furlongs, and once again shaped as though needing another furlong. Nurseries are now an option for her. (op 7-1 tchd 4-1)
Lambrini Lace(IRE) Official explanation: trainer said filly was unsuited by the track
Princess Rhianna(IRE) Official explanation: jockey said filly was always outpaced

4925 WAKEMAN STAYERS H'CAP 2m
5:00 (5:02) (Class 6) (0-65,65) 3-Y-O+ **£2,590** (£770; £385; £192) **Stalls** Low

Form RPR
5343 **1** **Golden Groom**[6] 4717 4-8-13 50 PaulFessey 14 59
(C W Fairhurst) *trckd ldrs: hdwy over 4f out: led over 3f out: rdn 2f out and styd on strly* **11/2**[3]
5353 **2** 2 1/2 **Mr Mischief**[9] 4638 7-9-2 58 RussellKennemore(5) 2 64
(M C Chapman) *hld up in rr: gd hdwy 6f out: chsd wnr over 3f out: rdn 2f out: drvn over 1f out and kpt on same pce fnl f* **8/1**
0500 **3** 2 1/2 **Foxxy**[25] 4139 3-7-13 50 oh4 ow1 JimmyQuinn 6 53
(J R Norton) *hld up: stdy hdwy 4f out: rdn to chse ldng pair over 2f out: sn drvn and no imp* **25/1**
6631 **4** hd **Karlani (IRE)**[20] 4280 4-10-0 65 (b) NCallan 8 68
(G A Swinbank) *hld up in rr: hdwy over 3f out: rdn along 2f out and plugged on same pce* **5/2**[1]
0051 **5** 8 **Erte**[15] 4451 6-8-13 53 (v) DominicFox(3) 9 46
(W Storey) *hld up in tch: pushed along and lost pl over 4f out: swtchd outside and rdn 3f out: kpt on u.p fnl 2f* **14/1**
5-50 **6** 1 1/4 **Kerry's Blade (IRE)**[9] 4638 5-8-12 49 oh1 SebSanders 1 41
(Micky Hammond) *towards rr tl styd on fnl 3f: nvr a factor* **25/1**
6132 **7** 2 **Josh You Are**[15] 4463 4-9-10 61 PatCosgrave 5 50
(D E Cantillon) *hld up in rr: hdwy 3f out: rdn along over 2f out and nvr a factor* **3/1**[2]
-543 **8** 8 **Blushing Hilary (IRE)**[14] 4475 4-9-8 59 TomEaves 3 39
(Miss J A Camacho) *in tch: hdwy to chse ldrs over 4f out: rdn along over 3f out and sn wknd* **10/1**
6-40 **9** 5 **Next Flight (IRE)**[15] 4451 8-8-12 49 oh4 PaulHanagan 10 23
(R E Barr) *prom: rdn along over 4f out: sn wknd* **28/1**
0050 **10** 3 **Zaville**[17] 4409 5-8-12 49 oh4 (p) DavidAllan 11 19
(J O'Reilly) *led 3f: cl up tl led again over 9f out: rdn along and hdd over 3f out: sn wknd* **25/1**
-063 **11** 9 **Sweet Lavinia**[15] 4451 4-8-9 49 oh4 AndrewElliott(3) 12 8
(J D Bethell) *cl up: led after 3f: hdd over 9f out: chsd ldrs tl rdn along over 4f out and sn wknd* **14/1**
0U-0 **12** 122 **Commander Wish**[12] 4534 4-8-12 49 oh1 TGMcLaughlin 4 —
(Lucinda Featherstone) *prom tl lost pl appr 1/2-way and sn bhd* **150/1**

3m 30.44s (-2.56) **Going Correction** -0.15s/f (Firm)
WFA 3 from 4yo+ 14lb **12 Ran SP% 118.1**
Speed ratings (Par 101): **100,98,97,97,93 92,91,87,85,83 79,—**
CSF £45.94 CT £1021.63 TOTE £6.60: £2.40, £2.90, £5.80; EX 58.00 Trifecta £241.10 Pool: £455.08 - 1.34 winning units. Place 6 £846.68, Place 5 £452.63.
Owner G H & S Leggott **Bred** G H And Simon Leggott **Trained** Middleham Moor, N Yorks

FOCUS
Moderate handicap form but a fair gallop and the form looks sound despite the third being out of the handicap.
T/Jkpt: Not won. T/Plt: £1,304.90 to a £1 stake. Pool: £96,355.15. 53.90 winning tickets. T/Qpdt: £755.20 to a £1 stake. Pool: £5,817.20. 5.70 winning tickets. JR

4926 - 4928a (Foreign Racing) - See Raceform Interactive

4869 BADEN-BADEN (L-H)
Tuesday, August 28

OFFICIAL GOING: Good

4929a DARELY OETTINGEN-RENNEN (GROUP 2) 1m
3:55 (4:00) 3-Y-O+ **£37,162** (£13,514; £6,757; £3,378)

RPR
1 **Mi Emma (GER)**[30] 4010 3-8-6 ABoschert 1 111
(A Wohler, Germany) *mde all: rdn 1f out: comf* **9/10**[1]
2 2 **Soldier Hollow**[30] 4013 7-9-7 AStarke 2 116
(P Schiergen, Germany) *racd in 2nd thrght: no imp on wnr fr over 1f out* **13/10**[2]
3 2 1/2 **Konig Turf (GER)**[23] 4217 5-9-1 TMundry 5 105
(C Sprengel, Germany) *racd in 3rd thrght: kpt on at one pce fnl 1 1/2f* **63/10**[3]
4 5 **Indochine (BRZ)**[30] 4012 4-8-10 ASuborics 4 90
(A De Royer-Dupre, France) *hld up in last: rdn and unable qck 2f out: wnt modest 4th over 1f out* **78/10**
5 7 **Imonso (GER)**[24] 4-9-1 THellier 3 81
(J Hirschberger, Germany) *racd in 4th: rdn 2f out: sn btn* **87/10**

1m 36.2s (-2.91)
WFA 3 from 4yo+ 6lb **5 Ran SP% 131.5**
PARI-MUTUEL (including 10 Euro stake): WIN 19; PL 12, 12; SF 29.
Owner Rennstall Darboven **Bred** Gestut Idee **Trained** Germany

4378 AYR (L-H)
Wednesday, August 29

OFFICIAL GOING: Good to firm (good in places; 7.7)
Wind: Breezy, half against

4930 COKE ZERO EUROPEAN BREEDERS' FUND MAIDEN STKS 7f 50y
2:30 (2:31) (Class 5) 2-Y-O **£4,210** (£1,252; £625; £312) **Stalls** Low

Form RPR
2 **1** **Dubai Time**[14] 4487 2-9-3 0 NCallan 1 83+
(K A Ryan) *pressed ldr: led gng wl over 2f out: shkn up and drew clr fr over 1f out: readily* **8/13**[1]
24 **2** 4 **Harrison George (IRE)**[11] 4611 2-9-3 0 PaulHanagan 9 70
(R A Fahey) *in tch: effrt over 2f out: chsd wnr over 1f out: kpt on: no imp* **9/1**[3]
3 3 **Pearl Trader (IRE)** 2-8-12 0 GregFairley 3 58+
(M Johnston) *prom: pushed along over 2f out: no imp over 1f out* **6/1**[2]
32 **4** 1/2 **Prince Kalamoun (IRE)**[12] 4578 2-9-3 0 PatCosgrave 4 61
(G A Swinbank) *chsd ldrs: edgd lft and chsd wnr over 2f out to over 1f out: sn no ex* **11/1**
06 **5** 3 **Livvy Inn (USA)**[14] 4495 2-9-3 0 DaleGibson 10 54
(Miss Lucinda V Russell) *s.i.s: rdn 3f out: nvr able to chal* **100/1**
55 **6** 1 **Howards Hope**[18] 4378 2-9-3 0 TomEaves 6 51
(I Semple) *towards rr: rdn 3f out: sn btn* **100/1**
0 **7** 3 1/2 **Terracos Do Pinhal**[35] 3842 2-9-3 0 PaulMulrennan 5 43
(M Johnston) *led to over 2f out: wknd over 1f out* **20/1**

1m 32.59s (-0.13) **Going Correction** -0.075s/f (Good) **7 Ran SP% 101.3**
Speed ratings (Par 94): **97,92,89,88,85 83,79**
CSF £4.76 TOTE £1.30: £1.30, £2.10; EX 4.40.
Owner Mrs M Forsyth, Hillen & Walsh **Bred** W And R Barnett Ltd **Trained** Hambleton, N Yorks
■ Mangham (7/1, reared over in stalls) & World Tour (28/1, upset in stalls) withdrawn. R4 applies, deduct 10p in the £.

FOCUS
Little strength in depth with just a fair pace and the level dictated by the fifth and sixth, but a decent performance from the winner, who should be able to hold his own in slightly better company.

NOTEBOOK
Dubai Time, who created a favourable impression on his debut at Beverley, bettered that effort with a fluent display. Although he had the rub of things in a race lacking strength, he impressed with the way he went about his business and he looks up to holding his own in stronger company. (op Evens)
Harrison George(IRE), not the most fluent of movers, had shown ability on his two previous starts and he again ran his race upped to this more suitable trip. He looks a good guide to the worth of this form, should stay 1m and is capable of picking up an ordinary event. (op 8-1)
Pearl Trader(IRE), a 200,000gns first foal of an Irish Oaks winner, is a leggy, unfurnished type and, although showing ability on this racecourse debut, she left the impression that a stiffer test of stamina would have been in her favour. She is entitled to improve for the experience and is likely to do better over middle distances in due course. (op 4-1 tchd 13-2)
Prince Kalamoun(IRE) had shown ability at an ordinary level on his two previous starts and he probably ran to a similar level in this better event. He is in good hands and may be seen to best effect in ordinary nursery company. (op 16-1)
Livvy Inn(USA) bettered the form of his two previous starts but this is modest form at best and he is likely to continue to look vulnerable in this type of event. (op 150-1 tchd 200-1)
Howards Hope was again below the form he showed on his debut but is now qualified for a handicap mark and may do better in ordinary nursery company.
Terracos Do Pinhal, well beaten in soft ground on his debut, took the eye in the paddock on this first run on a sound surface but he again proved a disappointment. However, given his physique and his connections, he would not be one to write off just yet. Official explanation: jockey said colt hung right-handed throughout (op 16-1)

4931 BLACK BOTTLE WHISKY H'CAP 7f 50y
3:00 (3:01) (Class 6) (0-65,63) 3-Y-O+ **£2,590** (£770; £385; £192) **Stalls** Low

Form RPR
6061 **1** **Joshua's Gold (IRE)**[12] 4562 6-9-12 63 (v) StephenDonohoe 2 72
(D Carroll) *prom: effrt 2f out: led ins fnl f: hld on wl* **6/1**[2]
0465 **2** shd **Spinning**[4] 4822 4-9-7 58 (b) PhillipMakin 4 67
(T D Barron) *midfield: effrt whn nt clr run over 2f out to over 1f out: edgd rt and kpt on wl fnl f: jst hld* **5/1**[1]
3511 **3** 1/2 **Kirkby's Treasure**[17] 4427 9-9-10 61 PatCosgrave 14 68
(G A Swinbank) *in tch: effrt over 2f out: kpt on fnl f: no ex towards fin* **8/1**

0215 **4** *nk* **Esoterica (IRE)**[19] 4353 4-9-6 **62**..............................(b) GaryBartley(5) 11 69
(J S Goldie) *bhd: pushed along over 2f out: gd hdwy fnl f: nrst fin* **13/2**[3]

0244 **5** *1* **Smart Pick**[23] 4223 4-8-12 **52**.............................. LiamJones(3) 12 56
(Mrs L Williamson) *s.i.s: bhd tl hdwy 2f out: kpt on: no imp wl ins fnl f* **33/1**

2433 **6** *1 3/4* **Another Genepi (USA)**[16] 4462 4-9-12 **63**..............................(b) NCallan 1 62
(K A Ryan) *led to ins fnl f: sn btn* **5/1**[1]

5-04 **7** *1* **Mineral Rights (USA)**[68] 2829 3-9-4 **60**.............................. TomEaves 7 54
(I Semple) *hld up: effrt over 2f out: kpt on fnl f: no imp* **25/1**

2220 **8** *hd* **Five Wishes**[15] 4480 3-9-3 **59**.............................. PaulMulrennan 3 53
(M Dods) *t.k.h: cl up tl rdn and no ex appr fnl f* **22/1**

4066 **9** *shd* **Hit's Only Money (IRE)**[7] 4706 7-9-2 **53**.............................. DaleGibson 10 49
(J S Goldie) *hld up: shkn up 2f out: nvr nrr* **16/1**

-066 **10** *1* **Redwood Rocks (IRE)**[15] 4477 6-9-9 **60**.............................. RoystonFfrench 8 53
(B Smart) *chsd ldrs tl rdn and wknd wl over 1f out* **6/1**[2]

2200 **11** *1* **Milson's Point (IRE)**[18] 4381 3-9-2 **58**.............................. GregFairley 13 46
(I Semple) *midfield: drvn over 2f out: sn outpcd* **33/1**

0050 **12** *3/4* **Crosby Vision**[7] 4704 4-9-12 **63**.............................. RichardMullen 6 51
(J R Weymes) *prom: effrt over 2f out: wknd over 1f out* **12/1**

4002 **13** *1/2* **Wisdom's Kiss**[23] 4223 3-9-1 **57**..............................(b) PaulHanagan 5 42
(J D Bethell) *t.k.h: chsd ldr tl wknd 2f out* **16/1**

1m 32.7s (-0.02) **Going Correction** -0.075s/f (Good)
WFA 3 from 4yo+ 5lb **13 Ran SP% 119.9**
Speed ratings (Par 101): **97,96,96,95,94 92,91,91,91,90 89,88,87**
CSF £34.62 CT £251.36 TOTE £7.80: £3.20, £2.20, £2.60; EX 48.00.
Owner Andy Helm, Simon Bean, David Jones **Bred** M G Masterson **Trained** Sledmere, E Yorks
FOCUS
A modest handicap in which the pace was soon sound. Solid form for the grade.
Redwood Rocks(IRE) Official explanation: jockey said gelding hung right-handed throughout

4932 WOODFORD RESERVE H'CAP 1m
3:30 (3:30) (Class 4) (0-80,80) 3-Y-0+ **£5,829** (£1,734; £866; £432) **Stalls** Low

Form RPR
0-60 **1** **Abbondanza (IRE)**[60] 3093 4-9-1 **68**..............................(p) TomEaves 8 75
(I Semple) *t.k.h: pressed ldr: led over 2f out: hrd pressed fnl f: hld on wl* **20/1**

2022 **2** *shd* **Society Music (IRE)**[19] 4353 5-9-4 **71**..............................(p) PhillipMakin 3 78
(M Dods) *prom: effrt 2f out: disp ld 1f out: kpt on wl: jst hld* **7/1**[3]

2312 **3** *3/4* **Bolton Hall (IRE)**[4] 4797 5-8-10 **63**..............................(p) PaulHanagan 2 68
(R A Fahey) *missed break: hld up: rdn over 2f out: r.o wl fnl f: jst hld* **7/2**[2]

3146 **4** *nk* **Champain Sands (IRE)**[4] 4820 8-8-13 **66**.............................. StephenDonohoe 5 71
(E J Alston) *hld up: rdn 2f out: kpt on fnl f: nrst fin* **7/1**[3]

-0S5 **5** *shd* **Isidore Bonheur (IRE)**[7] 4716 6-9-13 **80**.............................. NCallan 1 84
(G A Swinbank) *s.i.s: hld up in tch: effrt over 2f out: kpt on fnl f* **10/3**[1]

6024 **6** *1/2* **Shy Glance (USA)**[7] 4716 5-9-0 **70**.............................. MarkLawson(3) 6 73
(P Monteith) *prom: effrt over 2f out: kpt on same pce fnl f* **7/2**[2]

1002 **7** *nk* **Kenmore**[12] 4581 5-9-9 **76**.............................. RoystonFfrench 4 79
(J G Given) *hld up in tch: effrt over 2f out: no imp fnl f* **9/1**

/24- **8** *1 1/2* **Wind Shuffle (GER)**[330] 5761 4-8-6 **62** ow2.............................. GaryBartley(5) 7 63
(J S Goldie) *led to over 2f out: rallied: wknd fnl f* **20/1**

1m 42.01s (-1.48) **Going Correction** -0.075s/f (Good) **8 Ran SP% 112.0**
Speed ratings (Par 105): **104,103,103,102,102 102,101,100**
CSF £145.37 CT £614.94 TOTE £19.60: £3.90, £2.40, £1.30; EX 129.40.
Owner Joseph Leckie & Sons Ltd **Bred** M Nolan **Trained** Carluke, S Lanarks
FOCUS
An ordinary handicap in which the pace was fair but those held up were at a disadvantage. They finished in a bunch and the form is only moderate, if fairly sound.
Shy Glance(USA) Official explanation: jockey said race may have come too soon

4933 MORGANS SPICED RUM H'CAP 1m 2f
4:00 (4:02) (Class 4) (0-85,82) 3-Y-0+
£6,855 (£2,052; £1,026; £513; £256; £128) **Stalls** Low

Form RPR
2-53 **1** **King Of Rhythm (IRE)**[21] 4282 4-9-0 **68**.............................. NCallan 4 72
(D Carroll) *t.k.h: prom: effrt over 2f out: led ins fnl f: kpt on wl* **7/1**

153 **2** *3/4* **Just Lille (IRE)**[10] 4637 4-10-0 **82**..............................(p) RoystonFfrench 8 84
(Mrs A Duffield) *set stdy pce: rdn over 2f out: hdd ins fnl f: r.o same pce* **7/2**[2]

0260 **3** *1 1/4* **Pianoforte (USA)**[4] 4820 5-8-9 **63** oh6.............................. StephenDonohoe 3 63
(E J Alston) *dwlt: hld up: rdn over 2f out: hdwy over 1f out: kpt on: nt rch first two* **20/1**

2153 **4** *1* **Neil's Legacy (IRE)**[5] 4772 5-8-12 **66**.............................. GregFairley 6 64
(Miss L A Perratt) *chsd ldrs: effrt and ev ch over 1f out: no ex ins fnl f* **9/4**[1]

0105 **5** *hd* **Toshi (USA)**[83] 2391 5-8-11 **65**.............................. PhillipMakin 2 62
(P Monteith) *in tch: effrt 2f out: no imp fnl f* **6/1**

0311 **6** *1/2* **Hawkit (USA)**[14] 4497 6-9-6 **74**.............................. DaleGibson 7 70
(P Monteith) *t.k.h: cl up tl rdn and no ex over 1f out* **6/1**

0020 **7** *2 1/2* **Regent's Secret (USA)**[7] 4716 7-9-7 **75**.............................. PaulHanagan 5 66
(J S Goldie) *s.i.s: hld up: rdn over 2f out: n.d* **11/2**[3]

2m 14.35s (2.63) **Going Correction** -0.075s/f (Good) **7 Ran SP% 114.2**
Speed ratings (Par 105): **86,85,84,83,83 83,81**
CSF £31.50 CT £467.75 TOTE £7.50: £2.70, £1.90; EX 31.80.
Owner Miss C King **Bred** Illuminatus Investments **Trained** Sledmere, E Yorks
FOCUS
Few progressive sorts and the steady pace means this bare form may not be entirely reliable. The third was out of the weights which further holds down the form.

4934 MACLACHLAN'S BEST H'CAP 6f
4:30 (4:30) (Class 5) (0-70,75) 3-Y-0+ **£2,914** (£867; £433; £216) **Stalls** Low

Form RPR
0614 **1** **Ellens Academy (IRE)**[12] 4583 12-9-5 **70**.............................. GaryBartley(5) 3 77+
(E J Alston) *hld up: hdwy over 1f out: led ins fnl f: comf* **6/1**[3]

5006 **2** *1 1/4* **Oeuf A La Neige**[7] 4719 7-8-5 **51** oh4.............................. RichardMullen 5 54
(Miss L A Perratt) *in tch: effrt and hdwy over 1f out: chsd wnr wl ins fnl f: r.o* **10/1**

4021 **3** *1 1/4* **John Keats**[12] 4583 4-9-8 **68**.............................. PaulHanagan 2 67
(J S Goldie) *chsd ldrs: effrt and ch ins fnl f: kpt on same pce* **9/4**[1]

1044 **4** *1/2* **Charles Parnell (IRE)**[2] 4895 4-9-10 **70**.............................. PhillipMakin 4 67
(M Dods) *prom: effrt over 1f out: kpt on same pce fnl f* **5/2**[2]

-004 **5** *nk* **Indian Spark**[18] 4379 13-8-4 **55**.............................. KellyHarrison(5) 6 51
(J S Goldie) *hld up bhd ldng gp: effrt over 1f out: no imp fnl f* **14/1**

000 **6** *hd* **Seafield Towers**[5] 4773 7-8-6 **52** oh4 ow1..............(p) PaulMulrennan 10 48
(Miss L A Perratt) *led to ins fnl f: sn no ex* **25/1**

4033 **7** *2* **Cassie's Choice (IRE)**[9] 4658 3-9-4 **67**.............................. RoystonFfrench 1 56
(B Smart) *w ldr tl wknd over 1f out* **10/1**

6550 **8** *3 1/2* **Prospect Place**[34] 3885 3-9-6 **69**.............................. TomEaves 9 47
(M Dods) *hld up: drvn over 2f out: btn fnl f* **9/1**

-000 **9** *10* **Pays D'Amour (IRE)**[47] 3498 10-8-5 **51** oh6..................(tp) GregFairley 7 —
(D A Nolan) *prom tl wknd fr over 2f out* **125/1**

1m 12.16s (-1.51) **Going Correction** -0.225s/f (Firm)
WFA 3 from 4yo+ 3lb **9 Ran SP% 113.1**
Speed ratings (Par 103): **101,99,97,97,96 96,93,89,75**
CSF £62.57 CT £173.37 TOTE £9.20: £2.20, £2.40, £1.30; EX 68.10.
Owner K Lee And I Davies **Bred** Mrs Chris Harrington **Trained** Longton, Lancs
FOCUS
A run-of-the-mill sprint in which the field raced far side (stalls on that side). The pace was sound throughout. Modest form.

4935 TENNENTS LAGER H'CAP 5f
5:00 (5:00) (Class 6) (0-65,65) 3-Y-0 **£2,730** (£806; £403) **Stalls** Low

Form RPR
3462 **1** **Comptonspirit**[9] 4661 3-9-0 **58**..............................(p) PaulMulrennan 5 72
(B P J Baugh) *w ldr: led 2f out: rdn and r.o strly* **11/2**[3]

3634 **2** *1 3/4* **Princess Ellis**[25] 4158 3-9-0 **58**.............................. StephenDonohoe 11 66
(E J Alston) *led to 2f out: edgd lft: kpt on u.p fnl f* **4/1**[1]

4430 **3** *1 3/4* **Jojesse**[12] 4561 3-8-11 **55**.............................. PatCosgrave 6 57
(G A Swinbank) *midfield: rdn 1/2-way: hdwy over 1f out: r.o fnl f: nrst fin* **9/1**

0644 **4** *nk* **Beechside (IRE)**[18] 4384 3-8-2 **46** oh1.............................. DaleGibson 3 47
(W A Murphy, Ire) *s.i.s: bhd tl hdwy over 1f out: kpt on fnl f: no imp* **20/1**

2423 **5** *nk* **By The Edge (IRE)**[9] 4661 3-8-8 **52**.............................. PhillipMakin 9 52
(T D Barron) *in tch: drvn and outpcd 1/2-way: kpt on u.p fnl f* **5/1**[2]

0106 **6** *nk* **Rann Na Cille (IRE)**[7] 4714 3-9-7 **65**..............................(b[1]) NCallan 7 63
(K A Ryan) *cl up: rdn 2f out: no ex fnl f* **10/1**

301 **7** *nk* **Midnight Sky**[4] 4795 3-8-7 **51** 6ex.............................. RichardMullen 4 48
(Rae Guest) *prom: drvn 1/2-way: rallied: no ex appr fnl f* **4/1**[1]

-000 **8** *2 1/2* **Warm Tribute (USA)**[36] 3811 3-8-3 **47**.............................. PaulHanagan 8 35
(J S Goldie) *hld up: pushed along 1/2-way: n.d* **10/1**

3063 **9** *1* **Kilvickeon (IRE)**[13] 4536 3-7-13 **46** oh1.............................. LiamJones(3) 10 31
(Peter Grayson) *in tch: drvn 1/2-way: btn fnl f* **17/2**

0000 **10** *1 3/4* **Whats Your Game (IRE)**[18] 4384 3-7-11 **46** oh1........ KellyHarrison(5) 2 24
(A Berry) *bhd: struggling 1/2-way: n.d* **100/1**

5450 **11** *2* **Dotty's Daughter**[44] 3588 3-8-3 **47**..............................(p) RoystonFfrench 1 18
(Mrs A Duffield) *chsd ldrs: outpcd 1/2-way: sn btn* **20/1**

59.43 secs (-1.01) **Going Correction** -0.225s/f (Firm) **11 Ran SP% 121.3**
Speed ratings (Par 98): **99,96,93,92,92 91,91,87,85,83 79**
CSF £28.15 CT £204.23 TOTE £8.40: £2.70, £1.70, £3.10; EX 35.80.
Owner G B Hignett **Bred** Mrs F Wilson **Trained** Audley, Staffs
FOCUS
Another ordinary event but one in which the pace was sound throughout. Improved form from the winner, but the runner-up is a better guide.
Midnight Sky Official explanation: trainer's rep said filly lost a near-hind shoe
Warm Tribute(USA) Official explanation: jockey said gelding hung right-handed throughout
Whats Your Game(IRE) Official explanation: jockey said saddle slipped

4936 MAGNERS IRISH CIDER H'CAP 1m 2f
5:30 (5:32) (Class 6) (0-65,65) 3-Y-0 **£3,238** (£963; £481; £240) **Stalls** Low

Form RPR
-602 **1** **Zain (IRE)**[10] 4641 3-8-2 **46** oh1..............................(t) RoystonFrench 6 51+
(J G Given) *in tch: outpcd and lost pl 1/2-way: rallied 2f out: led ins fnl f: drvn out* **5/2**[1]

4060 **2** *nk* **Caviar Heights (IRE)**[17] 4424 3-8-4 **48** oh1 ow2............(b) GregFairley 4 52
(Miss L A Perratt) *s.i.s: sn prom: effrt over 2f out: ev ch ins fnl f: hld nr fin* **25/1**

0650 **3** *3/4* **Jane Of Arc (FR)**[12] 4579 3-8-5 **54**.............................. GaryBartley(5) 2 57
(J S Goldie) *cl up: led 1/2-way: rdn over 1f out: hdd ins fnl f: kpt on same pce* **12/1**

-040 **4** *3* **Peintre's Wonder (IRE)**[41] 3677 3-9-6 **64**.............................. RichardMullen 9 61
(E J O'Neill) *bhd: pushed along 1/2-way: hdwy outside 2f out: edgd lft and sn no imp* **7/1**

1005 **5** *3* **Skye But N Ben**[25] 4155 3-8-8 **59**..............................(b) DeanHeslop(7) 5 50
(T D Barron) *in tch: drvn over 3f out: no imp fr 2f out* **11/1**

0060 **6** *5* **Chookie Hamilton**[57] 3181 3-9-7 **65**..............................(p) TomEaves 7 46
(I Semple) *hld up: rdn 3f out: no imp fr 2f out* **12/1**

0116 **7** *nk* **Kiss Chase (IRE)**[18] 4382 3-9-2 **60**.............................. PaulHanagan 8 40
(J S Goldie) *in tch: rdn over 2f out: sn btn* **9/1**

5433 **8** *hd* **Grethel (IRE)**[2] 4902 3-8-4 **55**.............................. AdamCarter(7) 13 35
(A Berry) *midfield on outside: rdn over 2f out: sn btn* **12/1**

4066 **9** *nk* **Heaven's Gates**[2] 4902 3-8-8 **52**.............................. NCallan 12 31
(K A Ryan) *cl up: effrt over 3f out: wknd 2f out: eased whn no ch* **11/2**[3]

2365 **10** *4* **News Of The Day (IRE)**[14] 4499 3-9-2 **63**.............................. MarkLawson(3) 3 34
(P Monteith) *led to 1/2-way: cl up tl wknd fr 2f out* **5/1**[2]

2m 9.99s (-1.73) **Going Correction** -0.075s/f (Good) **10 Ran SP% 118.4**
Speed ratings (Par 98): **103,102,102,99,97 93,93,92,92,89**
CSF £75.04 CT £650.05 TOTE £2.80: £1.40, £6.00, £4.00; EX 64.40 Place 6 £94.94, Place 5 £74.03..
Owner Mrs G A Jennings **Bred** Mick McGinn And James Waldron **Trained** Willoughton, Lincs
FOCUS
A low-grade handicap in which the pace was sound and the time relatively quick. The front three pulled clear of the remainder, with the winner taking advantage of being well-in.
T/Jkpt: Not won. T/Plt: £66.60 to a £1 stake. Pool: £71,678.30. 784.75 winning tickets. T/Qpdt: £36.90 to a £1 stake. Pool: £3,207.90. 64.30 winning tickets. RY

4558 CATTERICK (L-H)
Wednesday, August 29

OFFICIAL GOING: Good to firm (8.6)
Wind: Virtually nil Weather: Fine and sunny

4937 OUSE MEDIAN AUCTION MAIDEN STKS 5f
2:20 (2:21) (Class 6) 2-Y-0 **£2,730** (£806; £403) **Stalls** Low

Form RPR
430 **1** **Van Bossed (CAN)**[12] 4578 2-9-3 **77**..............................(t) SilvestreDeSousa 5 84+
(D Nicholls) *dwlt and in rr: rapid hdwy to join ldr 1/2-way: rdn to ld over 1f out: kpt on wl* **7/2**[2]

254 **2** *2 1/2* **Grudge**[25] 4175 2-9-3 **68**.............................. TonyHamilton 2 71
(D W Barker) *led: rdn along 2f out: hdd over 1f out: kpt on same pce* **8/1**

3322 **3** *1 1/2* **Wotashirtfull (IRE)**[16] 4447 2-9-0 **79**.............................. AndrewMullen(3) 4 66
(K A Ryan) *trckd ldr: unbalanced and outpcd whn pce qcknd 1/2-way: sn rdn and kpt on same pce* **4/6**[1]

524 4 3/4 **Red Wings (IRE)**[13] 4522 2-8-9 72................................ PJMcDonald(3) 1 58
(G A Swinbank) *dwlt: sn trcking ldr: effrt 2f out: sn rdn along and wknd fr wl: over 1f out* **5/1**[3]

00 5 10 **Presidium Star**[10] 4636 2-8-9 0.................................... AndrewElliott(3) 3 22
(G M Moore) *s.i.s: a in rr: bhd fr 1/2-way* **80/1**

59.97 secs (-0.63) **Going Correction** -0.225s/f (Firm) **5** Ran SP% **111.2**
Speed ratings (Par 92): **96,92,89,88,72**
CSF £28.23 TOTE £5.80: £2.70, £3.00; EX 32.40.

Owner Mike & Maureen Browne **Bred** Bernard And Karen McCormack **Trained** Sessay, N Yorks

FOCUS
Not a bad maiden and the winner could be useful. The runner-up, however, appeared to run his race and could be the marker to the race.

NOTEBOOK
Van Bossed(CAN), taking a fairly big drop in trip and wearing a tongue tie for the first time, did not make the greatest of starts but came home strongly in the last two furlongs to win very nicely, still looking a bit green under pressure. He looks sure to make progress again and he will get 6f. (tchd 10-3, tchd 4-1 in places)

Grudge shows plenty of pace and did not quite get home as well as the winner did. He has shown more than enough form to suggest a small sprint race is within his scope. (op 9-1)

Wotashirtfull(IRE), a nice, big sort, once again managed to get placed without looking likely to win. There was a very small hint that he could have a few quirks under pressure. Official explanation: jockey said colt was unsuited by the track (op 8-11, tchd 5-6 in places)

Red Wings(IRE), who was entered in a seller the next day, did not really get involved and probably does not warrant her current mark. (op 9-2 tchd 11-2)

Presidium Star continued her poor record on the track with an uninspiring effort.

4938 WEATHERBYS BLOODSTOCK INSURANCE MAIDEN STKS 5f 212y
2:50 (2:56) (Class 5) 3-Y-0+ **£3,238** (£963; £481; £240) **Stalls** Low

Form RPR

2332 1 **Wolf River (USA)**[25] 4182 3-9-3 75.................................... SebSanders 5 72+
(D M Simcock) *trckd ldr: hdwy to ld over 1f out: pushed out* **4/11**[1]

-553 2 2 **Takanewa (IRE)**[51] 3372 4-8-10 48.................................... NeilBrown(5) 9 61
(J Howard Johnson) *led: rdn along 2f out: sn drvn and hdd over 1f out: kpt on same pce* **12/1**[3]

0043 3 6 **Nans Lady (IRE)**[13] 4545 4-9-1 63.................................... ChrisCatlin 6 42
(E J O'Neill) *chsd ldrs: pushed along and outpcd 3f out: styd on u.p appr fnl f: n.d* **7/2**[2]

50-0 4 hd **Swallow Senora (IRE)**[90] 2187 5-8-8 38.................... CharlotteKerton(7) 1 41
(M C Chapman) *chsd ldng pair: rdn along over 2f out: sn one pce* **200/1**

0 5 2 1/2 **Champagne Sue**[11] 4616 3-8-12 0.................................... TonyHamilton 3 33
(D W Barker) *in tch: rdn along 1/2-way: sn no hdwy* **66/1**

0200 6 1/2 **River Club**[7] 4706 3-9-0 57.................................... PJMcDonald(3) 12 36
(G A Swinbank) *a towards rr* **16/1**

0-50 7 5 **Mystic**[86] 2300 3-8-9 45.................................... AndrewMullen(3) 7 15
(D W Barker) *s.i.s: a in rr* **50/1**

000 8 4 **My Maite Mickey**[26] 4141 3-9-3 40....................................(v) PaulEddery 2 8
(R C Guest) *sn chsng ldrs: rdn along over 2f out and sn wknd* **50/1**

000 9 6 **Flying Princess (IRE)**[31] 3994 3-8-12 33.......................... PaddyAspell 11 —
(A Berry) *sn outpcd and bhd* **200/1**

0 10 2 1/2 **Rita Petite**[9] 4659 3-8-5 0.................................... DanielleMcCreery(7) 10 —
(D W Chapman) *s.i.s: a bhd* **200/1**

1m 13.19s (-0.81) **Going Correction** -0.05s/f (Good)
WFA 3 from 4yo+ 3lb **10** Ran SP% **116.0**
Speed ratings (Par 103): **103,100,92,92,88 88,81,76,68,64**
CSF £6.56 TOTE £1.40: £1.02, £2.10, £1.10; EX 5.70.

Owner The Anglo Americans **Bred** Liberation Farm & Cho Llc **Trained** Newmarket, Suffolk

FOCUS
A very moderate maiden won by a horse that should have bolted up. The proximity of the fourth is more worrying than the second.

4939 DERWENT H'CAP 5f
3:20 (3:24) (Class 6) (0-65,61) 3-Y-0+ **£2,730** (£806; £403) **Stalls** Low

Form RPR

4261 1 **Toy Top (USA)**[5] 4787 4-9-0 57....................................(b) NeilBrown(5) 4 67
(M Dods) *cl up: pushed along 2f out: sn rdn and styd on to ld ins fnl f: kpt on* **5/4**[1]

6423 2 1/2 **Blackheath (IRE)**[9] 4668 11-8-12 50.......................... SilvestreDeSousa 7 58
(D Nicholls) *chsd ldrs: rdn 2f out: kpt on u.p ins fnl f* **6/1**[3]

-400 3 nk **Trombone Tom**[12] 4561 4-8-4 45.................................... AndrewMullen(3) 3 52
(J R Norton) *cl up: rdn to ld wl over 1f out: drvn and hdd ins fnl f: no ex towards fin* **33/1**

0630 4 1/2 **Northern Chorus (IRE)**[4] 4822 4-9-1 60..............(v) JamesO'Reilly(7) 12 65+
(J O'Reilly) *sltly hmpd s and towards rr: hdwy on outer 1/2-way: sn rdn and styd on ins fnl f: nrst fin* **14/1**

0002 5 hd **Miacarla**[5] 4787 4-8-11 49.................................... LeeEnstone 2 53
(A Berry) *t.k.h: trckd ldrs: effrt 2f out and ev ch tl rdn and nt qckn ent fnl f* **8/1**

030 6 1/2 **Talcen Gwyn (IRE)**[8] 4689 5-9-8 60.................................... ChrisCatlin 1 63
(M F Harris) *led: rdn along and hdd wl over 1f out: one pce* **11/2**[2]

0040 7 nk **Sharp Hat**[5] 4773 13-8-3 48.................................... DanielleMcCreery(7) 14 50+
(D W Chapman) *wnt rt s and in rr: hdwy and rdn along 2f out: kpt on u.p ins fnl f: nrst fin* **50/1**

5050 8 3/4 **Jun Fan (USA)**[5] 4773 5-8-8 48 ow1......................(tp) JamieMoriarty(3) 8 48
(B Ellison) *dwlt: a in midfield* **14/1**

0500 9 hd **Stanley Wolfe (IRE)**[5] 4768 4-8-7 45.................................... PaulEddery 6 43
(Garry Moss) *chsd ldrs: rdn along 1/2-way: sn one pce* **40/1**

2605 10 1 **Bollin Franny**[38] 3763 3-9-6 60....................................(e) GrahamGibbons 10 55
(T D Easterby) *wnt rt s: chsd ldrs: rdn along over 2f out: grad wknd* **20/1**

0100 11 1/2 **Stir Crazy (IRE)**[2] 4896 3-9-5 59.................................... TPO'Shea 9 52
(M R Channon) *dwlt: a towards rr* **20/1**

0600 12 3/4 **Minimum Fuss (IRE)**[56] 3203 3-8-0 47.................. CharlotteKerton(7) 11 37
(M C Chapman) *hmpd s: a in rr* **100/1**

0000 13 3 1/2 **Navigation (IRE)**[69] 2791 5-8-4 45..........................(v) AndrewElliott(3) 13 22
(T J Etherington) *sltly hmpd s: a in rr* **33/1**

59.96 secs (-0.64) **Going Correction** -0.225s/f (Firm)
WFA 3 from 4yo+ 2lb **13** Ran SP% **119.4**
Speed ratings (Par 101): **96,95,94,93,93 92,92,91,90,89 88,87,81**
CSF £7.84 CT £170.63 TOTE £2.00: £1.10, £2.20, £6.80; EX 11.20 Trifecta £285.50 Part won. Pool £402.20 - 0.30 winning units..

Owner D Vic Roper **Bred** L Kengye **Trained** Denton, Co Durham

■ Stewards' Enquiry : Lee Enstone six-day ban: dropped hands and lost fourth place (Sep 9-14)

FOCUS
A modest-looking handicap at best. Straightforward form.

4940 WEATHERBYS FINANCE H'CAP 7f
3:50 (3:52) (Class 4) (0-80,77) 3-Y-0 **£5,181** (£1,541; £770; £384) **Stalls** Low

Form RPR

400 1 **Musical Beat**[12] 4566 3-9-2 77.................................... LukeMorris(5) 6 83
(Miss V Haigh) *trckd ldrs: gd hdwy over 2f out: rdn to ld over 1f out: drvn and edgd lft ins fnl f: eased nr fin* **13/2**[3]

6530 2 3/4 **Flying Valentino**[21] 4291 3-8-13 72.................................... PJMcDonald(3) 1 76
(G A Swinbank) *trckd ldrs on inner: effrt 2f out: sn swtchd rt and rdn: chsng wnr whn drvn and edgd lft ins fnl f: kpt on* **7/1**

5060 3 3/4 **Mundo's Magic**[17] 4425 3-8-10 66....................................(p) SebSanders 3 70+
(G M Moore) *sn cl up: effrt and ev ch 2f out: sn rdn and n.m.r jst ins fnl f: one pce* **16/1**

0050 4 nk **Hart Of Gold**[30] 4024 3-9-2 72.................................... ChrisCatlin 9 73
(M J Wallace) *hld up in rr: hdwy 2f out: rdn to chse ldrs ent fnl f: kpt on same pce* **12/1**

-466 5 1 **Ingleby Princess**[32] 3952 3-9-5 75.................................... PaulFessey 8 73
(T D Barron) *in tch: hdwy to chse ldrs over 2f out: sn rdn and no imp appr fnl f* **7/1**

5334 6 1/2 **Nufoudh (IRE)**[4] 4822 3-8-1 60 ow2.......................... AndrewElliott(3) 7 55
(Miss Tracy Waggott) *hld up in rr: hdwy on inner and nt clr run over 1f out: kpt on one pce* **9/2**[2]

4413 7 hd **Cheery Cat (USA)**[22] 4250 3-8-8 64..........................(p) TonyHamilton 4 61
(D W Barker) *led: rdn along over 2f out: drvn and hdd over 1f out: wknd ent fnl f* **11/4**[1]

1-40 8 3 1/2 **Tarraburn (USA)**[28] 4080 3-8-11 72.................................... NeilBrown(5) 5 59
(J Howard Johnson) *prom tl rdn along over 2f out and sn wknd* **10/1**

041- 9 16 **Messiah Garvey**[257] 6826 3-9-6 76.................................... TPO'Shea 2 20
(M R Channon) *chsd ldrs: rdn over 2f out and sn wknd* **15/2**

1m 26.41s (-0.95) **Going Correction** -0.05s/f (Good) **9** Ran SP% **117.6**
Speed ratings (Par 102): **103,102,101,100,99 99,99,95,76**
CSF £52.25 CT £708.49 TOTE £9.50: £3.20, £1.80, £3.80; EX 69.10.

Owner R J Budge **Bred** Juddmonte Farms Ltd **Trained** Wiseton, Notts

■ Stewards' Enquiry : Luke Morris three-day ban: careless riding (Sep 9-11)

FOCUS
A modest three-year-old handicap. The first four were closely covered at the finish, but the easing winner is value for plenty further than her winning margin. The form is rated through the fourth.

Nufoudh(IRE) Official explanation: jockey said gelding was denied a clear run

4941 SWALE H'CAP 1m 7f 177y
4:20 (4:21) (Class 5) (0-75,70) 3-Y-0+ **£3,412** (£1,007; £504) **Stalls** Low

Form RPR

1421 1 **Atlantic Coast (IRE)**[12] 4576 3-8-7 63..........................(v) SebSanders 1 73+
(M Johnston) *trckd ldng pair: hdwy 6f out: led over 3f out: rdn clr over 1f out: styd on* **1/2**[1]

0-05 2 3 **Young Scotton**[20] 4333 7-8-9 54 oh1.................................... AndrewElliott(3) 7 57
(J D Bethell) *hld up towards rr: hdwy 4f out: rdn along over 2f out: kpt on u.p appr fnl f* **28/1**

-656 3 hd **Parchment (IRE)**[14] 4493 5-8-13 55.................................... PaddyAspell 2 58
(A J Lockwood) *hld up in rr: hdwy 3f out: rdn along on outer wl over 1f out: styd on* **8/1**[3]

6505 4 nk **Square Dealer**[18] 4409 6-8-7 54 oh8..........................(b) NeilBrown(5) 8 56
(J R Norton) *hld up: hdwy 4f out: rdn to chse wnr over 2f out: sn drvn and wknd ins fnl f* **33/1**

3534 5 2 **Let It Be**[18] 4409 6-8-12 54 oh2.................................... KDarley 5 54
(K G Reveley) *trckd ldrs: effrt 3f out: rdn along over 2f out: drvn over 1f out and kpt on same pce* **5/1**[2]

4326 6 5 **Court Of Appeal**[12] 4558 10-9-11 70......................(tp) JamieMoriarty(3) 6 64
(B Ellison) *trckd ldrs: effrt 3f out and sn rdn along: drvn wl over 1f out and sn wknd* **9/1**

6544 7 1 1/2 **Red Sun**[4] 4521 10-8-12 54 oh2....................................(p) PaulEddery 3 46
(R C Guest) *led: rdn along and hdd over 3f out: drvn and wknd 2f out* **16/1**

0000 8 51 **College Rebel**[10] 4638 6-8-12 54 oh9.................................... ChrisCatlin 4 —
(J F Coupland) *chsd ldr: rdn along 1/2-way: sn lost pl and bhd* **100/1**

3m 30.24s (-1.16) **Going Correction** -0.05s/f (Good)
WFA 3 from 5yo+ 14lb **8** Ran SP% **117.7**
Speed ratings (Par 103): **100,98,98,98,97 94,94,68**
CSF £23.58 CT £68.63 TOTE £1.50: £1.10, £5.90, £1.70; EX 23.20.

Owner Atlantic Racing Limited **Bred** Gigginstown House **Trained** Middleham Moor, N Yorks

FOCUS
A moderate staying handicap. Dubious form, but the winner remains progressive although he did not have much to beat.

Let It Be Official explanation: jockey said mare was denied a clear run

4942 NIDD H'CAP 5f 212y
4:50 (4:50) (Class 5) (0-75,68) 3-Y-0+ **£3,238** (£963; £481; £240) **Stalls** Low

Form RPR

2332 1 **Ryedane (IRE)**[4] 4822 5-8-12 59..........................(b) DuranFentiman(3) 6 69
(T D Easterby) *cl up: rdn 2f out: led over 1f out and sn edgd lft: drvn and edgd rt ins fnl f: kpt on* **6/4**[1]

4004 2 1/2 **High Ridge**[5] 4767 8-9-7 65....................................(p) KDarley 3 73
(J M Bradley) *in tch: hdwy 2f out: rdn wl over 1f out: styd on to chal ent fnl f: sn drvn and nt qckn towards fin* **7/1**

2615 3 nk **Inca Soldier (FR)**[12] 4562 4-9-5 63.................................... PaulEddery 2 70
(R C Guest) *led: rdn along over 2f out: drvn and hdd over 1f out: kpt on u.p ins fnl f* **6/1**[3]

2005 4 3/4 **Summer Recluse (USA)**[10] 4634 8-9-0 63..................(t) LukeMorris(5) 8 70+
(J M Bradley) *s.i.s and bhd: hdwy over 2f out: sn rdn and styng on whn n.m.r ins fnl f* **11/1**

-001 5 nk **Hazelhurst (IRE)**[28] 4083 4-9-5 68.................................... NeilBrown(5) 7 72
(J Howard Johnson) *chsd ldrs on outer: effrt 2f out: sn rdn and kpt on u.p ins fnl f* **6/1**[3]

6000 6 1/2 **Mr Rooney (IRE)**[26] 4141 4-9-1 59..........................(t) SilvestreDeSousa 1 61
(D Nicholls) *chsd ldng pair: rdn along over 2f out: drvn and kpt on same pce fr wl over 1f out* **11/1**

0510 7 1 3/4 **Fern House (IRE)**[5] 4773 5-8-8 55.......................... JamieMoriarty(3) 4 51
(Garry Moss) *hld up: effrt 2f out: sn rdn and no imp* **11/2**[2]

1m 13.87s (-0.13) **Going Correction** -0.05s/f (Good) **7** Ran SP% **113.1**
Speed ratings (Par 103): **98,97,96,95,95 94,92**
CSF £12.32 CT £48.49 TOTE £2.20: £1.70, £3.00; EX 11.00.

Owner Ryedale Partners No 5 **Bred** Tally-Ho Stud **Trained** Great Habton, N Yorks

FOCUS
A moderate sprint handicap which saw a tight finish. The form looks straightforward enough, rated through the winner and second.

Summer Recluse(USA) Official explanation: jockey said gelding was denied a clear run inside final furlong

4943 FOSS H'CAP 1m 3f 214y
5:20 (5:21) (Class 6) (0-60,60) 3-Y-O £2,730 (£806; £403) Stalls Low

Form RPR
-405 1 **Sangfroid**[4] 4821 3-8-7 49 ow3 SebSanders 4 53
(Sir Mark Prescott) *in tch: hdwy & niggled along 4f out: rdn to chse ldrs 3f out: drvn to chse ldng pair 2f out & edgd lft: kpt on u.p to ld ins fnl f* 6/5[1]
0004 2 1 1/4 **Bond Casino**[21] 4283 3-8-7 49 GrahamGibbons 9 51
(G R Oldroyd) *chsd ldr: hdwy 3f out: rdn to ld wl over 1f out: drvn and hdd ins fnl f: no ex towards fin* 20/1
2006 3 1 **Sir Sandicliffe (IRE)**[21] 4282 3-8-13 60 LukeMorris(5) 8 60
(W M Brisbourne) *hld up in rr: stdy hdwy on inner 3f out: rdn to chse ldrs over 1f out: sn drvn and kpt on ins fnl f* 16/1
6000 4 hd **The Diamond Bond**[9] 4673 3-8-1 50 oh1 ow4 LanceBetts(7) 3 46
(G R Oldroyd) *hld up and bhd: pushed along 4f out: rdn and hdwy on outer 2f out: styd on under press ins fnl f: nrst fin* 16/1
0140 5 1/2 **Ellies Faith**[13] 4521 3-8-2 47 oh1 ow1 (b) AndrewElliott(3) 14 46
(N Bycroft) *led: rdn along over 3f out: drvn 2f out: sn hdd: wknd ins fnl f* 16/1
-006 6 2 **Bollin Freddie**[43] 3610 3-8-8 50 PaddyAspell 7 46
(A J Lockwood) *hld up: gd hdwy on outer to chse ldrs 1/2-way: rdn along over 2f out: drvn and one pce fr over 1f out* 18/1
0023 7 nk **Black Mogul**[8] 4687 3-8-11 53 (b) ChrisCatlin 12 49
(W R Muir) *chsd ldrs: rdn along 3f out: drvn and wknd fnl 2f* 17/2
U604 8 1 1/4 **Sky Chart (IRE)**[48] 3476 3-9-3 59 TonyHamilton 2 53
(N J Vaughan) *chsd ldrs: rdn over 2f out: sn drvn and wknd over 1f out* 13/2[3]
5446 9 3 **President Dan**[2] 4894 3-8-13 55 TPO'Shea 1 44
(M R Channon) *a towards rr* 4/1[2]
6000 10 10 **All Talk**[20] 4337 3-7-11 46 oh1 AmyBaker(7) 11 23
(M J Gingell) *a towards rr* 100/1
0000 11 hd **Ingleby Hill (IRE)**[4] 4821 3-8-4 46 PaulFessey 6 18
(T D Barron) *in tch: effrt over 3f out: sn rdn along and wknd over 2f out* 33/1
-000 12 28 **Averti Star**[42] 3639 3-8-5 50 AndrewMullen(3) 10 —
(Mrs A Duffield) *a towards rr* 66/1
006 13 1 3/4 **Elizabeth Garrett**[36] 3824 3-8-5 50 DuranFentiman(3) 13 —
(M J Gingell) *midfield: rdn along 5f out: sn lost pl and bhd* 100/1

2m 38.38s (-0.62) **Going Correction** -0.05s/f (Good) 13 Ran SP% 123.4
Speed ratings (Par 98): **100,99,98,98,98 96,96,95,93,87 86,68,67**
CSF £35.74 CT £290.92 TOTE £2.00: £1.30, £5.70, £4.70; EX 36.20 Place 6 £46.19, Place 5 £8.85.
Owner E B Rimmer-Osborne House **Bred** Miss K Rausing **Trained** Newmarket, Suffolk

FOCUS
A weak three-year-old handicap, run at an average pace. The race has been rated negatively, with only the front two in the market offering recent form.
T/Plt: £69.60 to a £1 stake. Pool: £50,364.10. 527.85 winning tickets. T/Qpdt: £12.60 to a £1 stake. Pool: £3,475.00. 203.30 winning tickets. JR

[4882]KEMPTON (A.W) (R-H)
Wednesday, August 29

OFFICIAL GOING: Standard
Wind: very modest across Weather: bright, mainly sunny

4944 MIX BUSINESS WITH PLEASURE H'CAP 5f (P)
2:10 (2:10) (Class 5) (0-70,68) 3-Y-O+ £3,238 (£963; £481; £240) Stalls High

Form RPR
5050 1 **What Do You Know**[30] 4024 4-9-9 68 (b[1]) RichardHughes 5 82
(A M Hales) *sn pushed into ld and crossed to rail: hdd ins jst ins fnl f: rdn to ld again last 100yds: r.o wl* 7/1[3]
51 2 1/2 **Even Bolder**[28] 4066 4-9-8 67 (p) LDettori 8 79
(R Simpson) *trckd ldrs: rdn to ld jst ins fnl f: hdd and no ex last 100yds* 10/3[1]
0000 3 2 1/2 **Azygous**[44] 3594 4-9-7 66 JimmyQuinn 4 69
(J Akehurst) *w ldrs: ev ch and rdn over 1f out: outpcd ins fnl f* 12/1
0000 4 1 **Smokin Beau**[15] 4486 10-9-1 65 PatrickHills(5) 1 65
(N P Littmoden) *chsd ldrs on outer: rdn wl over 1f out: kpt on same pce* 14/1
2600 5 1/2 **No Time (IRE)**[22] 4252 7-8-10 62 RobbieEgan(7) 12 60
(A J McCabe) *chsd ldrs: rdn over 2f out: kpt on same pce* 14/1
640 6 nk **Siraj**[87] 2272 8-9-4 63 (b) BrettDoyle 9 60+
(J Ryan) *bhd: rdn and kpt on wl over 1f out: n.d* 33/1
61 7 1/2 **King Egbert (FR)**[3] 4857 6-8-5 55 6ex TolleyDean(5) 11 50
(R J Price) *a bhd* 7/2[2]
2105 8 1 3/4 **Silver Prelude**[15] 4486 6-9-0 59 JimCrowley 3 48
(D K Ivory) *sn pressing ldrs: rdn wl over 1f out: sn wknd* 9/1
5245 9 3/4 **Scarlett Heart (IRE)**[5] 4759 3-9-7 68 TQuinn 7 54
(J Gallagher) *racd in midfield: rdn 1/2-way: n.d after* 25/1
0440 10 nk **Heavens Walk**[48] 3452 6-9-8 67 (b) MartinDwyer 2 52+
(P J Makin) *stdd and dropped in after s: t.k.h: a bhd: rdn over 1f out but little hdwy* 10/1
3540 11 1 3/4 **Millfields Dreams**[18] 4396 8-9-6 65 EddieAhern 10 44
(M G Quinlan) *racd in midfield: rdn and struggling 1/2-way* 7/1[3]
450 12 3 1/2 **Stoneacre Gareth (IRE)**[25] 4186 3-8-9 56 (b) LPKeniry 6 22
(Peter Grayson) *racd in midfield on outer: rdn and struggling 1/2-way: no ch last 2f* 40/1

59.28 secs (-1.12) **Going Correction** -0.10s/f (Stan)
WFA 3 from 4yo+ 2lb 12 Ran SP% 119.6
Speed ratings (Par 103): **104,103,99,97,96 96,95,92,91,91 88,82**
CSF £30.30 CT £283.27 TOTE £8.20: £3.60, £1.90, £5.80; EX 41.20.
Owner Brick Farm Racing **Bred** C G Reid **Trained** Preston Capes, Northants

FOCUS
A moderate handicap. The second course record to fall of the week here, with the first-time blinkered What Do You Know shaving virtually half a second under a fine front-running ride from Richard Hughes. Career-best form from the winner.
Heavens Walk Official explanation: jockey said gelding ran too free
Stoneacre Gareth(IRE) Official explanation: vet said gelding lost a hind shoe

4945 DAY TIME, NIGHT TIME, GREAT TIME, H'CAP 1m 2f (P)
2:40 (2:40) (Class 6) (0-50,50) 3-Y-O+ £2,047 (£604; £302) Stalls High

Form RPR
0455 1 **Fantasy Crusader**[3] 4850 8-9-0 50 DaneO'Neill 13 58
(R M H Cowell) *t.k.h: chsd ldrs: rdn over 2f out: chsd ldr over 1f out: kpt on steadily to ld fnl stride* 4/1[1]
4540 2 shd **Surdoue**[21] 4266 7-9-0 50 AdrianMcCarthy 6 58
(D Morris) *led: rdn 2f out: clr over 1f out: kpt on but worn down fnl stride* 28/1
6004 3 1/2 **Weet Yer Tern (IRE)**[14] 4488 5-8-11 47 RyanMoore 10 54+
(W M Brisbourne) *hld up towards rr: hdwy on rail over 2f out: swtchd lft over 1f out: styd on wl fnl f: nt quite rch ldrs* 10/1
0606 4 1 **Bowl Of Cherries**[20] 4340 4-8-13 49 (v) JamesDoyle 11 54
(I A Wood) *w.w wl in tch: effrt and rdn 2f out: kpt on same pce fnl f* 12/1
0445 5 3/4 **Magic Amigo**[14] 4517 6-9-0 50 (v) EddieAhern 12 54
(J R Jenkins) *t.k.h: wl in tch: rdn and effrt on outer 2f out: sn no imp* 13/2[3]
1000 6 nk **War Of The Roses (IRE)**[9] 4660 4-8-11 50 JerryO'Dwyer(3) 1 53
(R Brotherton) *hld up in midfield: rdn and hdwy on outer wl over 2f out: no imp over 1f out* 7/1
-064 7 1 3/4 **Kathleen Kennet**[13] 4533 7-8-13 49 RobertHavlin 14 48
(C Tinkler) *t.k.h: hld up in midfield: rdn and unable qck wl over 1f out: swtchd lft over 1f out: one pce* 11/1
0060 8 1 **Chapter (IRE)**[19] 4355 5-8-10 46 (p) JimCrowley 2 43
(Mrs A L M King) *stdd and dropped in after s: a bhd* 11/1
6000 9 3/4 **Mid Valley**[6] 4739 4-8-11 47 (v) PaulDoe 7 43
(J R Jenkins) *stdd s: hld up in rr: nvr on terms* 40/1
0520 10 1 **Smart Cat (IRE)**[27] 4112 4-8-11 47 (v) RichardHughes 4 41
(A P Jarvis) *t.k.h: chsd ldr tl over 1f out: eased whn btn ins fnl f* 11/2[2]
400 11 shd **Moonshine Creek**[4] 4802 5-8-12 48 LPKeniry 8 42
(P W Hiatt) *stdd sn after s: hld up in rr: nvr on terms* 9/1
0500 12 1 3/4 **Shadow Jumper (IRE)**[37] 3789 6-8-5 46 (v) RussellKennemore(5) 3 36
(J T Stimpson) *racd in midfield: rdn 3f out: wknd over 2f out* 25/1
00-6 13 7 **Future Deal**[210] 315 6-9-0 50 SimonWhitworth 5 26
(C A Horgan) *stdd s: hld up towards rr: n.d* 33/1
040 14 6 **Salisbury Plain**[47] 3487 6-8-11 47 MartinDwyer 9 11
(N I M Rossiter) *s.i.s: a last: lost tch 3f out* 11/1

2m 7.75s (-1.25) **Going Correction** -0.10s/f (Stan) 14 Ran SP% 125.7
Speed ratings (Par 101): **101,100,100,99,99 98,97,96,96,95 95,93,88,83**
CSF £133.06 CT £1085.42 TOTE £5.30: £1.40, £7.50, £2.80; EX 189.40.
Owner The Fantasy Fellowship **Bred** J R C And Mrs Wren **Trained** Six Mile Bottom, Cambs
■ Stewards' Enquiry : Adrian McCarthy four-day ban: used whip with excessive frequency and down the shoulder in the forehand position (Sep 9-12)

FOCUS
A drab handicap with 50 being the highest rating on offer and a race not to take much notice of with the future in mind. The form seems sound enough.
Chapter(IRE) Official explanation: jockey said gelding would not face the kickback
Smart Cat(IRE) Official explanation: jockey said filly had no more to give
Salisbury Plain Official explanation: jockey said horse was reluctant to race

4946 DIGIBET MAIDEN STKS (DIV I) 1m (P)
3:10 (3:11) (Class 4) 2-Y-O £3,238 (£963; £481; £240) Stalls High

Form RPR
04 1 **Palmerin**[13] 4540 2-9-3 0 RyanMoore 5 76
(R Hannon) *chsd ldr after 1f: ev ch and rdn over 2f out: led 1f out: hld on wl* 5/2[2]
4042 2 shd **Huzzah (IRE)**[26] 4121 2-9-3 76 MichaelHills 7 76
(B W Hills) *t.k.h: trckd ldrs on outer: rdn to ld narrowly over 2f out: hdd 1f out: unable qck* 4/6[1]
6 3 1 1/2 **Judgethemoment (USA)**[25] 4162 2-9-3 0 JohnEgan 8 73
(Jane Chapple-Hyam) *in tch: rdn over 2f out: chsd ldng pair over 1f out: kpt on* 8/1[3]
0 4 7 **Lord Of Esteem**[32] 3957 2-9-3 0 BrettDoyle 2 56
(J Ryan) *s.i.s: pushed up to ld after 1f and stdd pce: hdd and jinked lft over 2f out: sn wl btn* 33/1
0 5 5 **Ryan's Rock**[14] 4508 2-9-3 0 RobertHavlin 9 45
(T D McCarthy) *led for 1f: chsd ldrs: rdn wl over 2f out: sn wknd* 50/1
00 6 8 **Me Me Me**[28] 4070 2-9-3 0 VinceSlattery 10 27
(M J Wallace) *bhd: rdn and struggling 1/2-way: t.o last 2f* 33/1
00 7 3 **Mubher**[32] 3957 2-9-3 0 MartinDwyer 6 20
(J L Dunlop) *s.i.s: sn rdn: a bhd: lost tch 1/2-way: t.o* 8/1[3]
00 8 5 **Newcastle Sam**[14] 4500 2-9-3 0 FrankieMcDonald 4 8
(J J Bridger) *sn pushed along in rr: lost tch 1/2-way: t.o* 66/1
9 hd **Muga (SPA)** 2-8-9 0 AlanCreighton(3) 3 3
(E J Creighton) *racd in midfield: rdn and wknd qckly 1/2-way: t.o* 66/1

1m 42.65s (1.85) **Going Correction** -0.10s/f (Stan) 9 Ran SP% 121.6
Speed ratings (Par 96): **86,85,84,77,72 64,61,56,56**
CSF £4.70 TOTE £3.00: £1.10, £1.02, £2.30; EX 5.70.
Owner Mrs John Lee **Bred** London Thoroughbred S'Ces Ltd & West Blagdon Stud **Trained** East Everleigh, Wilts

FOCUS
The less interesting of the two divisions, it appeared to be a straight match on paper between Huzzah and Palmerin and that is how it turned out. Pretty solid form

NOTEBOOK
Palmerin battled on willingly and confirmed the promise of his recent Salisbury fourth. By champion sprinter Oasis Dream, there is stamina on the dam's side and he saw the 1m out extremely well. The obvious next step would be nurseries, but there was a suggestion from connections that he would not be seen out much more this season, as he is still quite weak and very much seen as more of a three-year-old prospect. (op 3-1, tchd 10-3 in a place)
Huzzah(IRE) really caught the eye with the way he flew home to snatch second off a mark of 73 in a competitive Goodwood nursery and, although by speedy first-season sire Acclamation, there is plenty of stamina on the dam's side and this step up to 1m was not expected to prove a problem. Drawing clear with the winner, he was edging nearer with every stride as they flashed past the post and clearly needs this trip, but the wait goes on for his first win. (tchd 8-13 and 8-11 and 4-5 in a place)
Judgethemoment(USA), who did not show much on his debut on turf at Lingfield, hanging under pressure and not looking an easy ride, really stepped up on that initial effort and, although no match for the front pair, will find easier opportunities. He is probably more of a nursery prospect. (op 12-1)
Lord Of Esteem was introduced in a warm Newmarket maiden and found this a bit easier, but will not be seen at his best until contesting handicaps. (op 50-1)

Mubher, who raced lazily in rear, could make no real headway in the straight and will not be at his best until tackling modest nurseries. (op 7-1)

4947 DIGIBET MAIDEN STKS (DIV II) 1m (P)
3:40 (3:44) (Class 4) 2-Y-O £3,238 (£963; £481; £240) Stalls High

Form RPR

04 **1** **City Of The Kings (IRE)**[12] 4586 2-9-3 0 .... RichardHughes 8 79
(R Hannon) *hld up in midfield: hdwy 3f out: drvn to ld ins fnl f: styd on wl* **10/3**[2]

0 **2** ½ **Yaddree**[19] 4362 2-9-3 0 .... PhilipRobinson 6 78
(M A Jarvis) *chsd ldrs: rdn to ld 2f out: hdd ins fnl f: unable qck* **6/1**[3]

0 **3** 1¾ **Conduit (IRE)**[19] 4362 2-9-3 0 .... RyanMoore 3 74+
(Sir Michael Stoute) *bhd: rdn 3f out: styd on u.p: chsd ldng pair ins fnl f: nvr pce to rch ldrs* **6/4**[1]

0 **4** 1½ **Stormy View (USA)**[18] 4402 2-8-12 0 .... JimmyFortune 10 66
(J H M Gosden) *chsd ldr: rdn and ev ch over 2f out: fdd ins fnl f* **12/1**

0 **5** 1¾ **Rampant Ronnie (USA)**[30] 4028 2-9-3 0 .... RobertHavlin 2 67
(P W D'Arcy) *led tl rdn and hdd 2f out: wknd over 1f out* **100/1**

450 **6** *hd* **Rockfield Tiger (IRE)**[76] 2600 2-9-3 77 .... (t) MartinDwyer 4 66
(J A Osborne) *hld up towards rr: rdn 3f out: kpt on same pce* **12/1**

6 **7** ½ **Aaim To Succeed (IRE)**[54] 3270 2-8-12 0 .... DarryllHolland 9 60
(M R Channon) *racd in midfield: rdn wl over 2f out: kpt on same pce* **6/1**[3]

8 5 **Jack Got Even (USA)** 2-9-3 0 .... SteveDrowne 1 54+
(B J Meehan) *sn pushed along on outer in midfield: wknd wl over 2f out* **16/1**

0 **9** *nk* **Pepper's Ghost**[30] 4028 2-9-0 0 .... JerryO'Dwyer(3) 7 54
(Miss J Feilden) *s.i.s: a bhd: rdn and struggling 3f out: no ch after* **66/1**

10 25 **Rock Me (IRE)** 2-9-3 0 .... EddieAhern 5 —
(N A Callaghan) *v.s.a: sn rdn and nvr gng in last: lost tch 3f out: t.o and eased fnl f* **33/1**

1m 40.65s (-0.15) **Going Correction** -0.10s/f (Stan) **10** Ran SP% **118.3**
Speed ratings (Par 96): **96,95,93,92,90 90,89,84,84,59**
CSF £24.04 TOTE £3.50: £1.40, £1.90, £1.10; EX 26.60.
Owner T Hyde **Bred** Tom McDonald **Trained** East Everleigh, Wilts

FOCUS
Probably the better of the two divisions, with several well bred individuals on show, and the time was significantly better.

NOTEBOOK
City Of The Kings(IRE), who improved on his debut effort when not beaten far in a decent 1m maiden at Newmarket earlier in the month, shaped that day as though already in need of 1m2f and he again gave that impression in winning, getting outpaced over 2f out before really coming home strongly and finishing nicely on top. He looks to have a bright future, with further improvement likely, and it will be interesting to see what sort of mark he gets for handicaps. (op 7-2 tchd 3-1 and 4-1 in a place)
Yaddree, boasting numerous big-race entries, including the Dewhurst, had a bit to find with Conduit on his Newmarket debut running, but he was always going to improve for this extra furlong and was able to reverse the form. Never far from the lead, he went on over a furlong out, but it soon became clear City Of The Kings had the move covered and he simply lacked that one's finishing kick. He should have little trouble winning a maiden and the sooner the 1m2f juvenile races come into effect the better for the son of Singspiel. (op 11-2 tchd 13-2)
Conduit(IRE), a Racing Post Trophy entrant who shaped as though the experience was needed on his debut at Newmarket, ahead of Yaddree, was expected to have improved a good deal on that effort, but still looked green in the preliminaries and never really looked likely to justify favouritism, getting going all too late. A close relation to Hard Top, he remains capable of better and is another unlikely to be troubled to find a standard maiden. (op 11-8 tchd 7-4)
Stormy View(USA), who is a half-sister to the yard's smart performer Asperity, improved on her initial effort at Newmarket and seemed quite happy on the surface. She will be qualified for a handicap mark following one more run. (op 16-1 tchd 20-1)
Rampant Ronnie(USA), who showed next to nothing on his debut at Yarmouth, stepped up significantly on that effort and there was no disgrace in being unable to hold off some well-bred individuals. He should find his level in nurseries.
Rockfield Tiger(IRE), fitted with a tongue tie for the first time on this return from a break, had some fair form to his name from early in the season, but seems to be going the wrong way and a mark of 77 will not make life any easier for him in handicaps. (tchd 14-1)
Aaim To Succeed(IRE) looked one of the more interesting ones, having shaped nicely on her debut at Sandown, and she had a good early sit, but did little once coming under pressure and may turn out to be more of a handicap prospect. (tchd 11-2)
Jack Got Even(USA) was eased right off and clearly failed to do himself justice on this racecourse debut. He looks sure to do better with time. (op 20-1 tchd 25-1)

4948 DIGIBET.COM MAIDEN STKS 1m 4f (P)
4:10 (4:12) (Class 5) 3-Y-O+ £3,238 (£963; £481; £240) Stalls Centre

Form RPR

32 **1** **Longspur**[18] 4403 3-9-3 0 .... LDettori 3 77
(Saeed Bin Suroor) *led over 10f out: mde rest: rdn over 2f out: battled on: all out* **11/8**[1]

42 **2** *nk* **Tropical Strait (IRE)**[18] 4392 4-9-13 0 .... FergusSweeney 8 76
(D W P Arbuthnot) *chsd ldrs: rdn to chse ldng pair 3f out: styd on u.p: wnt 2nd ins fnl f: kpt on* **5/1**[3]

0 **3** 1¼ **Out Of Court**[16] 4457 3-9-3 0 .... SimonWhitworth 5 74
(C A Cyzer) *t.k.h: led after 1f: sn hdd and chsd wnr after: rdn and ev ch over 2f out: no ex last 100yds* **28/1**

6 **4** 1½ **Bukit Tinggi (IRE)**[12] 4568 3-9-3 0 .... PhilipRobinson 2 72
(M A Jarvis) *chsd ldrs: rdn and chsd ldng trio wl over 2f out: sn hung rt and no imp tl styd on wl ins fnl f: nvr threatened ldrs* **11/2**

0 **5** 5 **Mounafes**[12] 4568 3-9-3 0 .... (b[1]) StephenCarson 12 64
(G A Butler) *chsd ldng pair tl 3f out: sn rdn and reluctant: no ch last 2f* **66/1**

06 **6** 3 **How's Business**[10] 4630 3-8-12 0 .... AdamKirby 13 54
(C A Cyzer) *off the pce in midfield: rdn and outpcd over 3f out: no ch after* **66/1**

0-4 **7** 1 **Theta**[12] 4568 3-8-12 0 .... TPQueally 6 52
(H R A Cecil) *bhd: reminder 8f out: nvr on terms* **8/1**

0-0 **8** 2 **Tejareb (IRE)**[55] 3236 4-9-8 0 .... RyanMoore 7 49
(C E Brittain) *racd in midfield: struggling over 3f out: no ch after* **33/1**

00 **9** 22 **Beths Choice**[10] 4630 6-9-8 0 .... KevinGhunowa(5) 1 19
(J M Bradley) *a towards rr: lost tch 4f out: virtually p.u fnl f: t.o* **100/1**

2 **10** ½ **Russian Invader (IRE)**[20] 4334 3-9-3 0 .... RichardHughes 14 18
(A King) *led for 1f: chsd ldrs tl rdn over 3f out: sn wknd: virtually p.u fnl f: t.o* **7/2**[2]

0 **11** 6 **Trigger's Friend**[13] 4541 3-8-12 0 .... MichaelHills 9 4
(Jamie Poulton) *s.i.s: sn rdn in last: t.o last 3f: virtually p.u fnl f* **50/1**

0 **12** 2½ **Moonshine Vixen**[55] 3236 6-9-1 0 .... WilliamCarson(7) 10 —
(P W Hiatt) *s.i.s: sn rdn in rr: lost tch 4f out: virtually p.u fnl f* **100/1**

05 **13** 4 **Hill Cloud**[12] 4563 5-9-13 0 .... EddieAhern 11 —
(W M Brisbourne) *chsd ldrs for 4f: bhd last 4f: virtually p.u fnl f: t.o* **100/1**

14 *shd* **Bold Josr** 3-9-3 0 .... TQuinn 4 —
(D J S Ffrench Davis) *a bhd: lost tch 4f out: virtually p.u fnl f: t.o* **66/1**

2m 33.68s (-3.22) **Going Correction** -0.10s/f (Stan)
WFA 3 from 4yo+ 10lb **14** Ran SP% **123.3**
Speed ratings (Par 103): **106,105,104,103,100 98,97,96,81,81 77,75,73,73**
CSF £8.60 TOTE £1.90: £1.10, £2.00, £5.10; EX 9.80.
Owner Godolphin **Bred** Darley **Trained** Newmarket, Suffolk

FOCUS
Only a handful could be given a chance in what was a modest middle-distance maiden. The winner did not need to improve and the race was dominated by prominent-racers.
Russian Invader(IRE) Official explanation: jockey said gelding had no more to give

4949 DIGIBET SPORTS BETTING H'CAP 7f (P)
4:40 (4:41) (Class 4) (0-85,85) 3-Y-O+ £4,728 (£1,406; £702; £351) Stalls High

Form RPR

210 **1** **Resplendent Nova**[21] 4268 5-9-12 85 .... JimmyQuinn 6 93
(P Howling) *mde all: rdn and qcknd over 2f out: r.o gamely: jst hld on* **14/1**

513 **2** *shd* **Blackat Blackitten (IRE)**[12] 4574 3-9-0 78 .... EddieAhern 8 84+
(G A Butler) *trckd ldrs on rail: rdn and hdwy over 1f out: styd on wl ins fnl f: jst failed* **11/4**[1]

1600 **3** *hd* **Carmenero (GER)**[26] 4135 4-9-1 74 .... MartinDwyer 5 81
(W R Muir) *t.k.h: pressed wnr: rdn and ev ch over 2f out: no ex towards fin* **25/1**

1230 **4** *nk* **Froissee**[25] 4166 3-8-13 77 .... JimmyFortune 2 81
(N A Callaghan) *bmpd s: hld up towards rr: rdn and hdwy 2f out: chsd ldrs 1f out: no imp last 50yds* **20/1**

0305 **5** ¾ **Marajaa (IRE)**[13] 4548 5-9-11 84 .... BrettDoyle 10 90+
(W J Musson) *hld up in last pair: hdwy 2f out: running on whn nt clr run ins fnl f: nt rcvr* **7/2**[2]

0463 **6** 1 **Bonnie Prince Blue**[13] 4548 4-9-4 77 .... MichaelHills 3 79
(B W Hills) *wnt lft s: snprom: rdn and ev ch over 2f out: wknd jst ins fnl f: eased towards fin* **4/1**[3]

2606 **7** ½ **Cape Of Luck (IRE)**[11] 4601 4-9-1 81 .... JackMitchell(7) 7 81
(P Mitchell) *w.win midfield: rdn and effrt 2f out: no imp* **15/2**

-110 **8** *nk* **One Night In Paris (IRE)**[181] 590 4-8-13 72 .... DaneO'Neill 9 71
(M J Wallace) *hld up in rr: c wd and rdn 2f out: kpt on but nvr pce to rch ldrs* **14/1**

0-04 **9** *shd* **Namid Reprobate (IRE)**[9] 4657 4-9-5 78 .... TQuinn 4 77
(P F I Cole) *t.k.h: in tch: rdn over 2f out: wknd over 1f out* **12/1**

0000 **10** 2 **Moayed**[14] 4515 8-9-7 80 .... (b) GeorgeBaker 1 74
(N P Littmoden) *dropped in after s: a bhd* **14/1**

1m 28.01s (1.21) **Going Correction** -0.10s/f (Stan)
WFA 3 from 4yo+ 5lb **10** Ran SP% **117.0**
Speed ratings (Par 105): **89,88,88,88,87 86,85,85,85,83**
CSF £52.70 CT £982.20 TOTE £21.30: £4.90, £1.80, £7.50; EX 68.70.
Owner Resplendent Racing Limited **Bred** A Turner **Trained** Newmarket, Suffolk
■ Stewards' Enquiry : Eddie Ahern six-day ban: used whip with excessive frequency without giving colt time to respond (Sep 10-15)

FOCUS
Largely exposed performers lined up for what was nothing more than a fair handicap, and not for the first time on the card, it was an advantage to race prominently. The form is rated through the third and fifth.
Marajaa(IRE) Official explanation: jockey said gelding suffered interference
Bonnie Prince Blue Official explanation: jockey said gelding was hampered in final furlong

4950 TFM NETWORKS H'CAP 6f (P)
5:10 (5:11) (Class 3) (0-95,92) 3-Y-O
£6,855 (£2,052; £1,026; £513; £256; £128) Stalls High

Form RPR

-211 **1** **Edge Closer**[32] 3944 3-9-4 89 .... RichardHughes 3 106+
(R Hannon) *trckd ldng pair: plld out over 2f out: led jst ins fnl f: in command after: comf* **11/10**[1]

6055 **2** ½ **Majuro (IRE)**[11] 4601 3-9-7 92 .... DarryllHolland 7 101
(M R Channon) *t.k.h: hld up towards rr: hdwy on rail 2f out: tried to chal wnr ins fnl f: a hld* **6/1**[3]

1034 **3** 2½ **Buxton**[19] 4360 3-8-8 79 .... RobertHavlin 4 80
(R Ingram) *chsd ldrs: rdn wl over 2f out: kpt on to go 3rd last 100yds: nt trble wnr* **14/1**

4220 **4** 1 **Mambo Spirit (IRE)**[26] 4123 3-9-3 88 .... TPQueally 2 86
(J G Given) *s.i.s: hdwy on outer over 3f out: rdn over 2f out: kpt on same pce fnl f* **12/1**

1002 **5** *nk* **Mac Gille Eoin**[4] 4806 3-9-4 89 .... JimCrowley 5 86
(J Gallagher) *w ldr: ev ch and rdn wl over 2f out: outpcd ins fnl f* **9/4**[2]

0000 **6** ½ **Luscivious**[7] 4726 3-9-1 86 .... (p) TQuinn 1 81
(A J McCabe) *led: rdn 2f out: hdd jst ins fnl f: sn fdd* **20/1**

3060 **7** ½ **Resplendent Alpha**[18] 4374 3-9-4 89 .... (t) JimmyQuinn 6 83
(P Howling) *v.s.a: nvr on terms* **25/1**

14 **8** 1 **Kelamon**[54] 3278 3-8-4 75 .... MartinDwyer 9 65
(M D I Usher) *outpcd in last pair: effrt u.p wl over 2f out: n.d* **25/1**

-001 **9** 5 **Guarantia**[13] 4530 3-9-5 90 .... RyanMoore 8 64
(C E Brittain) *racd in midfield: rdn wl over 2f out: wknd over 1f out* **10/1**

1m 11.87s (-1.83) **Going Correction** -0.10s/f (Stan) **9** Ran SP% **128.6**
Speed ratings (Par 104): **108,107,104,102,102 101,100,99,92**
CSF £9.75 CT £68.96 TOTE £2.10: £1.10, £2.20, £2.60; EX 10.60.
Owner Lady Whent And Friends **Bred** Caroline Wilson **Trained** East Everleigh, Wilts
■ Stewards' Enquiry : Jim Crowley one-day ban: careless riding (Sep 9)

FOCUS
Few could be ruled out in what was a tricky three-year-old sprint handicap, but it was the highly progressive Edge Closer who emerged a clear best. The time holds down the form, but the winner can rate higher.

NOTEBOOK
Edge Closer, in search of a hat-trick following back-to-back wins at Ascot, where he made all both times, was up a further 6lb here and had no previous experience of the sand, but quickened up well, having been forced to take a lead, and won with a bit to spare. He lost a shoe during the race, which makes the performance all the more creditable, and there is no reason why he cannot go on and make it five wins from six. (op 6-4)
Majuro(IRE) has shown all his best form in smallish fields and this was an awful lot easier than the races he has been contesting. Ridden with a bit more restraint on this occasion, he came to have every chance near the rail, but lacked the winner's pace and is likely to remain vulnerable off his current rating. (op 9-1)
Buxton was 8lb better off with Mac Gille Eoin for June's course form and he managed to reverse the placings, but lacked the pace to trouble the winner. (op 12-1)
Mambo Spirit(IRE), runner-up at here to the progressive King's Apostle on his only previous All-Weather start, is not the most consistent, but this was a fair enough effort. (op 14-1)

Mac Gille Eoin, 7lb higher than when winning over course and distance back in June, returned to form with a good effort behind Golden Dixie over 6f at Goodwood last time, but he was unable to build on that and proved most disappointing. (op 5-2 tchd 2-1)
Luscivious Official explanation: jockey said gelding suffered interference 1 1/2f out
Resplendent Alpha Official explanation: jockey said colt missed the break

4951 PANORAMIC BAR & RESTAURANT H'CAP 2m (P)
5:40 (5:41) (Class 5) (0-75,75) 3-Y-O **£3,238** (£963; £481; £240) **Stalls** High

Form				RPR
6522	1		**Shine And Rise (IRE)**[18] 4391 3-9-0 **68** PhilipRobinson 4 (C G Cox) *hld up in last: smooth hdwy to trck ldng pair over 3f out: led on bit over 1f out: cruised clr* **11/4**[2]	82+
4	2	5	**Kavaloti (IRE)**[14] 4511 3-9-7 **75** (b) RyanMoore 3 (G L Moore) *chsd ldr tl led over 7f out: rdn 3f out: hdd over 1f out: no ch w wnr:* **7/4**[1]	83
3506	3	7	**Sweetheart**[27] 4113 3-9-1 **69** RobertHavlin 5 (Jamie Poulton) *in rr: hdwy over 5f out: rdn to chse ldr 4f out tl wl over 1f out: sn totally outpcd* **11/1**	69
00	4	9	**Spinaimanwin (IRE)**[4] 4809 3-7-13 **56** oh6 WilliamBuick(3) 6 (Ian Williams) *rn in snatches: rdn 7f out: wknd 4f out: no ch after: wnt poor 4th ins fnl f* **25/1**	45
0063	5	2 1/2	**Fraternal**[19] 4357 3-9-4 **72** (b[1]) SteveDrowne 7 (R Charlton) *chsd ldrs: rdn over 4f out: wknd qckly over 3f out* **16/1**	58
3526	6	6	**I Predict A Riot (IRE)**[14] 4511 3-9-4 **72** EddieAhern 2 (J W Hills) *in tch: hdwy to trck ldng pair 6f out: wknd qckly over 3f out* **9/1**	51
3621	7	33	**Natural Action**[19] 4357 3-9-4 **72** DarryllHolland 1 (W Jarvis) *in tch: chsd ldr 7f out: rdn over 4f out: sn wknd: virtually p.u fnl last 2f: t.o* **11/2**[3]	11
2323	8	19	**Dansimar**[13] 4531 3-8-12 **66** RichardHughes 8 (M R Channon) *led tl rdn and hdd over 7f out: sn dropped out: virtually p.u last 2f: t.o* **6/1**	—

3m 27.36s (-4.04) **Going Correction** -0.10s/f (Stan) 8 Ran SP% **120.8**
Speed ratings (Par 100): **106,103,100,95,94 91,74,65**
CSF £8.53 CT £46.09 TOTE £3.30: £1.60, £1.10, £3.60; EX 10.10 Place 6 £21.88, Place 5 £9.76
.
Owner Gerald C S Siu **Bred** Freynestown Partners **Trained** Lambourn, Berks

FOCUS
A modest staying handicap in which the leaders went a bit too fast, and that led to the second course record on the card. With some of the fancied runners failing to run their race, there is a question mark over the merits of the form, but the winner did it well and is on the upgrade.
T/Plt: £10.10 to a £1 stake. Pool: £48,746.40. 3,510.95 winning tickets. T/Qpdt: £2.50 to a £1 stake. Pool: £3,308.50. 970.30 winning tickets. SP

4952 - 4956a (Foreign Racing) - See Raceform Interactive

4929 BADEN-BADEN (L-H)
Wednesday, August 29
OFFICIAL GOING: Good

4957a KABA BADENER STEHER-CUP (LISTED RACE) 1m 6f
2:45 (2:51) 3-Y-O+ **£10,135** (£4,054; £1,689; £1,014)

			RPR
1		**Brisant (GER)**[31] 5-9-4 ADeVries 5 (M Trybuhl, Germany)	106
2	1/2	**Jump For You (FR)**[31] 5-9-4 THellier 14 (W Baltromei, Germany)	105
3	nk	**Waldvogel (IRE)**[31] 3-8-7 JBojko 4 (A Wohler, Germany)	106
4	1 1/2	**Soul Of Magic (IRE)**[59] 8-8-9 TCastanheira 9 (Karin Suter, Switzerland)	94
5	1/2	**Dragon Fly (GER)**[46] 3565 5-9-4 AStarke 1 (Frau Jutta Mayer, Germany)	102
6	4	**Amoroso (GER)**[129] 6-9-0 TMundry 6 (P Rau, Germany)	93
7	5	**Bailamos (GER)**[283] 6529 7-9-0 RPiechulek 3 (C Von Der Recke, Germany)	86
8	hd	**Carus (GER)**[64] 2976 8-9-0 AHelfenbein 2 (D K Richardson, Germany)	86
9	shd	**La Grande Dame (GER)**[38] 5-8-9 EPedroza 7 (A Wohler, Germany)	81
10	11	**Majofils (FR)**[360] 4-9-0 SMaillot 11 (M Weiss, Switzerland)	72
11	12	**Alambic**[27] 4089 4-8-11 (b) DPMcDonogh 12 (Sir Mark Prescott) *led after 2f: 5 l clr 1/2-way: c bk to field over 4f out: hdd 3f out: 6th and btn st* **3/1**[1]	53
12	9	**Rhodesian Winner (GER)**[55] 8-9-0 (b) HGrewe 13 (Frau Marion Rotering, Germany)	44
13	25	**Potro Tell (ARG)**[216] 244 7-9-0 (b) J-PCarvalho 10 (W Hefter, Germany)	12

2m 51.37s (171.37)
WFA 3 from 4yo+ 12lb 13 Ran SP% **25.0**
(Including 10 Euros stake): WIN 111; PL 32, 45, 23; SF 1,408.
Owner Frau Maria M Holl **Bred** Dr Rolf Wilhelms **Trained** Germany

NOTEBOOK
Alambic had plenty of use made of her in the first-time blinkers, but she was caught with some way to go and was ultimately well beaten.

4958a FURSTENBERG-RENNEN (GROUP 3) 1m 2f
4:00 (4:11) 3-Y-O **£20,270** (£8,446; £3,378; £1,689)

			RPR
1		**Persian Storm (GER)**[59] 3146 3-9-0 THellier 1 (J Hirschberger, Germany) *mde all: 5 l clr 1/2-way: pushed along 1 1/2f out: r.o wl* **3/5**[1]	111
2	1 1/2	**Lord Hill (GER)**[93] 2102 3-8-12 J-PCarvalho 3 (C Zeitz) *prom in 2nd: pushed along st: nt pce of wnr fnl f* **124/10**	106
3	3	**Davidoff (GER)**[59] 3146 3-9-0 AStarke 4 (P Schiergen, Germany) *disp 3rd: 3rd and pushed along st: sn rdn: ev ch over 1f out: nt pce of wnr* **22/10**[2]	103
4	2 1/2	**Wassiljew (IRE)**[27] 3-8-12 ASuborics 5 (W Baltromei, Germany) *racd in 5th: 4th and drvn st: styd on u.p tl no ex fnl f* **58/10**[3]	97
5	6	**Monreale (GER)**[59] 3146 3-8-11 ow1 ADeVries 2 (T Horwart, Germany) *disp 3rd: 5th and pushed along st: nvr able to chal* **172/10**	85
6	16	**Integral (GER)**[77] 3-8-10 TMundry 6 (P Rau, Germany) *settled in last: pushed along st: n.d* **86/10**	55

2m 2.61s (-2.38) 6 Ran SP% **131.8**
WIN 16; PL 18, 29; SF 189.
Owner Baron G Von Ullmann **Bred** Dr Christoph Berglar **Trained** Germany

4914 LINGFIELD (L-H)
Thursday, August 30
OFFICIAL GOING: Turf course - good to firm (8.9); all-weather course - standard
Wind: Light, against Weather: Cloudy

4959 LINGFIELD PARK "THE PERFECT WEDDING VENUE" APPRENTICE H'CAP 1m 2f
2:20 (2:20) (Class 6) (0-65,62) 4-Y-O+ **£2,047** (£604; £302) **Stalls** Low

Form				RPR
0651	1		**Royal Indulgence**[3] 4878 7-9-4 **59** 6ex AlanRutter(3) 9 (W M Brisbourne) *hld up in cl tch: poised to chal over 2f out: shkn up to ld over 1f out: pushed clr* **2/1**[1]	66
60-3	2	1 1/2	**Measured Response**[48] 3487 5-9-1 **53** ThomasO'Brien 4 (J G M O'Shea) *t.k.h: hld up bhd ldrs: shkn up 3f out: nt qckn over 2f out: styd on fr over 1f out: to take 2nd nr fin* **5/1**[2]	57
5415	3	1/2	**Recalcitrant**[9] 4686 4-9-6 **58** JamieHamblett 6 (S Dow) *t.k.h: trckd ldr after 3f: narrow ld 2f out to over 1f out: hld fnl f: lost 2nd nr fin* **8/1**	61
0130	4	3/4	**General Flumpa**[23] 4253 6-9-6 **58** HaddenFrost 8 (Miss Tor Sturgis) *t.k.h: led after 2f: narrowly hdd 2f out: rdn and one pce* **11/2**[3]	60
0	5	3/4	**Beaver (AUS)**[41] 3721 8-9-10 **62** MCGeran 10 (J G M O'Shea) *hld up in 6th and sn wl off the pce: shkn up 3f out: clsd grad but nvr rchd ldrs* **11/1**	62
460	6	1 1/2	**Voice Mail**[9] 4686 8-8-2 **47** DavidProbert(7) 7 (A M Balding) *hld up in last pair and wl off the pce: pushed along 3f out: styd on fnl f: nrst fin* **11/1**	44
0010	7	shd	**Border Edge**[13] 4577 9-9-9 **61** (b) JackMitchell 1 (J J Bridger) *t.k.h: led 2f: cl up tl rdn and nt qckn over 2f out: fdd* **9/1**	58
4006	8	3/4	**Western Roots**[10] 4660 6-8-12 **50** WilliamCarson 3 (M Appleby) *dwlt: hld up in last trio and wl off the pce: rdn 3f out: nvr on terms:* **12/1**	45
-050	9	1 1/2	**Hey Presto**[19] 4395 7-8-2 **45** RichardRowe(5) 2 (R Rowe) *dwlt: a last: struggling fr 3f out* **50/1**	37

2m 13.41s (3.69) **Going Correction** +0.10s/f (Good) 9 Ran SP% **112.8**
Speed ratings (Par 101): **89,87,87,86,86 85,84,84,83**
CSF £11.37 CT £63.54 TOTE £3.00: £1.40, £1.40, £2.10; EX 11.20 Trifecta £80.40 Pool £313.96 - 2.77 wining units..
Owner P G Evans **Bred** P V And Mrs J P Jackson **Trained** Great Ness, Shropshire

FOCUS
A moderate handicap, run at a steady early pace and hard to rate positively.

4960 PUSHKABLUE H'CAP 1m 2f
2:50 (2:50) (Class 5) (0-75,74) 3-Y-O **£2,817** (£838; £418; £209) **Stalls** Low

Form				RPR
5453	1		**Shake On It**[21] 4313 3-9-9 **74** (t) StephenCarson 11 (Eve Johnson Houghton) *dwlt: hld up in last trio: prog and nt clr run 2f out: plld out and drvn jst over 1f out: r.o wl to ld last 100yds* **9/1**	82+
4210	2	1 1/4	**Four Miracles**[49] 3469 3-9-4 **69** JimmyQuinn 2 (M H Tompkins) *dwlt and rousted along early: prog fr rr on inner whn nt clr run and lost pl 2f out: rallied over 1f out: r.o wl to snatch 2nd last stride* **10/1**	74+
-050	3	shd	**Mardi**[22] 4277 3-9-2 **67** RHills 3 (W J Haggas) *trckd ldr: rdn to ld wl over 1f out to jst over 1f out: kpt on fnl f* **14/1**	72
0221	4	1/2	**Central Force**[20] 4365 3-9-8 **73** SebSanders 6 (E A L Dunlop) *hld up in rr: stdy prog fr 3f out: rdn to ld jst over 1f out: hdd & wknd last 100yds* **2/1**[1]	77
5663	5	2	**Willow Dancer (IRE)**[18] 4433 3-9-5 **70** AdamKirby 8 (W R Swinburn) *trckd ldrs: cl up over 2f out: hanging after and fnd nil* **13/2**[2]	70
351-	6	1/2	**Golan Way**[275] 6646 3-9-2 **74** JackMitchell(7) 9 (I A Wood) *hld up in last trio: rapid prog on wd outside 1/2-way: presseed ldrs 3f out: sn rdn: fdd over 1f out* **33/1**	73
6500	7	1/2	**Aegis (IRE)**[15] 4510 3-9-4 **69** MichaelHills 1 (B W Hills) *led: drvn and hdd wl over 1f out: wknd* **7/1**[3]	67
2200	8	1 1/4	**Castara Bay**[14] 4541 3-9-5 **70** RichardHughes 7 (R Hannon) *hld up in last pair: pushed along 3f out: sme prog 2f out but nvr on terms w ldrs: shkn up and one pce* **11/1**	66
2001	9	2	**Distiller (IRE)**[18] 4424 3-9-7 **72** RichardMullen 10 (W R Muir) *mostly in midfield: rdn over 2f out: no prog: wknd over 1f out* **14/1**	64
543	10	1	**Berry Hill Lass (IRE)**[38] 3794 3-9-0 **65** FergusSweeney 4 (J G M O'Shea) *pushed up to trck ldrs: cl up on inner 2f out: wknd over 1f out* **20/1**	55
000	11	3/4	**Putra Laju (IRE)**[28] 4111 3-8-9 **60** EddieAhern 14 (J W Hills) *hld up in rr: effrt on outer gng wl 3f out: wknd wl over 1f out* **40/1**	48
0-00	12	3/4	**Maid Of Ale (IRE)**[23] 4257 3-8-6 **57** SimonWhitworth 13 (A King) *pressed ldrs: stl cl up 3f out: wknd over 2f out* **40/1**	44
0600	13	2 1/2	**Opera Crown (IRE)**[12] 4603 3-8-8 **59** TQuinn 5 (P F I Cole) *chsd ldrs: rdn and lost pl 1/2-way: toiling 3f out* **12/1**	41

2m 10.7s (0.98) **Going Correction** +0.10s/f (Good) 13 Ran SP% **120.2**
Speed ratings (Par 100): **100,99,98,98,96 96,96,95,93,92 92,91,89**
CSF £93.05 CT £1257.78 TOTE £12.20: £2.30, £3.30, £4.50; EX 148.60 TRIFECTA Not won..
Owner Eden Racing (III) **Bred** Car Colston Hall Stud **Trained** Blewbury, Oxon

FOCUS
A fair three-year-old handicap, run at a solid pace and the form is sound rated around the third and fifth to recent form.
Castara Bay Official explanation: jockey said colt finished distressed

Opera Crown(IRE) Official explanation: jockey said gelding suffered interference in running

4961 LINGFIELDPARK.CO.UK (S) STKS — 1m 1f
3:20 (3:20) (Class 6) 3-Y-0+ — **£2,047** (£604; £302) **Stalls** Low

Form — RPR

5214 **1** **Treetops Hotel (IRE)**[61] 3083 8-9-7 53 .... RussellKennemore(5) 1 — 56
(B R Johnson) *chsd ldrs: clsd and rdn 2f out: plld out 1f out: r.o to ld last 100yds* — **13/8**[1]

0005 **2** ¾ **Give Evidence**[12] 4595 3-8-13 44 .... JimCrowley 8 — 48
(A P Jarvis) *pressed ldr: led wl over 1f out: hdd and outpcd last 100yds* — **10/1**

6052 **3** ¾ **Dr Dream (IRE)**[36] 3843 3-8-13 55 ....(v[1]) FergusSweeney 7 — 46
(J G M O'Shea) *led: drvn and hdd wl over 1f out: stl nrly upsides ent fnl f: one pce* — **8/1**

506 **4** 2 **Fine Art World (IRE)**[6] 4778 3-8-10 0 .... WilliamBuick(3) 3 — 42
(N A Callaghan) *hld up in last pair: effrt on inner and nt clr run over 2f out: styd on same pce after: nvr rchd ldrs* — **6/1**[3]

0530 **5** 2 **Hamilton House**[13] 4580 3-8-13 58 ....(b[1]) JimmyQuinn 9 — 38
(M H Tompkins) *cl up: rdn to chal 2f out: nt qckn and btn whn bmpd 1f out: wknd* — **9/4**[2]

0666 **6** 3½ **Acosta**[12] 4595 3-8-6 44 ....(v) MatthewCosham(7) 6 — 31
(Dr J R J Naylor) *nvr beyond midfield: rdn and struggling 3f out* — **33/1**

0000 **7** 1¼ **Miss Wolf**[47] 3549 7-8-8 35 .... MCGeran(7) 4 — 23
(G H Jones) *hld up in last pair: brought wd in st: sn btn* — **100/1**

4000 **8** 2 **Gala Jackpot (USA)**[62] 3063 4-9-6 35 .... TGMcLaughlin 2 — 24
(W M Brisbourne) *chsd ldrs 6f: struggling in rr 2f out* — **33/1**

0P30 **9** 2½ **Winds Of Kildare (IRE)**[22] 4272 4-9-6 44 ....(t) MartinDwyer 5 — 19
(C N Allen) *t.k.h: cl up tl wknd rapidly 2f out* — **16/1**

1m 58.82s (3.53) **Going Correction** +0.10s/f (Good)
WFA 3 from 4yo+ 7lb — **9** Ran SP% **116.1**
Speed ratings (Par 101): **88,87,86,84,83 80,78,77,74**
CSF £19.29 TOTE £2.70: £1.20, £2.30, £1.70; EX 25.80 Trifecta £135.50 Pool £717.76 - 3.76 winning units..There was no bid for the winner.
Owner Tann Racing **Bred** Miss Jill Finegan **Trained** Ashtead, Surrey

FOCUS
A dire affair rated around the second and fourth. The winner was the only horse in the line up to have previously won a race.
Miss Wolf Official explanation: jockey said mare hung right throughout

4962 WEATHERBYS BANK MEDIAN AUCTION MAIDEN STKS (DIV I) — 6f (P)
3:50 (3:50) (Class 6) 2-Y-0 — **£1,943** (£578; £288; £144) **Stalls** Low

Form — RPR

422 **1** **Rockfield Lodge (IRE)**[20] 4350 2-9-3 78 .... MartinDwyer 8 — 72+
(J A Osborne) *t.k.h early: trckd ldrs: shkn up and effrt 2f out: narrow ld over 1f out: rdn out to hold on* — **4/5**[1]

2 hd **Sunny Sprite** 2-9-3 0 .... KerrinMcEvoy 10 — 71
(J M P Eustace) *trckd ldr tl wd bnd 2f out: rdn to press wnr fnl f: jst hld* — **14/1**

60 **3** 1¼ **Alls Fair**[26] 4181 2-9-3 0 .... RichardHughes 7 — 68+
(R Hannon) *led at stdy pce: wd bnd 2f out: narrowly hdd over 1f out: one pce fnl f* — **5/2**[2]

4 2½ **Raiding Party (IRE)** 2-8-12 0 .... TQuinn 9 — 55
(J W Hills) *dwlt: in tch in rr: pushed along and sme prog over 1f out: kpt on: nvr threatened ldrs* — **50/1**

5 ¾ **Farpedon** 2-9-3 0 .... DaneO'Neill 1 — 58
(H Candy) *chsd ldrs: rdn and outpcd 2f out: kpt on one pce over 1f out* — **12/1**[3]

6 ¾ **Oceana Blue** 2-8-9 0 .... WilliamBuick(3) 6 — 51
(A M Balding) *dwlt: wl in rr: shkn up over 2f out: kpt on fnl f: n.d* — **14/1**

0 **7** nk **Peer Pressure**[36] 3856 2-8-10 0 .... JackMitchell(7) 4 — 55
(P Mitchell) *dwlt: sn in last pair: v wd bnd 2f out: kpt on fnl f* — **66/1**

0 **8** 1¼ **Master Of Arts (USA)**[7] 4733 2-9-3 0 .... SebSanders 2 — 51
(Sir Mark Prescott) *nvr bttr than midfield: shkn up over 2f out: hanging and no prog over 1f out* — **14/1**

0 **9** ¾ **Sweet Dane (IRE)**[14] 4537 2-8-12 0 .... EddieAhern 11 — 44
(V Smith) *chsd ldrs: wd and outpcd bnd 2f out: wknd fnl f* — **50/1**

00 **10** hd **Eastbourne**[31] 4016 2-9-3 0 .... StephenCarson 3 — 48
(Eve Johnson Houghton) *trckd ldng pair to 2f out: wknd on inner over 1f out* — **50/1**

11 7 **Imperial Mark (IRE)** 2-9-0 0 .... JerryO'Dwyer(3) 5 — 27
(P J O'Gorman) *s.s: rn green in last pair: bhd over 1f out* — **25/1**

1m 12.96s (0.15) **Going Correction** -0.15s/f (Stan) — **11** Ran SP% **123.0**
Speed ratings (Par 92): **93,92,91,87,86 85,85,83,82,82 73**
CSF £15.89 TOTE £2.00: £1.10, £3.30, £1.30; EX 17.10 Trifecta £75.50 Pool £336.20 - 3.16 winning unit..
Owner Michael O'Flynn & Mrs John Nesbitt **Bred** J & S Kelly **Trained** Upper Lambourn, Berks

FOCUS
A slowly-run first division of the juvenile maiden. The first pair came clear in a tight finish but the form is not that solid.

NOTEBOOK
Rockfield Lodge(IRE), despite taking time to settle, just did enough to edge it near the line and lose his maiden tag at the fourth attempt. He is a consistent performer and deserved this success, but will need to find some improvement if he is to progress now through the nursery ranks from his current mark. (op 10-11, evens in a place)
Sunny Sprite, half-brother to a 7f winner at three, only just failed to get off the mark at the first time of asking and deserves extra credit from his wide draw. He will get further before the year is out and, on this evidence, a similar event should be his for the taking in the coming weeks. (tchd 16-1)
Alls Fair, well backed, dictated from the front at just an ordinary pace and was found out when pressed for the lead nearing the final furlong. He was in turn clear of the remainder in third and should find life easier now he becomes eligible for a nursery mark. (op 7-2)
Raiding Party(IRE), a 20,000euros purchase whose dam scored over 12f at two, took time to get the hang of things and was keeping on with a degree of promise when the race was effectively over. She ought to improve a deal for this debut experience and will appreciate a stiffer test on this evidence.
Sweet Dane(IRE) Official explanation: jockey said filly hung right on final bend

4963 WEATHERBYS BANK MEDIAN AUCTION MAIDEN STKS (DIV II) — 6f (P)
4:20 (4:21) (Class 6) 2-Y-0 — **£1,943** (£578; £288; £144) **Stalls** Low

Form — RPR

04 **1** **Then 'n Now**[10] 4662 2-8-12 0 .... SimonWhitworth 10 — 68+
(C A Cyzer) *cl up: chsd ldng pair over 2f out: r.o fnl f to ld last 100yds* — **7/2**[2]

03 **2** ½ **Ike Quebec (FR)**[15] 4500 2-9-3 0 .... RichardHughes 5 — 72
(R Hannon) *led: rdn and hrd pressed 2f out: edgd rt fnl f: hdd and nt qckn last 100yds* — **4/5**[1]

03 **3** 2½ **Cordon Bleu (IRE)**[26] 4174 2-9-3 0 .... RHills 8 — 64+
(M Johnston) *pressed ldr: upsides 2f out tl hanging and v green over 1f out: nt rcvr* — **13/2**[3]

0 **4** ¾ **Plaka (FR)**[23] 4254 2-8-12 0 .... DaneO'Neill 3 — 57
(J A Osborne) *dwlt: in tch: green and outpcd over 2f out: styd on again fnl f* — **20/1**

060 **5** hd **Deckguard**[21] 4323 2-9-3 58 .... JohnEgan 4 — 61
(J S Moore) *chsd ldng pair to over 2f out: styd on inner and outpcd over 1f out* — **20/1**

0000 **6** 6 **Adam Eterno (IRE)**[62] 3065 2-9-0 49 .... RichardKingscote(3) 2 — 43
(Tom Dascombe) *sn wl outpcd in last: nvr a factor* — **50/1**

00 **7** ½ **Herrbee (IRE)**[15] 4500 2-9-3 0 .... KerrinMcEvoy 1 — 42
(M P Tregoning) *chsd ldrs: pushed along bef 1/2-way: wknd over 2f out* — **8/1**

00 **8** nk **Woodcote Wildcat (USA)**[45] 3589 2-8-9 0 .... WilliamBuick(3) 7 — 36
(N A Callaghan) *sn outpcd in 7th: nvr on terms* — **50/1**

1m 12.53s (-0.28) **Going Correction** -0.15s/f (Stan) — **8** Ran SP% **115.7**
Speed ratings (Par 92): **95,94,91,90,89 81,81,80**
CSF £6.53 TOTE £4.80: £1.40, £1.10, £1.40; EX 10.10 Trifecta £15.20 Pool £602.85 - 28.03 winning units..
Owner Mrs Charles Cyzer **Bred** C A Cyzer **Trained** Maplehurst, W Sussex

FOCUS
This could work out to be the stronger of the two juvenile divisions, despite still being only modest, and it was run at a sound enough pace and the form should prove solid enough.

NOTEBOOK
Then 'n Now, very well backed, rewarded her supporters with a dogged display to get up and lose her maiden tag at the third attempt. The switch to this surface proved right up her street - her half-brother Total Impact is a dual Polytrack winner - and she looked better the further she went, suggesting she could improve again when faced with another furlong. (op 6-1)
Ike Quebec(FR), making his All-Weather debut, had every chance from the front and was only picked off by the winner late in the day. He finished nicely clear of the rest and, now qualifying for nurseries, deserves to go one better now. (tchd 10-11 and evens in places)
Cordon Bleu(IRE), another making his All-Weather bow, showed up nicely until being put under pressure nearing the final furlong and eventually hung his chance away. He clearly needs more time and experience under hisr belt before coming into his own, but the talent is there and he now becomes eligible for a nursery mark. Official explanation: jockey said colt hung both ways (op 4-1)
Plaka(FR), having her first outing on this surface, again ran green and hit a flat spot at a crucial stage despite stepping up in trip here. She did run on when the race was effectively over, however, and looks one to be more interested in when qualifying for nurseries after his next outing. (tchd 22-1)
Deckguard posted his best effort to date on this switch to the Polytrack and left the impression he will be better off when faced with a stiffer test, although his pedigree does suggest he would relish another furlong.

4964 PUSHKABLUE NURSERY — 7f (P)
4:50 (4:51) (Class 5) 2-Y-0 — **£3,238** (£963; £481; £240) **Stalls** Low

Form — RPR

0356 **1** **Determind Stand (USA)**[15] 4501 2-8-7 **72** .... TedDurcan 7 — 76
(Sir Michael Stoute) *chsd ldng pair to 2f out: hrd rdn and rallied fnl f: r.o to ld last strides* — **11/2**[2]

0120 **2** nk **Sourire**[35] 3880 2-9-2 **81** .... SebSanders 1 — 84
(Sir Mark Prescott) *led: drvn 2f out: flashed tail but kpt on wl fnl f: hdd last strides* — **7/1**[3]

0033 **3** 1¼ **Howdigo**[29] 4076 2-8-12 **77** .... JimmyQuinn 6 — 77
(J R Best) *settled in rr: rdn and effrt over 1f out: prog and got through fnl f: styd on to take 3rd last 75yds* — **9/1**

5305 **4** nk **Gulf Coast**[17] 4461 2-7-9 **63** ....(v[1]) WilliamBuick(3) 13 — 62
(M Johnston) *racd on outer: prog into midfield 1/2-way: rdn over 2f out: styd on fnl f: nt pce to rch ldrs* — **8/1**

10 **5** shd **Flight Plan**[12] 4598 2-9-7 **86** .... SimonWhitworth 10 — 85
(C A Cyzer) *racd on outer: chsd ldrs: rdn over 2f out: styd on fnl f: nvr able to chal* — **10/1**

0640 **6** 1½ **Merchant Navy**[29] 4065 2-8-10 **75** .... TGMcLaughlin 2 — 70
(E A L Dunlop) *pressed ldr tl wknd ins fnl f* — **25/1**

040 **7** ½ **Tayarat (IRE)**[28] 4110 2-8-13 **78** .... RHills 9 — 72
(M P Tregoning) *s.i.s: wl in rr: nt clr run on inner wl over 1f out: taken to outer and styd on ins fnl f: no ch* — **9/2**[1]

0553 **8** hd **Deal Flipper**[17] 4453 2-8-7 **72** .... JimCrowley 5 — 65
(P Winkworth) *settled in midfield: rdn over 1f out: nt clr run briefly ent fnl f: kpt on last 100yds* — **11/1**

0260 **9** nk **Latin Scholar (IRE)**[20] 4364 2-8-7 **72** .... FergusSweeney 3 — 65
(A King) *t.k.h: trckd ldrs: 5th and rdn 2f out: nt qckn over 1f out: wl hld whn n.m.r ins fnl f* — **20/1**

310 **10** nk **Geoffdaw**[17] 4461 2-8-8 **73** .... EddieAhern 8 — 65
(M J Wallace) *dwlt: rcvrd to chse ldrs on inner: drvn into 3rd 2f out: wknd fnl f: eased* — **11/1**

654 **11** 1¾ **Jasmines Hero (USA)**[21] 4323 2-8-1 **66** .... RichardThomas 14 — 53
(J S Moore) *racd on outer: a in rr: no ch fnl 2f* — **8/1**

6241 **12** ½ **Mudhish (IRE)**[21] 4316 2-9-1 **80** .... KerrinMcEvoy 4 — 66
(C E Brittain) *chsd ldrs: rdn over 2f out: no prog over 1f out: wknd ins fnl f* — **12/1**

0430 **13** hd **Observatory Ridge**[15] 4501 2-7-6 **64** .... FrankiePickard(7) 11 — 49
(M D I Usher) *a in rr: rdn and struggling in last pair over 2f out* — **66/1**

003 **14** 1¼ **Stand In Flames**[21] 4310 2-7-12 **63** oh3 .... DavidKinsella 12 — 45
(Pat Eddery) *s.i.s: mostly last: no ch fnl 2f* — **25/1**

1m 25.01s (-0.88) **Going Correction** -0.15s/f (Stan) — **40** Ran SP% **125.7**
Speed ratings (Par 94): **99,98,97,96,96 95,94,94,93,93 91,91,90,89**
CSF £44.10 CT £364.52 TOTE £5.90: £2.50, £1.60, £3.80; EX 49.00 Trifecta £155.30 Pool £218.74 - 1.00 winning units..
Owner Saeed Suhail **Bred** Watership Down Stud **Trained** Newmarket, Suffolk

FOCUS
A tight nursery and the form looks fair for the grade and pretty sound.

NOTEBOOK
Determind Stand(USA), with the visor left off, just did enough to reel in the runner-up in the closing stages and was given a strong ride. He has now shown his best form on both his outings to date on Polytrack, this proves he is not ungenuine, and it would not be a surprise to see him go on from this now. Another furlong should also be within his compass before too long. (op 5-1)
Sourire, who shaped better than her finishing position suggests in Listed company last time, was representing a stable with a decent record in this event. She made full use of her inside draw and was only just denied, so looks to have found her level now and has more races of this nature within her grasp. (op 6-1 tchd 15-2)
Howdigo, making his All-Weather/nursery bow, was doing all of his best work at the finish and would have been better off under a more positive ride. He has now finished third on this last three outings, but is capable of a little better over this trip. (tchd 8-1 and 10-1)
Gulf Coast, with the visor replacing blinkers, showed improved form and left the impression he is worth riding more prominently over this trip in the future. He is still one to have reservations about. (tchd 9-1)

Flight Plan, dropping down from Listed company, was not helped by having to race wide throughout from his draw and should be rated better than the bare form. (op 11-1 tchd 9-1)
Merchant Navy paid for running too freely through the early parts on this step up a furlong, but this was a much more encouraging effort all the same. (op 20-1 tchd 18-1)
Tayarat(IRE), making his nursery debut, had to come from behind after a slow start and then found trouble on the inside when attempting to make up his ground. He found just the same pace when eventually switched wide, but is still better than his finishing position would indicate. Official explanation: jockey said colt missed the break (op 11-2)
Latin Scholar(IRE) Official explanation: jockey said colt was denied a clear run

4965 LINGFIELD PARK FOR CONFERENCES H'CAP — 6f (P)
5:20 (5:20) (Class 4) (0-80,80) 3-Y-0+ — **£4,857** (£1,445; £722; £360) **Stalls** Low

Form — RPR
6004 **1** **Little Edward**[15] 4507 9-9-8 **79** ... GeorgeBaker 3 — 88
(R J Hodges) *hld up in midfield: prog on outer wl over 1f out: cajoled along and styd on to ld last 75yds* **5/1**[2]
0411 **2** *nk* **Desert Dreamer (IRE)**[44] 3619 6-9-8 **79** ... EddieAhern 11 — 87+
(G A Butler) *settled in rr: prog on wd outside wl over 1f out: r.o to chal wl ins fnl f: jst hld* **10/3**[1]
1063 **3** *nk* **Fromsong (IRE)**[10] 4664 9-9-7 **78** ... RobertHavlin 12 — 85
(D K Ivory) *trckd ldrs: prog to ld 2f out: edgd rt u.p fnl f: hdd last 75yds* **20/1**
5050 **4** *1* **Mandarin Spirit (IRE)**[128] 1223 7-9-8 **79** ... (b) OscarUrbina 7 — 83
(G C H Chung) *hld up in midfield: prog 2f: rdn to chal ent fnl f: nt qckn last 100yds* **16/1**
006- **5** *1 3/4* **Bertie Southstreet**[379] 4481 4-9-4 **75** ... DaneO'Neill 6 — 73
(J R Best) *stdd s: plld hrd and hld up in last pair: rdn over 2f out: styd on: nvr rchd ldrs* **25/1**
3114 **6** *shd* **Quality Street**[31] 4024 5-9-2 **73** ... (p) RichardThomas 4 — 71
(P Butler) *chsd ldrs: u.p and struggling over 2f out: kpt on again ins fnl f* **6/1**[3]
400 **7** *3/4* **Total Impact**[61] 3080 4-9-9 **80** ... (b[1]) SimonWhitworth 9 — 76
(C A Cyzer) *t.k.h: prom: chal and upsides 2f out: wknd ins fnl f* **16/1**
0050 **8** *1/2* **Adantino**[17] 4456 8-9-2 **78** ... (b) JamesMillman(5) 8 — 72
(B R Millman) *outpcd and pushed along in last pair over 3f out: kpt on fnl f: n.d* **11/1**
1000 **9** *nk* **Mambazo**[19] 4397 5-8-12 **76** ... (e) WilliamCarson(7) 5 — 69
(S C Williams) *led for 2f: lost pl over 2f out: steadily fdd over 1f out* **16/1**
4002 **10** *1/2* **Teen Ager (FR)**[20] 4360 3-9-4 **78** ... JohnEgan 1 — 69
(J S Moore) *chsd ldrs on inner: lost pl 2f out: n.d after* **13/2**
2300 **11** *2* **George The Second**[12] 4594 4-9-0 **74** ... RichardKingscote(3) 10 — 59
(Mrs H Sweeting) *led after 2f to 2f out: wknd over 1f out* **13/2**
200 **12** *3 1/2* **Rosein**[34] 3920 5-9-6 **77** ... TedDurcan 2 — 51
(Mrs G S Rees) *dwlt: nvr beyond midfield on inner: struggling 2f out* **14/1**
1m 11.09s (-1.72) **Going Correction** -0.15s/f (Stan)
WFA 3 from 4yo+ 3lb — **12** Ran SP% **122.0**
Speed ratings (Par 105): **105,104,104,102,100 100,99,98,98,97 95,90**
CSF £22.67 CT £320.67 TOTE £5.60: £1.90, £2.40, £4.50; EX 24.80 Trifecta £139.90 Pool £490.90 - 2.49 winning units. Place 6 £ 46.96, Place 5 £30.79.
Owner J W Mursell **Bred** J W Mursell **Trained** Charlton Mackrell, Somerset
FOCUS
A fair sprint which saw a close finish between the first three. Solid form for the grade rated around the first three.
T/Plt: £39.20 to a £1 stake. Pool: £58,978.30. 1,095.65 winning tickets. T/Qpdt: £2.80 to a £1 stake. Pool: £3,739.30. 974.30 winning tickets. JN

4475 MUSSELBURGH (R-H)
Thursday, August 30
OFFICIAL GOING: Good to firm (good in places)
Wind: Slight, half against Weather: Sunny periods

4966 BANK OF IRELAND APPRENTICE H'CAP — 1m
2:10 (2:10) (Class 6) (0-60,60) 4-Y-0+ — **£2,590** (£770; £385; £192) **Stalls** High

Form — RPR
5200 **1** **Linden's Lady**[8] 4701 7-8-6 **47** ow1 ... (v) AlanCreighton 13 — 54
(J R Weymes) *stdd s: hld up in rr: hdwy on inner over 3f out: swtchd lft over 2f out: effrt to ld wl over 1f out: rdn ent fnl f & kpt on wl fin* **14/1**
3644 **2** *hd* **Miss Porcia**[10] 4663 6-8-0 **48** oh1 ow2 ... BrydieKilloran(7) 9 — 54
(P A Blockley) *a.p: rdn along and ev ch 2f out: kpt on ins fnl f: tl nt qckn nr fin* **9/1**
350 **3** *1/2* **Zabeel Tower**[26] 4156 4-8-11 **52** ... DuranFentiman 11 — 57
(R Allan) *cl up on inner: led after 3f: rdn along 2f out and sn hdd: rallied wl u.p ins fnl f: ev ch tl no ex nr fin* **8/1**
0300 **4** *1 1/4* **Anthemion (IRE)**[8] 4704 10-9-0 **55** ... AndrewMullen 12 — 57
(Mrs J C McGregor) *in tch on inner: hdwy to chse ldrs over 3f out: rdn along 2f out: swtchd lft and drvn over 1f out: kpt on same pce ins fnl f* **10/1**
5005 **5** *hd* **Lobengula (IRE)**[16] 4477 5-9-5 **60** ... AndrewElliott 10 — 62
(I W McInnes) *trckd ldrs: hdwy over 2f out: sn rdn and kpt on same pce appr fnl f* **5/1**[1]
1020 **6** *1* **Attacca**[13] 4562 6-8-13 **54** ... JamieMoriarty 8 — 53
(J R Weymes) *midfield: hdwy wl over 2f out: rdn to chse ldrs wl over 1f out: drvn and no imp appr fnl f* **7/1**[3]
5000 **7** *shd* **Adobe**[73] 2716 12-7-12 **46** ... Julie-AnneCumine(7) 5 — 45
(W M Brisbourne) *in rr: hdwy over 2f out: rdn and kpt on appr fnl f* **33/1**
0050 **8** *nk* **Gifted Flame**[8] 4701 8-9-3 **58** ... (p) NeilBrown 4 — 56
(T D Barron) *hld up: hdwy on outer over 2f out: rdn to chse ldrs wl over 1f out: edgd rt and wknd ent fnl f* **10/1**
-000 **9** *nk* **Mis Chicaf (IRE)**[14] 4525 6-8-2 **46** oh1 ... KellyHarrison(3) 6 — 44
(D Carroll) *nvr bttr than midfield* **16/1**
0300 **10** *1 3/4* **Barataria**[13] 4562 5-9-1 **56** ... MichaelJStainton 3 — 50
(R Bastiman) *a in rr* **6/1**[2]
0000 **11** *nk* **Brace Of Doves**[16] 4477 5-8-10 **51** ... GregFairley 7 — 44
(D W Whillans) *s.i.s: a in rr* **7/1**[3]
0564 **12** *2 1/2* **Jabraan (USA)**[42] 3675 5-8-2 **46** oh1 ... DanielleMcCreery(3) 2 — 33
(D W Chapman) *t.k.h: led 3f: prom tl rdn along 3f out and sn wknd* **22/1**
5/0- **13** *1 1/2* **Senor Eduardo**[305] 1198 10-8-7 **48** ... PJMcDonald 1 — 32
(Mrs H O Graham) *chsd ldrs on outer: rdn along over 3f out and sn wknd* **150/1**
1m 42.19s (-0.31) **Going Correction** +0.05s/f (Good) — **13** Ran SP% **115.7**
Speed ratings (Par 101): **103,102,102,101,100 99,99,99,99,97 97,94,93**
CSF £128.70 CT £748.58 TOTE £16.30: £3.80, £3.50, £3.30; EX 97.60.
Owner Edward Kingsley **Bred** Pigeon House Stud **Trained** Middleham Moor, N Yorks

FOCUS
A weak handicap best rated around the third.

4967 BANK OF IRELAND BUSINESS AND CORPORATE BANKING H'CAP — 5f
2:40 (2:40) (Class 5) (0-70,70) 3-Y-0+ — **£3,238** (£963; £481; £240) **Stalls** Low

Form — RPR
612 **1** **Methaaly (IRE)**[7] 4734 4-8-10 **64** ... SophieDoyle(7) 10 — 77+
(M Mullineaux) *hld up towards rr: hdwy on outer and nt clr run over 1f out: rdn and qcknd ins fnl f to ld nr fin* **3/1**[1]
4232 **2** *1/2* **Welcome Approach**[5] 4800 4-9-8 **69** ... PhillipMakin 6 — 76
(J R Weymes) *towards rr and rdn along after 2f: gd hdwy wl over 1f out: str run to ld wl ins fnl f: hdd and nt qckn nr fin* **3/1**[1]
2335 **3** *nk* **Malapropism**[15] 4507 7-9-9 **70** ... DarryllHolland 7 — 76
(M R Channon) *cl up: rdn to ld over 1f out: drvn and hdd ins fnl f: nt qckn* **5/1**[3]
5000 **4** *shd* **Strawberry Patch (IRE)**[6] 4773 8-8-4 **51** oh3 ... (p) ChrisCatlin 14 — 57
(J S Goldie) *towards rr: hdwy on outer wl over 1f out: sn rdn and styd on wl fnl f* **14/1**
0010 **5** *1 1/2* **Strensall**[8] 4703 10-9-9 **70** ... PaulHanagan 13 — 70
(R E Barr) *hld up in tch: hdwy on outer wl over 1f out: sn rdn and kpt on same pce ins fnl f* **16/1**
3015 **6** *1 3/4* **Rothesay Dancer**[6] 4787 4-9-2 **68** ... KellyHarrison(5) 1 — 62
(J S Goldie) *in rr: gd hdwy wl over 1f out: rdn to chse ldrs ent fnl f: kpt on same pce* **12/1**
0060 **7** *1 1/2* **Mutayam**[8] 4719 7-8-4 **51** oh6 ow3 ... (t) AndrewElliott(3) 11 — 42
(D A Nolan) *prom: rdn over 1f out and grad wknd* **125/1**
0000 **8** *1 1/4* **Compton Lad**[26] 4157 4-8-7 **54** oh6 ow3 ... GrahamGibbons 5 — 38
(D A Nolan) *prom: rdn along over 1f out and sn wknd* **100/1**
2611 **9** *2 1/2* **Toy Top (USA)**[1] 4939 4-8-11 **57** 6ex ... (b) NeilBrown(5) 9 — 38
(M Dods) *prom: rdn along over 1f out and sn wknd* **4/1**[2]
006 **10** *3/4* **Seafield Towers**[1] 4934 7-8-4 **51** oh4 ... (b[1]) GregFairley 12 — 23
(Miss L A Perratt) *sn led: rdn along 2f out: hdd over 1f out and sn wknd* **22/1**
000 **11** *6* **Sokoke**[89] 2244 6-8-8 **58** oh6 ow7 ... MarkLawson(3) 4 — 9
(D A Nolan) *a towards rr* **100/1**
0000 **12** *3* **Rosie's Result**[6] 4768 7-8-1 **51** oh6 ... AndrewMullen(3) 2 — —
(M Todhunter) *s.i.s: a in rr* **50/1**
60.88 secs (0.38) **Going Correction** +0.05s/f (Good) — **12** Ran SP% **116.0**
Speed ratings (Par 103): **98,97,96,96,94 91,88,86,82,81 72,67**
CSF £11.20 CT £42.84 TOTE £3.90: £1.30, £1.60, £2.00; EX 13.70.
Owner The Bellflower Methaaly Partnership **Bred** Scuderia Golden Horse S R L **Trained** Alpraham, Cheshire
FOCUS
A modest handicap run in a poor time, 0.38sec slower than the two-year-old seller and the form looks suspect.

4968 E.B.F./BANK OF IRELAND FILLIES' MEDIAN AUCTION MAIDEN STKS — 7f 30y
3:10 (3:11) (Class 5) 2-Y-O — **£3,238** (£963; £481; £240) **Stalls** High

Form — RPR
0030 **1** **Lady Bower**[10] 4669 2-9-0 58 ... GregFairley 2 — 62
(M Johnston) *mde all: rdn clr 3f over 3f out: drvn over 1f out: styd on wl* **13/2**
0 **2** *1* **Priceless Speedfit**[8] 4709 2-9-0 0 ... PaulHanagan 6 — 59
(G G Margarson) *in tch: hdwy to chse wnr 2f out and sn rdn: drvn and kpt on ins fnl f* **7/1**
0 **3** *hd* **Khandala (IRE)**[24] 4232 2-9-0 0 ... HayleyTurner 1 — 59
(M L W Bell) *stdd s and bhd: hdwy 3f out whn swtchd ins and rdn 2f out: nt clr run and swtchd lft over 1f out: drvn and styd on ins fnl f* **2/1**[2]
63 **4** *hd* **Heavenly Saint**[49] 3446 2-9-0 0 ... DarryllHolland 3 — 58
(M R Channon) *chsd ldrs: hdwy 3f out: rdn along on outer 2f out and sn edgd rt: drvn and hung rt ins fnl f: styd on* **15/8**[1]
000 **5** *1 1/2* **Kiwi Princess**[6] 4784 2-8-7 0 ... PatrickDonaghy(7) 4 — 54
(M Brittain) *chsd ldrs: rdn along and n.m.r 2f out: drvn and styng on whn hmpd and squeezed out ins fnl f* **33/1**
3 **6** *5* **Lady Of The Park (IRE)**[18] 4428 2-9-0 0 ... GrahamGibbons 5 — 41
(P A Blockley) *chsd wnr: rdn along and edgd lft over 2f out: drvn and wknd over 1f out: eased* **6/1**[3]
60 **7** *dist* **Robslastcall**[8] 4715 2-8-7 0 ... (b[1]) AdamCarter(7) 7 — —
(A Berry) *sn outpcd and wl bhd fr 1/2-way* **200/1**
1m 31.8s (1.86) **Going Correction** +0.05s/f (Good) — **7** Ran SP% **111.7**
Speed ratings (Par 91): **91,89,89,89,87 81,—**
CSF £47.68 TOTE £7.60: £2.90, £3.80; EX 51.40.
Owner Brian Yeardley Continental Ltd **Bred** Brian Yeardley Continental Ltd **Trained** Middleham Moor, N Yorks
FOCUS
A weak maiden won by a filly rated just 58 and basically plating-class form.
NOTEBOOK
Lady Bower, the most exposed runner in this line-up, has a rating of just 58, but this was a weak event and she was given an uncontested lead. She should pay her way at a lowly level in nursery company. (op 10-1)
Priceless Speedfit, whose dam was a 1m winner at three, showed more than on her debut in heavy ground. These conditions evidently suited her better. (op 8-1)
Khandala(IRE), who had shaped with promise on her debut at Windsor, did not really build on that effort as much as had looked likely despite the extra furlong playing to her strengths. (op 11-4)
Heavenly Saint, having her third run, hung under pressure inside the last and and did not build on her Folkestone effort. She is, however, now eligible to run in nurseries. (op 7-4)
Kiwi Princess is a half-sister to six winners, mostly sprinters, but she does not do anything quickly. (tchd 28-1)
Lady Of The Park(IRE) may prefer an easier surface. Official explanation: jockey said filly was unsuited by the good to firm (good in places) ground (op 7-2)

4969 BANK OF IRELAND GLOBAL MARKETS H'CAP — 1m 6f
3:40 (3:40) (Class 5) (0-75,73) 4-Y-0+ — **£3,886** (£1,156; £577; £288) **Stalls** High

Form — RPR
5265 **1** **Collette's Choice**[13] 4558 4-8-11 **61** ... (p) PaulHanagan 4 — 66
(R A Fahey) *hld up in tch: hdwy 3f out: rdn to chal 2f out: drvn and edgd rt ins fnl f: led last 50yds: jst hld on* **5/1**
3014 **2** *shd* **Cotton Eyed Joe (IRE)**[20] 4352 6-9-6 **73** ... PJMcDonald(3) 5 — 78
(G A Swinbank) *trckd ldrs: hdwy 3f out: led wl over 1f out and sn rdn: drvn ins fnl f: hdd last 50yds: rallied on line* **9/2**[3]
2305 **3** *3 1/2* **Campli (IRE)**[23] 4248 5-9-0 **67** ... MichaelJStainton(3) 3 — 67
(Micky Hammond) *t.k.h: hld up in tch: hdwy over 3f out: sn rdn along: drvn wl over 1f out: styd on ins fnl f: nrst fin* **14/1**

2110 **4** *hd* **Nero West (FR)**[29] 4056 6-9-8 **72**....(b) TomEaves 8 72
(I Semple) *led: clr 1/2-way: rdn along over 2f out: hdd over 1f out and grad wknd* **4/1**[2]
1321 **5** *nk* **Kyber**[16] 4475 6-8-6 **61**.... GaryBartley(5) 1 60
(J S Goldie) *hld up in rr: hdwy 3f out: rdn along over 2f out: styd on wl appr fnl f: nrst fin* **4/1**[2]
5416 **6** *5* **Danzatrice**[19] 4380 5-8-13 **63**.... DarryllHolland 2 55
(C W Thornton) *hld up: a in rr* **10/3**[1]
0001 **7** *1/2* **City Miss**[19] 4380 4-7-13 **54** oh3.... KellyHarrison(5) 7 46
(Miss L A Perratt) *chsd ldr: rdn along 3f out: sn drvn and wknd* **20/1**

3m 3.65s (-2.05) **Going Correction** +0.05s/f (Good) 7 Ran SP% **109.4**
Speed ratings (Par 103): **107,106,104,104,104 101,101**
CSF £25.05 CT £265.83 TOTE £6.40: £3.10, £2.10; EX 25.90.
Owner P D Smith Holdings Ltd **Bred** Highclere Stud Ltd **Trained** Musley Bank, N Yorks
■ Stewards' Enquiry : P J McDonald one-day ban:used whip without giving gelding time to respond (Sep 10)

FOCUS
An ordinary handicap and a hard race to rate positively.

4970 BANK OF IRELAND BUSINESS AND CORPORATE BANKING (S) STKS 5f
4:10 (4:10) (Class 6) 2-Y-O **£2,101** (£2,101; £481; £240) **Stalls** Low

Form RPR
0304 **1** **Rope Bridge (IRE)**[8] 4715 2-8-11 55....(b) DavidAllan 4 60
(T D Easterby) *disp ld tl led over 1f out: sn rdn and edgd lft: drvn and hung rt ins fnl f: hdd last 75yds: rallied post* **9/2**[2]
4500 **1** *dht* **Thomas Malory (IRE)**[23] 4255 2-8-11 53.... HayleyTurner 5 60
(Miss V Haigh) *in rr: pushed along and hdwy wl over 1f out: rdn and styd on ins fnl f to ld last 75yds: drvn and jnd on line* **8/1**
6000 **3** *2* **La Guancha**[8] 4715 2-8-6 53....(tp) GregFairley 3 48
(D A Nolan) *chsd ldrs: hdwy whn bmpd wl over 1f out: sn rdn and kpt on same pce ins fnl f* **50/1**
2430 **4** *1 3/4* **Shatter Resistant (IRE)**[11] 4629 2-8-11 72....(v[1]) DarryllHolland 1 47
(M R Channon) *disp ld: pushed along and edgd rt 1/2-way: sn rdn: hung rt and bmpd wl over 1f out: sn btn* **1/1**[1]
3303 **5** *1* **Next Best**[16] 4476 2-8-6 55.... PaulHanagan 6 38
(A Berry) *cl up on outer: effrt and ev ch 2f out: sn rdn and wknd appr fnl f* **11/2**
0040 **6** *7* **Victorian Princess (IRE)**[17] 4453 2-8-6 56.... ChrisCatlin 2 13
(E J O'Neill) *chsd ldrs: rdn along 2f out and sn wknd* **5/1**[3]

60.50 secs **Going Correction** +0.05s/f (Good) 6 Ran SP% **113.3**
Speed ratings (Par 92): **102,102,98,96,94 83**
WIN: Thomas Mallory 5.00, Rope Bridge £2.40; PL: TM £3.40, RB £2.10; EX: RP/TM £21.40, TM/RP £17.40; CSF: RP/TM £19.22, TM/RP £21.69.Thomas Mallory was bought in for £5,500; there was no bid for Rope Bridge.
Owner Habton Farms **Bred** Patrick F Kelly **Trained** Great Habton, N Yorks
Owner R J Budge **Bred** Ralph And Helen O'Brien **Trained** Wiseton, Notts
■ Stewards' Enquiry : David Allan one-day ban: used whip with excessive frequency (Sep 10)
Hayley Turner caution: used whip with excessive frequency

FOCUS
Moderate form with the favourite disappointing badly and the third along with the time sets the level. Due to technical difficulties and the judge not having a photo of the finish to view, he was forced to call a dead-heat.

NOTEBOOK
Rope Bridge(IRE) picked up late to share the spoils on the line. This better ground suited him but the form does not amount to much. (op 6-1 tchd 13-2)
Thomas Malory(IRE) was not sure to handle this shorter distance having tended to get outpaced over 6f in the past, but the drop in class proved the answer. (op 6-1 tchd 13-2)
La Guancha probably ran to her best form in third and will struggle to win a similar contest. (tchd 66-1)
Shatter Resistant(IRE) looked the one to beat on official ratings, and he had a visor on for the first time on this drop into selling company, but he has not looked the heartiest of battlers in the past and proved very disappointing here, hanging inside the final two furlongs. He looks one to avoid. Official explanation: jockey said gelding hung right-handed from halfway (op 11-10 tchd 10-11)
Next Best has been held on a number of occasions at this level and the quicker ground did not help her. (op 6-1)

4971 BANK OF IRELAND H'CAP 1m
4:40 (4:43) (Class 5) (0-70,68) 3-Y-O **£3,238** (£963; £481; £240) **Stalls** High

Form RPR
3300 **1** **Grand Diamond (IRE)**[8] 4701 3-9-1 **60**....(p) DanielTudhope 9 59
(J S Goldie) *trckd ldrs on inner: smooth hdwy to ld over 2f out: rdn wl over 1f out: drvn ins fnl f and styd on wl* **10/3**[1]
2055 **2** *1/2* **Crosby Jemma**[26] 4178 3-8-6 **51** oh2 ow2.... GrahamGibbons 8 49
(J R Weymes) *in tch on inner: hdwy 3f out: swtchd lft and rdn to chal over 1f out: sn drvn and ev ch: kpt on same pce towards fin* **10/1**
0000 **3** *1/2* **Gallows Hill (USA)**[16] 4480 3-8-4 **49** oh2....(v[1]) PaulHanagan 1 47+
(R A Fahey) *hld up in rr: hdwy 3f out: nt clr run wl over 1f out: swtchd rt and rdn ent fnl f: styd on towards fin* **12/1**
2515 **4** *1/2* **Mangano**[8] 4714 3-8-3 **55**.... DanielleMcCreery(7) 7 51
(A Berry) *in rr and rdn along 1/2-way: swtchd outside and hdwy over 2f out: styd on strly ins fnl f: nrst fin* **4/1**[2]
650 **5** *1/2* **Wilmington**[178] 624 3-9-4 **66**.... AndrewMullen(3) 5 60
(Mrs J C McGregor) *trckd ldrs: swtchd lft and hdwy over 2f out: rdn and ch wl over 1f out: sn drvn and kpt on same pce* **40/1**
6005 **6** *2 1/2* **Beck**[18] 4427 3-8-1 **49** oh3.... DuranFentiman(3) 2 38
(W M Brisbourne) *in tch on outer: hdwy to chse ldrs 3f out: sn rdn along and grad wknd fr wl over 1f out* **13/2**
0140 **7** *1/2* **Distant Pleasure**[22] 4287 3-9-4 **63**.... PhillipMakin 4 51
(M Dods) *prom: rdn along over 2f out: sn drvn and edgd rt: grad wknd* **9/2**[3]
5035 **8** *1/2* **Optical Illusion (USA)**[22] 4282 3-9-9 **68**.... TomEaves 3 54
(I Semple) *t.k.h: prom tl rdn along over 2f out and grad wknd* **7/1**
0000 **9** *4* **Senora Lenorah**[8] 4714 3-8-0 **50** oh4 ow1.... AnnStokell(5) 10 27
(D A Nolan) *led: hdd over 2f out: sn rdn and hung lft wl over 1f out: wknd* **125/1**

1m 42.77s (0.27) **Going Correction** +0.05s/f (Good) 9 Ran SP% **107.1**
Speed ratings (Par 100): **100,99,99,98,98 95,95,94,90**
CSF £32.51 CT £298.29 TOTE £3.50: £1.70, £2.40, £3.80; EX 38.90.
Owner Mrs M Craig **Bred** Newberry Stud Company **Trained** Uplawmoor, E Renfrews
■ Countess Majella was withdrawn (12/1, refused to enter stalls.) R4 applies, deduct 5p in the £.

FOCUS
A poor handicap in which the winner probably did not need to improve to score and hard to rate positively with the runner-up 4lb out of the handicap.

Distant Pleasure Official explanation: jockey said filly hung left-handed on bend turn into home straight

4972 BANK OF IRELAND GLOBAL MARKETS H'CAP 1m 4f
5:10 (5:10) (Class 6) (0-65,63) 3-Y-O+ **£2,590** (£770; £385; £192) **Stalls** High

Form RPR
-223 **1** **Princely Ted (IRE)**[22] 4267 6-9-4 **53**.... GrahamGibbons 8 62
(P A Blockley) *trckd ldrs: hdwy on inner to ld over 2f out: rdn over 1f out: styd on wl fnl f* **7/1**
0206 **2** *2* **Dance Sauvage**[16] 4475 4-8-11 **49**.... PJMcDonald(3) 13 55
(C W Thornton) *dwlt and towards rr: hdwy on inner 2f out: sn rdn and styd on wl fnl f* **10/1**
1600 **3** *nk* **Best Of The Lot (USA)**[13] 4582 5-10-0 **63**.... PaulHanagan 11 69
(R A Fahey) *a.p: cl up 1/2-way: rdn along and ev ch 2f out: drvn: hung rt and one pce ins fnl f* **6/1**[3]
0020 **4** *3/4* **Roman History (IRE)**[13] 4582 4-9-3 **52**....(p) SilvestreDeSousa 3 56
(Miss Tracy Waggott) *in tch: hdwy to chse ldrs over 2f out: sn rdn and kpt on same pce ent fnl f* **16/1**
5024 **5** *1 1/4* **Intavac Boy**[21] 4340 6-9-7 **59**.... MichaelJStainton(3) 12 61
(S P Griffiths) *led: rdn along over 3f out: hdd over 2f out: sn drvn and grad wknd fr over 1f out* **11/2**[2]
1401 **6** *nk* **Regency Red (IRE)**[14] 4521 9-9-0 **56**.... Julie-AnneCumine(7) 9 58
(W M Brisbourne) *hld up towards rr: hdwy on wd outside over 2f out: sn rdn and kpt on same pce appr fnl f* **10/1**
1040 **7** *3/4* **Rotuma (IRE)**[13] 4580 8-9-1 **50**....(b) TomEaves 4 51
(M Dods) *prom: rdn along wl over 2f out: drvn wl over 1f out and sn wknd* **25/1**
0065 **8** *1/2* **Borsch (IRE)**[16] 4475 5-8-5 **45**.... KellyHarrison(5) 1 45
(Miss L A Perratt) *hld up towards rr: gd hdwy on outer over 3f out: rdn along wl over 2f out: grad wknd* **66/1**
4001 **9** *shd* **Paparaazi (IRE)**[23] 4249 5-10-0 **63**.... DanielTudhope 5 63
(I W McInnes) *hld up in rr: hdwy on wd outside over 2f out: rdn and in tch over 1f out: snrdn and no imp* **12/1**
0162 **10** *1* **English Archer**[14] 4534 4-9-0 **49**.... DarryllHolland 14 47
(W M Brisbourne) *a towards rr* **9/2**[1]
3400 **11** *4* **Ho Pang Yau**[9] 3814 9-8-5 **45**.... GaryBartley(5) 7 37
(J S Goldie) *a towards rr* **12/1**
00 **12** *1* **Kyle Of Lochalsh**[11] 4096 7-8-10 **45**.... GregFairley 6 35
(Miss Lucinda V Russell) *a towards rr* **20/1**
00-3 **13** *nk* **Marvin Gardens**[22] 4294 4-8-10 **45**.... DavidAllan 10 35
(John Berry) *chsd ldrs: rdn along over 3f out: sn wknd* **10/1**
004/ **14** *16* **Royal Game**[75] 3816 5-8-10 **45**.... PhillipMakin 2 9
(M Todhunter) *a in rr: t.o fnl 3f* **25/1**

2m 38.48s (1.58) **Going Correction** +0.05s/f (Good) 14 Ran SP% **122.8**
Speed ratings (Par 101): **96,94,94,93,93 92,92,92,92,91 88,88,87,77**
CSF £73.75 CT £455.16 TOTE £10.10: £3.50, £3.80, £3.00; EX 117.10 Place 6 £4157.08, Place 5 £732.39.
Owner M S Heath **Bred** Thomas C Kerr **Trained** Lambourn, Berks

FOCUS
Modest form but sound enough rated through the third and fifth.
English Archer Official explanation: jockey said gelding failed to handle either bend
T/Plt: £2,454.30 to a £1 stake. Pool: £57,324.45. 17.05 winning tickets. T/Qpdt: £225.60 to a £1 stake. Pool: £3,171.70. 10.40 winning tickets. JR

4668 WOLVERHAMPTON (A.W) (L-H)
Thursday, August 30

OFFICIAL GOING: Standard
Wind: Fresh across Weather: Overcast

4973 SPONSOR A RACE BY CALLING 0870 220 2442 H'CAP 5f 20y(P)
2:30 (2:30) (Class 6) (0-50,54) 3-Y-O+ **£2,730** (£806; £403) **Stalls** Low

Form RPR
0023 **1** **Kennington**[19] 4397 7-9-3 **50**.... DMylonas 7 56
(Mrs C A Dunnett) *chsd ldrs: swtchd rt ins fnl f: rdn to ld towards fin* **13/2**
0050 **2** *1/2* **Meikle Barfil**[3] 4881 5-9-1 **48**....(tp) SteveDrowne 5 53
(J M Bradley) *hld up: hdwy over 1f out: hung lft ins fnl f: r.o* **6/1**[3]
6500 **3** *1/2* **Twinned (IRE)**[13] 4561 4-9-1 **48**.... LPKeniry 10 51
(M J Wilkinson) *mid-div: hdwy over 1f out: rdn to ld ins fnl f: hdd towards fin* **40/1**
0501 **4** *hd* **Arfinnit (IRE)**[10] 4668 6-9-4 **54** 6ex....(v) LiamJones(3) 6 56
(Mrs A L M King) *s.i.s: hdwy over 1f out: styd on* **5/1**[2]
5056 **5** *nk* **Violet's Pride**[2] 4795 3-8-8 **50**.... MatthewDavies(7) 4 51
(S Parr) *led: hdd over 3f out: led again 2f out: sn rdn: hdd and unable qckn ins fnl f* **20/1**
4010 **6** *hd* **He's A Rocket (IRE)**[34] 3921 6-8-9 **49**.... DeclanCannon(7) 2 49
(John R Upson) *chsd ldrs: hmpd 4f out: nt clr run over 2f out: r.o* **20/1**
6004 **7** *shd* **Mystery Pips**[6] 4787 7-9-1 **48**....(v) KimTinkler 1 48
(N Tinkler) *chsd ldrs: rdn 1/2-way: ev ch ins fnl f: styd on same pce* **10/1**
1405 **8** *1 1/2* **Elvina**[11] 4635 6-8-9 **47**.... PatrickHills(5) 3 41
(A G Newcombe) *chsd ldr tl led over 3f out: hdd 2f out: rdn and ev ch over 1f out: no ex ins fnl f* **4/1**[1]
0320 **9** *5* **Ruby's Dream**[13] 4561 5-8-13 **46**....(p) StephenDonohoe 8 22
(J M Bradley) *sn outpcd* **8/1**
0100 **10** *4* **Bee Magic**[10] 4668 4-9-3 **50**....(b) SamHitchcott 13 12
(C N Kellett) *mid-div: rdn over 3f out: wknd 2f out* **33/1**
0500 **11** *1/2* **Spirit Of Coniston**[18] 4423 4-9-3 **50**....(b) RoystonFfrench 11 10
(C J Teague) *sn outpcd* **5/1**[2]
00-0 **12** *6* **Diamond Josh**[8] 4706 5-9-0 **47**.... MickyFenton 12 —
(M Mullineaux) *s.s: outpcd* **25/1**

62.12 secs (-0.70) **Going Correction** -0.10s/f (Stan)
WFA 3 from 4yo+ 2lb 12 Ran SP% **119.9**
Speed ratings (Par 101): **101,100,99,99,98 98,98,95,87,81 80,70**
CSF £42.52 CT £1462.79 TOTE £9.30: £2.40, £2.60, £6.70; EX 60.20.
Owner Mrs Christine Dunnett **Bred** C J R Trotter **Trained** Hingham, Norfolk
■ Stewards' Enquiry : Patrick Hills caution: careless riding

FOCUS
A modest but competitive sprint handicap. They finished in a heap and, with the winning time 0.37 seconds slower than the following seller, the form rated through the fourth is probably not worth a great deal.

4974 STAY AT THE WOLVERHAMPTON HOLIDAY INN (S) STKS 5f 20y(P)
3:00 (3:01) (Class 5) 3-Y-O+ **£2,914** (£867; £433; £216) **Stalls** Low

Form RPR
2040 **1** **Desperate Dan**[24] 4233 6-8-12 78 (b) TPQueally 12 73+
(J A Osborne) *trckd ldrs: led ins fnl f: shkn up and r.o wl* **10/11**[1]
0660 **2** 3 ½ **Sofinella (IRE)**[9] 4689 4-8-2 44 LukeMorris(5) 3 55
(A W Carroll) *led: hdd over 3f out: led again over 1f out: rdn and hdd ins fnl f: unable qckn* **33/1**
3200 **3** 3 ½ **Luloah**[35] 3869 4-8-7 48 PaulEddery 9 42
(J G M O'Shea) *prom: rdn 1/2-way: wknd over 1f out* **25/1**
00- **4** 1 **Rag Tag (IRE)**[387] 4223 4-8-12 74 (t) LPKeniry 10 44
(A M Balding) *chsd ldr: led over 3f out: rdn and hdd over 1f out: wknd fnl f* **17/2**[3]
000 **5** 1 **Jessica Wigmo**[3] 4881 4-8-2 45 KevinGhunowa(5) 4 35
(A W Carroll) *hld up: hmpd over 3f out: n.d* **66/1**
2050 **6** shd **Nawayea**[16] 4471 4-8-10 45 ow3 (b) StephenDonohoe 13 38
(C N Allen) *mid-div: hdwy 1/2-way: rdn and wknd over 1f out* **33/1**
3500 **7** 1 **Tang**[24] 4226 3-8-2 48 LiamJones(3) 5 31
(W G M Turner) *chsd ldrs: lost pl over 3f out: n.d after* **33/1**
4645 **8** ¾ **Lady Hopeful (IRE)**[8] 4712 5-8-7 45 (b) AdrianMcCarthy 8 29
(Peter Grayson) *s.i.s: sn prom: bmpd over 3f out: rdn and wknd over 1f out* **20/1**
00-0 **9** 2 **Lord Blue Boy**[9] 4685 3-8-3 54 (v[1]) JackDean(7) 6 26
(W G M Turner) *sn outpcd* **66/1**
60- **10** ¾ **Saint Remus (IRE)**[332] 5735 3-8-10 0 BrettDoyle 2 24
(Peter Grayson) *hld up: a in rr* **66/1**
2000 **11** nk **North Fleet**[10] 4668 4-8-12 48 (b[1]) SteveDrowne 11 23
(J M Bradley) *s.i.s: hdwy and hung lft over 3f out: rdn and wknd 1/2-way* **25/1**
0000 **12** 2 ½ **Borzoi Maestro**[44] 3618 6-8-10 48 (p) MarkCoumbe(7) 7 19
(G F Bridgwater) *chsd ldrs: sn hung lft: hmpd and lost pl 4f out: sn bhd* **50/1**
3221 **R** **Danish Blues (IRE)**[16] 4478 4-9-3 59 AdrianTNicholls 1 —
(D Nicholls) *ref to r* **5/2**[2]

61.75 secs (-1.07) **Going Correction** -0.10s/f (Stan)
WFA 3 from 4yo+ 2lb **13** Ran SP% **119.2**
Speed ratings (Par 103): **104,98,92,91,89 89,87,86,83,82 81,77,—**
CSF £48.35 TOTE £1.90: £1.20, £9.10, £4.50; EX 46.10.The winner was sold to Andy Haynes for 12,000gns.
Owner Mountgrange Stud **Bred** Sheikh Amin Dahlawi **Trained** Upper Lambourn, Berks

FOCUS
A very moderate and uncompetitive seller, made even more so when second-favourite Danish Blues planted himself as the stalls opened, but the winning time was 0.37 seconds quicker than the preceding handicap. The winner is above average for the grade but the placed horses are the best guide to the level.
Jessica Wigmo Official explanation: jockey said filly suffered interference on the bend

4975 WOLVERHAMPTON-RACECOURSE.CO.UK NURSERY 5f 216y(P)
3:30 (3:33) (Class 4) 2-Y-O **£6,309** (£1,888; £944; £472; £235) **Stalls** Low

Form RPR
0150 **1** **Gin Genereux**[26] 4154 2-8-5 69 RoystonFfrench 8 76
(M Johnston) *mde all: edgd lft over 4f out: rdn out* **14/1**
4313 **2** 1 ¾ **Gross Prophet**[2] 4916 2-8-9 78 TolleyDean(5) 4 80
(Tom Dascombe) *chsd ldrs: rdn over 2f out: styd on* **9/2**
310 **3** ½ **Ten Meropa (USA)**[26] 4152 2-9-7 85 TPQueally 1 86+
(J A Osborne) *hld up in tch: hmpd over 4f out: rdn over 1f out: styd on same pce ins fnl f* **4/1**[3]
506 **4** 1 **Bermacha**[26] 4181 2-7-13 63 oh1 ow1 NickyMackay 6 61
(W R Muir) *chsd ldrs: lost pl over 4f out: rdn over 2f out: styd on fnl f* **20/1**
4620 **5** 1 ½ **Angle Of Attack (IRE)**[2] 4923 2-8-4 68 SaleemGolam 5 61
(R A Fahey) *chsd ldrs: nt clr run over 4f out: rdn over 2f out: styd on same pce appr fnl f* **8/1**
4456 **6** 2 ½ **Berrymead**[51] 3398 2-7-13 63 AdrianMcCarthy 7 49
(M W Easterby) *sn pushed along in rr: hdwy over 3f out: wknd 2f out* **20/1**
0100 **7** ½ **Bonny's Babe**[16] 4484 2-7-13 63 oh9 ow1 FrankieMcDonald 9 47
(B Smart) *s.i.s: outpcd* **40/1**
6400 **8** 3 **Fitolini**[6] 4775 2-7-11 66 LukeMorris(5) 2 41
(Mrs G S Rees) *dwlt: hdwy and hmpd over 4f out: rdn over 2f out: wknd over 1f out* **7/2**[2]
612 **9** 5 **Wise Son**[19] 4406 2-9-2 83 LiamJones(3) 3 43
(W J Haggas) *chsd ldrs: hmpd over 4f out: sn lost pl* **3/1**[1]

1m 14.43s (-1.38) **Going Correction** -0.10s/f (Stan) **9** Ran SP% **115.1**
Speed ratings (Par 96): **105,102,102,100,98 95,94,90,84**
CSF £73.75 CT £306.33 TOTE £14.30: £3.10, £1.70, £1.90; EX 68.40.
Owner Mrs R J Jacobs **Bred** Newsells Park Stud Limited **Trained** Middleham Moor, N Yorks

FOCUS
A decent and valuable nursery for the track, but it turned into a rather unsatisfactory affair as the winner caused problems in behind as he moved over to the rail half a mile from home. Nevertheless, the form looks solid enough with the placed horses rated to pre-race marks.

NOTEBOOK
Gin Genereux had been a bit disappointing in two starts since winning a Hamilton maiden, but he took well to the Polytrack at the first time of asking and put up a brave front-running display, although he did cause plenty of trouble in behind when moving to the far rail half a mile from home. There should be more to come from him if returning to this surface. (op 16-1)
Gross Prophet missed the early trouble and ran a decent race just two days after running well over 7f at Lingfield. Previously a winner over course and distance, he obviously likes it here. (op 3-1 tchd 11-4)
Ten Meropa(USA) ◆ was one of those hampered around half a mile from the finish but, after gathering himself together, he was travelling well on the inside turning for home and ran on to the line. He should be winning again before too long. (op 5-2 tchd 9-2)
Bermacha, making her nursery debut, stayed on late and again suggested that she really needs further. (tchd 22-1)
Angle Of Attack(IRE) did not enjoy the best of trips on his sand debut. (op 12-1 tchd 15-2)
Fitolini was one of those caught up in the trouble around half a mile from the finish. (op 5-1)
Wise Son, making his sand debut, could never get back into the race after the trouble and it may be best to forgive him this. (op 4-1)

4976 ENJOY THE HORIZONS RESTAURANT H'CAP 1m 4f 50y(P)
4:00 (4:00) (Class 4) (0-80,80) 3-Y-O+ **£6,309** (£1,888; £944; £472; £235) **Stalls** Low

Form RPR
-310 **1** **Chord**[32] 3993 3-9-1 76 (v) RyanMoore 2 87
(Sir Michael Stoute) *chsd ldr: led 2f out: rdn clr fnl f* **6/4**[1]
3153 **2** 3 ½ **Sister Maria (USA)**[12] 4615 3-9-2 77 RoystonFfrench 8 82
(E A L Dunlop) *prom: rdn over 2f out: edgd lft over 1f out: styd on same pce* **4/1**[2]
2412 **3** 1 **Lady Friend**[28] 4108 5-9-7 77 PatrickHills(5) 4 80
(J W Hills) *chsd ldrs: rdn over 1f out: styd on* **13/2**[3]
3120 **4** 1 ½ **El Toreador (USA)**[43] 3645 3-9-5 80 NickyMackay 1 81
(G A Butler) *chsd ldrs: rdn over 2f out: wknd ins fnl f* **9/1**
3060 **5** nk **Bull Market (IRE)**[12] 4597 4-10-0 79 TPQueally 3 80
(J A Osborne) *hld up: plld hrd: rdn over 1f out: nvr trbld ldrs* **10/1**
001 **6** nk **Global Traffic**[34] 3901 3-8-9 70 ow2 StephenDonohoe 7 70
(P D Evans) *s.i.s: hld up: rdn over 2f out: n.d* **14/1**
1000 **7** hd **Tromp**[21] 4318 6-9-6 71 SteveDrowne 5 71
(D J Coakley) *sn led: rdn and hdd 2f out: wknd fnl f* **10/1**
0440 **8** 8 **Desert Leader (IRE)**[10] 4672 6-9-8 73 MickyFenton 6 60
(R W Price) *hld up: rdn over 3f out: wknd over 2f out* **20/1**

2m 40.19s (-2.23) **Going Correction** -0.10s/f (Stan)
WFA 3 from 4yo+ 10lb **8** Ran SP% **112.9**
Speed ratings (Par 105): **103,100,100,99,98 98,98,93**
CSF £7.16 CT £28.38 TOTE £2.30: £1.40, £1.50, £1.60; EX 6.70.
Owner Cheveley Park Stud **Bred** Cheveley Park Stud Ltd **Trained** Newmarket, Suffolk

FOCUS
Another quite valuable and decent handicap, but the pace was modest and things did not quicken up appreciably until well past halfway. The placed horses set the standard.

4977 NAME A RACE TO ENHANCE YOUR BRAND MEDIAN AUCTION MAIDEN STKS 7f 32y(P)
4:30 (4:34) (Class 5) 3-5-Y-O **£3,886** (£1,156; £577; £288) **Stalls** High

Form RPR
6400 **1** **Memphis Marie**[15] 4518 3-8-12 47 StephenDonohoe 4 60
(C N Allen) *led 6f out: hdd over 3f out: led over 2f out: sn rdn: all out* **17/2**
-246 **2** nk **Six Of Trumps (IRE)**[21] 4321 3-9-3 62 TPQueally 1 64
(J A Osborne) *led: hdd 6f out: led again over 3f out: rdn and hdd over 2f out: stl ev ch tl nt qckn towards fin* **7/2**[2]
6 **3** 2 **Southwarknewsflash**[15] 4513 3-8-12 0 (t) DMylonas 7 54
(Mrs C A Dunnett) *s.i.s: in rr tl r.o ins fnl f: nrst fin* **66/1**
0- **4** 1 ¼ **Norman Tradition**[358] 5106 3-8-12 0 LPKeniry 3 50
(A M Balding) *prom: rdn over 2f out: sn outpcd* **16/1**
3-64 **5** shd **Beech Games**[10] 4659 3-9-3 77 (p) MickyFenton 11 55
(F Jordan) *s.i.s: hld up: hdwy over 2f out: rdn and hung lft over 1f out: nt run on* **8/1**
2200 **6** ½ **Sky Masterson**[72] 2749 3-9-3 70 (p) RyanMoore 10 54
(J H M Gosden) *hld up: hdwy over 2f out: sn rdn and no rspnse* **11/4**[1]
7 1 **Wattys The Craic** 3-9-3 0 SaleemGolam 12 51
(G Prodromou) *s.i.s: outpcd: mod late hdwy* **40/1**
05 **8** 2 **West End Lad**[10] 4659 4-9-8 0 PaulEddery 6 48
(S R Bowring) *s.i.s: hdwy over 5f out: lost pl over 3f out: n.d after* **66/1**
3-4 **9** 5 **Agitator**[10] 4671 3-9-3 0 BrettDoyle 5 32
(Mrs G S Rees) *chsd ldrs over 4f* **4/1**[3]
20 **10** 2 **Neboisha**[19] 4392 3-8-12 0 SteveDrowne 9 22
(P Howling) *prom: lost pl over 4f out: sn bhd* **8/1**
-060 **11** 9 **Esteemed Prince**[29] 4078 3-9-0 47 (e) DominicFox(3) 8 2
(D Shaw) *trckd ldrs: racd keenly: wknd over 2f out* **20/1**

1m 30.6s (0.20) **Going Correction** -0.10s/f (Stan)
WFA 3 from 4yo 5lb **11** Ran SP% **117.7**
Speed ratings (Par 103): **94,93,91,89,89 89,88,85,80,77 67**
CSF £37.55 TOTE £6.70: £1.70, £1.90, £9.40; EX 48.60.
Owner Black Star 2 **Bred** P Charles **Trained** Newmarket, Suffolk

FOCUS
Not a great maiden contested by some disappointing types and a few that have yet to show much ability. The winning time was 1.14 seconds slower than the following handicap and the form looks weak and somewhat dubious.

4978 RINGSIDE SUITE H'CAP 7f 32y(P)
5:00 (5:01) (Class 6) (0-60,60) 3-Y-O+ **£2,914** (£867; £433; £216) **Stalls** High

Form RPR
4106 **1** **Casablanca Minx (IRE)**[18] 4433 4-9-1 54 (v) StephenDonohoe 10 66+
(P D Evans) *s.i.s: hld up: hdwy and nt clr run over 1f out: swtchd rt: r.o u.p to ld post* **10/1**[3]
0661 **2** nk **Millfield (IRE)**[16] 4474 4-9-4 57 RyanMoore 3 68
(P R Chamings) *a.p: rdn to chse wnr and edgd lft over 1f out: styd on u.p to ld wl ins fnl f: hdd post* **11/4**[1]
3265 **3** ½ **Scuba (IRE)**[19] 4394 5-9-0 56 (b) TravisBlock(3) 6 66
(H Morrison) *chsd ldr: led over 2f out: sn rdn: hdd wl ins fnl f* **5/1**[2]
0150 **4** 2 ½ **Wodhill Schnaps**[19] 4395 6-9-2 55 (v) AdrianMcCarthy 4 58
(D Morris) *s.i.s: hld up: hdwy and nt clr run over 1f out: swtchd rt: r.o: nt trble ldrs* **16/1**
1000 **5** 1 **Night In (IRE)**[13] 4562 4-9-6 59 (t) KimTinkler 5 59
(N Tinkler) *hld up: plld hrd: hdwy over 1f out: sn rdn: styd on same pce ins fnl f* **50/1**
6541 **6** 1 ¼ **Burford Lass (IRE)**[35] 3873 4-9-4 57 SteveDrowne 12 54
(D K Ivory) *chsd ldrs: rdn over 2f out: wknd over 1f out* **20/1**
060P **7** 1 ½ **Grand Palace (IRE)**[62] 3064 4-8-12 54 (v) DominicFox(3) 1 47
(D Shaw) *prom: hung lft over 3f out: sn rdn: wknd fnl f* **25/1**
4320 **8** 1 **Green Pirate**[18] 4433 5-9-4 57 (p) RoystonFfrench 7 47
(W M Brisbourne) *s.i.s: hld up: hdwy over 2f out: rdn and wknd over 1f out* **5/1**[2]
0244 **9** ½ **Boreana**[45] 3599 4-9-4 57 PaulMulrennan 9 46
(Jedd O'Keeffe) *chsd ldrs: rdn over 2f out: wknd over 1f out* **12/1**
-000 **10** nk **Sovereignty (JPN)**[31] 4021 5-9-7 60 SaleemGolam 2 48
(D K Ivory) *led over 4f: wknd over 1f out* **20/1**
4021 **11** 2 **Blue Empire (IRE)**[17] 4449 6-9-4 60 (p) LiamJones(3) 11 43
(C R Dore) *s.i.s: hdwy 1/2-way: rdn and wknd 2f out* **5/1**[2]
0 **12** 3 ½ **Ashleigh Anderson (FR)**[50] 3421 3-9-2 60 MickyFenton 8 33
(Eamon Tyrrell, Ire) *mid-div: lost pl 1/2-way: wknd over 2f out* **25/1**

1m 29.46s (-0.94) **Going Correction** -0.10s/f (Stan)
WFA 3 from 4yo+ 5lb **12** Ran SP% **118.5**
Speed ratings (Par 101): **101,100,100,97,96 94,92,91,91,90 88,84**
CSF £35.06 CT £161.64 TOTE £15.30: £3.20, £1.40, £2.70; EX 57.20 Place 6 £140.85, Place 5 £30.79.

Owner J E Abbey **Bred** Airlie Stud And Widden Stud **Trained** Pandy, Monmouths

FOCUS
A modest handicap, but the winning time was 1.14 seconds quicker than the previous maiden and the form appears solid with the winner, third and fourth pretty reliable around this track.
Night In(IRE) Official explanation: jockey said gelding was struck into
Blue Empire(IRE) Official explanation: jockey said gelding never travelled
T/Jkpt: Not won. T/Plt: £110.60 to a £1 stake. Pool: £63,852.95. 421.15 winning tickets. T/Qpdt: £20.20 to a £1 stake. Pool: £4,391.80. 160.80 winning tickets. CR

4979 - 4988a (Foreign Racing) - See Raceform Interactive

4731 CHESTER (L-H)
Friday, August 31

OFFICIAL GOING: Good to firm (8.9)
15mm rain and watering over the previous week. The running rail was taken down and the ground was fast on the inside but dead four horses wide.
Wind: Moderate, half-against Weather: Overcast, changeable, light rain

4989 DAVID MCLEAN MAIDEN FILLIES' STKS — 1m 2f 75y
2:20 (2:21) (Class 5) 3-Y-0+ **£3,562** (£1,059; £529; £264) **Stalls** High

Form RPR
3002 **1** **Sues Surprise (IRE)**[19] 4430 3-8-12 100 (p) MichaelHills 2 84+
(B W Hills) *mde all: pushed clr over 1f out: eased towards fin* **8/13**[1]
024 **2** *10* **Demisemiquaver**[35] 3908 3-8-12 72 SebSanders 9 64
(J Noseda) *sn trcking ldrs: reminders over 4f out: showed clr 2nd over 1f out: wknd ins fnl f* **3/1**[2]
2025 **3** *1 3/4* **Cow Girl (IRE)**[10] 4684 3-8-12 62 DarryllHolland 3 60
(Miss Gay Kelleway) *t.k.h: hdwy to trck ldrs 7f out: chal 3f out: hung rt and lost pl over 1f out* **13/2**[3]
00 **4** *2* **Penang (IRE)**[14] 4568 3-8-12 0 TPQueally 7 56
(C E Brittain) *wnt lft s: hld up towards rr: hdwy to chse ldrs 4f out: kpt on same pce* **12/1**
000- **5** *11* **Taran Tregarth**[265] 6768 3-8-12 40 TGMcLaughlin 1 34
(W M Brisbourne) *trckd ldrs: drvn over 5f out: lost pl over 4f out* **50/1**
000 **6** *nk* **Lilymay**[22] 4334 7-8-13 30 SoniaEaton(7) 8 33
(B P J Baugh) *in rr: sn pushed along: lost pl over 4f out: sme hdwy on outer over 1f out: nvr on terms* **100/1**
0000 **7** *8* **Cardington Queen**[16] 4491 3-8-9 37 DominicFox(3) 5 17
(M Mullineaux) *hmpd s: sn chsng ldrs: outpcd over 4f out: sn lost pl and bhd* **80/1**
0/ **8** *23* **Mistblack**[1145] 3801 7-9-6 0 ChrisCatlin 4 —
(B P J Baugh) *wnt rt s: t.k.h: sn trcking ldrs: pushed along over 4f out: sn lost pl and bhd* **100/1**

2m 11.37s (-1.77) **Going Correction** -0.175s/f (Firm)
WFA 3 from 7yo 8lb **8** Ran SP% **113.1**
Speed ratings (Par 100): **100,92,90,89,80 79,73,55**
CSF £2.60 TOTE £1.60: £1.02, £1.10, £1.50; EX 2.50.
Owner John C Grant & A L R Morton **Bred** Bakewell Bloodstock And Freynestown Stud **Trained** Lambourn, Berks

FOCUS
A one-horse race, with the winner two stone superior on official figures. It was never in doubt, but she didn't need to be at her best..
Cow Girl(IRE) Official explanation: jockey said filly hung right

4990 TRITON HOLIDAYS H'CAP — 7f 2y
2:55 (2:55) (Class 3) (0-95,94) 3-Y-0+ **£9,463** (£2,832; £1,416; £708; £352) **Stalls** Low

Form RPR
1000 **1** **H Harrison (IRE)**[5] 4851 7-8-11 80 AndrewElliott(3) 4 90
(I W McInnes) *mde all: styd on strly* **9/1**
4235 **2** *1 1/2* **Trojan Flight**[9] 4703 6-9-0 80 PatCosgrave 1 86
(R A Fahey) *in rr whn hmpd on ins after 1f: gd hdwy over 1f out: fin wl to take 2nd nr line* **11/1**
5550 **3** *1/2* **The Kiddykid (IRE)**[13] 4601 7-9-6 86 TGMcLaughlin 10 91
(P D Evans) *chsd ldrs: kpt on same pce fnl f* **20/1**
0006 **4** *1/2* **Heywood**[20] 4374 3-9-3 88 DarryllHolland 9 89
(M R Channon) *chsd ldrs: wnt 2nd over 1f out: kpt on same pce* **25/1**
1202 **5** *nk* **White Deer (USA)**[5] 4851 3-9-9 94 SebSanders 2 94+
(M Johnston) *chsd ldrs: nt clr run over 1f out: styd on on ins fnl f: nt trble ldrs* **7/4**[1]
6526 **6** *hd* **Fiefdom (IRE)**[16] 4515 5-8-7 76 PatrickMathers(3) 11 78
(I W McInnes) *chsd ldrs: styd on same pce appr fnl f* **50/1**
6034 **7** *1* **Hiccups**[14] 4581 7-9-1 81 JimmyQuinn 6 80
(M Dods) *hld up towards rr: nt clr run over 1f out: styd on same pce* **11/1**
1050 **8** *shd* **Ektimaal**[34] 3943 4-9-7 87 (t) KDarley 5 86+
(E A L Dunlop) *hld up: hmpd on inner after 1f: hdwy over 1f out: sn nt clr run on ins: styd on ins fnl f* **17/2**
2402 **9** *1 1/4* **Gallantry**[26] 4195 5-9-5 88 DominicFox(3) 7 84
(D Shaw) *hld up in midfield: nt clr run over 1f out: kpt on: nvr nr ldrs* **8/1**[3]
2606 **10** *nk* **Qadar (IRE)**[14] 4567 5-9-13 93 ChrisCatlin 12 88
(N P Littmoden) *prom: effrt over 2f out: kpt on same pce* **33/1**
00 **11** *3/4* **Padrao Lima (BRZ)**[197] 472 4-9-10 90 TPQueally 8 83
(J S Moore) *prom: hung rt over 1f out: one pce* **66/1**
5-0B **12** *7* **Blades Girl**[28] 4119 4-9-8 91 (p) AndrewMullen(3) 14 65
(K A Ryan) *chsd wnr: wknd over 1f out* **66/1**
0014 **13** *39* **Jamieson Gold (IRE)**[13] 4601 4-9-7 87 MichaelHills 13 —
(B W Hills) *s.i.s: sn detached in last: bhd fnl 3f: t.o* **12/1**
110 **14** *9* **Orpsie Boy (IRE)**[13] 4614 4-9-11 94 WilliamBuick(3) 3 —
(N P Littmoden) *s.i.s: in rr and drvn along: lost tch 3f out: t.o* **5/1**[2]

1m 25.84s (-2.63) **Going Correction** -0.175s/f (Firm)
WFA 3 from 4yo+ 5lb **14** Ran SP% **125.5**
Speed ratings (Par 107): **108,106,105,105,104 104,103,103,101,101 100,92,48,37**
CSF £102.41 CT £1998.68 TOTE £9.90: £2.60, £3.70, £5.10; EX 141.80.
Owner David Lees **Bred** Margaret Conlon **Trained** Catwick, E Yorks

FOCUS
The quicker ground was on the inside against the running rail and the winner, who has a good record here, made all. There were plenty of traffic problems behind. The form seems sound.

NOTEBOOK
H Harrison(IRE), 4lb higher than when accounting for Gallantry by a head here in June, had an inside draw and was soon taking them along, racing on the quickest ground. In the end he did just enough. (tchd 10-1)
Trojan Flight, drawn one, was knocked over on the bend after the first furlong. He sprouted wings in the final furlong but the winner had poached sufficient lead. (op 12-1)
The Kiddykid(IRE), whose last success was in a Listed race here over a year ago, has slipped to a favourable mark and this was his best effort for quite some time. (op 25-1)
Heywood, just 2lb higher than when successful here in May, showed his liking for this track and after going in pursuit of the winner was only just run out of second.
White Deer(USA), making a quick return, is now a gelding. Lacking the basic pace to capitalise on an inside draw, he found himself short of racing room coming off the final bend. Sticking on at the finish, he is clearly in very good heart. (op 15-8 tchd 2-1)
Fiefdom(IRE) ran with credit, but his losing run now streches back 22 starts.
Hiccups looked at his very best and did well to finish as close as he did after meeting traffic problems coming off the final turn. (tchd 12-1)
Ektimaal, left short of room on the first bend, tried for an ambitious run up the inner once in line for home but he was continually baulked. He is clearly in very good form and may yet prove just as effective on turf as he is on Polytrack. Official explanation: jockey said gelding was denied a clear run (op 11-1 tchd 8-1)
Gallantry, closely matched with the winner on their running here in June, was left short of room at a crucial stage. (op 7-1)
Jamieson Gold(IRE) Official explanation: jockey said gelding was slowly away and outpaced
Orpsie Boy(IRE), well supported, missed a beat at the start and was soon well out of contention. Official explanation: vet said gelding had a fibrillating heart (op 13-2 tchd 7-1)

4991 SURRENDA-LINK NURSERY — 7f 2y
3:25 (3:26) (Class 3) 2-Y-0 **£9,067** (£2,697; £1,348; £673) **Stalls** Low

Form RPR
0336 **1** **Golan Knight (IRE)**[13] 4613 2-8-8 80 AndrewMullen(3) 4 88
(K A Ryan) *mde all: kpt on wl* **8/1**
361 **2** *1/2* **Alan Devonshire**[14] 4578 2-9-0 83 JimmyQuinn 2 90+
(M H Tompkins) *slipped s: hld up in rr: smooth hdwy over 2f out: wnt 2nd and hung lft over 1f out: styd on towards fin* **5/2**[1]
6401 **3** *4* **American Art (IRE)**[23] 4285 2-8-5 77 (t) WilliamBuick(3) 5 74
(B W Hills) *pushed along in rr: hdwy over 1f out: styd on to take modest 3rd nr fin* **10/3**[2]
1000 **4** *1/2* **Eileen's Violet (IRE)**[14] 4573 2-9-7 90 StephenDonohoe 3 86
(P D Evans) *in rr: hdwy on outer over 1f out: styd on same pce* **14/1**
2004 **5** *3/4* **Atheer Dubai (IRE)**[13] 4604 2-9-3 86 (b[1]) TPQueally 10 80
(C E Brittain) *sn chsng ldrs: styd on same pce appr fnl f* **16/1**
15 **6** *nk* **Firestreak**[34] 3938 2-9-4 87 DarryllHolland 9 80
(R Hannon) *swtchd lft after s: chsd ldrs: hung rt and kpt on same pce appr fnl f* **11/2**[3]
3561 **7** *3 1/2* **Casino Night**[7] 4770 2-8-0 72 6ex ow3 AndrewElliott(3) 1 56
(J R Weymes) *chsd ldrs: drvn over 3f out: lost pl over 1f out* **7/1**
0010 **8** *6* **Tamara Moon (IRE)**[23] 4278 2-8-3 72 DavidKinsella 7 41
(M R Channon) *rrd and v.s.a: nvr on terms* **25/1**
604 **9** *9* **Cosmea**[22] 4329 2-8-7 76 ow1 KDarley 8 23
(A King) *mid-div on outer: lost pl 2f out: sn bhd* **22/1**
100 **10** *shd* **Double Attack (FR)**[37] 3841 2-8-11 80 MichaelHills 12 26
(M Johnston) *chsd ldrs on outer: lost pl 2f out: sn bhd* **20/1**
5004 **11** *5* **Enodoc**[21] 4358 2-9-5 88 SebSanders 6 22
(W R Muir) *mid-div: t.k.h: lost pl 2f out: sn bhd* **16/1**

1m 26.01s (-2.46) **Going Correction** -0.175s/f (Firm) **11** Ran SP% **122.0**
Speed ratings (Par 98): **107,106,101,101,100 100,96,89,78,78 73**
CSF £28.63 CT £83.70 TOTE £10.30: £2.80, £1.70, £1.60; EX 44.60.
Owner S Carr **Bred** M J Halligan **Trained** Hambleton, N Yorks

FOCUS
Although the winner had the run of the race, both he and the runner-up did well to pull clear in what looked a decent nursery.

NOTEBOOK
Golan Knight(IRE), with the benefit of an inside draw, made every yard and in the end did just enough. He has plenty of size and scope and should continue to give a good account of himself. (op 10-1 tchd 11-1)
Alan Devonshire had an inside draw but it was negated when he slipped leaving the stalls. Travelling smoothly off the pace, he went in pursuit of the winner but hung in behind him. He was closing the gap at the line but never quite quickly enough. Official explanation: jockey said colt slipped on leaving stalls (op 10-3 tchd 7-2)
American Art(IRE) was soon making hard work of it, but stuck to his task and was rewarded with third spot near the line. He is crying out for a mile. (tchd 3-1 and 7-2)
Eileen's Violet(IRE), stepping up in trip and down in class, had an inside draw but she ended up having to come wide. Considering she was racing on slower ground than the three ahead of her at the line she deserves plenty of credit for this. (op 12-1)
Atheer Dubai(IRE), in first-time blinkers, did well from a wide draw. He can surely find a maiden race.
Firestreak had an outside draw and, switched inside soon after the start, did a lot of running early on. In the circumstances it was a highly creditable effort. Official explanation: jockey said colt hung right on turning into straight (op 4-1)
Tamara Moon(IRE) Official explanation: jockey said filly reared leaving stalls and was slowly away
Enodoc Official explanation: jockey said colt ran too freely

4992 EUROPEAN BREEDERS' FUND COMBERMERE FILLIES' CONDITIONS STKS — 6f 18y
4:00 (4:01) (Class 2) 2-Y-0 **£12,618** (£3,776; £1,888; £944; £470) **Stalls** Low

Form RPR
0 **1** **Dellini (IRE)**[13] 4602 2-8-12 0 DarryllHolland 3 84+
(M R Channon) *s.i.s: last and sn pushed along: hdwy on outer over 1f out: styd on strly ins fnl f: led last stride* **10/1**
1005 **2** *shd* **Fanatical**[14] 4573 2-9-1 96 ChrisCatlin 5 87
(E F Vaughan) *w ldr: led over 1f out: hdd post* **15/8**[1]
6025 **3** *1* **Kylayne**[20] 4400 2-9-1 97 KDarley 1 84
(P W D'Arcy) *smartly away: led: hdd over 1f out: kpt on same pce* **2/1**[2]
1122 **4** *nk* **Look Busy (IRE)**[3] 4921 2-8-12 88 PatrickMathers 6 80
(A Berry) *trckd ldng pair: effrt over 1f out: kpt on ins fnl f* **5/2**[3]
0 **5** *1 1/4* **Sweet Hope (USA)**[27] 4173 2-8-12 0 PatCosgrave 4 76
(K A Ryan) *chsd ldrs: sltly outpcd over 1f out: styd on ins fnl f* **8/1**

1m 14.26s (-1.39) **Going Correction** -0.175s/f (Firm) **5** Ran SP% **116.9**
Speed ratings (Par 97): **102,101,100,100,98**
CSF £30.88 TOTE £14.60: £3.70, £1.80; EX 32.00.
Owner Sheikh Ahmed Al Maktoum **Bred** Darley **Trained** West Ilsley, Berks
■ Qasayed was withdrawn (12/1, spread a plate). R4, deduct 5p in the £.

FOCUS
A good-class juvenile event, but it has been rated on the negative side as there is a suspicion the first two went off too fast and the third may be better at shorter.

NOTEBOOK
Dellini(IRE), whose dam won the Moyglare Stud Stakes, missed a beat at the start and was always racing towards the outer. She really found her stride inside the last and put her head in front right on the line. She will be even better suited by seven and looks a bright prospect. (old market op 12-1 tchd 9-1)
Fanatical matched strides with the leader. She took a narrow advantage once in line for home, only to be mugged right on the line. (old market op 15-8 tchd 5-2 in places, new market op 9-4)
Kylayne, drawn one, hit the boxes like a greyhound. She stuck to the rails like glue but was outgunned in the final furlong. (old market op 11-4)
Look Busy(IRE), making a quick return, was always racing three wide on the heels of the two leaders. She stuck on grimly inside the last and is all heart. (old market op 7-2 tchd 10-3 new market op 3-1)

Sweet Hope(USA) ♦, a Cheveley Park entry, showed a lot more than on her debut in maiden company at Thirsk a month earlier. Tapped for toe turning in, she was sticking on in solid fashion at the line and looks a ready-made winner in lesser company. (old market op 8-1 tchd 7-1)

4993 AUDI Q7 SEASON H'CAP — 1m 2f 75y

4:30 (4:31) (Class 3) (0-90,86) 3-Y-O

£9,348 (£2,799; £1,399; £700; £349; £175) Stalls High

Form — RPR

003 **1** **New Star (UAE)**[62] 3079 3-8-4 72 ..... LiamJones(3) 2 — 80
(W M Brisbourne) *led 1f: chsd ldrs: reminders 3f out: led over 1f out: kpt on wl* — 10/1

0000 **2** 1 ½ **Noticeable (IRE)**[27] 4147 3-9-1 80 ..... DarryllHolland 7 — 85
(M R Channon) *trckd ldrs: rdn 3f out: hung lft over 1f out: styd on same pce* — 8/1

0106 **3** 1 **Smokey Oakey (IRE)**[9] 4720 3-9-7 86 ..... JimmyQuinn 3 — 89
(M H Tompkins) *trckd ldrs: styd on same pce fnl f* — 7/2[2]

46-1 **4** ½ **Noisy Silence (IRE)**[18] 4457 3-9-4 83 ..... SebSanders 1 — 85
(E F Vaughan) *trckd ldrs: effrt over 2f out: kpt on same pce appr fnl f* 7/2[2]

3002 **5** hd **Old Romney**[26] 4197 3-8-13 78 ..... DavidKinsella 5 — 80
(G A Huffer) *hld up in rr: smooth hdwy over 2f out: edgd lft over 1f out: plld outside: styd on ins fnl f: lame* — 11/2[3]

610 **6** hd **Amanda Carter**[20] 4382 3-7-13 67 oh1 ..... AndrewMullen(3) 4 — 68
(R A Fahey) *in rr: sn pushed along: hdwy over 3f out: n.m.r on inner over 1f out: styd on ins fnl f* — 10/1

2011 **7** 7 **Ideally (IRE)**[19] 4419 3-9-6 85 ..... MichaelHills 6 — 72
(B W Hills) *led after 1f: hdd over 1f out: sn lost pl* — 5/2[1]

2m 11.04s (-2.10) **Going Correction** -0.175s/f (Firm) — 7 Ran SP% **117.7**
Speed ratings (Par 104): **101,99,99,98,98 98,92**
CSF £87.61 TOTE £15.20: £4.20, £4.30; EX 115.20.

Owner Shropshire Wolves **Bred** Darley **Trained** Great Ness, Shropshire

FOCUS

The progressive winner made a successful handicap bow, but the form does not look that solid. The riding of Old Romney came under scrutiny, but he was found to be lame afterwards.

NOTEBOOK

New Star(UAE), a Godolphin cast-off, has been making steady progress in maiden company and broke his duck on his handicap bow. He made hard work of it, but he was firmly in command at the line and is just the type his trainer does so well with. (op 11-1)

Noticeable(IRE), below his best on his four most recent starts, was given a most determined ride but he hung noticeably once in line for home and looked somewhat reluctant. Official explanation: jockey said colt hung left (op 12-1)

Smokey Oakey(IRE), having his first spin round here, ran right up to his best on ground possibly a fraction quicker than he prefers. (op 3-1)

Noisy Silence(IRE), stepping up in trip on his handicap bow, looked in tip-top condition and went down fighting. (tchd 4-1)

Old Romney, 3lb higher, didn't make the running this time. He looked to be travelling really well but edged in off the final bend and ran out of racing room. Pulled wide, he stayed on steadily and gave the impression he ought to have gone very close. It transpired that he was lame on his off-fore leg. Official explanation: vet said colt was lame on the off-fore (op 13-2)

Amanda Carter, suited by the fast ground, stuck to the inside and stayed on when it was all over. (op 7-1 tchd 13-2)

Ideally(IRE), 6lb higher, was hustled and harassed in the lead and did too much. In the end he was the only one to drop right out. Official explanation: jockey said gelding ran too freely and repeatedly raced on the leading rein (op 7-2)

4994 BOLLINGER CHAMPAGNE CHALLENGE SERIES H'CAP (FOR GENTLEMAN AMATEUR RIDERS) — 1m 4f 66y

5:05 (5:05) (Class 5) (0-75,74) 3-Y-O+ — £3,435 (£1,065; £532; £266) Stalls Low

Form — RPR

1 **Daryal (IRE)**[161] 6-11-3 72 ..... MrCPHuxley(5) 6 — 83
(A King) *mid-div: hdwy to chse ldrs over 3f out: led over 1f out: hld on wl* — 4/1[2]

1460 **2** ½ **Penang Cinta**[13] 4597 4-11-1 70 ..... RichardEvans(5) 2 — 80
(P D Evans) *trckd ldrs: chal 5f out: keeping on same pce whn rdr dropped whip towards fin* — 6/1[3]

3614 **3** 4 **Hugs Destiny (IRE)**[11] 4670 6-10-7 60 ..... (t) MrHHaynes(3) 4 — 64
(M A Barnes) *led tl over 1f out: kpt on same pce* — 6/1[3]

4033 **4** 1 **Agilete**[25] 4231 5-10-2 55 ..... MrSPearce(3) 5 — 57
(J Pearce) *hld up in rr: hdwy on inner over 2f out: kpt on same pce appr fnl f* — 6/1[3]

5433 **5** 2 ½ **Acuzio**[8] 4732 6-10-7 57 ..... MrSDobson 3 — 55
(W M Brisbourne) *t.k.h towards rr: gd hdwy on outer to join ldrs over 4f out: wknd appr fnl f* — 2/1[1]

2400 **6** 3 **Diktatorship (IRE)**[11] 4670 4-10-0 55 oh4 ..... MrPCollington(5) 1 — 48
(Jennie Candlish) *trckd ldrs: effrt over 2f out: one pce* — 14/1

1452 **7** 2 **Bavarica**[23] 4284 5-11-5 74 ..... MrRBirkett(5) 7 — 64
(Miss J Feilden) *trckd ldrs: t.k.h: hung rt and lost pl over 1f out* — 11/1

5500 **8** 14 **Royal Sailor (IRE)**[23] 4284 5-9-12 55 oh10 ..... (p) MrDavidMcMinn(7) 8 — 23
(J Ryan) *in rr: sme hdwy on wd outside over 4f out: sn lost pl and bhd* — 33/1

00/0 **9** 5 **Courant D'Air (IRE)**[15] 4535 6-10-0 55 oh10 ..... MrJPFeatherstone(5) 9 — 15
(Lucinda Featherstone) *chsd ldrs: drvn and lost pl over 4f out: sn bhd* — 66/1

2m 40.27s (-0.38) **Going Correction** -0.175s/f (Firm) — 9 Ran SP% **115.6**
Speed ratings (Par 103): **94,93,91,90,88 86,85,76,72**
CSF £28.30 CT £142.47 TOTE £4.70: £1.80, £2.60, £1.70; EX 37.10 Place 6 £837.05, Place 5 £796.07.

Owner Let's Live Racing **Bred** His Highness The Aga Khan's Studs S C **Trained** Barbury Castle, Wilts

FOCUS

A sound gallop and in the end the first two pulled clear. The form, rated through the third, is not that strong.

T/Plt: £691.30 to a £1 stake. Pool: £71,024.70. 75.00 winning tickets. T/Qpdt: £167.30 to a £1 stake. Pool: £4,002.70. 17.70 winning tickets. WG

[4713] HAMILTON (R-H)

Friday, August 31

OFFICIAL GOING: Good to firm (good in places; 8.8)

Wind: Fairly strong, half against Weather: Cloudy, bright

4995 GALA CASINO SAUCHIEHALL STREET NURSERY — 6f 5y

2:30 (2:30) (Class 5) 2-Y-O — £3,886 (£1,156; £577; £288) Stalls Low

Form — RPR

2523 **1** **Ramatni**[14] 4560 2-8-9 71 ..... RoystonFfrench 5 — 80+
(M Johnston) *mde all: pushed along over 2f out: edgd lft and kpt on strly fnl f* — 7/2[2]

11 **2** 3 **Only A Game (IRE)**[39] 3801 2-8-4 66 ..... PaulHanagan 3 — 66
(E J O'Neill) *cl up: effrt over 1f out: kpt on fnl f: nt rch wnr* — 4/1[3]

6320 **3** 1 ¾ **Stormy Journey**[13] 4611 2-8-7 69 ..... TomEaves 1 — 64
(Mrs K Walton) *in tch: effrt over 2f out: kpt on fnl f: nt rch front two* — 18/1

4102 **4** shd **Artsu**[7] 4775 2-8-11 73 ..... HayleyTurner 6 — 68+
(M L W Bell) *t.k.h: prom: effrt over 1f out: hung rt and sn one pce* — 13/8[1]

0200 **5** 1 ½ **Smileforawhile (IRE)**[32] 4020 2-8-9 71 ..... (p) PaulFessey 7 — 61
(K A Ryan) *s.i.s: sn wl bhd: gd hdwy over 1f out: nrst fin* — 40/1

0050 **6** 1 ¼ **Moonlight Gambler (IRE)**[15] 4524 2-7-9 60 oh8(b[1]) DuranFentiman(3) 2 — 46
(T D Easterby) *prom tl rdn and wknd over 1f out* — 40/1

412 **7** 1 ¼ **Thompsons Walls (IRE)**[6] 4819 2-9-7 83 ..... LeeEnstone 4 — 66
(P C Haslam) *prom: effrt over 2f out: wknd over 1f out* — 4/1[3]

1m 13.11s (0.01) **Going Correction** -0.175s/f (Firm) — 7 Ran SP% **110.5**
Speed ratings (Par 94): **92,88,85,85,83 81,80**
CSF £16.56 CT £202.24 TOTE £3.50: £1.40, £2.80; EX 12.30.

Owner Sheikh Ahmed Al Maktoum **Bred** Darley **Trained** Middleham Moor, N Yorks

FOCUS

A fair event run at a sound pace and this form looks solid and should stand up at a similar level.

NOTEBOOK

Ramatni, who looked better than the bare form of her previous start at Catterick where she stumbled at the start and ran wide on the home turn, proved much better suited to this track and turned in her best effort to beat a previous dual winner. She should stay 7f but life is going to be tougher after reassessment. (tchd 4-1)

Only A Game(IRE), up in grade after winning sellers on Polytrack and on quick ground, turned in his best effort yet on this nursery debut. He is worth a try over 7f and appeals as the sort to win more races. (op 7-2 tchd 9-2)

Stormy Journey, well beaten on his previous outing at Ripon, showed much more like his true form on this nursery debut. On this evidence he should stay 7f and, although he has had a few chances, may be capable of picking up a small event in the North. (tchd 16-1 and 22-1)

Artsu looked to have solid claims judging on his improved effort in soft ground in a valuable sales race at Newmarket on his previous start but he failed to settle and was below that level on this nursery debut and back on fast ground. Life is going to be tougher from a 9lb higher mark in future but he will be worth another chance returned to a soft surface. Official explanation: jockey said gelding was unsuited by the good to firm (good in places) ground (op 6-4 tchd 11-8 and 7-4)

Smileforawhile(IRE), soundly beaten in blinkers on his All-Weather debut on his previous start, fared much better back on turf and on this nursery debut in the first-time cheekpieces. The step up to 7f should suit but he looked a less than easy ride and it may be prudent to tread carefully with him until he gets his head in front where it matters. (op 28-1)

Moonlight Gambler(IRE), tried in blinkers for the return to sprint distances, was 8lb out of the handicap and did not really offer enough promise to suggest he will be of immediate interest from his proper mark.

Thompsons Walls(IRE), back in trip and turned out fairly quickly for this nursery debut, proved a disappointment. He does not look entirely straightforward and has little margin for error from his current mark. (op 5-1 tchd 11-2)

4996 WEATHERBYS PRINTING H'CAP — 5f 4y

3:05 (3:05) (Class 6) (0-55,61) 3-Y-O+ — £2,730 (£806; £403) Stalls Low

Form — RPR

0041 **1** **Making Music**[7] 4773 4-8-11 52 6ex ..... (b) DavidAllan 6 — 63
(T D Easterby) *mde all stands' side: rdn 2f out: hld on wl fnl f* — 5/1[1]

0201 **2** 1 ¼ **Briery Lane (IRE)**[12] 4635 6-9-6 61 6ex ..... PaulHanagan 1 — 67
(J M Bradley) *bhd stands' side: hdwy over 1f out: hung rt: chsd wnr ins fnl f: no imp* — 5/1[1]

0520 **3** ¾ **Highland Song (IRE)**[37] 3839 4-8-11 52 ..... PaulMulrennan 5 — 55
(R F Fisher) *chsd stands' side ldrs: effrt over 1f out: nt qckn fnl f* — 5/1[1]

0605 **4** 1 **Bond Becks (IRE)**[7] 4773 7-8-6 50 ..... MichaelJStainton(3) 2 — 50
(G R Oldroyd) *cl up stands' side: effrt over 1f out: no ex fnl f* — 6/1[2]

6043 **5** nk **Newkeylets**[16] 4494 4-8-8 49 ..... TomEaves 9 — 48
(I Semple) *in tch on outside of stands' side gp: effrt 2f out: no imp fnl f* — 12/1

0000 **6** nk **Alexia Rose (IRE)**[15] 4525 5-7-12 46 oh1 ..... (t) SophieDoyle(7) 14 — 44
(A Berry) *racd far side: sn rdn in rr: hdwy to ld that gp ins fnl f: no ch w stands' side* — 40/1

0060 **7** nk **Seafield Towers**[1] 4967 7-8-1 47 ..... (b) KellyHarrison(5) 4 — 43
(Miss L A Perratt) *bhd stands' side: effrt and edgd rt over 1f out: nvr rchd ldrs* — 20/1

0000 **8** shd **Rosie's Result**[1] 4967 7-7-12 46 oh1 ..... JamesRogers(7) 3 — 42
(M Todhunter) *sn drvn in midfield stands' side: no imp fr 2f out* — 100/1

0-00 **9** ¾ **Jadan (IRE)**[9] 4706 6-8-9 50 ..... JohnEgan 8 — 43
(E J Alston) *prom stands' side tl rdn and no ex over 1f out* — 16/1

0030 **10** 1 ¼ **Four Kings**[6] 4822 6-8-8 49 ..... PaulFessey 15 — 38
(Karen McLintock) *cl up far side tl rdn and no ex over 1f out* — 50/1

0000 **11** shd **Chairman Bobby**[21] 4351 9-8-5 46 oh1 ..... PaulQuinn 11 — 35
(D W Barker) *led far side to ins fnl f: sn btn* — 33/1

0000 **12** ½ **Sokoke**[1] 4967 6-8-9 53 oh1 ow7 ..... PJMcDonald(3) 7 — 40
(D A Nolan) *midfield stands' side: drvn and outpcd 1/2-way: sn btn* — 100/1

2500 **13** ¾ **Seven No Trumps**[4] 4881 10-8-1 49 ..... JakePayne(7) 13 — 33
(J M Bradley) *t.k.h: cl up far side tl wknd over 1f out* — 20/1

45 **14** 1 ½ **Throw The Dice**[24] 4252 5-8-8 49 ..... (v) RoystonFfrench 12 — 28
(A Berry) *chsd far side ldrs tl hung lft and wknd 2f out* — 6/1[2]

0036 **15** nk **Rare Breed**[7] 4773 4-8-6 54 ..... KristinStubbs(7) 10 — 32
(Mrs L Stubbs) *missed break: bhd stands' side: shortlived effrt over 2f out: sn btn* — 10/1[3]

59.95 secs (-1.25) **Going Correction** -0.175s/f (Firm) — 15 Ran SP% **120.1**
Speed ratings (Par 101): **103,101,99,98,97 97,96,96,95,93 93,92,91,88,88**
CSF £27.07 CT £133.71 TOTE £5.80: £2.10, £2.60, £1.70; EX 27.50.

Owner Jonathan Gill **Bred** Redmyre Bloodstock And Stuart McPhee **Trained** Great Habton, N Yorks

FOCUS

A run-of-the-mill sprint in which the stands' side group held the edge over the quintet that raced far side. The pace was sound and the form looks solid for the grade, rated around the placed horses.

Throw The Dice Official explanation: jockey said gelding hung left throughout

4997 KIER HOMES MEDIAN AUCTION MAIDEN STKS 1m 1f 36y
3:35 (3:35) (Class 6) 3-5-Y-0 £2,266 (£674; £337; £168) Stalls High

Form RPR
2325 1 **Arena's Dream (USA)**[19] 4424 3-9-0 71........................(p) PaulHanagan 3 59
(R A Fahey) *w ldr: led after 2f to over 2f out: sn drvn: rallied u.p to ld cl home* 1/2[1]
0505 2 *nk* **Mandarin Rocket (IRE)**[6] 4802 4-9-7 51.................. RoystonFfrench 2 58
(Miss L A Perratt) *cl up: led over 2f out: kpt on fnl f: hdd cl home* 9/1
3 *3 1/2* **Ezdeyaad (USA)** 3-8-11 0... PJMcDonald(3) 5 50
(G A Swinbank) *hld up in tch: stdy hdwy over 2f out: rdn over 1f out: sn no ex* 9/2[2]
5024 4 *1 1/2* **Musical Land (IRE)**[5] 4845 3-9-0 63.................................. PhillipMakin 4 47
(J R Weymes) *led 2f: cl up tl rdn and outpcd over 2f out: n.d after* 6/1[3]
4004 5 *5* **Cranworth Blaze**[20] 4411 3-8-9 45.................................(be) DavidAllan 7 31
(T J Etherington) *prom tl hung lft and wknd over 2f out* 50/1
1m 59.61s (-0.05) **Going Correction** -0.175s/f (Firm)
WFA 3 from 4yo 7lb 5 Ran SP% **111.1**
Speed ratings (Par 101): **93,92,89,88,83**
CSF £6.03 TOTE £1.40: £1.10, £2.70; EX 3.70.
Owner George Houghton **Bred** Lavin Bloodstock & Indian Creek **Trained** Musley Bank, N Yorks
FOCUS
A most uncompetitive maiden and one in which the pace was just fair, with the winner below form in getting off the mark.

4998 SITE SERVICES (PLANT) LTD H'CAP 1m 65y
4:10 (4:10) (Class 6) (0-65,69) 3-Y-0+ £2,730 (£806; £403) Stalls High

Form RPR
0062 1 **Oeuf A La Neige**[2] 4934 7-8-12 47.. PhillipMakin 9 55
(Miss L A Perratt) *hld up in midfield: hdwy to ld over 1f out: hld on wl fnl f* 10/1[3]
5010 2 *hd* **Alberts Story (USA)**[21] 4354 3-8-13 54........................ PaulHanagan 10 62
(R A Fahey) *in tch: effrt over 1f out: edgd rt: kpt on wl fnl f: jst hld* 11/1
4003 3 *nk* **Gala Sunday (USA)**[13] 4610 7-8-12 54.......................(bt) NSLawes(7) 5 61
(M W Easterby) *in tch: effrt over 2f out: hung rt: kpt on fnl f: nrst fin* 16/1
0050 4 *3/4* **Terenzium (IRE)**[25] 4219 5-8-13 48...........................(p) PaulMulrennan 8 53
(Micky Hammond) *hld up in midfield: effrt 2f out: swtchd and kpt on fnl f: nvr nrr* 33/1
6021 5 *shd* **Zain (IRE)**[2] 4936 3-8-10 51 6ex.................................(t) RoystonFfrench 14 56
(J G Given) *bhd: rdn 1/2-way: hdwy wl over 1f out: kpt on fnl f* 9/4[1]
2603 6 *nk* **Pianoforte (USA)**[2] 4933 5-9-8 57.. DavidAllan 1 61
(E J Alston) *bhd: hdwy whn n.m.r over 1f out: r.o fnl f: nrst fin* 16/1
-000 7 *nk* **Ulysees (IRE)**[16] 4496 8-8-12 50.............................. JamieMoriarty(3) 12 54
(J Barclay) *hld up: effrt whn nt clr run over 2f out and ins fnl f: kpt on nr fin* 25/1
0060 8 *3/4* **Just Dust**[14] 4581 3-9-9 64... DaleGibson 6 66
(M W Easterby) *prom: drvn over 3f out: rallied: one pce fnl f* 10/1[3]
1001 9 *nk* **Bold Indian (IRE)**[27] 4155 3-9-10 65.................................. TomEaves 16 66
(I Semple) *midfield: effrt over 2f out: nt clr run on ins fnl f: nvr rchd ldrs* 10/1[3]
3004 10 *3/4* **Anthemion (IRE)**[1] 4966 10-9-3 55.............................. PJMcDonald(3) 13 55
(Mrs J C McGregor) *set decent gallop to over 1f out: sn rdn and btn* 14/1
0-41 11 *shd* **Lauro**[40] 3765 7-9-6 62.. DawnRankin(7) 4 61
(Miss J A Camacho) *hld up: effrt on outside over 2f out: btn over 1f out* 16/1
5230 12 *1 3/4* **Goodwood Spirit**[15] 4532 5-8-10 50..............(v) RussellKennemore(5) 11 45
(J M Bradley) *hld up: stdy hdwy whn n.m.r 2f out: sn btn* 22/1
6442 13 *1/2* **Miss Porcia**[1] 4966 6-8-3 45.................................(p) SophieDoyle(7) 2 39
(P A Blockley) *chsd ldr tl wknd wl over 1f out* 10/1[3]
40 14 *2* **Moonstreaker**[30] 4081 4-9-3 55.......................... MichaelJStainton(3) 15 45
(R M Whitaker) *chsd ldrs tl wknd fr 2f out* 17/2[2]
3040 15 *3/4* **Howards Rocket**[9] 4704 6-8-13 53.......................... KellyHarrison(5) 3 41
(J S Goldie) *hld up: pushed along 3f out: sn btn* 66/1
1m 48.1s (-1.20) **Going Correction** -0.175s/f (Firm)
WFA 3 from 4yo+ 6lb 15 Ran SP% **122.9**
Speed ratings (Par 101): **99,98,98,97,97 97,97,96,96,95 95,93,92,90,90**
CSF £113.25 CT £1767.81 TOTE £12.60: £3.30, £5.10, £5.10; EX 87.60.
Owner Peter Tsim **Bred** Gainsborough Stud Management Ltd **Trained** Ayr, S Ayrshire
FOCUS
An ordinary handicap in which the pace was sound and straightforward form with the third to this year's best.
Bold Indian(IRE) Official explanation: jockey said gelding was denied a clear run
Miss Porcia Official explanation: jockey said mare ran flat
Howards Rocket Official explanation: jockey said gelding was unsuited by the good to firm (good in places) ground

4999 WEATHERBYS BANK H'CAP 6f 5y
4:45 (4:45) (Class 4) (0-80,77) 3-Y-0+ £6,477 (£1,927; £963; £481) Stalls Low

Form RPR
1232 1 **Rainbow Fox**[4] 4895 3-8-12 68.. PaulHanagan 11 77
(R A Fahey) *towards rr: hdwy over 1f out: qcknd between horses to ld nr fin* 11/2[3]
3232 2 *1/2* **Joyeaux**[9] 4719 5-8-4 60.. DuranFentiman(3) 3 67
(J Hetherton) *hld up in tch: effrt and edgd rt over 1f out: led briefly wl ins fnl f: kpt on* 10/1
1 3 *nk* **Haajes**[17] 4486 3-9-5 75.. JohnEgan 5 81
(D J Murphy) *prom: rdn to ld over 1f out: hdd wl ins fnl f: kpt on* 6/1
0456 4 *1 1/4* **Yorkshire Blue**[4] 4895 8-9-7 74.................................. DanielTudhope 9 76
(J S Goldie) *bhd and sn outpcd: plenty to do 1/2-way: gd hdwy over 1f out: nrst fin* 4/1[1]
6141 5 *nk* **Ellens Academy (IRE)**[2] 4934 12-9-4 76 6ex.................. GaryBartley(5) 7 77
(E J Alston) *hld up: hdwy over 1f out: kpt on: nvr able to chal* 6/1
120 6 *3/4* **Katie Boo (IRE)**[9] 4703 5-9-2 72.............................. JamieMoriarty(3) 6 71
(A Berry) *prom: effrt and edgd rt over 1f out: sn no ex* 9/1
5050 7 *1* **Stoic Leader (IRE)**[6] 4816 7-9-10 77................................ PhillipMakin 2 73
(R F Fisher) *chsd ldrs tl rdn and no ex over 1f out* 16/1
2100 8 *shd* **Steel Blue**[14] 4585 7-9-5 72.. PaulMulrennan 8 68
(R M Whitaker) *led to over 1f out: sn rdn and btn* 7/1
0513 9 *1 1/2* **Finsbury**[6] 4807 4-9-2 69.. RoystonFfrench 10 60
(J M Bradley) *bhd: drvn over 2f out: nvr on terms* 5/1[2]
6-40 10 *hd* **Opal Noir**[73] 2744 3-9-5 75.. TomEaves 4 65
(I Semple) *midfield: drvn over 2f out: hung rt: sn n.d* 33/1
2460 11 *3/4* **Wainwright (IRE)**[59] 3185 7-7-13 59 oh13 ow1........(t) BrydieKilloran(7) 1 47
(P A Blockley) *w ldr tl wknd over 1f out* 100/1
1m 11.14s (-1.96) **Going Correction** -0.175s/f (Firm)
WFA 3 from 4yo+ 3lb 11 Ran SP% **122.0**
Speed ratings (Par 105): **106,105,104,103,102 101,100,100,98,98 97**
CSF £61.97 CT £355.36 TOTE £7.50: £3.00, £2.20, £2.60; EX 47.60.
Owner Kevin Lee & David Barlow **Bred** Ms R A Myatt **Trained** Musley Bank, N Yorks
FOCUS
An ordinary handicap but one in which the pace was sound throughout and solid-looking form.
Katie Boo(IRE) Official explanation: trainer said mare finished lame

5000 COME RACING ON MONDAY H'CAP 1m 3f 16y
5:15 (5:15) (Class 6) (0-65,65) 3-Y-0+ £2,730 (£806; £403) Stalls High

Form RPR
0003 1 **Fadansil**[6] 4802 4-8-9 46 oh1.. PaulHanagan 5 55
(J Wade) *midfield: drvn over 3f out: rallied 2f out: led ins fnl f: styd on* 20/1
0045 2 *1* **Speagle (IRE)**[4] 4878 5-10-0 65................................. DanielTudhope 6 72
(D Carroll) *led: rdn over 2f out: hdd ins fnl f: kpt on* 5/2[1]
3000 3 *3 1/2* **Fenners (USA)**[21] 4352 4-9-9 60................................. PaulMulrennan 11 61
(M W Easterby) *prom: effrt over 2f out: one pce over 1f out* 11/2[3]
6065 4 *2* **Mayadeen (IRE)**[14] 4580 5-9-1 52...................................(b) PaulFessey 13 50
(I Semple) *bhd tl hdwy over 2f out: kpt on fnl f: nrst fin* 12/1
0660 5 *3* **Newcorp Lad**[9] 4717 7-8-9 46 oh1.................................. HayleyTurner 10 39
(Mrs G S Rees) *hld up towards rr: effrt u.p over 2f out: edgd rt: sn no imp* 14/1
2231 6 *1 1/4* **Princely Ted (IRE)**[1] 4972 6-9-1 59 6ex....................... BrydieKilloran(7) 1 49
(P A Blockley) *cl up: effrt and ev ch over 2f out: wknd over 1f out* 10/3[2]
00/0 7 *1/2* **Stravonian**[9] 4713 7-8-9 46 oh1....................................... DavidAllan 3 36
(D A Nolan) *midfield: drvn and outpcd 3f out: n.d after* 150/1
0400 8 *1/2* **Noble Edge**[27] 4177 4-9-1 52...(p) FTahir 2 41
(Karen McLintock) *prom tl wknd fr 2f out* 100/1
0604 9 *5* **Forrest Flyer (IRE)**[9] 4718 3-8-6 52.......................... RoystonFfrench 8 32
(Miss L A Perratt) *bhd: drvn over 4f out: n.d* 16/1
66-6 10 *1/2* **Rajam**[20] 4409 9-8-9 46 oh1...(v) LeeEnstone 4 25
(P C Haslam) *chsd ldrs tl wknd fr over 2f out* 14/1
000 11 *hd* **Kyle Of Lochalsh**[1] 4972 7-8-9 46 oh1............................ PaddyAspell 9 25
(Miss Lucinda V Russell) *chsd ldrs tl wknd over 3f out* 33/1
6505 12 *nk* **Alavana (IRE)**[9] 4705 3-8-4 50.. PaulQuinn 14 29
(D W Barker) *bhd: drvn over 4f out: sn btn* 33/1
4460 13 *5* **Grey Outlook**[9] 4717 4-8-11 48.. TomEaves 7 18
(Miss L A Perratt) *towards rr: rdn 4f out: nvr on terms* 12/1
6250 14 *20* **Advancement**[8] 4732 4-9-11 65............................... JamieMoriarty(3) 15 1
(R A Fahey) *in tch: n.m.r and lost pl 1/2-way: lost tch fnl 4f* 10/1
2m 23.21s (-3.05) **Going Correction** -0.175s/f (Firm)
WFA 3 from 4yo+ 9lb 14 Ran SP% **123.0**
Speed ratings (Par 101): **104,103,100,99,97 96,95,95,91,91 91,91,87,72**
CSF £69.63 CT £334.40 TOTE £23.80: £3.60, £2.20, £2.90; EX 61.20 Place 6 £169.85, Place 5 £62.71.
Owner John Wade **Bred** Kingwood Bloodstock **Trained** Mordon, Co Durham
FOCUS
An ordinary event in which the pace was sound and modest handicap form best rated around the placed horses.
Advancement Official explanation: jockey said gelding finished distressed
T/Plt: £72.00 to a £1 stake. Pool: £56,605.60. 573.15 winning tickets. T/Qpdt: £19.30 to a £1 stake. Pool: £2,605.40. 99.80 winning tickets. RY

4539 SALISBURY (R-H)
Friday, August 31

OFFICIAL GOING: Good to firm (9.1)
Wind: Virtually nil Weather: dry, overcast

5001 BATHWICK TYRES LADY RIDERS' SERIES H'CAP 1m
4:40 (4:42) (Class 5) (0-70,70) 3-Y-0+ £3,123 (£968; £484; £242) Stalls High

Form RPR
5322 1 **Gallego**[11] 4660 5-9-5 56.. MissABevan(5) 8 66
(R J Price) *hld up in last: swtchd to centre and stdy hdwy fr over 2f out: led ins fnl f: r.o: rdn out* 10/3[2]
1046 2 *nk* **Kavachi (IRE)**[11] 4667 4-9-13 64.......................... MissHayleyMoore(5) 13 73
(G L Moore) *mid-div: hdwy 3f out: led 2f out: sn rdn: no ex whn hdd ins fnl f* 3/1[1]
0006 3 *2 1/2* **Waterline Twenty (IRE)**[19] 4418 4-10-10 70................ MissEFolkes 14 74
(P D Evans) *hld up towards rr: weaved way through field fr 3f out: rdn over 1f out: wnt 3rd ent fnl f: kpt on* 14/1
0002 4 *1 1/4* **Batchworth Blaise**[4] 4908 4-8-12 51 oh6............. MissCNosworthy(7) 6 52
(E A Wheeler) *hld up towards rr: hdwy and nt clr run over 1f out: swtchd rt and sn rdn: styd on: nt rch ldrs* 20/1
2546 5 *1 1/2* **Colchium (IRE)**[48] 3555 3-9-13 70............................ MissVCartmel(5) 9 67
(H Morrison) *mid-div: rdn 3f out: styd on same pce fnl 2f* 5/1[3]
-640 6 *2 1/2* **Spice Bar**[53] 3367 3-9-7 62.. MissMSowerby(3) 11 53
(A M Balding) *stmbld leaving stalls: towards rr: rdn and hdwy 2f out: wknd fnl f* 8/1
-062 7 *1 1/4* **Mister Benedictine**[14] 4577 4-10-3 70........................ MissJJenner(7) 4 59
(B W Duke) *lw: sltly hmpd s: plld hrd: trckd ldrs after 2f: rdn over 2f out: wknd over 1f out* 10/1
1340 8 *nk* **Blue Line**[44] 3644 5-9-5 51 oh1.................................. MissSBrotherton 7 39
(M Madgwick) *mid-div: rdn over 2f out: wkng whn n.m.r ent fnl f* 11/1
0052 9 *1 1/4* **Bollywood (IRE)**[13] 4595 4-9-2 51 oh6............................ MissARyan(3) 12 36
(J J Bridger) *chsd ldrs: rdn and ev ch 2f out: hung lft and wknd fnl f* 25/1
2000 10 *1/2* **Theatre Royal**[28] 4131 4-9-10 56............................... MissFayeBramley 2 40
(Mouse Hamilton-Fairley) *led tl over 2f out: grad fdd* 20/1
5000 11 *2* **Compton Express**[59] 3186 4-9-0 51 oh6.......................... MissZoeLilly(5) 5 30
(Jamie Poulton) *a towards rr* 50/1
1320 12 *1 1/2* **Windy Prospect**[13] 4592 5-9-4 55.................................(p) MissAWallace(5) 10 31
(Mrs L J Mongan) *mid-div tl wknd over 2f out* 16/1
1040 13 *10* **Croft (IRE)**[4] 4880 4-9-7 53..(p) MissLEllison 3 6
(M S Saunders) *wnt rt s: chsd ldr: rdn over 3f out: sn btn* 33/1
00-0 14 *25* **Mocha Java**[198] 461 4-9-10 63.................................... MissLauraGray(7) 1 —
(B G Powell) *chsd ldrs: rdn 3f out: sn wknd: eased fnl 2f* 40/1
1m 44.85s (1.76) **Going Correction** +0.10s/f (Good)
WFA 3 from 4yo+ 6lb 14 Ran SP% **126.5**
Speed ratings (Par 103): **95,94,92,90,89 86,85,85,84,83 81,80,70,45**
CSF £13.31 CT £135.46 TOTE £3.60: £1.70, £2.00, £4.30; EX 16.30.
Owner My Left Foot Racing Syndicate **Bred** Mrs C C Regalado-Gonzalez **Trained** Ullingswick, H'fords

■ Stewards' Enquiry : Miss Zoe Lilly two-day ban: used whip when out of contention and filly showing no response (Sep 11,25)

FOCUS
A moderate handicap, but sound enough form. The winner apprciated the decent pace and was back to last year's best.

5002 SETSQUARE RECRUITMENT NOW IN SOUTHAMPTON NURSERY 1m
5:10 (5:12) (Class 5) 2-Y-O £3,238 (£963; £481; £240) Stalls High

Form RPR
4531 **1** **Siberian Tiger (IRE)**[28] 4130 2-9-3 **78**........................ RichardMullen 3 88+
(M R Channon) *hld up bhd ldrs: qcknd up wl to ld ent fnl f: r.o strly: readily* **3/1**[2]

5531 **2** 3 ½ **Mizooka**[16] 4501 2-8-10 **71**........................ EddieAhern 5 73
(R M Beckett) *lw: trckd ldrs: rdn to ld over 1f out: hdd ent fnl f and edgd rt: nt pce of wnr* **7/4**[1]

0440 **3** nk **Golden Penny**[28] 4121 2-8-11 **75**........................ TravisBlock(3) 4 77
(H Morrison) *trckd ldrs: rdn over 2f out: swtchd rt 1f out: wnt 3rd ent fnl f: kpt on same pce* **4/1**[3]

5360 **4** 1 ¾ **King Bathwick (IRE)**[26] 4202 2-8-3 **64**........................ AdrianMcCarthy 2 62
(B R Millman) *stdd s: pushed along over 3f out: swtchd lft wl over 1f out: styd on ins fnl f* **16/1**

006 **5** ½ **Space Pirate**[14] 4584 2-7-8 **60**........................ LukeMorris(5) 1 57
(M L W Bell) *hld up in last but in tch: hdwy over 3f out: rdn and ev ch 1f out: no ex* **8/1**

4030 **6** ¾ **Kyrie Eleison (IRE)**[28] 4121 2-8-9 **70**........................ KerrinMcEvoy 6 65
(R Hannon) *trckd ldr: rdn and ev ch jst ins 2f out: hld but cl up whn n.m.r ent fnl f: fdd* **6/1**

0505 **7** 4 **Abfabfong (IRE)**[32] 4022 2-7-12 **59** oh5........................ NickyMackay 8 45
(P F I Cole) *led: rdn and hdd over 1f out: wknd* **28/1**

1m 44.07s (0.98) **Going Correction** +0.10s/f (Good) 7 Ran SP% **116.1**
Speed ratings (Par 94): **99,95,95,93,92 92,88**
CSF £8.96 CT £20.34 TOTE £3.60: £1.90, £1.30; EX 5.90.
Owner Ridgeway Downs Racing **Bred** Ashley Guest And Mrs John Guest **Trained** West Ilsley, Berks

FOCUS
Solid form which should work out. The improving winner scored in style after travelling well.

NOTEBOOK
Siberian Tiger(IRE), off the mark in what was a modest maiden by Newmarket's standards, had previously shown useful form to finish third to the smart Fast Company at this course and he made a mockery of his mark of 78, quickening well from over a furlong out to win easily. This was a good performance from the son of Xaar, who clearly relished the extra furlong, and there may well be more to come. (op 5-2)
Mizooka, 5lb higher than when a course winner on her nursery debut, had an extra furlong to contend with here and she did not seem quite so effective. It was still a fair effort against a clearly well-handiapped rival though, and a return to 7f, possibly on easier ground, may bring about more improvement. (op 2-1 tchd 13-8)
Golden Penny, up to 1m having failed to make any impression on his nursery debut at Goodwood, looked awkward on the track, was found wanting for pace when it mattered and was another who possibly found this ground a shade lively. He remains capable of better and may be the type to improve dramatically for the softer ground in the coming months. (op 5-1 tchd 11-2)
King Bathwick(IRE) seemed suited to this rise in distance and ran one of his better races. (op 14-1)
Space Pirate, who had shown little in three maidens, was not certain to be suited to this longer trip and he appeared not to last home. A drop to 7f on a slower surface may see him in a better light. (tchd 15-2 and 9-1)
Kyrie Eleison(IRE) ran a bit better than his finishing position implies. (op 17-2 tchd 9-1)

5003 JAMES & SONS MAIDEN AUCTION STKS 6f
5:40 (5:45) (Class 5) 2-Y-O £3,238 (£963; £481; £240) Stalls High

Form RPR
1 **Max One Two Three (IRE)** 2-8-3 0........................ RichardKingscote(3) 6 74+
(Tom Dascombe) *unf: scope: hld up towards rr: hdwy over 3f out: nt clr run over over 1f out: swtchd lft: shkn up and str run ins fnl f: led nr fin: comf* **14/1**

0 **2** ¾ **Choiseau (IRE)**[14] 4571 2-8-11 0........................ RichardHughes 2 73
(Pat Eddery) *prom: led 2f out: sn rdn: hung rt 1f out: no ex whn hdd nr fin* **16/1**

3 nk **Dunn'o (IRE)** 2-9-2 0........................ AdamKirby 10 77
(C G Cox) *w'like: strong: trckd ldrs: rdn over 2f out: kpt on ins fnl f* **9/4**[1]

0 **4** 1 ¾ **Naughty Frida (IRE)**[30] 4061 2-8-11 0........................ KerrinMcEvoy 4 67
(E A L Dunlop) *trckd ldrs: rdn and ev ch 2f out: kpt on same pce fnl f* **14/1**

5 1 ¼ **Greek Theatre (USA)** 2-8-11 0........................ JimCrowley 5 63+
(Mrs A J Perrett) *unf: scope: hld up towards rr: hdwy over 2f out: sn rdn and edgd rt: styd on fnl f* **14/1**

63 **6** 1 ¾ **Sakhacity**[66] 2968 2-8-6 0 ow2........................ StephenCarson 9 53
(J R Jenkins) *led tl 2f out: sn rdn: wknd ins fnl f* **8/1**[2]

7 2 **Prince Afram** 2-8-13 0........................ EddieAhern 12 54
(R M Beckett) *w'like: unsettled stalls: hld up towards rr: hdwy 2f out: sn rdn: wknd fnl f* **20/1**

8 1 ½ **Buddy Holly** 2-8-9 0........................ RichardMullen 8 45
(Pat Eddery) *s.i.s: sn outpcd in rr: styd on past btn horses ins fnl f: nvr a factor* **50/1**

9 3 **Expediter** 2-8-6 0........................ FergusSweeney 7 33
(H Candy) *mid-div: rdn 3f out: wknd over 1f out* **25/1**

10 ¾ **Operachy** 2-8-13 0........................ AdrianMcCarthy 1 38
(B R Millman) *w'like: shortlived effrt over 2f out: mainly towards rr* **80/1**

11 2 ½ **Lady Van Gogh** 2-8-11 0........................ PatDobbs 3 29
(R Hannon) *w'like: s.i.s: a outpcd* **10/1**[3]

1m 15.91s (0.93) **Going Correction** +0.10s/f (Good) 11 Ran SP% **88.7**
Speed ratings (Par 94): **97,96,95,93,91 89,86,84,80,79 76**
CSF £108.62 TOTE £16.80: £4.30, £2.40, £1.40; EX 178.50.
Owner 123 Racing Partnership **Bred** P J Towell **Trained** Lambourn, Berks
■ Minshar (15/8F) was withdrawn after proving unruly in the stalls. R4 applies, deduct 30p in the £.

FOCUS
Difficult form to evaluate with confidence, as there is little to hang it on. The winner won cosily and looks capable of better.

NOTEBOOK
Max One Two Three(IRE) ◆, a relatively cheap purchase, would have been a most unlucky loser had she not got up as, having travelled strongly, she received no run over a furlong out and needed to be switched. She got there with plenty of time in the end, having really picked up once in the clear, and looks a useful prospect.
Choiseau(IRE), who shaped reasonably well on his debut at Newbury, had clearly learned plenty from that and looked the likliest winner when going to the front, but was cut down close home and forced to finish second. This represented an improved effort and he can win an ordinary maiden. (op 12-1)
Dunn'o(IRE), whose stable are more than capable of readying one first time up, was well supported in the market beforehand and held every chance, but could not quicken as well as the winner and was always just being held for second. This was a promising start and he is another who should find a standard maiden. (op 3-1 tchd 10-3)
Naughty Frida(IRE), last of fourteen on debut at Goodwood, stepped up significantly on that and was going on nicely close home. She will be qualified for a handicap mark after one more run and very much looks a nursery prospect. Official explanation: vet said filly lost a right hind shoe (tchd 12-1)
Greek Theatre(USA) ◆, bred to stay 1m in time, comes from a yard whose juveniles often need their first run and this American-bred colt was no different. He showed enough to suggest he can win a maiden, despite racing very greenly, and will be of interest next time over 7f. (op 9-1)

5004 WEATHERBYS BANK STONEHENGE STKS (LISTED RACE) 1m
6:10 (6:13) (Class 1) 2-Y-O
£12,775 (£4,842; £2,423; £1,208; £605; £303) Stalls High

Form RPR
31 **1** **McCartney (GER)**[16] 4495 2-8-13 0........................ GregFairley 2 102
(M Johnston) *lw: unf: scope: cl up: led 2f out: sn rdn and edgd rt: jst hld on* **13/8**[1]

0143 **2** hd **Scintillo**[13] 4598 2-8-13 96........................ RichardHughes 1 103+
(R Hannon) *lw: wnt lft s: hld up in last: smooth hdwy over 2f out: swtchd lft and rdn to chse wnr jst over 1f out: r.o strly: jst failed* **4/1**[2]

21 **3** 2 **Yahrab (IRE)**[26] 4199 2-8-13 0........................ KerrinMcEvoy 3 97
(C E Brittain) *lw: cl up: rdn over 2f out: styd on to go 3rd ins fnl f: nvr quite gng pce to chal* **4/1**[2]

3 **4** ¾ **Strategic Mover (USA)**[19] 4417 2-8-13 0........................(t) TQuinn 5 95
(P F I Cole) *w'like: strong: hmpd s: cl up: lost pl 4f out: swtchd lft and hdwy over 2f out: sn rdn: styd on* **14/1**

213 **5** shd **Donegal (USA)**[30] 4057 2-8-13 96........................ LPKeniry 7 95
(A M Balding) *led: rdn and hdd 2f out: kpt on same pce fnl f* **6/1**[3]

21 **6** ½ **Art Master**[37] 3842 2-8-13 87........................ EddieAhern 4 94
(S Kirk) *lw: trckd ldrs: rdn to chal over 2f out: fdd ins fnl f* **13/2**

21 **7** 16 **Quick Release (IRE)**[26] 4192 2-8-13 82........................ RichardMullen 6 57
(D M Simcock) *wnt lft s: racd keenly w ldr: restrained bhd ldr after 2f: rdn 3f out: sn wknd* **25/1**

1m 44.2s (1.11) **Going Correction** +0.10s/f (Good) 7 Ran SP% **116.2**
Speed ratings (Par 102): **98,97,95,95,94 94,78**
CSF £8.65 TOTE £2.50: £1.50, £2.70; EX 8.70.
Owner Sheikh Mohammed **Bred** Gestut Brummerhof **Trained** Middleham Moor, N Yorks

FOCUS
Plenty of smart form on offer for this Listed contest and the race should produce its share of winners. Another step forward from Mccartney.

NOTEBOOK
McCartney(GER), who looked a smart performer when demolishing the field in a novice stakes at Hamilton last time, was faced with a different calibre of oppositon here and did not have things his own way on this occasion, but still proved good enough and showed a determination typical of his trainer's horses. The Johnston juveniles are really in top form now and this son of In The Wings is likely to take in a Group contest next. (op Evens)
Scintillo has developed into a very useful juvenile and looked almost certain to improve for this first try at 1m. Held up right at the back early, he travelled strongly through the field to get within touching distance of the winner, but found the line coming too soon. He continues to progress and could be a force in the 1m2f races later in the season. (op 5-1)
Yahrab(IRE) was up in grade having won an uncompetitive novice stakes at Newbury, but he showed himself to be up to this level with a keeping-on third. He does not look the quickest and as with Scintillo, is likely to improve again when the 1m2f races start. (op 13-2)
Strategic Mover(USA), a well-held third over 7f at Leicester on debut, was impeded at the start and done no favours, but he recovered to race prominently. However, he soon found himself shuffled back through the field and by the time he got going again the race was all over. He can be rated a bit better than the bare form and should find a standard maiden for the taking. Official explanation: jockey said colt suffered interference at start (op 28-1)
Donegal(USA), who looked to have the beating of Scintillo on the evidence of his third placing in the Vintage Stakes, was soon in front and held every chance if good enough, but he began to look vulnerable from three furlongs out and could only find the one pace once headed. This was a bit disappointing. (tchd 5-1)
Art Master had plenty to find with the best of these and he was unable to cope. He is not going to be easy to place off his current mark. Official explanation: jockey said, regarding not riding out the colt, that he may have clipped the heels of Yahrab if he had continued (op 8-1)
Quick Release(IRE), ready winner of a Chester maiden, took a real grip early and failed to see it out, dropping right away in the end. He is clearly better than this, but has a bit to prove now. (op 33-1)

5005 FORD CIVIL ENGINEERING 25TH ANNIVERSARY MAIDEN STKS 1m 1f 198y
6:40 (6:42) (Class 5) 3-4-Y-O £4,857 (£1,445; £722; £360) Stalls High

Form RPR
-022 **1** **Demolition**[16] 4510 3-9-3 64........................ SimonWhitworth 9 78
(C A Cyzer) *mid-div: pushed along 4f out: hdwy 3f out: wnt 3rd wl over 1f out: styd on strly to ld ins fnl f: won gng away* **8/1**[3]

2 **2** 1 **Bright Mind**[14] 4568 3-9-3 0........................ RichardHughes 2 76
(J H M Gosden) *lw: in tch: tk clsr order 3f out: rdn to ld over 1f out: hdd ins fnl f: no ex* **4/11**[1]

0-33 **3** 3 **Harry Tricker**[45] 3621 3-9-3 79........................ JimCrowley 3 70
(Mrs A J Perrett) *trckd ldr: led over 2f out: rdn and hdd over 1f out: kpt on same pce* **7/1**[2]

6200 **4** 3 **Split The Wind (USA)**[16] 4504 3-8-12 60........................ StephenCarson 10 59
(Eve Johnson Houghton) *trckd ldrs: rdn 3f out: kpt on same pce fnl 2f* **66/1**

5 shd **Covert Mission**[105] 4-9-6 0........................ PatDobbs 5 59
(P D Evans) *leggy: hld up and bhd: rdn 3f out: styd on past btn horses ins fnl f: nvr a danger* **33/1**

4 **6** 1 ½ **Miss Habershon**[15] 4549 3-8-12 0........................ FergusSweeney 6 56
(A King) *neat: hld up towards rr: sme hdwy 3f out: sn rdn: one pce fnl 2f* **33/1**

7 2 **Wroughton (USA)** 3-9-3 0........................ SteveDrowne 7 57
(B J Meehan) *hld up towards rr: rdn and sme hdwy over 2f out: no further imp* **14/1**

0-04 **8** 1 ¼ **Elusory**[113] 1611 3-9-3 63........................ EddieAhern 11 54
(J L Dunlop) *lw: mid-div: rdn 3f out: wknd over 1f out: eased whn btn* **16/1**

40 **9** 1 ½ **Anna Towkaska**[78] 2597 3-8-12 0........................ AdamKirby 1 46
(W R Swinburn) *led tl over 2f out: wknd over 1f out* **25/1**

2m 10.81s (2.35) **Going Correction** +0.30s/f (Good)
WFA 3 from 4yo 8lb 9 Ran SP% **120.7**
Speed ratings (Par 103): **102,101,98,96,96 95,93,92,91**
CSF £11.66 TOTE £8.00: £1.80, £1.02, £1.90; EX 12.60.
Owner Mrs Charles Cyzer **Bred** P D And Mrs Player **Trained** Maplehurst, W Sussex

FOCUS
An uncompetitive maiden that looked Bright Mind's for the taking, but he was mowed down close home by the improved Demolition. The runner-up was clearly below form, but by how much is hard to say, so the overall level of the race is hard to pin down.

5006 STEPHEN & JENNIFER TILLEY MEMORIAL H'CAP 1m 4f
7:10 (7:10) (Class 4) (0-85,82) 3-Y-0 £5,181 (£1,541; £770; £384) Stalls High

Form RPR
1431 1 **Maid To Believe**[27] 4185 3-9-6 **81** EddieAhern 7 90
(J L Dunlop) *lw: mid-div: hdwy 3f out: chal 2f out: led jst ins fnl f: rdn clr: styd on wl* **8/1**

2120 2 3 **Fourteenth**[27] 4147 3-9-7 **82** SteveDrowne 6 86
(Sir Michael Stoute) *slowly away: sn led: rdn and hrd pressed fr over 2f out: hdd jst ins fnl f: no ex* **5/1**[2]

1344 3 ½ **Fretwork**[27] 4185 3-9-7 **82** RichardHughes 5 85
(R Hannon) *hld up: hdwy over 2f out: trcking ldrs and kpt in by wnr over 1f out: sn rdn: styd on ins fnl f: wnt 3rd fnl strides* **7/1**

2146 4 nk **Spiderback (IRE)**[98] 1987 3-9-4 **79** PatDobbs 3 82
(R Hannon) *hld up: hdwy over 2f out: cl up and nt clr run over 1f out: swtchd lft ent fnl f: styd on wl: wnt 4th fnl stride* **16/1**

2112 5 shd **Duty Free (IRE)**[16] 4511 3-9-0 **78** TravisBlock(3) 1 80
(H Morrison) *in tch: jnd ldrs 3f out: sn rdn: ev ch over 1f out: fdd fnl 100yds: lost 3rd fnl strides* **15/8**[1]

0010 6 ½ **Love Brothers**[14] 4558 3-8-11 **72** RichardMullen 10 74
(M R Channon) *hld up: rdn 3f out: no imp tl styd on ins fnl f* **16/1**

4-21 7 1 **Starry Messenger**[25] 4229 3-9-1 **76** TQuinn 2 76
(M P Tregoning) *lw: trckd ldrs: rdn and ev ch over 2f out: wknd fnl f* **6/1**[3]

3114 8 3 ½ **Down The Brick (IRE)**[18] 4458 3-8-10 **71** (b) FergusSweeney 9 65
(B R Millman) *plld hrd in mid-div: trckd ldrs after 4f: rdn 3f out: wknd over 1f out* **15/2**

2-04 9 5 **Lord Oroko**[42] 3722 3-8-8 **69** VinceSlattery 4 55
(J G M O'Shea) *mid-div: rdn over 3f out: wknd 2f out: eased ins fnl f* **33/1**

2m 38.54s (2.18) **Going Correction** +0.30s/f (Good) 9 Ran SP% **115.8**
Speed ratings (Par 102): **104,102,101,101,101 101,100,98,94**
CSF £47.83 CT £296.55 TOTE £8.90: £2.30, £2.20, £2.30; EX 40.70.

Owner Normandie Stud Ltd **Bred** Normandie Stud Ltd **Trained** Arundel, W Sussex

FOCUS
A decent three-year-old handicap. The favourite was a bit disappointing, but the form of the front three looks solid and the winner is clearly progressing.

Spiderback(IRE) Official explanation: jockey said gelding was denied a clear run

5007 WESTOVER GROUP H'CAP 1m 6f 21y
7:40 (7:40) (Class 5) (0-70,69) 3-Y-0+ £3,238 (£963; £481; £240) Stalls Far side

Form RPR
3003 1 **Synonymy**[18] 4463 4-8-10 **51** oh2 (b) NickyMackay 13 58
(M Blanshard) *trckd ldrs: rdn to chal over 2f out: led over 1f out: styd on: rdn out* **10/1**

0306 2 1 **Prince Of Medina**[15] 4534 4-8-7 **51** oh2 StephaneBreux(3) 8 56
(J R Best) *mid-div: rdn and hdwy fr over 2f out: styd on ins fnl f: gaining on wnr towards fin* **14/1**

3642 3 ½ **Sowdrey**[7] 4758 3-8-13 **66** RichardHughes 12 71
(M R Channon) *hld up towards rr: rdn and stdy hdwy fr over 2f out: styd on ins fnl f: nrst fin* **2/1**[1]

0020 4 shd **Valance (IRE)**[14] 4576 7-9-10 **65** (tp) SteveDrowne 5 69
(C R Egerton) *mid-div: hdwy after 5f to trck ldrs: rdn 3f out: styd on ins fnl f* **8/1**

3540 5 1 **Montjeu's Melody (IRE)**[32] 4019 3-9-1 **68** TQuinn 14 71
(J W Hills) *led: rdn and hrd pressed fr over 2f out: hdd over 1f out: no ex ins fnl f* **8/1**

2355 6 ¾ **Bob's Your Uncle**[14] 4576 4-9-3 **58** EddieAhern 1 60
(J G Portman) *in tch: rdn and effrt over 2f out: one pce fnl f* **6/1**[3]

0006 7 ¾ **Merchant Bankes**[34] 3969 4-8-6 **52** LukeMorris(5) 11 53
(W G M Turner) *t.k.h in midfield: hdwy 6f out: rdn 3f out: swtchd lft over 1f out: styng on whn bdly hmpd ins fnl f: nt rcvr* **28/1**

00/0 8 2 **Borora**[21] 4352 8-9-5 **60** JimCrowley 10 58
(R Lee) *a towards rr* **20/1**

0024 9 1 ½ **Mystic Storm**[13] 4597 4-10-0 **69** (t) PatDobbs 9 65
(Lady Herries) *lw: mid-div: hdwy over 3f out: effrt over 2f out: wknd over 1f out* **9/2**[2]

1400 10 2 ½ **Ronsard (IRE)**[14] 4576 5-9-5 **60** RichardMullen 2 53
(P D Evans) *hld up towards rr: swtchd lft and hdwy over 2f out: sn rdn: wknd over 1f out* **14/1**

0000 11 ¾ **Silver Surprise**[15] 4542 3-7-7 **51** oh6 NicolPolli(5) 6 42
(J J Bridger) *hmpd on rails 4f out: a towards rr* **80/1**

6/0- 12 ¾ **Absolutelythebest (IRE)**[89] 1502 6-9-12 **67** FergusSweeney 4 57
(J G M O'Shea) *prom: rdn 3f out: sn wknd* **25/1**

00-0 13 1 **Arch Folly**[15] 4521 5-8-6 **52** TolleyDean(5) 3 41
(R J Price) *prom: rdn 4f out: sn btn* **50/1**

600- 14 29 **Jubilee Dream**[408] 2132 5-8-10 **51** PaulDoe 7 —
(Mrs L J Mongan) *a towards rr: t.o* **40/1**

3m 9.97s (2.97) **Going Correction** +0.30s/f (Good)
WFA 3 from 4yo+ 12lb 14 Ran SP% **128.1**
Speed ratings (Par 103): **103,102,102,102,101 101,100,99,98,97 96,96,95,79**
CSF £141.27 CT £402.69 TOTE £11.50: £3.20, £4.30, £1.50; EX 186.90 Place 6 £14.31, Place 5 £8.16.

Owner G H Phillips,J M Beever & D G Chambers **Bred** Biddestone Stud **Trained** Upper Lambourn, Berks

FOCUS
A modest staying handicap. The form looks far from strong.

Merchant Bankes Official explanation: jockey said colt was denied a clear run

Absolutelythebest(IRE) Official explanation: jockey said gelding hung left-handed

T/Plt: £12.50 to a £1 stake. Pool: £39,755.95. 2,305.00 winning tickets. T/Qpdt: £7.80 to a £1 stake. Pool: £2,800.80. 264.25 winning tickets. TM

4546 SANDOWN (R-H)
Friday, August 31

OFFICIAL GOING: Round course - good (good to firm in places; 8.3); sprint course - good to firm (good in places; 8.4)
Wind: Moderate, against Weather: Cloudy

5008 BETFRED BINGO NURSERY 5f 6y
2:10 (2:13) (Class 4) 2-Y-0 £5,181 (£1,541; £770; £384) Stalls High

Form RPR
5035 1 **Thunder Bay**[13] 4605 2-9-2 **82** JimmyFortune 10 85
(M R Channon) *racd against far rail: w ldrs: led over 1f out: drvn fnl f: jst hld on* **5/1**[1]

5451 2 hd **Perfect Flight**[21] 4349 2-8-11 **77** TedDurcan 7 79
(M Blanshard) *hld up bhd ldrs: nt clr run wl over 1f out: got through to chse wnr last 150yds: clsng at fin* **5/1**[1]

045 3 shd **Lecanvey**[18] 4447 2-7-13 **65** SilvestreDeSousa 6 70+
(R A Fahey) *dwlt: pushed along in last after 1f: plld to outer and drvn over 1f out: styd on strly last 150yds: fin best of all* **11/2**[2]

01 4 nk **Royal Intruder**[36] 3878 2-9-7 **87** RyanMoore 1 88
(R Hannon) *dwlt: hld up in rr on outer: drvn over 1f out: styd on fnl f: nvr quite pce to chal* **11/2**[2]

4251 5 ¾ **Whispering Desert**[9] 4702 2-7-12 **64** 6ex FrankieMcDonald 2 62
(P T Midgley) *led to 1/2-way: sn drvn: styd pressing ldrs: kpt on same pce fnl f* **14/1**

5326 6 ½ **Ben**[18] 4459 2-8-10 **76** RobertHavlin 9 72
(P G Murphy) *racd against far rail: trckd ldrs: cl enough and effrt over 1f out: one pce fnl f* **14/1**

1163 7 ½ **Brassini**[13] 4605 2-9-4 **84** DaneO'Neill 8 79
(B R Millman) *w ldr: led 1/2-way to over 1f out: fdd ins fnl f* **5/1**[1]

2304 8 nk **Rio Princess (IRE)**[13] 4605 2-8-6 **72** RichardMullen 4 65
(T G Mills) *a towards rr: u.p fr 1/2-way: one pce and no imp* **11/1**[3]

0100 9 1 ½ **Presto Levanter**[27] 4168 2-8-4 **70** FrancisNorton 5 58
(R Hannon) *rdn to stay in tch over 3f out: struggling fnl 2f* **5/1**[1]

62.01 secs (-0.20) **Going Correction** -0.20s/f (Firm) 9 Ran SP% **119.1**
Speed ratings (Par 96): **93,92,92,92,90 90,89,88,86**
CSF £30.95 CT £145.83 TOTE £6.50: £2.40, £2.10, £2.60; EX 40.90.

Owner The Abercrombie Partnership **Bred** A C M Spalding **Trained** West Ilsley, Berks

FOCUS
They finished in a bit of a heap, but the form looks reasonably sound despite the winning time.

NOTEBOOK
Thunder Bay, who was behind the 7th and 8th last time, had the perfect sit throughout and did enough to win once under pressure. He has plenty of ability but was probably helped by hugging the favoured rail throughout. (op 6-1)
Perfect Flight, who had been raised 9lb for her last run, failed to obtain the best of runs, not for the first time, and can be counted an unlucky loser. (tchd 9-2)
Lecanvey ◆ did not get away that quickly and was still a length or two off the back of the field with around a furlong to go. However, he picked up to great effect and would have won in about 20 more yards. He is one to be with next time over further. Official explanation: jockey said colt ran green (op 8-1)
Royal Intruder was always chasing the leaders down the middle of the course and never quite got on terms under his big weight. It was a fair effort giving weight away but he is likely to struggle in similar company. (op 4-1)
Whispering Desert, who was officially 3lb well in, set a reasonable pace for part of the race and appeared to run up to scratch. A lesser grade is probably what is required. (op 12-1)
Ben was supported in the market before the off and did not have the best of runs when needed. However, he did find space in time and looked rather one paced under pressure. (op 20-1)
Brassini failed to get home after chasing the pace early. He was slightly hampered inside the final furlong, but it made no difference to the result. (op 11-2)
Presto Levanter Official explanation: trainer said filly was struck into

5009 HWFA WILLIAMS H'CAP 5f 6y
2:45 (2:47) (Class 5) (0-75,75) 3-Y-0+ £4,533 (£1,348; £674; £336) Stalls High

Form RPR
5303 1 **Canadian Danehill (IRE)**[7] 4780 5-9-9 **75** (p) LDettori 15 92
(R M H Cowell) *racd towards far side rail: mde virtually all: stretched clr over 1f out: comf* **7/1**

0010 2 2 ½ **Matsunosuke**[14] 4585 5-9-8 **74** JimmyFortune 10 82
(A B Coogan) *s.i.s: towards rr: prog 2f out: drvn and styd on to take 2nd last 100yds: no ch w wnr* **5/1**[2]

0352 3 ½ **Gwilym (GER)**[20] 4396 4-9-1 **72** AshleyHamblett(5) 8 78
(D Haydn Jones) *w wnr: led briefly 3f out: outpcd over 1f out: lost 2nd last 100yds* **10/1**

600 4 ½ **Pic Up Sticks**[13] 4606 8-9-2 **68** RyanMoore 16 72
(B G Powell) *racd against far side rail: hld up in midfield: trapped bhd rivals over 2f out to 1f out: styd on fnl f: no ch* **4/1**[1]

0063 5 hd **Musical Script (USA)**[7] 4767 4-8-4 **56** oh4 (b) FrankieMcDonald 11 60
(Mouse Hamilton-Fairley) *hld up in midfield: nt clr run over 2f out to 1f out: styd on same pce fnl f* **14/1**

000 6 ½ **Cerulean Rose**[15] 4545 8-8-4 **56** oh5 FrancisNorton 5 58
(A W Carroll) *dwlt: wl in rr on outer: styd on wl u.p on wd outside fnl f: nrst fin* **20/1**

3002 7 ½ **Brandywell Boy (IRE)**[7] 4767 4-8-5 **64** ow2 KylieManser(7) 14 64
(D J S Ffrench Davis) *chsd ldrs: urged along and no imp 2f out: plugged on* **14/1**

0000 8 nk **Oranmore Castle (IRE)**[28] 4122 5-9-9 **75** (t) TonyHamilton 6 74
(R A Fahey) *trckd ldrs: rdn wl over 1f out: folded tamely* **6/1**[3]

3041 9 1 ¼ **Jucebabe**[4] 4881 4-8-6 **63** 6ex ow2 (p) HaddenFrost(5) 2 58
(J L Spearing) *gd spd on outer: w ldrs to 1/2-way: wknd over 1f out* **10/1**

04 10 2 **Russian Gift (IRE)**[15] 4546 3-8-10 **64** AdamKirby 4 51
(C G Cox) *hld up in rr: rdn and struggling fr 1/2-way: no prog* **33/1**

4000 11 hd **Puskas (IRE)**[25] 4233 4-9-4 **70** (p) SteveDrowne 13 57
(J M Bradley) *mostly in last pair: rdn and no prog 2f out: v modest late hdwy* **20/1**

500 12 nk **Peopleton Brook**[26] 4204 5-9-4 **75** KevinGhunowa(5) 12 61
(J M Bradley) *racd against far side rail: prom: drvn and wknd over 1f out* **16/1**

0000 13 hd **Vanadium**[58] 3203 5-8-13 **65** FergusSweeney 7 50
(G L Moore) *settled in last pair: rdn and no prog 2f out: v modest late hdwy* **28/1**

300 14 1 ¾ **Detonate**[22] 4336 5-8-4 **56** oh11 SaleemGolam 1 34
(I A Wood) *dwlt: spd on outer: w ldrs to 1/2-way: wknd 2f out* **100/1**

23 **15** *shd* **One Way Ticket**[22] 4320 7-9-1 **67**....(p) DaneO'Neill 9 45
(J M Bradley) *nvr beyond midfield: u.p 1/2-way: sn wknd* **9/1**
60.46 secs (-1.75) **Going Correction** -0.20s/f (Firm)
WFA 3 from 4yo+ 2lb **15** Ran SP% **127.8**
Speed ratings (Par 103): **106,102,101,100,100 99,98,98,96,92 92,92,91,88,88**
CSF £41.79 CT £374.52 TOTE £6.40: £2.30, £2.70, £3.70; EX 46.40.
Owner T W Morley **Bred** Skymarc Farm Inc And Dr A J O'Reilly **Trained** Six Mile Bottom, Cambs
FOCUS
This featured plenty of old favourites and the form looks solid. High stalls had the call again.

5010 MONTY ALFORD EBF MAIDEN STKS (DIV I) 7f 16y
3:15 (3:16) (Class 4) 2-Y-0 **£4,533** (£1,348; £674; £336) **Stalls** High

Form RPR
60 **1** **Ridge Dance**[14] 4571 2-9-3 0.... JimmyFortune 10 83+
(J H M Gosden) *mde all: rdn over 1f out: styd on wl fnl f* **9/2**[1]
2 *1* **Emmrooz** 2-9-3 0.... LDettori 4 81+
(Saeed Bin Suroor) *dwlt: bucked sn after s and reminder: towards rr tl prog on outer 3f out: chsd wnr jst over 1f out: hung rt and nt qckn* **6/1**[3]
0 **3** *1 3/4* **Dr Livingstone (IRE)**[16] 4508 2-9-3 0.... RobertHavlin 8 76
(C R Egerton) *prom: effrt to dispute 2nd over 1f out: one pce fnl f* **50/1**
3 **4** *nk* **Black Dahlia**[14] 4565 2-8-12 0.... SteveDrowne 12 70
(A J McCabe) *chsd ldrs: rdn 2f out: styd on fr over 1f out: nt rch ldrs* **6/1**[3]
0 **5** *1 1/2* **Sinbad The Sailor**[21] 4362 2-9-3 0.... TQuinn 9 72
(J W Hills) *chsd ldrs: rdn over 2f out: styd on same pce* **14/1**
60 **6** *shd* **Irish Artist (FR)**[4] 4882 2-9-3 0.... RichardSmith 2 71
(R Hannon) *towards rr: shkn up over 2f out: kpt on fr over 1f out: n.d* **50/1**
3 **7** *1/2* **Funny Me**[49] 3478 2-9-3 0.... IanMongan 15 70
(P W Chapple-Hyam) *dwlt: towards rr: pushed along and kpt on fnl 2f: n.d* **11/2**[2]
8 *nk* **Nowaira (IRE)** 2-8-12 0.... DaneO'Neill 14 71+
(M Johnston) *settled in midfield: nt clr run fr over 2f out: no ch: gng on wl at fin* **14/1**
9 *hd* **Colony (IRE)** 2-9-3 0.... RyanMoore 3 69+
(Sir Michael Stoute) *chsd ldrs: shkn up 3f out: effrt 2f out: kpt on same pce after* **6/1**[3]
10 *nk* **Winged Legacy (USA)** 2-9-3 0.... RichardHughes 6 70+
(H R A Cecil) *chsd wnr to over 1f out: wkng whn n.m.r 150yds out: eased* **8/1**
11 *3/4* **Brexca (IRE)** 2-9-3 0.... AdamKirby 7 66+
(C G Cox) *dwlt: wl in rr: last over 1f out: shkn up and kpt on: n.d* **25/1**
12 *shd* **Colour Trooper (IRE)** 2-9-3 0.... JimCrowley 11 66
(P Winkworth) *cl up on inner: rdn over 2f out: fdd over 1f out* **50/1**
13 *nk* **Irish Mayhem (USA)** 2-9-3 0.... TedDurcan 5 65
(B J Meehan) *s.s: mostly in last trio: kpt on but no real prog fnl 2f* **12/1**
14 *1 1/4* **Pinnacle Point** 2-9-3 0.... GeorgeBaker 1 62
(G L Moore) *s.s: mostly in last pair: shkn up and no prog 3f out* **33/1**
1m 30.2s (0.86) **Going Correction** -0.125s/f (Firm) **14** Ran SP% **121.2**
Speed ratings (Par 96): **90,88,86,86,84 84,84,83,83,83 82,82,81,80**
CSF £29.93 TOTE £4.70: £1.70, £2.00, £11.20; EX 31.60.
Owner George Strawbridge **Bred** George Strawbridge **Trained** Newmarket, Suffolk
■ Stewards' Enquiry : L Dettori caution: careless riding
FOCUS
Unexceptional form, but the first two both look likely to go on and several of those behind look capable of much better in time.
NOTEBOOK
Ridge Dance made his experience tell and barely saw another rival. The trip definitely suited him, but it remains to be seen if he is up to justifying the fancy entries he has later this season. (op 11-2 tchd 4-1 in a place)
Emmrooz, who holds entries in the Royal Lodge and Mill Reef Stakes later this season, does not seem the most straightforward of characters but looks to have plenty of ability and came there looking the likely winner until inexperience and lack of peak fitness found him out. His next run will give us a clue as to which direction his temperament takes him, but he looks promising all the same. (op 9-2)
Dr Livingstone(IRE) improved on what he did on his debut and kept on well up the hill. An ordinary maiden looks well within his scope.
Black Dahlia ran another sound race but never really got on terms. She did well in a race of mostly colts and should have enough ability to win something this season, especially against her own sex. (op 13-2)
Sinbad The Sailor, who holds a Derby and Racing Post Trophy entry, is gradually getting the hang of things but is probably more a handicap sort, unless finding an average maiden next time. He also needs to settle much better during a race. (op 16-1)
Irish Artist(FR), who was quite free to post, probably ran as well as he has ever done despite still looking green. He is definitely one to note if turning up in a modest nursery. (tchd 33-1)
Funny Me kept on steadily up the hill and shaped like a horse who needs further. (op 9-2)
Nowaira(IRE) ◆ caught the eye in behind the leading bunch, as she had no room whatsoever to make a challenge when needed. She probably would have not troubled the first two but she can be rated much better than her final position suggests. (op 12-1)
Colony(IRE), the most expensive yearling colt sold from the sire's first crop, raced prominently early but was found wanting when the pace increased. (op 5-1)
Winged Legacy(USA) was prominent early on but started to lose places before a lack of room finished his chances altogether. A less-demanding track will probably see him in a better light. (tchd 9-1)
Brexca(IRE) moved well in the rear for a lot of the race and did not shape as badly as his final position suggests.
Colour Trooper(IRE) showed up nicely for a long way on his debut and ran better than his finishing position suggests. He is open to plenty of improvement. (op 33-1)
Irish Mayhem(USA) was making his debut and fluffed the start badly but did not run too badly thereafter. He has Group 1 entries and can be rated much better than this effort suggests. (op 25-1)

5011 MONTY ALFORD EBF MAIDEN STKS (DIV II) 7f 16y
3:50 (3:52) (Class 4) 2-Y-0 **£4,533** (£1,348; £674; £336) **Stalls** High

Form RPR
1 **Perfect Stride** 2-9-3 0.... RyanMoore 10 83+
(Sir Michael Stoute) *trckd ldrs: effrt 2f out: prog to chal ins fnl f: pushed along firmly and led last stride* **9/2**[2]
2 **2** *shd* **Bold Choice (IRE)**[35] 3896 2-9-3 0.... PhilipRobinson 9 81+
(M A Jarvis) *trckd ldng pair: rdn to ld 1f out: sn hrd pressed: hdd last stride* **6/5**[1]
3 **3** *nk* **Pinkindie (USA)**[34] 3958 2-9-3 0.... LDettori 2 80+
(E A L Dunlop) *hld up towards rr: stdy prog over 2f out: pressed ldrs and looked dangerous ins fnl f: no ex nr fin* **12/1**[3]
0 **4** *1 3/4* **Silver Regent (USA)**[14] 4571 2-9-3 0.... JimCrowley 14 76+
(Mrs A J Perrett) *trckd ldrs: rdn and sltly outpcd wl over 1f out: styd on again ins fnl f* **25/1**
5 *1/2* **Greylami (IRE)** 2-9-3 0.... JimmyFortune 8 75+
(T G Mills) *settled in midfield: prog 2f out: pressed ldrs 1f out: one pce fnl f* **33/1**
05 **6** *shd* **Jabal Tariq**[29] 4110 2-9-3 0.... RHills 12 74
(B W Hills) *w ldr: narrow ld 2f out: hdd and fdd 1f out* **9/2**[2]
6 **7** *3* **Metaphorical**[11] 4656 2-9-3 0.... DaneO'Neill 15 67
(M Johnston) *mde most to 2f out: stl w ldr jst over 1f out: wknd* **25/1**
4 **8** *1 1/2* **Highland Laddie**[26] 4198 2-9-3 0.... RobertHavlin 1 63
(C R Egerton) *settled in midfield: shkn up over 2f out: no prog* **50/1**
9 *1/2* **Inventor (IRE)** 2-9-3 0.... SteveDrowne 5 62
(B J Meehan) *s.s: wl in rr: rdn 3f out: kpt on fr over 1f out: n.d* **40/1**
5 **10** *3/4* **Landikhaya (IRE)**[78] 2596 2-9-3 0.... RichardHughes 13 60
(R Hannon) *a towards rr: pushed along and no prog over 2f out* **14/1**
11 *hd* **Manor Park (IRE)** 2-9-3 0.... TedDurcan 3 60
(C G Cox) *dwlt: rn green in rr: no real prog over 2f out* **25/1**
12 *1 3/4* **Hada Men (USA)** 2-9-3 0.... PaulFitzsimons 11 55
(M P Tregoning) *dwlt: a in rr: shkn up and struggling 3f out* **25/1**
00 **13** *shd* **Chrystal Venture (IRE)**[14] 4564 2-8-5 0.... RobbieEgan(7) 7 50
(A J McCabe) *rrd s: rn green and mostly last of main gp: nvr a factor* **66/1**
0 **14** *3/4* **Recoil (IRE)**[34] 3957 2-9-3 0.... PaulEddery 6 53
(Christian Wroe) *trckd ldrs tl rdn and wknd 2f out* **100/1**
15 *27* **Art Collector (USA)** 2-9-3 0.... GeorgeBaker 4 —
(G L Moore) *s.s: sn t.o* **40/1**
1m 29.4s (0.06) **Going Correction** -0.125s/f (Firm) **54** Ran SP% **123.8**
Speed ratings (Par 96): **94,93,93,91,90 90,87,85,85,84 84,82,81,81,50**
CSF £9.50 TOTE £6.10: £2.50, £1.40, £2.20; EX 14.50.
Owner Saeed Suhail **Bred** Bloomsbury Stud **Trained** Newmarket, Suffolk
FOCUS
This looked a decent maiden and was run in a quicker time than the first division. The winner looks a particularly good prospect and plenty of those behind will be doing better in time.
NOTEBOOK
Perfect Stride ◆, the most expensive purchase in the race, moved well under Ryan Moore before just getting the better of a decent-looking opponent in a tight finish. He was given quotes for next year's 2000 Guineas after this success and does hold two Group 1 entries this season, but he will obviously need to build on this at a higher level to justify his place in the Guineas market. Connections suggested the Horris Hill Stakes may come next. (tchd 11-2)
Bold Choice(IRE) ◆ ran another really promising race and was only mugged very late on. The winner could be pretty good and it may transpire that this was another solid effort. He holds an entry in the Royal Lodge Stakes at Ascot towards the end of September and could make up into a live contender for that, even if still a maiden going into the race. (op 10-11 tchd 4-5 and 5-4 in places)
Pinkindie(USA) clearly came on for his first run and just had the misfortune to run into two smart prospects. His turn will definitely come soon if maintaining this sort of form. He has an entry in the Redcar Two-Year-Old Trophy in early October that may look enticing on this effort. (op 11-1)
Silver Regent(USA) found this trip much more up his street and shaped with plenty of promise. A Derby entrant, he will appreciate a mile this season. (tchd 33-1)
Greylami(IRE), an already gelded son of Daylami, ran really nicely on his debut and looks sure to make up into a middle-distance performer in time, as his American dam stayed 1m3f. He might be more a long-term project than a sharp two-year-old sort.
Jabal Tariq, who cost a lot of money as a yearling and is related to some smart sorts, once again showed a degree of promise and looks the sort who may be better on a less demanding course. (op 9-1)
Metaphorical ran better than he had done on his debut and at least suggested that he is going the right way, without looking a potential star. (op 16-1)
Inventor(IRE), a 2008 Derby entrant, was a bit clueless early but kept on reasonably well when holding little chance. Time and experience will no doubt do him good. (op 33-1)

5012 U.A.E. H'CAP 1m 14y
4:20 (4:23) (Class 3) (0-90,88) 3-Y-0+ **£7,772** (£2,312; £1,155; £577) **Stalls** High

Form RPR
0212 **1** **Cactus Rose**[34] 3960 3-9-4 **85**.... SteveDrowne 13 96
(R Charlton) *settled bhd ldrs: prog 2f out: drvn to ld last 150yds: hld on wl* **4/1**[2]
3-1 **2** *nk* **Lang Shining (IRE)**[42] 3710 3-9-5 **86**.... RyanMoore 7 96
(Sir Michael Stoute) *dwlt: hld up in last quartet: rdn and prog fr over 2f out: pressed wnr last 100yds: jst hld* **11/4**[1]
-102 **3** *1* **Snaafy (USA)**[22] 4331 3-9-3 **84**.... RHills 9 92
(B W Hills) *mde most: rdn 2f out: hdd last 150yds: kpt on* **8/1**
3000 **4** *shd* **Irony (IRE)**[20] 4401 8-9-4 **79**.... FrancisNorton 6 86
(A M Balding) *w ldr: stl upsides 1f out: kpt on same pce* **50/1**
5004 **5** *hd* **South Cape**[20] 4377 4-9-10 **85**.... TedDurcan 12 92
(M R Channon) *trckd ldrs: rdn and nt qckn wl over 1f out: styd on fnl f: unable to chal* **7/1**
3-24 **6** *nk* **Ebert**[83] 2446 4-9-11 **86**.... JimmyFortune 3 92
(P J Makin) *dwlt: hld up in last: plenty to do whn effrt on outer over 2f out: drvn and styd on: nt rch ldrs* **6/1**[3]
0040 **7** *3/4* **Red Somerset (USA)**[27] 4184 4-8-10 **71**.... DaneO'Neill 1 76
(R J Hodges) *hld up in last pair: brought to wd outside and effrt over 2f out: kpt on fr over 1f out: nvr rchd ldrs* **22/1**
311 **8** *3/4* **Perfect Treasure (IRE)**[10] 4688 4-9-1 **76** 6ex.... RobertHavlin 10 79
(J A R Toller) *hld up in midfield: effrt over 2f out: no prog and btn jst over 1f out* **25/1**
0300 **9** *1 1/4* **Bustan (IRE)**[20] 4377 8-9-13 **88**.... LDettori 5 88
(G C Bravery) *hld up in last trio: effrt on outer and sme prog 2f out: no hdwy and btn over 1f out* **16/1**
0262 **10** *3/4* **Fabrian**[14] 4587 9-8-13 **74**.... JamesDoyle 4 72
(R J Price) *trckd ldng pair to 2f out: losing pl whn squeezed out over 1f out* **12/1**
2516 **11** *1* **Will He Wish**[80] 2536 11-9-7 **82**.... IanMongan 2 78
(S Gollings) *prom: rdn to go 3rd briefly 2f out: wknd over 1f out* **40/1**
401- **12** *1 1/4* **Kinsya**[328] 5810 4-9-12 **87**.... GeorgeBaker 8 80
(M H Tompkins) *dwlt: hld up in rr: shkn up over 2f out: hanging and no prog over 1f out* **16/1**
0023 **13** *nk* **Leptis Magna**[16] 4502 3-8-10 **77**.... OscarUrbina 11 69
(D R C Elsworth) *hld up in midfield: shkn up 2f out: no prog: eased whn no ch last 100yds* **12/1**
14 *6* **Jacquart (NZ)**[538] 5-9-5 **80**.... PhilipRobinson 14 59
(C G Cox) *t.k.h: cl up on inner: wknd rapidly 2f out* **66/1**
1m 41.32s (-2.63) **Going Correction** -0.125s/f (Firm)
WFA 3 from 4yo+ 6lb **14** Ran SP% **125.8**
Speed ratings (Par 107): **108,107,106,106,106 106,105,104,103,102 101,100,100,94**
CSF £15.43 CT £91.63 TOTE £4.90: £2.10, £1.60, £2.40; EX 13.90 Trifecta £190.90 Pool: £538.00 - 2.00 winning tickets..
Owner Thurloe Thoroughbreds XVIII **Bred** Langton Stud **Trained** Beckhampton, Wilts
FOCUS
A competitive handicap in which the finish was dominated by the less exposed three-year-olds. Good form.

NOTEBOOK
Cactus Rose was always in the right place to strike and did just enough to hold on. He is clearly improving with experience and can make up into a smart handicapper. Connections believe 1m2f is within his compass. (op 9-2)
Lang Shining(IRE) ◆ was given a very patient ride but improved to look the likely winner around a furlong from home before not quite finding quite as much as Cactus Rose, who had raced much more prominently in the early stages. He is still unexposed and the sort his trainer excels with, so it would be no surprise to see him make up into a smart performer with time. (op 9-4 tchd 3-1 in places)
Snaafy(USA) did well to finish as close as he did after forcing the pace with Irony. Much like the first two, he is an improving sort who has more to offer. (op 9-1)
Irony(IRE) is on a very handy mark now but remains very difficult to predict. If reproducing something close to this effort next time, he could be about to win again, especially if finding some slightly quicker ground. (op 66-1)
South Cape looked to be doing a bit too much during the early stages to have a telling burst left for the finish, despite the reasonable gallop being set by the leaders. (op 8-1 tchd 9-1)
Ebert, returning from a break, was given far too much to do under his big weight and will surely be ridden a touch more prominently next time. A slight ease in his handicap mark would obviously help. (op 5-1)
Red Somerset(USA) did not run badly but still looks in need of a bit more leniency. (op 20-1 tchd 25-1)
Bustan(IRE) Official explanation: jockey said gelding moved poorly
Jacquart(NZ), a dual winner in New Zealand over 6f and by one of the best southern hemisphere stallions, was very keen on his first run in England and could well need a run or two and a drop in trip before settling down.

5013 PADDOCK MAIDEN FILLIES' STKS 1m 14y
4:55 (5:01) (Class 5) 3-Y-O £4,533 (£1,348; £674; £336) Stalls High

Form RPR
5243 1 **Angel Kate (IRE)**[53] 3387 3-9-0 75 TedDurcan 3 74
(H R A Cecil) *mde all: 2 l clr 2f out: drvn fnl f: jst hld on* **10/3**[1]
502 2 shd **Meynell**[33] 4007 3-9-0 67 PhilipRobinson 10 74
(M A Jarvis) *trckd ldrs: wnt 2nd over 2f out: drvn and clsd grad fnl f: jst failed* **8/1**
2443 3 4 **Cassiara**[7] 4785 3-9-0 78 (p) FrancisNorton 8 65
(J Pearce) *hld up in midfield: rdn and prog to chse ldng pair wl over 1f out: no imp* **7/2**[2]
5-44 4 ½ **Satin Braid**[101] 1920 3-9-0 68 JamesDoyle 4 63
(A W Carroll) *chsd ldrs: rdn over 2f out: sn outpcd: styd on fr over 1f out* **14/1**
0- 5 hd **Change Course**[393] 4084 3-9-0 0 RyanMoore 9 63
(Sir Michael Stoute) *hld up in rr: shkn up and prog fr 2f out: styd on fnl f: nrst fin* **8/1**
0-0 6 3 ½ **Pink Salmon**[237] 55 3-9-0 0 IanMongan 7 55
(Mrs L J Mongan) *towards rr: rdn wl over 2f out: kpt on: n.d* **100/1**
36 7 nk **Blackberry Pie (USA)**[84] 2429 3-9-0 0 LDettori 1 54
(R Charlton) *hld up wl in rr: pushed along and modest prog on outer over 2f out: nvr nr ldrs* **5/1**[3]
8 2 ½ **Perfect Cause (USA)** 3-9-0 0 RobertHavlin 2 48
(J H M Gosden) *s.v.s: mostly in last pair: nudged along and sme prog fr over 2f out: bttr for experience* **14/1**
04 9 shd **With Confidence**[15] 4541 3-9-0 0 DaneO'Neill 11 48
(D R C Elsworth) *chsd wnr to over 2f out: wknd over 1f out* **22/1**
02 10 hd **Mini Mosa**[14] 4575 3-9-0 72 JimmyFortune 13 48
(J H M Gosden) *prom: rdn and 3rd briefly 2f out: sn btn: eased fnl f* **6/1**
5-00 11 6 **Full Of Promise (USA)**[99] 1961 3-9-0 62 OscarUrbina 12 34
(Mrs A J Perrett) *nvr beyond midfield: shkn up and no prog over 2f out: wknd over 1f out* **50/1**
0 12 1 ¼ **Pagan Rose (IRE)**[42] 3710 3-9-0 0 SaleemGolam 5 31
(J A R Toller) *a wl in rr: u.p and struggling 1/2-way* **66/1**
00 13 3 **Lady In Blue**[11] 4666 3-8-7 0 JackMitchell(7) 14 24
(T D McCarthy) *prom tl wknd rapidly over 2f out* **100/1**
-00 14 shd **Cadeaux Cerise (IRE)**[14] 4575 3-9-0 0 PaulEddery 6 24
(N I M Rossiter) *v s.i.s: sn last: a bhd* **100/1**
1m 42.15s (-1.80) **Going Correction** -0.125s/f (Firm) **14** Ran SP% **122.6**
Speed ratings (Par 97): **104,103,99,99,99 95,95,92,92,92 86,85,82,82**
CSF £30.45 TOTE £3.60: £1.50, £2.70, £1.90; EX 36.80.
Owner Plantation Stud **Bred** Dermot O'Rourke **Trained** Newmarket, Suffolk
FOCUS
Ordinary form, but there were a couple of pleasing performances.

5014 "TEXT BETFRED TO 83080" H'CAP 1m 2f 7y
5:25 (5:29) (Class 4) (0-80,80) 3-Y-O £6,477 (£1,927; £963; £481) Stalls High

Form RPR
00-6 1 **Nur Tau (IRE)**[27] 4147 3-9-5 78 LDettori 10 89
(M P Tregoning) *mde all: set decent pce: kicked on 2f out: styd on wl* **7/1**
0-31 2 1 ¼ **Sugar Ray (IRE)**[25] 4235 3-9-7 80 RyanMoore 5 89
(Sir Michael Stoute) *trckd ldng pair: rdn to chse wnr 2f out: styd on but nvr able to chal* **1/1**[1]
0214 3 1 ¾ **Risque Heights**[13] 4603 3-9-3 76 GeorgeBaker 6 81
(G A Butler) *s.i.s: hld up in last: stl there over 2f out: rdn and styd on strly fnl 2f: hopeless task* **16/1**
2042 4 2 **Highland Harvest**[18] 4455 3-9-2 75 AntonyProcter 12 76
(D R C Elsworth) *chsd wnr to 2f out: grad fdd* **14/1**
2012 5 3 ½ **Venir Rouge**[13] 4610 3-9-5 78 TedDurcan 1 72
(M Salaman) *hld up wl in rr: brought wd in st: rdn and plugged on one pce fnl 2f* **16/1**
2164 6 nk **Rock Anthem (IRE)**[22] 4318 3-9-4 77 DaneO'Neill 8 70
(J L Dunlop) *chsd ldng trio: rdn wl over 2f out: sn no imp and btn* **13/2**[3]
1601 7 shd **Malyana**[13] 4615 3-9-7 80 PhilipRobinson 4 73
(M A Jarvis) *hld up towards rr: shuffled along and limited prog over 2f out: no hdwy over 1f out: nvr nr ldrs* **6/1**[2]
0560 8 1 **Sir Liam (USA)**[16] 4510 3-8-3 69 (p) JackMitchell(7) 7 60
(P Mitchell) *chsd ldrs: rdn 3f out: sn lost pl and btn* **25/1**
000 9 1 ¼ **Kilburn**[29] 4111 3-9-2 75 OscarUrbina 9 64
(C G Cox) *nvr on terms w ldrs: u.p and struggling over 2f out* **25/1**
-360 10 ½ **Colonel Flay**[53] 3367 3-8-7 66 PaulEddery 2 54
(Mrs P N Dutfield) *nvr bttr than midfield: wknd over 2f out* **66/1**
102- 11 3 ½ **Minos (IRE)**[322] 5941 3-9-7 80 JimmyFortune 3 61
(R Hannon) *nvr bttr than midfield: wknd u.p over 2f out* **25/1**
2m 8.14s (-2.10) **Going Correction** -0.125s/f (Firm) **11** Ran SP% **121.6**
Speed ratings (Par 102): **103,102,100,99,96 95,95,95,94,93 90**
CSF £14.36 CT £118.55 TOTE £8.70: £2.20, £1.30, £4.40; EX 23.60 Place 6 £36.97, Place 5 £18.16.
Owner Nurlan Bizakov **Bred** C H Wacker Iii **Trained** Lambourn, Berks
FOCUS
The winner was given a terrific tactical ride from the front, but the form behind him looks solid.

T/Jkpt: Part won. £38,360.50 to a £1 stake. Pool: £54,029.00. 0.50 winning tickets. T/Plt: £40.50 to a £1 stake. Pool: £77,349.75. 1,393.30 winning tickets. T/Qpdt: £7.70 to a £1 stake. Pool: £3,917.10. 376.00 winning tickets. JN

[4973]WOLVERHAMPTON (A.W) (L-H)
Friday, August 31

OFFICIAL GOING: Standard
Wind: Fresh, half-behind Weather: Overcast

5015 WBX.COM WE'LL MATCH YOUR COMMISSION RATE CLAIMING STKS 5f 216y(P)
7:00 (7:01) (Class 5) 2-Y-O £3,238 (£963; £481; £240) Stalls Low

Form RPR
3130 1 **Lord Deevert**[8] 4737 2-8-7 74 JackDean(7) 11 68
(W G M Turner) *chsd ldr: led and edgd lft over 1f out: sn rdn: rdr dropped whip ins fnl f* **4/1**[1]
5504 2 1 **Liani (IRE)**[19] 4428 2-8-1 60 LiamJones(3) 12 55
(W M Brisbourne) *prom: led over 2f out: rdn and hdd over 1f out: styd on* **13/2**[2]
4 3 1 ¼ **One Called Alice**[18] 4459 2-8-9 0 TPQueally 9 56+
(J R Holt) *dwlt: outpcd: rdn over 1f out: r.o ins fnl f: nrst fin* **14/1**
00 4 1 ¼ **Desert Life (IRE)**[4] 4876 2-9-5 0 SebSanders 8 63
(R A Harris) *hld up in tch: rdn and hung lft over 1f out: styd on same pce* **4/1**[1]
01 5 ¾ **Smokeyourpipe (IRE)**[16] 4512 2-9-0 57 (v[1]) ChrisCatlin 3 55
(C Tinkler) *chsd ldrs: rdn over 1f out: styd on same pce* **10/1**
00 6 nk **Liz Long**[27] 4181 2-8-9 0 AmirQuinn 7 49
(P Howling) *led 5f out: propped at geese on trck: sn hdd: wknd ins fnl f* **66/1**
3000 7 ¾ **Carry On Cleo**[18] 4453 2-8-9 54 ow2 StephenDonohoe 1 47
(P D Evans) *s.i.s: outpcd: styd on ins fnl f* **11/1**
300 8 3 **Emef Princess**[9] 4702 2-8-6 0 (p) AndrewMullen(3) 10 38
(K A Ryan) *sn pushed along in rr: rdn over 2f out: n.d* **25/1**
1310 9 1 ¾ **Rio Taffeta**[28] 4136 2-8-12 68 BrettDoyle 4 36
(Peter Grayson) *led 1f: chsd ldrs: rdn and wknd over 1f out: eased* **4/1**[1]
4005 10 ½ **Miss Willoughby**[21] 4359 2-7-9 45 (e[1]) FrankiePickard(7) 2 24
(J Ryan) *s.s: outpcd* **40/1**
2404 11 nk **Alexander Monarchy (IRE)**[7] 4783 2-8-9 62 TonyHamilton 5 30
(D W Barker) *mid-div: hdwy over 3f out: rdn and wknd over 2f out* **7/1**[3]
1m 16.26s (0.45) **Going Correction** -0.25s/f (Stan) **11** Ran SP% **117.7**
Speed ratings (Par 94): **87,85,84,82,81 80,79,75,73,72 72**
CSF £29.77 TOTE £4.90: £1.90, £2.40, £2.30; EX 55.50.Liani was claimed by Diamond Racing Ltd for £5,000.
Owner Mrs M S Teversham **Bred** Mrs M S Teversham **Trained** Sigwells, Somerset
FOCUS
A reasonable claimer and certainly an eventful contest, with the field encountering a flock of wild Canada geese, two of which were killed, on the turn into the straight. The winner did not need to run to his best and the third is the improver.
NOTEBOOK
Lord Deevert benefited from the drop into claiming company and overcame his wide draw without too much fuss, proving too strong for ten rivals despite his apprentice dropping his whip inside the final furlong. This is his sort of level and he would probably struggle in nurseries off a mark in the 70s. (op 13-2)
Liani(IRE), a creditable fourth in a 7f maiden round here on her previous start, ran another decent race. She clearly has ability to win a small race, but it is worth remembering she has been beaten in sellers three times in the past. (op 9-1 tchd 6-1)
One Called Alice improved on the form she showed on her debut in a maiden round here, despite again starting slowly. She is only moderate, but is going the right way. (op 12-1)
Desert Life(IRE), dropped in trip and grade on his first start on sand, was short of room turning in and did not help his chance by hanging left in the straight. (op 5-1 tchd 7-2)
Smokeyourpipe(IRE), bought out of John Spearing's yard after winning a seller at Yarmouth on his previous start, was fitted with a visor for the first time and ran a respectable race in this tougher contest. (op 7-1 tchd 13-2)
Rio Taffeta was below form when a beaten favourite at Thirsk on his previous start and this was another disappointing effort. Official explanation: jockey said gelding hung right-handed (op 7-2 tchd 9-2)

5016 JOIN WBX.COM £150 FREE BETS H'CAP 5f 216y(P)
7:30 (7:34) (Class 6) (0-60,59) 3-Y-O+ £2,388 (£705; £352) Stalls Low

Form RPR
0643 1 **Tag Team (IRE)**[27] 4180 6-9-5 57 StephenDonohoe 10 67
(John A Harris) *chsd ldr: rdn to ld over 1f out: all out* **7/1**
1050 2 ½ **Silver Prelude**[2] 4944 6-9-7 59 SebSanders 2 67
(D K Ivory) *led: rdn and hdd over 1f out: styd on* **9/2**[1]
3200 3 hd **Green Pirate**[1] 4978 5-9-2 57 (p) LiamJones(3) 8 64
(W M Brisbourne) *hld up: hdwy over 1f out: r.o wl ins fnl f* **11/2**[2]
0430 4 ¾ **Registrar**[27] 4165 5-9-3 55 DMylonas 3 60
(Mrs C A Dunnett) *prom: outpcd 2f out: r.o ins fnl f* **12/1**
42-6 5 ½ **Murrisk**[15] 4529 3-8-13 57 JerryO'Dwyer(3) 1 60
(Eamon Tyrrell, Ire) *chsd ldrs: rdn over 1f out: styd on* **25/1**
0050 6 hd **Bond Playboy**[9] 4706 7-8-12 55 (p) SladeO'Hara(5) 11 58
(G R Oldroyd) *dwlt: in rr: r.o ins fnl f: nrst fin* **8/1**
0426 7 1 ¼ **Paddywack (IRE)**[6] 4800 10-8-12 57 (b) DanielleMcCreery(7) 7 56
(D W Chapman) *s.i.s: in rr: r.o ins fnl f: nvr nrr* **8/1**
0333 8 shd **Mistral Sky**[30] 4075 8-9-4 56 (v) MickyFenton 13 54
(Stef Liddiard) *chsd ldrs: rdn 1/2-way: outpcd over 2f out: styd on ins fnl f* **13/2**[3]
/000 9 ½ **Dorchester**[52] 3408 10-9-5 57 TGMcLaughlin 6 54
(W J Musson) *hld up: hdwy over 2f out: no imp fnl f* **28/1**
3060 10 2 **Royal Orissa**[20] 4394 5-9-1 53 BrettDoyle 5 43
(D Haydn Jones) *s.i.s: hdwy over 1f out: nvr trbld ldrs* **9/1**
0600 11 3 ½ **Muara**[19] 4423 5-9-3 55 TonyHamilton 12 34
(D W Barker) *chsd ldrs over 3f* **25/1**
4145 12 hd **Majestical (IRE)**[7] 4768 5-9-2 54 (p) DarryllHolland 4 33
(V Smith) *stdd s: sn outpcd: rdn and hung lft over 1f out: a in rr* **8/1**
0600 13 7 **Steeley Fox**[13] 4594 4-8-11 54 (t) KevinGhunowa(5) 9 10
(J M Bradley) *mid-div: rdn and wknd over 2f out* **66/1**
1m 14.43s (-1.38) **Going Correction** -0.25s/f (Stan)
WFA 3 from 4yo+ 3lb **13** Ran SP% **123.1**
Speed ratings (Par 101): **99,98,98,97,96 96,94,94,93,91 86,86,76**
CSF £38.39 CT £198.80 TOTE £9.70: £3.30, £2.20, £4.20; EX 74.30.
Owner Cleartherm Glass Sealed Units Ltd **Bred** Miss Sally Hodgins **Trained** Eastwell, Leics
FOCUS
A moderate sprint handicap but the form looks straightforward and sound, rated around the placved horses to their marks.

Paddywack(IRE) Official explanation: jockey said gelding was slowly away
Majestical(IRE) Official explanation: jockey said, regarding running and riding, that his orders were to miss the kick, abd come wide as the gelding dislikes running through horses, but it failed to pick up the bridle and ran flat; trainer added that gelding was unsuited by the delay to the start
Steeley Fox Official explanation: jockey said gelding never travelled

5017 BET NOW AT WBX.COM FILLIES' (S) STKS 5f 20y(P)
7:55 (7:58) (Class 6) 2-Y-O **£2,047** (£604; £302) **Stalls** Low

Form RPR
0330 **1** **Bahamarama (IRE)**[51] 3424 2-8-12 62 .... AmirQuinn 6 62
(J R Boyle) *chsd ldrs: rdn to ld over 1f out: drvn clr* **6/4**[1]
1544 **2** *6* **No Point (IRE)**[6] 4824 2-9-3 46 .... FrankieMcDonald 3 45
(P A Blockley) *led: rdn and hdd over 1f out: no ex fnl f* **15/2**
0500 **3** *½* **Star In The East**[9] 4715 2-8-12 58 .... (b[1]) BrettDoyle 2 39
(Peter Grayson) *chsd ldr: rdn to ld over 1f out: sn hdd and no ex* **5/1**[3]
4 *shd* **Little Cascade** 2-8-12 0 .... ChrisCatlin 1 38
(E S McMahon) *s.i.s: outpcd: nt clr run wl over 1f out: r.o ins fnl f: nrst fin* **9/1**
400 **5** *1 ½* **Dark Queen**[18] 4447 2-8-12 43 .... (v[1]) TPQueally 5 33
(D Carroll) *chsd ldrs: rdn 1/2-way: wknd fnl f* **25/1**
0000 **6** *½* **Mimton (IRE)**[20] 4405 2-8-5 39 .... LanceBetts(7) 12 31
(N Wilson) *mid-div: outpcd 1/2-way: n.d after* **66/1**
0422 **7** *nk* **Mama Leo**[45] 3626 2-8-12 59 .... (v) StephenDonohoe 10 30
(J G M O'Shea) *mid-div: rdn 1/2-way: wknd wl over 1f out* **3/1**[2]
0000 **8** *3* **Ephesian (IRE)**[43] 3673 2-8-5 54 .... JackDean(7) 11 19
(C L Popham) *mid-div: rdn 1/2-way: sn wknd* **25/1**
0040 **9** *7* **Poppy Perfect**[35] 3923 2-8-12 42 .... (b) JimmyQuinn 7 —
(J M P Eustace) *hld up: wknd 1/2-way* **33/1**

62.44 secs (-0.38) **Going Correction** -0.25s/f (Stan) **9** Ran SP% **115.6**
Speed ratings (Par 89): **93,83,82,82,80 79,78,73,62**
CSF £13.18 TOTE £2.70: £1.10, £2.30, £2.20; EX 18.70.The winner was sold to Ruth Serrell for 12,000gns.
Owner M Khan X2 **Bred** Hyde Park Stud & Stephen Hillen **Trained** Epsom, Surrey

FOCUS
A very moderate seller with an easy winner but the form is nothing special.

NOTEBOOK
Bahamarama(IRE) had shown ability in four starts in maiden company and was far too good for this moderate bunch dropped into selling grade. (op 9-4 tchd 5-2)
No Point(IRE), making her Polytrack debut, had no easy task under the penalty she picked for winning an atrocious race at Bath earlier in the season and she was well held back in second. (op 7-1 tchd 6-1)
Star In The East, fitted with blinkers for the first time, struggled in a battle with No Point for second and she looks very limited. (op 7-1)
Little Cascade, a 2,000gns daughter of Forzando and a half-sister to five winners, including dual 6f juvenile winner Red Typhoon, was never seen with a chance after starting slowly, but she made up some ground in the straight, despite not enjoying a clear run. There was degree of promise in this effort, but the bare form is extremely moderate. (op 7-1)
Mama Leo, now on her third trainer, ran no sort of race back on Polytrack and was a major disappointment. (op 7-2 tchd 11-4)
Poppy Perfect Official explanation: jockey said filly suffered interference at start

5018 PRELOK - THREAD LOCKING & SEALING H'CAP 1m 4f 50y(P)
8:25 (8:25) (Class 5) (0-70,69) 3-Y-0+ **£3,562** (£1,059; £529; £264) **Stalls** Low

Form RPR
0041 **1** **Mighty Kitchener (USA)**[11] 4670 4-9-8 63 6ex .... IanMongan 8 73
(P Howling) *mde all: rdn ins fnl f: jst hld on* **7/1**
0556 **2** *shd* **Ha'Penny Beacon**[18] 4463 4-9-2 57 .... (v[1]) StephenDonohoe 7 67
(D Carroll) *hld up: hdwy over 3f out: hrd rdn over 1f out: styd on wl* **12/1**
6402 **3** *1* **Art Professor (IRE)**[16] 4504 3-9-1 66 .... SebSanders 2 74
(J W Hills) *hld up in tch: rdn to chse wnr over 2f out: sn ev ch: hung lft and no ex ins fnl f* **5/2**[1]
2342 **4** *2* **Chia (IRE)**[21] 4355 4-9-11 66 .... FrancisNorton 5 71
(D Haydn Jones) *chsd ldrs: rdn over 2f out: styd on same pce appr fnl f* **8/1**
1100 **5** *7* **Royal Premier (IRE)**[21] 4365 4-9-9 67 .... (v) JerryO'Dwyer(3) 1 61
(H J Collingridge) *hld up in tch: lost pl over 4f out: n.d after* **16/1**
-002 **6** *5* **Sovereign Spirit (IRE)**[24] 4253 5-9-6 61 .... (t) DarryllHolland 10 47
(W R Swinburn) *chsd wnr: rdn over 2f out: sn wknd* **3/1**[2]
0000 **7** *1 ¼* **Colton**[13] 4610 4-9-6 61 .... JimmyQuinn 4 45
(J M P Eustace) *trckd ldrs: nt clr run over 3f out: wknd over 2f out* **14/1**
60/0 **8** *1 ¾* **Mighty Mover (IRE)**[65] 2981 5-8-2 50 oh3 .... JackDean(7) 9 31
(B Palling) *hld up: rdn and wknd over 2f out* **66/1**
006 **9** *1 ½* **Princess Aimee**[19] 4430 7-9-5 60 .... (p) MickyFenton 6 38
(D Burchell) *hld up: rdn over 5f out: wknd over 3f out* **33/1**
3032 **10** *7* **Moon Valley**[10] 4686 4-9-11 69 .... (b) LiamJones(3) 3 36
(W J Haggas) *s.s: hdwy 6f out: rdn and wknd over 2f out* **6/1**[3]

2m 38.52s (-3.90) **Going Correction** -0.25s/f (Stan)
WFA 3 from 4yo+ 10lb **10** Ran SP% **116.1**
Speed ratings (Par 103): **103,102,102,100,96 92,92,90,89,85**
CSF £87.05 CT £268.11 TOTE £9.00: £2.10, £5.20, £1.70; EX 163.30.
Owner S J Hammond **Bred** D Considine **Trained** Newmarket, Suffolk

FOCUS
A modest middle-distance handicap but a fair enough pace and the form looks sound.

5019 BET NOW AT WBX.COM MEDIAN AUCTION MAIDEN STKS 1m 1f 103y(P)
8:55 (8:56) (Class 6) 3-4-Y-0 **£2,388** (£705; £352) **Stalls** Low

Form RPR
2004 **1** **View From The Top**[10] 4686 3-9-3 70 .... SebSanders 5 60
(Sir Mark Prescott) *hld up: hdwy over 2f out: rdn to ld ins fnl f: r.o* **7/1**
5 **2** *2 ½* **Power Player**[44] 3651 3-9-3 0 .... JimmyQuinn 10 55
(D J Coakley) *dwlt: hld up: hdwy u.p over 1f out: edgd lft and r.o ins fnl f* **15/2**
3 **3** *shd* **Yab Adee**[205] 386 3-8-10 0 .... KatiaScallan(7) 1 55
(M P Tregoning) *w ldr: led over 6f out: hdd and unable qckn ins fnl f* **7/2**[2]
-006 **4** *2 ½* **Glenridding**[9] 4718 3-9-3 42 .... (b) TPQueally 9 49
(J G Given) *led: hdd over 6f out: rdn and ev ch over 1f out: edgd rt and wknd fnl f* **50/1**
-300 **5** *2 ½* **Geordie's Pool**[45] 3620 3-9-3 61 .... ChrisCatlin 3 44
(J W Hills) *mid-div: hdwy u.p over 2f out: wknd fnl f* **20/1**
50-3 **6** *2 ½* **Alecia (IRE)**[11] 4659 3-8-12 0 .... FrancisNorton 6 34
(A M Balding) *chsd ldrs: rdn over 2f out: wknd over 1f out* **9/4**[1]
6500 **7** *3* **Ionian**[18] 4462 4-9-7 68 .... WilliamBuick(3) 8 32
(Pat Eddery) *prom: rdn over 2f out: hung lft and wknd over 1f out* **6/1**[3]
2-0 **8** *½* **Ya Late Maite**[52] 3393 4-9-5 53 .... DarryllHolland 7 26
(E S McMahon) *hld up: rdn over 3f out: a in rr* **8/1**
0 **9** *13* **Llizaam**[19] 4430 3-8-12 0 .... SamHitchcott 4 —
(J T Stimpson) *bhd fr 1/2-way* **100/1**
62P0 **10** *132* **Mega Dame (IRE)**[19] 4430 3-8-12 64 .... (bt[1]) BrettDoyle 2 —
(D Haydn Jones) *chsd ldrs: hung lft and wknd over 4f out: eased* **16/1**

2m 0.91s (-1.71) **Going Correction** -0.25s/f (Stan)
WFA 3 from 4yo 7lb **10** Ran SP% **116.2**
Speed ratings (Par 101): **97,94,94,92,90 88,85,84,73,—**
CSF £57.46 TOTE £5.90: £2.40, £2.70, £1.80; EX 38.40.
Owner Mass Victory Racing **Bred** Hesmonds Stud Ltd **Trained** Newmarket, Suffolk

FOCUS
A weak maiden and modest form, with the form limited by the proximity of the fourth.
Mega Dame(IRE) Official explanation: jockey said filly lost its action

5020 WBX.COM WORLD BET EXCHANGE H'CAP 1m 141y(P)
9:20 (9:22) (Class 6) (0-65,65) 3-Y-0+ **£2,388** (£705; £352) **Stalls** Low

Form RPR
3122 **1** **Samuel Charles**[35] 3922 9-9-10 65 .... (p) LiamJones(3) 8 74
(C R Dore) *chsd ldr: led over 2f out: rdn over 1f out: jst hld on* **4/1**[3]
1061 **2** *nk* **Casablanca Minx (IRE)**[1] 4978 4-9-8 60 6ex .... (v) StephenDonohoe 12 68
(P D Evans) *dwlt: hld up: hdwy over 2f out: nt clr run over 1f out: swtchd lft and r.o wl ins fnl f* **13/2**
0305 **3** *1* **Lunar River (FR)**[17] 4472 4-9-11 63 .... (t) ChrisCatlin 1 69
(David Pinder) *chsd ldrs: rdn over 2f out: styd on* **16/1**
0204 **4** *nk* **Lord Of Dreams (IRE)**[19] 4433 5-9-12 64 .... SebSanders 5 69
(D W P Arbuthnot) *s.i.s: hld up: hdwy over 2f out: rdn over 1f out: styd on same pce towards fin* **10/3**[2]
2500 **5** *4* **Golden Spectrum (IRE)**[4] 4880 8-9-6 63 .... (b) KevinGhunowa(5) 3 59
(R A Harris) *chsd ldrs: rdn over 2f out: wknd over 1f out* **20/1**
0000 **6** *½* **Tabulate**[13] 4592 4-9-4 56 .... IanMongan 11 51
(P Howling) *hld up: hdwy and hung lft over 1f out: nt trble ldrs* **50/1**
5000 **7** *¾* **Linda's Colin (IRE)**[8] 4731 5-9-11 63 .... TPQueally 9 56
(R A Harris) *hld up: hdwy over 2f out: hung lft over 1f out: wknd ins fnl f* **16/1**
6022 **8** *5* **My Michelle**[15] 4532 6-9-8 63 .... RichardKingscote(3) 4 45
(B Palling) *led: rdn and hdd over 2f out: wknd fnl f* **3/1**[1]
0050 **9** *13* **Royal Amnesty**[22] 4340 4-9-13 65 .... OscarUrbina 6 19
(G C H Chung) *prom: rdn over 2f out: sn wknd* **7/1**
2050 **10** *3* **Under Fire (IRE)**[10] 4686 4-9-2 54 .... FrancisNorton 10 1
(A W Carroll) *hld up: rdn 1/2-way: a in rr* **14/1**
6000 **11** *44* **Tavares (IRE)**[11] 4660 4-9-8 60 .... (b[1]) SaleemGolam 2 —
(J Jay) *mid-div: sn drvn along: wknd over 4f out* **20/1**

1m 48.83s (-2.93) **Going Correction** -0.25s/f (Stan) **11** Ran SP% **123.8**
Speed ratings (Par 101): **103,102,101,101,98 97,96,92,80,78 39**
CSF £31.36 CT £398.29 TOTE £4.90: £1.70, £2.00, £5.10; EX 26.60 Place 6 £103.30, Place 5 £42.03 .
Owner Chris Marsh **Bred** Sheikh Mohammed Obaid Al Maktoum **Trained** West Pinchbeck, Lincs

FOCUS
A modest handicap and ordinary form for the grade, although solid enough rated through the runner-up and fourth.
Casablanca Minx(IRE) Official explanation: jockey said filly was denied a clear run
Royal Amnesty Official explanation: jockey said colt lost a front shoe
T/Plt: £244.80 to a £1 stake. Pool: £62,951.60. 187.70 winning tickets. T/Qpdt: £32.60 to a £1 stake. Pool: £5,050.50. 114.30 winning tickets. CR

5021 - 5027a (Foreign Racing) - See Raceform Interactive

4957 BADEN-BADEN (L-H)
Friday, August 31

OFFICIAL GOING: Good

5028a 134TH MAURICE LACROIX TROPHY (GROUP 3) 7f
4:00 (4:07) 2-Y-O **£37,162** (£13,514; £6,757; £3,378)

RPR
1 **Pomellato (GER)** 2-8-11 .... AStarke 10 103
(P Schiergen, Germany) *mde all: led narrowly tl rdn to increase advantage 1f out: hld on wl whn pressed ins fnl f* **33/10**[2]
2 *¾* **Peace Royale (GER)**[12] 2-8-8 ow1 .... EPedroza 2 98
(A Wohler, Germany) *midfield: 3rd and hdwy st: wnt 2nd 1f out: styd on* **6/4**[1]
3 *2* **Goose Bay (GER)**[26] 2-8-9 .... WMongil 1 94
(P Schiergen, Germany) *in tch in midfield: kpt on at same pce fnl 2f* **121/10**
4 *¾* **Diacaro** 2-8-11 .... FJohansson 6 94
(H Blume, Germany) *a in tch: cl 5th st: kpt on at one pce* **34/10**[3]
5 *5* **Every Day (GER)**[26] 2-8-7 .... ASuborics 7 78
(Mario Hofer, Germany) *trckd ldrs: wnt 2nd appr st: btn over 1f out* **101/10**
6 *1 ½* **Themelie Island (IRE)** 2-8-7 .... ABoschert 5 74
(A Trybuhl, Germany) *in tch: kpt to ins and cl 6th st: sn rdn and nt qckn* **171/10**
7 *nk* **Acotango (GER)** 2-8-11 .... J-PCarvalho 8 77
(Frau E Mader, Germany) *prom: pressed wnr on outside 3f out: 4th st: sn wknd* **193/10**
8 *nk* **Something Stupid (GER)** 2-9-0 .... ADeVries 4 79
(Mario Hofer, Germany) *pressed ldr to 1/2-way: btn over 2f out* **137/10**
9 *¾* **Sister Act (GER)**[48] 3563 2-8-7 .... AHelfenbein 3 71
(M Rulec, Germany) *s.s: wl in tch after 2f: wknd qckly over 1f out* **97/10**
10 *1 ½* **Bella Amica (GER)** 2-8-7 .... DPorcu 9 67
(Frau Marion Rotering, Germany) *sn outpcd: a bhd* **40/1**

1m 23.73s (-0.17) **10** Ran SP% **131.7**
PARI-MUTUEL (including 10 Euro stake): WIN 43; PL 16, 14, 25; SF 99.
Owner Gestut Ittlingen **Bred** Gestut Hof Ittlingen **Trained** Germany

[4989]CHESTER (L-H)

Saturday, September 1

OFFICIAL GOING: Good to firm (8.9)

Wind: Light, against Weather: Overcast

5029 BETTERBETCORBETT.CO.UK H'CAP 5f 16y

2:20 (2:21) (Class 4) (0-85,84) 3-Y-0+ **£5,829** (£1,734; £866; £432) **Stalls** Low

Form RPR

6502 **1** **Coconut Moon**[8] 4780 5-8-6 **74**.................................... WilliamBuick(3) 1 85
(E J Alston) *mde all: rdn over 1f out: r.o wl and in command whn pushed out towards fin* **5/2**[1]

2000 **2** *1 1/4* **Bluebok**[27] 4204 6-8-9 **79**..(t) TolleyDean(5) 3 86
(J M Bradley) *chsd ldrs: wnt 2nd 1/2-way: rdn over 1f out: kpt on ins fnl f: no imp on wnr towards fin* **15/2**

2211 **3** *1 1/2* **Cosmic Destiny (IRE)**[11] 4689 5-8-5 **70**........................ FrancisNorton 4 71
(E F Vaughan) *wnt rt s: hung rt thrght: in tch: rdn and styd on to chse ldrs over 1f out: kpt on same pce towards fin* **7/1**[3]

4000 **4** *1* **Misaro (GER)**[15] 4567 6-8-12 **82**..................................(b) LukeMorris(5) 10 80
(R A Harris) *midfield: rdn and hdwy 1f out: r.o and gng on at fin* **20/1**

0210 **5** *shd* **Peter Island (FR)**[15] 4567 4-9-0 **79**....................................(b) ChrisCatlin 5 76
(J Gallagher) *bmpd jst after s: towards rr: rdn and r.o fr over 1f out: nrst fin* **9/1**

3114 **6** *nk* **Bahamian Ballet**[12] 4664 5-9-5 **84**...................................... SebSanders 7 80
(E S McMahon) *prom: rdn over 1f out: no ex ins fnl f* **5/1**[2]

2242 **7** *shd* **Windjammer**[19] 4452 3-8-8 **74**...................................... GrahamGibbons 9 70
(T D Easterby) *chsd ldrs: rdn over 1f out: fdd ins fnl f* **14/1**

1501 **8** *1 1/2* **Drifting Gold**[28] 4186 3-8-9 **75**..(v[1]) EddieAhern 14 65
(C G Cox) *bhd after 2f: kpt on ins fnl f: nt pce to trble ldrs* **22/1**

0066 **9** *nk* **Royal Challenge**[10] 4703 6-8-10 **75**...................................... JimmyQuinn 8 64
(M H Tompkins) *s.i.s: bhd: nt clr run 1f out: nvr trbld ldrs* **12/1**

4000 **10** *shd* **Spanish Ace**[15] 4567 6-8-12 **82**.............................. KevinGhunowa(5) 15 71
(J M Bradley) *bhd: rdn over 1f out: kpt on ins fnl f: nt pce to chal* **50/1**

1515 **11** *hd* **The History Man (IRE)**[17] 4489 4-8-3 **71**....................(b) LiamJones(3) 6 59
(M Mullineaux) *bmpd jst after s: midfield: rdn and wknd over 1f out* **12/1**

0000 **12** *2* **Handsome Cross (IRE)**[38] 3836 6-9-3 **82**............ SilvestreDeSousa 12 63
(D Nicholls) *in tch: rdn and wknd 1/2-way* **16/1**

5521 **13** *nk* **Raccoon (IRE)**[15] 4561 7-8-8 **73**................................. PaulMulrennan 11 53
(D W Chapman) *midfield: rdn and wknd 1/2-way* **14/1**

60.43 secs (-1.62) **Going Correction** 0.0s/f (Good)

WFA 3 from 4yo+ 1lb **13** Ran SP% **125.2**

Speed ratings (Par 105): **112,110,107,106,105 105,105,102,102,102 101,98,98**

CSF £21.74 CT £115.87 TOTE £3.50: £1.60, £2.90, £2.10; EX 25.20 Trifecta £116.20 Pool £475.00 - 2.90 winning units..

Owner Valley Paddocks Racing Limited **Bred** Mrs R D Peacock **Trained** Longton, Lancs

FOCUS

The winner repeated her success of last year off a higher handicap mark. The form should prove fairly sound.

Cosmic Destiny(IRE) Official explanation: jockey said mare hung right

Drifting Gold Official explanation: jockey said filly was unsuited by the draw and denied a clear run

Royal Challenge Official explanation: jockey said gelding was denied a clear run

The History Man(IRE) Official explanation: jockey said gelding was hampered at start

5030 CALL 08000 568 621 CHESTER H'CAP (LISTED RACE) 1m 5f 89y

2:50 (2:51) (Class 1) (0-110,101) 3-Y-0+

£19,873 (£7,532; £3,769; £1,879; £941; £472) **Stalls** Low

Form RPR

1-02 **1** **Bauer (IRE)**[24] 4288 4-9-3 **93**... EddieAhern 3 104
(L M Cumani) *chsd ldrs: rdn over 1f out: led ins fnl f: r.o wl* **11/8**[1]

0624 **2** *2* **Lundy's Lane (IRE)**[21] 4388 7-9-5 **95**.............................. FrancisNorton 5 103
(A M Balding) *chsd ldrs: led over 3f out: rdn over 1f out: hdd ins fnl f: nt qckn* **13/2**[3]

6311 **3** *hd* **Sagredo (USA)**[30] 4105 3-8-12 **98**.................................. SebSanders 10 106
(Sir Mark Prescott) *s.s: hld up: hdwy over 3f out: rdn over 2f out: styd on ins fnl f* **9/2**[2]

0-20 **4** *1* **Mikao (IRE)**[70] 2859 6-9-1 **91**... JimmyQuinn 8 97
(M H Tompkins) *hld up: hdwy over 3f out: upsides over 2f out: rdn over 1f out: no ex ins fnl f* **25/1**

0501 **5** *hd* **Dansili Dancer**[21] 4388 5-9-10 **100**.............................. PaulMulrennan 6 106
(C G Cox) *midfield: outpcd over 2f out: styd on fr over 1f out: nvr able to chal* **10/1**

4140 **6** *1/2* **Ogee**[10] 4722 4-9-3 **93**..(v) WilliamBuick 9 98
(Sir Michael Stoute) *s.i.s: rn in snatches: in rr: struggling 7f out: rallied to chse ldrs over 3f out: outpcd 2f out: kpt on again ins fnl f* **10/1**

-505 **7** *10* **Gavroche (IRE)**[21] 4376 6-9-0 **90**.................................. NickyMackay 4 80
(J R Boyle) *s.i.s: hld up: hdwy 5f out: upsides 3f out: wknd over 1f out: eased whn btn ins fnl f* **16/1**

3004 **8** *12* **Galient (IRE)**[13] 4637 4-8-13 **89**... MichaelHills 2 61
(M A Jarvis) *midfield: pushed along and dropped to rr 5f out: eased whn btn ins fnl f* **11/1**

6102 **9** *22* **John Terry (IRE)**[21] 4376 4-9-3 **93**.................................. DarryllHolland 1 32
(Mrs A J Perrett) *led for 1f: chsd ldr: led over 4f out: hdd over 3f out: sn wknd: eased whn btn ins fnl f* **8/1**

6250 **10** *dist* **Solent (IRE)**[10] 4722 5-9-11 **101**................................. RichardHughes 7 —
(R Hannon) *rdn to ld after 1f: hdd over 4f out: wknd over 3f out: virtually p.u ins fnl f* **16/1**

2m 52.71s (-2.71) **Going Correction** 0.0s/f (Good)

WFA 3 from 4yo+ 10lb **10** Ran SP% **126.9**

Speed ratings (Par 111): **108,106,106,106,105 105,99,92,78,—**

CSF £12.09 CT £36.84 TOTE £2.30: £1.10, £2.50, £2.00; EX 15.20 Trifecta £36.20 Pool £423.30 - 8.30 winning units..

Owner Aston House Stud **Bred** Aston House Stud **Trained** Newmarket, Suffolk

FOCUS

A very competitive handicap won by an improving colt. The fourth and fifth are not well handicapped but the form appears solid with the runner-up and fifth close to recent Haydock form.

NOTEBOOK

Bauer(IRE) ◆, who missed the cut for the Ebor handicap recently, probably should have won last time but got back on the winning path with a clear-cut success. He is clearly improving with age, much like his sire, and he is definitely worth a chance in Group company now. (op 7-4)

Lundy's Lane(IRE) has been in fine fettle this season and ran another cracker over a trip he had yet to try. Placed in the Italian Derby as a three-year-old, he is not short of stamina and deserves a victory this season. The valuable John Smith's Handicap at Newbury later in the month might just be his day. (op 15-2)

Sagredo(USA), taking a big step up in distance, seemed to have no problem with the trip and deserves plenty of credit for a solid effort against his elders. It will be interesting to see what distance connections try him over next time and he remains a progressive-looking sort. (op 5-1 tchd 11-2)

Mikao(IRE) tried to stretch his rivals off the final bend but could not get away from them. He is high enough in the handicap now and will always been vulnerable to less-exposed sorts. (op 22-1)

Dansili Dancer, winner of the Old Newton Cup last time off a 5lb lower mark, never got into the race so it remains an unknown as to whether he stays this far. (op 12-1)

Ogee does not look an easy ride and was being niggled passing the winning post on their first circuit. (tchd 9-1)

Galient(IRE) was eased when his chance had gone and has seemingly completely lost the plot. Official explanation: jockey said gelding was unsuited by the good to firm ground (op 12-1)

Solent(IRE) Official explanation: jockey said saddle slipped

5031 BETTERBETCORBETT.CO.UK STKS (HERITAGE H'CAP) 7f 122y

3:25 (3:27) (Class 2) 3-Y-0+

£24,928 (£7,464; £3,732; £1,868; £932; £468) **Stalls** Low

Form RPR

4033 **1** **Vanderlin**[49] 3529 8-9-1 **100**... WilliamBuick(3) 12 108
(A M Balding) *chsd ldrs: rdn to ld jst over 1f out: jst hld on* **16/1**

1001 **2** *shd* **Laa Rayb (USA)**[31] 4062 3-8-11 **98**...................................... EddieAhern 6 105
(M Johnston) *midfield: hdwy over 2f out: plld out over 1f out: hung lft ins fnl f: fin strly: jst failed* **11/2**[2]

5266 **3** *nk* **Fiefdom (IRE)**[1] 4990 5-7-9 **82** oh4 ow2........................... LukeMorris(5) 9 89
(I W McInnes) *in tch: nt clr run 2f out: nt clr run again over 1f out: sn rdn: r.o ins fnl f: hld fnl strides* **25/1**

0115 **4** *hd* **Fremen (USA)**[9] 4745 7-8-7 **89**................................ SilvestreDeSousa 11 95
(D Nicholls) *midfield: hdwy 3f out: rdn to chse ldrs over 1f out: str chal ins fnl f: nt qckn fnl strides* **11/2**[2]

0001 **5** *nk* **H Harrison (IRE)**[1] 4990 7-8-1 **86** 6ex........................... AndrewElliott(3) 4 91
(I W McInnes) *led: rdn and hdd jst over 1f out: styd on ins fnl f* **8/1**

0100 **6** *3/4* **Capable Guest (IRE)**[73] 2755 5-8-9 **91**...........................(v) ChrisCatlin 16 94
(M R Channon) *in rr: hdwy over 2f out: nt clr run over 1f out: rdn and r.o ins fnl f: nt clr run towards fin* **28/1**

-231 **7** *1/2* **Robema**[27] 4195 4-8-1 **83**.. JimmyQuinn 2 85
(J J Quinn) *chsd ldrs: rdn over 1f out: styd on same pce ins fnl f* **6/1**[3]

21-5 **8** *1* **Beauchamp Viceroy**[161] 760 3-8-8 **95**............................... NickyMackay 7 95
(G A Butler) *prom: upsides over 1f out: fdd wl ins fnl f* **18/1**

2200 **9** *3/4* **Roman Maze**[14] 4614 7-8-7 **89**... FrancisNorton 5 87
(W M Brisbourne) *racd keenly: midfield: rdn over 2f out: no imp* **10/1**

3141 **10** *1 1/2* **Giganticus (USA)**[21] 4401 4-9-6 **102**................................. MichaelHills 3 96
(B W Hills) *midfield: rdn 2f out: nvr able to chal* **11/4**[1]

4040 **11** *1* **Dhaular Dhar (IRE)**[14] 4614 5-9-2 **98**............................. SaleemGolam 17 90
(J S Goldie) *hld up: rdn over 2f out: nvr on terms* **12/1**

6200 **12** *1 1/4* **Mezuzah**[9] 4745 7-8-1 **83**... AdrianMcCarthy 10 71
(M W Easterby) *midfield: sn niggled along: wknd over 1f out* **66/1**

/3-0 **13** *shd* **Cupid's Glory**[239] 43 5-9-4 **100**..................................(p) RichardHughes 8 88
(Mrs L C Jewell) *a towards rr* **40/1**

1660 **14** *3* **Countdown**[21] 4401 5-8-5 **87** ow1............................... GrahamGibbons 15 68
(T D Easterby) *swtchd lft s: a bhd* **50/1**

P **Markab**[405] 4-8-7 **89**.. PaulMulrennan 13 —
(K A Morgan) *a bhd: toiling 3f out: t.o and p.u ins fnl f* **66/1**

1m 33.37s (-1.38) **Going Correction** 0.0s/f (Good)

WFA 3 from 4yo+ 5lb **15** Ran SP% **125.4**

Speed ratings (Par 109): **106,105,105,105,105 104,103,102,102,100 99,98,98,95,—**

CSF £101.25 CT £2282.13 TOTE £21.20: £5.10, £2.50, £9.20; EX 123.00 Trifecta £4038.20 Pool £20,475.75 - 3.60 winning units..

Owner J C & S R Hitchins **Bred** Ellway Breeding **Trained** Kingsclere, Hants

FOCUS

A hot race featuring plenty of good handicap form but slightly messy and hard to rate positively.

NOTEBOOK

Vanderlin, a wonderful servant to connections who acts well around the course, was given a peach of a ride by his jockey from a very tricky draw. He was also helped by the questionable attitude of the runner-up, but very little should be taken away from this grand campaigner who may try and pick up a Listed race again. (op 25-1)

Laa Rayb(USA) was produced to have every chance in the latter stages but failed to impress with his head carriage under pressure. It is worth giving him another chance in case something was hurting him, because he had shown no sign of doing this in the past. (op 6-1)

Fiefdom(IRE), making a very swift reappearance, ran really well but was receiving lots of weight and may have been a bit flattered by the effort. It is difficult to believe the overweight the jockey put up cost him the race. (op 33-1)

Fremen(USA) ran another fine race but was not helped by racing wide throughout. (op 13-2)

H Harrison(IRE), a winner over the course the day before, ran really well but did not quite see out the extra distance. He is a real Chester specialist.

Capable Guest(IRE)stayed on nicely at the end of the race after finding trouble in running. He rarely runs two races alike and could not be guaranteed to reproduce this effort next time. (op 33-1)

Robema travelled really well during much of the race but found little when asked to quicken. (tchd 11-2 and 13-2)

Beauchamp Viceroy, not seen since March, was very keen towards the head of affairs and did not get home as a consequence. This run will do him a lot of good and he looks capable of winning on the turf after collecting all of his previous three successes at Wolverhampton. (op 20-1 tchd 16-1)

Roman Maze Official explanation: jockey said gelding ran too freely early on

Giganticus(USA) Official explanation: jockey said gelding suffered interference on the final bend

Mezuzah Official explanation: jockey said gelding never travelled

Cupid's Glory Official explanation: jockey said gelding was not moving well

Markab Official explanation: jockey said colt sustained an injury

5032 CALL 08000 568 621 E B F CONDITIONS STKS (C&G) 6f 18y

4:00 (4:01) (Class 2) 2-Y-0 **£9,778** (£2,926; £1,463; £731; £364) **Stalls** Low

Form RPR

2104 **1** **Imperial Mint (IRE)**[10] 4721 2-9-1 100.............................. JimmyQuinn 3 100
(K A Ryan) *a.p: led over 1f out: drvn out* **5/2**[1]

3103 **2** *1 3/4* **Fred's Lad**[10] 4724 2-9-8 95... PaulMulrennan 5 102
(M W Easterby) *led: rdn and hdd over 1f out: nt qckn ins fnl f* **7/1**[2]

6125 **3** *hd* **Nacho Libre**[10] 4721 2-9-1 98.. MichaelHills 2 94
(B W Hills) *hld up: hdwy on outside over 2f out: chsd ldrs over 1f out: styd on ins fnl f: nt pce of ldrs* **5/2**[1]

0050 **4** *2* **Carleton**[10] 4724 2-9-4 90.. DarryllHolland 1 91
(M R Channon) *handy: rdn over 1f out: outpcd after* **10/1**[3]

2106 **5** *18* **Supermassive Muse (IRE)**[7] 4823 2-8-12 81..............(bt[1]) ChrisCatlin 6 31+
(E S McMahon) *racd keenly: prom after 1f: rdn and wknd 2f out: eased whn btn ins fnl f* **28/1**

6116 **6** *5* **Sailor At Sea (USA)**[10] 4724 2-9-1 90........................ RichardHughes 4 19+
(R Charlton) *hld up in tch: pushed along 2f out: sn btn: eased ins fnl f* **5/2**[1]

1m 15.1s (-0.55) **Going Correction** 0.0s/f (Good) **6** Ran SP% **110.8**
Speed ratings (Par 101): **103,100,100,97,73 67**
CSF £20.35 TOTE £3.50: £1.80, £2.50; EX 20.20.
Owner David Fravigar, Kathy Dixon **Bred** Paul Starr **Trained** Hambleton, N Yorks

FOCUS
A decent conditions event for the juveniles touching on Listed race quality. The form has a solid look to it.

NOTEBOOK
Imperial Mint(IRE), fourth in the Gimcrack last time, enjoyed the drop in grade to win with something to spare. A nice sort, he holds an entry in the Middle Park Stakes and it would be no surprise to see him make the line up for that race. (op 2-1 tchd 11-4)
Fred's Lad did really well giving weight away but was comfortably held by the winner. He confirmed placings with Carleton and the unfortunate Sailor At Sea on their York meeting and remains a progressive juvenile. (tchd 11-2)
Nacho Libre finished behind the winner last time at York and did so again. It looks as though a step up in trip would pose him no problems, which would help him because he is not speedy enough for this distance in similar company. (op 9-4)
Carleton ran as well as could have been expected, failing to trouble the principals up the home straight. (op 12-1)
Supermassive Muse(IRE), wearing blinkers for the first time, ran no sort of race and was well out of his depth. (op 33-1 tchd 25-1)
Sailor At Sea(USA) ran very poorly but it transpired that he had lost his action and, although reported to have broken down, he was sound the following day. Official explanation: jockey said colt lost its action (op 3-1 tchd 9-4)

5033 RAYMOND CORBETT EBF MAIDEN STKS 7f 2y
4:35 (4:37) (Class 3) 2-Y-O **£6,800** (£2,023; £1,011; £505) **Stalls** Low

Form RPR

4522 **1** **Eastern Gift**[15] 4571 2-9-3 86........................ RichardHughes 5 85
(R Hannon) *chsd ldr: led over 3f out: rdn over 1f out: kpt on wl* **15/8**[2]

22 **2** *nk* **Bellomi (IRE)**[14] 4593 2-9-3 0........................ DarryllHolland 7 84
(M R Channon) *chsd ldrs: upsides in 2nd 3f out: rdn and edgd rt 1f out: sn edgd lft: edgd rt again wl ins fnl f: kpt on* **3/1**[3]

02 **3** *1* **Crystal Rock (IRE)**[19] 4454 2-9-3 0........................ MichaelHills 2 82+
(B W Hills) *s.i.s: chsd ldrs: running on whn edgd lft ins fnl f: sn bmpd: nt rcvr* **7/4**[1]

0 **4** *9* **Glittering Prize (UAE)**[8] 4781 2-8-12 0........................ EddieAhern 3 54
(M Johnston) *hld up: rdn and hdwy to chse ldrs over 3f out: wknd 1f out* **12/1**

3 **5** *¾* **Royal Applord**[25] 4247 2-9-3 0........................ PaulMulrennan 8 57
(K A Ryan) *s.i.s: rn green and pushed along thrght: a bhd* **11/1**

00 **6** *15* **Nothing To Add**[33] 4020 2-9-3 0........................ FrancisNorton 1 20
(K A Ryan) *rrd and s.s: a wl bhd* **25/1**

0 **7** *½* **Halton Castle**[17] 4487 2-9-3 0........................ GrahamGibbons 4 19
(E J Alston) *led: hdd over 3f out: rdn and wknd over 2f out* **25/1**

1m 28.33s (-0.14) **Going Correction** 0.0s/f (Good) **7** Ran SP% **119.9**
Speed ratings (Par 99): **100,99,98,88,87 70,69**
CSF £8.65 TOTE £2.90: £1.70, £2.20; EX 10.00.
Owner J A Lazzari **Bred** P And Mrs A G Venner **Trained** East Everleigh, Wilts
■ Hold The Gold was withdrawn (7/2, vet's advice). R4, deduct 20p in the £. New market formed.

FOCUS
Not an easy race to weigh up but the winner seemed to run right up to form. The first three were well clear of the rest, suggesting the form is solid.

NOTEBOOK
Eastern Gift was given a find ride around the bends and won a shade comfortably. He was racing off a fairly high handicap mark and will need to ply his trade at a decent level, which will not be easy for him despite his admirable attitude. (old market op 11-4 tchd 7-2, new market op 2-1)
Bellomi(IRE) was runner-up for the third time in a row and did hint at a bit of quirkiness in the final stages, although he was beaten fair and square by the winner. (old market op 7-2)
Crystal Rock(IRE), from a stable that had a terrific record in the race, stayed on really well after becoming outpaced off the final bend and was starting to bear down on the leader when receiving a bump from the runner-up. Still looking green himself, he seems sure to win a maiden and should get further this season. (old market op 5-2)
Glittering Prize(UAE), who was difficult to load, never really got involved at any stage and does not look about to win any sort of race soon. Official explanation: jockey said filly lost its action (old market op 20-1, new market op 14-1)
Royal Applord still looked in need of the run, even though he finished third on his debut, and will benefit greatly from this experience. (old market op 16-1, new market op 12-1)
Nothing To Add will have a nice handicap mark when he starts racing in that sphere after showing very little again. It seems unlikely that he is devoid of any ability considering his relations and connections. Official explanation: jockey said colt reared leaving stalls and was slowly away (old market op 40-1 tchd 28-1)
Halton Castle weakened alarmingly when joined for the lead and dropped right out. Official explanation: jockey said gelding lost its action (old market op 66-1 tchd 25-1)

5034 WILLIAM T CORBETT "IN RUNNING" H'CAP 1m 7f 195y
5:10 (5:11) (Class 4) (0-85,82) 3-Y-O+ **£5,829** (£1,734; £866; £432) **Stalls** Low

Form RPR

1405 **1** **Gee Dee Nen**[42] 3748 4-10-0 82........................ JimmyQuinn 2 87
(M H Tompkins) *chsd ldrs: rdn over 1f out: r.o to ld ins fnl f: all out* **4/1**[3]

1223 **2** *hd* **Jawaaneb (USA)**[17] 4511 3-8-10 77........................ EddieAhern 8 82
(J L Dunlop) *in tch: effrt 2f out: led over 1f out: hdd ins fnl f: r.o u.p* **3/1**[2]

14-3 **3** *shd* **Aphorism**[16] 4544 4-8-9 66........................ WilliamBuick(3) 4 71+
(J R Fanshawe) *s.i.s: hld up: nt clr run fr 2f out tl effrt and hdwy over 1f out: swtchd rt to chal 3 wd ins fnl f: fin strly: unlucky* **2/1**[1]

440- **4** *3½* **Merrymaker**[105] 5531 7-8-11 68........................ PatrickMathers(3) 5 69
(W M Brisbourne) *in rr: rdn over 3f out: hdwy over 1f out: one pce ins fnl f* **15/2**

1231 **5** *3* **Prelude**[9] 4732 6-9-0 71........................ LiamJones(3) 6 68
(W M Brisbourne) *led: rdn over 2f out: hdd over 1f out: wknd ins fnl f* **4/1**[3]

0540 **6** *11* **Mowadeh (IRE)**[7] 4809 3-7-12 65........................ AdrianMcCarthy 9 49
(M R Channon) *chsd ldr: rdn over 3f out: ev ch 2f out: wknd over 1f out* **14/1**

3m 31.65s (-1.95) **Going Correction** 0.0s/f (Good)
WFA 3 from 4yo+ 13lb **6** Ran SP% **116.8**
Speed ratings (Par 105): **104,103,103,102,100 95**
CSF £17.18 CT £30.56 TOTE £5.40: £2.70, £1.80; EX 24.10 Place 6 £109.68, Place 5 £60.18..
Owner David P Noblett **Bred** Kingwood Bloodstock **Trained** Newmarket, Suffolk

FOCUS
The early gallop was very moderate and it turned into a sprint up the home straight. The form is far from sound despite looking reasonable on paper.
Prelude Official explanation: jockey said mare was unsuited by the trip
T/Plt: £177.80 to a £1 stake. Pool: £102,438.65. 420.55 winning tickets. T/Qpdt: £65.90 to a £1 stake. Pool: £3,679.40. 41.30 winning tickets. DO

4966 MUSSELBURGH (R-H)
Saturday, September 1

OFFICIAL GOING: Good to firm (good in places) (8.1)
Wind: Moderate, half against Weather: Overcast, blustery

5035 TURFTV H'CAP 1m
5:30 (5:30) (Class 5) (0-75,73) 3-Y-O+ **£3,886** (£1,156; £577; £288) **Stalls** High

Form RPR

4463 **1** **Cool Ebony**[21] 4382 4-9-2 68........................ PhillipMakin 7 78
(M Dods) *chsd ldng pair: hdwy over 2f out: swtchd lft and effrt to ld wl over 1f out: rdn and edgd rt ent fnl f: sn drvn and hld on gamely* **6/1**[3]

5113 **2** *nk* **Kirkby's Treasure**[3] 4931 9-8-7 59........................ PatCosgrave 6 68
(G A Swinbank) *hld up: hdwy wl over 2f out: chsd ldrs over 1f out: rdn to chal ins fnl f and ev ch tl no ex towards fin* **2/1**[1]

-440 **3** *2* **Grand Opera (IRE)**[24] 4281 4-9-1 67........................(b[1]) TomEaves 8 71
(J Howard Johnson) *chsd ldng pair: hdwy over 2f out: rdn wl over 1f out: drvn and styng on whn n.m.r ent fnl f: drvn and kpt on same pce* **8/1**

0006 **4** *½* **She's Our Lass (IRE)**[5] 4880 6-9-4 70........................(v) DanielTudhope 2 73
(D Carroll) *hld up and bhd: hdwy on inner over 2f out: rdn and nt clr run over 1f out: swtchd lft and styd on strly ins fnl f: nrst fin* **7/1**

0040 **5** *2½* **Anthemion (IRE)**[1] 4998 10-8-4 59 oh6........................ AndrewMullen(3) 4 57
(Mrs J C McGregor) *led 3f: cl up tl rdn to ld again over 2f out: hdd wl over 1f out: sn drvn and grad wknd* **16/1**

0160 **6** *shd* **Tommy Tobougg**[10] 4701 3-8-4 61 oh1 ow2........................ GregFairley 3 58
(I Semple) *hld up: hdwy and in tch over 2f out: rdn wl over 1f out and no imp appr fnl f* **16/1**

0014 **7** *2* **Frank Crow**[10] 4704 4-9-2 73........................ GaryBartley(5) 1 66
(J S Goldie) *stdd s and bhd: stmbld home bnd: nvr a factor* **6/1**[3]

6160 **8** *6* **Kabis Amigos**[7] 4820 5-9-7 73........................(t) AdrianTNicholls 9 52
(D Nicholls) *cl up: led after 3f: rdn along and hdd over 2f out: drvn and wknd over 1f out* **9/2**[2]

0050 **9** *3* **Kadia**[42] 3754 4-8-7 59 oh14........................ DaleGibson 5 31
(P T Midgley) *in tch: rdn along 3f out and sn wknd* **66/1**

1m 40.93s (-1.57) **Going Correction** -0.10s/f (Good)
WFA 3 from 4yo+ 5lb **9** Ran SP% **117.0**
Speed ratings (Par 103): **103,102,100,100,97 97,95,89,86**
CSF £18.65 CT £98.33 TOTE £6.30: £2.00, £1.10, £2.40; EX 22.00.
Owner Wedgewood Estates **Bred** Wedgewood Estates **Trained** Denton, Co Durham

FOCUS
A modest handicap, run at a decent pace, which saw the first pair come clear. The form is solid rated through the runner-up backed up by the third.
Frank Crow Official explanation: jockey said gelding hit the rail turning into home straight

5036 SCOTTISH RACING MAIDEN STKS 1m
5:55 (5:56) (Class 5) 3-Y-O+ **£2,914** (£867; £433; £216) **Stalls** High

Form RPR

0 **1** **Chicken George (IRE)**[14] 4616 3-9-3 0........................ AdrianTNicholls 3 78
(D Nicholls) *chsd ldrs: rdn along over 2f out: swtchd lft and drvn over 1f out: styd on wl to ld ent fnl f: clr towards fin* **20/1**

0524 **2** *3* **Red Blossom**[15] 4575 3-8-12 70........................(v[1]) SebSanders 2 66
(Sir Mark Prescott) *led: rdn along over 2f out: sn drvn and hdd 2f out: kpt on reluctantly u.p fnl f* **9/4**[2]

0320 **3** *¾* **White Moss (IRE)**[15] 4582 3-8-7 60........................ PatrickHills(5) 8 64
(M H Tompkins) *trckd ldrs: smooth hdwy 3f out: sn chal and led 2f out: sn rdn and hung rt: drvn and hdd ent fnl f: wknd* **11/10**[1]

52-6 **4** *2½* **Divine Love (IRE)**[20] 4424 3-8-12 69........................(b[1]) PatCosgrave 7 58
(E J O'Neill) *trckd ldng pair tl rn green and wd bnd after 3f and sn lost pl: rdn along in midfield over 3f out: styd on fnl 2f: n.d* **4/1**[3]

5 *4* **Giant Star (USA)**[346] 5488 4-9-8 0........................ DanielTudhope 5 54
(J S Goldie) *hld up: hdwy 3f out: rdn 2f out and sn no imp* **12/1**

6 *1½* **Ancient Pride (IRE)** 3-9-0 0........................ PJMcDonald(3) 6 51
(Miss L A Perratt) *a towards rr* **50/1**

0 **7** *8* **Alimacdee**[34] 4000 3-8-12 0........................ TomEaves 1 27
(I Semple) *cl up: rdn along over 3f out and sn wknd* **33/1**

00/0 **8** *15* **Lexicon**[28] 4157 7-9-0 19........................ AndrewMullen(3) 9 —
(Mrs J C McGregor) *a in rr* **250/1**

1m 42.61s (0.11) **Going Correction** -0.10s/f (Good)
WFA 3 from 4yo+ 5lb **8** Ran SP% **116.1**
Speed ratings (Par 103): **95,92,91,88,84 83,75,60**
CSF £65.33 TOTE £15.00: £3.40, £1.10, £1.10; EX 78.20.
Owner Roses Partnership **Bred** Bryan Ryan **Trained** Sessay, N Yorks

FOCUS
A moderate maiden, run at at average pace. The winner rates full value for his winning margin although this was not the most solid of contests.
Divine Love(IRE) Official explanation: jockey said blinkers may have obscured filly's vision

5037 WEDDING VENUE H'CAP 7f 30y
6:25 (6:25) (Class 6) (0-55,57) 3-Y-O+ **£2,590** (£770; £385; £192) **Stalls** High

Form RPR

5002 **1** **No Grouse**[15] 4562 7-9-5 53........................ SebSanders 2 64
(E J Alston) *hld up towards rr: gd hdwy on outer over 2f out: rdn and str run to ld ent fnl f: drvn: edgd rt and styd on wl* **9/2**[1]

-440 **2** *1¼* **Sarraaf (IRE)**[18] 4477 11-9-7 55........................ TomEaves 9 63
(I Semple) *chsd ldr: hdwy to ld 2f out and sn rdn: hdd ent fnl f: sn drvn and kpt on same pce* **17/2**

0206 **3** *1¾* **Attacca**[2] 4966 6-9-6 54........................ PhillipMakin 11 57
(J R Weymes) *chsd ldrs: rdn along over 2f out: n.m.r over 1f out and ins fnl f: kpt on same pce* **5/1**[2]

5000 **4** *¾* **Playtotheaudience**[21] 4383 4-9-1 52........................ JamieMoriarty(3) 10 53
(R A Fahey) *midfield: hdwy 3f out: rdn along to chse ldrs 2f out: drvn and n.m.r over 1f out: kpt on u.p ins fnl f* **14/1**

2401 **5** *shd* **Lambency (IRE)**[8] 4768 4-9-4 57........................ GaryBartley(5) 13 58
(J S Goldie) *in tch: hdwy over 2f out: rdn wl over 1f out: n.m.r ins fnl f: swtchd lft and kpt on towards fin* **7/1**

1060 **6** *nk* **Coalite (IRE)**[12] 4668 4-8-10 49........................(p) NeilBrown(5) 14 49
(A D Brown) *led: rdn along 3f out: hdd 2f out and sn drvn: wknd ins fnl f* **11/1**

0006 **7** *nk* **Snow Bunting**[10] 4701 9-9-0 48........................ TonyHamilton 4 47
(Jedd O'Keeffe) *in tch on inner: hdwy wl over 2f out: sn rdn and wknd wl over 1f out* **13/2**[3]

06-0 **8** *3½* **Botham (USA)**[23] 4330 3-8-12 50........................(b[1]) AdrianTNicholls 6 40
(D J Murphy) *chsd ldrs: rdn along wl over 2f out: sn drvn: edgd rt and wknd wl over 1f out* **20/1**

0621 **9** ¾ **Oeuf A La Neige**[1] 4998 7-9-4 57 6ex.................................. GregFairley 1 40
(Miss L A Perratt) *s.i.s: a in rr* **7/1**

0042 **10** 1 ½ **Strife (IRE)**[20] 4416 4-8-13 50.. PJMcDonald(3) 8 34
(W M Brisbourne) *hld up: a in rr* **9/1**

0005 **11** ¾ **Cherri Fosfate**[6] 4842 3-9-2 54..................................(b) DanielTudhope 5 36
(D Carroll) *a bhd* **12/1**

1m 30.67s (0.73) **Going Correction** -0.10s/f (Good)
WFA 3 from 4yo+ 4lb 11 Ran SP% **121.2**
Speed ratings (Par 101): **91,89,87,86,86 86,85,81,81,79 78**
CSF £44.23 CT £206.19 TOTE £4.30: £1.80, £6.20, £2.10; EX 53.50.
Owner The Grumpy Old Geezers **Bred** Zubieta Ltd **Trained** Longton, Lancs

FOCUS
A poor handicap that was run at an average pace. The form is rated through the second and third and appears sound enough.
Cherri Fosfate Official explanation: jockey said gelding missed the break

5038 TURFTV MEDIAN AUCTION MAIDEN STKS 7f 30y
6:55 (6:57) (Class 6) 2-Y-O **£2,590** (£770; £385; £192) **Stalls** High

Form RPR

2 **1** **Sheekey (IRE)**[24] 4279 2-9-3 0.. PatCosgrave 5 73+
(G A Swinbank) *chsd ldr: hdwy over 2f out: effrt and hung rt wl over 1f out: styd on ent fnl f to ld last 100yds* **6/4**[1]

0 **2** ½ **Flight To Quality**[8] 4764 2-9-3 0.. GregFairley 2 72+
(M Johnston) *led: pushed clr 1/2-way: qcknd 3f out: rdn 2f out: drvn and wknd ins fnl f: hdd and edgd lft last 100yds* **6/4**[1]

0 **3** 9 **Xaravella (IRE)**[40] 3796 2-8-12 0.. TomEaves 3 43
(J G M O'Shea) *chsd ldng pair: rdn along over 2f out: kpt on same pce appr fnl f* **16/1**[3]

000 **4** ½ **Flashy Max**[14] 4612 2-9-3 45.. TonyHamilton 1 47
(Jedd O'Keeffe) *in rr: effrt and sme hdwy 3f out: sn rdn and no imp* **66/1**

5 2 **Bite The Boss** 2-9-3 0.. SebSanders 4 42
(E J O'Neill) *dwlt and sn pushed along: hdwy to chse ldng pair wl over 2f out: sn rdn: hung lft and rn green: wknd* **7/2**[2]

1m 31.19s (1.25) **Going Correction** -0.10s/f (Good) 5 Ran SP% **109.6**
Speed ratings (Par 93): **88,87,77,76,74**
CSF £3.91 TOTE £2.40: £1.60, £1.20; EX 4.10.
Owner Mrs J Porter **Bred** J McElroy **Trained** Melsonby, N Yorks

FOCUS
No strength in depth to this little juvenile maiden and the two market leaders came well clear.

NOTEBOOK
Sheekey(IRE), a runner-up on his debut at Newcastle 24 days previously, was doing all of his best work late on over this extra furlong and went one better in workmanlike fashion. He still looked green when asked to his effort, highlighted by him hanging right nearing the final furlong, and no doubt he will improve for this experience. It will be interesting to see how the Handicapper now rates him for nurseries. (op Evens tchd 13-8 in a place)
Flight To Quality ◆, distinctly green on debut over this trip at Newbury eight days previously, met plenty of support in the betting ring and improvement was clearly expected. He did put in a better showing, under a more positive ride, yet could not match the winner's speed at the business end and left the impression he may already need 1m. Well clear of the rest at the finish, he should not remain a maiden for too long. (op 11-4)
Xaravella(IRE) was left behind when the first pair locked horns entering the final furlong and ran below the level of her debut over 6f last time. She may not have really enjoyed this faster ground. (op 14-1 tchd 12-1)
Bite The Boss, a half-brother to winners from 5-13f, proved far too green to do himself justice on this racecourse bow. He should learn plenty for this experience. (op 100-30 tchd 3-1)

5039 SCOTTISH RACING YOUR BEST BET H'CAP 5f
7:25 (7:25) (Class 3) (0-95,96) 3-Y-0+ **£7,772** (£2,312; £1,155; £577) **Stalls** Low

Form RPR

603 **1** **Buachaill Dona (IRE)**[11] 4696 4-9-10 96.................... AdrianTNicholls 4 107
(D Nicholls) *hld up: swtchd rt and hdwy over 1f out: rdn ent fnl f and styd on to ld last 50yds* **10/3**[1]

6003 **2** ½ **Harry Up**[21] 4386 6-8-7 82.. AndrewMullen(3) 6 91
(K A Ryan) *chsd ldr: led wl over 1f out: rdn ent fnl f: hdd and nt qckn last 50yds* **11/2**[3]

401 **3** ¾ **Sunrise Safari (IRE)**[35] 3954 4-9-2 88..............................(v) TomEaves 5 94
(I Semple) *in tch: n.m.r and edgd rt wl over 1f out: sn rdn and styd on to chse ldng pair ins fnl f: sn drvn: hung lft and no ex* **5/1**[2]

0530 **4** 3 **Orientor**[34] 3990 9-9-9 95.. DanielTudhope 1 91
(J S Goldie) *hld up in rr: hdwy wl over 1f out: styd on ins fnl f: nrst fin* **20/1**

0530 **5** 2 **Mr Wolf**[30] 4095 6-8-13 85..(p) PatCosgrave 10 73
(D W Barker) *led: rdn along 2f out: sn hdd and grad wknd* **8/1**

146 **6** shd **Deserted Dane (USA)**[42] 3749 3-8-8 84.................... PJMcDonald(3) 7 72
(G A Swinbank) *chsd ldrs whn squeezed out after 1f: hdwy 2f out: sn rdn and n.m.r over 1f out: styd on ins fnl f: nrst fin* **16/1**

0000 **7** nk **Overstayed (IRE)**[11] 4696 4-8-8 80 ow1.......................(b[1]) PhillipMakin 8 67
(I Semple) *in tch: hdwy to chse ldrs wl over 1f out: sn rdn and kpt on same pce ent fnl f* **50/1**

-022 **8** nk **Sir Nod**[10] 4703 5-8-9 81.. TonyHamilton 9 67
(Miss J A Camacho) *prom: rdn along wl over 1f out and grad wknd* **6/1**

5520 **9** hd **Blazing Heights**[34] 3990 4-8-5 82 ow1.......................... GaryBartley(5) 2 67
(J S Goldie) *hld up in rr: swtchd rt and hdwy 2f out: nt clr run over 1f out: kpt on ins fnl f* **10/1**

-000 **10** shd **Yungaburra (IRE)**[10] 4726 3-8-12 85.............................. GregFairley 3 70
(D J Murphy) *a towards rr* **66/1**

6414 **11** 1 ¾ **Garstang**[17] 4489 4-8-4 76 oh4.................................(b) DaleGibson 14 54
(Peter Grayson) *t.k.h: chsd ldrs on outer: rdn along wl over 1f out: grad wknd appr fnl f* **14/1**

0200 **12** 2 **First Order**[29] 4140 6-8-7 82...............................(v) JamieMoriarty(3) 13 53
(I Semple) *chsd ldrs: rdn along wl over 1f out: sn wknd* **25/1**

253- **13** 5 **Argentine (IRE)**[313] 6146 3-8-11 84.......................... SebSanders 12 37
(L Lungo) *sn outpcd and a in rr* **18/1**

-020 **14** 8 **Ice Mountain**[50] 3493 3-8-7 85.. NeilBrown(5) 11 9
(B Smart) *sn rdn along and a in rr* **28/1**

59.45 secs (-1.05) **Going Correction** -0.10s/f (Good)
WFA 3 from 4yo+ 1lb 14 Ran SP% **122.9**
Speed ratings (Par 107): **104,103,102,97,94 93,93,92,92,92 89,86,78,65**
CSF £20.23 CT £94.30 TOTE £3.70: £2.20, £2.50, £2.10; EX 29.50.
Owner Mike Browne **Bred** John O Browne **Trained** Sessay, N Yorks

FOCUS
A decent sprint handicap that saw the first three come clear and sound form rated around the placed horses.

NOTEBOOK
Buachaill Dona(IRE) deservedly opened his account for the season and did the job in good style despite the burden of top weight. He is evidently coming right back to himself now, having taken time to find his feet this year, and looks worth a crack at something better again now. It would not be a surprise to see him head to the Ayr Gold Cup, but it should be noted that most of his best form is over this minimum trip. (op 3-1 tchd 7-2)
Harry Up was unable to dictate as he ideally prefers, but still ran another rock-solid race in defeat and did not go down without a fight. He really does deserve a winning turn. (op 15-2)
Sunrise Safari(IRE), raised 5lb, ran right up to his previous form and remains in great heart. He looks capable of a little better still, is best kept to this trip, and rates a sound benchmark for the form. (tchd 11-2 in a place)
Orientor was not surprisingly doing his best work late in the day over a trip plenty sharp enough for him nowadays. This was a decent run in the circumstances and he may still have a good race within his compass when reverting to a stiffer test on easier ground. (op 18-1)
Mr Wolf showed his customary early dash to bag the early lead, but he was done with before the final furlong and ran below his best. (tchd 9-1)
Deserted Dane(USA) endured a troubled passage when trying to make his challenge and must be rated better than the bare form.
Blazing Heights, whose jockey put up 1lb overweight, was another who suffered a troubled passage from off the pace and is better than he was able to show. Official explanation: jockey said gelding was denied a clear run

5040 FORTH ONE PARTY NIGHT H'CAP 1m 6f
7:55 (7:55) (Class 5) (0-70,69) 3-Y-O **£3,886** (£1,156; £577; £288) **Stalls** High

Form RPR

4002 **1** **Hurricane Thomas (IRE)**[7] 4821 3-9-7 69........................ GregFairley 2 77
(M Johnston) *trckd ldr: effrt over 2f out and sn ev ch: rdn wl over 1f out: drvn ins fnl f and styd on to ld last 75yds* **5/1**[3]

2511 **2** ¾ **Western Point (IRE)**[11] 4687 3-9-4 66.............................. SebSanders 3 73
(Sir Mark Prescott) *led: pushed along wl over 2f out: rdn wl over 1f out: drvn ins fnl f: hdd and no ex last 75yds* **11/10**[1]

0001 **3** ¾ **Sonara (IRE)**[7] 4821 3-9-1 68.. PatrickHills(5) 1 74
(M H Tompkins) *trckd ldrs: hdwy over 3f out: chsd ldng pair over 2f out: swtchd lft and rdn over 1f out: ch ins fnl f: sn drvn and one pce* **11/4**[2]

0560 **4** 7 **Salto Chico**[5] 4877 3-8-2 50 oh5.. DaleGibson 6 46
(W M Brisbourne) *chsd ldrs: rdn along over 3f out: drvn over 2f out and sn one pce* **22/1**

0602 **5** 2 ½ **Caviar Heights (IRE)**[3] 4936 3-8-0 51 oh5 ow1.....(b) AndrewMullen(3) 4 44
(Miss L A Perratt) *hld up in rr: effrt and sme hdwy over 3f out: sn rdn and btn* **12/1**

505 **6** 14 **Looktheotherway (IRE)**[40] 3794 3-9-0 62.......................... TomEaves 5 35
(J G M O'Shea) *hld up: a in rr* **12/1**

3m 7.01s (1.31) **Going Correction** -0.10s/f (Good) 6 Ran SP% **110.7**
Speed ratings (Par 101): **92,91,91,87,85 77**
CSF £10.68 TOTE £4.90: £1.50, £1.90; EX 13.20 Place 6 £5.64, Place 5 £3.24..
Owner P D Savill **Bred** P D Savill **Trained** Middleham Moor, N Yorks

FOCUS
A modest staying handicap. The form looks solid with the first three coming clear and the winner and third close to previous form.
Salto Chico Official explanation: jockey said gelding hung left-handed throughout
T/Plt: £5.80 to a £1 stake. Pool: £52,244.40. 6,519.80 winning tickets. T/Qpdt: £3.30 to a £1 stake. Pool: £3,964.60. 876.40 winning tickets. JR

4920 RIPON (R-H)
Saturday, September 1

OFFICIAL GOING: Good to firm (9.2)
After three dry days 8mm water was put on the track. The ground was described as 'quick but a good cover and no jar whatsoever'.
Wind: Moderate, half-behind Weather: Fine and breezy, becoming overcast

5041 MERVYN BELLAMY HAPPY BIRTHDAY APPRENTICE (S) STKS 6f
2:10 (2:12) (Class 6) 3-4-Y-O **£2,590** (£770; £385; £192) **Stalls** Low

Form RPR

1402 **1** **Orotund**[10] 4714 3-9-9 51.. KellyHarrison 10 61
(T D Easterby) *mde all far side: clr over 1f out: drvn out* **3/1**[1]

0-05 **2** 3 **Diamond Hurricane (IRE)**[22] 4351 3-9-4 64........................ MCGeran 2 46
(P D Evans) *w ldrs stands' side: hung bdly rt over 1f out and wnt to far side: kpt on to take 2nd ins fnl f* **3/1**[1]

5666 **3** ¾ **First Valentini**[6] 4842 3-8-13 45.............................. JamesO'Reilly 14 39
(N Bycroft) *racd far side: chsd wnr: kpt on same pce fnl 2f* **12/1**[3]

4550 **4** 1 ½ **Welsh Auction**[23] 4336 3-8-13 60.............................(b[1]) BradleyRoper(5) 1 39
(G A Huffer) *led stands' side gp of eight: kpt on same pce fnl 2f* **7/1**[2]

-300 **5** nk **Heidi Hi**[8] 4787 3-8-8 50.. JamesRogers(5) 4 33
(J R Turner) *racd stands' side: w ldrs on outer: hung rt over 2f out: ended in centre: kpt on same pce* **20/1**

4006 **6** 1 ½ **Didactic**[57] 3257 3-9-1 43.. SophieDoyle(3) 6 33
(A J McCabe) *in rr-div stands' side: kpt on fnl 2f: nt rch ldrs* **20/1**

6006 **7** hd **Signor Whippee**[18] 4478 4-9-6 45..........................(b) DanielleMcCreery 7 32
(A Berry) *in rr-div stands' side: kpt on fnl 2f: nvr a threat* **20/1**

3000 **8** ½ **Tenterhooks (IRE)**[6] 4842 3-8-10 43.......................(be) RobbieEgan(3) 8 26
(A J McCabe) *racd stands' side: chsd ldrs: hung rt over 2f out: one pce* **22/1**

0040 **9** shd **Flushed**[6] 4842 3-8-13 47..(be) SoniaEaton(5) 15 30
(A J McCabe) *stmbld: sddle slipped and almost uns rdr s: chsd ldrs far side: one pce fnl 2f* **50/1**

2500 **10** 1 ¼ **Almora Guru**[23] 4330 3-9-1 57.. DeanHeslop(3) 16 26
(W M Brisbourne) *racd far side: in tch: one pce fnl 2f* **7/1**[2]

0000 **11** shd **Harts In Mo Shun (IRE)**[10] 4713 3-8-13 42............(b) AdamCarter(5) 12 26
(A Berry) *racd far side: in rr: nvr a factor* **100/1**

-000 **12** 1 ¼ **College Land Boy**[13] 4642 3-9-4 55.............................. PJBenson 13 22
(J J Quinn) *prom far side: outpcd fnl 2f* **7/1**[2]

60 **13** 2 **Final Desire**[36] 3914 4-8-12 0.................................. PatrickDonaghy(3) 3 11
(M Brittain) *s.s: racd stands' side: a in rr* **100/1**

5-00 **14** 4 **Bidders Itch**[10] 4714 3-8-6 35.. PaulPickard(7) 11 —
(A Berry) *racd far side: chsd ldrs: wknd over 2f out* **100/1**

-000 **15** 10 **Littlemadgebob**[26] 4226 3-8-6 40..................................(b[1]) DavidHunt(7) 9 —
(J R Norton) *swtchd rt s and racd far side: in tch on outer: edgd bdly lft and lost pl over 2f out: sn bhd and eased* **100/1**

1m 13.23s (0.23) **Going Correction** +0.05s/f (Good)
WFA 3 from 4yo 2lb 15 Ran SP% **119.7**
Speed ratings (Par 101): **100,96,95,93,92 90,90,89,89,87 87,86,83,78,64**
CSF £9.43 TOTE £3.80: £1.70, £2.10, £3.80; EX 12.10 Trifecta £49.10 Part won. Pool £69.16 - 0.30 winning units..There was no bid for the winner. Diamond Hurricane was claimed by Mark Wellings for £6,000. Welsh Auction was claimed by K.J Burke for £6,000.
Owner Habton Farms **Bred** D R Botterill **Trained** Great Habton, N Yorks

FOCUS
A rock bottom apprentice selling stakes and the winner, an uncomplicated ride, made it look plain sailing but the form is rated fairly negatively. They originally split into two definite groups but in the end they raced here there and everywhere.
Diamond Hurricane(IRE) Official explanation: jockey said gelding hung right
Heidi Hi Official explanation: jockey said filly hung right
Flushed Official explanation: jockey said saddle slipped

5042 ARTHRITIS CARE NORTH ENGLAND DIAMOND JUBILEE MAIDEN STKS 6f
2:40 (2:44) (Class 5) 2-Y-O **£3,886** (£1,156; £577; £288) **Stalls** Low

Form RPR
45 **1** **Crystany (IRE)**[31] 4061 2-8-12 0 TedDurcan 7 84+
(H R A Cecil) *led on stands' side and overall ldr: styd on strly to forge clr fnl f* **3/1**[2]
05 **2** 3 1/2 **Hawk Eyed Lady (IRE)**[12] 4662 2-8-5 0 SophieDoyle(7) 9 74+
(J A Osborne) *racd stands' side: chsd wnr: kpt on wl ins fnl f to take 2nd last stride* **33/1**
5 **3** shd **First Trim (IRE)**[105] 1832 2-9-3 0 RobertHavlin 15 78
(B J Meehan) *chsd ldrs far side: led that gp 1f out: kpt on same pce: 1st of 6 that gp* **10/3**[3]
33 **4** 3 **Hunt The Bottle (IRE)**[37] 3878 2-9-3 0 MickyFenton 13 69
(B W Hills) *racd far side: trckd ldrs: outpcd fnl 2f: 2nd of 6 that gp* **11/2**
5 1 **Tiger Spice** 2-8-12 0 PaulHanagan 16 61
(W J Haggas) *racd far side: chsd ldrs: kpt on same pce fnl 2f* **20/1**
0 **6** nk **Bertie Vista**[49] 3560 2-9-3 0 LeeEnstone 10 65
(T D Easterby) *swvd rt s: racd stands' side: sn chsng ldrs: kpt on same pce fnl 2f* **100/1**
7 1/2 **Spice Trade** 2-9-3 0 TPQueally 8 64
(J Noseda) *chsd ldrs: kpt on same pce fnl 2f* **9/1**
8 hd **Ogre (USA)** 2-8-12 0 JamesDoyle 3 58
(J A Osborne) *swvd rt s: racd stands' side: hdwy on outer over 2f out: nvr nr ldrs* **66/1**
5 **9** 1/2 **Rio Sands**[13] 4636 2-9-0 0 MichaelJStainton(3) 5 62
(R M Whitaker) *dwlt: sn in tch: outpcd fnl 2f* **66/1**
26 **10** nk **Miesko (USA)**[15] 4571 2-9-3 0 J-PGuillambert 12 61
(M Johnston) *led far side tl hdd & wknd 1f out* **5/2**[1]
11 4 **Northern Bolt** 2-9-3 0 PaulQuinn 2 49
(D Nicholls) *s.s and rdr lost iron briefly: racd far side: hdwy on outer over 2f out: sn wknd* **25/1**
0 **12** 1 **Melwood Dreams**[9] 4733 2-8-12 0 RussellKennemore(5) 6 46
(Paul Green) *racd stands' side: mid-div: lost pl over 2f out* **100/1**
66 **13** 1 **When Yer Ready (IRE)**[14] 4612 2-9-3 0 DavidAllan 11 43
(T D Easterby) *racd far side: in tch: lost pl over 4f out: 5th of 6 that gp* **33/1**
14 8 **Liberode (IRE)** 2-8-12 0 PaulFessey 14 14
(K A Ryan) *s.s: racd far side: sn bhd: hung bdly lft* **100/1**
15 1/2 **Larkfield** 2-8-9 0 DuranFentiman(3) 4 12
(T D Easterby) *racd stands' side: chsd ldrs: lost pl over 2f out* **100/1**
0 **16** 6 **James's Lass (IRE)**[16] 4522 2-8-5 0 JamesRogers(7) 1 —
(R A Fahey) *in rr stands' side: bhd fnl 2f* **100/1**

1m 12.89s (-0.11) **Going Correction** +0.05s/f (Good) **16** Ran SP% **124.5**
Speed ratings (Par 95): **102,97,97,93,91 91,90,90,89,89 84,82,81,70,70 62**
CSF £110.13 TOTE £3.90: £1.60, £8.10, £1.80; EX 138.30 TRIFECTA Not won..
Owner Ballygallon Stud Limited **Bred** Watership Down Stud **Trained** Newmarket, Suffolk

FOCUS
An ordinary maiden but the winner scored well and the placed horses are capable of winning.

NOTEBOOK
Crystany(IRE), whose dam won the Fillies' Mile, is a smallish, close-coupled type. She dominated on the stands' side and in the end came away for a most decisive victory. She looks all speed and six may be as far as she wants to go this year. (op 9-4)
Hawk Eyed Lady(IRE), who stands over plenty of ground, ran her best race to date on her third start snatching second spot near the line and she appeals as a likely nursery type. (op 66-1)
First Trim(IRE), who has plenty of size and scope, took charge on the far side but in the end was no match for the winner. He can surely find an ordinary maiden. (op 9-2 tchd 5-1)
Hunt The Bottle(IRE), a keen type, kept on to finish second best on the far side. He too is now qualified for nurseries. (op 5-1)
Tiger Spice, who cost 55,000gns. as a yearling, is a close-coupled filly. She made a highly-satisfactory debut. (op 25-1)
Bertie Vista, quite a big type, showed a lot more than on his debut and should improve again.
Spice Trade, up in the air, showed ability on his debut and will improve given more time and a longer distance. (op 12-1 tchd 8-1)
Ogre(USA) Official explanation: jockey said filly ran green
Miesko(USA), who is only small, pinged the lids and took them along on the far side. He does not seem to be progressing and a drop back to five might aid his cause. (tchd 3-1)
Northern Bolt Official explanation: jockey said he lost an iron coming out of stalls
Liberode(IRE) Official explanation: jockey said filly hung right

5043 WENSLEYDALE H'CAP 1m 1f 170y
3:15 (3:15) (Class 4) (0-80,79) 3-Y-O **£6,309** (£1,888; £944; £472; £235) **Stalls** High

Form RPR
2414 **1** **Soul Mountain (IRE)**[14] 4615 3-9-4 **79** TedDurcan 2 86
(B W Hills) *trckd ldrs: styd on to ld jst ins fnl f: r.o* **3/1**[1]
4643 **2** 1 **Kalasam**[11] 4686 3-8-8 **69** TPQueally 5 74
(W R Muir) *trckd ldrs: rdn and chal over 2f out: led over 1f out: hdd and no ex jst ins fnl f* **11/2**
6014 **3** nk **Deadline (UAE)**[13] 4640 3-8-9 **70** MickyFenton 1 74
(P T Midgley) *hld up in rr: effrt 3f out: styd on wl fnl f* **7/1**
2224 **4** nk **Smugglers Bay (IRE)**[14] 4617 3-8-8 **72** DuranFentiman(3) 8 76
(T D Easterby) *trckd ldrs: effrt 3f out: kpt on wl fnl f* **9/2**[2]
4346 **5** shd **Rudry Dragon (IRE)**[21] 4387 3-8-9 **77** SophieDoyle(7) 3 81
(P A Blockley) *sn trcking ldrs on outside: edgd lft over 1f out: kpt on wl ins fnl f* **5/1**[3]
0120 **6** 6 **Tencendur (IRE)**[8] 4785 3-9-1 **76** PaulQuinn 7 68
(D Nicholls) *set mod gallop: qcknd over 3f out: hdd over 1f out: sn wknd and eased* **16/1**
21-0 **7** 3/4 **Dollar Chick (IRE)**[10] 4716 3-9-1 **76** J-PGuillambert 6 66
(M Johnston) *in rr: effrt 3f out: lost pl over 1f out* **12/1**
3241 **8** 8 **Jibajaba (USA)**[21] 4411 3-8-13 **74** PaulHanagan 4 48
(R A Fahey) *t.k.h in rr: effrt 3f out: lost pl 2f out: sn bhd* **13/2**

2m 5.28s (0.28) **Going Correction** +0.05s/f (Good) **8** Ran SP% **114.6**
Speed ratings (Par 103): **100,99,98,98,98 93,93,86**
CSF £19.74 CT £105.31 TOTE £3.80: £1.20, £2.10, £2.70; EX 19.30 Trifecta £141.70 Part won. Pool £199.66 - 0.70 winning units..
Owner Lady Bamford **Bred** Longueville B'Stk & H Lascelles B'Stk **Trained** Lambourn, Berks

FOCUS
A tactical affair but the winner was firmly in command at the line. The form makes sense rated around the placed horses.

5044 RIPON CATHEDRAL CITY OF THE DALES H'CAP 6f
3:50 (3:50) (Class 3) (0-90,90) 4-Y-O+
£11,217 (£2,519; £2,519; £840; £419; £210) **Stalls** Low

Form RPR
3200 **1** **Damika (IRE)**[34] 4006 4-8-12 **87** MichaelJStainton(3) 2 96
(R M Whitaker) *drvn along to chse ldrs: styd on to ld ins fnl f* **10/1**
0014 **2** 3/4 **Malcheek (IRE)**[14] 4614 5-9-3 **89** DavidAllan 5 96
(T D Easterby) *w ldr: hung rt and led 3f out: hdd over 1f out: styd on ins fnl f* **15/8**[1]
3010 **2** dht **Aegean Dancer**[21] 4386 5-8-12 **87** MarkLawson(3) 8 94
(B Smart) *chsd ldrs: led over 1f out: hdd ins fnl f: kpt on wl* **9/1**
1440 **4** 1 **Ice Planet**[14] 4614 6-9-4 **90** PaulQuinn 3 94
(D Nicholls) *sn in rr and pushed along: rdn over 2f out: n.m.r over 1f out: styd on ins fnl f* **9/2**[2]
4301 **5** 1/2 **Compton's Eleven**[14] 4606 6-9-0 **86** TedDurcan 9 88
(M R Channon) *s.i.s: hdwy on outer over 2f out: nvr really threatened* **7/1**[3]
0200 **6** 1/2 **Inter Vision (USA)**[11] 4696 7-8-7 **79** PaulHanagan 11 80
(A Dickman) *chsd ldrs on outer: one pce appr fnl f* **7/1**[3]
0000 **7** 1 **Captain Hurricane**[21] 4389 5-8-9 **81** (p) RobertHavlin 4 79
(B J Meehan) *led tl 3f out: rallied over 1f out: kpt on same pce* **16/1**
0000 **8** 2 **Distinctly Game**[15] 4567 5-8-10 **82** PaulFessey 10 74
(K A Ryan) *chsd ldrs: drvn over 2f out: lost pl over 1f out* **14/1**
2660 **9** 1 **Paris Bell**[14] 4606 5-8-1 **76** oh2 DuranFentiman(3) 7 65
(T D Easterby) *s.s: a in rr* **20/1**
4010 **10** 3 1/2 **Highland Warrior**[43] 3720 8-8-9 **81** MickyFenton 1 59
(P T Midgley) *hld up in rr: hmpd after 1f: nvr on terms: eased ins fnl f* **25/1**

1m 11.88s (-1.12) **Going Correction** +0.05s/f (Good) **10** Ran SP% **118.2**
Speed ratings (Par 107): **109,108,108,106,106 105,104,101,100,95**WIN: Damika £12.80. PL: £3.40, Malcheek £1.30, Aegean Dancer £2.60. EX: D/M £19.50, D/AD £66.80. CSF: D/M £14.74, D/AD £48.91. TC: D/M/AD £94.26, D/AD/M £125.65 TRIFECTA Part won. D/M/AD: £122.20 - 0.20 winning units; D/AD/M: Not won. Po27 Owner.

FOCUS
A decent sprint handicap in which they raced in one group towards the stands' side rail. The form looks rock solid rated around the dead-heaters.

NOTEBOOK
Damika(IRE), suited by the quick ground, bounced right back to his very best and recorded his first victory this year. (op 9-1)
Malcheek(IRE), 4lb higher than his win here two outings ago, tended to hang to his right but ran right up to his very best. (op 9-4 tchd 5-2 in places)
Aegean Dancer, who needed it last time after a break, went on looked the most likely winner but in the end the winner saw out the sixth furlong much the better. He is better over the minimum trip. (op 9-4 tchd 5-2 in places)
Ice Planet, who looked at his very best, was never going that well. He ran into traffic problems before putting in some solid late work. (op 6-1)
Compton's Eleven, 3lb higher, missed a beat at the start and had to make his effort on the outside. He deserves plenty of credit for this. (tchd 13-2)
Inter Vision(USA), who likes it here, had the ground to suit but was not helped by being worst drawn. (op 5-1)
Highland Warrior Official explanation: jockey said gelding lost its action

5045 WHARFEDALE MAIDEN STKS 1m 1f 170y
4:25 (4:29) (Class 5) 3-Y-O+ **£3,886** (£1,156; £577; £288) **Stalls** High

Form RPR
623 **1** **Double Doors**[13] 4641 3-9-3 74 RobertHavlin 8 81
(J H M Gosden) *trckd ldr: led over 3f out: rdn clr appr fnl f* **4/6**[1]
255 **2** 4 **Easterly Breeze (IRE)**[106] 1812 3-9-3 78 TedDurcan 9 73
(W R Muir) *dwlt: sn chsng ldrs: rdn and wnt 2nd over 2f out: no ch w wnr* **2/1**[2]
00 **3** 2 1/2 **King Zeal (IRE)**[7] 4815 3-9-3 0 TGMcLaughlin 7 68
(M Wigham) *s.i.s: sn trcking ldrs: nt clr run and swtchd outside over 1f out: kpt on same pce* **25/1**
40 **4** 5 **Allaire**[73] 2763 3-8-12 0 J-PGuillambert 4 52
(M Johnston) *led tl over 3f out: edgd lft and wknd over 1f out* **14/1**
563 **5** 7 **March Mate**[29] 4138 3-9-3 55 PaulHanagan 3 43
(B Ellison) *chsd ldrs: lost pl 2f out* **11/1**[3]
05 **6** 2 **Betterlatethanever (IRE)**[5] 4901 3-9-3 0 PaulQuinn 2 38
(C J Teague) *trckd ldrs: rdn 4f out: lost pl 2f out* **100/1**
00 **7** 5 **Hayfield Flyer**[36] 3914 3-8-7 0 RussellKennemore(5) 1 23
(Paul Green) *in rr snd sn pushed along: hdwy on outer over 5f out: lost pl over 3f out: sn bhd* **100/1**
8 hd **Serial Habit (IRE)** 4-8-12 0 PatrickDonaghy(7) 6 22
(M Brittain) *in rr: lost pl over 3f out: sn bhd* **100/1**

2m 6.29s (1.29) **Going Correction** +0.05s/f (Good)
WFA 3 from 4yo 7lb **8** Ran SP% **115.1**
Speed ratings (Par 103): **96,92,90,86,81 79,75,75**
CSF £2.18 TOTE £1.60: £1.02, £1.10, £6.10; EX 1.90 Trifecta £16.90 Pool £752.78 - 31.50 winning units..
Owner K Abdulla **Bred** Juddmonte Farms Ltd **Trained** Newmarket, Suffolk

FOCUS
A weak maiden run at just a steady pace with the betting suggesting just a two-horse race. The form may not prove that solid but is best rated at face value through the runner-up.

5046 COVERDALE H'CAP 1m
4:55 (4:55) (Class 5) (0-70,70) 3-Y-O **£3,886** (£1,156; £577; £288) **Stalls** High

Form RPR
3321 **1** **Ella Woodcock (IRE)**[16] 4538 3-9-4 **70** TPQueally 4 77
(J A Osborne) *trckd ldrs: wnt 2nd over 1f out: hung rt and styd on strly to ld towards fin* **11/4**[1]
2320 **2** 1 **Shotley Mac**[7] 4817 3-8-4 **56** oh1 (b) PaulFessey 6 61
(N Bycroft) *led: qcknd over 4f out: hdd and no ex wl ins fnl f* **16/1**
0206 **3** 2 **Mark Of Love (IRE)**[17] 4502 3-9-4 **70** TedDurcan 1 70
(M R Channon) *dwlt: hld up in rr: effrt over 2f out: wnt 3rd jst ins fnl f: nt rch 1st 2* **6/1**[3]
01 **4** 4 **Coppergirl (IRE)**[39] 3824 3-9-4 **70** MickyFenton 3 61
(G A Huffer) *sn trcking ldr: wkng whn n.m.r appr fnl f* **10/1**
6002 **5** 1/2 **Tri Chara (IRE)**[24] 4287 3-8-7 **64** RussellKennemore(5) 8 54
(R Hollinshead) *s.i.s: t.k.h in rr: effrt over 3f out: nvr trbld ldrs* **7/1**
-004 **6** nk **Tom Paris**[23] 4313 3-9-4 **70** (p) JamesDoyle 5 59
(W R Muir) *mid-div: effrt over 2f out: hung rt and one pce whn hmpd jst ins fnl f* **7/1**

5021 **7** *1* **Moheebb (IRE)**^{10} 4704 3-8-3 **62** PatrickDonaghy$^{(7)}$ 9 49
(D W Chapman) *s.i.s: hdwy on outer 4f out: edgd rt over 2f out: sn wknd* **11/2**^{2}

0216 **8** *shd* **Dancing Jest (IRE)**^{11} 4684 3-8-10 **62** PaulHanagan 7 48
(Rae Guest) *chsd ldrs: wknd over 1f out* **11/2**^{2}

6-06 **9** *9* **Bay Of Light**^{14} 4610 3-8-8 **67** MCGeran$^{(7)}$ 2 33
(P W Chapple-Hyam) *in tch: outpcd whn hmpd over 2f out: sn lost pl and eased* **20/1**

-040 **10** *9* **Sahara Dawn (IRE)**^{6} 4842 3-8-1 **56** oh11 DuranFentiman$^{(3)}$ 10 1
(D Carroll) *in tch: lost pl over 3f out: sn bhd and eased* **66/1**

1m 40.99s (-0.11) **Going Correction** +0.05s/f (Good) **10** Ran SP% **117.9**
Speed ratings (Par 101): **102,101,99,95,94 94,93,93,84,75**
CSF £52.52 CT £254.93 TOTE £3.50: £1.70, £4.50, £2.00; EX 46.10 Trifecta £189.80 Pool £532.18 - 1.99 winning units. Place 6 £23.62, Place 5 £13.44..
Owner Cavendish Star Racing **Bred** Pippa Hackett **Trained** Upper Lambourn, Berks

FOCUS
A tactical affair with the runner-up dictating the pace. The progressive winner was firmly in command at the line and the form is modest with the third to recent turf form.
Coppergirl(IRE) Official explanation: jockey said filly was denied a clear run
Tom Paris Official explanation: jockey said gelding hung right
T/Plt: £23.00 to a £1 stake. Pool: £61,020.80. 1,930.50 winning tickets. T/Qpdt: £4.60 to a £1 stake. Pool: £2,797.60. 449.00 winning tickets. WG

5008 SANDOWN (R-H)
Saturday, September 1

OFFICIAL GOING: Good to firm
Wind: Light, against Weather: Fine but cloudy

5047 VARIETY CLUB ATALANTA STKS (LISTED RACE) (F&M) 1m 14y
2:05 (2:07) (Class 1) 3-Y-0+

£14,762 (£5,595; £2,800; £1,396; £699; £351) **Stalls** High

Form RPR

0546 **1** **Sweet Lilly**^{13} 4654 3-8-9 **111** TPO'Shea 3 98
(M R Channon) *lw: wl away fr wd draw and trckd ldrs: prog to ld over 1f out: drvn and swished tail: kpt on wl* **6/1**^{2}

2236 **2** *3/4* **Heaven Sent**^{13} 4652 4-9-0 **106** RyanMoore 14 96
(Sir Michael Stoute) *lw: chsd ldrs: rdn and nt qckn over 2f out: styd on fr over 1f out: snatched 2nd last stride* **5/6**^{1}

-540 **3** *shd* **Basaata (USA)**^{13} 4633 3-8-9 **99** PatDobbs 4 96
(M P Tregoning) *racd wd in midfield: rdn 2f out: styd on fr over 1f out: clsng at fin* **16/1**

-405 **4** *shd* **Bicoastal (USA)**^{100} 1958 3-8-9 **103** (p) LDettori 1 96
(B J Meehan) *fast away fr wd draw: pressed ldr: upsides 2f out: chsd wnr over 1f out: a hld: lost 2 pls last strides* **20/1**

-300 **5** *nk* **Elusive Flash (USA)**^{35} 3961 3-8-9 **90** NelsonDeSouza 8 95
(P F I Cole) *awkward s: wl in rr: rdn 3f out: prog on outer fr 2f out: styd on wl fnl f: fin best of all* **100/1**

-146 **6** *1/2* **Italian Girl**^{28} 4148 3-8-9 **101** JimCrowley 11 94
(A P Jarvis) *warm: hld up in midfield: rdn and styd on fr 2f out: no imp on ldrs fnl f: kpt on* **15/2**^{3}

0500 **7** *1* **Satulagi (USA)**^{35} 3940 3-8-9 **94** JohnEgan 6 92
(J S Moore) *wl in rr: rdn and no prog over 2f out: kpt on fr over 1f out: nvr able to chal* **33/1**

1066 **8** *shd* **Chantilly Tiffany**^{35} 3961 3-8-9 **90** (b^{1}) SteveDrowne 16 91
(E A L Dunlop) *led at str pce: drvn and hdd over 1f out: wkng whn stmbld 75yds out* **66/1**

050 **9** *nk* **Lady Livius (IRE)**^{29} 4122 4-9-0 **87** DaneO'Neill 15 91
(R Hannon) *hld up in midfield: shkn up on inner over 2f out: nt pce to trble ldrs fr over 1f out* **66/1**

1331 **10** *nk* **Hansomelle (IRE)**^{14} 4596 5-9-0 **73** (p) NeilChalmers 5 90?
(Miss Sheena West) *swtg: mostly in last quartet: u.p wl over 2f out: styd on against ins rail fr over 1f out: nrst fin* **100/1**

5-00 **11** *1 1/4* **Tiana**^{17} 4503 4-9-0 **86** JimmyFortune 13 87
(Mrs A J Perrett) *hld up in midfield: effrt and n.m.r 2f out: rdn and nt qckn over 1f out* **66/1**

0363 **12** *1* **Ransom Captive (USA)**^{65} 3028 3-8-9 **91** RichardMullen 9 85
(M A Magnusson) *chsd ldrs: wknd 2f out* **66/1**

-110 **13** *1* **Tarteel (USA)**^{29} 4118 3-8-9 **98** RHills 12 82
(J L Dunlop) *lw: chsd ldrs: rdn and hanging rt 2f out: sn btn* **10/1**

2520 **14** *3/4* **In Safe Hands (IRE)**^{51} 3460 3-8-9 **92** PhilipRobinson 2 81
(C G Cox) *a in last quartet: rdn and hanging 2f out: no prog* **20/1**

-101 **15** *2 1/2* **Pintle**^{13} 4633 7-9-4 **90** KerrinMcEvoy 10 79
(J L Spearing) *chsd ldng pair to over 2f out: sn wknd* **14/1**

1m 41.03s (-2.92) **Going Correction** -0.125s/f (Firm) **15** Ran SP% **122.7**
WFA 3 from 4yo+ 5lb
Speed ratings (Par 111): **109,108,108,108,107 107,106,106,105,105 104,103,102,101,99**
CSF £10.77 TOTE £6.00: £1.80, £1.10, £4.80; EX 10.50 Trifecta £48.70 Pool £762.40 - 11.10 winning units.
Owner Jaber Abdullah **Bred** Red House Stud **Trained** West Ilsley, Berks

FOCUS
This looked a competitive Listed event, but the field finished tightly bunched, despite Chantilly Tiffany setting a fast early pace. Muddling form, with 73-rated Hansomelle finishing uncomfortably close. Neither of the first two were anywhere near their best.

NOTEBOOK
Sweet Lilly, a disappointment at Deauville last time when appearing not to handle the testing conditions, was back down in grade and seemed more at home on this faster surface. Always well placed, she did not look to be doing a great deal in front, swishing her tail, but it was enough to hold the favourite. The form does not look worth a great deal, with so many horses finishing close up, but she has already shown herself to be a bit better than this and it will be interesting to see whether or not she takes her place in the Prix De l'Opera. (op 4-1, tchd 7-1 in places)
Heaven Sent, a progressive filly who recorded a career-best effort when second to Championship Point at Royal Ascot, came into this having disappointed in a Group 2 at Deauville, but much better was expected on this faster surface. Although this is a race in her at this level, she was below her best and lacked the winner's pace. (op 11-10, tchd 5-4 in a place and 6-5 in places)
Basaata(USA), who ran a cracking race to finish fourth in a highly competitive listed event at Glorious Goodwood, flopped in a much weaker contest at Bath last time, but her trainer was inclined to put that down to the easier going and she had reportedly been working well again. Settled towards the outside of the main pack, she was edging nearer with every stride, but was never quite getting there in time. She is another who looks capable of winning at this level when granted her favoured conditions.
Bicoastal(USA), a blatant non-stayer over 1m2f at Goodwood when last seen back in May, overcame a tricky draw by using up plenty of gas early and it was no surprise to see it takes it toll late on, as she was just run out of the placings. This was a good effort in the first-time cheekpieces, but she remains hard to win with. (op 16-1)
Elusive Flash(USA) had it to do with the best of these and she appeared to run way above herself back in fifth, finishing fast and only just losing out on the places. She has yet to supplement last season's maiden win, but this was at least a step back in the right diection. (op 66-1)
Italian Girl, not far behind Basaata at Goodwood, does not seem to be progressing as well as once hoped, but she has yet to run a bad race and could be worth a try at 1m2f now. (op 8-1 tchd 9-1)
Satulagi(USA) has been struggling in handicaps and is not easy to place off her current mark, but this was a bit more promising. (op 50-1)
Chantilly Tiffany was responsible for the fast early gallop, but she was unable to sustain it and was already held when stumbling in the closing stages. (op 50-1)
Hansomelle(IRE), a winner off 61 at Lingfield the other day, had no chance with the worst of these and was undoubtedly flattered in finishing so close up. It is just hoped the Handicapper sees it this way.
Tiana Official explanation: jockey said filly was denied a clear run
Tarteel(USA), a dual handicap winner earlier in the season, has not gone on as expected since being upped to Listed level and the way she was hanging here was disconcerting. (op 11-1)

5048 IVECO SOLARIO STKS (GROUP 3) 7f 16y
2:35 (2:43) (Class 1) 2-Y-0

£21,008 (£7,962; £3,984; £1,986; £995; £499) **Stalls** High

Form RPR

11 **1** **Raven's Pass (USA)**^{35} 3938 2-9-0 0 JimmyFortune 1 115+
(J H M Gosden) *trckd ldrs: prog to ld 2f out: sn rdn wl clr: most impressive* **11/8**^{1}

1 **2** *7* **City Leader (IRE)**^{36} 3896 2-9-0 0 KDarley 8 98
(B J Meehan) *lw: trckd ldr: upsides 2f out: sn swept away by wnr: plugged on wl to hold on for 2nd* **8/1**

110 **3** *shd* **Gaspar Van Wittel (USA)**^{51} 3459 2-9-0 97 DaneO'Neill 4 97
(N A Callaghan) *dwlt: mostly in last pair tl rdn and prog 2f out: pressed for 2nd ins fnl f: kpt on* **12/1**

2 **4** *3/4* **Belgrave Square (USA)**^{28} 4151 2-9-0 0 JMurtagh 9 95
(A P O'Brien, Ire) *lw: dwlt: mostly in last pair: u.p and stl last over 2f out: kpt on fr over 1f out* **6/1**^{3}

21 **5** *1* **Pegasus Again (USA)**^{21} 4393 2-9-0 0 LDettori 5 93
(T G Mills) *hld up towards rr: rdn over 2f out: kpt on fr over 1f out: n.d* **6/1**^{3}

11 **6** *6* **Maze (IRE)**^{70} 2855 2-9-0 0 RoystonFfrench 7 78
(B Smart) *sweating: racd freely: led to 2f out: wknd rapidly fnl f* **4/1**^{2}

1002 **7** *hd* **Yem Kinn**^{27} 4199 2-9-0 95 TPO'Shea 6 77
(M R Channon) *t.k.h: cl up tl wknd rapidly 2f out* **25/1**

105 **8** *1/2* **Lindoro**^{51} 3462 2-9-0 83 AdamKirby 3 76
(W R Swinburn) *prom tl wknd rapidly wl over 1f out* **66/1**

01 **9** *10* **Ernie Owl (USA)**^{23} 4335 2-9-0 86 KerrinMcEvoy 10 51+
(B J Meehan) *t.k.h early: nvr beyond midfield: wkng whn hmpd on inner over 1f out: eased* **22/1**

1m 26.56s (-2.78) **Going Correction** -0.125s/f (Firm) 2y crse rec **9** Ran SP% **119.2**
Speed ratings (Par 105): **110,102,101,101,99 93,92,92,80**
CSF £13.81 TOTE £2.40: £1.10, £2.50, £4.00; EX 16.90 Trifecta £152.00 Pool £834.95 - 3.90 winning units..
Owner Stonerside Stable Llc **Bred** Stonerside Stable **Trained** Newmarket, Suffolk

FOCUS
A race with a poor recent history and this year's renewal was more like a Listed race. That said, Raven's Pass was massively impressive and hacked up, looking well worth his place in a Group 1.

NOTEBOOK
Raven's Pass(USA), a 20/1 winner of a decent maiden at Yarmouth on debut, showed it to be no fluke when bolting up over 7f at Ascot last time and this represented another big step forward. Although this was nothing more than a fair race for the grade, he was always travelling best and put daylight between himself and the others most impressively once coming through to lead just inside the two pole, smashing the two-year-old track record by 1.3sec in the process. He is clearly a colt of considerable potential, and his trainer is talking about aiming him at the very top, with the Grand Criterium or the Dewhurst (possibly both) on the agenda this year, and the 2000 Guineas the target in 2008. (op 6-4 tchd 7-4)
City Leader(IRE), ready winner of a decent Ascot madien on debut, was faced with stiffer opposition here and he coped well, but found the winner a class apart, being made to look paceless. He is clearly very useful, but it would be surprising to see him prove any better than Listed level in the long run. (tchd 10-1)
Gaspar Van Wittel(USA), a dual Chepstow winner before being found out behind Winker Watson in the July Stakes, was always going to be suited to this extra furlong and he kept on well to just miss out on second. Connections believe he will be suited by some give in the ground, but he too looks to have his limitations at this sort of level. (op 14-1, tchd 16-1 in places)
Belgrave Square(USA), a maiden in two starts coming into this, is clearly not one of his powerful stable's top juveniles and he was in trouble from quite a way out, but kept plugging away and was not too far off the placings in the end. He should find a maiden before long, possibly over 1m. (op 7-1 tchd 15-2, and 8-1 in places)
Pegasus Again(USA), who made a remarkable debut to run Maze close in the Chesham, ran out just a workmanlike winner of a modest Lingfield maiden over 1m last time and he was found out on this first try at Group level. The return to 1m is going to help and he may be capable of better in time. (op 17-2)
Maze(IRE), off since his narrow Chesham victory, was a big negative in the market beforehand, having got very warm, and then proceeded to race very freely during the race, ending any chance he had. He dropped out in the end and clearly failed to run his race, but is not going to find it easy at Group level. Official explanation: jockey said colt sweated up in the preliminaries and ran too free (op 3-1)
Yem Kinn has already had his limitations exposed and will find life easier returned to novice stakes. He is not going to be easy to place. (op 22-1 tchd 20-1)
Lindoro was always going to struggle and needs dropping in grade. Official explanation: jockey said colt hung right in straight (op 50-1)
Ernie Owl(USA), who made his debut in the Coventry, struggled when winning his maiden at Haydock and again fell woefully short on this return to Group level. He is evidently not as good as connections hoped. (op 25-1)

5049 TOTESPORT.COM H'CAP 1m 2f 7y
3:10 (3:13) (Class 2) (0-100,100) 3-Y-0+ **£11,658** (£3,468; £1,733; £865) **Stalls** High

Form RPR

5000 **1** **Impeller (IRE)**^{10} 4720 8-9-5 **94** JohnEgan 10 101
(J S Moore) *hld up in midfield: plld to outer and prog 2f out: chal fnl f: led nr fin* **8/1**

5504 **2** *shd* **Yarqus**^{10} 4720 4-8-12 **87** (t) KerrinMcEvoy 3 94
(C E Brittain) *hld up in tch: prog 3f out: led wl over 1f out: kpt on wl fnl f: hdd nr fin* **4/1**^{2}

1020 **3** *1* **Dan Dare (USA)**^{34} 3989 4-8-11 **86** (v) RyanMoore 7 91
(Sir Michael Stoute) *trckd ldrs: rdn and nt qckn over 2f out: hanging but plld out over 1f out: styd on fnl f* **4/1**^{2}

000 **4** *nk* **Bandama (IRE)**^{21} 4376 4-9-2 **91** JimCrowley 9 95
(Mrs A J Perrett) *trckd ldng pair: stl cl up but lost pl 3f out: drvn and chsng ldrs after: kpt on: unable to chal* **8/1**

6225 **5** *shd* **Pagan Sword**[5] 4888 5-8-11 **86** oh1 (p) JimmyFortune 2 90
(Mrs A J Perrett) *lw: s.s: hld up in rr: rdn and nt qckn over 2f out: styd on fr over 1f out: no threat* **11/1**

0540 **6** *hd* **Players Please (USA)**[10] 4720 3-8-7 **89** RHills 4 93
(M Johnston) *lw: hld up: prog 1/2-way: jnd ldrs 3f out: upsides 2f out and hanging rt: nt qckn: 3rd and hld whn short of room nr fin* **7/2**[1]

0306 **7** *2 1/2* **Wind Star**[11] 4690 4-8-13 **88** SteveDrowne 1 87
(G A Swinbank) *stdd s fr wd draw and hld up in last: rdn and no real prog over 2f out* **8/1**

610 **8** *2* **Strategic Mount**[10] 4722 4-9-11 **100** TQuinn 11 95
(P F I Cole) *led to over 2f out: wknd over 1f out* **15/2**[3]

-100 **9** *3/4* **Seal Point (USA)**[14] 4601 3-8-13 **95** PaulEddery 6 88
(Christian Wroe) *a in rr: rdn and struggling 3f out* **66/1**

0000 **10** *1/2* **Luberon**[10] 4720 4-9-3 **92** RoystonFfrench 5 84
(M Johnston) *swtg: pressed ldr: rdn to ld over 2f out to wl over 1f out: wknd rapidly* **25/1**

065 **11** *7* **Kew Green (USA)**[28] 4167 9-9-5 **94** DaneO'Neill 8 72
(P R Webber) *dwlt: a in rr: drvn and struggling 3f out: sn bhd* **40/1**

2m 6.59s (-3.65) **Going Correction** -0.125s/f (Firm)
WFA 3 from 4yo+ 7lb **11** Ran SP% **123.4**
Speed ratings (Par 109): **109,108,108,107,107 107,105,104,103,103 97**
CSF £41.69 CT £153.05 TOTE £13.10: £3.50, £2.00, £1.80; EX 59.20 Trifecta £340.80 Pool £720.10 - 1.50 winning units..
Owner Mrs Fitri Hay **Bred** P E Banahan **Trained** Upper Lambourn, Berks
■ Stewards' Enquiry : John Egan caution: careless riding; one-day ban: careless riding (Sep 12)

FOCUS
A reasonable handicap, but distinctly lacking in unexposed or progressive types.

NOTEBOOK
Impeller(IRE) has been a grand horse over the years and showed he is still capable of decent form when slightly unlucky not to get closer in a hugely competitive handicap at York last time. Again ridden under restraint, he began his run from well over two furlongs out and managed to get there in the final strides under a strong ride from Egan. He was just 1lb higher here than when last winning and should not go up too much for this, so can continue to pay his way. (op 11-1)
Yarqus has not won since dead-heating for the 2006 Esher Cup, but he has been running well and finished several places ahead of Impeller at York. Given a fine ride, he was sent to the front over a furlong out, but was just unable to hold on and the losing run continues. (tchd 9-2, and 5-1 in places)
Dan Dare(USA), back down to 1m2f, has generally struggled in handicaps, but this was a bit more promising and he was going on close home, albeit somewhat reluctantly. (op 5-1)
Bandama(IRE) has fallen to a reasonable mark now and this was his best run for a while, suggesting a return to winning ways may not be far away. He just lacks a bit of pace, however, and a return to 1m4f will help. (op 7-1)
Pagan Sword has been in decent form and he again ran well, going on close home having been given plenty to do. He is not the most straightforward though and would never be one to take a short price about. (op 12-1 tchd 10-1)
Players Please(USA), although running well in several hot handicaps this season, has not really progressed as expected and he did not look too keen to put his head down and battle having held every chance inside the final three furlongs. (op 9-2)
Strategic Mount, never involved on unsuitable ground in the Ebor, had his conditions here, but there was a big question mark as to whether he would have the speed to cope with this drop in distance and he found himself readily outpaced from two furlongs out. (op 5-1)

5050 VARIETY CLUB H'CAP — 5f 6y
3:45 (3:45) (Class 2) (0-100,100) 3-Y-0+
£11,217 (£3,358; £1,679; £840; £419; £210) **Stalls** High

Form RPR

0033 **1** **Indian Trail**[14] 4614 7-8-13 **94** (v) LDettori 14 108
(D Nicholls) *lw: hld up jst bhd ldrs: nt clr run fr 2f out: gap appeared 1f out and decisive burst to ld on inner: sn clr* **7/2**[1]

5600 **2** *1 3/4* **Fantasy Believer**[14] 4614 9-8-12 **93** JimmyFortune 7 101
(J J Quinn) *lw: wl in rr: last pair 2f out: plld to wd outside: r.o wl to take 2nd nr fin* **10/1**[3]

6113 **3** *1/2* **Rowe Park**[87] 2352 4-9-5 **100** LPKeniry 13 106
(Mrs L C Jewell) *w ldrs gng wl: led 2f out: drvn and hdd ent fnl f: kpt on u.p* **20/1**

2202 **4** *nk* **Hoh Hoh Hoh**[11] 4696 5-8-11 **92** TQuinn 12 97
(R J Price) *warm: dwlt: plld hrd and sn cl up: effrt to chal 1f out: nt qckn* **13/2**[2]

0050 **5** *shd* **The Tatling (IRE)**[9] 4746 10-9-3 **98** KDarley 10 103
(J M Bradley) *dwlt: sn towards rr: n.m.r fr 2f out: styd on wl fnl f: nt rch ldrs* **11/1**

240 **6** *1/2* **Tony The Tap**[29] 4122 6-8-5 **86** oh2 HayleyTurner 4 89
(W R Muir) *dwlt: wl in rr on inner: prog to chse ldrs over 1f out: keeping on but no ch whn no room nr fin* **33/1**

0060 **7** *1* **Ajigolo**[7] 4806 4-8-9 **90** TPO'Shea 2 89
(M R Channon) *wl in rr: nt clr run over 2f out to 1f out: styd on fnl 100yds: no ch* **25/1**

0400 **8** *hd* **Texas Gold**[7] 4806 9-8-5 **86** oh1 RichardMullen 5 85
(W R Muir) *lw: sn wl in rr: rdn and kpt on fnl 2f on outer: n.d* **25/1**

-141 **9** *nk* **Marozi (USA)**[29] 4123 3-8-5 **87** ow1 PhilipRobinson 3 84
(M A Jarvis) *lw: s.i.s: sn pressed ldrs on outer: cl up over 1f out: wknd tamely fnl f* **7/2**[1]

2301 **10** *hd* **Phantom Whisper**[19] 4456 4-8-11 **92** JimCrowley 11 89
(B R Millman) *w ldrs to over 1f out: steadily fdd* **11/1**

050 **11** *3/4* **Talbot Avenue**[11] 4696 9-8-5 **86** oh6 RoystonFfrench 8 80
(M Blanshard) *b. nvr beyond midfield: no prog over 1f out* **40/1**

0050 **12** *shd* **Dazed And Amazed**[10] 4726 3-8-13 **95** RyanMoore 6 89
(R Hannon) *lw: lost pl over 3f out and sn in rr: struggling fr 1/2-way* **25/1**

3000 **13** *nk* **Corridor Creeper (FR)**[11] 4696 10-8-8 **89** (p) StephenDonohoe 15 82
(J M Bradley) *mde most to 2f out: wknd fnl f* **25/1**

11-2 **14** *nk* **Oldjoesaid**[118] 1502 3-8-11 **93** DaneO'Neill 1 85
(H Candy) *s.i.s: rcvrd to press ldrs on outer: wknd wl over 1f out* **10/1**[3]

0500 **15** *nk* **Out After Dark**[28] 4150 6-8-12 **93** (p) AdamKirby 9 83
(C G Cox) *wl in rr on inner: nt clr run over 3f out and over 2f out whn pushed along: styng on but no ch whn hmpd last 75yds* **14/1**

60.10 secs (-2.11) **Going Correction** -0.15s/f (Firm)
WFA 3 from 4yo+ 1lb **15** Ran SP% **124.8**
Speed ratings (Par 109): **110,107,106,105,105 104,103,103,102,102 101,100,100,99,99**
CSF £37.25 CT £649.99 TOTE £4.30: £2.00, £4.10, £4.80; EX 55.80 Trifecta £1187.60 Part won. Pool £1,672.80 - 0.40 winning units..
Owner Martin Love **Bred** Whitsbury Manor Stud **Trained** Sessay, N Yorks

FOCUS
A hotly contested sprint handicap, but the frequently unlucky Indian Trail ran out a ready winner having quickened up smartly inside the final furlong. Solid form.

NOTEBOOK
Indian Trail has crept back up the weights following decent placed efforts at Goodwood and Ripon, but he had an excellent draw just one off the rail and booking of Dettori had to be significant. Always going strongly, he had to wait for his gap, but really picked up once it arrived and won comfortably. This win will see him pick up a 5lb for the Ayr Gold Cup and general quotes of 10/1 seem fair. (op 4-1, tchd 9-2 in places)
Fantasy Believer has been a grand servant to connections and he looked a big player here, having been running well in some decent handicaps, mainly over 6f. Unable to go the early gallop, he really began to fly once switched to the outside, but the winner had gone beyond recall. He will no doubt go close in his bid to repeat last year's winning effort in the Portland, now he has worked his way back down to a fair mark. (tchd 11-1)
Rowe Park, a really progressive sprinter earlier in the season, was giving weight to all his rivals and needed a career-best performance to win. Never far away, he was always going strongly, but the the winner's burst proved too much for him and he was then claimed for second by the fast-finishing runner-up. He looks well worth another try at Listed level on this evidence. (op 22-1)
Hoh Hoh Hoh has been in decent form without winning lately. He pulled hard but ran another fine race in defeat, without suggesting he is about to win off this mark. Official explanation: jockey said gelding jumped out slowly and pulled hard (op 15-2)
The Tatling(IRE) is well weighted these days and this was certainly an effort that suggested his winning days are not yet behind him.
Tony The Tap can be rated a little better than the bare form, but he has not won for well over three years and remains 6lb higher.
Ajigolo was certainly one of the unluckier ones, keeping on well close home having been denied a run through around two furlongs out.
Marozi(USA), a progressive and unexposed sprinter who won a hugely competitive handicap at Goodwood last time, was done no favours by the draw and faced a much stiffer test off a 7lb higher mark against his elders. Having been rushed up to hold a prominent position, he folded tamely, but he is clearly better than this and deserves another chance. (tchd 4-1 in places)

5051 GEOPOST H'CAP — 5f 6y
4:15 (4:19) (Class 4) (0-80,80) 3-Y-0
£5,181 (£1,541; £770; £384) **Stalls** High

Form RPR

2011 **1** **Day By Day**[9] 4740 3-8-7 **69** (b) StephenDonohoe 9 78
(B J Meehan) *lw: led 1f: w ldrs: led over 2f out: drvn clr over 1f out: edgd lft and stmbld jst ins fnl f: hld on wl* **7/1**

0005 **2** *3/4* **Cuppacocoa**[23] 4314 3-8-10 **72** PhilipRobinson 1 78
(C G Cox) *t.k.h: w ldrs: nt qckn over 1f out: chsd wnr fnl f: nvr quite able to chal* **11/1**

0500 **3** *3/4* **Sparkling Eyes**[17] 4489 3-8-12 **74** KerrinMcEvoy 2 77
(C E Brittain) *hld up: rdn on outer 2f out: styd on fnl f to take 3rd nr fin* **10/1**

6410 **4** *1/2* **Billy Red**[16] 4546 3-8-5 **67** ow1 (b) JohnEgan 7 69
(J R Jenkins) *hld up in tch: hanging rt and nt qckn over 1f out: kpt on fnl f* **20/1**

2431 **5** *3/4* **Gleaming Spirit (IRE)**[23] 4336 3-8-8 **70** JimCrowley 5 69+
(A P Jarvis) *lw: trckd ldrs: nt clr run 2f out to over 1f out: hmpd 1f out: nt rcvr* **4/1**[2]

0633 **6** *nk* **Bateleur**[20] 4425 3-9-1 **77** TPO'Shea 11 75
(M R Channon) *lw: chsd ldrs: rdn and n.d whn n.m.r on inner ins fnl f: one pce* **7/1**

6541 **7** *nk* **Golden Desert (IRE)**[22] 4360 3-9-4 **80** (v) AdamKirby 8 77
(T G Mills) *drvn to ld after 1f: hdd over 2f out: wknd fnl f* **5/2**[1]

420 **8** *hd* **My Love Thomas (IRE)**[22] 4360 3-9-0 **76** RyanMoore 3 72
(E A L Dunlop) *s.s: hld up in rr: outpcd fr 2f out* **5/1**[3]

0-00 **9** *2 1/2* **Vintage (IRE)**[16] 4541 3-8-4 **66** oh1 (t) RoystonFfrench 10 53
(P Mitchell) *sn rdn to chse ldrs: struggling fnl 2f* **50/1**

0002 **10** *hd* **Sacre Coeur**[24] 4269 3-9-3 **79** JimmyFortune 6 65
(J L Dunlop) *hld up: shkn up and wknd wl over 1f out* **14/1**

61.10 secs (-1.11) **Going Correction** -0.15s/f (Firm) **10** Ran SP% **121.1**
Speed ratings (Par 103): **102,100,99,98,97 97,96,96,92,92**
CSF £84.33 CT £794.47 TOTE £6.30: £2.00, £3.00, £3.40; EX 96.70.
Owner T G & Mrs M E Holdcroft **Bred** Bearstone Stud & T Herbert Jackson **Trained** Manton, Wilts

FOCUS
A trappy sprint handicap and ordinary form overall, although the winner is still very much on the upgrade.

5052 THAMESIDE AMATEUR DERBY (A H'CAP FOR GENTLEMAN AMATEUR RIDERS) — 1m 2f 7y
4:50 (4:50) (Class 4) (0-85,84) 4-Y-0+
£9,003 (£2,812; £1,405; £703; £351; £177) **Stalls** High

Form RPR

0002 **1** **Robustian**[5] 4909 4-11-6 **80** (b) MrLoekVanDerHam 8 89
(Eve Johnson Houghton) *t.k.h: hld up in last trio: prog over 4f out to chse clr ldr 3f out: grad clsd fr 2f out: led last strides* **10/3**[2]

1435 **2** *hd* **Prize Fighter (IRE)**[7] 4814 5-11-4 **78** (b) MrSWalker 2 87
(H R A Cecil) *led: drew clr over 4f out: abt 5 l up 2f out: tired over 1f out: collared last strides* **3/1**[1]

0215 **3** *2 1/2* **Sky Quest (IRE)**[22] 4365 9-10-12 **72** MrSDobson 3 76
(J R Boyle) *hld up: outpcd 4f out: wnt modest 3rd over 1f out: styd on: unable to chal* **11/2**[3]

5515 **4** *1/2* **Transvestite (IRE)**[23] 4318 5-11-4 **78** (v) MrDavidTurner 5 81
(J W Hills) *hld up in last: rdn and plenty to do over 2f out: styd on fr over 1f out* **17/2**

5100 **5** *nk* **Lucayan Dancer**[11] 4690 7-11-10 **84** MrJPMcKeown 1 86
(D Nicholls) *lw: chsd ldrs: no imp over 3f out: plugged on fr over 1f out* **12/1**

0560 **6** *nk* **Sienna Storm (IRE)**[14] 4609 4-11-2 **76** (b) MrLeeNewnes 9 78
(M H Tompkins) *chsd ldrs: outpcd 4f out: lost pl over 2f out: styd on again fnl f* **8/1**

-640 **7** *5* **Lilac Star**[19] 4449 4-10-10 **70** oh10 MrESelter 6 62
(T T Clement) *t.k.h: hld up in rr: sme prog 2f out but n.d: wknd and eased fnl f* **50/1**

0260 **8** *1/2* **Brief Goodbye**[28] 4184 7-11-5 **79** MrDWirenstal 7 70
(John Berry) *hld up and sn in last pair: bmpd along and no prog over 2f out* **7/1**

6012 **9** *4* **Uig**[16] 4551 6-10-10 **70** MrMRosport 4 53
(H S Howe) *chsd ldr to 3f out: wknd 2f out* **8/1**

2m 9.47s (-0.77) **Going Correction** -0.125s/f (Firm) **9** Ran SP% **118.4**
Speed ratings (Par 105): **98,97,95,95,95 94,90,90,87**
CSF £14.20 CT £53.85 TOTE £3.90: £1.50, £1.60, £2.40; EX 15.80.
Owner Michael Doran & R F Johnson Houghton **Bred** T J Cooper **Trained** Blewbury, Oxon
■ The first winner in Britain for Dutch rider Loek Van Der Ham.

FOCUS
The so-called 'amateurs' Derby', but a modest handicap in the broader context. Enterprising tactics only just failed on Prize Fighter.

5053 CAPITAL ENGINEERING GROUP NURSERY 7f 16y
5:25 (5:25) (Class 4) 2-Y-O £5,181 (£1,541; £770; £384) Stalls High

Form RPR
0040 1 **Indian Days**[8] 4776 2-8-0 **69** .... RoystonFfrench 10 73
(J G Given) *plld hrd: hld up in midfield: hit rail over 5f out: drvn and n.m.r over 2f out: looked to be struggling after: r.o fr over 1f out: sustained effrt to ld last strides* **14/1**
3224 2 *hd* **Always Ready**[8] 4776 2-8-8 **77** .... KerrinMcEvoy 3 81
(C E Brittain) *lw: trckd ldrs: prog over 2f out: drvn to ld last 150yds: hdd fnl strides* **7/2**[2]
3216 3 *1 1/2* **Fathsta (IRE)**[8] 4762 2-7-10 **72** .... KMay(7) 2 74+
(S Kirk) *in tch: prog over 2f out: chsd ldng pair jst over 1f out: trying to chal whn short of room last 100yds* **16/1**
61 4 *hd* **Arctic Cape**[21] 4378 2-9-2 **85** .... RHills 4 84
(M Johnston) *hld up in last pair: wd in st and stl last jst over 2f out: drvn and r.o: nrst fin* **5/2**[1]
2641 5 *nk* **High Days (IRE)**[24] 4274 2-8-7 **76** ow2 .... (t) RyanMoore 5 75
(Sir Michael Stoute) *chsd ldr: rdn and clsd to ld over 2f out: hdd and no ex last 150yds* **5/1**[3]
6412 6 *shd* **Sauze D'Oulx**[29] 4126 2-9-2 **90** .... JamesMillman(5) 6 88
(B R Millman) *hld up in rr: rdn over 2f out: kpt on fr over 1f out: nvr rchd ldrs* **8/1**
060 7 *1 3/4* **Classical Rhythm (IRE)**[15] 4571 2-8-0 **69** ow2 .... HayleyTurner 1 63
(J R Boyle) *dropped in last fr wd draw: rdn 2f out: kpt on fnl f: no ch* **40/1**
4150 8 *shd* **Sofia's Star**[29] 4121 2-9-3 **86** .... (b[1]) JimCrowley 12 80
(P Winkworth) *led at str pce to over 2f out: steadily wknd* **33/1**
6121 9 *shd* **What Katie Did (IRE)**[12] 4669 2-8-6 **75** .... JohnEgan 9 68
(J A Osborne) *lw: hld up in midfield: rdn whn n.m.r 2f out: btn after* **8/1**
1600 10 *1 1/2* **Stage Acclaim (IRE)**[21] 4372 2-8-9 **78** .... FergusSweeney 7 68
(B R Millman) *hld up in rr: nt clr run on inner in st: nvr nr ldrs* **20/1**
641 11 *shd* **Maybe I Will (IRE)**[45] 3643 2-8-5 **74** .... DavidKinsella 11 63+
(R Hannon) *trckd ldrs: lost pl over 2f out: repeatedly denied clr run after and lost all ch* **16/1**
4103 12 *1 3/4* **Legendary Guest**[7] 4823 2-8-11 **80** .... TPO'Shea 8 65
(M R Channon) *lw: prom: rdn to chal over 2f out: upsides 2f out: wknd rapidly* **16/1**

1m 28.59s (-0.75) **Going Correction** -0.125s/f (Firm) 12 Ran SP% **124.1**
Speed ratings (Par 97): **99,98,97,96,96 96,94,94,94,92 92,90**
CSF £64.48 CT £840.44 TOTE £18.40: £4.30, £1.60, £5.40; EX 85.10 Place 6 £100.38, Place 5 £76.05..
Owner D J Fish **Bred** Mrs C C Regalado-Gonzalez **Trained** Willoughton, Lincs
■ Stewards' Enquiry : James Millman caution: careless riding
Royston Ffrench caution: careless riding

FOCUS
A competitive nursery and a solid race, without looking anything special.

NOTEBOOK
Indian Days ◆, who ran much better than his finishing position suggested on his handicap debut at Newmarket, had been dropped 3lb for that and the only question mark seemed to be whether he had the speed to cope with this drop to 7f. The definitive answer was yes, as having pulled early and failed to settle, he burst through late on to nail Always Ready on the line, a smart effort considering he knocked into the rail down the back straight. There is no doubting the return to 1m will suit and the son of Daylami looks capable of further improvement. (op 16-1)
Always Ready, ahead of Indian Days at Newmarket, was worse off and unable to confirm the form, being nailed close home. He had been narrowly touched off by subsequent winner Siberian Tiger in a maiden earlier in the month, and second to Raven's Pass before that, so his turn should come sooner rather than later. (op 4-1 tchd 9-2)
Fathsta(IRE), a winner at Chester on his penultimate outing, was held off this mark at Newbury last time, but this step up in trip was always going to suit and he ran an improved race. He was still closing when he ran out of room and he seems to be progressing nicely. (op 12-1)
Arctic Cape, who improved on his initial effort to take an Ayr maiden, comes from a yard whose two-year-olds are going really well at the moment and he was made favourite to make a winning handicap debut off a mark of 85, which looked reasonable. However, he looked uncomfortable on this faster surface and, although making gradual inroads down the outside, he was never getting there in time. This trip should be fine on a slower surface and he remains capable of better. (op 2-1)
High Days(IRE), raised 5lb for his narrow Kempton victory, was done no favours by Moore putting up overweight, but would not have been good enough anyway and needs to improve to defy his current rating. (op 6-1 tchd 9-2)
Sauze D'Oulx looked vulnerable off a mark of 90, but he has been running well and the way he saw this out suggested 1m would not be out of range. (op 9-1 tchd 12-1)
T/Jkpt: Not won. T/Plt: £68.60 to a £1 stake. Pool: £141,554.95. 1,506.05 winning tickets.
T/Qpdt: £43.50 to a £1 stake. Pool: £4,367.50. 74.25 winning tickets. JN

5054 - 5057a (Foreign Racing) - See Raceform Interactive

3563 LONGCHAMP (R-H)
Saturday, September 1

OFFICIAL GOING: Good to soft

5058a PRIX DE LIANCOURT (LISTED RACE) (FILLIES) 1m 2f 110y
2:20 (9:20) 3-Y-O £17,568 (£7,027; £5,270; £3,514; £1,757)

RPR
1 **Hapsburg (FR)**[32] 4055 3-8-12 .... TJarnet 6 101
(E Libaud, France)
2 *1/2* **Mahara (USA)**[49] 3564 3-8-12 .... TGillet 10 100
(J E Hammond, France) **10/1**[1]
3 *3/4* **Bruxcalina (FR)**[100] 7-8-12 .... CSoumillon 1 91
(A Fabre, France)
4 *nse* **Beatrix Kiddo (FR)**[13] 4654 3-9-2 .... OPeslier 7 103
(Robert Collet, France)
5 *1 1/2* **Fontcia (FR)**[83] 2501 3-9-2 .... JVictoire 3 100
(D Sepulchre, France)
6 *hd* **Pinacotheque (IRE)**[57] 3-8-12 .... GFaucon 4 96
(E Lellouche, France)
7 *snk* **Sumarocca**[74] 3-8-12 .... MSautjeau 5 95
(J Van Handenhove, France)
8 *3/4* **Noble Ginger (FR)**[87] 2384 3-8-12 .... THuet 2 94
(J E Pease, France)
9 *1 1/2* **Toque De Queda**[62] 3148 3-9-2 .... WMongil 11 95
(M Delzangles, France)
10 *nk* **Thimble**[35] 3986 3-8-12 .... SPasquier 12 91
(Mme C Head-Maarek, France)
11 **Golding Star (FR)**[20] 3-9-2 .... C-PLemaire 9 95
(J C Lopera-Fernandez, France)
12 **Contentious (USA)**[34] 4005 3-8-12 .... DBonilla 8 91
(J L Dunlop) *racd keenly on outside in midfield tl wnt 4th after 2f: 3rd st on outside: sn rdn and wknd: eased fnl f* **13/1**[2]

2m 11.5s (-3.10)
WFA 3 from 7yo 7lb 12 Ran SP% **16.2**
PARI-MUTUEL: WIN 6.20; PL 2.10, 2.70, 1.80; DF 31.80.
Owner J Luck **Bred** Mickael M Kelly **Trained** France

NOTEBOOK
Contentious(USA), runner-up in a Listed race at Pontefract last time out, was disappointing, struggling to strike a blow after racing keenly.

4840 SARATOGA (R-H)
Saturday, September 1

OFFICIAL GOING: Fast

5059a WOODWARD STKS (GRADE 1) 1m 1f (D)
10:49 (10:58) 3-Y-O+

£153,061 (£51,020; £25,510; £12,755; £7,653; £1,701)

RPR
1 **Lawyer Ron (USA)**[35] 4-9-0 .... JRVelazquez 1 128
(T Pletcher, U.S.A) **3/4**[1]
2 *8 1/4* **Sun King (USA)**[35] 5-9-0 .... AGarcia 4 113
(N Zito, U.S.A) **135/10**
3 *1 1/4* **Diamond Stripes (USA)**[35] 4-9-0 .... (b) MLuzzi 2 111
(R Dutrow Jr, U.S.A) **73/10**[3]
4 *3/4* **Corinthian (USA)**[63] 4-9-0 .... KDesormeaux 5 110
(J Jerkens, U.S.A) **89/10**
5 *2* **Political Force (USA)**[63] 4-9-0 .... CVelasquez 7 106
(H A Jerkens, U.S.A) **67/10**[2]
6 *1/2* **Brass Hat (USA)**[35] 6-9-0 .... (b) WMartinez 8 105
(W Bradley, U.S.A) **27/1**
7 *9 1/4* **Wanderin Boy (USA)**[35] 6-9-0 .... RBejarano 6 88
(N Zito, U.S.A) **25/2**
8 *2* **Magna Graduate (USA)**[35] 5-9-0 .... GKGomez 3 85
(T Pletcher, U.S.A) **104/10**

1m 48.6s (108.60) 8 Ran SP% **118.9**
PARI-MUTUEL: WIN 3.50; PL 2.60, 7.70; SH 2.10, 4.70, 3.50.
Owner Hines Racing LLC **Bred** James T Hines Jr **Trained** USA

4707 FOLKESTONE (R-H)
Sunday, September 2

OFFICIAL GOING: Good to firm
Wind: Very modest, across Weather: bright, partly cloudy

5061 EBF CHECKMATE UK SUPPORTING DEMELZA MAIDEN FILLIES' STKS (DIV I) 7f (S)
2:00 (2:02) (Class 4) 2-Y-O £3,465 (£1,030; £515; £257) Stalls Low

Form RPR
02 1 **Presbyterian Nun (IRE)**[29] 4169 2-9-0 0 .... SebSanders 6 86+
(J L Dunlop) *mde all: rdn wl over 1f out: styd on gamely fnl f* **4/1**[2]
523 2 *nk* **Lady Deauville (FR)**[15] 4626 2-9-0 0 .... TPO'Shea 3 85
(P A Blockley) *trckd ldrs: rdn to chse wnr 2f out: ev ch u.p fnl f: unable qckn* **8/13**[1]
30 3 *6* **Jazz Jam**[31] 4102 2-9-0 0 .... TQuinn 2 70
(P F I Cole) *in tch on stands' rail: swtchd rt and hdwy 2f out: sn edgd rt: chsd ldng pair over 1f out: sn wl outpcd* **14/1**
40 4 *1* **Lille Tuva**[41] 3796 2-9-0 0 .... TedDurcan 5 67
(B R Millman) *prom: rdn jst over 2f out: outpcd over 1f out* **100/1**
0 5 *nk* **Smooth As Silk (IRE)**[27] 4232 2-9-0 0 .... RobertHavlin 14 66
(C R Egerton) *s.i.s: racd on outer in midfield: hdwy 1/2-way: rdn and wknd over 1f out* **66/1**
6 6 *1 1/4* **Darley Star**[16] 4565 2-9-0 0 .... HayleyTurner 10 63
(C E Brittain) *prom: rdn jst over 2f out: wknd wl over 1f out* **25/1**
00 7 *1/2* **True Time**[13] 4662 2-9-0 0 .... JimmyFortune 13 62
(E A L Dunlop) *hld up towards rr: hdwy 1/2-way: rdn and wknd 2f out* **20/1**
8 *2* **Amie Magnificent (IRE)** 2-9-0 0 .... JimCrowley 8 56
(P Winkworth) *chsd wnr tl 2f out: sn rdn and wknd* **66/1**
9 *nk* **Horticulture (USA)** 2-9-0 0 .... SteveDrowne 7 56
(R Charlton) *stdd s: hld up towards rr: hdwy 1/2-way: sn rdn: wknd jst over 2f out* **10/1**[3]
10 *3/4* **Siren Call** 2-9-0 0 .... DarryllHolland 4 54
(W J Haggas) *s.i.s: rn green in last pair: swtchd to outer and hdwy 1/2-way: sn btn* **22/1**
11 *1* **Skynda** 2-9-0 0 .... ChrisCatlin 9 51
(Rae Guest) *towards rr: rdn 4f out: wknd over 2f out* **50/1**
12 *2 1/2* **Here And How** 2-9-0 0 .... SaleemGolam 1 45
(M H Tompkins) *v.s.a: bhd but in tch: rdn and wknd 1/2-way* **66/1**
13 *16* **Lucky Danceuse (IRE)** 2-9-0 0 .... DaneO'Neill 11 —
(H J L Dunlop) *wnt rt s: bhd: pushed along after 2f: lost tch 1/2-way: t.o* **100/1**

1m 26.21s (-1.69) **Going Correction** -0.50s/f (Hard) 13 Ran SP% **119.1**
Speed ratings (Par 94): **89,88,81,80,80 78,78,76,75,74 73,70,52**
CSF £6.29 TOTE £4.50: £1.20, £1.10, £3.50; EX 8.70 Trifecta £17.80 Pool £112.94. - 4.50 winning units..
Owner The Earl Cadogan **Bred** The Earl Cadogan **Trained** Arundel, W Sussex

FOCUS
Strong maiden form for the track and the first two came nicely clear as the betting had suggested.

NOTEBOOK
Presbyterian Nun(IRE), runner-up to Sense Of Joy at Newmarket last time, looked the main danger to the odds-on favourite on that form, and that is how it turned out. She made every yard for a gritty success, and looks a useful type to go to war with in decent nursery company. (op 100-30 tchd 3-1)

Lady Deauville(FR), third in a Group 3 race in France last time out behind Classic hopes Proviso and Laureldean Gale, looked likely to take all the beating back in maiden company, but she was beaten by a useful rival who was also placed behind a Classic prospect on her previous start. Clear of the rest, she should find compensation soon. (op 4-5)

Jazz Jam had run with promise on her first two starts and this was another solid effort up a furlong in distance. The first two were in a different class, but she won the separate race for third well enough and can now be aimed at nurseries.

Lille Tuva, another stepping up a furlong in distance, appreciated the quicker ground and ran her best race to date. Another now eligible for a mark, she will have a better chance of success in nursery company.

Smooth As Silk(IRE), who cost 240,000euros and is a half-sister to Humungous, a dual 7f winner at two and also a 1m winner at four, showed a lot more than on her debut at Windsor, and appears to be progressing along the right lines.

Darley Star looks more of a three-year-old prospect. (op 33-1)

True Time Official explanation: jockey said filly stumbled

Horticulture(USA), a half-sister to Demonstrate, a useful multiple 7f winner, and Moratorium, a triple middle-distance winner, should derive plenty from this debut run. (tchd 9-1)

5062 HYTHE BAY SUPPORTING DEMELZA (S) STKS 7f (S)

2:30 (2:31) (Class 6) 3-Y-0+ **£2,047** (£604; £302) **Stalls** Low

Form RPR

0504 **1** **Hart Of Gold**[4] 4940 3-9-0 72 ChrisCatlin 13 61
(M J Wallace) *prom: chsd clr ldr 1/2-way: rdn wl over 2f out: led 1f out: r.o wl* **11/4**[2]

545 **2** *3/4* **Arctic Desert**[7] 4860 7-9-4 62 (t) JohnEgan 9 61
(Miss Gay Kelleway) *s.i.s: hld up in midfield: swtchd rt 1/2-way: nt clr run over 1f out: gd hdwy 1f out: chsd wnr last 100yds: hld towards fin* **5/2**[1]

0006 **3** *2* **Thomas Lawrence (USA)**[13] 4673 6-9-4 47 TPO'Shea 3 56
(P A Blockley) *chsd ldr tl led over 5f out: clr 1/2-way: faltered and rdn over 1f out: hdd 1f out: nt run on* **14/1**

300 **4** *1 1/4* **Jools**[12] 4685 9-9-9 52 RobertHavlin 10 57
(D K Ivory) *hld up in tch: rdn to chse ldrs wl over 2f out: no imp fnl f* **20/1**

00-0 **5** *1 1/2* **High Bray (GER)**[11] 4184 6-9-4 76 JimmyFortune 11 48
(J D Frost) *chsd ldrs: rdn 1/2-way: sn outpcd: kpt on same pce over 1f out* **6/1**[3]

6006 **6** *hd* **Simpleton**[10] 4741 4-9-1 44 StephaneBreux[(3)] 14 48
(J R Best) *dropped in after s: bhd on outer: hdwy u.p over 1f out: nvr threatened ldrs* **100/1**

0100 **7** *shd* **Ceredig**[47] 3619 4-9-9 55 IanMongan 5 52
(Mrs L J Mongan) *chsd ldrs: rdn and outpcd 1/2-way: rallied and edgd rt over 1f out: sn no imp* **33/1**

3000 **8** *1 1/2* **Brave Jack (IRE)**[15] 4591 3-9-0 45 (v) DaneO'Neill 1 41
(J R Best) *hld up in tch: rdn and outpcd 1/2-way: n.d after* **25/1**

100 **9** *2 1/2* **Convince (USA)**[82] 2540 6-9-9 56 (p) SteveDrowne 6 42
(J M Bradley) *hld in midfield: effrt and rdn 2f out: no hdwy over 1f out* **16/1**

0320 **10** *2 1/2* **Royal Guest**[9] 4759 3-9-0 52 DarryllHolland 7 28
(M R Channon) *hld up towards rr: hdwy to chse ldrs 1/2-way: sn rdn and btn* **12/1**

4050 **11** *1 1/4* **Lizarazu (GER)**[19] 4256 8-9-4 48 (p) SebSanders 12 26
(R A Harris) *dropped in after s: a bhd* **9/1**

0000 **12** *1/2* **North Fleet**[3] 4974 4-8-13 47 (p) TolleyDean[(5)] 2 25
(J M Bradley) *chsd ldrs tl rdn and wknd 1/2-way: no ch last 2f* **50/1**

5050 **13** *1 1/2* **Full Spate**[38] 3873 12-9-4 45 StephenDonohoe 8 21
(J M Bradley) *s.i.s: a bhd: rdn and no rspnse 1/2-way* **80/1**

0000 **14** *13* **Dumas (IRE)**[15] 4591 3-9-0 45 (p) JimCrowley 4 —
(A P Jarvis) *led tl over 5f out: chsd ldr tl 1/2-way: sn dropped out: t.o* **40/1**

1m 25.7s (-2.20) **Going Correction** -0.50s/f (Hard)

WFA 3 from 4yo+ 4lb **14** Ran SP% **117.9**

Speed ratings (Par 101): **92,91,88,87,85 85,85,83,80,77 76,75,74,59**

CSF £9.13 TOTE £3.50: £1.20, £1.70, £4.80; EX 10.30 Trifecta £138.10 Part won. Pool £194.54. - 0.10 winning units..The winner was sold to R A Harris for 10,200gns. Arctic Desert was claimed by R. A. Harris for £6,000.

Owner Hartshead Mob **Bred** Bearstone Stud **Trained** Newmarket, Suffolk

FOCUS

A run-of-the-mill seller and typically modest form.

High Bray(GER) Official explanation: jockey said gelding moved poorly

5063 EBF CHECKMATE UK SUPPORTING DEMELZA MAIDEN FILLIES' STKS (DIV II) 7f (S)

3:00 (3:01) (Class 4) 2-Y-0 **£3,465** (£1,030; £515; £257) **Stalls** Low

Form RPR

4 **1** **Dona Alba (IRE)**[31] 4094 2-9-0 0 SebSanders 12 79
(J L Dunlop) *racd far side: chsd ldrs: rdn to ld that gp over 1f out: styd on wl to ld nr fin* **9/4**[2]

05 **2** *hd* **Crying Aloud (USA)**[111] 1727 2-9-0 0 TPO'Shea 1 78
(P A Blockley) *led and clr of stands' side gp and overall: rdn 2f out: kpt on wl tl hdd towards fin* **8/1**[3]

40 **3** *1 1/4* **Patio**[37] 3895 2-9-0 0 JimCrowley 13 75
(Mrs A J Perrett) *hld up in rr of far side gp: hdwy over 2f out: rdn and chsd far side ldr over 1f out: kpt on same pce fnl f* **9/1**

0 **4** *5* **Miss Jolyon (USA)**[20] 4454 2-9-0 0 PhilipRobinson 11 62
(M A Jarvis) *led far side gp tl rdn and hdd over 1f out: sn wknd* **20/1**

0 **5** *nk* **L'Etincelle (IRE)**[16] 4564 2-9-0 0 TedDurcan 2 61
(H R A Cecil) *chsd ldng pair on stands' side: rdn and outpcd 1/2-way: n.d after* **16/1**

0 **6** *1/2* **Totem Flower (IRE)**[37] 3895 2-9-0 0 SteveDrowne 10 60+
(R Charlton) *chsd far side ldr: rdn over 2f out: wknd over 1f out* **6/4**[1]

45 **7** *5* **Pantherii (USA)**[88] 2365 2-9-0 0 TQuinn 5 47
(P F I Cole) *swtchd rt sn after s and racd far side: in tch: rdn 1/2-way: wknd over 2f out* **14/1**

0 **8** *1* **Fleur De Montjeu (IRE)**[22] 4402 2-9-0 0 AdamKirby 9 45
(W R Swinburn) *hld up in rr on far side: rdn wl over 2f out: sn wl btn* **25/1**

2400 **9** *4* **Nothing Likea Dame**[20] 4459 2-9-0 68 HayleyTurner 7 34
(D J Coakley) *swtchd rt sn after s and racd far side: t.k.h: in tch: rdn 1/2-way: sn btn* **22/1**

10 *2* **Dusk Ballet** 2-9-0 0 SaleemGolam 6 29
(S C Williams) *chsd ldr on stands' rail: rdn and struggling 1/2-way: no ch last 2f* **66/1**

P **Fathoming (USA)** 2-9-0 0 JimmyFortune 4 —
(E A L Dunlop) *stdd s: hld up in last of stands' side gp tl p.u and dismntd after 1f* **16/1**

1m 25.01s (-2.89) **Going Correction** -0.50s/f (Hard) **11** Ran SP% **124.8**

Speed ratings (Par 94): **96,95,94,88,88 87,82,80,76,74** —

CSF £21.41 TOTE £3.00: £1.30, £2.80, £2.30; EX 20.50 Trifecta £35.00 Pool £102.65. - 2.08 winning units..

Owner Windflower Overseas Holdings Inc **Bred** Windflower Overseas Holdings Inc **Trained** Arundel, W Sussex

FOCUS

The field split in two with the winner coming from the far-side group but the narrowly-beaten runner-up from the stands'-side group. The form looks solid with the front three clear.

NOTEBOOK

Dona Alba(IRE), who ran with plenty of promise on her debut at Goodwood, stayed on well to win her race on the far side, narrowly beating the winner on the stands' side in the process. She is undoubtedly going to be suited by stepping up to a mile in nursery company and will get much further again next year. (tchd 5-2)

Crying Aloud(USA) finished clear of her two rivals on the stands' side and was unfortunate to be beaten by something racing on the other side of the track. She has improved with every outing and now has the nursery option open to her. (op 14-1 tchd 13-2)

Patio, who was taking on lesser opposition than she encountered at Ascot last time, improved for the extra furlong, staying on well from off the pace to come home second on the far side. She is another now eligible for a mark. (op 10-1)

Miss Jolyon(USA), having learnt plenty from her debut, had the speed to lead on this occasion and ran a fair race before getting tired. A half-sister to Askham, a triple 1m to 1m2f winner, and Schapiro, 1m4f winner, a drop back to 6f should help her. (op 14-1)

L'Etincelle(IRE), a half-sister to Fashionable, a dual 1m to 1m2f winner, Artistic Style, a multiple 1m1f to 1m3f winner, and Fine Arts, a 7f winner, came home second on the stands' side. A longer trip is going to suit her in time. (op 18-1 tchd 20-1)

Totem Flower(IRE), who finished in front of Patio in a hot Ascot maiden on her debut, failed to build on that in this easier company. Perhaps the ground was faster than she would care for. (op 7-4 tchd 15-8 in a place)

Fathoming(USA) Official explanation: jockey said filly was lame

5064 SUNLEY GROUP SUPPORTING DEMELZA H'CAP 6f

3:30 (3:32) (Class 5) (0-75,74) 3-Y-0+ **£2,817** (£838; £418; £209) **Stalls** Low

Form RPR

0012 **1** **For Life (IRE)**[22] 4395 5-8-1 60 oh2 NataliaGemelova[(5)] 1 76
(J E Long) *mde all: pushed along and in command wl over 1f out: r.o strly* **4/1**[1]

4015 **2** *2 1/2* **Buy On The Red**[24] 4320 6-9-1 69 (p) RichardMullen 2 77
(W R Muir) *chsd wnr thrght: rdn over 2f out: kpt on same pce* **9/1**

0334 **3** *2* **Best One**[14] 4641 3-9-4 74 (t) TedDurcan 4 76
(C E Brittain) *w.w: hdwy over 2f out: rdn 2f out: kpt on steadily: no ch w wnr* **16/1**

0504 **4** *1* **Mandarin Spirit (IRE)**[3] 4965 7-9-4 72 (v[1]) OscarUrbina 6 71
(G C H Chung) *w.w in tch: rdn and effrt wl over 1f out: sn no imp* **13/2**[3]

240 **5** *nk* **Louphole**[34] 4024 5-9-5 73 SebSanders 5 71
(P J Makin) *hld up bhd: hdwy over 2f out: sn rdn and no imp* **15/2**

26-5 **6** *shd* **Lipizza (IRE)**[16] 4585 4-9-6 74 JimmyFortune 3 72
(N A Callaghan) *chsd ldng pair: rdn and tried to chal jst over 2f out: sn outpcd* **6/1**[2]

0046 **7** *1* **The Cayterers**[9] 4767 5-9-2 70 (p) SteveDrowne 11 65
(J M Bradley) *stdd s: bhd: rdn over 2f out: nvr nr ldrs* **10/1**

4046 **8** *1 3/4* **Mr Cellophane**[13] 4657 4-9-0 68 (v) DarryllHolland 12 58
(J R Jenkins) *racd solo on far side: in tch: rdn over 2f out: no ch fnl f* **11/1**

0042 **9** *1 3/4* **High Ridge**[4] 4942 8-8-9 63 (p) StephenDonohoe 8 47
(J M Bradley) *in tch in midfield: rdn wl over 2f out: n.d after* **13/2**[3]

010 **10** *6* **Sweet Pickle**[9] 4767 6-9-2 70 (e) JimCrowley 7 36
(J R Boyle) *hld up towards rr: rdn and no hdwy over 2f out* **20/1**

3600 **11** *7* **Connect**[6] 4895 10-8-11 70 (v) PatrickHills[(5)] 10 15
(M H Tompkins) *dropped in bhd after s: pushed along early: rdn over 2f out: no hdwy: eased whn no ch ins fnl f* **25/1**

6043 **12** *9* **Marko Jadeo (IRE)**[23] 4351 9-8-7 66 LukeMorris[(5)] 9 —
(R A Harris) *in tch tl rdn and lost pl over 3f out: eased whn no ch fnl f: t.o* **14/1**

1m 10.26s (-3.34) **Going Correction** -0.50s/f (Hard)

WFA 3 from 4yo+ 2lb **12** Ran SP% **121.3**

Speed ratings (Par 103): **102,98,96,94,94 94,92,90,88,80 70,58**

CSF £41.21 CT £412.22 TOTE £5.90: £2.40, £3.40, £3.50; EX 77.50 Trifecta £207.90 Pool £410.08. - 1.40 winning units..

Owner T H Bambridge **Bred** R N Auld **Trained** Caterham, Surrey

FOCUS

Modest handicap form dominated throughout by the improving For Life. Mr Cellophane went on his own to the far side but was well held at the line.

Lipizza(IRE) Official explanation: jockey said filly hung right and was unsuited by the good to firm ground

Mr Cellophane Official explanation: jockey said gelding hung left

5065 EASTWELL MANOR SUPPORTING DEMELZA MEDIAN AUCTION MAIDEN STKS 5f

4:00 (4:00) (Class 6) 2-Y-0 **£2,388** (£705; £352) **Stalls** Low

Form RPR

1 **Artistic License (IRE)** 2-8-12 0 DarryllHolland 3 65+
(M R Channon) *in tch: shkn up and hdwy over 1f out: led last 100yds: pushed out: readily* **8/1**

0234 **2** *1/2* **Magical Speedfit (IRE)**[29] 4181 2-9-3 78 TQuinn 2 68
(G G Margarson) *cl up: led 2f out: sn rdn: hdd and nt pce of wnr last 100yds* **5/4**[1]

5 **3** *1 1/2* **All In The Red (IRE)**[10] 4733 2-9-3 0 JohnEgan 7 63
(Miss Gay Kelleway) *sn rdn along in rr: hdwy on outer over 1f out: styd on u.p to chse ldng pair ins fnl f* **11/1**

3054 **4** *3/4* **The Magic Blanket (IRE)**[27] 4221 2-8-12 66 TolleyDean[(5)] 1 60
(Stef Liddiard) *prom: rdn 2f out: ev ch jst over 1f out: wknd last 100yds* **11/1**

04 **5** *1* **Wild Bill Tracey**[18] 4506 2-9-3 0 JimmyFortune 9 56
(M J Wallace) *t.k.h: led tl 2f out: sn hung rt and rdn: wknd over 1f out* **6/1**[3]

0 **6** *1/2* **Athboy Auction**[27] 4232 2-8-12 0 SebSanders 5 50
(H J Collingridge) *t.k.h: hld up in rr: shkn up and effrt over 1f out: nvr able to chal* **9/2**[2]

0620 **7** *3* **Lady Vibeeka**[14] 4629 2-8-5 68 KylieManser[(7)] 6 39
(Mrs H Sweeting) *in tch: rdn and wknd wl over 1f out* **20/1**

00 **8** *2* **Lady Of Passion (IRE)**[52] 3446 2-8-12 0 TPO'Shea 4 32
(M R Channon) *rrd leaving stalls: sn outpcd in last pair: no ch fr 1/2-way* **33/1**

9 *1 3/4* **Cherished Song** 2-8-12 0 DaneO'Neill 8 25
(N A Callaghan) *v.s.a: a outpcd in last: no ch fr 1/2-way* **33/1**

59.32 secs (-1.48) **Going Correction** -0.50s/f (Hard) **9** Ran SP% **115.3**

Speed ratings (Par 93): **91,90,87,86,85 84,79,76,73**

CSF £18.07 TOTE £10.30: £2.60, £1.10, £2.20; EX 25.00 Trifecta £109.30 Pool £275.71. - 1.79 winning units..

Owner Wood Street Syndicate IV **Bred** Mountarmstrong Stud **Trained** West Ilsley, Berks

FOCUS

With the favourite flattered by his current rating this race took little winning.

NOTEBOOK
Artistic License(IRE), a half-sister to Brandywell Boy, who also won over 5f at two, did not need to be anything too special to win this maiden, but she did it well and looks the type to pay her way in sprint handicaps. (op 13-2 tchd 6-1)
Magical Speedfit(IRE) has had a number of chances now and a mark of 78 clearly flatters him. (op 7-4)
All In The Red(IRE), dropping back to the minimum trip, found things happening a bit too quickly in the early stages but he made good late headway and a return to 6f is probably going to suit him. (op 10-1 tchd 9-1)
The Magic Blanket(IRE), who has changed stables, has shown himself to be just of modest ability, and perhaps low-grade nurseries will offer greater hope of a breakthrough. (op 12-1 tchd 16-1)
Wild Bill Tracey, too keen in front on this occasion, looks a nursery type now that he has his three runs under his belt. (tchd 5-1)
Athboy Auction, keen in rear, could never get close enough to throw down a challenge. She looks more of a longer-term prospect. (op 4-1)
Lady Of Passion(IRE) Official explanation: jockey said filly was slowly away

5066 PARKER STEEL SUPPORTING DEMELZA H'CAP 5f
4:30 (4:30) (Class 5) (0-75,72) 3-Y-O **£2,817** (£838; £418; £209) **Stalls** Low

Form RPR
-531 **1** **Millisecond**[29] 4164 3-9-4 **72** PhilipRobinson 3 81
(M A Jarvis) *chsd ldr: rdn to ld jst ins fnl f: r.o wl* **11/4**[2]
3003 **2** 1 3/4 **Rocker**[17] 4546 3-9-3 **71** SebSanders 1 74
(B R Johnson) *bmpd sltly s: chsd ldrs: rdn over 2f out: chsd wnr last 100yds: nvr able to chal* **9/4**[1]
0326 **3** 2 **Pretty Miss**[27] 4233 3-9-3 **71** (v[1]) JimCrowley 2 67
(H Candy) *wnt lft s: sn led: rdn 2f out: hdd jst ins fnl f: fdd last 100yds* **7/2**[3]
2002 **4** 2 1/2 **Bookiesindex Boy**[19] 4486 3-9-2 **70** TedDurcan 5 57
(J R Jenkins) *bhd: effrt 2f out: nvr threatened ldrs* **10/1**
3542 **5** 1 1/2 **Hythe Bay**[11] 4712 3-8-13 **67** DaneO'Neill 4 48
(J R Best) *chsd ldrs: rdn 1/2-way: wknd wl over 1f out* **5/1**
4403 **6** 3 **Perlachy**[8] 4801 3-8-4 **58** oh5 (v) HayleyTurner 6 29
(Mrs N Macauley) *sn rdn along: a struggling to go pce: no ch last 2f* **28/1**
2143 **7** 5 **Hereford Boy**[91] 2276 3-9-4 **72** RobertHavlin 7 25
(D K Ivory) *v.s.a: a outpcd in last* **12/1**
58.23 secs (-2.57) **Going Correction** -0.50s/f (Hard) course record **7** Ran SP% **116.6**
Speed ratings (Par 101): **100,97,94,90,87 82,74**
CSF £9.75 CT £21.45 TOTE £3.10: £2.20, £2.00; EX 11.30 Trifecta £47.00 Pool £369.23. - 5.57 winning units..
Owner Helena Springfield Ltd **Bred** Meon Valley Stud **Trained** Newmarket, Suffolk
FOCUS
Just an ordinary handicap but they went a decent pace on this quick ground and the winner set a new course record.
Hereford Boy Official explanation: jockey said gelding missed the break

5067 EBF GALLAGHER GROUP SUPPORTING DEMELZA FILLIES' H'CAP 1m 1f 149y
5:00 (5:00) (Class 3) (0-90,87) 3-Y-O+
£8,724 (£2,612; £1,306; £653; £326; £163) **Stalls** Low

Form RPR
6001 **1** **Free Offer**[28] 4205 3-9-0 **78** DaneO'Neill 7 84
(J L Dunlop) *trckd ldrs: rdn wl over 1f out: swtchd lft jst over 1f out: r.o wl u.p to ld towards fin* **7/2**[2]
1454 **2** 1/2 **Vale De Lobo**[30] 4128 5-9-2 **73** TedDurcan 2 78
(B R Millman) *led: rdn 2f out: battled on gamely tl hdd and no ex towards fin* **13/2**
5-05 **3** nk **Postage Stampe**[82] 2543 4-9-6 **77** RichardMullen 5 81
(D M Simcock) *w.w in last trio: rdn over 2f out: swtchd lft over 1f out: r.o strly ins fnl f: nt rch ldrs* **14/1**
-016 **4** 2 **Miss Marvellous (USA)**[38] 3871 3-8-8 **72** OscarUrbina 3 72
(J R Fanshawe) *t.k.h: chsd ldrs: hdwy to chal 2f out: rdn and fnd little over 1f out: fdd last 100yds* **11/1**
0051 **5** nk **Samdaniya**[24] 4327 3-8-4 **68** HayleyTurner 6 68
(C E Brittain) *t.k.h: chsd ldr: rdn and ev ch 2f out: wknd jst ins fnl f: btn and edgd rt nr fin* **5/1**[3]
-031 **6** 1 1/4 **Sunlight (IRE)**[24] 4331 3-9-9 **87** PhilipRobinson 4 84
(M A Jarvis) *dwlt: hld up in last: rdn and effrt 2f out: nvr able to chal* **6/4**[1]
300 **7** 7 **Love On Sight**[31] 4093 3-9-3 **81** SebSanders 1 63
(A P Jarvis) *t.k.h: hld up in last pair: rdn and effrt 2f out: wknd over 1f out: eased whn btn ins fnl f* **16/1**
2m 4.46s (-0.77) **Going Correction** 0.0s/f (Good)
WFA 3 from 4yo+ 7lb **7** Ran SP% **113.1**
Speed ratings (Par 104): **103,102,102,100,100 99,93**
CSF £25.49 TOTE £4.90: £2.70, £3.60; EX 30.20.
Owner The Earl Cadogan **Bred** The Earl Cadogan **Trained** Arundel, W Sussex
FOCUS
A competitive handicap but the pace was not strong.
NOTEBOOK
Free Offer defied a 5lb higher mark than at Newbury and is clearly on an upward curve. She picked up well once switched and that turn of speed will stand her in good stead as she rises up the ratings. (op 9-2)
Vale De Lobo enjoyed the run of the race out in front and was only denied close home. This was a sound effort considering that the Handicapper has been in charge since her win in May. (op 7-1)
Postage Stampe stayed on well from off the pace in a race that was not run at a strong gallop. She could be interesting now that she is finally on a fair mark, and it is worth remembering that she is proven on Polytrack, too. (op 11-1)
Miss Marvellous(USA), who failed to progress from her Yarmouth maiden win at Bath last time, had quicker ground to deal with here and raced keenly off the ordinary gallop. (tchd 12-1)
Samdaniya was another who did not help her chance by failing to settle. (op 15-2 tchd 9-2)
Sunlight(IRE), stepping up in trip, never got into it from off the pace and was unsuited by the way the race was run. (op 5-4)

5068 "DREAMS" OF EASTWELL MANOR SUPPORTING DEMELZA H'CAP 1m 4f
5:30 (5:30) (Class 6) (0-65,66) 3-Y-O **£2,047** (£604; £302) **Stalls** Low

Form RPR
0600 **1** **Hermanita**[30] 4139 3-8-9 **56** SteveDrowne 2 61
(G Wragg) *hld up towards rr: hdwy wl over 1f out: swtchd lft over 1f out: styd on wl u.p to ld nr fin* **22/1**
5053 **2** 1/2 **Barbs Pink Diamond (USA)**[17] 4534 3-8-8 **55** JimCrowley 10 59
(Mrs A J Perrett) *chsd ldrs: rdn over 2f out: ev ch u.p 1f out: no ex nr fin* **14/1**
21U1 **3** shd **Chant De Guerre (USA)**[19] 4472 3-8-8 **62** JackMitchell[(7)] 1 66
(P Mitchell) *hld up in last early: gd hdwy 6f out: chsd ldr 4f out: rdn to ld narrowly over 2f out: hdd and no ex nr fin* **8/1**[3]
0550 **4** 1 **Paymaster General (IRE)**[23] 4355 3-8-10 **57** HayleyTurner 8 59
(M D I Usher) *t.k.h: hld up in rr: rdn over 2f out: styd on u.p fnl f: nt rch ldrs* **12/1**
0016 **5** nk **Mayireneyrbel**[19] 4472 3-8-8 **55** NickyMackay 3 57
(J Akehurst) *chsd ldr tl 4f out: rdn over 2f out: kpt on same pce fnl f* **40/1**
0005 **6** 3/4 **Cavalry Twill (IRE)**[29] 4172 3-9-4 **65** (b) TQuinn 5 66
(P F I Cole) *led tl hdd over 2f out: ev ch after tl fdd jst ins fnl f* **12/1**
430 **7** nk **Woolfall Rose**[46] 3651 3-9-2 **63** OscarUrbina 9 63
(G G Margarson) *hld up in midfield: rdn over 2f out: kpt on same pce* **14/1**
-600 **8** 1 3/4 **Bring It On Home**[32] 4069 3-9-4 **65** AdamKirby 6 62
(G L Moore) *s.i.s: sn in tch in midfield: rdn wl over 2f out: sn struggling* **12/1**
3504 **9** 1 1/4 **She's So Pretty (IRE)**[24] 4327 3-9-1 **62** (p) TedDurcan 7 57
(W R Swinburn) *chsd ldrs tl lost pl over 3f out: rdn and btn over 2f out: eased ins fnl f* **9/2**[2]
0341 **10** 3/4 **Blue Space**[10] 4742 3-9-5 **66** SebSanders 4 60
(P J Makin) *t.k.h early: settled in rr: pushed along wl over 2f out: sme hdwy u.p over 1f out: sn no imp* **6/5**[1]
2m 40.8s (0.30) **Going Correction** 0.0s/f (Good) **10** Ran SP% **117.9**
Speed ratings (Par 99): **99,98,98,97,97 97,95,95,94**
CSF £299.22 CT £2676.49 TOTE £27.30: £3.10, £2.00, £2.80; EX 162.00 Trifecta £243.80 Part won. Pool £343.51. - 0.10 winning units. Place 6 £15.69. Place 5 £13.70..
Owner Miss K Rausing **Bred** Miss K Rausing **Trained** Newmarket, Suffolk
FOCUS
A steadily-run handicap which turned into something of a sprint in the straight.
Blue Space Official explanation: trainer said filly was found to be jarred up the following morning
T/Plt: £16.40 to a £1 stake. Pool: £64,943.80. 2,874.95 winning tickets. T/Qpdt: £11.50 to a £1 stake. Pool: £2,778.90. 177.50 winning tickets. SP

5069 - (Foreign Racing) - See Raceform Interactive

4829 CURRAGH (R-H)
Sunday, September 2

OFFICIAL GOING: Good (good to firm in places on round course)

5070a GO AND GO ROUND TOWER STKS (GROUP 3) 6f
2:35 (2:36) 2-Y-O **£35,189** (£10,324; £4,918; £1,675)

RPR
1 **Norman Invader (USA)**[24] 4347 2-9-1 CO'Donoghue 4 108
(K J Condon, Ire) *hld up in rr: hdwy on outer under 2f out: 2nd and chal 1f out: led 100yds out: kpt on wl* **14/1**
2 hd **Perfect Polly**[8] 4829 2-8-12 NGMcCullagh 7 104
(Andrew Oliver, Ire) *cl up on outer: led travelling wl 2f out: rdn and strly pressed over 1f out: hdd 100yds out: kpt on u.p* **25/1**
3 nk **Great Barrier Reef (USA)**[11] 4721 2-9-1 KFallon 9 107
(A P O'Brien, Ire) *hld up in 7th: 5th u.p 2f out: 3rd and styd on ins fnl f* **2/5**[1]
4 2 1/2 **Rock Moss (IRE)**[9] 4789 2-9-1 KJManning 3 99
(J S Bolger, Ire) *prom: 3rd bef 1/2-way: rdn and lost pl under 2f out: kpt on same pce fr over 1f out* **12/1**[3]
5 hd **Domingues**[27] 4242 2-9-1 JMurtagh 1 98
(Edward Lynam, Ire) *sn led on stands' rail: hdd 2f out: kpt on same pce u.p* **12/1**[3]
6 shd **Dedo (IRE)**[10] 4743 2-9-1 DPMcDonogh 2 98
(Kevin Prendergast, Ire) *sn 2nd: 3rd and rdn 2f out: no imp: kpt on same pce* **12/1**[3]
7 2 **Going Public (IRE)**[60] 3221 2-9-1 PJSmullen 5 92
(D K Weld, Ire) *trckd ldrs in 5th: lost pl 2f out: sn no ex* **7/1**[2]
8 2 **Another Express (IRE)**[63] 3141 2-9-1 WMLordan 8 86
(T Stack, Ire) *chsd ldrs in 6th: rdn and lost pl over 2f out: last and no ex fr 1 1/2f out* **16/1**
1m 12.12s (-2.38) **Going Correction** -0.175s/f (Firm) **9** Ran SP% **123.4**
Speed ratings: **108,107,107,104,103 103,100,98**
CSF £308.40 TOTE £26.20: £2.80, £3.70, £1.10; DF 969.50.
Owner A Gannon **Bred** Flaxman Holdings Ltd **Trained** Fairstown Co Kildare
FOCUS
All sorts of improvers suggest there is a fair chance that this race has been overrated, although for now it has been rated through the third to his Gimcrack run.
NOTEBOOK
Norman Invader(USA), who arrived on the outside with a sustained challenge to seize the initiative inside the last half-furlong, went into this race with form that tied in two of the best juveniles seen out in Ireland this season. He ran second to the talented Bruges in a maiden at The Curragh on his second start, and was not disgraced when third of four behind New Approach in the Group 3 Tyros Stakes at Leopardstown. Tried over an extended 7f at Tipperary last month, he was more effective back at 6f here and has the makings of a genuine Group 3-standard horse.
Perfect Polly, running just eight days after a maiden victory over the course and distance, looked for a while as if she was about to bring off one of the shocks of the season. She was going easily when taken into the lead two furlongs out and maintained her effort well without having enough in reserve to repel the winner. With average luck she should continue to be a fine standard bearer for an emerging stable.
Great Barrier Reef(USA) was a warm order on the strength of his debut second in the Gimcrack. He got fairly close in the end, but never gave the impression that he was travelling particularly well, and it took him a while to crank up an effort. It looks as if he has failed to make any significant progress from the York race, or perhaps this came just a bit soon for him. (op 1/2)
Rock Moss(IRE) ran as well he was entitled to after being a beaten favourite in a nursery at Tralee.
Domingues was found wanting after running out in front through the first half-mile, and will need to improve to make an impact at Pattern level.
Dedo(IRE) is worthy of similar comments. (op 10/1)
Going Public(IRE) might have been expected to do better after his run behind Bruges in a 7f Listed race at Leopardstown. There was always a possibility that the drop back in trip might not be ideal, but it was disappointing that he failed to manage any sort of counter-attack after dropping off the pace two furlongs down. (op 11/2)
Another Express(IRE) looked out of his depth.

5073a MOYGLARE STUD STKS (GROUP 1) (FILLIES) 7f
4:05 (4:06) 2-Y-O
£115,945 (£38,918; £18,648; £6,486; £4,459; £2,432)

RPR
1 **Saoirse Abu (USA)**[21] 4437 2-8-12 (b) KJManning 3 110+
(J S Bolger, Ire) *trckd ldrs in 3rd: impr into 2nd after 1/2-way: rdn to chal 2f out: led over 1f out: styd on wl cl home: comf* **13/2**[3]
2 1 1/2 **Listen (IRE)**[21] 4440 2-8-12 KFallon 2 106
(A P O'Brien, Ire) *hld up: 7th 1/2-way: swtchd lft 2f out: 3rd over 1f out: 2nd and kpt on wl ins fnl f wout threatening wnr* **4/5**[1]

3 ½ **Mad About You (IRE)**[46] 3659 2-8-12 .... PJSmullen 8 105
(D K Weld, Ire) *trckd ldrs: 6th 1/2-way: 4th whn nt clr run 2f out: kpt on u.p ins fnl f* **7/1**

4 1 **Albabilia (IRE)**[22] 4400 2-8-12 .... KerrinMcEvoy 5 103
(C E Brittain) *settled 2nd: led 1/2-way: strly pressed 2f out: hdd over 1f out: no ex ins fnl f* **7/2**[2]

5 2 **Allicansayis Wow (USA)**[60] 3221 2-8-12 .... FMBerry 7 98
(J S Bolger, Ire) *trckd ldrs: 4th 1/2-way: 3rd and rdn 2f out: 5th and no ex fr over 1f out* **40/1**

6 2½ **Solas Na Greine (IRE)**[7] 4862 2-8-12 .... DJMoran 4 91
(J S Bolger, Ire) *hld up in tch: 5th after 1/2-way: no imp fr 2f out: one pce* **16/1**

7 hd **Queen Jock (USA)**[53] 3438 2-8-12 .... PShanahan 1 91
(Tracey Collins, Ire) *chsd ldrs in 6th: effrt 2f out: sn no ex* **25/1**

8 2 **Juniper Berry (IRE)**[12] 4697 2-8-12 .... WMLordan 6 86
(John Joseph Murphy, Ire) *led: rdn and hdd 1/2-way: sn no ex and wknd* **66/1**

9 6 **Miss Red Eye (IRE)**[21] 4434 2-8-12 .... FranciscoDaSilva 9 71
(Luke Comer, Ire) *a bhd: wknd fr 1/2-way* **200/1**

1m 25.01s (-2.49) **Going Correction** -0.175s/f (Firm) **9** Ran SP% **117.8**
Speed ratings: **107,105,104,103,101 98,98,95,89**
CSF £12.30 TOTE £7.50: £2.10, £1.10, £2.60; DF 13.40.
Owner Ennistown Stud **Bred** White Cloud B'Sk,Omar Trevino&N&PP **Trained** Coolcullen, Co Carlow

FOCUS
Solid enough form for the grade, with the winner confirming her Phoenix Stakes success was no fluke.

NOTEBOOK
Saoirse Abu(USA) was allowed to go off at an almost insulting price. Those who kept faith with the Phoenix Stakes heroine were rewarded with a performance that marks her out as a juvenile talent to match some of the best that her trainer has handled. Having beaten the Royal Ascot winners Henrythenavigator and Elletelle in the Phoenix, one could argue that she was faced with less substantial opponents here, but there was an infectious degree of confidence behind the favourite in the light of a near-miss in the Group 2 Debutante Stakes, and Clive Brittain, so often in the limelight with horses apparently running above their station, had come this time with a filly of proven substance at Group 3 level. Viewed in that perspective, there was an appropriate quality to this renewal. Always well positioned, and right in the firing line when asked to raise the tempo two furlongs down, she stuck to her task with relish after edging into the lead from over a furlong out. For a stride or two it looked as if Listen might close the gap significantly after being switched to the outer, but the winner asserted strongly in the closing stages and accomplished her task with a fair bit to spare in the end. A tough sort who gives an impression that she will prove durable, she is versatile in terms of ground and is another fine advertisement for her sire Mr Greeley. (op 11/2)
Listen(IRE), of which much was expected following her run in the Debutante, is clearly a very smart filly. In the context of previous form involving the experienced Tuscan Evening she surpassed her two previous efforts here and there is sound reason to believe that she can mature into a Classic-standard filly. (op 4/5 tchd 4/6)
Mad About You(IRE), who had finished in front of a below-par Saoirse Abu in a Listed race at Leopardstown, enhanced her reputation with an excellent third. She suffered in some bunching in behind the leaders around two furlongs out and stayed on in a manner that augurs well for her prospects of getting a mile in due course.
Albabilia(IRE), winner of the Sweet Solera, seemed to be beaten fair and square, and her performance helps to give a preliminary view of the relative merits of the British and Irish juvenile fillies. After running in second, she took over at around the halfway stage but failed to maintain the momentum of her challenge and was a lost cause through the final furlong. (op 3/1 tchd 4/1)
Allicansayis Wow(USA) was flying high at this level, but it is realistic to regard her as a filly who could make a telling impression in Listed races. (op 33/1)
Queen Jock(USA) should be able to win a maiden if building on this effort. (op 33/1)

5075a NOLAN & BROPHY AUCTIONEERS FLYING FIVE (GROUP 3) 5f
5:05 (5:06) 3-Y-0+ **£32,939** (£9,628; £4,560; £1,520)

RPR

1 **Benbaun (IRE)**[75] 2733 6-9-5 ....(b) PJSmullen 8 123
(M J Wallace) *cl up in 3rd: 2nd 2f out: sn chal: led 1f out: kpt on wl u.p: all out to hold on nr fin* **10/3**[2]

2 hd **Dandy Man (IRE)**[10] 4746 4-9-2 116.................................. PShanahan 5 119
(Tracey Collins, Ire) *cl 2nd: led over 2f out: sn rdn and strly pressed: hdd 1f out: rallied u.p: jst failed* **11/10**[1]

3 1¾ **Moss Vale (IRE)**[28] 4214 6-9-2 .... KFallon 10 113
(D Nicholls) *trckd ldrs in 5th: impr into 3rd under 2f out: sn chal: no imp ins fnl f* **4/1**[3]

4 2 **Senor Benny (USA)**[7] 4864 8-9-2 104........................... DPMcDonogh 1 106
(M McDonagh, Ire) *towards rr: last 2f out: rdn and r.o wl fnl f* **16/1**

5 1 **Snaefell (IRE)**[49] 3573 3-9-1 106... JMurtagh 9 102
(M Halford, Ire) *hld up: prog on outer under 2f out: mod 4th 1f out: kpt on same pce* **10/1**

6 nk **Moone Cross (IRE)**[14] 4639 4-8-13 100........................ NGMcCullagh 6 98
(Mrs John Harrington, Ire) *chsd ldrs: mod 4th over 1f out: sn no ex* **50/1**

7 4½ **Peak District (IRE)**[11] 4726 3-9-1 95................................ WMLordan 11 85
(David Wachman, Ire) *chsd ldrs: mod 5th 1 1/2f out: no ex fnl f* **14/1**

8 1½ **Osterhase (IRE)**[7] 4864 8-9-2 106.....................................(b) FMBerry 3 79
(J E Mulhern, Ire) *led: hdd over 2f out: sn no ex and wknd* **16/1**

9 1 **Leitra (IRE)**[88] 2379 4-8-13 100.. RPCleary 4 73
(M Halford, Ire) *s.i.s: sn chsd ldrs in 4th: wknd fr 2f out* **33/1**

58.79 secs (-2.51) **Going Correction** -0.175s/f (Firm)
WFA 3 from 4yo+ 1lb **11** Ran SP% **123.1**
Speed ratings: **113,112,109,106,105 104,97,95,93**
CSF £7.91 TOTE £4.70: £1.60, £1.20, £1.40; DF 10.00.
Owner Ransley, Birks, Hillen **Bred** Dr T A Ryan **Trained** Newmarket, Suffolk

FOCUS
Solid form for the grade and a third win in this race for Benbaun.

NOTEBOOK
Benbaun(IRE) was winning the race for the third time, and had to call on all his battling qualities to hold off the gallant runner-up. A relatively fresh horse making his first appearance since failing to run up his best in the King's Stand, he was having only his third race of the season, having begun the campaign with a victory in the 6f Greenlands Stakes at this venue. He has improved with age and brings a brand of seasoned professionalism to his racing that is the hallmark of a sprinter only a little short of the highest class. (op 5/2)
Dandy Man(IRE) deserves some sympathy as he has experienced ill-fortune with the draw in some top races in Britain and this time the rain did him no favours, perhaps slowing the ground just enough to blunt his speed. He still had every chance as they scrapped it out through an exciting final furlong, but there was a definite sense that he was not quite as effective as might have been the case had the change in the weather not occurred. (op 5/4 tchd 7/4)
Moss Vale(IRE), beaten by Benbaun in the Greenlands, again had to settle for a minor role but gave a typically honest performance, securing third without much fuss, ahead of the essentially journeymen Irish sprinters who made up the rest of the field. (op 9/2 tchd 5/1)
Senor Benny(USA) did best of the rest, running on powerfully from the rear.

5074 - 5076a (Foreign Racing) - See Raceform Interactive

5028 BADEN-BADEN (L-H)
Sunday, September 2

OFFICIAL GOING: Good

5077a 135TH GROSSER PREIS VON BADEN (GROUP 1) 1m 4f
4:00 (4:08) 3-Y-0+ **£101,351** (£40,541; £16,892; £10,135)

RPR

1 **Quijano (GER)**[28] 5-9-6 .... AStarke 7 122
(P Schiergen, Germany) *disp 4th: wnt 2nd wl over 2f out: led 1 1/2f out: rdn and hung rt appr fnl f: drvn out* **59/10**

2 nk **Adlerflug (GER)**[63] 3146 3-8-9 .... FJohansson 9 120
(J Hirschberger, Germany) *in tch: cl 6th st and brought to outside: sn drvn: chal appr fnl f: ev ch tl unable qck last strides* **22/10**[1]

3 3½ **Egerton (GER)**[21] 4442 6-9-6 .... TMundry 4 116
(P Rau, Germany) *hld up: clsd up over 3f out: styd towards ins and 5th st: hrd rdn wl over 1f out: kpt on u.p* **26/1**

4 hd **Youmzain (IRE)**[36] 3942 4-9-6 .... RichardHughes 6 116
(M R Channon) *hld up in rr: clsd up on outside wl over 2f out: 6th and c wdst st: sn outpcd: hrd rdn over 1f out: kpt on u.p* **37/10**[3]

5 1½ **Axxos (GER)**[50] 3566 3-8-9 .... EPedroza 2 111
(P Schiergen, Germany) *trckd ldr: led and qcknd 3f out: hdd 1 1/2f out: carried rt by wnr appr fnl f: kpt on one pce* **88/10**

6 ¾ **First Stream (GER)**[21] 4442 3-8-9 .... C-PLemaire 8 110
(Mario Hofer, Germany) *disp 6th: cl 8th st: rdn over 1f out: one pce fnl f* **16/1**

7 1 **Prince Flori (GER)**[36] 3942 4-9-6 .... ADeVries 1 110
(S Smrczek, Germany) *hld up in rr: last st and styd on ins: effrt over 2f out: sn rdn: btn over 1f out* **13/2**

8 1 **Mountain High (IRE)**[70] 2925 5-9-6 .... RyanMoore 3 109
(Sir Michael Stoute) *a cl up: 3rd st: hrd rdn 2f out: wkng whn hmpd appr fnl f* **28/10**[2]

9 15 **Sommertag (GER)**[35] 4013 4-9-6 .... THellier 5 85
(J Hirschberger, Germany) *led to 3f out: 4th st: eased* **27/1**

2m 28.19s (-5.27)
WFA 3 from 4yo+ 9lb **9** Ran SP% **130.0**
TOTE (including ten euro stake) WIN 69; PL 20, 17, 37; SF 224.
Owner Stiftung Gestut Fahrhof **Bred** Stiftung Gestut Fahrhof **Trained** Germany

NOTEBOOK
Quijano(GER), who enjoyed such a good time of it in Dubai earlier in the year, relished the fast ground and got the better of a final-furlong duel with the German Derby winner Adlerflug. His connections are now planning some more foreign travel with him, with the Canadian International and Japan Cup serious options.
Adlerflug(GER), last seen out winning the German Derby in July, would probably not have been ideally suited by the fast ground, but he only went down narrowly after a battle royale inside the last. He is now done for the year but will return as a four-year-old, and he looks just the type to improve again next season.
Youmzain(IRE) tried to come from the back of the field but that proved difficult on this sharp track and, with the early pace having not been that strong, he was never going to get there. He remains a possible for the Arc.
Mountain High(IRE), whose rider reported that the five-year-old would not let himself down on the fast ground, was unable to show his best form.

4995 HAMILTON (R-H)
Monday, September 3

OFFICIAL GOING: Good to firm (good in places; 8.5)
Wind: Breezy, half against Weather: Cloudy, bright

5081 WBX.COM £25 FREE BET FOR NEW ACCOUNTS TWO YEAR OLD CLAIMING STKS 6f 5y
2:20 (2:21) (Class 6) 2-Y-0 **£2,266** (£674; £337; £168) **Stalls** Low

Form RPR

1 1 **Genethni**[54] 3410 2-8-4 0... AndrewMullen(3) 11 61+
(K A Ryan) *racd in midfield on outside: effrt over 2f out: hung rt: led ins fnl f: kpt on wl* **8/1**[3]

5640 2 nk **Atephobia**[23] 4406 2-8-9 63.. AndrewElliott(3) 5 65
(K R Burke) *led to ins fnl f: kpt on towards fin* **5/2**[2]

5636 3 5 **Elusive Lady (IRE)**[10] 4770 2-8-3 56 ow1................ PatrickMathers(3) 4 44
(J R Weymes) *prom: effrt over 2f out: outpcd over 1f out* **9/1**

00 4 shd **Tommytush (IRE)**[9] 4818 2-9-0 0...................................... MickyFenton 7 52
(E J Alston) *w ldr: rdn and edgd rt over 2f out: no ex over 1f out* **16/1**

00 5 shd **Scientific**[17] 4578 2-8-8 0... TonyHamilton 2 45
(R A Fahey) *bhd and sn outpcd: hdwy over 1f out: nrst fin* **40/1**

5350 6 shd **Duke Of Touraine (IRE)**[30] 4892 2-9-3 75........................ LeeEnstone 10 54
(P C Haslam) *prom: drvn and outpcd over 2f out: n.d after* **15/8**[1]

0050 7 1½ **Miss Willoughby**[3] 5015 2-8-4 45 ow2.....................(e) AdrianTNicholls 1 37
(J Ryan) *towards rr: hung rt thrght: no imp fr 1/2-way* **50/1**

063 8 6 **Jazz Stick (IRE)**[12] 4715 2-8-8 59..(v) TomEaves 6 23
(I Semple) *s.i.s: rdn in rr 1/2-way: nvr on terms* **8/1**[3]

066 9 1¾ **Abbey Express**[28] 4221 2-9-0 62..................................(b[1]) PhillipMakin 3 23
(M Dods) *chsd ldrs tl wknd over 2f out* **33/1**

10 16 **Aberlady Lad** 2-8-10 0... GregFairley 9 —
(B Mactaggart) *s.i.s: a outpcd* **100/1**

660 11 13 **Royal Sovereign (IRE)**[30] 4173 2-9-3 61......................... PaulMulrennan 8 —
(J Howard Johnson) *plld hrd to post: towards rr: rdn after 2f: sn struggling* **20/1**

1m 13.73s (0.63) **Going Correction** -0.125s/f (Firm) **11** Ran SP% **114.6**
Speed ratings (Par 93): **90,89,82,82,82 82,80,72,70,48 31**
CSF £26.55 TOTE £6.90: £2.40, £1.20, £2.50; EX 24.00.
Owner H B Hughes **Bred** H B Hughes **Trained** Hambleton, N Yorks

FOCUS
A weak juvenile event which saw the first pair pull clear. The runner-up was back to his best and helps set the standard.

NOTEBOOK
Genethni, winner of a Catterick seller on her debut in July, raced down the middle of the track and dug deep when put under pressure to follow up for a narrow success. She wanted to hang right inside the final 2f, but that was likely down to her racing alone for most of the way and she saw out the extra furlong really well. While she may have beaten little in her two starts to date, plus she is clearly not that straightforward, it is hard to crab an unbeaten horse and she looks worth a crack in nurseries now. (op 7-1)

Atephobia, well backed, appreciated the drop into this class and turned in a bold effort from the front on the stands'-side rail. He was only picked off late on and evidently has one of these within his compass, as he finished well clear of the remainder. (op 10-3)
Elusive Lady(IRE) turned in a more encouraging effort, but simply did not prove that suited by the drop back a furlong (op 10-1 tchd 8-1)
Tommytush(IRE) ran close to his recent level on his first outing in this lower grade and left the definite impression he will be suited by a return to 5f now. (tchd 14-1)
Scientific, down in trip/class, took an age to hit his full stride and by the time he got the hang of things the race was effectively over. It is hard to know what his ideal trip is at present and he is still very much learning his trade.
Duke Of Touraine(IRE), who held an obvious chance on official figures, failed to raise his game for the drop in class and was found out soon after passing the 2f pole. He probably finds this trip too sharp now, however. (op 13-8 tchd 2-1 in places)
Royal Sovereign(IRE) Official explanation: jockey said gelding ran too free to post

5082 WBX.COM 0% COMMISSION ON DAY'S BIG MAIDEN STKS 6f 5y
2:50 (2:51) (Class 5) 3-4-Y-O **£3,238** (£963; £481; £240) **Stalls** Low

Form RPR
2300 **1** **Zamalik (USA)**[12] 4704 4-9-5 65 MickyFenton 11 76
(E J Alston) *mde all: rdn and forged clr fnl f: readily* **6/4**[1]
2 **2** 7 **Alto Vertigo**[9] 4795 4-9-5 0 LeeEnstone 2 55
(P C Haslam) *w ldrs: rdn and edgd rt 2f out: kpt on fnl f: no ch w wnr* **4/1**[2]
6 **3** 2 **Ancient Pride (IRE)**[2] 5036 3-9-0 0 PJMcDonald(3) 8 49
(Miss L A Perratt) *bhd and hung rt: hdwy over 1f out: nrst fin* **50/1**
0 **4** 1 **Van Ruymbeke (IRE)**[116] 1605 3-9-3 0 (t) GregFairley 10 46
(D J Murphy) *t.k.h: chsd ldrs: effrt over 2f out: sn one pce* **7/1**
4040 **5** 4 **Splendidio**[20] 4478 3-8-12 45 PaulMulrennan 7 29
(Mrs Marjorie Fife) *t.k.h: w ldrs tl wknd fr 2f out* **50/1**
-056 **6** ¾ **Golden Topaz (IRE)**[33] 4079 3-8-9 62 AndrewMullen(3) 3 27
(J Howard Johnson) *cl up tl rdn and wknd fr 2f out* **11/2**
0350 **7** 2 **Optical Illusion (USA)**[4] 4971 3-9-3 68 (p) TomEaves 9 26
(I Semple) *bhd: drvn along 1/2-way: nvr on terms* **9/2**[3]
65 **8** ¾ **Bovered (IRE)**[96] 2135 3-8-9 0 PatrickMathers(3) 4 19
(A Berry) *towards rr: drvn 1/2-way: sn btn* **100/1**
0 **9** 3 **Bella Grande**[61] 3202 3-8-12 0 PhillipMakin 5 10
(Garry Moss) *cl up tl rdn and wknd over 2f out* **100/1**
4 **10** 1¾ **Champagne Mindy**[40] 3846 3-8-9 0 AndrewElliott(3) 1 4
(Garry Moss) *s.i.s: a bhd* **33/1**
4-40 **11** 4 **Craig Y Nos**[30] 4178 3-8-12 29 TonyHamilton 6 —
(A Berry) *s.i.s: nvr on terms* **150/1**
1m 12.19s (-0.91) **Going Correction** -0.125s/f (Firm)
WFA 3 from 4yo 2lb 11 Ran SP% **115.6**
Speed ratings (Par 103): **101,91,89,87,82 81,78,77,73,71 66**
CSF £7.30 TOTE £2.50: £1.30, £1.80, £7.80; EX 9.90.
Owner M R Johnson and A Draper **Bred** Darley **Trained** Longton, Lancs
FOCUS
A weak maiden in which the field finished fairly strung out behind the well-backed winner. He did not have much to beat but this was an improved effort.

5083 WBX.COM FREE FOOTBALL SHIRT FOR NEW ACCOUNTS CLAIMING STKS 6f 5y
3:20 (3:20) (Class 6) 3-Y-O+ **£2,388** (£705; £352) **Stalls** Low

Form RPR
4564 **1** **Yorkshire Blue**[3] 4999 8-9-4 74 DanielTudhope 10 76
(J S Goldie) *towards rr: drvn 1/2-way: hdwy centre to ld 1f out: styd on strly* **11/8**[1]
0000 **2** ½ **Guto**[13] 4696 4-9-1 84 AndrewMullen(3) 3 74
(K A Ryan) *prom: effrt and ev ch over 1f out: kpt on fnl f* **4/1**[2]
0201 **3** 1¾ **Razzano (IRE)**[25] 4321 3-8-1 52 AndrewElliott(3) 15 57
(A M Hales) *cl up: led 2f to 1f out: one pce ins fnl f* **16/1**
6045 **4** 5 **Following Flow (USA)**[7] 4891 5-8-8 43 (p) GregFairley 14 44
(R Allan) *bhd: drvn 1/2-way: sme late hdwy: n.d* **100/1**
0220 **5** 1 **Gifted Heir (IRE)**[11] 4735 3-8-11 59 MickyFenton 9 46
(A Bailey) *in tch: effrt over 2f out: wknd over 1f out* **25/1**
0000 **6** ¾ **Chairman Bobby**[3] 4996 9-8-8 45 PaulQuinn 8 39
(D W Barker) *w ldrs tl edgd rt and wknd fr 2f out* **50/1**
-600 **7** 1¾ **Chookie Heiton (IRE)**[16] 4614 9-9-7 85 (p) TomEaves 5 47
(I Semple) *in tch: effrt and edgd rt over 2f out: btn over 1f out* **8/1**
0204 **8** 1 **Regal Raider (IRE)**[12] 4719 4-8-11 58 PhillipMakin 12 34
(I Semple) *led to 2f out: sn rdn and btn* **15/2**
0300 **9** nk **Frimley's Matterry**[9] 4822 7-8-1 48 DanielleMcCreery(7) 13 30
(R E Barr) *towards rr: drvn 1/2-way: sn btn* **50/1**
6000 **10** 1 **Polish Emperor (USA)**[17] 4583 7-8-8 45 (b) TonyHamilton 1 27
(D W Barker) *s.i.s: nvr on terms* **50/1**
530 **11** 1¼ **Brut**[46] 3676 5-9-1 68 (p) PJMcDonald(3) 11 33
(D W Barker) *cl up tl rdn and wknd over 2f out* **6/1**[3]
0-00 **12** shd **Wolf Pack**[19] 4499 5-8-1 33 (t) PaulPickard(7) 2 23
(D A Nolan) *s.i.s: nvr on terms* **200/1**
50-0 **13** 4 **Geordie Dancer (IRE)**[27] 4251 5-8-7 37 (b) PatrickMathers(3) 6 13
(A Berry) *midfield: drvn over 2f out: sn wknd* **100/1**
0000 **14** 3 **Underthemistletoe (IRE)**[30] 4178 5-8-0 44 (v) DuranFentiman(3) 7 —
(R E Barr) *s.i.s: nvr on terms* **100/1**
5000 **15** 14 **Bandos**[10] 4768 7-9-0 43 PaulMulrennan 4 —
(M Smith) *midfield: drvn along 1/2-way: sn wknd* **100/1**
1m 11.94s (-1.16) **Going Correction** -0.125s/f (Firm)
WFA 3 from 4yo+ 2lb 15 Ran SP% **119.3**
Speed ratings (Par 101): **102,101,99,92,91 90,87,86,85,84 82,82,77,73,54**
CSF £6.22 TOTE £2.70: £1.50, £1.80, £3.30; EX 12.30.
Owner Great Northern Partnership 1 **Bred** R T And Mrs Watson **Trained** Uplawmoor, E Renfrews
■ Stewards' Enquiry : Paul Pickard caution: used whip when out of contention
FOCUS
A pretty typical claimer and the form is fair for the class. The first two were both below their best with the third and fourth helping set the standard.

5084 WBX.COM 0% COMMISSION ON DAY'S BIG MATCH H'CAP 1m 65y
3:50 (3:50) (Class 6) (0-60,60) 3-Y-O **£2,266** (£674; £337; £168) **Stalls** High

Form RPR
2000 **1** **Milson's Point (IRE)**[5] 4931 3-8-13 58 JamieMoriarty(3) 4 63
(I Semple) *prom: led over 3f out to over 1f out: rallied fr 1f out to ld wl ins fnl f* **25/1**
0452 **2** nk **Lady Valentino**[8] 4842 3-8-7 49 PaulMulrennan 5 54
(M Dods) *in tch: drvn and outpcd over 2f out: rallied ins fnl f: jst hld* **5/1**[2]
1063 **3** nk **Muncaster Castle (IRE)**[52] 3497 3-8-12 54 SilvestreDeSousa 2 58
(R F Fisher) *cl up: ev ch over 3f out: led over 1f out to wl ins fnl f: no ex* **9/2**[1]
0056 **4** ½ **Beck**[4] 4971 3-8-4 46 PaulQuinn 12 49
(W M Brisbourne) *in tch: hdwy over 2f out: edgd rt over 1f out: ev ch ins fnl f: no ex last 50yds* **12/1**
-030 **5** 1 **Pegasus Prince (USA)**[83] 2538 3-8-8 50 MickyFenton 3 51
(Miss J A Camacho) *hld up on outside: rdn and hung rt over 2f out: kpt on fnl f: nrst fin* **12/1**
0552 **6** nk **Crosby Jemma**[4] 4971 3-8-2 47 AndrewMullen(3) 13 47
(J R Weymes) *hld up: rdn over 2f out: kpt on: nvr rchd ldrs* **9/2**[1]
-060 **7** ½ **Wee Ellie Coburn**[18] 4526 3-8-2 51 DanielleMcCreery(7) 7 50
(M Mullineaux) *bhd: rdn over 3f out: nvr rchd ldrs* **14/1**
4203 **8** 1 **Fistral**[12] 4714 3-8-6 48 (b) GregFairley 8 44
(J Hetherton) *towards rr: drvn over 3f out: n.d* **10/1**
5000 **9** 3 **Stepaside (IRE)**[15] 4642 3-8-12 54 PhillipMakin 10 44
(A D Brown) *towards rr: pushed along over 3f out: nvr on terms* **66/1**
0564 **10** hd **Miss Percy**[11] 4735 3-8-13 55 (p) TonyHamilton 9 44
(R A Fahey) *chsd ldrs tl rdn and wknd over 2f out* **11/2**[3]
2150 **11** 14 **Sophie's Dream**[173] 676 3-9-1 60 AndrewElliott(3) 11 17
(A M Hales) *led to over 3f out: sn rdn and wknd* **25/1**
430- **U** **Stay Active (USA)**[353] 5334 3-9-4 60 TomEaves 6 —
(I Semple) *hld up: checked, sprawled bdly and uns rdr 7f out* **14/1**
1m 48.4s (-0.90) **Going Correction** -0.125s/f (Firm) 12 Ran SP% **115.4**
Speed ratings (Par 99): **99,98,98,97,96 96,96,95,92,91 77,—**
CSF £140.51 CT £543.98 TOTE £30.50: £6.60, £1.70, £2.00; EX 238.60.
Owner D G Savala **Bred** John B O'Connor **Trained** Carluke, S Lanarks
■ Stewards' Enquiry : Paul Quinn six-day ban: used whip with excessive frequency (Sep 14-19)
FOCUS
A moderate handicap, run at a fair pace. The first four were closely covered at the finish and the form seems sound enough.
Milson's Point(IRE) Official explanation: trainer's rep said, regarding apparent improvement in form, that the gelding was better suited by being dropped in.

5085 WBX.COM £25 FREE BET FOR NEW ACCOUNTS H'CAP 5f 4y
4:20 (4:20) (Class 6) (0-65,62) 4-Y-O+ **£2,590** (£770; £385; £192) **Stalls** Low

Form RPR
50 **1** **Throw The Dice**[3] 4996 5-8-2 49 (v) PatrickMathers(3) 5 60
(A Berry) *mde all: rdn and r.o wl fnl f* **9/1**
-000 **2** 1¾ **Jadan (IRE)**[3] 4996 6-8-4 48 AdrianTNicholls 9 53
(E J Alston) *bhd: hdwy whn nt clr run over 1f out to ins fnl f: nt rch wnr* **13/2**[3]
5203 **3** 1¾ **Highland Song (IRE)**[3] 4996 4-8-8 52 PaulMulrennan 4 50
(R F Fisher) *w ldrs: rdn and edgd rt over 1f out: no ex* **9/4**[1]
4663 **4** ¾ **Nusoor (IRE)**[11] 4734 4-9-4 62 (b) TonyHamilton 10 58
(Peter Grayson) *in tch: effrt outside over 2f out: no imp over 1f out* **7/2**[2]
0600 **5** ¾ **Mutayam**[4] 4967 7-8-4 48 oh3 (t) GregFairley 6 41
(D A Nolan) *prom: drvn over 2f out: no ex over 1f out* **33/1**
000 **6** ¾ **The Keep**[33] 4079 5-8-1 48 oh3 (v) DuranFentiman(3) 11 38
(R E Barr) *sn outpcd and drvn on outside: sme late hdwy: nvr on terms* **100/1**
00 **7** hd **Law Maker**[55] 3396 7-8-7 51 (v) MickyFenton 8 41
(A Bailey) *prom tl edgd rt and no ex wl over 1f out* **9/1**
6054 **8** 3 **Bond Becks (IRE)**[3] 4996 7-8-10 54 ow2 PhillipMakin 3 33
(G R Oldroyd) *cl up tl rdn and wknd over 1f out* **7/1**
2000 **9** ½ **Falmassim**[10] 4773 4-8-11 55 (b) TomEaves 7 32
(Miss J A Camacho) *w wnr tl wknd over 1f out* **8/1**
60.06 secs (-1.14) **Going Correction** -0.125s/f (Firm) 9 Ran SP% **113.9**
Speed ratings (Par 101): **104,101,98,97,96 94,94,89,88**
CSF £65.17 CT £177.41 TOTE £10.80: £2.20, £2.60, £1.30; EX 97.40.
Owner E Nisbet **Bred** N E Poole And Paul Trickey **Trained** Cockerham, Lancs
FOCUS
A very weak sprint handicap, with recent form in short supply. The winner bounced back to form and reversed previous course-and-distance running with several rivals.

5086 WBX.COM 0% COMMISSION ON DAY'S BIG H'CAP 1m 3f 16y
4:50 (4:50) (Class 5) (0-75,69) 4-Y-O+ **£4,533** (£1,348; £674; £336) **Stalls** High

Form RPR
5045 **1** **Doctor Scott**[10] 4786 4-9-3 68 GregFairley 6 80
(M Johnston) *prom: rdn over 3f out: led over 2f out: styd on strly to go clr over 1f out* **2/1**[1]
00-0 **2** 6 **Farne Island**[17] 4582 4-8-9 60 DanielTudhope 3 62
(Micky Hammond) *prom: effrt over 2f out: chsd wnr over 1f out: kpt on: nt pce to chal* **8/1**
302 **3** nk **Red Chairman**[10] 4772 5-8-7 63 (p) KellyHarrison(5) 2 64
(R Johnson) *t.k.h: led to over 2f out: kpt on same pce over 1f out* **13/2**
6021 **4** 3½ **Dark Charm (FR)**[12] 4716 8-9-1 69 (p) JamieMoriarty(3) 5 65
(R A Fahey) *bhd: pushed along 1/2-way: kpt on fr 2f out: n.d* **5/1**[3]
0431 **5** 4 **Princess Lavinia**[19] 4517 4-9-2 67 TonyHamilton 8 56
(G Wragg) *chsd ldr: chal 3f out: sn rdn: wknd over 1f out* **3/1**[2]
-064 **6** 6 **Miss Sure Bond (IRE)**[9] 4802 4-8-1 55 oh3 DuranFentiman(3) 4 34
(G R Oldroyd) *hld up: rdn 4f out: n.d* **16/1**
0100 **7** 8 **Ignition**[28] 4219 5-8-8 59 TomEaves 7 24
(W M Brisbourne) *t.k.h: chsd ldrs tl rdn and wknd fr over 2f out* **14/1**
2m 23.67s (-2.59) **Going Correction** -0.125s/f (Firm) 7 Ran SP% **112.0**
Speed ratings (Par 103): **104,99,99,96,93 89,83**
CSF £17.89 CT £85.75 TOTE £3.10: £1.50, £4.70; EX 18.20.
Owner Irene White And Helen Bogie **Bred** The Kingwood Partnership **Trained** Middleham Moor, N Yorks
FOCUS
A modest handicap, run at a sound pace. The winner took full advantage of a lenient mark.

5087 WBX.COM FREE FOOTBALL SHIRT FOR NEW ACCOUNTS AMATEUR RIDERS' H'CAP 1m 5f 9y
5:20 (5:20) (Class 6) (0-65,63) 4-Y-O+ **£2,307** (£709; £354) **Stalls** High

Form RPR
2230 **1** **Rare Coincidence**[21] 4463 6-11-4 63 (p) MrHHaynes(3) 8 75
(R F Fisher) *mde all: rdn and kpt on strly fr 2f out* **8/1**
2062 **2** 4 **Dance Sauvage**[4] 4972 4-10-7 49 MrSDobson 6 55
(C W Thornton) *hld up: pushed along over 3f out: kpt on wl fr 2f out: tk 2nd nr fin: no ch w wnr* **4/1**[3]
-013 **3** ½ **Hi Dancer**[59] 3280 4-11-1 57 MissLEllison 10 62
(P C Haslam) *hld up in tch: effrt over 2f out: no imp over 1f out* **9/4**[2]
140/ **4** shd **Red Opera**[705] 5550 5-10-12 59 MrCWallis(5) 9 64
(D E Pipe) *chsd wnr: drvn 1/2-way: one pce fr 2f out* **2/1**[1]
0000 **5** 1 **The Dunion**[20] 4475 4-10-0 49 oh4 (b[1]) MrGRSmith(7) 3 53
(Miss L A Perratt) *hld up: effrt and hdwy over 2f out: no imp over 1f out* **100/1**

6426 **6** *1* **Andorran (GER)**[8] 4860 4-10-1 **50**............................ MissRLLockie(7) 11 52
(A Bailey) *s.i.s: bhd tl hdwy over 2f out: no ex appr fnl f* **25/1**

0/64 **7** *8* **Named At Dinner**[23] 4380 6-10-7 **49** oh2................(v) MissSBrotherton 4 39
(Miss Lucinda V Russell) *prom tl rdn and wknd over 2f out* **33/1**

-650 **8** *shd* **Front Rank (IRE)**[32] 4096 7-10-3 **52**............................ MissNSayer(7) 13 42
(Mrs Dianne Sayer) *prom tl rdn and wknd fr 3f out* **20/1**

0006 **9** *10* **Twilight Avenger (IRE)**[46] 3679 4-10-7 **49** oh4................ MrsCBartley 2 24
(W M Brisbourne) *bhd: pushed along 4f out: nvr on terms* **100/1**

36/4 **10** *3 1/2* **Prince Among Men**[15] 1888 10-10-4 **53**................ MissJRRichards(7) 1 23
(N G Richards) *bhd: rdn along 4f out: nvr on terms* **33/1**

0000 **11** *hd* **Missouri (USA)**[10] 4772 4-10-2 **49** oh4.............(t) MissAngelaBarnes(5) 7 18
(M A Barnes) *midfield: drvn and wknd over 3f out* **100/1**

504- **12** *1/2* **Lake Wakatipu**[317] 6108 5-10-11 **58**.................... MissMMullineaux(5) 5 27
(M Mullineaux) *dwlt: nvr on terms* **14/1**

5000 **13** *23* **Royal Sailor (IRE)**[3] 4994 5-10-0 **49** oh4..........(p) MrDavidMcMinn(7) 12 —
(J Ryan) *prom tl hung rt and wknd fr 4f out* **100/1**

2m 52.53s (-0.87) **Going Correction** -0.125s/f (Firm) **13** Ran SP% **120.3**
Speed ratings (Par 101): **97,94,94,94,93 92,88,87,81,79 79,79,65**
CSF £38.39 CT £97.28 TOTE £9.50: £2.50, £1.30, £1.50; EX 36.60 Place 6 £ 25.78, Place 5 £ 9.08.

Owner A Kerr **Bred** D R Tucker **Trained** Ulverston, Cumbria

■ Stewards' Enquiry : Mr C Wallis ten-day ban: failed to ride out for third place (Sep 25, Oct 3,16, Nov 8,12,21,27, Dec 3-4,10)
Mr David McMinn caution: used whip when out of contention

FOCUS
A moderate staying handicap, confined to amateur riders, run at an uneven gallop. A career best from the winner, but weakish form, rated at face value through the runner-up.
T/Plt: £98.00 to a £1 stake. Pool: £54,140.85. 403.20 winning tickets. T/Qpdt: £14.10 to a £1 stake. Pool: £3,779.10. 197.90 winning tickets. RY

4959 LINGFIELD (L-H)
Monday, September 3

OFFICIAL GOING: Turf course - good to firm (8.7); all-weather - standard
Turf course: There was a huge bias towards those who raced against the stands'-side rail, although not many of the jockeys seemed to realise this.
Wind: Moderate, against Weather: Fine

5088 HAPPY BIRTHDAY BOB HACKING MAIDEN STKS (DIV I) 7f
1:40 (1:40) (Class 5) 2-Y-O **£2,730** (£806; £403) **Stalls** High

Form RPR

24 **1** **Mujaadel (USA)**[54] 3435 2-9-3 0.. RHills 1 82+
(E A L Dunlop) *rrd s: w ldrs: led over 2f out: in n.d after: comf* **1/3**[1]

2 *2* **Bullet Man (USA)** 2-9-3 0.. DarryllHolland 10 72+
(L M Cumani) *dwlt: rn green but wl in tch: shkn up over 2f out: chsd wnr over 1f out: styd on but no ch* **7/2**[2]

0 **3** *4* **Bathwick Man**[18] 4539 2-9-3 0... JimCrowley 9 62
(B R Millman) *mde most at stdy pce to over 2f out: sn outpcd: kpt on* **33/1**

4 *hd* **Fearless Warrior** 2-9-3 0.. DaneO'Neill 2 61
(J L Dunlop) *t.k.h: trckd ldrs: shkn up and outpcd 2f out: kpt on fr over 1f out* **25/1**

0 **5** *2* **Tobago Bay**[10] 4761 2-9-3 0.. TPO'Shea 6 56
(M R Channon) *w ldr to over 2f out: sn rdn and btn* **20/1**

00 **6** *1 1/4* **Colmar Magic (IRE)**[16] 4602 2-8-12 0........................... RichardSmith 5 48
(R Hannon) *w ldrs to 1/2-way: sn rdn and struggling* **50/1**

04 **7** *1* **Thunder Gorge (USA)**[21] 4454 2-9-3 0.......................... FergusSweeney 4 50
(Mouse Hamilton-Fairley) *plld hrd: cl up tl wknd wl over 1f out* **12/1**[3]

8 *6* **Bute Street** 2-9-3 0.. RobertHavlin 7 35
(R J Hodges) *dwlt: last but in tch tl wknd over 2f out* **33/1**

1m 26.05s (1.84) **Going Correction** -0.10s/f (Good) **8** Ran SP% **121.4**
Speed ratings (Par 95): **85,82,78,77,75 74,73,66**
CSF £1.86 TOTE £1.30: £1.02, £1.40, £9.80; EX 2.60 Trifecta £45.00 Pool: £338.64, 5.34 winning units.

Owner Hamdan Al Maktoum **Bred** L Goichman **Trained** Newmarket, Suffolk

FOCUS
An uncompetitive maiden and the winning time was 1.43 seconds slower than the second division, but Mujaadel set a useful standard on the form of his two previous runs. The first two can do better on the bare form.

NOTEBOOK
Mujaadel(USA) had shown plenty of ability in a couple of decent Newmarket maidens and found this a suitable opportunity to get off the mark, coming clear of his seven rivals without having to be given a hard time. The winning time did not compare favourably with the second division, but he is clearly useful and will have to be worthy of respect in future. (op 2-5 tchd 4-9 in a place)
Bullet Man(USA), an 88,000gns son of sire of the moment Mr Greeley, half-brother to three winners in the US, including one on turf, out of a 1m juvenile winner, made an encouraging debut behind the comfortable winner. He showed real signs of inexperience, and could not pose a threat to the eventual winner, but there was a lot to like about the way he kept on for second. The bare form is probably not that strong, but he is open to plenty of improvement. (op 10-3 tchd 3-1)
Bathwick Man had the benefit of the favoured stands' rail to run against and is possibly a touch flattered, but was still a big improvement on the form he showed when down the field on his debut at Salisbury. He should find his level once handicapped. (op 50-1)
Fearless Warrior, a gelded son of Erhaab, brother to 1m6f winner Queen Of Iceni, half-brother to several winners, notably top-class stayer Give Notice, out of a 1m winner at two and three, showed ability on his racecourse debut. He should come into his own over much further in handicaps next year. (op 33-1)
Tobago Bay improved on the form he showed when failing to beat a rival on his debut at Newbury. (op 33-1)
Thunder Gorge(USA) was far too keen on this step up in trip and was below the form of his two previous starts. Official explanation: jockey said colt ran too free (op 14-1)

5089 PLAY GOLF AT LINGFIELD PARK NURSERY 6f
2:10 (2:11) (Class 6) (0-65,64) 2-Y-O **£3,238** (£963; £481; £240) **Stalls** High

Form RPR

2545 **1** **Carrickmacross (IRE)**[24] 4349 2-9-7 **64**....................... RichardMullen 7 67
(E S McMahon) *a w ldrs: drvn and upsides fnl f: led nr fin* **7/1**[3]

0365 **2** *shd* **Richardthesecond (IRE)**[10] 4762 2-9-5 **62**.................. MartinDwyer 11 65
(R M Beckett) *w ldrs: narrow advantage over 1f out: hdd nr fin: styd on* **11/2**[1]

5001 **3** *1 1/2* **Thomas Malory (IRE)**[4] 4970 2-8-11 **59** 6ex................ LukeMorris(5) 17 62+
(Miss V Haigh) *racd against nrside rail: hld up early: prog 2f out: clsng whn nt clr run and swtchd lft 1f out: styd on* **7/1**[3]

0500 **4** *1 1/4* **Orpen's Art (IRE)**[16] 4605 2-8-10 **53**........................ StephenDonohoe 15 47
(N A Callaghan) *racd against nrside rail: led or disp to jst over 1f out: edgd lft and fdd* **11/1**

0012 **5** *hd* **Llab Nala**[23] 4405 2-9-1 **58**.. TPO'Shea 18 52+
(M R Channon) *racd against nrside rail: sn in rr: outpcd over 2f out: hanging but drvn and styd on wl fnl f* **12/1**

3400 **6** *nk* **Pretty Bonnie**[22] 4428 2-9-0 **57**... JamesDoyle 10 50
(J G Portman) *trckd ldrs: stl cl up over 1f out: one pce u.p after* **33/1**

5400 **7** *1 3/4* **New Balls Please (IRE)**[51] 3524 2-9-0 **57**...............(p) FergusSweeney 1 45
(P M Phelan) *racd on outer: w ldrs to jst over 1f out: wknd* **66/1**

015 **8** *1* **Smokeyourpipe (IRE)**[3] 5015 2-8-11 **57**...........(v) RichardKingscote(3) 6 42
(C Tinkler) *w ldrs over 2f: sn lost pl: rdn wl over 2f out: kpt on same pce* **20/1**

0332 **9** *nk* **Culzean Bay**[19] 4512 2-8-5 **51**.. NeilChalmers(3) 9 35
(Miss Diana Weeden) *dwlt: in tch: losing pl whn hmpd over 1f out: swtchd to nrside rail and styd on fnl f* **33/1**

6040 **10** *shd* **Don't Tell Anna (IRE)**[21] 4453 2-8-13 **61**.................. HaddenFrost(5) 2 45
(R Hannon) *racd on outer: nvr on terms w ldrs: no real prog fnl 2f* **25/1**

400 **11** *1/2* **Whiskey Creek**[68] 2984 2-9-3 **60**...................................... SteveDrowne 14 42
(Miss Tor Sturgis) *pushed along in last pair bef 1/2-way: nvr on terms: plugged on* **8/1**

000 **12** *shd* **Tiger's Rocket (IRE)**[57] 3348 2-9-6 **63**................................ RyanMoore 5 45
(R Hannon) *in tch towards rr: rdn over 2f out: no prog* **16/1**

000 **13** *1 3/4* **Una Auroraborealis**[10] 4776 2-8-9 **52**.......................... TGMcLaughlin 3 28
(J Ryan) *racd on outer: chsd ldrs: u.p over 2f out: sn btn* **50/1**

6504 **14** *1* **Leading Edge (IRE)**[7] 4903 2-9-7 **64**............................ DarryllHolland 16 37
(M R Channon) *hld up in rr: nt clr run repeatedly fr over 2f out: nvr nr ldrs* **13/2**[2]

006 **15** *1/2* **Mandarinka**[16] 4593 2-9-5 **62**.. JimCrowley 8 34
(P Winkworth) *trckd ldrs: rdn and stl cl up over 2f out: wknd over 1f out* **10/1**

065 **16** *1* **Eye Catching**[77] 2717 2-9-6 **63**.. JohnEgan 12 32
(J R Jenkins) *a in rr: rdn and no prog wl over 2f out* **12/1**

0304 **17** *2* **Kintyre Lass (IRE)**[26] 4265 2-8-13 **56**.......................... StephenCarson 13 19
(B R Millman) *chsd ldrs 2f: struggling in rr fr 1/2-way* **14/1**

1m 11.93s (0.26) **Going Correction** -0.10s/f (Good) **17** Ran SP% **128.1**
Speed ratings (Par 93): **94,93,91,90,89 89,87,85,85,85 84,84,82,80,80 78,76**
CSF £44.29 CT £302.58 TOTE £8.90: £2.40, £1.40, £2.20, £4.00; EX 48.50 TRIFECTA Not won..

Owner J C Fretwell **Bred** Vincent Dunne **Trained** Lichfield, Staffs

FOCUS
Just a modest nursery and the form looks nothing to get excited about. Five of the first six home came from a double-figure stall and those who raced close to the stands' rail were at an advantage.

NOTEBOOK
Carrickmacross(IRE) had not really had things go his way lately, including in a first-time visor over 5f at Haydock on his previous start, but he was given a positive ride stepped back up to 6f and battled on well to gain his first success at the sixth attempt, proving himself a better horse without the headgear. This was a good effort considering he came from a single-figure stall, but a rise in the weights will force him up in grade and that should be enough to stop him following up. (op 8-1)
Richardthesecond(IRE) did not run badly in a better nursery than this at Newbury on his previous start and he only just failed off a 3lb lower mark. He could pick up a similar event. (tchd 5-1)
Thomas Malory(IRE), who dead-heated in a seller at Musselburgh on his previous start, had to be switched out wide with his effort, but he was not unlucky.
Orpen's Art(IRE), without the blinkers this time, raced against the favoured stands' rail and can have no excuses. (tchd 12-1)
Llab Nala had the benefit of the rail to run against, but he found himself further back than was ideal and was denied a clear run when trying to stay on. (tchd 10-1)
Culzean Bay Official explanation: jockey said filly suffered interference in running
Don't Tell Anna(IRE) ◆ raced ridiculously wide throughout, even allowing for her low draw, and considering how much of an advantage it was to race close to the stands' rail, she did well to finish so close. Quite an attractive sort, she has yet to fulfil her potential, but on the evidence of this performance she is not one to give up on just yet. (op 20-1)
Leading Edge(IRE) was denied a clear run when trying to stay on and is better than she showed. Official explanation: jockey said filly was denied a clear run (op 7-1 tchd 6-1)
Eye Catching Official explanation: jockey said filly was unsuited by the good to firm ground

5090 LINGFIELD PARK FOR WEDDINGS H'CAP 6f
2:40 (2:42) (Class 6) (0-50,50) 3-Y-0+ **£2,730** (£806; £403) **Stalls** High

Form RPR

0533 **1** **Viewforth**[8] 4857 9-9-0 **50**...(b) RyanMoore 18 63
(M A Buckley) *racd against nr side rail: mde all and sn clr: drvn over 1f out: unchal* **10/3**[2]

3050 **2** *3* **Inscribed (IRE)**[35] 4029 4-8-11 **47**................................ TGMcLaughlin 11 51
(G A Huffer) *prom in chsng gp: wnt 2nd 2f out: hrd rdn and styd on: no ch w wnr* **20/1**

-061 **3** *1 3/4* **Contented (IRE)**[8] 4853 5-8-8 **49**...................................(p) SCreighton(5) 9 48
(Mrs L C Jewell) *cl up in chsng gp: effrt 2f out: styd on fr over 1f out: no ch w wnr* **7/4**[1]

0324 **4** *nk* **Willofcourse**[8] 4853 6-8-7 **50**.. AmyScott(7) 5 48
(H Candy) *racd on outer: prom in chsng gp: nudged along and kpt on steadily: no threat to wnr* **13/2**[3]

005 **5** *shd* **Half A Tsar (IRE)**[30] 4182 3-8-7 **50**................................ TolleyDean(5) 17 48
(Mark Gillard) *racd towards nr side: prom in chsng gp: chsd wnr over 3f out to 2f out: fdd fnl f* **33/1**

6U01 **6** *hd* **Double Valentine**[11] 4741 4-8-5 **48**.............................. HarryPoulton(7) 7 45
(R Ingram) *settled in rr and off the pce: sme prog 2f out: rdn and styd on fr over 1f out: nrst fin* **14/1**

6000 **7** *hd* **Enjoy The Buzz**[16] 4594 8-8-11 **47**........................(p) StephenDonohoe 15 43
(J M Bradley) *s.v.s: bhd against nr side rail tl styd on fr 2f out: clsng on plcd horses nr fin* **20/1**

005 **8** *1 1/2* **Riolo (IRE)**[13] 4688 5-8-8 **49**...................................(b) KevinGhunowa(5) 10 41
(K F Clutterbuck) *chsd ldrs: hrd rdn and no prog over 2f out* **16/1**

6030 **9** *1 1/2* **Blue Knight (IRE)**[13] 4685 8-9-0 **50**................................(p) AmirQuinn 8 37
(P Howling) *struggling in rr after 2f: nvr a factor: kpt on fnl f* **16/1**

5-00 **10** *3/4* **Royal Senga**[90] 2334 4-8-12 **48**.. FergusSweeney 3 33
(C A Horgan) *dwlt: rcvrd to chse ldrs on outer: no prog over 1f out: fdd* **33/1**

0000 **11** *1 1/2* **Shortcake**[25] 4324 3-8-11 **49** ow1.. DaneO'Neill 13 30
(M R Hoad) *nvr on terms w ldrs: struggling towards rr over 2f out* **50/1**

0U45 **12** *1/2* **Mister Elegant**[8] 4853 5-8-6 **49**...................................... JamieHamblett(7) 1 28
(J L Spearing) *racd on outer: nvr quite on terms w ldrs: wknd over 1f out* **10/1**

000- **13** *1/2* **Aboyne (IRE)**[308] 6033 4-8-4 **47**....................................... MCGeran(7) 12 25
(K F Clutterbuck) *struggling in rr by 1/2-way: sn no ch* **50/1**

0500 **14** *hd* **Princely Vale (IRE)**[20] 4471 5-8-4 **47**...........................(p) JackDean(7) 4 24
(W G M Turner) *racd on outer: nvr on terms struggling over 2f out* **25/1**

040 **15** 2 1/2 **Batchworth Fleur**[8] 4853 4-9-0 **50** StephenCarson 14 20
(E A Wheeler) *racd towards nr side: chsd wnr to over 3f out: wknd over 2f out* **14/1**

6040 **16** 3/4 **Flower Of Cork (IRE)**[15] 4635 3-8-9 **47** (p) JamesDoyle 6 14
(I A Wood) *nvr btr than midfield: wknd 2f out* **33/1**

4000 **17** 1/2 **Must Be Keen**[26] 4296 8-8-7 **46** (v) NeilChalmers(3) 2 12
(Miss Diana Weeden) *s.s: in tch in rr to over 2f out: wknd* **50/1**

1m 11.06s (-0.61) **Going Correction** -0.10s/f (Good) 17 Ran SP% **135.0**
WFA 3 from 4yo+ 2lb
Speed ratings (Par 101): **100,96,93,93,93 92,92,90,88,87 85,84,84,84,80 79,79**
CSF £81.00 CT £167.95 TOTE £3.10: £1.20, £6.10, £1.40, £1.70; EX 100.00 TRIFECTA Not won..
Owner Chris Handley **Bred** Britton House Stud And R J Gorringe **Trained** Castle Bytham, Lincs
■ Cayman Breeze was withdrawn (12/1, arrived at start without declared cheekpieces). R4 applies, deduct 5p in the £.

FOCUS
A moderate sprint handicap and, with the winner at a huge advantage racing against the stands' rail, the form wants treating with caution. Decent form for the grade.
Blue Knight(IRE) Official explanation: jockey said gelding never travelled
Aboyne(IRE) Official explanation: jockey said gelding was denied a clear run
Batchworth Fleur Official explanation: trainer said filly bled from the nose

5091 HAPPY BIRTHDAY BOB HACKING MAIDEN STKS (DIV II) 7f
3:10 (3:11) (Class 5) 2-Y-O **£2,730** (£806; £403) **Stalls** High

Form RPR

03 **1** **Hustle (IRE)**[29] 4201 2-9-3 0 RyanMoore 1 74+
(R Hannon) *mde virtually all and sn crossed to nrside rail: rdn and jnd 2f out: styd on wl fr over 1f out* **6/4**[1]

6 **2** 1 **Hamalka (IRE)**[47] 3643 2-8-12 0 MichaelHills 5 66+
(B W Hills) *cl up but nt clr run twice bef 1/2-way: plld out and styd on wl to go 2nd ins fnl f: no real ch w wnr* **7/1**[2]

3 1 1/4 **Sea Admiral** 2-9-0 0 RichardKingscote(3) 6 68+
(R Charlton) *hld up in tch: outpcd over 2f out: pushed along and styd on steadily fnl f: gng on at fin* **16/1**[3]

4 3/4 **Tasdeer (USA)** 2-9-3 0 RHills 9 66
(M A Jarvis) *cl up: jnd wnr gng strly over 2f out: rn green and hanging lft after: btn over 1f out: fdd and lost 2 pls ins fnl f* **6/4**[1]

00 **5** 3/4 **Sabre Light**[7] 4883 2-8-10 0 JemmaMarshall(7) 7 64
(G L Moore) *hld up in tch: chsd clr ldng pair over 2f out: pushed along and no imp: one pce* **40/1**

6 1 1/4 **Leitmotif (USA)** 2-9-3 0 J-PGuillambert 10 61+
(J L Dunlop) *hld up in rr: shkn up over 2f out: kpt on same pce fr over 1f out* **20/1**

7 1/2 **Rosentraub** 2-9-3 0 DaneO'Neill 8 60
(H J L Dunlop) *dwlt: hld up in tch: chsd ldng trio over 2f out: pushed along and fdd fnl f* **40/1**

0 **8** 2 1/2 **Little Evie**[10] 4756 2-8-12 0 RobertHavlin 3 48
(R J Hodges) *prom: lost pl and rdn over 2f out: sn btn* **100/1**

9 8 **Beneath The Trees (USA)** 2-9-3 0 MartinDwyer 2 32
(J A Osborne) *dwlt: racd on outer: t.k.h and hld up in tch: wknd wl over 2f out* **20/1**

1m 24.62s (0.41) **Going Correction** -0.10s/f (Good) 9 Ran SP% **113.8**
Speed ratings (Par 95): **93,91,90,89,88 87,86,83,74**
CSF £12.46 TOTE £2.50: £1.10, £1.80, £3.20; EX 11.00 Trifecta £54.20 Pool: £518.39, 6.79 winning units.
Owner Highclere Thoroughbred Racing (Tamarisk) **Bred** Gigginstown House Stud **Trained** East Everleigh, Wilts
■ Stewards' Enquiry : Ryan Moore three-day ban: careless riding (Sep 14,16,17)

FOCUS
Just an ordinary maiden and the winning time was modest, despite being 1.43 seconds quicker than the first division. The principals should prove better than the bare form.

NOTEBOOK
Hustle(IRE) improved on the form he showed when third at Ascot on his previous start, although the bare form wants treating with caution as he was the only horse to race tight against the favoured stands' rail. It was quite clear in the previous race, won by Viewforth, that the rail was the place to be, but Ryan Moore was the only jockey who seemed to have noticed and he was able to amble over to the stands' side, despite being drawn lowest of all, putting his colleagues to shame. (op 13-8 tchd 11-8, 7-4 in places)
Hamalka(IRE) ◆ confirmed the promise she showed on her debut at Kempton and may well have won under a better ride. She broke well enough, but soon gave up pole position to the eventual winner and ended up racing keenly in that one's slipstream. She then lost her position again when switched left with her challenge and was left with plenty to do. Despite all that, she stuck on well without being given too hard a time and was closing the gap on Hustle, who was racing on quicker ground. (op 5-1)
Sea Admiral, a 60,000gns gelded son of Sinndar, half-brother to Summer Of Love, who was placed over 1m1f-1m4f, out of a mare who was placed over 1m4f, made a satisfactory debut and is open to a fair amount of improvement. (op 20-1)
Tasdeer(USA), a Rahy colt, who is closely related to among others high-class dual 1m2f winner Najah, out of Irish 1000 Guineas winner Mehthaaf, has been given an entry in the Royal Lodge. He looked the most likely winner when travelling strongly into the final couple of furlongs, but he hung when first coming under pressure and failed to pick up. (tchd 15-8, 2-1 in a place)
Sabre Light ran a respectable race and will have more options now he is qualified for a handicap mark. (op 33-1)

5092 LINGFIELDPARK.CO.UK H'CAP 7f
3:40 (3:40) (Class 4) (0-85,83) 3-Y-O **£5,181** (£1,541; £770; £384) **Stalls** High

Form RPR

2005 **1** **Captain Jacksparra (IRE)**[37] 3944 3-9-3 **82** DarryllHolland 5 91
(K A Ryan) *taken down early: sn led and racd against nrside rail: edgd lft and hrd pressed over 1f out: kpt on wl u.p* **7/2**[2]

0014 **2** 1 1/4 **Nadawat (USA)**[17] 4589 3-9-3 **82** RHills 3 88
(J L Dunlop) *sn trckd wnr: rdn to chal over 1f out: nt qckn and a jst hld fnl f* **2/1**[1]

5-00 **3** 2 **Abunai**[16] 4607 3-9-0 **79** SteveDrowne 6 79
(R Charlton) *hld up in last: prog to chse ldng pair 2f out: kpt on same pce and no imp after* **5/1**[3]

4010 **4** hd **Buckie Massa**[17] 4574 3-8-12 **77** RyanMoore 8 77
(S Kirk) *settled in last pair: rdn over 2f out: styd on fr over 1f out: nvr able to chal* **8/1**

4400 **5** 3 **Roodolph**[17] 4574 3-8-9 **74** (t) StephenCarson 4 66
(Eve Johnson Houghton) *trckd ldrs: rdn and no rspnse over 2f out: wl btn over 1f out* **10/1**

0310 **6** 3 **Satyricon**[30] 4170 3-8-6 **76** (b) NicolPolli(5) 1 59
(M Botti) *hld up bhd ldrs: n.m.r 3f out: wknd over 1f out* **12/1**

6035 **7** 8 **Averticus**[88] 2395 3-8-11 **76** MichaelHills 7 38
(B W Hills) *prom tl wknd rapidly 2f out: eased: sddle slipped* **9/1**

2-30 **8** 4 **Baylini**[30] 4170 3-9-4 **83** JamesDoyle 2 34
(Ms J S Doyle) *racd on outer: chsd ldrs: rdn 1/2-way: sn wknd rapidly: t.o* **20/1**

1m 22.05s (-2.16) **Going Correction** -0.10s/f (Good) 8 Ran SP% **114.9**
Speed ratings (Par 103): **108,106,104,104,100 97,88,83**
CSF £10.99 CT £33.73 TOTE £3.60: £1.20, £1.20, £2.10; EX 9.90 Trifecta £33.60 Pool: £595.04, 12.55 winning units.
Owner J Duddy,B McDonald,A Heeney,M McMenamin **Bred** Quay Bloodstock **Trained** Hambleton, N Yorks

FOCUS
This was run at a decent pace and the final time was very creditable for a race of its type. Despite that it suited those that raced handily and it proved very hard for those trying to come from off the pace. The form is rated through the second.
Averticus Official explanation: jockey said saddle slipped

5093 ARENALEISUREPLC.COM H'CAP 1m 4f (P)
4:10 (4:10) (Class 5) (0-70,69) 3-Y-O+ **£3,238** (£963; £481; £240) **Stalls** Low

Form RPR

3230 **1** **Apache Fort**[17] 4576 4-9-0 **60** NickyMackay 6 70
(T Keddy) *trckd ldrs: effrt 2f out: rdn to ld jst over 1f out: styd on wl and in command fnl f* **11/4**[2]

0446 **2** 1 1/4 **Amwell Brave**[38] 3912 6-9-1 **61** JohnEgan 2 69
(J R Jenkins) *hld up in last pair: effrt over 2f out: drvn and styd on to take 2nd last 75yds: nvr able to chal* **12/1**

4002 **3** 3/4 **Ross Moor**[16] 4609 5-9-9 **69** JamesDoyle 5 76
(Mike Murphy) *trckd ldr 2f: styd cl up: rdn and effrt whn hmpd over 1f out: styd on again to take 3rd last stride* **5/1**[3]

0436 **4** hd **Trifti**[6] 4915 6-9-1 **66** PatrickHills(5) 4 72
(C A Cyzer) *hld up: prog and prom 5f out: rdn to ld 2f out: hdd jst over 1f out: wknd last 100yds* **9/1**

2150 **5** 1 1/2 **Watchmaker**[60] 3249 4-9-5 **65** FergusSweeney 1 69
(Miss Tor Sturgis) *hld up in rr: effrt on inner 2f out: no real imp on ldrs fr over 1f out* **12/1**

4 **6** 1 1/4 **Kerayasi (FR)**[18] 4544 5-9-4 **64** RyanMoore 8 66
(G L Moore) *dwlt: trckd ldr after 2f: rdn to chal and upsides 2f out: fdd fnl f* **9/4**[1]

2510 **7** 1 3/4 **Pothos Way (GR)**[21] 4458 4-9-4 **64** JimCrowley 7 63
(P R Chamings) *led to 2f out: wknd fnl f* **15/2**

-300 **8** 13 **King's Spear (IRE)**[160] 805 4-9-2 **62** DaneO'Neill 3 40
(Miss J R Tooth) *in tch: rdn over 3f out: wknd over 2f out: t.o* **40/1**

2m 34.15s (-0.24) **Going Correction** -0.20s/f (Stan) 8 Ran SP% **113.7**
Speed ratings (Par 103): **92,91,90,90,89 88,87,78**
CSF £34.69 CT £156.15 TOTE £3.80: £1.10, £2.00, £1.50; EX 37.90 Trifecta £248.20 Pool: £552.55, 1.58 winning units.
Owner Andrew Duffield **Bred** Juddmonte Farms Ltd **Trained** Newmarket, Suffolk

FOCUS
They went a very steady early pace in this and things did not quicken up until around half a mile from home. As a result the winning time was moderate for a race of its class. The form appears pretty solid.

5094 LINGFIELD PARK FOR EXHIBITIONS H'CAP 1m (P)
4:40 (4:40) (Class 6) (0-55,55) 3-Y-O+ **£2,730** (£806; £403) **Stalls** High

Form RPR

3015 **1** **Blue Quiver (IRE)**[54] 3419 7-9-4 **55** JimCrowley 3 65
(C A Horgan) *dwlt: sn chsd ldrs: drvn and effrt 2f out: wnt 2nd ins fnl f: styd on to ld last strides* **8/1**

0404 **2** nk **King After**[23] 4394 5-9-2 **53** (v) DaneO'Neill 2 62
(J R Best) *trckd ldng pair: effrt to ld wl over 1f out and kicked on: worn down last strides* **5/1**[2]

5400 **3** 1 **Greenmeadow**[25] 4327 5-9-4 **55** RyanMoore 8 62
(S Kirk) *hld up in rr: pushed along over 4f out: nt clr run over 2f out: drvn and styd on wl fr over 1f out: gaining on ldng pair fin* **15/2**

4060 **4** 1/2 **Roman Boy (ARG)**[190] 556 8-8-10 **52** TolleyDean(5) 11 58
(Stef Liddiard) *hld up in last trio: effrt on outer over 2f out: drvn and styd on fr over 1f out: nrst fin* **10/1**

6002 **5** 2 1/2 **Briery Blaze**[11] 4736 4-9-1 **52** TGMcLaughlin 7 52
(J W Unett) *t.k.h early: hld up in midfield: outpcd 3f out: plugged on fr over 1f out: n.d* **16/1**

0-05 **6** hd **Terminate (GER)**[14] 4667 5-9-1 **52** StephenDonohoe 12 52
(N A Callaghan) *dwlt: hld up in last trio: outpcd wl over 2f out: rdn and kpt on fr over 1f out: no ch* **8/1**

0000 **7** 3/4 **Golden Square**[7] 4880 5-9-1 **52** (b) JohnEgan 5 50
(A W Carroll) *pressed ldr: rdn to ld briefly 2f out: wknd and eased fnl f* **28/1**

5100 **8** 1 1/4 **Tipsy Lad**[12] 4294 5-9-2 **53** (t) DarryllHolland 10 48
(D J S Ffrench Davis) *trckd ldng trio: rdn 3f out: btn 2f out: fdd* **20/1**

2603 **9** 4 **Milton's Keen**[7] 4879 4-8-13 **55** LukeMorris(5) 6 41
(M Salaman) *s.i.s: plld hrd in midfield early: pushed along in rr sn after 1/2-way: n.d* **6/1**[3]

3064 **10** hd **Exotic Venture**[35] 4023 4-9-2 **53** MartinDwyer 9 38
(R M Beckett) *hld up in last trio: u.p and struggling over 3f out* **8/1**

2000 **11** nk **Charlie Bear**[77] 2722 6-9-1 **52** AdrianMcCarthy 4 37
(Miss Z C Davison) *led to 2f out: wknd rapidly* **25/1**

6024 **12** 2 **Postmaster**[23] 4395 5-9-4 **55** (v) RobertHavlin 1 35
(R Ingram) *trckd ldrs on inner: rdn and losing pl whn n.m.r over 2f out: nt run on* **9/2**[1]

1m 37.51s (-1.92) **Going Correction** -0.20s/f (Stan) 12 Ran SP% **121.3**
Speed ratings (Par 101): **101,100,99,99,96 96,95,94,90,90 90,88**
CSF £47.71 CT £325.00 TOTE £7.30: £2.40, £2.20, £4.00; EX 50.60 Trifecta £277.50 Part won. Pool: £390.91, 0.10 winning units..
Owner C A Horgan **Bred** Mrs B Sumner **Trained** Uffcott, Wilts

FOCUS
A modest handicap, though competitive enough and the pace was solid. Sound form.
Milton's Keen Official explanation: jockey said gelding did not handle the kickback
Postmaster Official explanation: trainer had no explanation for the poor form shown

5095 HOTEL ON IT'S WAY HERE CLASSIFIED STKS 1m 2f (P)
5:10 (5:10) (Class 6) 3-Y-O+ **£2,047** (£604; £302) **Stalls** Low

Form RPR

0035 **1** **Picky**[11] 4742 3-8-12 51 (v) FergusSweeney 5 62
(C Tinkler) *trckd ldrs: rdn and prog to chal wl over 1f out: led ins fnl f: drvn out* **13/2**

0000 **2** 1 1/4 **Almahaza (IRE)**[9] 4809 3-8-12 50 (b) JimCrowley 4 60
(Mrs A J Perrett) *trckd ldng pair: drvn and effrt to ld jst over 2f out: sn pressed: hdd ins fnl f: wknd nr fin* **14/1**

0604 **3** 1¼ **Polyquest (IRE)**[11] 4742 3-8-12 54 NickyMackay 1 57
(G A Butler) *hld up in midfield: prog to chse ldrs over 1f out but outpcd: kpt on same pce* **7/2**[2]

6-30 **4** 1 **Papradon**[65] 3082 3-8-12 53 DaneO'Neill 13 55
(J R Best) *hld up towards rr: prog on outer 3f out: chsng ldrs but outpcd over 1f out: kpt on* **7/1**

0000 **5** 2 **Beckenham's Secret**[10] 4760 3-8-12 50 DarryllHolland 14 51
(B R Millman) *stdd s: hld up in last: effrt on wd outside 3f out: v wd bnd 2f out: no ch after: plugged on* **14/1**

6 ¾ **Matarazzo (IRE)**[72] 5-9-5 55 RyanMoore 2 50
(G L Moore) *led for 1f: chsd ldr to over 2f out: sn btn: wknd fnl f* **11/4**[1]

00-0 **7** 1½ **Cosimo Primo**[107] 1839 3-8-9 49 TravisBlock(3) 7 47
(J A Geake) *s.i.s: hld up in rr: effrt on outer 3f out: nt pce to make prog over 2f out: plugged on fnl f* **33/1**

060 **8** ¾ **Holyfield Warrior (IRE)**[26] 4292 3-8-12 55 JamesDoyle 11 45
(I A Wood) *t.k.h: hld up in rr: effrt on outer 3f out: lost pl bef 2f out: n.d after* **50/1**

5603 **9** 2 **Law Of The Land (IRE)**[10] 4763 3-8-12 52 RichardMullen 8 41
(W R Muir) *t.k.h: hld up in rr: effrt 3f out: no prog sn after: no ch whn hmpd over 1f out* **6/1**[3]

0000 **10** ¾ **Time For Change (IRE)**[11] 4742 3-8-12 54 (p) SteveDrowne 12 40
(P G Murphy) *hld up but sn in midfield: lost pl on inner over 2f out: wknd tamely* **14/1**

-604 **11** 6 **Mirko**[18] 4530 3-8-12 54 (t) RobertHavlin 6 28
(B R Millman) *t.k.h: led after 1f: clr 1/2-way: hdd & wknd rapidly jst over 2f out* **16/1**

2m 7.22s (-0.57) **Going Correction** -0.20s/f (Stan)
WFA 3 from 4yo+ 7lb **11** Ran SP% **119.8**
Speed ratings (Par 101): **94,93,92,91,89 89,87,87,85,85 80**
CSF £95.47 TOTE £9.30: £2.30, £4.00, £1.80; EX 160.40 TRIFECTA Not won. Place 6 £ 10.70, Place 5 £ 9.62.
Owner Colin Tinkler **Bred** T C Ellis **Trained** Compton, Berks

FOCUS
A poor contest and although the early pace looked decent, the final winning time was modest. Dubious form, with little recent form to go on.
Beckenham's Secret Official explanation: jockey said gelding hung left and ran too free
Holyfield Warrior(IRE) Official explanation: jockey said gelding resented being crowded
T/Jkpt: £4,182.90 to a £1 stake. Pool: £55,968.75. 9.50 winning tickets. T/Plt: £5.00 to a £1 stake. Pool: £61,554.45. 8,826.10 winning tickets. T/Qpdt: £2.50 to a £1 stake. Pool: £3,022.20. 887.70 winning tickets.

5015 WOLVERHAMPTON (A.W) (L-H)

Monday, September 3

OFFICIAL GOING: Standard
Wind: Light across Weather: Fine

5096 LADBROKES YOUR BEST BET NURSERY 5f 20y(P)
2:30 (2:31) (Class 6) (0-65,65) 2-Y-0 **£2,388** (£705; £352) **Stalls** Low

Form RPR

001 **1** **Fabuleux Cherie**[9] 4824 2-8-13 **57** RichardHughes 6 64
(W R Muir) *w ldr: rdn 2f out: led wl ins fnl f: r.o* **8/1**[2]

5414 **2** ¾ **Choisette**[17] 4560 2-9-7 **65** RoystonFfrench 1 69
(B Smart) *led: rdn wl over 1f out: hdd and nt qckn wl ins fnl f* **5/2**[1]

1055 **3** 1¾ **Weet A Surprise**[30] 4175 2-9-7 **65** LPKeniry 3 63
(R Hollinshead) *chsd ldrs: rdn wl over 1f out: kpt on same pce fnl f* **10/1**

006 **4** 3 **Maccabeus**[16] 4604 2-9-1 **62** JerryO'Dwyer(3) 2 49
(P J O'Gorman) *t.k.h: sn in tch: rdn 2f out: wknd ins fnl f* **17/2**[3]

02 **5** 1 **Mister Beano (IRE)**[60] 3246 2-9-2 **60** TedDurcan 9 44
(V Smith) *towards rr: rdn over 3f out: hdwy on ins wl over 1f out: nvr trbld ldrs* **8/1**[2]

400 **6** 1½ **Erin Thomas (IRE)**[35] 4026 2-8-13 **57** (p) TPQueally 10 35
(M G Quinlan) *mid-div: rdn over 2f out: no hdwy* **66/1**

060 **7** shd **Flying Indian**[11] 4737 2-9-6 **64** SebSanders 12 42
(A M Balding) *towards rr: rdn and c wd ent st: sme late hdwy* **8/1**[2]

0656 **8** 1¼ **Biased Opinion (IRE)**[14] 4669 2-9-3 **61** (v[1]) FrancisNorton 13 34
(H J L Dunlop) *prom: hung lft fr over 2f out: wknd wl over 1f out* **11/1**

6221 **9** 1 **Shepherds Warning (IRE)**[114] 1674 2-9-1 **59** ChrisCatlin 11 29
(N J Vaughan) *a bhd* **12/1**

600 **10** 1 **Diamond Soles (IRE)**[10] 4755 2-8-11 **55** (b[1]) KDarley 4 21
(B J Meehan) *a bhd* **22/1**

0640 **11** ¾ **Our Kally**[33] 4065 2-9-0 **58** HayleyTurner 5 21
(M D I Usher) *s.i.s: rdn over 3f out: a bhd* **16/1**

200 **12** 1¾ **Vixens Daughter**[21] 4454 2-8-9 **53** DaleGibson 8 10
(R T Phillips) *prom tl wknd over 2f out* **16/1**

62.15 secs (-0.67) **Going Correction** -0.125s/f (Stan) **12** Ran SP% **115.2**
Speed ratings (Par 93): **100,98,96,91,89 87,87,85,83,81 80,77**
CSF £27.29 CT £207.75 TOTE £10.00: £2.50, £1.40, £2.80; EX 31.50.
Owner David & Gwyn Joseph **Bred** J K Beckitt And Son **Trained** Lambourn, Berks

FOCUS
A decent winning time for this tightly-knit low-grade nursery. Pretty good form for the grade, with the winner progressing.

NOTEBOOK
Fabuleux Cherie justified the decision to retain her for 7,400gns after she won a Windsor seller last time. She seems to be going the right way. (op 11-2)
Choisette appeared to appreciate a return to the minimum trip but could not quite hold the winner. (op 3-1)
Weet A Surprise seems worth another try at 6f. (op 14-1)
Maccabeus eventually paid the penalty for racing too freely on this drop back from six. (op 12-1)
Mister Beano(IRE) was having his first run for new connections and will appreciate a return to six. (op 12-1)
Biased Opinion(IRE) Official explanation: jockey said colt hung left-handed
Diamond Soles(IRE) Official explanation: jockey said filly ran too freely

5097 LADBROKES IN THE COMMUNITY CHARITABLE TRUST MAIDEN AUCTION STKS 5f 216y(P)
3:00 (3:01) (Class 5) 2-Y-0 **£2,914** (£867; £433; £216) **Stalls** Low

Form RPR

1 **Zaskar** 2-8-6 0 HayleyTurner 8 67+
(Tom Dascombe) *s.i.s: bhd tl hdwy over 2f out: rdn over 1f out: led wl ins fnl f: r.o* **7/1**[3]

644 **2** ¾ **Gower Belle**[25] 4310 2-8-10 69 ow1 RichardHughes 4 69
(W R Muir) *w ldr: rdn over 2f out: ev ch over 1f out: kpt on towards fin* **4/1**[2]

2332 **3** hd **Bookiebasher Dude**[10] 4755 2-9-0 75 SebSanders 5 72
(M Quinn) *led: rdn over 2f out: hdd and nt qckn wl ins fnl f* **5/4**[1]

0 **4** 6 **Shakespeare's Son**[18] 4527 2-8-11 0 ChrisCatlin 13 51
(H J Evans) *bhd: rdn and hdwy over 1f out: nvr trbld ldrs* **50/1**

5 1 **Heron (IRE)** 2-9-1 0 IanMongan 10 52
(N P Littmoden) *prom: rdn over 2f out: wknd wl over 1f out* **25/1**

0 **6** ¾ **Albany Becky (IRE)**[26] 4273 2-8-2 0 LiamJones(3) 3 40
(M G Quinlan) *prom: rdn 3f out: sn wknd* **40/1**

063 **7** ½ **Ever Hopeful**[15] 4629 2-8-7 64 TedDurcan 12 41
(H J L Dunlop) *hld up in tch: rdn over 3f out: wkng whn hung bdly rt bnd over 2f out* **10/1**

0 **8** hd **Stellar Rose (USA)**[18] 4540 2-8-6 0 ow1 KDarley 11 39
(B J Meehan) *bhd fnl 3f* **16/1**

9 ¾ **Mad Man Will (IRE)** 2-9-0 0 SaleemGolam 2 45
(S C Williams) *mid-div: wknd over 2f out* **25/1**

10 ¾ **Topflightrebellion** 2-8-5 0 DaleGibson 9 34
(Mrs G S Rees) *sn outpcd* **40/1**

11 1½ **Copperbottomed (IRE)** 2-9-1 0 PaulEddery 7 39
(R Hollinshead) *prom: rdn over 2f out: wkng whn edgd rt over 1f out* **16/1**

12 2 **Sunshine Lady (IRE)** 2-8-9 0 FrancisNorton 1 27
(D Haydn Jones) *s.i.s: a bhd* **20/1**

13 9 **Jazz Romance (IRE)** 2-8-7 0 DominicFox(3) 6 1
(D Shaw) *s.i.s: a in rr* **100/1**

1m 15.21s (-0.60) **Going Correction** -0.125s/f (Stan) **13** Ran SP% **118.1**
Speed ratings (Par 95): **99,98,97,89,88 87,86,86,85,84 82,79,67**
CSF £32.47 TOTE £8.60: £2.60, £1.60, £1.10; EX 50.90.
Owner P A Deal **Bred** Darley **Trained** Lambourn, Berks

FOCUS
The first three finished clear in this modest maiden and there was little strength in depth, but the form looks sound.

NOTEBOOK
Zaskar ◆, described as a bit of a madam by her trainer, played up after being mounted in the paddock. She did nothing wrong in the race and did well to overcome missing the break. Well regarded, she can score again in modest company. (op 8-1 tchd 13-2)
Gower Belle made her debut over 7f and ran as if she is now worth another try at that trip. (op 5-1)
Bookiebasher Dude deserves full marks for his consistency but is looking increasingly vulnerable. (op 13-8)
Shakespeare's Son stepped up on his Chepstow debut and gave the impression he will appreciate a longer trip. (op 40-1)
Heron(IRE) appeared to be unfancied on his debut and should be better for the experience. (op 20-1)

5098 LADBROKES SERIOUS ABOUT BUSINESS CLASSIFIED STKS 7f 32y(P)
3:30 (3:30) (Class 6) 3-Y-0+ **£2,047** (£604; £302) **Stalls** High

Form RPR

000 **1** **Bold Cross (IRE)**[42] 3799 4-9-2 52 PaulFitzsimons 11 58
(E G Bevan) *hld up and bhd: hdwy over 2f out: sn rdn: c wd st: r.o to ld nr fin* **7/1**[3]

000 **2** ¾ **Western Land**[72] 2894 3-8-12 44 TPQueally 7 54
(B Smart) *a.p: rdn over 2f out: ev ch wl ins fnl f: kpt on* **33/1**

6100 **3** shd **Hayley's Flower (IRE)**[79] 2668 3-8-12 54 PatDobbs 3 54
(J C Fox) *hld up in mid-div: rdn over 2f out: ev ch wl ins fnl f: nt qckn* **14/1**

3033 **4** shd **Chalentina**[26] 4295 4-9-2 55 IanMongan 2 55
(P Howling) *sn led: hrd rdn over 1f out: hdd nr fin* **7/2**[1]

0000 **5** 3½ **Musicmaestroplease (IRE)**[12] 4701 4-8-9 54 MatthewDavies(7) 8 46
(S Parr) *bhd tl styd on fnl f: nvr nrr: fin lame* **10/1**

0-44 **6** shd **Tumbelini**[33] 4066 3-8-12 55 TedDurcan 12 44
(C F Wall) *prom: rdn and swtchd lft wl over 1f out: wknd ins fnl f* **4/1**[2]

-024 **7** 1 **Rock Diva (IRE)**[12] 4705 3-8-9 54 LiamJones(3) 5 41
(P C Haslam) *prom: rdn over 3f out: wknd wl over 1f out* **4/1**[2]

2030 **8** nk **Kassuta**[22] 4416 3-8-12 55 (v) SaleemGolam 4 40
(John A Harris) *n.m.r and lost pl bnd after 1f: nvr nr ldrs* **18/1**

0060 **9** nk **Early Promise (IRE)**[24] 4361 3-8-12 53 SebSanders 1 39
(Mrs A L M King) *led early: prom: hrd rdn wl over 1f out: wknd fnl f* **9/1**

6650 **10** ½ **Red Barnet**[27] 4250 3-8-12 53 DaleGibson 6 38
(M W Easterby) *prom 3f* **16/1**

000- **11** 2½ **Munster Mountain (IRE)**[7] 6534 3-8-12 54 (p) RoystonFfrench 10 31
(James Moffatt) *a bhd* **100/1**

-600 **12** 14 **Shantina's Dream (USA)**[59] 3281 3-8-12 55 PatCosgrave 9 —
(J R Boyle) *rrd stalls and s.v.s: a wl bhd* **33/1**

1m 30.61s (0.21) **Going Correction** -0.125s/f (Stan)
WFA 3 from 4yo 4lb **12** Ran SP% **118.5**
Speed ratings (Par 101): **93,92,92,91,87 87,86,86,85,85 82,66**
CSF £218.55 TOTE £8.80: £3.00, £15.90, £5.50; EX 425.90.
Owner E G Bevan **Bred** M Hosokawa **Trained** Ullingswick, H'fords

FOCUS
Ordinary form for the weak grade, but fairly sound.
Musicmaestroplease(IRE) Official explanation: trainer said colt finished lame

5099 LADBROKES IN WOLVERHAMPTON H'CAP 1m 1f 103y(P)
4:00 (4:00) (Class 4) (0-85,83) 3-Y-0+ **£4,857** (£1,445; £722; £360) **Stalls** Low

Form RPR

1522 **1** **Veiled Applause**[24] 4365 4-9-3 **76** SebSanders 6 85
(R M Beckett) *chsd ldr: led over 3f out: rdn wl over 1f out: edgd lft cl home: drvn out* **3/1**[1]

6505 **2** 1¼ **Kildare Sun (IRE)**[28] 4228 5-8-13 **72** DaleGibson 4 78
(J Mackie) *hld up in tch: rdn over 2f out: kpt on ins fnl f* **7/1**

2500 **3** hd **Master Pegasus**[9] 4827 4-9-7 **80** GeorgeBaker 2 86
(C F Wall) *hld up: rdn and hdwy wl over 1f out: swtchd lft jst ins fnl f: nt qckn whn n.m.r on ins nr fin* **8/1**

5566 **4** ½ **Call My Bluff (FR)**[40] 3854 4-8-12 **71** ChrisCatlin 1 76
(Rae Guest) *hld up in rr: rdn and hdwy on side over 1f out: styng on whn nt clr run ins fnl f* **9/1**

0-51 **5** hd **First To Call**[94] 2196 3-9-3 **82** TedDurcan 7 86
(P J Makin) *led: hdd over 5f out: rdn over 3f out: hld whn nt clr run ins fnl f* **6/1**[3]

003 **6** nk **Aegean Prince**[18] 4551 3-9-2 **81** (p) RichardHughes 5 84
(W R Muir) *stdd s: hld up: rdn over 2f out: swtchd lft wl over 1f out: styd on towards fin: n.d* **6/1**[3]

1031 **7** 1¼ **Just Bond (IRE)**[14] 4672 5-9-5 **83** SladeO'Hara(5) 8 84
(G R Oldroyd) *prom: led over 5f out tl over 3f out: rdn and wknd over 1f out* **9/2**[2]

1300 **8** *15* **Beau Sancy**[8] 4847 3-8-11 **79** LiamJones(3) 3 48
(R A Harris) *hld up: rdn over 3f out: sn struggling: eased whn no ch over 1f out* **16/1**

2m 2.65s (0.03) **Going Correction** -0.125s/f (Stan)
WFA 3 from 4yo+ 6lb 8 Ran SP% **111.2**
Speed ratings (Par 105): **94,92,92,92,92 91,90,77**
CSF £22.89 CT £144.98 TOTE £4.20: £1.10, £2.70, £2.90; EX 21.30.
Owner The Wright And Wrong Partnership **Bred** P J McCalmont **Trained** Whitsbury, Hants
■ Stewards' Enquiry : George Baker two-day ban: careless riding (Sep 14,16)

FOCUS
This slowly-run, messy affair resulted in a very modest winning time for the grade. The winner keeps improving but this overall form is not sure to prove reliable.

5100 LADBROKES HOME OF FOOTBALL BETTING MAIDEN FILLIES' STKS 1m 141y(P)
4:30 (4:31) (Class 5) 2-Y-O **£2,968** (£876; £438) **Stalls** Low

Form RPR
05 **1** **Step This Way (USA)**[17] 4565 2-9-0 0 RoystonFfrench 6 80+
(M Johnston) *sn led: rdn clr over 1f out: r.o wl* **7/1**
624 **2** *3 1/2* **Altitude**[39] 3874 2-9-0 81 SebSanders 9 71
(Sir Mark Prescott) *chsd wnr: rdn and ev ch over 2f out: one pce* **5/4**[1]
00 **3** *1 1/4* **Beat The Rain**[17] 4564 2-9-0 0 RichardHughes 3 68
(J H M Gosden) *hld up in tch: rdn over 2f out: one pce* **6/1**[3]
4 *hd* **Dramatic Solo** 2-9-0 0 KDarley 4 68
(K R Burke) *s.i.s: hld up: rdn over 3f out: hdwy wl over 1f out: one pce fnl f* **16/1**
5 *1 1/2* **Keep Your Head (USA)** 2-9-0 0 TPQueally 5 65
(J A Osborne) *hld up and bhd: hdwy on outside wl over 1f out: no imp whn rn green and hung lft ins fnl f* **20/1**
0 **6** *3 1/2* **Sparkling Montjeu (IRE)**[23] 4402 2-9-0 0 ChrisCatlin 7 57
(J W Hills) *hld up in tch: rdn and wknd over 2f out* **33/1**
6 **7** *1* **Ruby Light**[30] 4169 2-9-0 0 TedDurcan 1 55
(Sir Michael Stoute) *led early: prom: rdn and wknd over 2f out* **11/4**[2]
0000 **8** *17* **Cottam Breeze**[9] 4796 2-9-0 35 DaleGibson 10 20
(M W Easterby) *bhd: rdn over 5f out: lost tch fnl 3f* **125/1**

1m 51.42s (-0.34) **Going Correction** -0.125s/f (Stan) 8 Ran SP% **112.3**
Speed ratings (Par 92): **96,92,91,91,90 87,86,71**
CSF £15.62 TOTE £7.20: £1.60, £1.10, £2.00; EX 17.50.
Owner S R Counsell **Bred** Crescent Hill Farm & Dr W A Rood **Trained** Middleham Moor, N Yorks

FOCUS
The first three were all up in distance in this ordinary maiden. Tricky to rate, the second and third helping set the level.

NOTEBOOK
Step This Way(USA) ◆ relished the step up from 7f and proved far too good for the favourite once in the home straight. She can go on from here. (op 13-2 tchd 6-1 and 8-1)
Altitude, back on Polytrack, was also trying a longer trip but could not go with the winner in the final quarter of a mile. (tchd 11-10 and 11-8)
Beat The Rain kept on at the same pace on this first attempt at a mile. (op 8-1)
Dramatic Solo showed signs of ability on her debut against some more experienced rivals. (op 12-1)
Keep Your Head(USA) is another newcomer who should be better for the experience. (tchd 25-1)

5101 LADBROKES SERIOUS ABOUT BUSINESS H'CAP 1m 4f 50y(P)
5:00 (5:00) (Class 4) (0-85,85) 3-Y-O **£4,857** (£1,445; £722; £360) **Stalls** Low

Form RPR
31 **1** **Opal Haze (USA)**[48] 3621 3-9-4 **85** RichardHughes 6 90+
(J H M Gosden) *sn led: rdn wl over 1f out: r.o* **6/4**[1]
4140 **2** *1/2* **Vallemeldee (IRE)**[37] 3964 3-8-5 **72** FrancisNorton 4 76
(P W D'Arcy) *led early: chsd wnr: ev ch over 2f out: rdn wl over 1f out: nt qckn ins fnl f* **9/1**[2]
3302 **3** *1 3/4* **Maslak (IRE)**[12] 4707 3-8-8 **75** ChrisCatlin 5 76
(P W Hiatt) *hld up: rdn and hdwy on ins wl over 1f out: no ex ins fnl f* **11/1**
5651 **4** *1* **Veenwouden**[18] 4542 3-9-0 **81** SebSanders 3 81
(E F Vaughan) *hld up in tch: hdwy over 3f out: ev ch over 2f out: rdn wl over 1f out: one pce* **6/4**[1]
0010 **5** *8* **History Boy**[55] 3407 3-9-4 **85** TedDurcan 2 72
(D J Coakley) *hld up in rr: rdn over 2f out: sn struggling* **10/1**[3]

2m 39.5s (-2.92) **Going Correction** -0.125s/f (Stan) 5 Ran SP% **107.4**
Speed ratings (Par 103): **104,103,102,101,96**
CSF £14.65 TOTE £2.40: £1.40, £5.40; EX 15.30.
Owner K Abdulla **Bred** Juddmonte Farms Inc **Trained** Newmarket, Suffolk

FOCUS
They went a respectable pace despite the small field. Pretty ordinary form for the grade, but the winner could be capable of better.

5102 LADBROKES IN WOLVERHAMPTON MEDIAN AUCTION MAIDEN STKS 1m 1f 103y(P)
5:30 (5:32) (Class 6) 3-5-Y-O **£2,047** (£604; £302) **Stalls** Low

Form RPR
1 **Velma Kelly** 3-8-12 0 AdamKirby 7 56
(W R Swinburn) *stdd s: hld up: hdwy over 2f out: c wd st: rdn over 1f out: r.o to ld post* **16/1**
6-64 **2** *shd* **Auntie Mame**[37] 3948 3-8-12 60 TPQueally 3 56
(D J Coakley) *hld up in tch: rdn over 2f out: edgd lft and led wl ins fnl f: hdd post* **14/1**
005 **3** *1 1/4* **Silent Beauty (IRE)**[14] 4673 3-8-12 42 ChrisCatlin 2 53
(S C Williams) *prom: rdn and outpcd over 2f out: rallied ins fnl f* **13/2**
3400 **4** *hd* **House Maiden (IRE)**[17] 4579 3-8-5 57 KirstyMilczarek(7) 5 53
(D M Simcock) *led: rdn over 1f out: hdd and no ex wl ins fnl f* **9/1**
0642 **5** *2 1/2* **Split Briefs (IRE)**[16] 4591 3-8-12 65 SebSanders 4 48
(D J Daly) *chsd ldr: ev ch 2f out: rdn over 1f out: wknd wl ins fnl f* **15/8**[1]
033 **6** *2 1/2* **Le Singe Noir**[55] 3406 3-9-3 70 OscarUrbina 8 47
(M Botti) *hld up and bhd: rdn and shortlived effrt on outside 3f out* **9/4**[2]
-000 **7** *22* **Soylent Green**[22] 4426 3-8-12 25 PaulEddery 6 —
(S Parr) *a bhd: lost tch 4f out: t.o* **200/1**
5 **8** *1 3/4* **King Of Connacht**[87] 2433 4-9-9 0 GeorgeBaker 1 —
(J W Unett) *hld up: rdn over 5f out: sn struggling: t.o* **6/1**[3]

2m 1.11s (-1.51) **Going Correction** -0.125s/f (Stan)
WFA 3 from 4yo 6lb 8 Ran SP% **116.2**
Speed ratings (Par 101): **101,100,99,99,97 95,75,74**
CSF £214.44 TOTE £27.60: £3.80, £3.50, £1.60; EX 219.20 Place 6 £ 56.72, Place 5 £ 33.41.
Owner Mr & Mrs W R Swinburn **Bred** Rockwell Bloodstock **Trained** Aldbury, Herts

FOCUS
They went a decent clip in this weak maiden. Shaky form, rated through the runner-up.
T/Plt: £248.60 to a £1 stake. Pool: £49,972.90. 146.70 winning tickets. T/Qpdt: £66.80 to a £1 stake. Pool: £3,701.60. 41.00 winning tickets. KH

5103 - 5108a (Foreign Racing) - See Raceform Interactive

4847 GOODWOOD (R-H)
Tuesday, September 4

OFFICIAL GOING: Good to firm (good in places; 8.7)
Wind: Virtually nil Weather: Dry

5109 ELECTROLUX PROFESSIONAL NURSERY STKS (H'CAP) 1m
2:00 (2:01) (Class 4) (0-85,82) 2-Y-O **£2,941** (£2,941; £674; £336) **Stalls** High

Form RPR
0042 **1** **Townkab (IRE)**[11] 4776 2-8-0 **64** LiamJones(3) 1 66
(N P Littmoden) *a.p: 4l clr w ldr 3f out: led 2f out: sn rdn: all out: jnd on line* **9/1**
1 **1** *dht* **Goodwood Starlight (IRE)**[19] 4539 2-9-3 **78** KerrinMcEvoy 5 80
(J L Dunlop) *trckd ldrs: rdn and hung lft fr 3f out: str run on stands' side rails ins fnl f: jnd ldr on line* **3/1**[2]
4225 **3** *nk* **Bailey (IRE)**[11] 4776 2-9-3 **78** TedDurcan 6 79
(B J Meehan) *t.k.h early: hld up: stdy prog fr 3f out: rdn ent fnl f: r.o wl: jst hld* **13/2**
41 **4** *shd* **Ghetto**[66] 3095 2-9-7 **82** RichardHughes 8 83
(R Hannon) *hld up bhd ldrs: tk clsr order 3f out: rdn whn swtchd lft wl over 1f out: r.o ins fnl f: jst hld* **5/2**[1]
2003 **5** *3* **Marning Star**[8] 4892 2-8-11 **72** TPO'Shea 2 66
(M R Channon) *s.i.s: hld up: rdn 3f out: nvr gng pce to chal fnl 2f* **9/1**
6410 **6** *3/4* **Maybe I Will (IRE)**[3] 5053 2-8-13 **74** SebSanders 9 66
(R Hannon) *led: 4 l clr w wnr 3f out: rdn and hdd 2f out: rallied tl wknd ins fnl f* **9/1**
010 **7** *3/4* **Classical World (USA)**[11] 4776 2-9-0 **75** RyanMoore 7 66
(Sir Michael Stoute) *prom for over 4f: chsd ldrs and rdn 3f out: wknd fnl f* **11/2**[3]

1m 40.52s (0.25) **Going Correction** -0.10s/f (Good) 7 Ran SP% **112.3**
Speed ratings (Par 97): **94,94,93,93,90 89,89**
TRIFECTA W: GS £1.60, T £4.90. P: GS £1.60, T £4.00. Ex: GS/T £15.60, T/GS £12.80. CSF: GS/T £14.11, T/GS £17.40. Tcst: GS/T/B £80.22, T/GS/.
Owner Goodwood Racehorse Owners Group Fourteen **Bred** Lynn Lodge Stud **Trained** Arundel, W Sussex
Owner Trojan Racing **Bred** J Turley **Trained** Newmarket, Suffolk

FOCUS
A fair nursery, but the gallop was just ordinary and the first four home finished in a bunch, despite that the form appears sound.

NOTEBOOK
Townkab(IRE) was only 1lb higher than when second in a similar event at Newmarket on his previous start and he made the most of both his light weight and Goodwood Starlight's wayward course, despite being left in front much sooner than was probably ideal. The ground was much faster than on his previous start, but he handled the conditions well and confirmed he is progressing into a fair sort. He should continue to run well in similar company and looks the type to train on. (op 8-1)
Goodwood Starlight(IRE) ◆'s debut success in a 7f maiden at Salisbury represented just fair form, but there was plenty to like about that success considering he was the only horse to make up ground from off the pace and he confirmed himself a useful individual on his nursery debut. The step up to 1m would have been in his favour, but he did not seem at home on the quick ground or the track - which is ironic considering his name - and he nearly threw this away by hanging badly left. He must have lost several lengths when wandering under pressure and he did not look to be letting himself down for much of the way up the straight, but he eventually ran on when almost against the stands' rail, just doing enough to share the spoils. He should be capable of even better on a galloping track and is a fine middle-distance prospect for next year. (op 8-1)
Bailey(IRE) did not get home under a positive ride at Newmarket on his previous start and more patient tactics suited much better, although he was still unable to reverse form with Townkab. He was a little keen under restraint, but had plenty left for the business end and picked up well from the pace to take a close third. (op 7-1)
Ghetto, the winner of a 7f maiden on soft ground on the July course on his previous start, did not seem totally comfortable back on a faster surface and failed to show his best. It is to his credit he was still not beaten that far and he will be one to keep on side when there is a little more give underfoot. (tchd 11-4 in places)
Marning Star did not really build on his recent third at Newcastle. (tchd 10-1 and 8-1 in places)
Maybe I Will(IRE) is not progressing and is another who may go better on slightly easier ground. (op 11-1 tchd 12-1)
Classical World(USA) looked to have conditions to suit, but he failed to perform and was disappointing. (op 13-2)

5110 R.H. HALL EUROPEAN BREEDERS' FUND MEDIAN AUCTION MAIDEN FILLIES' STKS 6f
2:35 (2:35) (Class 5) 2-Y-O **£3,886** (£1,156; £577; £288) **Stalls** Low

Form RPR
00 **1** **The Jostler**[17] 4602 2-9-0 0 MichaelHills 10 78
(B W Hills) *in tch: swtchd lft 2f out: r.o strly to ld ent fnl f: sn clr: readily* **13/2**[3]
0 **2** *2* **Ochoa (IRE)**[19] 4527 2-9-0 0 PhilipRobinson 20 72
(C G Cox) *a.p: led 2f out: sn rdn: hdd ent fnl f: nt pce of wnr* **16/1**
3 *shd* **Mille Feuille (IRE)** 2-9-0 0 SebSanders 1 72
(R M Beckett) *in tch: rdn over 2f out: styd on strly ins fnl f: wnt 3rd nr nr fin* **5/1**[2]
434 **4** *3/4* **Candle Sahara (IRE)**[23] 4422 2-9-0 83 TPO'Shea 18 70
(M R Channon) *trckd ldrs: rdn over 2f out: ev ch jst over 1f out: no ex: lost 3rd nr fin* **2/1**[1]
0 **5** *1 1/2* **Red Amaryllis**[55] 3417 2-8-11 0 RichardKingscote(3) 4 65
(H J L Dunlop) *bmpd s: sn chsng ldrs: rdn wl over 2f out: kpt on same pce fnl f* **66/1**
6 *nk* **Night Premiere (IRE)** 2-9-0 0 RichardHughes 14 64
(R Hannon) *s.i.s: bhd: swtchd lft fr over 2f out: styd on ins fnl f: nrst fin* **12/1**
60 **7** *3/4* **Ava Gee**[20] 4506 2-9-0 0 DavidKinsella 8 62
(B De Haan) *chsd ldrs: rdn over 2f out: kpt on same pce* **25/1**
06 **8** *shd* **The Hoofer (IRE)**[19] 4537 2-9-0 0 TedDurcan 17 62
(J L Dunlop) *in tch: rdn 2f out: one pce fnl f* **50/1**
9 *nk* **Miss Poppy** 2-9-0 0 JimCrowley 19 61
(P R Chamings) *towards rr: rdn over 2f out: sme late progres: nvr trbld ldrs* **22/1**
04 **10** *hd* **Plaka (FR)**[5] 4963 2-9-0 0 TPQueally 6 60
(J A Osborne) *bmpd s: nvr bttr than mid-div* **25/1**
0 **11** *3/4* **Miss Mozart**[15] 4662 2-8-11 0 TravisBlock(3) 3 58
(H Morrison) *mainly towards rr* **66/1**
06 **12** *1 1/4* **Compton Abbess**[70] 2969 2-9-0 0 FergusSweeney 11 54
(B R Millman) *led: rdn and hung rt over 2f out: sn hdd: wknd* **33/1**

The Form Book, Raceform Ltd, Compton, RG20 6NL

00 **13** *1* **Futune (IRE)**[8] 4883 2-9-0 0 RHills 13 51
(B J Meehan) *a towards rr* **66/1**
30 **14** *½* **Coral Shores**[8] 4904 2-9-0 0 JimmyFortune 7 50
(P W Chapple-Hyam) *wnt lft s: nvr bttr than mid-div* **9/1**
0 **15** *½* **Lella Beya**[106] 1896 2-9-0 0 KerrinMcEvoy 12 48
(S Kirk) *mid-div tl 2f out* **12/1**
00 **16** *1¾* **Lady Maya**[20] 4500 2-8-9 0 KevinGhunowa(5) 16 43
(Dr J R J Naylor) *chsd ldrs: rdn over 2f out: sn wknd* **100/1**
0 **17** *3* **Our Tallulah (IRE)**[11] 4755 2-9-0 0 ChrisCatlin 9 34
(C G Cox) *a towards rr* **66/1**
00 **18** *8* **Kili Links (IRE)**[11] 4774 2-9-0 0 RyanMoore 2 10
(R Hannon) *a bhd* **25/1**

1m 12.25s (-0.60) **Going Correction** -0.30s/f (Firm) **18** Ran SP% **122.3**
Speed ratings (Par 92): **92,89,89,88,86 85,84,84,84,84 83,81,80,79,78 76,72,61**
CSF £94.72 TOTE £8.10: £2.40, £6.40, £1.80; EX 140.10.
Owner Burton Agnes Bloodstock **Bred** Burton Agnes Stud Co Ltd **Trained** Lambourn, Berks

FOCUS
Plenty of runners, but this looked like a modest fillies' maiden. They were well spread out across the middle of the track.

NOTEBOOK
The Jostler did not show much on her debut over course and distance, but she put up an improved effort when mid-division at Newbury on her previous start and progressed again to get off the mark in convincing fashion. It remains to be seen what the form is worth, but she is coming along nicely and will have to be respected in future. (tchd 7-1)
Ochoa(IRE) attracted market support on her debut, which probably had a lot to do with Robinson going on from another meeting to take a rare ride at Chepstow, but she showed absolutely nothing. That experience was clearly not lost on her, though, and she produced a much-improved effort to take second. Much better away from the gates than on her debut, she was soon in a good rhythm up front and her challenge only flattened out inside the final furlong. This was not much of a race, but at least she is going the right way. (tchd 14-1)
Mille Feuille(IRE), a 110,000euros daughter of Choisir, half-sister to among others 1m4f winner Feed The Meter, out of a fairly useful dual 7f winner at two, attracted support on her debut and shaped well in third. She should improve and should be placed to advantage before the season is out. (op 7-1)
Candle Sahara(IRE) was well below form when a beaten favourite at Redcar on her previous start and she once again failed to produce her best, running well below her official mark of 83. This ground was probably much quicker than she would have liked and she can be given another chance back on an easier surface. (op 15-8 tchd 7-4)
Red Amaryllis improved significantly on the form she showed when beating just one home on her debut at Kempton.
Night Premiere(IRE), an 80,000gns daughter of Night Shift, first foal of an unraced sister to high-class juvenile/sprinter Land Of Dreams, was never really involved after starting slowly, but there was a lot to like about the way she kept on and she is open to plenty of improvement. (op 11-1)
Kili Links(IRE) Official explanation: jockey said filly missed the break

5111 TETLEY TEA STKS (H'CAP) 2m
3:10 (3:10) (Class 5) (0-70,68) 3-Y-0+ **£3,238** (£963; £481; £240) **Stalls** High

Form RPR
3131 **1** **Franchoek (IRE)**[8] 4877 3-9-3 67 6ex JimmyFortune 2 80+
(A King) *hld up bhd ldng trio: clsd on ldrs 3f out: rdn to ld 1f out: edgd lft: styd on wl: rdn out* **6/4**[1]
4212 **2** *1¾* **Strobe**[8] 4906 3-9-4 68 TPQueally 5 79
(J A Osborne) *chsd ldrs: wnt 2nd 6f out: rdn to ld over 2f out: hdd 1f out: kpt on but sn hld by wnr* **13/2**
40-3 **3** *½* **French Opera**[54] 3448 4-9-8 59 JamieSpencer 1 69
(N J Henderson) *hld up in mid-div: clsd on ldrs and travelling wl fr 3f out: shkn up to chal over 1f out: nt qckn* **11/4**[2]
0050 **4** *5* **Mostarsil (USA)**[26] 4318 9-9-7 58 (p) RyanMoore 7 62
(G L Moore) *hld up: hdwy over 3f out: sn rdn: one pce fnl 2f out: wnt 4th ins fnl f: fin lame* **5/1**[3]
3033 **5** *½* **Noddies Way**[34] 4056 4-9-11 65 LiamJones(3) 9 68
(J F Panvert) *s.i.s: sn pushed along to chse ldr after 1f: niggled along to ld over 6f out: drvn and hdd over 2f out: wknd ins fnl f* **12/1**
5431 **6** *2½* **Treason Trial**[9] 4859 6-9-3 59 6ex TolleyDean(5) 6 59
(Stef Liddiard) *hld up bhd: hdwy over 3f out: sn rdn for effrt: wknd ent fnl f* **16/1**
-640 **7** *3½* **Tivers Song (USA)**[24] 4391 3-8-11 61 (t) JimCrowley 8 57
(Mrs A J Perrett) *mid-div: wnt 3rd over 3f out: sn rdn: wknd over 1f out* **20/1**
6-00 **8** *101* **Divine River**[32] 4128 4-9-11 65 RichardKingscote(3) 3 —
(J G Portman) *plld hrd: led tl over 6f out: sn wknd: virtually p.u fr 3f out* **66/1**

3m 27.89s (-2.90) **Going Correction** -0.10s/f (Good)
WFA 3 from 4yo+ 13lb **8** Ran SP% **116.5**
Speed ratings (Par 103): **103,102,101,99,99 97,96,—**
CSF £12.43 CT £25.03 TOTE £2.30: £1.10, £1.80, £1.60; EX 10.70.
Owner David Mason **Bred** 6c Stallions Ltd **Trained** Barbury Castle, Wilts

FOCUS
A fair race for the grade, run at a strong pace. The front pair are progressive and the third not fully exposed, and they finished clear.
Mostarsil(USA) Official explanation: vet said gelding returned lame
Divine River Official explanation: jockey said filly ran too free

5112 CHARLTON HUNT SUPREME STKS (GROUP 3) 7f
3:45 (3:45) (Class 1) 3-Y-0+
£28,390 (£10,760; £5,385; £2,685; £1,345; £675) **Stalls** High

Form RPR
3111 **1** **Lovelace**[17] 4601 3-8-9 96 JamieSpencer 3 112
(M Johnston) *trckd ldrs: tk narrow advantage 2f out: sn hrd pressed: battled on gamely u.str.p: drvn out* **5/1**
534 **2** *nk* **Dunelight (IRE)**[10] 4805 4-8-13 110 (v) PhilipRobinson 10 111
(C G Cox) *hd on floor leaving stalls: sn rcvrd to chse ldr: rdn and ev ch thrght fnl 2f: hld nr fin* **9/4**[1]
-460 **3** *nk* **Bygone Days**[30] 4214 6-8-13 110 KerrinMcEvoy 5 110+
(Saeed Bin Suroor) *hld up in last pair: pushed along and stdy prog fr over 2f out: rdn over 1f out: styd on to go 3rd nr fin: nt quite rch ldng pair* **9/2**[3]
3066 **4** *hd* **Mac Love**[24] 4401 6-8-13 99 SebSanders 8 110
(J Noseda) *trckd ldrs: rdn in cl 4th 2f out: swtchd lft jst ins fnl f: r.o fnl 50yds* **14/1**
0001 **5** *¾* **Beckermet (IRE)**[10] 4813 5-8-13 109 ChrisCatlin 2 108
(R F Fisher) *led: rdn and hdd narrowly 2f out: raiiled gamely: no ex ins fnl f* **25/1**
5000 **6** *hd* **Areyoutalkingtome**[12] 4747 4-8-13 105 SimonWhitworth 6 107
(C A Cyzer) *hld up: rdn to chse ldrs over 2f out: kpt on same pce ins fnl f* **50/1**
0523 **7** *½* **Racer Forever (USA)**[12] 4747 4-8-13 108 (b) JimmyFortune 1 106+
(J H M Gosden) *hld up last: nt clr run and swtchd lft over 1f out: rdn and swtchd rt ins fnl f: styd on: nvr trbld ldrs* **7/2**[2]
0-00 **8** *nk* **Tawaassol (USA)**[10] 4798 4-8-13 98 (t) RHills 7 105
(Sir Michael Stoute) *mid-div: hdwy over 2f out: cl 5th and sn rdn: fdd ins fnl f* **25/1**
0405 **9** *½* **Assertive**[23] 4438 4-8-13 106 RichardHughes 4 104
(R Hannon) *hld up: rdn and effrt over 2f out: one pce fnl f* **12/1**
0014 **10** *hd* **Presto Shinko (IRE)**[10] 4813 6-8-13 108 RyanMoore 9 103
(R Hannon) *hld up: rdn 3f out: kpt on same pce: nvr trbld ldrs* **33/1**

1m 25.11s (-2.93) **Going Correction** -0.10s/f (Good)
WFA 3 from 4yo+ 4lb **10** Ran SP% **114.8**
Speed ratings (Par 113): **112,111,111,111,110 110,109,109,108,108**
CSF £15.78 TOTE £4.60: £1.90, £1.40, £2.10; EX 12.00.
Owner Hamad Suhail **Bred** Mrs Mary Taylor **Trained** Middleham Moor, N Yorks

FOCUS
A competitive Group 3 contest with little between the entire field on ratings and they were covered by around three lengths at the line. Ordinary form for the grade, a progressive 3yo beating his elders.

NOTEBOOK
Lovelace, a rapidly progressive colt who came into this in search of a four-timer following a tidy win in slow ground at Newbury, was making the step up from handicap company, but looked well worth his place in this field and soon held a good position just behind the leaders. Ridden to lead over two furlongs out, he found plenty for pressure and was always just doing enough. This son of Royal Applause is as tough as they come and he now has either the Group 1 Prix de la Foret or the Group 2 Challenge Stakes later in the season as his main target. (op 4-1)
Dunelight(IRE), back down in trip having failed to last home in the Celebration Mile, seems to enjoy it around here and he was understandably made favourite. He had his head down leaving the gates though and could not lead as he likes to, but still held every chance in the straight and was simply not as good as the winner. This is about his level, but he has become quite exposed now. (tchd 5-2 and 11-4 in places)
Bygone Days, outclassed in a couple of Group 1 events most recently, was well off the pace early and did not appear to be going well, but he stuck on really well in the final furlong and was closing fast as the line came. It is possible he was feeling the ground, but he has become tricky to win with and would never be one to take too short a price about. (op 4-1)
Mac Love, a formerly smart sort who won this in 2004, has been performing well in handicaps off his declining mark and ran his best race for a while here with a keeping-on fourth, but it will do his rating no good with regards to a return to handicaps. (op 18-1)
Beckermet(IRE), who ended a lengthy losing run when bolting up in soft ground at Newmarket the other day, was back up in trip on much faster ground here, but he ran well for a long way and it was only in the final half-furlong he could offer no more. A return to 6f will suit and he is clearly on good terms with himself at present. (tchd 20-1)
Areyoutalkingtome, a prolific winner on Polytrack earlier in the season, has struggled back on turf since being outclassed in the Dubai Golden Shaheen back in March, but this represented an improved effort. That said, he is not going to be easy to win with off his current mark and is likely to continue to find a few too good at this level. (tchd 66-1)
Racer Forever(USA), who has rightly had his attitude questioned on more than one occasion, found the race was all over by the time he got into the clear, but there had to be a doubt anyway as to whether he would have had the resolution to get past the winner. (op 11-2)

5113 SALAD MAKERS MAIDEN STKS 1m 1f 192y
4:20 (4:22) (Class 5) 3-Y-O **£3,238** (£963; £481; £240) **Stalls** High

Form RPR
00 **1** **Give Me A Break**[10] 4815 3-9-3 0 TedDurcan 7 80
(P W Chapple-Hyam) *trckd ldrs: rdn to chal 2f out: kpt on u.str.p ins fnl f: led fnl strides* **9/2**[3]
3203 **2** *hd* **Coyote Creek**[24] 4403 3-9-3 78 JimmyFortune 5 80
(E F Vaughan) *sn led at stdy pce: rdn and hrd pressed fr over 2f out: kpt on u.str.p ins fnl f: ct fnl strides* **11/10**[1]
3 *10* **Whenever** 3-9-3 0 JimCrowley 6 60
(R T Phillips) *racd green: s.i.s: bhd: pushed along after 3f: rdn wl over 3f out: styd on past btn horses ins fnl f: nvr trbld ldng pair* **33/1**
04P0 **4** *1¾* **Restless Soul**[12] 4748 3-8-12 58 SebSanders 3 52
(C A Cyzer) *hld up bhd ldrs: rdn 3f out: wkng whn lft 3rd briefly jst ins fnl f* **8/1**
5 *3½* **Istibian (IRE)**[383] 3-8-10 0 KylieManser(7) 2 50
(Mrs H Sweeting) *t.k.h in tch: wnt 3rd 4f out: rdn 3f out: wknd over 1f out* **66/1**
0 **6** *3* **Park Valley Prince**[100] 2059 3-9-3 0 RichardHughes 4 44
(W R Muir) *hld up: hdwy 5f out: effrt 3f out: wknd over 1f out* **20/1**
03 **7** *5* **Out Of Court**[6] 4948 3-9-3 0 SimonWhitworth 8 74+
(C A Cyzer) *trckd ldr: ev ch over 2f out: sn rdn: stl chalng whn lost action jst over 1f out: immediately eased* **5/2**[2]

2m 8.25s (0.50) **Going Correction** -0.10s/f (Good) **7** Ran SP% **114.7**
Speed ratings (Par 101): **94,93,85,84,81 79,75**
CSF £9.95 TOTE £5.90: £2.40, £1.40; EX 13.60.
Owner R J Arculli **Bred** Easton Park Stud **Trained** Newmarket, Suffolk

FOCUS
A weak maiden and the winning time was moderate. ordinary form, rated around the runner-up, with the winner up 12lb.

5114 BETTING SHOPS BACK TURFTV STKS (H'CAP) 1m
4:55 (4:55) (Class 4) (0-80,80) 3-Y-0+ **£5,181** (£1,541; £770; £384) **Stalls** High

Form RPR
0063 **1** **Don't Panic (IRE)**[41] 3857 3-9-7 80 KerrinMcEvoy 3 90
(P W Chapple-Hyam) *hld up towards rr: swtchd lft and hdwy 2f out: sn rdn: chal ins fnl f: led fnl stride* **7/1**[3]
5203 **2** *shd* **Salient**[27] 4268 3-9-7 80 PaulDoe 5 90
(J Akehurst) *mid-div: swtchd lft and hdwy jst over 2f out: rdn to ld over 1f out: sn edgd rt: hdd fnl stride* **12/1**
3301 **3** *1¼* **Titan Triumph**[10] 4807 3-9-3 76 (t) RichardHughes 7 83
(W J Knight) *hld up towards rr: swtchd lft and hdwy 2f out: sn rdn: styd on to go 3rd ins fnl f* **9/4**[1]
0050 **4** *¾* **Lazy Darren**[17] 4608 3-9-3 76 RyanMoore 10 82+
(R Hannon) *unsettled stalls: mid-div: hdwy over 2f out: styng on whn nt clr run over 1f out: swtchd lft and kpt on again fnl 100yds* **14/1**
0612 **5** *½* **Minnis Bay (CAN)**[8] 4889 3-9-4 77 SebSanders 11 81
(E F Vaughan) *mid-div: hdwy 3f out: rdn to press ldr over 1f out: hld whn sltly hmpd ins fnl f: no ex* **5/1**[2]
060 **6** *2½* **Music Note (IRE)**[19] 4548 4-9-2 75 (t) NicolPolli(5) 9 75
(Miss Gay Kelleway) *chsd ldrs: rdn to ld briefly wl over 1f out: wknd fnl f* **20/1**
4610 **7** *½* **Murrin (IRE)**[47] 3689 3-9-5 78 JimmyFortune 8 75
(T G Mills) *s.i.s: bhd: swtchd lft 3f out: sn rdn: styd on past btn horses ins fnl f: nvr on terms* **7/1**[3]

3310 **8** *1 1/4* **Hansomelle (IRE)**[3] 5047 5-9-2 **73**............................(p) NeilChalmers(3) 2 68
(Miss Sheena West) *mid-div: pushed along 5f out: no further imp fr 3f out* **7/1**[3]

6301 **9** *5* **Glencalvie (IRE)**[29] 4234 6-9-5 **76**....................(p) RichardKingscote(3) 6 60
(J Akehurst) *prom: led 4f out: rdn and hdd over 1f out: wknd* **12/1**

6413 **10** *1 1/4* **Empire Dancer (IRE)**[12] 4731 4-8-8 **65**.................... MarcHalford(3) 4 46
(C N Allen) *led for 4f: prom: rdn and ev ch 3f out tl 2f out: wknd* **25/1**

2221 **11** *3 1/2* **Spriggan**[15] 4671 3-9-5 **78**... FergusSweeney 1 51
(C G Cox) *trckd ldrs: rdn 3f out: wknd over 1f out* **16/1**

1m 38.09s (-2.18) **Going Correction** -0.10s/f (Good)
WFA 3 from 4yo+ 5lb 11 Ran SP% **121.5**
Speed ratings (Par 105): **106,105,104,103,103 100,100,99,94,92 89**
CSF £90.94 CT £252.59 TOTE £7.30: £2.20, £3.60, £1.70; EX 68.80.
Owner A B S Webb **Bred** Bernard Colclough **Trained** Newmarket, Suffolk

FOCUS
A fairly competitive handicap. Ordinary form for the grade, but sound enough.
Lazy Darren Official explanation: jockey said gelding was denied a clear run
Spriggan Official explanation: jockey said colt had no more to give

5115 BEST UK RACING ON TURFTV STKS (H'CAP) 7f
5:30 (5:31) (Class 4) (0-85,85) 3-Y-0+ **£5,181** (£1,541; £770; £384) **Stalls** High

Form RPR

3310 **1** **Ivory Lace**[9] 4851 6-9-7 **85**.. JimCrowley 10 97
(S Woodman) *hld up towards rr: swtchd lft over 2f out: rdn and hdwy over 1f out: r.o strly to ld fnl 75yds: rdn out* **12/1**

3430 **2** *1* **Lavenham (IRE)**[18] 4589 4-8-10 **74**.................................... RyanMoore 8 83
(R Hannon) *hld up bhd: swtchd lft wl over 1f out: sn rdn and hdwy: r.o: wnt 2nd fnl stride: nt rch wnr* **10/1**[3]

2440 **3** *shd* **Lunces Lad (IRE)**[10] 4811 3-8-12 **80**.................................... TPO'Shea 9 87
(M R Channon) *in tch: rdn and swtchd lft over 2f out: led 1f out: hdd fnl 75yds: lost 2nd fnl stride* **16/1**

1113 **4** *2 1/2* **Super Frank (IRE)**[22] 4455 4-8-7 **71**.................................... TPQueally 5 73
(J Akehurst) *led: rdn and hdd 1f out: no ex* **5/1**[2]

4600 **5** *nk* **Grizedale (IRE)**[19] 4548 8-8-7 **71**..(t) PaulDoe 6 72
(J Akehurst) *hld up towards rr: hdwy over 3f out: rdn to chse ldrs over 2f out: kpt on same pce fnl f* **50/1**

3006 **6** *3/4* **Rubenstar (IRE)**[8] 4889 4-8-6 **75**.................................... PatrickHills(5) 4 74
(M H Tompkins) *mid-div: tk clsr order over 2f out: sn rdn: kpt on same pce* **14/1**

0052 **7** *nk* **Trimlestown (IRE)**[19] 4548 4-9-1 **79**.................................... FergusSweeney 3 78
(H Candy) *mid-div: hdwy over 2f out: sn rdn: fdd ins fnl f* **9/2**[1]

6000 **8** *1* **Phluke**[17] 4601 6-9-7 **85**.. StephenCarson 12 81
(Eve Johnson Houghton) *chsd ldrs: rdn over 2f out: wknd fnl f* **12/1**

2653 **9** *nk* **Blue Java**[15] 4657 6-8-6 **73**..(t) TravisBlock(3) 7 68
(H Morrison) *chsd ldrs: rdn and effrt over 2f out: wknd ent fnl f* **5/1**[2]

2122 **10** *3 1/2* **Yandina (IRE)**[18] 4589 4-9-4 **82**.................................... MichaelHills 11 68
(B W Hills) *mainly in rr* **9/2**[1]

0000 **11** *4* **Royal Storm (IRE)**[10] 4806 8-8-10 **74**.................................... TedDurcan 2 49
(Mrs A J Perrett) *chsd ldrs: effrt 3f out: wknd 2f out* **25/1**

0051 **12** *2 1/2* **Tara Too (IRE)**[9] 4855 4-8-12 **76** 6ex....................(b) FrankieMcDonald 1 44
(J G Portman) *in tch on outer: rdn over 3f out: sn btn* **16/1**

1m 25.89s (-2.15) **Going Correction** -0.10s/f (Good)
WFA 3 from 4yo+ 4lb 12 Ran SP% **118.4**
Speed ratings (Par 105): **108,106,106,103,103 102,102,101,100,96 92,89**
CSF £126.53 CT £1932.84 TOTE £12.60: £3.10, £3.00, £5.10; EX 91.20 Place 6 £39.01, Place 5 £9.31..
Owner Sally Woodman J Lenaghan D Mortimer **Bred** D R Tucker **Trained** East Lavant, W Sussex

FOCUS
A fair handicap likely to produce the odd winner. Fairly sound form, Ivory Lace producing a clear best.
Yandina(IRE) Official explanation: jockey said filly was unsuited by the track
Tara Too(IRE) Official explanation: trainer said filly was unsuited by the good to firm (good in places) ground
T/Jkpt: Not won. T/Plt: £58.80 to a £1 stake. Pool: £83,355.80. 1,033.85 winning tickets. T/Qpdt: £4.00 to a £1 stake. Pool: £5,882.10. 1,066.00 winning tickets. TM

5088 LINGFIELD (L-H)
Tuesday, September 4

OFFICIAL GOING: Standard
Wind: Moderate, against Weather: Partly cloudy with bright spells

5116 WILLIAM HILL 0800 44 40 40 MAIDEN AUCTION STKS 1m (P)
2:10 (2:13) (Class 5) 2-Y-0 **£2,968** (£876; £438) **Stalls** High

Form RPR

54 **1** **Cheque**[8] 4904 2-8-10 0.. MartinDwyer 12 73+
(J A Osborne) *prom: chsd ldr 5f out: led 3f out: clr over 1f out: pushed out: readily* **7/2**[1]

04 **2** *2* **City Hustler (USA)**[19] 4539 2-8-11 0.................................... JohnEgan 3 69
(J S Moore) *chsd ldr tl 5f out: rdn and swtchd rt 2f out: styd on to chse wnr last 100yds* **9/1**

4 **3** *1/2* **Moment's Notice**[13] 4709 2-9-0 0.. PatDobbs 11 71
(S Kirk) *t.k.h: in tch: hdwy 3f out: rdn to chse wnr 2f out: kpt on but no imp on wnr: lost 2nd last 100yds* **6/1**[2]

24 **4** *1/2* **Spiritofthetiger (USA)**[26] 4316 2-8-7 0.................................... LPKeniry 2 63
(R A Teal) *awkward leaving stalls: in tch in midfield: rdn over 2f out: hdwy wl over 1f out: styd on nt pce to trble wnr* **7/2**[1]

5 *3/4* **Silk Hall (UAE)** 2-9-2 0.. JamesDoyle 7 70
(D W P Arbuthnot) *bhd: in tch: rdn 3f out: hdwy wl over 1f out: styd on steadily: nt threaten ldrs* **16/1**

6 *3* **Everybody Knows** 2-9-3 0.. DarryllHolland 6 64
(M L W Bell) *t.k.h early: stdd towards rr after 2f: effrt whn sltly hmpd 2f out: kpt on: n.d* **10/1**

0 **7** *3* **All Lit Up**[24] 4393 2-9-1 0.. DaneO'Neill 8 56
(A King) *in tch: hdwy to chse ldrs 3f out: rdn and struggling whn sltly hmpd 2f out: n.d after* **25/1**

0 **8** *shd* **Bid To The Beat**[32] 4130 2-8-11 0.................................... JerryO'Dwyer(3) 10 54
(H J Collingridge) *sn outpcd and pushed along in rr: sme late hdwy: n.d* **66/1**

0 **9** *3/4* **Mujahope**[8] 4883 2-8-12 0.. OscarUrbina 4 51
(M Botti) *sn led: hdd 3f out: sn rdn: wknd wl over 1f out* **33/1**

0 **10** *1 1/4* **Shishio**[17] 4598 2-8-6 0.. DominicFox(3) 1 45
(W De Best-Turner) *v.s.a: hdwy on outer over 4f out: btn whn hmpd and stmbld 2f out: n.d after* **100/1**

50 **11** *1 3/4* **Shadows Fall (USA)**[9] 4852 2-9-3 0.. TQuinn 5 49
(P F I Cole) *chsd ldrs: rdn 3f out: edgd rt and hmpd rivals 2f out: sn btn and eased* **7/1**[3]

12 *6* **Miss Okaloosa** 2-8-11 0.. RichardMullen 9 29
(D M Simcock) *s.i.s: rn green towards rr on outer: hdwy 4f out: rdn and hung rt bnd over 2f out: sn btn: eased ins fnl f* **7/1**[3]

1m 38.61s (-0.82) **Going Correction** -0.20s/f (Stan) 12 Ran SP% **118.0**
Speed ratings (Par 95): **96,94,93,93,92 89,86,86,85,84 82,76**
CSF £35.42 TOTE £3.60: £2.20, £2.40, £2.00; EX 27.50 Trifecta £168.80 Part won. Pool £237.76. - 0.34 winning units..
Owner E S G Faber **Bred** Downclose Stud **Trained** Upper Lambourn, Berks

FOCUS
No more than modest maiden form. The first three all showed improvement.

NOTEBOOK
Cheque appreciated the step up to a mile on this third outing and ran out a comfortable winner in the end. He might not have had to improve to win this and the Handicapper should not be too harsh so he could be able to win a nursery. (tchd 4-1)
City Hustler(USA), who did not go unbacked prior to running with promise at Salisbury last time, built on that effort up a furlong in distance. He is now eligible for a mark. (op 8-1 tchd 10-1)
Moment's Notice who did not run badly at Folkestone on his debut despite being green, had different conditions to deal with here and shaped well. He looks to be progressing along the right lines. (op 7-1 tchd 15-2)
Spiritofthetiger(USA) again failed to run up to the level of her debut effort at Kempton. She is, however, now eligible for a mark, and if she can regain that early form she might well end up favourably handicapped. (tchd 10-3)
Silk Hall(UAE), a 22,000gns son of Halling, shaped with a bit of promise and looks the type to derive plenty of benefit from this debut experience. (tchd 14-1)
Everybody Knows, a half-brother to Ecologically Right, a 6f winner at two, Logsdail, a multiple winner at up to 1m1f, Royal Rationale, a 1m1f winner, and Rationale, a winner at up to 1m6f, looks the type to do better with this run under his belt, as most of his stable's juveniles do. Official explanation: jockey said colt was hampered in running (tchd 12-1)
Shadows Fall(USA) Official explanation: jockey said colt lost its action

5117 BET ONLINE @ WILLIAMHILL.CO.UK NURSERY 7f (P)
2:45 (2:45) (Class 6) (0-65,65) 2-Y-0 **£2,388** (£705; £352) **Stalls** Low

Form RPR

006 **1** **Princess India (IRE)**[15] 4662 2-9-7 **65**.................................... IanMongan 5 72
(P Winkworth) *in tch: hdwy 3f out: swtchd rt 2f out: rdn to ld ins fnl f: readily drew clr* **12/1**

640 **2** *2 1/2* **Greystoke Prince**[19] 4527 2-9-7 **65**.................................... AdamKirby 4 66
(W R Swinburn) *in tch: hdwy to chal over 2f out: led over 1f out: rdn and hdd ins fnl f: nt pce of wnr* **6/1**[2]

0600 **3** *1 1/2* **Flying Applause**[11] 4762 2-9-7 **65**.................................... DaneO'Neill 11 62
(A King) *taken down early: stdd s: bhd: hdwy on rail over 4f out: rdn 3f out: styd on u.p last 2f: nt rch ldrs* **13/2**[3]

6020 **4** *shd* **Bridge Of Fermoy (IRE)**[11] 4776 2-9-4 **62**........................(t) JohnEgan 6 58
(Miss Gay Kelleway) *racd in midfield: effrt and rdn wl over 2f out: hanging lft over 1f out: r.o ins fnl f: nvr threatened ldrs* **10/1**

0001 **5** *nk* **Loose Caboose (IRE)**[25] 4359 2-8-7 **58**....................(p) RobbieEgan(7) 3 54
(A J McCabe) *sn rdn to ld: hdd after 1f: w ldr tl led briefly again over 1f out: wknd ins fnl f* **20/1**

5400 **6** *1* **Rubytwosox (IRE)**[27] 4265 2-9-2 **60**.................................... SamHitchcott 7 53
(W R Muir) *sn rdn: chsd ldrs: drvn 3f out: kpt on same pce after* **66/1**

055 **7** *1 1/4* **Too Grand**[26] 4310 2-8-13 **60**.. NeilChalmers(3) 8 50
(A M Balding) *s.i.s: bhd: hdwy into midfield over 3f out: sn rdn: no hdwy last 2f* **14/1**

6366 **8** *1 1/4* **Sheik'N'Knotsterd**[45] 3734 2-9-5 **63**.................................... MartinDwyer 9 49
(J Akehurst) *hld up in rr: nvr on terms* **25/1**

045 **9** *nk* **A Dream Come True**[27] 4273 2-9-7 **65**.................................... RobertHavlin 12 51
(D K Ivory) *stdd and dropped in after s: a bhd* **25/1**

1 **10** *1 1/2* **Steal My Fire (IRE)**[24] 4405 2-9-6 **64**.................................... RichardMullen 2 46
(E J O'Neill) *sn rdn to chse ldr: led after 1f: rdn and hdd over 1f out: sn wknd* **5/4**[1]

040 **11** *2* **Rosy Dawn**[31] 4162 2-9-2 **60**.. PaulDoe 10 37
(H J L Dunlop) *sn rdn to chse ldrs: lost pl after 2f: wl bhd after* **33/1**

0021 **12** *nk* **Never Sold Out (IRE)**[67] 3065 2-8-8 **59**.................................... MCGeran(7) 13 35
(J G M O'Shea) *a bhd: no ch fr 1/2-way* **25/1**

0630 **13** *7* **Spinning Ridge (IRE)**[14] 4683 2-9-1 **59**.................................... SteveDrowne 1 17
(R A Harris) *chsd ldrs tl 1/2-way: wknd qckly over 2f out: eased ins fnl f* **11/1**

1m 25.18s (-0.71) **Going Correction** -0.20s/f (Stan) 13 Ran SP% **124.6**
Speed ratings (Par 93): **96,93,91,91,90 89,88,86,86,84 82,82,74**
CSF £79.38 CT £540.93 TOTE £17.00: £3.40, £2.20, £4.30; EX 145.40 TRIFECTA Not won..
Owner The Hon Mrs C Cameron **Bred** C H Wacker Iii **Trained** Chiddingfold, Surrey

FOCUS
Just an ordinary nursery, but the form should work out.

NOTEBOOK
Princess India(IRE), who caught the eye at Windsor on her last outing, was in a handicap for the first time and ran out a clear winner. She had shaped as though in need of this extra furlong and it certainly proved to be an advantage, as did the surface - two of her previous three starts had been on unsuitably soft ground. (op 10-1)
Greystoke Prince, another running in a nursery for the first time and stepping up a furlong in distance, may have hit the front too soon, but essentially he did not do a lot wrong and simply ran into a better handicapped rival. (op 7-1)
Flying Applause, stepping up to 7f for the first time on his Polytrack debut, got the trip well, and this consistent performer looks the best guide to the level of the form. (op 5-1)
Bridge Of Fermoy(IRE), dropping back from a mile, seemed better suited by this surface than the soft ground he raced on last time. Official explanation: jockey said colt hung left (op 14-1)
Loose Caboose(IRE), winner of a seller over a furlong shorter here last time, did not see this longer trip out as well in this stronger company. (op 16-1)
Steal My Fire(IRE), winner of a seller at Redcar on his debut, was a well-backed favourite but he did not get home over this longer trip. (op 11-8 tchd 13-8 and 6-4 in places)

5118 CHIPS @ WILLIAMHILLCASINO.COM H'CAP 7f (P)
3:20 (3:22) (Class 6) (0-65,64) 3-Y-0+ **£1,547** (£1,547; £352) **Stalls** Low

Form RPR

4042 **1** **King After**[1] 5094 5-8-11 **53**..(v) DaneO'Neill 12 63
(J R Best) *t.k.h: hld up in midfield: rdn and hdwy over 2f out: styng on whn bmpd ins fnl f: kpt on to force dead heat last stride* **7/2**[2]

4350 **1** *dht* **Magroom**[26] 4313 3-8-7 **53**.. SteveDrowne 6 61
(R J Hodges) *chsd ldrs: rdn over 2f out: styng on whn sltly hmpd ins fnl f: kpt on to force dead heat on line* **33/1**

0034 **3** *shd* **Confucius Classic (IRE)**[8] 4907 3-8-10 **56**.................... RichardMullen 4 64+
(J R Boyle) *t.k.h: w ldr tl led narrowly 2f out: sn rdn: edgd rt briefly ins fnl f: kpt on tl hdd last stride* **3/1**[1]

0004 **4** *1* **Treasure House (IRE)**[10] 4797 6-9-0 **56** DaleGibson 8 63
(M Blanshard) *t.k.h: hld up towards rr: rdn and hdwy over 2f out: r.o u.p fnl f: nt rch ldrs* **13/2**[3]

0003 **5** *nk* **Nikki Bea (IRE)**[25] 4361 4-9-4 **60** PaulDoe 2 66
(Jamie Poulton) *s.i.s: sn in midfield: hdwy and rdn over 2f out: chal ent fnl f: no ex last 100yds* **16/1**

-000 **6** *2 1/2* **Zabeel House**[41] 3851 4-9-8 **64** GeorgeBaker 11 63
(J A R Toller) *dropped in bhd after s: hld up in last pair: rdn and effrt over 2f: no imp over 1f out* **8/1**

3400 **7** *1* **Blue Line**[4] 5001 5-8-13 **58** MarcHalford(3) 9 55
(M Madgwick) *sn rdn in last: hdwy u.p over 2f out: n.d* **25/1**

3040 **8** *nk* **Fateful Attraction**[9] 4856 4-9-6 **62** (b) JamesDoyle 3 58
(I A Wood) *led for 1f: chsd ldrs: rdn wl over 2f out: wknd 2f out* **20/1**

4603 **9** *shd* **Strut The Stage (IRE)**[19] 4529 3-8-9 **62** JackDean(7) 7 56
(B W Duke) *in tch in midfield: rdn over 2f out: wknd wl over 1f out* **22/1**

1126 **10** *1 3/4* **Bucharest**[28] 4250 4-9-8 **64** NickyMackay 13 55
(M Wigham) *t.k.h: led after 1f tl rdn and hdd 2f out: wknd qckly over 1f out* **7/1**

1m 24.57s (-1.32) **Going Correction** -0.20s/f (Stan)
WFA 3 from 4yo+ 4lb 10 Ran SP% **105.9**
Speed ratings (Par 101): **99,99,98,97,97 94,93,93,92,90**
, £2.40 Trifecta £82.60 W: KA £1.90, M £16.50. P: KA £1.20, M £4.80. E: KA/M £80.90, M/KA £58.60. CSF: KA/M £49.36, M/KA £57.82. T: KA/M/CC £145.42, M/KA/CC £178.47.
Owner Miss Sara Furnival **Bred** Mrs J McCreery **Trained** Hucking, Kent
■ Sands Of Barra was withdrawn (15/2, vet's advice). R4, deduct 10p in the £.
Owner Mrs A Hart Mrs A Hodges Mrs C Penny **Bred** Mrs M Chaworth-Musters **Trained** Charlton Mackrell, Somerset
■ Sands Of Barra was withdrawn (15/2, vet's advice). R4, deduct 10p in the £.

FOCUS
A modest handicap producing a dead-heat and a stewards' enquiry into interference between the first three near the line. Dead-heater King After is probably the best guide to the form, which looks sound.
Confucius Classic(IRE) Official explanation: jockey said gelding lost a near front shoe

5119 HEADS-UP @ WILLIAM HILL POKER H'CAP 6f (P)
3:55 (3:56) (Class 4) (0-80,85) 3-Y-0+ **£5,181** (£1,541; £770; £384) **Stalls** Low

Form RPR

0540 **1** **Capricorn Run (USA)**[52] 3525 4-9-2 **76** (v) SteveDrowne 8 89
(A J McCabe) *v.s.a: wl bhd: hdwy on outer 2f out: r.o strly to ld last 50yds* **9/1**

0041 **2** *3/4* **Little Edward**[5] 4965 9-9-11 **85** 6ex GeorgeBaker 12 96
(R J Hodges) *t.k.h: hld up in tch on outer: hdwy to chse ldrs 2f out: rdn to ld ins fnl f: hdd and no ex last 50yds* **5/1**[2]

6432 **3** *1 1/4* **Tous Les Deux**[22] 4462 4-8-13 **73** BrettDoyle 2 80
(Peter Grayson) *in tch: rdn over 2f out: swtchd rt wl over 1f out: styd on wl ins fnl f: wnt 3rd towards fin* **11/2**[3]

0633 **4** *1/2* **Fromsong (IRE)**[5] 4965 9-9-4 **78** RobertHavlin 9 84
(D K Ivory) *prom: ev ch and drvn over 1f out: no ex last 100yds* **6/1**

2350 **5** *shd* **Dvinsky (USA)**[26] 4320 6-8-12 **72** IanMongan 5 77
(P Howling) *chsd ldr: rdn to ld over 1f out: hdd ins fnl f: no ex* **14/1**

1415 **6** *1/2* **Everygrainofsand (IRE)**[32] 4140 4-9-3 **77** DaneO'Neill 6 81
(J R Best) *led tl rdn and hdd over 1f out: fdd last 100yds* **4/1**[1]

000 **7** *1/2* **Total Impact**[5] 4965 4-9-6 **80** (b) MartinDwyer 7 82
(C A Cyzer) *plld hrd in midfield: rdn and effrt over 2f out: kpt on same pce fnl f* **10/1**

1146 **8** *3/4* **Quality Street**[5] 4965 5-8-13 **73** (p) RichardThomas 4 73
(P Butler) *chsd ldrs: rdn over 2f out: wknd ent fnl f* **12/1**

2004 **9** *nk* **Romany Nights (IRE)**[26] 4320 7-8-13 **73** (bt) JohnEgan 11 72
(Miss Gay Kelleway) *a bhd: drvn and no hdwy over 2f out* **14/1**

1340 **10** *14* **Silent Storm**[13] 4716 7-9-1 **75** LPKeniry 1 32
(Peter Grayson) *in tch tl lost pl qckly 1/2-way: t.o fnl f* **25/1**

1m 11.56s (-1.25) **Going Correction** -0.20s/f (Stan) 10 Ran SP% **110.3**
Speed ratings (Par 105): **100,99,97,96,96 95,95,94,93,75**
CSF £48.35 CT £241.45 TOTE £10.60: £2.60, £1.80, £1.70; EX 66.80 Trifecta £321.50 Part won. Pool £452.82. - 0.34 winning units..
Owner Paul J Dixon And Placida Racing **Bred** Santa Rosa Partners **Trained** Babworth, Notts
■ His Master's Voice was withdrawn (12/1, unruly in stalls). R4, deduct 5p in the £.

FOCUS
Sound handicap form rated through the reliable third.
Total Impact Official explanation: jockey said gelding ran too free
Romany Nights(IRE) Official explanation: jockey said gelding was denied a clear run shortly before line
Silent Storm Official explanation: jockey said gelding never travelled

5120 PLAY BACKGAMMON @ WILLHILL.COM H'CAP 1m 4f (P)
4:30 (4:30) (Class 6) (0-60,60) 3-Y-0+ **£2,388** (£705; £352) **Stalls** Low

Form RPR

0602 **1** **Magic Show**[9] 4858 3-9-1 **60** JohnEgan 14 69
(Jane Chapple-Hyam) *w.w in midfield: hdwy over 3f out: rdn to ld wl over 1f out: hld on wl ins fnl f* **9/4**[1]

0006 **2** *nk* **War Of The Roses (IRE)**[6] 4945 4-9-0 **50** DaneO'Neill 4 59
(R Brotherton) *hld up in midfield: hdwy on outer over 3f out: rdn to chal ins fnl f: hld last 50yds* **11/1**

1420 **3** *2 1/2* **Featherlight**[34] 4069 3-8-11 **56** IanMongan 8 61
(Jamie Poulton) *wnt rt s: w.w in midfield: hdwy over 4f out: ev ch and rdn over 2f out: outpcd ins fnl f* **13/2**[3]

0005 **4** *nk* **Sopran Gath (ITY)**[12] 4739 4-9-9 **59** JamesDoyle 10 64
(J W Hills) *hld up in rr: stdy hdwy 3f out: chsd ldrs 2f out: sn rdn: kpt on same pce ins fnl f* **20/1**

5341 **5** *shd* **Spritza (IRE)**[13] 4718 3-9-1 **60** HayleyTurner 16 64
(M L W Bell) *t.k.h: mostly 2nd tl led 2f out: sn hdd and rdn: one pce ins fnl f* **11/2**[2]

6103 **6** *1 3/4* **Zalkani (IRE)**[12] 4739 7-9-9 **59** GeorgeBaker 12 61
(J Pearce) *hld up in rr: hdwy wl over 3f out: trckd ldrs over 2f out: rdn and one pce over 1f out* **13/2**[3]

-600 **7** *1 1/4* **Mystical Moon**[20] 4518 3-9-1 **60** (b[1]) PatDobbs 5 60
(Lady Herries) *t.k.h: chsd ldrs: rdn wl over 2f out: kpt on same pce last 2f* **33/1**

-000 **8** *3* **Nothing Is Forever (IRE)**[24] 4391 3-8-12 **57** DarryllHolland 13 52
(Mrs A J Perrett) *t.k.h: prom on outer: led 5f out: hdd 2f out: sn btn* **12/1**

6364 **9** *2* **Blackmail (USA)**[12] 4739 9-9-5 **55** (b) TQuinn 1 47
(P Mitchell) *in tch in midfield: rdn and struggling whn bmpd over 2f out: no ch after* **16/1**

06-0 **10** *6* **Papeete (GER)**[131] 291 6-9-2 **57** JamesMillman(5) 11 39
(Mrs N Smith) *hld up in rr: rdn over 4f out: n.d* **33/1**

652 **11** *1 1/4* **Lady Ambitious**[75] 2800 4-9-0 **50** RobertHavlin 15 30
(D K Ivory) *stdd after s: hld up in rr: hdwy on outer over 3f out: wknd over 2f out* **33/1**

00-0 **12** *3* **You Live And Learn**[15] 4660 4-9-6 **56** SteveDrowne 9 31
(H Morrison) *bmpd s: t.k.h and sn chsng ldrs: rdn and wknd qckly 3f out* **10/1**

-006 **13** *7* **Ground Patrol**[12] 4739 6-8-12 **55** JackDean(7) 3 19
(W G M Turner) *led tl 5f out: rdn and wknd qckly 3f out: eased ins fnl f* **25/1**

0005 **14** *1/2* **Sterling Moll**[12] 4738 4-8-11 **50** DominicFox(3) 2 13
(W De Best-Turner) *bhd and rdn whn hit rail 5f out: no ch last 3f: eased fnl f* **66/1**

600/ **15** *8* **Paula Lane**[818] 321 7-8-12 **48** DaleGibson 6 —
(R Curtis) *chsd ldrs tl lost pl 5f out: no ch last 3f: t.o and eased fnl f* **66/1**

2m 32.11s (-2.28) **Going Correction** -0.20s/f (Stan)
WFA 3 from 4yo+ 9lb 15 Ran SP% **124.2**
Speed ratings (Par 101): **99,98,97,96,96 95,94,92,91,87 86,84,80,79,74**
CSF £27.55 CT £149.27 TOTE £3.10: £2.00, £5.20, £2.50; EX 53.80 Trifecta £258.80 Part won. Pool £364.59. - 0.99 winning units..
Owner Franconson Partners **Bred** The Earl Of Halifax **Trained** Newmarket, Suffolk

FOCUS
A big field, but still a moderate handicap. The pace was fair, but as is usually the case over middle-distances here the finish was dominated by those held up. The form seems sound enough.
Blackmail(USA) Official explanation: jockey said gelding was hampered approaching final bend
Paula Lane Official explanation: jockey said mare lost its action

5121 CALL HOUSE @ WILLIAMHILLBINGO.COM CLASSIFIED STKS 1m (P)
5:05 (5:05) (Class 7) 3-Y-0+ **£2,047** (£604; £302) **Stalls** High

Form RPR

0065 **1** **Charlottebutterfly**[17] 4596 7-9-5 45 IanMongan 7 56
(P J McBride) *w.w in tch: hdwy to trck ldr wl over 2f out: rdn to ld wl over 1f out: r.o wl* **10/1**

0030 **2** *1 1/2* **Sion Hill (IRE)**[19] 4526 6-9-5 45 (p) JimmyQuinn 9 53
(John A Harris) *t.k.h: chsd ldrs: led 5f out: rdn and hdd wl over 1f out: kpt on same pce* **20/1**

0423 **3** *2 1/2* **Prince Valentine**[21] 4469 6-9-5 45 (p) GeorgeBaker 2 47
(G L Moore) *hld up: hdwy over 3f out: rdn to chse ldng pair wl over 1f out: no imp* **9/4**[1]

0024 **4** *2 1/2* **Slavonic Lake**[27] 4292 3-9-0 45 (t) JamesDoyle 3 41
(I A Wood) *taken down early: in tch: rdn and outpcd 3f out: kpt on past btn horses fnl f: no ch* **13/2**[3]

4003 **5** *1/2* **Dexileos (IRE)**[15] 4673 8-9-0 45 KevinGhunowa(5) 5 40
(David Pinder) *chsd ldr tl led over 5f out: sn hdd: styd handy tl rdn and wknd over 1f out* **10/1**

0500 **6** *3/4* **Fun In The Sun**[11] 4760 3-9-0 45 (v) SteveDrowne 11 38
(P D Evans) *sn bhd and rdn: nvr on terms* **12/1**

0500 **7** *2 1/2* **Lizarazu (GER)**[2] 5062 8-9-5 45 (p) JohnEgan 1 32
(R A Harris) *led tl over 5f out: chsd ldrs tl rdn and wknd over 2f out* **11/1**

2000 **8** *3* **Sharpattack**[26] 4337 3-9-0 45 OscarUrbina 10 26
(M Botti) *t.k.h: hld up in midfield on outer: hdwy over 3f out: chsd ldrs and rdn over 2f out: sn wl hld* **66/1**

0005 **9** *3/4* **Baarrij**[20] 4516 3-9-0 45 MickyFenton 4 24
(G A Huffer) *sn bhd and rdn: nvr on terms* **28/1**

0000 **10** *3 1/2* **Edin Burgher (FR)**[161] 797 6-9-5 45 TGMcLaughlin 12 16
(T T Clement) *hld up in rr: rdn over 3f out: sn no ch* **20/1**

0 **11** *6* **Abtak (IRE)**[121] 1501 7-9-5 45 TQuinn 6 —
(P Burgoyne) *plld hrd: chsd ldrs tl wknd qckly 2f out* **20/1**

0002 **P** **Fancy (IRE)**[15] 4673 4-8-12 45 SophieDoyle(7) 8 —
(R A Farrant) *bhd: rdn and no rspnse wl over 2f out: wl bhd whn p.u and dismntd wl over 1f out* **7/2**[2]

1m 38.26s (-1.17) **Going Correction** -0.20s/f (Stan)
WFA 3 from 4yo+ 5lb 12 Ran SP% **119.8**
Speed ratings (Par 97): **97,95,93,90,90 89,86,83,83,79 73,—**
CSF £198.97 TOTE £12.00: £2.40, £6.00, £1.10; EX 216.80 Trifecta £223.80 Pool £343.60 - 1.09 winning units..
Owner Future Electrical Services Ltd **Bred** J T O'Neill **Trained** Newmarket, Suffolk

FOCUS
Weak form, even for a race at the lowest level, though the pace was solid enough. The form has been rated through the winner.
Lizarazu(GER) Official explanation: jockey said gelding hung right

5122 PLAY GAMES @ WILLIAMHILLARCADE.COM H'CAP 1m (P)
5:40 (5:40) (Class 5) (0-75,75) 3-Y-O **£3,071** (£680; £680) **Stalls** High

Form RPR

0-16 **1** **Mount Hermon (IRE)**[133] 1228 3-9-4 **75** SteveDrowne 12 81+
(H Morrison) *t.k.h: hld up on outer towards rr: hdwy 2f out: styd on wl u.p fnl f to ld nr fin* **5/1**[2]

3414 **2** *1/2* **Divertimenti (IRE)**[8] 4884 3-9-4 **75** GeorgeBaker 7 80
(C R Dore) *t.k.h: hld up in tch: hdwy to trck ldrs 2f out: rdn and effrt ent fnl f: styd on* **5/1**[2]

15 **2** *dht* **Tremelo Pointe (IRE)**[154] 904 3-8-10 **67** MickyFenton 10 72
(H Morrison) *cl up: chsd ldr 4f out: led 3f out: rdn and kpt on wl fr 2f out tl hdd and no ex nr fin* **20/1**

2452 **4** *hd* **Nicada (IRE)**[26] 4313 3-8-8 **70** (p) TolleyDean(5) 8 74
(J S Moore) *t.k.h: trckd ldrs: rdn to chse ldr over 2f out: ev ch tl unable qck wl ins fnl f* **16/1**

1342 **5** *1 1/2* **Zelos (IRE)**[11] 4760 3-8-10 **67** (b) TQuinn 4 68
(D J S Ffrench Davis) *plld hrd: trckd ldrs: rdn and effrt on rail ent fnl f: no imp last 100yds* **12/1**

1406 **6** *shd* **Proper (IRE)**[8] 4884 3-8-6 **70** MatthewDavies(7) 5 71
(M R Channon) *hld up in tch: rdn 3f out: outpcd 2f out: rallied ins fnl f: r.o nt rch ldrs* **16/1**

501 **7** *shd* **Elusive Dreams (USA)**[19] 4541 3-8-13 **70** RobertHavlin 9 71
(J H M Gosden) *s.i.s: sn in tch in midfield: rdn and chsd ldrs over 2f out: unable qck fnl f* **8/1**

0036 **8** *nk* **Effigy**[36] 4015 3-8-9 **66** DaneO'Neill 3 66
(H Candy) *chsd ldr tl 4f out: rdn and wknd over 2f out* **7/1**[3]

366 **9** *3* **Winning Show**[28] 4258 3-9-2 **73** JohnEgan 11 66
(R A Harris) *stdd sn after s: hld up in rr: rdn 3f out: nvr able to chal* **33/1**

2012 **10** *1/2* **The Fifth Member (IRE)**[10] 4807 3-9-0 **71** DarryllHolland 2 63
(J R Boyle) *chsd ldrs tl lost pl and dropped to rr over 4f out: rdn 3f out: nvr able to chal* **11/4**[1]

3000 **11** *hd* **Resplendent Ace (IRE)**[27] 4276 3-9-4 **75** JimmyQuinn 6 66
(P Howling) *led tl rdn and hdd 3f out: wknd 2f out* **20/1**

100 **12** *2* **Dansil In Distress**[14] 4684 3-8-9 **66**............ PatDobbs 1 53
(S Kirk) *a bhd: rdn 3f out: n.d* **25/1**

1m 37.56s (-1.87) **Going Correction** -0.20s/f (Stan) **12** Ran SP% **119.4**
Speed ratings (Par 101): **101,100,100,100,98 98,98,98,95,94 94,92**
TOTE £6.30: £2.00 TRIFECTA P:D £2.80, TP £6.90. E: MH/D £18.50, MH/TP £55.70. CSF: MH/D £14.39, MH/TP £53.15. T: MH/D/TP £236.87, MH/TP/D £269.57. P6 £65.67,.
Owner Wood Street Syndicate III **Bred** Illumnatus Investments And Elite Bloodst **Trained** East Ilsley, Berks
■ Stewards' Enquiry : Jimmy Quinn two-day ban: careless riding (Sep 16-17)

FOCUS
An ordinary handicap run at just a fair pace and the winning time was 0.7 seconds quicker than the preceding event, though given the difference in class that was no more than would have been expected. Fair form, if not easy to rate. The winner and dead-heater for second Tremelo Pointe, both trained by Hughie Morrison, were both up 6lb and may do better.
The Fifth Member(IRE) Official explanation: jockey said colt never travelled
T/Plt: £93.60 to a £1 stake. Pool: £53,642.05. 418.30 winning tickets. T/Qpdt: £16.10 to a £1 stake. Pool: £3,634.80. 166.80 winning tickets. SP

5123 - 5125a (Foreign Racing) - See Raceform Interactive

4944 KEMPTON (A.W) (R-H)
Wednesday, September 5

OFFICIAL GOING: Standard
Wind: Virtually nil

5126 EUROPEAN BREEDERS' FUND MEDIAN AUCTION MAIDEN STKS 6f (P)
6:20 (6:21) (Class 6) 2-Y-O £2,730 (£806; £403) Stalls High

Form RPR
43 **1** **Lodi (IRE)**[12] 4764 2-9-3 0............ RichardHughes 4 81
(B J Meehan) *b.hind: lw: chsd ldrs: wnt 2nd 2f out: sn drvn along: str run on ins fnl f: led last strides* **4/9**[1]
2 *nk* **Blue Eyed Miss (IRE)** 2-8-12 0............ FrankieMcDonald 10 75
(P A Blockley) *w'like: b.hind: led: t.k.h: rdn and styd on wl fnl 2f: ct last strides* **12/1**[3]
3 *2* **Paco Boy (IRE)** 2-9-3 0............ RyanMoore 9 74
(R Hannon) *w'like: bit bkwd: s.i.s: sn mid-div: styd on fnl 2f and kpt on ins fnl f but nvr gng pce to rch ldng duo* **11/2**[2]
0 **4** *3* **Southern Mistral**[28] 4285 2-9-3 0............ TPQueally 1 65
(W J Haggas) *w'like: chsd ldrs: rdn and edgd rt ins fnl 2f: styd on same pce* **16/1**
00 **5** *1* **In A Pickle**[12] 4761 2-8-12 0............ DaneO'Neill 7 57
(H J L Dunlop) *chsd ldrs: rdn 3f out: no ch fnl 2f* **40/1**
0 **6** *1 ¼* **Charlevoix (IRE)**[79] 2724 2-8-12 0............ TedDurcan 5 53
(C F Wall) *w'like: chsd ldrs early: outpcd 1/2-way: n.d after* **12/1**[3]
7 *1 ½* **Our Lament** 2-9-3 0............ J-PGuillambert 6 54
(G C Bravery) *w'like: in rr: rdn 1/2-way: mod prog fnl f* **100/1**
0 **8** *¾* **Mio Fiore**[20] 4540 2-8-12 0............ JimmyQuinn 11 47
(M Blanshard) *in tch: rdn 3f out: sn btn* **50/1**
9 *½* **Pretty Officer (USA)** 2-8-12 0............ ChrisCatlin 8 45
(Rae Guest) *leggy: unf: s.i.s: outpcd* **33/1**
00 **10** *nk* **Enchanted Lady**[15] 4683 2-8-12 0............ RobertHavlin 3 44
(H J L Dunlop) *swtg: chsd ldrs tl bmpd and wknd ins fnl 2f* **100/1**
00 **11** *1 ¾* **Master Of Arts (USA)**[6] 4962 2-9-3 0............ SebSanders 12 44
(Sir Mark Prescott) *s.i.s: outpcd* **25/1**
00 **12** *13* **Follow The Band**[19] 4571 2-9-3 0............ RichardSmith 2 —
(R Hannon) *early spd: sn outpcd* **20/1**

1m 13.76s (0.06) **Going Correction** -0.175s/f (Stan) **12** Ran SP% **123.8**
Speed ratings (Par 93): **92,91,88,84,83 81,79,78,78,77 75,58**
CSF £7.30 TOTE £1.40: £1.02, £4.50, £2.00; EX 11.20.
Owner 6C Racing & Attenborough,Mann & Maynard **Bred** Allevamento Gialloblu S R L **Trained** Manton, Wilts

FOCUS
An ordinary maiden in which they bet 16/1 bar three and the result was pretty much as the market indicated. The winner looks the best guide to the level.

NOTEBOOK
Lodi(IRE), in the frame in maidens at Newbury and Newmarket over 7f, was keen to post and went off odds-on but was made to work hard to get off the mark at the third attempt. He was always in the right position, but Hughes had to get serious with the colt to catch the runner-up in the dying strides. He should be competitive in nurseries off a mark in the low 70s. (op 1-2)
Blue Eyed Miss(IRE) ♦, a debutante who clearly knew her job, made full use of her high draw, trying to lead throughout. She was only caught in the last few strides and should not be long in gaining compensation. (op 11-1 tchd 14-1)
Paco Boy(IRE), quite a strong, good-bodied half-brother to several winners at 7f-1m2f, made a promising debut, being the only one to come from off the pace. He should be better for the experience and a step up in trip is likely to be in his favour. (op 13-2)
Southern Mistral had clearly improved from his debut and showed up well until finding no extra inside the last quarter-mile. (op 20-1)

5127 BETRESCUE ANTEPOSTMAG.COM NURSERY 1m (P)
6:50 (6:53) (Class 6) (0-65,65) 2-Y-O £2,047 (£604; £302) Stalls High

Form RPR
300 **1** **King Supreme (IRE)**[12] 4777 2-9-5 **63**............ RyanMoore 10 69
(R Hannon) *sn reminders to chse ldrs: rdn over 3f out: chsd wnr appr fnl f: led last half f: readily* **5/1**[2]
0406 **2** *1* **Synge Street**[31] 4202 2-9-3 **61**............ RichardHughes 7 65
(R Hannon) *in rr: stl last 3f out: rapid hdwy over 1f out: str run fnl f and qcknd to chse wnr cl home but a hld* **9/2**[1]
000 **3** *2* **Dawn Wind**[49] 3643 2-9-2 **60**............ JamesDoyle 8 59
(I A Wood) *lw: in rr: hdwy fr 2f out: styd on wl fr over 1f out and gng on cl home but nvr gng pce to ldng duo* **14/1**
046 **4** *hd* **Smith Esquire (USA)**[55] 3471 2-9-5 **63**............ AdamKirby 6 62
(W R Swinburn) *lw: chsd ldrs: rdn to dispute 2nd 2f out: outpcd ins fnl f* **7/1**
000 **5** *hd* **Danamight (IRE)**[32] 4162 2-9-7 **65**............ MartinDwyer 3 63
(G G Margarson) *s.i.s: bhd: n.m.r over 2f out: styd on wl fnl f but nvr gng pce to be competitive* **20/1**
0301 **6** *½* **Lady Bower**[6] 4968 2-9-3 **61** 6ex............ J-PGuillambert 9 58
(M Johnston) *lw: led: rdn over 2f out: hdd & wknd last half f* **6/1**[3]
5011 **7** *1 ½* **Marmite (IRE)**[40] 3923 2-9-7 **65**............(v) LPKeniry 1 58
(E F Vaughan) *in rr: rdn and hdwy on outside bnd 3f out: kpt on fnl f but nvr in contention* **13/2**
0500 **8** *½* **Titfer (IRE)**[24] 4417 2-8-12 **61**............ LukeMorris[(5)] 2 53
(A W Carroll) *in rr tl sme prog fr over 1f out* **66/1**
560 **9** *nk* **Xtravaganza (IRE)**[32] 4181 2-9-6 **64**............ GeorgeBaker 5 56
(J W Hills) *chsd ldrs: rdn over 2f out: wknd over 1f out* **18/1**
060 **10** *shd* **Ovthenight (IRE)**[20] 4547 2-9-6 **64**............ MickyFenton 13 55
(Mrs P Sly) *a towards rr* **14/1**
006 **11** *1* **Singer Of Songs (IRE)**[40] 3902 2-8-13 **62**............ KevinGhunowa[(5)] 11 51
(P A Blockley) *chsd ldr: rdn over 3f out: wknd over 1f out* **25/1**
000 **12** *½* **I Certainly May**[32] 4151 2-9-7 **65**............ DaneO'Neill 12 53
(S Dow) *in rr: sme hdwy whn n.m.r ins fnl 2f: n.d after* **12/1**
060 **13** *1 ¼* **Air Chief**[34] 4110 2-9-7 **65**............ SebSanders 4 50
(H J L Dunlop) *in tch: rdn and effrt 3f out: nvr rchd ldrs: wknd 2f out* **14/1**
2504 **14** *nk* **Valhillen**[37] 4022 2-9-0 **61**............ JamieMoriarty[(3)] 14 45
(M J Wallace) *chsd ldrs: rdn 3f out: wknd fr 2f out* **10/1**

1m 40.66s (-0.14) **Going Correction** -0.175s/f (Stan) **14** Ran SP% **127.1**
Speed ratings (Par 93): **93,92,90,89,89 89,87,87,86,86 85,85,83,83**
CSF £28.89 CT £311.77 TOTE £7.30: £2.90, £1.80, £3.70; EX 43.10.
Owner Brian C Oakley **Bred** Miss Joan Murphy **Trained** East Everleigh, Wilts
■ Stewards' Enquiry : Richard Hughes caution: careless riding

FOCUS
An open-looking nursery featuring plenty of unexposed sorts making their handicap debuts. The form looks reasonable rated around the third and fourth.

NOTEBOOK
King Supreme(IRE), making his handicap debut having not really gone on from his promising first start, was well backed and got off the mark at the fourth attempt. He was backed against his stablemate and favourite Synge Street and, getting first run on that rival, he collared the long-time leader inside the last to win well. He will be aimed at similar races at Doncaster and Newmarket this backend. (op 10-1)
Synge Street had to come from virtually last turning in but eventually got a clear passage in the wake of his stablemate and chased him home. He can be considered slightly unlucky but he was not closing the gap appreciably in the last half-furlong. (op 4-1)
Dawn Wind, another making her handicap debut, stayed on steadily in the final furlong and seemed to appreciate the step up in trip.
Smith Esquire(USA), who was ridden more positively on this step up in trip, was just run out of the places after being close up throughout. (op 8-1)
Danamight(IRE) was again slowly away but, on her handicap and Polytrack debut, did best of those drawn low. (op 16-1)
Lady Bower, who made all when winning her maiden on fast ground at Musselburgh, adopted similar tactics and was clear early in the straight. However, she weakened in the last furlong and was swallowed up by the closers, suggesting this trip was too far at this stage of her career. (op 4-1 tchd 13-2)
Marmite(IRE), a dual selling winner, on this surface last time, had to race wide throughout and, although briefly making headway off the turn, never really figured. (op 8-1)

5128 DIGIBET CASINO CLAIMING STKS 1m (P)
7:20 (7:22) (Class 6) 3-5-Y-O £2,047 (£604; £302) Stalls High

Form RPR
6030 **1** **Russki (IRE)**[18] 4608 3-9-2 76............(b) JimCrowley 8 74
(Mrs A J Perrett) *towards rr but in tch: hdwy over 3f out: led 2f out and sn drvn clr: comf* **7/2**[2]
0151 **2** *3* **Norisan**[12] 4778 3-9-5 95............(b) RyanMoore 7 70
(R Hannon) *lw: chsd ldrs: drvn along 3f out: styd on to chse wnr fnl f but nvr any ch* **5/6**[1]
3400 **3** *1 ¾* **Sweet World**[21] 4518 3-9-2 60............ SebSanders 6 63
(A P Jarvis) *led 2f: styd chsng ldr tl led 3f out: hdd 2f out: outpcd sn after and lost 2nd fnl f* **16/1**
455 **4** *¾* **Silver Blue (IRE)**[19] 4577 4-8-6 58............ HaddenFrost[(5)] 11 53
(R Hannon) *towards rr but in tch: hdwy on ins 3f out: sn rdn: styd on fr over 1f out but nvr in contention* **6/1**[3]
-640 **5** *¾* **Franky'N'Jonny**[41] 3868 4-8-7 35............(p) PaulFitzsimons 9 47
(M J Attwater) *chsd ldrs: rdn over 2f out: little rspnse* **66/1**
0010 **6** *nk* **Vietnam**[10] 4856 3-8-8 55............(b) FrancisNorton 3 51
(G A Huffer) *towards rr but in tch: rdn 3f out: nvr in contention* **25/1**
0000 **7** *1 ½* **Ninth House (USA)**[9] 4889 5-9-5 80............(bt) TolleyDean[(5)] 2 60
(N P Littmoden) *a towards rr* **7/1**
1000 **8** *5* **Tipsy Lad**[2] 5094 5-8-11 53............(t) ChrisCatlin 1 35
(D J S Ffrench Davis) *sn rdn: a in rr* **33/1**
0106 **9** *3* **Joint Expectations (IRE)**[40] 3918 3-8-11 48............(b) DMylonas 5 32
(Mrs C A Dunnett) *w ldr: led after 2f tl hdd 3f out: sn wknd* **50/1**

1m 39.06s (-1.74) **Going Correction** -0.175s/f (Stan)
WFA 3 from 4yo+ 5lb **9** Ran SP% **119.7**
Speed ratings (Par 101): **101,98,96,95,94 94,92,87,84**
CSF £6.91 TOTE £4.10: £1.10, £1.10, £3.40; EX 9.00.Norisan was claimed by Alan Edward Jones for £18,000. Russki was claimed by D. M. I. Simcock for £15,000. Silver Blue was claimed by C. R. Dore for £5,000.
Owner John E Bodie **Bred** Mark Commins **Trained** Pulborough, W Sussex

FOCUS
An uncompetitive claimer run 1.6secs faster than the preceding nursery and the form looks sound rated around the third and fifth.

5129 DIGIBET MEDIAN AUCTION MAIDEN STKS 7f (P)
7:50 (7:52) (Class 6) 3-5-Y-O £2,047 (£604; £302) Stalls High

Form RPR
5-23 **1** **Gilded Youth**[11] 4808 3-9-3 70............ DaneO'Neill 7 68
(H Candy) *mde all: drvn and styd on strly fnl 2f: unchal* **9/4**[1]
0-50 **2** *1 ¼* **Touch Of Style (IRE)**[11] 4811 3-9-3 78............ RyanMoore 3 65
(J R Boyle) *chsd ldrs: rdn over 2f out and sn one pce: styd on again fnl f to take 2nd cl home but nvr any ch w wnr* **3/1**[2]
3-6P **3** *nk* **Towy Girl (IRE)**[29] 4257 3-8-7 67............ LukeMorris[(5)] 12 59
(A W Carroll) *chsd ldrs: wnt 2nd over 2f out and sn hrd drvn: nvr any ch w wnr: edgd lft ins fnl f: ct for 2nd cl home* **11/1**
0043 **4** *¾* **Task Complete**[39] 3966 4-9-2 45............ StephenCarson 8 59
(Jean-Rene Auvray) *sn chsng wnr tl 2f out: one pce u.p sn after* **16/1**
0-5 **4** *dht* **Far Seeking**[125] 1433 3-9-3 0............ RichardHughes 6 62+
(Mrs A J Perrett) *chsd ldrs: rdn 2f out: on pce whn n.m.r ins fnl f and nvr a danger after* **9/2**[3]
5 **6** *3 ½* **Compulsion**[97] 2173 4-9-2 0............ MartinDwyer 9 50
(Pat Eddery) *t.k.h early: chsd ldrs: pushed along over 2f out: wknd fnl f* **9/2**[3]
0 **7** *1 ¼* **Tiger Trail (GER)**[20] 4541 3-9-3 0............ JamesDoyle 11 49
(Mrs N Smith) *a towards rr* **50/1**
0000 **8** *2 ½* **Polish Prospect (IRE)**[50] 3619 3-8-12 43............ JimmyQuinn 1 37
(H S Howe) *in tch over 4f* **100/1**
0 **9** *¾* **Lady Lorins**[20] 4530 3-8-9 0............ JerryO'Dwyer[(3)] 5 35
(Andrew Turnell) *leggy: a towards rr* **100/1**
00 **10** *1 ¾* **Forever Bold**[16] 4666 3-9-3 0............ VinceSlattery 2 36
(J G Portman) *w'like: slowly away: rdn and effrt on outside over 3f out: sn wknd* **100/1**

11 3/4 **Rollin 'n Tumblin** 3-9-3 0 .... SebSanders 10 34
(W Jarvis) *leggy: rdn and green in rr thrght* **16/1**

1m 26.0s (-0.80) **Going Correction** -0.175s/f (Stan)
WFA 3 from 4yo 4lb 11 Ran SP% **117.2**
Speed ratings (Par 101): **97,95,95,94,94 90,88,86,85,83 82**
CSF £8.96 TOTE £3.30: £1.30, £1.50, £3.20; EX 12.60.
Owner Girsonfield Ltd **Bred** Girsonfield Ltd **Trained** Kingston Warren, Oxon

FOCUS
A modest all-aged maiden limited by the proximity of the 45-rated dead-heating fourth and little solidity to the form.

5130 DIGIBET.COM H'CAP 6f (P)
8:20 (8:23) (Class 6) (0-65,65) 3-Y-O+ **£2,047** (£604; £302) **Stalls** High

Form RPR

6600 1 **Hollow Jo**[18] 4594 7-9-3 **62** .... MickyFenton 1 74
(J R Jenkins) *hld up in rr: rapid hdwy over 1f out to ld ins fnl f: hld on wl* **14/1**

6406 2 *nk* **Nautical**[18] 4606 9-8-9 **59** .... LukeMorris(5) 6 70
(A W Carroll) *in rr: rdn and hung rt ins fnl 2f: stl plenty to do over 1f out: rapid hdwy ins fnl f: fin strly: nt quite get up* **11/2**[2]

5235 3 *nk* **Norcroft**[18] 4594 5-8-10 **62** .... (p) KirstyMilczarek(7) 3 72
(Mrs C A Dunnett) *chsd ldrs: rdn 2f out: styd on to chal ins fnl f: no ex cl home* **5/1**[1]

6356 4 1 1/4 **Drumming Party (USA)**[25] 4396 5-8-13 **58** .... (t) LPKeniry 8 64
(A M Balding) *b.hind: lw: trckd ldrs: hdwy on ins 2f out: led 1f out: hdd ins fnl f: wknd cl home* **13/2**[3]

2324 5 *hd* **Make My Dream**[11] 4808 4-9-4 **63** .... JimCrowley 9 69
(J Gallagher) *chsd ldrs: led 2f out: hdd 1f out: wknd cl home* **5/1**[1]

0400 6 2 **Guildenstern (IRE)**[28] 4296 5-9-6 **65** .... IanMongan 5 65
(P Howling) *chsd ldrs: rdn over 2f out: styd on same pce fnl f* **12/1**

6005 7 1/2 **No Time (IRE)**[7] 4944 7-8-10 **62** .... RobbieEgan(7) 12 60
(A J McCabe) *chsd ldrs: rdn 3f out: wknd fnl f* **14/1**

406 8 *nk* **Siraj**[7] 4944 8-9-4 **63** .... (p) BrettDoyle 4 60
(J Ryan) *in tch: rdn over 2f out: n.d* **11/2**[2]

0100 9 *hd* **Kind Of Fizzy**[27] 4326 3-9-3 **64** .... ChrisCatlin 2 61
(Rae Guest) *outpcd most of way* **33/1**

0050 10 *nk* **Kingscross**[19] 4585 9-9-5 **64** .... JimmyQuinn 7 60
(M Blanshard) *in rr: sme hdwy on ins 3f out but nvr gng pce to be competitive* **12/1**

1240 11 7 **Currency**[10] 4853 10-9-2 **61** .... RyanMoore 11 36
(J M Bradley) *outpcd most of way* **8/1**

0-00 12 3 1/2 **Mother's Day**[11] 4828 4-8-8 **60** .... (p) HarryPoulton(7) 10 24
(L A Dace) *led tl hdd 2f out: wknd qckly* **100/1**

1m 12.14s (-1.56) **Going Correction** -0.175s/f (Stan)
WFA 3 from 4yo+ 2lb 12 Ran SP% **121.2**
Speed ratings (Par 101): **103,102,102,100,100 97,96,96,96,95 86,81**
CSF £91.23 CT £457.68 TOTE £18.60: £4.60, £3.30, £2.10; EX 119.80.
Owner Jim McCarthy **Bred** K J Reddington **Trained** Royston, Herts

FOCUS
A modest handicap run 1.62sec faster than the opening juvenile maiden and solid enough with the fourth and fifth close to recent form.

5131 WOODFORD RESERVE H'CAP 1m 4f (P)
8:50 (8:50) (Class 5) (0-75,72) 3-Y-O **£2,914** (£867; £433; £216) **Stalls** Centre

Form RPR

3241 1 **Silver Mitzva (IRE)**[27] 4339 3-8-10 **69** .... (b) AshleyHamblett(5) 1 78
(M Botti) *chsd ldr: led 2f out: kpt slt advantage u.p thrght fnl f: all out* **15/2**

2012 2 *shd* **Raise The Goblet (IRE)**[21] 4518 3-9-1 **72** .... LiamJones(3) 8 80
(W J Haggas) *mde most tl hdd 2f out: rallied to chal thrght fnl f: no ex last strides* **9/2**[2]

2414 3 1/2 **Music Review**[14] 4717 3-8-13 **70** .... JamieMoriarty(3) 5 78
(R A Fahey) *towards rr but in tch: hdwy 3f out: chsd ldrs 2f out: styd on strly thrght fnl f but nvr quite gng pce to press ldng duo* **8/1**

0612 4 2 **Tebee**[32] 4185 3-9-2 **70** .... RobertHavlin 7 74
(J H M Gosden) *lw: chsd ldrs: rdn 3f out: one pce fnl 2f* **2/1**[1]

0356 5 1 1/2 **Best Selection**[56] 3421 3-9-0 **68** .... SebSanders 4 70
(A P Jarvis) *towards rr: rdn over 3f out: sme hdwy fnl 2f but nvr in contention* **16/1**

3605 6 2 1/2 **Dan Tucker**[21] 4511 3-9-3 **71** .... RichardHughes 3 69
(B J Meehan) *chsd ldrs: rdn over 2f out: wknd over 1f out* **6/1**[3]

-340 7 1 1/4 **Limbo King**[16] 4667 3-9-4 **72** .... RyanMoore 6 68
(J R Fanshawe) *a towards rr* **15/2**

5-03 8 2 1/2 **Verbatim**[25] 4392 3-8-13 **67** .... FrancisNorton 2 59
(A M Balding) *plld hrd: pressed wnr after 2f to 7f out: wknd fr 3f out* **14/1**

2m 34.25s (-2.65) **Going Correction** -0.175s/f (Stan) 8 Ran SP% **113.0**
Speed ratings (Par 101): **101,100,100,99,98 96,95,94**
CSF £40.08 CT £276.76 TOTE £7.00: £2.10, £1.80, £2.70; EX 32.90.
Owner A Nencini **Bred** Soc Finanza Locale Consulting Srl **Trained** Newmarket, Suffolk
■ Stewards' Enquiry : Ashley Hamblett caution: used whip down the shoulder in forehand position

FOCUS
A moderate handicap that produced a desperate finish but the form looks straightforward rated around the placed horses.

5132 FOLLOW YOUR MEETING WITH EVENING RACING H'CAP 1m 3f (P)
9:20 (9:21) (Class 6) (0-60,60) 3-Y-O+ **£2,047** (£604; £302) **Stalls** High

Form RPR

0022 1 **Little Carmela**[15] 4687 3-9-0 **58** .... SaleemGolam 13 70
(S C Williams) *sn chsng ldr: led 2f out: drvn 3l clr sn after: hld on u.p thrght fnl f* **7/2**[2]

5644 2 3/4 **Mae Cigan (FR)**[21] 4504 4-9-6 **56** .... RyanMoore 6 66
(M Blanshard) *towards rr: rapid hdwy fr 2f out: str run thrght fnl f to chse wnr wl ins fnl f but a jst hld* **3/1**[1]

661 3 3/4 **Ile Michel**[74] 2875 10-9-10 **60** .... SebSanders 5 69
(Lady Herries) *lw: chsd ldrs: outpcd 4f out: rdn and styd on again fr 2f out: kpt on ins fnl f but nvr quite gng pce to rr ldng duo* **6/1**[3]

0045 4 3/4 **Sir Haydn**[18] 4592 7-9-8 **58** .... (v) MickyFenton 10 66
(J R Jenkins) *in tch tl outpcd 4f out: rallied 3f out to chse wnr ins fnl 2f: wknd ins fnl f* **16/1**

6064 5 3 **Bowl Of Cherries**[7] 4945 4-8-13 **49** .... (v) JamesDoyle 14 52
(I A Wood) *chsd ldrs: rdn 3f out: wknd over 1f out* **7/1**

4000 6 1 **Maria Antonia (IRE)**[28] 4297 4-8-11 **52** .... KevinGhunowa(5) 7 53
(P A Blockley) *chsd ldrs: rdn over 3f out: wknd over 1f out* **20/1**

4035 7 *nk* **Snake Skin**[12] 4766 4-9-5 **58** .... JerryO'Dwyer(3) 11 58
(J Gallagher) *sn led: hdd & wknd 2f out* **8/1**

6400 8 3/4 **Lilac Star**[4] 5052 4-9-3 **53** .... (p) TGMcLaughlin 9 52
(T T Clement) *t.k.h: chsd ldrs to 3f out: wknd 2f out* **25/1**

0600 9 3 **Ganache (IRE)**[18] 4592 5-9-3 **53** .... GeorgeBaker 8 47
(P R Chamings) *a towards rr* **7/1**

-000 10 1 3/4 **Lynford Lady**[16] 4670 4-9-0 **50** .... (v[1]) RobertHavlin 4 41
(P W D'Arcy) *nvr bttr than mid-div* **50/1**

0000 11 8 **Soizic (NZ)**[19] 4577 5-9-1 **58** .... HarryPoulton(7) 2 35
(L A Dace) *towards rr: sme hdwy 5f out: sn wknd* **100/1**

0060 12 *hd* **Dictatrix**[10] 4856 4-9-10 **60** .... (p) AdamKirby 1 37
(C R Dore) *a in rr* **40/1**

5635 13 1/2 **Snowflight**[14] 4718 3-8-11 **58** .... JamieMoriarty(3) 12 34
(R A Fahey) *chsd ldrs 1m* **14/1**

2m 21.11s (-1.57) **Going Correction** -0.175s/f (Stan)
WFA 3 from 4yo+ 8lb 13 Ran SP% **124.2**
Speed ratings (Par 101): **98,97,96,96,94 93,93,92,90,89 83,83,82**
CSF £14.39 CT £64.09 TOTE £4.90: £1.60, £2.00, £2.10; EX 24.60 Place 6 £24.97, Place 5 £21.23.
Owner O Pointing **Bred** O Pointing **Trained** Newmarket, Suffolk

FOCUS
A moderate handicap run at a steady early pace but the first four were clear and the form is rated slightly positively.
T/Plt: £54.60 to a £1 stake. Pool: £64,369.10. 859.50 winning tickets. T/Qpdt: £10.60 to a £1 stake. Pool: £4,118.30. 285.10 winning tickets. ST

5116 LINGFIELD (L-H)
Wednesday, September 5

OFFICIAL GOING: Turf course - good to firm; all-weather - standard
Wind: Almost nil Weather: Fine

5133 PLAY GOLF @ LINGFIELD PARK (S) STKS 6f (P)
2:10 (2:10) (Class 6) 2-Y-O **£2,047** (£604; £302) **Stalls** Low

Form RPR

556 1 **Sharps Gold**[11] 4810 2-8-1 45 .... (t) LukeMorris(5) 8 45
(P J McBride) *dwlt: hld up in last pair: prog on outer 2f out: drvn to chal fnl f: led last stride* **16/1**

2 2 *shd* **Bollywood Style**[26] 4359 2-8-6 0 .... JimCrowley 4 45
(P Winkworth) *trckd ldrs: effrt 2f out: drvn to ld narrowly ins fnl f: hdd post* **7/2**[3]

0000 3 3/4 **Mairead's Boy (IRE)**[11] 4824 2-8-6 45 .... (b[1]) TolleyDean(5) 6 48
(J S Moore) *prog to press ldrs over 3f out: drvn to chal 1f out: upsides ins fnl f: nt qckn* **25/1**

060 4 *hd* **Chemise (IRE)**[17] 4629 2-8-6 55 .... FrancisNorton 9 42
(R J Hodges) *led after 1f and set mod pce: hrd pressed over 1f out: hdd and no ex ins fnl f* **8/1**

0266 5 2 **Tenjack Queen (IRE)**[26] 4359 2-8-6 65 .... ChrisCatlin 5 36
(Miss Tor Sturgis) *hld up in tch: rdn whn nt clr run jst over 1f out: one pce fnl f* **10/3**[2]

000 6 *nk* **Korcula**[62] 3246 2-8-11 41 .... DaneO'Neill 2 40
(M J Wallace) *hld up bhd ldrs: rdn and n.m.r over 1f out: nt qckn fnl f* **66/1**

0003 7 1 3/4 **Seventh Cloud (IRE)**[11] 4824 2-8-6 51 .... SimonWhitworth 7 30
(A P Jarvis) *led 1f: pressed ldr tl wknd ent fnl f* **7/1**

5003 8 1 3/4 **Star In The East**[5] 5017 2-8-6 53 .... (b) LPKeniry 1 25
(Peter Grayson) *cl up on inner tl wknd over 1f out* **16/1**

9 3 **To The Dance (IRE)** 2-8-11 0 .... RichardMullen 3 21
(E J O'Neill) *dwlt: rn green in rr: shkn up on inner over 2f out: no prog: eased whn no ch fnl f* **7/4**[1]

1m 13.2s (0.39) **Going Correction** -0.25s/f (Stan) 9 Ran SP% **122.4**
Speed ratings (Par 93): **87,86,85,85,82 82,80,77,73**
CSF £75.74 TOTE £26.20: £5.20, £1.80, £5.90; EX 114.70 TRIFECTA Not won..There was no bid for the winner. Bollywood Style was claimed by J Best for £6,000.
Owner R Nunn **Bred** J M Beever **Trained** Newmarket, Suffolk

FOCUS
A dire juvenile event, even by selling standards, and the first four were closely covered at the finish. A candidate for worst juvenile event of the year.

NOTEBOOK
Sharps Gold, making her All-Weather bow, relished the drop back down in grade and came home for a last-gasp win. She did well to overcome a sluggish start and showed a good attitude when asked to make up her ground in the final 2f. She is evidently going the right way, but this is still very much her level. (op 20-1)
Bollywood Style again was well backed and was produced with what appeared to be a winning move inside the final furlong. She eventually found the post coming a touch too late, however, and again managed to find one too good. She was later claimed to join John Best and it will be surprising if she cannot go one better before long in this sort of class. (op 5-1)
Mairead's Boy(IRE) showed his best form to date on this switch to the All-Weather and the application of first-time blinkers had a positive effect. He got the extra furlong without much fuss.
Chemise(IRE), back up in trip, was another to show improved form on this All-Weather bow. However, she had very much the run of the race out in front and is clearly flattered by her current mark of 55. (op 16-1)
Tenjack Queen(IRE), making her debut for a new trainer, would have been a bit closer with a better passage nearing the final furlong. She is no doubt greatly flattered by her current official mark, however. (op 3-1 tchd 5-2 and 7-2 in places)
To The Dance(IRE), a 35,000gns half-brother to course-and-distance winner Golden Desert, was all the rage in the betting ring ahead of this racecourse bow and was clearly "expected". However, after missing the kick he proved far too green to do himself any justice and his supporters knew their fate from an early stage. He now has a deal to prove. (tchd 3-1 and 7-2 in a place)

5134 LINGFIELDPARK.CO.UK H'CAP 6f (P)
2:40 (2:40) (Class 5) (0-70,70) 3-Y-O **£2,817** (£838; £418; £209) **Stalls** Low

Form RPR

0151 1 **Lord Of The Reins (IRE)**[8] 4919 3-8-9 **61** 6ex .... DaneO'Neill 5 68+
(D Shaw) *settled in midfield: prog over 2f out: rdn to ld last 100yds: kpt on wl* **9/2**[3]

3660 2 3/4 **Gimme Some Lovin (IRE)**[12] 4759 3-8-4 **56** oh1 .... FrancisNorton 4 61
(D W P Arbuthnot) *w ldrs: upsides over 2f out: nt qckn on inner wl over 1f out: styd on again ins fnl f* **8/1**

31 3 *shd* **Blackmalkin (USA)**[132] 1267 3-8-11 **63** .... SebSanders 9 68
(C E Brittain) *w ldrs on outer: rdn to ld wl over 1f out: fnd little in front: hdd and nt qckn last 100yds* **7/2**[1]

1260 4 3/4 **Riverside Dancer (USA)**[13] 4740 3-9-2 **68** .... RichardHughes 8 70
(G A Huffer) *stdd s: hld up in last: effrt 2f out: hanging lft but styd on fr over 1f out: nt rch ldrs* **7/2**[1]

0151 5 1 1/4 **Pragmatist**[20] 4545 3-8-10 **62** .... JimCrowley 7 60
(P Winkworth) *w ldrs: led 1/2-way to wl over 1f out: wknd ins fnl f* **4/1**[2]

0205 **6** *nk* **Emma Jean Lad (IRE)**[8] 4919 3-8-5 **57**.................... SimonWhitworth 2 54
(J S Moore) *settled in rr: pushed along over 2f out: kpt on fr over 1f out: n.d* **10/1**

6120 **7** *hd* **Polish World (USA)**[103] 1994 3-8-13 **70**................... JamesMillman(5) 6 67
(T J Etherington) *a towards rr: pushed along bef 1/2-way: effrt 2f out: kpt on same pce fr over 1f out* **10/1**

0000 **8** *8* **Land Ahoy**[12] 4759 3-8-4 **56** oh2................................ FrankieMcDonald 1 27
(D W P Arbuthnot) *led to 1/2-way: losing pl whn hmpd* **50/1**

4065 **9** *1 1/4* **Kondakova (IRE)**[20] 4546 3-8-13 **70**..........................(v) LukeMorris(5) 3 37+
(M L W Bell) *trckd ldrs: cl up on inner whn bdly hmpd over 2f out: nt rcvr* **14/1**

1m 11.55s (-1.26) **Going Correction** -0.25s/f (Stan) **9** Ran SP% **120.5**
Speed ratings (Par 101): **98,97,96,95,94 93,93,82,81**
CSF £42.16 CT £143.94 TOTE £3.50: £1.70, £2.30, £1.60; EX 47.00 Trifecta £310.30 Part won. Pool £437.16 - 0.88 winning units..
Owner Danethorpe Racing Partnership **Bred** C Farrell **Trained** Danethorpe, Notts
■ Stewards' Enquiry : Francis Norton four-day ban: careless riding (Sep 16-19)
Luke Morris three-day ban: careless riding (Sep 16-18)

FOCUS
A modest sprint which saw the first four come clear. The winner looks the type to do a bit better.

5135 WAYMENT FLOORING NOVICE STKS 7f (P)
3:15 (3:15) (Class 4) 2-Y-O **£3,886** (£1,156; £577; £288) **Stalls** Low

Form RPR

1030 **1** **Meeriss (IRE)**[12] 4776 2-9-5 86...................................... DarryllHolland 2 93
(M R Channon) *pressed ldr: rdn 2f out: looked hld 1f out: styd on to ld last 100yds: drvn out* **5/1**[3]

1202 **2** *nk* **Sourire**[6] 4964 2-8-11 81.. SebSanders 3 84
(Sir Mark Prescott) *mde most: drvn and looked in command over 1f out: idled fnl f: hdd last 100yds: kpt on* **6/4**[1]

4021 **3** *nk* **Harlech Castle**[12] 4762 2-9-0 88.................................(b) TolleyDean(5) 4 91
(P F I Cole) *dwlt: chsd ldng pair: rdn 3f out: nt qckn and looked btn 2f out: styd on again fnl f* **6/1**

63 **4** *2* **Fool's Wildcat (USA)**[19] 4571 2-8-12 0...................... RichardHughes 1 79
(B J Meehan) *hld up in 4th: drvn 3f out: chsd ldng pair over 2f out: clsd and disp 2nd 1f out: nt qckn and hld whn n.m.r sn after* **15/8**[2]

5 *10* **Minjim** 2-8-8 0.. TedDurcan 5 49
(C E Brittain) *a last: lost tch over 2f out* **25/1**

1m 24.79s (-1.10) **Going Correction** -0.25s/f (Stan) **5** Ran SP% **109.6**
Speed ratings (Par 97): **96,95,95,93,81**
CSF £12.90 TOTE £6.40: £2.70, £1.10; EX 14.00.
Owner Sheikh Ahmed Al Maktoum **Bred** Hugo Lascelles **Trained** West Ilsley, Berks

FOCUS
A good little novice event. The first three came clear in a bobbing finish and the form is sound.

NOTEBOOK
Meeriss(IRE), having his first outing on the All-Weather, showed his true colours on this return to a sounder surface and gamely resumed winning ways. This was a decent effort at the weights and 7f looks to be his optimum trip at present. (op 6-1 tchd 9-2)
Sourire, just touched off over course and distance six days previously, was again given an aggressive ride and again just managed to find one too good for her after idling in front. She is holding her form very well at present and deserves to go one better again now. (tchd 7-4)
Harlech Castle, off the mark at Newbury last time out, had the blinkers back on for this All-Weather bow and first outing over the extra furlong. He hit a flat spot before staying on again with purpose at the business end and was not beaten at all far. This trip now looks to be his optimum and he can go in again when reverting to a more galloping track. (op 3-1)
Fool's Wildcat(USA), well backed for this All-Weather debut, came through on the home turn to have his chance yet was found out when the gun was put to his head. This was no disgrace and he should fare a little better when switching to nurseries. (op 5-2)
Minjim, a 50,000gns purchase related to winners from 5f-1m2f, looked clueless for most of the way and this debut run was clearly much needed. He is at least entitled to come on for the experience.

5136 BOOK YOUR CHRISTMAS PARTY HERE H'CAP 7f (P)
3:45 (3:46) (Class 6) (0-65,65) 3-Y-O **£2,817** (£838; £418; £209) **Stalls** Low

Form RPR

-412 **1** **Shaded Edge**[8] 4919 3-8-9 **56**.. JamesDoyle 14 63
(D W P Arbuthnot) *prom: w ldng pair 3f out: sn outpcd and rdn: no imp tl styd on fnl f: led nr fnish* **7/2**[2]

2156 **2** *shd* **Excessive**[20] 4545 3-9-1 **62**.. TedDurcan 8 69
(W Jarvis) *hld up early: chsd ldrs 1/2-way: rdn and nt on terms over 2f out: styd on u.p over 1f out: tk 2nd last strides: jst hld* **7/1**

3321 **3** *1/2* **Glencal**[20] 4529 3-8-9 **59**.. TravisBlock(3) 2 65+
(H Morrison) *led 1f: pressed ldr: rdn to ld over 2f out: wknd and hdd nr fin* **9/4**[1]

6040 **4** *1 1/4* **Dance Of Dreams**[12] 4760 3-8-8 **60**............................ LukeMorris(5) 6 62
(N P Littmoden) *wl in rr: u.p and no prog 3f out: styd on wl fnl f: nrst fin* **20/1**

2-30 **5** *hd* **The Cool Sandpiper**[55] 3447 3-9-4 **65**............................. JimCrowley 1 67
(P Winkworth) *pushed along and wl in rr: struggling fr 3f out: styd on over 1f out: nrst fin* **20/1**

0040 **6** *shd* **Grand Lucre**[61] 3286 3-9-0 **61**...................................... StephenCarson 9 63+
(G A Butler) *v s.i.s: wl bhd tl stdy prog 1/2-way: outpcd over 2f out: styd on fr over 1f out* **14/1**

5004 **7** *hd* **Ede's Dot Com (IRE)**[20] 4538 3-9-1 **62**.......................... IanMongan 12 63
(P M Phelan) *led after 1f to over 2f out: hld by ldr over 1f out: wknd ins fnl f* **12/1**

6035 **8** *3/4* **Flying Encore (IRE)**[9] 4884 3-9-4 **65**..........................(e[1]) AdamKirby 7 64
(W R Swinburn) *chsd ldrs: outpcd 3f out: drvn and no imp on inner over 1f out: one pce* **13/2**[3]

0530 **9** *3/4* **Scarlet Oak**[26] 4361 3-9-2 **63**.. LPKeniry 5 60
(D J S Ffrench Davis) *nvr bttr than midfield: no prog over 2f out: kpt on same pce fnl f* **15/2**

200 **10** *6* **Dancing Duo**[86] 2515 3-8-13 **60**....................................(v) DaneO'Neill 13 41
(D Shaw) *s.v.s: a wl bhd* **50/1**

2000 **11** *21* **Nashharry (IRE)**[13] 4740 3-8-13 **60**.............................. RichardHughes 3 —
(S Kirk) *prom early: dropped away fr 3f out: sn eased: t.o* **33/1**

1m 24.02s (-1.87) **Going Correction** -0.25s/f (Stan) **11** Ran SP% **119.4**
Speed ratings (Par 99): **100,99,99,97,97 97,97,96,95,88 64**
CSF £27.40 CT £68.63 TOTE £4.30: £1.60, £2.70, £1.50; EX 34.60 Trifecta £76.90 Pool £224.47 - 2.07 winning units..
Owner Lady Whent And Friends **Bred** Lady Whent **Trained** Compton, Berks

FOCUS
A moderate handicap run at a strong pace. The first three are progressive and a positive view has been taken of the form.

Nashharry(IRE) Official explanation: jockey said filly stopped quickly

5137 LINGFIELD PARK FOR CONFERENCES MAIDEN STKS 1m 3f 106y
4:20 (4:20) (Class 5) 3-Y-O+ **£2,817** (£838; £418; £209) **Stalls** High

Form RPR

32 **1** **Hibiki (IRE)**[30] 4235 3-8-12 0... TolleyDean(5) 6 71
(J S Moore) *hld up in tch: prog to chse clr ldr over 3f out: clsd to ld 2f out: kpt on wl* **3/1**[2]

4504 **2** *1* **Vanquisher (IRE)**[40] 3919 3-9-3 72................................(p) SebSanders 5 69
(W J Haggas) *led: drew clr over 4f out: drvn and one pce 3f out: hdd 2f out: plugged on* **8/11**[1]

05 **3** *7* **Mounafes**[7] 4948 3-9-3 0... StephenCarson 4 57
(G A Butler) *mostly chsd ldr to over 3f out: sn btn* **16/1**[3]

0063 **4** *11* **Winforjoe (IRE)**[16] 4663 3-8-12 45.......................... FrankieMcDonald 2 34
(J J Bridger) *mostly chsd ldng pair to over 4f out: wknd 3f out* **66/1**

5 *3 1/2* **Valassini**[33] 7-8-13 0... KylieManser(7) 3 28
(B G Powell) *dwlt: a in last pair: lost tch 4f out* **25/1**

00 **6** *40* **Lady Pomerol**[25] 4392 3-8-12 0.. IanMongan 7 —
(Lady Herries) *sn last: lost tch over 4f out: t.o* **50/1**

2m 32.71s (2.79) **Going Correction** +0.35s/f (Good)
WFA 3 from 7yo 8lb **6** Ran SP% **96.1**
Speed ratings (Par 103): **103,102,97,89,86 57**
CSF £3.88 TOTE £3.00: £1.20, £1.20; EX 4.20.
Owner Albert Conneally **Bred** Albert Conneally **Trained** Upper Lambourn, Berks
■ Hareem was withdrawn on vet's advice (5/1, deduct 15p in the £.)

FOCUS
A weak, uncompetitive maiden. The winner improved to the tune of 5lb.
Lady Pomerol Official explanation: jockey said filly hung right; vet said filly was stiff on return

5138 LINGFIELD PARK FOR WEDDINGS H'CAP 2m
4:50 (4:50) (Class 6) (0-65,63) 3-Y-O+ **£2,047** (£604; £302) **Stalls** Low

Form RPR

3022 **1** **Right Option (IRE)**[9] 4877 3-8-1 **54** ow1.................. KevinGhunowa(5) 6 61
(J L Flint) *t.k.h: hld up tl led 1/2-way: hrd pressed fr over 2f out: kpt on wl* **4/1**[3]

2163 **2** *1/2* **Mister Completely (IRE)**[9] 4906 6-10-0 **63**..................(v) JamesDoyle 5 69
(Ms J S Doyle) *mde most to 1/2-way: styd cl up: rdn to chal over 2f out: kpt on but a hld fnl f* **3/1**[2]

0556 **3** *hd* **Sir Duke (IRE)**[21] 4518 3-8-7 **55**.. RobertHavlin 8 61
(P W D'Arcy) *hld up: prog to chse wnr 5f out: rdn to chal 3f out: wandered and fnd nil: a hld after* **9/2**

-605 **4** *1* **Top Trees**[14] 3467 9-9-1 **50**... FrancisNorton 1 55
(W S Kittow) *t.k.h: hld up in tch: prog to press ldrs 2f out: nt qckn fnl f* **6/1**

0000 **5** *7* **Silver Dreamer (IRE)**[20] 4531 5-8-11 **46** oh1............ AdrianMcCarthy 4 42
(H S Howe) *hld up: in tch over 3f out: sn btn* **33/1**

0540 **6** *19* **Screenplay**[35] 4056 6-9-12 **61**.......................................(p) GeorgeBaker 3 34
(G L Moore) *prom: lost pl 6f out: last and struggling over 4f out: sn wl bhd: lame* **9/4**[1]

250 **7** *12* **Nod's Star**[27] 4322 6-8-11 **46** oh1......................................(t) ChrisCatlin 7 5
(Mrs L C Jewell) *in tch: prog to chse wnr over 6f out to 5f out: sn wknd: t.o* **16/1**

3m 41.05s (7.79) **Going Correction** +0.35s/f (Good)
WFA 3 from 5yo+ 13lb **7** Ran SP% **117.1**
Speed ratings (Par 101): **94,93,93,93,89 80,74**
CSF £17.09 CT £56.14 TOTE £4.80: £2.70, £2.20; EX 11.80 TRIFECTA Pool £326.88 - 5.89 winning units. Place 6 £46.15, Place 5 £7.77..
Owner Roy Mathias **Bred** Paul Monaghan, R Berns And P Sexton **Trained** Kenfig Hill, Bridgend

FOCUS
A moderate staying handicap and, with the pace just steady, the winning time was ordinary for the grade. The form makes sense at face value.
Screenplay Official explanation: vet said gelding was lame in front
T/Plt: £15.60 to a £1 stake. Pool: £53,009.45. 2,474.75 winning tickets. T/Qpdt: £3.10 to a £1 stake. Pool: £3,332.90. 774.20 winning tickets. JN

4743 YORK (L-H)
Wednesday, September 5

OFFICIAL GOING: Good to firm
There was a huge bias towards front-runners with five winners making all and another was in front at halfway. Therefore the form may not be totally reliable.
Wind: Moderate, half against Weather: Fine and sunny

5139 CSL SCAFFOLDING APPRENTICE STKS (H'CAP) 5f
2:00 (2:00) (Class 5) (0-70,70) 3-Y-O **£5,181** (£1,541; £770; £384) **Stalls** Centre

Form RPR

5503 **1** **Zahour Al Yasmeen**[27] 4330 3-8-11 **69**.................... MatthewDavies(7) 4 79
(M R Channon) *cl up: led 1/2-way: pushed clr over 1f out: sn rdn and styd on strly* **7/1**[3]

3004 **2** *1 3/4* **Valley Of The Moon (IRE)**[24] 4425 3-9-5 **70**............... JamieMoriarty 7 74
(R A Fahey) *in tch: hdwy wl over 1f out: rdn to chse wnr ent fnl f: kpt on* **7/1**[3]

6654 **3** *3/4* **Baybshambles (IRE)**[9] 4896 3-8-5 **56** oh2...................... AndrewElliott 1 57
(R E Barr) *in rr: hdwy on wd outside wl over 1f out: sn rdn and styd on ins fnl f: nrst fin* **14/1**

4621 **4** *nk* **Comptonspirit**[7] 4935 3-9-1 **69** 6ex..................(p) RussellKennemore(3) 6 69
(B P J Baugh) *cl up: rdn along and ch 2f out: edgd rt appr fnl f and sn one pce* **13/2**[2]

0365 **5** *shd* **Triple Shadow**[9] 4896 3-8-8 **62**....................................... NeilBrown(3) 2 62
(T D Barron) *towards rr: hdwy wl over 1f out: sn rdn and styd on ins fnl f* **7/1**[3]

6050 **6** *2 1/2* **Bollin Franny**[7] 4939 3-8-4 **60**...................................(e) KellyHarrison(5) 5 51
(T D Easterby) *chsd ldrs: rdn along 2f out: drvn and one pce appr fnl f* **14/1**

0400 **7** *hd* **Frisky Talk (IRE)**[25] 4396 3-8-13 **67**............................... PatrickHills(3) 3 57
(B W Hills) *chsd ldrs: rdn along wl over 1f out: wknd ent fnl f* **9/1**

6024 **8** *nk* **Feelin Foxy**[12] 4759 3-8-12 **68**.......................................(v) GaryBartley(5) 11 57
(D Shaw) *in tch: rdn along and sltly outpcd 2f out: kpt on u.p fnl f* **14/1**

4030 **9** *2 1/2* **Durova (IRE)**[9] 4896 3-9-1 **66**...................................(e[1]) DuranFentiman 12 46
(T D Easterby) *cl up: rdn along 2f out: grad wknd* **20/1**

0024 **10** *nk* **Bookiesindex Boy**[3] 5066 3-9-0 **70**............................ HarryPoulton(5) 14 49
(J R Jenkins) *cl up opn stands' rail: rdn along over 2f out and grad wknd* **16/1**

0354 **11** *shd* **Hawaii Prince**[23] 4452 3-9-0 **65**...................................... GregFairley 10 43
(S T Mason) *led: hdd 1/2-way: sn rdn along and wknd over 1f out* **6/1**[1]

22 **12** *1* **Croeso Bach**[12] 4759 3-8-0 56 oh2 SophieDoyle(5) 13 31
(J L Spearing) *cl up: rdn along 2f out: grad wknd* **14/1**
62-0 **13** *3 1/2* **Centreboard (USA)**[18] 4606 3-8-11 **69** NSLawes(7) 9 31
(M W Easterby) *a towards rr: rdn along and bhd fr 1/2-way* **33/1**
5000 **14** *nk* **Sunley Sovereign**[9] 4896 3-8-2 **58** DanielleMcCreery(5) 8 19
(D W Chapman) *s.i.s: a in rr* **50/1**
58.77 secs (-0.55) **Going Correction** -0.075s/f (Good) **14** Ran SP% **117.3**
Speed ratings (Par 101): **101,98,97,96,96 92,92,91,87,87 86,85,79,79**
CSF £52.84 CT £690.02 TOTE £6.90: £3.00, £2.70, £5.00; EX 35.40.
Owner Jaber Abdullah **Bred** Gainsborough Stud Management Ltd **Trained** West Ilsley, Berks

FOCUS
A competitive sprint that was won in good fashion by Zahour Al Yasmeen. The form looks sound through the runner-up and fourth.
Hawaii Prince Official explanation: vet said gelding lost an off-fore shoe
Croeso Bach Official explanation: jockey said filly hung left-handed from halfway

5140 E B F PRINCE OF WALES'S OWN REGIMENT OF YORKSHIRE MAIDEN STKS 7f
2:30 (2:31) (Class 3) 2-Y-O **£7,124** (£2,119; £1,059; £529) **Stalls** Low

Form RPR
0 **1** **Giant Love (USA)**[14] 4725 2-9-3 0 GregFairley 1 78
(M Johnston) *mde all: pushed along and edgd rt over 2f out: rdn and hung rt wl over 1f out and again ins fnl f: drvn and styd on gamely towards fin* **2/1**[1]
0 **2** *nk* **Beetuna (IRE)**[12] 4784 2-9-3 0 TomEaves 2 77
(B Smart) *a.p: cl up 1/2-way: rdn and ev ch whn n.m.r fr wl over 1f out tl ins fnl f: kpt on gamely* **50/1**
6 **3** *3/4* **Deira Dubai**[19] 4564 2-8-12 0 RHills 4 70
(B W Hills) *hld up: effrt and rn green over 2f out: sn rdn: hdwy on outer over 1f out: styd on and ch ins fnl f: no ex towards fin* **3/1**[3]
5 **4** *nk* **Thunderstruck**[45] 3760 2-9-3 0 NCallan 3 74
(K A Ryan) *in tch: hdwy to chse ldng pair over 2f out: rdn wl over 1f out: kpt on u.p ins fnl f* **10/1**
3 **5** *nk* **Military Power**[34] 4110 2-9-3 0 MichaelHills 6 74
(J W Hills) *trckd ldrs: hdwy 2f out: rdn and nt mcuh room over 1f out: swtchd lft and drvn ins fnl f: kpt on same pce* **9/4**[2]
45 **6** *2* **Diamond Lass (IRE)**[26] 4350 2-8-12 0 PaulHanagan 7 64
(R A Fahey) *chsd ldrs: rdn along over 2f out: sn one pce* **12/1**
7 *1* **Intabih (USA)** 2-9-3 0 KerrinMcEvoy 5 66
(C E Brittain) *a in rr* **16/1**
00 **8** *7* **Fantastic Lass**[19] 4565 2-8-9 0 JamieMoriarty(3) 8 43
(R A Fahey) *a in rr* **100/1**
1m 24.69s (-0.71) **Going Correction** -0.075s/f (Good) **8** Ran SP% **114.7**
Speed ratings (Par 99): **101,100,99,99,99 96,95,87**
CSF £92.05 TOTE £3.20: £1.20, £9.20, £1.70; EX 115.60.
Owner Crone Stud Farms Ltd **Bred** Swettenham Stud **Trained** Middleham Moor, N Yorks
■ Stewards' Enquiry : Greg Fairley caution: used whip down the shoulder in forehand position

FOCUS
A decent maiden run in a decent time and likely to produce its share of winners.

NOTEBOOK
Giant Love(USA), too green and inexperienced over an inadequate 6f on his debut at the Ebor meeting, knew much more on this occasion and was soon in front. He got warm beforehand, but on a day where it was a huge advantage to race on the pace, he was not for passing, battling on strongly under a fine ride from Fairley. He is going to stay 1m in time and this Group 2 Beresford Stakes entry looks capable of further improvement. (tchd 9-4 and 5-2 in places)
Beetuna(IRE), never involved following a slow start on his Thirsk debut, comes from a stable whose juveniles have had another excellent season and it was no surprise to see him step up significantly on his initial effort. Like the winner, he knew his job much better on this occasion and he went down fighting, so should have no trouble finding an ordinary maiden.
Deira Dubai, a promising sixth on her debut at Doncaster, came to have her chance, but still hinted at signs of greenness and she was unable to get to the winner. This was an improved effort and she is another who looks capable of winning a small maiden. Official explanation: jockey said filly was too free to post (op 11-4 tchd 2-1)
Thunderstruck was another to step up on his initial effort, but he was uanble to get close enough to throw down a serious challenge and may be more of a nursery type. (op 9-1)
Military Power, a most promising third on his debut at Sandown, was subsequently purchased by Princess Haya of Jordan and looked one of the more interesting ones. Never too far away, he was switched to have every chance, but could not quicken sufficiently and was made to look paceless. He may be more of a nursery type. (op 5-2 tchd 3-1)
Intabih(USA) Official explanation: jockey said colt moved poorly throughout

5141 UBS GARROWBY STKS (H'CAP) 1m 4f
3:05 (3:06) (Class 2) (0-100,98) 3-Y-O **£11,658** (£3,468; £1,733; £865) **Stalls** Centre

Form RPR
-030 **1** **Philanthropy**[13] 4749 3-8-5 **85** JohnEgan 2 96
(K A Ryan) *led: pushed along and qcknd clr over 3f out: rdn and wandered over 2f out: kpt on wl u.p fr wl over 1f out* **25/1**
3441 **2** *2 1/2* **Sanbuch**[32] 4147 3-8-13 **93** JamieSpencer 7 100+
(L M Cumani) *hld up in rr: niggled along 5f out: hdwy over 3f out: rdn over 2f out: hung lftover 1f out: drvn and hung lft ent fnl f: styd on u.p: nt rch wnr* **5/2**[1]
4411 **3** *2 1/2* **Tifernati**[18] 4597 3-8-1 **84** oh3 LiamJones(3) 3 87
(W J Haggas) *t.k.h: cl up: rdn along over 3f out: drvn over 2f out and sn one pce* **6/1**
1-50 **4** *4* **Proponent (IRE)**[34] 4092 3-9-0 **94** SteveDrowne 8 91
(R Charlton) *hld up in tch: hdwy 4f out: rdn 3f out: sn drvn and no imp fnl 2f* **3/1**[2]
102 **5** *1 3/4* **Rosbay (IRE)**[18] 4617 3-8-8 **88** RyanMoore 5 82
(T D Easterby) *hld up in rr: hdwy over 3f out: sn rdn along and no imp* **4/1**[3]
6101 **6** *nk* **Horseford Hill**[18] 4609 3-8-4 **84** oh1 PaulHanagan 1 77
(D R C Elsworth) *t.k.h: chsd ldng pair: effrt over 3f out: sn rdn along and wknd over 2f out* **9/1**
0053 **7** *12* **Always Fruitful**[18] 4617 3-8-8 **88** GregFairley 6 62
(M Johnston) *chsd ldng pair: rdn along over 3f out: sn drvn along and wknd* **9/1**
2m 29.46s (-5.14) **Going Correction** -0.075s/f (Good) **7** Ran SP% **111.7**
Speed ratings (Par 107): **114,112,110,108,106 106,98**
CSF £83.13 CT £432.50 TOTE £23.40: £5.80, £1.90; EX 109.10.
Owner N Cable & M Smith **Bred** Darley **Trained** Hambleton, N Yorks

FOCUS
A decent handicap run at a sound gallop resulting in a very decent time for the type of contest. As with much of the card, front-runners appeared to have an edge so the winner might be a little bit flattered, although the form looks reasonable rated through the third.

NOTEBOOK
Philanthropy, who had sweated up before the race, kept on in determined style after making every yard of the running. He is not an easy horse to catch right and was gelded before his last run, but clearly has plenty of ability when conditions are right for him. Official explanation: trainer said, regarding apparent improvement in form, that the gelding was previously unsuited by the step up in trip
Sanbuch is a talented if quirky individual, who never gave the impression he was enjoying it again even without the visor he wore to victory last time. It probably was not a bad effort in the circumstances but one suspects he is not one to trust. (tchd 11-4 in places)
Tifernati, running off a 12lb higher mark than last time, chased the winner throughout but could not find another gear from the two-furlong pole. He did, however, keep on respectably and may stay a bit further in time. (op 15-2 tchd 8-1 in a place)
Proponent(IRE), trying this trip for the first time, has not built on any of the promise he showed last season, which saw him quoted in the Derby betting, and does not look well handicapped after this effort. (op 11-4)
Rosbay(IRE) was pushed along rounding the final bend and never managed to get on terms. He probably stays 1m4f but all of his very-best form has come over shorter and this race was turn at a sound gallop. (op 5-1)
Horseford Hill looked very one-paced under pressure and is more likely to be seen to better effect at a stiffer course. He can make up into a nice stayer next season. (op 8-1 tchd 15-2)

5142 TURFTV STRENSALL STKS (GROUP 3) 1m 208y
3:35 (3:36) (Class 1) 3-Y-O+ **£29,635** (£11,205; £5,600; £2,800) **Stalls** Low

Form RPR
0-41 **1** **Echo Of Light**[21] 4520 5-9-8 116 (p) LDettori 6 118
(Saeed Bin Suroor) *mde all: qcknd clr over 3f out: rdn 2f out and styd on strly* **5/4**[1]
0501 **2** *2 1/2* **Halicarnassus (IRE)**[25] 4387 3-9-2 111 TPO'Shea 5 113
(M R Channon) *hld up in rr: hdwy 3f out: rdn wl over 1f out: styd on fnl f: nt rch wnr* **9/1**
3565 **3** *3/4* **Kandidate**[25] 4387 5-9-8 112 (t) RyanMoore 1 111
(C E Brittain) *chsd ldng pair: headway on inner to chse wnr 2f out: sn rdn and kpt on same pce* **12/1**
0120 **4** *1 1/4* **Royal Oath (USA)**[36] 4045 4-9-4 112 (b) JimmyFortune 4 105
(J H M Gosden) *hld up in tch: hdwy 3f out: rdn wl over 1f out: kpt on same pce* **10/3**[2]
2-23 **5** *nk* **Mullins Bay**[158] 858 6-9-4 0 JMurtagh 7 104
(M F De Kock, South Africa) *trckd ldrs: hdwy 3f out: rdn along 2f out: sn drvn and wknd over 1f out* **10/1**
0S22 **6** *10* **Formal Decree (GER)**[25] 4387 4-9-8 112 KerrinMcEvoy 8 87
(Saeed Bin Suroor) *hld up in rr: sme hdwy on outer over 2f out: nvr a factor* **9/2**[3]
0246 **7** *6* **Flying Clarets (IRE)**[10] 4849 4-9-1 92 PaulHanagan 2 67
(R A Fahey) *chsd wnr: rdn along 3f out: sn wknd* **66/1**
1m 46.76s (-4.23) **Going Correction** -0.075s/f (Good) course record
WFA 3 from 4yo+ 6lb **7** Ran SP% **114.0**
Speed ratings (Par 113): **115,112,112,111,110 101,96**
CSF £13.82 TOTE £2.10: £1.50, £3.00; EX 14.00.
Owner Godolphin **Bred** Kilcarn Stud **Trained** Newmarket, Suffolk

FOCUS
A very solid winning time for a Group 3 allowing for the conditions, with Echo Of Light taking 2.23 seconds off the old course record. The runner-up is rated as having run his best race.

NOTEBOOK
Echo Of Light, who won this last year, has often fallen short at the top level, but he is a solid performer in Group2/3 company, as he showed when winning over 1m2f in the first-time cheekpieces at Deauville last time. He was always going to take some stopping, being the only recognised front-runner in the field, and having led at a decent gallop, he ran on strongly for a comfortable victory. He will have to step back up to Group 2 level now and is likely to head to Longchamp next for the Prix Daniel Wildenstein. (op 11-8 after 13-8 in a place and 6-4 in places)
Halicarnassus(IRE), a ready winner at Haydock last time, swooping late to win going away, faced a stiffer task here, especially with the drop in trip looking unlikely to suit, and he was always going to be at a disadvantage in being held up on a day when it paid to race on the pace. He came through late, but the winner had flown, and remains capable of better back up in trip. (op 15-2)
Kandidate, a winner at Nad Al Sheba earlier in the year, has not been running badly in the face of several stiffish tasks since returning to Britain and he seemed to appreciate this slightly easier assignment. He ran well, but gives the impression he is likely to continue to find at least a couple too good at this level. (op 14-1 tchd 16-1 in a place)
Royal Oath(USA), a progressive handicapper who has not been running badly in competitive Group 2s, never really got into it on a day when it was hard to make ground and can be rated a bit better than the bare form. (op 3-1 tchd 7-2)
Mullins Bay was running well for current connections at Nad Al Sheba back in the spring, but this was his first run for a while and he shaped as though the run was needed. (tchd 9-1)
Formal Decree(GER) was expected to provide Godolphin with a solid second-string, but he never really threatened having been in rear early and proved most disappointing. He is better than this, but is not finding it easy to win at this level. Official explanation: trainer had no explanation for the poor form shown (op 11-2)
Flying Clarets(IRE) had it to do with all of these at the weights and she was found wanting when things hotted up. (tchd 80-1)

5143 CHERRIES PROMOTIONS MAIDEN AUCTION STKS 6f
4:10 (4:11) (Class 4) 2-Y-O **£6,541** (£1,946; £972; £485) **Stalls** Centre

Form RPR
6 **1** **Captain Macarry (IRE)**[17] 4636 2-9-1 0 TomEaves 11 76
(B Smart) *mde all: rdn wl over 1f out: drvn ins fnl f and styd on gamely* **11/1**
05 **2** *1 1/4* **Gala Casino Star (IRE)**[18] 4612 2-8-13 0 DaleGibson 10 70
(R A Fahey) *prom: rdn along and outpcd 2f out: styd on wl u.p ins fnl f* **25/1**
654 **3** *shd* **Misplaced Fortune**[11] 4818 2-8-6 68 ow1 KDarley 9 63
(N Tinkler) *a.p: rdn wl over 1f out: kpt on u.p ins fnl f* **5/1**[3]
4 *nk* **Flowing Cape (IRE)** 2-9-2 0 KerrinMcEvoy 2 72+
(R Hollinshead) *hld up: effrt and nt clr run wl over 1f out: rdn and squeezed through ins fnl f: nrst fin* **7/1**
5 *nk* **Govenor Eliott (IRE)** 2-9-3 0 GregFairley 12 72
(M Johnston) *prom: rdn along 2f out: wknd ins fnl f* **7/2**[1]
30 **6** *3/4* **Society Venue**[12] 4782 2-9-3 0 PaulMulrennan 1 70
(Jedd O'Keeffe) *hld up: hdwy on outer 2f out: rdn ent fnl f and kpt on same pce* **20/1**
7 *3/4* **Karmei** 2-9-0 0 MichaelHills 6 65
(J W Hills) *wnt rt and dwlt s: bhd tl gd hdwy on stands' rails 2f out: rdn over 1f out: wknd ins fnl f* **14/1**
8 *2 1/2* **Bluejain** 2-8-10 0 JohnEgan 8 53
(Miss Gay Kelleway) *trckd ldrs: hdwy 1/2-way: rdn and ev ch wl over 1f out: wknd ins fnl f* **7/1**

9 2 **Gunner Fly (IRE)** 2-8-11 0 .... PaulHanagan 3 48
(R A Fahey) *hmpd and dwlt s: towards rr tl gd hdwy 2f out: sn rdn and wknd appr fnl f* **8/1**

10 2 **Wimoweh (IRE)** 2-8-8 0 .... DuranFentiman(3) 5 42
(T D Easterby) *s.i.s: a in rr* **28/1**

11 1 1/4 **Sylvias Grove** 2-8-11 0 .... JamieSpencer 4 38
(D Carroll) *dwlt: sn swtchd rt and hdwy to chse ldrs 1/2-way: rdn wl over 1f out and sn wknd* **4/1**[2]

1m 12.92s (0.36) **Going Correction** -0.075s/f (Good) **11** Ran SP% **122.1**
Speed ratings (Par 97): **94,92,92,91,91 90,89,86,83,80 79**
CSF £265.09 TOTE £17.40: £4.20, £6.50, £2.00; EX 296.40.
Owner Anthony D Gee **Bred** Humphrey Okeke **Trained** Hambleton, N Yorks

FOCUS
Probably an ordinary maiden for the track and the fourth consecutive race at the meeting where the winner made all. The 68-rated third sets the standard in a low-grade contest for the track.

NOTEBOOK
Captain Macarry(IRE), well beaten on his Pontefract debut, was ridden very differently this time and on a day when those that were ridden positively were hugely favoured, he showed the right attitude to keep his rivals at bay. The track bias means that the form may not be totally reliable, but he obviously has ability and his breeding suggests that he is a sprinter.

Gala Casino Star(IRE) stayed on again having been off the bridle for some time and, as at Ripon last time, gave the strong impression that he needs further now even though this was his best effort yet. Nurseries now become an option for him. (op 22-1)

Misplaced Fortune, the most experienced in the field and carrying 1lb overweight, was always there or thereabouts and kept on right to the line. Already with an official mark of 68, she will always be vulnerable to less-exposed types in races like this and would probably be better off in nurseries. (op 4-1 tchd 7-2)

Flowing Cape(IRE) ◆, who fetched 40,000gns as a two-year-old, is a full-brother to a winning juvenile and a half-brother to two other winners, including a fair sort in Danjet. He did not have a great deal of room to play with when trying to get closer over the last couple of furlongs, but was staying on nicely at the line and still emerged best of the newcomers. Improvement can be expected and his pedigree suggests that he will come into his own once stepped up to 1m. (op 9-1)

Govenor Eliott(IRE), a 60,000euros half-brother to a winner at up to 1m 4f, had every chance and showed enough to suggest he can win races once stepped up to a more suitable trip. (tchd 4-1 and 9-2 in a place)

Society Venue ◆, rather drawn in no man's land out towards the middle of the track, was far from disgraced and gave himself every chance until done for foot over the last furlong or so. Having looked to need every yard of the 7f on his debut, he has been rather surprisingly dropped to 6f for his two starts since and has not been suited by it. He now qualifies for nurseries and is well worth watching out for if contesting one of those and/or stepping back up in trip in the near future.

Karmei, a 30,000gns yearling out of a winner at up to 1m2f, came out of the stalls sideways and immediately gave himself plenty to do, but stayed on against the stands' rail later on and looks the type that will come into his own over much further in due course. (op 20-1)

Sylvias Grove, a 36,000gns two-year-old out of a half-sister to Branston Abby and Desert Deer, fluffed the start and her efforts to get back into the contest eventually told. Her position in the market suggests she is thought capable of much better. (op 10-3 tchd 3-1 in a place)

5144 PD PORTS STKS (H'CAP) 1m 6f
4:40 (4:41) (Class 4) (0-85,81) 3-Y-O+ **£6,477** (£1,927; £963; £481) **Stalls** Low

Form RPR

2031 1 **Generous Jem**[12] 4766 4-9-1 **68** .... JohnEgan 4 81+
(G G Margarson) *hld up in rr: smooth hdwy over 4f out: chal 2f out: rdn to ld over 1f out: drvn and edgd lft ins fnl f: hld on wl* **13/8**[1]

0543 2 nk **Mighty Moon**[29] 4248 4-9-6 **73** .... (t) JamieSpencer 2 86
(J O'Reilly) *trckd ldrs: hdwy to ld 3f out: rdn 2f out: hdd over 1f out: drvn and rallied ins fnl f: no ex towards fin* **10/3**[2]

6143 3 11 **Hugs Destiny (IRE)**[5] 4994 6-8-2 **62** oh3 .... (t) SophieDoyle(7) 5 60
(M A Barnes) *led: rdn along 4f out: hdd 3f out and grad wknd* **5/1**[3]

2651 4 14 **Collette's Choice**[6] 4969 4-9-0 **67** 6ex .... (p) PaulHanagan 6 45
(R A Fahey) *trckd ldrs: effrt over 3f out: sn rdn and btn* **11/2**

0010 5 39 **Blue Jet (USA)**[38] 3993 3-8-3 **70** .... DuranFentiman(3) 7 —
(R M Whitaker) *prom: rdn along over 5f out: wknd 4f out* **20/1**

3616 6 10 **King's Ransom**[13] 4732 4-9-6 **73** .... NCallan 3 —
(S Gollings) *in tch: rdn along 5f out: sn wknd* **7/1**

2m 57.66s (-1.84) **Going Correction** -0.075s/f (Good)
WFA 3 from 4yo+ 11lb **6** Ran SP% **110.5**
Speed ratings (Par 105): **102,101,95,87,65 59**
CSF £6.95 CT £19.16 TOTE £2.40: £1.50, £1.90; EX 7.00.
Owner Norcroft Park Stud **Bred** Norcroft Park Stud **Trained** Newmarket, Suffolk
■ Stewards' Enquiry : John Egan caution: used whip with excessive frequency

FOCUS
They went just a fair pace in this, but that was still enough to make it too much of a test of stamina for some and there were some very big margins separating those behind the front pair. The winner bucked the trend for the day by coming from off the pace and the runner-up is rated to this year's form.

5145 BOLLINGER CHAMPAGNE CHALLENGE SERIES STKS (FOR GENTLEMAN AMATEUR RIDERS) (H'CAP) 1m 4f
5:10 (5:10) (Class 4) (0-80,80) 4-Y-O+ **£6,246** (£1,937; £968; £484) **Stalls** Centre

Form RPR

2225 1 **Sporting Gesture**[13] 4732 10-10-5 **68** .... MrCCollins(7) 6 75
(M W Easterby) *mde all: pushed clr over 2f out: sn rdn and kpt on ins fnl f: jst lasted* **7/1**

6216 2 3/4 **Jack Rolfe**[30] 1813 5-10-11 **72** .... MrRBirkett(5) 3 78
(G L Moore) *trckd ldrs on inner: effrt and n.m.r over 2f out: sn rdn and styd on to chse wnr ent fnl f: kpt on: nt rch wnr* **12/1**

1 3 shd **Daryal (IRE)**[5] 4994 6-11-3 **78** 6ex .... MrCPHuxley(5) 8 84
(A King) *hld up: hdwy 3f out: swtchd outside and rdn over 1f out: kpt on ins fnl f* **5/2**[1]

6630 4 1/2 **Torrens (IRE)**[18] 4597 5-11-3 **78** .... MrBMcHugh(5) 7 83
(R A Fahey) *hld up: hdwy 3f out: effrt and nt clr run over 1f out and ins fnl f: swtchd rt and styd on towards fin* **14/1**

3065 5 1 1/2 **Hue**[14] 4717 6-10-10 **66** .... (b) MrSWalker 4 68
(B Ellison) *trckd ldrs: effrt and hdwy over 2f out: rdn wl over 1f out and sn one pce* **9/1**

1532 6 hd **Just Lille (IRE)**[7] 4933 4-11-7 **80** .... (p) MrHHaynes(3) 9 82
(Mrs A Duffield) *trckd ldrs on outer: rdn along 3f out: drvn and one pce fnl 2f* **11/2**[3]

6300 7 2 **Top Spec (IRE)**[32] 4171 6-10-9 **68** .... MrSPearce(3) 10 67
(J Pearce) *hld up: a in rr* **16/1**

6003 8 2 **Best Of The Lot (USA)**[6] 4972 5-10-7 **66** oh3 .... FelixDeGiles(3) 5 62
(R A Fahey) *chsd wnr: rdn along over 3f out: grad wknd fnl 2f* **10/1**

2135 9 4 **Tcherina (IRE)**[70] 2987 5-11-9 **79** .... MrSDobson 1 68
(T D Easterby) *hld up: effrt and hdwy 3f out: sn rdn along and btn over 2f out* **4/1**[2]

2m 33.02s (-1.58) **Going Correction** -0.075s/f (Good) **9** Ran SP% **115.8**
Speed ratings (Par 105): **102,101,101,101,100 99,98,97,94**
CSF £86.71 CT £267.84 TOTE £8.80: £1.80, £3.70, £1.40; EX 87.10 Place 6 £116.44, Place 5 £28.09..
Owner Steve Hull **Bred** C C Bromley And Son **Trained** Sheriff Hutton, N Yorks

FOCUS
Just a fair pace for this amateur contest and another winner to make all - the fifth of the seven at the meeting - which makes the form rather suspect, although on paper it looks sound enough.
Torrens(IRE) Official explanation: trainer said gelding ran without declared tongue-strap because it snapped and could not be refitted
T/Jkpt: Not won. T/Plt: £109.60 to a £1 stake. Pool: £90,681.00. 603.60 winning tickets. T/Qpdt: £13.80 to a £1 stake. Pool: £4,790.00. 256.60 winning tickets. JR

5146 - 5149a (Foreign Racing) - See Raceform Interactive

5107 CHANTILLY (R-H)
Wednesday, September 5

OFFICIAL GOING: Good to soft

5150a PRIX DES TOURELLES (LISTED RACE) (F&M) 1m 4f
2:05 (2:05) 3-Y-O+ **£17,568** (£7,027; £5,270; £3,514; £1,757)

RPR

1 **King Luna (FR)**[41] 3893 4-9-2 .... CSoumillon 5 103
(A Fabre, France)

2 1/2 **Doe Ray Me**[27] 3-8-7 .... (p) SPasquier 2 102
(H-A Pantall, France) **6/1**[1]

3 nk **Sureyya (GER)**[23] 4-9-2 .... GFaucon 4 102
(E Lellouche, France)

4 hd **La Boum (GER)**[15] 4-9-2 .... OPeslier 5 102
(Robert Collet, France)

5 1 **Kasatana (IRE)** 3-8-7 .... FDiFede 8 100
(A De Royer-Dupre, France)

6 nk **Dance The Classics (IRE)**[30] 4238 3-8-7 .... (b) IMendizabal 6 100
(J L Dunlop) *pressed ldr tl led after 5f: hdd over 1f out: one pce* **20/1**[2]

7 3 **Miss Clem's (FR)**[53] 4-9-2 .... TThulliez 3 95
(P Bary, France)

8 1 1/2 **Crumpett (IRE)**[109] 4-9-2 .... JAuge 7 93
(J E Hammond, France)

9 8 **Kankakee (USA)**[31] 4215 4-9-2 .... DBonilla 1 81
(J E Pease, France)

2m 29.8s (-3.60)
WFA 3 from 4yo 9lb **9** Ran SP% **19.0**
PARI-MUTUEL: WIN 2.10 (coupled with Kasatana); PL 1.20, 1.80, 1.90;DF 10.20.
Owner H H Aga Khan **Bred** Snc Lagardere Elevage **Trained** Chantilly, France

NOTEBOOK
Kasatana(IRE)
Dance The Classics(IRE) put up a good performance although out of the frame. Second early, she was taken into the lead just under a mile from home and held the advantage until the furlong marker before staying on at the one pace. It looks as if she will stay even further and softer ground would definitely have been an advantage.

5151 - 5152a (Foreign Racing) - See Raceform Interactive

4817 REDCAR (L-H)
Thursday, September 6

OFFICIAL GOING: Good to firm (firm in places; 10.2)
After a dry spell 1" water was put on the track over the previous five days resulting in 'quick ground, no jar and a very good cover of grass'.
Wind: Light, half-against Weather: Fine

5153 WEDDINGS AT REDCAR NURSERY 7f
2:00 (2:00) (Class 5) 2-Y-O **£2,817** (£838; £418; £209) **Stalls** Centre

Form RPR

052 1 **Joinedupwriting**[19] 4612 2-8-11 **71** .... PaulMulrennan 10 73
(R M Whitaker) *in rr and sn drvn along: hdwy over 2f out: styd on wl to ld towards fin* **7/1**[3]

0210 2 1/2 **Willyn (IRE)**[13] 4770 2-7-12 **63** .... KellyHarrison(5) 3 64
(J S Goldie) *hld up in rr: hdwy on wd outside 3f out: led over 1f out: hdd and no wl ins fnl f* **50/1**

5340 3 3/4 **Kinout (IRE)**[41] 3925 2-9-1 **75** .... DO'Donohoe 6 74
(K A Ryan) *chsd ldrs: upsides 1f out: no ex ins fnl f* **14/1**

320 4 shd **Suzi Spends (IRE)**[13] 4769 2-8-8 **68** .... RoystonFfrench 4 67
(M Johnston) *in rr and sn drvn along: hdwy over 2f: styd on fnl f* **11/1**

3040 5 hd **Elusive Deal (USA)**[34] 4126 2-7-13 **59** .... PaulHanagan 9 57
(R A Fahey) *in rr: rdn and outpcd 3f out: hdwy over 1f out: fin strly* **25/1**

4310 6 1 1/2 **Menadha (USA)**[22] 4501 2-9-7 **81** .... DarryllHolland 8 75
(M R Channon) *chsd ldrs: chal over 2f out: fdd appr fnl f* **4/1**[2]

0000 7 1 1/2 **Tikinheart (IRE)**[13] 4775 2-7-9 **58** oh3 .... DuranFentiman(3) 2 48
(T D Easterby) *dwlt: hld up in rr: smooth hdwy on outer to ld 3f out: hdd over 1f out: sn wknd* **20/1**

566 8 1 **The Last Bottle (IRE)**[22] 4487 2-8-7 **67** .... MickyFenton 11 55
(T P Tate) *prom: effrt over 2f out: outpcd appr fnl f* **7/1**[3]

000 9 1 **Battlecruiser (IRE)**[19] 4604 2-8-0 **60** ow2 .... (b[1]) AdrianTNicholls 7 45
(M Johnston) *led tl 3f out: wknd wl over 1f out* **11/1**

641 10 nk **Coffee Cup (IRE)**[13] 4783 2-8-6 **66** .... KerrinMcEvoy 12 50
(G A Swinbank) *in rr: effrt over 2f out: nvr on terms* **9/4**[1]

1465 11 1/2 **Charlotti Carlotti (IRE)**[23] 4476 2-9-0 **74** .... TomEaves 13 57
(T D Barron) *hld up in rr: rdn and hung rt over 2f out: nvr on terms* **14/1**

0640 12 1 1/4 **Northgate Lodge (USA)**[29] 4278 2-7-12 **58** .... DaleGibson 1 38
(M Brittain) *chsd ldrs: rdn and wknd 2f out* **100/1**

0056 13 4 **Hildegarde (IRE)**[10] 4897 2-7-13 **59** oh4 ow1 .... (p) PaulFessey 5 29
(T D Easterby) *chsd ldrs: lost pl over 2f out* **100/1**

1m 24.62s (-0.28) **Going Correction** -0.15s/f (Firm) **13** Ran SP% **118.3**
Speed ratings (Par 95): **95,94,93,93,93 91,89,88,87,87 86,85,80**
CSF £331.23 CT £4846.68 TOTE £9.50: £2.30, £9.10, £4.80; EX 254.60.
Owner R C Dollar **Bred** Ink Pot Partnership **Trained** Scarcroft, W Yorks

FOCUS
An ordinary nursery but the form has a solid look about it with those in the frame behind the winner close to their marks. They went a strong gallop and Kinout deserves credit, he did easily best of those who raced up with the pace.

NOTEBOOK

Joinedupwriting, improving with every outing, appreciated the step up to seven and showed battling qualities to show ahead near the line. (tchd 8-1)

Willyn(IRE) showed much improved form on her second outing for this yard. She moved up on the outer to show ahead only to be mugged near the line.

Kinout(IRE), 4lb lower than when making his nursery bow after being gelded, was in the firing line throughout. He was the only one who raced up with the pace to be still involved at the finish. (op 16-1 tchd 12-1)

Suzi Spends(IRE) put a poor effort last time behind her and she will be even better suited by a mile. (op 10-1 tchd 12-1)

Elusive Deal(USA), who is only small, was racing from a 5lb lower mark. She stayed on from way off the pace and finished with a real flourish. (op 33-1)

Menadha(USA), who looked a picture of health, continually swished his tail beforehand. Suited by this fast ground, he looked a major threat at one stage but in the end others saw out the final furlong better. (op 9-2 tchd 5-1 and 7-2)

Tikinheart(IRE), 3lb out of the handicap, is only small and has presumably given problems in the stalls in the past. After missing a beat he came there on the bridle to take charge but in the end the seventh furlong seemed beyond him. (op 22-1 tchd 25-1)

Coffee Cup(IRE), on her toes beforehand, was most disappointing on her nursery debut. Official explanation: trainer had no explanation for the poor form shown (op 5-2)

5154 DAVID BOSOMWORTH CHAMPAGNE MAIDEN AUCTION STKS 5f

2:30 (2:31) (Class 6) 2-Y-0 **£2,047** (£604; £302) **Stalls** Centre

Form				RPR
	1		**Yankee Bravo (USA)** 2-9-1 0 ... RoystonFfrench 9 (Mrs A Duffield) *dwlt: sn chsng ldrs: led 1f out: wnt clr: v readily* **6/1**[3]	85+
5234	**2**	*6*	**Upstanding**[9] 4924 2-8-4 66 ... DaleGibson 8 (M Brittain) *chsd ldrs: led over 1f out: sn hdd: no ch w wnr* **11/8**[1]	52
	3	*¾*	**Kyllis** 2-8-4 0 ... PaulHanagan 4 (B Smart) *sn outpcd and in midfield: edgd lft over 1f out: kpt on wl* **4/1**[2]	49
00	**4**	*2 ½*	**Piccolo Pete**[13] 4770 2-8-11 0 ... PatCosgrave 2 (J J Quinn) *sn outpcd on outer: hung lft thrght: hdwy over 1f out: styd on wl* **25/1**	47
00	**5**	*shd*	**Son Of Spartacus (IRE)**[13] 4784 2-8-13 0 ... (b[1]) TomEaves 6 (Mrs L Stubbs) *sn outpcd and in rr: hdwy over 1f out: styd on wl* **11/1**	49
0	**6**	*hd*	**Lunar Lass**[43] 3833 2-8-4 0 ... AdrianTNicholls 10 (G Woodward) *chsd ldrs: fdd appr fnl f* **20/1**	39
05	**7**	*¾*	**Just Sam (IRE)**[13] 4781 2-8-7 0 ow1 ... MickyFenton 3 (D Carroll) *led tl hdd & wknd over 1f out* **6/1**[3]	40
00	**8**	*1 ¾*	**Brough (IRE)**[22] 4487 2-8-8 0 ow4 ... JamesO'Reilly(7) 5 (J O'Reilly) *rrd s: sn chsng ldrs: fdd appr fnl f* **100/1**	41
000	**9**	*nk*	**Eternal Optimist (IRE)**[9] 4924 2-8-7 0 ow1 ... PaulMulrennan 7 (C W Thornton) *sn chsng ldrs: outpcd over 2f out: wknd over 1f out* **33/1**	32
606	**10**	*4*	**Penny Arcade**[20] 4559 2-7-11 35 ... DeclanCannon(7) 1 (M E Sowersby) *w ldrs: rdn 2f out: sn wknd* **125/1**	15
	11	*nk*	**Ruby's Rainbow (IRE)** 2-8-1 0 ... PatrickMathers(3) 11 (J Balding) *s.s: bhd and hung lft: nvr on terms* **25/1**	14

58.68 secs (-0.02) **Going Correction** -0.15s/f (Firm) 11 Ran SP% **116.2**
Speed ratings (Par 93): **94,84,83,79,79 78,77,74,74,67 67**
CSF £13.65 TOTE £8.10: £2.20, £1.40, £1.60; EX 20.90.
Owner Middleham Park Racing I **Bred** Tommy Burberry And Barry Hay **Trained** Constable Burton, N Yorks

FOCUS

A weak maiden auction race lacking any strength in depth but a wide-margin winner of some potential who could rate considerably higher.

NOTEBOOK

Yankee Bravo(USA), a 16,500gns purchase at the breeze-up sales, has size and scope but he did not look fully wound up. He came right away in the final furlong and looks a decent prospect. (op 5-1)

Upstanding, having his eighth start, is standing up to her racing really well. Rated 66, she proved no match whatsoever for the winner. (op 13-8 tchd 7-4 in a place)

Kyllis, an April foal, looked very inexperienced going to post. She stayed on from an unpromising position and this will have taught her plenty. (op 7-2)

Piccolo Pete, having his third outing, struggled to go the pace and showed a marked tendency to hang left. He was putting in all his best work at the finish and this opens up the nursery route for him.

Son Of Spartacus(IRE), tried in blinkers, stayed on when it was all over and he too can now compete in nursery company. (op 14-1)

Lunar Lass, who hung and finished last on her debut six weeks earlier, showed a fair bit more this time. (tchd 16-1)

Just Sam(IRE), who made his debut two outings ago over seven, showed bags of toe before falling in a heap. (op 7-1)

5155 STOREYS:SSP 50 YEARS ON TEESSIDE H'CAP 6f

3:00 (3:00) (Class 5) (0-75,78) 3-Y-0+ **£2,817** (£838; £418; £209) **Stalls** Centre

Form				RPR
0213	**1**		**John Keats**[8] 4934 4-9-1 **68** ... DanielTudhope 1 (J S Goldie) *outpcd and drvn over 3f out: hdwy on outside over 2f out: led 1f out: edgd lft: hld on towards fin* **4/1**[2]	79
0303	**2**	*hd*	**Guest Connections**[10] 4895 4-9-6 **73** ... (v) AdrianTNicholls 8 (D Nicholls) *in rr: reminders after 2f: hdwy over 2f out: upsides ins fnl f: no ex nr fin* **6/1**[3]	83
1101	**3**	*hd*	**Dakota Rain (IRE)**[10] 4895 5-9-8 **78** 6ex ... LiamTreadwell(3) 2 (Jennie Candlish) *w ldrs: led 3f out: hdd 1f out: rallied ins fnl f: r.o* **9/4**[1]	87
0000	**4**	*1 ½*	**Circuit Dancer (IRE)**[41] 3921 7-9-5 **72** ... SilvestreDeSousa 4 (D Nicholls) *chsd ldrs: sn drvn along: kpt on same pce fnl 2f* **11/1**	77
3346	**5**	*hd*	**Nufoudh (IRE)**[8] 4940 3-8-4 **59** oh2 ... RoystonFfrench 5 (Miss Tracy Waggott) *led tl 3f out: kpt on same pce* **8/1**	63
0603	**6**	*1 ¼*	**Mundo's Magic**[8] 4940 3-8-11 **66** ... (p) SebSanders 3 (G M Moore) *dwlt: hdwy over 2f out: sn rdn and edgd rt: wknd over 1f out* **6/1**[3]	67
0606	**7**	*6*	**Just Joey**[10] 4898 3-9-5 **74** ... PhillipMakin 7 (J R Weymes) *in rr: rdn over 2f out: sn wknd* **28/1**	57
4336	**8**	*shd*	**Another Genepi (USA)**[8] 4931 4-8-10 **63** ... (b) DO'Donohoe 9 (K A Ryan) *racd isolated stands' side: edgd lft and lost pl over 2f out* **8/1**	45
060U	**9**	*6*	**Howards Princess**[96] 2249 5-8-6 **59** oh14 ... PaulHanagan 6 (J O'Reilly) *chsd ldrs: lost pl over 2f out* **100/1**	23

1m 10.98s (-0.72) **Going Correction** -0.15s/f (Firm)
WFA 3 from 4yo+ 2lb 9 Ran SP% **114.3**
Speed ratings (Par 103): **98,97,97,95,95 93,85,85,77**
CSF £27.93 CT £65.98 TOTE £4.50: £1.70, £2.00, £1.50; EX 33.20.
Owner Tough Construction Ltd **Bred** R Preece **Trained** Uplawmoor, E Renfrews

FOCUS

A fair handicap and pretty sound form rated around the third.

5156 JOHN SMITH'S REDCAR STRAIGHT-MILE CHAMPIONSHIP (QUALIFIER) (H'CAP) 1m

3:30 (3:30) (Class 4) (0-85,84) 3-Y-0 **£4,728** (£1,406; £702; £351) **Stalls** Centre

Form				RPR
111	**1**		**Caravel (IRE)**[11] 4847 3-9-5 **84** 6ex ... SebSanders 5 (Sir Mark Prescott) *sn chsng ldrs: edgd lft 3f out: rdn to ld over 1f out: styd on strly ins fnl f* **8/13**[1]	97+
154	**2**	*1 ½*	**Fragrancy (IRE)**[13] 4785 3-9-3 **82** ... PhilipRobinson 3 (M A Jarvis) *w ldr: led 4f out: hdd over 1f out: kpt on same pce ins fnl f* **3/1**[2]	90
20	**3**	*2 ½*	**Ghafeer (USA)**[23] 4479 3-8-6 **71** ... (p) TomEaves 1 (B Ellison) *hld up wl in tch: rdn over 3f out: sn outpcd: kpt on same pce fnl 2f* **66/1**	73
2063	**4**	*nk*	**Mark Of Love (IRE)**[5] 5046 3-8-5 **70** ... PaulHanagan 2 (M R Channon) *trckd ldrs: t.k.h: effrt over 2f out: kpt on same pce* **16/1**	72
0143	**5**	*3 ½*	**Deadline (UAE)**[5] 5043 3-8-5 **70** ... PaulFessey 6 (P T Midgley) *chsd ldrs: effrt over 3f out: lost pl over 1f out* **18/1**	64
6055	**6**	*1 ¼*	**Voodoo Moon**[13] 4785 3-9-4 **83** ... RoystonFfrench 4 (M Johnston) *led tl 4f out: lost pl over 1f out* **15/2**[3]	74

1m 35.45s (-2.35) **Going Correction** -0.15s/f (Firm) 6 Ran SP% **111.3**
Speed ratings (Par 103): **105,103,101,100,97 95**
CSF £2.63 TOTE £1.80: £1.80, £1.20; EX 2.50.
Owner Neil Greig - Osborne House **Bred** G A M Grothier **Trained** Newmarket, Suffolk

FOCUS

A decent handicap run at a strong pace although the winner did not need to improve on previous efforts and the form is best rated through the fourth to recent form.

Ghafeer(USA) Official explanation: trainer said gelding had a breathing problem

5157 STOREYS:SSP IAN BATTLE MEMORIAL MAIDEN STKS 1m 1f

4:00 (4:02) (Class 5) 3-Y-0+ **£2,817** (£838; £418; £209) **Stalls** Low

Form				RPR
	1		**Arqaam** 3-9-3 0 ... KerrinMcEvoy 5 (Saeed Bin Suroor) *trckd ldrs: hdwy over 3f out: led over 1f out: smoothly* **4/7**[1]	83+
3362	**2**	*5*	**Ashmal (USA)**[29] 4282 3-8-12 65 ... (b) SebSanders 3 (J L Dunlop) *trckd ldrs: chal over 2f out: kpt on to take 2nd last 100yds: no ch w wnr* **11/4**[2]	58
05	**3**	*1*	**Passing True (IRE)**[28] 4334 3-8-12 0 ... RoystonFfrench 1 (M Johnston) *t.k.h: w ldr: led after 2f: hdd over 1f out: one pce* **10/1**[3]	56
2-00	**4**	*5*	**Macaroni Gin (IRE)**[22] 4499 3-9-3 62 ... TomEaves 2 (J Howard Johnson) *led 2f: trckd ldrs: rdn 3f out: wknd over 1f out* **14/1**	50
50	**5**	*14*	**Island King (IRE)**[18] 4641 4-9-9 0 ... PatCosgrave 6 (R Bastiman) *s.i.s: drvn over 4f out: lost pl over 3f out: sn bhd* **150/1**	19
	6	*9*	**North Stars (IRE)** 3-8-10 0 ... JamesO'Reilly(7) 4 (J O'Reilly) *chsd ldrs: rdn over 3f out: sn lost pl* **80/1**	—
0-0	**7**	*19*	**Tyrone Lady (IRE)**[170] 714 4-9-1 0 ... JerryO'Dwyer(3) 7 (M C Chapman) *swvd bdly rt s: in rr: bhd fnl 4f* **150/1**	—

1m 51.84s (-1.56) **Going Correction** -0.10s/f (Good)
WFA 3 from 4yo 6lb 7 Ran SP% **108.6**
Speed ratings (Par 103): **102,97,96,92,79 71,54**
CSF £2.04 TOTE £1.50: £1.10, £1.30; EX 2.20.
Owner Godolphin **Bred** Shadwell Estate Company Limited **Trained** Newmarket, Suffolk

FOCUS

A weak maiden but a very comfortable winner in newcomer Arqaam, but difficult to know what he beat.

5158 CHRISTMAS DISCO PARTY NIGHTS H'CAP 1m 6f 19y

4:30 (4:32) (Class 6) (0-65,65) 3-Y-0+ **£2,047** (£604; £302) **Stalls** Low

Form				RPR
5345	**1**		**Let It Be**[8] 4941 6-9-1 **52** ... PhillipMakin 8 (K G Reveley) *trckd ldr: led and qcknd over 2f out: styd on ins fnl f* **7/1**[3]	62
0066	**2**	*1*	**Chunky's Choice (IRE)**[12] 4821 3-8-12 **60** ... KerrinMcEvoy 10 (J Noseda) *hld up in mid-div: stdy hdwy over 3f out: wnt 2nd 2f out: no ex ins fnl f* **7/1**[3]	69
3532	**3**	*2 ½*	**Mr Mischief**[9] 4925 7-9-2 **56** ... JerryO'Dwyer(3) 12 (M C Chapman) *hld up in rr: hdwy on outer over 4f out: hung lft and wnt 3rd over 1f out: kpt on same pce* **4/1**[2]	62
6563	**4**	*4*	**Parchment (IRE)**[8] 4941 5-9-4 **55** ... PaddyAspell 4 (A J Lockwood) *mid-div: hdwy and edgd rt over 3f out: kpt on: nvr trbld ldrs* **8/1**	55
-000	**5**	*hd*	**On Every Street**[59] 3371 6-8-9 **46** oh1 ... (vt) RoystonFfrench 2 (R Bastiman) *hmpd and reminders sn after s: sn chsng ldrs: one pce fnl 3f* **100/1**	46
0503	**6**	*4*	**Cecina Marina**[21] 4521 4-8-6 **46** oh1 ... PJMcDonald(3) 11 (C W Thornton) *mid-div: effrt over 3f out: nvr nr ldrs* **33/1**	40
0500	**7**	*1 ¼*	**Zaville**[9] 4925 5-8-8 **52** oh1 ow6 ... (b) JamesO'Reilly(7) 3 (J O'Reilly) *led: clr after 2f: hdd over 2f out: sn wknd* **66/1**	44
0455	**8**	*¾*	**The Pen**[22] 4493 5-9-5 **56** ... PaulMulrennan 5 (C W Fairhurst) *wnt lft s: chsd ldrs: effrt 4f out: one pce* **10/1**	47
0004	**9**	*¾*	**The Diamond Bond**[8] 4943 3-7-12 **46** oh1 ... PaulHanagan 9 (G R Oldroyd) *sn bhd: kpt on fnl 2f: nvr on terms* **15/2**	36
4051	**10**	*1 ½*	**Sangfroid**[8] 4943 3-8-7 **55** 6ex ow3 ... SebSanders 13 (Sir Mark Prescott) *hld up in rr: hdwy 7f out: effrt over 3f out: hung lft and no imp: no ch whn eased ins fnl f* **2/1**[1]	46
4056	**11**	*1*	**Ninetyninetreble (IRE)**[39] 4003 4-9-11 **65** ... MarkLawson(3) 6 (Grant Tuer) *sn chsng ldrs: drvn over 5f out: lost pl over 2f out* **25/1**	52
/0-0	**12**	*15*	**Southern Bazaar (USA)**[10] 3610 6-8-6 **46** oh1 ... DominicFox(3) 1 (M C Chapman) *hmpd s: in rr: drvn 7f out: sn bhd* **100/1**	12

3m 2.92s (-2.10) **Going Correction** -0.10s/f (Good)
WFA 3 from 4yo+ 11lb 12 Ran SP% **120.6**
Speed ratings (Par 101): **102,101,100,97,97 95,94,94,93,92 92,83**
CSF £54.90 CT £226.44 TOTE £8.30: £1.90, £1.90, £1.40; EX 55.40.
Owner A Frame **Bred** Sir Eric Parker **Trained** Lingdale, Redcar & Cleveland

FOCUS

A low-grade handicap not run at a strong pace but the form looks sound rated around the winner and third.

Sangfroid Official explanation: trainer's representative had no explanation for the poor form shown

5159 GO RACING AT THIRSK ON SATURDAY APPRENTICE H'CAP 7f

5:00 (5:01) (Class 5) (0-70,70) 3-Y-0+ **£2,817** (£838; £418; £209) **Stalls** Centre

Form				RPR
2154	1		**Esoterica (IRE)**^{8} 4931 4-9-0 **62**...(b) GaryBartley$^{(5)}$ 2 (J S Goldie) *hld up: effrt over 2f out: styd on strly to ld jst ins fnl f: sn clr* **9/2**^{2}	75
0020	2	3	**Tour D'Amour (IRE)**^{25} 4427 4-8-8 **58**... LanceBetts$^{(7)}$ 4 (R Craggs) *hld up in rr: hdwy over 2f out: n.m.r over 1f out: styd on to snatch 2nd post* **33/1**	63
5600	3	shd	**Malinsa Blue (IRE)**^{21} 4526 5-9-5 **62**...(p) PJMcDonald 3 (B Ellison) *w ldrs: led over 1f out: hdd jst ins fnl f: kpt on same pce* **12/1**	67
0000	4	¾	**Lincolneurocruiser**^{20} 4587 5-9-3 **60**...(v) StephaneBreux 12 (Mrs N Macauley) *in tch: effrt and c to r alone stands' side over 2f out: kpt on wl fnl f* **50/1**	63
0004	5	nk	**Uhuru Peak**^{31} 4219 6-8-2 **52** oh1...(bt) NSLawes$^{(7)}$ 14 (M W Easterby) *led tl over 1f out: one pce* **25/1**	54
5002	6	½	**Petite Mac**^{13} 4768 7-8-10 **53**... MarkLawson 10 (N Bycroft) *mid-div: rdn over 2f out: styd on fnl f* **14/1**	53
2635	7	hd	**Aussie Blue (IRE)**^{27} 4354 3-8-2 **56**...(b) DeclanCannon$^{(7)}$ 1 (R M Whitaker) *slowly away and swvd lft s: sn chsng ldrs: hung rt and one pce over 1f out* **8/1**	54
100	8	¾	**Turn Me On (IRE)**^{26} 4390 4-9-0 **62**... KellyHarrison$^{(5)}$ 5 (T D Walford) *hld up in mid-div: effrt over 2f out: nvr nr ldrs* **13/2**^{3}	60
1041	9	hd	**Pay Time**^{15} 4705 8-9-6 **63**... DuranFentiman 13 (R E Barr) *hld up in mid-div: effrt over 2f out: nvr trbld ldrs* **12/1**	60
0350	10	nk	**Sunnyside Tom (IRE)**^{10} 4898 3-9-9 **70**...(p) JamieMoriarty 6 (R A Fahey) *t.k.h towards rr: effrt over 2f out: nvr a factor* **14/1**	65
4504	11	1	**Davaye**^{11} 4842 3-8-10 **64** ow2... JBrennan$^{(7)}$ 7 (K R Burke) *chsd ldrs: wknd 2f out* **40/1**	56
4652	12	¾	**Spinning**^{8} 4931 4-8-10 **56**...(b) NeilBrown$^{(3)}$ 9 (T D Barron) *chsd ldrs: wknd over 1f out* **15/8**^{1}	48
0005	13	nk	**Sea Frolic (IRE)**^{24} 4464 6-8-4 **52** oh7... JamieHamblett$^{(5)}$ 11 (Jennie Candlish) *hld up towards rr: lost pl over 2f out* **100/1**	43
0-00	14	23	**Lord Conyers (IRE)**^{26} 4410 8-8-4 **52** oh7... PatrickDonaghy$^{(5)}$ 8 (G Woodward) *in rr: hung lft over 3f out: ended up alone far side: sn bhd: t.o* **125/1**	—

1m 23.57s (-1.33) **Going Correction** -0.15s/f (Firm)
WFA 3 from 4yo+ 4lb **14** Ran SP% **119.1**
Speed ratings (Par 103): **101,97,97,96,96 95,95,94,94,94 92,92,91,65**
CSF £158.36 CT £1167.74 TOTE £5.80: £2.30, £8.00, £4.80; EX 200.70 Place 6 £22.96, Place 5 £2.66.
Owner Mrs S E Bruce **Bred** A Lyons Bloodstock **Trained** Uplawmoor, E Renfrews

FOCUS
A modest handicap run at a strong pace and in the end a most decisive winner. The race has been rated through the runner-up and the form is straightforward and solid.
Spinning Official explanation: trainer's representative had no explanation for the poor form shown
T/Plt: £26.00 to a £1 stake. Pool: £50,284.60. 1,408.95 winning tickets. T/Qpdt: £4.60 to a £1 stake. Pool: £3,470.50. 551.00 winning tickets. WG

5001 SALISBURY (R-H)

Thursday, September 6

OFFICIAL GOING: Good to firm (good in places; 8.9)
Wind: Virtually nil Weather: warm and dry

5160 SYDENHAMS H'CAP 5f

2:10 (2:13) (Class 5) (0-70,72) 3-Y-0+ **£3,238** (£963; £481; £240) **Stalls** High

Form				RPR
004	1		**Pic Up Sticks**^{6} 5009 8-9-3 **68**... RyanMoore 12 (B G Powell) *b: hld up in mid-div: swtchd lft and hdwy over 1f out: r.o strly: led fnl 30yds: rdn out* **3/1**^{1}	80+
512	2	nk	**Even Bolder**^{8} 4944 4-8-9 **67**...(p) SophieDoyle$^{(7)}$ 14 (R Simpson) *lw: a.p: led over 1f out: sn rdn and edgd lft: ct fnl 30yds* **5/1**^{2}	78+
0006	3	1½	**Dancing Mystery**^{16} 4689 13-8-2 **56**...(b) LiamJones$^{(3)}$ 10 (E A Wheeler) *chsd ldrs: rdn and ev ch over 1f out: kpt on but nt pce of ldng pair* **33/1**	62
5601	4	1½	**Kings College Boy**^{12} 4800 7-9-2 **67**...(b) PaulDoe 13 (R A Fahey) *in tch: rdn and cl up whn bdly hmpd 1f out: r.o but no ch after* **14/1**	74+
3353	5	nk	**Malapropism**^{7} 4967 7-9-5 **70**... TPO'Shea 8 (M R Channon) *mid-div: hdwy over 2f out: sn rdn: kpt on same pce fnl f* **8/1**	69
3125	6	shd	**Roman Quintet (IRE)**^{26} 4390 7-9-2 **67**... TQuinn 6 (R J Price) *led: rdn and hdd over 1f out: no ex* **8/1**	66
4330	7	1½	**Caustic Wit (IRE)**^{13} 4767 9-9-0 **65**... RichardHughes 7 (M S Saunders) *nvr bttr than mid-div* **12/1**	58
1224	8	shd	**Ocean Blaze**^{42} 3870 3-9-3 **69**... FergusSweeney 9 (B R Millman) *squeezed out s: steadily rcvrd into mid-div: rdn over 2f out: one pce fnl f* **22/1**	62
6121	9	hd	**Methaaly (IRE)**^{7} 4967 4-9-0 **72** 6ex... DanielleMcCreery$^{(7)}$ 2 (M Mullineaux) *s.i.s: a towards rr* **13/2**^{3}	64
0003	10	1½	**Azygous**^{8} 4944 4-9-1 **66**... SimonWhitworth 11 (J Akehurst) *chsd ldrs: rdn over 2f out: wknd over 1f out* **16/1**	53
2012	11	1¼	**Briery Lane (IRE)**^{6} 4996 6-8-9 **60**... SteveDrowne 1 (J M Bradley) *a towards rr* **11/1**	42
230	12	½	**One Way Ticket**^{6} 5009 7-9-2 **67**...(p) JimmyFortune 5 (J M Bradley) *prom: rdn and ev ch 2f out: sn btn* **16/1**	48
5000	13	3½	**Figaro Flyer (IRE)**^{13} 4780 4-9-1 **66**... AmirQuinn 3 (P Howling) *stdd s: a bhd* **20/1**	34

61.31 secs (-0.28) **Going Correction** +0.025s/f (Good)
WFA 3 from 4yo+ 1lb **13** Ran SP% **123.7**
Speed ratings (Par 103): **103,102,100,97,97 97,94,94,94,91 89,89,83**
CSF £17.10 CT £367.42 TOTE £3.20: £1.40, £3.00, £9.10; EX 25.40.
Owner Mrs P Jubert **Bred** J P Coggan **Trained** Lambourn, Berks

FOCUS
A modest, but open sprint for the class in which it paid to be drawn high. The first pair came clear and the runner-up sets the level.

Figaro Flyer(IRE) Official explanation: jockey said gelding was never travelling

5161 WILTSHIRE LIFE E B F NOVICE STKS 1m

2:40 (2:44) (Class 4) 2-Y-0 **£5,181** (£1,541; £770; £384) **Stalls** High

Form				RPR
246	1		**Ramona Chase**^{19} 4598 2-8-12 **95**... RyanMoore 3 (S Kirk) *trckd ldrs: shkn up to chal ins 3f out: led 2f out: drvn clr fnl f* **1/3**^{1}	95
0122	2	6	**Unnefer (FR)**^{23} 4482 2-9-5 **88**... TedDurcan 2 (H R A Cecil) *lw: led: rdn and hdd 2f out: eased whn btn ins fnl f* **3/1**^{2}	88
	3	2	**Monashee Rock (IRE)** 2-8-5 0 ow2... SimonWhitworth 4 (M Salaman) *w'like: plld hrd: trckd ldr tl rdn over 2f out: kpt on same pce* **66/1**	70
	4	10	**Red Leaves** 2-8-5 0... LiamJones$^{(3)}$ 5 (P F I Cole) *w'like: str: chsd ldrs tl outpcd over 3f* **14/1**^{3}	50
00	5	40	**Aries Magic**^{54} 3552 2-8-7 0... FergusSweeney 1 (S C Burrough) *chsd ldrs tl 4f out: sn wl bhd* **200/1**	—

1m 43.64s (0.55) **Going Correction** +0.025s/f (Good) **5** Ran SP% **108.7**
Speed ratings (Par 97): **98,92,90,80,40**
CSF £1.56 TOTE £1.50: £1.02, £1.60; EX 1.60.
Owner Norman Ormiston **Bred** Ridgecourt Stud **Trained** Upper Lambourn, Berks

FOCUS
No real strength in depth to this novice event and the winner did not need to be at his best to score at the weights with the runner-up to his mark.

NOTEBOOK
Ramona Chase, not beaten at all far in Listed company the last twice, relished the drop into this easier grade and duly opened his account at the fourth attempt. He took time to pick up once asked for his effort, and did not totally convince with his attitude, but his class told going into the final furlong, with this extra furlong looking right up his street. He still looks to be very much learning his trade, and appears most likely to come into his own as a three-year-old, but he is certainly worth another try in better company before the season's end now his confidence will have been boosted. It would not be a surprise to see him turn up in the 1m Group 3 Autumn Stakes at Ascot in October in a bid try and emulate his stable companion Caldra who won that event last season. (op 4-11 tchd 2-5 in a place)
Unnefer(FR), disappointing on softer ground last time, was given a more positive ride on this switch to a quicker surface and was not disgraced in giving the winner 7lb. He has not quite gone on as could have been expected, and looks more of a handicapper in the making, but he is still holding his form well all the same. (op 11-4)
Monashee Rock(IRE) ◆, half-sister to a 1m2f three-year-old winner, was warm and on her toes beforehand, but she posted a pleasing debut effort and only paid entering the final furlong for running too freely through the early parts. She has scope and looks likely to make up into a better three-year-old, but her connections will likely be keen to find a maiden after this and she looks sure to benefit for the experience. A drop back to 7f may also help in the short term.
Red Leaves, a 42,000gns half-brother to high-class juvenile winner Lady Lahar among others, started to feel the pinch passing the halfway stage and eventually dropped out from the 3f pole. This experience will not be lost on him. (tchd 12-1)

5162 EUROPEAN BREEDERS' FUND QUIDHAMPTON MAIDEN FILLIES' STKS 6f 212y

3:10 (3:16) (Class 2) 2-Y-0 **£7,772** (£2,312; £1,155; £577) **Stalls** High

Form				RPR
0	1		**Joffe's Run (USA)**^{41} 3895 2-9-0 0... IanMongan 12 (B J Meehan) *lw: mde all: rdn clr over 1f out: unchal* **5/1**^{2}	88+
	2	3½	**Shamayel** 2-9-0 0... RHills 15 (B W Hills) *leggy: lw: b.hind: s.i.s: sn in tch: rdn to chse wnr over 1f out: kpt on but no further imp on wnr* **7/2**^{1}	79+
	3	1¾	**Snowy Indian** 2-9-0 0... RyanMoore 16 (Sir Michael Stoute) *w'like: lengthy: bit bkwd: mid-div: stdy prog fr 3f out: wnt 3rd ent fnl f: styd on* **6/1**^{3}	74
55	4	1½	**Sahaadi**^{13} 4774 2-9-0 0... RichardHughes 6 (R Hannon) *in tch: rdn over 2f out: styd on to go 4th ent fnl f but nvr quite able to chal* **5/1**^{2}	70
	5	3½	**Gaabal (IRE)** 2-9-0 0... J-PGuillambert 11 (C E Brittain) *w'like: scope: lengthy: chsd wnr: rdn over 2f out: wknd ent fnl f* **11/1**	61
	6	nk	**Secret Gem (IRE)** 2-9-0 0... JimmyFortune 4 (C G Cox) *w'like: bit bkwd: mid-div: rdn 3f out: kpt on same pce fnl 2f* **8/1**	61
0	7	¾	**Cheviot Red**^{19} 4602 2-9-0 0... NelsonDeSouza 1 (B J Meehan) *w'like: chsd ldrs: rdn over 2f out: wknd over 1f out* **100/1**	59
	8	shd	**Jollyhockeysticks** 2-9-0 0... SamHitchcott 17 (M R Channon) *leggy: awkward leaving stalls: towards rr: hdwy over 3f out: sn rdn: no further imp* **40/1**	58
00	9	¾	**Politeia (USA)**^{35} 4094 2-9-0 0... JimCrowley 3 (R Hannon) *towards rr: sme late prog: nvr a factor* **18/1**	56
	10	1	**Mount Lavinia (IRE)** 2-9-0 0... FergusSweeney 10 (R M Beckett) *athletic: lw: s.i.s: towards rr: sme prog over 1f out: no further imp fnl f* **20/1**	54
	11	1¼	**Karate Queen** 2-9-0 0... FrancisNorton 7 (A M Balding) *leggy: b.hind: nvr bttr than mid-div* **50/1**	51
	12	2	**Daisy Nook** 2-9-0 0... JDSmith 5 (S Kirk) *leggy: alway towards rr* **100/1**	45
	13	2	**Balletic (IRE)** 2-9-0 0... TQuinn 9 (S Kirk) *w'like: str: bit bkwd: wnt rt s: mid-div: rdn over 3f out: wknd wl over 1f out* **33/1**	40
	14	hd	**Kalokairi (IRE)** 2-9-0 0... TedDurcan 2 (J L Dunlop) *w'like: bit bkwd: s.i.s: hmpd wl over 2f out: a towards rr* **16/1**	40
	15	1½	**Dance Easily** 2-9-0 0... PaulDoe 8 (J L Dunlop) *w'like: leggy: bit bkwd: s.i.s: sn pushed along: a towards rr* **66/1**	36
	16	3½	**Bobby Darling (IRE)** 2-9-0 0... TPO'Shea 13 (M R Channon) *w'like: a towards rr* **16/1**	27
	17	5	**Lady Selkirk** 2-9-0 0... SteveDrowne 18 (R Charlton) *w'like: str: hld up towards rr: making sme hdwy whn bdly hmpd wl over 2f out: nt rcvr and eased* **14/1**	14+
	18	12	**Apple Pie Order (IRE)** 2-9-0 0... MatthewHenry 14 (R J Hodges) *w'like: mid-div: rdn and swtchd rt wl over 2f out: sn wknd* **100/1**	—

1m 28.7s (-0.36) **Going Correction** +0.025s/f (Good) **18** Ran SP% **129.5**
Speed ratings (Par 98): **103,99,97,95,91 90,90,89,89,87 86,84,81,81,80 76,70,56**
CSF £22.96 TOTE £5.50: £2.10, £1.90, £2.10; EX 29.50.
Owner Andrew Rosen **Bred** Dr Masatake Iida **Trained** Manton, Wilts
■ Stewards' Enquiry : Matthew Henry three-day ban: careless riding (Sep 17-19)

FOCUS
A race that can throw up the odd smart performer and the winning time was fair for a race of its type. The fourth helps set the standard.

NOTEBOOK

Joffe's Run(USA), whose debut eighth at Ascot has worked out exceptionally well, winner and third going on to Listed and Group 2 success respectively, pinged out of the gates and Mongan was quick to ensure he bagged the far rail. Leading at a decent pace throughout, she went clear racing into the final quarter mile and galloped on resolutely to win with plenty in hand. This was a smart performance from the daughter of Giant's Causeway and, given this race has been won by some smart performers over the years, it would not surprise to see her go on to taste success at Pattern level. She holds a Group 1 Fillies' Mile entry. (op 7-1 tchd 8-1)

Shamayel, a 380,000gns daughter of Pivotal, holds no big-race entries, but she had clearly been showing something at home as she was supported into favouritism. Sluggish out of the stalls, she quickly recovered, but the winner simply knew too much and she was unable to get anywhere near that rival. Winning an ordinary maiden should prove a formality and she may well benefit from slightly easier ground. (op 5-1)

Snowy Indian ◆, a sister to the high-class Snow Ridge, is another lacking big-race entries, but having been outpaced she really came home nicely and gave the impression the experience would not be lost on her. She too is likely to appreciate a bit of juice in the ground and winning a maiden should prove a formality, with the step up to 1m likely to suit in time. (op 5-1 tchd 9-2)

Sahaadi had already fallen short in a couple of lesser maidens and it would have been a surprise had she proved good enough. Now qualified for nurseries, she can be expected to win in that sphere. (tchd 4-1)

Gaabal(IRE), a daughter of Frenchmans Bay, offered only limited promise for the future, but she comes from a yard whose juveniles often benefit from a run and as a result it would not surprise to see her improve next time. (op 8-1 tchd 15-2)

Secret Gem(IRE), whose trainer is more than capable of readying one to win first time, never really threatened to challenge on this racecourse debut and kept on in a manner to suggest she will benefit from 1m in time. (op 15-2 tchd 7-1)

Daisy Nook was on her toes and looked quite fit.

Dance Easily is a very good walker.

Lady Selkirk, a 170,000gns daughter of Selkirk, was just beginning to get going when badly hampered and she was eased right off afterwards. She would have been an awful lot closer and can safely be given another chance to display her capabilities. (op 16-1 tchd 20-1)

5163 EUROPEAN BREEDERS' FUND LOCHSONG FILLIES' STKS (H'CAP) 6f 212y

3:40 (3:46) (Class 2) (0-100,95) 3-Y-0+

£14,956 (£4,478; £2,239; £1,120; £559; £280) **Stalls** High

Form / RPR

5122 **1** **Perfect Star**[22] 4509 3-8-13 **86** SteveDrowne 8 — 94
(C G Cox) *mde all: rdn and edgd lft over 1f out: kpt on gamely: drvn out* **10/3**[1]

2242 **2** ½ **Miss Lucifer (FR)**[25] 4420 3-9-3 **90** RyanMoore 1 — 97
(B W Hills) *hld up in last pair: swtchd lft over 2f out: sn rdn: r.o strly fnl 100yds: wnt 2nd towards fin* **10/3**[1]

6200 **3** ¾ **Regal Quest (IRE)**[11] 4848 3-8-5 **78** FrancisNorton 7 — 83
(S Kirk) *trckd ldrs: rdn and nt clr run 2f out: str chal and ch jst ins fnl f: no ex fnl 75yds* **25/1**

6143 **4** nk **Steam Cuisine**[20] 4589 3-9-0 **87** TedDurcan 6 — 91+
(M G Quinlan) *trckd ldrs: swtchd lft over 2f out: sn rdn: ch over 1f out: kpt on but no ex* **5/1**[3]

1115 **5** ½ **Our Faye**[18] 4633 4-9-4 **87** GeorgeBaker 2 — 92
(S Kirk) *hld up in last: swtchd lft over 2f out: sn rdn: kpt on but nt pce to chal* **4/1**[2]

231 **6** ½ **Medley**[40] 3961 3-9-8 **95** RichardHughes 5 — 96
(R Hannon) *lw: trckd wnr: rdn to chal 2f out: no ex ent fnl f* **5/1**[3]

2000 **7** 2 **Gaelic Princess**[21] 4551 7-8-8 **77** oh3 FergusSweeney 4 — 75
(A G Newcombe) *hld up in last trio: rdn and effrt over 2f out: one pce fnl f* **8/1**

1m 27.33s (-1.73) **Going Correction** +0.025s/f (Good)
WFA 3 from 4yo+ 4lb — **7** Ran SP% **114.4**
Speed ratings (Par 96): **110,109,108,108,107 107,104**
CSF £14.64 CT £232.41 TOTE £4.30: £2.50, £1.30; EX 13.30 Trifecta £218.60 Pool: £307.95 - 1.00 winning tickets..
Owner Dr Bridget Drew & E E Dedman **Bred** Mrs A M Jenkins And E D Kessly **Trained** Lambourn, Berks

FOCUS

A decent fillies' handicap, run at a solid pace. Sound form set and limited by the placed horses.

NOTEBOOK

Perfect Star, a runner-up to the progressive Shevchenko at Sandown the last twice, ran out a determined winner from the front on this return to racing against her own sex. She is in the form of her life at present, has developed into a very likeable filly, and will now likely go in search of some all-important black type at Doncaster's St Leger meeting. (op 9-2 tchd 5-1 in places)

Miss Lucifer(FR), ridden with more patience this time, got going all too late in the day and again found one too good. She rates a decent benchmark for the form and may be worth trying over a stiffer test now, in a bid to gain a much-deserved first success of the current campaign. (op 7-2)

Regal Quest(IRE), who did not get the best of runs when trying to get in the clear around 2f out, returned to something like her best and was only found out at the business end. It is hard to know whether she will repeat this sort of form next time, however, as she has been inconsistent this term and she will probably go up again a pound for two for this. (tchd 33-1)

Steam Cuisine ran her usual race and did nothing wrong in defeat, but the Handicapper does look in charge of her now. She is another who helps to set the standard of this form. (tchd 6-1)

Our Faye, back down in grade, could muster only the same pace when asked for her effort and her progression looks to have levelled out for now. (op 7-2)

Medley, 2lb higher, was not disgraced under top weight from her new mark and can have no excuses. (op 4-1)

Gaelic Princess, who took this race last season from a 1lb higher mark, has been struggling for form of late and never seriously threatened from off the pace. (op 9-1 tchd 11-1)

5164 EUROPEAN BREEDERS' FUND DICK POOLE FILLIES' STKS (LISTED RACE) 6f

4:10 (4:17) (Class 1) 2-Y-0

£15,614 (£5,918; £2,961; £1,476; £739; £371) **Stalls** High

Form / RPR

216 **1** **Fashion Rocks (IRE)**[14] 4744 2-8-12 100 JimmyFortune 5 — 97
(B J Meehan) *lw: wnt rt s: trckd ldrs: led wl over 1f out: sn hrd pressed: drifted lft ent fnl f: drvn out* **11/8**[1]

61 **2** nk **Vive Les Rouges**[19] 4593 2-8-12 79 IanMongan 8 — 96
(C F Wall) *t.k.h trcking ldrs: gng wl and ev ch fr over 2f out: rdn wl over 1f out: str chal thrght fnl f: hld nr fin* **11/1**

13 **3** ¾ **Raymi Coya (CAN)**[28] 4329 2-8-12 86 TedDurcan 6 — 94
(M Botti) *bmpd s: in last trio: hdwy 3f out: sn rdn: drifted rt 1f out: kpt on* **16/1**

2 **4** 3 **Dubai Power**[22] 4506 2-8-12 0 RyanMoore 7 — 85
(C E Brittain) *trckd ldrs: outpcd 3f out: swtchd lft jst over 2f out: hdwy over 1f out: wnt 4th ent fnl f: no further imp* **7/1**[3]

0253 **5** 2½ **Kylayne**[6] 4992 2-8-12 97 (b[1]) TQuinn 1 — 77
(P W D'Arcy) *led: rdn and hdd wl over 1f out: fdd ins fnl f* **10/1**

12U1 **6** nk **Ocean Transit (IRE)**[24] 4453 2-8-12 77 JackDean 3 — 76
(W G M Turner) *hld up: effrt over 2f out: one pce fnl f* **40/1**

2510 **7** hd **Shamrock Lady (IRE)**[42] 3880 2-8-12 79 JimCrowley 4 — 76
(Pat Eddery) *in last pair: rdn 3f out: nvr gng pce to chal* **25/1**

42 **8** 14 **Fifty (IRE)**[26] 4402 2-8-12 0 RichardHughes 2 — 34
(R Hannon) *lw: chsd ldrs: rdn over 2f out: wknd over 1f out: eased fnl f* **3/1**[2]

2450 **9** shd **Romantic Destiny**[14] 4744 2-8-12 95 (b) FrancisNorton 9 — 34
(K A Ryan) *prom tl over 2f out: eased fnl f* **11/1**

1m 15.0s (0.02) **Going Correction** +0.025s/f (Good) — **9** Ran SP% **117.5**
Speed ratings (Par 100): **100,99,98,94,91 90,90,71,71**
CSF £18.97 TOTE £2.40: £1.20, £3.00, £5.10; EX 22.10.
Owner Andrew Rosen **Bred** Swordlestown Stud **Trained** Manton, Wilts
■ Stewards' Enquiry : Jimmy Fortune one-day ban: used whip with excessive force (Sep 17)

FOCUS

An average renewal of this juvenile fillies' Listed prize, run at a decent pace. The first three came clear and the sixth is the best guide to the level.

NOTEBOOK

Fashion Rocks(IRE), not beaten too far when sixth in the Lowther last time, gave that form a boost and resumed winning ways in dogged fashion on this drop down in class. She was made to work hard by the runner-up close home, but was always holding that rival and left the impression she may now require a stiffer test. Therefore it would be little surprise to see her back up in class in the Rockfel at Newmarket next month. (tchd 5-4 and 6-4 in a place)

Vive Les Rouges ◆, a narrow winner of a Lingfield maiden 19 days previously, was on her toes beforehand, but she stepped up on that form in this much better company and made the winner work all the way to the line. She looks somewhat headstrong, but is yet another of her first-season sire's progeny to advertise a liking for fast ground and clearly is up to winning at this level when consenting to settle better. (op 9-1 tchd 12-1)

Raymi Coya(CAN), done no favours by the eventual winner at the start, put in a much more encouraging effort on this debut in Listed company and readily reversed her Haydock form with the fifth. She was not beaten at all far, clearly stays all of this trip now, and a more positive ride in the future could see her bag something similar. (op 20-1)

Dubai Power ◆, second on debut at Sandown last time, was representing a stable with a decent past record in this event. She ultimately lost out through her inexperience on this marked step up in class and shaped as though an easier surface may suit better in due course, but no doubt got the extra furlong here. A return to maiden company should see her shed her maiden tag. (op 15-2)

Kylayne, equipped with first-time blinkers, again tried to make all yet was a sitting duck nearing the final furlong. She still looks flattered by her current official rating and it is hard to know whether the blinkers helped or not. (op 11-1 tchd 12-1)

Fifty(IRE), back in trip and up in class, dropped out tamely when push came to shove. Her rider later reported that she had lost her action. Official explanation: jockey said filly lost its action (op 7-2 tchd 4-1 in places)

Romantic Destiny Official explanation: jockey said filly ran flat

5165 "MIKE SHEP" MEMORIAL PERSIAN PUNCH CONDITIONS STKS 1m 6f 21y

4:40 (4:42) (Class 2) 3-Y-0+ **£9,971** (£2,985; £1,492; £747; £372) **Stalls** Far side

Form / RPR

5100 **1** **Tranquil Tiger**[15] 4722 3-9-2 106 RichardHughes 4 — 113+
(H R A Cecil) *lw: hld up in last: hdwy to trck ldr after 4f: led 3f out: in command fr 2f out: edgd sltly lft ins fnl f: comf* **5/2**[1]

6130 **2** 2 **Munsef**[34] 4117 5-9-9 105 RHills 2 — 105
(J L Dunlop) *lw: hld up bhd ldrs: rdn and hdwy 3f out: wnt 2nd over 2f out: kpt on but a hld by wnr* **6/1**

3414 **3** 1¾ **Sunley Peace**[14] 4749 3-8-5 93 MarcHalford 3 — 96
(D R C Elsworth) *hld up bhd ldrs: swtchd lft and rdn wl over 2f out: styd on to go 3rd ent fnl f: nt rch ldng pair* **7/2**[3]

0033 **4** 2 **Land 'n Stars**[12] 4803 7-9-2 102 PaulDoe 1 — 93
(R A Fahey) *lw: led at stdy pce: steadily qckned pce fr 6f out: rdn and hdd 3f out: wknd ent fnl f* **4/1**

3300 **5** 11 **Bulwark (IRE)**[35] 4091 5-9-2 102 (be) RyanMoore 5 — 77
(Mrs A J Perrett) *trckd ldr for 4f: cl up: rdn 3f out: eased whn btn over 1f out* **11/4**[2]

3m 10.99s (3.99) **Going Correction** +0.025s/f (Good)
WFA 3 from 5yo+ 11lb — **5** Ran SP% **111.7**
Speed ratings (Par 109): **89,87,86,85,79**
CSF £17.22 TOTE £2.80: £2.50, £3.50; EX 21.10.
Owner K Abdulla **Bred** Juddmonte Farms Ltd **Trained** Newmarket, Suffolk

FOCUS

A very slow winning time for the class of contest and the form is probably unreliable, at the moment the third is the best guide.

NOTEBOOK

Tranquil Tiger, a generally progressive sort who took the Bahrain Trophy earlier in the season, found himself outclassed in the Gordon Stakes before running disappointingly in the Ebor, but this represented a more simple task and he seemed well suited to the smaller field. Last early on, he made gradual headway through the field and found himself in front three out having headed Land 'n Stars. He ran on strongly once asked for maximum effort and was always doing enough to hold Munsef, but at this stage looks no better than Listed level and will probably make up into a better four-year-old. (op 11-4)

Munsef set too fast a gallop when disappointing in a listed contest at Goodwood last time, but he reverted to his old tactics of being held up here and ran much better, seeming to appreciate having the blinkers left off. He is no longer progressing and it will not be easy for him to find races, but is really a happier horse over a sharper test. (op 5-1 tchd 7-1)

Sunley Peace, an easy winner over 2m at Newmarket last month, ran well in a hotly-contested Melrose Handicap at York last time and he looked a player at the weights. However, as was expected, he lacked the pace of these on the ground and could only make laboured headway into third. He may get away with this trip on easier ground, but there is no doubting 2m, or even further, suits the son of Lomitas and it would not surprise to see him take his chance in the Cesarewitch later in the season. (op 4-1)

Land 'n Stars has not won for well over a year and having made the early running he was readily brushed aside from over three furlongs out. (tchd 7-2)

Bulwark(IRE) has always been capable of smart form, despite being a renowned 'character', but he looks to have lost the plot completely now and was going nowhere in last place when being eased off by Moore. He is one to have extreme reservations about. (op 3-1 tchd 5-2)

5166 DANCO MARQUEES H'CAP 1m

5:10 (5:15) (Class 5) (0-70,70) 3-Y-0+ **£3,238** (£963; £481; £240) **Stalls** High

Form / RPR

6060 **1** **Tyzack (IRE)**[162] 809 6-9-6 **67** GeorgeBaker 1 — 81+
(Stef Liddiard) *confidently rdn: settled in last: gd hdwy fr over 2f out: shkn up to ld jst ins fnl f: r.o:* **16/1**

6630 **2** 1½ **Piper's Song (IRE)**[20] 4587 4-9-6 **67** (v[1]) FergusSweeney 16 — 78
(H Candy) *led: rdn over 1f out: hdd ins fnl f: no ex* **9/2**[2]

3001 **3** 3½ **Feolin**[16] 4684 3-9-1 **70** TravisBlock(3) 14 — 72
(H Morrison) *trckd ldr: rdn over 2f out: no ex ins fnl f* **10/1**

-263 **4** shd **Silent Applause**[20] 4587 4-9-8 **69** TedDurcan 9 — 72
(Dr J D Scargill) *lw: mid-div: hdwy fr 2f out: edgd rt u.p fnl f: styd on* **5/1**[3]

2111 **5** 3/4 **Ellen's Girl (IRE)**[12] 4828 4-9-3 **64**........................ RichardHughes 8 65
(R Hannon) *in tch: rdn over 3f out: no ex ent fnl f* **3/1**[1]
1405 **6** *hd* **Aggravation**[24] 4455 5-9-6 **70**........................ MarcHalford(3) 2 71
(D R C Elsworth) *hld up towards rr: rdn over 2f out: hdwy over 1f out: styd on fnl f* **8/1**
30-0 **7** 1 3/4 **Moorlander (USA)**[22] 4502 3-9-1 **67**........................(t) JimCrowley 13 63
(Mrs A J Perrett) *mid-div: effrt 3f out: one pce fr over 1f out* **25/1**
0100 **8** 1/2 **Border Edge**[7] 4959 9-9-0 **61**........................(b) PaulDoe 15 56
(J J Bridger) *chsd ldrs: rdn over 3f out: wknd over 1f out* **16/1**
0100 **9** 1 1/2 **Mythical Charm**[11] 4850 8-8-11 **58**........................(t) J-PGuillambert 12 50
(J J Bridger) *chsd ldrs: rdn 3f out: wknd over 1f out* **33/1**
5364 **10** 1 **Gracie's Gift (IRE)**[22] 4505 5-8-13 **60**........................ AmirQuinn 3 50
(A G Newcombe) *rdn over 2f out: nt clr run over 1f out: mainly towards rr* **12/1**
6002 **11** 1 3/4 **Shouldntbethere (IRE)**[36] 4064 3-8-4 **56** oh1........................ RichardThomas 6 41
(Mrs P N Dutfield) *a towards rr* **33/1**
602 **12** *nk* **Dirty Dancing**[40] 3968 3-8-12 **64**........................ TQuinn 5 48
(B W Hills) *a towards rr* **7/1**
6310 **13** 3 **Outer Hebrides**[14] 4731 6-9-9 **70**........................(v) RyanMoore 7 48
(J M Bradley) *mid-div tl wknd 2f out* **12/1**

1m 42.76s (-0.33) **Going Correction** +0.025s/f (Good)
WFA 3 from 4yo+ 5lb 13 Ran SP% **129.4**
Speed ratings (Par 103): **102,100,97,96,96 95,94,93,92,91 89,89,86**
CSF £92.45 CT £819.05 TOTE £22.50: £5.60, £2.60, £4.50; EX 341.90 Place 6 £16.42, Place 5 £8.08.
Owner Mrs S J Roberts **Bred** Rabea Syndicate **Trained** Great Shefford, Berks

FOCUS
A modest handicap, run at a sound pace.
T/Plt: £19.20 to a £1 stake. Pool: £59,904.35. 2,276.55 winning tickets. T/Qpdt: £12.40 to a £1 stake. Pool: £3,095.20. 184.45 winning tickets. TM

4903 WARWICK (L-H)
Thursday, September 6

OFFICIAL GOING: Good to firm (8.2) (meeting abandoned after race 2 (2.50) due to unsafe ground)
Only the first two races on the card were run following a watering error that led to there being a stretch of false ground between the three and two pole.
Wind: Nil

5167 WARWICK NURSERY 5f 110y
2:20 (3:00) (Class 5) (0-75,75) 2-Y-O **£3,238** (£963; £481; £240) **Stalls** Centre

Form RPR
042 **1** **Enactment**[29] 4285 2-9-7 **75**........................ JamieSpencer 3 78+
(Sir Michael Stoute) *hld up in rr: smooth hdwy fr 2f out to ld ins fnl f: idled and edgd rt cl home: readily* **11/4**[1]
5662 **2** *nk* **Mistress Cooper**[10] 4903 2-8-8 **62** ow2........................ JohnEgan 2 64
(W J Musson) *sn led: hdd ins fnl f: rallied u.p and kpt on wl but a jst hld by wnr* **5/1**[2]
6405 **3** *nk* **Miss Firefly**[13] 4755 2-9-0 **68**........................ ChrisCatlin 12 69
(M R Channon) *chsd ldrs: rdn over 2f out: styd on to chal fnl f: no ex cl home* **12/1**
6224 **4** 1/2 **Style Award**[11] 4844 2-9-1 **72**........................ AndrewMullen(3) 5 71
(W J H Ratcliffe) *chsd ldrs: rdn over 2f out: styd on fnl f but nvr gng pce of wnr* **11/1**
3600 **5** 1/2 **Bazguy**[13] 4775 2-9-1 **69**........................ TGMcLaughlin 1 67
(P D Evans) *chsd ldrs: rdn and ev ch over 1f out: one pce u.p ins fnl f* **33/1**
4000 **6** 3 1/2 **Whiskey Creek**[3] 5089 2-8-7 **61** ow1........................ KDarley 9 47
(Miss Tor Sturgis) *in rr: rdn over 2f out: styd on thrght fnl f but nvr in contention* **25/1**
4102 **7** 3/4 **Penrice Castle**[24] 4453 2-9-4 **72**........................ PatDobbs 10 56
(R Hannon) *in rr: rdn over 2f out: kpt on thrght fnl f but nvr in contention* **10/1**
1501 **8** 3/4 **Gin Genereux**[7] 4975 2-9-7 **75** 6ex........................ GregFairley 7 56
(M Johnston) *broke wl: outpcd after 2f: kpt on fnl f but nvr a threat* **15/2**
112 **9** *nk* **Only A Game (IRE)**[6] 4995 2-8-12 **66**........................ RichardMullen 8 46
(E J O'Neill) *chsd ldrs: rdn 3f out: wknd over 1f out* **6/1**[3]
3203 **10** *nk* **Stormy Journey**[6] 4995 2-8-10 **69**........................ LukeMorris(5) 4 48
(Mrs K Walton) *chsd ldrs: rdn 3f out: wknd over 1f out* **18/1**
364 **11** 3 1/2 **Lekin Sedona (IRE)**[18] 4636 2-7-12 **57**........................ NataliaGemelova(5) 15 25
(J M Saville) *in tch: wknd fr 2f out* **33/1**
4105 **12** 1 1/4 **Ramblin Bob**[30] 4255 2-9-2 **70**........................ MartinDwyer 11 34
(R M Beckett) *sn outpcd* **12/1**
000 **13** 3/4 **Victoria Valentine**[19] 4602 2-9-6 **74**........................ MichaelHills 17 35
(B W Hills) *chsd ldrs: rn wd and unbalanced: sn wknd* **25/1**
203 **14** 2 1/2 **Rebel Aclaim (IRE)**[30] 4254 2-9-1 **69**........................ BrettDoyle 13 22
(M G Quinlan) *bhd fr 1/2-way* **20/1**

66.29 secs (0.40) **Going Correction** -0.35s/f (Firm) 14 Ran SP% **125.8**
Speed ratings (Par 95): **83,82,82,81,80 76,75,74,73,73 68,67,66,62**
CSF £15.10 CT £151.89 TOTE £2.80: £1.40, £2.10, £4.20; EX 18.20.
Owner Gainsborough **Bred** Gainsborough Stud Management Ltd **Trained** Newmarket, Suffolk
■ Stewards' Enquiry : Jamie Spencer caution: careless riding

FOCUS
A modest nursery, but Enactment was value for more than the winning margin and survived the Stewards' enquiry. The form looks solid at this level.

NOTEBOOK
Enactment improved with each run in maidens and it was not hard to see why he was made favourite for this nursery debut off a mark of 75. In rear early, he was delivered with a well-timed challenge under Spencer and looked value for a bit more than the official winning margin. He had to survive a Stewards' enquiry, but the best horse won and there may well be more to come as he steps back up in trip. (tchd 3-1)
Mistress Cooper, runner-up over course and distance just the other day, ran a gallant race from the front and may well have won had her rider not put up 2lb overweight. She clearly posseses plenty of speed and would not be inconvenienced by a drop to the bare 5f. (tchd 9-2, 11-2 in places)
Miss Firefly seems to have benefited from being dropped back down in distance and this was easily her best effort to date. She is only modest, but can find a race eventually. (op 16-1 tchd 11-1)
Style Award, a dual winner already this season, has been running well without winning in handicaps and it was a similar story here. Never far away, she ran on well under pressure, but lacked the speed of the principals and may benefit from a full 6f next time. (op 12-1)
Bazguy, well down the field in the St Leger Yearling Stakes at Newmarket last time, found this a bit easier and ran above himself. He was a few lengths clear of the rest.
Only A Game(IRE), a dual winner in sellers earlier in the season, ran well to finish second off this mark on his recent handicap debut at Hamilton, but he was unable to build on that and dropped out disappointingly. (op 13-2 tchd 11-2)

5168 BOTT LTD H'CAP 6f
2:50 (3:36) (Class 4) (0-85,85) 3-Y-O+ **£6,477** (£1,927; £963; £481) **Stalls** Centre

Form RPR
0502 **1** **Barons Spy (IRE)**[17] 4657 6-8-5 **75**........................ RussellKennemore(5) 1 84
(R J Price) *in tch: hdwy to trck ldrs 2f out: led appr fnl f: r.o strly* **11/1**
0002 **2** 1 **Who's Winning (IRE)**[28] 4320 6-8-10 **78**........................ RichardKingscote(3) 7 84
(B G Powell) *w ldr tl slt advantage ins fnl 2f: hdd appr fnl f: kpt on but nt pce of wnr* **6/1**[1]
000 **3** 3/4 **Rainbow Mirage (IRE)**[35] 4093 3-9-3 **84**........................ RichardMullen 3 88
(E S McMahon) *mid-div: hdwy 2f out: styd on u.p to take 3rd fnl f but nvr gng pce to chal* **8/1**[2]
0003 **4** *nk* **Bazroy (IRE)**[26] 4389 3-8-12 **79**........................ TGMcLaughlin 5 82
(P D Evans) *in tch: rdn and effrt over 1f out: swtchd rt ins fnl f and fin wl but nvr in contention* **10/1**
0221 **5** 3/4 **Shes Minnie**[17] 4664 4-9-5 **84**........................ JamieSpencer 2 85
(J G M O'Shea) *chsd ldrs: ev ch 2f out: one pce fnl f* **8/1**[2]
0343 **6** *shd* **Buxton**[8] 4950 3-8-8 **75**........................ RobertHavlin 4 75
(R Ingram) *pressed ldrs: rdn over 2f out: one pce ins fnl f* **14/1**
1415 **7** 1 3/4 **Whitbarrow (IRE)**[31] 4227 8-9-1 **85**........................(b) JamesMillman(5) 10 80
(B R Millman) *slt ld tl hdd ins fnl 2f: wknd fnl f* **8/1**[2]
2305 **8** 1 **King's Bastion (IRE)**[20] 4574 3-8-11 **78**........................ HayleyTurner 12 70
(M L W Bell) *chsd ldrs: rdn and no imp fnl 2f* **14/1**
1040 **9** *shd* **Keyaki (IRE)**[26] 4373 6-9-0 **84**........................ PatrickHills(5) 6 76
(C F Wall) *pressed ldrs: rdn 3f out: wknd appr fnl f* **10/1**
4003 **10** *hd* **Everymanforhimself (IRE)**[10] 4898 3-9-3 **84**........................ TPQueally 8 75
(J G Given) *outpcd tl sme prog fnl f* **8/1**[2]
1045 **11** *shd* **Stamford Blue**[12] 4806 6-9-0 **84**........................(b) LukeMorris(5) 11 75
(R A Harris) *s.i.s: outpcd* **8/1**[2]
0000 **12** 1 **Spanish Ace**[5] 5029 6-8-12 **82**........................ KevinGhunowa(5) 9 70
(J M Bradley) *spd to 1/2-way* **20/1**
0660 **13** *hd* **Royal Challenge**[5] 5029 6-8-10 **75**........................ JimmyQuinn 13 62
(M H Tompkins) *outpcd* **17/2**[3]

1m 11.33s (-2.95) **Going Correction** -0.35s/f (Firm) course record
WFA 3 from 4yo+ 2lb 13 Ran SP% **125.0**
Speed ratings (Par 105): **105,103,102,102,101 101,98,97,97,97 96,95,95**
CSF £79.19 CT £594.92 TOTE £16.00: £4.30, £1.10, £7.80; EX 118.60 Place 6 £4.93, Place 5 £2.86.
Owner Barry Veasey **Bred** Tally-Ho Stud **Trained** Ullingswick, H'fords

FOCUS
A competitive sprint handicap and straightforward form with the runner-up a solid guide..
Stamford Blue Official explanation: jockey said gelding missed the break and was never travelling
Spanish Ace Official explanation: jockey said gelding slipped on the bend

5169 EUROPEAN BREEDERS' FUND MAIDEN STKS (C&G) 7f 26y
() (Class 5) 2-Y-O £

5170 EUROPEAN BREEDERS' FUND MAIDEN FILLIES' STKS 7f 26y
() (Class 5) 2-Y-O £

5171 PAULA ROSA KITCHENS H'CAP 2m 39y
() (Class 5) (0-75,) 3-Y-O+ £

5172 KGM MOTOR INSURANCE MEDIAN AUCTION MAIDEN STKS 1m 22y
() (Class 6) 3-4-Y-O £

5173 GO>DIRECT TO THE BEST DSA SUPPLIERS APPRENTICE H'CAP 1m 2f 188y
() (Class 6) (0-58,) 3-Y-O+ £

T/Jkpt: £248.00 to a £1 stake. Pool: £22,888.00. 65.50 winning tickets. T/Plt: £5.70 to a £1 stake. Pool: £45,768.00. 5,797.35 winning tickets. ST

5096 WOLVERHAMPTON (A.W) (L-H)
Thursday, September 6

OFFICIAL GOING: Standard to fast
Wind: Almost nil Weather: Fine

5174 CREDIT CARDS @ MONEYGEM.COM H'CAP 5f 20y(P)
6:50 (6:51) (Class 6) (0-60,60) 3-Y-O+ **£1,943** (£578; £288; £144) **Stalls** Low

Form RPR
200 **1** **Multahab**[16] 4689 8-9-5 **60**........................(t) JimmyQuinn 9 73
(M Wigham) *chsd ldrs: wnt 2nd over 2f out: hrd rdn to ld last strides* **16/1**
0502 **2** *hd* **Silver Prelude**[6] 5016 6-9-4 **59**........................ NCallan 2 71
(D K Ivory) *led: rdn over 1f out: hdd last strides* **15/8**[1]
1023 **3** 1 1/4 **Rosie Cross (IRE)**[13] 4759 3-8-11 **58**........................ PatrickHills(5) 4 66
(Eve Johnson Houghton) *mid-div: hdwy wl over 1f out: sn rdn and edgd lft: kpt on ins fnl f* **8/1**[3]
0231 **4** 1 1/2 **Kennington**[7] 4973 7-9-1 **56** 6ex........................ DMylonas 1 58
(Mrs C A Dunnett) *towards rr: hdwy on ins whn swtchd rt over 1f out: kpt on ins fnl f* **8/1**[3]
0030 **5** 3/4 **Swing On A Star (IRE)**[10] 4885 3-9-4 **60**........................ AdamKirby 5 60
(W R Swinburn) *mid-div: hdwy over 2f out: rdn over 1f out: one pce fnl f* **14/1**
4260 **6** *nk* **Paddywack (IRE)**[6] 5016 10-8-12 **60**........................(v[1]) DanielleMcCreery(7) 3 59
(D W Chapman) *s.i.s: outpcd: hdwy fnl f: nvr nrr* **12/1**
5061 **7** *nk* **Blessed Place**[14] 4734 7-9-0 **55**........................(t) JamieSpencer 12 53
(D J S Ffrench Davis) *chsd ldr over 2f: hung lft and wknd over 1f out* **4/1**[2]
006 **8** 1 1/4 **Charming Ballet (IRE)**[11] 4853 4-9-5 **60**........................(b) JamesDoyle 8 53
(N P Littmoden) *mid-div: rdn over 2f out: swtchd rt wl over 1f out: no hdwy* **9/1**
P-40 **9** 1 1/4 **Fast Freddie**[21] 4546 3-9-4 **60**........................(b[1]) JohnEgan 7 49
(D J Murphy) *prom: rdn over 2f out: wknd wl over 1f out* **14/1**
000 **10** 2 **Avoca Dancer (IRE)**[52] 3594 4-9-0 **55**........................ PaulEddery 6 36
(M Wigham) *a bhd* **40/1**
0050 **11** *shd* **Pride Of Joy**[43] 3853 4-9-1 **56**........................ RichardMullen 10 37
(M A Buckley) *chsd ldrs tl wknd over 1f out* **25/1**
5600 **12** 5 **Futuristic Dragon (IRE)**[9] 4919 3-8-12 **59**........................(t) KevinGhunowa(5) 11 22
(P A Blockley) *outpcd* **40/1**

61.46 secs (-1.36) **Going Correction** -0.25s/f (Stan)
WFA 3 from 4yo+ 1lb 12 Ran SP% **122.6**
Speed ratings (Par 101): **100,99,97,95,94 93,93,91,89,85 85,77**
CSF £47.17 CT £279.48 TOTE £19.70: £6.60, £1.10, £3.20; EX 91.70.

Owner P J Burke and Dave Anderson **Bred** Shadwell Estate Company Limited **Trained** Newmarket, Suffolk

FOCUS
A routine and modest sprint handicap for the track but solid form rated around the placed horses. With several front-runners in opposition there was always going to be plenty of early pace on and not that many got into the contest.

5175 LOANS @ MONEYGEM.COM MEDIAN AUCTION MAIDEN STKS 5f 216y(P)
7:20 (7:22) (Class 6) 3-5-Y-0 **£2,047** (£604; £302) **Stalls** Low

Form RPR

63 **1** **Southwarknewsflash**[7] 4977 3-8-12 0..............................(t) DMylonas 3 58
(Mrs C A Dunnett) *hld up in mid-div: rdn whn swtchd rt and hdwy wl over 1f out: rdn to ld wl ins fnl f: r.o wl* **14/1**

0000 **2** *1¼* **Kindallachan**[16] 4689 4-9-0 43.............................JohnEgan 13 54
(G C Bravery) *led early: hld up in tch: rdn wl over 1f out: led ins fnl f: sn hdd: nt qckn* **33/1**

00 **3** *¾* **White's Ruby**[33] 4157 3-8-12 0.............................PaulEddery 10 52
(B Smart) *sn w ldr: led over 2f out: rdn wl over 1f out: edgd rt and hdd ins fnl f: nt qckn* **28/1**

0-30 **4** *nk* **Call Me Rosy (IRE)**[66] 3168 3-8-9 60.......................LiamJones(3) 8 51
(C F Wall) *hld up in mid-div: c wd st: rdn and hdwy over 1f out: edgd lft ins fnl f: kpt on same pce* **5/1**[3]

0600 **5** *3½* **Esteemed Prince**[7] 4977 3-9-3 47........................(e) AdamKirby 11 44
(D Shaw) *outpcd and bhd: hdwy whn edgd lft and bmpd jst over 1f out: nvr trbld ldrs* **66/1**

60-0 **6** *nk* **Saint Remus (IRE)**[7] 4974 3-9-3 0............................BrettDoyle 2 43+
(Peter Grayson) *prom: lost pl over 2f out: nt clr run wl over 1f out: sme late hdwy* **66/1**

5500 **7** *½* **Darling Belinda**[9] 4919 3-8-12 58.......................(p) AdrianMcCarthy 6 37
(D K Ivory) *hld up in tch: ev ch over 2f out: sn rdn: wknd over 1f out* **16/1**

-400 **8** *½* **Pont Wood**[33] 4163 3-9-3 55.............................JimmyQuinn 4 40
(M Blanshard) *outpcd: kpt on fnl f: n.d* **20/1**

5000 **9** *¾* **Diksie Dancer**[15] 4705 3-8-12 59.............................NCallan 5 33
(K A Ryan) *prom: rdn over 1f out: wknd fnl f* **9/4**[2]

0505 **10** *½* **Compton Special**[14] 4741 3-8-12 44.............................TPQueally 1 31
(J G Given) *prom: nt clr run on ins over 2f out: swtchd rt wl over 1f out: sn rdn: wkng whn bmpd over 1f out* **18/1**

0- **11** *3* **Bathwick Leti (IRE)**[423] 3344 3-8-12 0.............................ChrisCatlin 7 22
(A M Balding) *outpcd* **20/1**

5202 **12** *6* **Orchestrator (IRE)**[17] 4671 3-9-3 69.............................RobertHavlin 9 —
(T G Mills) *sn led: rdn and hdd over 2f out: wknd wl over 1f out* **7/4**[1]

00 **13** *6* **Rita Petite**[8] 4938 3-8-5 0.............................DanielleMcCreery(7) 12 —
(D W Chapman) *s.i.s: outpcd* **100/1**

1m 14.39s (-1.42) **Going Correction** -0.25s/f (Stan)
WFA 3 from 4yo 2lb **13** Ran SP% **121.5**
Speed ratings (Par 101): **99,97,96,95,91 90,90,89,88,87 83,75,67**
CSF £412.00 TOTE £12.60: £1.60, £7.80, £8.20; EX 371.60.

Owner Southwark News Racing Club **Bred** Franconson Partners **Trained** Hingham, Norfolk

FOCUS
The market suggested this was a three-horse race, so the fact that none of them made the first three suggests the form is modest, especially with the runner-up rated just 43.

Rita Petite Official explanation: jockey said filly missed the break

5176 MORTGAGES @ MONEYGEM.COM MEDIAN AUCTION MAIDEN STKS 5f 20y(P)
7:50 (7:50) (Class 5) 2-Y-0 **£2,914** (£867; £433; £216) **Stalls** Low

Form RPR

4320 **1** **Our Acquaintance**[13] 4775 2-9-3 76.............................RichardMullen 3 73
(W R Muir) *chsd ldrs: wnt 2nd wl over 1f out: rdn to ld ins fnl f: r.o wl* **13/8**[1]

402 **2** *2½* **Lavande**[35] 4097 2-8-12 69.............................JamieSpencer 4 59
(M J Wallace) *chsd ldrs: rdn over 2f out: hung rt wl over 1f out: hung lft ent fnl f: kpt on to take 2nd nr post* **3/1**[3]

6622 **3** *hd* **Rathmolyon**[13] 4756 2-8-12 77.............................RobertHavlin 6 58
(D Haydn Jones) *chsd ldr tl rdn wl over 1f out: edgd lft ins fnl f: kpt on* **9/4**[2]

4 *1¼* **Wiseman's Diamond (USA)** 2-8-12 0.............................NCallan 8 54
(K A Ryan) *s.i.s: rdn wl over 1f out: kpt on fnl f* **10/1**

0600 **5** *nk* **Frizzini**[24] 4459 2-9-3 50.............................JohnEgan 9 58+
(N Tinkler) *led: rdn over 1f out: hdd ins fnl f: 4th and btn whn eased nr fin* **33/1**

020 **6** *½* **Kaystar Ridge**[33] 4181 2-9-3 71.............................AdrianMcCarthy 7 56
(D K Ivory) *mid-div: rdn over 2f out: hung lft wl over 1f out: no real prog* **14/1**

40 **7** *5* **Silver Deal**[36] 4074 2-8-12 0.............................JimmyQuinn 1 33
(J A Pickering) *bhd: short-lived effrt on ins over 2f out* **40/1**

8 *1¼* **Captain Crooner (IRE)** 2-9-3 0.............................AdamKirby 10 33
(D Shaw) *s.i.s: a bhd* **33/1**

62.24 secs (-0.58) **Going Correction** -0.25s/f (Stan) **8** Ran SP% **117.9**
Speed ratings (Par 95): **94,90,89,87,87 86,78,76**
CSF £7.02 TOTE £3.60: £1.10, £1.50, £1.10; EX 9.50.

Owner Quaintance Partnership **Bred** S R Hope **Trained** Lambourn, Berks

FOCUS
A modest maiden rated around the fifth and could be slightly better.

NOTEBOOK
Our Acquaintance had shown fair placed form in maidens prior to finishing down the field in the St Leger Yearling Stakes at Newmarket, and this was always going to be a lot easier. Always going well, he surged ahead inside the final furlong and won with plenty in hand, suggesting he could make his mark in handicaps. (op 9-4 tchd 5-2 in places)

Lavande looked a player at the weights and had shown fair form in defeat behind Cute Ass at Musselburgh last month. However, she ruined her chance by hanging all over the place and was unable to get near the winner. She clearly has ability, but could not be backed with any confidence next time. Official explanation: jockey said filly hung right (tchd 11-4)

Rathmolyon was another who came into this with claims on the best of her form, but she was readily left trailing by the winner and was claimed on the line by Lavande for second. She is likely to remain vulnerable to improvers in maidens. (op 5-2)

Wiseman's Diamond(USA), an Amercian-bred filly from a yard that is capable of readying a newcomer, is bred to need further than this in time and a slow start ended her chances. She kept on nicely enough in the straight though and should be winning once upped in trip. (op 13-2)

Frizzini was responsible for the early pace, but he could not sustain it and was swamped in the final furlong. He will find life easier in handicaps. Official explanation: jockey said gelding lost its action in the closing stages (op 40-1)

5177 FREE BETS @ FREEBETS.CO.UK H'CAP 7f 32y(P)
8:20 (8:20) (Class 5) (0-70,70) 3-Y-0+ **£2,914** (£867; £433; £216) **Stalls** High

Form RPR

216 **1** **Napoleon Dynamite (IRE)**[26] 4394 3-9-3 **69**.............................JamieSpencer 11 75
(J W Hills) *hld up towards rr: hdwy on outside over 2f out: rdn wl over 1f out: led and hung lft jst ins fnl f: jst hld on* **9/2**[1]

50-0 **2** *hd* **Dance Spirit (IRE)**[34] 3907 4-9-0 **62**.............................RichardMullen 4 69
(W R Muir) *a.p: rdn 2f out: r.o wl towards fin: jst failed* **16/1**

2330 **3** *¾* **Carcinetto (IRE)**[82] 2655 5-9-3 **65**.............................TGMcLaughlin 7 70
(P D Evans) *a.p: rdn over 2f out: r.o ins fnl f* **11/2**[3]

0003 **4** *½* **Red Contact (USA)**[17] 4672 6-9-8 **70**.............................(p) DanielTudhope 5 74
(A Dickman) *led after 1f: rdn over 1f out: hdd jst ins fnl f: nt qckn* **13/2**

0210 **5** *nk* **Moheebb (IRE)**[5] 5046 3-8-7 **62**.............................LiamJones(3) 8 63
(D W Chapman) *mid-div: rdn over 4f out: hdwy over 1f out: kpt on ins fnl f* **5/1**[2]

1000 **6** *hd* **Charlie Delta**[13] 4767 4-8-12 **60**.............................(v[1]) NCallan 2 62
(J M Bradley) *broke wl: hld up in tch: nt clr run briefly 2f out: rdn over 1f out: one pce fnl f* **9/1**

-600 **7** *shd* **Swiper Hill (IRE)**[48] 3723 4-9-0 **62**.............................(t) GregFairley 12 64
(B Ellison) *hld up and bhd: rdn over 2f out: hdwy over 1f out: nvr trbld ldrs* **14/1**

-505 **8** *1* **Tanforan**[15] 4719 5-9-0 **62**.............................(p) ChrisCatlin 10 61
(B P J Baugh) *hld up towards rr: rdn over 3f out: styd on fnl f: n.d* **8/1**

0-00 **9** *4* **Global Guest**[49] 3682 3-8-3 **62**.............................MarkCoumbe(7) 6 49
(A J Chamberlain) *a towards rr* **100/1**

0150 **10** *1½* **Middle Eastern**[10] 4884 5-8-10 **58**.............................(p) TPO'Shea 3 42
(P A Blockley) *mid-div: rdn over 2f out: nt clr run over 1f out: n.d after* **15/2**

1550 **11** *hd* **Gilded Cove**[38] 4024 7-8-13 **66**.............................RussellKennemore(5) 9 50
(R Hollinshead) *s.i.s: effrt on ins whn bdly hmpd over 1f out: nt rcvr* **10/1**

060 **12** *7* **Lithaam (IRE)**[30] 4258 3-8-6 **65**.............................BarrySavage(7) 1 28
(J M Bradley) *t.k.h: led 1f: prom: rdn over 2f out: wkng whn hung lft over 1f out* **100/1**

1m 29.0s (-1.40) **Going Correction** -0.25s/f (Stan)
WFA 3 from 4yo+ 4lb **12** Ran SP% **120.1**
Speed ratings (Par 103): **98,97,96,96,96 95,95,94,89,88 88,80**
CSF £78.92 CT £416.15 TOTE £4.60: £2.10, £7.50, £1.60; EX 102.40.

Owner Richard Tufft and Partners **Bred** Humphrey Okeke **Trained** Upper Lambourn, Berks

FOCUS
An ordinary handicap and the early pace looked solid enough, but they eventually finished in a bit of a heap and the final time was modest. The form looks straightforward rated around the runner-up and the fifth.

Global Guest Official explanation: jockey said colt hung left throughout

5178 FREE CASINO CHIPS @ FREEBETS.CO.UK H'CAP 1m 1f 103y(P)
8:50 (8:50) (Class 5) (0-75,75) 3-Y-0+ **£2,914** (£867; £433; £216) **Stalls** Low

Form RPR

6040 **1** **Merrymadcap (IRE)**[10] 4889 5-9-3 **69**.............................FrancisNorton 7 76+
(M Blanshard) *hld up and bhd: hdwy over 2f out: rdn and r.o to ld post* **7/1**

0040 **2** *shd* **New World Order (IRE)**[41] 3919 3-9-1 **73**.............................(t) RichardMullen 10 79
(K R Burke) *a.p: wnt 2nd 5f out: rdn wl over 1f out: led nr fin: hdd post* **11/1**

0015 **3** *hd* **Queen Noverre (IRE)**[25] 4429 3-8-13 **71**.............................(p) JamesDoyle 8 77
(J W Hills) *a.p: rdn to ld 1f out: hdd nr fin* **25/1**

005 **4** *1½* **Garden Party**[73] 2944 3-8-8 **66**.............................JamieSpencer 6 69
(Sir Michael Stoute) *hld up in mid-div: hdwy 5f out: rdn and hung lft over 1f out: edgd rt ins fnl f: one pce* **3/1**[1]

3455 **5** *¾* **Scamperdale**[25] 4418 5-9-7 **73**.............................(p) TPQueally 5 74+
(B P J Baugh) *hld up and bhd: rdn and hdwy on outside wl over 1f out: hung rt ins fnl f: one pce* **5/1**[3]

4542 **6** *½* **The Grey One (IRE)**[10] 4880 4-8-11 **63**.............................(p) NCallan 3 63
(J M Bradley) *plld hrd: prom: rdn wl over 1f out: no ex ins fnl f* **4/1**[2]

4126 **7** *1¼* **Tizzy May (FR)**[15] 4716 7-9-2 **68**.............................GregFairley 2 66
(B Ellison) *led: rdn over 2f out: hdd 1f out: wknd ins fnl f* **8/1**

3053 **8** *hd* **Lunar River (FR)**[6] 5020 4-8-11 **63**.............................(t) ChrisCatlin 9 60
(David Pinder) *hld up towards rr: hdwy over 2f out: wkng whn edgd lft over 1f out* **11/1**

9 *2½* **Manathon (FR)**[165] 4-9-9 **75**.............................RobertHavlin 4 67
(A E Jones) *bhd fnl 5f* **33/1**

0050 **10** *3* **Where's Broughton**[13] 4766 4-8-13 **65**.............................BrettDoyle 1 51
(W J Musson) *prom 5f* **9/1**

2m 0.08s (-2.54) **Going Correction** -0.25s/f (Stan)
WFA 3 from 4yo+ 6lb **10** Ran SP% **118.7**
Speed ratings (Par 103): **101,100,100,99,98 98,97,97,94,92**
CSF £82.66 CT £1825.56 TOTE £7.90: £2.10, £4.90, £13.10; EX 114.30.

Owner Mrs N L Young **Bred** Wickfield Farm Partnership **Trained** Upper Lambourn, Berks

FOCUS
An ordinary handicap and a very open one with seven horses stretched across the track entering the last furlong. The winning time was 0.33 seconds faster than the following lower-grade handicap over the same trip and there are slight questions over the form.

Queen Noverre(IRE) Official explanation: jockey said filly lost a near-fore shoe

5179 £2000 FREE BETS @ FREEBETS.CO.UK H'CAP 1m 1f 103y(P)
9:20 (9:20) (Class 6) (0-50,56) 3-Y-0+ **£2,047** (£604; £302) **Stalls** Low

Form RPR

0043 **1** **Weet Yer Tern (IRE)**[8] 4945 5-9-0 **47**.............................JamieSpencer 1 57+
(W M Brisbourne) *hld up in mid-div: hdwy over 2f out: nt clr run and swtchd lft wl over 1f out: rdn to ld cl home* **2/1**[1]

4000 **2** *½* **Bobering**[126] 1435 7-8-7 **47**.............................SoniaEaton(7) 7 55
(B P J Baugh) *hld up towards rr: hdwy on ins wl over 1f out: sn rdn: led ins fnl f: hdd cl home* **15/2**[3]

5533 **3** *1¼* **Beamsley Beacon**[24] 4449 6-9-1 **48**.............................PaddyAspell 6 53
(S T Mason) *chsd ldr: led 4f out: rdn over 1f out: hdd ins fnl f: nt qckn* **8/1**

0-00 **4** *2½* **Proud Scholar (USA)**[154] 496 5-9-3 **50**.............................TPQueally 3 50
(M A Magnusson) *a.p: rdn 4f out: wknd ins fnl f* **12/1**

00-3 **5** *½* **Slo Mo Shun**[16] 4684 3-8-11 **50**.............................JimmyQuinn 4 49
(H J L Dunlop) *t.k.h: prom: rdn over 1f out: wknd ins fnl f* **12/1**

0231 **6** *1½* **Moonlight Fantasy (IRE)**[9] 4920 4-9-9 **56** 6ex.............................TGMcLaughlin 9 52
(Lucinda Featherstone) *hld up and bhd: hdwy on outside over 2f out: btn over 1f out* **15/2**[3]

2300 **7** 1 **Goodwood Spirit**[6] 4998 5-8-12 **50**........................(v) KevinGhunowa(5) 8 44
(J M Bradley) *t.k.h in mid-div: hdwy over 3f out: rdn and wknd over 1f out* **20/1**

0040 **8** 1 1/4 **King Of Knight (IRE)**[21] 4533 6-9-3 **50**............................ DMylonas 12 41
(G Prodromou) *nvr trbld ldrs* **10/1**

5402 **9** 3/4 **Surdoue**[8] 4945 7-9-3 **50**.. AdrianMcCarthy 2 40
(D Morris) *led: hdd 4f out: rdn wl over 1f out: wknd ent fnl f* **7/1**[2]

/0-0 **10** 7 **New Diamond**[10] 4880 8-8-11 **47**..................................... MarcHalford(3) 5 22
(Mrs P Ford) *rdn over 3f out: a bhd* **100/1**

5030 **11** 7 **Show Me The Lolly (FR)**[11] 4856 7-8-13 **46**.............. RichardMullen 11 6
(S W Hall) *hld up in mid-div: rdn over 3f out: sn bhd* **20/1**

0036 **12** 4 **Crush On You**[24] 4449 4-8-9 **47**......................... RussellKennemore(5) 13 —
(R Hollinshead) *prom: rdn 4f out: wknd over 2f out* **14/1**

0-64 **13** 15 **Flaming Cat (IRE)**[13] 4771 4-9-3 **50**.........................(p) GregFairley 10 —
(F Watson) *hld up in mid-div: rdn 4f out: sn bhd* **25/1**

2m 0.41s (-2.21) **Going Correction** -0.25s/f (Stan)
WFA 3 from 4yo+ 6lb **13** Ran SP% **126.0**
Speed ratings (Par 101): **99,98,97,95,94 93,92,91,90,84 78,74,61**
CSF £17.18 CT £108.31 TOTE £2.70: £1.30, £3.10, £2.70; EX 27.30 Place 6 £1,093.02, Place 5 £541.80.
Owner Ed Weetman (haulage & Storage) Ltd **Bred** E O'Leary **Trained** Great Ness, Shropshire

FOCUS
A modest handicap in which the winning time was 0.33 seconds slower than the preceding Class 5 handicap. The pace was only fair but the form looks sound enough rated through the third to recent turf form.
Crush On You Official explanation: jockey said filly hung right throughout
T/Plt: £1,981.50 to a £1 stake. Pool: £90,663.10. 33.40 winning tickets. T/Qpdt: £92.00 to a £1 stake. Pool: £7,285.70. 58.60 winning tickets. KH

5180 - 5183a (Foreign Racing) - See Raceform Interactive

LAYTOWN (L-H)
Thursday, September 6
OFFICIAL GOING: Standard

5184a HIBERNIA STEEL (Q.R.) H'CAP 7f
4:15 (4:15) (50-80,80) 4-Y-0+ **£6,069** (£1,414; £623; £360)

RPR

1 **Quai Du Roi (IRE)**[20] 4566 5-11-13 75...................... MrDerekO'Connor 88+
(D Nicholls) *cl 2nd and disp ld: led 2f out: drew clr over 1f out: easily* **5/1**[2]

2 3 1/2 **Keen Look (IRE)**[29] 4308 8-11-9 76..................................... MrATDuff(5) 79
(Gerard Keane, Ire) *chsd ldrs: prog after 1/2-way: 4th 2f out: mod 2nd over 1f out: kpt on* **10/1**

3 2 **Five Two**[35] 4116 4-11-7 74.......................................(t) MrRPMcNamara(5) 72
(A J Martin, Ire) *trckd ldrs in 6th: 5th 1/2-way: 4th and rdn under 2f out: no imp: kpt on same pce* **7/4**[1]

4 1 **Sling Back (IRE)**[4] 5074 6-11-13 80.................................. MrPRoche(5) 75
(Eamon Tyrrell, Ire) *cl up: 3rd after 1/2-way: 2nd and rdn to chal 2f out: mod 3rd and no ex 1f out: one pce* **8/1**

5 1/2 **Closetocrazy (IRE)**[74] 2918 7-11-12 74......................... MissNCarberry 68
(Ms Joanna Morgan, Ire) *chsd ldrs: 3rd early: rdn after 1/2-way: 5th 2f out: kpt on same pce* **6/1**[3]

6 1 3/4 **Islandbane (IRE)**[59] 3390 5-10-12 65.......................... MrBTO'Connell(5) 54
(H Rogers, Ire) *chsd ldrs: 6th after 1/2-way: no imp fr 1 1/2f out: one pce* **8/1**

7 3 **Mill House Girl (IRE)**[31] 1760 6-11-2 69.................... MrCMotherway(5) 50
(S Donohoe, Ire) *hld up: no imp fr over 2f out* **5/1**[2]

8 2 1/2 **Pennyforurthoughts (IRE)**[127] 4917 5-11-5 70................ JPO'Farrell(3) 44
(James McAuley, Ire) *towards rr: rdn and outpcd over 2f out: sn no ex* **20/1**

9 2 **Dapple Dawn (IRE)**[166] 771 4-11-7 74..................... MrJPMcKeown(5) 43
(Garvan Donnelly, Ire) *led and disp: hdd 2f out: sn wknd* **12/1**

10 shd **Classic Croco (GER)**[36] 3254 6-10-12 65...............(t) MrColmSharkey(5) 33
(T Hogan, Ire) *bhd: trailing bef 1/2-way: sme prog 2f out: no imp fr over 1f out* **10/1**

1m 22.6s (82.60) **10** Ran SP% **136.8**
CSF £64.31 TOTE £7.40: £2.70, £3.10, £1.90; DF 102.90.
Owner D Nicholls F Devaney **Bred** Twelve Oaks Stud **Trained** Sessay, N Yorks
■ Quai Du Roi is the first ever British-trained winner, and runner, on the beach at Laytown.

NOTEBOOK
Quai Du Roi(IRE), who has had problems with the stalls back in Britain, appreciated the fact that this race was started by flag and won easily. He could have a good campaign over hurdles this winter. (op 7/2)

5185 - (Foreign Racing) - See Raceform Interactive

4875 CHEPSTOW (L-H)
Friday, September 7
OFFICIAL GOING: Good to firm
Wind: virtually nil Weather: Sunny

5186 BETDIRECT.COM MAIDEN AUCTION STKS 1m 14y
2:10 (2:10) (Class 6) 2-Y-0 **£2,202** (£655; £327; £163) **Stalls** High

Form RPR

62 **1** **Trenchtown (IRE)**[12] 4852 2-9-2 0................................. SebSanders 12 86+
(R Charlton) *a.p: rdn to ld over 1f out: rdn out* **4/11**[1]

0 **2** 2 **No To Trident**[14] 4755 2-8-9 0.............................. StephenDonohoe 5 74
(P D Evans) *s.i.s: hld up towards rr: hdwy over 2f out: edgd lft fr over 1f out: wnt 2nd ins fnl f: nt trble wnr* **66/1**

03 **3** 3 **Loyal Knight (IRE)**[23] 4508 2-8-13 0............................ LPKeniry 14 71
(S Kirk) *t.k.h: w ldr: led over 3f out: rdn and hdd over 1f out: no ex ins fnl f* **7/2**[2]

65 **4** 3 1/2 **Bozeman Trail**[34] 4162 2-9-2 0............................... NelsonDeSouza 13 66
(P F I Cole) *t.k.h in tch: rdn over 3f out: wknd over 2f out* **25/1**

00 **5** hd **Cool The Heels (IRE)**[27] 4393 2-8-11 0......................... JamesDoyle 4 61
(J S Moore) *prom tl rdn and wknd over 2f out* **40/1**

00 **6** 2 1/2 **Lenouska (IRE)**[18] 4662 2-8-8 0.............................. FergusSweeney 8 52
(B De Haan) *mid-div: rdn over 3f out: btn over 2f out* **40/1**

0 **7** shd **Balais Folly (FR)**[18] 4656 2-8-11 0.............................. DavidKinsella 7 55
(B Palling) *dwlt: nvr nr ldrs* **66/1**

0 **8** shd **Dubai Land**[14] 4764 2-9-2 0..................................... FrancisNorton 2 59
(M R Channon) *bhd: sme hdwy over 2f out: n.d* **18/1**[3]

06 **9** nk **Bahamian Blue (IRE)**[29] 4325 2-8-13 0............................ JimmyQuinn 9 56
(H J L Dunlop) *t.k.h: led: hdd over 3f out: sn rdn: wknd 2f out* **22/1**

0046 **10** 1 3/4 **Friction**[28] 4363 2-8-4 46... FrankieMcDonald 11 43
(J G Portman) *mid-div: rdn over 3f out: sn struggling* **80/1**

00 **11** 5 **Zarees**[22] 4537 2-8-9 0... BrettDoyle 1 36
(J S Moore) *a towards rr* **66/1**

0 **12** 2 1/2 **Les Allues (IRE)**[11] 4875 2-8-4 0.............................. AdrianMcCarthy 15 25
(H S Howe) *plld hrd: sn prom: rdn and hung lft over 3f out: sn wknd* **80/1**

0000 **13** 13 **Virtual Paddy**[57] 3465 2-8-11 52..................................... PaulDoe 6 —
(M Blanshard) *a bhd* **100/1**

00 **14** 3 **Paul The Carpet (UAE)**[27] 4393 2-8-6 0.......................... TolleyDean(5) 10 —
(P F I Cole) *rdn 4f out: a bhd* **80/1**

1m 36.22s (0.22) **Going Correction** -0.075s/f (Good) **14** Ran SP% **123.0**
Speed ratings (Par 93): **95,93,90,86,86 83,83,83,83,81 76,74,61,58**
CSF £66.83 TOTE £1.30: £1.02, £20.70, £1.10; EX 153.10 Trifecta £161.30 Part won. Pool £227.20 - 0.64 winning units..
Owner David & Paul Hearson **Bred** Granham Farm And P Hearson Bloodstock **Trained** Beckhampton, Wilts

FOCUS
A moderate maiden and the form looks reasonable, although the runner-up sounds a note of caution.

NOTEBOOK
Trenchtown(IRE) had less to do this time but had to be sent about his business to assert. Well on top in the end, he is considered a middle-distance prospect for next year. (op 1-2)
No To Trident ◆ left the form of his debut behind with the help of a longer trip. He will eventually stay further and a reproduction of this effort should enable him to take a similar event. (tchd 80-1)
Loyal Knight(IRE) ran freely down the hill in the first three furlongs on this step up to a mile and that may have caught up with him in the closing stages. (tchd 10-3)
Bozeman Trail, previously trained by Mick Channon, was another who did not help his cause by being difficult to settle. (op 20-1)
Cool The Heels(IRE) did not run so freely this time but the end result was much the same. (op 50-1)
Bahamian Blue(IRE) Official explanation: jockey said colt ran too keen
Les Allues(IRE) Official explanation: jockey said filly hung left
Virtual Paddy Official explanation: jockey said gelding hung left

5187 BETDIRECT GET INVOLVED CLAIMING STKS 1m 4f 23y
2:45 (2:45) (Class 6) 3-Y-0+ **£2,072** (£616; £308; £153) **Stalls** Low

Form RPR

003 **1** **Noora (IRE)**[10] 4915 6-9-1 70..(v) SebSanders 5 54
(C G Cox) *s.s and carried rt: bhd tl swtchd rt and hdwy on outside over 3f out: rdn over 2f out: led ins fnl f: drvn out* **9/4**[1]

0005 **2** 1/2 **Beckenham's Secret**[4] 5095 3-8-7 50........................ FergusSweeney 8 55
(B R Millman) *hld up and bhd: hdwy over 2f out: sn hung lft: r.o ins fnl f* **8/1**

2050 **3** 1 **My Legal Eagle (IRE)**[11] 4906 13-8-9 48...................... LukeMorris(5) 11 51
(E G Bevan) *hld up and bhd: swtchd lft and hdwy over 2f out: sn rdn: r.o ins fnl f* **10/1**

4024 **4** 1/2 **Tiegs (IRE)**[10] 4914 5-8-8 42... MarcHalford(3) 4 47
(P W Hiatt) *wnt rt s: prom: chsd ldr over 3f out: rdn over 2f out: no ex fnl f* **14/1**

0000 **5** 1 3/4 **Rosie's Glory (USA)**[12] 4843 3-8-8 69.......................(b[1]) JimmyQuinn 3 50
(B J Meehan) *led: hrd rdn and hdd ins fnl f: no ex* **7/1**[3]

000/ **6** 1 3/4 **Perfect Storm**[188] 6475 8-9-5 75.................................... JackDean(7) 7 57
(W G M Turner) *mid-div: hdwy over 2f out: one pce fnl f* **12/1**

0060 **7** 1 1/2 **Princess Aimee**[7] 5018 7-8-7 55.....................................(v[1]) AlanDaly 14 35
(D Burchell) *prom tl rdn and wknd over 2f out* **20/1**

\- **8** 1/2 **Jajoleen (IRE)**[79] 2781 4-8-9 45................................ StephenDonohoe 2 36
(P A Blockley) *hld up in tch: rdn over 3f out: wknd over 2f out* **28/1**

1462 **9** 4 **Missie Baileys**[30] 4267 5-8-13 49.................................(p) IanMongan 6 34
(Mrs L J Mongan) *mid-div: rdn over 3f out: sn lost pl* **4/1**[2]

3003 **10** nk **Ranavalona**[10] 4920 3-8-2 47...(t) AdrianMcCarthy 1 32
(C Smith) *hld up in tch: rdn and wknd over 3f out* **20/1**

40-0 **11** 2 1/2 **First Slip**[20] 3473 4-9-0 62.. LPKeniry 10 31
(Jonjo O'Neill) *mid-div: rdn and wknd over 2f out* **28/1**

6-06 **12** 13 **Miss Glory Be**[198] 517 9-8-8 43..............................(p) HaddenFrost(5) 16 9
(C J Down) *t.k.h: prom tl wknd over 2f out* **33/1**

-000 **13** 3 **Sparkbridge (IRE)**[16] 3868 4-9-4 43.......................(bt) FrankieMcDonald 9 9
(S C Burrough) *s.i.s: sn mid-div: rdn over 4f out: sn bhd* **100/1**

0150 **14** 1 3/4 **Diamond Key (IRE)**[42] 3907 3-8-12 50.......................(b) PatCosgrave 17 9
(M G Quinlan) *slipped ent st over 4f out: a bhd* **12/1**

00 **15** 1 1/2 **Moonshine Vixen**[9] 4948 6-8-8 0............................. WilliamCarson(7) 15 1
(P W Hiatt) *dwlt: a bhd* **66/1**

2m 38.55s (-0.17) **Going Correction** +0.05s/f (Good)
WFA 3 from 4yo+ 9lb **15** Ran SP% **127.4**
Speed ratings (Par 101): **102,101,101,100,99 98,97,97,94,94 92,83,81,80,79**
CSF £20.25 TOTE £3.00: £1.20, £2.70, £3.50; EX 41.50 TRIFECTA Not won..Beckenham's Secret was claimed by R Buckland for £7,000.
Owner P G Jacobs & Partners **Bred** Shadwell Estate Company Limited **Trained** Lambourn, Berks

FOCUS
A poor claimer with little solid and the third possibly the best guide.
Miss Glory Be Official explanation: jockey said mare ran very keen in the early stages and he thought saddle was slipping
Sparkbridge(IRE) Official explanation: jockey said gelding was unsuited by the good to firm ground
Diamond Key(IRE) Official explanation: jockey said filly slipped on the bend

5188 BETDIRECTPOKER.COM H'CAP 1m 2f 36y
3:20 (3:21) (Class 6) (0-62,62) 3-Y-0+ **£2,590** (£770; £385; £192) **Stalls** Low

Form RPR

5543 **1** **Spunger**[11] 4878 4-9-2 **57**..(v) SebSanders 3 67
(H J L Dunlop) *hld up in mid-div: stdy hdwy over 3f out: led jst over 1f out: rdn and edgd rt wl ins fnl f: r.o* **7/1**[3]

2100 **2** 1 1/4 **Red Current**[20] 4591 3-8-9 **57**.. LPKeniry 16 64
(R A Harris) *hld up in mid-div: hdwy over 3f out: rdn and r.o ins fnl f* **50/1**

5 **3** 1/2 **Our Kes (IRE)**[12] 4856 5-9-3 **58**.. AmirQuinn 9 64
(P Howling) *hld up towards rr: hdwy over 2f out: rdn over 1f out: swtchd lft ins fnl f: kpt on* **9/2**[2]

0422 **4** 2 **Libre**[12] 4856 7-9-2 **57**.. DavidKinsella 8 59
(F Jordan) *plld hrd in mid-div: hdwy on ins over 2f out: rdn over 1f out: kpt on same pce fnl f* **8/1**

30-0 **5** 1 3/4 **Sekula Pata (NZ)**[67] 3149 8-9-2 **62**.............................(b) SCreighton(5) 14 61
(E J Creighton) *a.p: led 3f out: rdn and hdd jst over 1f out: no ex ins fnl f* **66/1**

6104 **6** hd **Trevian**[11] 4878 6-9-0 **55**... StephenDonohoe 5 53
(J M Bradley) *hld up and bhd: rdn and hdwy over 1f out: nvr trbld ldrs* **14/1**

6511 **7** *shd* **Royal Indulgence**[8] 4959 7-8-11 **59** 6ex........................ AlanRutter(7) 13 57+
(W M Brisbourne) *stdd s: hld up in rr: hdwy over 2f out: swtchd lft over 1f out: swtchd rt ins fnl f: nvr able to chal* **2/1**[1]

0-03 **8** *2 1/2* **Ernmoor**[16] 4707 5-8-10 **51** oh1.......................... PatCosgrave 6 44
(J R Jenkins) *led: hdd 3f out: sn rdn: wknd 1f out* **80/1**

0-32 **9** *1 1/4* **Measured Response**[8] 4959 5-8-5 **53**.................. ThomasO'Brien(7) 7 43
(J G M O'Shea) *s.i.s: hld up and bhd: hdwy on ins 3f out: rdn over 2f out: sn wknd* **7/1**[3]

10 *3* **Tullythered (IRE)**[75] 2915 3-8-3 **51**.............................. FrancisNorton 2 35
(K R Burke) *hld up in tch: rdn and wknd 2f out* **20/1**

0520 **11** *nk* **Mango Masher (IRE)**[11] 4879 3-8-7 **60**..............(p) KevinGhunowa(5) 11 44
(J M Bradley) *a bhd* **50/1**

3500 **12** *2* **Cat Six (USA)**[19] 4632 3-8-5 **60**.............................. JackDean(7) 4 40
(T Wall) *hld up in tch: rdn over 4f out: wknd over 3f out* **66/1**

6-24 **13** *4* **Soviet Sceptre (IRE)**[31] 4253 6-8-13 **54**..................(t) FergusSweeney 1 26
(Evan Williams) *prom tl rdn and wknd over 2f out* **7/1**[3]

3000 **14** *23* **King's Spear (IRE)**[4] 5093 4-9-7 **62**......................(b[1]) PaulFitzsimons 10 —
(Miss J R Tooth) *chsd ldr 5f: rdn and wknd qckly over 3f out: t.o* **66/1**

2-60 **15** *2 1/2* **Vehari**[26] 4421 4-8-12 **60**.. MarkCoumbe(7) 15 —
(G F Bridgwater) *s.i.s: a in rr: t.o fnl 4f* **100/1**

2m 10.26s (0.36) **Going Correction** +0.05s/f (Good)
WFA 3 from 4yo+ 7lb **15** Ran SP% **122.2**
Speed ratings (Par 101): **100,99,98,97,95 95,95,93,92,89 89,88,84,66,64**
CSF £332.36 CT £1761.99 TOTE £6.90: £1.80, £7.80, £2.10; EX 338.40 Trifecta £262.90 Part won. Pool £370.36 - 0.10 winning units..
Owner Barry Marsden **Bred** The Complimentary Pass Partnership **Trained** Lambourn, Berks
■ Stewards' Enquiry : L P Keniry one-day ban: used whip with excessive frequency (Sep 18)

FOCUS
A modest handicap but the form makes sense, although not cast iron.
Our Kes(IRE) Official explanation: jockey said mare was struck into on the right-hind leg
Soviet Sceptre(IRE) Official explanation: jockey said gelding lost its action
Vehari Official explanation: jockey said gelding was never travelling

5189 BETDIRECT.COM H'CAP 1m 14y
3:55 (3:57) (Class 6) (0-65,66) 3-Y-0+ **£2,590** (£770; £385; £192) **Stalls** High

Form RPR

5212 **1** **Wrighty Almighty (IRE)**[17] 4688 5-9-5 **61**.............................. PaulDoe 3 70
(P R Chamings) *a.p: led over 2f out: rdn over 1f out: drvn out* **11/2**[3]

0351 **2** *1 1/4* **Red Rudy**[11] 4879 5-9-10 **66** 6ex.......................... SebSanders 7 72
(A W Carroll) *chsd ldrs: rdn and ev ch wl over 1f out: nt qckn ins fnl f* **4/1**[2]

3501 **3** *hd* **Corrib (IRE)**[21] 4577 4-9-7 **63**.............................. DavidKinsella 1 69
(B Palling) *chsd ldrs: rdn 2f out: kpt on ins fnl f* **11/1**

5503 **4** *shd* **The Gaikwar (IRE)**[12] 4850 8-9-2 **63**..................(b) KevinGhunowa(5) 13 68
(R A Harris) *hld up in mid-div: rdn over 1f out: styd on fnl f* **8/1**

-610 **5** *hd* **Dancing Storm**[31] 4257 4-9-0 **56**.............................. FergusSweeney 8 61
(W S Kittow) *a.p: ev ch over 2f out: rdn over 1f out: nt qckn ins fnl f* **8/1**

6004 **6** *shd* **Isphahan**[11] 4879 4-9-4 **60**.............................(p) FrancisNorton 5 65
(A M Balding) *a.p: rdn and sltly outpcd over 2f out: kpt on ins fnl f* **14/1**

0024 **7** *1 3/4* **Batchworth Blaise**[7] 5001 4-8-6 **51** oh6...................... TravisBlock(3) 10 52
(E A Wheeler) *hld up towards rr: rdn and hdwy over 1f out: one pce fnl f* **14/1**

5564 **8** *1 3/4* **Emily's Place (IRE)**[11] 4880 4-9-9 **65**.......................... BrettDoyle 6 62
(J Pearce) *mid-div: swtchd lft over 2f out: rdn over 1f out: no hdwy* **10/1**

0006 **9** *2 1/2* **Huxley (IRE)**[17] 4685 8-8-9 **51** oh6..................(t) SimonWhitworth 12 42
(D J Wintle) *s.i.s: n.d* **28/1**

0060 **10** *4* **Dora Explora**[17] 4686 3-9-4 **65**.............................. StephenDonohoe 11 47
(D J Wintle) *rdn 3f out: a bhd* **25/1**

3000 **11** *1 1/2* **Goodwood Spirit**[1] 5179 5-8-9 **51** oh1.....................(v) LPKeniry 2 29
(J M Bradley) *dwlt: sn hld up in mid-div: rdn 2f out: sn wknd* **20/1**

0000 **12** *23* **Linda's Colin (IRE)**[7] 5020 5-9-6 **62**.......................... AmirQuinn 4 —
(R A Harris) *led: hdd over 2f out: wknd qckly: b.b.v* **50/1**

4222 **13** *21* **Chief Exec**[11] 4879 5-8-9 **56**.............................. HaddenFrost(5) 9 —
(B J Llewellyn) *s.i.s: in rr whn hung lft over 5f out: sn lost tch: t.o* **7/2**[1]

1m 35.38s (-0.62) **Going Correction** -0.075s/f (Good)
WFA 3 from 4yo+ 5lb **13** Ran SP% **124.6**
Speed ratings (Par 101): **100,98,98,98,98 98,96,94,92,88 86,63,42**
CSF £27.86 CT £252.84 TOTE £6.10: £1.20, £2.30, £3.00; EX 28.10 Trifecta £193.30 Pool £604.63 - 2.22 winning units..
Owner The Boccy Hall Evans Tyrrell Partnership **Bred** P Heffernan **Trained** Baughurst, Hants

FOCUS
A low-grade handicap but the form looks solid with the placed horses close to their latest marks.
Linda's Colin(IRE) Official explanation: vet said gelding bled from the nose
Chief Exec Official explanation: jockey said gelding reared and was unsettled in the stalls and lost its action coming out

5190 BETDIRECT.COM GET INVOLVED H'CAP 7f 16y
4:25 (4:28) (Class 6) (0-60,60) 3-Y-0+ **£2,590** (£770; £385; £192) **Stalls** High

Form RPR

U0 **1** **Trinculo (IRE)**[34] 4165 10-8-7 **50**.............................(b) HaddenFrost(5) 15 67
(R A Harris) *mde all: clr over 2f out: edgd lft ins fnl f: r.o wl* **20/1**

0001 **2** *4* **Bold Cross (IRE)**[4] 5098 4-9-6 **58** 6ex...................... PaulFitzsimons 17 64
(E G Bevan) *a.p: rdn and r.o one pce fnl f* **9/1**

3652 **3** *shd* **Tilsworth Charlie**[12] 4855 4-9-2 **54**.......................(b) PatCosgrave 14 60
(J R Jenkins) *hld up and bhd: hdwy on stands' rail over 2f out: rdn and r.o one pce fnl f* **9/1**

0061 **4** *3* **Ten To The Dozen**[17] 4685 4-9-1 **53**.............................. LPKeniry 4 51
(P W Hiatt) *mid-div: rdn 3f out: rdn and hdwy over 1f out: one pce fnl f* **14/1**

034 **5** *hd* **Vogarth**[34] 4182 3-9-2 **58**.............................. FergusSweeney 10 55
(B R Millman) *chsd wnr tl rdn and wknd ins fnl f* **16/1**

0004 **6** *1 1/2* **Tibinta**[29] 4312 3-8-6 **48**.............................. SimonWhitworth 16 41
(P D Evans) *hld up towards rr: hdwy over 3f out: rdn over 2f out: wknd fnl f* **25/1**

0446 **7** *shd* **Buzzin'Boyzee (IRE)**[147] 1027 4-8-10 **48**................. StephenDonohoe 1 41
(P D Evans) *prom: rdn over 2f out: wknd over 1f out* **20/1**

6505 **8** *3/4* **Machinate (USA)**[32] 4223 5-8-8 **51**.............................. LukeMorris(5) 6 42
(W M Brisbourne) *nvr nr ldrs* **10/1**

0334 **9** *hd* **Chalentina**[4] 5098 4-9-3 **55**.............................. IanMongan 8 45
(P Howling) *hld up in tch: rdn over 3f out: wknd over 2f out* **7/1**[3]

1000 **10** *1 1/2* **Convince (USA)**[5] 5062 6-8-13 **56**.....................(p) KevinGhunowa(5) 2 42
(J M Bradley) *hld up towards rr* **66/1**

6612 **11** *1* **Millfield (IRE)**[8] 4978 4-9-5 **57**.............................. GeorgeBaker 5 40
(P R Chamings) *s.i.s: a bhd* **11/4**[1]

0045 **12** *1* **Moon Forest (IRE)**[13] 4807 5-8-3 **48**.....................(p) PietroRomeo(7) 9 29
(J M Bradley) *bhd fnl 3f* **11/2**[2]

0050 **13** *1 1/2* **Cayman Breeze**[86] 2576 7-8-5 **48**..............................(p) TolleyDean(5) 3 25
(J M Bradley) *a bhd* **25/1**

006 **14** *nk* **Cerulean Rose**[7] 5009 8-8-13 **51**.............................. FrancisNorton 13 27
(A W Carroll) *hld up in mid-div: wknd over 2f out* **14/1**

0000 **15** *10* **Imperial Gain (USA)**[27] 4395 4-9-1 **60**.....................(v) BarrySavage(7) 11 9
(J M Bradley) *prom tl rdn and wknd over 2f out* **33/1**

1m 22.67s (-0.63) **Going Correction** -0.075s/f (Good)
WFA 3 from 4yo+ 4lb **15** Ran SP% **124.5**
Speed ratings (Par 101): **100,95,95,91,91 89,89,88,88,87 85,84,83,82,71**
CSF £182.95 CT £1142.76 TOTE £22.60: £7.10, £3.60, £3.90; EX 441.80 TRIFECTA Not won..
Owner Peter A Price **Bred** Humphrey Okeke **Trained** Earlswood, Monmouths

FOCUS
This did not take much winning and turned into something of a one-horse race with the winner on a good mark and the placed horses to recent levels.
Millfield(IRE) Official explanation: jockey said gelding failed to handle the loose ground coming down the hill

5191 BETDIRECT H'CAP 6f 16y
4:55 (5:02) (Class 6) (0-60,60) 3-Y-0+ **£2,590** (£770; £385; £192) **Stalls** High

Form RPR

2104 **1** **Dematraf (IRE)**[11] 4881 5-9-6 **59**.............................. StephenDonohoe 1 69
(P D Evans) *a.p: rdn to ld 2f out: r.o* **9/1**

0410 **2** *nk* **Support Fund (IRE)**[34] 4165 3-9-0 **60**.......................... PatrickHills(5) 6 69
(Eve Johnson Houghton) *hld up in mid-div: rdn over 2f out: hdwy over 1f out: edgd lft ins fnl f: r.o* **16/1**

0523 **3** *1 1/4* **Endless Summer**[11] 4881 10-9-5 **58**.............................. FrancisNorton 14 63
(A W Carroll) *bhd tl gd hdwy fnl f: r.o* **4/1**[2]

4600 **4** *1/2* **Slipasearcher (IRE)**[11] 4879 3-9-3 **58**......................(v) GeorgeBaker 15 62
(P D Evans) *bhd: rdn and hdwy over 1f out: r.o ins fnl f* **20/1**

0466 **5** *hd* **Duke Of Milan (IRE)**[30] 4296 4-8-13 **52**.......................... IanMongan 3 55
(G C Bravery) *hld up and bhd: hdwy and edgd lft over 1f out: rdn and r.o ins fnl f* **10/1**

4502 **6** *1* **Digital**[11] 4881 10-8-12 **58**.............................(v) MatthewDavies(7) 5 58
(M R Channon) *hld up in mid-div: rdn and hdwy wl over 1f out: one pce ins fnl f* **7/1**

0635 **7** *nk* **Musical Script (USA)**[7] 5009 4-8-10 **52**..................(b) TravisBlock(3) 16 51
(Mouse Hamilton-Fairley) *prom: ev ch wl over 1f out: sn rdn and hung rt: wknd ins fnl f* **13/2**[3]

3300 **8** *1 1/4* **Peruvian Style (IRE)**[11] 4881 6-8-6 **52**.......................... BarrySavage(7) 4 48
(J M Bradley) *hld up in tch: rdn 2f out: wknd ins fnl f* **33/1**

0345 **9** *nk* **Hello Roberto**[11] 4881 6-8-10 **54**..........................(p) KevinGhunowa(5) 7 49
(R A Harris) *prom: rdn over 2f out: wknd ins fnl f* **16/1**

100 **10** *1/2* **Piccostar**[11] 4881 4-9-1 **54**.............................(b) SamHitchcott 2 47
(A B Haynes) *led: rdn and hdd 2f out: wknd ins fnl f* **40/1**

4-30 **11** *nk* **Unlimited**[52] 3613 5-8-10 **56**.............................(p) SophieDoyle(7) 8 48
(R Simpson) *stdd s: sn prom: wknd 2f out* **16/1**

0004 **12** *2 1/2* **Minnie Mill**[22] 4529 3-8-12 **53**.............................. PatCosgrave 10 38
(B P J Baugh) *a bhd* **50/1**

4-00 **13** *1/2* **Stargazy**[113] 1786 3-8-12 **60**.............................. JackDean(7) 13 43
(W G M Turner) *t.k.h in tch: rdn over 2f out: wknd wl over 1f out* **33/1**

10-0 **14** *1/2* **Two Acres (IRE)**[165] 787 4-9-1 **54**.............................. LPKeniry 9 36
(A G Newcombe) *bhd fnl 2f* **33/1**

0650 **15** *2* **Ensign's Trick**[12] 4855 3-9-0 **60**.............................. LukeMorris(5) 11 36
(W M Brisbourne) *prom tl rdn and wknd 2f out* **18/1**

0011 **16** *3 1/2* **Jabbara (IRE)**[22] 4525 4-9-4 **57**.............................. SebSanders 12 22
(C E Brittain) *chsd ldrs: rdn over 2f out: sn wknd: eased whn btn fnl f* **3/1**[1]

1m 11.92s (-0.48) **Going Correction** -0.075s/f (Good)
WFA 3 from 4yo+ 2lb **16** Ran SP% **130.8**
Speed ratings (Par 101): **100,99,97,97,97 95,95,93,93,92 92,88,88,87,84 80**
CSF £145.93 CT £710.09 TOTE £12.30: £2.00, £3.30, £1.50, £3.50; EX 211.50 TRIFECTA Not won..
Owner T V Cullen **Bred** Edward Ryan **Trained** Pandy, Monmouths

FOCUS
A tightly-knit basement level contest that is rated at face value for now through the third and fourth.
Musical Script(USA) Official explanation: jockey said gelding hung right
Unlimited Official explanation: jockey said gelding was unsuited by the good to frim ground
Jabbara(IRE) Official explanation: jockey said filly lost its action
T/Jkpt: Not won. T/Plt: £249.00 to a £1 stake. Pool: £62,506.10. 183.20 winning tickets. T/Qpdt: £174.40 to a £1 stake. Pool: £3,464.90. 14.70 winning tickets. KH

4385 HAYDOCK (L-H)
Friday, September 7

OFFICIAL GOING: Good to firm (good in places; 7.0)
Wind: light, half-against Weather: Overcast

5192 WILLIE MCKAY SPORTS MANAGEMENT EBF MAIDEN STKS 5f
2:00 (2:03) (Class 5) 2-Y-0 **£3,238** (£963; £481; £240) **Stalls** Centre

Form RPR

1 **Inxile (IRE)** 2-9-3 0.............................. AdrianTNicholls 11 87
(D Nicholls) *mde all: rdn over 1f out: kpt on wl* **33/1**

43 **2** *3/4* **Hammadi (IRE)**[16] 4725 2-9-3 0.............................. NCallan 8 84
(K A Ryan) *a pressing wnr: rdn over 1f out: ev ch thrght fnl f: nt qckn towards fin* **11/4**[2]

0 **3** *hd* **Hamish McGonagall**[160] 845 2-9-3 0.............................. DavidAllan 9 83+
(T D Easterby) *sn in midfield: hdwy over 1f out: r.o ins fnl f: clsng at fin* **50/1**

4 **4** *2 1/2* **No Page (IRE)**[32] 4232 2-8-12 0.............................. TedDurcan 6 69
(B W Hills) *midfield: effrt and hdwy 2f out: kpt on ins fnl f: nt pce of ldrs* **14/1**

5 *1 1/2* **Writingonthewall (IRE)** 2-9-3 0.............................. HayleyTurner 10 69+
(M L W Bell) *towards rr: rn green: kpt on fr 2f out: should improve* **40/1**

435 **6** *1* **Chivola (IRE)**[14] 4782 2-9-3 75.............................. RoystonFfrench 12 65
(B Smart) *trckd ldrs: rdn 1/2-way: wknd over 1f out* **10/1**[3]

5 **7** *1/2* **Silvanus (IRE)**[16] 4725 2-9-3 0.............................. PaulMulrennan 2 63
(W J Haggas) *in tch: pushed along 1/2-way: sn outpcd* **4/5**[1]

45 **8** *1 3/4* **Not My Choice (IRE)**[121] 1580 2-9-3 0.....................(t) JohnEgan 4 57
(D J Murphy) *midfield: outpcd fr 1/2-way* **12/1**

0 **9** *6* **Silken Spell**[26] 4422 2-8-12 0.............................. TPQueally 7 31
(Mrs A Duffield) *dwlt: a outpcd and bhd* **100/1**

0 **10** *3 1/2* **Kiowa Princess**[22] 4522 2-8-12 0.............................. PhillipMakin 5 18
(M Dods) *chsd ldrs tl rdn and wknd 1/2-way* **100/1**

11 10 **Charlie Oxo** 2-9-3 0 GrahamGibbons 3 —
(B P J Baugh) *dwlt: a outpcd and bhd* **200/1**

61.71 secs (1.59) **Going Correction** +0.325s/f (Good) **11** Ran SP% **115.5**
Speed ratings (Par 95): **100,98,98,94,92 90,89,86,77,71 55**
CSF £120.70 TOTE £26.40: £5.20, £1.10, £6.00; EX 64.20.

Owner Peter Brice **Bred** Denis And Mrs Teresa Bergin **Trained** Sessay, N Yorks

FOCUS

A fair juvenile maiden, run at a solid pace with the runner-up to previous York form.

NOTEBOOK

Inxile(IRE), an 80,000gns half-brother to his yard's smart sprinter Tax Free, made just about every yard to get his career off to a perfect start. He knuckled down well to repel the more experienced runner-up at the business end and is clearly a very speedy individual. With improvement likely for this debut experience, his connections look to have a potentially smart prospect on their hands, and it will be very interesting to see where he is sent next. (op 22-1)

Hammadi(IRE) came there with every chance when it mattered, but could not get on top of the debutant winner try as he might and did not prove that suited by the drop back in trip. He is now qualified for nurseries, but does have a maiden within his grasp when reverting to 6f and is certainly not one to abandon yet. (op 9-4)

Hamish McGonagall ◆, not seen since finishing midfield on his debut 160 days previously, took time to hit full stride and was doing all of his best work inside the final furlong. He looks to have grown since his absence from the track and, considering he probably needed this run, it has to rate a promising return to action. Another furlong will now suit and he looks sure to lose his maiden tag before long.

No Page(IRE), fourth on debut at Windsor against her own sex 32 days previously, raced a touch freely through the early parts and simply lacked the pace to trouble the principals on this drop back to the minimum trip. She ought to benefit again for this experience and will be eligible for nurseries after her next assignment. (op 11-1)

Writingonthewall(IRE), a 160,000gns half-brother to Dunelight, ran distinctly green on this racecourse bow and the run was clearly needed. He was keeping on with some promise late on and should prove a lot sharper with this experience under his belt. (op 33-1)

Chivola(IRE) failed to raise his game for the drop back a furlong and posted a fairly tame effort. He now has a little to prove, but really wants 6f. (op 11-1)

Silvanus(IRE), all the rage in the betting ring, failed to run near to the level of his promising York debut behind Hammadi and has to rate very disappointing. He did not prove suited by the shorter trip, but was still beaten a long way out and his Group 1 entry looks very ambitious. Official explanation: trainer was unable to explain the poor form shown (op 6-5 tchd 5-4 in places)

5193 PFA CENTENARY E B F MAIDEN STKS (DIV I) 6f

2:35 (2:35) (Class 5) 2-Y-O **£2,590** (£770; £385; £192) **Stalls** Centre

Form				RPR
5	**1**		**Striking Spirit**[21] 4571 2-9-3 0 TedDurcan 10 (B W Hills) *dwlt: hld up: hdwy over 3f out: rdn over 1f out: r.o to ld wl ins fnl f: on top towards fin* **11/10**[1]	78+
	2	1 ½	**Beacon Lodge (IRE)** 2-9-3 0 PaulMulrennan 2 (C G Cox) *racd keenly: led: hdd over 4f out: remained prom: rdn to regain ld over 1f out: sn hung lft: hdd wl ins fnl f: hld after* **7/1**	74
	3	shd	**Tawzeea (IRE)** 2-9-3 0 RHills 9 (M Johnston) *prom: led over 4f out: rdn and hdd over 1f out: sn hung lft: nt qckn wl ins fnl f* **9/1**	73
	4	1 ¼	**Classic Descent** 2-9-3 0 NCallan 3 (P J Makin) *hld up: hdwy 1/2-way: chsd ldrs over 1f out: cl up in 4th whn sltly short of room wl ins fnl f: sn eased* **13/2**[3]	70+
022	**5**	1 ¾	**Call For Liberty (IRE)**[14] 4781 2-9-3 85 RoystonFfrench 1 (B Smart) *in tch: rdn 1/2-way: outpcd over 1f out* **4/1**[2]	64
	6	hd	**Dazzling Colours** 2-9-3 0 TPQueally 6 (J Noseda) *in rr: rdn over 4f out: kpt on fr over 1f out: nt rch ldrs* **12/1**	64
	7	nk	**Viscaya (IRE)** 2-8-9 0 AndrewMullen(3) 11 (Mrs A Duffield) *s.i.s: outpcd: kpt on fr 2f out: nt rch ldrs* **100/1**	58
	8	9	**Babilu** 2-8-12 0 J-PGuillambert 5 (J G Given) *trckd ldrs tl rdn and wknd qckly over 2f out* **66/1**	31
	9	4	**John Potts** 2-9-3 0 DanielTudhope 7 (B P J Baugh) *rn green and a bhd* **150/1**	24
00	**10**	9	**Kalanda Kurl (IRE)**[13] 4796 2-8-12 0 GrahamGibbons 8 (J J Quinn) *prom tl wknd 1/2-way* **150/1**	—

1m 15.64s (1.75) **Going Correction** +0.325s/f (Good) **10** Ran SP% **115.0**
Speed ratings (Par 95): **101,99,98,97,94 94,94,82,76,64**
CSF £9.53 TOTE £1.90: £1.30, £2.30, £2.00; EX 11.50.

Owner K Abdulla **Bred** Juddmonte Farms Ltd **Trained** Lambourn, Berks

■ Stewards' Enquiry : R Hills caution: careless riding

FOCUS

A good first divison of this juvenile maiden, run at a sound pace. The form is not as strong as it could have been but should work out.

NOTEBOOK

Striking Spirit confirmed the promise of his Newbury debut effort 21 days previously and readily got off the mark at the second attempt. He took time to get on top and needed a reminder or two entering the final furlong, but was well on top at the finish. The step up to 7f should see him in an even better light in due course, although his pedigree does not scream stamina, and he looks sure to improve again for this experience. It will be very interesting to see where he is pitched in next as he holds entries in the Group 2 Mill Reef and Group 1 Middle Park Stakes. (op 11-8 tchd 6-4 in places)

Beacon Lodge(IRE) ◆, a 150,000gns purchase related to numerous winners at around 1m, showed definite ability on this racecourse debut yet hung his chance away under maximum pressure inside the final furlong. He should learn a good deal from this experience and obviously has a future, with a similar race looking sure to come his way. (op 5-1)

Tawzeea(IRE) ◆, bred to come into his own over a stiffer test next year, clearly knew his job and was soon racing on the early pace. He tended to hang left with the runner-up late on, but was just held at the time and left the impression he may already want 1m. This was a very pleasing debut effort. (op 11-2 tchd 10-1)

Classic Descent ◆, half-brother to Irish 1000 Guineas heroine Saoire, posted a solid effort in defeat and must be rated a bit better than the bare form as he was tight for room behind the principals at the business end. He has scope and looks sure to improve for the run, so ought not to be long in finding a winning opportunity. (op 12-1)

Call For Liberty(IRE), officially rated 85 after his three previous outings, was feeling the pinch passing the halfway stage and was never a serious player. He ran a little below his best here, and is now looking fully exposed, but he does rate a sound benchmark for this form all the same. (tchd 9-2)

Dazzling Colours, a 110,000gns purchase whose dam won over 1m at three, ran distinctly green through the early stages and is clearly a lazy sort. He picked up when the race was effectively over, however, and did more than enough to suggest he will come on a deal for this debut experience. It may also be that he prefers an easier surface and a seventh furlong should be well within his compass before the year is out. (op 14-1 tchd 11-1)

Viscaya(IRE), half-sister to this season's winning three-year-old sprinter Mandurah, took an age to get the hang of things and was doing all of her best work too late in the day. She is one to keep an eye on when switching to one of the smaller tracks. (tchd 150-1)

5194 PFA CENTENARY E B F MAIDEN STKS (DIV II) 6f

3:10 (3:11) (Class 5) 2-Y-O **£2,590** (£770; £385; £192) **Stalls** Centre

Form				RPR
2	**1**		**Errigal Lad**[37] 4076 2-9-3 0 NCallan 8 (K A Ryan) *chsd ldrs: rdn over 1f out: sn led: r.o ins fnl f* **7/1**[3]	79
4	**2**	½	**Glorious Gift (IRE)**[16] 4725 2-9-3 0 TedDurcan 7 (P W Chapple-Hyam) *midfield: hdwy whn nt clr run over 1f out: r.o ins fnl f: gng on at fin* **6/5**[1]	80+
40	**3**	¾	**Birkintastic**[14] 4775 2-9-3 0 JohnEgan 9 (B J Meehan) *hld up: rdn and hdwy over 1f out: styd on ins fnl f* **16/1**	75+
	4	hd	**Fabreze** 2-9-3 0 DO'Donohoe 2 (P J Makin) *in rr: rn green: drifted lft whn hdwy over 1f out: styd on ins fnl f: promising* **50/1**	74+
4	**5**	½	**Almoutaz (USA)**[21] 4571 2-9-3 0 RHills 3 (B W Hills) *midfield: hdwy to ld jst under 2f out: rdn and hdd 1f out: no ex towards fin* **9/4**[2]	73+
	6	2	**Hieroglyph** 2-8-12 0 J-PGuillambert 4 (M Johnston) *w ldr: rdn and ev ch 2f out: n.m.r whn hld over 1f out* **16/1**	62+
	7	¾	**Sweet Mind** 2-8-12 0 PaulHanagan 5 (R A Fahey) *midfield: rdn over 1f out: green and kpt on fnl f: should improve* **100/1**	59+
	8	¾	**Silk Gallery (USA)** 2-8-12 0 HayleyTurner 10 (M L W Bell) *in tch: rdn 2f out: wknd ins fnl f* **80/1**	57
2	**9**	2	**Bahamian Lad**[35] 4125 2-9-3 0 PaulEddery 1 (R Hollinshead) *broke wl: wnt rt s: in tch: rdn 2f out: wknd ent fnl f* **12/1**	56
00	**10**	1 ¼	**Melwood Dreams**[6] 5042 2-8-10 0 FrankiePickard(7) 6 (Paul Green) *upset in stalls bef s: led: rdn and hdd jst under 2f out: wknd over 1f out* **200/1**	52

1m 16.07s (2.18) **Going Correction** +0.325s/f (Good) **10** Ran SP% **112.9**
Speed ratings (Par 95): **98,97,96,96,95 92,91,90,88,86**
CSF £15.34 TOTE £7.70: £1.80, £1.10, £4.00; EX 20.60.

Owner Errigal Racing **Bred** R Lawson **Trained** Hambleton, N Yorks

FOCUS

A fair juvenile maiden and it looked the weaker of the two divisons. The form looks straightforward.

NOTEBOOK

Errigal Lad, a close second on debut 37 days previously, did the job in determined fashion and went one better in this higher grade. He is clearly an improving juvenile who looks a sprinter through-and-through and can expect an official mark in the 80s after this. (op 8-1)

Glorious Gift(IRE), a promising fourth at York on his debut 16 days previously, found the winner drifting across him entering the final furlong and, as was the case last time, did not get a clear passage when it mattered. He stayed on when in the clear only to find that rival gone beyond recall and has to rate somewhat unfortunate not to have lost his maiden tag. It may well prove that he will now enjoy a seventh furlong however, and he is well worth another chance. (op 5-6 tchd 5-4 in places)

Birkintastic, well beaten in a valuable race at Newmarket on soft ground last time, raced lazily through the early parts yet was staying on with purpose inside the final furlong and posted his best effort to date. He is now qualifies for nurseries, looked happier on the faster surface, and will appreciate another furlong now. (op 25-1)

Fabreze, whose dam was a dual 6f-1m winner, was allowed to go off at massive odds on this racecourse bow yet belied his price with a promising effort in defeat. Having proved very green early on, he picked up nicely when switched to the far rail and left the impression he will learn plenty for this experience. (op 100-1)

Almoutaz(USA), who played up at the start, raced a little freely early on the outside of the field and could find just the one pace when put under pressure after hitting the front near 2f out. He ran a little below his debut form here and his pre-race antics cannot have helped. (tchd 15-8 and 5-2 in places)

5195 PFA CENTENARY E B F CLASSIFIED STKS 6f

3:45 (3:46) (Class 3) 3-Y-O+ **£9,715** (£2,890; £1,444; £721) **Stalls** Centre

Form				RPR
0000	**1**		**One More Round (USA)**[20] 4614 9-8-13 90 (b) RoystonFfrench 3 (N P Littmoden) *bhd: swtchd rt and hdwy over 1f out: r.o to ld wl ins fnl f* **14/1**	100
0020	**2**	½	**Come Out Fighting**[27] 4389 4-8-13 90 GrahamGibbons 4 (P A Blockley) *led: rdn over 1f out: hdd wl ins fnl f: r.o u.p* **15/2**	98
6031	**3**	1 ½	**High Curragh**[27] 4389 4-8-13 89 NCallan 10 (K A Ryan) *hld up: hdwy 1/2-way: rdn and hung lft over 1f out: styd on same pce ins fnl f* **5/2**[1]	93
0600	**4**	3 ½	**Ajigolo**[6] 5050 4-8-13 90 TPO'Shea 5 (M R Channon) *midfield: hdwy 1/2-way: effrt to chse ldrs over 2f out: one pce ins fnl f* **5/1**[3]	82
0400	**5**	1 ¼	**Angus Newz**[48] 3749 4-8-10 88 (v) J-PGuillambert 9 (M Quinn) *prom: rdn and carried hd high whn lost pl over 1f out: n.d after* **16/1**	75
0010	**6**	2 ½	**Continent**[17] 4696 10-8-13 89 PaulHanagan 1 (D Nicholls) *plld hrd: in tch: stdd off pce over 3f out: effrt over 1f out: wknd ins fnl f* **22/1**	70
0142	**7**	6	**Malcheek (IRE)**[6] 5044 5-8-13 89 DavidAllan 2 (T D Easterby) *w ldr: rdn and wknd over 1f out: eased whn btn ins fnl f* **11/4**[2]	51
0005	**8**	4	**Fire Up The Band**[17] 4696 8-8-13 87 AdrianTNicholls 6 (D Nicholls) *awkward leaving stalls: hld up: rdn over 2f out: no imp: eased whn btn ins fnl f* **9/1**	38
402-	**9**	1 ½	**Godfrey Street**[335] 5807 4-8-13 88 DO'Donohoe 8 (K A Ryan) *prom: rdn 1/2-way: wknd 2f out* **33/1**	33

1m 14.74s (0.85) **Going Correction** +0.325s/f (Good)
WFA 3 from 4yo+ 2lb **9** Ran SP% **113.5**
Speed ratings (Par 107): **107,106,104,99,98 94,86,81,79**
CSF £112.29 TOTE £20.80: £4.10, £3.20, £1.30; EX 116.40.

Owner Nigel Shields **Bred** Kenneth L Ramsey And Sarah K Ramsey **Trained** Newmarket, Suffolk

FOCUS

A typically tight classified stakes that was run at a strong pace. The form is worth treating with some caution with the third the best guide.

NOTEBOOK

One More Round(USA)was taken off his feet through the first 2f and looked to have it all do passing halfway. However, the strong early pace clearly played into his hands and he emerged to join the leaders full of running inside the final furlong before going on to score readily in the end. This signalled a massive return to form for the nine-year-old, who does find winning hard these days, which does not really say a great deal for the overall strength of this form. (op 12-1 tchd 10-1)

Come Out Fighting, who proved restless in the stalls, made a bold bid under a positive ride yet it was clear in the final 100 yards he was going to play second fiddle to the winner. He had his ideal conditions this time and it was a much more encouraging effort in defeat, but he is very hard to catch right all the same. (op 6-1 tchd 8-1)
High Curragh, back to winning ways over course and distance 27 days previously, came there with every chance nearing the final furlong yet eventually hung when put under maximum pressure and was well held at the finish. This was no disgrace. (op 7-2)
Ajigolo, back up in trip after an unlucky-in-running effort over 5f last time, found just the same pace when the gun was put to his head yet still ran close to his recent level. He helps to set the standard of this form. (op 11-2)
Malcheek(IRE) dropped out most tamely around 2f out and ran miles below his recent best. Something was clearly amiss. Official explanation: jockey said gelding was never travelling (op 3-1 tchd 5-2)
Fire Up The Band Official explanation: jockey said gelding lost its action

5196 PFA ONE GOAL ONE MILLION CHARITY H'CAP 1m 30y
4:15 (4:15) (Class 4) (0-85,84) 3-Y-0+ **£5,505** (£1,637; £818; £408) **Stalls** Low

Form RPR
2540 **1** **Orpen Wide (IRE)**[10] 4922 5-9-1 **83**.................(b) RussellKennemore(5) 1 92
(M C Chapman) *mde all: rdn 2f out: qcknd ins fnl f: r.o* **11/2**[3]
1234 **2** *2* **Flighty Fellow (IRE)**[11] 4900 7-9-2 **79**..............................(b) DavidAllan 9 83
(T D Easterby) *chsd wnr after 1f: rdn 2f out: nt qckn ins fnl f* **5/1**[2]
0310 **3** *1* **Just Bond (IRE)**[4] 5099 5-8-13 **76**............................. DanielTudhope 2 78
(G R Oldroyd) *hld up: rdn and hdwy over 1f out: styd on ins fnl f: nt pce to rch front pair* **9/1**
0240 **4** *1/2* **Wheels In Motion (IRE)**[40] 4006 3-8-8 **76**......................... TedDurcan 5 77
(T P Tate) *hld up: rdn 2f out: hdwy over 1f out: styd on ins fnl f* **6/1**
4000 **5** *2* **Kings Point (IRE)**[15] 4745 6-9-7 **84**................................ PaulHanagan 3 80
(R A Fahey) *chsd wnr for 1f: chsd ldrs after: rdn over 2f out: one pce fr over 1f out* **6/1**
0004 **6** *1/2* **Bobski (IRE)**[33] 4195 5-9-3 **80**.. NCallan 8 75
(G A Huffer) *midfield: hdwy 2f out: rdn over 1f out: hung rt ins fnl f: sn no ex* **4/1**[1]
00-5 **7** *1/2* **Sea Storm (IRE)**[11] 4100 9-8-9 **72**..................................... PhillipMakin 7 66
(James Moffatt) *in tch: rdn over 2f out: wknd fnl f* **16/1**
6100 **8** *2 1/2* **Spume (IRE)**[12] 4847 3-8-11 **79**..(t) JohnEgan 6 67
(D J Murphy) *hld up: rdn 3f out: hung lft fr 2f out: eased whn no imp ins fnl f* **16/1**
1060 **9** *4* **Wovoka (IRE)**[15] 4745 4-9-6 **83**... TPO'Shea 4 62
(M R Channon) *midfield: effrt and hdwy over 3f out: wknd over 1f out* **8/1**
1m 45.72s (0.21) **Going Correction** +0.175s/f (Good)
WFA 3 from 4yo+ 5lb 9 Ran SP% **113.5**
Speed ratings (Par 105): **105,103,102,101,99 99,98,96,92**
CSF £32.50 CT £242.96 TOTE £6.30: £2.80, £1.40, £2.90; EX 24.10.
Owner Andy & Bev Wright **Bred** Mrs Marian Maguire **Trained** Market Rasen, Lincs
FOCUS
A fair handicap for the grade where the front runners seemed favoured. It was run at an uneven pace, however, and the form should be treated with a degree of caution.

5197 PFA BILLY MEREDITH CENTENARY H'CAP 1m 3f 200y
4:45 (4:45) (Class 4) (0-85,83) 3-Y-0+ **£5,505** (£1,637; £818; £408) **Stalls** High

Form RPR
3423 **1** **Bajan Parkes**[11] 4909 4-9-4 **76**... DavidAllan 8 84
(E J Alston) *mde all: rdn over 2f out: r.o wl* **6/1**
2114 **2** *1 3/4* **Sadler's Kingdom (IRE)**[29] 4332 3-8-9 **76**...................... PaulHanagan 5 81+
(R A Fahey) *chsd ldrs: outpcd over 4f out: rallied to take 2nd over 1f out: nt rch wnr* **7/1**
061 **3** *3* **Riguez Dancer**[32] 4230 3-8-2 **72**............................... AndrewMullen(3) 2 72
(P C Haslam) *in tch: rdn over 3f out: chsd wnr over 2f out tl over 1f out: one pce ins fnl f* **7/2**[1]
5016 **4** *2 1/2* **Sforzando**[14] 4772 6-8-11 **69** oh1.. TomEaves 4 65
(Mrs L Stubbs) *midfield: rdn over 2f out: one pce* **12/1**
3113 **5** *1 1/4* **Mirthful (USA)**[14] 4779 3-9-1 **82**.................................... TedDurcan 7 77
(B W Hills) *s.i.s: hld up: rdn over 2f out: nt trble ldrs* **4/1**[2]
0014 **6** *7* **United Nations**[13] 4820 6-8-12 **70**.............................. PaulMulrennan 1 53
(M W Easterby) *hld up: rdn over 2f out: no imp* **11/2**
1112 **7** *4* **Olimpo (FR)**[24] 4483 6-9-6 **83**..................................... JamesMillman(5) 3 60
(B R Millman) *racd keenly: chsd wnr: rdn over 3f out: lost 2nd over 2f out: wknd over 1f out* **9/2**[3]
2m 35.08s (0.09) **Going Correction** +0.175s/f (Good)
WFA 3 from 4yo+ 9lb 7 Ran SP% **110.3**
Speed ratings (Par 105): **106,104,102,101,100 95,93**
CSF £43.01 CT £158.40 TOTE £7.40: £3.40, £3.30; EX 41.60.
Owner Joseph Heler **Bred** Joseph Heler **Trained** Longton, Lancs
FOCUS
A fair handicap that saw the field finish fairly strung out behind the winner, who readily made all. The runner-up to his best sets the level.
Olimpo(FR) Official explanation: jockey said gelding had no more to give

5198 PFA CENTENARY H'CAP (FOR GENTLEMAN AMATEUR RIDERS) 1m 2f 120y
5:15 (5:15) (Class 5) (0-75,74) 3-Y-0+ **£2,717** (£842; £421; £210) **Stalls** High

Form RPR
6633 **1** **Rawdon (IRE)**[23] 4517 6-10-11 **66**...............................(v) MrCPHuxley(5) 4 73
(M L W Bell) *chsd ldr: rdn 2f out: nosed ahd over 1f out: kpt on whn continually pressed ins fnl f* **4/1**[2]
0005 **2** *hd* **Mulaazem**[32] 4230 4-10-12 **62**.. MrSDobson 8 69
(J Mackie) *led at stdy pce: rdn 2f out: hdd narrowly over 1f out: continued to press wnr thrght fnl f* **15/2**
0411 **3** *2 1/2* **Snark (IRE)**[12] 4850 4-11-7 **71** 6ex................................... MrSWalker 6 73
(P J Makin) *chsd ldrs: rdn over 1f out: kpt on wout troubling front pair* **11/4**[1]
3221 **4** *1/2* **Gallego**[7] 5001 5-10-7 **64** 6ex.. MrMPrice(7) 3 65+
(R J Price) *lost 7l s: racd keenly: hld up and sn in main gp due to stdy pce: rdn and hdwy on outside over 1f out: styd on ins fnl f* **7/1**[3]
5002 **5** *1/2* **Calculating (IRE)**[66] 3176 3-10-12 **70**.......................... MrLeeNewnes 7 70
(M D I Usher) *hld up: hdwy over 4f out: rdn 2f out: styd on same pce fr over 1f out* **11/1**
0052 **6** *1/2* **Sol Rojo**[22] 4526 5-10-12 **65**.....................................(v) MrSPearce(3) 2 64
(J Pearce) *lost 6l s: racd keenly and sn in midfield: pushed along over 3f out: outpcd over 2f out: n.d after* **8/1**
4520 **7** *1* **Bavarica**[7] 4994 5-11-5 **74**.. MrRBirkett(5) 1 71
(Miss J Feilden) *chsd ldrs: rdn 2f out: wknd ins fnl f* **9/1**
3123 **8** *nk* **Bolton Hall (IRE)**[9] 4932 5-10-11 **64**.........................(p) FelixDeGiles(3) 9 60
(R A Fahey) *lost 18l s: sn in rr of main gp due to stdy pce: effrt 2f out: wknd ins fnl f* **15/2**
0500 **9** *5* **Daniel Thomas (IRE)**[25] 4455 5-10-13 **70**.................... MrOJMurphy(7) 5 56
(Mrs A L M King) *hld up: rdn over 2f out: no imp* **20/1**
2m 24.5s (8.36) **Going Correction** +0.175s/f (Good)
WFA 3 from 4yo+ 8lb 9 Ran SP% **116.9**
Speed ratings (Par 103): **76,75,74,73,73 72,72,72,68**
CSF £34.50 CT £96.19 TOTE £5.40: £1.60, £2.70, £1.80; EX 43.20 Place 6 £413.98, Place 5 £110.94.
Owner Edward J Ware **Bred** Hascombe And Valiant Studs **Trained** Newmarket, Suffolk
FOCUS
A modest handicap, confined to amateur riders, that was run at a steady early pace. The form gallop was slow and consequently the form looks dubious.
T/Plt: £172.10 to a £1 stake. Pool: £55,014.55. 233.30 winning tickets. T/Qpdt: £32.70 to a £1 stake. Pool: £4,022.40. 90.95 winning tickets. DO

5126 KEMPTON (A.W) (R-H)
Friday, September 7

OFFICIAL GOING: Standard
Wind: Almost nil Weather: Sunny, warm

5199 CELTIC CONTRACTORS NURSERY 6f (P)
6:20 (6:21) (Class 6) (0-70,70) 2-Y-0 **£2,047** (£604; £302) **Stalls** High

Form RPR
0500 **1** **Asian Power (IRE)**[14] 4776 2-9-4 **67**................................ OscarUrbina 11 70
(P J O'Gorman) *settled in midfield on inner: rdn and prog fr 2f out: styd on wl fnl f to ld last strides* **10/1**
404 **2** *hd* **Wreningham**[22] 4527 2-9-1 **67**...................................... JerryO'Dwyer(3) 6 69
(T Keddy) *led: kicked 2l clr 2f out: looked wnr tl tired last 100yds: hdd fnl strides* **16/1**
0544 **3** *1/2* **The Magic Blanket (IRE)**[5] 5065 2-9-3 **66**..................... MickyFenton 5 67
(Stef Liddiard) *chsd ldr: rdn and no imp 2f out: lost 2nd last 100yds: styd on* **12/1**
2522 **4** *nk* **Natmana**[12] 4844 2-9-7 **70**... DarryllHolland 3 70
(M R Channon) *lw: dwlt: sn trckd ldrs: rdn over 2f out and hanging rt: no real imp tl styd on ins fnl f* **11/4**[1]
5535 **5** *1* **Choisky (IRE)**[17] 4683 2-9-6 **69**... TQuinn 1 66+
(J Akehurst) *racd wd in rr: rdn over 2f out: styd on fr wl over 1f out: nrst fin* **10/1**
0000 **6** *shd* **Tiger's Rocket (IRE)**[4] 5089 2-9-0 **63**................................ RyanMoore 2 60
(R Hannon) *wl in rr and sn pushed along: styd on u.p fr over 1f out: nrst fin* **16/1**
305 **7** *1* **Towy Boy (IRE)**[19] 4629 2-9-4 **67**....................................... JamesDoyle 7 61
(I A Wood) *settled in midfield: pushed along over 2f out: nt clr run wl over 1f out: kpt on fnl f: n.d* **33/1**
1 **8** *3/4* **Little Firecracker**[80] 2738 2-9-5 **68**.................................... PatDobbs 12 59
(L M Cumani) *unf: cl up on inner: rdn wl over 2f out: no prog: fdd fnl f* **11/2**[2]
4500 **9** *1* **Andrasta**[11] 4903 2-9-6 **69**..(p) RichardHughes 4 57
(B J Meehan) *trckd ldrs: hanging and nt qckn over 2f out: losing pl whn n.m.r over 1f out* **25/1**
063 **10** *nk* **No Nines**[106] 1975 2-9-4 **67**.. MichaelHills 8 55
(B W Hills) *dwlt: mostly in last: detached over 2f out: kpt on fnl f* **13/2**[3]
6224 **11** *3* **Alabama Spirit (USA)**[25] 4453 2-9-7 **70**........................ SteveDrowne 9 49
(D Shaw) *awkward s: hld up in rr: effrt on inner 2f out: sn no prog: wknd fnl f* **8/1**
030 **12** *nk* **Keeparryappy (IRE)**[25] 4459 2-9-3 **66**.......................... JimmyFortune 10 44
(K R Burke) *t.k.h: hld up towards rr: pushed along 2f out: no prog: wknd fnl f* **8/1**
1m 13.68s (-0.02) **Going Correction** -0.10s/f (Stan) 12 Ran SP% **122.0**
Speed ratings (Par 93): **96,95,95,94,93 93,91,90,89,89 85,84**
CSF £164.09 CT £1976.92 TOTE £17.00: £4.50, £7.20, £5.20; EX 446.00.
Owner N S Yong **Bred** Luke O'Reilly **Trained** Newmarket, Suffolk
FOCUS
Just a modest nursery but solid-enough form. The winning time was 0.40 seconds slower than the later fillies' maiden.
NOTEBOOK
Asian Power(IRE), although well held on his six previous starts, he had hinted at ability and, dropped significantly in trip and switched to Polytrack for the first time, he landed a bit of a gamble. He responded well to pressure to get up in the shadow of the post and this experience could bring him on again. (op 20-1)
Wreningham was nibbled at in the market on his nursery debut and he ran a blinder in second, just being reeled in late on. His running style is well suited to Kempton and he will be one to keep on-side round here. (op 25-1)
The Magic Blanket(IRE), upped in trip and switched to Polytrack for the first time on his nursery debut, ran right up to his best and can have few excuses. (op 14-1)
Natmana, back up in trip and switched to Polytrack for the first time, did not help his chance by hanging and failed to justify favouritism. Official explanation: jockey said colt hung right (op 7-2)
Choisky(IRE) ran well considering he had the worst draw of all. (op 12-1)
Little Firecracker, bought out of George Moore's yard after winning a weak seller at Thirsk on her debut, found this a lot tougher and was readily held. (op 11-4)

5200 E B F LETCHWORTH COURIERS MAIDEN STKS 1m (P)
6:50 (6:57) (Class 4) 2-Y-0 **£4,695** (£1,397; £698; £348) **Stalls** High

Form RPR
2364 **1** **Ordinance (USA)**[27] 4372 2-9-3 85.. JohnEgan 4 80+
(T G Mills) *lw: hld up bhd ldng pair: led and qcknd over 4f out: mde rest: drvn and styd on wl fnl f* **7/2**[2]
3 **2** *3/4* **Aboriginie (USA)**[27] 4393 2-9-3 0................................... JimmyFortune 8 78
(J H M Gosden) *w'like: athletic: str: disp ld at slow pce to over 4f out: chsd wnr after: rdn and cl enough over 1f out: a hld fnl f* **8/11**[1]
6 **3** *1 3/4* **Formation (USA)**[76] 2885 2-9-3 0..................................... SteveDrowne 11 74
(E A L Dunlop) *bit bkwd: settled in midfield: outpcd and pushed along 1/2-way: prog over 2f out: wnt 3rd and rn green over 1f out: no imp* **33/1**
60 **4** *1 1/4* **Hit The Roof**[14] 4761 2-9-3 0.. RichardHughes 7 71
(R Hannon) *disp ld at slow pce to over 4f out: snatched up sn after: chsd ldng pair to over 1f out: one pce* **16/1**[3]
5 *nk* **Quam Celerrime** 2-9-3 0.. FrankieMcDonald 2 70+
(P A Blockley) *leggy: dwlt: wl in rr: rdn and styd on fr over 2f out: n.d but kpt on* **100/1**
0 **6** *1 1/4* **Wabbraan (USA)**[22] 4540 2-9-3 0..................................... RichardMullen 6 68
(D M Simcock) *reluctant to enter stalls: towards rr: rdn and kpt on fnl 2f: n.d* **66/1**
06 **7** *hd* **Nikolaievich (IRE)**[11] 4876 2-9-3 0..................................... TQuinn 12 67
(P F I Cole) *chsd ldrs: shkn up over 2f out: hanging over 1f out: one pce and no imp* **50/1**

	8 5	**Averoo** 2-9-3 0 TGMcLaughlin 5 (E A L Dunlop) *lw: bit bkwd: s.v.s: wl in rr: brief effrt on inner over 2f out: sn btn* **33/1**	56
	9 1 3/4	**Slip** 2-9-3 0 DarryllHolland 10 (M P Tregoning) *leggy: in tch but rn green: struggling and wknd wl over 2f out* **50/1**	52
	10 9	**St Michael's Mount** 2-9-3 0 PatDobbs 13 (M P Tregoning) *w'like: dwlt: sn trckd ldrs: gng wl enough 3f out: wknd over 2f out* **33/1**	31
	11 9	**Fongster** 2-9-0 0 JerryO'Dwyer(3) 3 (A M Hales) *leggy: angular: reluctant to enter stalls: rel to r and rousted along: in tch to over 3f out: t.o* **100/1**	10
00	12 2 1/2	**Cocktail Shaker (USA)**[23] 4508 2-9-3 0 RobertHavlin 1 (B J Meehan) *a in rr: bhd fnl 3f: t.o* **100/1**	4

1m 41.38s (0.58) **Going Correction** -0.10s/f (Stan) **12** Ran SP% **103.2**
Speed ratings (Par 97): **93,92,90,89,88 87,87,82,80,71 62,60**
CSF £4.57 TOTE £3.50: £1.10, £1.02, £9.20; EX 6.30.
Owner J Daniels **Bred** S Peskoff & Gainesway Thoroughbreds Ltd **Trained** Headley, Surrey
■ Tenjack King (9/2) was withdrawn on vet's advice. Deduct 15p in the £ under Rule 4.
■ Stewards' Enquiry : John Egan two-day ban: careless riding (Sep 18-19)

FOCUS
A fair maiden but the time was modest, so the form has been rated negatively.

NOTEBOOK
Ordinance(USA) looked to becoming a little frustrating, but he was well suited by the step up to 1m on his return maiden company and he proved too strong for the favourite, benefiting from an enterprising ride from Egan, who kicked on around half a mile from the finish. (op 11-4)
Aboriginie(USA) confirmed the promise he showed when third on his debut at Lingfield, but the winner got first run and that proved crucial. He should prove hard to beat in similar company next time. (op Evens)
Formation(USA) showed just modest form on his debut over 7f at Newmarket back in June, but this was a lot more encouraging. He still looked a little backward and there could be more to come. (op 40-1)
Hit The Roof's two outings at Newbury represented just moderate form, but this was a creditable effort. He will have more options now he is qualified for a handicap mark. (op 20-1)
Quam Celerrime, a 65,000euros son of Xaar, half-brother to among others triple sprint winner Joyeaux, looked in need of the experience, but he was noted doing some good late work and should improve a fair bit next time.

5201 E B F PRUDENTIAL MAIDEN FILLIES' STKS 6f (P)
7:20 (7:28) (Class 4) 2-Y-O **£4,695** (£1,397; £698; £348) **Stalls** High

Form			RPR
	1	**Dream Day** 2-9-0 0 RyanMoore 12 (R Hannon) *athletic: lw: led 1f: pressed ldr: led 2f out: rdn and hld on wl fnl f* **9/4**[2]	77+
5	2 hd	**Ceka Dancer (IRE)**[21] 4564 2-9-0 0 RichardMullen 3 (E J O'Neill) *w'like: str: led after 1f: hdd 2f out: drvn to chal fnl f: styd on wl but jst hld* **7/4**[1]	76
	3 2	**Lady Sorcerer** 2-9-0 0 TQuinn 6 (A P Jarvis) *w'like: bit bkwd: trckd ldrs: shkn up and outpcd 2f out: styd on wl again to take 3rd last 75yds* **20/1**	70+
0	4 1	**Tense (IRE)**[14] 4756 2-9-0 0 JimmyFortune 7 (J A Osborne) *w'like: prom: rdn to chse ldng pair 2f out: one pce and no imp over 1f out: lost 3rd last 75yds* **13/2**[3]	67
	5 1 1/4	**Danvers** 2-9-0 0 SteveDrowne 4 (J L Dunlop) *leggy: bit bkwd: s.s: prog fr rr over 3f out: shkn up to chse ldrs over 1f out: fdd ins fnl f* **8/1**	63
	6 3 1/2	**Street Diva (USA)** 2-9-0 0 FrankieMcDonald 10 (P A Blockley) *w'like: s.s: nvr on terms w ldrs: sme late prog* **16/1**	53
0	7 4	**Regal Veil**[12] 4854 2-9-0 0 SaleemGolam 2 (S C Williams) *w'like: bit bkwd: dwlt: rcvrd into midfield: wknd over 1f out* **66/1**	41
0	8 4	**Racey Rachel (IRE)**[22] 4537 2-9-0 0 DarryllHolland 9 (E F Vaughan) *leggy: chsd ldrs: rdn over 2f out: wknd over 1f out* **16/1**	29
0	9 1/2	**Jazz Romance (IRE)**[4] 5097 2-9-0 0 OscarUrbina 1 (D Shaw) *w'like: str: wnt bdly lft s: hanging lft and a bhd* **66/1**	27
06	10 2 1/2	**Albany Becky (IRE)**[4] 5097 2-8-11 0 JerryO'Dwyer(3) 5 (M G Quinlan) *awkward s: chsd ldrs: hrd rdn over 2f out: wknd wl over 1f out* **33/1**	20
	11 1/2	**Faraami (IRE)** 2-9-0 0 PatDobbs 11 (Pat Eddery) *w'like: s.s: v green in last: a wl bhd* **20/1**	18

1m 13.28s (-0.42) **Going Correction** -0.10s/f (Stan) **11** Ran SP% **118.8**
Speed ratings (Par 94): **98,97,95,93,92 87,82,76,76,72 72**
CSF £6.23 TOTE £3.90: £1.50, £1.10, £6.90; EX 7.80.
Owner R Barnett **Bred** W And R Barnett Ltd **Trained** East Everleigh, Wilts

FOCUS
Just a fair fillies' maiden run in a time 0.40 seconds quicker than the earlier 0-70 nursery and the form is ordinary but solid.

NOTEBOOK
Dream Day ◆, a daughter of Oasis Dream, half-sister to quite useful triple 6f-1m winner Sabbeeh, out of the smart dual 7f-1m winner Capistrano Day, who was fourth in the 1000 Guineas, knew her job and proved good enough to make a successful debut. There may not be that much bare improvement to come, but she can still be expected to progress with racing and it would be no surprise to see her develop into a very useful filly in time. (op 7-4 tchd 3-1)
Ceka Dancer(IRE) confirmed the promise she showed on her debut over 7f at Doncaster, and she had sufficient pace to come with the drop in trip, but the Hannon newcomer was too strong. She was clear of the remainder and clearly has the ability to win a similar race. (op 11-4 tchd 11-8)
Lady Sorcerer, a 10,000gns daughter of Diktat, half-sister to Ms Rainbow Runner, a winner over 1m2f at two, out of a dual sprint juvenile scorer, shaped nicely on her racecourse debut. She took a while to respond when first coming under pressure, but there was a lot to like about the way she stayed once finally understanding what was required.
Tense(IRE) improved significantly on the form she showed on her debut over 5f at Bath. She is open to further improvement and could come into her own when handicapped. (op 11-2)
Danvers, a Cape Cross, first foal of a dual 7f winner, showed ability on her racecourse debut and will have learnt plenty from this. She should do well over a little further next year. (op 9-1)
Albany Becky(IRE) Official explanation: jockey said filly lost her action

5202 E B F CELTIC CONTRACTORS FILLIES' CONDITIONS STKS 7f (P)
7:50 (7:54) (Class 3) 2-Y-O **£7,478** (£2,239; £1,119; £560; £279; £140) **Stalls** High

Form			RPR
2	1	**Annie Skates (USA)**[14] 4774 2-8-12 0 JohnEgan 1 (Jane Chapple-Hyam) *w'like: str: lw: t.k.h: trckd ldng pair: shkn up to go 2nd 2f out: led over 1f out: styd on wl* **4/9**[1]	77+
	2 2	**Island Vista** 2-8-12 0 RyanMoore 3 (M A Jarvis) *leggy: chsd ldr to 2f out: styd on to take 2nd again wl ins fnl f: no ch w wnr* **4/1**[2]	72
	3 1/2	**My Aunt Fanny** 2-8-9 0 NeilChalmers(3) 5 (A M Balding) *unf: scope: dwlt: t.k.h and hld up in last pair: outpcd 3f out: green but styd on fnl 2f: snatched 3rd last strides* **20/1**	71
00	4 nk	**Mollyatti**[14] 4784 2-8-12 0 MickyFenton 4 (Miss V Haigh) *w'like: led: rdn and hdd over 1f out: wknd and lost 2 pls last 75yds* **25/1**	70
	5 hd	**Bushy Dell (IRE)** 2-8-9 0 JerryO'Dwyer(3) 7 (Miss J Feilden) *leggy: in tch: effrt over 2f out: styd on fr over 1f out but nvr able to chal* **33/1**	69
	6 7	**Rowan Dancer** 2-8-12 0 SteveDrowne 8 (J R Boyle) *w'like: cl up on inner tl wknd 2f out: eased fnl f* **20/1**	51
	7 1 3/4	**Stones Of Venice (IRE)** 2-8-12 0 OscarUrbina 6 (J R Fanshawe) *leggy: in tch tl wknd rapidly over 2f out* **5/1**[3]	47
	8 2 1/2	**Amouretta** 2-8-12 0 TGMcLaughlin 2 (T T Clement) *w'like: a in rr: wknd over 2f out* **33/1**	40

1m 27.13s (0.33) **Going Correction** -0.10s/f (Stan) **8** Ran SP% **125.2**
Speed ratings (Par 96): **94,91,91,90,90 82,80,77**
CSF £2.79 TOTE £1.50: £1.02, £2.00, £3.60; EX 4.10.
Owner Michael H Watt **Bred** Liberation Farm & Oratis Thoroughbreds **Trained** Newmarket, Suffolk

FOCUS
It is hard to know what to make of this fillies' conditions contest, with the first three home making plenty of appeal, but the fourth, and possibly even the fifth, suggesting the bare form is just ordinary. It would probably be wise to keep an open mind until we learn more.

NOTEBOOK
Annie Skates(USA) confirmed the ability she showed when second of 17 on her debut on the July course, running out a most decisive winner on this switch to sand. Only time will tell what this form is really worth, but she is held in very high regard and may now be aimed at the Prix Marcel Boussac at Longchamp, with her connections hoping the ground will not be too soft. (op 8-13)
Island Vista ◆, a daughter of Montjeu, half-sister to high-class dual 7f juvenile winner Mudeer, dual middle-distance scorer Durable, and multiple middle-distance/staying winner Amir Zaman, has been given an entry in the Fillies' Mile. This was a pleasing debut behind the highly-regarded winner and, with improvement to come, she could pick up a maiden this year, but she is likely to come into her own when tackling further next season and beyond.
My Aunt Fanny, a Nayef half-sister to triple 1m-1m2f winner Kingsholm, out of a useful triple 1m-1m2f scorer, shaped with plenty of promise on her racecourse debut behind a couple of potentially useful fillies, despite showing signs of inexperience. Like the runner-up, she can be expected to improve when sent over further in time. (op 25-1)
Mollyatti's proximity casts doubts over the strength of the form, for having shown ability on her debut at Doncaster, her last run at Thirsk was a poor effort. We should learn more about her now she is qualified for an official mark, but the Handicapper is unlikely to go easy on her.
Bushy Dell(IRE), an 11,000gns daughter of King Charlemagne, and a half-sister to 2m winner Spectested, showed plenty of ability on her racecourse debut. It is hard to say exactly what she achieved, but this was a promising start and she should do better over longer distances in time. (op 50-1)
Stones Of Venice(IRE), a 65,000gns daughter of Barathea, and half-sister to among others high-class German filly Moonlady, a multiple 1m3f-1m6f winner, dropped our rather tamely on her racecourse debut. (op 4-1)

5203 WEATHERBYS PRINTING APPRENTICE H'CAP (FINAL ROUND) 1m (P)
8:20 (8:20) (Class 4) (0-85,82) 3-Y-O+ **£6,232** (£1,866; £933; £467; £233; £117) **Stalls** High

Form			RPR
2051	1	**Officer**[39] 4018 3-8-12 **75** (v) JamieHamblett 4 (Sir Michael Stoute) *t.k.h: led: narrowly hdd jst over 2f out: shkn up and pressed ldr after: styd on to ld last 100yds* **3/1**[1]	83
1313	2 1 1/4	**Le Chiffre (IRE)**[30] 4272 5-8-13 **71** (p) WilliamCarson 2 (S Curran) *b: pressed ldr: effrt to ld narrowly jst over 2f out: kpt on but hdd and hld last 100yds* **9/2**[2]	77
0000	3 nk	**The Snatcher (IRE)**[38] 4049 4-9-8 **80** HaddenFrost 6 (R Hannon) *chsd ldrs: lost pl 1/2-way: effrt again over 2f out: wnt 3rd wl ins fnl f: clsng at fin* **11/2**[3]	85+
0323	4 1	**Tender The Great (IRE)**[13] 4827 4-9-2 **77** KylieManser(3) 5 (B G Powell) *hld up in rr: outpcd over 2f out: shuffled along and kpt on fnl 2f: nvr rchd ldrs* **15/2**	80
0-00	5 1 1/4	**Kingsholm**[113] 1791 5-9-3 **82** DavidProbert(7) 9 (A M Balding) *b.hind: stdd s: hld up: prog to chse clr ldng pair over 3f out: no imp: lost 2 pls ins fnl f* **20/1**	82
6-00	6 1	**Strawberry Lolly**[128] 1414 4-9-4 **76** KirstyMilczarek 7 (M Botti) *in tch: c wd bnd 3f out: outpcd and hung lft over 2f out: no ch after* **14/1**	74
-400	7 hd	**Tempsford Flyer (IRE)**[11] 4889 4-9-4 **76** MCGeran 3 (J W Hills) *t.k.h: chsd ldng pair to over 3f out: outpcd over 2f out: fdd* **15/2**	73
4066	8 shd	**Proper (IRE)**[3] 5122 3-8-2 **70** MatthewDavies(5) 8 (M R Channon) *swtg: chsd ldrs: outpcd on inner wl over 2f out: fdd* **7/1**	66
4603	9 1/2	**Boundless Prospect (USA)**[23] 4496 8-8-10 **68** JackMitchell 1 (Miss Gay Kelleway) *t.k.h: hld up in last: wd bnd over 3f out: no prog sn after* **12/1**	64

1m 39.36s (-1.44) **Going Correction** -0.10s/f (Stan)
WFA 3 from 4yo+ 5lb **9** Ran SP% **113.7**
Speed ratings (Par 105): **103,101,101,100,99 98,98,97,97**
CSF £15.94 CT £69.73 TOTE £4.20: £1.20, £1.50, £1.90; EX 9.00.
Owner Cheveley Park Stud **Bred** Cheveley Park Stud Ltd **Trained** Newmarket, Suffolk

FOCUS
A fair handicap restricted to apprentices who had not ridden more than 25 winners. The form is rated at face value through the runner-up.

5204 CASHSCORE H'CAP 2m (P)
8:50 (8:51) (Class 5) (0-70,70) 4-Y-O+ **£2,914** (£867; £433; £216) **Stalls** High

Form			RPR
2003	1	**Critical Stage (IRE)**[32] 3969 8-8-7 **61** HaddenFrost(5) 1 (J D Frost) *sn cl up: in ldng trio after 6f: led over 2f out: drvn and hld on fnl f* **8/1**	70
-101	2 nk	**Dhehdaah**[48] 2887 6-9-7 **70** MickyFenton 12 (Mrs P Sly) *hld up towards rr: prog 5f out: rdn to chse wnr 2f out: no imp tl clsd grad fnl f: jst hld* **4/1**[2]	78
2200	3 2 1/2	**Teorban (POL)**[123] 1526 8-8-10 **59** ow3 StephenDonohoe 14 (Mrs N S Evans) *chsd ldr 5f: styd prom: rdn fr 5f out: kpt on wl u.p fr over 2f out* **33/1**	64
2640	4 1	**Carlton Scroop (FR)**[94] 2332 4-8-2 **58** MCGeran(7) 10 (J Jay) *reluctant to enter stalls: hld up in rr: prog over 4f out: chsd ldrs 2f out: hung rt and nt qckn sn after* **15/2**	62
0063	5 3/4	**Follow On**[30] 4297 5-8-5 **54** RichardMullen 7 (A P Jarvis) *dwlt: sn wl plcd: rdn and chsng ldrs over 2f out: limited rspnse and no imp* **11/2**[3]	57

06 **6** *10* **Dream Mountain**[57] 3457 4-7-10 **52**..........................(p) SophieDoyle(7) 9 43
(Ms J S Doyle) *t.k.h: cl up on inner: lost pl over 3f out: bmpd along and n.d after* **25/1**

2430 **7** *nk* **Dark Parade (ARG)**[32] 3273 6-8-11 **65**........................ JamieJones(5) 11 56
(G L Moore) *wl in rr: detached fr main gp and struggling 4f out: plugged on* **8/1**

-002 **8** *hd* **Ardent Prince**[18] 4670 4-8-7 **56**.. TQuinn 5 47
(Heather Dalton) *t.k.h: led to over 2f out: wknd rapidly* **16/1**

24-2 **9** *shd* **Land Of Light**[10] 4917 4-9-4 **67**.. RyanMoore 13 58
(G L Moore) *b: settled in midfield: effrt over 4f out: chsng ldrs over 2f out: sn wknd* **7/2**[1]

2025 **10** *13* **Galantos (GER)**[109] 1888 6-8-4 **53**............................. FrankieMcDonald 4 28
(Jane Southcombe) *nvr gng wl: reminder after 5f: struggling fr 1/2-way* **8/1**

0224 **11** *14* **Daring Racer (GER)**[44] 3858 4-9-0 **63**................................. IanMongan 6 21
(S Dow) *lw: chsd ldr after 5f to over 3f out: wknd rapidly: t.o* **16/1**

000- **12** *12* **Our Choice (IRE)**[328] 5971 5-8-9 **58**............................... RichardHughes 2 2
(C J Mann) *wl in tch tl wknd rapidly over 4f: sn eased and t.o* **25/1**

-600 **13** *6* **Versatile**[166] 775 4-8-9 **58**...(t) OscarUrbina 8 —
(G A Ham) *in tch tl wknd rapidly 6f out: t.o* **50/1**

3m 28.01s (-3.39) **Going Correction** -0.10s/f (Stan) **13** Ran SP% **127.1**
Speed ratings (Par 103): **104,103,102,102,101 96,96,96,96,89 82,76,73**
CSF £41.33 CT £1049.21 TOTE £9.10: £2.00, £1.50, £13.40; EX 55.60.
Owner Le Rochjobi Partnership **Bred** Park Place International Ltd **Trained** Scorriton, Devon

FOCUS
A modest staying handicap and solid form with the winner to his winter course and distance mark backed up by the runner-up.
Land Of Light Official explanation: jockey said gelding hung right throughout
Galantos(GER) Official explanation: jockey said gelding did not face the kickback

5205 MICHAEL O'LEARY H'CAP 1m 3f (P)
9:20 (9:20) (Class 3) (0-90,88) 3-Y-0+
£6,855 (£2,052; £1,026; £513; £256; £128) **Stalls** High

Form RPR

4320 **1** **Coeur De Lionne (IRE)**[15] 4749 3-9-2 **86**....................... SteveDrowne 5 99+
(R Charlton) *lw: trckd ldng pair: prog to ld jst over 2f out: hung lft over 1f out: rdn and wl in command fnl f* **3/1**[2]

3501 **2** *1 ½* **Boot 'n Toot**[10] 4917 6-8-10 **77** 6ex.................................. PatrickHills(5) 7 84
(C A Cyzer) *hld up in rr: smooth prog 3f out: chsd wnr 2f out: sn rdn and no imp* **16/1**

0610 **3** *1 ½* **Invasian (IRE)**[17] 4690 6-9-11 **87**....................................(e) RobertHavlin 4 92
(P W D'Arcy) *led at decent pce: rdn and hdd jst over 2f out: no ch w ldng pair after: kpt on* **14/1**

1-00 **4** *shd* **Tommy Toogood (IRE)**[13] 4814 4-9-8 **84**......................... MichaelHills 8 89
(B W Hills) *t.k.h: hld up in tch: cl up over 2f out: sn rdn and one pce* **16/1**

1464 **5** *1 ¾* **Spiderback (IRE)**[7] 5006 3-8-9 **79**.............................. RichardHughes 2 81
(R Hannon) *stdd s: hld up in last trio: effrt 3f out: hanging and nt qckn 2f out: kpt on same pce* **13/2**

2103 **6** *½* **Multicultural**[112] 1819 4-8-12 **74** oh1............................ RichardMullen 3 75
(D M Simcock) *lw: mostly in last: rdn over 3f out: kpt on one pce fnl 2f: n.d* **14/1**

3101 **7** *1 ¾* **Chord**[8] 4976 3-8-12 **82** 6ex...(v) RyanMoore 9 80
(Sir Michael Stoute) *lw: chsd ldrs but nvr gng wl: u.p over 4f out: struggling over 2f out* **15/8**[1]

5252 **8** *3 ½* **I Have Dreamed (IRE)**[11] 4888 5-9-12 **88**...............................(b) TQuinn 1 80
(T G Mills) *hld up in tch: rdn and no rspnse over 2f out: sn wknd* **4/1**[3]

6000 **9** *3* **Mahmjra**[25] 4458 5-8-13 **75**.. StephenDonohoe 6 62
(C N Allen) *chsd ldr to 3f out: wknd* **50/1**

2m 19.22s (-3.46) **Going Correction** -0.10s/f (Stan)
WFA 3 from 4yo+ 8lb **9** Ran SP% **120.2**
Speed ratings (Par 107): **108,106,105,105,104 104,102,100,98**
CSF £51.93 CT £598.73 TOTE £4.40: £1.60, £2.30, £3.60; EX 58.30.
Owner Mountgrange Stud **Bred** Hawthorn Villa Stud **Trained** Beckhampton, Wilts

FOCUS
A good middle-distance handicap and decent form for the grade backed up by a sound gallop.

NOTEBOOK
Coeur De Lionne(IRE) ◆ had been winless on turf since landing his maiden over course and distance back in April, but the return to Polytrack did the trick. This was a very useful effort and he looks well worth persevering with on sand. (tchd 11-4)
Boot 'n Toot has not always been the most consistent, but she returned to form when winning over 1m5f at Lingfield on her previous start and this was another good effort behind a very useful type, especially considering she as 2lb wrong under her penalty. (tchd 18-1)
Invasian(IRE) looks high enough in the weights now, but this track has been suiting front runners lately and he ran up to his best in third.
Tommy Toogood(IRE) ran a creditable race and has yet to finish out of the first four on sand. (op 14-1)
Spiderback(IRE) struggled to land a telling blow and it would be no surprise to see him connections reach for the headgear again at some point. (op 10-1 tchd 11-1)
Chord was 3lb well-in under the penalty he picked up for his recent Wolverhampton success, but he failed to run his race. Perhaps he just a better horse at Dunstall Park. (op 7-4 tchd 2-1)
I Have Dreamed(IRE) was 2lb lower than in future, but he is beginning to look a difficult ride and was well beaten this time. (op 9-2 tchd 3-1)
T/Plt: £255.80 to a £1 stake. Pool: £66,449.50. 189.60 winning tickets. T/Qpdt: £7.10 to a £1 stake. Pool: £7,400.40. 764.20 winning tickets. JN

4761 NEWBURY (L-H)
Friday, September 7

OFFICIAL GOING: Good to firm (7.7)
Wind: moderate, half-behind

5206 AXMINSTER CARPETS E B F MAIDEN STKS 1m (S)
1:50 (1:52) (Class 4) 2-Y-0 **£6,477** (£1,927; £963; £481) **Stalls** High

Form RPR

3 **1** **Alfathaa**[18] 4656 2-9-3 0.. MartinDwyer 11 90+
(W J Haggas) *w'like: lw: trckd ldr: led ins fnl 2f: c clr fnl f: easily* **8/1**[2]

5 **2** *5* **Slam**[20] 4598 2-9-3 0... RichardHughes 8 79+
(B W Hills) *unf: scope: stdd s: plld hrd in mid-div: shake up and hdwy 2f out: chsd wnr over 1f out but nvr any imp and one pce* **1/2**[1]

3 *1 ¾* **Mushtaaq (USA)** 2-9-3 0.. MichaelHills 1 74+
(M A Jarvis) *w'like: str: bit bkwd: chsd ldrs: pushed along 3f out: styd on fnl 2f but nvr gng pce to be competitive* **25/1**

4 *2* **Love Galore (IRE)** 2-9-3 0.. GregFairley 5 70
(M Johnston) *w'like: scope: str: swtg: led: pushed along 3f out: hdd ins fnl 2f: wknd fnl f* **8/1**[2]

5 *2* **Daddy's Boy** 2-9-3 0.. JimCrowley 3 65
(Mrs A J Perrett) *tall: scope: bit bkwd: s.i.s: sn in tch: pushed along 3f out: styd on fr over 1f out but nvr in contention* **66/1**

6 *½* **Mashrai (IRE)** 2-9-3 0.. DarryllHolland 4 64
(M R Channon) *leggy: chsd ldrs: rdn 3f out: wknd fr 2f out* **33/1**

7 *¾* **General Tufto** 2-9-3 0.. SteveDrowne 6 62+
(R Charlton) *unf: scope: bit bkwd: slowly away: a bhd* **50/1**

5 **8** *4* **Dusk**[28] 4362 2-9-3 0... KerrinMcEvoy 12 53
(J L Dunlop) *w'like: chsd ldrs: rdn 3f out: wknd over 2f out* **8/1**[2]

0 **9** *2 ½* **Ice Choice (IRE)**[11] 4875 2-8-9 0.................................. DominicFox(3) 10 42
(Mark Gillard) *w'like: chsd ldrs: rdn over 3f out: wknd qckly 2f out* **125/1**

10 *12* **Opera Prince** 2-9-3 0... JamieSpencer 13 20
(S Kirk) *unf: leggy: hld up in rr: wknd and lost tch over 1f out* **16/1**[3]

1m 40.05s (-0.57) **Going Correction** -0.225s/f (Firm) **10** Ran SP% **116.9**
Speed ratings (Par 97): **93,88,86,84,82 81,81,77,74,62**
CSF £12.26 TOTE £7.80: £2.00, £1.02, £5.20; EX 14.80.
Owner Hamdan Al Maktoum **Bred** Miss G Abbey **Trained** Newmarket, Suffolk

FOCUS
This looked like quite a good maiden beforehand, but they finished surprisingly well strung out considering the early pace was pretty steady, suggesting a few of these are probably longer-term prospects, although the form should be at least this good. They raced against the stands'-side rail.

NOTEBOOK
Alfathaa ◆ shaped nicely in what looked an above-average maiden at Leicester over 7f on his debut and he confirmed that promise with a pretty impressive display to get off the mark at the second attempt, proving well suited by this longer trip. Having tracked the early leader for much of the way, he picked up well off the modest gallop to pull nicely clear of his nine rivals, despite still displaying signs of greenness. He has a really powerful action when in full flight, but he galloped like a horse still very much learning what the game is all about - he also pricked his ears near the finish - and there should be a lot more to come as he gains further experience. He promises to progress into a smart three-year-old, but may not be finished with for the year just yet and he holds entries in both the Royal Lodge and the Racing Post Trophy. (op 7-1)
Slam had shaped really well when a running-on fifth on his debut in a 7f Listed race here, but he was too keen for his own good this time stepped up in trip. The steady gallop was totally against him and, having been left with plenty to do when the pace finally quickened, he never really looked like getting to the winner. There is no getting away from the encouragement of his first run, but he will need to learn to settle better in future. (op 8-13)
Mushtaaq(USA), a Dynaformer colt, half-brother to among others Mahara, a useful 1m4f winner in France, out of a decent 1m2f scorer, has been given an entry in the Royal Lodge and he shaped with some promise in third. He stuck on at the one pace after coming under pressure a little way from the finish and should come into his own over further next year. (op 22-1)
Love Galore(IRE), a Galileo colt, half-brother to nine winners, notably very smart multiple 7f winner at two and three Lil's Jessy, has been given an entry in the Group 2 Beresford Stakes. He was left alone up front, but was a touch keen through the first furlong or so and could only find the one pace once let down. (op 12-1)
Daddy's Boy ◆, a gelded son of Selkirk, half-brother to triple 1m winner Pretence, was caught a little wide towards the back of the pace for much of the way, but he was noted keeping on near the finish. He can build on this.
Mashrai(IRE), a 55,000gns son of Dubai Destination, first foal of a dual middle-distance winner, has no fancy entries. This was a respectable debut and he is open to improvement.
General Tufto ◆, a son of Fantastic Light, out of 6f juvenile winner who later scored over 1m, was still last with two furlongs left to run, but he gradually got the hang of the things and was keeping on in the closing stages. He should be capable of a lot better in time.
Dusk was well below the form he showed on his debut at Newmarket and was disappointing. (op 7-1)

5207 JAMES COWPER NURSERY 6f 8y
2:20 (2:23) (Class 4) (0-85,84) 2-Y-0 **£4,533** (£1,348; £674; £336) **Stalls** High

Form RPR

3132 **1** **Gross Prophet**[8] 4975 2-9-0 **80**............................ RichardKingscote(3) 5 88
(Tom Dascombe) *lw: sn led: hdd 3f out: rdn and outpcd 2f out: rallied styd on over 1f out to regain slt ld fnl 100yds: all out* **8/1**

3100 **2** *nk* **Silver Wind**[17] 4695 2-9-2 **79**.......................................(b) JimmyFortune 8 86
(P D Evans) *chsd ldrs: led 3f out: rdn and hung lft 2f out: hdd last half f: rallied gamely: no ex nr fin* **14/1**

0053 **3** *2* **Fervent Prince**[11] 4903 2-8-10 **73**.................................... SteveDrowne 4 74
(H Morrison) *swtg: in tch: hdwy to press ldrs 2f out: kpt on fnl f but nvr gng pce of ldng duo* **7/1**

5514 **4** *½* **River Bounty**[14] 4762 2-8-8 **71**... JamieSpencer 3 71
(A P Jarvis) *chsd ldrs: rdn 2f out: styd on same pce fnl f* **11/2**[3]

001 **5** *¾* **Harry Gee**[15] 4733 2-9-3 **80**... RichardMullen 6 77
(W R Muir) *in rr: drvn along fr 4f out: styd on appr fnl f and gng on cl home but nvr gng pce to be competitive* **25/1**

5201 **6** *nk* **Hobson**[19] 4629 2-9-0 **77**.. StephenCarson 9 73
(Eve Johnson Houghton) *s.i.s: hld up in rr: rapid hdwy 2f out to chse ldrs 1f out: wknd last half f* **16/1**

3221 **7** *hd* **Nawaaff**[34] 4174 2-9-7 **84**... DarryllHolland 1 80
(M R Channon) *towards rr but in tch: hrd drvn and effrt over 2f out: nvr gng pce to rch ldrs and styd on same pce* **8/1**

531 **8** *hd* **Good Gorsoon (USA)**[14] 4755 2-9-7 **84**.......................... MichaelHills 7 79
(B W Hills) *hld up in rr: rapid hdwy to chse ldrs jst ins fnl f: wknd qckly fnl 100yds* **7/2**[1]

425 **9** *nk* **Blues Minor (IRE)**[13] 4810 2-8-11 **74**............................... RyanMoore 2 68
(R Hannon) *chsd ldrs: rdn over 2f out: wknd fnl f* **12/1**

4130 **10** *7* **Rocking**[21] 4573 2-9-1 **81**..(b[1]) LiamJones(3) 11 54
(W J Haggas) *s.i.s: sn rcvrd and in tch: rdn over 2f out: wknd fnl f* **25/1**

5231 **11** *1 ½* **Ramatni**[7] 4995 2-9-0 **77** 6ex... GregFairley 10 46
(M Johnston) *lw: chsd ldrs: rdn over 2f out: sn btn* **5/1**[2]

1m 13.5s (-0.82) **Going Correction** -0.225s/f (Firm) **11** Ran SP% **116.9**
Speed ratings (Par 97): **96,95,92,92,91 90,90,90,89,80 78**
CSF £113.55 CT £818.00 TOTE £9.90: £2.60, £3.90, £3.80; EX 120.50.
Owner Alan Solomon **Bred** A D Solomon **Trained** Lambourn, Berks

FOCUS
A good, competitive nursery and, with the pace decent throughout, the form looks solid. They raced up the middle of the track through the early stages, but were spread out all over the place at the line.

NOTEBOOK
Gross Prophet was 2lb higher than when second at Wolverhampton on his previous start, but he improved on that form with a determined effort, battling back well to get the better of Silver Wind after leading to halfway and then getting outpaced. He has been kept busy lately, but is clearly a tough sort and there should be more to come.
Silver Wind had lost his way since winning a novice event at Folkestone earlier in the year, but he had been given a bit of a chance by the Handicapper and returned to his best with blinkers replacing the visor. He seemed to be hanging slightly under pressure, but it did not cost him any momentum. (op 20-1)
Fervent Prince, who looked unlucky at Warwick on his previous start, lost an off-fore shoe at the start and may be a little bit better than he was able to show. Official explanation: jockey said colt hung left (op 9-2)

River Bounty looked to run to the same sort of form she showed when fourth in a similar event over course and distance on her previous start. (op 6-1 tchd 5-1)
Harry Gee seemed to find this trip on the short side, which is a little surprising considering he had the pace to win round Chester and there is plenty of speed in his pedigree. (tchd 28-1)
Hobson, on his toes beforehand, found this tougher than the Bath maiden he won on his previous start. (op 20-1 tchd 22-1)
Good Gorsoon(USA), the winner of a Bath maiden on his previous start, was the slowest to find his stride and met trouble two furlongs from the finish. He began to pick up when switched into the clear, but his effort petered out rather tamely near the line and it is interesting to note he suffered from a breathing problem on his debut. (op 4-1)
Ramatni was 3lb well-in under the penalty she picked up for winning at Hamilton on her previous start, but she failed to run her race. (op 9-2)

5208 CHRISTAL CONSTRUCTION MANAGEMENT H'CAP 1m 2f 6y
2:55 (2:56) (Class 3) (0-90,90) 3-Y-O **£7,124** (£2,119; £1,059; £529) **Stalls** Centre

Form RPR
2602 1 **Gulf Express (USA)**[20] 4603 3-9-0 **86** RyanMoore 8 96+
(Sir Michael Stoute) *hld up in rr: stdy hdwy fr 3f out: drvn and qcknd to ld jst ins fnl f: r.o strly* **15/8**[1]
3240 2 1 3/4 **Warm Embraces (IRE)**[13] 4799 3-8-6 **78** TQuinn 5 84
(D R C Elsworth) *mid-div: hdwy 3f out: drvn to ld over 1f out: hdd jst ins fnl f: kpt on same pce* **5/1**[3]
2023 3 1 **King Charles**[13] 4814 3-9-4 **90** JimmyFortune 6 94
(E A L Dunlop) *chsd ldrs: drvn to chal 2f out: kpt on same pce ins fnl f* **4/1**[2]
4000 4 shd **Opera Music**[56] 3480 3-8-12 **84** JamieSpencer 7 88
(S Kirk) *hld up in rr: stl wl off pce 3f out: hdwy over 1f out: kpt on wl thrght fnl f but nt rch ldrs* **12/1**
3500 5 1/2 **Eager Igor (USA)**[23] 4510 3-8-5 **77** RichardMullen 2 80
(Eve Johnson Houghton) *chsd ldrs: rdn 3f out: one pce fr over 1f out* **20/1**
4665 6 2 **Woodcraft**[40] 4004 3-8-5 **77** MartinDwyer 4 76
(B W Hills) *swtg: chsd ldr: led 3f out: hdd over 1f out: wknd ins fnl f* **10/1**
4531 7 3/4 **Shake On It**[8] 4960 3-8-8 **80** 6ex (t) StephenCarson 3 77
(Eve Johnson Houghton) *hld up towards rr: hdwy 3f out: chsd ldrs and n.m.r 2f out: wknd fnl f* **8/1**
0002 8 3 1/2 **Noticeable (IRE)**[7] 4993 3-8-8 **80** DarryllHolland 1 70
(M R Channon) *led: hdd 3f out: wknd fr 2f out* **17/2**
02-0 9 22 **Minos (IRE)**[7] 5014 3-8-8 **80** RichardHughes 9 26
(R Hannon) *t.k.h: racd on outside tl wknd qckly 3f out* **33/1**

2m 8.25s (-0.46) **Going Correction** +0.10s/f (Good) **9 Ran SP% 117.6**
Speed ratings (Par 105): **105,103,102,102,102 100,100,97,79**
CSF £11.60 CT £34.15 TOTE £2.80: £1.50, £1.80, £1.50; EX 14.30.
Owner Saeed Suhail **Bred** Gracefield And Brad Ray **Trained** Newmarket, Suffolk

FOCUS
A decent three-year-old handicap run at a fair pace. The winning time was 2.06 seconds quicker than the later 71-85 fillies' contest and the form looks reasonable rated around the third and fifth.

NOTEBOOK
Gulf Express(USA) stepped up on the form he showed when second in a slightly muddling event over course and distance on his previous start with a decisive success. The return to quick ground posed him no problems at all and he picked up in good style from off the pace to win going away. He is a typical Sir Michael Stoute improver and has to be kept on-side. (op 7-4 tchd 2-1 in places)
Warm Embraces(IRE) could not hold off the winner's strong challenge, but he stuck on well to take second and this was a solid effort in defeat. He again shaped as though he will stay further. (op 6-1)
King Charles continues to run well in defeat, but he does not have much in hand of the Handicapper. (tchd 7-2)
Opera Music ◆, last year's Horris Hill fourth, had shown very little in the face of some stiff tasks so far this year, but he has been gelded since he was last seen and this was a very promising return from almost two months off the track. Trying his furthest trip to date, he was held up last of all for much of the way, but ran on nicely past beaten horses close home and this should have provided him with a nice confidence boost. He was racing off a mark 13lb lower than at the beginning of the year and could be one to look out for in the coming weeks. (op 14-1)
Eager Igor(USA) has lost his way a touch lately and his pedigree suggests he may appreciate a return to shorter trips. (op 25-1)
Shake On It was 2lb well-in under the penalty he picked up for winning at Lingfield on his previous start, but he was not at his best, even allowing for him being a little short of room with two furlongs left to run. (op 15-2)
Noticeable(IRE) could not take advantage of a mark 2lb lower than in future. Official explanation: jockey said colt hung left (op 14-1 tchd 16-1 in places)
Minos(IRE) was due to be dropped 6lb. Official explanation: jockey said colt stopped quickly (op 40-1)

5209 INKERMAN LONDON H'CAP 6f 8y
3:30 (3:30) (Class 3) (0-95,95) 3-Y-O+ **£7,124** (£2,119; £1,059; £529) **Stalls** High

Form RPR
0552 1 **Beaver Patrol (IRE)**[25] 4456 5-9-6 **95** (v1) StephenCarson 5 108
(Eve Johnson Houghton) *mde virtually all: rdn and kpt on gamely fr over 1f out* **9/2**[2]
2121 2 1 3/4 **Genki (IRE)**[27] 4374 3-9-2 **93** SteveDrowne 8 101
(R Charlton) *lw: hld up towards rr: drvn and gd hdwy fr 2f out to chse wnr ins fnl f but a readily hld* **15/8**[1]
2002 3 3/4 **Ceremonial Jade (UAE)**[27] 4401 4-9-1 **90** (t) OscarUrbina 1 96
(M Botti) *b: lw: chsd ldrs: rdn to go 2nd wl over 1f out but no imp: one pce and dropped to 3rd ins fnl f* **15/2**
0200 4 3/4 **Go On Be A Tiger (USA)**[20] 4601 3-8-9 **86** DarryllHolland 2 89
(M R Channon) *in rr: rdn and hdwy over 2f out: kpt on fnl f but nvr gng pce to be competitive* **25/1**
6426 5 1/2 **Obe Gold**[25] 4456 5-8-10 **85** (v) RichardHughes 4 87
(M R Channon) *chsd ldrs: rdn 3f out: outpcd 2f out: kpt on again ins fnl f but nvr gng pce to be competitive* **11/1**
1201 6 3 **Barney McGrew (IRE)**[21] 4585 4-8-13 **88** JimmyFortune 7 81
(J A R Toller) *chsd ldrs: rdn 3f out: wknd ins fnl 2f* **17/2**
1000 7 hd **My Gacho (IRE)**[27] 4389 5-8-4 **82** (b) LiamJones(3) 3 74
(T D Barron) *chsd wnr: chal 3f out to 2f out: wknd over 1f out* **14/1**
5543 8 3 1/2 **Greenslades**[13] 4806 8-9-3 **92** RyanMoore 6 74
(P J Makin) *in rr: rdn over 2f out: no rspnse* **6/1**[3]
5503 9 2 1/2 **The Kiddykid (IRE)**[7] 4990 7-8-11 **86** TGMcLaughlin 9 60
(P D Evans) *sn rdn and bhd* **12/1**

1m 11.83s (-2.49) **Going Correction** -0.225s/f (Firm)
WFA 3 from 4yo+ 2lb **9 Ran SP% 116.1**
Speed ratings (Par 107): **107,104,103,102,102 98,97,93,89**
CSF £13.40 CT £62.00 TOTE £5.40: £1.70, £1.10, £3.70; EX 12.10.
Owner G C Stevens **Bred** Kevin B Lynch **Trained** Blewbury, Oxon

FOCUS
Not that big a field for a sprint, but this still a decent enough contest and seems sound enough rated through the third. They raced up the middle early on, but were spread out across the track at the line.

NOTEBOOK
Beaver Patrol(IRE), who ran a blinder in first-time blinkers when fifth in the Stewards' Cup two starts previously but was a beaten favourite without the headgear at Windsor last time, took well to the fitting of a visor and ran out a clear-cut winner. This was a good effort, but this is the highest mark he has ever won off and, with the headgear no sure thing to work as well in future, he appeals as one to take on next time. He is entered in the Ayr Gold Cup, but has picked up a 5lb penalty. (tchd 5-1 in places)
Genki(IRE), racing off a mark 7lb higher than when winning the Shergar Cup Sprint at Ascot on his previous start, ran on well from the back of the back when switched towards the stands' rail, but he was always being held by Beaver Patrol, who was lit up by a first-time visor. A highly-progressive young sprinter, he is very much one to keep on the right side of and, like the winner, he is entered in the Ayr Gold Cup, although he is not sure to make the cut. (op 2-1 tchd 11-4)
Ceremonial Jade(UAE), having his first run over a trip this short, travelled like the winner just in behind Beaver Patrol for much of the way, but he looked to be hanging slightly and did not find as much as expected once let down. (op 8-1)
Go On Be A Tiger(USA), dropping back to 6f for the first time, kept on towards the far side of the track in the closing stages, but he could make no real impression and continues to underachieve. (op 33-1)
Obe Gold did not run badly, but his frustrating losing run continues. (op 16-1)
My Gacho(IRE) Official explanation: jockey said gelding reared as stalls openend
Greenslades could not build on the promise of his recent Goodwood third. Official explanation: jockey said horse was never travelling (op 8-1 tchd 11-2)

5210 NEWBURY GROUNDSTAFF FILLIES' H'CAP 1m 2f 6y
4:05 (4:05) (Class 4) (0-85,84) 3-Y-O+ **£4,857** (£1,445; £722; £360) **Stalls** Centre

Form RPR
4316 1 **Viva La Flag (USA)**[20] 4603 3-9-2 **79** (t) JimmyFortune 8 89
(J L Dunlop) *trckd ldrs: chal 2f out: sn led: drvn 2l clr 1f out: hld on wl* **12/1**
0324 2 nk **Ronaldsay**[12] 4849 3-9-7 **84** RichardHughes 11 94+
(R Hannon) *hld up in rr: sme hdwy whn hmpd 2f out: swtchd to qckn through gap ins fnl f: r.o strly fnl 100yds* **9/2**[2]
6535 3 1 1/4 **Voliere**[18] 4665 4-9-4 **74** KerrinMcEvoy 10 81
(S C Williams) *hld up in rr: swtchd rt to outside 2f out: rdn: hdwy and hung lft ins fnl f and sn chsng wnr: no imp and lost 2nd nr fin* **14/1**
0034 4 nk **Going To Work (IRE)**[55] 3555 3-8-10 **73** TQuinn 9 79
(D R C Elsworth) *t.k.h in rr: hdwy 3f out: drvn to chse ldrs ins fnl 2f: one pce fnl f* **12/1**
6146 5 3/4 **Arabian Treasure (USA)**[53] 3591 3-8-10 **73** RyanMoore 2 78
(Sir Michael Stoute) *lw: t.k.h: chsd ldr: drvn to chal appr fnl 2f: outpcd ins fnl f* **4/1**[1]
-105 6 1/2 **Royal Fantasy (IRE)**[27] 4404 4-9-3 **73** OscarUrbina 7 77
(J R Fanshawe) *swtg: hld up in rr: hdwy on outside fr 3f out: styng on whn hmpd jst ins fnl f: nt rcvr* **13/2**
3011 7 hd **Gib (IRE)**[43] 3871 3-8-10 **73** MichaelHills 5 77
(B W Hills) *swtg: led tl hdd jst ins fnl 2f: wknd fnl f* **7/1**
504/ 8 shd **Capitana (GER)**[20] 3195 6-9-8 **78** SteveDrowne 6 81
(N J Henderson) *in tch: rdn to chse ldrs 2f out: one pce whn hmpd jst ins fnl f: nvr in contention after* **5/1**[3]
0-26 9 1 **Josephine Malines**[40] 3992 3-9-0 **77** DaneO'Neill 4 78
(C G Cox) *chsd ldrs: rdn 3f out: wknd ins fnl 2f* **12/1**
-520 10 18 **Home Sweet Home (IRE)**[37] 4060 4-9-9 **79** DarryllHolland 3 44
(L M Cumani) *in rr: shkn up and effrt 3f out: little rspnse and sn dropped away* **9/1**

2m 10.31s (1.60) **Going Correction** +0.10s/f (Good)
WFA 3 from 4yo+ 7lb **10 Ran SP% 120.4**
Speed ratings (Par 102): **97,96,95,95,94 94,94,94,93,79**
CSF £67.52 CT £785.56 TOTE £15.20: £3.90, £1.50, £3.90; EX 94.70.
Owner Phipps Stable **Bred** Phipps Stable **Trained** Arundel, W Sussex
■ Stewards' Enquiry : Kerrin McEvoy one-day ban: careless riding (Sep 18)

FOCUS
A fair fillies' handicap on paper, but they went a steady pace for much of the way, resulting in something of a sprint finish, and the form, rated around the third and fourth, wants treating with a little caution. The winning time was 2.06 seconds slower than the earlier 76-90.
Going To Work(IRE) Official explanation: jockey said filly hung right
Arabian Treasure(USA) Official explanation: jockey said filly ran too free

5211 G4S APPRENTICE H'CAP 1m 4f 5y
4:35 (4:35) (Class 5) (0-75,73) 3-Y-O+ **£3,071** (£906; £453) **Stalls** Centre

Form RPR
2000 1 **Mister Right (IRE)**[18] 4667 6-9-11 **70** AshleyHamblett(3) 2 77+
(D J S Ffrench Davis) *lw: s.i.s: in rr: stdy hdwy fr 6f out: chal over 3f out: led wl over 2f out: rdn and styd on wl fnl f* **9/2**[3]
3040 2 1 **Love Always**[11] 4909 5-9-9 **70** JamieHamblett(5) 3 75
(S Dow) *swtg: led after 1f: hdd wl over 2f out: styd chsng wnr and kpt on fnl f but a hld* **8/1**
0604 3 nk **Prime Number (IRE)**[36] 4108 5-9-11 **67** RichardKingscote 4 72
(J Akehurst) *led 1f: styd chsng ldr: rdn and effrt 3f out: kpt on same pce fnl f* **5/1**
0532 4 2 **Pretty Demanding (IRE)**[12] 4843 3-9-8 **73** JamieMoriarty 6 74+
(M G Quinlan) *hld up in tch: riddn and effrt over 2f out: nvr gng pce to rch ldrs and sn outpcd* **5/2**[1]
3252 5 3 1/2 **Sharmy (IRE)**[33] 4200 11-9-1 **57** GregFairley 5 53
(Ian Williams) *chsd ldrs: rdn 3f out: wknd ins fnl 2f* **8/1**
0-31 6 4 **Darghan (IRE)**[29] 4340 7-9-8 **64** LiamJones 1 53
(W J Musson) *lw: rdn 3f out: a in rr* **11/4**[2]

2m 41.09s (5.10) **Going Correction** +0.10s/f (Good)
WFA 3 from 5yo+ 9lb **6 Ran SP% 112.3**
Speed ratings (Par 103): **87,86,86,84,82 79**
CSF £37.84 TOTE £5.30: £2.20, £4.60; EX 32.70 Place 6 £190.19, Place 5 £143.74..
Owner Miss A Jones **Bred** Joe Rogers **Trained** Lambourn, Berks

FOCUS
A modest middle-distance handicap restricted to apprentices who had not ridden more than 50 winners. The pace was just ordinary and the form looks doubtful rated around then placed horses.
T/Plt: £280.10 to a £1 stake. Pool: £62,025.85. 161.60 winning tickets. T/Qpdt: £73.00 to a £1 stake. Pool: £3,667.10. 37.15 winning tickets. ST

5192 HAYDOCK (L-H)

Saturday, September 8

OFFICIAL GOING: Good to firm (good in places; 7.9)

Many trainers and jockeys felt the ground was much softer than the official description and thought the track had been overwatered. Times backed this up.

Wind: Light, half-against Weather: Overcast

5212 BETFREDBINGO BE FRIENDLY H'CAP 5f

2:05 (2:06) (Class 2) (0-100,102) 3-Y-O+

£18,696 (£5,598; £2,799; £1,401; £699; £351) **Stalls** Centre

Form RPR

0331 **1** **Indian Trail**[7] 5050 7-9-7 **102**.................(v) LDettori 11 113
(D Nicholls) *hld up: swtchd lft and hdwy over 1f out: r.o ins fnl f to ld cl home* **3/1**[1]

3016 **2** *hd* **Judd Street**[18] 4696 5-9-5 **100**.................. StephenCarson 10 110
(Eve Johnson Houghton) *a.p: rdn over 1f out: led briefly wl ins fnl f: hld fnl strides* **11/1**

2024 **3** *nk* **Hoh Hoh Hoh**[7] 5050 5-8-11 **92**.................. SebSanders 5 101
(R J Price) *in tch: hdwy to ld wl over 1f out: hdd wl ins fnl f: nt qckn fnl strides* **7/1**[2]

0400 **4** *3/4* **Tabaret**[14] 4798 4-8-12 **93**.................. TomEaves 13 99
(R M Whitaker) *a.p: rdn over 1f out: styd on same pce towards fin* **16/1**

0000 **5** *3/4* **Corridor Creeper (FR)**[7] 5050 10-8-5 **86**..........(p) RichardMullen 12 90
(J M Bradley) *hld up: rdn and hdwy over 1f out: r.o ins fnl f: nrst fin* **33/1**

4564 **6** *shd* **The Jobber (IRE)**[14] 4798 6-9-5 **100**.................. TedDurcan 7 103
(M Blanshard) *racd keenly: trckd ldrs: rdn whn nt clr run ent fnl f: sn swtchd lft: no ex towards fin* **8/1**[3]

2252 **7** *3/4* **Special Day**[17] 4726 3-8-10 **92**.................. MichaelHills 16 92
(B W Hills) *in rr: rdn over 1f out: r.o fnl f: nt rch ldrs* **9/1**

6300 **8** *1/2* **Invincible Force (IRE)**[17] 4726 3-9-0 **96**.................. SteveDrowne 8 95
(Paul Green) *dwlt: in rr: rdn and hdwy over 1f out: one pce whn eased fnl 100yds* **33/1**

5021 **9** *1 1/4* **Coconut Moon**[7] 5029 5-8-5 **86** oh6.................. ChrisCatlin 2 80
(E J Alston) *led: rdn and hdd wl over 1f out: wknd fnl f* **28/1**

5020 **10** *nk* **Cape Royal**[18] 4696 7-8-6 **92**..........(bt) KevinGhunowa(5) 9 85
(J M Bradley) *handy: rdn over 1f out: wknd ins fnl f* **16/1**

-004 **11** *1* **Northern Empire (IRE)**[18] 4696 4-8-9 **90**.................. NCallan 1 79
(K A Ryan) *prom: rdn and ev ch wl over 1f out: wknd ins fnl f* **9/1**

1353 **12** *shd* **Jack Rackham**[22] 4567 3-8-5 **87**.................. PaulHanagan 3 76
(B Smart) *in midfield: clipped heels and lost pl 3f out: rdn and sme hdwy over 1f out: eased whn no imp ins fnl f* **14/1**

0500 **13** *hd* **Elhamri**[17] 4726 3-8-13 **95**.................. MartinDwyer 14 83
(S Kirk) *prom: rdn over 1f out: wknd ins fnl f* **33/1**

0311 **14** *nk* **Golden Dixie (USA)**[14] 4806 8-9-2 **97**.................. KerrinMcEvoy 4 84
(R A Harris) *sn pushed along and outpcd* **12/1**

5200 **15** *nk* **Blazing Heights**[7] 5039 4-8-5 **86** oh7.................. SaleemGolam 15 72
(J S Goldie) *dwlt: swtchd lft s: rdn over 1f out: a in rr* **20/1**

1300 **16** *1 3/4* **Dig Deep (IRE)**[22] 4567 5-8-4 **88**.................. LiamJones(3) 17 68
(W J Haggas) *in tch: rdn 2f out: wknd over 1f out* **16/1**

60.62 secs (0.50) **Going Correction** +0.30s/f (Good)

WFA 3 from 4yo+ 1lb **16** Ran SP% **126.0**

Speed ratings (Par 109): **108,107,107,106,104 104,103,102,100,100 98,98,98,97,97 94**

CSF £35.23 CT £219.50 TOTE £3.70: £1.50, £3.80, £1.90, £4.60; EX 54.00 Trifecta £155.50 Pool £720.66. - 3.29 winning units..

Owner Martin Love **Bred** Whitsbury Manor Stud **Trained** Sessay, N Yorks

FOCUS

A very good, typically competitive sprint handicap and this race also provided some of Ayr Gold Cup clues with the time good and the form looking solid. They were spread out across the track for much of the way, but the principals ended up towards the far side, so it was surprising that those drawn in double-figure stalls dominated.

NOTEBOOK

Indian Trail had not been enjoying much luck in-running in some big sprint handicaps for most of the season, but he finally got it right when Dettori took over at Sandown on his previous start and, back in the winning habit, he was able to follow up off an 8lb higher mark, with the former champion again doing the steering. This was a very smart effort indeed conceding weight all round off a mark of 102 and, such is the lack of strength in depth in the sprint division, he would not have much to find to be competitive in Listed and Group races. In the meantime, he is likely to take his chance in the Ayr Gold Cup and he will be well-in with his 8lb penalty set to put him on the same mark he just won off, although Dettori, who clearly gets the best out of him, is no sure thing to be available. (op 7-2, tchd 4-1 in a place)

Judd Street is at the top of his game right now and he looked to post a career-best effort in defeat. He is also in the Ayr Gold Cup, but he has yet to prove himself fully effective over 6f. (tchd 12-1)

Hoh Hoh Hoh could not reverse recent Sandown form with Indian Trail, but he fared best of those in a single-figure stall and this was a terrific race in defeat. Currently 10lb higher than when last winning, he clearly does not have much in hand of the Handicapper, but he is in great form and, like the first two, he is entered in the Ayr Gold Cup. (op 15-2)

Tabaret is a smart sprinter when on a going day and this one of his better efforts. (op 14-1 tchd 18-1)

Corridor Creeper(FR) ◆ was rated 112 at his peak but, although clearly nowhere near as good these days, this was an encouraging effort. He is beginning to look very attractively handicapped and appeals as one to keep on-side in the coming weeks. (tchd 40-1)

The Jobber(IRE) had no easy task off a mark of 100, but he ran well and continues in good form. He was a little short of room around a furlong out, but was not unlucky. (tchd 15-2)

Special Day was found out by a 6lb rise in the weights for her recent York second thrown in against her elders for the first time. (op 10-1)

5213 BETFREDPOKER SUPERIOR MILE (LISTED RACE) 1m 30y

2:35 (2:35) (Class 1) 3-Y-O+

£19,873 (£7,532; £3,769; £1,879; £941; £472) **Stalls** Low

Form RPR

-150 **1** **Harvest Queen (IRE)**[43] 3897 4-9-0 103.................. SebSanders 9 110
(P J Makin) *hld up in last pl: swtchd rt 3f out: hdwy on outside over 2f out: r.o to ld ins fnl f: pushed out towards fin* **12/1**

15-0 **2** *1 1/4* **Smart Enough**[16] 4745 4-9-2 101.................. SteveDrowne 1 109
(M A Magnusson) *led: rdn over 1f out: hdd ins fnl f: nt qckn towards fin* **17/2**

11-4 **3** *1/2* **Caldra (IRE)**[23] 4543 3-8-11 109.................. NCallan 8 107
(S Kirk) *trckd ldrs: rdn over 2f out: hung lft ins fnl f: r.o same pce* **4/1**[3]

3002 **4** *shd* **Metropolitan Man**[35] 4167 4-9-2 102.................. MartinDwyer 5 108
(D M Simcock) *in midfield: rdn 2f out: styd on ins fnl f: nt pce to chal ldrs* **16/1**

0020 **5** *1* **Appalachian Trail (IRE)**[43] 3894 6-9-2 106.................. TomEaves 6 106
(I Semple) *hld up: effrt over 1f out: one pce ins fnl f* **16/1**

-453 **6** *nk* **Olympian Odyssey**[23] 4543 4-9-2 114.................. LDettori 4 105
(Saeed Bin Suroor) *trckd ldrs: rdn to chal 1f out: btn ins fnl f* **9/4**[1]

/142 **7** *1* **Winged Cupid (IRE)**[14] 4826 4-9-5 110.................. KerrinMcEvoy 7 106
(Saeed Bin Suroor) *prom: rdn over 1f out: wknd ins fnl f* **11/4**[2]

5605 **8** *3/4* **Azarole (IRE)**[16] 4747 6-9-2 100.................. JimmyFortune 2 101
(J S Moore) *in midfield: rdn over 1f out: nvr able to chal: eased whn n.d wl ins fnl f* **20/1**

606 **9** *2* **Tell**[70] 3103 4-9-2 98.................. TedDurcan 3 96
(J L Dunlop) *hld up: rdn and swtchd rt over 1f out: nvr on terms* **33/1**

1m 43.58s (-1.93) **Going Correction** +0.075s/f (Good)

WFA 3 from 4yo+ 5lb **9** Ran SP% **115.1**

Speed ratings (Par 111): **112,110,110,110,109 108,107,107,105**

CSF £108.65 TOTE £22.00: £3.30, £1.80, £1.40; EX 176.60 Trifecta £229.40 Part won. Pool £323.20. - 0.50 winning units..

Owner Bakewell Bloodstock Ltd **Bred** Bakewell Bloodstock **Trained** Ogbourne Maisey, Wilts

FOCUS

A good Listed race on paper but, although the winner managed to come from last, one suspects some of these would have preferred a stronger gallop, and the bare form probably wants treating with some caution.

NOTEBOOK

Harvest Queen(IRE) had not had things go her way in a couple of starts since winning impressively in this grade at Goodwood earlier in the season, but everything fell kindly for her this time and she returned to her very best. Dropped in from her wide draw, she travelled with ease throughout and made smooth progress into a challenging position before bounding clear when asked. It would probably be unwise to get carried away with the bare form, as a few of her rivals seemed to under-perform, but she is clearly smart when everything goes her way. It would be no surprise to see her make an impression in Pattern company against her own sex and the Group 1 Sun Chariot Stakes at Newmarket is said to be her next target. (op 16-1)

Smart Enough seemed badly in need of the run on his return from almost a year off the track at York last time, but that outing clearly brought him on significantly and this was much better. Allowed the run of the race out in front, he stuck to his task well in the straight and found only one too strong. He is entitled to come on again for this and deserves another shot in similar company. (op 10-1 tchd 11-1 and 8-1)

Caldra(IRE) confirmed the promise he showed on his belated reappearance at Salisbury with another solid effort in defeat. He suffered a serious injury last year, but clearly retains plenty of ability and could be capable of even better when there is more juice in the ground. (tchd 9-2)

Metropolitan Man is a very smart horse and this was a respectable effort in defeat, but he always seems to fall just short of this sort of level.

Appalachian Trail(IRE), stepped back up in trip with the blinkers left off, is often seen at his best finishing off a strong pace, so he did not really have the race run to suit.

Olympian Odyssey could not confirm Salisbury form with Caldra and was disappointing. He would probably have preferred a stronger pace. Official explanation: trainer had no explanation for the poor form shown (op 13-8)

Winged Cupid(IRE), like his stablemate Olympian Odyssey, he failed to show his best form and was unsuited by the way the race was run. (op 7-2)

5214 BETFRED SPRINT CUP (GROUP 1) 6f

3:10 (3:10) (Class 1) 3-Y-O+

£179,027 (£67,852; £33,957; £16,931; £8,481; £4,256) **Stalls** Centre

Form RPR

0434 **1** **Red Clubs (IRE)**[16] 4746 4-9-3 114.................. MichaelHills 6 122
(B W Hills) *in midfield: rdn and hdwy over 1f out: led ins fnl f: r.o* **9/1**

0141 **2** *3/4* **Marchand D'Or (FR)**[34] 4214 4-9-3 0.................. DBonilla 1 120
(F Head, France) *hld up: hdwy over 2f out: sn edgd lft: rdn to ld over 1f out: hdd ins fnl f: nt pce of wnr towards fin* **13/2**[3]

0162 **3** *1/2* **Balthazaar's Gift (IRE)**[14] 4813 4-9-3 114.................. JimmyFortune 7 119
(L M Cumani) *awkward s: bhd: rdn and hdwy over 1f out: fin wl* **11/1**

00 **4** *1 1/4* **Mutawaajid (AUS)**[39] 4045 4-9-3 110.................. DarryllHolland 14 115
(M R Channon) *chsd ldr: rdn and ev ch over 1f out: styd on same pce ins fnl f* **33/1**

1111 **5** *nk* **Sakhee's Secret**[57] 3506 3-9-1 120.................. SteveDrowne 2 114
(H Morrison) *hld up: hdwy 2f out: rdn to chal over 1f out: no ex wl ins fnl f* **11/8**[1]

1362 **6** *1* **Asset (IRE)**[39] 4045 4-9-3 115..........(b[1]) LDettori 12 111
(R Hannon) *hld up: rdn 2f out: hdwy over 1f out: styd on ins fnl f: nt pce to rch ldrs* **6/1**[2]

0245 **7** *nk* **Wi Dud**[16] 4746 3-9-1 109.................. DO'Donohoe 9 110
(K A Ryan) *awkward s: in midfield: rdn over 2f out: hdwy to chse ldrs over 1f out: one pce ins fnl f* **33/1**

1066 **8** *2 1/2* **Scarlet Runner**[36] 4118 3-8-12 107.................. SebSanders 10 99
(J L Dunlop) *in midfield: rdn 2f out: one pce fnl f* **66/1**

4-60 **9** *2 1/2* **Somnus**[16] 4747 7-9-3 110.................. RichardMullen 15 95
(T D Easterby) *towards rr: rdn 2f out: sme hdwy over 1f out: nt pce to trble ldrs* **100/1**

5002 **10** *nk* **Advanced**[16] 4747 4-9-3 105.................. PatCosgrave 3 94
(K A Ryan) *gd spd: rdn 2f out: wknd over 1f out* **100/1**

1500 **11** *2 1/2* **Sierra Vista**[16] 4746 7-9-0 109.................. PaulHanagan 11 84
(D W Barker) *led: rdn and hdd over 1f out: wknd fnl f* **50/1**

1000 **12** *1 1/2* **Amadeus Wolf**[16] 4746 4-9-3 114.................. NCallan 5 82
(K A Ryan) *prom: rdn over 2f out: wkng whn n.m.r over 1f out: eased whn btn ins fnl f* **16/1**

16 **13** *nk* **Per Incanto (USA)**[21] 4600 3-9-1 112.................. MartinDwyer 13 81
(J L Dunlop) *in tch: rdn over 2f out: sn wknd* **20/1**

4-01 **14** *1/2* **Hellvelyn**[14] 4798 3-9-1 112.................. TedDurcan 16 80
(B Smart) *hld up in midfield: hdwy 1/2-way: rdn and wknd over 1f out: eased ins fnl f* **15/2**

1m 13.11s (-0.78) **Going Correction** +0.30s/f (Good)

WFA 3 from 4yo+ 2lb **14** Ran SP% **121.8**

Speed ratings (Par 117): **117,116,115,113,113 111,111,108,104,104 101,99,98,98**

CSF £64.66 TOTE £11.60: £2.90, £1.80, £4.00; EX 103.30 Trifecta £3655.50 Pool £5,148.66. - 1 winning unit..

Owner R J Arculli **Bred** J Fike **Trained** Lambourn, Berks

FOCUS

As well as no foreign challengers, the likes of Dutch Art, Soldier's Tale and last year's winner, Reverence were all missing, and this looked a decidedly ordinary renewal of this Group 1 sprint. There was also some controversy afterwards, with Hughie Morrison, trainer of the red-hot favourite Sakhee's Secret, among many who felt the ground had been overwatered. The pace was strong throughout, with Sierra Vista soon blasting off in front, and the first three home came from a long way back with the first two close to July Cup form. They raced up the middle of the track.

NOTEBOOK

Red Clubs(IRE) had not won since landing last year's Diadem Stakes, but he had run several fine races in defeat this term, including when third in the July Cup and fourth in the Nunthorpe on his two most recent outings, and this was a deserved first Group 1 success. Having struggled to hold his position, he only looked to have two or three rivals behind him at about halfway, and he was briefly denied a clear run when trying to stay on, but he found a gap in plenty of time, picking up well to ultimately run out quite a convincing winner. He is likely to be retired to the Tally-Ho Stud in Ireland at the end of the season, but is not finished with just yet and could be aimed at races such as the Prix de l'Abbaye and the Hong Kong Sprint. He would obviously be worthy of his place in the big sprint in France on Arc day, but he could manage only ninth last year, and one just feels he needs 6f to be seen at his best. (op 10-1 tchd 11-1)

Marchand D'Or(FR) came into this off the back of a tremendous success in the Group 1 Prix Maurice de Gheest (a race he also won last year) and, although unable to reverse July Cup form with Red Clubs, this was another terrific effort, confirming himself one of the best sprinters in Europe. He may even have the given the winner a little more to think about had he not edged left when first produced with his challenge. He looks the type to do even better as he continues to strengthen up and will be one to keep in mind for next year. In the shorter term, he could now take his chance in the Prix de la Foret. (op 7-1 tchd 11-2 and 15-2 in a place)

Balthazaar's Gift(IRE) ◆ failed to run up to his best in a somewhat muddling Listed contest on the July course on his previous start, but this was much more like it. He was soon towards the rear after starting a little awkwardly, but the strong pace played into his hands and he came home in good style to take third. He just seemed to lack the mid-race speed of the winner, allowing that one first run, and it is no surprise his two best efforts have come at Ascot, a noticeably stiff track. He is now likely to go for the Diadem Stakes and he should take all the beating, especially if there is some ease in the ground. (op 14-1)

Mutawaajid(AUS) ◆ had failed to make much impression in his two runs in this country since coming over from Australia, but this was a blinding effort in defeat. He fared best of those to chase the frantic early gallop and emerges with a great deal of credit. On the evidence of this performance, he looks capable of picking up a big prize. (op 40-1)

Sakhee's Secret confirmed himself a top-class sprinter when landing the July Cup on his previous start, where he had no fewer than seven of today's rivals behind, but he needs genuinely fast ground to be seen at his best and, below form this time, his connections were adamant the ground had been overwatered. Well off the pace early on, he briefly looked threatening around two furlongs form the finish, but he could find only the one pace under pressure and his rider reported afterwards that he knew after a furlong that he was struggling to handle the conditions. His trainer was furious afterwards, claiming far too much water had been put on the track, and that view was backed up by several other racing professionals, as well as the race times. Official explanation: trainer said colt was unsuited by the good to firm (firm in places) ground, which he believed was slower than the official description (op 5-4 tchd 6-4)

Asset(IRE), although running some good races in defeat lately, he had not really gone on from his impressive Newmarket Listed success earlier in the season and his connections opted for first-time blinkers. The headgear failed to improve him though, and he is so far struggling to break through at this sort of level. (op 7-1 tchd 15-2 and 8-1 in a place)

Wi Dud has so far fallen just short of this level, but this was a creditable effort considering he was awkward away from the stalls.

Scarlet Runner looked to have plenty to find in this company, but she ran quite well in defeat. (tchd 80-1)

Somnus would not have minded the heavily watered track, but he is probably not good enough for these sorts of races any more.

Advanced had plenty to find at this level and he was unable to sustain his effort after showing bright early pace.

Sierra Vista had won her last four starts at this track, but she is a better mare over the minimum trip and was unable to maintain her challenge after going off very quickly.

Amadeus Wolf looked set for a very good season after bolting up in the Duke of York Stakes (Red Clubs second) back in May, but he has not gone on as one might have expected.

Per Incanto(USA)'s connections were not happy afterwards, having supplemented their horse at a of £17,500, only to find the ground was totally unsuitable following the heavy watering.

Hellvelyn ran no sort of race and his trainer felt the watered ground was against him. (op 10-1)

5215 BETFREDCASINO.COM OLD BOROUGH CUP (HERITAGE H'CAP) 1m 6f

3:40 (3:40) (Class 2) (0-105,101) 3-Y-O+ **£48,577** (£14,452; £7,222; £3,607) **Stalls** Low

Form				RPR
2601	1		**Regal Flush**[38] 4059 3-9-0 **101** ... LDettori 4 (Sir Michael Stoute) *hld up in last pl: hdwy over 2f out: led over 1f out: in command ins fnl f* **4/1**[1]	112+
2122	2	2	**Samurai Way**[39] 4047 5-9-3 **93** ... JimmyFortune 5 (L M Cumani) *in tch: rdn over 2f out: led wl over 1f out: sn hdd: edgd lft ins fnl f: nt qckn towards fin* **4/1**[1]	101
5015	3	¾	**Dansili Dancer**[7] 5030 5-9-10 **100** ... SteveDrowne 3 (C G Cox) *chsd ldrs: rdn 2f out: ev ch and str chal over 1f out: nt qckn ins fnl f* **20/1**	107
3303	4	¾	**Tilt**[39] 4047 5-8-10 **86** ... (p) TomEaves 6 (B Ellison) *hld up in midfield: rdn and hdwy over 2f out: styd on and clsd on ldrs ins fnl f* **20/1**	92
0002	5	¾	**Cape Secret (IRE)**[28] 4398 4-8-10 **86** ... MartinDwyer 12 (R M Beckett) *led: rdn and hdd over 2f out: kpt on same pce ins fnl f* **16/1**	91
6202	6	¾	**Whispering Death**[22] 4569 5-8-12 **88** ... (v) KerrinMcEvoy 1 (W J Haggas) *s.i.s: in midfield: hdwy 3f out: ev ch and str chal fr 2f out: no ex wl ins fnl f* **11/1**	92
4231	7	1 ¾	**Bajan Parkes**[1] 5197 4-8-7 **83** 6ex ... MatthewHenry 11 (E J Alston) *chsd ldr: rdn to ld over 2f out: hdd wl over 1f out: sn wknd* **28/1**	84
3113	8	shd	**Sagredo (USA)**[7] 5030 3-8-13 **100** ... SebSanders 14 (Sir Mark Prescott) *hld up: hdwy into midfield 3f out: rdn and hung lft over 2f out: no further prog* **6/1**[3]	101
1000	9	½	**Greenwich Meantime**[28] 4375 7-9-7 **97** ... PaulHanagan 10 (R A Fahey) *hld up: rdn 2f out: hdwy over 1f out: one pce fnl f* **16/1**	98
3606	10	nk	**Lets Roll**[28] 4375 6-8-8 **84** ... SaleemGolam 15 (C W Thornton) *in midfield: hdwy 5f out: rdn and lost pl over 3f out: n.d after* **25/1**	84
6510	11	4	**Record Breaker (IRE)**[14] 4799 3-7-13 **89** ... LiamJones(3) 8 (M Johnston) *chsd ldrs but nvr travelling: lost pl 6f out: no imp after* **5/1**[2]	84
0013	12	1 ¾	**Inchnadamph**[22] 4569 7-8-9 **85** ... (t) RichardMullen 7 (T J Fitzgerald) *hld up: rdn and hdwy over 2f out: wknd over 1f out* **28/1**	77
/240	13	14	**Clueless**[57] 3509 5-8-9 **85** ... (b) NCallan 9 (N G Richards) *racd keenly: in midfield: hdwy 7f out: wknd 3f out* **22/1**	57
000-	14	3	**Savannah Bay**[434] 3078 8-8-10 **86** ... (b) PatCosgrave 13 (B Ellison) *bmpd s: sn rdn and nt keen: hdwy after 6f: rdn and wknd 4f out* **100/1**	54
2143	15	4	**Misty Dancer**[28] 4388 8-9-0 **90** ... TedDurcan 2 (Miss Venetia Williams) *in tch: rdn and wknd 3f out* **16/1**	53

3m 4.26s (-2.03) **Going Correction** +0.075s/f (Good)
WFA 3 from 4yo+ 11lb **15** Ran SP% **122.5**
Speed ratings (Par 109): **108,106,106,106,105 105,104,104,103,103 101,100,92,90,88**
CSF £17.37 CT £295.57 TOTE £3.60: £1.60, £2.30, £4.80; EX 18.60 Trifecta £284.80 Pool £1,195.68. - 2.98 winning units..
Owner Cheveley Park Stud **Bred** Cheveley Park Stud Ltd **Trained** Newmarket, Suffolk

FOCUS

A very good renewal of this valuable handicap and, with the pace strong from the outset, the form looks solid rated around the four immediately behind the principals.

NOTEBOOK

Regal Flush ◆ gave the impression he would benefit from a step up in trip when getting on top in the closing stages in a 1m4f handicap at Goodwood on his previous start and that proved to be the case as he was able to defy 9lb rise in the weights. He was held up a long way last for much of the way, and only had one rival behind him passing the three-furlong marker, but he really stretched out when switched to the centre of the track, ultimately taking this in most convincing fashion. He looks a Group-horse in the making and his connections later took decision to supplement him for the following weekend's St Leger at Doncaster at a cost of £40,000. That will obviously be a lot tougher, but such is the rate at which he is progressing, he will be well worth his place in the line up. (tchd 9-2 in places)

Samurai Way, racing off a mark 2lb higher than when second over this trip at Goodwood on his previous start, did everything right but was just beaten by a better horse on the day. He could well go up in the weights again. (tchd 9-2)

Dansili Dancer had no easy task off top weight, but he ran right up to his best stepped up to his furthest trip to date.

Tilt was unable to reverse recent Goodwood form with Samurai Way, but ran well nevertheless and remain in good order.

Cape Secret(IRE) set a good gallop from the outset, but he was always going to struggle to maintain his challenge and see off some strong finishers. Still, this was not a bad effort in the circumstances.

Whispering Death got a dream run up the far rail in the straight and moved into contention looking dangerous, but his effort soon flattened out. (op 14-1)

Bajan Parkes, trying this trip for the first time, could not defy a 7lb higher mark than when winning over 1m4f here the previous day, but he ran considering this probably came soon enough. (op 25-1)

Sagredo(USA) hung under pressure and could make no impression on the leaders. It is possible this came a little too soon after his recent Chester third and he is not one to give up on just yet. (op 13-2)

Record Breaker(IRE), stepped up to his furthest trip to date, looked in trouble a fair way out and was probably beaten before his stamina was tested. (op 11-2 tchd 6-1)

5216 BETFRED FORTY YEARS OLD THIS WEEK NURSERY 6f

4:10 (4:11) (Class 2) 2-Y-O

£12,464 (£3,732; £1,866; £934; £466; £234) **Stalls** Centre

Form				RPR
0531	1		**Mr Keppel (IRE)**[18] 4683 2-8-3 **73** ... DavidKinsella 3 (J A Osborne) *hld up: hdwy 1/2-way: led over 2f out: sn edgd lft: clr over 1f out: edgd rt ins fnl f: r.o* **16/1**	82+
3313	2	1 ¼	**Art Sale**[11] 4921 2-9-5 **89** ... JimmyFortune 12 (G L Moore) *hld up: rdn and hdwy over 1f out: r.o and edgd lft ins fnl f: nt rch wnr* **6/1**[3]	94
6345	3	nk	**Eastern Romance**[66] 3200 2-8-4 **74** ... RichardMullen 16 (K A Ryan) *a.p: rdn over 1f out: nt qckn ins fnl f* **20/1**	78
0100	4	2 ½	**Vhujon (IRE)**[14] 4832 2-9-5 **89** ... (t) StephenDonohoe 8 (P D Evans) *led: hdd over 2f out: rdn over 1f out: kpt on same pce ins fnl f* **28/1**	86
2221	5	hd	**Victorian Bounty**[22] 4560 2-8-12 **82** ... ChrisCatlin 7 (E J O'Neill) *chsd ldrs: rdn over 1f out: kpt on same pce ins fnl f* **9/1**	78
2214	6	1	**Guertino (IRE)**[18] 4695 2-9-5 **89** ... TedDurcan 6 (B Smart) *in midfield: rdn 2f out: one pce ins fnl f* **7/2**[1]	82
121	7	½	**Little Big Boy (IRE)**[21] 4605 2-8-9 **79** ... MartinDwyer 10 (R Hannon) *racd keenly: hld up: rdn and nt clr run wl over 1f out: hdwy ent fnl f: kpt on: nt pce to rch ldrs* **11/2**[2]	71+
605	8	½	**Dome Rock (IRE)**[24] 4506 2-8-10 **80** ... SebSanders 13 (L M Cumani) *in midfield: rdn over 2f out: nvr able to chal* **10/1**	70
0013	9	½	**Thomas Malory (IRE)**[5] 5089 2-7-13 **69** oh9 ow1 ... FrankieMcDonald 9 (Miss V Haigh) *chsd ldrs: rdn 2f out: wknd over 1f out* **66/1**	58
5560	10	1 ½	**Southwest Star (IRE)**[14] 4832 2-7-12 **68** oh1 ... AdrianMcCarthy 11 (J S Moore) *in midfield: rdn over 2f out: no hdwy* **22/1**	52
0453	11	½	**Lecanvey**[8] 5008 2-7-12 **68** oh2 ... PaulHanagan 2 (R A Fahey) *in midfield: outpcd over 2f out* **7/1**	51
3201	12	1 ¾	**Fitzroy Crossing (USA)**[30] 4328 2-9-5 **89** ... KerrinMcEvoy 15 (M Johnston) *hld up: outpcd 1/2-way* **14/1**	67
1310	13	2	**Pelican Prince**[16] 4743 2-9-1 **85** ... PatCosgrave 4 (K R Burke) *bhd: effrt and hdwy over 1f out: wknd ent fnl f: sn eased* **11/1**	57
232	14	6	**Feisty Royale**[45] 3834 2-8-0 **73** ... LiamJones(3) 1 (M Johnston) *prom tl rdn and wknd over 3f out* **16/1**	27

1m 15.07s (1.18) **Going Correction** +0.30s/f (Good) **14** Ran SP% **124.3**
Speed ratings (Par 101): **104,102,101,98,98 97,96,95,95,93 92,90,87,79**
CSF £108.58 CT £2021.52 TOTE £29.00: £7.10, £2.30, £6.40; EX 254.60.
Owner Mountgrange Stud **Bred** Mrs C F Van Straubenzee And Miss A Gibson Flemi **Trained** Upper Lambourn, Berks

FOCUS

The top weight raced off a mark of 91 and this looked like a decent nursery with the good time suggesting the form is strong. They tended to race up the middle of the track.

NOTEBOOK

Mr Keppel(IRE) ◆ only scraped home in a maiden at Brighton on his previous start, but the 7f trip looked to stretch him that day and, handicapped on the bare form of that success, it turned out he was thrown in on his nursery debut, with the return to sprinting bringing about a much-improved performance. He appeared to hit the front plenty soon enough, but he was able to take a good three or so lengths out of the field inside the final couple of furlongs and, although getting a little lonely, he maintained a decent advantage all the way to the line. He can be rated even better than the bare form and looks capable of progressing into a useful sprinter.

Art Sale appreciated the step back up in trip having seemed to find 5f too short in a conditions race at Ripon on his previous start, but he probably just bumped into a well-handicapped rival. (op 12-1)

Eastern Romance is not badly handicapped on the pick of her form and this was a respectable effort stepped up to 6f for the first time off the back of a 66-day break. (op 16-1)

Vhujon(IRE) was unsuited by soft ground in a sales races at the Curragh on his previous start, but this was a lot better. He is all speed and probably needs to be able to get a good breather in to be fully effective over this trip in this sort of company. (op 25-1)

Victorian Bounty ran with credit off a mark 7lb higher than when winning at Catterick on his previous start. (op 12-1)

Guertino(IRE) did not look to have too many excuses and basically gave the impression he is plenty high enough in the weights. (tchd 4-1)

Little Big Boy(IRE) was just 2lb higher than when winning a weak nursery over 5f on the July course on his previous start, but he raced a little keenly through the early stages and was also denied a clear run when trying to get involved. He is better than he was able to show. (tchd 9-2)

Pelican Prince Official explanation: jockey said colt lost its action

5217 TEXT BETFRED TO 83080 FOR MOBILE BETTING CONDITIONS STKS 1m 30y

4:40 (4:41) (Class 2) 2-Y-O **£12,954** (£3,854; £1,926; £962) **Stalls** Low

Form RPR

14 **1** **Campanologist (USA)**[18] 4694 2-8-12 0 KerrinMcEvoy 3 90
(M Johnston) *a.p: led over 1f out: edgd lft ins fnl f: a in command after* **11/4**[2]

0004 **2** ½ **Eileen's Violet (IRE)**[8] 4991 2-8-13 90 StephenDonohoe 4 90
(P D Evans) *hld up: rdn over 2f out: swtchd rt and hdwy over 1f out: r.o cl home but no ch w wnr* **20/1**

1361 **3** ¾ **Dan Tucket**[14] 4812 2-8-12 85 DarryllHolland 8 87
(M R Channon) *trckd ldrs: rdn to chal over 1f out: one pce towards fin* **11/2**

21 **4** ½ **Dubai Time**[10] 4930 2-8-12 0 NCallan 6 86
(K A Ryan) *led: rdn and hdd over 1f out: kpt on same pce ins fnl f* **9/4**[1]

521 **5** *nk* **Jedediah**[23] 4547 2-8-12 92 MartinDwyer 1 85
(A M Balding) *in tch: rdn over 2f out: kpt on same pce ins fnl f* **7/2**[3]

6 2 ½ **North Parade** 2-8-9 0 (t) SteveDrowne 5 79+
(B J Meehan) *s.i.s: a niggled along and bhd: nvr on terms* **28/1**

4126 **7** *shd* **Sauze D'Oulx**[7] 5053 2-8-12 90 JamesMillman 7 79
(B R Millman) *in tch: effrt to chal 3f out: wknd 1f out* **16/1**

0 **8** 7 **Jack Got Even (USA)**[10] 4947 2-8-12 0 MichaelHills 2 63
(B J Meehan) *rdn over 4f out: a bhd* **14/1**

1m 47.23s (1.72) **Going Correction** +0.075s/f (Good) **8** Ran SP% **115.8**
Speed ratings (Par 101): **94,93,92,92,91 89,89,82**
CSF £54.77 TOTE £3.50: £1.40, £3.70, £1.80; EX 47.80.

Owner Sheikh Mohammed **Bred** Darley **Trained** Middleham Moor, N Yorks

FOCUS
This looked like a good juvenile conditions event and although it looks sound enough on paper the time limits confidence.

NOTEBOOK
Campanologist(USA), a winner on his debut before running a shade keen but still faring best of those to race handy in the 7f Group 3 Acomb Stakes on his next start, took advantage of this drop in grade, getting this longer trip without any problems. Having had to be encouraged to adopt a prominent position, he was soon in a good rhythm just in behind Dubai Time and picked up best of all in the straight. He only had half a length to spare at the line, but he never looked in any danger close home and, with his rider not giving him an unnecessarily hard time, he looks better than the bare form suggests. Physically he looks the type who can strength up over the winter and make a nice three-year-old. (op 5-2 tchd 3-1)

Eileen's Violet(IRE), stepped up to 1m for the first time, took an age to get going and, although eventually staying on, the line was always going to come too soon. This was a blinding effort in defeat considering she was a filly conceding weight all round, but one suspects she might just benefit from the fitting of some headgear to help her concentrate. (op 16-1)

Dan Tucket, the winner of a 7f Newmarket nursery off a mark of 81 on his previous start, was produced with every chance and can have few excuses. (op 8-1)

Dubai Time did not run a bad race back in fourth, but it still easy to be disappointed considering how good he looked when winning his maiden at Ayr the previous week. He appeared to get a soft enough lead, but perhaps he was doing more in front than it looked at the first glance, and the heavily-watered track may also have been against him. (op 5-2, tchd 11-4 in a place)

Jedediah was below the form he had shown on his three previous starts, only managing to find the one pace in the straight and never looking likely to get involved. (op 10-3 tchd 3-1)

North Parade, a 70,000gns son of Nayef, half-brother to the multiple 7f-1m winner Minority Report, out of a smart triple sprint winner at two and three, faced a stiff task on his debut, but he showed ability. (op 33-1 tchd 25-1)

Sauze D'Oulx was effectively 5lb wrong with his apprentice unable to claim his allowance. (op 12-1)

5218 BETFRED 700 SHOPS NATIONWIDE H'CAP 1m 2f 120y

5:15 (5:15) (Class 4) (0-85,83) 3-Y-O **£6,477** (£1,927; £963; £481) **Stalls** High

Form RPR

232 **1** **Seeking The Buck (USA)**[21] 4597 3-9-1 **80** (bt) KerrinMcEvoy 3 93+
(M A Magnusson) *hld up: hdwy 3f out: led over 1f out: rdn clr ins fnl f: eased cl home* **7/4**[1]

1520 **2** 4 **Hurlingham**[17] 4720 3-9-3 **82** LDettori 9 87+
(M W Easterby) *hld up: hdwy over 2f out: edgd rt whn chalng over 1f out: sn in 2nd: no ch w wnr ins fnl f* **13/2**

066 **3** 3 **Lord Theo**[14] 4811 3-8-10 **75** JamesDoyle 8 74
(N P Littmoden) *a.p: led over 2f out: rdn and hdd over 1f out: sn btn* **16/1**

2105 **4** 1 ¼ **Gold Prospect**[27] 4419 3-9-1 **80** JimmyFortune 5 76
(M L W Bell) *s.s: in rr: hdwy to chse ldrs over 1f out: sn rdn and one pce* **7/1**

1204 **5** 3 **El Toreador (USA)**[9] 4976 3-9-0 **79** StephenCarson 6 70
(G A Butler) *trckd ldrs: effrt whn n.m.r and hmpd over 1f out: sn btn* **18/1**

0000 **6** ¾ **Kilburn**[8] 5014 3-8-6 **71** FrankieMcDonald 1 61
(C G Cox) *hld up: pushed along over 3f out: no imp* **12/1**

2051 **7** 5 **Honorable Love**[36] 4128 3-8-8 **73** TedDurcan 4 54
(M Dods) *led: hdd over 2f out: wkng whn n.m.r and hmpd over 1f out* **5/1**[3]

-002 **8** 15 **Five A Side**[33] 4228 3-9-4 **83** MichaelHills 2 37
(M Johnston) *prom: rdn over 3f out: sn wknd: eased fnl f* **9/2**[2]

2m 14.5s (-1.64) **Going Correction** +0.075s/f (Good) **8** Ran SP% **115.9**
Speed ratings (Par 103): **108,105,102,102,99 99,95,84**
CSF £13.92 CT £137.36 TOTE £2.70: £1.10, £1.70, £4.90; EX 14.30 Place 6 £517.77, Place 5 £232.70..

Owner Eastwind Racing Ltd and Martha Trussell **Bred** Flaxman Holdings Ltd **Trained** Upper Lambourn, Berks

FOCUS
A fair handicap run at an even gallop with the runner-up a little off his spring form but the time suggests the race is worth taking a positive view about.

T/Jkpt: Not won. T/Plt: £2,104.90 to a £1 stake. Pool: £150,662.16. 52.25 winning tickets. T/Qpdt: £138.90 to a £1 stake. Pool: £6,480.40. 34.50 winning tickets. DO

5199 KEMPTON (A.W) (R-H)

Saturday, September 8

OFFICIAL GOING: Standard
Wind: Moderate across Weather: Overcast but warm

5219 TOTESCOOP6 SIRENIA STKS (GROUP 3) 6f (P)

2:20 (2:21) (Class 1) 2-Y-O
£21,008 (£7,962; £3,984; £1,986; £995; £499) **Stalls** High

Form RPR

120 **1** **Philario (IRE)**[16] 4743 2-9-0 90 FergusSweeney 4 104
(K R Burke) *sn led: mde rest: rdn and forged 2l clr 2f out: r.o wl: edgd lft nr fin* **16/1**

2312 **2** 1 **Red Alert Day**[14] 4812 2-9-0 95 BrettDoyle 6 101+
(N A Callaghan) *bdly hmpd s: bhd: hdwy wl over 1f out: r.o strly: wnt 2nd wl ins fnl f: nt rch wnr* **13/2**[3]

6310 **3** *hd* **Lady Aquitaine (USA)**[41] 3988 2-8-11 85 IanMongan 12 97
(B J Meehan) *lw: hld up towards rr on inner: hdwy and swtchd lft over 2f out: chsd wnr over 1f out: kpt on: lost 2nd wl ins fnl f* **14/1**

11 **4** 1 ¾ **Sporting Art (USA)**[21] 4613 2-9-0 92 GeorgeBaker 9 95
(G L Moore) *t.k.h: in tch tl hung lft and lost pl bnd 4f out: drvn over 2f out: styd on u.p: nt rch ldrs* **9/2**[2]

214 **5** *nk* **Naomh Geileis (USA)**[21] 4626 2-8-11 0 J-PGuillambert 10 91
(M Johnston) *towards rr: drvn wl over 2f out: swtchd rt and hdwy over 1f out: styd on: nt rch ldrs* **9/1**

3103 **6** *hd* **Ten Meropa (USA)**[9] 4975 2-9-0 85 DaneO'Neill 5 94
(J A Osborne) *hmpd s: bhd: rdn wl over 2f out: styd on u.p: nt rch ldrs* **14/1**

1 **7** *hd* **Lytton**[26] 4454 2-9-0 0 AdamKirby 1 93
(W R Swinburn) *w'like: str: lw: dropped in after s: bhd: rdn over 2f out: kpt on: unable to chal* **8/1**

1032 **8** *hd* **Fred's Lad**[7] 5032 2-9-0 95 PaulMulrennan 11 92
(M W Easterby) *chsd ldrs on inner: rdn over 2f out: no ex fnl f* **10/1**

6300 **9** 1 **Cee Bargara**[16] 4743 2-9-0 97 JimCrowley 8 89
(J A Osborne) *in tch: rdn wl over 2f out: kpt on same pce u.p* **20/1**

12 **10** 1 ½ **Reel Gift**[41] 3988 2-8-11 0 PatDobbs 3 82
(R Hannon) *b: in tch: rdn over 2f out: sn no hdwy: kpt on one pce* **4/1**[1]

3165 **11** ½ **Master Chef (IRE)**[14] 4812 2-9-0 95 (b) RobertHavlin 7 83
(J H M Gosden) *wnt bdly lft s and hmpd rivals: hdwy to chse ldrs 4f out: rdn wl over 2f out: wknd 1f out* **9/1**

2160 **12** 3 ½ **Spanish Bounty**[12] 4899 2-9-0 95 TPQueally 2 73+
(J G Portman) *lw: pressed wnr: rdn over 2f out: wknd ent fnl f: eased whn btn wl ins fnl f* **66/1**

1m 12.25s (-1.45) **Going Correction** -0.025s/f (Stan) **12** Ran SP% **117.2**
Speed ratings (Par 105): **108,106,106,104,103 103,103,102,101,99 98,94**
CSF £115.27 TOTE £25.20: £6.10, £2.50, £4.60; EX 164.10 TRIFECTA Not won..

Owner Philip Richards **Bred** David Barry **Trained** Middleham Moor, N Yorks

FOCUS
No more than a fair renewal of this juvenile Group 3. It was run at a sound pace and the first three came clear, with the runner-up helping to set the level, although not totally convincing.

NOTEBOOK
Philario(IRE), making his All-Weather debut, proved rejuvenated for the switch to this sounder surface and produced a clear personal-best effort to score. He was given an aggressive ride, which suited, and his rider's decision to kick on for home around 2f out paid dividends. On this evidence he should get another furlong in time, but is best kept to this trip for now and it would not be a surprise to see him try on build on this in the Group 2 Mill Reef Stakes later in the month. (op 20-1)

Red Alert Day has to rate unfortunate on this return to Group company as he lost more ground when hampered at the start than he was eventually beaten. He stayed on well from an unpromising position when asked for maximum effort, but the winner had gone beyond recall. This switch to this surface suited and he is developing into a most consistent performer, so rates a sound-enough benchmark even though he should be rated better than the bare form. Official explanation: jockey said colt suffered interference shortly after start (op 15-2)

Lady Aquitaine(USA), who ran no sort of race in the Group 3 Princess Margaret last time, showed her true colours on this return to a sounder surface and posted a sound effort in defeat, picking up some valuable black type in the process. A more positive ride over this trip may see her in an even better light. (op 16-1 tchd 20-1 and 12-1)

Sporting Art(USA), unbeaten in two previous outings on turf, did not help his cause by refusing to settle early on having got a bit warm beforehand and then did not handle the home turn very well. He stayed on for pressure, however, and left the impression he can build on this when reverting to a more galloping circuit. (op 4-1)

Naomh Geileis(USA), fourth in a decent Group 3 against her own sex in France last time, was given a more patient ride on this All-Weather debut and drop back a furlong. She did not prove suited by the change in tactics, however, and can be rated a little better than the bare form. (op 8-1)

Ten Meropa(USA) was another not done any favours at the start and was not at all disgraced in the circumstances on this marked step up in class. (op 33-1)

Lytton, a taking Windsor maiden winner on debut 26 days previously, was soon restrained from his outside draw and was never really looking that happy on this All-Weather bow. He kept on nicely enough in the home straight, however, and was still not beaten far. (tchd 7-1)

Fred's Lad, having his first outing on the All-Weather, ran his race and was probably a little below his recent level on turf. (op 11-1 tchd 12-1)

Reel Gift, the Princess Margaret second, failed to land any sort of blow on this return to Polytrack and ran someway below her previous best. She has something to prove now. (op 5-2)

5220 TOTEPOOL SEPTEMBER STKS (GROUP 3) 1m 4f (P)

2:50 (2:50) (Class 1) 3-Y-O+
£26,686 (£10,114; £5,061; £2,523; £1,264; £634) **Stalls** Centre

Form RPR

1300 **1** **Steppe Dancer (IRE)**[58] 3461 4-9-4 104 TPQueally 6 114
(D J Coakley) *lw: t.k.h early: stdd after 1f and hld up in last pair: hdwy over 3f out: rdn to ld ent fnl f: r.o wl* **8/1**

5101 **2** 1 ½ **Al Tharib (USA)**[12] 4887 3-8-9 101 PhilipRobinson 7 111
(Sir Michael Stoute) *lw: led: rdn wl over 2f out: hdd ent fnl f: kpt on one pce* **11/4**[1]

-145 **3** *shd* **Lion Sands**[39] 4044 3-8-9 109 NickyMackay 5 111
(L M Cumani) *swtg: s.i.s: t.k.h early: chsd ldr after 1f: rdn and ev ch jst over 2f out: kpt on but nt pce of wnr* **10/3**[2]

0323 **4** ½ **Imperial Star (IRE)**[14] 4825 4-9-4 109 (v[1]) RobertHavlin 1 110
(J H M Gosden) *swtg: t.k.h: hld up in last pair: hdwy over 3f out: chsd ldrs and rdn over 2f out: kpt on same pce* **13/2**

2453 **5** 2 ½ **Grand Passion (IRE)**[43] 3912 7-9-4 106 WilliamBuick 4 106
(G Wragg) *trckd ldng pair: rdn and effrt over 2f out: outpcd wl over 1f out* **20/1**

2422 **6** *2* **Shahin (USA)**[21] 4599 4-9-4 113 .... PatDobbs 3 103
(M P Tregoning) *in tch: shkn up 1/2-way: rdn 4f out: dropped to last over 3f out: one pce u.p after* **7/2**[3]

-010 **7** *shd* **Great Hawk (USA)**[17] 4720 4-9-4 98 .... (v) GeorgeBaker 2 103
(Sir Michael Stoute) *hld up in tch: hdwy to chse ldrs over 3f out: rdn over 2f out: wknd wl over 1f out* **10/1**

2m 31.58s (-5.32) **Going Correction** -0.025s/f (Stan)
WFA 3 from 4yo+ 9lb 7 Ran SP% **110.3**
Speed ratings (Par 113): **116,115,114,114,112 111,111**
CSF £28.09 TOTE £12.30: £3.20, £2.30; EX 25.50.

Owner Chris Van Hoorn **Bred** Maggiorelli Ice Guarnieri **Trained** West Ilsley, Berks
■ Trainer Denis Coakley's first Group winner.

FOCUS
A decent and open Group 3, that featured plenty of previous All-Weather form and a solid-looking contest. It was run in a course record time and the winner produced a career-best effort to score on a surface he clearly loves.

NOTEBOOK
Steppe Dancer(IRE), despite taking a keen early hold, emerged from off the pace to win this going away and produced a lifetime-best effort on a surface he clearly adores. He showed a right turn of foot when asked to pick up his rivals and has now won his last four races on this surface. No doubt he is still improving, but this looks to be his optimum trip and surface, so it looks wise for his connections to swerve a step up in class in the Irish St Leger as that would represent a much stiffer task over the longer trip. It would probably also come a little too soon. (op 11-1)
Al Tharib(USA), a ready winner over a little shorter at this venue 12 days previously, again set out to make it a decent test from the front. He eventually proved a sitting duck for the winner at the business end, but this was still another solid effort and he looks the type to continue improving as a four-year-old. (op 5-2)
Lion Sands, having his first taste of the All-Weather, was slowly into his stride and then proved hard to settle through the first furlong or so. He was still in with every chance passing the 2f pole, but his early exertions eventually told when it really mattered. This son of Montjeu is capable of better on his day, but he is another who appeals as the type to really come into his own next year. (op 7-2)
Imperial Star(IRE) was very keen in the first-time visor and, despite coming from a similar position as the winner around 3f out, he could not match that rival for speed when it mattered. He is not proving easy to win with in this sort of company, and has a little to prove again after this, but no doubt he can do better when consenting to settle again. (op 9-2)
Grand Passion(IRE), back on his favoured surface, has always looked a better horse over a shorter trip yet he no doubt stayed the distance. He simply lacked the required speed when it mattered. (op 14-1)
Shahin(USA), with the visor left off for this All-Weather debut, was beaten a long way out and never looked like confirming his Newmarket form with the winner. It later transpired, however, that he finished lame in front and he has to really be excused this effort. Official explanation: jockey said colt ran flat; vet said colt was lame in front (op 4-1 tchd 3-1)
Great Hawk(USA), a winner over 10f at the track on his only previous outing on Polytrack, faced a stiff task at the weights on this debut in Group company and was not surprisingly found out. He still did not really convince with his attitude, however. (op 11-1)

5221 TOTESPORT.COM LONDON MILE H'CAP (SERIES FINAL) 1m (P)
3:25 (3:28) (Class 2) 3-Y-0+

£46,245 (£13,920; £6,960; £3,472; £1,740; £877) **Stalls** High

Form RPR

1033 **1** **Magical Music**[20] 4632 4-9-1 **82** .... JimmyQuinn 13 91
(J Pearce) *lw: racd in midfield: hdwy over 2f out: styd on wl u.p fr over 1f out: led towards fin* **33/1**

2014 **2** *nk* **Evident Pride (USA)**[26] 4455 4-9-2 **83** .... DaneO'Neill 1 91
(B R Johnson) *in tch: hdwy wl over 2f out: ev ch over 1f out: no ex last strides* **8/1**[3]

0111 **3** *shd* **Samarinda (USA)**[52] 3650 4-9-10 **91** .... MickyFenton 4 99
(Mrs P Sly) *lw: in midfield early: hdwy to chse ldrs 1/2-way: led narrowly wl over 2f out: kpt on u.p tl hdd and lost 2 pls nr fin* **14/1**

141 **4** *½* **Cape Hawk (IRE)**[31] 4276 3-8-12 **84** .... JimCrowley 14 91+
(R Hannon) *in tch: hdwy to chse ldrs over 2f out: sn hrd rdn: n.m.r 1f out tl fnl 100yds: styd on cl home* **8/1**[3]

2122 **5** *nk* **Electric Warrior (IRE)**[28] 4385 4-9-2 **86** .... AndrewElliott(3) 15 92
(K R Burke) *lw: s.i.s: sn chsng ldrs: rdn jst over 2f out: kpt on u.p fnl 100yds* **10/1**

2136 **6** *¾* **Unshakable (IRE)**[36] 4119 8-9-10 **91** .... PaulEddery 7 96
(Bob Jones) *chsd ldr: ev ch 3f out: sn rdn: no ex fnl 100yds* **8/1**[3]

3055 **7** *shd* **Marajaa (IRE)**[10] 4949 5-9-3 **84** .... BrettDoyle 9 88
(W J Musson) *hld up in rr: hdwy on outer wl over 2f out: chse ldrs over 1f out: no imp fnl 100yds* **9/1**

0120 **8** *1 ¾* **Karoo Blue (IRE)**[21] 4608 3-9-2 **88** .... J-PGuillambert 16 87
(C E Brittain) *lw: led tl hdd wl over 2f out: sn rdn: wknd 1f out* **16/1**

4020 **9** *½* **Gallantry**[8] 4990 5-9-6 **87** .... OscarUrbina 5 86
(D Shaw) *in tch in midfield: rdn and outpcd 3f out: kpt on u.p fnl f: nt threaten ldrs* **25/1**

3335 **10** *3* **Granston (IRE)**[22] 4566 6-9-8 **89** .... (p) AdamKirby 2 81
(J D Bethell) *swtg: in tch on outer: hdwy 4f out: chsd ldrs and rdn wl over 2f out: sn struggling* **16/1**

4004 **11** *shd* **Councellor (FR)**[31] 4268 5-9-2 **83** .... (t) RobertHavlin 11 75
(Stef Liddiard) *t.k.h: hld up in midfield: rdn wl over 3f out: sn outpcd and n.d after* **33/1**

1300 **12** *½* **Killena Boy (IRE)**[36] 4119 5-9-9 **90** .... PaulDoe 12 81
(W Jarvis) *hld up in midfield on inner: effrt 3f out: no imp over 2f out: sn wl btn* **14/1**

-116 **13** *1* **Atlantic Story (USA)**[35] 4176 5-9-2 **83** .... (t) PaulMulrennan 6 72
(M W Easterby) *swtg: chsd ldrs early: sn pulling hrd and stdd to rr: bhd and rdn over 3f out: no real hdwy* **7/1**[2]

0230 **14** *¾* **Mataram (USA)**[14] 4797 4-9-1 **82** .... TPQueally 10 69
(W Jarvis) *hld up in rr: n.d* **14/1**

0255 **15** *2 ½* **Montpellier (IRE)**[36] 4119 4-9-9 **90** .... TGMcLaughlin 8 71
(E A L Dunlop) *lw: hld up bhd: rdn over 2f out: no rspnse* **5/1**[1]

1m 38.22s (-2.58) **Going Correction** -0.025s/f (Stan)
WFA 3 from 4yo+ 5lb 15 Ran SP% **123.1**
Speed ratings (Par 109): **111,110,110,110,109 109,108,107,106,103 103,103,102,101,98**
CSF £280.33 CT £3961.52 TOTE £34.80: £9.00, £3.20, £2.70; EX 625.90 Trifecta £7909.20 Pool £24,507.60. - 2.20 winning units..

Owner Killarney Glen & Mrs E M Clarke **Bred** Peter Taplin **Trained** Newmarket, Suffolk
■ Stewards' Enquiry : Paul Eddery one-day ban: not riding to draw (Sep 19)

FOCUS
A really strong All-Weather handicap, run at a decent pace. Solid form and the race should work out.

NOTEBOOK
Magical Music, in good form on the turf of late, relished the return to her favoured surface and resumed winning ways under a well-judged ride from Quinn. This has to rate her best effort to date and she does look much more at home on the All-Weather - this being her first win at the track - yet she is currently rated 21lb lower on grass, so surely her connections will now be looking to exploit that mark.
Evident Pride(USA), unbeaten in two previous outings over course and distance, almost made it three wins from as many starts at this venue and was only just reeled back near the line. He deserves extra credit as he was drawn widest of all.
Samarinda(USA), unbeaten in his last four outings on this surface, was racing from another 3lb higher mark and posted a brave effort under top weight. He was only beaten in a tight finish and this rates a rock-solid effort. While has had been a revelation since switching to Polytrack, he is currently rated 7lb lower on turf and it would be little surprise to see him back on grass now. (op 11-1)
Cape Hawk(IRE), whose previous course-and-distance figures read 211, was racing from a 3lb higher mark than when scoring last time and posted another improved effort in defeat. He continues in top form and it rates a decent performance against his elders. Official explanation: jockey said gelding lost a hind shoe (tchd 9-1)
Electric Warrior(IRE), whose previous record at the track read 2212, had to overcome a slow start and turned in another sound effort in defeat. He is most consistent and rates a decent benchmark for the form. (op 9-1)
Unshakable(IRE), a runner-up at the track on his only previous All-Weather outing, was given a prominent ride and this likeable eight-year-old was only found out at the business end. He will likely take up his entry in the Cambridgeshire. (op 10-1)
Marajaa(IRE) fared best of those to race from off the pace and ran respectably. He was later found to have been struck into. Official explanation: vet said gelding had been struck into (op 8-1)
Killena Boy(IRE), who took this race last year from an 8lb lower mark, was never a serious player from off the pace and was some way below his best. (op 16-1)
Atlantic Story(USA), easy to back, began to run too freely when restained to the rear after a decent break and that cost him any real chance he may have held. He is not straightforward by any means, but is certainly capable of a lot better when in the mood. Official explanation: trainer said, regarding the poor form shown, that gelding ran too free (op 11-2)
Montpellier(IRE) needed a blanket for stalls entry and is clearly a quirky customer. That does still not excuse this lifeless effort, however, and he is one to tread carefully with. Official explanation: trainer had no explanation for the poor form shown (op 7-1)

5222 TOTESPORT 0800 221 221 CONDITIONS STKS (C&G) 7f (P)
3:55 (3:57) (Class 3) 2-Y-0

£6,232 (£1,866; £933; £467; £233; £117) **Stalls** High

Form RPR

4 **1** **Kal Barg**[15] 4782 2-8-12 0 .... PhilipRobinson 1 77+
(M A Jarvis) *unf: scope: tall: s.i.s: sn chsng ldrs: wnt 2nd over 2f out: rdn and ev ch over 1f out: r.o gamely to ld fnl 100yds* **5/4**[1]

2 *nk* **Prohibit** 2-8-12 0 .... RobertHavlin 7 77
(J H M Gosden) *w'like: bit bkwd: hld up in tch on rail: plld out over 2f out: pushed along and qcknd to ld 1f out: hdd and no ex fnl 100yds* **9/2**[3]

2 **3** *1* **Tension Mounts (IRE)**[12] 4883 2-8-12 0 .... TPQueally 2 74
(J A Osborne) *athletic: lw: t.k.h: hld up: hdwy on outer over 2f out: rdn and chsd ldrs over 1f out: kpt on same pce ins fnl f* **4/1**[2]

041 **4** *hd* **Palmerin**[10] 4946 2-9-2 0 .... DaneO'Neill 5 77
(R Hannon) *led: rdn over 2f out: hdd 1f out: kpt on same pce u.p* **9/2**[3]

5 *3 ½* **King Columbo (IRE)** 2-8-9 0 .... JerryO'Dwyer(3) 4 64
(Miss J Feilden) *unf: hld up wl in tch: rdn over 2f out: sn outpcd* **25/1**

5 **6** *1 ½* **Gardes (IRE)**[19] 4656 2-8-12 0 .... IanMongan 3 60
(Jane Chapple-Hyam) *leggy: scope: lw: t.k.h: chsd ldr tl over 2f out: wknd over 1f out* **12/1**

7 *3* **Romford Car Two** 2-8-5 0 .... AmyBaker(7) 6 53
(Miss J Feilden) *w'like: str: bit bkwd: hld up in last: rdn 3f out: sn struggling* **40/1**

1m 27.7s (0.90) **Going Correction** -0.025s/f (Stan) 7 Ran SP% **114.8**
Speed ratings (Par 99): **93,92,91,91,87 85,82**
CSF £7.35 TOTE £2.70: £3.80, £1.10; EX 8.70.

Owner Sheikh Ahmed Al Maktoum **Bred** Mrs C G Gardiner **Trained** Newmarket, Suffolk

FOCUS
An interesting conditions stakes, run at a fair pace. The form looks solid enough with the first pair coming clear.

NOTEBOOK
Kal Barg, fourth at Thirsk on debut 15 days previously, showed battling qualities and got off the mark at the second attempt on this All-Weather bow. He evidently appreciated the extra furlong, and can be rated a little better than the bare margin as he blew the start, but while he is open to plenty of improvement his Group 1 entry does look very ambitious. His trainer later reported he is a more likely a nursery type. (tchd 11-8)
Prohibit ♦, whose dam was a useful 6f winner at two, turned in a very promising display and was only just denied a winning start. He looked the most likely winner entering the final furlong, but he proved unable to cope with the renewed challenge of the winner and left the impression he would enjoy racing over 6f in the short term. This son of his yard's former sprinting star Oasis Dream should soon be going one better. (op 11-2 tchd 6-1)
Tension Mounts(IRE), a runner-up over course and distance on his debut 12 days previously, hampered his cause by refusing to settle under restraint yet still ran close to his debut level in defeat. He only paid late on for his early exertions and looks to have a maiden well within his grasp. (op 7-2 tchd 3-1)
Palmerin, off the mark over 1m at this venue ten days previously, had his chance from the front and was only found out by his 4lb penalty. This was a solid effort. (op 5-1 tchd 11-2 and 6-1 in a place)

5223 TOTEEXACTA H'CAP 7f (P)
4:25 (4:26) (Class 4) (0-80,82) 3-Y-0+ **£4,728** (£1,406; £702; £351) **Stalls** High

Form RPR

0300 **1** **Alfresco**[12] 4889 3-9-0 **76** .... (b) PatDobbs 4 84
(Pat Eddery) *hld up bhd: hdwy 2f out: rdn over 1f out: r.o to ld towards fin* **16/1**

0301 **2** *nk* **Landucci**[12] 4884 6-8-12 **75** .... (p) PatrickHills(5) 11 84
(J W Hills) *hld up in tch: hdwy over 2f out: swtchd lft over 1f out: rdn to ld ins fnl f: hdd and no ex towards fin* **11/2**[2]

1306 **3** *1 ¼* **Indian's Feather (IRE)**[19] 4665 6-9-2 **74** .... IanMongan 12 80
(N Tinkler) *led for 1f: rdn 3f out: led again over 1f out: hdd ins fnl f: kpt on same pce* **22/1**

4636 **4** *½* **Bonnie Prince Blue**[10] 4949 4-9-2 **77** .... WilliamBuick(3) 2 81
(B W Hills) *lw: in tch: chsd ldrs 4f out: rdn 2f out: ch 1f out: no ex* **11/2**[2]

4260 **5** *1 ¼* **Sailor King (IRE)**[17] 4657 5-9-6 **78** .... RobertHavlin 10 79
(D K Ivory) *t.k.h: hld up: hdwy 3f out: chsd ldrs u.p 2f out: no hdwy* **12/1**

112 **6** *nk* **Desert Dreamer (IRE)**[9] 4965 6-9-10 **82** .... NickyMackay 1 82
(G A Butler) *dropped in after s: hld up in rr: hdwy on outer 1/2-way: kpt on but nvr rchd ldrs* **6/1**[3]

1100 **7** *nk* **One Night In Paris (IRE)**[10] 4949 4-8-13 **71** .... DaneO'Neill 7 70
(M J Wallace) *in tch: rdn wl over 2f out: kpt on same pce* **12/1**

0260 **8** *1* **Roman Quest**[24] 4505 4-8-6 **67**.......................... TravisBlock(3) 8 64
(H Morrison) *lw: stdd s: t.k.h: hld up in rr: swtchd lft and rdn 2f out: nvr on terms* **11/1**

43-0 **9** *hd* **Onenightinlisbon (IRE)**[29] 4360 3-8-13 **75**................. J-PGuillambert 6 69
(K R Burke) *t.k.h and chsd ldrs early: steadily lost pl: bhd and rdn wl over 2f out: n.d after* **33/1**

0500 **10** *hd* **Adantino**[9] 4965 8-9-3 **75**..(b) JimCrowley 3 71
(B R Millman) *led and crossed to rail after 1f: hdd over 1f out: sn wknd* **16/1**

3234 **11** *2 1/2* **Stonecrabstomorrow (IRE)**[14] 4816 4-9-1 **73**............... JimmyQuinn 9 62
(R A Fahey) *s.i.s: hdwy into midfield on rail 1/2-way: sn rdn: n.d after* **4/1**[1]

1050 **12** *shd* **Rabbit Fighter (IRE)**[56] 3556 3-8-9 **74**..................... AndrewElliott(3) 5 61
(D Shaw) *t.k.h: hld up in rr: rdn and struggling 1/2-way: no ch after* **18/1**

2626 **13** *3/4* **Rydal Mount (IRE)**[58] 3472 4-9-0 **72**........................ FergusSweeney 13 59
(W S Kittow) *chsd ldrs on inner: rdn over 2f out: sn wknd* **14/1**

1m 25.78s (-1.02) **Going Correction** -0.025s/f (Stan)
WFA 3 from 4yo+ 4lb **13** Ran SP% **119.8**
Speed ratings (Par 105): **104,103,102,101,100 99,99,98,98,97 95,94,94**
CSF £101.91 CT £2026.49 TOTE £21.50: £6.70, £2.50, £6.90; EX 138.40.
Owner Pat Eddery Racing (Caerleon) **Bred** Usk Valley Stud **Trained** Nether Winchendon, Bucks
■ Stewards' Enquiry : Jim Crowley one-day ban: careless riding (Sep 19)
Pat Dobbs one-day ban: used whip in a wrong place (Sep 19)

FOCUS
A fair and open handicap for the grade. The first two pulled clear and the form is ordinary rated through the runner-up.

5224 TOTE TEXT BETTING 60021 H'CAP 2m (P)
5:00 (5:00) (Class 4) (0-80,76) 3-Y-O **£4,728** (£1,406; £702; £351) **Stalls** High

Form RPR

2122 **1** **Strobe**[4] 5111 3-9-1 **70**.. JimCrowley 5 76
(J A Osborne) *chsd ldr after 2f: rdn to ld wl over 2f out: styd on wl and a holding rivals after* **10/3**[2]

221 **2** *1* **Shine And Rise (IRE)**[10] 4951 3-9-7 **76**...................... PhilipRobinson 2 81
(C G Cox) *t.k.h: hld up in last: crept clsr on outer 3f out: rdn jst over 1f out: kpt on one pce: wnt 2nd on post* **4/6**[1]

0106 **3** *hd* **Love Brothers**[8] 5006 3-9-2 **71**.................................. DaneO'Neill 4 76
(M R Channon) *hld up in last pair: rdn and effrt wl over 2f out: kpt on u.p to chse wnr ins fnl f: a hld: lost 2nd on post* **16/1**

542 **4** *1 1/4* **Golden Wave (IRE)**[64] 3284 3-8-10 **65**............................... TPQueally 3 68
(J Noseda) *lw: chsd ldr for 2f: in tch: plld out and rdn over 2f out: chsd wnr over 1f out tl ins fnl f: one pce* **10/1**

5322 **5** *2 1/2* **Plane Painter (IRE)**[16] 4732 3-9-6 **75**........................ J-PGuillambert 1 75
(M Johnston) *led: rdn and hdd wl over 2f out: wknd 1f out* **6/1**[3]

3m 33.92s (2.52) **Going Correction** -0.025s/f (Stan) **5** Ran SP% **112.3**
Speed ratings (Par 103): **92,91,91,90,89**
CSF £6.16 TOTE £4.00: £1.70, £1.10; EX 4.60.
Owner Kerr-Dineen Pallett Tullett **Bred** Old Mill Stud **Trained** Upper Lambourn, Berks

FOCUS
A fair three-year-old staying race, run at an average gallop. The form looks straightforward enough rated around the placed horses.

5225 IT'S WARMER UP NORTH H'CAP 1m 3f (P)
5:30 (5:33) (Class 4) (0-85,85) 3-Y-0+ **£4,728** (£1,406; £702; £351) **Stalls** High

Form RPR

3212 **1** **Pivotal Answer (IRE)**[49] 3731 3-8-11 **78**.......................... TPQueally 5 90+
(J Noseda) *w.w in midfield on outer: hdwy 3f out: led gng wl 2f out: hdd ins fnl f: rdn and fnd ex to assert nr fin* **9/2**[2]

11/ **2** *3/4* **Desert D'Argent (IRE)**[686] 6016 4-9-5 **78**..................... RobertHavlin 6 89
(H Morrison) *w.w in midfield: rdn and hdwy wl over 2f out: led briefly ins fnl f: hdd and nt pce of wnr wl ins fnl f* **8/1**[3]

1513 **3** *1 3/4* **Kingscape (IRE)**[21] 4609 4-8-11 **73**........................ WilliamBuick(3) 15 83+
(J R Fanshawe) *hld up in midfield: nt clr run briefly over 2f out: sn swtchd rt: kpt on to go 3rd ins fnl f: nt rch ldrs* **7/2**[1]

0041 **4** *1/2* **Mustajed**[12] 4888 6-9-7 **80**.. JimCrowley 12 87
(B R Millman) *chsd ldrs: rdn wl over 2f out: ev ch u.p over 1f out: one pce fnl f* **9/2**[2]

5120 **5** *1 1/4* **Crossbow Creek**[21] 4171 9-9-12 **85**.................................. DaneO'Neill 9 90
(M G Rimell) *lw: t.k.h: hld up towards rr: hdwy over 2f out: kpt on u.p: nt rch ldrs* **10/1**

4000 **6** *nk* **Krugerrand (USA)**[12] 4909 8-9-3 **76**.................................. NeilPollard 2 80+
(W J Musson) *hld up in rr: weaved thrugh and gd hdwy 2f out: chsd ldrs 1f out: sn no imp* **14/1**

0166 **7** *nk* **Ocean Avenue (IRE)**[33] 4231 8-8-13 **72**.................. SimonWhitworth 7 76
(C A Horgan) *taken down early: mostly 2nd: rdn and led briefly over 2f out: wknd over 1f out* **16/1**

4400 **8** *3/4* **Desert Leader (IRE)**[9] 4976 6-8-12 **71**........................ NickyMackay 1 74
(R W Price) *hld up in rr: effrt and hdwy on outer 3f out: kpt on but n.d* **25/1**

5060 **9** *1* **Daring Affair**[42] 3972 6-8-12 **71**.................................... J-PGuillambert 8 72
(K R Burke) *t.k.h: hld up towards rr: hdwy 4f out: no imp over 2f out* **25/1**

2503 **10** *nk* **Cavallini (USA)**[45] 3858 5-8-13 **72**............................ FergusSweeney 14 72
(G L Moore) *chsd ldrs: rdn over 3f out: wkng whn swtchd rt over 2f out: sn wl btn* **10/1**

2034 **11** *1 1/2* **Magic Mountain (IRE)**[15] 4763 3-8-4 **71**........................ JimmyQuinn 11 69
(R Hannon) *chsd ldrs: rdn wl over 2f out: wknd wl over 1f out* **20/1**

4550 **12** *2* **Polish Power (GER)**[21] 4597 7-9-7 **83**...................... AndrewElliott(3) 10 77
(J S Moore) *lw: in tch tl lost pl and pushed along over 6f out: swtchd rt and drvn over 2f out: no imp* **16/1**

4420 **13** *3 1/2* **Prince Nureyev (IRE)**[22] 4572 7-9-6 **79**........................ GeorgeBaker 4 67
(B R Millman) *dropped in after s: hld up in last: n.d* **8/1**[3]

000 **14** *13* **Kervriou (FR)**[23] 4551 4-8-12 **71** oh2.............................. PatDobbs 3 37
(A M Balding) *swtg: v.s.a: rapid hdwy on outer to ld 7f out tl over 2f out: sn wknd* **40/1**

-P20 **15** *3* **Fear To Tread (USA)**[31] 4288 4-9-9 **82**........................ MickyFenton 13 43
(Mrs P Sly) *swtg: led tl 7f out: styd prom tl wknd qckly wl over 2f out* **33/1**

2m 20.34s (-2.34) **Going Correction** -0.025s/f (Stan)
WFA 3 from 4yo+ 8lb **15** Ran SP% **135.3**
Speed ratings (Par 105): **107,106,105,104,103 103,103,102,102,101 100,99,96,87,85**
CSF £43.09 CT £150.95 TOTE £5.80: £2.30, £3.70, £2.20; EX 67.80 Place 6 £482.38, Place 5 £99.83..
Owner Tom Ludt **Bred** Pontchartrain Stud **Trained** Newmarket, Suffolk

FOCUS
Another fair handicap and solid form that should work out. The first pair came clear and look progressive.
T/Plt: £1,016.90 to a £1 stake. Pool: £77,526.90. 55.65 winning tickets. T/Qpdt: £50.10 to a £1 stake. Pool: £4,186.20. 61.80 winning tickets. SP

4781 THIRSK (L-H)
Saturday, September 8

OFFICIAL GOING: Good to firm
Wind: Nil Weather: Fine and sunny

5226 SCARBOROUGH CASTLE MAIDEN AUCTION STKS 7f
2:00 (2:01) (Class 5) 2-Y-O **£3,886** (£1,156; £577; £288) **Stalls** Low

Form RPR

04 **1** **Veronicas Way**[21] 4612 2-8-1 0.............................. AndrewMullen(3) 8 61
(G M Moore) *chsd ldr: hdwy to chal 2f out: sn rdn and edgd rt over 1f out: drvn and hung rt ent fnl f: styd on u.p to ld cl home* **7/1**

56 **2** *nk* **Grand Value (USA)**[15] 4769 2-8-4 0.................................. PaulFessey 5 60
(T D Barron) *led: rdn along over 2f out: drvn over 1f out: hdd and no ex nr fin* **6/1**[3]

02 **3** *2* **Priceless Speedfit**[9] 4968 2-8-4 0.................................. HayleyTurner 9 55
(G G Margarson) *trckd ldng pair: hdwy 3f out: rdn and carried rt ent fnl f: sn drvn and one pce* **7/2**[2]

00 **4** *5* **Shot Through (USA)**[21] 4611 2-8-9 0.............................. LeeEnstone 3 47
(P C Haslam) *in tch: hdwy 3f out: rdn to chse ldrs over 2f out: sn one pce* **33/1**

5 *1 1/4* **Defies Logic** 2-8-13 0.. DaleGibson 6 48
(J G Given) *s.i.s: sn in tch: rdn along wl over 2f out and no imp* **13/2**

0556 **6** *1 3/4* **Invincible Rose (IRE)**[42] 3951 2-7-11 **48**.............. AndrewHeffernan(7) 4 34
(M Brittain) *t.k.h: towards rr: rn wd home bnd: hdwy over 2f out: sn rdn and no imp* **10/1**

7 *nk* **Kavinsky** 2-8-13 0... GregFairley 2 42
(M Johnston) *chsd ldrs: pushed along 3f out: rdn over 2f out and sn wknd* **2/1**[1]

8 *20* **Indigo Mail (IRE)** 2-8-9 0.. RoystonFfrench 1 —
(M Brittain) *dwlt: sn rdn along: green and outpcd: a bhd* **11/1**

1m 28.8s (1.70) **Going Correction** +0.10s/f (Good) **8** Ran SP% **116.0**
Speed ratings (Par 95): **94,93,91,85,84 82,81,59**
CSF £48.99 TOTE £7.40: £1.70, £2.80, £1.50; EX 41.50.
Owner J Stevenson **Bred** A C Birkle **Trained** Middleham Moor, N Yorks

FOCUS
A moderate juvenile maiden which saw the first two come clear, but the pair had looked limited prior to this so the form is rated on the negative side.

NOTEBOOK
Veronicas Way, easy to back, found the step up to this extra furlong much to her liking and narrowly opened her account. She has improved with each of her three outings to date, but still looked green here as she continually hung right when under pressure and it may prove that she is happiest on slightly easier ground in the future - like her sprinting half-brother Mormeatmic. (op 4-1)
Grand Value(USA), back up in trip, was given a positive ride and proved game under maximum pressure. She only just failed, finishing nicely clear in second, and now has the option of nurseries. (op 7-1)
Priceless Speedfit, a market drifter, found just the one pace when it mattered and ran close her to Musselburgh form. She is probably worth a trying over 1m before long and now becomes eligible for a nursery mark. (op 9-4)
Shot Through(USA) turned in a rather laboured effort, but still showed by far his best form to date and now qualifies for nurseries. (op 25-1)
Defies Logic, who cost 21,000gns, met support in the betting ring ahead of this racecourse bow. He did not help his chances with a slow start, however, and his effort ultimately proved short-lived in the home straight. Presumably he is though capable of better and he should learn from the experience at least. (op 10-1)
Invincible Rose(IRE) Official explanation: jockey said filly ran too free; trainer later said filly had been struck into
Kavinsky, well backed, is related to winners from 6-12f and is from a stable whose juveniles are really now starting to fire. He proved too green to do himself full justice, however, and was made to look one paced under pressure. (op 11-4)
Indigo Mail(IRE) Official explanation: jockey said gelding was never travelling

5227 EUROPEAN BREEDERS' FUND MAIDEN STKS 1m
2:30 (2:31) (Class 4) 2-Y-O **£5,181** (£1,541; £770; £384) **Stalls** Low

Form RPR

52 **1** **Dr Faustus (IRE)**[19] 4656 2-9-3 0.. KDarley 6 85+
(Sir Michael Stoute) *mde all: pushed along over 2f out: rdn over 1f out: styd on ins fnl f: comf* **10/11**[1]

30 **2** *1* **Funny Me**[8] 5010 2-8-10 0.. MCGeran(7) 11 83
(P W Chapple-Hyam) *trckd ldrs: hdwy wl over 2f out: rdn wl over 1f out: drvn to chse wnr and edgd lft ins fnl f: kpt on* **14/1**

02 **3** *2* **Meer Kat (IRE)**[12] 4876 2-9-0 0.............................. RichardKingscote(3) 4 78+
(R Charlton) *towards rr: hdwy on outer over 3f out: chsd ldrs 2f out: sn rdn and kpt on same pce ent fnl f* **9/4**[2]

6 **4** *1 1/4* **Lanterns Of Gold**[14] 4796 2-8-12 0.............................. RoystonFfrench 10 70
(Mrs A Duffield) *chsd wnr: rdn along over 2f out: drvn over 1f out and grad wknd* **14/1**

5 *1 1/2* **Muzmin (USA)** 2-9-3 0.. GregFairley 1 72+
(M Johnston) *chsd ldrs on inner: rdn along over 3f out: wknd over 2f out* **12/1**[3]

00 **6** *3* **Terracos Do Pinhal**[10] 4930 2-9-0 0.............................. AndrewMullen(3) 3 65
(M Johnston) *towards rr: hdwy 3f out: rdn to chse ldrs 2f out: wknd ent fnl f* **50/1**

0560 **7** *5* **Harlequinn Danseur (IRE)**[15] 4781 2-9-3 **60**.....................(t) KimTinkler 9 53
(N Tinkler) *t.k.h: chsd ldrs to 1/2-way: sn wknd* **66/1**

8 *hd* **Whaston (IRE)** 2-9-3 0.. PaulFessey 2 53
(J D Bethell) *a in rr* **25/1**

6 **9** *9* **Desert Lark**[38] 4077 2-9-0 0.. PJMcDonald(3) 8 32
(G A Swinbank) *in midfield: rdn along 3f out: sn wknd* **25/1**

10 *49* **Wadi Raider** 2-9-3 0.. TPO'Shea 5 —
(M R Channon) *v.s.a and a bhd* **12/1**[3]

1m 39.59s (-0.11) **Going Correction** +0.10s/f (Good) **10** Ran SP% **123.0**
Speed ratings (Par 97): **104,103,101,99,98 95,90,90,81,32**
CSF £17.58 TOTE £1.90: £1.10, £2.60, £1.10; EX 14.70.
Owner Gainsborough **Bred** Gainsborough Stud Management Ltd **Trained** Newmarket, Suffolk

FOCUS
This could prove to be a fair juvenile maiden for the track. The form is straightforward with the winner and third close to form, and should work out.

NOTEBOOK

Dr Faustus(IRE), who caught a tartar on easy ground at Leicester when turned over at odds on last time, made amends with a straightforward display to shed his maiden tag at the third time of asking. The positive tactics certainly suited him over this extra furlong and he looks to be coming into his own now, so it will be very interesting to see whether his leading trainer takes the nursery route or opts to have a crack in Pattern company - he holds an entry in the Group 2 Royal Lodge. (op 6-5 tchd 5-4 in a place)

Funny Me posted a much more encouraging effort in defeat over this longer trip and was nicely clear of the remainder in second. He is developing into a fair sort, has more to offer, and now becomes eligible for a nursery mark.

Meer Kat(IRE) was again given a very patient ride and was forced to race wide, despite being drawn in stall four. He kept on once more without posing a serious threat and, now that he is eligible for a nursery mark, it will not be at all surprising to see him fare better under a more prominent ride in that sphere. (op 2-1)

Lanterns Of Gold failed to see out the extra furlong like the principals, but still improved on the level of his Beverley debut a fortnight previously and will be of greater interest when qualifying for a nursery mark after his next assignment. (op 12-1)

Muzmin(USA), half-brother to four winners in the US, showed up well enough until tiring approaching the final furlong. He may be best off dropping to 7f for the short term and should come on a deal for this debut experience. (op 11-1)

Desert Lark Official explanation: jockey said colt was unsuited by the good to firm going

Wadi Raider Official explanation: jockey said colt missed the break

5228 ERA LOCKS H'CAP — 1m

3:00 (3:00) (Class 5) (0-75,72) 3-Y-0+ — **£3,886** (£1,156; £577; £288) **Stalls** Low

Form — RPR

1541 **1** **Esoterica (IRE)**[2] 5159 4-8-13 **62**.....(b) DanielTudhope 5 — 68+
(J S Goldie) *dwlt and bhd: hmpd bnd after 3f: hdwy wl over 2f out: swtchd rt over 1f out and sn rdn: styd on gamely ins fnl f to ld on line* **13/8**[1]

4631 **2** *shd* **Cool Ebony**[7] 5035 4-9-9 **72**..... PhillipMakin 9 — 78
(M Dods) *trckd ldrs: hdwy 3f out: rdn to ld 1f out: drvn ins fnl f: hdd on line* **5/1**[2]

5043 **3** *1/2* **Efidium**[14] 4820 9-9-0 **68**..... NeilBrown(5) 7 — 73
(N Bycroft) *in midfield: gd hdwy on outer 3f out: chal 2f out: sn rdn and ev ch tl drvn and nt qckn wl ins fnl f* **10/1**

053 **4** *2* **Titinius (IRE)**[17] 4704 7-8-13 **62**..... KDarley 11 — 62
(Micky Hammond) *chsd ldrs: hdwy 3f out: rdn to ld 2f out: drvn and hdd 1f out: kpt on same pce* **14/1**

0500 **5** *shd* **Crocodile Bay (IRE)**[22] 4581 4-9-6 **69**..... AdrianTNicholls 12 — 69+
(D Nicholls) *stdd s: hld up in rr: gd hdwy on outer wl over 2f out: rdn ent fnl f and kpt on same pce* **15/2**[3]

0640 **6** *2* **Tough Love**[28] 4407 8-9-4 **67**.....(p) DavidAllan 4 — 63
(T D Easterby) *hld up: hdwy on inner 3f out: swtchd rt and rdn 2f out: styd on same pce appr fnl f* **8/1**

0063 **7** *1 3/4* **Waterline Twenty (IRE)**[8] 5001 4-9-2 **70**..... GaryBartley(5) 3 — 62
(P D Evans) *in tch: effrt over 3f out: sn rdn and wknd over 2f out* **11/1**

0000 **8** *hd* **Mis Chicaf (IRE)**[9] 4966 6-8-9 **58** oh13..... GrahamGibbons 1 — 49
(D Carroll) *led: rdn along 3f out: hdd 2f out and sn wknd* **66/1**

0400 **9** *2* **Sahara Dawn (IRE)**[7] 5046 3-8-4 **58** oh13..... HayleyTurner 10 — 44
(D Carroll) *prom: rdn along 3f out: grad wknd* **100/1**

0000 **10** *nk* **It's A Dream (FR)**[22] 4581 4-9-5 **68**..... DaleGibson 8 — 54
(M W Easterby) *a in rr* **11/1**

0200 **11** *8* **Heureux (USA)**[41] 3998 4-9-6 **69**.....(v) RoystonFfrench 6 — 36
(J Howard Johnson) *prom: rdn along over 3f out and sn wknd* **14/1**

40-0 **12** *5* **Kaymich Perfecto**[14] 4820 7-9-4 **70**..... MichaelJStainton(3) 2 — 26
(R M Whitaker) *a in rr* **20/1**

1m 39.62s (-0.08) **Going Correction** +0.10s/f (Good)
WFA 3 from 4yo+ 5lb — **12** Ran SP% **124.0**
Speed ratings (Par 103): **104,103,103,101,101 99,97,97,95,95 87,82**
CSF £9.74 CT £66.99 TOTE £2.80: £1.70, £2.70, £2.30; EX 13.50.
Owner Mrs S E Bruce **Bred** A Lyons Bloodstock **Trained** Uplawmoor, E Renfrews
■ Stewards' Enquiry : Daniel Tudhope two-day ban: careless riding (Sep 19-20)

FOCUS
A moderate handicap, run at a sound pace, which saw the first three come clear. The form is rated around the placed horses to their recent marks.

5229 SKYBET.COM HAMBLETON CUP (H'CAP) — 1m 4f

3:30 (3:30) (Class 4) (0-80,79) 3-Y-0+ — **£6,477** (£1,927; £963; £481) **Stalls** Low

Form — RPR

0311 **1** **Generous Jem**[3] 5144 4-9-3 **74** 6ex..... NeilBrown(5) 5 — 83+
(G G Margarson) *hld up in rr: hdwy on outer 3f out: rdn and hung lft ent fnl f: sn drvn and styd on wl to ld last 75yds* **11/4**[1]

115 **2** *1 1/4* **Ravenna**[21] 4597 3-8-11 **72**..... HayleyTurner 2 — 79
(M P Tregoning) *prom: hdwy to chse ldr 3f out: rdn to ld over 1f out: drvn ins fnl f: hdd and no ex last 75yds* **11/2**

2013 **3** *2 1/2* **Hypoteneuse (IRE)**[50] 3719 3-9-3 **78**..... KDarley 1 — 81
(Sir Michael Stoute) *led: rdn along 3f out: drvn and hdd over 1f out: kpt on same pce* **9/2**[2]

0451 **4** *2 1/2* **Doctor Scott**[5] 5086 4-9-8 **74** 6ex..... GregFairley 7 — 73
(M Johnston) *in tch: rdn along to chse ldrs over 3f out: drvn 2f out and kpt on same pce* **11/4**[1]

-052 **5** *nk* **Go Tech**[11] 4922 7-9-13 **79**..... DavidAllan 3 — 78
(T D Easterby) *hld up: hdwy over 2f out: sn rdn and no imp* **5/1**[3]

3600 **6** *1 1/4* **Stretton (IRE)**[16] 4732 9-9-10 **76**..... RoystonFfrench 4 — 73
(J D Bethell) *hld up: effrt over 3f out: sn rdn along and btn 2f out* **14/1**

4330 **7** *1* **Moonwalking**[21] 4617 3-8-12 **73**..... DanielTudhope 6 — 68
(Jedd O'Keeffe) *chsd ldr: rdn along 3f out: sn wknd* **20/1**

2m 35.61s (0.41) **Going Correction** +0.10s/f (Good)
WFA 3 from 4yo+ 9lb — **7** Ran SP% **115.0**
Speed ratings (Par 105): **102,101,99,97,97 96,96**
CSF £18.61 TOTE £3.70: £1.80, £3.20; EX 24.50.
Owner Norcroft Park Stud **Bred** Norcroft Park Stud **Trained** Newmarket, Suffolk

FOCUS
A good handicap for the class with the third the best guide to the level. It was run at an ordinary gallop, however, so the progressive winner deserves extra credit.

5230 BDO STOY HAYWARD FILLIES' STKS (H'CAP) — 1m

4:00 (4:00) (Class 4) (0-85,84) 3-Y-0+ — **£5,181** (£1,541; £770; £384) **Stalls** Low

Form — RPR

0222 **1** **Society Music (IRE)**[10] 4932 5-8-11 **72**.....(p) NeilBrown(5) 6 — 79
(M Dods) *trckd ldrs: hdwy 2f out: sn rdn: styd on to ld ins fnl f: styd on wl* **15/2**

1116 **2** *nk* **Sam's Secret**[28] 4407 5-9-4 **77**..... PJMcDonald(3) 3 — 83
(G A Swinbank) *hld up towards rr: smooth hdwy over 2f out: swtchd outside and rdn to chal ent fnl f: ev ch tl drvn and nt qckn nr fin* **7/1**[3]

0533 **3** *hd* **Millestan (IRE)**[13] 4848 3-9-9 **84**..... KDarley 11 — 89
(H R A Cecil) *trckd ldrs: hdwy to ld over 1f out: drvn and hdd ins fnl f: kpt on wl u.p* **7/2**[1]

1043 **4** *1* **Onatopp (IRE)**[17] 4705 3-8-7 **68**..... DavidAllan 9 — 71
(T D Easterby) *stdd s and hld up in rr: hdwy on outer 3f out: rdn to chse ldrs over 1f out: drvn and kpt on same pce ins fnl f* **12/1**

0064 **5** *nk* **She's Our Lass (IRE)**[7] 5035 6-9-0 **70**.....(v) GrahamGibbons 5 — 73
(D Carroll) *in rr and pushed along 1/2-way: rdn and hdwy 2f out: swtchd lft over 1f out: styd on wl u.p ins fnl f: nrst fin* **7/1**[3]

3004 **6** *1* **Rakata (USA)**[54] 3591 5-9-3 **78**..... TolleyDean(5) 4 — 79
(P F I Cole) *led: rdn along over 2f out: drvn over 1f out: hdd appr last and one pce* **15/2**

0000 **7** *hd* **Hula Ballew**[14] 4820 7-9-4 **74**..... PhillipMakin 8 — 74
(M Dods) *cl up: rdn along 2f out and ev ch tl drvn and wknd appr fnl f* **8/1**

4001 **8** *1 1/4* **Musical Beat**[10] 4940 3-9-0 **80**..... LukeMorris(5) 7 — 76
(Miss V Haigh) *in midfield: hdwy over 2f out: rdn to chse ldrs over 1f out: wknd ins fnl f* **12/1**

5510 **9** *3/4* **Wasalat (USA)**[73] 2985 5-9-1 **71**..... RoystonFfrench 2 — 67
(D W Barker) *s.i.s: in midfield and rdn along on inner 1/2-way: sn wknd* **16/1**

1101 **10** *11* **Rhuepunzel**[19] 4665 3-9-5 **80**..... HayleyTurner 1 — 49
(G A Butler) *trckd ldrs on inner: rdn along over 2f out and sn wknd* **6/1**[2]

-600 **11** *10* **Lakshmi (IRE)**[121] 1610 3-9-4 **79**..... TPO'Shea 10 — 25
(M R Channon) *in midfield: rdn along on outer 1/2-way: sn wknd* **20/1**

1m 39.24s (-0.46) **Going Correction** +0.10s/f (Good)
WFA 3 from 5yo+ 5lb — **11** Ran SP% **122.2**
Speed ratings (Par 102): **106,105,105,104,104 103,103,101,101,90 80**
CSF £61.65 CT £225.01 TOTE £11.50: £3.80, £2.20, £1.90; EX 92.10.
Owner Henry Hewitson **Bred** John Weld **Trained** Denton, Co Durham

FOCUS
A fair fillies' handicap that was run at a solid pace and the form is rated around the winner and fifth.
Rhuepunzel Official explanation: jockey said filly was unsuited by the good to firm going

5231 RJF HOMES MAIDEN STKS — 6f

4:35 (4:36) (Class 5) 3-Y-0+ — **£3,886** (£1,156; £577; £288) **Stalls** High

Form — RPR

40 **1** **Haedi**[71] 3051 3-8-12 0.....(t) KDarley 2 — 56+
(Saeed Bin Suroor) *in tch: hdwy over 2f out: rdn to ld appr fnl f: kpt on* **9/2**[2]

3304 **2** *3/4* **Slip Star**[16] 4736 4-9-0 48..... GregFairley 12 — 52
(T J Etherington) *prom: led 1/2-way: rdn and hdd appr fnl f: kpt on same pce* **6/1**[3]

0000 **3** *1 1/2* **Boppys Dream**[14] 4801 5-8-11 42.....(p) JamieMoriarty(3) 15 — 47
(P T Midgley) *chsd ldrs: rdn along 2f out: drvn and kpt on same pce fnl f* **18/1**

4 *hd* **Royal Encore** 3-8-12 0..... RoystonFfrench 4 — 47+
(J R Fanshawe) *dwlt and in rr: hdwy on outer and rn green over 2f out: sn rdn: styd on ins fnl f: nrst fin* **6/1**[3]

5 *1 1/2* **Thermidor (USA)** 4-9-2 0..... RichardKingscote(3) 13 — 47+
(R Charlton) *s.i.s and bhd: hdwy 2f out: styd on ins fnl f: nrst fin* **9/2**[2]

04 **6** *2* **Van Ruymbeke (IRE)**[5] 5082 3-8-10 0.....(t) JamesO'Reilly(7) 10 — 40
(D J Murphy) *in rr tl styd on fnl 2f* **12/1**

22 **7** *nk* **Alto Vertigo**[5] 5082 4-9-5 0..... LeeEnstone 7 — 39
(P C Haslam) *chsd ldrs: rdn along 2f out: kpt on same pce* **4/1**[1]

0006 **8** *3/4* **Ducal Regancy Red**[14] 4801 3-8-12 37..... PaulQuinn 14 — 32
(C J Teague) *chsd ldrs: rdn along over 2f out: sn no imp* **50/1**

04/0 **9** *3/4* **High Window (IRE)**[105] 2027 7-8-12 36..... NSLawes(7) 8 — 35
(G P Kelly) *a in rr* **50/1**

40 **10** *1 1/2* **Johnston's Glory (IRE)**[16] 4736 3-8-7 0..... GaryBartley(5) 5 — 25
(E J Alston) *a towards rr* **12/1**

002 **11** *3/4* **Cumberland Road**[24] 4494 4-8-12 45.....(v) SophieDoyle(7) 3 — 27
(C A Mulhall) *a towards rr* **12/1**

600 **12** *7* **Rose Of Inchinor**[36] 4141 4-8-11 43.....(v[1]) DuranFentiman(3) 9 — —
(R E Barr) *led: hdd 1/2-way: sn rdn along and wknd* **25/1**

0 **R** **Florentine Lady**[21] 4616 4-8-11 0..... DominicFox(3) 1 — —
(D Shaw) *veered sharply lft s and ref to r* **66/1**

1m 13.45s (0.95) **Going Correction** +0.10s/f (Good)
WFA 3 from 4yo+ 2lb — **13** Ran SP% **122.5**
Speed ratings (Par 103): **97,96,94,93,91 89,88,87,86,84 83,74,—**
CSF £31.98 TOTE £5.80: £2.40, £3.00, £5.60; EX 44.10.
Owner Godolphin **Bred** Gainsborough Stud Management Ltd **Trained** Newmarket, Suffolk

FOCUS
A very weak maiden. The winner is value for a bit further than her winning margin.
Van Ruymbeke(IRE) Official explanation: jockey said colt was denied a clear run
Alto Vertigo Official explanation: jockey said gelding was never travelling

5232 RACE AGAIN ON 18TH SEPTEMBER H'CAP — 6f

5:10 (5:10) (Class 5) (0-75,74) 3-Y-0+ — **£3,886** (£1,156; £577; £288) **Stalls** High

Form — RPR

3000 **1** **Cornus**[14] 4800 5-8-5 **66**.....(be) RobbieEgan(7) 10 — 76
(A J McCabe) *dwlt and towards rr: hdwy over 2f out: swtchd lft and rdn to chal ent fnl f: edgd lft and styd on to ld last 75yds* **9/1**[3]

0000 **2** *hd* **Oranmore Castle (IRE)**[8] 5009 5-9-2 **73**..... JamieMoriarty(3) 11 — 82
(R A Fahey) *led: rdn along 2f out: drvn and edgd rt ins fnl f: hdd and nt qckn last 75yds* **11/2**[2]

1010 **3** *hd* **Choysia**[20] 4639 4-9-6 **74**..... RoystonFfrench 6 — 82
(D W Barker) *chsd ldrs: hdwy 2f out: sn rdn and ev ch ins fnl f: drvn and kpt on* **9/1**[3]

440 **4** *1 3/4* **Mulligan's Gold (IRE)**[14] 4800 4-8-3 **60**.....(p) DuranFentiman(3) 9 — 63
(T D Easterby) *towards rr: hdwy 2f out: sn rdn and kpt on ins fnl f: nrst fin* **14/1**

221R **5** *hd* **Danish Blues (IRE)**[9] 4974 4-8-6 **60** oh1..... SilvestreDeSousa 12 — 62
(D Nicholls) *cl up: rdn along and ev ch 2f out: drvn over 1f out and kpt on same pce* **11/1**

4020 **6** *shd* **Pickering**[12] 4898 3-9-3 **73**..... DavidAllan 3 — 75
(E J Alston) *swtchd rt s and bhd: hdwy 2f out: rdn and kpt on ins fnl f: nrst fin* **20/1**

1000 **7** *3* **Steel Blue**[8] 4999 7-9-2 **70**..... HayleyTurner 13 — 62
(R M Whitaker) *trckd ldrs: hdwy on stands' rail 2f out: rdn over 1f out and sn wknd* **7/2**[1]

6060 **8** *3 1/2* **Just Joey**[2] 5155 3-9-4 **74**..... PhillipMakin 7 — 55
(J R Weymes) *in midfield: hdwy to chse ldrs 2f out: sn rdn and btn* **18/1**

2110 **9** *1/2* **Makabul**[19] 4664 4-9-6 **74**..... GrahamGibbons 1 — 53
(B R Millman) *chsd ldrs on outer: rdn along over 2f out: sn wknd* **10/1**

3263 **10** *2* **Choreography**[14] 4822 4-8-8 **62**.....(v) AdrianTNicholls 5 — 35
(D Nicholls) *rdn along and bhd fr 1/2-way* **7/2**[1]

3030 **11** *6* **Bahamian Duke**[17] 4703 4-8-1 **62** DeclanCannon[(7)] 8 16
(K R Burke) *chsd ldrs to 1/2-way: sn wknd* **20/1**

4665 **12** *1 1/4* **Ingleby Princess**[10] 4940 3-9-2 **72** PaulFessey 4 22
(T D Barron) *racd wd: bhd fr 1/2-way* **12/1**

1m 12.25s (-0.25) **Going Correction** +0.10s/f (Good)
WFA 3 from 4yo+ 2lb **12** Ran SP% **126.4**
Speed ratings (Par 103): **105,104,104,102,101 101,97,93,92,89 81,80**
CSF £61.88 CT £475.87 TOTE £13.00: £3.60, £3.20, £2.50; EX 94.50 Place 6 £53.60, Place 5 £17.67..
Owner Club ROA **Bred** G Russell **Trained** Babworth, Notts
■ Stewards' Enquiry : Robbie Egan two-day ban: used whip with excessive frequency (Sep 19-20)
Jamie Moriarty two-day ban: used whip with excessive frequency (Sep 19-20)

FOCUS
A modest, yet open sprint for the class with the runner-up setting the standard. Again a high draw was an advantage and the first three came clear.
Choreography Official explanation: jockey said gelding was never travelling
T/Plt: £42.00 to a £1 stake. Pool: £55,548.00. 964.90 winning tickets. T/Qpdt: £31.50 to a £1 stake. Pool: £2,249.80. 52.80 winning tickets. JR

5174 WOLVERHAMPTON (A.W) (L-H)
Saturday, September 8

OFFICIAL GOING: Standard

5233 BRINDLEY CITROEN CLAIMING STKS 7f 32y(P)
7:00 (7:00) (Class 5) 3-Y-0+ **£3,071** (£906; £453) **Stalls** High

Form RPR

0404 **1** **Megalo Maniac**[17] 4701 4-9-4 62 PaulHanagan 2 72
(R A Fahey) *hld up in tch: lost pl over 4f out: hdwy on ins to ld over 1f out: drvn out* **4/1**[2]

362- **2** *nk* **Ask The Clerk (IRE)**[12] 6-8-9 68 VinceSlattery 6 62
(Mrs J L Le Brocq, Jersey) *hld up in mid-div: rdn and hdwy over 1f out: r.o ins fnl f* **33/1**

0000 **3** *3/4* **Autograph Hunter**[40] 4021 3-8-5 72 AdrianMcCarthy 3 58
(Peter Grayson) *s.i.s: hld up in rr: rdn and hdwy over 1f out: r.o ins fnl f* **14/1**

3223 **4** *1* **Million Percent**[29] 4353 8-9-7 71 LiamJones[(3)] 7 72
(C R Dore) *a.p: rdn and one pce fnl f: fin lame* **2/1**[1]

2040 **5** *1* **Regal Raider (IRE)**[5] 5083 4-9-7 73 TomEaves 1 67
(I Semple) *led early: prom: rdn over 1f out: no ex ins fnl f* **4/1**[2]

5040 **6** *3/4* **Ocean Gift**[14] 4822 5-9-1 59 KimTinkler 9 59
(N Tinkler) *hld up and bhd: hdwy over 5f out: ev ch wl over 1f out: sn rdn: wknd 1f out* **8/1**[3]

2200 **7** *2 1/2* **Local Poet**[28] 4381 6-9-7 69 (b) PaulMulrennan 8 58
(I Semple) *hld up in mid-div: hdwy over 4f out: wknd over 2f out* **9/1**

0600 **8** *3/4* **Alfredian Park**[24] 4505 3-8-11 68 (b[1]) LPKeniry 4 48
(S Kirk) *t.k.h: sn led: rdn whn hung lft and hdd over 1f out: sn wknd* **20/1**

0050 **9** *3/4* **Cherri Fosfate**[7] 5037 3-9-0 62 (b) StephenDonohoe 10 49
(D Carroll) *s.s: rdn over 3f out: a in rr* **12/1**

1m 29.03s (-1.37) **Going Correction** -0.275s/f (Stan)
WFA 3 from 4yo+ 4lb **9** Ran SP% **116.5**
Speed ratings (Par 103): **96,95,94,93,92 91,88,87,87**
CSF £119.91 TOTE £6.70: £2.70, £9.50, £4.10; EX 206.20.
Owner A Long **Bred** E R W Stanley And New England Stud Farm Ltd **Trained** Musley Bank, N Yorks

FOCUS
A modest claimer best rated through the winner with little solid in behind.
Million Percent Official explanation: jockey said gelding was lame on the right foreleg
Cherri Fosfate Official explanation: jockey said gelding missed the break

5234 BRINDLEY FIRST FOR FLEET H'CAP 5f 216y(P)
7:30 (7:31) (Class 6) (0-65,65) 3-Y-0+ **£2,388** (£705; £352) **Stalls** Low

Form RPR

6634 **1** **Nusoor (IRE)**[5] 5085 4-9-3 **62** (b) BrettDoyle 11 72
(Peter Grayson) *t.k.h: hdwy over 4f out: rdn to ld over 1f out: hdd ins fnl f: led last strides* **11/2**[2]

2353 **2** *hd* **Norcroft**[3] 5130 5-8-10 **62** (p) KirstyMilczarek[(7)] 6 71
(Mrs C A Dunnett) *led 1f: a.p: rdn over 1f out: led ins fnl f: hdd last strides* **11/8**[1]

1260 **3** *1* **Bucharest**[4] 5118 4-9-5 **64** PaulEddery 4 70
(M Wigham) *hld up in tch: squeezed through over 1f out: rdn and ev ch whn edgd lft ins fnl f: nt qckn* **10/1**

5066 **4** *1 1/4* **Chatshow (USA)**[30] 4320 6-9-6 **65** AdamKirby 8 67
(A W Carroll) *hld up in mid-div: swtchd lft and hdwy over 1f out: rdn ins fnl f: one pce* **8/1**

4006 **5** *hd* **Guildenstern (IRE)**[3] 5130 5-9-6 **65** IanMongan 12 67
(P Howling) *a.p: led 2f out: rdn and hdd over 1f out: no ex ins fnl f* **7/1**[3]

320 **6** *3/4* **Bluebelle Dancer (IRE)**[13] 4848 3-9-3 **64** RichardMullen 5 63
(W R Muir) *s.i.s: bhd: rdn and hung lft fr over 1f out: styng on whn bdly bmpd wl ins fnl f* **10/1**

00 **7** *shd* **Law Maker**[5] 5085 7-9-0 **62** (v) NeilChalmers[(3)] 3 61
(A Bailey) *led after 1f: rdn and hdd 2f out: wkng whn n.m.r and swtchd rt ins fnl f: sn hung bdly rt* **28/1**

0433 **8** *1 1/4* **Nans Lady (IRE)**[10] 4938 4-9-4 **63** ChrisCatlin 2 58
(E J O'Neill) *sn bhd* **16/1**

0004 **9** *5* **James Street (IRE)**[72] 3036 4-9-4 **63** LPKeniry 9 43
(Peter Grayson) *hld up in tch: lost pl over 3f out: sn rdn: n.d after* **16/1**

224 **10** *6* **Ellablue**[137] 1207 3-9-2 **63** PaulHanagan 13 25
(Rae Guest) *sn bhd* **20/1**

1m 14.04s (-1.77) **Going Correction** -0.275s/f (Stan)
WFA 3 from 4yo+ 2lb **10** Ran SP% **119.3**
Speed ratings (Par 101): **100,99,98,96,96 95,95,93,87,79**
CSF £13.73 CT £79.02 TOTE £8.50: £2.80, £1.10, £4.60; EX 16.00.
Owner R Teatum And Mrs S Grayson **Bred** Shadwell Estate Company Limited **Trained** Formby, Lancs
■ Stewards' Enquiry : Neil ChalmersM three-day ban: careless riding (Sep 19-21)
Paul EdderyM caution: careless riding
Richard MullenM three-day ban: hit rival horse with whip (Sep 19-21)

FOCUS
A very tight handicap, with only 4lb between top and bottom weight. The form looks sound enough rated around the placed horses.
Bluebelle Dancer(IRE) Official explanation: jockey said filly hung left
Law Maker Official explanation: jockey said gelding hung right
Ellablue Official explanation: jockey said filly hung right

5235 ANTHONY AND ALAN'S 40TH B'DAY CELEBRATION (S) STKS 1m 4f 50y(P)
7:55 (7:55) (Class 6) 3-5-Y-0 **£2,047** (£604; £302) **Stalls** Low

Form RPR

3303 **1** **Brastar Jelois (FR)**[13] 4846 4-8-8 59 (p) RussellKennemore[(5)] 1 52+
(R Hollinshead) *hld up and bhd: stdy hdwy on ins whn nt clr run briefly over 2f out: shkn up to ld jst over 1f out: sn clr: r.o wl* **7/2**[2]

003 **2** *2 1/2* **Hook Money (IRE)**[23] 4528 3-8-4 50 KevinGhunowa[(5)] 10 53
(J L Flint) *hld up in tch: rdn over 2f out: styd on wl ins fnl f: nt trble wnr* **28/1**

0063 **3** *2 1/2* **Flashing Floozie**[12] 4-8-11 36 MarkCoumbe[(7)] 6 49
(Mrs J L Le Brocq, Jersey) *led: rdn over 2f out: hdd over 1f out: no ex ins fnl f* **33/1**

0005 **4** *2* **Cool Isle**[26] 4460 4-8-13 40 (b) IanMongan 3 41
(P Howling) *hld up in mid-div: hdwy on ins 4f out: rdn wl over 1f out: wknd ins fnl f* **16/1**

6060 **5** *2 1/2* **Figaro's Quest (IRE)**[13] 4859 5-9-4 44 (b) SamHitchcott 4 42
(C N Kellett) *hld up in mid-div: lost pl over 4f out: rdn and hdwy on outside wl over 1f out: sn no imp* **22/1**

50-4 **6** *8* **Forever Autumn**[15] 4757 4-9-4 58 ChrisCatlin 11 29
(D G Bridgwater) *hld up in tch: rdn and wknd over 3f out* **20/1**

0523 **7** *shd* **Dr Dream (IRE)**[9] 4961 3-8-9 57 (v) FergusSweeney 12 29
(J G M O'Shea) *hld up in mid-div: rdn and shortlived effrt on outside over 3f out* **8/1**[3]

5500 **8** *5* **Ten Black**[32] 4256 3-8-9 43 StephenDonohoe 2 21
(R Brotherton) *hld up and bhd: hdwy on ins over 2f out: rdn and wknd over 1f out* **66/1**

2150 **9** *5* **Soldiers Quest**[17] 4713 3-9-0 86 LPKeniry 8 18
(Peter Grayson) *prom: chsd ldr 7f out tl rdn and wknd over 2f out: fin lame* **9/4**[1]

600 **10** *1/2* **Screaming Reel**[13] 4856 4-9-4 48 AdamKirby 5 12
(M Wellings) *rdn over 4f out: a bhd* **66/1**

2066 **11** *1 1/2* **Rock Haven (IRE)**[23] 4526 5-9-4 55 TGMcLaughlin 7 10
(J W Unett) *a bhd* **7/2**[2]

0044 **12** *shd* **Leprechaun's Gold (IRE)**[11] 4920 3-8-7 48 ow3 HaddenFrost[(5)] 9 12
(B J Llewellyn) *hld ldr 5f: prom tl rdn and wknd over 2f out* **14/1**

2m 40.28s (-2.14) **Going Correction** -0.275s/f (Stan)
WFA 3 from 4yo+ 9lb **12** Ran SP% **117.4**
Speed ratings (Par 101): **96,94,92,91,89 84,84,80,77,77 76,76**
CSF £106.71 TOTE £4.60: £1.30, £6.80, £5.20; EX 124.70.There was no bid for the winner. Hook Money was claimed by A. J. McCabe for £6,000
Owner Phil Pye **Bred** M Guillois & Roger Jean **Trained** Upper Longdon, Staffs

FOCUS
A weak seller run at a modest pace and rated around the placed horses, although not that solid.
Soldiers Quest Official explanation: vet said colt finished lame behind
Screaming Reel Official explanation: jockey said gelding was never travelling

5236 BRINDLEY HONDA NOVICE AUCTION STKS 1m 141y(P)
8:25 (8:26) (Class 5) 2-Y-0 **£3,238** (£963; £481; £240) **Stalls** Low

Form RPR

245 **1** **Abolition (USA)**[55] 3574 2-8-11 0 KDarley 6 85+
(M Johnston) *chsd ldr: led 3f out: rdn over 1f out: edgd lft ins fnl f: r.o* **5/6**[1]

223 **2** *3* **Graceful Descent (FR)**[13] 4852 2-8-6 74 PaulHanagan 5 74
(R A Fahey) *led: hdd 3f out: sn rdn: hld whn swtchd rt ins fnl f* **2/1**[2]

13 **3** *7* **Semah Harold**[25] 4482 2-9-1 82 RichardMullen 4 68
(E S McMahon) *chsd ldrs: rdn 3f out: wknd over 2f out* **5/1**[3]

00 **4** *19* **Ba Speedbird (IRE)**[91] 2443 2-8-6 0 ChrisCatlin 2 19
(M R Channon) *in rr: pushed along over 4f out: sn struggling* **25/1**

1m 49.41s (-2.35) **Going Correction** -0.275s/f (Stan) **4** Ran SP% **108.4**
Speed ratings (Par 95): **99,96,90,73**
CSF £2.76 TOTE £1.80; EX 2.60.
Owner Joy And Valentine Feerick **Bred** B C Jones **Trained** Middleham Moor, N Yorks

FOCUS
Not a very competitive novice race with half the original line-up withdrawn. The runner-up is the most reliable guide to the level.

NOTEBOOK
Abolition(USA) did not cut much ice in a Group 3 event at the Curragh last time, but this represented a much easier task and he ran out a clear winner. A son of Halling, he appreciated the step up in trip, and look the type to make up into a useful three-year-old next season. (op 6-5)
Graceful Descent(FR), who had put up consistent efforts in maiden company without winning, shaped well up in grade, and ran a perfectly respectable race. She should be competitive in nurseries if not put up for this. (op 5-2)
Semah Harold, who had to give weight to the rest, made a winning debut over 7f here in July, but he has been held in better company since and does not seem to get home over a mile plus at present. (op 11-4 tchd 11-2)

5237 BRINDLEY FIRST FOR HONDA H'CAP 1m 141y(P)
8:55 (8:56) (Class 6) (0-60,64) 3-Y-0+ **£2,388** (£705; £352) **Stalls** Low

Form RPR

4421 **1** **Bethanys Boy (IRE)**[23] 4533 6-9-7 **57** VinceSlattery 11 64
(D J Daly) *chsd ldrs: rdn to ld jst over 1f out: jst hld on* **5/1**[2]

53 **2** *hd* **October Ben**[22] 4577 4-9-1 **58** FrankiePickard[(7)] 2 65
(M D I Usher) *s.i.s: hld up and bhd: rdn over 1f out: str run ins fnl f: jst failed* **10/1**

0612 **3** *3/4* **Casablanca Minx (IRE)**[8] 5020 4-9-13 **63** (v) StephenDonohoe 9 68
(P D Evans) *hld up and bhd: hdwy wl over 1f out: swtchd lft ins fnl f: r.o* **4/1**[1]

0-00 **4** *nk* **George's Flyer (IRE)**[25] 4477 4-9-2 **52** (v) PaulHanagan 10 56
(R A Fahey) *a.p: rdn over 2f out: r.o one pce fnl f* **33/1**

2003 **5** *3/4* **Green Pirate**[8] 5016 5-9-5 **58** (p) LiamJones[(3)] 4 60
(W M Brisbourne) *hld up in mid-div: hdwy 2f out: rdn over 1f out: one pce* **6/1**[3]

3606 **6** *shd* **Bold Saxon (IRE)**[86] 2593 3-9-4 **60** RichardSmith 12 62
(M D I Usher) *chsd ldr: led 2f out: rdn and hdd jst over 1f out: no ex towards fin* **33/1**

5040 **7** *2* **Soldier Field**[29] 4354 3-9-3 **59** LPKeniry 3 57
(A M Balding) *chsd ldrs: rdn and edgd lft fr jst over 1f out: wknd ins fnl f* **9/1**

0006 **8** *3* **Blue Bird's Dream**[12] 4905 4-9-4 **57** TravisBlock[(3)] 6 48
(E J Alston) *led: rdn and hdd 2f out: wknd jst over 1f out* **25/1**

2451 **9** *shd* **Hits Only Cash**[13] 4856 5-10-0 **64** BrettDoyle 13 54
(J Pearce) *hld up and bhd: rdn over 3f out: a bhd* **13/2**

-004 **10** *3/4* **Da Bookie (IRE)**[32] 4256 7-9-1 **51** TPO'Shea 1 40
(P A Blockley) *s.i.s: a bhd* **10/1**

06-0 **11** *10* **Hurricane Coast**[183] 650 8-9-8 **58**................................(b) AdamKirby 7 24
(K McAuliffe) *a bhd* **9/1**
060- **12** *2* **Pearl Of Esteem**[311] 6289 4-9-7 **57**................................ TGMcLaughlin 8 18
(Mrs C A Dunnett) *s.i.s: n.m.r on ins over 6f out: a towards rr* **100/1**
5-03 **13** *3 1/2* **Kings Topic (USA)**[21] 4592 7-9-10 **60**............................ SamHitchcott 5 13
(A B Haynes) *hld up in mid-div: rdn over 4f out: wknd over 2f out* **12/1**

1m 49.18s (-2.58) **Going Correction** -0.275s/f (Stan)
WFA 3 from 4yo+ 6lb **13** Ran SP% **120.9**
Speed ratings (Par 101): **100,99,99,98,98 98,96,93,93,92 84,82,79**
CSF £53.50 CT £229.86 TOTE £6.00: £1.70, £3.70, £2.70; EX 71.70.
Owner Ms S Hamilton **Bred** K And Mrs Cullen **Trained** Newmarket, Suffolk

FOCUS
There are doubts over the form with 33-1 shots too close for comfort, but overall it looks solid enough for the grade.
Da Bookie(IRE) Official explanation: jockey said gelding had no more to give
Kings Topic(USA) Official explanation: jockey said gelding was never travelling

5238 BRINDLEY FLEET H'CAP 7f 32y(P)
9:20 (9:21) (Class 5) (0-75,75) 3-Y-O **£3,238** (£963; £481; £240) **Stalls** High

Form RPR
4433 **1** **Giant Slalom**[14] 4811 3-9-0 **74**........................... LiamJones(3) 7 83+
(W J Haggas) *sn led: rdn over 1f out: r.o* **15/8**[1]
0106 **2** *3/4* **All You Need (IRE)**[16] 4740 3-8-11 **68**.............................. LPKeniry 5 75
(R Hollinshead) *chsd ldrs: wnt 2nd over 2f out: rdn over 1f out: kpt on ins fnl f* **11/1**
0046 **3** *1 1/4* **Tom Paris**[7] 5046 3-9-1 **72**.............................. RichardMullen 1 76
(W R Muir) *hld up and bhd: hdwy on ins wl over 1f out: r.o ins fnl f* **7/1**[3]
161 **4** *3/4* **Napoleon Dynamite (IRE)**[2] 5177 3-9-4 **75** 6ex................. TPO'Shea 2 77
(J W Hills) *hld up towards rr: hdwy on ins over 2f out: rdn over 1f out: one pce fnl f* **9/2**[2]
6134 **5** *hd* **Gap Princess (IRE)**[13] 4848 3-8-9 **66**.............................. PaulHanagan 11 67
(R A Fahey) *hld up in mid-div: hdwy over 2f out: rdn over 1f out: one pce* **10/1**
2555 **6** *1* **Telltime (IRE)**[27] 4420 3-9-0 **74**.............................. NeilChalmers(3) 4 73
(A M Balding) *led early: sn mid-div: no hdwy fnl 2f* **9/2**[2]
0004 **7** *hd* **Jord (IRE)**[12] 4885 3-8-8 **72**.............................. RobbieEgan(7) 6 70
(A J McCabe) *hld up towards rr: rdn and c wd st: nvr trbld ldrs* **25/1**
6106 **8** *1 3/4* **Tipsy Prince**[23] 4538 3-9-1 **72**.............................. ChrisCatlin 3 65
(David Pinder) *hld up towards rr: nt clr run briefly wl over 1f out: n.d* **33/1**
1002 **9** *1/2* **Chattan Clan**[16] 4740 3-9-1 **72**..............................(t) FergusSweeney 9 64
(R A Kvisla) *chsd ldrs: rdn over 3f out: wknd over 2f out* **20/1**
2-00 **10** *3 1/2* **Trickle (USA)**[13] 4855 3-8-10 **67**.............................. PaulEddery 12 50
(Miss D Mountain) *s.i.s: a bhd* **33/1**
0160 **11** *6* **Leonard Charles**[29] 4354 3-9-1 **72**..............................(b) AdamKirby 10 38
(C R Dore) *chsd ldrs: rdn over 2f out: wknd wl over 1f out* **18/1**

1m 28.08s (-2.32) **Going Correction** -0.275s/f (Stan) **11** Ran SP% **120.8**
Speed ratings (Par 101): **102,101,99,98,98 97,97,95,94,90 83**
CSF £24.39 CT £125.82 TOTE £3.30: £1.70, £2.70, £3.40; EX 43.60 Place 6 £ 135.46, Place 5 £ 23.67.
Owner B Smith,A Duke,J Netherthorpe,G Goddard **Bred** Old Mill Farm **Trained** Newmarket, Suffolk

FOCUS
An ordinary handicap run at a good clip. The form looks solid rated around the third and fourth.
T/Plt: £320.90 to a £1 stake. Pool: £79,242.15. 180.25 winning tickets. T/Qpdt: £50.50 to a £1 stake. Pool: £5,010.30. 73.40 winning tickets. KH

4643 LEOPARDSTOWN (L-H)
Saturday, September 8

OFFICIAL GOING: Good to firm

5240a STARAIR KILTERNAN STKS (GROUP 3) 1m 2f
2:10 (2:13) 3-Y-O+ **£43,918** (£12,837; £6,081; £2,027)

RPR
1 **Hearthstead Maison (IRE)**[18] 4692 3-9-1 .... RyanMoore 6 114
(M Johnston) *chsd ldrs in 6th: 5th and drvn along 3f out: hdwy early st: led over 1f out: styd on wl* **9/2**[2]
2 *1 1/2* **Arch Rebel (USA)**[20] 4647 6-9-8 108..................................(p) FMBerry 1 111
(Noel Meade, Ire) *dwlt: hld up towards rr: last but in tch appr st: prog 2f out: 4th 1f out: kpt on u.p* **10/1**
3 *nk* **Regime (IRE)**[21] 4627 3-9-4 .... JamieSpencer 3 113
(M L W Bell) *hld up in rr: 7th 3f out: hdwy early st: 3rd over 1f out: kpt on same pce u.p* **7/2**[1]
4 *1* **Ferneley (IRE)**[80] 2752 3-9-1 108.............................. RichardHughes 4 108+
(Francis Ennis, Ire) *trckd ldrs in 4th: nt clr run st: 6th whn swtchd rt under 1f out: rdn and kpt on wl cl home* **6/1**[3]
5 *shd* **Cougar Bay (IRE)**[14] 4826 4-9-8 109.............................. DPMcDonogh 8 108
(David Wachman, Ire) *cl 2nd: rdn to ld ent st: hdd over 1f out: sn no ex* **9/2**[2]
6 *3* **Brave Tin Soldier (USA)**[118] 1703 3-9-1 107.......................... KFallon 7 102
(A P O'Brien, Ire) *trckd ldrs in 3rd: rdn to chal ent st: wknd fr 1 1/2f out* **7/1**
7 *4* **Flamingo Guitar (USA)**[9] 4985 4-9-5 89..............................(t) WMLordan 5 91
(David Wachman, Ire) *chsd ldrs: 5th 1/2-way: 6th 3f out: wknd st* **40/1**
8 *12* **Truly Mine (IRE)**[70] 3117 3-8-12 103.................................. PJSmullen 2 67
(D K Weld, Ire) *led: rdn and hdd ent st: sn wknd: eased over 1f out* **7/1**

2m 3.12s (-7.28) **Going Correction** -0.35s/f (Firm)
WFA 3 from 4yo+ 7lb **8** Ran SP% **109.4**
Speed ratings: **115,113,113,112,112 110,107,97**
CSF £43.70 TOTE £4.90: £2.20, £2.00, £1.60; DF 46.50.
Owner Hearthstead Homes Ltd **Bred** T Nakata **Trained** Middleham Moor, N Yorks

FOCUS
A competitive Group 3 event best rated through the runner-up.

NOTEBOOK
Hearthstead Maison(IRE), dropping back to the trip at which he gained his two handicap wins at Newmarket, recorded his first success at Pattern level. He had to be driven along around three furlongs out, but like so many of his stablemates over the years he does not lack determination and he kept on well after getting to the front over a furlong out. It looked as if he failed to stay when tried over 1m4f in the Great Voltigeur, and having flopped badly over 2m in the Queen's Vase, it seems fair to assume that this distance is close to his optimum. (op 5/1)
Arch Rebel(USA), who recorded two of his three Listed wins last season at this venue, has gone through this season without managing to add to his tally but had shown signs of a return to peak form with his third placing in a Group 3 over two furlongs further here last month. Held up at the rear of the field, he was still at the back on the approach to the straight before staying on with a sustained run. This was a livelier performance than his fourth in the corresponding race last season, and especially praiseworthy considering that his best form has come with plenty of ease in the ground.
Regime(IRE), who had run with credit in two Group 2 races in France since contesting the Derby, was also held up but failed to quicken appreciably having begun to wind up his effort before Arch Rebel's challenge started to gain momentum. It looked a rather flat effort from a horse with smart form at Pattern level. Official explanation: jockey said colt hung left under pressure (op 11/4)
Ferneley(IRE), making his first appearance since finishing in midfield in the Jersey Stakes, did not get the run of the race in the straight and was visibly unlucky not to finish closer, staying on late after being switched out. Last season, he won twice and was Group 2-placed behind Teofilo, and with a clearer passage here he might have matched his early-sesson effort in taking second place in the Ballysax Stakes over the course and trip. He can be rated a genuine Group 3 horse. Official explanation: jockey said colt was short of room in the straight but eventually ran on strongly (op 5/1)
Cougar Bay(IRE), second in this event 12 months ago, has rarely run a bad race despite being a hard horse to win with. However, he had a bit of on off-day here, fading from over a furlong out after a spell in the lead. (op 5/1)
Brave Tin Soldier(USA), a Listed winner at two, had not run since contesting the Poule d'Essai des Poulains on his seasonal debut. He dropped away when the heat was turned on after showing up prominently, and though it is quite possible that he will come on from the run, he remains a difficult horse to assess.
Flamingo Guitar(USA) was out of her depth in this company. (op 33/1)
Truly Mine(IRE) failed to do justice to her ability and was eased to finish detached. (op 6/1)

5241a COOLMORE FUSAICHI PEGASUS MATRON STKS (GROUP 1) (F&M) 1m
2:40 (2:41) 3-Y-O+ **£109,797** (£32,094; £15,202; £5,067)

RPR
1 **Echelon**[14] 4805 5-9-3 .... RyanMoore 2 118+
(Sir Michael Stoute) *trckd ldrs in 4th: 3rd and hdwy ent st: led 1f out: r.o wl: comf* **9/4**[1]
2 *1 1/2* **Red Evie (IRE)**[21] 4600 4-9-3 .... JamieSpencer 3 114
(M L W Bell) *hld up in tch on inner: 7th after 1/2-way: 4th and hdwy early st: 3rd under 1f out: kpt on u.p* **7/2**[3]
3 *nk* **Arch Swing (USA)**[59] 3433 3-8-12 113.................................. MJKinane 1 115+
(John M Oxx, Ire) *cl 2nd and disp ld: rdn and hdd ent st: sn sltly hmpd: hmpd again 1f out: swtchd and kpt on: fin 4th: plcd 3rd* **11/4**[2]
4 *nk* **Eastern Appeal (IRE)**[20] 4648 4-9-3 107.............................. RPCleary 7 113
(M Halford, Ire) *led and disp: slt advantage st: wandered abt u.p: hdd 1f out: kpt on: fin 3rd: disqualified and plcd 4th* **40/1**
5 *2 1/2* **Sweet Lilly**[7] 5047 3-8-12 .... KFallon 4 106
(M R Channon) *settled 3rd: dropped to 5th ent st: kpt on same pce* **10/1**
6 *hd* **Modeeroch (IRE)**[66] 3222 4-9-3 105....................................(t) KJManning 6 106
(J S Bolger, Ire) *hld up in tch: 7th 1/2-way: no imp st* **20/1**
7 *1 1/4* **She's Our Mark**[9] 4985 3-8-12 106.. DMGrant 9 103
(Patrick J Flynn, Ire) *trckd ldrs on outer: 5th 1/2-way: no imp st* **25/1**
8 *nk* **Evening Time (IRE)**[27] 4438 3-8-12 108.......................... DPMcDonogh 8 102
(Kevin Prendergast, Ire) *chsd ldrs: sltly hmpd early: 6th and drvn along after 1/2-way: no ex st* **12/1**
9 *1* **Barshiba (IRE)**[24] 4503 3-8-12 .... TQuinn 5 100
(D R C Elsworth) *a in rr* **14/1**

1m 39.52s (-4.88) **Going Correction** -0.35s/f (Firm)
WFA 3 from 4yo+ 5lb **9** Ran SP% **114.2**
Speed ratings: **110,108,107,108,105 105,103,103,102**
CSF £9.90 TOTE £3.90: £1.80, £1.80, £1.10; DF 12.90.
Owner Cheveley Park Stud **Bred** Cheveley Park Stud Ltd **Trained** Newmarket, Suffolk

FOCUS
While several of these were flying high at this level, a smart standard was supplied by the duo who ended up taking the second and third placings, and the form looks solid for the grade.

NOTEBOOK
Echelon won with a fair degree of ease with the help of a well-executed race plan. She has now surpassed the exploits of her half-sister Chic, who went close to Group 1 glory in two clashes with the brilliant Attraction, in the 2004 Sun Chariot and in this event in 2005. The daughter of Danehill had emulated Chic by landing the Celebration Mile at Goodwood last month, earning herself a supplementary entry for this, after initial thoughts had been to leave the race off her schedule, in the wake of a below-par effort on a previous visit to Ireland. That was on soft ground in the Pretty Polly, and while she managed to cope with an easy surface when winning the Princess Elizabeth Stakes at Epsom, she has a definite preference for quicker ground. There is no shortage of Group 1 opportunities for fillies and mares these days. (op 11/4)
Red Evie(IRE), last year's winner, had bounced back from a couple of disapointments when landing the Hungerford Stakes at Newbury, and she was not far below her best in staying on for second after the winner had taken command a furlong down.
Arch Swing(USA), not the first time, found trouble in running. She was coming back at the finish after recovering from the interference that resulted from a prolonged tussle with Eastern Appeal. If she had been at the top of her form one would have expected her to have brushed aside that rival with some conviction, but she was already starting to feel the heat early in the straight. (op 5/2 tchd 3/1)
Eastern Appeal(IRE) ran the race of her life to pass the post in third, only to be demoted a place after an enquiry called to investigate interference that she had caused to Arch Swing by running around a bit under pressure a furlong out. There can be no real argument that the interference cost Arch Swing third place, but nothing should be taken away from a gallant effort by the Michael Halford-trained filly, winner of the Group 3 Athasi Stakes earlier in the season but the rank outsider of the field here. (op 33/1)
Sweet Lilly has struggled at Group 1 level in the past, and it was very much the same story here.
Modeeroch(IRE), consistent at Group 3 level, was found wanting on her first run in a Group 1since contesting the Cheveley Park in 2005. (op 20/1 tchd 25/1)
She's Our Mark, who has enjoyed such a progressive campaign, found this grade too demanding.
Evening Time(IRE), twice successful in Listed races over 6f, was unable to make any significant impact on her first attempt at this trip. Her cause was possibly done some damage when she was slightly hampered in the early stages of the race.
Barshiba(IRE) failed to stamp her presence on the race, a performance more in keeping with a poor run at Salisbury last month than her excellent fourth to Darjina in the Prix d'Astarte. (op 16/1)

5242a OLIVER FREANEY & COMPANY SEPTEMBER H'CAP (PREMIER HANDICAP) 7f
3:15 (3:16) 3-Y-O+ **£52,783** (£15,486; £7,378; £2,513)

RPR
1 **Thoughtless Moment (IRE)**[9] 4985 3-8-7 90.................... PJSmullen 8 101+
(D K Weld, Ire) *towards rr: hdwy on inner early st: 5th 1f out: r.o strly to ld cl home* **14/1**
2 *3/4* **Excelerate (IRE)**[6] 5074 4-9-3 96.. KFallon 5 105
(Edward Lynam, Ire) *towards rr: 16th and drvn along appr st: hdwy on outer 2f out: styd on wl fnl f* **12/1**
3 *1* **Miss Gorica (IRE)**[10] 4954 3-8-7 90.................................. WMLordan 12 96
(Ms Joanna Morgan, Ire) *5th early: 3rd 1/2-way: rdn to ld ent st: kpt on wl: hdd cl home* **12/1**
4 *1/2* **Newgate Lodge (IRE)**[20] 4646 3-8-7 90.............................. RPCleary 11 95
(M Halford, Ire) *mid-div: 8th appr st: 5th under 2f out: kpt on u.p* **16/1**

The Form Book, Raceform Ltd, Compton, RG20 6NL

5 shd **Dynamo Dancer (IRE)**[6] 5074 4-9-5 98 .... WJSupple 1 103
(G M Lyons, Ire) *hld up: 9th and drvn along appr st: kpt on wl fr over 1f out* **20/1**

6 1 **Empirical Power (IRE)**[83] 2701 6-9-2 95 .... DPMcDonogh 6 97
(Edward Lynam, Ire) *led: rdn and hdd ent st: no ex fnl f* **11/2**[1]

7 nk **Ireland's Call (IRE)**[13] 4864 6-8-6 90 .... OCasey(5) 2 91
(Peter Casey, Ire) *prom: 4th and rdn 1/2-way: kpt on same pce st* **16/1**

8 3/4 **Kyles Bay (IRE)**[20] 4646 4-8-13 92 .... JAHeffernan 15 91
(Ms Caroline Hutchinson, Ire) *towards rr: prog into 11th appr st: kpt on same pce fr over 1 1/2f out* **12/1**

9 nk **King Of Tory (IRE)**[6] 5074 5-9-1 94 ....(b) CDHayes 10 92
(Edward Lynam, Ire) *hld up: kpt on same pce st* **10/1**[3]

10 2 1/2 **Tajneed (IRE)**[34] 4211 4-8-6 88 ....(bt) SMGorey(3) 4 80
(D K Weld, Ire) *chsd ldrs: 7th 1/2-way: 4th and effrt ent st: sn no ex* **20/1**

11 1 1/4 **Crossing**[9] 4985 6-9-5 98 ....(t) PShanahan 14 86
(William J Fitzpatrick, Ire) *in rr of mid-div: sme prog on outer 3f out: no ex early st* **14/1**

12 1 1/4 **Namaya (IRE)**[13] 4864 4-10-2 109 .... KJManning 9 94
(J S Bolger, Ire) *in rr of mid-div: 10th appr st: no imp fr over 1f out* **14/1**

13 3/4 **Baggio (IRE)**[43] 3929 6-9-3 96 ....(b) FMBerry 18 79
(Charles O'Brien, Ire) *towards rr: no imp st* **12/1**

14 1 1/2 **Bolodenka (IRE)**[12] 4900 5-8-13 92 .... TonyHamilton 13 71
(R A Fahey) *trckd ldrs: 5th after 1/2-way: rdn and no imp ent st: sn wknd* **6/1**[2]

15 nk **Bush Maiden (IRE)**[425] 3371 7-9-5 98 .... MJKinane 3 76
(Mrs Seamus Hayes, Ire) *a towards rr* **20/1**

16 1 3/4 **Worldly Wise**[13] 4867 4-8-13 92 .... DMGrant 7 65
(Patrick J Flynn, Ire) *chsd ldrs: 6th 1/2-way: wknd appr st* **12/1**

17 1 **Regional Counsel**[69] 3139 3-8-10 96 .... CPGeoghegan(3) 16 67
(Kevin Prendergast, Ire) *nvr a factor: wknd appr st* **25/1**

18 12 **An Tadh (IRE)**[13] 4864 4-10-0 107 .... JamieSpencer 17 45
(G M Lyons, Ire) *cl 2nd: rdn and wknd ent st: sn eased* **12/1**

1m 24.37s (-7.83) **Going Correction** -0.875s/f (Hard)
WFA 3 from 4yo+ 4lb **18** Ran SP% **134.8**
Speed ratings: **109,108,107,106,106 105,104,103,103,100 99,97,97,95,95 93,91,78**
CSF £178.31 CT £2181.66 TOTE £19.80: £4.20, £3.90, £4.00, £3.40; DF 327.10.
Owner Moyglare Stud Farm **Bred** Moyglare Stud Farm Ltd **Trained** The Curragh, Co Kildare

NOTEBOOK
Baggio(IRE) Official explanation: jockey said gelding ran out of room in the straight
Bolodenka(IRE) was being scrubbed along almost from the start and was always struggling to get into the race. (op 7/1)

5243a TATTERSALLS MILLIONS IRISH CHAMPION STKS (GROUP 1) 1m 2f
3:50 (3:50) 3-Y-0+

£404,729 (£127,702; £60,135; £19,594; £12,837; £6,081)

RPR

1 **Dylan Thomas (IRE)**[18] 4693 4-9-7 127 .... KFallon 5 126+
(A P O'Brien, Ire) *trckd ldrs in 4th: 3rd and hdwy appr st: led over 1f out: styd on wl: eased nr fin: easily* **8/15**[1]

2 1 1/2 **Duke Of Marmalade (IRE)**[18] 4693 3-9-0 120 .... JAHeffernan 3 122
(A P O'Brien, Ire) *trckd ldr in 2nd: rdn to ld ent st: hdd over 1f out: kpt on* **15/2**[3]

3 2 **Red Rock Canyon (IRE)**[42] 3983 3-9-0 104 .... CO'Donoghue 1 118
(A P O'Brien, Ire) *led: hdd ent st: kpt on same pce u.p fr 2f out* **100/1**

4 2 1/2 **Red Rocks (IRE)**[80] 2754 4-9-7 .... RichardHughes 4 113+
(B J Meehan) *dwlt: hld up in rr: 5th and prog ent st: mod 4th and no imp fr over 1 1/2f out* **10/1**

5 3 1/2 **Maraahel (IRE)**[42] 3942 6-9-7 ....(b) RHills 2 106+
(Sir Michael Stoute) *trckd ldrs in 3rd: dropped to 4th bef st: sn no ex* **14/1**

6 1 3/4 **Finsceal Beo (IRE)**[78] 2814 3-8-11 119 .... KJManning 6 100+
(J S Bolger, Ire) *hld up in 5th: last and rdn ent st: no imp: eased cl home* **5/1**[2]

2m 2.27s (-8.13) **Going Correction** -0.35s/f (Firm)
WFA 3 from 4yo+ 7lb **6** Ran SP% **110.4**
Speed ratings: **118,116,115,113,110 109**
CSF £5.05 TOTE £1.30: £1.10, £3.00; DF 6.50.
Owner Mrs John Magnier **Bred** Tower Bloodstock **Trained** Ballydoyle, Co Tipperary

FOCUS
Not the strongest renewal of a Group 1 event that has provided some wonderful battles in the past, but nonetheless it produced a memorable result, involving an historic repeat of last year's victory for the excellent Dylan Thomas and a superb one-two-three for Aidan O'Brien's Ballydoyle stable.

NOTEBOOK
Dylan Thomas(IRE) confirmed what everyone must have already known, that he is a devastating performer on his favoured quick ground and stands comparison with many of the great horses that have won this race in the past. A colt of the very highest calibre over both 1m2f and 1m4f, he is blessed with qualities of physique and temperament to match his ability. Kieren Fallon, who stressed in his post-race assessment his mount's relish for quick ground, also observed that Dylan Thomas had given him no worries through the race but is actually an easier horse to ride going right-handed. (op 1/2 tchd 4/7)

Duke Of Marmalade(IRE), who had also played a notable part in one of this season's O'Brien monopolies when second in the St James's Palace, has established a fine record at Group 1 level. He finished closer to Dylan Thomas than when fourth to Authorized on his first attempt against older horses in the Juddmonte International, and there is a range of international options open to him at around this trip and a little shorter. (op 7/1)

Red Rock Canyon(IRE) began the season with a reputation as a useful if somewhat untrustworthy maiden with a rating of 104. He had slumped to a modest 88 until put back on his original mark after his second to Fracas in the Meld Stakes. Not only did he play a significant part in determining the shape of the race, he produced a display that gives him a strong claim to the title of best maiden in training. As to whether or not he can be found a winning opportunity before the end of the season, that may be another matter. (op 66/1)

Red Rocks(IRE) may appear to have run below his best but he was not beaten much further here by Dylan Thomas than in the Prince Of Wales's Stakes. (op 8/1)

Maraahel(IRE) produced a disappointingly tame effort. At this stage there is almost overwhelming evidence to suggest that he will struggle to win a Group 1 event, though some of his form certainly allows for the possibility. (op 14/1 tchd 16/1)

Finsceal Beo(IRE) did not recapture her early-season brilliance on her first run back after a break and on her first attempt at the trip. Held up at the back, she never looked like getting seriously involved and was eased before the finish. (op 6/1)

5244 - 5246a (Foreign Racing) - See Raceform Interactive

4412 ARLINGTON (L-H)
Saturday, September 8

OFFICIAL GOING: Fast

5247a ARLINGTON-WASHINGTON LASSIE STKS (GRADE 3) (FILLIES) 1m (D)
11:24 (11:33) 2-Y-0

£45,918 (£153,068; £8,418; £4,592; £2,296; £510)

RPR

1 **Dreaming Of Liz (USA)** 2-8-4 .... EBaird 11 97
(W Catalano, U.S.A) **6/4**[1]

2 2 1/2 **Rasierra (USA)** 2-8-5 ow1 ....(b) HTheriot 1 93
(Ray E Tracy Jr, U.S.A) **57/1**

3 2 1/2 **Minewander (USA)** 2-8-6 ow2 .... ERazoJr 6 89
(D Vance, U.S.A) **285/10**

4 1 **Love Buzz (USA)**[63] 2-8-5 ow1 .... MGuidry 4 86
(Dale Romans, U.S.A) **162/10**

5 1/2 **Honest To Betsy (USA)**[24] 2-8-4 .... RRDouglas 7 84
(Dale Romans, U.S.A) **6/1**[3]

6 1/2 **Startswampindowski (USA)** 2-8-4 .... CEmigh 2 83
(S Asmussen, U.S.A) **206/10**

7 1 1/4 **Pretty Persuasion (USA)** 2-8-4 .... JesseMCampbell 5 81
(M Stidham, U.S.A) **96/10**

8 2 1/4 **Wonderful Luck (USA)**[21] 2-8-6 .... RAlbarado 3 78
(S Asmussen, U.S.A) **22/10**[2]

9 14 **Pegasus Prospect (USA)** 2-8-7 ow3 .... CNakatani 8 51
(Terry Gestes, U.S.A) **34/1**

10 5 1/4 **Eat Pie (USA)**[59] 3432 2-8-4 .... JamesGraham 10 38
(M J Wallace) *tracked leaders til weakening quickly over 2f out* **136/10**

11 3 1/4 **La Wildcat (CAN)** 2-8-4 ....(b) EPerez 9 31
(B Flint, U.S.A) **73/1**

1m 37.08s (-40.92) **11** Ran SP% **121.6**
PARI-MUTUEL: WIN 5.00; PL (1-2) 3.80, 35.60; SHOW (1-2-3) 3.20, 14.40,11.20; SF 159.80.
Owner Frank C Calabrese **Bred** F Calabrese **Trained** USA

NOTEBOOK
Eat Pie(USA) was attempting further than 6f for the first time and patently failed to stay.

3810 BELMONT PARK (L-H)
Saturday, September 8

OFFICIAL GOING: Turf course - firm; dirt course - fast

5248a GARDEN CITY STKS (GRADE 1) (FILLIES) (TURF) 1m 1f (T)
9:08 (9:12) 3-Y-0

£76,531 (£25,510; £12,755; £6,378; £3,827; £510)

RPR

1 **Alexander Tango (IRE)**[27] 4435 3-8-6 .... SXBridgmohan 7 107
(T Stack, Ire) *hld up: racing in 9th to fnl turn: hdwy on outside and 5th st: r.o wl to ld wl ins fnl f: drvn out* **58/10**[3]

2 3/4 **Bit Of Whimsy (USA)**[49] 3-8-6 .... JCastellano 5 105
(B Tagg, U.S.A) **143/10**

3 nse **Sharp Susan (USA)**[22] 3-8-8 .... KDesormeaux 2 107
(W Mott, U.S.A) **68/10**

4 nse **Costume**[36] 4118 3-8-4 .... RBejarano 4 103
(J H M Gosden) *a in tch: 6th st: moved outside: r.o: nrest at fin* **124/10**

5 1 1/4 **Chestoria (USA)** 3-8-4 .... ECoa 9 101
(B Levine, U.S.A) **37/1**

6 nk **Valbenny (IRE)**[21] 3-8-8 .... ASolis 6 104
(P Gallagher, U.S.A) **52/10**[2]

7 hd **Missvinski (USA)**[41] 4010 3-8-4 .... C-PLemaire 1 100
(J-C Rouget, France) **82/10**

8 nk **Street Sounds (CAN)**[42] 3-8-6 .... JRVelazquez 3 101
(M Matz, U.S.A) **21/1**

9 hd **New Edition (USA)**[22] 3-8-4 .... CVelasquez 8 99
(J Larry Jones, U.S.A) **23/1**

10 2 3/4 **Rutherienne (USA)**[21] 3-8-10 .... GKGomez 10 99
(Christophe Clement, U.S.A) **8/5**[1]

1m 48.97s (108.97) **10** Ran SP% **118.3**
PARI-MUTUEL (including $2 stakes): WIN 13.60; PL (1-2) 8.90, 13.00; SHOW (1-2-3) 5.60, 6.60, 5.70; SF 231.00.
Owner Noel O'Callaghan **Bred** Philip Brady **Trained** Golden, Co Tipperary

NOTEBOOK
Alexander Tango(IRE), a consistent filly in Pattern company in Ireland this year including when finishing fourth in the Irish 1,000 Guineas, managed to gain a famous victory even though the slow pace would not have been ideal for her. She will likely stay here for the Grade 1 Flower Bowl at the end of the month.
Costume, trying her longest trip to date, was doing her best work late but could not get there in time.

5250a MAN O'WAR STKS (GRADE 1) (TURF) 1m 3f (T)
10:12 (10:18) 3-Y-0+

£153,061 (£51,020; £25,510; £12,755; £7,653; £2,551)

RPR

1 **Doctor Dino (FR)**[28] 4414 5-9-0 .... OPeslier 1 119
(R Gibson, France) *trckd ldrs on ins: moved outside over 3f out: 2nd st: drvn to ld wl ins fnl f* **77/20**[3]

2 hd **Sunriver (USA)**[28] 4414 4-9-0 .... GKGomez 2 119
(T Pletcher, U.S.A) **26/10**[2]

3 3 1/4 **Grand Couturier**[28] 4415 4-9-0 .... CHBorel 3 114
(R Ribaudo, U.S.A) **84/10**

4 1/2 **Trippi's Storm (USA)**[28] 4415 4-9-0 .... JCastellano 4 113
(S Hough, U.S.A) **137/10**

5 3 **Shamdinan (FR)**[28] 4412 3-8-9 .... JRLeparoux 5 111
(Doug O'Neill, U.S.A) **63/10**

6 3/4 **Yellowstone (IRE)**[18] 4692 3-8-9 .... JMurtagh 7 110
(A P O'Brien, Ire) *led or disp to 3f out: 3rd st: sn btn* **21/10**[1]

7 3 ¾ **Marsh Side (USA)**[48] 4-9-0 .... KDesormeaux 6 101
(M Dickinson, U.S.A) 141/10

2m 12.26s (-2.79)
WFA 3 from 4yo+ 8lb 7 Ran SP% **118.4**
PARI-MUTUEL: WIN 9.70; PL (1-2) 4.30, 3.90; SHOW (1-2-3) 2.90, 2.90, 4.60; SF 31.20.
Owner J Martinez Salmean **Bred** Ecurie Pelder **Trained** Lamorlaye, France

NOTEBOOK
Doctor Dino(FR), third in the Arlington Million, got the timing right this time and battled on well to score. He is not Breeders' Cup nominated so is more likely to head for Hong Kong.
Yellowstone(IRE) was rather surprisingly given a positive ride, but was off the bridle a long way out and the tactic clearly did not work. His rider reported that he was never comfortable at any stage.

5139 YORK (L-H)
Sunday, September 9

OFFICIAL GOING: Good to firm (8.9)
After three dry days 3mm was put on the back straight and 6mm on the straight track resulting in 'quick ground but level and no jar whatsoever'.
Wind: Fresh, 1/2 against Weather: Fine but overcast, breezy and cool

5251 HSS.COM STKS (NURSERY H'CAP) 7f
2:20 (2:20) (Class 4) (0-85,84) 2-Y-0 **£6,477** (£1,927; £963; £481) **Stalls** Low

Form RPR
13 1 **Choose Your Moment**[22] 4613 2-9-7 **84** .... JamieSpencer 6 94+
(P C Haslam) *hld up in rr: hdwy over 2f out: wnt 2nd 1f out: led last 100yds: styd on strly* **15/8**[1]
2110 2 3 **La Chicaluna**[37] 4121 2-9-1 **78** .... PaulHanagan 2 80
(J G Given) *led: hdd and no ex ins fnl f* **6/1**[3]
00 3 3 ½ **Geordie Girl**[23] 4560 2-8-1 **64** ow1 .... PaulFessey 3 57
(R C Guest) *chsd ldrs: one pce whn edgd rt jst ins fnl f* **16/1**
006 4 nk **Johnny Friendly**[65] 3256 2-7-12 **61** oh1 .... DavidKinsella 4 53
(K R Burke) *t.k.h: w ldrs: fading whn sltly hmpd jst ins fnl f* **40/1**
6336 5 ½ **Woodford Regen**[14] 4844 2-7-13 **62** ow1 .... JimmyQuinn 8 53
(M W Easterby) *chsd ldrs: kpt on wl fnl f* **16/1**
3040 6 1 ½ **Bahama Baileys**[19] 4695 2-9-0 **77** .... GregFairley 10 64
(M Johnston) *chsd ldrs: rdn over 2f out: hung lft and and wknd fnl f* **7/1**
605 7 1 ¾ **Marlena (IRE)**[28] 4422 2-7-9 **61** oh2 .... DuranFentiman(3) 1 43
(T D Easterby) *hld up: hdwy over 2f out: nvr trbld ldrs* **20/1**
0066 8 2 **Prince Desire (IRE)**[16] 4776 2-8-6 **69** .... TedDurcan 5 46
(B W Hills) *dwlt: in rr and sn pushed along: kpt on fnl f: nvr a factor* **2/1**[2]
0136 9 2 ½ **Natural Rhythm (IRE)**[13] 4892 2-8-0 **63** .... DaleGibson 7 34
(D W Chapman) *sn pushed along: prom: lost pl over 4f out: sn in rr* **22/1**
6400 10 8 **Northgate Lodge (USA)**[3] 5153 2-7-9 **65** oh3 ow4(b[1]) AndrewHeffernan(7) 9 15
(M Brittain) *chsd ldrs on outer: lost pl over 3f out: sn bhd* **100/1**

1m 24.93s (-0.47) **Going Correction** 0.0s/f (Good) 10 Ran SP% **119.2**
Speed ratings (Par 97): **102,98,94,94,93 91,89,87,84,75**
CSF £13.62 CT £142.50 TOTE £2.50: £1.20, £2.00, £3.80; EX 13.40.
Owner Mr & Mrs Duncan Davidson **Bred** Alpha Bloodstock Limited **Trained** Middleham Moor, N Yorks

FOCUS
A solid looking nursery in which the winner did well to come from off the pace and in the end won going away. He is highly progressive and the runner-up emerges with credit.

NOTEBOOK
Choose Your Moment, easily the biggest in the line-up, looked to have been given plenty to do but he showed a good turn of foot and in the end won going away. There may be even better to come. (op 2-1)
La Chicaluna, freshened up by a five-week break, took them along and looked to have poached a winning lead but in the end she was readily cut down by the progressive winner. She deserves to win another nursery. (tchd 13-2)
Geordie Girl, dropped 2lb, was stepping up to seven furlongs for the first time. (op 14-1)
Johnny Friendly, back after a two-month break, was very fresh and would not settle. He was fast coming to the end of his tether when tightened up by the third just inside the last. (tchd 33-1)
Woodford Regen, suited by this longer trip, was putting in his best work in the closing stages and is now ready to try a mile.
Bahama Baileys, with the blinkers left off, was dropping back in trip but does not seem to be progressing at all. (op 11-1)
Prince Desire(IRE) missed a beat at the start and never went a yard. Out of luck at Newmarket on his previous start, he can surely do a lot better than this. (op 9-4)

5252 HSS MEDIAN AUCTION MAIDEN STKS 5f 89y
2:50 (2:50) (Class 4) 2-Y-0 **£6,541** (£1,946; £972; £485) **Stalls** Low

Form RPR
4 1 **Excitement (IRE)**[17] 4733 2-8-12 0 .... PaulHanagan 8 85+
(R A Fahey) *mid-div: hdwy over 2f out: shkn up to ld 75yds out: r.o strly* **6/1**[3]
422 2 2 ½ **Tugalu (IRE)**[16] 4782 2-9-3 76 .... JamieSpencer 9 79
(K A Ryan) *trckd ldrs: led over 2f out: hdd and no ex ins fnl f* **6/4**[1]
00 3 ½ **Bahamian Ballad**[22] 4611 2-8-12 0 .... JimmyQuinn 6 72
(J D Bethell) *s.i.s: hdwy over 2f out: styd on ins fnl f* **22/1**
2 4 1 ¼ **Love Of Dubai (USA)**[12] 4924 2-8-12 0 .... SebSanders 3 68
(C E Brittain) *w ldrs: kpt on same pce fnl f* **15/8**[2]
2342 5 2 ½ **Upstanding**[3] 5154 2-8-5 66 .... PatrickDonaghy(7) 11 60
(M Brittain) *mid-div: effrt over 2f out: nvr trbld ldrs* **10/1**
00 6 1 ½ **Miss Olivia**[12] 4924 2-8-12 0 .... StephenDonohoe 5 55
(P W Chapple-Hyam) *in rr: edgd rt and kpt on appr fnl f* **25/1**
0060 7 3 **Astrol**[23] 4578 2-8-12 40 .... TedDurcan 7 45+
(T D Easterby) *sn outpcd in rr: kpt on fnl 2f: nvr nr ldrs* **80/1**
0064 8 2 **Maccabeus**[6] 5096 2-9-0 62 .... JerryO'Dwyer(3) 10 44
(P J O'Gorman) *led after 1f: hdd over 2f out: sn wknd* **20/1**
5 9 nk **Lujiana**[153] 972 2-8-5 0 .... AndrewHeffernan(7) 2 38
(M Brittain) *mid-div: effrt over 2f out: sn outpcd* **66/1**
0 10 ½ **Captain Turbot (IRE)**[21] 4636 2-9-3 0 .... TonyHamilton 4 41
(D W Barker) *led 1f: outpcd and lost pl over 3f out* **50/1**
000 11 3 **Miss Deeds (IRE)**[15] 4810 2-8-12 46 .... TGMcLaughlin 1 27
(N P Littmoden) *in rr: sme hdwy over 2f out: sn lost pl* **25/1**

64.88 secs (-0.12) 11 Ran SP% **119.6**
CSF £14.75 TOTE £6.10: £1.60, £1.10, £6.00; EX 16.20.
Owner R A Fahey **Bred** E Tynan **Trained** Musley Bank, N Yorks

FOCUS
A fair maiden that seems solid enough but the third seemed to improve dramatically and the exposed seventh has an official rating of just 40.

NOTEBOOK
Excitement(IRE), a lot wiser after making her debut at Chester, looked to be going nowhere at the halfway mark and was matched at 48 on the exchanges. She came there strongly and with the winner in her sights and in the end won going right away. She will improve again. (op 5-1 tchd 9-2)
Tugalu(IRE) really took the eye in the paddock but in the end was swept aside. He thoroughly deserves to go one better. (tchd 13-8, after 2-1 and 7-4 in a place)
Bahamian Ballad, a half-sister to Moorhouse Lad, stepped up considerably on her first two efforts. Unlike him she seems to need a sixth furlong. (op 25-1 tchd 33-1)
Love Of Dubai(USA), reappearing after finishing runner-up on her debut just 12 days earlier, seemed to run rather flat. (op 9-4)
Upstanding is fully exposed and had finished just behind Love Of Dubai at Ripon two outings ago. (op 12-1)
Miss Olivia, very edgy beforehand, will appreciate seven furlongs plus. (op 28-1 tchd 33-1)
Astrol, well beaten on four previous starts, would have a good chance if connections can get her a place in a nursery over the next 12 days before her mark shoots up. (op 100-1)

5253 SYMPHONY STKS (H'CAP) 7f
3:25 (3:25) (Class 5) (0-75,75) 3-Y-0+ **£5,181** (£1,541; £770; £384) **Stalls** Low

Form RPR
3054 1 **Neon Blue**[29] 4407 6-9-1 **68** .... (v) HayleyTurner 7 77
(R M Whitaker) *trckd ldrs: led over 2f out: hld on wl towards fin* **5/1**[1]
0500 2 nk **Sedge (USA)**[15] 4797 7-8-9 **62** .... (p) MickyFenton 2 70
(P T Midgley) *chsd ldrs: wnt 2nd 1f out: no ex clsng stages* **16/1**
6350 3 1 **Aussie Blue (IRE)**[3] 5159 3-7-13 **61** oh5 .... NataliaGemelova(5) 6 64
(R M Whitaker) *prom: effrt over 2f out: styd on same pce fnl f* **33/1**
1425 4 1 **Charlie Tipple**[13] 4898 3-9-3 **74** .... DavidAllan 3 75+
(T D Easterby) *hld up in rr: hdwy 2f out: styd on strly ins fnl f* **8/1**
0030 5 nk **Grey Boy (GER)**[13] 4880 6-8-8 **68** .... MarkCoumbe(7) 8 70
(A W Carroll) *w ldrs: chal over 2f out: kpt on same pce appr fnl f* **20/1**
0060 6 ½ **King Harson**[35] 4195 8-9-3 **70** .... TedDurcan 10 70
(J D Bethell) *led tl over 2f out: kpt on same pce* **20/1**
0004 7 1 ¼ **Lincolneurocruiser**[3] 5159 5-8-5 **61** oh1 .... (v) StephaneBreux(3) 12 58
(Mrs N Macauley) *mid-div: c wd to r alone stands' side over 2f out: kpt on same pce appr fnl f* **20/1**
1012 8 shd **High Ambition**[93] 2414 4-9-8 **75** .... (v) PaulHanagan 1 72
(R A Fahey) *in rr: styd on wl fnl 2f: nvr nr ldrs* **11/2**[2]
1603 9 ½ **Zennerman (IRE)**[15] 4797 4-9-8 **75** .... (b) JamieSpencer 5 70
(K A Ryan) *hld up in rr: hdwy over 2f out: hrd rdn over 1f out: wknd last 100yds* **11/2**[2]
5156 10 2 **Dorn Dancer (IRE)**[15] 4822 5-8-9 **62** .... PatCosgrave 11 52
(D W Barker) *rr-div: kpt on fnl 2f: nvr a factor* **25/1**
0611 11 shd **Joshua's Gold (IRE)**[11] 4931 6-8-13 **66** .... (v) StephenDonohoe 15 56
(D Carroll) *chsd ldrs on outer: wknd over 1f out* **13/2**[3]
4300 12 nk **Dispol Isle (IRE)**[18] 4705 5-9-1 **68** .... PhillipMakin 14 57
(T D Barron) *prom: wknd fnl 2f* **25/1**
0500 13 1 **Paraguay (USA)**[14] 4850 4-8-8 **64** .... (v[1]) LiamJones(3) 4 50
(Miss V Haigh) *dwlt: hdwy on ins 4f out: wknd over 1f out* **20/1**
0021 14 nk **No Grouse**[8] 5037 7-8-8 **61** oh3 .... JimmyQuinn 17 46
(E J Alston) *hld up in rr: swtchd lft after 1f: nvr a factor* **10/1**
2440 15 nk **Sake (IRE)**[15] 4820 5-8-12 **65** .... (v[1]) KimTinkler 13 50
(N Tinkler) *in rr: effrt on outer 3f out: nvr on terms* **20/1**
3465 16 1 ¼ **Nufoudh (IRE)**[3] 5155 3-8-4 **61** oh4 .... PaulFessey 9 39
(Miss Tracy Waggott) *trckd ldrs: t.k.h: wknd fnl 2f* **33/1**
10-0 17 2 **Elusive Warrior (USA)**[23] 4581 4-8-9 **62** .... (p) TonyHamilton 18 37
(R A Fahey) *hld up on outside: lost pl over 4f out* **33/1**

1m 24.43s (-0.97) **Going Correction** 0.0s/f (Good)
WFA 3 from 4yo+ 4lb 17 Ran SP% **127.2**
Speed ratings (Par 103): **105,104,103,102,102 101,100,99,99,97 96,96,95,95,94 92,90**
CSF £74.31 CT £2407.28 TOTE £7.80: £2.10, £5.60, £8.40, £1.90; EX 113.80.
Owner Country Lane Partnership **Bred** R And Mrs Watson & Mrs A J Ralli **Trained** Scarcroft, W Yorks

FOCUS
A modest but tight-knit handicap where it paid to race up with the pace but the front pair are pretty solid performers. The first five home had single-figure draws.
Nufoudh(IRE) Official explanation: jockey said gelding ran too free

5254 HSS HIRE STKS (H'CAP) 6f
3:55 (3:55) (Class 2) (0-100,100) 3-Y-0+ **£12,954** (£3,854; £1,926; £962) **Stalls** Low

Form RPR
1131 1 **King's Apostle (IRE)**[22] 4607 3-8-7 **91** .... LiamJones(3) 3 104
(W J Haggas) *trckd ldrs: smooth hdwy over 2f out: shkn up to ld over 1f out: pushed out* **7/1**[3]
1202 2 1 ¼ **Lipocco**[29] 4374 3-9-5 **100** .... SebSanders 1 109
(R M Beckett) *led: hdd over 1f out: kpt on wl* **4/1**[1]
0004 3 1 **Wyatt Earp (IRE)**[15] 4806 6-8-9 **88** .... PaulHanagan 7 94+
(R A Fahey) *in rr: hdwy 2f out: styd on wl ins fnl f* **4/1**[1]
-434 4 2 ½ **Celtic Sultan (IRE)**[60] 3431 3-9-0 **95** .... MickyFenton 9 93
(T P Tate) *sn w ldrs: kpt on same pce fnl 2f* **7/1**[3]
2000 5 ½ **Roman Maze**[8] 5031 7-8-9 **88** .... TedDurcan 8 84
(W M Brisbourne) *hld up towards rr: hdwy 2f out: kpt on: nvr trbld ldrs* **25/1**
0033 6 1 **Partners In Jazz (USA)**[22] 4601 6-9-4 **97** .... PhillipMakin 2 90
(T D Barron) *chsd ldrs: one pce fnl 2f* **10/1**
2001 7 3 **Damika (IRE)**[8] 5044 4-8-9 **91** .... MichaelJStainton(3) 4 74
(R M Whitaker) *chsd ldrs: drvn over 3f out: outpcd fnl 2f* **12/1**
0300 8 ½ **Ingleby Arch (USA)**[29] 4401 4-8-6 **85** .... PaulFessey 11 67
(T D Barron) *sn outpcd and in rr: nvr a factor* **16/1**
0005 9 ¾ **Fayr Jag (IRE)**[15] 4798 8-9-6 **99** .... DavidAllan 10 78
(T D Easterby) *mid-div: drvn and outpcd over 3f out: no threat after* **15/2**
6050 10 1 ¼ **Burning Incense (IRE)**[22] 4601 4-8-13 **95** .... (b) RichardKingscote(3) 5 70
(R Charlton) *chsd ldrs: hung rt and lost pl over 1f out* **6/1**[2]
1000 11 17 **Desert Commander (IRE)**[34] 4227 5-8-8 **87** .... (b) DO'Donohoe 6 8
(K A Ryan) *chsd ldrs: lost pl over 2f out: sn bhd* **33/1**

1m 10.99s (-1.57) **Going Correction** 0.0s/f (Good)
WFA 3 from 4yo+ 2lb 11 Ran SP% **120.5**
Speed ratings (Par 109): **110,108,107,103,103 101,97,97,96,94 71**
CSF £36.05 CT £133.18 TOTE £7.80: £2.50, £1.90, £1.90; EX 30.80 Trifecta £100.80 Pool: £1,348.76 - 9.50 winning units..
Owner Wentworth Racing (pty) Ltd **Bred** Wentworth Racing **Trained** Newmarket, Suffolk

FOCUS
A seemingly highly-competitive sprint handicap run at a good gallop and the form is sound. Three-year-olds filled three of the first four places and the fast-improving winner did it in style.

NOTEBOOK
King's Apostle(IRE), much improved since being dropped back to six, defied another 4lb weight rise. He travelled as sweet as a nut and had only to be sent about his job to put a seal on it.

Lipocco, who likes to bounce off fast ground, took them along and kept on strongly but in the end his fellow three-year-old swept past him in a matter of strides. (op 9-2)
Wyatt Earp(IRE), on the same mark as his win over this course and distance in May, was attempting to make it four victories here from just seven starts. He was sticking on strongly at the finish and there will be another opportunity for him here next month. (tchd 9-2)
Celtic Sultan(IRE), back after an enforced two-month break, matched strides with the leader. Keeping on in his own time, he may well be worth another try over seven. (op 12-1)
Roman Maze, who has not shone on his last three outings, seems better suited by seven these days. (op 20-1)
Partners In Jazz(USA), not seen out last year after his Victoria Cup success in the spring, has struggled this time and this was his first try over six furlongs since 2005. (op 11-1 tchd 12-1)
Burning Incense(IRE) Official explanation: jockey said gelding was unsuited by the good to firm ground

5255 DRS TELEVISION FOR SONY CLAIMING STKS 1m 2f 88y
4:30 (4:30) (Class 4) 3-Y-0+ **£5,181** (£1,541; £770; £384) **Stalls Low**

Form RPR
1500 **1** **Realism (FR)**[19] 4690 7-9-8 86....(p) PaulHanagan 2 84
(R A Fahey) *trckd ldrs: led 2f out: styd on wl* **5/2**[1]
5606 **2** *4* **Sienna Storm (IRE)**[8] 5052 4-9-4 74....(v[1]) JimmyQuinn 11 73
(M H Tompkins) *sn trcking ldrs: wnt 2nd over 1f out: no imp* **8/1**
6114 **3** *1 1/4* **Inside Story (IRE)**[23] 4577 5-9-2 76....(b) SebSanders 9 68
(N Wilson) *hld up in rr: hdwy over 2f out: styd on wl to take 3rd last 100yds* **11/2**
5001 **4** *1* **El Coto**[18] 4713 7-9-3 81....(p) JamieSpencer 6 67
(K A Ryan) *hld up in rr: hdwy and c outside over 2f out: kpt on wl fnl f* **5/1**[3]
3202 **5** *1 3/4* **Shotley Mac**[8] 5046 3-8-7 59....(b) NeilBrown(5) 3 66
(N Bycroft) *led tl 2f out: wknd ins fnl f* **16/1**
6-00 **6** *3* **Lago D'Orta (IRE)**[74] 2985 7-9-1 70....(t) AdrianTNicholls 1 56
(D Nicholls) *s.s: hdwy on ins over 3f out: wknd over 1f out* **20/1**
5300 **7** *1 1/4* **Fairy Monarch (IRE)**[15] 4797 8-8-12 50....(p) MickyFenton 4 51
(P T Midgley) *trckd ldrs: t.k.h: wknd over 2f out* **66/1**
5600 **8** *2 1/2* **Moving Story**[18] 4704 4-8-12 46.... FrankieMcDonald 5 46
(P T Midgley) *prom: drvn over 3f out: lost pl over 1f out* **100/1**
0006 **9** *1 1/4* **Corriolanus (GER)**[29] 4376 7-9-8 93.... TedDurcan 7 54
(A M Balding) *hld up in mid-div: effrt over 2f out: wknd and eased 1f out* **3/1**[2]
0452 **10** *nk* **Speagle (IRE)**[9] 5000 5-9-1 69.... StephenDonohoe 10 46
(D Carroll) *chsd ldrs: lost pl over 2f out* **12/1**
30- **11** *1/2* **Typhoon Ginger (IRE)**[359] 5354 12-8-6 60 ow1.. RichardKingscote(3) 8 39
(G Woodward) *hld up in rr: nvr on terms* **20/1**
0-05 **12** *2 1/2* **Epicurean**[43] 3956 5-8-6 52 ow1....(p) PJMcDonald(3) 12 35
(Mrs K Walton) *hld up in rr: effrt 4f out: nvr a factor* **66/1**

2m 11.79s (-0.71) **Going Correction** 0.0s/f (Good)
WFA 3 from 4yo+ 7lb **12** Ran SP% **123.8**
Speed ratings (Par 105): **102,98,97,97,95 93,92,90,89,88 88,86**
CSF £23.65 TOTE £3.90: £2.00, £2.90, £2.20; EX 27.20.Inside Story was claimed by M. W. Easterby for £18,000. Realism was claimed by M. W. Easterby for £30,000.
Owner G H Leatham **Bred** Darley Stud Management Co Ltd **Trained** Musley Bank, N Yorks

FOCUS
A decent claimer but the proximity of the long-standing maiden Shotley Mac, rated just 59, ties down the overall value of the form, although it is rated at face value for now.
Corriolanus(GER) Official explanation: jockey said gelding lost its action

5256 LAYERTHORPE VW STKS (H'CAP) 2m 88y
5:00 (5:00) (Class 4) (0-85,81) 3-Y-0+ **£7,772** (£2,312; £1,155; £577) **Stalls Low**

Form RPR
0036 **1** **Mister Arjay (USA)**[13] 4893 7-9-6 73.... TonyHamilton 7 81
(B Ellison) *led: clr tl 11f out: qcknd over 4f out: hld on gamely* **20/1**
0006 **2** *1/2* **Missoula (IRE)**[32] 4288 4-9-1 68.... JimmyQuinn 8 75
(M H Tompkins) *trckd ldrs: chal 3f out: no ex wl ins fnl f* **16/1**
0513 **3** *3 1/2* **Abstract Folly (IRE)**[16] 4786 5-8-11 67.... PJMcDonald(3) 3 70
(J D Bethell) *hld up in rr: hdwy over 3f out: kpt on to take 3rd towards fin* **12/1**
1025 **4** *3/4* **Industrial Star (IRE)**[25] 4490 6-9-4 71....(p) JamieSpencer 1 73
(Micky Hammond) *chsd ldrs: kpt on one pce fnl 2f* **7/1**[2]
4211 **5** *1 3/4* **Atlantic Coast (IRE)**[11] 4941 3-8-1 67....(v) PaulHanagan 6 67
(M Johnston) *trckd ldrs: drvn over 5f out: rdn over 3f out: put hd in air: nvr doing eough to seriously chal* **10/11**[1]
1560 **6** *3* **Mind How You Go (FR)**[50] 1793 9-9-6 73.... TedDurcan 2 69
(J R Best) *prom: effrt on ins over 3f out: wknd over 1f out* **10/1**
0360 **7** *10* **Kyoto Summit**[19] 4690 4-10-0 81.... PaulMulrennan 10 65
(M W Easterby) *hld up in rr: brief effrt 4f out: sn lost pl* **10/1**
2365 **8** *4* **Great As Gold (IRE)**[23] 4569 8-9-11 78.... TomEaves 5 57
(B Ellison) *in rr: hdwy to chse ldrs 8f out: lost pl over 3f out: sn bhd* **14/1**
0200 **9** *75* **Noble Minstrel**[23] 4569 4-9-5 72....(t) SebSanders 9 —
(S C Williams) *prom: lost pl over 3f out: sn bhd: virtually p.u: t.o* **8/1**[3]

3m 36.78s (216.78)
WFA 3 from 4yo+ 13lb **9** Ran SP% **119.2**
CSF £304.99 CT £3976.27 TOTE £31.20: £4.90, £4.50, £2.50; EX 717.60.
Owner Keith Middleton **Bred** Barbara Hunter **Trained** Norton, N Yorks

FOCUS
A fair staying handicap and the winner is at his best when allowed to dominate and things fell perfectly into place with him here. Difficult to say how solid this is but rated at face value through the runner-up for now, with the fourth close to form.
Mister Arjay(USA) Official explanation: trainer said, regarding the apparent improvement in form, that gelding was able to dictate and had the run of the race today.

5257 JINNAH RESTAURANTS APPRENTICE STKS (H'CAP) 1m 6f
5:30 (5:30) (Class 5) (0-70,67) 4-Y-0+ **£5,181** (£1,541; £770; £384) **Stalls Low**

Form RPR
-234 **1** **Casual Affair**[25] 4493 4-9-1 61.... NeilBrown(3) 1 71+
(J D Bethell) *hld up in rr: stdy hdwy on ins over 3f out: led over 1f out: rdn out* **12/1**
2330 **2** *3* **Boxhall (IRE)**[36] 4179 5-9-2 66.... LanceBetts(7) 11 71
(N Wilson) *led after 1f: hdd over 3f out: kpt on wl fnl 2f* **9/1**
0655 **3** *1* **Hue**[4] 5145 6-9-9 66....(b) JamieMoriarty 10 70
(B Ellison) *trckd ldrs: smooth hdwy to ld over 3f out: fnd little and hdd over 1f out* **15/2**
0-25 **4** *2 1/2* **Mcqueen (IRE)**[13] 4906 7-8-13 59.... RussellKennemore(3) 7 60
(J T Stimpson) *led 1f: chsd ldrs: rdn over 3f out: kpt on same pce fnl 2f* **18/1**
4166 **5** *1* **Danzatrice**[10] 4969 5-9-5 62.... GregFairley 8 61
(C W Thornton) *pushed along in rr: hdwy over 1f out: edgd lft and kpt on same pce fnl 2f* **13/2**[3]
0234 **6** *hd* **Vice Admiral**[21] 4638 4-8-7 57.... NSLawes(7) 2 56
(M W Easterby) *chsd ldrs: drvn over 4f out: one pce* **7/1**
6314 **7** *1 1/4* **Karlani (IRE)**[12] 4925 4-9-7 64.... PJMcDonald 4 61
(G A Swinbank) *hld up in rr: hdwy and prom over 5f out: one pce fnl 3f* **4/1**[1]
3-60 **8** *14* **El Alamein (IRE)**[21] 4638 4-9-5 62.... StephenDonohoe 12 39
(Sir Mark Prescott) *hld up in rr: rdn over 3f out: sn lost pl* **11/2**[2]
1021 **9** *nk* **Takes Tutu (USA)**[17] 4739 8-9-1 58....(p) LiamJones 3 35
(C R Dore) *hld up towards rr: hdwy and prom 7f out: lost pl over 3f out* **9/1**
1433 **10** *nk* **Hugs Destiny (IRE)**[4] 5144 6-8-11 59....(t) SophieDoyle(5) 5 36
(M A Barnes) *trckd ldrs: lost pl over 2f out* **17/2**
3053 **11** *hd* **Campli (IRE)**[10] 4969 5-9-10 67.... MichaelJStainton 9 43
(Micky Hammond) *t.k.h towards rr: hdwy to trck ldrs 9f out: lost pl over 2f out* **16/1**

3m 0.74s (1.24) **Going Correction** 0.0s/f (Good) **11** Ran SP% **122.3**
Speed ratings (Par 103): **96,94,93,92,91 91,90,82,82,82 82**
CSF £120.18 CT £882.15 TOTE £13.70: £3.50, £3.80, £2.70; EX 190.80 Place 6 £361.35, Place 5 £191.90.
Owner Peter J Mitchell **Bred** Ian Neville Marks **Trained** Middleham Moor, N Yorks

FOCUS
A low-grade handicap run at a strong pace and the winner came from last to first in the home straight. The form is rated around the placed horses and the winner could improve again.
Hugs Destiny(IRE) Official explanation: jockey said gelding had no more to give
T/Jkpt: Not won. T/Plt: £538.40 to a £1 stake. Pool: £94,087.95. 127.55 winning tickets. T/Qpdt: £121.80 to a £1 stake. Pool: £4,710.40. 28.60 winning tickets. WG

5058 LONGCHAMP (R-H)
Friday, September 7

OFFICIAL GOING: Good to soft

5258a QATAR PRIX DE LUTECE (GROUP 3) 1m 7f
2:50 (2:50) 3-Y-0 **£27,027** (£10,811; £8,108; £5,405; £2,703)

RPR
1 **Coastal Path**[30] 3-8-9.... SPasquier 3 114+
(A Fabre, France) *in tch: disputing 4th 1/2-way: 4th and hdwy st: led over 1f out: pushed out* **4/5**[1]
2 *4* **Dancing Lady (FR)**[22] 4557 3-8-8.... OPeslier 7 108
(J-M Beguigne, France) *led after 3f: pushed along st: hdd over 1f out: styd on at one pce* **61/10**[3]
3 *1* **Royal And Regal (IRE)**[68] 3142 3-8-11.... JAuge 6 110
(A Fabre, France) *racd in 3rd: 2nd and pushed along st: u.p 2f out: styd on at one pce fnl 1 1/2f* **23/10**[2]
4 *3* **Gat (FR)**[50] 3-8-9.... CNora 5 104
(Mme C Dufreche, France) *plld early: last 1/2-way: pushed along bef st: n.d* **79/10**
5 *1* **Noble Prince (GER)**[26] 4446 3-8-9.... CSoumillon 8 103
(A Fabre, France) *plld early: led 2f to 3f: 2nd 1/2-way: 3rd st: sn no ex* **23/10**[2]
6 *2* **Dilshaan's Prize (IRE)**[26] 4446 3-8-9....(b) DBonilla 4 101
(R Pritchard-Gordon, France) *in tch: disputing 4th 1/2-way: 5th st: sn btn* **18/1**

3m 7.80s (-10.60) **6** Ran SP% **146.7**
PARI-MUTUEL: WIN 1.80; PL 1.30, 2.20; SF 6.90.
Owner K Abdulla **Bred** Juddmonte Farms Ltd **Trained** Chantilly, France

NOTEBOOK
Coastal Path is something out of the ordinary. He did not start his career until this season and is now unbeaten in three races. Never far from the leaders, he was cantering throughout and took command of the race early in the straight. He then strode clear to pass the post alone and was in a class of his own. Further improvement can be guaranteed and he now heads for the Hubert de Chaudenay on October 6 over this course and distance. He may well turn into a top class cup horse next year.
Dancing Lady(FR) ran a brave race and tried to make most of the running. Set a sensible pace but could not fend off the challenge of the winner when it came early in the straight. She just stayed on one paced throughout the final furlong and a half.
Royal And Regal(IRE), well up from the start, made his final effort from two out but looked very one paced throughout the final furlong and a half. He has been a little disappointing since winning a Listed race at this track back in the spring.
Gat(FR) ran very free in the early part of this race and was last at the half way stage. He had plenty to do at the entrance to the straight but ran on well in the closing stages.

5258 LONGCHAMP (R-H)
Sunday, September 9

OFFICIAL GOING: Good

5259a QATAR AIRWAYS PRIX DU PIN (GROUP 3) 7f
2:20 (2:22) 3-Y-0+ **£27,027** (£10,811; £8,108; £5,405; £2,703)

RPR
1 **Sabana Perdida (IRE)**[81] 2753 4-8-11.... C-PLemaire 8 108
(A De Royer-Dupre, France) *settled in mid-div: in tch in 7th st: hdwy 2f out on outside: styd on to ld cl home: comf* **7/2**[2]
2 *1 1/2* **King Jock (USA)**[88] 2586 6-9-1.... PShanahan 2 108
(R J Osborne, Ire) *racd in 2nd: led 2 1/2f out: rdn and r.o 2f out: hdd cl home* **16/1**
3 *nse* **Bertranicus (FR)**[42] 4012 4-9-1.... CSoumillon 3 108
(L Urbano-Grajales, France) *mid-div: disputing 8th on ins st: rdn and hdwy 2f out: disputing 2nd 1f out: kpt on* **4/1**[3]
4 *snk* **Satri (IRE)**[35] 4214 5-9-1.... KFallon 9 108
(J-M Beguigne, France) *prom: 3rd st: pushed along to chse ldr over 2f out: rdn and no ex fr over 1f out* **10/3**[1]
5 *2* **Impressionnante**[42] 4010 4-8-11.... OPeslier 1 98
(C Laffon-Parias, France) *in tch: cl 4th st: pushed along 2f out: nt pce of ldrs* **9/2**
6 *snk* **Winter Fashion (FR)**[43] 3986 3-8-8.... TThulliez 7 97
(F Head, France) *sn led: hdd 2 1/2f out and wknd* **14/1**
7 *shd* **Loda (FR)**[68] 4-8-11.... JVictoire 6 98
(C Baillet, France) *mid-div: disputing 5th st: n.d* **40/1**
8 *2 1/2* **Law Lord**[60] 3445 3-8-11.... LDettori 10 93
(A Fabre, France) *hld up in last: nvr a factor* **12/1**

9 ½ **Sabasha (FR)**[14] 4871 4-8-11 .... TJarnet 4 89
(F Rohaut, France) *mid-div: disputing 5th st: nvr in chalng position* **16/1**

10 3 **Grand Vista**[35] 4216 3-8-11 .... SPasquier 5 83
(A Fabre, France) *settled towards rr: disputing 8th st: n.d* **9/1**

1m 19.8s (-2.60) **Going Correction** -0.025s/f (Good)
WFA 3 from 4yo+ 4lb **10** Ran SP% **122.0**
Speed ratings: **113,111,111,111,108 108,108,105,105,101**
PARI-MUTUEL: WIN 5.30; PL 1.80, 4.80, 1.30; DF 70.80.
Owner Scuderia Zaro Snc **Bred** Musaed Abo Salim **Trained** Chantilly, France

NOTEBOOK

Sabana Perdida(IRE) is a top class performer when the ground is good or faster, but she is kilos inferior on testing going. She was dropped out in the early part of this seven-furlong event and still had plenty to do at the entrance of the straight. Her jockey bided his time and brought the filly with a sweeping late run which took her into the lead inside the final furlong. She then drew clear to win with something in hand. This filly has now been marked down for the Prix de la Foret but will only be raced on good or firmer ground in the future.

King Jock(USA) put up an excellent display and he is a very consistent performer. He was well up from the start and stayed in second place until taking the advantage on the rail half way up the straight. He stuck to his task in a brave manner but did not have the acceleration of the winner. He could turn out for the Park Stakes at Doncaster next Saturday and the alternative is the Solonaway Stakes at the Curragh the following day.

Bertranicus(FR) was given every possible chance, having been in mid division in the early part of the race and brought with a run from one and a half out. He battled well to the line and was only beaten by inches for second place. Always puts in a decent performance. He now goes for the Foret.

Satri(IRE), smartly into his stride, sat behind the runner up for much of this race. He was given every possible chance, was slightly unlucky in the straight and was only narrowly beaten for third place. This was a slightly disappointing effort from this five-year-old who is another who will line up for the Foret at the beginning of next month.

5260a QATAR PRIX LA ROCHETTE (GROUP 3) 7f
2:55 (2:53) 2-Y-O **£27,027** (£10,811; £8,108; £5,405; £2,703)

RPR

1 **Young Pretender (FR)**[22] 4604 2-8-11 .... LDettori 3 105+
(J H M Gosden) *4th st: 3rd and rdn wl over 1f out: r.o fnl f: drvn to ld cl home* **9/4**[2]

2 ½ **Shediak (FR)**[33] 2-8-11 .... CSoumillon 2 104+
(A Fabre, France) *trckd ldr: led wl over 2f out tl unable qck and ct cl home* **6/4**[1]

3 1 ½ **Stern Opinion (USA)**[42] 4009 2-8-11 .... SPasquier 1 100
(P Bary, France) *wnt lft s: plld v hrd early and sn disputing 2nd: 3rd st: 2nd and rdn over 1f out: one pce fnl f* **5/2**[3]

4 3 **Salut L'Africain (FR)**[22] 4625 2-8-11 .... OPeslier 4 92
(Robert Collet, France) *5th st: 4th and rdn over 2f out: no hdwy* **14/1**

5 1 ½ **Emirati (IRE)**[4] 2-8-11 .... J-BHamel 5 88?
(Robert Collet, France) *led to st: hung lft over 3f out: hdd and hung bdly lft wl over 2f out: sn wknd* **66/1**

6 1 ½ **Timbo Timbo (FR)**[7] 2-8-11 .... JVictoire 6 85
(H-A Pantall, France) *s.i.s: last thrght* **33/1**

1m 21.9s (-0.50) **Going Correction** -0.025s/f (Good) **6** Ran SP% **110.4**
Speed ratings: **101,100,98,95,93 91**
PARI-MUTUEL: WIN 4.50; PL 1.70, 1.10; SF 7.10.
Owner H R H Princess Haya Of Jordan **Bred** Carl Holt **Trained** Newmarket, Suffolk

NOTEBOOK

Young Pretender(FR) is beginning to look like a Classic prospect and he earned at a 20-1 quote for next seasons 2000 Guineas after this effort. Now unbeaten in two races, he was not hussled along in the early stages of this seven furlong event and still had plenty to do with a furlong and a half left to run. He engaged top gear a furlong out and then went to the head of affairs in the last 50 yards. Was running on really well at the finish and he will now come back to run over the course and distance again in the Prix Jean-Luc Lagardere on Arc day.

Shediak(FR) is an imposing individual and looked the likely winner when he went into the lead at the two furlong marker. He stayed on but could not quicken in the same way as the winner inside the final furlong. The colt was totally unsuited by a lack of early pace which led to him running free for part of the race. He was also left in the lead when the long time leader dropped out rapidly. Certainly a high class individual who needs a longer trip. He could have another run this season but connections might leave him alone until next year.

Stern Opinion(USA) was slowly into his stride and took a real keen grip early, as there was no early pace. He was soon in third position and was another to run a little free. He made a challenge for the lead with the winner but it did not last until the bitter end. He just stayed on and is not quite up to this class.

Salut L'Africain(FR) was never seen with a real chance. He made some late progress but was still well adrift from the first three past the post as the race came to an end. Consistent but not up to this level.

5261a QATAR PRIX DU MOULIN DE LONGCHAMP (GROUP 1) (C&F) 1m
3:25 (3:29) 3-Y-O+ **£154,433** (£61,784; £32,197; £15,433; £7,730)

RPR

1 **Darjina (FR)**[42] 4010 3-8-8 .... CSoumillon 3 124
(A De Royer-Dupre, France) *racd in 3rd: pushed along and wnt 2nd 2f out: chal 1 1/2f out: led appr fnl f: r.o wl* **9/2**[3]

2 2 **Ramonti (FR)**[39] 4058 5-9-2 .... LDettori 5 123
(Saeed Bin Suroor) *racd in cl 2nd: led 2f out: rdn 1 1/2f out: hdd appr fnl f: kpt on* **9/4**[2]

3 1 **George Washington (IRE)**[64] 3331 4-9-2 .... KFallon 7 121+
(A P O'Brien, Ire) *hld up: 7th st: effrt 1 1/2f out: styd on fnl f: tk 3rd cl home* **6/4**[1]

4 1 **Linngari (IRE)**[133] 5-9-2 .... RyanMoore 2 118
(A De Royer-Dupre, France) *mid-div: disputing 5th st: drvn to chse ldrs and wnt 3rd over 1f out: no ex fnl stages* **25/1**

5 2 ½ **Archipenko (USA)**[39] 4058 3-8-11 .... JAHeffernan 1 112
(A P O'Brien, Ire) *led: pushed along st: hdd 2f out: styd on tl outpcd fnl f* **40/1**

6 2 **Holocene (USA)**[28] 4445 3-8-11 .... C-PLemaire 6 107
(P Bary, France) *hld up in last: pushed along st: n.d* **20/1**

7 nk **Astronomer Royal (USA)**[63] 3362 3-8-11 .... CO'Donoghue 9 107
(A P O'Brien, Ire) *hld up: 8th and pushed along st: rdn 1 1/2f out: no imp* **16/1**

8 snk **Turtle Bowl (IRE)**[28] 4445 5-9-2 .... OPeslier 4 107
(F Rohaut, France) *mid-div: disputing 5th st: pushed along 2f out: unable qck* **12/1**

9 1 **Golden Titus (IRE)**[63] 3362 3-8-11 .... SPasquier 8 104
(A Renzoni, Italy) *in tch: 4th on outside st: sn pushed along: rdn and btn over 1 1/2f out* **40/1**

1m 36.8s (-5.60) **Going Correction** -0.275s/f (Firm)
WFA 3 from 4yo+ 5lb **9** Ran SP% **116.0**
Speed ratings: **117,115,114,113,110 108,108,108,107**
PARI-MUTUEL: WIN 4.90; PL 1.30, 1.10, 1.10; DF 5.80.
Owner Princess Zahra Aga Khan **Bred** Princess Zahra Aga Khan **Trained** Chantilly, France

NOTEBOOK

Darjina(FR) gave some top performers a real hiding by this filly who really appealed when walking around the paddock. She has improved throughout the season and completely redeemed her reputation by this superlative effort. The only time she failed to win came when the ground went very soft at Ascot in June. She has now won all her five races in France and is certainly improving with every outing. Smartly away, she settled beautifully in third position before challenging for the lead at the furlong and a half marker. From this point on she lengthened her stride and never looked likely to taste defeat. Good ground is definitely an advantage and even further improvement can be expected. Connections have time to announce her next race. Options include the Queen Elizabeth II Stakes (a supplement would be necessary), the Sun Chariot Stakes or the Prix de L'Opera. Her jockey feels she would definitely stay 10 furlongs and the filly is very likely to stay in training next year.

Ramonti(FR) was taken down to the start early and virtually took no part in the preliminaries. His jockey dismounted at the start and waited for the other to arrive. The five-year-old did nothing wrong in the race and was simply beaten by a better horse on the day. Settled in second place, he went to the head of affairs at the two furlong marker and stayed there until passed the winner a short time after. He kept up the good work until the bitter end and there were no excuses. He is likely to go back to Ascot and try and win his second Group 1 race in the Queen Elizabeth II Stakes.

George Washington(IRE) was taken back from his wide draw and raced for much of this race on the rail. Coming into the straight he still had an enormous amount of ground to make out on the winner and runner up who were about to set the race alight. He was still well adrift running into the final furlong but finished best of all and was rapidly cutting down the runner up inside the final furlong. His trainer had wished for a faster pace and he was coming back to a mile. The colt may now try and go for back-to-back wins in the Queen Elizabeth II at the end of the month. Should certainly not be written off for his second career at the racetrack.

Linngari(IRE) put up a very decent performance considering he had not been out since April and was running for the first time for a new trainer. He was given a great ride by his jockey and always in a decent position. Third just over a furlong out, he just blew up as the race came to an end. He can only strip much fitter next time out and he may next be seen over a mile again in the Prix Daniel Wildenstein on October 5th.

Archipenko(USA) has not gone on from his Derrinstown victory and not for the first time seemed to be sacrificed as a pacemaker.

Astronomer Royal(USA), shock winner of the French 2000 Guineas earlier in the season, found himself too far back and could never get into it. He is better than this run suggests.

2548 TABY (R-H)
Sunday, September 9

OFFICIAL GOING: Turf course - good; all-weather - easy

5262a NICATOR TABY OPEN SPRINT CHAMPIONSHIP (GROUP 3) 5f 165y
2:45 (2:48) 3-Y-O+ **£30,405** (£15,203; £7,297; £4,865; £3,041)

RPR

1 **Francis**[38] 9-9-4 .... ESki 9 —
(Niels Petersen, Norway) *mid-div: r.o to chal fnl f: led 50yds out (exact SP 11.81-1)* **118/10**

2 ½ **Solvana (IRE)**[28] 5-9-0 .... FJohansson 10 —
(Wido Neuroth, Norway) *mid-div: prog 1/2-way to ld 2f out: hdd 50yds out* **9/2**[2]

3 1 **Berri Chis (ARG)**[28] 5-9-4 .... FDiaz 3 —
(Vanja Sandrup, Sweden) *prom: chal and ev ch fnl f: kpt on at one pce* **117/10**

4 1 ½ **Completo (IRE)**[28] 4-9-4 .... (b) NCordrey 6 —
(F Castro, Sweden) *led to 2f out: one pce fnl f* **66/10**

5 hd **King Quantas (IRE)**[84] 9-9-4 .... JimmyFortune 4 —
(B Bo, Sweden) *last to 1/2-way: sme late hdwy* **124/10**

6 1 **Muskateer Steel (IRE)**[38] 6-9-4 .... P-AGraberg 8 —
(B Bo, Sweden) *bhd: n.d* **18/10**[1]

7 3 **Waquaas**[364] 5225 11-9-4 .... KAndersen 7 —
(B Bo, Sweden) *nvr bttr than mid-div* **58/10**

8 ½ **Steve's Champ (CHI)**[38] 7-9-4 .... (b) JJohanson 1 —
(Rune Haugen, Norway) *racd in 3rd to 1/2-way: wknd 2f out* **52/10**[3]

9 nk **Bellamont Forest (USA)**[38] 11-9-4 .... DinaDanekilde 2 —
(O Larsen, Sweden) *a bhd* **20/1**

1m 11.2s (4.50) **9** Ran SP% **125.8**
(Including Skr1 stake): WIN 12.81; PL 3.26, 1.90, 2.73; DF 83.07.
Owner Oslo Racing Stables AS **Bred** Fares Stables Ltd **Trained** Norway

5263a NICATOR STOCKHOLM CUP INTERNATIONAL (GROUP 3) 1m 4f
3:15 (3:16) 3-Y-O+ **£33,784** (£15,203; £7,297; £4,865; £3,041)

RPR

1 **Appel Au Maitre (FR)**[14] 3-8-9 .... FJohansson 3 104
(Wido Neuroth, Norway) *mid-div: hdwy 4f out: r.o to ld 2f out: wnt clr fnl f: easily (exact SP 1.26-1)* **5/4**[1]

2 8 ½ **Peas And Carrots (DEN)**[35] 4218 4-9-4 .... MSantos 9 91
(L Reuterskiold, Sweden) *mid-div: r.o to take 2nd 2f out: no ch w wnr* **121/10**

3 3 **Jagodin (IRE)**[75] 2976 7-9-4 .... (b) CLopez 2 87
(B Neuman, Sweden) *prom: kpt on fnl 2f but nt pce of ldng pair* **53/1**

4 ½ **Alnitak (USA)**[35] 4218 6-9-4 .... (b) KAndersen 10 86
(B Olsen, Norway) *towards rr: stdy hdwy fr 4f out: tk 4th fnl strides* **37/1**

5 shd **Angel De Madrid (CHI)**[14] 4874 6-9-4 .... JohnFortune 4 86
(Rune Haugen, Norway) *last to 1/2-way: r.o 2f out: wnt 4th ins fnl f: lost pl fnl strides* **25/1**

6 2 **Equip Hill (SWE)**[35] 4218 5-9-4 .... (b) P-AGraberg 6 83
(B Bo, Sweden) *a mid-div* **56/10**[3]

7 5 **Miss The Boat**[14] 5-9-0 .... JJohanson 7 71
(A Lund, Norway) *prom: 3rd 1/2-way: wknd fr 3f out* **116/10**

8 1 **Farouge (FR)**[94] 6-9-4 .... YvonneDurant 8 74
(Yvonne Durant, Sweden) *a towards rr* **122/10**

9 dist **Steelwolf**[35] 4218 6-9-4 .... LVillarroel 1 —
(B Bo, Sweden) *led to 2f out: wknd and eased fnl f* **48/1**

10 3 **Sudan (IRE)**[84] 2706 4-9-4 .... RichardHughes 5 —
(M A Jarvis) *mid-div: rdn and wknd 4f out: dropped to last: virtually p.u fnl f* **2/1**[2]

2m 36.5s (7.30)
WFA 3 from 4yo+ 9lb **10** Ran SP% **126.4**
WIN 2.26; PL 1.25, 2.32, 4.51; DF 36.45.
Owner Stall Perlen **Bred** Gilles & Aliette Forien **Trained** Norway

NOTEBOOK
Sudan(IRE), last seen winning the Group 1 Gran Premio di Milano for Elie Lellouche in June, was making his debut for the Jarvis yard but ran too badly to be true and something was clearly amiss.

VELIEFENDI (R-H)

Sunday, September 9

OFFICIAL GOING: Good

5264a BOSPHORUS CUP 1m 4f

2:30 (2:32) 3-Y-0+ **£204,082** (£81,633; £40,816; £20,408)

RPR

1 **Bussoni (GER)**[28] 4442 6-9-6 .... (t) ASuborics 4 115
(H Blume, Germany) *mde all: 2 l clr ent st: rdn 1 1/2f out: 1 l up ins fnl f: drew away again clsng stages* **9/4**[2]

2 2 **Pressing (IRE)**[29] 4414 4-9-6 .... NCallan 2 112
(M A Jarvis) *hld up: 6th st on outside: hdwy to go 2nd ins fnl f: nt pce of wnr* **137/10**

3 1/2 **Laverock (IRE)**[28] 4442 5-9-6 .... KerrinMcEvoy 1 111
(Saeed Bin Suroor) *in tch: 3rd st on ins: wnt 2nd against ins rail jst over 1f out: one pce and lost 2nd ins fnl f* **23/10**[3]

4 1 1/2 **Tiramisu (TUR)** 4-9-3 .... (b) SKaya 8 106
(S Tasbek, Turkey) *cl up: 2nd st: sn rdn: lost 2nd jst over 1f out: wknd* **68/10**

5 1 1/2 **Annosh (TUR)** 4-9-3 .... ECankilic 7 103
(M Yigiter, Turkey) *hld up: last st: swtchd to outside over 2f out: wnt 5th ins fnl f: r.o* **54/10**

6 10 **Prince Of Eulleup (TUR)**[21] 4-9-6 .... HKaratas 6 90
(A Guven, Turkey) *in tch: 4th st: wknd 2f out* **68/10**

7 1 1/2 **Runaway**[74] 3011 5-9-6 .... (t) DBonilla 5 88
(R Pritchard-Gordon, France) *hld up in rr: 5th st: sn btn* **17/10**[1]

2m 31.28s (2.48)
WFA 3 from 4yo+ 9lb **7** Ran SP% **146.2**
(including 1YTL stake): WIN 3.25; no place betting; DF 9.05; SF 13.15.
Owner Stall Kaiserberg **Bred** Gestut Karlshof **Trained** Germany

NOTEBOOK
Pressing(IRE) came from off the pace and had every chance, but this trip appears to stretch him and he could make little impression on the winner.
Laverock(IRE) had every chance and there appeared to be no real excuses.

5265a TOPKAPI TROPHY (GROUP 2) 1m

3:30 (3:34) 3-Y-0+ **£280,158** (£122,449; £61,224; £30,612)

RPR

1 **Sabirli (TUR)**[21] 6-9-6 .... HKaratas 13 113
(C Kurt, Turkey) *hld up: hdwy towards centre over 1f out: led 150yds out: drvn out* **17/4**[3]

2 1 **Ribella (IRE)**[343] 8-9-3 .... SKaya 9 108
(S Tasbek, Turkey) *hld up: hdwy over 1f out: wnt 2nd 150yds out: kpt on* **72/10**

3 1/2 **Trip To The Moon**[42] 4010 4-9-3 .... J-LMartinez 8 107
(M Delzangles, France) *hld up: swtchd outside and hdwy 1f out: fin wl* **32/10**[2]

4 1/2 **Caradak (IRE)**[22] 4600 6-9-6 .... KerrinMcEvoy 3 109
(Saeed Bin Suroor) *hld up: n.m.r over 2f out: hdwy towards ins to go 3rd briefly 1f out: one pce* **17/10**[1]

5 nse **Banknote**[57] 3523 5-9-6 .... FrancisNorton 1 109
(A M Balding) *racd in 3rd: led 1 1/2f out: hdd 150yds out: lost 3rd cl home* **64/10**

6 1 3/4 **Aspectus (IRE)**[35] 4217 4-9-6 .... ASuborics 2 105
(H Blume, Germany) *in tch: hdwy to go 2nd briefly 1f out: one pce* **11/2**

7 1 **Sahnur (TUR)** 3-8-9 .... BKurdu 6 97
(Enver Mutlu, Turkey) *hld up in rr: styd on wl down outside fnl f* **159/10**

8 hd **Traffic Guard (USA)**[36] 4148 3-8-12 .... (p) JohnEgan 5 100
(J S Moore) *racd in 4th: remained prom tl wknd 1f out* **27/1**

9 4 **Topor (TUR)** 3-8-12 .... MKaya 11 92
(B Tosun, Turkey) *racd in 2nd: one pce fnl 1 1/2f* **149/10**

10 6 **Dubai's Touch**[22] 4600 3-8-12 .... RoystonFfrench 7 80
(M Johnston) *hld up in rr: nvr a factor* **27/1**

11 2 **Cincinnati Kid (TUR)**[21] 5-9-6 .... EYavuz 12 79
(I Eser, Turkey) *in tch: 5th over 1f out: wknd* **162/10**

12 6 **Lovely Doyoun (TUR)**[21] 4-9-3 .... GYildiz 4 64
(A K Aksoy, Turkey) *led to 1 1/2f out: wknd* **29/1**

13 dist **Fairson (TUR)**[213] 399 4-9-6 .... SBoyraz 10 —
(K Tekdogan, Turkey) *t.o fnl 2f* **121/10**

1m 36.24s (0.91)
WFA 3 from 4yo+ 5lb **13** Ran SP% **157.1**
TOTE: WIN 5.25; no place betting; DF 10.20; SF 19.65.
Owner Aydogan San **Bred** A San **Trained** Turkey

NOTEBOOK
Caradak(IRE) started favourite despite finishing last in the Hungerford on his recent return from ten months off. He was a little short of room entering the home straight, but he still had every chance and it probably did not make the difference between victory and defeat.
Banknote, who can be keen on his races, was ridden prominently and was still in front entering the last furlong so was very unfortunate to finish out of the money.
Traffic Guard(USA) was in a good position early, but did not get home on this occasion.
Dubai's Touch, who tends to be found out when raised outside Listed company, was never in the race and failed to confirm Goodwood form with Traffic Guard.

4755 BATH (L-H)

Monday, September 10

OFFICIAL GOING: Firm
Wind: virtually nil

5267 RANDSTAD WORK SOLUTIONS MAIDEN AUCTION FILLIES' STKS 5f 11y

2:10 (2:11) (Class 6) 2-Y-O **£2,072** (£616; £308; £153) **Stalls** Centre

Form RPR

63 1 **Heaven**[17] 4755 2-8-3 0 .... ChrisCatlin 5 65
(P J Makin) *disp ld tl slt advantage 3f out: rdn 2f out: narrowly hdd 1f out: styd chalng tl led last stride* **3/1**[3]

062 2 shd **Blue Zenith (IRE)**[22] 4629 2-8-3 67 .... JimmyQuinn 4 65
(J S Moore) *disp ld to 3f out: styd upsides tl slt ld 1f out: styd on u.p tl ct last stride* **11/4**[2]

3 1 3/4 **Solo River** 2-8-3 0 .... MartinDwyer 8 59
(P J Makin) *slowly away: green and wl in rr early: styd on wl fr 2f out: squeezed through and qcknd to go 3rd ins fnl f: gaining on ldng duo cl home* **12/1**

240 4 1 **Ronsai (USA)**[32] 4310 2-8-7 68 .... RyanMoore 2 59
(R Hannon) *chsd ldrs: rdn over 2f out: wknd ins fnl f* **5/2**[1]

5 hd **Eastern Pride** 2-8-3 0 .... FrankieMcDonald 9 54
(P A Blockley) *s.i.s: green and bhd: sme hdwy on outside fr 2f out: nvr quite gng pce to rch ldrs: one pce ins fnl f* **40/1**

00 6 2 **Bathwick Icon (IRE)**[14] 4904 2-8-7 0 .... SteveDrowne 1 51
(A B Haynes) *in rr: sme prog whn sltly hmpd on rails jst ins fnl f: nvr a factor after* **15/2**

0300 7 1 1/4 **Structura (USA)**[18] 4737 2-8-11 67 .... StephenCarson 3 50
(J S Moore) *chsd ldrs in 3rd: rdn 1/2-way: wknd fnl f* **16/1**

000 8 hd **April's Quest (IRE)**[29] 4428 2-8-7 45 .... FergusSweeney 6 45
(David Pinder) *spd 3f* **100/1**

06 9 2 1/2 **Oronsay**[25] 4540 2-8-9 0 .... TQuinn 7 38
(B R Millman) *in tch to 1/2-way* **20/1**

63.19 secs (0.69) **Going Correction** -0.05s/f (Good) **9** Ran SP% **113.8**
Speed ratings (Par 90): **92,91,89,87,87 83,81,81,77**
CSF £11.31 TOTE £3.90: £1.20, £1.30, £4.80; EX 8.40.
Owner Wedgewood Estates **Bred** Mrs D O Joly **Trained** Ogbourne Maisey, Wilts

FOCUS
A weak juvenile maiden and modest form.

NOTEBOOK
Heaven improved on the form of her recent course third with a narrow victory. She is likely to find things tougher from now on, but she has progressed with every run so far. (tchd 5-2)
Blue Zenith(IRE) probably ran to the same sort of form she showed when second over course and distance on her previous start and she was just denied. (op 5-2 tchd 7-2)
Solo River, a cheaply-bought daughter of Averti, ran green through the early stages, but she came home well and offered promise. She is open to plenty of improvement, but is it worth remembering this was a modest contest. (tchd 10-1)
Ronsai(USA), who returned lame when running here last time, fared better this time, although she was below her official mark of 68. Official explanation: jockey said filly was unsuited by the firm ground (op 7-2)
Eastern Pride, the first foal of a mare who was placed over 6f at three, looked in need of the experience, but she showed ability and can improve. (op 28-1)
Oronsay struggled to go the pace and can do better over further now she is qualified for a handicap mark. (op 16-1 tchd 12-1)

5268 WESTERN DAILY PRESS NURSERY 1m 5y

2:40 (2:42) (Class 5) (0-75,73) 2-Y-O **£3,238** (£963; £481; £240) **Stalls** Low

Form RPR

3140 1 **Palm Court**[16] 4812 2-9-7 **73** .... SteveDrowne 8 77+
(R Charlton) *trckd ldrs: wnt 2nd ins fnl 3f: led ins fnl 2f: pushed along and styd on strly fnl thrght fnl f* **3/1**[2]

455 2 1 1/2 **Feasible**[62] 3404 2-9-0 **66** .... JamesDoyle 1 67
(J G Portman) *led: hdd ins fnl 2f: kpt on wl to hold 2nd but no ch w ready wnr* **12/1**

0030 3 2 **Hyper Viper (IRE)**[42] 4022 2-8-8 **60** .... (b) JimmyQuinn 5 56
(J S Moore) *chsd ldrs: rdn and kpt on u.p fnl 2f but nvr gng pce of ldng duo* **7/1**[3]

4100 4 3/4 **Yes Meg**[42] 4022 2-8-8 **60** .... TQuinn 14 55
(P F I Cole) *chsd ldr and upsides fr 6f out to 4f out: rdn 3f out: one pce fnl 2f* **20/1**

0304 5 shd **Kristal Glory (IRE)**[26] 4501 2-8-5 **57** .... DavidKinsella 2 51
(J L Dunlop) *t.k.h: chsd ldrs: rdn and kpt on same pce fnl 2f* **11/4**[1]

0400 6 3/4 **Blandys Wood**[42] 4022 2-8-8 **60** .... MartinDwyer 15 53
(M R Channon) *s.i.s: bhd: hdwy on outside over 2f out: kpt on wl fnl f but nvr in contention* **16/1**

4005 7 1 1/4 **Alfredtheordinary**[17] 4783 2-8-4 **56** .... ChrisCatlin 13 46
(M R Channon) *in rr: rdn over 3f out: styd on fnl 2f but nvr in contention* **8/1**

0050 8 3 1/2 **Ostinata (IRE)**[30] 4393 2-8-0 **52** .... WandersonD'Avila 16 34
(B W Duke) *in tch: pushed along 3f out: wknd fr 2f out* **40/1**

000 9 1/2 **Just Jimmy (IRE)**[29] 4417 2-8-6 **57** ow1 .... StephenCarson 10 39
(P D Evans) *s.i.s: bhd: sme hdwy whn nt clr run 1f out: kpt on again cl home* **14/1**

000 10 3/4 **Agon Eyes (USA)**[32] 4310 2-8-2 **54** .... FrankieMcDonald 3 33
(D J Coakley) *t.k.h: chsd ldrs: rdn 3f out: wknd 2f out* **18/1**

0400 11 1 1/4 **Dhaka Dazzle**[17] 4770 2-7-11 **56** .... MatthewDavies(7) 6 32
(M R Channon) *in rr: mod prog fr over 1f out* **66/1**

000 12 nk **Holy Storm (IRE)**[36] 4201 2-8-1 **53** ow3 .... NelsonDeSouza 7 28
(Eve Johnson Houghton) *chsd ldrs: rdn 3f out: sn btn* **33/1**

0000 13 2 1/2 **Mister Cafnex (IRE)**[20] 4683 2-7-7 **50** oh1 .... NicolPolli(5) 12 20
(B W Duke) *mid-div whn rn wd bnd 4f out: sn bhd* **50/1**

600 14 2 **Charlie Be (IRE)**[90] 2539 2-8-7 **59** .... FergusSweeney 4 24
(Mrs P N Dutfield) *s.i.s: a towards rr* **22/1**

4255 15 34 **Midnite Blews (IRE)**[32] 4316 2-8-12 **69** .... KevinGhunowa(5) 9 —
(A B Haynes) *sddle slipped sn after s: t.o* **14/1**

1m 41.24s (0.14) **Going Correction** -0.05s/f (Good) **15** Ran SP% **125.4**
Speed ratings (Par 95): **97,95,93,92,92 91,90,87,86,85 84,84,81,79,45**
CSF £37.85 CT £251.00 TOTE £3.90: £1.80, £3.70, £3.00; EX 42.90.
Owner B E Nielsen **Bred** B E Nielsen **Trained** Beckhampton, Wilts

FOCUS
Plenty of runners, but this looked a pretty modest nursery. The winner looks well handicapped and the runner-up would have been a clear-cut winner without him.

NOTEBOOK

Palm Court ran no sort of race on soft ground in first-time blinkers at Newmarket on his previous start, but the return to a fast surface suited and he had no problems with the step up to 1m. He should remain competitive under similar conditions provided he is kept to a sensible level. (op 2-1)
Feasible had shown ability in three runs in maiden company and this was a creditable effort on his nursery debut off the back of a two-month break. (tchd 14-1)
Hyper Viper(IRE) ran with credit stepped up to 1m for the first time, but this was just a modest race and it is probably worth noting he has been entered for a seller. (op 14-1)
Yes Meg, back on turf with the ground in her favour, was trying this trip for the first time and did not fare too badly. Official explanation: jockey said filly hung left-handed (op 16-1)
Kristal Glory(IRE) failed to build on his recent Salisbury fourth over 7f, despite being able to race off a 3lb lower mark. (op 3-1)
Just Jimmy(IRE) Official explanation: jockey said gelding ran too free
Charlie Be(IRE) Official explanation: jockey said gelding hung right-handed
Midnite Blews(IRE) Official explanation: jockey said saddle slipped

5269 WESTERNDAILYPRESS.CO.UK (S) STKS — 1m 5y
3:10 (3:16) (Class 6) 3-4-Y-0 — **£1,943** (£578; £288; £144) **Stalls** Low

Form — RPR
5424 **1** **The Jailer**[77] 2938 4-8-6 44 ....(p) MCGeran(7) 9 — 53
(J G M O'Shea) *led 1f: styd w ldr tl led again over 3f out: pushed clr over 1f out: readily* **6/1**[3]
0420 **2** 3 **Strife (IRE)**[9] 5037 4-9-4 48 .... GeorgeBaker 8 — 51
(W M Brisbourne) *in rr: hdwy over 3f out: rdn and styd on to go 2nd appr fnl f but nvr any ch w wnr* **9/2**[1]
5006 **3** 1 ½ **Fun In The Sun**[6] 5121 3-8-13 45 ....(b[1]) StephenDonohoe 16 — 47
(P D Evans) *in rr: rdn and stl plenty to do on outside over 2f out: kpt on fr over 1f out and fin strly: nt rch ldng duo* **10/1**
0 **4** shd **Hawridge Miss**[25] 4541 3-8-6 0 ow1 .... RichardKingscote(3) 4 — 42
(B R Millman) *in rr and wd into st over 3f out: styd on fnl 2f but nvr in contention* **20/1**
0000 **5** nk **Polish Prospect (IRE)**[5] 5129 3-8-8 43 .... JimmyQuinn 1 — 41
(H S Howe) *chsd ldrs: rdn over 3f out: wknd fnl f* **40/1**
-040 **6** 1 ½ **Buckle And Hyde**[21] 4673 4-8-13 41 .... JamesDoyle 12 — 38
(Mrs A L M King) *in rr: rdn and styd on fnl 2f: nt rch ldrs* **33/1**
3300 **7** 1 **Valeesha**[27] 4471 3-8-2 44 ow1 .... JackDean(7) 5 — 36
(W G M Turner) *slowly away: hdwy on ins over 3f out: outpcd over 2f out: styd on again ins fnl f* **66/1**
0500 **8** nk **Kyburg**[33] 4270 3-8-8 42 .... TQuinn 14 — 34
(P F I Cole) *chsd ldrs: rdn and hmpd ins fnl 2f: no ch aftrer* **28/1**
0025 **9** shd **Briery Blaze**[7] 5094 4-8-13 52 .... SteveDrowne 3 — 35
(J W Unett) *chsd ldrs: rdn and hmpd ins fnl 2f: n.d after* **11/2**[2]
0034 **10** ½ **Meadfoot**[23] 4591 3-8-8 51 .... FergusSweeney 11 — 33
(B R Millman) *chsd ldrs: rdn 3f out: wknd 2f out* **7/1**
2000 **11** ½ **Lay The Cash (USA)**[14] 4885 3-8-13 54 ....(b) MartinDwyer 6 — 37
(J S Moore) *led after 1f: hdd over 3f out: wknd appr fnl f* **8/1**
0006 **12** 1 **Salvestro**[14] 4532 4-8-11 45 .... MarkCoumbe(7) 15 — 35
(A W Carroll) *sddle slipped a in rr* **11/1**
0050 **13** 3 **It's No Problem (IRE)**[17] 4766 3-8-13 47 ....(t) J-PGuillambert 2 — 27
(M Salaman) *chsd ldrs: rdn and wknd over 2f out* **6/1**[3]
0400 **14** 2 ½ **Croft (IRE)**[10] 5001 4-9-9 49 ....(v) TGMcLaughlin 10 — 28
(M S Saunders) *a towards rr* **22/1**
0060 **15** ¾ **Spirit Rising**[32] 4321 3-8-8 42 ....(p) KevinGhunowa(5) 7 — 20
(J M Bradley) *a towards rr* **80/1**

1m 40.37s (-0.73) **Going Correction** -0.05s/f (Good)
WFA 3 from 4yo 5lb — **15** Ran SP% **123.8**
Speed ratings (Par 101): **101,98,96,96,96 94,93,93,93,92 92,91,88,85,84**
CSF £31.70 TOTE £7.60: £1.90, £2.80, £3.80; EX 47.80.There was no bid for the winner.
Owner N M Lowe **Bred** D R Tucker **Trained** Elton, Gloucs

FOCUS
Very moderate form, as one would expect for the level, with the fourth, fifth and sixth far from solid. The runner-up is close to form.
Kyburg Official explanation: jockey said filly suffered interference in running
Briery Blaze Official explanation: jockey said filly suffered interference in running
Lay The Cash(USA) Official explanation: jockey said gelding lost its action
Salvestro Official explanation: jockey said saddle slipped

5270 JOHN SMITH'S EXTRA SMOOTH MAIDEN STKS — 5f 161y
3:40 (3:47) (Class 5) 3-Y-0+ — **£2,849** (£847; £423; £211) **Stalls** Centre

Form — RPR
25 **1** **Oystermouth**[40] 4066 3-8-9 0 .... RichardKingscote(3) 4 — 65+
(R Charlton) *chsd ldrs: chal 2f out: led appr fnl f: drvn out* **3/1**[2]
3 **2** ¾ **O Fourlunda**[26] 4513 3-8-12 0 .... J-PGuillambert 2 — 62+
(C E Brittain) *chsd ldrs: drien along over 2f out: styd on strly to take 2nd ins fnl f but nvr quite gng pce to rch wnr* **13/2**
6065 **3** 1 ¼ **Star Strider**[23] 4606 3-9-3 68 ....(p) MartinDwyer 9 — 62
(A M Balding) *in rr but in tch: hdwy on outside over 2f out: chsd wnr ins fnl f but no imp: wknd and lost 2nd nr fin* **2/1**[1]
4000 **4** 2 **Punching**[81] 2799 3-9-3 52 .... StephenCarson 10 — 56
(Eve Johnson Houghton) *pressed ldrs: led jst ins fnl 2f: hdd appr fnl f: wknd ins fnl f* **14/1**
3660 **5** ¾ **Winning Show**[6] 5122 3-9-3 73 .... RyanMoore 7 — 53
(R A Harris) *chsd ldrs: rdn over 2f out: wknd ins fnl f* **7/2**[3]
0000 **6** 1 ¾ **The Carpet Man**[112] 1883 3-8-10 42 .... MarkCoumbe(7) 5 — 48
(A W Carroll) *in rr: rdn and sme hdwy over 1f out: sn hung lft and no further prog* **100/1**
0-00 **7** 4 **Our Archie**[56] 3597 3-9-3 37 ....(p) PaulFitzsimons 12 — 34
(M J Attwater) *chsd ldrs: rdn 3f out: wknd ins fnl 2f* **150/1**
4000 **8** 2 **Damhsoir (IRE)**[30] 4397 3-8-12 45 .... JimmyQuinn 13 — 23
(H S Howe) *led tl hdd & wknd ins fnl 2f* **16/1**
0 **9** 1 ¼ **Ring Of Charm**[14] 4905 5-8-9 0 .... KevinGhunowa(5) 6 — 19
(C J Down) *slowly away: outpcd most of way* **100/1**
6-65 **10** ½ **One White Sock**[241] 108 3-8-9 48 .... MarcHalford(3) 8 — 17
(J L Spearing) *chsd ldrs: rdn 3f out: sn btn* **33/1**
000 **11** nk **Silver Flame**[20] 4684 3-8-12 44 ....(b[1]) JamesDoyle 3 — 16
(A W Carroll) *early spd: bhd fr 1/2-way* **66/1**
-000 **12** 1 ½ **Stargazy**[3] 5191 3-8-10 60 ....(b) JackDean(7) 1 — 16
(W G M Turner) *prssed ldrs to 1/2-way* **25/1**
00 **13** 27 **Pathway To Glory**[45] 3924 3-9-3 0 .... ChrisCatlin 11 — —
(M Quinn) *sn wl bhd* **100/1**

1m 10.93s (-0.27) **Going Correction** -0.05s/f (Good)
WFA 3 from 5yo 2lb — **13** Ran SP% **118.4**
Speed ratings (Par 103): **99,98,96,93,92 90,85,82,80,80 79,77,41**
CSF £22.18 TOTE £4.60: £1.80, £2.10, £1.30; EX 16.00.
Owner D J Deer **Bred** D J And Mrs Deer **Trained** Beckhampton, Wilts

FOCUS
A modest maiden with the third and fourth not up to their ratings and the sixth and seventh anchoring the form.
Ring Of Charm Official explanation: jockey said mare stumbled on leaving stalls

5271 WEATHERBYS BLOODSTOCK INSURANCE MAIDEN FILLIES' STKS — 1m 3f 144y
4:10 (4:13) (Class 5) 3-Y-0+ — **£2,849** (£847; £423; £211) **Stalls** Low

Form — RPR
2442 **1** **Thinking Positive**[18] 4738 3-8-12 74 .... JimmyFortune 5 — 77
(J H M Gosden) *chsd ldrs: wnt 2nd over 5f out: drvn to ld ins fnl 2f and sn edgd lft: rdn clr fnl f* **11/8**[1]
2344 **2** 1 ½ **Snake's Head**[31] 4357 3-8-12 67 .... JimmyQuinn 6 — 73
(J L Dunlop) *led tl hdd ins fnl 2f: hmpd on rail sn after: kpt on but no ch w wnr* **8/1**
0242 **3** 4 **Sweet Request**[14] 4878 3-8-12 68 .... MartinDwyer 9 — 66
(R M Beckett) *in rr: hdwy fr 3f out: styd on to go 3rd ins fnl 2f but nvr any ch w ldng duo* **6/1**[3]
042 **4** 1 ¼ **Adorabella (IRE)**[22] 4630 4-9-7 65 .... FergusSweeney 7 — 64
(A King) *chsd ldrs: rdn over 3f out: wknd 2f out* **4/1**[2]
0 **5** 4 **Aquamarine Beauty (FR)**[47] 3847 3-8-12 0 .... RyanMoore 8 — 57
(Sir Michael Stoute) *chsd ldr tl over 5f out: wknd fr 3f out* **6/1**[3]
5 **6** 1 ½ **Covert Mission**[10] 5005 4-9-7 0 .... StephenDonohoe 10 — 55
(P D Evans) *in rr tl modest prog fnl 2f* **28/1**
6-65 **7** 5 **Indigo Rose (IRE)**[17] 4765 3-8-12 66 .... DavidKinsella 4 — 46
(J H M Gosden) *t.k.h: chsd ldrs to 3f out* **16/1**

2m 28.7s (-1.60) **Going Correction** -0.05s/f (Good)
WFA 3 from 4yo 9lb — **7** Ran SP% **111.1**
Speed ratings (Par 100): **103,102,99,98,95 94,91**
CSF £12.47 TOTE £1.90: £1.90, £2.80; EX 12.10.
Owner George Strawbridge **Bred** George Strawbridge **Trained** Newmarket, Suffolk

FOCUS
A modest middle-distance fillies' maiden and a race that is unlikely to produce too many future winners. The form is rated through the far-from-solid runner-up to her previous course and distance effort with the winner to form.
Covert Mission Official explanation: jockey said filly missed the break and hung right-handed

5272 EVENING POST H'CAP — 5f 161y
4:40 (4:40) (Class 5) (0-75,74) 3-Y-0+ — **£2,979** (£886; £442; £221) **Stalls** Centre

Form — RPR
5026 **1** **Digital**[3] 5191 10-8-8 **60** ....(v) ChrisCatlin 12 — 68
(M R Channon) *in rr: hdwy on outside over 1f out: str run and edgd lft ins fnl f: led last strides* **8/1**
1000 **2** nk **Stir Crazy (IRE)**[12] 4939 3-8-4 **58** oh1 .... JimmyQuinn 6 — 65
(M R Channon) *chsd ldrs: hdwy fr 2f out to ld ins fnl f: ct last strides* **50/1**
0041 **3** 1 ½ **Pic Up Sticks**[4] 5160 8-9-8 **74** 6ex .... RyanMoore 2 — 82+
(B G Powell) *s.i.s: bhd: hdwy over 1f out: styng on ins fnl f whn nt clr run: kpt on again cl home but nt a threat to ldng duo* **5/2**[1]
306 **4** ½ **Talcen Gwyn (IRE)**[12] 4939 5-8-6 **58** ....(v) FergusSweeney 11 — 58
(M F Harris) *chsd ldrs: led ins fnl 2f: hdd ins fnl f: sn one pce* **8/1**
0401 **5** shd **Desperate Dan**[11] 4974 6-8-10 **67** ....(b) KevinGhunowa(5) 9 — 67
(A B Haynes) *trckd ldrs: rdn and edgd lft over 1f out: no ex u.p fnl f* **10/1**
0052 **6** nk **Cuppacocoa**[9] 5051 3-9-6 **74** .... MartinDwyer 8 — 77+
(C G Cox) *chsd ldrs: rdn and stl wl there whn hmpd over 1f out: nt rcvr* **11/2**[3]
0054 **7** ¾ **Summer Recluse (USA)**[12] 4942 8-8-10 **62** ....(t) SteveDrowne 1 — 66+
(J M Bradley) *in rr: hdwy whn hmpd over 1f out: styng on whn hmpd again ins fnl f and nt rcvr* **14/1**
300 **8** 2 ½ **One Way Ticket**[4] 5160 7-8-13 **65** ....(p) TQuinn 5 — 53
(J M Bradley) *chsd ldrs: rdn over 2f out: wknd fnl f* **20/1**
0420 **9** 2 **High Ridge**[8] 5064 8-9-0 **66** ....(p) JimmyFortune 3 — 48
(J M Bradley) *outpcd most of way* **10/1**
1041 **10** ½ **Dematraf (IRE)**[3] 5191 5-8-13 **65** 6ex .... StephenDonohoe 7 — 45
(P D Evans) *s.i.s: outpcd* **5/1**[2]
2200 **11** ½ **Willhewiz**[75] 2982 7-8-10 **62** .... TGMcLaughlin 10 — 40
(M S Saunders) *led tl hdd & wknd ins fnl 2f* **16/1**

1m 10.17s (-1.03) **Going Correction** -0.05s/f (Good)
WFA 3 from 5yo+ 2lb — **11** Ran SP% **120.3**
Speed ratings (Par 103): **104,103,101,100,100 100,99,96,93,92 92**
CSF £337.19 CT £1315.17 TOTE £11.40: £2.90, £9.20, £1.60; EX 187.50.
Owner W G R Wightman **Bred** W G R Wightman **Trained** West Ilsley, Berks
■ Stewards' Enquiry : Chris Catlin one-day ban: careless riding (Sep 21)

FOCUS
A routine Bath sprint handicap full of the usual suspects and although slightly messy the form appears reasonably sound.
Pic Up Sticks Official explanation: jockey said gelding was denied a clear run
Cuppacocoa Official explanation: jockey said filly suffered interference in running
Summer Recluse(USA) Official explanation: jockey said gelding was denied a clear run
Dematraf(IRE) Official explanation: jockey said mare was unsuited by the firm ground

5273 BOLLINGER CHAMPAGNE CHALLENGE SERIES MAIDEN H'CAP (FOR GENTLEMAN AMATEUR RIDERS) — 1m 5f 22y
5:10 (5:10) (Class 5) (0-70,67) 3-Y-0+ — **£2,810** (£871; £435; £217) **Stalls** High

Form — RPR
-040 **1** **Lord Oroko**[10] 5006 3-10-8 **64** .... FelixDeGiles(3) 5 — 71
(J G M O'Shea) *in rr: drvn along over 3f out: styd on fr over 2f out: chsd ldr over 1f out: led fnl half f: rdn out* **12/1**
0242 **2** ¾ **Prince Zafonic**[47] 3858 4-11-10 **67** ....(t) MrSWalker 1 — 73
(Miss Gay Kelleway) *led: drvn 3l clr over 2f out: hdd and no ex fnl half f* **3/1**[2]
-065 **3** 7 **Magnum Opus (IRE)**[15] 4859 5-10-9 **57** ....(t) MrNKinnon(5) 4 — 52
(D J Murphy) *chsd ldr: rdn and no imp fnl 3f: lost 2nd over 1f out: wknd ins fnl f* **14/1**
6-62 **4** 1 ¼ **Mexican Bob**[14] 4333 4-11-5 **67** .... MrCPHuxley(5) 7 — 60
(A King) *in rr but in tch: hdwy and rdn over 3f out: nvr gng pce to be competitive: wknd fr 2f out* **6/5**[1]
0500 **5** hd **Kingsmead (USA)**[48] 3825 3-9-9 **53** oh3 ....(vt[1]) MrRBirkett(5) 6 — 46
(Miss J Feilden) *chsd ldrs: rdn 4f out: wknd 2f out* **25/1**
6000 **6** 1 ½ **Bring It On Home**[8] 5068 3-10-9 **65** .... MrDHutchison(3) 2 — 56
(G L Moore) *chsd ldrs tl wknd fr 3f out* **15/2**[3]
0060 **7** 9 **Merchant Bankes**[10] 5007 4-10-10 **53** oh1 .... MrJJDoyle 3 — 30
(W G M Turner) *in rr: lost tch fnl 3f* **15/2**[3]

2m 51.15s (-0.35) **Going Correction** -0.05s/f (Good)
WFA 3 from 4yo+ 10lb — **7** Ran SP% **112.2**
Speed ratings (Par 103): **99,98,94,93,93 92,86**
CSF £46.09 TOTE £18.80: £4.80, £1.50; EX 50.40 Place 6 £47.00, Place 5 £18.77.
Owner Alan G Craddock **Bred** A M Tombs **Trained** Elton, Gloucs

The Form Book, Raceform Ltd, Compton, RG20 6NL

FOCUS
A maiden handicap for amateur riders, but the winning time stood up well enough considering the type of contest and the race is rated at face value through the runner-up.
T/Plt: £33.20 to a £1 stake. Pool: £53,257.15. 1,169.60 winning tickets. T/Qpdt: £5.40 to a £1 stake. Pool: £3,462.80. 468.90 winning tickets. ST

5061 FOLKESTONE (R-H)

Monday, September 10

OFFICIAL GOING: Good to firm (9.1)
Wind: virtually nil Weather: mainly overcast

5274 ARENALEISUREPLC.COM MEDIAN AUCTION MAIDEN STKS — 7f (S)

2:20 (2:20) (Class 5) 2-Y-O — £2,914 (£867; £433; £216) Stalls Low

Form — RPR

22 **1** **Billion Dollar Kid**[67] 3238 2-9-3 0 RichardHughes 9 85+
(R Hannon) *mde all: rdn clr wl over 1f out: styd on wl ins fnl f* **3/1**[2]

024 **2** ¾ **Nezami (IRE)**[24] 4584 2-9-3 81 RobertHavlin 5 83
(B J Meehan) *t.k.h: chsd ldrs: chsd wnr over 1f out: swtchd rt ins fnl f and tried to chal: no imp last 100yds* **4/1**[3]

3 **3** 7 **Mon Plaisir (USA)**[24] 4584 2-9-3 0 SebSanders 11 65
(J L Dunlop) *chsd wnr: rdn wl over 2f out: ev ch 2f out: sn demoted and outpcd by ldng pair* **9/4**[1]

0 **4** 2 **Langham House**[43] 3991 2-9-3 0 PaulDoe 3 60+
(J R Jenkins) *hld up in tch: rdn and edgd lft wl over 1f out: plugged on but no ch w ldrs* **40/1**

00 **5** 1 **It's My Day (IRE)**[55] 3625 2-9-0 0 LiamJones(3) 13 57
(Jane Chapple-Hyam) *pushed along early but sn prom: rdn wl over 2f out: sn outpcd: plugged on* **66/1**

0 **6** ½ **Pediment**[14] 4882 2-8-12 0 JamieSpencer 1 51
(J R Fanshawe) *stdd s: hld up in rr: swtchd to outer and effrt over 2f out: no prog over 1f out and wl hld after* **4/1**[3]

03 **7** 3½ **Little Toto**[17] 4761 2-9-3 0 PhilipRobinson 7 47
(C G Cox) *t.k.h: chsd ldrs: rdn over 2f out: wkng whn sltly hmpd wl over 1f out* **11/1**

0506 **8** 1½ **Altercation**[32] 4315 2-8-12 53 TedDurcan 4 38
(W Jarvis) *hld up in midfield: rdn wl over 2f out: sn btn* **40/1**

9 1¼ **Desert Thistle (IRE)** 2-9-3 0 IanMongan 10 40
(H J L Dunlop) *sn pushed along in rr: nvr on terms: sme modest late hdwy* **66/1**

00 **10** 1½ **Peer Pressure**[11] 4962 2-8-10 0 JackMitchell(7) 6 36
(P Mitchell) *t.k.h: in tch: effrt on outer over 2f out: wknd wl over 1f out* **100/1**

05 **11** 4 **Tobago Bay**[7] 5088 2-9-3 0 TPO'Shea 2 25
(M R Channon) *a bhd: rdn 1/2-way: sn lost tch: t.o* **25/1**

5050 **12** 3 **Fraamington**[30] 4405 2-9-3 38 SamHitchcott 8 18
(M R Channon) *a bhd: no ch last 3f: t.o* **100/1**

13 ½ **Fort Hull (IRE)** 2-9-3 0 JimCrowley 12 16
(Mrs A J Perrett) *sn bhd and rdn: no ch fr 1/2-way* **50/1**

1m 25.68s (-2.22) **Going Correction** -0.425s/f (Firm) 13 Ran SP% 119.8
Speed ratings (Par 95): **95,94,86,83,82 82,78,76,75,73 68,65,64**
CSF £14.90 TOTE £4.40: £1.40, £1.60, £1.10; EX 19.30 Trifecta £26.40 Pool £264.58 - 7.11 winning units..
Owner M Sines **Bred** Catridge Farm Stud & Mrs J Hall **Trained** East Everleigh, Wilts

FOCUS
A modest maiden, but the front pair drew clear and the form rated around those two.

NOTEBOOK
Billion Dollar Kid, who failed to last home in the soft ground at Warwick last time, had been given a break and the faster ground on this occasion proved much more suitable. Soon in front, he was always doing enough and it will be interesting to see whether he improves again for a move into handicaps. (tchd 11-4)
Nezami(IRE), placed over 1m earlier in the season, fell short in a fair maiden at Newmarket last time and he found this a bit easier, finishing clear of the third. He was never getting to the winner and may find it easier in handicaps. (op 7-2)
Mon Plaisir(USA), one place behind Nezami at Newmarket last time, made a pleasing start that day and he was understandably made favourite, but failed to build on that and finished up well beaten back in third. This was disappointing, but he deserves another chance. (tchd 5-2 and 2-1 in places)
Langham House improved on his initial effort, but was still beaten quite a way and is likely to do better in low-grade handicaps in time. (op 66-1)
It's My Day(IRE) has now finished down the field in three maidens, but his trainer is capable of doing well with her juveniles and he could be the type to do better in nurseries. (op 80-1)
Pediment failed to improve on her initial effort and is clearly one of her trainer's lesser lights. Official explanation: jockey said filly became upset in stalls (op 5-1)
Little Toto Official explanation: jockey said colt hung right

5275 CONGRATULATIONS LORNA & PHILIP MARRIED HERE TODAY H'CAP — 7f (S)

2:50 (2:52) (Class 6) (0-65,64) 3-Y-O+ — £2,590 (£770; £385; £192) Stalls Low

Form — RPR

0403 **1** **Whistleupthewind**[15] 4855 4-8-8 50 HayleyTurner 3 60
(J M P Eustace) *trckd ldrs on stands' rail: drvn and swtchd rt over 1f out: styd on wl u.p to ld wl ins fnl f* **7/1**

4423 **2** nk **Young Bertie**[15] 4853 4-9-6 62 (v) RobertHavlin 9 72
(H Morrison) *chsd ldr on stands' side: drvn and ev ch 2f out: kpt on unable qck wl ins fnl f: wnt 2nd fnl strides* **5/1**[1]

5345 **3** hd **Metropolitan Chief**[25] 4538 3-8-3 56 (b[1]) KirstyMilczarek(7) 4 63
(D M Simcock) *led on stands' side and overall: rdn wl over 1f out: hdd and no ex wl ins fnl f* **9/1**

0030 **4** 3½ **Scarlet Knight**[16] 4807 4-9-7 63 IanMongan 8 63
(P Mitchell) *in tch on stands' side: rdn 3f out: hdwy and ev ch 2f out: outpcd fnl f* **14/1**

3006 **5** 1 **Golden Brown (IRE)**[13] 4919 3-9-3 63 JimCrowley 5 58
(David Pinder) *chsd ldrs on stands' side: rdn 1/2-way: no imp over 1f out* **40/1**

0450 **6** 1 **Convivial Spirit**[16] 4807 3-8-11 60 (t) TravisBlock(3) 1 52
(E F Vaughan) *hld up on stands' rail: swtchd rt over 2f out: sn rdn and hung bdly rt: nvr trbld ldrs* **8/1**

452 **7** 1¾ **Arctic Desert**[8] 5062 7-9-6 62 (t) RichardHughes 2 51
(R A Harris) *stdd s: hld up in rr on stands' side: hdwy and rdn 2f out: sn no imp* **11/2**[2]

5606 **8** 1½ **Supercast (IRE)**[18] 4731 4-9-5 61 JamieSpencer 13 51+
(W M Brisbourne) *led far side quartet for 1f: led far side again over 2f out: sn rdn and ev ch: btn and eased ins fnl f* **6/1**[3]

3200 **9** 1¼ **Royal Guest**[8] 5062 3-8-6 52 TPO'Shea 11 32
(M R Channon) *racd far side: rdn and struggling wl over 2f out: no ch after* **20/1**

0006 **10** 1 **Charlie Delta**[4] 5177 4-9-3 64 (v) TolleyDean(5) 7 43
(J M Bradley) *in tch on stands' side: rdn 3f out: no ch last 2f* **14/1**

410 **11** ½ **Reigning Monarch (USA)**[30] 4397 4-9-0 56 SamHitchcott 6 34
(Miss Z C Davison) *hld up on stands' side: rdn wl over 2f out: sn wl btn* **15/2**

3003 **12** 7 **Fantasy Defender (IRE)**[20] 4685 5-8-8 50 oh5 RichardMullen 10 9
(R M H Cowell) *racd far side: led that gp after 1f tl over 2f out: sn wl btn* **22/1**

0-00 **13** 17 **Mocha Java**[10] 5001 4-9-4 60 TedDurcan 12 —
(B G Powell) *a last of far side quartet: lost tch 3f out: eased over 1f out: t.o* **33/1**

1m 24.55s (-3.35) **Going Correction** -0.425s/f (Firm)
WFA 3 from 4yo+ 4lb 13 Ran SP% 119.5
Speed ratings (Par 101): **102,101,101,97,96 95,93,91,90,88 88,80,60**
CSF £40.05 CT £334.58 TOTE £9.20: £3.60, £2.10, £4.30; EX 45.50 TRIFECTA Not won..
Owner Blue Peter Racing 6 **Bred** Baydon House Stud **Trained** Newmarket, Suffolk
■ Stewards' Enquiry : Jamie Spencer caution: allowed mount to coast home

FOCUS
A moderate handicap and not form to have total faith in with the first three possibly favoured by the draw.

5276 NEXT MEETING SEPTEMBER 25TH CLASSIFIED STKS — 6f

3:20 (3:22) (Class 7) 3-Y-O+ — £2,047 (£604; £302) Stalls Low

Form — RPR

3040 **1** **Tuscan Flyer**[27] 4471 9-9-0 44 (b) SaleemGolam 14 51
(R Bastiman) *mde all on far side and overall: rdn 2f out: hld on gamely u.p* **20/1**

0400 **2** hd **Knead The Dough**[14] 4881 6-8-9 44 NataliaGemelova(5) 13 50
(A E Price) *w wnr on far side: ev chand rdn 2f out: a jst hld: 2nd of 4 in gp* **20/1**

0000 **3** shd **Brave Jack (IRE)**[8] 5062 3-8-9 45 WilliamBuick(3) 4 50+
(J R Best) *hld up on stands' side: swtchd rt and bmpd rival over 1f out: styd on u.p: wnt 3rd nr fin: 1st of 10 in gp* **8/1**

040 **4** hd **Lawdy Miss Clawdy**[16] 4801 3-8-12 45 JimCrowley 2 49
(D W P Arbuthnot) *prom on stands' side: ev ch u.p over 2f out: led stands' side gp last 100yds tl nr fin: 2nd of 10 in gp* **16/1**

0000 **5** ½ **Campeon (IRE)**[86] 2652 5-9-0 43 HayleyTurner 1 48
(J M Bradley) *led stands' side gp: rdn 2f out: hdd last 100yds: no ex: 3rd of 10 in gp* **33/1**

0506 **6** hd **Nawayea**[11] 4974 4-8-7 45 (t) KirstyMilczarek(7) 3 47+
(C N Allen) *in tch on stands' rail: shkn up and nt clr run and unable to chal fr over 1f out: 4th of 10 in gp* **16/1**

0000 **7** ½ **Only If I Laugh**[30] 4397 6-9-0 45 (v) IanMongan 10 45
(M J Attwater) *bhd on stands' side: rdn and hdwy 2f out: no imp last 100yds: 5th of 10 in gp* **12/1**

3363 **8** 1¾ **Foreland Sands (IRE)**[143] 1119 3-8-12 45 TedDurcan 5 40
(J R Best) *trckd ldrs on stands' side: rdn 2f out: no hdwy 1f out: 6th of 10 in gp* **7/2**[1]

6665 **9** hd **Valiant Romeo**[15] 4857 7-9-0 45 SebSanders 7 40
(R Bastiman) *prom on stands' side: rdn 1/2-way: wknd 1f out: 7th of 10 in gp* **7/1**

4600 **10** ½ **Wainwright (IRE)**[10] 4999 7-9-0 45 (t) TPO'Shea 12 38
(P A Blockley) *chsd ldrs on far side: effrt and rdn over 2f out: btn 1f out: 3rd of 4 in gp* **11/2**[2]

0060 **11** 3 **She Wont Wait**[25] 4536 3-8-9 45 (b) NeilChalmers(3) 11 29
(T M Jones) *s.i.s: a struggling on far side: 4th of 4 in gp* **66/1**

4300 **12** 2½ **Laith (IRE)**[101] 2220 4-8-11 45 LiamJones(3) 8 22
(Miss V Haigh) *rdr struggled to remove blinds and v.s.a: nvr on terms on stands' side: 8th of 10 in gp* **9/1**

0044 **13** nk **Beverley Beau**[18] 4741 5-8-7 45 KristinStubbs(7) 9 21
(Mrs L Stubbs) *a bhd on stands' side: 9th of 10 in gp* **10/1**

6000 **14** 8 **My Tiger Lilly**[32] 4317 3-8-12 45 JamieSpencer 6 —
(R A Teal) *in tch on stands' side: rdn over 2f out: wkng whn bmpd over 1f out: btn and eased after: 10th of 10 in gp* **13/2**[3]

1m 12.1s (-1.50) **Going Correction** -0.425s/f (Firm)
WFA 3 from 4yo+ 2lb 14 Ran SP% 127.1
Speed ratings (Par 97): **93,92,92,92,91 91,90,88,88,87 83,80,79,69**
CSF £376.23 TOTE £27.40: £7.20, £5.80, £2.70; EX 230.80 TRIFECTA Not won..
Owner John Endersby **Bred** F Hines **Trained** Cowthorpe, N Yorks

FOCUS
A moderate sprint handicap in which the far side prevailed and the form rated around the principals with the third doing best of the stands'-side group.
Campeon(IRE) Official explanation: jockey said gelding hung right
Laith(IRE) Official explanation: jockey said gelding was slowly away due to problems removing blindfold
My Tiger Lilly Official explanation: jockey said filly suffered interference in running

5277 FOLKESTONE RACECOURSE FOR EXHIBITIONS NOVICE STKS — 6f

3:50 (3:50) (Class 4) 2-Y-O — £3,886 (£1,156; £577; £288) Stalls Low

Form — RPR

1 **Keep Discovering (IRE)** 2-8-9 0 ow1 LDettori 4 76+
(Saeed Bin Suroor) *t.k.h: chsd ldrs: wnt 2nd over 2f out: led over 1f out: rdn 1f out: kpt on: in command last 50yds* **11/8**[1]

01 **2** nk **Mesmerize Me**[46] 3866 2-9-0 87 RichardMullen 2 80
(E S McMahon) *t.k.h: chsd ldr tl led wl over 2f out: hdd over 1f out: kpt on same pce u.p* **2/1**[2]

6 **3** nk **Clifton Four (USA)**[23] 4602 2-8-7 0 FrancisNorton 5 72
(R Hannon) *bmpd s: pushed along 3f out: hdwy to chse ldrs wl over 1f out: swished tail u.p: nt qckn ins fnl f* **14/1**

3042 **4** ½ **Mansii**[13] 4923 2-8-12 75 HayleyTurner 3 76
(C E Brittain) *chsd ldrs: rdn and outpcd 3f out: swtchd rt and hdwy over 1f out: keeping on same pce whn n.m.r ins fnl f* **11/1**

60 **5** ½ **Acquifer**[23] 4602 2-8-7 0 SebSanders 6 69
(J L Dunlop) *wnt lft and bmpd rival s: outpcd in last pair: swtchd rt and gd hdwy 2f out: chsd ldrs over 1f out: one pce* **10/1**

00 **6** 6 **Vilna (USA)**[17] 4777 2-8-12 0 SimonWhitworth 7 56
(N A Callaghan) *stdd s: sn outpcd in last: nvr on terms* **66/1**

0016 **7** 3 **Rough Rock (IRE)**[17] 4775 2-8-12 75 (bt) TedDurcan 1 47
(Miss Gay Kelleway) *sn pushed into ld: rdn and hdd wl over 2f out: wknd 2f out* **7/1**[3]

1m 11.96s (-1.64) **Going Correction** -0.425s/f (Firm) 7 Ran SP% 113.5
Speed ratings (Par 97): **93,92,92,91,90 82,78**
CSF £4.22 TOTE £2.00: £1.40, £2.00; EX 3.30.
Owner Godolphin **Bred** Kilfrush Stud **Trained** Newmarket, Suffolk

FOCUS
A competitive little novice stakes but the form is rather muddling with the first five in a heap.

NOTEBOOK
Keep Discovering(IRE), a 550,000gns son of Oasis Dream, was making his debut at an ordinary level and is clearly no star, but he showed a good attitude in winning and certainly shaped as though he would stay further. He holds several big-race entries, but may be best off trying his luck in something a bit smaller first. (op 6-4 tchd 13-8)
Mesmerize Me, a ready winner in soft ground at Bath, was always going to prove vulnerable if the winner was useful and he was simply unable to concede the weight. He may improve again for a return to a slower surface. (op 5-2 tchd 11-4)
Clifton Four(USA), a promising sixth on debut at Newmarket, stepped up on that effort and seemed to appreciate the fast ground. He was not beaten far at the line and should have little trouble finding a standard maiden. (op 9-1)
Mansii, second off a mark of 73 on his recent handicap debut, ran just as well and was edging nearer with every stride at the line, suggesting a step up in trip would help. (op 8-1 tchd 12-1)
Acquifer ran his best race to date, finishing close up in third, and is now qualified for nurseries. He will be interesting in that division, assuming he is fairly treated. (op 9-1 tchd 8-1)
Vilna(USA) was never going the gallop and strikes as the type to do better in handicaps.
Rough Rock(IRE), a winner in selling company two starts back, ran well for a long way in the St Leger Yearling Stakes at Newmarket last time, but he failed to run his race here and dropped right away. (op 8-1 tchd 13-2)

5278 INVICTA MOTORS H'CAP — 5f
4:20 (4:20) (Class 4) (0-85,83) 3-Y-O+ **£4,857** (£1,445; £722; £360) **Stalls** Low

Form — RPR
0044 **1** **Loch Verdi**[24] 4567 4-9-5 **83** ... FrancisNorton 8 — 93
(A M Balding) *mde all: rdn and drew clr 1f out: sn in command: comf* **7/2**[2]
4000 **2** 1 1/2 **Texas Gold**[9] 5050 9-9-5 **83** ... RichardMullen 7 — 88
(W R Muir) *racd in midfield: hdwy 2f out: drvn to chse wnr ins fnl f: no imp* **10/1**
0102 **3** shd **Matsunosuke**[10] 5009 5-8-11 **75** ... JamieSpencer 3 — 79+
(A B Coogan) *stdd s: hld up in last swtchd rt 2f out: nt clr run over 1f out tl last 100yds: pushed along and nrly snatched 2nd: no ch wnr* **3/1**[1]
3535 **4** 3/4 **Malapropism**[4] 5160 7-8-6 **70** ... (v[1]) TPO'Shea 5 — 72
(M R Channon) *t.k.h: chsd wnr for 1f: styd prom: rdn 2f out: one pce* **10/1**
1616 **5** nk **Safari Mischief**[39] 4095 4-8-12 **79** ... LiamJones(3) 9 — 79
(P Winkworth) *chsd wnr after 1f: rdn wl over 1f out: outpcd by wnr 1f out: sn lost 2nd and one pce* **8/1**
6040 **6** 3/4 **Bridge It Jo**[14] 4898 3-8-12 **77** ... SebSanders 6 — 75
(G G Margarson) *towards rr: hdwy and rdn wl over 1f out: chsd ldrs 1f out: wknd ins fnl f* **12/1**
0002 **7** hd **Bluebok**[9] 5029 6-8-11 **80** ... (t) TolleyDean(5) 4 — 77
(J M Bradley) *bhd: rdn 1/2-way: modest hdwy and nt clr run briefly ins fnl f: nvr trbld ldrs* **11/2**
0004 **8** 2 1/2 **Misaro (GER)**[9] 5029 6-8-11 **80** ... (b) HaddenFrost(5) 2 — 68
(R A Harris) *bhd: rdn 2f out: no hdwy* **9/2**[3]
600 **9** 5 **Daddy Cool**[38] 4123 3-8-12 **77** ... (p) SaleemGolam 1 — 47
(W G M Turner) *chsd ldrs tl 1/2-way: sn dropped out: eased whn no ch ins fnl f* **33/1**

58.25 secs (-2.55) **Going Correction** -0.425s/f (Firm) course record
WFA 3 from 4yo+ 1lb — **9** Ran SP% **120.7**
Speed ratings (Par 105): **103,100,100,99,98 97,97,93,85**
CSF £40.24 CT £120.11 TOTE £3.70: £1.50, £2.50, £1.70; EX 20.90 Trifecta £145.00 Pool £408.52 - 2.00 winning units..
Owner J C Smith **Bred** Littleton Stud **Trained** Kingsclere, Hants
■ Stewards' Enquiry : Francis Norton one-day ban: failed to ride to draw (Sep 21)

FOCUS
A fair sprint handicap with the winner back to three-year-old form and possibly value for a little more.
Matsunosuke Official explanation: jockey said gelding was denied a clear run

5279 FOLKESTONE-RACECOURSE.CO.UK H'CAP — 1m 4f
4:50 (4:50) (Class 5) (0-70,70) 3-Y-O **£2,914** (£867; £433; £216) **Stalls** Low

Form — RPR
4-35 **1** **Tonnante**[32] 4339 3-8-10 **62** ... SebSanders 9 — 71+
(Sir Mark Prescott) *led for 1f: chsd ldr after: rdn 2f out: led ins fnl f: wandered u.p: styd on* **4/1**[3]
0-00 **2** 1 1/4 **Aphrodisia**[78] 2913 3-8-6 **58** ... SaleemGolam 2 — 65+
(S C Williams) *pushed into ld after 1f: rdn 2f out: hdd ins fnl f: one pce* **3/1**[1]
0-16 **3** 3 **Sumner (IRE)**[23] 4617 3-9-4 **70** ... TedDurcan 7 — 72
(M H Tompkins) *chsd ldrs: rdn 2f out: kpt on one pce and no imp* **7/2**[2]
0165 **4** 3/4 **Mayireneyrbel**[8] 5068 3-8-1 **56** oh1 ... WilliamBuick(3) 6 — 57
(J Akehurst) *bhd: pushed along 7f out: hdwy u.p on outer wl over 2f out: kpt on steadily: nvr able to chal* **22/1**
0501 **5** nk **Up In Arms (IRE)**[17] 4763 3-8-11 **63** ... JimCrowley 5 — 64
(P Winkworth) *racd in midfield off the pce: rdn over 3f out: kpt on: nvr trbld ldrs* **8/1**
3232 **6** 1 1/2 **Lapina (IRE)**[15] 4859 3-8-13 **65** ... (b) IanMongan 1 — 63
(Pat Eddery) *dropped in after s: hld up in last: rdn and modest hdwy 2f out: n.d* **9/2**
7 7 **Confirm (IRE)**[7] 5106 3-8-9 **61** ... (b) TPO'Shea 3 — 48
(H Rogers, Ire) *hld up: hdwy on outer 7f out: chsd ldrs and rdn 4f out: wknd 2f out* **16/1**
-266 **8** 7 **Lindy Lou**[17] 4763 3-8-13 **65** ... (t) SimonWhitworth 8 — 41
(C A Cyzer) *t.k.h: hld up in midfield: rdn wl 2f out: sn wl btn* **33/1**
2530 **9** 3 **Iolanthe**[22] 4632 3-9-1 **67** ... RobertHavlin 4 — 38
(B J Meehan) *hld up in rr: rdn and struggling whn n.m.r over 2f out: eased fnl f: t.o* **12/1**

2m 35.89s (-4.61) **Going Correction** -0.425s/f (Firm) — **9** Ran SP% **117.4**
Speed ratings (Par 101): **98,97,95,94,94 93,88,84,82**
CSF £16.75 CT £46.04 TOTE £5.50: £3.20, £3.40, £1.50; EX 27.00 Trifecta £169.10 Part won. Pool £238.30 - 0.34 winning units..
Owner Miss K Rausing **Bred** Miss K Rausing **Trained** Newmarket, Suffolk

FOCUS
A modest handicap in which the front two came clear and the form is rated around the third and fourth.

5280 FOLKESTONE RACECOURSE FOR WEDDINGS H'CAP — 1m 1f 149y
5:20 (5:21) (Class 6) (0-65,65) 3-Y-O+ **£2,590** (£770; £385; £192) **Stalls** Low

Form — RPR
4326 **1** **Blu Manruna**[15] 4850 4-8-12 **55** ... (b) PaulDoe 12 — 63
(J Akehurst) *mde all: rdn over 2f out: sn hrd pressed: edgd lft briefly ins fnl f: forged ahd last 100yds* **12/1**
6422 **2** 1 1/2 **Billy One Punch**[26] 4517 5-9-8 **65** ... JamieSpencer 11 — 70
(G G Margarson) *trckd ldng pair: wnt 2nd over 2f out: upsides wnr 2f out: sn rdn and fnd little: bmpd ins fnl f: sn btn* **6/4**[1]
2000 **3** nk **Stark Contrast (USA)**[36] 4197 3-8-12 **65** ... WilliamBuick(3) 7 — 69
(J Akehurst) *in tch: hdwy to chse ldng pair 2f out: kpt on u.p:* **22/1**
5300 **4** 2 **Postsprofit (IRE)**[15] 4858 3-8-11 **61** ... JimCrowley 2 — 61+
(N A Callaghan) *s.i.s: plld hrd and hld up wl in rr: c v wd and hdwy 2f out: r.o wl: nt rch ldrs* **25/1**
0544 **5** 2 **Moyoko (IRE)**[25] 4532 4-8-8 **51** ... FrancisNorton 5 — 47
(M Blanshard) *in tch in midfield: rdn and hdwy on rail over 2f out: kpt on u.p but nvr threatened ldrs* **12/1**
4551 **6** 3/4 **Fantasy Crusader**[12] 4945 8-8-10 **53** ... TedDurcan 6 — 48
(R M H Cowell) *chsd ldrs: rdn over 2f out: sn struggling: wl btn 1f out* **12/1**
2006 **7** hd **Golden Platitude (IRE)**[86] 2667 4-9-5 **62** ... (t) AdamKirby 8 — 57
(W R Swinburn) *t.k.h: hld up wl bhd: rdn and hdwy over 2f out: kpt on steadily: nvr nr ldrs* **20/1**
0604 **8** 3/4 **Roman Boy (ARG)**[7] 5094 8-8-9 **52** ... HayleyTurner 13 — 45
(Stef Liddiard) *stdd s: hld up wl in rr: rdn over 2f out: kpt on but nvr on terms* **9/1**[3]
4153 **9** 1 **Recalcitrant**[11] 4959 4-9-2 **59** ... SebSanders 3 — 50
(S Dow) *chsd ldr tl over 2f out: sn outpcd: no ch fnl f* **9/1**[3]
5426 **10** 1 3/4 **The Grey One (IRE)**[4] 5178 4-9-3 **65** ... (p) TolleyDean(5) 10 — 53
(J M Bradley) *hld up in rr: hdwy wl over 3f out: rdn wl over 2f out: sn no imp* **14/1**
0006 **11** nk **Montchara (IRE)**[19] 4708 4-9-5 **62** ... RobertHavlin 1 — 49
(G Wragg) *in tch: rdn over 2f out: sn struggling and wl btn* **12/1**
0-06 **12** 16 **Pink Salmon**[10] 5013 3-8-9 **59** ... SamHitchcott 4 — 14
(Mrs L J Mongan) *racd in midfield: rdn 3f out: sn lost pl: no ch and eased fnl f: t.o* **50/1**
13 1 1/4 **Crowning Moment (IRE)**[141] 1183 3-8-2 **52** ... TPO'Shea 9 — 4
(H Rogers, Ire) *bhd: rdn 6f out: t.o last 3f* **9/2**[2]

2m 1.60s (-3.63) **Going Correction** -0.425s/f (Firm)
WFA 3 from 4yo+ 7lb — **13** Ran SP% **130.5**
Speed ratings (Par 101): **97,95,95,93,92 91,91,91,90,88 88,75,74**
CSF £31.87 CT £445.66 TOTE £15.10: £4.30, £1.50, £7.60; EX 56.10 Trifecta £233.30 Part won. Pool £328.61 - 0.40 winning units. Place 6 £45.25, Place 5 £34.22..
Owner Canisbay Bloodstock **Bred** Canisbay Bloodstock Ltd **Trained** Epsom, Surrey

FOCUS
A moderate handicap rated around the first two and the fourth the only one to make ground from the rear.
Golden Platitude(IRE) Official explanation: jockey said gelding was denied a clear run
Pink Salmon Official explanation: jockey said saddle slipped
T/Plt: £239.50 to a £1 stake. Pool: £63,664.45. 194.05 winning tickets. T/Qpdt: £118.80 to a £1 stake. Pool: £2,826.60. 17.60 winning tickets. SP

4890 NEWCASTLE (L-H)
Monday, September 10
OFFICIAL GOING: Good to firm (firm in places on round course; 8.7)
Wind: Breezy, half-against Weather: Cloudy, fine

5281 EBF CLASSIC EXCEL MAIDEN STKS — 6f
2:30 (2:30) (Class 4) 2-Y-O **£4,100** (£1,227; £613; £306; £152) **Stalls** Low

Form — RPR
4222 **1** **Atabaas Pride**[37] 4152 2-9-3 79 ... GregFairley 11 — 78+
(M Johnston) *prom: shkn up to ld over 1f out: edgd lft over 1f out: kpt on wl* **1/2**[1]
00 **2** 2 1/2 **Andaman Sunset**[41] 4048 2-9-3 0 ... DarryllHolland 10 — 71
(G Wragg) *towards rr: rdn along 1/2-way: hdwy over 1f out: kpt on fnl f: wnt 2nd cl home* **7/1**[2]
3 3/4 **Orchestrion** 2-8-12 0 ... PatCosgrave 12 — 63
(G A Swinbank) *midfield: effrt over 2f out: chsd wnr ins fnl f: one pce and lost 2nd nr fin* **12/1**[3]
63 **4** hd **On Instinct (IRE)**[25] 4522 2-8-12 0 ... TomEaves 8 — 63
(B Smart) *bhd: pushed along 1/2-way: kpt on wl fr 2f out: nrst fin* **12/1**[3]
0 **5** 1 1/2 **Arcetri (IRE)**[45] 3916 2-8-12 0 ... DO'Donohoe 1 — 58
(K A Ryan) *cl up: ev ch over 2f out: no ex ins fnl f* **7/1**[2]
0 **6** 4 **Bond Scissorsister (IRE)**[38] 4125 2-8-12 0 ... PaulMulrennan 9 — 46
(G R Oldroyd) *sn outpcd and drvn along: sme late hdwy: nvr on terms* **100/1**
3660 **7** 5 **Handsinthemist (IRE)**[17] 4783 2-8-12 50 ... MickyFenton 4 — 31
(P T Midgley) *led to over 2f out: sn rdn and btn* **100/1**
60 **8** 1/2 **Lamistrelle (IRE)**[24] 4564 2-8-12 0 ... (v[1]) RoystonFfrench 7 — 30
(Mrs A Duffield) *cl up tl rdn and wknd over 2f out* **25/1**
0 **9** 9 **Kyzer Chief**[16] 4818 2-9-0 0 ... MarkLawson(3) 3 — 8
(R E Barr) *dwlt: sn chsng ldrs: rdn and wknd over 2f out* **200/1**
10 shd **Spooky** 2-9-0 0 ... DominicFox(3) 13 — 7
(W Storey) *s.s: a wl bhd* **100/1**
11 6 **Benitez Bond** 2-9-3 0 ... DanielTudhope 2 — —
(G R Oldroyd) *sn drvn along towards rr: struggling fr: 1/2-way* **66/1**
00 **12** 6 **Latin Dancer**[109] 1963 2-9-3 0 ... (p) PaulHanagan 6 — —
(B S Rothwell) *chsd ldrs to 1/2-way: sn rdn and struggling* **100/1**

1m 15.89s (0.80) **Going Correction** -0.025s/f (Good) — **12** Ran SP% **116.8**
Speed ratings (Par 97): **93,89,88,88,86 81,74,73,61,61 53,45**
CSF £4.34 TOTE £1.50: £1.02, £2.40, £3.00; EX 5.40.
Owner Mrs R J Jacobs & Mrs D Imholz **Bred** Newsells Park Stud Limited **Trained** Middleham Moor, N Yorks

FOCUS
A modest juvenile maiden in which the winner did not need to have to run up to his best to score.

NOTEBOOK
Atabaas Pride, third on his last three outings, had been found an ideal opportunity on this return to maiden company and he duly lost his maiden tag with a clear-cut success. It took him time to really get going, but once he hit full stride the race was soon in the bag and he did look better the further he went. A typically hardy horse from his stable, a step up to 7f could now bring about further improvement, but it is most likely that he will only really come into his own as a three-year-old. (op 8-15 tchd 4-7)
Andaman Sunset again ran green through the first half of the race, but the penny dropped inside the final 2f and he was noted staying on with some promise without ever threatening the winner. He is going the right way and now has the option of nurseries, so it would be no surprise to see him upped to another furlong once switching to that sphere. (op 8-1)
Orchestrion, bred to make her mark at two over sprint distances, posted a pleasing-enough debut effort and acted well on the ground. She ought to come on plenty from this debut experience, but could be worth dropping back to 5f for the short term. (op 10-1)

On Instinct(IRE), up in trip, needed to be ridden from an early stage and eventually got going all too late. She stayed this trip without much fuss and now becomes eligible for a nursery mark, but does not look that straightforward. (tchd 14-1)
Arcetri(IRE), easy to back on this drop in trip, was made to look one paced and did not prove that suited by the sharper test. Having the far rail enabled her to keep a straight line this time and it was still a step in the right direction, but she already looks more of a nursery type - for which she will be eligible after her next outing. (op 6-1)

5282 CPD DISTRIBUTION MAIDEN STKS 5f
3:00 (3:00) (Class 5) 3-Y-O+ **£3,785** (£1,132; £566; £283; £141) **Stalls** Low

Form RPR
6444 **1** **Beechside (IRE)**[12] 4935 3-8-12 0 DaleGibson 13 50
(W A Murphy, Ire) *t.k.h: hld up in midfield: rdn over 2f out: rallied over 1f out: led ins fnl f: r.o wl* **6/1**[2]
4306 **2** *1* **Mickleberry (IRE)**[43] 4001 3-8-12 54 DarryllHolland 9 46
(J D Bethell) *chsd ldrs: rdn and led over 1f out: hdd ins fnl f: r.o* **7/1**[3]
0402 **3** *nk* **The Cube**[16] 4801 3-9-3 49 PaulHanagan 5 50+
(J Balding) *bhd and outpcd: gd hdwy over 1f out: nrst fin* **11/2**[1]
0050 **4** *nk* **Yorke's Folly (USA)**[17] 4787 6-8-13 44 (b) PaulFessey 2 44
(C W Fairhurst) *midfield: pushed along 1/2-way: kpt on fnl f: nvr rchd ldrs* **15/2**
0000 **5** *½* **Whats Your Game (IRE)**[12] 4935 3-9-0 40 PatrickMathers(3) 11 47
(A Berry) *in tch on outside: effrt and edgd lft over 1f out: kpt on same pce ins fnl f* **66/1**
60-0 **6** *¾* **Piccolo Diamante (USA)**[23] 4616 3-9-3 45 AdrianTNicholls 1 45
(D J Murphy) *prom tl rdn and nt qckn over 1f out* **16/1**
4 **7** *1 ¼* **Tumbleweed Di**[16] 4801 3-8-5 0 LanceBetts(7) 3 35+
(G R Oldroyd) *towards rr: stdy hdwy over 1f out: nvr rchd ldrs* **9/1**
600 **8** *hd* **Nabra**[14] 4896 3-8-12 55 PaulMulrennan 6 35
(M Brittain) *hmpd sn after s: rdn in rr 1/2-way: sme late hdwy: nvr on terms* **10/1**
000 **9** *shd* **Archimage (USA)**[79] 2894 3-9-3 50 PhillipMakin 8 39
(T D Barron) *bhd and sn outpcd: kpt on fnl f: n.d* **8/1**
0000 **10** *2 ½* **Compton Lad**[11] 4967 4-9-4 41 GregFairley 12 30
(D A Nolan) *chsd clr ldr: ev ch over 1f out: wknd ins fnl f* **66/1**
400 **11** *2* **Fast Freddie**[4] 5174 3-8-10 60 (b) JamesO'Reilly(7) 7 23
(D J Murphy) *led and sn clr: hdd over 1f out: sn btn* **6/1**[2]
3540 **12** *2* **Optical Seclusion (IRE)**[161] 892 4-9-4 47 (be) RoystonFfrench 10 16
(T J Etherington) *in tch: drvn over 2f out: wknd over 1f out* **15/2**
05 **13** *3* **Champagne Sue**[12] 4938 3-8-12 0 TonyHamilton 4 —
(D W Barker) *in tch: drvn 1/2-way: sn struggling* **25/1**

62.49 secs (0.99) **Going Correction** -0.025s/f (Good)
WFA 3 from 4yo+ 1lb **13 Ran SP% 122.9**
Speed ratings (Par 103): **91,89,88,88,87 86,84,84,83,79 76,73,68**
CSF £48.74 TOTE £10.10: £3.30, £3.30, £1.90; EX 58.90.
Owner Thomas P Waters **Bred** Ms Catheryn Jones **Trained** Carbury, Co Kildare

FOCUS
A very weak maiden and it was a moderate winning time, even for a race like this with the fourth setting the level.

5283 USG H'CAP 2m 19y
3:30 (3:30) (Class 6) (0-65,63) 3-Y-O+ **£3,154** (£944; £472; £236; £117) **Stalls** Centre

Form RPR
3431 **1** **Golden Groom**[13] 4925 4-9-4 53 PaulFessey 15 64+
(C W Fairhurst) *a.p: wnt 2nd over 6f out: rdn and led wl over 1f out: hld on wl fnl f* **9/2**[1]
23 **2** *½* **Balakar (IRE)**[30] 4380 11-9-6 55 (p) PaulMulrennan 2 64
(J J Lambe, Ire) *hld up: rdn and hdwy over 3f out: chsd wnr 1f out: kpt on u.p* **8/1**
2412 **3** *3* **Sharaab (USA)**[14] 4451 6-9-7 56 (t) DaleGibson 8 61
(D E Cantillon) *bhd tl styd on wl fr 2f out: nt rch front two* **9/2**[1]
4424 **4** *½* **Sa Nau**[14] 4906 4-9-6 55 NickyMackay 3 60
(T Keddy) *hld up in tch: drvn over 4f out: kpt on fnl 2f: nrst fin* **5/1**[2]
3023 **5** *1 ¼* **Red Chairman**[7] 5086 5-9-9 63 (p) KellyHarrison(5) 7 66
(R Johnson) *led and sn clr: hdd wl over 1f out: no ex ins fnl f* **18/1**
4206 **6** *½* **Great Quest (IRE)**[19] 4717 5-10-0 63 RoystonFfrench 17 68+
(James Moffatt) *bhd: hdwy 2f out: n.m.r ins fnl f: nrst fin* **12/1**
5003 **7** *1 ¼* **Foxxy**[13] 4925 3-7-9 46 oh1 DuranFentiman(3) 6 47
(J R Norton) *bhd tl kpt on fr 2f out: nvr rchd ldrs* **14/1**
-052 **8** *½* **Young Scotton**[12] 4941 7-9-2 54 AndrewElliott(3) 1 55
(J D Bethell) *chsd ldrs tl rdn and wknd over 1f out* **12/1**
0411 **9** *nk* **Mighty Kitchener (USA)**[10] 5018 4-9-6 55 AmirQuinn 4 55
(P Howling) *hld up in tch: stdy hdwy 3f out: rdn and wknd over 1f out* **7/1**[3]
0650 **10** *1 ¼* **Borsch (IRE)**[11] 4972 5-8-11 46 oh1 TomEaves 11 45
(Miss L A Perratt) *prom: rdn 3f out: wknd over 1f out* **50/1**
0515 **11** *1* **Erte**[13] 4925 6-8-13 51 (v) DominicFox(3) 12 49
(W Storey) *midfield: drvn 4f out: outpcd over 2f out* **25/1**
0005 **12** *1 ½* **The Dunion**[7] 5087 4-8-8 46 oh1 (b) AndrewMullen(3) 13 42
(Miss L A Perratt) *dwlt: bhd: short-lived effrt over 3f out: sn btn* **50/1**
-506 **13** *3* **Kerry's Blade (IRE)**[13] 4925 5-8-11 46 oh1 (p) PaulHanagan 9 38
(Micky Hammond) *midfield: drvn over 4f out: edgd lft and wknd over 2f out* **40/1**
0010 **14** *2 ½* **City Miss**[11] 4969 4-8-12 50 JamieMoriarty(3) 14 39
(Miss L A Perratt) *bhd: pushed along over 4f out: nvr on terms* **40/1**
3-00 **15** *25* **Compton Eclaire (IRE)**[28] 4451 7-9-1 50 DanielTudhope 16 9
(N Wilson) *racd wd in midfield: lost pl over 6f out: n.d after* **33/1**
5-30 **16** *35* **Soubriquet (IRE)**[17] 4771 4-9-4 53 (t) GregFairley 10 —
(M A Barnes) *chsd clr ldr to over 6f out: wknd over 4f out* **25/1**
00/0 **17** *16* **Forever My Lord**[27] 4475 9-8-11 46 oh1 AdrianTNicholls 5 —
(W A Murphy, Ire) *bhd: struggling over 6f out: eased whn no ch ent st* **100/1**

3m 33.42s (-1.78) **Going Correction** -0.025s/f (Good)
WFA 3 from 4yo+ 13lb **17 Ran SP% 124.4**
Speed ratings (Par 101): **103,102,101,101,100 100,99,99,99,98 97,97,95,94,81 64,56**
CSF £38.10 CT £177.59 TOTE £4.60: £1.30, £2.60, £2.00, £1.60; EX 35.50.
Owner G H & S Leggott **Bred** G H And Simon Leggott **Trained** Middleham Moor, N Yorks

FOCUS
A moderate staying handicap, run at a solid pace. The form looks sound with the first pair coming clear and the third and fourth to form.

5284 BRITISH GYPSUM H'CAP 6f
4:00 (4:00) (Class 6) (0-55,55) 3-Y-O+ **£3,238** (£963; £481; £240) **Stalls** Low

Form RPR
3105 **1** **Quicks The Word**[19] 4706 7-8-11 52 GregFairley 17 63
(T A K Cuthbert) *mde all stands' side: rdn over 2f out: hld on wl fnl f* **10/1**
3423 **2** *½* **Conjecture**[19] 4706 5-9-0 55 RoystonFfrench 5 64
(R Bastiman) *led far side gp: rdn 2f out: kpt on wl fnl f: jst hld by stands' side wnr: 1st of 10 in gp* **9/2**[1]
6210 **3** *nk* **Oeuf A La Neige**[9] 5037 7-8-10 51 PhillipMakin 13 59
(Miss L A Perratt) *in tch stands' side: rdn over 2f out: rallied over 1f out: chsd wnr ins fnl f: kpt on: 2nd of 7 in gp* **9/1**
3503 **4** *1 ¼* **Zabeel Tower**[11] 4966 4-8-9 53 AndrewElliott(3) 12 57
(R Allan) *chsd stands' side ldrs: effrt and chsd wnr over 1f out tl ins fnl f: no ex: 3rd of 7 in gp* **12/1**
3000 **5** *¾* **Frimley's Matterry**[7] 5083 7-8-7 48 PaddyAspell 4 50
(R E Barr) *chsd far side ldrs: wnt 2nd that gp over 2f out: kpt on u.p fnl f: 2nd of 10 in gp* **33/1**
0000 **6** *¾* **Falmassim**[7] 5085 4-9-0 55 (p) TomEaves 2 54+
(Miss J A Camacho) *bhd far side: hdwy over 1f out: kpt on fnl f: nrst fin: 3rd of 10 in gp* **25/1**
045 **7** *¾* **Littledodayno (IRE)**[15] 4855 4-9-0 55 NickyMackay 1 52
(M Wigham) *midfield far side: drvn over 2f out: rallied over 1f out: no imp ins fnl f: 4th of 10 in gp* **7/1**[2]
0522 **8** *1 ¼* **High Five Society**[21] 4658 3-8-7 50 (b) PaulEddery 15 43
(S R Bowring) *chsd stands' side ldrs: rdn over 2f out: sn one pce: 4th of 7 in gp* **11/1**
1600 **9** *hd* **Bold Haze**[29] 4423 5-9-0 55 (v) PaulMulrennan 16 47
(Miss S E Hall) *in tch stands' side: rdn over 2f out: sn no imp: 5th of 7 in gp* **16/1**
6603 **10** *1 ¼* **Princess Cleo**[17] 4787 4-8-9 50 (p) PaulHanagan 11 38
(T D Easterby) *w wnr stands' side tl edgd lft and wknd fr 2f out: 6th of 7 in gp* **15/2**[3]
0045 **11** *½* **Indian Spark**[12] 4934 13-8-6 52 GaryBartley(5) 10 39
(J S Goldie) *midfield far side: pushed along over 2f out: sn no imp: 5th of 10 in gp* **16/1**
0500 **12** *½* **Gifted Flame**[11] 4966 8-8-9 55 (p) NeilBrown(5) 3 40
(T D Barron) *towards rr far side: drvn 1/2-way: n.d: 6th of 10 in gp* **16/1**
2022 **13** *shd* **Miss Taboo (IRE)**[37] 4178 3-8-10 53 (p) MickyFenton 6 38
(P T Midgley) *prom far side tl rdn and no ex fr 2f out: 7th of 10 in gp* **16/1**
0660 **14** *nk* **Hit's Only Money (IRE)**[12] 4931 7-8-10 51 (p) DanielTudhope 14 35
(J S Goldie) *bhd stands' side: rdn and edgd lft over 2f out: nvr on terms: last of 7 in gp* **14/1**
6356 **15** *5* **Compton Plume**[29] 4423 7-8-12 53 DaleGibson 7 21
(M W Easterby) *chsd far side ldrs to 2f out: eased whn btn: 8th of 10 in gp* **16/1**
5006 **16** *1 ¾* **Vondova**[17] 4787 5-8-9 50 ow1 PatCosgrave 9 12
(D A Nolan) *prom far side to 1/2-way: sn wknd: 9th of 10 in gp* **40/1**
1000 **17** *1 ¼* **Greek Secret**[16] 4822 4-8-8 54 ow2 (b) JamesO'Reilly(7) 8 14
(J O'Reilly) *bhd far side: drvn outside of that gp over 2f out: sn btn: last of 10 in gp* **14/1**

1m 14.44s (-0.65) **Going Correction** -0.025s/f (Good)
WFA 3 from 4yo+ 2lb **17 Ran SP% 129.5**
Speed ratings (Par 101): **103,102,101,100,99 98,97,95,95,93 93,92,92,91,85 82,81**
CSF £56.42 CT £456.52 TOTE £11.90: £2.30, £1.90, £2.10, £3.90; EX 93.80.
Owner W Hurst **Bred** Roy Matthews **Trained** Little Corby, Cumbria

FOCUS
A moderate sprint which saw the first two home drawn on opposite sides of the track. The runner-up sets the level.
Compton Plume Official explanation: jockey said gelding had no more to give

5285 ARMSTRONG MAIDEN STKS 1m (R)
4:30 (4:33) (Class 5) 3-Y-O+ **£3,785** (£1,132; £566; £283; £141) **Stalls** Centre

Form RPR
0 **1** **Bankable (IRE)**[16] 4815 3-9-3 0 NickyMackay 2 81+
(L M Cumani) *chsd ldrs: wnt 2nd 3f out: sn rdn: styd on wl fnl f to ld nr fin* **11/8**[1]
224 **2** *1* **Trees Of Green (USA)**[52] 3710 3-9-3 75 DO'Donohoe 5 78
(Saeed Bin Suroor) *set stdy pce: rdn over 2f out: edgd lft ins fnl f: hdd nr fin* **3/1**[3]
6- **3** *9* **Inner Voice (USA)**[457] 2465 4-9-8 0 PaulMulrennan 3 57
(J J Lambe, Ire) *chsd ldr tl outpcd fr over 2f out* **20/1**
5333 **4** *2* **Alpes Maritimes**[24] 4568 3-9-3 76 (p) DarryllHolland 1 53
(G Wragg) *unruly in stalls: t.k.h in tch: rdn 3f out: sn btn* **7/4**[2]
63 **5** *9* **Ancient Pride (IRE)**[7] 5082 3-9-3 0 TomEaves 4 32
(Miss L A Perratt) *prom tl rdn and wknd fr 3f out* **50/1**

1m 42.75s (-0.73) **Going Correction** -0.025s/f (Good)
WFA 3 from 4yo 5lb **5 Ran SP% 110.2**
Speed ratings (Par 103): **102,101,92,90,81**
CSF £5.92 TOTE £2.20: £1.60, £1.40; EX 5.40.
Owner JMC Breed & Race Limited **Bred** Barronstown Stud And Cobra **Trained** Newmarket, Suffolk

FOCUS
An average maiden, run at an ordinary early pace. The first pair came well clear with the runner-up the best guide and the winner could rate higher.

5286 SHEFFIELD INSULATIONS H'CAP 1m 2f 32y
5:00 (5:00) (Class 6) (0-60,60) 3-Y-O+ **£3,238** (£963; £481; £240) **Stalls** Centre

Form RPR
4400 **1** **Garibaldi (GER)**[26] 4493 5-8-9 51 (b) JamesO'Reilly(7) 4 60
(J O'Reilly) *hld up ins: smooth hdwy over 2f out: rdn to ld wl ins fnl f: r.o* **20/1**
4151 **2** *1* **Dechiper (IRE)**[17] 4772 5-9-4 60 PatrickDonaghy(7) 13 67+
(R Johnson) *hld up outside: smooth hdwy over 2f out: effrt and ev ch ins fnl f: kpt on fin* **7/2**[1]
2000 **3** *nk* **Eijaaz (IRE)**[24] 4582 6-9-5 54 PaulFessey 2 60
(G A Harker) *midfield: effrt over 2f out: led briefly ins fnl f: hld cl home* **7/1**[3]
0204 **4** *nk* **Roman History (IRE)**[11] 4972 4-9-3 52 (p) SilvestreDeSousa 1 57
(Miss Tracy Waggott) *chsd ldrs: led over 2f out to ins fnl f: no ex* **12/1**
0415 **5** *1 ¼* **Awaken**[15] 4846 6-9-5 54 PhillipMakin 6 57
(Miss Tracy Waggott) *midfield: effrt over 2f out: rallied over 1f out: kpt on wl fnl f* **20/1**
0-02 **6** *3* **Farne Island**[7] 5086 4-9-11 60 DanielTudhope 17 57
(Micky Hammond) *hld up: effrt over 2f out: no imp over 1f out* **8/1**
5052 **7** *1 ½* **Mandarin Rocket (IRE)**[10] 4997 4-9-3 52 RoystonFfrench 9 46
(Miss L A Perratt) *towards rr: drvn over 2f out: kpt on fnl f: n.d* **16/1**
4630 **8** *nk* **Royal Citadel (IRE)**[15] 4846 4-8-10 50 KellyHarrison(5) 12 43
(Mrs L B Normile) *chsd ldrs tl rdn and wknd over 1f out* **28/1**
0336 **9** *nk* **Waterloo Corner**[19] 4704 5-9-5 54 TomEaves 5 47
(R Craggs) *chsd ldrs: drvn over 2f out: wknd over 1f out* **11/1**
4244 **10** *2* **Colditz (IRE)**[49] 3785 3-9-1 57 (p) TonyHamilton 8 46
(D W Barker) *led to over 2f out: wknd over 1f out* **11/1**

6503 **11** *1 1/4* **Jane Of Arc (FR)**[12] 4936 3-8-10 **57**............................ GaryBartley(5) 10 43
(J S Goldie) *hld up: drvn over 2f out: nt pce to chal* **9/1**
3-00 **12** *2 1/2* **Captain Nemo (USA)**[15] 4842 3-8-11 **60**.................... DeanHeslop(7) 7 41
(T D Barron) *bhd: struggling over 3f out: kpt on fnl f: nvr on terms* **33/1**
1150 **13** *nk* **Whittinghamvillage**[19] 4705 6-9-0 **52**....................... AndrewElliott(3) 15 33
(J P L Ewart) *chsd ldr: rdn over 2f out: wknd over 1f out* **16/1**
0245 **14** *1* **Intavac Boy**[11] 4972 6-9-6 **58**.................................. MichaelJStainton(3) 3 37
(S P Griffiths) *t.k.h: hmpd sn after s: midfield: rdn over 2f out: sn btn* **13/2**[2]
15 *2 1/2* **Spa Wells (IRE)**[14] 4912 6-9-6 **55**..............................(v[1]) PatCosgrave 14 29
(Barry Potts, Ire) *in tch outside tl wknd over 2f out* **25/1**
0-43 **16** *14* **Hunting Haze**[61] 3415 4-9-8 **57**.................................... MickyFenton 11 3
(Miss S E Hall) *in tch tl rdn and lost pl over 2f out* **16/1**

2m 10.43s (-1.37) **Going Correction** -0.025s/f (Good)
WFA 3 from 4yo+ 7lb **16** Ran SP% **130.9**
Speed ratings (Par 101): **104,103,102,102,101 99,98,97,97,96 95,93,92,92,90 78**
CSF £89.89 CT £576.84 TOTE £26.00: £4.20, £1.10, £2.40, £3.20; EX 359.80 Place 6 £15.15, Place 5 £12.55.
Owner D & S L Tanker Transport Limited **Bred** Gestut Hof Eichenstein **Trained** Doncaster, S Yorks

FOCUS
A moderate handicap, run at a solid pace. The form is rated around the fourth.
Garibaldi(GER) Official explanation: trainer said, regarding apparent improvement in form, that his runners are returning to form after being affected by a virus.
T/Jkpt: Not won. T/Plt: £8.80 to a £1 stake. Pool: £67,149.35. 5,562.00 winning tickets. T/Qpdt: £6.60 to a £1 stake. Pool: £3,010.60. 335.70 winning tickets. RY

5287 - 5292a (Foreign Racing) - See Raceform Interactive

5060 WOODBINE (R-H)
Sunday, September 9

OFFICIAL GOING: Firm

5293a NATALMA STKS (GRADE 3) 1m (T)
9:25 (9:25) 2-Y-O
£39,474 (£17,544; £7,237; £3,947; £1,974; £175)

RPR
1 **Clearly Foxy (USA)**[34] 2-8-2 .... JCJones 7 100
(M Casse, Canada) **171/10**
2 *3 1/2* **Nite In Rome (CAN)** 2-8-2 .... MESmith 4 92
(M Casse, Canada) **12/1**
3 *1 1/2* **Lickety Lemon (USA)** 2-8-2 .... PHusbands 9 88
(M Casse, Canada) **4/5**[1]
4 *1* **Lacadena (USA)**[84] 2-8-2 .... TKabel 10 86
(Josie Carroll, Canada) **96/10**
5 *2* **Remarkable Remy (USA)** 2-8-2 .... ECastro 3 81
(J Kimmel, U.S.A) **101/20**[2]
6 *1* **Honour Fulfilled (CAN)**[34] 2-8-2 .... SCallaghan 8 79
(Michael J Doyle, U.S.A) **78/1**
7 *1 1/2* **Bar City (USA)** 2-8-2 ....(b) DavidClark 6 76
(Linda Rice, U.S.A) **68/10**[3]
8 *3/4* **Star Of Jove (USA)** 2-8-2 ....(b) EmmaJayneWilson 5 74
(J Wilson, Canada) **323/10**
9 *2 1/2* **Raw Possibility (CAN)** 2-8-2 .... CMontpellier 1 68
(Don Pleterski, Canada) **76/10**
10 *7 3/4* **Waveline (USA)**[36] 4152 2-8-4 ....(b) ERamsammy 2 52
(B J Meehan) *driven to race in touch after slow start, 6th half-way, weakened 2f out, last and beaten straight* **43/4**

1m 36.12s (96.12) **10** Ran SP% **132.0**
PARI-MUTUEL (Including C$2 stake): WIN 36.30; PL (1-2) 16.50, 12.40;SHOW (1-2-3) 5.70, 5.40, 2.70; SF 294.30.
Owner Charles Laloggia **Bred** Hopewell Investments LLC & Tim Kegel **Trained** North America

NOTEBOOK
Waveline(USA), tried in blinkers and racing beyond 6f for the first time, had to use up a lot of energy to get into midfield after missing the break, but that eventually took its toll and her stamina gave out completelely.

4841 BEVERLEY (R-H)
Tuesday, September 11

OFFICIAL GOING: Good to firm (9.5)
No rain since the previous meeting. 30mm of water was put on in the last week resulting in 'good to firm ground but loose on top and patchy'.
Wind: light 1/2 against Weather: Fine and sunny

5294 WESTWOOD MAIDEN AUCTION STKS 1m 100y
2:30 (2:32) (Class 6) 2-Y-O **£2,914** (£867; £433; £216) **Stalls** High

Form RPR
0 **1** **Flying Time**[16] 4852 2-8-4 0.. PaulHanagan 10 66
(M R Channon) *trckd ldrs: wnt 2nd over 1f out: led fnl 150yds: hld on towards fin* **7/1**
2 *3/4* **Synergistic (IRE)** 2-9-0 0.. KDarley 7 75
(M Johnston) *s.i.s: in rr and sn pushed along: hdwy and nt clr run over 2f out: swtchd lft and hdwy appr fnl f: fin strly* **7/1**
04 **3** *3/4* **Reel Buddy Blaze**[45] 3951 2-8-11 0.......................... MickyFenton 9 70
(T P Tate) *led: qcknd over 3f out: hdd and no ex ins fnl f* **8/1**
324 **4** *1* **Prince Kalamoun (IRE)**[13] 4930 2-8-7 74.................. PJMcDonald(3) 3 67
(G A Swinbank) *dwlt: sn chsng ldrs: effrt on outer 3f out: styd on same pce appr fnl f* **11/4**[2]
042 **5** *2* **City Hustler (USA)**[7] 5116 2-8-10 0................................ JohnEgan 5 63
(J S Moore) *trckd ldr: rdn 3f out: fdd fnl f* **5/2**[1]
2656 **6** *4* **Eager Diva (USA)**[14] 4923 2-8-8 73.......................... DO'Donohoe 4 52+
(K A Ryan) *sn trcking ldrs on outer: wd bnd 4f out: wkng whn bmpd appr fnl f* **11/2**[3]
06 **7** *1 1/4* **Blazing Mask (IRE)**[15] 4890 2-8-6 0........................ RoystonFfrench 2 48
(Mrs A Duffield) *in rr and sn pushed along: nvr a factor* **66/1**
00 **8** *1/2* **Pret A Tout**[33] 4335 2-8-2 0................................ DuranFentiman(3) 8 46
(P J McBride) *prom: drvn 3f out: sn lost pl* **100/1**
9 *3/4* **Bobal Girl** 2-7-11 0.. MCGeran(7) 6 43
(E F Vaughan) *s.i.s: a in rr* **20/1**

1m 48.8s (1.40) **Going Correction** 0.0s/f (Good) **9** Ran SP% **114.0**
Speed ratings (Par 93): **93,92,91,90,88 84,83,82,82**
CSF £53.37 TOTE £8.50: £2.20, £2.20, £2.50; EX 36.50.
Owner Jaber Abdullah **Bred** Whitson Bloodstock Limited **Trained** West Ilsley, Berks

FOCUS
Probably just an ordinary maiden auction event with the fourth the best guide to the overall value of the form.

NOTEBOOK
Flying Time showed the benefit of her first outing and challenging one off the favoured running rail, in the end the post came just in time. She should be able to make her mark in nursery company. (op 9-1 tchd 10-1)
Synergistic(IRE) ♦, out of a tough racemare that won at up to a mile six, was coltish and very noisy in the paddock. He was fairly clueless but when pulled wide coming to the final furlong he finished with a real flourish and would have made it in a few more strides. Hopefully this will help him keep his mind on the job and he looks sure to improve and win races. (op 6-1)
Reel Buddy Blaze had the run of the race but in the end the first two proved simply too good. A well-made type he will be seen to better advantage at three. (op 7-1)
Prince Kalamoun(IRE), who continually swished his tail in the paddock, does not seem to be improving with racing. (op 10-3)
City Hustler(USA), who has size and scope, looked at sea on this track and in the end could not see it out. Official explanation: trainer said colt was unsuited by the track (op 7-2)
Eager Diva(USA) tended to race away from the favoured inside rail and his chance had gone when pushed sideways by the runner-up. (op 7-2)
Blazing Mask(IRE) Official explanation: jockey said filly never travelled

5295 RACING AGAIN NEXT WEDNESDAY H'CAP 5f
3:00 (3:02) (Class 6) (0-50,54) 3-Y-O+ **£2,266** (£674; £337; £168) **Stalls** High

Form RPR
5331 **1** **Viewforth**[8] 5090 9-9-2 **54** 6ex...(b) KDarley 16 63
(M A Buckley) *chsd ldrs: styd on on ins to ld ins fnl f: kpt on wl* **4/1**[1]
6650 **2** *1/2* **Valiant Romeo**[1] 5276 7-8-8 **46** oh1.................................. GregFairley 15 53
(R Bastiman) *led: edgd lft over 1f out: hdd and no ex ins fnl f* **15/2**
3433 **3** *1/2* **Miss Daawe**[18] 4773 3-8-9 **48**....................................... RoystonFfrench 4 53+
(B Ellison) *in rr: hdwy over 1f out: fin wl* **13/2**[3]
0000 **4** *1/2* **Desert Hunter (IRE)**[20] 4701 4-8-8 **46** oh1................... PatCosgrave 17 50
(Micky Hammond) *chsd ldrs on ins: kpt on wl fnl f* **12/1**
0600 **5** *1 1/4* **Seafield Towers**[11] 4996 7-8-8 **46** oh1..............................(p) TomEaves 9 45+
(Miss L A Perratt) *stmbld s: in rr: hdwy over 1f out: swtchd lft ins fnl f: styd on strly* **22/1**
01 **6** *shd* **Throw The Dice**[8] 5085 5-8-10 **51** 6ex..................(v) PatrickMathers(3) 14 50
(A Berry) *chsd ldrs: kpt on same pce appr fnl f* **9/2**[2]
0044 **7** *hd* **Larky's Lob**[20] 4706 8-8-7 **52** ow3............................ JamesO'Reilly(7) 6 50
(J O'Reilly) *mid-div: kpt on fnl 2f: nvr trbld ldrs* **7/1**
3010 **8** *2 1/2* **Midnight Sky**[13] 4935 3-8-11 **50**...................................... MickyFenton 10 39
(Rae Guest) *mid-div: n.m.r over 2f out: kpt on: nvr a threat* **10/1**
0000 **9** *nk* **The Thrifty Bear**[25] 4583 4-8-3 **46** oh1.....................(b) KellyHarrison(5) 5 34
(C W Fairhurst) *mid-div: hdwy over 2f out: wknd over 1f out* **80/1**
0004 **10** *2* **Strawberry Patch (IRE)**[12] 4967 8-8-12 **50**...............(p) DanielTudhope 1 31
(J S Goldie) *swvd lft s: racd alone stands' side: nvr on terms* **16/1**
2460 **11** *4* **Spinning Game**[18] 4787 3-8-2 **48**.....................(v[1]) DanielleMcCreery(7) 8 14
(D W Chapman) *s.v.s: detached and bhd: kpt on fnl 2f: nvr on terms* **50/1**
0565 **12** *nk* **Violet's Pride**[12] 4973 3-8-4 **50**................................ MatthewDavies(7) 2 15
(S Parr) *chsd ldrs: wknd 2f out* **100/1**
0540 **13** *1 1/4* **Bond Becks (IRE)**[8] 5085 7-8-9 **50**...................... MichaelJStainton(3) 13 11
(G R Oldroyd) *tubed: chsd ldrs: lost pl 2f out: sn bhd* **12/1**
0040 **14** *1/2* **Mystery Pips**[12] 4973 7-8-10 **48**..(v) KimTinkler 12 7
(N Tinkler) *chsd ldrs: wknd and wandered 2f out: sn bhd* **33/1**

64.47 secs (0.47) **Going Correction** 0.0s/f (Good)
WFA 3 from 4yo+ 1lb **14** Ran SP% **117.6**
Speed ratings (Par 101): **96,95,94,93,91 91,91,87,86,83 77,76,74,73**
CSF £31.89 CT £197.29 TOTE £4.10: £1.60, £2.40, £2.20; EX 28.80.
Owner Chris Handley **Bred** Britton House Stud And R J Gorringe **Trained** Castle Bytham, Lincs

FOCUS
As usual on fast ground here it paid to race as close as possible to the far rail. The form is straightforward rated through the winner and the third deserves plenty of credit in the circumstances.
Seafield Towers Official explanation: jockey said gelding was denied a clear run in home straight
Strawberry Patch(IRE) Official explanation: jockey said gelding hung left-handed
Spinning Game Official explanation: jockey said filly was slowly away

5296 WEATHERBYS PRINTING H'CAP 1m 1f 207y
3:30 (3:30) (Class 4) (0-80,80) 3-Y-O+ **£6,477** (£1,927; £963; £481) **Stalls** High

Form RPR
6635 **1** **Gloucester**[18] 4772 4-8-10 **67**...................................... GrahamGibbons 10 77
(J J Quinn) *trckd ldrs: c outside over 2f out: styd on to ld fnl stride* **7/1**
1206 **2** *shd* **Little Jimbob**[14] 4922 6-8-13 **70**...................................... PaulHanagan 12 80
(R A Fahey) *led 1f: trckd ldrs: led over 1f out: hdd post* **8/1**
2244 **3** *1 3/4* **Smugglers Bay (IRE)**[10] 5043 3-8-4 **71**.................... DuranFentiman(3) 6 78
(T D Easterby) *in tch: sn drvn along: kpt on wl fnl 2f: nvr able to chal* **9/2**[2]
5211 **4** *2 1/2* **Ahlawy (IRE)**[17] 4817 4-9-9 **80**.. PaulMulrennan 1 82
(M W Easterby) *hld up in rr: hdwy on outer over 3f out: kpt on fnl 2f: nvr rchd ldrs* **6/1**[3]
0200 **5** *shd* **Regent's Secret (USA)**[13] 4933 7-9-3 **74**..................(p) DanielTudhope 2 75
(J S Goldie) *s.s: hdwy on wd outside over 2f out: nvr nr ldrs* **25/1**
2412 **6** *nk* **Motafarred (IRE)**[17] 4820 5-8-13 **70**............................ PatCosgrave 11 71
(Micky Hammond) *in rr: hdwy over 6f out: kpt on same pce fnl 2f* **6/1**[3]
6311 **7** *5* **Suits Me**[14] 4922 4-9-5 **76**.. MickyFenton 3 67
(T P Tate) *trckd ldrs: led over 2f out: hdd over 1f out: wknd rapidly fnl 150yds* **7/2**[1]
2600 **8** *1 1/2* **Riley Boys (IRE)**[15] 4900 6-9-8 **79**.. TPQueally 5 67
(J G Given) *hld up in rr: hdwy and nt clr run over 2f out: hung lft over 1f out: edgd rt andwknd fnl f* **20/1**
1534 **9** *3* **Neil's Legacy (IRE)**[13] 4933 5-8-9 **66** oh1........................ GregFairley 9 48
(Miss L A Perratt) *chsd ldrs: wknd over 1f out: eased ins fnl f* **12/1**
3360 **10** *8* **El Dececy (USA)**[16] 4847 3-8-13 **77**.......................................(b[1]) JohnEgan 4 43
(D J Murphy) *led after 1f: t.k.h: clr over 4f out: hdd over 2f out: wknd qckly: bhd whn eased ins fnl f* **16/1**

2m 5.25s (-2.05) **Going Correction** 0.0s/f (Good)
WFA 3 from 4yo+ 7lb **10** Ran SP% **114.8**
Speed ratings (Par 105): **108,107,106,104,104 104,100,99,96,90**
CSF £60.83 CT £279.99 TOTE £7.40: £2.10, £3.10, £2.10; EX 82.80.
Owner Ross Harmon **Bred** Juddmonte Farms Ltd **Trained** Settrington, N Yorks

FOCUS
A fair handicap run at a strong gallop yet it was hard to make ground from off the pace. However, the form looks sound rated around the placed horses.

The Form Book, Raceform Ltd, Compton, RG20 6NL

Suits Me Official explanation: trainer had no explanation for the poor form shown

5297 BEVERLEY ANNUAL BADGEHOLDERS H'CAP 5f

4:00 (4:02) (Class 5) (0-70,72) 3-Y-O+ **£3,886** (£1,156; £577; £288) **Stalls** High

Form RPR

0411 **1** **Making Music**[11] 4996 4-8-8 **58**....(b) DavidAllan 9 66
(T D Easterby) *led: clr over 1f out: hld on towards fin* **6/1**[3]

0112 **2** *nk* **Lake Chini (IRE)**[18] 4773 5-9-4 **68**....(b) DaleGibson 7 75
(M W Easterby) *sn chsng ldrs: styd on wl ins fnl f: jst hld* **9/1**

4443 **3** *hd* **Hotham**[17] 4800 4-9-0 **64**.... PatCosgrave 5 70+
(N Wilson) *mid-div: effrt over 2f out: kpt on wl fnl f* **9/2**[1]

0025 **4** *1* **Miacarla**[13] 4939 4-8-3 **56** oh3 ow1.... PatrickMathers(3) 11 66+
(A Berry) *hmpd s: hld up in midfield: nt clr run over 2f out and 1f out: siwtched ins fnl f: styd on strly: no room last 75yds: nt rcvr* **14/1**

0001 **5** *1* **Cornus**[3] 5232 5-9-1 **72** 6ex....(be) RobbieEgan(7) 1 71+
(A J McCabe) *swvd lft s: swtchd rt after s: in rr: n.m.r 2f out: styd on wl fnl f* **11/1**

-100 **6** *nk* **Steel City Boy (IRE)**[28] 4486 4-9-1 **65**.... StephenDonohoe 4 63
(D Carroll) *chsd ldrs: kpt on same pce fnl 2f* **25/1**

2606 **7** *shd* **Paddywack (IRE)**[5] 5174 10-8-3 **60**....(b) DanielleMcCreery(7) 3 57
(D W Chapman) *in rr: hdwy over 1f out: styd on wl towards fin* **11/1**

5210 **8** *hd* **Raccoon (IRE)**[10] 5029 7-9-2 **69**.... PJMcDonald(3) 10 66
(D W Chapman) *chsd ldrs: kpt on same pce fnl 2f* **5/1**[2]

0304 **9** *2* **Henry Hall (IRE)**[18] 4773 11-8-5 **55** oh1.... KimTinkler 6 44
(N Tinkler) *mid-div: outpcd over 2f out: no threat* **16/1**

6014 **10** *½* **Kings College Boy**[5] 5160 7-9-3 **67**....(b) PaulHanagan 2 55
(R A Fahey) *a in rr* **7/1**

60U0 **11** *1 ½* **Howards Princess**[5] 5155 5-7-12 **55** oh10....(b) MCGeran(7) 12 37
(J O'Reilly) *swvd lft s: in rr: n.m.r over 2f out: no ch* **100/1**

0214 **12** *1 ¾* **Never Without Me**[17] 4800 7-9-5 **69**.... TPQueally 8 45
(J F Coupland) *chsd ldrs: hung lft over 1f out: sn wknd* **8/1**

00-0 **13** *12* **Golband**[252] 8 5-8-6 **57** oh10 ow1.... JohnEgan 13 —
(J O'Reilly) *chsd ldrs: lost pl over 2f out: bhd and eased ins fnl f* **80/1**

63.57 secs (-0.43) **Going Correction** 0.0s/f (Good) **13** Ran SP% **118.0**
Speed ratings (Par 103): **103,102,102,100,99 98,98,98,94,94 91,88,69**
CSF £57.96 CT £268.50 TOTE £7.10: £2.40, £3.00, £1.80; EX 37.90.
Owner Jonathan Gill **Bred** Redmyre Bloodstock And Stuart McPhee **Trained** Great Habton, N Yorks

FOCUS
It again paid to race as close as possible to the far-side rail. The fourth should have gone very close and along with the third helps set the standard.
Miacarla Official explanation: jockey said filly was denied a clear run
Howards Princess Official explanation: jockey said mare was denied a clear run
Golband Official explanation: jockey said mare lost its action

5298 GMTV AND BRILLIANT MEDIA NURSERY 7f 100y

4:30 (4:31) (Class 6) (0-65,64) 2-Y-O **£3,238** (£963; £481; £240) **Stalls** High

Form RPR

6025 **1** **Destinys Dream (IRE)**[16] 4841 2-9-7 **64**.... RoystonFfrench 8 71
(Mrs A Duffield) *prom: str run to ld 1f out: sprinted clr* **8/1**

1360 **2** *4* **Natural Rhythm (IRE)**[2] 5251 2-9-6 **63**.... DanielTudhope 14 61
(D W Chapman) *mid-div: hdwy over 2f out: styd on wl fnl f: tk 2nd nr line* **9/1**

0005 **3** *hd* **Kiwi Princess**[12] 4968 2-9-0 **57**.... DaleGibson 2 55
(M Brittain) *led tl 1f out: kpt on same pce* **66/1**

545 **4** *½* **Countrywide Comet (IRE)**[104] 2147 2-9-2 **59**.... DO'Donohoe 11 55
(K A Ryan) *chsd ldrs: styd on same pce fnl f* **12/1**

3054 **5** *½* **Gulf Coast**[12] 4964 2-9-5 **62**....(v) GregFairley 5 57
(M Johnston) *prom: rdn over 2f out: kpt on wl fnl f* **4/1**[1]

005 **6** *shd* **Sand Maiden (IRE)**[18] 4784 2-9-2 **59**.... DavidAllan 16 54
(T D Easterby) *prom: effrt on inner over 2f out: kpt on wl ins fnl f* **12/1**

000 **7** *1* **Jafra (IRE)**[44] 4002 2-8-9 **55**.... MichaelJStainton(3) 4 48
(R M Whitaker) *dwlt: hdwy on wd outside 4f out: hung rt over 1f out: nvr nr ldrs* **18/1**

004 **8** *nk* **Dream Bee**[21] 4683 2-9-7 **64**.... StephenDonohoe 3 56
(E A L Dunlop) *s.i.s: hdwy on outer and hung lft over 2f out: kpt on fnl f* **9/1**

0506 **9** *¾* **Hurstpierpoint (IRE)**[26] 4524 2-8-11 **54**.... PaulHanagan 10 44
(R A Fahey) *hld up in mid-div: effrt over 2f out: kpt on fnl f* **5/1**[2]

0000 **10** *3 ½* **Galley Slave (IRE)**[25] 4584 2-8-8 **56**.... RussellKennemore(5) 12 38
(M C Chapman) *in rr: swtchd lft over 1f out: nvr on terms* **15/2**[3]

030 **11** *hd* **Black Duke**[67] 3283 2-8-11 **61**.... MCGeran(7) 1 42
(M G Quinlan) *chsd ldrs: wknd 2f out* **28/1**

003 **12** *½* **Buju**[18] 4770 2-9-1 **58**.... KDarley 15 38
(N Tinkler) *mid-div: wknd 3f out* **20/1**

000 **13** *1* **Mganga**[15] 4904 2-9-7 **64**.... TomEaves 13 42+
(M R Channon) *in rr: sme hdwy on inner whn n.m.r 2f out: nvr on terms* **12/1**

004 **14** *nk* **Imaginemysurprise**[18] 4755 2-8-7 **57**.... KirstyMilczarek(7) 9 34
(J A Geake) *in rr: effrt on outside over 2f out: nvr on terms* **20/1**

040 **15** *shd* **Powys Lad**[70] 3192 2-9-3 **60**.... PhillipMakin 6 37
(K R Burke) *sn chsng ldrs: lost pl over 2f out* **33/1**

0040 **16** *6* **Zaplamation (IRE)**[63] 3398 2-8-12 **55**.... TonyHamilton 7 18
(D W Barker) *chsd ldrs: lost pl over 2f out: sn bhd* **50/1**

1m 35.32s (1.01) **Going Correction** 0.0s/f (Good) **16** Ran SP% **127.2**
Speed ratings (Par 93): **94,89,89,88,88 87,86,86,85,81 81,80,79,79,79 72**
CSF £75.91 CT £4655.39 TOTE £8.50: £2.10, £2.40, £6.50, £3.60; EX 101.70.
Owner Destiny Racing Club **Bred** Sean Burke **Trained** Constable Burton, N Yorks

FOCUS
A modest nursery but a clear-cut winner and the level looks solid through those in the frame behind the winner.

NOTEBOOK
Destinys Dream(IRE), a half-sister to six winners including the multiple winner Jack Dawson, had run well over course and distance on her nursery debut and showed her liking for the track by sweeping through to score decisively. She will continue at this level, should stay further, and connections will be hoping the Handicapper does not over-react to this clear-cut victory. (op 7-1)
Natural Rhythm(IRE), who took a seller at around this trip when in the care of today's winning trainer, ran arguably his best race for new connections, staying on without ever looking likely to trouble the winner (op 16-1)
Kiwi Princess was given a positive ride on this handicap debut and it seemed to suit her, as she repelled all challengers bar the winner and only lost second near the finish. She is not badly treated at present and may be capable of staying in front on a less-stiff track. (tchd 80-1)
Countrywide Comet(IRE), another making his handicap debut, was also returning from a three and a half-month break. He seemed much sharper than in the spring and ran well before fading in the last furlong. He can be expected to come on for the outing and may be up to winning a small race. (op 14-1)
Gulf Coast, who has had plenty of experience in handicaps, was reverting to turf after a couple of decent efforts on Polytrack. He was always struggling and, although staying on late, looks better on the artificial surface. (tchd 10-3)
Sand Maiden(IRE), making her handicap debut, seems to be progressing with racing and is one to keep an eye on, although the best of her may not be seen until next season.
Dream Bee Official explanation: jockey said filly hung left-handed throughout
Hurstpierpoint(IRE), who was 11lb better off with today's winner for a beating of just under five lengths here recently, was never really going having been settled off the pace. She seems a little inconsistent but that may be due to immaturity. (op 7-1)
Galley Slave(IRE), another who was held up off the pace, failed to get in a blow. He has had quite a few chances now but may be worth trying on an artifical surface. (op 8-1)
Black Duke Official explanation: jockey said colt had no more to give
Buju Official explanation: jockey said gelding lost its action on the bend

5299 BEVERLEY-RACECOURSE.CO.UK CLASSIFIED STKS 1m 100y

5:00 (5:02) (Class 6) 3-Y-O+ **£2,730** (£806; £403) **Stalls** High

Form RPR

4330 **1** **Grethel (IRE)**[13] 4936 3-8-5 55.... DanielleMcCreery(7) 16 58
(A Berry) *hld up in rr: hdwy and swtchd lft over 2f out: str run appr fnl f: led post* **12/1**

4000 **2** *hd* **Monsieur Dumas (IRE)**[26] 4526 3-8-12 54.... PatCosgrave 12 58
(R Bastiman) *hld up: hdwy over 4f out: styd on to ld jst ins fnl f: hdd towards fin* **15/2**

2053 **3** *1 ¾* **Cap St Jean (IRE)**[32] 4354 3-8-7 55.... RussellKennemore(5) 9 54+
(R Hollinshead) *mid-div: hdwy and nt clr run over 2f out: styd on fnl f to take 3rd nr line* **3/1**[1]

5000 **4** *hd* **Murrumbidgee (IRE)**[16] 4850 4-9-3 54....(p) KDarley 2 55
(J W Hills) *chsd ldrs: wd bnd 4f out: chal jst ins fnl f: no ex* **4/1**[2]

404 **5** *1* **Papa's Princess**[20] 4713 3-8-12 54.... DanielTudhope 8 51
(J S Goldie) *bmpd s: sn chsng ldrs: upsides jst ins fnl f: one pce* **5/1**[3]

000 **6** *1 ¼* **Summer Gift**[16] 4846 4-9-3 53.... DavidAllan 11 49
(J O'Reilly) *chsd ldrs: almost upsides on inner whn n.m.r jst ins fnl f: kpt on one pce* **100/1**

5300 **7** *1 ½* **Forced Upon Us**[16] 4856 3-8-9 54....(b[1]) DuranFentiman(3) 6 45
(P J McBride) *trckd ldrs: led 3f out: hdd & wknd jst ins fnl f* **10/1**

6500 **8** *shd* **Red Barnet**[8] 5098 3-8-12 53.... PaulMulrennan 13 45
(M W Easterby) *mid-div: kpt on fnl 2f: nvr rchd ldrs* **25/1**

0-00 **9** *1 ½* **Bold Nevison (IRE)**[115] 1850 3-8-12 49.... RoystonFfrench 5 41
(B Smart) *t.k.h in rr: sme hdwy over 2f out: nvr nr ldrs* **40/1**

000 **10** *1* **Simba's Pride**[20] 4713 3-8-12 40.... GregFairley 14 39
(Miss L A Perratt) *in rr: nvr a factor* **100/1**

5154 **11** *4* **Mangano**[12] 4971 3-8-9 55.... PatrickMathers(3) 3 30
(A Berry) *chsd ldrs: rn wd bnd 4f out: sn lost pl* **8/1**

0400 **12** *¾* **Grey Vision**[20] 4705 4-9-3 48.... DaleGibson 10 29
(M Brittain) *chsd ldrs: drvn over 4f out: lost pl 3f out* **33/1**

606P **13** *1 ¼* **Cape Dancer (IRE)**[59] 3540 3-8-12 55....(p) PaddyAspell 7 25
(J S Wainwright) *swvd rt s: sn chsng ldrs: wknd 2f out* **40/1**

0000 **14** *3* **Sunley Sovereign**[6] 5139 3-8-12 55.... TomEaves 17 18
(D W Chapman) *mde most tl 3f out: lost pl over 1f out* **22/1**

00/0 **15** *11* **Dashing Dane**[22] 4673 7-9-0 40.... JamieMoriarty(3) 1 —
(Mrs Marjorie Fife) *chsd ldrs: lost pl over 2f out: sn bhd* **100/1**

1m 48.75s (1.35) **Going Correction** 0.0s/f (Good)
WFA 3 from 4yo+ 5lb **15** Ran SP% **120.3**
Speed ratings (Par 101): **93,92,91,90,89 88,87,87,85,84 80,79,78,75,64**
CSF £93.23 TOTE £13.50: £3.90, £2.90, £1.30; EX 121.50.
Owner Mrs Linda White **Bred** Liam Queally **Trained** Cockerham, Lancs

FOCUS
A competitive-looking classified event but run in a moderate time, even for a race like this. The form looks weak with the third the best guide to the level.
Cap St Jean(IRE) Official explanation: jockey said filly was denied a clear run

5300 SAWFISH SOFTWARE H'CAP (FOR LADY AMATEUR RIDERS) 1m 4f 16y

5:30 (5:30) (Class 6) (0-65,69) 3-Y-O+ **£3,123** (£968; £484; £242) **Stalls** High

Form RPR

5634 **1** **Parchment (IRE)**[5] 5158 5-9-12 **55**....(b) MissADeniel 12 64
(A J Lockwood) *hld up in rr: stdy hdwy on ins 3f out: styd on to ld ins fnl f* **9/2**[1]

0034 **2** *1 ¼* **Falcon's Fire (IRE)**[15] 4894 3-9-1 **56**.... MissJAKidd(3) 5 63
(Mrs A Duffield) *sn in tch: hdwy over 3f out: kpt on to take 2nd wl ins fnl f* **11/1**

2301 **3** *nk* **Rare Coincidence**[8] 5087 6-10-12 **69** 6ex....(p) MrsCBartley 8 76
(R F Fisher) *led: hdd and no ex ins fnl f* **11/2**[2]

5323 **4** *1 ½* **Mr Mischief**[5] 5158 7-9-6 **56**.... MissSEilbeck(7) 1 60
(M C Chapman) *chsd ldrs: chal 3f out: edgd lft and one pce appr fnl f* **9/1**

0003 **5** *2 ½* **Fenners (USA)**[11] 5000 4-9-11 **59**....(b[1]) MissJoannaMason(5) 9 59
(M W Easterby) *hld up in mid-div: hdwy over 2f out: kpt on fnl f* **11/1**

0033 **6** *½* **Gala Sunday (USA)**[11] 4998 7-9-13 **56**....(bt) MissSBrotherton 10 55
(M W Easterby) *hld up in midfield: hdwy 3f out: hung rt over 1f out: nvr threatened ldrs* **7/1**

3542 **7** *hd* **Moment Of Clarity**[17] 4802 5-9-5 **51**.... MissMSowerby(3) 7 50
(R C Guest) *hld up towards rr: hdwy over 2f out: kpt on: nvr nr ldrs* **13/2**[3]

4252 **8** *1* **William John**[17] 4817 4-9-12 **55**....(tp) MissLEllison 4 52
(B Ellison) *hld up in midfield: hdwy to chse ldrs over 4f out: one pce* **13/2**[3]

-054 **9** *¾* **Bollin Dolly**[16] 4846 4-10-4 **64**.... MissJCoward(3) 3 60
(T D Easterby) *chsd ldr: wknd over 1f out* **10/1**

/466 **10** *12* **Oniz Tiptoes (IRE)**[24] 4096 6-9-10 **60** oh2 ow10..(v) MissFRodmell(7) 11 37
(J S Wainwright) *in rr: bhd fnl 3f* **14/1**

30/3 **11** *5* **Skiddaw Jones**[17] 4817 7-9-2 **50** oh5....(t) MissAngelaBarnes(5) 2 19
(M A Barnes) *s.s: hdwy over 5f out: wd and lost pl 3f out: sn bhd* **40/1**

0060 **12** *20* **Inchloss (IRE)**[63] 3397 6-9-7 **50** oh5.... MissFayeBramley 6 —
(S Parr) *hld up in rr: t.o 4f out* **100/1**

2m 39.37s (-0.84) **Going Correction** 0.0s/f (Good)
WFA 3 from 4yo+ 9lb **12** Ran SP% **118.6**
Speed ratings (Par 101): **102,101,100,99,98 97,97,97,96,88 85,72**
CSF £54.76 CT £281.71 TOTE £6.30: £2.50, £3.50, £2.50; EX 85.90 Place 6 £ 416.93, Place 5 £ 90.19.
Owner A J Lockwood **Bred** Wickfield Farm Partnership **Trained** Brawby, N Yorks

FOCUS
A moderate amateurs' event run at a sound gallop but very few got involved from off the pace. The form is rated through the third and could go a little higher.
T/Jkpt: Not won. T/Plt: £475.30 to a £1 stake. Pool: £67,650.90. 103.90 winning tickets. T/Qpdt: £40.80 to a £1 stake. Pool: £4,369.70. 79.10 winning tickets. WG

4656 LEICESTER (R-H)

Tuesday, September 11

OFFICIAL GOING: Good to firm (firm in places)

Wind: Light, across Weather: Cloudy with sunny spells

5301 EBF FILBERT MAIDEN FILLIES' STKS 1m 60y

2:20 (2:21) (Class 4) 2-Y-O **£4,857** (£1,445; £722; £360) **Stalls** High

Form RPR

0 **1** **Nowaira (IRE)**[11] 5010 2-9-0 0 JamieSpencer 6 74
(M Johnston) *trckd ldrs: rdn and edgd rt over 1f out: led ins fnl f: all out* **2/1**[1]

00 **2** *shd* **Baraari (USA)**[40] 4094 2-9-0 0 RichardMullen 14 74
(J L Dunlop) *chsd ldrs: rdn over 1f out: r.o* **11/1**

04 **3** *½* **Trinkila (USA)**[15] 4875 2-9-0 0 TQuinn 8 73
(P F I Cole) *hld up: hdwy over 3f out: led over 2f out: sn rdn: hdd and unable qckn ins fnl f* **40/1**

5 **4** *½* **Burn The Breeze (IRE)**[31] 4402 2-9-0 0 TedDurcan 11 72
(H R A Cecil) *prom: nt clr run over 1f out: swtchd rt: styd on same pce towards fin* **9/4**[2]

5 *2* **Sweet Sara** 2-9-0 0 FrancisNorton 10 67
(C E Brittain) *s.i.s: sn pushed along in rr: r.o ins fnl f: nt trble ldrs* **100/1**

34 **6** *nk* **Black Dahlia**[11] 5010 2-9-0 0 LDettori 4 67
(A J McCabe) *hld up: hdwy 3f out: rdn and edgd rt fr over 1f out: styd on same pce* **5/1**[3]

7 *1 ½* **Italian Goddess** 2-9-0 0 HayleyTurner 9 63
(M L W Bell) *mid-div: sn pushed along: hdwy 3f out: wknd ins fnl f* **80/1**

8 *shd* **Sendefaa (IRE)** 2-8-9 0 AshleyHamblett(5) 3 63
(M Botti) *s.i.s: hld up: hdwy 3f out: hung rt and wknd fnl f* **66/1**

053 **9** *¾* **Hasty Lady**[24] 4611 2-9-0 73 NCallan 13 61
(K A Ryan) *chsd ldrs: rdn over 2f out: wknd fnl f* **9/1**

0 **10** *2* **Anamarka**[15] 4875 2-9-0 0 FergusSweeney 5 57
(H Candy) *hld up: rdn 1/2-way: a in rr* **100/1**

00 **11** *2* **Fareeha**[31] 4402 2-9-0 0 MartinDwyer 12 53
(J H M Gosden) *chsd ldrs: rdn and ev ch over 2f out: wknd over 1f out* **14/1**

0 **12** *2* **Skynda**[9] 5061 2-9-0 0 ChrisCatlin 2 48
(Rae Guest) *hld up: rdn 1/2-way: a in rr* **150/1**

6 **13** *2* **Shaama Rose (FR)**[15] 4875 2-9-0 0 DarryllHolland 7 44
(M R Channon) *sn outpcd: bhd fr 1/2-way* **25/1**

00 **14** *2* **Spanish Heroine**[70] 3187 2-9-0 0 (p) StephenCarson 1 39
(P Winkworth) *led over 5f: wknd over 1f out* **200/1**

1m 45.38s (0.08) **Going Correction** -0.05s/f (Good) **14** Ran SP% **117.9**

Speed ratings (Par 94): **97,96,96,95,93 93,92,92,91,89 87,85,83,81**

CSF £24.40 TOTE £3.10: £1.60, £4.00, £10.90; EX 28.60 Trifecta £187.60 Part won. Pool: £264.26 - 0.34 winning units..

Owner Sheikh Ahmed Al Maktoum **Bred** Darley **Trained** Middleham Moor, N Yorks

FOCUS

A competitive little maiden rated around the principals and likely to produce its share of winners.

NOTEBOOK

Nowaira(IRE), a well-bred daughter of Daylami who was unlucky not to finish a fair bit closer on her recent debut over 7f at Sandown, was always going to relish this extra distance and the booking of Spencer was significant, the rider having recently struck up a good relationship with the stable's smart Lovelace. Never too far from the lead, she raced a shade keenly and looked vulnerable from two furlongs out, being strongly ridden, but kept finding in a manner typical of her trainer's horses and just did enough, snatching it on the bob. She already looks in need of 1m2f and rates as a promising handicap prospect. (tchd 9-4 in places)

Baraari(USA) was found wanting for speed over 6f and 7f on her two previous starts, but this stiffer test saw the daughter of Nayef in a much better light and she very nearly snatched it from the winner. Finding an ordinary maiden at this distance should not prove too difficult, but connections will now also have the options of handicaps. Either way she looks one to keep on-side. (op 16-1)

Trinkila(USA) had looked a filly of limited ability in two previous attempts, but she showed greatly improved form here and very nearly caused a huge shock. In rear early, she made gradual headway through the field to take it up racing into the final quarter mile, but could not repel the dour winner. She is another likely to be winning once sent handicapping. (op 66-1)

Burn The Breeze(IRE), a pleasing fifth over 7f on debut at Newmarket, did not get the gap when she wanted it, but would still have won if she had that much in hand as, having been switched, she could only cough up the one pace. A fine, big filly, she still looked unsure of what was required and an ordinary maiden should be within her capabilities. (tchd 5-2)

Sweet Sara, a 27,000gns daughter of Mark Of Esteem, hails from a yard whose juveniles often need a run to set them straight, so this has to go down as a pleasing debut. She showed distinct signs of greeness before running on and can be expected to know much more next time. (op 80-1 tchd 66-1)

Black Dahlia had displayed a fair level of form in two previous attempts and she was always going to be thereabouts, but was found wanting for a change of speed when it mattered and she may be best off going down the handicap route now. (op 6-1 tchd 9-2)

5302 RANCLIFFE (S) STKS 7f 9y

2:50 (2:53) (Class 6) 2-Y-O **£2,590** (£770; £385; £192) **Stalls** Low

Form RPR

0 **1** **Mwindaji**[25] 4571 2-8-12 0 DarryllHolland 5 64
(M R Channon) *s.i.s: hdwy over 2f out: rdn and hung rt fr over 1f out: styd on to ld cl home* **3/1**[1]

60 **2** *¾* **Ten Pole Tudor**[15] 4904 2-8-12 0 (b[1]) MartinDwyer 16 62
(J A Osborne) *s.i.s: hdwy over 4f out: led over 2f out: rdn clr and hung rt fr over 1f out: hdd cl home* **11/1**

400 **3** *¾* **Novestar (IRE)**[17] 4818 2-8-12 50 NCallan 8 60+
(Mrs A Duffield) *s.i.s and wnt lft s: in rr whn hmpd 4f out: r.o ins fnl f: nt rch ldrs* **25/1**

40 **4** *6* **The Willowy Wigeon**[15] 4904 2-8-7 0 StephenCarson 3 39
(P Winkworth) *chsd ldrs: rdn over 2f out: wknd over 1f out* **13/2**[2]

3520 **5** *nk* **La Belle Joannie**[15] 4883 2-8-4 53 LiamJones(3) 12 39
(S Curran) *hld up: hmpd 5f out: n.d* **17/2**

3040 **6** *¾* **Kintyre Lass (IRE)**[8] 5089 2-8-7 56 (b[1]) FergusSweeney 6 37+
(B R Millman) *led over 4f: wkng whn hmpd over 1f out* **25/1**

0000 **7** *1 ½* **Bantham Bay**[18] 4783 2-8-7 50 TedDurcan 14 33
(B J Meehan) *hld up: rdn 1/2-way: sme hdwy u.p over 1f out: n.d* **50/1**

065 **8** *3 ½* **Victorian Cape (IRE)**[32] 4363 2-8-12 60 (b[1]) ChrisCatlin 17 29
(E J O'Neill) *chsd ldrs: rdn over 2f out: sn wknd* **7/1**[3]

0006 **9** *1* **Adam Eterno (IRE)**[12] 4963 2-8-12 49 HayleyTurner 4 26
(Tom Dascombe) *sn pushed along in rr: sme hdwy over 2f out: sn wknd* **16/1**

4005 **10** *3* **Baby Jack**[20] 4715 2-8-12 57 JamesDoyle 13 18
(D Nicholls) *chsd ldrs over 4f* **7/1**[3]

0225 **11** *1 ½* **Ten On Line (IRE)**[48] 3835 2-8-9 55 TravisBlock(3) 2 14
(J G M O'Shea) *prom over 4f* **14/1**

12 *8* **Reel Madam** 2-8-7 0 FrancisNorton 7 —
(K A Ryan) *s.s: outpcd* **25/1**

0060 **13** *nk* **Goldhill Fair**[62] 3423 2-8-5 46 (p) JackDean(7) 1 —
(W G M Turner) *chsd ldrs over 4f* **80/1**

6332 **14** *hd* **Shipboard Romance (IRE)**[25] 4559 2-8-8 50 ow1 JamieSpencer 9 —
(P D Evans) *prom 5f* **8/1**

0 **15** *hd* **April Reigns**[18] 4756 2-8-7 0 RichardThomas 15 —
(D Burchell) *prom to 1/2-way* **100/1**

000 **16** *4* **Somarini**[18] 4770 2-8-7 52 RichardMullen 18 —
(J G Given) *chsd ldrs over 4f* **66/1**

1m 25.47s (-0.63) **Going Correction** -0.25s/f (Firm) **16** Ran SP% **123.1**

Speed ratings (Par 93): **93,92,91,84,84 83,81,77,76,72 71,62,61,61,61 56**

CSF £35.88 TOTE £3.90: £1.40, £4.70, £9.30; EX 48.50 TRIFECTA Not won..The winner was sold to John Kettle for 10,500gns. Novestar (IRE) was claimed by G. L. Moore for £6,000. Ten Pole Tudor was claimed by C. R. Dore for £6,000

Owner M Channon **Bred** Mike Channon Bloodstock Ltd **Trained** West Ilsley, Berks

■ Stewards' Enquiry : Liam Jones caution (reduced from one-day ban on appeal): entered wrong stall

FOCUS

Not a bad seller with each of the front three, who drew clear, dropping to this level for the first time. The form looks decent for the grade.

NOTEBOOK

Mwindaji, always outpaced in a decent maiden at Newbury on debut, was always going to be suited by this extra furlong and he did enough to win with a bit in hand. Still green under pressure, he is likely to prove better than this grade and can make his mark in handicaps. (op 4-1 tchd 9-2)

Ten Pole Tudor left his recent dismal effort at Warwick well behind in the first-time blinkers and kept finding under pressure to hold off all bar the winner. There is clearly a race in him at this level. Official explanation: jockey said gelding hung right-handed

Novestar(IRE) showed improved form as a result of the drop in grade/rise in distance and was arguably unlucky not to finish even closer, having been slowly away and then impeded mid-race. He is another who can find a race at this level. Official explanation: jockey said colt suffered interference in running

The Willowy Wigeon was a little disappointing on this drop in grade, having previously shaped well in a couple of modest maidens, and perhaps a return to 6f is required. (op 4-1)

La Belle Joannie never really threatened to play a leading role having been impeded after a couple of furlongs and can be given another chance at this level. (op 11-1)

Reel Madam Official explanation: jockey said filly became upset in stalls and missed the break

Shipboard Romance(IRE) Official explanation: jockey said filly had no more to give

5303 RACECOURSE VIDEO SERVICES H'CAP 7f 9y

3:20 (3:21) (Class 5) (0-70,76) 3-Y-O+ **£3,238** (£963; £481; £240) **Stalls** Low

Form RPR

3030 **1** **Torquemada (IRE)**[34] 4295 6-9-4 63 NCallan 12 71+
(J Akehurst) *racd centre: hld up in tch: hit over hd by rivals whip 1f out: led ins fnl f: r.o* **5/1**[2]

5041 **2** *½* **Hart Of Gold**[9] 5062 3-9-8 76 6ex HaddenFrost(5) 11 81
(R A Harris) *racd centre: chsd ldrs: led overall over 1f out: rdn and hdd ins fnl f: kpt on:* **9/1**

4021 **3** *½* **Fleuret**[17] 4808 3-9-4 67 StephenCarson 4 70
(Eve Johnson Houghton) *racd stands' side: hld up: hdwy over 1f out: styd on* **5/1**[2]

5-1 **4** *1 ¾* **Red Blooded Woman (USA)**[19] 4736 3-9-6 69 TedDurcan 10 68
(J Noseda) *racd centre: trckd ldrs: rdn and edgd lft over 1f out: styd on same pce* **9/2**[1]

2006 **5** *nk* **Material Witness (IRE)**[17] 4807 10-9-8 67 MartinDwyer 7 67
(W R Muir) *racd stands' side: led that gp 6f out: rdn: hung rt and ev ch over 1f out: no ex ins fnl f* **13/2**[3]

0-60 **6** *2 ½* **Middleton Grey**[24] 4606 9-9-7 66 (b) FergusSweeney 1 59
(A G Newcombe) *s.s: racd stands' side: bhd tl styd on ins fnl f: nvr nr to chal* **12/1**

-105 **7** *nk* **Blue Bamboo**[90] 2571 3-9-3 66 DarryllHolland 9 56
(Mrs A J Perrett) *overall ldr in centre over 5f: wknd ins fnl f* **20/1**

0010 **8** *hd* **Meditation**[16] 4855 5-9-8 67 JamesDoyle 2 59
(I A Wood) *led stands' side 1f: chsd ldrs: rdn over 2f out: wknd fnl f* **11/1**

0026 **9** *4* **Lady Edge (IRE)**[21] 4688 5-8-4 54 (v) KevinGhunowa(5) 5 35
(A W Carroll) *racd stands' side: prom: rdn 1/2-way: wknd over 1f out* **33/1**

0050 **10** *12* **Major League (USA)**[19] 4731 5-8-8 56 LiamJones(3) 6 4
(D Morris) *racd stands' side: chsd ldrs: rdn 1/2-way: wknd over 1f out* **14/1**

5006 **11** *6* **Franksalot (IRE)**[17] 4797 7-9-2 66 TolleyDean(5) 8 —
(I W McInnes) *racd stands' side: prom: rdn 1/2-way: wknd 2f out* **17/2**

1000 **12** *2* **Mujart**[22] 4661 3-8-4 53 oh3 ChrisCatlin 3 —
(J A Pickering) *racd stands' side: chsd ldrs: rdn 1/2-way: wknd 2f out* **80/1**

1m 24.5s (-1.60) **Going Correction** -0.25s/f (Firm)

WFA 3 from 5yo+ 4lb **12** Ran SP% **117.0**

Speed ratings (Par 103): **99,98,97,95,95 92,92,92,87,73 66,64**

CSF £48.02 CT £241.21 TOTE £6.10: £1.90, £3.10, £1.70; EX 42.30 Trifecta £208.20 Part won. Pool: £293.30 - 0.98 winning units..

Owner Canisbay Bloodstock **Bred** Oak Lodge Stud/hamford Stud/lileagh Fox **Trained** Epsom, Surrey

FOCUS

A modest handicap in which those who raced towards the centre of the track prevailed. The winner has now taken this event three times in the past four seasons and sets the standard.

Middleton Grey Official explanation: jockey said gelding missed the break

Franksalot(IRE) Official explanation: jockey said gelding hung right-handed from 3f out

5304 ISHERWOOD MCCANN MAIDEN STKS 1m 1f 218y

3:50 (3:50) (Class 5) 3-Y-O+ **£3,238** (£963; £481; £240) **Stalls** High

Form RPR

4-33 **1** **Teodora Adivina**[18] 4765 3-8-12 68 TedDurcan 2 61+
(H R A Cecil) *led early: chsd ldr tl led: over 1f out: sn rdn and edgd rt: styd on wl: eased nr fin* **5/6**[1]

2 *1 ½* **Sun Lane**[108] 3-8-12 0 DarryllHolland 5 54
(W R Swinburn) *sn led: rdn and hdd over 1f out: styd on same pce* **25/1**

3000 **3** *1 ¾* **New Light**[26] 4532 3-8-12 47 StephenCarson 4 50
(Eve Johnson Houghton) *chsd ldrs: rdn over 1f out: styd on same pce* **50/1**

4 *2* **Prairie Tiger (GER)** 3-9-3 0 LDettori 6 51
(N J Vaughan) *s.s: hdwy 3f out: sn rdn: styng on same pce whn edgd rt over 1f out* **6/4**[2]

5 1 1/4 **Eco Sympathy** 3-9-3 0 NCallan 1 49
(M L W Bell) *hld up in tch: racd keenly: rdn over 2f out: wknd fnl f* **10/1**3
6 27 **Fashion Accessory** 3-9-12 0 ChrisCatlin 3 —
(M Appleby) *bhd fr 1/2-way* **150/1**
2m 8.33s (0.03) **Going Correction** -0.05s/f (Good) **6** Ran SP% **110.1**
Speed ratings (Par 103): **97,95,94,92,91 70**
CSF £20.31 TOTE £1.70: £1.10, £5.70; EX 10.50.
Owner Felipe Hinojosa **Bred** Chevington Stud **Trained** Newmarket, Suffolk
FOCUS
A moderate maiden, run at an ordinary gallop. The 68-rated winner is value for plenty further than her winning margin with the far -from solid third setting the level.

5305 PRESTWOLD CONDITIONS STKS 5f 2y
4:20 (4:20) (Class 4) 3-Y-0+ **£6,232** (£1,866; £933; £467; £233) **Stalls** Low

Form RPR
2454 1 **Siren's Gift**52 3746 3-8-1 93 FrancisNorton 1 102
(A M Balding) *trckd ldr: led over 1f out: rdn out* **3/1**2
5646 2 nk **The Jobber (IRE)**3 5212 6-8-7 100 TedDurcan 4 106
(M Blanshard) *trckd ldrs: racd keenly: rdn and ev ch ins fnl f: styd on* **13/8**1
1-03 3 3/4 **Riotous Applause**94 2450 4-8-7 92 JamieSpencer 3 103
(J R Fanshawe) *s.i.s: hld up: hdwy over 1f out: sn rdn: r.o* **9/2**3
3300 4 1 1/2 **Bond City (IRE)**38 4150 5-8-7 102 (p) ChrisCatlin 2 98
(G R Oldroyd) *chsd ldrs: rdn 1/2-way: styd on same pce appr fnl f* **5/1**
0200 5 1 **Cape Royal**3 5212 7-8-2 92 (bt) TolleyDean(5) 5 94
(J M Bradley) *led: rdn and hdd over 1f out: wknd ins fnl f* **8/1**
58.40 secs (-2.50) **Going Correction** -0.25s/f (Firm)
WFA 3 from 4yo+ 1lb **5** Ran SP% **109.1**
Speed ratings (Par 105): **110,109,108,105,104**
CSF £8.15 TOTE £3.90: £1.80, £1.60; EX 9.00.
Owner J C Smith **Bred** Littleton Stud **Trained** Kingsclere, Hants
FOCUS
A decent conditions stakes, run at a solid pace. The first three came clear and the form looks sound and fair for the grade.

5306 EUROPEAN BREEDERS' FUND APOLLO MAIDEN STKS 7f 9y
4:50 (4:51) (Class 4) 2-Y-0 **£4,857** (£1,445; £722; £360) **Stalls** Low

Form RPR
4 1 **Ibn Khaldun (USA)**16 4854 2-9-3 0 LDettori 7 83+
(Saeed Bin Suroor) *hld up: racd keenly: hdwy 1/2-way: led over 1f out: edgd lft: r.o wl: eased nr fin* **4/9**1
2 1 1/4 **Forsyte Saga** 2-8-12 0 JamieSpencer 2 69
(M Johnston) *chsd ldrs: rdn to ld 2f out: sn hdd: styd on same pce ins fnl f* **9/1**2
5 3 1 1/4 **King's Wonder**109 1989 2-9-3 0 RichardMullen 9 71
(W R Muir) *hld up in tch: rdn over 1f out: styd on same pce* **10/1**3
0 4 4 **St Jean Cap Ferrat**52 3747 2-9-3 0 DarryllHolland 11 61
(G Wragg) *hld up: rdn over 2f out: hdwy over 1f out: hung lft and no ex fnl f* **9/1**2
0 5 2 1/2 **Looter (FR)**26 4540 2-9-3 0 MartinDwyer 5 54
(J L Dunlop) *hld up: rdn over 2f out: n.d* **28/1**
00 6 nk **Morestead (IRE)**18 4761 2-9-3 0 TQuinn 3 53
(B G Powell) *s.i.s: hdwy over 2f out: hung rt and wknd over 1f out* **40/1**
7 3/4 **Royal Manor** 2-8-12 0 ChrisCatlin 6 46
(N J Vaughan) *s.i.s: hld up: plld hrd: effrt over 2f out: wknd over 1f out* **25/1**
8 3 **Abeyance (IRE)** 2-9-3 0 TedDurcan 1 44
(J Noseda) *sn pushed along and prom: lost pl 3f out: sn bhd* **33/1**
5000 9 1 **Amwell House**32 4363 2-8-12 42 HaddenFrost(5) 4 41
(J R Jenkins) *led: rdn and hdd 2f out: wkng whn n.m.r sn after* **250/1**
10 10 **Novas (IRE)** 2-9-3 0 NCallan 10 15
(M R Channon) *plld hrd and prom: rdn and wknd over 1f out* **33/1**
1m 25.88s (-0.22) **Going Correction** -0.25s/f (Firm) **10** Ran SP% **114.4**
Speed ratings (Par 97): **91,89,88,83,80 80,79,76,74,63**
CSF £4.27 TOTE £1.40: £1.02, £2.40, £1.90; EX 6.00 Trifecta £25.00 Pool: £545.72 - 15.44 winning units..
Owner Godolphin **Bred** Darley **Trained** Newmarket, Suffolk
FOCUS
A modest winning time, 0.41 seconds slower than the earlier juvenile seller which helps to limit the form.
NOTEBOOK
Ibn Khaldun(USA) ◆ confirmed the promise of his Yarmouth debut fourth on easier ground and opened his account with a deal left up his sleeve at the finish. He ran freely off the ordinary early pace and his rider's decision to allow him his head from halfway proved a wise move. The race was sewn up soon after he hit the front and there was plenty to like about the manner of his success, with the step up to this extra furlong proving right up his street. He is choicely bred, should get 1m before the season is out and has a host of Group race entries so it will be fascinating to see how he copes when upped to Pattern company as he looks assured to improve plenty again for this experience. (op 1-2 tchd 8-15 in a place)
Forsyte Saga ◆, a half-sister to this season's progressive Irish-trained three-year-old Many Colours, was suited by racing up with the pace and clearly knew her job. She not surprisingly lacked the speed required to go with the winner as that rival went for home, but was staying on again at the business end and evidently got every yard of this trip. A maiden looks hers for the taking in the coming weeks. (op 6-1 tchd 11-2 and 10-1)
King's Wonder, fifth on debut at Goodwood 109 days previously, came through to post an improved effort over this exra furlong and finished clear of the remainder in third. He can be ridden more prominently in the future and clearly has a future. (op 11-1 tchd 9-1)
St Jean Cap Ferrat, a slow starter on his debut at Newmarket 52 days previously, ran a fair race in defeat without ever seriously threatening and showed improved form. He may just be better off reverting to 6f for the short term and, considering he still looked green, should come on again for this experience. (op 25-1)
Looter(FR) got going too late in the day and is clearly still learning his trade. He will be eligible for a nursery mark after his next outing, but does look the type to make up into a better three-year-old. (tchd 25-1 and 33-1)

5307 STAG APPRENTICE H'CAP 1m 1f 218y
5:20 (5:20) (Class 5) (0-70,70) 3-Y-0+ **£3,238** (£963; £481; £240) **Stalls** High

Form RPR
6432 1 **Kalasam**10 5043 3-9-0 68 TolleyDean(3) 3 77
(W R Muir) *chsd ldrs: led over 1f out: rdn out* **5/1**2
6043 2 1 1/4 **Prime Number (IRE)**4 5211 5-9-4 67 JackMitchell(5) 1 74
(J Akehurst) *chsd ldrs: led and hung rt over 2f out: rdn and hdd over 1f out: styd on same pce* **9/2**1
0050 3 3/4 **Jackie Kiely**16 4850 6-9-4 65 (t) NeilBrown(3) 7 70
(R Brotherton) *hld up: rdn over 2f out: hdwy and hung rt fr over 1f out: nt rch ldrs* **9/1**
4411 4 4 **Majehar**19 4739 5-8-12 56 oh1 TravisBlock 5 53
(A G Newcombe) *hld up: styd on ins fnl f: nvr nrr* **5/1**2
5000 5 nk **Aegis (IRE)**12 4960 3-8-12 66 PatrickHills(3) 10 62
(B W Hills) *chsd ldr: rdn and ev ch over 2f out: wknd fnl f* **5/1**2
0006 6 3 1/2 **King's Majesty (IRE)**40 4107 5-9-7 70 KMay(5) 2 59
(V R A Dartnall) *led: sddle slipped sn after s: hdd over 2f out: wknd fnl f* **13/2**3
30-0 7 nk **Malech (IRE)**18 4772 4-8-13 62 JamieHamblett(5) 8 51
(K G Reveley) *prom: rdn over 3f out: wknd over 2f out* **28/1**
5005 8 1 **Golden Spectrum (IRE)**11 5020 8-8-11 60 (b) HaddenFrost(5) 6 47
(R A Harris) *hld up in tch: rdn and wknd over 2f out* **16/1**
5110 9 3 **Royal Indulgence**4 5188 7-9-7 65 LiamJones 9 46
(W M Brisbourne) *s.i.s: hld up: rdn over 4f out: wknd 3f out* **9/2**1
2m 5.51s (-2.79) **Going Correction** -0.05s/f (Good)
WFA 3 from 4yo+ 7lb **9** Ran SP% **119.0**
Speed ratings (Par 103): **109,108,107,104,103 101,100,100,97**
CSF £28.73 CT £200.56 TOTE £4.50: £1.80, £2.50, £3.20; EX 26.00 Trifecta £150.50 Part won. Pool: £212.00 - 0.34 winning units. Place 6 £ 22.59, Place 5 £ 9.12.
Owner A J De V Patrick & M J Caddy **Bred** C I T Racing Ltd **Trained** Lambourn, Berks
FOCUS
A modest handicap, confined to apprentice riders. It was a decent winning time for a race like this, 2.82 seconds quicker than the earlier maiden, and the form is rated around the runner-up.
Majehar Official explanation: jockey said gelding slipped on the bend
Golden Spectrum(IRE) Official explanation: vet said gelding finished distressed
T/Plt: £48.00 to a £1 stake. Pool: £53,807.80. 816.95 winning tickets. T/Qpdt: £4.30 to a £1 stake. Pool: £3,194.50. 547.60 winning tickets. CR

5133 LINGFIELD (L-H)
Tuesday, September 11
OFFICIAL GOING: Turf course - good to firm; all-weather - standard
Wind: Light, against Weather: Sunny, warm

5308 EUROPEAN BREEDERS' FUND MAIDEN FILLIES' STKS (DIV I) 7f (P)
1:40 (1:42) (Class 5) 2-Y-0 **£3,465** (£1,030; £515; £257) **Stalls** Low

Form RPR
00 1 **Blue Rhapsody**22 4662 2-9-0 0 KerrinMcEvoy 8 75+
(L M Cumani) *trckd ldng pair: effrt 2f out: shkn up to ld jst over 1f out: sn in command: idled and rdn out nr fin* **15/2**3
2 1 **Red Icon** 2-9-0 0 SebSanders 9 72
(R M Beckett) *leggy: lw: rn green in midfield and sn pushed along: prog u.p fr over 2f out: styd on wl fnl f to take 2nd nr fin* **4/1**1
3 shd **Riverscape (IRE)** 2-9-0 0 JimCrowley 7 72
(Mrs A J Perrett) *w'like: scope: sn chsd ldng trio but nt on terms: rdn and effrt over 2f out: green over 1f out: styd on wl fnl f: tk 3rd nr fin* **14/1**
0 4 hd **Magical Fantasy (USA)**31 4402 2-9-0 0 RichardHughes 1 72
(J Nicol) *led to 4f out: led again over 2f out: hrd rdn and hdd jst over 1f out: one pce and lost 2 pls nr fin* **7/1**2
5 1 1/4 **Vallani (IRE)** 2-9-0 0 AdamKirby 12 68
(W R Swinburn) *lengthy: unf: b.hind: dwlt: hld up in rr and wl off the pce: rdn 1/2-way: no real prog tl r.o fr over 1f out: nrst fin* **10/1**
006 6 1/2 **Exodia**15 4883 2-9-0 67 (p) MichaelHills 11 67
(Jane Chapple-Hyam) *w ldr: led 4f out to over 2f out: stl nrly upsides over 1f out: wknd ins fnl f* **4/1**1
0 7 2 1/2 **Lavender And Lace**31 4402 2-9-0 0 RyanMoore 10 61
(Sir Michael Stoute) *w'like: sn wl off the pce: rdn and sme prog fr 3f out: nvr rchd ldrs* **4/1**1
00 8 6 **Mia Haria**15 4875 2-9-0 0 DaneO'Neill 5 45
(B R Millman) *rdn and lost pl after 2f: struggling in rr after* **80/1**
00 9 1/2 **Latimer House (IRE)**30 4428 2-9-0 0 RobertHavlin 2 44
(Dr J D Scargill) *sn off the pce towards rr: rdn 1/2-way: no ch after* **100/1**
10 13 **Sue's Hawk (IRE)** 2-8-11 0 AndrewElliott(3) 3 10
(A P Jarvis) *lw: free to post: pild hrd and hld up: wknd 3f out: t.o* **20/1**
11 17 **Nouvelle Nova (IRE)** 2-9-0 0 JimmyQuinn 6 —
(G G Margarson) *w'like: scope: b.bkwd: v green and sn wl t.o* **10/1**
1m 25.26s (-0.63) **Going Correction** -0.175s/f (Stan) **11** Ran SP% **116.1**
Speed ratings (Par 92): **96,94,94,94,93 92,89,82,82,67 47**
CSF £36.71 TOTE £7.80: £3.10, £1.70, £4.80; EX 25.30.
Owner JMC Breed & Race Limited **Bred** Ronchalon Racing (uk) Ltd **Trained** Newmarket, Suffolk
FOCUS
The seemed to go a fair pace in this with Magic Fantasy and Exodia duelling from the start. As a result the winning time was 0.94 seconds faster than the second division but the form looks limited and has been rated conservatively.
NOTEBOOK
Blue Rhapsody, well beaten in a couple of turf maidens that have each produced a few subsequent winners, was always in a good position behind the leaders and initially found plenty when pulled out for her effort, but seemed to think she had done enough once in front. She probably has more improvement in her and where she goes next may depend on what mark she gets after this. (op 11-2 tchd 5-1)
Red Icon ◆, out of a winner over 1m 3f in France, took a while to realise what was required, but came home in good style and was closing down the admittedly idling winner near the line. She should come on for this and an extra furlong would not hurt. (op 7-2)
Riverscape(IRE), a half-sister to a couple of winners over middle-distances, was another that took a while to realise what was required but was finishing in pleasing style. Her pedigree suggests the best of her will be seen over much further than this, probably next year.
Magical Fantasy(USA), who was given a much more positive ride than on her Newmarket debut, was not given a lot of peace by Exodia though to her credit she lasted the longer of the pair. There should be a small race in her, possibly after one more run when she will qualify for a mark. (op 6-1 tchd 11-2)
Vallani(IRE) ◆, a 32,000euros filly out of a winner over 1m 2f, is from a yard not renowned for winning debutants but was noted staying on well against the inside rail late on. The distaff side of her pedigree is all stamina, so she can be expected to improve over further in due course. (op 16-1)
Exodia, the most experienced filly in the line up, tried to make use of that under a positive ride, but she and Magical Fantasy rather took each other on and she came out worst of that duel. Her mark of 67 gives some guide to the form, but she does not appear to be progressing herself and may be better off in nurseries. (op 7-1)
Lavender And Lace, easy to back, never really got involved and finished exactly the same distance behind Magical Fantasy as she did on her Newmarket debut despite starting the shorter price of the pair for this rematch. (op 11-4)
Sue's Hawk(IRE) Official explanation: jockey said filly ran too free

Nouvelle Nova(IRE), a half-sister to a couple of winning sprinters, was backed at fancy odds but her supporters soon knew their fate. (op 40-1)

5309 EUROPEAN BREEDERS' FUND MAIDEN FILLIES' STKS (DIV II) 7f (P)
2:10 (2:12) (Class 5) 2-Y-O **£3,465** (£1,030; £515; £257) **Stalls** Low

Form RPR

3230 **1** **Romany Princess (IRE)**[38] 4152 2-9-0 77 RichardHughes 7 75
(R Hannon) *hld up in tch gng wl: wnt 3rd over 2f out: effrt on inner and squeezed through to ld jst ins fnl f: sn clr* **7/2**[2]

0200 **2** *1 ¾* **Thought Is Free**[19] 4744 2-9-0 95 LPKeniry 10 70
(J S Moore) *lw: trckd ldr after 2f: led wl over 2f out: drvn and hdd jst ins fnl f: one pce* **5/4**[1]

60 **3** *1 ¾* **Private Code**[144] 1123 2-9-0 0 RyanMoore 3 66
(B J Meehan) *lw: lost prom pl after 2f and dropped to rr: effrt again over 2f out: styd on to take 3rd ins fnl f* **8/1**[3]

4 *1* **Bookish** 2-9-0 0 J-PGuillambert 6 63
(M Johnston) *lengthy: bit bkwd: led to wl over 2f out: sn rdn and outpcd: kpt on again fnl f* **11/1**

5 *1 ¾* **Qasayed (USA)** 2-9-0 0 KerrinMcEvoy 2 59
(C E Brittain) *w'like: towards rr: rdn 3f out: styd on fr over 1f out: n.d* **25/1**

06 **6** *shd* **Siryena**[34] 4293 2-9-0 0 SteveDrowne 5 58
(E A L Dunlop) *hld up towards rr on outer: outpcd over 2f out: styd on fr over 1f out: n.d* **33/1**

7 *nk* **Capefly** 2-9-0 0 SebSanders 8 58
(P F I Cole) *leggy: wnt prom after 2f: jnd ldr over 2f out: wknd rapidly jst over 1f out* **16/1**

00 **8** *5* **Fernlawn Hope (IRE)**[17] 4796 2-9-0 0 JimCrowley 9 45
(J A Osborne) *nvr on terms: struggling in rr fnl 3f* **66/1**

0 **9** *½* **Teadancer (IRE)**[20] 4709 2-8-11 0 RichardKingscote(3) 1 43
(J G Portman) *b.hind: w'like: s.i.s: prom to 1/2-way: sn wknd* **100/1**

00 **10** *1 ½* **Sweet Dane (IRE)**[12] 4962 2-8-11 0 JerryO'Dwyer(3) 11 40
(V Smith) *dwlt: a last: struggling fr 1/2-way* **100/1**

1m 26.2s (0.31) **Going Correction** -0.175s/f (Stan) **48** Ran SP% **102.3**
Speed ratings (Par 92): **91,89,87,85,83 83,83,77,77,75**
CSF £6.37 TOTE £3.70: £1.10, £1.10, £2.40; EX 7.40.
Owner M Sines **Bred** St Simon Foundation **Trained** East Everleigh, Wilts
■ Lekita was withdrawn (6/1, refused to enter stalls.) R4 applies, deduct 10p in the £.

FOCUS
Nothing like as competitive as the first division, made even less so when the third-favourite Lekita was withdrawn. The finish was dominated by the two market leaders, but a modest early pace meant that the winning time was 0.94 seconds slower than division one and the winner is the best guide.

NOTEBOOK
Romany Princess(IRE), trying this trip for the first time on this switch to sand, was always stalking her market rival, but took the brave route up the inside rail when asked for her effort. She had very little room to play with at one stage, but she proved the stronger physically by nudging the favourite out of the way and then quickening clear. As she was officially rated 18lb inferior to the runner-up in a her fate now lies in the hands of the Handicapper, which could be a problem as she has already been beaten twice in nurseries off similar marks. (tchd 9-2)
Thought Is Free, who has contested the Cherry Hinton and the Lowther since finishing runner-up in a Newmarket Listed contest, was presumably coming here in search of a confidence-boosting victory, but after taking it up on the home bend she could never stamp her authority on the contest and was literally bullied out of the way by her market rival. Unless the change of surface was not to her liking she is not going to be easy to place, but in any case she did not run to anything like her mark here. (op 11-8 tchd 13-8)
Private Code, not seen since showing a little ability in a couple of 5f maidens in April which were both won by horses that have gone on to be successful in Pattern company, rather ran in snatches over this longer trip but was going forward at the line and will have more opportunities now that she qualifies for a mark. (op 6-1 tchd 5-1)
Bookish, out of a half-sister to a couple of winners in France and to the dam of Silkwood, was given a positive ride and to her credit did not drop away as might have been expected once the favourite had gone past her. She can be expected to come on for this. (op 10-1)
Qasayed(USA), a 32,000gns filly out of a half-sister to a winner in France and to the dam of Carry On Katie, never really got involved but did show a little ability as the race progressed and it would be no surprise to see her do better with this experience under her belt. (tchd 22-1)
Siryena did not improve for the switch to sand, but does at least now qualify for a mark.
Capefly, a 110,000gns foal and a half-sister to a couple of winners including Mashaahed, showed up for a long way before appearing to blow up. She should last a bit longer next time. (tchd 14-1)
Sweet Dane(IRE) Official explanation: jockey said filly never travelled

5310 LINGFIELD PARK FOR CONFERENCES (S) STKS 1m 2f (P)
2:40 (2:40) (Class 6) 3-Y-O+ **£2,047** (£604; £302) **Stalls** Low

Form RPR

1005 **1** **Birkside**[18] 4763 4-9-9 70 PaulDoe 13 61
(S Dow) *racd wd in tch: prog 3f out: led over 2f out and sn kicked wl clr: kpt on fnl f: unchal* **9/2**[2]

0-05 **2** *1 ¾* **Sekula Pata (NZ)**[4] 5188 8-9-1 62 (b) AlanCreighton(3) 14 53
(E J Creighton) *trckd ldrs: drvn to chse clr wnr over 1f out: styd on: nvr able to chal* **14/1**

030 **3** *nk* **Mr Napoleon (IRE)**[27] 4517 5-9-4 58 J-PGuillambert 6 52
(G Prodromou) *hld up in rr: nt clr run wl over 2f out and sn swtchd to outer: drvn and r.o fr over 1f out: nrst fin* **8/1**[3]

2044 **4** *hd* **Lord Of Dreams (IRE)**[11] 5020 5-9-4 64 SebSanders 3 52+
(D W P Arbuthnot) *hld up towards rr: nt clr run fr wl over 2f out to jst over 1f out: no ch after: r.o wl fnl f* **11/10**[1]

0060 **5** *1 ¼* **Mamichor**[28] 4469 4-9-9 43 RichardSmith 8 54
(B R Johnson) *hld up wl in rr: prog on outer fr 3f out: pressed for 2nd 1f out: kpt on same pce after* **25/1**

5400 **6** *1 ¼* **Fairly Honest**[27] 4491 3-8-4 54 WilliamCarson(7) 2 47+
(P W Hiatt) *hld up wl in rr: trapped on inner fr 3f out tl over 1f out: r.o fnl f: no ch* **16/1**

0052 **7** *hd* **Give Evidence**[12] 4961 3-8-8 48 AndrewElliott(3) 7 46
(A P Jarvis) *lw: disp ld to over 4f out: rdn to ld briefly wl over 2f out: chsd wnr to over 1f out: wknd rapidly fnl f* **14/1**

-000 **8** *2 ½* **Ron In Ernest**[18] 4758 3-8-11 52 SteveDrowne 12 41
(J A Geake) *prom: rdn and n.m.r over 2f out: wknd over 1f out* **66/1**

4000 **9** *1 ¼* **Fulvio (USA)**[14] 4914 7-9-4 41 (v) IanMongan 9 39
(P Howling) *hld up towards rr: nt clr run on inner over 2f out and over 1f out: nvr any ch* **40/1**

5305 **10** *nk* **Hamilton House**[12] 4961 3-8-11 56 JimmyQuinn 11 38
(M H Tompkins) *in tch: chsng ldrs and rdn over 2f out: sn wknd* **16/1**

4420 **11** *5* **Miss Porcia**[11] 4998 6-8-13 50 TPO'Shea 5 23
(P A Blockley) *lw: prom tl wknd u.p 3f out* **9/1**

300 **12** *5* **Kastan**[24] 4591 3-8-11 43 DavidKinsella 1 18
(B Palling) *disp ld tl def advantage over 4f out: hdd wl over 2f out: wknd rapidly over 1f out* **66/1**

0000 **13** *4* **Veba (USA)**[16] 4853 4-8-11 40 GHannon(7) 10 10
(M D I Usher) *s.v.s: sn in tch in rr: wknd 3f out* **40/1**

0000 **14** *1 ¼* **Rose Muwasim**[17] 4802 4-8-10 40 (p) DominicFox(3) 4 3
(S Parr) *b.hind: a in rr: no ch fnl 3f* **100/1**

2m 6.54s (-1.25) **Going Correction** -0.175s/f (Stan)
WFA 3 from 4yo+ 7lb **14** Ran SP% **124.7**
Speed ratings (Par 101): **98,96,96,96,95 94,94,92,91,90 86,82,79,78**
CSF £65.86 TOTE £5.20: £1.80, £3.10, £3.40; EX 75.70.The winner was bought in for £6,400.
Lord of Dreams (IRE) was claimed by G. L. Moore for £6,000
Owner I Hedgecock **Bred** Pendley Farm **Trained** Epsom, Surrey

FOCUS
A routine seller run at an ordinary pace and the finish was dominated by those most favoured by the weights with the form rated around the first three. Only two of these had previously been successful this year, including the winner, and in such a big field there was always the possibility that a few could find traffic problems.
Lord Of Dreams(IRE) Official explanation: jockey said horse was denied a clear run
Veba(USA) Official explanation: trainer said gelding finished distressed

5311 BOOK YOUR TICKETS ONLINE MEDIAN AUCTION MAIDEN STKS 1m 4f (P)
3:10 (3:10) (Class 6) 3-4-Y-O **£2,730** (£806; £403) **Stalls** Low

Form RPR

6-0 **1** **Valrhona (IRE)**[94] 2455 3-8-12 0 SebSanders 6 80+
(J Noseda) *lw: hld up in tch: pressed ldr over 4f out: led over 2f out: rdn clr over 1f out* **9/2**[3]

4-22 **2** *5* **Gordonsville**[62] 3415 4-9-12 74 RyanMoore 5 76
(A M Balding) *reluctant to enter stalls: trckd ldr after 2f: led over 4f out: drvn and hdd over 2f out: no ch w wnr over 1f out* **15/8**[1]

02-0 **3** *5* **River Deuce**[136] 1289 3-9-3 70 JimmyQuinn 4 68
(M H Tompkins) *hld up bhd ldrs: effrt to go 3rd over 3f out: outpcd and no ch after* **15/2**

52 **4** *8* **Power Player**[11] 5019 3-9-3 0 TPO'Shea 1 55
(D J Coakley) *led 1f: restrained: last 1/2-way: trapped bhd wkng rivals over 4f out to over 3f out and no ch after: no imp fnl 2f* **7/1**

025 **5** *6* **Precept**[31] 4403 3-8-12 75 DaneO'Neill 2 41
(H Candy) *cl up: rdn over 4f out: sn struggling and btn* **9/4**[2]

6666 **6** *3 ½* **Acosta**[12] 4961 3-8-10 40 MatthewCosham(7) 3 40
(Dr J R J Naylor) *led after 1f to over 4f out: sn wknd* **100/1**

2m 31.65s (-2.74) **Going Correction** -0.175s/f (Stan)
WFA 3 from 4yo 9lb **6** Ran SP% **109.0**
Speed ratings (Par 101): **102,98,95,90,86 83**
CSF £12.59 TOTE £5.10: £1.70, £1.20; EX 13.40.
Owner Ballygallon Stud Limited **Bred** Ballygallon Stud **Trained** Newmarket, Suffolk

FOCUS
A maiden lacking strength in depth, but the pace was more solid that is often the case for races over this trip here, especially given the small field, and they finished strung out like yesterday's washing. The form is rated through the runner-up but without much confidence.

5312 LINGFIELDPARK.CO.UK H'CAP 7f (P)
3:40 (3:41) (Class 4) (0-80,80) 3-Y-O+ **£4,857** (£1,445; £722; £360) **Stalls** Low

Form RPR

0014 **1** **Hessian (IRE)**[15] 4889 3-8-5 **67** JimmyQuinn 9 74
(P Howling) *lw: settled in midfield: prog on outer over 2f out: drvn to chal over 1f out: led ins fnl f: styd on wl* **20/1**

0400 **2** *¾* **Russian Symphony (USA)**[45] 3943 6-9-6 **78** RobertHavlin 10 85
(C R Egerton) *lw: prom: rdn to chse ldr jst over 2f out: led 1f out: sn hdd: styd on* **25/1**

0000 **3** *shd* **Yaroslav (USA)**[17] 4811 3-9-3 **79** (b) SteveDrowne 13 84+
(R Charlton) *hld up in last trio: prog on outer 2f out: r.o wl fnl f: too much to do* **11/2**[3]

6003 **4** *1* **Carmenero (GER)**[13] 4949 4-9-3 **75** SaleemGolam 1 79
(W R Muir) *lw: awkward s: sn trckd ldrs: rdn and cl up over 1f out: styd on same pce* **20/1**

1141 **5** *nk* **Cativo Cavallino**[24] 4594 4-8-9 **72** NataliaGemelova(5) 3 75
(J E Long) *lw: mde most: drvn and hdd 1f out: one pce fnl f* **7/1**

6403 **6** *hd* **Swinbrook (USA)**[17] 4816 6-9-6 **78** SebSanders 5 80
(J A R Toller) *lw: settled in midfield on inner: rdn over 2f out: drvn and chsng ldrs fnl f: one pce nr fin* **4/1**[2]

0000 **7** *nk* **Moayed**[13] 4949 8-9-3 **75** (b) IanMongan 6 77
(N P Littmoden) *rousted along to rch midfield: drvn over 2f out: one pce and no prog* **20/1**

266- **8** *shd* **Sophia Gardens**[330] 6018 3-8-2 **67** WilliamBuick(3) 7 66
(D W P Arbuthnot) *a abt same pl: rdn and nt qckn 2f out: kpt on fnl f* **50/1**

4016 **9** *1 ¼* **Coeur Courageux (FR)**[22] 4672 5-9-8 **80** (t) RyanMoore 12 81+
(G L Moore) *lw: stdd s: hld up in last: lft bhd over 2f out: prog 1f out: styng on wl but no ch whn eased fnl 75yds* **10/3**[1]

0032 **10** *3 ½* **Rocker**[9] 5066 3-8-9 **71** (v) DaneO'Neill 11 58
(B R Johnson) *t.k.h: hld up in rr: no prog over 2f out* **20/1**

1354 **11** *nk* **Classira (IRE)**[20] 4710 3-9-1 **77** (p) PhilipRobinson 2 63
(M A Jarvis) *lw: w ldr to over 2f out: wknd over 1f out* **9/1**

-060 **12** *nk* **St Petersburg**[164] 848 7-9-6 **78** AmirQuinn 4 65
(J R Boyle) *taken down early: dwlt: hld up in rr: pushed along and no prog on inner fnl 2f: nvr nr ldrs* **25/1**

565 **13** *2 ½* **Sun Catcher (IRE)**[18] 4767 4-9-0 **72** (b) RichardHughes 8 52
(R Hannon) *dwlt: a in rr: rdn and struggling 3f out* **8/1**

1m 23.92s (-1.97) **Going Correction** -0.175s/f (Stan)
WFA 3 from 4yo+ 4lb **13** Ran SP% **120.8**
Speed ratings (Par 105): **104,103,103,101,101 101,100,100,99,95 95,94,91**
CSF £417.83 CT £2040.40 TOTE £30.30: £7.50, £9.70, £2.10; EX 805.50.
Owner Miss T J Fitzgerald **Bred** Rathbarry Stud **Trained** Newmarket, Suffolk

FOCUS
A typical Lingfield Polytrack handicap over this sort of trip with little covering the principals at the line. The form is rated at face value but does not look the most solid.

5313 EUROPEAN BREEDERS' FUND MEDIAN AUCTION MAIDEN STKS 6f
4:10 (4:12) (Class 6) 2-Y-O **£2,914** (£867; £433; £216) **Stalls** High

Form RPR

2 **1** **Missit (IRE)**[145] 1101 2-8-12 0 TPO'Shea 10 86+
(M R Channon) *w ldr: led 1/2-way: drew clr fr 2f out: comf* **11/8**[1]

2 *5* **Elizabeth Swann** 2-8-12 0 RichardHughes 4 71
(R Hannon) *leggy: scope: w ldng pair: chsd wnr fnl 2f: kpt on but no ch* **5/1**

4244 **3** *1 ¾* **Freudian Slip**[15] 4882 2-8-12 65 PaulDoe 12 66
(S Curran) *leggy: racd against nr side rail: mde most to 1/2-way: outpcd fr 2f out: hrd rdn and plugged on* **33/1**

2 **4** *shd* **Sunny Sprite**[12] 4962 2-9-3 0 KerrinMcEvoy 6 70
(J M P Eustace) *lw: cl up: pushed along 2f out: sn outpcd: chal for 3rd fnl f: kpt on* **8/1**

43 **5** *1* **Carnival Queen**[41] 4077 2-8-12 0 RyanMoore 9 62
(J R Fanshawe) *b. bit bkwd: in tch in midfield: effrt over 2f out: one pce and n.d over 1f out* **9/2**[3]

0 **6** *1* **Eseej (USA)**[20] 4725 2-9-3 0 RHills 1 64
(B W Hills) *racd towards outer: w ldrs 4f: green and fdd* **7/2**[2]

406 **7** *1* **Janet's Delight**[30] 4417 2-8-5 50 WilliamCarson(7) 13 56
(S Curran) *w'like: cl up: rdn and fdd fr 2f out* **100/1**

0 **8** *5* **Imperial Mark (IRE)**[12] 4962 2-9-0 0 JerryO'Dwyer(3) 5 46
(P J O'Gorman) *t.k.h: hld up in tch: struggling and btn wl over 2f out* **100/1**

9 *2 1/2* **Lady Docker (IRE)** 2-8-12 0 DaneO'Neill 11 34
(H J L Dunlop) *leggy: bit bkwd: s.s: nvr on terms: bhd fr over 2f out* **50/1**

10 *5* **Man Appeal** 2-8-12 0 SteveDrowne 3 19
(B J Meehan) *w'like: b.hind: racd on outer: nvr on terms: bhd fnl 2f* **66/1**

000 **11** *2 1/2* **Newcastle Sam**[13] 4946 2-9-3 30 FrankieMcDonald 8 16
(J J Bridger) *toiling in rr after 2f: bhd after* **100/1**

12 *12* **Milloaks (IRE)** 2-8-9 0 AlanCreighton(3) 2 —
(E J Creighton) *wnt lft s: nvr on terms: bhd fr 1/2-way: t.o* **100/1**

69.78 secs (-1.89) **Going Correction** -0.325s/f (Firm) **12** Ran SP% **120.6**
Speed ratings (Par 93): **99,92,90,89,88 87,85,79,75,69 65,49**
CSF £8.92 TOTE £2.50: £1.10, £2.40, £4.40; EX 11.10.
Owner Tim Corby **Bred** Churchtown House Stud **Trained** West Ilsley, Berks

FOCUS
Probably only an average maiden and not as competitive as the numbers might suggest, but the time was decent and the winner looks above average with the form capable of being rated higher. The front three held those positions virtually throughout and little else ever got into it.

NOTEBOOK
Missit(IRE), not seen since finishing runner-up in a maiden at the Newmarket Craven meeting - a race that has produced a handful of subsequent winners including Romany Princess who was successful earlier on this card - was always to the fore and when asked to go and win her race she fairly bolted clear. She clearly has a bright future and is in the Cheveley Park, but whether she is up to that is debatable and the £250000 Tattersalls October Auction Stakes on the same day may be a more tempting target. (op 5-4 tchd 13-8)
Elizabeth Swann, a 45,000gns filly out of a mare that was successful over this trip, was soon in a handy position and although she could not cope with the winner she was very much second best. She will not always come up against the likes of the winner and her pedigree suggests this sort of trip will always suit her best. (op 6-1 tchd 9-2 and 4-1 in a place)
Freudian Slip, down in trip, was soon able to bag the favoured stands' rail and that probably helped her keep on going to make the frame. She is more exposed than most, but this was not the first time she has run better than might be anticipated in races like this. She would be even more interesting if contesting a nursery off her current mark.
Sunny Sprite, narrowly beaten on his debut over this trip on the Polytrack here, looked to need further then and this performance merely confirmed that view. (op 13-2 tchd 10-1)
Carnival Queen never got involved, but she needed this for a mark and that opens up plenty more options for her. (op 5-1 tchd 6-1)
Eseej(USA), who got a bit warm beforehand, was the only one of those that showed up early not to figure in the finish, but he had it to from his draw in any case and rather found himself exposed on the outside of the field. He still looked to need this experience and the fact that he attracted market support again suggests he is thought capable of much better. (op 9-2 tchd 3-1)
Lady Docker(IRE) Official explanation: jockey said filly missed the break

5314 LINGFIELD PARK FOR WEDDINGS NURSERY 7f
4:40 (4:41) (Class 5) (0-75,75) 2-Y-O **£3,238** (£963; £481; £240) **Stalls** High

Form RPR

035 **1** **Clifton Dancer**[18] 4775 2-9-1 **72** RichardKingscote(3) 7 79
(Tom Dascombe) *mde virtually all: drvn over 1f out: jst hld on* **11/2**[1]

055 **2** *shd* **Shadow Cabinet (IRE)**[15] 4883 2-8-10 **67** AndrewElliott(3) 10 74
(M L W Bell) *prom: rdn to chse wnr 2f out: str chal fnl f: jst failed* **10/1**

6003 **3** *1 1/4* **Flying Applause**[7] 5117 2-8-11 **65** RichardHughes 6 68
(A King) *taken down early: cl up: rdn over 2f out: nrly upsides ins fnl f: no ex* **10/1**

006 **4** *3* **Gipsy Prince**[34] 4279 2-8-12 **66** JimmyQuinn 14 62
(M G Quinlan) *cl up on nr side: nt qckn 2f out: kpt on one pce after* **8/1**[3]

5040 **5** *3/4* **Leading Edge (IRE)**[8] 5089 2-8-10 **64** TPO'Shea 12 58
(M R Channon) *lw: w wnr to over 2f out: grad fdd u.p* **20/1**

0600 **6** *1 1/2* **Classical Rhythm (IRE)**[10] 5053 2-8-11 **65** AmirQuinn 16 55
(J R Boyle) *wl in rr: rdn and last of main gp 1/2-way: prog u.p 2f out: kpt on* **14/1**

000 **7** *1 3/4* **Kashmina**[18] 4774 2-9-0 **68** SteveDrowne 5 53+
(M R Channon) *dwlt: last and sn detached: t.o 1/2-way: styd on fr 2f out: no ch but clsng whn eased 1f out: shkn up and r.o nr fin* **50/1**

000 **8** *hd* **Weight In Gold**[48] 3849 2-7-12 **52** NickyMackay 17 37
(P J McBride) *racd nr side: nvr bttr than midfield: struggling u.p over 2f out* **9/1**

1210 **9** *1/2* **What Katie Did (IRE)**[10] 5053 2-9-7 **75** JimCrowley 4 58
(J A Osborne) *lw: racd on outer: wl in tch: nt on terms fr over 2f out: no ch after* **10/1**

0421 **10** *3 1/2* **Townkab (IRE)**[7] 5109 2-9-2 **70** 6ex TGMcLaughlin 8 44
(N P Littmoden) *racd on outer: in tch to 1/2-way: nt on terms after: wknd* **7/1**[2]

226 **11** *2 1/2* **Harbour Blues**[34] 4273 2-9-2 **70** KerrinMcEvoy 13 38
(C E Brittain) *nvr on terms w ldrs: rdn and hanging bdly lft fr over 2f out* **9/1**

4106 **12** *2 1/2* **Maybe I Will (IRE)**[7] 5109 2-9-3 **71** DaneO'Neill 9 32
(R Hannon) *nvr beyond midfield: rdn and btn over 2f out: wknd over 1f out* **20/1**

464 **13** *5* **Captain Esteem**[78] 2949 2-9-7 **75** MichaelHills 2 23
(B W Hills) *lw: racd on outer: wl in tch to 3f out: eased whn no ch wl over 1f out* **16/1**

033 **14** *2 1/2* **Cordon Bleu (IRE)**[12] 4963 2-9-2 **70** J-PGuillambert 1 12+
(M Johnston) *racd on wd outside: in tch to 3f out: wknd and eased over 2f out* **20/1**

4246 **15** *3* **Ruby Delta**[20] 4709 2-9-3 **71** SebSanders 15 5+
(P D Cundell) *racd against nrside rail: cl up tl wknd wl over 2f out: sn eased* **8/1**[3]

1m 22.97s (-1.24) **Going Correction** -0.325s/f (Firm) **15** Ran SP% **126.2**
Speed ratings (Par 95): **94,93,92,89,88 86,84,84,83,79 76,73,68,65,61**
CSF £59.17 CT £555.21 TOTE £6.90: £2.30, £4.30, £4.60; EX 80.70.
Owner Clifton Partners **Bred** Redmyre Bloodstock & Stuart McPhee **Trained** Lambourn, Berks

FOCUS
An ordinary nursery in which the front three pulled clear. As is often the case on the straight turf track here, those that raced closest to the stands' rail were at an advantage. The form looks solid but is ordinary.

NOTEBOOK
Clifton Dancer, making her nursery debut over an extra furlong after running so well in a decent little sales race at Newmarket last time, was soon in front and was able to gradually edge across to the stands' rail as the race progressed. That may have been crucial, as she managed to just about hold on to win with nothing to spare and had the runner-up been racing against the rail, the result would probably have been different. (op 6-1)
Shadow Cabinet(IRE), another making his nursery debut, put in a determined late effort but the favourite had the advantage of the rail and he could never quite get there. There should be a similar race in him. (tchd 12-1)
Flying Applause had every chance on this return to turf and posted another decent effort. He seems to be gradually improving with racing and looks to have the ability to win a race like this. (op 12-1 tchd 14-1)
Gipsy Prince, unplaced in three maidens and trying his longest trip to date on this nursery debut, was well supported in the market. Racing on the best part of the track, he ran his best race so far and was not beaten through lack of stamina. (op 9-2)
Leading Edge(IRE), trying her longest trip to date on her seventh outing, was not ridden as though stamina was going to be an issue but she performed as though she did not see it out, at least when ridden this way. (tchd 16-1)
Classical Rhythm(IRE) conceded any advantage he may have had from his draw by being dropped out and, as was the case at Sandown, did not get going until it was too late. Official explanation: jockey said colt never travelled
Kashmina, unplaced at big prices in three turf maidens, ran a strange race on this nursery debut as she threatened to finish tailed off at halfway, but then consented to run on past beaten horses late. She may not be entirely straightforward, but may have a bit more ability than she has shown thus far.
Harbour Blues Official explanation: jockey said colt hung left; vet said colt returned lame behind
Ruby Delta Official explanation: jockey said colt hung left

5315 LINGFIELDPARK.CO.UK MAIDEN STKS 7f
5:10 (5:15) (Class 5) 3-Y-0+ **£2,817** (£838; £418; £209) **Stalls** High

Form RPR

1 **Hucking Heist** 3-9-3 0 SteveDrowne 1 74+
(J R Best) *w'like: free to post: rn green and sn wl bhd in last: rapid prog on outer fr 2f out: str run to ld ins fnl f: sn clr* **16/1**

-032 **2** *1 1/4* **Laura's Best (IRE)**[27] 4514 3-8-12 64 JimCrowley 5 66
(W J Haggas) *hld up on outer: stdy prog fr over 2f out: rdn to ld 1f out: hdd and outpcd ins fnl f* **7/4**[1]

5242 **3** *1 3/4* **Red Blossom**[10] 5036 3-8-12 67 SebSanders 2 61
(Sir Mark Prescott) *wnt lft s: racd against r nrside rail and trckd ldrs: prog to chal 2f out: upsides 1f out but looked most reluctant: sn btn* **5/2**[2]

- **4** *1 1/4* **Cinnamon Hill** 3-8-12 0 RyanMoore 3 58
(Eve Johnson Houghton) *w'like: unruly bhd stalls: s.s: bhd in last pair: prog over 2f out: swtchd lft over 1f out: nudged along and styd on* **8/1**

6-5 **5** *3/4* **Edge End**[17] 4808 3-9-3 0 PaulDoe 6 61
(R A Farrant) *mde most: drvn 2f out: hdd 1f out: wknd* **20/1**

0-3 **6** *2* **Capania (IRE)**[15] 4905 3-8-12 0 DaneO'Neill 4 50
(Pat Eddery) *b. t.k.h: racd on outer: hld up bhd ldrs: fdd fr over 2f out: eased fnl f* **6/1**[3]

0 **7** *nk* **Smash Hit (IRE)**[22] 4666 4-9-4 0 NeilChalmers(3) 10 57
(David Pinder) *w'like: w ldrs to over 2f out: wknd over 1f out* **40/1**

0 **8** *1 1/4* **Barbar**[15] 4908 4-9-7 0 IanMongan 9 53
(Eve Johnson Houghton) *lw: w ldrs to 2f out: wknd rapidly jst over 1f out* **33/1**

6030 **9** *7* **Shavoulin (USA)**[26] 4541 3-9-3 78 PaulEddery 8 32
(Christian Wroe) *chsd ldrs: rdn 3f out: sn struggling* **10/1**

00 **10** *1 1/2* **Abtak (IRE)**[7] 5121 7-9-2 45 LPKeniry 7 25
(P Burgoyne) *chsd ldrs: rdn 3f out: wknd over 2f out* **100/1**

11 *9* **Tinsy** 3-8-12 0 KerrinMcEvoy 11 —
(J L Spearing) *w'like: bit bkwd: free to post: w ldrs 2f: cl up tl wknd wl over 2f out: t.o* **14/1**

1m 23.34s (-0.87) **Going Correction** -0.325s/f (Firm)
WFA 3 from 4yo+ 4lb **11** Ran SP% **123.1**
Speed ratings (Par 103): **91,89,87,86,85 83,82,81,73,71 61**
CSF £45.51 TOTE £15.30: £3.90, £1.20, £1.30; EX 65.70 Place 6 £ 118.85, Place 5 £ 46.16.
Owner Hucking Horses **Bred** Miss S N Ralphs **Trained** Hucking, Kent

FOCUS
An extraordinary race with the winner coming from a tailed-off last to score. However, the winning time was moderate, 0.37 seconds slower than the preceding nursery, which may put a question mark against the form, which is best rated through the runner-up.
T/Plt: £184.60 to a £1 stake. Pool: £52,210.15. 206.40 winning tickets. T/Qpdt: £180.40 to a £1 stake. Pool: £2,707.00. 11.10 winning tickets. JN

5316 - 5320a (Foreign Racing) - See Raceform Interactive

4564 DONCASTER (L-H)
Wednesday, September 12

OFFICIAL GOING: Good to firm (good in places; 9.0)
After a mainly dry time 60mm water was put down on the track over the previous month resulting in ' nice quick ground, a lovely surface'.
Wind: almost nil Weather: Fine and warm

5321 TORNE VALLEY LTD E B F AHT MAIDEN STKS 1m (S)
2:05 (2:09) (Class 4) 2-Y-O **£6,477** (£1,927; £963; £481) **Stalls** High

Form RPR

2 **1** **Kandahar Run**[27] 4547 2-9-3 0 TedDurcan 6 89
(H R A Cecil) *trckd ldng pair: hdwy over 2f out: led wl over 1f out: rdn and edgd lft ent fnl f: styd on wl* **7/2**[2]

2 *1 1/4* **Tiger Dream** 2-9-3 0 NCallan 3 86+
(K A Ryan) *lengthy: scope: midfield: gd hdwy on outer over 2f out: rdn to chse wnr ent fnl f: kpt on wl* **5/1**[3]

2 **3** *1 3/4* **Rochefort (IRE)**[19] 4777 2-9-3 0 JimmyFortune 5 82
(J H M Gosden) *trckd ldrs: hdwy over 2f out: rdn wl over 1f out: kpt on same pce* **15/8**[1]

5 **4** *1 3/4* **Piermarini**[29] 4482 2-9-3 0 GregFairley 10 78
(M Johnston) *cl up: led after 3f: rdn along over 2f out: hdd wl over 1f out and grad wknd* **28/1**

02 **5** *3 1/2* **Moville (IRE)**[26] 4586 2-9-3 0 MichaelHills 11 70
(B W Hills) *led 3f: cl up tl rdn wl over 2f out and grad wknd* **15/2**

6 *3/4* **Angel Rock (IRE)** 2-9-3 0 RyanMoore 4 68
(P W Chapple-Hyam) *leggy: scope: towards rr: effrt over 2f out: sn rdn along and styd on ins fnl f* **14/1**

7 *hd* **Mikhail Fokine (IRE)**[24] 4645 2-9-3 0 JMurtagh 8 68
(A P O'Brien, Ire) *cmpt: chsd ldrs: rdn along over 2f out and sn btn* **7/1**

0 **8** *1/2* **Ablaan (USA)**[26] 4584 2-9-3 0 DarryllHolland 9 67
(M F De Kock, South Africa) *rangy: scope: in tch: rdn along wl over 2f out: sn one pce* **50/1**

9 *1* **Full Speed (GER)** 2-9-3 0.. JamieSpencer 1 64
(G A Swinbank) *rangy: scope: wnt lft s and s.i.s: a in rr* **33/1**

10 *¾* **House Of Tudor** 2-9-3 0.. KerrinMcEvoy 2 63
(J H M Gosden) *rangy: unf: wnt lft s: a in rr* **33/1**

11 *8* **Real Pearl** 2-9-3 0.. RichardMullen 7 44
(T D Easterby) *rangy: unf: a in rr* **100/1**

1m 39.0s (-2.51) **Going Correction** -0.425s/f (Firm) **11** Ran SP% **116.9**
Speed ratings (Par 97): **95,93,92,90,86 86,85,85,84,83 75**
CSF £20.42 TOTE £3.90: £1.50, £1.80, £1.40; EX 22.40 Trifecta £213.10 Pool £402.31 - 1.34 winning units..

Owner Ammerland Verwaltung GmbH & Co KG **Bred** Britton House Stud **Trained** Newmarket, Suffolk

FOCUS

This looked like a decent maiden, although the early pace was just ordinary, and the winner is rated a slight improver on his debut in a strong race, so the form should work out. They raced against the stands'-side rail.

NOTEBOOK

Kandahar Run ◆ finished well clear of the remainder when second in a good maiden at Sandown on his debut and he showed he has gone the right way since then with a convincing success in what looked another decent contest. He got first run on the eventual runner-up, but found extra when that one moved to within about a length inside the final furlong and displayed a likeably attitude under pressure. He is entered in both the Royal Lodge and the Racing Post Trophy, but his trainer suggested he may look for a conditions race instead if he decides a Group race will come a little soon in this horse's development. Henry Cecil also said he expects the winner to be a "much better horse next year". (op 9-4)

Tiger Dream ◆, a 195,000euros yearling, 150,000gns two-year-old, son of Oasis Dream, and half-brother to the top-class Italian performer Distant Way, a 15-time winner at around 7f-1m2f, out of a high-class multiple 1m2f-1m3f winner in Italy, is entered in both the Royal Lodge and the Racing Post Trophy. Considering his sire it was a little surprising to see him make his racecourse debut over a trip this far, but he shaped very promisingly indeed behind the potentially smart winner. Having been ridden with restraint, he showed a good change of pace when asked to move into a challenging position and he briefly looked a real threat, although his effort flattened out late on, with the winner possibly finding more in front. He looks a serious prospect. (op 11-2)

Rochefort(IRE), a promising third when favourite on soft ground over 7f on the July on his debut, confirmed the ability he showed there with a useful effort in defeat. Admittedly he was again a beaten favourite, but he did not look to do too much wrong. (op 9-4 tchd 5-2 in a place)

Piermarini was well held in a good race on his debut at Nottingham, but this was a lot better. He should come into his own when sent over further next year. (op 25-1)

Moville(IRE) could not match the form he showed when second on the July course on his previous start, but he was not given a hard time once his chance had gone and, now qualified for a nursery mark, he could be one to keep an eye on. (op 7-1)

Angel Rock(IRE), a son of Rock Of Gibraltar, half-brother to high-class miler Spirit Of Desert, has been entered in the Racing Post Trophy. This was a respectable debut and he should know more next time. (op 16-1)

Mikhail Fokine(IRE) failed to confirm the promise he showed when third on his debut over 7f at Leopardstown and this was disappointing. (op 6-1)

Ablaan(USA) showed a little more than on his debut at Newmarket, but he was still well held.

5322 EUROPEAN BREEDERS' FUND CARRIE RED FILLIES' NURSERY 6f 110y

2:40 (2:40) (Class 2) 2-Y-O **£25,908** (£7,708; £3,852; £1,924) **Stalls** High

Form RPR

2521 **1** **Royal Confidence**[28] 4506 2-8-2 **84**............................ WilliamBuick(3) 16 90
(B W Hills) *a.p stands' side: hdwy to ld and overall ldr over 2f out: rdn over 1f out: drvn ins fnl f and hld on wl* **5/1**[1]

451 **2** *hd* **Crystany (IRE)**[11] 5042 2-8-6 **85** ow1............................ TedDurcan 11 90
(H R A Cecil) *lw: hld up towards rr stands' side: hdwy 2f out: rdn to chal ins fnl f and ev ch tl drvn and nt qckn nr fin* **6/1**[2]

0613 **3** *¾* **Cristal Clear (IRE)**[16] 4899 2-8-7 **86**............................ DavidAllan 19 89
(T D Easterby) *in rr stands' side: swtchd lft and gd hdwy wl over 1f out: str run ent fnl f: sn rdn: carried hd high and hung lft ins fnl f: no ex towards fin* **15/2**

124 **4** *nk* **Broken Applause (IRE)**[37] 4225 2-8-6 **85**............................ PaulHanagan 9 87
(R A Fahey) *in rr stands' side: gd hdwy wl over 1f out: rdn and styng on wl whn hmpd ins fnl f: no ex towards fin* **20/1**

510 **5** *¾* **Serena's Storm (IRE)**[45] 3988 2-8-0 **79**............................ JimmyQuinn 2 79
(J J Quinn) *hld up far side: hdwy 2f out: sn rdn and styd on strly ins fnl f: nrst fin* **20/1**

2011 **6** *½* **Sophie's Girl**[15] 4923 2-7-9 **81**............................ MCGeran(7) 20 80
(P W Chapple-Hyam) *in tch stands' side: hdwy over 2f out: rdn and edgd rt over 1f out: kpt on u.p ins fnl f* **13/2**[3]

1435 **7** *hd* **Miss Bootylishes**[18] 4819 2-8-2 **86** oh5 ow9.......... KevinGhunowa(5) 13 84
(A B Haynes) *hmpd s and in rr stands' side: rdn along and hdwy 2f out: styd on u.p ins fnl f: nrst fin* **100/1**

041 **8** *nk* **Close To Paradise (IRE)**[42] 4074 2-7-12 **77**............................ PaulFessey 14 74
(E A L Dunlop) *in tch stands' side: hdwy over 2f out: rdn to chal over 1f out: drvn and wknd ins fnl f* **33/1**

1530 **9** *nk* **Kay Es Jay (FR)**[25] 4626 2-9-7 **100**............................ MichaelHills 18 97
(B W Hills) *towards rr stands' side: hdwy over 2f out: rdn and edgd rt over 1f out: nt rch ldrs* **16/1**

0201 **10** *1 ¼* **Dresden Doll (USA)**[19] 4756 2-7-9 **79**............................ LukeMorris(5) 17 72
(M L W Bell) *prom stands' side: rdn along over 2f out: sn drvn and grad wknd appr fnl f* **20/1**

122 **11** *shd* **Anosti**[16] 4899 2-8-13 **92**............................ NCallan 3 85
(K A Ryan) *hld up far side: effrt over 2f out: sn rdn and no imp* **8/1**

524 **12** *nk* **Geestring (IRE)**[19] 4775 2-7-12 **77** oh2............................ FrancisNorton 12 69
(R Hannon) *wnt rt s and sn led: rdn along and hdd over 2f out: drvn and wkng whn hung rt appr fnl f* **12/1**

1005 **13** *½* **Jennifers Joy (IRE)**[20] 4737 2-7-12 **77** oh1............................ NickyMackay 21 68
(M R Channon) *cl up stands' rail: rdn along 2f out: wkng whn hmpd ent fnl f* **33/1**

6214 **14** *shd* **Mey Blossom**[15] 4921 2-8-0 **84**............................ NataliaGemelova(5) 6 74
(R M Whitaker) *trckd ldrs far side: hdwy over 2f out: rdn and ch over 1f out: sn wknd* **50/1**

1102 **15** *1 ¼* **La Chicaluna**[3] 5251 2-7-13 **78**............................ PaulQuinn 7 65
(J G Given) *prom far side: led that gp after 2f: rdn and ch 2f out: sn drvn and wknd over 1f out* **12/1**

4053 **16** *nk* **Miss Firefly**[6] 5167 2-8-2 **81** oh9 ow4............................ TPO'Shea 1 67
(M R Channon) *prom far side tl rdn wl over 2f out and sn wknd* **50/1**

052 **17** *3* **Hawk Eyed Lady (IRE)**[11] 5042 2-7-12 **77** oh2............................ DavidKinsella 4 55
(J A Osborne) *led far side gp 2f: prom tl rdn along over 2f out and grad wknd* **20/1**

4613 **18** *¾* **Bohobe (IRE)**[32] 4406 2-7-12 **77** oh4............................ JamieMackay 5 53
(J G Given) *prom far side: rdn along wl over 2f out and sn wknd* **50/1**

000 **19** *12* **Amazing Spirit**[48] 3884 2-7-12 **77** oh32............................ FrankieMcDonald 8 20
(Miss V Haigh) *s.i.s and a bhd far side* **200/1**

1m 17.42s (-3.06) **Going Correction** -0.425s/f (Firm) 2y crse rec **19** Ran SP% **120.7**
Speed ratings (Par 98): **100,99,98,98,97 97,96,96,96,94 94,94,93,93,92 91,88,87,73**
CSF £28.17 CT £233.70 TOTE £6.30: £2.10, £2.30, £2.10, £5.90; EX 28.30 Trifecta £88.80 Pool £563.08 - 4.50 winning units..

Owner D M James **Bred** D M James **Trained** Lambourn, Berks

FOCUS

A very good, competitive fillies' nursery, although the field split into two groups and those in the larger bunch on the stands' side seemed to be at an advantage, with nine of the first ten home emerging form that group, despite the principals edging towards the centre of the course. The winning time, a new course record, was 0.09 seconds quicker than the later sales race and the form looks solid rated through the third.

NOTEBOOK

Royal Confidence ◆, off the mark at the fourth attempt over 5f at Sandown on her previous start, was able to race off a mark 1lb lower than in future and she produced her best effort yet to follow up on her nursery debut. Having raced without any cover for much of the way on the stands' side of the track, she found herself in front plenty soon enough, but battled on well when strongly challenged by Crystany. On this evidence she can prove just as effective back over shorter and she looks a smart sprinter in the making. She is now likely to go for the Firth Of Clyde Stakes at Ayr. (op 6-1)

Crystany(IRE) ◆, the convincing winner of a Ripon maiden on her previous start, ran a good race switched to nursery company and was just unable to reverse earlier Goodwood form with Royal Confidence. She got a good lead off the eventual winner and, having shown real guts to take a tight gap around a furlong from the finish, she was just held. Her rider put up 1lb overweight, but it is debatable whether that cost her the race. A Cheveley Park entry, she is clearly well regarded and appeals as one to keep on-side. (op 11-2)

Cristal Clear(IRE), third in a weak Listed race at Ripon on her previous start, ran well off a 6lb higher mark than when winning a nursery at York prior to that. She hung to her left close home and, having got involved in a real barging match with fourth-placed Broken Applause, she could be considered very fortunate to hang onto third. She carried her head a little high, but it did not seem to slow her down. (op 8-1)

Broken Applause(IRE) returned to her best following a disappointing effort at Ripon last time. She was badly hampered by Cristal Clear near the line before trying to get in a good bump of her own and she could be considered a little unlucky not to get third in the Stewards' room.

Serena's Storm(IRE) ◆, dropped in class having failed to make an impression in a Group 3 at Ascot on her previous start, was 1lb lower than in future and she ran a blinder to win her race on the far side of the track. She was the only horse in the first ten to race far side and she appeals as one to keep on-side off her current sort of mark.

Sophie's Girl, bidding for the hat-trick off a mark 5lb higher than when winning at Ripon on her previous start, ran a respectable race faced with her toughest task to date.

Miss Bootylishes was 5lb out of the handicap and her rider also put up 9lb overweight, so her proximity is a slight concern considering she was beaten off a mark of 71 two starts back.

Anosti fared second best of those to race on the far side, although she compromised her chance by hanging right towards the centre of the track. (op 7-1)

5323 ANIMAL HEALTH TRUST CONDITIONS STKS 7f

3:10 (3:11) (Class 4) 2-Y-O

£6,232 (£1,866; £933; £467; £233; £117) **Stalls** High

Form RPR

1 **1** **Newly Elected (IRE)**[26] 4571 2-9-2 0............................ JMurtagh 5 91
(C G Cox) *bdly hmpd and carried lft s: sn trcking ldrs: led over 2f out: r.o strly fnl f* **3/1**[2]

2 *1 ¼* **Internationaldebut (IRE)** 2-8-9 0............................ JamieSpencer 4 81+
(D J Murphy) *rangy: scope: dwlt: hld up: nt clr run over 2f out: rdn to chal over 1f out: kpt on same pce ins fnl f* **14/1**

0 **3** *hd* **Bazergan (IRE)**[19] 4777 2-8-12 0............................ KerrinMcEvoy 1 83
(C E Brittain) *dwlt: in rr: hdwy on ins over 2f out: nt clr run over 1f out: edgd lft and styd on strly ins fnl f* **33/1**

0 **4** *1 ½* **Cigalas**[43] 4048 2-8-12 0............................ MichaelHills 7 79
(B W Hills) *t.k.h in rr: hdwy over 4f out: chal over 1f out: hung rt and wknd ins fnl f* **3/1**[2]

6020 **5** *½* **Woolfall Treasure**[25] 4625 2-8-12 90............................ NCallan 3 78
(G G Margarson) *bdly hmpd s: sn trcking ldrs: effrt over 2f out: wknd over 1f out* **20/1**

6 *shd* **Ascot Lime** 2-8-9 0............................ RyanMoore 2 75
(Sir Michael Stoute) *rangy: scope: hmpd s: in rr: drvn over 3f out: nvr a threat* **15/8**[1]

105 **7** *1 ¼* **Flight Plan**[13] 4964 2-8-12 85............................ SimonWhitworth 6 75
(C A Cyzer) *swvd violently lft out of stalls: t.k.h and led over 5f out: hdd over 2f out: wknd over 1f out* **10/1**[3]

1m 26.8s (-0.97) **Going Correction** -0.425s/f (Firm) **7** Ran SP% **108.2**
Speed ratings (Par 97): **88,86,86,84,84 83,82**
CSF £37.42 TOTE £3.40: £2.00, £3.30; EX 29.60.

Owner One Carat Partnership **Bred** R Ernst And Castletown Stud **Trained** Lambourn, Berks

FOCUS

A good conditions contest on paper, although the early pace was just steady, unsurprisingly resulting in a moderate time for the grade, and the bare form wants treating with some caution. It is worth noting that Flight Plan veered badly left on leaving the stalls, badly hampering Newly Elected, Bazergan, Woolfall Treasure and Ascot Lime, although most of them seemed to recover quite quickly.

NOTEBOOK

Newly Elected(IRE) ◆, bought out of Ed McMahon's yard after winning a 6f Newbury maiden on his debut, followed up in convincing fashion over this extra furlong. Always well placed in a race run at a moderate gallop having recovered from the trouble at the start, he was a class apart late on and was always holding the fast-finishing runner-up. One suspects he is a fair bit better than the bare form suggests and he looks a Pattern-class performer in the making, although he is set to continue his career in Hong Kong sooner rather than later. (tchd 11-4)

Internationaldebut(IRE), a 225,000euros son of High Chaparral out of a 7f winner at three, holds entries in the Dewhurst and the Racing Post Trophy. He seemed to get a little bit warm beforehand, but he shaped very well in the race itself, picking up from a little way off the moderate gallop to case home a very useful type. He looks a useful individual in the making, provided of course he goes the right way. (op 20-1)

Bazergan(IRE) ◆ improved on the form he showed when mid-division in a Newmarket maiden on his debut. He was outpaced a crucial stage before running on close home and he gave the impression he will benefit from both a stronger pace and a longer trip. He looks a very nice three-year-old in the making. Official explanation: jockey said colt was denied a clear run (op 50-1)

Cigalas, who shaped nicely on his debut over 6f at Goodwood, was too keen for his own good on this step up in trip. He avoided the trouble at the start, but pulled throughout and it is to his credit he finished so close. He is clearly full of potential, but will need to learn to settle better and a stronger-run race is likely to help. (op 9-4)

Woolfall Treasure, dropped in trip and grade, was one of those caught up in the trouble at the start and he was below his official mark of 90. (op 25-1)

Ascot Lime, a Pivotal first foal of a 6f juvenile winner who was useful over 7f at three, has no Group-race entries, but he was very popular in the market. He never seemed to be going after being badly hampered at the start and he was probably the worst affected considering this was his first experience of a racecourse. (op 2-1)

The Form Book, Raceform Ltd, Compton, RG20 6NL

Flight Plan veered badly left as soon as the stalls opened, almost wiping out over half the field, and he then raced keenly when re-joining the main bunch. He actually did well to finish so close all things considered, but then again this was a steadily-run race. (tchd 11-1)

5324 SAMSUNG £300000 ST LEGER 2-Y-O STKS 6f 110y

3:45 (3:48) (Class 2) 2-Y-O

£191,533 (£76,613; £38,306; £19,133; £9,566; £9,566) **Stalls** High

Form RPR

4633 **1** **Dream Eater (IRE)**[32] 4372 2-8-12 99 FrancisNorton 7 98+
(A M Balding) *racd far side: hld up: hdwy over 2f out: led 1f out: drvn out: 1st of 10 that gp* **15/2**[3]

140 **2** *1 1/4* **Achilles Of Troy (IRE)**[85] 2737 2-9-2 0 JMurtagh 20 99
(A P O'Brien, Ire) *rangy: scope: racd stands' side: hld up towards rr: hdwy and nt clr run over 2f out: swtchd wd and wandered: styd on strly to take 2nd nr fin: 1st of 12 that gp* **10/1**

451 **3** *hd* **Copywriter**[16] 4883 2-8-12 0 JimmyFortune 13 94
(J H M Gosden) *racd stands' side: mid-div: hdwy over 2f out: led that gp jst ins fnl f: styd on same pce: 2nd of 12 that gp* **16/1**

120 **4** *1 1/4* **Reel Gift**[4] 5219 2-7-12 0 WilliamBuick 18 77
(R Hannon) *racd stands' side: trckd ldr: led that side over 2f out tl jst ins fnl f: kpt on same pce: 3rd of 12 that gp* **5/1**[1]

1050 **5** *1* **Lindoro**[11] 5048 2-9-0 83 (t) AdamKirby 19 90
(W R Swinburn) *racd stands' side: chsd ldrs: kpt on same pce fnl 2f: 4th of 12 that gp* **66/1**

312 **6** *nk* **Oasis Wind**[22] 4695 2-9-2 88 JamieSpencer 6 91
(P F I Cole) *racd far side: w ldrs: led that side over 2f out: hdd 1f out: no ex: 2nd of 10 that gp* **11/2**[2]

5616 **7** *nk* **Paveroc**[21] 4721 2-9-0 93 (p) NCallan 14 88
(J S Moore) *racd stands' side: chsd ldrs on outer: styd on same pce fnl 2f: 5th of 12 that gp* **66/1**

5 **8** *1/2* **Leandros (FR)**[17] 4863 2-9-2 0 WJSupple 2 89
(G M Lyons, Ire) *cmpt: racd far side: chsd ldrs: kpt on same pce fnl 2f: 3rd of 10 that gp* **25/1**

1035 **9** *hd* **Mister Hardy**[20] 4743 2-8-12 91 PaulHanagan 12 84
(R A Fahey) *racd stands' side: mid-div: nt clr run over 2f out: styd on fnl f: 6th of 12 that gp* **25/1**

6110 **10** *shd* **Johar Jamal (IRE)**[20] 4743 2-7-12 84 JimmyQuinn 1 70
(M R Channon) *racd far side: chsd ldrs: n.m.r over 1f out: swtchd rt jst ins fnl f: styd on: 4th of 10 that gp* **8/1**

144 **11** *1/2* **Nikindi (IRE)**[18] 4832 2-8-6 0 StephenCarson 22 77
(J S Moore) *led stands' side gp: hdd over 2f out: wknd over 1f out: 7th of 12 that gp* **20/1**

0504 **12** *nk* **Carleton**[11] 5032 2-8-3 90 RichardMullen 5 73
(M R Channon) *racd far side: chsd ldrs: edgd rt and one pce fnl 2f: 5th of 10 that gp* **33/1**

3320 **13** *shd* **Quest For Success (IRE)**[20] 4743 2-8-9 82 TonyHamilton 4 79
(R A Fahey) *racd far side: chsd ldrs: outpcd fnl 2f: 6th of 10 that gp* **100/1**

01 **14** *1 1/4* **Dellini (IRE)**[12] 4992 2-8-11 0 DarryllHolland 15 77
(M R Channon) *racd stands' side: in rr and sn pushed along: edgd lft and styd on over 1f out: nvr on terms: 8th of 12 that gp* **9/1**

2315 **15** *nk* **Tadalavil**[15] 4921 2-8-9 86 TedDurcan 16 74
(M R Channon) *racd stands' side: hld up: hdwy over 2f out: wknd over 1f out: 9th of 12 that gp* **100/1**

4403 **16** *1 1/2* **Cordell (IRE)**[28] 4506 2-9-2 83 RyanMoore 21 77
(R Hannon) *racd stands' side: chsd ldrs: wknd 2f out: 10th of 12 that gp* **50/1**

135 **17** *1/2* **Ellmau**[42] 4057 2-8-9 98 ChrisCatlin 11 69
(E J O'Neill) *racd stands' side: mid-div on outer: drvn 3f out: sn lost pl: 11th of 12 that gp* **14/1**

0351 **18** *nk* **Thunder Bay**[12] 5008 2-8-3 82 TPO'Shea 9 62
(M R Channon) *racd far side: hld up: hdwy over 2f out: wknd over 1f out: 7th of 10 that gp* **66/1**

0140 **19** *1/2* **Grylls (USA)**[20] 4743 2-8-9 84 PatDobbs 8 67
(R Hannon) *racd far side: chsd ldrs: lost pl over 1f out: 8th of 10 that gp* **100/1**

2100 **20** *nk* **Jebel Tara**[61] 3504 2-8-9 86 KerrinMcEvoy 17 66
(C E Brittain) *racd stands' side: trckd ldrs: lost pl over 1f out: last of 12 that gp* **50/1**

303 **21** *1* **Honey Monster (IRE)**[35] 4286 2-8-9 82 TPQueally 3 63
(Miss V Haigh) *led far side: hdd over 2f out: lost pl over 1f out: 9th of 10 that gp* **100/1**

1253 **22** *hd* **Nacho Libre**[11] 5032 2-8-12 98 MichaelHills 10 65
(B W Hills) *racd far side: hld up: hdwy over 2f out: lost pl over 1f out: last of 10 that gp* **10/1**

1m 17.51s (-2.97) **Going Correction** -0.425s/f (Firm) 2y crse rec **22** Ran SP% **123.4**
Speed ratings (Par 101): **99,97,97,95,94 94,94,93,93,93 92,92,92,90,90 88,88,87,87,86 85,85**
CSF £72.19 TOTE £9.20: £2.80, £3.90, £4.70; EX 138.80 Trifecta £729.40 Part won. Pool £1,027.46 - 0.49 winning units..
Owner J C Smith **Bred** Stone Ridge Farm **Trained** Kingsclere, Hants

FOCUS

An extremely valuable sales race and unsurprisingly some very useful types turned out. They split into two groups and, although the winner raced far side, the next four home emerged from the opposite side of the track, suggesting the stands' side was slightly favoured, just as had appeared the case in the earlier nursery. However, the winning time was 0.09 seconds slower than the nursery and the bare form is no better than Listed level.

NOTEBOOK

Dream Eater(IRE) ◆, although failing to win prior to this, had been promising to progress into a smart type with some very useful efforts in defeat and he has clearly got his act together now. The evidence of the earlier nursery suggested the stands' side was the favoured part of the track, and the fact the next four home in this contest also raced stands' side suggested that, in sticking to the far side, he won against the bias, making this a particularly noteworthy effort. Having travelled very strongly indeed, he probably found himself in front a little sooner than was ideal and he did not seem to do a great deal once there, but he was still far too good for his 21 rivals. Clearly a very smart individual, he is entered in both the Mill Reef and the Middle Park and must not be underestimated, although a strong pace looks important. (op 8-1)

Achilles Of Troy(IRE) lost his way after bolting up in a maiden at Newmarket much earlier in the season, but he has clearly benefited from a near three-month break. He took a little while to pick up when first coming under pressure and the winner was long gone by the time he was switched with his challenge. On this evidence he will benefit from a step up to 7f. (op 12-1)

Copywriter, off the mark in a 7f maiden on the Polytrack at Kempton on his previous start, produced an improved effort to take third.

Reel Gift ran better than when down the field in a Group 3 at Kempton four days earlier, but she was still below the form she showed when second at Ascot two starts back. This was a fair effort off her light weight, but she could not quite sustain his challenge and gave the impression this trip just stretched her. (op 4-1)

Lindoro has faced some tough tasks since winning on his debut at Goodwood, but this was a useful effort and the first-time tongue-tie seemed to help.

Oasis Wind gave the impression he would benefit from a drop back to 5f when just pegged back in a 6f nursery at York on his previous start, but one can understand why his connections opted go for such a valuable prize and he ran well to take second on the far side. (op 7-1)

Paveroc ran close to his best in first-time cheekpieces.

Leandros(FR), off the mark on the sand at Dundalk on his previous start, posted a useful effort in defeat in this much tougher contest, taking third on the far side.

Mister Hardy would have been closer with a clearer run.

Johar Jamal(IRE) endured a troubled passage on the far side of the track and is better than she was able to show.

5325 ALTIUM SCARBROUGH STKS (LISTED RACE) 5f

4:20 (4:21) (Class 1) 2-Y-O+ **£17,781** (£6,723; £3,360; £1,680) **Stalls** High

Form RPR

/213 **1** **Galeota (IRE)**[16] 4907 5-9-9 107 RyanMoore 5 111
(R Hannon) *chsd ldng pair: rdn wl over 1f out: styd on u.p ins fnl f to ld last 75yds* **5/1**[2]

2443 **2** *nk* **Peace Offering (IRE)**[18] 4798 7-10-0 108 AdrianTNicholls 9 115
(D Nicholls) *cl up: rdn to ld over 1f out: drvn and edgd lft ins fnl f: hdd and nt qckn last 75yds* **7/1**[3]

0505 **3** *2 1/2* **Conquest (IRE)**[18] 4813 3-9-8 107 (t) JimmyFortune 6 101
(W J Haggas) *hld up towards rr: hdwy 2f out: sn rdn and kpt on ins fnl f* **8/1**

6010 **4** *3/4* **Green Manalishi**[20] 4746 6-9-12 104 NCallan 8 101
(K A Ryan) *chsd ldng pair: rdn wl over 1f out: kpt on same pce* **9/2**[1]

5005 **5** *3/4* **Drayton (IRE)**[38] 4196 3-9-8 0 JMurtagh 4 96
(M F De Kock, South Africa) *towards rr: rdn along and hdwy 2f out: kpt on same pce* **5/1**[2]

1160 **6** *nk* **Pivotal's Princess (IRE)**[18] 4798 5-9-4 100 DarryllHolland 2 90
(E S McMahon) *sn outpcd and a in rr* **9/1**

1040 **7** *shd* **Hogmaneigh (IRE)**[45] 3990 4-9-9 104 JamieSpencer 7 94
(S C Williams) *hld up in rr: effrt and sme hdwy 2f out: sn rdn and no imp* **5/1**[2]

3224 **8** *nk* **Morinqua (IRE)**[21] 4726 3-9-3 95 TPQueally 1 88
(J G Given) *led: rdn along and hung lft 2f out: sn hdd & wknd over 1f out* **11/1**

2031 **9** *nk* **Perfect Paula (USA)**[20] 4737 2-7-12 98 JimmyQuinn 3 82
(B J Meehan) *chsd ldrs: rdn along over 2f out and sn wknd* **16/1**

57.77 secs (-3.65) **Going Correction** -0.425s/f (Firm)
WFA 2 from 3yo 22lb 3 from 4yo+ 1lb **9** Ran SP% **116.0**
Speed ratings: **112,111,107,106,105 104,104,104,103**
CSF £39.98 TOTE £5.90: £2.10, £2.50, £3.10; EX 41.50 Trifecta £3036.20 Pool £4,404.71 - 1.03 winning units..
Owner Robin Blunt **Bred** W Maxwell Ervine **Trained** East Everleigh, Wilts

FOCUS

A Listed sprint run at a break-neck pace.

NOTEBOOK

Galeota(IRE) ◆, a failure at stud and now a gelding, recaptured his smart three-year-old form, swooping through on the inner to nail Peace Offering. The Diadem is under consideration and there is no reason he should not keep on competing in top sprints for several more years now. (tchd 11-2)

Peace Offering(IRE), conceding weight all round, went head-to-head with the pacesetter but he was always inclined to edge away from the stands' rail and out to the middle. In the end he was just edged out.

Conquest(IRE), having his second outing since being gelded, had the blinkers left off and his tongue tied-down. He stuck on despite carrying his head high and, though talented, is clearly a complex character.

Green Manalishi is all speed and under his penalty probably ran right up to his very best. (op 5-1)

Drayton(IRE) struggled to go the pace. Putting in all his best work at the finish he may well be worth another try over six, at least when the ground is quick. (op 6-1 tchd 13-2 in a place)

Pivotal's Princess(IRE), who met slight interference at the start, has not shone in her last three starts now after winning her first two this year. Official explanation: jockey said mare suffered interference shortly after leaving stalls

Hogmaneigh(IRE) could never take a serious hand and he prefers much easier ground. (op 9-2)

Morinqua(IRE), who had a fair bit to find, has blinding speed and took them along but she tended to hang out to the centre and in the end did not last home. (op 12-1)

Perfect Paula(USA) was taking on plenty and was in trouble at the halfway mark.

5326 BRONCROFT AHT H'CAP 1m 2f 60y

4:55 (4:56) (Class 2) (0-110,105) 3-Y-O+**£19,431** (£5,781; £2,889; £1,443) **Stalls** Low

Form RPR

21-1 **1** **Red Gala**[144] 1149 4-8-13 **93** RyanMoore 2 107+
(Sir Michael Stoute) *lw: hld up in rr: hdwy on outer over 2f out: rdn over 1f out: styd on strly ins fnl f to ld last 100yds* **7/4**[1]

-133 **2** *1* **Fairmile**[188] 645 5-9-11 **105** KerrinMcEvoy 1 117
(Saeed Bin Suroor) *trckd ldrs: hdwy over 2f out: swtchd rt and rdn over 1f out: ev ch ins fnl f tl drvn and no ex towards fin* **5/1**[3]

3030 **3** *1/2* **Ladies Best**[41] 4092 3-8-6 **93** ow1 TedDurcan 7 104+
(Sir Michael Stoute) *hld up in rr: hdwy wl over 2f out: rdn wl over 1f out: styd on ins fnl f: nrst fin* **10/1**

0502 **4** *hd* **All The Good (IRE)**[17] 4867 4-9-2 **96** JMurtagh 3 107
(G A Butler) *a.p: led over 2f out: rdn wl over 1f out: drvn and hdd last 100yds: no ex nr fin* **9/1**

3316 **5** *4* **Benandonner (USA)**[20] 4745 4-8-11 **91** PaulHanagan 4 94
(R A Fahey) *led: rdn along over 3f out: hdd over 2f out and grad wknd* **11/1**

21-0 **6** *2 1/2* **Heaven Knows**[21] 4720 4-8-11 **91** RHills 5 89
(W J Haggas) *swtg: trckd ldrs: hdwy 4f out: rdn 2f out and sn btn* **7/2**[2]

0010 **7** *1 1/4* **Star Of Light**[21] 4720 6-9-1 **95** JimmyFortune 6 90
(B J Meehan) *chsd ldrs: rdn along over 4f out and sn wknd* **14/1**

0-40 **8** *4* **Chantaco (USA)**[107] 2093 5-8-8 **91** WilliamBuick(3) 8 78
(A M Balding) *sn prom: rdn along over 3f out and sn wknd* **14/1**

2m 4.81s (-7.02) **Going Correction** -0.425s/f (Firm) course record
WFA 3 from 4yo+ 7lb **8** Ran SP% **116.0**
Speed ratings (Par 109): **111,110,109,109,106 104,103,100**
CSF £10.96 CT £67.64 TOTE £2.20: £1.40, £1.80, £2.80; EX 10.10 Trifecta £51.40 Pool £768.11- 10.60 winning units..
Owner Cheveley Park Stud **Bred** Cheveley Park Stud Ltd **Trained** Newmarket, Suffolk

FOCUS

A competitive handicap run at a strong pace and the winner can take yet another climb up the ladder. Red Gala took 0.67 seconds off the course record which had stood for 12 years.

NOTEBOOK

Red Gala, absent since April, resumed from a 9lb higher mark. He had to work hard but was firmly in command at the line. There may be another valuable handicap to be won with him this time and he will make an even better five-year-old. (op 15-8)

Fairmile, who had three runs in Dubai in the winter, was having his first start under the Godolpin banner and his first outing since March. He looked very light and gave problems in the stalls but, travelling strongly and forced to switch, he went down fighting.
Ladies Best stayed on in willing fashion down the wide outside. She looks right back to her best.
All The Good(IRE) went on travelling well within himself. He dug deep but over this trip was outspeeded inside the last and lost third place right on the line. (op 10-1)
Benandonner(USA) took them along but, hard at work once in line for home, found this mark, 6lb higher than Ascot, and this company simply too tough.
Heaven Knows, very warm beforehand, hardly advertised his Cambridgeshire chances. (op 4-1)

5327 UNICORN ASSET MANAGEMENT AHT CLASSIFIED STKS 1m 2f 60y
5:30 (5:30) (Class 3) 3-Y-O+

£11,217 (£3,358; £1,679; £840; £419; £210) **Stalls** Low

Form RPR
4056 **1** **Buccellati**[41] 4092 3-8-8 85 (v) WilliamBuick(3) 1 97+
(A M Balding) *s.i.s: hdwy to trck ldrs after 2f: nt clr run on ins over 2f out tl jst ins fnl f: squeezed through: edgd lft and led post* **7/2**[2]
2010 **2** *shd* **Soft Morning**[39] 4147 3-8-8 85 SebSanders 7 91
(Sir Mark Prescott) *led: qcknd over 3f out: hrd rdn fnl f: hdd post* **7/1**
2340 **3** *1 ¾* **Lisathedaddy**[27] 4551 5-8-12 80 RichardKingscote(3) 3 87
(B G Powell) *hld up in rr: hdwy on outside over 2f out: styd on same pce ins fnl f* **20/1**
3633 **4** *nk* **Resonate (IRE)**[16] 4888 9-9-4 85 TPQueally 9 90
(A G Newcombe) *lw: trckd ldrs: chal over 3f out: keeping on same pce whn sltly hmpd nr fin* **25/1**
0500 **5** *1* **Fusili (IRE)**[17] 4849 4-9-1 85 NCallan 11 85
(N P Littmoden) *trckd ldrs: effrt over 2f out: kpt on same pce* **33/1**
6605 **6** *1* **Hassaad**[46] 3959 4-9-4 85 (t) RHills 6 86
(W J Haggas) *s.s: in rr: drvn over 3f out: hdwy on outside fnl f: nvr nr ldrs* **8/1**
3060 **7** *nk* **Collateral Damage (IRE)**[21] 4720 4-9-4 82 (t) DavidAllan 2 85
(T D Easterby) *edgy in stalls: sn trcking ldrs: effrt 3f out: kpt on same pce* **16/1**
3121 **8** *¾* **Parisian Dream**[24] 4640 3-8-11 85 JamieSpencer 12 84
(B W Hills) *swtchd lft after s: hld up in rr: effrt over 3f out: nvr rchd ldrs* **5/1**[3]
0200 **9** *½* **Along The Nile**[105] 2136 5-9-4 81 PaulHanagan 8 83
(K G Reveley) *hld up in mid-div: effrt over 2f out: kpt on fnl f: nvr a threat* **40/1**
2311 **10** *1 ½* **Ravarino (USA)**[27] 4523 3-8-8 85 RyanMoore 10 77
(Sir Michael Stoute) *hld up in tch: effrt 4f out: rdn aover 2f out: nvr really threatened: wknd and eased fnl f* **9/4**[1]
300 **11** *2 ½* **Blue Spinnaker (IRE)**[16] 4900 8-8-11 82 NSLawes(7) 4 75
(M W Easterby) *t.k.h in rr: drvn over 3f out: no rspnse* **33/1**
1005 **12** *nk* **Lucayan Dancer**[11] 5052 7-9-4 82 AdrianTNicholls 14 74
(D Nicholls) *sn trcking ldrs on outer: lost pl over 1f out* **33/1**

2m 7.59s (-4.24) **Going Correction** -0.425s/f (Firm)
WFA 3 from 4yo+ 7lb 12 Ran SP% **119.0**
Speed ratings (Par 107): **99,98,97,97,96 95,95,94,94,93 91,91**
CSF £25.80 TOTE £4.20: £1.50, £2.50, £4.10; EX 32.60 Trifecta £615.40 Part won. Pool £866.79 - 0.34 winning units. Place 6 £171.08, Place 5 £137.41..
Owner P C & Mrs J A McMahon **Bred** Burton Agnes Stud Co Ltd **Trained** Kingsclere, Hants

FOCUS
A tightly-knit classified stakes and the winner would have been an unlucky loser. The winning time was moderate for the class and 2.78 seconds slower than the preceding contest.

NOTEBOOK
Buccellati, whose style of running lends itself to traffic problems, would have been a most unlucky loser. He was trapped on the inner with nowhere to go and was matched at 50 on the exchanges. He wriggled through a narrow gap to put his head in front on the line. (op 4-1 tchd 9-2 in places)
Soft Morning, whose rider had enjoyed success at Haydock earlier in the day, took them along and wound it up in the home straight. She did not really deserve to miss out but the winner had traffic problems to overcome. (op 15-2 tchd 8-1 in a place)
Lisathedaddy, whose four wins have been on the Polytrack at Lingfield, stayed on down the outside. She was keeping on at the finish without ever looking likely to seriously trouble the first two.
Resonate(IRE), who really took the eye in the paddock, kept tabs on the leader but was held when tightened up by the winner near the line.
Fusili(IRE), having her second outing in two weeks after a break, has four career wins to her credit, all on the All-Weather. She ran really well here on ground plenty quick enough for her.
Hassaad, who gave away three or four lengths at the start, was in the rear and going nowhere until staying on down the wide outside late on. His temperament is under suspicion. Official explanation: jockey said gelding missed the break
Collateral Damage(IRE), who was edgy in the stalls, gave a good account of himself on ground plenty quick enough for him.
Ravarino(USA), who looked in fine fettle, was in trouble the minute the runner-up stepped up the pace. She never really threatened and in the end Moore threw in the towel. She is a lot better than this and well worth another chance. (op 15-8 tchd 5-2 in places)
Lucayan Dancer Official explanation: jockey said gelding had no more to give
T/Jkpt: £13,298.10 to a £1 stake. Pool: £56,189.50. 3.00 winning tickets. T/Plt: £81.10 to a £1 stake. Pool: £111,941.45. 1,006.45 winning tickets. T/Qpdt: £26.70 to a £1 stake. Pool: £4,247.00. 117.65 winning tickets. JR

5212 HAYDOCK (L-H)
Wednesday, September 12

OFFICIAL GOING: Good to firm (good in places; 8.0)
Wind: Light against Weather: Fine and sunny

5328 EUROPEAN BREEDERS' FUND MEDIAN AUCTION MAIDEN STKS (DIV I) 7f 30y
2:00 (2:06) (Class 5) 2-Y-O

£2,590 (£578; £578; £192) **Stalls** Low

Form RPR
1 **Maryqueenofscots (IRE)** 2-8-12 0 HayleyTurner 3 68
(M L W Bell) *s.s: towards rr and green: hdwy over 2f out: r.o to ld ins fnl f: rdn out* **13/2**
04 **2** *¾* **Ballochroy (IRE)**[19] 4761 2-9-3 0 MartinDwyer 11 71
(B W Hills) *chsd ldrs: wnt 2nd over 3f out: led 2f out: rdn over 1f out: hdd ins fnl f: nt qckn* **5/1**[2]
5 **2** *dht* **Boy Blue**[26] 4578 2-9-3 0 AdrianTNicholls 6 71
(D Nicholls) *racd keenly: chsd ldrs: lost pl 3f out: sn outpcd: swtchd rt to rally over 1f out: r.o ins fnl f to dispute 2nd on line* **3/1**[1]
0 **4** *1 ¾* **Blindspin**[40] 4125 2-9-3 0 PhillipMakin 9 67
(M Dods) *midfield: hdwy 3f out: rdn whn chsd ldrs over 1f out: styd on same pce ins fnl f* **50/1**
5 *3* **Incarnation (IRE)** 2-8-12 0 TomEaves 2 54
(J G Given) *chsd ldr tl over 3f out: outpcd 2f out: no imp on ldrs after* **6/1**[3]
6 *hd* **Seta Pura** 2-8-12 0 RoystonFfrench 8 54
(Mrs A Duffield) *racd keenly in midfield: hdwy 3f out: rdn and rn green whn chsd ldrs over 1f out: edgd lft ins fnl f: sn no ex* **13/2**
00 **7** *1 ½* **Potemkin (USA)**[16] 4904 2-9-3 0 FergusSweeney 4 55
(A King) *sn pushed along towards rr: hdwy into midfield over 3f out: no imp on ldrs* **12/1**
8 *nk* **Love Valentine (IRE)** 2-8-12 0 J-PGuillambert 5 49
(M Johnston) *pushed along in midfield and green: outpcd over 3f out* **13/2**
00 **9** *5* **Halton Castle**[11] 5033 2-8-12 0 GaryBartley(5) 1 42
(E J Alston) *led: hdd 2f out: wknd over 1f out* **100/1**
05 **10** *1 ½* **Trip The Light**[35] 4285 2-9-0 0 JamieMoriarty(3) 7 38
(R A Fahey) *broke loose on way to post: midfield: lost pl 3f out: nvr a danger* **9/1**
11 *22* **Ugly Betty** 2-8-9 0 NeilChalmers(3) 10 —
(Garry Moss) *s.i.s: a bhd* **100/1**

1m 32.84s (0.78) **Going Correction** +0.025s/f (Good) 11 Ran SP% **117.6**
Speed ratings (Par 95): **96,95,95,93,89 89,87,87,81,80 54**
PL: Ballochroy Boy £1.70; Boy Blue £150; EX: Maryqueenofscots/BY £23.10, MS/BB £17.10; CSF: MS/BY £19.50, MS/BB £13.14. CSF £13.14 TOTE £9.40: £9.40, £2.40; EX 17.10.
Owner Mrs Melba Bryce **Bred** Keith Wills **Trained** Newmarket, Suffolk

FOCUS
An average juvenile maiden and probably the weaker of the two divisions with those having form only ordinary.

NOTEBOOK
Maryqueenofscots(IRE), a 65,000gns purchase bred to stay further in time, overcame distinct greeness through the early stages and came though from off the pace to win at the first time of asking. The fast ground proved to her liking and she was well on top at the finish, suggesting another furlong should be within her range before long. She clearly has a future and rates a nice handicap prospect. (op 9-1)
Ballochroy(IRE), friendless in the betting ring, was always handy and did nothing wrong in defeat. He now looks ready to tackle 1m and has the option of nurseries. (op 10-3 tchd 11-2)
Boy Blue, fifth on debut at Newcastle 26 days previously, got a little warm beforehand and raced too freely through the first couple of furlongs. He hit a flat spot when the race became really serious, but picked up again for pressure and was coming back at the first pair near the finish. This was another step in the right direction and he looks sure to make his mark in nurseries in due course. (op 10-3 tchd 11-2)
Blindspin, a slow starter on his debut over 6f at this venue 40 days previously, showed the benefit of that experience and travelled nicely through most of the race. He was found wanting at the business end, but this was a pleasing effort and he is no doubt going the right way now.
Incarnation(IRE), a half-sister to high-class middle-distance performer Norse Dancer among others, was the subject of market support ahead of this racecourse debut. She ultimately lacked the pace to get serious over this trip, but still showed ability and left the impression she would benefit for the experience. (op 10-1)
Seta Pura, whose dam has produced seven previous winners, proved too green to do herself full justice on this racecourse bow. She will also have to learn to settle better, but is fully entitled to do so and she is one to keep an eye on. (op 7-1 tchd 6-1)
Love Valentine(IRE), bred to make her mark at two, proved far too green through the early stages and clearly needed the run. She got the hang of things late on and should be capable of leaving this form behind as she becomes more streetwise. (op 5-1 tchd 7-1)

5329 EUROPEAN BREEDERS' FUND MEDIAN AUCTION MAIDEN STKS (DIV II) 7f 30y
2:30 (2:32) (Class 5) 2-Y-O

£2,590 (£770; £385; £192) **Stalls** Low

Form RPR
1 **Brasingaman Hifive** 2-8-12 0 GrahamGibbons 1 76
(Mrs G S Rees) *midfield: rdn and hdwy over 2f out: r.o to ld ins fnl f: pushed out towards fin* **100/1**
2 **2** *1* **Bonny Rose**[18] 4818 2-8-12 0 J-PGuillambert 4 73
(M Johnston) *led: rdn whn pressed over 2f out: hdd ins fnl f: nt qckn* **7/4**[1]
3 *½* **All The Aces (IRE)** 2-9-3 0 PhilipRobinson 6 77+
(M A Jarvis) *trckd ldrs: upsides fr over 3f out: rdn over 2f out: hld in 3rd whn sltly short of room cl home* **7/2**[3]
2 **4** *1* **Copperwood**[19] 4761 2-9-3 0 SebSanders 10 74
(M Blanshard) *racd keenly: midfield: rdn over 2f out: hdwy over 1f out: styd on ins fnl f: nt pce to chal ldrs* **11/4**[2]
0 **5** *5* **Warsaw Waltz**[47] 3916 2-8-12 0 TomEaves 5 57
(J G Given) *trckd ldrs tl rdn and wknd over 1f out* **80/1**
0 **6** *nk* **Oxbridge**[19] 4761 2-9-3 0 RobertHavlin 11 61
(B J Meehan) *midfield: rdn over 2f out: hung lft whn no imp over 1f out: nvr able to chal* **33/1**
55 **7** *½* **Green Earrings (IRE)**[16] 4875 2-8-12 0 SteveDrowne 9 55
(R Charlton) *prom: chalng 3f out: wknd over 1f out* **7/1**
0 **8** *shd* **Feeling Fresh (IRE)**[96] 2432 2-8-12 0 RussellKennemore(5) 7 60
(Paul Green) *dwlt: hld up in rr: rdn 2f out: nvr on terms w ldrs* **50/1**
9 *½* **Better In Heaven** 2-9-3 0 DaneO'Neill 2 58
(H J L Dunlop) *dwlt: towards rr: pushed along 4f out: rdn and sme hdwy 2f out: wknd fnl f* **20/1**
10 *3 ½* **Pentandra (IRE)** 2-8-12 0 RoystonFfrench 8 45
(J G Given) *dwlt: pushed along and rn green 4f out: a bhd* **80/1**
0 **11** *nk* **Love Cat (USA)**[18] 4819 2-9-3 0 DO'Donohoe 3 49
(K A Ryan) *dwlt: a bhd* **20/1**

1m 32.52s (0.46) **Going Correction** +0.025s/f (Good) 11 Ran SP% **115.6**
Speed ratings (Par 95): **98,96,96,95,89 89,88,88,87,83 83**
CSF £262.03 TOTE £120.20: £17.20, £1.20, £1.60; EX 721.80.
Owner R Morgan **Bred** Mrs Heather Morgan **Trained** Sollom, Lancs

FOCUS
This was the stronger of the two divisions and the form, rated around the runner-up and fourth, looks sound with the first four coming clear, despite the winner defying odds of 100/1.

NOTEBOOK
Brasingaman Hifive, the first known foal of an unraced mare, defied her massive odds and got her career off to a perfect start. She travelled kindly into the race around the 2f pole, showed a decent attitude when asked for her effort, and could be called the winner soon after entering the final furlong. Considering her stable is not renowned for debut winners and her sire's progeny generally progress with age, this has to bode well for her future prospects. She also clearly stays well and it will be interesting to see what handicap mark she is now allotted. (op 66-1)
Bonny Rose, runner-up on debut at Redcar 18 days previously, was given a positive ride over this extra furlong and posted a slightly improved effort, only to again find one too good. She helps to set the level of this form and should have little trouble in going one better before the season's end. (op 2-1 tchd 9-4)
All The Aces(IRE) ◆, a 95,000gns purchase, found support in the betting ring and posted a solid debut effort. He clearly knew his job and momentarily looked the winner when making his effort passing the 2f pole, but he eventually had no more to give at the business end. With improvement looking assured for this experience, he is probably the one to take from the race with the immediate future in mind. (tchd 5-1)

 The Form Book, Raceform Ltd, Compton, RG20 6NL

Copperwood, narrowly denied a winning debut at Newbury 19 days previously, proved too free for his own good through the early parts and eventually stayed on too late. He still ran close to his previous level and clearly has a future, but that looks sure to lie with the Handicapper and he will be eligible for nurseries after his next outing. (op 7-2 tchd 5-2)

Green Earrings(IRE) dropped out somewhat disappointingly when the gun was put to her head. She still performed close to her previous level, however, and can be expected to enjoy a return to easier ground in due course. Nurseries are also now an option. (op 5-1)

5330 RACING WELFARE H'CAP 1m 30y
3:00 (3:00) (Class 5) (0-70,70) 3-Y-0+ **£3,011** (£896; £447; £223) **Stalls** Low

Form RPR

3044 **1** **Jawaab (IRE)**[19] 4778 3-9-1 **67** MartinDwyer 14 73+
(M A Buckley) *hld up: hdwy whn nt clr run 2f out: prog on rail over 1f out: str run to ld fnl strides* **10/1**

-000 **2** *nk* **Kansas Gold**[91] 2576 4-8-12 **59** RoystonFfrench 9 65
(J Mackie) *midfield: rdn over 4f out: hdwy over 2f out: hung lft over 1f out: upsides ins fnl f: r.o u.p* **33/1**

1101 **3** *shd* **Dudley Docker (IRE)**[40] 4129 5-9-8 **69** PhilipRobinson 6 75
(C R Dore) *midfield: hdwy gng wl over 2f out: r.o to ld narrowly wl ins fnl f: hdd fnl strides* **7/2**[1]

5005 **4** *shd* **Crocodile Bay (IRE)**[4] 5228 4-9-8 **69** SilvestreDeSousa 3 75
(D Nicholls) *in tch: effrt over 2f out: led over 1f out: hdd wl ins fnl f: r.o u.p* **7/2**[1]

0600 **5** *½* **Blues In The Night (IRE)**[60] 3525 4-9-9 **70** SebSanders 8 75
(P J Makin) *in tch: effrt over 2f out: swtchd rt wl ins fnl f: r.o towards fin* **7/1**[2]

6036 **6** *1 ½* **Pianoforte (USA)**[12] 4998 5-8-10 **62** GaryBartley(5) 16 63
(E J Alston) *stdd s: hld up: nt clr run 2f out: rdn and swtchd rt over 1f out: styd on ins fnl f: nt rch ldrs* **14/1**

3205 **7** *1 ¾* **Just Oscar (GER)**[20] 4731 3-8-10 **62** DaneO'Neill 10 58
(W M Brisbourne) *midfield: rdn over 2f out: one pce fnl f* **16/1**

216 **8** *½* **Dressed To Dance (IRE)**[30] 4450 3-9-2 **68** PhillipMakin 17 63
(N Tinkler) *hld up: rdn over 2f out: hdwy over 1f out: one pce ins fnl f* **25/1**

0000 **9** *hd* **Foreign Edition (IRE)**[19] 4768 5-9-1 **62** TomEaves 5 58
(Miss J A Camacho) *towards rr: rdn over 2f out: kpt on fnl f: nvr able to chal* **33/1**

6102 **10** *1 ¾* **Legal Lover (IRE)**[29] 4469 5-9-0 **66** RussellKennemore(5) 7 58
(R Hollinshead) *chsd ldrs: wnt 2nd over 3f out: rdn to ld 2f out: hdd over 1f out: wknd ins fnl f* **10/1**

000- **11** *1* **Kirstys Lad**[316] 6279 5-8-2 **56** oh11 SophieDoyle(7) 12 45?
(M Mullineaux) *midfield: hung lft u.p over 1f out: nvr on terms* **100/1**

4134 **12** *2* **Benny The Bus**[64] 3409 5-9-1 **62** GrahamGibbons 2 47
(Mrs G S Rees) *chsd ldr tl over 3f out: rdn and wknd over 1f out* **16/1**

0340 **13** *2 ½* **Ming Vase**[21] 4713 5-8-9 **56** oh6 MickyFenton 4 35
(P T Midgley) *midfield: lost pl over 3f out: nt clr run whn u.p over 1f out: n.d* **25/1**

4010 **14** *2 ½* **Wahoo Sam (USA)**[18] 4820 7-9-2 **66** (p) AndrewMullen(3) 13 39
(D W Barker) *led: rdn and hdd 2f out: wknd over 1f out* **16/1**

4004 **15** *3 ½* **Lady Aspen (IRE)**[24] 4632 4-8-11 **58** FergusSweeney 1 23
(Ian Williams) *chsd ldrs tl rdn and wknd over 2f out* **8/1**[3]

1m 44.01s (-1.50) **Going Correction** +0.025s/f (Good)
WFA 3 from 4yo+ 5lb **15** Ran SP% **125.1**
Speed ratings (Par 103): **108,107,107,107,107 105,103,103,103,101 100,98,95,93,89**
CSF £324.14 CT £1432.73 TOTE £12.90: £3.10, £15.40, £2.10; EX 490.20.
Owner C C Buckley **Bred** Hascombe And Valiant Studs **Trained** Castle Bytham, Lincs

FOCUS
A modest handicap which saw the first five come clear in a blanket finish. It was a fair winning time for the grade.
Ming Vase Official explanation: jockey said gelding hung right-handed
Lady Aspen(IRE) Official explanation: jockey said filly lost its action

5331 SHAMMAH NICHOLLS CORPORATE DEPARTMENT NURSERY 6f
3:35 (3:36) (Class 4) (0-85,85) 2-Y-0 **£5,181** (£1,541; £770; £384) **Stalls** Centre

Form RPR

331 **1** **Craggy Cat (IRE)**[18] 4818 2-9-0 **78** SebSanders 2 90+
(L M Cumani) *chsd ldr: rdn to ld and edgd rt over 1f out: r.o and in command ins fnl f* **2/1**[1]

0250 **2** *2 ½* **Russian Reel**[20] 4743 2-9-7 **85** PatCosgrave 12 90+
(K A Ryan) *a.p: rdn and edgd rt over 1f out: sn on stands' rail: nt pce of wnr ins fnl f* **8/1**

4512 **3** *2 ½* **Perfect Flight**[12] 5008 2-9-0 **78** SteveDrowne 3 75
(M Blanshard) *hld up: rdn and hdwy over 1f out: styd on ins fnl f: nt trble front pair* **13/2**[3]

0451 **4** *nk* **Ridge Wood Dani (IRE)**[16] 4903 2-8-3 **67** MatthewHenry 9 63
(E J Alston) *midfield: rdn and hdwy over 1f out: styd on ins fnl f: nt pce of ldrs* **12/1**

5412 **5** *3* **Chatham Islands (USA)**[19] 4762 2-8-13 **77** J-PGuillambert 1 64
(M Johnston) *led: rdn and hdd over 1f out: wknd ins fnl f* **9/2**[2]

6000 **6** *nk* **Stage Acclaim (IRE)**[11] 5053 2-8-11 **75** GrahamGibbons 8 61
(B R Millman) *midfield: rdn 2f out: kpt on fnl f: nt pce to chal* **10/1**

2210 **7** *1 ¼* **Rievaulx Valentino**[23] 4669 2-8-12 **76** DO'Donohoe 10 58
(K A Ryan) *prom: rdn 1/2-way: wknd over 1f out* **18/1**

3603 **8** *2 ½* **Narmeen**[16] 4890 2-8-5 **69** MartinDwyer 6 44
(M R Channon) *midfield: rdn over 2f out: nvr able to chal: wknd fnl f* **25/1**

2201 **9** *1 ¾* **Irving Place**[29] 4484 2-9-1 **79** HayleyTurner 5 49
(M L W Bell) *hld up: effrt 2f out: no imp* **14/1**

0060 **10** *3* **Falcon Speed**[21] 4715 2-7-9 **62** oh15 DuranFentiman(3) 4 23
(P T Midgley) *a outpcd* **100/1**

6001 **11** *shd* **Fyodorovich (USA)**[19] 4781 2-9-0 **78** (v) MickyFenton 14 38
(J S Wainwright) *s.s and wnt rt leaving stalls: racd keenly: hld up: impr to midfield over 4f out: wknd 2f out* **20/1**

3210 **12** *5* **Brixworth Scribe**[29] 4484 2-8-7 **74** MarkLawson(3) 13 19
(B Smart) *upset in stalls: s.s: a bhd* **25/1**

314 **13** *¾* **The Real Guru**[29] 4476 2-9-0 **78** RoystonFfrench 11 21
(Mrs A Duffield) *prom tl rdn and wknd over 2f out* **20/1**

1m 13.8s (-0.09) **Going Correction** +0.025s/f (Good) **13** Ran SP% **122.9**
Speed ratings (Par 97): **101,97,94,93,89 89,87,84,82,78 78,71,70**
CSF £17.57 CT £96.89 TOTE £2.60: £1.30, £2.60, £2.30; EX 22.70.
Owner JMC Breed & Race Limited **Bred** Ian Fair **Trained** Newmarket, Suffolk

FOCUS
A strong nursery for the grade which saw the field spread across the track and it was run at a decent pace. The progressive winner scored with something to spare and the runner-up sets the standard.

NOTEBOOK
Craggy Cat(IRE) ◆, narrowly off the mark at the third attempt 18 days previously, showed himself to be a rapidly-improving juvenile with a clear-cut success on this nursery bow. He was always travelling like the winner and had a deal left up his sleeve at the finish, this being by far his best effort to date. The Handicapper will no doubt now hike him up in the weights, but it may still not prove enough to stop him following up - he would look a "good thing" under a penalty - and he did enough here to suggest another furlong will be well within his compass. (op 9-4)
Russian Reel enjoyed the drop into this grade and ran a solid race in defeat on the stands' side, finishing nicely clear in second. He probably faced an impossible task in giving 7lb to the winner and this was a very pleasing effort under top weight. (op 9-1)
Perfect Flight got going too late on this return to 6f and was never a serious threat to the first pair. This was still another sound effort however, and she rates a decent benchmark for the form. (op 11-2 tchd 7-1 in places)
Ridge Wood Dani(IRE), back up 7lb in the weights for his Warwick success 16 days previously, lacked the required pace to land a significant blow and may just be held by the Handicapper again now. This was still no disgrace, however. (op 14-1)
Chatham Islands(USA) had no more to give when pressed for the lead and probably went off too fast for her own good. (tchd 5-1)
Stage Acclaim(IRE) Official explanation: jockey said colt stumbled leaving stalls
Brixworth Scribe Official explanation: jockey said gelding missed the break

5332 KING'S REGIMENT CUP H'CAP 5f
4:10 (4:10) (Class 4) (0-80,80) 3-Y-0+ **£6,477** (£1,927; £963; £481) **Stalls** Centre

Form RPR

250 **1** **Bo McGinty (IRE)**[28] 4489 6-8-11 **75** (b) JamieMoriarty(3) 9 87
(R A Fahey) *a.p: r.o to ld ins fnl f: drvn out* **7/1**[3]

1350 **2** *1* **Mimi Mouse**[26] 4567 5-9-4 **79** KDarley 2 87
(T D Easterby) *led main gp: overall ld 2f out: rdn over 1f out: hdd ins fnl f: nt qckn* **8/1**

0000 **3** *1 ¼* **Yungaburra (IRE)**[11] 5039 3-9-4 **80** (t) GrahamGibbons 12 84
(D J Murphy) *chsd ldrs: rdn 2f out: styd on same pce ins fnl f* **33/1**

1620 **4** *¾* **Elkhorn**[37] 4227 5-9-5 **80** (b) TomEaves 8 81
(Miss J A Camacho) *in rr: rdn and hdwy over 1f out: kpt on ins fnl f: nvr able to chal* **9/2**[1]

53-0 **5** *nk* **Argentine (IRE)**[11] 5039 3-9-3 **79** GregFairley 15 79
(L Lungo) *racd on stands' rail: overall ld to 2f out: rdn over 1f out kpt on same pce fnl f* **20/1**

0020 **6** *shd* **Bluebok**[2] 5278 6-9-0 **80** (t) TolleyDean(5) 7 80
(J M Bradley) *chsd ldrs: rdn 1/2-way: no ex ins fnl f* **5/1**[2]

0000 **7** *nk* **Spanish Ace**[6] 5168 6-9-4 **79** SteveDrowne 6 78
(J M Bradley) *bhd: outpcd 1/2-way: kpt on ins fnl f: nt pce to chal* **11/1**

6520 **8** *shd* **Darcy's Pride (IRE)**[21] 4703 3-8-11 **73** PatCosgrave 3 71
(D W Barker) *prom: rdn over 1f out: wknd ins fnl f* **18/1**

00 **9** *nk* **Peopleton Brook**[12] 5009 5-8-4 **72** (p) BarrySavage(7) 1 69
(J M Bradley) *in tch: rdn over 1f out: nt pce of ldrs ins fnl f* **14/1**

3403 **10** *hd* **Pegasus Dancer (FR)**[16] 4896 3-8-6 **68** (p) DO'Donohoe 4 65
(K A Ryan) *hld up: rdn 1/2-way: outpcd over 1f out* **11/1**

2106 **11** *nk* **Bold Minstrel (IRE)**[19] 4780 5-9-3 **78** RobertHavlin 14 73
(M Quinn) *chsd ldr on stands' side: rdn over 1f out: wknd ins fnl f* **14/1**

4140 **12** *hd* **Garstang**[11] 5039 4-8-10 **71** (b) LPKeniry 13 66
(Peter Grayson) *wnt rt leaving stalls: racd keenly: hld up: rdn over 1f out: nvr on terms* **5/1**[2]

60.46 secs (0.34) **Going Correction** +0.025s/f (Good)
WFA 3 from 4yo+ 1lb **12** Ran SP% **118.1**
Speed ratings (Par 105): **98,96,94,93,92 92,92,91,91,91 90,90**
CSF £61.82 CT £1765.78 TOTE £8.60: £2.30, £2.90, £5.20; EX 62.80.
Owner Paddy McGinty & Bo Turnbull **Bred** Stephen Breen **Trained** Musley Bank, N Yorks

FOCUS
Ordinary sprint handicap form.

5333 BET365 H'CAP 1m 6f
4:45 (4:45) (Class 4) (0-80,75) 3-Y-0 **£6,477** (£1,927; £963; £481) **Stalls** Low

Form RPR

0321 **1** **Irish Quest (IRE)**[18] 4809 3-9-5 **73** PhilipRobinson 7 84+
(M A Jarvis) *chsd ldr: led 3f out: rdn over 2f out: styd on wl* **7/4**[1]

0003 **2** *1 ¼* **Spanish Diva**[28] 4518 3-9-3 **71** RoystonFfrench 6 81+
(S C Williams) *midfield: lost pl over 7f out: hdwy over 2f out: styd on to take 2nd whn edgd lft and rdr dropped rein ent fnl f: nt rch wnr* **8/1**[3]

1402 **3** *4* **Vallemeldee (IRE)**[9] 5101 3-8-10 **64** KDarley 5 68
(P W D'Arcy) *hld up: hdwy after 6f: rdn over 2f out: one pce ins fnl f* **20/1**

0013 **4** *1 ¼* **Sonara (IRE)**[11] 5040 3-9-2 **70** TomEaves 9 72
(M H Tompkins) *chsd ldrs: rdn over 2f out: one pce fnl f* **11/1**

3234 **5** *¾* **Louviere**[24] 4630 3-9-5 **73** DaneO'Neill 4 74
(Pat Eddery) *rrd bef s: led: hdd 3f out: rdn over 2f out: wknd over 1f out* **14/1**

3451 **6** *1* **Hatton Flight**[19] 4758 3-8-7 **61** (b) SteveDrowne 10 61
(A M Balding) *hld up: rdn over 2f out: no imp on ldrs* **5/1**[2]

1433 **7** *hd* **Abounding**[19] 4766 3-8-12 **69** PJMcDonald(3) 8 69
(R M Beckett) *s.v.s: detached tl after 4f: in rr: effrt over 2f out: no real imp* **9/1**

0021 **8** *½* **Hurricane Thomas (IRE)**[11] 5040 3-9-6 **74** GregFairley 3 73
(M Johnston) *chsd ldrs: rdn over 4f out: wknd over 1f out* **8/1**[3]

1140 **9** *2 ½* **Down The Brick (IRE)**[12] 5006 3-9-2 **70** FergusSweeney 1 65
(B R Millman) *hld up: rdn 4f out: nvr on terms* **16/1**

4421 **10** *40* **Atayeb (USA)**[20] 4738 3-9-7 **75** MartinDwyer 2 14
(M P Tregoning) *hld up: hdwy after 6f: rdn and wknd 4f out: virtually p.u fnl f* **10/1**

3m 3.53s (-2.76) **Going Correction** +0.025s/f (Good) **10** Ran SP% **120.0**
Speed ratings (Par 103): **108,107,105,104,103 103,103,102,101,78**
CSF £16.95 CT £218.75 TOTE £2.70: £1.10, £2.60, £4.70; EX 22.40.
Owner A D Spence **Bred** Epona Bloodstock Ltd **Trained** Newmarket, Suffolk

FOCUS
They did not go that quick early but the pace picked up and the final time was fair for the grade.
Atayeb(USA) Official explanation: trainer's rep said, regarding running, that the filly was heavily in season

5334 WILLIAMHILLCASINO.COM H'CAP 1m 3f 200y
5:15 (5:15) (Class 4) (0-85,84) 3-Y-0+ **£6,477** (£1,927; £963; £481) **Stalls** High

Form RPR

6231 **1** **Double Doors**[11] 5045 3-9-1 **78** RobertHavlin 5 83
(J H M Gosden) *chsd ldrs: rdn to nose ahd jst over 1f out: leant on rival whn a doing enough towards fin* **7/2**[2]

3-00 **2** *hd* **Leslingtaylor (IRE)**[24] 4637 5-9-6 **74** GrahamGibbons 7 79
(J J Quinn) *chsd ldr: led over 2f out: rdn and hdd narrowly jst over 1f out: bmpd towards fin: a jst hld* **10/3**[1]

2241 **3** 1 **Yossi (IRE)**[26] 4563 3-9-3 **80** .... TomEaves 4 83
(M H Tompkins) *in tch: rdn and ev ch over 1f out: sn nt qckn: swtchd rt wl ins fnl f: r.o towards fin: nt pce to chal front pair* **11/2**

0340 **4** 1 1/2 **Baan (USA)**[17] 4843 4-9-3 **71** .... J-PGuillambert 3 72
(M Johnston) *led: rdn and hdd over 2f out: styd on same pce ins fnl f* **9/1**

3310 **5** 1/2 **Heathyards Pride**[24] 4637 7-9-11 **79** .... LPKeniry 2 79
(R Hollinshead) *hld up: hdwy into midfield 7f out: rdn over 1f out: kpt on same pce* **14/1**

60-6 **6** 1 **Free To Air**[172] 753 4-9-5 **73** .... SteveDrowne 8 72
(A M Balding) *hld up: rdn over 1f out: nvr able to chal* **20/1**

0035 **7** hd **Fossgate**[18] 4817 6-8-13 **70** .... AndrewElliott(3) 1 68
(J D Bethell) *midfield: rdn 4f out: one pce fnl f* **10/1**

53-0 **8** 1 1/4 **King Kasyapa (IRE)**[10] 4231 5-8-12 **69** .... JamieMoriarty(3) 6 65
(P Bowen) *hld up: carried lft whn no imp 2f out: nvr a danger* **16/1**

4110 **9** 1 3/4 **Rhaam**[20] 4749 3-9-7 **84** .... MartinDwyer 9 77
(B W Hills) *hld up: rdn and hung lft 2f out: nvr on terms* **4/1**[3]

2m 35.48s (0.49) **Going Correction** +0.025s/f (Good)
WFA 3 from 4yo+ 9lb **9** Ran SP% **117.1**
Speed ratings (Par 105): **99,98,98,97,96 96,96,95,94**
CSF £15.88 CT £62.95 TOTE £3.30: £1.40, £1.80, £2.10; EX 9.40.
Owner K Abdulla **Bred** Juddmonte Farms Ltd **Trained** Newmarket, Suffolk
■ Stewards' Enquiry : Robert Havlin caution: careless riding

FOCUS
The hold-up horses struggled to get into this competitive handicap.

5335 RACING WELFARE CHARITY DAY MAIDEN STKS 1m 2f 120y
5:45 (5:46) (Class 5) 3-Y-0+ **£2,817** (£838; £418; £209) **Stalls** High

Form RPR

2 **1** **Royal Jasra**[19] 4771 3-9-3 0 .... SteveDrowne 3 78
(E A L Dunlop) *trckd ldrs: rdn to ld over 1f out: r.o and in command ins fnl f* **1/1**[1]

5-4 **2** 1 1/4 **Pearl (IRE)**[45] 4007 3-8-12 0 .... J-PGuillambert 5 71
(W J Haggas) *led: rdn and hdd over 1f out: nt qckn* **10/1**

20 **3** 2 1/2 **Russian Invader (IRE)**[14] 4948 3-9-3 0 .... FergusSweeney 4 71
(A King) *midfield: rdn over 2f out: hdwy to chse ldng pair over 1f out: kpt on ins fnl f: nt pce of ldrs* **7/2**[2]

04 **4** 2 1/2 **Granary**[19] 4765 3-8-12 0 .... DaneO'Neill 9 62
(H Candy) *midfield: rdn 2f out: sme hdwy over 1f out: edgd lft and one pce ins fnl f* **8/1**

0 **5** 2 **Mysterious World (IRE)**[24] 4641 3-9-0 0 .... PJMcDonald(3) 2 63
(Mrs K Walton) *trckd ldrs: rdn over 2f out: wknd over 1f out* **100/1**

0- **6** nk **Still Calm**[368] 5168 3-9-3 0 .... DO'Donohoe 10 62
(N J Vaughan) *broke loose on way to post: racd keenly: prom: rdn 3f out: wknd over 1f out* **25/1**

7 1 1/2 **Emily's Rainbow (IRE)** 3-8-12 0 .... RobertHavlin 11 54
(W J Haggas) *hld up: rdn over 1f out: nvr able to chal* **14/1**

8 3 1/2 **Refinement (IRE)**[139] 8-9-3 0 .... JamieMoriarty(3) 8 48
(Jonjo O'Neill) *s.i.s: hdwy into midfield after 2f: rdn and outpcd 3f out: n.d after* **9/2**[3]

00 **9** 2 1/2 **Llizaam**[12] 5019 3-8-12 0 .... LPKeniry 6 43
(J T Stimpson) *hld up: rdn over 4f out: nvr on terms* **100/1**

00- **10** 23 **Fara's Kingdom**[316] 6284 3-9-3 0 .... TomEaves 7 —
(Miss J A Camacho) *racd keenly: a bhd: rdn over 4f out: t.o* **66/1**

2m 17.44s (1.30) **Going Correction** +0.025s/f (Good)
WFA 3 from 8yo 8lb **10** Ran SP% **124.6**
Speed ratings (Par 103): **96,95,93,91,90 89,88,86,84,67**
CSF £14.35 TOTE £2.00: £1.10, £2.70, £1.50; EX 14.90 Place 6 £69.38, Place 5 £46.19.
Owner Abdul Rahman Al Khalifa **Bred** Rockdown Investments **Trained** Newmarket, Suffolk

FOCUS
An ordinary maiden run at a steady early gallop.
T/Plt: £111.60 to a £1 stake. Pool: £52,316.90. 342.10 winning tickets. T/Qpdt: £38.70 to a £1 stake. Pool: £2,410.20. 46.00 winning tickets. DO

5219 KEMPTON (A.W) (R-H)
Wednesday, September 12

OFFICIAL GOING: Standard
Wind: Virtually nil

5336 KIRSTY PRICE 21ST BIRTHDAY H'CAP 7f (P)
6:20 (6:20) (Class 6) (0-50,50) 3-Y-0+ **£2,047** (£604; £302) **Stalls** High

Form RPR

3004 **1** **Jools**[10] 5062 9-8-12 **48** oh1 .... PatrickHills(5) 7 60
(D K Ivory) *hld up towards rr but in tch: smooth hdwy to chse wnr 1f out: led last half f: sn clr: comf* **6/1**[2]

0066 **2** 1 1/2 **Laphonic (USA)**[37] 4223 4-9-3 **48** .... TQuinn 13 56
(T J Etherington) *led: rdn 2f out: hdd and nt pce of wnr last half f* **8/1**

0401 **3** 1 1/2 **Parthenope**[29] 4469 4-8-12 **50** .... JackDean(7) 9 54
(J A Geake) *in rr: hdwy over 3f out: chsd ldrs fr over 1f out: kpt on same pce* **9/1**

0244 **4** 1 1/4 **Shunkawakhan (IRE)**[35] 4294 4-8-10 **48** .... (p) AmyBaker(7) 8 49
(G C H Chung) *s.i.s: in rr: hdwy 2f out: hmpd whn styng on appr fnl f: kpt on again cl home* **9/2**[1]

0560 **5** shd **Time To Regret**[28] 4488 7-9-3 **48** .... (p) DanielTudhope 14 48
(I W McInnes) *chsd ldrs: wnt 2nd over 1f out: no imp on ldrs ins fnl f and one pce* **9/2**[1]

U016 **6** hd **Double Valentine**[9] 5090 4-8-10 **48** .... HarryPoulton(7) 2 48
(R Ingram) *in rr: hdwy on ins 3f out: chsd ldrs over 1f out: no imp and sn outpcd* **14/1**

P300 **7** 5 **Winds Of Kildare (IRE)**[13] 4961 4-9-3 **48** .... (t) StephenDonohoe 3 34
(C N Allen) *in rr: styd on fnl 2f: nvr in contention* **22/1**

/06- **8** hd **Sir Mikeale**[585] 298 4-9-5 **50** .... SaleemGolam 10 36
(G Prodromou) *chsd ldr to 3f out: wknd 2f out* **50/1**

0502 **9** shd **Inscribed (IRE)**[9] 5090 4-9-3 **48** oh1 .... TGMcLaughlin 6 33
(G A Huffer) *chsd ldrs: wnt 2nd over 3f out: rdn and hung lft over 1f out: sn wknd* **13/2**[3]

00-0 **10** 3/4 **Diamond World**[175] 723 4-9-3 **48** oh1 .... JimCrowley 1 31
(C A Horgan) *a towards rr* **20/1**

0300 **11** 1/2 **Blue Knight (IRE)**[9] 5090 8-9-5 **50** .... (p) AmirQuinn 11 32
(P Howling) *chsd ldrs 4f* **14/1**

0000 **12** 1 3/4 **Tamatave (IRE)**[83] 2795 5-9-3 **48** oh1 .... (e[1]) PaulMulrennan 4 25
(M W Easterby) *in tch: effrt over 3f out: sn wknd* **8/1**

1m 25.57s (-1.23) **Going Correction** -0.175s/f (Stan) **12** Ran SP% **120.6**
Speed ratings (Par 101): **100,98,96,95,95 94,89,88,88,87 87,85**
CSF £53.19 CT £444.61 TOTE £6.30: £2.00, £3.80, £3.40; EX 83.20.
Owner Dean Ivory **Bred** Tsarina Stud **Trained** Radlett, Herts

FOCUS
A race full of moderate and exposed individuals, so the value of the form is highly debateable. Jools was beaten in a seller last time.
Time To Regret Official explanation: jockey said gelding suffered interference in running

5337 COA SOLUTIONS MAIDEN STKS 7f (P)
6:50 (6:51) (Class 5) 2-Y-0 **£2,914** (£867; £433; £216) **Stalls** High

Form RPR

2 **1** **Iguazu Falls (USA)**[21] 4725 2-9-3 0 .... LDettori 9 90+
(Saeed Bin Suroor) *mde all: strode clr over 1f out: sn clr on bit: impressive* **30/100**[1]

2 3 1/2 **Oarsman** 2-9-3 0 .... ChrisCatlin 1 70
(R Charlton) *s.i.s: t.k.h and sn chsng ldrs: styd on fr over 1f out to chse wnr ins fnl f but nvr the remotest ch* **9/1**[3]

04 **3** 1/2 **Southern Mistral**[7] 5126 2-9-0 0 .... LiamJones(3) 5 69
(W J Haggas) *wnt rt s: sn chsd ldrs: wnt 2nd 2f out but nvr any ch w facile wnr: lost outpcd into 3rd ins fnl f* **33/1**

4 1/2 **Autumn Blades (IRE)** 2-9-3 0 .... TQuinn 4 68
(J W Hills) *in rr: sn pushed along: styd on fr 2f out and kpt on ins fnl f: nvr in contention* **50/1**

5 hd **Haydens Mark** 2-9-3 0 .... OscarUrbina 2 67
(W J Haggas) *in rr: pushed along and hdwy ins fnl 2f: gng on cl home but gng pce to be competitive* **66/1**

6 1/2 **Earlsmedic** 2-8-10 0 .... WilliamCarson(7) 8 66
(S C Williams) *hmpd s: bhd: hdwy 2f out: kpt on fnl f: nvr in contention* **66/1**

50 **7** nk **Landikhaya (IRE)**[12] 5011 2-9-3 0 .... GeorgeBaker 11 65
(R Hannon) *chsd ldrs: rdn 3f out: wknd over 1f out* **33/1**

8 1/2 **Bronze Cannon (USA)** 2-9-3 0 .... DavidKinsella 10 64
(J H M Gosden) *s.i.s: towards rr: pushed along over 3f out: styd on fr over 1f out: nvr gng pce to be competitive* **14/1**

9 2 1/2 **Special Branch Ami (IRE)** 2-9-3 0 .... JimCrowley 3 57
(C R Egerton) *s.i.s: a towards rr* **12/1**

0 **10** 1/2 **Prime Aspiration (USA)**[28] 4500 2-9-3 0 .... PaulEddery 7 56
(Christian Wroe) *hmpd s: sn rcvrd to chse ldrs: rdn over 2f out: wknd wl over 1f out* **33/1**

06 **11** nk **Distant Diamond (IRE)**[19] 4761 2-9-3 0 .... SaleemGolam 6 55+
(W R Swinburn) *hmpd s: in rr: pushed along and sme hdwy whn hmpd 1f out: nt rcvr* **66/1**

5 **12** 1/2 **Charmel's Lad**[27] 4540 2-9-3 0 .... AdamKirby 13 54
(W R Swinburn) *pressed wnr 2f: styd 2nd to 2f out: wknd qckly* **8/1**[2]

0 **13** 1/2 **Pure Scandal**[21] 4725 2-9-3 0 .... PaulMulrennan 12 53
(M W Easterby) *a in rr* **66/1**

1m 26.56s (-0.24) **Going Correction** -0.175s/f (Stan) **13** Ran SP% **129.1**
Speed ratings (Par 95): **94,90,89,88,88 88,87,87,84,83 83,82,82**
CSF £4.41 TOTE £1.20: £1.02, £2.40, £6.90; EX 7.20.
Owner Godolphin **Bred** Darley **Trained** Newmarket, Suffolk

FOCUS
A lopsided race due to the impressive nature of victory by Iguazu Falls, who can go on to better things. Quite a few looked in need of the experience and shaped with promise for the future.

NOTEBOOK
Iguazu Falls(USA) kept on really well at York on his debut to trouble Moynahan in the latter stages, and looked ready for a step up in trip. Entered in two Group 1s this season, the seventh furlong proved well within his compass, as it should have on pedigree, and he won easily. We learnt nothing here about how good he actually is but he remains a progressive individual that should operate at a higher level. (op 1-3 tchd 4-11)
Oarsman was most notably a half-brother to Lateen Sails, a horse Godolphin did so well with in the past. He was green in the early stages but really stuck to his task well under pressure and should be all the better for the run.
Southern Mistral is bred to be fairly useful but is very much one to be interested in when moved into handicap company. He was never far away but was readily put in his place up the straight.
Autumn Blades(IRE) ◆, a 35,000euros half-brother to winning sprinter Gallery Girl, kept on nicely from off the pace and was hardly given a hard time on his debut. That kindness can be repaid next time.
Haydens Mark ◆ shaped with lots of promise, albeit off a slow pace, and was noted staying on strongly in the latter stages.
Earlsmedic ◆ is a name well worth remembering for the future after a highly-promising effort. He finished really well after meeting some trouble up the home straight.
Landikhaya(IRE) ◆ was not beaten far and should find his level in handicaps now.
Bronze Cannon(USA) ◆ was doing nothing fast at the beginning of the race but caught the eye late on. Under a considerate ride, he shaped as though capable of much better with time. (op 16-1)
Prime Aspiration(USA) Official explanation: jockey said colt had no more to give
Distant Diamond(IRE) Official explanation: jockey said colt jumped right on leaving stalls and was denied a clear run in the straight

5338 DIGIBET.COM CLAIMING STKS 1m (P)
7:20 (7:20) (Class 6) 3-Y-0+ **£2,047** (£604; £302) **Stalls** High

Form RPR

1100 **1** **Logsdail**[39] 4153 7-9-12 **74** .... (p) GeorgeBaker 8 74
(G L Moore) *hld up in rr: hdwy to trck ldrs over 3f out: drvn to ld over 1f out: styd on wl* **2/1**[1]

2000 **2** 1 1/2 **Langford**[18] 4827 7-9-3 **76** .... PatrickHills(5) 9 67
(M H Tompkins) *chsd ldrs: led 3f out: hdd over 1f out: kpt on same pce* **5/2**[2]

6030 **3** 1 **Boundless Prospect (USA)**[5] 5203 8-9-7 **68** .... NicolPolli(5) 4 68
(Miss Gay Kelleway) *s.i.s: in rr: rdn 3f out: hdwy fr 2f out: styd on to take 3rd ins fnl f but nvr gng pce to be competitive* **8/1**

2600 **4** 1 **Henry The Seventh**[17] 4858 3-9-7 **70** .... TQuinn 5 65
(J W Hills) *chsd ldrs: rdn over 2f out: styd on same pce fr over 1f out* **13/2**[3]

6405 **5** 1 **Franky'N'Jonny**[7] 5128 4-8-5 **35** .... (p) PaulFitzsimons 10 43
(M J Attwater) *in rr: hdwy on outside 3f out: styd on same pce fnl 2f* **40/1**

5504 **6** 2 **Welsh Auction**[11] 5041 3-8-1 **55** .... BrydieKilloran(7) 12 45
(K J Burke) *chsd ldrs: rdn over 2f out: wknd over 1f out* **25/1**

3450 **7** 3 **Music Celebre (IRE)**[34] 4319 7-8-11 **49** .... (b) WilliamCarson(7) 1 44
(S Curran) *in rr: wd into st 3f out: nvr in contention* **20/1**

2230 **8** shd **Our Herbie**[25] 4591 3-9-7 **62** .... (v) RichardHughes 11 51
(J W Hills) *stdd s: shkn up over 2f out: no rspnse* **10/1**

1060 **9** 1/2 **Joint Expectations (IRE)**[7] 5128 3-8-9 **48** .... DMylonas 3 38
(Mrs C A Dunnett) *led 1f: styd w ldr to 1/2-way: wknd over 2f out* **66/1**

1500 **10** 9 **Sophie's Dream**[9] 5084 3-8-3 **60** .... ChrisCatlin 7 11
(A M Hales) *stdd towards rr sn after s: rdn 3f out and styd there* **16/1**

0330 11 2 1/2 **Crafty Fox**[17] 4856 4-9-4 55........(b1) StephenDonohoe 13 16
(John A Harris) *led after 1f: hdd 3f out: sn btn* **16/1**

1m 39.28s (-1.52) **Going Correction** -0.175s/f (Stan)
WFA 3 from 4yo+ 5lb 11 Ran SP% **119.7**
Speed ratings (Par 101): **100,98,97,96,95 93,90,90,89,80 78**
CSF £6.83 TOTE £3.10: £1.60, £1.50, £2.80; EX 9.30.
Owner D T L Limited **Bred** Stetchworth Park Stud Ltd **Trained** Woodingdean, E Sussex

FOCUS
The best two horses in the race dominated the finish.
Crafty Fox Official explanation: jockey said gelding lost its action

5339 DIGIBET CASINO H'CAP 1m (P)
7:50 (7:52) (Class 5) (0-75,75) 3-Y-O+ **£2,914** (£867; £433; £216) **Stalls** High

Form RPR
-016 1 **Lawyers Choice**[51] 3798 3-8-10 69........ PaulEddery 2 79
(Pat Eddery) *chsd ldrs: rdn to ld 2f out: drvn out fnl f* **25/1**
4210 2 1 **Reeling N' Rocking (IRE)**[32] 4394 4-9-0 68........ ChrisCatlin 4 76
(B W Hills) *chsd ldrs tl drvn and outpcd 3f out: styd on u.p fr 2f out to chse wnr ins fnl f but no imp* **11/2**[3]
2403 3 3/4 **Fealeview Lady (USA)**[34] 4338 3-8-8 70........ TravisBlock(3) 7 75
(H Morrison) *in rr: drvn along on outside 3f out: styd on fr over 1f out: gng on ins fnl f to take 3rd but nvr quite gng pce to rch ldng duo* **12/1**
4560 4 shd **Katiypour (IRE)**[35] 4266 10-8-13 67........ TQuinn 5 73
(P Mitchell) *in rr: pushed along and hdwy fr 2f out: styd on ins fnl f and gng on cl home but nvr gng pce to be competitive* **12/1**
4011 5 1 3/4 **Im Ova Ere Dad (IRE)**[16] 4880 4-9-3 71........ RichardHughes 12 73+
(D E Cantillon) *plld hrd: hld up in rr: hdwy on ins over 2f out: chsd wnr 1f out but no imp: wknd fnl 100yds* **2/1**[1]
2630 6 hd **Doyles Lodge**[25] 4610 3-8-4 68........ LukeMorris(5) 6 69
(H Candy) *mid-div whn drvn along over 2f out: kpt on fnl f but nvr in contention* **33/1**
-100 7 1/2 **Tasweet (IRE)**[175] 725 3-8-13 72........(v) AdamKirby 10 71
(T G Mills) *led: hdd 2f out: wknd fnl f* **16/1**
1200 8 1/2 **Polish World (USA)**[7] 5134 3-8-11 70........ SaleemGolam 3 68
(T J Etherington) *in tch: hdwy to chse ldrs 3f out: wknd ins fnl 2f* **50/1**
0550 9 1/2 **Gavarnie Beau (IRE)**[16] 4884 4-8-7 61 oh1........ JimmyQuinn 9 59
(M Blanshard) *chsd ldrs: rdn over 2f out: wknd over 1f out* **25/1**
-662 10 nk **Reballo (IRE)**[16] 4884 4-9-0 68........ OscarUrbina 11 65
(J R Fanshawe) *in tch: rdn to chse ldrs over 2f out: no imp: wknd over 1f out* **11/4**[2]
0005 11 1/2 **Exit Smiling**[18] 4820 5-8-10 64........ MickyFenton 8 60
(P T Midgley) *t.k.h: hld up in rr: rdn and hung rt bnd 3f out: sn no ch* **6/1**

1m 38.61s (-2.19) **Going Correction** -0.175s/f (Stan)
WFA 3 from 4yo+ 5lb 11 Ran SP% **123.5**
Speed ratings (Par 103): **103,102,101,101,99 99,98,98,97,97 96**
CSF £160.60 CT £1808.47 TOTE £19.60: £4.30, £1.70, £4.60; EX 162.40.
Owner Raymond Tooth **Bred** Chippenham Lodge Stud & Rathbarry Stud **Trained** Nether Winchendon, Bucks
■ Stewards' Enquiry : Paul Eddery caution: careless riding

FOCUS
There was a distinct lack of pace in the early stages, which saw a mad rush for the line start at the top of the home straight.
Gavarnie Beau(IRE) Official explanation: jockey said gelding hung left-handed
Exit Smiling Official explanation: jockey said gelding was denied a clear run

5340 DIGIBET SPORTS BETTING H'CAP 6f (P)
8:20 (8:20) (Class 6) (0-60,60) 3-Y-O+ **£2,047** (£604; £302) **Stalls** High

Form RPR
0000 1 **Anfield Dream**[123] 1681 5-9-1 55........ MickyFenton 10 67
(J R Jenkins) *chsd ldrs: drvn to ld ins fnl 2f: rdn and hld on wl thrght fnl f* **25/1**
6350 2 1 **Musical Script (USA)**[5] 5191 4-8-7 54........(b) JamieHamblett(7) 9 63
(Mouse Hamilton-Fairley) *towards rr: hdwy on ins 3f out: ev ch over 2f out: styd on fnl f but a hld by wnr* **8/1**
1004 3 hd **Jayanjay**[25] 4594 8-9-2 56........ TQuinn 11 64
(P Mitchell) *chsd ldrs: drvn to chal over 2f out: kpt on same pce u.p ins fnl f* **12/1**
4062 4 1/2 **Nautical**[7] 5130 9-9-0 59........ LukeMorris(5) 6 66
(A W Carroll) *in rr: hdwy on outside and hung rt ins fnl 3f: styd on ins fnl f but nvr gng pce to rch ldrs* **13/8**[1]
6431 5 1 1/2 **Tag Team (IRE)**[12] 5016 6-9-6 60........ StephenDonohoe 7 62
(John A Harris) *chsd ldrs: rdn 3f out: wknd fnl f* **9/2**[2]
5014 6 nk **Arfinnit (IRE)**[13] 4973 6-8-12 55........(v) LiamJones(3) 1 57
(Mrs A L M King) *in rr: drvn along over 3f out: styd on appr fnl f and gng on cl home but nvr in contention* **5/1**[3]
0000 7 nk **Sovereignty (JPN)**[13] 4978 5-8-11 56........ PatrickHills(5) 4 59+
(D K Ivory) *chsd ldrs: rdn and hung rt over 1f out: no imp: eased whn hld last half f* **16/1**
2206 8 1 3/4 **Bodden Bay**[139] 1262 5-9-3 57........ DanielTudhope 2 52
(I W McInnes) *in rr: rdn and effrt on outside 3f out: nvr in contention and sn btn* **33/1**
4304 9 3/4 **Registrar**[12] 5016 5-9-1 55........ DMylonas 8 48
(Mrs C A Dunnett) *in rr most of way* **8/1**
66-6 10 2 **Fastrac Boy**[229] 251 4-9-2 56........ GeorgeBaker 12 43
(J R Best) *led tl hdd ins fnl 2f: wkng whn n.m.r over 1f out* **14/1**

1m 12.46s (-1.24) **Going Correction** -0.175s/f (Stan) 10 Ran SP% **122.2**
Speed ratings (Par 101): **101,99,99,98,96 96,95,93,92,89**
CSF £221.67 CT £1694.64 TOTE £24.30: £8.80, £5.10, £2.80; EX 270.00.
Owner The Saints Partnership **Bred** Michael Ng **Trained** Royston, Herts
■ Stewards' Enquiry : Micky Fenton two-day ban: careless riding (Sep 23-24)

FOCUS
The pace was good and the form looks sound for the level.
Sovereignty(JPN) Official explanation: jockey said gelding hung both ways

5341 AZURE HOSPITALITY H'CAP 1m 4f (P)
8:50 (8:50) (Class 6) (0-60,59) 3-Y-O+ **£2,047** (£604; £302) **Stalls** Centre

Form RPR
2141 1 **Treetops Hotel (IRE)**[13] 4961 8-9-6 59........ RussellKennemore(5) 8 66
(B R Johnson) *s.i.s: hld up in rr tl drvn and str run on outside fr over 2f out to ld fnl 100yds: hld on all out* **13/2**
0454 2 shd **Sir Haydn**[7] 5132 7-9-10 58........(v) MickyFenton 2 65
(J R Jenkins) *s.i.s: in rr: hdwy on outside over 2f out: str run u.p to chal fnl 100yds: no ex last strides* **6/1**[3]
3005 3 1/2 **Geordie's Pool**[12] 5019 3-9-1 58........ TQuinn 11 64
(J W Hills) *led 2f: styd chsng ldr: rdn over 2f out: led ins fnl f: hdd a no ex fnl 100yds* **25/1**
0026 4 nk **Sovereign Spirit (IRE)**[12] 5018 5-9-11 59........(t) AdamKirby 4 65
(W R Swinburn) *in rr: hdwy over 2f out: str run u.p into last and clsng on ldng trio fnl 100yds but nvr quite gng pce to chal* **6/1**[3]
000 5 shd **Lord Laing (USA)**[41] 4108 4-8-12 46........ PatDobbs 14 52
(H J Collingridge) *mid-div: hdwy 3f out: qcknd to chal ins fnl f: no ex nr fin* **20/1**
0532 6 1 1/4 **Barbs Pink Diamond (USA)**[10] 5068 3-8-12 55........ JimCrowley 6 59
(Mrs A J Perrett) *chsd ldrs: rdn fr 3f out: styd on same pce fnl 2f* **5/1**[1]
2304 7 nk **Ja Myford**[37] 4229 3-8-13 56........(p) PaulMulrennan 10 59
(P T Midgley) *chsd ldrs: rdn 3f out: wknd fnl f* **12/1**
0101 8 3/4 **Icannshift (IRE)**[21] 4708 7-9-1 52........ NeilChalmers(3) 1 54
(T M Jones) *drvn to ld after 2f: kpt slt ld whn chal fr 2f out tl hdd ins fnl f and sn btn* **9/1**
3640 9 nk **Blackmail (USA)**[8] 5120 9-9-7 55........ JimmyQuinn 7 56
(P Mitchell) *in tch: hdwy over 4f out: chsd ldrs fr 3f out: rdn: n.m.r and wknd jst ins fnl f* **16/1**
0023 10 3 **Credential**[17] 4860 5-9-10 58........ StephenDonohoe 13 55
(John A Harris) *in rr: rdn over 3f out: wknd over 2f out* **7/1**
0010 11 8 **Paparaazi (IRE)**[13] 4972 5-9-4 52........ DanielTudhope 9 36
(I W McInnes) *s.i.s: mid-div: hdwy to chse ldrs 3f out: sn btn* **11/2**[2]
554 12 2 1/2 **Silver Blue (IRE)**[7] 5128 4-9-7 58........ LiamJones(3) 5 38
(C R Dore) *a in rr* **12/1**
305 13 hd **Benellino**[35] 4290 4-8-11 50........ HaddenFrost(5) 12 29
(R M Stronge) *chsd ldrs over 1m* **33/1**

2m 34.21s (-2.69) **Going Correction** -0.175s/f (Stan)
WFA 3 from 4yo+ 9lb 13 Ran SP% **129.3**
Speed ratings (Par 101): **101,100,100,100,100 99,99,98,98,96 91,89,89**
CSF £48.23 CT £958.15 TOTE £8.80: £3.00, £3.10, £10.50; EX 73.10.
Owner Tann Racing **Bred** Miss Jill Finegan **Trained** Ashtead, Surrey

FOCUS
Icannshift, as usual, helped to set the early gallop, which looked reasonable enough despite quite a few of the field racing a bit keenly throughout.
Silver Blue(IRE) Official explanation: jockey said gelding never travelled

5342 DAY TIME, NIGHT TIME, GREAT TIME, H'CAP 1m 3f (P)
9:20 (9:20) (Class 6) (0-65,65) 3-Y-O **£2,047** (£604; £302) **Stalls** High

Form RPR
2220 1 **Potentiale (IRE)**[16] 4878 3-9-3 64........(p) ChrisCatlin 3 66
(J W Hills) *in rr: rdn over 3f out: str run u.p fr 2f out to ld ins fnl f: hld on wl u.p* **7/2**[2]
6545 2 1/2 **Motarjm (USA)**[17] 4858 3-9-4 65........(t) MickyFenton 5 66
(H J Collingridge) *in rr: pushed along and hdwy on outside fr 2f out: styd on strly ins fnl f: gng on cl home but nt quite get to wnr* **8/1**
6030 3 hd **Driving Miss Suzie**[19] 4766 3-8-12 62........(b) NeilChalmers(3) 8 63
(A M Balding) *trckd ldrs: n.m.r whn rdn jst ins fnl f: sn qcknd to chal: no ex cl home* **10/1**
05-2 4 shd **Perfect Reward**[23] 4667 3-9-3 64........ JimCrowley 14 64
(Mrs A J Perrett) *chsd ldr: rdn and ev ch ins fnl f: no ex cl home* **3/1**[1]
0056 5 1 1/4 **Cavalry Twill (IRE)**[10] 5068 3-9-4 65........(b) TQuinn 4 63
(P F I Cole) *led: rdn over 2f out: kpt slt advantage tl hdd & wknd ins fnl f: sn outpcd* **12/1**
0620 6 1/2 **Spinal Tap (IRE)**[72] 3150 3-9-0 61........(p) DavidKinsella 10 59
(C R Egerton) *s.i.s: hdwy on outside over 2f out: kpt on fr over 1f out but nvr gng pce to rch ldrs* **4/1**[3]
5-P0 7 1/2 **Go Dude**[17] 4858 3-9-1 65........(p) LiamJones(3) 7 62
(J Ryan) *in rr: rdn and kpt on fr over 1f out: kpt on cl home but nt a danger* **33/1**
6562 8 hd **Run For Ede'S**[15] 4918 3-9-3 64........(p) IanMongan 13 60
(P M Phelan) *t.k.h: chsd ldrs: rdn to chal fr 2f out: wknd ins fnl f* **16/1**
5040 9 nk **She's So Pretty (IRE)**[10] 5068 3-9-1 62........(v) SaleemGolam 12 58
(W R Swinburn) *chsd ldrs: rdn and outpcd 3f out: styd on again fnl f* **16/1**
-000 10 nk **Christalini**[42] 4064 3-9-1 62........ PatDobbs 11 57
(J C Fox) *chsd ldrs: rdn over 2f out: wknd fnl f* **33/1**
0330 11 1 3/4 **Lemon Silk (IRE)**[40] 4127 3-9-4 65........(t) GeorgeBaker 6 57
(K J Burke) *s.i.s: a towards rr* **12/1**
0215 12 1/2 **Zain (IRE)**[12] 4998 3-8-11 58........ JamieMackay 2 49
(J G Given) *chsd ldrs over 1m* **8/1**

2m 23.33s (0.65) **Going Correction** -0.175s/f (Stan) 12 Ran SP% **131.6**
Speed ratings (Par 99): **90,89,89,89,88 88,87,87,87,87 85,85**
CSF £36.03 CT £272.71 TOTE £5.50: £2.20, £3.20, £2.30; EX 44.40 Place 6 £669.10, Place 5 £206.37.
Owner J W Hills **Bred** Copperhead Stable **Trained** Upper Lambourn, Berks

FOCUS
They went a very steady early pace here and as a result the winning time was very moderate, even for a race of this class. A whole host of horses came to have a chance with a furlong to go but it was Potentiale who showed the best turn of foot to gain the day.
Driving Miss Suzie Official explanation: jockey said filly was denied a clear run
Cavalry Twill(IRE) Official explanation: jockey said gelding hung left-handed
Go Dude Official explanation: jockey said gelding was denied a clear run
T/Plt: £365.90 to a £1 stake. Pool: £58,355.65. 116.40 winning tickets. T/Qpdt: £272.90 to a £1 stake. Pool: £4,758.60. 12.90 winning tickets. ST

5186 CHEPSTOW (L-H)
Thursday, September 13

OFFICIAL GOING: Good to firm (8.9)
The ground had been well watererd and the jockeys considered it to be a shade slower than the official description.
Wind: Nil Weather: Sunny

5343 JOIN WBX.COM FOR FREE FOOTBALL SHIRT/E.B.F. MAIDEN STKS 7f 16y
2:30 (2:30) (Class 5) 2-Y-O **£3,562** (£1,059; £529; £264) **Stalls** High

Form RPR
0 1 **Confidence Trick (USA)**[20] 4777 2-9-3 0........ JDSmith 14 80+
(Sir Michael Stoute) *hld up in tch: rdn to ld ins fnl f: r.o wl* **9/4**[2]
00 2 2 1/2 **Connor's Choice**[59] 3589 2-9-0 0........ RichardKingscote(3) 7 74
(Andrew Turnell) *w ldrs: led over 2f out: rdn and edgd lft over 1f out: hdd ins fnl f: sn edgd rt: nt qckn* **50/1**
60 3 1/2 **Maximus Aurelius (IRE)**[31] 4454 2-8-12 0........ LukeMorris(5) 8 73
(J Jay) *trckd ldrs: rdn and styd on whn carried rt cl home* **17/2**
622 4 1 **Barliffey (IRE)**[17] 4904 2-9-3 79........ AdamKirby 5 70+
(D J Coakley) *s.i.s: t.k.h: sn mid-div: swtchd rt and rdn over 2f out: styd on ins fnl f* **7/4**[1]

35 **5** 1½ **We'Re Delighted**[20] [4761] 2-9-3 0 .... JimmyQuinn 6 66
(M R Channon) *hld up in tch: rdn over 2f out: no ex fnl f* **8/1**
6 *shd* **Always Certain (USA)** 2-9-3 0 .... J-PGuillambert 13 66
(M Johnston) *led: hdd over 2f out: sn rdn: wknd fnl f* **13/2**[3]
7 3 **Celt** 2-9-3 0 .... NickyMackay 9 59+
(L M Cumani) *s.i.s and sltly hmpd s: hld up: rdn over 2f out: sme hdwy fnl f: n.d* **20/1**
00 **8** *nk* **Recoil (IRE)**[13] [5011] 2-9-3 0 .... PaulEddery 4 58
(Christian Wroe) *hld up towards rr: rdn over 3f out: sme hdwy 2f out: no further prog* **100/1**
00 **9** *nk* **Zabeel Tiger**[20] [4782] 2-9-3 0 .... SamHitchcott 11 57
(M R Channon) *w ldr: rdn 2f out: wknd over 1f out* **50/1**
10 3½ **Saafend Geezer** 2-9-3 0 .... IanMongan 12 48
(B J Meehan) *s.s: hdwy over 3f out: sn rdn: wknd wl over 1f out* **25/1**
0 **11** *nk* **Ray Diamond**[29] [4508] 2-9-3 0 .... JamesDoyle 1 48
(N P Littmoden) *bhd: hdwy over 4f out: rdn over 3f out: wknd over 2f out* **100/1**
00 **12** ½ **Talon (IRE)**[29] [4487] 2-9-3 0 .... OscarUrbina 15 46
(W J Haggas) *a bhd* **33/1**
50 **13** *nk* **Seconds Out (IRE)**[78] [2991] 2-9-3 0 .... JamieMackay 10 46
(Sir Mark Prescott) *a bhd* **66/1**
06 **14** 1¾ **Khana Ras (IRE)**[17] [4904] 2-9-3 0 .... ChrisCatlin 3 41
(E J O'Neill) *hld up in tch: wknd 3f out* **33/1**
15 1 **Avril Valley** 2-8-12 0 .... PatDobbs 2 34
(D J S Ffrench Davis) *a bhd* **100/1**
16 9 **Restless Swallow** 2-8-12 0 .... KevinGhunowa[(5)] 16 16
(C J Down) *s.s: a wl in rr* **150/1**

1m 23.14s (-0.16) **Going Correction** -0.175s/f (Firm) **16** Ran SP% **125.6**
Speed ratings (Par 95): **93,90,89,88,86 86,83,82,82,78 78,77,77,75,74 63**
CSF £130.42 TOTE £3.80: £1.60, £10.60, £2.50; EX 117.50.
Owner Gainsborough **Bred** Gainsborough Farm Inc **Trained** Newmarket, Suffolk

FOCUS
An ordinary maiden but reasonable form rated around the placed horses.

NOTEBOOK
Confidence Trick(USA), whose trainer's previous winners of this race include the subsequent 2000 Guineas winner Golan, still holds an entry in the Dewhurst. There was plenty of support for him in the market throughout the day to improve on his ninth in a Newmarket maiden on his debut, and the quicker ground suited him. He won easily in the end, and there should be better to come. (op 5-2)
Connor's Choice, despite having plenty of speed in his pedigree, had shaped as though he would be suited by a step up in trip, and he duly improved on his previous efforts to win the separate race for second. He is now eligible for a mark and should pay his way in handicap company.
Maximus Aurelius(IRE) must show plenty at home as he was backed again, this time from 25-1. He ran well over this extra furlong and has a race in him, but handicaps might offer a better opportunity to get off the mark than maidens (op 25-1)
Barliffey(IRE) set no more than a fair standard to aim at, having finished runner-up in auction maidens at Brighton and Warwick the last twice. He did not get away that well though, and raced keenly before staying on late. He is probably capable of a bit better than he showed here but the Handicapper is starting to get to know him quite well now. (op 5-2 tchd 11-4 in places)
We'Re Delighted has failed to build on the promise of his debut effort, but at least he now has the option of handicaps. Softer ground might suit him. Official explanation: jockey said colt stumbled on leaving stalls (tchd 15-2)
Always Certain(USA), a half-brother to Marty's Legend, a multiple sprint winner in the US, made much of the running and is entitled to come on for his debut. (op 4-1)
Celt, a half-brother to Pukka, a quite useful dual middle-distance winner, Pongee, high-class over middle distances, Garhoud, a 1m4f winner, and Lion Sands, a 1m4f winner, will do better in time. (op 16-1)

5344 WBX.COM £25 BET FOR NEW ACCOUNTS MEDIAN AUCTION MAIDEN STKS 1m 14y
3:00 (3:03) (Class 5) 2-Y-O **£2,914** (£867; £433; £216) **Stalls High**

Form RPR
05 **1** **Black Jacari (IRE)**[17] [4876] 2-9-0 0 .... RichardKingscote[(3)] 7 78
(A King) *hld up towards rr: rdn and hdwy 2f out: swtchd rt over 1f out: led ins fnl f: r.o* **8/1**[3]
0 **2** *nk* **Downhiller (IRE)**[29] [4508] 2-9-3 0 .... JimmyQuinn 8 77
(J L Dunlop) *hld up towards rr: rdn and hdwy over 2f out: ev ch whn edgd rt wl ins fnl f: r.o* **16/1**
3 **3** *nk* **Tenjack King**[17] [4882] 2-9-3 0 .... PatDobbs 9 77
(J A Osborne) *s.i.s: hdwy over 3f out: rdn over 2f out: ev ch whn bmpd wl ins fnl f: kpt on* **7/2**[2]
33 **4** *nk* **Stop On**[18] [4841] 2-9-3 0 .... ChrisCatlin 12 76
(M R Channon) *w ldr: led jst over 2f out: sn rdn and edgd lft: hdd ins fnl f: nt qckn* **12/1**
64 **5** 2 **Hampstead Heath (IRE)**[29] [4487] 2-9-3 0 .... J-PGuillambert 2 71
(M Johnston) *t.k.h: prom: led over 5f out: rdn and hdd jst over 2f out: sn carried lft: no ex ins fnl f* **10/11**[1]
0 **6** 2½ **Addikt (IRE)**[46] [3991] 2-9-3 0 .... LPKeniry 5 66
(S Kirk) *prom: rdn over 2f out: wknd fnl f* **10/1**
00 **7** 1¾ **Got Green (FR)**[94] [2504] 2-8-7 0 .... HaddenFrost[(5)] 3 57
(R Hannon) *nvr trbld ldrs* **66/1**
00 **8** 1 **Graylyn Ruby (FR)**[27] [4584] 2-9-3 0 .... MatthewHenry 14 59
(J Jay) *n.d* **100/1**
9 2 **Tepee** 2-8-12 0 .... NickyMackay 11 50
(L M Cumani) *s.i.s: hdwy over 3f out: sn rdn: wknd over 2f out* **33/1**
000 **10** 1½ **Orbital Orchid**[57] [3648] 2-8-12 52 .... AdamKirby 1 46
(W S Kittow) *hld up: rdn and hdwy 3f out: wknd 3f out* **100/1**
0 **11** 1¼ **Has To Be Abacus (IRE)**[76] [3043] 2-8-12 0 .... KevinGhunowa[(5)] 10 48
(A B Haynes) *in tch 3f* **150/1**
12 6 **Captain Mainwaring** 2-9-3 0 .... JamesDoyle 4 35
(N P Littmoden) *a bhd* **66/1**
13 ¾ **Dancing Sword** 2-9-3 0 .... IanMongan 13 33
(H J L Dunlop) *prom: rdn over 3f out: sn wknd* **50/1**
00 **14** 9 **Lancaster Lad (IRE)**[17] [4904] 2-9-3 0 .... SamHitchcott 6 12
(A B Haynes) *led over 2f: rdn over 3f out: wknd over 2f out* **150/1**

1m 34.89s (-1.11) **Going Correction** -0.175s/f (Firm) **14** Ran SP% **119.6**
Speed ratings (Par 95): **98,97,97,97,95 92,90,89,87,86 85,79,78,69**
CSF £123.63 TOTE £9.60: £2.40, £4.80, £1.50; EX 153.80.
Owner David Bellamy & Alan King **Bred** Allevamento Gialloblu S R L **Trained** Barbury Castle, Wilts

FOCUS
A bunched finish to this average maiden and, although the time was good there were a couple of improvers close up plus the favourite disappointed.

NOTEBOOK
Black Jacari(IRE), fifth in a better race over the course and distance last time, came from well off the pace to lead late on and get off the mark at the third attempt. He is by Black Sam Bellamy, has bags of stamina and will be suited by much further next year. (op 7-1 tchd 10-1)
Downhiller(IRE) showed a lot more than on his debut over 7f and was only beaten narrowly. He shapes as though he needs even further already and is likely to make a stayer next year. (op 12-1)
Tenjack King, another who stayed on well from off the pace, had every chance. He looks just as effective on turf as he is on Polytrack. (op 5-2 tchd 4-1)
Stop On, not beaten far, has now had the requisite three runs for a mark. Official explanation: jockey said colt hung when under pressure (tchd 9-1)
Hampstead Heath(IRE), sent off favourite for the third time in three starts, once again let his supporters down. He must learn to settle if he is to fulfil his potential. (op 13-8 tchd 5-6)
Lancaster Lad(IRE) Official explanation: jockey said colt was hanging left-handed

5345 WBX.COM 0% COMMISSION ON BIG RACES (S) STKS 1m 2f 36y
3:35 (3:36) (Class 6) 3-Y-O+ **£1,943** (£578; £288; £144) **Stalls Low**

Form RPR
424 **1** **Rowan Lodge (IRE)**[18] [4860] 5-8-12 59 .... HarryPoulton[(7)] 4 62
(J R Boyle) *plld hrd: mde all: c centre st: swvd lft over 2f out and wl over 1f out: r.o* **9/4**[2]
0320 **2** 1½ **Stagehand (IRE)**[16] [4915] 3-8-12 64 .... ChrisCatlin 11 59
(B R Millman) *t.k.h: a.p: rdn to chse wnr over 2f out: kpt on ins fnl f* **5/4**[1]
0500 **3** 4 **Summer Bounty**[18] [4860] 11-9-5 46 .... TGMcLaughlin 8 51
(F Jordan) *s.s: hld up and bhd: stdy hdwy over 3f out: rdn and one pce fnl f* **20/1**
606 **4** *nk* **Voice Mail**[14] [4959] 8-8-12 45 .... (p) DavidProbert[(7)] 10 50
(A M Balding) *hld up towards rr: rdn and hdwy 3f out: one pce fnl f* **9/1**
0060 **5** 2½ **Salvestro**[3] [5269] 4-9-0 45 .... LukeMorris[(5)] 6 45
(A W Carroll) *s.s: bhd tl hdwy on ins over 3f out: swtchd rt 2f out: no imp fnl f* **7/1**[3]
5000 **6** 2 **Ten Black**[5] [5235] 3-8-12 43 .... AdamKirby 13 41
(R Brotherton) *hld up in mid-div: rdn and hdwy 3f out: wknd ins fnl f* **40/1**
0005 **7** 2½ **Yenaled**[36] [4267] 10-8-12 43 .... PietroRomeo[(7)] 7 36
(J M Bradley) *hld up in mid-div: rdn and hdwy on ins 3f out: wknd fnl f* **33/1**
3000 **8** 6 **Snake Hips**[20] [4757] 3-8-9 47 .... (b) RichardKingscote[(3)] 2 24
(B Palling) *t.k.h: w wnr tl rdn over 3f out: wknd wl over 1f out* **14/1**
000- **9** 2 **Balfour House**[441] [3006] 4-9-5 35 .... RichardThomas 1 20
(C Roberts) *a bhd* **100/1**
5 **10** 2 **Valassini**[8] [5137] 7-8-7 0 .... KylieManser[(7)] 12 11
(B G Powell) *s.s: hdwy over 5f out: rdn and wknd over 2f out* **50/1**
000 **11** 1¼ **Borita (IRE)**[25] [4630] 4-9-0 50 .... VinceSlattery 9 9
(M Scudamore) *bhd fnl 5f* **66/1**
030- **12** 1 **Shaaban (IRE)**[17] [3386] 6-9-0 40 .... TolleyDean[(5)] 5 12
(R J Price) *prom: rdn 4f out: sn wknd* **50/1**
0600 **13** 5 **Spirit Rising**[3] [5269] 3-8-12 42 .... (p) LPKeniry 3 2
(J M Bradley) *prom: rdn over 3f out: sn wknd* **66/1**

2m 10.75s (0.85) **Going Correction** 0.0s/f (Good)
WFA 3 from 4yo+ 7lb **13** Ran SP% **122.4**
Speed ratings (Par 101): **96,94,91,91,89 87,85,80,79,77 76,75,71**
CSF £5.24 TOTE £3.40: £1.10, £1.30, £5.40; EX 7.10.The winner was bought in for 6,000gns.
Owner M Khan X2 **Bred** M P B Bloodstock Ltd **Trained** Epsom, Surrey
■ Stewards' Enquiry : Harry Poulton one-day ban: breach of Rule 153, improper riding (Sep 24)

FOCUS
Ordinary selling-grade form rated around the first two but limited by those immediately behind.
Ten Black Official explanation: jockey said gelding hung left-handed

5346 WBX.COM 0% COMMISSION ON BIG FOOTBALL MATCHES MAIDEN STKS 1m 4f 23y
4:10 (4:11) (Class 5) 3-Y-O **£2,914** (£867; £433; £216) **Stalls Low**

Form RPR
0-40 **1** **Theta**[15] [4948] 3-8-12 65 .... JimmyQuinn 7 66
(H R A Cecil) *mde all: rdn over 1f out: drvn out* **4/1**[2]
2 ¾ **Vivacita** 3-8-12 0 .... ChrisCatlin 5 65
(E J O'Neill) *hld up towards rr: hdwy over 5f out: rdn wl over 1f out: kpt on ins fnl f* **25/1**
2552 **3** 3 **Easterly Breeze (IRE)**[12] [5045] 3-9-3 74 .... SamHitchcott 9 65
(W R Muir) *chsd wnr: rdn and ev ch over 2f out: no ex ins fnl f* **15/8**[1]
3503 **4** 2 **Apache Chant (USA)**[17] [4877] 3-8-12 50 .... LukeMorris[(5)] 3 62
(A W Carroll) *hld up in tch: rdn over 3f out: one pce fnl 2f* **8/1**
40 **5** 5 **Meon Mix**[33] [4392] 3-8-12 0 .... OscarUrbina 8 49
(J R Fanshawe) *hld up in mid-div: rdn over 3f out: hung lft over 2f out: no imp* **13/2**
6 1 **Hareem (IRE)** 3-9-3 0 .... PatDobbs 2 52
(J A Osborne) *s.s: a bhd* **9/2**[3]
5430 **7** *hd* **Berry Hill Lass (IRE)**[14] [4960] 3-8-5 63 .... ThomasO'Brien[(7)] 4 47
(J G M O'Shea) *hld up towards rr: hdwy over 5f out: rdn over 3f out: sn wknd* **12/1**
8 ½ **Icansingarainbow** 3-8-12 0 .... RussellKennemore[(5)] 1 51
(R Hollinshead) *rdn over 4f out: a bhd* **66/1**
0 **9** 2½ **Wroughton (USA)**[13] [5005] 3-9-3 0 .... IanMongan 6 47
(B J Meehan) *prom: rdn over 2f out: sn wknd* **14/1**

2m 38.32s (-0.40) **Going Correction** 0.0s/f (Good) **9** Ran SP% **117.1**
Speed ratings (Par 101): **101,100,98,97,93 93,93,92,91**
CSF £96.03 TOTE £6.00: £1.50, £4.40, £1.30; EX 117.60.
Owner Niarchos Family **Bred** Mrs B V Chennells **Trained** Newmarket, Suffolk

FOCUS
Poor maiden form and not a race to be with.
Meon Mix Official explanation: jockey said filly hung left-handed

5347 MASKREYS H'CAP 1m 2f 36y
4:45 (4:46) (Class 6) (0-65,64) 3-Y-O **£2,590** (£770; £385; £192) **Stalls Low**

Form RPR
1002 **1** **Red Current**[6] [5188] 3-8-11 **57** .... LPKeniry 5 65
(R A Harris) *prom: lost pl over 5f out: hdwy over 3f out: rdn over 1f out: led wl ins fnl f: r.o* **9/2**[2]
-606 **2** 1 **Danehill Silver**[21] [4742] 3-8-6 **57** .... RussellKennemore[(5)] 13 63
(R Hollinshead) *hld up: hdwy over 5f out: led over 2f out: sn rdn: hdd wl ins fnl f: nt qckn* **20/1**
050 **3** 1¼ **Ravenhill Ralph (IRE)**[66] [3365] 3-7-13 **50** .... LukeMorris[(5)] 9 54
(J G M O'Shea) *hld up and bhd: rdn over 5f out: hdwy on outside over 2f out: edgd lft 1f out: one pce* **66/1**
-606 **4** ½ **Joyful Tears (IRE)**[18] [4855] 3-9-4 **64** .... TGMcLaughlin 4 67
(M G Quinlan) *s.i.s: hld up and bhd: hdwy 3f out: rdn over 1f out: one pce* **25/1**
5540 **5** ½ **Irish Dancer**[73] [3150] 3-9-3 **63** .... (b[1]) J-PGuillambert 2 65
(J L Dunlop) *hld up towards rr: rdn and hdwy 2f out: one pce fnl f* **8/1**[3]
-450 **6** *nk* **Spirit Of Adjisa (IRE)**[115] [1887] 3-9-4 **64** .... PatDobbs 8 65
(Pat Eddery) *a.p: rdn and one pce fnl 2f* **9/1**

0406 **7** *2* **Palanoverre (IRE)**[20] 4766 3-8-0 **53**......................(p) ThomasO'Brien(7) 7 50
(D J S Ffrench Davis) *hld up in tch: rdn over 2f out: no hdwy* **14/1**

3214 **8** *2 ½* **Bidable**[20] 4760 3-9-0 **63**....................................... RichardKingscote(3) 14 55
(B Palling) *led after 1f: rdn and hdd over 2f out: wknd over 1f out* **10/3**[1]

0041 **9** *2* **View From The Top**[13] 5019 3-9-4 **64**.............................. JamieMackay 6 52
(Sir Mark Prescott) *prom: rdn and n.m.r on ins over 2f out: sn wknd* **9/2**[2]

1005 **10** *shd* **Blue Mistral (IRE)**[20] 4760 3-9-0 **60**..............................(t) JimmyQuinn 1 48
(W J Knight) *nvr trbld ldrs* **11/1**

2-64 **11** *9* **Divine Love (IRE)**[12] 5036 3-9-4 **64**..............................(b) ChrisCatlin 11 34
(E J O'Neill) *prom: rdn over 2f out: wknd wl over 1f out* **20/1**

00-6 **12** *shd* **Ceris Star (IRE)**[22] 4707 3-8-6 **52**............................... PaulFitzsimons 16 22
(B R Millman) *hld up in tch: rdn over 3f out: wknd over 2f out* **33/1**

5200 **13** *¾* **Mango Masher (IRE)**[6] 5188 3-8-9 **60**......................(p) TolleyDean(5) 15 28
(J M Bradley) *a bhd* **25/1**

000 **14** *nk* **Stafford Will (IRE)**[108] 2081 3-7-12 **51** ow1............. JosephWalsh(7) 10 18
(J G M O'Shea) *a towards rr* **66/1**

000- **15** *hd* **Classic Blue (IRE)**[300] 6504 3-8-9 **55**............................ OscarUrbina 12 22
(Ian Williams) *led 1f: w ldr tl rdn and wknd wl over 2f out* **33/1**

00U0 **16** *½* **Come On Nellie (IRE)**[52] 3794 3-7-11 **50** oh2................. MCGeran(7) 3 16
(J G M O'Shea) *a bhd* **66/1**

2m 9.65s (-0.25) **Going Correction** 0.0s/f (Good) **16** Ran SP% **123.1**
Speed ratings (Par 99): **101,100,99,98,98 98,96,94,92,92 85,85,85,84,84 84**
CSF £99.15 CT £5181.47 TOTE £5.30: £1.30, £4.00, £12.40, £6.00; EX 171.30.
Owner Leeway Group Limited **Bred** Wretham Stud **Trained** Earlswood, Monmouths

FOCUS
A moderate but competitive handicap rated around the first two and backed up by the fifth and sixth.
Bidable Official explanation: jockey said filly had no more to give
Mango Masher(IRE) Official explanation: jockey said colt never travelled

5348 LETHEBY & CHRISTOPHER H'CAP 1m 14y
5:20 (5:23) (Class 6) (0-65,65) 3-Y-0+ **£2,590** (£770; £385; £192) **Stalls High**

Form RPR

4224 **1** **Libre**[6] 5188 7-9-4 **59**.. TGMcLaughlin 5 69
(F Jordan) *hld up and bhd: rdn and hdwy over 1f out: led ins fnl f: r.o* **13/2**[3]

5013 **2** *nk* **Corrib (IRE)**[6] 5189 4-9-5 **63**................................... RichardKingscote(3) 6 72
(B Palling) *hld up in tch: rdn to ld 1f out: sn hdd: r.o* **5/1**[2]

0046 **3** *¾* **Isphahan**[6] 5189 4-9-3 **58**...(p) LPKeniry 7 65
(A M Balding) *a.p: rdn and ev ch over 1f out: nt qckn ins fnl f* **7/1**

066 **4** *2* **Imperium**[65] 3396 6-9-7 **62**..................................... FrankieMcDonald 10 65
(Jean-Rene Auvray) *hld up and bhd: rdn and hung lft over 1f out: hdwy fnl f: r.o* **18/1**

0200 **5** *hd* **Puissant Princess (IRE)**[23] 4684 3-9-2 **62**..................... JamesDoyle 8 64
(J W Hills) *hld up: hdwy over 3f out: rdn over 1f out: one pce fnl f* **33/1**

-500 **6** *½* **Royal Tavira Girl (IRE)**[30] 4469 4-8-5 **51**.................... TolleyDean(5) 9 52
(M G Quinlan) *s.i.s: hld up in rr: hdwy over 1f out: nt rch ldrs* **66/1**

6030 **7** *nk* **Milton's Keen**[10] 5094 4-8-8 **54**................................ HaddenFrost(5) 2 54
(M Salaman) *led: rdn and hdd 1f out: wknd* **8/1**

5034 **8** *nk* **The Gaikwar (IRE)**[6] 5189 8-9-4 **64**...........................(b) LukeMorris(5) 4 64
(R A Harris) *hld up in tch: rdn over 2f out: wkng whn hung lft ins fnl f* **9/2**[1]

0150 **9** *2 ½* **Foolish Groom**[17] 4880 6-9-3 **58**................................(v) VinceSlattery 13 52
(R Hollinshead) *a bhd* **8/1**

5000 **10** *shd* **Tahdeed**[17] 4885 3-9-5 **65**...(t) JDSmith 3 59
(Sir Michael Stoute) *s.i.s: hld up in mid-div: hdwy over 2f out: rdn over 1f out: btn whn hmpd ins fnl f* **14/1**

0053 **11** *8* **Alasil (USA)**[18] 4856 7-8-5 **51**............................ RussellKennemore(5) 1 26
(R J Price) *prom tl wknd 2f out* **5/1**[2]

404 **12** *4* **Allaire**[12] 5045 3-8-12 **58**.. J-PGuillambert 12 24
(M Johnston) *w ldr tl rdn over 3f out: wknd over 2f out* **20/1**

0500 **13** *½* **Divine White**[37] 4257 4-8-9 **50** oh1.................................. ChrisCatlin 11 15
(P Bowen) *hld up in tch: rdn and wknd over 2f out* **100/1**

1m 34.74s (-1.26) **Going Correction** -0.175s/f (Firm)
WFA 3 from 4yo+ 5lb **13** Ran SP% **121.7**
Speed ratings (Par 101): **99,98,97,95,95 95,94,94,92,92 84,80,79**
CSF £38.82 CT £241.30 TOTE £7.70: £2.50, £1.80, £2.70; EX 51.80.
Owner On The Up Partnership **Bred** J C S Wilson Bloodstock **Trained** Adstone, Northants
■ Stewards' Enquiry : T G McLaughlin two-day ban: excessive use of the whip (Sep 24-25)

FOCUS
Moderate handicap form but, following Red Current's success earlier on the card, this was another boost for the form of the 1m2f handicap that was run here six days earlier. The form is solid and straightforward rated around the placed horses.
Milton's Keen Official explanation: jockey said gelding ran too freely
The Gaikwar(IRE) Official explanation: jockey said gelding hung left-handed
Alasil(USA) Official explanation: jockey said gelding ran too freely

5349 LETHEBY & CHRISTOPHER CATERING MADE SPECIAL H'CAP 5f 16y
5:50 (5:54) (Class 6) (0-65,66) 3-Y-0+ **£2,590** (£770; £385; £192) **Stalls High**

Form RPR

0060 **1** **Cerulean Rose**[6] 5190 8-8-0 **53**.............................. KirstyMilczarek(7) 2 61
(A W Carroll) *hld up and bhd: rdn and hdwy over 1f out: led ins fnl f: r.o* **14/1**

0261 **2** *nk* **Digital**[3] 5272 10-9-6 **66** 6ex...(v) ChrisCatlin 7 73
(M R Channon) *hld up in mid-div: rdn over 2f out: hdwy fnl f: fin wl* **8/1**[3]

064 **3** *hd* **Talcen Gwyn (IRE)**[3] 5272 5-8-12 **58**..........................(v) JimmyQuinn 8 64
(M F Harris) *chsd ldrs: led jst over 1f out: hdd ins fnl f: r.o* **9/2**[2]

3450 **4** *nk* **Hello Roberto**[6] 5191 6-8-2 **53**.............................(p) KevinGhunowa(5) 4 58
(R A Harris) *chsd ldrs: rdn and ev ch ins fnl f: kpt on* **14/1**

000 **5** *½* **One Way Ticket**[3] 5272 7-9-5 **65**..............................(p) J-PGuillambert 13 68
(J M Bradley) *a.p: rdn and ev ch 1f out: kpt on* **12/1**

5233 **6** *hd* **Endless Summer**[6] 5191 10-8-11 **57**............................. DavidKinsella 5 61+
(A W Carroll) *hld up and bhd: hdwy over 2f out: rdn over 1f out: ev ch ins fnl f: hld whn hmpd cl home* **3/1**[1]

0540 **7** *½* **Summer Recluse (USA)**[3] 5272 8-8-9 **62**..............(t) BarrySavage(7) 12 63
(J M Bradley) *hld up and bhd: rdn over 1f out: late hdwy: nrst fin* **14/1**

3564 **8** *½* **Drumming Party (USA)**[8] 5130 5-8-12 **58**.......................(t) LPKeniry 14 57
(A M Balding) *s.i.s: hld up and bhd: stdy hdwy over 2f out: one pce fnl f* **9/2**[2]

10 **9** *shd* **King Egbert (FR)**[15] 4944 6-8-2 **53**............................. TolleyDean(5) 6 51
(R J Price) *chsd ldrs: rdn over 2f out: one pce fnl f* **8/1**[3]

0005 **10** *nk* **Campeon (IRE)**[3] 5276 5-8-5 **51** oh6.............................. JamesDoyle 3 48
(J M Bradley) *chsd ldr tl rdn over 1f out: sn btn* **50/1**

0000 **11** *1 ¾* **Maktavish**[150] 1065 8-8-0 **53**..(b) SophieDoyle(7) 1 44
(R Brotherton) *led: rdn and hdd jst over 1f out: fdd ins fnl f* **25/1**

6050 **12** *1 ¾* **Whistler**[17] 4881 10-8-5 **51** oh4.................................(b) RichardThomas 11 36
(Miss J R Tooth) *a towards rr* **33/1**

0000 **13** *nk* **Enjoy The Buzz**[10] 5090 8-7-12 **51** oh4..............................(p) MCGeran(7) 9 35
(J M Bradley) *a bhd* **66/1**

0000 **14** *7* **Ballybunion (IRE)**[24] 4668 8-8-0 **51** oh6........................ LukeMorris(5) 15 9
(R A Harris) *a bhd* **33/1**

59.07 secs (-0.53) **Going Correction** -0.175s/f (Firm) **14** Ran SP% **123.6**
Speed ratings (Par 101): **97,96,96,95,94 94,93,93,92,92 89,86,86,75**
CSF £121.13 CT £615.60 TOTE £14.00: £4.00, £2.20, £2.30; EX 173.40 Place 6 £134.05, Place 5 £50.85.
Owner Rob Willis **Bred** J And Mrs Bowtell **Trained** Cropthorne, Worcs

FOCUS
A moderate handicap run at a good pace and sound but ordinary form for the grade rated around the third and fourth.
T/Plt: £109.20 to a £1 stake. Pool: £49,851.20. 333.20 winning tickets. T/Qpdt: £7.70 to a £1 stake. Pool: £3,281.60. 313.40 winning tickets. KH

5321 DONCASTER (L-H)
Thursday, September 13

OFFICIAL GOING: Good to firm (9.4)
After more dry weather the ground had dried out and was described as 'good to firm, quicker than the previous day but with no jar whatsoever'.
Wind: Light, half-against Weather: Fine, sunny and warm

5350 FOUNTAIN SPA AT BARRINGTON HOUSE NURSERY 1m (S)
2:05 (2:08) (Class 2) 2-Y-0 **£16,192** (£4,817; £2,407; £1,202) **Stalls High**

Form RPR

504 **1** **Jack Dawkins (USA)**[41] 4130 2-8-10 **75**.............................. TedDurcan 16 83
(H R A Cecil) *racd stands' side: hld up in rr: hdwy over 2f out: led and edgd lft 1f out: styd on wl to ld overall towards fin: 1st of 9 that gp* **8/1**[3]

053 **2** *½* **Stubbs Art (IRE)**[28] 4539 2-8-6 **71**.. TQuinn 8 78
(D R C Elsworth) *racd far side: chsd ldrs: led that gp and overall over 1f out: hdd towards fin: 1st of 10 that gp* **12/1**

0326 **3** *½* **Ellemujie**[19] 4812 2-9-5 **84**.. LDettori 14 90
(D K Ivory) *racd stands' side: in rr: hdwy over 2f out: styd on strly ins fnl f: 2nd of 9 that gp* **20/1**

5153 **4** *1 ¼* **The Betchworth Kid**[20] 4776 2-9-3 **82**........................... HayleyTurner 15 85
(M L W Bell) *lw: racd stands' side: chsd ldrs: edgd lft over 1f out: styd on same pce: 3rd of 9 that gp* **13/2**[2]

010 **5** *¾* **Ernie Owl (USA)**[12] 5048 2-9-7 **86**....................................... MJKinane 18 87
(B J Meehan) *lw: racd stands' side: chsd ldrs: effrt over 2f out: styd on same pce appr fnl f: 4th of 9 that gp* **50/1**

3561 **6** *shd* **Determind Stand (USA)**[14] 4964 2-8-11 **76**................... RyanMoore 21 77
(Sir Michael Stoute) *lw: racd stands' side: chsd ldrs: kpt on same pce appr fnl f: 5th of 9 that gp* **14/1**

0233 **7** *nk* **Talk Of Saafend (IRE)**[19] 4812 2-8-9 **74**........................ SebSanders 1 74
(R Hannon) *racd far side: chsd ldrs: kpt on same pce appr fnl f: 2nd of 10 that gp* **16/1**

2163 **8** *nk* **Fathsta (IRE)**[12] 5053 2-8-9 **74**.. MartinDwyer 20 73
(S Kirk) *lw: racd stands' side: chsd ldrs: kpt on same pce appr fnl f: 6th of 9 that gp* **33/1**

5311 **9** *shd* **Siberian Tiger (IRE)**[13] 5002 2-9-7 **86**......................... RichardMullen 3 85
(M R Channon) *racd far side: chsd ldrs: chal over 1f out: kpt on same pce: 3rd of 10 that gp* **6/1**[1]

0034 **10** *hd* **Dalkey Girl (IRE)**[19] 4812 2-9-2 **81**............................... JamieSpencer 5 80
(V Smith) *hmpd s: racd far side: sn chsng ldrs: one pce fnl 2f: 4th of 10 that gp* **25/1**

414 **11** *2* **Ghetto**[9] 5109 2-9-3 **82**.. JimmyFortune 6 76
(R Hannon) *lw: led far side tl over 1f out: sn wknd: 5th of 10 that gp* **9/1**

41 **12** *hd* **Blue Sky Basin**[17] 4882 2-8-11 **76**................................ FrancisNorton 13 70
(A M Balding) *racd stands' side: t.k.h: w ldrs: led that gp over 2f out: hdd & wknd 1f out: 7th of 9 that gp* **25/1**

41 **13** *2 ½* **Annaliesse (IRE)**[53] 3761 2-8-7 **72**................................ PaulHanagan 10 60
(R A Fahey) *racd far side: hld up towards rr: effrt 2f out: sn wknd: 6th of 10 that gp* **33/1**

002 **14** *3* **Doctor Robert**[20] 4764 2-8-10 **75**................................ SteveDrowne 19 56
(R Charlton) *led stands' side tl over 2f out: lost pl over 1f out: 8th of 9 that gp* **8/1**[3]

3235 **15** *shd* **Transmission (IRE)**[36] 4278 2-8-12 **77**............................... TomEaves 7 58
(B Smart) *racd far side: in rr and sn drvn along: nvr a factor: 7th of 10 that gp* **100/1**

023 **16** *nk* **Crystal Rock (IRE)**[12] 5033 2-9-2 **81**............................... MichaelHills 12 61
(B W Hills) *swtchd rt and racd stands' side: t.k.h: sn trcking ldrs: wknd over 1f out: last of 9 that gp* **14/1**

3411 **17** *3* **Cobo Bay**[20] 4776 2-9-4 **83**.. NCallan 2 56
(K A Ryan) *racd far side: chsd ldrs: lost pl over 1f out: 8th of 10 that gp* **14/1**

6612 **18** *¾* **Welcome Return (IRE)**[17] 4892 2-8-10 **75**..................(b) DavidAllan 4 47
(T D Easterby) *racd far side: prom on outer: lost pl over 1f out: 9th of 10 that gp* **40/1**

21 **19** *2* **Bonjour Allure (IRE)**[29] 4487 2-9-1 **80**.................. RoystonFfrench 9 47
(Mrs A Duffield) *racd far side: w ldrs: lost pl over 2f out: last of 10 that gp* **14/1**

1m 38.68s (-2.83) **Going Correction** -0.325s/f (Firm) **19** Ran SP% **123.8**
Speed ratings (Par 101): **101,100,100,98,98 97,97,97,97,97 95,94,92,89,89 88,85,85,83**
CSF £91.76 CT £1918.53 TOTE £12.00: £3.20, £3.60, £3.60, £2.70; EX 193.80 TRIFECTA Not won..
Owner Mark & Sue Harniman **Bred** Clovelly Farms **Trained** Newmarket, Suffolk

FOCUS
A very competitive nursery in which the field predictably split into two. The ten drawn lowest all went far side whilst the other nine came stands' side and there never seemed to be a great deal between the two groups throughout the contest, though ultimately five of the first six came from the stands'-side group. The pace was solid and the winning time was about what you would expect for a race like this with the form rated positively and should throw up plenty of winners.

NOTEBOOK
Jack Dawkins(USA) ◆, making his nursery debut and 11lb better off with Siberian Tiger after finishing just over a length behind him at Newmarket last time, was given a patient ride in the nearside group but took off when switched wide for his effort and flew home to nail the leader on the other flank. The extra furlong and decent gallop suited him down to the ground and he can win again. (tchd 17-2)
Stubbs Art(IRE) ◆, another making his nursery debut over an extra furlong, could hardly have done much more without breaking his duck as he put clear daylight between himself and the others in the far-side group, only to get mugged by a strong-finishing rival on the other flank. He would only need repeat this in order to get off the mark. (op 11-1)

Ellemujie ◆, another stepping up in trip, was noted finishing very strongly in the nearside group. He is a bit more exposed than the pair that beat him, but is certainly still capable of winning a nursery off this sort of mark. (op 25-1)

The Betchworth Kid ◆, whose stamina for this trip was not in doubt, did not do a lot wrong having been there or thereabouts in the stands'-side group throughout, but the quicker ground meant that this was probably an insufficient test. With the ground between now and the end of the season likely to become more testing, there should be other days. (op 7-1 tchd 15-2)

Ernie Owl(USA), making his nursery debut after finishing last in the Solario, found that the solid pace gave him less of a chance to pull and he ran with credit in the nearside group. He has probably been handicapped on the basis that he has run twice in Group races and beaten a 92-rated rival in his maiden, but he may need to drop a little bit in order to be successful in races like this.

Determind Stand(USA), raised 4lb for his Lingfield victory, had every chance in the nearside group but so far his best efforts have come on Polytrack.

Talk Of Saafend(IRE), raised another 2lb for her possibly unlucky effort at Newmarket, was staying on in fair fashion over on the far side of the track to finish second of that group, albeit a respectful distance behind Stubbs Art. The trip was not a problem, but she is continually creeping up the weights despite still being a maiden after eight attempts.

Siberian Tiger(IRE) had been raised 8lb for his easy victory in a nursery over this trip at Salisbury, but that meant he was 11lb worse off with Jack Dawkins whom he had beaten by just over a length in his previous outing at Newmarket. That gave an indication as to the task he faced in his bid for a hat-trick and he was not up to it, although he did threaten to get into the argument over on the far side at one stage and finished third of that group. (op 13-2)

Ghetto took the far-side group along for much of the contest before fading, but is still worth another chance back on an easier surface. (op 8-1)

Blue Sky Basin, making his nursery debut after winning a Polytrack maiden, did his chances no good by taking a keen grip at the front of the nearside group and duly paid for it later on. He was one of the least exposed in the field so is worth another chance over this sort of trip, especially when he learns to settle better. Official explanation: jockey said gelding ran too free (op 28-1)

Doctor Robert, making his nursery debut, led the stands'-side group for a long way but appeared not to see out the extra furlong. (op 15-2 tchd 7-1)

5351 CROWNHOTEL-BAWTRY.COM CONDITIONS STKS — 1m 2f 60y

2:40 (2:40) (Class 2) 3-5-Y-O

£12,464 (£3,732; £1,866; £934; £466; £234) **Stalls** Low

Form — RPR

431- **1** — **Kirklees (IRE)**[333] [6003] 3-8-9 111 .... LDettori 3 — 113+
(Saeed Bin Suroor) *hld up in tch: smooth hdwy on outer 3f out: led 2f out: sn qcknd clr: eased ins fnl f* — **7/4**[1]

5051 **2** *2 1/2* **Many Volumes (USA)**[34] [4366] 3-9-1 96 .... TPQueally 2 — 111
(H R A Cecil) *hld up in tch: hdwy 3f out: n.m.r and swtchd rt 2f out: sn rdn and chsd wnr over 1f out: no imp* — **11/2**[3]

2160 **3** *1 1/4* **Salford Mill (IRE)**[83] [2813] 3-9-3 111 .... TedDurcan 6 — 111
(D R C Elsworth) *hld up in rr: hdwy on outer over 3f out: rdn along over 2f out: drvn and no imp fr wl over 1f out* — **11/4**[2]

-250 **4** *1 1/4* **Gravitas**[189] [645] 4-9-2 109 .... JamieSpencer 7 — 100
(Saeed Bin Suroor) *led: rdn along 3f out: hdd 2f out and grad wknd* — **6/1**

0603 **5** *3/4* **Duke Of Tuscany**[17] [4887] 3-8-9 96 .... (p) RyanMoore 4 — 99
(R Hannon) *chsd ldr: effrt over 2f out: sn rdn and wknd wl over 1f out* — **20/1**

3160 **6** *shd* **Big Robert**[19] [4803] 3-8-13 107 .... (t) MartinDwyer 5 — 102
(W R Muir) *hld up: a in rr* — **18/1**

005 **7** *nk* **Dont Dili Dali**[40] [4149] 4-8-11 107 .... (p) SebSanders 1 — 93
(J S Moore) *prom: rdn along over 3f out: wknd over 2f out* — **10/1**

2m 6.01s (-5.82) **Going Correction** -0.325s/f (Firm)
WFA 3 from 4yo 7lb — **7** Ran SP% **111.8**
Speed ratings (Par 109): **110,108,107,106,105 105,105**
CSF £11.31 TOTE £2.50: £1.70, £3.50; EX 11.20.

Owner Godolphin **Bred** Darley **Trained** Newmarket, Suffolk

FOCUS

A decent little conditions event with five of the seven runners rated 107 or higher and Gravitas made sure the pace was even. However, this was turned into a rout by the winner who looks capable of holding his own back in much better company.

NOTEBOOK

Kirklees(IRE) ◆, not seen since winning the Gran Criterium at San Siro for Mark Johnston 11 months ago, was making his first start for Godolphin and stepping up two furlongs in trip. The market suggested he was not expected to need it and that was proved correct, as he travelled like a dream and when asked to go and win his race produced a very impressive turn of foot to put his rivals to the sword. He could have won by even further had he wanted and he can make his mark back in Group company. (op 2-1 tchd 9-4 in places)

Many Volumes(USA) had plenty to find with most of these at the weights, but at least he came into this in form and the conditions were ideal. He stayed on well once switched out for his effort, but the winner was in a completely different league. Where he goes next may depend to a certain extent on whether the Handicapper takes this form at face value.

Salford Mill(IRE), down in class after contesting the Epsom Derby and King Edward VII at Royal Ascot, was given a patient ride but when pulled out and asked for his effort his response was rather slow and laboured. The drop back in trip may not have been ideal, but he is not progressing and may continue to be a difficult horse to place. (tchd 3-1)

Gravitas, formerly with Andre Fabre and not seen since the third of three outings for Godolphin at Nad Al Sheba in March, was having his first start in this country. Whether by accident or design, he did a good job of pacemaking but this performance told us very little about him. (op 7-1)

Duke Of Tuscany, who had plenty on at these weights, showed up for a long way but has become a very hard horse to place. (op 16-1)

Big Robert was briefly off the bridle just after exiting the stalls and things never really got much better for him. Apart from winning a virtual match at Leicester in July, he is another that is beginning to look a 'twilight' horse. (op 14-1)

Dont Dili Dali, must have an iron constitution given her busy schedule, but even though this should have been easier than many of her tasks this season she was still well and truly put in her place. (op 9-1)

5352 GOFFS/DBS PARK HILL STKS (GROUP 2) (F&M) — 1m 6f 132y

3:10 (3:12) (Class 1) 3-Y-O+

£56,780 (£21,520; £10,770; £5,370; £2,690; £1,350) **Stalls** Low

Form — RPR

5111 **1** — **Hi Calypso (IRE)**[42] [4089] 3-8-7 106 ow1 .... RyanMoore 1 — 111
(Sir Michael Stoute) *lw: hld up in rr: stdy hdwy on outer over 3f out: chsd ldrs 2f out: rdn to ld ent fnl f: sn drvn: edgd lft and kpt on* — **9/2**[3]

2323 **2** *nk* **All My Loving (IRE)**[60] [3576] 3-8-6 0 .... MJKinane 3 — 110
(A P O'Brien, Ire) *trckd ldng pair: hdwy 4f out: led over 2f out: rdn wl over 1f out: drvn and hdd ent fnl f: kpt on* — **9/4**[1]

0442 **3** *3/4* **Brisk Breeze (GER)**[21] [4748] 3-8-6 101 .... TedDurcan 2 — 109
(H R A Cecil) *trckd ldrs: n.m.r on inner and swtchd rt 2f out: sn rdn and ev ch ent fnl f: drvn and no ex last 100yds* — **33/1**

61 **4** *1 1/2* **Synopsis (IRE)**[28] [4557] 3-8-6 0 .... SPasquier 10 — 107
(A Fabre, France) *rangy: midfield: hdwy over 4f out: chsd ldrs 3f out: rdn over 2f out: kpt on same pce appr fnl f* — **9/2**[3]

4234 **5** *shd* **Under The Rainbow**[22] [4723] 4-9-4 100 .... (p) LDettori 6 — 107
(B W Hills) *hld up towards rr: stdy hdwy 4f out: chsd ldrs whn n.m.r and swtchd rt over 2f out: sn rdn and kpt on same pce* — **20/1**

1-10 **6** *2* **Kayah**[104] [2211] 3-8-6 96 .... MartinDwyer 4 — 104
(R M Beckett) *midfield: hdwy 3f out: rdn along and kpt on fnl 2f: nt rch ldrs* — **33/1**

0033 **7** *3 1/2* **Trick Or Treat**[22] [4723] 4-9-4 102 .... TPQueally 5 — 99
(J G Given) *led 4f: chsd ldr tl led again 4f out: rdn 3f out: drvn and hdd over 2f out: grad wknd* — **25/1**

2321 **8** *hd* **Wannabe Posh (IRE)**[21] [4748] 4-9-4 104 .... SebSanders 14 — 99
(J L Dunlop) *hld up: hdwy on outer 1/2-way: chsd ldrs 4f out: sn rdn along and wknd fnl 2f* — **10/1**

05-0 **9** *hd* **Guilia**[21] [4748] 4-9-4 96 .... DarryllHolland 9 — 98
(Rae Guest) *s.i.s and bhd tl sme late hdwy* — **66/1**

111 **10** *6* **Turbo Linn**[54] [3744] 4-9-7 110 .... NCallan 11 — 93
(G A Swinbank) *lw: in tch: hdwy 4f out: pushed along to chse ldrs 3f out: rdn and btn 2f out* — **3/1**[2]

0042 **11** *4* **Lady Dedlock**[19] [4809] 3-8-6 53 .... SimonWhitworth 13 — 84?
(C A Cyzer) *a in rr* — **200/1**

1602 **12** *10* **Wassfa**[39] [4203] 4-9-4 85 .... PhilipRobinson 12 — 70
(C E Brittain) *a in rr* — **100/1**

0-03 **13** *7* **Mussoorie (FR)**[21] [4748] 4-9-4 103 .... JimmyFortune 7 — 61
(J H M Gosden) *chsd ldrs: rdn along 4f out: sn wknd* — **50/1**

2006 **14** *3* **High Heel Sneakers**[21] [4748] 4-9-4 104 .... (b) TQuinn 8 — 56
(P F I Cole) *chsd ldr: led after 4f: rdn along and hdd 4f out: sn wknd* — **100/1**

3m 1.07s (-8.67) **Going Correction** -0.325s/f (Firm) course record
WFA 3 from 4yo 12lb — **14** Ran SP% **121.6**
Speed ratings (Par 115): **110,109,109,108,108 107,105,105,105,102 100,94,91,89**
CSF £14.28 TOTE £6.10: £2.00, £1.50, £8.10; EX 21.00 Trifecta £416.30 Pool: £996.90 - 1.70 winning tickets..

Owner Philip Newton **Bred** Philip Newton **Trained** Newmarket, Suffolk

FOCUS

A decent-sized field for the Park Hill and, with High Heel Sneakers and Trick Or Treat taking each other on for the lead from the start, the early pace was a good one and the form looks reasonable. The winner Hi Calypso took 1.15 seconds off the course record which had stood for 15 years, but when assessed alongside the rest of the meeting the winning time was just fair for a race of its stature.

NOTEBOOK

Hi Calypso(IRE), whose stamina for this was not in doubt, jumped the path after they had gone a furlong in a style of which Istabraq would have been proud. She did not appear to be going that well turning for home either, but once into the straight she was back on the bridle down the outside of the track and, when asked to go and win her race, maintained her effort to just get the better of the very brave runner-up. She is likely to be put away now and is very much one to look forward to next season. (tchd 5-1 in a place)

All My Loving(IRE), placed in the English and Irish Oaks' plus the Ribblesdale in her last three outings, was not ridden as though the longer trip was going to be an issue, racing in a clear third for much of the way. She hit the front halfway up the home straight and fought back in tenacious style even after being headed, thereby proving her stamina. She more than deserves to win a Group race, but there are not that many opportunities left this season for those fillies just short of Group 1 class, though the Princess Royal Stakes at Ascot could be a possibility. (op 3-1 tchd 10-3 in a place)

Brisk Breeze(GER) had to change course halfway up the home straight, but still came through to hold every chance and ran a cracker. She finished a bit closer to Hi Calypso than she did at Goodwood early last month and reversed the form of that race with both Trick Or Treat and Wannabe Posh. This consistent filly deserves to win a Listed contest at least.

Synopsis(IRE), still comparatively lightly raced, had every chance entering the last couple of furlongs, but lacked the pace to get in an effective blow. The fast ground may have inconvenienced her more than the longer trip. (op 4-1)

Under The Rainbow ran her usual sort of race, plugging on after being switched wide but never looking like getting to the leaders. She is not short of stamina, but she is short of pace and is now without a win in nearly two years.

Kayah, not seen since finishing well beaten in the Oaks, lacked the pace to get to the principals but was by no means disgraced. Her Lingfield Oaks Trial victory over Brisk Breeze earlier in the season showed how well she acts with cut, so with this effort likely to have brought her on there may still be an opportunity waiting for her.

Guilia Official explanation: jockey said filly was slowly away due to one side of the gate opening slowly

Turbo Linn, bidding to extend her unbeaten winning sequence to nine, did not pick up under pressure in the same way she has been doing and ended up well beaten. The fact that fillies she had previously beaten comfortably finished well ahead of her here shows how far below form she ran. It may be that the quick ground found her out in this grade, even though she has won on it in much lesser company, but she owes no-one anything and will hopefully return better than ever next term. Official explanation: jockey said filly was outpaced on fast ground (tchd 10-3, 7-2 in a place)

5353 FRENCHGATE FIRST FOR FASHION MAY HILL STKS (GROUP 2) (FILLIES) — 1m (S)

3:45 (3:45) (Class 1) 2-Y-O

£42,585 (£16,140; £8,077; £4,027; £2,017; £1,012) **Stalls** High

Form — RPR

1 **1** — **Spacious**[24] [4656] 2-8-12 0 .... JamieSpencer 5 — 107+
(J R Fanshawe) *stdd s: hld up in rr: smooth hdwy over 2f out: shkn up to ld jst ins fnl f: edgd rt: hld on towards fin* — **9/4**[1]

1 **2** *1/2* **Kotsi (IRE)**[20] [4774] 2-8-12 0 .... LDettori 11 — 104
(E F Vaughan) *hld up in rr: hdwy over 2f out: styd on wl ins fnl f* — **10/1**

612 **3** *hd* **Celtic Slipper (IRE)**[19] [4804] 2-8-12 99 .... SebSanders 7 — 103
(R M Beckett) *hld up in midfield: hdwy over 2f out: led over 1f out: hdd jst ins fnl f: kpt on same pce* — **16/1**

2 **4** *1 1/4* **Sugar Mint (IRE)**[27] [4565] 2-8-12 0 .... MichaelHills 3 — 101
(B W Hills) *hld up: hdwy over 2f out: styd on same pce fnl f* — **12/1**

1 **5** *1* **Lady Jane Digby**[27] [4564] 2-8-12 0 .... GregFairley 10 — 98
(M Johnston) *chsd ldrs: qcknd and led over 3f out tl over 1f out: styd on same pce* — **8/1**[3]

11 **6** *5* **Step Softly**[35] [4329] 2-8-12 0 .... RyanMoore 12 — 87
(R Hannon) *mid-div: effrt 3f out: wknd over 1f out* — **14/1**

12 **7** *1 1/4* **Don't Forget Faith (USA)**[33] [4400] 2-8-12 0 .... PhilipRobinson 2 — 84
(C G Cox) *chsd ldrs: wknd over 1f out* — **5/2**[2]

0 **8** *1* **Soinlovewithyou (USA)**[25] [4644] 2-8-12 0 .... TedDurcan 4 — 82
(A P O'Brien, Ire) *mid-div: effrt over 2f out: no imp* — **66/1**

5 **9** *3/4* **Prima Luce (IRE)**[19] [4834] 2-8-12 0 .... KJManning 8 — 80
(J S Bolger, Ire) *rangy: scope: chsd ldrs: lost pl over 1f out* — **18/1**

3 **10** *1* **Sweet Kiss (USA)**[62] 3507 2-8-12 0 MJKinane 13 78
(B J Meehan) *chsd ldrs: lost pl 2f out* **12/1**

4 **11** *5* **Ariege (USA)**[32] 4440 2-8-12 0 WMLordan 6 66
(T Stack, Ire) *lengthy: scope: sn trcking ldrs: hung lft thrght: lost pl 2f out* **20/1**

2044 **12** *4* **Miss Emma May (IRE)**[20] 4774 2-8-12 81 TQuinn 9 57
(D R C Elsworth) *t.k.h: led tl over 3f out: wknd 2f out* **100/1**

1m 37.58s (-3.93) **Going Correction** -0.325s/f (Firm) **12** Ran SP% **120.0**
Speed ratings (Par 104): **106,105,105,104,103 98,96,95,95,94 89,85**
CSF £25.97 TOTE £3.20: £1.50, £2.70, £4.70; EX 42.90 Trifecta £559.40 Part won. Pool: £788.00 - 0.84 winning tickets..
Owner Cheveley Park Stud **Bred** Cheveley Park Stud Ltd **Trained** Newmarket, Suffolk
■ Stewards' Enquiry : Jamie Spencer one-day ban: careless riding (Sep 24)

FOCUS
A competitive May Hill, run at a decent pace and the first four were all held up. Most of the runners raced towards the stands' rail, though one was kept wider than the others early. The winning time was perfectly creditable for a race like this, 1.1 seconds faster than the earlier nursery and the form looks sound enough.

NOTEBOOK
Spacious ◆, easy winner of a Leicester maiden on her debut in which the pair that chased her home have both gone in since, was ridden with all the confidence in the world right out the back. She cruised right around the whole field to hit the front down the outside coming to the last furlong, but once there she started to idle and hung away to her right, hampering the runner-up as she did so. Given her lack of experience she can be forgiven for that and she was the best filly in the race. She will apparently be put away now and be trained for the 1000 Guineas, and on this evidence she will go there with a major chance provided she trains on and all goes well. (op 2-1)
Kotsi(IRE) ◆, successful from a subsequent winner on her Newmarket debut last month, was given a more patient ride this time. Produced with her effort between horses, she was finishing strongly when carried away to her right by the hanging favourite and she would have gone even closer with a clear run. She is likely to be given a chance at the top level before the end of the season, but would need to be supplemented for both the Fillies' Mile and Prix Marcel Boussac. (op 14-1)
Celtic Slipper(IRE) ◆, already placed in Group company, came through to hold every chance and kept on battling right to the line even though she was done few favours by being nudged towards the stands'-rail near the line in the chain reaction started by the hanging winner. She is more exposed than the pair that beat her, but looks up to winning a Listed race at least on this evidence. (op 20-1)
Sugar Mint(IRE), who ran well despite being a beaten favourite on her debut here last month, came through to hold every chance down the wide outside, but was only fighting for places when having to check slightly as the winner ran across her half a furlong from home. She is bred to get further and will have no difficulty in winning races. (op 10-1 tchd 14-1)
Lady Jane Digby, successful on her debut here last month, was always up there and, although she was done for speed late on, still did best of those that raced handily and pulled right away from the others. Her talented siblings tended to improve with age, so the future does look bright for her. (op 12-1)
Step Softly, winner of her first two starts, though neither contest has worked out that well, was taking a big step up in class. However, a mid-race move came to little and a combination of the stiffer company and longer trip seemed to find her out, even though she should get it on pedigree.
Don't Forget Faith(USA) was kept noticably wide of her rivals in the early stages, but was right up with the pace until coming under pressure and dropping tamely away over a furlong from home. Perhaps she saw too much daylight and her rider reported that she did not enjoy the ground, but even so the Sweet Solera form is starting to look a little suspect. Official explanation: jockey said filly was unsuited by the good to firm ground (op 11-4)

5354 JAPAN RACING ASSOCIATION SCEPTRE STKS (LISTED RACE) (F&M) 7f
4:20 (4:20) (Class 1) 3-Y-0+ **£17,781** (£6,723; £3,360; £1,680) **Stalls** High

Form RPR

2316 **1** **Medley**[7] 5163 3-8-10 95 RyanMoore 3 92
(R Hannon) *hld up towards rr: gd hdwy over 2f out: rdn to chse ldrs over 1f out: drvn and styd on strly ins fnl f to ld post* **14/1**

1155 **2** *hd* **Our Faye**[7] 5163 4-9-0 87 JamieSpencer 8 93
(S Kirk) *hld up in rr: gd hdwy on outer over 2f out: hung rt: rdn and edgd rt 1f out: led wl ins fnl f: hdd on post* **16/1**

0410 **3** *½* **Passion Fruit**[27] 4581 6-9-0 83 PaulMulrennan 9 92
(C W Fairhurst) *hld up and bhd: gd hdwy on outer over 2f out: rdn to chse ldrs over 1f out: kpt on u.p ins fnl f* **66/1**

1205 **4** *hd* **Majestic Roi (USA)**[41] 4118 3-9-1 108 DarryllHolland 13 96+
(M R Channon) *hld up in rr: hdwy and nt clr run over 1f out: swtchd lft and rdn ins fnl f: kpt on wl towards fin* **5/2**[1]

-305 **5** *1* **Rahiyah (USA)**[40] 4148 3-8-10 111 TedDurcan 2 87
(J Noseda) *chsd ldrs: hdwy over 2f out: rdn to ld 1f out: sn drvn: hdd wl ins fnl f and no ex towards fin* **11/4**[2]

500 **6** *1* **Lady Livius (IRE)**[12] 5047 4-9-0 89 JimmyFortune 7 86
(R Hannon) *cl up: led wl over 1f out: sn rdn: hdd ent fnl f: sn drvn: edgd rt and wknd* **66/1**

4030 **7** *nk* **Daniella**[39] 4196 5-9-0 76 (b) NCallan 11 85
(Rae Guest) *hld up towards rr: hdwy 2f out: rdn to chse ldrs whn hmpd ent fnl f: swtchd lft and styd on wl towards fin* **100/1**

6050 **8** *1* **Vital Statistics**[41] 4118 3-8-10 102 TQuinn 5 81
(D R C Elsworth) *nvr bttr than midfield* **7/1**[3]

-115 **9** *1 ¾* **Para Siempre**[76] 3059 3-8-10 95 (b) RoystonFfrench 15 76
(B Smart) *chsd ldrs: rdn along 3f out: grad wknd* **66/1**

2221 **10** *hd* **Awwal Malika (USA)**[22] 4711 3-8-10 70 PhilipRobinson 1 75
(C E Brittain) *cl up: rdn along wl over 2f out and grad wknd* **66/1**

20-0 **11** *shd* **Wid (USA)**[145] 1146 3-8-10 100 MartinDwyer 10 75
(J L Dunlop) *t.k.h: chsd ldrs: rdn along wl over 2f out and sn wknd* **16/1**

6002 **12** *½* **Sesmen**[25] 4633 3-8-10 100 (t) LDettori 4 74
(M Botti) *led 3f: rdn along wl over 2f out and sn wknd* **8/1**

2-00 **13** *2* **Silk Blossom (IRE)**[83] 2814 3-8-10 107 MichaelHills 14 68
(B W Hills) *n.d* **12/1**

1210 **14** *2 ½* **Expensive**[85] 2753 4-9-3 98 GeorgeBaker 6 67
(C F Wall) *prom: led after 3f: rdn over 2f out: hdd wl over 1f out and sn wknd* **14/1**

0660 **15** *26* **Chantilly Tiffany**[12] 5047 3-8-10 90 (b) SteveDrowne 12 —
(E A L Dunlop) *dwlt: sn cl up on stands' rail: rdn along 3f out and sn wknd: bhd and eased wl over 1f out* **40/1**

1m 24.82s (-2.95) **Going Correction** -0.325s/f (Firm)
WFA 3 from 4yo+ 4lb **15** Ran SP% **121.0**
Speed ratings (Par 111): **103,102,102,101,100 99,99,98,96,95 95,95,93,90,60**
CSF £215.98 TOTE £17.50: £5.50, £4.40, £13.90; EX 118.80 TRIFECTA Not won..
Owner The Queen **Bred** The Queen **Trained** East Everleigh, Wilts

FOCUS
They went a very strong gallop and it paid to come from off the pace. The race has been rated around the placed horses but overall the form has a doubtful look about it.

NOTEBOOK
Medley, who had something to find, showed a very willing spirit to snatch the spoils near the line. She may now continue her racing career in America before going to a stallion over there. (op 12-1)
Our Faye, who had a lot to find, hung right under pressure but she battled hard and only lost out near the line. Official explanation: jockey said filly hung right-handed (op 18-1)
Passion Fruit, who had a mountain to climb, sat last. She made ground on the wide outside and in the end only just missed out. She has proved a grand servant and is a credit to connections. (op 100-1)
Majestic Roi(USA), who seems to need to come from the rear, met all sorts of traffic problems and may well have been unlucky not to pull it off (op 11-4)
Rahiyah(USA), who had a genuine excuse at Goodwood, hit her head in the stalls. Only found wanting in the closing stages she was reported to have returned with a head injury. Official explanation: jockey said filly hit her head in stalls; vet said filly returned injured (op 5-2 tchd 3-1)
Lady Livius(IRE), out of sorts since her Polytrack success in March, made no appeal beforehand but seemed to run out of her skin. (op 100-1)
Daniella, a candidate for last place on official ratings, belied her extreme odds. (op 80-1)
Vital Statistics Official explanation: vet said filly had lost right-fore shoe
Sesmen Official explanation: jockey said filly lost its action
Chantilly Tiffany Official explanation: trainer's rep said filly finished distressed

5355 WEATHERBYS INSURANCE H'CAP 7f
4:55 (4:56) (Class 2) (0-100,100) 3-Y-O
£12,464 (£3,732; £1,866; £934; £466; £234) **Stalls** High

Form RPR

2110 **1** **Danehillsundance (IRE)**[25] 4640 3-8-7 **89** ow1 RyanMoore 12 100
(R Hannon) *hld up and bhd: gd hdwy 2f out: swtchd lft and rdn over 1f out: str run to ld ins fnl f: kpt on wl* **8/1**

2422 **2** *shd* **Miss Lucifer (FR)**[7] 5163 3-8-8 **90** LDettori 5 101
(B W Hills) *hld up in rr: effrt whn nt clr run over 2f out: gd hdwy over 1f out: rdn and ev ch ent fnl f: drvn and kpt on wl* **5/2**[1]

0552 **3** *2 ½* **Majuro (IRE)**[15] 4950 3-9-0 **96** DarryllHolland 11 100
(M R Channon) *trckd ldrs: hdwy 2f out: rdn to ld over 1f out: sn drvn: hdd & wknd wl ins fnl f* **17/2**

0003 **4** *1 ½* **Fares (IRE)**[32] 4420 3-8-7 **89** ow1 PhilipRobinson 6 89
(C E Brittain) *chsd ldng pair: rdn along and ev ch 2f out: sn drvn and one pce ins fnl f* **16/1**

2611 **5** *1* **Medicea Sidera**[27] 4589 3-8-4 **86** MartinDwyer 1 84
(E F Vaughan) *sn led: rdn along wl over 1f out: sn hdd and one pce* **7/1**[3]

4-30 **6** *3 ½* **Evens And Odds (IRE)**[131] 1473 3-9-1 **97** NCallan 7 85
(K A Ryan) *hld up: hdwy over 2f out: styng on to chse ldrs whn hmpd over 1f out: nt rcvr* **8/1**

3100 **7** *3* **El Bosque (IRE)**[26] 4607 3-9-3 **99** GrahamGibbons 4 79
(B R Millman) *cl up: rdn 2f out: grad wknd* **28/1**

200- **8** *hd* **Sadeek**[349] 5653 3-9-4 **100** RoystonFfrench 9 79
(B Smart) *nvr bttr than midfield* **33/1**

0-00 **9** *1 ¾* **Zafonical Storm (USA)**[25] 4648 3-9-1 **97** TedDurcan 13 72
(B W Duke) *hld up: effrt and sme hdwy 1/2-way: sn rdn along and btn: b.b.v* **50/1**

2025 **10** *½* **White Deer (USA)**[13] 4990 3-8-13 **95** GregFairley 10 68
(M Johnston) *chsd ldrs: rdn along and wandered over 2f out: sn wknd* **9/2**[2]

11 *14* **Fan Club**[44] 3-7-12 **87** DanielleMcCreery(7) 3 23
(D W Chapman) *chsd ldrs to 1/2-way: sn wknd* **50/1**

1062 **12** *2 ½* **Folly Lodge**[26] 4601 3-8-7 **89** ow2 MichaelHills 2 18
(B W Hills) *a towards rr* **7/1**[3]

1m 23.82s (-3.95) **Going Correction** -0.325s/f (Firm) **12** Ran SP% **120.7**
Speed ratings (Par 107): **109,108,106,104,103 99,95,95,93,92 76,74**
CSF £28.14 CT £183.14 TOTE £11.90: £3.00, £1.20, £3.10; EX 32.10 Trifecta £595.10 Part won. Pool: £838.17 - 0.64 winning tickets..
Owner J P Hardiman **Bred** J P Hardiman **Trained** East Everleigh, Wilts
■ Stewards' Enquiry : Ryan Moore two-day ban: careless riding (Sep 24-25)

FOCUS
They went a strong gallop and the winner came from last to first. The form looks rock solid rated around the first four.

NOTEBOOK
Danehillsundance(IRE), on his toes beforehand, had the ground he likes this time and he came from last to first but at the line it was touch and go. (op 10-1)
Miss Lucifer(FR), runner-up four times in all this year, had to wait for a run. She drew upsides a furlong out but in the end just missed out. She richly deserves to go one better. (op 7-2)
Majuro(IRE), back up in trip, showed ahead coming to the final furlong but in the end did not see it out nearly as well as the first two. This was his best effort so far on turf. (op 12-1 tchd 8-1)
Fares(IRE), who is not very big, again had the blinkers left off. (op 20-1)
Medicea Sidera, who lacks size and scope, took them along at a sound pace but the 5lb hike in the ratings found her out in the end. (op 6-1 tchd 11-2)
Evens And Odds(IRE), absent since finishing down the track in the 2000 Guineas, moved poorly to post and was going nowhere when the winner brushed past him. (tchd 9-1)
Zafonical Storm(USA) Official explanation: trainer said colt had bled from the nose
White Deer(USA) was one of the first to come under pressure and this must go down as a disappointing effort. (op 4-1 tchd 5-1)

5356 MILLER HOMES YORKSHIRE H'CAP 6f
5:30 (5:30) (Class 3) (0-90,89) 3-Y-0+ **£9,715** (£2,890; £1,444; £721) **Stalls** High

Form RPR

1415 **1** **Ellens Academy (IRE)**[13] 4999 12-8-6 **75** DavidAllan 17 86
(E J Alston) *racd stands' side: hld up in rr: gd hdwy over 1f out: styd on wl to ld last 50yds: 1st of 12 that gp* **16/1**

0-11 **2** *1* **Tamagin (USA)**[34] 4367 4-9-2 **85** NCallan 15 93
(K A Ryan) *led stands' side: edgd lft appr fnl f: hdd towards fin: 2nd of 12 that gp* **8/1**[3]

2126 **3** *1 ¼* **Bel Cantor**[33] 4381 4-8-1 **77** (p) LanceBetts(7) 12 81
(W J H Ratcliffe) *racd stands' side: chsd ldrs: styd on same pce ins fnl f: 3rd of 12 that gp* **28/1**

3000 **4** *½* **Ingleby Arch (USA)**[4] 5254 4-9-2 **85** (v) JimmyFortune 16 88
(T D Barron) *racd stands' side: chsd ldrs: kpt on wl fnl f: 4th of 12 that gp* **14/1**

13 **5** *nk* **Haajes**[13] 4999 3-8-1 **75** DuranFentiman(3) 20 77
(D J Murphy) *racd stands' side: chsd ldrs: kpt on same pce appr fnl f: 5th of 12 that gp* **17/2**

2204 **6** *½* **Mambo Spirit (IRE)**[15] 4950 3-9-2 **87** TPQueally 19 87
(J G Given) *racd stands' side: hld up: hdwy 2f out: nt clr run and swtchd lft ins fnl f: r.o: 6th of 12 that gp* **40/1**

0-10 **7** *1 ¼* **Maker's Mark (IRE)**[22] 4726 3-8-13 **84** FergusSweeney 14 81
(H Candy) *racd stands' side: in rr: kpt on fnl 2f: nvr rchd ldrs: 7th of 12 that gp* **14/1**

6-52 **8** *1 1/4* **Joseph Henry**[41] 4122 5-9-6 **89** AdrianTNicholls 7 82
(D Nicholls) *racd far side: mid-div: styd on appr fnl f: led that side towards fin: 1st of 8 that gp* **11/2**[2]

2110 **9** *nk* **Express Wish**[64] 3431 3-9-4 **89** LDettori 3 84+
(J Noseda) *led far side: edgd rt fnl f: lost ld that side nr fin: 2nd of 8 that gp* **9/2**[1]

6000 **10** *nk* **Pretty Majestic (IRE)**[18] 4848 3-8-11 **82** (v) DarryllHolland 18 73
(M R Channon) *racd stands' side: chsd ldrs: kpt on same pce fnl 2f: 8th of 12 that gp* **33/1**

1100 **11** *1/2* **Makabul**[5] 5232 4-8-6 **75** oh1 HayleyTurner 4 65
(B R Millman) *racd far side: chsd ldrs: hung rt and lost pl over 1f out: 3rd of 8 that gp* **66/1**

041 **12** *1* **Lady Lily (IRE)**[32] 4425 3-9-1 **86** TedDurcan 5 73
(H R A Cecil) *racd far side: chsd ldrs: wknd and eased fnl f: 4th of 8 that gp* **11/1**

5136 **13** *shd* **Daaweitza**[75] 3091 4-8-13 **82** GregFairley 2 68
(B Ellison) *racd far side: chsd ldrs: wknd over 1f out: 5th of 8 that gp* **33/1**

-050 **14** *1 3/4* **Mango Music**[62] 3489 4-8-13 **82** MartinDwyer 9 63
(M R Channon) *racd stands' side: chsd ldrs: wknd over 1f out: 9th of 12 that gp* **33/1**

1064 **15** *nk* **Baltimore Jack (IRE)**[17] 4898 3-8-11 **82** PaulMulrennan 11 62
(M W Easterby) *racd stands' side: a in rr: 10th of 12 that gp* **66/1**

0400 **16** *shd* **Charles Darwin (IRE)**[70] 3240 4-9-0 **83** RyanMoore 6 63
(M Blanshard) *racd far side: chsd ldrs: wknd over 1f out: 6th of 8 that gp* **11/1**

000 **17** *hd* **Zanida (IRE)**[22] 4726 3-8-9 **80** (b) PatCosgrave 21 59
(K R Burke) *racd stands' side: mid-div: nvr a factor: 11th of 12 that gp* **50/1**

0403 **18** *3/4* **Our Blessing (IRE)**[27] 4585 3-8-6 **80** AndrewElliott(3) 10 57
(A P Jarvis) *dwlt: racd stands' side: sn chsng ldrs on outer: edgd lft and lost pl over 1f out: last of 12 that gp* **50/1**

5401 **19** *5* **Capricorn Run (USA)**[9] 5119 4-8-13 **82** 6ex (v) SteveDrowne 1 44
(A J McCabe) *s.v.s: racd far side: a detached: 7th of 8 that gp* **16/1**

2352 **20** *1 3/4* **Trojan Flight**[13] 4990 6-8-12 **81** PaulHanagan 8 38
(R A Fahey) *racd far side: hld up in rr: bhd fnl 2f: b.b.v: last of 8 that gp* **8/1**[3]

1m 11.62s (-2.68) **Going Correction** -0.325s/f (Firm)
WFA 3 from 4yo+ 2lb **20** Ran SP% **129.7**
Speed ratings (Par 107): **104,102,101,100,99 99,97,95,95,95 94,93,93,90,90 90,89,88,82,79**
CSF £135.40 CT £3601.03 TOTE £23.40: £4.70, £2.70, £12.60, £3.50; EX 93.60 TRIFECTA Not won. Place 6 £684.80, Place 5 £151.04.
Owner K Lee And I Davies **Bred** Mrs Chris Harrington **Trained** Longton, Lancs

FOCUS
They split into two groups but the first seven home raced on the stands' side. The winner had a dream run up the favoured stands' side rail and is back to the very best he showed last year.

NOTEBOOK
Ellens Academy(IRE), twice the age of any other runner, came from last to first with a sweeping run down the stands' side rail. This was his 11th career success on his 102nd start and he is a credit to his trainer.
Tamagin(USA), 5lb higher, dominated on the stands' side but he edged away from the rail and left the door open for the winner. He is proving a grand servant for this yard.
Bel Cantor, with the cheekpieces retained, put a poor run last time behind him on ground plenty fast enough for him. (op 50-1)
Ingleby Arch(USA), with the visor back on, ran one of his better races especially considering the flat track and fast ground did not play to his strengths.
Haajes, 6lb higher than Hamilton, again ran well. (op 9-1)
Mambo Spirit(IRE), tackling older sprinters for the first time, did not enjoy the best of luck otherwise he must have finished a bit closer. Official explanation: jockey said gelding was denied a clear run (op 50-1)
Joseph Henry, 4lb higher, is still well treated compared with his prime and he led them home on the far side, but that group seemed to be at a disadvantage of almost a stone. (tchd 6-1)
Express Wish, 5lb higher than Haydock, had Dettori back on board and took them along on the far side. He tended to drift towards the centre and ended up only eased second best on that side. (op 11-2 tchd 6-1)
Makabul Official explanation: jockey said gelding hung right-handed
Capricorn Run(USA) Official explanation: jockey said gelding dwelt leaving stalls
Trojan Flight Official explanation: jockey said gelding bled from the nose
T/Jkpt: Not won. T/Plt: £1,010.70 to a £1 stake. Pool: £135,130.05. 97.60 winning tickets. T/Qpdt: £149.70 to a £1 stake. Pool: £5,715.85. 28.25 winning tickets. JR

5047 SANDOWN (R-H)

Thursday, September 13

OFFICIAL GOING: Round course - good (good to firm in places); sprint course - good to firm
Wind: Almost nil Weather: Fine, warm

5357 H & V NEWS MEDIAN AUCTION MAIDEN FILLIES' STKS — 5f 6y
2:20 (2:21) (Class 5) 2-Y-O — **£3,886** (£1,156; £577; £288) **Stalls** High

Form — RPR

2 **1** **Blue Eyed Miss (IRE)**[8] 5126 2-9-0 0 FrankieMcDonald 9 84+
(P A Blockley) *lw: b. mde virtually all: drew clr wl over 1f out: in n.d after: rdn out* **7/1**

350 **2** *2* **Honky Tonk Sally**[21] 4744 2-9-0 87 JimCrowley 12 77
(M L W Bell) *taken down early: w wnr to 1/2-way: outpcd wl over 1f out: no ch after: kpt on* **7/4**[1]

4 **3** *shd* **Kalligal**[19] 4810 2-9-0 0 RobertHavlin 8 76
(R Ingram) *chsd ldrs: effrt but outpcd wl over 1f out: kpt on to press for 2nd ins fnl f* **40/1**

23 **4** *1 1/2* **Divine Power**[24] 4662 2-9-0 0 KerrinMcEvoy 4 71
(R M Beckett) *lw: chsd ldrs: n.m.r after 2f and again 2f out: sn outpcd: kpt on* **11/4**[2]

06 **5** *1* **Athboy Auction**[11] 5065 2-9-0 0 MickyFenton 7 67
(H J Collingridge) *settled towards rr: wl outpcd fr 1/2-way: pushed along and styd on steadily fr over 1f out: nvr nrr* **40/1**

6 *1 1/4* **Ma Al Salamah (IRE)** 2-9-0 0 RHills 2 63+
(C E Brittain) *leggy: scope: b.bkwd: s.i.s: rn green in last pair and racd on outer: pushed along and styd on steadily fnl 2f* **20/1**

7 *hd* **Badoura** 2-9-0 0 StephenCarson 3 62
(G A Butler) *w'like: hld up in midfield on outer: pushed along and outpcd 2f out: kpt on steadily after* **40/1**

6 **8** *1 1/2* **Night Premiere (IRE)**[9] 5110 2-9-0 0 RichardHughes 1 57
(R Hannon) *dwlt: rcvrd to press ldrs: rdn 1/2-way: wknd over 1f out* **6/1**[3]

600 **9** *3/4* **Ava Gee**[9] 5110 2-9-0 0 DavidKinsella 11 54
(B De Haan) *w ldrs for 2f: sn lost pl and struggling* **28/1**

6003 **10** *2 1/2* **Evenstorm (USA)**[21] 4737 2-8-11 64 WilliamBuick(3) 10 45
(B Gubby) *b. w ldrs over 1f: sn lost pl and struggling* **16/1**

6400 **11** *1 1/2* **Our Kally**[10] 5096 2-9-0 58 RichardSmith 6 40
(M D I Usher) *rdn in rr over 3f out: a struggling* **100/1**

12 *1/2* **Mythical Fosroc (USA)** 2-9-0 0 JohnEgan 5 38
(J S Moore) *outpcd and struggling over 3f out: nvr a factor* **33/1**

13 *7* **The Dragon (IRE)** 2-9-0 0 TPO'Shea 13 13
(M Quinn) *w'like: leggy: sn t.o* **40/1**

60.86 secs (-1.35) **Going Correction** -0.325s/f (Firm) **13** Ran SP% **117.6**
Speed ratings (Par 92): **97,93,93,91,89 87,87,84,83,79 77,76,65**
CSF £17.94 TOTE £8.40: £2.40, £1.10, £7.00; EX 22.60.
Owner M J Wiley **Bred** Mrs Monica Hackett **Trained** Lambourn, Berks
■ Stewards' Enquiry : Frankie McDonald one-day ban: careless riding (Oct 8)

FOCUS
A fair fillies' sprint maiden. The form looks solid, with second and fourth both close to their pre-race marks, and it is likely to produce its share of winners.

NOTEBOOK
Blue Eyed Miss(IRE), down in trip having shown plenty of speed when second over 6f on debut at Kempton, was quickly into stride and again showed plenty of early pace, leading throughout and willingly coming clear under pressure. Speed is evidently her main weapon and, although connections have no major plans, there are surely more races to be won with her. (op 6-1)
Honky Tonk Sally, outclassed in the Lowther latest, had previously shown some fair placed form, but all her prior efforts had been over 6f and she was found wanting for pace at the business end on this drop in trip. Soon prominent on the rail, she had her chance, but Blue Eyed Miss readily outspeeded her when it mattered and a return to 6f looks in order. (op 6-4 tchd 15-8 tchd 2-1 in places)
Kalligal, who did not run too badly in a decent Newmarket maiden on debut, was down in trip and faced with much faster conditions here, but she confirmed that initial promise and stuck on well under pressure to just miss out on second. She should have little trouble finding an ordinary maiden on this evidence.
Divine Power, another dropping in trip having twice been placed over 6f, did not get the best of runs through, but in the end it was her lack of speed that cost her. She may get away with this trip in slower ground, but a return to further will suit eventually and connections now have the option of nurseries. (op 4-1 tchd 5-2)
Athboy Auction has progressed a little with each run and the way in which she saw out her race will give connections hope that she will be winning races once venturing into handicaps, with a step back up to 6f likely to see her in a better light.
Ma Al Salamah(IRE), a 38,000gns daughter of Noverre, is a half-sister to Makshoof, a dual 6f winner, and she herself shaped as though it will not be long before she is winning races. Slowly away, she showed distinct signs of greeness, but came home nicely under a tender ride and is going to appreciate the step up to 6f. (op 22-1)
Badoura, a 50,000gns daughter of Dr Fong, comes from a yard whose juveniles often need a run and she shaped well back in seventh, keeping on steadily having been outpaced early. Better can be expected now she has the run under her belt, with the step up to 6f also likely to suit. (op 33-1)
Night Premiere(IRE) failed to confirm the promise of her initial effort at Goodwood and may now be more of a nursery prospect. (op 5-1)
Evenstorm(USA) Official explanation: jockey said filly was hampered

5358 FLAKT WOODS H'CAP — 5f 6y
2:50 (2:53) (Class 4) (0-85,84) 3-Y-O — **£5,181** (£1,541; £770; £384) **Stalls** High

Form — RPR

5031 **1** **Zahour Al Yasmeen**[8] 5139 3-8-4 **70** oh1 TPO'Shea 1 79
(M R Channon) *lw: wl in tch: prog to chse ldr 2f out: drvn and narrow ld fnl f: jst hld on* **5/1**[2]

0111 **2** *shd* **Day By Day**[12] 5051 3-8-9 **75** (b) RobertHavlin 7 84
(B J Meehan) *led: drvn and narrowly hdd fnl f: kpt on wl: jst failed* **6/1**[3]

3440 **3** *1 1/4* **Rasaman (IRE)**[22] 4726 3-9-3 **83** RichardHughes 6 87
(M A Jarvis) *chsd ldr to 2f out: styd on same pce u.p after* **3/1**[1]

114 **4** *hd* **Back In The Red (IRE)**[16] 4919 3-8-9 **75** JohnEgan 2 78
(R A Harris) *chsd ldr to 2f out: drvn and kpt on same pce after* **8/1**

0034 **5** *hd* **Bazroy (IRE)**[7] 5168 3-8-13 **79** (b) StephenDonohoe 4 82
(P D Evans) *mostly in 6th or 7th: rdn 1/2-way: no imp tl styd on fnl f: unable to chal* **13/2**

5003 **6** *hd* **Sparkling Eyes**[12] 5051 3-8-8 **74** KerrinMcEvoy 5 76
(C E Brittain) *lw: settled in last: rdn over 1f out: styd on wl fnl f: nt rch ldrs* **9/1**

0000 **7** *3/4* **He's A Humbug (IRE)**[22] 4726 3-9-4 **84** (p) DO'Donohoe 9 83
(K A Ryan) *trckd ldrs on inner: nt clr run and hit rail over 1f out* **20/1**

0-00 **8** *1/2* **Oi Vay Joe (IRE)**[19] 4806 3-8-11 **80** LiamJones(3) 8 77
(W Jarvis) *mostly in 6th or 7th: shkn up 2f out: one pce and no prog* **11/1**

0526 **9** *1/2* **Cuppacocoa**[3] 5272 3-8-8 **74** JimCrowley 3 70
(C G Cox) *a in last pair: rdn and no prog 1/2-way: one pce* **10/1**

60.41 secs (-1.80) **Going Correction** -0.325s/f (Firm) **9** Ran SP% **112.6**
Speed ratings (Par 103): **101,100,98,98,98 97,96,95,95**
CSF £33.93 CT £104.53 TOTE £5.40: £2.00, £1.70, £2.00; EX 14.80.
Owner Jaber Abdullah **Bred** Gainsborough Stud Management Ltd **Trained** West Ilsley, Berks

FOCUS
A typically competitive three-year-old sprint handicap in which two red-hot fillies dominated. Solid enough form.
Sparkling Eyes Official explanation: jockey said filly was denied a clear run

5359 FUJITSU FORTUNE STKS (LISTED RACE) — 7f 16y
3:25 (3:29) (Class 1) 3-Y-O+
£14,762 (£5,595; £2,800; £1,396; £699; £351) **Stalls** High

Form — RPR

0104 **1** **Eisteddfod**[18] 4871 6-9-2 103 NelsonDeSouza 8 114
(P F I Cole) *lw: reluctant to enter stalls: mde all: set stdy pce for 4f: rdn and styd on wl fnl 2f* **16/1**

4603 **2** *1 1/4* **Bygone Days**[9] 5112 6-9-2 110 KerrinMcEvoy 3 111
(Saeed Bin Suroor) *t.k.h: hld up in tch: rdn to chse wnr over 2f out: nt qckn over 1f out: nvr able to chal after* **11/8**[1]

4050 **3** *shd* **Assertive**[9] 5112 4-9-5 106 DaneO'Neill 10 113
(R Hannon) *lw: trckd ldrs: effrt on inner 2f out: drvn and styd on: unable to chal* **12/1**

5230 **4** *nk* **Racer Forever (USA)**[9] 5112 4-9-2 108 (b) RobertHavlin 7 110
(J H M Gosden) *hld up in midfield: effrt wl over 1f out: hanging and nt qckn: styd on fnl f: unable to chal* **4/1**[3]

5045 **5** *1/2* **Thousand Words**[28] 4543 3-8-12 110 RichardHughes 6 108
(B W Hills) *lw: t.k.h: hld up in last pair: effrt over 1f out: reminder and styd on fnl f: hopeless task* **5/2**[2]

-000 **6** *1 1/4* **Tiana**[12] 5047 4-8-11 86 (b[1]) RHills 4 100
(Mrs A J Perrett) *s.i.s: hld up in last pair: shkn up over 2f out: kpt on same pce* **66/1**

0300 **7** *1/2* **Royal Power (IRE)**[21] 4747 4-9-2 100 TPO'Shea 2 103
(M R Channon) *mostly chsd wnr to over 2f out: nt qckn u.p: fdd fnl f* **33/1**

3101 **8** ½ **Ivory Lace**[9] 5115 6-8-11 85 .... JimCrowley 5 97
(S Woodman) *wl in tch: rdn over 2f out: grad fdd* **20/1**

1m 29.49s (0.15) **Going Correction** -0.10s/f (Good)
WFA 3 from 4yo+ 4lb 8 Ran SP% **113.4**
Speed ratings (Par 111): **95,93,93,93,92 91,90,89**
CSF £37.99 TOTE £17.90: £2.20, £1.10, £2.50; EX 31.90.
Owner Elite Racing Club **Bred** Elite Racing Club **Trained** Whatcombe, Oxon
■ Stewards' Enquiry : Richard Hughes caution: careless riding

FOCUS
There was just a steady gallop on up front and the winning time was very slow as a result, some 1.28 seconds slower than the following Class 4 handicap for three-year-olds. The winner had the run of the race and the form is dubious.

NOTEBOOK
Eisteddfod, not beaten far in a Group 3 at Deauville last month, was a winner over this distance earlier in the season and he caused a minor shock in scoring, having the run of things from the front and keeping on well under pressure. He was undoubtedly flattered, but did well on ground he would have found quicker than ideal and De Souza has now won on six of his eight rides on the gelding. (tchd 12-1)
Bygone Days, who got going too late when third behind Lovelace at Goodwood the other day, seems to find winning hard these days and, although running well in second, the winner was simply allowed too much rope. He is always going to be short in these sort of races and remains one to continue to take on. (op 5-4)
Assertive, a winner in this grade back in June, has since struggled to make an impact in Group races and finished behind Bygone Days at Goodwood the other day. He ran much better here though and seems more at home in this grade.
Racer Forever(USA) is a horse with tons of ability, but not for the first time this season, he seemed reluctant to put it all in when asked for maximum effort. He is capable of finding a race, having run some big races in defeat this season, but connections must be coming towards the end of their tether with him. (tchd 5-1)
Thousand Words could be the one to take from the race. Having gone off too fast over 1m at Salisbury last time, he was dropped in here over 7f and again raced keenly off the steady gallop. Given too much to do, he was edging nearer with every stride and can be rated a fair bit better than the form. (op 3-1)

5360 ANDREWS AIR CONDITIONING H'CAP — 7f 16y
4:00 (4:00) (Class 4) (0-80,80) 3-Y-O £5,181 (£1,541; £770; £384) Stalls High

Form RPR
2032 **1** **Salient**[9] 5114 3-9-4 80 .... PaulDoe 12 93+
(J Akehurst) *lw: mde all: shkn up and drew clr 2f out: rdn out* **2/1**[1]
3040 **2** 3 ½ **Okikoki**[22] 4710 3-9-0 76 .... SaleemGolam 7 79
(W R Muir) *t.k.h: prom: rdn to chse wnr over 1f out: no imp* **16/1**
2160 **3** nk **Gentle Guru**[18] 4848 3-9-2 78 .... JohnEgan 8 80
(R T Phillips) *hld up towards rr: prog over 2f out: drvn to press for 2nd fnl f: no ch w wnr* **6/1**[3]
6336 **4** 2 **Bateleur**[12] 5051 3-9-0 76 .... RichardHughes 16 73+
(M R Channon) *hld up in rr: nt clr run over 2f out to over 1f out: shkn up and styd on: no ch* **10/1**
5225 **5** ½ **Princess Zada**[29] 4502 3-8-6 68 .... AdrianMcCarthy 3 63
(B R Millman) *lw: t.k.h: cl up on outer: rdn and one pce fnl 2f* **25/1**
41-0 **6** nk **Messiah Garvey**[15] 4940 3-8-11 73 .... DaneO'Neill 2 68
(M R Channon) *t.k.h: chsd wnr to over 1f out: wknd last 100yds* **50/1**
010 **7** 1 **Pagan Belief**[55] 3707 3-8-10 72 .... RobertHavlin 5 64
(J A R Toller) *settled in midfield: hrd rdn and no prog over 2f out: one pce* **16/1**
4403 **8** shd **Lunces Lad (IRE)**[9] 5115 3-9-4 80 .... TPO'Shea 15 77+
(M R Channon) *hld up in last trio: modest prog and no ch whn nt clr run 1f out: kpt on* **15/2**
2-61 **9** 1 ½ **Social Rhythm**[142] 1219 3-8-11 76 .... MarcHalford(3) 11 64
(H J Collingridge) *hld up in last trio: brought v wd in st: plugged on one pce: n.d* **16/1**
2020 **10** nk **The Jay Factor (IRE)**[21] 4740 3-7-12 67 ....(p) KMay(7) 10 54
(Pat Eddery) *cl up on inner: wknd over 1f out* **16/1**
0031 **11** ½ **Lordship (IRE)**[22] 4710 3-8-2 71 ow4 .... MarkCoumbe(7) 4 56+
(A W Carroll) *dwlt: t.k.h: hld up in last trio: rdn and no prog over 2f out* **16/1**
3-60 **12** ½ **My Learned Friend (IRE)**[143] 1202 3-8-12 77 .... WilliamBuick(3) 13 61
(A M Balding) *chsd ldrs: lost pl over 2f out: sn btn* **11/2**[2]
0000 **13** nk **Prince Of Elegance**[18] 4847 3-9-3 79 ....(b[1]) JimCrowley 9 62
(Mrs A J Perrett) *hld up in rr: rdn on outer and no prog over 2f out: fdd* **50/1**

1m 28.21s (-1.13) **Going Correction** -0.10s/f (Good) 13 Ran SP% **121.0**
Speed ratings (Par 103): **102,98,97,95,94 94,93,93,91,91 90,90,89**
CSF £38.96 CT £172.31 TOTE £2.70: £1.40, £4.50, £2.80; EX 45.00.
Owner Canisbay Bloodstock **Bred** Hesmonds Stud Ltd **Trained** Epsom, Surrey

FOCUS
An average handicap, lacking in obvious improvers, and while the time was faster than the earlier Listed race it was by no means strongly run. The winner had the run of the race, but the form makes sense.

5361 MAIN E B F MAIDEN STKS — 1m 14y
4:35 (4:35) (Class 4) 2-Y-O £4,533 (£1,348; £674; £336) Stalls High

Form RPR
04 **1** **Silver Regent (USA)**[13] 5011 2-9-3 0 .... JimCrowley 8 83+
(Mrs A J Perrett) *rousted along early: sn prom: effrt to ld narrowly 2f out: rdn clr fnl f* **16/1**
2 **2** 2 **Rattan (USA)**[29] 4508 2-9-3 0 .... RichardHughes 11 78
(H R A Cecil) *lw: led: hdd and shkn up 2f out: pressed wnr tl one pce fnl f* **15/8**[1]
04 **3** ½ **Summon Up Theblood**[17] 4876 2-9-3 0 .... TPO'Shea 9 77
(M R Channon) *prom: rdn and cl up 2f out: nt qckn sn after: kpt on* **20/1**
4 nk **Rock Peak (IRE)** 2-9-3 0 .... MickyFenton 3 77
(H Morrison) *w'like: bit bkwd: dwlt: wl in rr: stdy prog fr over 2f out: pushed along and styd on fnl f: nrst fin* **33/1**
04 **5** 1 **Tyrrells Wood (IRE)**[28] 4547 2-9-3 0 .... JohnEgan 1 74
(T G Mills) *prom on outer: rdn and cl up 2f out: one pce after* **20/1**
43 **6** ½ **Sainglend**[17] 4876 2-9-3 0 .... DaneO'Neill 12 73
(H Candy) *mostly pressed ldr to over 2f out: fdd fnl f* **9/1**
0 **7** shd **Yathreb (USA)**[48] 3896 2-9-3 0 .... RHills 10 73
(J L Dunlop) *dwlt: wl in rr: effrt on outer over 2f out: v green and awkward over 1f out: no prog* **9/4**[2]
8 nk **Blue Citadel (USA)** 2-9-3 0 .... RobertHavlin 6 72
(J H M Gosden) *strong: bit bkwd: dwlt: trckd ldrs on inner: pushed along and outpcd fr 2f out* **33/1**
9 nk **Houghton (IRE)** 2-9-0 0 .... WilliamBuick(3) 7 72+
(Sir Michael Stoute) *w'like: bit bkwd: settled in rr: shkn up over 2f out and rn green: styd on fnl f: n.d* **16/1**
10 2 ½ **Sleepy Hollow** 2-9-0 0 .... TravisBlock(3) 13 66
(H Morrison) *w'like: bit bkwd: dwlt: wl off the pce in last pair: sme prog on outer over 2f out: sn no hdwy* **100/1**
11 1 ¼ **World Of Choice (USA)** 2-9-3 0 .... KerrinMcEvoy 4 63
(Saeed Bin Suroor) *lw: w'like: settled in midfield: shkn up and wknd 2f out* **5/1**[3]
0 **12** 7 **Pinnacle Point**[13] 5010 2-8-10 0 .... JemmaMarshall(7) 2 47
(G L Moore) *dwlt: a towards rr: wknd 2f out* **100/1**
13 5 **Tasheba** 2-9-0 0 .... LiamJones(3) 5 35
(P W Chapple-Hyam) *strong: bit bkwd: sn last and struggling: a bhd* **50/1**

1m 42.84s (-1.11) **Going Correction** -0.10s/f (Good) 13 Ran SP% **123.3**
Speed ratings (Par 97): **101,99,98,98,97 96,96,96,96,93 92,85,80**
CSF £45.62 TOTE £22.20: £3.40, £1.50, £5.60; EX 54.40.
Owner P Graham, R D Hubbard And R Masterson **Bred** R D Hubbard And R Masterson **Trained** Pulborough, W Sussex

FOCUS
A solid maiden likely to produce its share of winners.

NOTEBOOK
Silver Regent(USA) stepped up on his debut effort when a keeping-on fourth over 7f at the course last time and this extra furlong proved to be the making of him. Sluggish out of the gates, he had to be driven to obtain a prominent position, but he saw his race out with relish and was well on top at the line. He has plenty of scope for further improvement and it will be interesting to see what mark he gets for handicaps. (op 12-1)
Rattan(USA), second in a 7f course maiden on debut, set the standard, but his lack of big-race entries was slightly off-putting and it was no real surprise to see him again find one too good. He did not necessarily seem to improve for this extra furlong, but has done enough to win an ordinary maiden at one of the lesser tracks. (op 9-4 tchd 13-8)
Summon Up Theblood had already shown a fair level of form when placed in a 1m maiden at Chepstow and it was no surprise to see him run better than his 20/1 odds suggest. Stamina is clearly his forte at this stage and he has already shown enough to suggest an ordinary maiden will come his way. (op 16-1)
Rock Peak(IRE) ◆, a son of Dalakhani who holds a Derby entry, comes from a yard whose juveniles often need a run and as a result this has to go down as a highly promising debut. In rear early, he made good late progress despite running green and natural progression should see him winning a standard maiden. (op 22-1)
Tyrrells Wood(IRE) ran his best race to date and strikes as the type to do better in nurseries, for which he is now qualified. Official explanation: jockey said colt slipped on leaving stalls
Sainglend, a place ahead of Summon Up Theblood at Chepstow, failed to get home having showed up well to a point, but he is at least now qualified for nurseries. (op 8-1)
Yathreb(USA), who shaped better than his finishing position suggested when eighth in a decent Ascot maiden on debut, holds numerous big-race entries and it was no surprise to see him strongly supported in the market throughout the day, with the step up in trip almost certain to suit. However, having been sluggish out of the stalls and forced to race wide towards the rear, he could not pick up in the straight and still looked unsure of what was required of him. This was obviously disappointing and it may now be that we do not see the best of him until he is sent handicapping. (op 11-4 tchd 3-1)
Blue Citadel(USA), a 75,000gns son of Dubai Destination, was evidently not fancied to do much on this debut, but he did not shape without promise and can be expected to come on for this initial experience. (op 20-1)
Houghton(IRE), a 140,000gns son of Sadler's Wells and a half-brother to Yellowstone, looked badly in need of the experience, running green under pressure. He can be expected to improve significantly. (op 14-1)
World Of Choice(USA), who holds numerous big-race entries, was a costly purchase at $700,000, but he offered very little on this racecourse debut, dropping away disappointingly under pressure. He is evidently thought capable of better. (op 8-1)
Tasheba Official explanation: jockey said colt never travelled

5362 VAILLANT H'CAP — 1m 2f 7y
5:10 (5:12) (Class 3) (0-90,90) 3-Y-O+ £7,772 (£2,312; £1,155; £577) Stalls High

Form RPR
1-36 **1** **Seabow (USA)**[40] 4166 4-9-10 89 ....(t) KerrinMcEvoy 9 99+
(Saeed Bin Suroor) *lw: trckd ldr: effrt to chal over 2f out: cajoled along and led over 1f out: grad asserted* **6/4**[1]
3014 **2** ½ **Press The Button (GER)**[19] 4814 4-9-3 82 .... JimCrowley 7 91
(J R Boyle) *led: set stdy pce to 1/2-way: clr w wnr 2f out: hdd over 1f out: no ex last 150yds* **9/2**[2]
0600 **3** 2 ½ **Del Mar Sunset**[17] 4909 8-8-8 76 .... LiamJones(3) 8 80+
(W J Haggas) *swtg: dwlt: hld up in last: gng wl enough 3f out: plld out and effrt 2f out: styd on to take 3rd ins fnl f: no ch of rching ldng pair* **6/1**[3]
2600 **4** 1 **Brief Goodbye**[12] 5052 7-8-11 76 oh2 .... MickyFenton 1 78
(John Berry) *lw: chsd ldng pair: outpcd fr 2f out* **12/1**
6440 **5** ½ **Active Asset (IRE)**[16] 4917 5-9-0 79 .... RobertHavlin 5 80
(M Quinn) *hld up bhd ldrs: rdn over 3f out: no real prog* **11/1**
0005 **6** nk **Folio (IRE)**[28] 4551 7-9-3 82 .... NeilPollard 2 82
(W J Musson) *trckd ldrs: outpcd fr 2f out: fdd* **16/1**
34-2 **7** 3 **Zonergem**[28] 4523 9-9-11 90 ....(p) JohnEgan 6 84
(Lady Herries) *hld up in rr: shkn up and no rspnse 3f out: no prog after: eased fnl f* **15/2**
2255 **8** 4 **Pagan Sword**[12] 5049 5-9-0 86 ....(v) KMay(7) 4 72
(Mrs A J Perrett) *dwlt: hld up in rr: rdn 3f out: wknd 2f out* **10/1**

2m 10.53s (0.29) **Going Correction** -0.10s/f (Good)
WFA 3 from 4yo+ 7lb 8 Ran SP% **115.2**
Speed ratings (Par 107): **94,93,91,90,90 90,87,84**
CSF £8.33 CT £31.11 TOTE £2.00: £1.20, £1.50, £1.80; EX 10.00 Place 6 £12.96, Place 5 £6.60.
Owner Godolphin **Bred** Gainsborough Farm Llc **Trained** Newmarket, Suffolk

FOCUS
A very moderate time for a race of its class,and steadily run. The third was the only one to make any ground from off the pace.

NOTEBOOK
Seabow(USA) failed to build on his reappearance third when flopping on fast ground at Newmarket last time, but he had been given a short break and managed to return to something like his best here, sticking on under pressure to grind out the result. Rated a general 25/1 chance for the Cambridgeshire, he looks capable of only limited improvement and, if anything, a step up to 1m4f may help. (op 2-1)
Press The Button(GER), 4lb higher than when winning at Bath two starts back, was responsible for the early pace and he had an easy time of it on the front end, but could not repel the winner's late challenge and was forced to settle for second. He is clearly in good nick at the minute. (tchd 5-1)
Del Mar Sunset ◆, a pound lower than when winning at Newmarket back in May, was always travelling well enough, but he found himself too far back and could not make up the ground. A stronger pace would have helped and he will be of obvious interest next time. (op 8-1)
Brief Goodbye has slipped back down to a fair mark and this was a reasonable effort from 2lb out of the handicap. (op 10-1)
Active Asset(IRE) never really got going having been in rear early on and could have done with a faster pace. (op 16-1)
T/Plt: £9.40 to a £1 stake. Pool: £68,221.65. 5,263.60 winning tickets. T/Qpdt: £4.60 to a £1 stake. Pool: £2,786.50. 442.35 winning tickets. JN

[5233]WOLVERHAMPTON (A.W) (L-H)

Thursday, September 13

OFFICIAL GOING: Standard

Wind: Light, behind Weather: Fine

5363 DINE IN THE HORIZONS RESTAURANT MEDIAN AUCTION MAIDEN STKS 5f 216y(P)

7:00 (7:03) (Class 5) 2-Y-O **£2,914** (£867; £433; £216) **Stalls** Low

Form RPR

4 **1** **Raiding Party (IRE)**[14] 4962 2-8-12 0 SebSanders 5 74
(J W Hills) *a.p: chsd ldr over 3f out: rdn to ld and edgd rt ins fnl f: r.o* **4/1**[3]

260 **2** 1 **Miesko (USA)**[12] 5042 2-9-0 77 AndrewMullen(3) 11 76
(M Johnston) *trckd ldr: led over 3f out: rdn over 1f out: hdd and unable qckn ins fnl f* **6/4**[1]

3 ½ **Just Like A Woman** 2-8-12 0 JamieSpencer 7 70
(M L W Bell) *s.i.s: hld up: hdwy over 1f out: r.o* **6/1**

03 **4** 3½ **Highland Love**[31] 4459 2-9-3 0 TonyHamilton 6 64
(Jedd O'Keeffe) *broke wl: sn lost pl: hdwy and hung lft over 1f out: nt rch ldrs* **7/2**[2]

004 **5** hd **Desert Life (IRE)**[13] 5015 2-9-3 68 (p) AmirQuinn 9 63
(R A Harris) *hld up: hdwy and nt clr run over 2f out: rdn over 1f out: nt trble ldrs* **16/1**

60 **6** ½ **Fu Wa (USA)**[43] 4077 2-8-12 0 DaleGibson 8 57
(M W Easterby) *sn led: hdd over 3f out: rdn and wknd over 1f out* **100/1**

7 1½ **Woodland Mist** 2-8-12 0 PhillipMakin 4 52
(M Dods) *mid-div: rdn 1/2-way: sn lost pl* **40/1**

0 **8** 5 **Captain Crooner (IRE)**[7] 5176 2-9-3 0 AdamKirby 12 42
(D Shaw) *chsd ldrs: rdn over 3f out: hung lft and wknd wl over 1f out* **125/1**

0 **9** ¾ **Sunshine Lady (IRE)**[10] 5097 2-8-12 0 FrancisNorton 3 35
(D Haydn Jones) *chsd ldrs over 3f* **33/1**

060 **10** 2 **Albany Becky (IRE)**[6] 5201 2-8-12 0 StephenDonohoe 13 29
(M G Quinlan) *mid-div: rdn over 3f out: sn wknd* **66/1**

11 5 **Flex** 2-9-3 0 IanMongan 10 19
(D J Murphy) *s.i.s: sn prom: rdn 1/2-way: sn wknd* **25/1**

00 **12** ½ **Jazz Romance (IRE)**[6] 5201 2-8-9 0 DominicFox(3) 2 13
(D Shaw) *dwlt: outpcd* **100/1**

13 3 **Abitofafath (IRE)** 2-9-3 0 TomEaves 1 9
(J G Given) *sn outpcd* **16/1**

1m 15.24s (-0.57) **Going Correction** -0.175s/f (Stan) **13 Ran SP% 121.8**
Speed ratings (Par 95): **96,94,94,89,89 88,86,79,78,76 69,68,64**
CSF £10.29 TOTE £4.20: £1.20, £1.20, £2.30; EX 15.20.
Owner Donald M Kerr **Bred** Airlie Stud **Trained** Upper Lambourn, Berks

FOCUS
A pretty ordinary maiden with the runner-up setting the standard and the fourth and fifth backing up the form.

NOTEBOOK
Raiding Party(IRE) improved on the form she showed when fourth on her debut at Lingfield to get off the mark at the second attempt. The form does not look anything special, with the runner-up below his official mark of 77, but she should continue to progress and ought to stay further. (tchd 5-1)
Miesko(USA) found one too good and has now been a beaten favourite on three of his four starts. He did not look to run up to his mark of 77 and is not progressing. (op 15-8 tchd 11-8)
Just Like A Woman, a daughter of Observatory, sister to Halfwaytoparadise, who was placed over 6f-7f at two and three, half-sister to multiple 7f-1m winner Dr Thong, out of a multiple 6f scorer, showed plenty of ability on her racecourse debut. She was asked to make her move very wide off the final turn, but was noted to be travelling quite well and she finished strongly when getting the hang of things in the straight. This is ordinary form, but she should improve and can find a small race or two. (op 11-4)
Highland Love stayed on from well off the pace after losing his position. He should benefit from a step up in trip and is now qualified for a handicap mark. (op 11-1)
Desert Life(IRE), beaten in claiming company on his previous start, was well below form in first-time cheekpieces and has plenty to prove now. (tchd 20-1)

5364 STAY AT THE WOLVERHAMPTON HOLIDAY INN H'CAP 1m 5f 194y(P)

7:30 (7:32) (Class 6) (0-65,65) 3-Y-O+ **£2,047** (£604; £302) **Stalls** Low

Form RPR

2610 **1** **Adage**[43] 4067 4-9-4 57 (t) NeilChalmers(3) 10 65
(David Pinder) *hld up: hdwy and edgd lft over 2f out: rdn to ld ins fnl f: styd on* **13/2**

0031 **2** ¾ **Synonymy**[13] 5007 4-9-9 59 (b) NickyMackay 2 66
(M Blanshard) *led over 12f out: hdd over 10f out: led again over 2f out: sn rdn: hdd ins fnl f: kpt on* **5/2**[1]

5562 **3** 1¼ **Ha'Penny Beacon**[13] 5018 4-9-9 59 (v) StephenDonohoe 8 64
(D Carroll) *hld up: hdwy 6f out: rdn whn hmpd and lost pl over 2f out: styd on u.p fnl f* **8/1**

6450 **4** 2 **Pertemps Power**[17] 4877 3-8-6 53 ow1 SaleemGolam 11 55
(A D Smith) *s.i.s: hld up: hdwy over 4f out: rdn and ev ch over 2f out: no ex fnl f* **66/1**

0006 **5** ¾ **Regal Ovation**[17] 4877 3-8-3 50 FrancisNorton 3 51
(W R Muir) *trckd ldrs: rdn and n.m.r over 2f out: edgd lft over 1f out: styd on same pce* **20/1**

3343 **6** ¾ **Pairumani Princess (IRE)**[18] 4859 3-9-4 65 SebSanders 4 65
(E A L Dunlop) *hld up: nt clr run and lost pl over 3f out: rdn over 2f out: nt trble ldrs* **9/2**[2]

5430 **7** 1½ **Blushing Hilary (IRE)**[16] 4925 4-9-10 60 (p) TomEaves 9 58
(Miss J A Camacho) *led: hdd over 12f out: led again over 6f out: rdn and hdd over 2f out: wknd over 1f out* **25/1**

3340 **8** 1½ **Thorny Mandate**[17] 4910 5-10-0 64 JamieSpencer 6 60
(W M Brisbourne) *hld up: nt clr run over 2f out: sn rdn and swtchd rt: n.d* **6/1**[3]

4505 **9** 3 **Always Best**[17] 4894 3-8-0 50 AndrewMullen(3) 13 42
(M Johnston) *chsd ldrs: led over 10f out: hdd over 6f out: rdn and wknd over 1f out* **9/1**

0020 **10** 5 **Ardent Prince**[6] 5204 4-9-6 56 GeorgeBaker 7 41
(Heather Dalton) *hld up: rdn over 2f out: a in rr* **18/1**

-410 **11** 5 **I'll Do It Today**[142] 1222 6-9-8 58 TonyHamilton 12 36
(J M Jefferson) *chsd ldrs: rdn over 3f out: wknd over 2f out* **14/1**

50-0 **12** dist **Crystal Annie**[22] 4718 4-9-2 52 AdamKirby 1 —
(Heather Dalton) *chsd ldrs: rdn and wknd over 3f out: eased fnl 2f* **66/1**

3m 5.24s (-2.13) **Going Correction** -0.175s/f (Stan)
WFA 3 from 4yo+ 11lb **12 Ran SP% 119.0**
Speed ratings (Par 101): **99,98,97,96,96 95,95,94,92,89 86,—**
CSF £22.44 CT £134.70 TOTE £9.60: £3.00, £1.60, £3.60; EX 31.50.
Owner Ms L Burns **Bred** Side Hill Stud **Trained** Kingston Lisle, Oxon

FOCUS
A moderate staying handicap in which the third sets the standard but the fourth tends to raise doubts.
Ardent Prince Official explanation: jockey said gelding hung right
Crystal Annie Official explanation: jockey said filly moved badly on final bend

5365 HOTEL & CONFERENCING AT WOLVERHAMPTON RACECOURSE NURSERY 5f 20y(P)

7:55 (7:58) (Class 5) (0-75,75) 2-Y-O **£2,914** (£867; £433; £216) **Stalls** Low

Form RPR

4142 **1** **Choisette**[10] 5096 2-8-9 63 RoystonFfrench 1 66
(B Smart) *chsd ldrs: rdn over 3f out: edgd rt and styd on u.p to ld wl ins fnl f* **11/10**[1]

5004 **2** ½ **Orpen's Art (IRE)**[10] 5089 2-7-10 53 WilliamBuick(3) 4 54
(N A Callaghan) *hmpd s: sn led: rdn and hdd wl ins fnl f* **8/1**[3]

0636 **3** ½ **Myriola**[28] 4527 2-8-7 64 RichardKingscote(3) 3 53
(B Palling) *hmpd s: chsd ldrs: lost pl 4f out: styd on u.p fr over 1f out* **50/1**

3301 **4** shd **Bahamarama (IRE)**[13] 5017 2-8-10 64 AmirQuinn 2 52
(R A Harris) *hld up: hdwy over 1f out: nrst fin* **12/1**

2600 **5** nk **Baytown Blaze**[26] 4605 2-9-7 75 TGMcLaughlin 6 62
(Miss K B Boutflower) *chsd ldrs: rdn 1/2-way: styd on same pce fnl f* **33/1**

3652 **6** ½ **Richardthesecond (IRE)**[10] 5089 2-8-8 62 SebSanders 12 47
(R M Beckett) *chsd ldrs: rdn 1/2-way: no ex fnl f* **8/1**[3]

5450 **7** nk **Diademas (USA)**[17] 4903 2-8-10 71 (b) RobbieEgan(7) 5 55+
(J A Osborne) *wnt lft s: in rr: effrt and nt clr run over 1f out: n.d* **33/1**

5431 **8** 2½ **Speedy Senorita (IRE)**[22] 4715 2-8-12 66 FrancisNorton 13 41
(K R Burke) *chsd ldrs over 3f* **8/1**[3]

630 **9** ½ **Rightcar Ellie (IRE)**[45] 4020 2-8-7 61 LPKeniry 8 34
(Peter Grayson) *mid-div: rdn 1/2-way: n.d* **50/1**

6005 **10** 8 **Frizzini**[7] 5176 2-7-5 52 oh2 DanielleMcCreery(7) 9 —
(N Tinkler) *sn w ldr: rdn 1/2-way: hung lft and wknd over 1f out* **22/1**

3633 **11** 1¼ **Paddy Jack**[22] 4702 2-9-1 69 JamieSpencer 7 9
(J R Weymes) *mid-div: rdn 1/2-way: sn wknd: eased fnl f* **5/1**[2]

400 **12** nk **Only In Jest**[35] 4315 2-9-7 75 (t) SaleemGolam 10 14
(W G M Turner) *s.i.s: a in rr* **40/1**

4360 **13** 3 **Maracana Boy (IRE)**[42] 4098 2-9-0 68 (t) PhillipMakin 11 —
(M Dods) *sn outpcd* **40/1**

62.45 secs (-0.37) **Going Correction** -0.175s/f (Stan) **13 Ran SP% 124.3**
Speed ratings (Par 95): **95,94,88,88,87 87,86,82,81,69 67,66,61**
CSF £10.44 CT £305.97 TOTE £2.40: £1.02, £3.40, £17.90; EX 13.90.
Owner Pinnacle Choisir Partnership **Bred** M R M Bloodstock **Trained** Hambleton, N Yorks

FOCUS
A modest sprint nursery and the form is solid enough for the level.

NOTEBOOK
Choisette was 2lb lower than when second over course and distance on her previous start and she took full advantage. This looks as good as she is and a significant rise in the weights may be enough to stop her following up. (op 5-4 tchd 11-8, 6-4 in places)
Orpen's Art(IRE) showed good speed dropped back to the minimum trip on his Polytrack debut, but the way he stayed on again when headed suggests he might have been saving something for himself, and it would be no surprise to see headgear reached for again at some point. (op 10-1)
Myriola came out on top in the bunch for third and this was a good effort considering she was hampered at the start. (op 66-1)
Bahamarama(IRE) found this tougher than the course-and-distance seller she won for Jim Boyle on her previous start. (op 10-1 tchd 14-1)
Baytown Blaze did not run a bad race off joint top weight. (op 25-1)
Richardthesecond(IRE) could not take advantage of a mark 4lb lower than in future. (op 7-1)
Speedy Senorita(IRE) Official explanation: jockey said filly hung right
Frizzini, despite racing from out of the handicap, was 13lb lower than in future, but he is going to struggle off his new mark on this evidence. (op 20-1)
Paddy Jack Official explanation: jockey said gelding charged the gate, resented the kickback and never travelled

5366 RINGSIDE SUITE CLASSIFIED STKS 1m 1f 103y(P)

8:25 (8:25) (Class 6) 3-Y-O+ **£2,047** (£604; £302) **Stalls** Low

Form RPR

0006 **1** **Alfie Tupper (IRE)**[17] 4879 4-9-4 55 SimonWhitworth 1 62
(S Kirk) *hld up: racd keenly: hdwy over 1f out: rdn to ld ins fnl f: edgd lft: r.o* **13/2**[3]

5-00 **2** ½ **Ardmaddy (IRE)**[19] 4815 3-8-12 55 TPO'Shea 10 61
(J A R Toller) *hld up: hdwy over 2f out: sn rdn: r.o* **12/1**

0646 **3** 2 **Miss Sure Bond (IRE)**[10] 5086 4-8-13 52 (p) SladeO'Hara(5) 4 57
(G R Oldroyd) *chsd ldr: rdn and ev ch ins fnl f: styd on same pce* **16/1**

0403 **4** 3½ **Fantastic Delight**[32] 4426 4-9-4 43 GeorgeBaker 13 49
(B G Powell) *hld up: hdwy u.p and hung lft over 1f out: nt rch ldrs* **9/2**[1]

0064 **5** nk **Glenridding**[13] 5019 3-8-12 50 (b) SebSanders 5 49
(J G Given) *led: rdn over 1f out: hdd & wknd ins fnl f* **9/2**[1]

053 **6** 2½ **Silent Beauty (IRE)**[10] 5102 3-8-12 42 ChrisCatlin 2 44
(S C Williams) *mid-div: rdn 1/2-way: hmpd over 1f out: n.d* **5/1**[2]

006- **7** 2½ **The Great Delaney**[268] 6870 4-9-4 54 JamieSpencer 3 38
(K McAuliffe) *chsd ldrs: rdn over 2f out: hung lft and wknd over 1f out* **8/1**

-506 **8** 4 **Over Ice**[11] 3427 4-9-1 55 (p) RichardKingscote(3) 6 30
(Karen George) *awkward leaving stalls: mid-div: rdn over 3f out: sn wknd* **16/1**

-320 **9** 7 **Measured Response**[6] 5188 5-8-11 55 (p) ThomasO'Brien(7) 9 15
(J G M O'Shea) *chsd ldrs 7f* **5/1**[2]

3430 **10** 3½ **Musical Locket (IRE)**[119] 1782 3-8-12 55 BThomas 8 8
(J C Fox) *s.i.s: hld up: hdwy over 5f out: wknd over 2f out* **33/1**

2m 1.81s (-0.81) **Going Correction** -0.175s/f (Stan)
WFA 3 from 4yo+ 6lb **10 Ran SP% 116.5**
Speed ratings (Par 101): **96,95,93,90,90 88,85,82,76,73**
CSF £81.37 TOTE £10.60: £3.30, £3.80, £4.90; EX 171.30.
Owner Eamon McCay and John Sanders **Bred** Stone Ridge Farm **Trained** Upper Lambourn, Berks

FOCUS
A moderate handicap run at a fair pace and rated slightly positively with the form rated around the third, fourth and fifth.

5367 WOLVERHAMPTON-RACECOURSE.CO.UK H'CAP 1m 141y(P)

8:55 (8:55) (Class 5) (0-75,75) 3-Y-O **£2,914** (£867; £433; £216) **Stalls** Low

Form RPR

1011 **1** **Mountain Cat (IRE)**[32] 4433 3-9-2 73 TPO'Shea 8 82
(W J Musson) *mde all: rdn over 1f out: edgd rt ins fnl f: r.o u.p* **9/4**[1]

503 **2** 1¼ **Cape Velvet (IRE)**[19] 4828 3-8-9 66 SebSanders 5 72
(J W Hills) *hld up in tch: rdn over 1f out: r.o* **10/1**

2305 **3** *hd* **Pivotalia (IRE)**[17] 4889 3-8-7 **64** ..... SaleemGolam 3 69
(W R Swinburn) *chsd wnr: reminders over 3f out: hrd rdn fr over 1f out: ev ch ins fnl f: edgd rt and unable qckn towards fin* **8/1**

4142 **4** *1 1/4* **Divertimenti (IRE)**[9] 5122 3-9-4 **75** ..... GeorgeBaker 1 77
(C R Dore) *hld up and bhd: hdwy over 1f out: rdn and ev ch ins fnl f: no ex whn nt clr run towards fin* **5/2**[2]

3330 **5** *1/2* **Areyaam (USA)**[42] 4112 3-9-0 **71** ..... JamieSpencer 2 72
(L M Cumani) *hld up and bhd: rdn and hung lft over 2f out: styd on fr over 1f out: nt rch ldrs* **9/2**[3]

0500 **6** *1/2* **Cherri Fosfate**[5] 5233 3-8-5 **62** ..... ChrisCatlin 6 62
(D Carroll) *chsd ldrs: rdn over 3f out: no ex fnl f* **33/1**

2105 **7** *5* **Moheebb (IRE)**[7] 5177 3-8-2 **62** ..... LiamJones(3) 7 51
(D W Chapman) *chsd ldrs: rdn and edgd lft over 3f out: wknd over 1f out* **7/1**

1m 48.89s (-2.87) **Going Correction** -0.175s/f (Stan) 7 Ran SP% **113.2**
Speed ratings (Par 101): **105,103,103,102,102 101,97**
CSF £24.51 CT £151.68 TOTE £3.10: £2.10, £4.50; EX 35.90.
Owner S Rudolf **Bred** Mrs Mary Gallagher **Trained** Newmarket, Suffolk

FOCUS
A fair handicap but not rock solid with the runner-up and fourth to recent form.
Areyaam(USA) Official explanation: jockey said filly hung left

5368 COME EVENING RACING TOMORROW CLASSIFIED STKS 1m 141y(P)
9:20 (9:21) (Class 7) 3-Y-0+ **£1,706** (£503; £252) **Stalls** Low

Form RPR

0302 **1** **Sion Hill (IRE)**[9] 5121 6-9-4 45 .....(p) JamieSpencer 2 51
(John A Harris) *trckd ldr: plld hrd: led over 3f out: hrd rdn and hung lft fr over 1f out: all out* **9/2**[2]

0651 **2** *nk* **Charlottebutterfly**[9] 5121 7-9-10 45 ..... IanMongan 9 56
(P J McBride) *hld up: hdwy over 1f out: r.o wl* **6/1**

0035 **3** *hd* **Dexileos (IRE)**[9] 5121 8-9-4 45 ..... ChrisCatlin 6 50
(David Pinder) *chsd ldrs: rdn over 2f out: r.o* **12/1**

5000 **4** *1/2* **Shadow Jumper (IRE)**[15] 4945 6-8-13 44 ..... RussellKennemore(5) 12 48
(J T Stimpson) *led: hdd over 3f out: rdn and ev ch over 1f out: styd on same pce ins fnl f* **16/1**

4241 **5** *3 1/2* **The Jailer**[3] 5269 4-9-3 44 .....(p) MCGeran(7) 4 46
(J G M O'Shea) *bhd: hdwy u.p over 1f out: nrst fin* **11/4**[1]

0000 **6** *hd* **Only If I Laugh**[3] 5276 6-9-4 45 ..... PaulFitzsimons 3 40
(M J Attwater) *chsd ldrs: rdn over 3f out: styd on same pce fnl 2f* **16/1**

0060 **7** *1 1/2* **Altos Reales**[18] 4846 3-8-9 45 ..... DominicFox(3) 11 36
(D Shaw) *s.i.s: sn mid-div: rdn 1/2-way: sme hdwy over 2f out: nt trble ldrs* **33/1**

6-60 **8** *5* **Mr Belvedere**[4] 2595 6-9-4 44 .....(p) SaleemGolam 10 25
(A J Lidderdale) *chsd ldrs: rdn over 3f out: wknd over 2f out* **11/2**[3]

0-06 **9** *shd* **Saint Remus (IRE)**[7] 5175 3-8-12 45 ..... LPKeniry 7 25
(Peter Grayson) *hld up: rdn over 3f out: a in rr* **16/1**

2001 **10** *1 3/4* **Linden's Lady**[14] 4966 7-9-4 45 .....(v) SebSanders 5 21
(J R Weymes) *hld up: rdn over 2f out: n.d* **11/2**[3]

-000 **11** *1 3/4* **Penny Glitters**[40] 4177 4-9-4 44 .....(v[1]) PaulEddery 8 17
(S Parr) *s.i.s: hld up: n.d* **40/1**

0000 **12** *1* **Mostanad**[17] 4905 5-9-1 44 .....(p) LiamJones(3) 13 14
(R A Harris) *mid-div: hdwy over 2f out: sn wknd* **50/1**

0000 **13** *8* **Glenargo (USA)**[31] 2652 4-8-11 44 ..... DanielleMcCreery(7) 1 —
(S T Lewis) *mid-div: rdn over 3f out: sn wknd* **66/1**

1m 50.89s (-0.87) **Going Correction** -0.175s/f (Stan)
WFA 3 from 4yo+ 6lb 13 Ran SP% **124.1**
Speed ratings (Par 97): **96,95,95,95,92 91,90,86,85,84 82,81,74**
CSF £32.52 TOTE £4.30: £2.20, £3.10, £5.20; EX 37.10 Place 6 £209.58, Place 5 £148.88.
Owner Peter Taylor **Bred** Joe Rogers **Trained** Eastwell, Leics

FOCUS
A very moderate classified contest and the form looks sound for the grade.
T/Plt: £102.00 to a £1 stake. Pool: £94,306.30. 674.85 winning tickets. T/Qpdt: £106.90 to a £1 stake. Pool: £4,451.80. 30.80 winning tickets. CR

5369 - 5372a (Foreign Racing) - See Raceform Interactive

5150 CHANTILLY (R-H)
Thursday, September 13

OFFICIAL GOING: Good

5373a PRIX D'ARENBERG (GROUP 3) 5f 110y
1:20 (1:20) 2-Y-0 **£27,027** (£10,811; £8,108; £5,405; £2,703)

RPR

1 **Starlit Sands**[27] 4573 2-8-8 ..... J-BEyquem 5 105
(Sir Mark Prescott) *disp ld against ins rail tl led 2f out: sn rdn: drvn clr ins fnl f* **62/10**[3]

2 *2* **Wilki (FR)**[39] 2-8-8 ..... OPeslier 6 98
(A De Royer-Dupre, France) *disp ld tl hdd 2f out: remained pressing wnr tl one pce ins fnl f* **5/1**[2]

3 *2* **Galaktea (IRE)**[15] 2-8-8 ..... MBlancpain 1 92
(C Laffon-Parias, France) *racd in 5th on ins rail: wnt 3rd over 2 1/2f out: rdn 2f out: no ex over 1f out: jst hld on for 3rd* **37/1**

4 *nk* **Untitled Blues (USA)**[29] 4519 2-8-8 ..... DBoeuf 3 91
(D Smaga, France) *hld up in rr: hdwy 2 1/2f out: hrd rdn 2f out: kpt on fnl f* **15/1**

5 *shd* **Etenia (USA)**[25] 4653 2-8-8 ..... DBonilla 2 90
(S Wattel, France) *racd in 3rd: one pce fnl 2 1/2f* **20/1**

6 *1* **Rey Davis (IRE)**[18] 4870 2-8-11 ..... J-BHamel 4 90
(Robert Collet, France) *racd in 6th: rdn 2 1/2f out: kpt on at one pce* **33/1**

7 *3* **Minted (FR)**[33] 2-8-11 ..... CSoumillon 7 80
(A Fabre, France) *cl up in 4th on outside tl shkn up and nt qckn over 2f out: sn btn: eased fnl f* **3/5**[1]

8 *1 1/2* **Faslen (USA)**[29] 4519 2-8-8 ..... C-PLemaire 9 72
(J-C Rouget, France) *a in rr* **28/1**

9 *3* **Mystic Spirit (IRE)**[29] 4519 2-8-8 ..... TThulliez 8 62
(N Clement, France) *racd in 7th: rdn 3f out: sn btn* **18/1**

62.20 secs (-4.00) 9 Ran SP% **118.4**
PARI-MUTUEL: WIN 7.20; PL 4.20, 2.30, 8.50; DF 18.00.
Owner Miss K Rausing **Bred** Miss K Rausing **Trained** Newmarket, Suffolk

NOTEBOOK
Starlit Sands returned to form following a below-par run at Newbury. Having raced on the rails, away from the main group, she was smartly away and was always going well within herself. She looked to win with something in hand.
Wilki(FR) took command of this race soon after the start and quickened things up with two furlongs left to run, but the winner was just too good. This was her first run for her new trainer and it was a promising effort.
Galaktea(IRE), always close to the stands' rail, she began to run on from two out but never looked like getting there.
Untitled Blues(USA), slowly away with plenty to do at the halfway stage, she began to run on from the furlong marker and only failed to catch third place by a narrow distance.

5350 DONCASTER (L-H)
Friday, September 14

OFFICIAL GOING: Good to firm (9.2)
5mm water was put on overnight resulting in 'lovely quick ground'.
Wind: Moderate half against Weather: Overcast and breezy

5374 FRANK WHITTLE PARTNERSHIP NURSERY 7f
1:35 (1:35) (Class 3) (0-95,85) 2-Y-0 **£9,715** (£2,890; £1,444; £721) **Stalls** High

Form RPR

1035 **1** **Dubai Dynamo**[24] 4695 2-8-11 **75** ..... JohnEgan 3 84
(J S Moore) *sn led: qcknd over 2f out: rdn wl over 1f out: kpt on strly ins fnl f* **11/2**[3]

1 **2** *1 1/2* **Perfect Act**[21] 4764 2-8-13 **77** ..... AdamKirby 9 82
(C G Cox) *lw: trckd ldrs: swtchd lft and hdwy over 2f out: challenegd wl over 1f out: sn rdn and nt qckn ins fnl f* **5/2**[2]

5100 **3** *3/4* **Hansinger (IRE)**[21] 4775 2-8-9 **76** ..... WilliamBuick(3) 7 79
(B I Case) *hld up: hdwy wl over 2f out: rdn to chse ldrs over 1f out: kpt on u.p ins fnl f* **66/1**

21 **4** *nk* **Winter Bloom (USA)**[33] 4422 2-9-2 **80** ..... RichardHughes 2 82
(H R A Cecil) *lw: leggy: scope: hld up in rr: swtchd lft and hdwy over 2f out: rdn to chse ldng pair ent fnl f: sn one pce* **9/4**[1]

0422 **5** *4* **Huzzah (IRE)**[16] 4946 2-8-12 **76** ..... MichaelHills 4 68
(B W Hills) *chsd ldrs: effrt over 2f out: sn rdn and wknd appr fnl f* **7/1**

0641 **6** *1 1/2* **Relative Order**[34] 4372 2-9-1 **79** ..... TedDurcan 1 67
(J R Best) *hld up towards rr: effrt on outer over 2f out: sn rdn and btn* **11/2**[3]

6230 **7** *1* **Kersaint (IRE)**[24] 4695 2-9-7 **85** ..... DO'Donohoe 5 70
(K A Ryan) *prom: rdn along wl over 2f out and sn wknd* **20/1**

0644 **8** *3* **Higgy's Boy (IRE)**[100] 2353 2-8-12 **76** ..... PatDobbs 8 54
(R Hannon) *chsd ldrs: pushed along 3f out: sn wknd* **33/1**

1m 25.94s (-1.83) **Going Correction** -0.35s/f (Firm) 8 Ran SP% **111.8**
Speed ratings (Par 99): **96,94,93,93,88 86,85,82**
CSF £18.70 CT £796.08 TOTE £7.00: £1.50, £1.50, £5.10; EX 23.50 Trifecta £519.60 Part won. Pool £731.90 - 0.44 winning units..
Owner Mrs Fitri Hay **Bred** T K And Mrs P A Knox **Trained** Upper Lambourn, Berks

FOCUS
Not a strong nursery run at just a steady pace and the winner largely had his own way out in front. It is doubtful if he had to improve much on his York effort and the form is rated around the third and fourth.

NOTEBOOK
Dubai Dynamo had a lot more use made of him. He tended to hang left but stuck on in most willing fashion. He has a round action and will be even better with some ease in the ground. (op 7-1)
Perfect Act, winner of her only previous starts, worked her way almost upsides coming to the final furlong but in the end was very much second best. There was no disgrace in this. (op 2-1)
Hansinger(IRE), back up in trip, ran a lot better and seems suited by fast ground.
Winter Bloom(USA), who is up in the air, showed a moderate action. She made hard work of entering the argument and never really threatened. She should do better next year when she has strengthened to her frame. (tchd 5-2)
Huzzah(IRE) dropped away in disappointing fashion. (op 9-1 tchd 10-1)
Relative Order, 5lb higher, showed a very scratchy action. (tchd 5-1)

5375 LADBROKES MALLARD STKS (H'CAP) 1m 6f 132y
2:05 (2:05) (Class 2) (0-110,103) 3-Y-0+**£32,385** (£9,635; £4,815; £2,405) **Stalls** Low

Form RPR

3025 **1** **Dansant**[22] 4749 3-8-3 **93** ..... WilliamBuick(3) 6 102+
(G A Butler) *lw: trckd ldng pair: hdwy 3f out: led over 2f out: rdn and edgd lft over 1f out and ins fnl f: kpt on wl* **5/2**[1]

6062 **2** *1 1/4* **Kasthari (IRE)**[18] 4893 8-9-6 **95** ..... TedDurcan 2 102
(J D Bethell) *trckd ldr: hdwy to ld over 3f out: rdn and hdd over 2f out: rallied u.p ins fnl f* **14/1**

2026 **3** *1/2* **Whispering Death**[6] 5215 5-8-10 **88** .....(b) LiamJones(3) 4 94
(W J Haggas) *hld up in rr: hdwy on outer 3f out: rdn to chse ldng pair wl over 1f out: drvn and kpt on same pce ins fnl f* **9/2**[2]

0000 **4** *2 1/2* **Greenwich Meantime**[6] 5215 7-9-8 **97** ..... PaulHanagan 7 100
(R A Fahey) *hld up in rr: effrt 3f out: rdn along wl over 2f out: kpt on ins fnl f: nrst fin* **8/1**

1406 **5** *2 1/2* **Ogee**[13] 5030 4-9-4 **93** ..... LDettori 5 92
(Sir Michael Stoute) *trckd ldrs: effrt 3f out: sn rdn along and btn 2f out* **9/2**[2]

2100 **6** *1/2* **Castle Howard (IRE)**[23] 4722 5-9-6 **95** ..... TPQueally 9 94
(W J Musson) *hld up: hdwy 3f out: swtchd lft and rdn to chse ldrs 2f out: sn btn* **7/1**[3]

3340 **7** *3* **Golden Quest**[28] 4569 6-9-6 **95** ..... RoystonFfrench 3 89
(M Johnston) *led: rdn along 4f out: sn hdd & wknd* **8/1**

3005 **8** *5* **Bulwark (IRE)**[8] 5165 5-9-13 **102** ..... JimCrowley 1 89
(Mrs A J Perrett) *lw: in tch: rdn along over 3f out and sn wknd* **14/1**

3m 3.99s (-5.75) **Going Correction** -0.35s/f (Firm)
WFA 3 from 4yo+ 12lb 8 Ran SP% **113.0**
Speed ratings (Par 109): **101,100,100,98,97 97,95,92**
CSF £38.58 CT £148.39 TOTE £3.50: £1.50, £2.50, £1.80; EX 42.90 Trifecta £119.60 Pool £931.66 - 5.53 winning units..
Owner Damiano Drago **Bred** Mrs Cino Del Duca **Trained** Blewbury, Oxon
■ The eighth three-year-old winner of this race in the last 11 years.

FOCUS
A good handicap in which the winner advertised the Melrose form. The older second and third ran to their pre-race marks.

NOTEBOOK
Dansant, the only three-year-old in the line-up, travelled strongly. He lengthened rather than quickened and was firmly in command at the line, winning in the style of a progressive young stayer. His rider has made exceptional progress since he rode his first winner just a year ago. (op 10-3 tchd 7-2)
Kasthari(IRE), 3lb higher and dropping back in trip, pushed the winner hard all the way to the line. He likes it here. (op 10-1)
Whispering Death jumped off on terms this time. He looked a possible threat coming to the final furlong but at the end of the day could only keep on in his own time. He really needs further. (op 5-1 tchd 11-2 in a place)

Greenwich Meantime, 4lb higher than his Chester Cup success, had the ground in his favour but these days this trip looks his bare minimum. (op 15-2)
Ogee went to post in good style but, reunited with Dettori, in truth he found little when the gun was put to his head. (op 5-1 tchd 4-1)
Castle Howard(IRE), who had run so well in the Ebor, did not shine on ground plenty fast enough for him. (op 11-2 tchd 5-1)

5376 GNER DONCASTER CUP (GROUP 2) 2m 2f
2:40 (2:40) (Class 1) 3-Y-0+

£56,780 (£21,520; £10,770; £5,370; £2,690; £1,350) **Stalls** Low

Form RPR
-121 **1** **Septimus (IRE)**[24] 4691 4-9-4 0 .... JMurtagh 8 124+
(A P O'Brien, Ire) *lw: trckd ldng pair: hdwy over 3f out: led over 2f out: shkn up and qckd clr appr fnl f: easily* **11/10**[1]
5225 **2** *5* **Geordieland (FR)**[43] 4091 6-9-1 114 .... TPQueally 5 116
(J A Osborne) *lw: hld up in rr: hdwy on bit to chal over 2f out and ev ch until rdn and one pce over 1f out* **7/1**[3]
1012 **3** *½* **Allegretto (IRE)**[23] 4723 4-9-1 114 .... LDettori 6 115
(Sir Michael Stoute) *hld up: hdwy 5f out: effrt over 2f out: rdn wl over 1f out and kpt on same pce* **7/2**[2]
3-04 **4** *1 ¾* **Distinction (IRE)**[24] 4691 8-9-1 112 .... OPeslier 4 113
(Sir Michael Stoute) *lw: hld up in tch: hdwy 4f out: rdn along over 2f out and plugged on same pce* **8/1**
4433 **5** *5* **Finalmente**[43] 4091 5-9-1 111 ....(p) RichardHughes 2 108
(N A Callaghan) *led and sn clr: rdn along over 4f out: hdd over 2f out and sn wknd* **14/1**
1142 **6** *6* **Balkan Knight**[24] 4691 7-9-1 112 .... TedDurcan 1 101
(D R C Elsworth) *b.hind: hld up: a in rr* **12/1**
0334 **7** *1 ¼* **Land 'n Stars**[8] 5165 7-9-1 102 .... PaulHanagan 7 100
(R A Fahey) *chsd clr ldr: rdn along over 4f out and sn wknd* **50/1**
2020 **8** *127* **Baddam**[43] 4091 5-9-1 105 .... IanMongan 3 —
(M R Channon) *lw: chsd ldrs: rdn along over 5f out and sn wknd* **33/1**
3m 48.41s (-9.52) **Going Correction** -0.35s/f (Firm) course record **8** Ran SP% **112.7**
Speed ratings (Par 115): **107,104,104,103,101 98,98,—**
CSF £9.22 TOTE £2.00: £1.10, £1.60, £1.50; EX 8.40 Trifecta £26.30 Pool £1,531.13 - 41.19 winning units..
Owner D Smith, Mrs J Magnier, M Tabor **Bred** Barronstown Stud & Orpendale **Trained** Ballydoyle, Co Tipperary

FOCUS
A decent renewal of this important stayers' race. with an end-to-end gallop resulting in a record time. The winner looks a top-class stayer, a successor possibly to Yeats.

NOTEBOOK
Septimus(IRE), given a patient ride, really put his foot on the gas and came right away. The fast ground was no problem and he seemed suited by the extended trip. The Prix du Cadran could be next for this top-class stayer. (op 5-4 tchd Evens in a place)
Geordieland(FR), who looked at his very best, travelled strongly and looked a real threat when moving upsides but in the end the winner proved far too tough. He empties so fast he must have a physical problem.
Allegretto(IRE), who went to post with real relish, had the visor left off again. She ran somewhere near her best and is very tough and versatile. (tchd 10-3)
Distinction(IRE), struggling to regain his best form after a tendon injury, looked really well but this may be as good as he is now. (op 9-1)
Finalmente took them along in record-breaking time and it was no surprise to see him fall in a heap when the winner went on and struck for home. (op 12-1 tchd 16-1 in a place)
Balkan Knight, who pushed the winner hard over shorter at York, never entered the argument.
Land 'n Stars paid the price for being the only one to keep close tabs on the pacesetter.
Baddam, the first to come under serious pressure, dropped right out once in line for home and walked over the line.

5377 POLYPIPE FLYING CHILDERS STKS (GROUP 2) 5f
3:10 (3:15) (Class 1) 2-Y-0

£42,585 (£16,140; £8,077; £4,027; £2,017; £1,012) **Stalls** High

Form RPR
113 **1** **Fleeting Spirit (IRE)**[22] 4744 2-8-11 109 .... LDettori 4 112+
(J Noseda) *lw: prom: effrt 2f out: rdn to ld over 1f out: kpt on wl fnl f* **5/4**[1]
1306 **2** *1 ¾* **Spirit Of Sharjah (IRE)**[45] 4046 2-9-0 100 .... RichardHughes 3 109
(P W Chapple-Hyam) *lw: dwlt: hld up in rr: hdwy 2f out: rdn to chse wnr ins fnl f: no imp* **15/2**
2412 **3** *¾* **Cute Ass (IRE)**[28] 4573 2-8-11 99 .... TedDurcan 6 103
(K R Burke) *chsd ldrs: hdwy 2f out: sn rdn and kpt on same pce ent fnl f* **28/1**
1131 **4** *¾* **Captain Gerrard (IRE)**[23] 4724 2-9-0 108 .... RichardMullen 1 103
(B Smart) *lw: led: rdn along 2f out: drvn and hdd over 1f out: wknd ins fnl f* **7/2**[2]
2534 **5** *nk* **The Loan Express (IRE)**[33] 4437 2-8-11 0 .... WJLee 7 99
(T Stack, Ire) *towards rr: hdwy 2f out: sn rdn and styd on ins fnl f: nrst fin* **16/1**
1054 **6** *2* **Warsaw (IRE)**[20] 4833 2-9-0 0 .... JMurtagh 2 95
(A P O'Brien, Ire) *lw: in tch: rdn along over 2f out and sn btn* **12/1**
1041 **7** *shd* **Dark Angel (IRE)**[22] 4743 2-9-0 105 .... MichaelHills 9 95
(B W Hills) *cl up: rdn along over 2f out and sn wknd* **5/1**[3]
5012 **8** *shd* **Cake (IRE)**[23] 4724 2-8-11 100 .... PatDobbs 5 91
(R Hannon) *t.k.h: cl up: rdn along over 2f out and sn wknd* **20/1**
58.46 secs (-2.96) **Going Correction** -0.35s/f (Firm) **8** Ran SP% **116.9**
Speed ratings (Par 107): **109,106,105,103,103 100,99,99**
CSF £12.01 TOTE £2.20: £1.20, £2.40, £2.80; EX 16.20 Trifecta £341.30 Pool £1,476.10 - 3.07 winning units..
Owner The Searchers **Bred** Mrs Bernadette Hayden **Trained** Newmarket, Suffolk
■ Proud Linus was withdrawn 25/1, bolted and injured rdr O. Peslier bef s.) No Rule 4

FOCUS
A good quality renewal and another boost for the form of the Molecomb Stakes, with the form looking solid if unspectacular.

NOTEBOOK
Fleeting Spirit(IRE) found 6f just too far in the Lowther but she was always going to take a deal of beating back over the minimum trip. Always well placed, she picked up well when asked to go and win her race and scored comfortably in the end. Given the ease of success of Kingsgate Native (whom she beat in the Molecomb) in the Nunthorpe, it is no surprise that connections are now considering supplementing her to take on the older horses in the Abbaye. (op 11-8 tchd 6-4)
Spirit Of Sharjah(IRE), who has joined Peter Chapple-Hyam since finishing sixth behind Fleeting Spirit in the Molecomb, stayed on well from the back of the field to chase the fairly easy winner home. On this evidence he might be worth another try over 6f. (op 8-1 tchd 10-1)
Cute Ass(IRE), who stepped up on her previous efforts when runner-up in a Listed race at Newbury last time, showed that run was no fluke with a solid effort in this higher grade. (op 40-1)
Captain Gerrard(IRE) was beaten a little further by Fleeting Spirit here than he was in the Molecomb, where his trainer thought that the colt did not act on the track and, while he is a smart sprinting juvenile, he may need some give underfoot to be seen at his best.
The Loan Express(IRE), third in the Queen Mary and fourth in the Phoenix Stakes, ran as though finding this distance too short now. She could well pop up in a Listed or Group 3 race when returned to 6f on quick ground.
Warsaw(IRE), used as a pacemaker for Henrythenavigator on his last two starts, got to race for himself here but was well held. (op 16-1 tchd 11-1)
Dark Angel(IRE), who won a valuable sales race last time out, had more to do against higher-rated rivals back in Group company. He is also probably more effective over 6f these days as well. (op 6-1)
Cake(IRE), keen in the early stages, did too much too soon against this stronger opposition and paid the price in the latter part of the race. (op 28-1)

5378 INSPIREPAC CONDITIONS STKS 1m (S)
3:45 (3:45) (Class 2) 3-Y-0 **£18,696** (£5,598; £2,799; £1,401) **Stalls** High

Form RPR
0153 **1** **Tobosa**[41] 4148 3-8-11 111 .... MichaelHills 4 97+
(W Jarvis) *lw: chsd clr ldr: hdwy to ld over 2f out: sn rdn clr* **2/5**[1]
2 *7* **Rock Of Veio (IRE)**[152] 3-9-0 0 .... TedDurcan 2 90
(P W Chapple-Hyam) *w'like: hld up: hdwy 3f out: chsd wnr wl over 1f out: no imp* **14/1**[3]
1-31 **3** *20* **Mount Hadley (USA)**[190] 641 3-9-0 104 ....(vt[1]) LDettori 3 38+
(Saeed Bin Suroor) *led and sn clr: rdn along and hdd over 2f out: wknd qckly and eased* **5/2**[2]
034 **4** *40* **Little Darlin**[28] 4588 3-8-6 0 .... PaulHanagan 1 —
(G J Smith) *sn outpcd and a bhd* **150/1**
1m 36.86s (-4.65) **Going Correction** -0.35s/f (Firm) **4** Ran SP% **107.3**
Speed ratings (Par 107): **109,102,82,42**
CSF £6.84 TOTE £1.40; EX 5.30.
Owner Collins, Randall, Rich & Turnbull **Bred** G S Shropshire **Trained** Newmarket, Suffolk

FOCUS
An uncompetitive conditions race and the form looks dubious with the placed horses eased.

NOTEBOOK
Tobosa, who would probably have won at Goodwood last time under a stronger rider, was strongly favoured by the race conditions and it would have been a big surprise had he not collected. This taught us nothing we did not already know, and he remains capable of winning a Listed contest this season, although he may apparently be put away for the year now. (op 4-9)
Rock Of Veio(IRE), who was previously trained in Italy, was having his first outing for his new stable and shaped with promise. Not given a hard ride to secure second place, he should improve for this first run since April, and easier ground might suit him this autumn. (op 12-1 tchd 11-1)
Mount Hadley(USA), wearing a visor and a tongue tie for the first time, looked the only danger to the favourite on the ratings and he set out to make every yard, but was headed with a quarter mile to run and soon beat a retreat. He had not run since winning in Dubai in March but fitness is rarely an issue with representatives from the Godolphin stable. Official explanation: jockey said colt ran too free (op 9-4)
Little Darlin keeps running in races she has absolutely no chance of winning, but is picking up some nice prizemoney along the way for just turning up. (op 100-1)

5379 ULTIMATE PACKAGING H'CAP 5f
4:20 (4:20) (Class 4) (0-85,85) 3-Y-0+ **£6,477** (£1,927; £963; £481) **Stalls** High

Form RPR
2006 **1** **Inter Vision (USA)**[13] 5044 7-8-11 77 .... DanielTudhope 9 95
(A Dickman) *hld up in rr stands' side: gd hdwy wl over 1f out: rdn to ld ent fnl f: sn drvn and hld on wl* **12/1**
0003 **2** *shd* **Yungaburra (IRE)**[2] 5332 3-8-13 80 ....(t) AdamKirby 13 97
(D J Murphy) *hld up in rr stands' side: swtchd to stands' rail 2f out: rdn & hdwy whn sddle slipped over 1f out: styd on ins fnl f: jst failed* **12/1**
3031 **3** *hd* **Canadian Danehill (IRE)**[14] 5009 5-9-3 83 ....(p) LDettori 17 100
(R M H Cowell) *hld up stands' side: hdwy 2f out: rdn ent fnl f: sn ev ch: drvn and nt qckn nr fin* **3/1**[1]
0032 **4** *3 ½* **Harry Up**[13] 5039 6-9-5 85 .... DO'Donohoe 16 89
(K A Ryan) *lw: overall ldr stands' side: rdn wl over 1f out: hdd ent fnl f: sn drvn and wknd* **6/1**[2]
6334 **5** *hd* **Fromsong (IRE)**[10] 5119 9-8-10 76 .... JohnEgan 11 79
(D K Ivory) *hld up stands' side: hdwy 2f out: rdn to chse ldrs ent fnl f: sn drvn and one pce* **14/1**
0002 **6** *nk* **Oranmore Castle (IRE)**[6] 5232 5-8-7 73 .... PaulHanagan 15 75
(R A Fahey) *prom stands' side: rdn along 2f out: drvn and kpt on same pce ent fnl f* **6/1**[2]
2000 **7** *hd* **First Order**[13] 5039 6-8-8 77 ....(v) JamieMoriarty[(3)] 10 78
(I Semple) *midfield stands' side: hdwy 2f out: sn rdn to chse ldrs: kpt on same pce ins fnl f* **25/1**
135 **8** *¾* **Haajes**[1] 5356 3-8-8 75 .... AdrianTNicholls 5 74
(D J Murphy) *chsd ldrs stands' side: rdn along wl over 1f out: drvn and one pce ent fnl f* **10/1**[3]
00 **9** *½* **Kay Two (IRE)**[47] 3990 5-8-12 83 .... RussellKennemore[(5)] 7 80
(R J Price) *prom stands' side: rdn along 2f out: drvn and wknd appr fnl f* **16/1**
0000 **10** *½* **Distinctly Game**[13] 5044 5-8-10 79 .... AndrewMullen[(3)] 1 74
(K A Ryan) *chsd ldrs far side: hdwy 2f out: rdn to ld that gp ins fnl f: no ch w stands' side* **20/1**
3060 **11** *nk* **The Nifty Fox**[23] 4726 3-9-0 81 ....(b[1]) TedDurcan 3 75
(T D Easterby) *chsd ldr far side: led that gp 2f out: sn rdn and kpt on same pce: no ch w stands' side* **50/1**
2000 **12** *¾* **Gallery Girl (IRE)**[24] 4696 4-9-2 82 .... DavidAllan 8 73
(T D Easterby) *chsd ldrs stands' side: rdn along 2f out: grad wknd* **14/1**
1146 **13** *nk* **Bahamian Ballet**[13] 5029 5-9-3 83 .... GrahamGibbons 6 73
(E S McMahon) *prom stands' side: rdn along 2f out: grad wknd* **16/1**
5305 **14** *hd* **Mr Wolf**[13] 5039 6-9-3 83 .... PatCosgrave 14 73
(D W Barker) *lw: prom stands' side: rdn along 2f out: wknd over 1f out* **14/1**
0100 **15** *3 ½* **Highland Warrior**[13] 5044 8-9-0 80 .... MickyFenton 4 57
(P T Midgley) *racd far side: a towards rr* **50/1**
0000 **16** *shd* **Overstayed (IRE)**[13] 5039 4-8-11 77 ....(b) PhillipMakin 2 54
(I Semple) *led far side gp: rdn and hdd 2f out: sn wknd* **100/1**
00-5 **17** *5* **Wicked Uncle**[147] 1121 8-8-9 75 ow1 ....(v) MichaelHills 12 34
(S Gollings) *s.i.s: a bhd* **40/1**
58.62 secs (-2.80) **Going Correction** -0.35s/f (Firm)
WFA 3 from 4yo+ 1lb **17** Ran SP% **125.8**
Speed ratings (Par 105): **108,107,107,101,101 101,100,99,98,98 97,96,95,95,89 89,81**
CSF £144.67 CT £572.63 TOTE £17.80: £3.40, £2.60, £1.40, £2.00; EX 193.20 Trifecta £1015.20 Part won. Pool £1,429.89 - 0.30 winning units. Place 6 £16.06, Place 5 £5.12.
Owner Mrs D Hodgkinson **Bred** W A Carl **Trained** Sandhutton, N Yorks

FOCUS
The bigger stands'-side group had the edge in this competitive handicap and the form could be rated higher with the first three clear.
Yungaburra(IRE) Official explanation: jockey said saddle slipped

The Form Book, Raceform Ltd, Compton, RG20 6NL

T/Jkpt: £4,652.60 to a £1 stake. Pool: £19,659.00. 3.00 winning tickets. T/Plt: £16.80 to a £1 stake. Pool: £130,660.25. 5,650.35 winning tickets. T/Qpdt: £2.90 to a £1 stake. Pool: £5,215.45. 1,289.10 winning tickets. JR

5357 SANDOWN (R-H)

Friday, September 14

OFFICIAL GOING: Good to firm (good in places; 9.4)
Wind: virtually nil

5380 UKN GROUP MANAGED IT EBF MAIDEN STKS — 5f 6y
2:20 (2:21) (Class 5) 2-Y-0 — **£3,886** (£1,156; £577; £288) Stalls High

Form — RPR

5202 **1** — **Kashoof**[27] 4605 2-8-12 84 .... MartinDwyer 2 — 85+
(J L Dunlop) *mde all: drvn and styd on strly fnl f: unchal* — **8/13**[1]

66 **2** 4 **Wavertree Princess (IRE)**[21] 4755 2-8-12 0 .... JamesDoyle 5 — 71
(N P Littmoden) *in tch: rdn: n.m.r and edgd lft over 1f out: styd on to take 2nd cl home but no ch w wnr* — **25/1**

3 ½ **Your Pleasure (USA)** 2-8-12 0 .... FrancisNorton 8 — 69
(A M Balding) *chsd ldrs: flashed tail: rdn to chse wnr over 1f out: no imp and lost 2nd cl home* — **9/1**[3]

63 **4** ¾ **Mayaar (USA)**[55] 3750 2-8-12 0 .... AdrianMcCarthy 3 — 67
(P W Chapple-Hyam) *chsd ldrs: rdn 1/2-way: one pce fr over 1f out* **11/2**[2]

00 **5** 1 ½ **Sistos Fascination**[36] 4323 2-9-3 0 .... (p) OscarUrbina 9 — 66
(M Botti) *chsd ldrs: rdn and hmpd over 1f out: sn btn* — **66/1**

6 ½ **Barbary Boy (FR)** 2-9-3 0 .... HayleyTurner 6 — 64
(M L W Bell) *s.i.s: sme hdwy 2f out: nvr in contention* — **10/1**

0 **7** ¾ **Karmei**[9] 5143 2-9-3 0 .... KerrinMcEvoy 7 — 62
(J W Hills) *s.i.s: outpcd* — **12/1**

8 10 **Warden Fizz** 2-9-3 0 .... DaneO'Neill 4 — 26
(D R C Elsworth) *slowly away: a in rr* — **33/1**

9 1 ¼ **Ubiquitous Bounty** 2-9-3 0 .... FergusSweeney 1 — 21
(G L Moore) *slowly away: sn hung bdly lft and styd wl bhd* — **33/1**

61.76 secs (-0.45) **Going Correction** -0.15s/f (Firm) — **9** Ran SP% **115.3**
Speed ratings (Par 95): **97,90,89,88,86 85,84,68,66**
CSF £25.19 TOTE £1.60: £1.02, £5.50, £2.60; EX 13.20.
Owner Hamdan Al Maktoum **Bred** Shadwell Estate Company Limited **Trained** Arundel, W Sussex

FOCUS
An uncompetitive sprint maiden in which the winner did not need to reproduce her best form..

NOTEBOOK
Kashoof, whose recent second off a mark of 84 in a Newmarket handicap set a strong standard, was soon in front and rarely had a moment's worry, running on strongly for pressure and winning easily. We learned nothing knew about the daughter of Green Desert, but this should give her the confidence to go on to better things back in handicaps. (op 4-6, tchd 8-11 in a place)
Wavertree Princess(IRE) had not shown a great deal in two previous starts, but this was certainly an improved effort and, although proving no match for the winner, she gave the impression there will be more to come once stepping up to 6f. She is now qualified for nurseries and should fare better in that sphere. (op 28-1)
Your Pleasure(USA), a half-sister to a useful 6-9f winner, comes from a yard whose juveniles often need a run to set them straight, but this one seemed to know her job and she showed a bit of early speed. However, she was readily left trailing by the winner and it was a bit disconcerting to see her flash her tail even before she came under pressure. (tchd 10-1)
Mayaar(USA), faced with this sort of ground for the first time, failed to improve as much as anticipated and lacked the speed to challenge. She is now qualified for a handicap mark and should do better in that sphere, with a return to 6f likely to suit. (op 9-2)
Sistos Fascination had beaten a combined total of one horse in two previous attempts, the first-time tongue tie failing to bring about any improvement at Folkestone last time, but the cheekpieces had more of an effect and he was arguably unlucky not to finish a bit closer. He should fare better in low-grade nurseries. (op 50-1)
Barbary Boy(FR), a son of Rock Of Gibraltar, could make only limited headway having been slowly away, but it is safe to assume he will be capable of better as he steps up in distance. (op 12-1)

5381 LONDON STOCK EXCHANGE H'CAP — 5f 6y
2:50 (2:51) (Class 4) (0-80,79) 3-Y-0+ — **£5,181** (£1,541; £770; £384) Stalls High

Form — RPR

1023 **1** — **Matsunosuke**[4] 5278 5-9-1 75 .... KerrinMcEvoy 1 — 88
(A B Coogan) *hld up in rr but in tch: hdwy 2f out: qckd to ld fnl 100yds: readily* — **9/4**[1]

3523 **2** 1 **Gwilym (GER)**[14] 5009 4-8-7 72 .... AshleyHamblett(5) 4 — 81
(D Haydn Jones) *pressed ldr: led 2f out: rdn and hung lft ins fnl f: hdd and outpcd fnl 100yds* — **4/1**[3]

6165 **3** ½ **Safari Mischief**[4] 5278 4-8-12 79 .... JackMitchell(7) 2 — 86
(P Winkworth) *chsd ldrs: drvn to chal fr over 2f out: kpt on ins fnl f but outpcd fnl 100yds* — **12/1**

0413 **4** 1 ½ **Pic Up Sticks**[4] 5272 8-8-11 74 6ex .... RichardKingscote(3) 6 — 76
(B G Powell) *t.k.h: chsd ldrs: rdn 2f out: styd on same pce fnl f* — **3/1**[2]

2060 **5** nk **Rainbow Bay**[23] 4703 4-8-8 68 .... (v) StephenDonohoe 3 — 69
(P D Evans) *in rr: rdn and hdwy over 1f out: gng on cl home but nt rch ldrs* — **20/1**

5044 **6** 2 **Mandarin Spirit (IRE)**[12] 5064 7-8-12 72 .... (b) OscarUrbina 7 — 66
(G C H Chung) *chsd ldrs: rdn over 2f out: wknd fnl f* — **12/1**

0140 **7** 1 **Kings College Boy**[3] 5297 7-8-7 67 .... (b) DaleGibson 9 — 57
(R A Fahey) *chsd ldrs: rdn 1/2-way: wknd fnl f* — **9/1**

0-00 **8** ¾ **Avening**[25] 4664 7-8-12 72 .... (bt) StephenCarson 8 — 59
(Eve Johnson Houghton) *s.i.s: outpcd* — **10/1**

1460 **9** 2 **Quality Street**[10] 5119 5-8-13 73 .... (p) RichardThomas 5 — 53
(P Butler) *led tl hdd 2f out: sn btn* — **33/1**

61.21 secs (-1.00) **Going Correction** -0.15s/f (Firm) — **9** Ran SP% **117.9**
Speed ratings (Par 105): **102,100,99,97,96 93,91,90,87**
CSF £11.73 CT £88.91 TOTE £3.10: £1.40, £1.70, £3.50; EX 12.50.
Owner A B Coogan **Bred** R Coogan **Trained** Soham, Cambs

FOCUS
A typically competitive sprint handicap. Straightforward form.
Avening Official explanation: jockey said gelding missed the break

5382 AIM H'CAP — 1m 14y
3:20 (3:20) (Class 3) (0-90,88) 3-Y-0
£7,478 (£2,239; £1,119; £560; £279; £140) Stalls High

Form — RPR

411 **1** — **Amarna (USA)**[18] 4889 3-9-0 84 .... KerrinMcEvoy 2 — 95+
(Saeed Bin Suroor) *trckd ldrs: qcknd to ld over 1f out: pushed out ins fnl f: readily* — **9/4**[1]

1151 **2** 1 **Padlocked (IRE)**[30] 4502 3-9-4 88 .... FergusSweeney 6 — 94
(D M Simcock) *t.k.h early: chsd ldrs: outpcd and pushed along over 2f out: styd on fnl f to take 2nd cl home but no imp on wnr* — **5/1**[3]

-104 **3** nk **First Buddy**[36] 4331 3-8-9 79 .... OscarUrbina 4 — 84
(W J Haggas) *sn led: rdn over 2f out: sn narrowly hdd: styd on but nt pce of wnr: ct for 2nd cl home* — **16/1**

5421 **4** 2 **Safwa (IRE)**[29] 4549 3-8-10 80 .... MartinDwyer 8 — 80
(Sir Michael Stoute) *t.k.h early: chsd ldr: led 2f out: hdd over 1f out: edgd rt u.p ins fnl f and sn wknd* — **5/1**[3]

1120 **5** ¾ **Bajan Pride**[20] 4827 3-8-11 81 .... SteveDrowne 5 — 80
(R Hannon) *in rr: drvn along 3f out: styd on fnl f but nvr in contention* **14/1**

3304 **6** 2 **Kyle (IRE)**[27] 4607 3-8-9 84 .... HaddenFrost(5) 1 — 78
(R Hannon) *in rr: pushed along 4f out: mod prog fnl f* — **14/1**

221 **7** shd **Pillar Of Hercules (IRE)**[37] 4290 3-9-3 87 .... DaneO'Neill 9 — 81
(H R A Cecil) *chsd ldrs: rdn and one pce over 2f out: wknd fnl f* — **11/4**[2]

0060 **8** 1 **Cesc**[20] 4811 3-9-3 87 .... AmirQuinn 7 — 79
(P J Makin) *hld up in rr: rdn and no prog over 2f out* — **20/1**

1m 40.9s (-3.05) **Going Correction** -0.15s/f (Firm) — **8** Ran SP% **114.7**
Speed ratings (Par 105): **109,108,107,105,104 102,102,101**
CSF £14.01 CT £142.25 TOTE £3.20: £1.40, £1.90, £2.80; EX 14.70.
Owner Godolphin **Bred** Darley **Trained** Newmarket, Suffolk

FOCUS
A decent handicap. The first two are progressive and the third and fourth look pretty solid.

NOTEBOOK
Amarna(USA), up 8lb for his recent Kempton victory, is clearly a progressive handicapper and, although taking his time to reach top stride, he was nicely on top close home. He gives every indication an extra quarter mile will suit and it would not surprise to see the son of Danzig go on to further success, with a crack at something a bit bigger no doubt on the cards. (tchd 2-1)
Padlocked(IRE), whose only previous defeat in four attempts came when not appearing to stay 1m2f at Goodwood in June, returned to winning ways over 1m at Salisbury last time and he again looked a player off a 5lb higher mark. He took a keen grip early, but still came to have every chance and was simply unable to match the highly-progressive winner. (op 11-2)
First Buddy was down in trip having failed to see out 1m2f on his recent handicap debut, but having taken them along early he found himself done for speed. Perhaps a more patient ride over further is the answer, as he clearly has a race in him off this sort of mark. (op 14-1)
Safwa(IRE), ready winner of a course and distance maiden last time, took a bit of a grip early on and having gone to the front racing into the final quarter mile, it was no surprise to see her fade out of it. She would have benefited from a better gallop and can be given another chance. Official explanation: jockey said filly hung right (tchd 9-2)
Bajan Pride remains 8lb higher than when last winning and he again gave the impression this mark is currently beyond him. (op 11-1)
Pillar Of Hercules(IRE), off the mark at the third attempt in a weak Pontefract maiden last time, looked to be starting out his handicap career off a stiff mark and having held a prominent early position he gradually faded out of it. (op 3-1)
Cesc Official explanation: jockey said colt stumbled in back straight

5383 MAIN MARKET H'CAP — 1m 14y
3:55 (3:55) (Class 4) (0-80,80) 3-Y-0+ — **£5,181** (£1,541; £770; £384) Stalls High

Form — RPR

-040 **1** — **Namid Reprobate (IRE)**[16] 4949 4-9-0 76 .... TolleyDean(5) 7 — 86
(P F I Cole) *in rr: hdwy on outside over 3f out: led ins fnl 2f: drvn out ins fnl f* — **33/1**

4122 **2** ½ **Optimus (USA)**[19] 4850 5-9-1 72 .... OscarUrbina 9 — 81
(B G Powell) *hld up in rr: hdwy over 2f out: styd on to chse wnr fnl f but a jst hld* — **5/1**[1]

0630 **3** nk **Waterline Twenty (IRE)**[6] 5228 4-8-13 70 .... StephenDonohoe 2 — 78
(P D Evans) *in rr: stl plenty to do over 2f out: rdn and styd on wl fr over 1f out: styd on to chse ldrs ins fnl f but a jst hld* — **25/1**

0004 **4** 1 ¼ **Irony (IRE)**[14] 5012 8-9-8 79 .... FrancisNorton 8 — 84
(A M Balding) *chsd ldrs: drvn to chal over 2f out: outpcd ins fnl f* — **6/1**[3]

0504 **5** ½ **Lazy Darren**[10] 5114 3-9-0 76 .... SteveDrowne 12 — 83+
(R Hannon) *hld up in rr: nt clr run over 2f out and again over 1f out: rdn and styd on strly fnl f: gng on cl home* — **11/2**[2]

1430 **6** 3 **Scarlet Flyer (USA)**[37] 4268 4-9-4 75 .... (v[1]) LPKeniry 6 — 72
(G L Moore) *in tch: rdn and hdwy on outside to chse ldrs over 1f out: no ex ins fnl f* — **16/1**

2620 **7** 1 ¼ **Fabrian**[14] 5012 9-9-1 72 .... JamesDoyle 4 — 69+
(R J Price) *chsd ldrs: rdn and one pce whn n.m.r over 1f out: n.d* — **12/1**

1060 **8** shd **Bold Diktator**[18] 4672 5-9-3 77 .... RichardKingscote(3) 13 — 71
(Tom Dascombe) *chsd ldrs: rdn along over 3f out: wknd appr fnl f* — **15/2**

1000 **9** ½ **Spume (IRE)**[7] 5196 3-9-1 77 .... (t) TPO'Shea 1 — 69
(D J Murphy) *w ldr: led 6f out: hdd ins fnl 2f: wknd fnl f* — **25/1**

3020 **10** 1 ½ **Laish Ya Hajar (IRE)**[69] 3299 3-8-12 74 .... DaneO'Neill 15 — 63
(P R Webber) *chsd ldrs: rdn 3f out: wknd over 1f out* — **12/1**

5160 **11** 1 **Will He Wish**[14] 5012 11-9-6 80 .... PJMcDonald(3) 10 — 67
(S Gollings) *mid-div: sme prog to get in tch w ldrs whn n.m.r 2f out: sn btn* — **33/1**

6000 **12** ¾ **Symbol Of Peace (IRE)**[17] 4922 4-9-2 73 .... (b[1]) MartinDwyer 5 — 59
(J W Unett) *s.i.s: pushed along 3f out: nvr in contention* — **66/1**

2153 **13** 1 ¾ **Sky Quest (IRE)**[13] 5052 9-9-1 72 .... KerrinMcEvoy 11 — 54+
(J R Boyle) *mid-div: effrt whn nt clr run over 2f out: nvr a factor after* **11/1**

135- **14** shd **First Mate (IRE)**[372] 5133 3-9-0 76 .... J-PGuillambert 17 — 56
(M Johnston) *led 2f: styd pressing ldr to 2f out: sn wknd* — **11/2**[2]

5052 **15** 2 ½ **Kildare Sun (IRE)**[11] 5099 5-9-1 72 .... DaleGibson 14 — 48
(J Mackie) *in rr: effrt and nt clr run over 2f out: n.d after* — **14/1**

0030 **16** nk **Glenmuir (IRE)**[39] 4234 4-8-13 70 .... HayleyTurner 16 — 45+
(B R Millman) *mid-div: nt clr run on ins fnl 3f: nt rcvr and eased fnl f* **16/1**

1m 41.33s (-2.62) **Going Correction** -0.15s/f (Firm)
WFA 3 from 4yo+ 5lb — **16** Ran SP% **130.7**
Speed ratings (Par 105): **107,106,106,104,104 101,100,100,99,98 97,96,94,94,92 91**
CSF £197.89 CT £4305.11 TOTE £61.20: £9.50, £1.80, £3.20, £2.10; EX 515.10.
Owner Mrs J M Haines **Bred** A P Jarvis **Trained** Whatcombe, Oxon

FOCUS
Just a modest handicap and the fast early pace played into the hands of those who were held up.
Lazy Darren Official explanation: jockey said gelding was denied a clear run
Fabrian Official explanation: jockey said gelding was denied a clear run
Glenmuir(IRE) Official explanation: jockey said gelding was denied a clear run

5384 BGC SUPPORTING SPARKS MAIDEN STKS — 1m 2f 7y
4:30 (4:30) (Class 5) 3-4-Y-0 — **£3,886** (£1,156; £577; £288) Stalls High

Form — RPR

00 **1** — **Kaateb (IRE)**[20] 4815 4-9-10 0 .... MartinDwyer 11 — 76+
(W J Haggas) *mde all: rdn over 2f out: styd on str fr over 1f out: unchal* — **11/1**

2- **2** 1 ¼ **Sharp Dresser (USA)**[323] 6187 3-8-12 0 .... SteveDrowne 6 — 67
(Mrs A J Perrett) *t.k.h: chsd wnr tl ins fnl 2f: sn rdn: rallied to retake 2nd fnl f but a readily hld* — **7/2**[3]

-052 **3** 1 1/4 **Timber Treasure (USA)**[18] 4901 3-9-3 72......................(v) DaneO'Neill 9 69
(H R A Cecil) *chsd ldrs: rdn over 2f out: kpt on ins fnl f and gng on cl home but nvr gng pce to to press ldng duo* **8/1**

0 **4** hd **Al Naahadth (USA)**[32] 4457 3-9-3 0......................(v¹) KerrinMcEvoy 4 69
(Saeed Bin Suroor) *chsd ldrs: rdn and styd on to go 2nd ins fnl 2f: sn no imp on wnr: fnd little ins fnl f and sn btn* **3/1**[2]

3 **5** nk **Viva Vettori**[20] 4815 3-9-3 0...................... AntonyProcter 3 68+
(D R C Elsworth) *t.k.h: hld up in rr: stl plenty to do whn shkn up over 2f out: hdwy over 1f out: swtchd rt ins fnl f: r.o and edgd rt cl home: nt rch ldrs* **15/8**[1]

6 1 1/4 **Mythical Story (IRE)** 3-8-12 0...................... OscarUrbina 8 63+
(J R Fanshawe) *chsd ldrs: rdn over 2f out: one pce and hld whn hmpd on rails cl home* **25/1**

46 **7** 1/2 **Miss Habershon**[14] 5005 3-8-12 0...................... FergusSweeney 2 60?
(A King) *mid-div: rdn 3f out: no imp on ldrs 2f out: kpt on same pce* **66/1**

56 **8** 3 1/2 **Covert Mission**[4] 5271 4-9-5 0...................... StephenDonohoe 7 53
(P D Evans) *s.i.s: t.k.h in rr: sme prog fnl 2f* **33/1**

9 8 **Heavenward** 3-8-10 0...................... JamieHamblett(7) 1 42
(Sir Michael Stoute) *rdn over 3f out: a in rr* **12/1**

06 **10** 5 **Welsh Guard (USA)**[35] 4357 4-9-10 0...................... SimonWhitworth 10 32
(G P Enright) *s.i.s: sme prog 1/2-way: sn wknd* **100/1**

2m 13.37s (3.13) **Going Correction** -0.15s/f (Firm)
WFA 3 from 4yo 7lb **10** Ran SP% **118.4**
Speed ratings (Par 103): **81,80,79,78,78 77,77,74,68,64**
CSF £49.40 TOTE £14.50: £3.40, £1.50, £2.10; EX 54.60.
Owner Hamdan Al Maktoum **Bred** Shadwell Estate Company Limited **Trained** Newmarket, Suffolk

FOCUS
Not a strong maiden and muddling form. Only a couple of these make any appeal with the future in mind.
Welsh Guard(USA) Official explanation: jockey said gelding was unsuited by the slow early pace

5385 SUNGARD H'CAP — 1m 2f 7y
5:05 (5:06) (Class 4) (0-85,84) 3-Y-O — **£5,181** (£1,541; £770; £384) **Stalls** High

Form — RPR

0-10 **1** **Venerable**[112] 1987 3-9-0 **80**...................... SteveDrowne 10 90
(J H M Gosden) *t.k.h: sn led: drvn along whn chal ins fnl 2f: asserted ins fnl f: pushed out: readily* **10/1**

3102 **2** 3/4 **Jamboretta (IRE)**[19] 4847 3-9-2 **82**...................... KerrinMcEvoy 7 91
(Sir Michael Stoute) *trckd ldrs: drvn and qcknd to chal ins fnl 2f: stl upsides u.p ins fnl f: no ex fnl 100yds* **15/8**[1]

1023 **3** 1 **Snaafy (USA)**[14] 5012 3-9-4 **84**...................... MartinDwyer 5 91
(B W Hills) *in tch: hdwy to chse ldrs over 2f out: rdn: hung rt u.p and one pce ins fnl f* **7/2**[2]

0004 **4** 1 1/2 **Opera Music**[7] 5208 3-9-4 **84**...................... LPKeniry 3 88
(S Kirk) *in rr: rdn over 2f out: hdwy on outside over 1f out and kpt on ins fnl f: nt rch ldrs* **13/2**[3]

0150 **5** shd **Hunting Tower**[19] 4847 3-9-4 **84**...................... DaneO'Neill 4 88
(R Hannon) *hld up in rr: hdwy fr 2f out: kpt on ins fnl f but nt pce to rch ldrs* **12/1**

0221 **6** 3/4 **Demolition**[14] 5005 3-8-12 **78**...................... SimonWhitworth 8 80
(C A Cyzer) *t.k.h: hld up in rr: rdn and sme hdwy on ins 2f out: no imp on ldrs fnl f* **12/1**

4331 **7** 2 **Rowan River**[27] 4610 3-8-8 **74**...................... NickyMackay 1 72
(M H Tompkins) *in rr: rdn and sme progrss over 2f out: no imp on ldrs whn hmpd 1f out* **9/1**

0-06 **8** shd **Simba Sun (IRE)**[20] 4827 3-8-13 **82**...................... PJMcDonald(3) 9 80
(R M Beckett) *s.i.s: sme hdwy 4f out: nvr rchd ldrs* **10/1**

-260 **9** nk **Josephine Malines**[7] 5210 3-8-11 **77**...................... FergusSweeney 6 74
(C G Cox) *chsd ldrs: rdn 3f out: wknd ins fnl 2f* **25/1**

0040 **10** 1/2 **Frosty Night (IRE)**[22] 4735 3-8-4 **70**...................... GregFairley 2 66
(M Johnston) *chsd ldrs tl wknd ins fnl 2f* **25/1**

2m 8.58s (-1.66) **Going Correction** -0.15s/f (Firm) **10** Ran SP% **121.6**
Speed ratings (Par 103): **100,99,98,97,97 96,95,95,94,94**
CSF £30.38 CT £82.38 TOTE £14.60: £3.80, £1.30, £1.60; EX 39.60 Place 6 £39.84, Place 5 £29.53..
Owner K Abdulla **Bred** Juddmonte Farms Ltd **Trained** Newmarket, Suffolk

FOCUS
A decent three-year-old handicap run at a better pace than the earlier maiden, the time being almost five seconds faster. The winner was another to make all, and the second and third were always handy too. The next three all ran close to their marks.
T/Plt: £28.70 to a £1 stake. Pool: £70,472.40. 1,792.30 winning tickets. T/Qpdt: £13.60 to a £1 stake. Pool: £2,799.00. 152.00 winning tickets. ST

5363 WOLVERHAMPTON (A.W) (L-H)
Friday, September 14

OFFICIAL GOING: Standard
Wind: fresh across

5386 PARADE RESTAURANT CLASSIFIED STKS — 5f 216y(P)
7:00 (7:00) (Class 6) 3-Y-0+ — **£2,388** (£705; £352) **Stalls** Low

Form — RPR

6602 **1** **Gimme Some Lovin (IRE)**[9] 5134 3-8-12 55...................... TedDurcan 13 64
(D W P Arbuthnot) *mid-div: hdwy on outside 2f out: drvn out fnl f: jst hld on* **7/2**[1]

5416 **2** shd **Burford Lass (IRE)**[15] 4978 4-9-0 55...................... JimCrowley 12 64
(D K Ivory) *in tch early on outside: hdwy over 2f out: swtchd rt 1f out: r.o jst failed* **13/2**

0000 **3** 2 1/2 **Suhayl Star (IRE)**[97] 2444 3-8-9 54...................... WilliamBuick(3) 9 56
(S W Hall) *in tch: hdwy on outside 2f out: led over 1f out: hung lft and hdd ins fnl f: no ex* **5/1**[3]

-446 **4** 5 **Bonnet O'Bonnie**[109] 2080 3-8-12 53...................... RoystonFfrench 3 41
(J Mackie) *slowly away: mde sme late hdwy but nvr on terms* **14/1**

0040 **5** 1 **Minnie Mill**[7] 5191 3-8-12 53...................... PaulEddery 8 38
(B P J Baugh) *towards rr: mde mod late hdwy* **40/1**

5054 **6** nk **Time Share (IRE)**[23] 4711 3-8-12 54......................(bt) RichardMullen 4 37
(Miss K B Boutflower) *a.p: led 1/2-way: rdn and hdd over 1f out: wknd* **12/1**

0600 **7** hd **Early Promise (IRE)**[11] 5098 3-8-7 53...................... LukeMorris(5) 6 37
(Mrs A L M King) *mid-div: making sme hdwy whn sltly hmpd 1f out: sn btn* **28/1**

5033 **8** 1/2 **Tenancy (IRE)**[20] 4795 3-8-5 54...................... RobbieEgan(7) 10 35
(A J McCabe) *prom tl wknd appr fnl f* **11/2**

050 **9** nk **Anne Bonney**[65] 3427 3-8-12 54...................... ChrisCatlin 7 34
(E J O'Neill) *slowly away: t.k.h: nvr on terms* **16/1**

0-00 **10** 5 **Dhurwah (IRE)**[18] 4908 4-8-11 42...................... EmmettStack(3) 11 19
(T Keddy) *a bhd* **150/1**

055 **11** nk **Half A Tsar (IRE)**[11] 5090 3-8-6 50 ow1...................... JackDean(7) 5 19
(Mark Gillard) *in tch: rdn over 2f out: wknd fnl f* **18/1**

0000 **12** nk **Sunley Sovereign**[3] 5299 3-8-12 55...................... PaulMulrennan 1 18
(D W Chapman) *sn led: hdd 1/2-way: wknd* **33/1**

0300 **13** 22 **Royal Envoy (IRE)**[65] 3419 4-9-0 55...................... JimmyQuinn 2 —
(D Shaw) *slowly away: sn wl bhd: t.o* **9/2**[2]

1m 14.84s (-0.97) **Going Correction** -0.325s/f (Stan)
WFA 3 from 4yo 2lb **13** Ran SP% **120.8**
Speed ratings (Par 101): **93,92,89,82,81 81,80,80,79,73 72,72,43**
CSF £25.97 TOTE £5.90: £2.20, £2.30, £1.40; EX 37.50.
Owner Christopher Wright **Bred** Stratford Place Stud **Trained** Compton, Berks

FOCUS
A modest handicap in which a wide draw was no disadvantage.
Royal Envoy(IRE) Official explanation: jockey said gelding had no more to give

5387 DTE LEONARD CURTIS H'CAP — 5f 216y(P)
7:30 (7:30) (Class 5) (0-70,70) 3-Y-0+ — **£3,071** (£906; £453) **Stalls** Low

Form — RPR

3321 **1** **Ryedane (IRE)**[16] 4942 5-8-9 **62**......................(b) DuranFentiman(3) 10 75
(T D Easterby) *mde all: drvn out fnl f* **7/1**

1233 **2** 1 1/4 **Ebraam (USA)**[18] 4884 4-9-3 **67**...................... JimmyQuinn 4 77
(D Shaw) *t.k.h: a.p: chsd wnr 1f out: no imp wl ins fnl f* **10/3**[1]

1210 **3** hd **Methaaly (IRE)**[8] 5160 4-8-11 **68**...................... SophieDoyle(7) 7 77
(M Mullineaux) *prom: chsd wnr to 2f out: rdn and one pce fnl f* **9/2**[3]

2603 **4** 2 1/2 **Bucharest**[6] 5234 4-9-0 **64**...................... PaulEddery 2 66
(M Wigham) *prom: rdn and hung lft over 1f out: one pce after* **9/1**

6340 **5** 3/4 **After The Show**[20] 4816 6-9-3 **67**...................... TedDurcan 5 66
(Rae Guest) *towards rr: effrt and hdwy over 2f out: kpt on one pce* **11/1**

6610 **6** nk **Mr Loire**[26] 4634 3-8-10 **69**...................... MarkCoumbe(7) 1 67
(A J Chamberlain) *towards rr: rdn 1/2-way: styd on on ins fr over 1f out: n.d* **50/1**

1062 **7** hd **All You Need (IRE)**[6] 5238 3-8-11 **68**...................... RussellKennemore(5) 3 66
(R Hollinshead) *mid-div: rdn over 2f out: one pce after* **4/1**[2]

0020 **8** 3 **Brandywell Boy (IRE)**[14] 5009 4-8-5 **62**...................... KylieManser(7) 12 51
(D J S Ffrench Davis) *in tch on outside: rdn and wknd 2f out* **16/1**

6001 **9** 3/4 **Hollow Jo**[9] 5130 7-9-4 **68** 6ex...................... MickyFenton 8 55
(J R Jenkins) *in tch: rdn and lost pl 1/2-way: n.d after* **12/1**

0350 **10** nk **Speed Dial Harry (IRE)**[192] 629 5-9-1 **70**......................(b) LukeMorris(5) 13 56
(C R Dore) *a bhd* **20/1**

60 **11** 2 **Siraj**[9] 5130 8-8-9 **62**......................(p) MarcHalford(3) 6 42
(J Ryan) *hld up: bhd whn hung bdly rt turning into st: no ch after* **25/1**

3330 **12** 2 **Overwing (IRE)**[21] 4787 4-9-2 **66**...................... RichardMullen 9 40
(R M H Cowell) *slowly away: bhd whn carried wd into st* **22/1**

-006 **13** 6 **Crow's Nest Lad**[61] 3568 3-9-0 **66**...................... PaulMulrennan 11 22
(T D Easterby) *trckd ldrs tl rdn and weakaned over 2f out* **66/1**

1m 13.57s (-2.24) **Going Correction** -0.325s/f (Stan)
WFA 3 from 4yo+ 2lb **13** Ran SP% **122.1**
Speed ratings (Par 103): **101,99,99,95,94 94,94,90,89,88 86,83,75**
CSF £29.52 CT £125.05 TOTE £8.90: £1.80, £1.60, £2.00; EX 26.00.
Owner Ryedale Partners No 5 **Bred** Tally-Ho Stud **Trained** Great Habton, N Yorks

FOCUS
A run-of-the-mill handicap but those racing up with the pace seemed to have the edge.
All You Need(IRE) Official explanation: jockey said gelding ran flat

5388 JOIN WBX.COM FOR FREE FOOTBALL SHIRT H'CAP — 1m 4f 50y(P)
7:55 (7:55) (Class 6) (0-65,65) 3-Y-O — **£3,071** (£906; £453) **Stalls** Low

Form — RPR

635 **1** **Calzaghe (IRE)**[28] 4570 3-8-13 **63**......................(v) WilliamBuick(3) 4 75
(A M Balding) *t.k.h: in tch: sltly short of room over 1f out: swtchd rt wl over 1f out: edgd rt and rdn to ld wl ins fnl f* **11/10**[1]

0042 **2** 1 1/2 **Bond Casino**[16] 4943 3-8-4 **51**...................... ChrisCatlin 7 61
(G R Oldroyd) *trckd ldrs rdn to ld 2f out: hdd wl ins fnl f: no ex* **16/1**

0040 **3** 5 **Bold Adventure**[36] 4339 3-8-4 **51** oh5...................... PaulEddery 10 53
(W J Musson) *t.k.h: rdn and hdwy 2f out: styd on but edgd lft ins fnl f and nvr nr to chal* **12/1**

0063 **4** 3 **Sir Sandicliffe (IRE)**[16] 4943 3-8-8 **60**...................... LukeMorris(5) 12 57
(W M Brisbourne) *in rr: hdwy on ins over 2f out: hung lft: wknd ins fnl f* **16/1**

0446 **5** 1 **Treasure Isle**[39] 4230 3-8-4 **51** oh1...................... PaulHanagan 8 46
(R A Fahey) *in rr: sme late hdwy but n.d* **12/1**

000 **6** 3/4 **Slip Silver**[21] 4765 3-8-4 **51** oh6......................(p) RichardMullen 6 45
(P J Makin) *prom: sn led: rdn and hdd 2f out: sn wknd* **50/1**

0062 **7** 2 **Kimono My House**[19] 4846 3-8-7 **54**...................... TPQueally 11 45
(J G Given) *in rr: hdwy over 5f out: chal on outside over 2f out: wknd appr fnl f* **7/1**[3]

0002 **8** 1/2 **Centenary (IRE)**[18] 4902 3-8-9 **56**......................(p) GrahamGibbons 1 46
(J J Quinn) *mid-div: wknd wl over 2f out* **14/1**

600 **9** 1 1/2 **Present**[41] 4172 3-8-4 **51** oh5...................... AdrianMcCarthy 2 39
(D Morris) *trckd ldr for 3f: prom tl rdn 3f out: sn wknd* **50/1**

1010 **10** 1 1/4 **Miss Havisham (IRE)**[28] 4582 3-8-6 **53**...................... DO'Donohoe 5 39
(J R Weymes) *a towards rr* **18/1**

2536 **11** 8 **Pugnacious Lady**[20] 4809 3-9-4 **65**...................... TedDurcan 9 38
(J W Hills) *wnt 2nd after 3f: prom tl wknd over 2f out* **11/2**[2]

2m 39.27s (-3.15) **Going Correction** -0.325s/f (Stan) **11** Ran SP% **118.5**
Speed ratings (Par 99): **97,96,92,90,90 89,88,87,86,86 80**
CSF £22.36 CT £148.41 TOTE £2.00: £1.30, £2.30, £5.20; EX 21.80.
Owner Calzaghe Partnership **Bred** Wentworth Racing Pty Ltd **Trained** Kingsclere, Hants

FOCUS
Another ordinary handicap in which the pace was just fair.

5389 JOIN WBX.COM FOR £150 FREE BETS H'CAP — 1m 4f 50y(P)
8:25 (8:25) (Class 6) (0-50,50) 3-Y-0+ — **£2,047** (£604; £302) **Stalls** Low

Form — RPR

250- **1** **Royal Melbourne (IRE)**[167] 6158 7-8-10 **46**...................... SilvestreDeSousa 5 65+
(A D Brown) *in tch: gd hdwy to ld over 2f out: rdn clr: easily* **20/1**

1-43 **2** 8 **Master Nimbus**[6] 4230 7-8-11 **47**...................... GrahamGibbons 3 53
(J J Quinn) *trckd ldrs wnt 2nd over 5f out: clr 2nd but no ch w wnr fr over 1f out* **9/4**[1]

1-05 **3** 1 1/4 **Saameq (IRE)**[205] 514 6-8-11 **50**...................... PatrickMathers(3) 8 54
(D W Thompson) *hld up: hdwy to chse ldrs over 3f out: wknd fnl f* **10/1**

4266 **4** nk **Andorran (GER)**[11] 5087 4-9-0 **50**...................... MickyFenton 12 54
(A Bailey) *in rr: rdn and hdwy on outside over 3f out: kpt on one pce* **14/1**

3002 **5** 2 1/2 **Cragganmore Creek**[17] 4914 4-8-6 **47**......................(b) LukeMorris(5) 4 47
(D Morris) *in rr: rdn and hdwy over 2f out: one pce after* **11/2**[3]

/0-0 **6** *4* **Francescas Boy (IRE)**[38] 4249 4-8-7 46 .... AndrewMullen(3) 11 39
(P D Niven) *in rr: mde mod late hdwy* **100/1**

0062 **7** *5* **War Of The Roses (IRE)**[10] 5120 4-9-0 50 .... RoystonFfrench 9 35
(R Brotherton) *hld up: effrt over 3f out: wknd wl over 1f out* **4/1**[2]

0645 **8** *3/4* **Bowl Of Cherries**[9] 5132 4-8-13 49 .... (v) PaulHanagan 10 33
(I A Wood) *in tch tl rdn and wknd 3f out* **8/1**

520 **9** *9* **Lady Ambitious**[10] 5120 4-9-0 50 .... JimCrowley 1 20
(D K Ivory) *mid-div: rdn over 3f out: sn wknd* **40/1**

-004 **10** *5* **Proud Scholar (USA)**[8] 5179 5-9-0 50 .... (b[1]) TPQueally 2 12
(M A Magnusson) *led tl rdn and hdd over 2f out: wknd appr fnl f* **8/1**

003 **11** *8* **Investment Pearl (IRE)**[21] 4757 4-9-0 50 .... FrancisNorton 7 —
(D R Gandolfo) *trckd ldr to over 5f out: wknd over 3f out* **40/1**

0-60 **12** *9* **Scott**[122] 1752 6-9-0 50 .... ChrisCatlin 6 —
(J Jay) *in tch to 1/2-way: sn bhd* **22/1**

2m 37.15s (-5.27) **Going Correction** -0.325s/f (Stan) **12** Ran SP% **119.1**
Speed ratings (Par 101): **104,98,97,97,95 93,89,89,83,80 74,68**
CSF £63.14 CT £504.79 TOTE £19.20: £6.70, £1.20, £4.70; EX 152.00.
Owner S Pedersen **Bred** Mrs S Camacho **Trained** Pickering, York

FOCUS
A modest handicap and an improved effort from Royal Melbourne on this first run for new connections.
Francescas Boy(IRE) Official explanation: jockey said gelding never travelled
War Of The Roses(IRE) Official explanation: jockey said gelding never travelled

5390 NAME A RACE TO ENHANCE YOUR BRAND MEDIAN AUCTION MAIDEN STKS 1m 141y(P)
8:55 (8:56) (Class 6) 3-5-Y-0 £2,388 (£705; £352) Stalls Low

Form RPR

0402 **1** **New World Order (IRE)**[8] 5178 3-9-3 73 .... (t) RichardMullen 3 79
(K R Burke) *led for 1f: trckd ldr: rdn 3f out: strly rdn to ld again ins fnl f* **3/1**[2]

2-3 **2** *1* **Gemology (USA)**[204] 527 3-9-3 .... TedDurcan 5 77
(Saeed Bin Suroor) *led after 1f: shkn up 2f out: hdd ins fnl f: no ex* **1/2**[1]

0 **3** *8* **Princess Danehill (IRE)**[67] 3387 3-8-7 .... (b[1]) TolleyDean(5) 2 53
(P F I Cole) *t.k.h: trckd ldrs: no imp on first two fr over 1f out* **33/1**

4 *1* **Fair Sailing (IRE)** 3-8-12 .... JamesDoyle 8 51
(J W Hills) *in tch: rdn to chse ldrs over 2f out: wknd appr fnl f* **20/1**

33 **5** *nk* **Yab Adee**[14] 5019 3-8-10 .... KatiaScallan(7) 6 55
(M P Tregoning) *t.k.h: in tch: rdn 2f out: fdd fnl f* **10/1**[3]

-645 **6** *3/4* **Beech Games**[15] 4977 3-9-3 61 .... (b) JimmyQuinn 7 54
(F Jordan) *in tch: rdn 3f out: n.d after* **33/1**

7 *1 1/2* **Oat Cuisine** 3-8-12 .... HayleyTurner 1 45
(M L W Bell) *a towards rr* **33/1**

0 **8** *9* **Wattys The Craic**[15] 4977 3-9-3 .... IanMongan 9 29
(G Prodromou) *in rr and nvr on terms* **100/1**

4000 **9** *nk* **Pont Wood**[8] 5175 3-9-3 55 .... FrancisNorton 12 29
(M Blanshard) *a in rr* **50/1**

10 *1 1/2* **Mark Of The Fen** 3-9-3 .... (e[1]) ChrisCatlin 10 25
(Rae Guest) *slowly away: a bhd* **40/1**

06 **11** *6* **I'm Agenius**[25] 4659 4-9-4 .... JimCrowley 11 6
(C Roberts) *a bhd* **100/1**

0-0 **12** *1 1/2* **Balanchine Moon**[18] 4905 3-8-12 .... PaulFitzsimons 4 3
(M P Tregoning) *trckd ldrs: tl rdn and wknd over 2f out* **40/1**

0 **13** *1 1/4* **Lily La Belle**[18] 4905 3-8-7 .... LukeMorris(5) 13 —
(A W Carroll) *a bhd* **125/1**

1m 48.85s (-2.91) **Going Correction** -0.325s/f (Stan)
WFA 3 from 4yo 6lb **13** Ran SP% **124.0**
Speed ratings (Par 101): **99,98,91,90,89 89,87,79,79,78 72,71,70**
CSF £4.68 TOTE £5.00: £1.40, £1.02, £15.00; EX 7.60.
Owner Mrs Maura Gittins **Bred** Tullamaine Castle Stud **Trained** Middleham Moor, N Yorks

FOCUS
Little strength in depth but the two market leaders pulled a long way clear of the remainder.
Wattys The Craic Official explanation: jockey said colt hung right
I'm Agenius Official explanation: jockey said filly was unsteerable and hanging badly right

5391 WBX.COM £25 FREE BET FOR NEW ACCOUNTS H'CAP 7f 32y(P)
9:20 (9:20) (Class 6) (0-55,55) 3-Y-0+ £2,388 (£705; £352) Stalls High

Form RPR

3453 **1** **The City Kid (IRE)**[32] 4460 4-9-1 53 .... TedDurcan 5 65
(S C Williams) *in rr: hdwy on ins over 2f out: strly rdn to ld ins fnl f* **6/1**[3]

5320 **2** *2* **Bens Georgie (IRE)**[48] 3950 5-9-1 53 .... JimCrowley 2 60
(D K Ivory) *mid-div: rdn and hdwy over 2f out: r.o fnl f to go 2nd cl home* **13/2**

2440 **3** *1/2* **Boreana**[15] 4978 4-9-0 55 .... TravisBlock(3) 3 60
(Jedd O'Keeffe) *broke wl: trckd ldr: chal appr fnl f: no ex and lost 2nd nr fin* **10/1**

3660 **4** *nk* **Marmooq**[34] 4395 4-9-1 53 .... PaulFitzsimons 8 57
(M J Attwater) *sn led: rdn 2f out: hdd ins fnl f and no ex* **20/1**

3340 **5** *3* **Chalentina**[7] 5190 4-9-3 55 .... IanMongan 1 51
(P Howling) *chsd ldrs: rdn 1/2-way: one pce fr over 1f out* **14/1**

1030 **6** *1 1/2* **Ermine Grey**[18] 4878 6-8-12 55 .... (b) LukeMorris(5) 9 47
(A W Carroll) *bhd: sme late hdwy but nvr nr to chal* **18/1**

0602 **7** *hd* **Regal Dream (IRE)**[22] 4731 5-9-1 53 .... GrahamGibbons 4 45
(J W Unett) *in tch: effrt over 1f out: no ex* **7/2**[1]

1504 **8** *1* **Wodhill Schnaps**[15] 4978 6-9-1 53 .... (v) AdrianMcCarthy 6 42
(D Morris) *bhd: effrt on ins over 1f out: sn btn* **15/2**

3042 **9** *shd* **General Feeling (IRE)**[23] 4701 6-8-12 53 .... (t) DuranFentiman(3) 11 42
(S T Mason) *v.s.a: a bhd* **11/2**[2]

2063 **10** *1 1/4* **Attacca**[13] 5037 6-9-1 53 .... DO'Donohoe 12 38
(J R Weymes) *a bhd* **9/1**

0000 **11** *1 1/4* **Tipsy Lad**[9] 5128 5-9-1 53 .... (b) ChrisCatlin 7 35
(D J S Ffrench Davis) *mid-div: rdn over 2f out: sn wknd* **33/1**

000- **12** *3 1/2* **Jonny Ebeneezer**[386] 4730 8-9-2 54 .... (b) TPQueally 10 27
(K McAuliffe) *trckd ldrs: rdn and wknd wl over 1f out* **20/1**

1m 28.14s (-2.26) **Going Correction** -0.325s/f (Stan) **12** Ran SP% **120.5**
Speed ratings (Par 101): **99,96,96,95,92 90,90,89,89,87 86,82**
CSF £44.36 CT £391.69 TOTE £7.20: £2.70, £3.50, £3.40; EX 39.20 Place 6 £26.68, Place 5 £15.21.
Owner Luke McGarrigle **Bred** T B And Mrs T B Russell **Trained** Newmarket, Suffolk

FOCUS
Modest stuff, but a race run at a decent gallop.
General Feeling(IRE) Official explanation: jockey said gelding missed the break
T/Plt: £48.70 to a £1 stake. Pool: £86,167.05. 1,289.50 winning tickets. T/Qpdt: £15.80 to a £1 stake. Pool: £5,273.70. 246.10 winning tickets. JS

5069 CURRAGH (R-H)
Friday, September 14

OFFICIAL GOING: Good to firm

5392a ONE 51 RACE 6f
2:30 (2:30) 3-Y-0+ £13,195 (£3,871; £1,844; £628)

RPR

1 **Abraham Lincoln (IRE)**[173] 780 3-8-13 99 .... KFallon 3 96+
(A P O'Brien, Ire) *hld up towards rr: 5th and hdwy on outer 2f out: sn chal: led 1f out: r.o wl* **5/1**[2]

2 *1 3/4* **Inourthoughts (IRE)**[19] 4861 3-8-9 86 .... DJMoran(3) 6 88
(Francis Ennis, Ire) *trckd ldrs: 4th and hdwy 2f out: 3rd and chal over 1f out: 2nd and kpt on u.p fnl f* **12/1**

3 *shd* **Dimenticata (IRE)**[15] 4985 3-8-12 112 .... CDHayes 1 88
(Kevin Prendergast, Ire) *hld up towards rr: 8th under 2f out: r.o wl fnl f* **5/1**[2]

4 *2* **Murfreesboro**[19] 4864 4-9-5 95 .... JAHeffernan 7 87
(M Halford, Ire) *led: rdn and strly pressed fr 2f out: hdd under 1f out: no ex* **16/1**

5 *hd* **Fleeting Shadow (IRE)**[34] 4412 3-9-3 99 .... (b) PJSmullen 9 86
(D K Weld, Ire) *cl 2nd: rdn to chal fr 2f out: stl in tch whn checked 1f out: kpt on same pce* **7/1**

6 *hd* **Mutamared (USA)**[18] 4886 7-9-5 .... DPMcDonogh 2 86
(K A Ryan) *trckd ldrs on stand's rail: 5th 2f out: in tch whn hmpd and checked 1f out: no ex* **6/1**[3]

7 *1* **Johnstown Lad (IRE)**[14] 5023 3-9-3 87 .... (t) MJKinane 10 83
(Niall Moran, Ire) *trckd ldrs in 3rd: 4th under 2f out: no ex fr over 1f out* **20/1**

8 *nk* **That's Hot (IRE)**[19] 4864 4-9-0 104 .... JamieSpencer 8 77
(G M Lyons, Ire) *Fhld up: 6th and effrt on outer under 2f out: no ex fr over 1f out* **9/4**[1]

9 *hd* **Pelican Waters (IRE)**[48] 3981 3-8-8 81 .... NGMcCullagh 5 72
(Mrs John Harrington, Ire) *hld up in rr: kpt on same pce fr 1 1/2f out* **25/1**

10 *1/2* **Nanny McPhee (IRE)** 3-8-8 .... MCHussey 4 71
(Dermot Murphy, Ire) *chsd ldrs: 5th 1/2-way: wknd fr 2f out* **100/1**

1m 11.4s (-3.10) **Going Correction** -0.525s/f (Hard)
WFA 3 from 4yo+ 2lb **11** Ran SP% **114.1**
Speed ratings: **99,96,96,93,93 93,92,91,91,90**
CSF £60.13 TOTE £3.70: £1.50, £3.00, £1.60; DF 121.30.
Owner Mrs John Magnier **Bred** Quay Bloodstock & Samac Ltd **Trained** Ballydoyle, Co Tipperary

NOTEBOOK
Mutamared(USA), reined back after being prominent early, was coming with a challenge when badly squeezed out over a furlong out. He was unlucky not to run into a place, but he will not find many better opportunities than this. (op 5/1)

5393a SPORTSMAN'S CHALLENGE 6f
3:00 (3:03) 2-Y-0
£39,864 (£12,837; £6,081; £2,702; £1,351; £675)

RPR

1 **Lucies Pride (IRE)**[33] 4434 2-8-12 .... FMBerry 9 78
(M Halford, Ire) *hld up in tch: 4th and hdwy 2f out: 2nd and chal over 1f out: led ins fnl f: kpt on wl u.p: all out* **9/4**[1]

2 *nk* **Our Jo Jo (IRE)**[50] 3890 2-8-12 .... (b[1]) KFallon 3 77
(J C Hayden, Ire) *dwlt: hld up on stands' rail: swtchd 2f out: 6th 1f out: r.o wl: nrest at fin* **5/1**[2]

3 *shd* **Tina's Best (IRE)**[36] 4315 2-8-12 .... JimmyFortune 10 77
(R Hannon) *cl up: rdn to ld 2f out: sn strly pressed: hdd ins fnl f: kpt on u.p* **14/1**

4 *1/2* **Harrison George (IRE)**[16] 4930 2-9-3 .... TonyHamilton 2 80
(R A Fahey) *chsd ldrs: 6th after 1/2-way: rdn 2f out: kpt on u.p ins fnl f* **7/1**

5 *3/4* **Moura Praia (IRE)**[20] 4829 2-8-12 .... JAHeffernan 4 73
(M Halford, Ire) *chsd ldrs: rdn under 2f out: 5th 1f out: kpt on same pce* **10/1**

6 *nk* **Concertmaster**[27] 4605 2-9-3 .... SebSanders 7 77
(R M Beckett) *prom on stands' rail: 2nd 1/2-way: rdn to chal 2f out: no ex fnl f* **13/2**[3]

7 *2 1/2* **Iamagrey (IRE)**[48] 3947 2-8-12 .... (p) PJSmullen 8 59
(J S Moore) *led: hdd 2f out: sn wknd: passed the post eighth: promoted to seventh* **16/1**

8 *1 1/2* **Soca Warrior (IRE)**[14] 5021 2-9-3 .... NGMcCullagh 12 59
(M J Grassick, Ire) *hld up in tch: effrt on outer 2f out: sn no ex: passed the post ninth: promoted to eighth* **25/1**

9 *1 3/4* **Lady Schmuck (IRE)**[117] 1864 2-8-12 .... PShanahan 11 49
(Tracey Collins, Ire) *s.i.s: towards rr on outer: no ex fr 2f out: eased fnl f: passed the post tenth: promoted to ninth* **10/1**

10 *1/2* **Tucum (IRE)**[16] 4952 2-8-12 .... WMLordan 1 47
(Edgar Byrne, Ire) *chsd ldrs on stands' rail: 5th 1/2-way: no ex fr under 2f out: passed the post eleventh: promoted to tenth* **50/1**

11 *nk* **Swift Acclaim (IRE)**[34] 4378 2-8-12 .... KDarley 6 47
(K R Burke) *hld up: no imp fr 2f out: passed the post twelfth: promoted to eleventh* **25/1**

D *2 1/2* **Red Key (IRE)** 2-8-12 .... DPMcDonogh 5 66
(Edward Lynam, Ire) *s.i.s and hld up: swtchd rt 1/2-way: mod 7th 1f out: kpt on: passed the post seventh: disqualified and plcd last* **10/1**

1m 12.9s (-1.60) **Going Correction** -0.525s/f (Hard) **12** Ran SP% **122.7**
Speed ratings: **89,88,88,87,86 86,79,77,75,74 74,83**
CSF £13.05 TOTE £2.60: £1.50, £1.70, £5.80; DF 9.90.
Owner C Glynn **Bred** Newtown Stud **Trained** the Curragh, Co Kildare
■ Stewards' Enquiry : D P McDonogh caution: failed to weigh-in

NOTEBOOK
Tina's Best(IRE), readily held off a mark of 66 on her recent handicap debut at Brighton, showed quite a bit of improvement here and the stiff 6f clearly had a bit to do with that. She kept on well from a prominent position and might be good enough to win a nursery at home.
Harrison George(IRE), readily brushed aside by the smart-looking Dubai Time at Ayr latest, ran on well to finish fourth and shaped as though a return to 7f would suit. He is still a maiden, but should put that right back home.
Concertmaster could have been expected to run a bit better than he did, dropping away from a prominent position inside the final furlong. (op 6/1)
Iamagrey(IRE), sporting first-time cheekpieces, took them along early and ran well to a point, but she remains a maiden and will find easier opportunities. (op 14/1)

Swift Acclaim(IRE) showed little on her debut at Ayr, but she managed to step up on that and could become of interest once qualified for nurseries.

5394a WILLIAM FRY H'CAP (PREMIER HANDICAP) 5f
3:30 (3:32) 3-Y-0+ **£30,790** (£9,033; £4,304; £1,466)

RPR

1 **Invincible Force (IRE)**[6] 5212 3-9-5 94 FMBerry 3 101+
(Paul Green) *hld up in tch: 6th 1 1/2f out: 5th and rdn to chal over 1f out: led wl ins fnl f: all out to hold on nr fin* **7/1**[3]

2 *hd* **Mist And Stone (IRE)**[19] 4861 4-8-9 83 JamieSpencer 2 89+
(G M Lyons, Ire) *outpcd early: in rr after 1/2-way: r.o strly ins fnl f: jst failed* **6/1**[2]

3 *nk* **If Paradise**[54] 3769 6-8-8 82 NGMcCullagh 6 87
(M Halford, Ire) *cl up and disp ld: 2nd and chal over 1f out: ev ch: kpt on u.p* **14/1**

4 *1/2* **Flash McGahon (IRE)**[19] 4864 3-9-8 97 MJKinane 13 100
(John M Oxx, Ire) *prom on outer: 4th 1/2-way: sn rdn to chal: 2nd over 1f out: led briefly under 1f out: no ex cl home* **11/1**

5 *1 1/4* **Girl Power (IRE)**[15] 4982 3-8-4 79 (t) CDHayes 8 78
(Edward Lynam, Ire) *trckd ldrs: 7th under 2f out: kpt on same pce fr over 1f out* **12/1**

6 *hd* **Shinko Dancer (IRE)**[14] 5023 4-8-2 79 DJMoran(3) 12 77
(H Rogers, Ire) *cl up: 2nd and rdn 2f out: sn led: hdd under 1f out: no ex cl home* **16/1**

7 *nk* **Benwilt Breeze (IRE)**[19] 4864 5-9-13 101 (t) WJSupple 1 98
(G M Lyons, Ire) *trckd ldrs: 6th travelling wl whn nt clr run 1f out: sn checked: no ex* **6/1**[2]

8 *hd* **Seven Gold Rings (IRE)**[1] 5372 4-8-5 79 (p) WMLordan 9 75
(Ms Joanna Morgan, Ire) *chsd ldrs on outer: no imp fr 1 1/2f out* **14/1**

9 *nk* **Leitra (IRE)**[12] 5075 4-9-7 95 JAHeffernan 7 90
(M Halford, Ire) *hld up: sme prog after 1/2-way: no ex fr over 1f out* **14/1**

10 *1 1/4* **Contest (IRE)**[90] 2672 3-9-13 102 (p) KFallon 11 93
(David Wachman, Ire) *towards rr: no imp fr 2f out* **11/4**[1]

11 *3/4* **Divert (IRE)**[14] 5023 3-8-11 86 (p) PJSmullen 4 74
(Edward Lynam, Ire) *led and disp on stand's rail: hdd under 2f out: wknd fr over 1f out* **12/1**

57.50 secs (-3.80) **Going Correction** -0.525s/f (Hard)
WFA 3 from 4yo+ 1lb **13** Ran SP% **117.3**
Speed ratings: **109,108,108,107,105 105,104,104,103,101 100**
CSF £48.57 CT £577.79 TOTE £9.60: £2.30, £2.00, £5.80; DF 49.10.
Owner Terry Cummins **Bred** Robert Wilson **Trained** Lydiate, Merseyside

NOTEBOOK
Invincible Force(IRE), winner of the Tattersalls Breeders' Stakes at this meeting a year ago, was held up behind the leaders and quickened through the gap when it appeared a furlong out, running on well to score by a head. It was a good ride by Berry on an individual who has enough ability to win another stakes race on his day. (op 8/1)

5395a PARKNASILLA HOTEL GOFFS FILLIES MILLION 7f
4:10 (4:16) 2-Y-0
£665,540 (£192,567; £91,216; £43,918; £20,945; £6,081)

RPR

1 **Lush Lashes** 2-9-0 KJManning 17 97
(J S Bolger, Ire) *a.p: 2nd bef 1/2-way: led 2f out: rdn and styd on wl fr over 1f out* **10/1**

2 *1 1/2* **Rinterval (IRE)**[27] 4602 2-9-0 JimmyFortune 14 93
(R Hannon) *a.p: 3rd 1/2-way: 2nd and rdn under 2f out: kpt on u.p* **7/1**[3]

3 *1* **Carribean Sunset (IRE)**[24] 4697 2-9-0 PShanahan 5 90
(D K Weld, Ire) *towards rr: hdwy on outer over 2f out: 8th 1 1/2f out: kpt on wl u.p ins fnl f* **25/1**

4 *shd* **Zeu Tin Tin (IRE)**[28] 4564 2-9-0 TQuinn 16 90
(R A Kvisla) *prom: 5th 2f out: kpt on u.p fnl f* **33/1**

5 *3/4* **Campfire Glow (IRE)**[33] 4440 2-9-0 107 PJSmullen 10 88
(D K Weld, Ire) *prom: 4th 1/2-way: 3rd and rdn under 2f out: no ex ins fnl f* **3/1**[1]

6 *3/4* **Amylee (IRE)**[27] 4602 2-9-0 PhilipRobinson 23 86
(C G Cox) *prom on far side: 5th 1/2-way: 4th and rdn 2f out: kpt on same pce u.p* **16/1**

7 *2* **Temecula (IRE)**[26] 4644 2-9-0 JAHeffernan 15 81
(M Halford, Ire) *mid-div: rdn 2f out: 7th 1 1/2f out: kpt on same pce u.p* **50/1**

8 *shd* **Eva's Request (IRE)**[20] 4804 2-9-0 DarryllHolland 22 81
(M R Channon) *hld up: kpt on u.p fr 1 1/2f out* **14/1**

9 *hd* **Allicansayis Wow (USA)**[12] 5073 2-9-0 101 (p) DJMoran 3 80
(J S Bolger, Ire) *towards rr: rdn 2 1/2f out: kpt on same pce fr 1 1/2f out* **16/1**

10 *shd* **Shaker (IRE)**[50] 3880 2-9-0 RobertHavlin 2 80
(M L W Bell) *towards rr: kpt on wout threatening fr 1 1/2f out* **25/1**

11 *hd* **Spinning Lucy (IRE)**[132] 1469 2-9-0 RHills 7 80
(B W Hills) *towards rr: kpt on same pce fr under 2f out* **20/1**

12 *hd* **Precipice**[50] 3890 2-9-0 83 NGMcCullagh 18 79
(Declan Gillespie, Ire) *cl up early: dropped to 7th bef 1/2-way: kpt on same pce fr 1 1/2f out* **25/1**

13 *1/2* **Beatrix Potter (IRE)**[12] 5076 2-9-0 WJSupple 20 78
(Francis Ennis, Ire) *mid-div: prog on far side after 1/2-way: 6th 1 1/2f out: sn no ex* **50/1**

14 *2* **Value Of Time (IRE)**[24] 4697 2-9-0 74 CO'Donoghue 6 73
(K J Condon, Ire) *in rr of mid-div thrght* **50/1**

15 *3/4* **Graceful Star (IRE)**[11] 5103 2-9-0 MJKinane 8 71
(D K Weld, Ire) *a towards rr* **20/1**

16 *nk* **Dramatic Solo**[11] 5100 2-9-0 KDarley 12 70
(K R Burke) *chsd ldrs on outer: rdn 1/2-way: sn no ex* **33/1**

17 *3/4* **Hollow Hill (IRE)**[17] 4926 2-9-0 77 (p) CDHayes 21 68
(Brian Nolan, Ire) *s.i.s: hld up: sme prog on far rail whn hmpd under 1 1/2f out: no ex* **33/1**

18 *3/4* **Casa Catalina (IRE)**[32] 4448 2-9-0 KFallon 19 66
(M Johnston) *led: rdn and hdd 2f out: sn wknd* **12/1**

19 *1/2* **Toberanthawn (IRE)**[12] 5076 2-9-0 DPMcDonogh 9 65
(K J Condon, Ire) *in rr of mid-div: no ex fr 2f out* **40/1**

20 *1* **Kingsdalemillenium (IRE)**[37] 4299 2-9-0 64 MCHussey 4 62
(W M Roper, Ire) *a bhd* **66/1**

21 *3/4* **Ochoa (IRE)**[10] 5110 2-9-0 FMBerry 13 60
(C G Cox) *a bhd* **40/1**

22 *18* **Albabilia (IRE)**[12] 5073 2-9-0 SebSanders 1 13
(C E Brittain) *a bhd: rdn and no imp 1/2-way: eased fr 1 1/2f out* **5/1**[2]

1m 24.3s (-3.20) **Going Correction** -0.525s/f (Hard) **23** Ran SP% **131.5**
Speed ratings: **97,95,94,94,93 92,90,89,89,89 89,89,88,86,85 85,84,83,82,81 80,60**
CSF £65.78 TOTE £11.90: £2.20, £2.30, £4.40, £9.30; DF 109.20.
Owner Mrs J S Bolger **Bred** Mrs A M Jenkins **Trained** Coolcullen, Co Carlow

NOTEBOOK
Lush Lashes, a newcomer by Derby hero Galileo, clearly knew her job and she was soon well positioned under Manning. Always travelling strongly, she went to the front two out and always looked to be doing enough, really running on willingly. Her trainer rates her on a par with Finsceal Beo, but whether she herself goes on to reach those heights is open to question. The Group 3 C L Weld Park Stakes is next, as she holds no big-race entries, and quotes of 16/1 for next season's 1000 Guineas seem no more than fair.
Rinterval(IRE), fair winner of a standard Newbury maiden, stepped up significantly on that effort with a staying-on effort in second. The step up to 7f clearly suited and connections believe she could develop into a 1000 Guineas filly next season. (op 8/1)
Carribean Sunset(IRE), the Weld second-string, finished second in a 1m heavy-ground maiden at Tralee last time and she stepped up markedly on that with a keeping-on effort back in third. Winning a maiden should prove a formality.
Zeu Tin Tin(IRE), placed in Newmarket and Doncaster maidens on her two previous starts, ran a cracker back in fourth and gave the form of Sense Of Joy, whom she finished well behind on debut, a nice form boost in the process. She should find a race before long.
Campfire Glow(IRE), narrow winner of the Group 2 Debutante Stakes over course and distance last time, was always close up and had every chance before failing to raise her effort from over a furlong out. This was her first run on ground without some degree of ease, and her jockey reported that she did not enjoy the ground. She can be given another chance. (op 5/2 tchd 7/2)
Amylee(IRE), runner-up to Rinterval in that Newbury maiden, showed up well for a long way and seemed to run above herself back in sixth. She is another who should find a maiden before long.
Eva's Request(IRE), third to Sense Of Joy in the Prestige Stakes, made some good late headway and should be capable of finding a Listed contest.
Shaker(IRE) failed to cope with the rise in grade when well down the field in a Listed contest at Sandown last time, but she bounced back from that on this return from a break and now looks ready for 1m. (op 33/1)
Spinning Lucy(IRE), touted by many as a Queen Mary filly following a slightly unlucky debut at Newmarket, was unable to build on that effort when disappointing next time, a common trait with progeny of Spinning World, but had been off since and could hardly have faced a stiffer test on this return. She was not disgraced and will find easier opportunities.
Casa Catalina(IRE), ready winner of a Thirsk maiden, was responsible for the early gallop, but she stopped very quickly once headed and seemed to find this all too competitive.
Ochoa(IRE), runner-up in a 6f Goodwood maiden last time, was always going to find this a good deal harder and she never got involved.
Albabilia(IRE) looked the main danger to the favourite, having won a Newmarket Group 3 before finishing fourth in the Moyglare, but she was behind all the way and reported to be "clinically abnormal" following examination by the Turf Club veterinary officer. Official explanation: vet said filly was clinically abnormal post-race (op 5/1 tchd 11/2)

5396a IRISH NATIONAL STUD BLANDFORD STKS (GROUP 2) (F&M) 1m 2f
4:45 (4:47) 3-Y-0+ **£54,898** (£16,047; £7,601; £2,533)

RPR

1 **Four Sins (GER)**[61] 3576 3-8-12 106 MJKinane 8 110
(John M Oxx, Ire) *led early: settled 2nd: led again over 2f out: strly pressed fnl f: kpt on wl u.p: jst hld on* **9/4**[1]

2 *shd* **Queen's Best**[20] 4826 4-9-5 JamieSpencer 6 110
(Sir Michael Stoute) *hld up towards rr: prog early st: 3rd under 2f out: 2nd and chal fnl f: ev ch: kpt on wl: jst failed* **9/4**[1]

3 *2* **Dalvina**[23] 4723 3-8-12 JimmyFortune 10 106
(E A L Dunlop) *trckd ldrs on inner: 4th 1/2-way: 5th into st: prog into 2nd under 2f out: 3rd and no ex fnl f* **7/1**[3]

4 *hd* **Uimhir A Haon (IRE)**[26] 4649 3-8-12 100 JAHeffernan 11 106
(A P O'Brien, Ire) *mid-div: 7th 1/2-way: 6th over 1f out: kpt on u.p* **20/1**

5 *2* **Bahia Breeze**[26] 4652 5-9-5 106 PJSmullen 2 102
(Rae Guest) *prom: 3rd 1/2-way: 2nd and rdn 2f out: 4th and no ex 1f out* **6/1**[2]

6 *3/4* **Darrfonah (IRE)**[23] 4723 3-8-12 (t) SebSanders 5 100
(C E Brittain) *hld up towards rr: kpt on wout threatening fr 2f out* **20/1**

7 *3* **Sina Cova (IRE)**[12] 5071 5-9-5 105 KJManning 9 94
(Peter Casey, Ire) *chsd ldrs: 5th 1/2-way: 4th and rdn ent st: sn no ex* **20/1**

8 *1/2* **Mango Mischief (IRE)**[26] 4652 6-9-5 KDarley 7 93
(M R Channon) *sn led: hdd 2f out: wkng whn sltly hmpd 1f out* **33/1**

9 *hd* **Navajo Moon (IRE)**[12] 5071 3-8-12 102 KFallon 3 93
(David Wachman, Ire) *hld up in tch: sme prog after 1/2-way: 6th and rdn ent st: sn no ex* **8/1**

10 *8* **Wait Watcher (IRE)**[146] 1146 3-8-12 DPMcDonogh 1 77
(P A Blockley) *hld up: wknd fr 4f out: trailing st* **25/1**

2m 9.30s **Going Correction** +0.30s/f (Good)
WFA 3 from 4yo+ 7lb **11** Ran SP% **120.5**
Speed ratings: **112,111,110,110,108 107,105,105,105,98**
CSF £6.49 TOTE £3.00: £1.70, £1.30, £2.00; DF 6.40.
Owner H H Aga Khan **Bred** Graf U Grafin V Stauffenberg **Trained** Currabeg, Co Kildare

NOTEBOOK
Four Sins(GER), fourth in the Oaks before finishing down the field in heavy ground in the Irish version, raced prominently from the outset and knuckled down bravely under a vintage Kinane ride to narrowly snatch the verdict on the line. She had been "thriving" according to her trainer, who has no firm plans for the daughter of Sinndar. (op 9/4)
Queen's Best, hailing from a yard that has won this race for the last two years, made a bold bid to complete her hat-trick. She has progressed very nicely since winning an Ascot handicap off 79 almost 12 months ago and was just unfortunate to come up against another decent filly. This ground may have been just too lively for her and she can hopefully be winning again before long. (op 5/2)
Dalvina, who had her limitations ruthlessly exposed against some of the best fillies around earlier in the season, found the going tough after getting into a challenging position passing the two-furlong pole. She had finished behind Four Sins after meeting with interference at Epsom, but overall she has failed to confirm the promise shown in winning the Pretty Polly Stakes over this trip at Newmarket in May.
Uimhir A Haon(IRE) was staying on well under pressure at the death and may well appreciate a step back up to 1m4f on this evidence.
Bahia Breeze was outclassed when asked for her effort. She looked another who might appreciate some ease after her gallant runner-up effort in a similar contest on soft at Deauville last month. (op 11/2)
Darrfonah(IRE) has seemingly failed to last home over 1m4f, but she scored in a 1m2f Listed contest at Newbury in between and it was no surprise to see her run better back at this distance.
Mango Mischief(IRE) has been running above herself in Group races and having cut out much of the early running, she soon dropped back through the field. (op 33/1 tchd 40/1)

Wait Watcher(IRE), disqualified from first place in last season's fillies' Goffs Million, showed little in the Fred Darling on her seasonal reappearance and again did little on this return from another lengthy break.

5397a PARKNASILLA HOTEL GOFFS (C & G) MILLION 7f

5:30 (5:31) 2-Y-O

£665,540 (£192,567; £91,216; £43,918; £20,945; £6,081)

RPR

1 **Luck Money (IRE)**[87] 2732 2-9-0 .... TQuinn 4 106
(P F I Cole) *mde all: edgd clr 2f out: kpt on wl u.p ins fnl f* **9/2**[1]

2 2 1/2 **Hitchens (IRE)**[24] 4695 2-9-0 .... KFallon 1 100
(G L Moore) *hld up towards rr: hdwy on outer 2f out: 2nd and chal 1f out: no imp: kpt on u.p* **9/1**

3 1 1/4 **Major Willy**[27] 4593 2-9-0 .... JAHeffernan 19 96
(W Jarvis) *mid-div on far rail: prog after 1/2-way: 2nd and rdn 2f out: 3rd and no imp fnl f: kpt on* **33/1**

4 2 **Lisvale (IRE)**[36] 4347 2-9-0 106 .... WMLordan 17 91+
(David Wachman, Ire) *chsd ldrs on far side: rdn 2f out: 7th 1 1/2f out: kpt on ins fnl f* **7/1**[2]

5 shd **Mr Medici (IRE)**[19] 4863 2-9-0 .... DPMcDonogh 2 91
(Kevin Prendergast, Ire) *chsd ldrs: 6th after 1/2-way: mod 4th over 1f out: kpt on same pce* **25/1**

6 1/2 **Fireside** 2-9-0 .... JamieSpencer 5 92+
(P W Chapple-Hyam) *slowly away: hld up towards rr: 9th and hdwy on inner 1 1/2f out: sn short of room and swtchd: kpt on ins fnl f* **7/1**[2]

7 nk **Feared In Flight (IRE)**[63] 3504 2-9-0 .... MJKinane 15 89
(B W Hills) *hld up: kpt on u.p fr under 2f out* **10/1**

8 shd **Redolent (IRE)**[30] 4508 2-9-0 .... JimmyFortune 7 88
(R Hannon) *prom: 3rd 1/2-way: rdn over 2f out: kpt on same pce* **14/1**

9 1 1/2 **Pittori (IRE)**[23] 4727 2-9-0 89 ....(tp) KJManning 6 85
(J S Bolger, Ire) *chsd ldrs: 4th u.p after 1/2-way: no ex fr under 2f out* **10/1**

10 3/4 **Calmdownmate (IRE)**[24] 4694 2-9-0 .... KDarley 13 83
(K R Burke) *mid-div: kpt on same pce fr under 2f out* **20/1**

11 1 1/4 **Better Built**[12] 5076 2-9-0 .... FMBerry 14 79
(Declan Gillespie, Ire) *dwlt: bhd and drvn along 1/2-way: kpt on same pce* **66/1**

12 1 1/2 **Chun Tosaigh (USA)**[26] 4645 2-9-0 ....(tp) DJMoran 9 75
(J S Bolger, Ire) *nvr bttr than mid-div* **50/1**

13 1 **Doon Haymer (IRE)**[30] 4495 2-9-0 .... TomEaves 12 73
(I Semple) *a towards rr* **50/1**

14 1/2 **Hawaana (IRE)**[33] 4417 2-9-0 .... RHills 3 72
(B W Hills) *chsd ldrs on outer: 7th and rdn over 2f out: sn short of room and no ex* **8/1**[3]

15 1 3/4 **Bold Choice (IRE)**[14] 5011 2-9-0 .... PhilipRobinson 10 67
(M A Jarvis) *chsd ldrs to 1/2-way: sn no ex* **14/1**

16 1 3/4 **Flag Of Honour (IRE)**[15] 4986 2-9-0 .... NGMcCullagh 16 62
(D T Hughes, Ire) *nvr a factor* **100/1**

17 1 3/4 **Unquenchable Fire (IRE)**[37] 4298 2-9-0 .... PShanahan 8 58
(D K Weld, Ire) *a towards rr* **16/1**

18 1 1/4 **Artic Cry (USA)**[117] 1864 2-9-0 87 ....(b[1]) PJSmullen 18 55
(D K Weld, Ire) *prom: 2nd 1/2-way: rdn and wknd fr over 2f out: eased fnl f* **12/1**

19 1/2 **Accused (IRE)**[20] 4818 2-9-0 .... SebSanders 11 53
(J Noseda) *a bhd* **12/1**

1m 23.3s (-4.20) **Going Correction** -0.525s/f (Hard) **19** Ran SP% **135.0**
Speed ratings: **103,100,98,96,96 95,95,95,93,92 91,89,88,87,85 83,81,80,79**
CSF £45.67 TOTE £5.30: £2.40, £3.00, £5.00, £2.10; DF 69.60.

Owner Mrs Stephanie Smith **Bred** Mrs Chris Harrington **Trained** Whatcombe, Oxon

NOTEBOOK

Luck Money(IRE) had somewhat spoiled his chance in the Coventry Stakes by hanging to his left, but his good third in that race set the form standard and, if anything, he bettered that display with a commanding performance. Bounced out in front, he gradually wound it up from beyond halfway, and when the eventual runner-up came with a strong challenge inside the final furlong, he found plenty and drew clear to win comfortably. He really seemed to relish the step up in trip and there is no reason why he will not stay 1m in time. (op 4/1)

Hitchens(IRE) had to improve to get into the shake-up and duly did. Held up early, he came sweeping through on the stands' side and briefly looked dangerous until the winner went away from him again. He also had a tendency to lug to his right inside the final furlong. His pedigree suggests that he might be more effective over sprint trips, but this was a career-best effort and there is no reason to think that he did not stay, he was just beaten by a superior horse.

Major Willy made it a clean sweep for the visitors. He was another one who would have needed to find improvement to be involved at the business end and he ran on well to claim third, but proved no match for the classy winner.

Fireside, a newcomer by Dr Fong, ran a very eye-catching race on this racecourse debut. After missing the break, he found himself well behind early, and when starting to make headway he met trouble in running on more than one occasion. It was an excellent effort in the circumstances, and winning a maiden should be a mere formality before he goes on to better things. (op 7/1 tchd 8/1)

Feared In Flight(IRE) has had his limitations exposed in Pattern company the last twice and he could only keep on at the one pace here, having been held up early. (op 10/1 tchd 12/1)

Redolent(IRE), ready winner of a 7f Sandown maiden, was prominent from the outset, but he could not quicken on with the principals. He will find easier opportunities.

Calmdownmate(IRE), outclassed behind Fast Company in the Acomb latest, again found this a bit too competitive and the way he was keeping on suggests the step up to 1m may suit.

Doon Haymer(IRE), back down to 7f having been slammed by McCartney at Hamilton last time, found this all a bit too hot and he needs dropping back into maiden company.

Hawaana(IRE), ready winner of 7f Leicester maiden, had his chance if good enough, but he faded out of it late on and was already beaten when squeezed for room late on. (op 10/1)

Bold Choice(IRE), narrowly denied in a 7f Sandown maiden latest, found this a bit too competitive and will find easier opportunities back in maidens. (op 12/1)

Accused(IRE), a promising third over 6f on debut at Redcar, looked one of the more interesting ones, but he never threatened to get into it. (op 14/1)

5398 - (Foreign Racing) - See Raceform Interactive

5029 CHESTER (L-H)

Saturday, September 15

OFFICIAL GOING: Good to firm (9.0)

Wind: Light, accross Weather: Fine and sunny

5399 HEATHCOTES E B F MAIDEN STKS 7f 2y

1:50 (1:51) (Class 4) 2-Y-O **£5,505** (£1,637; £818; £408) **Stalls** Low

Form RPR

222 1 **Bellomi (IRE)**[14] 5033 2-9-3 83 .... RichardMullen 1 84+
(M R Channon) *broke wl: trckd ldrs: chal 3 wd 2f out: sn led: qcknd clr over 1f out: eased down towards fin* **8/13**[1]

62 2 3 1/2 **Hamalka (IRE)**[12] 5091 2-8-12 0 .... KDarley 4 68
(B W Hills) *led for 1f: remained w ldr: regained ld 2f out: sn hdd: no ch w wnr fnl f* **4/1**[2]

3 2 **Try Me (UAE)** 2-8-12 0 .... SebSanders 6 63
(C E Brittain) *rdn along most of way and green: in tch: chsd ldng duo over 1f out: nvr able to chal* **16/1**

0 4 3/4 **Sergeant Sharpe**[38] 4293 2-9-3 0 .... JimmyQuinn 2 66
(M H Tompkins) *s.s: bhd: rdn on outside over 1f out: nvr on terms* **50/1**

6 5 nk **Afton View (IRE)**[23] 4733 2-9-3 0 .... FrancisNorton 3 65
(D J Murphy) *fractious bef r: s.i.s: pushed along early: in rr: effrt on ins 2f out: no imp* **16/1**

62 6 12 **Art Currency (USA)**[25] 4683 2-9-3 0 .... PatCosgrave 5 34
(M J Wallace) *led after 1f: pushed along and hdd 2f out: sn wknd: eased whn wl btn ins fnl f* **6/1**[3]

1m 27.47s (-1.00) **Going Correction** -0.15s/f (Firm) **6** Ran SP% **109.9**
Speed ratings (Par 97): **99,95,92,91,91 77**
CSF £3.18 TOTE £1.60: £1.20, £2.20; EX 2.90.
Owner Sheikh Ahmed Al Maktoum **Bred** Barronstown Stud **Trained** West Ilsley, Berks

FOCUS

An ordinary maiden at the mercy of the useful Bellomi, who had previous course experience to call upon. The form looks solid backed up by the time.

NOTEBOOK

Bellomi(IRE), who has an official rating of 83, set a decent standard. He was always well positioned tracking the pace and had no trouble picking up and going clear once in line for home. Nurseries will be more competitive but he has the potential to improve. (op 4-5)

Hamalka(IRE), representing a stable that always has to be respected at this track, ran her best race to date but the winner was just too good for her. She is now eligible for nurseries and things should be easier in that sphere. (op 11-4)

Try Me(UAE), whose dam won over a mile in a light career at three, did not have a clue for most of the race but kept on to finish an honourable third. Given her inexperience this was a fair effort, and there should be plenty of improvement to come. (tchd 14-1)

Sergeant Sharpe, who lost ground with a slow start, made some late ground round the outside and was not disgraced. He looks more of a handicap type after one more run. (op 66-1)

Afton View(IRE), a half-brother to Apache Red, who won over 7f and 1m, and Bed Fellow, a dual 1m winner at two, got worked up before the start and never really got competitive after being slowly away. (op 14-1)

Art Currency(USA) showed early speed but dropped away tamely after being headed two furlongs out. This was a step backwards but he is at least now eligible for a mark, and he could do better in handicap company. (op 15-2 tchd 8-1 and 11-2)

5400 CHESHIRE LIFE NURSERY 7f 2y

2:20 (2:20) (Class 3) (0-95,87) 2-Y-O **£9,463** (£2,832; £1,416; £708; £352) **Stalls** Low

Form RPR

041 1 **City Of The Kings (IRE)**[17] 4947 2-8-10 76 .... FrancisNorton 5 82
(R Hannon) *sn chsd ldr: lost pl and nt clr run over 2f out: rallied over 1f out: r.o to ld wl ins fnl f* **4/1**[2]

3612 2 3/4 **Alan Devonshire**[15] 4991 2-9-7 87 .... JimmyQuinn 3 91
(M H Tompkins) *chsd ldrs: led over 2f out: rdn over 1f out: hdd wl ins fnl f: nt qckn towards fin* **11/8**[1]

2022 3 nk **Sourire**[10] 5135 2-9-4 84 .... SebSanders 2 87
(Sir Mark Prescott) *led early: sn dropped bk to chse ldrs: n.m.r and hmpd over 2f out: rdn over 1f out: r.o ins fnl f* **5/1**[3]

0015 4 1 3/4 **Harry Gee**[8] 5207 2-8-13 79 ....(b[1]) RichardMullen 6 78
(W R Muir) *racd keenly early: bhd: rdn 4f out: hdwy over 1f out: kpt on: nt pce to trble ldrs* **12/1**

3150 5 3 **Tadalavil**[3] 5324 2-9-5 85 .... PatCosgrave 1 76
(M R Channon) *s.i.s: towards rr: hdwy 3f out: chsd ldr over 2f out tl over 1f out: wknd ins fnl f* **17/2**

1030 6 34 **Legendary Guest**[14] 5053 2-8-12 78 .... KerrinMcEvoy 4 —
(M R Channon) *sn pushed along: hung rt thrght: a bhd: lost tch and eased over 1f out: t.o* **12/1**

1004 P **Vhujon (IRE)**[7] 5216 2-9-6 86 .... KDarley 7 —
(P D Evans) *racd freely: sn led and clr: hung rt thrght: hdd over 2f out: wknd qckly: eased over 1f out: t.o whn p.u ins fnl f: sddle slipped* **10/1**

1m 26.92s (-1.55) **Going Correction** -0.15s/f (Firm) **7** Ran SP% **113.8**
Speed ratings (Par 99): **102,101,100,98,95 56,—**
CSF £9.82 TOTE £5.40: £2.30, £1.40; EX 9.80.
Owner T Hyde **Bred** Tom McDonald **Trained** East Everleigh, Wilts

FOCUS

A fairly competitive nursery run at a decent pace and sound enough form that should work out with the first three close to their marks.

NOTEBOOK

City Of The Kings(IRE) was far from overburdened on his handicap debut, but the drop back to 7f was a concern as he had, if anything, looked to be crying out for further than a mile when winning at Kempton. There was a decent gallop though, and that suited him well, allowing him to use his stamina to rally in the latter stages. He will be very much suited by a return to a mile and, as the Handicapper cannot put him up too much for this, will have an excellent chance of notching the hat-trick. (op 11-2)

Alan Devonshire, who was a beaten favourite over this course and distance last time out, again found one too good. He did not do a lot wrong as he looked the winner kicking off the bend into the straight, but he simply ran out of gas close home. He may remain vulnerable to slightly better-handicapped rivals in this sphere. (op 6-5)

Sourire, just touched off in a decent little race on the Polytrack at Lingfield last time, would no doubt have liked to have been given a free hand in front, but Darley was keen to lead on Vhujon and she was denied that role. She did run on late, though, suggesting that a mile will be within her compass. (op 9-2 tchd 4-1)

Harry Gee was a bit too keen in the first-time blinkers even though the pace was good, and although he ran on a bit late in the day, he was never really a threat. (op 20-1 tchd 11-1)

Tadalavil, down the field in a sales race last time out, was stepping up in distance and he did not appear to get home. (op 8-1 tchd 10-1)

Legendary Guest did not handle the track at all and it will be a big surprise if he ever returns to the Roodeye. Official explanation: jockey said colt hung right-handed throughout; vet said colt finished lame on its off-fore leg (tchd 11-1)

Vhujon(IRE), who was keen to lead, went a decent gallop in front but his chance went when his saddle slipped. Official explanation: jockey said colt had a breathing problem (op 11-1)

5401 CO-OPERATIVE FINANCIAL SERVICES CHARITY OF THE YEAR H'CAP 5f 16y

2:50 (2:50) (Class 4) (0-85,85) 3-Y-0+ **£5,829** (£1,734; £866; £432) **Stalls** Low

Form RPR

0004 **1** **Circuit Dancer (IRE)**[9] 5155 7-8-5 **71** oh1............... SilvestreDeSousa 2 80
(D Nicholls) *chsd ldrs: wnt 2nd 2f out: rdn over 1f out: r.o to ld wl ins fnl f* **3/1**[2]

0210 **2** ¾ **Coconut Moon**[7] 5212 5-9-0 **80**............... KDarley 1 86
(E J Alston) *broke wl: led: rdn over 1f out: hdd wl ins fnl f* **2/1**[1]

0560 **3** *nk* **Merlin's Dancer**[25] 4696 7-9-5 **85**............... SebSanders 6 90
(S Dow) *in tch: effrt to chse ldng pair over 1f out: edgd rt ins fnl f: r.o towards fin* **13/2**

2105 **4** 2½ **Peter Island (FR)**[14] 5029 4-8-12 **78**...............(b) JimCrowley 3 74
(J Gallagher) *disp 2nd to 2f out: sn rdn: outpcd over 1f out* **4/1**[3]

4121 **5** ½ **Melalchrist**[31] 4489 5-9-5 **85**...............(b) PatCosgrave 8 79
(K A Ryan) *disp 2nd to 2f out: sn rdn: outpcd over 1f out* **11/2**

6214 **6** 2 **Comptonspirit**[10] 5139 3-7-11 **71** oh4...............(p) SoniaEaton[(7)] 9 58
(B P J Baugh) *rdn over 1f out: a in last pl* **25/1**

60.47 secs (-1.58) **Going Correction** -0.15s/f (Firm)
WFA 3 from 4yo+ 1lb **6** Ran SP% **110.9**
Speed ratings (Par 105): **106,104,104,100,99 96**
CSF £9.19 CT £32.07 TOTE £3.60: £1.70, £1.60; EX 6.00.
Owner David Fish **Bred** Michael Staunton **Trained** Sessay, N Yorks

FOCUS
A fairly tight little handicap run at a good pace and the form is rated through the runner-up.

5402 CARLSBERG STAND CUP (LISTED RACE) 1m 4f 66y

3:25 (3:25) (Class 1) 3-Y-0+ **£15,410** (£5,826; £2,912; £1,456) **Stalls** Low

Form RPR

5246 **1** **Hattan (IRE)**[25] 4693 5-9-1 110............... SebSanders 1 111+
(C E Brittain) *racd keenly: hld up: hdwy over 2f out: rdn and hung lft fr over 1f out: r.o to ld wl ins fnl f: on top towards fin* **11/4**[1]

3560 **2** 1 **Foxhaven**[44] 4091 5-9-1 108...............(v[1]) JimCrowley 3 109
(P R Chamings) *trckd ldrs: led over 2f out: rdn over 1f out: hdd wl ins fnl f: hld fnl strides* **11/2**

6242 **3** 2 **Lundy's Lane (IRE)**[14] 5030 7-9-1 97............... FrancisNorton 6 106
(A M Balding) *racd keenly: hld up: rdn 2f out: hdwy to chse ldng pair 1f out: kpt on but nt pce to chal* **11/2**

113- **4** ½ **Linas Selection**[410] 4024 4-9-1 110............... KDarley 2 105
(M Johnston) *led: rdn and hdd over 2f out: kpt on same pce fnl f* **10/3**[3]

6210 **5** 3½ **Book Of Music (IRE)**[191] 648 4-9-1 112............... KerrinMcEvoy 7 100
(Saeed Bin Suroor) *hld up in rr: hdwy 4f out: rdn and wknd over 1f out* **3/1**[2]

4-06 **6** 20 **Cresta Gold**[112] 2036 4-8-10 93............... RichardMullen 5 63
(A Bailey) *prom: rdn 3f out: wknd over 2f out* **25/1**

2m 37.11s (-3.54) **Going Correction** -0.15s/f (Firm)
WFA 3 from 4yo+ 9lb **6** Ran SP% **109.4**
Speed ratings (Par 111): **105,104,103,102,100 87**
CSF £16.97 TOTE £3.60: £2.00, £2.80; EX 18.40.
Owner Saeed Manana **Bred** Darley **Trained** Newmarket, Suffolk

FOCUS
A race made up mainly of horses who find winning opportunities thin on the ground. The form is ordinary for the grade with the runner-up setting the level.

NOTEBOOK
Hattan(IRE), who won the Chester Vase over this course and distance earlier in his career and was far from disgraced when not beaten far in the Group 3 Huxley Stakes over a less favourable shorter trip here at the May meeting this year, clearly likes it here and had conditions to suit. He wore down Foxhaven in the closing stages to record a deserved second career win at Pattern level. (op 10-3)
Foxhaven, visored for the first time, was well positioned behind the leader for most of the race and, when he kicked for home it looked a race-winning move, but he was run out of it close home. He has not scored since winning a slightly weaker renewal of this race 12 months ago, and is very much a twilight horse. (tchd 9-2 and 6-1)
Lundy's Lane(IRE) had quite a bit to find strictly on the ratings with most of his rivals, but he ran well behind Bauer here last time and course form has always counted for plenty at this track. This was a good effort but he is another likely to find winning opportunities hard to come by. (op 7-1)
Linas Selection, absent for over a year since finishing third to Sixties Icon in last year's Gordon Stakes, was allowed the run of the race out in front and, had he already had a race, it would have been easy to see him make every yard. As it was, lack of a recent outing seemed to find him out. He should come on for this and will be interesting in similar company next time. (op 3-1 tchd 11-4 and 7-2)
Book Of Music(IRE), who had not been seen out since running at the Dubai Carnival in the spring, was held up in last place and made a challenging move turning into the straight. It did not come to anything though, and he dropped out disappointingly. (op 5-2)
Cresta Gold, running for the first time since May, finished well beaten and is another who is very hard to place off her current mark. (tchd 16-1)

5403 BETDAQ THE BETTING EXCHANGE HENRY GEE FILLIES' STKS (LISTED RACE) 6f 18y

4:00 (4:00) (Class 1) 3-Y-0+
£14,762 (£5,595; £2,800; £1,396; £699; £351) **Stalls** Low

Form RPR

3045 **1** **Blue Echo**[24] 4726 3-8-12 92............... KDarley 2 91
(M A Jarvis) *mde all: rdn over 1f out: r.o wl and in command fnl f* **3/1**[1]

6122 **2** 3 **Diamond Diva**[27] 4639 3-8-12 94............... JamesDoyle 8 82
(J W Hills) *missed break: hdwy 4f out: wnt 2nd 2f out: nt pce of wnr fnl f* **9/2**[3]

0650 **3** *nk* **Kondakova (IRE)**[10] 5134 3-8-12 70...............(v) HayleyTurner 3 82
(M L W Bell) *racd keenly: hld up: hdwy over 1f out: sn hung lft: styd on ins fnl f* **50/1**

0103 **4** ½ **Choysia**[7] 5232 4-9-0 74............... TonyHamilton 6 80
(D W Barker) *prom: rdn over 2f out: sn hung rt: kpt on same pce fr over 1f out* **25/1**

2001 **5** 1¾ **Ripples Maid**[27] 4639 4-9-3 100............... SebSanders 10 78
(J A Geake) *stdd s: hld up: hdwy 3f out: rdn over 1f out: no ex ins fnl f* **7/2**[2]

1206 **6** 2 **Katie Boo (IRE)**[15] 4999 5-9-0 71............... FrancisNorton 5 69
(A Berry) *prom: lost pl over 4f out: n.m.r and hmpd whn in midfield over 1f out: n.d after* **10/1**

0000 **7** *nk* **Folga**[21] 4798 5-9-0 90............... JimmyQuinn 4 68
(J G Given) *in rr: rdn over 1f out: nvr on terms* **16/1**

1P10 **8** ½ **Song Of Passion (IRE)**[27] 4639 4-9-0 100...............(b[1]) RichardMullen 7 66
(R Hannon) *pushed along s: hdwy to chse wnr over 4f out: rdn over 2f out: sn lost 2nd: wknd over 1f out* **9/2**[3]

3604 **9** 1 **Pusey Street Lady**[27] 4639 3-8-12 83............... JimCrowley 1 63
(J Gallagher) *chsd ldrs: pushed along over 3f out: sn lost pl: n.d after* **8/1**

1m 13.64s (-2.01) **Going Correction** -0.15s/f (Firm)
WFA 3 from 4yo+ 2lb **9** Ran SP% **115.5**
Speed ratings (Par 108): **107,103,102,101,99 96,96,95,94**
CSF £16.73 TOTE £4.10: £1.50, £1.60, £8.60; EX 21.10.
Owner Mrs Mary Taylor **Bred** Mrs M F Taylor And James F Taylor **Trained** Newmarket, Suffolk

FOCUS
Not strong form for the grade rated through the third and fourth and the latter limits things.

NOTEBOOK
Blue Echo, who is known for her early speed, got out of the traps quickly and was soon in front. Dominating throughout, she kicked again entering the straight and finished up good value for her three-length winning margin. This would not be the strongest Listed race ever run but she is clearly in good form, and a trip to Ayr for the Gold Cup, where she will have a 5lb penalty, could now be on the cards. (op 7-2)
Diamond Diva, second behind Ripples Maid in similar company at Pontefract last time, has developed into a consistent performer and she did well to overcome a wide draw and briefly pose the only possible threat to the winner. (op 11-2 tchd 6-1)
Kondakova(IRE) only has a rating of 70 so her performance does not do a lot for the value of the form, but she is without doubt at her best coming from off the pace in a strongly-run race, and that is what she got here. Her connections will no doubt be thrilled to have got some black type with her.
Choysia, another whose mark in the 70s puts a limit on the value of the form, finished well behind Ripples Maid at Pontefract two starts back, but this quicker ground was much more in her favour. (op 33-1)
Ripples Maid was forced to race wide throughout from her wide draw and that cost her dearly around here. (op 10-3 tchd 4-1)
Katie Boo(IRE) looked beaten when hampered inside the final two furlongs. (op 16-1 tchd 8-1)
Song Of Passion(IRE), blinkered for the first time, was rousted along to go prominent, but she had her work cut out to do that from her wide stall and she ended up racing wide and using up too much energy in the early stages. Easier ground suits her best, too. Official explanation: jockey said filly's blinkers came loose 2f out (op 7-2)

5404 HEATHCOTES OUTSIDE H'CAP 1m 7f 195y

4:30 (4:31) (Class 4) (0-80,77) 3-Y-0+ **£5,829** (£1,734; £866; £432) **Stalls** High

Form RPR

0062 **1** **Missoula (IRE)**[6] 5256 4-9-7 **68**............... JimmyQuinn 8 76
(M H Tompkins) *hld up: hdwy 4f out: r.o to ld ins fnl f: drvn out* **5/1**

2232 **2** ½ **Jawaaneb (USA)**[14] 5034 3-9-3 **77**............... SebSanders 3 84
(J L Dunlop) *chsd ldrs: rdn over 1f out: str chal and ev ch ins fnl f: hld fnl strides* **5/2**[1]

-061 **3** *nk* **Sivota (IRE)**[31] 4490 3-8-5 **65**............... RichardMullen 1 72
(T P Tate) *led: hdd 4f out: regained ld 2f out: sn rdn: hdd ins fnl f: styd on same pce towards fin* **11/4**[2]

0-12 **4** *nk* **Hawridge King**[19] 4910 5-9-9 **75**............... JamesMillman[(5)] 4 82
(W S Kittow) *hld up: nt clr run wl over 1f out: sn rdn: r.o wl towards fin* **7/2**[3]

1632 **5** ½ **Mister Completely (IRE)**[10] 5138 6-9-3 **64**...............(v) JamesDoyle 6 70
(Ms J S Doyle) *chsd ldrs: led 4f out: rdn and hdd 2f out: stl chalng and ch ent fnl f: no ex towards fin* **11/1**

40-4 **6** 8 **Merrymaker**[14] 5034 7-9-3 **67**............... PatrickMathers[(3)] 5 63
(W M Brisbourne) *s.s: in rr: effrt over 4f out: no real imp: wknd 3f out* **10/1**

0240 **7** 5 **York Cliff**[26] 4670 9-8-13 **60**............... DavidAllan 7 50
(W M Brisbourne) *chsd ldr tl rdn 4f out: wknd over 3f out* **22/1**

3m 28.11s (-5.49) **Going Correction** -0.15s/f (Firm)
WFA 3 from 4yo+ 13lb **7** Ran SP% **115.9**
Speed ratings (Par 105): **107,106,106,106,106 102,99**
CSF £18.44 CT £41.10 TOTE £6.40: £3.10, £2.00; EX 20.50.
Owner Pollards Bloodstock **Bred** Pollards Stables **Trained** Newmarket, Suffolk

■ Stewards' Enquiry : Jimmy Quinn one-day ban: used whip with excessive frequency (Sep 26)
Seb Sanders caution: used whip with excessive frequency

FOCUS
An ordinary handicap in which they did not go a mad gallop here and it turned into something of a sprint off the final bend. However, despite the bunched finish all five were close to form.

5405 HEATHCOTES H'CAP 1m 2f 75y

5:05 (5:06) (Class 5) (0-75,75) 3-Y-0 **£3,562** (£1,059; £529; £264) **Stalls** High

Form RPR

2166 **1** **Wise Little Girl**[31] 4510 3-9-3 **74**............... KDarley 3 81
(M A Jarvis) *chsd ldr: led over 2f out: qcknd clr over 1f out: r.o wl* **5/1**[3]

3400 **2** 2 **Snow Dancer (IRE)**[62] 3570 3-8-7 **67**............... PatrickMathers[(3)] 1 70
(A Berry) *in midfield: rdn and hdwy over 1f out: wnt 2nd ins fnl f: no ch w wnr* **14/1**

51-6 **3** 1¼ **Golan Way**[16] 4960 3-9-3 **74**............... FrancisNorton 4 74
(I A Wood) *chsd ldrs: rdn over 2f out: styd on same pce fr over 1f out* **8/1**

0010 **4** *shd* **Distiller (IRE)**[16] 4960 3-9-0 **71**............... RichardMullen 6 71
(W R Muir) *hld up: rdn and hdwy over 1f out: styd on ins fnl f* **16/1**

6312 **5** 1¾ **La Vecchia Scuola (IRE)**[19] 4894 3-8-4 **66**...............(v) KellyHarrison[(5)] 2 62
(R Johnson) *led: hdd over 2f out: sn n.m.r: wknd ins fnl f* **9/2**[2]

2511 **6** 3 **Grand Art (IRE)**[41] 4197 3-9-4 **75**............... SebSanders 8 65
(M H Tompkins) *in midfield: rdn over 2f out: no imp whn hung lft over 1f out* **5/4**[1]

3301 **7** ¾ **Grethel (IRE)**[4] 5299 3-7-11 **61** 6ex............... DanielleMcCreery[(7)] 7 50
(A Berry) *plld hrd in rr: nvr on terms* **25/1**

0336 **8** 2½ **Milliegait**[29] 4579 3-9-4 **75**............... DavidAllan 5 59
(T D Easterby) *chsd ldrs: rdn over 2f out: wknd over 1f out* **10/1**

2m 11.54s (-1.60) **Going Correction** -0.15s/f (Firm) **8** Ran SP% **115.9**
Speed ratings (Par 101): **100,98,97,97,95 93,92,90**
CSF £71.06 CT £552.63 TOTE £4.90: £1.40, £3.00, £2.50; EX 70.60 Place 6 £10.31, Place 5 £9.08..
Owner Sheikh Mohammed **Bred** Darley **Trained** Newmarket, Suffolk

FOCUS
An ordinary handicap but a nice performance from the winner, who, while undoubtedly getting the run of the race, looks to be improving. The placed horses set the level for the form.

T/Plt: £14.20 to a £1 stake. Pool: £70,333.05. 3,595.40 winning tickets. T/Qpdt: £7.10 to a £1 stake. Pool: £2,151.30. 223.00 winning tickets. DO

5374 DONCASTER (L-H)

Saturday, September 15

OFFICIAL GOING: Good to firm (9.0)

3mm water was put down all round overnight. The ground was described as 'good to firm, quicker than the previous three days'.

Wind: moderate 1/2 against Weather: Fine

5406 URBAN-I CHAMPAGNE STKS (GROUP 2) (C&G) 7f

2:10 (2:11) (Class 1) 2-Y-O

£56,780 (£21,520; £10,770; £5,370; £2,690; £1,350) **Stalls** High

Form RPR

311 **1** **McCartney (GER)**[15] 5004 2-8-12 0 RyanMoore 9 115+
(M Johnston) *lw: led 1f: cl up tl led again over 2f out: sn rdn clr: comf* **8/1**

1 **2** *2 1/2* **Alexander Castle (USA)**[19] 4890 2-8-12 0 DO'Donohoe 10 108+
(K A Ryan) *unf: scope: chsd ldrs: pushed along and outpcd 1/2-way: rdn along and hdwy 2f out: styd on to chse wnr ent fnl f: no imp* **22/1**

3 **3** *1 1/4* **One Great Cat (USA)**[43] 4120 2-8-12 0 MJKinane 1 105
(A P O'Brien, Ire) *hld up in rr: hdwy on outer over 2f out: sn rdn and styd on ins fnl f: nrst fin* **25/1**

1 **4** *1 1/4* **Tajdeef (USA)**[41] 4198 2-8-12 0 RHills 8 102
(B W Hills) *hld up: gd hdwy on outer 3f out: rdn to chal wl over 1f out: sn rdn and wknd appr fnl f* **6/1**[3]

341 **5** *1/2* **Let Us Prey**[57] 3718 2-8-12 97 StephenDonohoe 4 100
(N A Callaghan) *hld up: hdwy over 2f out: sn rdn and kpt on ins fnl f* **25/1**

1 **6** *1/2* **Atlantic Sport (USA)**[48] 3991 2-8-12 0 TPO'Shea 6 99
(M R Channon) *lw: trckd ldrs: hdwy 1/2-way: rdn along over 2f out and sn one pce* **5/2**[2]

2 **7** *4* **Lucifer Sam (USA)**[25] 4694 2-8-12 0 JMurtagh 3 89
(A P O'Brien, Ire) *chsd ldrs: rdn along wl over 2f out and sn wknd* **20/1**

12 **8** *1/2* **River Proud (USA)**[65] 3459 2-8-12 0 TQuinn 2 87
(P F I Cole) *hld up in tch: effrt on outer 1/2-way: sn rdn along and wknd 2f out* **9/4**[1]

1531 **9** *2* **Strike The Deal (USA)**[43] 4120 2-9-1 107 JimmyFortune 11 85
(J Noseda) *t.k.h: trckd ldrs: rdn along wl over 2f out and sn wknd* **10/1**

116 **10** *3* **Maze (IRE)**[14] 5048 2-8-12 0 RoystonFfrench 7 74
(B Smart) *swtg: plld hrd: led after 1f: rdn along and hdd over 2f out: wknd qckly* **33/1**

1m 25.04s (-2.73) **Going Correction** -0.175s/f (Firm) **10** Ran SP% **113.6**
Speed ratings (Par 107): **108,105,103,102,101 101,96,96,93,90**
CSF £166.33 TOTE £11.50: £2.50, £5.00, £4.10; EX 210.60 Trifecta £1083.10 Part won. Pool: £1,525.61 - 0.30 winning units..
Owner Sheikh Mohammed **Bred** Gestut Brummerhof **Trained** Middleham Moor, N Yorks

FOCUS

A race that usually throws up a Classic contender or two and, although neither of the front two in the betting lived up to expectations, the first three all look horses of substantial quality and the form appears sound. It was a big step up from the winner, but no fluke, while the runner-up is a highly regarded colt from a top stable.

NOTEBOOK

McCartney(GER), a typically progressive sort from the yard who followed up his Hamilton win with a narrow victory in a Listed contest at Salisbury, had a bit to prove on this drop back to 7f, but Moore ensured he was made plenty of use of and he sat just in behind the hard-pulling Maze, having allowed him to stride on after a furlong. A strong traveller, he came through to regain the lead just over two furlongs out and quickly stamped his class, pulling away to win impressively against the stands' rail. This was a smart effort from the son of In The Wings and connections are now eyeing a return to Doncaster for next month's Racing Post Trophy. He was cut into a general 16/1 chance for next season's 2000 Guineas following this. (op 9-1)

Alexander Castle(USA), an American-bred colt who ran out an impressive winner of a 7f Newcastle maiden on debut, comes from a yard that is no stranger to housing a smart juvenile and on this evidence that is exactly what they have. Though no match for the powerful winner, the way in which he stayed on having been outpaced pointed strongly towards a step up to 1m suiting and it would come as no surprise to see him reoppose the winner in the Racing Post Trophy, a race his trainer having won with Palace Episode a couple of years back.

One Great Cat(USA), who lacked the speed to make a serious impact in the Richmond Stakes behind Strike The Deal at Glorious Goodwood, was always going to improve markedly for this extra furlong and it was a surprise to see him so readily dismissed in the market, especially considering his connections. In rear early, he began to make headway just over two furlongs out, but did not get the clearest of runs and had to wait to come with his challenge, in the end getting going all too late. He can be rated a bit better than the bare form, especially as he raced away from the favoured stands' rail.

Tajdeef(USA), ready winner of a 6f Newbury maiden on debut, was representing a yard that took this contest twice in the late 90s and he looked to hold sound claims. He started to come with a run towards the outer, but it was clear from a furlong out he was making no further inroads and in the end he was run out of the placings. Clearly a horse with plenty of speed, his dam was a useful sprinter, he looks likely to prove best at 6f. (op 5-1 tchd 9-2)

Let Us Prey, ready winner of his maiden at Pontefract last time, had already run well in a Group race, having finished fourth behind Hatta Fort in the Superlative Stakes, but this represented a stiffer test and it was surprising to see him do so well. The way in which he was keeping on suggests 1m will suit in time and he looks capable of landing a Listed race. (op 40-1)

Atlantic Sport(USA), although clearly well thought of, seemed very short in the betting for what he had actually achieved, scraping home in a 6f Ascot maiden, and it was no real surprise to see him come up short. He simply lacked a change of pace when it was required, surprising considering there is plenty of speed in the pedigree, and he is another who may find things easier down in grade. (op 9-4)

Lucifer Sam(USA) had already had his limitations exposed behind Fast Company in the Acomb Stakes at York and this effort confirmed him to be one of the Ballydoyle lesser lights. He will find easier opportunities back home in Ireland. (op 16-1)

River Proud(USA) was the main disappointment of the race. An impressive maiden winner, he just lost out to Winker Watson on his first try at this level when second in the July Stakes and that piece of form seemed to set a high standard. He was never really going though and it was clear from well over two furlongs out that he was not going to be winning. This was clearly not his form, but it cannot solely be blamed on the step up in trip. It was reported afterwards he had banged his head in the stalls. Official explanation: jockey said colt became upset and hit its head in stalls (tchd 5-2 in places)

Strike The Deal(USA) showed plenty of pace when quickening up to win the Richmond, but this new distance seemed to prove beyond him and it was no surprise to see One Great Cat comprehensively reverse the form.

Maze(IRE) has completely lost the plot since his hard-fought Chesham victory and for the second consecutive race he boiled over before the start and then failed to settle during the race. He is one to avoid at all costs. Official explanation: jockey said colt ran too free

5407 LADBROKES PORTLAND (HERITAGE H'CAP) 5f 140y

2:40 (2:43) (Class 2) 3-Y-O+

£46,740 (£13,995; £6,997; £3,502; £1,747; £877) **Stalls** High

Form RPR

0100 **1** **Fullandby (IRE)**[28] 4614 5-8-13 **97** PJMcDonald(3) 21 109
(T J Etherington) *racd stands' side: hld up: hdwy over 2f out: wnt 2nd appr fnl f: r.o to ld nr fin: 1st of 12 that gp* **20/1**

5306 **2** *hd* **Paradise Isle**[98] 2450 6-9-7 **102** RichardHughes 11 113
(C F Wall) *lw: swtchd rt s and racd stands' side: trckd ldrs: led over 1f out: hdd towards fin: 2nd of 12 that gp* **25/1**

1031 **3** *1* **Pearly Wey**[43] 4122 4-9-0 **95** PhilipRobinson 14 103+
(C G Cox) *hdw: racd stands' side: hld up: hdwy over 2f out: kpt on wl fnl f: 3rd of 12 that gp* **7/1**[3]

1100 **4** *1 1/4* **Orpsie Boy (IRE)**[15] 4990 4-8-8 **94** LukeMorris(5) 12 98
(N P Littmoden) *racd stands' side: hld up in rr: hdwy over 2f out: edgd rt and kpt on wl fnl f: 4th of 12 that gp* **28/1**

5005 **5** *shd* **Gift Horse**[29] 4567 7-8-12 **93** (v) StephenDonohoe 13 96
(D Nicholls) *racd stands' side: hld up in rr: hdwy 2f out: kpt on wl ins fnl f: 5th of 12 that gp* **7/1**[3]

0104 **6** *1 3/4* **Green Manalishi**[3] 5325 6-9-2 **104** PTownend(7) 16 101
(K A Ryan) *lw: racd stands' side: chsd ldrs: kpt on same pce fnl 2f: 6th of 12 that gp* **20/1**

6001 **7** *shd* **River Falcon**[25] 4696 7-9-4 **99** TQuinn 15 100+
(J S Goldie) *racd stands' side: hld up in rr: hdwy and n.m.r over 1f out: kpt on steadily: 7th of 12 that gp* **25/1**

5304 **8** *1/2* **Orientor**[14] 5039 9-8-12 **93** DanielTudhope 20 88
(J S Goldie) *racd stands' side: hld up in mid-div: nt clr run on inner over 1f out: swtchd lft and styd on: 8th of 12 that gp* **33/1**

6060 **9** *shd* **Qadar (IRE)**[15] 4990 5-8-8 **92** (b) WilliamBuick(3) 18 87
(N P Littmoden) *racd stands' side: chsd ldrs: one pce fnl 2f: 9th of 12 that gp* **33/1**

0162 **10** *shd* **Judd Street**[7] 5212 5-9-9 **104** StephenCarson 2 99
(Eve Johnson Houghton) *racd far side: chsd ldrs: led that side jst ins fnl f: kpt on: 1st of 9 that gp* **18/1**

0001 **11** *hd* **One More Round (USA)**[8] 5195 9-8-12 **93** (b) RoystonFfrench 3 87
(N P Littmoden) *s.s: racd far side: hdwy over 2f out: styd on wl ins fnl f: 2nd of 9 that gp* **33/1**

031 **12** *hd* **Buachaill Dona (IRE)**[14] 5039 4-9-7 **102** AdrianTNicholls 7 96
(D Nicholls) *racd far side: hld up in mid-div: hdwy 2f out: hung rt and kpt on wl fnl f: 3rd of 9 that gp* **9/1**

6002 **13** *shd* **Fantasy Believer**[14] 5050 9-8-13 **94** JimmyFortune 17 87
(J J Quinn) *lw: racd stands' side: in tch: effrt over 2f out: hmpd ins fnl f: nvr trbld ldrs: 10th of 12 that gp* **13/2**[2]

4004 **14** *hd* **Tabaret**[7] 5212 4-8-12 **93** TomEaves 22 86
(R M Whitaker) *lw: led stands' side: led: hdd & wknd over 1f out: 11th of 12 that gp* **16/1**

1202 **14** *dht* **Off The Record**[28] 4607 3-9-0 **97** TPQueally 8 90
(J G Given) *led far side: hdd & wknd jst ins fnl f: 4th of 9 that gp* **12/1**

0000 **16** *1* **King Orchisios (IRE)**[42] 4150 4-9-5 **100** (p) PaulMulrennan 4 89
(K A Ryan) *racd far side: w ldrs: wknd over 1f out: 5th of 9 that gp* **66/1**

2022 **17** *3/4* **Lipocco**[6] 5254 3-9-3 **100** GeorgeBaker 19 87
(R M Beckett) *lw: w ldrs stands' side: wknd over 1f out: last of 12 that gp* **6/1**[1]

0243 **18** *hd* **Hoh Hoh Hoh**[7] 5212 5-9-0 **95** JMurtagh 10 81
(R J Price) *racd far side: hld up in rr: nvr a factor: 6th of 9 that gp* **12/1**

1030 **19** *nk* **Green Park (IRE)**[25] 4696 4-8-13 **94** PaulHanagan 9 79
(R A Fahey) *mid-div: lost pl 2f out: 7th of 9 that gp* **50/1**

3110 **20** *2 1/2* **Golden Dixie (USA)**[7] 5212 8-9-2 **97** RyanMoore 5 74
(R A Harris) *racd far side: chsd ldrs: wknd fnl f: 8th of 9 that gp* **20/1**

0536 **21** *5* **Bounty Quest**[21] 4798 5-9-3 **98** DO'Donohoe 1 58
(K A Ryan) *racd far side: chsd ldrs: lost pl 2f out: last of 9 that gp* **66/1**

66.63 secs (-1.37) **Going Correction** -0.175s/f (Firm)
WFA 3 from 4yo+ 2lb **21** Ran SP% **128.3**
Speed ratings (Par 109): **102,101,100,98,98 96,96,95,95,95 94,94,94,94,94 92,91,91,91,87 81**
CSF £437.86 CT £3902.93 TOTE £28.60: £7.10, £4.80, £2.10, £11.40; EX 1735.90 Trifecta £14079.90 Part won. Pool: £19,830.94 - 0.40 winning units..
Owner Miss M Greenwood **Bred** Mrs A Haskell Ellis **Trained** Norton, N Yorks

■ Stewards' Enquiry : William Buick 12-day ban (takes into account earlier offences, two days deferred): careless riding (Oct 5-14)

Luke Morris two-day ban; careless riding (Sep 26-27)

FOCUS

A traditionally competitive sprint handicap and also a sound trial for the Ayr Gold Cup. The first nine home raced on the stands' side and a personal best from the winner and the third deserves plenty of credit.

NOTEBOOK

Fullandby(IRE), drawn on the wrong side at Ripon, handles quicker ground better as he gets older. He came with a sustained run to put his head in front almost on the line. He will now carry his 5lb penalty at Ayr and the double has been done before.

Paradise Isle, who looked at her very best, has struggled to find top form since her return from Dubai. She travelled supremely well but possibly hit the front sooner than ideal and she missed out in the final strides. She deserves a ninth career success this backend.

Pearly Wey ◆, 5lb higher than Goodwood, looks to have thrived in the interim. He ended up racing wide of the first two and deserves plenty of praise. There may well be another good handicap to be won with him this time. (op 17-2)

Orpsie Boy(IRE), who was found to have an irregular heartbeat after running badly at Chester, ran a lot better but he came off a straight line late on, getting in the way of Fantasy Believer.

Gift Horse, who had the visor retained, again showed that he is far from being a back-number. (tchd 8-1 in a place)

Green Manalishi, full of himself beforehand, gave a good account of himself for a second time at this meeting. (op 22-1)

River Falcon, 7lb higher, was racing from a career mark and the ground was plenty quick enough for him. He met traffic problems and connection will be hoping for better luck at Ayr. Official explanation: jockey said gelding was denied a clear run

Orientor, on a three-year losing run, was staying on to some purpose when Qadar got in his way. He goes to Ayr in great heart.

Qadar(IRE) has five career wins to his credit but they have all been on the All-Weather. (op 28-1)

Judd Street, 4lb higher, ran out of his skin, first home on the far side. Now rated 104, he should be able to make his mark in Listed company. (op 16-1)

One More Round(USA), slowly away, would have been first home on the far side in a few more strides.

Buachaill Dona(IRE), gaelic for Naughty Boy, lived up to his name hanging left and proving a tricky ride. He was beaten just two heads on the far side. Official explanation: jockey said gelding hung right (op 8-1)

Fantasy Believer, who took this when it was run at York 12 months ago, had not shone in this when it was run here in each of the previous years. (tchd 6-1)

Tabaret took them along at a fierce gallop down the stands' side but he is better over the bare five.

Lipocco, making a quick return, paid a heavy price for attempting to match strides with Tabaret at the head of affairs down the favoured stands' side. Official explanation: jockey said gelding ran flat (op 7-1)

5408 LADBROKES ST LEGER STKS (GROUP 1) (ENTIRE COLTS & FILLIES) 1m 6f 132y

3:15 (3:22) (Class 1) 3-Y-O

£303,914 (£115,185; £57,646; £28,742; £14,398; £7,225) **Stalls** Low

Form RPR

4241 **1** **Lucarno (USA)**[25] 4692 3-9-0 113 ..... JimmyFortune 8 121+
(J H M Gosden) *lw: hld up in tch gng wl: smooth hdwy over 3f out: chal on bit wl over 1f out: sn led: rdn and edgd lft ins fnl f: styd on* **7/2[2]**

015 **2** *1* **Mahler**[25] 4692 3-9-0 0 ..... MJKinane 3 119
(A P O'Brien, Ire) *swtg: led: rdn along wl over 2f out: drvn: hdd and jinked over 1f out: kpt on u.p ins fnl f* **13/2[3]**

12 **3** *¾* **Honolulu (IRE)**[24] 4722 3-9-0 0 ..... JMurtagh 7 118
(A P O'Brien, Ire) *lw: hld up in rr: hdwy over 4f out: rdn and edgd lft wl over 1f out: drvn and kpt on same pce ins fnl f* **13/8[1]**

6011 **4** *nk* **Regal Flush**[7] 5215 3-9-0 101 ..... RyanMoore 5 117
(Sir Michael Stoute) *lw: hld up and bhd: hdwy on outer 3f out: rdn along and edgd lft 2f out: styd on u.p ins fnl f: nrst fin* **13/2[3]**

1122 **5** *shd* **Veracity**[44] 4091 3-9-0 112 ..... PhilipRobinson 1 116
(M A Jarvis) *lw: trckd ldng pair: effrt to chse ldr over 4f out: rdn along 3f out: drvn wl over 1f out: kpt on same pce* **16/1**

333 **6** *nk* **Macarthur**[25] 4692 3-9-0 0 ..... CSoumillon 2 116+
(A P O'Brien, Ire) *lw: hld up towards rr: hdwy whn n.m.r wl over 1f out: swtchd lft and styng on whn nt clr run ins fnl f: drvn and kpt on same pce* **17/2**

3002 **7** *¾* **Celestial Halo (IRE)**[23] 4749 3-9-0 100 ..... RHills 4 115+
(B W Hills) *hld up in rr: hdwy whn n.m.r over 2f out: sn rdn: edgd lft and no imp* **66/1**

204 **8** *1 ¼* **Acapulco (IRE)**[25] 4692 3-9-0 0 ..... CO'Donoghue 9 113
(A P O'Brien, Ire) *swtg: trckd ldr: effrt over 3f out: sn rdn along: drvn and wknd over 2f out* **25/1**

3232 **9** *12* **Samuel**[21] 4803 3-9-0 105 ..... TQuinn 6 96
(J L Dunlop) *lw: chsd ldrs: rdn along over 3f out: sn wknd* **40/1**

1203 **10** *16* **Raincoat**[46] 4044 3-9-0 109 ..... RichardHughes 10 74
(J H M Gosden) *trckd ldrs: effrt 4f out: sn rdn along and wknd wl over 2f out* **12/1**

3m 1.90s (-7.84) **Going Correction** -0.175s/f (Firm) course record **10** Ran SP% **118.9**
Speed ratings (Par 115): **113,112,112,111,111 111,111,110,104,95**
CSF £26.83 TOTE £4.40: £1.60, £2.60, £1.30; EX 35.60 Trifecta £80.80 Pool: £5,892.25 - 51.74 winning units..

Owner George Strawbridge **Bred** Augustin Stable **Trained** Newmarket, Suffolk

■ There was a stalls malfunction and the race had to be hand timed. Jimmy Fortune's first Classic winner.

FOCUS

Not a vintage renewal, with Soldier Of Fortune and the injured Aqaleem notable absentees, the 13/8 favourite Honolulu contesting a Group contest for the first time and something of a bunch finish, but it produced a good winner in the highly-progressive Lucarno. Mahler was responsible for the pace, but there were several in behind whose connections claimed a faster gallop would have seen them finish closer. Macarthur was the only one who never had a chance to show what he could do, twice meeting trouble in running. Only Lucarno looks capable of making it as a top-class middle-distance performer next season, but the likes of Mahler and Veracity should develop into Cup horses, whilst Honolulu, Regal Flush and Macarthur can do well at just short of the top level.

NOTEBOOK

Lucarno(USA), the outstanding candidate following a remarkable first season which has seen him finish fourth in the Derby, was not stopping when running out a ready winner of the Great Voltigeur, often the key trial for this contest, and it simply looked a case of if he stays, he wins. Settled in off the steady early pace set by Mahler, he started to come with his run as they raced into the final half mile and none was going better as he eased into the lead a furlong out. He had to knuckle down, with the persistent O'Brien pair ensuring he did not have it easy, but he found plenty and layed to rest any doubts surrounding his ability to last the distance. It would be unwise to get carried away with the form, with two horses stepping up from handicaps finishing third and fourth, but he has already proven himself to be just short of top class at 1m4f and this big, scopey son of Dynaformer may well improve enough from three to four to make it at the very top level over middle-distances next season. (op 9-2)

Mahler showed himself to be a high-class stayer when running away with the Queen's Vase, and was unsurprisingly found wanting for pace back at 1m4f in the Great Voltigeur last time. Sent straight to the front by Kinane, he gradually upped the tempo and kept grinding away, despite seeming to stumble over a furlong out, but in the end was found out by the classy winner's superior pace. He did enough to hold off his better-fancied stable companion though and is going to relish the return to 2m, but whilst it is tempting to say he could develop into a Gold Cup horse, Ballydoyle already have the likes of Yeats, Septimus and possibly even Scorpion for the staying races, so it is hard to see where he will fit into their plans. Official explanation: jockey said colt lost its action (op 15-2)

Honolulu(IRE) has quickly progressed through the ranks, winning his maiden, a Listed race, and then finding only Purple Moon too good off a mark of 111 in the Ebor. This was his hardest test yet however and, although holding outstanding claims on the ratings, there were several in here who could have achieved something similar had they been asked to. Well supported in the market throughout the past couple of weeks, he was again ridden with plenty of restraint and began to follow the winner through, but as was the case in the Ebor he did not look to be fully concentrating when asked for maximum effort and in the end he could only keep on at the one pace. It would be silly to mark this down as a disappointing, if anything it was a cracking run from one so inexperienced, and the son of Montjeu can continue to progress, with a return to slower ground likely to suit. (op 15-8, tchd 2-1 in places)

Regal Flush, another stepping up from handicaps, has really got his act together of late and the way in which he won off 101 at Haydock last week entitled him to take his chance in this, for which he was supplemented for £40,000. Another ridden under restraint, he came through behind Honolulu, but like that one found the line coming too soon and Sir Michael Stoute's misery in this race continues. Moore thought a faster early pace would have seen him finish a bit closer, but this was a still career-best effort and further progress is likely. (op 7-1, tchd 8-1 in a place)

Veracity, another to have progressed from handicaps, proved no match for Mahler in the Queen's Vase at Royal Ascot, but he bettered that effort when running a huge race for a three-year-old to finish second to Allegretto in the Goodwood Cup and he certainly looked one of the likelier outsiders. However, having tracked the early leaders, he simply lacked the pace to stay in the mix as they raced into the final quarter mile and in hindsight his rider would have pressed on a lot earlier. Stamina is his strong point and he could develop into a Cup regular over the next couple of years.

Macarthur, favourite for the Derby earlier in the season, has not lived up to lofty expectations, but his staying-on Great Voltigeur third, when returning from a lengthy break, pointed to this step up in trip suiting and he provided Ballydoyle with a most valid third-string. However, things never happened for him as, having been in rear early, he started to make ground against the rail, but soon found the door shut and he again met trouble when switched. He would not have been far away had he found an uninterrupted passage and was certainly the hard-luck story of the race. The return to softer ground in future will suit and he remains open to improvement. Official explanation: jockey said colt was denied a clear run (op 15-2 tchd 9-1)

Celestial Halo(IRE), not up to the task when tried in Group company earlier in the season, returned to form when second in a hotly-contested handicap at York last time, but he was only ever going to play a minor role here and it was surprising to see him beat as many as three horses home. He is not going to be easy to place.

Acapulco(IRE), a close-up fourth behind Lucarno in the Voltigeur, was the one with most to find of the Ballydoyle quartet and, having sat just off stablemate Mahler early, he quickly fell back through the field when things began to hot up. This was only the fifth start of his career and he gives the impression he is not quite ready for this sort of test yet. He has only won a maiden and could be one to work his way up next season.

Samuel, who is still a maiden, has been progressing well without winning, but even on the best of his efforts, which included a second to Tungsten Strike in a Listed contest at Goodwood last time, he had plenty to find and he gradually faded out of it having held a prominent early position. This should not be held against him and the priority now is to win a maiden. He is likely to be a much better horse next year. (op 33-1)

Raincoat was the only disappointment among the seven who had realistic claims. Runner-up to Authorized in the Dante earlier in the season, he had reportedly been trained with this race in mind and did not have that much to find on the form of his Gordon Stakes third to Yellowstone, but having failed to settle and been exposed with no cover, he quickly dropped away and plainly failed to give his true running. (op 9-1)

5409 GNER PARK STKS (GROUP 2) 7f

3:50 (3:53) (Class 1) 3-Y-O+

£56,780 (£21,520; £10,770; £5,370; £2,690; £1,350) **Stalls** High

Form RPR

2135 **1** **Arabian Gleam**[46] 4045 3-8-12 109 ..... JMurtagh 1 115
(J Noseda) *trckd ldng pair: hdwy over 2f out: rdn over 1f out: styd on u.p ins fnl f to ld last 100yds* **5/2[2]**

-431 **2** *nk* **Duff (IRE)**[23] 4747 4-9-2 0 ..... RyanMoore 6 115
(Edward Lynam, Ire) *led 2f: cl up tl qckned to ld again wl over 1f out and sn rdn: drvn and hung lft ins fnl f: hdd and no ex last 100yds* **11/4[3]**

1414 **3** *2 ½* **Wake Up Maggie (IRE)**[28] 4600 4-8-13 115 ..... GeorgeBaker 5 105
(C F Wall) *lw: hld up in rr: hdwy over 2f out: rdn to chse ldng pair and hung lft ent fnl f: one pce* **2/1[1]**

3452 **4** *1 ¾* **King Jock (USA)**[6] 5259 6-9-2 0 ..... PShanahan 4 104
(R J Osborne, Ire) *chsd ldrs: rdn along 2f out: kpt on same pce* **11/1**

0664 **5** *3 ½* **Mac Love**[11] 5112 6-9-2 107 ..... TPQueally 7 94
(J Noseda) *lw: hld up: effrt over 2f out: sn rdn and btn* **9/1**

31-6 **6** *12* **Captain Marvelous (IRE)**[147] 1147 3-8-12 117 ..... CSoumillon 3 62
(B W Hills) *dwlt: hdwy to ld after 2f: rdn along over 2f out: hdd wl over 1f out and sn wknd* **14/1**

1m 24.24s (-3.53) **Going Correction** -0.175s/f (Firm)
WFA 3 from 4yo+ 4lb **6** Ran SP% **113.6**
Speed ratings (Par 115): **113,112,109,107,103 90**
CSF £10.02 TOTE £3.50: £2.30, £2.00; EX 10.20.

Owner Saeed Suhail **Bred** P And Mrs A G Venner **Trained** Newmarket, Suffolk

FOCUS

Not a particularly strong race for the race, but two progressive sorts fought out the finish, pulling a little way clear.

NOTEBOOK

Arabian Gleam has quickly developed into a very smart performer, finishing third behind Tariq in the Jersey Stakes on only his third start, and then receiving little luck in running when reopposing Peter Chapple-Hyam's colt in the Betfair Cup at Goodwood. This seemed very winnable and, having held a stalking early position, he went in pursuit of Duff from over two furlongs out and gradually wore him down, despite being away from the favoured stands' rail. Although by top-class sprinter Kyllachy, there is plenty of stamina in his pedigree and he may well improve again for the step up to 1m, although connections may resist for the time being and keep him back for the Challenge Stakes at Newmarket on Champions Day. (op 2-1, tchd 11-4 in places)

Duff(IRE), who led throughout for a narrow victory in a 7f Listed contest at York last time, had more to do here, but he launched his challenge against the favoured stands' rail and it momentarily looked as though he has stolen it. The three-year-old wore him down in the end, but this still has to go down as a personal best from the progressive four-year-old. (op 4-1,)

Wake Up Maggie(IRE) has come right back to her best of late, winning a Group 3 at Goodwood before finishing a close-up fourth to Red Evie in the Hungerford Stakes, so this has to go down as a little disappointing. She was unable to make up the ground having allowed the front pair first run and there was a suggestion she has had enough for the season. (tchd 9-4)

King Jock(USA) is a little short of this grade and fourth was about as good as he could have hoped for. He had run well to finish second in a French Group 3 last time and a return to that level will give him more of a chance. (tchd 10-1 and 12-1)

Mac Love is past his best these days, but his recent effort behind Lovelace at Goodwood entitled him to some respect. Held up, he briefly threatened to make a run, but soon flattened out and is likely to continue to struggle to get his head in front. (op 10-1 tchd 8-1)

Captain Marvelous(IRE), a Group 2 winner at Maisons-Laffitte as a juvenile, finished a long last of six behind Major Cadeaux on his seasonal reappearance in the Greenham and had been off since. He showed up well to a point, but stopped very quickly once headed and clearly is still some way below his juvenile form. (op 12-1)

5410 EMBERS PLUMBING AND HEATING SHOP CONDITIONS STKS 6f

4:20 (4:20) (Class 2) 2-Y-O

£11,217 (£3,358; £1,679; £840; £419; £210) **Stalls** High

Form RPR

1104 **1** **Spitfire**[34] 4431 2-8-13 87 ..... PaulHanagan 4 98
(J R Jenkins) *in tch: hdwy 2f out: swtchd lft and rdn over 1f out: styd on ins fnl f to ld last 75yds* **25/1**

3132 **2** *nk* **Art Sale**[7] 5216 2-8-11 89 ..... JimmyFortune 9 95
(G L Moore) *lw: trckd ldrs: swtchd lft and gd hdwy wl over 1f out: rdn to ld ent fnl f: sn drvn: hdd and no ex last 75yds* **11/4[2]**

4611 **3** *1 ½* **Taurian**[22] 4769 2-8-11 91 ..... TomEaves 3 91
(Mrs L Stubbs) *lw: hld up: hdwy over 2f out: nt clr run wl over 1f out: rdn and styd on strly ins fnl f: nrst fin* **9/1**

1 **4** *nk* **Ancien Regime (IRE)**[20] 4854 2-8-13 0 ..... PhilipRobinson 11 92
(M A Jarvis) *unf: scope: led: rdn wl over 1f out: drvn and hdd ent fnl f: kpt on same pce* **9/4[1]**

3321 **5** *shd* **Al Muheer (IRE)**[42] 4162 2-8-11 95 ..... JMurtagh 5 89
(C E Brittain) *in tch: hdwy over 2f out: rdn to chse ldrs over 1f out: one pce ins fnl f* **9/2[3]**

2160 **6** 1 ½ **Mazzanti**[23] 4743 2-8-11 87 .... DO'Donohoe 2 89+
(K A Ryan) *sn rdn along and bhd: hdwy over 2f out: swtchd to stands' rail wl over 1f out: styd on strly ins fnl f: nrst fin* **25/1**
156 **7** 11 **Firestreak**[15] 4991 2-8-13 85 .... RyanMoore 1 54
(R Hannon) *hld up: swtchd outside and gd hdwy 2f out: sn rdn and ch wl over 1f out: sn wknd* **9/1**
021 **8** 8 **Mister Fips (IRE)**[27] 4636 2-8-13 85 .... TGMcLaughlin 8 30
(Jane Chapple-Hyam) *chsd ldrs: rdn along 1/2-way: sn wknd* **18/1**
61 **9** nk **Captain Macarry (IRE)**[10] 5143 2-8-13 0 .... RoystonFfrench 10 29
(B Smart) *cl up: rdn along wl over 2f out: sn wknd* **22/1**
1166 **10** 7 **Sailor At Sea (USA)**[14] 5032 2-8-13 90 .... RichardHughes 6 8
(R Charlton) *lw: prom: rdn along 1/2-way: sn wknd* **14/1**

1m 12.6s (-1.70) **Going Correction** -0.175s/f (Firm) **10** Ran SP% **119.6**
Speed ratings (Par 101): **104,103,101,101,101 99,84,73,73,64**
CSF £93.68 TOTE £22.90: £4.00, £1.80, £2.10; EX 161.80 Trifecta £916.40 Part won. Pool: £1,290.76 - 0.35 winning units..
Owner The Spitfire Partnership **Bred** R B Hill **Trained** Royston, Herts

FOCUS
A decent conditions stakes in which the winner may have been a surprise but it was certainly no fluke. The placed horses set the standard for now.

NOTEBOOK
Spitfire, matched at 65 on the exchanges, bounced back really knuckling down to show ahead near the line. He now has the Redcar Two-Year-Old Trophy in his sights. sdf sdf sdfsdf sd, matched at 65 on the exchanges, bounced back really knuckling down to show ahead near the line. He now has the Redcar Two-Year-Old Trophy in his sights. (tchd 22-1)
Art Sale, clearly going the right away, looked nailed on when storming to the front but he was worn down near the line. (op 3-1 tchd 10-3)
Taurian, the biggest in the line-up, gets better with every outing and he was unlucky not to give the first two more to do. (tchd 8-1 and 10-1)
Ancien Regime(IRE), a Dewhurst entry, took them along but in the end he was outspeeded by the first three. He looks the type to make a better three-year-old, but under whose banner? (op 5-2 tchd 11-4)
Al Muheer(IRE), best of those with an official rating, was given a more patient ride over this extended trip and it may not have suited him. (tchd 5-1)
Mazzanti, out of luck in the big sales race at York, stayed on really well when switched to the stands' side rail and now may be the time to give him a try over seven. Certainly we have yet to see the best of him.

5411 DONCASTER AUDI STKS (H'CAP) 1m 4f
4:55 (4:55) (Class 2) (0-110,110) 3-Y-0+**£17,487** (£5,202; £2,600; £1,298) **Stalls** Low

Form RPR
-521 **1** **Galactic Star**[25] 4690 4-8-11 96 oh3 .... RyanMoore 4 113+
(Sir Michael Stoute) *lw: hld up in rr: gd hdwy 3f out: rdn to ld over 1f out: styd on wl* **5/4**[1]
211- **2** 2 ½ **New Guinea**[385] 4791 4-8-12 97 .... DO'Donohoe 2 106
(Saeed Bin Suroor) *prom: hdwy to chse ldr over 4f out: led over 2f out and sn rdn: drvn and hdd appr fnl f: kpt on same pce* **8/1**
2002 **3** 6 **Camrose**[29] 4588 6-8-13 98 .... (b) JimmyFortune 1 97
(J L Dunlop) *hld up: hdwy 3f out: rdn 2f out: styd on same pce* **14/1**
-105 **4** nk **Rayhani (USA)**[21] 4803 4-8-10 98 .... WilliamBuick(3) 7 97
(M P Tregoning) *lw: in tch: hdwy on outer over 3f out: rdn over 2f out and sn no imp* **7/1**[3]
/12- **5** 5 **Rampallion**[315] 6337 4-8-12 97 .... RHills 8 88
(Saeed Bin Suroor) *hld up: hdwy on outer over 3f out: rdn along wl over 2f out and sn btn* **9/2**[2]
1020 **6** ½ **Lake Poet (IRE)**[24] 4722 4-9-5 104 .... JMurtagh 5 94
(C E Brittain) *trckd ldrs: hdwy over 3f out: rdn along over 2f out and sn btn* **8/1**
1152 **7** 3 ½ **Classic Punch (IRE)**[21] 4825 4-9-11 110 .... TQuinn 6 95
(D R C Elsworth) *led: rdn along over 3f out: drvn and hdd over 2f out: sn wknd* **10/1**
3- **8** 30 **Britannic**[153] 5584 4-9-6 105 .... PaulHanagan 3 42
(T P Tate) *slipped s: plld hrd and sn chsng ldr: rdn along over 4f out: sn wknd and bhd* **25/1**

2m 28.58s (-6.95) **Going Correction** -0.175s/f (Firm) **8** Ran SP% **117.0**
Speed ratings (Par 109): **116,114,110,110,106 106,104,84**
CSF £12.58 CT £98.84 TOTE £2.10: £1.20, £2.20, £2.60; EX 14.30 Trifecta £71.00 Pool: £1,412.60 - 14.12 winning units..
Owner Saeed Suhail **Bred** Hascombe And Valiant Studs **Trained** Newmarket, Suffolk

FOCUS
A good handicap and although not a great deal solid here the highly-progressive winner was value for a bit further and looks a Group horse in the making.

NOTEBOOK
Galactic Star, who had an unhappy time in the stalls and needed surgery at two, is improving fast. Out of the handicap and in effect 11lb higher, he was given a most confident ride and in the end won going away. There is even better to come. (op 11-8, tchd 6-4 in places)
New Guinea, absent for over a year, was having his first run for Godolpin. Very fit, he went on but it was a question of time before the highly-progressive winner cut him down to size.
Camrose, without a win for over two years, ran one of his better races without ever threatening real danger. (tchd 11-1)
Rayhani(USA), 9lb higher than when successful at Newmarket in may, has been highly tried since. He had the quick ground he needs but was simply not good enough.
Rampallion, absent since being pipped at Windsor in November, looked very fit but he had neither the ground nor the trip in his favour. (op 11-2 tchd 6-1)
Lake Poet(IRE) possibly found the Ebor trip beyond him but this was not one of his better efforts.

5412 1STSECURITYSOLUTIONS.CO.UK H'CAP 1m (S)
5:30 (5:30) (Class 2) (0-110,110) 3-Y-0+**£19,431** (£5,781; £2,889; £1,443) **Stalls** High

Form RPR
0411 **1** **The Illies (IRE)**[23] 4745 3-8-2 95 .... WilliamBuick(3) 8 102+
(B W Hills) *lw: trckd ldrs: rdn to ld 1f out: hld on towards fin* **10/11**[1]
0024 **2** hd **Metropolitan Man**[7] 5213 4-9-5 104 .... GeorgeBaker 6 111
(D M Simcock) *hld up in rr: nt clr run over 2f out tl over 1f out: styd on wl to go 2nd ins fnl f: no ex towards fin* **16/1**
3100 **3** 1 ¾ **Eddie Jock (IRE)**[42] 4148 3-9-6 110 .... RichardHughes 9 112
(M L W Bell) *led: qcknd over 3f out: hdd 1f out: kpt on same pce* **14/1**
1020 **4** 1 **Humungous (IRE)**[23] 4745 4-9-3 102 .... RyanMoore 2 103
(C R Egerton) *hood removed v late: missed break sltly: hdwy to chse ldrs over 2f out: one pce appr fnl f* **4/1**[2]
3000 **5** shd **Vortex**[43] 4119 8-9-6 105 .... (t) JMurtagh 5 105
(Miss Gay Kelleway) *trckd ldrs: nt clr run over 2f out: styd on same pce fnl f* **11/1**
6004 **6** 1 ¼ **Mine (IRE)**[23] 4747 9-9-7 106 .... (v) TQuinn 7 104
(J D Bethell) *hld up in rr: effrt over 2f out: edgd lft: nvr trbld ldrs* **10/1**
2030 **7** ¾ **Flipando (IRE)**[23] 4745 6-9-1 100 .... JimmyFortune 3 96
(T D Barron) *rrd s: sn chsng ldrs: wknd over 1f out* **7/1**[3]
0103 **8** 5 **Rio Riva**[51] 3887 5-9-3 102 .... TomEaves 4 86
(Miss J A Camacho) *trckd ldrs: wkng whn sltly hmpd and stmbld appr fnl f* **16/1**

1m 38.22s (-3.29) **Going Correction** -0.175s/f (Firm)
WFA 3 from 4yo+ 5lb **8** Ran SP% **120.7**
Speed ratings (Par 109): **109,108,107,106,105 104,103,98**
CSF £20.27 CT £142.56 TOTE £1.90: £1.30, £3.90, £2.80; EX 21.20 Trifecta £149.00 Pool: £1,383.79 - 6.59 winning units. Place 6 £577.25, Place 5 £59.22..
Owner John C Grant **Bred** Glashare House Stud **Trained** Lambourn, Berks

FOCUS
A good contest but a somewhat messy affair. The winner is better than he showed on the day, the race has been rated through the third who had the run of the race.

NOTEBOOK
The Illies(IRE), 6lb higher, completed the hat-trick but in the end he had to dig deep. A much stronger pace plays to his strengths and he should give a good account of himself in the Cambridgeshire. (op 11-8 tchd 4-5)
Metropolitan Man, raised 2lb after Haydock, had the quick ground he needs. He had to wait his turn but in the end he was just held. (op 12-1)
Eddie Jock(IRE), 6lb higher than his shock Royal Ascot success, took them along in his own time. He wound up the pace from the halfway mark but in the end was simply not good enough. (op 11-1 tchd 10-1)
Humungous(IRE), with the blinkers left off, had an outside draw. The hood was left on in the stalls until the last possible moment and as a result he missed a beat at the start. He never really threatened and a return to front-running tactics might prove the answer. (tchd 11-2)
Vortex, with the eyeshields back on, put his unhappy Goodwood experience behind him. He owes connections nothing. (op 12-1)
Mine(IRE) did not have the end-to-end gallop he needs.
T/Jkpt: Not won. T/Plt: £522.50 to a £1 stake. Pool: £187,150.84. 261.45 winning tickets. T/Qpdt: £8.70 to a £1 stake. Pool: £7,756.90. 657.25 winning tickets. JR

5109 GOODWOOD (R-H)
Saturday, September 15

OFFICIAL GOING: Good to firm (9.0)
The inside of the home straight was railed off by 6 metres until 2 furlongs from home, with a cutaway then creating extra room on the far side.
Wind: virtually nil Weather: bright

5413 SHELL HOUSE STKS (H'CAP) 7f
2:25 (2:27) (Class 2) (0-100,95) 3-Y-0+
£11,217 (£3,358; £1,679; £840; £419; £210) **Stalls** High

Form RPR
0045 **1** **South Cape**[15] 5012 4-8-12 85 .... DarryllHolland 6 95
(M R Channon) *hld up wl bhd: gd hdwy on rail wl over 1f out: styd on u.p to ld last stride* **7/1**[3]
3003 **2** shd **Presumptive (IRE)**[49] 3943 7-9-5 92 .... SteveDrowne 1 102
(R Charlton) *hld up wl bhd: rdn and hdwy on outer wl over 1f out: edgd rt and ld last 100yds: hdd last stride* **10/1**
0060 **3** 1 **Jedburgh**[20] 4851 6-9-5 92 .... (b) MartinDwyer 2 99
(J L Dunlop) *hld up wl bhd: rdn and hdwy 2f out: kpt on u.p fnl f: snatched 3rd on line* **17/2**
0000 **4** shd **Prince Of Thebes (IRE)**[20] 4851 6-8-8 81 .... PaulDoe 8 88
(J Akehurst) *mostly chsd ldr: rdn over 2f out: led 1f out: hdd and no ex last 100yds* **10/1**
3015 **5** 1 **Compton's Eleven**[14] 5044 6-8-5 85 .... MatthewDavies(7) 4 89
(M R Channon) *hld up in rr: rdn and hdwy jst over 2f out: styng on whn short of room ins fnl f: kpt on* **33/1**
6060 **6** 1 ¾ **Cape Of Luck (IRE)**[17] 4949 4-8-7 87 .... JackMitchell(7) 9 86
(P Mitchell) *hld up in rr: swtchd to outer and rdn 2f out: kpt on: nt rch ldrs* **20/1**
0000 **7** nk **King's Caprice**[28] 4601 6-9-4 94 .... (vt[1]) TravisBlock(3) 10 92
(J A Geake) *taken down early: led: clr 1/2-way: rdn 2f out: hdd 1f out: fdd last 100yds* **20/1**
1110 **8** shd **Guilded Warrior**[45] 4068 4-9-2 89 .... FergusSweeney 5 87
(W S Kittow) *in tch: rdn 2f out: kpt on same pce u.p* **20/1**
0500 **9** nk **Ektimaal**[15] 4990 4-9-0 87 .... (t) DaneO'Neill 13 84
(E A L Dunlop) *trckd ldrs on rail: rdn to chal 2f out: ev ch tl wknd ins fnl f* **9/1**
3030 **10** 2 ½ **Minority Report**[20] 4851 7-9-8 95 .... JamieSpencer 12 108+
(L M Cumani) *racd in midfield: rdn and nt clr run over 2f out: nt clr run and swtchd rt over 1f out: running on whn nt clr run last 100yds and heavily eased* **11/4**[1]
2663 **11** 4 **Fiefdom (IRE)**[14] 5031 5-8-9 82 .... ChrisCatlin 11 62
(I W McInnes) *chsd ldrs: rdn 2f out: sn struggling* **16/1**
0015 **12** 7 **H Harrison (IRE)**[14] 5031 7-8-10 86 .... AndrewElliott(3) 7 47
(I W McInnes) *prom on outer: rdn and wknd wl over 2f out: eased whn wl btn ins fnl f* **18/1**
0-30 **13** 1 ½ **Desert Chief**[101] 2374 5-9-6 93 .... LDettori 3 50
(Saeed Bin Suroor) *chsd ldrs tl wknd wl over 2f out: sn wknd: eased ins fnl f* **6/1**[2]

1m 26.3s (-1.74) **Going Correction** +0.025s/f (Good) **13** Ran SP% **120.5**
Speed ratings (Par 109): **110,109,108,108,107 105,105,105,104,101 97,89,87**
CSF £71.52 CT £613.41 TOTE £8.80: £2.80, £3.00, £3.00; EX 100.60 Trifecta £478.60 Pool: £674.12, 1.00 w/u.
Owner Heart Of The South Racing **Bred** John And Mrs Caroline Penny **Trained** West Ilsley, Berks
■ Stewards' Enquiry : Jamie Spencer caution: allowed gelding to coast home with no assistance

FOCUS
A decent competitive race of its type.

NOTEBOOK
South Cape stays a mile, but has yet to win beyond 7f and was dropped back in trip here. Taking advantage of the cutaway running rail in the last 2f, he found a nice run up the inside to get there in the nick of time. (op 10-1)
Presumptive(IRE) is only just above his winning mark, and on the evidence is capable of winning off it, having been nailed right on the line. (tchd 11-1)
Jedburgh has not won for over a year, but a fast-ground 7f is perfect for him, and he looks back in form now. He is handicapped to win, and can do so if conditions continue to suit. (op 8-1)
Prince Of Thebes(IRE) is really well-handicapped at present, and this signalled a major return to form. He can win over 7f or a mile if keeping up the good work. (op 11-1)
Compton's Eleven has done pretty well in his last three races, and proved again that he is effective over this trip as well as 6f.
Cape Of Luck(IRE) is working his way back down to an attractive mark, and is capable of striking on either turf or Polytrack. (tchd 22-1)
King's Caprice, winner of this last year and off the same mark here, ran freely in the first-time visor. However, it was his best effort race for some time, and he could yet make some appeal if able to save a bit more for the finish.

Guilded Warrior is higher in the weights now, but ran a fair race on much faster ground than he had won on earlier in the season.
Ektimaal is battling with the Handicapper at present, but ran well enough to prove he is not just an All-Weather horse these days.
Minority Report ◆ had a terrible run through, even with the false running rail allowing the runners to fan out in the last 2f, and might well have gone close with better luck. His final position is irrelevant, and the market support suggests he can find compensation. Official explanation: jockey said gelding was denied a clear run (op 5-2, tchd 3-1 in places)
H Harrison(IRE) Official explanation: jockey said gelding ran flat
Desert Chief Official explanation: jockey said horse pulled up lame

5414 STAY TUNED FOR BETFAIR TURBO TENNIS STARDOM STKS (LISTED RACE) 1m

2:55 (2:59) (Class 1) 2-Y-O **£12,491** (£4,734; £2,369; £1,181; £591) **Stalls** High

Form RPR
0301 **1** **Meeriss (IRE)**[10] 5135 2-9-0 86 .... DarryllHolland 3 98
(M R Channon) *led at stdy pce: rdn over 2f out: narrowly hdd 2f out: led again 1f out: r.o gamely* **15/2**
5221 **2** *nk* **Eastern Gift**[14] 5033 2-9-0 85 .... SteveDrowne 6 97
(R Hannon) *chsd ldrs: swtchd to rail and effrt over 2f out: ev ch 1f out: unable qck last 100yds* **8/1**
021 **3** *½* **Dauberval (IRE)**[20] 4852 2-9-0 89 .... JamieSpencer 2 96
(S Kirk) *chsd ldr: rdn to ld narrowly 2f out: hdd 1f out: no ex last 100yds* **9/2**[3]
114 **4** *¾* **Sporting Art (USA)**[7] 5219 2-9-0 92 .... FergusSweeney 5 94
(G L Moore) *t.k.h: hld up in last pair: effrt and rdn 2f out: kpt on same pce fnl f* **3/1**[2]
1 **5** *1 ½* **Tanweer (USA)**[36] 4362 2-9-0 0 .... MartinDwyer 4 91
(Sir Michael Stoute) *t.k.h: hld up in last pair: drvn and outpcd over 2f out: kpt on ins fnl f: nt pce to trble ldrs* **6/4**[1]

1m 42.58s (2.31) **Going Correction** +0.025s/f (Good) 5 Ran SP% **106.1**
Speed ratings (Par 103): **89,88,88,87,85**
CSF £53.25 TOTE £9.50: £2.30, £2.90; EX 52.40.
Owner Sheikh Ahmed Al Maktoum **Bred** Hugo Lascelles **Trained** West Ilsley, Berks
■ Stewards' Enquiry : Darryll Holland three-day ban: used whip down the shoulder in the forehand position (Sep 26-28)

FOCUS
A decent field, but not form to put too much faith in owing to the modest pace and tactical nature of the race.

NOTEBOOK
Meeriss(IRE) gets this trip well, and is progressing well with racing. Holland was impressed, reporting that he is an adaptable horse with a good attitude and a touch of class, so a step into Group company may follow before long. (op 11-1)
Eastern Gift was not certain to get the mile on breeding, but he had a good crack at it and only gave best in the last half-furlong. It was an excellent effort in this company, and he is improving race by race. (op 9-1)
Dauberval(IRE) had already proved that he gets this trip, having won over course and distance three weeks earlier, and showed he is worth another go at this level. (tchd 4-1)
Sporting Art(USA), upped from 6f, had every chance of getting the mile on breeding. In the end, he was not quite good enough rather than failing to stay. (op 9-4)
Tanweer(USA) fell short of expectations, but would have appreciated a stronger pace. He has big-race entries, and can be given another chance if not aimed too high. Official explanation: jockey said colt ran too free (op 15-8)

5415 GUNCAST POOLS STKS (H'CAP) 1m 4f

3:30 (3:34) (Class 4) (0-85,85) 3-Y-O+ **£7,772** (£2,312; £1,155; £577) **Stalls** High

Form RPR
63-1 **1** **Kahara**[22] 4765 3-8-8 73 ow1 .... JamieSpencer 4 82+
(L M Cumani) *t.k.h early: chsd ldrs tl stdd in midfield 1/2-way: hdwy 3f out: chal u.p & edgd rt wl over 1f out: led ins fnl f: asserted nr fin* **6/5**[1]
0224 **2** *½* **Prince Sabaah (IRE)**[32] 4483 3-9-6 85 .... PatDobbs 5 92
(R Hannon) *chsd ldr tl 7f out: styd handy: rdn and ev ch over 2f out tl unable qck fnl 50yds* **6/1**[2]
2160 **3** *shd* **Bergonzi (IRE)**[80] 2999 3-9-5 84 .... RobertHavlin 7 90
(J H M Gosden) *led at stdy pce tl 7f out: led again over 2f out: sn rdn: hdd ins fnl f: unable qck fnl 50yds* **6/1**[2]
0001 **4** *shd* **Mister Right (IRE)**[8] 5211 6-8-11 72 .... AshleyHamblett(5) 2 78
(D J S Ffrench Davis) *stdd s and s.i.s: hld up in rr: swtchd lft and hdwy on outer 2f out: chal and hung rt ins fnl f: no imp last 50yds* **10/1**[3]
0125 **5** *2* **Venir Rouge**[15] 5014 3-8-8 78 .... HaddenFrost(5) 8 81
(M Salaman) *in tch: outpcd over 3f out: swtchd lft and hdwy 2f out: styd on wl fnl f: nt rch ldrs* **33/1**
-600 **6** *shd* **Nordwind (IRE)**[119] 1844 6-9-13 83 .... DarryllHolland 9 86
(W R Swinburn) *t.k.h: stdd s: hld up in rr: swtchd lft and hdwy over 2f out: hdwy and hanging rt ent fnl f: no hdwy last 100yds* **14/1**
4602 **7** *3* **Penang Cinta**[15] 4994 4-9-3 73 .... SteveDrowne 3 71
(P D Evans) *in tch: rdn and effrt on inner 2f out: wknd over 1f out* **16/1**
1-65 **8** *3* **Height Of Fury (IRE)**[101] 2367 4-9-3 73 .... MartinDwyer 11 66
(J L Dunlop) *stdd s: t.k.h: hld up in rr tl hdwy 8f out: led 7f out tl over 2f out: sn wknd* **16/1**
3035 **9** *shd* **Nawamees (IRE)**[25] 4690 9-9-13 83 ....(p) FergusSweeney 6 76
(G L Moore) *hld up in tch: hdwy 5f out: rdn over 2f out: wknd wl over 1f out* **11/1**
0023 **10** *4* **Ross Moor**[12] 5093 5-8-13 69 oh1 .... DaneO'Neill 10 56
(Mike Murphy) *chsd ldrs: rdn over 2f out: wknd over 1f out* **40/1**
0135 **11** *28* **Inchinata (IRE)**[28] 4617 3-8-12 77 .... ChrisCatlin 1 19
(B W Hills) *in tch tl lost pl 5f out: rdn and lost tch over 3f out: eased fnl f: t.o* **20/1**

2m 38.14s (-0.78) **Going Correction** +0.025s/f (Good)
WFA 3 from 4yo+ 9lb 11 Ran SP% **120.0**
Speed ratings (Par 105): **103,102,102,102,101 101,99,97,97,94 75**
CSF £8.42 CT £33.64 TOTE £2.10: £1.40, £2.40, £2.30; EX 11.60.
Owner Fittocks Stud & Mrs John Magnier **Bred** Fittocks Stud **Trained** Newmarket, Suffolk

FOCUS
A competitive race of a respectable standard, but the favourite was an alarmingly short price for what should have been a competitive handicap. She made hard work of it but remains capable of much better.
Nordwind(IRE) Official explanation: jockey said gelding hung both ways
Height Of Fury(IRE) Official explanation: jockey said gelding ran too free

5416 GUIDO'S 40TH BIRTHDAY STARLIT STKS (LISTED RACE) 6f

4:05 (4:05) (Class 1) 3-Y-O+
£15,898 (£6,025; £3,015; £1,503; £753; £378) **Stalls** Low

Form RPR
0015 **1** **Beckermet (IRE)**[11] 5112 5-9-4 109 .... ChrisCatlin 6 114
(R F Fisher) *mde all: rdn over 2f out: edgd rt but r.o strly fnl f* **12/1**
2131 **2** *1* **Galeota (IRE)**[3] 5325 5-9-4 107 .... PatDobbs 7 111
(R Hannon) *chsd wnr thrght: rdn 2f out: kpt on u.p but a hld fnl f* **9/2**[3]
5000 **3** *1 ¾* **Grantley Adams**[28] 4614 4-9-0 100 .... DarryllHolland 8 102
(M R Channon) *hld up bhd: rdn and outpcd over 2f out: styd on u.p fnl f: wnt 3rd nr fin: nt trble ldrs* **10/1**
0006 **4** *nk* **Areyoutalkingtome**[11] 5112 4-9-0 105 .... SimonWhitworth 5 101
(C A Cyzer) *in tch: hdwy to chse ldng pair over 2f out: sn rdn: outpcd fnl f: lost 3rd nr fin* **16/1**
3-40 **5** *1 ¾* **Pivotal Point**[88] 2733 7-9-0 108 .... LDettori 1 96
(P J Makin) *trckd ldrs: rdn wl over 1f out: wknd jst over 1f out* **5/1**
1013 **6** *2 ½* **Shmookh (USA)**[44] 4093 3-8-12 99 .... MartinDwyer 2 88
(J L Dunlop) *hld up in tch in rr: rdn wl over 1f out: sn btn* **3/1**[2]
010- **7** *hd* **Aeroplane**[336] 5962 4-9-0 105 .... JamieSpencer 4 88
(P W Chapple-Hyam) *w.w in tch: rdn 2f out: wknd over 1f out: eased wl ins fnl f* **2/1**[1]
0600 **8** *9* **Resplendent Alpha**[17] 4950 3-8-12 87 .... SteveDrowne 3 61
(P Howling) *v.s.a: a struggling in last: t.o* **66/1**

69.90 secs (-2.95) **Going Correction** -0.20s/f (Firm)
WFA 3 from 4yo+ 2lb 8 Ran SP% **117.3**
Speed ratings (Par 111): **111,109,107,106,104 101,101,89**
CSF £66.76 TOTE £12.70: £2.60, £1.80, £2.80; EX 34.60.
Owner Great Head House Taylor Nash Edwards **Bred** Fritz Von Ball Moss **Trained** Ulverston, Cumbria

FOCUS
A good-quality sprint in which the winner made all at a decent pace.

NOTEBOOK
Beckermet(IRE) was given an excellent front-running ride, wth Catlin going a decent sprint gallop but judging the pace perfectly and leaving plenty for the final dash. A genuine sort, he is right back to form at present, reminding everyone that he is a smart sprinter at his best. The Diadem Stakes at Ascot is his next target.. (op 11-1)
Galeota(IRE) was making a quick reappearance after his Doncaster win earlier in the week and kept up the excellent work of recent outings as there was no disgrace in being beaten by the back-to-form winner. He is effective from 5f to 7f, so has plenty of options. (op 10-3)
Grantley Adams just about ran his race on official figures, having been forced to run at this level because he is weighted up to his best in handicaps at present. However, he has been running better than his form figures suggest, and is now likely to go back to handicapping in the Ayr Gold Cup.
Areyoutalkingtome is slightly more effective on Polytrack, but again showed he is capable of a decent show on turf, if falling a bit short against some speedy sorts.
Pivotal Point, a high-class sprinter at his best, was still top-rated of these despite being lightly-raced this season. He ran a fair race, but will not be easy to place unless stepping up a bit on this effort. (op 8-1)
Shmookh(USA), stepping up from handicaps, ran very modestly. He is surely capable of better. (tchd 11-4 and 7-2 in places)
Aeroplane went off a very short price considering his two wins were at 7f. He fell well short of expectations, but the weight of money suggests he is worth another chance if returning to the longer trip. Official explanation: jockey said colt was unsuited by the good to firm ground (op 9-4 tchd 5-2 and 11-4 in a place)
Resplendent Alpha Official explanation: jockey said colt missed the break

5417 MARK HUTCHINSON CELEBRATION EUROPEAN BREEDERS' FUND MAIDEN STKS 1m

4:40 (4:40) (Class 4) 2-Y-O **£5,505** (£1,637; £818; £408) **Stalls** High

Form RPR
2 **1** **Emmrooz**[15] 5010 2-9-3 0 .... LDettori 7 92
(Saeed Bin Suroor) *in tch: qcknd to ld 2f out: edgd rt sn after: r.o strly: eased nr fin* **15/8**[2]
2 *¾* **Green Wadi** 2-9-3 0 .... DarryllHolland 5 90
(M R Channon) *stdd s: hld up: stdy hdwy 1/2-way: rdn to chse ldng pair wl over 1f out: kpt on to go 2nd wl ins fnl f:* **12/1**
04 **3** *¾* **Bouguereau**[28] 4625 2-9-3 0 .... JamieSpencer 4 89
(P W Chapple-Hyam) *trckd ldrs: rdn and hdwy on rail over 2f out: sn ev ch: btn whn swtchd lft ins fnl f: lost 2nd towards fin* **11/8**[1]
34 **4** *6* **Strategic Mover (USA)**[15] 5004 2-9-3 0 ....(t) SteveDrowne 3 75
(P F I Cole) *pressed ldr: rdn wl over 2f out: sltly hmpd: edgd rt and bmpd rival wl over 1f out: wl btn after* **7/2**[3]
0 **5** *¾* **Hada Men (USA)**[15] 5011 2-9-3 0 .... DaneO'Neill 2 73
(M P Tregoning) *stdd s: hld up in rr: rdn wl over 2f out: sn outpcd* **50/1**
65 **6** *2 ½* **Al Azy (IRE)**[30] 4547 2-9-3 0 .... MartinDwyer 6 67
(J L Dunlop) *sn led: rdn and hdd 2f out: wkng whn bmpd wl over 1f out: no ch after* **20/1**
000 **7** *3* **Follow The Band**[10] 5126 2-9-3 61 .... RichardSmith 8 60
(R Hannon) *prom tl stdd to rr after 2f: rdn over 2f out: sn wl outpcd* **66/1**
8 *¾* **Cape Colony** 2-9-3 0 .... PatDobbs 1 59
(R Hannon) *hld up in rr: rdn 2f out: sn wl btn* **50/1**

1m 40.71s (0.44) **Going Correction** +0.025s/f (Good) 8 Ran SP% **117.0**
Speed ratings (Par 97): **98,97,96,90,89 87,84,83**
CSF £23.24 TOTE £2.60: £1.30, £1.80, £1.20; EX 22.50.
Owner Godolphin **Bred** Darley **Trained** Newmarket, Suffolk

FOCUS
This looked a decent race of its type, with the first three home all having significant potential. The winner stepped up on a promising debut, and the runner-up looks a ready made winner at this level.

NOTEBOOK
Emmrooz was still a bit green, but stepped up on his first effort to win convincingly enough. Dettori opted for caution afterwards, saying he would leave the horse to do the talking for the time being, but he has entries for the Dewhurst and Racing Post Trophy and is certainly going in the right direction. (op 13-8 tchd 2-1)
Green Wadi ◆, a 70,000gns son of Dansili with winners in the family from 6f to 1m4f, was expected to need the run. In the event, he made a most encouraging debut and this Racing Post Trophy entry should win his maiden before going on to better things. (tchd 11-1)
Bouguereau was unable to justify favouritism, but the two who finished in front of him are probably decent sorts. He is well up to winning a typical maiden, but connections will be hoping he improves enough to make the step back into Listed company at least. (op 13-8 tchd 7-4 and 15-8 in a place)
Strategic Mover(USA) is certainly capable of winning a maiden at least and, though beaten a long way here, can do much better. On the evidence of his previous two efforts, it would be a surprise if he could not find a suitable opportunity. (tchd 9-2)
Hada Men(USA), a $300,000 yearling whose sire Dynaformer stayed 1m2f, is from a good American family up to 1m1f. He stepped up quite a bit on his debut, and nurseries will be available after one more run, so should find some suitable opportunities. (tchd 66-1)

Al Azy(IRE) is entered for the Royal Lodge and Derby, but handicaps look to be his future. (op 25-1)

5418 GOODWOOD RACEHORSE OWNERS GROUP STKS (H'CAP) 5f
5:15 (5:15) (Class 5) (0-75,82) 3-Y-O **£3,238** (£963; £481; £240) **Stalls** Low

Form RPR

2240 **1** **Ocean Blaze**[9] 5160 3-8-10 **67**.. DarryllHolland 7 76
(B R Millman) *led after 1f: mde rest: edgd rt over 1f out: kpt on wl* **10/1**

3263 **2** ½ **Pretty Miss**[13] 5066 3-8-12 **69**.. FergusSweeney 8 76
(H Candy) *hld up in tch: plld out and rdn over 1f out: kpt on u.p: nt quite rch wnr* **11/2**[3]

0311 **3** *nk* **Zahour Al Yasmeen**[2] 5358 3-9-4 **82** 6ex................ MatthewDavies(7) 3 88
(M R Channon) *led for 1f: chsd ldr after: rdn 2f: kpt on same pce: lost 2nd wl ins fnl f* **5/1**[2]

5311 **4** 2½ **Millisecond**[13] 5066 3-9-7 **78**.. MartinDwyer 5 75
(M A Jarvis) *chsd ldrs: rdn over 2f out: no hdwy: wl btn fnl f* **5/4**[1]

4000 **5** ½ **Frisky Talk (IRE)**[10] 5139 3-8-7 **64**.. ChrisCatlin 1 59
(B W Hills) *in tch: rdn 3f out: outpcd over 2f out: plugged on fnl f* **16/1**

5010 **6** ¾ **Drifting Gold**[14] 5029 3-9-4 **75**..(b) LDettori 4 67
(C G Cox) *pressed ldrs: rdn 2f out: wknd jst over 1f out* **11/2**[3]

2416 **7** ¾ **Dualagi**[19] 4896 3-8-12 **69**.. SimonWhitworth 6 59
(J S Moore) *hmpd sn after s: hanging rt thrght and a bhd* **14/1**

57.92 secs (-1.13) **Going Correction** -0.20s/f (Firm) **7** Ran SP% **113.5**
Speed ratings (Par 101): **101,100,99,95,94 93,92**
CSF £61.94 CT £309.21 TOTE £12.10: £3.90, £2.30.

Owner Ocean View Properties International Ltd **Bred** Longdon Stud And Robin Lawson **Trained** Kentisbeare, Devon

FOCUS
Only fillies ended up in this fair-quality handicap following the withdrawal of Double Bill, with the winner making most at a strong pace.

Dualagi Official explanation: jockey said filly suffered interference at the start

5419 PICNIC STKS (H'CAP) 1m 1f
5:45 (5:45) (Class 2) (0-100,96) 3-Y-O+
£12,464 (£3,732; £1,866; £934; £466; £234) **Stalls** High

Form RPR

336 **1** **Escape Route (USA)**[20] 4851 3-8-12 **91**........................ RobertHavlin 9 104+
(J H M Gosden) *chsd ldrs: hdwy on rail over 2f out: rdn to ld wl over 1f out: in command whn edgd lft nr fin* **5/2**[1]

00 **2** 1 **Formax (FR)**[28] 4601 5-8-12 **85**.. PatDobbs 2 96
(M P Tregoning) *stdd and dropped in after s: hld up wl bhd: plld out and gd hdwy jst over 1f out: chsd wnr wl ins fnl f: hld last 50yds* **33/1**

-246 **3** ¾ **Ebert**[15] 5012 4-8-13 **86**..(b[1]) LDettori 6 95
(P J Makin) *s.i.s: hld up in last: hdwy on rail over 3f out: chsd wnr u.p 1f out: no ex and lost 2nd wl ins fnl f* **9/2**[2]

4006 **4** 1½ **Regal Parade**[19] 4900 3-8-10 **89**.. GregFairley 7 95+
(M Johnston) *racd in midfield: rdn over 4f out: lost pl and nt clr run over 2f out: swtchd rt over 1f out: kpt on u.p fnl f: nt trble ldrs* **8/1**

-303 **5** *hd* **Mesbaah (IRE)**[29] 4566 3-9-3 **96**.. MartinDwyer 5 101
(M A Jarvis) *chsd ldrs: rdn and ev ch 2f out: wknd over 1f out* **13/2**

0123 **6** ½ **Ace Of Hearts**[19] 4900 8-9-1 **95**.. JackMitchell(7) 3 99
(C F Wall) *chsd ldrs: hdwy over 3f out: ev ch: rdn and edgd rt wl over 2f out: wknd over 1f out* **5/1**[3]

1023 **7** *hd* **Emerald Wilderness (IRE)**[18] 4922 3-8-13 **92**............ SteveDrowne 4 96+
(E A L Dunlop) *w.w in midfield: effrt whn nt clr run and bmpd 2f out: swtchd lft ins fnl f: kpt on* **8/1**

1006 **8** ½ **Capable Guest (IRE)**[14] 5031 5-9-4 **91**........................(v) ChrisCatlin 10 94
(M R Channon) *hld up towards rr: rdn and n.m.r briefly over 2f out: n.d* **10/1**

3630 **9** 2 **Ransom Captive (USA)**[14] 5047 3-8-10 **89**................(t) DarryllHolland 8 87
(M A Magnusson) *led: rdn over 2f out: hdd wl over 1f out: sn wknd: eased ins fnl f* **25/1**

0554 **10** 9 **Bahar Shumaal (IRE)**[151] 1082 5-9-6 **93**........................ PaulDoe 1 71
(C E Brittain) *pressed ldr: effrt and upsides over 4f out: sn rdn: wknd over 2f out: eased fnl f* **33/1**

1m 54.92s (-1.94) **Going Correction** +0.025s/f (Good)
WFA 3 from 4yo+ 6lb **10** Ran SP% **117.8**
Speed ratings (Par 109): **109,108,107,106,105 105,105,104,103,95**
CSF £101.05 CT £365.23 TOTE £3.80: £1.80, £8.50, £2.00; EX 111.90 Place 6 £1,360.10, Place 5 £388.11..

Owner H R H Princess Haya Of Jordan **Bred** R N Clay & Serengeti Stable **Trained** Newmarket, Suffolk

FOCUS
A decent-quality race, and competitive too.

NOTEBOOK
Escape Route(USA) seems to have put his starting stalls phobia behind him following a spell with horse whisperer Gary Witheford, and should now be capable of showing his full potential. He needed to pick up a penalty here to get a run in the Cambridgeshire, and after winning decisively enough despite idling in front he is now generally favourite for that race at around 8-1 or 10-1. It will be much tougher there obviously, but the longer trip clearly suits him and he remains capable of better than he has shown so far. (op 9-4 tchd 11-4 in places)

Formax(FR) ran by far his best race since arriving from France, and should be able to win a race over this sort of trip. However, he will not start as generous a price again in similar company.

Ebert, blinkered for the first time, continues to run well without winning. He is on a stiffish mark at present, but any leniency would bring him right into it. (op 5-1 tchd 11-2 and 6-1 in places)

Regal Parade looked well suited by the longer trip, running his best race for some time in the process, and may even stay 1m2f. (op 12-1)

Mesbaah(IRE) was trying a longer trip, but his stamina for the extra furlong still needs to convince.

Ace Of Hearts did not have things all his own way, as when winning here at the Glorious meeting, but ran with credit without being good enough. (op 6-1)

Emerald Wilderness(IRE) has had a great season, but this mark looks just beyond him. (tchd 15-2)

Bahar Shumaal(IRE) raced without the tongue tie that had been declared. Official explanation: did not wear declared tongue strap, whch did not affect its performance (tchd 25-1)

T/Plt: £569.40 to a £1 stake. Pool: £87,206.60. 111.80 winning tickets. T/Qpdt: £28.10 to a £1 stake. Pool: £3,736.55. 98.30 winning tickets. SP

5336 KEMPTON (A.W) (R-H)
Saturday, September 15

OFFICIAL GOING: Standard
Wind: Nil

5420 DIGIBET.COM H'CAP 5f (P)
6:20 (6:20) (Class 6) (0-60,60) 3-Y-O **£2,047** (£604; £302) **Stalls** High

Form RPR

0233 **1** **Rosie Cross (IRE)**[9] 5174 3-8-11 **58**........................ PatrickHills(5) 5 67
(Eve Johnson Houghton) *mde all: drvn and styd on wl fnl f: unchal* **5/2**[1]

6340 **2** 2 **Smirfys Gold (IRE)**[26] 4661 3-8-11 **53**....................(v) GrahamGibbons 9 55
(E S McMahon) *chsd wnr most of way: rdn over 2f out and no imp* **5/1**[2]

0002 **3** 1¾ **Stir Crazy (IRE)**[5] 5272 3-9-1 **57**.. TPO'Shea 4 53
(M R Channon) *chsd ldrs: rdn 2f out: kpt on same pce* **5/1**[2]

0606 **4** ½ **Minnow**[19] 4885 3-9-3 **59**..(v[1]) SaleemGolam 8 53
(S C Williams) *s.i.s: bhd: hdwy fr 2f out: kpt on ins fnl f: nvr gng pce to trble ldng trio* **13/2**[3]

0630 **5** ¾ **Inquisitress**[25] 4684 3-8-13 **55**.. FrankieMcDonald 10 46+
(J J Bridger) *in rr: rdn along over 2f out: r.o ins fnl f but nvr in contention* **12/1**

0000 **6** *hd* **Polish Prize**[18] 4919 3-8-11 **53**.. AdamKirby 7 43
(W R Swinburn) *chsd ldrs tl wknd fnl f* **20/1**

000 **7** *shd* **Fast Freddie**[5] 5282 3-8-11 **53**.. MickyFenton 2 43
(D J Murphy) *in rr: rdn over 2f out: mod prog fnl f* **16/1**

5350 **8** *nk* **The Geester**[26] 4661 3-8-10 **52**..(b) PaulEddery 3 41
(S R Bowring) *chsd ldrs: rdn over 2f out: wknd fnl f* **25/1**

-000 **9** ¾ **Vintage (IRE)**[14] 5051 3-9-4 **60**.. StephenDonohoe 11 46
(P Mitchell) *a towards rr* **16/1**

0015 **10** *nk* **Come What May**[82] 2939 3-9-4 **60**..(bt) DaneO'Neill 12 45
(Rae Guest) *a towards rr* **10/1**

2000 **11** 1¼ **Royal Guest**[5] 5275 3-8-12 **54**..(v[1]) SamHitchcott 1 35
(M R Channon) *s.i.s: wd and a outpcd* **14/1**

0546 **12** *shd* **Time Share (IRE)**[1] 5386 3-8-5 **54**..(bt) MCGeran(7) 6 34
(Miss K B Boutflower) *in rr: rdn and hung rt ins fnl 2f: nt run on* **16/1**

60.15 secs (-0.25) **Going Correction** -0.175s/f (Stan) **12** Ran SP% **124.9**
Speed ratings (Par 99): **95,91,89,88,87 86,86,86,84,84 82,82**
CSF £15.15 CT £62.90 TOTE £4.40: £1.50, £2.20, £1.40; EX 26.80.

Owner Club ROA **Bred** Century Farms **Trained** Blewbury, Oxon

FOCUS
A moderate sprint handicap in which the pace held up and the winner scored emphatically.

Polish Prize Official explanation: jockey said colt hung right and did not face the kickback

5421 DIGIBET POKER H'CAP 1m 2f (P)
6:50 (6:51) (Class 6) (0-50,57) 3-Y-O+ **£2,047** (£604; £302) **Stalls** High

Form RPR

0033 **1** **Boz**[19] 4894 3-8-12 **50**.. JamieSpencer 3 67+
(L M Cumani) *chsd ldrs: rdn on outside 2f out: led wl over 1f out: sn clr: eased cl home* **9/4**[1]

0431 **2** 4 **Weet Yer Tern (IRE)**[9] 5179 5-9-8 **53**.. DaneO'Neill 5 58
(W M Brisbourne) *in tch: hdwy 3f out: drvn and styd on to chse wnr ins fnl f but nvr any ch* **9/2**[2]

-605 **3** ½ **Noah Jameel**[30] 4533 5-9-3 **48**.. FergusSweeney 2 52
(A G Newcombe) *in rr: rdn and styd on fnl 2f but nvr gng pce to be competitive* **6/1**[3]

4455 **4** ½ **Magic Amigo**[17] 4945 6-9-4 **49**..(v) MickyFenton 6 52
(J R Jenkins) *rrd stalls: bhd: rdn 3f out: styd on fr over 1f out but nt trble ldrs* **6/1**[3]

4620 **5** *shd* **Missie Baileys**[8] 5187 5-9-3 **48**..(p) IanMongan 12 51
(Mrs L J Mongan) *chsd ldr: chal 5f out to 3f out: wknd fnl f* **10/1**

0-60 **6** ½ **Future Deal**[17] 4945 6-9-3 **48**.. SimonWhitworth 13 50
(C A Horgan) *led: rdn 3f out: hdd wl over 1f out: sn wknd* **33/1**

0050 **7** 1½ **Band**[30] 4532 7-9-5 **50**.. GrahamGibbons 8 49
(E S McMahon) *chsd ldrs: rdn 3f out: wknd appr fnl f* **9/1**

5-46 **8** *nk* **Abbeygate**[33] 4464 6-8-12 **46**.. EmmettStack(3) 9 44
(T Keddy) *in rr: rdn and hung rt ins fnl 2f: mod prog fnl f* **10/1**

0400 **9** 2 **King Of Knight (IRE)**[9] 5179 6-9-2 **47**.. OscarUrbina 10 41
(G Prodromou) *mid-div: rdn over 3f out: nvr in contention* **10/1**

000- **10** ¾ **Vettori Dancer**[457] 2592 4-9-3 **48**.. NeilPollard 7 41
(G G Margarson) *chsd ldrs tl wknd over 2f out* **66/1**

-005 **11** 1½ **Doonigan (IRE)**[30] 4550 3-8-12 **50**.. StephenDonohoe 14 40
(A M Balding) *chsd ldrs tl wknd over 2f out* **22/1**

000 **12** 17 **Ridgeway Star**[178] 720 3-8-12 **50**..(b[1]) RichardThomas 11 6
(R Ingram) *s.i.s: rdn asnd lost tch over 4f out* **40/1**

000- **13** 48 **Twentyfirst Dansar**[485] 1799 4-8-12 **48**.. HaddenFrost(5) 1 —
(A D Smith) *chsd ldrs to 1/2-way: t.o* **40/1**

2m 7.71s (-1.29) **Going Correction** -0.175s/f (Stan)
WFA 3 from 4yo+ 7lb **13** Ran SP% **128.5**
Speed ratings (Par 101): **98,94,94,94,93 93,92,92,90,89 88,75,—**
CSF £12.42 CT £58.88 TOTE £2.60: £1.10, £2.50, £2.50; EX 13.80.

Owner Aston House Stud **Bred** Aston House Stud **Trained** Newmarket, Suffolk

FOCUS
Essentially a banded race and the form is not solid with the form rated around the second and fourth.

Magic Amigo Official explanation: jockey said gelding reared up on leaving stalls

Twentyfirst Dansar Official explanation: trainer said gelding made a noise and never travelled

5422 DIGIBET SPORTS BETTING CLAIMING STKS 1m 3f (P)
7:20 (7:22) (Class 6) 3-Y-O+ **£2,047** (£604; £302) **Stalls** High

Form RPR

5150 **1** **Atlantic Gamble (IRE)**[39] 4249 7-9-4 60....................(p) AndrewElliott(3) 5 68
(K R Burke) *chsd ldr: led appr fnl 2f: drvn out* **16/1**

5012 **2** *hd* **Boot 'n Toot**[8] 5205 6-9-2 79.. PatrickHills(5) 3 67
(C A Cyzer) *in rr: hdwy on outside over 2f out: styd on to chse wnr fnl f: gng on cl home but a hld* **4/5**[1]

004 **3** 1½ **Fantasy Ride**[28] 4610 5-9-6 64.. JamieSpencer 8 64
(J Pearce) *in rr: hdwy on outside over 2f out and hung lft: styd on fnl f but nvr rch ldng duo* **15/2**[3]

0434 **4** 1¾ **Turner's Touch**[18] 4915 5-9-12 68..(b) FergusSweeney 9 67
(G L Moore) *in rr: hdwy over 2f out: styd on fnl f but nvr gng pce to chal* **8/1**

5200 **5** 1½ **Key Partners (IRE)**[35] 4383 6-9-4 56.. TPO'Shea 4 56
(P A Blockley) *in rr: hdwy 5f out: chsd ldrs over 3f out: styd on same pce fnl 2f* **33/1**

0340 **6** ½ **Magic Mountain (IRE)**[7] 5225 3-9-0 66 .... DaneO'Neill 2 59
(R Hannon) *chsd ldrs rdn 3f out: wknd over 1f out* **10/1**

0032 **7** 2 **Hook Money (IRE)**[7] 5235 3-8-1 52 .... (p) RobbieEgan(7) 10 49
(A J McCabe) *in rr: rdn 5f out: mod prog fnl 2f* **40/1**

0500 **8** 1 **Royal Amnesty**[15] 5020 4-9-9 63 .... OscarUrbina 1 55
(G C H Chung) *sn led: hdd appr fnl 2f: wknd over 1f out* **16/1**

0301 **9** 1 ½ **Musango**[18] 4915 4-9-8 68 .... (t) RichardSmith 12 51
(B R Johnson) *chsd ldrs: rdn over 2f out: wknd over 1f out* **11/2**[2]

0000 **10** 2 ½ **Compton Express**[6] 5001 4-8-10 43 .... (b[1]) SimonWhitworth 11 34
(Jamie Poulton) *chsd ldrs 7f* **66/1**

0444 **11** 18 **Hot Property (IRE)**[45] 4073 3-9-0 56 .... SaleemGolam 7 14
(W R Muir) *a in rr: wl bhd fnl 3f* **20/1**

2m 20.53s (-2.15) **Going Correction** -0.175s/f (Stan)
WFA 3 from 4yo+ 8lb 11 Ran SP% **126.3**
Speed ratings (Par 101): **100,99,98,97,96 96,94,93,92,90 77**
CSF £30.84 TOTE £22.10: £5.40, £1.10, £2.40; EX 67.60.
Owner R G Greaney **Bred** Larry Ryan **Trained** Middleham Moor, N Yorks

FOCUS
A reasonable claimer.
Musango Official explanation: trainer said gelding made a noise
Hot Property(IRE) Official explanation: jockey said gelding hung left

5423 DIGIBET NURSERY 1m (P)
7:50 (7:54) (Class 6) (0-65,68) 2-Y-O £2,047 (£604; £302) **Stalls** High

Form RPR

0204 **1** **Bridge Of Fermoy (IRE)**[11] 5117 2-9-3 61 .... (t) MickyFenton 6 64
(Miss Gay Kelleway) *chsd ldrs: wnt 2nd over 3f out: led over 2f out: styd on wl u.p fnl f: in command cl home* **10/1**

0000 **2** 1 **I Certainly May**[10] 5127 2-9-4 62 .... DaneO'Neill 10 63
(S Dow) *drvn to chse ldrs: outpcd over 3f out: styd on again fr 2f out: kpt on u.p to take 2nd last stride but no imp on wnr* **20/1**

0005 **3** shd **Danamight (IRE)**[10] 5127 2-9-2 65 .... NeilBrown(5) 3 66
(G G Margarson) *in rr: hdwy on outside 3f out: styd on u.p to chse wnr insde fnl f: no imp and ct for 2nd last stride* **14/1**

0601 **4** nk **Ambrose Princess (IRE)**[19] 4897 2-8-13 57 .... LPKeniry 2 57
(J S Moore) *in rr: hdwy 3f out: drvn and qcknd to press ldrs ins fnl 2f: kpt on same pce ins fnl f* **12/1**

3604 **5** ½ **King Bathwick (IRE)**[15] 5002 2-9-4 62 .... ChrisCatlin 1 61
(B R Millman) *in rr: hdwy on ins whn hmpd over 1f out: kpt on again ins fnl f but nvr gng pce to press ldrs* **8/1**[3]

0405 **6** nk **Elusive Deal (USA)**[9] 5153 2-8-13 60 .... JamieMoriarty(3) 11 58
(R A Fahey) *in rr: hrd drvn over 2f out: styd on fr over 1f out: gng on ins fnl f but nt rch ldrs* **9/1**

500 **7** 1 ¾ **Sarah Park (IRE)**[63] 3550 2-9-0 58 .... StephenDonohoe 8 52
(B J Meehan) *in rr and rdn 4f out: styd on fnl 2f but nt rch ldrs* **20/1**

056 **8** shd **Ras Laffan**[22] 4784 2-9-6 64 .... GrahamGibbons 5 58
(E S McMahon) *in tch: rdn and effrt 3f out: outpcd 2f out: kpt on again ins fnl f* **16/1**

3001 **9** ½ **King Supreme (IRE)**[10] 5127 2-9-10 68 .... SteveDrowne 14 61
(R Hannon) *led 1f: styd chsng ldrs: one pce whn hmpd ins fnl 2f* **2/1**[1]

634 **10** 1 **Heavenly Saint**[16] 4968 2-9-4 62 .... DarryllHolland 4 53
(M R Channon) *in tch: hdwy 4f out: chsd ldrs 3f out: wknd over 1f out* **8/1**[3]

5600 **11** 2 **Harlequinn Danseur (IRE)**[7] 5227 2-9-2 60 .... (t) IanMongan 13 46
(N Tinkler) *chsd ldrs tl wknd fr 2f out* **20/1**

000 **12** 2 **Anabaa's Secret (IRE)**[57] 3712 2-9-2 60 .... JamieSpencer 9 41
(J A Osborne) *in tch: rdn: n.m.r and wknd ins fnl 3f* **5/1**[2]

4006 **13** 5 **Blandys Wood**[5] 5268 2-9-2 60 .... (v[1]) TPO'Shea 12 30
(M R Channon) *led after 1f: hdd over 3f out: wknd and hmpd sn after* **16/1**

0056 **14** 1 ¾ **Frammenti**[34] 4428 2-8-7 58 .... (p) RobbieEgan(7) 7 24
(A J McCabe) *a outpcd* **66/1**

1m 40.76s (-0.04) **Going Correction** -0.175s/f (Stan) 14 Ran SP% **133.2**
Speed ratings (Par 93): **93,92,91,91,91 90,89,88,88,87 85,83,78,76**
CSF £212.58 CT £2909.04 TOTE £12.90: £2.70, £7.70, £5.70; EX 473.90.
Owner T & Z Racing Club **Bred** Tally-Ho Stud **Trained** Exning, Suffolk

FOCUS
A modest nursery and the usual strong pace made this a real test. The form is modest but solid.

NOTEBOOK
Bridge Of Fermoy(IRE), beaten in a seller earlier in the season, had looked an improved performer on softer ground in a hot nursery two runs ago, so the surface was a concern. However, under a more positive ride over a furlong further, he came good in game fashion. He has a bit of scope and could win again. (op 14-1)
I Certainly May was scrubbed along after a slow start to get a midfield position before staying on for an improved effort, having failed to trouble the judge previously. He looks like taking after his dam, who won over 1m4f. (op 33-1)
Danamight(IRE) ◆ was rushed up widest out around the home bend to look a danger into the final furlong but, not surprisingly, her run flattened out. She is looking an improved performer on Polytrack and, a strapping filly, she can continue to progress. (tchd 16-1)
Ambrose Princess(IRE) found this tougher than the seller she won on her previous start. (op 8-1)
King Bathwick(IRE), making his Polytrack debut, was doing his best work late on and he looks a stayer in the making. (op 10-1)
Elusive Deal(USA) was the one to keep on out of the pack in the straight. This was a fair sighter of the All-Weather and she can build on the form. (op 7-1)
King Supreme(IRE) managed to win a similar event over course and distance on his previous start, but he was never really going this time, failing to defy a 5lb rise. Official explanation: jockey said colt never travelled (op 10-3)
Anabaa's Secret(IRE) Official explanation: jockey said gelding had no more to give

5424 DIGIBET SPORTS BETTING H'CAP 1m (P)
8:20 (8:22) (Class 5) (0-70,69) 3-Y-O+ £2,914 (£867; £433; £216) **Stalls** High

Form RPR

-430 **1** **Desert Island Miss**[20] 4860 4-8-12 60 .... AdamKirby 5 71
(W R Swinburn) *in tch: chsd ldrs 3f out: drvn to ld ins fnl 2f: drvn out fnl f* **8/1**

4364 **2** 1 ¾ **Trifti**[12] 5093 6-8-12 65 .... PatrickHills(5) 9 72
(C A Cyzer) *in rr: hdwy 3f out: styd on fnl f to go 2nd cl home but a readily hld by wnr* **8/1**

1221 **3** 1 ¾ **Samuel Charles**[15] 5020 9-9-4 69 .... (p) LiamJones(3) 10 73
(C R Dore) *pressed ldr tl slt ld over 3f out: sn rdn: hdd ins fnl 2f: outpcd ins fnl f: eased last strides and jst hld on for 3rd* **9/2**[2]

1160 **4** shd **Silca Key**[28] 4615 3-8-13 66 .... TPO'Shea 6 68+
(M R Channon) *s.i.s: in rr: rdn 3f out: styd on fr over 1f out: fin wl: gng on cl home* **12/1**

1145 **5** 1 **Azreme**[52] 3855 7-8-9 57 .... AmirQuinn 1 57
(P Howling) *mid-div: rdn 3f out: styd on fnl 2f but nvr in contention* **10/1**

2316 **6** 1 ¼ **Princely Ted (IRE)**[15] 5000 6-8-10 58 .... (v) GrahamGibbons 11 55
(D Burchell) *led tl hdd over 3f out: styd pressing ldr to 2f out: wknd fnl f* **8/1**

4160 **7** hd **Copper King**[19] 4880 3-9-1 68 .... (p) JamesDoyle 12 65
(J W Hills) *in tch: hdwy 3f out: drvn to chse ldrs over 2f out: wknd fnl f* **20/1**

0-02 **8** 1 ¾ **Dance Spirit (IRE)**[9] 5177 4-9-1 63 .... SaleemGolam 3 56
(W R Muir) *chsd ldrs: rdn 3f out: wknd appr fnl f* **7/1**[3]

0600 **9** ½ **Seneschal**[19] 4879 6-9-5 67 .... SamHitchcott 4 58
(A B Haynes) *in rr: rdn over 3f out: sme prog fnl f* **25/1**

000 **10** 2 ½ **Putra Laju (IRE)**[16] 4960 3-9-0 67 .... DarryllHolland 13 53
(J W Hills) *mid-div: hdwy over 3f out: chsd ldrs 2f out: sn wknd* **25/1**

-504 **11** 3 ½ **Pirouetting**[21] 4828 4-9-6 68 .... JamieSpencer 8 46
(B W Hills) *in rr: rdn and sme prog on outside over 2f out: nvr gng pce to be competitive* **3/1**[1]

2000 **12** 2 **Cavort (IRE)**[21] 4828 3-9-1 68 .... DaneO'Neill 2 41
(Pat Eddery) *s.i.s: a towards rr* **20/1**

6364 **13** nk **Haasem (USA)**[24] 4707 4-9-6 68 .... MickyFenton 14 40
(J R Jenkins) *chsd ldrs over 5f* **16/1**

000 **14** 16 **Trickle (USA)**[7] 5238 3-8-9 62 .... PaulEddery 7 —
(Miss D Mountain) *slowly away: a in rr* **66/1**

1m 38.12s (-2.68) **Going Correction** -0.175s/f (Stan)
WFA 3 from 4yo+ 5lb 14 Ran SP% **130.4**
Speed ratings (Par 103): **106,104,102,102,101 100,99,98,97,95 91,89,89,73**
CSF £71.98 CT £337.57 TOTE £11.20: £4.00, £3.30, £1.70; EX 100.70.
Owner Kempton Park Punters' Club **Bred** Pendley Farm **Trained** Aldbury, Herts

FOCUS
An ordinary handicap but sound enough form for the grade.
Pirouetting Official explanation: jockey said filly never travelled

5425 DIGIBET CASINO H'CAP 6f (P)
8:50 (8:53) (Class 6) (0-50,58) 3-Y-O+ £2,047 (£604; £302) **Stalls** High

Form RPR

3244 **1** **Willofcourse**[12] 5090 6-8-9 48 .... AmyScott(7) 8 61
(H Candy) *trckd ldrs: led appr fnl 2f: pushed clr fnl f* **7/2**[2]

0002 **2** 2 ½ **Kindallachan**[9] 5175 4-9-8 54 .... DarryllHolland 2 59
(G C Bravery) *chsd ldrs: hrd rdn and styd on to chse wnr fnl f but no ch* **20/1**

6022 **3** 1 **Master Malarkey**[20] 4857 4-9-4 50 .... (b) ChrisCatlin 11 52
(Mrs C A Dunnett) *led tl hdd appr fnl f 2f: outpcd fnl f* **8/1**

05 **4** ½ **Silver Hotspur**[85] 2837 3-9-2 50 .... OscarUrbina 5 50
(M Wigham) *hld up in mid-div: rdn and kpt on fr over 1f out: nvr rchd ldrs* **3/1**[1]

6060 **5** ¾ **Supreme Kiss**[52] 3853 4-8-11 50 .... (p) SophieDoyle(7) 9 48
(Mrs N Smith) *in rr: hrd drvn fr 2f out: kpt on ins fnl f but nvr in contention* **20/1**

0166 **6** ½ **Double Valentine**[3] 5336 4-8-9 48 .... HarryPoulton(7) 10 44
(R Ingram) *in rr: rdn and hdwy over 2f out: nt rch ldrs and wknd fnl f* **9/1**

01 **7** 1 ½ **Trinculo (IRE)**[8] 5190 10-9-7 58 .... (b) HaddenFrost(5) 3 49
(R A Harris) *chsd ldrs: rdn over 2f out: wknd fnl f* **9/2**[3]

0-60 **8** 2 ½ **Silver Appraisal**[28] 4606 3-9-2 50 .... PaulEddery 1 33
(Pat Eddery) *s.i.s: sn rdn: a outpcd* **12/1**

-000 **9** 1 ¼ **Marker**[31] 4505 7-9-3 49 .... (p) NelsonDeSouza 6 28
(J D Frost) *nvr gng pce to be competitive* **12/1**

0-00 **10** 5 **Clearing Sky (IRE)**[28] 4606 6-9-4 50 .... JamieSpencer 4 13
(J R Boyle) *chsd ldrs over 3f* **7/1**

/04- **11** 10 **Pix**[612] 83 4-9-3 49 .... GrahamGibbons 12 —
(Michael McElhone, Ire) *a bhd* **33/1**

1m 12.73s (-0.97) **Going Correction** -0.175s/f (Stan)
WFA 3 from 4yo+ 2lb 11 Ran SP% **126.9**
Speed ratings (Par 101): **99,95,94,93,92 92,90,86,85,78 71**
CSF £79.54 CT £562.21 TOTE £5.50: £1.70, £4.10, £2.20; EX 77.50.
Owner Henry Candy **Bred** H Candy & R S A Urquhart **Trained** Kingston Warren, Oxon

FOCUS
There was a strong pace to sort out this moderate bunch with maidens dominating the finish.

5426 DIGIBET H'CAP 2m (P)
9:20 (9:20) (Class 6) (0-60,65) 3-Y-O+ £2,047 (£604; £302) **Stalls** High

Form RPR

4203 **1** **Featherlight**[11] 5120 3-8-11 56 .... (b) RobertHavlin 12 69+
(Jamie Poulton) *hld up in mid-div: hdwy on bit 3f out: nt clr run over 2f out: drvn and qcknd to ld appr fnl f: rdn out* **12/1**

0004 **2** 1 ¾ **Composing (IRE)**[21] 4809 3-8-11 56 .... (t) SteveDrowne 3 63
(H Morrison) *chsd ldrs: led over 2f out: sn rdn: hdd appr fnl f: styd on same pce* **4/1**[2]

0031 **3** 1 ½ **Critical Stage (IRE)**[8] 5204 8-10-0 65 .... HaddenFrost(5) 10 70
(J D Frost) *in tch: hdwy 3f out: drvn to chse ldr 2f out: no imp and one pce fnl f* **3/1**[1]

5060 **4** 2 **Arabian Sun**[37] 4322 3-9-1 60 .... ChrisCatlin 14 63
(M J Attwater) *mid-div: hrd drvn and hdwy over 2f out: styd on fnl f but nvr in contention* **66/1**

60-2 **5** 1 ¾ **Living On A Prayer**[32] 4475 4-9-4 50 .... JamieSpencer 8 51
(Michael McElhone, Ire) *in rr: rdn 3f out: styd on fr over 1f out: nvr gng pce to be competitive* **4/1**[2]

0265 **6** 2 ½ **Madiba**[33] 4463 8-9-7 53 .... IanMongan 1 51
(P Howling) *chsd ldrs: wnt 2nd 7f out: rdn 3f out: wknd fr 2f out* **16/1**

6-03 **7** 2 **Golden Folly**[31] 4491 3-8-3 51 .... AndrewElliott(3) 11 46
(Lady Herries) *towards rr: hdwy 4f out: chsd ldrs and rdn over 2f out: sn wknd* **16/1**

6000 **8** 1 ¼ **Mystical Moon**[11] 5120 3-8-13 58 .... (b) DarryllHolland 6 52
(Lady Herries) *led 10f out: hdd over 2f out and sn wknd* **12/1**

06/0 **9** 12 **Revelino (IRE)**[146] 623 8-10-0 60 .... StephenDonohoe 4 39
(Mrs N S Evans) *a towards rr* **50/1**

0-06 **10** 2 **Explosive Fox (IRE)**[24] 3598 6-9-3 49 .... (p) PaulDoe 13 26
(S Curran) *nvr bttr than mid-div* **25/1**

-254 **11** shd **Mcqueen (IRE)**[6] 5257 7-9-8 59 .... RussellKennemore(5) 2 36
(J T Stimpson) *led 6f: wknd 4f out* **12/1**

0653 **12** nk **Magnum Opus (IRE)**[5] 5273 5-9-11 57 .... (t) GrahamGibbons 7 33
(D J Murphy) *chsd ldrs: rdn 4f out: wknd 3f out* **33/1**

3556 **13** 6 **Bob's Your Uncle**[15] 5007 4-9-13 59 .... JamesDoyle 5 28
(J G Portman) *a in rr* **7/1**[3]

3m 28.25s (-3.15) **Going Correction** -0.175s/f (Stan)
WFA 3 from 4yo+ 13lb 13 Ran SP% **122.6**
Speed ratings (Par 101): **100,99,98,97,96 95,94,93,87,86 86,86,83**
CSF £59.82 CT £188.51 TOTE £10.80: £2.20, £1.90, £2.10; EX 76.10 Place 6 £240.08, Place 5 £162.13..
Owner Jirena Partnership **Bred** Keith Wills **Trained** Whitcombe, Dorset

FOCUS
A modest handicap but there was a decent pace and the form looks sound rated through the third.
Living On A Prayer Official explanation: jockey said filly was unsuited by the trip
Bob's Your Uncle Official explanation: jockey said gelding never travelled
T/Plt: £239.80 to a £1 stake. Pool: £70,299.75. 214.00 winning tickets. T/Qpdt: £100.50 to a £1 stake. Pool: £4,266.20. 31.40 winning tickets. ST

5167 WARWICK (L-H)

Saturday, September 15

OFFICIAL GOING: Good to firm (firm in places; 8.7)
Wind: Nil Weather: Sunny

5427 BETTERBET.COM CLAIMING STKS — 1m 4f 134y
2:00 (2:00) (Class 5) 3-Y-0+ **£3,562** (£1,059; £529; £264) **Stalls** Low

Form RPR
5443 **1** **Salute (IRE)**[32] 4483 8-9-13 82 TedDurcan 3 59
(P G Murphy) *hld up in tch: rdn over 2f out: edgd rt over 1f out: led ent fnl f: drvn out* **1/2**[1]
0503 **2** *nk* **My Legal Eagle (IRE)**[8] 5187 13-8-12 50 TolleyDean(5) 2 49
(E G Bevan) *hld up in mid-div: rdn 3f out: hdwy on ins over 1f out: ev ch ins fnl f: kpt on* **17/2**[3]
0230 **3** *1* **Black Mogul**[17] 4943 3-9-0 50 (b) SamHitchcott 10 54
(W R Muir) *a.p: rdn over 2f out: led over 1f out tl ent fnl f: nt qckn* **25/1**
600- **4** *¾* **Trackattack**[11] 3592 5-8-12 42 (p) NeilChalmers(3) 12 44
(M Appleby) *led: rdn over 2f out: hdd over 1f out: one pce fnl f* **100/1**
0025 **5** *¾* **Joy In The Guild (IRE)**[78] 3047 4-9-0 50 LPKeniry 1 42
(W S Kittow) *hld up in mid-div: swtchd rt over 2f out: rdn and hdwy on outside over 1f out: one pce fnl f* **15/2**[2]
00/6 **6** *1 ½* **Perfect Storm**[8] 5187 8-9-1 65 JackDean(7) 6 48
(W G M Turner) *hld up towards rr: hdwy 4f out: rdn and one pce fnl 2f* **10/1**
0633 **7** *3* **Flashing Floozie**[7] 5235 4-8-4 48 MarkCoumbe(7) 7 32
(A W Carroll) *chsd ldr: rdn and ev ch 2f out: wknd fnl f* **18/1**
0600 **8** *7* **Chapter (IRE)**[17] 4945 5-9-5 45 (p) AmirQuinn 4 29
(Mrs A L M King) *s.i.s: nvr nr ldrs* **25/1**
9 *2 ½* **Bythehokey (IRE)**[105] 2637 6-9-2 45 MarcHalford(3) 8 25
(W M Brisbourne) *n.m.r over 3f out: a bhd* **28/1**
0-00 **10** *6* **Young Valentino**[6] 181 5-8-12 34 RussellKennemore(5) 11 13
(M Appleby) *s.i.s: sn hld up in mid-div: rdn over 3f out: sn bhd* **150/1**
0030 **11** *2* **Padre Nostro (IRE)**[14] 3901 8-9-4 44 (t) VinceSlattery 5 11
(M Sheppard) *a bhd* **33/1**
0 **12** *45* **Crescentia**[34] 4430 4-8-11 0 LiamJones(3) 9 —
(Jane Chapple-Hyam) *s.i.s: a in rr: t.o fnl 6f* **40/1**

2m 44.86s (1.26) **Going Correction** +0.05s/f (Good)
WFA 3 from 4yo+ 10lb **12** Ran SP% **121.5**
Speed ratings (Par 103): **98,97,97,96,96 95,93,89,87,83 82,55**
CSF £5.17 TOTE £1.60: £1.02, £2.60, £6.20; EX 7.80.
Owner The Golden Anorak Partnership **Bred** Ahmed M Foustok **Trained** East Garston, Berks

FOCUS
This weak claimer looked a golden opportunity for Salute to return to winning ways, being miles clear on the ratings, but he made mightily hard work of it. The form looks dubious given the proximity of the fourth, although the placed horses were close to form.

5428 BET WITH BETTER ON 08000 89 88 87 MAIDEN STKS — 6f
2:30 (2:33) (Class 5) 2-Y-0 **£4,533** (£1,348; £674; £336) **Stalls** Centre

Form RPR
1 **Hurricane Hymnbook (USA)** 2-9-3 0 NickyMackay 8 78
(B J Meehan) *hld up in mid-div: rdn and hdwy over 1f out: r.o to ld last strides* **16/1**[2]
305 **2** *nk* **Pha Mai Blue**[30] 4539 2-9-3 77 LPKeniry 5 77
(W J Knight) *led: hrd rdn fnl f: edgd lft and ct last strides* **7/2**[1]
05 **3** *¾* **Red Amaryllis**[11] 5110 2-8-12 0 RichardKingscote 9 70
(H J L Dunlop) *chsd ldr: rdn over 1f out: kpt on ins fnl f* **16/1**[2]
30 **4** *1 ¼* **Park Royal (UAE)**[24] 4725 2-8-12 0 J-PGuillambert 14 66
(M Johnston) *chsd ldrs: rdn over 2f out: kpt on ins fnl f* **7/2**[1]
56 **5** *nk* **Moral Duty (USA)**[33] 4454 2-9-3 0 PaulEddery 3 70
(Pat Eddery) *hld up in tch: rdn over 2f out: one pce fnl f* **7/2**[1]
04 **6** *nk* **Tense (IRE)**[8] 5201 2-8-5 0 RobbieEgan(7) 11 64
(J A Osborne) *hld up in mid-div: rdn 2f out: kpt on towards fin* **18/1**[3]
7 *shd* **Counterclaim** 2-8-12 0 TedDurcan 4 64+
(Saeed Bin Suroor) *s.i.s: bhd: sme hdwy on ins whn swtchd rt over 1f out: nvr nrr: should improve* **7/2**[1]
8 *shd* **Carole Os (IRE)** 2-8-5 0 JCorrigan(7) 6 64
(S W Hall) *s.s: hdwy on ins 2f out: sn rdn: one pce fnl f* **100/1**
06 **9** *¾* **Minwir (IRE)**[20] 4854 2-9-3 0 MatthewHenry 16 66
(M A Jarvis) *prom: rdn over 1f out: wknd ins fnl f* **16/1**[2]
0 **10** *¾* **Ogre (USA)**[14] 5042 2-8-12 0 DavidKinsella 12 59
(J A Osborne) *hld up in mid-div: hdwy over 2f out: rdn and wkng whn edgd lft over 1f out* **20/1**
11 *½* **Santa Clara** 2-8-9 0 LiamJones(3) 10 58
(Jane Chapple-Hyam) *dwlt and wnt rt s: hdwy on outside over 2f out: c wd st: rdn over 1f out: wknd fnl f* **25/1**
05 **12** *nk* **Rampant Ronnie (USA)**[17] 4947 2-9-3 0 RichardThomas 2 62
(P W D'Arcy) *prom: rdn over 2f out: sn wknd* **33/1**
000 **13** *5* **Wynberg (IRE)**[38] 4285 2-8-10 0 BradleyRoper(7) 15 47
(N A Callaghan) *s.i.s: a bhd* **100/1**
0 **14** *3 ½* **Daggerman**[19] 4882 2-9-3 0 FrankieMcDonald 13 36
(P A Blockley) *a towards rr* **80/1**
0 **15** *½* **Faraami (IRE)**[8] 5201 2-8-12 0 SamHitchcott 1 30
(Pat Eddery) *sn outpcd* **40/1**
16 *2* **Emir Bagatelle** 2-9-3 0 DaleGibson 17 29
(H Morrison) *s.i.s and wnt rt: a in rr* **50/1**

1m 11.22s (-3.06) **Going Correction** +0.05s/f (Good) 2y crse rec **16** Ran SP% **131.0**
Speed ratings (Par 95): **95,94,93,91,91 91,91,90,89,88 88,87,81,76,75 73**
CSF £73.37 TOTE £21.50: £5.80, £1.50, £4.80; EX 214.50.
Owner Bill Hinge & John Searchfield **Bred** Respite Farm Inc **Trained** Manton, Wilts

FOCUS
Not a bad maiden rated around the principals to pre-race marks and it should produce the odd winner.

NOTEBOOK
Hurricane Hymnbook(USA), a costly American-bred, comes from a yard whose juveniles often need a run, but he overcame inexperience to get up close home and deny Pha Mai Blue. This was a fair effort first time up and, although he holds no big-race entries, there is going to be more to come as he steps up in distance.
Pha Mai Blue, a disappointment on easy ground at Salisbury last time, was down to 6f for the first time and the son of leading first-season sire Acclamation looked to have it won until Hurricane Hymnbook really got motoring. A sound surface is clearly key to him and he will find a race before long. (op 6-1)
Red Amaryllis showed bright early speed and kept on well under pressure, but gives the impression she is going to remain vulnerable to improvers in maidens. She is now qualified for nurseries and should fare better in that sphere. (op 14-1)
Park Royal(UAE), who ran as though something was amiss when last of 13 at York last time, had shaped most promisingly over 7f on debut at Goodwood and, although running better here, she gave the impression a return to the longer distance would help. (op 5-1 tchd 10-3)
Moral Duty(USA) ran his best race to date, keeping on late to claim fifth, but he is now qualified for handicaps and can be expected to do better in that sphere, with a step up to 7f likely to suit. (op 5-1)
Tense(IRE) has improved a little with each run and the way she kept on here implied that a step up to 7f will suit in nurseries. (op 16-1)
Counterclaim, a 250,000gns daughter of Pivotal, lost her race coming out of the stalls, being slowly away and failing to obtain a good position. The race was all over by the time she got going, but she is going to benefit from the combination of an extra furlong on slower ground and should find an ordinary maiden. Official explanation: jockey said filly had run green (op 11-4)
Santa Clara Official explanation: jockey said filly had run freely to post

5429 WATCH GOODWOOD LIVE AT BETTER MAIDEN AUCTION STKS — 5f
3:05 (3:05) (Class 5) 2-Y-0 **£3,562** (£1,059; £529; £264) **Stalls** Centre

Form RPR
1 **Ocean Glory (IRE)** 2-8-10 0 LPKeniry 2 68
(Peter Grayson) *hld up in tch: rdn to ld over 1f out: drvn out* **12/1**
0630 **2** *1 ¼* **Ever Hopeful**[12] 5097 2-8-7 64 TedDurcan 4 60
(H J L Dunlop) *t.k.h: w ldr: rdn and ev ch over 1f out: kpt on same pce fnl f* **5/1**[3]
3266 **3** *nk* **Ben**[15] 5008 2-8-10 74 DavidKinsella 7 62
(P G Murphy) *a.p: rdn and ev ch over 1f out: nt qckn ins fnl f* **11/10**[1]
0 **4** *½* **Cherished Song**[13] 5065 2-8-1 0 KirstyMilczarek(7) 3 58
(N A Callaghan) *led: rdn and hdd over 1f out: one pce fnl f* **25/1**
4 **5** *nk* **Wiseman's Diamond (USA)**[9] 5176 2-8-1 0 AndrewMullen(3) 6 53
(K A Ryan) *s.i.s: hld up: effrt on outside over 2f out: rdn over 1f out: one pce* **9/4**[2]
000 **6** *2 ½* **Eastbourne**[16] 4962 2-8-12 55 (b[1]) IanMongan 5 52
(Eve Johnson Houghton) *t.k.h in tch: rdn over 1f out: no rspnse* **16/1**

60.65 secs (1.25) **Going Correction** +0.05s/f (Good) **6** Ran SP% **112.5**
Speed ratings (Par 95): **92,90,89,88,88 84**
CSF £68.61 TOTE £13.60: £5.20, £3.10; EX 158.30.
Owner Lloyd Partnership **Bred** Tally-Ho Stud **Trained** Formby, Lancs

FOCUS
A weak maiden and the time was modest and the form is limited by the runner-up with the sixth not beaten far.

NOTEBOOK
Ocean Glory(IRE), a gelded son of Redback, was making his debut in only a moderate maiden and he proved good enough to run out a ready winner. He had reportedly been working well at home and showed a bright change of speed to win going away. It will be interesting to see what mark he gets for handicaps. (op 16-1)
Ever Hopeful could be given a chance on last month's Bath third, but she ran poorly over 6f at Wolverhampton last time and lacked the pace of the winner. It may take a drop in grade for her to get off the mark. (op 9-2 tchd 4-1)
Ben looks to have missed the boat as far as maidens go, having numerous close misses earlier in the season, and he again fell short. He is not progressing. (op 11-8)
Cherished Song improved on her initial effort, showing plenty of early speed and only being brushed aside in the final furlong. She is likely to continue to fall short in maidens, but could be of interest once qualified for nurseries. (op 16-1)
Wiseman's Diamond(USA) was the disappointment of the race, failing to really improve on her initial effort and again looking to find this an inadequate test of stamina. The step up to 6f is going to suit and she could be worth another chance. (tchd 5-2)
Eastbourne Official explanation: jockey said colt had run too freely

5430 WATCH GOODWOOD 4.05 LIVE AT BETTER H'CAP — 5f
3:40 (3:41) (Class 5) (0-70,70) 3-Y-0+ **£3,886** (£1,156; £577; £288) **Stalls** Centre

Form RPR
0063 **1** **Dancing Mystery**[9] 5160 13-8-6 **57** ow1 (b) LPKeniry 1 68
(E A Wheeler) *mde all: rdn and hung rt to stands' rail fr over 1f out: drvn out* **7/1**
5000 **2** *¾* **Calabaza**[38] 4296 5-7-12 **56** oh5 (p) KirstyMilczarek(7) 9 65
(J Akehurst) *hld up in mid-div: rdn and hdwy over 1f out: kpt on ins fnl f* **12/1**
6342 **3** *1* **Princess Ellis**[17] 4935 3-8-6 **58** DaleGibson 5 63
(E J Alston) *s.i.s: sn prom: chsd wnr over 2f out: rdn and hung lft over 1f out: nt qckn ins fnl f* **9/2**[3]
0146 **4** *½* **Arfinnit (IRE)**[3] 5340 6-8-6 **57** oh1 ow1 (b) RichardKingscote 3 60
(Mrs A L M King) *chsd ldrs: rdn 2f out: one pce fnl f* **8/1**
1256 **5** *2* **Roman Quintet (IRE)**[9] 5160 7-8-9 **65** RussellKennemore(5) 6 61
(R J Price) *s.i.s: hld up and bhd: rdn 2f out: sme hdwy over 1f out: nvr trbld ldrs* **3/1**[1]
000 **6** *½* **Coseadrom (IRE)**[21] 4800 5-9-0 **70** KevinGhunowa(5) 7 64
(M F Harris) *bhd: rdn and hung lft jst over 1f out: no real prog* **6/1**
100 **7** *3* **King Egbert (FR)**[2] 5349 6-8-5 **56** oh3 NickyMackay 2 39
(R J Price) *s.i.s: hld up: rdn over 2f out: no rspnse* **10/3**[2]
0-00 **8** *1 ¾* **Diamond Josh**[16] 4973 5-8-2 **56** oh11 LiamJones(3) 4 33
(M Mullineaux) *chsd wnr over 2f: sn rdn and wknd* **40/1**
-000 **9** *4* **Lindbergh**[26] 4664 5-9-4 **69** DavidKinsella 8 32
(A J Lidderdale) *outpcd* **25/1**

58.59 secs (-0.81) **Going Correction** +0.05s/f (Good)
WFA 3 from 5yo+ 1lb **9** Ran SP% **118.1**
Speed ratings (Par 103): **108,106,105,104,101 100,95,92,86**
CSF £88.49 CT £426.05 TOTE £7.00: £2.50, £3.10, £1.40; EX 110.00.
Owner Astrod TA Austin Stroud & Co **Bred** Mrs D Price **Trained** Whitchurch-on-Thames, Oxon

FOCUS
A moderate handicap sprint with the winner up slightly on recent form, but the runner-up putting some poor form behind him.
Roman Quintet(IRE) Official explanation: jockey said gelding anticipated start and hit the gates

5431 WATCH CHESTER 4.30 LIVE AT BETTER H'CAP — 1m 22y
4:15 (4:15) (Class 2) (0-100,99) 3-Y-0 **£12,464** (£3,732; £1,866; £934) **Stalls** Low

Form RPR
6112 **1** **Ragheed (USA)**[19] 4900 3-8-10 **94** LiamJones(3) 6 105+
(W J Haggas) *mde all: rdn over 1f out: r.o wl* **13/8**[1]
0514 **2** *2* **Guacamole**[28] 4608 3-8-4 **85** oh1 DaleGibson 1 90
(B W Hills) *a.p: rdn to chse wnr over 1f out: no imp fnl f* **9/2**[3]

0012 **3** *1 ¾* **Laa Rayb (USA)**[14] 5031 3-9-4 **99** .... J-PGuillambert 2 100
(M Johnston) *hld up: rdn and carried hd awkwardly over 1f out: wnt 3rd and hld whn edgd lft ins fnl f* **15/8**[2]

1211 **4** *2* **Lap Of Honour (IRE)**[21] 4811 3-7-11 **85** oh1 .... KMay(7) 5 81
(N A Callaghan) *chsd wnr tl rdn over 1f out: wknd fnl f* **5/1**

1m 37.75s (-1.85) **Going Correction** +0.05s/f (Good) **4** Ran SP% **107.7**
Speed ratings (Par 107): **111,109,107,105**
CSF £8.64 TOTE £2.00; EX 10.90.
Owner Hamdan Al Maktoum **Bred** Swordlestown Stud **Trained** Newmarket, Suffolk

FOCUS
A steadily-run race and the progressive Ragheed had the run of things from the front. The form is not the most solid.

NOTEBOOK
Ragheed(USA), a most progressive colt who only failed by a head when bidding for the hat-trick at Ripon last time, was up another 3lb, but he was bounced straight into the lead by Jones and gradually wound it up to win going away. He was undoubtedly suited by the way things worked out, but continues to progress and would pick up a 4lb penalty if going for the Cambridgeshire. (op 15-8 tchd 11-8)
Guacamole, a winner at Newmarket back in August, was a bit unlucky back there next time when bidding to defy a 4lb rise, behind Lap Of Honour, but she had every chance here and was simply unable to match the winner. She continues to head in the right direction. (op 6-1 tchd 7-1)
Laa Rayb(USA) has his quirks, but should have won when flying home for second at Chester last time and it was a surprise to see him again held up. His best performance this season came when racing prominently throughout at Goodwood back in August and he failed to pick up here having been asked for his effort from the turn into the straight. He deserves another chance under a more positive ride. (op 13-8)
Lap Of Honour(IRE), a progressive gelding on a slow surface who has won three of his last four, was up a further 7lb and he was unable to prove as effective on this fast surface. (op 9-2 tchd 11-2)

5432 BETTER BETTING ON 08000 89 88 87 H'CAP — 1m 2f 188y
4:45 (4:47) (Class 4) (0-85,85) 3-Y-O **£7,570** (£2,265; £1,132; £566; £282) **Stalls** Low

Form RPR

2402 **1** **Warm Embraces (IRE)**[8] 5208 3-8-12 **79** .... LPKeniry 1 87
(D R C Elsworth) *hld up in mid-div: rdn and hdwy to ld over 1f out: drvn out* **9/4**[1]

240 **2** *1* **Can Can Star**[34] 4419 4-8-9 **73** .... RussellKennemore(5) 2 79
(A W Carroll) *hld up in rr: rdn and hdwy wl over 1f out: chsd wnr fnl f: nt qckn* **20/1**

6044 **3** *1 ¾* **Arctic Wings (IRE)**[19] 4910 3-8-4 **71** oh3 .... NickyMackay 8 74
(W R Muir) *a.p: rdn 3f out: carried sltly rt wl over 1f out: one pce fnl f* **14/1**

104 **4** *¾* **Snowed Under**[18] 4922 6-8-11 **75** .... NeilBrown(5) 7 77
(J D Bethell) *led 1f: hld up in mid-div: rdn and hdwy on outside whn carried rt wl over 1f out: one pce fnl f* **10/1**

0116 **5** *¾* **Calabash Cove (USA)**[57] 3709 3-9-3 **84** .... (t) TedDurcan 5 84
(Saeed Bin Suroor) *led after 1f: rdn and hung lft 2f out: hdd over 1f out: wknd ins fnl f* **4/1**[2]

4044 **6** *1 ¼* **Counsel's Opinion (IRE)**[19] 4909 10-9-7 **80** .... J-PGuillambert 3 78
(C F Wall) *hld up and bhd: rdn over 2f out: nvr trbld ldrs* **8/1**

0021 **7** *nk* **Robustian**[14] 5052 4-9-12 **85** .... (b) IanMongan 4 83
(Eve Johnson Houghton) *hld up and bhd: rdn over 2f out: swtchd lft jst over 1f out: n.d* **15/2**

5221 **8** *nk* **Veiled Applause**[12] 5099 4-9-6 **79** .... RichardKingscote 9 76
(R M Beckett) *chsd ldr after 1f: rdn whn carried sltly rt wl over 1f out: wknd ent fnl f* **11/2**[3]

0031 **9** *8* **New Star (UAE)**[15] 4993 3-8-8 **78** .... LiamJones(3) 6 61
(W M Brisbourne) *t.k.h: prom: pushed along 4f out: rdn over 2f out: wknd over 1f out* **12/1**

2m 19.21s (-0.19) **Going Correction** +0.05s/f (Good)
WFA 3 from 4yo+ 8lb **9** Ran SP% **117.2**
Speed ratings (Par 105): **102,101,100,99,98 98,97,97,91**
CSF £52.65 CT £525.20 TOTE £2.70: £1.50, £4.40, £3.90; EX 59.00.
Owner Gordon Li **Bred** Zapping Syndicate **Trained** Newmarket, Suffolk

FOCUS
A fair handicap but ordinary form with the third to his best from out of the handicap and the runner-up back to form.

5433 BETTERCASINO.COM H'CAP — 7f 26y
5:20 (5:20) (Class 6) (0-60,60) 3-Y-O+ **£3,238** (£963; £481; £240) **Stalls** Low

Form RPR

0012 **1** **Bold Cross (IRE)**[8] 5190 4-9-7 **59** .... PaulFitzsimons 2 68
(E G Bevan) *t.k.h: sn in tch: hdwy to ld over 1f out: rdn out* **4/1**[2]

066 **2** *½* **Airman (IRE)**[19] 4908 4-9-5 **60** .... MarcHalford(3) 7 68
(W M Brisbourne) *hld up in mid-div: rdn and hdwy over 1f out: kpt on ins fnl f* **28/1**

0614 **3** *shd* **Ten To The Dozen**[8] 5190 4-9-0 **52** .... AdrianMcCarthy 5 59
(P W Hiatt) *s.i.s: bhd: rdn over 2f out: hdwy on outside over 1f out: edgd lft ins fnl f: kpt on* **9/1**

010 **4** *2 ½* **Poppets Sweetlove**[35] 4395 3-9-4 **60** .... J-PGuillambert 1 59
(A B Haynes) *sn prom: rdn 2f out: one pce fnl f* **12/1**

0260 **5** *1* **Lady Edge (IRE)**[4] 5303 5-8-11 **54** .... KevinGhunowa(5) 11 52
(A W Carroll) *hld up and bhd: rdn 3f out: styd on fnl f: nvr nrr* **28/1**

-000 **6** *nk* **Sagunt (GER)**[19] 4884 4-9-6 **58** .... AmirQuinn 4 55
(S Curran) *hld up and bhd: hdwy over 1f out: nt clr run briefly ins fnl f: styd on: nt rch ldrs* **14/1**

0000 **7** *shd* **Rigat**[21] 4822 4-9-0 **57** .... NeilBrown(5) 12 54
(T D Barron) *s.i.s: hld up and bhd: rdn 2f out: styd on fnl f: nt rch ldrs* **15/2**[3]

0204 **8** *½* **Maison Dieu**[23] 4731 4-9-6 **58** .... DaleGibson 10 54
(E J Alston) *t.k.h in mid-div: rdn 2f out: no real prog fnl f* **8/1**

6020 **9** *1* **Regal Dream (IRE)**[1] 5391 5-9-6 **58** .... RichardKingscote 3 51
(J W Unett) *chsd ldrs: rdn over 2f out: wknd ins fnl f* **11/4**[1]

6120 **10** *1 ¾* **Millfield (IRE)**[8] 5190 4-9-8 **60** .... LPKeniry 14 48
(P R Chamings) *prom: rdn and ev ch wl over 1f out: wknd ent fnl f* **15/2**[3]

4050 **11** *1* **Fluttering Rose**[23] 4740 3-9-4 **60** .... (b[1]) TedDurcan 6 43
(R M Beckett) *prom: rdn to ld 2f out: sn hdd: eased whn btn ins fnl f* **14/1**

0500 **12** *5* **Under Fire (IRE)**[15] 5020 4-8-9 **54** .... MarkCoumbe(7) 13 26
(A W Carroll) *bhd fnl 4f* **40/1**

-000 **13** *7* **Mootamaress (IRE)**[57] 3713 3-8-13 **60** .... (v[1]) TolleyDean(5) 8 11
(Mrs A L M King) *led: rdn and hdd 2f out: sn wknd and eased* **40/1**

1m 24.13s (-0.07) **Going Correction** +0.05s/f (Good)
WFA 3 from 4yo+ 4lb **13** Ran SP% **124.1**
Speed ratings (Par 101): **102,101,101,98,97 96,96,96,95,93 92,86,78**
CSF £122.91 CT £973.93 TOTE £6.10: £1.90, £9.70, £4.70; EX 115.00 Place 6 £533.13, Place 5 £419.53..
Owner E G Bevan **Bred** M Hosokawa **Trained** Ullingswick, H'fords

FOCUS
A moderate handicap and sound form, backed up by the time.
Regal Dream(IRE) Official explanation: jockey said gelding had run flat
Mootamaress(IRE) Official explanation: jockey said gelding had had no more to give
T/Plt: £679.40 to a £1 stake. Pool: £38,809.95. 41.70 winning tickets. T/Qpdt: £131.40 to a £1 stake. Pool: £1,545.60. 8.70 winning tickets. KH

5434 - (Foreign Racing) - See Raceform Interactive

5392 CURRAGH (R-H)
Saturday, September 15

OFFICIAL GOING: Good to firm (firm in places)

5435a FLAME OF TARA EUROPEAN BREEDERS' FUND STKS (LISTED RACE) (FILLIES) — 6f
2:35 (2:39) 2-Y-O **£32,989** (£9,679; £4,611; £1,570)

RPR

1 **Forthefirstime**[21] 4834 2-8-12 .... FMBerry 5 98
(John M Oxx, Ire) *hld up towards rr: 8th appr 1/2-way: hdwy on outer under 2f out: 3rd and chal over 1f out: kpt on wl u.p to ld cl home* **7/2**[1]

2 *nk* **Longing To Dance**[21] 4829 2-8-12 .... WMLordan 8 97
(David Wachman, Ire) *trckd ldrs on outer: 5th appr 1/2-way: impr to chal 2f out: led under 1 1/2f out: rdn and hdd 1f out: kpt on u.p* **5/1**[2]

3 *nk* **Bett's Spirit (IRE)**[16] 4983 2-8-12 .... JAHeffernan 4 96
(M J Grassick, Ire) *disp ld: led 2f out: hdd under 1 1/2f out: regained ld 1f out: kpt on u.p: hdd cl home* **14/1**

4 *3 ½* **Sweeter Still (IRE)** 2-8-12 .... SMLevey 2 86
(A P O'Brien, Ire) *lost grnd s: towards rr: sme prog whn nt clr run 1 1/2f out: 5th 1f out: kpt on* **25/1**

5 *nk* **Solas Na Greine (IRE)**[13] 5073 2-8-12 **92** .... KJManning 7 85
(J S Bolger, Ire) *cl 4th: 2nd and chal 2f out: no imp fr over 1f out: one pce* **7/1**[3]

6 *2 ½* **Sudden Impact (IRE)**[21] 4832 2-8-12 .... NGMcCullagh 1 77
(Paul Green) *disp ld: rdn 1/2-way: hdd 2f out: no ex fr over 1f out* **7/2**[1]

7 *1* **Capall An Ibre (IRE)**[13] 5076 2-8-12 .... (t) PJSmullen 9 74
(Edward Lynam, Ire) *towards rr: no imp fr under 2f out* **12/1**

8 *hd* **Savethisdanceforme (IRE)**[69] 3354 2-8-12 .... KFallon 3 74
(A P O'Brien, Ire) *chsd ldrs in 6th: rdn and no imp fr under 2f out* **5/1**[2]

9 *½* **Crying Aloud (USA)**[13] 5063 2-8-12 .... DPMcDonogh 6 72
(P A Blockley) *disp ld to 1/2-way: sn wknd* **16/1**

1m 11.6s (-2.90) **Going Correction** -0.425s/f (Firm) **9** Ran SP% **114.4**
Speed ratings: **102,101,101,96,96 92,91,91,90**
CSF £20.72 TOTE £3.40: £1.50, £2.10, £2.80; DF 27.80.
Owner Byerley Racing **Bred** Glebe Stud & J F Dean **Trained** Currabeg, Co Kildare

NOTEBOOK
Sweeter Still(IRE) Official explanation: jockey said filly ran short of room and had to be switched wide in the latter stages of the race
Sudden Impact(IRE), winner of a valuable sales race at the course last time, was quite keen early but had a good position on the stands' rail. He was in trouble just beyond halfway and was disappointingly soon beaten. Official explanation: jockey said filly did not handle the ground (op 3/1 tchd 4/1)
Crying Aloud(USA), narrowly touched off in a 7f Folkestone maiden latest, found this company too hot to handle and will find easier opportunities.

5436a ST JOVITE RENAISSANCE STKS (GROUP 3) — 6f
3:05 (3:05) 3-Y-O+ **£32,939** (£9,628; £4,560; £1,520)

RPR

1 **Benbaun (IRE)**[13] 5075 6-9-8 .... (b) PJSmullen 2 123
(M J Wallace) *led: hdd 2f out: regained ld under 1f out: styd on wl u.p* **5/4**[1]

2 *¾* **Moss Vale (IRE)**[13] 5075 6-9-3 .... JohnEgan 6 116
(D Nicholls) *cl 2nd: rdn to ld 2f out: hdd under 1f out: kpt on u.p* **10/3**[2]

3 *2 ½* **Prime Defender**[44] 4090 3-9-1 .... MichaelHills 1 109+
(B W Hills) *hld up in rr: mod 5th 1 1/2f out: r.o wl fr over 1f out wout threatening* **10/3**[2]

4 *1 ½* **Absolutelyfabulous (IRE)**[94] 2586 4-9-0 **100** .... KFallon 5 101
(David Wachman, Ire) *chsd ldrs: 4th u.p 2f out: no imp: kpt on same pce* **14/1**[3]

5 *1* **Senor Benny (USA)**[13] 5075 8-9-3 **104** .... DPMcDonogh 4 101
(M McDonagh, Ire) *chsd ldrs: 4th 1/2-way: 3rd u.p 2f out: sn no ex* **16/1**

6 *nk* **Snaefell (IRE)**[13] 5075 3-9-1 **106** .... RPCleary 3 100
(M Halford, Ire) *towards rr: no imp fr 2f out* **16/1**

7 *11* **Moone Cross (IRE)**[13] 5075 4-9-0 **98** .... NGMcCullagh 7 64
(Mrs John Harrington, Ire) *chsd ldrs in 3rd: wknd after 1/2-way: eased cl home* **33/1**

69.97 secs (-4.53) **Going Correction** -0.425s/f (Firm)
WFA 3 from 4yo+ 2lb **7** Ran SP% **112.0**
Speed ratings: **113,112,108,106,105 104,90**
CSF £5.31 TOTE £1.50: £1.40, £2.10; DF 3.50.
Owner Ransley, Birks, Hillen **Bred** Dr T A Ryan **Trained** Newmarket, Suffolk

NOTEBOOK
Benbaun(IRE), who really likes it at this course, gradually wound it up from before halfway, and he just seemed to toy a bit with Moss Vale, letting him lead two furlongs out until inside the final furlong, before drawing ahead inside the final furlong. The winning trainer said that he has kept the winner's campaign a good bit quieter this year as he intends to go travelling over the winter. He is a horse that travels so well in his races that he should be capable of holding his own in some of those Australian or Far Eastern sprints. (op 11/10)
Moss Vale(IRE) has a fair record at this track as well. It developed into more or less a two-horse race from halfway, but he had no real answer when the winner found a good deal more inside the last furlong. He has not quite been at his best this season but this was probably as good as he has done this year. (op 3/1 tchd 7/2)
Prime Defender, subject to a change in tactics on this occasion, looked beaten at halfway despite the rider not having made any sort of move, and when asked for an effort the first and second had well and truly flown. Whether a more positive ride would have made any difference we will never know, but he was left with too much to do and was very much nearest at the finish. (op 7/2)

5437a IRISH FIELD ST. LEGER (GROUP 1) — 1m 6f
3:35 (3:37) 3-Y-O+
£115,945 (£38,918; £18,648; £6,486; £4,459; £2,432)

RPR

1 **Yeats (IRE)**[86] 2787 6-9-11 **121** .... KFallon 4 122+
(A P O'Brien, Ire) *trckd ldrs in 4th: drvn along appr st: impr into mod 2nd 2f out: chal ins fnl f: styd on wl to ld cl home* **4/7**[1]

The Form Book, Raceform Ltd, Compton, RG20 6NL

2 1/2 **Scorpion (IRE)**[49] 3942 5-9-11 120 JAHeffernan 3 121
(A P O'Brien, Ire) *sn led: rdn clr ent st: strly pressed whn wandered abt u.p wl ins fnl f: hdd cl home* **7/2**[2]
3 4 1/2 **Mores Wells**[27] 4647 3-9-0 112 (t) DPMcDonogh 7 115
(Kevin Prendergast, Ire) *trckd ldrs in 3rd: 4th and rdn early st: mod 3rd and kpt on fr 1 1/2f out* **8/1**[3]
4 1 1/2 **Macorville (USA)**[49] 3973 4-9-11 FMBerry 5 113?
(G M Moore) *settled in 2nd: outpcd early st: 3rd 2f out: sn no ex* **100/1**
5 3/4 **Mighty**[84] 2856 4-9-11 JohnEgan 1 112
(Jane Chapple-Hyam) *trckd ldrs on outer: 5th 1/2-way: rdn ent st: no imp fr 2f out* **20/1**
6 6 **Galistic (IRE)**[59] 3664 4-9-8 100 DMGrant 6 100
(Patrick J Flynn, Ire) *towards rr: sme prog ent st: no imp fr under 2f out* **50/1**
7 2 1/2 **Steppe Dancer (IRE)**[7] 5220 4-9-11 KJManning 2 100
(D J Coakley) *towards rr: sme prog ent st: no ex fr over 2f out* **25/1**
8 2 1/2 **The Whistling Teal**[28] 4599 11-9-11 WJSupple 8 96
(G Wragg) *chsd ldrs: 7th and pushed along 1/2-way: dropped to rr appr st: no ex* **66/1**
9 5 1/2 **Bellamy Cay**[168] 861 5-9-11 PJSmullen 9 89
(D K Weld, Ire) *racd in 6th: plld hrd to after 1/2-way: wknd early st: eased fr 1 1/2f out* **16/1**

3m 3.40s (1.10) **Going Correction** +0.525s/f (Yiel)
WFA 3 from 4yo+ 11lb **9 Ran SP% 115.9**
Speed ratings: **117,116,114,113,112 109,108,106,103**
CSF £2.59 TOTE £2.00: £1.10, £1.40, £1.90; DF 2.60.
Owner Mrs John Magnier **Bred** Barrowsdale Stud & Orpendale **Trained** Ballydoyle, Co Tipperary
■ Aidan O'Brien's first Irish St Leger winner, completing a full house of the English and Irish Classics.

FOCUS
Sound form, with Yeats rated to this year's best and Scorpion to this year's best form.

NOTEBOOK
Yeats(IRE), dual winner of the Ascot Gold Cup, looked briefly in trouble before the turn in, but class prevailed in the end and he finally won the Irish St Leger after being a beaten favourite in the race for the last two years. Having been held up in mid-division, he looked to be briefly in trouble when his stable companion kicked half a mile out, but he gradually wore down the wandering Scorpion inside the last two furlongs to get up close home, despite lugging a bit towards the far rail. The race worked out pretty well for him in the end, as over this shorter trip he had a lead until well inside the final furlong and that may have proved crucial. (op 1/2)
Scorpion(IRE) has won his Group 1 this year, but he has also had his share of bad luck, and this was nearly a carbon copy of the Irish Derby of 2005 when he was cut down close home by Fallon on Hurricane Run. Heffernan could not have done any more, trying to make all, and he kicked for home half a mile out, but the horse started to wander inside the last furlong. He carried his head slightly awkwardly, drifted off the rail and changed his legs as if he was feeling the ground. Even so, it was a good performance.
Mores Wells, the only three-year-old in the line-up, ran a cracker and performed as well as he was entitled to. Indeed, he travelled probably better than anything up to half a mile from the finish, but was feeling the pinch from there before staying on well enough to be an excellent third, albeit no match in the end for the two Ballydoyle horses.
Macorville(USA) came into the race with a BHB rating of 95. You can say that his prominent effort in this Group 1 speaks volumes about the strength in depth of the race, but he kept on gamely in the straight to beat horses rated a good bit higher than him seemingly fair and square. It will be interesting to see if he can repeat this performance off whatever his revised mark will be. (op 66/1)
Mighty did not quite run up to his best on his first try at this distance. He was unable to improve his position from half a mile out while running respectably, and whether he stayed or not is inconclusive.
Steppe Dancer(IRE) was always in the rear group and never threatened to get involved. This was a disappointing effort.
The Whistling Teal is past his best and he was always going to struggle to make an impact at this level. (op 50/1)

5438 - 5441a (Foreign Racing) - See Raceform Interactive

5267 BATH (L-H)
Sunday, September 16

OFFICIAL GOING: Firm (11.3)
Wind: Brisk, ahead

5442 WILLIAMHILLCASINO.COM MAIDEN FILLIES' STKS 5f 161y
2:25 (2:26) (Class 5) 2-Y-O £3,562 (£1,059; £529; £264) **Stalls** Centre

Form RPR
03 1 **Floristry**[32] 4487 2-9-0 0 SebSanders 8 82+
(Sir Michael Stoute) *trckd ldrs tl led ins fnl 2f: c readily clr over 1f out: v easily* **2/9**[1]
2 6 **Toasted Special (USA)** 2-9-0 0 SteveDrowne 2 62+
(B J Meehan) *sn led: rdn and hdd ins fnl 2f: kpt on wl for clr 2nd but no ch w extremely easy wnr* **6/1**[2]
0000 3 2 1/2 **Polish Priory (IRE)**[22] 4832 2-9-0 65 TGMcLaughlin 5 53
(P D Evans) *awkward stalls: rdn and in tch 1/2-way: styd on for mod 3rd fnl f* **16/1**[3]
00 4 1 **Little Evie**[13] 5091 2-9-0 0 DavidKinsella 3 50
(R J Hodges) *pressed ldr: upsides and rdn over 2f out: wknd fnl f* **33/1**
00 5 1 1/4 **Willit (IRE)**[19] 4924 2-8-7 0 ThomasO'Brien(7) 6 45
(M R Channon) *plunged as stalls opened: sn in tch: rdn: effrt and edgd rt over 1f out: nvr in contention* **25/1**
6 1/2 **Nancymay** 2-8-7 0 FrankiePickard(7) 4 44
(J Ryan) *chsd ldrs to 1/2-way* **66/1**
000 7 3/4 **Enchanted Lady**[11] 5126 2-9-0 50 EddieAhern 1 41
(H J L Dunlop) *s.i.s: a outpcd* **33/1**
8 nk **Amber Bamber** 2-9-0 0 RichardThomas 7 40
(D Burchell) *a in rr* **100/1**

1m 11.08s (-0.12) **Going Correction** -0.075s/f (Good) **8 Ran SP% 114.2**
Speed ratings (Par 92): **97,89,85,84,82 82,81,80**
CSF £1.81 TOTE £1.20: £1.02, £1.10, £2.60; EX 2.40 Trifecta £16.50 Pool £193.06 - 8.29 winning units..
Owner Gainsborough **Bred** Gainsborough Stud Management Ltd **Trained** Newmarket, Suffolk

FOCUS
A very uncompetitive fillies' maiden and not an easy race to rate.

NOTEBOOK
Floristry stood out on the form of her two previous efforts and was far too good for this lot. She was actually dropping back in trip, but she showed plenty of speed and took this in effortless fashion. She will find things harder from now on, but at least she is going the right way. (op 4-9)
Toasted Special(USA), a 165,000gns daughter of Johannesburg, half-sister to among others quite useful 6f juvenile scorer Shuhrah, out of a dual 7f-1m winner, made a respectable debut, but she was no match for the easy winner. (op 9-2)
Polish Priory(IRE) did not look to run up to her official mark of 65 and is not progressing.
Little Evie did not run a bad race and, now qualified for a handicap mark, she will have more options. Official explanation: jockey said filly hung right-handed throughout (op 25-1)
Willit(IRE) was well beaten after leaving the stalls very awkwardly, but she is another now qualified for a handicap mark. (op 16-1 tchd 14-1)
Enchanted Lady Official explanation: jockey said filly stumbled badly on leaving stalls
Amber Bamber Official explanation: jockey said filly hung right throughout

5443 WILLIAM HILL 0800 44 40 40 NURSERY (FILLIES) 1m 5y
3:00 (3:01) (Class 3) 2-Y-O £6,309 (£1,888; £944; £472; £235) **Stalls** Low

Form RPR
0100 1 **Tamara Moon (IRE)**[16] 4991 2-9-3 71 ChrisCatlin 2 75
(M R Channon) *mde all: rdn over 2f out: styd on strly thrght fnl f* **6/1**
1000 2 1 **Double Attack (FR)**[16] 4991 2-9-7 75 RoystonFfrench 1 77
(M Johnston) *wore net muzzle: t.k.h: in rr but in tch: rdn and hdwy over 2f out: styd on u.p to go 2nd ins fnl f but no imp on wnr* **7/1**
4220 3 1 1/2 **Quick Sands (IRE)**[32] 4501 2-9-5 73 PatDobbs 3 71
(R Hannon) *chsd ldrs: drvn to dispute 2nd 2f out but nvr gng pce to trble wnr: wknd ins fnl f* **5/2**[1]
030 4 1/2 **Neve Lieve (IRE)**[22] 4796 2-8-12 66 (p) EddieAhern 6 63
(M Botti) *chsd ldr: rdn over 2f out: wknd ins fnl f* **5/1**[3]
404 5 3 1/2 **Lille Tuva**[14] 5061 2-9-1 69 FergusSweeney 7 58
(B R Millman) *chsd ldrs: rdn to dispute 2nd 2f out but nvr gng pce to trble wnr: wknd fnl f* **5/1**[3]
0550 6 7 **Too Grand**[12] 5117 2-8-1 58 WilliamBuick(3) 5 31
(A M Balding) *s.i.s: in rr: hdwy on outside 4f out: rdn and hung rt 3f out: wknd over 2f out: eased whn no ch ins fnl f* **11/4**[2]
4000 7 4 **Bold Diva**[20] 4875 2-7-12 52 oh7 (b) DavidKinsella 4 16
(A W Carroll) *a in rr* **50/1**

1m 40.3s (-0.80) **Going Correction** -0.075s/f (Good) **7 Ran SP% 117.3**
Speed ratings (Par 96): **101,100,98,98,94 87,83**
CSF £48.17 TOTE £6.20: £2.70, £3.30; EX 32.40.
Owner Jaber Abdullah **Bred** Ms Sheila Lavery **Trained** West Ilsley, Berks

FOCUS
A modest nursery and the form looks ordinary but solid enough rated through the placed horses and backed up by the time.

NOTEBOOK
Tamara Moon(IRE) had not shown much on his last couple of starts but, upped to 1m for the first time, he was able to dominate and returned to his best. (op 5-1 tchd 7-1)
Double Attack(FR) failed to progress after winning on her debut at Hamilton earlier in the season, but this represented a return to form, despite her taking quite a grip early on. Official explanation: jockey said filly ran too free (op 11-2 tchd 5-1)
Quick Sands(IRE), still a maiden, ran a creditable race upped to 1m for the first time. (op 10-3 tchd 7-2)
Neve Lieve(IRE), fitted with cheekpieces for the first time on her nursery debut, finished up well held and looks high enough in the weights on this evidence. (op 6-1 tchd 7-1)
Lille Tuva was disappointing stepped up in trip on her nursery debut. (op 6-1 tchd 9-2)
Too Grand ran no sort of race on this step up in trip. Official explanation: jockey said filly missed the break (op 10-3 tchd 7-2)

5444 WILLIAMHILLPOKER.COM CONDITIONS STKS 1m 5y
3:35 (3:35) (Class 4) 3-Y-O+ £5,181 (£1,541; £770; £384) **Stalls** Low

Form RPR
060 1 **Tell**[8] 5213 4-9-0 98 (b) SebSanders 1 105
(J L Dunlop) *mde all: hrd rdn ins fnl 2f: styd on gamely whn strly chal thrght fnl f: hld on all out* **12/1**
513- 2 shd **Kilworth (IRE)**[324] 6203 4-9-0 106 EddieAhern 2 105
(Saeed Bin Suroor) *trckd wnr: rdn and qcknd to chal ins fnl f: r.o cl home but nt quite get up* **10/11**[1]
0050 3 3 1/2 **Dont Dili Dali**[3] 5351 4-8-9 107 (p) SteveDrowne 3 92
(J S Moore) *racd in 3rd: rdn and effrt 2f out: nvr gng pce of ldng duo: wknd ins fnl f* **10/3**[3]
0033 4 7 **Pentecost**[36] 4377 8-8-11 93 (p) WilliamBuick(3) 4 81
(A M Balding) *a in last pl: rdn over 3f out: sn no ch* **3/1**[2]

1m 39.19s (-1.91) **Going Correction** -0.075s/f (Good) **4 Ran SP% 108.2**
Speed ratings (Par 105): **106,105,102,95**
CSF £23.92 TOTE £11.20; EX 34.10.
Owner Prince A A Faisal **Bred** Nawara Stud Co Ltd **Trained** Arundel, W Sussex
■ Stewards' Enquiry : Seb Sanders one-day ban: used whip with excessive frequency (Sep 27)

FOCUS
A decent conditions contest on paper, but both Dont Dili Dali and Pentecost failed to run to form and the outsider of the four proved good enough.
Kilworth(IRE) Official explanation: jockey said colt was unsuited by the firm ground and hung right-handed

5445 BET LIVE @ WILLIAMHILL.COM H'CAP 1m 2f 46y
4:10 (4:12) (Class 2) (0-100,89) 3-Y-O£10,094 (£3,020; £1,510; £755; £376) **Stalls** Low

Form RPR
4130 1 **Six Of Diamonds (IRE)**[22] 4799 3-9-1 89 WilliamBuick(3) 1 99
(J A Osborne) *mde virtually all: set modest pce first 2f: qcknd fr over 3f out: rdn 2f out: r.o gamely whn 2nd c upsides thrght fnl f: edgd lft last stride* **3/1**[2]
1166 2 shd **Gold Hush (USA)**[22] 4799 3-9-1 86 SebSanders 3 96
(Sir Michael Stoute) *hld up in tch: hdwy over 2f out: pressed wnr over 1f out and upsides thrght fnl f: styd on wl: bmpd and no ex last stride* **10/11**[1]
0011 3 1 1/4 **Free Offer**[14] 5067 3-8-12 83 EddieAhern 5 90
(J L Dunlop) *in rr but in tch: hdwy to chse ldrs over 2f out: outpcd appr fnl f* **10/1**
4141 4 3 **Soul Mountain (IRE)**[15] 5043 3-8-10 81 MichaelHills 4 82
(B W Hills) *trckd ldrs in 3rd: rdn and effrt over 2f out: nvr quite gng pce to chal: wknd fnl f* **4/1**[3]
5310 5 3 **Shake On It**[9] 5208 3-8-10 81 (t) StephenCarson 6 76
(Eve Johnson Houghton) *in rr: rdn and no imp fr 3f out: wknd 2f out* **10/1**
0020 6 1 3/4 **Noticeable (IRE)**[9] 5208 3-8-10 81 ChrisCatlin 2 73
(M R Channon) *chsd wnr to 2f out: sn wknd* **16/1**

2m 9.72s (-1.28) **Going Correction** -0.075s/f (Good) **6 Ran SP% 121.4**
Speed ratings (Par 107): **102,101,100,98,96 94**
CSF £4.48 TOTE £2.10: £1.10, £2.40; EX 9.80.
Owner Booth,Durkan,Mountgrange&Wood Hall Studs **Bred** Tally-Ho Stud **Trained** Upper Lambourn, Berks
■ Stewards' Enquiry : William Buick one-day ban: careless riding (Sep 27)

FOCUS
Just the six runners and the top weight was rated 11lb below the ceiling of 100. A controversial race, with the first past the post, Six Of Diamonds, originally demoted to second place having been adjudged to have tightened up Gold Hush. The result was reinstated after an appeal by Six Of Diamonds' connections.

NOTEBOOK

Six Of Diamonds(IRE) returned to his best having been allowed his own way up front, but he edged left close home and, having past the post in front, he was demoted to second place. The Stewards reasoned that he tightened up Gold Hush, preventing Sanders from using his whip properly, but that looked a harsh decision, and it was overturned following an appeal. (op 5-1 tchd 11-2)

Gold Hush(USA) found this easier than her last couple of assignments and was awarded the race in the Stewards' room having originally failed by a short-head. The Stewards felt Seb Sanders was prevented from using his whip properly close home, but the decision was reversed following an appeal. (op 5-4)

Free Offer was bidding for the hat-trick off a mark 5lb higher than when winning at Folkestone on her previous start, but the front two were just too strong. (op 15-2)

Soul Mountain(IRE) could not defy a 2lb rise in the weights for her recent Ripon success and she looked to find this ground plenty quick enough. (op 9-2 tchd 6-1)

Shake On It has not gone on since winning at Lingfield two starts back. (op 17-2 tchd 8-1 and 14-1)

5446 WILLIAMHILLBINGO.COM H'CAP 2m 1f 34y

4:45 (4:46) (Class 2) (0-100,91) 3-Y-0+ **£10,094** (£3,020; £1,510; £755) **Stalls** Low

Form RPR

0-32 **1** **Caracciola (GER)**[36] 4375 10-9-11 **88** .... EddieAhern 3 95
(N J Henderson) *trcked ldrs in 3rd: wnt 2nd 2f out: drvn and styd on to ld fnl 110yds: kpt on wl* **5/1**

0103 **2** *nk* **Colloquial**[36] 4375 6-10-0 **91** ....(v) FergusSweeney 4 98
(H Candy) *trckd ldr: led ins fnl 3f: sn drvn: hdd and no ex fnl 110yds* **3/1**[3]

1641 **3** *5* **Secret Ploy**[46] 4056 7-9-1 **78** .... SteveDrowne 2 79
(H Morrison) *led: nudged along 1/2-way: drvn along fr 7f out: hdd ins fnl 3f: sn btn* **11/8**[1]

4220 **4** *9* **Serpentaria**[24] 4749 3-8-7 **82** .... SebSanders 1 72
(Sir Mark Prescott) *hld up in last pl but wl in tch: rdn 3f out: no rspnse and sn btn* **11/4**[2]

3m 47.59s (-2.01) **Going Correction** -0.075s/f (Good)
WFA 3 from 6yo+ 12lb **4** Ran SP% **110.4**
Speed ratings (Par 109): **101,100,98,94**
CSF £19.15 TOTE £5.70; EX 15.00.
Owner P J D Pottinger **Bred** Frau I U A Brunotte **Trained** Upper Lambourn, Berks

FOCUS

A decent handicap but just the four runners and the form is not strong for the level.

NOTEBOOK

Caracciola(GER), runner-up in the Shergar Cup stayers' event on his previous start, defied a 1lb rise in the weights for that effort with a narrow victory. Better known as a hurdler/chaser, this was his first win on the Flat since he was successful in Germany back in 2001, but he is clearly very capable and he holds an entry in the Cesarewitch. (op 4-1)

Colloquial had conditions to suit, but he does not have much in hand of the Handicapper and he was just held. Like the winner, he is entered in the Cesarewitch. (op 4-1)

Secret Ploy could not match the form he showed when winning over 2m5f at Goodwood on his previous start and was a touch disappointing. Perhaps this ground was a little faster than he really wants. (op 13-8 tchd 7-4)

Serpentaria is another who may have found this ground too quick. (op 5-2)

5447 WILLIAMHILLARCADE.COM H'CAP 5f 161y

5:20 (5:20) (Class 4) (0-85,84) 3-Y-0+ **£4,857** (£1,445; £722; £360) **Stalls** Centre

Form RPR

0412 **1** **Little Edward**[12] 5119 9-9-4 **82** .... SteveDrowne 5 98+
(R J Hodges) *hld up in tch: hdwy fr 2f out to ld ins fnl f: readily* **4/1**[2]

122 **2** *2* **Even Bolder**[10] 5160 4-8-1 **72** ....(p) SophieDoyle(7) 1 78
(R Simpson) *led tl hdd ins fnl f: kpt on but nt pce of wnr* **6/1**[3]

0002 **3** *1 1/4* **Texas Gold**[6] 5278 9-9-5 **83** .... SebSanders 8 85
(W R Muir) *in rr: hdwy over 1f out: sn n.m.r: styd on ins fnl f but nvr gng pce of ldng duo* **5/2**[1]

3402 **4** *1 1/4* **Holbeck Ghyll (IRE)**[36] 4389 5-8-12 **79** .... NeilChalmers(3) 2 77
(A M Balding) *chsd ldrs: rdn 2f out: sn outpcd* **5/2**[1]

0040 **5** *nk* **Misaro (GER)**[6] 5278 6-8-9 **80** ....(b) MatthewDavies(7) 4 77
(R A Harris) *pressed ldr after 2f: rdn 2f out: wknd fnl f* **20/1**

406 **6** *3* **Tony The Tap**[15] 5050 6-9-6 **84** .... EddieAhern 7 71
(W R Muir) *rdn 1/2-way: a outpcd* **13/2**

0501 **7** *6* **What Do You Know**[18] 4944 4-8-10 **74** ....(b) ChrisCatlin 3 41
(A M Hales) *chsd ldrs: chal over 2f out: wknd wl over 1f out* **16/1**

69.64 secs (-1.56) **Going Correction** -0.075s/f (Good) **7** Ran SP% **115.4**
Speed ratings (Par 105): **107,104,102,101,100 96,88**
CSF £28.34 CT £71.17 TOTE £5.30: £3.70, £3.80; EX 41.10 Trifecta £191.60 Part won. Pool £269.95 - 0.20 winning units. Place 6 £6,065.29, Place 5 £6,009.94..
Owner J W Mursell **Bred** J W Mursell **Trained** Charlton Mackrell, Somerset

FOCUS

A fair sprint handicap.

What Do You Know Official explanation: jockey said gelding slipped on leaving stalls

T/Plt: £770.00 to a £1 stake. Pool: £54,748.85. 51.90 winning tickets. T/Qpdt: £285.80 to a £1 stake. Pool: £2,472.50. 6.40 winning tickets. ST

5413 GOODWOOD (R-H)

Sunday, September 16

OFFICIAL GOING: Good to firm (9.4)

Wind: Fresh, half against Weather: partly cloudy with bright spells

5448 CELER ET AUDAX EUROPEAN BREEDERS' FUND MAIDEN STKS 6f

2:00 (2:01) (Class 4) 2-Y-0 **£4,857** (£1,445; £722; £360) **Stalls** Low

Form RPR

2 **1** **Sam's Cross (IRE)**[39] 4286 2-9-3 0 .... KerrinMcEvoy 2 86+
(W R Swinburn) *chsd ldr: hdwy and upsides 2f out: rdn 1f out: led last 50yds: pushed out* **9/4**[2]

2 *nk* **Shabiba (USA)** 2-8-12 0 .... RHills 3 80+
(M P Tregoning) *w'like: strong: w.w in tch: swtchd lft and hdwy wl over 1f out: rdn to ld ins fnl f: hdd and no ex last 50yds* **7/1**

53 **3** *1 1/2* **First Trim (IRE)**[15] 5042 2-9-3 0 .... JamieSpencer 1 81
(B J Meehan) *lw: led: rdn wl over 1f out: hdd ins fnl f: wknd last 50yds* **3/1**[3]

02 **4** *2 1/2* **House**[29] 4604 2-9-3 0 .... TedDurcan 6 73+
(M R Channon) *sn pushed along: chsd ldrs: rdn over 2f out: wknd jst over 1f out: eased last 50yds* **15/8**[1]

5 **5** *3* **Greek Theatre (USA)**[16] 5003 2-9-3 0 .... JimCrowley 9 64
(Mrs A J Perrett) *lw: in tch: rdn over 2f out: sn outpcd* **16/1**

6 *3/4* **Shanzu** 2-8-12 0 .... DaneO'Neill 7 57
(H Candy) *w'like: leggy: sn bustled along: in tch in midfield to 1/2-way: sn lost tch* **50/1**

6 **7** *5* **Whitcombe Flyer (USA)**[43] 4160 2-9-3 0 ....(t) IanMongan 8 47
(Jamie Poulton) *sn rdn along in rr: wl bhd last 2f* **66/1**

03 **8** *8* **Spic 'n Span**[39] 4273 2-9-3 0 .... SimonWhitworth 4 23
(C A Cyzer) *lw: v.s.a: a wl detached in last: t.o* **25/1**

1m 11.82s (-1.03) **Going Correction** -0.075s/f (Good) **8** Ran SP% **116.2**
Speed ratings (Par 97): **103,102,100,97,93 92,85,74**
CSF £18.47 TOTE £3.20: £1.40, £2.00, £1.50; EX 20.50.
Owner Owen O'Brien **Bred** Gainsborough Stud Management Ltd **Trained** Aldbury, Herts

FOCUS

A fair maiden and sound enough form.

NOTEBOOK

Sam's Cross(IRE), a promising runner-up on his debut, stayed on well to collar Shabiba close home. He shapes as though he needs further than 6f now and will be interesting in nursery company. Easier ground is expected to suit him in future. (op 11-4)

Shabiba(USA), whose dam won the Nell Gwyn, is entered in the Cheveley Park Stakes and Fillies' Mile so is evidently well regarded. She looked the likely winner when hitting the front inside the last, but she was too green to see it out successfully. Sure to improve for the run, she looks a ready-made winner of a similar event and will surely be racing in Pattern company before long. (tchd 6-1)

First Trim(IRE) ran another good race, leading for most of the way, and an average maiden should be within his ability, although connections may now opt to go the nursery route with him. (op 7-2 tchd 4-1 in places)

House, runner-up to a colt who went on to win a French Group 3 last time out, struggled a bit with the early pace but finished clear of the rest despite being eased close home, and is another now eligible for a mark. (op 7-4 tchd 9-4)

Greek Theatre(USA) needs further than this and looks more of a handicap sort after one more run.

Spic 'n Span Official explanation: jockey said colt missed the break

5449 DENNIS EDE'S BIG 70TH BIRTHDAY CELEBRATION STKS (H'CAP) 6f

2:35 (2:35) (Class 2) (0-100,97) 3-Y-0+

£11,217 (£3,358; £1,679; £840; £419; £210) **Stalls** Low

Form RPR

0025 **1** **Mac Gille Eoin**[18] 4950 3-8-11 **90** .... JimCrowley 7 100
(J Gallagher) *lw: bhd and sn pushed along: hdwy over 1f out: rdn to chse wnr ins fnl f: styd on wl to ld fnl stride* **9/1**

2121 **2** *shd* **Esteem Machine (USA)**[22] 4816 3-8-7 **86** .... KerrinMcEvoy 5 96
(R A Teal) *lw: chsd ldr tl led over 3f out: rdn over 1f out: kpt on wl tl hdd last stride* **15/8**[1]

0600 **3** *2* **Baron's Pit**[36] 4401 7-9-4 **95** ....(b) JimmyFortune 2 99
(E F Vaughan) *b. racd stands' side: effrt 2f out: rdn to chse overall ldr over 1f out: sn edgd lft: lost 2nd ins fnl f: outpcd last 100yds* **5/1**[2]

6004 **4** *3/4* **Dingaan (IRE)**[20] 4886 4-8-6 **83** oh2 .... LPKeniry 9 84
(A M Balding) *w.w in tch: rdn and effrt over 1f out: outpcd fnl f* **8/1**[3]

6004 **5** *shd* **Ajigolo**[9] 5195 4-8-9 **86** .... TPO'Shea 4 87
(M R Channon) *lw: trckd ldrs: rdn over 1f out: outpcd fnl f* **9/1**

0600 **6** *5* **Mujood**[22] 4806 4-8-7 **84** ow1 ....(v) MickyFenton 1 70
(Eve Johnson Houghton) *sn pushed along: led stands' side pair tl over 1f out: sn wknd* **12/1**

0251 **7** *2 1/2* **Diane's Choice**[20] 4886 4-8-10 **87** .... NickyMackay 6 66
(J Akehurst) *prom: chsd ldr 3f out tl over 1f out: sn wknd* **8/1**[3]

0505 **8** *1 1/2* **The Tatling (IRE)**[15] 5050 10-9-6 **97** .... KDarley 3 71
(J M Bradley) *in tch: rdn and effrt 2f out: sn btn* **8/1**[3]

0150 **9** *hd* **H Harrison (IRE)**[1] 5413 7-8-6 **86** .... AndrewElliott(3) 10 60
(I W McInnes) *w ldrs tl 1/2-way: sn dropped out* **16/1**

000 **10** *1 1/2* **Padrao Lima (BRZ)**[16] 4990 4-8-5 **87** .... TolleyDean(5) 8 56
(J S Moore) *led tl over 3f out: styd prom tl wknd qckly 2f out* **66/1**

1m 11.0s (-1.85) **Going Correction** -0.075s/f (Good)
WFA 3 from 4yo+ 2lb **10** Ran SP% **119.8**
Speed ratings (Par 109): **109,108,106,105,105 98,95,93,92,90**
CSF £26.97 CT £101.88 TOTE £11.90: £3.00, £1.40, £2.00; EX 32.40.
Owner M C S D Racing Partnership **Bred** M C S D Racing Ltd **Trained** Moreton-in-Marsh, Gloucs

FOCUS

A competitive sprint handicap run at a good pace.

NOTEBOOK

Mac Gille Eoin, only 1lb higher than when runner-up over this course and distance last month, stayed on late to grab the front-running Esteem Machine on the line. This track seems to bring out the best in him and it is easy to see him developing into a Stewards' Cup candidate next season. (op 10-1 tchd 11-1)

Esteem Machine(USA), 8lb higher than when successful at Newmarket last time, was a well-backed favourite but had quicker ground to deal with this time. He showed great pace throughout and almost made every yard, but he was just denied by the strong finish of Mac Gille Eoin on the line. He remains on the upgrade. (op 9-4 tchd 5-2 in a place)

Baron's Pit finised well up the stands' side while the first two came up the centre. He was arguably at a disadvantage where he raced so this was a fair effort, and his handicap mark has fallen to a level he can be expected to be able to win off. (tchd 11-2)

Dingaan(IRE) was 2lb wrong at the weights but he has won over this course and distance in the past off a 1lb higher mark. He ran well enough but did not find as much off the bridle as had looked likely. (op 9-1)

Ajigolo keeps edging down the weights but looks no nearer winning. (op 17-2 tchd 8-1)

Mujood, back on the same mark as when successful over this course and distance earlier in the year, was rousted along in the early stages to go prominent, but he was probably at a disadvantage racing nearer the stands' side and he could never dominate. (op 16-1)

5450 ADENSTAR MAIDEN STKS 1m 3f

3:10 (3:11) (Class 5) 3-Y-0 **£3,238** (£963; £481; £240) **Stalls** Low

Form RPR

1 **Watchful (IRE)** 3-8-12 0 .... JimmyFortune 6 75+
(L M Cumani) *w'like: strong: bit bkwd: chsd ldng pair: rdn to chse ldr over 2f out: chal over 1f out: led last 100yds: drvn out* **13/2**

0-52 **2** *1* **Unreachable Star**[66] 3476 3-8-12 75 .... JimCrowley 5 73
(Mrs A J Perrett) *chsd ldr tl led wl over 2f out: rdn 2f out: hdd last 100yds: one pce* **1/1**[1]

-245 **3** *4* **Inchlaggan (IRE)**[30] 4568 3-9-3 74 .... RHills 2 71
(B W Hills) *t.k.h: hld up bhd: 3f out: rdn and edgd rt over 1f out: no imp after: wnt 3rd wl ins fnl f* **6/1**[3]

5523 **4** *3/4* **Easterly Breeze (IRE)**[3] 5346 3-9-3 74 .... MartinDwyer 4 70
(W R Muir) *w.w in midfield: hdwy over 3f out: rdn to chse ldng pair 2f out: sn no imp: lost 3rd wl ins fnl f* **7/2**[2]

0000 **5** *13* **Silver Surprise**[16] 5007 3-8-12 42 .... DaneO'Neill 7 43?
(J J Bridger) *led tl wl over 3f out: sn wknd* **100/1**

4 **6** *nk* **Kokkokila**[114] 1988 3-8-12 0 .... JamieSpencer 3 42
(Lady Herries) *hld up in midfield: hdwy to trck ldrs 5f out: rdn over 3f out: btn and eased fr 2f out* **7/1**

5 **7** ½ **Highest Esteem**[31] 4541 3-9-3 0 .... TedDurcan 1 47
(G L Moore) *hld up in rr: rdn and lost tch over 3f out: no ch after: eased* **14/1**

2m 29.55s (2.34) **Going Correction** +0.075s/f (Good) 7 Ran SP% **120.0**
Speed ratings (Par 101): **94,93,90,89,80 80,79**
CSF £14.41 TOTE £9.10: £3.00, £1.80; EX 20.60.
Owner De La Warr Racing **Bred** Neville O'Byrne **Trained** Newmarket, Suffolk

FOCUS
Not a great maiden and the early pace was far from frenetic, but the winner, the only newcomer in the field, did it nicely enough and can only improve.
Easterly Breeze(IRE) Official explanation: jockey said colt was unsuited by the good to firm ground

5451 SELECT RACING UK ON SKY 432 STKS (GROUP 3) 1m 1f 192y
3:45 (3:46) (Class 1) 3-Y-0+
£28,390 (£10,760; £5,385; £2,685; £1,345; £675) **Stalls** High

Form RPR
-203 **1** **Stotsfold**[44] 4117 4-9-0 104 .... AdamKirby 3 113
(W R Swinburn) *stdd s: hld up in rr: hdwy on outer over 2f out: rdn and edgd rt u.p fr over 1f out: led last 100yds: r.o wl* **7/1**[3]

1113 **2** ½ **Zaham (USA)**[36] 4387 3-8-8 108 .... RHills 1 112
(M Johnston) *led: clr tl 3f out: hdd 2f out: sn swtchd lft: rallied u.p fnl f: r.o to go 2nd nr fin* **9/4**[1]

-235 **3** shd **Mullins Bay**[11] 5142 6-9-0 0 .... (t) JamieSpencer 2 112
(M F De Kock, South Africa) *b. lw: chsd ldr: hdwy over 3f out: rdn to ld 2f out: hung to rail: hdd last 100yds: carried hd awkwardly & nt qckn: lost 2nd nr fin* **8/1**

5403 **4** 1 **Basaata (USA)**[15] 5047 3-8-5 100 .... MartinDwyer 4 107
(M P Tregoning) *t.k.h: hld up in midfield: drvn and unable qck 2f out: styd on ins fnl f: nt rch ldrs* **16/1**

5012 **5** hd **Halicarnassus (IRE)**[11] 5142 3-8-11 111 .... TPO'Shea 6 112
(M R Channon) *hld up in last pair: rdn over 2f out: grad edgd lft: styd on u.p fnl f: nt rch ldrs* **4/1**[2]

1213 **6** ½ **Blue Ksar (FR)**[22] 4805 4-9-0 112 .... (t) KerrinMcEvoy 7 108
(Saeed Bin Suroor) *lw: s.i.s: chsd ldng pair after 2f: rdn to chse ldr over 1f out tl 1f out: wknd last 100yds* **9/4**[1]

2m 6.56s (-1.19) **Going Correction** +0.075s/f (Good)
WFA 3 from 4yo+ 6lb 6 Ran SP% **111.0**
Speed ratings (Par 113): **107,106,106,105,105 105**
CSF £22.62 TOTE £8.80: £3.70, £1.60; EX 26.00.
Owner Mrs P W Harris **Bred** Pendley Farm **Trained** Aldbury, Herts
■ Walter Swinburn's first Group winner as a trainer.

FOCUS
The early pace could have been stronger, but the form still looks solid for the level.

NOTEBOOK
Stotsfold, who did not get the clearest of runs behind subsequent Ebor winner Purple Moon in a Listed race here last month, had conditions to suit and posted a career-best effort to win this Group 3 event. He stayed on well down the outside to get up inside the last and clearly remains an improving sort. As he needs fast conditions opportunities may be thin on the ground for the rest of the season, but connections are apparently considering sending him to the Dubai carnival early next year. (op 6-1 tchd 15-2)
Zaham(USA) again had the opportunity to make every yard but, just as at Haydock, his rider failed to go quick enough in the early stages on him. He rode him as though worried about his stamina, but in each of his hat-trick of wins on turf earlier this year he stayed on strongly at the finish, and it was the same again this time as he battled back after being headed. It is puzzling, and a more forceful ride should pay dividends at this level. (op 11-4)
Mullins Bay, not disgraced last time behind Echo Of Light at York on his return from a five-month absence, took it up travelling well two furlongs out but he hung under pressure and did not look too keen about things in the closing stages. He look one to leave alone despite his obvious ability. (op 10-1)
Basaata(USA), stepping up in distance, was held up and raced keenly, but she stayed on well, albeit without ever having a chance of catching the principals in the closing stages, suggesting a stronger pace would have suited. There could well be a Listed or even a Group 3 race in her over this trip back against her own sex. (op 14-1)
Halicarnassus(IRE) could not confirm York form with Mullins Bay and was a bit disappointing. One could argue that he too would have been better suited by a stronger gallop, but his wins this term have come when quickening off a fairly steady early gallop. (op 7-2 tchd 3-1)
Blue Ksar(FR) has done all his winning on easier ground than this and that looks the likeliest reason for this disappointing effort. (tchd 5-2)

5452 COUNTRYSIDE ALLIANCE NURSERY STKS (H'CAP) 5f
4:20 (4:20) (Class 5) (0-75,75) 2-Y-0 **£3,238** (£963; £481; £240) **Stalls** Low

Form RPR
0430 **1** **Piscean (USA)**[22] 4812 2-9-2 70 .... (b[1]) MickyFenton 7 76
(T Keddy) *v.s.a and wnt rt s: sn bustled along: hdwy to chse ldrs 1/2-way: led ent fnl f: hung lft: rdn out* **9/2**[2]

4100 **2** 1 ¼ **Cocabana**[20] 4903 2-8-13 67 .... JamesDoyle 2 69
(J G Portman) *b.hind: led for 1f: prom: ev ch and rdn wl over 1f out: nt pce of wnr last 100yds* **10/1**

2605 **3** ¾ **Hucking Harmony (IRE)**[48] 4026 2-8-6 63 .... StephaneBreux(3) 11 62
(J R Best) *wnt rt s: sn chsng ldrs: rdn and ev ch over 1f out: no ex last 100yds* **22/1**

2200 **4** nk **Barraland**[30] 4560 2-9-7 75 .... TPO'Shea 9 73
(M R Channon) *prom: rdn to ld over 1f out: hdd ent fnl f: one pce* **7/1**

0622 **5** shd **Blue Zenith (IRE)**[6] 5267 2-8-8 67 .... TolleyDean(5) 1 64
(J S Moore) *chsd ldrs: rdn 3f out: kpt on same pce u.p fnl f* **9/1**

501 **6** 1 ¼ **Mac Dalia**[50] 3947 2-9-5 73 .... TedDurcan 10 66
(M G Quinlan) *taken down early: hld up in tch travelling wl: swtchd lft wl over 1f out: rdn over 1f out: fnd little* **11/1**

2300 **7** 1 **Party In The Park**[23] 4762 2-9-5 73 .... (b[1]) JimmyFortune 4 62
(R Hannon) *lw: prom: led after 1f tl over 1f out: sn hrd rdn: wknd ins fnl f* **11/2**[3]

044 **8** 2 ½ **Caradoc Place**[48] 4014 2-9-2 70 .... MartinDwyer 8 50
(M P Tregoning) *chsd ldrs: rdn and struggling over 2f out: btn whn hung rt over 1f out: eased ins fnl f* **7/1**

6420 **9** 2 **Splash The Cash**[24] 4737 2-9-3 71 .... JimCrowley 5 44
(P Winkworth) *w ldrs: rdn 2f out: wknd over 1f out* **20/1**

1524 **10** 30 **Attribution**[20] 4903 2-8-11 65 .... JamieSpencer 3 —
(A B Haynes) *bhd: lost tch and eased fr 1/2-way: t.o* **10/3**[1]

59.92 secs (0.87) **Going Correction** -0.075s/f (Good) 10 Ran SP% **118.2**
Speed ratings (Par 95): **90,88,86,86,86 84,82,78,75,27**
CSF £49.67 CT £921.88 TOTE £7.90: £2.60, £4.80, £6.70; EX 57.10.
Owner Andrew Duffield **Bred** And Mrs C & J Iacuone **Trained** Newmarket, Suffolk

FOCUS
A competitive nursery run at a good gallop.

NOTEBOOK
Piscean(USA), wearing blinkers for the first time on this drop back in trip, was slowly away as usual, but he came to challenge travelling well and finished to some effect to win well in the end. He was very much suited by these faster conditions. (tchd 5-1 after 11-2 in a place)
Cocabana ran well considering she raced nearer the seemingly unfavoured stands'-side rail, and this sharp five clearly suited her.
Hucking Harmony(IRE) was well drawn to race up the centre of the track but unfortunately she has a tendency to hang right, and that was always going to be a problem without a rail to race against. Her rider was always struggling to keep her in a straight line but she still ran well to finish third, and could yet win a similar contest when she gets a right-hand rail to run against. (op 25-1)
Barraland showed speed from his good draw but he is beginning to look exposed. (tchd 6-1 and 15-2)
Blue Zenith(IRE), running in a handicap for the first time, was another possibly disadvantaged by a low draw as the main action unfolded up the centre. (op 15-2 tchd 10-1)
Mac Dalia, another handicap debutante, found disappointingly little after travelling kindly, which is worth bearing in mind for in-running purposes. (op 10-1)
Caradoc Place Official explanation: jockey said gelding was unsuited by the good to firm ground
Attribution Official explanation: jockey said colt lost its action

5453 COUNTRY PARK STKS (H'CAP) 2m
4:55 (4:56) (Class 6) (0-65,65) 4-Y-0+ **£3,238** (£963; £481; £240) **Stalls** High

Form RPR
0030 **1** **Go Amwell**[19] 4914 4-7-13 46 oh1 .... LiamJones(3) 12 55
(J R Jenkins) *t.k.h: hld up in rr: hdwy 5f out: rdn and effrt on outer over 2f out: hung rt but styd on to ld ins fnl f: rdn out* **20/1**

0335 **2** 1 ¾ **Noddies Way**[12] 5111 4-9-4 62 .... JimCrowley 1 69
(J F Panvert) *lw: led: rdn and pushed on 5f out: hdd 2f out: led again ent fnl f: hdd and one pce ins fnl f* **4/1**[2]

6054 **3** ¾ **Top Trees**[11] 5138 9-8-6 50 .... TPO'Shea 11 56
(W S Kittow) *swtg: s.i.s: t.k.h: hld up towards rr: gd hdwy over 4f out: ev ch and rdn 2f out: btn whn short of room wl ins fnl f* **7/1**

6404 **4** 3 **Carlton Scroop (FR)**[9] 5204 4-9-0 58 .... (b) PaulEddery 9 61
(J Jay) *hld up towards rr: drvn and effrt on outer wl over 2f out: hung rt u.p: kpt on: nvr trbld ldrs* **9/1**

0/2- **5** 2 ½ **Jockser (IRE)**[127] 5587 6-9-2 65 .... HaddenFrost(5) 4 65
(J W Mullins) *racd in midfield: rdn along over 4f out: outpcd over 3f out: n.d after* **3/1**[1]

0/65 **6** shd **Neckar Valley (IRE)**[31] 4534 8-8-7 51 .... NickyMackay 2 50
(J G Portman) *t.k.h: chsd ldrs: rdn to chal 4f out: wknd over 2f out* **20/1**

4650 **7** 1 ¼ **Lysander's Quest (IRE)**[38] 4322 9-8-2 46 oh1 .... NelsonDeSouza 8 44
(R Ingram) *plld hrd: hld up in midfield: rdn and outpcd 4f out: n.d after* **11/1**

0/65 **8** 1 ¾ **Honour High**[98] 2493 5-8-4 48 oh1 ow2 .... MartinDwyer 3 49+
(Lady Herries) *t.k.h: chsd ldr after 2f tl 4f out: short of room briefly over 3f out: btn and eased last 2f* **5/1**

0504 **9** 7 **Mostarsil (USA)**[12] 5111 9-9-0 58 .... (p) JimmyFortune 5 64
(G L Moore) *b. chsd ldr for 2f: chsd ldrs after tl hdwy on rail to ld 2f out: sn rdn: hdd 1f out: lost action and virtually p.u ins fnl f* **9/2**[3]

-000 **10** 38 **St Fris**[21] 4859 4-8-4 48 oh1 ow2 .... (v) SimonWhitworth 6 —
(J A R Toller) *a last and nvr gng wl: t.o last 3f* **40/1**

3m 33.63s (2.84) **Going Correction** +0.075s/f (Good) 10 Ran SP% **122.6**
Speed ratings (Par 101): **95,94,93,92,91 90,90,89,85,66**
CSF £101.50 CT £642.61 TOTE £26.10: £6.80, £1.30, £2.40; EX 173.10.
Owner Robin Stevens **Bred** Michael Ng **Trained** Royston, Herts

FOCUS
A weak event run at a crawl early.
Honour High Official explanation: jockey said gelding lost its action
Mostarsil(USA) Official explanation: jockey said gelding finished lame

5454 SUSSEX MILITIA STKS (H'CAP) 1m 1f 192y
5:30 (5:30) (Class 5) (0-75,75) 3-Y-0+ **£3,886** (£1,156; £577; £288)

Form RPR
-333 **1** **Harry Tricker**[16] 5005 3-9-4 75 .... JimCrowley 3 88+
(Mrs A J Perrett) *lw: hld up in midfield: hdwy over 2f out: rdn over 1f out: led jst ins fnl f: r.o strly* **10/1**

314 **2** 2 ½ **Shadow The Wind (IRE)**[65] 3480 3-9-3 74 .... KerrinMcEvoy 7 82
(E F Vaughan) *lw: hld up rr: hdwy over 2f out: outpcd briefly 2f out: rdn & flashed tail over 1f out: pushed along & styd on fnl f: nt trble wnr* **4/1**[1]

2301 **3** shd **Apache Fort**[13] 5093 4-9-0 65 .... NickyMackay 5 73
(T Keddy) *chsd ldrs: rdn to chal over 2f out: led narrowly jst over 1f out: hdd ins fnl f: no ch w wnr: lost 2nd on line* **4/1**[1]

0000 **4** 2 ½ **Art Modern (IRE)**[31] 4551 5-9-10 75 .... (b) JimmyFortune 4 78
(G L Moore) *b.hind: t.k.h: chsd ldr for 2f and again 3f out: ev ch and rdn 2f out: wknd fnl f* **9/1**

3415 **5** 1 ½ **Nightspot**[31] 4523 6-9-9 74 .... KDarley 6 74
(Eve Johnson Houghton) *led: rdn and hrd pressed over 2f out: hdd jst over 1f out: wknd* **5/1**[2]

0036 **6** 1 ½ **Little Miss Tara (IRE)**[26] 4686 3-8-5 67 .... (v) KevinGhunowa(5) 10 64
(A B Haynes) *hld up bhd: rdn and n.m.r over 2f out: n.d* **50/1**

3253 **7** 1 **Haarth Sovereign (IRE)**[83] 2945 3-9-3 74 .... AdamKirby 2 69
(W R Swinburn) *lw: hld up in rr: rn wd bnd 5f out: n.d* **5/1**[2]

105 **8** nk **Siena Star (IRE)**[39] 4266 9-9-2 67 .... MickyFenton 9 61
(Stef Liddiard) *chsd ldrs: rdn over 2f out: sn btn* **14/1**

264 **9** 2 **Professor Twinkle**[52] 3877 3-8-13 70 .... (v) DaneO'Neill 1 60
(W J Knight) *w.w in midfield: hdwy 4f out: rdn and wknd over 2f out* **16/1**

3261 **10** 7 **Blu Manruna**[6] 5280 4-8-10 61 6ex .... (b) PaulDoe 11 37
(J Akehurst) *s.i.s: hdwy on outer to chse ldr after 2f tl 3f out: wkng whn n.m.r over 2f out: wl btn after: eased ins fnl f* **15/2**[3]

-000 **11** 5 **Trepa (USA)**[44] 4135 3-8-12 69 .... MartinDwyer 8 35
(W Jarvis) *t.k.h: hld up towards rr: lost pl over 4f out: rdn wl over 2f out: sn lost tch: eased ins fnl f: t.o* **16/1**

2m 6.90s (-0.85) **Going Correction** +0.075s/f (Good)
WFA 3 from 4yo+ 6lb 11 Ran SP% **124.6**
Speed ratings (Par 103): **106,104,103,101,100 99,98,98,96,91 87**
CSF £52.87 CT £195.26 TOTE £8.80: £2.20, £2.30, £2.20; EX 45.00 Place 6 £98.00, Place 5 £55.95..
Owner J H Richmond-Watson **Bred** Lawn Stud **Trained** Pulborough, W Sussex

FOCUS
A problem with the stalls led to this race being started by flag and the form has to be treated with caution as a result.
Haarth Sovereign(IRE) Official explanation: jockey said colt never travelled
T/Plt: £255.60 to a £1 stake. Pool: £72,897.30. 208.15 winning tickets. T/Qpdt: £157.40 to a £1 stake. Pool: £3,362.20. 15.80 winning tickets. SP

5455 - (Foreign Racing) - See Raceform Interactive

[5434] CURRAGH (R-H)

Sunday, September 16

OFFICIAL GOING: Good to firm

5456a ROSALEEN KELLY BLENHEIM STKS (LISTED RACE) 6f
2:10 (2:11) 2-Y-O **£24,192** (£7,097; £3,381; £1,152)

RPR

1 **Rock Of Rochelle (USA)**[14] 5076 2-9-1 ....(t) VRDeSouza 6 99
(A Kinsella, Ire) *cl up: 3rd and rdn 1/2-way: 2nd and chal fnl f: led cl home: drvn out and kpt on wl* **15/2**

2 *shd* **Domingues**[14] 5070 2-9-1 95.. DPMcDonogh 5 99
(Edward Lynam, Ire) *lost grnd s: sn cl up in 4th: led 2f out: rdn and strly pressed fnl f: hdd cl home: kpt on u.p* **5/1**[3]

3 *3/4* **Deal Breaker**[17] 4983 2-9-1 95..(t) PJSmullen 4 97
(Edward Lynam, Ire) *chsd ldrs: 6th 1/2-way: sn rdn: 5th under 2f out: kpt on u.p fnl f* **12/1**

4 *nk* **Slam Dunk (USA)**[14] 5076 2-9-1 .... WJSupple 3 96
(G M Lyons, Ire) *cl 2nd: rdn to chal fr under 2f out: 3rd ins fnl f: no ex cl home* **6/1**

5 *1/2* **South Dakota (IRE)**[63] 3574 2-9-1 102........................... JAHeffernan 1 94
(A P O'Brien, Ire) *trckd ldrs in 5th: lost pl briefly under 2f out: kpt on fnl f* **4/1**[2]

6 *1/2* **Great Rumpuscat (USA)** 2-9-1 .... KFallon 7 93+
(A P O'Brien, Ire) *outpcd early: towards rr 1/2-way: prog 2f out: 5th 1f out: sn no ex* **7/2**[1]

7 *1 3/4* **Victorian Bounty**[8] 5216 2-9-1 .... WMLordan 2 88
(E J O'Neill) *led: rdn and hdd 2f out: no ex fr over 1f out* **20/1**

8 *1 3/4* **Capt Chaos (IRE)**[38] 4347 2-9-1 .... FMBerry 8 82
(Edward Lynam, Ire) *hld up in tch: effrt on outer over 2f out: no imp: wknd fnl f: eased cl home* **5/1**[3]

1m 12.2s (-2.30) **Going Correction** -0.30s/f (Firm) **8** Ran SP% **114.1**
Speed ratings: **103,102,101,101,100 100,97,95**
CSF £44.37 TOTE £7.60: £2.30, £2.20, £3.30; DF 91.20.
Owner Her Diamond Necklace Farms FZE **Bred** Beau Cheval Llc **Trained** Athy, Co. Kildare

FOCUS
The form is nothing special for the grade.

NOTEBOOK
Rock Of Rochelle(USA) had Slam Dunk a bit further behind than when winning a maiden over course and distance earlier this month. (op 8/1)
Victorian Bounty, a winner off 75 at Catterick two starts back, failed to handle a 7lb rise when fifth at Haydock last time and she failed to last home on this rise in grade.

5458a BANK OF SCOTLAND (IRELAND) NATIONAL STKS (GROUP 1) (ENTIRE COLTS & FILLIES) 7f
3:10 (3:11) 2-Y-O
£115,810 (£38,783; £18,513; £6,351; £4,324; £2,297)

RPR

1 **New Approach (IRE)**[22] 4833 2-9-1 115........................... KJManning 7 123+
(J S Bolger, Ire) *mde all: rdn and edgd clr fr over 2f out: styd on wl fnl f: comf* **9/4**[1]

2 *1 3/4* **Rio De La Plata (USA)**[46] 4057 2-9-1 .... LDettori 5 118+
(Saeed Bin Suroor) *hld up: 7th and hdwy 2f out: impr into mod 2nd under 1f out: rdn and kpt on wl wout threatening wnr: eased nr fin* **5/2**[2]

3 *1 3/4* **Myboycharlie (IRE)**[28] 4653 2-9-1 122.. KFallon 8 114
(T Stack, Ire) *hld up in 6th: hdwy into 4th 2f out: sn rdn: 3rd and kpt on fnl f* **5/2**[2]

4 *1 1/2* **Lizard Island (USA)**[46] 4057 2-9-1 108........................... JAHeffernan 9 110
(A P O'Brien, Ire) *trckd ldrs in 3rd: rdn 2 1/2f out: 2nd under 2f out: no imp: 4th and no ex fnl f* **25/1**

5 *3* **Great Barrier Reef (USA)**[14] 5070 2-9-1 .... CO'Donoghue 3 102
(A P O'Brien, Ire) *cl 2nd: rdn over 2f out: sn outpcd: 5th and no ex fr over 1f out* **25/1**

6 *2* **Famous Name**[67] 3438 2-9-1 .... PJSmullen 1 97
(D K Weld, Ire) *trckd ldrs in 5th: rdn over 2f out: no imp: one pce* **8/1**[3]

7 *1 3/4* **Minneapolis**[50] 3980 2-9-1 102.. DPMcDonogh 2 92
(A P O'Brien, Ire) *chsd ldrs in 7th: no imp fr over 2f out* **100/1**

8 *5* **Magna Cum Laude (IRE)**[8] 5245 2-9-1 86........................... FMBerry 4 79
(A P O'Brien, Ire) *in rr: trailing fr 1/2-way* **100/1**

9 *shd* **Via Galilei (IRE)**[8] 5245 2-9-1 .... DJMoran 6 79
(J S Bolger, Ire) *chsd ldrs in 4th: rdn 1/2-way: wknd fr 2 1/2f out* **33/1**

1m 23.5s (-4.00) **Going Correction** -0.30s/f (Firm) **9** Ran SP% **111.6**
Speed ratings: **110,108,106,104,100 98,96,90,90**
CSF £7.50 TOTE £2.90: £1.30, £1.50, £1.50; DF 9.10.
Owner Mrs J S Bolger **Bred** Lodge Park Stud **Trained** Coolcullen, Co Carlow

FOCUS
Outstanding form, New Approach putting up a performance worthy of champion two-year-old status as he continued down the route taken by stablemate Teofilo last year. Rio De La Plata was given plenty to do and would be fancied to get closer another time. Myboycharlie was a little below the form he showed in France.

NOTEBOOK
New Approach(IRE), taking the same route as the stable's Champion juvenile of last season, Teofilo, put a high-class field to the sword in the manner of a juvenile champion elect. Controlling the race from the start, he looked a class apart when sent about his business in the final furlong, and everything about him suggests that he is going to be a three-year-old of the very highest calibre. The lessons of what happened with Teofilo, whose career-path has been followed to the letter by New Approach, is a harsh reminder of what can go wrong with any horse, but this majestic victory sets a current standard that will be hard to match. With Manning judging the pace of the race perfectly, the winner possibly benefited to some degree from getting first run, Manning taking him a few lengths clear at a stage when his principal rivals had yet to be asked to lift the tempo. However, the way in which he raised his game through the final furlong left absolutely no room for excuses for the beaten horses. The Galileo colt has bundles of pace, is now proven on a range of surfaces and will surely be suited by middle distances next season. He is a firm favourite at the head of the 2000 Guineas market. (op 2/1)
Rio De La Plata(USA), a supplementary entry, came here as a worthy standard-bearer for top-level British form by virtue of his Goodwood win. His running relative to the fourth horse indicates that he produced a similar display. Held up in the early stages, he started to pick up really well on the outside from around two furlongs out and gave a strong visual impression of accleration. The fact that this could be the case and that he was unable to get to grips with the front-runner, only serves to emphasise the quality of the New Approach's performance. It goes without saying that the Godolphin colt is amongst the very best of his age-group, and remains a serious Classic contender. (op 2/1)
Myboycharlie(IRE) lost his unbeaten record, but he gave a fine account of himself on ground that contrasted sharply with anything that he had dealt with before. The Prix Morny winner was held up to get the trip and travelled well to improve into fourth two furlongs out. Thereafter he could not manage to match Rio De La Plata, and it will be no surprise if he finds his forte as a sprinter next season. He has enjoyed an excellent campaign and is a colt of genuine Group 1 standard. (op 9/4)
Lizard Island(USA), runner-up to Rio De La Plata at Goodwood, was never far from the pace and he had his chance. There was no disgrace in finding three quality colts too good and he will find easier opportunities. (op 16/1)
Great Barrier Reef(USA), runner-up to Sir Gerry in the Gimcrack on debut, failed to build on that when third at odds of 2/5 at the course last time, and it was always unlikely he was going to be breaking his maiden here. He will see the trip out better in a maiden and should be winning before long. (op 20/1)
Famous Name, impressive winner on debut at Naas, failed to cope with the sharp rise in grade and is not the first Abdulla-owned Weld runner to not improve on their winning debut.

5459a LADBROKES.COM SOLONAWAY STKS (GROUP 3) 1m
3:40 (3:42) 3-Y-O+ **£32,939** (£9,628; £4,560; £1,520)

RPR

1 **Jumbajukiba**[41] 4237 4-9-5 111..(b) FMBerry 1 115+
(Mrs John Harrington, Ire) *mde all: rdn clr fr under 2f out: styd on wl: comf* **11/4**[1]

2 *1 3/4* **Cougar Bay (IRE)**[8] 5240 4-9-5 107........................... NGMcCullagh 8 110
(David Wachman, Ire) *chsd ldrs in 3rd: 4th and rdn after 1/2-way: 5th early st: styd on u.p fr over 1f out* **7/1**

3 *1/2* **Lord Admiral (USA)**[28] 4648 6-9-8 111........................(b) MJKinane 9 112
(Charles O'Brien, Ire) *trckd ldrs in 5th: 4th and hdwy ent st: 3rd over 1f out: kpt on same pce u.p* **7/1**

4 *2* **Thoughtless Moment (IRE)**[8] 5242 3-8-12 98................. PJSmullen 6 101
(D K Weld, Ire) *hld up in 7th: 6th st: 5th and no imp fr 1 1/2f out: kpt on ins fnl f* **5/1**[3]

5 *2 1/2* **Namaya (IRE)**[8] 5242 4-9-5 108.. KJManning 5 99
(J S Bolger, Ire) *trckd ldrs: 3rd 1/2-way: 2nd and rdn over 2f out: no imp: no ex ins fnl f* **10/1**

6 *1 3/4* **Decado (IRE)**[35] 4435 4-9-8 110.. DPMcDonogh 7 98
(Kevin Prendergast, Ire) *settled 2nd: rdn ent st: 3rd 2f out: sn no ex* **4/1**[2]

7 *hd* **Black Cat Crossing (USA)** 3-9-1 .... JAHeffernan 2 94
(A P O'Brien, Ire) *in rr: rdn and swished tail st: kpt on fr over 1f out* **14/1**

8 *10* **Anna Karenina (IRE)**[28] 4648 4-9-2 102.. KFallon 3 68
(David Wachman, Ire) *towards rr: no imp early st: eased over 1f out* **7/1**

9 *1 3/4* **Dapple Grey (IRE)**[63] 3578 4-9-2 85.. WMLordan 4 64
(T Stack, Ire) *chsd ldrs in 6th: rdn and wknd ent st: eased fr over 1f out* **33/1**

1m 36.2s (-5.90) **Going Correction** -0.30s/f (Firm)
WFA 3 from 4yo+ 4lb **9** Ran SP% **119.5**
Speed ratings: **117,115,114,112,110 108,108,98,96**
CSF £23.56 TOTE £3.10: £1.60, £2.70, £2.50; DF 25.90.
Owner J P O'Flaherty **Bred** Woodcote Stud Ltd **Trained** Moone, Co Kildare

NOTEBOOK
Jumbajukiba has made an amazingly effective transition from handicapping and ran out a very easy winner here from rivals who would mostly have been considered much superior to him a relatively short time ago. He dictated the pace, and the vastly-improved four-year-old had all his pursuers in trouble from well over a furlong out. (op 3/1)
Cougar Bay(IRE) continues to fall short in the face of stiff tasks, but he again ran well and it is surely a matter of time before he wins at Listed/Group 3 level. (op 10/1)
Lord Admiral(USA), a 7f Group 3 winner at Leopardstown earlier in the season, tends to give his running more often than not and he kept on well enough in third.

5460a ANGLESEY LODGE EQUINE HOSPITAL H'CAP 7f
4:10 (4:14) (50-80,80) 3-Y-O+ **£6,769** (£1,577; £695; £401)

RPR

1 **Sedna (IRE)**[28] 4643 5-10-0 79.. CO'Donoghue 8 95
(W T Farrell, Ire) *towards rr: hdwy on stands' side 2f out: led under 1f out: sn drew clr* **10/1**[3]

2 *3* **Katirisa (IRE)**[14] 5069 3-9-12 80..(b) MJKinane 4 88
(John M Oxx, Ire) *hld up on stands' side: hdwy over 2f out: 3rd and chal over 1f out: 2nd and no imp wl ins fnl f* **3/1**[1]

3 *hd* **Zhukhov (IRE)**[39] 4308 4-9-9 74.. WMLordan 2 81
(T G McCourt, Ire) *hld up on stands' side: hdwy over 2f out: 5th 1f out: kpt on* **12/1**

4 *1 1/4* **Diamonds For Luck (IRE)**[42] 4210 5-8-9 60................. DPMcDonogh 9 64
(Desmond McDonogh, Ire) *prom in centre: 3rd bef 1/2-way: rdn to chal over 2f out: led under 2f out: hdd under 1f out: kpt on* **20/1**

5 *hd* **Accentuate (IRE)**[28] 4650 3-9-8 76........................... NGMcCullagh 22 79
(Charles O'Brien, Ire) *in rr of mid-div: hdwy on far side 1 1/2f out: 3rd and chal under 1f out: no ex cl home* **20/1**

6 *3/4* **Reload (IRE)**[21] 4866 4-8-3 64.. JPFahy(10) 6 65
(Thomas Mullins, Ire) *towards rr on stands' side: rdn after 1/2-way: r.o wl fr over 1f out* **33/1**

7 *1/2* **Collingwood (IRE)**[10] 5185 5-8-10 61........................... JAHeffernan 14 61
(T M Walsh, Ire) *trckd ldrs: impr into 3rd and chal 1 1/2f out: 5th under 1f out: no ex* **8/1**[2]

8 *1 3/4* **Bold Heta (IRE)**[41] 4241 4-8-2 60.. CO'Farrell(7) 3 55
(Sabrina J Harty, Ire) *chsd ldrs on stands' side: 5th and rdn 2f out: no imp fr over 1f out* **25/1**

9 *hd* **Itsabeautifulday (IRE)**[46] 4085 3-8-7 61........................(t) RPCleary 21 55
(M Halford, Ire) *in rr of mid-div: rdn and styd on fr under 2f out* **25/1**

10 *nk* **Tornadodancer (IRE)**[23] 4792 4-8-4 62....... AmyKathleenParsons(7) 29 56
(T G McCourt, Ire) *led: strly pressed fr 2 1/2f out: hdd under 2f out: sn no ex* **50/1**

11 *1/2* **Blue Mountie (IRE)**[35] 4439 3-8-4 58.. MCHussey 27 50
(Edward P Harty, Ire) *trckd ldrs on far side: effrt 2f out: no imp fr over 1f out* **20/1**

12 *hd* **Kilmannin (IRE)**[53] 3862 7-8-13 64..(bt) CDHayes 13 56
(H Rogers, Ire) *mid-div: rdn and kpt on same pce fr under 2f out* **20/1**

13 *3/4* **Ludwigshafen (IRE)**[22] 4836 3-8-13 70................. CPGeoghegan(3) 26 60
(John Geoghegan, Ire) *towards rr on far side: kpt on fr over 1f out* **20/1**

14 *3/4* **Almazaal (IRE)**[169] 855 3-9-12 80.. PJSmullen 16 67
(D K Weld, Ire) *towards rr: kpt on same pce fr 1 1/2f out* **12/1**

15 *1* **Set Fire (IRE)**[17] 4985 4-9-7 79.. SFoley(7) 23 64
(M Halford, Ire) *cl up in 2nd: chal 2 1/2f out: no ex fr under 2f out* **33/1**

16 *3/4* **Jilly Why (IRE)**[22] 4836 6-9-13 78..(b) DJCondon 15 61
(Paul Green) *mid-div: no imp fr 2f out* **8/1**[2]

17 *3/4* **Kerama (GER)**[38] 4348 6-8-4 58..(t) DJMoran(3) 18 38
(H Rogers, Ire) *nvr bttr than mid-div* **50/1**

18 *shd* **Espartano**^{16} [5023] 3-9-4 72 .... KFallon 12 52
(R McGlinchey, Ire) *towards rr: kpt on same pce fr 2f out* **16/1**
19 *1/2* **Hypocrisy**^{184} [692] 4-9-12 77 .... WJSupple 17 56
(Garvan Donnelly, Ire) *nvr a factor* **25/1**
20 *shd* **Fabled (IRE)**^{11} [5149] 3-8-4 58 .... (p) FranciscoDaSilva 11 36
(Ms Joanna Morgan, Ire) *nvr a factor* **33/1**
21 *1/2* **Five Two**^{10} [5184] 4-8-13 74 .... (t) EJMcNamara$^{(10)}$ 10 51
(A J Martin, Ire) *towards rr: no imp fr over 2f out* **10/1**^{3}
22 *nk* **Impossible Dream (IRE)**^{17} [4984] 3-9-12 80 .... VRDeSouza 1 56
(A Kinsella, Ire) *mid-div: rdn 2 1/2f out: sn wknd* **20/1**
23 *1* **Rookwith (IRE)**^{10} [5182] 7-8-5 59 .... SMGorey$^{(3)}$ 30 32
(T G McCourt, Ire) *chsd ldrs on far rail: no ex fr 1 1/2f out* **20/1**
24 *8* **Australia Day (IRE)**^{132} [1551] 4-9-11 76 .... FMBerry 25 27
(Charles O'Brien, Ire) *nvr a factor* **14/1**
25 *1/2* **The Real Thing (IRE)**^{13} [5104] 3-9-10 78 .... (b) PShanahan 7 28
(Tracey Collins, Ire) *chsd ldrs early: bhd fr over 2f out: eased 1 1/2f out* **33/1**
26 *nk* **Misima Sunrise (IRE)**^{41} [4245] 5-8-9 60 ow1 .... WJLee 5 8
(Timothy Doyle, Ire) *in rr of mid-div: no ex fr 2 1/2f out* **50/1**
27 *1/2* **Bobbish**^{39} [4304] 3-9-2 77 .... PTownend$^{(7)}$ 24 24
(J E Mulhern, Ire) *chsd ldrs: 5th 1/2-way: rdn and wknd 2 1/2f out* **25/1**
28 *1* **Jazabelle (IRE)**^{10} [5182] 4-8-2 56 .... (bt^{1}) PBBeggy$^{(3)}$ 28 1
(Tracey Collins, Ire) *chsd ldrs on far side: reminders early: wknd fr 1/2-way: eased ins fnl f* **33/1**
29 *3/4* **Fastnowfast (IRE)**^{47} [4054] 3-7-13 58 .... HelenKeohane$^{(5)}$ 19 —
(F Costello, Ire) *mid-div: wknd fr over 2f out* **25/1**
30 *3 1/2* **Bring Back Matron (IRE)**^{21} [4868] 3-9-10 78 .... KJManning 20 11
(J S Bolger, Ire) *a bhd: eased over 1f out* **16/1**

1m 23.8s (-3.70) **Going Correction** -0.30s/f (Firm)
WFA 3 from 4yo+ 3lb **30** Ran SP% **172.4**
Speed ratings: **109,105,105,103,103 102,102,100,100,99 99,98,98,97,96 95,94,94,93,93 92,92,91,82,81 81,80,79,**
CSF £41.14 CT £430.44 TOTE £13.10: £3.40, £1.60, £2.60, £5.70; DF 65.10.
Owner Mrs Alan Dargan **Bred** Alan Dargan **Trained** Curragh, Co Kildare

NOTEBOOK
Sedna(IRE), who defied topweight, has improved with every start this term. (op 8/1)
Jilly Why(IRE), up 10lb for her recent course and distance success, did not prove so effective on this faster surface and could only plod on at the one pace. Official explanation: trainer said filly was showing signs of being in season post-race (op 7/1 tchd 9/1)

5461 - (Foreign Racing) - See Raceform Interactive

3778 DUSSELDORF (R-H)
Sunday, September 16

OFFICIAL GOING: Soft

5462a BBAG AUKTIONSRENNEN DUSSELDORF (FILLIES) 7f
2:35 (2:40) 2-Y-O
£16,892 (£7,432; £4,054; £2,703; £1,351; £1,351)

RPR
1 **Peace Royale (GER)**^{16} [5028] 2-9-2 .... AStarke 3 89+
(A Wohler, Germany) **1/10**^{1}
2 *5* **Sina (GER)**^{22} [4837] 2-9-2 .... AHelfenbein 6 76
(W Hickst, Germany) **59/10**^{2}
3 *shd* **Time To Beat (GER)** 2-9-0 .... ASuborics 2 74
(W Baltromei, Germany) **103/10**^{3}
4 *nk* **Easy Wonder (GER)**^{22} [4837] 2-8-12 .... THellier 5 71
(I A Wood) *broke wl: chsd easy wnr tl appr fnl f: tired last 100yds: lost 2nd cl home* **126/10**
5 *3* **Sacota**^{22} [4837] 2-8-12 .... JiriPalik 4 64
(E Kurdu, Germany) **36/1**
6 *nse* **Have A Nice Day (GER)** 2-8-12 .... HGrewe 8 63
(S Smrczek, Germany) **46/1**
7 *7* **Ischka (GER)** 2-8-12 .... WPanov 7 46
(M Sowa, Germany) **36/1**
8 *8* **Tapisserie (GER)** 2-8-12 .... APietsch 1 26
(C Von Der Recke, Germany) **33/1**

1m 26.96s (86.96) **8** Ran SP% **132.1**
(including 10 euro stake): WIN 11; PL 10, 12, 12; SF 26.
Owner Filly Syndicate **Bred** Gestut Etzean **Trained** Germany

NOTEBOOK
Easy Wonder(GER), a British raider who was fourth in a similar event over 6f at Baden-Baden on her previous start, ran another decent race in defeat. The well-regarded winner was in a different league, but she was only run out of second close home and, on this evidence, she may appreciate a return to slightly shorter.

5463a JUNIOREN-PREIS (LISTED RACE) 1m
3:40 (4:04) 2-Y-O **£8,784** (£4,054; £2,703; £1,351)

RPR
1 **Idonea (CAN)** 2-8-7 .... AHelfenbein 6 97
(Mario Hofer, Germany) **34/10**^{3}
2 *3 1/2* **Larella (GER)** 2-8-7 .... AStarke 8 89
(P Rau, Germany) **11/10**^{1}
3 *3 1/2* **Maybe (GER)** 2-8-5 .... ASuborics 5 80
(H Blume, Germany) **68/10**
4 *hd* **Sarkando (GER)** 2-8-9 .... JiriPalik 2 83
(E Kurdu, Germany) **15/1**
5 *nk* **Violet Sky (IRE)** 2-8-5 .... PVanDeKeere 4 78
(C Von Der Recke, Germany) **14/1**
6 *7* **Keenes Day (FR)**^{21} [4841] 2-9-0 .... J-PGuillambert 7 72
(M Johnston) *in rr whn reminder 1/2-way: last st: brought wd st: sn hrd rdn and no hdwy* **24/10**^{2}
7 *12* **Trigger Shot (IRE)** 2-8-7 .... JBojko 3 39
(M Weiss, Switzerland) **13/1**

1m 39.02s (-2.14) **7** Ran SP% **132.6**
WIN 44; PL 13, 12, 13; SF 83.
Owner Stall Mercurius **Bred** Anderson Farms Inc & Dr J Storer **Trained** Germany

NOTEBOOK
Keenes Day(FR), the narrow winner of a Beverley maiden last time at the third attempt, was again held up but found this step up in grade too much and never figured after coming wide turning for home.

3581 FRANKFURT (L-H)
Sunday, September 16

OFFICIAL GOING: Good

5464a MERRILL LYNCH EURO-CUP (GROUP 3) 1m 2f
3:55 (4:14) 3-Y-O+ **£21,622** (£6,757; £3,378; £2,027)

RPR
1 **Shrek (GER)**^{77} [3146] 3-8-10 .... EPedroza 7 112
(A Wohler, Germany) *racd in 4th: clsd up over 2f out: 3rd st: remained on rails: rdn dist: led ins fnl f: drvn out* **9/5**^{2}
2 *1/2* **Persian Storm (GER)**^{18} [4958] 3-8-10 .... TPQueally 6 111
(J Hirschberger, Germany) *led: hung rt and c to middle over 1f out: hdd ins fnl f: r.o u.p* **5/2**^{3}
3 *hd* **Wiesenpfad (FR)**^{22} [4838] 4-9-4 .... ADeVries 5 113
(W Hickst, Germany) *hld up in 5th: hdwy on outside and cl 4th st: carried rt by 2nd over 1f out: ev ch ins fnl f: unable qck last 100yds* **8/5**^{1}
4 *2 1/2* **Charlie Cool**^{22} [4805] 4-9-2 .... (v) PaulMulrennan 3 106
(W J Haggas) *disp 2nd: 2nd and pushed along over 2f out: hrd rdn over 1f out: one pce fnl f* **106/10**
5 *5* **Wassiljew (IRE)**^{18} [4958] 3-8-8 .... ABoschert 2 94
(W Baltromei, Germany) *last to st: nvr a factor* **24/1**
6 *4* **Fighting Johan (GER)**^{119} [1875] 3-8-8 .... (b) J-PCarvalho 4 86
(H Blume, Germany) *6th st: a in rr* **23/2**
7 *8* **Lord Hill (GER)**^{18} [4958] 3-8-8 .... FilipMinarik 8 70
(C Zeitz) *trckd ldr tl wl over 2f out: 5th and btn st* **99/10**

2m 3.26s (-5.31)
WFA 3 from 4yo+ 6lb **7** Ran SP% **132.5**
(including ten euro stakes): WIN 28; PL 10,10, 10 (i.e. money back for all three): SF 72.
Owner Frau C Ostermann-Richter **Bred** Frau C Ostermann-Richter **Trained** Germany

NOTEBOOK
Charlie Cool has been struggling in Group 2 company in Britain of late and this drop in grade helped him run better, but he failed to find an extra gear after having his chance.

5259 LONGCHAMP (R-H)
Sunday, September 16

OFFICIAL GOING: Good

5465a PRIX VERMEILLE LUCIEN BARRIERE (GROUP 1) (F&M) 1m 4f
2:25 (2:26) 3-Y-O+ **£115,420** (£46,338; £23,169; £11,574; £5,797)

RPR
1 **Mrs Lindsay (USA)**^{31} [4557] 3-8-9 ow1 .... JMurtagh 2 116
(F Rohaut, France) *racd in 2nd: led 3 1/2f out: rdn st: r.o gamely u.p to line: rdn out* **16/1**
2 *3/4* **West Wind**^{78} [3117] 3-8-8 .... JVictoire 9 114+
(H-A Pantall, France) *hld up: 9th st: swtchd to centre 1 1/2f out: rdn and rapid hdwy over 1f out: wnt 2nd 50yds out: nrest at fin* **4/1**^{2}
3 *3/4* **Passage Of Time**^{107} [2211] 3-8-8 .... RichardHughes 11 113
(H R A Cecil) *prom: 3rd st: rdn to chse ldr 1 1/2f out: kpt on at one pce* **4/1**^{2}
4 *1* **Legerete (USA)**^{28} [4654] 3-8-8 .... OPeslier 6 111
(A Fabre, France) *mid-div: pushed along and disputing 5th st: rdn 1 1/2f out: styd on steadily to line* **14/1**
5 *nk* **Macleya (GER)**^{42} [4215] 5-9-2 .... JAuge 1 111
(A Fabre, France) *prom: 4th st: pushed along 2f out: rdn 1 1/2f out: styd on but nt pce of ldng pair* **16/1**
6 *1 1/2* **Montare (IRE)**^{42} [4215] 5-9-2 .... C-PLemaire 10 108
(J E Pease, France) *hld up in last: effrt over 1f out: sme late hdwy but nvr a factor* **14/1**
7 *2* **Diyakalanie (FR)**^{28} [4654] 3-8-8 .... TThulliez 4 105
(J Boisnard, France) *prom early: disputing 5th st: drvn 2f out: unable qck* **33/1**
8 *2* **Tashelka (FR)**^{28} [4654] 3-8-8 .... SPasquier 7 101
(A Fabre, France) *mid-div: disputing 7th st: unable qck fr 1 1/2f out* **11/2**^{3}
9 *snk* **Vadapolina (FR)**^{47} [4055] 3-8-8 .... CSoumillon 8 101
(A Fabre, France) *hld up in mid-div: disputing 7th st: pushed along 2f out and hdwy in centre tl rdn and no ex fr 1f out* **15/8**^{1}
10 *dist* **Takaniya (IRE)**^{96} [2547] 3-8-8 .... MSautjeau 3 —
(A Fabre, France) *led: hdd 3 1/2f out: pushed along st: sn btn: eased fnl 1 1/2f* **66/1**

2m 27.0s (-8.00) **Going Correction** -0.325s/f (Firm)
WFA 3 from 5yo 8lb **10** Ran SP% **119.7**
Speed ratings: **113,112,112,111,111 110,108,107,107,—**
PARI-MUTUEL: WIN 19.30; PL 4.40, 2.50, 3.60; DF 42.20.
Owner Mme B Jenney **Bred** Derry Meeting Farm **Trained** Sauvagnon, France

NOTEBOOK
Mrs Lindsay(USA) had been aimed at this race all season and she completely reversed the form of the Prix de Diane. She basically stole this under an enterprising ride from Murtagh, who kicked her into a clear lead early in the straight and she just held on. She is not entered in the Arc de Triomphe and is unlikely to be supplemented, but there was some talk afterwards of the Breeders' Cup Fillies & Mares Turf.
West Wind was none too well away from her outside draw and still had plenty to do in the straight. She had to wait for a gap before starting her run but flew home once in the clear and looked a most unlucky loser. It would be no surprise to see her take her chance in the Prix de l'Opera.
Passage Of Time posted a decent effort considering this was her first run for over three months after a serious illness. She was always close to the winner but couldn't quicken in the same manner when things warmed up in the straight and this ground was probably plenty quick enough. This outing will have undoubtedly brought her on a lot and she should strip much fitter next time out. The Arc, the Opera and the Breeders' Cup are all options for her.
Legerete(USA), a great disappointment in the Prix de la Nonnette at Deauville, posted a better effort. She will not run in the Arc and there are no immediate plans.

5466a PRIX NIEL CASSINO BARRIERE D'ENGHIEN (GROUP 2) (C&F) 1m 4f
3:00 (3:00) 3-Y-O **£50,068** (£19,324; £9,223; £6,149; £3,074)

RPR
1 **Soldier Of Fortune (IRE)**^{77} [3142] 3-9-2 .... JMurtagh 5 126
(A P O'Brien, Ire) *racd in 2nd: 3rd 1/2-way: 2nd st: led over 2f out: r.o wl to line: drvn out* **9/4**^{2}

2 1½ **Sagara (USA)**^{21} 4872 3-9-2 .... TGillet 6 123
(J E Pease, France) *hld up in last: pushed along 2f out: r.o to go 3rd 1 1/2f out: styd on and tk 2nd 50yds out* **20/1**

3 ¾ **Zambezi Sun**^{64} 3566 3-9-2 .... SPasquier 2 123+
(P Bary, France) *disp 4th: 5th 1/2-way: 3rd and shkn up st: drvn and wnt 2nd 2f out: no imp on wnr fnl f and lost 2nd 50yds out* **11/8**^{1}

4 6 **Sageburg (IRE)**^{49} 4011 3-9-2 .... CSoumillon 1 112
(A Fabre, France) *disp 4th: 4th 1/2-way: pushed along on outside 2f out: one pce fnl f* **5/2**^{3}

5 8 **Spirit One (FR)**^{29} 4627 3-9-2 .... DBoeuf 3 98
(P Demercastel, France) *racd in 3rd: 2nd 1/2-way: cl 4th and rdn st: last and btn 2f out* **33/1**

6 5 **Song Of Hiawatha**^{26} 4693 3-9-2 .... DavidMcCabe 4 90
(A P O'Brien, Ire) *led: pushed along 4f out: hdd over 2f out: sn wknd and eased fnl f* **100/1**

2m 25.6s (-9.40) **Going Correction** -0.325s/f (Firm) **6** Ran SP% **110.1**
Speed ratings: **118,117,116,112,107 103**
PARI-MUTUEL: WIN 3.30 (coupled with Song Of Hiawatha); PL 3.20, 5.80; SF 34.70.
Owner Mrs John Magnier, M Tabor & D Smith **Bred** J S Bolger **Trained** Ballydoyle, Co Tipperary
■ Eight of the last ten Arc winners ran here. Sagamix, Montjeu, Sinndar, Dalakhani, Hurricane Run and Rail Link won both races.

NOTEBOOK
Soldier Of Fortune(IRE) ◆, an impressive winner of the Irish Derby on really testing ground, confirmed himself top class on all kinds of surfaces, winning in straightforward fashion in a very good time. Having followed his lead horse until the beginning of the straight, he soon took control and strode out well. He will probably be even better back on easier ground and will now be aimed at the Prix de l'Arc de Triomphe, in which the recent winners of this trial have a superb record.
Sagara(USA)'s connections have been waiting for him to show this kind of form for some time. He had been unlucky in the Grand Prix de Paris and disappointed when only fifth in the Grand Prix de Deauville, but this was more like it. Dropped out last in the early part of the race, he came with a run up the far rail and took second place well inside the final furlong. Still on the upgrade, it would be no surprise if his connections let him take his chance in the Arc.
Zambezi Sun's trainer stated that he would need the outing and afterwards he added that he definitely needed the run. He had not been seen out since strolling home in a controversial Grand Prix and he had been given a nice break in the meantime. He was in fifth place in the long descent towards the straight and appeared to be going nicely with a furlong and a half left to run. However, his stride then began to shorten inside the final furlong and he was never touched with the whip. He can be expected to come on a bundle for this and should not be underestimated in the Arc.
Sageburg(IRE) ran way below the expectations of his connections and other racing professionals. Having not for the first time got very warm in the preliminaries, he never really appeared to be going that well in the race itself and, under pressure early in the straight, he was soon beaten. It is possible this ground was a little too fast.

5467a PRIX FOY GRAY D'ALBION BARRIERE (GROUP 2) (C&F) 1m 4f
3:30 (3:30) 4-Y-O+ **£50,068** (£19,324; £9,223; £6,149; £3,074)

RPR

1 **Manduro (GER)**^{35} 4445 5-9-2 .... SPasquier 4 126+
(A Fabre, France) *disp 3rd early: 3rd 1/2-way: 2nd st: led gng easily over 1 1/2f out: pushed out* **4/11**^{1}

2 2½ **Mandesha (FR)**^{43} 4149 4-8-13 .... CSoumillon 1 119+
(A De Royer-Dupre, France) *racd in last: 4th st: pushed along to go 2nd 1 1/2f out: no imp on wnr* **11/4**^{2}

3 3 **Dragon Dancer**^{22} 4825 4-9-2 .... DarryllHolland 5 116
(G Wragg) *disp 3rd early: 4th 1/2-way: last on ins st: pushed along over 1 1/2f out: styd on to take 3rd* **25/1**

4 ½ **Sommertag (GER)**^{14} 5077 4-9-2 .... JVictoire 3 115?
(J Hirschberger, Germany) *led: pushed along appr st: hdd over 1 1/2f out: one pce* **150/1**

5 4 **Distant Way (USA)**^{126} 1700 6-9-2 .... MDemuro 2 108
(L Brogi, Italy) *prom in 2nd: pressing ldr appr st: cl 3rd st: unable qckn fr 2f out* **20/1**^{3}

2m 28.8s (-6.20) **Going Correction** -0.325s/f (Firm) **5** Ran SP% **109.3**
Speed ratings: **107,105,103,103,100**
PARI-MUTUEL: WIN 1.40 (coupled with Sommertag); PL 1.10, 1.10; SF 1.90.
Owner Baron G Von Ullmann **Bred** Rolf Brunner **Trained** Chantilly, France

NOTEBOOK
Manduro(GER), racing over 1m4f for the first time, won with real authority, although this was a slowly-run race and the winning time was 3.2 seconds slower than Prix Niel. He raced a little freely through the early stages, but was well placed throughout and, having taken over at the two-furlong marker, he came clear in impressive fashion. His odds were immediately cut for the Arc de Triomphe, but bad news was to follow after the race. His trainer looked anxious in the winner's enclosure and it was later announced that the horse had sustained a fracture to his off-hind fetlock. His retirement has been confirmed and the racing world has been robbed of a real star.
Mandesha(FR) raced very freely early on when only a moderate pace was set by the lead horse. Dropped out last, she began her effort from one and a half out, but the winner was long gone and she was by no means given a hard time. Despite being looked after, she carried her head a little high and did not totally convince with her attitude. Her connections seemed happy with the run, but it would be no surprise if she was fitted with cheekpieces in the Prix de l'Arc de Triomphe, her next intended target, as it is felt she lacks a little concentration when put under pressure.
Dragon Dancer, finally off the mark in a Listed event at Windsor last month, was denied a clear run when trying to stay on and probably should finished a little closer. His trainer was well pleased with this run and he will be allowed to take his chance in the Arc.
Sommertag(GER) set just a steady gallop in his role as pacemaker and he looks flattered by his proximity.

5468a PRIX DU PETIT COUVERT CASINO BARRIERE DE DINARD (GROUP 3) 5f (S)
4:00 (4:01) 3-Y-O+ **£27,027** (£10,811; £8,108; £5,405; £2,703)

RPR

1 **Tax Free (IRE)**^{45} 4090 5-9-2 .... AdrianTNicholls 5 113
(D Nicholls) *disp ld tl narrow ldr 1/2-way: fnd more fnl f: drvn out* **1/1**^{1}

2 snk **Derison (USA)**^{29} 5-8-13 .... (b) DBonilla 2 109
(P Van De Poele, France) *disp ld: cl 2nd 1/2-way: rdn over 1f out: r.o to line but a jst hld by wnr* **12/1**

3 1½ **Kourka (FR)**^{67} 3445 5-8-9 .... RonanThomas 1 100
(J-M Beguigne, France) *mid-div: 5th 1/2-way: rdn over 1 1/2f out on rail: styd on to take 3rd on line* **8/1**^{3}

4 nse **Only Answer**^{43} 4190 3-8-8 .... OPeslier 3 100
(A Fabre, France) *prom: 3rd 1/2-way: rdn to chse ldrs 1 1/2f out: no imp on ldng pair* **5/2**^{2}

5 hd **Place Vendome (FR)**^{23} 3-8-8 .... TJarnet 4 99
(Mlle S-V Tarrou, France) *mid-div: 4th 1/2-way: effrt fnl f and disputing 3rd 100yds out: styd on* **14/1**

6 ¾ **Kocooning (IRE)**^{43} 4190 4-8-9 .... CSoumillon 6 96
(Robert Collet, France) *mid-div: 6th 1/2-way: n.d* **14/1**

7 4 **Deauville (GER)**^{16} 4-8-10 ow1 .... FSpanu 7 83
(Frau E Mader, Germany) *bhd: last 1/2-way: nvr a factor* **33/1**

55.80 secs (-3.00) **Going Correction** -0.325s/f (Firm)
WFA 3 from 4yo+ 1lb **7** Ran SP% **113.6**
Speed ratings: **111,110,108,108,107 106,100**
PARI-MUTUEL: WIN 2.20; PL 1.60, 2.80; SF 10.60.
Owner Ian Hewitson **Bred** Denis & Mrs Teresa Bergin **Trained** Sessay, N Yorks

NOTEBOOK
Tax Free(IRE), smartly into his stride, was soon at the head of affairs with the runner-up and they had the race to themselves from some way out. Asked to quicken at the furlong marker, he responded well and was game to the bitter end. His connections had to wait for a worrying 20 minutes before the Stewards confirmed the result, however. This thoroughly genuine five-year-old may well come back for the Prix de l'Abbaye de Longchamp on October 7.
Derison(USA), also smartly into his stride, raced with the winner throughout. He came under strong pressure one and a half out, but could never quite make it to the head of affairs. The time was fast and this gelding may well be allowed to take his chance in the Abbaye.
Kourka(FR) never looked like taking a hand in the battle for first place. Fourth early on, she just ran on one paced but was game until the end and snatched third place in the last few strides. She is not really up to this level and a longer distance would be better.
Only Answer, well backed, was third early on but she found nothing when asked to close on the winner and runner up. She will probably benefit from a longer trip.

5469a PRIX GLADIATEUR ROYAL THALASSO BARRIERE (GROUP 3) 1m 7f 110y
4:30 (4:32) 4-Y-O+ **£27,027** (£10,811; £8,108; £5,405; £2,703)

RPR

1 **Varevees**^{28} 4655 4-8-8 .... TJarnet 5 112
(J Boisnard, France) *settled in last: 4th st: sn pushed along: r.o to ld 1 1/2f out: styd on wl fnl f: drvn out* **43/10**^{3}

2 nk **Getaway (GER)**^{28} 4655 4-9-4 .... SPasquier 4 122
(A Fabre, France) *racd in 3rd: 4th 1/2-way: last st: nt clr run on rails 2f out: drvn and r.o wl 1 1/2f out: wnt 2nd fnl f: nrst at fin* **3/5**^{1}

3 5 **Le Miracle (GER)**^{28} 4655 6-9-2 .... DBoeuf 1 114
(W Baltromei, Germany) *led 6f: 2nd 1/2-way: 3rd st: rdn 1 1/2f out: styd on at one pce* **32/10**^{2}

4 2½ **Latin Mood (FR)**^{28} 4655 4-8-11 .... OPeslier 3 106
(P Demercastel, France) *racd in 2nd: led after 6f: rdn over 1 1/2f out: hdd 1 1/2f out: one pce* **15/1**

5 20 **Mudawin (IRE)**^{25} 4722 6-8-11 .... JohnEgan 2 82
(Jane Chapple-Hyam) *racd in 4th: 3rd 1/2-way: wnt 2nd 5f out: pushed along appr st: u.p 2f out: sn btn* **19/1**

3m 15.0s (-11.60) **Going Correction** -0.325s/f (Firm) **5** Ran SP% **116.4**
Speed ratings: **116,115,113,112,102**
PARI-MUTUEL: WIN 5.30; PL 1.70, 1.20; SF 8.90.
Owner J Uzel **Bred** Daniel Cherdo **Trained** France

NOTEBOOK
Varevees reversed the form with the runner-up on their running in Deauville, despite this not being her favoured surface. Settled in fourth position on the far side, she took control of the race at the furlong marker and ran on bravely to hold off the favourite by a narrow margin. She was giving her trainer his first Group success and will be allowed to take her chance in the Prix du Cadran when it is hoped there will be more cut in the ground.
Getaway(GER) really hated the fast going and it was a worry before the race as he has been jarred up in the past. He dropped back into last position on the downhill section before the straight and did not look at all at ease when starting his challenge and, although eventually running on, he was definitely feeling the ground. Hopefully he will come out of the race in good condition and if all goes well he will go for the Cadran.
Le Miracle(GER) won this race last year but he could only manage a moderate third on this occasion. He usually comes with a late run but he could only stay on one pace this time. He was not fitted with ear plugs and his jockey felt that it made him more nervous than usual. He is another marked down for the Cadran.
Latin Mood(FR), a supplementary entry, recovered his owner's money and more. Having raced in second early on, he took over the running on the far side and stayed at the head of affairs until halfway up the straight. He was then passed by three of the other runners while staying on at the one pace and is not really up to this class.
Mudawin(IRE) seemed to hate the fast ground, but he probably was not up to this level anyway.

5301 LEICESTER (R-H)
Monday, September 17
OFFICIAL GOING: Firm (good to firm in places; 9.7)
Wind: Light across Weather: Overcast with a light shower between races 4 and 5

5470 LADBROKES.COM IBSTOCK MAIDEN AUCTION STKS 5f 218y
2:30 (2:32) (Class 5) 2-Y-O **£3,238** (£963; £481; £240) **Stalls** Low

Form RPR

43 1 **Suzi's Decision**^{26} 4709 2-8-1 0 .... LiamJones(3) 2 67
(P W D'Arcy) *chsd ldrs: led 2f out: sn rdn and hung rt: r.o* **5/1**^{2}

5 2 2 **Balata**^{147} 1201 2-9-0 0 .... SimonWhitworth 7 71
(B R Millman) *chsd ldrs: rdn and ev ch over 1f out: styd on same pce ins fnl f* **16/1**

3 1¼ **La Famiglia** 2-8-4 0 .... HayleyTurner 1 57
(H Candy) *sn pushed along in rr: hung rt fr 1/2-way: hdwy over 1f out: nrst fin* **16/1**

3 4 nk **Solo River**^{7} 5267 2-8-4 0 .... MartinDwyer 10 56
(P J Makin) *prom: rdn over 2f out: styd on same pce fnl f* **7/1**

5 5 hd **Blitzen (IRE)**^{26} 4702 2-8-12 0 .... RichardMullen 6 63
(E S McMahon) *trckd ldr: rdn over 2f out: sn hung rt: styd on same pce fnl f* **5/2**^{1}

044 6 ¾ **Always Brave**^{22} 4852 2-8-11 75 .... EddieAhern 5 60
(M Johnston) *led 4f: styd on same pce fnl f* **13/2**^{3}

240 7 3 **I Dont Do Walkin (USA)**^{93} 2651 2-8-10 70 .... SteveDrowne 12 50
(B J Meehan) *chsd ldrs: rdn over 2f out: wknd fnl f* **8/1**

0000 8 1 **Holy Storm (IRE)**^{7} 5268 2-8-13 50 .... (b^{1}) StephenCarson 13 50
(Eve Johnson Houghton) *hld up: rdn over 2f out: n.d* **100/1**

00 9 hd **Halsion Challenge**^{26} 4709 2-8-11 0 .... DaneO'Neill 14 47
(J R Best) *s.s: hdwy over 3f out: rdn and wknd over 1f out* **25/1**

10 shd **Reve Vert (FR)** 2-9-0 0 .... JimCrowley 9 50
(A W Carroll) *s.s: outpcd: nvr nrr* **40/1**

0 11 shd **Our Lament**^{12} 5126 2-8-13 0 .... OscarUrbina 8 49
(G C Bravery) *sn outpcd* **100/1**

6 12 1½ **Magical Song**^{68} 3424 2-8-9 0 .... PaulEddery 4 40
(E J O'Neill) *chsd ldrs: lost pl 4f out: sn bhd* **25/1**

553 **13** *shd* **Faber Hall Flyer**[22] 4854 2-8-11 78........................(t) DMylonas 11 42
(Mrs C A Dunnett) *mid-div: hdwy over 3f out: wknd 2f out* **13/2**[3]

14 *24* **Casual Garcia** 2-9-3 0........................ JamieMackay 3 —
(Sir Mark Prescott) *s.s: outpcd* **100/1**

1m 12.97s (-0.23) **Going Correction** -0.15s/f (Firm) **14** Ran SP% **120.4**
Speed ratings (Par 95): **95,92,90,90,90 89,85,83,83,83 83,81,81,49**
CSF £78.29 TOTE £7.70: £1.60, £6.30, £5.10; EX 122.80 TRIFECTA Not won..

Owner Greenstead Hall Racing **Bred** David And Mrs Vicki Fleet **Trained** Newmarket, Suffolk

FOCUS
A weak maiden run in a modest time. The eighth limits the form.

NOTEBOOK
Suzi's Decision ◆ did not seem to appreciate the testing ground at Folkestone on her previous start and the return to a quick surface suited. She had actually been shaping as though she would appreciate a step up to 1m, but she displayed plenty of speed on this drop in trip and was a convincing winner. She is bred to stay further and could progress into a useful type in time.
Balata, gelded since his debut at Windsor back in April, made a respectable return to action. He is open to improvement.
La Famiglia, a daughter of Tobougg, half-sister to multiple 6f-7f winner Cativo Cavallino, showed real signs of greenness, but she gradually got the hang of things and finished well. She should improve plenty and ought to find a similar race.
Solo River, whose debut third at Bath represented just modest form, found this tougher. (op 9-1)
Blitzen(IRE), who got going too late when a beaten favourite on his debut over 5f at Carlisle, was again strongly supported on this step up in trip, but this time he failed to see out his race after showing good early speed. One suspects he works quite well at home, but he is not doing it on the track at the moment. Official explanation: jockey said colt was unsuited by the firm ground (op 6-1)
Always Brave showed good early speed, but he failed to sustain his challenge and was below his official mark of 75. (op 3-1)
Magical Song Official explanation: jockey said colt was unsuited by the firm ground

5471 LADBROKES.COM DESFORD NURSERY 7f 9y
3:00 (3:01) (Class 4) (0-85,77) 2-Y-O **£3,886** (£1,156; £577; £288) **Stalls** Low

Form RPR
006 **1** **Rich Kid (IRE)**[43] 4198 2-8-9 **65**........................ MartinDwyer 4 66
(R Hannon) *chsd ldrs: led over 2f out: sn rdn: all out* **4/1**[2]

0333 **2** *shd* **Howdigo**[18] 4964 2-9-7 **77**........................ DaneO'Neill 6 78
(J R Best) *trckd ldrs: rdn and ev ch fr over 1f out: r.o* **9/4**[1]

3204 **3** *3/4* **Suzi Spends (IRE)**[11] 5153 2-8-13 **69**........................ EddieAhern 2 68
(M Johnston) *chsd ldrs: rdn and ev ch over 1f out: styd on same pce ins fnl f* **6/1**

5001 **4** *1* **Asian Power (IRE)**[10] 5199 2-9-1 **71**........................ OscarUrbina 3 67
(P J O'Gorman) *hld up in tch: rdn over 1f out: styd on same pce fnl f* **11/2**[3]

0030 **5** *3 1/2* **Bid Art (IRE)**[66] 3508 2-8-9 **68**........................ WilliamBuick(3) 8 55
(A M Balding) *hld up: racd keenly: hdwy u.p 2f out: edgd lft and wknd fnl f* **13/2**

5610 **6** *1/2* **Casino Night**[17] 4991 2-8-8 **67**........................ PatrickMathers(3) 1 53
(J R Weymes) *led: rdn and hdd over 2f out: wknd over 1f out* **12/1**

060 **7** *6* **The Hoofer (IRE)**[13] 5110 2-8-9 **65**........................ TedDurcan 7 35
(J L Dunlop) *s.i.s: hld up: racd keenly: effrt over 2f out: wknd over 1f out: eased ins fnl f* **10/1**

1m 26.55s (0.45) **Going Correction** -0.15s/f (Firm) **7** Ran SP% **110.6**
Speed ratings (Par 97): **91,90,90,88,84 84,77**
CSF £12.50 CT £48.46 TOTE £6.30: £3.70, £1.30; EX 14.10 Trifecta £102.60 Pool £193.74 - 1.34 winning units..

Owner M Sines **Bred** R Goodwin **Trained** East Everleigh, Wilts

FOCUS
A modest nursery, but sound form with improvement from the winner.

NOTEBOOK
Rich Kid(IRE) had shown just moderate form in sprint maidens, but he was not too hardly treated on his nursery debut and improved for the step up in trip. He should remain competitive in similar company. (op 3-1)
Howdigo, racing off the same mark at when third on the Polytrack at Lingfield on his previous start, had every chance and just failed. (op 3-1)
Suzi Spends(IRE) again gave the impression she is ready for 1m. (tchd 7-1)
Asian Power(IRE), who arrived late on the scene to get off the mark in a nursery on the Polytrack at Kempton on his previous start, could not defy a 4lb rise in the weights back up in trip and returned to turf. He briefly looked dangerous, but his effort eventually flattened out. (op 7-1)
Bid Art(IRE) offered disappointingly little. (tchd 6-1 and 7-1)

5472 LADBROKESCASINO.COM CLAIMING STKS 1m 1f 218y
3:30 (3:30) (Class 5) 3-Y-O+ **£2,914** (£867; £433; £216) **Stalls** High

Form RPR
2000 **1** **Castara Bay**[18] 4960 3-9-1 68........................ HaddenFrost(5) 4 76
(R Hannon) *broke wl: sn lost pl: bhd 1/2-way: r.o fr over 1f out: hung rt and led wl ins fnl f: sn clr* **9/1**[3]

4062 **2** *3* **Tufton**[24] 4763 4-9-7 77........................(t) AshleyHamblett(5) 2 70
(M Botti) *trckd ldrs: led 8f out: clr 3f out: rdn over 1f out: hdd and no ex wl ins fnl f* **15/8**[1]

0005 **3** *3/4* **Rosie's Glory (USA)**[10] 5187 3-8-8 62 ow1........................(b) JamieSpencer 9 57
(B J Meehan) *led after 1f: hdd 8f out: chsd ldrs: rdn over 3f out: sn hung rt: styd on same pce ins fnl f* **5/1**[2]

6200 **4** *1/2* **Fabrian**[3] 5383 9-9-6 72........................ JamesDoyle 8 62
(R J Price) *led 1f: trckd ldrs: rdn over 3f out: styd on same pce appr fnl f* **15/8**[1]

066- **5** *3* **Bamboo Banks (IRE)**[342] 5887 4-9-4 57........................ TedDurcan 1 54
(J L Dunlop) *hld up: rdn over 3f out: sme hdwy over 1f out: n.d* **20/1**

5-50 **6** *9* **Francesco**[12] 2105 3-8-8 54........................(vt) LPKeniry 6 32
(Evan Williams) *prom 6f* **40/1**

44-3 **7** *8* **Hall Of Fame**[16] 392 3-9-0 72........................ EddieAhern 5 22
(C J Mann) *bhd fr 1/2-way* **9/1**[3]

0000 **8** *12* **Princess Arwen**[86] 2870 5-8-8 37........................ AnnStokell(5) 3 —
(Mrs Barbara Waring) *a in rr: wknd 4f out* **100/1**

2m 5.98s (-2.32) **Going Correction** -0.10s/f (Good)
WFA 3 from 4yo+ 6lb **8** Ran SP% **114.4**
Speed ratings (Par 103): **105,102,102,101,99 92,85,76**
CSF £26.13 TOTE £10.90: £3.00, £1.60, £1.40; EX 35.70 Trifecta £243.60 Part won. Pool £343.23 - 0.95 winning units..Tufton was claimed by I Williams for £18,000.

Owner J R Shannon **Bred** J R Shannon **Trained** East Everleigh, Wilts

FOCUS
An ordinary claimer run at a strong pace. The form is rated through the winner.

Hall Of Fame Official explanation: jockey said gelding was unsuited by the firm ground

5473 WEATHERBYS PRINTING H'CAP 5f 218y
4:00 (4:00) (Class 4) (0-85,82) 3-Y-O **£6,309** (£1,888; £944; £472; £235) **Stalls** Low

Form RPR
0030 **1** **Everymanforhimself (IRE)**[11] 5168 3-9-4 **82**........................(b) JimCrowley 6 93
(J G Given) *chsd ldr tl led over 1f out: rdn out* **14/1**

0020 **2** *2 1/2* **Sacre Coeur**[16] 5051 3-9-0 **78**........................ EddieAhern 8 81
(J L Dunlop) *led: rdn and hdd over 1f out: edgd rt and styd on same pce ins fnl f* **16/1**

3135 **3** *2 1/2* **Flying Goose (IRE)**[23] 4811 3-9-3 **81**........................ JamieSpencer 4 77
(L M Cumani) *hld up: hdwy over 2f out: rdn over 1f out: no ex fnl f* **1/1**[1]

2321 **4** *2* **Rainbow Fox**[17] 4999 3-8-7 **71**........................ DaleGibson 7 61
(R A Fahey) *hld up: hdwy over 2f out: sn rdn: wknd ins fnl f* **4/1**[2]

3050 **5** *1 1/2* **King's Bastion (IRE)**[11] 5168 3-8-11 **75**........................(v[1]) HayleyTurner 2 60
(M L W Bell) *trckd ldrs: rdn over 2f out: wknd over 1f out* **9/1**

0345 **6** *1/2* **Bazroy (IRE)**[4] 5358 3-9-1 **79**........................(b) TGMcLaughlin 1 63
(P D Evans) *chsd ldrs: rdn over 2f out: wknd over 1f out* **7/1**[3]

5100 **7** *shd* **Castano**[44] 4186 3-8-4 **68** oh1........................ AdrianMcCarthy 5 51
(B R Millman) *s.i.s: hdwy over 2f out: rdn and wknd over 1f out* **28/1**

0200 **8** *1 1/4* **Ice Mountain**[16] 5039 3-9-1 **82**........................ MarkLawson(3) 3 61
(B Smart) *s.i.s: hdwy over 2f out: sn rdn: edgd rt and wknd over 1f out* **66/1**

0653 **9** *10* **Star Strider**[7] 5270 3-8-4 **68**........................(p) MartinDwyer 9 17
(A M Balding) *prom over 3f* **12/1**

1m 11.39s (-1.81) **Going Correction** -0.15s/f (Firm) **9** Ran SP% **117.7**
Speed ratings (Par 103): **106,102,99,96,94 94,93,92,78**
CSF £216.06 CT £432.93 TOTE £24.30: £4.60, £3.80, £1.10; EX 218.70 Trifecta £471.70 Pool £757.51 - 1.14 winning units..

Owner Cavan Pickering & Stewart Whitehead **Bred** Denis McDonnell **Trained** Willoughton, Lincs

FOCUS
A fair sprint handicap. The form has been rated at face value but may not prove that sound.

Bazroy(IRE) Official explanation: jockey said colt never travelled
Ice Mountain Official explanation: jockey said gelding missed the break

5474 LADBROKES.COM MAIDEN STKS 1m 3f 183y
4:30 (4:31) (Class 5) 3-Y-O+ **£3,238** (£963; £481; £240) **Stalls** High

Form RPR
0-24 **1** **Grand Heights (IRE)**[142] 1290 3-8-12 80........................ TedDurcan 1 69+
(J L Dunlop) *trckd ldr: led over 4f out: clr fnl 2f* **1/16**[1]

2 *10* **Optimistic Alfie**[42] 7-9-6 0........................ GeorgeBaker 3 53
(B G Powell) *dwlt: bhd: hdwy over 3f out: sn rdn and edgd rt: styng on same pce whn wnt 2nd over 1f out* **20/1**[2]

00 **3** *7* **Pagan Rose (IRE)**[17] 5013 3-8-7 0........................ RobertHavlin 4 37
(J A R Toller) *prom: chsd wnr over 3f out: sn rdn: wknd over 1f out: eased ins fnl f* **25/1**[3]

000- **4** *45* **Sharpe Image (IRE)**[441] 3145 4-9-1 51........................ TGMcLaughlin 2 —
(G Woodward) *led: hung lft 5f out: sn hdd: wknd over 3f out* **100/1**

2m 34.4s (-0.10) **Going Correction** -0.10s/f (Good)
WFA 3 from 4yo+ 8lb **4** Ran SP% **103.7**
Speed ratings (Par 103): **96,89,84,54**
CSF £1.81 TOTE £1.10; EX 2.50.

Owner Windflower Overseas Holdings Inc **Bred** Windflower Overseas **Trained** Arundel, W Sussex

FOCUS
Very uncompetitive and not a race to dwell on, with the winner a class above his rivals.

5475 LADBROKES.COM H'CAP 1m 60y
5:00 (5:00) (Class 5) (0-75,72) 3-Y-O **£3,238** (£963; £481; £240) **Stalls** High

Form RPR
-322 **1** **Princess Taylor**[31] 4579 3-9-4 **72**........................(t) TedDurcan 11 79
(M Botti) *a.p: chsd ldr 3f out: rdn over 1f out: styd on to ld post* **9/1**

0663 **2** *shd* **Lord Theo**[9] 5218 3-9-4 **72**........................ JamesDoyle 1 79
(N P Littmoden) *unruly in stalls: led: rdn over 1f out: hdd post* **5/1**[1]

0463 **3** *1 1/2* **Tom Paris**[9] 5238 3-9-0 **68**........................ RichardMullen 9 72
(W R Muir) *hld up: hdwy over 3f out: rdn and nt clr run over 1f out: r.o* **11/2**[2]

1060 **4** *1/2* **Zonta Zitkala**[22] 4848 3-9-3 **71**........................ MartinDwyer 7 73+
(R M Beckett) *rrd s: bhd: hdwy and nt clr run over 1f out: swtchd lft: r.o wl* **10/1**

0420 **5** *1 1/2* **Golden Prospect**[23] 4807 3-9-3 **71**........................ EddieAhern 10 70
(J W Hills) *chsd ldrs: rdn over 2f out: styd on same pce ins fnl f* **7/1**[3]

360 **6** *3/4* **Blackberry Pie (USA)**[17] 5013 3-9-0 **68**........................ SteveDrowne 12 65
(R Charlton) *hld up: hdwy over 2f out: rdn over 1f out: styd on same pce* **7/1**[3]

6020 **7** *1/2* **Dirty Dancing**[11] 5166 3-8-4 **61**........................ WilliamBuick(3) 2 57
(B W Hills) *hld up: rdn over 2f out: r.o ins fnl f: nt rch ldrs* **8/1**

0003 **8** *shd* **Apollo Five**[24] 4760 3-8-8 **62**........................ HayleyTurner 3 58
(D J Coakley) *hld up in tch: rdn over 3f out: wknd ins fnl f* **9/1**

0252 **9** *hd* **Carlitos Spirit (IRE)**[26] 4710 3-8-8 **62**........................ SimonWhitworth 4 57
(B R Millman) *trckd ldr: plld hrd: rdn over 2f out: edgd lft and wknd fnl f* **10/1**

-444 **10** *nk* **Satin Braid**[17] 5013 3-8-13 **67**........................ JimCrowley 13 62
(A W Carroll) *hld up in tch: rdn over 2f out: wknd fnl f* **10/1**

1m 44.13s (-1.17) **Going Correction** -0.10s/f (Good) **10** Ran SP% **115.4**
Speed ratings (Par 101): **101,100,99,98,97 96,96,96,95,95**
CSF £53.04 CT £280.03 TOTE £7.00: £2.20, £2.00, £2.10; EX 37.50 Trifecta £151.70 Pool £467.94 - 2.19 winning units. Place 6 £325.25, Place 5 £4.68 .

Owner Rothmere Racing Limited **Bred** Blenheim Bloodstock **Trained** Newmarket, Suffolk

FOCUS
A modest handicap run at a fair pace. Sound but ordinary form.

Zonta Zitkala Official explanation: jockey said filly reared on leaving stalls
Golden Prospect Official explanation: jockey said colt was unsuited by the firm ground

T/Plt: £83.10 to a £1 stake. Pool: £56,958.50. 500.05 winning tickets. T/Qpdt: £5.60 to a £1 stake. Pool: £3,585.50. 465.80 winning tickets. CR

[5035]MUSSELBURGH (R-H)

Monday, September 17

OFFICIAL GOING: Good to soft (good in places; 7.5)

Wind: Moderate half-against Weather: Overcast and showers

5476 SCOTTISH WHOLESALE ASSOCIATION H'CAP 7f 30y
2:20 (2:21) (Class 6) (0-65,64) 3-Y-0+ £2,590 (£770; £385; £192) Stalls High

Form RPR

1132 1 **Kirkby's Treasure**[16] [5035] 9-9-2 62 .... PJMcDonald(3) 8 70+
(G A Swinbank) *towards rr: hdwy 2f out: n.m.r and swtchd lft 1f out: sn rdn and styd on strly to ld nr fin* 3/1[1]

0001 2 nk **Sands Of Barra (IRE)**[25] [4731] 4-9-5 62 .... RoystonFfrench 11 69
(I W McInnes) *trckd ldrs on inner: effrt and n.m.r 2f out: sn rdn and squeezed through on inner ent fnl f: ev ch tl drvn and nt qckn nr fin* 7/1[3]

0630 3 hd **Attacca**[3] [5391] 6-8-10 53 .... DavidAllan 13 59
(J R Weymes) *chsd ldrs: hdwy 2f out: swtchd lft and rdn ent fnl f: sn ev ch tl drvn and nt qckn towards fin* 6/1[2]

2103 4 1/2 **Oeuf A La Neige**[7] [5284] 7-8-8 51 .... SilvestreDeSousa 2 56
(Miss L A Perratt) *hld up in rr: hdwy on wd outside over 2f out: rdn and ev ch ent fnl f tl drvn and nt qckn towards fin* 16/1

5034 5 1/2 **Zabeel Tower**[7] [5284] 4-8-7 53 .... (p) AndrewElliott(3) 3 57
(R Allan) *trckd ldrs: hdwy 3f out: led 2f out: rdn over 1f out: drvn ent fnl f: hdd and no ex last 100yds* 10/1

2630 6 3/4 **Choreography**[9] [5232] 4-9-3 60 .... AdrianTNicholls 1 62
(D Nicholls) *trckd ldrs: hdwy over 2f out: rdn and ev ch over 1f out: drvn and one pce ins fnl f* 8/1

5500 7 1/2 **Monashee Brave (IRE)**[23] [4800] 4-9-3 60 .... GrahamGibbons 10 61
(J J Quinn) *cl up: rdn along and ev ch 2f out tl drvn and wknd ent fnl f* 22/1

6506 8 2 **Caluba**[26] [4705] 3-8-8 54 .... J-PGuillambert 4 48
(K R Burke) *in tch: hdwy on outer to chse ldrs 2f out: sn rdn: edgd lft and wknd appr fnl f* 100/1

6520 9 1/2 **Spinning**[11] [5159] 4-9-3 60 .... (b) PhillipMakin 6 54
(T D Barron) *hld up in rr: sme hdwy over 2f out: sn rdn and no imp* 9/1

0405 10 2 1/2 **Anthemion (IRE)**[16] [5035] 10-8-10 53 .... PaulHanagan 14 41
(Mrs J C McGregor) *sn led: rdn along 3f out: hdd 2f out and sn wknd* 16/1

-040 11 1 3/4 **Mineral Rights (USA)**[19] [4931] 3-8-12 58 .... TomEaves 5 40
(I Semple) *chsd ldrs: rdn along wl over 2f out and grad wknd* 25/1

000 12 2 1/2 **Turn Me On (IRE)**[11] [5159] 4-8-13 61 .... (b[1]) KellyHarrison(5) 12 38
(T D Walford) *dwlt: effrt and sme hdwy on inner 1/2-way: sn rdn along and wknd* 12/1

0410 13 2 **Pay Time**[11] [5159] 8-9-1 63 .... NataliaGemelova(5) 7 34
(R E Barr) *dwlt: a in rr* 22/1

5000 14 12 **Paraguay (USA)**[8] [5253] 4-9-7 64 .... (v) SebSanders 9 4
(Miss V Haigh) *hld up: a bhd* 11/1

1m 31.16s (1.22) **Going Correction** +0.30s/f (Good)
WFA 3 from 4yo+ 3lb 14 Ran SP% **123.3**
Speed ratings (Par 101): **105,104,104,103,103 102,101,99,99,96 94,91,89,75**
CSF £22.66 CT £124.22 TOTE £3.30: £1.30, £3.10, £2.40; EX 21.70.
Owner Kirkby Lonsdale Racing **Bred** Mrs J M Berry **Trained** Melsonby, N Yorks

FOCUS

A moderate handicap. Pretty solid form with the second and third both pretty close to their marks.

5477 TURFTV (S) STKS 7f 30y
2:50 (2:55) (Class 5) 2-Y-0 £3,238 (£963; £481; £240) Stalls High

Form RPR

1 **Stevie Thunder** 2-8-8 0 .... PJMcDonald(3) 12 61
(G A Swinbank) *in rr and sn pushed along: niggled and rn greeen 3f out: hdwy and swtchd outside wl over 1f out: rdn ent fnl f and styd on strly to ld nr fin* 10/1

40 2 1/2 **Thanxforthat (USA)**[30] [4612] 2-8-11 0 .... GrahamGibbons 3 60
(J J Quinn) *sn led: rdn along and hdd wl over 2f out: rallied to ld again over 1f out: drvn ins fnl f: hdd and nt qckn nr fin* 5/1[2]

6363 3 3/4 **Elusive Lady (IRE)**[14] [5081] 2-8-3 53 .... AndrewElliott(3) 10 53
(J R Weymes) *trckd ldrs: hdwy 3f out: rdn wl over 1f out: drvn and kpt on same pce ins fnl f* 12/1

35 4 shd **Prunes**[110] [2138] 2-8-7 0 ow1 .... SebSanders 1 54
(Sir Mark Prescott) *prom: led wl over 2f out: rdn wl over 1f out: sn drvn and hdd appr fnl f: wknd* 10/11[1]

0006 5 2 1/2 **Eboracum Dream**[32] [4522] 2-8-7 52 ow1 .... (b) DavidAllan 4 48
(T D Easterby) *in tch: hdwy to chse ldrs over 2f out: sn rdn and kpt on same pce appr fnl f* 20/1

0 6 11 **Reel Madam**[6] [5302] 2-8-6 0 .... DO'Donohoe 6 19
(K A Ryan) *towards rr: sme hdwy over 2f out: sn rdn and nvr a factor* 66/1

6046 7 4 **Rich James (IRE)**[44] [4154] 2-8-11 58 .... DarrylHolland 2 14
(J D Bethell) *chsd ldr: rdn along over 2f out and sn one pce* 6/1[3]

0630 8 6 **Jazz Stick (IRE)**[14] [5081] 2-8-11 55 .... (v) TomEaves 5 —
(I Semple) *midfield: hdwy on outer to chse ldrs 1/2-way: sn rdn and btn 2f out* 20/1

005 9 1 **Scientific**[14] [5081] 2-8-11 54 .... PaulHanagan 9 —
(R A Fahey) *a towards rr* 20/1

5 10 1 3/4 **Jendas Jem**[31] [4559] 2-8-6 0 .... RoystonFfrench 11 —
(Mrs A Duffield) *midfield: rdn along 3f out: sn wknd* 40/1

4605 11 16 **Limestone**[66] [3499] 2-8-11 51 .... (b) PhillipMakin 8 —
(J R Weymes) *a in rr* 66/1

5040 12 5 **Lavemill (IRE)**[35] [4461] 2-8-6 37 .... AdrianTNicholls 7 —
(R F Fisher) *chsd ldrs: n.m.r wl over 2f out: sn wknd and eased* 80/1

1m 33.4s (3.46) **Going Correction** +0.30s/f (Good) 12 Ran SP% **121.1**
Speed ratings (Par 95): **92,91,90,90,87 75,70,63,62,60 42,36**
CSF £56.84 TOTE £11.00: £3.00, £1.80, £2.50; EX 93.40.The winner was bought in for 8,000gns.
Owner Steve Gray **Bred** Sir Eric Parker **Trained** Melsonby, N Yorks

FOCUS

A weak race, with the third and fifth, along with the time, setting the level of the form.

NOTEBOOK

Stevie Thunder, a 20,000gns son of top-class middle-distance performer Storming Home, was introduced at a lowly level and he managed to overcome early greenness to win going away. He is likely to go on to prove better than this level and it will be interesting to see what mark he gets for handicaps. (op 17-2 tchd 8-1)

Thanxforthat(USA), down in grade having failed to make an impact in sprint maidens, proved suited by the combination of a drop in grade/rise in distance and gave it a bold stab under a positive ride, keeping on well once headed. There is a race in him at this level. (op 4-1 tchd 11-2)

Elusive Lady(IRE), narrowly touched off in this grade back in August, has found it tougher going in claimers the last twice and this effort seemed to confirm this is her level. (op 14-1)

Prunes, a speedily-bred daughter of Cadeaux Genereux who disappointed in soft ground at Brighton last time, was rightly made favourite on this drop in grade, but having gone to the front two out she failed to last the 7f distance and proved disappointing. (op 5-4 tchd 4-5)

Eboracum Dream ran her best race to date and was clearly suited by the drop in grade. She needs to find more before she can be considered a likely winner though.

Limestone Official explanation: jockey said gelding moved poorly throughout

Lavemill(IRE) Official explanation: jockey said filly lost its action

5478 CMYK H'CAP 1m 6f
3:20 (3:21) (Class 4) (0-80,74) 3-Y-0+ £5,505 (£1,637; £818; £408) Stalls High

Form RPR

3015 1 **Toparudi**[54] [3858] 6-9-13 73 .... RoystonFfrench 6 87
(M H Tompkins) *hld up and bhd: stdy hdwy on inner 3f out: rdn to ld appr fnl f: styd on* 13/2[2]

062- 2 1 1/4 **Sharp Reply (USA)**[144] [5815] 5-9-6 69 .... PJMcDonald(3) 8 81
(Mrs S C Bradburne) *trckd ldrs: rdn 3f out: drvn over 1f out: styd on ins fnl f* 7/1[3]

-351 3 shd **Tonnante**[7] [5279] 3-8-12 68 6ex .... SebSanders 2 80
(Sir Mark Prescott) *trckd ldng pair: hdwy to ld over 2f out: rdn and hdd appr fnl f: sn drvn and kpt on same pce* 11/8[1]

3225 4 2 **Plane Painter (IRE)**[9] [5224] 3-9-4 74 .... J-PGuillambert 1 83
(M Johnston) *trckd ldr: led over 3f out: rdn and hdd over 2f out: drvn and kpt on same pce appr fnl f* 7/1[3]

460 5 8 **Grizebeck (IRE)**[45] [4124] 5-9-8 68 .... PaulHanagan 3 66
(R F Fisher) *in tch: rdn along 3f out: sn wknd* 18/1

5216 6 1 1/4 **Nimra (USA)**[51] [3963] 4-10-0 74 .... (b) DavidAllan 4 70
(G A Butler) *sxoon pushed along in rr: effrt and sme hdwy over 3f out: sn rdn and btn* 9/1

3215 7 1 1/4 **Kyber**[18] [4969] 6-9-1 61 .... DanielTudhope 5 55
(J S Goldie) *hld up: effrt and sme hdwy over 3f out: sn rdn and btn* 8/1

0404 8 28 **Nelsons Column (IRE)**[22] [4843] 4-10-0 74 .... TomEaves 7 29
(G M Moore) *led: rdn along and hdd over 3f out: sn wknd* 14/1

3m 6.53s (0.83) **Going Correction** +0.30s/f (Good)
WFA 3 from 4yo+ 10lb 8 Ran SP% **113.5**
Speed ratings (Par 105): **109,108,108,107,102 101,101,85**
CSF £50.05 CT £97.11 TOTE £8.40: £1.70, £1.90, £1.50; EX 58.80.
Owner M P Bowring **Bred** M P Bowring **Trained** Newmarket, Suffolk

FOCUS

A modest staying handicap, run at a good pace. The form is sound, with a career best from winner Toparudi and the second entitled to rate at least this high on jumps form.

5479 GOOSE GREEN CLAIMING STKS 1m 1f
3:50 (3:50) (Class 6) 3-Y-0+ £2,590 (£770; £385; £192) Stalls Far side

Form RPR

0005 1 **Kings Point (IRE)**[10] [5196] 6-10-0 82 .... (p) PaulHanagan 6 82
(R A Fahey) *mde all: rdn 2f out: styd on strly* 9/4[2]

0014 2 1 1/2 **El Coto**[8] [5255] 7-9-10 81 .... (p) DO'Donohoe 1 75
(K A Ryan) *hld up towards rr: gd hdwy wl over 2f out: rdn to chse wnr over 1f out: sndrvn: edgd rt and one pce* 9/2[3]

6062 3 4 **Sienna Storm (IRE)**[8] [5255] 4-9-12 74 .... (v) SebSanders 9 69
(M H Tompkins) *trckd ldrs: effrt over 2f out: sn rdn and one pce* 2/1[1]

4402 4 1 1/4 **Sarraaf (IRE)**[16] [5037] 11-9-2 57 .... TomEaves 5 56
(I Semple) *prom: effrt to chal 3f out: sn rdn along and wknd wl over 1f out* 8/1

-006 5 2 1/2 **Lago D'Orta (IRE)**[8] [5255] 7-9-10 70 .... AdrianTNicholls 3 59
(D Nicholls) *hld up in rr: swtchd rt and hdwy wl over 2f out: sn rdn and no impfr wl over 1f out* 11/1

3000 6 shd **Procrastinate (IRE)**[41] [4250] 5-9-0 45 .... PhillipMakin 4 49
(R F Fisher) *in tch: rdn along 3f out and sn wknd* 100/1

0-00 7 5 **Insubordinate**[46] [4099] 6-9-0 48 .... DanielTudhope 7 38
(J S Goldie) *s.i.s: in rr tl hdwy 3f out: rdn along and edgd lft over 2f out: nvr a factor* 66/1

2002 8 3/4 **Yo Pedro (IRE)**[21] [4891] 5-9-0 58 .... (b) StephenDonohoe 8 36
(D Carroll) *hld up in tch: rdn along wl over 2f out and sn btn* 20/1

2044 9 16 **Roman History (IRE)**[7] [5286] 4-9-3 52 .... (v[1]) SilvestreDeSousa 2 6
(Miss Tracy Waggott) *prom: rdn along 1/2-way and sn wknd* 16/1

1m 57.14s (3.28) **Going Correction** +0.30s/f (Good) 9 Ran SP% **114.9**
Speed ratings (Par 101): **97,95,92,91,88 88,84,83,69**
CSF £12.66 TOTE £3.80: £1.50, £1.80, £1.30; EX 14.00.The winner was claimed by D Nicholls for £20,000.
Owner David M Knaggs & Mel Roberts **Bred** John Costello **Trained** Musley Bank, N Yorks

FOCUS

A decent claimer containing several that were formerly useful but are on the downgrade. It was run at a steady pace and the sixth limits the form.

5480 BETFAIR NURSERY 5f
4:20 (4:23) (Class 3) (0-95,94) 2-Y-0
£9,971 (£2,985; £1,492; £747; £372; £187) Stalls Low

Form RPR

4222 1 **Know No Fear**[26] [4702] 2-7-12 71 oh2 .... PaulHanagan 5 75
(J J Quinn) *trckd ldrs: swtchd rt and hdwy over 1f out: rdn to chal ent fnl f: styd on to ld last 100yds* 17/2

3510 2 nk **Thunder Bay**[5] [5324] 2-8-11 84 .... DarryllHolland 4 87
(M R Channon) *hld up in rr: swtchd wd and hdwy wl over 1f out: rdn to chal ins fnl f and ev ch tl drvn and nt qckn nr fin* 11/2

311 3 3/4 **Secret Asset (IRE)**[22] [4844] 2-9-7 94 .... DavidAllan 7 94
(W M Brisbourne) *led: rdn along over 1f out: drvn ins fnl f: hdd and no ex last 100yds* 7/2[2]

2502 4 1/2 **Russian Reel**[5] [5331] 2-8-12 85 .... DO'Donohoe 6 87+
(K A Ryan) *dwlt and wnt rt s: in rr tl hdwy 2f out: rdn and nt clr run over 1f out: kpt on u.p ins fnl f* 2/1[1]

5100 5 2 **Liberty Belle (IRE)**[79] [3096] 2-8-3 79 .... StephaneBreux(3) 2 70
(J R Best) *pushed along and outpcd in rr 1/2-way: rdn along wl over 1f out: kpt on ins fnl f* 8/1

1200 6 3/4 **Bespoke Boy**[26] [4724] 2-9-5 92 .... LeeEnstone 1 80
(P C Haslam) *cl up: rdn and ev ch over 1f out: drvn and wknd ent fnl f* 9/2[3]

0003 7 7 **La Guancha**[18] [4970] 2-7-12 71 oh23 .... (tp) SilvestreDeSousa 8 34
(D A Nolan) *chsd ldrs: rdn along 1/2-way: sn wknd* 100/1

0040 8 8 **Enodoc**[17] [4991] 2-8-13 86 .... SebSanders 3 20
(W R Muir) *cl up: rdn along 2f out: sn drvn and wknd* 20/1

61.14 secs (0.64) **Going Correction** +0.225s/f (Good) 8 Ran SP% **116.5**
Speed ratings (Par 99): **103,102,101,100,97 96,84,72**
CSF £55.40 CT £196.42 TOTE £7.10: £2.50, £2.00, £1.40; EX 41.30.
Owner F D C Racing Club **Bred** B Bargh **Trained** Settrington, N Yorks

FOCUS
A fair sprint nursery, and solid with the principals close to form.

NOTEBOOK
Know No Fear, narrowly touched off in a 5f maiden at Carlisle last time, looked to be on a fair mark for this handicap debut and he ran on strongly close home to deny Thunder Bay. There could be more to come and he will stay 6f in time. (op 11-1)
Thunder Bay, who had the benefit of the far rail when winning at Sandown two starts back, failed to last home in last week's valuable sales race at Doncaster, but he was seen to much better effect back at the minimum distance, just losing out to the winner's challenge. (op 15-2 tchd 8-1 and 5-1)
Secret Asset(IRE), a progressive sort who came into this in search of a hat-trick, was up 6lb for his Beverley win and found the rise beyond him, being unable to hold off the front pair. He has tons of speed and will find more races. (op 5-2)
Russian Reel, back down to the minimum distance having found only the progressive Craggy Cat too good at Haydock last time, again ran well, but just lacked the pace of the principals. (op 9-4 tchd 15-8)
Liberty Belle(IRE), a maiden winner at Newmarket back in May, has failed to make an impact in much stiffer company, but she stood more of a chance here off 79 and ran well. The return to 6f should suit. (tchd 9-1, tchd 10-1 in a place)

5481 RECTANGLE GROUP H'CAP 5f
4:50 (4:52) (Class 4) (0-80,80) 3-Y-0+ **£5,505** (£1,637; £818; £408) **Stalls** Low

Form RPR
1104 **1** **Divine Spirit**[26] 4703 6-9-3 **74** RoystonFfrench 2 67
(M Dods) *trckd ldrs: hdwy wl over 1f out: sn rdn and styd on to ld wl ins fnl f* **13/2**
0105 **2** *nk* **Strensall**[18] 4967 10-8-11 **68** PaulHanagan 9 59
(R E Barr) *in tch: hdwy wl over 1f out: rdn ent fnl f: edgd lft and kpt on wl towards fin* **12/1**
2322 **3** *½* **Welcome Approach**[18] 4967 4-9-0 **71** PhillipMakin 5 61+
(J R Weymes) *dwlt and towards rr: gd hdwy over 2f out: rdn to chse ldrs over 1f out: swtchd rt and drvn and ev ch ins fnl f: nt qckn towards fin* **7/2**[1]
0220 **4** *½* **Sir Nod**[16] 5039 5-9-9 **80** TomEaves 4 68
(Miss J A Camacho) *trckd ldrs: hdwy 2f out: rdn to ld over 1f out: drvn and hdd wl ins fnl f: no ex towards fin* **6/1**
2000 **5** *nk* **Blazing Heights**[9] 5212 4-9-8 **79** DanielTudhope 10 66+
(J S Goldie) *dwlt and bhd whn hmpd after 1f: gd hdwy whn nt clr run and swtchd rt over 1f out: nt clr run ins fnl f: swtchd rt again and styng on whn hmpd towards fin* **4/1**[2]
0060 **6** *½* **Vondova**[7] 5284 5-8-8 **68** oh12 ow7 (p) PJMcDonald(3) 6 53
(D A Nolan) *in tch: rdn along wl over 1f out: kpt on u.p ins fnl f* **100/1**
0000 **7** *½* **Compton Lad**[7] 5282 4-8-3 **63** oh16 ow2 AndrewElliott(3) 8 46
(D A Nolan) *led: rdn along 2f out: drvn and hdd over 1f out: wknd* **150/1**
6005 **8** *1 ¼* **Mutayam**[14] 5085 7-8-4 **61** oh16 (t) SilvestreDeSousa 7 40
(D A Nolan) *cl up: rdn along 2f out: sn wknd* **100/1**
0156 **9** *1* **Rothesay Dancer**[18] 4967 4-8-5 **67** KellyHarrison(5) 12 42
(J S Goldie) *in rr and swtchd lft s: a bhd* **14/1**
0000 **10** *1 ¾* **Handsome Cross (IRE)**[16] 5029 6-9-8 **79** AdrianTNicholls 3 48
(D Nicholls) *prom: rdn along 1/2-way: sn wknd* **5/1**[3]
0050 **11** *1 ¼* **Alfie Lee (IRE)**[34] 4478 10-7-12 **62** oh16 ow1 (t) PaulPickard(7) 11 26
(D A Nolan) *towards rr fr 1/2-way* **150/1**
2420 **12** *nk* **Windjammer**[16] 5029 3-9-1 **73** DavidAllan 1 36
(T D Easterby) *prom: rdn along and ev ch over 1f out: sn drvn and wknd* **7/1**

61.52 secs (1.02) **Going Correction** +0.225s/f (Good)
WFA 3 from 4yo+ 1lb **12 Ran SP% 116.7**
Speed ratings (Par 105): **100,99,98,97,97 96,95,93,92,89 87,86**
CSF £80.69 CT £321.21 TOTE £8.20: £2.80, £3.90, £1.10; EX 76.20.
Owner The Newcastle Racing Club **Bred** S R Hope And D Erwin Bloodstock **Trained** Denton, Co Durham

FOCUS
A typically competitive sprint handicap but the form looks dubious with the Nolan-trained trio finishing sixth, seventh and eighth from a long way out of the weights.

5482 SCOTTISH RACING H'CAP 1m 4f
5:20 (5:20) (Class 6) (0-65,64) 3-Y-0+ **£2,590** (£770; £385; £192) **Stalls** High

Form RPR
5105 **1** **Elopement (IRE)**[45] 4128 5-9-8 **58** GrahamGibbons 10 67
(W M Brisbourne) *mde all: qcknd clr 2f out: sn rdn and styd on strly ins fnl f* **10/1**
0342 **2** *2 ½* **Falcon's Fire (IRE)**[6] 5300 3-8-12 **56** (p) RoystonFfrench 14 61
(Mrs A Duffield) *trckd ldrs: hdwy over 2f out: rdn to chse wnr ent fnl f: sn drvn and no imp* **9/4**[1]
4016 **3** *¾* **Regency Red (IRE)**[18] 4972 9-9-5 **55** SebSanders 3 59
(W M Brisbourne) *hld up and bhd: gd hdwy on outer 3f out: rdn to chse wnr over 1f out: sn drvn and kpt on same pce* **13/2**[3]
3434 **4** *1 ½* **Star Of Angels**[23] 4817 3-8-13 **57** (b) J-PGuillambert 8 58+
(M Johnston) *in tch: hdwy to chse ldrs wl over 2f out: sn rdn and kpt on same pce fr wl over 1f out* **11/2**[2]
6350 **5** *1 ¾* **Snowflight**[12] 5132 3-8-12 **56** PaulHanagan 9 55
(R A Fahey) *in tch: hdwy 3f out: sn rdn along and no imp fr wl over 1f out* **16/1**
6 *nk* **Puy D'Arnac (FR)**[104] 4-9-11 **64** PJMcDonald(3) 7 62
(G A Swinbank) *hld up: hdwy on bridle to trck ldrs over 2f out: one pce appr fnl f* **16/1**
0031 **7** *2* **Fadansil**[17] 5000 4-9-2 **52** TomEaves 4 47
(J Wade) *in tch: hdwy to chse ldrs 3f out: rdn along 2f out and sn one pce* **7/1**
0244 **8** *15* **Musical Land (IRE)**[17] 4997 3-9-1 **59** DarryllHolland 13 30
(J R Weymes) *a towards rr* **20/1**
3-00 **9** *2 ½* **Wise Choice**[220] 215 4-9-3 **53** StephenDonohoe 5 20
(Mrs L B Normile) *prom: chsd wnr over 4f out: rdn along wl over 2f out: sn drvn and wknd* **28/1**
053 **10** *¾* **Mounafes**[12] 5137 3-9-1 **59** PhillipMakin 11 25
(G A Butler) *a towards rr* **15/2**
350- **11** *24* **Stainley (IRE)**[145] 5173 4-9-12 **62** DO'Donohoe 6 —
(Mrs S C Bradburne) *chsd lwnr: pushed along over 4f out: rdn along over 3f out and grad wknd* **25/1**
0502 **12** *10* **Frith (IRE)**[48] 3538 5-9-9 **59** AdrianTNicholls 1 —
(Mrs L B Normile) *a in rr* **28/1**

2m 42.06s (5.16) **Going Correction** +0.30s/f (Good)
WFA 3 from 4yo+ 8lb **12 Ran SP% 120.1**
Speed ratings (Par 101): **94,92,91,90,89 89,88,78,76,75 59,53**
CSF £31.65 CT £162.68 TOTE £10.60: £2.70, £1.60, £2.00; EX 41.40 Place 6 £55.47, Place 5 £34.17.
Owner Stratford Bards Racing **Bred** Haras Du Mezeray **Trained** Great Ness, Shropshire

FOCUS
A moderate handicap in which the winner set a good pace but was allowed his own way in front. The form looks solid enough.
Stainley(IRE) Official explanation: jockey said gelding hung badly right throughout
T/Jkpt: Not won. T/Plt: £30.70 to a £1 stake. Pool: £62,948.45. 1,492.70 winning tickets. T/Qpdt: £4.10 to a £1 stake. Pool: £3,703.60. 654.45 winning tickets. JR

5153 REDCAR (L-H)
Monday, September 17

OFFICIAL GOING: Firm (good to firm in places; 10.9)
After a dry spell the ground was described as 'very firm, bordering on hard'.
Wind: Fresh half-against Weather: Overcast, cool and breezy

5483 EUROPEAN BREEDERS' FUND MAIDEN FILLIES' STKS 6f
2:10 (2:12) (Class 5) 2-Y-O **£3,141** (£934; £467; £233) **Stalls** Centre

Form RPR
4 **1** **Maramba (USA)**[68] 3417 2-9-0 KDarley 7 81+
(Sir Michael Stoute) *chsd ldrs: shkn up to ld over 1f out: pushed clr* **5/1**[3]
3 **2** *3* **Tobar Suil Lady (IRE)**[20] 4924 2-8-11 AndrewMullen(3) 6 72+
(K A Ryan) *w ldrs: led over 2f out: hdd over 1f out: no ex* **6/1**
36 **3** *4* **Tudor Court (IRE)**[66] 3507 2-9-0 GregFairley 5 60
(M Johnston) *led: hung lft and hdd over 2f out: fdd over 1f out* **7/4**[1]
0 **4** *1 ¾* **Madam Carwell**[31] 4565 2-9-0 TPQueally 10 55
(J G Given) *mid-div: kpt on fnl 2f: nvr trbld ldrs* **33/1**
00 **5** *1 ¾* **Honeycott (IRE)**[35] 4448 2-9-0 KerrinMcEvoy 13 50
(J D Bethell) *in rr: kpt on fnl 2f: nvr nr ldrs* **66/1**
0 **6** *1 ¼* **Viscaya (IRE)**[10] 5193 2-9-0 PaulMulrennan 12 46
(Mrs A Duffield) *s.i.s: bhd tl sme hdwy fnl 2f* **25/1**
00 **7** *1* **Killer Class**[56] 3781 2-8-9 GaryBartley(5) 1 43
(J S Goldie) *stmbld s: bhd tl kpt on fnl 2f* **66/1**
52 **8** *¾* **Ceka Dancer (IRE)**[10] 5201 2-9-0 ChrisCatlin 2 41
(E J O'Neill) *w ldrs: lost pl over 2f out* **3/1**[2]
0 **9** *4* **Dawn Whisper**[111] 2115 2-9-0 PaddyAspell 8 29
(M E Sowersby) *in tch: lost pl 3f out: sn bhd* **100/1**
00 **10** *hd* **Miss Skycat (USA)**[36] 4422 2-9-0 PaulFessey 3 28
(T D Barron) *chsd ldrs: hung lft and lost pl over 2f out: sn bhd* **33/1**
0 **11** *1* **Larkfield**[16] 5042 2-8-11 (b[1]) DuranFentiman(3) 9 25
(T D Easterby) *sn outpcd and in rr* **100/1**

1m 13.51s (1.81) **Going Correction** +0.175s/f (Good) **11 Ran SP% 107.0**
Speed ratings (Par 92): **94,90,84,82,80 78,77,76,70,70 69**
CSF £28.49 TOTE £4.70: £1.30, £1.50, £1.20; EX 38.20.
Owner Philip Newton **Bred** Philip Newton **Trained** Newmarket, Suffolk
■ Orchestrion was withdrawn (10/1, burst out of stalls). R4 applies, deduct 5p in the £.

FOCUS
A reasonable race for the track and grade and an unexposed winner of some potential.

NOTEBOOK
Maramba(USA), on the sidelines since Kempton in July, travelled best and had only needed a shake of the reins to come clear. She will be even better suited by 7f. (op 10-3)
Tobar Suil Lady(IRE), quite a tall filly, knew what was required this time but in the end met one much too good. She can surely find a race. (op 7-1 tchd 11-2)
Tudor Court(IRE), absent for two months, is not that big. She ran as if she was feeling the very firm ground and she might just have been in need of it. She must not be written off yet. (op 2-1)
Madam Carwell, an attractive, good-topped filly, showed a bit more than on her debut but she will not be seen to best effect until tackling much further next year.
Honeycott(IRE) still looked as if the outing would do her good and this was her first real sign of ability. She can do even better in time.
Killer Class Official explanation: jockey said filly stumbled leaving stalls
Ceka Dancer(IRE) seems to have overcome her problem with the stalls but this was a most disappointing effort, dropping right away before the race had begun in earnest. (op 7-2)

5484 HERALD & POST NURSERY 5f
2:40 (2:43) (Class 6) (0-65,65) 2-Y-O **£1,943** (£578; £288; £144) **Stalls** Centre

Form RPR
6600 **1** **Handsinthemist (IRE)**[7] 5281 2-8-7 **51** ow1 (p) MickyFenton 6 53
(P T Midgley) *chsd ldrs: styd on appr fnl f: led nr fin* **16/1**
3320 **2** *nk* **Culzean Bay**[14] 5089 2-7-12 **49** FrankiePickard(7) 9 50
(Miss Diana Weeden) *s.s: hdwy over 2f out: no ex ins fnl f* **12/1**
0000 **3** *shd* **Tikinheart (IRE)**[11] 5153 2-8-8 **55** DuranFentiman(3) 11 56
(T D Easterby) *w ldr: led over 2f out: hdd towards fin* **7/2**[1]
0630 **4** *3* **Linnet Park**[38] 4349 2-9-5 **63** TPQueally 8 53
(J G Given) *led: hdd over 2f out: fdd fnl f* **13/2**[3]
004 **5** *hd* **Tommytush (IRE)**[14] 5081 2-9-3 **61** (t) KDarley 2 50
(E J Alston) *chsd ldrs: kpt on same pce fnl 2f* **6/1**[2]
030 **6** *shd* **She's Our Dream**[37] 4406 2-9-1 **64** NeilBrown(5) 4 53
(R C Guest) *mid-div: styd on fnl f: nvr nr ldrs* **12/1**
000 **7** *1 ¾* **Miss Sunshine**[56] 3781 2-8-6 **55** GaryBartley(5) 7 37
(J S Goldie) *s.i.s: kpt on fnl 2f: nvr nr ldrs* **11/1**
2030 **8** *1 ½* **Rebel Aclaim (IRE)**[11] 5167 2-9-4 **65** JerryO'Dwyer(3) 14 42
(M G Quinlan) *racd wd: chsd ldrs: rdn and wknd over 1f out* **6/1**[2]
0506 **9** *1 ¾* **Caprima (IRE)**[38] 4349 2-8-3 **54** AndrewHeffernan(7) 13 24
(M Brittain) *racd wd: chsd ldrs: lost pl 2f out* **20/1**
004 **10** *nk* **Piccolo Pete**[11] 5154 2-8-11 **55** (v[1]) PatCosgrave 1 24
(J J Quinn) *chsd ldrs: reminders over 3f out: sn lost pl* **20/1**
050 **11** *hd* **Tafira (IRE)**[29] 4636 2-8-5 **49** ChrisCatlin 5 17
(K R Burke) *chsd ldrs: lost pl over 1f out* **11/1**
4306 **12** *3 ½* **Rocheport**[26] 4702 2-9-6 **64** (b[1]) PaulMulrennan 3 19
(J Howard Johnson) *stmbld and almost fell s: nt rcvr: a bhd* **8/1**
6060 **13** *1 ¼* **Penny Arcade**[11] 5154 2-7-8 **45** (t) DeclanCannon(7) 12 —
(M E Sowersby) *racd wd: chsd ldrs: lost pl over 1f out* **66/1**

60.75 secs (2.05) **Going Correction** +0.175s/f (Good) **13 Ran SP% 124.2**
Speed ratings (Par 93): **90,89,89,84,84 84,81,78,76,75 75,69,67**
CSF £198.78 CT £840.70 TOTE £22.20: £5.90, £3.10, £2.30; EX 411.60.
Owner J F Wright **Bred** Dr P Hackett **Trained** Westow, N Yorks

FOCUS
A low-grade nursery in which the first three finished in a heap.

NOTEBOOK
Handsinthemist(IRE), who has already been tried over 7f, stuck on in willing fashion in first-time cheekpieces to put her head in front right on the line. She looks a very laid-back individual.
Culzean Bay, having her second outing for this stable, lost ground at the start. In the end she was just found lacking with her rider's inexperience showing. (op 10-1)
Tikinheart(IRE), dropping back in trip, was heavily supported. He went on looking all over a winner only to narrowly miss out in the end. His turn will come. (op 6-1)
Linnet Park is all speed but in the end she could not see it out. (op 6-1 tchd 11-2)
Tommytush(IRE), in a first-time tongue tie, was dropping back in trip on his nursery debut. (op 7-1)

She's Our Dream, with the tongue tie left off, was very edgy beforehand. (op 10-1)
Rocheport Official explanation: jockey said gelding stumbled at start

5485 EUROPEAN BREEDERS' FUND - DOUBLE TRIGGER MAIDEN STKS (FOR THE DOUBLE TRIGGER TROPHY) 1m 1f

3:10 (3:10) (Class 5) 2-Y-0 **£3,141** (£934; £467; £233) **Stalls** Low

Form RPR

64 **1** **Lanterns Of Gold**[9] 5227 2-8-12 0 ... KDarley 1 71
(Mrs A Duffield) *chsd ldrs: drvn over 3f out: swtchd outside over 2f out: hung lft and led ins fnl f: styd on wl* **5/4**[1]

64 **2** *1* **Elk Trail (IRE)**[22] 4841 2-9-3 0 ... MickyFenton 3 74
(T P Tate) *led: shkn up over 3f out: hdd ins fnl f: no ex* **13/2**[3]

5 **3** *1 1/4* **Bite The Boss**[16] 5038 2-9-3 0 ... ChrisCatlin 2 72
(E J O'Neill) *sn chsng ldrs: shkn up over 5f out: styd on ins fnl f* **12/1**

00 **4** *1 1/4* **Dubai Land**[10] 5186 2-9-3 0 ... TPO'Shea 7 69
(M R Channon) *hld up in rr: smooth hdwy 4f out: rdn and edgd lft over 2f out: one pce appr fnl f* **8/1**

3 **5** *shd* **Pearl Trader (IRE)**[19] 4930 2-8-12 0 ... GregFairley 4 64
(M Johnston) *w ldr: effrt over 3f out: one pce whn sltly hmpd ins fnl f* **9/4**[2]

0 **6** *17* **Wimoweh (IRE)**[12] 5143 2-9-0 0 ... DuranFentiman(3) 8 35
(T D Easterby) *s.i.s: swtchd lft after s: bhd fnl 3f* **33/1**

0 **7** *3/4* **Miss Holderness**[33] 4487 2-8-9 0 ow2 ... JamesO'Reilly(5) 6 30
(J O'Reilly) *chsd ldrs: lost pl over 2f out: sn bhd* **100/1**

1m 54.59s (1.19) **Going Correction** +0.025s/f (Good) **7** Ran SP% **111.3**
Speed ratings (Par 95): **95,94,93,91,91 76,76**
CSF £9.61 TOTE £2.30: £1.20, £3.00; EX 13.40.
Owner A Mordain **Bred** Mrs D O Joly **Trained** Constable Burton, N Yorks

FOCUS
Not a strong pace but in the end a convincing winner. Probably not a race to get behind.

NOTEBOOK
Lanterns Of Gold, stepping up in trip, made hard work of it but scored in decisive fahsion in the end despite looking a shade unhappy on the very firm ground. On the leg, she will make a better three-year-old. (op 7-4)
Elk Trail(IRE), a big, rangy type, found the very fast ground no problem. He wound it up from the front but in the end the winner was too good for him. He will make a better three-year-old. (op 7-1 tchd 15-2)
Bite The Boss, loaded with a blanket, knew a lot more this time. Sticking on strongly at the finish, he should improve again. (op 8-1)
Dubai Land, who lacks size, showed a lot more than on his first two outings and he is now qualified for a handicap mark. (op 9-1)
Pearl Trader(IRE), out of Irish Oaks winner Vintage Tipple, continually swished her tail in the paddock. She was safely held when the winner went across her bows inside the last. (op 15-8 tchd 7-4)

5486 EVENING GAZETTE H'CAP 1m 6f 19y

3:40 (3:41) (Class 5) (0-70,69) 3-Y-0+ **£2,817** (£838; £418; £209) **Stalls** Low

Form RPR

0061 **1** **Double Banded (IRE)**[21] 4894 3-8-6 **57** ... KerrinMcEvoy 1 73+
(J L Dunlop) *trckd ldrs gng wl: smooth hdwy to go 2nd over 2f out: shkn up to ld over 1f out: qcknd clr: smoothly* **5/2**[2]

3451 **2** *3 1/2* **Let It Be**[11] 5158 6-9-1 **56** ... PatCosgrave 11 61
(K G Reveley) *led 1f: chsd ldrs: led 3f out tl over 1f out: no ch w wnr* **11/2**[3]

-000 **3** *3* **Zefooha (FR)**[22] 4843 3-9-2 **67** ... KDarley 10 68
(T D Walford) *sn w ldrs: one pce fnl 2f* **18/1**

05-4 **4** *2* **Categorical**[119] 1890 4-10-0 **69** ... TonyHamilton 14 67
(K G Reveley) *sn chsng ldrs: drvn over 4f out: one pce fnl 2f* **28/1**

2341 **5** *1 1/4* **Casual Affair**[8] 5257 4-9-1 **61** ... NeilBrown(5) 6 57
(J D Bethell) *hld up: detached in rr: hdwy 3f out: sn rdn and hung lft over 2f out: nvr on terms* **13/8**[1]

0520 **6** *shd* **Maneki Neko (IRE)**[104] 2342 5-9-9 **67** ... JamieMoriarty(3) 7 63
(E W Tuer) *sn trcking ldrs: effrt over 3f out: hung lft and one pce over 1f out* **16/1**

6341 **7** *1 1/4* **Parchment (IRE)**[6] 5300 5-9-4 **59** 6ex ... (b) PaddyAspell 2 54
(A J Lockwood) *hld up detached in rr: effrt over 3f out: hopeless task* **7/1**

4666 **8** *7* **Qaasi (USA)**[28] 4670 5-8-10 **51** ... TPQueally 12 36
(M Brittain) *led after 1f tl 3f out: sn lost pl* **14/1**

0-50 **9** *8* **Starbougg**[24] 4771 3-8-9 **60** ... PaulFessey 8 34
(K G Reveley) *detached in rr: pushed along 8f out: bhd whn eased 1f out* **40/1**

3m 4.37s (-0.65) **Going Correction** +0.025s/f (Good)
WFA 3 from 4yo+ 10lb **9** Ran SP% **118.3**
Speed ratings (Par 103): **102,100,98,97,96 96,95,91,87**
CSF £17.34 CT £205.81 TOTE £3.10: £1.40, £1.70, £4.20; EX 14.40.
Owner Sir Thomas Pilkington **Bred** Sir Thomas Pilkington **Trained** Arundel, W Sussex

FOCUS
A steady gallop to this modest handicap. Double Banded was an effortless winner, value at least double the actual margin, and is clearly a fast-improving young stayer. The placed horses ran to form.
Casual Affair Official explanation: jockey said gelding was unsuited by the firm (good to firm places) ground
Parchment(IRE) Official explanation: trainer said gelding lost a near-fore shoe
Qaasi(USA) Official explanation: jockey said gelding was unsuited by the firm (good to firm places) ground

5487 GRAHAM REGAN (S) STKS 1m 2f

4:10 (4:12) (Class 6) 3-5-Y-0 **£2,047** (£604; £302) **Stalls** Low

Form RPR

0600 **1** **Contemplation**[28] 4660 4-9-3 48 ... PatCosgrave 13 62+
(G A Swinbank) *hld up in rr: stdy hdwy and n.m.r over 3f out: squeezed through on inner to go 2nd over 1f out: led ins fnl f: drvn clr* **13/2**[3]

4-00 **2** *2 1/2* **Mister Fizzbomb (IRE)**[15] 3204 4-9-3 53 ... (v) TPQueally 14 57
(J S Wainwright) *led: drvn clr 3f out: hung rt over 1f out: hdd and no ex ins fnl f* **11/1**

2440 **3** *2* **Colditz (IRE)**[7] 5286 3-8-11 57 ... (p) TonyHamilton 9 53
(D W Barker) *sn chsng ldrs: wnt 2nd 5f out: rdn over 3f out: one pce fnl 2f* **11/2**[2]

0030 **4** *2* **Ranavalona**[10] 5187 3-8-6 45 ... (t) GregFairley 11 44
(C Smith) *in rr: hdwy over 3f out: one pce fnl 2f* **20/1**

2000 **5** *1 1/4* **Falimar**[22] 4846 3-8-8 56 ow2 ... (v[1]) PaddyAspell 2 44
(Miss J A Camacho) *trckd ldrs: hung rt over 2f out: one pce* **8/1**

6000 **6** *nk* **Moving Story**[8] 5255 4-9-3 46 ... MickyFenton 4 46
(P T Midgley) *hld up in mid-div: effrt over 3f out: kpt on same pce fnl 2f* **12/1**

0004 **7** *1 3/4* **Playtotheaudience**[16] 5037 4-9-0 50 ... JamieMoriarty(3) 3 42
(R A Fahey) *in rr: effrt over 3f out: one pce whn n.m.r on ins 1f out* **4/1**[1]

0-00 **8** *1/2* **Malech (IRE)**[6] 5307 4-9-3 62 ... KDarley 7 41
(K G Reveley) *s.s: sme hdwy 3f out: nvr a factor* **7/1**

4000 **9** *2 1/2* **Grey Vision**[6] 5299 4-8-5 48 ... AndrewHeffernan(7) 10 31
(M Brittain) *in rr and sn pushed along: sme hdwy 3f out: nvr a factor* **50/1**

665 **10** *1 1/2* **Miss Lovat**[20] 4920 4-8-9 48 ... (t) DuranFentiman(3) 6 28
(W M Brisbourne) *chsd ldrs: wknd over 2f out* **20/1**

1405 **11** *1 1/4* **Ellies Faith**[19] 4943 3-8-6 46 ... (b) PaulFessey 12 26
(N Bycroft) *chsd ldrs: lost pl 2f out* **16/1**

6000 **12** *shd* **Ocean Of Champagne**[21] 3636 3-8-6 44 ... (v) PaulMulrennan 8 26
(Micky Hammond) *mid-div: rdn 4f out: sn btn* **25/1**

-000 **13** *1/2* **Captain Nemo (USA)**[7] 5286 3-8-7 60 ow1 ... NeilBrown(5) 5 31
(T D Barron) *s.s: sme hdwy on outside over 3f out: nvr a factor* **12/1**

224- **14** *7* **Lansdown**[426] 3619 3-7-13 54 ... (p) PatrickDonaghy(7) 1 11
(R Johnson) *chsd ldrs: lost pl over 3f out: sn bhd* **16/1**

0-00 **15** *27* **Kyrhena**[23] 4821 3-8-6 38 ... (b[1]) ChrisCatlin 15 —
(C W Thornton) *in rr: bhd and hung rt over 2f out: t.o* **100/1**

2m 5.55s (-1.25) **Going Correction** +0.025s/f (Good)
WFA 3 from 4yo 6lb **15** Ran SP% **124.1**
Speed ratings (Par 101): **106,104,102,100,99 99,98,97,95,94 93,93,93,87,65**
CSF £73.72 TOTE £7.20: £2.40, £3.40, £2.60; EX 104.10.There was no bid for the winner.
Owner R L Crowe **Bred** Darley **Trained** Melsonby, N Yorks

FOCUS
An ordinary seller, run at a decent pace. Contemplation returned to form back with the Swinbank yard, with the third and fourth the best guides here.

5488 MARKET CROSS JEWELLERS MAIDEN STKS 7f

4:40 (4:41) (Class 5) 3-Y-0+ **£2,817** (£838; £418; £209) **Stalls** Centre

Form RPR

1 **Step In Line (USA)** 3-9-3 0 ... KerrinMcEvoy 2 65+
(Saeed Bin Suroor) *quite keen and led after 1f: shkn up and hung lft ins fnl f: kpt on wl* **4/9**[1]

4433 **2** *1 1/4* **Cassiara**[17] 5013 3-8-12 78 ... (p) KDarley 4 57+
(J Pearce) *trckd ldrs: drvn 1f out: edgd lft and kpt on: no real imp* **2/1**[2]

3 *1 1/2* **Bretwalda (IRE)** 4-9-6 0 ... MickyFenton 3 58
(P T Midgley) *s.s: hdwy over 3f out: kpt on same pce fnl f: n.m.r towards fin* **66/1**

6663 **4** *4* **First Valentini**[16] 5041 3-8-7 43 ... NeilBrown(5) 1 42
(N Bycroft) *chsd ldrs: effrt over 2f out: wknd over 1f out* **20/1**

0003 **5** *5* **Boppys Dream**[9] 5231 5-8-12 45 ... (p) JamieMoriarty(3) 5 29
(P T Midgley) *led 1f: chsd ldrs: wknd 2f out* **16/1**[3]

006 **6** *4* **Oriental Gift (FR)**[21] 4901 3-9-3 33 ... PaddyAspell 6 23
(J R Norton) *chsd ldrs: rdn over 3f out: edgd lft: lost pl 2f out* **100/1**

7 *6* **Shady Bay** 3-8-5 0 ... DanielleMcCreery(7) 7 2
(D W Chapman) *s.s: in rr: wknd over 2f out* **100/1**

6 **8** *2 1/2* **North Stars (IRE)**[11] 5157 3-8-12 0 ... JamesO'Reilly(5) 8 —
(J O'Reilly) *w ldrs: drvn over 3f out: lost pl 2f out* **100/1**

1m 26.76s (1.86) **Going Correction** +0.175s/f (Good)
WFA 3 from 4yo+ 3lb **8** Ran SP% **117.7**
Speed ratings (Par 103): **96,94,92,88,82 78,71,68**
CSF £1.63 TOTE £1.40: £1.02, £1.10, £9.30; EX 2.10.
Owner Godolphin **Bred** Gainsborough Farm Llc **Trained** Newmarket, Suffolk
■ Stewards' Enquiry : K Darley caution: careless riding

FOCUS
A weak and slowly-run maiden in which the fourth to sixth limit the form. The Godolphin newcomer could do no more than asked and could have been rated a stone or so higher.

5489 GO RACING AT THIRSK TOMORROW APPRENTICE H'CAP 6f

5:10 (5:10) (Class 5) (0-70,69) 3-Y-0+ **£2,817** (£838; £418; £209) **Stalls** Centre

Form RPR

0000 **1** **Greek Secret**[7] 5284 4-8-8 **54** ... JamesO'Reilly 5 61
(J O'Reilly) *hld up in rr: hdwy 2f out: r.o to ld last 75yds* **11/1**

0026 **2** *1/2* **Petite Mac**[11] 5159 7-8-7 **53** oh1 ... DanielleMcCreery 9 59
(N Bycroft) *mid-div: hdwy to ld over 1f out: edgd lft: hdd and no ex wl ins fnl f* **10/1**

4015 **3** *1 1/4* **Lambency (IRE)**[16] 5037 4-8-11 **57** ... GaryBartley 1 59
(J S Goldie) *hld up towards rr: hdwy over 1f out: styd on same pce ins fnl f* **8/1**

0-00 **4** *1 1/2* **Elusive Warrior (USA)**[8] 5253 4-8-11 **62** ... (p) JamesRogers(5) 2 60
(R A Fahey) *hld up in rr: hdwy and edgd rt over 1f out: kpt on: nvr rchd ldrs* **18/1**

5214 **5** *3/4* **Beautiful Madness (IRE)**[32] 4536 3-9-7 **69** ... JamieJones 6 64
(M G Quinlan) *hld up in midfield: effrt 2f out: kpt on: nvr threatened* **10/1**

3001 **6** *1* **Zamalik (USA)**[14] 5082 4-9-5 **65** ... MCGeran 4 57
(E J Alston) *led 1f: w ldrs: fdd fnl f* **5/4**[1]

4021 **7** *shd* **Orotund**[16] 5041 3-8-9 **57** ... SladeO'Hara 10 49
(T D Easterby) *w ldrs: led after 1f tl over 1f out: edgd lft and fdd* **15/2**[3]

3655 **8** *5* **Triple Shadow**[12] 5139 3-8-9 **60** ... DeanHeslop(3) 7 37
(T D Barron) *dwlt: hld up in rr: lost pl over 1f out* **13/2**[2]

-000 **9** *1 3/4* **Silidan**[38] 4353 4-9-0 **65** ... AndrewHeffernan(5) 8 37
(M Brittain) *w ldrs: rdn over 2f out: sn lost pl* **50/1**

5532 **10** *4* **Takanewa (IRE)**[19] 4938 4-8-3 **54** ... NSLawes(5) 3 14
(J Howard Johnson) *w ldrs: wknd 2f out* **12/1**

1m 13.81s (2.11) **Going Correction** +0.175s/f (Good)
WFA 3 from 4yo+ 2lb **10** Ran SP% **122.1**
Speed ratings (Par 103): **92,91,89,87,86 85,85,78,76,70**
CSF £120.98 CT £962.81 TOTE £16.80: £6.00, £2.40, £3.30; EX 129.40 Place 6 £38.91, Place 5 £27.05..
Owner The Boot & Shoe Ackworth Partnership **Bred** James Clark **Trained** Doncaster, S Yorks

FOCUS
A low-grade apprentices' handicap in which it is doubtful if the winner had to match this year's form.
Greek Secret Official explanation: trainer had no explanation for the apparent improvement in form
Zamalik(USA) Official explanation: trainer had no explanation for the poor form shown

T/Plt: £109.90 to a £1 stake. Pool: £55,616.35. 369.40 winning tickets. T/Qpdt: £12.50 to a £1 stake. Pool: £3,002.20. 176.90 winning tickets. WG

5373 CHANTILLY (R-H)

Monday, September 17

OFFICIAL GOING: Good

5493a PRIX D'AUMALE (GROUP 3) (FILLIES) 1m
2:05 (2:16) 2-Y-O **£27,027** (£10,811; £8,108; £5,405; £2,703)

RPR

1 **Top Toss (IRE)**[20] 2-8-9 .... CSoumillon 2 100+
(Y De Nicolay, France) *racd in 2nd: jnd ldr early st: led appr fnl f: drvn and styd on wl to line* **38/10**[3]

2 ½ **Mousse Au Chocolat (USA)**[36] 4444 2-8-9 .... C-PLemaire 3 99
(J-C Rouget, France) *led and set stdy pce: jnd early st: hdd appr fnl furlnog: nt pce of wnr fnl f* **26/10**[1]

3 snk **African Rose**[45] 2-8-9 .... SPasquier 4 99
(Mme C Head-Maarek, France) *hld up in 4th: pushed along and wnt 3rd 1 1/2f out: rdn to chse ldr fnl f: nvr nrr* **27/10**[2]

4 nk **Belle Allure (IRE)**[32] 2-8-9 .... DBonilla 1 98
(R Pritchard-Gordon, France) *hld up in last: drvn on outside over 1f out: nvr able to chal* **147/10**

5 4 **Yacht Woman (USA)**[29] 2-8-9 .... MMonteriso 5 89
(E Borromeo, Italy) *racd in 3rd tl pushed along and outpcd over 1 1/2f out* **67/10**

1m 40.9s (0.60) 5 Ran SP% **95.0**
PARI-MUTUEL: WIN 4.80; PL 1.90, 2.00; SF 13.40.
Owner Ecurie Skymarc Farm **Bred** Ecurie Skymarc Farm **Trained** France

NOTEBOOK
Top Toss(IRE), a filly with plenty of scope, may well stay further than a mile. She was settled in second place for much of the race before taking the advantage a furlong and a half out, then battled well to the line. Her trainer has no plans for the moment and she may well not be seen out until next season.
Mousse Au Chocolat(USA) tried to make every yard of the running and quickened the race up early in the straight. Once passed she fought back and was staying on until the end.
African Rose ran very free early on as the pace was not strong for the first few furlongs. She came with a promising run but she did not carry it through until the end and is still rather a green individual.
Belle Allure(IRE), held up last for much of this mile, began her run from one and a half out and was putting in her best work at the finish.

5308 LINGFIELD (L-H)

Tuesday, September 18

OFFICIAL GOING: Standard
Wind: Light, against Weather: Fine

5494 KINGSTON SMITH LLP CHALLENGE MAIDEN STKS (DIV I) 1m (P)
1:50 (1:50) (Class 5) 3-Y-O+ **£2,169** (£645; £322; £161) **Stalls** High

Form RPR

1 **Gold Sovereign (IRE)** 3-9-3 0 .... TedDurcan 2 91+
(Saeed Bin Suroor) *w'like: scope: lw: prom: trckd ldr 1/2-way: rdn to ld over 1f out: r.o wl and drew clr fnl f: promising* **5/2**[2]

430 2 2½ **Axiom**[41] 4275 3-9-3 70 .... RyanMoore 11 85
(E A L Dunlop) *lw: led: kicked on over 2f out: rdn and hdd over 1f out: clr of rest fnl f but redily hld by wnr* **11/2**[3]

0322 3 6 **Laura's Best (IRE)**[7] 5315 3-8-12 68 .... EddieAhern 10 69
(W J Haggas) *hld up in midfield: prog to go 3rd over 2f out: no ch w ldng pair but clr of rest 1f out: eased last 100yds* **10/1**

50 4 2½ **Dream Of Fortune (IRE)**[60] 3710 3-9-3 0 .... DarryllHolland 4 65+
(J Noseda) *in tch: rdn and struggling in rr over 3f out: no ch over 2f out: pushed along and kpt on steadily to take 4th nr fin* **9/4**[1]

5 shd **Bochinche (USA)** 3-8-12 0 .... MartinDwyer 1 60
(Saeed Bin Suroor) *str: s.i.s: sn cl up: shkn up and outpcd fr wl over 2f out* **16/1**

4- 6 3 **Royal Choir**[327] 6186 3-8-12 0 .... SebSanders 6 53
(C E Brittain) *chsd ldrs: wl outpcd fr over 2f out* **8/1**

-620 7 nk **Convallaria (FR)**[86] 2905 4-9-2 62 .... SteveDrowne 3 52
(G Wragg) *nvr bttr than midfield: wl outpcd fr 3f out* **16/1**

03- 8 1½ **Lascelles**[261] 6998 3-9-3 0 .... JimCrowley 5 54
(J A Osborne) *dwlt: plld hrd and hld up in rr: lft bhd fr 3f out* **16/1**

0 9 hd **Rollin 'n Tumblin**[13] 5129 3-9-3 0 .... PaulDoe 7 54
(W Jarvis) *s.i.s: prog on outer to chse ldrs 1/2-way: sn rdn: lft bhd fr 3f out* **100/1**

0 10 1 **Beau Bramble**[22] 4908 3-9-3 0 .... GeorgeBaker 9 51
(C F Wall) *leggy: chsd ldr to 1/2-way: styd prom tl wknd over 2f out* **66/1**

6 11 11 **Quicklime**[52] 3948 3-8-12 0 .... SimonWhitworth 8 21
(Jamie Poulton) *leggy: plld hrd: hld up in last: bhd fr 1/2-way: t.o* **66/1**

1m 36.59s (-2.84) **Going Correction** -0.175s/f (Stan)
WFA 3 from 4yo 4lb 11 Ran SP% **116.5**
Speed ratings (Par 103): **107,104,98,96,95 92,92,91,90,89 78**
CSF £16.64 TOTE £4.60: £1.90, £2.00, £1.80; EX 22.70.
Owner Godolphin **Bred** Sunderland Holdings **Trained** Newmarket, Suffolk

FOCUS
Strong form for the grade, and the winner created a good impression. With the pace good, the winning time was 0.78 seconds quicker than the second division. A race to be with.
Lascelles Official explanation: jockey said colt hung right

5495 BETFAIR APPRENTICE H'CAP (PART OF THE BETFAIR "APPRENTICE TRAINING RACE" SERIES) 6f (P)
2:20 (2:21) (Class 5) (0-75,75) 3-Y-O **£2,817** (£838; £418; £209) **Stalls** Low

Form RPR

3321 1 **Wolf River (USA)**[20] 4938 3-9-5 75 .... KirstyMilczarek 4 80
(D M Simcock) *lw: t.k.h: mde virtually all: rdn and def advantage over 1f out: kpt on fnl f: hld on* **7/2**[1]

0040 2 nk **Ede's Dot Com (IRE)**[13] 5136 3-8-5 61 .... JackMitchell 1 65
(P M Phelan) *trckd ldrs: rdn to chse wnr 1f out: styd on: a jst hld* **12/1**

1511 3 ¾ **Lord Of The Reins (IRE)**[13] 5134 3-8-9 65 .... MCGeran 2 67+
(D Shaw) *stdd s: t.k.h and hld up in last trio: nt clr run briefly over 1f out: prog to chse ldng pair fnl f: nt qckn last 100yds* **9/2**[3]

1163 4 nk **Nouveau (GER)**[22] 4885 3-8-7 70 .... CharlesEddery(7) 8 71+
(R Hannon) *s.s: rushed up on wd outside after 2f: w ldrs 1/2-way: wd bnd 2f out and lost grnd: kpt on* **9/2**[3]

0040 5 ¾ **Jord (IRE)**[10] 5238 3-8-11 70 .... RobbieEgan(3) 11 69
(A J McCabe) *pressed wnr: upsides 1/2-way to wl over 1f out: nt qckn and btn after: fdd fnl f* **25/1**

0020 6 ¾ **Chattan Clan**[10] 5238 3-9-1 71 .... (t) ThomasO'Brien 6 67
(R A Kvisla) *mostly in last trio: rdn over 2f out: styd on fnl f: nrst fin* **8/1**

125 7 1½ **Expensive Art (IRE)**[41] 4295 3-8-6 67 .... BradleyRoper(5) 5 59
(N A Callaghan) *dwlt: hld up and mostly last: effrt on inner over 1f out: no prog and btn fnl f* **4/1**[2]

4305 8 2½ **Hucking Hope (IRE)**[40] 4324 3-8-1 64 .... KierenFox(7) 3 48
(J R Best) *racd wd: in tch: outpcd over 2f out: swtchd to inner over 1f out: no prog* **9/1**

500- 9 shd **Earl Compton (IRE)**[347] 5784 3-8-5 61 .... (t) WilliamCarson 7 45
(P F I Cole) *prom: w wnr on outer 1/2-way to 2f out: wknd over 1f out* **25/1**

1m 12.03s (-0.78) **Going Correction** -0.175s/f (Stan) 9 Ran SP% **115.1**
Speed ratings (Par 101): **98,97,96,96,95 94,92,88,88**
CSF £46.01 CT £188.91 TOTE £5.30: £2.60, £3.20, £1.20; EX 42.40.
Owner The Anglo Americans **Bred** Liberation Farm & Cho Llc **Trained** Newmarket, Suffolk

FOCUS
A fair three-year-old sprint handicap restricted to apprentices who had not ridden more than 20 winners. Just ordinary form, but a race that should produce some winners in similar company.

5496 KINGSTON SMITH LLP CHALLENGE NURSERY 6f (P)
2:50 (2:50) (Class 5) (0-75,75) 2-Y-O **£3,238** (£963; £481; £240) **Stalls** Low

Form RPR

3100 1 **Geoffdaw**[19] 4964 2-9-2 70 .... EddieAhern 5 76+
(M J Wallace) *trckd ldng pair: effrt to ld wl over 1f out and drvn: drew clr fnl f* **7/1**

041 2 2 **Then 'n Now**[19] 4963 2-9-3 71 .... SimonWhitworth 12 71+
(C A Cyzer) *hld up in last trio: prog over 2f out: rdn to chse wnr fnl f: no imp* **7/1**

004 3 ½ **Mollyatti**[11] 5202 2-9-6 74 .... SebSanders 6 73
(Miss V Haigh) *pressed ldr: led after 2f to wl over 1f out: nt qckn fnl f* **16/1**

6552 4 ½ **Replicator**[41] 4274 2-9-0 71 .... WilliamBuick(3) 8 68
(Pat Eddery) *bit bkwd: racd wd: in tch: nt qckn wl over 1f out: kpt on fnl f* **9/2**[3]

0006 5 ¾ **Stage Acclaim (IRE)**[6] 5331 2-9-2 75 .... JamesMillman(5) 7 70
(B R Millman) *lw: reminder in last after 1f: outpcd 2f out: plugged on fnl f: n.d* **4/1**[2]

0424 6 ¾ **Mansii**[8] 5277 2-9-7 75 .... RyanMoore 3 68
(C E Brittain) *led for 2f: styd prom but racd awkwardly after: wknd fnl f* **3/1**[1]

1301 7 ½ **Lord Deevert**[18] 5015 2-8-11 72 .... JackDean(7) 9 63
(W G M Turner) *dwlt: hld up in last pair: rdn and no prog 2f out: kpt on* **20/1**

4242 8 hd **Far Gone**[26] 4733 2-9-4 72 .... HayleyTurner 1 62
(M L W Bell) *lw: t.k.h: hld up bhd ldrs: effrt on inner over 1f out: wknd fnl f* **13/2**

1m 12.65s (-0.16) **Going Correction** -0.175s/f (Stan) 8 Ran SP% **112.2**
Speed ratings (Par 95): **94,91,90,90,89 88,87,87**
CSF £52.50 CT £754.40 TOTE £9.10: £2.40, £2.20, £4.70; EX 38.80.
Owner Mike & Denise Dawes **Bred** Barton Stud Partnership **Trained** Newmarket, Suffolk

FOCUS
Just a fair nursery and they finished in a bunch behind the clear-cut winner. The form looks quite solid.

NOTEBOOK
Geoffdaw had not shown much in a couple of Polytrack nurseries over 7f since landing a gamble in a Folkestone maiden earlier in the year, but the return to sprinting clearly suited and he ran out a most decisive winner. He finished nicely clear and should remain competitive off higher marks. (op 8-1 tchd 17-2)
Then 'n Now, off the mark in a course-and-distance maiden on her previous start, travelled quite well just in behind the pace and looked a real danger at the top of the straight, but she proved no match for the winner. (op 4-1)
Mollyatti's breeding hardly screams 'sprinter', but she ran well dropped in trip on her nursery debut. This effort helps boost the form of her previous fourth at Kempton, a race that proved difficult to get a handle on at the time.
Replicator was not helped by racing wide and was also reported to have lost a shoe, so he is probably a little better than he was able to show. He is still a maiden, but he should win a small race when everything falls into place and he may be suited by a drop back to 5f. Official explanation: jockey said colt pulled off near-fore shoe (tchd 4-1 and 5-1)
Stage Acclaim(IRE) was well backed on his Polytrack debut, but he was never going. (op 11-2)
Mansii, who was a bit on his toes beforehand, never looked comfortable and, just as he had on his only previous start on Polytrack, he was well beaten. He basically just looks a turf horse. Official explanation: jockey said colt hung right throughout (op 7-2 tchd 4-1 and 11-4)

5497 LINGFIELD PARK FOR CONFERENCES (S) STKS 1m 2f (P)
3:20 (3:20) (Class 6) 3-Y-O+ **£2,047** (£604; £302) **Stalls** Low

Form RPR

0444 1 **Lord Of Dreams (IRE)**[7] 5310 5-8-9 64 .... JamieJones(5) 5 71+
(G L Moore) *hld up wl off the pce: prog over 3f out: led wl over 1f out: rdn and in command fnl f* **11/8**[1]

2 2 **Drizzi (IRE)**[27] 6-9-5 0 .... (tp) GeorgeBaker 7 72
(Aldo Locatelli, Italy) *w'like: b: b.hind: lw: hld up last of main gp: gd prog on outer fr 4f out: led 2f out: hdd & nt look keen: easily hld by wnr fnl f* **11/4**[2]

-056 3 2½ **Terminate (GER)**[15] 5094 5-9-0 50 .... StephenDonohoe 6 62
(N A Callaghan) *hld up in main gp: rdn and prog 3f out: chsd ldng pair over 1f out: kpt on same pce* **3/1**[3]

0063 4 8 **Fun In The Sun**[8] 5269 3-8-8 43 .... (b) SteveDrowne 11 46
(P D Evans) *hld up in rr of main gp: sme prog fr 3f out but nvr on terms w ldrs* **16/1**

2003 5 shd **Sahara Prince (IRE)**[33] 4532 7-8-9 46 .... (p) TolleyDean(5) 8 46
(K A Morgan) *b: chsd clr ldr and wl clr of rest: wknd 2f out* **20/1**

0405 6 8 **Kirkhammerton (IRE)**[27] 4713 5-8-7 48 .... (b) RobbieEgan(7) 10 30
(A J McCabe) *blazed off in clr ld: drvn and reluctant 4f out: hdd & wknd rapidly u.p 2f out* **16/1**

0020 7 2½ **Anatolian Prince**[25] 4763 3-8-8 48 .... (t) HayleyTurner 2 25
(J M P Eustace) *prom in main gp: wknd 3f out: t.o* **33/1**

0066 8 1½ **Simpleton**[16] 5062 4-9-0 44 .... DaneO'Neill 1 22
(J R Best) *dwlt: in rr of main gp: u.p and no prog over 3f out: t.o* **50/1**

0044 9 1½ **Meeting Of Minds**[28] 4684 3-8-4 50 ow1 .... MartinDwyer 9 15
(W Jarvis) *lft 20 l: detached in last tl sme prog fr 4f out: no ch: wknd over 1f out: t.o* **14/1**

0500 10 8 **It's No Problem (IRE)**[8] 5269 3-8-8 47 .... SimonWhitworth 3 —
(M Salaman) *prom in main gp tl wknd 3f out: t.o* **33/1**

0406 **11** *1 ½* **Buckle And Hyde**[8] [5269] 4-8-9 41 .... EddieAhern 4 —
(Mrs A L M King) *lw: prom in main gp tl wknd over 3f out: t.o* **50/1**

2m 5.88s (-1.91) **Going Correction** -0.175s/f (Stan)
WFA 3 from 4yo+ 6lb **11** Ran SP% **126.8**
Speed ratings (Par 101): **100,98,96,90,89 83,81,80,79,72 71**
CSF £5.49 TOTE £2.20: £1.10, £1.50, £2.00; EX 10.10.The winner was bought in for 8,000gns. Drizzi was claimed by J. T. Billson for £6,000. Terminate was claimed by Ian Williams for £6,000.
Owner N J Jones **Bred** B Ryan **Trained** Woodingdean, E Sussex
■ Jamie Jones's first winner since returning to the saddle after six months out of racing.

FOCUS
Not a bad seller, but the leader went off ridiculously fast and set the race up for those held up. The third looks the best guide and the winner did not really need to improve.
Meeting Of Minds Official explanation: jockey said filly missed the break
Buckle And Hyde Official explanation: jockey said filly lost its action

5498 EUROPEAN BREEDERS' FUND MAIDEN STKS 7f (P)
3:50 (3:51) (Class 5) 2-Y-O **£3,141** (£934; £467; £233) **Stalls** Low

Form RPR
6 **1** **Sky Dive**[25] [4777] 2-9-3 0 .... NickyMackay 14 85+
(L M Cumani) *w'like: scope: str: prom: rdn to chse ldr over 1f out: r.o to ld last 100yds: readily* **10/1**
2 *1* **Adversity** 2-9-3 0 .... RyanMoore 4 78+
(Sir Michael Stoute) *leggy: athletic: settled in midfield: shkn up and prog over 2f out: styd on wl fr over 1f out to take 2nd nr fin* **6/1**[3]
0 **3** *½* **Lemon N Sugar (USA)**[47] [4094] 2-8-12 0 .... DarryllHolland 9 72
(J Noseda) *lw: mde most: rdn over 1f out: hdd last 100yds: lost 2nd nr fin* **7/2**[2]
6 **4** *½* **Hieroglyph**[11] [5194] 2-8-12 0 .... EddieAhern 6 71
(M Johnston) *leggy: prom: rdn to chse ldr briefly wl over 1f out: kpt on same pce fnl f* **14/1**
00 **5** *1* **Mystic Art (IRE)**[32] [4571] 2-9-3 0 .... RobertHavlin 8 73
(C R Egerton) *dwlt: settled in rr: stdy prog on inner fr 2f out: shuffled along and styd on fnl f: improve* **100/1**
2 **6** *shd* **Prohibit**[10] [5222] 2-9-3 0 .... RichardHughes 3 73
(J H M Gosden) *lw: trckd ldrs: effrt 2f out: one pce fr over 1f out* **6/5**[1]
0 **7** *5* **Slip**[11] [5200] 2-9-3 0 .... MartinDwyer 13 60
(M P Tregoning) *settled in midfield: outpcd over 2f out: pushed along and plugged on one pce after* **40/1**
0 **8** *½* **Oli James (USA)**[45] [4151] 2-9-3 0 .... NelsonDeSouza 12 59
(P F I Cole) *hld up in midfield: gng wl enough 3f out: outpcd over 2f out* **14/1**
9 *½* **Krisnando** 2-8-12 0 .... PaulDoe 2 52
(W J Knight) *w'like: scope: str: s.v.s: wl in rr: prog on wd outside 3f out: nvr rchd ldrs: no hdwy over 1f out* **25/1**
6 **10** *1 ½* **Lyrical Symphony**[54] [3874] 2-8-9 0 .... WilliamBuick(3) 11 48
(W J Knight) *leggy: w ldr to 3f out: chsng after tl wknd rapidly wl over 1f out: eased fnl f* **28/1**
11 *2* **Rough Sketch (USA)** 2-9-3 0 .... JamieMackay 5 48
(Sir Mark Prescott) *w'like: scope: bit bkwd: s.s: sn last and rn v green: nvr a factor* **66/1**
12 *1* **General Ting (IRE)** 2-9-3 0 .... SebSanders 10 46
(Sir Mark Prescott) *w'like: lengthy: bit bkwd: dwlt: racd wd: a in rr: struggling over 2f out* **33/1**
00 **13** *2* **Jevington Star (IRE)**[22] [4882] 2-9-3 0 .... IanMongan 7 40
(R M Flower) *nvr beyond midfield: rdn 3f out: wknd over 2f out* **100/1**
2550 **14** *4* **Midnite Blews (IRE)**[8] [5268] 2-9-3 69 .... SteveDrowne 1 30
(A B Haynes) *sn wl in rr: last and losing tch 1/2-way: sn wl bhd* **66/1**

1m 25.29s (-0.60) **Going Correction** -0.175s/f (Stan) **14** Ran SP% **122.0**
Speed ratings (Par 95): **96,94,94,93,92 92,86,86,85,83 81,80,78,73**
CSF £66.79 TOTE £15.30: £2.80, £1.40, £2.10; EX 113.10.
Owner Fittocks Stud **Bred** Fittocks Stud Ltd **Trained** Newmarket, Suffolk

FOCUS
Some good stables were represented and this looked a decent maiden.

NOTEBOOK
Sky Dive improved on the form he showed on his debut at Newmarket to get off the mark at the second attempt. This looked a reasonable race and he should not be underestimated in better company. (op 9-1 tchd 11-1)
Adversity ◆, an 88,000gns foal, 140,000gns two-year-old, son of Oasis Dream, is a half-brother to numerous winners, including the high-class 1m-1m2f performer Desert Deer, as well as very smart sprinter Branston Abby, out of a dual 5f winner at two and three. Racing in the colours of Sir Alex Ferguson, he showed plenty of ability on his racecourse debut and could even be considered a little unlucky as Sky Dive, who had the benefit of previous experience, was able to get first run. He does not hold any big-race entries, but he can be expected to come on for the experience and should progress into a very useful sort in time. (op 8-1)
Lemon N Sugar(USA) showed ability on her debut at Goodwood at the beginning of August and this was another promising effort. She knew her job much better this time, but just tired in the straight and can be expected to improve again. (op 3-1 tchd 11-4)
Hieroglyph showed ability on her debut over 6f at Haydock and this was another reasonable effort. She could pick up an ordinary maiden, but will also have the options of nurseries/handicaps after one more run. (op 16-1)
Mystic Art(IRE) ◆ had shown just moderate form in a couple of 6f maidens on turf, but he was a real eye-catcher stepped up in trip and switched to sand. Having been settled well off the pace, he was noted doing some good late work, despite not being knocked about, and will be one to watch now he is qualified for a handicap mark.
Prohibit shaped well in a reasonable race at Kempton on his debut, but he failed to confirm that promise and was a little disappointing. (op 5-4 tchd 11-8 and 11-10)
Krisnando Official explanation: jockey said filly missed the break
Lyrical Symphony Official explanation: jockey said filly had no more to give
Midnite Blews(IRE) Official explanation: jockey said gelding ran too free

5499 KINGSTON SMITH LLP CHALLENGE MAIDEN STKS (DIV II) 1m (P)
4:20 (4:20) (Class 5) 3-Y-0+ **£2,169** (£645; £322; £161) **Stalls** High

Form RPR
5-02 **1** **Rhyming Slang (USA)**[29] [4666] 3-9-3 76 .... DarryllHolland 9 83+
(J Noseda) *lw: settled in rr: rapid prog on outer 1/2-way to join ldrs 3f out: led 2f out: drvn clr fr over 1f out* **5/2**[1]
6 **2** *3* **Zero Cool (USA)**[24] [4815] 3-9-3 0 .... RobertHavlin 2 73
(J H M Gosden) *w'like: str: prom: lost pl sltly 3f out: renewed effrt 2f out: drvn and rdn on to take 2nd last strides* **3/1**[2]
5022 **3** *hd* **Meynell**[18] [5013] 3-8-12 75 .... PhilipRobinson 8 68
(M A Jarvis) *prom: led over 3f out: drvn and hdd 2f out: no ch w wnr fnl f: lost 2nd last strides* **5/2**[1]
6 **4** *3* **Fixation**[29] [4666] 3-9-3 0 .... RichardHughes 4 66
(Mrs A J Perrett) *w'like: sn w ldrs: hrd rdn over 2f out: one pce fnl 2f* **16/1**
- **5** *2 ½* **Beautiful Dancer (IRE)** 3-8-12 0 .... NickyMackay 7 55
(L M Cumani) *unf: mostly in midfield: pushed along 3f out: outpcd over 2f out: kpt on steadily* **16/1**
6 *½* **Kissing** 3-8-12 0 .... SebSanders 3 54
(Sir Mark Prescott) *w'like: lengthy: bit bkwd: dwlt: rn in snatches: sme prog fr rr 2f out: no hdwy after* **10/1**[3]
0 **7** *5* **Impenetrable (USA)**[29] [4666] 3-9-3 0 .... TedDurcan 11 47
(Saeed Bin Suroor) *w'like: scope: rdn towards rr over 4f out: struggling over 3f out: n.d after* **12/1**
4/0- **8** *2 ½* **Maraagel (USA)**[371] [5272] 4-9-0 0 .... WilliamCarson(7) 1 41
(S C Williams) *b: mde most to over 3f out: wknd rapidly over 2f out* **50/1**
06 **9** *nk* **Park Valley Prince**[14] [5113] 3-9-3 0 .... MartinDwyer 5 41
(W R Muir) *chsd ldr to 1/2-way: wknd over 2f out: b.b.v* **66/1**
00 **10** *½* **Amichi**[36] [4457] 3-8-12 0 .... RyanMoore 10 35
(G L Moore) *leggy: a in last pair and nvr gng wl* **50/1**
-030 **11** *6* **Serene Dancer**[33] [4545] 4-9-2 52 .... FergusSweeney 6 21
(Mrs P N Dutfield) *a in rr: no ch over 2f out: virtually p.u nr fin: lame* **66/1**

1m 37.37s (-2.06) **Going Correction** -0.175s/f (Stan)
WFA 3 from 4yo 4lb **46** Ran SP% **117.6**
Speed ratings (Par 103): **103,100,99,96,94 93,88,86,86,85 79**
CSF £10.00 TOTE £3.50: £1.50, £1.50, £1.30; EX 11.50.
Owner Sheikh Marwan Al Maktoum **Bred** J Kerber And Iveta Kerber **Trained** Newmarket, Suffolk

FOCUS
The winning time was 0.78 seconds slower than the first division and this looked an ordinary maiden. The form seems sound enough though.
Impenetrable(USA) Official explanation: trainer's rep said colt had breathing problems
Park Valley Prince Official explanation: trainer said colt had bled
Serene Dancer Official explanation: vet said filly returned lame

5500 PLAY GOLF @ LINGFIELD PARK H'CAP 1m 4f (P)
4:50 (4:50) (Class 5) (0-75,75) 3-Y-0+ **£2,817** (£838; £418; £209) **Stalls** Low

Form RPR
4102 **1** **Elegant Hawk**[25] [4766] 3-9-9 75 .... PaulDoe 11 85+
(W J Knight) *hld up in midfield: nt clr run briefly over 2f out: prog wl over 1f out: led jst ins fnl f: rdn clr* **6/1**[2]
5504 **2** *1 ½* **Paymaster General (IRE)**[16] [5068] 3-9-6 72 .... DaneO'Neill 15 78
(M D I Usher) *plld hrd early: hld up towards rr: prog on outer fr 3f out: rdn and r.o fr over 1f out: snatched 2nd on post* **66/1**
-242 **3** *hd* **Fringe**[25] [4765] 4-9-12 70 .... JimCrowley 3 76
(Jane Chapple-Hyam) *lw: led for 3f: prom: drvn wl over 3f out: outpcd over 2f out: styd on wl again fnl f* **7/2**[1]
0242 **4** *shd* **Red Wine**[27] [4717] 8-8-11 62 .... RobbieEgan(7) 13 70+
(A J McCabe) *hld up in last trio: prog whn nt clr run and swtchd rt over 1f out: r.o wl fnl f: too much to do* **11/1**
4-20 **5** *½* **Land Of Light**[11] [5204] 4-9-9 67 .... GeorgeBaker 12 72
(G L Moore) *lw: settled in midfield: prog fr 3f out: rdn to ld over 1f out: hdd jst ins fnl f: lost 3 pls nr fin* **14/1**
3023 **6** *hd* **Maslak (IRE)**[15] [5101] 3-9-5 74 .... TravisBlock(3) 7 78+
(P W Hiatt) *trckd ldrs: lost pl 3f out: nt clr run several times after: r.o wl fnl f: fin wl* **25/1**
4462 **7** *3* **Amwell Brave**[15] [5093] 6-9-3 61 .... DarryllHolland 1 61
(J R Jenkins) *hld up in rr: last 4f out: prog on inner 2f out: nt clr run 1f out: swtchd rt and styd on: no ch* **10/1**
1505 **8** *nk* **Watchmaker**[15] [5093] 4-9-6 64 .... FergusSweeney 9 63
(Miss Tor Sturgis) *lw: racd on outer in midfield: reminder over 4f out: effrt and chsng ldrs over 1f out: wknd fnl f* **20/1**
0/6- **9** *1 ½* **Cash On (IRE)**[349] [1927] 5-9-12 70 .... (p) RichardHughes 5 67
(Karen George) *dwlt: hld up in rr: effrt on outer 3f out: outpcd over 2f out: n.d after* **33/1**
0000 **10** *¾* **Tromp**[19] [4976] 6-9-11 69 .... TedDurcan 10 65
(D J Coakley) *prom: rdn over 3f out: wknd over 1f out* **20/1**
-320 **11** *hd* **Abyla**[44] [4205] 3-9-1 67 .... MartinDwyer 4 62
(M P Tregoning) *t.k.h: led after 3f to wl over 3f out: wknd wl over 1f out* **13/2**[3]
-504 **12** *1 ¼* **Captain General**[21] [4917] 5-9-10 68 .... EddieAhern 2 61
(J A R Toller) *cl up: rdn on inner over 2f out: stl wl in tch whn tightened up over 1f out: wknd* **15/2**
5221 **13** *2* **Selkirk Grace**[24] [4802] 7-8-13 62 .... (p) TolleyDean(5) 8 52
(K A Morgan) *prom: led wl over 3f out to over 1f out: wknd rapidly* **10/1**
3015 **14** *1 ¼* **Muraco**[22] [4910] 3-9-4 70 .... SebSanders 14 58
(R M Beckett) *racd on outer in midfield: u.p over 3f out: wknd 2f out* **14/1**
01-0 **15** *10* **Maximix**[218] [89] 4-9-6 64 .... RyanMoore 6 36
(G L Moore) *nvr bttr than midfied on inner: wknd 4f out: t.o* **10/1**

2m 32.61s (-1.78) **Going Correction** -0.175s/f (Stan)
WFA 3 from 4yo+ 8lb **15** Ran SP% **128.3**
Speed ratings (Par 103): **98,97,96,96,96 96,94,94,93,92 92,91,90,89,82**
CSF £390.71 CT £1632.89 TOTE £8.40: £2.60, £12.40, £1.70; EX 548.10 Place 6 £58.40, Place 5 £27.80.
Owner Hesmonds Stud **Bred** Hesmonds Stud Ltd **Trained** Patching, W Sussex

FOCUS
A fair middle-distance handicap in which they finished in a bit of a heap behind the unexposed winner. The form seems sound.
Land Of Light Official explanation: jockey said gelding hung left
Amwell Brave Official explanation: jockey said gelding was denied a clear run
T/Plt: £64.90 to a £1 stake. Pool: £55,594.95. 624.45 winning tickets. T/Qpdt: £21.60 to a £1 stake. Pool: £2,800.20. 95.80 winning tickets. JN

5226 THIRSK (L-H)
Tuesday, September 18

OFFICIAL GOING: Good to firm
Wind: Slight, half behind Weather: Sunny

5501 INGLEBOROUGH MEDIAN AUCTION MAIDEN STKS 6f
2:00 (2:01) (Class 6) 2-Y-O **£2,730** (£806; £403) **Stalls** High

Form RPR
5 **1** **Writingonthewall (IRE)**[11] [5192] 2-9-3 0 .... JamieSpencer 9 79
(M L W Bell) *trckd ldrs: hdwy over 2f out: rdn to chal and wandered appr fnl f: styd on to ld last 100yds* **5/4**[1]
0 **2** *nk* **Actabou**[22] [4890] 2-9-3 0 .... PhillipMakin 14 78
(M Dods) *cl up: led over 2f out: sn rdn: drvn ins fnl f: hdd and no ex last 100yds* **33/1**
0 **3** *1* **Unbreak My Heart (IRE)**[59] [3747] 2-9-3 0 .... PaulHanagan 11 75
(R Charlton) *trckd ldrs: hdwy over 2f out: rdn and hung lft ent fnl f: n.m.r and kpt on* **11/8**[2]

The Form Book, Raceform Ltd, Compton, RG20 6NL

6 **4** *2* **Doric Dream**[49] 4041 2-8-12 0 RoystonFfrench 12 64
(B Smart) *sn pushed along in rr: hdwy over 2f out: rdn over 1f out: kpt on ins fnl f: nrst fin* **10/1**

4235 **5** *1* **Carnival Dream**[32] 4560 2-8-9 69 PatrickMathers(3) 10 61
(A Berry) *wnt rt s: sn led: rdn along and hdd over 2f out: grad wknd* **13/2**[3]

6 *2* **Casa Mia (IRE)** 2-8-12 0 TonyHamilton 13 55
(R A Fahey) *dwlt: sn in tch: hdwy to chse ldrs over 2f out: rdn and no imp over 1f out* **33/1**

000 **7** *4* **Latin Dancer**[8] 5281 2-9-3 0 (p) DO'Donohoe 2 48
(B S Rothwell) *bhd tl sme late hdwy* **100/1**

8 *½* **Petidium** 2-8-5 0 DanielleMcCreery(7) 1 42
(N Bycroft) *dwlt: sn in tch on outer: rdn along 1/2-way and sn wknd* **80/1**

00 **9** *1* **Kyzer Chief**[8] 5281 2-9-3 0 TomEaves 4 44
(R E Barr) *prom: rdn along wl over 2f out sn wknd* **100/1**

00 **10** *2½* **Chica Guapa (IRE)**[99] 2504 2-8-7 0 RussellKennemore(5) 7 31
(Paul Green) *hmpd s: a in rr* **100/1**

11 *3* **Primer Lugar** 2-8-9 0 AndrewMullen(3) 6 22
(W J H Ratcliffe) *hmpd s: a in rr* **100/1**

500 **12** *1½* **Sandies Choice**[89] 2803 2-8-5 45 PatrickDonaghy(7) 8 18
(M Brittain) *wnt lft s: a in rr* **100/1**

0 **13** *1¼* **Ruby's Rainbow (IRE)**[12] 5154 2-8-12 0 MickyFenton 5 14
(J Balding) *a towards rr* **100/1**

1m 12.12s (-0.38) **Going Correction** -0.40s/f (Firm) **13** Ran SP% **122.0**
Speed ratings (Par 93): **86,85,84,81,80 77,72,71,70,66 62,60,59**
CSF £54.13 TOTE £2.10: £1.10, £6.30, £1.10; EX 42.10.
Owner Michael Tabor **Bred** D And Ms B Egan **Trained** Newmarket, Suffolk

FOCUS
Not a great maiden, with two horses attracting the bulk of market support. Improved form from the first three.

NOTEBOOK
Writingonthewall(IRE) was too green on his debut at Haydock but that experience had clearly done him some good and he appreciated the extra furlong. He cannot be rated too highly for this narrow success, and that should mean he will be competitive in nursery company. (op 11-10 tchd 5-6)
Actabou did not show a great deal on his debut at Newcastle but this was far more promising. Despite being coltish beforehand, he gave the favourite a real race having bagged the favoured stands'-side rail and, being by Tobougg, he might appreciate easier ground this autumn. (op 28-1)
Unbreak My Heart(IRE) had finished ninth in a stronger maiden at Newmarket on his debut and did not need to improve a great deal for that to be involved here. He came up short but would have probably finished second with a clearer run, and he too might be suited by easier ground. (op 15-8 tchd 2-1 and 9-4 in a place)
Doric Dream, who did not run too badly from a poor draw at Beverley on her debut back in July, struggled to go the early pace but was keeping on well at the end. She looks one for nurseries after one more run. (op 11-1)
Carnival Dream is beginning to look exposed but is probably the best guide to the level of the form. (tchd 7-1)
Casa Mia(IRE), a half-sister to winners abroad, shaped with some promise on her debut and should come on for the run.
Kyzer Chief was on his toes beforehand.

5502 HYGICARE MAIDEN STKS 7f
2:30 (2:31) (Class 5) 2-Y-0 **£3,562** (£1,059; £529; £264) **Stalls** Low

Form RPR

.42 **1** **Inspector Clouseau (IRE)**[22] 4890 2-9-3 0 MickyFenton 6 66+
(T P Tate) *led over 2f: cl up tl led again over 2f out: sn rdn clr: comf* **3/1**[3]

00 **2** *1¾* **Mahadee (IRE)**[34] 4487 2-9-3 0 SilvestreDeSousa 3 61
(C E Brittain) *prom: rdn along 3f out: kpt on u.p to chse wnr wl over 1f out: one pce* **33/1**

0000 **3** *¾* **Eternal Optimist (IRE)**[12] 5154 2-8-12 40 DanielTudhope 4 54
(C W Thornton) *in rr: hdwy over 3f out: rdn along 2f out: kpt on same pce appr fnl f* **100/1**

02 **4** *nk* **Beetuna (IRE)**[13] 5140 2-9-3 0 TomEaves 5 58
(B Smart) *trckd ldrs: effrt over 2f out: sn rdn and kpt on same pce* **85/40**[2]

5 **5** *2* **Govenor Eliott (IRE)**[13] 5143 2-9-3 0 JamieSpencer 1 53
(M Johnston) *sn cl up: led over 4f out: rdn along and hdd over 2f out: sn wknd* **11/10**[1]

0 **6** *1½* **Snickers First**[53] 3916 2-8-12 0 PaulMulrennan 8 44
(M W Easterby) *chsd ldrs: rdn along and outpcd fr 1/2-way* **100/1**

000 **7** *1½* **Maahe (IRE)**[51] 3995 2-8-9 50 JamieMoriarty(3) 7 40
(R A Fahey) *sn outpcd and bhd: sme hdwy over 2f out: nvr a factor* **40/1**

1m 27.38s (0.28) **Going Correction** -0.175s/f (Firm) **7** Ran SP% **112.0**
Speed ratings (Par 95): **91,89,88,87,85 83,82**
CSF £64.66 TOTE £3.40: £1.70, £5.10; EX 108.00.
Owner T P Tate **Bred** P Byrne, Eimear Mulhern & B Grassick **Trained** Tadcaster, N Yorks

FOCUS
Modest maiden form based on the performances of the placed horses, which seem to have shown dubious improvement.

NOTEBOOK
Inspector Clouseau(IRE) was always in control and won comfortably in the end, only having to be pushed out to score. This was a poor race, though, evidenced by the performance of the 40-rated third, so the Handicapper might not go overboard. (op 10-3 tchd 5-2 and 7-2 in a place)
Mahadee(IRE), noisy in the paddock, had shown very little in his previous two starts and, while this was better, the form is not worth a hill of beans. Low-grade nurseries are now an option for him. (op 50-1)
Eternal Optimist(IRE), exposed as a very moderate performer over 5f, improved for the step up in trip, but his performance still makes the form look pretty weak.
Beetuna(IRE), on his toes beforehand, failed to replicate his York form but is at least now eligible for a mark. (op 15-8 tchd 11-4)
Govenor Eliott(IRE), sent off favourite again, was on his toes beforehand and had every chance, but came up short. This was a step backwards. (op 6-5 tchd 5-4, 10-11 and 11-8 in a place)

5503 WHERNSIDE H'CAP 1m
3:00 (3:00) (Class 6) (0-50,52) 3-Y-0+ **£1,943** (£578; £288; £144) **Stalls** Low

Form RPR

003 **1** **Grandad Bill (IRE)**[82] 3042 4-8-13 49 DanielTudhope 6 55
(J S Goldie) *in tch: hdwy to trck ldrs 3f out: rdn over 1f out: styd on to ld last 100yds: jst hld on* **4/1**[1]

0003 **2** *shd* **Domesday (UAE)**[22] 4891 6-8-8 47 DuranFentiman(3) 12 53
(W G Harrison) *a.p: rdn wl over 1f out: kpt on ins fnl f: jst hld* **28/1**

5400 **3** *nk* **Zhitomir**[32] 4562 9-8-13 49 PhillipMakin 11 54
(M Dods) *midfield: hdwy over 2f out: sn rdn and edgd lft: stayed on wl u.p ins fnl f* **20/1**

5605 **4** *½* **Time To Regret**[6] 5336 7-8-12 48 (p) PaulHanagan 8 52
(I W McInnes) *led: rdn along 2f out: drvn ent fnl f: hdd and one pce last 100yds* **8/1**[3]

2445 **5** *1¼* **Smart Pick**[20] 4931 4-9-0 50 TonyHamilton 3 51
(Mrs L Williamson) *s.i.s: hdwy 3f out: nt clr 2f out: swtchd rt and rdn over 1f out: styd on ins fnl f* **10/1**

0420 **6** *1* **Passionately Royal**[22] 4891 5-8-10 46 AdrianTNicholls 15 45
(M Brittain) *chsd ldrs: rdn along 2f out: drvn and hung lft ent fnl f: one pce* **33/1**

5000 **7** *½* **Counterfactual (IRE)**[97] 2582 4-8-13 49 RoystonFfrench 1 50+
(B Smart) *hld up towards rr: hdwy 2f out: sn hmpd: styd on ins fnl f: nrst fin* **14/1**

0504 **8** *hd* **Terenzium (IRE)**[18] 4998 5-8-12 48 (p) PaulMulrennan 9 45
(Micky Hammond) *hld up in rr: hdwy on inner 2f out: sn rdn: kpt on appr fnl f: nrst fin* **11/1**

5000 **9** *½* **The Bonus King**[33] 4533 7-8-11 47 JamieSpencer 4 43
(J Jay) *nvr bttr than midfield* **8/1**[3]

0050 **10** *¾* **Jalamid (IRE)**[32] 4580 5-8-11 47 (t) GregFairley 10 42
(M A Barnes) *hld up: swtchd outside and hdwy wl over 2f oiut: sn rdn along and no imp fr over 1f out* **11/1**

0005 **11** *shd* **Baby Barry**[36] 4449 10-8-8 47 DominicFox(3) 7 41
(S Parr) *prom: rdn along 3f out: sn drvn and wknd 2f out* **20/1**

0035 **12** *nk* **Green Pirate**[10] 5237 5-8-10 52 PJMcDonald(3) 13 43
(W M Brisbourne) *s.i.s: a in rr* **7/1**[2]

0010 **13** *2* **Linden's Lady**[5] 5368 7-8-11 50 (v) AlanCreighton(3) 18 39
(J R Weymes) *chsd ldrs on outer: rdn along 3f out: grad wknd* **20/1**

0000 **14** *shd* **Brace Of Doves**[19] 4966 5-8-9 48 (p) AndrewMullen(3) 2 37
(D W Whillans) *a towards rr* **14/1**

0005 **15** *3* **Frimley's Matterry**[8] 5284 7-8-12 48 PaddyAspell 5 30
(R E Barr) *chsd ldng pair: rdn along 3f out: wknd 2f out* **20/1**

0606 **16** *2½* **Coalite (IRE)**[17] 5037 4-8-12 48 DO'Donohoe 14 24
(A D Brown) *chsd ldrs: rdn along over 2f out and sn wknd* **20/1**

3000 **17** *2* **Fairy Monarch (IRE)**[9] 5255 8-9-0 50 (b) MickyFenton 16 22
(P T Midgley) *a in rr* **16/1**

000 **18** *4* **Nortelco (IRE)**[21] 4920 4-8-11 47 (t) PatCosgrave 17 9
(Micky Hammond) *a in rr* **80/1**

1m 39.33s (-0.37) **Going Correction** -0.175s/f (Firm) **18** Ran SP% **131.1**
Speed ratings (Par 101): **94,93,93,93,91 90,90,90,89,88 88,88,86,86,83 80,78,74**
CSF £137.45 CT £2096.26 TOTE £5.50: £2.20, £4.80, £5.30, £2.10; EX 204.80.
Owner Tough Construction Ltd **Bred** M Hosokawa **Trained** Uplawmoor, E Renfrews

FOCUS
A bunch finish to this competitive but very moderate handicap. Effectively banded form.
Counterfactual(IRE) Official explanation: jockey said gelding ran too free early
Green Pirate Official explanation: jockey said gelding missed the break

5504 HYGICARE H'CAP 1m 4f
3:30 (3:30) (Class 3) (0-95,91) 3-Y-0+ **£7,124** (£2,119; £1,059; £529) **Stalls** Low

Form RPR

5406 **1** **Players Please (USA)**[17] 5049 3-9-4 89 GregFairley 6 100
(M Johnston) *cl up: led after 2f: rdn and qcknd over 2f out: styd on strly* **7/2**[2]

3111 **2** *3* **Generous Jem**[10] 5229 4-8-13 81 NeilBrown(5) 3 87+
(G G Margarson) *hld up: hdwy over 3f out: rdn to chse wnr over 1f out: sn drvn and no imp* **9/4**[1]

0301 **3** *1½* **Philanthropy**[13] 5141 3-9-6 91 DO'Donohoe 7 95
(K A Ryan) *trckd ldng pair: hdwy to chse wnr 5f out: rdn along over 2f out: sn one pce* **11/2**[3]

0033 **4** *1¼* **Habalwatan (IRE)**[24] 4799 3-9-2 87 JamieSpencer 8 89+
(C E Brittain) *hld up in rr: effrt and hdwy over 2f out: sn rdn and no imp* **9/4**[1]

0250 **5** *1¼* **Luna Landing**[26] 4732 4-9-7 84 PaulMulrennan 5 84
(Jedd O'Keeffe) *led 2f: cl up: rdn along over 3f out and sn wknd* **20/1**

2400 **6** *8* **Clueless**[10] 5215 5-9-3 83 JamieMoriarty(3) 1 70
(N G Richards) *chsd ldrs: rdn along 1/2-way: sn outpcd and bhd* **11/1**

2m 35.11s (-0.09) **Going Correction** -0.175s/f (Firm)
WFA 3 from 4yo+ 8lb **6** Ran SP% **112.2**
Speed ratings (Par 107): **93,91,90,89,88 83**
CSF £11.81 CT £40.24 TOTE £4.60: £2.40, £1.50; EX 13.70.
Owner N N Browne **Bred** 6 C Racing Limited **Trained** Middleham Moor, N Yorks

FOCUS
Decent handicap form. The winner had the run of things and there is a slight doubt over what he achieved here.

NOTEBOOK
Players Please(USA) found the drop in class just what he needed and was able to dominate this small field throughout. He deserved this as he has run well in some good handicaps this season, and it also proved that he gets 1m4f well. (op 3-1)
Generous Jem, another 7lb higher, is a hold-up performer reliant on others to set a good gallop for her, so the fact that Players Please got to set his own pace out in front was always going to be against her. She ran a solid race in the circumstances, but may now be in the Handicapper's grip. (op 2-1 tchd 5-2 in a place)
Philanthropy got the run of the race at York last time, but with Players Please in the field he was denied the chance to make all again. (op 5-1)
Habalwatan(IRE) has been in good form of late but he is another who could have done with a stronger pace. At least he shows he stays 1m4f. (op 3-1 tchd 10-3 and 7-2 in a place)
Luna Landing has largely struggled since winning over this course and distance in June. (op 16-1)

5505 SHIRLEY CARTER H'CAP 6f
4:00 (4:01) (Class 3) (0-90,89) 3-Y-0+ **£7,124** (£2,119; £1,059; £529) **Stalls** High

Form RPR

0061 **1** **Inter Vision (USA)**[4] 5379 7-9-0 83 6ex DanielTudhope 11 99+
(A Dickman) *hld up in rr: swtchd lft and gd hdwy 2f out: shkn up over 1f out: qcknd to ld ins fnl f: comf* **2/1**[1]

3032 **2** *2½* **Guest Connections**[12] 5155 4-8-6 75 (v) AdrianTNicholls 2 84
(D Nicholls) *in tch: hdwy 2f out: rdn over 1f out: kpt on u.p ins fnl f* **13/2**[2]

1013 **3** *nk* **Dakota Rain (IRE)**[12] 5155 5-8-11 80 GregFairley 4 88
(Jennie Candlish) *led: rdn along wl over 1f out: drvn and hdd ins fnl f: one pce* **15/2**[3]

0313 **4** *2* **High Curragh**[11] 5195 4-9-6 89 (p) DO'Donohoe 6 91
(K A Ryan) *prom: rdn along wl over 1f out: kpt on same pce* **13/2**[2]

0040 **5** *shd* **Romany Nights (IRE)**[14] 5119 7-8-6 75 oh1 (b) PaulHanagan 9 76
(Miss Gay Kelleway) *hld up: pushed along 1/2-way: swtchd lft and rdn 2f out: styd on same pce ins fnl f* **9/1**

0002 **6** *1¾* **Guto**[15] 5083 4-8-5 77 AndrewMullen(3) 5 73
(W J H Ratcliffe) *chsd ldrs: rdn along 2f out: grad wknd* **14/1**

3502 **7** *1* **Avertuoso**[22] 4898 3-8-13 84 TomEaves 8 77
(B Smart) *s.i.s: a towards rr* **8/1**

6446 **8** *2* **Musca (IRE)**[32] 4581 3-8-7 78 PaulMulrennan 3 65
(J Wade) *a towards rr* **16/1**

0000 **9** *1* **Swing The Ring (IRE)**[38] 4389 4-8-8 **80**................ PatrickMathers(3) 10 64
(A Berry) *chsd ldrs: rdn along over 2f out: sn wknd and in rr whn hmpd over 1f out* **25/1**

0050 **10** *nk* **Fire Up The Band**[11] 5195 8-8-10 **86**.............................. OliveGaule(7) 7 69
(D Nicholls) *prom: rdn along over 2f out: sn wknd* **14/1**

69.91 secs (-2.59) **Going Correction** -0.40s/f (Firm)
WFA 3 from 4yo+ 2lb **10** Ran SP% **115.9**
Speed ratings (Par 107): **101,97,97,94,94 92,90,88,86,86**
CSF £14.75 CT £83.16 TOTE £2.80: £2.10, £1.80, £2.30; EX 16.00.
Owner Mrs D Hodgkinson **Bred** W A Carl **Trained** Sandhutton, N Yorks

FOCUS
There was a good pace to this fair sprint handicap, and the form looks rock solid.

NOTEBOOK
Inter Vision(USA), who won narrowly over 5f at Doncaster last time, had the race very much run to suit as the leaders set a decent pace and he was able to come through and win quite comfortably in the end, despite having a 6lb penalty to shoulder. He is clearly right at the top of his game. (tchd 9-4 in a place)
Guest Connections has been running well lately but is just lacking that little bit extra to get his head in front. On this occasion he bumped into a well-handicapped rival in top form and there was no disgrace in finishing second. (op 11-2)
Dakota Rain(IRE) showed good early speed to lead and kept on well to take third, but the impression left is that he is held off his current mark. Official explanation: trainer said gelding finished distressed (op 8-1)
High Curragh, wearing cheekpieces for the first time, ran on late but was never a threat to the principals. He had a draw advantage when winning at Haydock last month. (op 6-1 tchd 7-1)
Romany Nights(IRE), 1lb wrong at the weights, went without the usual tongue tie and could never land a blow. (tchd 8-1)
Guto achieved little when runner-up in a claimer last time and this performance confirmed his continued decline. (op 16-1)
Avertuoso Official explanation: jockey said gelding reared in stalls as gates opened
Swing The Ring(IRE) Official explanation: jockey said colt suffered interference in running

5506 WHITE SWAN AT AMPLEFORTH H'CAP 5f
4:30 (4:30) (Class 4) (0-85,85) 3-Y-O **£5,505** (£1,637; £818; £408) **Stalls** High

Form RPR
4021 **1** **Ishetoo**[36] 4452 3-9-1 **85**.. MichaelJStainton(3) 3 92
(A Dickman) *trckd ldrs: pushed along wl over 1f out: rdn to ld appr fnl f: styd on u.p* **85/40**[2]

0030 **2** *1 1/4* **Valery Borzov (IRE)**[27] 4726 3-8-13 **80**...................... AdrianTNicholls 7 83
(D Nicholls) *hld up: pushed along and sltly outpcd 2f out: sn rdn and edgd lft over 1f out: styd on ins fnl f* **11/8**[1]

4030 **3** *shd* **Pegasus Dancer (FR)**[6] 5332 3-8-4 **71** oh3................(b[1]) DO'Donohoe 4 73
(K A Ryan) *cl up: rdn wl over 1f out and ev ch and nt qckn ins fnl f* **28/1**

3540 **4** *1* **Hawaii Prince**[13] 5139 3-8-4 **71** oh9.......................... SilvestreDeSousa 6 70
(S T Mason) *prom: rdn along 2f out: sn drvn and one pce ent fnl f* **20/1**

0406 **5** *1* **Bridge It Jo**[8] 5278 3-8-7 **79** ow2...................................... NeilBrown(5) 5 74
(G G Margarson) *led: rdn along 2f out: drvn and hdd over 1f out: wknd* **8/1**

466 **6** *1 3/4* **Deserted Dane (USA)**[17] 5039 3-8-12 **82**.................. PJMcDonald(3) 1 71
(G A Swinbank) *chsd ldrs: rdn along 2f out: sn drvn and wknd* **9/2**[3]

57.61 secs (-2.29) **Going Correction** -0.40s/f (Firm) **6** Ran SP% **111.6**
Speed ratings (Par 103): **102,100,99,98,96 93**
CSF £5.36 CT £51.04 TOTE £3.00: £1.60, £1.10; EX 5.20.
Owner John H Sissons **Bred** Longdon Stud Ltd **Trained** Sandhutton, N Yorks

FOCUS
Not many of these arrived here in good form and the proximity of Hawaii Prince (9lb wrong at the weights) at the finish casts doubt on the value of the form. The winner is progressive.

5507 RACE AT PONTEFRACT ON SEPTEMBER 20TH H'CAP 5f
5:00 (5:02) (Class 6) (0-65,65) 3-Y-O+ **£2,047** (£604; £302) **Stalls** High

Form RPR
0254 **1** **Miacarla**[7] 5297 4-8-3 **52**.. PatrickMathers(3) 19 64+
(A Berry) *trckd ldrs stands' rail: hdwy and squeezed through ins fnl f: qcknd to ld last 75yds* **4/1**[1]

0050 **2** *1 1/2* **No Time (IRE)**[13] 5130 7-8-8 **54**...................................... PatCosgrave 20 61
(A J McCabe) *cl up stands' rail: rdn to ld briefly ins fnl f: edgd lft and hdd last 75yds* **13/2**[2]

4303 **3** *3/4* **Jojesse**[20] 4935 3-8-6 **53**.. PaulHanagan 13 57+
(G A Swinbank) *hld up stands' side: hdwy and nt clr run over 1f out: styd on ins fnl f* **13/2**[2]

0006 **4** *hd* **Mr Rooney (IRE)**[20] 4942 4-8-11 **57**............................ AdrianTNicholls 14 60
(D Nicholls) *overall ldr stands' side: rdn wl over 1f out: drvn and hdd ins fnl f: kpt on* **12/1**

1066 **4** *dht* **Rann Na Cille (IRE)**[20] 4935 3-8-13 **63**................(b) AndrewMullen(3) 17 66
(K A Ryan) *trckd ldrs: hdwy over 1f out: rdn and styng on whn hit over hd w rivals whip: kpt on wl towards fin* **33/1**

0-00 **6** *hd* **Niteowl Lad (IRE)**[24] 4800 5-9-2 **62**.............................. TomEaves 15 65
(J Balding) *cl up stands' side: rdn over 1f out: edgd lft ent fnl f and one pce* **33/1**

6304 **7** *3/4* **Northern Chorus (IRE)**[20] 4939 4-8-8 **59**.............(v) JamesO'Reilly(5) 3 59
(J O'Reilly) *led far side: rdn wl over 1f out and ev ch: kpt on ins fnl f: no ch w stands' side* **11/1**

3040 **8** *nk* **Henry Hall (IRE)**[7] 5297 11-8-8 **54**.................................... KimTinkler 12 53
(N Tinkler) *chsd ldrs stands' side: swtchd lft anmd hdwy 2f out: sn rdn and kpt on same pce ins fnl f* **14/1**

6110 **9** *hd* **Toy Top (USA)**[19] 4967 4-9-3 **63**................................(b) PhillipMakin 10 61
(M Dods) *cl up stands' side: rdn along wl over 1f out: sn wknd* **10/1**

1006 **10** *nk* **Steel City Boy (IRE)**[7] 5297 4-9-0 **65**...................... KellyHarrison(5) 18 62
(D Carroll) *cl up: rdn wl over 1f out: wkng whn n.m.r ent fnl f* **9/1**

0300 **11** *1/2* **Durova (IRE)**[13] 5139 3-8-13 **62**...........................(e) DuranFentiman(3) 9 58
(T D Easterby) *hld up stands' side: swtchd lft and hdwy 2f out: sn rdn and wknd ent fnl f* **33/1**

0000 **12** *nk* **Smiddy Hill**[25] 4787 5-8-5 **51** oh1............................ RoystonFfrench 16 45
(R Bastiman) *in tch stands' side: rdn along wl over 1f out and sn wknd* **8/1**[3]

5430 **13** *1 3/4* **Hamaasy**[162] 967 6-8-6 **52**.................................... SilvestreDeSousa 8 40
(D Nicholls) *chsd ldrs stands' side: rdn along 2f out: grad wknd* **11/1**

0560 **14** *nk* **It's Unbelievable (USA)**[24] 4800 4-8-8 **54** ow1............(p) MickyFenton 5 41
(P T Midgley) *in tch far side: rdn along 2f out and sn wknd* **20/1**

2-00 **15** *1* **Centreboard (USA)**[13] 5139 3-9-3 **64**.............................. PaulMulrennan 2 47
(M W Easterby) *prom far side: rdn along 1/2-way: sn wknd* **50/1**

6005 **16** *1 3/4* **Seafield Towers**[7] 5295 7-8-5 **51** oh6............................(p) GregFairley 4 30
(Miss L A Perratt) *a in rr far side* **18/1**

000 **17** *6* **Mint**[25] 4768 4-8-6 **52**..(p) TonyHamilton 7 9
(D W Barker) *a in rr far side* **50/1**

58.21 secs (-1.69) **Going Correction** -0.40s/f (Firm)
WFA 3 from 4yo+ 1lb **17** Ran SP% **130.7**
Speed ratings (Par 101): **97,94,93,93,93 92,91,91,90,90 89,89,86,85,84 82,72**
PL: Rann Na Cille £2.00, Mr Rooney £1.50 CSF £28.49 CT £181.40 TOTE £5.30: £1.40, £2.80, £2.60; EX 30.70 Place 6 £56.24, Place 5 £45.93.
Owner J D Riches **Bred** Primrose Cottage **Trained** Cockerham, Lancs

FOCUS
A moderate sprint handicap in which a high draw was an advantage. Probably fair form for the grade, and solid enough.
Smiddy Hill Official explanation: jockey said mare missed the break
Mint Official explanation: jockey said filly missed the break
T/Jkpt: £5,612.40 to a £1 stake. Pool: £51,381.50. 6.50 winning tickets. T/Plt: £39.40 to a £1 stake. Pool: £63,305.00. 1,170.15 winning tickets. T/Qpdt: £6.70 to a £1 stake. Pool: £3,552.70. 388.40 winning tickets. JR

4854 YARMOUTH (L-H)
Tuesday, September 18

OFFICIAL GOING: Good
Wind: Fresh, across Weather: Cloudy

5508 EVEN MORE SPORTS LIVE - "BETLIVE" @ WILLIAMHILL.COM CLAIMING STKS 1m 3y
2:10 (2:10) (Class 5) 3-Y-O **£4,731** (£1,416; £708; £354; £176) **Stalls** High

Form RPR
3211 **1** **Ella Woodcock (IRE)**[17] 5046 3-8-13 77............................. TPQueally 5 85
(J A Osborne) *trckd ldrs: led over 1f out: rdn out* **9/4**[1]

513 **2** *1 1/2* **Getrah**[54] 3889 3-8-5 76.. LiamJones(3) 9 77
(W J Haggas) *chsd ldrs: led 2f out: sn edgd lft: styd on same pce fnl f* **9/4**[1]

0000 **3** *3 1/2* **Bed Fellow (IRE)**[31] 4608 3-9-0 72................................. JimmyFortune 6 75
(A P Jarvis) *hld up: hdwy over 2f out: n.m.r and hung lft over 1f out: no ex ins fnl f* **5/1**[2]

3004 **4** *2 1/2* **Postsprofit (IRE)**[8] 5280 3-8-9 61.. LDettori 7 64
(N A Callaghan) *dwlt: hld up: hdwy over 2f out: rdn over 1f out: wknd ins fnl f* **13/2**[3]

3530 **5** *6* **Grand Symphony**[88] 2834 3-8-4 65............................... RichardMullen 1 45
(W Jarvis) *led 6f: wknd fnl f* **14/1**

0100 **6** *1 1/4* **Lawyer To World**[56] 3825 3-8-9 47....................................... DMylonas 2 48
(Mrs C A Dunnett) *prom: rdn over 2f out: wknd over 1f out* **40/1**

0660 **7** *3/4* **Proper (IRE)**[11] 5203 3-8-13 75.. TPO'Shea 8 50
(M R Channon) *hld up in tch: rdn over 2f out: wknd over 1f out* **12/1**

1600 **8** *5* **All Of Me (IRE)**[55] 3857 3-8-11 72.................................. AdamKirby 11 36
(T G Mills) *hld up: rdn and wknd over 1f out* **16/1**

3306 **9** *3 1/2* **Flamestone**[40] 4337 3-7-12 43........................... NataliaGemelova(5) 10 20
(A E Price) *chsd ldrs: rdn and hung rt over 2f out: wknd wl over 1f out* **100/1**

R000 **10** *72* **Supercraft (IRE)**[91] 2747 3-8-3 25.....................................(b) ChrisCatlin 4 —
(M Quinn) *s.s: bhd fnl 5f* **200/1**

1m 40.98s (1.08) **Going Correction** +0.15s/f (Good) **10** Ran SP% **115.7**
Speed ratings (Par 101): **100,98,95,92,86 85,84,79,76,4**
CSF £6.77 TOTE £3.10: £1.10, £1.20, £2.40; EX 9.20 Trifecta £17.80 Pool: £319.59 - 12.68 winning units..Getrah was claimed by N. Wilson for £19,000.
Owner Cavendish Star Racing **Bred** Pippa Hackett **Trained** Upper Lambourn, Berks

FOCUS
A fair claimer run at a steady pace. The winner is progressing but the sixth does limit the form.
Grand Symphony Official explanation: jockey said filly was unsuited by the good ground

5509 TACKLE THE RUGBY ODDS "BETLIVE" @ WILLIAMHILL.COM NURSERY (FOR THE JACK LEADER CHALLENGE TROPHY) 7f 3y
2:40 (2:41) (Class 4) (0-85,80) 2-Y-O **£5,047** (£1,510; £755; £377; £188) **Stalls** High

Form RPR
601 **1** **Ridge Dance**[18] 5010 2-9-7 80... JimmyFortune 2 93+
(J H M Gosden) *racd centre: s.i.s: hld up: hdwy to ld that gp 2f out: edgd lft: overall ldr over 1f out: shkn up and r.o wl* **4/6**[1]

0065 **2** *5* **Space Pirate**[18] 5002 2-7-12 57.. JimmyQuinn 6 57
(M L W Bell) *racd centre: mde most in that gp tl 2f out: sn rdn: styd on same pce* **8/1**[3]

510 **3** *nk* **Farsighted**[36] 4453 2-9-0 73... DaleGibson 3 72
(J M P Eustace) *swtchd to r alone far side: led and sn wl clr: rdn and hdd over 1f out: hung rt and no ex ins fnl f* **22/1**

011 **4** *1* **Tuanku (IRE)**[22] 4892 2-8-12 71.. TPO'Shea 4 68
(M R Channon) *racd centre: chsd ldrs: rdn and ev ch that gp over 2f out: no ex fnl f* **9/2**[2]

5330 **5** *1/2* **Ezthegezza**[24] 4832 2-8-9 68... JamesDoyle 1 63
(J S Moore) *racd centre: chsd ldrs: rdn over 2f out: no ex fnl f* **14/1**

4221 **6** *29* **Rockfield Lodge (IRE)**[19] 4962 2-9-7 80............................ TPQueally 5 —
(J A Osborne) *stdd s: racd centre: hld up: rdn: hung lft and wknd over 2f out: eased fnl f* **11/1**

1m 27.96s (1.36) **Going Correction** +0.15s/f (Good) **6** Ran SP% **108.6**
Speed ratings (Par 97): **98,92,91,90,90 57**
CSF £6.16 TOTE £1.60: £1.20, £2.90; EX 4.70.
Owner George Strawbridge **Bred** George Strawbridge **Trained** Newmarket, Suffolk

FOCUS
A fair maiden dominated by a horse who will probably handle himself in Stakes company.

NOTEBOOK
Ridge Dance, whose victory in a maiden last time has been boosted a couple of times recently, was not the quickest away but travelled smoothly down the centre of the course and eventually won going away. It will be interesting to see what the trainer does with him next, considering his entries, but he looks capable of holding his own in Stakes company. (op 8-11 tchd 4-5 in places)
Space Pirate was beaten a respectable distance by the improving winner and ought to be found an opportunity unless the Handicapper takes a really dim view of his position.
Farsighted was taken to the inside rail, away from her rivals, and set what looked a fair gallop. However, as the race unfolded she was quickly reeled in and she failed to gain a signifcant advantage for that early move. (op 16-1)
Tuanku(IRE), up 4lb in the weights and dropping down in trip, never really got involved and is probably better than he showed. A larger field may suit him better. (op 6-1)
Ezthegezza was pushed along from an early stage and never really got on terms. A horse with a bit of size, he will be better suited by further and may make a reasonable handicapper next season. (op 10-1)

Rockfield Lodge(IRE) never looked to be going that well and gave the impression he was hanging. The jockey eased right off in the final furlong and his beaten distance was exaggerated. Official explanation: jockey said colt lost its action 1 1/2f out (op 9-1)

5510 THOMAS PRIOR MEMORIAL MAIDEN STKS — 6f 3y
3:10 (3:12) (Class 5) 3-Y-O+ **£3,562** (£1,059; £529; £264) **Stalls** High

Form RPR

4002 **1** **Knead The Dough**[8] 5276 6-9-0 44 .... NataliaGemelova(5) 4 63
(A E Price) *led: hdd over 4f out: led again over 2f out: rdn and hung rt fr over 1f out: styd on* **33/1**

4-20 **2** 3 ½ **Prince Of Delphi**[113] 2088 4-9-5 72 .... LDettori 7 53
(R M Beckett) *trckd ldrs: rdn over 1f out: no ex ins fnl f* **10/11**[1]

32 **3** 1 **O Fourlunda**[8] 5270 3-8-12 0 .... AdamKirby 6 45
(C E Brittain) *hld up: rdn and hung lft over 2f out: styd on ins fnl f: nt trble ldrs* **11/2**[3]

0350 **4** 1 **Appleby**[80] 3087 3-8-12 70 .... JimmyFortune 1 42
(J H M Gosden) *chsd ldrs: rdn and hung lft over 1f out: wknd ins fnl f* **8/1**

0-54 **5** 1 ¾ **Land's End (IRE)**[80] 3102 3-9-3 65 .... TPQueally 5 41
(J Noseda) *w wnr tl led over 4f out: hung rt and hdd over 2f out: hrd rdn and wknd fnl f* **4/1**[2]

0406 **6** 3 **Nothingtodeclaire**[57] 3800 3-8-10 60 .... EddieSemaan(7) 8 32
(G A Huffer) *prom over 3f* **100/1**

0000 **7** nk **Leg Sweep**[34] 4505 3-9-3 60 .... TQuinn 3 31
(D R C Elsworth) *hld up in tch: rdn and wknd over 2f out* **22/1**

60 **8** 1 ¾ **Iguacu**[22] 4908 3-9-0 0 .... LiamJones(3) 9 26
(J L Spearing) *sn pushed along in rr: hung lft and wknd over 2f out* **12/1**

1m 14.78s (1.08) **Going Correction** +0.15s/f (Good)
WFA 3 from 4yo+ 2lb **8** Ran SP% **114.9**
Speed ratings (Par 103): **98,93,92,90,88 84,83,81**
CSF £63.95 TOTE £32.20: £4.40, £1.10, £1.80; EX 87.80 Trifecta £404.80 Pool: £906.70 - 1.59 winning units..
Owner N Field **Bred** C L B Racing Ltd **Trained** Leominster, H'fords

FOCUS
A very moderate maiden landed by a 6yo who was rated 44 and having his 35th race. Improved form from him, but the favourite was very disappointing.
Leg Sweep Official explanation: jockey said gelding had stumbled on the good ground

5511 EVERY MINUTE EVERY MATCH "BETLIVE" @ WILLIAMHILL.COM (S) STKS — 7f 3y
3:40 (3:41) (Class 6) 3-Y-O **£1,943** (£578; £288; £144) **Stalls** High

Form RPR

3240 **1** **Candyland (IRE)**[21] 4918 3-8-7 58 .... ChrisCatlin 8 55
(M Quinn) *chsd ldr: led over 2f out: rdn and hung lft fr over 1f out: styd on* **13/2**

0223 **2** 1 ¼ **Calloff The Search**[37] 4416 3-8-12 53 ....(v) SaleemGolam 5 57
(W G M Turner) *hld up: hdwy over 2f out: sn rdn: kpt on* **7/2**[2]

0-50 **3** 2 ½ **Persian Fox (IRE)**[41] 4270 3-8-12 61 .... JimmyFortune 1 50
(G A Huffer) *prom: rdn over 1f out: no ex fnl f* **7/4**[1]

0520 **4** 3 **Give Evidence**[7] 5310 3-8-12 48 .... RichardMullen 7 42
(A P Jarvis) *led: hdd 5f out: outpcd over 2f out: styd on ins fnl f* **8/1**

6-45 **5** hd **Ardennes (IRE)**[50] 4021 3-8-7 52 ....(p) AshleyHamblett(5) 4 42
(M Botti) *s.i.s: hld up: plld hrd: hdwy to ld 5f out: hdd over 2f out: wknd over 1f out* **9/2**[3]

0000 **6** 14 **Pixie Princess (IRE)**[27] 4718 3-8-0 30 .... SophieDoyle(7) 2 —
(Miss V Haigh) *chsd ldrs over 4f* **100/1**

6560 **7** ½ **Storm Mission (USA)**[43] 4220 3-8-12 45 ....(p) TPQueally 3 2
(J Mackie) *chsd ldrs over 4f* **11/1**

3000 **8** ¾ **Valeesha**[8] 5269 3-8-4 44 .... LiamJones(3) 9 —
(W G M Turner) *hld up: plld hrd early: rdn over 4f out: wknd 1/2-way* **33/1**

1m 28.64s (2.04) **Going Correction** +0.15s/f (Good) **8** Ran SP% **113.5**
Speed ratings (Par 99): **94,92,89,86,86 70,69,68**
CSF £29.03 TOTE £5.90: £1.60, £2.00, £1.10; EX 19.80 Trifecta £36.90 Pool: £629.33 - 12.08 winning units..The winner was sold to Mrs C A Dunnett for 9,200gns.
Owner Steven Astaire **Bred** Darley **Trained** Newmarket, Suffolk

FOCUS
A bad race that is very unlikely to prove informative at any level. The second is probably the best guide to the form.

5512 ATTHERACES.COM FREE RACE REPLAYS CONDITIONS STKS — 6f 3y
4:10 (4:11) (Class 3) 3-Y-O+ **£7,790** (£2,332; £1,166; £583; £291) **Stalls** High

Form RPR

0130 **1** **Greek Renaissance (IRE)**[194] 644 4-8-9 107 .... LDettori 3 106+
(Saeed Bin Suroor) *hld up: hdwy over 2f out: rdn to ld ins fnl f: r.o* **6/5**[2]

4343 **2** ¾ **Masta Plasta (IRE)**[35] 4485 4-8-9 98 .... TQuinn 1 104
(D Nicholls) *w ldr tl led 1/2-way: rdn and hdd ins fnl f: unable qck* **17/2**[3]

3430 **3** ½ **Something (IRE)**[45] 4150 5-8-9 105 .... AdamKirby 4 103
(T G Mills) *trckd ldrs: rdn fnl f: nt qckn* **11/10**[1]

6000 **4** 4 **Resplendent Alpha**[3] 5416 3-8-7 87 .... JimmyQuinn 2 91
(P Howling) *prom: rdn and hung rt over 1f out: sn wknd* **66/1**

1500 **5** 1 ¾ **H Harrison (IRE)**[2] 5449 7-8-6 86 .... AndrewElliott(3) 5 85
(I W McInnes) *led to 1/2-way: wknd over 1f out* **33/1**

1m 12.84s (-0.86) **Going Correction** +0.15s/f (Good)
WFA 3 from 4yo+ 2lb **5** Ran SP% **108.0**
Speed ratings (Par 107): **111,110,109,104,101**
CSF £10.76 TOTE £2.40: £1.30, £3.40; EX 7.10.
Owner Godolphin **Bred** Ballymacoll Stud Farm Ltd **Trained** Newmarket, Suffolk

FOCUS
A decent sprint run at a good pace. The winner and third were not at their best but the second and fourth improved by a length on their recent form.

NOTEBOOK
Greek Renaissance(IRE), having his first run since Dubai in March, took a while to get on top but eventually won with a bit to spare. He always looked like making a good sprinter when trained by Marcus Tregoning in the early stages of last season, and can make his mark in a higher grade. He should have little problem staying another furlong but a race like the Diadem Stakes at Ascot is probably a realistic target next. (tchd Evens and 5-4)
Masta Plasta(IRE) showed good pace throughout and was clear second best in the race. He has been coasting along nicely throughout the season, picking up place money in conditions races, but this could have been a handy sharpener for the Ayr Gold Cup this weekend and, with a decent draw, he could be a very difficult horse to beat off a realistic weight. (op 9-1 tchd 15-2)
Something(IRE) would not be the easiest horse to place considering his handicap mark and was the first beaten of the big three in the race. He will find things tough for a while untill coming down the weights but he has the size to make improvement again next season and could develop into a stronger horse. (tchd 5-4)
Resplendent Alpha had no business getting involved in the finish but did at least get the better of H Harrison for fourth-place money.
H Harrison(IRE) is high in the weights now and could do with coming down the handicap. Running in these sorts of races will do him no harm in the short term unless he gets close to a much higher-rated rival. (op 25-1)

5513 MAKING SPORT MORE EXCITING "BETLIVE" @ WILLIAMHILL.COM SPRINT H'CAP — 5f 43y
4:40 (4:41) (Class 4) (0-85,85) 3-Y-O+
£6,232 (£1,866; £933; £467; £233; £117) **Stalls** High

Form RPR

0313 **1** **Canadian Danehill (IRE)**[4] 5379 5-9-3 83 ....(p) LDettori 4 90
(R M H Cowell) *trckd ldrs: rdn to ld wl ins fnl f* **1/1**[1]

4005 **2** ½ **Angus Newz**[11] 5195 4-9-3 83 ....(v) ChrisCatlin 3 88
(M Quinn) *led: rdn and edgd lft over 2f out: hdd wl ins fnl f* **9/1**

066 **3** nk **Tony The Tap**[2] 5447 6-9-4 84 .... RichardMullen 2 88
(W R Muir) *prom: rdn 1/2-way: r.o* **11/2**[3]

3000 **4** 1 **Dig Deep (IRE)**[10] 5212 5-9-5 85 .... JimmyFortune 7 86
(W J Haggas) *s.i.s: hld up: nt clr run over 1f out: r.o wl ins fnl f: nt rch ldrs* **9/2**[2]

0005 **5** 1 ¾ **Corridor Creeper (FR)**[10] 5212 10-8-12 85 ....(p) BarrySavage(7) 1 79
(J M Bradley) *chsd ldrs: rdn over 1f out: wknd wl ins fnl f* **15/2**

3000 **6** 2 **Laith (IRE)**[8] 5276 4-7-12 71 oh26 .... SophieDoyle(7) 5 58?
(Miss V Haigh) *prom: rdn whn hmpd over 1f out: hung lft and wknd fnl f* **150/1**

05-P **7** 1 **Mr Lambros**[222] 396 6-9-0 80 ....(t) JimmyQuinn 6 63
(Miss Gay Kelleway) *s.i.s: sn prom: rdn and hmpd over 1f out: wknd ins fnl f* **14/1**

62.37 secs (-0.43) **Going Correction** +0.15s/f (Good) **7** Ran SP% **112.7**
Speed ratings (Par 105): **109,108,107,106,103 100,98**
CSF £10.85 TOTE £1.70: £1.30, £2.70; EX 8.60.
Owner T W Morley **Bred** Skymarc Farm Inc And Dr A J O'Reilly **Trained** Six Mile Bottom, Cambs

FOCUS
A good handicap sprint run at a fair gallop. The runner-up looks poised to strike soon and the fourth looked a bit unlucky.
Mr Lambros Official explanation: jockey said gelding became unbalanced about 1 1/2f out

5514 VAUXHALL HOLIDAY PARK H'CAP — 1m 3f 101y
5:10 (5:12) (Class 5) (0-70,70) 3-Y-O+ **£4,210** (£1,252; £625; £312) **Stalls** Low

Form RPR

6021 **1** **Magic Show**[14] 5120 3-9-0 66 .... LDettori 7 81+
(Jane Chapple-Hyam) *hld up: hdwy over 3f out: led over 1f out: styd on wl* **7/4**[1]

6204 **2** 3 **Tafiya**[26] 4738 4-9-4 63 .... ChrisCatlin 11 71
(J W Hills) *chsd ldrs: led over 3f out: rdn and hdd over 1f out: styd on same pce* **22/1**

4222 **3** 4 **Billy One Punch**[8] 5280 5-9-6 65 .... JimmyQuinn 1 66
(G G Margarson) *chsd ldrs: rdn over 2f out: wknd fnl f* **4/1**[2]

1005 **4** 1 **Royal Premier (IRE)**[18] 5018 4-9-2 64 ....(v) JerryO'Dwyer(3) 15 64
(H J Collingridge) *hld up: rdn and hung lft over 3f out: styd on ins fnl f: n.d* **25/1**

1322 **5** 1 ¼ **Bienheureux**[27] 4708 6-9-1 65 ....(t) NicolPolli(5) 13 62
(Miss Gay Kelleway) *hld up: rdn over 2f out: r.o ins fnl f: nvr nrr* **9/1**[3]

6400 **6** hd **Cortesia (IRE)**[32] 4576 4-9-6 65 .... RichardMullen 12 62
(P W Chapple-Hyam) *chsd ldr tl led over 4f out: hdd over 3f out: rdn and wknd over 1f out* **25/1**

316 **7** ½ **Darghan (IRE)**[11] 5211 7-9-5 64 .... TPO'Shea 8 60
(W J Musson) *hld up: nvr nr to chal* **10/1**

-350 **8** 3 ½ **Barry Island**[201] 594 8-9-3 62 .... TQuinn 9 52
(D R C Elsworth) *hld up: effrt over 2f out: n.d* **16/1**

0402 **9** 1 **Love Always**[11] 5211 5-9-4 70 .... JamieHamblett(7) 10 59
(S Dow) *chsd ldrs: rdn over 2f out: sn hung lft and wknd* **12/1**

1304 **10** nk **General Flumpa**[19] 4959 6-8-5 57 .... LauraReynolds(7) 2 45
(Miss Tor Sturgis) *s.i.s: hld up: a in rr* **16/1**

014 **11** 7 **Coppergirl (IRE)**[17] 5046 3-9-2 68 ....(b1) JimmyFortune 3 44
(G A Huffer) *hld up in tch: rdn over 2f out: sn wknd* **14/1**

0000 **12** 3 **Faith And Reason (USA)**[31] 4610 4-8-13 58 .... TPQueally 5 29
(B J Curley) *led: hdd over 4f out: wknd over 2f out* **16/1**

0515 **13** 1 **Samdaniya**[16] 5067 3-9-1 67 .... AdamKirby 4 36
(C E Brittain) *chsd ldrs: rdn over 4f out: wknd over 2f out* **14/1**

2m 28.75s (1.25) **Going Correction** +0.15s/f (Good)
WFA 3 from 4yo+ 7lb **13** Ran SP% **126.2**
Speed ratings (Par 103): **101,98,95,95,94 94,93,91,90,90 85,83,82**
CSF £53.65 CT £148.20 TOTE £3.00: £1.40, £4.60, £1.60; EX 50.90 Trifecta £261.10 Pool: £643.73 - 1.75 winning units. Place 6 £6.57, Place 5 £5.48.
Owner Franconson Partners **Bred** The Earl Of Halifax **Trained** Newmarket, Suffolk

FOCUS
A very modeste race full of largely exposed and badly-handicapped horses. The winner did not fit that profile, however, and looks on to keep on the right side of. The form is rated through the fourth and fifth.
Barry Island Official explanation: jockey said gelding ran too free early
General Flumpa Official explanation: jockey said gelding missed the break and was denied a clear run
T/Plt: £4.80 to a £1 stake. Pool: £59,463.35. 8,919.40 winning tickets. T/Qpdt: £3.00 to a £1 stake. Pool: £3,035.00. 738.00 winning tickets. CR

5515 - (Foreign Racing) - See Raceform Interactive

5490 LISTOWEL (L-H)
Tuesday, September 18
OFFICIAL GOING: Good to firm (firm in places on jumps courses)

5516a GOFFS AUTUMN BONUS — 6f 60y
2:55 (2:59) 2-Y-O **£21,959** (£6,418; £3,040; £1,013)

RPR

1 **Lilleshall (IRE)**[41] 4306 2-8-12 58 ....(t) CO'Donoghue 8 79
(K J Condon, Ire) *sn led: rdn clr ent st: kpt on wl ins fnl f* **20/1**

2 1 ¾ **The Quiet Enforcer (IRE)**[29] 4680 2-9-3 93 .... WJSupple 10 82+
(Andrew Oliver, Ire) *reluctant to load: chsd ldrs: 3rd and drvn along after 1/2-way: rdn and no imp st: kpt on u.p ins fnl f* **9/4**[2]

3 1 **Princess India (IRE)**[14] 5117 2-8-12 .... KJManning 11 71
(P Winkworth) *prom: 2nd bef 1/2-way: rdn and outpcd early st: 3rd and kpt on same pce fnl f* **7/4**[1]

4 1 **Valentine Hill (IRE)**[10] 5239 2-8-12 .... WMLordan 9 68
(Adrian Maguire, Ire) *chsd ldrs in 7th: prog into 4th ent st: kpt on same pce* **14/1**

5 2 **Her Name Is Rio (IRE)**[60] 3718 2-8-12 .... PJSmullen 4 62
(J S Moore) *prom: 4th 1/2-way: 5th and no imp st* **8/1**

6 3 **Miranda's Girl (IRE)**[21] 4926 2-8-12 68..................(p) RPCleary 1 54
(Thomas Cleary, Ire) *chsd ldrs: 6th and rdn st: no imp* **8/1**

7 4 **Elusive Beau (IRE)**[3] 5434 2-9-3 .... MCHussey 2 47
(James Bernard McCabe, Ire) *s.i.s and hld up: kpt on same pce fr 1/2-way* **50/1**

8 5 **Lady Nova (IRE)**[46] 4121 2-8-12 .... DPMcDonogh 7 28
(J S Moore) *bhd: trailing thrght* **12/1**

9 nk **Mis Fancy That (IRE)** 2-8-12 ....(t) KFallon 5 27
(W P Mullins, Ire) *a bhd: trailing thrght* **7/1**[3]

10 hd **First In Command (IRE)**[44] 4206 2-9-3 .... JAHeffernan 3 31
(Daniel Mark Loughnane, Ire) *chsd ldrs: 5th early: wknd st* **33/1**

11 1 3/4 **Mr Mylerstown (IRE)**[27] 4727 2-9-3 .... FMBerry 6 26
(Joseph Crowley, Ire) *a bhd: trailing thrght* **25/1**

1m 24.4s (84.40) **11** Ran SP% **129.7**
CSF £69.68 TOTE £43.80: £7.90, £1.50, £1.40; DF 144.30.
Owner Thomas P O'Leary **Bred** Patrick Cummins **Trained** Fairstown Co Kildare

NOTEBOOK
Princess India(IRE), the winner of a Polytrack nursery last time off a mark of 65, was dropping in trip but went off favourite. She ran pretty well but got outpaced turning in and needed the extra furlong. (op 4/1)
Her Name Is Rio(IRE), whose best previous effort came on easy ground, was tackling fast going for the first time and performed creditably. (op 7/1)
Lady Nova(IRE) finished much further behind her stable companion than she had at Goodwood and a return to easier ground is required.

5294 BEVERLEY (R-H)

Wednesday, September 19

OFFICIAL GOING: Good to firm (9.7)
12mm of water had been put on the track since last week's meeting, resulting in ground the 'quick side of good but very loose on top'.
Wind: breezy half-against Weather: Fine, overcast and cool. Rain race 5 onwards.

5520 BEVERLEY ANNUAL BADGEHOLDERS (S) NURSERY 5f
2:00 (2:00) (Class 6) (0-65,60) 2-Y-O **£3,071** (£906; £453) **Stalls** High

Form RPR

2205 1 **Prigsnov Dancer (IRE)**[26] 4770 2-9-7 **60**....................(p) LeeEnstone 10 65
(P C Haslam) *mde virtually all: 3l clr over 1f out: hld on towards fin* **7/2**[1]

2405 2 nk **Best Suited**[23] 4897 2-9-3 **56**...................................... GrahamGibbons 8 60
(J J Quinn) *chsd ldrs: wnt 2nd over 1f out: styd on ins fnl f: jst hld* **7/2**[1]

0500 3 6 **Fraamington**[9] 5274 2-8-6 **45**...................................... PaulHanagan 13 27
(M R Channon) *chsd ldrs: one pce fnl 2f* **10/1**[3]

U043 4 3 1/2 **Mill Creek**[23] 4897 2-8-6 **45**..............................(b[1]) RoystonFfrench 2 15+
(B Smart) *hmpd s and bdly hmpd sn after: swtchd rt after s: detached in rr tl styd on fnl 2f: snatched modest 4th nr fin* **12/1**

005 5 1/2 **Son Of Spartacus (IRE)**[13] 5154 2-9-4 **57**..................(b) TomEaves 11 25
(Mrs L Stubbs) *slowly away: hdwy 3f out: nvr nr ldrs* **10/1**[3]

0030 6 1 **Star In The East**[14] 5133 2-8-8 **47**.................................(b) LPKeniry 7 11
(Peter Grayson) *chsd ldrs: wknd 2f out* **12/1**

5442 7 1 3/4 **No Point (IRE)**[19] 5017 2-9-0 **53**.......................... FrankieMcDonald 12 11
(P A Blockley) *s.i.s: hung rt and nvr on terms* **5/1**[2]

050 8 1 3/4 **Just Sam (IRE)**[13] 5154 2-9-2 **55**.........................(v[1]) StephenDonohoe 3 7+
(D Carroll) *swvd lft and bdly hmpd s: nvr on terms: hung bdly rt 1f out* **18/1**

0060 9 3 **Carlton Mac**[26] 4770 2-8-6 **45**.. PaulFessey 1 —
(N Bycroft) *swvd rt and bdly hmpd s: a bhd* **80/1**

0600 10 1/2 **Falcon Speed**[7] 5331 2-8-5 **47**...............................(p) DuranFentiman[(3)] 6 —
(P T Midgley) *w wnr: wknd 2f out* **18/1**

0050 11 42 **Baby Jack**[8] 5302 2-9-4 **57**.......................................(b[1]) AdrianTNicholls 5 —
(D Nicholls) *chsd ldrs: wkng whn blinkers c loose and swvd lft 2f out: virtually p.u: t.o* **10/1**[3]

5050 U **Little Finch (IRE)**[33] 4559 2-8-6 **45**............................(b) PaulMulrennan 4 —
(R C Guest) *swvd violently lft and uns rdr sn after s* **28/1**

65.76 secs (1.76) **Going Correction** +0.125s/f (Good) **12** Ran SP% **119.0**
Speed ratings (Par 93): **90,89,79,74,73 71,69,66,61,60** —,—
CSF £14.79 CT £113.44 TOTE £3.80: £1.70, £1.90, £4.30; EX 20.20.There was no bid for the winner.
Owner Middleham Park Racing Xxiv **Bred** Tom Radley **Trained** Middleham Moor, N Yorks

FOCUS
A poor selling nursery with a fair amount of mayhem leaving the stalls. The front two, who finished well clear, were both helped by a high draw. The form looks weak with the messy start not helping.

NOTEBOOK
Prigsnov Dancer(IRE), the biggest in the line-up, looked home and dried when holding a useful lead coming to the final furlong but in the end he was praying for the line. (op 5-1)
Best Suited, back in trip, went in pursuit of the winner and was fast closing him down at the line. She is well worth another try over six. (op 4-1)
Fraamington, who unseated his rider on the way down, started on terms this time but was left for dead by the winner. (op 14-1)
Mill Creek, tried in blinkers this time, was brought almost to a standstill leaving the stalls. Switched to the favoured far-side rail, she made up a deal of ground under a considerate ride to take fourth place. She must have troubled the first two with better luck. Official explanation: jockey said filly was hampered at start (op 11-1)
Son Of Spartacus(IRE), with the blinkers retained and on his toes beforehand, missed the kick at the start. He does not have the speed to be effective over 5f even in company as poor as he encountered here. (op 17-2 tchd 8-1)
No Point(IRE) was on his toes beforehand. Official explanation: jockey said filly hung right-handed throughout (op 9-2)
Just Sam(IRE) Official explanation: jockey said filly was hampered at start
Carlton Mac Official explanation: jockey said gelding was hampered at start
Baby Jack, dropping back to the minimum trip and on his toes beforehand, could not see where he was going when his blinkers worked loose. Official explanation: jockey said blinkers came loose (op 9-1)

5521 BRECKS CHEVROLET MAIDEN STKS 5f
2:35 (2:38) (Class 5) 2-Y-O **£3,238** (£963; £481; £240) **Stalls** High

Form RPR

3453 1 **Eastern Romance**[11] 5216 2-8-12 76.......................... PaulMulrennan 9 81+
(K A Ryan) *w ldrs: shkn up to ld over 1f out: drvn clr* **10/11**[1]

0 2 3 1/2 **Terry's Tip (IRE)**[107] 2297 2-9-3 0...................................... TomEaves 5 74
(Mrs L Stubbs) *chsd ldrs: clr 2nd over 1f out: no ch w wnr* **18/1**

2223 3 3 1/2 **Foreign Rhythm (IRE)**[37] 4447 2-8-12 75............................ KDarley 6 56
(N Tinkler) *chsd ldrs: one pce fnl 2f* **10/3**[2]

4 hd **Lu's Woman** 2-8-12 0.. DaleGibson 13 55
(M W Easterby) *s.s: detached in rr: hdwy over 1f out: fin strly* **40/1**

0 5 hd **Copperbottomed (IRE)**[16] 5097 2-9-3 0...................... RoystonFfrench 4 60
(R Hollinshead) *swtchd rt s: in rr: hdwy 3f out: nvr nr ldrs* **28/1**

65 6 1 1/4 **Afton View (IRE)**[4] 5399 2-9-3 0... LPKeniry 8 55
(D J Murphy) *chsd ldrs: one pce fnl 2f* **14/1**

6 7 nk **Smarterthanuthink (USA)**[26] 4781 2-9-3 0................. PaulHanagan 12 54
(R A Fahey) *in tch: wnt lft jst ins fnl f* **11/2**[3]

6 8 shd **Admiralcollingwood**[52] 3995 2-9-3 0........................ GrahamGibbons 7 54
(J J Quinn) *in rr: kpt on fnl 2f: nvr a factor* **16/1**

000 9 1 1/4 **Lucky Stream**[93] 2710 2-8-5 40............................ PatrickDonaghy[(7)] 17 44
(M Brittain) *prom: lost pl over 3f out: no threat after* **100/1**

0 10 1 **Flex**[6] 5363 2-8-12 0... JamesO'Reilly[(5)] 11 46+
(D J Murphy) *mid-div: hdwy over 2f: wkng whn hmpd jst ins fnl f* **50/1**

00 11 2 **Joint Agency (IRE)**[34] 4522 2-8-5 0........................... LanceBetts[(7)] 16 33
(N Wilson) *led tl hdd & wknd qckly over 1f out* **66/1**

12 4 **Senora's Best** 2-8-9 0.. AndrewMullen[(3)] 3 19
(M W Easterby) *s.i.s: a bhd* **100/1**

13 shd **Phoenix Bay** 2-8-12 0.. PatCosgrave 10 19
(J J Quinn) *dwlt: a bhd* **50/1**

65.21 secs (1.21) **Going Correction** +0.125s/f (Good) **13** Ran SP% **121.9**
Speed ratings (Par 95): **95,89,83,83,83 81,80,80,78,76 73,67,67**
CSF £22.75 TOTE £1.80: £1.20, £5.00, £1.20; EX 28.40.
Owner T G & Mrs M E Holdcroft **Bred** Bearstone Stud **Trained** Hambleton, N Yorks

FOCUS
No strength in depth in this ordinary maiden and the winner was not breaking her duck out of turn. It is hard to rate the form any higher than it has been with the time so moderate.

NOTEBOOK
Eastern Romance, rated 76, looked to have been found a good opportunity and made no mistake, breaking her duck at the sixth attempt. (op 6-4 tchd 5-6)
Terry's Tip(IRE), not the best of movers, had an outside draw. He went in pursuit of the winner but was never going to get close enough to bother her. (op 16-1)
Foreign Rhythm(IRE), who had just 1lb to find with the winner on official ratings, has had plenty of chances now. On her toes beforehand, she never looked like being seriously involved. (op 7-2 tchd 9-2 and 3-1)
Lu's Woman, a May foal, has size and scope. Slowly away and detached in the rear, she made up a deal of late ground but will not be the finished article until next year. (op 20-1)
Copperbottomed(IRE), drawn wide, was switched across the field after the start. He stuck on in his own time and should be capable of better given a little more time. (op 25-1)
Afton View(IRE), making a quick return, again showed ability and will be suited by a fair bit further in nursery company. (op 10-1)
Smarterthanuthink(USA), dropping back in trip, still looked very inexperienced. He can do a fair bit better in time. (op 6-1 tchd 5-1)
Admiralcollingwood, a 14,000gns gelding out of a winner in Belgium and France, is a big sort and needs more time.

5522 HAPPY 40TH BIRTHDAY MARK HIELDS H'CAP 5f
3:10 (3:11) (Class 5) (0-75,75) 3-Y-O+ **£3,562** (£1,059; £529; £264) **Stalls** High

Form RPR

5354 1 **Malapropism**[9] 5278 7-8-13 **68**.................................(v) DarryllHolland 12 86
(M R Channon) *smartly away: mde all: shkn up and clr over 1f out: drvn out: unchal* **7/2**[1]

201 2 4 **Royal Composer (IRE)**[25] 4801 4-8-5 **60** oh1.............(b) PaulHanagan 7 64
(T D Easterby) *dwlt: hdwy to chse ldrs over 3f out: styd on wl fnl f: tk 2nd nr line* **10/1**

3223 3 1/2 **Welcome Approach**[2] 5481 4-9-2 **71**................................ PhillipMakin 6 73
(J R Weymes) *chsd ldrs: wnt 2nd over 1f out: kpt on same pce* **4/1**[2]

0020 4 1 1/4 **Soto**[25] 4822 4-8-9 **64**... PaulMulrennan 10 67+
(M W Easterby) *chsd ldrs: nt clr run over 2f out tl over 1f out: swtchd ins and styd on ins fnl f* **9/1**

4565 5 shd **Winthorpe (IRE)**[43] 4251 7-8-7 **62**.......................... GrahamGibbons 8 59
(J J Quinn) *chsd ldrs: one pce fnl 2f* **8/1**[3]

1122 6 1 1/4 **Lake Chini (IRE)**[8] 5297 5-8-13 **68**..................................(b) DaleGibson 5 61
(M W Easterby) *mid-div: sn drvn along: kpt on fnl 2f: nvr a threat* **7/2**[1]

6036 7 hd **Mundo's Magic**[13] 5155 3-8-9 **65**.............................. RoystonFfrench 11 57
(G M Moore) *in rr: sme drvn along: kpt on fnl 2f: nvr a factor* **9/1**

00 8 2 1/2 **Danum Dancer**[23] 4898 3-9-0 **75**.................................(b) NeilBrown[(5)] 9 58
(N Bycroft) *chsd ldrs: wknd appr fnl f* **9/1**

0100 9 4 **Morristown Music (IRE)**[34] 4525 3-8-9 **65**...................... PaddyAspell 1 34
(J S Wainwright) *swtchd rt s: hld up in rr: bhd fnl 2f* **66/1**

0-4 10 3 **Rag Tag (IRE)**[20] 4974 4-8-12 **67**......................................(t) LPKeniry 4 25
(A M Balding) *t.k.h in rr: hdwy on outer 3f out: sn rdn and btn* **28/1**

0000 11 3 1/2 **Signor Panettiere**[173] 835 6-8-13 **68**.............................(t) TomEaves 3 13
(A D Brown) *hld up in rr: effrt on wd outside over 2f out: sn wknd* **66/1**

63.43 secs (-0.57) **Going Correction** +0.125s/f (Good)
WFA 3 from 4yo+ 1lb **11** Ran SP% **121.1**
Speed ratings (Par 103): **109,102,101,99,99 97,97,93,86,82 76**
CSF £40.52 CT £151.40 TOTE £4.50: £1.40, £2.60, £1.70; EX 46.80.
Owner Michael A Foy **Bred** Michael A Foy **Trained** West Ilsley, Berks

FOCUS
A modest handicap in which the winner had the plum draw and had this won from start to finish. The form is rated at face value through the runner-up.

5523 BRECKS SAAB H'CAP 1m 4f 16y
3:45 (3:45) (Class 4) (0-85,76) 3-Y-O **£6,477** (£1,927; £963; £481) **Stalls** High

Form RPR

4143 1 **Music Review**[14] 5131 3-9-0 **72**....................................... PaulHanagan 2 80
(R A Fahey) *trckd ldrs: effrt over 3f out: squeezed through on inner to ld over 1f out: rdn clr* **7/2**[3]

2411 2 2 1/2 **Silver Mitzva (IRE)**[14] 5131 3-8-9 **72**...................(b) AshleyHamblett[(5)] 5 76
(M Botti) *trckd ldr: effrt over 2f out: hrd rdn wnt 2nd: hung lft and rt and carried hd high over 1f out: no imp* **3/1**[2]

6105 3 3/4 **Its Moon (IRE)**[24] 4843 3-9-0 **72**................................ GrahamGibbons 4 75
(T D Walford) *led: qcknd over 3f out: edgd lft and hdd over 1f out: kpt on same pce* **11/2**

0011 4 1/2 **Paradise Walk**[24] 4846 3-8-13 **71**................................ PaulMulrennan 3 73
(E W Tuer) *t.k.h in rr: effrt over 2f out: swtchd lft over 1f out: kpt on same pce* **10/1**

152 5 nk **Ravenna**[11] 5229 3-9-4 **76**.. KDarley 1 78
(M P Tregoning) *hld up: hdwy to trck ldrs 7f: effrt over 3f out: keeping on same pce whn sltly hmpd over 1f out* **5/2**[1]

1063 6 6 **Love Brothers**[11] 5224 3-9-0 **72**................................ DarryllHolland 6 64
(M R Channon) *hld up in last: hdwy 5f out: drvn 3f out: fnd little and lost pl over 1f out* **8/1**

2m 41.88s (1.67) **Going Correction** +0.175s/f (Good) **6** Ran SP% **111.4**
Speed ratings (Par 103): **101,99,98,98,98 94**
CSF £14.12 TOTE £5.00: £2.10, £1.80; EX 19.30.

Owner R A Fahey **Bred** Darley **Trained** Musley Bank, N Yorks

FOCUS

A tight little handicap but they went no gallop and the winner was the only one to quicken from off the pace. The form is hard to rate more positively but looks sound enough with the third, fourth and fifth close to their marks.

5524 E B F SILVER JUBILEE MAIDEN FILLIES' STKS 7f 100y

4:20 (4:21) (Class 5) 2-Y-O **£4,210** (£1,252; £625; £312) **Stalls** High

Form RPR

403 **1** **Patio**[17] 5063 2-9-0 77 ... DaleGibson 1 77
(Mrs A J Perrett) *trckd ldr: led over 1f out: drvn out* **4/1**[3]

2 **2** *1 1/4* **Forsyte Saga**[8] 5306 2-9-0 0 ... RoystonFfrench 7 74
(M Johnston) *led: hdd over 1f out: styd on same pce* **5/4**[1]

34 **3** *3/4* **Dream Sea**[46] 4169 2-9-0 0 ... DarryllHolland 8 72
(M R Channon) *trckd ldrs: effrt over 2f out: kpt on same pce fnl f* **85/40**[2]

4 *nk* **Wusuul** 2-9-0 0 ... J-PGuillambert 2 72
(C E Brittain) *s.i.s: hdwy over 2f out: styd on fnl f* **20/1**

5 *7* **Volvoretas Rainbow** 2-9-0 0 ... KDarley 4 55
(P C Haslam) *s.i.s: in rr and drvn over 5f out: nvr on terms* **18/1**

6 *1/2* **Saratee** 2-9-0 0 ... AdrianTNicholls 3 54
(C E Brittain) *mid-div: drvn and sme hdwy 5f out: wknd over 1f out* **28/1**

7 *12* **Bollin Greta** 2-9-0 0 ... GrahamGibbons 9 26
(T D Easterby) *rrd and s.v.s: sme hdwy over 5f out: lost pl 3f out: sn bhd* **20/1**

4550 **8** *33* **Arabian Fern**[60] 3751 2-9-0 48 ... PaulMulrennan 5 —
(M E Sowersby) *chsd ldrs: lost pl over 3f out: sn bhd: t.o* **100/1**

1m 36.31s (2.00) **Going Correction** +0.175s/f (Good) **8** Ran SP% **115.7**

Speed ratings (Par 92): **95,93,92,92,84 83,70,32**

CSF £9.21 TOTE £4.40: £1.30, £1.10, £1.20; EX 9.90.

Owner K Abdulla **Bred** Juddmonte Farms Ltd **Trained** Pulborough, W Sussex

FOCUS

A modest-looking maiden rated around the principals. The first three home were in the same positions throughout the race but the form should prove sound enough.

NOTEBOOK

Patio, one of the most experienced in the field, chased her market rival throughout before getting the better of her inside the final furlong. She ought to stay a mile. (op 7-2)

Forsyte Saga tried to burn off her rivals from the front but merely set the race up for Patio. One suspects she will appreciate further. (op 11-8, tchd 6-4 in a place)

Dream Sea, who ran in a maiden last time that has worked out really well, did not run badly at all and looks more than capable of winning a similar race. (op 15-8 tchd 7-4)

Wusuul was green in the early stages but picked up well once straightened out and may have troubled the winner in another half a furlong. It was a promising debut. Official explanation: jockey said filly ran green (op 25-1)

Volvoretas Rainbow, out of an Arc runner-up, was slowly away and could not pick up when asked to quicken. She will be better for the experience. (op 22-1)

Saratee, noisy in the paddock, travelled nicely in the early stages but weakened quickly under pressure. (op 33-1)

Bollin Greta, a half-sister to three winners including the St Leger winner Bollin Eric, was green and noisy in the paddock. She had no chance after walking out of the stalls, but it is too soon to write her off completely. Official explanation: jockey said filly reared leaving stalls and was slowly away

5525 MAC AND LENI MEMORIAL H'CAP 1m 100y

4:55 (4:56) (Class 6) (0-55,55) 3-Y-0+ **£3,238** (£963; £481; £240) **Stalls** High

Form RPR

3351 **1** **Myfrenchconnection (IRE)**[24] 4842 3-8-13 **54** ... FrankieMcDonald 6 64
(P T Midgley) *sn trcking ldrs on outer: led over 1f out: kpt on wl* **9/1**

0500 **2** *1 1/2* **Ours (IRE)**[44] 4223 4-9-1 **52** ... RoystonFfrench 10 59+
(John A Harris) *in rr: gd hdwy 2f out: fin fast to snatch 2nd towards fin* **12/1**

0045 **3** *3/4* **Uhuru Peak**[13] 5159 6-9-0 **51** ...(bt) PaulMulrennan 13 56
(M W Easterby) *led tl over 1f out: kpt on same pce* **7/1**[2]

000 **4** *5* **Anything Once (USA)**[22] 4920 4-9-0 **51** ...(b) StephenDonohoe 5 45
(D Carroll) *in rr: hdwy over 1f out: styd on wl to take modest 4th post* **66/1**

1345 **5** *shd* **Top Dirham**[28] 4701 9-9-3 **54** ... DaleGibson 17 48
(M W Easterby) *in rr: hdwy and n.m.r 2f out: styd on fnl f* **6/1**[1]

5000 **6** *1 3/4* **Gifted Flame**[9] 5284 8-9-4 **55** ...(p) PhillipMakin 9 45
(T D Barron) *in rr: effrt over 2f out: kpt on fnl f* **11/1**

542 **7** *1/2* **Apache Point (IRE)**[33] 4580 10-8-13 **50** ... KimTinkler 1 38
(N Tinkler) *dwlt: in rr: kpt on fnl 2f: nvr nr ldrs* **16/1**

5440 **8** *hd* **Volaticus (IRE)**[46] 4156 6-9-1 **52** ... TonyHamilton 15 40
(A D Brown) *chsd ldrs: rdn and hung rt over 2f out: lost pl over 1f out* **6/1**[1]

0006 **9** *1/2* **Summer Gift**[8] 5299 4-8-11 **53** ... JamesO'Reilly[(5)] 12 40
(J O'Reilly) *chsd ldrs: wknd over 1f out* **33/1**

5333 **10** *2* **Beamsley Beacon**[13] 5179 6-8-12 **49** ... PaddyAspell 4 31
(S T Mason) *chsd ldrs: wknd 2f out* **25/1**

003 **11** *hd* **Gallows Hill (USA)**[20] 4971 3-8-8 **49** ...(b[1]) PaulHanagan 3 31+
(R A Fahey) *mid-div: sn pushed along: outpcd fnl 2f* **14/1**

0050 **12** *2* **Hello Nod**[47] 4137 3-8-10 **51** ... TomEaves 11 28
(Miss J A Camacho) *awkward to load: sn chsng ldrs: edgd lft over 3f out: sn btn* **12/1**

1030 **13** *1 1/4* **Drink To Me Only**[36] 4477 4-8-9 **46** ... DarryllHolland 8 20
(J R Weymes) *in rr-div: hdwy on outer over 4f out: lost pl over 2f out* **8/1**[3]

0000 **14** *2* **Stepaside (IRE)**[16] 5084 3-8-5 **49** ... AndrewMullen[(3)] 7 19
(A D Brown) *in rr: hdwy 4f out: lost pl over 2f out* **100/1**

0046 **15** *8* **Ammeyrr**[26] 4771 3-8-4 **50** ...(b[1]) KellyHarrison[(5)] 14 —
(A Crook) *prom: lost pl over 2f out: sn bhd* **40/1**

0460 **16** *20* **King's Account (USA)**[90] 2810 5-9-1 **52** ...(p) PatCosgrave 16 —
(S Gollings) *mid-div: sn drvn along: lost pl over 4f out: sn bhd: t.o* **7/1**[2]

000 **17** *10* **Straight Face (IRE)**[22] 4918 3-8-9 **50** ... AdrianTNicholls 2 —
(M Wigham) *restless in stalls: chsd ldrs: hung lft: wknd and eased over 2f out: sn bhd: t.o* **25/1**

1m 48.8s (1.40) **Going Correction** +0.175s/f (Good)

WFA 3 from 4yo+ 4lb **17** Ran SP% **126.5**

Speed ratings (Par 101): **100,98,97,92,92 90,90,90,89,87 87,85,84,82,74 54,44**

CSF £110.45 CT £846.32 TOTE £11.70: £3.00, £3.30, £2.20, £13.60; EX 184.60.

Owner J F Wright **Bred** Mrs Stephanie Winters **Trained** Westow, N Yorks

FOCUS

A moderate handicap in which the first three finished clear. The third to this year;s form sets the standard.

Top Dirham Official explanation: jockey said gelding was struck into

Hello Nod Official explanation: trainer's representative said gelding didn't stay the trip

Drink To Me Only Official explanation: jockey said gelding was unsuited by the good to firm (loose) ground

Straight Face(IRE) Official explanation: jockey said gelding hung left

5526 GOOD LUCK LOUISE AND PAUL MAIDEN AUCTION STKS 7f 100y

5:25 (5:27) (Class 6) 2-Y-O **£2,590** (£770; £385; £192) **Stalls** High

Form RPR

54 **1** **Thunderstruck**[14] 5140 2-9-1 0 ... PaulMulrennan 8 74
(K A Ryan) *mde all: edgd lft over 1f out: hld on wl towards fin* **10/3**[2]

446 **2** *1 1/2* **Celtic Strand (IRE)**[25] 4819 2-9-1 70 ... PaulHanagan 2 70
(T P Tate) *w wnr: chal over 2f out: sn rdn and edgd lft: pushed wd over 1f out: no ex wl ins fnl f* **7/1**[3]

0030 **3** *1* **Stand In Flames**[20] 4964 2-8-4 59 ... DavidKinsella 3 57
(Pat Eddery) *chsd ldrs: styd on same pce fnl f* **18/1**

2 **4** *1 3/4* **Synergistic (IRE)**[8] 5294 2-9-1 0 ... KDarley 6 64
(M Johnston) *chsd ldrs: sn drvn along: rdn over 3f out: kpt on same pce appr fnl f* **5/6**[1]

0 **5** *hd* **Locum**[92] 2746 2-8-9 0 ... TomEaves 9 58
(M H Tompkins) *hld up in tch: effrt and edgd rt over 2f out: kpt on same pce appr fnl f* **28/1**

50 **6** *7* **Warming Up (IRE)**[35] 4508 2-8-13 0 ... DarryllHolland 7 45
(C E Brittain) *dwlt: in rr and sn pushed along: sme hdwy 2f out: nvr a factor* **7/1**[3]

600 **7** *5* **Mujinda**[53] 3951 2-8-4 43 ... DaleGibson 10 24
(M Brittain) *prom: outpcd over 3f out: wknd over 2f out* **100/1**

0600 **8** *5* **Kingstyle (IRE)**[42] 4279 2-8-9 52 ... RoystonFfrench 1 18
(M Brittain) *in rr: bhd fnl 3f* **100/1**

060 **9** *1 1/4* **Viscount Monty**[47] 4136 2-8-9 46 ...(v[1]) PhillipMakin 11 15
(N Tinkler) *hld up in tch: effrt over 2f out: sn lost pl* **150/1**

10 *1/2* **Reel Classy** 2-8-0 0 ow3 ... DeanHeslop[(7)] 4 11
(M A Peill) *s.i.s: mid-div: lost pl over 3f out: sn bhd* **66/1**

1m 36.6s (2.29) **Going Correction** +0.175s/f (Good) **10** Ran SP% **115.5**

Speed ratings (Par 93): **93,91,90,88,87 79,74,68,67,66**

CSF £26.02 TOTE £4.30: £1.30, £2.00, £3.30; EX 23.50 Place 6 £32.46, Place 5 £18.70.

Owner Paul J Dixon **Bred** Mrs Yvette Dixon **Trained** Hambleton, N Yorks

FOCUS

The first four home raced in the first four throughout. The form is not up to much but is solid, with the first three all near their marks.

NOTEBOOK

Thunderstruck, a big strong colt, had shown more than enough in two previous runs to be a major player in this and, despite edging right over to the stands'-side rail under pressure, never gave his rivals any hope after making all of the running. He will need to up his game now but looks likely to stay a bit further. (op 9-4)

Celtic Strand(IRE) chased the winner throughout but just could not force his way past in the last two furlongs. His effort helps to set the level of the form. (op 9-1)

Stand In Flames, who ran dreadfully on Polytrack last time, kept on really well up the home straight on this return to turf over a slightly longer trip. (op 20-1 tchd 22-1)

Synergistic(IRE), a narrow sort who still looked in need of the outing and was coltish in the paddock, sat third for most of the race but got outpaced off the final bend. He only kept on steadily once his chance is gone. (op 10-11)

Locum, given a break since his first run over 5f, stayed on really well up the home straight to give his connections hope for the future. (op 33-1)

Warming Up(IRE), a big sort, was never racing on an even keel after missing the break and failed to get involved. (op 8-1)

T/Jkpt: Not won. T/Plt: £43.80 to a £1 stake. Pool: £58,000.30. 965.30 winning tickets. T/Qpdt: £23.60 to a £1 stake. Pool: £2,786.20. 87.10 winning tickets. WG

5420 KEMPTON (A.W) (R-H)

Wednesday, September 19

OFFICIAL GOING: Standard

Wind: Moderate, across Weather: Overcast

5527 EUROPEAN BREEDERS' FUND MEDIAN AUCTION MAIDEN FILLIES' STKS 1m (P)

6:20 (6:22) (Class 6) 2-Y-O **£2,047** (£604; £302) **Stalls** High

Form RPR

0 **1** **Love Valentine (IRE)**[7] 5328 2-9-0 0 ... GregFairley 4 66
(M Johnston) *trckd ldr: led wl over 2f out: sn pressed: drvn and kpt on fnl f: jst hld on* **12/1**

033 **2** *shd* **La Columbina**[23] 4875 2-9-0 73 ... RichardHughes 13 66+
(R Hannon) *rousted along early and in rr: rdn on inner over 2f out: swtchd lft over 1f out: r.o fnl f: jst failed* **4/6**[1]

5064 **3** *1/2* **Bermacha**[20] 4975 2-8-11 60 ... WilliamBuick[(3)] 8 65
(W R Muir) *chsd ldrs: rdn over 2f out: styd on u.p to cl on ldng pair over 1f out: kpt on but a jst hld* **6/1**[3]

4 *hd* **Spiritofthestorm (USA)** 2-9-0 0 ... ChrisCatlin 1 65
(R A Teal) *t.k.h: prom: pressed wnr over 2f out: nt qckn and hld fnl f: lost 2 pls nr fin* **50/1**

0 **5** *5* **Amie Magnificent (IRE)**[17] 5061 2-9-0 0 ... StephenCarson 7 53
(P Winkworth) *chsd ldrs: rdn over 2f out: readily outpcd fr wl over 1f out* **33/1**

0000 **6** *hd* **Treacle Noir (IRE)**[31] 4629 2-9-0 50 ... RichardKingscote 2 53
(Tom Dascombe) *led to wl over 2f out: wknd over 1f out* **40/1**

0 **7** *1 1/2* **Milanollo**[69] 3446 2-9-0 0 ... HayleyTurner 12 49
(M L W Bell) *nvr beyond midfield: rdn and no prog over 2f out: fdd* **12/1**

05 **8** *2* **L'Etincelle (IRE)**[17] 5063 2-9-0 0 ... TedDurcan 6 45+
(H R A Cecil) *nvr beyond midfield: rdn over 2f out: no prog: eased whn btn fnl f* **9/2**[2]

0 **9** *3* **Here And How**[17] 5061 2-9-0 0 ... SaleemGolam 5 38
(M H Tompkins) *stdd after 100yds: a towards rr and wd: rdn and no prog over 2f out: wknd* **66/1**

0 **10** *1 1/4* **Zarene**[26] 4774 2-9-0 0 ...(v[1]) DaneO'Neill 11 35
(P W D'Arcy) *rdn in rr early: nvr on terms: no ch fnl 2f* **80/1**

0 **11** *nk* **Lady Cobra**[34] 4537 2-9-0 0 ... MartinDwyer 9 34
(C E Brittain) *snatched up after 1f: a in rr after: struggling over 2f out* **50/1**

12 *hd* **Recast (IRE)** 2-9-0 0 ... RichardSmith 3 34
(R Hannon) *s.i.s: a wl in rr: struggling 3f out* **33/1**

5 **13** *24* **Our Joan**[117] 2009 2-9-0 0 ... MickyFenton 10 —
(P T Midgley) *chsd ldrs to 1/2-way: wknd rapidly: t.o* **66/1**

1m 41.07s (0.27) **Going Correction** -0.225s/f (Stan) **13** Ran SP% **124.3**

Speed ratings (Par 90): **89,88,88,88,83 83,81,79,76,75 74,74,50**

CSF £20.79 TOTE £13.30: £2.70, £1.10, £2.20; EX 33.50.

Owner Crone Stud Farms Ltd **Bred** Crone Stud Farms Ltd **Trained** Middleham Moor, N Yorks

FOCUS

A modest maiden for fillies limited by the third and sixth.

NOTEBOOK
Love Valentine(IRE) was well placed throughout and did just enough to hold on in the final stages. The runner-up did look unlucky and would have one in a couple more strides, but she was not doing too much once in front and could be better than the bare result. (op 10-1 tchd 14-1)
La Columbina got going far too late and would have won in another stride. Although disappointing for the second time in a row, she really should be winning soon and could be of some interest if taking her place in the Watership Down Stud Sales Race at Ascot on the 28th September . (op 4-5)
Bermacha, taking a step up in trip, is a consistent sort who is a decent marker to the level of the form. She always runs well but is finding something to beat her every time. (op 7-1)
Spiritofthestorm(USA), an American-bred filly, showed a fair degree of ability on her debut and shaped promisingly. She looks promising enough and should go close in a similar event.
Amie Magnificent(IRE) does not look devoid of ability and should make her mark in handicap company in due course.
L'Etincelle(IRE) did not improve for the step up in trip and move to the Polytrack. On the positive side, she should be given a very moderate handicap mark. (tchd 5-1)

5528 PETER BROMWICH 60TH BIRTHDAY H'CAP — 1m (P)
6:50 (7:00) (Class 6) (0-60,60) 3-Y-O — **£2,047** (£604; £302) **Stalls** High

Form — RPR
6305 **1** **Inquisitress**[4] 5420 3-8-13 **55**.......... EddieAhern 10 — 62
(J J Bridger) *dwlt: stdy prog on inner fr rr 1/2-way: effrt and got through to ld 1f out: rdn clr* **13/2**[3]
0406 **2** 1 1/2 **Grand Lucre**[14] 5136 3-9-4 **60**.......... StephenCarson 9 — 64
(G A Butler) *pressed ldr: narrow ld over 2f out: hdd 1f out: kpt on same pce* **11/1**
0053 **3** hd **Six Of Hearts**[32] 4591 3-9-4 **60**..........(p) MartinDwyer 4 — 64
(J A Osborne) *w ldng pair: pressed ldr over 2f out: upsides 1f out: kpt on one pce* **15/2**
3501 **4** nk **Magroom**[15] 5118 3-8-9 **56**.......... HaddenFrost(5) 2 — 59
(R J Hodges) *trapped out wd in midfield: drvn over 2f out and off the pce: styd on fr over 1f out: nrst fin* **3/1**[1]
0200 **5** 3 **Path To Glory**[42] 4277 3-8-10 **52**.......... AdrianMcCarthy 8 — 48
(Miss Z C Davison) *snatched up on outer after 1f: outpcd in midfield 3f out: kpt on fr over 1f out: nt rch ldrs* **20/1**
0404 **6** 5 **Dance Of Dreams**[14] 5136 3-8-13 **60**..........(p) LukeMorris(5) 7 — 44
(N P Littmoden) *towards rr: u.p whn nt clr run over 2f out and again sn after: plugged on* **11/1**
0440 **7** shd **Hope Your Safe**[32] 4596 3-8-11 **53**.......... DaneO'Neill 11 — 37
(J R Best) *s.i.s: sn trckd ldrs: rdn and hd high over 2f out: sn outpcd* **16/1**
200 **8** 1/2 **Neboisha**[20] 4977 3-8-10 **52**.......... IanMongan 12 — 35
(P Howling) *led to over 2f out: sn wknd* **50/1**
6066 **9** hd **Bold Saxon (IRE)**[11] 5237 3-9-4 **60**.......... RichardSmith 14 — 43
(M D I Usher) *trckd ldrs on inner tl wknd 2f out* **12/1**
6600 **10** hd **Hannahbecc**[22] 4918 3-9-4 **60**.......... SaleemGolam 5 — 42
(S C Williams) *trckd ldrs: rdn over 2f out: sn wknd* **6/1**[2]
-026 **11** 11 **Iron Dancer (IRE)**[145] 1281 3-8-8 **55**.......... KevinGhunowa(5) 3 — 12
(P A Blockley) *a towards rr: wknd 2f out: sn bhd* **50/1**
0000 **12** 18 **My Spring Rose**[27] 4742 3-8-10 **52**.......... TedDurcan 13 — —
(J R Jenkins) *s.i.s: a in rr: rdn 1/2-way: sn wknd and eased: t.o* **33/1**
2-35 **13** 3 1/2 **The Slider**[176] 794 3-8-11 **53**.......... ChrisCatlin 6 — —
(Mrs L C Jewell) *t.k.h: lost pl over 5f out: towards rr after: wknd 3f out: t.o* **20/1**

1m 40.02s (-0.78) **Going Correction** -0.225s/f (Stan) — **13** Ran SP% **111.0**
Speed ratings (Par 99): **94,92,92,92,89 84,83,83,83,83 72,54,50**
CSF £59.34 CT £418.31 TOTE £6.50: £1.60, £4.50, £2.30; EX 67.60.
Owner C Marshall T Wallace J J Bridger **Bred** A Saccomando **Trained** Liphook, Hants
■ Dragon Flower was withdrawn (13/2, burst out of stalls.) R4 applies, deduct 10p in the £.

FOCUS
An ordinary handicap, but pretty straightforward form rated around the third and fourth. As in the first race, the first four finished clear of the rest, who were well strung out.

5529 DIGIBET.COM NURSERY — 6f (P)
7:20 (7:27) (Class 6) (0-65,65) 2-Y-O — **£2,047** (£604; £302) **Stalls** High

Form — RPR
1320 **1** **We Have A Dream**[26] 4762 2-9-4 **62**.......... MartinDwyer 11 — 66
(W R Muir) *w ldr: led on inner wl over 2f out: drvn over 1f out: styd on wl* **7/2**[1]
0400 **2** 3/4 **Don't Tell Anna (IRE)**[16] 5089 2-8-12 **56**.......... RichardHughes 12 — 58
(R Hannon) *chsd ldrs: effrt over 2f out: drvn to take 2nd 1f out: styd on but a hld* **8/1**
0006 **3** nk **Whiskey Creek**[13] 5167 2-8-11 **55**.......... ChrisCatlin 3 — 56
(Miss Tor Sturgis) *fast away fr wd draw: mde most to wl over 2f out: chsd wnr to 1f out: styd on u.p* **14/1**
600 **4** 1 1/4 **Flying Indian**[16] 5096 2-9-3 **64**.......... WilliamBuick(3) 10 — 61
(A M Balding) *chsd ldrs: drvn over 2f out: kpt on same pce u.p* **15/2**
0060 **5** nk **Mandarinka**[16] 5089 2-8-9 **60**..........(b[1]) JackMitchell(7) 2 — 56
(P Winkworth) *s.v.s: stdy prog on inner fr 4f out: drvn to chse ldrs over 1f out: kpt on: no imp ins fnl f* **25/1**
0405 **6** 2 1/2 **Leading Edge (IRE)**[8] 5314 2-9-6 **64**.......... TPO'Shea 8 — 53
(M R Channon) *pressed ldrs: rdn and nt qckn over 2f out: steadily fdd* **7/1**[3]
2515 **7** 2 **Whispering Desert**[19] 5008 2-9-7 **65**.......... MickyFenton 5 — 48
(P T Midgley) *cl up: rdn and nt qckn over 2f out: wknd* **7/1**[3]
0130 **8** 1/2 **Thomas Malory (IRE)**[11] 5216 2-9-1 **59**.......... HayleyTurner 6 — 40
(Miss V Haigh) *a in rr: rdn and struggling bef 1/2-way* **4/1**[2]
060 **9** 1 **Bahamian Blue (IRE)**[12] 5186 2-9-6 **64**.......... EddieAhern 9 — 42+
(H J L Dunlop) *a towards rr: rdr looking down fr over 2f out: eased over 1f out* **12/1**
0150 **10** 1 1/2 **Smokeyourpipe (IRE)**[16] 5089 2-8-13 **60**..........(v) LiamJones(3) 7 — 34
(C Tinkler) *sn bhd: t.o in last over 3f out: plugged on over 1f out* **20/1**
000 **11** 8 **Mr Funshine**[65] 3589 2-9-1 **59**.......... FergusSweeney 1 — 9
(Mrs P N Dutfield) *chsd ldrs on outer tl wknd over 2f out* **33/1**
0650 **12** 7 **Eye Catching**[16] 5089 2-9-5 **63**.......... TedDurcan 4 — —
(J R Jenkins) *a in rr: wknd over 2f out: sn wl bhd* **16/1**

1m 13.36s (-0.34) **Going Correction** -0.225s/f (Stan) — **12** Ran SP% **121.9**
Speed ratings (Par 93): **93,92,91,89,89 86,83,82,81,79 68,59**
CSF £32.01 CT £365.68 TOTE £4.30: £1.70, £2.20, £3.60; EX 33.50.
Owner The Dreaming Squires **Bred** Whitsbury Manor Stud **Trained** Lambourn, Berks

FOCUS
A moderate nursery in which the first two home emerged from the top two boxes but the form is rated slightly negatively.

NOTEBOOK
We Have A Dream found this easier than the Newbury nursery he contested on his previous start and doubled his career tally in straightforward fashion, benefiting from a positive ride from his favourable draw. (op 4-1)
Don't Tell Anna(IRE) was caught very wide from a poor draw on the turf at Lingfield on her previous start, but she had been dropped 5lb for that effort and showed much more this time, taking well to Polytrack at the first attempt. Much better drawn, she was kept on well in the straight having tracked the pace and gave the impression she may have given the winner even more to think about had she been ridden more forcefully from the gates.
Whiskey Creek, racing off a mark 6lb lower than at Warwick on his previous start, emerges with plenty of credit on his Polytrack debut considering he had a wide draw to overcome.
Flying Indian did not run badly, but she is already exposed as modest and does not appeal as one to be following. (op 7-1 tchd 8-1)
Mandarinka, fitted with blinkers for the first time, must have lost a good five or so lengths with a very slow start, but he was noted doing some good work in the straight. He could well find a similar race if managing to get away on terms. (tchd 33-1)

5530 DIGIBET MEDIAN AUCTION MAIDEN STKS — 1m 4f (P)
7:50 (7:54) (Class 6) 3-4-Y-O — **£2,047** (£604; £302) **Stalls** Centre

Form — RPR
30-6 **1** **Yeoman Spirit (IRE)**[49] 4072 4-9-11 70.......... MartinDwyer 1 — 70
(A M Balding) *mde all: drvn over 2f out: styd on wl: gng away last 100yds* **2/1**[1]
2-03 **2** 2 1/2 **River Deuce**[8] 5311 3-9-3 70.......... TedDurcan 3 — 66
(M H Tompkins) *trckd ldng pair tl wnt 2nd over 3f out: rdn to chal over 2f out: nt qckn: stl cl enough 1f out: sn btn* **11/4**[2]
3 3 1/2 **Dart** 3-8-12 0.......... JamieSpencer 7 — 57
(J R Fanshawe) *trckd ldng trio tl wnt 3rd over 3f out: sn shkn up: no imp last 2f* **11/4**[2]
-002 **4** 8 **Dream Master (IRE)**[24] 4860 4-9-11 46.......... MickyFenton 2 — 48
(J Ryan) *chsd wnr to over 3f out: sn wknd u.p* **14/1**
646- **5** 3 **Poyle Kiera**[323] 6284 3-8-12 49.......... TQuinn 4 — 38
(M Blanshard) *a 5th: pushed along after 4f: lost tch over 3f out* **33/1**
0003 **6** 1 1/2 **New Light**[8] 5304 3-8-12 47.......... StephenCarson 6 — 35
(Eve Johnson Houghton) *a in last pair: lost tch over 3f out* **12/1**[3]
500- **7** 3 **Henry Holmes**[427] 3650 4-9-11 55.......... AlanDaly 5 — 36
(Mrs L Richards) *a in last pair: lost tch over 3f out* **50/1**

2m 34.08s (-2.82) **Going Correction** -0.225s/f (Stan)
WFA 3 from 4yo 8lb — **7** Ran SP% **105.9**
Speed ratings (Par 101): **100,98,96,90,88 87,85**
CSF £6.50 TOTE £3.00: £1.60, £1.70; EX 8.50.
Owner Yeoman Homes Limited **Bred** Mrs S Dalton **Trained** Kingsclere, Hants
■ Act Three was withdrawn (14/1, refused to enter stalls.) R4 applies, deduct 5p in the £.

FOCUS
A weak, uncompetitive maiden, although the winning time was 0.40 seconds quicker than the following 46-60. The form looks sound with the first two to this year's marks.
Poyle Kiera Official explanation: jockey said filly was never travelling

5531 DIGIBET CASINO H'CAP — 1m 4f (P)
8:20 (8:23) (Class 6) (0-60,65) 3-Y-O+ — **£2,047** (£604; £302) **Stalls** Centre

Form — RPR
3415 **1** **Spritza (IRE)**[15] 5120 3-9-4 **60**.......... HayleyTurner 1 — 68
(M L W Bell) *sn trckd ldr: t.k.h fr 1/2-way: led gng easily over 2f out: pressed and rdn wl over 1f out: styd on wl fnl f* **8/1**
-002 **2** nk **Aphrodisia**[9] 5279 3-9-2 **58**.......... SaleemGolam 6 — 66+
(S C Williams) *t.k.h: sn trckd ldng pair: drvn to press wnr wl over 1f out: styd on but a hld* **2/1**[1]
60-5 **3** 1/2 **Group Force (IRE)**[154] 1092 3-8-13 **55**.......... MartinDwyer 11 — 62
(M H Tompkins) *trckd ldrs: effrt over 2f out: drvn and styd on to press ldng pair fnl f: a hld* **25/1**
1036 **4** 1/2 **Zalkani (IRE)**[15] 5120 7-9-7 **58**.......... WilliamBuick(3) 10 — 64
(J Pearce) *hld up towards rr: prog over 2f out: drvn to chse ldrs 1f out: nt qckn* **14/1**
1411 **5** 3/4 **Treetops Hotel (IRE)**[7] 5341 8-9-12 **65** 6ex.......... RussellKennemore(5) 7 — 70
(B R Johnson) *hld up in last quartet: rdn on wd outside 3f out: kpt on fnl 2f: nt pce to rch ldrs* **11/1**
6442 **6** 2 **Mae Cigan (FR)**[14] 5132 4-9-10 **58**.......... TedDurcan 14 — 60
(M Blanshard) *hld up in midfield on inner: rdn over 2f out: plugged on one pce: n.d* **9/2**[2]
4542 **7** 1 1/2 **Sir Haydn**[7] 5341 7-9-9 **57**..........(v) MickyFenton 12 — 57
(J R Jenkins) *hld up in last pair: hanging and nt qckn over 2f out: kpt on fr over 1f out: n.d* **7/1**[3]
602- **8** 1/2 **Mutamaasek (USA)**[355] 5652 5-9-12 **60**.......... JamieSpencer 3 — 59
(Lady Herries) *led to over 2f out: wknd rapidly ins fnl f* **8/1**
0/4 **9** shd **Slew Charm (FR)**[144] 830 5-9-9 **57**..........(t) SamHitchcott 5 — 56
(Noel T Chance) *racd on outer in midfield: rdn over 3f out: no prog over 2f out: fdd* **8/1**
0006 **10** 1/2 **Tabulate**[19] 5020 4-9-5 **53**.......... IanMongan 2 — 51
(P Howling) *hld up in last pair: rdn 3f out: no real prog* **66/1**
0440 **11** 1 1/2 **Ashmolian (IRE)**[54] 3901 4-8-13 **47**.......... AdrianMcCarthy 4 — 42
(Miss Z C Davison) *t.k.h: trckd ldrs on outer: rdn 3f out: sn btn* **66/1**
0351 **12** nk **Picky**[16] 5095 3-9-1 **57**..........(v) FergusSweeney 9 — 52
(C Tinkler) *trckd ldrs on inner tl wknd 2f out* **25/1**
6001 **13** 6 **Hermanita**[17] 5068 3-9-4 **60**.......... EddieAhern 13 — 45+
(G Wragg) *hld up in last quartet: trying to make prog on inner but plenty to do whn hmpd over 1f out: nt rcvr* **20/1**
6 **14** 1 1/2 **Matarazzo (IRE)**[16] 5095 5-9-5 **53**..........(b) RichardHughes 8 — 36
(G L Moore) *trckd ldng pair to over 2f out: sn wknd: heavily eased fnl f* **20/1**

2m 34.48s (-2.42) **Going Correction** -0.225s/f (Stan)
WFA 3 from 4yo+ 8lb — **14** Ran SP% **132.5**
Speed ratings (Par 101): **99,98,98,98,97 96,95,94,94,94 93,93,89,88**
CSF £25.09 CT £423.86 TOTE £11.70: £2.50, £1.60, £11.50; EX 42.10.
Owner The Royal Ascot Racing Club **Bred** Pat Garvey **Trained** Newmarket, Suffolk
■ Stewards' Enquiry : Saleem Golam one-day ban: used whip with excessive frequency (Sep 30)

FOCUS
Unlike in the earlier maiden over this trip, they went only steadily and the winning time was 0.40 seconds slower. Overall the form is sound.
Hermanita Official explanation: jockey said filly was denied a clear run
Matarazzo(IRE) Official explanation: jockey said gelding stopped quickly

5532 MANSARD HOMES H'CAP — 7f (P)
8:50 (8:52) (Class 5) (0-75,75) 3-Y-O+ — **£2,914** (£867; £433; £216) **Stalls** High

Form — RPR
3234 **1** **Tender The Great (IRE)**[12] 5203 4-9-7 **75**.......... TQuinn 14 — 87
(B G Powell) *hld up in rr: prog on wd outside over 2f out: rdn to ld over 1f out: hung lft but sn wl in command: eased fnl 50yds* **10/1**
1013 **2** 2 **Dudley Docker (IRE)**[7] 5330 5-9-3 **74**.......... LiamJones(3) 9 — 81
(C R Dore) *t.k.h: hld up bhd ldrs: effrt to chal over 1f out: sn outpcd by wnr: kpt on to take 2nd nr fin* **7/2**[2]

-6P3 **3** *nk* **Towy Girl (IRE)**[14] 5129 3-8-8 **65** JamieSpencer 13 71
(A W Carroll) *s.i.s and rousted along early: sn t.k.h and hld up: prog on outer over 2f out: chsd wnr 1f out: no imp: lost 2nd nr fin* **12/1**

0034 **4** *1 1/4* **Carmenero (GER)**[8] 5312 4-9-7 **75** MartinDwyer 5 78
(W R Muir) *hld up in midfield: trckd ldrs 2f out and nt clr run briefly: kpt on fnl f: nt pce to chal* **8/1**

0 **5** *shd* **Jacquart (NZ)**[19] 5012 5-9-7 **75** AdamKirby 2 78
(C G Cox) *trckd ldrs: prog on outer to ld 2f out: hdd over 1f out: fdd fnl f* **66/1**

0000 **6** *1* **Resplendent Ace (IRE)**[15] 5122 3-9-1 **72** ChrisCatlin 11 72
(P Howling) *sn pushed along in last trio: effrt u.p on outer over 2f out: kpt on: no real threat* **25/1**

3063 **7** *shd* **Indian's Feather (IRE)**[11] 5223 6-9-6 **74** IanMongan 3 74
(N Tinkler) *prom: rdn over 2f out: sn lost pl: plugged on fr over 1f out* **7/1**

4-00 **8** *1 1/2* **Bonne D'Argent (IRE)**[61] 3710 3-8-10 **67** FergusSweeney 10 63
(J R Boyle) *t.k.h early: hld up in rr: prog on inner 2f out: no hdwy fnl f* **50/1**

3140 **9** *1 1/4* **Oscarshall (IRE)**[48] 4111 3-8-8 **65** JimmyQuinn 12 57
(M H Tompkins) *s.i.s and sltly hmpd: sn rousted along in last: sme prog on inner 2f out: no hdwy jst over 1f out* **16/1**

-231 **10** *3* **Gilded Youth**[14] 5129 3-9-4 **75** DaneO'Neill 4 59
(H Candy) *led at fast pce to 2f out: wknd fnl f* **13/2**[3]

4130 **11** *1* **Empire Dancer (IRE)**[15] 5114 4-8-10 **64** EddieAhern 7 45
(C N Allen) *pressed ldr: upsides 2f out: wkng whn n.m.r 1f out* **10/1**

34-1 **12** *6* **Subadar**[148] 1215 3-9-2 **73** RichardHughes 6 38
(R Charlton) *hld up in rr: rdn over 2f out: hanging and nt qckn: btn after: eased ins fnl f* **3/1**[1]

-502 **13** *shd* **Touch Of Style (IRE)**[14] 5129 3-9-0 **71** AmirQuinn 8 36
(J R Boyle) *cl up on inner but sn pushed along: stl wl in tch 2f out: wknd rapidly over 1f out* **16/1**

1m 24.69s (-2.11) **Going Correction** -0.225s/f (Stan)
WFA 3 from 4yo+ 3lb **13** Ran SP% **129.1**
Speed ratings (Par 103): **103,100,100,98,98 97,97,95,94,91 89,83,82**
CSF £48.20 CT £452.18 TOTE £12.10: £2.80, £2.30, £5.70; EX 55.40.
Owner Miss Kwok-Mei Ada Yip **Bred** Y Wai Kwan **Trained** Lambourn, Berks

FOCUS
A fair handicap run at a good pace but run at face value and not entirely solid rated through the third.
Subadar Official explanation: trainer's representative had no explanation for the poor form shown
Touch Of Style(IRE) Official explanation: jockey said gelding was never travelling

5533 WOODEN SPOON H'CAP 2m (P)
9:20 (9:20) (Class 6) (0-65,65) 3-Y-0+ **£2,047** (£604; £302) **Stalls** High

Form RPR

0403 **1** **Bold Adventure**[5] 5388 3-7-12 **47** oh1 AdrianMcCarthy 5 61+
(W J Musson) *hld up wl in rr: smooth prog on outer fr 4f out: led over 2f out: at least 3l clr fnl f: heavily eased nr fin* **8/1**[3]

000- **2** *1/2* **Hora**[309] 6475 3-7-13 **48** JamieMackay 10 57
(Sir Mark Prescott) *prom: trckd ldr 1/2-way: led over 3f out to over 2f out: sn outpcd: kpt on but flattered by proximity to wnr* **10/1**

066 **3** *shd* **How's Business**[21] 4948 3-8-4 **53** ow3 SimonWhitworth 8 62
(C A Cyzer) *trckd ldrs: rdn over 2f out: styd on fr over 1f out: flattered by proximity to wnr* **40/1**

2326 **4** *3 1/2* **Lapina (IRE)**[9] 5279 3-9-2 **65** (b) DaneO'Neill 9 70
(Pat Eddery) *t.k.h: hld up in midfield: effrt over 2f out: drvn and kpt on one pce: n.d* **14/1**

0221 **5** *1 3/4* **Right Option (IRE)**[14] 5138 3-8-2 **56** KevinGhunowa[(5)] 3 59
(J L Flint) *cl up: rdn to chse ldr briefly 3f out: sn outpcd: one pce u.p after* **10/1**

031 **6** *2* **Noora (IRE)**[12] 5187 6-10-0 **65** (v) AdamKirby 2 65
(C G Cox) *dwlt: hld up in rr: rdn 3f out: sn outpcd: plugged on fnl 2f: n.d* **25/1**

5204 **7** *1 1/2* **Tobougg Welcome (IRE)**[23] 4877 3-7-12 **47** oh2 JimmyQuinn 14 45
(S C Williams) *trckd ldrs on inner: rdn and outpcd over 2f out: no ch after* **25/1**

6500 **8** *2 1/2* **Lysander's Quest (IRE)**[3] 5453 9-8-10 **47** oh2 FergusSweeney 12 42
(R Ingram) *nvr bttr than midfield: effrt on inner but no prog whn nt clr run 2f out: no ch after* **25/1**

6206 **9** *5* **Spinal Tap (IRE)**[7] 5342 3-8-9 **61** (p) WilliamBuick[(3)] 1 50
(C R Egerton) *pressed ldr to 1/2-way: lost pl and rdn 6f out: wknd over 3f out* **14/1**

111 **10** *8* **Colwyn Bay (IRE)**[34] 4544 5-9-13 **64** (p) JamieSpencer 7 44
(Jane Chapple-Hyam) *hld up in rr: effrt over 3f out: rdn and no imp on ldrs over 2f out: 7th and btn whn virtually p.u over 1f out* **11/8**[1]

0312 **11** *1* **Synonymy**[6] 5364 4-9-8 **59** (b) NickyMackay 4 38
(M Blanshard) *led to over 3f out: wknd rapidly and eased: t.o* **7/2**[2]

3206 **12** *2 1/2* **Squirtle (IRE)**[23] 4906 4-8-12 **52** LiamJones[(3)] 11 28
(W M Brisbourne) *chsd ldrs: wknd over 3f out: eased fnl 2f: t.o* **20/1**

4300 **13** *1* **Dark Parade (ARG)**[12] 5204 6-9-7 **63** (b) JamieJones[(5)] 13 37
(G L Moore) *s.s and reluctant: in tch to 4f out: wknd and eased: t.o* **25/1**

3m 27.22s (-4.18) **Going Correction** -0.225s/f (Stan)
WFA 3 from 4yo+ 12lb **13** Ran SP% **129.5**
Speed ratings (Par 101): **101,100,100,98,98 97,96,95,92,88 88,86,86**
CSF £84.25 CT £3080.56 TOTE £20.40: £5.40, £2.40, £7.10 Place 6 £96.91, Place 5 £74.74.
Owner Mustard Cord Cads **Bred** Bricklow Ltd **Trained** Newmarket, Suffolk

FOCUS
A low-grade staying handicap won in a very quick time. The form should be sound at this level rated through the fourth.
Colwyn Bay(IRE) Official explanation: jockey said gelding was never travelling
T/Plt: £75.10 to a £1 stake. Pool: £71,557.50. 694.70 winning tickets. T/Qpdt: £33.00 to a £1 stake. Pool: £4,048.30. 90.60 winning tickets. JN

5380 SANDOWN (R-H)
Wednesday, September 19

OFFICIAL GOING: Good to firm (9.1)
Wind: Virtually nil

5534 SPEEDY NURSERY 5f 6y
2:20 (2:21) (Class 5) (0-75,75) 2-Y-0 **£4,533** (£1,348; £674; £336) **Stalls** High

Form RPR

6622 **1** **Mistress Cooper**[13] 5167 2-8-10 **64** TedDurcan 5 70
(W J Musson) *hld up in rr: hdwy over 1f out: hrd rdn and styd on to ld fnl 100yds* **7/1**

4514 **2** *1* **Ridge Wood Dani (IRE)**[7] 5331 2-8-13 **67** JimmyFortune 12 69
(E J Alston) *s.i.s: in rr: rdn and hdwy over 1f out styd on wl thrght fnl f to take 2nd last stride but nt rch wnr* **9/2**[2]

011 **3** *shd* **Fabuleux Cherie**[16] 5096 2-8-8 **62** MartinDwyer 6 64
(W R Muir) *chsd ldrs: drvn to chal jst ins fnl f: sn slt advantage: hdd and outpcd fnl 100yds: lost 2nd last stride* **8/1**

2004 **4** *3/4* **Barraland**[3] 5452 2-9-7 **75** TPO'Shea 15 74
(M R Channon) *pressed ldr tl led jst over 1f out: hdd ins fnl f: one pce fnl 100yds* **8/1**

2016 **5** *1/2* **Hobson**[12] 5207 2-9-7 **75** StephenCarson 8 73
(Eve Johnson Houghton) *chsd ldrs: rdn 2f out: one pce ins fnl f* **13/2**[3]

0000 **6** *nk* **Running Buck (USA)**[23] 4903 2-7-9 **54** ow1 (b[1]) LukeMorris[(5)] 16 50
(N P Littmoden) *s.i.s: in rr: hdwy over 1f out: r.o ins fnl f but nt pce to rch ldrs* **22/1**

2600 **7** *3/4* **Advertisement**[23] 4903 2-9-0 **68** DaneO'Neill 13 62
(C G Cox) *in tch: pushed along 1/2-way: styd on fnl f but nvr gng pce to trble ldrs* **16/1**

1020 **8** *hd* **Penrice Castle**[13] 5167 2-9-3 **71** RichardHughes 9 64
(R Hannon) *hld up in rr: effrt and n.m.r 2f out: styd on fnl f but nvr in contention* **12/1**

0606 **9** *1* **Maybe I Wont**[27] 4737 2-8-13 **67** PaulFitzsimons 7 56
(S Dow) *chsd ldrs: rdn 1/2-way: styd on same pce ins fnl f* **20/1**

0125 **10** *shd* **Llab Nala**[16] 5089 2-8-4 **58** ChrisCatlin 3 47
(M R Channon) *in rr: rdn 3f out: styd on fnl f: nvr in contention* **16/1**

000 **11** *1/2* **Ile Royale**[39] 4402 2-8-1 **60** KirstyMilczarek[(5)] 11 47
(C N Allen) *s.i.s: outpcd tl mod late prog* **50/1**

0042 **12** *1 1/4* **Orpen's Art (IRE)**[6] 5365 2-7-9 **52** oh1 WilliamBuick[(3)] 14 35
(N A Callaghan) *led tl hdd jst over 1f out: wknd rapidly* **4/1**[1]

060 **13** *9* **Compton Abbess**[15] 5110 2-8-10 **64** (b[1]) FergusSweeney 10 14+
(B R Millman) *chsd ldrs 3f: wknd qckly: eased whn no ch fnl f* **40/1**

61.99 secs (-0.22) **Going Correction** -0.025s/f (Good) **13** Ran SP% **119.2**
Speed ratings (Par 95): **100,98,98,97,96 95,94,94,92,92 91,89,75**
CSF £36.86 CT £270.15 TOTE £8.80: £2.50, £2.20, £2.50; EX 48.00.
Owner Mrs Rita Brown **Bred** R F And S D Knipe **Trained** Newmarket, Suffolk

FOCUS
A modest but competitive nursery run at a decent pace and the form looks solid rated through the consistent fourth.

NOTEBOOK
Mistress Cooper shaped as though she would appreciate the drop back to the bare 5f when second over slightly further at Warwick on her previous start and she ran out a clear-cut winner, picking up well from off the decent pace. She has a bit of size and could progress into a fair sprinter. (tchd 13-2 and 8-1)
Ridge Wood Dani(IRE) was left with plenty to do after starting slowly, but he came home well to take second. On this evidence, he probably wouldn't mind a return to 6f.
Fabuleux Cherie, bidding for the hat-trick, ran well off a mark 5lb higher than when winning a lesser event at Wolverhampton on her previous start. She is only modest, but is in great form.
Barraland showed good speed and this was a reasonable effort from the top of the weights. He may do even better over an easier 5f. (op 10-1)
Hobson did not run a bad race, but he continues to look high enough in the weights. (op 6-1)
Orpen's Art(IRE) once again showed plenty of early pace, but he did not see his race out. (op 9-2)
Compton Abbess Official explanation: jockey said filly hung right

5535 EXECUTIVE HIRE SHOW CLAIMING STKS 5f 6y
2:55 (2:56) (Class 5) 3-Y-0+ **£3,238** (£963; £481; £240) **Stalls** High

Form RPR

6000 **1** **Connect**[17] 5064 10-8-7 65 (b) TedDurcan 4 61+
(M H Tompkins) *sn pushed along in rr: impr and nt clr run 2f out: hdwy on rails whn nt clr run fr ins fnl f tl qcknd smartly fnl 50yds to ld last strides* **14/1**

20/2 **2** *nk* **Rydal (USA)**[40] 4351 6-8-13 69 MartinDwyer 10 66
(J A Osborne) *chsd ldrs: chal over 1f out: led ins fnl f and styd on wl: edgd lft cl home: ct last strides* **11/2**[3]

5000 **3** *1/2* **Pieter Brueghel (USA)**[53] 3954 8-9-7 77 JimmyFortune 1 72
(D Nicholls) *hld up trcking ldrs: drvn to take slt advantage appr fnl f: hdd ins fnl f and edgd rt: no ex nr fin* **8/1**

5400 **4** *nk* **Millfields Dreams**[21] 4944 8-8-9 62 EddieAhern 6 59
(M G Quinlan) *in rr: hdwy over 1f out: styd on and edgd rt ins fnl f: nt pce to chal fnl 100yds* **12/1**

0000 **5** *1 1/2* **Lindbergh**[4] 5430 5-9-4 69 (p) WilliamBuick[(3)] 8 66
(A J Lidderdale) *chsd ldrs: rdn and one pce over 1f out: no imp on ldrs whn n.m.r ins fnl f* **33/1**

0022 **6** *1 3/4* **Who's Winning (IRE)**[13] 5168 6-9-5 79 TQuinn 9 57
(B G Powell) *w ldrs: slt advantage 2f out: hdd appr fnl f: sn n.m.r: wknd ins fnl f* **2/1**[1]

4150 **7** *hd* **Whitbarrow (IRE)**[13] 5168 8-9-2 84 (b) JamesMillman[(5)] 7 59
(B R Millman) *sn drvn to ld: hdd 2f out: wkng whn n.m.r 1f out* **3/1**[2]

-000 **8** *2* **Our Archie**[9] 5270 3-8-6 37 (p) PaulFitzsimons 2 38
(M J Attwater) *outpcd thrght* **100/1**

0-00 **9** *1* **Two Acres (IRE)**[12] 5191 4-8-7 50 FergusSweeney 5 34
(A G Newcombe) *chsd ldrs: wknd fnl f* **66/1**

21R5 **R** **Danish Blues (IRE)**[11] 5232 4-8-7 58 SilvestreDeSousa 3 —
(D Nicholls) *ref to r* **8/1**

61.89 secs (-0.32) **Going Correction** -0.025s/f (Good)
WFA 3 from 4yo+ 1lb **10** Ran SP% **115.7**
Speed ratings (Par 103): **101,100,99,99,96 94,93,90,88,—**
CSF £87.96 TOTE £16.80: £3.60, £1.70, £2.50; EX 87.80.
Owner Mrs P R Bowring **Bred** J A E Hobby **Trained** Newmarket, Suffolk

FOCUS
A good claimer but the time was only slightly quicker than the preceding nursery and with doubts over plenty formwise coming into this race.

5536 PERI FORMWORK & SCAFFOLDING NOVICE STKS 7f 16y
3:30 (3:35) (Class 3) 2-Y-0
£7,478 (£2,239; £1,119; £560; £279; £140) **Stalls** High

Form RPR

221 **1** **Billion Dollar Kid**[9] 5274 2-9-2 0 RichardHughes 6 88
(R Hannon) *w ldr tl led 2f out: hrd drvn and styd on wl fnl f* **3/1**[1]

13 **2** *1 1/2* **Hobby**[55] 3880 2-8-11 0 MartinDwyer 1 80
(R M Beckett) *in rr: drvn along over 3f out: styd on u.p fr over 1f out: hung rt last strides and tk 2nd but a hld by wnr* **7/2**[2]

601 **3** *hd* **Aye Aye Digby (IRE)**[34] 4540 2-9-2 85 DaneO'Neill 4 84
(H Candy) *chsd ldrs: rdn to go 2nd appr fnl f: nvr quite gng pce of wnr: lost 2nd wl ins fnl f* **4/1**[3]

06 **4** *nk* **Maxwil**[34] 4547 2-8-12 0 FergusSweeney 8 79
(G L Moore) *hld up in rr but in tch: hdwy and nt clr run ins fnl 2f: n.m.r jst ins fnl f and kpt on wl fnl 100yds: gng on cl home* **33/1**

2311 **5** *nk* **Solent Ridge (IRE)**[22] 4916 2-9-4 85........................... JimmyFortune 7 85+
(J S Moore) *chsd ldrs: rdn and styd on fr 2f out: one pce whn hmpd last strides* **7/1**

0020 **6** *shd* **Yem Kinn**[18] 5048 2-9-4 95.. TPO'Shea 10 84
(M R Channon) *mde most tl hdd 2f out: one pce ins fnl f* **8/1**

01 **7** *1 3/4* **Giant Love (USA)**[14] 5140 2-9-4 81................................ GregFairley 2 80
(M Johnston) *chsd ldrs: rdn 3f out: wknd over 1f out* **5/1**

5 **8** *7* **Heart Of Dubai (USA)**[22] 4916 2-8-9 0...................... WilliamBuick(3) 5 56
(C E Brittain) *rdn over 3f out: a towards rr* **33/1**

9 *7* **Royal Tartan (USA)** 2-8-4 0.. ChrisCatlin 3 31
(G L Moore) *s.i.s: a in rr* **66/1**

1m 29.23s (-0.11) **Going Correction** -0.025s/f (Good) **9** Ran SP% **114.9**
Speed ratings (Par 99): **99,97,97,96,96 96,94,86,78**
CSF £13.40 TOTE £3.70: £1.40, £1.60, £2.00; EX 12.60.
Owner M Sines **Bred** Catridge Farm Stud & Mrs J Hall **Trained** East Everleigh, Wilts
■ Stewards' Enquiry : Richard Hughes two-day ban: careless riding (Sep 30-Oct 1)

FOCUS
A good novice event but they finished in a heap and the form is rated around the third, fifth and seventh.

NOTEBOOK
Billion Dollar Kid ◆ produced an improved performance when winning at Folkestone on his previous start and he confirmed himself very much on the up, following up in determined fashion. He looks the type to keep improving as he strengthens. (op 9-2, tchd 5-1 in places)
Hobby managed third in a Listed race over course and distance nearly two months previously, but that was a weak race for the level and she found one too good on this drop in grade. She gives the impression she wouldn't mind a little bit of cut in the ground and might find things easier against her own sex. (op 9-4)
Aye Aye Digby(IRE) was well held in two runs on fast ground, and then won his maiden when encountering a bit of give underfoot, so it was a real surprise to see this son of the mud-loving Captain Rio back on a quick surface. He is better than he was able to show, but needs easy ground to be seen at his best. (op 11-2)
Maxwil ◆, despite finishing up well held on his two previous start, had shown ability and this was an eye-catching run. Having been settled out the back, he lacked the pace to pose a serious threat and was also briefly denied a clear run over a furlong from the finish, but he kept on well under just hands and heels riding. The Handicapper will not have missed this, so he is unlikely to get off lightly, but he shapes as though he can step forward again when upped in trip. In the longer term, he should do well over middle-distances. (op 25-1)
Solent Ridge(IRE) came into this bidding for a hat-trick, but this was tougher than the novice event he landed at Lingfield and he was comfortably held. (tchd 13-2)
Yem Kinn was beaten when hampered on the rail over a furlong from home. (tchd 15-2)
Giant Love(USA), whose York win represented just fair form, was well held in this tougher heat. (op 9-2)

5537 B&CE BENEFIT SCHEMES FILLIES' H'CAP 1m 14y
4:05 (4:07) (Class 4) (0-85,85) 3-Y-O **£6,477** (£1,927; £963; £481) **Stalls** High

Form RPR

-122 **1** **Ventura (USA)**[53] 3970 3-9-4 **85**.............................. RichardHughes 1 94+
(Mrs A J Perrett) *trckd ldr: chal fr 3f out tl slt ld 1f out: sn edgd rt: continued to hang rt u.p but a in command: pushed out* **15/8**[1]

542 **2** *nk* **Fragrancy (IRE)**[13] 5156 3-9-3 **84**............................. PhilipRobinson 2 92
(M A Jarvis) *led: rdn and styd on whn chal fr 3f out: hdd 1f out: sn bmpd: continued to be pushed rt but a hld* **11/4**[2]

0-26 **3** *1 1/4* **World's Heroine (IRE)**[33] 4589 3-9-0 **81**........................ EddieAhern 6 86
(G A Butler) *in tch: hdwy over 2f out: chsd ldng duo fnl f but a hld* **11/2**

2304 **4** *3/4* **Froissee**[21] 4949 3-8-7 **77**..........................(b[1]) WilliamBuick(3) 3 80
(N A Callaghan) *in rr: rdn and n.m.r over 2f out: styd on u.p fnl f but nvr in contention* **11/1**

300 **5** *nk* **Baylini**[16] 5092 3-8-7 **81**... SophieDoyle(7) 7 84
(Ms J S Doyle) *chsd ldrs: rdn 3f out: wknd fnl f* **66/1**

4611 **6** *4* **Nice To Know (FR)**[24] 4848 3-8-9 **76**........................ FergusSweeney 5 70
(G L Moore) *rdn over 2f out: a in rr* **9/2**[3]

-620 **7** *1 1/2* **Ficoma**[24] 4848 3-8-7 **74**.. TQuinn 4 64
(C G Cox) *chsd ldrs: rdn 3f out: wknd ins fnl 2f* **12/1**

1m 42.79s (-1.16) **Going Correction** -0.025s/f (Good) **7** Ran SP% **112.5**
Speed ratings (Par 100): **104,103,102,101,101 97,95**
CSF £6.95 TOTE £2.50: £1.50, £1.80; EX 5.80.
Owner K Abdulla **Bred** Juddmonte Farms Inc **Trained** Pulborough, W Sussex

FOCUS
A decent fillies' handicap run at a reasonable gallop but the form is relatively ordinary rated through the runner-up.
Nice To Know(FR) Official explanation: jockey said filly ran flat

5538 GENSET EBF MAIDEN STKS 1m 14y
4:40 (4:42) (Class 4) 2-Y-O **£5,181** (£1,541; £770; £384) **Stalls** High

Form RPR

0 **1** **Hawaass (USA)**[125] 1792 2-9-3 0.................................. GregFairley 2 82
(M Johnston) *trckd ldrs: styd on u.p fr over 1f out: wnt 2nd ins fnl f: edge rt fnl 100yds: led last stride* **12/1**[3]

02 **2** *shd* **Yaddree**[21] 4947 2-9-3 0.. PhilipRobinson 3 82
(M A Jarvis) *chased ldrs: wnt 2nd 2f out: styd on u.p to ld jst ins fnl f: carried rt fnl 100yds: ct last stride* **5/2**[2]

0 **3** *1 1/2* **Irish Mayhem (USA)**[19] 5010 2-9-3 0............................... TedDurcan 1 78+
(B J Meehan) *s.i.s: sn drvn along to get in tch w ldrs: kpt on u.p ins fnl f: gng on cl home* **12/1**[3]

0 **4** *1* **Brexca (IRE)**[19] 5010 2-9-3 0....................................... DaneO'Neill 7 76+
(C G Cox) *in rr: pushed along over 2f out: styd on fnl f and gng on cl home but nvr gng pce to be competitive* **25/1**

32 **5** *1* **Aboriginie (USA)**[12] 5200 2-9-3 0.............................. JimmyFortune 9 74
(J H M Gosden) *slt ld: drvn along over 2f out: hrd rdn and hdd jst ins fnl f: wknd fnl 100yds* **4/6**[1]

6 *2 1/2* **Patkai (IRE)** 2-9-3 0.. JDSmith 5 68
(Sir Michael Stoute) *in rr: pushed along 2f out: styd on ins fnl f: nvr in contention* **20/1**

7 *nk* **Ragamuffin Man (IRE)** 2-9-3 0.. PaulDoe 10 67
(W J Knight) *v green in rr and stl carrying hd high over 2f out: styd on fr over 1f out but nvr in contention* **50/1**

05 **8** *nk* **Sinbad The Sailor**[19] 5010 2-9-3 0..................................... TQuinn 6 67
(J W Hills) *w ldr: rdn 3f out: wknd 2f out* **14/1**

0 **9** *10* **Lady Van Gogh**[19] 5003 2-8-12 0................................ RichardSmith 4 39
(R Hannon) *chsd ldrs: rdn 3f out: wknd qckly over 2f out* **66/1**

1m 44.12s (0.17) **Going Correction** -0.025s/f (Good) **9** Ran SP% **122.7**
Speed ratings (Par 97): **98,97,96,95,94 91,91,91,81**
CSF £43.87 TOTE £14.20: £2.70, £1.20, £3.40; EX 34.50.
Owner Sheikh Ahmed Al Maktoum **Bred** Darley **Trained** Middleham Moor, N Yorks

FOCUS
A fair-looking maiden run at only a moderate pace. The time was slower than the preceding three-year-old fillies' handicap but still acceptable and the form looks reasonable.

NOTEBOOK
Hawaass(USA), not seen since only a fair debut effort four months ago, stuck to his task really well to edge out his owner's first string close to the line - a Stewards' enquiry was called but the result remained unaltered. A half-brother to Kabool, who did so well for Godolphin in the past, he is sure to have a decent future in front of him. (op 11-1)
Yaddree, who was difficult to load in the stalls, only just got outstayed in the final furlong and, some would say, was possibly unlucky not to get the result in the Stewards' room. It should not be too long before he wins his race. (op 11-4 tchd 9-4)
Irish Mayhem(USA) ◆ was not that quickly away again but travelled like a good horse once on terms and was unlucky not to get closer after being stopped in his run up the home straight. He appears to have more than enough ability to win a race soon. (tchd 14-1)
Brexca(IRE) ◆ shaped well once again but may be more the sort for handicaps in time. That said, if an ordinary maiden can be found for him over at least a mile, he ought to be competitive.
Aboriginie(USA) was made a really short-priced favourite on the strength of two runs on the Polytrack, but could not reproduce that promise on turf. The way he was supported in the market suggests he is considered a very nice sort and he is not one to give up on quite yet. (op 10-11, tchd evens in a place)
Patkai(IRE), who holds an entry in next year's Derby, was too green on his debut to have much impact. He should stay well in time, as his dam was an unraced sister to the top-class Islington. (op 16-1)
Ragamuffin Man(IRE) was extremely green on his debut, presumably why his head was carried in an awkward position under pressure, and should be better for the first run. (op 40-1)
Sinbad The Sailor helped to set a medium pace before dropping out quickly up the home straight. (op 12-1)

5539 ROYAL BANK OF SCOTLAND H'CAP 1m 2f 7y
5:15 (5:15) (Class 4) (0-80,78) 3-Y-O+ **£5,181** (£1,541; £770; £384) **Stalls** High

Form RPR

0153 **1** **Queen Noverre (IRE)**[13] 5178 3-8-13 **73**............................(p) TQuinn 2 82
(J W Hills) *chsd ldr after 2f: rdn to ld over 1f out: edgd rt ins fnl f and hld on wl* **14/1**

66-3 **2** *3/4* **Qualify**[28] 4708 4-8-13 **67**... DaneO'Neill 12 74
(Miss Sheena West) *in tch: rdn 2f out: styd on fnl f to take 2nd cl home but a hld by wnr* **14/1**

4321 **3** *nk* **Kalasam**[8] 5307 3-8-3 **68**... TolleyDean(5) 9 74
(W R Muir) *chsd ldrs: rdn to chal ins fnl 2f: styd on wel but nt pce on wnr ins fnl f* **9/4**[1]

3500 **4** *nk* **Dragon Slayer (IRE)**[25] 4814 5-9-9 **77**............................. TPO'Shea 6 83
(P A Blockley) *sn led: rdn over 2f out: hdd over 1f out: wknd and lost 2nd wl ins fnl f whn carried rt* **14/1**

0302 **5** *2 1/2* **Don Pietro**[31] 4631 4-9-6 **74**..................................... EddieAhern 10 80+
(D J Coakley) *chsd ldrs: outpcd 2f out: styng on again ins fnl f whn no much room and no further prog* **4/1**[2]

0366 **6** *3/4* **Pianoforte (USA)**[7] 5330 5-8-10 **64** oh2..................... PhilipRobinson 4 63
(E J Alston) *in rr: pushed along over 2f out: styd on fr over 1f out but nt trble ldrs* **13/2**[3]

6004 **7** *1 1/4* **Brief Goodbye**[6] 5362 7-9-6 **74**.................................... MickyFenton 7 71
(John Berry) *towards rr most of way* **13/2**[3]

5005 **8** *1* **Eager Igor (USA)**[12] 5208 3-9-2 **76**............................. StephenCarson 3 71
(Eve Johnson Houghton) *t.k.h in rr: hdwy 3f out: pressed ldrs 2f out: wknd over 1f out* **15/2**

U065 **9** *1 1/4* **Harvest Joy (IRE)**[46] 4185 3-9-0 **74**........................... FergusSweeney 8 66
(J Gallagher) *in rr: rdn 5f out: sme prog 3f out: nt rch ldrs and wknd 2f out* **33/1**

00-0 **R** **Willhego**[34] 4551 6-9-7 **78**................................... StephaneBreux(3) 5 —
(J R Best) *ref to r: tk no part* **18/1**

2m 9.95s (-0.29) **Going Correction** -0.025s/f (Good)
WFA 3 from 4yo+ 6lb **10** Ran SP% **117.4**
Speed ratings (Par 105): **100,99,99,98,96 96,95,94,93,—**
CSF £194.49 CT £610.03 TOTE £14.50: £2.70, £3.70, £1.70; EX 173.90 Place 6 £96.11, Place 5 £39.45.
Owner Jerry Jamgotchian **Bred** W Lazy T Ranch **Trained** Upper Lambourn, Berks

FOCUS
A fair handicap run at a sedate pace and the form does not look that solid, with the third the best guide but several close up being out of form prior to this.
T/Plt: £81.20 to a £1 stake. Pool: £65,248.85. 585.90 winning tickets. T/Qpdt: £7.10 to a £1 stake. Pool: £4,019.20. 413.10 winning tickets. ST

5508 YARMOUTH (L-H)
Wednesday, September 19

OFFICIAL GOING: Good (8.0)
Wind: Fresh across Weather: Overcast

5540 EUROPEAN BREEDERS' FUND/BENNETTS ELECTRICAL MAIDEN FILLIES' STKS 6f 3y
2:10 (2:11) (Class 4) 2-Y-O **£4,731** (£1,416; £708; £354; £176) **Stalls** High

Form RPR

22 **1** **Street Star (USA)**[24] 4854 2-9-0 0.............................. JamieSpencer 13 85
(J R Fanshawe) *w'like: lengthy: lw: mde all: rdn and hung lft ins fnl f: r.o* **10/3**[2]

3 **2** *shd* **Applauded (IRE)**[32] 4602 2-9-0 0............................... SteveDrowne 12 85
(B J Meehan) *w'like: str: lw: a.p: chsd wnr over 1f out: sn rdn and ev ch: hung lft ins fnl f: r.o* **4/6**[1]

3 *3 1/2* **Diamond Yas (IRE)** 2-9-0 0.. LDettori 3 75+
(H R A Cecil) *w'like: leggy: hld up: hdwy over 1f out: nt trble ldrs* **12/1**[3]

4 *1 1/2* **Klarity** 2-9-0 0.. JimmyQuinn 10 70
(J Pearce) *leggy: s.i.s: hld up: plld hrd: hdwy over 3f out: rdn over 1f out: styd on same pce* **66/1**

5 *1* **Meydan Princess (IRE)** 2-9-0 0.................................... TPQueally 5 67+
(J Noseda) *w'like: trckd ldrs: racd keenly: rdn over 1f out: sn outpcd* **12/1**[3]

6 *2* **Wannabe Free** 2-9-0 0.. AdamKirby 1 61+
(J Noseda) *w'like: bit bkwd: dwlt: hld up: styd on ins fnl f: nvr nrr* **40/1**

6 **7** *nk* **Ma Al Salamah (IRE)**[6] 5357 2-9-0 0............................... RyanMoore 2 60
(C E Brittain) *chsd ldrs: rdn over 2f out: wknd over 1f out* **14/1**

8 *1* **Hawa Khana (IRE)** 2-9-0 0... TGMcLaughlin 9 57+
(N P Littmoden) *w'like: chsd ldrs: rdn over 2f out: wknd fnl f* **100/1**

9 *shd* **Rossini Byline (IRE)** 2-8-11 0.................................. LiamJones(3) 11 57
(J L Spearing) *leggy: chsd ldrs 4f* **100/1**

0 **10** *hd* **Payne Relief (IRE)**[24] 4854 2-9-0 0.................................... RHills 8 56
(M L W Bell) *unf: hld up: a in rr* **66/1**

11 *3/4* **Fandangerina** 2-9-0 0.. SebSanders 7 54
(Sir Mark Prescott) *w'like: str: bit bkwd: sn pushed along in rr: wknd over 2f out* **33/1**

12 *nk* **Clean Sheet (USA)** 2-9-0 0 KerrinMcEvoy 6 53
(W J Haggas) *unf: s.i.s: hld up: hdwy 1/2-way: wknd over 1f out* **25/1**

1m 14.51s (0.81) **Going Correction** +0.225s/f (Good) **12** Ran SP% **119.3**
Speed ratings (Par 94): **103,102,98,96,94 92,91,90,90,90 89,88**
CSF £5.70 TOTE £3.90: £1.10, £1.10, £2.60; EX 7.00 Trifecta £26.80 Pool £341.60 - 8.84 winning units..
Owner Mrs C C Regalado-Gonzalez **Bred** Rose Hill Farm **Trained** Newmarket, Suffolk

FOCUS
A fair fillies' maiden with the time decent and the form horses clear, so should prove sound.

NOTEBOOK
Street Star(USA), who failed to build on her initial effort when second over course and distance last time, seemed to appreciate the faster going and she led throughout for a narrow success, just managing to hang on from the hot favourite. She shows plenty of speed, but is bred to stay further in time and it will be interesting to see what sort of mark she gets for handicaps. (op 3-1 tchd 4-1)
Applauded(IRE), a promising third in a fair maiden on her debut at Newbury, was understandably made favourite in what was a weaker contest, but she was unable to get past the winner, still showing signs of greenness under pressure. She will find a race before long. (op 10-11 tchd Evens in places)
Diamond Yas(IRE), a 5,000euros daughter of Mull Of Kintyre, comes from a yard whose juveniles often need a run and, having been held up early on, she ran on nicely to claim third. The step up to 7f will suit in time and she should be up to winning an ordinary maiden. (op 9-1 tchd 14-1)
Klarity, a half-sister to the useful Johnny Jumpup, comes from a yard who are hardly renowned for their success with two-year-olds, but she shaped most promisingly back in fourth and can be expected to improve for this initial experience. (op 50-1)
Meydan Princess(IRE), a daughter of first-season sire Choisir, was never far from the lead and seemed to know her job, but she was found wanting for a change of gear when it mattered. She can be expected to improve for this initial experience. (tchd 17-2 and 14-1)
Wannabe Free, an attractive half-sister to useful handicapper King Of Argos, is likely to need further in time and it was no surprise to see her doing her best work late. She could be one for a similar race. (op 33-1)

5541 EUROPEAN BREEDERS' FUND/JERRY GARCIA MEMORIAL MAIDEN STKS 7f 3y
2:45 (2:46) (Class 4) 2-Y-O **£4,731** (£1,416; £708; £354; £176) **Stalls** High

Form RPR
4 **1** **Tasdeer (USA)**[16] 5091 2-9-3 0 RHills 13 86+
(M A Jarvis) *w'like: str: lw: a.p: chsd ldr over 2f out: led over 1f out: sn pushed clr* **9/4**[1]
2 *4* **City Stable (IRE)** 2-9-3 0 RyanMoore 4 71
(Sir Michael Stoute) *w'like: hld up: hdwy over 1f out: no ch w wnr* **10/3**[2]
02 **3** *1 3/4* **Green Diamond**[26] 4784 2-9-3 0 JamieSpencer 10 66
(M Johnston) *unf: scope: chsd ldrs: rdn over 2f out: no ex fnl f* **10/3**[2]
0 **4** *2 1/2* **Calypso Charms**[39] 4402 2-8-12 0 JamieMackay 1 59+
(M L W Bell) *leggy: hld up: plld hrd: styd on fr over 1f out: nvr nrr* **40/1**
000 **5** *hd* **High Standing (USA)**[46] 4160 2-9-3 38 VinceSlattery 5 59
(N A Callaghan) *w'like: hld up: hdwy and hung lft fr over 2f out: wknd fnl f* **150/1**
6 *1/2* **Bianca Capello** 2-8-12 0 OscarUrbina 7 53
(J R Fanshawe) *leggy: narrow: s.i.s: hld up: hdwy and edgd lft over 2f out: wknd fnl f* **28/1**
0000 **7** *3/4* **Galley Slave (IRE)**[8] 5298 2-8-10 56 CharlotteKerton(7) 11 56
(M C Chapman) *chsd ldr: rdn over 2f out: wknd fnl f* **200/1**
00 **8** *1/2* **Any Given Day (IRE)**[34] 4539 2-9-3 0 TGMcLaughlin 6 54
(D M Simcock) *sn outpcd: hdwy over 1f out: nt clr run ent fnl f: nvr nrr* **100/1**
0 **9** *nk* **Grand Cuvee**[34] 4537 2-9-3 0 TPQueally 14 54
(D M Simcock) *w'like: mid-div: rdn 1/2-way: wknd 2f out* **40/1**
10 *1* **Skycruiser (IRE)** 2-9-3 0 LDettori 9 51
(Saeed Bin Suroor) *str: dwlt: hld up: hdwy over 2f out: wknd over 1f out* **6/1**[3]
06 **11** *1 1/2* **Dorso Rosso (IRE)**[22] 4916 2-8-10 0 JCorrigan(7) 8 47
(Mrs C A Dunnett) *w'like: led: clr 4f out: hung lft over 2f out: hdd & wknd over 1f out* **200/1**
12 *1/2* **Iron Cross (IRE)** 2-9-3 0 SebSanders 12 46
(Sir Mark Prescott) *w'like: lengthy: bit bkwd: s.s: rdn 1/2-way: a in rr* **12/1**
5 **13** *hd* **Minjim**[14] 5135 2-9-3 0 AdamKirby 2 45
(C E Brittain) *leggy: sn outpcd* **66/1**
14 *3 1/2* **Muharjam** 2-9-3 0 KerrinMcEvoy 3 36
(C E Brittain) *w'like: bit bkwd: hld up: wknd over 2f out* **16/1**

1m 27.85s (1.25) **Going Correction** +0.225s/f (Good) **14** Ran SP% **117.3**
Speed ratings (Par 97): **101,96,94,91,91 90,89,89,89,87 86,85,85,81**
CSF £9.10 TOTE £3.60: £1.40, £1.60, £1.60; EX 13.60 Trifecta £23.80 Pool £347.88 - 10.61winning units..
Owner Hamdan Al Maktoum **Bred** Shadwell Farm LLC **Trained** Newmarket, Suffolk

FOCUS
A fair maiden likely to produce winners but the form is limited by the proximity of the fifth and seventh.

NOTEBOOK
Tasdeer(USA), caught out by inexperience on his Lingfield debut, knew his job much better this time and, having gone on a furlong out, he quickly put daylight between himself and the rest. This was a smart performance from the son of Rahy and, with 1m likely to bring about further improvement, he looks one to keep on side. (op 11-4 tchd 3-1 in places)
City Stable(IRE), a son of Machiavellian, holds a Derby entry and is unlikely to be seen at his best until tackling middle-distances next season, but he did best of the remainder here and, although no match for the winner, he should find an ordinary maiden over 1m. (op 11-2)
Green Diamond, run out of it late on at Thirsk last time, was always likely to prove vulnerable to an improver and he once again failed to see out his race as strongly as one would have liked. He could be worth trying back over 6f. (op 2-1)
Calypso Charms improved on her initial effort at Newmarket, keeping on quite well despite pulling early on, and will be qualified for handicaps after one more run, a sphere she should do well in. (op 50-1)
High Standing(USA), handed a rating of 38 following three dismal efforts in maidens, appeared to run above himself back in fifth and will find easier opportunities at selling level. (op 100-1)
Skycruiser(IRE), a 625,000gns son of Dubai Destination, would ordinarily have been strongly fancied for an event such as this, but it was significant he holds no big-race entries and he shaped with only limited promise. (op 7-2 tchd 7-1)
Minjim Official explanation: jockey said colt was unbalanced over 3f out

5542 DANNY WRIGHT MEMORIAL (S) STKS 1m 2f 21y
3:20 (3:21) (Class 6) 3-4-Y-0 **£1,943** (£578; £288; £144) **Stalls** Low

Form RPR
6000 **1** **Present**[5] 5388 3-8-7 46 TPQueally 6 53
(D Morris) *s.i.s: rcvrd to ld over 8f out: hdd over 3f out: rallied to ld over 1f out: hrd rdn and hung rt ins fnl f: all out* **7/1**
0030 **2** *hd* **Dot's Delight**[41] 4340 3-8-7 59 JimmyQuinn 4 53
(M H Tompkins) *s.i.s: hld up: hdwy over 3f out: rdn over 1f out: ev ch and hung rt ins fnl f: styd on* **7/4**[1]
0054 **3** *4* **Cool Isle**[11] 5235 4-8-10 40 (b) TravisBlock(3) 2 45
(P Howling) *hld up: rdn over 3f out: carried hd high fr over 1f out: no ex ins ins fnl f: nt trble ldrs* **6/1**
0044 **4** *2* **Brierley Lil**[11] 3244 3-8-4 50 LiamJones(3) 3 41
(J L Spearing) *led: hdd over 8f out: chsd ldr tl led over 3f out: sn rdn: hdd over 1f out: wknd ins fnl f* **4/1**[3]
060 **5** *1 3/4* **Elizabeth Garrett**[21] 4943 3-8-4 44 (v) AndrewElliott(3) 1 38
(M J Gingell) *chsd ldrs: rdn over 3f out: wknd over 1f out* **40/1**
6030 **6** *1 1/4* **Law Of The Land (IRE)**[16] 5095 3-8-12 52 SebSanders 8 40
(W R Muir) *hld up: rdn over 2f out: sn hung lft and nt run on* **3/1**[2]
00- **7** *7* **Fantasy Legend (IRE)**[280] 6812 4-9-4 43 (b) JamesDoyle 7 26
(N P Littmoden) *chsd ldrs over 7f* **33/1**
00-0 **8** *21* **Aboyne (IRE)**[16] 5090 4-8-11 45 MCGeran(7) 5 —
(K F Clutterbuck) *hld up: rdn over 4f out: sme hdwy over 2f out: sn wknd* **66/1**

2m 11.75s (3.65) **Going Correction** +0.225s/f (Good)
WFA 3 from 4yo 6lb **8** Ran SP% **115.0**
Speed ratings (Par 101): **94,93,90,89,87 86,81,64**
CSF £19.74 TOTE £7.70: £2.40, £1.10, £2.40; EX 23.20 Trifecta £303.30 Pool £529.80 - 1.24 winning units..The winner was sold to M Hole for 7,200gns.
Owner Miss S Graham **Bred** Bloomsbury Stud **Trained** Newmarket, Suffolk

FOCUS
A desperate contest but sound enough for the level.

5543 WBX.COM £25 BET FOR NEW ACCOUNTS H'CAP (FOR THE GOLDEN JUBILEE TROPHY) 1m 2f 21y
3:55 (3:55) (Class 3) (0-90,89) 3-Y-O+ **£8,096** (£2,408; £1,203; £601) **Stalls** Low

Form RPR
2204 **1** **Gyroscope**[25] 4827 3-8-13 84 RyanMoore 3 94
(Sir Michael Stoute) *lw: chsd ldr: rdn to ld ins fnl f: r.o* **4/1**[2]
5353 **2** *1 3/4* **Voliere**[12] 5210 4-8-10 75 oh1 JamieSpencer 7 82
(S C Williams) *hld up: hdwy over 2f out: edgd lft fr over 1f out: styd on same pce ins fnl f* **18/1**
5005 **3** *3/4* **Fusili (IRE)**[7] 5327 4-9-1 85 PatrickHills(5) 1 90
(N P Littmoden) *lw: led: clr 1/2-way: rdn over 1f out: hdd and no ex ins fnl f* **28/1**
1215 **4** *2* **Le Soleil (GER)**[53] 3978 6-8-12 77 TPQueally 4 78
(B J Curley) *hld up: outpcd over 2f out: hdwy over 1f out: nt trble ldrs* **11/1**
3060 **5** *1/2* **Wind Star**[18] 5049 4-9-4 86 PJMcDonald(3) 6 86
(G A Swinbank) *chsd ldrs: rdn and hung lft over 2f out: styd on same pce appr fnl f* **9/1**
5042 **6** *1/2* **Yarqus**[18] 5049 4-9-10 89 (t) SebSanders 8 88
(C E Brittain) *lw: hld up: nt clr run over 2f out: swtchd rt: rdn and hung lft over 1f out: n.d* **9/2**[3]
2321 **7** *nk* **Seeking The Buck (USA)**[11] 5218 3-9-2 87 (bt) KerrinMcEvoy 5 85
(M A Magnusson) *hld up: hdwy 3f out: hmpd 2f out: wknd ins fnl f* **5/4**[1]
4405 **8** *3/4* **Active Asset (IRE)**[6] 5362 5-9-0 79 RobertHavlin 2 76
(M Quinn) *chsd ldrs: rdn whn hmpd over 2f out: wknd over 1f out* **18/1**

2m 9.72s (1.62) **Going Correction** +0.225s/f (Good)
WFA 3 from 4yo+ 6lb **8** Ran SP% **114.9**
Speed ratings (Par 107): **102,100,100,98,98 97,97,96**
CSF £70.30 CT £1761.92 TOTE £4.90: £1.40, £3.00, £5.50; EX 49.80 Trifecta £640.50 Part won. Pool £902.24 - 0.35 winning units..
Owner Cheveley Park Stud **Bred** The Niarchos Family **Trained** Newmarket, Suffolk
■ Stewards' Enquiry : Jamie Spencer one-day ban: careless riding (Sep 30)

FOCUS
A fair handicap but not that strong and best rated around the first two.

NOTEBOOK
Gyroscope had become a bit disappointing, but this first try at 1m2f brought about the necessary improvement and she kept on strongly for what was ultimately a cosy victory. She will need to progress again to defy a rise, and could be one to take on at a short price next time. (op 5-1 tchd 7-2)
Voliere showed improved form for the step up in trip when third in a fair handicap at Newbury last time and she confirmed the promise of that effort with a keeping-on effort in second. It is surely a matter of time before she finds a similar race. (op 20-1 tchd 25-1)
Fusili(IRE), now 6lb lower than when last winning, was responsible for the early pace and she went into a clear lead at past halfway, but was unable to sustain the gallop and could find no more. This was a still a reasonable effort. (op 25-1 tchd 33-1)
Le Soleil(GER) did not prove quite so effective back at this distance and he could only keep on at the one pace under pressure. (op 15-2)
Wind Star is slowly beginning to creep back down to a more realistic mark and the way he was keeping on here suggests a return to winning ways may not be far off. (op 17-2 tchd 8-1)
Seeking The Buck(USA), an easy winner at Haydock last time, was up 7lb and looked a major player, but he was hampered when trying to come with a challenge and was never really going thereafter. He could be worth another chance. Official explanation: jockey said colt ran flat; trainer later said colt scoped dirty and was found to have an irregular blood count (op 11-8 tchd 6-5, 6-4 in places)

5544 E B F ATTHERACES.COM BEST ODDS JOHN MUSKER FILLIES' STKS (LISTED RACE) 1m 2f 21y
4:30 (4:31) (Class 1) 3-Y-O+
£15,046 (£5,702; £2,854; £1,423; £712; £357) **Stalls** Low

Form RPR
1201 **1** **Samira Gold (FR)**[24] 4849 3-8-13 99 SebSanders 6 107
(L M Cumani) *lw: s.i.s: sn pushed into mid-div: hdwy over 3f out: led over 2f out: hung lft ins fnl f: drvn out* **11/4**[2]
-404 **2** *1 1/2* **Shorthand**[35] 4503 3-8-9 99 RyanMoore 10 100
(Sir Michael Stoute) *hld up: hdwy over 2f out: rdn over 1f out: edgd lft: styd on same pce ins fnl f* **10/1**
122- **3** *shd* **Reunite (IRE)**[389] 4818 4-9-1 107 LDettori 5 100
(Saeed Bin Suroor) *lw: trckd ldrs: ev ch fr over 2f out tl rdn and no ex ins fnl f* **2/1**[1]
0122 **4** *3/4* **Sell Out**[35] 4503 3-8-9 91 SteveDrowne 11 99+
(G Wragg) *hld up: nt clr run over 2f out: swtchd rt over 1f out: rdn and edgd lft ins fnl f: styd on* **25/1**
-253 **5** *1/2* **Mont Etoile (IRE)**[45] 4203 4-9-1 99 (v[1]) TPQueally 13 97
(W J Haggas) *lw: hld up: r.o ins fnl f: nt trble ldrs* **18/1**
/31- **6** *shd* **Lake Toya (USA)**[319] 6333 5-9-1 103 KerrinMcEvoy 1 97
(Saeed Bin Suroor) *lw: chsd ldr 4f: rdn over 2f out: styd on same pce fnl f* **6/1**[3]

2254 **7** *1* **Sudoor**[31] 4633 3-8-9 100 RHills 3 95
(J L Dunlop) *hld up in tch: nt clr run 2f out: swtchd lft: no ex ins fnl f* **14/1**
2033 **8** *½* **Russian Rosie (IRE)**[24] 4849 3-8-9 96 JamesDoyle 7 94
(J G Portman) *prom: chsd ldr 6f out: ev ch over 2f out: wknd ins fnl f* **25/1**
0-50 **9** *½* **Chatila (USA)**[24] 4849 4-9-1 86 RobertHavlin 2 93
(J H M Gosden) *hld up: hdwy over 3f out: wknd ins fnl f* **66/1**
3536 **10** *1 ¼* **Glitter Baby (IRE)**[44] 4238 4-9-1 91 JimmyQuinn 12 91
(M G Quinlan) *chsd ldrs: rdn and ev ch over 2f out: wknd fnl f* **100/1**
0316 **11** *2 ½* **Sunlight (IRE)**[17] 5067 3-8-9 87 LiamJones 14 86
(M A Jarvis) *s.i.s: hld up: rdn and hung lft over 2f out: n.d* **66/1**
5642 **12** *1* **Marzelline (IRE)**[23] 4887 3-8-9 100 AdamKirby 4 84
(W R Swinburn) *lw: sn led: rdn and hdd over 2f out: wknd over 1f out* **25/1**
220 **13** *3* **Athenian Way (IRE)**[66] 3576 3-8-9 0 JamieSpencer 9 78
(J R Fanshawe) *hld up: rdn over 3f out: hung lft: wknd over 1f out: eased fnl f* **15/2**

2m 7.31s (-0.79) **Going Correction** +0.225s/f (Good)
WFA 3 from 4yo+ 6lb **13** Ran SP% **122.6**
Speed ratings (Par 108): **112,110,110,110,109 109,108,108,108,107 105,104,101**
CSF £29.64 TOTE £4.40: £1.50, £4.30, £1.70; EX 34.10 Trifecta £195.00 Pool £519.19 - 1.89 winning units..
Owner Jaber Abdullah **Bred** L L C Woodside Farms **Trained** Newmarket, Suffolk
■ Stewards' Enquiry : Ryan Moore caution: careless riding

FOCUS
Solid enough Listed-race form rated around the runner-up and fourth and backed up by a decent time.

NOTEBOOK
Samira Gold(FR), who won nicely at Goodwood last time, looks a progressive filly and was put in a position where she could wind up her challenge from a long way out. She came unstuck when unlucky in running over this course and distance back in July, but got a clear run this time and won well. Another two furlongs will not inconvenience her and she can win at Group 3 level. (op 5-2)
Shorthand, ridden more patiently this time, had enough ease in the ground to return to her best and post a sound effort. She has not hit the heigths some expected this season but is still capable of winning at this level, and softer ground this autumn could see her off the mark for the year. (op 11-1 tchd 9-1)
Reunite(IRE) was runner-up in a Group 3 race on her final start last season and looked the one to beat at this level despite not having run since. She ran well and, if her trainer can get any improvement out of her for this outing, she could well be winning again soon. (op 9-4 tchd 11-4, 3-1 in places)
Sell Out, runner-up at this level at Salisbury last time, does not mind a bit of give in the ground and, although she had a bit to find strictly on the ratings, she has progressed into a very useful filly this season and put up another fine performance. (op 28-1 tchd 20-1)
Mont Etoile(IRE), visored for the first time, has not run to the level that saw her win the Ribblesdale last term for a while now. This trip is on the short side for her and, although she was staying on well at the finish, she never got a sniff at a place. (op 14-1)
Lake Toya(USA), another Godolphin inmate making a belated seasonal reappearance, had every chance based on her win in similar company last autumn, but softer ground suits her ideally and she came up short. She is capable of better than this and might improve for the run. (op 15-2 tchd 11-2)
Sudoor, whose season has tailed off rather, did not enjoy the best of luck in running. (op 16-1)
Chatila(USA) shaped a bit better than her finishing position suggests and always has the option of returning to handicap company.

5545 SEA-DEER H'CAP — 1m 3y
5:05 (5:05) (Class 4) (0-85,85) 3-Y-0+
£6,232 (£1,866; £933; £467; £233; £117) **Stalls** High

Form RPR
4323 **1** **Fondled**[32] 4608 3-8-13 80 JamieSpencer 1 91
(J R Fanshawe) *s.i.s: hld up: hdwy over 1f out: rdn to ld ins fnl f: r.o* **3/1**[2]
0310 **2** *½* **Trivia (IRE)**[33] 4587 3-7-11 71 KMay(7) 6 81
(N A Callaghan) *lw: hld up: hdwy and nt clr run over 1f out: r.o wl* **50/1**
0511 **3** *½* **Officer**[12] 5203 3-8-12 79 (v) RyanMoore 4 88
(Sir Michael Stoute) *lw: chsd ldr: led and hung lft fr over 2f out: sn rdn: hdd and hung rt ins fnl f: styd on same pce* **15/8**[1]
0303 **4** *½* **Boundless Prospect (USA)**[7] 5338 8-8-3 71 oh3 NicolPolli(5) 11 79
(Miss Gay Kelleway) *hld up: hdwy over 3f out: ev ch over 2f out: no ex ins fnl f* **33/1**
0-01 **5** *nk* **Habshan (USA)**[102] 2469 7-9-8 85 GeorgeBaker 10 92
(C F Wall) *hld up: r.o ins fnl f: nt rch ldrs* **10/1**
1162 **6** *¾* **Sam's Secret**[11] 5230 5-8-12 78 PJMcDonald(3) 5 83
(G A Swinbank) *lw: hld up in tch: rdn over 1f out: styd on* **15/2**[3]
4331 **7** *¾* **Sonny Parkin**[33] 4587 5-8-6 76 (v) EddieSemaan(7) 3 80
(G A Huffer) *hld up: hdwy over 2f out: rdn and hung lft over 1f out: no ex fnl f* **20/1**
6155 **8** *3 ½* **Furbeseta**[24] 4848 3-8-11 78 SebSanders 2 74
(L M Cumani) *chsd ldrs: rdn and ev ch over 2f out: wknd fnl f* **17/2**
0040 **9** *nk* **Councellor (FR)**[11] 5221 5-8-10 73 (t) TPQueally 12 68
(Stef Liddiard) *trckd ldrs: plld hrd: rdn over 2f out: wknd over 1f out* **12/1**
101 **10** *½* **Resplendent Nova**[21] 4949 5-8-13 76 JimmyQuinn 7 70
(P Howling) *chsd ldrs: rdn whn hmpd over 2f out: wknd over 1f out* **14/1**
0230 **11** *¾* **Leptis Magna**[19] 5012 3-8-6 76 MarcHalford(3) 9 68
(D R C Elsworth) *hld up: rdn over 2f out: sn edgd lft and wknd* **20/1**
0060 **12** *½* **Valdan (IRE)**[23] 4898 3-8-11 78 (t) SteveDrowne 13 69
(M A Barnes) *led over 5f: wknd over 1f out* **66/1**

1m 41.08s (1.18) **Going Correction** +0.225s/f (Good)
WFA 3 from 5yo+ 4lb **12** Ran SP% **121.4**
Speed ratings (Par 105): **103,102,102,101,101 100,99,96,95,95 94,94**
CSF £164.61 CT £366.14 TOTE £5.60: £1.90, £10.20, £1.40; EX 209.80 Trifecta £301.80 Pool £573.97 - 1.35 winning units..
Owner Cheveley Park Stud **Bred** Cheveley Park Stud Ltd **Trained** Newmarket, Suffolk

FOCUS
A fairly competitive handicap with the first three relatively unexposed and the form rated positively around the fourth and fifth.
Valdan(IRE) Official explanation: jockey said gelding felt wrong in closing stages

5546 WORDINGHAM PLANT HIRE H'CAP — 7f 3y
5:35 (5:35) (Class 6) (0-60,60) 3-Y-0+ **£2,914** (£867; £433; £216) **Stalls** High

Form RPR
3060 **1** **Border Artist**[23] 4879 8-8-13 52 JimmyQuinn 4 65
(J Pearce) *hld up: hdwy over 1f out: led ins fnl f: r.o wl* **15/2**[3]
200 **2** *3 ½* **Mugeba**[24] 4856 6-8-10 54 (t) NicolPolli(5) 10 58
(Miss Gay Kelleway) *dwlt: hld up: rdn 2f out: hdwy and hung rt over 1f out: r.o* **8/1**
0040 **3** *shd* **Lincolneurocruiser**[10] 5253 5-9-7 60 (v) RHills 9 64
(Mrs N Macauley) *hld up: racd keenly: lost pl whn hmpd 1/2-way: hdwy over 1f out: r.o* **8/1**
5330 **4** *nk* **Oh So Saucy**[41] 4326 3-9-0 56 TPQueally 8 59
(C F Wall) *prom: rdn over 2f out: styd on* **16/1**
644 **5** *hd* **Pride Of Northcare (IRE)**[173] 826 3-8-11 60 EddieSemaan(7) 2 62
(G A Huffer) *mid-div: hdwy over 4f out: rdn over 1f out: styd on same pce ins fnl f* **25/1**
3660 **6** *½* **Feelin Irie (IRE)**[42] 4294 4-8-6 52 (p) HarryPoulton(7) 1 53
(J R Boyle) *racd alone far side tl jnd main gp 3f out: chsd ldrs: led over 2f out: rdn over 1f out: hdd and no ex ins fnl f* **20/1**
0240 **7** *1 ¼* **Postmaster**[16] 5094 5-8-9 48 RobertHavlin 3 46
(R Ingram) *hld up: hdwy over 2f out: no etxra fnl f* **17/2**
5006 **8** *½* **Royal Tavira Girl (IRE)**[6] 5348 4-8-12 51 TGMcLaughlin 14 47
(M G Quinlan) *dwlt: hld up: rdn over 2f out: n.d* **20/1**
2004 **9** *shd* **Favouring (IRE)**[50] 4042 5-8-4 46 (v) DominicFox(3) 11 42
(M C Chapman) *led over 4f: wknd fnl f* **20/1**
6004 **10** *nk* **Sea Willow (IRE)**[24] 4856 3-9-1 57 SteveDrowne 7 52
(D R C Elsworth) *chsd ldrs: lost pl 1/2-way: n.d after* **14/1**
4031 **11** *1 ¼* **Whistleupthewind**[9] 5275 4-9-3 56 6ex SebSanders 13 48
(J M P Eustace) *hld up: hdwy over 2f out: rdn and hung lft over 1f out: sn wknd* **4/1**[1]
-051 **12** *2 ½* **Wickedish**[41] 4337 3-8-13 55 (t) OscarUrbina 5 40
(M J Gingell) *chsd ldrs: hung lft over 4f out: rdn and wknd over 1f out* **10/1**
2010 **13** *2 ½* **Life's A Whirl**[42] 4295 5-9-6 59 (p) DMylonas 12 37
(Mrs C A Dunnett) *chsd ldrs: rdn 1/2-way: wknd wl over 1f out* **12/1**
2060 **14** *11* **Bodden Bay**[7] 5340 5-9-1 57 AndrewElliott(3) 6 6
(I W McInnes) *chsd ldr: rdn 1/2-way: wknd 2f out* **20/1**
60-0 **15** *14* **Pearl Of Esteem**[11] 5237 4-8-9 55 JCorrigan(7) 15 —
(Mrs C A Dunnett) *s.s: outpcd* **80/1**
0U30 **16** *¾* **Petito (IRE)**[23] 4879 4-9-5 58 JamesDoyle 17 —
(J L Spearing) *s.i.s: a in rr: rdn and wknd over 2f out* **7/1**[2]

1m 27.64s (1.04) **Going Correction** +0.225s/f (Good)
WFA 3 from 4yo+ 3lb **16** Ran SP% **130.5**
Speed ratings (Par 101): **103,99,98,98,98 97,96,95,95,95 93,91,88,75,59 58**
CSF £64.38 CT £515.30 TOTE £8.60: £2.80, £3.80, £3.30, £6.40; EX 57.20 Trifecta £188.00 Part won. Pool £264.80 - 0.10 winning units. Place 6 £13.14, Place 5 £11.69.
Owner B & G Racing & Friends **Bred** Chippenham Lodge Stud Ltd **Trained** Newmarket, Suffolk

FOCUS
Moderate handicap form in which the principals came from off the pace. Nevetheless, it looks sound enough with the third, fourth and fifth close to their marks.
Bodden Bay Official explanation: jockey said gelding hung left-handed throughout
Petito(IRE) Official explanation: jockey said gelding had no more to give
T/Plt: £20.90 to a £1 stake. Pool: £65,915.00. 2,293.50 winning tickets. T/Qpdt: £16.00 to a £1 stake. Pool: £3,023.10. 139.50 winning tickets. CR

5547 - 5549a (Foreign Racing) - See Raceform Interactive

4930 AYR (L-H)
Thursday, September 20

OFFICIAL GOING: Good to soft (good in places) changing to soft after race 6 (5.20)
The ground deteriorated and 'soft' on the round course, it soon turned 'good to soft or even softer' on the straight course.
Wind: Fresh, half against Weather: Overcast

5550 YOU CAN'T PREDICT FA MAIDEN AUCTION STKS — 6f
2:20 (2:22) (Class 5) 2-Y-0 **£3,886** (£1,156; £577; £288) **Stalls** High

Form RPR
0 **1** **Northern Bolt**[19] 5042 2-8-13 0 AdrianTNicholls 6 85+
(D Nicholls) *mde all: rdn 2f out: r.o strly fnl f* **12/1**
2 **2** *2* **Elizabeth Swann**[9] 5313 2-8-11 0 RyanMoore 2 77+
(R Hannon) *a cl up: effrt over 2f out: kpt on ins fnl f: nt rch wnr* **7/2**[2]
6434 **3** *3* **Daring Dream (GER)**[48] 4126 2-9-2 68 PatCosgrave 16 73
(T D Easterby) *chsd ldrs: rdn over 2f out: kpt on same pce over 1f out* **14/1**
03 **4** *1* **Hamish McGonagall**[13] 5192 2-8-11 0 DavidAllan 9 68+
(T D Easterby) *in tch: nt clr run fr 3f to 2f out: hdwy and swtchd lft over 1f out: kpt on: no imp* **13/8**[1]
5 *4* **Piverina (IRE)** 2-8-11 0 PhillipMakin 5 53+
(T D Barron) *s.i.s: sn in midfield: shkn up over 2f out: sn no imp* **33/1**
05 **6** *1 ½* **Safari Dancer (IRE)**[24] 4890 2-8-11 0 TomEaves 13 55+
(I Semple) *dwlt: hld up: shkn up 2f out: nvr nr ldrs* **20/1**
0 **7** *¾* **Sweet Mind**[13] 5194 2-8-6 0 PaulHanagan 1 41
(R A Fahey) *racd wd in midfield: rdn and wknd wl over 1f out* **33/1**
4230 **8** *1 ¼* **Dream Express (IRE)**[24] 4892 2-8-13 73 (b[1]) PaulMulrennan 3 45+
(M Dods) *dwlt: t.k.h and sn chsng ldrs: wkng whn n.m.r over 1f out* **14/1**
9 *1* **Emperors Jade** 2-8-13 0 AndrewElliott(3) 8 45
(A P Jarvis) *uns rdr to post: prom: pushed along and lost pl after 2f: n.d after* **7/1**[3]
00 **10** *½* **Kiowa Princess**[13] 5192 2-8-11 0 TonyHamilton 10 38
(M Dods) *hld up: shkn up over 2f out: n.d* **150/1**
11 *nk* **Forrest Star** 2-8-3 0 AndrewMullen(3) 15 32
(Miss L A Perratt) *missed break: a bhd* **80/1**
12 *5* **Riverside** 2-8-6 0 JimmyQuinn 4 17
(M Brittain) *missed break: nvr on terms* **100/1**
13 *½* **Chanteuse De Rue (IRE)** 2-8-6 0 GregFairley 11 16
(M Johnston) *bhd and sn outpcd: no ch fr 1/2-way* **11/1**
000 **14** *shd* **Magnushomestwo (IRE)**[45] 4221 2-8-6 41 PatrickMathers(3) 12 18
(A Berry) *in tch: n.m.r over 2f out: sn btn* **150/1**
15 *2* **Ridley Didley (IRE)** 2-8-11 0 GrahamGibbons 7 14
(N Wilson) *s.i.s: sn chsng ldrs: rdn and wknd fr 2f out* **66/1**
000 **16** *½* **Big Slick (IRE)**[84] 3024 2-8-9 51 DarryllHolland 14 11
(M Brittain) *chsd ldrs: n.m.r and lost pl over 4f out: no ch after* **100/1**

1m 13.18s (-0.49) **Going Correction** -0.025s/f (Good) **16** Ran SP% **118.9**
Speed ratings (Par 95): **102,99,95,94,88 86,85,84,82,82 81,74,74,74,71 70**
CSF £50.55 TOTE £20.80: £7.00, £1.60, £4.20; EX 137.70.
Owner Jim Dale/Jason Berry **Bred** Mrs C Regalado-Gonzalez **Trained** Sessay, N Yorks

FOCUS
An ordinary bunch on looks but an improved performance from the winner, who may be capable of better and the form looks solid rated through the third.

NOTEBOOK
Northern Bolt, who shaped as though a bit better than his debut form, jumped off on terms this time and left that form a long way behind. He should have no problems with 7f and is the type to improve again. (op 14-1)
Elizabeth Swann, who shaped well on her debut at Lingfield, ran up to that level on this easier surface. She should stay 7f and, although vulnerable to the more progressive types in this grade, she looks capable of winning a race. (op 5-2 tchd 9-4)

Daring Dream(GER) has had a few chances but is essentially a consistent sort and he looks a good guide to the worth of this form. He should have no problems with 7f and is capable of picking up a run-of-the-mill event. (op 25-1)

Hamish McGonagall, upped to 6f for the first time, did not enjoy the run of the race and he looks a fair bit better than the bare form of this contest. He is well worth another chance in similar company and looks sure to win a race. (op 6-4 tchd 7-4)

Piverina(IRE), the third foal of a 1m1f winner, was easy to back but was far from disgraced on this racecourse debut. She should be suited by the step up to 7f and will be of interest in ordinary handicap company in due course. (tchd 28-1)

Safari Dancer(IRE) ◆, dropped in trip, caught the eye without being knocked about and he is now qualified for a handicap mark. The return to 7f will be in his favour and, although his form so far is modest, he is one to keep an eye on. (op 25-1)

Dream Express(IRE) Official explanation: jockey said gelding ran too free in first-time blinkers

Ridley Didley(IRE) Official explanation: jockey said gelding ran too free early

Big Slick(IRE) Official explanation: jockey said colt suffered interference shortly after start

5551 TOTESPORT 0800 221 221 EBF NOVICE STKS 1m

2:50 (2:51) (Class 4) 2-Y-O **£5,829** (£1,734; £866; £432) **Stalls** Low

Form RPR

2232 **1** **Graceful Descent (FR)**[12] 5236 2-8-7 78 .... PaulHanagan 4 74
(R A Fahey) *led tl over 2f out: rallied fnl f: led last strides* **11/4**[2]

66 **2** *shd* **Ivestar (IRE)**[26] 4818 2-8-12 0 .... AdrianTNicholls 7 79
(D Nicholls) *chsd ldrs: hung rt bnd over 3f out: led jst ins fnl f: hdd post* **16/1**

4240 **3** *1 1/4* **Aaim To Storm (USA)**[50] 4057 2-9-0 83 .... DarryllHolland 2 78
(M R Channon) *trckd ldrs: t.k.h: effrt 3f out: led appr fnl f: hdd jst ins fnl f: nt qckn* **13/2**[3]

2210 **4** *1 1/4* **Shepherds Warning (IRE)**[17] 5096 2-8-3 55 ow1 .... SCreighton(5) 3 69
(N J Vaughan) *trckd ldrs: led over 2f out: hdd appr fnl f: kpt on same pce* **50/1**

5 *3* **Pondapie (IRE)** 2-8-5 0 .... MichaelJStainton(3) 9 62
(R M Whitaker) *s.i.s: in tch whn hmpd and lost pl after 2f: hdwy 2f out: styng on at fin* **18/1**

1 **6** *10* **Danzig Fox**[74] 3341 2-8-13 0 .... PJMcDonald(3) 8 48
(M Mullineaux) *hld up in rr: hmpd and lost pl after 2f: no threat after* **12/1**

7 *3/4* **Ibrox (IRE)** 2-8-8 0 .... PaulMulrennan 5 39
(R M Whitaker) *s.s: in rr: bhd fnl 3f* **50/1**

01 **F** **Redesignation (IRE)**[34] 4584 2-9-5 84 .... RyanMoore 1 —
(R Hannon) *hld up: trcking ldrs whn stmbld bdly and fell after 2f* **10/11**[1]

1m 45.34s (1.85) **Going Correction** +0.225s/f (Good) **8** Ran SP% **115.1**

Speed ratings (Par 97): **99,98,97,96,93 83,82,—**

CSF £45.16 TOTE £3.60: £1.10, £3.30, £1.50; EX 52.20.

Owner Miss S Bowles **Bred** Castleton Group **Trained** Musley Bank, N Yorks

FOCUS

With the favourite on the ground at an early stage this did not take a deal of winning with the fourth rated just 55. The race has been rated negatively round the first three.

NOTEBOOK

Graceful Descent(FR) is not very big but all heart. After making the running she fought back in the bravest possible fashion to snatch the prize almost on the line. Stamina will prove her strong point. (op 10-3 tchd 7-2)

Ivestar(IRE), taking a step up in trip and encountering much softer ground, gave a problem or two turning for home. He worked his way to the front only to miss out on the line. (op 12-1)

Aaim To Storm(USA), gelded since Goodwood, was keen to get on with it. After taking a narrow advantage in the end the first two proved too tough. He has had plenty of chances and looks something of a professional loser. (op 5-1 tchd 7-1)

Shepherds Warning(IRE), whose previous five outings were over the minimum trip, is only small. She went on and stuck on all the way to the line, and stamina was certainly not a problem.

Pondapie(IRE), who has plenty of size and scope, missed the break and was then knocked right back in the melee. He made up a fair amount of late ground and clearly possesses ability. (op 14-1)

Danzig Fox, who had stamina to prove, was effectively put out of the race at an early stage. (op 10-1)

Redesignation(IRE), noisy in the paddock, was quite keen to post. He took a tug and clipped heels and came down after two furlongs. (op 5-4 tchd 5-6 and 11-8 in places)

5552 YOU CAN'T PREDICT FA H'CAP 5f

3:20 (3:25) (Class 5) (0-70,70) 3-Y-O+ **£5,181** (£1,541; £770; £384) **Stalls** High

Form RPR

0444 **1** **Charles Parnell (IRE)**[22] 4934 4-9-3 **68** .... PhillipMakin 9 78
(M Dods) *in tch stands' side: hdwy over 1f out: led ins fnl f: hld on wl* **11/1**

4433 **2** *3/4* **Hotham**[9] 5297 4-8-13 **64** .... JimmyQuinn 7 71
(N Wilson) *midfield stands' side: effrt 2f out: rdr dropped whip ent fnl f: sn chsng wnr: kpt on fin* **8/1**[3]

2513 **3** *shd* **Howards Tipple**[29] 4719 3-9-0 **66** ....(p) TomEaves 16 73
(I Semple) *bhd stands' side: gd hdwy over 1f out: r.o fnl f: nrst fin* **12/1**

300 **4** *3/4* **Brut**[17] 5083 5-9-0 **65** ....(p) TonyHamilton 8 69
(D W Barker) *led stands' side tl hung lft and hdd ins fnl f: kpt on same pce* **33/1**

016 **5** *3/4* **Throw The Dice**[9] 5295 5-8-2 **56** oh2 ....(v) PatrickMathers(3) 1 58+
(A Berry) *racd w one other far side: gd spd thrght: no imp on stands' side ldrs last 75yds* **33/1**

2316 **6** *nk* **Funfair Wane**[28] 4734 8-9-0 **65** .... AdrianTNicholls 5 65+
(D Nicholls) *racd centre: gd spd tl edgd rt and no ex ent fnl f* **6/1**[1]

0153 **7** *1/2* **Lambency (IRE)**[3] 5489 4-8-1 **57** .... KellyHarrison(5) 11 56
(J S Goldie) *hld up: hdwy on stands' side over 1f out: nrst fin* **20/1**

0630 **8** *nk* **Ashes (IRE)**[35] 4525 5-8-8 **59** .... PaulMulrennan 12 57
(K R Burke) *chsd stands' side ldrs tl rdn and no ex over 1f out* **22/1**

3414 **9** *1* **Spiritual Peace (IRE)**[57] 3837 4-9-0 **65** ....(p) DarryllHolland 15 59
(K A Ryan) *midfield stands' side: drvn over 2f out: nvr rchd ldrs* **14/1**

0040 **10** *nk* **Strawberry Patch (IRE)**[9] 5295 8-8-5 **56** oh6 ....(p) GregFairley 17 49
(J S Goldie) *bhd on stands' side: rdn 1/2-way: sme late hdwy: nvr on terms* **25/1**

56 **11** *1* **Sandwith**[90] 2830 4-8-6 **60** ....(p) PJMcDonald(3) 18 49
(J S Wainwright) *prom stands' side tl no ex over 1f out* **11/1**

0050 **12** *nk* **Seafield Towers**[2] 5507 7-8-2 **56** oh11 ....(p) AndrewElliott(3) 19 44
(Miss L A Perratt) *chsd stands' side ldrs tl wknd fr 2f out* **28/1**

1034 **13** *nk* **Oeuf A La Neige**[3] 5476 7-8-2 **56** oh5 .... AndrewMullen(3) 3 43
(Miss L A Perratt) *racd w one other on far side: no imp fr 2f out* **22/1**

1560 **14** *1/2* **Rothesay Dancer**[3] 5481 4-8-11 **67** .... GaryBartley(5) 13 52
(J S Goldie) *hld up stands' side: rdn over 1f out: n.d* **25/1**

1400 **15** *shd* **Kings College Boy**[6] 5381 7-9-2 **67** ....(b) PaulHanagan 4 52
(R A Fahey) *prom centre: rdn over 2f out: no ex over 1f out* **20/1**

4005 **16** *hd* **Bond Boy**[27] 4780 10-9-0 **70** ....(p) SladeO'Hara(5) 2 54
(G R Oldroyd) *cl up centre tl wknd fr 2f out* **12/1**

0002 **17** *3/4* **Jadan (IRE)**[17] 5085 6-8-6 **57** oh8 ow1 .... DavidAllan 14 39
(E J Alston) *bhd on outside of stands' side gp: rdn 2f out: n.d* **12/1**

5150 **18** *2 1/2* **The History Man (IRE)**[19] 5029 4-9-0 **70** ....(b) SCreighton(5) 6 43
(M Mullineaux) *dwlt: racd centre to far side: a bhd* **9/1**

4315 **19** *9* **Gleaming Spirit (IRE)**[19] 5051 3-9-4 **70** .... PatCosgrave 10 10
(A P Jarvis) *prom on outside of stands' side gp tl wknd qckly fr 2f out* **15/2**[2]

60.85 secs (0.41) **Going Correction** -0.025s/f (Good)

WFA 3 from 4yo+ 1lb **19** Ran SP% **128.8**

Speed ratings (Par 103): **95,93,93,92,91 90,89,89,87,87 85,85,84,84,83 83,82,78,63**

CSF £85.70 CT £1127.02 TOTE £12.70: £2.60, £3.20, £2.90, £8.80; EX 129.50.

Owner C A Lynch **Bred** R And Mrs R Hodgins **Trained** Denton, Co Durham

FOCUS

An ordinary handicap in which the bulk of the runners came stands' side. The pace was sound throughout and the form looks solid rated around the first two.

Gleaming Spirit(IRE) Official explanation: jockey said gelding was unsuited by the good to soft ground

5553 JOHN SMITH'S EXTRA SMOOTH (S) STKS 1m 2f

3:50 (3:52) (Class 4) 3-Y-O+ **£6,477** (£1,927; £963; £481) **Stalls** Low

Form RPR

4003 **1** **Sweet World**[15] 5128 3-8-10 60 .... AndrewElliott(3) 11 69
(A P Jarvis) *mde all: edgd rt over 1f out: styd on wl towards fin* **10/1**

3031 **2** *1 1/4* **Brastar Jelois (FR)**[12] 5235 4-9-0 59 ....(p) GrahamGibbons 7 61
(R Hollinshead) *hld up in mid-div: hdwy over 3f out: wnt 2nd over 1f out: no ex ins fnl f* **5/1**[3]

4130 **3** *1 3/4* **Top Jaro (FR)**[29] 4716 4-9-5 66 .... TonyHamilton 8 63
(D W Barker) *sn chsng ldrs: styd on same pce appr fnl f* **11/2**

1260 **4** *1/2* **Tizzy May (FR)**[14] 5178 7-9-5 71 ....(p) TomEaves 13 62
(B Ellison) *chsd wnr: kpt on same pce appr fnl f* **10/3**[1]

062 **5** *1 1/4* **Prince Noel**[23] 4920 3-8-10 52 ....(b) JimmyQuinn 5 56
(N Wilson) *s.v.s: hdwy on wd outside over 2f out: nvr rchd ldrs* **11/1**

0600 **6** *2* **Daring Affair**[12] 5225 6-9-0 68 .... PaulMulrennan 2 50
(K R Burke) *trckd ldrs: one pce fnl 2f* **9/2**[2]

0214 **7** *1* **Dark Charm (FR)**[17] 5086 8-9-5 69 ....(p) PaulHanagan 12 53
(R A Fahey) *trckd ldrs: effrt over 2f out: nvr really threatened* **5/1**[3]

0604 **8** *3* **Touch Of Ivory (IRE)**[24] 4383 4-8-8 50 ....(b) PatrickMathers(3) 1 39
(P Monteith) *in rr: drvn over 4f out: nvr a factor* **14/1**

-640 **9** *3* **Flaming Cat (IRE)**[14] 5179 4-9-2 50 ....(p) PaddyAspell 4 38
(F Watson) *s.i.s: nvr on terms* **66/1**

3006 **10** *2* **Modarab**[90] 2824 5-8-13 56 .... PJMcDonald(3) 14 34
(Mrs L B Normile) *in rr: bhd fnl 3f* **33/1**

5020 **11** *43* **Frith (IRE)**[3] 5482 5-9-2 59 ....(p) PatCosgrave 3 —
(Mrs L B Normile) *chsd ldrs: reminders 7f out: lost pl 3f out: sn bhd: t.o* **40/1**

2m 12.78s (1.06) **Going Correction** +0.225s/f (Good)

WFA 3 from 4yo+ 6lb **11** Ran SP% **120.9**

Speed ratings (Par 105): **104,103,101,101,100 98,97,95,93,91 57**

CSF £60.65 TOTE £11.80: £2.80, £1.70, £2.20; EX 78.10.The winner was bought in for £10,500

Owner Geoffrey Bishop and Ann Jarvis **Bred** Natton House Thoroughbreds **Trained** Twyford, Bucks

FOCUS

A mixed bag in this much better than average seller and the first three home did not have obvious chances on their official ratings. The proximity of slow starter Prince Noel casts a big cloud over the exact value of the form.

Prince Noel Official explanation: jockey said gelding missed the break

Daring Affair Official explanation: jockey said mare was unsuited by the good to soft ground

5554 KNIGHT FRANK H'CAP (FOR THE KILKERRAN CUP) 1m 2f

4:20 (4:20) (Class 2) (0-100,97) 3-Y-O+ **£12,954** (£3,854; £1,926; £962) **Stalls** Low

Form RPR

1163 **1** **The Grey Berry**[32] 4640 3-8-5 **86** .... PaulHanagan 7 99+
(T D Walford) *hld up: hdwy whn n.m.r 2f out and appr fnl f: kpt on wl to ld cl home* **7/1**[3]

0600 **2** *nk* **Best Prospect (IRE)**[35] 4523 5-8-8 **83** oh1 ....(t) PhillipMakin 4 93
(M Dods) *hld up: smooth hdwy over 2f out: edgd lft and led ins fnl f: hdd nr fin* **13/2**[2]

2160 **3** *2* **Very Wise**[28] 4745 5-9-6 **95** .... PaulMulrennan 8 101
(W J Haggas) *in tch: effrt and edgd rt 2f out: ev ch ins fnl f: no ex last 75yds* **18/1**

1063 **4** *shd* **Smokey Oakey (IRE)**[20] 4993 3-8-5 **86** .... JimmyQuinn 11 92
(M H Tompkins) *chsd ldrs: effrt and led appr fnl f to ins fnl f: no ex* **7/2**[1]

0100 **5** *1* **Pevensey (IRE)**[29] 4722 5-9-8 **97** .... GrahamGibbons 5 101
(J J Quinn) *s.i.s: sn pushed along in rr: gd hdwy fnl 2f: nrst fin* **12/1**

44- **6** *nk* **Peculiar Prince (IRE)**[18] 5074 5-8-8 **83** .... PatCosgrave 1 86
(Liam McAteer, Ire) *cl up: led over 2f out to appr fnl f: no ex* **40/1**

0203 **7** *6* **Dan Dare (USA)**[19] 5049 4-8-11 **86** ....(v) TomEaves 3 77
(Sir Michael Stoute) *chsd ldrs: rdn and edgd lft 2f out: sn btn* **7/2**[1]

1025 **8** *1 1/4* **Rosbay (IRE)**[15] 5141 3-8-5 **86** .... DavidAllan 9 75
(T D Easterby) *set decent gallop to over 2f out: wknd over 1f out* **7/1**[3]

/400 **9** *8* **Troubadour (IRE)**[24] 4900 6-8-12 **90** .... PJMcDonald(3) 10 63
(W Jarvis) *midfield: drvn over 3f out: sn btn* **50/1**

10-3 **10** *1* **Descartes**[231] 329 5-9-7 **96** .... DarryllHolland 6 67
(Saeed Bin Suroor) *hld up: drvn along over 3f out: sn btn* **8/1**

3455 **11** *5* **Nanton (USA)**[29] 4720 5-8-3 **85** .... LanceBetts(7) 2 46
(N Wilson) *towards rr: rdn along 1/2-way: sn btn* **12/1**

2m 11.24s (-0.48) **Going Correction** +0.225s/f (Good)

WFA 3 from 4yo+ 6lb **11** Ran SP% **118.9**

Speed ratings (Par 109): **110,109,108,108,107 107,102,101,94,94 90**

CSF £52.68 CT £795.81 TOTE £8.30: £2.50, £2.00, £4.10; EX 60.40.

Owner N J Maher **Bred** G Deacon **Trained** Sheriff Hutton, N Yorks

FOCUS

A fair handicap in which the pace was sound throughout. The first two came from behind and the fourth is rated to form.

NOTEBOOK

The Grey Berry ◆ has progressed well this year and he turned in his best effort up to this trip for the first time. He is ideally suited by some cut in the ground and he is the type to win a decent handicap around this trip in due course. (op 8-1 tchd 10-1 in a place)

Best Prospect(IRE) had not been anywhere near his best this year but he had slipped to a very attractive mark and he was well supported. With the familiar patient tactics adopted once more after a surprisingly forceful ride at Beverley the time before he duly returned to form, but having cruised through looking sure to win he was caught close home, just as he had been in this race in 2006. He may not be entirely straightforward but is more than capable of winning a similar event. (op 6-1 tchd 7-1 in a place)

Very Wise, who went off too quickly at York on his previous start, was dropped out this time and returned to form. He goes well with give in the ground but has little margin for error from his current mark. (op 16-1 tchd 20-1)

Smokey Oakey(IRE), from a stable in tremendous form, had conditions to suit and ran up to his best. He fared the best of those ridden close to the decent gallop and is more than capable of winning a similar event around this trip from his current mark. (op 4-1 tchd 9-2 in a place)
Pevensey(IRE) ◆ shaped with a fair bit of promise over a trip that is a bare minimum. He will be suited by the return to 1m4f and, although having little margin for error from his current mark of 97, will be of interest in similar company back over that trip or when returned to hurdles. (op 11-1)
Peculiar Prince(IRE) returned to this trip for the first time since winning at the Curragh on his reappearance, fared a bit better than the bare form as he was up with the strong pace throughout. He may be best suited by a sound surface.
Dan Dare(USA), back on easy ground, was a disappointment and he looked anything but straightforward. He has the ability to win races from his current mark but does not look one to be placing too much faith in. (tchd 4-1 in a place)
Descartes ran a stinker, even allowing for the fact that he had been off the track since the Dubai Carnival. Official explanation: jockey said horse hung right-handed throughout (op 7-1 tchd 6-1)

5555 W&D MCCULLOCH RAIL DIVISION H'CAP — 1m
4:50 (4:52) (Class 5) (0-70,67) 3-Y-O — **£4,533** (£1,348; £674; £336) **Stalls** Low

Form — RPR
1 **Nans Best (IRE)**[15] 5149 3-9-4 **67** PatCosgrave 11 — 75
(Liam McAteer, Ire) *trckd ldrs: hdwy 3f out: led jst ins fnl f: edgd lft: hld on towards fin* **18/1**
0040 2 ½ **Dark Energy**[67] 3570 3-8-13 **62** PaulHanagan 9 — 69
(B Smart) *s.i.s: hdwy over 3f out: chsng ldrs 1f out: kpt on towards fin* **14/1**
326 3 2 **Ducal Pip Squeak**[53] 3997 3-9-2 **65** PhillipMakin 12 — 67
(M Dods) *chsd ldrs: led over 1f out: hdd jst ins fnl f: no ex* **9/1**
3010 4 1 ¼ **Grethel (IRE)**[5] 5405 3-8-12 **61** 6ex TonyHamilton 8 — 61
(A Berry) *prom: effrt on outside 3f out: styd on same pce appr fnl f* **50/1**
0010 5 shd **Bold Indian (IRE)**[20] 4998 3-9-2 **65** TomEaves 6 — 64
(I Semple) *mid-div: hdwy 3f out: styd on fnl f* **10/1**
-165 6 ½ **Vesuvio**[37] 4480 3-8-8 **60** PJMcDonald(3) 4 — 58
(C W Thornton) *chsd ldrs: effrt on ins over 2f out: one pce* **7/1**[3]
505 7 1 **Wilmington**[21] 4971 3-8-12 **64** AndrewMullen(3) 5 — 60
(Mrs J C McGregor) *chsd ldrs: one pce fnl 2f* **100/1**
2060 8 ½ **Run Free**[38] 4450 3-9-2 **65** GrahamGibbons 2 — 60
(N Wilson) *led tl over 1f out: wknd ins fnl f* **20/1**
110 9 4 **Tina's Ridge (IRE)**[33] 4287 3-8-13 **62** (p) JimmyQuinn 13 — 47
(R Hollinshead) *in rr: hdwy over 2f out: wknd appr fnl f* **16/1**
0134 10 nk **Kunte Kinteh**[37] 4480 3-9-2 **65** AdrianTNicholls 3 — 50
(D Nicholls) *chsd ldr: rdn 3f out: hung rt: wknd 1f out* **7/1**[3]
152 11 5 **Tremelo Pointe (IRE)**[16] 5122 3-9-4 **67** DarryllHolland 10 — 40
(H Morrison) *sn trcking ldrs: effrt over 2f out: hung lft and sn btn* **9/4**[1]
0434 12 12 **Onatopp (IRE)**[12] 5230 3-9-4 **67** DavidAllan 7 — 13
(T D Easterby) *in rr: sn drvn along: bhd fnl 2f* **6/1**[2]
1160 13 1 ¼ **Kiss Chase (IRE)**[22] 4936 3-8-6 **60** (b) GaryBartley(5) 1 — 3
(J S Goldie) *in rr: rdn over 3f out: sn bhd* **12/1**
30-U 14 20 **Stay Active (USA)**[17] 5084 3-8-11 **60** PaulMulrennan 14 — —
(I Semple) *swtchd lft s: in rr: bhd fnl 3f: t.o* **50/1**

1m 45.69s (2.20) **Going Correction** +0.225s/f (Good) **14** Ran SP% **124.3**
Speed ratings (Par 101): **98,97,95,94,94 93,92,92,88,87 82,70,69,49**
CSF £252.14 CT £2436.66 TOTE £16.70: £3.70, £3.90, £3.40; EX 242.30.
Owner Frank Cosgrove **Bred** Mrs Brid Cosgrove **Trained** Navan, Co Meath
■ There was a downpour before this race and the jockeys reported the ground on the round course had turned soft.

FOCUS
A low-grade handicap not much better than a seller and rated around the placed horses.
Kunte Kinteh Official explanation: jockey said gelding hung right-handed in home straight
Tremelo Pointe(IRE) Official explanation: jockey said filly hung left

5556 BURNS MALL KILMARNOCK H'CAP — 7f 50y
5:20 (5:21) (Class 5) (0-70,74) 3-Y-O+ — **£4,533** (£1,348; £674; £336) **Stalls** Low

Form — RPR
0012 1 **Sands Of Barra (IRE)**[3] 5476 4-8-10 **62** AndrewElliott(3) 5 — 75+
(I W McInnes) *prom gng wl: led on bit 2f out: rdn and r.o wl fnl f* **10/3**[1]
0054 2 1 ¾ **Crocodile Bay (IRE)**[8] 5330 4-9-5 **68** AdrianTNicholls 8 — 76
(D Nicholls) *hld up in midfield: hdwy to chal over 1f out: kpt on same pce ins fnl f* **13/2**[3]
0122 3 2 ½ **Mystical Ayr (IRE)**[29] 4716 5-9-2 **65** PhillipMakin 13 — 67
(Miss L A Perratt) *hld up: hdwy over 2f out: chsd ldrs over 1f out: kpt on same pce* **6/1**[2]
5411 4 nk **Esoterica (IRE)**[12] 5228 4-9-1 **69** (b) GaryBartley(5) 12 — 70
(J S Goldie) *bhd and sn drvn along: hdwy on outside 2f out: kpt on fnl f: nrst fin* **8/1**
6150 5 nk **Poppy's Rose**[32] 4642 3-8-12 **64** PaulMulrennan 14 — 64
(I W McInnes) *hld up: hdwy over 2f out: hung lft over 1f out: no imp* **33/1**
0541 6 ½ **Neon Blue**[11] 5253 6-9-8 **74** 6ex (v) MichaelJStainton(3) 4 — 73+
(R M Whitaker) *prom: rdn and hung lft whn n.m.r over 2f out: sddle slipped and eased fnl f* **8/1**
1560 7 nk **Dorn Dancer (IRE)**[11] 5253 5-8-13 **62** PatCosgrave 11 — 60
(D W Barker) *hld up: hdwy over 2f out: no further imp over 1f out* **16/1**
0-50 8 1 **Sea Storm (IRE)**[13] 5196 9-9-4 **70** PJMcDonald(3) 10 — 66
(James Moffatt) *in tch: lost pl 1/2-way: rallied over 1f out: nt pce to chal* **28/1**
0020 9 3 ½ **Fair Shake (IRE)**[53] 3999 7-8-12 **61** (v) GregFairley 2 — 48
(Karen McLintock) *bhd: rdn over 3f out: nvr rchd ldrs* **16/1**
-400 10 ¾ **Opal Noir**[20] 4999 3-9-4 **70** TomEaves 9 — 55
(I Semple) *prom: rdn over 3f out: wknd over 1f out* **20/1**
0110 11 hd **Mozakhraf (USA)**[40] 4381 5-9-2 **65** DarryllHolland 3 — 49
(K A Ryan) *chsd ldr tl wknd fr 2f out* **12/1**
1345 12 2 **Gap Princess (IRE)**[12] 5238 3-8-13 **65** PaulHanagan 1 — 44
(R A Fahey) *in tch on ins: rdn whn n.m.r over 2f out: wknd over 1f out* **8/1**
0000 13 1 ¼ **Campo Bueno (FR)**[53] 4006 5-8-10 **62** (b) PatrickMathers(3) 6 — 38
(A Berry) *towards rr: drvn over 3f out: nvr on terms* **25/1**
0100 14 3 ½ **Wahoo Sam (USA)**[8] 5330 7-9-3 **66** (p) TonyHamilton 7 — 33
(D W Barker) *led to 2f out: sn rdn and wknd* **25/1**

1m 33.96s (1.24) **Going Correction** +0.225s/f (Good)
WFA 3 from 4yo+ 3lb **14** Ran SP% **122.3**
Speed ratings (Par 103): **101,99,96,95,95 94,94,93,89,88 88,86,84,80**
CSF £22.52 CT £132.57 TOTE £4.70: £2.50, £2.40, £2.20; EX 37.50 Place 6 £2221.32, Place 5 £ 718.32.
Owner Wold Construction Company **Bred** Sunderland Holdings Inc **Trained** Catwick, E Yorks

FOCUS
An ordinary handicap and one in which the pace was soon sound. The form looks solid with the runner-up to recent form.
Neon Blue Official explanation: jockey said saddle slipped
T/Jkpt: Not won. T/Plt: £1,704.50 to a £1 stake. Pool: £76,938.75. 32.95 winning tickets. T/Qpdt: £259.60 to a £1 stake. Pool: £4,701.30. 13.40 winning tickets. RY

[4636] PONTEFRACT (L-H)
Thursday, September 20

OFFICIAL GOING: Firm (good to firm in places; 8.8)
Wind: Virtually nil Weather: Sunny periods

5557 BETFAIR.COM APPRENTICE SERIES (ROUND 4) H'CAP — 1m 2f 6y
2:30 (2:30) (Class 5) (0-70,70) 3-Y-O+ — **£3,886** (£1,156; £577; £288) **Stalls** Low

Form — RPR
-163 1 **Sumner (IRE)**[10] 5279 3-9-2 **70** AshleyMorgan(7) 7 — 79+
(M H Tompkins) *trckd ldrs: smooth hdwy 3f out: led over 1f out: clr ins fnl f: styd on wl* **5/1**[2]
3-00 2 3 **Boppys Pride**[27] 4772 4-8-11 **55** JamesRogers(3) 9 — 58
(R A Fahey) *chsd ldrs: rdn along and sltly outpcd over 2f out: styd on on inner appr fnl f: kpt on wl u.p towards fin* **9/1**
0503 3 shd **Jackie Kiely**[9] 5307 6-9-10 **65** (t) WJCafferty 3 — 68
(R Brotherton) *hld up: hdwy and pushed along 4f out: hdwy on wd outside wl over 1f out: styd on ins fnl f* **9/2**[1]
5420 4 nk **Moment Of Clarity**[9] 5300 5-8-11 **52** oh1 (p) DanielleMcCreery 12 — 54
(R C Guest) *hld up in rr: stdy hdwy over 3f out: rdn to chse ldrs over 1f out: kpt on u.p ins fnl f* **10/1**
3621 5 nk **Thornaby Green**[34] 4582 6-9-8 **63** DeanHeslop 1 — 65
(T D Barron) *led: clr after 3f: rdn along 2f out: hdd over 1f out: sn drvn and wknd ins fnl f* **5/1**[2]
4012 6 1 ¼ **Kindlelight Blue (IRE)**[28] 4742 3-9-8 **69** MCGeran 8 — 68
(N P Littmoden) *stdd s: hld up and bhd tl styd on fnl 2f* **7/1**[3]
6530 7 hd **Magnum Opus (IRE)**[5] 5426 5-9-2 **57** (bt[1]) SophieDoyle 11 — 56
(D J Murphy) *bhd tl sme late hdwy* **25/1**
0004 8 7 **Anything Once (USA)**[1] 5525 4-8-4 **52** oh1 (b) GaryWales(7) 5 — 37
(D Carroll) *chsdc ldrs: rdn along over 3f out and sn wknd* **16/1**
5515 9 9 **Nota Liberata**[24] 4197 3-9-4 **65** (t) WilliamCarson 2 — 32
(G M Moore) *chsd ldng pair: rdn along 3f out: wknd over 2f out* **17/2**
206 10 ¾ **Emperor's Well**[26] 4817 8-9-8 **66** NSLawes(3) 10 — 31
(M W Easterby) *chsd ldrs: rdn along over 2f out: sn wknd* **12/1**
4006 11 20 **Fairly Honest**[9] 5310 3-8-7 **54** JamieHamblett 6 — —
(P W Hiatt) *chsd clr ldr: rdn along wl over 2f out: sn wknd* **14/1**

2m 12.24s (-1.84) **Going Correction** -0.125s/f (Firm)
WFA 3 from 4yo+ 6lb **11** Ran SP% **117.7**
Speed ratings (Par 103): **102,99,99,99,99 98,97,92,85,84 68**
CSF £49.65 CT £218.93 TOTE £6.60: £2.00, £3.10, £1.70; EX 55.10.
Owner Mrs Beryl Lockey **Bred** Liam Ormsby **Trained** Newmarket, Suffolk
■ Ashley Morgan was riding his first winner.

FOCUS
It seemed to be an advantage to race prominently in what was modest handicap but with the pace reasonable the form looks sound rated around the third and fourth.
Kindlelight Blue(IRE) Official explanation: jockey said gelding missed the break and stumbled 2 1/2f out
Fairly Honest Official explanation: vet said gelding was struck into

5558 READ HUNT INSURANCE BROKERS MEDIAN AUCTION MAIDEN STKS — 5f
3:00 (3:01) (Class 5) 2-Y-O — **£3,886** (£1,156; £577; £288) **Stalls** Low

Form — RPR
1 **Candela Bay (IRE)** 2-8-12 0 SebSanders 3 — 74+
(W J Haggas) *trckd ldr: hdwy 2f out: swtchd rt and rdn to chal over 1f out: led ins fnl f: pushed out* **10/3**[2]
6330 2 1 **Paddy Jack**[7] 5365 2-9-3 69 TPQueally 2 — 72
(J R Weymes) *led: rdn along 2f out: drvn and hdd ins fnl f: kpt on* **3/1**[1]
0 3 3 ½ **Resounding Glory (USA)**[50] 4076 2-9-3 0 StephenDonohoe 1 — 59
(R A Fahey) *towards rr: hdwy over 2f out: sn rdn and styd on ins fnl f: nrst fin* **5/1**
4 5 **Bourbon Balistic** 2-9-3 0 RoystonFfrench 5 — 41
(Mrs A Duffield) *prom: rdn along over 2f out: sn wknd* **4/1**[3]
5 hd **Laureldean Breeze (USA)** 2-8-12 0 DaleGibson 9 — 36
(R A Fahey) *dwlt and bhd: hdwy 2f out: sn rdn and no imp* **16/1**
0 6 3 ½ **Steph The Ref**[124] 1848 2-8-7 0 NataliaGemelova(5) 4 — 23
(R M Whitaker) *prom: rdn along over 2f out: sn wknd* **20/1**
00 7 3 **James's Lass (IRE)**[19] 5042 2-8-12 0 SilvestreDeSousa 7 — 12
(R A Fahey) *outpcd and bhd: hmpd wl over 1f out: nvr a factor* **50/1**
8 8 **Fantasy Fighter (IRE)** 2-9-3 0 MickyFenton 8 — —
(J J Quinn) *s.i.s: a bhd* **17/2**
00 P **Memphis Kate**[63] 3687 2-8-12 0 KDarley 6 — —
(M L W Bell) *chsd ldrs: rdn along over 2f out: hung rt and lost action wl over 1f out: sn p.u: dead* **8/1**

63.26 secs (-0.54) **Going Correction** -0.125s/f (Firm) **9** Ran SP% **119.0**
Speed ratings (Par 95): **99,97,91,83,83 77,73,60,—**
CSF £14.29 TOTE £3.40: £1.50, £1.40, £1.40; EX 11.20.
Owner Mrs A Goddard & M Hawkes **Bred** Piercetown Stud **Trained** Newmarket, Suffolk
■ Stewards' Enquiry : T P Queally caution: used whip with excessive force

FOCUS
A moderate maiden rated through the runner-up and backed up by the time.

NOTEBOOK
Candela Bay(IRE), a half-sister to Baron's Pit, comes from a yard whose juveniles often need a run to set them straight, but looked fit enough for this debut. She had been found a weak opening and picked up well once switched to win a shade comfortably. She is unlikely to prove anything other than useful, but could progress further in handicaps. (op 7-2 tchd 3-1)
Paddy Jack flopped on his recent handicap debut at Wolverhampton, but he was able to dominate in this less-competitive contest and ran well, just finding the one too good. He can he given another chance back in nurseries. (op 7-2)
Resounding Glory(USA), a big strong type who showed bright early speed before fading over 6f on debut, soon found himself towards the rear this time, but he ran on nicely in the straight and is likely to prove suited by a return to further. He could be one for nurseries. (op 7-1)
Bourbon Balistic, a 20,000gns son of Piccolo, looked as though he would be better for the race and ran well to a point, but is bred to stay further than this in time and it is likely the run was needed. (op 3-1 tchd 9-2)
Laureldean Breeze(USA), the Fahey second-string, looked as though the race would do her good and she showed her inexperience early, but did not shape too badly in the end and a step up in distance is going to be a big help.
Fantasy Fighter(IRE), noisy in the paddock, gave the impression he would be better for the race. (op 9-1 tchd 8-1)

Memphis Kate had not shown a great deal in two previous runs and she again looked likely to play a minor role. Soon prominent, she lost her action over a furlong out and her rider was quick to pulled her up. Sadly she had to be put down. (op 17-2 tchd 9-1)

5559 SUBSCRIBE TO RACING UK ON 08700 50 69 57 H'CAP 1m 4y
3:30 (3:42) (Class 5) (0-75,73) 3-Y-0+ **£5,181** (£1,541; £770; £384) **Stalls** Low

Form RPR

6003 **1** **Malinsa Blue (IRE)**[14] 5159 5-8-12 **63**........................(p) J-PGuillambert 3 72
(B Ellison) *trckd ldrs on inner: hdwy 2f out: rdn over 1f out: led wl ins fnl f: kpt on* **8/1**

0534 **2** *1/2* **Titinius (IRE)**[12] 5228 7-8-10 **61**.............................. KDarley 6 69
(Micky Hammond) *trckd ldrs: swtchd lft 2f out and sn rdn along: hdwy on inner to chal ins fnl f: ev ch tl drvn: hdd and nt qckn towards fin* **16/1**

4056 **3** *3/4* **Aggravation**[14] 5166 5-9-1 **69**.............................. MarcHalford(3) 11 75+
(D R C Elsworth) *dwlt and hld up in rr: hdwy 2f out: rdn and styd on ins fnl f: nrst fin* **14/1**

4311 **4** *3/4* **Palmetto Point**[23] 4918 3-8-12 **70**........................(p) TravisBlock(3) 12 74
(H Morrison) *cl up: effrt over 2f out: rdn over 1f out and ev ch tl drvn and one pce ins fnl f* **13/2**[2]

0000 **5** *nk* **Hula Ballew**[12] 5230 7-9-7 **72**.............................. TPQueally 4 76
(M Dods) *in tch: pushed along and outpcd over 2f out: swtchd outside and rdn over 1f out: styd on ins fnl f: nrst fin* **8/1**

0050 **6** *nk* **Exit Smiling**[8] 5339 5-9-8 **73**.............................. MickyFenton 14 76
(P T Midgley) *sn led: rdn over 2f out: drvn over 1f out: hdd & wknd wl ins fnl f* **12/1**

2634 **7** *hd* **Silent Applause**[14] 5166 4-8-12 **68**........................(v) LukeMorris(5) 15 71
(Dr J D Scargill) *chsd ldrs on outer: rdn along over 2f out: sn drvn and kpt on same pce* **15/2**[3]

0000 **8** *1/2* **Happy As Larry (USA)**[156] 1083 5-9-3 **73**..............(t) JamesO'Reilly(5) 1 74+
(D J Murphy) *towards rr: hdwy on inner whn hmpd 2f out: sn rdn and kpt on same pce ins fnl f* **22/1**

1464 **9** *2 1/2* **Champain Sands (IRE)**[22] 4932 8-9-0 **65**.............. StephenDonohoe 8 61
(E J Alston) *in rr tl styd on fnl 2f: nvr a factor* **11/1**

3425 **10** *1/2* **Zelos (IRE)**[16] 5122 3-8-2 **64**........................(b) MCGeran(7) 2 59
(D J S Ffrench Davis) *a towards rr* **12/1**

5100 **11** *3 1/2* **Wasalat (USA)**[12] 5230 5-9-5 **70**.............................. RoystonFfrench 13 56
(D W Barker) *a towards rr* **40/1**

5003 **12** *3/4* **Personify**[24] 4880 5-9-4 **69**........................(p) AdamKirby 5 54
(C G Cox) *prom: rdn along 3f out: wknd wl over 1f out: b.b.v* **11/2**[1]

4315 **13** *3* **Princess Lavinia**[17] 5086 4-9-2 **67**.............................. SebSanders 9 45
(G Wragg) *prom: rdn along over 3f out and sn wknd* **12/1**

6406 **14** *1/2* **Tough Love**[12] 5228 8-8-11 **65**........................(tp) DuranFentiman(3) 7 42
(T D Easterby) *in tch: rdn along over 2f out: grad wknd* **25/1**

0000 **15** *1* **It's A Dream (FR)**[12] 5228 4-8-13 **64**.............................. DaleGibson 10 38
(M W Easterby) *a towards rr* **16/1**

1m 44.42s (-1.28) **Going Correction** -0.125s/f (Firm)
WFA 3 from 4yo+ 4lb **15 Ran SP% 123.2**
Speed ratings (Par 103): **101,100,99,99,98 98,98,97,95,94 91,90,87,86,85**
CSF £129.21 CT £1817.60 TOTE £10.50: £3.20, £4.90, £5.10; EX 191.40.
Owner Mrs Andrea M Mallinson **Bred** Martin Donovan **Trained** Norton, N Yorks
■ Stewards' Enquiry : M C Geran one-day ban: careless riding (Oct 1)

FOCUS
A modest but competitive handicap and once again there seemed to be an advantage for those who raced prominently. The form is rated at face value despite doubts about its solidity.
Personify Official explanation: trainer's rep said gelding had bled from the nose

5560 PONTEFRACT PARK FILLIES' H'CAP 6f
4:00 (4:07) (Class 3) (0-90,86) 3-Y-0+
£9,348 (£2,799; £1,399; £700; £349; £175) **Stalls** Low

Form RPR

410 **1** **Lady Lily (IRE)**[7] 5356 3-9-6 **86**.............................. TPQueally 6 91
(H R A Cecil) *a.p: effrt to chal wl over 1f out: rdn to ld ins fnl f: sn drvn and hld on gamely* **9/2**[3]

0500 **2** *hd* **Mango Music**[7] 5356 4-9-4 **82**.............................. LDettori 2 87
(M R Channon) *led: qcknd 2f out: jnd and rdn over 1f out: hdd ins fnl f: rallied and ev ch tl drvn and no ex nr fin* **11/2**

110 **3** *3* **Perfect Treasure (IRE)**[20] 5012 4-8-11 **75**.............................. RobertHavlin 5 70
(J A R Toller) *hld up in tch: hdwy 2f out: sn rdn and kpt on same pce ent fnl f* **7/1**

0142 **4** *nk* **Nadawat (USA)**[17] 5092 3-9-5 **85**.............................. SebSanders 7 79
(J L Dunlop) *hld up in tch: effrt and hdwy over 2f out: sn rdn and no imp fr over 1f out* **2/1**[1]

0015 **5** *1/2* **Hazelhurst (IRE)**[22] 4942 4-8-6 **70** oh2.............................. RoystonFfrench 4 63
(J Howard Johnson) *prom: rdn along over 3f out: wknd over 2f out* **16/1**

-102 **6** *3 1/2* **La Matanza**[37] 4479 4-8-13 **77**.............................. PaulFessey 1 59
(T D Barron) *trckd ldng pair: pushed along over 2f out: rdn and edgd lft 1 1/2f out: sn wknd* **5/1**[3]

0400 **7** *1* **Keyaki (IRE)**[14] 5168 6-8-13 **82**.............................. PatrickHills(5) 8 60+
(C F Wall) *s.i.s and bhd: sme hdwy on inner whn hmpd 1 1/2f out: n.d* **8/1**

1m 15.12s (-2.28) **Going Correction** -0.125s/f (Firm)
WFA 3 from 4yo+ 2lb **7 Ran SP% 113.1**
Speed ratings (Par 104): **110,109,105,105,104 100,98**
CSF £28.36 CT £168.66 TOTE £5.30: £2.10, £3.10; EX 32.20.
Owner Diamond Racing Ltd **Bred** Owen Bourke **Trained** Newmarket, Suffolk
■ Stewards' Enquiry : Paul Fessey one-day ban: careless riding (Oct 1)

FOCUS
Just a fair sprint handicap and despite the good time few got into it and there is a slight doubt over the form.

NOTEBOOK
Lady Lily(IRE), a winner off 82 at Redcar two starts back, found it all a bit too competitive off this mark in a big-field handicap at Doncaster last time, but this was easier and she soon held a good position. Driven into the lead racing inside the final furlong, she showed a good attitude to hang on from the persistent Mango Music and fully deserved the win. Things will only get harder though and she will be doing well to defy a rise of any significance. (op 4-1)
Mango Music was soon in front under Dettori and tried to get away turning into the straight, but Lady Lily would not let her go and, try though she did, the winner was not for passing close home. This was a fine effort, finishing clear of the third, and certainly a step back in the right direction following a poor spell. (tchd 6-1)
Perfect Treasure(IRE) allowed the front pair a bit too much rope and was unable to make any serious impression in the final quarter mile. She will benefit from a return to further. (op 9-1)
Nadawat(USA), 11lb higher than when winning at Lingfield last month, has been running creditably in defeat since, but this drop back to 6f did not work in her favour and she could only offer the one pace. This mark may prove beyond her for the time being. (op 9-4)
Hazelhurst(IRE) has looked an improved performer of late, but she may have found this a bit too competitive and there will be easier opportunities.
La Matanza was always well positioned, but she failed to respond to pressure and dropped away disappointingly. (op 6-1)
Keyaki(IRE) lost her race at the start, being slowly away and then impeded when trying to come with a run inside the final quarter mile. (op 5-1)

5561 PONTEFRACT STAYERS CHAMPIONSHIP H'CAP (ROUND 6) 2m 1f 22y
4:30 (4:32) (Class 5) (0-75,74) 3-Y-0+ **£2,521** (£2,521; £577; £288) **Stalls** Low

Form RPR

1221 **1** **Strobe**[12] 5224 3-9-1 **73**.............................. TPQueally 6 81
(J A Osborne) *set stdy pce: jnd and qcknd 3f out: rdn 2f out: drvn and hdd ent fnl f: rallied to ld last 50yds: jnd on line* **6/5**[1]

3402 **1** *dht* **Indonesia**[27] 4786 5-10-0 **74**.............................. KDarley 8 82
(T D Walford) *t.k.h: hld up in rr: gd hdwy 4f out: chal 3f out: rdn over 1f out: led ent fnl f: sn drvn and hdd last 50yds: rallied to join rival on line* **11/4**[3]

6212 **3** *7* **Last Flight (IRE)**[54] 3976 3-9-2 **74**.............................. SebSanders 5 74
(J L Dunlop) *trckd ldrs: hdwy to chal over 4f out: rdn along and n.m.r 3f out: sn one pce* **9/4**[2]

5060 **4** *6* **Kerry's Blade (IRE)**[10] 5283 5-8-10 **56** oh11.................... MickyFenton 1 49
(Micky Hammond) *in tch: rdn along over 4f out: sn drvn and plugged on same pce* **50/1**

-003 **5** *hd* **Matinee Idol**[34] 4563 4-8-10 **56** oh6.............................. PaulFessey 7 49
(Mrs S Lamyman) *chsd ldrs: rdn along 7f out and sn wknd* **100/1**

5440 **6** *2* **Red Sun**[22] 4941 10-8-10 **56** oh6..............................(tp) PaulEddery 4 46
(R C Guest) *plld hrd: chsd ldrs: rdn along over 4f out and sn wknd* **25/1**

0300 **7** *5* **High Frequency (IRE)**[37] 4475 6-8-3 **56** oh11..........(b) DeanHeslop(7) 2 40
(A Crook) *prom: rdn along over 4f out and sn wknd* **100/1**

3m 56.21s (5.71) **Going Correction** -0.125s/f (Firm)
WFA 3 from 4yo+ 12lb **7 Ran SP% 110.7**
Speed ratings (Par 103): **81,81,77,74,74 73,71**
TRIFECTA Tote Win I 1.90, S 1.10; Pl I 3.70, S 1.10; Ex I-S 2.40; S-I 3.00; CSF I-S 3.02, S-I 2.24; T/C I-S-LF 3.42, S-I-LF 2.66.
Owner Miss P A & P J Carnaby **Bred** Old Mill Stud **Trained** Upper Lambourn, Berks
Owner G E Dempsey **Bred** Darley **Trained** Sheriff Hutton, N Yorks

FOCUS
A hugely uncompetitive contest and the front pair, who could not be separated at the line, drew well clear. The form is not strong with all but the first three racing from out of the handicap.
Red Sun Official explanation: jockey said gelding hung right-handed throughout

5562 PONTEFRACT-RACES.CO.UK MAIDEN STKS 1m 2f 6y
5:00 (5:01) (Class 5) 3-Y-0+ **£3,886** (£1,156; £577; £288) **Stalls** Low

Form RPR

1 **Bold Glance** 3-9-3 0.............................. KDarley 2 80+
(Saeed Bin Suroor) *trckd ldrs: hdwy and pushed along over 2f out: swtchd rt and rdn over 1f out: drvn and hdd ins fnl f: no ex towards fin* **8/1**

35 **2** *1/2* **Abydos**[26] 4815 3-9-3 0.............................. LDettori 6 79
(Saeed Bin Suroor) *cl up: rdn to ld over 1f out: drvn and hdd ins fnl f: no ex towards fin* **8/11**[1]

3242 **3** *1 1/4* **Know The Law**[26] 4815 3-9-3 76.............................. SebSanders 3 79+
(D R C Elsworth) *hld up: hdwy over 2f out: chsd ldrs and n.m.r over 1f out: sn rdn and kpt on same pce ins fnl f* **9/4**[2]

0- **4** *shd* **Wraith**[362] 5537 3-9-3 0.............................. TPQueally 11 76
(H R A Cecil) *hld up: hdwy 3f out: rdn wl over 1f out: kpt on u.p ins fnl f* **7/1**[3]

05 **5** *11* **Mysterious World (IRE)**[8] 5335 3-9-3 0.................... RoystonFfrench 1 54
(Mrs K Walton) *sn led: rdn along over 2f out: hdd over 1f out and grad wknd* **50/1**

6 *5* **Lady Killer Queen** 3-8-12 0.............................. StephenDonohoe 8 39
(D Carroll) *s.i.s: a in rr* **100/1**

7 *3* **Camerooney**[244] 4-9-9 0.............................. SilvestreDeSousa 4 38
(A D Brown) *dwlt and in rr: hdwy to chse ldrs 1/2-way: rdn along and wknd over 3f out* **100/1**

00 **8** *21* **Rosemary And Thyme**[103] 2477 3-8-12 0.............................. PaulFessey 9 —
(Mrs S Lamyman) *a in rr* **100/1**

2m 13.32s (-0.76) **Going Correction** -0.125s/f (Firm)
WFA 3 from 4yo 6lb **8 Ran SP% 117.2**
Speed ratings (Par 103): **98,97,96,96,87 83,81,64**
CSF £14.97 TOTE £9.50: £2.70, £1.10, £1.10; EX 14.10.
Owner Godolphin **Bred** Belgrave Bloodstock Ltd **Trained** Newmarket, Suffolk

FOCUS
Only four counted in what was an uncompetitive maiden but the form looks sound with the third to his mark.
Rosemary And Thyme Official explanation: jockey said filly had no more to give

5563 GO RACING AT CATTERICK ON SATURDAY H'CAP 1m 4y
5:30 (5:30) (Class 6) (0-65,65) 3-Y-0+ **£3,238** (£963; £481; £240) **Stalls** Low

Form RPR

4232 **1** **Young Bertie**[10] 5275 4-9-5 **62**........................(v) TravisBlock(3) 5 72
(H Morrison) *trckd ldrs: hdwy 3f out: chal over 1f out and sn rdn: drvn to ld wl ins fnl f: styd on* **3/1**[1]

1544 **2** *1/2* **Keisha Kayleigh (IRE)**[34] 4582 4-9-3 **57**........................(v) TPQueally 11 66
(B Ellison) *hld up in rr: hdwy and in tch 3f out: niggled along and sltly outpcd over 2f out: sn chsng ldrs: rdn wl over 1f out and styd on ins fnl f: nrst fin* **4/1**[2]

5204 **3** *1* **Astroangel**[34] 4579 3-8-12 **61**.............................. PatrickHills(5) 12 68
(M H Tompkins) *trckd ldrs on inner: hdwy to ld wl over 1f oiut: sn rdn and hdd wl ins fnl f: kpt on* **10/1**

0253 **4** *3/4* **Cow Girl (IRE)**[20] 4989 3-9-4 **62**.............................. MickyFenton 7 67
(Miss Gay Kelleway) *hld up in rr: hdwy over 2f out: rdn wl over 1f out: styd on ins fnl f: nrst fin* **11/1**

2214 **5** *nk* **Gallego**[13] 5198 5-9-1 **60**.............................. RussellKennemore(5) 15 64
(R J Price) *s.i.s and bhd: stdy hdwy on outer over 2f out: rdn over 1f out and kpt on ins fnl f: nrst fin* **9/2**[3]

2160 **6** *3 1/2* **Dancing Jest (IRE)**[19] 5046 3-8-10 **61**.................... WilliamCarson(7) 9 57
(Rae Guest) *chsd ldrs: rdn along over 3f out: sn drvn and kpt on same pce* **20/1**

5526 **7** *2* **Crosby Jemma**[17] 5084 3-8-7 **51**.............................. PaulQuinn 17 42
(J R Weymes) *midfield: hdwy over 2f out: sn rdn along and no imp* **33/1**

3400 **8** *1 1/4* **Ming Vase**[8] 5330 5-8-10 **50**.............................. FrankieMcDonald 1 39
(P T Midgley) *led: rdn along over 2f out: drvn and hdd wl over 1f out: wknd* **14/1**

1131 **9** *3* **Mister Jingles**[26] 4797 4-9-8 **62**........................(b[1]) J-PGuillambert 4 44
(R M Whitaker) *cl up: rdn along over 2f out and ev ch tl wknd over 1f out* **6/1**

0600 **10** *7* **Just Dust**[20] 4998 3-9-4 **62**.............................. DaleGibson 16 28
(M W Easterby) *in tch: hdwy on outer to chse ldrs 1/2-way: rdn along wl: over 2f out and sn wknd* **14/1**

2450 **11** *18* **Wells Of Badr (IRE)**[28] 4736 3-9-6 **64**......................... AdrianMcCarthy 6 —
(P W Chapple-Hyam) *chsd ldrs: rdn along over 2f out and sn wknd* **25/1**
-300 **12** *18* **Spirit Of Ecstacy**[92] 2760 3-9-0 **58**..................................(t) PaulFessey 8 —
(G M Moore) *cl up: rdn along over 3f out and sn wknd* **66/1**
1m 43.96s (-1.74) **Going Correction** -0.125s/f (Firm)
WFA 3 from 4yo+ 4lb 12 Ran SP% **121.3**
Speed ratings (Par 101): **103,102,101,100,100 96,94,93,90,83 65,47**
CSF £14.41 CT £111.15 TOTE £4.70: £1.90, £2.00, £3.10; EX 20.00 Place 6 £ 82.86, Place 5 £ 46.92.
Owner M T Bevan **Bred** Red House Stud **Trained** East Ilsley, Berks

FOCUS
A moderate handicap and good form for the grade rated around the winner and fourth and backed up by the time.
Dancing Jest(IRE) Official explanation: trainer's rep said filly lost its near-fore shoe
Ming Vase Official explanation: jockey said gelding hung right throughout
Just Dust Official explanation: jockey said gelding slipped
Spirit Of Ecstacy Official explanation: jockey said filly had no more to give
T/Plt: £74.30 to a £1 stake. Pool: £58,085.35. 570.40 winning tickets. T/Qpdt: £22.90 to a £1 stake. Pool: £2,808.00. 90.70 winning tickets. JR

5386 WOLVERHAMPTON (A.W) (L-H)
Thursday, September 20

OFFICIAL GOING: Standard
Wind: Moderate behind Weather: Fine

5564 SPONSOR A RACE BY CALLING 0870 220 2442 H'CAP — 5f 20y(P)
6:50 (6:50) (Class 6) (0-50,50) 3-Y-0+ **£2,047** (£604; £302) **Stalls** Low

Form RPR
6602 **1** **Sofinella (IRE)**[21] 4974 4-8-12 **50**.................................... LukeMorris(5) 8 64
(A W Carroll) *mde all: rdn and edgd lft over 1f out: drvn out* **9/1**
5003 **2** *½* **Twinned (IRE)**[21] 4973 4-9-2 **49**.................................... FergusSweeney 2 61
(M J Wilkinson) *t.k.h: a.p: wnt 2nd 2f out: sn rdn: kpt on towards fin* **5/1**[2]
6066 **3** *1 ½* **Hephaestus**[76] 3281 3-9-0 **48**.. LPKeniry 1 55
(Peter Grayson) *a.p: pushed along over 2f out: rdn wl over 1f out: kpt on same pce fnl f* **15/2**
3300 **4** *½* **Mister Always**[25] 4842 3-9-1 **49**.......................................(b[1]) ChrisCatlin 3 54
(K McAuliffe) *n.m.r s: hld up: hdwy over 2f out: rdn wl over 1f out: one pce fnl f* **10/1**
4050 **5** *2 ½* **Elvina**[21] 4973 6-9-0 **47**.. DaneO'Neill 4 43
(A G Newcombe) *t.k.h early: chsd ldrs: rdn and no hdwy fnl 2f* **13/2**
0000 **6** *shd* **Avoca Dancer (IRE)**[14] 5174 4-9-3 **50**......................... TGMcLaughlin 11 46
(M Wigham) *outpcd: nvr nrr* **25/1**
0400 **7** *shd* **Mystery Pips**[9] 5295 7-9-1 **48**...(v) KimTinkler 9 43
(N Tinkler) *chsd wnr 3f: rdn and wknd wl over 1f out* **16/1**
0106 **8** *nk* **He's A Rocket (IRE)**[21] 4973 6-8-9 **49**..................(b) DeclanCannon(7) 5 43
(John R Upson) *s.i.s: bhd: rdn over 2f out: nvr trbld ldrs* **9/1**
4665 **9** *4* **Duke Of Milan (IRE)**[13] 5191 4-9-0 **50**....................... MarcHalford(3) 10 30
(G C Bravery) *rdn over 2f out: a towards rr* **3/1**[1]
0502 **10** *¾* **Meikle Barfil**[21] 4973 5-9-3 **50**...(tp) JamesDoyle 6 27
(J M Bradley) *a towards rr* **11/2**[3]
45-0 **11** *nk* **Ten For Tosca (IRE)**[23] 4919 3-8-11 **50**...............(t) KevinGhunowa(5) 13 26
(R A Harris) *s.s: sn swtchd lft: rdn over 2f out: short-lived effrt on ins wl over 1f out* **50/1**
62.30 secs (-0.52) **Going Correction** -0.025s/f (Stan)
WFA 3 from 4yo+ 1lb 11 Ran SP% **122.9**
Speed ratings (Par 101): **103,102,99,99,95 94,94,94,87,86 86**
CSF £56.13 CT £372.47 TOTE £14.30: £6.60, £1.30, £3.70; EX 63.20.
Owner Serafino Agodino **Bred** Dr Paschal Carmody **Trained** Cropthorne, Worcs

FOCUS
A tightly-knit low-grade contest but rated positively around the first two and solid for the grade.

5565 DINE IN THE HORIZONS RESTAURANT H'CAP — 5f 20y(P)
7:20 (7:20) (Class 6) (0-65,65) 3-Y-0+ **£2,218** (£654; £327) **Stalls** Low

Form RPR
5022 **1** **Silver Prelude**[14] 5174 6-9-3 **63**.. SebSanders 4 71
(D K Ivory) *led 1f: led 3f out: rdn wl over 1f out: drvn out* **7/4**[1]
0000 **2** *½* **Triskaidekaphobia**[79] 3190 4-8-8 **54**..............................(t) JamesDoyle 5 60
(Miss J R Tooth) *a.p: rdn over 2f out: edgd lft over 1f out: r.o ins fnl f* **10/1**
1450 **3** *shd* **The Fisio**[121] 1914 7-9-2 **62**..(v) ChrisCatlin 1 68
(S Gollings) *towards rr: rdn over 2f out: hdwy on ins over 1f out: r.o ins fnl f* **12/1**
300- **4** *nk* **Obe Royal**[346] 5866 3-9-0 **61**.. TGMcLaughlin 2 66+
(P D Evans) *outpcd in rr: rdn and swtchd rt over 1f out: gd hdwy fnl f: r.o* **33/1**
0210 **5** *1 ¼* **Our Fugitive (IRE)**[37] 4486 5-9-5 **65**...........................(b) FrancisNorton 9 65
(A W Carroll) *led after 1f to 3f out: w wnr whn hung rt bnd over 2f out: rdn over 1f out: no ex ins fnl f* **10/1**
000 **6** *nk* **Stoneacre Boy (IRE)**[72] 3396 4-8-13 **59**............................ AdamKirby 3 58
(Peter Grayson) *hld up towards rr: hdwy on ins over 2f out: rdn and swtchd rt wl over 1f out: one pce fnl f* **25/1**
4504 **7** *1 ½* **Hello Roberto**[7] 5349 6-8-1 **52**.................................(p) KevinGhunowa(5) 8 46
(R A Harris) *chsd ldrs: rdn over 2f out: wknd over 1f out* **8/1**[3]
4315 **8** *1 ¼* **Tag Team (IRE)**[8] 5340 6-9-0 **60**...................................... StephenDonohoe 7 49
(John A Harris) *chsd ldrs: rdn over 2f out: wknd wl over 1f out* **6/1**[2]
1464 **9** *1* **Arfinnit (IRE)**[5] 5430 6-8-4 **55**...............................(b) LukeMorris(5) 12 40
(Mrs A L M King) *towards rr: rdn over 2f out: c wd st: n.d* **16/1**
2541 **10** *2* **Miacarla**[2] 5507 4-8-5 **58** 6ex...................................... DeclanCannon(7) 10 36
(A Berry) *hld up in mid-div: hdwy on outside over 2f out: sn rdn: wknd wl over 1f out* **6/1**[2]
0040 **11** *1 ¾* **James Street (IRE)**[12] 5234 4-9-0 **60**.................................(b) LPKeniry 11 32
(Peter Grayson) *rdn 3f out: a towards rr* **50/1**
-200 **12** *1 ½* **Cadwell**[29] 4701 3-8-13 **60**...(bt) DaneO'Neill 6 27
(D J Murphy) *s.i.s: rdn over 3f out: a bhd* **20/1**
62.60 secs (-0.22) **Going Correction** -0.025s/f (Stan)
WFA 3 from 4yo+ 1lb 12 Ran SP% **121.3**
Speed ratings (Par 101): **100,99,99,98,96 96,93,91,90,86 84,81**
CSF £20.12 CT £172.09 TOTE £3.00: £1.10, £8.30, £1.80; EX 47.90.
Owner Mrs A Shone **Bred** Bearstone Stud **Trained** Radlett, Herts

FOCUS
A modest sprint handicap rated through the winner and backed up by the placed horses.

5566 BOOK YOUR CHRISTMAS PARTY NOW CLASSIFIED STKS — 5f 216y(P)
7:50 (7:52) (Class 7) 3-Y-0+ **£1,911** (£564; £282) **Stalls** Low

Form RPR
4006 **1** **Avontuur (FR)**[27] 4768 5-8-7 45...........................(b) DanielleMcCreery(7) 7 54
(D W Chapman) *t.k.h in rr: hdwy over 1f out: sn rdn: r.o to ld last strides* **20/1**
0000 **2** *shd* **Wodhill Be**[25] 4855 7-8-9 45... LukeMorris(5) 2 54
(D Morris) *hld up towards rr: rdn and hdwy over 1f out: edgd rt and led wl ins fnl f: hdd last strides* **6/1**[3]
5003 **3** *nk* **Obe One**[27] 4768 7-9-0 45...(b) FrancisNorton 3 53
(A Berry) *hld up in mid-div: rdn and hdwy over 2f out: ev ch wl ins fnl f: kpt on* **5/1**[1]
0002 **4** *1* **Miss Mujahid Times**[28] 4741 4-9-0 45.................(p) SilvestreDeSousa 10 50
(A D Brown) *chsd ldrs: rdn over 3f out: ev ch wl ins fnl f: nt qckn* **11/2**[2]
0000 **5** *1* **Damhsoir (IRE)**[10] 5270 3-8-12 45.. DaneO'Neill 9 46
(H S Howe) *sn chsng ldrs: rdn over 2f out: no ex ins fnl f* **16/1**
5066 **6** *½* **Nawayea**[10] 5276 4-9-0 45..(t) StephenDonohoe 11 45
(C N Allen) *towards rr: rdn 3f out: kpt on ins fnl f: nvr nrr* **7/1**
0000 **7** *nk* **Creme Brulee**[31] 4668 4-9-0 45.. RobertHavlin 1 44
(P T Dalton) *sn led: rdn 2f out: hdd wl ins fnl f: fdd* **25/1**
0020 **8** *1* **Sydneyroughdiamond**[24] 3686 5-9-0 45........................... ChrisCatlin 4 41
(M Mullineaux) *chsd ldrs: rdn over 2f out: wknd over 1f out* **8/1**
6450 **9** *½* **Lady Hopeful (IRE)**[21] 4974 5-9-0 45.................................(b) LPKeniry 5 39
(Peter Grayson) *hld up and bhd: sme hdwy over 1f out: no further prog* **12/1**
4033 **10** *3* **A Teen**[28] 4741 9-9-0 45.. AdamKirby 12 29
(P Howling) *broke wl: led early: stdd into mid-div: rdn over 2f out: sn bhd* **15/2**
0000 **11** *¾* **Must Be Keen**[17] 5090 8-9-0 45...................................(v) FergusSweeney 8 27
(Miss Diana Weeden) *s.i.s: a bhd* **33/1**
0400 **12** *1 ¼* **Sharp Hat**[22] 4939 13-8-11 45.. MarcHalford(3) 13 23
(D W Chapman) *a bhd* **12/1**
0005 **13** *¾* **Jessica Wigmo**[21] 4974 4-9-0 45.. SebSanders 6 21
(A W Carroll) *hld up in mid-div: rdn over 2f out: wknd wl over 1f out* **8/1**
1m 16.0s (0.19) **Going Correction** -0.025s/f (Stan)
WFA 3 from 4yo+ 2lb 13 Ran SP% **125.6**
Speed ratings (Par 97): **97,96,96,95,93 93,92,91,90,86 85,84,83**
CSF £140.06 TOTE £19.50: £10.40, £2.60, £1.70; EX 745.50.
Owner David W Chapman **Bred** Haras D'Etreham **Trained** Stillington, N Yorks

FOCUS
This weak event produced a cracking finish and rated at face value around the first two and the fourth.
Sharp Hat Official explanation: jockey said gelding stumbled leaving stalls

5567 STAY AT THE WOLVERHAMPTON HOLIDAY INN MAIDEN STKS — 7f 32y(P)
8:20 (8:23) (Class 5) 3-Y-0+ **£2,914** (£867; £433; £216) **Stalls** High

Form RPR
400 **1** **Pivotal Truth**[61] 3743 3-8-12 70.. ChrisCatlin 6 71
(B W Hills) *a.p: led over 4f out tl over 3f out: rdn wl over 1f out: led ins fnl f: r.o* **7/1**[3]
0-0 **2** *1 ¼* **Juzilla (IRE)**[31] 4666 3-8-12 0.. AdamKirby 1 68
(W R Swinburn) *hld up in mid-div: rdn and hdwy 2f out: r.o ins fnl f* **12/1**
4520 **3** *1 ½* **Al Badeya (IRE)**[70] 3447 3-8-12 70.. KDarley 12 64
(Sir Michael Stoute) *a.p: led over 3f out: rdn 2f out: hdd ins fnl f: nt qckn* **4/1**[2]
00 **4** *1 ¾* **Smash Hit (IRE)**[9] 5315 4-9-6 0...................................... FergusSweeney 9 64
(David Pinder) *hld up and bhd: rdn and hdwy over 2f out: one pce fnl f* **25/1**
00 **5** *3* **Lily La Belle**[6] 5390 3-8-12 0.. JamesDoyle 2 51
(A W Carroll) *hld up in mid-div: rdn and hdwy on ins wl over 1f out: no imp fnl f* **40/1**
25- **6** *1 ½* **The Tyke**[287] 6738 4-9-6 0.. DaneO'Neill 8 52
(C G Cox) *prom: rdn over 2f out: wknd over 1f out* **12/1**
7 *1 ½* **Just Crystal** 3-8-12 0.. TGMcLaughlin 11 43
(B P J Baugh) *s.s: nvr nr ldrs* **66/1**
2242 **8** *½* **Trees Of Green (USA)**[10] 5285 3-9-3 75..................(v[1]) KerrinMcEvoy 7 46
(Saeed Bin Suroor) *led after 1f tl over 4f out: rdn 2f out: wknd over 1f out* **8/13**[1]
60 **9** *½* **Reddy Ronnie (IRE)**[32] 4641 3-9-3 0...................... StephenDonohoe 10 45
(D Carroll) *outpcd* **50/1**
00 **10** *10* **Newgate Parisien**[31] 4659 4-9-6 0... LPKeniry 3 18
(Mark Campion) *led 1f: rdn over 3f out: wknd over 2f out* **100/1**
0R **11** *5* **Florentine Lady**[12] 5231 4-8-12 0.................................. DominicFox(3) 4 —
(D Shaw) *s.s: a wl in rr* **100/1**
1m 30.0s (-0.40) **Going Correction** -0.025s/f (Stan)
WFA 3 from 4yo 3lb 11 Ran SP% **121.5**
Speed ratings (Par 103): **101,99,97,95,92 90,89,88,87,76 70**
CSF £83.57 TOTE £10.90: £3.90, £9.70, £1.80; EX 56.70.
Owner D J Deer **Bred** D J And Mrs Deer **Trained** Lambourn, Berks

FOCUS
This modest maiden may not have taken much winning after the odds-on favourite flopped. The form is not easy to rate and the the proximity of the fifth raises doubts.
Trees Of Green(USA) Official explanation: trainer's rep had no explanation for the poor form shown

5568 ENJOY EVENING RACING AT WOLVERHAMPTON H'CAP — 1m 141y(P)
8:50 (8:51) (Class 5) (0-75,73) 3-Y-0+ **£3,562** (£1,059; £529; £264) **Stalls** Low

Form RPR
1043 **1** **Red Birr (IRE)**[169] 921 6-9-8 **72**.. ChrisCatlin 11 82+
(P R Webber) *hld up in tch: rdn whn nt clr run and swtchd rt over 1f out: r.o to ld nr fin* **13/2**
353 **2** *½* **Paradise Dancer (IRE)**[34] 4575 3-8-13 **68**........................ DaneO'Neill 8 74
(Pat Eddery) *hld up in mid-div: hdwy 2f out: rdn over 1f out: led wl ins fnl f: hdd nr fin* **11/1**
5324 **3** *¾* **War Anthem**[24] 4902 3-8-12 **67**...(b) RobertHavlin 2 71
(C R Egerton) *sn led: hrd rdn over 1f out: hdd and nt qckn wl ins fnl f* **7/1**
0401 **4** *1 ¼* **Merrymadcap (IRE)**[14] 5178 5-9-8 **72**................................ FrancisNorton 3 74
(M Blanshard) *hld up in mid-div: hdwy on ins 2f out: rdn over 1f out: nt qckn ins fnl f* **7/2**[1]
3605 **5** *1 ¼* **Hoh Wotanite**[31] 4672 4-9-3 **72**............................(p) RussellKennemore(5) 7 76+
(R Hollinshead) *hld up towards rr: swtchd lft and hdwy on ins whn nt clr run over 1f out: swtchd rt ins fnl f: nt rcvr* **5/1**[3]

3501 **6** *hd* **Pitbull**[29] 4701 4-8-9 **59** oh3 (p) RoystonFfrench 10 57
(Mrs G S Rees) *s.i.s: hld up in rr: rdn over 2f out: swtchd rt wl over 1f out: edgd lft ins fnl f: nvr trbld ldrs* **10/1**

4006 **7** *½* **Dream Catcher (SWE)**[64] 3641 4-9-5 **69** (t) FergusSweeney 9 66
(R A Kvisla) *hld up and bhd: rdn over 2f out: c wd st: n.d* **16/1**

4003 **8** *½* **Wodhill Gold**[52] 4023 6-8-9 **59** oh5 (v) AdrianMcCarthy 4 55
(D Morris) *led early: chsd ldr: rdn over 2f out: wknd ins fnl f* **20/1**

4000 **9** *2* **Tempsford Flyer (IRE)**[13] 5203 4-9-9 **73** JamesDoyle 1 65
(J W Hills) *prom: rdn over 2f out: wknd fnl f* **10/1**

3512 **10** *5* **Red Rudy**[13] 5189 5-9-2 **66** SebSanders 6 47
(A W Carroll) *hld up in mid-div: hdwy over 5f out: rdn over 2f out: wkng whn n.m.r ent st* **9/2**[2]

0500 **11** *13* **Rabbit Fighter (IRE)**[12] 5223 3-8-10 **70** KevinGhunowa[(5)] 5 22
(D Shaw) *rdn 4f out: a bhd* **20/1**

1m 49.35s (-2.41) **Going Correction** -0.025s/f (Stan)
WFA 3 from 4yo+ 5lb **11** Ran SP% **124.8**
Speed ratings (Par 103): **109,108,107,106,105 105,105,104,102,98 86**
CSF £80.84 CT £532.44 TOTE £6.50: £1.02, £7.10, £3.00; EX 82.00.
Owner John Nicholls (Trading) Ltd **Bred** Mrs Ellen Lyons **Trained** Mollington, Oxon

FOCUS
An open-looking little handicap and with the exception of the third the form looks sound.
Hoh Wotanite Official explanation: jockey said colt was denied a clear run
Pitbull Official explanation: jockey said colt missed the break
Wodhill Gold Official explanation: jockey said gelding had no more to give
Tempsford Flyer(IRE) Official explanation: jockey said gelding hung left

5569 SATURDAY NIGHT IS PARTY NIGHT AT WOLVERHAMPTON H'CAP 1m 1f 103y(P)
9:20 (9:20) (Class 6) (0-65,65) 3-Y-0+ **£2,047** (£604; £302) **Stalls** Low

Form RPR

0002 **1** **Kansas Gold**[8] 5330 4-9-3 **59** RoystonFfrench 8 69
(J Mackie) *chsd ldr: led wl over 2f out: rdn wl over 1f out: drvn out* **8/1**

2241 **2** *1* **Libre**[7] 5348 7-9-8 **64** 6ex TGMcLaughlin 3 72
(F Jordan) *hld up in tch: rdn and wnt 2nd 1f out: kpt on* **8/1**

0530 **3** *1* **Lunar River (FR)**[14] 5178 4-9-7 **63** (t) FergusSweeney 10 69
(David Pinder) *hld up towards rr: hdwy wl over 1f out: sn rdn: kpt on same pce ins fnl f* **16/1**

6123 **4** *1¼* **Casablanca Minx (IRE)**[12] 5237 4-9-9 **65** (b) StephenDonohoe 9 68+
(P D Evans) *hld up and bhd: n.m.r jst over 1f out: styd on ins fnl f: nrst fin* **6/1**[3]

5431 **5** *nk* **Spunger**[13] 5188 4-9-7 **63** (v) SebSanders 4 66
(H J L Dunlop) *hld up towards rr: hdwy on ins wl over 1f out: rdn and edgd rt jst over 1f out: one pce* **7/2**[2]

3166 **6** *hd* **Princely Ted (IRE)**[5] 5424 6-9-2 **58** DaneO'Neill 1 60
(D Burchell) *set slow pce: hdd wl over 2f out: sn rdn: wknd fnl f* **6/1**[3]

-052 **7** *nk* **Sekula Pata (NZ)**[9] 5310 8-9-0 **59** (b) AlanCreighton[(3)] 11 61
(E J Creighton) *hld up and bhd: rdn wl over 1f out: late hdwy: nvr nrr* **20/1**

0655 **8** *2* **Odessa Star (USA)**[162] 1002 4-9-9 **65** JamesDoyle 12 62
(J G Portman) *hld up in rr: rdn whn nt clr run and swtchd rt jst over 1f out: n.d* **16/1**

5000 **9** *1¼* **Don Pasquale**[31] 4660 5-8-6 **53** (t) RussellKennemore[(5)] 2 48
(J T Stimpson) *s.i.s: sn prom: rdn over 2f out: wknd over 1f out* **25/1**

0306 **10** *1¼* **Ermine Grey**[6] 5391 6-8-8 **55** (v) LukeMorris[(5)] 13 47
(A W Carroll) *plld hrd: hdwy 6f out: rdn and lost pl over 3f out: sn bhd* **10/1**

4211 **11** *½* **Bethanys Boy (IRE)**[12] 5237 6-9-5 **61** VinceSlattery 6 52
(D J Daly) *t.k.h in tch: rdn 2f out: sn wknd: carried sltly rt jst over 1f out* **10/3**[1]

2m 3.27s (0.65) **Going Correction** -0.025s/f (Stan)
WFA 3 from 4yo+ 5lb **11** Ran SP% **125.6**
Speed ratings (Par 101): **96,95,94,93,92 92,92,90,89,88 87**
CSF £75.55 CT £1027.82 TOTE £10.10: £2.70, £2.50, £5.50; EX 109.20 Place 6 £ 918.18, Place 5 £ 302.70.
Owner A J Winterton **Bred** Coln Valley Stud **Trained** Church Broughton , Derbys

FOCUS
A slowly-run minor handicap with several coming into the race in decent form. The form is rated at face value around the first three, despite the modest time.
Bethanys Boy(IRE) Official explanation: jockey said gelding was unsuited by the slow pace
T/Plt: £1,308.20 to a £1 stake. Pool: £91,665.55. 51.15 winning tickets. T/Qpdt: £125.30 to a £1 stake. Pool: £6,758.10. 39.90 winning tickets. KH

5540 YARMOUTH (L-H)
Thursday, September 20

OFFICIAL GOING: Good to firm (good in places) changing to good after race 6 (4.40)
The ground was reported by riders to be a little loose on top.
Wind: Fresh across Weather: Cloudy with sunny spells until turning showery after race 4

5570 EUROPEAN BREEDERS' FUND / CUSTOM KITCHENS MAIDEN STKS 1m 3y
2:10 (2:13) (Class 4) 2-Y-0 **£4,857** (£1,445; £722; £360) **Stalls** High

Form RPR

33 **1** **Pinkindie (USA)**[20] 5011 2-9-3 0 JimmyFortune 6 74+
(E A L Dunlop) *trckd ldrs: plld hrd: rdn to chse ldr over 1f out: styd on u.p to ld nr fin* **8/13**[1]

2 *nk* **Robby Bobby** 2-9-3 0 EddieAhern 4 73+
(M Johnston) *hld up in tch: hung lft and led 2f out: sn rdn: hung rt ins fnl f: hdd nr fin* **10/1**[3]

3 *2½* **Top Ticket (IRE)** 2-9-3 0 GeorgeBaker 3 68+
(D M Simcock) *chsd ldrs: ev ch 2f out: styd on same pce fnl f* **20/1**

3 **4** *hd* **Mushtaaq (USA)**[13] 5206 2-9-3 0 RHills 5 67+
(M A Jarvis) *trckd ldr: ev ch over 2f out: sn outpcd: styd on ins fnl f* **9/4**[2]

0 **5** *5* **Aim**[31] 4656 2-9-3 0 TPO'Shea 7 56
(J R Jenkins) *led 6f: wknd over 1f out* **150/1**

6 *28* **Palmer's Green** 2-8-10 0 JCorrigan[(7)] 1 —
(Mrs C A Dunnett) *wnt lft s: outpcd* **100/1**

7 *1* **Where To Now** 2-8-12 0 DMylonas 2 —
(Mrs C A Dunnett) *chsd ldrs over 4f* **100/1**

1m 43.16s (3.26) **Going Correction** +0.225s/f (Good) **7** Ran SP% **109.2**
Speed ratings (Par 97): **92,91,89,89,84 56,55**
CSF £7.13 TOTE £1.90: £1.10, £2.70; EX 7.40.
Owner C Cornes **Bred** Liberation Farm & Oratis Thoroughbreds **Trained** Newmarket, Suffolk

FOCUS
A steadily-run maiden and not easy to rate but initially set lower than expected.

NOTEBOOK
Pinkindie(USA) was third in maidens at Newmarket and Sandown on his first two starts, finishing one place ahead of subsequent winner Silver Regent on the latter occasion. Taking a tug in the early parts, he settled by halfway and came through to chase the leader going to the final furlong, but really had to knuckle down to get his head in front late on. He will be seen in a better light granted a truly-run race over this trip. (op 5-6 tchd 10-11 in places)
Robby Bobby ◆, a half-brother to smart middle-distance performer Foxhaven, made a promising debut and would have prevailed had he not proved so green. With normal improvement to come this Royal Lodge entry should soon open his account. (op 8-1 tchd 11-1)
Top Ticket(IRE), a half-brother to winning miler Tumbleweed Glory, could not go with the first two in the final quarter mile but made a pleasing debut nonetheless. (op 25-1)
Mushtaaq(USA) was slightly short of room with around two furlongs to run and soon lost his pitch, but was staying on again in the final furlong and almost salvaged third. He looks the type for middle-distance handicaps next season. (op 15-8)
Aim, last of ten after a slow start on his debut, knew more this time and took a step in the right direction, but still has to show further improvement if he is to win a race. (op 100-1)

5571 ATTHERACES.COM FREE VIDEO NURSERY 1m 3y
2:40 (2:42) (Class 4) (0-85,81) 2-Y-0 **£6,309** (£1,888; £944; £472; £235) **Stalls** High

Form RPR

0400 **1** **Tayarat (IRE)**[21] 4964 2-9-4 **78** RHills 8 81
(M P Tregoning) *mde all: rdn out* **11/2**[3]

2242 **2** *½* **Always Ready**[19] 5053 2-9-7 **81** JimmyFortune 4 83
(C E Brittain) *a.p: nt clr run 2f out: hrd rdn ins fnl f: styd on* **10/3**[1]

001 **3** *nk* **Dancer's Legacy**[24] 4904 2-9-2 **76** (t) TGMcLaughlin 7 77
(E A L Dunlop) *hld up: rdn over 2f out: hdwy over 1f out: styd on* **20/1**

010 **4** *2½* **Imperial Decree**[26] 4832 2-9-2 **76** FrancisNorton 2 71
(John Berry) *s.i.s: hld up: hdwy over 2f out: rdn and hung lft over 1f out: styd on* **8/1**

064 **5** *1¾* **Spent**[36] 4500 2-9-0 **74** TedDurcan 11 65+
(R M Beckett) *hmpd s: in rr: styd on fr over 1f out: nvr nrr* **7/1**

1401 **6** *nk* **Palm Court**[10] 5268 2-9-5 **79** 6ex SteveDrowne 10 70+
(R Charlton) *hmpd s: hld up in tch: rdn and edgd rt over 1f out: wknd ins fnl f* **4/1**[2]

5450 **7** *4* **Timewatch**[41] 4364 2-8-8 **68** EddieAhern 6 49
(M Johnston) *chsd ldr: rdn over 2f out: wknd over 1f out* **14/1**

000 **8** *nk* **Isander (USA)**[54] 3958 2-8-8 **68** JimCrowley 3 49
(Mrs A J Perrett) *hld up in tch: rdn and wknd over 1f out* **33/1**

004 **9** *½* **Ski School (IRE)**[42] 4335 2-8-9 **72** LiamJones[(3)] 9 52
(W J Haggas) *wnt rt s: prom: racd keenly: rdn and wknd over 1f out* **15/2**

000 **10** *1½* **American Welcome (IRE)**[27] 4781 2-8-0 **60** NickyMackay 5 36
(B J Meehan) *mid-div: rdn over 3f out: wknd over 2f out* **14/1**

0500 **11** *18* **Miss Willoughby**[17] 5081 2-7-5 **58** oh13 (e) FrankiePickard[(7)] 1 —
(J Ryan) *chsd ldrs over 5f* **125/1**

1m 41.13s (1.23) **Going Correction** +0.225s/f (Good) **11** Ran SP% **115.7**
Speed ratings (Par 97): **102,101,101,98,96 96,92,92,91,90 72**
CSF £23.34 CT £341.88 TOTE £6.70: £2.70, £1.70, £4.00; EX 28.00 Trifecta £139.20 Pool: £402.06, 2.05 winning units.
Owner Hamdan Al Maktoum **Bred** Golden Garden Stud **Trained** Lambourn, Berks

FOCUS
A reasonable nursery, and the fastest of the three races over this trip. The form looks straightforward.

NOTEBOOK
Tayarat(IRE) had been slowly away on three of his first four runs, including his nursery/Polytrack bow last time, but he had no such problems this time. Travelling well in front, he held on well as the placed horses closed on him inside the last. He is bred to stay further, being out of a 1m4f winner who was a half-sister to the dam of Sinndar. (op 5-1 tchd 6-1)
Always Ready, raised 4lb after his decent effort at Sandown, ran another solid race and was staying on in determined fashion, but again found one too good on the day. He deserves a change of luck. (op 5-1)
Dancer's Legacy , upped in trip after his surprise win in a Warwick maiden, went after the winner with over a furlong to run but had no more to give in the final 50 yards. He is on the upgrade. (op 14-1)
Imperial Decree finished ninth in a valuable sales race over 6f at the Curragh last time. Back up in trip and on faster ground, she made late gains after being switched left despite not really helping her jockey. (op 15-2)
Spent, stepping up in trip on his nursery debut after three runs in 6f maidens, was having his first run on a sound surface. Finding himself in rear after being slightly hampered leaving the stalls, he stayed on late but was never going to get to the leaders. (op 8-1)
Palm Court, officially 2lb well in under the penalty he incurred for his Bath win, was done no favours leaving the stalls and, although soon racing in touch, lacked the necessary pace when the pressure was on. (op 10-3 tchd 3-1)

5572 BACK YOUR TEAM AND "BETLIVE" @ WILLIAMHILL.COM (S) NURSERY 1m 3y
3:10 (3:12) (Class 6) (0-65,60) 2-Y-0 **£1,943** (£578; £288; £144) **Stalls** High

Form RPR

0060 **1** **Adam Eterno (IRE)**[9] 5302 2-8-10 49 (t) RichardKingscote 10 50
(Tom Dascombe) *chsd ldr: led over 1f out: rdn and edgd rt fnl f: r.o* **16/1**

0303 **2** *nk* **Hyper Viper (IRE)**[10] 5268 2-9-7 60 (b) JohnEgan 12 60
(J S Moore) *s.i.s: hld up: hdwy over 3f out: rdn and ev ch fnl f: r.o* **5/2**[2]

0060 **3** *1¾* **Blandys Wood**[5] 5423 2-9-7 60 TPO'Shea 9 56
(M R Channon) *hld up: hdwy u.p over 1f out: hung lft: styd on* **8/1**[3]

4003 **4** *3* **Novestar (IRE)**[9] 5302 2-8-6 50 JamieJones[(5)] 5 39+
(G L Moore) *trckd ldrs: plld hrd: rdn over 2f out: hmpd 1f out: styd on same pce* **11/8**[1]

0030 **5** *2½* **Buju**[9] 5298 2-9-5 58 EddieAhern 8 42
(N Tinkler) *hld up in tch: outpcd over 2f out: styd on ins fnl f* **16/1**

030 **6** *nk* **Ochenvay**[39] 4428 2-9-1 54 FrancisNorton 6 37
(M Quinn) *s.i.s: sn prom: rdn and ev ch 2f out: wknd ins fnl f* **14/1**

0000 **7** *shd* **Weight In Gold**[9] 5314 2-8-13 52 HayleyTurner 7 35
(P J McBride) *hld up: rdn over 1f out: n.d* **10/1**

0000 **8** *4* **Premier Class (IRE)**[54] 3951 2-9-1 54 JimCrowley 4 28
(J S Wainwright) *led: rdn and hdd over 1f out: wknd fnl f* **16/1**

0000 **9** *hd* **Bantham Bay**[9] 5302 2-8-11 50 (b[1]) TedDurcan 2 23
(B J Meehan) *chsd ldrs: rdn half way: wknd over 1f out* **50/1**

4000 **10** *1¾* **Dhaka Dazzle**[10] 5268 2-9-3 56 (v[1]) SteveDrowne 3 25
(M R Channon) *hld up: rdn over 2f out: wknd over 1f out* **50/1**

1m 44.3s (4.40) **Going Correction** +0.225s/f (Good) **10** Ran SP% **119.1**
Speed ratings (Par 93): **87,86,84,81,79 79,79,75,74,73**
CSF £57.30 CT £311.99 TOTE £25.40: £3.90, £1.20, £2.50; EX 102.70 TRIFECTA Not won..The winner was bought in for 4,800gns. Hyper Viper (IRE) was claimed by Steve Wilson for £5,000. Novestar (IRE) was claimed by Graham Smith for £5,000
Owner Alan Solomon **Bred** R N Auld **Trained** Lambourn, Berks
■ Stewards' Enquiry : T P O'Shea caution: careless riding

FOCUS
Unsurprisingly, the slowest of the three mile races for juveniles and the form looks weak.
NOTEBOOK
Adam Eterno(IRE) had not troubled the judge in six prior runs but, off bottom weight, he proved good enough to land this low-grade affair. The step up to a mile and the application of a tongue tie seemed the key reasons for this improved effort. (op 14-1)
Hyper Viper(IRE), a creditable third in a non-selling nursery last time, issued his challenge to the winner with over a furlong to run but could not quite get by. He is probably up to winning a similar race. (op 10-3 tchd 7-2)
Blandys Wood, who was due to be dropped 4lb before this, was without the visor. Drifting to her left in the latter stages but closing at the end, she ran close to her Bath form with the runner-up. (op 14-1)
Novestar(IRE) was having his first run since being claimed at Leciester, where he finished a long way in front of today's winner. Officially 10lb well in, he seemed to stay this longer trip but was held when done no favours by the third with a furlong to run. On this evidence he will struggle from his new mark. (op 5-4 tchd 11-10 and 6-4 in places)
Buju, down in this grade for the first time, was doing his best work when it was all over. (op 25-1)

5573 STEWART BULLARD & SON GROUNDS MAINTENANCE H'CAP 2m
3:40 (3:40) (Class 5) (0-70,69) 3-Y-0+
£4,985 (£1,492; £746; £373; £186; £93) **Stalls** High

Form RPR
2115 **1** **Atlantic Coast (IRE)**[11] 5256 3-9-0 **67**............................(v) EddieAhern 3 81
(M Johnston) *led 1f: chsd ldrs: led over 3f out: rdn and hdd over 1f out: rallied to ld ins fnl f: styd on* **15/8**[1]
2422 **2** *nk* **Prince Zafonic**[10] 5273 4-9-12 **67**..(t) JohnEgan 1 80
(Miss Gay Kelleway) *hld up in tch: racd keenly: rdn to ld over 1f out: hung rt and hdd ins fnl f: kpt on* **9/2**[2]
0502 **3** *11* **High Point (IRE)**[34] 4576 9-10-0 **69**.......................... SimonWhitworth 4 69
(G P Enright) *hld up: hdwy 9f out: rdn over 3f out: outpcd fnl 2f* **15/2**
5563 **4** *2* **Sir Duke (IRE)**[15] 5138 3-8-0 **56**...................................(v) LiamJones(3) 8 54
(P W D'Arcy) *chsd ldrs: rdn over 3f out: wknd over 1f out* **10/1**
0635 **5** *shd* **Follow On**[13] 5204 5-8-12 **53**... SteveDrowne 5 50
(A P Jarvis) *s.s: hld up: hdwy u.p over 2f out: wknd over 1f out* **14/1**
0020 **6** *nk* **Ashwell Rose**[27] 4766 5-9-3 **58**.....................................(v) GeorgeBaker 2 55
(J R Jenkins) *hld up: rdn over 3f out: n.d* **28/1**
6451 **7** *nk* **Rajayoga**[18] 4531 6-8-10 **51** oh1....................................... SaleemGolam 6 48
(M H Tompkins) *chsd ldrs: rdn over 4f out: hung lft and wknd 3f out* **11/1**
6426 **8** *1 3/4* **Esclarmonde (IRE)**[27] 4758 3-9-1 **68**.............................. NickyMackay 9 63
(L M Cumani) *s.i.s: sn prom: reminder 1/2-way: rdn and wknd over 2f out* **13/2**[3]
502 **9** *5* **Mabel (IRE)**[65] 3630 4-9-6 **61**.. TedDurcan 7 50
(S C Williams) *led after 1f: hdd over 3f out: wknd wl over 1f out* **15/2**
0044 **10** *31* **Wavertree One Off**[25] 4859 5-8-10 **51** oh6...............(p) JamieMackay 10 —
(J Ryan) *hld up: hdwy 11f out: wknd over 3f out* **100/1**
3m 30.01s (-1.40) **Going Correction** 0.0s/f (Good)
WFA 3 from 4yo+ 12lb **10** Ran SP% **118.4**
Speed ratings (Par 103): **103,102,97,96,96 96,96,95,92,77**
CSF £10.19 CT £52.43 TOTE £2.90: £1.10, £1.80, £2.70; EX 18.90 Trifecta £84.90 Pool: £365.00 - 3.05 winning units.
Owner Atlantic Racing Limited **Bred** Gigginstown House **Trained** Middleham Moor, N Yorks
FOCUS
The pace was just steady in this ordinary handicap. The first two pulled well clear and the winner looks progressive.
Wavertree One Off Official explanation: trainer said gelding was found to be suffering from colic after the race

5574 HALLS GROUP "VICTORY VASE" H'CAP (FOR THE VICTORY VASE) 1m 6f 17y
4:10 (4:12) (Class 2) (0-100,98) 3-Y-0+
£12,464 (£3,732; £1,866; £934; £466; £234) **Stalls** High

Form RPR
1633 **1** **Aajel (USA)**[43] 4288 3-8-11 **90**... RHills 2 100
(M P Tregoning) *mde all: rdn over 1f out: styd on* **15/2**
3211 **2** *1/2* **Irish Quest (IRE)**[8] 5333 3-7-11 **79** 6ex........................ WilliamBuick(3) 5 88
(M A Jarvis) *chsd wnr: rdn over 2f out: styd on* **2/1**[1]
4643 **3** *hd* **Metaphoric (IRE)**[28] 4749 3-9-5 **98**...............................(t) JimmyFortune 10 107
(M L W Bell) *chsd ldrs: rdn over 2f out: styd on* **9/2**[3]
4311 **4** *6* **Ajaan**[27] 4779 3-8-11 **90**...(b) TedDurcan 9 90
(H R A Cecil) *trckd ldrs: rdn over 3f out: styd on same pce fnl 2f* **7/2**[2]
3120 **5** *5* **Camps Bay (USA)**[28] 4749 3-9-0 **93**.................................. JimCrowley 11 86
(Mrs A J Perrett) *hld up: rdn and hung lft over 3f out: nvr trbld ldrs* **7/1**
5520 **6** *1 1/4* **Futun**[30] 4690 4-10-0 **97**.. EddieAhern 6 89
(L M Cumani) *hld up: effrt over 2f out: n.d* **10/1**
1334 **7** *7* **Dundry**[80] 3153 6-8-12 **81**..(p) SteveDrowne 7 63
(G L Moore) *hld up: rdn and wknd over 3f out* **40/1**
300/ **8** *7* **Inchpast**[705] 5903 6-8-9 **78** oh1.....................................(b) SaleemGolam 1 50
(M H Tompkins) *chsd ldrs: rdn over 3f out: wknd over 2f out* **50/1**
1124 **9** *5* **Mull Of Dubai**[30] 4690 4-9-8 **91**.. JohnEgan 8 56
(J S Moore) *hld up: rdn over 3f out: wknd over 2f out: eased fnl f* **12/1**
3m 2.28s (-3.02) **Going Correction** 0.0s/f (Good)
WFA 3 from 4yo+ 10lb **9** Ran SP% **119.2**
Speed ratings (Par 109): **108,107,107,104,101 100,96,92,89**
CSF £23.68 CT £78.56 TOTE £9.70: £2.60, £1.30, £1.80; EX 26.00 Trifecta £121.00 Pool: £443.43 - 2.60 winning units.
Owner Hamdan Al Maktoum **Bred** Shadwell Farm LLC **Trained** Lambourn, Berks
FOCUS
A valuable and competitive handicap in which the winner set a decent gallop. The form is rated fairly positively around the third and fourth.
NOTEBOOK
Aajel(USA) benefited from a fine front-running ride to post his second career victory. This giant grey was well suited by the change to forcing tactics and saw out the longer trip well. (tchd 7-1 and 8-1)
Irish Quest(IRE), 2lb well in under his penalty, made a bold bid for the hat-trick but, try as he might, he could not get past the winner, a much bigger individual than he is. There was no disgrace in this. (op 9-4)
Metaphoric(IRE), again equipped with the tongue tie, was once more staying on at the death. He looks ready for another try at 2m, his only previous run at that trip having been in the Group 3 Queen's Vase. (op 5-1 tchd 6-1)
Ajaan, attempting a three-timer, had today's winner behind when scoring at Pontefract but was 7lb worse off here. He was never quite able to make his presence felt, and although that Pontefract win came on firm ground he is probably happier on an easier surface. (op 9-2)
Camps Bay(USA) has yet to really prove that he stays this far. (op 10-1)
Futun, trying his longest trip to date, was held up as usual. He did pass a few rivals in the straight but was never a factor. (op 17-2 tchd 8-1)
Mull Of Dubai Official explanation: jockey said gelding was unsuited by the good to firm (good in places) ground

5575 DON'T MISS THE SCRUM - "BETLIVE" @ WILLIAMHILL.COM MAIDEN STKS 6f 3y
4:40 (4:42) (Class 5) 2-Y-0 **£3,886** (£1,156; £577; £288) **Stalls** High

Form RPR
3 **1** **Manassas (IRE)**[33] 4604 2-9-3 0.................................... SteveDrowne 10 83+
(B J Meehan) *chsd ldrs: led over 1f out: r.o wl* **5/2**[1]
04 **2** *2 1/2* **Naughty Frida (IRE)**[20] 5003 2-8-12 0.......................... JimmyFortune 8 71
(E A L Dunlop) *hld up in tch: racd keenly: rdn over 1f out: styd on* **15/2**[3]
3 *1 1/4* **Danish Art (IRE)** 2-9-0 0.. WilliamBuick(3) 1 72+
(J A R Toller) *chsd ldrs: led wl over 1f out: sn hdd: edgd rt and no ex ins fnl f* **14/1**
4 *3/4* **Torch Of Freedom (IRE)** 2-9-3 0.................................. JamieMackay 2 70
(Sir Mark Prescott) *s.s: outpcd: swtchd rt over 1f out: r.o ins fnl f: nvr nrr* **33/1**
5 *nk* **Dan Chillingworth (IRE)** 2-9-3 0.................................. OscarUrbina 12 69+
(J R Fanshawe) *s.i.s: hld up: hdwy over 1f out: nt trble ldrs* **11/1**
02 **6** *1/2* **Mandelieu (IRE)**[58] 3823 2-9-0 0...................................... LiamJones(3) 7 67+
(W J Haggas) *led: racd keenly: rdn and hdd wl over 1f out: styng on same pce whn hmpd ins fnl f* **6/1**[2]
3225 **7** *nk* **Aaim For Applause**[23] 4923 2-9-3 80.................................... TPO'Shea 9 66
(M R Channon) *chsd ldrs: rdn over 2f out: wknd ins fnl f* **5/2**[1]
8 *1/2* **Young Ivanhoe** 2-9-3 0...(t) JohnEgan 11 65
(P J McBride) *hld up: hdwy and hung lft over 1f out: nt trble ldrs* **50/1**
9 *1/2* **Bairag (USA)** 2-9-3 0... DMylonas 3 63
(Mrs C A Dunnett) *s.i.s and wnt lft s: hdwy 1/2-way: rdn over 1f out: sn wknd* **33/1**
10 *11* **Dual Faith (IRE)** 2-9-3 0... TedDurcan 5 30+
(B J Meehan) *mid-div: rdn 1/2-way: wknd over 2f out* **28/1**
11 *1 3/4* **Topazes** 2-9-3 0.. HayleyTurner 6 25
(M L W Bell) *prom: rdn and lost pl over 4f out: sn bhd* **12/1**
1m 15.74s (2.04) **Going Correction** +0.225s/f (Good) **11** Ran SP% **117.2**
Speed ratings (Par 95): **95,91,90,89,88 87,87,86,86,71 69**
CSF £21.67 TOTE £3.20: £1.90, £2.20, £3.50; EX 22.30 Trifecta £362.60 Part won. Pool: £510.83 - 0.90 winning units..
Owner Mrs R Philipps **Bred** Mrs Rebecca Philipps **Trained** Manton, Wilts
FOCUS
There was a heavy shower prior to this race. A reasonable maiden with the winner rated to Newmarket form backed up by the runner-up.
NOTEBOOK
Manassas(IRE), third on his debut in a Newmarket maiden won by subsequent Group 3 scorer Young Pretender, ran here in preference to the weekend's Mill Reef Stakes at Newbury. He quickened up well to assert in the final half-furlong and there should be a good deal better to come from him. (op 2-1 tchd 15-8)
Naughty Frida(IRE) stayed on in good style inside the last, if no match for the winner. She is now qualified for handicaps and should pay her way in that sphere. (op 7-1 tchd 8-1)
Danish Art(IRE), a half-brother to three winners, two of them in Italy, cost 57,000gns as a yearling. He showed plenty of ability on this debut and was only run out of second place inside the last. (op 16-1)
Torch Of Freedom(IRE) ◆ is a half-brother to six winners out of a smart 7-10f performer who was a half-sister to Salsabil and Marju. Slow to break and racing at the back of the field, he made steady progress inside the last after being switched to the stands' side and was going on at the finish. This was certainly an eye-catching introduction and there should be much better to come from him in time.
Dan Chillingworth(IRE), whose dam was a smart performer at 5-7f for Jim Bolger, made 120,000gns as a yearling. He was not knocked about when held on this debut and there should be improvement to come. (op 16-1)
Mandelieu(IRE), a half-brother to useful sprinter Knot In Wood, has been gelded since his last run. He again made the running but could not hold on over this longer trip. (tchd 11-2 and 7-1)
Aaim For Applause, back in maiden company and without the visor, disappointed again and continues to prove expensive to follow. (op 11-4 tchd 9-4)

5576 BE IN THE GAME "BETLIVE" @ WILLIAMHILL.COM H'CAP 6f 3y
5:10 (5:11) (Class 6) (0-60,64) 3-Y-0+ **£3,238** (£963; £481; £240) **Stalls** High

Form RPR
4605 **1** **Wadnagin (IRE)**[35] 4529 3-8-11 52............................ RichardThomas 11 62
(I A Wood) *sn outpcd: hdwy u.p over 1f out: r.o to ld post* **33/1**
4333 **2** *shd* **Miss Daawe**[9] 5295 3-8-4 48.. WilliamBuick(3) 13 58
(B Ellison) *prom: reminder after 1f: rdn to ld over 1f out: edgd lft: hdd post* **7/2**[1]
2612 **3** *1 1/4* **Digital**[7] 5349 10-9-11 64 6ex..(v) TPO'Shea 3 70
(M R Channon) *hld up: hdwy over 1f out: sn rdn: r.o* **9/2**[2]
2314 **4** *3/4* **Kennington**[14] 5174 7-9-2 55... HayleyTurner 17 59
(Mrs C A Dunnett) *chsd ldrs: rdn over 2f out: ev ch over 1f out: no ex ins fnl f* **8/1**
0230 **5** *1* **Lost All Alone**[79] 3178 3-8-1 49............................. ThomasO'Brien(7) 9 49
(D M Simcock) *edgd rt s: sn mid-div: outpcd 1/2-way: hdwy u.p over 1f out: r.o* **40/1**
-600 **6** *1/2* **Storm Petrel**[44] 4257 3-9-4 59..(t) GeorgeBaker 6 58
(R M Beckett) *dwlt: outpcd: r.o ins fnl f: nvr nrr* **33/1**
0440 **7** *3/4* **Larky's Lob**[9] 5295 8-8-10 49.. JohnEgan 12 45
(J O'Reilly) *chsd ldrs: rdn over 2f out: no ex fnl f* **12/1**
3130 **8** *3/4* **Xalted**[36] 4514 3-8-10 51.. RichardKingscote 4 45
(S C Williams) *s.i.s: hld up: hdwy over 1f out: nt trble ldrs* **12/1**
5441 **9** *1 1/2* **Limonia (GER)**[29] 4712 5-8-9 53.................................... TolleyDean(5) 2 42
(Mike Murphy) *led: rdn and hdd over 1f out: wknd ins fnl f* **10/1**
0540 **10** *1* **Monashee Prince (IRE)**[50] 4083 5-9-4 57..................... SteveDrowne 10 43
(J R Best) *hmpd s: hdwy 1/2-way: wknd fnl f* **16/1**
3532 **11** *shd* **Norcroft**[12] 5234 5-9-1 59..............................(p) KirstyMilczarek(5) 15 45
(Mrs C A Dunnett) *chsd ldrs: rdn over 2f out: wknd fnl f* **5/1**[3]
3311 **12** *9* **Viewforth**[9] 5295 9-9-11 64 6ex......................................(b) JimCrowley 5 21
(M A Buckley) *w ldr tl rdn and hung rt over 2f out: wknd over 1f out* **12/1**
0150 **13** *3* **Gone'N'Dunnett (IRE)**[30] 4689 8-8-13 52.........................(p) DMylonas 8 —
(Mrs C A Dunnett) *mid-div: rdn over 3f out: sn wknd* **12/1**
1m 14.44s (0.74) **Going Correction** +0.225s/f (Good)
WFA 3 from 4yo+ 2lb **13** Ran SP% **122.2**
Speed ratings (Par 101): **104,103,102,101,99 99,98,97,95,93 93,81,77**
CSF £147.75 CT £668.46 TOTE £37.70: £9.20, £2.30, £1.80; EX 187.30 Trifecta £326.50 Part won. Pool: £459.89 - 0.10 winning units. Place 6 £ 22.48, Place 5 £ 15.17.
Owner Jim Browne **Bred** Kilnamoragh Stud **Trained** Upper Lambourn, Berks
FOCUS
A moderate handicap rated around the first two and the fourth but limited by the proximity of the fifth and sixth.
Norcroft Official explanation: jockey said gelding was unsuited by the ground

The Form Book, Raceform Ltd, Compton, RG20 6NL

T/Plt: £41.70 to a £1 stake. Pool: £65,475.60. 1,144.40 winning tickets. T/Qpdt: £12.50 to a £1 stake. Pool: £3,350.40. 197.10 winning tickets. CR

5577 - 5579a (Foreign Racing) - See Raceform Interactive

[5550]AYR (L-H)

Friday, September 21

OFFICIAL GOING: Soft

10mm rain since the start of racing the previous day. 'Heavy' in the back straight, 'soft and patchy' in the home straight was the riders' verdict.
Wind: Moderate half-against

5580 ROBB FERGUSON CA EUROPEAN BREEDERS' FUND MAIDEN STKS 7f 50y
2:20 (2:22) (Class 4) 2-Y-O £5,181 (£1,541; £770; £384) Stalls Low

Form RPR
52 **1** **Boy Blue**[9] 5328 2-9-3 0 AdrianTNicholls 11 85+
(D Nicholls) *mde all: rdn 2f out: kpt on strly fnl f* **8/1**[3]
3 **2** ½ **Lady Sorcerer**[14] 5201 2-8-9 0 AndrewElliott(3) 9 79+
(A P Jarvis) *a cl up: effrt and chsd wnr over 1f out: kpt on fnl f* **16/1**
0 **3** 7 **Blue Citadel (USA)**[8] 5361 2-9-3 0 RobertHavlin 2 67+
(J H M Gosden) *hld up: rdn over 2f out: hdwy on outside over 1f out: kpt on: nt rch first two* **5/1**[2]
63 **4** shd **Shaloo Diamond**[27] 4819 2-9-0 0 MichaelJStainton(3) 12 67
(R M Whitaker) *prom on outside: effrt and edgd lft over 2f out: sn one pce* **40/1**
5 1¼ **Sir Royal (USA)** 2-9-0 0 PJMcDonald(3) 13 64
(G A Swinbank) *towards rr: hdwy over 1f out: no imp fnl f* **25/1**
2 **6** 2 **Azure Mist**[53] 4028 2-8-12 0 JimmyQuinn 7 54+
(M H Tompkins) *t.k.h: chsd ldrs: rdn whn hmpd over 2f out: sn btn* **10/1**
6 **7** 1½ **Silent Master (USA)**[28] 4782 2-9-3 0 GregFairley 4 56
(M Johnston) *midfield: drvn fr 3f out: no imp fnl 2f* **8/1**[3]
8 1 **Princess Maria (USA)** 2-8-12 0 PaulHanagan 6 48
(R A Fahey) *midfield: drvn over 2f out: btn over 1f out* **40/1**
9 1 **Arganil (USA)** 2-9-3 0 PatCosgrave 8 51+
(K A Ryan) *towards rr: pushed along over 2f out: btn whn n.m.r over 1f out* **9/1**
10 2½ **Supporting Role (IRE)** 2-9-3 0 GrahamGibbons 10 45
(E S McMahon) *prom: effrt whn checked over 2f out: sn btn* **20/1**
0 **11** 2 **Jetta Joy (IRE)**[39] 4448 2-8-12 0 RoystonFfrench 5 35
(Mrs A Duffield) *towards rr: drvn along 3f out: nvr on terms* **100/1**
3 **12** 10 **Manuka Bee**[70] 3510 2-9-3 0 TomEaves 3 16
(J Howard Johnson) *bhd: struggling 1/2-way: nvr on terms* **20/1**
2 **13** 2½ **Internationaldebut (IRE)**[9] 5323 2-9-3 0 JohnEgan 1 10
(D J Murphy) *cl up tl rdn and wknd qckly fr 2f out* **2/1**[1]

1m 36.6s (3.88) **Going Correction** +0.50s/f (Yiel) **13 Ran SP% 116.4**
Speed ratings (Par 97): **97,96,88,88,86 84,82,81,80,77 75,64,61**
CSF £113.37 TOTE £7.20: £2.00, £4.20, £2.30; EX 65.80.
Owner Ian Bishop **Bred** G Russell **Trained** Sessay, N Yorks

FOCUS
An ordinary event and only a fair gallop but the first two did well to pull clear in the last quarter mile. The form looks strong and could be rated a little higher but treated with caution in view of the ground.

NOTEBOOK
Boy Blue ◆ has improved with every outing and turned in his best effort on this first run on an easy surface. He will have no problems with a mile and appeals as the sort to win in handicap company. (op 10-1 tchd 15-2)
Lady Sorcerer ◆, who shaped well on her debut over 6f on Polytrack, bettered that effort over this longer trip for this turf debut. She pulled well clear of the remainder and looks sure to win a similar event at the very least. (op 25-1)
Blue Citadel(USA), who was far from disgraced on his debut at Sandown, ran to a similar level back in trip and in softer ground to fare the best of those attempting to come from off the pace. He will be suited by the return to 1m and is sure to win a race in nursery company. (op 9-2)
Shaloo Diamond, who showed improved form behind an impressive winner at Redcar on his previous start, again showed ability. He is likely to continue to look vulnerable in this type of event, though, and will be seen to better effect in ordinary handicap company. (tchd 50-1)
Sir Royal(USA), a half-brother to a couple of winners abroad, was easy to back and was not disgraced on this racecourse debut. He will stay further and is in good hands but appeals as the type to fare better once handicapped.
Azure Mist, who shaped well over this trip on quick ground on her debut, proved far too keen in these much softer conditions and was well below that level after meeting trouble. She should be suited by the return to quick ground but is going to have to settle better if she is to progress. (op 9-1)
Internationaldebut(IRE), who shaped with a good deal of promise on his debut at Doncaster, looked to have fair claims in this lesser event turned out fairly quickly but proved a big disappointment in these much softer conditions. He should be suited by the return to a sound surface and is well worth another chance in similar company. Official explanation: jockey said colt was unsuited by the soft ground (op 5-2 tchd 11-4 in places)

5581 HBG PROPERTIES H'CAP 5f
2:55 (2:56) (Class 4) (0-85,84) 3-Y-O+ £6,477 (£1,927; £963; £481) Stalls High

Form RPR
1041 **1** **Divine Spirit**[4] 5481 6-9-1 80 6ex RoystonFfrench 16 89
(M Dods) *chsd ldrs: styd on wl to ld post* **7/1**[3]
2211 **2** shd **Swift Princess (IRE)**[32] 4658 3-8-8 77 (v) AndrewElliott(3) 15 86
(K R Burke) *w ldrs: led over 2f out: hdd last stride* **13/2**[2]
4610 **3** 1¼ **Compton Classic**[30] 4703 5-8-7 77 GaryBartley(5) 11 81
(J S Goldie) *in rr: hdwy and nt clr run over 1f out: swtchd lft ins fnl f: styd on: nt rch 1st 2* **7/1**[3]
1000 **4** 2 **Highland Warrior**[7] 5379 8-9-1 80 MickyFenton 4 77+
(P T Midgley) *in rr: hdwy on wd outside 2f out: kpt on: nvr rchd ldrs* **20/1**
0000 **5** hd **Distinctly Game**[7] 5379 5-8-11 79 AndrewMullen(3) 20 75
(K A Ryan) *in rr-div: hdwy and swtchd lft over 1f out: styd on wl ins fnl f* **16/1**
1431 **6** 1 **Glasshoughton**[30] 4703 4-9-5 84 PhillipMakin 18 77
(M Dods) *led tl over 2f out: wknd over 1f out* **13/2**[2]
1500 **7** hd **The History Man (IRE)**[1] 5552 4-8-2 72 ow2 (b) SCreighton(5) 17 64
(M Mullineaux) *w ldrs: one pce fnl 2f* **16/1**
5600 **8** nk **Rothesay Dancer**[1] 5552 4-8-0 70 oh3 KellyHarrison(5) 5 61
(J S Goldie) *in rr: hdwy 2f out: nvr nr ldrs* **50/1**
0322 **9** ½ **Guest Connections**[3] 5505 4-8-10 75 (v) AdrianTNicholls 1 64
(D Nicholls) *chsd ldrs: outpcd over 2f out: hung rt and lost pl over 1f out* **8/1**
6621 **10** 2 **Word Perfect**[30] 4719 5-8-7 72 (b) DaleGibson 9 54
(M W Easterby) *chsd ldrs: lost pl over 1f out* **17/2**
2131 **11** shd **John Keats**[15] 5155 4-8-7 72 TonyHamilton 13 53
(J S Goldie) *in rr: nvr a factor* **25/1**
0032 **12** 1½ **Yungaburra (IRE)**[7] 5379 3-9-0 80 JohnEgan 14 56
(D J Murphy) *chsd ldrs: rdn and carried hd high over 1f out: sn lost pl* **11/2**[1]
35- **13** hd **Poisiedon (IRE)**[26] 4861 3-8-11 77 PatCosgrave 7 52
(Liam McAteer, Ire) *s.i.s: hdwy 3f out: lost pl over 1f out* **28/1**
02-0 **14** 8 **Godfrey Street**[14] 5195 4-9-4 83 PaulMulrennan 2 30
(K A Ryan) *chsd ldrs: lost pl over 1f out: sn bhd and eased* **25/1**

61.31 secs (0.87) **Going Correction** +0.225s/f (Good)
WFA 3 from 4yo+ 1lb **14 Ran SP% 118.3**
Speed ratings (Par 105): **102,101,99,96,96 94,94,93,93,89 89,87,87,74**
CSF £47.59 CT £335.11 TOTE £8.30: £2.70, £2.20, £3.30; EX 45.20.
Owner The Newcastle Racing Club **Bred** S R Hope And D Erwin Bloodstock **Trained** Denton, Co Durham

FOCUS
A fair handicap and despite the winner being back to his best at face value there are doubts about the form.
Guest Connections Official explanation: jockey said gelding hung right-handed
Yungaburra(IRE) Official explanation: jockey said gelding was unsuited by the soft ground

5582 WEST SOUND & WEST FM NURSERY 6f
3:30 (3:31) (Class 4) (0-85,85) 2-Y-O £6,477 (£1,927; £963; £481) Stalls High

Form RPR
1 **1** **Cape Vale (IRE)**[28] 4782 2-9-1 79 AdrianTNicholls 5 84+
(D Nicholls) *t.k.h early: hld up: swtchd lft and hdwy over 2f out: led appr fnl f: hld on wl* **11/2**[2]
3520 **2** nk **Rubirosa (IRE)**[31] 4695 2-9-5 83 PhillipMakin 12 87+
(M Dods) *hld up: nt clr run over 3f out to over 1f out: rdn and kpt on strly fnl f: jst hld* **7/1**
001 **3** shd **Upton Grey (IRE)**[27] 4810 2-9-7 85 RobertHavlin 8 89
(J H M Gosden) *stdd s: hdwy and cl up 1/2-way: led briefly over 1f out: kpt on fnl f: hld nr fin* **11/4**[1]
0133 **4** 1½ **Ginger Pickle**[26] 4844 2-8-13 77 GrahamGibbons 3 77
(J R Weymes) *chsd ldrs: drvn 1/2-way: rallied: one pce fnl f* **16/1**
3403 **5** 1¼ **Kinout (IRE)**[15] 5153 2-8-12 76 JohnEgan 2 72
(K A Ryan) *prom: rdn and led over 2f out to over 1f out: one pce* **20/1**
1230 **6** 1 **Nine Stories (IRE)**[29] 4743 2-9-6 84 TomEaves 15 77
(J Howard Johnson) *chsd ldrs: outpcd over 2f out: kpt on fnl f: no imp* **9/1**
040 **7** shd **Red Skipper (IRE)**[27] 4818 2-8-0 64 JimmyQuinn 11 56
(N Wilson) *bhd: bmpd over 4f out: effrt outside over 2f out: sn no imp* **20/1**
2102 **8** ¾ **Willyn (IRE)**[15] 5153 2-7-11 66 KellyHarrison(5) 1 56
(J S Goldie) *bhd: bmpd over 4f out: rdn over 2f out: nvr rchd ldrs* **40/1**
4160 **9** hd **Dark Tara**[31] 4695 2-8-12 76 (b[1]) PaulHanagan 13 66
(R A Fahey) *early reminders in rr: wnt sharply lft over 4f out: effrt over 2f out: n.d* **13/2**[3]
5224 **10** 5 **Natmana**[14] 5199 2-8-9 73 PatCosgrave 10 48
(M R Channon) *cl up: ev ch over 2f out: wknd over 1f out* **11/1**
2030 **11** nk **Fulford**[24] 4923 2-7-13 63 DaleGibson 6 37
(M Brittain) *chsd ldrs: ev ch over 2f out: sn wknd* **40/1**
532 **12** 7 **River Gleam (IRE)**[34] 4611 2-8-5 72 AndrewElliott(3) 14 25
(A P Jarvis) *led to over 2f out: sn btn* **9/1**

1m 15.2s (1.53) **Going Correction** +0.225s/f (Good) **12 Ran SP% 116.5**
Speed ratings (Par 97): **98,97,97,95,93 92,92,91,91,84 84,74**
CSF £40.93 CT £129.24 TOTE £5.20: £2.40, £2.40, £1.80; EX 50.50.
Owner Lady O'Reilly **Bred** Derek Veitch **Trained** Sessay, N Yorks
■ Stewards' Enquiry : Adrian T Nicholls caution: used whip down shoulder in forehand position
Robert Havlin caution: used whip with excessive frequency

FOCUS
A fair nursery in which the pace was sound and the form looks solid enough. The field raced stands' side.

NOTEBOOK
Cape Vale(IRE) ◆, who created a favourable impression on his debut on quick ground, bettered that form in this fair nursery in these much softer conditions. He travelled strongly for much of the way before showing the right attitude under pressure and he appeals strongly as the type to win more races. (op 5-1 tchd 9-2)
Rubirosa(IRE) ◆, a consistent performer who has only raced so far over 6f, looked a shade unfortunate not to add to his debut success as he was short of room for over a furlong around halfway. He looks well worth a try over 7f and is the sort to win more races. (op 15-2 tchd 13-2)
Upton Grey(IRE), who showed much improved form when scoring over this trip and in soft ground on his previous start, seemed to give it his best shot on this nursery debut. He seems best with give underfoot and is capable of further success. (op 5-2 tchd 3-1, 7-2 in a place)
Ginger Pickle, back over 6f, was one of the first off the bridle but kept responding to pressure and left the impression that he would be worth another try over 7f. He is a consistent sort who should continue to give a good account. (op 20-1)
Kinout(IRE), has yet to win a race but is a consistent sort on turf and he proved his effectiveness with give in the ground. He looks worth another try over 7f but on the evidence so far, has little margin for error from this mark. (tchd 18-1)
Nine Stories(IRE), back in handicap company, left the impression that the return to 7f and beyond would be in his favour but he is going to have to improve to defy his current mark of 84 in competitive handicap company. (op 20-1)
Dark Tara Official explanation: jockey said filly never travelled

5583 JAMES BARR CHARTERED SURVEYORS HARRY ROSEBERY STKS (FOR THE SOUTH AYRSHIRE CUP) (LISTED RACE) 5f
4:05 (4:05) (Class 1) 2-Y-O
£17,034 (£6,456; £3,231; £1,611; £807; £405) Stalls High

Form RPR
1314 **1** **Captain Gerrard (IRE)**[7] 5377 2-9-6 108 TomEaves 1 107
(B Smart) *swtchd rt after s: mde all: shkn up and r.o strly ins fnl f* **5/6**[1]
1224 **2** 2 **Look Busy (IRE)**[21] 4992 2-8-12 88 PatrickMathers 5 92
(A Berry) *n.m.r sn after s: hdwy over 2f out: hung lft and wnt 2nd 1f out: kpt on: no imp* **12/1**
5040 **3** ¾ **Carleton**[9] 5324 2-9-3 91 PaulHanagan 10 94
(M R Channon) *hld up towards rr: hdwy 2f out: styd on ins fnl f* **12/1**
124 **4** 1½ **Lesson In Humility (IRE)**[25] 4899 2-8-12 84 PhillipMakin 8 84
(K R Burke) *hmpd s: chsd ldrs: kpt on wl fnl f* **10/1**[3]
012 **5** 3 **Mesmerize Me**[11] 5277 2-9-3 87 GrahamGibbons 6 78
(E S McMahon) *chsd ldrs: sn drvn along: lost pl over 1f out* **12/1**
4260 **6** nk **New Jersey (IRE)**[29] 4743 2-9-3 97 JimmyQuinn 4 77
(K A Ryan) *trckd ldrs: effrt over 1f out: sn wknd* **5/1**[2]
2535 **7** 3½ **Kylayne**[15] 5164 2-8-12 92 JohnEgan 7 59
(P W D'Arcy) *chsd ldrs: wknd over 1f out: eased* **14/1**
3000 **8** 5 **Cee Bargara**[13] 5219 2-9-3 96 RobertHavlin 2 46
(J A Osborne) *chsd ldrs: wknd over 1f out: eased* **22/1**

4500 **9** *hd* **Romantic Destiny**[15] 5164 2-8-12 95........................(b) RoystonFfrench 9 41
(K A Ryan) *swvd lft s: drvn along in rr: nvr wnt pce* **40/1**
60.71 secs (0.27) **Going Correction** +0.225s/f (Good) **9** Ran SP% **116.8**
Speed ratings (Par 103): **106,102,101,99,94 93,88,80,80**
CSF £12.83 TOTE £1.80: £1.20, £2.80, £3.30; EX 12.70.
Owner R C Bond **Bred** Alan Dargan **Trained** Hambleton, N Yorks

FOCUS
Not that strong a Listed race in which Captain Gerrard had easily the strongest claims and ran out a most decisive winner. The form loos sound though.

NOTEBOOK
Captain Gerrard(IRE), worst drawn, is all speed and was soon showing them a clean pair of heels. He loves to get his toe in the ground and has a splendid attitude. (op 4-5 tchd 8-11 and Evens)
Look Busy(IRE) had 12lb to find with the winner. Squeezed out soon after the start and showing a marked tendency to hang, she stuck on grimly to claim second spot. (tchd 14-1)
Carleton looked at his very best and showed a return to form. He stuck on in willing fashion and is clearly at his best in the mud. (op 16-1)
Lesson In Humility(IRE), dropping back in trip and encountering soft ground for the first time, took a bump at the start. She stuck on in goood style and is clearly going the right way. (op 9-1)
Mesmerize Me was tackling much stronger company and was not up to it. (op 18-1)
New Jersey(IRE) took the eye in the paddock. He travelled strongly but in the end was firmly put in his place. (op 11-2 tchd 9-2)
Cee Bargara Official explanation: jockey said colt was unsuited by the soft ground

5584 TOTESPORT.COM AYR SILVER CUP (H'CAP) 6f
4:40 (4:40) (Class 2) 3-Y-0+
£21,812 (£6,531; £3,265; £1,634; £815; £409) **Stalls** High

Form RPR
1-03 **1** **Utmost Respect**[72] 3431 3-9-6 **93**.................................. PaulHanagan 15 113+
(R A Fahey) *trckd stands' side ldr: shkn up to ld 1f out: pushed out: readily* **11/4**[1]
3123 **2** *1 ½* **Northern Dare (IRE)**[34] 4607 3-8-11 **84**................ SilvestreDeSousa 16 95
(D Nicholls) *led stands' side to 1f out: kpt on fnl f: 2nd of 14 in gp* **14/1**
1111 **3** *2 ½* **Sundae**[55] 3952 3-9-7 **94**.................................. GeorgeBaker 20 98
(C F Wall) *trckd stands' side ldrs: rdn over 2f out: one pce fnl f: 3rd of 14 in gp* **9/1**[3]
013 **4** *2* **Sunrise Safari (IRE)**[20] 5039 4-9-3 **88**...........................(v) TomEaves 27 86+
(I Semple) *bhd stands' side tl hdwy over 1f out: kpt on: nrst fin: 4th of 14 in gp* **16/1**
0106 **5** *¾* **Continent**[14] 5195 10-9-4 **89**... JimmyQuinn 25 84
(D Nicholls) *hld up stands' side: effrt and hdwy over 1f out: kpt on: 5th of 14 in gp* **25/1**
6110 **6** *½* **Balakiref**[35] 4581 8-8-12 **83**.. PhillipMakin 18 77
(M Dods) *midfield stands' side: rdn and hdwy 2f out: kpt on same pce fnl f: 6th of 14 in gp* **33/1**
5626 **7** *½* **Geojimali**[27] 4816 5-8-11 **82**... DanielTudhope 23 74
(J S Goldie) *dwlt: bhd stands' side: hdwy over 1f out: nvr rchd ldrs: 7th of 14 in gp* **10/1**
6105 **8** *½* **Commando Scott (IRE)**[26] 4851 6-9-2 **87**................. RoystonFfrench 5 78
(I W McInnes) *hld up bhd far side ldrs: effrt 2f out: led that gp wl ins fnl f: no ch w stands' side: 1st of 11 in gp* **9/1**[3]
3030 **9** *shd* **Caribbean Coral**[35] 4567 8-9-6 **91**......................... GrahamGibbons 26 81
(J J Quinn) *hld up stands' side: effrt 2f out: no imp: 8th of 14 in gp* **33/1**
0055 **10** *1* **Gift Horse**[6] 5407 7-9-5 **93**..(v) PJMcDonald[(3)] 7 80
(D Nicholls) *prom far side: led that gp over 2f out to wl ins fnl f: no ex: 2nd of 11 in gp* **17/2**[2]
0432 **11** *nk* **Imperial Echo (USA)**[69] 3559 6-9-0 **85**........................... PaulFessey 22 72
(T D Barron) *bhd stands' side tl hdwy over 1f out: n.d: 9th of 14 in gp* **16/1**
5000 **12** *nk* **Out After Dark**[20] 5050 6-9-8 **93**..................................(p) PaulMulrennan 4 79
(C G Cox) *chsd far side ldrs: drvn over 2f out: one pce fnl f: 3rd of 11 in gp* **25/1**
0000 **13** *½* **Pacific Pride**[27] 4806 4-8-9 **80**.. PatCosgrave 28 64
(J J Quinn) *hld up stands' side: drvn over 2f out: n.d: 10th of 14 in gp* **33/1**
6040 **14** *½* **Pusey Street Lady**[6] 5403 3-8-10 **83**............................. RobertHavlin 19 66
(J Gallagher) *chsd stands' side ldrs tl wknd fr 2f out: 11th of 14 in gp* **100/1**
0300 **15** *nk* **Green Park (IRE)**[6] 5407 4-9-6 **94**............................. JamieMoriarty[(3)] 8 76
(R A Fahey) *hld up far side: hdwy over 2f out: no imp fnl f: 4th of 11 in gp* **33/1**
3134 **16** *¾* **High Curragh**[3] 5505 4-9-1 **89**..............................(b[1]) AndrewMullen[(3)] 11 69
(K A Ryan) *racd alone centre: no imp fr 2f out* **40/1**
0040 **17** *shd* **Northern Empire (IRE)**[13] 5212 4-9-5 **90**.......................... JohnEgan 9 69
(K A Ryan) *spd far side gp tl no ex fnl f: 5th of 11 in gp* **50/1**
0005 **18** *½* **Blazing Heights**[4] 5481 4-8-6 **82** ow1........................... GaryBartley[(5)] 3 60
(J S Goldie) *hld up far side: effrt and hdwy over 1f out: no ex fnl f: 6th of 11 in gp* **25/1**
-106 **19** *¾* **Makshoof (IRE)**[30] 4726 3-8-10 **83**................................ GregFairley 6 58
(K A Ryan) *prom far side tl rdn and no ex over 1f out: 7th of 11 in gp* **40/1**
0010 **20** *nk* **Damika (IRE)**[12] 5254 4-9-4 **92** 5ex..................... MichaelJStainton[(3)] 14 67
(R M Whitaker) *dwlt: bhd stands' side: effrt on outside 1/2-way: btn over 1f out: 12th of 14 in gp* **66/1**
3050 **21** *2* **Mr Wolf**[7] 5379 6-9-0 **85**..(p) TonyHamilton 12 54
(D W Barker) *led far side to over 2f out: btn over 1f out: 8th of 11 in gp* **66/1**
4024 **22** *½* **Curtail (IRE)**[28] 4780 4-9-2 **87**...(v[1]) LeeEnstone 2 54
(I Semple) *in tch far side tl wknd over 2f out: 9th of 11 in gp* **80/1**
000 **23** *nk* **Varadouro (BRZ)**[35] 4567 5-8-12 **83**.................................... DavidAllan 1 49
(D Nicholls) *prom far side tl rdn and wknd over 2f out: 10th of 11 in gp* **66/1**
0000 **24** *2 ½* **Coleorton Dancer**[117] 2058 5-9-0 **85**.............................. MickyFenton 10 44
(K A Ryan) *chsd far side ldrs tl wknd fnl 2f: last of 11 in gp* **33/1**
0000 **25** *¾* **Dickie Le Davoir**[74] 3380 3-8-12 **88**......................... AndrewElliott[(3)] 13 44
(K R Burke) *prom stands' side tl edgd lft and wknd wl over 1f out: 13th of 14 in gp* **100/1**
2601 **26** *5* **Northern Fling**[30] 4726 3-9-10 **97**................................ AdrianTNicholls 21 38
(D Nicholls) *dwlt: a bhd stands' side: eased whn no ch fnl f: last of 14 in gp* **20/1**
1m 13.7s (0.03) **Going Correction** +0.225s/f (Good)
WFA 3 from 4yo+ 2lb **105** Ran SP% **130.3**
Speed ratings (Par 109): **108,106,102,100,99 98,97,97,96,95 95,94,94,93,93 92,91,91,90,89 87,86,86,82,81 75**
CSF £34.28 CT £330.86 TOTE £3.70: £1.90, £3.60, £3.00, £4.90; EX 70.70 Trifecta £476.40 Pool £1,946.16 - 2.90 winning units..
Owner The Rumpole Partnership **Bred** Mrs H B Raw **Trained** Musley Bank, N Yorks

FOCUS
A competitive handicap run at a decent gallop but one in which the stands' side held the clear edge, with the first seven home racing on that part of the track. The form is rated around the placed horses although not totally solid.

NOTEBOOK
Utmost Respect ◆, who looked a fair bit better than the bare form of his two previous runs this year, confirmed he was a smart performer with his best effort yet, winning this competitive affair in style. A strong traveller who relishes give underfoot, he should have no problems with 7f and is open to plenty of further improvement. He remains an exciting prospect and appeals strongly as the sort to win another decent handicap granted suitable conditions. Indeed, he is not far off Pattern class on this evidence. (op 10-3 tchd 7-2 in places)
Northern Dare(IRE), from a stable whose runners at this meeting have been performing with credit, is a progressive sprinter who turned in his best effort against a most progressive rival. He beat the rest comprehensively enough and, although he will be up in the weights again, he should continue to give a good account over sprint distances. (op 16-1)
Sundae, who has improved markedly this year, found his winning sequence coming to an end but, although he enjoyed the run of the race, he ran right up to his best from his decent draw. This trip with give in the ground are his requirements and this relatively lightly-raced sort looks the sort to win more races. (op 10-1)
Sunrise Safari(IRE) ran creditably back up in trip and in softer ground and may be better than the bare form in a race where it paid to race prominently but, although he is a proven performer at this distance, all of his best form has been over the minimum trip in strongly run races.
Continent, who won this race six years ago and who has already been on the mark twice this year, had conditions to suit and ran creditably from his decent draw against three progressive three-year-olds. However, he is always going to look vulnerable against the more progressive or better handicapped sorts in this type of event. (op 28-1)
Balakiref, not at his best over 7f at Newcastle on his previous start, fared better back in trip under ideal conditions. He has already had a good season with three wins but has little margin for error from his current mark.
Geojimali, the winner of this race last year, was not disgraced in a race where those held up were not seen to best effect but he is the type that needs things to drop just right. (tchd 11-1)
Commando Scott(IRE) ◆, who attracted plenty of support, looks better than the bare form as he finished best of those to race on the far-side group. Equally effective over this trip or 7f with give in the ground, he is capable of winning more races. (op 10-1 tchd 8-1)
Gift Horse ran better than the distance beaten suggests when finishing second in the far-side group but, given he has not won since lifting the Stewards Cup in 2005, remains one to tread carefully with at single-figure odds from his current mark in this type of event. (op 15-2)
Pusey Street Lady Official explanation: jockey said filly hung left-handed from halfway
Northern Fling Official explanation: jockey said gelding ran flat

5585 BOON HOMES H'CAP 1m
5:15 (5:15) (Class 4) (0-85,85) 3-Y-0+ **£6,477** (£1,927; £963; £481) **Stalls** Low

Form RPR
1040 **1** **Wigwam Willie (IRE)**[27] 4827 5-9-3 **80**............................(p) JohnEgan 12 92
(K A Ryan) *pushed along and prom 5f out: led appr fnl f: drvn out* **4/1**[1]
2000 **2** *1 ¾* **Mezuzah**[20] 5031 7-9-3 **80**... PaulMulrennan 14 89
(M W Easterby) *sn trcking ldrs: chal over 2f out: no ex ins fnl f* **12/1**
2562 **3** *1 ¾* **Osteopathic Remedy (IRE)**[28] 4785 3-9-0 **81**............ PaulHanagan 10 85
(M Dods) *trckd ldrs: t.k.h: led 2f out: hdd and no ex appr fnl f* **15/2**[3]
0125 **4** *shd* **Gunfighter (IRE)**[70] 3512 4-8-9 **75**........................... PJMcDonald[(3)] 1 80
(J S Wainwright) *hld up in rr: hdwy on ins over 2f out: styd on fnl f* **10/1**
5112 **5** *1* **Gleneagles (IRE)**[51] 4080 3-8-6 **80**................................ LanceBetts[(7)] 2 82
(N Wilson) *chsd ldrs: one pce fnl 2f* **17/2**
4004 **6** *1* **Emerald Bay (IRE)**[37] 4497 5-9-2 **79**.................................. TomEaves 6 80
(I Semple) *chsd ldrs: one pce fnl 2f* **16/1**
1000 **7** *shd* **Bold Marc (IRE)**[27] 4827 5-8-12 **82**.......................... DeclanCannon[(7)] 13 83
(K R Burke) *hld up in rr: hdwy over 3f out: kpt on fnl 2f: nvr a threat* **14/1**
1000 **8** *1 ¼* **Vicious Warrior**[24] 4922 8-9-5 **85**......................... MichaelJStainton[(3)] 5 83
(R M Whitaker) *w ldr: led 3f out: hdd 2f out: wknd jst ins fnl f* **6/1**[2]
2440 **9** *¾* **Cross The Line (IRE)**[52] 4049 5-9-4 **81**........................... RobertHavlin 9 78
(A P Jarvis) *hld up in rr: hdwy on outside over 2f out: nvr rchd ldrs* **8/1**
2310 **10** *6* **Robema**[20] 5031 4-9-5 **82**... GrahamGibbons 7 67
(J J Quinn) *prom: drvn over 5f out: wknd appr fnl f* **8/1**
0562 **11** *3 ½* **Prince Samos (IRE)**[30] 4713 5-8-12 **75**.................... SilvestreDeSousa 3 53
(D Nicholls) *led tl 3f out: sn wknd* **12/1**
000 **12** *6* **Love On Sight**[19] 5067 3-8-10 **80**................................ AndrewElliott[(3)] 4 45
(A P Jarvis) *in rr: detached over 3f out* **66/1**
4R01 **R** **Quai Du Roi (IRE)**[15] 5184 5-9-5 **82**........................... AdrianTNicholls 11 —
(D Nicholls) *ref to r: tk no part* **20/1**
1m 46.23s (2.74) **Going Correction** +0.50s/f (Yiel)
WFA 3 from 4yo+ 4lb **13** Ran SP% **122.1**
Speed ratings (Par 105): **106,104,102,102,101 100,100,99,98,92 88,82,—**
CSF £54.69 CT £286.32 TOTE £3.80: £1.90, £4.90, £2.50; EX 65.10.
Owner Neil & Anne Dawson Partnership **Bred** Mrs Margaret Christie **Trained** Hambleton, N Yorks

FOCUS
An ordinary handicap run at a steady pace but sound form rated through the runner-up and fifth.
Cross The Line(IRE) Official explanation: jockey said gelding was unsuited by the soft ground
Robema Official explanation: jockey said filly was unsuited by the soft ground
Love On Sight Official explanation: jockey said filly was unsuited by the soft ground

5586 BRIGHT PURPLE H'CAP (FOR THE EGLINTON & WINTON CHALLENGE CUP) 2m 1f 105y
5:50 (5:50) (Class 5) (0-75,71) 4-Y-0+ **£5,181** (£1,541; £770; £384) **Stalls** Low

Form RPR
232 **1** **Balakar (IRE)**[11] 5283 11-8-9 **59**..................................(p) PaulMulrennan 2 66
(J J Lambe, Ire) *hld up: reminders over 6f out: rallied and led over 2f out: hung lft: hld on wl fnl f* **11/2**[3]
-223 **2** *2 ½* **Kristiansand**[33] 2825 7-8-4 **54**... PaulFessey 12 59
(P Monteith) *hld up: hdwy and prom over 6f out: effrt and ev ch over 1f out: no ex ins fnl f* **5/1**[2]
230/ **3** *4* **Tangible**[21] 5027 5-8-11 **61**.. PatCosgrave 1 61
(Liam McAteer, Ire) *chsd ldrs: effrt over 2f out: no ex over 1f out* **9/2**[1]
1104 **4** *11* **Nero West (FR)**[22] 4969 6-9-7 **71**..(b) TomEaves 3 60
(I Semple) *chsd ldrs: drvn over 3f out: wknd fr 2f out* **5/1**[2]
0400 **5** *10* **Quicuyo (GER)**[41] 4380 4-7-13 **52** oh6..................... AndrewMullen[(3)] 6 31
(P Monteith) *in tch: rdn over 5f out: wknd over 3f out* **20/1**
203- **6** *14* **Calatagan (IRE)**[153] 4252 8-9-2 **66**................................ PaulHanagan 4 31
(J M Jefferson) *led to over 2f out: sn btn* **5/1**[2]
06-0 **7** *8* **Vicious Prince (IRE)**[127] 1598 8-8-11 **64**........... MichaelJStainton[(3)] 16 21
(R M Whitaker) *bhd: lost tch 1/2-way: nvr on terms* **20/1**
0100 **8** *30* **City Miss**[11] 5283 4-7-11 **52** oh4................................ KellyHarrison[(5)] 11 —
(Miss L A Perratt) *chsd ldrs tl wknd over 7f out* **18/1**
4600 **9** *1 ½* **Grey Outlook**[21] 5000 4-8-2 **52** oh7........................... RoystonFfrench 10 —
(Miss L A Perratt) *in tch tl wknd over 6f out: t.o* **11/1**

2664 **10** *75* **Andorran (GER)**[7] 5389 4-8-2 **52** oh4................................ JimmyQuinn 8 —
(A Bailey) *midfield: struggling 1/2-way: virtually p.u* **9/1**

4m 5.51s (10.74) **Going Correction** +0.50s/f (Yiel) **10** Ran SP% **116.7**
Speed ratings (Par 103): **94,92,90,85,81 74,70,—,—,—**
CSF £33.20 CT £132.03 TOTE £5.10: £1.90, £1.70, £2.30; EX 31.50 Place 6 £58.67, Place 5 £13.90.
Owner D M Robb **Bred** His Highness The Aga Khan's Studs S C **Trained** Dungannon, Co. Tyrone
■ Stewards' Enquiry : Paul Mulrennan two-day ban; used whip with excessive frequency (Oct 2-3)

FOCUS
A low-grade event but, although the pace was only modest, conditions placed the emphasis firmly on stamina. The form is rated at face value through the runner-up.
T/Jkpt: £9,375.90 to a £1 stake. Pool: £13,205.50. 0.50 winning tickets. T/Plt: £75.80 to a £1 stake. Pool: £108,034.30. 1,039.30 winning tickets. T/Qpdt: £6.80 to a £1 stake. Pool: £5,736.40. 617.60 winning tickets. WG

5206 NEWBURY (L-H)
Friday, September 21

OFFICIAL GOING: Good to firm (8.3)
Wind: Brisk across

5587 DUBAI DUTY FREE GOLF WORLD CUP MAIDEN STKS (DIV I) 6f 8y
1:40 (1:40) (Class 4) 2-Y-O **£5,829** (£1,734; £866; £432) **Stalls** Centre

Form RPR
1 **Stimulation (IRE)** 2-9-3 0.. SteveDrowne 5 87+
(H Morrison) *s.i.s: sn in tch: drvn and qcknd to chse ldr over 1f out: led ins fnl f: nudged out: comf* **6/1**[3]
4 **2** *nk* **Flowing Cape (IRE)**[16] 5143 2-9-3 0......................... JimmyFortune 10 86
(R Hollinshead) *chsd ldrs: led 2f out: rdn over 1f out: hdd ins fnl f: kpt on wl but a hld by wnr* **17/2**
2 **3** *3 1/2* **Alsadeek (IRE)**[105] 2424 2-9-3 0.. RHills 3 76
(J L Dunlop) *chsd ldrs: rdn and ev ch 2f out: wknd fnl f* **7/4**[1]
4 *2 1/2* **Cotton Reel** 2-9-3 0.. TQuinn 6 68+
(P F I Cole) *chsd ldrs: rdn and ev ch appr fnl 2f: wknd over 1f out* **7/2**[2]
220 **5** *2 1/2* **Redsensor**[30] 4725 2-9-3 78... RichardHughes 9 61
(R Hannon) *led tl hdd 2f out: wknd over 1f out* **7/2**[2]
6 *shd* **Lord Sandicliffe (IRE)** 2-9-3 0.................................. JMurtagh 7 60
(B W Hills) *chsd ldrs: rdn and wknd over 2f out* **25/1**
7 *2* **Last Of The Line** 2-9-3 0.. IanMongan 1 54
(H J L Dunlop) *sn rdn in rr: modest prog fnl f* **25/1**
8 *5* **Tiepie** 2-9-3 0.. StephenCarson 4 39
(J Akehurst) *sn rdn: a in rr* **100/1**

1m 13.56s (-0.76) **Going Correction** -0.075s/f (Good) **8** Ran SP% **114.3**
Speed ratings (Par 97): **102,101,96,93,90 90,87,80**
CSF £53.41 TOTE £7.50: £1.90, £2.10, £1.40; EX 70.10.
Owner Michael Kerr-Dineen **Bred** Illuminatus Investments **Trained** East Ilsley, Berks

FOCUS
Quite a decent maiden with the time good, and an impressive winner who seems sure to do better. The runner-up built on a pleasing debut, but the third failed to come on for a pleasing start.

NOTEBOOK
Stimulation(IRE) ◆, a 92,000gns son of the top Australian sprinter Choisir, has winners in the family up to 1m2f, so may stay a bit farther than his sire in due course. A big juvenile with plenty of scope, he won with a bit to spare, and Drowne - who reported him to be "a bit green" - rates him an exciting prospect with plenty of improvement to come. (op 11-1)
Flowing Cape(IRE) seemed to come on quite a bit for his initial outing, and is certainly up to winning a maiden before going on to better things. The winner looks a smart prospect, so this was an excellent effort. (op 9-1 tchd 10-1)
Alsadeek(IRE), off the track for three months since his debut, made an encouraging reappearance. He is good enough to win a typical maiden, and should improve with experience. (tchd 13-8 and 2-1)
Cotton Reel, a 48,000gns Cape Cross colt out of the sprinter Cotton House, showed promise on this debut, with his dam's speed suggesting he could handle a drop down to 5f. He should leave this behind. (op 11-4 tchd 9-4)
Redsensor has done reasonably well in maidens, but now looks ready for a switch to nurseries. (tchd 4-1 and 9-2 in a place)
Lord Sandicliffe(IRE), a 26,000gns son of the top-class juvenile Spartacus, from a speedy family, ran reasonably for a while without setting the world alight. (tchd 22-1)
Last Of The Line, an Efisio colt, is a half-brother to many winners including French 1000 Guineas winner Danseuse Du Soir, but will come into own over 7f and beyond. (op 33-1 tchd 40-1)

5588 DUBAI DUTY FREE CUP (LISTED RACE) 7f (S)
2:10 (2:11) (Class 1) 3-Y-O+
£14,762 (£5,595; £2,800; £1,396; £699; £351) **Stalls** Centre

Form RPR
6-00 **1** **Hotel Du Cap**[27] 4826 4-9-2 95... SteveDrowne 1 103
(G Wragg) *in rr: outpcd and drvn along 1/2-way: styd on wl fr 2f out to ld jst ins fnl f: drvn out* **25/1**
3626 **2** *1/2* **Asset (IRE)**[13] 5214 4-9-2 114......................................(b) RichardHughes 3 102
(R Hannon) *hld up in tch: hdwy on bridle fr 2f out to chal appr fnl f: styd on u.p tl no imp on wnr fnl 100yds* **4/6**[1]
0 **3** *3* **Miyasaki (CHI)**[21] 5-9-2 0...(bt) JJohansen 10 94
(Rune Haugen, Norway) *led tl hdd jst ins fnl f: styd on same pce: wknd fnl 100yds* **66/1**
0343 **4** *nk* **Confucius Classic (IRE)**[17] 5118 3-8-13 59.............. FergusSweeney 6 92
(J R Boyle) *t.k.h: chsd ldrs: drvn to chal appr fnl f: wknd ins fnl f* **100/1**
0151 **5** *1 3/4* **Beckermet (IRE)**[6] 5416 5-9-2 109.................................. RyanMoore 8 88
(R F Fisher) *trckd ldrs: shkn up and n.m.r 1f out: sn no ch* **7/2**[2]
0005 **6** *5* **Vortex**[6] 5412 8-9-2 105...(e) JMurtagh 9 75
(Miss Gay Kelleway) *in rr but in tch: rdn over 2f out and sme prog over 1f out: nvr in contention: wknd fnl f* **8/1**[3]
3200 **7** *3* **Levera**[52] 4045 4-9-2 104.. JimmyFortune 2 66
(A King) *sn in rr: rdn and sme hdwy 3f out: nt rch ldrs and wknd ins fnl 2f* **11/1**
3423 **8** *15* **Lone Wolfe**[47] 4216 3-8-13 97... IanMongan 7 25
(Jane Chapple-Hyam) *chsd ldr to 2f out: sn wknd qckly over 1f out* **16/1**

1m 25.03s (-1.97) **Going Correction** -0.075s/f (Good)
WFA 3 from 4yo+ 3lb **8** Ran SP% **113.9**
Speed ratings (Par 111): **108,107,104,103,101 95,92,75**
CSF £42.34 TOTE £25.70: £5.40, £1.10, £10.00; EX 56.10.
Owner J L C Pearce **Bred** J L C Pearce **Trained** Newmarket, Suffolk

FOCUS
The Norwegian challenger Miyasaki ensured this decent Listed event was run at a strong pace. Hot favourite Asset had run in Group 1 and 2 company of late, but he was not at his best here, and nor were those who looked likeliest to give him a race. With a horse rated just 59 in fourth this is hard form to weigh up and is best treated with caution.

NOTEBOOK
Hotel Du Cap's only previous win was over 1m4f on Polytrack, but he had been struggling over middle distances this season, and the drop in trip paid handsome dividends. It seems likely that he will continue to be campaigned at 7f or a mile. (op 33-1)
Asset(IRE) travelled best of all, and was still on the bit a furlong from home, but his finishing effort did not quite match the promise. Though undoubtedly very smart, he was the one to beat given the big drop in class, but is becoming rather hard to win with. (tchd 8-11 and 4-5 in a place)
Miyasaki(CHI) has won six times up to a mile in Chile and Norway, but had been out of form in recent races. However, this trip to Britain was a revelation and further trips from Scandanivia can be expected if this is any guide. (tchd 50-1)
Confucius Classic(IRE) had a hopeless task at the weights, but ran a blinder. He is obviously capable of winning races, but this will have done his handicap mark no favours and connections will have to search the programme book to find something suitable.
Beckermet(IRE) stays this trip, but he is best at 6f, and at this level the final furlong was one too many.
Vortex is still capable of running a big race, but he has not been firing with any consistency of late. Official explanation: jockey said gelding lost its action (op 13-2)
Levera can be dangerous from the front, but on this occasion was never going well enough to have any hope of making it, with the ground probably faster than ideal. He is now likely to head to the sales. (op 12-1)
Lone Wolfe Official explanation: jockey said colt lost its action

5589 DUBAI DUTY FREE ARC TRIAL (GROUP 3) 1m 3f 5y
2:45 (2:45) (Class 1) 3-Y-O+
£26,686 (£10,114; £5,061; £2,523; £1,264; £634) **Stalls** Centre

Form RPR
0125 **1** **Halicarnassus (IRE)**[5] 5451 3-8-13 111................................. TPO'Shea 5 117
(M R Channon) *4th but in tch: rdn over 3f out: styd on wl fr 2f out and str run ins fnl f to ld last stride* **9/1**
115- **2** *nk* **Soapy Danger**[395] 4678 4-9-3 119... KDarley 6 113
(M Johnston) *trckd ldr: chal fr 4f out tl drvn to take narrow advantage ins fnl 2f: kpt on u.p tl ct last strides* **9/1**
4511 **3** *shd* **Papal Bull**[34] 4599 4-9-8 118.. RyanMoore 3 118
(Sir Michael Stoute) *hld up in rr: pushed along over 3f out: rdn and hdwy over 1f out: hd sltly to one stride but str run ins fnl f: fin wl but nt quite get up* **11/10**[1]
1603 **4** *1 1/4* **Salford Mill (IRE)**[8] 5351 3-8-10 111... TQuinn 1 111
(D R C Elsworth) *trckd ldrs in 3rd: rdn to chal between horses over 1f out: n.m.r but kpt on tl outpcd ins fnl f* **13/2**[3]
5240 **5** *2 1/2* **Admiral's Cruise (USA)**[71] 3461 5-9-3 111................(b) JimmyFortune 4 107
(B J Meehan) *slowly away: sn pushed along but in tch: rdn 4f out: hdwy 3f out: effrt 2f out but nvr gng pce to rch ldrs: wknd and hung lft wl ins fnl f* **14/1**
-021 **6** *6* **Bauer (IRE)**[20] 5030 4-9-3 103... JMurtagh 2 97
(L M Cumani) *led: rdn over 3f out: hdd ins fnl 2f: wknd over 1f out: eased wn btn fnl f* **10/3**[2]

2m 18.11s (-4.16) **Going Correction** -0.05s/f (Good)
WFA 3 from 4yo+ 7lb **6** Ran SP% **110.7**
Speed ratings (Par 113): **113,112,112,111,109 105**
CSF £77.80 TOTE £10.10: £3.00, £2.80; EX 67.50.
Owner Box 41 **Bred** Yeomanstown Lodge Stud **Trained** West Ilsley, Berks
■ Stewards' Enquiry : T P O'Shea caution: used whip with excessive frequency

FOCUS
A decent enough Group 3, but not really a trial for the Arc. The form is rated around the third and fourth but cannot really be taken at face value.

NOTEBOOK
Halicarnassus(IRE) is improving with time, and now looks a solid Group 3 performer following a second victory at this level. Though only just forging ahead near the line, this tough sort needs at least 1m2f to bring out the best in him these days, and his battling qualities did the rest. Fast ground suits him ideally, and he is an ideal type for the Dubai Carnival next spring. In the meantime he might go to Hong Kong. (op 10-1 tchd 17-2)
Soapy Danger, off the track since fracturing a pastern last August, made a highly-creditable reappearance, only to be touched off near the line. Already a winner in Group 2 company, he will be a dangerous opponent in Pattern races from now on if recovering from this first run following a long absence. (op 13-2)
Papal Bull took an age to get going, and for much of the home straight looked as if he might finish last. He needs at least this trip these days, and ideally 1m4f or beyond, but he is not easiest of rides and needs a certain amount of humouring. (op Evens tchd 10-11 and 6-5 in places)
Salford Mill(IRE) just lacked the pace to take advantage of a promising position a furlong out, giving the impression that he was beaten on merit. However, he remains a decent performer at Group 3 level and shapes as if he will appreciate a return to 1m4f. (op 8-1 tchd 9-1)
Admiral's Cruise(USA) had the blinkers re-applied, but he has been disappointing in his last two races and needs to show more signs of form before inspiring confidence again. (tchd 16-1)
Bauer(IRE) went off second favourite, despite needing to improve to beat these better opponents, but in the event he was not up to it and Murtagh eased him down in the last 200 yards. In any case, he would benefit from a return to a longer trip. (op 4-1)

5590 HAYNES, HANSON & CLARK CONDITIONS STKS 1m (S)
3:20 (3:21) (Class 2) 2-Y-O
£11,217 (£3,358; £1,679; £840; £419; £210) **Stalls** Centre

Form RPR
31 **1** **Centennial (IRE)**[35] 4586 2-9-2 83.................................. JimmyFortune 1 96+
(J H M Gosden) *in tch: pushed along and hdwy 2f out: styng on whn rdr dropped whip over 1f out: drvn to ld jst ins fnl f: r.o strly* **9/4**[2]
6 **2** *1* **North Parade**[13] 5217 2-8-12 0..(t) IanMongan 10 90+
(B J Meehan) *chsd ldrs: drvn to ld over 1f out: hdd ins fnl f and showed signs of greenness: kpt on but nt pce of wnr* **28/1**
63 **3** *3 1/2* **Judgethemoment (USA)**[23] 4946 2-8-12 0.......................... JMurtagh 2 82
(Jane Chapple-Hyam) *in tch: rdn and outpcd over 2f out: rdn: rallied and kpt on fr over 1f out: fin wl but nt trble ldng duo* **33/1**
04 **4** *1 1/4* **Talayeb**[48] 4151 2-8-12 0...(b[1]) PatDobbs 8 79
(M P Tregoning) *led tl hdd over 3f out: styd chsng ldrs: rdn over 2f out: wknd fnl f* **6/1**[3]
2451 **5** *1* **Abolition (USA)**[13] 5236 2-8-12 89... KDarley 3 77
(M Johnston) *chsd ldrs: drvn along fr 3f out: wknd appr fnl f* **15/2**
241 **6** *4* **Mujaadel (USA)**[18] 5088 2-9-2 87.. RHills 4 72+
(E A L Dunlop) *chsd ldrs: led over 3f out: sn drvn along: hdd over 1f out: sn wknd* **7/1**
7 *12* **Askar Tau (FR)** 2-8-12 0.. RichardHughes 9 40
(M P Tregoning) *slowly away: green and a in rr* **20/1**
00 **8** *10* **Shishio**[17] 5116 2-8-12 0... FrankieMcDonald 7 17
(W De Best-Turner) *veered lft s: plld hrd and continued to hang lft: lost tch fr 1/2-way* **100/1**

2461 **U** **Ramona Chase**[15] 5161 2-9-2 95 .... RyanMoore 6 —
(S Kirk) *carried lft s and plld hrd tl stmbld and uns rdr over 6f out* **15/8**[1]

1m 40.08s (-0.54) **Going Correction** -0.075s/f (Good) **9** Ran SP% **116.2**
Speed ratings (Par 101): **99,98,94,93,92 88,76,66,—**
CSF £67.59 TOTE £3.00: £1.60, £5.20, £4.00; EX 72.40.
Owner Michael O'Flynn **Bred** W Lazy T Ltd **Trained** Newmarket, Suffolk

FOCUS
A race with a rich tradition - Authorized was third last year - and although this does not look a vintage renewal it has been rated reasonably positively. The winner built on his good Newmarket win, and it was a good effort from the runner-up, who should have no trouble winning a maiden.

NOTEBOOK
Centennial(IRE) ◆ continues to come on with every race, and is developing into a high-class juvenile. His trainer has a fine team of two-year-olds this season, but this expensive colt is likely to be one of the best. He is expected to stay 1m4f next year and is now as short as 25-1 for the Derby. (op 2-1 tchd 15-8)
North Parade ◆ came on a bundle from his first run, and on this evidence is going to make up into a smart sort. Although his dam, Queen Sceptre, was a sprinter, he looks more likely to take after his sire Nayef, and his half-brothers Unfuwain and Nashwan, all of whom were top-class over middle distances. (op 50-1)
Judgethemoment(USA) ran really well in this better company. Effective on both Polytrack and turf, he is progressing with every race and gets a mile really well, with trips up to 1m2f on the cards as he matures. (op 66-1)
Talayeb, with blinkers applied for this third outing, ran well without suggesting he is a Group-class horse in the making. However, he should make a decent handicapper if continuing to respond to the headgear. (op 15-2 tchd 9-2)
Abolition(USA) was taking on better horses here, but can be placed to win again in lesser company. (tchd 8-1)
Mujaadel(USA) fell short among these decent sorts, and looked as if a drop back to 7f would suit for the time being. (tchd 15-2)
Ramona Chase unluckily dumped his rider after clipping heels early on, but the weight of money tells the rest of of the story, and he is worth another chance in decent company. (op 2-1 tchd 11-4 and 3-1 in places)

5591 DUBAI DUTY FREE GOLF WORLD CUP MAIDEN STKS (DIV II) 6f 8y
3:55 (3:56) (Class 4) 2-Y-O **£5,829** (£1,734; £866; £432) **Stalls** Centre

Form RPR
3 **1** **Paco Boy (IRE)**[16] 5126 2-9-3 0 .... RyanMoore 6 88+
(R Hannon) *trckd ldrs: led over 2f out: rdn over 1f out and styd on strly fnl f* **2/1**[1]
2 *2½* **Storm Sir (USA)** 2-9-3 0 .... JMurtagh 7 81+
(J Noseda) *chsd ldrs: wnt 2nd 2f out: rdn: over 1f out: green and edgd lft ins fnl f: styd on wl but a hld by wnr* **4/1**[3]
3 *2½* **Danseuse Volante (IRE)** 2-8-12 0 .... TQuinn 3 68+
(J W Hills) *in rr but in tch: rdn and hdwy 2f out: styd on to go 3rd fnl f but no imp on ldng duo* **20/1**
4 *2½* **Thannaan (USA)** 2-9-3 0 .... RHills 4 66+
(B W Hills) *s.i.s: sn rcvrd: drvn to chse ldrs over 2f out: nvr gng pce to chal: wknd over 1f out* **7/2**[2]
5 *3* **Bombardier Wells** 2-9-3 0 .... StephenCarson 5 57+
(Eve Johnson Houghton) *in rr but in tch: hdwy over 2f out: sn rdn and nvr in contention: kpt on same pce ins fnl f* **8/1**
0 **6** *1* **Operachy**[21] 5003 2-9-3 0 .... FergusSweeney 2 54
(B R Millman) *led tl hdd over 2f out: wknd wl over 1f out* **33/1**
0 **7** *1¼* **Drumhallagh (IRE)**[28] 4755 2-9-3 0 .... RichardKingscote 9 50
(Tom Dascombe) *outpcd most of way* **14/1**
0 **8** *¾* **Reel Man**[43] 4328 2-9-3 0 .... RichardHughes 8 48
(R Hannon) *chsd ldr over 3f: wknd fr 2f out* **6/1**
0 **9** *13* **Novas (IRE)**[10] 5306 2-9-3 0 .... TPO'Shea 1 9
(M R Channon) *chsd ldrs: rdn 3f out and sn wknd* **33/1**

1m 13.22s (-1.10) **Going Correction** -0.075s/f (Good) **41** Ran SP% **118.3**
Speed ratings (Par 97): **104,100,97,94,90 88,87,86,68**
CSF £10.18 TOTE £3.00: £1.60, £1.60, £4.40; EX 8.10.
Owner The Calvera Partnership **Bred** Mrs Joan Browne **Trained** East Everleigh, Wilts

FOCUS
Not much to go on, but the time was a little faster than the first division and, while four newcomers followed him home, the winner appeared to step up significantly on his Polytrack debut and the race should produce winners.

NOTEBOOK
Paco Boy(IRE) had shown promise on Polytrack first time and, with the runner-up in that race having gone on to win since, had obvious prospects here if making the switch to turf. In the event, he came through with flying colours and looks sure to improve again, with 7f likely to suit both on breeding and running style. (op 9-4 tchd 7-4 and 5-2 in a place)
Storm Sir(USA), a $270,000 son of Johannesburg out of an unsuccessful but well-related middle-distance mare, made an encouraging debut and should have no problem going one better. He should get 7f before long, and looks a decent prospect up to a mile in the long run. (op 9-4)
Danseuse Volante(IRE), a half-sister to Castle Howard, has stamina on the dam's side, but her sire was the speedy Danehill Dancer. Though it is not obvious what her best trip will be, she showed enough on this debut to suggest she will win races. (op 12-1)
Thannaan(USA)'s sire was high-class up to a mile on dirt and turf in the USA, and her dam a smart miler in Canada, so she has a decent North American pedigree. She should improve with experience, and get a bit farther in due course. (op 4-1 tchd 5-1)
Bombardier Wells, a 40,000euro Red Ransom colt out of a disappointing mare but from a good family, made a satisfactory if unspectacular debut. He should stay 7f no problem. (op 20-1)
Operachy, a 32,000gns Kyllachy colt, is not as precocious as some of his progeny, but he is showing some signs of ability and should be more effective when qualified for handicaps. There is some stamina on his dam's side, so he should stay a bit farther than his sire as he matures.
Reel Man is proving somewhat disappointing in maidens, but the market support suggests he has ability, and handicaps are only one race away now. (op 10-1)

5592 DUBAI DUTY FREE FULL OF SURPRISES EBF FILLIES' CONDITIONS STKS 7f (S)
4:30 (4:32) (Class 2) 2-Y-O
£11,217 (£3,358; £1,679; £840; £419; £210) **Stalls** Centre

Form RPR
1 **1** **Rosa Grace**[28] 4784 2-8-12 79 .... PhilipRobinson 5 82+
(Rae Guest) *hld up in rr but in tch: gd hdwy over 1f out: styd on wl fnl f but stl sltly green: led fnl 100yds: readily* **10/3**[3]
1 **2** *¾* **Dream Day**[14] 5201 2-9-2 0 .... RyanMoore 9 84
(R Hannon) *chsd ldrs: led over 1f out: kpt on wl tl hdd fnl 100yds and styd on same pce* **11/4**[1]
1 **3** *¾* **Max One Two Three (IRE)**[21] 5003 2-8-12 0 .... RichardKingscote 7 78
(Tom Dascombe) *chsd ldrs: led jst ins fnl 2f: hdd over 1f out: styd on u.p but no ex fnl 100yds* **3/1**[2]
4 *5* **King's Kazeem** 2-8-12 0 .... JMurtagh 4 65
(B W Hills) *t.k.h: hld up in rr but in tch: hdwy 2f out: hung lft u.p fnl f and no ch w ldng trio* **20/1**
5 *2* **Madame Hoi (IRE)** 2-8-12 0 .... TPO'Shea 3 60
(M R Channon) *t.k.h: chsd ldrs: rdn over 2f out: wknd appr fnl f* **7/1**
01 **6** *3½* **Marchpane**[28] 4761 2-8-12 81 .... AdamKirby 8 51
(R M Beckett) *led tl hdd ins fnl 2f: sn btn* **11/1**
7 *2* **Io (IRE)** 2-8-12 0 .... TQuinn 6 46
(J L Dunlop) *slowly away: effrt 1/2-way: nvr in contention and sn towards rr* **50/1**
00 **8** *7* **Ice Choice (IRE)**[14] 5206 2-8-12 0 .... JackDean 10 27
(Mark Gillard) *bhd most of way* **125/1**
9 *10* **Sepia** 2-8-12 0 .... RichardHughes 2 —
(B W Hills) *chsd ldrs 4f: wknd 2f out: eased whn no ch fnl f* **5/1**

1m 27.37s (0.37) **Going Correction** -0.075s/f (Good) **9** Ran SP% **119.8**
Speed ratings (Par 98): **94,93,92,86,84 80,78,70,58**
CSF £13.38 TOTE £3.70: £1.30, £2.00, £1.50; EX 15.70.
Owner E P Duggan **Bred** Worksop Manor Stud **Trained** Newmarket, Suffolk

FOCUS
Debut winners filled the first three places here, all three of them improving as they pulled clear of the rest. The form should prove at least this good.

NOTEBOOK
Rosa Grace again looked to have a bit to learn, but she stepped up nicely from her debut victory and is progressive. The second and third had also both made successful first appearances, so the form looks solid, and her entries in the Irish 1000 Guineas and Irish Oaks suggest she is highly thought of. (op 7-2 tchd 4-1 and 3-1)
Dream Day showed she is at least as effective on turf as Polytrack, and the extra furlong proved not to be a problem even though she was edged out of it late on. This was good effort conceding weight, and there are other races to be won with her. (op 5-1)
Max One Two Three(IRE) had won on her debut, but this was a much stronger race. She stayed the 7f well and, with the fourth horse finishing some way behind the first three, it looked a good effort despite still showing signs of inexperience. (tchd 7-2)
King's Kazeem, a daughter of King's Best, has winners in the family even though her dam was unplaced up to 1m2f, and her half-sister Azeema won over 7f. Making a more than satisfactory debut here, in decent company behind three previous winners, she will find her level and win races. Official explanation: jockey said filly hung left-handed (op 25-1)
Madame Hoi(IRE), a 46,000gns daughter of Hawk Wing, has many good winners in the family, and should improve enough to win races up to a mile. (op 6-1)
Marchpane found this company much harder, as the betting suggested, and was just not good enough. (op 10-1 tchd 9-1 and 12-1)
Sepia Official explanation: jockey said filly lost its action behind

5593 DUBAI DUTY FREE FINEST SURPRISE STKS (H'CAP) 1m 2f 6y
5:05 (5:05) (Class 4) (0-85,83) 3-Y-O+ **£5,505** (£1,637; £818; £408) **Stalls** Centre

Form RPR
0-46 **1** **Peppertree**[118] 2047 4-9-7 **82** .... FergusSweeney 15 92
(E F Vaughan) *trckd ldr 7f out: slt advantage fr 3f out: styd on u.p fnl 2f: edgd lft fnl 100yds: kpt on wl* **14/1**
3403 **2** *1* **Lisathedaddy**[9] 5327 5-9-5 **80** .... RichardKingscote 5 88
(B G Powell) *in rr: hdwy 3f out: chsd ldrs 2f out: rdn and kpt on fnl f: tk 2nd cl home but nt rch wnr* **9/2**[1]
0525 **3** *nk* **Go Tech**[13] 5229 7-9-3 **78** .... JimmyFortune 14 86
(T D Easterby) *sn led: narrowly hdd 3f out but styd upsides wnr tl outpcd ins fnl f and hmpd fnl 100yds: lost 2nd cl home* **5/1**[2]
6003 **4** *¾* **Del Mar Sunset**[8] 5362 8-9-1 **76** .... LiamJones 6 82
(W J Haggas) *t.k.h: hld up in rr: hdwy 3f out: styd on u.p fnl 2f and kpt on cl home: nt pce to trble ldng trio* **8/1**[3]
6026 **5** *1* **Zaif (IRE)**[27] 4814 4-9-6 **81** .... AntonyProcter 8 85
(D R C Elsworth) *in rr: hdwy fr 3f out: srated on fr over 1f out and kpt on ins fnl f: nvr gng pce to be competitive* **11/1**
06 **6** *1½* **Cool Box (USA)**[51] 4068 3-8-12 **79** .... JMurtagh 13 80
(Mrs A J Perrett) *in tch: hdwy and n.m.r over 2f out: sn rdn and no imp on ldrs* **8/1**[3]
0003 **7** *nk* **The Snatcher (IRE)**[14] 5203 4-9-5 **80** .... RyanMoore 9 80
(R Hannon) *in rr: drvn along 3f out: sme prog 2f out: sn one pce* **9/2**[1]
1145 **8** *nk* **Apex**[69] 3527 6-9-3 **83** .... HaddenFrost(5) 10 83
(M Hill) *chsd ldr 3f: styd front rnk: rdn 3f out: wknd ins fnl f* **9/1**
5154 **9** *2½* **Transvestite (IRE)**[20] 5052 5-8-10 **76** ....(v) PatrickHills(5) 12 71
(J W Hills) *in rr: hdwy on outside 4f out: nvr rchd ldrs: wknd 2f out* **8/1**[3]
10-0 **10** *17* **Pagan Crest**[139] 1470 4-8-11 **72** .... KDarley 16 33
(Mrs A J Perrett) *chsd ldrs: rdn 3f out: wknd qckly over 2f out* **20/1**

2m 7.99s (-0.72) **Going Correction** -0.05s/f (Good)
WFA 3 from 4yo+ 6lb **10** Ran SP% **116.1**
Speed ratings (Par 105): **100,99,98,98,97 96,96,95,93,80**
CSF £75.71 CT £366.24 TOTE £21.90: £3.50, £1.80, £1.90; EX 134.40.
Owner Wood Hall Stud Limited **Bred** Wood Hall Stud **Trained** Newmarket, Suffolk

FOCUS
Just a fair race of its type for the course, with nobody wanting to make it until Go Tech took over and controlled an ordinary pace. The form looks solid rated around the first three.
The Snatcher(IRE) Official explanation: jockey said colt was unsuited by the good to firm ground
Pagan Crest Official explanation: jockey said gelding hung right-handed throughout

5594 DUBAI DUTY FREE FOUNDATION H'CAP 1m 4f 5y
5:35 (5:35) (Class 4) (0-85,85) 3-Y-O+ **£5,505** (£1,637; £818; £408) **Stalls** Centre

Form RPR
2162 **1** **Jack Rolfe**[16] 5145 5-9-0 **73** .... RyanMoore 11 81
(G L Moore) *in tch chsd ldrs ½-way: rdn to ld appr fnl 2f: styd on wl thrght fnl f* **3/1**[1]
425- **2** *½* **Counting House (IRE)**[189] 3974 4-9-5 **78** .... JMurtagh 5 85
(J A B Old) *chsd ldrs: rdn over 2f out: kpt on to chse wnr fnl f but a jst hld* **8/1**
-016 **3** *shd* **Mirin**[47] 4203 3-8-9 **76** .... SteveDrowne 7 83
(G Wragg) *in rr: hdwy on outside fr 3f out: kpt on u.p to go 3rd and dispute 2nd ins fnl f: nvr quite gng pce to rch wnr* **8/1**
1060 **4** *1* **Galianna (IRE)**[37] 4511 3-8-9 **76** .... PatDobbs 12 81
(Pat Eddery) *sn chsng ldr: rdn over 2f out: edgd lft 1f out: one pce ins fnl f* **9/1**
321 **5** *1* **Hibiki (IRE)**[16] 5137 3-8-6 **73** .... StephenCarson 2 78
(J S Moore) *in rr but in tch: hdwy on ins whn n.m.r over 1f out and jst ins fnl f: kpt on same pce* **13/2**[3]
04/0 **6** *shd* **Capitana (GER)**[14] 5210 6-9-4 **77** .... TQuinn 10 81
(N J Henderson) *t.k.h in rr: rdn and hdwy over 2f out: nvr gng pce to rch ldrs and kpt on same pce fnl f* **7/2**[2]
1255 **7** *1* **Venir Rouge**[6] 5415 3-8-11 **78** .... TPO'Shea 3 80
(M Salaman) *in rr: rdn and effrt over 3f out: nvr in contention and one pce fnl 2f* **13/2**[3]
8 *2* **Magic Clover (ARG)**[532] 6-9-12 **85** .... RichardHughes 6 84
(P R Webber) *led tl hdd appr fnl 2f: wkng whn hmpd 1f out* **20/1**

0105 **9** ¾ **History Boy**[18] 5101 3-9-1 **82**.................................... KDarley 8 80
(D J Coakley) *plld hrd in rr: rdn and effrt 3f out: nvr in contention* **16/1**

2m 33.3s (-2.69) **Going Correction** -0.05s/f (Good)
WFA 3 from 4yo+ 8lb **9** Ran SP% **116.8**
Speed ratings (Par 105): **106,105,105,104,104 104,103,102,101**
CSF £27.92 CT £175.76 TOTE £3.50: £1.40, £2.60, £3.10; EX 18.60 Place 6 £189.12, Place 5 £101.09.
Owner Mrs Sarah Diamandis & Mrs Celia Woollett **Bred** W H F Carson **Trained** Woodingdean, E Sussex

FOCUS
An ordinary race for the course, with part-time hurdlers filling the first two places. The form looks solid enough rated around the placed horses.
Venir Rouge Official explanation: trainer later said colt was found to have a throat infection after the race
Magic Clover(ARG) Official explanation: jockey said horse was hanging left-handed
T/Plt: £93.90 to a £1 stake. Pool: £57,832.65. 449.25 winning tickets. T/Qpdt: £53.80 to a £1 stake. Pool: £2,749.70. 37.80 winning tickets. ST

4810 NEWMARKET (ROWLEY) (R-H)

Friday, September 21

OFFICIAL GOING: Good to firm (firm in places; 10.1)
A meeting consisting entirely of races for two-year-olds.
Wind: Fresh across Weather: Cloudy with sunny spells

5595 LAKENHAM ICE CREAM MEDIAN AUCTION MAIDEN STKS 6f
2:00 (2:02) (Class 4) 2-Y-O **£4,533** (£1,348; £674; £336) **Stalls** Centre

Form RPR
0 **1** **Red Rumour (IRE)**[37] 4500 2-9-3 0.................................... SebSanders 12 83+
(R M Beckett) *lengthy: scope: lw: chsd ldr: rdn to ld 1f out: r.o wl* **11/2**[3]
2 2½ **Ramaad** 2-9-3 0.................................... MartinDwyer 10 76
(W J Haggas) *w'like: hld up: hdwy over 2f out: rdn over 1f out: styd on same pce* **9/1**
00 **3** hd **Manhattan Dream (USA)**[28] 4774 2-8-12 0.................... MichaelHills 13 70
(B W Hills) *sn led: rdn and hdd 1f out: styd on same pce* **10/3**[2]
035 **4** 1½ **Superduper**[39] 4454 2-8-12 **76**.................................... TedDurcan 11 65
(R Hannon) *w'like: cl cpld: chsd ldrs: rdn over 2f out: styd on same pce appr fnl f* **13/2**
4 **5** ½ **Mcconnell (USA)**[43] 4325 2-9-0 0.................... StephaneBreux(3) 8 69+
(J R Best) *str: chsd ldrs: outpcd 2f out: styd on fnl f* **16/1**
6 nk **Doric Lady** 2-8-12 0.................................... EddieAhern 9 63
(J A R Toller) *w'like: s.i.s: hdwy over 2f out: rdn over 1f out: wknd ins fnl f* **33/1**
7 ½ **Lord Snooty (IRE)** 2-9-3 0.................................... KerrinMcEvoy 1 67+
(P W Chapple-Hyam) *w'like: scope: bit bkwd: hld up: hdwy over 2f out: sn rdn: styd on same pce: b.b.v* **11/4**[1]
03 **8** ½ **Khandala (IRE)**[22] 4968 2-8-12 0.................................... HayleyTurner 5 60
(M L W Bell) *w'like: b: chsd ldrs: rdn over 2f out: wknd fnl f* **16/1**
9 2½ **Racie Gracie** 2-8-12 0.................................... AdrianMcCarthy 2 53
(John Berry) *w'like: leggy: mid-div: rdn 1/2-way: wkng whn hung rt 2f out* **100/1**
10 2 **Clear Daylight** 2-9-3 0.................................... JimCrowley 6 52
(J R Best) *w'like: bit bkwd: s.i.s: outpcd* **16/1**
11 ½ **Hits Only Time** 2-9-3 0.................................... J-PGuillambert 4 50
(J Pearce) *w'like: str: bit bkwd: hld up: bhd fr 1/2-way* **66/1**
12 4 **Mexican Venture** 2-9-3 0.................................... DarryllHolland 14 38
(W Jarvis) *w'like scope: bit bkwd: s.i.s: a in rr* **50/1**
00 **13** ½ **Peas In A Pod**[26] 4854 2-9-3 0.................................... JamieSpencer 3 37
(J R Fanshawe) *str: hld up: rdn and wknd over 2f out* **28/1**
14 1¾ **Star Grazer** 2-8-12 0.................................... TPQueally 7 26
(C F Wall) *neat: bit bkwd: on toes: sn pushed along in rr: bhd fr 1/2-way* **33/1**

1m 12.86s (-0.24) **Going Correction** -0.25s/f (Firm) **14** Ran SP% **119.9**
Speed ratings (Par 97): **91,87,87,85,84 84,83,83,79,77 76,71,70,68**
CSF £51.66 TOTE £6.20: £2.10, £2.70, £1.90; EX 47.60.
Owner R Roberts **Bred** Tally-Ho Stud **Trained** Whitsbury, Hants

FOCUS
There was a fairly strong cross-wind and, as in all of the other races, the field came down the centre of the track. A fairly good maiden that could rate a little higher.

NOTEBOOK
Red Rumour(IRE), who showed ability despite running green in a Salisbury maiden that is not working out, was nevertheless supported in the ring and that was justified. Always up with the pace, he found plenty under pressure and was going away near the finish. There is plenty of speed in his pedigree and he can go on from this. (op 6-1 tchd 13-2 and 5-1)
Ramaad, a medium-sized, gelded son of Dr Fong from the family of Ardkinglass, looked fit for this debut and was held up, but ran on quite well in the closing stages and will be better for the experience. (op 16-1)
Manhattan Dream(USA), a half-sister to Maids Causeway with two previous outings under her belt, tried to put that experience to good use and made the running. She could not shake off the winner however, and had nothing in reserve on the climb to the line. (op 4-1)
Superduper, another with plenty of previous experience but still on the weak side, showed up well enough but may be better off in handicaps. She helps set the level for the form. (op 6-1 tchd 7-1)
Mcconnell(USA), whose debut form could have worked out better, ran reasonably but looks as if he needs more time and a longer trip. (op 25-1)
Doric Lady, quite a plain filly out of a half-sister to Latino Magic, looked fit enough but missed the break then picked up to challenge going into the dip before fading up the hill. She will be sharper next time. (op 40-1)
Lord Snooty(IRE), an athletic half-brother to Shamrock City and several other winners, was an easy-to-back favourite, was held up at the back but never got into contention but reportedly broke a blood-vessel. The fact that he was short in the marked suggests that he has shown something at home and if the bleeding problem can be sorted out he can be expected to do a lot better in the future. Official explanation: vet said colt had bled from the nose (op 2-1 tchd 3-1)
Khandala(IRE) whose effort over 7f last time did not suggest that this drop in trip would suit her, dropped away in the closing stages but now qualifies for a handicap mark. (op 12-1)

5596 TRADITIONAL PIE AND PASTY EBF MAIDEN FILLIES' STKS 1m
2:35 (2:38) (Class 4) 2-Y-O **£5,181** (£1,541; £770; £384) **Stalls** Centre

Form RPR
1 **Makaaseb (USA)** 2-9-0 0.................................... MartinDwyer 14 93+
(M A Jarvis) *tall: rangy: scope: chsd ldrs: led over 2f out: rdn out* **7/4**[1]
2 ¾ **Queen Of Naples** 2-9-0 0.................................... DavidKinsella 1 91+
(J H M Gosden) *w'like: str: bit bkwd: hld up: hdwy over 3f out: chsd wnr over 1f out: r.o* **11/1**
3 6 **Saleima (IRE)** 2-9-0 0.................................... TPQueally 2 76
(J Noseda) *unf: bit bkwd: prom: led 3f out: sn rdn: edgd rt and hdd: outpcd fr over 1f out* **25/1**
0 **4** 1¾ **Star Of Gibraltar**[28] 4774 2-9-0 0.................................... EddieAhern 13 72
(J L Dunlop) *str: lw: chsd ldrs: rdn over 2f out: styd on same pce* **7/2**[2]
5 ½ **Flam** 2-9-0 0.................................... JamieSpencer 9 71
(J R Fanshawe) *unf: scope: bit bkwd: s.i.s: hld up: hdwy over 2f out: nt trble ldrs* **12/1**
60 **6** hd **Aaim To Succeed (IRE)**[23] 4947 2-9-0 0.................... DarryllHolland 7 71
(M R Channon) *lw: sn led: hdd over 3f out: rdn and wknd over 1f out* **33/1**
7 2 **Rabeera** 2-9-0 0.................................... LPKeniry 8 66
(A M Balding) *w'like: scope: hld up: rdn over 3f out: n.d* **66/1**
8 hd **Hamsat Elqamar** 2-9-0 0.................................... MichaelHills 15 66
(J H M Gosden) *unf: lengthy: scope: bit bkwd: dwlt: drvn along thrght: n.d* **7/1**[3]
0 **9** 3 **Kalokairi (IRE)**[15] 5162 2-9-0 0.................................... TedDurcan 4 59
(J L Dunlop) *w'like: cl cpld: edgy: s.s: hld up: hdwy 3f out: sn rdn and wknd* **40/1**
10 1 **Forgive Me** 2-9-0 0.................................... J-PGuillambert 11 57
(C E Brittain) *athletic: sn pushed along: a in rr* **66/1**
11 nk **Houri (IRE)** 2-9-0 0.................................... SebSanders 10 56
(R M Beckett) *str: bit bkwd: mid-div: rdn over 3f out: wknd over 2f out* **16/1**
12 ¾ **Shraayef** 2-9-0 0.................................... OscarUrbina 12 55
(M Botti) *unf: bit bkwd: hld up: rdn and wknd over 2f out* **50/1**
13 4 **Appointment** 2-9-0 0.................................... JimCrowley 6 46
(Mrs A J Perrett) *unf: lengthy: scope: mid-div: rdn and wknd over 2f out* **25/1**
00 **14** 2 **Free Fallin**[27] 4796 2-9-0 0.................................... KerrinMcEvoy 3 42
(P W Chapple-Hyam) *w'like: chsd ldr tl led over 3f out: sn hdd: wknd 2f out* **10/1**

1m 37.65s (-1.72) **Going Correction** -0.25s/f (Firm) **14** Ran SP% **120.1**
Speed ratings (Par 94): **98,97,91,89,89 88,86,86,83,82 82,81,77,75**
CSF £21.38 TOTE £2.50: £1.50, £3.10, £4.30; EX 26.10.
Owner Hamdan Al Maktoum **Bred** Fred M Allor **Trained** Newmarket, Suffolk

FOCUS
There could be a couple of useful performers in this maiden with the first two clear and the time decent for the grade, 0.68sec faster than the later maiden over the same trip.

NOTEBOOK
Makaaseb(USA) ♦, a $370,000 foal from a decent American family, was a well-backed favourite and duly justified confidence. Always close up, she soon settle the issue when asked running into the dip and only the tendency to run green and idle in the closing stages meant the winning margin was fairly narrow. She is unlikely to take up her Fillies' Mile entry and will probably not run again, but looks a good prospect and has been quoted for the Oaks, although her pedigree suggests 8-10f may be her optimum trip. (op 13-8 tchd 11-8, 15-8 in a place)
Queen Of Naples ♦, a 190,000gns daughter of Singspiel from the family of Oath, showed plenty of promise on this debut and, after getting briefly outpaced when the winner went for home, picked up well on the climb to the line, suggesting she will appreciate a longer trip in time. She was well clear of the rest and the time was decent so she will not be long in winning and may have a better chance of staying the Oaks trip next season than the winner. (op 10-1 tchd 14-1)
Saleima(IRE), an 80,000gns daughter of a dual middle-distance winner, raced in company with the runner-up and went to the front travelling well. However, she was brushed aside by the first two and tended to run green under pressure. She should be capable of winning races with this experience behind her. (tchd 33-1)
Star Of Gibraltar, out of a triple winner at up to a mile from the family of Nashwan, faced very different ground to the soft surface she encountered but showed the benefit of that outing with a fair effort. Although she looks very unlikely to take up her Fillies' Mile entry, she is likely to find a race before too long. (tchd 10-3)
Flam ♦, a Singspiel half-sister to three winners including Delsarte, is bred to appreciate middle distances and looked in need of the experience. She should come into her own next season. (tchd 11-1 and 14-1)
Aaim To Succeed(IRE), having her third run but encountering fast turf for the first time, showed a bit more this time but may well have come up against some potentially useful performers and is likely to find her level in handicaps.
Rabeera, a 60,000gns half-sister to Chivalry among others, was green beforehand and ran on late without really figuring but, being from a yard whose youngsters are rarely ready first time, she can be expected to step up on this in the future.
Hamsat Elqamar, a Nayef half-sister to Yazamaan, was backed beforehand and after missing the break tended to see too much daylight on the outside of her field and ran green. She looks open to a good deal of improvement, and the fact she was better backed than the runner-up suggests she has been showing a fair amount at home. She looks one to bear in mind. (op 9-1 tchd 10-1)

5597 EXPRESS CAFES LTD NURSERY 7f
3:10 (3:11) (Class 3) (0-95,95) 2-Y-O **£7,772** (£2,312; £1,155; £577) **Stalls** Centre

Form RPR
062 **1** **Noble Citizen (USA)**[25] 4882 2-8-1 **75**.................................... HayleyTurner 3 82
(D M Simcock) *chsd ldrs: rdn to ld over 1f out: styd on u.p* **9/2**[2]
0340 **2** 2½ **Dalkey Girl (IRE)**[8] 5350 2-8-2 **83**.................... AshleyMorgan(7) 5 83
(V Smith) *lw: hld up: rdn over 2f out: r.o ins fnl f: nt rch wnr* **20/1**
3613 **3** hd **Dan Tucket**[13] 5217 2-9-0 **88**.................................... DarryllHolland 7 87
(M R Channon) *chsd ldrs: rdn over 2f out: no ex* **11/2**[3]
031 **4** ¾ **Hustle (IRE)**[18] 5091 2-8-5 **79**.................................... MartinDwyer 9 77
(R Hannon) *led 1f: chsd ldr: led again over 2f out: rdn: edgd lft and hdd over 1f out: no ex ins fnl f* **11/2**[3]
3263 **5** 3 **Ellemujie**[8] 5350 2-8-10 **84**.................................... SebSanders 2 74
(D K Ivory) *lw: hld up: rdn over 2f out: wknd ins fnl f* **11/4**[1]
1650 **6** 2½ **Master Chef (IRE)**[13] 5219 2-9-7 **95**.................(b) KerrinMcEvoy 6 78
(J H M Gosden) *lw: led 6f out: hdd over 2f out: wknd fnl f* **7/1**
4350 **7** 2½ **Miss Bootylishes**[9] 5322 2-7-12 **72**.................................... DavidKinsella 4 49
(A B Haynes) *sn outpcd: hung lft fr 1/2-way* **9/2**[2]

1m 24.63s (-1.87) **Going Correction** -0.25s/f (Firm) **7** Ran SP% **111.1**
Speed ratings (Par 99): **100,97,96,96,92 89,86**
CSF £76.24 CT £484.87 TOTE £6.10: £2.80, £9.20; EX 98.20.
Owner Khalifa Dasmal **Bred** Don M Robinson **Trained** Newmarket, Suffolk
■ Stewards' Enquiry : Hayley Turner caution: used whip in incorrect place

FOCUS
A fair nursery run at a decent gallop and the time was 1.38sec faster than the following maiden. The form looks solid rated around the placed horses.

NOTEBOOK
Noble Citizen(USA), making his handicap debut after running well on Polytrack last time, had previously shown promise in two runs on the July course. He was always travelling well and, going on coming out of the dip, was always in control thereafter. He should still be reasonably handicapped after re-assessment. (op 11-2 tchd 4-1)
Dalkey Girl(IRE), who has had plenty of experience, was able to reverse previous form with Dan Tucket on 4lb better terms. She came from well back to snatch second place from her old rival but the winner was already home. (op 28-1 tchd 33-1)

Dan Tucket ran his race and performed pretty close to the form he showed when winning a valuable nursery on the July course on a line through the runner-up. The pair help give this form a solid appearance. (tchd 7-1)

Hustle(IRE), who got off the mark on his first try at this trip at Lingfield last time, was unable to dominate as he did there with Master Chef running too free and, although eventually getting to the head of affairs, was run out of it up the hill. Official explanation: jockey said colt was unsuited by the good to firm (firm in places) ground (op 11-4)

Ellemujie, was 7lb better off for a three and a half-length beating on soft ground on the July course, but was made favourite on the strength of better efforts on fast going. However, he never got competitive having been held up at the rear. (op 10-3)

Master Chef(IRE) ran quite free again and paid the penalty but at least ensured a good strong gallop and a decent time. (op 9-1 tchd 10-1)

Miss Bootylishes, who is due to go up 13lb from tomorrow following a good effort at Doncaster the previous week, looked theoretically well in. However, she was always struggling to go the pace and hanging left to the stands rail effectively ended her chance. The Handicapper may well be re-adjusting her figure after this performance and she may need a return to softer ground. Official explanation: jockey said filly hung left (tchd 4-1)

5598 EXPRESS COFFEE CARS EBF MAIDEN STKS — 7f

3:45 (3:46) (Class 4) 2-Y-O — **£5,181** (£1,541; £770; £384) **Stalls** Centre

Form	Pos	Dist	Horse / Trainer / Comment	Jockey	RPR
	1		**Fr Dominic (USA)** 2-9-3 0 (R M Beckett) *w'like: str: scope: chsd ldrs: led 1/2-way: rdn: hung lft and hdd over 1f out: rallied to ld ins fnl f: r.o* **10/1**	SebSanders 6	82+
	2	1/2	**Virtual** 2-9-3 0 (J H M Gosden) *athletic: bit bkwd: chsd ldrs: led and hung lft fr over 1f out: hdd ins fnl f: styd on* **11/2**[1]	DavidKinsella 4	81+
	3	3/4	**Aromatherapy** 2-8-12 0 (H R A Cecil) *w'like: hld up in tch: rdn over 1f out: styd on* **15/2**	EddieAhern 11	74+
00	4	4	**Perks (IRE)**[28] 4777 2-9-3 0 (J L Dunlop) *chsd ldrs: rdn over 2f out: wknd fnl f* **11/2**[1]	TedDurcan 12	69+
0	5	nk	**Tevez**[62] 3747 2-9-3 0 (M H Tompkins) *neat: str: prom: shkn up and hung rt fr over 1f out: wknd fnl f* **22/1**	NickyMackay 3	68
	6	1 3/4	**Blue Admiral** 2-9-3 0 (M H Tompkins) *athletic: leggy: s.s: outpcd: styd on ins fnl f: nvr nrr* **40/1**	MichaelHills 1	63+
	7	1/2	**Cassablanca** 2-8-12 0 (M L W Bell) *w'like: chsd ldrs over 5f* **6/1**[2]	JamieSpencer 13	57+
	8	1/2	**Deo Valente (IRE)** 2-9-3 0 (B J Meehan) *w'like: leggy: prom: rdn and lost pl 1/2-way: n.d after* **15/2**	StephenDonohoe 10	60
	9	hd	**Jaser** 2-9-3 0 (P W Chapple-Hyam) *lengthy: str: dwlt: hld up: rdn over 2f out: n.d* **12/1**	KerrinMcEvoy 8	60+
04	10	nk	**St Jean Cap Ferrat**[10] 5306 2-9-3 0 (G Wragg) *str: lw: hld up in tch: edgd rt and wknd over 1f out* **10/1**	DarryllHolland 9	59
	11	shd	**Trawlerman (IRE)** 2-9-3 0 (M H Tompkins) *leggy: s.s: rn green: nt clr run over 1f out: n.d* **50/1**	SaleemGolam 7	59+
0	12	1 3/4	**Abeyance (IRE)**[10] 5306 2-9-3 0 (J Noseda) *w'like: str: bit bkwd: led to 1/2-way: wknd over 1f out* **28/1**	TPQueally 5	54
	13	1 1/4	**Tajweed (IRE)** 2-9-3 0 (M Johnston) *athletic: bit bkwd: s.s: outpcd* **13/2**[3]	MartinDwyer 2	51+

1m 26.01s (-0.49) **Going Correction** -0.25s/f (Firm) — **13** Ran SP% **120.0**

Speed ratings (Par 97): **92,91,90,86,85 83,83,82,82,81 81,79,78**

CSF £62.39 TOTE £14.20: £3.40, £2.80, £2.80; EX 132.80.

Owner R A Pegum **Bred** Kenneth C Duncan & Neal R Phelps **Trained** Whitsbury, Hants

FOCUS

An open-looking maiden with pre-race favouritism changing several times. The time was 1.38sec slower than the preceding nursery but there could be a few winners come from the race.

NOTEBOOK

Fr Dominic(USA), who fetched 50,000gns when re-sold earlier this year after being bought in America for $72,000 as a yearling, emulated his stable companion earlier in the day, showing up throughout and then finding enough under pressure to hold off the runner-up. He is likely to be be put away until next season, when he will be suited by a mile plus, but the experience should not be lost on him. (op 12-1)

Virtual ◆, an attractive home-bred colt closely related to Iceman, was backed in to joint favourite just before the off. He showed up throughout but ran green and wandered under pressure, and in the end found the winner just too strong. He should have learnt plenty and will be winning his maiden given normal progression. (op 13-2 tchd 15-2)

Aromatherapy, an attractive filly out of a half-sister to Distant Music who won over 10f, was another to run well despite showing her inexperience. She is likely to be placed to win races, and may be better off against her own sex. (op 8-1 tchd 10-1)

Perks(IRE), on his toes in the paddock, had shown promise in a couple of maidens on softer ground, was encountering a surface this fast for the first time and appeared to have his chance but was left behind up the hill. He sets a modest standard for the form and is likely to be seen to better effect in handicaps in due course. (op 13-2)

Tevez, a half-brother to Benayoun from the family of Summoner, is bred to win as a juvenile on his dam's side. He showed considerable improvement on his debut and, like his namesake, should be scoring before too long. (op 20-1)

Blue Admiral ◆, related to sprinters and out of a sprinter, but with the stout stayer Sadeem further back on the dam's side, looked really green on this debut after badly missing the break. However, he stayed on at the end and can be given credit for finishing as close as he did. (op 33-1)

Cassablanca, an attractive half-sister to Captain Hurricane from the family of Niche, drifted out from favourite and ran her race in a similar fashion. She showed up well enough before fading out of contention up the hill, but Spencer was not hard on her once she was beaten and she can be expected to show the benefit in due course. (op 5-1)

Deo Valente(IRE), who made less as a yearling than as a foal, has a Derby entry and attracted some money beforehand. However, after showing up early he lost his place around the halfway mark and just kept on past beaten rivals. (op 10-1 tchd 7-1)

5599 WARRENS OF WARWICK MEDIAN AUCTION MAIDEN STKS — 1m

4:20 (4:23) (Class 4) 2-Y-O — **£4,533** (£1,348; £674; £336) **Stalls** Centre

Form	Pos	Dist	Horse / Trainer / Comment	Jockey	RPR
3	1		**Tomintoul Flyer**[35] 4586 2-9-3 0 (H R A Cecil) *w'like: mde all: edgd rt ins fnl f: rdn out* **6/4**[1]	TedDurcan 18	88+
	2	2	**Mystery Star (IRE)** 2-9-3 0 (M H Tompkins) *w'like: a.p: rdn to chse wnr over 1f out: styd on same pce ins fnl f* **50/1**	NickyMackay 14	83+
0	3	1/2	**Inventor (IRE)**[21] 5011 2-9-3 0 (B J Meehan) *lw: hld up: hdwy and hung rt over 1f out: r.o wl* **7/1**[3]	StephenDonohoe 1	82+
4	4	5	**Fearless Warrior**[18] 5088 2-9-3 0 (J L Dunlop) *w'like: chsd ldrs: rdn over 2f out: wknd over 1f out* **11/1**	EddieAhern 10	71
0	5	hd	**Kabuku**[35] 4584 2-9-3 0 (M H Tompkins) *w'like: leggy: dwlt: hld up: hdwy over 1f out: nvr nrr* **100/1**	SaleemGolam 4	70+
0	6	1	**General Tufto**[14] 5206 2-9-3 0 (R Charlton) *w'like: bit bkwd: s.i.s: hdwy over 3f out: wknd over 1f out* **11/1**	MartinDwyer 17	68+
50	7	3	**Dusk**[14] 5206 2-9-3 0 (J L Dunlop) *lw: chsd ldrs: rdn over 2f out: wknd over 1f out* **8/1**	SebSanders 13	61
00	8	1/2	**Pepper's Ghost**[23] 4947 2-8-10 0 (Miss J Feilden) *leggy: mid-div: rdn 1/2-way: wknd over 2f out* **66/1**	AmyBaker[(7)] 8	60
0	9	1 3/4	**Sonny Sam (IRE)**[25] 4890 2-9-3 0 (M H Tompkins) *w'like: str: prom 6f* **40/1**	TPQueally 16	56
0	10	nk	**Siren Call**[19] 5061 2-8-12 0 (W J Haggas) *leggy: hld up: racd keenly: swtchd rt 3f out: n.d* **33/1**	MichaelHills 6	50+
04	11	1/2	**Lord Of Esteem**[23] 4946 2-9-3 0 (J Ryan) *leggy: s.i.s: hld up: a in rr* **66/1**	BrettDoyle 5	54
	12	hd	**Arrewig Lissome (USA)** 2-9-3 0 (A M Balding) *str: bit bkwd: dwlt: sn chsng ldrs: wknd over 2f out* **33/1**	LPKeniry 12	54
0	13	5	**Captain Mainwaring**[8] 5344 2-9-3 0 (N P Littmoden) *w'like: str: bit bkwd: chsd ldrs over 5f* **100/1**	JamesDoyle 9	42
	14	nk	**Great Charm (IRE)** 2-9-3 0 (M L W Bell) *str: bit bkwd: hld up: wknd over 2f out* **33/1**	HayleyTurner 15	41
0	15	1 3/4	**Wadi Raider**[13] 5227 2-9-3 0 (M R Channon) *athletic: hld up: bhd fr 1/2-way* **40/1**	DarryllHolland 3	37
	16	2 1/2	**Trudder (USA)** 2-9-3 0 (P W Chapple-Hyam) *athletic: bit bkwd: hld up: rdn and wknd over 2f out: eased fnl f* **12/1**	KerrinMcEvoy 7	32+
60	P		**Metaphorical**[21] 5011 2-9-3 0 (M Johnston) *chsd wnr tl rdn and hung rt over 1f out: 3rd whn p.u sn after: dead* **4/1**[2]	JamieSpencer 11	—

1m 38.33s (-1.04) **Going Correction** -0.25s/f (Firm) — **17** Ran SP% **128.6**

Speed ratings (Par 97): **95,93,92,87,87 86,83,82,81,80 80,80,75,74,73 70,—**

CSF £120.61 TOTE £2.20: £1.60, £14.60, £2.30; EX 102.60.

Owner Angus Dundee Distillers plc **Bred** Whitsbury Manor Stud **Trained** Newmarket, Suffolk

FOCUS

Just a fair maiden and run 0.68 sec slower than the earlier fillies' race over the same trip. The form looks strong enough.

NOTEBOOK

Tomintoul Flyer, an attractive colt whose debut effort was given a boost when the winner of that race scored at Newbury earlier in the day, was given a confident ride from the front and was always in control. He drew away up the hill and looks the sort who can go on to better things. (op 7-4 tchd 15-8 in places)

Mystery Star(IRE), a medium-sized colt, is by Kris Kin but related to several performers who scored at 6-8f. He has a Derby entry and ran in the manner of a stayer, being the only one to seriously threaten the winner in the last quarter-mile. He should be able to win a maiden on this evidence. (op 40-1)

Inventor(IRE) was the real eyecatcher, finishing best of all having been held up. Another with the Derby entry, he built on his effort in a Sandown maiden that is beginning to work out reasonably well and looks the sort who will make his mark over middle-distances next season. (op 14-1)

Fearless Warrior, who is bred to stay really well, again showed ability and is another who will come into his own over longer trips, probably in handicaps. (op 16-1)

Kabuku, who finished last in what looks an ordinary maiden on the July course on his debut, improved on that but was well beaten and needs more time and further.

General Tufto again missed the break but got onto the heels of the leaders at one point before fading out of contention. He is likely to make his mark in handicaps in due course. (op 10-1 tchd 12-1)

Dusk ran close to previous form with General Tufto, but has not really built on his debut in a fair Newbury maiden. However, he does now qualify for handicaps.

Metaphorical, who had progressed from his debut, was in the process of improving again and looked booked for third place when sadly going wrong with fatal results.

5600 MC SEAFOOD AND ORIENTAL FOODS NURSERY — 1m 1f

4:55 (4:55) (Class 4) (0-85,79) 2-Y-O — **£6,477** (£1,927; £963; £481) **Stalls** Centre

Form	Pos	Dist	Horse / Trainer / Comment	Jockey	RPR
0532	1		**Stubbs Art (IRE)**[8] 5350 2-9-2 **72** (D R C Elsworth) *lw: hld up in tch: racd keenly: led over 3f out: hung rt fr over 1f out: drvn out* **8/13**[1]	SebSanders 2	83+
4210	2	4	**Townkab (IRE)**[10] 5314 2-8-9 **65** (N P Littmoden) *hld up: rdn over 2f out: hdwy to chse wnr over 1f out: no imp* **13/2**[3]	TGMcLaughlin 6	66
000	3	1 3/4	**Cocktail Shaker (USA)**[14] 5200 2-8-6 **62** (b[1]) (B J Meehan) *led: hdd over 6f out: rdn over 2f out: styd on same pce appr fnl f* **33/1**	NickyMackay 5	60
3134	4	4	**Relinquished**[25] 4892 2-9-3 **73** (J Noseda) *lw: prom: jnd ldrs over 3f out: rdn and wknd over 1f out* **11/2**[2]	TPQueally 4	63
541	5	4	**Cheque**[17] 5116 2-9-7 **77** (J A Osborne) *wnt rt s: sn chsng ldrs: lost pl over 4f out: wknd over 2f out* **8/1**	MartinDwyer 9	59
0026	6	1 1/2	**Elegant Step**[26] 4852 2-9-0 **70** (A P Jarvis) *chsd ldr tl led over 6f out: hdd over 3f out: wknd over 2f out* **25/1**	DarryllHolland 3	49

1m 52.59s (0.64) **Going Correction** 0.0s/f (Good) — **6** Ran SP% **108.5**

Speed ratings (Par 97): **97,93,91,88,84 83**

CSF £4.70 CT £49.36 TOTE £1.60: £1.10, £2.70; EX 4.30 Place 6 £89.71, Place 5 £33.27.

Owner Matthew Green **Bred** Grenane House Stud, Steve Hillen & Sean Graham **Trained** Newmarket, Suffolk

FOCUS

A fair nursery run at an ordinary gallop but they finished well strung out and the form is straightforward despite there not being much strength in depth.

NOTEBOOK

Stubbs Art(IRE) has progressed steadily with racing and distance and, already due to go up 4lb, justified favouritism decisively. He was keen throughout over the longest trip he has tried to date, but he picked up well when asked to come right away. He may need to improve again, but could be worth a tilt at the Zetland Stakes over 10f here at the end of the season. (op 4-6)

Townkab(IRE) bounced back from a below-par effort on this step back up in distance. He never really troubled the winner, but stayed on past tiring rivals in the manner which suggests he will get further next season. (op 8-1)

Cocktail Shaker(USA), making his handicap debut having shown little in maidens at 7-8f, had blinkers on for the first time. The headgear resulted in an improved effort, as he made the early running and then kept going after being headed. (op 25-1)

Relinquished, who brought plenty of reasonable nursery form into this, tried to go with the winner when that rival made his effort, but she faded up the hill as if this extra furlong found her out stamina-wise. (tchd 13-2)

Cheque, who got off the mark in an ordinary Polytrack maiden, failed to build on that and was in trouble some way from home. Official explanation: jockey said gelding lost its action (op 13-2)

Elegant Step set the pace but was soon done with once the race began in earnest. (op 20-1 tchd 16-1)

T/Plt: £613.90 to a £1 stake. Pool: £56,895.40. 67.65 winning tickets. T/Qpdt: £122.40 to a £1 stake. Pool: £3,135.20. 18.95 winning tickets. CR

The Form Book, Raceform Ltd, Compton, RG20 6NL

5564 WOLVERHAMPTON (A.W) (L-H)

Friday, September 21

OFFICIAL GOING: Standard

Wind: Virtually nil Weather: Fine

5601 WILLIAM HILL 0800 44 40 40 NURSERY 7f 32y(P)

7:00 (7:01) (Class 5) (0-75,75) 2-Y-O £3,071 (£906; £453) Stalls High

Form RPR

056 **1** **Dancing Marabout (IRE)**[43] 4323 2-9-3 **71**............... NelsonDeSouza 6 73
(C R Egerton) *chsd ldr: rdn over 2f out: r.o to ld wl ins fnl f* **17/2**

4235 **2** *1 ¼* **Lady Rochbonne**[40] 4428 2-8-10 **69**...................... AshleyHamblett(5) 11 68
(Mrs G S Rees) *led: rdn over 1f out: hdd and nt qckn wl ins fnl f* **12/1**

6020 **3** *nk* **Bencorr (USA)**[25] 4892 2-9-2 **70**.................................... JamieSpencer 2 68
(M J Wallace) *hld up and bhd: c wd st: hdwy and hung lft fnl f: nrst fin* **3/1**[1]

6442 **4** *1 ¼* **Gower Belle**[18] 5097 2-9-2 **70**.. SamHitchcott 7 65
(W R Muir) *hld up in tch: rdn and hdwy over 2f out: hung lft jst over 1f out: one pce* **8/1**

5235 **5** *hd* **Betty Burke**[24] 4924 2-8-12 **66**... DaneO'Neill 5 61
(H J L Dunlop) *t.k.h early: a.p: rdn over 2f out: one pce fnl f* **14/1**

2100 **6** *¾* **What Katie Did (IRE)**[10] 5314 2-9-0 **75**...................... RobbieEgan(7) 12 68
(J A Osborne) *prom: rdn 2f out: swtchd rt jst over 1f out: one pce* **6/1**[3]

030 **7** *½* **Home**[37] 4500 2-9-0 **68**.. J-PGuillambert 4 59
(E A L Dunlop) *hld up in tch: nt clr run ins fnl f: nvr able to chal* **4/1**[2]

0560 **8** *1* **Frammenti**[6] 5423 2-7-11 **58**................................. DanielleMcCreery(7) 10 47
(A J McCabe) *s.i.s: sme late hdwy* **100/1**

3040 **9** *hd* **Rio Princess (IRE)**[21] 5008 2-9-0 **71**........................... WilliamBuick(3) 9 59
(T G Mills) *t.k.h towards rr: hdwy over 2f out: rdn and wknd wl over 1f out* **17/2**

500 **10** *hd* **Intersky Melody (USA)**[39] 4448 2-9-0 **68**......................... JimCrowley 1 56
(R M Whitaker) *broke wl: lost pl over 5f out: bhd fnl 3f* **12/1**

2240 **11** *hd* **Alabama Spirit (USA)**[14] 5199 2-8-12 **69**..................... DominicFox(3) 3 56
(D Shaw) *a towards rr* **25/1**

000 **12** *4* **Chrystal Venture (IRE)**[21] 5011 2-8-11 **68**................ JerryO'Dwyer(3) 8 45
(A J McCabe) *hld up towards rr: short-lived effrt over 2f out* **66/1**

1m 30.05s (-0.35) **Going Correction** -0.30s/f (Stan) 12 Ran SP% **119.8**
Speed ratings (Par 95): **90,88,88,86,86 85,85,84,83,83 83,78**
CSF £106.32 CT £386.02 TOTE £15.40: £7.40, £3.60, £1.10; EX 152.60.

Owner Allsopp, Astor, Broughton & Drummond I **Bred** Edgeridge Ltd & Lynch Bages Ltd **Trained** Chaddleworth, Berks

FOCUS

A run-of-the-mill event and several unexposed sorts on show here, but the winning time was ordinary and the placed horses dictate the level.

NOTEBOOK

Dancing Marabout(IRE) was making his All-Weather debut and having his first handicap run after three unplaced efforts in turf maidens. Always tracking the pace, he got on top in the last 100 yards and looks the type to go on improving for a while yet. (op 14-1)

Lady Rochbonne, who had raced too keenly here last time, was allowed a soft lead on this occasion and did not give up without a fight when taken on by the winner. She is evidently coming to hand and should be able to pick up a similar event. (op 10-1)

Bencorr(USA), who had failed to get home over a 1m at Newcastle last time, came from a long way back on this occasion and finished to good effect, despite going left under pressure. A stronger-run 7f will probably suit him better. (op 4-1 tchd 11-4)

Gower Belle, who was stepping up from 6f, was also inclined to hang left when asked for her effort, but she showed enough to suggest she can find a race as she gains experience. (op 7-1 tchd 17-2)

Betty Burke did not help her chances of seeing out this longer trip by taking a grip early. (tchd 16-1)

What Katie Did(IRE), 6lb higher than when winning here on his last visit, raced wide from his high draw and could never land an effective blow. (op 13-2 tchd 8-1)

Home did not have a lot of racing room in the closing stages and is probably a bit better than he was able to show here. Official explanation: jockey said colt was denied a clear run (op 11-2)

5602 BET ONLINE @ WILLIAMHILL.CO.UK H'CAP 7f 32y(P)

7:30 (7:30) (Class 6) (0-60,60) 3-Y-O £2,388 (£705; £352) Stalls High

Form RPR

3453 **1** **Metropolitan Chief**[11] 5275 3-8-9 56.....................(b) KirstyMilczarek(5) 2 67
(D M Simcock) *a.p: edgd lft over 1f out: rdn to ld ins fnl f: edgd lft: r.o* **3/1**[1]

5143 **2** *1 ¼* **Luck Will Come (IRE)**[24] 4919 3-9-3 59..................... JamieSpencer 10 67
(M J Wallace) *led early: chsd ldr: rdn to ld wl over 1f out: hdd ins fnl f: flashed tail whn hit w whip: kpt on* **7/2**[2]

0065 **3** *3 ½* **Golden Brown (IRE)**[11] 5275 3-9-1 57........................... JimCrowley 5 56
(David Pinder) *chsd ldrs: rdn over 2f out: edgd lft jst over 1f out: one pce* **10/1**

2-65 **4** *hd* **Murrisk**[21] 5016 3-8-11 56... JerryO'Dwyer(3) 11 54
(Eamon Tyrrell, Ire) *sn led: rdn and hdd wl over 1f out: wknd ins fnl f* **15/2**

400- **5** *1 ¼* **Torver**[316] 6416 3-8-10 55... WilliamBuick(3) 4 50
(Dr J D Scargill) *wnt sltly lft s: hld up in mid-div: rdn over 2f out: hdwy on ins wl over 1f out: sn hung rt: no imp fnl f* **16/1**

-500 **6** *2* **Amber Isle**[46] 4224 3-9-1 57...................................... StephenDonohoe 7 46
(D Carroll) *hld up and bhd: rdn over 2f out: sme hdwy on ins wl over 1f out: n.d* **9/1**

-045 **7** *1* **Izabela Hannah**[86] 3000 3-9-4 60....................................(b) SebSanders 6 47
(R M Beckett) *hld up towards rr: rdn over 2f out: nvr nr ldrs* **8/1**

3010 **8** *nk* **Karmest**[75] 3342 3-9-2 58... DaneO'Neill 3 44
(A D Brown) *sltly hmpd s: hld up towards rr: hdwy over 3f out: wknd 2f out* **14/1**

1003 **9** *1 ¼* **Hayley's Flower (IRE)**[18] 5098 3-8-13 55.......................... LPKeniry 12 37
(J C Fox) *chsd ldrs: rdn over 3f out: wknd wl over 1f out* **20/1**

-000 **10** *2 ½* **Global Guest**[15] 5177 3-8-9 58...................................... MarkCoumbe(7) 1 34
(A J Chamberlain) *a in rr* **80/1**

631 **11** *3* **Southwarknewsflash**[15] 5175 3-9-0 56................................ DMylonas 9 24
(Mrs C A Dunnett) *hld up in mid-div: wknd over 2f out* **7/1**[3]

1m 28.64s (-1.76) **Going Correction** -0.30s/f (Stan) 11 Ran SP% **120.2**
Speed ratings (Par 99): **98,96,92,92,90 88,87,87,85,82 79**
CSF £13.65 CT £96.75 TOTE £3.90: £1.50, £2.00, £3.40; EX 27.80.

Owner The Metropolitans **Bred** J A Prescott And C M Oakshott **Trained** Newmarket, Suffolk

■ Stewards' Enquiry : Mark Coumbe caution: used whip when out of contention

FOCUS

This modest event was run at a decent pace, which evidently suited the winner. The first pair were clear and the form looks reasonable with the runner-up to her best.

5603 CHIPS @ WILLIAMHILLCASINO.COM MEDIAN AUCTION MAIDEN FILLIES' STKS 5f 216y(P)

7:55 (8:00) (Class 6) 2-Y-O £2,388 (£705; £352) Stalls Low

Form RPR

22 **1** **Our Piccadilly (IRE)**[32] 4662 2-9-0 0...................................... LPKeniry 8 74
(W S Kittow) *a.p: rdn to ld wl ins fnl f: drvn out* **2/1**[2]

5 **2** *nk* **Showtime Ice**[28] 4756 2-9-0 0...................................... JamieSpencer 9 73
(M J Wallace) *led: rdn and hung rt fr over 1f out: hdd wl ins fnl f: kpt on* **10/1**

2 **3** *3* **Change Tack (USA)**[104] 2457 2-9-0 0.............................. JimCrowley 5 64
(Mrs A J Perrett) *hld up in tch: rdn over 1f out: one pce* **7/4**[1]

4060 **4** *1 ¾* **Janet's Delight**[10] 5313 2-8-7 50.............................. WilliamCarson(7) 3 59
(S Curran) *hld up towards rr: rdn over 1f out: r.o ins fnl f: nvr nrr* **100/1**

43 **5** *½* **One Called Alice**[21] 5015 2-9-0 0...................................... TPQueally 12 58
(J R Holt) *a.p: ev ch over 2f out: rdn wl over 1f out: sn wknd* **20/1**

6 *½* **Concealment (IRE)** 2-9-0 0.. SebSanders 6 56
(R M Beckett) *hld up in mid-div: rdn over 2f out: edgd lft over 1f out: no hdwy* **16/1**

4 **7** *hd* **Little Cascade**[21] 5017 2-9-0 0................................. StephenDonohoe 2 55
(E S McMahon) *hld up in mid-div: rdn over 1f out: no imp* **50/1**

0 **8** *1 ¼* **Carole Os (IRE)**[6] 5428 2-8-7 0.. JCorrigan(7) 1 52
(S W Hall) *bhd: rdn over 2f out: nvr nr ldrs* **33/1**

45 **9** *1 ¾* **Weet By Far**[25] 4904 2-9-0 0... PaulEddery 4 46
(R Hollinshead) *prom tl rdn and wknd over 1f out* **9/1**[3]

10 *6* **Bahamian Princess** 2-8-9 0.......................... RussellKennemore(5) 10 28
(E S McMahon) *s.i.s: sn mid-div: rdn over 3f out: hdwy and hung rt over 2f out: rn wd ent st: sn wknd* **20/1**

2443 **11** *1 ¾* **Freudian Slip**[10] 5313 2-9-0 69.. PaulDoe 11 23
(S Curran) *racd wd: sn bhd: eased whn no ch wl over 1f out* **12/1**

0000 **12** *20* **April's Quest (IRE)**[11] 5267 2-9-0 45.............................. DaneO'Neill 13 —
(David Pinder) *a bhd: eased whn no ch fnl 2f* **100/1**

1m 15.01s (-0.80) **Going Correction** -0.30s/f (Stan) 12 Ran SP% **118.8**
Speed ratings (Par 90): **93,92,88,86,85 84,84,83,80,72 70,43**
CSF £20.87 TOTE £2.70: £1.10, £2.80, £1.10; EX 28.20.

Owner J Hopkins, S Kittow, R Perry **Bred** Mrs Hopkins, Mr Kittow And Mrs Perry **Trained** Blackborough, Devon

■ Stewards' Enquiry : L P Keniry one-day ban: used whip with excessive frequency (Oct 2)
Jamie Spencer caution: used whip with excessive frequency

FOCUS

A fair maiden but the fourth horse was rated just 50 otherwise the form could have rated higher.

NOTEBOOK

Our Piccadilly(IRE) showed a good attitude to wear down the runner-up who had hung across her approaching the furlong mark leaving her with work to do, but she buckled down well to her work in the last 150 yards to gain the day. She may improve again over further. (op 5-2)

Showtime Ice, who had been slowly away and ran green on her debut over 5f at Bath last month, proved much sharper here but threw her race away by hanging in the straight, and she may not be entirely straightforward. Official explanation: jockey said filly was hanging badly right-handed (op 11-1)

Change Tack(USA) , not seen since running second in a 6f Lingfield maiden in June, was never far away but she lacked the speed to get in a blow in the straight and probably already needs a stiffer test. (op 13-8 tchd 15-8)

Janet's Delight, who has not been getting home in her races, was more patiently ridden on this occasion and derived the benefit as she kept on through beaten horses in the final furlong. She may be worth a try in a nursery off her current modest mark.

One Called Alice did not step up on her previous creditable efforts at this track though she was not well drawn. She now qualifies for a mark. (op 28-1 tchd 18-1)

Freudian Slip for some reason ran way below form, certainly well below her current mark. She is better than this. (tchd 14-1)

5604 HEADS-UP @ WILLIAMHILLPOKER.COM H'CAP 1m 4f 50y(P)

8:25 (8:25) (Class 5) (0-75,74) 3-Y-O £3,071 (£906; £453) Stalls Low

Form RPR

2205 **1** **Aypeeyes (IRE)**[31] 4687 3-8-11 67.. LPKeniry 1 74
(S Kirk) *hld up in mid-div: hdwy on ins wl over 1f out: sn rdn: swtchd rt ins fnl f: sn led: r.o wl* **9/1**

0236 **2** *1 ¾* **Maslak (IRE)**[3] 5500 3-9-4 74.. DaneO'Neill 9 78
(P W Hiatt) *hld up towards rr: hdwy on outside 3f out: rdn 2f out: edgd lft 1f out: r.o one pce* **15/2**[3]

5112 **3** *1 ¼* **Western Point (IRE)**[20] 5040 3-8-13 69............................ SebSanders 4 71
(Sir Mark Prescott) *sn chsng ldr: led 8f out: rdn over 1f out: hdd and no ex wl ins fnl f* **5/4**[1]

4241 **4** *1* **Magdalene**[26] 4858 3-8-13 69.. JamieSpencer 8 70
(Rae Guest) *s.i.s: sn swtchd lft: hld up and bhd: rdn and hung lft fr over 1f out: styd on ins fnl f* **7/2**[2]

1006 **5** *shd* **Iceman George**[29] 4735 3-8-10 66..............................(v) TGMcLaughlin 2 67
(D Morris) *led early: a.p: rdn and wnt 2nd 2f out: nt qckn whn n.m.r and squeezed out ins fnl f* **33/1**

5600 **6** *3 ½* **Troialini**[63] 3709 3-9-0 73... JerryO'Dwyer(3) 3 68
(S W Hall) *hld up: hdwy over 8f out: chsd ldr over 5f out tl rdn 2f out: sn n.m.r and wknd* **10/1**

6635 **7** *3 ½* **Willow Dancer (IRE)**[22] 4960 3-9-0 70.................................. AdamKirby 5 59
(W R Swinburn) *hld up: rdn over 3f out: hdwy whn nt clr run over 2f out: wknd wl over 1f out* **8/1**

-430 **8** *13* **Steel Silk (IRE)**[25] 4902 3-8-8 67 ow2.......................... MarkLawson(3) 7 35
(B Smart) *sn led: hdd 8f out: rdn over 5f out: wknd 4f out* **40/1**

0200 **9** *1 ¼* **Sularno**[47] 4197 3-8-11 70... TravisBlock(3) 6 36
(H Morrison) *hld up in tch: rdn and wknd over 2f out* **16/1**

2m 38.76s (-3.66) **Going Correction** -0.30s/f (Stan) 9 Ran SP% **119.9**
Speed ratings (Par 101): **100,98,98,97,97 94,92,83,83**
CSF £77.25 CT £143.42 TOTE £22.00: £2.70, £1.80, £1.10; EX 96.00.

Owner The www.mortgages.tv Partnership **Bred** John Malone **Trained** Upper Lambourn, Berks

FOCUS

A modest handicap with no pace on early here, and rather a messy affair in the straight. The form seems to make sense, though.

5605 PLAY BACKGAMMON @ WILLHILL.COM MEDIAN AUCTION MAIDEN STKS 1m 141y(P)

8:55 (8:56) (Class 6) 2-Y-O £2,388 (£705; £352) Stalls Low

Form RPR

043 **1** **Trinkila (USA)**[10] 5301 2-8-7 0.. TolleyDean(5) 3 71
(P F I Cole) *w ldr: led over 6f out: rdn over 1f out: r.o* **11/2**[2]

0 **2** *1 1/4* **Samurai Warrior**[28] 4764 2-9-3 0 SebSanders 4 73
(P J Makin) *a.p: rdn 2f out: hung lft over 1f out: kpt on ins fnl f: nt trble wnr* **8/1**

6 **3** *1 1/4* **Oceana Blue**[22] 4962 2-8-9 0 WilliamBuick(3) 2 66
(A M Balding) *led: hdd over 6f out: chsd wnr: rdn 2f out: no imp whn rdr dropped whip ins fnl f* **12/1**

23 **4** *1 1/4* **Tension Mounts (IRE)**[13] 5222 2-9-3 0 TPQueally 10 68
(J A Osborne) *hld up in mid-div: hdwy whn hung lft over 1f out: hung rt ins fnl f: one pce* **7/4**[1]

02 **5** *2* **No To Trident**[14] 5186 2-9-3 0 StephenDonohoe 8 64
(P D Evans) *hld up and bhd: c wd st: styng on whn hung lft ins fnl f: nvr trbld ldrs* **6/1**[3]

0 **6** *1 1/2* **Reel Star**[28] 4761 2-9-3 0 LPKeniry 11 61
(S Kirk) *nvr nr ldrs* **25/1**

06 **7** *hd* **Redesdale**[84] 3043 2-9-3 0 J-PGuillambert 7 60
(P W D'Arcy) *hld up in tch: rdn over 3f out: hung rt bnd over 2f out: sn wknd* **6/1**[3]

0000 **8** *1/2* **Saturday Boy**[36] 4524 2-8-12 51 RussellKennemore(5) 9 59
(Paul Green) *hld up in mid-div: rdn over 2f out: wknd over 1f out* **100/1**

355 **9** *1/2* **We'Re Delighted**[8] 5343 2-9-3 0 SamHitchcott 12 58
(M R Channon) *hld up and bhd: hdwy on outside over 3f out: rdn over 2f out: wknd over 1f out* **7/1**

10 *2 1/2* **Cherokee Star** 2-9-0 0 MarkLawson(3) 6 53
(C C Bealby) *mid-div: rdn 5f out: sn bhd* **150/1**

00 **11** *11* **Whodouthinkur (IRE)**[55] 3962 2-9-3 0 (p) TGMcLaughlin 5 30
(Mrs C A Dunnett) *prom: rdn over 3f out: wknd over 2f out* **100/1**

12 *11* **Silver Sprite** 2-9-3 0 DaneO'Neill 1 7
(D Shaw) *a in rr* **50/1**

1m 51.63s (-0.13) **Going Correction** -0.30s/f (Stan) **12** Ran SP% **120.1**
Speed ratings (Par 93): **88,86,85,84,82 81,81,80,80,78 68,58**
CSF £48.86 TOTE £7.70: £2.20, £2.00, £3.40; EX 57.90.

Owner D S Lee **Bred** B Wayne Hughes **Trained** Whatcombe, Oxon

■ Stewards' Enquiry : T P QueallyG one-day ban: improper riding (Oct 2)

FOCUS
A modest maiden, the form limited by the eighth. The winner ran close to her latest form.

NOTEBOOK
Trinkila(USA) had improved steadily with each of her three runs on turf and she got off the mark on this Polytrack debut. Given a positive ride, she was always holding the pack at bay in the straight and should continue to progress. (op 10-3 tchd 6-1)

Samurai Warrior, who could never make an impression on his debut at Newbury last month, found the competition more to his liking here and plugged on under pressure for a fair second. On this evidence, he looks a middle-distance performer in the making. (op 12-1)

Oceana Blue stepped up on her debut sixth over 6f at Lingfield and is evidently going the right way. (op 8-1)

Tension Mounts(IRE), who had run creditably in a couple of 7f events at Kempton, was unable to build on that promise here and, after being forced wide on the home turn, was inclined to run about under pressure in the straight. (op 5-2)

No To Trident, runner-up at Chepstow last time, could never get into the action on this All-Weather debut. He is now qualified for handicaps. (tchd 5-1 and 13-2)

5606 CALL HOUSE @ WILLIAMHILLBINGO.COM CLASSIFIED STKS 1m 1f 103y(P)
9:20 (9:21) (Class 7) 3-Y-O+ **£1,911** (£564; £282) **Stalls** Low

Form RPR

004 **1** **Private Soldier**[37] 4492 4-9-3 44 SamHitchcott 9 59
(N J Vaughan) *hld up towards rr: gd hdwy on outside to ld over 2f out: rdn and hung lft fr over 1f out: r.o* **25/1**

0244 **2** *1 1/4* **Slavonic Lake**[17] 5121 3-8-12 45 (t) SebSanders 8 56
(I A Wood) *hld up and bhd: rdn and hdwy over 2f out: styd on wl to take 2nd nr post* **5/1**[2]

0460 **3** *nk* **Justcallmehandsome**[35] 4577 5-8-10 45 (v) SophieDoyle(7) 13 55
(D J S Ffrench Davis) *hld up in mid-div: hdwy over 2f out: ev ch over 1f out: nt qckn ins fnl f* **25/1**

0600 **4** *6* **Altos Reales**[8] 5368 3-8-9 45 DominicFox(3) 1 43
(D Shaw) *bhd: rdn over 5f out: c wd and hdwy wl over 1f out: styng on whn hung lft ins fnl f: n.d* **33/1**

3630 **5** *2* **Foreland Sands (IRE)**[11] 5276 3-8-12 45 DaneO'Neill 3 39
(J R Best) *prom: rdn over 2f out: wknd over 1f out* **4/1**[1]

/00- **6** *1/2* **Pips Assertive Way**[5] 166 6-8-10 45 MarkCoumbe(7) 7 38
(A W Carroll) *hld up and bhd: rdn and hdwy wl over 1f out: nvr nr ldrs* **16/1**

0353 **7** *1 3/4* **Dexileos (IRE)**[8] 5368 8-9-0 45 TravisBlock(3) 5 35
(David Pinder) *t.k.h in mid-div: rdn over 3f out: n.m.r over 2f out: n.d after* **11/2**[3]

6064 **8** *1* **Voice Mail**[8] 5345 8-8-10 45 (v) DavidProbert(7) 4 33
(A M Balding) *hld up in mid-div: lost pl and n.m.r over 2f out: n.d after* **15/2**

25-0 **9** *5* **Ai Hawa (IRE)**[36] 4532 4-9-0 45 (b1) JerryO'Dwyer(3) 12 23
(Eamon Tyrrell, Ire) *prom: wnt 2nd 7f out: led 3f out: sn hdd: wknd wl over 1f out* **16/1**

0004 **10** *2* **Shadow Jumper (IRE)**[8] 5368 6-8-12 44 (b) RussellKennemore(5) 2 19
(J T Stimpson) *led 1f: prom: wkng whn nt clr run over 2f out* **12/1**

01-0 **11** *shd* **Guadiana (GER)**[142] 1406 5-9-3 44 JimCrowley 6 19
(A W Carroll) *a bhd* **7/1**

-546 **12** *2 1/2* **Musical Gift**[38] 2980 7-8-12 44 HaddenFrost(5) 10 14
(M Hill) *t.k.h: chsd ldrs: rdn and wknd over 2f out* **8/1**

0000 **13** *11* **Gary's Indian (IRE)**[36] 4532 4-9-3 45 (p) PaulEddery 11 —
(B P J Baugh) *led after 1f to 3f out: sn wknd* **100/1**

2m 0.59s (-2.03) **Going Correction** -0.30s/f (Stan)
WFA 3 from 4yo+ 5lb **13** Ran SP% **118.5**
Speed ratings (Par 97): **97,95,95,90,88 88,86,85,81,79 79,77,67**
CSF £141.77 TOTE £19.50: £9.50, £2.40, £6.40; EX 142.40 Place 6 £129.98, Place 5 £51.24.

Owner Owen Promotions Limited **Bred** Owen Promotions Ltd **Trained** Malpas, Cheshire

FOCUS
Obviously limited form, but the first three finished clear and it seems sound for the grade.

T/Plt: £150.10 to a £1 stake. Pool: £97,654.65. 474.90 winning tickets. T/Qpdt: £17.70 to a £1 stake. Pool: £6,248.90. 260.60 winning tickets. KH

5607 - 5612a (Foreign Racing) - See Raceform Interactive

5580 AYR (L-H)
Saturday, September 22

OFFICIAL GOING: Good to soft
After a dry night the ground was reckoned 'very tacky, patchy and very soft and loose on the home turn. Awful ground'.
Wind: Moderate, half against Weather: Fine, sunny and warm

5613 YOU CAN'T PREDICT FA NURSERY 1m
1:50 (1:51) (Class 2) (0-95,85) 2-Y-O
£12,464 (£3,732; £1,866; £934; £466; £234) **Stalls** Low

Form RPR

4110 **1** **Cobo Bay**[9] 5350 2-9-6 **84** DarryllHolland 7 92+
(K A Ryan) *mde all: pushed along 2f out: hld on wl fnl f* **14/1**

4343 **2** *1 3/4* **Daring Dream (GER)**[2] 5550 2-8-6 **70** ow2 GrahamGibbons 8 74
(T D Easterby) *sn midfield: drvn and outpcd over 3f out: rallied to chse wnr ins fnl f: kpt on* **20/1**

21 **3** *1 1/4* **Sheekey (IRE)**[21] 5038 2-9-0 **78** PatCosgrave 5 79
(G A Swinbank) *lw: hld up: hdwy over 1f out: edgd lft: kpt on fnl f: nrst fin* **8/1**

410 **4** *nk* **Annaliesse (IRE)**[9] 5350 2-8-6 **70** PaulHanagan 10 71
(R A Fahey) *t.k.h: prom: effrt over 2f out: no ex ins fnl f* **14/1**

022 **5** *4* **Soggy Dollar**[31] 4709 2-8-13 **77** JimmyQuinn 2 69
(M H Tompkins) *lw: in midfield: drvn and outpcd 2f out: no imp fnl f* **9/1**

3310 **6** *nk* **Montaquila**[71] 3504 2-9-7 **85** TomEaves 12 76
(J Howard Johnson) *t.k.h: cl up tl rdn and wknd over 1f out* **12/1**

6120 **7** *1 1/2* **Welcome Return (IRE)**[9] 5350 2-8-9 **73** (b) DavidAllan 13 61
(T D Easterby) *in midfield on outside: drvn and outpcd 1/2-way: kpt on fnl f: no imp* **33/1**

51 **8** *1 3/4* **Bencoolen (IRE)**[26] 4876 2-9-7 **85** SteveDrowne 6 69
(R Charlton) *lw: in tch: effrt over 2f out: btn over 1f out* **5/1**[2]

3224 **9** *1 1/4* **Rub Of The Relic (IRE)**[59] 3841 2-8-9 **73** TPO'Shea 4 54
(P A Blockley) *lw: chsd ldrs tl rdn and wknd wl over 1f out* **20/1**

0223 **10** *2 1/2* **Ink Spot**[81] 3192 2-9-0 **78** JamieSpencer 11 54
(M L W Bell) *dwlt: hld up: pushed along over 2f out: nvr on terms* **13/2**[3]

5312 **11** *nk* **Mizooka**[22] 5002 2-8-8 **72** SebSanders 1 47
(R M Beckett) *lw: hld up: pushed along over 2f out: nvr on terms* **4/1**[1]

634 **12** *4* **Parliamentary (JPN)**[41] 4417 2-8-11 **75** RoystonFfrench 9 41
(M Johnston) *bhd and sn drvn along: no ch fr 1/2-way* **10/1**

0521 **13** *2* **Joinedupwriting**[16] 5153 2-8-12 **76** KDarley 3 38
(R M Whitaker) *s.i.s: drvn in rr 3f out: sn btn* **16/1**

1m 46.35s (2.86) **Going Correction** +0.40s/f (Good) **13** Ran SP% **119.6**
Speed ratings (Par 101): **101,99,98,97,93 93,91,90,88,86 86,82,80**
CSF £270.19 CT £2392.98 TOTE £13.40: £3.80, £5.30, £2.80; EX 377.00.

Owner The C H F Partnership **Bred** The C H F Partnership **Trained** Hambleton, N Yorks

FOCUS
A fair event but one run at a fair gallop and the first four were clear, suggesting the form is solid.

NOTEBOOK
Cobo Bay, well beaten at Doncaster on fast ground, appreciated the return to this easy surface and returned to his best to notch his third win from his last four starts. He was allowed to do his own thing in front to a large extent but he showed a good attitude for pressure and should continue to give a good account. (op 16-1 tchd 18-1)

Daring Dream(GER), back in nursery company and over this trip for the first time, ran his best race yet with his rider posting 2lb of overweight. He shapes as though an even stiffer test of stamina would be to his liking and he is sure to win in ordinary company. (op 16-1)

Sheekey(IRE) ◆, off the mark in uncompetitive nursery company at Musselburgh, bettered that form on this nursery debut and may be a bit better than the bare form as he fared the best of those held up. A stronger overall gallop would have suited and this lightly-raced sort looks capable of further progress. (op 13-2 tchd 6-1)

Annaliesse(IRE), back on an easy surface, failed to settle and in the circumstances did well to last as long as she did. A stronger gallop and more cover might see her in a better light and she is worth another chance in similar company.

Soggy Dollar had shown fair form in maidens and was not disgraced from a stiffish mark on this nursery debut and first run over this trip. A stronger gallop would have suited and he may be capable of a bit better. (op 12-1)

Montaquila, out of his depth in Group 2 company at Newmarket last time, was on his toes in the paddock and failed to get home after racing keenly on his first start over this trip. He is going to have to improve to win races from his current mark of 85. (op 14-1 tchd 16-1)

Bencoolen(IRE), on edge in the paddock, Official explanation: jockey said colt was unsuited by the good to soft ground (op 9-2)

Ink Spot Official explanation: jockey said colt was unsuited by the good to soft ground

Mizooka has been running consistently well but was well beaten for no apparent reason back on an easy surface. She is worth another chance in ordinary company. (op 5-1)

Parliamentary(JPN) Official explanation: jockey said colt never travelled

5614 LAUNDRY COTTAGE STUD FIRTH OF CLYDE STKS (GROUP 3) (FILLIES) 6f
2:20 (2:24) (Class 1) 2-Y-O
£34,068 (£12,912; £6,462; £3,222; £1,614; £810) **Stalls** High

Form RPR

2134 **1** **Unilateral (IRE)**[30] 4744 2-8-12 106 LDettori 10 103
(B Smart) *lw: chsd ldrs stands' side: rdn to ld over 1f out: edgd lft: hld on wl fnl f* **5/1**[2]

1244 **2** *3/4* **Broken Applause (IRE)**[10] 5322 2-8-12 85 PaulHanagan 8 102+
(R A Fahey) *in tch stands' side: drvn and outpcd 1/2-way: rallied over 1f out: chsd wnr ins fnl f: kpt on* **7/1**[3]

130 **3** *1 1/2* **Highland Daughter (IRE)**[55] 3988 2-8-12 91 PhilipRobinson 11 96
(C G Cox) *bhd stands' side: outpcd 1/2-way: gd hdwy fnl f: r.o wl* **14/1**

5232 **4** *1 1/4* **Lady Deauville (FR)**[20] 5061 2-8-12 99 EddieAhern 3 93+
(P A Blockley) *cl up centre: ev ch tl no ex fnl f* **10/1**

6133 **5** *1 1/4* **Cristal Clear (IRE)**[10] 5322 2-8-12 86 DavidAllan 13 89
(T D Easterby) *bhd stands' side: hdwy and edgd lft fr over 1f out: no imp fnl f* **8/1**

120 **6** *1/2* **Lady Avenger (IRE)**[94] 2756 2-8-12 96 SebSanders 1 87
(J M P Eustace) *lw: cl up centre: effrt and ev ch over 1f out: no ex ent fnl f* **7/1**[3]

216 **7** *shd* **Gone Fast (USA)**[42] 4400 2-8-12 92 JamieSpencer 14 87
(J R Fanshawe) *bhd stands' side: rdn 1/2-way: hdwy over 1f out: n.d* **4/1**[1]

1044 **8** *nk* **Loch Jipp (USA)**[55] 3988 2-8-12 102 KDarley 7 86
(J S Wainwright) *cl up stands' side: ev ch over 1f out: sn btn* **9/1**

51 **9** *9* **Irish Pearl (IRE)**[33] 4662 2-8-12 87 PhillipMakin 5 59
(K R Burke) *led stands' side to over 1f out: sn btn* **14/1**

010 **10** *shd* **Dellini (IRE)**[10] 5324 2-8-12 93 (v[1]) DarryllHolland 2 59
(M R Channon) *s.i.s: bhd centre: rdn over 2f out: sn wknd* **28/1**

21 **11** *1 1/2* **Blue Eyed Miss (IRE)**[9] 5357 2-8-12 0 FrankieMcDonald 4 54
(P A Blockley) *lw: spd centre tl wknd fr 2f out* **16/1**

1m 14.31s (0.64) **Going Correction** +0.175s/f (Good) **11** Ran SP% **114.5**
Speed ratings (Par 102): **102,101,99,97,95 95,94,94,82,82 80**
CSF £37.22 TOTE £4.80: £2.10, £2.40, £3.60; EX 37.70 Trifecta £300.00 Part won. Pool: £422.64 - 0.80 winning tickets..
Owner Prime Equestrian **Bred** Gaines-Gentry Thoroughbred & Tower Bloodstock **Trained** Hambleton, N Yorks
■ Edge Of Light was withdrawn (12/1, refused to enter stalls). R4, deduct 5p in the £.

FOCUS
A fair event and one in which the gallop was sound. The field split into two - and the larger group raced on the stands' rail. The form is rated through the winner to her Lowther mark with the fourth close to her best.

NOTEBOOK
Unilateral(IRE), who turned in an improved effort in Group company in the Lowther at York last time, had the race run to suit and she did not really have to improve too much to beat an 85-rated rival this time. She should have no problems with 7f and should continue to give a good account. (op 9-2 tchd 4-1, 6-1 and 11-2 in places)
Broken Applause(IRE) ◆, who shaped well in a competitive nursery at Doncaster, turned in an improved performance on this first venture into Group company. She shapes as though the step up to 7f will suit and, although her handicap mark will be taking a fair rise after this, she is in very good hands and looks capable of scoring in minor Pattern company. (op 9-1)
Highland Daughter(IRE), who has only raced on an easy surface to date, confirmed herself a useful performer with this career-best effort. She is bred to stay further and appeals as the sort to win in minor Group company. (op 20-1)
Lady Deauville(FR) has yet to win a race but turned in a fair performance dropped in trip and may be better than the bare form as she fared the best of those up with the strong pace and was the best of those to race in the centre. She looks sure to win a minor event at the very least. (op 11-1 tchd 12-1)
Cristal Clear(IRE) has had a busy time of it this year but she is holding her form well and was she ran creditably in the face of a stiff task, despite edging away from the stands' rail. She will be up in the weights for this and, although worth a try over 7f, may not be the easiest to place successfully after reassessment. (op 12-1)
Lady Avenger(IRE) was far from disgraced but failed to improve for the step up to this trip on this first start after three months. She may be suited by the return to 5f and a sound surface and is worth another chance. (op 15-2 tchd 8-1)
Gone Fast(USA), back in trip and back on an easy surface, again had her limitations exposed in Group company. She shaped as though the return to further would suit and, as she is in very good hands, is not one to write off yet. (tchd 9-2, 5-1 in places)

5615 TOTESCOOP6 AYRSHIRE H'CAP 1m
2:50 (2:51) (Class 2) (0-100,98) 3-Y-0+
£15,580 (£4,665; £2,332; £1,167; £582; £292) **Stalls** Low

Form RPR

1154 **1** **Fremen (USA)**[21] 5031 7-9-3 89 AdrianTNicholls 9 104+
(D Nicholls) *lw: t.k.h in rr: hdwy over 2f out: led over 1f out: r.o strly* **7/1[2]**

01-0 **2** *2 1/2* **Kinsya**[22] 5012 4-9-1 87 JimmyQuinn 5 94
(M H Tompkins) *hld up in rr: hdwy over 4f out: styd on to take 2nd ins fnl f* **12/1**

3130 **3** *1 1/4* **Vainglory (USA)**[45] 4276 3-8-7 83 PaulHanagan 7 87
(D M Simcock) *lw: trckd ldrs: led over 2f out tl over 1f out: kpt on same pce* **12/1**

-111 **4** *nk* **Mutajarred**[64] 3715 3-9-8 98 RHills 10 101
(W J Haggas) *b: lw: mid-div: hdwy to trck ldrs over 4f out: styd on same pce fnl 2f* **13/8[1]**

2405 **5** *8* **Nevada Desert (IRE)**[26] 4900 7-8-11 86 MichaelJStainton(3) 8 71
(R M Whitaker) *chsd ldrs: wknd over 1f out* **25/1**

-504 **6** *1 3/4* **Proponent (IRE)**[17] 5141 3-9-2 92 SteveDrowne 1 73
(R Charlton) *lw: sn chsng ldrs: wknd and eased over 1f out* **7/1[2]**

1204 **7** *3/4* **Moody Tunes**[53] 4051 4-9-2 88 PatCosgrave 3 67
(K R Burke) *in rr-div: effrt 3f out: lost pl over 1f out* **9/1**

5000 **8** *1/2* **My Paris**[30] 4745 6-9-4 93 AndrewMullen(3) 4 71
(K A Ryan) *w ldr: led over 5f out: styd far side: hdd over 2f out: wknd over 1f out* **8/1[3]**

0250 **9** *1 3/4* **White Deer (USA)**[9] 5355 3-9-5 95 RoystonFfrench 12 69
(M Johnston) *in rr: sn drvn along: nvr a factor* **28/1**

3004 **10** *3/4* **Royal Dignitary (USA)**[30] 4745 7-9-3 89 SilvestreDeSousa 2 61
(D Nicholls) *t.k.h: led tl over 5f out: styd far side: lost pl over 2f out* **25/1**

0045 **11** *2 1/2* **Wavertree Warrior (IRE)**[28] 4827 5-8-12 84 (b) LDettori 11 51
(N P Littmoden) *in tch: effrt on wd outside over 2f out: sn wknd* **11/1**

1m 44.2s (0.71) **Going Correction** +0.40s/f (Good)
WFA 3 from 4yo+ 4lb **11** Ran SP% **119.1**
Speed ratings (Par 109): **112,109,108,107,99 98,97,96,95,94 91**
CSF £86.61 CT £1000.26 TOTE £7.20: £2.10, £3.80, £3.10; EX 98.70 TRIFECTA Not won..
Owner Miss C King Mrs A Seed Ms Finola Devaney **Bred** Flaxman Holdings Ltd **Trained** Sessay, N Yorks

FOCUS
A decent handicap and solid form rated through the placed horses. The winner looks better than ever.

NOTEBOOK
Fremen(USA) continues in fine form and stayed on in willing fashion to forge clear. He deserves to take his chance in the Cambridgeshire under a 4lb penalty. (op 8-1 tchd 13-2)
Kinsya showed the benefit of his Sandown return. He likes to get his toe in and should be able to add to his three wins last year. (tchd 11-1)
Vainglory(USA), full of himself after a six-week break, handles soft ground and should continue to give a good account of himself this backend. (op 9-1)
Mutajarred, 20lb higher than his first handicap success two outings ago, was back after a two-month break. He gave a good account of himself from a much higher mark on much less-testing ground. (op 5-2 tchd 6-4)
Nevada Desert(IRE) has been in good form this summer but he looks to have gone slightly off the boil.
Proponent(IRE), taking a big drop back in trip, dropped away in a matter of strides and connections must be scratching their heads. What do they try next? (op 11-2 tchd 8-1)
White Deer(USA) Official explanation: jockey said gelding never travelled
Wavertree Warrior(IRE) Official explanation: jockey said gelding lost its action

5616 TOTESPORT.COM AYR GOLD CUP (HERITAGE H'CAP) 6f
3:30 (3:30) (Class 2) 3-Y-0+
£75,407 (£22,578; £11,289; £5,650; £2,819; £1,415) **Stalls** High

Form RPR

0020 **1** **Advanced**[14] 5214 4-9-9 109 JamieSpencer 22 119
(K A Ryan) *lw: chsd stands' side ldrs: rdn to ld that gp and edgd rt ins fnl f: kpt on strly and overall ldr nr fin* **20/1**

5020 **2** *nk* **Benwilt Breeze (IRE)**[8] 5394 5-8-12 98 (t) EddieAhern 6 107
(G M Lyons, Ire) *str: chsd far side ldrs: led that gp over 1f out: hung rt: kpt on: hdd by stands' side wnr nr fin: 1st of 14 in gp* **22/1**

3500 **3** *1 3/4* **Patavellian (IRE)**[97] 2695 9-9-0 100 (b) SteveDrowne 9 104
(R Charlton) *chsd far side ldrs: ev ch that gp over 1f out: one pce ins fnl f: 2nd of 14 in gp* **100/1**

5521 **4** *1/2* **Beaver Patrol (IRE)**[15] 5209 5-9-0 100 5ex (v) KDarley 18 102
(Eve Johnson Houghton) *cl up stands' side: rdn and ev ch that gp over 1f out: one pce ins fnl f: 2nd of 14 in gp* **20/1**

2066 **5** *nk* **Fonthill Road (IRE)**[30] 4747 7-9-0 100 PaulHanagan 7 101+
(R A Fahey) *lw: bhd far side: hdwy over 1f out: kpt on: nrst fin: 3rd of 14 in gp* **12/1**

0010 **6** *nk* **River Falcon**[7] 5407 7-8-13 99 DanielTudhope 2 99+
(J S Goldie) *bhd far side tl hung rt and styd on fr over 1f out: nrst fin: 4th of 14 in gp* **50/1**

4344 **7** *shd* **Majestic Times (IRE)**[27] 4864 7-9-0 100 PatCosgrave 25 100
(Liam McAteer, Ire) *led stands' side gp to ins fnl f: no ex: 3rd of 14 in gp* **16/1**

3311 **8** *hd* **Indian Trail**[14] 5212 7-9-2 102 8ex (v) LDettori 23 101
(D Nicholls) *in midfield gng wl stands' side: effrt over 1f out: one pce fnl f: 4th of 14 in gp* **8/1[3]**

0205 **9** *shd* **Appalachian Trail (IRE)**[14] 5213 6-9-6 106 (b) TomEaves 19 105
(I Semple) *cl up stands' side: ev ch and rdn that gp over 1f out: sn no ex whn hmpd ins fnl f: 5th of 14 in gp* **33/1**

3432 **9** *dht* **Masta Plasta (IRE)**[4] 5512 4-8-12 98 DavidAllan 13 97
(D Nicholls) *in tch far side: effrt over 1f out: one pce fnl f: 5th of 14 in gp* **40/1**

2016 **11** *nk* **Zomerlust**[35] 4614 5-8-12 98 (v) GrahamGibbons 1 96
(J J Quinn) *prom far side: drvn over 2f out: one pce over 1f out: 6th of 14 in gp* **20/1**

0406 **12** *shd* **Rising Shadow (IRE)**[28] 4813 6-9-5 105 SebSanders 17 103
(T D Barron) *dwlt: bhd stands' side tl hdwy over 1f out: nvr rchd ldrs: 6th of 14 in gp* **28/1**

0336 **13** *1/2* **Partners In Jazz (USA)**[13] 5254 6-8-11 97 PhillipMakin 27 93
(T D Barron) *prom stands' side: drvn over 2f out: sn one pce: 7th of 14 in gp* **20/1**

-600 **14** *nk* **Steenberg (IRE)**[56] 3941 8-8-11 97 JimmyQuinn 21 92
(M H Tompkins) *lw: bhd stands' side tl hdwy fnl f: n.d: 8th of 14 in gp* **33/1**

1001 **15** *shd* **Fullandby (IRE)**[7] 5407 5-8-13 102 5ex PJMcDonald(3) 8 97
(T J Etherington) *lw: bhd far side: rdn and hdwy over 1f out: no imp: 7th of 14 in gp* **12/1**

6200 **16** *1 1/2* **Turnkey**[35] 4614 5-8-4 97 AdeleRothery(7) 12 88
(D Nicholls) *bhd far side: sme hdwy over 1f out: no imp: 8th of 14 in gp* **50/1**

3040 **17** *nk* **Orientor**[7] 5407 9-8-9 95 RobertHavlin 10 85
(J S Goldie) *bhd far side: drvn over 2f out: nt pce to chal: 9th of 14 in gp* **50/1**

3R0 **18** *nk* **Skhilling Spirit**[35] 4614 4-8-7 98 NeilBrown(5) 15 87
(T D Barron) *missed break: racd alone centre to 1/2-way: outpcd w far side gp fnl 2f: 10th of 14 in gp* **50/1**

0022 **19** *hd* **Borderlescott**[28] 4798 5-9-12 112 RoystonFfrench 28 100
(R Bastiman) *cl up stands' side tl rdn and no ex over 1f out: 9th of 14 in gp* **5/1[1]**

30-3 **20** *1/2* **Dream Theme**[158] 1082 4-8-13 99 SilvestreDeSousa 11 86
(D Nicholls) *bhd far side: drvn over 2f out: no imp: 11th of 14 in gp* **66/1**

0000 **21** *shd* **King Orchisios (IRE)**[7] 5407 4-8-11 100 (p) MichaelJStainton(3) 3 86
(K A Ryan) *led far side gp to over 1f out: sn btn: 12th of 14 in gp* **100/1**

0003 **22** *3/4* **Grantley Adams**[7] 5416 4-9-0 100 DarryllHolland 26 84
(M R Channon) *bhd stands' side: n.m.r over 2f out: n.d: 10th of 14 in gp* **14/1**

6013 **23** *1 1/4* **Knot In Wood (IRE)**[49] 4150 5-9-0 103 JamieMoriarty(3) 4 83
(R A Fahey) *cl up far side tl wknd over 1f out: 11th of 14 in gp* **13/2[2]**

0310 **24** *1* **Buachaill Dona (IRE)**[7] 5407 4-9-1 101 5ex AdrianTNicholls 20 78
(D Nicholls) *prom on outside of stands' side gp tl hung rt and wknd over 1f out: 11th of 14 in gp* **20/1**

0400 **25** *1 1/2* **Dhaular Dhar (IRE)**[21] 5031 5-8-7 98 GaryBartley(5) 24 71
(J S Goldie) *bhd stands' side: n.m.r over 2f out to over 1f out: n.d: 12th of 14 in gp* **25/1**

1500 **26** *shd* **Mecca's Mate**[30] 4746 6-8-10 99 AndrewMullen(3) 14 72
(D W Barker) *chsd stands' side ldrs tl wknd fr 2f out: 13th of 14 in gp* **50/1**

0313 **27** *1 1/4* **Pearly Wey**[7] 5407 4-8-9 95 PhilipRobinson 16 64
(C G Cox) *dwlt: bhd stands' side: rdn over 2f out: nvr on terms: last of 14 in gp* **16/1**

1002 **28** *27* **Obe Brave**[35] 4614 4-9-3 103 TPO'Shea 5 —
(M R Channon) *sn cl up far side: rdn: hung rt and wknd fr over 2f out: eased whn no ch: last of 14 in gp* **40/1**

1m 12.91s (-0.76) **Going Correction** +0.175s/f (Good) **28** Ran SP% **134.4**
Speed ratings (Par 109): **112,111,109,108,108 107,107,107,107,107 106,106,106,105,105 103,103,102,102,101 101,100,99,97,**
CSF £398.77 CT £34708.63 TOTE £25.70: £5.60, £6.20, £20.10, £4.90; EX 1308.70 Trifecta £32456.20 Part won. Pool: £45,712.99 - 0.30 winning tickets..
Owner T Doherty and McHeen **Bred** Gestut Gorlsdorf **Trained** Hambleton, N Yorks
■ Stewards' Enquiry : Eddie Ahern two-day ban: used whip with excessive frequency (Oct 3-4)
Jamie Spencer two-day ban: careless riding (Oct 3-4)

FOCUS
A tremendously competitive handicap run at a sound pace throughout and one in which there was little difference between the stands'-side group and those that raced centre to far side. Strong form, best rated through the fourth.

NOTEBOOK
Advanced, out of his depth in the Group 1 Betfred Sprint Cup at Haydock, looked in tremendous shape and returned to his very best back in handicap company to better his excellent third placing in this race last year. He is worth another chance in Listed or minor Group company and he is capable of winning more races. (tchd 25-1 in a place)
Benwilt Breeze(IRE) ◆ has developed into a smart sprinter and, after very much taking the eye in the preliminaries, ran as well as he ever has done to be touched off by the stands'-side winner. It would have been even closer had he kept straight in the closing stages and the gelding, who is effective on faster ground and on Polytrack, is capable of landing a decent handicap over sprint distances.
Patavellian(IRE) has only won once since landing the Abbaye four years ago but he confirmed he is a smart performer over sprint distances with his best effort of the year. This was his first run in handicap company for four years and, although vulnerable to the more progressive and better-handicapped sorts in this type of event, looks capable of winning a conditions or Listed event around this trip. (op 80-1)

Beaver Patrol(IRE), from a stable that has created a favourable impression this year, is a most consistent sort who seemed to give it his best shot under his penalty and he looks a good guide to the worth of this form. He is equally effective on quicker ground and should continue to give a good account. (tchd 22-1)
Fonthill Road(IRE) has not won since winning this race last year but he has shown he retains plenty of ability this year and he ran right up to his recent best. He is ideally suited by a bit of give in the ground but looks vulnerable against the more progressive types in this grade and has had a few chances without winning in Listed and Group company. (op 14-1)
River Falcon, 7lb higher than his York win over 5f, had conditions to suit and turned in another creditable effort He has not been the most predictable but is a capable sort when in the mood. Official explanation: jockey said gelding hung right-handed (op 40-1)
Majestic Times(IRE), a useful sprinter who was just touched off in this race in 2005, finished a similar margin behind Benwilt Breeze as he had on Polytrack at Dundalk last month. Best when allowed to lead, he should continue to give a good account in decent handicap company.
Indian Trail ◆, in good form over 5f on a sound surface, travelled really strongly for much of the way but did not find as much as expected once asked for an effort. He will be suited by the return to the minimum trip and fast ground and is capable of adding to his tally before the season is out. (op 17-2 tchd 9-1 and 10-1 in places)
Borderlescott, who turned in a fine effort when just touched off in this race last year, had the run of the race against the stands' rail but, although he looked in really good nick, he turned in a rare below-par performance. He is usually a model of consistency though, and is well worth another chance. Official explanation: trainer had no explanation for the poor form shown (op 13-2 tchd 7-1 in places)
Grantley Adams Official explanation: jockey said gelding was unsuited by the good to soft ground
Knot In Wood(IRE) looked to have plenty in his favour regarding trip and ground but he proved a disappointment on this occasion. His record has been one of steady improvement though, and he is well worth another chance. (op 7-1 tchd 10-1 in a place)
Buachaill Dona(IRE) Official explanation: jockey said gelding hung right-handed
Dhaular Dhar(IRE) Official explanation: jockey said horse was denied a clear run
Mecca's Mate Official explanation: jockey said mare never travelled
Pearly Wey Official explanation: jockey said gelding was unsuited by the good to soft ground
Obe Brave Official explanation: jockey said gelding hung right-handed

5617 KELVIN KBB H'CAP (FOR THE WEIR MEMORIAL TROPHY) 7f 50y
4:05 (4:05) (Class 3) (0-90,87) 3-Y-O+

£11,217 (£3,358; £1,679; £840; £419; £210) **Stalls** Low

Form				RPR
1050	**1**		**Commando Scott (IRE)**[1] 5584 6-9-7 **87** ... RoystonFfrench 10 (I W McInnes) *t.k.h in midfield: effrt over 2f out: r.o to ld nr fin* **7/2**[1]	98
032	**2**	½	**Heroes**[28] 4827 3-9-3 **86** ... SebSanders 5 (G A Huffer) *lw: trckd ldrs: led jst ins fnl f: hdd and no ex towards fin* **9/2**[2]	95
4020	**3**	1 ½	**Shot To Fame (USA)**[71] 3512 8-8-13 **79** ... (t) AdrianTNicholls 13 (D Nicholls) *led tl jst ins fnl f: styd on same pce* **14/1**	85
1106	**4**	1 ¼	**Balakiref**[1] 5584 8-9-3 **83** ... PhillipMakin 2 (M Dods) *chsd ldrs: styd on same pce fnl 2f* **11/1**	86
2-10	**5**	2 ½	**Fifty Cents**[57] 3900 3-8-13 **82** ... SteveDrowne 11 (R Charlton) *lw: hld up in rr: effrt over 3f out: kpt on fnl f: nvr a factor* **8/1**[3]	77+
4320	**6**	1 ¼	**Imperial Echo (USA)**[1] 5584 6-9-0 **85** ... NeilBrown(5) 9 (T D Barron) *hld up in rr: hdwy over 4f out: sn chsng ldrs: hung bdly lft over 1f out: kpt on one pce* **17/2**	78
126	**7**	2	**Desert Dreamer (IRE)**[14] 5223 6-8-13 **79** ... EddieAhern 12 (G A Butler) *in tch: effrt over 2f out: one pce* **14/1**	67
6600	**8**	2 ½	**Countdown**[21] 5031 5-9-5 **85** ... DavidAllan 3 (T D Easterby) *in rr: sn drvn along: nvr a factor* **10/1**	66
0340	**9**	nk	**Hiccups**[22] 4990 7-9-0 **80** ... PhilipRobinson 6 (M Dods) *rrd s: hld up in rr: nvr on terms* **8/1**[3]	61
0062	**10**	1	**Grimes Faith**[176] 833 4-8-12 **78** ... PatCosgrave 8 (K A Ryan) *chsd ldrs: wknd over 1f out* **25/1**	56
0-26	**11**	4	**Stonehaugh (IRE)**[108] 2374 4-8-13 **79** ... (t) TomEaves 14 (J Howard Johnson) *t.k.h: trckd ldr: lost pl 2f out* **40/1**	47
4265	**12**	hd	**Obe Gold**[15] 5209 5-9-3 **83** ... (v) DarryllHolland 4 (M R Channon) *in rr: drvn over 3f out: nvr on terms* **9/1**	50

1m 34.81s (2.09) **Going Correction** +0.40s/f (Good)
WFA 3 from 4yo+ 3lb **12** Ran SP% **120.2**
Speed ratings (Par 107): **104,103,101,100,97 96,93,90,90,89 84,84**
CSF £18.78 CT £203.69 TOTE £4.90: £1.70, £1.80, £4.70; EX 18.80.
Owner Mrs Ann Morris **Bred** Noel Finegan **Trained** Catwick, E Yorks

FOCUS
A competitive handicap run at a sound pace. The form looks rock solid rated through the third and fourth.

NOTEBOOK
Commando Scott(IRE), first home on the far side in the Silver Cup the previous day, stuck on bravely to show ahead near the finish. The seventh furlong was no problem. (op 4-1 tchd 9-2 in places)
Heroes, loaded with a blanket, was racing from a 2lb higher mark. He worked hard to take a narrow advantage only to miss out near the finish. (op 7-2)
Shot To Fame(USA), without a win for over three years, took them along and to his credit on this occasion stuck on all the way to the line.
Balakiref, sixth on the stands' side in the Silver Cup here the previous day, continues in fine form but he is now 6lb higher than for his last success. (op 10-1 tchd 12-1)
Fifty Cents, anchored in the rear, made hard work of it once in line for home but was the only runner to make significant ground from off the pace.
Imperial Echo(USA), well beaten in the Silver Cup 24r hours earlier, ran much better but gave his rider real problems hanging badly left. (op 10-1 tchd 11-1)
Hiccups reared leaving the stalls and lost a shoe in running. Official explanation: trainer said gelding lost a near-fore shoe (op 9-1 tchd 10-1)

5618 DOONSIDE CUP STKS (LISTED RACE) 1m 2f
4:40 (4:40) (Class 1) 3-Y-O+

£28,390 (£10,760; £5,385; £2,685; £1,345; £675) **Stalls** Low

Form				RPR
-123	**1**		**Anna Pavlova**[32] 4691 4-8-13 **110** ... PaulHanagan 12 (R A Fahey) *hld up in tch: smooth hdwy to ld appr fnl f: rdn and drifted lft ins fnl f: kpt on strly* **4/1**[2]	113+
1302	**2**	1 ¾	**Dunaskin (IRE)**[32] 4690 7-9-0 **100** ... KDarley 3 (Karen McLintock) *led to appr fnl f: kpt on u.p fnl f: nt rch wnr* **50/1**	110
1154	**3**	½	**Ivy Creek (USA)**[28] 4803 4-9-4 **112** ... SteveDrowne 6 (G Wragg) *s.i.s: sn midfield: hdwy and ev ch over 1f out: no ex ins fnl f* **9/1**	113
3110	**4**	4	**Blythe Knight (IRE)**[28] 4805 7-9-7 **110** ... GrahamGibbons 10 (J J Quinn) *lw: in tch: effrt over 2f out: chsng ldrs over 1f out: sn no ex* **25/1**	108
2304	**5**	1	**Sunshine Kid (USA)**[28] 4826 3-8-8 **107** ... RobertHavlin 13 (J H M Gosden) *prom: rdn over 2f out: edgd lft and no ex wl over 1f out* **16/1**	99
1546	**6**	nk	**Spice Route**[32] 4692 3-8-8 **108** ... EddieAhern 14 (M L W Bell) *racd wd in midfield: rdn and outpcd over 2f out: n.d after* **10/1**	98
2416	**7**	1 ¼	**Charlie Tokyo (IRE)**[56] 3974 4-9-0 **107** ... (v) JamieMoriarty 8 (R A Fahey) *hld up: pushed along over 2f out: n.d* **33/1**	96
1-54	**8**	1 ½	**Into The Dark**[113] 2216 6-9-0 **107** ... (t) LDettori 7 (Saeed Bin Suroor) *hld up: short-lived effrt over 2f out: nvr rchd ldrs* **8/1**[3]	93
0610	**9**	3	**Group Captain**[31] 4722 5-9-0 **110** ... JamieSpencer 5 (R Charlton) *lw: bhd: hdwy 1/2-way: rdn over 2f out: sn btn* **14/1**	87
1-43	**10**	¾	**Caldra (IRE)**[14] 5213 3-8-8 **105** ... PhilipRobinson 2 (S Kirk) *chsd ldrs tl rdn and wknd over 2f out* **9/1**	85
1146	**11**	12	**Championship Point (IRE)**[28] 4826 4-9-4 **114** ... DarryllHolland 11 (M R Channon) *bhd: rdn over 3f out: nvr on terms* **14/1**	65
1-00	**12**	5	**Wait Watcher (IRE)**[8] 5396 3-8-3 **98** ... TPO'Shea 9 (P A Blockley) *pressed ldr tl wknd fr 2f out* **100/1**	46
552-	**13**	hd	**Confidential Lady**[335] 6124 4-8-9 **113** ... SebSanders 4 (Sir Mark Prescott) *trckd ldrs: rdn and edgd lft over 2f out: sn wknd* **2/1**[1]	46

2m 13.56s (1.84) **Going Correction** +0.40s/f (Good)
WFA 3 from 4yo+ 6lb **13** Ran SP% **122.5**
Speed ratings (Par 111): **108,106,106,103,102 101,100,99,97,96 87,83,83**
CSF £208.06 TOTE £5.50: £1.70, £7.20, £3.00; EX 199.50.
Owner Galaxy Racing **Bred** Raymond Cowie **Trained** Musley Bank, N Yorks

FOCUS
This attracted a decent field, much more competitive than usual. Although the market leader disappointed, this was a smart performance from the winner, who is a most versatile sort. Decent listed form.

NOTEBOOK
Anna Pavlova ◆, a fine third to subsequent Doncaster Cup winner Septimus at York last time, was not in the least bit inconvenienced by the return to this trip and, although showing her usual tendency to drift left, she travelled strongly before beating Dunaskin with more in hand than the official margin suggests. She goes particularly well with give in the ground and she is well worth another try in Group company either over this trip or over another quarter-mile (tchd 9-2, 5-1 in places)
Dunaskin(IRE), back over 1m2f, had plenty to find on these terms but was allowed his own way in front and showed a good attitude in the closing stages to regain second spot. Life is going to be tougher after reassessment but he may be able to pick up a conditions event/minor Listed event when allowed to set his own pace.
Ivy Creek(USA), a dual 1m4f Listed winner this year, ran creditably dropped to this trip. He left the impression that a stiffer test of stamina would have been in his favour and he should continue to give a good account in this type of event. (op 17-2 tchd 10-1)
Blythe Knight(IRE), a Listed and Group 3 winner over 1m this year, was far from disgraced back up in trip in a race run at less than a true pace. The return to that shorter trip and a more end-to-end gallop are likely to be in his favour. (op 20-1)
Sunshine Kid(USA) had run creditably in Group company on his last three starts and was not disgraced in this fair Listed event after having the run of the race. (op 25-1)
Spice Route, dropped in distance and grade and drawn on the outside, shaped as though the return to middle distances would suit after getting tapped for toe early in the straight. He is going to have to improve to win in competitive Listed or minor Group company. (op 12-1)
Charlie Tokyo(IRE) is an improved performer this year and was not disgraced in the face of a stiff task in a race that was not really run to suit those held up. A more strongly-run race would be to his liking. (op 28-1)
Confidential Lady, who looked fit enough beforehand, escaped a penalty for her win in the French Oaks last year and had reportedly been working extremely well at home but she proved a big disappointment on this belated reappearance. She is obviously capable of better but will have to show more before she is a solid betting proposition. Official explanation: trainer had no explanation for the poor form shown (op 11-4 tchd 3-1 in places)

5619 MERLO UK H'CAP 1m 5f 13y
5:15 (5:15) (Class 3) (0-90,90) 3-Y-O+ **£11,658** (£3,468; £1,733; £432; £432) **Stalls** Low

Form				RPR
3101	**1**		**Black Rock (IRE)**[35] 4617 3-9-7 **90** ... PhilipRobinson 8 (M A Jarvis) *lw: trckd ldrs: racd wd: led over 2f out: styd on strly: drvn out* **9/2**[3]	99
2301	**2**	1 ¼	**Sphinx (FR)**[39] 4483 9-9-13 **87** ... (b) SteveDrowne 9 (Jamie Poulton) *b: hld up in rr: hdwy and nt clr run 2f out: wnt 2nd over 1f out: no imp* **8/1**	95
1130	**3**	5	**Bollin Felix**[30] 4749 3-8-10 **79** ... (b) DavidAllan 5 (T D Easterby) *hld up in rr: hdwy over 4f out: styd on down wd outside to take 3rd nr fin* **15/2**	79
311	**4**	hd	**Opal Haze (USA)**[19] 5101 3-9-7 **90** ... RobertHavlin 4 (J H M Gosden) *led: qcknd over 3f out: hdd over 2f out: kpt on same pce* **10/1**	90
6060	**4**	dht	**Lets Roll**[14] 5215 6-9-8 **82** ... DanielTudhope 7 (C W Thornton) *sn trcking ldrs: effrt over 3f out: rdr dropped whip over 2f out: kpt on one pce* **11/4**[1]	82
13-6	**6**	1 ¼	**St Savarin (FR)**[34] 4637 6-10-0 **88** ... PaulHanagan 1 (R A Fahey) *t.k.h in rr: effrt 3f out: nvr nr ldrs* **33/1**	86
2413	**7**	3	**Yossi (IRE)**[10] 5334 3-8-12 **81** ... (b[1]) EddieAhern 6 (M H Tompkins) *hld up in midfield: effrt 3f out: wknd appr fnl f* **12/1**	74
00	**8**	½	**Southern Regent (IND)**[25] 4922 6-9-10 **87** ... PJMcDonald(3) 2 (G A Swinbank) *hld up in rr: effrt 3f out: nvr on terms* **16/1**	80
-413	**9**	16	**Furmigadelagiusta**[58] 3883 3-9-6 **89** ... JamieSpencer 3 (L M Cumani) *lw: trckd ldrs: effrt 3f out: edgd rt and sn lost pl: eased* **10/3**[2]	58

3m 1.66s (5.05) **Going Correction** +0.40s/f (Good)
WFA 3 from 6yo+ 9lb **9** Ran SP% **116.4**
Speed ratings (Par 107): **100,99,96,96,96 95,93,93,83**
CSF £40.56 CT £265.43 TOTE £4.90: £1.90, £2.50, £2.30; EX 52.90.
Owner A D Spence **Bred** Rockhart Trading Ltd **Trained** Newmarket, Suffolk

FOCUS
A very moderate pace. The winner is progressive and the first two finished clear. The race has been rated through the third for the time being.

NOTEBOOK
Black Rock(IRE), 6lb higher, was kept wide in the back straight in search of less-testing ground. He struck for home and his rider left nothing to chance. He is a grand type who is clearly going the right way. (op 7-2)
Sphinx(FR), 4lb higher, met traffic problems but was definitely only second best anyway.
Bollin Felix, 12lb higher than his last win, stuck on to snatch third spot and now may be the time to step him up in trip again. (op 11-1 tchd 12-1)
Lets Roll, attempting a hat-trick in this event, never really looked like pulling it off and he was going up and down on the spot when his rider dropped his whip. (op 8-1 tchd 7-1)
Opal Haze(USA), loaded with a blanket, was racing from a 5lb higher mark back on turf. She stepped up the pace coming off the home turn but in the end was not nearly good enough. (op 8-1 tchd 7-1)
St Savarin(FR), having just his second outing this time, was again keen to get on with it. He kept on in his own time and should be cherry ripe next time. (tchd 28-1)

Furmigadelagiusta, proven in soft ground, dropped right out and virtually walked over the line. This was simply too bad to be true. Official explanation: jockey said colt lost its action (op 7-2 tchd 4-1)

5620 JOHN SMITH'S EXTRA SMOOTH H'CAP — 1m 2f

5:45 (5:45) (Class 5) (0-75,75) 3-Y-0+

£4,985 (£1,492; £746; £373; £186; £93) **Stalls** Low

Form — RPR

0645 **1** **She's Our Lass (IRE)**[14] 5230 6-9-4 **69** .... DavidAllan 1 — 80
(D Carroll) *hld up in mid-div: hdwy to chse ldr over 2f out: led 1f out: styd on wl* **9/1**

1150 **2** 1¾ **Magic Echo**[52] 4080 3-9-4 **75** .... PhillipMakin 4 — 82
(M Dods) *sn led: qcknd clr over 3f out: hdd 1f out: no ex* **12/1**

0064 **3** 2 **Trouble Mountain (USA)**[29] 4772 10-8-13 **64** ....(t) JimmyQuinn 3 — 67
(M W Easterby) *hld up in rr: hdwy 4f out: wnt 3rd over 1f out: styd on same pce* **11/1**

0224 **4** 5 **Superior Star**[61] 3793 4-9-1 **69** ....(b) JamieMoriarty(3) 7 — 62
(R A Fahey) *chsd ldrs: hung lft over 3f out: hrd rdn: wknd fnl f* **20/1**

2410 **5** nk **Jibajaba (USA)**[21] 5043 3-9-1 **72** .... PaulHanagan 2 — 64
(R A Fahey) *hld up in rr: hdwy 3f out: carried hd high and no threat* **16/1**

-642 **6** 1¾ **Moonhawk**[62] 3764 4-8-13 **69** .... NeilBrown(5) 13 — 58
(J Howard Johnson) *hld up in rr: hdwy on outer over 4f out: wknd appr fnl f* **8/1**

0003 **7** ½ **Hannicean**[35] 4603 3-9-3 **74** .... PhilipRobinson 9 — 62
(M A Jarvis) *lw: racd wd: chsd ldrs: lost pl over 1f out* **4/1**[2]

0424 **8** 28 **Highland Harvest**[22] 5014 3-9-4 **75** .... SteveDrowne 14 — 7
(D R C Elsworth) *chsd ldrs: lost pl over 2f out: bhd whn eased over 1f out: t.o* **9/1**

6-60 **9** 2 **Thumpers Dream**[125] 1862 4-9-10 **75** .... DanielTudhope 10 — 3
(I W McInnes) *led early: lost pl over 4f out: t.o 2f out* **28/1**

0006 **F** **Krugerrand (USA)**[14] 5225 8-9-10 **75** .... EddieAhern 6 — —
(W J Musson) *hld up towards rr: slipped and fell over 5f out* **7/2**[1]

0531 **F** **Prime Powered (IRE)**[33] 4667 6-9-9 **74** .... DarrylHolland 8 — —
(R M Beckett) *mid-div: effrt on outer whn fell over 2f out: dead* **5/1**[3]

2m 16.51s (4.79) **Going Correction** +0.40s/f (Good)
WFA 3 from 4yo+ 6lb — **11** Ran SP% **120.1**
Speed ratings (Par 103): **96,94,93,89,88 87,86,64,62,— —**
CSF £114.34 CT £1212.53 TOTE £10.50: £2.60, £4.50, £3.90 Place 6 £4,184.00, Place 5 £565.44..
Owner We-Know Partnership **Bred** Illuminatus Investments **Trained** Sledmere, E Yorks

■ A sad end to the three-day Western meeting with the jockeys highly critical of the ground, especially on the round course.

■ Stewards' Enquiry : Jamie Moriarty one-day ban: used whip with excessive frequency (Oct 3)

FOCUS
Not strong form overall but the first two ran to their pre-race marks.
T/Jkpt: Not won. T/Plt: £8,085.80 to a £1 stake. Pool: £163,932.30. 14.80 winning tickets. T/Qpdt: £287.90 to a £1 stake. Pool: £8,445.30. 21.70 winning tickets. RY

4937 CATTERICK (L-H)

Saturday, September 22

OFFICIAL GOING: Good (good to firm in places; 8.5)
Wind: Virtually nil Weather: Sunny

5621 EUROPEAN BREEDERS' FUND MAIDEN STKS — 5f 212y

2:25 (2:25) (Class 5) 2-Y-0 — **£3,562** (£1,059; £529; £264) **Stalls** Low

Form — RPR

432 **1** **Hammadi (IRE)**[15] 5192 2-9-3 84 .... PaulMulrennan 1 — 92+
(K A Ryan) *mde all: pushed clr wl over 1f out: easily* **5/6**[1]

3 **2** 10 **Tawzeea (IRE)**[15] 5193 2-9-3 0 .... GregFairley 2 — 59
(M Johnston) *trckd wnr: effrt over 2f out: rdn along and hung lft wl over 1f out: sn one pce* **5/4**[2]

60 **3** 3 **Mr Lu**[72] 3465 2-9-3 0 .... DaleGibson 6 — 50
(G A Swinbank) *chsd ldrs: rdn along over 2f out: drvn and hanging lft wl over 1f out: one pce* **33/1**

6030 **4** 1¾ **Narmeen**[10] 5331 2-8-12 66 .... ChrisCatlin 4 — 40
(M R Channon) *chsd ldng pair: rdn along 1/2-way: drvn over 2f out and sn one pce* **14/1**[3]

06 **5** 6 **Viscaya (IRE)**[5] 5483 2-8-12 0 .... SaleemGolam 7 — 22
(Mrs A Duffield) *v.s.a and wl bhd tl styd on fnl 2f* **33/1**

6 hd **Rascasse** 2-9-0 0 .... MarkLawson(3) 8 — 26
(Garry Moss) *s.i.s: sn chsng ldrs: rdn along 1/2-way and wknd wl over 2f out* **100/1**

7 3½ **Lechero (IRE)** 2-9-3 0 .... PaddyAspell 9 — 16
(Ian Williams) *s.i.s: a outpcd and bhd* **50/1**

1m 14.34s (0.34) **Going Correction** +0.175s/f (Good) — **7** Ran SP% **114.5**
Speed ratings (Par 95): **104,90,86,84,76 76,71**
CSF £2.11 TOTE £1.60: £1.02, £1.90; EX 2.60.
Owner Malih L Al Basti **Bred** Peter Hodgson And Star Pointe Limited **Trained** Hambleton, N Yorks

FOCUS
An uncompetitive maiden won in a canter by Hammadi who could be Listed class. The form is rated through the third.

NOTEBOOK
Hammadi(IRE) coped just fine with the drop to 5f when second at Haydock earlier in the month, but this step back up in trip was always going to suit and he simply possessed too much speed for his only market rival, leading throughout and cantering clear for an easy victory. It is difficult to say whether or not this represented improved form, but he remains capable of better. (tchd 10-11, Evens in a place)
Tawzeea(IRE), who showed up well over this trip on his Haydock debut, found himself woefully done for speed by the winner and ended up being beaten a long way. Bred to appreciate 1m, he will benefit from the step up to 7f first of all and can find an ordinary maiden before eventually going handicapping. (op 11-8 tchd 6-4)
Mr Lu had previously shown little, but he stuck on well for third, albeit a remote one, and is now qualified for nurseries. He should fare better in that sphere. Official explanation: jockey said gelding hung left throughout
Narmeen failed to improve when recently tried in a handicap and she was always likely to fall short on this return to maiden company. She looks worth another try at 7f back in handicaps. (op 20-1)
Viscaya(IRE) lost any chance she had with a very slow start, but she was at least going on towards the end of her race and is the type to fare better in low-grade handicaps. Official explanation: jockey said filly missed the break

5622 JACQUELINE & JULIE CLARKE BIRTHDAY (S) STKS — 1m 5f 175y

3:00 (3:00) (Class 6) 3-Y-0 — **£2,730** (£806; £403) **Stalls** Low

Form — RPR

3462 **1** **Lady Pickpocket**[33] 4663 3-8-5 49 .... SaleemGolam 8 — 49
(M H Tompkins) *hld up: gd hdwy 4f out: led wl over 1f out: sn rdn and kpt on u.p fnl f* **9/4**[1]

2 1 **Katesville (IRE)**[146] 1331 3-8-5 0 .... GregFairley 4 — 47
(R Ford) *hld up: hdwy over 3f out: rdn to chse ldrs 2f out: swtchd lft and drvn ins fnl f: kpt on: nrst fin* **7/1**[3]

0065 **3** 2 **Regal Ovation**[9] 5364 3-8-10 49 .... ChrisCatlin 6 — 49
(W R Muir) *trckd ldrs: cl up 1/2-way: led 5f out: rdn along 2f out: sn hdd: drvn and edgd rt ent fnl f: one pce* **9/4**[1]

-000 **4** 3½ **Kyrhena**[5] 5487 3-8-8 38 ow3 .... PaddyAspell 2 — 42
(C W Thornton) *hld up: stdy hdwy over 3f out: rdn over 2f out: kpt on u.p appr fnl f* **66/1**

0000 **5** 10 **Ocean Of Champagne**[5] 5487 3-8-5 44 ....(v) DaleGibson 1 — 24
(Micky Hammond) *chsd ldrs: rdn along 1/2-way: wknd 4f out* **16/1**

0000 **6** 3 **Soylent Green**[19] 5102 3-8-2 25 .... DominicFox(3) 9 — 19
(S Parr) *sn led: rdn along and hdd 5f out: drvn along 3f out and sn wknd* **100/1**

-030 **7** 2 **Strathaird (IRE)**[26] 2389 3-8-10 46 .... LeeEnstone 5 — 21
(P C Haslam) *a in rr* **17/2**

0050 **8** 8 **Alloro**[46] 4256 3-8-7 44 .... PatrickMathers(3) 7 — 9
(D W Thompson) *t.k.h: hld up: rapid hdwy to join ldrs 1/2-way: rdn along over 4f out: sn wknd* **16/1**

0000 **9** 6 **Captain Nemo (USA)**[5] 5487 3-8-10 55 .... PaulMulrennan 3 — —
(T D Barron) *trckd ldrs: hdwy and cl up 1/2-way: rdn along 4f out: sn wknd* **6/1**[2]

3m 6.85s (2.35) **Going Correction** +0.175s/f (Good) — **9** Ran SP% **113.1**
Speed ratings (Par 99): **100,99,98,96,90 88,87,83,79**
CSF £18.81 TOTE £3.10: £1.20, £2.80, £1.10; EX 27.40.The winner was sold to F Murtagh for 7,500gns.
Owner Les Stirling **Bred** A D G Oldrey **Trained** Newmarket, Suffolk

FOCUS
A poor seller in which the winner did not need to improve. The form seems sound.

5623 CONSTANT SECURITY SEPTEMBER STKS (H'CAP) — 1m 3f 214y

3:35 (3:35) (Class 3) (0-90,86) 3-Y-0+ — **£7,124** (£2,119; £1,059; £529) **Stalls** High

Form — RPR

025 **1** **Dzesmin (POL)**[34] 4637 5-9-3 **79** ....(p) ChrisCatlin 8 — 89+
(R C Guest) *hld up in rr: smooth hdwy 1/2-way: led wl over 1f out and sn rdn: drvn ent fnl f and kpt on wl* **11/4**[1]

5001 **2** nk **Realism (FR)**[13] 5255 7-9-10 **86** .... PaulMulrennan 1 — 95
(M W Easterby) *trckd ldrs: effrt whn bmpd over 2f out: sn rdn and ev ch: drvn ins fnl f and kpt on wl* **6/1**

1315 **3** 7 **Osolomio (IRE)**[25] 4917 4-9-7 **83** .... DaleGibson 6 — 81
(G A Swinbank) *led: rdn along over 3f out: drvn and hdd wl over 1f out: sn drvn and kpt on one pce* **3/1**[2]

5432 **4** 1 **Mighty Moon**[17] 5144 4-8-13 **80** ....(t) JamesO'Reilly(5) 4 — 76
(J O'Reilly) *chsd ldrs: rdn along 3f out: sn one pce* **9/2**[3]

0446 **5** 3½ **Cripsey Brook**[120] 2011 9-8-8 **77** ....(t) DanielleMcCreery(7) 2 — 68
(K G Reveley) *in tch: rdn along over 4f out: sn wknd* **12/1**

0020 **6** 3½ **Five A Side**[14] 5218 3-8-11 **81** ....(b[1]) GregFairley 3 — 66
(M Johnston) *cl up: rdn along over 3f out: wknd over 2f out* **15/2**

5440 **7** nk **Harvest Warrior**[25] 4922 5-9-0 **79** .... DuranFentiman(3) 5 — 64
(T D Easterby) *t.k.h: hld up: a towards rr* **16/1**

461- **8** 45 **Trew Style**[515] 1213 5-8-13 **75** .... SaleemGolam 7 — —
(M H Tompkins) *t.k.h: chsd ldrs on outer: pushed along 5f out: sn wknd and bhd whn virtually p.u over 1f out* **12/1**

2m 37.76s (-1.24) **Going Correction** +0.175s/f (Good)
WFA 3 from 4yo+ 8lb — **8** Ran SP% **117.2**
Speed ratings (Par 107): **111,110,106,105,103 100,100,70**
CSF £20.30 CT £52.75 TOTE £4.20: £1.90, £2.50, £1.60; EX 29.00.
Owner JAS Partnership **Bred** Marian Pokrywka **Trained** Carburton, Notts

■ Richard Guest's first winner and runner from his new yard in Nottinghamshire.

FOCUS
An ordinary handicap in which the front two drew clear. The form is rated through the runner-up.

NOTEBOOK
Dzesmin(POL), never involved in a decent handicap at Pontefract last time, had previously run well to finish second in heavy ground at York and he travelled much more kindly on this occasion. Sent on a furlong out, he ran on well to hold the persistent Realism and fully deserved this first win in over a year. He is just as effective with plenty of cut and is the type to pay his way in the coming weeks. Official explanation: trainer said, regarding apparent improvement in form, that he was disappointed with the gelding's run last time and allowed it a short break, adding that the change to his new stable facility had appeared to freshen it up. (op 10-3)
Realism(FR), ready winner of a York claimer latest, has not won a handicap in almost two years, but he is now 9lb lower and this was a sound effort under a big weight. He was clear of the third and could be of interest for a similar contest. (op 11-2 tchd 5-1)
Osolomio(IRE), 3lb higher than when making all at this track two starts back, was unable to repeat those tactics on the Ppolytrack last time and he was again readily brushed aside. He tends to run his race more often than not, but he just be a few pounds too high at present. (op 7-2)
Mighty Moon, raised a harsh 7lb for his recent York second, seemed to find the rise beyond him and he was readily left trailing by the front duo. (op 4-1)
Cripsey Brook, in decent form back in the spring, is beginning to creep back down the weights, but needs to show more.
Five A Side has failed to build on a promising effort at Ripon two starts back and the first-time blinkers did not have the desired effect. (tchd 13-2)

5624 DON'T MISS TOTESPORT SATURDAY 20TH OCTOBER NURSERY — 7f

4:10 (4:10) (Class 4) (0-85,85) 2-Y-0 — **£5,181** (£1,541; £770; £384) **Stalls** Low

Form — RPR

603 **1** **Maximus Aurelius (IRE)**[9] 5343 2-8-3 **72** .... LukeMorris(5) 3 — 74+
(J Jay) *trckd ldrs: hdwy 2f out: swtchd lft and rdn over 1f out: squeezed through on inner to ld ins fnl f: styd on wl* **5/2**[1]

13 **2** 1½ **Grand Fleet**[120] 2009 2-9-6 **84** .... GregFairley 4 — 82
(M Johnston) *cl up: led 1/2-way: rdn over 2f out: drvn over 1f out: hdd ins fnl f and kpt on same pce* **7/2**[2]

4260 **3** nk **Creative (IRE)**[28] 4832 2-8-7 **71** .... SaleemGolam 6 — 68
(M H Tompkins) *t.k.h: prom: effrt 2f out: sn rdn and chal over 1f out: ev ch tl drvn and one pce ins fnl f* **6/1**

0050 **4** *hd* **Jennifers Joy (IRE)**[10] 5322 2-8-11 **75** ChrisCatlin 5 72
(M R Channon) *hld up in rr: hdwy on outer wl over 1f out: sn rdn and styd on ins fnl f: nrst fin* **9/2**[3]

6106 **5** *1 1/4* **Casino Night**[5] 5471 2-8-2 **69** ow2 PatrickMathers(3) 1 63
(J R Weymes) *t.k.h: hld up: effrt and rdn 2f out: styd on appr fnl f: nvr nr ldrs* **12/1**

0530 **6** *hd* **Hasty Lady**[11] 5301 2-8-8 **72** PaulMulrennan 7 65
(K A Ryan) *led: rdn along and hdd 1/2-way: cl up tl drvn wl over 1f out and grad wknd* **15/2**

135 **7** *nk* **Soopacal (IRE)**[26] 4899 2-9-4 **85** MarkLawson(3) 8 77
(B Smart) *chsd ldrs: rdn along wl over 2f out: sn drvn and wknd* **7/1**

1m 28.85s (1.49) **Going Correction** +0.175s/f (Good) **7** Ran SP% **115.2**
Speed ratings (Par 97): **98,96,95,95,94 94,93**
CSF £11.59 CT £46.35 TOTE £3.40: £2.20, £2.30; EX 14.30.
Owner K Snell **Bred** Denis Brosnan And Patsy Byrne **Trained** Newmarket, Suffolk

FOCUS
A modest but competitive nursery. The form seems sound, but is nothing to get excited about.

NOTEBOOK
Maximus Aurelius(IRE), who improved for the step up to 7f when third at Chepstow last time, was understandably made favourite off a mark of 72 on this handicap debut and, having taken plenty of time to hit top gear, he came through towards the inside to win comfortably in the end. The step up to 1m should bring about further improvement in time and he looks one to keep on-side for the time being. (op 3-1)
Grand Fleet, not seen since disappointing at Pontefract back in May, was making his handicap debut off a stiff mark of 84, but the step up to 7f brought about an improved effort and he only found the lightly-weighted winner too good. His dam was a 1m4f winner and he should improve again for 1m. (tchd 3-1, 4-1 in a place)
Creative(IRE), never involved in an ultra-competitive sales contest at the Curragh the other day, made a pleasing switch to handicaps and momentarily looked as though he was going to swoop for the victory. He should find a small race off this sort of mark. (op 8-1)
Jennifers Joy(IRE) has found it tough going in handicaps, but she is beginning to edge back down to a reasonable mark and this was certainly a more promising effort. (op 13-2)
Casino Night has gained her only victory to date at claiming level and she continues to fall short in handicaps. (op 11-1 tchd 14-1)
Hasty Lady was responsible for the early pace, but she probably did a bit too much and faded in the last home. (tchd 6-1 and 8-1)
Soopacal(IRE) has struggled since making a winning debut in a weak race at Beverley and this mark proved beyond him on this handicap debut. Official explanation: jockey said colt was unsuited by the track (op 9-2)

5625 BOOK RACEDAY HOSPITALITY ON 01748 810165 MAIDEN STKS 7f
4:45 (4:45) (Class 5) 3-4-Y-O **£3,238** (£963; £481; £240) **Stalls** Low

Form RPR

360 **1** **Singleb (IRE)**[121] 1976 3-9-3 55 LeeEnstone 6 66
(T D Barron) *a.p: cl up 1/2-way: rdn over 1f out: drvn to ld ent fnl f: kpt on wl* **25/1**

4332 **2** *nk* **Cassiara**[5] 5488 3-8-12 78 (b[1]) ChrisCatlin 4 60
(J Pearce) *dwlt: sn trcking ldrs: hdwy to chse ldng pair 2f out and sn rdn: swtchd outside and drvn over 1f out: styd on ins fnl f* **10/11**[1]

0040 **3** *2 1/2* **Umpa Loompa (IRE)**[26] 4896 3-9-3 49 (v) PaddyAspell 15 58+
(D Nicholls) *led: rdn along over 2f out: drvn over 1f out: hdd & wknd ent fnl f* **14/1**

0220 **4** *2* **Miss Taboo (IRE)**[12] 5284 3-8-12 50 PaulMulrennan 7 48
(P T Midgley) *prom: rdn along wl over 2f out: drvn and one pce fnl 2f* **13/2**[3]

0060 **5** *3/4* **Summer Gift**[3] 5525 4-8-10 51 JamesO'Reilly(5) 2 46
(J O'Reilly) *midfield: hdwy on inner 2f out: sn rdn and kpt on same pce appr fnl f* **14/1**

0564 **6** *4* **Beck**[19] 5084 3-9-3 45 PaulQuinn 14 40
(W M Brisbourne) *towards rr: rdn along 2f out: styd on appr fnl f: nvr nr ldrs* **12/1**

203 **7** *1/2* **Ghafeer (USA)**[16] 5156 3-9-3 70 (vt[1]) GregFairley 13 38
(B Ellison) *in tch on outer: rdn along over 2f out and sn no imp* **10/3**[2]

000- **8** *3/4* **Inchmarlow (IRE)**[312] 6480 4-9-3 40 DuranFentiman(3) 11 36
(T H Caldwell) *chsd ldrs: rdn along 3f out: sn drvn and wknd 2f out* **66/1**

0-06 **9** *3/4* **Chilsdown**[61] 3789 4-9-6 42 JamieMackay 12 34
(J G Given) *a in midfield* **40/1**

0-05 **10** *6* **Lauder**[33] 4658 3-8-9 43 PatrickMathers(3) 9 13
(J Balding) *a in rr* **66/1**

00 **11** *nk* **Bella Grande**[19] 5082 3-8-9 0 MarkLawson(3) 8 12
(Garry Moss) *a in rr* **100/1**

00 **12** *1 3/4* **Own Gift**[49] 4178 3-8-9 0 DominicFox(3) 5 8
(S Parr) *chsd ldrs: rdn along 1/2-way: sn wknd* **100/1**

0 **13** *11* **Bovered (IRE)**[19] 5082 3-8-5 45 AdamCarter(7) 3 —
(A Berry) *dwlt: a in rr* **100/1**

14 *dist* **Power Trip (IRE)** 3-9-3 0 AdrianMcCarthy 1 —
(Miss V Haigh) *s.i.s: green and outpcd: sn wl bhd* **25/1**

1m 27.99s (0.63) **Going Correction** +0.175s/f (Good)
WFA 3 from 4yo 3lb **14** Ran SP% **125.9**
Speed ratings (Par 103): **103,102,99,97,96 92,91,90,89,82 82,80,68,—**
CSF £49.68 TOTE £40.50: £5.80, £1.20, £4.50; EX 93.00.
Owner JTM **Bred** Spratstown Stud Gm **Trained** Maunby, N Yorks
■ Stewards' Enquiry : Paul Quinn one-day ban: careless riding (Oct 3)

FOCUS
A poor maiden, but the time was not bad. Improvement by the winner on his poor sand form.
Power Trip(IRE) Official explanation: vet said gelding pulled up lame

5626 RICHMOND H'CAP 1m 7f 177y
5:20 (5:21) (Class 6) (0-65,65) 3-Y-O+ **£2,730** (£806; £403) **Stalls** Low

Form RPR

4512 **1** **Let It Be**[5] 5486 6-9-7 **56** GregFairley 8 64
(K G Reveley) *trckd ldr: hdwy to ld 4f out: rdn 2f out: drvn and styd on wl fnl f* **7/4**[1]

0-34 **2** *1/2* **Born West (USA)**[44] 4339 3-9-2 **63** AdrianMcCarthy 13 71
(P W Chapple-Hyam) *hld up in tch: hdwy 3f out and sn chsng wnr: rdn wl over 1f out: kpt on ins fnl f* **7/1**[3]

3230 **3** *1 1/2* **Dansimar**[24] 4951 3-9-4 **65** ChrisCatlin 4 71+
(M R Channon) *hld up towards rr: hdwy 5f out: rdn to chse ldng pair 2f out: drvn and kpt on same pce ins fnl f* **11/2**[2]

6106 **4** *5* **Jenny Soba**[25] 4920 4-8-10 **48** NeilChalmers(3) 6 48
(Lucinda Featherstone) *hld up towards rr: hdwy over 4f out: rdn along over 2f out: sn drvn and no imp appr fnl f* **28/1**

6660 **5** *1* **Qaasi (USA)**[5] 5486 5-9-2 **51** (v) DaleGibson 7 50
(M Brittain) *hld up towards rr: stdy hdwy 6f out: rdn to chse ldrs over 2f out: sn drvn and kpt on one pce* **25/1**

0520 **6** *nk* **Young Scotton**[12] 5283 7-9-3 **52** PaulMulrennan 12 50
(J D Bethell) *hld up towards rr: tk clsr order over 4f out: hdwy on outer to chse ldrs 3f out: sn rdn and btn wl over 1f out* **10/1**

6404 **7** *3/4* **Green Day Packer (IRE)**[26] 4491 3-8-9 **56** LeeEnstone 15 54
(P C Haslam) *hld up towards rr: hdwy 4f out: rdn over 2f out and sn no imp* **12/1**

-003 **8** *nk* **Emotive**[46] 4246 4-9-4 **53** SaleemGolam 3 50
(F P Murtagh) *in tch: effrt 4f out: sn rdn along and kpt on same pce fr over 2f out* **28/1**

5150 **9** *nk* **Erte**[12] 5283 6-8-10 **48** (v) DominicFox(3) 1 45
(W Storey) *hld up and bhd: sme hdwy on inner over 3f out: sn rdn: nvr nr ldrs* **16/1**

5054 **10** *1 1/4* **Square Dealer**[24] 4941 6-9-3 **52** (b) PaddyAspell 2 47
(J R Norton) *chsd ldrs on inner: rdn along over 3f out: drvn and wknd fnl 2f* **20/1**

/004 **11** *4* **Top Tenor (IRE)**[49] 4179 7-8-8 **50** SophieDoyle(7) 9 41
(W Storey) *a in rr* **28/1**

0560 **12** *hd* **Ninetyninetreble (IRE)**[16] 5158 4-9-11 **63** MarkLawson(3) 14 53
(Grant Tuer) *chsd ldng pair: rdn along over 4f out and sn wknd* **40/1**

2346 **13** *9* **Vice Admiral**[13] 5257 4-8-13 **55** NSLawes(7) 10 34
(M W Easterby) *led: rdn along and hdd 4f out: sn wknd* **7/1**[3]

-640 **14** *7* **Gigi Glamor**[61] 3803 5-8-12 **47** PaulQuinn 11 18
(W M Brisbourne) *chsd ldrs: rdn along 5f out and sn wknd* **25/1**

3m 37.02s (5.62) **Going Correction** +0.175s/f (Good)
WFA 3 from 4yo+ 12lb **14** Ran SP% **124.7**
Speed ratings (Par 101): **92,91,91,88,88 87,87,87,87,86 84,84,79,76**
CSF £12.92 CT £61.57 TOTE £2.40: £1.30, £2.40, £1.60; EX 16.70.
Owner A Frame **Bred** Sir Eric Parker **Trained** Lingdale, Redcar & Cleveland

FOCUS
The front three came clear in what was a moderate staying handicap. Not a lot came into this in much form. The form has been rated through the winner, who won this event off a 3lb higher mark last year.

5627 CATTERICKBRIDGE.CO.UK FILLIES' H'CAP 7f
5:55 (5:56) (Class 6) (0-60,59) 3-Y-O+ **£2,730** (£806; £403) **Stalls** Low

Form RPR

0325 **1** **Dasheena**[43] 4361 4-8-6 **51** (be) SophieDoyle(7) 14 61
(A J McCabe) *fly j. s and towards rr: gd hdwy on wd outside over 2f out: rdn to ld ent fnl f: kpt on wl* **17/2**

6523 **2** *nk* **Tilsworth Charlie**[15] 5190 4-9-4 **56** (b) ChrisCatlin 3 65
(J R Jenkins) *hld up in tch: hdwy 3f out: rdn and ev ch ent fnl f: drvn: edgd lft and no ex towards fin* **3/1**[1]

2013 **3** *2 1/2* **Razzano (IRE)**[19] 5083 3-8-11 **55** NeilChalmers(3) 6 56
(A M Hales) *chsd ldrs: hdwy over 2f out: rdn to chal wl over 1f out and ev ch tl drvn and one pce ins fnl f* **8/1**

0210 **4** *1 1/4* **Smash N'Grab (IRE)**[27] 4842 3-9-1 **56** (p) PaulMulrennan 15 54
(K A Ryan) *led: rdn along 2f out: drvn over 1f out: hdd ent fnl f: wknd* **11/1**

0202 **5** *3/4* **Tour D'Amour (IRE)**[16] 5159 4-9-7 **59** PaddyAspell 1 56
(R Craggs) *chsd ldrs: n.m.r on inner after 1f: rdn along over 2f out and kpt on same pce* **9/2**[2]

0410 **6** *1 3/4* **Missus Molly Brown**[31] 4706 3-8-9 **50** SaleemGolam 12 41
(R A Fahey) *s.i.s and bhd: rdn and hdwy over 2f out: kpt on appr fnl f: nrst fin* **8/1**

6500 **7** *nk* **Ensign's Trick**[15] 5191 3-8-11 **57** LukeMorris(5) 11 47
(W M Brisbourne) *midfield: hdwy on outer to chse ldrs 3f out: rdn 2f out and sn no imp* **18/1**

450 **8** *1/2* **Sparky Vixen**[49] 4180 3-8-12 **53** DaleGibson 2 42
(G A Swinbank) *hld up towards rr: hdwy 3f out: sn rdn and n.d* **14/1**

3400 **9** *nk* **Cadogen Square**[28] 4822 5-8-7 **52** DanielleMcCreery(7) 4 41
(D W Chapman) *midfield: n.m.r and hmpd on inner after 1f: bhd after* **14/1**

466 **10** *hd* **Safranine (IRE)**[26] 4907 10-8-11 **54** AnnStokell(5) 13 42
(Miss A Stokell) *cl up: rdn along over 2f out and sn wknd* **40/1**

6000 **11** *3/4* **Nabra**[12] 5282 3-8-11 **55** MarkLawson(3) 7 40
(M Brittain) *a in rr* **40/1**

3005 **12** *shd* **Heidi Hi**[21] 5041 3-8-5 **46** AdrianMcCarthy 9 31
(J R Turner) *chsd ldrs: rdn over 2f out and sn wknd* **50/1**

0100 **13** *1/2* **Linden's Lady**[4] 5503 7-8-9 **50** (v) AlanCreighton(3) 10 35
(J R Weymes) *midfield: rdn along over 2f out and nvr a factor* **16/1**

3042 **14** *1 1/2* **Slip Star**[14] 5231 4-8-12 **50** GregFairley 5 31
(T J Etherington) *a towards rr* **7/1**[3]

245 **15** *2 1/2* **Lan Kwai Fong**[38] 4492 3-8-2 **46** (b[1]) DuranFentiman(3) 8 19
(T D Easterby) *s.i.s: a bhd* **25/1**

1m 29.31s (1.95) **Going Correction** +0.175s/f (Good)
WFA 3 from 4yo+ 3lb **15** Ran SP% **131.9**
Speed ratings (Par 98): **95,94,91,90,89 87,87,86,86,86 85,85,84,82,79**
CSF £36.33 CT £233.47 TOTE £9.80: £2.60, £1.70, £2.30; EX 53.20 Place 6 £3.50, Place 5 £3.39..
Owner Paul J Dixon **Bred** Mrs Yvette Dixon **Trained** Babworth, Notts

FOCUS
Weak handicap form, rated through the second and third.
Missus Molly Brown Official explanation: jockey said filly missed the break
Nabra Official explanation: jockey said filly suffered interference shortly after start
Slip Star Official explanation: jockey said filly was denied a clear run
Lan Kwai Fong Official explanation: jockey said filly slipped at the start
T/Plt: £3.50 to a £1 stake. Pool: £45,918.45. 9,435.30 winning tickets. T/Qpdt: £3.20 to a £1 stake. Pool: £2,087.20. 482.10 winning tickets. JR

5587 NEWBURY (L-H)
Saturday, September 22

OFFICIAL GOING: Good to firm (firm in places; 8.3)
Wind: Slight, across

5628 E B F DUBAI TENNIS CHAMPIONSHIPS MAIDEN STKS (DIV I) 7f (S)
1:35 (1:37) (Class 4) 2-Y-O **£5,829** (£1,734; £866; £432) **Stalls** Centre

Form RPR

634 **1** **Fool's Wildcat (USA)**[17] 5135 2-9-3 82 (b[1]) JimmyFortune 5 87+
(B J Meehan) *mde all: drvn along 2f out: forged clr fnl f: unchal* **7/1**[3]

2 *4* **Confront** 2-9-3 0 RyanMoore 2 76+
(Sir Michael Stoute) *in tch: hdwy 3f out: drvn and styd on to chse wnr over 1f out: kpt on for clr 2nd but a readily hld* **15/8**[1]

05 **3** *2* **Sweet Hope (USA)**[22] 4992 2-8-12 0 DO'Donohoe 6 66
(K A Ryan) *rdn along in mid-div 1/2-way: styd on fr 2f out to go 3rd ins fnl f but no ch w ldng duo* **8/1**

06 **4** *shd* **Musashi (IRE)**[38] 4500 2-9-3 0 .... JohnEgan 8 71
(J S Moore) *in tch: rdn fr 3f out: styd on to chse ldrs fnl 2f: one pce ins fnl f* **14/1**

0 **5** *½* **Penchesco (IRE)**[110] 2303 2-9-3 0 .... PaulEddery 10 69
(Pat Eddery) *in rr: rdn and hdwy 3f out: chsd ldrs 2f out: no ex ins fnl f* **66/1**

6 *1 ½* **Garland** 2-8-12 0 .... TedDurcan 13 61+
(R Hannon) *t.k.h: chsd ldrs: rdn over 2f out: kpt on same pce fr over 1f out* **16/1**

7 *¾* **Tourist** 2-9-3 0 .... RichardHughes 9 64+
(B W Hills) *s.i.s: hdwy into mid-div 3f out: shkn up 2f out: wknd fnl f* **7/2**[2]

500 **8** *5* **Talamahana**[35] 4602 2-8-12 56 .... LPKeniry 1 46
(S Kirk) *chsd ldrs tl wknd ins fnl 2f* **100/1**

9 *nk* **Cape Rock** 2-9-3 0 .... SimonWhitworth 7 50
(C A Horgan) *s.i.s: nvr in contention* **20/1**

3 **10** *½* **Boot Strap Bill**[26] 4904 2-9-3 0 .... JamesDoyle 11 49
(Miss J R Tooth) *chsd ldrs: wnt 2nd over 3f out: wknd over 2f out* **14/1**

11 *½* **Dark Camellia** 2-8-12 0 .... JMurtagh 4 42
(H J L Dunlop) *s.i.s: outpcd* **33/1**

12 *4* **Mazara (IRE)** 2-9-3 0 .... MartinDwyer 3 37
(J L Dunlop) *sn rdn: a wl bhd* **12/1**

1m 25.54s (-1.46) **Going Correction** -0.275s/f (Firm) **12** Ran SP% **117.7**
Speed ratings (Par 97): **97,92,90,90,89 87,86,81,80,80 79,75**
CSF £19.78 TOTE £6.50: £2.10, £1.30, £2.50; EX 21.70.
Owner Favourites Racing XXV **Bred** Summer Wind Farm **Trained** Manton, Wilts
■ Stewards' Enquiry : James Doyle jockey said gelding hung left-handed

FOCUS
An impressive win from Fool's Wildcat, who stepped up on his previous form and can do better still, but overall this did not look a strong race.

NOTEBOOK
Fool's Wildcat(USA) showed just fair form in his first three starts, including on Polytrack last time, but was something of a revelation here in the first-time blinkers. Adopting forcing tactics, he quickened right away in the final furlong to score impressively. He is on the upgrade, but he did not beat a great deal here and is unlikely to be taking up his entries in the Dewhurst and the Racing Post Trophy. (op 9-2)
Confront ◆ is a half-brother to decent French 1m2f performer Nearby, out of an unraced half-sister to Oaks winner Reams Of Verse. Held up on the far side of the bunch, he kept on nicely to move into second but the winner had already gone clear. He should soon go one better in ordinary company. (op 7-4 tchd 9-4)
Sweet Hope(USA) came under pressure at halfway before staying on to secure a modest third close home. She appreciated this extra furlong and is now qualified for a handicap mark. (op 15-2 tchd 7-1)
Musashi(IRE) got away on terms this time and was staying on at the end over this extra furlong. He is now eligible for nurseries. (op 11-1)
Penchesco(IRE), out of a half-sister to Group 3 Prestige Stakes winner Gracefully, is a half-brother to a middle-distance winner in Italy. Off the track since finishing last on his debut over 5f at Leicester in June, he showed much more on this much quicker surface and was only run out of third place inside the last. (op 50-1)
Garland is a half-sister to three minor winners out of a mare who won in Spain and was a half-sister to Champion Stakes winner Legal Case. She flashed her tail in the preliminaries but shaped with a bit of promise and should improve for the experience. (op 12-1 tchd 11-1 and 20-1)
Tourist, whose dam, an unraced half-sister to the US Grade 1 winner Tinners Way, has produced three previous winners, was not knocked about and can be expected to improve. (op 8-1)
Boot Strap Bill Official explanation: jockey said gelding hung left-handed

5629 USK VALLEY STUD NURSERY 6f 8y
2:05 (2:07) (Class 2) 2-Y-O

£12,464 (£3,732; £1,866; £700; £700; £234) **Stalls** Centre

Form RPR

5311 **1** **Mr Keppel (IRE)**[14] 5216 2-8-10 **80** .... TPQueally 4 88+
(J A Osborne) *trckd ldrs: led over 1f out: hrd rdn and r.o strly fnl f* **5/1**[3]

1002 **2** *1 ¾* **Silver Wind**[15] 5207 2-9-0 **84** ....(b) JimmyFortune 6 87
(P D Evans) *chsd ldrs: drvn to chal over 1f out: kpt on u.p ins fnl f but nt pce of wnr* **10/1**

6113 **3** *hd* **Taurian**[7] 5410 2-9-7 **91** .... JMurtagh 12 94
(Mrs L Stubbs) *s.i.s: in rr: hdwy over 2f out: kpt on to chse ldng duo ins fnl f but nvr gng pce to chal* **7/1**

6225 **4** *½* **Blue Zenith (IRE)**[6] 5452 2-7-7 **68** .... NataliaGemelova(5) 5 69+
(J S Moore) *broke wl: stdd towards rr: hdwy and n.m.r ins fnl 2f: nt clr run and swtchd lft 1f out: fin wl and gng on cl home* **66/1**

0421 **4** *dht* **Enactment**[16] 5167 2-8-8 **78** .... RyanMoore 8 79
(Sir Michael Stoute) *in tch: rdn and hdwy 2f out: kpt in fnl f but nvr gng pce to rch ldrs* **4/1**[1]

004P **6** *nk* **Vhujon (IRE)**[7] 5400 2-9-2 **86** ....(t) JohnEgan 10 86
(P D Evans) *led after 1f: styd ahd tl hung rt and hdd over 1f out: styd on same pce ins fnl f* **20/1**

3165 **7** *½* **Barbarossa**[39] 4484 2-8-6 **76** .... FrancisNorton 15 78+
(R Hannon) *in rr: drvn along 1/2-way: r.o ins fnl f: gng on cl home* **25/1**

5123 **8** *½* **Perfect Flight**[10] 5331 2-8-8 **78** .... TedDurcan 11 75
(M Blanshard) *chsd ldrs: rdn 2f out: kpt on same pce ins fnl f* **33/1**

3214 **9** *½* **Zippi Jazzman (USA)**[30] 4737 2-8-8 **78** .... MartinDwyer 13 74
(R M Beckett) *chsd ldrs: rdn over 2f out: one pce ins fnl f: wknd cl home* **14/1**

001 **10** *1* **The Jostler**[18] 5110 2-8-9 **79** .... MichaelHills 2 72
(B W Hills) *in rr: hdwy to chse ldrs ins fnl 3f: wknd fnl f* **12/1**

2410 **11** *½* **Mudhish (IRE)**[23] 4964 2-8-7 **77** .... KerrinMcEvoy 14 68
(C E Brittain) *chsd ldrs: rdn over 2f out: wknd appr fnl f* **66/1**

0351 **12** *2* **Clifton Dancer**[11] 5314 2-8-7 **77** .... RichardKingscote 1 62
(Tom Dascombe) *led 1f: styd chsng ldrs to 2f out: sn wknd* **9/1**

431 **13** *1 ½* **Lodi (IRE)**[17] 5126 2-8-10 **80** .... RichardHughes 7 61+
(B J Meehan) *plld hrd early: rdn and effrt fr 3f out: nvr in contention* **9/2**[2]

1001 **14** *nk* **Geoffdaw**[4] 5496 2-8-2 **77** 6ex ow1 .... TolleyDean(5) 3 57
(M J Wallace) *chsd ldrs: rdn 1/2-way: sn wknd* **16/1**

1630 **15** *1 ¼* **Brassini**[22] 5008 2-8-13 **83** .... JimCrowley 9 59
(B R Millman) *in tch to 1/2-way* **50/1**

1m 12.12s (-2.20) **Going Correction** -0.275s/f (Firm) **15** Ran SP% **123.2**
Speed ratings (Par 101): **103,100,100,99,99 99,98,98,97,96 95,92,90,90,88**
CSF £52.00 CT £366.85 TOTE £5.30: £2.30, £3.10, £2.50; EX 62.80 Trifecta £403.70 Pool: £966.74 - 1.70 winning tickets..
Owner Mountgrange Stud **Bred** Mrs C F Van Straubenzee And Miss A Gibson Fleming **Trained** Upper Lambourn, Berks
■ Stewards' Enquiry : Tolley Dean jockey said gelding never travelled
John Egan jockey said colt hung right-handed
Martin Dwyer jockey said colt hung left-handed

FOCUS
Very solid nursery form. Mr Keppel is progressive, and the runner-up performed to the level of his previous course run.

NOTEBOOK
Mr Keppel(IRE) shrugged off the 7lb rise for his Haydock win to complete a hat-trick, pulling away from the runner-up in the final furlong. He is set to be raised in class now, and might return here for the Horris Hill Stakes, as that Group 3 event is sponsored by his owner. (op 4-1)
Silver Wind, runner-up to Gross Prophet in a similar event over course and distance, was put up 5lb for that but ran another solid race. He could not go with the winner inside the final furlong but stuck on to hold second. (op 16-1)
Taurian, a progressive gelding who was 11lb higher than when he last in a nursery, ran another good race under topweight without quite getting to the first two. (op 13-2 tchd 15-2)
Blue Zenith(IRE), back up in trip, came home in taking style once switched to race on the far side of the bunch. She remains in good order. (op 5-1)
Enactment, whose Warwick victory has been franked by the subsequent win of runner-up Mistress Cooper, had no real excuse off this 3lb higher mark. He was briefly in third place inside the last but was never going to get to the leading pair. (op 5-1)
Vhujon(IRE), a stablemate of the runner-up, showed good pace but hung over to the stands' rail and could not hold on to his lead. Official explanation: jockey said colt hung right-handed (op 25-1)
Barbarossa, dropped a further 2lb, was doing some sterling late work and looks the type to win a nursery if upped to 7f. (op 33-1)
Zippi Jazzman(USA) Official explanation: jockey said colt hung left-handed
Lodi(IRE), whose Kempton Polytrack form has been franked by third home Paco Boy, was too free on this nursery debut. (op 13-2)
Geoffdaw Official explanation: jockey said gelding was never travelling

5630 DUBAI DUTY FREE MILL REEF STKS (GROUP 2) 6f 8y
2:35 (2:39) (Class 1) 2-Y-O

£36,907 (£13,988; £7,000; £3,490; £1,748; £877) **Stalls** Centre

Form RPR

0410 **1** **Dark Angel (IRE)**[8] 5377 2-9-1 105 .... MichaelHills 1 108
(B W Hills) *mde all: rdn appr fnl f: hld on gamely whn strly chal fnl 100yds* **9/4**[1]

5310 **2** *nk* **Strike The Deal (USA)**[7] 5406 2-9-4 107 .... JMurtagh 2 110
(J Noseda) *trckd ldrs: wnt 2nd ins fnl 2f: r.o u.p and str chal thrght fnl f: nt quite get up* **5/2**[2]

3414 **3** *¾* **Berbice (IRE)**[30] 4743 2-9-1 91 .... RyanMoore 5 105
(R Hannon) *trckd ldrs: rdn & hdwy over 1f out: styd on wl thrght fnl f but nvr quite gng pce to rch ldrs* **4/1**[3]

1201 **4** *hd* **Philario (IRE)**[14] 5219 2-9-1 90 .... FergusSweeney 7 104
(K R Burke) *chsd wnr tl ins fnl 2f: styd on u.p ins fnl f but nvr quite gng pce of ldng duo* **9/2**

110 **5** *2* **Easy Target (FR)**[31] 4721 2-9-1 99 .... PaulEddery 4 98
(B Smart) *s.i.s: in rr: rdn and no prog fnl 2f* **9/1**

1000 **6** *½* **Jebel Tara**[10] 5324 2-9-1 86 .... JimmyFortune 6 97
(C E Brittain) *rdn over 3f out: nvr gng pce of ldrs* **22/1**

1m 11.68s (-2.64) **Going Correction** -0.275s/f (Firm) **6** Ran SP% **111.9**
Speed ratings (Par 107): **106,105,104,104,101 101**
CSF £8.12 TOTE £3.10: £1.60, £1.80; EX 6.10.
Owner The Hon Mrs J M Corbett & C Wright **Bred** Yeomanstown Stud **Trained** Lambourn, Berks

FOCUS
A weak renewal on pre-race figures, and that impression was confirmed as they finished in a heap. Dark Angel ran to the level of his July Stakes fourth and the runner-up to his Richmond win.

NOTEBOOK
Dark Angel(IRE) was found wanting in the Flying Childers last time but bounced back over his optimum trip. Making all, and the last to come off the bridle, he edged slightly to his right but was always holding the runner-up's sustained challenge. He has had a fine season, but this was a weak Group 2 and he may struggle to build on this. (op 5-2, tchd 11-4 in places)
Strike The Deal(USA), carrying a Group 2 penalty for his Richmond Stakes win, was back down in trip after 7f appeared too far for him at Doncaster, where he was hampered early on according to his trainer. He was closing on the winner throughout the final furlong but the line was always going to beat him. (op 15-8)
Berbice(IRE), fourth to Dark Angel in the big sales race at York, kept trying and could be worth a step up to 7f now. (op 13-2)
Philario(IRE), winner of the Group 3 Sirenia Stakes on the Kempton Polytrack on his latest start, ran to a similar level of form on this return to turf. (tchd 5-1)
Easy Target(FR) had his excuses in the Gimcrack but there appeared none here, although he still produced a respectable effort. (op 8-1 tchd 15-2)
Jebel Tara has been well beaten in three runs at this level now, but he did post an improved effort form-wise here. (op 33-1)

5631 JOHN SMITH'S STKS (HERITAGE H'CAP) 1m 2f 6y
3:10 (3:10) (Class 2) (0-105,102) 3-Y-O+

£62,320 (£18,660; £9,330; £4,670; £2,330; £1,170) **Stalls** Centre

Form RPR

3122 **1** **Monte Alto (IRE)**[28] 4799 3-8-10 **92** .... JMurtagh 19 108+
(L M Cumani) *stdd s: hld up in rr on rails tl eased to outside and stdy hdwy ins fnl 3f: led jst ins fnl f: rdn and edgd lft: kpt on wl* **9/2**[2]

0040 **2** *1 ¼* **Speedy Sam**[53] 4043 4-8-9 **88** .... AndrewElliott(3) 17 100
(K R Burke) *in rr: rdn over 4f out: stl plenty to do u.p 2f out: styd on strly u.p fnl f: tk 2nd cl home but no ch w wnr* **20/1**

1451 **3** *½* **Greek Well (IRE)**[31] 4720 4-9-1 **91** ....(v) RyanMoore 8 102
(Sir Michael Stoute) *hld up in rr: stdy hdwy over 3f out to ld jst ins fnl f: sn rdn: hdd jst ins fnl f: one pce and ct for 2nd cl home* **4/1**[1]

0010 **4** *1 ¼* **Bolodenka (IRE)**[14] 5242 5-9-3 **93** 5ex .... TonyHamilton 9 101
(R A Fahey) *towards rr: rdn and hdwy 3f out: chsd ldrs tl press over 1f out: kpt on same pce ins fnl f* **25/1**

6103 **5** *2* **Invasian (IRE)**[15] 5205 6-8-11 **87** ....(e) MickyFenton 5 91
(P W D'Arcy) *t.k.h: led after 1f: hdd ins fnl 3f: styd presing ldrs: wknd fnl half f* **25/1**

4000 **6** *½* **Eradicate (IRE)**[32] 4690 3-9-0 **96** .... RichardMullen 18 99
(M Johnston) *chsd ldrs: slt ld ins fnl 3f: hdd ins fnl 2f: wknd fnl f* **22/1**

0001 **7** *nk* **Impeller (IRE)**[21] 5049 8-9-9 **99** 5ex .... JohnEgan 2 101
(J S Moore) *chsd ldrs: rdn fr 3f out: one pce fr over 1f out* **20/1**

2550 **8** *hd* **Pagan Sword**[9] 5362 5-8-9 **85** ....(p) TedDurcan 6 87
(Mrs A J Perrett) *in rr: rdn and styd on fr 2f out: kpt on ins fnl f: nvr in contention* **33/1**

004 **9** *nk* **Bandama (IRE)**[21] 5049 4-9-1 **91** ....(v[1]) JimCrowley 10 92
(Mrs A J Perrett) *chsd ldrs: drvn to chal 3f out: wknd appr fnl f* **10/1**

3165 **10** *1 ¼* **Benandonner (USA)**[10] 5326 4-9-1 **91** .... MartinDwyer 13 90
(R A Fahey) *chsd ldrs: rdn and ev ch 3f out: wknd over 1f out* **20/1**

2042 **11** *hd* **Mr Aviator (USA)**[51] 4092 3-8-9 **91** .... RichardHughes 12 90
(R Hannon) *t.k.h: in tch: rdn and effrt 3f out: wknd over 1f out* **11/2**

2460 **12** *½* **Flying Clarets (IRE)**[17] 5142 4-9-2 **92** .... DO'Donohoe 1 90
(R A Fahey) *chsd ldrs: rdn over 2f out: wknd fnl f* **40/1**

3332 **13** *1 ¾* **Peruvian Prince (USA)**[31] 4720 5-9-1 **91** .... TQuinn 7 85
(R A Fahey) *in tch: rdn 3f out: n.d after* **5/1**[3]

4061 **14** *3* **Players Please (USA)**[4] 5504 3-8-12 **94** 5ex.................... DaneO'Neill 3 82
(M Johnston) *led 1f: styd chsng ldrs: rdn 3f out: wknd over 2f out* **8/1**

0300 **15** *3* **Flipando (IRE)**[7] 5412 6-9-10 **100**....................................... PaulFessey 4 82
(T D Barron) *t.k.h: prom 6f* **33/1**

2m 3.95s (-4.76) **Going Correction** -0.225s/f (Firm)
WFA 3 from 4yo+ 6lb **15** Ran SP% **125.1**
Speed ratings (Par 109): **110,109,108,107,106 105,105,105,104,103 103,103,102,99,97**
CSF £98.00 CT £402.36 TOTE £5.60: £1.70, £5.20, £2.10; EX 124.00 Trifecta £742.70 Part won. Pool: £1,046.10 - 0.40 winning tickets..
Owner Timothy Steel **Bred** C H Wacker Iii **Trained** Newmarket, Suffolk
■ Stewards' Enquiry : Paul Fessey jockey said gelding ran too free early stages

FOCUS
Several non-runners, but still a competitive handicap run at a good pace. Solid form with the winner and third progressive and the second and fourth on good marks. The principals came from the back of the field.

NOTEBOOK
Monte Alto(IRE) ◆ was dropped in from his wide draw and raced at the back of the field. Still last turning into the long home straight, he was soon moved to the outside and came with a steady run to show in front entering the last, scoring readily despite wandering a little. This progressive colt looks a realistic candidate for the Cambridgeshire, a race he should get into under the 4lb penalty he picked up here. (op 4-1 tchd 5-1)
Speedy Sam, who has edged down the weights this term despite a couple of encouraging efforts, was held up at the back in common with the winner and third. He was under pressure early in the home straight, but responded to his rider's urgings and stayed on to go second near the line. (op 28-1)
Greek Well(IRE), up 5lb and visored again, ran another solid race. He made good progress from the rear to lead inside the last but was soon tackled by the winner and was unable to put up a great deal of resistance. The ground was a shade faster than he would have cared for. (op 7-2)
Bolodenka(IRE), well beaten over 7f at Leopardstown last time, was running over this far for only the second time and he seemed to stay well enough, if lacking a change of gear late on. (tchd 28-1)
Invasian(IRE) ran his usual race from the front but, although anything but disgraced, it does look as if the Handicapper has his measure now. (op 33-1)
Eradicate(IRE) had become most disappointing, but this was a step back in the right direction. (op 25-1)
Bandama(IRE) travelled well in the first-time visor but failed to find much once coming off the bridle. (op 12-1 tchd 9-1)
Mr Aviator(USA), 4lb higher than when runner-up at Glorious Goodwood, failed to settle and was disappointing, although the drying ground would not have been in his favour. (op 7-1)
Flipando(IRE) Official explanation: jockey said gelding ran too free in the early stages

5632 DUBAI INTERNATIONAL AIRPORT WORLD TROPHY (GROUP 3) 5f 34y
3:45 (3:45) (Class 1) 3-Y-0+
£26,686 (£10,114; £5,061; £2,523; £1,264; £634) **Stalls** Centre

Form RPR

1133 **1** **Rowe Park**[21] 5050 4-9-0 100.. LPKeniry 7 115
(Mrs L C Jewell) *trckd ldrs: led appr fnl f: rdn and hld on wl thrght fnl f* **25/1**

1542 **2** *½* **Enticing (IRE)**[51] 4090 3-8-10 110..................................... MichaelHills 1 111
(W J Haggas) *chsd ldrs: rdn to chal over 1f out: kpt on ins fnl f but a hld by wnr* **5/2**[2]

1620 **3** *1* **Judd Street**[7] 5407 5-9-0 104....................................... StephenCarson 11 110
(Eve Johnson Houghton) *trckd ldrs: travelleing wl ins fnl 2f: rdn appr fnl f and kpt on same pce* **10/1**

004 **4** *nk* **Mutawaajid (AUS)**[14] 5214 4-9-5 110.......................... JimmyFortune 10 114
(M R Channon) *towards rr but in tch: hrd rdn and hdwy over 1f out: kpt on u.p but nvr gng pce to be competitive* **3/1**[3]

3602 **5** *nk* **Desert Lord**[30] 4746 7-9-0 113..(b) DO'Donohoe 5 108
(K A Ryan) *led tl hdd appr fnl f: outpcd ins fnl f* **9/4**[1]

4541 **6** *2 ½* **Siren's Gift**[11] 5305 3-8-10 93.. FrancisNorton 6 96
(A M Balding) *in rr: sme hdwy whn pushed lft jst ins fnl f: nvr in contention after* **14/1**

1105 **7** *10* **Bertoliver**[50] 4133 3-8-13 88.. JohnEgan 9 63
(D K Ivory) *chsd ldrs: rdn 2f out: wknd ins fnl 2f* **33/1**

6462 **8** *2 ½* **The Jobber (IRE)**[11] 5305 6-9-0 99.. TedDurcan 4 54
(M Blanshard) *s.i.s: sn in tch: wknd fr 2f out* **8/1**

60.18 secs (-2.38) **Going Correction** -0.275s/f (Firm)
WFA 3 from 4yo+ 1lb **8** Ran SP% **118.0**
Speed ratings (Par 113): **108,107,105,105,104 100,84,80**
CSF £90.11 TOTE £28.10: £4.00, £1.50, £2.90; EX 103.70.
Owner Mrs Sue Ashdown And Mrs Lesley Hammond **Bred** J Baker **Trained** Sutton Valence, Kent
■ The first Group winner for both Linda Jewell and Liam Keniry.

FOCUS
Not a strong Group 3 although the form has been rated at face value through the third, with another step up from the progressive Rowe Park.

NOTEBOOK
Rowe Park, who won a Wolverhampton handicap off a mark of just 59 on New Year's Eve, has made remarkable progress this season and was successful on this first foray into Group company. There was no fluke about it and connections are considering supplementing him for the Prix de l'Abbaye, where he would not be without a chance. (op 20-1 tchd 18-1)
Enticing(IRE), with ground conditions to suit, had every chance from her low draw but the winner always had her measure.
Judd Street, who ran a cracker from an unfavourable draw in the Portland, is a progressive sprinter and this was another excellent effort. He is well capable of winning in this grade or at Listed level. (op 12-1 tchd 14-1)
Mutawaajid(AUS), conceding 5lb all round, ran a decent race on this drop in grade but will be happier back over 6f on this evidence. (op 10-3 tchd 7-2 and 4-1 in places)
Desert Lord had found only juvenile Kingsgate Native too good for him in the Nunthorpe last time but was below his best here, fading late on after showing good pace to lead. (op 15-8 tchd 11-4)
Siren's Gift, winner of a conditions event at Leicester, was again found wanting in higher grade but would have finished slightly closer had she not been hampered by Mutawaajid entering the final furlong. (op 12-1)

5633 E B F DUBAI TENNIS CHAMPIONSHIPS MAIDEN STKS (DIV II) 7f (S)
4:20 (4:21) (Class 4) 2-Y-0
£5,829 (£1,734; £866; £432) **Stalls** Centre

Form RPR

1 **Mystery Sail (USA)** 2-8-12 0...................................... RichardHughes 3 74
(Mrs A J Perrett) *in tch: hdwy 2f out: n.m.r and green appr fnl f: str run ins fnl f: got up last strides* **7/1**[2]

5 **2** *hd* **Lord Peter Flint (IRE)**[29] 4777 2-9-3 0.......................... JimmyFortune 5 78
(B J Meehan) *w ldr 3f: styd front rnk: rdn to chal jst ins fnl f: led fnl 75yds: ct last strides* **2/1**[1]

3 **3** *hd* **Monashee Rock (IRE)**[16] 5161 2-8-12 0................................... TQuinn 10 72+
(M Salaman) *t.k.h: chsd ldrs: rdn and one pce 2f out: styd on u.p fnl f: fin wl: nt quite get to ldng duo* **10/1**

4 *hd* **Tathkaar** 2-8-12 0.. JohnEgan 7 72
(C E Brittain) *chsd ldrs: led 2f out: rdn over 1f out: hdd fnl 75yds: no ex cl home* **25/1**

3 **5** *½* **Mountain Pride (IRE)**[29] 4777 2-9-3 0................................ TedDurcan 2 76
(J L Dunlop) *chsd ldrs: rdn 2f out: styd on ins fnl f but nvr gng pce to chal* **2/1**[1]

0 **6** *1* **Seventh Hill**[70] 3552 2-9-3 0.. DaneO'Neill 6 73
(M Blanshard) *in rr: drvn along over 2f out: styd on wl thrght fnl f: fin wl* **33/1**

7 *2 ½* **Provision** 2-8-12 0.. FrancisNorton 4 62+
(A M Balding) *s.i.s: in rr: hdwy over 2f out: chsd ldrs over 1f out: edgd lft and wknd fnl f* **8/1**[3]

0 **8** *2* **Lady Selkirk**[16] 5162 2-8-12 0................................. RichardKingscote 13 56+
(R Charlton) *s.i.s: in rr: rdn and green 1/2-way: nvr in contention* **14/1**

03 **9** *nk* **Bathwick Man**[19] 5088 2-9-3 0... JimCrowley 12 61
(B R Millman) *chsd ldrs: rdn over 2f out: wknd over 1f out* **14/1**

10 *3* **Artistic Light** 2-8-12 0... RichardMullen 11 48
(W R Muir) *slt ld tl hdd 2f out: sn wknd* **33/1**

0 **11** *1* **Desert Thistle (IRE)**[12] 5274 2-9-3 0.................................. IanMongan 8 50
(H J L Dunlop) *chsd ldrs: rdn 1/2-way: sn wknd* **50/1**

12 *3* **Lawton** 2-9-3 0.. JamesDoyle 1 42
(Miss J R Tooth) *in tch: rdn 3f out: edgd lft: green and sn wknd* **66/1**

1m 26.72s (-0.28) **Going Correction** -0.275s/f (Firm) **12** Ran SP% **125.9**
Speed ratings (Par 97): **90,89,89,89,88 87,84,82,82,78 77,74**
CSF £22.03 TOTE £11.70: £2.80, £1.20, £2.50; EX 36.90.
Owner K Abdulla **Bred** Juddmonte Farms Inc **Trained** Pulborough, W Sussex

FOCUS
A sedate pace and a bunch finish with just heads between the first four. A pretty modest event for the track all told rated around the third and fifth.

NOTEBOOK
Mystery Sail(USA), out of a mare who won over 1m in France, is half-sister to a middle-distance winner. Her inexperience was plain for all to see on this debut, but she finally put her head down and ran in the last furlong, snatching the race almost on the line. (op 11-1)
Lord Peter Flint(IRE), who made an encouraging debut in soft ground at Newmarket, was always up on the speed. He battled his way to the front inside the last but was caught in the last couple of strides. (op 3-1 tchd 10-3)
Monashee Rock(IRE), who again pulled hard, as on her Salisbury debut, finished in good style but just too late. She will not be inconvenienced by a return to a mile. (op 8-1 tchd 15-2)
Tathkaar, who refused to go in the stalls on her intended debut here in June, is bred to stay, being out of a 1m6f winner whose dam Indian Queen won the Gold Cup at Ascot. She took a narrow lead with a quarter of a mile to run and refused to give way, but after looking sure to be placed at least she had to settle for fourth. (op 14-1)
Mountain Pride(IRE) had finished two places ahead of today's runner-up Lord Peter Flint when they made their respective debuts at Newmarket, but could not quite confirm the form on this faster ground. He really needs a stiffer test of stamina. (op 6-4)
Seventh Hill, a half-brother to five winners, showed more than he had on his debut at Salisbury two months ago and was putting in some decent late work. (op 40-1)
Provision, a half-sister to her connections' smart miler Banknote, was slowly away on this debut but showed ability, and should improve with the experience behind her. (op 16-1)

5634 JOHN SMITH'S EXTRA COLD CONDITIONS STKS 1m 1f
4:55 (4:55) (Class 3) 3-Y-0+ **£6,855** (£2,052; £1,026; £513; £256) **Stalls** Centre

Form RPR

101- **1** **Multidimensional (IRE)**[399] 4623 4-9-3 111....................... TedDurcan 5 113+
(H R A Cecil) *hld up in last pl: styd on over 1f out: str run fr ins fnl f: shkn up to ld last strides* **5/2**[1]

3226 **2** *nk* **Oracle West (SAF)**[125] 1877 6-8-11 0.................................. JMurtagh 6 106
(M F De Kock, South Africa) *racd in 4th: rdn and hdwy 2f out: styd on u.p to ld jst ins fnl f: kpt on: ct last strides* **11/4**[2]

4536 **3** *2* **Olympian Odyssey**[14] 5213 4-8-11 112.....................(v[1]) KerrinMcEvoy 4 102
(Saeed Bin Suroor) *led 1f: chsd ldr tl led 3f out: rdn over 1f out: hung rt and hdd jst ins fnl f: fnd nil* **5/2**[1]

0100 **4** *2 ½* **Great Hawk (USA)**[14] 5220 4-9-6 98..................................(v) RyanMoore 3 106
(Sir Michael Stoute) *chsd ldrs in 3rd: rdn over 2f out: no rspnse and nvr in contention* **4/1**[3]

1500 **5** *9* **New Seeker**[30] 4747 7-9-6 106......................................(b) JimmyFortune 7 87
(P F I Cole) *led after 1f: hdd 3f out: wknd qckly over 2f out* **11/1**

1m 51.2s (-3.39) **Going Correction** -0.225s/f (Firm)
WFA 3 from 4yo+ 5lb **5** Ran SP% **112.1**
Speed ratings (Par 107): **106,105,103,101,93**
CSF £9.88 TOTE £2.80: £1.70, £1.90; EX 6.20.
Owner Niarchos Family **Bred** The Niarchos Family **Trained** Newmarket, Suffolk
■ Stewards' Enquiry : Jimmy Fortune jockey said gelding ran too free

FOCUS
An interesting conditions event, but one in which there were question marks over each of the runners. The fourth limits the form, but take nothing away from Multidimensional who looks to have more improvement to come.

NOTEBOOK
Multidimensional(IRE) won three of his four starts last season, culminating in the Group 2 Prix Guillaume d'Ornano at Deauville, but suffered a hairline fracture of the pelvis earlier this year. Held up at the back, and still last with two furlongs left, he came with a good run between horses inside the last to get on top close home. Set to take his chance in the Champion Stakes now, he will be fresher than most at Newmarket and easier ground will help his cause. (op 2-1 tchd 11-4)
Oracle West(SAF), who showed high-class form in Dubai earlier this year, finishing second to Vengeance Of Rain in the Sheema Classic, was appearing for the first time for four months. After staying on from the rear to take a narrow lead inside the last, he was cut down near the line. (op 5-2 tchd 10-3 and 7-2 in places)
Olympian Odyssey, who was visored for the first time, had not run outside Group or Listed company since he was a two-year-old. Back in front with three to run, he drifted across the track under pressure and was immediately beaten once headed. (op 3-1 tchd 9-4)
Great Hawk(USA), who normally runs over further, could never get into contention. (op 15-2 tchd 8-1)
New Seeker raced too freely in front and failed to see out this longer trip. Official explanation: jockey said gelding ran too free (op 8-1 tchd 7-1 and 12-1)

5635 WESTON-SUPER-MARE WORKING MENS CLUB H'CAP 7f (S)
5:25 (5:25) (Class 4) (0-85,85) 3-Y-0 **£4,857** (£1,445; £722; £360) **Stalls** Centre

Form RPR

-510 **1** **Premio Loco (USA)**[119] 2045 3-9-2 **83**............................ GeorgeBaker 18 98+
(C F Wall) *trckd ldrs: led jst ins fnl f: r.o strly* **10/1**

1211 **2** *1 ¾* **Big Noise**[49] 4170 3-9-2 **83**.. TedDurcan 19 93+
(Dr J D Scargill) *trckd ldrs: travelling wl fr 2f out: drvn to chal jst ins fnl f: sn nt pce of wnr but r.o wl for clr 2nd* **5/2**[1]

-003 **3** *1 ¼* **Abunai**[19] 5092 3-8-11 **78**.. RichardKingscote 6 85
(R Charlton) *chsd ldrs: rdn to ld wl over 1f out: hdd jst ins fnl f: kpt on same pce* **14/1**

633 **4** *1* **Summer Dancer (IRE)**[31] 4710 3-8-9 **76** TQuinn 17 80
(D R C Elsworth) *s.i.s: hld up in rr: hdwy over 2f out: r.o wl fnl f but nvr gng pce to trble ldrs* **8/1**

0631 **5** *½* **Don't Panic (IRE)**[18] 5114 3-9-2 **83** KerrinMcEvoy 8 86
(P W Chapple-Hyam) *chsd ldrs: rdn 2f out: wknd ins fnl f* **5/1**[2]

0350 **6** *hd* **Averticus**[19] 5092 3-8-8 **75** (b[1]) MichaelHills 4 77
(B W Hills) *in rr: hdwy over 2f out: styd on wl fnl f but nvr gng pce to rch ldrs* **33/1**

4656 **7** *½* **Shustraya**[27] 4848 3-8-13 **80** JimCrowley 2 81
(P J Makin) *chsd ldrs: rdn to chal over 2f out: wknd ins fnl f* **20/1**

3120 **8** *1* **Masai Moon**[28] 4811 3-8-13 **85** JamesMillman[(5)] 20 83
(B R Millman) *led 1f: styd pressing ldr and stl ev ch 2f out: wknd fnl f* **25/1**

6450 **9** *½* **Manchurian**[28] 4799 3-9-3 **84** JMurtagh 14 81
(M J Wallace) *s.i.s: in rr: hdwy fr 2f out: styd on fnl f but nvr in contention* **9/1**

003 **10** *½* **Rainbow Mirage (IRE)**[16] 5168 3-9-3 **84** RichardMullen 3 80
(E S McMahon) *s.i.s: in rr: hdwy 3f out: chsd ldrs 2f out: wknd ins fnl f* **14/1**

4410 **11** *1 ¼* **Handsome Falcon**[49] 4176 3-8-9 **76** TonyHamilton 5 68
(R A Fahey) *chsd ldrs: hrd rdn and wknd ins fnl 2f* **33/1**

4500 **12** *shd* **Soviet Palace (IRE)**[26] 4898 3-8-13 **80** DO'Donohoe 7 72
(K A Ryan) *led after 1f: kpt slt ld tl hdd & wknd qckly wl over 1f out* **50/1**

2003 **13** *½* **Regal Quest (IRE)**[16] 5163 3-8-10 **77** RichardHughes 1 68+
(S Kirk) *hld up in rr: hdwy and nt clr run 2f out and again over 1f out: kpt on but nt rcvr* **16/1**

3046 **14** *nk* **Kyle (IRE)**[8] 5382 3-9-2 **83** RyanMoore 10 73
(R Hannon) *trckd ldrs: wknd ins fnl 2f* **7/1**[3]

0-10 **15** *3* **Expensive Detour (IRE)**[47] 4222 3-8-11 **78** DaneO'Neill 15 60
(Mrs L Stubbs) *chsd ldrs over 4f* **33/1**

0412 **16** *2 ½* **Hart Of Gold**[11] 5303 3-8-11 **78** (p) JohnEgan 9 53
(R A Harris) *chsd ldrs over 4f* **14/1**

1m 24.35s (-2.65) **Going Correction** -0.275s/f (Firm) **16** Ran SP% **133.2**
Speed ratings (Par 103): **104,102,100,99,98 98,98,96,96,95 94,94,93,93,89 87**
CSF £35.94 CT £399.87 TOTE £16.80: £3.10, £1.70, £4.00, £2.60; EX 55.30 Place 6 £57.86, Place 5 £38.90..
Owner Bernard Westley **Bred** Kidder, Cole & Griggs **Trained** Newmarket, Suffolk

FOCUS
Those drawn high held the call in this fair handicap. The form looks sound and the first two may do better.
T/Plt: £40.90 to a £1 stake. Pool: £91,642.30. 1,632.60 winning tickets. T/Qpdt: £15.50 to a £1 stake. Pool: £3,627.70. 172.40 winning tickets. ST

5595 NEWMARKET (ROWLEY) (R-H)

Saturday, September 22

OFFICIAL GOING: Good to firm (firm in places) changing to firm after race 2 (2.45)

The rescheduled 'Lester Piggott Day' which had been cancelled in the spring following the former champion jockey's health scare.

Wind: Light, across Weather: Cloudy with sunny spells

5636 VCBET.COM EUROPEAN ASSOCIATION OF RACING SCHOOLS CREPELLO APPRENTICE H'CAP 1m 2f

2:10 (2:10) (Class 5) (0-70,72) 3-Y-0+ **£6,477** (£1,927; £963; £481) **Stalls** Centre

Form RPR

3620 **1** **Candy Mountain**[29] 4766 3-9-11 **70** ConcettoSantangelo 3 76+
(L M Cumani) *chsd ldrs: led over 1f out: rdn out* **5/1**[3]

2145 **2** *hd* **Gallego**[2] 5563 5-9-7 **60** FLeroy 8 66
(R J Price) *s.s: hld up: racd keenly: hdwy over 3f out: ev ch whn rdr dropped whip over 1f out: r.o* **11/4**[2]

3213 **3** *1 ¼* **Kalasam**[3] 5539 3-9-13 **72** JamieHamblett 6 76
(W R Muir) *a.p: rdn over 1f out: styd on same pce* **9/4**[1]

1530 **4** *3 ½* **Recalcitrant**[12] 5280 4-9-4 **57** LisaKrullmann 1 54
(S Dow) *led: hdd over 7f out: led again over 2f out: rdn and hdd over 1f out: wknd ins fnl f* **11/1**

1100 **5** *nk* **Royal Indulgence**[11] 5307 7-9-10 **63** KTO'Neill 2 59
(W M Brisbourne) *hld up: plld hrd: rdn over 1f out: nvr trbld ldrs* **12/1**

050 **6** *1* **Siena Star (IRE)**[6] 5454 9-10-0 **67** CO'Farrell 7 61
(Stef Liddiard) *s.i.s: hld up: rdn over 2f out: n.d* **8/1**

5516 **7** *2* **Fantasy Crusader**[12] 5280 8-8-13 **52** FXWeissmeier 4 42
(R M H Cowell) *trckd ldrs: racd keenly: rdn and wknd over 1f out* **14/1**

040/ **8** *6* **New Wave**[100] 5537 5-9-9 **62** AndreaDeias 5 40
(R Lee) *hld up: rdn over 2f out: sn hung rt and wknd* **50/1**

50-0 **9** *5* **Only Hope**[109] 2335 3-9-0 **59** EBureller 9 27
(Miss Diana Weeden) *chsd ldr: led over 7f out: hdd over 2f out: sn wknd* **33/1**

2m 5.48s (-0.23) **Going Correction** -0.025s/f (Good)
WFA 3 from 4yo+ 6lb **9** Ran SP% **112.8**
Speed ratings (Par 103): **99,98,97,95,94 94,92,87,83**
CSF £18.62 CT £38.38 TOTE £4.50: £1.40, £1.70, £1.20; EX 18.70.
Owner Lady Carolyn Warren **Bred** Highclere Stud **Trained** Newmarket, Suffolk
■ A winner on his first ride in Britain for Italian apprentice Concetto Santangelo.

FOCUS
A race for apprentices from across Europe that sadly failed to attract as many runners as organisers hoped. The early pace was steady. Modest form, but the winner could have further improvement in her.
Only Hope Official explanation: trainer's rep said filly was found to be in season

5637 VC BET 08000 787878 SIR IVOR MAIDEN STKS 1m 4f

2:45 (2:47) (Class 5) 3-4-Y-0 **£4,533** (£1,348; £674; £336) **Stalls** Centre

Form RPR

5042 **1** **Vanquisher (IRE)**[17] 5137 3-9-3 71 (p) LiamJones 1 71+
(W J Haggas) *trckd ldrs: led over 3f out: drvn out* **11/4**[2]

5266 **2** *2 ½* **I Predict A Riot (IRE)**[24] 4951 3-9-0 70 (p) WilliamBuick[(3)] 2 67
(J W Hills) *lft in ld over 10f out: drvn along 1/2-way: hdd over 3f out: styd on same pce appr fnl f* **10/3**[3]

3 *18* **World Beat (GER)** 3-8-12 0 J-PGuillambert 7 33
(M Johnston) *chsd ldrs: rdn 1/2-way: wknd over 3f out* **6/1**

0 **4** *18* **Perfect Cause (USA)**[22] 5013 3-8-12 0 DavidKinsella 3 4
(J H M Gosden) *chsd ldrs: rdn over 4f out: wknd over 3f out* **9/4**[1]

5 *48* **Jollys Joy** 3-8-7 0 KevinGhunowa[(5)] 4 —
(K F Clutterbuck) *hld up: hmpd by loose rail over 10f out: lost tch fnl 7f* **66/1**

0034 **R** **Two Timer (IRE)**[42] 4403 3-9-3 80 AntonyProcter 5 —
(D R C Elsworth) *led: hung rt and rn out over 10f out* **11/2**

2m 31.28s (-2.22) **Going Correction** -0.025s/f (Good) **6** Ran SP% **111.7**
Speed ratings (Par 103): **106,104,92,80,48** —
CSF £12.16 TOTE £3.70: £2.00, £2.10; EX 10.90.
Owner Ian and Christine Beard **Bred** Ennistown Stud **Trained** Newmarket, Suffolk

FOCUS
A very modest maiden for the track and made less competitive by the early departure of Two Timer. The winner did not need to be at his best.

5638 VCBET.COM HUMBLE DUTY H'CAP 6f

3:20 (3:22) (Class 4) (0-85,88) 3-Y-0+ **£5,181** (£1,541; £770; £384) **Stalls** Centre

Form RPR

4010 **1** **Capricorn Run (USA)**[9] 5356 4-9-3 **82** (p) AdamKirby 9 96
(A J McCabe) *prom: rdn to chse ldr over 1f out: led ins fnl f: r.o* **16/1**

-112 **2** *2* **Tamagin (USA)**[9] 5356 4-9-4 **88** PatrickHills[(5)] 3 96
(K A Ryan) *led: clr 1/2-way: rdn over 1f out: hdd and unable qckn ins fnl f* **10/3**[1]

5021 **3** *1 ¼* **Barons Spy (IRE)**[16] 5168 6-8-7 **79** MCGeran[(7)] 5 83
(R J Price) *hld up: hdwy 2f out: sn rdn: r.o: nt rch ldrs* **5/1**[2]

0000 **4** *1* **Pretty Majestic (IRE)**[9] 5356 3-8-6 **80** MatthewDavies[(7)] 1 81
(M R Channon) *chsd ldr tl rdn over 1f out: styd on same pce* **14/1**

0200 **5** *nk* **Gallantry**[14] 5221 5-9-6 **85** OscarUrbina 11 85
(D Shaw) *s.i.s: hld up: hdwy over 1f out: nt rch ldrs* **13/2**

0226 **6** *2 ½* **Who's Winning (IRE)**[3] 5535 6-8-8 **80** ow1 KylieManser[(7)] 6 72
(B G Powell) *mid-div: hdwy 1/2-way: rdn 2f out: wknd fnl f* **10/1**

4151 **7** *¾* **Ellens Academy (IRE)**[9] 5356 12-8-13 **81** WilliamBuick[(3)] 12 70
(E J Alston) *hld up: rdn over 2f out: a in rr* **6/1**[3]

4020 **8** *¾* **Certain Justice (USA)**[26] 4884 9-8-6 **71** NickyMackay 7 58
(Stef Liddiard) *s.i.s: hld up: rdn over 2f out: a in rr* **8/1**

6-56 **9** *1 ¾* **Lipizza (IRE)**[20] 5064 4-8-7 **72** PatDobbs 8 53
(N A Callaghan) *hld up: rdn over 2f out: a in rr* **16/1**

0000 **10** *3* **My Gacho (IRE)**[15] 5209 5-9-0 **79** (b) J-PGuillambert 10 51
(T D Barron) *chsd ldrs 4f* **9/1**

1m 10.37s (-2.73) **Going Correction** -0.275s/f (Firm)
WFA 3 from 4yo+ 2lb **10** Ran SP% **116.0**
Speed ratings (Par 105): **107,104,102,101,100 97,96,95,93,89**
CSF £68.59 CT £320.96 TOTE £23.20: £4.40, £1.50, £2.20; EX 125.90.
Owner Paul J Dixon And Placida Racing **Bred** Santa Rosa Partners **Trained** Babworth, Notts

FOCUS
The going description was changed from good to firm to firm before this race. A decent handicap run at a strong gallop and very few got into contention. The form seems sound enough.
Certain Justice(USA) Official explanation: jockey said gelding was unsuited by the firm ground

5639 VICTOR CHANDLER NIJINSKY H'CAP 1m 2f

3:55 (3:55) (Class 2) (0-100,97) 3-Y-0 **£12,954** (£3,854; £1,926; £962) **Stalls** Centre

Form RPR

401 **1** **Teslin (IRE)**[28] 4799 3-9-4 **97** J-PGuillambert 8 109+
(B Ellison) *hld up: hdwy over 1f out: rdn to ld ins fnl f: r.o* **5/2**[1]

510 **2** *¾* **Urban Spirit**[51] 4092 3-8-7 **86** OscarUrbina 5 93
(B W Hills) *hld up: plld hrd: hdwy over 1f out: r.o: nt rch wnr* **13/2**[3]

0230 **3** *1* **Emerald Wilderness (IRE)**[7] 5419 3-8-13 **92** StephenDonohoe 3 97
(E A L Dunlop) *trckd ldrs: led over 1f out: sn rdn: hdd and unable qckn ins fnl f* **6/1**[2]

3161 **4** *½* **Viva La Flag (USA)**[15] 5210 3-8-4 **83** oh1 (t) NickyMackay 2 87
(J L Dunlop) *chsd ldrs: rdn and edgd rt over 1f out: styd on same pce* **13/2**[3]

4021 **5** *3 ½* **Warm Embraces (IRE)**[7] 5432 3-8-1 **83** WilliamBuick[(3)] 7 80
(D R C Elsworth) *chsd ldr: led over 2f out: rdn and hdd over 1f out: sn wknd* **6/1**[2]

0-61 **6** *4* **Nur Tau (IRE)**[22] 5014 3-8-7 **86** PatDobbs 4 75
(M P Tregoning) *led over 7f: sn rdn: wknd over 1f out* **5/2**[1]

2m 4.65s (-1.06) **Going Correction** -0.025s/f (Good) **6** Ran SP% **112.4**
Speed ratings (Par 107): **103,102,101,101,98 95**
CSF £19.32 CT £85.92 TOTE £2.60: £1.90, £3.00; EX 22.90 Trifecta £122.80 Pool: £225.00 - 1.30 winning tickets..
Owner Mr & Mrs D A Gamble **Bred** Saud Bin Saad **Trained** Norton, N Yorks

FOCUS
A decent handicap but the early pace was steady. Teslin is progressing and the form is rated through the third and fourth.

NOTEBOOK
Teslin(IRE) ◆, who was gelded after being bought out of Mark Johnston's yard for 65,000gns in the spring, has really found his form for new connections and followed up his recent Beverley win, where he beat Monte Alto, who scored at Newbury earlier in the afternoon. He beat no less than Aqaleem and Authorized at Newbury last season so has the potential to be a Pattern-race performer, but for now he will go for the Cambridgeshire back here in a fortnight, and the 4lb penalty he earned may not be enough to stop him. (op 2-1 tchd 15-8)
Urban Spirit, who was awash with sweat at the start, was keen under restraint but then ran on well at the finish to hunt up the winner. He has maintained a decent level of form this season and goes well here, so it would be no surprise if he returned before the season is out, and he looks to have a good handicap in him. (op 8-1)
Emerald Wilderness(IRE), another bringing solid form into this contest, had his chance but found the principals too strong on the climb to the line. He is pretty high in the handicap now, but is consistent and may well appreciate returning to a turning track. (op 13-2 tchd 8-1)
Viva La Flag(USA), who just got home over this trip at Newbury, had her chance again but the males ran her out of it up the hill. She may appreciate a return to a mile and easier ground. (op 5-1 tchd 6-1 and 11-2 in a place)
Warm Embraces(IRE), 4lb higher for his recent Warwick victory, as a result was meeting the winner on the same terms as at Beverley and finished further behind this time. However, he did take a keen hold and the winner looks to be on the upgrade. (op 7-1)
Nur Tau(IRE), who made all when winning at Sandown last time, adopted the same tactics but his limitations were exposed off an 8lb higher mark against better rivals. (op 7-2)

5640 VC BET 08000 787878 FAIRY FOOTSTEPS "PREMIER" CLAIMING STKS 1m 4f

4:30 (4:30) (Class 4) 3-5-Y-0 **£6,477** (£1,927; £963; £481) **Stalls** Centre

Form RPR

-010 **1** **Nobelix (IRE)**[42] 4375 5-9-1 87 WilliamBuick[(3)] 11 61+
(J R Fanshawe) *chsd ldrs: led over 1f out: shkn up and styd on wl* **8/11**[1]

6200 **2** *2* **Baizically (IRE)**[51] 4091 4-9-7 89 RobbieEgan[(7)] 1 68
(J A Osborne) *plld hrd: hdd over 3f out: rdn and ev ch over 1f out: styd on same pce* **8/1**

4614 **3** *nk* **Hot Diamond**[27] 4858 3-9-6 76 AntonyProcter 9 67
(D R C Elsworth) *s.i.s: hld up: hdwy over 4f out: led wl over 1f out: sn edgd rt and hdd: styd on same pce* **6/1**[3]

1006 **4** 3/4 **Lawyer To World**^{4} 5508 3-8-6 47 DMylonas 10 52
(Mrs C A Dunnett) *prom: lost pl over 4f out: hdwy over 2f out: styd on same pce fnl f* **50/1**
043 **5** 1 3/4 **Fantasy Ride**^{7} 5422 5-8-13 61 OscarUrbina 6 48
(J Pearce) *chsd ldr 5f: rdn over 2f out: no ex fnl f* **14/1**
0060 **6** 1 **Etoile D'Or (IRE)**^{26} 4894 3-7-12 54 NickyMackay 5 40
(M H Tompkins) *hld up in tch: plld hrd: trckd ldr 7f out: led over 3f out: rdn and hdd wl over 1f out: n.m.r sn after: wknd ins fnl f* **20/1**
0200 **7** shd **Art Investor**^{35} 4610 4-9-1 56 (b) StephenDonohoe 7 48
(D R C Elsworth) *hld up: rdn over 2f out: nt trble ldrs* **33/1**
0503 **8** 13 **Mardi**^{23} 4960 3-8-3 70 LiamJones 4 24
(W J Haggas) *trckd ldrs: plld hrd: rdn over 3f out: wknd over 2f out* **5/1**^{2}

2m 34.03s (0.53) **Going Correction** -0.025s/f (Good)
WFA 3 from 4yo+ 8lb **8** Ran SP% **116.3**
Speed ratings (Par 105): **97,95,95,94,93 93,93,84**
CSF £7.47 TOTE £1.70: £1.10, £2.20, £1.60; EX 9.00.The winner was claimed by A. B. Haynes for £30,000.
Owner Rupert Hambro **Bred** Horst Rapp And Dieter Burkle **Trained** Newmarket, Suffolk
■ Stewards' Enquiry : Robbie Egan caution: careless riding

FOCUS
A valuable claimer but a two-horse race judged on official ratings and they finished first and second, although the time was moderate, 2.75sec slower than the earlier maiden, and the proximity of the fourth raises doubts about the form.

5641 ANTEPOSTMAG.COM SHADEED H'CAP 1m
5:05 (5:05) (Class 3) (0-90,89) 3-Y-O+ **£7,772** (£2,312; £1,155; £577) **Stalls** Centre

Form RPR
0001 **1** **Persian Express (USA)**^{40} 4455 4-9-2 83 OscarUrbina 1 94
(B W Hills) *trckd ldrs: rdn to ld ins fnl f: r.o* **11/2**^{3}
0451 **2** 1 1/2 **South Cape**^{7} 5413 4-9-1 89 MatthewDavies(7) 3 97
(M R Channon) *led: rdn over 1f out: hdd and unable qckn ins fnl f* **5/1**^{2}
321 **3** nk **King's Event (USA)**^{33} 4666 3-8-12 86 WilliamBuick(3) 2 93
(Sir Michael Stoute) *hld up in tch: rdn over 2f out: hung lft over 1f out: styd on* **10/11**^{1}
1360 **4** 1/2 **Daaweitza**^{9} 5356 4-8-10 80 JerryO'Dwyer(3) 8 86
(B Ellison) *chsd ldr: rdn and ev ch over 1f out: no ex ins fnl f* **7/1**
5455 **5** 5 **Goodbye Mr Bond**^{25} 4922 7-9-6 87 StephenDonohoe 6 82
(E J Alston) *hld up: rdn over 1f out: sn outpcd* **7/1**
-050 **6** 38 **To The Max (IRE)**^{98} 2671 3-9-0 85 DMylonas 7 —
(Mrs C A Dunnett) *plld hrd and prom: lost pl over 5f out: wknd 3f out* **33/1**

1m 36.86s (-2.51) **Going Correction** -0.275s/f (Firm)
WFA 3 from 4yo+ 4lb **6** Ran SP% **112.4**
Speed ratings (Par 107): **101,99,99,98,93 55**
CSF £32.18 CT £45.93 TOTE £7.10: £2.80, £2.40; EX 22.10.
Owner D M James **Bred** Kingswood Farm **Trained** Lambourn, Berks

FOCUS
A good handicap run at an ordinary gallop with the first four coming clear. The winner is rated to his sand best but it remains to be seen how solid the form proves.

NOTEBOOK
Persian Express(USA) ◆, who tends to hit form in the late summer/early autumn, has done so again and followed up her recent Windsor win off a 3lb higher mark. She was well suited by the fast ground and scored in good fashion, suggesting a hat-trick is on the cards. She also has the option of swiching to Polytrack, having scored three times on that surface last autumn. (op 15-2)
South Cape made the running and, 4lb higher for his recent Goodwood success, lost little in defeat. However, he has yet to win over this trip and a return to his optimum distance of 7f looks sure to suit. (op 7-2)
King's Event(USA), a lightly-raced colt, got a good lead from the runner-up but did not looked entirely happy on the ground when asked to stretch and only ran on once meeting the rising ground. His win was on soft ground and a return to that sort of surface is likely to be in his favour, so he could be one to consider for a handicap at one of the several meetings here before the end of the season. (op 11-8, tchd 6-4 in a place)
Daaweitza had had a break since showing good form in the spring and on his second run back had trip and ground to suit. He ran reasonably well but seems best suited by a turning track and has the option of returning to the All-Weather. (tchd 8-1)
Goodbye Mr Bond probably needs an extra furlong or so these days and is still 2lb above his last winning mark. He was left behind up the hill on this occasion. (op 5-1)
To The Max(IRE) Official explanation: jockey said colt lost its action

5642 NGK SPARK PLUGS RODRIGO DE TRIANO H'CAP 5f
5:35 (5:35) (Class 5) (0-75,82) 3-Y-O+ **£3,886** (£1,156; £577; £288) **Stalls** Centre

Form RPR
3541 **1** **Malapropism**^{3} 5522 7-8-13 75 6ex (v) MatthewDavies(7) 4 89
(M R Channon) *led 3f: rdn to ld wl ins fnl f: r.o* **5/1**^{2}
0231 **2** 1/2 **Matsunosuke**^{8} 5381 5-9-10 82 LiamTreadwell(3) 12 94+
(A B Coogan) *hld up: hdwy over 1f out: r.o* **11/4**^{1}
0200 **3** nk **Brandywell Boy (IRE)**^{8} 5387 4-8-6 61 oh1 RichardThomas 3 72
(D J S Ffrench Davis) *mid-div: sn pushed along: hdwy and hung rt fr over 1f out: r.o* **16/1**
3300 **4** shd **Overwing (IRE)**^{8} 5387 4-8-7 62 OscarUrbina 7 73
(R M H Cowell) *chsd ldrs: rdn over 1f out: r.o* **25/1**
2401 **5** 1/2 **Ocean Blaze**^{7} 5418 3-9-2 72 BrettDoyle 8 81
(B R Millman) *chsd ldr: led 2f out: rdn and hdd wl ins fnl f* **12/1**
2632 **6** 1/2 **Pretty Miss**^{7} 5418 3-9-2 72 FergusSweeney 6 79
(H Candy) *mid-div: hdwy over 1f out: r.o* **15/2**
0030 **7** 1 1/2 **Azygous**^{16} 5160 4-8-8 63 NickyMackay 13 65
(J Akehurst) *mid-div: hdwy 2f out: sn rdn: no ex ins fnl f* **14/1**
2001 **8** 1/2 **Multahab**^{16} 5174 8-8-10 65 (t) AdamKirby 5 65
(M Wigham) *hld up in tch: rdn over 1f out: wknd ins fnl f* **20/1**
0015 **9** shd **Cornus**^{11} 5297 5-8-8 70 (be) RobbieEgan(7) 10 69
(A J McCabe) *s.i.s: outpcd: nvr nrr* **12/1**
0065 **10** 1 **Guildenstern (IRE)**^{14} 5234 5-8-10 65 ow2 StephenDonohoe 9 61
(P Howling) *hld up: rdn over 1f out: a in rr* **18/1**
0221 **11** 4 **Silver Prelude**^{2} 5565 6-8-3 63 PatrickHills(5) 2 44
(D K Ivory) *chsd ldrs over 3f* **13/2**^{3}
0320 **12** 1 3/4 **Rocker**^{11} 5312 3-9-1 71 (v) PatDobbs 1 46
(B R Johnson) *s.s: outpcd* **14/1**
1430 **13** 5 **Hereford Boy**^{20} 5066 3-8-11 70 JerryO'Dwyer(3) 11 27
(D K Ivory) *sn outpcd* **50/1**

58.35 secs (-2.12) **Going Correction** -0.275s/f (Firm)
WFA 3 from 4yo+ 1lb **13** Ran SP% **118.9**
Speed ratings (Par 103): **105,104,103,103,102 101,99,98,98,97 90,87,79**
CSF £18.49 CT £215.23 TOTE £6.20: £2.10, £1.80, £5.40; EX 17.40 Place 6 £46.08, Place 5 £38.17..
Owner Michael A Foy **Bred** Michael A Foy **Trained** West Ilsley, Berks

FOCUS
A fair sprint handicap run at a good gallop. Solid form, with a career best from the runner-up.
Hereford Boy Official explanation: jockey said gelding never travelled

T/Plt: £31.60 to a £1 stake. Pool: £63,292.75. 1,459.90 winning tickets. T/Qpdt: £10.70 to a £1 stake. Pool: £3,309.80. 227.50 winning tickets. CR

5601 WOLVERHAMPTON (A.W) (L-H)
Saturday, September 22

OFFICIAL GOING: Standard
Wind: Light, behind Weather: Fine

5643 WOLVERHAMPTON-RACECOURSE.CO.UK H'CAP 7f 32y(P)
7:00 (7:00) (Class 6) (0-65,65) 3-Y-O+ **£2,388** (£705; £352) **Stalls** High

Form RPR
1562 **1** **Excessive**^{17} 5136 3-9-3 64 TPQueally 2 72
(W Jarvis) *a.p: rdn and edgd rt over 1f out: sn led: drvn out* **10/3**^{1}
0350 **2** 1/2 **Green Pirate**^{4} 5503 5-9-0 58 (p) LiamJones 6 66
(W M Brisbourne) *s.i.s: hld up and bhd: hdwy 2f out: rdn and r.o ins fnl f* **11/2**
24-4 **3** 1/2 **Flaxby**^{26} 5-8-11 55 (b) VinceSlattery 10 62
(Mrs J L Le Brocq, Jersey) *s.i.s: hld up in rr: rdn and hdwy on ins over 2f out: ev ch 1f out: nt qckn* **33/1**
/3-5 **4** hd **Robinzal**^{26} 5-9-1 59 (t) MickyFenton 5 65
(Mrs J L Le Brocq, Jersey) *a.p: intimidated and carried rt over 1f out: rdn and kpt on same pce fnl f* **5/1**^{3}
6000 **5** 1 **Swiper Hill (IRE)**^{16} 5177 4-9-2 60 (t) SamHitchcott 1 63
(B Ellison) *wnt lft s: sn hld up in mid-div: rdn and hdwy whn edgd lft jst over 1f out: one pce ins fnl f* **13/2**
2653 **6** 3 1/2 **Scuba (IRE)**^{23} 4978 5-8-11 58 (b) TravisBlock(3) 11 52
(H Morrison) *hld up and bhd: rdn and c wd st: hung lft fr over 1f out: n.d* **4/1**^{2}
1340 **7** 1/2 **Benny The Bus**^{10} 5330 5-9-4 62 J-PGuillambert 3 55
(Mrs G S Rees) *led: rdn and hdd over 1f out: eased whn btn wl ins fnl f* **8/1**
004 **8** 5 **Karma Llama (IRE)**^{96} 2713 3-9-0 61 PaulEddery 12 39
(B Smart) *sn chsng ldrs: rdn and wknd over 2f out* **20/1**
350 **9** 1/2 **Loves Bidding**^{29} 4759 3-9-1 62 DavidKinsella 4 39
(R Ingram) *w ldrs tl rdn 2f out: sn wknd* **33/1**
200- **10** 5 **Surely Truly (IRE)**^{281} 6833 4-8-11 55 LPKeniry 8 19
(A E Jones) *a bhd* **100/1**
3165 **11** 14 **Matterofact (IRE)**^{84} 3086 4-9-2 65 HaddenFrost(5) 7 —
(M S Saunders) *a towards rr* **16/1**

1m 28.79s (-1.61) **Going Correction** -0.20s/f (Stan)
WFA 3 from 4yo+ 3lb **11** Ran SP% **117.1**
Speed ratings (Par 101): **101,100,99,99,98 94,93,88,87,81 65**
CSF £20.96 CT £525.00 TOTE £3.60: £2.20, £3.70, £8.50; EX 29.30.
Owner Mrs Susan Davis **Bred** John And Susan Davis **Trained** Newmarket, Suffolk

FOCUS
A modest handicap but the form looks sound rated through the runner-up.
Swiper Hill(IRE) Official explanation: jockey said gelding hung left
Loves Bidding Official explanation: jockey said gelding failed to handle the bend
Matterofact(IRE) Official explanation: jockey said filly failed to stay the trip

5644 HADLEY GROUP (S) STKS 7f 32y(P)
7:30 (7:30) (Class 6) 2-Y-O **£2,047** (£604; £302) **Stalls** High

Form RPR
6 **1** **Ten Spot (IRE)**^{45} 4265 2-8-7 0 ow1 (b^{1}) TPQueally 1 59+
(J A Osborne) *s.i.s: sn rcvrd: nt clr run on ins and dropped to rr bnd after 1f: rdn over 2f out: c wd st: edgd lft and hdwy over 1f out: str run to ld last strides* **5/1**^{2}
5060 **2** nk **Hurstpierpoint (IRE)**^{11} 5298 2-8-6 54 PaulDoe 12 54
(R A Fahey) *sn chsng ldrs: rdn 3f out: led wl ins fnl f: hdd last strides* **8/1**^{3}
354 **3** 1 **Prunes**^{5} 5477 2-8-6 0 J-PGuillambert 5 52
(Sir Mark Prescott) *led: rdn wl over 1f out: hdd wl ins fnl f: no ex* **11/8**^{1}
0 **4** 1 1/4 **Dusk Ballet**^{20} 5063 2-8-6 0 DavidKinsella 7 48
(S C Williams) *hld up: hdwy 3f out: rdn 2f out: one pce fnl f* **22/1**
5 1 1/4 **Brick (IRE)** 2-8-6 0 FrancisNorton 10 45
(J A Osborne) *hld up and bhd: hdwy over 2f out: rdn over 1f out: one pce fnl f* **11/1**
0000 **6** 1 3/4 **Carry On Cleo**^{22} 5015 2-8-7 53 ow1 (v^{1}) LPKeniry 11 42
(P D Evans) *bhd: rdn over 3f out: kpt on fnl f: n.d* **16/1**
1000 **7** 2 1/2 **Bonny's Babe**^{23} 4975 2-8-11 53 PaulEddery 8 40
(B Smart) *prom: rdn 2f out: wknd 1f out* **17/2**
2250 **8** 1 **Ten On Line (IRE)**^{11} 5302 2-8-11 53 TGMcLaughlin 4 37
(J G M O'Shea) *prom: lost pl over 5f out: rdn and bhd fnl 3f* **8/1**^{3}
500 **9** 1/2 **La Varrosa**^{58} 3866 2-8-6 55 ow3 TravisBlock(3) 9 34
(Mrs P N Dutfield) *hld up in mid-div: rdn over 2f out: sn wknd* **33/1**
006 **10** 1 1/4 **Liz Long**^{22} 5015 2-8-6 55 LiamJones 6 28
(P Howling) *prom tl rdn and wknd over 2f out* **16/1**
0 **11** 3 1/2 **Muga (SPA)**^{24} 4946 2-8-3 0 ow2 SCreighton(5) 3 21
(E J Creighton) *w ldr tl wknd over 3f out* **100/1**

1m 30.88s (0.48) **Going Correction** -0.20s/f (Stan) **11** Ran SP% **119.9**
Speed ratings (Par 93): **89,88,87,86,84 82,79,78,78,76 72**
CSF £45.03 TOTE £6.00: £1.80, £3.20, £1.10; EX 35.40.The winner was bought in for 8,500gns. Brick was claimed by Bellflower Racing Ltd for £6,000. Prunes was claimed by E. Nisbet for £6,000.
Owner Peter Bennett-Jones And Ten **Bred** Kilshannig Stud **Trained** Upper Lambourn, Berks

FOCUS
A poor seller with those with official ratings in the mid-50s. The form is weak with the runner-up the guide to the level.

NOTEBOOK
Ten Spot(IRE) was tried in blinkers and dropped in class after disappointing on her Brighton debut. She had to overcome plenty of adversity after again missing the break and she did well to come through to win given the way things worked out. (op 11-2 tchd 6-1)
Hurstpierpoint(IRE), down in grade for this switch to sand, could not withstand the winner's strong finish after striking the front late on. (op 7-1 tchd 9-1)
Prunes, trying her luck on sand, again had her limitations exposed in selling company. (op 15-8)
Dusk Ballet stepped up on his Folkestone debut at the beginning of the month with the help of a drop in class. (op 20-1)
Brick(IRE), a half-sister to a five-furlong juvenile scorer, was apparently a less-fancied stable companion of the winner. (op 9-1)

The Form Book, Raceform Ltd, Compton, RG20 6NL

Carry On Cleo got going too late in the first-time visor despite the extra furlong. (op 12-1)

5645 JOIN WBX.COM FOR FREE FOOTBALL SHIRT H'CAP 1m 141y(P)
7:55 (7:55) (Class 5) (0-70,68) 3-Y-0+ **£3,071** (£906; £453) **Stalls** Low

Form RPR
4510 **1** **Hits Only Cash**[14] 5237 5-9-4 **63**.............................. TPQueally 8 73
(J Pearce) *hld up in rr: hdwy wl over 1f out: rdn to ld ins fnl f: r.o wl* **7/1**
4560 **2** *1 ¾* **Cinematic (IRE)**[26] 4889 4-9-9 **68**.............................. AmirQuinn 5 74
(J R Boyle) *sn led: hdd over 6f out: rdn 2f out: kpt on one pce fnl f* **8/1**
2121 **3** *nk* **Wrighty Almighty (IRE)**[15] 5189 5-9-2 **61**.............................. PaulDoe 4 66
(P R Chamings) *dwlt: sn prom: led 3f out: rdn wl over 1f out: hdd ins fnl f: one pce* **7/2**[2]
130 **4** *1* **Encores**[67] 3622 3-8-9 **62**.............................. WilliamBuick(3) 2 65
(N A Callaghan) *hld up: hdwy over 2f out: swtchd rt ent st: rdn and one pce fnl f* **8/1**
0006 **5** *1* **Zabeel House**[18] 5118 4-9-3 **62**.............................. MickyFenton 6 63
(J A R Toller) *hld up and bhd: carried v wd ent st: rdn over 1f out: styd on towards fin* **12/1**
0121 **6** *1* **Bold Cross (IRE)**[7] 5433 4-9-4 **63**.............................. PaulFitzsimons 3 62
(E G Bevan) *hld up: hdwy over 3f out: rdn whn carried rt ent st: sn btn* **5/1**[3]
5050 **7** *6* **Tanforan**[16] 5177 5-8-7 **59**..............................(p) SoniaEaton(7) 7 45
(B P J Baugh) *plld hrd: led over 6f out to 3f out: rdn and wknd over 1f out* **16/1**
032 **8** *3* **Cape Velvet (IRE)**[9] 5367 3-9-2 **66**.............................. SebSanders 1 45
(J W Hills) *led early: hld up in tch: rdn 3f out: wknd 2f out* **11/4**[1]

1m 50.22s (-1.54) **Going Correction** -0.20s/f (Stan)
WFA 3 from 4yo+ 5lb **8** Ran SP% **113.9**
Speed ratings (Par 103): **98,96,96,95,94 93,88,85**
CSF £60.36 CT £230.37 TOTE £11.20: £2.50, £1.90, £1.50; EX 105.00.
Owner Clive Whiting **Bred** G S Shropshire **Trained** Newmarket, Suffolk
■ Stewards' Enquiry : William Buick caution: careless riding

FOCUS
A competitive little handicap but slightly messy and best rated through the fifth.

5646 EUROPEAN BREEDERS' FUND MAIDEN STKS 1m 141y(P)
8:25 (8:25) (Class 5) 2-Y-0 **£3,886** (£1,156; £577; £288) **Stalls** Low

Form RPR
03 **1** **Conduit (IRE)**[24] 4947 2-9-3 0.............................. JamieSpencer 1 83
(Sir Michael Stoute) *hld up: c wd st: rdn and hdwy whn hung lft over 1f out: led ins fnl f: r.o* **10/11**[1]
2 *¾* **Oberlin (USA)** 2-9-3 0.............................. J-PGuillambert 2 81
(M Johnston) *a.p: rdn over 2f out: ev ch whn edgd rt ins fnl f: nt qckn* **7/1**
33 **3** *1* **Tenjack King**[9] 5344 2-9-3 0.............................. TPQueally 5 79
(J A Osborne) *led: rdn over 2f out: hdd and edgd rt ins fnl f: no ex* **7/2**[2]
0 **4** *3 ½* **Lacala (IRE)**[33] 4656 2-8-12 0.............................. LiamJones 6 67
(Jane Chapple-Hyam) *prom: chsd ldr over 6f out tl rdn wl over 1f out: wknd fnl f* **100/1**
6242 **5** *¾* **Altitude**[19] 5100 2-8-12 **78**.............................. SebSanders 7 65
(Sir Mark Prescott) *hld up: hdwy over 5f out: rdn 3f out: wknd over 1f out* **4/1**[3]
6 *8* **Caltire (GER)** 2-9-0 0.............................. WilliamBuick(3) 3 54
(J A Osborne) *in rr: pushed along over 5f out: no ch fnl 2f* **33/1**

1m 49.6s (-2.16) **Going Correction** -0.20s/f (Stan) **6** Ran SP% **111.0**
Speed ratings (Par 95): **101,100,99,96,95 88**
CSF £7.99 TOTE £2.00: £1.30, £4.00; EX 11.30.
Owner Ballymacoll Stud **Bred** Ballymacoll Stud Farm Ltd **Trained** Newmarket, Suffolk

FOCUS
A fair maiden and decent form with the third to his pre-race mark.

NOTEBOOK
Conduit(IRE) had less to do than when third in quite a hot contest at Kempton and had matters under control after hanging left when asked for his effort. (op 5-4)
Oberlin(USA) ◆, a well-bred colt, made a highly satisfactory debut and normal improvement should soon see him go one better. (op 5-1)
Tenjack King adopted totally different tactics in this small field and was eventually found wanting. (tchd 3-1)
Lacala(IRE) ran a lot better than on her debut at Leicester and gave the impression she will be suited by a return to seven.
Altitude is proving expensive to follow and may have had more to do than when second over course and distance on her previous outing.

5647 WBX.COM £25 FREE BET FOR NEW ACCOUNTS H'CAP 1m 4f 50y(P)
8:55 (8:55) (Class 6) (0-60,62) 3-Y-0+ **£2,388** (£705; £352) **Stalls** Low

Form RPR
0331 **1** **Boz**[7] 5421 3-9-4 **60**.............................. JamieSpencer 7 70+
(L M Cumani) *chsd ldr: led 2f out: rdn and edgd rt over 1f out: r.o wl* **6/5**[1]
0000 **2** *1 ¼* **Heights Of Golan**[30] 4742 3-8-11 **53**.............................. LPKeniry 8 58+
(I A Wood) *hld up in tch: nt clr run briefly 2f out: rdn and swtchd lft over 1f out: r.o ins fnl f: nt trble wnr* **14/1**
346- **3** *¾* **Carr Hall (IRE)**[26] 4-9-11 **59**.............................. VinceSlattery 12 63
(Mrs J L Le Brocq, Jersey) *hld up towards rr: rdn and hdwy over 2f out: nt qckn ins fnl f* **25/1**
0163 **4** *1* **Regency Red (IRE)**[5] 5482 9-9-7 **55**.............................. SebSanders 1 57
(W M Brisbourne) *hld up in mid-div: hdwy on ins wl over 1f out: sn rdn: one pce fnl f* **5/1**[2]
0320 **5** *hd* **Hook Money (IRE)**[7] 5422 3-8-1 **50**..............................(b[1]) RobbieEgan(7) 4 52
(A J McCabe) *bhd: rdn over 5f out: hdwy on ins whn nt clr run wl over 1f out: styd on same pce ins fnl f* **14/1**
5623 **6** *½* **Ha'Penny Beacon**[9] 5364 4-10-0 **62**..............................(v) TPQueally 3 63
(D Carroll) *hld up towards rr: hdwy over 1f out: sn rdn: one pce fnl f* **7/1**
4000 **7** *4* **Croft (IRE)**[12] 5269 4-8-13 **47**.............................. TGMcLaughlin 11 42
(M S Saunders) *hld up and bhd: nvr nr ldrs* **80/1**
50-1 **8** *2* **Royal Melbourne (IRE)**[8] 5389 7-9-12 **60**.............................. SilvestreDeSousa 9 52
(A D Brown) *t.k.h: prom: rdn wl over 1f out: wknd fnl f* **11/2**[3]
5005 **9** *1 ½* **Kingsmead (USA)**[12] 5273 3-8-7 **49**..............................(vt) FrancisNorton 10 38
(Miss J Feilden) *hld up in mid-div: pushed along over 3f out: bhd fnl 2f* **28/1**
4-00 **10** *1 ¼* **Port Macquairie (IRE)**[13] 267 3-8-8 **50**..............................(p) MickyFenton 2 37
(J W Mullins) *led: rdn and hdd 2f out: wknd over 1f out* **80/1**
0536 **11** *9* **Silent Beauty (IRE)**[9] 5366 3-8-13 **55**.............................. J-PGuillambert 6 28
(S C Williams) *sn prom: rdn over 2f out: wknd wl over 1f out* **22/1**
000 **12** *¾* **Sierra Rose**[28] 4815 3-9-0 **59**.............................. WilliamBuick(3) 5 31
(P J McBride) *in rr: eased whn no ch wl over 1f out* **25/1**

2m 40.21s (-2.21) **Going Correction** -0.20s/f (Stan)
WFA 3 from 4yo+ 8lb **12** Ran SP% **121.3**
Speed ratings (Par 101): **99,98,97,97,96 96,93,92,91,90 84,84**
CSF £19.89 CT £301.42 TOTE £1.90: £1.20, £3.90, £4.50; EX 34.40.
Owner Aston House Stud **Bred** Aston House Stud **Trained** Newmarket, Suffolk

FOCUS
Not many could be seriously fancied in this basement-level handicap and not the most solid, although the winner could be a cut above these.
Silent Beauty(IRE) Official explanation: jockey said filly lost her action
Sierra Rose Official explanation: jockey said filly had no more to give

5648 WBX.COM 0% COMMISSION ON BIG RACES H'CAP 5f 216y(P)
9:20 (9:21) (Class 5) (0-75,75) 3-Y-0+ **£3,071** (£906; £453) **Stalls** Low

Form RPR
3303 **1** **Carcinetto (IRE)**[16] 5177 5-8-10 **65**.............................. TGMcLaughlin 12 76
(P D Evans) *hld up in mid-div: rdn and c wd st: str run to ld cl home* **20/1**
3505 **2** *1 ¼* **Dvinsky (USA)**[18] 5119 6-9-1 **70**.............................. IanMongan 8 77
(P Howling) *chsd ldrs: rdn to ld wl over 1f out: hdd cl home* **10/1**
6401 **3** *nk* **Minaash (USA)**[26] 4885 3-8-12 **74**.............................. KirstyMilczarek(5) 3 80
(D M Simcock) *hld up in mid-div: rdn and hdwy wl over 1f out: nt qckn ins fnl f* **7/1**[3]
0605 **4** *½* **Rainbow Bay**[8] 5381 4-8-6 **66**..............................(v) TolleyDean(5) 11 70
(P D Evans) *outpcd in rr: hdwy on ins over 1f out: r.o ins fnl f* **25/1**
4015 **5** *shd* **Desperate Dan**[12] 5272 6-9-0 **74**..............................(b) KevinGhunowa(5) 5 78
(A B Haynes) *led: edgd rt and hdd wl over 1f out: no ex towards fin* **14/1**
0664 **6** *nk* **Chatshow (USA)**[14] 5234 6-8-8 **63**.............................. FrancisNorton 1 66
(A W Carroll) *hld up and bhd: rdn and hdwy over 1f out: kpt on ins fnl f* **13/2**[2]
5000 **7** *hd* **Adantino**[14] 5223 8-8-12 **72**..............................(b) JamesMillman(5) 4 75
(B R Millman) *hld up towards rr: rdn over 1f out: kpt on ins fnl f* **11/1**
2103 **8** *1* **Methaaly (IRE)**[8] 5387 4-9-0 **69**.............................. LiamJones 9 68
(M Mullineaux) *chsd ldrs: rdn over 1f out: edgd lft ins fnl f: one pce* **9/2**[1]
100 **9** *hd* **Sweet Pickle**[20] 5064 6-8-11 **69**..............................(e) WilliamBuick(3) 7 68
(J R Boyle) *hld up towards rr: c v wd st: n.d* **16/1**
4323 **10** *1* **Tous Les Deux**[18] 5119 4-9-3 **72**.............................. LPKeniry 6 67
(Peter Grayson) *s.i.s: towards rr: rdn over 2f out: short-lived effrt over 1f out* **9/2**[1]
6341 **11** *1 ½* **Nusoor (IRE)**[14] 5234 4-8-12 **67**..............................(b) BrettDoyle 13 58
(Peter Grayson) *t.k.h: chsd ldrs: wnt 2nd over 3f out: wknd wl over 1f out* **12/1**
6003 **12** *2 ½* **Aye Aye Definitely (IRE)**[42] 4379 3-8-8 **65**.............................. TonyHamilton 10 48
(R A Fahey) *s.i.s: a in rr* **33/1**
0206 **13** *2 ½* **Namir (IRE)**[38] 4489 5-9-1 **75**..............................(vt) PatrickHills(5) 2 50
(D Shaw) *led to s: chsd ldrs: rdn over 2f out: eased whn btn ins fnl f* **9/1**

1m 14.05s (-1.76) **Going Correction** -0.20s/f (Stan)
WFA 3 from 4yo+ 2lb **13** Ran SP% **121.4**
Speed ratings (Par 103): **103,101,100,100,100 99,99,98,97,96 94,91,87**
CSF £207.12 CT £1612.53 TOTE £20.50: £6.50, £2.50, £3.20; EX 182.10 Place 6 £108.85, Place 5 £47.83.
Owner Mrs Sally Edwards **Bred** M A Doyle **Trained** Pandy, Monmouths

FOCUS
A strongly-run typically open sprint handicap run at a good pace and rated positively with some solid recent formlines and the third and fourth to recent form.
Minaash(USA) Official explanation: jockey said colt was outpaced early
T/Plt: £97.80 to a £1 stake. Pool: £88,372.70. 659.45 winning tickets. T/Qpdt: £70.00 to a £1 stake. Pool: £4,489.40. 47.45 winning tickets. KH

5649 - 5659a (Foreign Racing) - See Raceform Interactive

5465 LONGCHAMP (R-H)
Saturday, September 22

OFFICIAL GOING: Good to soft

5660a PRIX DES CHENES (GROUP 3) (C&G) 1m
2:50 (2:51) 2-Y-0 **£27,027** (£10,811; £8,108; £5,405; £2,703)

RPR
1 **Blue Chagall (FR)**[35] 4625 2-9-2 .... JVictoire 4 106+
(H-A Pantall, France) *racd in 2nd: chal over 1 1/2f out: led over 1f out: pushed clr fnl f: readily* **64/10**[3]
2 *2 ½* **Dubai Time**[14] 5217 2-9-2 .... SPasquier 6 101
(K A Ryan) *racd in 4th: prog appr st: 3rd st: drvn 1 1/2f out: styd on to take 2nd fnl f* **19/1**
3 *1* **Beret Rouge (IRE)**[19] 2-9-2 .... CSoumillon 2 98
(A Fabre, France) *racd freely early in 3rd: 4th st: rdn 1 1/2f out: styd on at one pce to take 3rd but nvr pce of ldrs* **1/2**[1]
4 *¾* **Salsalavie (FR)**[27] 4870 2-9-2 .... OPeslier 1 97
(P Demercastel, France) *hld up in last on ins: pushed along st: kpt on at one pce on outside fr over 1f out* **12/1**
5 *1* **Flying Blue (FR)**[34] 4653 2-9-2 .... IMendizabal 5 94
(R Martin-Sanchez, Spain) *racd in 5th: pushed along st: n.d* **24/1**
6 *½* **Yorktown (FR)**[25] 2-9-2 .... C-PLemaire 3 93
(J-C Rouget, France) *led: pressed over 1 1/2f out: hdd over 1f out: no ex* **41/10**[2]

1m 40.8s (-1.60) **Going Correction** -0.075s/f (Good) **6** Ran SP% **116.5**
Speed ratings: **105,102,101,100,99 99**
PARI-MUTUEL: WIN 7.40; PL 4.00, 8.20; SF 79.40.
Owner W-J Preston **Bred** Mme Antoinette Tamagni-Bodmer **Trained** France

NOTEBOOK
Blue Chagall(FR) is a most imposing individual and he was the pick of the paddock. He had a completely trouble-free run throughout and was settled in second place before taking control of the race halfway up the straight. He has considerable scope for improvement, but his handler feels he needs time to develop more physically so another run this season may not be on the cards. If he does reappear it will be in the Criterium de Saint-Cloud but the colt will not be risked on very soft ground. Certainly an individual worth keeping in the notebook.
Dubai Time lost nothing in defeat. He was never far from the leader and raced on the outside for much of the mile. He went in pursuit of the winner more than a furlong out and stayed on well to hold second place. A longer distance could be an advantage in the future and he will now be aimed at the Gran Criterium at San Siro next month.
Beret Rouge(IRE) can safely be described as a very disappointing favourite. He was raced close to the rail in fourth place for much of the time, but appeared completely outpaced in the straight before running on again inside the final furlong. Possibly this colt has been overrated, but certainly a longer trip could be an advantage in the future.

Salsalavie(FR), dropped out in the early stages, made some late progress up the centre of the track but never looked likely to make the first three. He is a consistent individual but probably only at Listed level.

5661a PRIX DU PRINCE D'ORANGE (GROUP 3) 1m 2f
3:20 (3:21) 3-Y-O **£27,027** (£10,811; £8,108; £5,405; £2,703)

RPR

1 **Literato (FR)**[35] 4627 3-9-2 .... C-PLemaire 6 117
(J-C Rouget, France) *hld up: 5th 1/2-way: 4th st: 3rd and gng easily 1 1/2f out: pushed along to ld 1f out: comf* **1/2**[1]

2 ¾ **Indian Choice (USA)**[24] 3-8-11 .... SPasquier 5 111
(P Bary, France) *racd in 3rd: pushed along and disputing ld st: drvn 2f out: led 1 1/2f out to 1f out: kpt on* **87/10**[3]

3 nk **Anabaa's Creation (IRE)**[104] 2501 3-8-8 .... CSoumillon 1 107
(A De Royer-Dupre, France) *racd in 2nd: dropped to 5th but in tch st: shkn up 2f out: rdn and styd on 1 1/2f out: wnt 3rd 100yds out* **41/10**[2]

4 2 **All Is Vanity (FR)**[55] 4010 3-8-12 .... FBlondel 7 107
(W J S Cargeeg, France) *led: jnd st: pushed along 2f out: hdd 1 1/2f out: no ex fnl f* **19/1**

5 3 **Not Just Swing (IRE)**[28] 4839 3-8-11 .... JVictoire 3 100
(A Fabre, France) *4th 1/2-way: 3rd st: drvn on outside over 1 1/2f out: outpcd* **13/1**

6 8 **Selinka**[28] 4805 3-8-8 .... TThulliez 2 81
(R Hannon) *sn in last: u.p 3 1/2f out: btn st* **12/1**

2m 7.30s (-0.70) **Going Correction** -0.075s/f (Good) 6 Ran SP% **116.4**
Speed ratings: **99,98,98,96,94 87**
PARI-MUTUEL: WIN 1.50; PL 1.20, 2.30; SF 6.00.
Owner H Morin **Bred** Bsh Of Administrativa **Trained** Pau, France

NOTEBOOK
Literato(FR) outclassed his rivals in this Group 3 event, but did give his connections slight cause for concern inside the final furlong when he began to idle in front. Although waited with, he was in fourth position for most of the 1m2f before being extracted to challenge halfway up the straight. He has never been out of the first two in ten races and will now go on to the Emirates Airlines Champion Stakes.
Indian Choice(USA), dropped in behind the leaders, this gelding ran a very sound race considering he was tackling a Group event for the first time. He was moved up to second place at the entrance to the straight and held the advantage for a short time before the final furlong. He then stayed on bravely and made the winner pull out all the stops in the last 50 yards. He was fitted with cheekpieces and should be capable of winning a race in this class later in his career.
Anabaa's Creation(IRE), who had been off track for three months, put up a fine performance. She was mid-division early on, before staying on strongly up the centre of the track. The filly is said to prefer a flat track so Longchamp would not be ideal for her to show her best. She is now an intended runner in the E. P. Taylor Stakes at Woodbine next month.
All Is Vanity(FR) was soon at the head of affairs and took the field along at a sensible gallop. She gave up her lead before the final furlong and then stayed on one paced, but this was a much better performance than she put up at Deauville and the filly will definitely be running over a shorter trip next time out.
Selinka was last throughout before finishing a detached. This was a most disappointing effort and she will now be put away for the season before a decision about her future racing career is made.

5081 HAMILTON (R-H)
Sunday, September 23
OFFICIAL GOING: Good (good to soft in places; 7.8)
Wind: Breezy, across Weather: Overcast

5662 TOTEPLACEPOT H'CAP 6f 5y
2:10 (2:14) (Class 5) (0-75,74) 3-Y-O **£4,533** (£1,348; £674; £336) **Stalls** Centre

Form RPR

0240 1 **Feelin Foxy**[18] 5139 3-8-10 **66** .... TPQueally 12 73
(J G Given) *t.k.h: sn cl up: led over 1f out: drvn out* **25/1**

1505 2 ¾ **Poppy's Rose**[3] 5556 3-8-8 **64** .... RoystonFfrench 5 69
(I W McInnes) *prom: effrt over 1f out: chsd wnr ins fnl f: r.o* **10/1**

6241 3 nk **Distant Sun (USA)**[32] 4714 3-9-4 **74** .... TomEaves 6 78
(I Semple) *hld up: hdwy over 1f out: kpt on fnl f: nrst fin* **8/1**

504 4 nk **Farefield Lodge (IRE)**[37] 4574 3-9-0 **70** .... PhilipRobinson 13 73
(C G Cox) *disp ld to over 1f out: kpt on same pce ins fnl f* **7/2**[1]

3214 5 1 **Rainbow Fox**[6] 5473 3-9-1 **71** .... PaulHanagan 11 71
(R A Fahey) *hld up: rdn over 2f out: hdwy over 1f out: nrst fin* **9/2**[2]

1-33 6 ½ **Bussel (USA)**[30] 4778 3-9-0 **70** .... PaulMulrennan 7 69
(W J Haggas) *bhd tl hdwy over 1f out: kpt on fnl f: no imp* **13/2**[3]

132 7 nk **Cha Cha Cha**[129] 1786 3-9-3 **73** .... DO'Donohoe 8 71
(K A Ryan) *unruly bef s: prom: effrt over 2f out: one pce appr fnl f* **9/1**

0100 8 hd **Equuleus Pictor**[37] 4574 3-8-12 **68** .... FrancisNorton 4 65
(J L Spearing) *trckd ldrs: effrt over 1f out: no ex fnl f* **33/1**

6550 9 hd **Triple Shadow**[6] 5489 3-8-4 **60** .... JimmyQuinn 2 57
(T D Barron) *prom: rdn over 2f out: one pce fnl f* **12/1**

3412 10 2 **Mandurah (IRE)**[27] 4896 3-9-2 **72** .... AdrianTNicholls 3 63
(D Nicholls) *t.k.h: slt ld to over 1f out: sn btn* **8/1**

0-00 11 shd **Kerry's Dream**[32] 4703 3-9-4 **74** .... DavidAllan 10 64
(T D Easterby) *bhd: drvn 1/2-way: n.d* **33/1**

5500 12 4 **Prospect Place**[25] 4934 3-8-9 **65** .... DaleGibson 1 43
(M Dods) *dwlt: a bhd* **16/1**

0-00 13 13 **Lafontaine Bleu**[152] 1219 3-8-4 **60** .... PaulFessey 9 —
(I Semple) *bhd and sn outpcd: nvr on terms* **66/1**

1m 12.4s (-0.70) **Going Correction** -0.125s/f (Firm) 13 Ran SP% **119.8**
Speed ratings (Par 101): **99,98,97,97,95 95,94,94,94,91 91,86,68**
CSF £252.50 CT £2273.10 TOTE £32.50: £8.00, £3.30, £2.90; EX 360.10.
Owner Danethorpe Racing Partnership **Bred** Bearstone Stud **Trained** Willoughton, Lincs

FOCUS
An ordinary handicap in which the field raced in the centre. The pace was sound. Not strong form, with the winner more exposed than most.
Mandurah(IRE) Official explanation: jockey said gelding hung left-handed final 2f
Lafontaine Bleu Official explanation: jockey said filly hung right-handed throughout

5663 ALWAYS TRYING EBF MAIDEN STKS 1m 65y
2:40 (2:42) (Class 5) 2-Y-O **£3,886** (£1,156; £577; £288) **Stalls** High

Form RPR

4 1 **Love Galore (IRE)**[16] 5206 2-9-3 0 .... GregFairley 3 85+
(M Johnston) *mde all: shkn up over 2f out: r.o strly* **4/7**[1]

52 2 6 **The Riddler (IRE)**[28] 4841 2-9-3 0 .... TPQueally 2 72
(J A Osborne) *chsd wnr: effrt over 2f out: wandered u.p and sn no imp* **15/8**[2]

5 3 8 **World Tour**[39] 4495 2-9-3 0 .... TomEaves 1 54
(I Semple) *unruly bef s: hld up: drvn and outpcd 1/2-way: no imp fnl 3f* **14/1**[3]

0 4 2½ **Social Spirit (IRE)**[37] 4578 2-8-12 0 .... JimmyQuinn 4 44
(J R Weymes) *in tch to 1/2-way: sn outpcd: n.d after* **50/1**

60 5 hd **Next Of Kin (IRE)**[36] 4611 2-9-0 0 .... PJMcDonald(3) 5 48
(G A Swinbank) *in tch to 1/2-way: sn rdn and no imp* **25/1**

1m 47.74s (-1.56) **Going Correction** -0.125s/f (Firm) 5 Ran SP% **110.9**
Speed ratings (Par 95): **102,96,88,85,85**
CSF £1.89 TOTE £1.40: £1.02, £1.50; EX 2.20.
Owner Crone Stud Farms Ltd **Bred** Razza Pallorsi **Trained** Middleham Moor, N Yorks

FOCUS
An uncompetitive event but a fair performance from Love Galore, who is the sort to win more races for his current stable.
NOTEBOOK
Love Galore(IRE) ◆, who shaped well in a much stronger maiden than this on his debut, fully confirmed that promise to pull clear of his only serious rival in the closing stages. Stamina looks his strong suit and he appeals as the type to hold his own in stronger company. (tchd 4-6 and 8-11 in places)
The Riddler(IRE), edgy and sweating in the paddock, again failed to run in a straight line once pressure was applied but he was beaten with no excuses against a potentially fair sort. He is capable of winning an uncompetitive race in this grade, though. (op 7-4 tchd 13-8 and 2-1 in places)
World Tour, who had two handlers in the paddock, was reluctant to enter the stalls but, although not totally disgraced in the face of a stiff task, may do better once handicapped. (op 18-1 tchd 20-1)
Social Spirit(IRE) faced a stiff task on these terms and was soundly beaten. Her future lies in low-grade handicaps in due course.
Next Of Kin(IRE) again had his limitations exposed in this type of event but he is in very good hands and may progress in ordinary handicap company in due course. (op 28-1)

5664 TOTEQUADPOT "PREMIER" CLAIMING STKS 1m 1f 36y
3:10 (3:10) (Class 4) 3-5-Y-O **£5,181** (£1,541; £770; £384) **Stalls** High

Form RPR

2111 1 **Ella Woodcock (IRE)**[5] 5508 3-9-1 77 .... TPQueally 2 75
(J A Osborne) *hld up in tch: stdy hdwy over 3f out: effrt over 1f out: edgd rt and led wl ins fnl f: r.o* **9/4**[1]

4021 2 ¾ **New World Order (IRE)**[9] 5390 3-9-1 77 ....(t) AndrewElliott(3) 6 76
(K R Burke) *cl up: chal after 4f: led over 2f out to wl ins fnl f: kpt on* **5/1**

3666 3 1¾ **Pianoforte (USA)**[4] 5539 5-9-3 60 .... DavidAllan 1 66
(E J Alston) *bhd: rdn over 4f out: edgd lft and styd on wl fr over 1f out: nt rch first two* **20/1**

0246 4 1½ **Shy Glance (USA)**[25] 4932 5-9-1 69 .... DaleGibson 7 61
(P Monteith) *hld up in tch: outpcd over 3f out: rallied over 1f out: no imp* **10/1**

6304 5 ¾ **Torrens (IRE)**[18] 5145 5-9-2 78 .... PaulHanagan 5 60
(R A Fahey) *t.k.h: trckd ldrs: effrt over 2f out: one pce over 1f out* **5/2**[2]

-005 6 shd **Kingsholm**[16] 5203 5-9-3 80 .... FrancisNorton 3 61
(A M Balding) *t.k.h: led to over 2f out: btn fnl f* **9/2**[3]

5500 7 77 **Kames Park (IRE)**[27] 4893 5-9-6 80 .... PJMcDonald(3) 4 —
(Mrs H O Graham) *sn chsng ldrs: drvn and wknd over 3f out: virtually p.u* **25/1**

1m 58.34s (-1.32) **Going Correction** -0.125s/f (Firm)
WFA 3 from 5yo 5lb 7 Ran SP% **111.9**
Speed ratings (Par 105): **100,99,97,96,95 95,27**
CSF £13.30 TOTE £2.40: £1.70, £2.80; EX 7.70.The winner was claimed by E. J. Alston for £29,000.
Owner Cavendish Star Racing **Bred** Pippa Hackett **Trained** Upper Lambourn, Berks

FOCUS
A fair event of its type and one in which the pace was sound. The third limits the form and the winner did not need to improve.

5665 TOTESPORT.COM NURSERY 6f 5y
3:40 (3:40) (Class 3) (0-95,91) 2-Y-O **£7,772** (£2,312; £1,155; £577) **Stalls** Centre

Form RPR

0242 1 **Nezami (IRE)**[13] 5274 2-8-11 **81** .... RobertHavlin 6 86
(B J Meehan) *t.k.h: chsd ldrs: rdn to ld appr fnl f: edgd lft ins fnl f: r.o* **9/4**[1]

2120 2 1 **Lady Benjamin**[44] 4364 2-8-0 **73** .... AndrewElliott(3) 5 75
(P C Haslam) *led to appr fnl f: rallied: kpt on ins fnl f* **9/2**[3]

1100 3 2 **Burnwynd Boy**[43] 4372 2-9-7 **91** .... TomEaves 7 87
(I Semple) *cl up: effrt and ev ch over 1f out: one pce ins fnl f* **4/1**[2]

0406 4 1¾ **Bahama Baileys**[14] 5251 2-8-5 **75** .... RoystonFfrench 4 66
(M Johnston) *cl up tl rdn and no ex over 1f out* **7/1**

1334 5 1¼ **Ginger Pickle**[2] 5582 2-8-7 **77** .... JimmyQuinn 1 64
(J R Weymes) *bhd and sn pushed along: effrt 2f out: sn no imp* **11/2**

41 6 3 **Whiteoak Lady (IRE)**[58] 3902 2-8-8 **78** .... FrancisNorton 2 56
(J L Spearing) *dwlt: sn chsng ldrs: rdn and wknd over 1f out* **10/1**

0306 7 1¼ **She's Our Dream**[6] 5484 2-7-12 **68** oh4 .... PaulHanagan 8 42
(R C Guest) *hld up: effrt over 2f out: btn over 1f out* **22/1**

030 8 11 **Honey Monster (IRE)**[11] 5324 2-8-12 **82** .... TPQueally 3 23
(Miss V Haigh) *prom: outpcd after 2f: sn struggling* **18/1**

1m 12.34s (-0.76) **Going Correction** -0.125s/f (Firm) 8 Ran SP% **115.5**
Speed ratings (Par 99): **100,98,96,93,92 88,86,71**
CSF £12.67 CT £37.79 TOTE £2.90: £1.50, £1.70, £1.30; EX 15.50.
Owner Ed McCormack **Bred** Falah Ithnein **Trained** Manton, Wilts

FOCUS
A fair event which was run at a decent gallop. The field again raced in the centre. Sound form.
NOTEBOOK
Nezami(IRE), dropped in trip for this first venture into nursery company, failed to settle but showed a good attitude in the closing stages to get off the mark. He should not be going up too much for this workmanlike success and may well be capable of a bit better. (tchd 5-2, 11-4 in places)
Lady Benjamin, who did not get home over 7f on her previous start, ran right up to her best back at this course and back over this trip. She is a good guide to the worth of this form and she should continue to give a good account. (op 6-1)
Burnwynd Boy, dropped in trip, ran his best race since scoring at Pontefract in May but his current mark of 91 means he is likely to remain vulnerable to the more progressive sorts in this type of event. (tchd 9-2)
Bahama Baileys, returned to sprinting, was not disgraced but again had his limitations exposed in nursery company and he is going to have to improve if he is to win races in this sphere from his mark in the mid-70s. (op 8-1)
Ginger Pickle, turned out quickly after a fair run against a couple of progressive types at Ayr, was far from disgraced and left the impression that the return to 7f would be in his favour. (op 7-1)
Whiteoak Lady(IRE), edgy in the preliminaries, was easy to back and failed to build on her maiden success from a stiff looking mark on this nursery debut on this first run after a short break. She will have to show more before she is worth a bet. (op 8-1)

Honey Monster(IRE) Official explanation: jockey said colt was unsuited by the good (good to soft places) ground

5666 EUROPEAN BREEDERS' FUND FLOWER OF SCOTLAND STKS (LISTED RACE) (F&M) 5f 4y

4:10 (4:11) (Class 1) 3-Y-0+

£17,034 (£6,456; £3,231; £1,611; £807; £405) **Stalls** Centre

Form RPR

0441 **1** **Loch Verdi**[13] 5278 4-8-13 83 .... FrancisNorton 1 95
(A M Balding) *mde all stands' rail: rdn and kpt on strly fnl f* **6/1**

1606 **2** *1* **Pivotal's Princess (IRE)**[11] 5325 5-8-13 100 .... GregFairley 2 92
(E S McMahon) *prom: effrt over 1f out: sn chsng wnr: kpt on fnl f* **11/2**[3]

0-30 **3** *¾* **Blue Rocket (IRE)**[140] 1496 3-8-12 95 .... JohnEgan 5 89
(D J Murphy) *towards rr: hdwy over 1f out: kpt on ins fnl f* **12/1**

-033 **4** *shd* **Riotous Applause**[12] 5305 4-8-13 92 .... JimmyQuinn 7 89
(J R Fanshawe) *t.k.h in tch: effrt and swtchd rt over 1f out: kpt on u.p fnl f* **7/2**[1]

1112 **5** *¾* **Day By Day**[10] 5358 3-8-12 75 .... (b) RobertHavlin 9 86
(B J Meehan) *prom: rdn over 2f out: one pce over 1f out* **22/1**

2066 **6** *½* **Katie Boo (IRE)**[8] 5403 5-8-13 71 .... TomEaves 6 84
(A Berry) *prom: outpcd after 2f: rallied fnl f: no imp* **66/1**

2166 **7** *nk* **Final Dynasty**[35] 4639 3-8-12 97 .... PaulHanagan 8 83
(Mrs G S Rees) *prom: drvn 1/2-way: one pce over 1f out* **6/1**

2215 **8** *½* **Shes Minnie**[17] 5168 4-8-13 84 .... FergusSweeney 12 81
(J G M O'Shea) *bhd: shortlived effrt 2f out: sn no imp* **33/1**

0010 **9** *½* **Cashel Mead**[69] 3586 7-8-13 87 .... AdrianTNicholls 11 79
(J L Spearing) *bhd tl hdwy over 1f out: nvr rchd ldrs* **25/1**

3502 **10** *2½* **Mimi Mouse**[11] 5332 5-8-13 79 .... DavidAllan 4 70
(T D Easterby) *chsd ldrs tl rdn and wknd over 1f out* **66/1**

0451 **11** *¾* **Blue Echo**[8] 5403 3-9-2 92 .... PhilipRobinson 10 72
(M A Jarvis) *cl up tl edgd rt and wknd over 1f out* **4/1**[2]

2240 **12** *7* **Morinqua (IRE)**[11] 5325 3-8-12 95 .... TPQueally 3 42
(J G Given) *cl up tl wknd qckly wl over 1f out* **7/1**

59.32 secs (-1.88) **Going Correction** -0.125s/f (Firm)
WFA 3 from 4yo+ 1lb **12** Ran SP% **120.5**
Speed ratings (Par 111): **110,108,107,107,105 105,104,103,102,98 97,86**
CSF £37.88 TOTE £6.80: £2.10, £2.60, £4.80; EX 46.10.

Owner J C Smith **Bred** Littleton Stud **Trained** Kingsclere, Hants

FOCUS

A fair event of its type but an improved effort from Loch Verdi, who raced on the stands rail just away from the remainder of the field, who congregated in the centre. The sixth does hold down the form.

NOTEBOOK

Loch Verdi, edgy in the preliminaries, is an improved performer of late who turned in a career best effort to notch her second win over course and distance and her first in Listed company. She may well have been helped by racing closest to the stands' rail but she is getting better as she matures and may well be capable of better. (op 7-1)

Pivotal's Princess(IRE), on an easy surface for the first time this year, ran her best race since winning at Beverley in May. She is a strong-travelling sort who may well be capable of picking up a similar event before the season is out. (tchd 13-2)

Blue Rocket(IRE), soundly beaten upped to 1m in the 1000 Guineas, ran creditably dropped sharply in distance on this first run since. The return to 6f will be to her liking and she is worth another chance in similar company. (op 14-1)

Riotous Applause, who very much took the eye in the preliminaries, is a relatively lightly raced sort who turned in another creditable display and she left the strong impression that the return to 6f would be in her favour. (tchd 10-3)

Day By Day has progressed nicely in handicaps since the blinkers have been fitted and she ran a fine race in defeat in the face of a stiff task. This will not have done her handicap mark much good but she should continue to give a good account. (op 25-1 tchd 20-1)

Katie Boo(IRE) ran another solid race in the face of a stiff task and she has been a model of consistency this year. She will be much more at home returned to handicap company but is likely to find things tougher after reassessment. (tchd 50-1)

Blue Echo, who returned to winning ways on quick ground at Hamilton, looked to have plenty in her favour regarding trip and ground but she proved a disappointment for no apparent reason after enjoying the run of the race. Official explanation: jockey said race may have come too soon for filly, having raced eight-days earlier (op 7-2)

5667 TOTESPORT 0800 221 221 H'CAP 5f 4y

4:40 (4:41) (Class 4) (0-80,85) 3-Y-0+ **£6,477** (£1,927; £963; £481) **Stalls** Centre

Form RPR

2322 **1** **Joyeaux**[23] 4999 5-8-0 **61** .... DuranFentiman(3) 3 73
(J Hetherton) *trckd ldrs: led over 1f out: rdn and r.o wl* **7/2**[2]

2501 **2** *¾* **Bo McGinty (IRE)**[11] 5332 6-9-9 **81** .... (b) PaulHanagan 10 90
(R A Fahey) *cl up: rdn 2f out: kpt on ins fnl f* **5/1**[3]

6204 **3** *hd* **Elkhorn**[11] 5332 5-9-7 **79** .... (b) TomEaves 2 87
(Miss J A Camacho) *trckd ldrs: effrt over 1f out: kpt on u.p fnl f* **3/1**[1]

3-05 **4** *1¾* **Argentine (IRE)**[11] 5332 3-9-4 **77** .... GregFairley 7 79
(L Lungo) *wnt lft s: in tch: effrt over 1f out: kpt on same pce fnl f* **7/1**

0020 **5** *¾* **Jadan (IRE)**[3] 5552 6-8-3 **61** oh13 .... JimmyQuinn 11 60
(E J Alston) *t.k.h: in tch: rdn 2f out: one pce appr fnl f* **11/1**

300 **6** *nk* **Ashes (IRE)**[3] 5552 5-8-0 **61** oh2 .... AndrewElliott(3) 1 59
(K R Burke) *led to over 1f out: nt qckn* **15/2**

0041 **7** *2* **Circuit Dancer (IRE)**[8] 5401 7-9-3 **75** .... AdrianTNicholls 6 66
(D Nicholls) *hmpd s: hld up: rdn and edgd rt 2f out: sn n.d* **5/1**[3]

0606 **8** *3* **Vondova**[6] 5481 5-8-9 **70** oh16 ow9 .... (p) PJMcDonald(3) 4 50
(D A Nolan) *hmpd s: bhd: rdn and struggling 1/2-way: nvr on terms* **66/1**

0050 **9** *½* **Mutayam**[6] 5481 7-8-3 **61** oh16 .... (t) PaulFessey 12 39
(D A Nolan) *hld up on wd outside: rdn over 2f out: btn over 1f out* **100/1**

59.74 secs (-1.46) **Going Correction** -0.125s/f (Firm)
WFA 3 from 5yo+ 1lb **9** Ran SP% **115.6**
Speed ratings (Par 105): **106,104,104,101,100 100,96,92,91**
CSF £21.47 CT £58.17 TOTE £5.30: £1.50, £1.70, £1.80; EX 18.90 Place 6 £70.84, Place 5 £8.17..

Owner PSB Holdings Ltd **Bred** Mrs Ann Jarvis **Trained** Norton, N Yorks

FOCUS

A run-of-the-mill sprint in which the pace was sound throughout. The winner is rated to his best form of the past year or so, but the proximity of the fifth is a slight concern.

Circuit Dancer(IRE) Official explanation: jockey said gelding suffered interference on leaving stalls

T/Plt: £66.50 to a £1 stake. Pool: £70,576.60. 774.05 winning tickets. T/Qpdt: £12.60 to a £1 stake. Pool: £3,898.70. 227.45 winning tickets. RY

5668 - (Foreign Racing) - See Raceform Interactive

4442 COLOGNE (R-H)

Sunday, September 23

OFFICIAL GOING: Good

5669a IVG - EUROSELECT-PREIS (LISTED RACE) (F&M) 1m 4f

2:05 (2:08) 3-Y-0+ **£8,784** (£2,703; £1,351; £676)

RPR

1 **Souvenance**[29] 4803 4-9-5 .... THellier 3 97
(Sir Mark Prescott) *mde virtually all: rn wd first turn: 5 l clr 3f out: 3 l clr 1f out: rdn out* **48/10**[3]

2 *¾* **Rinconada (GER)**[483] 6-9-5 .... ABoschert 10 96
(Dr A Bolte, Germany) **16/1**

3 *¾* **Lemonette (USA)**[27] 4909 4-9-5 .... RyanMoore 9 94
(J W Hills) *hld up: 9th st: hdwy 2f out: styd on u.p: nrest at fin* **53/10**

4 *hd* **Guardia (GER)**[21] 3-8-9 .... SPasquier 6 92
(J Hirschberger, Germany) **39/10**[2]

5 *1¼* **Avanti Polonia (GER)**[35] 4651 3-8-9 .... AStarke 2 90
(P Schiergen, Germany) **9/5**[1]

6 *½* **Rhapsody In Blue (GER)**[78] 4-9-5 .... PHeugl 7 91
(D K Richardson, Germany) **58/1**

7 *5* **Wutzeline (GER)**[21] 3-8-10 ow1 .... ADeVries 4 82
(A Trybuhl, Germany) **117/10**

8 *4* **La Grande Dame (GER)**[25] 4957 5-9-5 .... EPedroza 5 77
(A Wohler, Germany) **31/1**

9 *4½* **Nebiola (GER)**[70] 3-8-9 .... (b) ASuborics 1 68
(W Hickst, Germany) **116/10**

10 *3* **Nouvelle Europe (GER)**[21] 3-8-9 .... ABest 8 63
(P Rau, Germany) **37/1**

11 *18* **Gaggia (GER)**[98] 3-8-9 .... TMundry 12 34
(P Rau, Germany) **74/10**

2m 29.27s (-3.63)
WFA 3 from 4yo+ 8lb **11** Ran SP% **130.3**
(including ten euro stakes): WIN 58; PL 26, 38, 22; SF 1683.

Owner Miss K Rausing **Bred** Miss K Rausing **Trained** Newmarket, Suffolk

NOTEBOOK

Souvenance, who was unsuited by the tactical nature of the race at Goodwood, was sent out in front and made almost all the running. She got tired towards the finish and the pack closed in, but she had enough in hand at the line to hold on. It is likely that she will go to the paddocks now.

Lemonette(USA), who won a handicap off 80 last time out, was staying on well at the death but could not quite reel in the front-running leader. She is worth persevering with in similar races on the continent.

5670a CHRISTLACKE EUROPA MEILE (GROUP 2) 1m

3:40 (3:47) 3-Y-0+ **£27,027** (£10,135; £4,054; £2,703)

RPR

1 **Konig Turf (GER)**[26] 4929 5-9-1 .... TMundry 6 106
(C Sprengel, Germany) *hld up: last but wl in tch st: swtchd outside: hdwy fr 2f out: rdn fnl f: r.o to ld last strides* **33/10**[2]

2 *shd* **Apollo Star (GER)**[49] 4217 5-9-4 .... AHelfenbein 1 109
(Mario Hofer, Germany) *led tl ct last strides* **9/10**[1]

3 *nse* **Santiago (GER)**[23] 5-9-1 .... ASuborics 3 106
(H Blume, Germany) *racd in 5th to st: swtchd outside 2f out: rdn and r.o fnl f: fin strly* **36/10**[3]

4 *1¾* **Idealist (GER)**[21] 5-9-1 .... SPasquier 2 102
(J Hirschberger, Germany) *disp 2nd: 3rd st: one pce fr dist* **56/10**

5 *¾* **Simple Exchange (IRE)**[29] 4838 6-9-1 .... AStarke 5 100
(A Savujev, Czech Republic) *disp 2nd on outside: 2nd st: rdn 2f out: no ex fr dist* **99/10**

6 *hd* **Igor Protti**[98] 5-9-1 .... (b) EPedroza 4 99
(A Wohler, Germany) *racd in 4th to st: one pce fr over 1f out* **96/10**

1m 35.41s (-2.98) **6** Ran SP% **131.4**
WIN 43; PL 16, 15; SF 59.

Owner Stall Route 66 **Bred** Gestut Elsetal **Trained** Germany

5671a IVG - PREIS VON EUROPA (GROUP 1) 1m 4f

4:15 (4:22) 3-Y-0+ **£67,568** (£22,297; £10,135; £4,730)

RPR

1 **Schiaparelli (GER)**[63] 3778 4-9-6 .... AStarke 6 116
(P Schiergen, Germany) *trckd ldr to st: led over 1f out: drvn out* **6/5**[1]

2 *¾* **Poseidon Adventure (IRE)**[29] 4838 4-9-6 .... (b) ADeVries 2 115
(W Figge, Germany) *hld up in 6th: last st: swtchd outside over 2f out: stl last 1 1/2f out: r.o wl fnl f: nrest at fin* **39/1**

3 *nk* **Ioannina**[35] 4651 4-9-2 .... SPasquier 5 111
(J Hirschberger, Germany) *led to over 1f out: r.o same pce* **98/10**

4 *¾* **First Stream (GER)**[21] 5077 3-8-10 .... AHelfenbein 3 111
(Mario Hofer, Germany) *racd in 3rd to st: disputing 3rd whn n.m.r 1f out: rallied to take 4th last stride* **9/2**

5 *hd* **Egerton (GER)**[21] 5077 6-9-6 .... TMundry 7 113
(P Rau, Germany) *racd in 4th to st: rdn and disputing 3rd ins fnl f: no ex and lost 4th last stride* **39/10**[3]

6 *3½* **Hearthstead Maison (IRE)**[15] 5240 3-8-10 .... RyanMoore 1 105
(M Johnston) *hld up in 5th: rdn 2f out: one pce* **28/10**[2]

7 *1* **Dickens (GER)**[39] 4520 4-9-6 .... ASuborics 4 106
(H Blume, Germany) *hld up in rr: wnt 6th on ins st: disp 5th 2f out: sn one pce* **97/10**

2m 29.7s (-3.20)
WFA 3 from 4yo+ 8lb **7** Ran SP% **131.5**
WIN 22; PL 12, 30, 18; SF 518.

Owner Stall Blankenese **Bred** Gestut Karlshof **Trained** Germany

NOTEBOOK

Hearthstead Maison(IRE), winner of a Group 3 event at the Curragh last time out, needs quick ground to be seen at his best and conditions were simply not fast enough for him. He may now be rested and brought back for a campaign in Dubai early next year.

[5662]HAMILTON (R-H)

Monday, September 24

OFFICIAL GOING: Good to soft (soft in places)

Wind: Fresh, half-behind Weather: Overcast, raining

5672 PRESTIGE SCOTLAND H'CAP 5f 4y

2:10 (2:10) (Class 5) (0-70,65) 3-Y-O+ **£3,238** (£963; £481; £240) **Stalls** Low

Form RPR

004 **1** **Brut**[4] 5552 5-9-8 **65**........(p) TonyHamilton 9 75
(D W Barker) *mde all: clr 1f out: hld on wl* **6/1**

0205 **2** ½ **Jadan (IRE)**[1] 5667 6-8-5 **48**........ AdrianTNicholls 2 56
(E J Alston) *hld up in tch: hdwy and hung rt over 1f out: chsd wnr ent fnl f: r.o* **4/1**[1]

0316 **3** 1½ **The Salwick Flyer (IRE)**[35] 4668 4-8-10 **53**........ TomEaves 3 56
(I Semple) *chsd ldrs: effrt over 1f out: edgd rt: kpt on same pce fnl f* **9/2**[2]

0165 **4** ½ **Throw The Dice**[4] 5552 5-8-8 **54**........(v) PatrickMathers[(3)] 4 55
(A Berry) *dwlt: effrt and hdwy over 1f out: kpt on fnl f: no imp* **5/1**[3]

3040 **5** 3½ **George The Best (IRE)**[33] 4706 6-8-10 **53**........ PaulHanagan 11 41
(Micky Hammond) *prom tl rdn and wknd over 1f out* **5/1**[3]

5000 **6** 3 **Stanley Wolfe (IRE)**[26] 4939 4-8-3 **46** oh1........ RoystonFfrench 12 24
(Garry Moss) *towards rr on outside: rdn 1/2-way: n.d* **50/1**

0400 **7** nk **Strawberry Patch (IRE)**[4] 5552 8-8-5 **48**........(p) MartinDwyer 7 25
(J S Goldie) *bhd and outpcd: hung rt u.p 1/2-way: nvr on terms* **17/2**

3310 **8** ¾ **Dodaa (USA)**[193] 680 4-7-13 **49** oh1 ow3........ LanceBetts[(7)] 8 23
(N Wilson) *chsd ldrs tl wknd over 1f out* **10/1**

0000 **9** 2 **Town House**[63] 3782 5-8-3 **46** oh1........ DaleGibson 5 13
(B P J Baugh) *prom tl rdn and wknd fr 2f out* **20/1**

0500 **10** hd **Seafield Towers**[4] 5552 7-8-0 **46** oh1........(p) DuranFentiman[(3)] 6 12
(Miss L A Perratt) *dwlt: a outpcd and bhd* **20/1**

0000 **11** 1 **Compton Lad**[7] 5481 4-8-9 **55** oh1 ow9........ PJMcDonald[(3)] 10 17
(D A Nolan) *chsd ldrs tl rdn and wknd fr 2f out* **66/1**

61.14 secs (-0.06) **Going Correction** +0.125s/f (Good) **11 Ran SP% 114.6**
Speed ratings (Par 103): **105,104,101,101,95 90,90,88,85,85 83**
CSF £28.79 CT £119.97 TOTE £5.30: £2.00, £2.00, £2.00; EX 35.60.
Owner D W Barker **Bred** Mrs Deborah O'Brien **Trained** Scorton, N Yorks

FOCUS
A weak handicap but run at a reasonable gallop and the form looks solid rated around the first three.

5673 TOTESPORT CONDITIONS STKS 6f 5y

2:40 (2:40) (Class 2) 3-Y-O+

£12,464 (£3,732; £1,866; £934; £466; £234) **Stalls** Low

Form RPR

0-54 **1** **Opera Cape**[60] 3887 4-8-9 102........(t) LDettori 4 107
(Saeed Bin Suroor) *hld up in tch: stdy hdwy 1/2-way: effrt and rdn over 1f out: led ins fnl f: kpt on strly* **9/2**[2]

0202 **2** 2 **Come Out Fighting**[17] 5195 4-8-9 91........ GrahamGibbons 6 101
(P A Blockley) *pressed ldr: rdn and ev ch over 1f out: kpt on same pce fnl f* **14/1**

0030 **3** 1 **Strike Up The Band**[30] 4798 4-8-9 105........ AdrianTNicholls 5 98
(D Nicholls) *led tl edgd rt and hdd ins fnl f: kpt on same pce* **14/1**

2150 **4** 2 **Shes Minnie**[1] 5666 4-8-4 84........ PaulHanagan 8 87
(J G M O'Shea) *bhd and sn outpcd: hdwy over 1f out: kpt on: nt rch ldrs* **40/1**

10-0 **5** 2 **Big Timer (USA)**[184] 760 3-9-0 102........ TomEaves 1 93
(I Semple) *chsd ldrs: outpcd over 2f out: n.d after* **8/1**[3]

0342 **6** ¾ **Welsh Emperor (IRE)**[37] 4600 8-9-2 113........ MartinDwyer 2 91
(T P Tate) *chsd ldrs: drvn over 2f out: wknd over 1f out* **1/2**[1]

6060 **7** 9 **Vondova**[1] 5667 5-8-9 49 ow5........(p) PJMcDonald 7 57?
(D A Nolan) *in tch tl rdn and wknd over 3f out* **200/1**

1m 12.5s (-0.60) **Going Correction** +0.125s/f (Good)
WFA 3 from 4yo+ 2lb **7 Ran SP% 112.2**
Speed ratings (Par 109): **109,106,105,102,99 98,86**
CSF £58.93 TOTE £3.60: £2.50, £5.30; EX 52.90.
Owner Godolphin **Bred** Littleton Stud **Trained** Newmarket, Suffolk

FOCUS
A decent little conditions event but the form is rated at face value though the runner-up with the form limited by the fourth.

NOTEBOOK
Opera Cape, a formerly high-class juvenile, has not achieved much in a handful of runs for current connections, but he was dropping to this trip for the first time and the ease in the ground helped. He took a while to hit top stride, but was well on top at the line and this was a step back in the right direction. The return to 7f may bring about further progress and, although he is highly unlikely to reach the heights he once promised, he could do well now the ground has come in his favour. (tchd 5-1)
Come Out Fighting, a useful sprint-handicapper, is not the most consistent, but he ran above himself in second and there was no disgrace and finding the classy winner too strong. He has not won for over a year, but is only a few pounds higher and certainly deserves to find another race. (op 18-1 tchd 12-1)
Strike Up The Band has had a pretty miserable season, but this second start back from a break was certainly more promising. He is likely to remain hard to place and these conditions races are going to continues to be his best opportunity. (op 12-1)
Shes Minnie, a useful sprinter, had it all to do with the best of these at the weights, but appeared to run above herself. It is hoped though the Handicapper does not overreact to this. (op 50-1)
Big Timer(USA), winner of the Group 3 Acomb Stakes as a juvenile, has not really gone on since and showed little on his reappearance at Lingfield in March. This was his first start since and once again he shaped with limited potential. (op 13-2)
Welsh Emperor(IRE), a tough and consistent sort who was narrowly touched off by Red Evie in the Group 2 Hungerford Stakes last time, is just as effective at this shorter distance and he looked set to take an awful lot of beating. However, he was never really travelling and dropped out as though something had gone amiss. He is much better than this and can safely have the run ignored. Official explanation: jockey said gelding had never been travelling and had no more to give (op 8-13 tchd 4-6 in places)

5674 TOTEPOOL SERIES FINAL (H'CAP) 1m 1f 36y

3:10 (3:10) (Class 3) 3-Y-O+ **£9,715** (£2,890; £1,444; £721) **Stalls** High

Form RPR

340 **1** **Neil's Legacy (IRE)**[13] 5296 5-8-5 **64**........ RoystonFfrench 8 72
(Miss L A Perratt) *prom: smooth hdwy to ld over 2f out: sn rdn: hld on wl fnl f* **9/1**

1223 **2** 1 **Mystical Ayr (IRE)**[4] 5556 5-8-7 **66** ow1........ TonyHamilton 5 72
(Miss L A Perratt) *midfield: smooth hdwy and ev ch over 2f out: sn rdn along: kpt on fnl f* **9/2**[2]

2660 **3** 2 **Barbirolli**[38] 4582 5-8-4 **63**........ MartinDwyer 9 64
(W M Brisbourne) *hld up: hdwy and in tch over 2f out: sn rdn: r.o ins fnl f* **4/1**[1]

2221 **4** 3 **Society Music (IRE)**[16] 5230 5-8-10 **74**........(p) NeilBrown[(5)] 7 69
(M Dods) *hld up: stdy hdwy to chse ldrs over 2f out: sn rdn and edgd rt: one pce over 1f out* **5/1**[3]

2005 **5** 3 **Regent's Secret (USA)**[13] 5296 7-8-13 **72**........(p) DanielTudhope 3 60
(J S Goldie) *s.i.s: bhd and pushed along: hdwy over 2f out: n.d* **8/1**

3116 **6** 6 **Hawkit (USA)**[26] 4933 6-9-1 **74**........ DaleGibson 6 49
(P Monteith) *bhd: rdn over 3f out: nvr rchd ldrs* **15/2**

0520 **7** nk **Mandarin Rocket (IRE)**[14] 5286 4-7-9 **57** oh7........ DuranFentiman[(3)] 2 31
(Miss L A Perratt) *led 1f: pressed ldr: ev ch over 2f out: sn rdn and wknd over 1f out* **33/1**

2140 **8** 3½ **Dark Charm (FR)**[4] 5553 8-8-7 **69**........(p) JamieMoriarty[(3)] 12 36
(R A Fahey) *bhd: pushed along 4f out: nvr on terms* **10/1**

1000 **9** 4 **Ignition**[21] 5086 5-7-12 **57**........ PaulQuinn 4 15
(W M Brisbourne) *chsd ldrs tl rdn and wknd over 2f out* **16/1**

0030 **10** 11 **Best Of The Lot (USA)**[19] 5145 5-8-5 **64**........ PaulHanagan 11 —
(R A Fahey) *led after 1f to over 2f out: sn wknd* **13/2**

4500 **11** 5 **The Mighty Ogmore**[16] 4582 3-7-13 **63** oh13 ow1........(p) PaulFessey 1 —
(R C Guest) *midfield: outpcd 1/2-way: sn struggling* **100/1**

2m 1.00s (1.34) **Going Correction** +0.375s/f (Good)
WFA 3 from 4yo+ 5lb **11 Ran SP% 120.0**
Speed ratings (Par 107): **109,108,106,103,101 95,95,92,88,78 74**
CSF £50.30 CT £192.72 TOTE £11.40: £3.90, £2.30, £1.60; EX 38.10.
Owner Terry & Mrs Linda Pardoe **Bred** Patrick M Ryan **Trained** Ayr, S Ayrshire
■ Stewards' Enquiry : Dale Gibson caution: careless riding

FOCUS
A competitive handicap that looks sound enough with the first two rated as achieving personal bests.

NOTEBOOK
Neil's Legacy(IRE), who beat only the one home when stopping quickly as Beverley last time, bounced right back to her best here and stuck on strongly once getting to the front. The slight ease in the going obviously suited, but it would take an improved effort for her to follow up. Official explanation: trainer had no explanation for the apparent improvement in form (op 8-1)
Mystical Ayr(IRE), a consistent stable companion of the winner, was back up in trip having finished third over 7f at Ayr last time, but having travelled well she could not match the winner. She should continue to pay her way. (op 5-1)
Barbirolli, still 4lb higher than when last winning over course and distance this time last year, ran his best race for a while and could be edging back to something like his best. (op 7-1)
Society Music(IRE), nudged up just 2lb for his recent Thirsk victory, did not prove quite so effective on this slower surface and could never really reach a threatening position having been in rear early. (op 11-2)
Regent's Secret(USA) has not been in particularly good form and he never threatened to get involved. (op 7-1)

5675 PRESTIGE SCOTLAND E B F MEDIAN AUCTION MAIDEN STKS 6f 5y

3:40 (3:40) (Class 5) 2-Y-O **£3,886** (£1,156; £577; £288) **Stalls** Low

Form RPR

4 **1** **C'Mon You Irons (IRE)**[33] 4702 2-9-3 0........ TomEaves 7 76
(B Smart) *cl up: chal 1/2-way: led ins fnl f: rdn out* **9/4**[2]

22 **2** nk **Bonny Rose**[12] 5329 2-8-12 0........ RoystonFfrench 4 70
(M Johnston) *led: rdn and edgd rt over 1f out: hdd ins fnl f: rallied* **8/11**[1]

3 3 **Safebreaker** 2-9-3 0........ MartinDwyer 6 66
(M Johnston) *dwlt: hdwy on outside to chse ldrs over 1f out: sn one pce* **6/1**[3]

0065 **4** 4 **Amber Ridge**[39] 4527 2-9-3 56........ DaleGibson 5 54
(B P J Baugh) *trckd ldrs tl rdn and outpcd fr 2f out* **25/1**

00 **5** 16 **Northwest**[69] 3606 2-9-0 0........ PatrickMathers[(3)] 1 6
(A Berry) *chsd ldrs tl wknd over 2f out* **125/1**

6 26 **Becky Quick (IRE)** 2-8-12 0........ PaulHanagan 3 —
(Garry Moss) *t.k.h: prom tl lost tch fr 1/2-way* **33/1**

0 **7** ½ **Aberlady Lad**[21] 5081 2-9-0 0........ PJMcDonald[(3)] 2 —
(B Mactaggart) *bhd and outpcd: no ch fr 1/2-way* **125/1**

1m 14.91s (1.81) **Going Correction** +0.125s/f (Good) **7 Ran SP% 111.3**
Speed ratings (Par 95): **92,91,87,82,60 26,25**
CSF £4.00 TOTE £2.20: £1.50, £1.20; EX 6.40.
Owner Hintlesham Racing **Bred** Airlie Stud **Trained** Hambleton, N Yorks

FOCUS
An uncompetitive maiden and the form is limited by the fourth.

NOTEBOOK
C'Mon You Irons(IRE), who made a highly promising debut over 5f at Carlisle, was doing his best work late that day and this additional furlong was always going to play to his strengths. Soon prominent, he kept finding under pressure and just did enough to hold the favourite, still looking a bit green in the process. There should still be more to come and he may stay further in time. (op 7-2)
Bonny Rose has now finished second on all three starts. There is nothing wrong with her attitude, but she continues to just find one too good and perhaps the step back up in trip will suit. (op 8-13 tchd 4-7, 4-5 and 5-6 in places)
Safebreaker, bread to appreciate trips in excess of 7f in time, comes from a stable whose juveniles often benefit from a run and he shaped well considering. Natural progression should see him winning an ordinary maiden. (op 5-1)
Amber Ridge is exposed as a very moderate performer and he will find easier opportunities at selling level. (tchd 20-1 and 33-1)

5676 TOTEEXACTA APPRENTICE SERIES H'CAP (FINAL OF THE HAMILTON PARK APPRENTICE SERIES) 1m 3f 16y

4:10 (4:11) (Class 6) (0-65,64) 3-Y-O+ **£2,590** (£770; £385; £192) **Stalls** High

Form RPR

1051 **1** **Elopement (IRE)**[7] 5482 5-9-13 **64** 6ex........ DeanHeslop[(3)] 9 74
(W M Brisbourne) *mde all: rdn over 2f out: edgd lft fnl f: hld on gamely* **4/1**[1]

0-60 **2** nk **Tiger King (GER)**[36] 3343 6-9-10 **58**........ JamesMillman 3 68
(P Monteith) *dwlt: early reminders in rr: outpcd 1/2-way: gd hdwy outside over 2f out: chsd wnr ins fnl f: kpt on: jst hld* **6/1**[3]

0060 **3** 2½ **Wulimaster (USA)**[66] 3722 4-9-10 **58**........ NeilBrown 13 63
(D W Barker) *prom: effrt over 2f out: kpt on same pce fnl f* **12/1**

3031 **4** hd **Desert Hawk**[29] 4860 6-9-5 **56**........ PatrickDonaghy[(3)] 5 61
(W M Brisbourne) *hld up: hdwy over 2f out: kpt on fnl f: no imp* **12/1**

05 **5** shd **Beaver (AUS)**[25] 4959 8-9-7 **60**........ LanceBetts[(5)] 8 65
(J G M O'Shea) *in tch: drvn 3f out: kpt on same pce fnl f* **8/1**

0405 **6** shd **Thunderwing (IRE)**[64] 3764 5-9-2 **55**........ NSLawes[(5)] 7 60
(James Moffatt) *midfield: rdn and outpcd over 2f out: swtchd lft and rallied fnl f: nrst fin* **20/1**

4344 **7** shd **Star Of Angels**[7] 5482 3-9-2 **57**........(b) RussellKennemore 14 61
(M Johnston) *cl up: drvn over 3f out: one pce over 1f out* **9/2**[2]

0654 **8** *5* **Mayadeen (IRE)**[24] 5000 5-9-4 **52**....................(b) GaryBartley 1 48
(I Semple) *hld up: pushed along over 3f out: nvr rchd ldrs* **9/1**

0400 **9** *hd* **Howards Rocket**[24] 4998 6-9-2 **50**.................... KellyHarrison 2 46
(J S Goldie) *cl up tl rdn and wknd fr 2f out* **40/1**

0310 **10** *9* **Fadansil**[7] 5482 4-8-11 **50**.................... JamesRogers(5) 12 30
(J Wade) *hld up: rdn over 3f out: btn 2f out* **8/1**

5004 **11** *7* **Blushing Prince (IRE)**[15] 4580 9-8-13 **47**............(t) DanielleMcCreery 6 15
(R C Guest) *towards rr: drvn over 4f out: btn over 2f out* **28/1**

0000 **12** *9* **Ulysees (IRE)**[24] 4998 8-9-2 **50**.................... KMay 11 3
(J Barclay) *t.k.h in midfield: rdn over 3f out: sn btn* **25/1**

0100 **13** *19* **Miss Havisham (IRE)**[10] 5388 3-8-7 **53**.................... MatthewDavies(5) 4 —
(J R Weymes) *hld up: rdn over 3f out: sn btn: t.o* **25/1**

43-0 **14** *55* **Robbie Scott**[43] 4424 3-9-3 **58**.................... SladeO'Hara 10 —
(M Johnston) *towards rr and sn pushed along: lost tch fr 1/2-way: t.o* **20/1**

2m 30.76s (4.50) **Going Correction** +0.375s/f (Good)
WFA 3 from 4yo+ 7lb **14** Ran SP% **123.2**
Speed ratings (Par 101): **98,97,95,95,95 95,95,91,91,85 80,73,59,19**
CSF £25.48 CT £274.73 TOTE £4.50: £2.00, £2.60, £4.80; EX 39.90.
Owner Stratford Bards Racing **Bred** Haras Du Mezeray **Trained** Great Ness, Shropshire

FOCUS
A moderate handicap with the fourth a solid guide to the level.
Fadansil Official explanation: jockey said gelding had been unsuited by the the good to soft, soft in places going

5677 TOTESPORT.COM BUTTONHOOK H'CAP 1m 5f 9y
4:40 (4:40) (Class 3) (0-95,88) 3-Y-0+
£11,217 (£3,358; £1,679; £840; £419; £210) **Stalls** High

Form RPR

1142 **1** **Sadler's Kingdom (IRE)**[17] 5197 3-8-10 **79**.................... PaulHanagan 1 96+
(R A Fahey) *hld up in tch: effrt over 2f out: led ins fnl f: hld on wl* **11/4**[1]

1 **2** *1/2* **Dustoori**[36] 4630 3-8-7 **76**.................... MartinDwyer 6 92+
(Saeed Bin Suroor) *t.k.h: cl up: led 4f out to ins fnl f: kpt on u.p* **10/3**[3]

3012 **3** *5* **Sphinx (FR)**[2] 5619 9-9-8 **87**....................(b) RussellKennemore(5) 9 96
(Jamie Poulton) *hld up: smooth hdwy and prom over 3f out: outpcd over 1f out* **3/1**[2]

3034 **4** *2 1/2* **Tilt**[16] 5215 5-9-11 **88**....................(p) JamieMoriarty(3) 2 93
(B Ellison) *hld up: effrt whn drifted to stands' side 4f out: hung rt wl over 1f out: sn no imp* **9/2**

2310 **5** *3* **Bajan Parkes**[16] 5215 4-9-8 **82**.................... KDarley 3 83
(E J Alston) *led 2f: cl up tl rdn and wknd over 2f out* **14/1**

0142 **6** *4* **Cotton Eyed Joe (IRE)**[25] 4969 6-8-13 **76**.................... PJMcDonald(3) 5 71
(G A Swinbank) *in tch tl rdn and wknd over 2f out* **16/1**

4514 **7** *nk* **Doctor Scott**[16] 5229 4-9-2 **76**.................... RoystonFfrench 4 70
(M Johnston) *chsd ldrs: pushed along over 4f out: wknd over 2f out* **14/1**

00-0 **8** *nk* **Savannah Bay**[16] 5215 8-9-8 **82**.................... TomEaves 7 76
(B Ellison) *led after 2f to 4f out: rdn and wknd over 2f out* **66/1**

9 *2 1/2* **Los Nadis (GER)**[107] 3-8-8 **77**.................... PaulFessey 8 67
(P Monteith) *prom: ev ch 4f out: wknd wl over 2f out* **100/1**

2m 55.27s (1.87) **Going Correction** +0.375s/f (Good)
WFA 3 from 4yo+ 9lb **9** Ran SP% **114.6**
Speed ratings (Par 107): **109,108,105,104,102 99,99,99,97**
CSF £12.07 CT £28.23 TOTE £4.30: £1.80, £1.70, £1.20; EX 14.60.
Owner J J Staunton **Bred** Tower Bloodstock **Trained** Musley Bank, N Yorks
■ Stewards' Enquiry : Martin Dwyer two-day ban: careless riding (Oct 8-9)

FOCUS
A decent handicap in which two progressive sorts pulled clear and, with the time good and the fourth a decent guide, the form looks useful.

NOTEBOOK
Sadler's Kingdom(IRE), a winner off 55 at Beverley back in May, has progressed rapidly since, scoring at Galway in July, and he looked a major contender here with the return to a slower surface likely to suit. Always going strongly, he got the better of the lightly-raced Dustoori in a tussle, despite being carried left, and that extra stamina saw him through. He gives every indication there is more to come and he may well stay even further. (op 3-1 tchd 5-2)
Dustoori, a workmanlike winner on debut at Bath, had slower ground to contend with here, but he looked fairly weighted off 76 and it was only that lack of experience that cost him. He was clear of the third and rates as a handicapper to follow. (op 11-4 tchd 7-2)
Sphinx(FR) is a most useful handicapper when the ground is slow and he did nothing wrong in defeat against the progressive Black Rock at Ayr the other day. Evidently thought none the worse for those exertions, he travelled with his usual exuberance, but two younger, more progressive sorts had too much pace for him where it mattered. (op 4-1)
Tilt is not easy to win with, but he rarely runs poorly and as a result the Handicapper has not eased him. This, however, was not one of his better efforts.
Bajan Parkes, who had things go his way when beating Sadler's Kingdom at Haydock two starts back, was unable to confirm the form and has gone the wrong way since that victory. (tchd 12-1)

5678 CHRIS'S HAPPY MEMORIES MAIDEN STKS 1m 1f 36y
5:10 (5:11) (Class 5) 3-4-Y-O **£3,238** (£963; £481; £240) **Stalls** High

Form RPR

-330 **1** **Monsoon Wedding**[54] 4072 3-8-12 69.................... RoystonFfrench 3 72
(M Johnston) *mde all: rdn over 2f out: hld on gamely fnl f* **7/2**[3]

0322 **2** *1 1/4* **Muqadam (IRE)**[29] 4845 3-9-3 72....................(v[1]) MartinDwyer 9 74
(Sir Michael Stoute) *t.k.h: chsd ldrs: effrt and ev ch over 1f out: kpt on: no ex wl ins fnl f* **5/2**[1]

0-53 **3** *5* **Hint Of Spring**[135] 1676 3-8-12 66.................... LDettori 1 58
(Saeed Bin Suroor) *cl up: ev ch over 3f out: outpcd over 1f out* **11/4**[2]

4 *2* **Accusation (IRE)** 3-8-12 0.................... KDarley 6 54
(L M Cumani) *in tch: rdn and outpcd over 2f out: no imp after* **7/1**

0 **5** *3* **Soul Angel**[74] 3447 3-9-3 0.................... PaddyAspell 7 52
(Miss S E Forster) *chsd ldrs tl wknd over 2f out* **125/1**

6300 **6** *1 1/2* **Royal Citadel (IRE)**[14] 5286 4-8-12 48.................... KellyHarrison(5) 8 44
(Mrs L B Normile) *hld up: rdn over 3f out: sn btn* **66/1**

0- **7** *3/4* **Zawariq (IRE)**[333] 6186 3-8-12 0.................... GrahamGibbons 10 42
(E J O'Neill) *in tch tl rdn and wknd over 2f out* **12/1**

3500 **8** *5* **Optical Illusion (USA)**[21] 5082 3-9-3 58.................... TomEaves 5 36
(I Semple) *stdd s: rdn in rr over 3f out: sn btn* **25/1**

4060 **9** *9* **Musical Giant (USA)**[73] 3497 4-9-8 42....................(t) PaulHanagan 4 16
(J Wade) *bhd: rdn and hung rt 4f out: sn btn* **100/1**

2m 3.31s (3.65) **Going Correction** +0.375s/f (Good)
WFA 3 from 4yo 5lb **9** Ran SP% **104.8**
Speed ratings (Par 103): **98,96,92,90,88 86,86,81,73**
CSF £10.34 TOTE £4.70: £1.20, £1.20, £1.20; EX 11.90 Place 6 £28.28, Place 5 £15.85.Schoenberg was withdrawn. Price at time of withdrawal 7/1. Rule 4 applies to all bets. Deduction 10p in the pound.
Owner Helena Springfield Ltd **Bred** Meon Valley Stud **Trained** Middleham Moor, N Yorks
■ Schoenberg was withdrawn because the ground was unsuitable (7/1, deduct 10p in the £ under Rule 4.)

FOCUS
A hugely uncompetitive maiden with the time modest and the form looks suspect and best rated through the runner-up.
Musical Giant(USA) Official explanation: jockey said gelding hung right throughout
T/Plt: £107.60 to a £1 stake. Pool: £66,491.00. 450.95 winning tickets. T/Qpdt: £9.00 to a £1 stake. Pool: £4,313.10. 352.70 winning tickets. RY

5527 KEMPTON (A.W) (R-H)
Monday, September 24

OFFICIAL GOING: Standard
Wind: Strong across

5679 BALLYMORE PROPERTIES EBF MAIDEN STKS (DIV I) 1m (P)
1:50 (1:52) (Class 4) 2-Y-O **£4,210** (£1,252; £625; £312) **Stalls** High

Form RPR

4030 **1** **Cordell (IRE)**[12] 5324 2-9-3 79.................... PatDobbs 2 78
(R Hannon) *led 2f: styd w ldr and led again over 2f out: hdd ins fnl 2f: rallied to ld again ins fnl f and styd on wl* **12/1**

5 **2** *1/2* **Greylami (IRE)**[24] 5011 2-9-3 0.................... AdamKirby 5 77
(T G Mills) *chsd ldrs: led ins fnl 2f: sn rdn: hdd ins fnl f: nt pce of wnr nr fin* **7/2**[2]

23 **3** *1 1/4* **Rochefort (IRE)**[12] 5321 2-9-3 0.................... JimmyFortune 6 74
(J H M Gosden) *chsd ldrs: rdn over 2f out: styd on same pce ins fnl f* **1/2**[1]

5 **4** *2* **Silk Hall (UAE)**[20] 5116 2-9-3 0.................... JamesDoyle 3 70
(D W P Arbuthnot) *s.i.s: sn rcvrd: hdwy 3f out: rdn and styd on fr over 1f out but nt pce to rch ldrs* **20/1**

0 **5** *1 1/4* **Averoo**[17] 5200 2-9-3 0.................... SteveDrowne 7 67
(E A L Dunlop) *led after 2f: kpt slt advantage tl hdd over 2f out: wknd fnl f* **33/1**

6 *2 1/2* **Redarsene** 2-8-12 0.................... JamieJones(5) 11 62+
(M G Quinlan) *in rr but in tch: hdwy over 2f out: nvr nr ldrs and one pce fr over 1f out* **16/1**

7 *8* **Grapes Of Wrath (UAE)** 2-8-12 0.................... J-PGuillambert 1 39
(M Johnston) *chsd ldrs tl wknd fr 3f out* **7/1**[3]

0000 **8** *8* **Virtual Paddy**[17] 5186 2-9-3 52.................... LPKeniry 4 26
(M Blanshard) *a towards rr* **66/1**

9 *10* **Warren Bank** 2-9-3 0.................... VinceSlattery 10 4
(Mrs Mary Hambro) *sn bhd* **66/1**

10 *8* **Amphibalus (IRE)** 2-9-3 0.................... JimCrowley 8 —
(D K Ivory) *slowly away: a wl bhd* **50/1**

1m 40.31s (-0.49) **Going Correction** -0.125s/f (Stan) **10** Ran SP% **127.6**
Speed ratings (Par 97): **97,96,95,93,92 89,81,73,63,55**
CSF £57.29 TOTE £16.00: £3.10, £1.40, £1.02; EX 56.70.
Owner Mrs J Wood **Bred** Scea Haras De La Poterie **Trained** East Everleigh, Wilts

FOCUS
An ordinary maiden and the winning time was 0.35 seconds slower than the second division. There was not much encouragement from those outside the first four.

NOTEBOOK
Cordell(IRE), one of the most experienced in the field, was stepping up significantly in trip and his stamina was truly tested, as he was in and out of the lead throughout the contest and showed a good attitude to wrestle back the advantage from the runner-up. Having proved he stays, this opens up a few more options for him and his mark of 79 provides a good benchmark to the form. (op 14-1)
Greylami(IRE), stepping up a furlong from his debut in a Sandown maiden that has worked out pretty well, looked to have hit the front at just the right time but the more streetwise winner just had his measure late on. He continues to go the right way, but the best of him will likely be seen next season. (op 5-2)
Rochefort(IRE), making his Polytrack debut after being placed in two turf maidens, was in a good position throughout but when pulled out for his effort was make to look rather one paced. This was disappointing, but given the promise he has already shown it is too early to write him off. Perhaps he needs an even stiffer test. (op 4-6)
Silk Hall(UAE) was always having to race wide of the field from his low draw and therefore covering more ground. He kept on going right to the line though, backing up the promise he showed on his debut, and remains one to be interested in for middle-distance handicaps in due course.
Averoo was ridden totally differently to his debut over course and distance earlier in the month, but did not get home. His speedy pedigree and the way he performed here suggested he may be worth dropping in trip.
Redarsene, a half-brother to two winners over 7f, was backed at long odds beforehand, probably by Arsenal supporters. He tried to get into the race turning for home, but could never land a blow though at least he did fare best of the newcomers. (op 33-1)

5680 BALLYMORE PROPERTIES EBF MAIDEN STKS (DIV II) 1m (P)
2:20 (2:20) (Class 4) 2-Y-O **£4,210** (£1,252; £625; £312) **Stalls** High

Form RPR

0 **1** **Bronze Cannon (USA)**[12] 5337 2-9-3 0.................... JimmyFortune 3 77
(J H M Gosden) *in tch: hdwy 4f out: drvn to ld insde fnl 2f: pushed along ins fnl f and a jst holding styng on 2nd* **9/2**[3]

5 **2** *1/2* **Quam Celerrime**[17] 5200 2-9-3 0.................... FrankieMcDonald 4 76
(P A Blockley) *chsd ldrs: rdn over 2f out: swtchd rt 1f out and styd on strly ins fnl f but a jst hld by wnr* **7/1**

604 **3** *2* **Hit The Roof**[17] 5200 2-9-3 76.................... PatDobbs 6 71
(R Hannon) *led 2f: styd w ldr tl rdn to ld again over 2f out: hdd ins fnl quarter m: outpcd ins fnl f* **9/1**

4 *nk* **Dandy Erin (IRE)** 2-9-3 0.................... TPQueally 7 71+
(J A Osborne) *in rr but in tch: hdwy 3f out: rdn and styd on fr 2f out: kpt on ins fnl f but nvr gng pce to be competitive* **20/1**

5 *6* **Highly Regal (IRE)** 2-9-3 0.................... EddieAhern 2 57
(R A Teal) *in rr: rdn over 4f out: mod prog fnl 2f* **20/1**

0 **6** *1/2* **Celt**[11] 5343 2-8-12 0.................... AshleyHamblett(5) 1 56
(L M Cumani) *s.i.s: sn rcvrd and in tch: wknd 3f out* **13/2**

043 **7** *6* **Dubai Samurai**[39] 4540 2-9-3 82.................... SebSanders 10 42
(J W Hills) *w ldr: led after 2f: kpt slt ld tl hdd over 2f out and sn wknd* **2/1**[1]

8 *5* **Robbmaa (FR)** 2-9-3 0.................... PhilipRobinson 8 30
(M A Jarvis) *slowly away: sn rdn: green and a wl bhd* **7/2**[2]

00 **9** *1/2* **Pure Scandal**[12] 5337 2-9-3 0.................... DO'Donohoe 5 29
(M W Easterby) *chsd ldrs: rdn along after 2f: wknd 1/2-way* **66/1**

0 **10** *3/4* **Casual Garcia**[7] 5470 2-9-3 0.................... JamieMackay 9 27
(Sir Mark Prescott) *s.i.s: no ch fr 1/2-way* **66/1**

1m 39.96s (-0.84) **Going Correction** -0.125s/f (Stan) **10** Ran SP% **122.1**
Speed ratings (Par 97): **99,98,96,96,90 89,83,78,78,77**
CSF £36.34 TOTE £6.30: £2.40, £2.60, £2.20; EX 38.40.
Owner A E Oppenheimer **Bred** Hascombe And Valiant Studs **Trained** Newmarket, Suffolk

FOCUS
This looked the stronger of the two divisions, especially as the pace seemed quicker and the winning time was 0.35 seconds faster. The form looks sound, the leading quartet pulled right away from the others and each probably has a future.

NOTEBOOK
Bronze Cannon(USA), an eye-catcher on his debut here, proved well suited by this extra furlong and was much sharper this time. He impressed with the way he knuckled down to repel the runner-up in the latter stages and should continue to progress, whilst his pedigree suggests he will get a bit further. (op 2-1)
Quam Celerrime ◆, who showed promise on his debut over course and distance earlier in the month, reversed the form of that race with Hit The Roof and was putting in a spirited late effort tight against the inside rail, which is never the easiest thing to do here. Despite the way he finished, his breeding suggests this may be as far as he wants but in any case it should not be long before he gets off the mark. (op 8-1)
Hit The Roof was always thereabouts and had every chance, but he lacks the scope of a few of these and failed to confirm recent course form with Quam Celerrime. Already officially rated 76, it may be worth switching him into a nursery. (op 10-1)
Dandy Erin(IRE) ◆, out of a half-sister to Lugana Beach and the dam of The Tatling, appeared to be travelling well on the outside turning for home and kept on to record a very promising debut effort. He can only improve and should find an opportunity before too long.
Highly Regal(IRE), a half-brother to three winners, was never in the hunt and given how far he finished adrift of the front four it is hard to know what he achieved. There is a blend of speed and stamina in his pedigree and, whatever the merit of the performance, he is at least entitled to have learned something from this debut.
Celt did not step forward much from his Chepstow debut, but is more of a handicap prospect for next season in any case. (op 8-1)
Dubai Samurai boasted some decent turf form coming into this, but after making much of the running he eventually dropped out very tamely. The different surface and longer trip may have been part of the reason for his disappointing effort, but either way he now has questions to answer. Official explanation: jockey had no explanation for the poor form shown (tchd 7-4)
Robbmaa(FR), a 220,000euros half-brother to three winners including Tahreeb and Ihtiyati, was expected to put in a big effort on this debut if the market support was anything to go by, but he proved as green as grass almost straight away and was under the cosh in a detached last racing down the back straight. He did eventually pass the two rags, but he will need to have grown up a lot after this if he is to start justifying his purchase price. (op 6-1)

5681 AVANTA EBF MAIDEN FILLIES' STKS (DIV I) 7f (P)
2:50 (2:52) (Class 4) 2-Y-O **£4,210** (£1,252; £625; £312) **Stalls** High

Form RPR
2 **1** **Shamayel**18 5162 2-9-0 0 .... RHills 11 74+
(B W Hills) *trckd ldr: shkn up to ld appr fnl 2f: styd on strly ins fnl f* **4/6**1
2 *2* **Freedom Song** 2-9-0 0 .... SteveDrowne 3 69+
(R Charlton) *s.i.s: bhd: drvn and rapid hdwy over 1f out: str run to take 2nd wl ins fnl f but nt rch wnr* **14/1**
6 **3** *nk* **La Rosa Nostra**28 4882 2-9-0 0 .... AdamKirby 7 68
(W R Swinburn) *in rr: pshd along over 2f out: rapid hdwy over 1f out: str run ins fnl f to press for 2nd cl home but nt trble wnr* **7/2**2
6 **4** *½* **Trumpet Lily**31 4774 2-9-0 0 .... EddieAhern 4 67
(J G Portman) *in tch: rdn over 2f out: chsd ldrs and disp 2nd 1f out: outpcd ins fnl f* **8/1**3
6 **5** *1* **Street Diva (USA)**17 5201 2-9-0 0 .... FrankieMcDonald 10 64
(P A Blockley) *led tl hdd appr fnl 2f: styd chsng wnr tl jst ins fnl f: wknd fnl 100yds* **16/1**
6 *1¼* **Koraleva Tectona (IRE)** 2-9-0 0 .... PaulEddery 5 61
(Pat Eddery) *slowly away: sn in tch: rdn 2f out: wknd fnl f* **20/1**
7 *nk* **Where's Susie** 2-9-0 0 .... RobertHavlin 9 60
(D K Ivory) *chsd ldrs: rdn over 2f out: wknd ins fnl f* **50/1**
0 **8** *5* **Balletic (IRE)**18 5162 2-9-0 0 .... LPKeniry 1 48
(S Kirk) *chsd ldrs: rdn over 2f out: wknd over 1f out* **33/1**
9 *1½* **Crimsonwing (IRE)** 2-9-0 0 .... TPQueally 2 44
(A M Hales) *a outpcd* **33/1**
10 *2½* **Bona Fidelis (IRE)** 2-8-11 0 .... WilliamBuick(3) 6 38
(A J McCabe) *chsd ldrs tl wknd over 2f out* **33/1**
11 *hd* **Corking (IRE)** 2-9-0 0 .... StephenCarson 8 37
(Eve Johnson Houghton) *a in rr* **25/1**
1m 27.57s (0.77) **Going Correction** -0.125s/f (Stan) **11** Ran SP% **125.3**
Speed ratings (Par 94): **90,87,87,86,85 84,83,78,76,73 73**
CSF £12.51 TOTE £1.60: £1.10, £3.50, £1.60; EX 12.10.
Owner Hamdan Al Maktoum **Bred** Tarworth Bloodstock Investments Ltd **Trained** Lambourn, Berks

FOCUS
Despite the winning time being 0.36 seconds faster than the second division, this looked an ordinary fillies' maiden and it lacked strength in depth. There may be some improvement to come from the principals, however.

NOTEBOOK
Shamayel had learnt from her debut effort and, after being up with the pace throughout, saw it out well when asked. She may not have beaten much, but is entitled to improve again and, with a price tag of 380,000gns, a victory of any sort is important with her long-term future in mind.
Freedom Song ◆, a half-sister to a couple of winners including the high-class Luvah Girl, took a while to realise what was required but the way she came home could not be faulted. She should not take long in going one better. (tchd 16-1)
La Rosa Nostra, who showed promise on her debut over course and distance last month, was given a patient ride. She did not have a lot of room to play with when trying to get closer halfway up the home straight, but it did not affect her chances of winning. This was still another solid effort though and, as with most youngsters from the yard, she is likely to continue to progress over time. (tchd 10-3 and 4-1)
Trumpet Lily, as on her debut, ran with credit on this switch to sand but shapes as though she needs a stiffer test now. (op 9-1 tchd 7-1)
Street Diva(USA), up a furlong from her debut here earlier in the month, was ridden totally differently this time but although she tried to hang on to the favourite after she had gone past, her efforts to do so eventually told. She seems to have some ability and there should be a race for her on this surface somewhere down the line.

5682 AVANTA EBF MAIDEN FILLIES' STKS (DIV II) 7f (P)
3:20 (3:21) (Class 4) 2-Y-O **£4,210** (£1,252; £625; £312) **Stalls** High

Form RPR
0 **1** **Albaraari**37 4602 2-9-0 0 .... RHills 3 74+
(Sir Michael Stoute) *s.i.s: hdwy 4f out: drvn and qcknd to ld wl over 1f out: pushed out fnl f: readily* **2/1**1
04 **2** *1* **Miss Jolyon (USA)**22 5063 2-9-0 0 .... PhilipRobinson 7 70
(M A Jarvis) *led 1f: styd pressing ldr and drvn to chal fr 2f out: kpt on ins fnl f and hld 2nd but nvr gng pce of wnr* **10/1**
244 **3** *nk* **Spiritofthetiger (USA)**20 5116 2-9-0 69 .... EddieAhern 1 69
(R A Teal) *in rr but in tch: rdn over 2f out: str run fr over 1f out and fin wl: nt rch wnr* **10/1**
0 **4** *nk* **Tepee**11 5344 2-8-9 0 .... AshleyHamblett(5) 10 68+
(L M Cumani) *trckd ldrs: hdwy on ins and nt clr run appr fnl f: swtchd lft and r.o ins fnl f: gng on cl home* **14/1**
00 **5** *¾* **Lella Beya**20 5110 2-9-0 0 .... LPKeniry 6 66+
(S Kirk) *chsd ldrs: drvn to chal 2f out: wknd ins fnl f* **33/1**
63 **6** *¾* **Clifton Four (USA)**14 5277 2-9-0 0 .... PatDobbs 11 65
(R Hannon) *led after 1f: kpt narrow ld tl hdd wl over 1f out: wknd fnl f* **6/1**3
03 **7** *¾* **Redeemed**44 4402 2-9-0 0 .... StephenDonohoe 9 63
(B J Meehan) *s.i.s: in rr: rdn 3f out: styd on fnl f but nvr in contention* **3/1**2
50 **8** *nk* **Double On Red**38 4564 2-9-0 0 .... HayleyTurner 2 62
(J M P Eustace) *in tch: chsd ldrs and rdn over 2f out: sn outpcd* **8/1**
0 **9** *nk* **Fandangerina**5 5540 2-9-0 0 .... SebSanders 8 61+
(Sir Mark Prescott) *in rr: shkn up and kpt on fnl f: nvr in contention* **20/1**
66 **10** *1* **Darley Star**22 5061 2-9-0 0 .... TPQueally 4 59
(C E Brittain) *chsd ldrs: hung lft over 2f out: sn btn* **16/1**
1m 27.93s (1.13) **Going Correction** -0.125s/f (Stan) **10** Ran SP% **122.2**
Speed ratings (Par 94): **88,86,86,86,85 84,83,83,82,81**
CSF £25.04 TOTE £3.20: £1.10, £2.80, £2.20; EX 30.00.
Owner Hamdan Al Maktoum **Bred** Grangecon Stud **Trained** Newmarket, Suffolk

FOCUS
As was the case in the first division, this did not look a strong maiden and the pace was modest, but a couple are entitled to improve. The winning time was 0.36 seconds slower and the third sets the standard.

NOTEBOOK
Albaraari, up a furlong from her Newbury debut, again fluffed the start but these rivals were much more modest and she got away with it, eventually weaving her way through for a comfortable success. The form looks ordinary and she does not look the best two-year-old filly in the yard, but as was the case with the winner of the first division, in the same ownership, this victory was important given her 200,000gns purchase price. She is entitled to improve again, especially when she learns to break on terms. (op 11-4)
Miss Jolyon(USA) was again given a positive ride and never stopped trying. She should be able to find an ordinary maiden, but nurseries are also an option for her now. (op 8-1)
Spiritofthetiger(USA), who has already run well on this surface, did not appear to be helped by dropping back in trip and her late effort was never going to be in time. Already rated 69, she could be of interest in a nursery back over further. (tchd 9-1)
Tepee ◆, well beaten on her Chepstow debut, ran out of room when trying to creep up the inside of Lella Beya over a furlong from home before staying on again once switched and would probably have made the first three with a clear run. She should continue to progress with racing and, as she has plenty of stamina in her pedigree, should eventually make her name as a middle-distance handicapper. Official explanation: jockey said filly was denied a clear run (op 12-1)
Lella Beya, up in trip and on sand for the first time, ran well for a long way and, even in this ordinary contest, this was a marked improvement on her two previous efforts. She now qualifies for a mark. (op 25-1)
Clifton Four(USA), another stepping up in trip on this switch to sand, was given a positive ride but did not get home. She is another that now qualifies for nurseries. (tchd 13-2)
Redeemed never got into the race at all after missing the break and has to be rated disappointing. Despite a speedy pedigree, this performance suggested he found this much too sharp. (op 11-4 tchd 5-2)

5683 KENMORE PROPERTY GROUP MAIDEN STKS 1m 4f (P)
3:50 (3:51) (Class 4) 3-4-Y-O **£4,728** (£1,406; £702; £351) **Stalls** Centre

Form RPR
22 **1** **Tropical Strait (IRE)**26 4948 4-9-11 71 .... SebSanders 3 91+
(D W P Arbuthnot) *in tch: qcknd to ld 4f out: clr over 2f out: v easily* **6/4**1
2 *12* **Srikuantan (IRE)** 3-9-3 0 .... TQuinn 1 69
(P F I Cole) *in rr but in tch: hdwy over 3f out: chsd v easy wnr fr over 2f out and nvr any ch: hld on wl for 2nd ins fnl f* **12/1**
646 **3** *½* **Hesivorthedriver (GER)**59 3908 3-9-3 78 .... JimCrowley 7 68+
(Mrs A J Perrett) *chsd ldrs tl n.m.r and lost pl 4f out: sn rdn: styd on again fnl 2f and pressed for mod 2nd wl ins fnl f* **9/2**3
4 *½* **Power Shared (IRE)**87 3074 3-9-3 0 .... RobertHavlin 4 67
(P G Murphy) *chsd ldrs 1/2-way: styd on same pce fr over 2f out* **33/1**
4-24 **5** *½* **Coastal Command**109 2402 3-9-3 76 .... SteveDrowne 8 67
(R Charlton) *s.i.s: t.k.h in rr after 4f: stl keen whn rapid hdwy to chse ldrs 4f out: chsd wnr 3f out but nvr any ch: wknd over 1f out* **9/4**2
64 **6** *3½* **Bukit Tinggi (IRE)**26 4948 3-9-3 0 .... PhilipRobinson 2 61
(M A Jarvis) *chsd ldrs: led over 4f out: sn hdd: no ch w wnr over 2f out: sn btn* **5/1**
2 **7** *nk* **Sun Lane**13 5304 3-8-12 65 .... AdamKirby 5 56
(W R Swinburn) *chsd ldrs: rdn over 3f out: sn btn* **20/1**
00 **8** *22* **Wroughton (USA)**11 5346 3-9-3 0 .... StephenDonohoe 6 25
(B J Meehan) *chsd ldrs to 4f out: sn wknd* **33/1**
0000 **9** *33* **Classic Hall (IRE)**39 4535 4-9-6 37 .... PaulDoe 9 —
(T Keddy) *led tl hdd over 4f out: sn wknd: t.o* **100/1**
2m 32.65s (-4.25) **Going Correction** -0.125s/f (Stan)
WFA 3 from 4yo 8lb **9** Ran SP% **124.9**
Speed ratings (Par 105): **109,101,100,100,100 97,97,82,60**
CSF £22.99 TOTE £2.30: £1.40, £1.80, £1.80; EX 27.00.
Owner Francis Ward and Anthony Ward **Bred** George Ward **Trained** Compton, Berks

FOCUS
A very uncompetitive maiden and ultimately a one-horse race. The winning time was very good for a race like this, but the form of those behind the winner looks moderate, although the fourth and seventh were close to their marks.
Bukit Tinggi(IRE) Official explanation: jockey said colt had a breathing problem

5684 AVANTA H'CAP 6f (P)
4:20 (4:20) (Class 4) (0-85,84) 3-Y-O **£4,728** (£1,406; £702; £351) **Stalls** High

Form RPR
024 **1** **Crystal Gazer (FR)**56 4017 3-9-0 **80** .... EddieAhern 5 88
(R Hannon) *hld up in rr: hdwy fr 2f out: rdn and qcknd over 1f out to ld wl ins fnl f: readily* **3/1**1
4042 **2** *1* **Hucking Hill (IRE)**28 4885 3-8-3 **72** .... (b) StephaneBreux(3) 10 77
(J R Best) *s.i.s: in rr: hdwy over 1f out: styd on wl fnl f to take 2nd cl home but nt pce of wnr* **6/1**3
5410 **3** *1¼* **Golden Desert (IRE)**23 5051 3-9-4 **84** .... (v) AdamKirby 7 85
(T G Mills) *pressed ldr: rdn over 3f out: led over 1f out: hdd & wknd wl ins fnl f* **11/2**2
1443 **4** *nk* **Goodbye Cash (IRE)**81 3240 3-9-0 **80** .... StephenDonohoe 2 80
(P D Evans) *s.i.s: in rr: hdwy over 1f out: styd on wl fnl f but nt rch ldrs* **12/1**
3110 **5** *1½* **Diminuto**52 4123 3-8-5 **78** .... FrankiePickard(7) 4 74
(M D I Usher) *in rr: rdn over 2f out: r.o fnl f but nvr in contention* **16/1**
1-00 **6** *½* **Estimator**135 1660 3-8-13 **79** .... (b1) DaneO'Neill 6 73
(Pat Eddery) *chsd ldrs: rdn over 2f out: wknd ins fnl f* **9/1**
0000 **7** *½* **He's A Humbug (IRE)**11 5358 3-9-3 **83** .... (b1) DO'Donohoe 9 76
(K A Ryan) *mde most tl hdd over 1f out and sn wknd* **14/1**

0104 **8** 1¼ **Buckie Massa**[21] 5092 3-8-7 **76**........ WilliamBuick(3) 11 65
(S Kirk) *outpcd most of way* **6/1**[3]
0660 **9** 1½ **College Scholar (GER)**[30] 4811 3-9-4 **84**........(b¹) SebSanders 8 69
(E A L Dunlop) *chsd ldrs: rdn over 2f out: wknd over 1f out* **11/2**[2]
-000 **10** ½ **Oi Vay Joe (IRE)**[11] 5358 3-8-11 **77**........ TPQueally 3 60
(W Jarvis) *in rr: sme hdwy 3f out: hung bdly rt onto ins rail over 1f out: nt rcvr and wknd rapidly* **12/1**
1m 12.84s (-0.86) **Going Correction** -0.125s/f (Stan) **10** Ran SP% **122.3**
Speed ratings (Par 103): **100,98,97,96,94 93,93,91,89,88**
CSF £22.10 CT £100.33 TOTE £3.70: £1.80, £2.20, £2.00; EX 19.40.
Owner A F Merritt **Bred** Cheik Sultan B K B Z Al Nahyan **Trained** East Everleigh, Wilts
FOCUS
A fair handicap in which they went off at a furious pace in this and at least ten lengths covered the field before halfway, but they could never maintain it and the race was set up for the closers. As a result the form should be treated with a little caution.
Oi Vay Joe(IRE) Official explanation: jockey said gelding hung right throughout

5685 PROPERTY SHUTTLE H'CAP 1m (P)
4:50 (4:50) (Class 4) (0-85,85) 3-Y-0+ **£4,728** (£1,406; £702; £351) **Stalls** High

Form RPR
5132 **1** **Blackat Blackitten (IRE)**[26] 4949 3-8-12 **79**........ EddieAhern 10 98+
(G A Butler) *broke wl: stdd after 2f: rdn and rapid hdwy over 1f out: str run to ld fnl 100yds: readily* **11/2**[2]
0400 **2** 1¼ **Tumbleweed Glory (IRE)**[59] 3900 4-9-3 **80**........ RobertHavlin 8 90
(B J Meehan) *in rr: hdwy 3f out: rdn and hung rt 2f out: drvn to chal ins fnl f: outpcd fnl 100yds* **25/1**
0142 **3** 1¼ **Evident Pride (USA)**[16] 5221 4-9-8 **85**........ DaneO'Neill 5 92
(B R Johnson) *chsd ldr: led ins fnl 2f: hdd & wknd fnl 100yds* **5/2**[1]
1160 **4** 3 **Atlantic Story (USA)**[16] 5221 5-9-4 **81**........(t) SebSanders 12 81
(M W Easterby) *chsd ldrs: rdn and styd on same pce fnl 2f* **15/2**[3]
1600 **5** 1½ **Will He Wish**[10] 5383 11-9-1 **78**........ IanMongan 14 75
(S Gollings) *chsd ldrs: rdn 3f out: wknd fnl f* **33/1**
1102 **6** *shd* **Dichoh**[155] 1180 4-9-7 **84**........ PhilipRobinson 11 81
(M A Jarvis) *chsd ldrs: rdn and hung rt 2f out: wknd over 1f out* **15/2**[3]
4140 **7** *nk* **Sign Of The Cross**[65] 3745 3-8-11 **78**........ OscarUrbina 2 74+
(J R Fanshawe) *in rr: effrt and hmpd bnd 3f out: styd on fr over 1f out but nvr in contention* **14/1**
6125 **8** *hd* **Minnis Bay (CAN)**[20] 5114 3-8-12 **79**........ LPKeniry 9 74
(E F Vaughan) *led tl hdd ins fnl 2f: sn wknd* **10/1**
1001 **9** *nk* **Logsdail**[12] 5338 7-8-11 **74**........(p) PatDobbs 13 69
(G L Moore) *s.i.s: in rr: hdwy on ins over 2f out but nvr in contention* **20/1**
0160 **10** 1 **Coeur Courageux (FR)**[13] 5312 5-9-2 **79**........(t) TPQueally 6 71
(G L Moore) *in rr: rdn and mod prog fnl 2f* **8/1**
0401 **11** *shd* **Namid Reprobate (IRE)**[10] 5383 4-8-13 **81**........ TolleyDean(5) 1 73
(P F I Cole) *in rr: sme prog on outside over 3f out: n.d* **16/1**
051- **12** 1 **Grande Caiman (IRE)**[279] 6867 3-8-11 **78**........ JimCrowley 7 68
(R Hannon) *bhd most of way* **20/1**
206 **13** 6 **Masterofthecourt (USA)**[36] 4631 4-9-3 **80**........ SteveDrowne 3 56
(H Morrison) *sn bhd* **12/1**
0500 **14** 1¾ **Mubaashir (IRE)**[40] 4502 3-9-1 **82**........ StephenDonohoe 4 54
(E A L Dunlop) *chsd ldrs over 5f* **33/1**
1m 38.32s (-2.48) **Going Correction** -0.125s/f (Stan)
WFA 3 from 4yo+ 4lb **14** Ran SP% **127.2**
Speed ratings (Par 105): **107,105,104,101,100 99,99,99,99,98 98,97,91,89**
CSF £149.39 CT £437.30 TOTE £5.10: £2.40, £6.00, £1.80; EX 230.50.
Owner Beetle N Wedge Partnership **Bred** Conor Murphy **Trained** Blewbury, Oxon
■ Stewards' Enquiry : Robert Havlin caution: used whip with excessive frequency
Oscar Urbina one-day ban: careless riding (Oct 8)
Jim Crowley one-day ban: careless riding (Oct 8)
FOCUS
A good, competitive handicap run at a proper gallop and the form looks rock solid rated around the placed horses.

5686 EXPEDITE H'CAP 1m 4f (P)
5:20 (5:20) (Class 3) (0-95,92) 3-Y-0+
£6,855 (£2,052; £1,026; £513; £256; £128) **Stalls** Centre

Form RPR
3201 **1** **Coeur De Lionne (IRE)**[17] 5205 3-9-4 **92**........ SteveDrowne 6 109
(R Charlton) *chsd ldrs: wnt 2nd 4f out: led ins fnl 3f: hrd drvn and hung rt ins fnl f: hld on all out* **11/4**[2]
2121 **2** *shd* **Pivotal Answer (IRE)**[16] 5225 3-8-11 **85**........ TPQueally 2 102
(J Noseda) *in tch: hdwy 4f out: chsd ldrs over 3f out: wnt 2nd over 2f out: str chal thrght fnl f: no ex cl home* **5/2**[1]
1004 **3** 8 **Kerriemuir Lass (IRE)**[28] 4888 4-9-7 **87**........(p) PhilipRobinson 4 91
(M A Jarvis) *chsd ldr: led over 5f out: rdn and hdd ins fnl 3f: wknd appr fnl 2f* **10/1**
5352 **4** 1½ **Night Hour (IRE)**[36] 4637 5-9-8 **88**........(p) RobertHavlin 5 90
(J H M Gosden) *hld up in rr: sme hdwy over 3f out: rdn and hung rt sn after and nvr in contention* **3/1**[3]
6000 **5** 25 **Shimoni**[60] 3883 3-8-8 **82**........ PaulDoe 3 44
(W J Knight) *in tch: rdn 4f out: wknd ins fnl 3f* **33/1**
026 **6** 8 **Oh Glory Be (USA)**[53] 4089 4-9-7 **92**........ HaddenFrost(5) 1 41
(R Hannon) *a in rr: lost tch 3f out* **8/1**
4156 **7** *nk* **Madaarek (USA)**[38] 4572 3-8-8 **82**........(t) RHills 7 31
(E A L Dunlop) *in tch: rdn 1/2-way: sn wknd* **10/1**
0110 **8** 29 **Ideally (IRE)**[24] 4993 3-8-11 **85**........ MichaelHills 8 —
(B W Hills) *led tl hdd over 5f out: wknd qckly* **16/1**
2m 31.49s (-5.41) **Going Correction** -0.125s/f (Stan)
WFA 3 from 4yo+ 8lb **8** Ran SP% **118.4**
Speed ratings (Par 107): **113,112,107,106,89 84,84,65**
CSF £10.53 CT £59.64 TOTE £3.20: £1.10, £1.40, £2.20; EX 8.40 Place 6 £16.20, Place 5 £13.76.
Owner Mountgrange Stud **Bred** Hawthorn Villa Stud **Trained** Beckhampton, Wilts
FOCUS
A cracking finish to a race run at a very strong pace and the two market leaders pulled a mile clear of the rest. Coeur De Lionne took 9/100ths of a second off the course record set by Steppe Dancer in the Group 3 September Stakes earlier in the month. The two principals are well worth keeping on-side with the next two backing up the form.
NOTEBOOK
Coeur De Lionne(IRE) ◆, a winner on his last two visits here and 6lb higher than when successful over a furlong shorter earlier in the month, was sent for home soon after turning in. He hung over to the inside rail as the favourite was brought with her effort, but he never gave up and managed to hold on with little to spare. He is beginning to look a very smart sand performer, but it remains to be seen if he can transfer this sort of form back on to turf. (op 7-4 tchd 3-1 in place)
Pivotal Answer(IRE) ◆, 7lb higher than when successful over a furlong shorter here earlier in the month, was ridden with plenty of patience. She was produced with her effort in good time and did nothing wrong, but found the gelding was in no mood to give in. She is still lightly raced and should find more opportunities on this surface. (op 2-1)
Kerriemuir Lass(IRE), tried in cheekpieces, was given her usual positive ride but thanks to Ideally was unable to lead on her own. She did her best to see it out, but was ultimately swept away by a couple of progressive three-year-olds.
Night Hour(IRE), on sand for the first time and with the cheekpieces reapplied, was switched off out the back and followed the eventual runner-up through as the field turned for home. However, once there he hung yet again and did not seem to be giving it everything. He cannot really be trusted. (op 4-1)
Shimoni, who has faced some impossible tasks this year, was beaten out of sight once again and is obviously nothing like as good as was once thought.
Oh Glory Be(USA), last of 12 in her only previous try on Polytrack, was back in more realistic company after contesting a Group race last time and was a springer in the market, but she never gave her supporters much hope. (op 14-1)
Madaarek(USA) Official explanation: jockey said colt had a breathing problem
T/Plt: £15.30 to a £1 stake. Pool: £52,097.60. 2,473.10 winning tickets. T/Qpdt: £4.00 to a £1 stake. Pool: £3,220.30. 586.00 winning tickets. ST

5470 LEICESTER (R-H)
Monday, September 24

OFFICIAL GOING: Good (good to firm patches)
Many of the jockeys felt the ground was riding much easier than the official description.
Wind: Fresh behind Weather: Cloudy with sunny spells

5687 PERTEMPS PEOPLE DEVELOPMENT "HANDS AND HEELS" APPRENTICE SERIES H'CAP 7f 9y
2:30 (2:31) (Class 5) (0-70,70) 3-Y-0+ **£3,238** (£963; £481; £240) **Stalls** Low

Form RPR
6302 **1** **Piper's Song (IRE)**[18] 5166 4-9-4 **70**........(v) AmyScott(3) 11 84
(H Candy) *chsd ldr: led over 1f out: edgd rt: pushed clr* **9/2**[2]
2220 **2** 4 **Chief Exec**[17] 5189 5-8-5 **59**........ DavidProbert(5) 4 62
(B J Llewellyn) *sn outpcd: hdwy over 1f out: chsd wnr ins fnl f: no imp* **9/1**
0500 **3** 1¾ **Kingscross**[19] 5130 9-8-10 **62**........ LauraReynolds(3) 5 60
(M Blanshard) *dwlt: outpcd: hdwy over 1f out: nrst fin* **25/1**
66-0 **4** 2 **Sophia Gardens**[13] 5312 3-9-0 **66**........ RobbieEgan 10 59
(D W P Arbuthnot) *in rr: hmpd 6f out: hdwy over 1f out: nvr nrr* **10/1**
0651 **5** *hd* **Viable**[28] 4294 5-8-6 **58**........ JosephWalsh(3) 2 50
(Mrs P Sly) *prom: pushed along 3f out: styd on same pce fnl 2f* **6/1**[3]
010 **6** ½ **Trinculo (IRE)**[9] 5425 10-8-9 **58**........(b) WilliamCarson 13 49
(R A Harris) *led over 5f: wknd ins fnl f* **17/2**
0030 **7** 1 **Quantum Leap**[28] 4884 10-8-4 **56** oh1........(p) ThomasBubb(3) 3 44
(S Dow) *sn outpcd: nvr nrr* **16/1**
0420 **8** 1½ **Goose Green (IRE)**[46] 4326 3-8-13 **65**........ HaddenFrost 1 49
(R J Hodges) *chsd ldrs: pushed along 1/2-way: wknd wl over 1f out* **8/1**
3100 **9** 1¾ **Outer Hebrides**[18] 5166 6-9-2 **68**........(v) BarrySavage(3) 8 48
(J M Bradley) *sn pushed along in rr: n.d* **25/1**
000 **10** 7 **King Egbert (FR)**[9] 5430 6-8-7 **56** oh4........ JackDean 12 17
(R J Price) *chsd ldrs over 4f* **20/1**
0301 **11** 1 **Torquemada (IRE)**[13] 5303 6-9-6 **69**........ JackMitchell 6 27
(J Akehurst) *s.i.s: hld up: hdwy over 2f out: wknd over 1f out* **10/3**[1]
000U **12** 16 **Danehill Warrior (IRE)**[27] 4920 3-8-2 **59** oh11 ow3........(p) ABetts(5) 7 —
(R C Guest) *mid-div: wknd over 2f out* **100/1**
1m 25.48s (-0.62) **Going Correction** -0.075s/f (Good)
WFA 3 from 4yo+ 3lb **12** Ran SP% **115.6**
Speed ratings (Par 103): **100,95,93,91,90 90,89,87,85,77 76,58**
CSF £41.52 CT £919.45 TOTE £4.40: £1.30, £2.30, £5.00; EX 37.20 TRIFECTA Not won..
Owner Mrs J Graham & Partners **Bred** Patrick M Ryan **Trained** Kingston Warren, Oxon
FOCUS
A moderate 'hands and heels' apprentice handicap restricted to riders who, at the start of the season, had not ridden more than ten winners. The form is rated around the placed horses but slightly below recent marks.

5688 GOLDEN HAND (S) STKS 7f 9y
3:00 (3:02) (Class 6) 3-Y-O **£2,590** (£770; £385; £192) **Stalls** Low

Form RPR
0660 **1** **Montemayorprincess (IRE)**[31] 4759 3-8-8 45 ow2........(p) TedDurcan 1 54
(D Haydn Jones) *sn outpcd: hdwy over 1f out: edgd rt and r.o to ld wl ins fnl f* **33/1**
0003 **2** 1 **Brave Jack (IRE)**[14] 5276 3-8-11 45........ JohnEgan 7 54
(J R Best) *in rr: hdwy 1/2-way: rdn to ld and edgd rt over 1f out: hdd wl ins fnl f* **15/2**
04 **3** 1¼ **Hawridge Miss**[14] 5269 3-8-6 0........ RichardKingscote 9 46
(B R Millman) *s.i.s: sn prom: chsd ldr over 2f out: rdn and ev ch over 1f out: styd on same pce ins fnl f* **12/1**
2232 **4** 2 **Calloff The Search**[6] 5511 3-8-11 53........(v) SaleemGolam 15 45
(W G M Turner) *s.i.s: hdwy over 5f out: led 3f out: rdn and hdd over 1f out: no ex ins fnl f* **6/1**[2]
1300 **5** *nk* **Xalted**[4] 5576 3-8-4 51........ WilliamCarson(7) 11 44
(S C Williams) *hld up in tch: rdn over 2f out: styd on* **13/2**[3]
0-35 **6** 1½ **Slo Mo Shun**[18] 5179 3-8-6 49........ JimmyQuinn 6 37
(H J L Dunlop) *hld up: hdwy over 2f out: wknd fnl f* **4/1**[1]
0066 **7** ¾ **Didactic**[23] 5041 3-8-4 43........ RobbieEgan(7) 3 38
(A J McCabe) *sn outpcd: hdwy over 1f out: nrst fin* **50/1**
2104 **8** 6 **Smash N'Grab (IRE)**[2] 5627 3-8-8 56........(p) AndrewMullen(3) 14 22
(K A Ryan) *led: hdd 5f out: rdn 1/2-way: wknd over 1f out* **4/1**[1]
0000 **9** *nk* **Royal Guest**[9] 5420 3-8-11 50........(v) TPO'Shea 5 21
(M R Channon) *dwlt: outpcd: hdwy over 2f out: wknd over 1f out* **16/1**
0003 **10** 1¾ **Suhayl Star (IRE)**[10] 5386 3-9-2 54........(p) NickyMackay 2 22
(S W Hall) *chsd ldrs over 4f* **16/1**
5040 **11** 2 **Davaye**[18] 5159 3-8-8 58........ AndrewElliott(3) 10 11
(K R Burke) *prom over 4f* **8/1**
4000 **12** 13 **Mr Chocolate Drop (IRE)**[28] 3950 3-8-11 49........ SamHitchcott 17 —
(Miss M E Rowland) *mid-div: rdn 1/2-way: sn wknd* **100/1**
-650 **13** 2½ **One White Sock**[14] 5270 3-8-3 43........(b) MarcHalford(3) 4 —
(J L Spearing) *led 5f out: hdd 3f out: sn rdn and wknd* **66/1**
-305 **14** 1½ **Aggbag**[234] 335 3-8-9 54........ JackMitchell(7) 18 —
(B P J Baugh) *prom 4f* **66/1**
6000 **15** 1¼ **Pat Will (IRE)**[38] 4561 3-8-6 44........(b) RichardMullen 12 —
(P D Evans) *chsd ldrs over 4f* **66/1**

0 **16** *33* **Bit Of A Monkey**[39] 4530 3-8-6 0 KevinGhunowa(5) 8 —
(L P Grassick) *edgd rt s: sn hung rt and outpcd* **100/1**

0-0 **17** *9* **Out Of Town**[43] 4426 3-8-11 0 PaulMulrennan 16 —
(R C Guest) *chsd ldrs to 1/2-way* **100/1**

1m 26.42s (0.32) **Going Correction** -0.075s/f (Good) **17** Ran SP% **122.3**
Speed ratings (Par 99): **95,93,92,90,89 88,87,80,80,78 75,60,58,56,54 17,6**
CSF £264.22 TOTE £36.50: £9.80, £3.40, £4.50; EX 437.50 TRIFECTA Not won..The winner was bought in for 5,600gns. Smash N Grab was claimed by J Jenkins for £6,000.
Owner R Phillips **Bred** Thomas Morrin **Trained** Efail Isaf, Rhondda C Taff

FOCUS
A typical seller with the winner back to juvenile form and the runner-up slightly up on his recent effort.

5689 CLUB ROOM PRIVATE HIRE H'CAP 5f 2y
3:30 (3:30) (Class 3) (0-95,92) 3-Y-0 **£6,939** (£2,076; £1,038; £519; £258) **Stalls** Low

Form RPR

00 **1** **Kay Two (IRE)**[10] 5379 5-8-7 **80** (p) JimmyQuinn 10 89
(R J Price) *led to 1/2-way: rdn to ld ins fnl f: r.o* **8/1**

2005 **2** *shd* **Cape Royal**[13] 5305 7-8-11 **89** (bt) KevinGhunowa(5) 2 98
(J M Bradley) *chsd wnr: led and hung rt fr 1/2-way: rdn and hdd ins fnl f: r.o* **16/1**

2312 **3** *hd* **Matsunosuke**[2] 5642 5-8-9 **82** KerrinMcEvoy 12 90+
(A B Coogan) *chsd ldrs: rdn ins fnl f: r.o* **7/2**[1]

0102 **4** *1* **Aegean Dancer**[23] 5044 5-8-12 **88** MarkLawson(3) 6 93
(B Smart) *chsd ldrs: rdn 1/2-way: styd on* **9/2**[2]

-100 **5** *nk* **Maker's Mark (IRE)**[11] 5356 3-8-9 **83** FergusSweeney 13 87
(H Candy) *wnt rt s: sn outpcd: hdwy over 1f out: r.o* **12/1**

4104 **6** *nk* **Border Music**[42] 4456 6-9-3 **90** (b) FrancisNorton 11 93
(A M Balding) *trckd ldrs: rdn over 1f out: styd on* **13/2**

1215 **7** *¾* **Melalchrist**[9] 5401 5-8-9 **85** (b) AndrewMullen(3) 3 85
(K A Ryan) *chsd ldrs: rdn and edgd rt over 1f out: styd on same pce* **12/1**

0150 **8** *1 ¼* **Ishi Adiva**[30] 4806 3-9-1 **89** RichardKingscote 7 84
(Tom Dascombe) *hld up: rdn over 1f out: nt trble ldrs* **22/1**

3010 **9** *shd* **Phantom Whisper**[23] 5050 4-9-5 **92** TedDurcan 8 87+
(B R Millman) *chsd ldrs: lost pl over 3f out: nt clr run over 1f out: n.d after* **16/1**

0023 **10** *3* **Texas Gold**[8] 5447 9-8-11 **84** RichardMullen 9 68
(W R Muir) *hld up: effrt over 1f out: wknd ins fnl f* **16/1**

4121 **11** *1* **Little Edward**[8] 5447 9-9-1 **88** 6ex GeorgeBaker 1 69
(R J Hodges) *hld up: a in rr* **5/1**[3]

59.11 secs (-1.79) **Going Correction** -0.075s/f (Good) **11** Ran SP% **118.9**
WFA 3 from 4yo+ 1lb
Speed ratings (Par 107): **111,110,110,108,108 107,106,104,104,99 98**
CSF £129.61 CT £540.89 TOTE £9.70: £3.30, £5.60, £1.60; EX 154.50 TRIFECTA Not won..
Owner H McGahon, D McCarthy & B Llewellyn **Bred** Roger A Ryan **Trained** Ullingswick, H'fords

FOCUS
A decent sprint handicap and the winning time was good. The form looks reasonable despite nothing getting into the race from the rear, with the runner-up, fourth and fifth setting the level.

NOTEBOOK
Kay Two(IRE) had been proving very frustrating so far this season, but the easing in the ground was in his favour and, with first-time cheekpieces applied to help him concentrate, he gamely recorded his first success of the campaign. He looked vulnerable when strongly challenged inside the final couple of furlongs, but he really stuck his neck out. He is well suited by a bit of give in the ground and could be in for a good autumn. (op 12-1)
Cape Royal had dropped to a mark 1lb lower than when successful at Epsom earlier in the season and he ran close to his best in defeat. (op 14-1)
Matsunosuke travelled quite smoothly, but some of his best efforts have come on a stiff track when the leaders are stopping in front and on this occasion Kay Two failed to come back in time. The easing of the ground was probably not ideal. (tchd 10-3 and 4-1)
Aegean Dancer would not have minded the return to the minimum trip, but he is another who probably would not have appreciated the easing in the ground. (op 6-1 tchd 13-2)
Maker's Mark(IRE) struggled to land a telling blow and may be worth a try back over 6f on quicker ground. (tchd 14-1)
Border Music probably needs quicker ground. (op 6-1 tchd 11-2 and 7-1)
Texas Gold Official explanation: jockey said gelding found the good ground too slow
Little Edward has been in great form lately, but he never looked like defying a 6lb penalty for his recent Bath success. Official explanation: jockey said gelding found the good ground too slow (op 9-2 tchd 11-2)

5690 HENRY ALKEN CLAIMING STKS 1m 1f 218y
4:00 (4:00) (Class 6) 3-4-Y-0 **£2,590** (£770; £385; £192) **Stalls** High

Form RPR

0051 **1** **Birkside**[13] 5310 4-9-1 62 JohnEgan 5 60
(S Dow) *hld up: hdwy u.p 2f out: styd on to ld wl ins fnl f* **13/8**[1]

1500 **2** *½* **Diamond Key (IRE)**[17] 5187 3-8-6 47 (b) JimmyQuinn 6 56
(M G Quinlan) *chsd ldrs: led 3f out: rdn over 1f out: hdd wl ins fnl f* **8/1**

-000 **3** *2 ½* **Divine River**[20] 5111 4-8-8 60 TPO'Shea 2 47
(J G Portman) *hld up: hdwy over 3f out: rdn over 1f out: styd on same pce fnl f* **9/1**

2300 **4** *1 ¼* **Our Herbie**[12] 5338 3-8-11 59 TedDurcan 4 54
(J W Hills) *hld up in tch: rdn over 2f out: hung rt fr over 1f out: styd on same pce* **11/4**[2]

3000 **5** *¾* **Arabellas Homer**[27] 4920 3-8-1 42 ow1 AndrewElliott(3) 1 45
(Mrs N Macauley) *led: hdd over 7f out: chsd ldr: ev ch 3f out: sn rdn: no ex fnl f* **33/1**

0005 **6** *5* **Polish Prospect (IRE)**[14] 5269 3-8-0 40 AdrianMcCarthy 8 31
(H S Howe) *chsd ldrs: rdn over 2f out: wknd over 1f out* **18/1**

0006 **7** *1* **Fancy You (IRE)**[28] 3612 4-8-3 38 LukeMorris(5) 7 31
(A W Carroll) *hld up: racd keenly: rdn over 2f out: wknd over 1f out* **66/1**

-000 **8** *39* **Pertemps Green**[44] 4395 4-9-1 52 GeorgeBaker 3 —
(Stef Liddiard) *s.s: plld hrd: hdwy to ld over 7f out: hdd & wknd 3f out* **5/1**[3]

2m 10.87s (2.57) **Going Correction** +0.25s/f (Good)
WFA 3 from 4yo 6lb **8** Ran SP% **112.2**
Speed ratings (Par 101): **99,98,96,95,95 91,90,59**
CSF £15.07 TOTE £2.20: £1.10, £2.20, £2.00; EX 14.80 Trifecta £49.80 Pool £348.73 - 4.97 winning units..The winner was claimed by Declan Carroll for £10,000.
Owner S Dow **Bred** Pendley Farm **Trained** Epsom, Surrey

FOCUS
A moderate claimer that was steadily run and the form is not solid.

Pertemps Green Official explanation: jockey said gelding ran very free early

5691 E B F KEGWORTH NOVICE STKS 7f 9y
4:30 (4:30) (Class 4) 2-Y-0 **£5,047** (£1,510; £755; £377) **Stalls** Low

Form RPR

2010 **1** **Fitzroy Crossing (USA)**[16] 5216 2-9-2 86 GregFairley 3 90
(M Johnston) *chsd ldr tl rdn over 2f out: nt clr run and outpcd sn after: hung lft over 1f out: rallied to ld towards fin* **12/1**[3]

1 **2** *½* **Perfect Stride**[24] 5011 2-9-5 0 KerrinMcEvoy 1 92
(Sir Michael Stoute) *chsd ldrs: led ins fnl f: sn rdn and hung lft: hdd towards fin* **1/4**[1]

1321 **3** *3* **Gross Prophet**[17] 5207 2-9-9 86 RichardKingscote 4 88
(Tom Dascombe) *led: rdn and hung rt over 2f out: hdd and no ex ins fnl f* **6/1**[2]

210 **4** *2* **Quick Release (IRE)**[24] 5004 2-9-5 82 RichardMullen 2 79
(D M Simcock) *s.i.s: hld up in tch: rdn over 2f out: wknd fnl f* **22/1**

1m 25.61s (-0.49) **Going Correction** -0.075s/f (Good) **4** Ran SP% **106.3**
Speed ratings (Par 97): **99,98,95,92**
CSF £16.06 TOTE £12.70; EX 19.90.
Owner Favourites Racing XXIII **Bred** Diamond G Ranch, Inc **Trained** Middleham Moor, N Yorks

FOCUS
A good novice event, but not the result many expected. The form looks solid enough despite the small field.

NOTEBOOK
Fitzroy Crossing(USA) did not put up much of a show in a Haydock nursery on his previous start, but this step up in trip clearly suited and he turned over the odds-on favourite. He appeared at an advantage racing against the stands' rail in the closing stages, with Perfect Stride more towards the centre of the track for much of the way, and the bare result probably flatters him, but he is obviously still very useful when everything falls right. (op 10-1 tchd 14-1)
Perfect Stride looked a serious prospect when winning on his debut over this trip at Sandown, and the form of that race has been working out well, so this has to be considered disappointing. His jockey looked confident for much of the way, just encouraging his mount with hands and heels when initially trying to make a move, but one got the impression McEvoy did not spot Fitzroy Crossing against the stands' rail until well inside the final furlong. When finally put under serious pressure, Perfect Stride still looked green and hung to his left. A Dewhurst and Racing Post Trophy entrant, he is highly regarded and, likely to leave this form behind as he matures, he is certainly not one to give up on just yet. (op 2-7 tchd 2-9)
Gross Prophet would have found this tougher than the 6f Newbury nursery he won off a mark of 80 on his previous start, but this trip seemed to stretch him in any case. He can do better when returned to sprint trips. Official explanation: jockey said gelding hung right (tchd 15-2)
Quick Release(IRE) was disappointing in a Listed race at Salisbury on his previous start and this was another ordinary effort. (op 14-1)

5692 ASTON FLAMVILLE FILLIES' NURSERY 5f 218y
5:00 (5:01) (Class 4) (0-85,83) 2-Y-0 **£3,886** (£1,156; £577; £288) **Stalls** Low

Form RPR

2320 **1** **Feisty Royale**[16] 5216 2-8-10 **72** GregFairley 1 75
(M Johnston) *led: rdn and hung rt fr over 2f out: hdd over 1f out: rallied to ld wl ins fnl f* **8/1**[3]

2U16 **2** *hd* **Ocean Transit (IRE)**[18] 5164 2-8-9 **78** JackDean(7) 9 80
(W G M Turner) *chsd ldrs: hrd rdn to ld over 1f out: hdd wl ins fnl f* **12/1**

0210 **3** *1 ½* **Meridian Line (IRE)**[29] 4844 2-9-7 **83** RichardKingscote 4 81
(J G Portman) *chsd ldrs: rdn 2f out: sn outpcd: hung rt and styd on ins fnl f* **14/1**

5310 **4** *shd* **Nylla**[31] 4762 2-8-13 **75** TPO'Shea 7 73
(M R Channon) *chsd ldrs: rdn and ev ch over 1f out: styd on same pce ins fnl f* **17/2**

01 **5** *hd* **Jennifer's Dream (IRE)**[27] 4924 2-9-2 **81** AndrewMullen(3) 8 78
(K A Ryan) *hld up: n.m.r sn after s: hdwy over 2f out: rdn and ev ch over 1f out: edgd lft and no ex ins fnl f* **10/1**

10 **6** *1* **Little Firecracker**[17] 5199 2-8-6 **68** NickyMackay 10 62
(L M Cumani) *hld up: hdwy over 2f out: rdn and styng on whn n.m.r towards fin* **17/2**

1346 **7** *1* **Longoria (IRE)**[38] 4560 2-8-0 **69** MCGeran(7) 2 61+
(M G Quinlan) *s.i.s: hld up: hdwy 2f out: styng on whn hmpd ins fnl f* **17/2**

0043 **8** *¾* **Mollyatti**[6] 5496 2-8-8 **75** LukeMorris(5) 3 64
(Miss V Haigh) *prom: rdn 1/2-way: styd on same pce fnl f* **20/1**

003 **9** *2 ½* **Bahamian Ballad**[15] 5252 2-8-7 **69** JimmyQuinn 11 50
(J D Bethell) *prom: rdn over 2f out: wknd over 1f out* **11/2**[2]

0003 **10** *shd* **Polish Priory (IRE)**[8] 5442 2-8-6 **68** RichardMullen 12 49
(P D Evans) *w ldrs: rdn over 2f out: wknd over 1f out* **33/1**

0410 **11** *shd* **Close To Paradise (IRE)**[12] 5322 2-9-1 **77** TedDurcan 6 58+
(E A L Dunlop) *chsd ldrs: rdn over 2f out: edgd rt and wknd over 1f out* **11/4**[1]

1m 13.32s (0.12) **Going Correction** -0.075s/f (Good) **11** Ran SP% **115.9**
Speed ratings (Par 94): **96,95,93,93,93 92,90,89,86,86 86**
CSF £98.47 CT £1349.06 TOTE £8.90: £3.60, £3.80, £4.70; EX 110.00 Trifecta £214.60 Part won. Pool £302.34 - 0.35 winning units..
Owner T T Bloodstocks **Bred** Aston Mullins Stud **Trained** Middleham Moor, N Yorks

FOCUS
A pretty ordinary fillies' nursery for the grade and the form is rated around the principals.

NOTEBOOK
Feisty Royale failed to beat a rival on her handicap debut at Haydock, but she left that form behind to get off the mark at the fifth attempt. She battled on well, as so many from her stable do, and she should remain competitive in similar company. (op 9-1 tchd 10-1)
Ocean Transit(IRE) did not run too badly in a Listed race at Salisbury on her previous start, but this was more realistic and she was just held. (tchd 14-1)
Meridian Line(IRE) looked on a stiff enough mark, but she ran well conceding weight all round. (op 12-1)
Nylla could make little impression in a nursery at Newbury on her previous start, but this was a little more encouraging. (op 9-1 tchd 8-1)
Jennifer's Dream(IRE)'s maiden success came over 5f on quick ground and she did not run badly under these different conditions. (op 8-1)
Longoria(IRE) Official explanation: jockey said filly was denied a clear run
Close To Paradise(IRE) seemed to travel quite well for much of the way, but she failed to see her race out and was disappointing. (op 3-1 tchd 10-3)

5693 HIGHFIELDS H'CAP 1m 60y
5:30 (5:30) (Class 5) (0-75,74) 3-Y-0+ **£3,238** (£963; £481; £240) **Stalls** High

Form RPR

0400 **1** **Red Somerset (USA)**[24] 5012 4-9-3 **69** FrancisNorton 10 80
(R J Hodges) *mde all: rdn over 1f out: styd on wl* **7/2**[1]

0066 **2** *1 ½* **Rubenstar (IRE)**[20] 5115 4-9-7 **73** JimmyQuinn 7 80+
(M H Tompkins) *hld up: hdwy over 2f out: rdn and hung rt ins fnl f: r.o* **13/2**

0441 **3** *shd* **Jawaab (IRE)**[12] 5330 3-8-13 **69** RichardMullen 5 76+
(M A Buckley) *hld up: nt clr run over 3f out: r.o ins fnl f: nvr nrr* **11/2**
0601 **4** *1* **Tyzack (IRE)**[18] 5166 6-9-8 **74** GeorgeBaker 12 79
(Stef Liddiard) *trckd ldrs: racd keenly: rdn over 1f out: styd on same pce* **9/2**[3]
6312 **5** *1 1/2* **Cool Ebony**[16] 5228 4-9-8 **74** (p) PhillipMakin 8 75
(M Dods) *chsd wnr: rdn over 2f out: no ex fnl f* **4/1**[2]
0101 **6** *1* **Grand Vizier (IRE)**[59] 3926 3-9-0 **70** LiamJones 6 69
(C F Wall) *chsd ldrs: rdn over 2f out: no ex fnl f* **12/1**
0300 **7** *nk* **Glenmuir (IRE)**[10] 5383 4-9-2 **68** TedDurcan 1 66
(B R Millman) *hld up: hdwy u.p and hung rt fr over 1f out: nt trble ldrs* **16/1**
4010 **8** *11* **Coup D'Etat**[30] 4807 5-9-1 **72** (b) KevinGhunowa(5) 9 45
(R A Harris) *hld up in tch: racd keenly: wknd over 2f out* **18/1**
0340 **9** *2 1/2* **The Gaikwar (IRE)**[11] 5348 8-8-6 **63** (b) LukeMorris(5) 3 30
(R A Harris) *hld up: rdn over 3f out: nt run on* **25/1**
0000 **10** *13* **Happy As Larry (USA)**[4] 5559 5-9-7 **73** (t) JohnEgan 2 10
(D J Murphy) *mid-div: shkn up 1/2-way: wknd wl over 1f out* **20/1**

1m 46.26s (0.96) **Going Correction** +0.25s/f (Good)
WFA 3 from 4yo+ 4lb **10** Ran SP% **116.6**
Speed ratings (Par 103): **105,103,103,102,100 99,99,88,86,73**
CSF £26.53 CT £126.04 TOTE £4.60: £1.90, £1.60, £2.60; EX 27.10 Trifecta £44.60 Place 6 £11,358.39, Place 5 £3,195.13. Pool £188.59 - 3.00 winning units..
Owner Fieldspring Racing **Bred** Haras D'Etreham **Trained** Charlton Mackrell, Somerset

FOCUS
A fair handicap, but the winner was allowed the run of the race in front. The fourth to latest form is the best guide to the level.
Happy As Larry(USA) Official explanation: jockey said gelding found the good ground too slow
T/Jkpt: Not won. T/Plt: £9,278.10 to a £1 stake. Pool: £74,352.60. 5.85 winning tickets. T/Qpdt: £371.20 to a £1 stake. Pool: £3,662.70. 7.30 winning tickets. CR

4465 BALLINROBE (R-H)
Monday, September 24

OFFICIAL GOING: Yielding

5696a IRELAND'S LAKE DISTRICT RACE 1m 1f
3:45 (3:48) 3-Y-0+ **£7,003** (£1,631; £719; £415)

RPR
1 **Caravel (IRE)**[18] 5156 3-9-9 DPMcDonogh 2 88
(Sir Mark Prescott) *reluctant to load: sn trckd ldrs in 3rd: rdn to chal fr over 2f out: sn 2nd: led and wandered sltly ins fnl f: kpt on wl* **4/7**[1]
2 *hd* **Princely Hero (IRE)**[28] 4911 3-9-6 84 (b) PJSmullen 5 85
(D K Weld, Ire) *trckd ldr in 2nd: rdn to chal and dispute ld 2 1/2f out: sn narrowly in front: strly pressed and jst hdd ins fnl f: sltly hmpd: kpt on wl* **15/8**[2]
3 *6* **Invincible Star (IRE)**[9] 5440 3-8-3 66 ow1 (t) OCasey(5) 4 60
(Peter Casey, Ire) *chsd ldrs: no imp u.p fr over 3f out: mod 4th and kpt on same pce fr 2 1/2f out* **16/1**
4 *nk* **Barndeh (IRE)**[13] 5318 4-9-0 62 (b[1]) DJMoran(3) 14 64
(R McGlinchey, Ire) *led: strly pressed and jnd fr 2 1/2f out: 3rd and no ex fr 1 1/2f out: kpt on same pce* **25/1**
5 *18* **Masriyna's Heiress (IRE)**[25] 4984 6-8-12 44 (p) DMGrant 10 21
(Daniel J P Barry, Ire) *prom: rdn 1/2-way: sn mod 4th and no imp: 5th and kpt on same pce fr 2 1/2f out* **100/1**
6 *4* **Golden Banjo (IRE)**[342] 6042 3-8-12 CDHayes 6 18
(Ms Joanna Morgan, Ire) *towards rr: kpt on wout threatening u.p fr over 3f out* **50/1**
7 *3/4* **Cnoc Rua (IRE)**[48] 3010 3-9-6 74 WJSupple 11 24
(Timothy Doyle, Ire) *chsd ldrs: 7th 1/2-way: no imp u.p and kpt on same pce fr over 3f out* **12/1**[3]
8 *1* **Black Wish (IRE)**[463] 2373 8-8-12 43 FranciscoDaSilva 13 9
(L Young, Ire) *mid-div: 8th and rdn 1/2-way: no imp and kpt on same pce fr over 3f out* **100/1**
9 *7* **Merry Moon (IRE)**[350] 5860 3-8-8 PBBeggy(3) 8 —
(R J Osborne, Ire) *towards rr: no imp u.p and kpt on same pce fr over 3f out* **50/1**
10 *nk* **Major Melody (IRE)**[13] 5319 5-9-0 SMGorey(3) 7 —
(J J Lennon, Ire) *mid-div: 9th 1/2-way: no imp u.p fr over 3f out* **66/1**
11 *2 1/2* **Karagan (FR)**[5] 5547 5-8-10 AmyKathleenParsons(7) 12 —
(T G McCourt, Ire) *v.s.a: a bhd* **66/1**
12 *3* **Assir**[36] 2449 5-8-5 BACurtis(7) 9 —
(C Hennessy, Ire) *in rr of mid-div: mod 11th appr 1/2-way: no ex u.p fr over 3f out* **20/1**
13 *2 1/2* **The Card Shark (IRE)**[1112] 5430 7-9-3 JAHeffernan 1 —
(Vivian J Noone, Ire) *in rr of mid-div: mod 10th 1/2-way: no ex u.p fr over 3f out* **66/1**
14 *2 1/2* **Sean Og Coulston (IRE)**[2] 5651 3-8-12 MCHussey 3 —
(John J Coleman, Ire) *chsd ldrs: mod 5th fr sn after 1/2-way: sn no ex u.p* **33/1**

2m 6.30s (-0.20)
WFA 3 from 4yo+ 5lb **14** Ran SP% **133.9**
CSF £1.96 TOTE £1.50: £1.10, £1.70, £10.30; DF 1.80.
Owner Neil Greig - Osborne House **Bred** G A M Grothier **Trained** Newmarket, Suffolk

NOTEBOOK
Caravel(IRE), a typically progressive Sir Mark Prescott-trained three-year-old, came into this in search of a five-timer and was made to work a lot harder than would have been expected, not doing a lot in front and nearly throwing it away. His trainer does expectionally well as placing his horses in Ireland and he may well go on and make it six. (op 9/10 tchd 1/1)

5697 - (Foreign Racing) - See Raceform Interactive

5520 BEVERLEY (R-H)
Tuesday, September 25

OFFICIAL GOING: Good (good to soft in places in home straight; 8.5)
Wind: Moderate, half against Weather: Sunny periods

5698 HAPPY BIRTHDAY EMMA (S) STKS 1m 4f 16y
2:00 (2:00) (Class 5) 3-4-Y-0 **£2,914** (£867; £433; £216) **Stalls** High

Form RPR
-002 **1** **Mister Fizzbomb (IRE)**[8] 5487 4-9-2 53 (v) GrahamGibbons 2 59
(J S Wainwright) *cl up: led after 2f: rdn clr 2f out: styd on wl* **3/1**[1]
0440 **2** *5* **Leprechaun's Gold (IRE)**[17] 5235 3-8-8 46 FrancisNorton 5 51
(B J Llewellyn) *hld up: stdy hdwy over 3f out: rdn to chse wnr wl over 1f out: kpt on u.p ins fnl f* **12/1**
P50 **3** *4* **Everyman**[47] 4333 3-8-8 46 LiamJones 10 45
(A W Carroll) *bhd: hdwy 4f out: rdn along over 2f out: styd on appr fnl f: nrst fin* **13/2**[3]
5036 **4** *1 1/4* **Cecina Marina**[19] 5158 4-8-11 44 PaulMulrennan 11 38
(C W Thornton) *trckd ldrs: effrt 3f out: rdn along over 2f out: wknd ent fnl f* **5/1**[2]
0520 **5** *3* **Namarian (IRE)**[45] 4391 3-8-3 44 (b) RoystonFfrench 1 33
(T D Easterby) *hld up in tch: effrt and sme hdwy 4f out: rdn along over 2f out: sn one pce* **5/1**[2]
0304 **6** *12* **Ranavalona**[8] 5487 3-8-1 45 ow1 (t) AndrewElliott(3) 6 15
(C Smith) *midfield: hdwy on outer to chse ldrs 4f out: rdn along 3f out and sn btn* **8/1**
5-00 **7** *nk* **Gavanello**[102] 1376 4-9-2 30 StephenDonohoe 9 18
(M C Chapman) *a in rr* **150/1**
6330 **8** *4* **Flashing Floozie**[10] 5427 4-8-11 46 LukeMorris(5) 8 12
(A W Carroll) *prom: rdn along 3f out: sn drvn and wknd* **7/1**
4050 **9** *4* **Ellies Faith**[8] 5487 3-8-8 46 (b) PaulFessey 7 5
(N Bycroft) *led 2f: prom tl rdn along 4f out and grad wknd frm over 2f out* **11/1**
0400 **10** *18* **Mister Maq**[55] 4082 4-9-2 42 (b) PaulHanagan 12 —
(A Crook) *a in rr* **66/1**

2m 43.75s (3.54) **Going Correction** +0.325s/f (Good)
WFA 3 from 4yo 8lb **10** Ran SP% **113.5**
Speed ratings (Par 103): **101,97,95,94,92 84,83,81,78,66**
CSF £40.22 TOTE £3.90: £1.30, £3.90, £2.70; EX 37.30.There was no bid for the winner.
Owner S Enwright **Bred** Remora Bloodstock Ltd **Trained** Kennythorpe, N Yorks

FOCUS
A weak seller but run in a reasonable time and the third sets the standard.

5699 NUFFIELD HOSPITALS 50TH ANNIVERSARY CELEBRATION NOVICE STKS 5f
2:30 (2:32) (Class 4) 2-Y-0 **£4,210** (£1,252; £625; £312) **Stalls** High

Form RPR
1365 **1** **In Uniform**[60] 3910 2-9-0 96 RichardMullen 4 86+
(E S McMahon) *mde all: qcknd 2f out: rdn over 1f out: kpt on ins fnl f* **11/10**[1]
010 **2** *3* **Baldemar**[32] 4775 2-9-5 77 PhillipMakin 6 80
(K R Burke) *a.p: chsd wnr fr 1/2-way: rdn over 1f out and kpt on same pce* **11/2**[3]
1 **3** *1 3/4* **Prime Performer (IRE)**[122] 2021 2-9-0 0 TomEaves 5 69
(B Smart) *chsd ldrs: rdn along wl over 1f out and sn one pce* **5/2**[2]
4 *7* **Tittle** 2-8-3 0 FrancisNorton 1 33
(H Candy) *chsd ldrs: rn green and outpcd 1/2-way: pushed along and styd on appr fnl f: nrst fin* **11/2**[3]
00 **5** *shd* **Flex**[6] 5521 2-8-12 0 GrahamGibbons 2 41
(D J Murphy) *cl up: rdn along over 2f out: wknd wl over 1f out* **100/1**
000 **6** *12* **Howe's Jack (IRE)**[39] 4586 2-8-12 40 LiamJones 3 —
(M C Chapman) *sn outpcd and bhd fr 1/2-way* **200/1**

64.79 secs (0.79) **Going Correction** +0.15s/f (Good) **6** Ran SP% **108.4**
Speed ratings (Par 97): **99,94,91,80,80 60**
CSF £7.23 TOTE £1.90: £1.70, £1.30; EX 6.30.
Owner J C Fretwell **Bred** Mrs H B Raw **Trained** Lichfield, Staffs

FOCUS
Not strong form for the grade with the winner not needing to be at his best to score and the race could be rated higher.

NOTEBOOK
In Uniform was very much the one to beat in this grade and his rider did the wise thing and sent him out to make every yard. The drop back to the minimum trip suited him but the softish ground did not, and it was his class that saw him through in the end. He is now off to the sales. (tchd 10-11 and 6-5)
Baldemar, well held in a sales race last time out, has a rating of 77 and had plenty to find with the winner, especially as he had to give him 5lb. He is by Namid though, and the easing ground was more in his favour than the winner. (op 7-1 tchd 15-2)
Prime Performer(IRE), who won a maiden over this course and distance back in May, had a problem afterwards, hence the absence. Weak in the market for this return to action, she was a shade disappointing, but could be the type who needs another year overn her back to be seen at her best. (op 15-8 tchd 13-8)
Tittle, whose dam was a dual winner over 5f and is a half-sister to champion older sprinter Kyllachy, was too green to do herself justice on this debut. She was not given a hard race though, and will improve a good deal for the experience. (op 7-1 tchd 8-1)

5700 VIOLET AND EDDIE SMITH MEMORIAL CONDITIONS STKS 5f
3:00 (3:01) (Class 3) 3-Y-0+
£6,855 (£2,052; £1,026; £513; £256; £128) **Stalls** High

Form RPR
0-40 **1** **Philharmonic**[38] 4614 6-8-9 96 PaulHanagan 2 104
(R A Fahey) *trckd ldrs: hdwy 1/2-way: rdn over 1f out: drvn and kpt on wl to ld last 75yds* **11/4**[1]
3004 **2** *3/4* **Bond City (IRE)**[14] 5305 5-8-9 98 (p) DanielTudhope 4 101
(G R Oldroyd) *cl up: led after 1 1/2f: rdn 2f out: drvn ins fnl f: hdd and nt qckn last 75yds* **5/1**
2430 **3** *nk* **Hoh Hoh Hoh**[10] 5407 5-8-9 94 J-PGuillambert 7 100
(R J Price) *hld up in rr: hdwy 2f out: effrt to chal ent fnl f: sn rdn and ev ch tl drvn and nt qckn last 100yds* **10/3**[2]
0600 **4** *2* **Tournedos (IRE)**[58] 3990 5-8-9 89 AdrianTNicholls 9 93
(D Nicholls) *cl up on inner: effrt 2f out and ev ch tl rdn and wknd ent fnl f* **9/1**
0040 **5** *nk* **Tabaret**[10] 5407 4-8-9 92 TomEaves 1 92
(R M Whitaker) *chsd ldrs on outer: rdn along 2f out: kpt on u.p ins fnl f* **13/2**
0425 **6** *7* **The Trader (IRE)**[30] 4871 9-8-10 100 ow1 (b) NCallan 5 68
(M Blanshard) *wnt rt s: chsd ldrs: rdn along 2f out and grad wknd* **9/2**[3]
032- **7** *2* **Stolt (IRE)**[430] 3720 3-8-8 89 GrahamGibbons 8 59
(N Wilson) *led 1 1/2f: cl up tl rdn along 1/2-way and sn wknd* **40/1**
6000 **8** *6* **Minimum Fuss (IRE)**[27] 4939 3-7-10 45 CharlotteKerton(7) 6 33
(M C Chapman) *hmpd s: a outpcd and bhd* **200/1**

64.07 secs (0.07) **Going Correction** +0.15s/f (Good)
WFA 3 from 4yo+ 1lb **8** Ran SP% **110.9**
Speed ratings (Par 107): **105,103,103,100,99 88,85,75**
CSF £15.77 TOTE £4.00: £1.80, £1.80, £1.30; EX 20.70.
Owner R Cowie **Bred** Raymond Cowie **Trained** Musley Bank, N Yorks

FOCUS
A competitive little conditions race made up mainly of hard-to-place types. The third looks the best guide to the form.

NOTEBOOK
Philharmonic won this race last year and, by finishing strongly to repeat that victory, he improved his course record to 2111. He appreciates the stiff finish here and the bit of ease in the ground was in his favour too. (op 3-1)
Bond City(IRE) showed good pace from the off and made a bold bid. Only collared by the winner well inside the last, this was a rare good opportunity for him as he is difficult to place off his current mark. (tchd 11-2)
Hoh Hoh Hoh, who was drawn on the wrong side in the Portland last time, came through to have his chance travelling well, but he did not find a great deal off the bridle. (op 3-1 tchd 11-4)
Tournedos(IRE), who has gone backwards this season, seeing his mark drop from three figures to 89, is better suited by a sharper track. (op 8-1)
Tabaret probably wants quicker ground than this, but he has become a difficult horse to win with over the last two years. (op 7-1 tchd 8-1)
The Trader(IRE) was best in at the weights according to official figures but he seems to be on the downgrade now.

5701 MKM BUILDING SUPPLIES H'CAP — 7f 100y
3:30 (3:30) (Class 5) (0-75,73) 3-Y-O+ — **£3,238** (£963; £481; £240) **Stalls** High

Form — RPR
6550 **1** **Nuit Sombre (IRE)**[29] 4891 7-9-5 **70**............................(p) PaulFessey 10 — 78
(G A Harker) *mde all: pushed clr over 2f out: rdn wl over 1f out: drvn ins fnl f and styd on gamely* **33/1**
6110 **2** *shd* **Joshua's Gold (IRE)**[16] 5253 6-9-1 **66**..................(v) StephenDonohoe 5 — 74
(D Carroll) *hld up in midfield: hdwy over 2f out: rdn to chse wnr over 1f out: drvn and styd on strly ins fnl f: jst hld* **13/2[3]**
0060 **3** *1* **Crow's Nest Lad**[11] 5387 3-8-7 **61** ow1............................... DavidAllan 4 — 66+
(T D Easterby) *in rr: swtchd outside and hdwy 2f out: sn rdn and styd on strly ins fnl f: nrst fin* **50/1**
3000 **4** *2½* **Dispol Isle (IRE)**[16] 5253 5-8-10 **66**............................... NeilBrown(5) 12 — 65
(T D Barron) *hld up in tch: hdwy to chse ldrs 2f out: sn rdn and kpt on same pce* **13/2[3]**
4006 **5** *¾* **Tracer**[90] 3003 3-8-9 **63**.. DaleGibson 1 — 59+
(M W Easterby) *towards rr: hdwy 2f out: rdn and n.m.r over 1f out: styd on strly ins fnl f: nrst fin* **50/1**
4130 **6** *shd* **Cheery Cat (USA)**[27] 4940 3-8-10 **64**.......................(p) TonyHamilton 13 — 60
(D W Barker) *chsd wnr: rdn along 3f out: drvn wl over 1f out and grad wknd* **11/2[1]**
5002 **7** *1* **Sedge (USA)**[16] 5253 7-8-13 **64**....................................(p) MickyFenton 6 — 59
(P T Midgley) *midfield: effrt and sme hdwy over 2f out: sn rdn and no imp appr fnl f* **13/2[3]**
2240 **8** *1¾* **Kashmir Lady (FR)**[30] 4848 3-9-2 **70**............................... DaneO'Neill 7 — 59
(H Candy) *chsd ldrs: rdn along over 2f out: sn edgd lft and grad wknd* **6/1[2]**
-000 **9** *5* **Marshman (IRE)**[63] 3828 8-8-11 **69**........................... AshleyMorgan(7) 9 — 47
(M H Tompkins) *dwlt: a in rr* **11/1**
0000 **10** *3* **Mis Chicaf (IRE)**[17] 5228 6-8-7 **58** oh13.......................... JamesDoyle 8 — 28
(D Carroll) *prom: rdn along over 2f out: sn drvn and grad wknd* **80/1**
0060 **11** *2½* **Franksalot (IRE)**[14] 5303 7-8-12 **63**............................... RoystonFfrench 14 — 27
(I W McInnes) *stmbld s: sn chsng ldrs: rdn along wl over 2f out and sn wknd* **15/2**
0000 **12** *1½* **Foreign Edition (IRE)**[13] 5330 5-8-8 **59**....................... PaulHanagan 11 — 19
(Miss J A Camacho) *s.i.s: a in rr* **8/1**
0000 **13** *1* **Spume (IRE)**[11] 5383 3-9-5 **73**..................................... GrahamGibbons 3 — 30
(D J Murphy) *dwlt: a in rr* **12/1**

1m 36.74s (2.43) **Going Correction** +0.325s/f (Good)
WFA 3 from 4yo+ 3lb — **13** Ran SP% **116.7**
Speed ratings (Par 103): **99,98,97,94,94 93,92,90,85,81 78,77,75**
CSF £229.13 CT £10679.04 TOTE £52.30: £11.70, £2.80, £14.00; EX 395.00.
Owner P I Harker **Bred** M P B Bloodstock Ltd **Trained** Thirkleby, N Yorks
■ Stewards' Enquiry : Stephen Donohoe two-day ban: used whip with excessive frequency (Oct 8-9)

FOCUS
An ordinary handicap rated around the runner-up but with little solid behind.

5702 EBF BEVERLEY ANNUAL BADGEHOLDERS MEDIAN AUCTION MAIDEN STKS — 7f 100y
4:00 (4:00) (Class 6) 2-Y-O — **£3,412** (£1,007; £504) **Stalls** High

Form — RPR
02 **1** **Flight To Quality**[24] 5038 2-9-3 0............................... RoystonFfrench 5 — 72
(M Johnston) *mde all: rdn along 2f out and hung bdly lft to stands' rail: drvn ins fnl f and kpt on wl* **2/1[1]**
0 **2** *1½* **Long Distance (FR)**[39] 4584 2-9-3 0............................... OscarUrbina 8 — 69
(J R Fanshawe) *in tch: hdwy to chse ldrs 3f out: rdn along wl over 1f out and ev ch tl drvn and no ex wl ins fnl f* **7/2[2]**
63 **3** *1¼* **Formation (USA)**[18] 5200 2-9-3 0.................................... PaulHanagan 9 — 66
(E A L Dunlop) *trckd ldrs on inner: hdwy over 2f out: rdn over 1f out and ev ch tl no ex wl ins fnl f* **2/1[1]**
4 *3½* **My Shadow** 2-9-3 0.. RichardMullen 3 — 58+
(E S McMahon) *s.i.s and outpcd in rr: stdy hdwy 1/2-way: rdn along 2f out: styd on appr fnl f: nrst fin* **12/1**
0000 **5** *¾* **Aquarian Dancer**[48] 4278 2-8-12 45............................ PaulMulrennan 6 — 51
(Jedd O'Keeffe) *chsd ldrs: rdn along 3f out: kpt on same pce fnl 2f* **100/1**
043 **6** *12* **Reel Buddy Blaze**[14] 5294 2-9-3 73.............................. MickyFenton 7 — 28
(T P Tate) *prom: rdn along 3f out and sn wknd* **11/2[3]**
7 *14* **Stealth Project** 2-9-3 0.. StephenDonohoe 2 — —
(A M Hales) *a in rr* **66/1**
8 *2* **Ursus** 2-9-3 0... TonyHamilton 4 — —
(C R Wilson) *a in rr* **150/1**
00 **9** *19* **Miss Holderness**[8] 5485 2-8-12 0...................................... DavidAllan 1 — —
(J O'Reilly) *cl up: rdn along 1/2-way: sn wknd* **200/1**

1m 38.0s (3.69) **Going Correction** +0.325s/f (Good) — **9** Ran SP% **115.6**
Speed ratings (Par 93): **91,89,87,83,83 69,53,51,29**
CSF £9.55 TOTE £3.00: £1.10, £1.50, £1.10; EX 9.50.
Owner Markus Graff **Bred** P And Mrs A G Venner **Trained** Middleham Moor, N Yorks

FOCUS
Modest maiden form rated through the winner to his mark but limited by the proximity of the fifth.

NOTEBOOK
Flight To Quality had shaped with plenty of promise in his previous two starts and and looked likely to take some catching around here, with the extra bit of distance only going to help. He hung badly over to the stands' rail in the straight but had enough in hand to win well, and looks likely to be the sort who just keeps on improving as he steps up in trip. (op 15-8 tchd 13-8)
Long Distance(FR) improved on his debut effort at Newmarket and he is another who will be more the finished article next year when he will get to run over middle distances. (op 9-2)
Formation(USA) was a bit disappointing on this return to the turf but quicker ground might have suited him. He did swish his tail under pressure, though. Handicaps are now an option for him. (op 5-2 tchd 11-4)
My Shadow, who is out of a well-related mare, was slowly away and struggled in the early part of the race before getting the hang of things late in the day. He should have learnt plenty from this. (op 10-1)
Aquarian Dancer, well held in her previous four starts, has an official mark of 45 so her relative proximity does not do a lot for the value of the form.

5703 BRIAN AND JASON MERRINGTON MEMORIAL H'CAP — 1m 100y
4:30 (4:31) (Class 5) (0-75,74) 3-Y-O — **£3,238** (£963; £481; £240) **Stalls** High

Form — RPR
1050 **1** **Moheebb (IRE)**[12] 5367 3-8-4 **60**... LiamJones 6 — 69
(D W Chapman) *midfield: hdwy 3f out: rdn to chse ldr wl over 1f out: edgd lft and styd on u.p to ld ins fnl f* **20/1**
3500 **2** *2* **Sunnyside Tom (IRE)**[19] 5159 3-8-11 **67**....................... PaulHanagan 2 — 71
(R A Fahey) *towards rr: hdwy over 2f out: rdn over 1f out: styd on strly ins fnl f: nrst fin* **16/1**
3520 **3** *hd* **Sonning Star (IRE)**[39] 4568 3-9-2 **72**............................... DaneO'Neill 8 — 76
(D R C Elsworth) *midfield: hdwy 1/2-way: rdn to chse ldrs wl over 1f out: drvn and styd on ins fnl f: nrst fin* **15/2**
2025 **4** *nk* **Shotley Mac**[16] 5255 3-8-4 **60** oh1....................................(b) PaulFessey 7 — 63
(N Bycroft) *led: rdn 2f out: drvn and wandered over 1f out: edgd lft and hdd ins fnl f: wknd towards fin* **12/1**
4254 **5** *1¾* **Charlie Tipple**[16] 5253 3-9-3 **73**....................................... DavidAllan 5 — 72
(T D Easterby) *towards rr: hdwy on outer wl over 21f out: sn rdn and styd on ins fnl f: nrst fin* **7/1[3]**
1435 **6** *½* **Deadline (UAE)**[19] 5156 3-8-13 **69**................................... MickyFenton 10 — 67
(P T Midgley) *chsd ldr: rdn along over 2f out: sn drvn and grad wknd* **13/2[2]**
0310 **7** *2½* **Lordship (IRE)**[12] 5360 3-8-6 **67**.................................... LukeMorris(5) 14 — 60
(A W Carroll) *t.k.h: trckd ldrs: hdwy 3f out: rdn to chse ldr over 2f out: sn drvn and wknd* **12/1**
4033 **8** *1¼* **Fealeview Lady (USA)**[13] 5339 3-8-11 **70**................. TravisBlock(3) 13 — 60
(H Morrison) *nvr bttr than midfield* **15/2**
4002 **9** *6* **Snow Dancer (IRE)**[10] 5405 3-8-13 **69**.......................... FrancisNorton 11 — 46
(A Berry) *a towards rr* **10/1**
35-0 **10** *2½* **First Mate (IRE)**[11] 5383 3-9-4 **74**................................. J-PGuillambert 3 — 45
(M Johnston) *in tch: rdn along 3f out: sn wknd* **10/1**
3600 **11** *4* **El Dececy (USA)**[14] 5296 3-9-4 **74**...(b) NCallan 1 — 37
(D J Murphy) *stdd s: hld up and a in rr* **33/1**
0025 **12** *4* **Tri Chara (IRE)**[24] 5046 3-8-7 **63** ow1......................... GrahamGibbons 9 — 17
(R Hollinshead) *chsd ldrs: rdn along wl over 2f out and sn wknd* **20/1**
6632 **13** *7* **Lord Theo**[8] 5475 3-9-2 **72**.. JamesDoyle 4 — 10
(N P Littmoden) *rrd s: a in rr* **9/2[1]**
000 **14** *29* **Coconut Queen (IRE)**[43] 4450 3-9-0 **70**.................(p) RoystonFfrench 12 — —
(Mrs A Duffield) *chsd ldrs on inner: rdn along 1/2-way: sn wknd* **25/1**

1m 49.93s (2.53) **Going Correction** +0.325s/f (Good) — **14** Ran SP% **123.3**
Speed ratings (Par 101): **100,98,97,97,95 95,92,91,85,83 79,75,68,39**
CSF £303.81 CT £2692.01 TOTE £29.00: £7.80, £5.90, £2.90; EX 527.30.
Owner Michael Hill **Bred** Hascombe & Valiant Studs **Trained** Stillington, N Yorks

FOCUS
A fair handicap and sound form rated around the third.
Moheebb(IRE) Official explanation: trainer had no explanation for the apparent improvement in form
Tri Chara(IRE) Official explanation: jockey said the colt was unsuited by the good (good to soft places) ground
Lord Theo Official explanation: jockey said gelding missed the break
Coconut Queen(IRE) Official explanation: jockey said filly was unsuited by the good (good to soft places) ground

5704 COME DANCING WITH THE AMATEUR JOCKEYS AMATEUR RIDERS' H'CAP — 1m 1f 207y
5:00 (5:00) (Class 6) (0-60,59) 3-Y-O+ — **£3,123** (£968; £484; £242) **Stalls** High

Form — RPR
0055 **1** **Lobengula (IRE)**[26] 4966 5-11-7 **58**.................................. MrSDobson 17 — 67
(I W McInnes) *mde all: rdn and edgd lft to stands' rail 2f out: kpt on u.p ins fnl f* **17/2**
-363 **2** *2* **Harry The Hawk**[67] 3721 3-11-2 **59**..................................... MrSWalker 1 — 64+
(T D Walford) *towards rr: hdwy on outer 3f out: rdn to chse ldrs wl over 1f out: drvn and edgd rt ins fnl f: one pce towards fin* **6/1[2]**
0501 **3** *½* **Penel (IRE)**[29] 4891 6-10-8 **52**...................................(p) MissWGibson(7) 9 — 56
(P T Midgley) *a.p: rdn along to chal over 2f out: kpt on same pce ins fnl f* **28/1**
0102 **4** *3* **Alberts Story (USA)**[25] 4998 3-10-9 **57**..................... MrBMcHugh(5) 16 — 55
(R A Fahey) *hld up towards rr: stdy hdwy 3f out: rdn to chse ldrs over 1f out: kpt on u.p ins fnl f: nrst fin* **4/1[1]**
0003 **5** *nk* **Eijaaz (IRE)**[15] 5286 6-11-4 **55**..(p) MrsCBartley 2 — 52
(G A Harker) *hld up: stdy hdwy over 3f out: rdn to chse ldrs 2f out: drvn and one pce ent fnl f* **9/1**
0336 **6** *2½* **Gala Sunday (USA)**[14] 5300 7-11-4 **55**.................(bt) MissSBrotherton 3 — 47+
(M W Easterby) *s.i.s and hld up towards rr: hdwy 3f out: swtchd to far rail and rdn wl over 1f out: kpt on same pce ent fnl f* **6/1[2]**
3410 **7** *1½* **Parchment (IRE)**[8] 5486 5-11-7 **58**.............................(b) MissADeniel 12 — 47
(A J Lockwood) *bhd hdwy over 2f out: sn rdn and styd on: nt rch ldrs* **11/1**
5300 **8** *1½* **Magnum Opus (IRE)**[5] 5557 5-11-3 **54**.......................(bt) MrMSeston 11 — 40
(D J Murphy) *in rr: effrt and sme hdwy 3f out and sn drvn along: nvr nr ldrs* **14/1**
5 **9** *2* **Pertemps Networks**[72] 3260 3-11-0 **57**........................... MrTGreenall 10 — 39
(M W Easterby) *hld up: a towards rr* **12/1**
3040 **10** *hd* **General Flumpa**[7] 5514 6-11-1 **57**............................... MrCPHuxley(5) 13 — 39
(Miss Tor Sturgis) *dwlt: sn chsng ldrs: rdn along wl over 2f out and grad wknd over 1f out* **10/1**
0005 **11** *1* **Scotty's Future (IRE)**[34] 4704 9-11-0 **54**.................... MissARyan(3) 14 — 34
(A Berry) *s.i.s: a in rr* **16/1**
2316 **12** *8* **Moonlight Fantasy (IRE)**[19] 5179 4-10-13 **55**.... MrJPFeatherstone(5) 8 — 19
(Lucinda Featherstone) *plld hrd: chsd ldrs on outer: rdn along over 2f out and sn wknd* **33/1**
4001 **13** *7* **Garibaldi (GER)**[15] 5286 5-11-1 **55**..........................(b) MrOWilliams(3) 15 — 5
(J O'Reilly) *plld hrd: hld up: a in rr* **8/1[3]**

-000 **14** *1* **Oh Danny Boy**88 2831 6-10-7 **51** MissSEilbeck(7) 6 —
(M C Chapman) *chsd ldrs on inner: rdn along over 3f out and sn wknd* **66/1**

2m 14.62s (7.32) **Going Correction** +0.325s/f (Good)
WFA 3 from 4yo+ 6lb **14** Ran SP% **125.8**
Speed ratings (Par 101): **83,81,81,78,78 76,75,73,72,72 71,65,59,58**
CSF £60.81 CT £1408.69 TOTE £11.90: £4.00, £2.00, £6.40; EX 91.50 Place 6 £209.30, Place 5 £98.17.
Owner Colin G R Booth **Bred** A S O'Brien And Lars Pearson **Trained** Catwick, E Yorks
■ Stewards' Enquiry : Mr S Dobson one-day ban: careless riding (Oct 16)
Mr M Seston four-day ban: used whip with excessive frequency (Oct 16, Nov 8, 12 & 21)

FOCUS
A modest handicap and not run at a strong pace. The first three all ended up on the stands' side in the closing stages, carried there by the hanging winner. The form is rated through the third backed up by the runner-up.
T/Plt: £467.40 to a £1 stake. Pool: £58,434.20. 91.25 winning tickets. T/Qpdt: £459.90 to a £1 stake. Pool: £3,480.40. 5.60 winning tickets. JR

4683 BRIGHTON (L-H)
Tuesday, September 25

OFFICIAL GOING: Good (8.6)
Wind: Moderate, half against Weather: Fine

5705 H.B.L.B. NURSERY 5f 213y
2:10 (2:10) (Class 4) (0-85,82) 2-Y-0 **£5,678** (£1,699; £637; £637; £211) **Stalls** Low

Form RPR

2446 **1** **Kaldoun Kingdom (IRE)**29 4903 2-8-7 **68** JimmyQuinn 1 72
(E A L Dunlop) *chsd ldrs: led over 1f out: hrd rdn and hung lft ins fnl f: jst hld on* **6/1**

1160 **2** *shd* **Elna Bright**31 4812 2-9-4 **82** WilliamBuick(3) 7 86
(R Hannon) *nvr gng wl and sn bhd: 10l bhd wnr over 1f out: rapid hdwy fnl f: jst failed* **10/3**2

0533 **3** *1* **Fervent Prince**18 5207 2-8-12 **73** (b1) SebSanders 8 74
(H Morrison) *s.s: sn in tch: hrd rdn over 2f out: hung bdly lft: kpt on* **3/1**1

5355 **3** *dht* **Choisky (IRE)**18 5199 2-7-12 **59** NickyMackay 6 61+
(J Akehurst) *fair 6th tl swtchd to rail and hdwy 2f out: cl 2nd whn hmpd ins fnl f: one pce* **12/1**

2602 **5** *3* **Miesko (USA)**12 5363 2-9-1 **76** GregFairley 2 68
(M Johnston) *pressed ldr: led over 2f out tl over 1f out: no ex* **5/1**3

4640 **6** *3 ½* **Captain Esteem**14 5314 2-8-12 **73** JimCrowley 4 54
(B W Hills) *dwlt: a bhd: no ch fr 1/2-way* **12/1**

4042 **7** *½* **Wreningham**18 5199 2-8-9 **70** TPQueally 5 49
(T Keddy) *slt ld tl over 2f out: hung lft and wknd wl over 1f out* **10/1**

0530 **8** *shd* **Miss Firefly**13 5322 2-8-8 **69** TPO'Shea 9 48
(M R Channon) *prom tl hung bdly lft and wknd wl over 1f out* **11/1**

69.52 secs (-0.58) **Going Correction** -0.05s/f (Good) **8** Ran SP% **111.8**
Speed ratings (Par 97): **101,100,99,99,95 90,90,90**
PL: Fervent Prince £0.70, Choisky £1.90; TRICAST: Fervent Prince £35.27, Choisky £114.55 CSF £25.11 TOTE £7.70: £2.00, £1.60; EX 29.70.
Owner Mohammed Jaber **Bred** Gainsborough Stud Management Ltd **Trained** Newmarket, Suffolk
■ Stewards' Enquiry : Seb Sanders one-day ban: careless riding (Oct 8)
Jimmy Quinn four-day ban: careless riding (Oct 8-11)

FOCUS
An ordinary nursery for the grade but the time was good for the grade and the form could be better than rated.

NOTEBOOK
Kaldoun Kingdom(IRE) failed to make much impression at Warwick on his previous start, but he had been dropped 2lb and just proved good enough to gain his first success at the sixth attempt. He was treading water in front though, and would have been passed in another stride. (op 11-2 tchd 5-1)
Elna Bright, dropping in trip, was going nowhere for much of the way and was still a good eight to ten lengths down at the furlong pole, but he fairly flew home and would have got up in another stride. On this evidence he will benefit from a return to 7f, but there is lots of speed in his pedigree and it might just be that he is not putting it all in. He may well benefit from some headgear just to help him concentrate. (tchd 5-2 and 7-2)
Fervent Prince did not look happy in first-time blinkers and hung badly to his left in the straight, costing him any chance he may have had of winning. He then got rid of Seb Sanders after the line when proving hard to pull up, suggesting he had plenty left in the locker. He looks best left for the time being. Official explanation: jockey said filly hung left (op 16-1)
Choisky(IRE), still a maiden, was bidding to take advantage of a mark 10lb lower than on sand and he may well have been second had he not been hampered inside the final furlong. (op 16-1)
Miesko(USA) had no easy task off a mark of 76 and he did not look happy on the track. (op 4-1 tchd 6-1)
Captain Esteem Official explanation: jockey said gelding hung left-handed
Miss Firefly Official explanation: jockey said filly hung left-handed

5706 ENTREMETTIER (S) STKS 5f 59y
2:40 (2:40) (Class 6) 2-Y-0 **£2,072** (£616; £308; £153) **Stalls** Low

Form RPR

4310 **1** **Speedy Senorita (IRE)**12 5365 2-8-11 66 LeeEnstone 6 65+
(K R Burke) *mde all: hrd rdn 2f out: styd on wl fnl f: readily* **9/4**1

006 **2** *2* **Golden Dane (IRE)**37 4629 2-8-11 62 SebSanders 7 58
(I A Wood) *chsd wnr: hrd rdn wl over 1f out: hung lft: nt qckn* **7/1**

5042 **3** *1 ¾* **Liani (IRE)**25 5015 2-8-6 58 HayleyTurner 9 47
(P D Evans) *chsd ldrs: hrd rdn and hung lft ins fnl 2f: styd on same pce* **8/1**

0000 **4** *hd* **Enchanted Lady**9 5442 2-8-6 50 JimmyQuinn 10 46
(H J L Dunlop) *wnt rt s: towards rr: rdn over 2f out: styd on fnl f* **33/1**

3504 **5** *1 ¾* **Fox's Den**59 3947 2-8-11 69 (v1) AdamKirby 1 44
(R M Beckett) *chsd ldrs: hrd rdn over 1f out: no ex* **6/1**3

3050 **6** *nk* **Iamagrey (IRE)**11 5393 2-8-6 65 (p) JohnEgan 8 38+
(J S Moore) *in tch: effrt and hung bdly lft ins fnl 2f: hld whn hmpd on rail 1f out* **11/4**2

4006 **7** *hd* **Pretty Bonnie**22 5089 2-8-6 55 TPO'Shea 2 38+
(J G Portman) *mid-div: no imp whn n.m.r on rail ins fnl 2f* **15/2**

0 **8** *7* **Ubiquitous Bounty**11 5380 2-8-11 0 (b1) JimCrowley 5 17
(G L Moore) *s.s: a bhd: no ch fr 1/2-way* **20/1**

6 **9** *3 ½* **Nancymay**9 5442 2-8-6 0 ChrisCatlin 4 —
(J Ryan) *sn wl bhd* **50/1**

62.01 secs (-0.29) **Going Correction** -0.05s/f (Good) **9** Ran SP% **116.8**
Speed ratings (Par 93): **100,96,94,93,90 90,90,78,73**
CSF £18.57 TOTE £3.00: £1.20, £2.50, £2.10; EX 24.20.The winner was bought in for 6,400gns.
Owner F D C Racing Club **Bred** R McEnery And Vincent Millett **Trained** Middleham Moor, N Yorks

FOCUS
A reasonable seller and the form looks solid rated around the runner-up and fourth.

NOTEBOOK
Speedy Senorita(IRE) could make little impression in a nursery at Wolverhampton on her previous start, but this was a lot easier and she doubled her career tally in straightforward fashion. She is better than this grade and will be worth another try in nurseries or claimers. (tchd 2-1 and 5-2)
Golden Dane(IRE) ran well returned to selling company, but he was always being held by the eventual winner and did not help his chances by hanging left. (op 9-1)
Liani(IRE) did not improve for the drop back to 5f on her return to selling company. (op 9-1)
Enchanted Lady gave the impression she will benefit from a return to 6f. (tchd 40-1)
Fox's Den ran nowhere near his official mark of 69 and seems to be regressing. (op 8-1 tchd 9-1)
Iamagrey(IRE) is another who is struggling to build on earlier promise. Official explanation: jockey said filly hung left (op 9-4 tchd 3-1, 7-2 in a place)

5707 EUROPEAN BREEDERS' FUND MAIDEN STKS 6f 209y
3:10 (3:20) (Class 5) 2-Y-0 **£3,497** (£1,040; £520; £259) **Stalls** Low

Form RPR

554 **1** **Sahaadi**19 5162 2-8-12 77 PatDobbs 4 65+
(R Hannon) *mde all: set modest pce: rdn and qcknd clr fnl 2f: readily* **2/1**1

602 **2** *2* **Ten Pole Tudor**14 5302 2-9-3 64 JohnEgan 9 65
(R A Harris) *hld up in rr: rdn and r.o fnl 2f: wnt 2nd ins fnl f: nt rch wnr* **25/1**

000 **3** *1* **Ledgerwood**71 3592 2-9-3 50 TPO'Shea 7 62
(J W Hills) *chsd wnr: hrd rdn 2f out: one pce* **66/1**

43 **4** *½* **Moment's Notice**21 5116 2-9-3 0 SimonWhitworth 6 61
(S Kirk) *hld up in rr: hdwy and in tch over 2f out: one pce appr fnl f* **14/1**

6 **5** *1* **Wannarock (IRE)**108 2478 2-9-3 0 JimmyQuinn 10 59
(E A L Dunlop) *t.k.h: in tch: effrt over 2f out: no imp* **13/2**

05 **6** *3* **Cryptonite Diamond (USA)**50 4232 2-8-12 0 AdamKirby 5 46
(W R Swinburn) *in tch: effrt and nt clr run over 2f out: sn outpcd* **9/1**

2050 **7** *hd* **Swindon Town Flyer (IRE)**62 3849 2-8-12 71 KevinGhunowa(5) 8 50
(A B Haynes) *t.k.h: prom tl wknd over 2f out* **33/1**

0520 **8** *½* **Hawk Eyed Lady (IRE)**13 5322 2-8-12 75 TPQueally 1 44+
(J A Osborne) *chsd ldrs: 4th and btn whn hmpd on rail over 1f out* **7/2**2

0 **9** *2 ½* **Arab League (IRE)**142 1498 2-9-3 0 GregFairley 2 42
(M Johnston) *chsd ldrs: rdn 3f out: sn wknd* **7/1**

053 **10** *¾* **Red Amaryllis**10 5428 2-8-12 73 SebSanders 3 35
(H J L Dunlop) *in rr: sme hdwy whn n.m.r on rail 2f out: hung lft: sn wknd* **6/1**3

1m 23.16s (0.46) **Going Correction** -0.05s/f (Good) **10** Ran SP% **120.6**
Speed ratings (Par 95): **95,92,91,91,89 86,86,85,82,81**
CSF £62.17 TOTE £3.40: £1.30, £3.90, £13.10; EX 58.60.
Owner Mrs James Wigan **Bred** Mrs James Wigan **Trained** East Everleigh, Wilts

FOCUS
A modest maiden and hardly an ideal situation for these inexperienced two-year-olds, with the race delayed for over ten minutes by a couple of intruders on motorbikes down by the start. The form has been rated negatively with the runner-up basically to form.

NOTEBOOK
Sahaadi was allowed her own way out in front, albeit she did take a little bit of a grip, and she proved far too good for this lot. She is likely to find things tougher from now on, and will not always get things her own way, but she is progressing. (op 9-4 tchd 5-2)
Ten Pole Tudor, cast out of Jamie Osborne's yard after running second in a seller at Leicester on his previous start, had plenty to find with the favourite on official figures and he ran about as well as could have been expected with the blinkers left off this time. (tchd 28-1)
Ledgerwood did not show much in three runs in sprint maidens earlier in the season, but he has been gelded since he was last seen and produced an improved effort stepped up in trip off the back of a 71-day break. He has ruined what would have been a very attractive handicap mark having come into this rated just 50, but that is not to say he cannot be placed to advantage at some point.
Moment's Notice proved unsuited by the drop in trip, but he will be one to keep an eye on now he is qualified for a handicap mark. (tchd 16-1)
Wannarock(IRE) failed to confirm the promise he showed on his debut at Windsor back in June. (op 15-2 tchd 6-1)
Cryptonite Diamond(USA) is now qualified for a handicap mark and it would be no surprise to see her improve when stepped up in trip. (op 8-1 tchd 10-1)
Swindon Town Flyer(IRE) Official explanation: jockey said gelding ran too free
Hawk Eyed Lady(IRE), returned to maiden company, did not appear to stay and may do better back over sprint trips. (op 4-1)

5708 BRAKES FRESH IDEAS MEMORIAL H'CAP 7f 214y
3:40 (3:46) (Class 6) (0-60,60) 3-Y-0+ **£2,266** (£674; £337; £168) **Stalls** Low

Form RPR

4233 **1** **Prince Valentine**21 5121 6-8-11 **49** (p) JimCrowley 1 59
(G L Moore) *hld up towards rr: rdn and hdwy over 2f out: led jst ins fnl f: drvn out* **6/1**3

6143 **2** *1* **Ten To The Dozen**10 5433 4-9-2 **54** ChrisCatlin 4 62
(P W Hiatt) *led 3f: led over 1f out tl jst ins fnl f: kpt on same pce* **4/1**2

0314 **3** *1 ¾* **Pelham Crescent (IRE)**38 4592 4-9-8 **60** SebSanders 2 64
(B Palling) *t.k.h: in tch: effrt over 2f out: one pce appr fnl f* **5/2**1

4000 **4** *1* **Blue Line**21 5118 5-8-6 **47** MarcHalford(3) 8 51+
(M Madgwick) *mid-div: drvn along 3f out: styd on fnl f* **16/1**

4506 **5** *hd* **Convivial Spirit**15 5275 3-9-3 **59** (t) TPO'Shea 7 60
(E F Vaughan) *hdwy to chse ldrs 5f out: n.m.r 2f out: styd on same pce* **17/2**

6040 **6** *nk* **Roman Boy (ARG)**15 5280 8-8-8 **51** (v) TolleyDean(5) 10 51
(Stef Liddiard) *mid-div: rdn to chse ldrs 2f out: one pce* **20/1**

2605 **7** *nk* **Lady Edge (IRE)**10 5433 5-8-9 **52** KevinGhunowa(5) 12 52
(A W Carroll) *prom: hrd rdn 2f out: no ex over 1f out* **16/1**

6200 **8** *½* **Hucking Heat (IRE)**29 4884 3-9-0 **59** StephaneBreux(3) 5 57
(J R Best) *hld up towards rr: shkn up and styd on fnl 2f: nvr nrr* **14/1**

0000 **9** *hd* **Theatre Royal**25 5001 4-8-8 **53** (b1) JamieHamblett(7) 11 51
(Mouse Hamilton-Fairley) *prom: led after 3f tl over 1f out: wknd fnl f* **20/1**

0000 **10** *hd* **Adobe**26 4966 12-8-8 **46** oh1 JohnEgan 6 43
(W M Brisbourne) *hld up towards rr: rdn and sme hdwy 2f out: wknd over 1f out* **20/1**

6300 **11** *6* **A Nod And A Wink (IRE)**57 4025 3-8-5 **47** BThomas 3 31
(J C Fox) *a bhd* **40/1**

0030 **12** *15* **Fantasy Defender (IRE)**15 5275 5-8-8 **46** oh1 JimmyQuinn 14 —
(R M H Cowell) *t.k.h: in tch: rdn and lost pl 5f out: n.d fnl 3f: eased whn no ch over 1f out* **16/1**

0000 **13** *12* **Shortcake**22 5090 3-8-5 **47** PaulDoe 13 —
(M R Hoad) *plld hrd: w ldrs tl wknd qckly 3f out: eased whn no ch fnl 2f* **50/1**

1m 35.24s (0.20) **Going Correction** -0.05s/f (Good)
WFA 3 from 4yo+ 4lb **13** Ran SP% **124.1**
Speed ratings (Par 101): **97,96,94,93,93 92,92,91,91,91 85,70,58**
CSF £30.20 CT £78.44 TOTE £5.60: £1.40, £2.10, £1.70; EX 19.30.
Owner D R Hunnisett **Bred** Mrs E Y Hunnisett **Trained** Woodingdean, E Sussex

FOCUS
A moderate handicap run at a good pace and straightforward form with the first two close to previous course form and the third to his mark.
Fantasy Defender(IRE) Official explanation: jockey said gelding moved poorly throughout
Shortcake Official explanation: jockey said filly lost its action

5709 HOP H'CAP 1m 3f 196y
4:10 (4:19) (Class 6) (0-65,63) 3-Y-0+ £2,396 (£712; £356; £177) Stalls High

Form RPR
0662 1 **Chunky's Choice (IRE)**[19] 5158 3-9-3 **62** TPQueally 2 74
(J Noseda) *dwlt: sn in midfield: effrt and swtchd wd over 2f out: led 1f out: drvn out* **9/2**[3]
0410 2 1 1/4 **View From The Top**[12] 5347 3-9-1 **60** SebSanders 11 70
(Sir Mark Prescott) *hld up towards rr: hdwy over 2f out: drvn to chal over 1f out: nt qckn fnl f* **6/1**
0054 3 2 1/2 **Sopran Gath (ITY)**[21] 5120 4-9-8 **59** TPO'Shea 4 65
(J W Hills) *hld up in midfield: hdwy to ld over 2f out: hdd and no ex 1f out* **11/1**
5326 4 1 3/4 **Barbs Pink Diamond (USA)**[13] 5341 3-8-11 **56** JimCrowley 1 59
(Mrs A J Perrett) *led tl 4f out: w ldrs tl edgd lft and wknd over 1f out* **11/1**
3225 5 1 1/4 **Bienheureux**[7] 5514 6-9-7 **63** (t) NicolPolli[(5)] 9 64
(Miss Gay Kelleway) *hld up towards rr: rdn and hdwy 2f out: no imp over 1f out* **7/2**[2]
6041 6 1 3/4 **Susie May**[42] 4473 3-8-13 **58** SimonWhitworth 8 56
(C A Cyzer) *hdwy and in tch 5f out: rdn and btn over 2f out* **10/3**[1]
6400 7 1 3/4 **Blackmail (USA)**[13] 5341 9-9-1 **52** (b) PaulDoe 10 48
(P Mitchell) *wd: sn prom: led 4f out tl over 2f out: sn wknd* **20/1**
00-0 8 2 **My Monna**[255] 116 3-8-5 **50** ChrisCatlin 3 42
(Miss Sheena West) *prom tl wknd over 2f out* **25/1**
0510 9 3 **Orphina (IRE)**[32] 4766 4-8-7 **51** KylieManser[(7)] 13 39
(B G Powell) *s.s: a bhd* **16/1**
0/00 10 14 **Mighty Mover (IRE)**[25] 5018 5-8-7 **49** oh3 PatrickHills[(5)] 7 14
(B Palling) *t.k.h: in tch: wknd 3f out: eased whn wl btn 1f out* **50/1**
0-00 11 20 **Tejareb (IRE)**[27] 4948 4-8-13 **50** JohnEgan 5 —
(C E Brittain) *prom to 1/2-way: grad lost pl: bhd and eased fnl 2f* **20/1**
2m 33.8s (1.60) **Going Correction** -0.05s/f (Good)
WFA 3 from 4yo+ 8lb 11 Ran SP% **115.6**
Speed ratings (Par 101): **92,91,89,88,87 86,85,83,81,72 59**
CSF £31.55 CT £289.86 TOTE £4.40: £1.80, £2.10, £4.10; EX 21.80.
Owner C Fox & J Wright **Bred** John Davison **Trained** Newmarket, Suffolk
■ Golden Platitude was withdrawn (ref to enter stalls, 12/1.) R4, deduct 5p in the £.
FOCUS
A modest middle-distance handicap but solid form best rated through the fourth.
Tejareb(IRE) Official explanation: jockey said filly oost its action

5710 MASCOL PRODUCTIONS LTD H'CAP 1m 1f 209y
4:40 (4:50) (Class 6) (0-60,60) 3-Y-0 £2,396 (£712; £356; £177) Stalls High

Form RPR
0050 1 **Blue Mistral (IRE)**[12] 5347 3-9-2 **58** (vt) PaulDoe 3 66
(W J Knight) *dwlt: in rr: rdn 4f out: gd hdwy to ld over 1f out: styd on wl* **10/1**
0066 2 2 **Djalalabad (FR)**[30] 4856 3-8-13 **55** JohnEgan 1 59
(Mrs C A Dunnett) *hld up and bhd: gd hdwy to ld briefly wl over 1f out: nt qckn fnl f* **20/1**
4400 3 3 **Astrolibra**[103] 2609 3-8-10 **52** JimmyQuinn 8 50
(M H Tompkins) *in tch: rdn to chse ldng pair over 1f out: one pce* **9/1**
064 4 1 1/2 **Withywood (USA)**[28] 4918 3-8-4 **46** ChrisCatlin 7 41
(G L Moore) *plld hrd: sn stdd towards rr: rdn and styd on fnl 3f: nvr nrr* **7/1**[2]
0040 5 1 1/2 **Kyloe Belle (USA)**[32] 4766 3-9-0 **56** (bt[1]) JimCrowley 11 48
(Mrs A J Perrett) *dwlt and hmpd s: chsd ldrs tl outpcd fnl 2f* **7/1**[2]
0105 6 2 1/2 **Bathwick Breeze**[32] 4758 3-9-1 **57** (b) TPQueally 5 44
(A B Haynes) *led: hrd rdn and hdd wl over 1f out: sn wknd* **15/2**[3]
400 7 3 **Anna Towkaska**[25] 5005 3-9-0 **56** (t) AdamKirby 15 37
(W R Swinburn) *prom tl hrd rdn and wknd 2f out* **16/1**
6000 8 4 **Hannahbecc**[6] 5528 3-9-4 **60** (t[1]) SaleemGolam 13 33
(S C Williams) *hmpd s: towards rr: sme hdwy on outside 4f out: wknd over 2f out* **25/1**
004 9 3/4 **Penang (IRE)**[25] 4989 3-9-2 **58** HayleyTurner 14 30
(C E Brittain) *chsd ldrs 4f: sn lost pl* **16/1**
0000 10 9 **For Eileen**[33] 4530 3-7-11 **46** oh1 SophieDoyle[(7)] 6 —
(G C H Chung) *chsd ldrs 7f* **66/1**
0020 11 6 **Kings Art (IRE)**[30] 4858 3-8-5 **52** PatrickHills[(5)] 2 —+
(W M Brisbourne) *chsd ldrs: bdly hmpd by loose horse bnd over 3f out: nt rcvr: bhd whn virtually p.u fnl f* **8/1**
6062 U **Danehill Silver**[12] 5347 3-8-13 **60** RussellKennemore[(5)] 10 —
(R Hollinshead) *stmbld and uns rdr leaving stalls* **10/3**[1]
2m 3.01s (0.41) **Going Correction** -0.05s/f (Good) 12 Ran SP% **111.9**
Speed ratings (Par 99): **96,94,92,90,89 87,85,82,81,74 69,—**
CSF £176.67 CT £1601.77 TOTE £12.30: £4.40, £6.00, £3.80; EX 246.80.
Owner Angmering Park Thoroughbreds **Bred** Blue Bloodstock Limited **Trained** Patching, W Sussex
■ Roxy Singer was withdrawn (ref to enter stalls, 12/1.) R4, deduct 5p in the £.
FOCUS
A moderate handicap rated through the winner to form, but little solid behind.
Djalalabad(FR) Official explanation: vet said filly had lost a shoe
Bathwick Breeze Official explanation: jockey said gelding hung left

5711 WEATHERBYS PRINTING H'CAP 5f 213y
5:10 (5:16) (Class 5) (0-70,69) 3-Y-0+ £3,154 (£944; £472; £236; £117) Stalls Low

Form RPR
0121 1 **For Life (IRE)**[23] 5064 5-9-0 **68** NataliaGemelova[(5)] 9 78
(J E Long) *w ldr: led after 2f: hld on wl fnl f* **7/2**[1]
0152 2 1/2 **Buy On The Red**[23] 5064 6-9-6 **69** (p) SaleemGolam 4 78
(W R Muir) *prom: wnt 2nd 2f out: hrd rdn over 1f out: kpt on: a hld* **9/2**[2]
5400 3 shd **Summer Recluse (USA)**[12] 5349 8-8-11 **60** (t) JimCrowley 5 68
(J M Bradley) *hld up towards rr: rdn and hdwy over 1f out: r.o wl fnl f: clsng at fin* **15/2**
313 4 shd **Goodenough Mover**[38] 4594 11-9-3 **66** HayleyTurner 6 74
(Andrew Turnell) *in tch: drvn to chse ldrs over 1f out: kpt on* **10/1**
0344 5 1 **Lii Najma**[31] 4807 4-9-1 **64** AdamKirby 3 69
(C E Brittain) *chsd ldrs: rdn over 2f out: one pce* **13/2**
3051 6 shd **Plateau**[31] 4822 8-9-3 **66** JohnEgan 11 72+
(C R Dore) *bhd: rdn and hdwy over 1f out: disputing 5th and hld but styng on whn n.m.r and eased nr fin* **10/1**
0006 7 4 **Laith (IRE)**[7] 5513 4-7-13 **55** oh10 (p) SophieDoyle[(7)] 10 48
(Miss V Haigh) *mid-div: hrd rdn over 2f out: sn outpcd* **50/1**
0664 8 1/2 **Imperium**[12] 5348 6-8-12 **61** (p) FrankieMcDonald 12 52
(Jean-Rene Auvray) *outpcd and bhd: nvr rchd ldrs* **16/1**
0023 9 1/2 **Stir Crazy (IRE)**[10] 5420 3-8-8 **59** TPO'Shea 13 49
(M R Channon) *chsd ldrs: hrd rdn 2f out: wknd over 1f out* **12/1**
144 10 nk **Exit Strategy (IRE)**[61] 3872 3-8-11 **67** (b) HaddenFrost[(5)] 7 56
(R A Harris) *sn towards rr: rdn and n.d fnl 2f* **20/1**
1500 11 2 **Gone'N'Dunnett (IRE)**[5] 5576 8-8-6 **55** oh3 (v) ChrisCatlin 8 38
(Mrs C A Dunnett) *led 2f: wknd wl over 1f out* **33/1**
4102 12 6 **Support Fund (IRE)**[18] 5191 3-8-7 **63** PatrickHills[(5)] 1 28
(Eve Johnson Houghton) *mid-div on rail: rdn 3f out: no imp whn hmpd over 1f out: eased* **11/2**[3]
69.47 secs (-0.63) **Going Correction** -0.05s/f (Good)
WFA 3 from 4yo+ 2lb 12 Ran SP% **122.3**
Speed ratings (Par 103): **102,101,101,101,99 99,94,93,92,92 89,81**
CSF £19.03 CT £116.72 TOTE £3.90: £1.80, £2.10, £2.60; EX 16.60 Place 6 £174.42, Place 5 £122.04.
Owner T H Bambridge **Bred** R N Auld **Trained** Caterham, Surrey
■ Stewards' Enquiry : Chris Catlin two-day ban: careless riding (Oct 8-9)
FOCUS
A modest but very competitive sprint handicap and solid form with te five immediately behind the winner close to recent marks.
T/Jkpt: £14,791.50 to a £1 stake. Pool: £41,666.25. 2.00 winning tickets. T/Plt: £166.50 to a £1 stake. Pool: £72,456.65. 317.60 winning tickets. T/Qpdt: £91.40 to a £1 stake. Pool: £4,721.70. 38.20 winning tickets. LM

5274 FOLKESTONE (R-H)
Tuesday, September 25

OFFICIAL GOING: Firm (10.1)
Wind: Virtually nil Weather: bright spells but partly cloudy

5712 WEATHERBYS INSURANCE H'CAP 7f (S)
2:20 (2:21) (Class 4) (0-85,85) 3-Y-0+ £4,857 (£1,445; £722; £360) Stalls Low

Form RPR
6530 1 **Blue Java**[21] 5115 6-8-7 **71** SteveDrowne 11 79
(H Morrison) *racd in far side pair: chsd ldr: rdn to chal over 1f out: led last stride* **9/2**[1]
6006 2 shd **Mujood**[9] 5449 4-9-5 **83** (b) StephenCarson 12 91
(Eve Johnson Houghton) *led far side pair and overall: rdn wl over 1f out: kpt on wl tl hdd last stride* **10/1**
1130 3 5 **Purus (IRE)**[56] 4049 5-9-5 **83** GeorgeBaker 3 77
(R A Teal) *hld up on stands' side: hdwy and nt clr run over 2f out: kpt on u.p: no ch w far side: 1st of 8 in gp* **11/2**[3]
1220 4 shd **Yandina (IRE)**[21] 5115 4-9-4 **82** MichaelHills 6 76
(B W Hills) *w.w on stands' side: hdwy 3f out: rdn to chse far side pair over 1f out: kpt on but nvr trbld ldng pair: 2nd of 8 in gp* **5/1**[2]
6630 5 2 **Fiefdom (IRE)**[10] 5413 5-9-0 **81** PatrickMathers[(3)] 2 70
(I W McInnes) *chsd ldr on stands' side: rdn 2f out: kpt on same pce: no ch w far side: 3rd of 8 in gp* **14/1**
4356 6 shd **Bold Abbott (USA)**[54] 4111 3-8-12 **79** (v[1]) EddieAhern 4 67
(Mrs A J Perrett) *t.k.h: trckd ldrs on stands' side: rdn wl over 1f out: kpt on same pce: no ch w far side: 4th of 8 in gp* **9/1**
06-5 7 1 **Bertie Southstreet**[26] 4965 4-8-11 **75** TedDurcan 8 61
(J R Best) *stdd s: hld up in last: rdn and hdwy 3f out: hung lft over 1f out: no imp after: 5th of 8 in gp* **14/1**
0606 8 1 1/4 **Cape Of Luck (IRE)**[10] 5413 4-9-0 **85** JackMitchell[(7)] 5 67
(P Mitchell) *in tch: hdwy over 3f out: rdn to ld stands' side 3f out tl over 1f out: sn wknd: 6th of 8 in gp* **8/1**
4306 9 1 1/4 **Scarlet Flyer (USA)**[11] 5383 4-8-9 **73** (b) FergusSweeney 1 52
(G L Moore) *hld up in tch on stands' side: rdn wl over 1f out: keeping on same pce whn sltly hmpd over 1f out: no ch: 7th of 8 in gp* **13/2**
3010 10 5 **Glencalvie (IRE)**[21] 5114 6-8-12 **76** (p) TQuinn 10 41
(J Akehurst) *led stands' side tl rdn and hdd 3f out: wknd 2f out: eased whn no ch ins fnl f: 8th of 8 in gp* **10/1**
1m 24.4s (-3.50) **Going Correction** -0.60s/f (Hard)
WFA 3 from 4yo+ 3lb 10 Ran SP% **116.2**
Speed ratings (Par 105): **96,95,90,90,87 87,86,85,83,77**
CSF £49.39 CT £259.74 TOTE £5.40: £1.70, £3.20, £2.40; EX 44.50 Trifecta £186.00 Part won. Pool: £262.00 - 0.35 winning units..
Owner Pangfield Partners **Bred** T J Billington **Trained** East Ilsley, Berks
FOCUS
A competitive race for the grade, but the two that went far side had a massive advantage. The form is rated through the winner, with the stands'-side group better than the bare form.
Fiefdom(IRE) Official explanation: jockey said gelding hung right

5713 LOOKOUT RESTAURANT NOVICE STKS 6f
2:50 (2:50) (Class 4) 2-Y-0 £3,886 (£1,156; £577; £288) Stalls Low

Form RPR
14 1 **Dubai Princess (IRE)**[130] 1821 2-8-11 87 JamieSpencer 1 86+
(J A Osborne) *hld up: hdwy and swtchd rt over 1f out: pushed into ld and edgd lft jst ins fnl f: pushed out* **4/11**[1]
1400 2 1 1/4 **Grylls (USA)**[13] 5324 2-9-2 80 TedDurcan 5 82
(R Hannon) *led: rdn 2f out: hdd jst ins fnl f: no ch w wnr* **4/1**[2]
0 3 1 3/4 **Capefly**[14] 5309 2-8-0 0 RobbieEgan[(7)] 4 68
(P F I Cole) *prom: chsd ldr over 4f out: ev ch over 2f out: outpcd last 100yds* **16/1**
2210 4 5 **Sinead Of Aglish (IRE)**[32] 4762 2-9-0 79 SteveDrowne 2 60
(A B Haynes) *chsd ldr tl over 4f out: last fr 1/2-way: no ch fnl f* **10/1**[3]
1m 11.21s (-2.39) **Going Correction** -0.60s/f (Hard) 4 Ran SP% **108.3**
Speed ratings (Par 97): **91,89,87,80**
CSF £2.14 TOTE £1.50; EX 2.40.
Owner A F O'Callaghan **Bred** Darley **Trained** Upper Lambourn, Berks
FOCUS
A fair juvenile contest for the track with the winner not needing to be at her best and the form rated around the runner-up and fourth.
NOTEBOOK
Dubai Princess(IRE) ◆ cannot be easy to train, considering the lack of races she has had, but looks to have plenty of ability. She definitely won with something in hand after her lengthy absence but whether she is good enough to take up her Cheveley Park entry is debatable at the moment. That race is very much on the agenda though. (op 1-4)
Grylls(USA) set the pace in front but was readily brushed aside by the winner one she loomed up. He kept on quite well though and certainly looks capable of winning again this season. (op 5-1)
Capeflylooked to be very keen during the race and did well to be competitive at the end of the race. She appears to be progressing with racing, although it should be noted that she was receiving a lot of weight. (op 28-1)

Sinead Of Aglish(IRE) tried to keep tabs on her rivals when the pace increase but dropped out quickly under pressure. (op 14-1 tchd 9-1)

5714 BACK HERE OCTOBER 9TH MAIDEN STKS 6f
3:20 (3:20) (Class 5) 3-Y-O+ **£2,914** (£867; £433; £216) **Stalls** Low

Form RPR

2-45 **1** **Salsa Steps (USA)**[58] 3992 3-8-12 77..........................(t) SteveDrowne 3 77+
(H Morrison) *in tch: chsd ldr over 2f out: led over 1f out: sn clr: eased towards fin* **13/8**[1]

4302 **2** *5* **Hazytoo**[29] 4905 3-9-3 72.. JamieSpencer 7 59
(N A Callaghan) *chsd ldr tl led over 3f out: rdn over 2f out: hdd over 1f over: no ch w wnr* **7/2**[2]

0004 **3** *1* **Punching**[15] 5270 3-9-3 59... StephenCarson 9 56
(Eve Johnson Houghton) *chsd ldrs: rdn 2f out: sn outpcd: plugged on* **25/1**

5 **4** *shd* **Thermidor (USA)**[17] 5231 4-9-5 0............................. RichardKingscote 6 56
(R Charlton) *stdd s: hld up in last: hdwy wl over 1f out: kpt on steadily: n.d* **8/1**

0200 **5** *3/4* **The Jay Factor (IRE)**[12] 5360 3-9-3 65...........................(p) EddieAhern 1 53
(Pat Eddery) *chsd ldrs: reminders 1/2-way: rdn over 2f out: outpcd wl over 1f out* **13/2**[3]

0000 **6** *5* **She's Dunnett**[47] 4336 4-8-9 40..............................(t) KirstyMilczarek(5) 5 32
(Mrs C A Dunnett) *bhd: rdn and struggling 1/2-way: no ch after* **100/1**

2225 **7** *shd* **Tarkamara (IRE)**[31] 4801 3-8-12 64.......................................(t) TQuinn 8 32
(P F I Cole) *s.i.s: racd in midfield on outer: effrt u.p over 2f out: wl outpcd 2f out* **8/1**

6605 **8** *1 3/4* **Winning Show**[15] 5270 3-9-3 65.. TedDurcan 2 31
(R A Harris) *sn pushed into ld: hdd over 3f out: wknd over 2f out* **16/1**

4-6 **9** *hd* **Royal Choir**[7] 5494 3-8-12 0.. KerrinMcEvoy 4 26
(C E Brittain) *a bhd: rdn 4f out: no ch fr 1/2-way* **11/1**

1m 10.23s (-3.37) **Going Correction** -0.60s/f (Hard)
WFA 3 from 4yo 2lb **9** Ran SP% **114.9**
Speed ratings (Par 103): **98,91,90,89,88 82,82,79,79**
CSF £7.12 TOTE £2.90: £1.30, £1.20, £5.90; EX 8.40 Trifecta £123.50 Part won. Pool: £174.02. - 0.90 winning units..

Owner Ben & Sir Martyn Arbib **Bred** M Arbib **Trained** East Ilsley, Berks

FOCUS
A modest maiden in which the winner probably ran close to her mark, but the rest are moderate. The whole field stayed to the stands' side early before coming up the middle.

Hazytoo Official explanation: jockey said colt hung right

5715 LADBROKES £500 SLOT JACKPOT NURSERY 5f
3:50 (3:52) (Class 6) (0-65,64) 2-Y-O **£2,914** (£867; £433; £216) **Stalls** Low

Form RPR

6300 **1** **Rightcar Ellie (IRE)**[12] 5365 2-9-1 **58**............................(b[1]) LPKeniry 9 61
(Peter Grayson) *mde all on far side: rdn wl over 1f out: kpt on: 1st of 3 in gp* **18/1**

4000 **2** *3/4* **New Balls Please (IRE)**[22] 5089 2-8-8 **51**....................(p) TedDurcan 11 51
(P M Phelan) *a chsng wnr on far side: effrt and edgd lft over 1f out: kpt on: nt quite rch wnr: 2nd of 3 in gp* **8/1**

113 **3** *hd* **Fabuleux Cherie**[6] 5534 2-9-5 **62**................................... KerrinMcEvoy 1 64+
(W R Muir) *chsd ldrs on stands' side: short of room and swtchd rt over 1f out: r.o: nt rch wnr: 1st of 8 in gp* **13/8**[1]

1300 **4** *hd* **Thomas Malory (IRE)**[6] 5529 2-9-2 **59**.......................... JamieSpencer 8 60
(Miss V Haigh) *hld up in rr on stands' side: hdwy u.p over 1f out: r.o fnl f: nt rch wnr: 2nd of 8 in gp* **4/1**[2]

6560 **5** *1* **Biased Opinion (IRE)**[22] 5096 2-9-1 **58**..........................(v) EddieAhern 6 55
(H J L Dunlop) *led stands' side gp after 1f: rdn 2f out: lost stands' side ld ins fnl f: one pce: 3rd of 8 in gp* **11/1**

000 **6** *1 1/4* **Honest Value (IRE)**[31] 4823 2-9-2 **59**........................ RichardThomas 10 50
(Mrs L C Jewell) *racd far side: a last of trio: sme hdwy over 1f out: nvr able to chal: 3rd of 3 in gp* **25/1**

0604 **7** *shd* **Chemise (IRE)**[20] 5133 2-8-8 **51**...................................... SteveDrowne 2 44+
(R J Hodges) *racd stands' side: led that gp for 1f: chsd ldr tl over 1f out: wknd ins fnl f: 4th of 8 in gp* **25/1**

0300 **8** *hd* **Black Duke**[14] 5298 2-8-8 **58**.. MCGeran(7) 4 50
(M G Quinlan) *chsd ldrs on stands' side: rdn over 2f out: wknd over 1f out: 5th of 8 in gp* **20/1**

3202 **9** *4* **Culzean Bay**[8] 5484 2-8-7 **50** ow1................................ FergusSweeney 7 27
(Miss Diana Weeden) *chsd ldrs on stands' side tl rdn and wknd qckly over 1f out: 6th of 8 in gp* **14/1**

0000 **10** *1 1/4* **In Decorum**[75] 3446 2-8-5 **48**.. DavidKinsella 3 21
(J A Geake) *s.i.s: a bhd on stands' side: 7th of 8 in gp* **40/1**

000 **11** *2* **Zabeel Tiger**[12] 5343 2-9-7 **64**.. TQuinn 5 30
(M R Channon) *racd stands' side: sn rdn along: bhd fr 1/2-way: 8th of 8 in gp* **13/2**[3]

59.34 secs (-1.46) **Going Correction** -0.60s/f (Hard) **11** Ran SP% **117.7**
Speed ratings (Par 93): **87,85,85,85,83 81,81,81,74,72 69**
CSF £147.70 CT £374.76 TOTE £20.00: £6.20, £5.00, £1.10; EX 235.90 Trifecta £273.30 Part won. Pool: £384.99 - 0.10 winning units..

Owner S Kamis And Mrs S Grayson **Bred** L Cashman And M Fahy **Trained** Formby, Lancs

■ Stewards' Enquiry : Eddie Ahern one-day ban: careless riding (Oct 8)

FOCUS
A moderate race and, although the form could prove solid, the form is modest at best.

NOTEBOOK

Rightcar Ellie(IRE) took the preferred route down the far side and did enough to hold the late thrust of the runner-up. The blinkers could have helped but the part of the track she came down probably made the biggest difference and is not one to go overboard about next time. (op 14-1)

New Balls Please(IRE) followed the winner down the rail early but drifted into the centre of the course one under pressure. He does not look an easy ride and is not one to have much confidence in. (op 17-2 tchd 9-1)

Fabuleux Cherie was the first home down the stands' side and finished strongly inside the final furlong. She is probably still in form. (tchd 11-8 tchd 2-1 in place)

Thomas Malory(IRE) kept on strongly down the stands' side after being behind early. A bit further would have helped him. (op 5-1 tchd 11-2)

Biased Opinion(IRE) set the pace down the stands' side and ran up to his best. He is pretty exposed now. (op 16-1)

Chemise(IRE) Official explanation: jockey said filly hung left

Zabeel Tiger, dropped back in trip, proved very disappointing and never threatened to take a hand. (tchd 7-1)

5716 LADBROKES JACKS OR BETTER 97% POKER CLASSIFIED STKS 5f
4:20 (4:21) (Class 7) 3-Y-O+ **£2,047** (£604; £302) **Stalls** Low

Form RPR

0405 **1** **Splendidio**[22] 5082 3-8-12 45.. SteveDrowne 13 55
(Mrs Marjorie Fife) *chsd ldr on far side: shkn up to ld ins fnl f: sn in command: 1st of 7 in gp* **12/1**

0106 **2** *3* **Savanagh Forest (IRE)**[41] 4514 3-8-12 45.............. FergusSweeney 12 44
(M Quinn) *chsd ldrs on far side: rdn wl over 1f out: kpt on: wnt 2nd nr fin: no ch w wnr: 2nd of 7 in gp* **25/1**

0000 **3** *1/2* **Smart Cassie**[37] 4635 4-8-6 45.................................(b) RobbieEgan(7) 14 42
(H J Evans) *led on far side and overall: rdn 2f out: hdd ins fnl f: no ch w wnr: 3rd of 7 in gp* **12/1**

0-06 **4** *shd* **Piccolo Diamante (USA)**[15] 5282 3-8-12 45.........................(t) TQuinn 8 42
(D J Murphy) *v free to post: prom on far side: rdn 2f out: kpt on same pce: 4th of 7 in gp* **25/1**

0021 **5** *1 3/4* **Knead The Dough**[7] 5510 6-9-0 44........................... KirstyMilczarek(5) 3 42+
(A E Price) *racd stands' side: w ldr of that gp: led that side wl over 1f out: kpt on but no ch w far side: 1st of 6 in gp* **2/1**[1]

5000 **6** *shd* **Tang**[26] 4974 3-8-5 45... JackDean(7) 10 35
(W G M Turner) *chsd ldrs on far side: drvn over 2f out: sn outpcd: 5th of 7 in gp* **40/1**

4500 **7** *nk* **Lady Hopeful (IRE)**[5] 5566 5-8-13 45.................................(b) LPKeniry 7 34
(Peter Grayson) *chsd ldrs on far side: rdn wl over 1f out: no imp after: 6th of 7 in gp* **12/1**

6000 **8** *1 3/4* **Mannello**[47] 4336 4-8-13 45......................................(b[1]) RichardThomas 2 28+
(Jim Best) *s.i.s: racd stands' side: drvn and hdwy over 2f out: kpt on but no ch w far side: 2nd of 6 in gp* **7/2**[2]

400 **9** *nk* **Shevalina (IRE)**[43] 4464 5-8-10 45................................. JerryO'Dwyer(3) 9 27
(Adrian Sexton, Ire) *a outpcd on far side: 7th of 7 in gp* **12/1**

0404 **10** *1* **Lawdy Miss Clawdy**[15] 5276 3-8-12 45................................ TedDurcan 4 23
(D W P Arbuthnot) *led stands' side tl wl over 1f out: sn wknd: 3rd of 6 in gp* **7/1**[3]

0630 **11** *shd* **Kilvickeon (IRE)**[27] 4935 3-8-12 45...................................... BrettDoyle 5 23
(Peter Grayson) *chsd ldrs on stands' side: rdn and disp ld on that side wl over 1f out: wknd fnl f: 4th of 6 in gp* **16/1**

0400 **12** *3* **Flower Of Cork (IRE)**[22] 5090 3-8-12 45....................(p) DavidKinsella 1 12
(I A Wood) *a struggling on stands' side: 5th of 6 in gp* **40/1**

6605 **13** *1/2* **Chingford (IRE)**[40] 4536 3-8-12 45..............................(b) EddieAhern 6 10
(J G Portman) *a bhd on stands' side: 6th of 6 in gp* **20/1**

58.43 secs (-2.37) **Going Correction** -0.60s/f (Hard) course record
WFA 3 from 4yo+ 1lb **13** Ran SP% **122.0**
Speed ratings (Par 97): **94,89,88,88,85 85,84,82,81,79 79,74,74**
CSF £291.24 TOTE £17.20: £3.60, £8.00, £5.00; EX 58.80 Trifecta £143.60 Part won. Pool: £202.27 - 0.10 winning units..

Owner R W Fife **Bred** D D And Mrs Jean P Clee **Trained** Stillington, N Yorks

FOCUS
A poor contest and, not for the first time, on the straight course the far side enjoyed a considerable advantage. As a result the form looks dubious with the stands' side group clearly better than the bare form.

5717 FOLKESTONE RACECOURSE FOR CHRISTMAS PARTIES H'CAP 1m 1f 149y
4:50 (4:50) (Class 3) (0-90,89) 3-Y-O+ **£6,855** (£2,052; £1,026; £513; £256) **Stalls** Low

Form RPR

0142 **1** **Press The Button (GER)**[12] 5362 4-9-9 **85**.................. KerrinMcEvoy 1 92+
(J R Boyle) *mde all: rdn wl over 1f out: kpt on wl: eased towards fin* **9/2**[3]

0206 **2** *1 1/4* **Noticeable (IRE)**[9] 5445 3-8-13 **81**................................. JamieSpencer 4 85
(M R Channon) *chsd ldrs: disp 2nd 7f out: rdn 2f out: kpt on but a hld by wnr* **14/1**

1301 **3** *1/2* **Six Of Diamonds (IRE)**[9] 5445 3-9-0 **89**..................... RobbieEgan(7) 6 92+
(J A Osborne) *t.k.h: chsd wnr: plld out and rdn 2f out: nt clr run and bmpd wl over 1f out: sn swtchd rt: kpt on same pce u.p fnl f* **10/11**[1]

2463 **4** *nk* **Ebert**[10] 5419 4-9-10 **86**...(p) EddieAhern 7 88
(P J Makin) *t.k.h: hld up: effrt on outer jst over 2f out: hanging rt and nt qckn after* **9/4**[2]

5 *6* **Marsam (IRE)**[135] 4854 4-9-6 **82**... TedDurcan 5 72
(M G Quinlan) *hld up in last: rdn and effrt 2f out: no real hdwy: eased wl ins fnl f* **25/1**

2m 5.61s (0.38) **Going Correction** -0.325s/f (Firm)
WFA 3 from 4yo+ 6lb **5** Ran SP% **111.8**
Speed ratings (Par 107): **85,84,83,83,78**
CSF £51.56 TOTE £6.10: £2.10, £3.50; EX 36.40 Trifecta £39.30 Pool: £285.03 - 5.14 winning units..

Owner Brian McAtavey **Bred** Gestut Sommerberg **Trained** Epsom, Surrey

■ Stewards' Enquiry : Robbie Egan two-day ban: careless riding (Oct 8-9)

FOCUS
A fair handicap but a moderate pace and the form looks dubious with the runner-up having very little recent form.

NOTEBOOK

Press The Button(GER) has taken a while to find his best form this season, but he was a winner at Bath a few starts back and his most recent effort when second to Seabow at Sandown pointed to an imminent return to winning ways. Soon in front, he dominated throughout under McEvoy and won comfortably, being eased close home. There is no denying he had the run of the race, but he should continue to pay his way. (tchd 5-1)

Noticeable(IRE), who won his maiden at the track earlier in the season, has not really gone on as expected since being touched off on his handicap debut at Goodwood, but this was one of his better efforts. He is still quite a raw type and it would not surprise to see him progress quite a bit from three to four. (tchd 16-1)

Six Of Diamonds(IRE), narrowly touched off at Bath last time, looked the one to beat off the same mark, but he did not get the best of rides and, having met trouble, was unable to pick up as his rider would have hoped. He is better than this and can be given another chance. (op Evens tchd 5-4 and 11-10 in a place)

Ebert, back to form in the first-time blinkers at Goodwood last time, exchanged them for the cheekpieces on this occasion, but having come to have a chance, he began to hang and his losing run continues. (tchd 5-2 and 3-1 in a place)

Marsam(IRE), a formerly useful Flat racer for Dermot Weld, went the wrong way over hurdles and he looked to be starting out handicap life over here off a stiff mark. He ran a little better than his finishing position suggests and will be capable of better in time. (op 33-1)

5718 FOLKESTONE RACECOURSE FOR WEDDINGS H'CAP 1m 4f

5:20 (5:22) (Class 3) (0-95,85) 3-Y-O **£6,855** (£2,052; £1,026; £513; £256) **Stalls** Low

Form				RPR
1305	1		**Samsons Son**[30] 4847 3-9-2 **83** JamieSpencer 5 (J R Best) *trckd ldrs: shkn up and effrt on rail over 1f out: led 1f out: r.o strly* **15/8**[2]	88+
2000	2	1 1/2	**Mutadarrej (IRE)**[38] 4609 3-9-0 **81** KerrinMcEvoy 3 (J L Dunlop) *led: rdn and qcknd over 2f out: hdd 1f out: kpt on but nt pce of wnr* **7/2**[3]	84
1-40	3	hd	**Wait For The Light**[108] 2448 3-9-0 **81** (p) SteveDrowne 1 (E A L Dunlop) *pressed ldr thrght: rdn and evry ch 2f out: kpt on same pce* **8/1**	84
4645	4	nk	**Spiderback (IRE)**[18] 5205 3-8-11 **78** TedDurcan 6 (R Hannon) *hld up in last: plld out and rdn 2f out: hung rt after: kpt on same pce* **7/4**[1]	80+
1300	5	3 1/2	**Surrey Spinner**[38] 4603 3-9-2 **83** (b[1]) EddieAhern 4 (Mrs A J Perrett) *awkward leaving stalls: t.k.h: hld up in tch: rdn wl over 1f out: fnd little: wl hld fnl f* **12/1**	80

2m 41.36s (0.86) **Going Correction** -0.325s/f (Firm) **5** Ran SP% **112.2**
Speed ratings (Par 105): **84,83,82,82,80**
CSF £8.96 TOTE £2.60: £1.50, £1.60; EX 10.50 Place 6 £422.26, Place 5 £196.22.
Owner M Folan **Bred** J R Best **Trained** Hucking, Kent

FOCUS
They went just a modest gallop in what was a fair handicap and that played into the hands of Samsons Son. The form looks rather messy and as a result cannot be rated too positively.

NOTEBOOK
Samsons Son, who was keeping on well towards the end on his recent venture over 1m1f, looked worth a try at this distance and he saw it out really well, always doing too much for the runner-up once hitting the front. He remains open to further improvement, but connections are planning on sending him to the horses-in-training sales next month. He might make a hurdler. (op 7-4 tchd 9-4)
Mutadarrej(IRE) has not progressed the way connections would have hoped this season, failing to adapt to the blinkers the last twice, but he had the headgear left off here and seemed to enjoy bowling along in front. He tried to up the tempo from over two furlongs out, but in the end the winner's superior speed found him out. He may be worth trying over 1m6f. (op 9-2 tchd 5-1)
Wait For The Light, who made a pleasing reappearance behind Bergonzi at Windsor back in May, ran as though something was a amiss at Haydock last time and had been given a break since. Wearing first-time cheekpieces here, he showed his true form and is another who could be worth a try over further. (op 7-1 tchd 11-2)
Spiderback(IRE), whose only victory to date came in a maiden, has been running reasonably well in similarly modest handicaps, but he failed to give his running here and seemed to find this firm ground against him, judging by the way he hung under pressure. (op 2-1)
Surrey Spinner, trying this trip for the first time, raced keenly in the first-time blinkers and he failed to get home, stopping very quickly under pressure. He is clearly one to be wary of. (op 8-1)
T/Plt: £952.90 to a £1 stake. Pool: £57,569.30. 44.10 winning tickets. T/Qpdt: £339.80 to a £1 stake. Pool: £3,214.70. 7.00 winning tickets. SP

3986 MAISONS-LAFFITTE (R-H)

Tuesday, September 25

OFFICIAL GOING: Good to soft

5719a LA COUPE DE MAISONS-LAFFITTE (GROUP 3) (STRAIGHT COURSE) 1m 2f (S)

2:20 (2:25) 3-Y-O+ **£27,027** (£10,811; £8,108; £5,405; £2,703)

Form				RPR
	1		**Musical Way (FR)**[20] 5151 5-8-10 RonanThomas 7 (P Van De Poele, France) *pressed ldr tl led narrowly over 1f out: drvn out* **28/10**[3]	106
	2	1/2	**Kocab**[23] 5078 5-9-0 SPasquier 4 (A Fabre, France) *set stdy pce: pushed along over 2f out: jinked rt over 1 1/2f out: hdd over 1f out: r.o* **17/10**[1]	109
	3	1 1/2	**Fontcia (FR)**[24] 5058 3-8-5 JVictoire 5 (D Sepulchre, France) *racd in 4th: rdn over 2f out and sn disputing 3rd: tk 3rd over 1 1/2f out: styd on u.str.p to hold 3rd* **13/1**	103
	4	1/2	**Atlantic Air (FR)**[41] 4520 5-9-3 TThulliez 3 (Y De Nicolay, France) *trckd ldr on ins in 3rd: n.m.r whn hmpd and lost 3rd over 1 1/2f out: kpt on u.p fnl f* **21/10**[2]	108
	5	1/2	**Miss Salvador (FR)**[199] 663 4-8-10 TJarnet 2 (S Wattel, France) *racd in 5th thrght: kpt on fnl 2f* **10/1**	100
	6	15	**Shades Of Beige (UAE)**[72] 5-8-10 EPedroza 1 (Frau E Mader, Germany) *s.s: sn rcvrd to r in tch in last: outpcd fr over 2f out* **18/1**	70

2m 3.20s (-6.20)
WFA 3 from 4yo+ 6lb **6** Ran SP% **117.1**
PARI-MUTUEL: WIN 3.80; PL 1.90, 1.70; SF 10.20.
Owner S Constantinidis **Bred** Sarl Haras Du Tallis **Trained** France

NOTEBOOK
Musical Way(FR), a consistent mare, thoroughly deserved her second victory in this Group 3 event. She seems to peek at this time of year as this success came after a Listed win at Chantilly. Always close up, she raced close to the long-time leader before taking the advantage with half a furlong left to run. She lengthened her stride well and was not put under undue pressure during the final stages. If the ground remains good, she may well turn out for either the Prix Dollar or Prix de l'Opera during the Arc weekend. A longer term plan is the Premio Lydia Tesio in Rome
Kocab stays 1m 4f well, so it was no surprise to see him taking the field along in the early stages. He was travelling well within himself at the two-furlong marker and lengthened his stride when asked, but over this distance he did not quite have the pace to go with the winner inside the final furlong.
Fontcia(FR), the only three-year-old in the race, did not put up a bad effort. She was putting in her best work at the finish and took second place inside the final furlong.
Atlantic Air(FR) was always behind the leading group, but was hemmed in a furlong and a half out. Even so he failed to run on in the final stages and did not really have an excuse. There was an enquiry, but the result remained unchanged.

5448 GOODWOOD (R-H)

Wednesday, September 26

OFFICIAL GOING: Good to soft (good in places; 7.7)
Wind: Strong, across Weather: Fine,cold

5720 ONLY ON TURFTV MEDIAN AUCTION MAIDEN STKS 7f

2:20 (2:23) (Class 5) 2-Y-O **£3,238** (£963; £481; £240) **Stalls** High

Form				RPR
04	1		**Silver Rime (FR)**[33] 4777 2-9-3 0 RyanMoore 14 (R Hannon) *dwlt: sn rcvrd to chse ldrs on inner: prog 3f out: drvn to ld over 1f out: styd on wl* **15/8**[1]	79+
6	2	2	**Shanzu**[10] 5448 2-8-12 0 DaneO'Neill 9 (H Candy) *led to 1/2-way: w ldr after: kpt on wl fnl f but readily hld by wnr* **16/1**	69
4	3	3/4	**Especially (IRE)**[95] 2888 2-8-12 0 J-PGuillambert 2 (M Johnston) *scratchy to post: hld up in midfield: nt clr run wl over 2f out: prog wl over 1f out: styd on wl to take 3rd last 100yds* **15/2**	67+
00	4	2	**Grand Cuvee**[7] 5541 2-9-3 0 TPO'Shea 1 (D M Simcock) *towards rr on outer: drvn fr 1/2-way: hanging rt but styd on wl fnl 2f: nrst fin* **66/1**	67
	5	1/2	**Morocchius (USA)** 2-9-3 0 SebSanders 3 (R M Beckett) *w ldr: narrow ld 1/2-way to over 1f out: wknd fnl f* **4/1**[3]	66
0	6	1 1/2	**Luminous Gold**[68] 3706 2-8-12 0 EddieAhern 16 (C F Wall) *trckd ldng pair: outpcd fr over 2f out: steadily fdd* **22/1**	57
0	7	1 1/4	**Valentine Blue**[151] 1291 2-9-3 0 SamHitchcott 6 (A B Haynes) *rdn and wl in rr bef 1/2-way: no prog tl kpt on fr over 1f out* **100/1**	59
	8	1 1/4	**Epsom Salts** 2-9-3 0 IanMongan 11 (P M Phelan) *mostly in midfield: outpcd over 2f out: no imp on ldrs after* **100/1**	56
	9	3	**Valento** 2-9-3 0 StephenCarson 13 (Eve Johnson Houghton) *settled in midfield: outpcd and shkn up over 2f out: no ch after* **40/1**	48
02	10	nk	**Our Chairman (IRE)**[41] 4527 2-9-3 0 PatDobbs 5 (R Hannon) *nvr beyond midfield: shkn up 3f out: sn outpcd and btn* **7/2**[2]	48
6	11	nk	**Gunnadoit (USA)**[41] 4539 2-9-3 0 PhilipRobinson 10 (C G Cox) *pushed along in rr after 2f: nvr on terms: lft bhd fr over 2f out* **16/1**	47
55	12	1	**Greek Theatre (USA)**[10] 5448 2-9-3 0 JimCrowley 8 (Mrs A J Perrett) *free to post: awkward s: prom tl wknd over 2f out* **20/1**	44+
0	13	1/2	**Follow Your Spirit**[30] 4876 2-9-3 0 RichardKingscote 7 (B Palling) *racd on outer: nvr bttr than midfield: rdn 3f out: wknd 2f out* **66/1**	43
0	14	hd	**Saafend Geezer**[13] 5343 2-9-3 0 SteveDrowne 4 (B J Meehan) *dwlt: a in last trio: nvr a factor* **33/1**	43
0	15	1 1/2	**Dance Easily**[20] 5162 2-8-12 0 PaulDoe 15 (J L Dunlop) *hld up in last pair: pushed along 3f out: no prog* **25/1**	34
00	16	3	**Mio Fiore**[21] 5126 2-8-12 0 RobertHavlin 12 (M Blanshard) *prom early: losing pl steadily after 3f: wl in rr fnl 2f* **100/1**	26

1m 29.76s (1.72) **Going Correction** +0.225s/f (Good) **16** Ran SP% **124.8**
Speed ratings (Par 95): **99,96,95,93,93 91,89,88,85,84 84,83,82,82,80 77**
CSF £35.12 TOTE £2.50: £1.40, £5.20, £2.10; EX 36.50.
Owner Fieldspring Racing **Bred** Jean-Philippe Dubois **Trained** East Everleigh, Wilts

FOCUS
A modest-looking maiden and the form does not look strong for the track. Slightly improved form from winner Silver Rime.

NOTEBOOK
Silver Rime(FR) took his time to get to the front but won going away as they passed the line. Another furlong will easily be within his scope this season if connections can fit in another race, but he may be put away now until next season. (tchd 7-4 and 2-1)
Shanzu did all of the early work and responded well to pressure to hold her place during the final stages. She stays well and will be hard to beat next time if given a realistic target, especially if found a race confined to her own sex. (op 14-1)
Especially(IRE) ◆, who did not take the eye in the paddock, took time to warm to her task but kept on well in the final stages. She is getting better with experience and should win any ordinary maiden. (op 13-2)
Grand Cuvee stayed on reasonably well in the final two furlongs to catch the eye to some extent. He now has the option of handicaps and is likely to find his level in that sphere. (op 50-1)
Morocchius(USA) ◆, who was free to post and attracted support in the market before the race, showed plenty of ability and only weakened out of the argument in the last furlong. He should go very close to winning next time if not regressing for this first run. (op 6-1)
Luminous Gold, having her first run since late July, was close to the pace throughout the early part of the race and shaped nicely before fitness became an issue. She looks the sort for handicaps once qualified. (op 25-1 tchd 20-1)
Our Chairman(IRE) never got involved after being settled in midfield. This was a most disappointing effort. (op 4-1)
Greek Theatre(USA) Official explanation: jockey said colt had no more to give having bolted to post
Follow Your Spirit Official explanation: jockey said colt had no more to give

5721 E B F CHICHESTER CITY MAIDEN STKS 1m 1f

2:55 (2:56) (Class 4) 2-Y-O **£4,857** (£1,445; £722; £360) **Stalls** High

Form				RPR
302	1		**Funny Me**[18] 5227 2-9-3 86 JimmyFortune 8 (P W Chapple-Hyam) *prom: trckd ldr 1/2-way: led main gp to nr side in st: drvn and in clr command over 1f out: styd on wl* **1/1**[1]	81+
0335	2	3 1/2	**Benhavis**[31] 4852 2-9-3 83 (t) EddieAhern 3 (J L Dunlop) *led: styd alone far side in st: no ch w wnr fr over 1f out: but clr of rest of nr side gp* **5/1**[2]	74+
04	3	1 3/4	**Havanavich**[30] 4883 2-9-3 0 GeorgeBaker 6 (S Kirk) *in rr of main gp: prog fr 1/2-way: chsd wnr on nr side 2f out: no imp* **14/1**	71
0	4	1 1/4	**Jollyhockeysticks**[20] 5162 2-8-12 0 SamHitchcott 10 (M R Channon) *s.i.s: pushed up to midfield: effrt to chse wnr nr side 3f out to 2f out: one pce* **10/1**	63
0	5	5	**House Of Tudor**[14] 5321 2-9-3 0 KerrinMcEvoy 2 (J H M Gosden) *wl in tch: cl up in chsng gp 3f out: pushed along and wknd 2f out* **11/1**	58
6406	6	1 3/4	**Nathan Dee**[44] 4461 2-8-10 52 KylieManser[(7)] 5 (Mrs H Sweeting) *racd wd in tch: cl enough 3f out: sn pushed along: wknd 2f out* **80/1**	55
	7	9	**Shaftesbury (IRE)** 2-9-3 0 J-PGuillambert 1 (M Johnston) *chsd ldr to 1/2-way: sn rdn: lost pl and struggling 3f out* **9/1**	37

0 **8** ½ **Bobby Darling (IRE)**[20] 5162 2-8-12 0 TPO'Shea 4 31
(M R Channon) *in tch to 4f out: struggling after* **50/1**

9 ½ **High Dee Jay (IRE)** 2-9-3 0 RyanMoore 9 35
(R Hannon) *s.s: a in last pair: shkn up and no prog over 3f out: bhd after* **7/1**[3]

0 **10** 25 **Fongster**[19] 5200 2-9-0 0 JerryO'Dwyer(3) 7 —
(A M Hales) *prom 3f: lost pl rapdily: eased whn no ch 2f out: t.o* **100/1**

1m 58.91s (2.05) **Going Correction** +0.225s/f (Good) **10** Ran SP% **117.4**
Speed ratings (Par 97): **99,95,94,93,88 87,79,78,78,56**
CSF £6.19 TOTE £1.80: £1.10, £1.50, £3.60; EX 6.90.

Owner Mrs Susan Roy **Bred** Lady Davis **Trained** Newmarket, Suffolk

■ Stewards' Enquiry : Sam Hitchcott two-day ban: careless riding (Oct 8-9)

FOCUS

An ordinary maiden with the moderate sixth limiting the form and the winner not up to previous form in success.

NOTEBOOK

Funny Me set the standard on the evidence of his recent second to Dr Faustus at Thirsk and he ultimately ran out a ready winner. Spearheading the move across to the stands' side, he kept galloping right the way to the line and gave every indication he will stay further in time. He will need to progress again for handicaps, but that is entirely possible. (op 10-11 tchd 5-4)

Benhavis, reported to having a breathing problem when not lasting home over 1m at the course last time, was aided with a tongue tie on this occasion and he showed his true form in second. He was the only one who elected to stay far side, but whether he would have finished any closer had joined the pack on the stands' side remains open to debate. (op 6-1)

Havanavich looked far from certain to be suited by this step up in trip, having run well over 7f at Kempton last time, but he actually stuck on better than most. He was no match for the winner on his side, but is now qualified for nurseries and should do better in that sphere. (tchd 16-1)

Jollyhockeysticks, strongly supported in the market beforehand, improved on her initial effort when down the field at Salisbury and kept plugging away under pressure, but lacked the pace to mount a serious challenge. A daughter of Fantastic Light, she is going to appreciate middle-distances next season and is another who will do better once handicapping. (op 14-1 tchd 8-1)

House Of Tudor, never involved on his debut at Doncaster, looked green that day, but this step up in trip looked far from certain to suit and he appeared not to last home. He is clearly a horse of limited ability. (op 12-1 tchd 10-1)

Shaftesbury(IRE), whose stable's juveniles have really hit top form now, gave mixed messages on the breeding as his dam was a sprinter, and he never really threatened to get involved. (tchd 8-1)

High Dee Jay(IRE), a son of High Chaparral, never recovered from a slow start and can be expected to improve on this. (tchd 15-2)

5722 JOIN GOODWOOD OWNERS GROUP STKS (H'CAP) 6f

3:30 (3:30) (Class 4) (0-80,80) 3-Y-0+ **£4,857** (£1,445; £541; £541) **Stalls** Low

Form RPR

3002 **1** **Don Pele (IRE)**[37] 4664 5-9-6 **79** (p) RyanMoore 18 87
(R A Harris) *hld up last of far side quartet: prog to chse ldr jst over 1f out: drvn to ld last 50yds: jst prevailed* **8/1**[3]

-142 **2** shd **Dixieland Boy (IRE)**[38] 4634 4-8-11 **70** SteveDrowne 7 78+
(P J Makin) *trckd nr side ldrs: prog to ld gp over 1f out: drvn fnl f: jst hld on in gp: jst failed overall* **8/1**[3]

46-3 **3** shd **Grand Show**[42] 4507 5-9-5 **78** AdamKirby 9 86+
(W R Swinburn) *settled in rr nr side: prog over 2f out: pressed ldr fnl f: jst hld* **13/2**[2]

5002 **3** dht **Mango Music**[6] 5560 4-9-6 **79** LDettori 17 87
(M R Channon) *pressed far side ldr: led quartet wl over 1f out: hdd last 50yds: kpt on wl* **4/1**[1]

2600 **5** 1 ½ **Roman Quest**[18] 5223 4-8-6 **65** LPKeniry 13 68
(H Morrison) *s.i.s: racd on outer of nr side gp: wl in rr: prog over 1f out: styd on: nrst fin* **9/1**

4410 **6** ½ **Angel Sprints**[32] 4816 5-9-1 **77** WilliamBuick(3) 16 79
(C J Down) *chsd ldng pair far side: one pce u.p over 1f out* **14/1**

0405 **7** 1 **Misaro (GER)**[10] 5447 6-8-11 **77** (b) MatthewDavies(7) 14 76
(R A Harris) *mde most nr side to over 1f out: edgd lft sn after: wknd fnl f* **33/1**

0026 **8** ½ **Oranmore Castle (IRE)**[12] 5379 5-9-2 **75** TonyHamilton 6 72
(R A Fahey) *w nr side ldrs 2f: lost pl: stl chsng over 1f out: fdd* **12/1**

2540 **9** nk **Linda Green**[32] 4816 6-8-12 **71** TPO'Shea 11 67+
(M R Channon) *hld up in last pair nr side: effrt 2f out: kpt on one pce and n.d to ldrs* **25/1**

5232 **10** nk **Gwilym (GER)**[12] 5381 4-9-2 **75** RobertHavlin 5 70
(D Haydn Jones) *prom nr side: lost pl and drvn 2f out: hld whn hmpd jst over 1f out* **16/1**

0006 **11** ½ **Cheap Street**[35] 4710 3-9-2 **77** (b) JimmyFortune 19 71
(J G Portman) *led far side quartet to wl over 1f out: wknd* **25/1**

1415 **12** ½ **Cativo Cavallino**[15] 5312 4-8-8 **72** NataliaGemelova(5) 8 64
(J E Long) *cl up nr side: rdn to chal and upsides 2f out: wknd over 1f out* **10/1**

0000 **13** 2 **Spanish Ace**[14] 5332 6-9-4 **77** JimCrowley 10 63
(J M Bradley) *racd on outer of nr side gp: nvr bttr than midfield: fdd wl over 1f out* **40/1**

0103 **14** ½ **Mason Ette**[103] 2629 3-9-5 **80** PhilipRobinson 2 65
(C G Cox) *racd against nr side rail: cl up tl fdd 2f out* **14/1**

-000 **15** nk **Avening**[12] 5381 7-8-8 **67** StephenCarson 3 51
(Eve Johnson Houghton) *nvr beyond midfield nr side: no prog 2f out: wknd over 1f out* **25/1**

0405 **16** 1 ½ **Romany Nights (IRE)**[8] 5505 7-9-1 **74** (bt) JohnEgan 4 54
(Miss Gay Kelleway) *s.i.s: a towards rr nr side: rdn and no prog bef 1/2-way* **16/1**

0000 **17** 3 **Fairfield Princess**[40] 4574 3-8-12 **73** FergusSweeney 1 44
(M S Saunders) *racd against nr side rail: a wl in rr* **66/1**

0000 **18** 7 **River Kirov (IRE)**[61] 3911 4-9-5 **78** PaulDoe 15 28
(M Wigham) *racd on outer of nr side gp: nvr beyond midfield: wknd 2f out* **33/1**

1m 13.19s (0.34) **Going Correction** +0.225s/f (Good)
WFA 3 from 4yo+ 2lb **18** Ran SP% **128.8**
Speed ratings (Par 105): **106,105,105,105,103 103,101,101,100,100 99,98,96,95,95 93,89,79**
PL: Mango Music £1.50, Grand Show £2.10; TC: Don Pele/Dixieland Boy/MM £157.14, DP/DB/GS £235.51. CSF £68.93 TOTE £11.60: £2.70, £2.20; EX 92.30 Trifecta £244.20 Part won. Pool £688.10 - 0.50 winning units..

Owner Robert & Nina Bailey **Bred** John J Cosgrave **Trained** Earlswood, Monmouths

■ Stewards' Enquiry : Matthew Davies one-day ban: careless riding (Oct 8)

FOCUS

An ultra competitive sprint handicap in which the first four home were split by two short heads. The far side appeared to be advantaged. Sound form.

5723 CHARLES JAMES HOMES FOUNDATION STKS (LISTED RACE) 1m 1f 192y

4:05 (4:05) (Class 1) 3-Y-0+ **£15,898** (£6,025; £3,015; £1,503; £753) **Stalls** High

Form RPR

31-1 **1** **Kirklees (IRE)**[13] 5351 3-8-8 111 LDettori 2 119+
(Saeed Bin Suroor) *trckd ldr: clsd to ld 2f out: drvn clr fr jst over 1f out* **8/11**[1]

125 **2** 3 **Ordnance Row**[32] 4826 4-9-0 107 RyanMoore 1 113
(R Hannon) *hld up in last: rdn 3f out: styd on fr over 1f out to take 2nd last 100yds: no ch w wnr* **8/1**

142- **3** ¾ **Windsor Knot (IRE)**[347] 5968 5-9-0 111 KerrinMcEvoy 4 112
(Saeed Bin Suroor) *led at decent pce: rdn and hdd 2f out: fdd fnl f* **11/2**[3]

3421 **4** hd **Illustrious Blue**[124] 1985 4-9-0 109 PaulDoe 5 111
(W J Knight) *dwlt: t.k.h: hld up: rdn and nt qckn over 2f out: plugged on fnl f* **9/2**[2]

S226 **5** 1 ¾ **Formal Decree (GER)**[21] 5142 4-9-3 112 MartinDwyer 3 111
(Saeed Bin Suroor) *hld up in tch: rdn over 2f out: wknd over 1f out* **14/1**

2m 7.99s (0.24) **Going Correction** +0.225s/f (Good)
WFA 3 from 4yo+ 6lb **5** Ran SP% **109.2**
Speed ratings (Par 111): **108,105,105,104,103**
CSF £7.05 TOTE £1.50: £1.20, £2.50; EX 7.40.

Owner Godolphin **Bred** Darley **Trained** Newmarket, Suffolk

FOCUS

This looked up to the standard one would expect for a Listed contest. Kirkless was given a nice lead by a stablemate and won comfortably in the end, producing a career-best mark.

NOTEBOOK

Kirklees(IRE) ◆ had the race set up for him by one of his stablemates and he only needed nudging out to follow up his recent comeback victory. He has made a pleasing return to the track after being absent for a long time and, one suspects, he can ply his trade in a slightly higher grade. The Darley Stakes at Newmarket in October could be a realistic target. (op 4-6 tchd 4-5 in places)

Ordnance Row has been a grand servant to connections this season and posted another solid effort after being at the rear early. He handles ease in the ground so could be the sort that a few jumps trainers have their eye on. (op 11-1)

Windsor Knot(IRE) made a satisfactory return to the track but did look like a horse sent out to make a decent gallop for his more fancied stable companion. He stays further than 10f and will probably be stepped back up to that sort of trip next time. (op 13-2 tchd 5-1)

Illustrious Blue, absent since picking up an injury earlier in the season, was keen for much of the race and ran well until getting understandably tired late on. He can improve for the run and could be another from this race to find his way to the Darley Stakes at Newmarket next time. (tchd 5-1)

Formal Decree(GER), who was the third-string for Godolphin under his Group 3 penalty, does not look straightforward and started to look a bit awkward rounding the bend. His slip at Longchamp earlier in the the year may have affected his confidence and he would be of some interested if found a race on a straight track. The Joel Stakes at Newmarket could be the race for him. (op 10-1 tchd 16-1)

5724 GOODWOOD HOUSE STKS (H'CAP) 1m 3f

4:40 (4:40) (Class 4) (0-85,85) 3-Y-0 **£4,857** (£1,445; £722; £360) **Stalls** Low

Form RPR

3331 **1** **Harry Tricker**[10] 5454 3-9-0 **81** 6ex JimCrowley 8 90+
(Mrs A J Perrett) *hld up in tch: prog over 2f out: led over 1f out: styd on strly fnl f* **9/2**

1603 **2** 2 **Bergonzi (IRE)**[11] 5415 3-9-4 **85** (v[1]) JimmyFortune 5 91
(J H M Gosden) *cl up: trckd ldr over 4f out: led jst over 2f out to over 1f out: kpt on but readily outpcd by wnr* **4/1**[3]

001 **3** 2 ½ **Ezdiyaad (IRE)**[32] 4815 3-9-1 **82** RHills 1 87+
(M P Tregoning) *cl up: hmpd on inner wl over 2f out: effrt to chse ldng pair jst over 1f out: no imp* **3/1**[2]

6236 **4** 1 ¼ **Eglevski (IRE)**[62] 3883 3-9-4 **85** EddieAhern 3 85
(J L Dunlop) *led after 2f to jst over 2f out: sn one pce u.p and btn* **11/4**[1]

2216 **5** ½ **Demolition**[12] 5385 3-8-9 **76** SimonWhitworth 2 75+
(C A Cyzer) *trckd ldrs: n.m.r on inner wl over 2f out: kpt on one pce fnl 2f: n.d* **12/1**

51-0 **6** 3 **Grande Caiman (IRE)**[2] 5685 3-8-11 **78** RyanMoore 6 72
(R Hannon) *sn restrained to last pair: pushed along and no prog over 2f out: sn btn* **14/1**

10-0 **7** ½ **One To Follow**[110] 2426 3-9-0 **81** PhilipRobinson 4 74
(C G Cox) *led for 2f: chsd ldr to over 4f out: wknd 2f out* **40/1**

515 **8** 1 ¾ **First To Call**[23] 5099 3-9-1 **82** SebSanders 7 72
(P J Makin) *hld up in rr but in tch: rdn and no prog 3f out: eased whn btn over 1f out* **16/1**

2m 29.06s (1.85) **Going Correction** +0.225s/f (Good) **8** Ran SP% **112.5**
Speed ratings (Par 103): **102,100,98,97,97 95,94,93**
CSF £22.07 CT £60.92 TOTE £5.80: £1.70, £1.40, £1.60; EX 8.90.

Owner J H Richmond-Watson **Bred** Lawn Stud **Trained** Pulborough, W Sussex

■ Stewards' Enquiry : Eddie Ahern two-day ban: careless riding (Oct 9-10)
R Hills caution: careless riding

FOCUS

A decent handicap won readily by the progressive Harry Tricker. The runner-up ran up to his recent course mark.

5725 TURFTV FOR BETTING SHOPS STKS (H'CAP) 1m 4f

5:15 (5:17) (Class 4) (0-80,79) 3-Y-0+ **£4,857** (£1,445; £722; £360) **Stalls** Low

Form RPR

5133 **1** **Kingscape (IRE)**[18] 5225 4-9-7 **74** KerrinMcEvoy 11 85+
(J R Fanshawe) *trckd ldrs: clsd 3f out: plld out gng wl 2f out: rdn to ld jst ins fnl f: kpt on wl* **7/2**[2]

6463 **2** ½ **Chocolate Caramel (USA)**[29] 4917 5-9-12 **79** JimCrowley 8 89
(Mrs A J Perrett) *trckd ldng pair: clsd over 2f out: chal and upsides 1f out: hld by wnr last 100yds* **12/1**

4113 **3** 1 **Snark (IRE)**[19] 5198 4-9-1 **68** JimmyFortune 7 76
(P J Makin) *trckd ldr: grabbed nr side rail and narrow ld 3f out: drvn and hdd jst ins fnl f: one pce* **6/1**

1021 **4** 1 **Elegant Hawk**[8] 5500 3-9-4 **79** 6ex PaulDoe 10 86
(W J Knight) *trckd ldng trio: cl enough but rdn over 2f out: one pce after and nvr able to chal* **11/4**[1]

0344 **5** nk **Going To Work (IRE)**[19] 5210 3-8-12 **73** SebSanders 1 79
(D R C Elsworth) *hld up in last pair: prog on outer 3f out: chsd ldrs over 1f out: nt qckn* **8/1**

-026 **6** 1 ¼ **Is It Me (USA)**[30] 4910 4-9-6 **73** AdamKirby 4 77
(A W Carroll) *led at gd pce: narrowly hdd 3f out: steadily lost pl fnl 2f* **20/1**

-104 **7** nk **Mandragola**[140] 1584 3-9-1 **76** RyanMoore 9 80
(B W Hills) *hld up in last pair: pushed along and no prog 3f out: sme hdwy fnl 2f: nvr a threat* **14/1**

2340 **8** 2 ½ **Great View (IRE)**[39] 4597 8-9-3 **73**........................(v) WilliamBuick(3) 3 73
(Mrs A L M King) *towards rr: rdn 3f out: no prog 2f out: n.d after* **33/1**

3140 **9** *shd* **Muhannak (IRE)**[32] 4799 3-9-3 **78**................................ EddieAhern 6 78
(G A Butler) *settled in midfield: gng wl enough 3f out: pushed along and lost grnd 2f out: rdn and no prog over 1f out* **11/2**[3]

-005 **10** *11* **Zabeel Palace**[137] 1668 5-9-9 **76**................................ TPQueally 5 58
(B J Curley) *mostly in midfield: rdn and lost pl over 3f out: wknd over 2f out* **18/1**

3310 **11** *12* **Rowan River**[12] 5385 3-8-11 **72**................................ MartinDwyer 2 35
(M H Tompkins) *chsd ldrs tl wknd 3f out: t.o* **16/1**

2m 43.34s (4.42) **Going Correction** +0.225s/f (Good)
WFA 3 from 4yo+ 8lb **11** Ran SP% **122.9**
Speed ratings (Par 105): **94,93,93,92,92 91,91,89,89,82 74**
CSF £47.77 CT £253.53 TOTE £3.70: £1.90, £3.10, £2.20; EX 53.40.
Owner Mrs V Shelton **Bred** E Tynan **Trained** Newmarket, Suffolk

FOCUS
Only a fair handicap full of mainly exposed horses. Is It Me set a decent pace and the whole field came stands' side up the straight. Solid form.

5726 RACING UK ON SKY 432 APPRENTICE STKS (H'CAP) 5f
5:50 (5:50) (Class 5) (0-70,81) 3-Y-0+ **£3,238** (£963; £481; £240) **Stalls** Low

Form RPR

5411 **1** **Malapropism**[4] 5642 7-9-10 **81** 12ex....................(v) MatthewDavies(7) 4 89
(M R Channon) *mde virtually all: hrd pressed fr 2f out: def advantage ins fnl f: hld on wl* **6/1**[3]

2113 **2** ½ **Cosmic Destiny (IRE)**[25] 5029 5-9-6 **70**................ RichardKingscote 2 76
(E F Vaughan) *hld up bhd ldrs gng wl: effrt against nr side rail 1f out: styd on but nt rch wnr* **9/2**[1]

0643 **3** *nk* **Talcen Gwyn (IRE)**[13] 5349 5-8-2 **59**....................(v) JosephWalsh(7) 14 64
(M F Harris) *racd towards outer: trckd ldrs: clsd to chal over 1f out: pushed along and kpt on same pce* **12/1**

0/22 **4** *hd* **Rydal (USA)**[7] 5535 6-9-5 **69**................................ WilliamBuick 8 73
(J A Osborne) *sn outpcd in last trio and bhd: prog over 1f out: styd on fnl f: nrst fin* **9/2**[1]

0300 **5** *hd* **Azygous**[4] 5642 4-8-12 **65** ow2.................................. JamesMillman(3) 3 69
(J Akehurst) *pressed wnr: upsides 2f out to 1f out: fdd fnl f* **15/2**

2336 **6** *nk* **Endless Summer**[13] 5349 10-8-7 **57**.............................. LiamJones 10 59
(A W Carroll) *outpcd in last trio: styd on fr over 1f out: nrst fin* **11/2**[2]

0601 **7** ¾ **Cerulean Rose**[13] 5349 8-8-1 **56** oh1.......................... KirstyMilczarek(5) 12 56
(A W Carroll) *outpcd early: sme prog 3f out: rdn on outer and no imp on ldrs over 1f out* **11/1**

0410 **8** 1 ¾ **Jucebabe**[26] 5009 4-8-9 **59**..(p) MarcHalford 15 52
(J L Spearing) *racd on outer: in tch: rdn 1/2-way: no prog over 1f out* **16/1**

0002 **9** *shd* **Calabaza**[11] 5430 5-8-5 **58**..(p) TolleyDean(3) 11 51
(J Akehurst) *w ldrs to over 1f out: wknd* **9/1**

0000 **10** ½ **Puskas (IRE)**[26] 5009 4-9-1 **65**................................ TravisBlock 6 56
(J M Bradley) *struggling in last trio 1/2-way: no prog after* **25/1**

6-60 **11** ¾ **Fastrac Boy**[14] 5340 4-8-6 **56** oh3................................ StephaneBreux 7 45
(J R Best) *chsd ldrs tl wknd over 1f out* **33/1**

1650 **12** *3* **Matterofact (IRE)**[4] 5643 4-8-12 **65**............................ HaddenFrost(3) 1 43
(M S Saunders) *trckd ldrs against nr side rail: wknd wl over 1f out* **16/1**

59.73 secs (0.68) **Going Correction** +0.225s/f (Good) **12** Ran SP% **122.4**
Speed ratings (Par 103): **103,102,101,101,101 100,99,96,96,95 94,89**
CSF £34.30 CT £328.60 TOTE £4.30: £2.50, £2.20, £3.00; EX 18.60 Place 6 £28.08, Place 5 £14.27.
Owner Michael A Foy **Bred** Michael A Foy **Trained** West Ilsley, Berks

FOCUS
They all elected to stay stands' side for what was a fair handicap sprint. Malapropism defied a double penalty and the form is solid.
Cerulean Rose Official explanation: jockey said mare was outpaced early

T/Jkpt: £645.40 to a £1 stake. Pool: £10,000.00. 11.00 winning tickets. T/Plt: £9.30 to a £1 stake. Pool: £74,435.40. 5,790.45 winning tickets. T/Qpdt: £6.40 to a £1 stake. Pool: £3,709.60. 424.95 winning tickets. JN

5679 KEMPTON (A.W) (R-H)
Wednesday, September 26

OFFICIAL GOING: Standard
Wind: Fresh, half against Weather: partly cloudy with bright spells but a chilly wind

5727 KEMPTON.CO.UK MEDIAN AUCTION MAIDEN FILLIES' STKS 1m (P)
6:20 (6:21) (Class 6) 2-Y-0 **£2,047** (£604; £302) **Stalls** High

Form RPR

02 **1** **Ballora (FR)**[30] 4875 2-9-0 0................................ RichardHughes 12 73+
(S Kirk) *sn w ldrs: chsd ldr 5f out: led wl over 1f out: sn pushed clr: readily* **8/13**[1]

06 **2** 1 ¾ **Pediment**[16] 5274 2-9-0 0.. OscarUrbina 1 69+
(J R Fanshawe) *w.w in midfield: swtchd lft and hdwy over 2f out: styd on to go 2nd ins fnl f: no ch w wnr* **7/1**[3]

3 *nk* **Shy** 2-9-0 0.. StephenCarson 9 68
(P Winkworth) *led for 1f: chsd ldrs: rdn to chse wnr over 1f out: kpt on but no ch w wnr: lost 2nd ins fnl f* **50/1**

0 **4** 2 ½ **Tamdiid (USA)**[53] 4169 2-9-0 0................................ JohnEgan 4 63+
(C E Brittain) *hld up bhd: rdn and hdwy over 2f out: kpt on steadily: nt trble ldrs* **25/1**

5 *3* **Bluebell Ridge (IRE)** 2-9-0 0.................................... JamesDoyle 10 56
(D W P Arbuthnot) *s.i.s: sn rcvrd and in midfield: rdn and effrt over 2f out: nvr able to chal* **80/1**

5 **6** ½ **Keep Your Head (USA)**[23] 5100 2-9-0 0........................ TPQueally 5 55+
(J A Osborne) *t.k.h: hld up in tch: rdn and hanging rt 2f over 2f out: swtchd lft wl over 1f out: kpt on but nvr threatened ldrs* **20/1**

7 *1* **Express Princess (IRE)** 2-8-9 0.......................... AshleyHamblett(5) 11 53
(M Botti) *trckd ldrs: rdn and effrt on rail jst over 2f out: wknd over 1f out* **33/1**

0400 **8** *hd* **Rosy Dawn**[22] 5117 2-9-0 56..(v[1]) DaneO'Neill 7 53
(H J L Dunlop) *led after 1f: clr 1/2-way: hdd wl over 1f out: sn wknd* **100/1**

9 *1* **Bitooh** 2-9-0 0...(t) LDettori 3 50
(Saeed Bin Suroor) *chsd ldrs: rdn 3f out: sn struggling:* **9/2**[2]

6340 **10** ½ **Heavenly Saint**[11] 5423 2-9-0 60.................................. TPO'Shea 2 49
(M R Channon) *hld up bhd: rdn wl over 2f out: no hdwy* **25/1**

0 **11** *14* **Avril Valley**[13] 5343 2-9-0 0.. TQuinn 6 18
(D J S Ffrench Davis) *bhd after 3f: t.o* **100/1**

12 3 ½ **Evette** 2-9-0 0.. SebSanders 8 11
(M Johnston) *s.i.s: nvr gng and a wl bhd: rn wd bnd 3f out: t.o* **12/1**

1m 38.94s (-1.86) **Going Correction** -0.25s/f (Stan) **12** Ran SP% **120.9**
Speed ratings (Par 90): **99,97,96,94,91 90,89,89,88,88 74,70**
CSF £5.12 TOTE £1.60: £1.02, £2.30, £21.60; EX 6.70.
Owner The Hon Mrs J M Corbett & C Wright **Bred** G And Mrs Forien **Trained** Upper Lambourn, Berks

FOCUS
This looked no more than an average-standard maiden with the winner not needing to be at her best to score but the winning time was marginally quicker than the following older-horse maiden.

NOTEBOOK
Ballora(FR) had appreciated the step up in trip and drop in grade when runner-up at Chepstow over this distance last month, and was not pressed to justify odds-on favouritism. Always handy, she was sent to the front just inside the two-furlong pole and quickly put the race to bed. She should have no problem staying further in time, and was simply much better than her rivals. (op 4-5 tchd 8-11 in places)
Pediment, representing Cheveley Park, who can do little wrong with fillies, was up a furlong on this nursery qualifying run. She appreciated the trip, keeping on well, and she can certainly be placed to win. (op 8-1 tchd 9-1)
Shy, a half-sister to a dual 6f winner, belied odds of 50-1 to post an encouraging debut effort and is likely to benefit for the experience.
Tamdiid(USA), dropping in class after finishing last on her debut behind Sense Of Joy, appreciated the easier grade and waiting ride and kept on takingly. (tchd 20-1)
Bluebell Ridge(IRE), who has plenty of speed in her immediate pedigree, ran well on her debut after a slow start. (op 66-1)
Bitooh, a 340,000gns yearling from the family of Puce and Alexandrova, did not run like a second favourite but may do better on soft turf. Official explanation: jockey said filly had no more to give (op 11-4)
Heavenly Saint looked to have fair each-way prospects, given her experience, but was disappointing. (op 20-1)
Evette Official explanation: jockey said filly hung left-handed

5728 STEVE EDKINS SAYS GOODBYE TO DST MEDIAN AUCTION MAIDEN STKS 1m (P)
6:50 (6:52) (Class 6) 3-5-Y-0 **£2,047** (£604; £302) **Stalls** High

Form RPR

4- **1** **Power Ballad**[426] 3868 3-8-12 0.................................. SebSanders 8 59+
(W J Knight) *mde all: rdn 2f out: edgd lft but sn in command: readily* **7/1**[3]

0 **2** 2 ½ **Oat Cuisine**[12] 5390 3-8-12 0.................................. HayleyTurner 14 53
(M L W Bell) *chsd ldrs: rdn to chse wnr over 1f out: outpcd by wnr fnl f* **12/1**

5622 **3** *nk* **Handset (USA)**[37] 4659 3-8-12 68.............................. RichardHughes 11 53
(H R A Cecil) *hld up in midfield: rdn over 2f out: kpt on steadily u.p: nt pce to trble wnr* **5/4**[1]

2004 **4** *nk* **Split The Wind (USA)**[26] 5005 3-8-12 60.................... StephenCarson 3 52
(Eve Johnson Houghton) *a.p: rdn over 2f out: kpt on same fnl f* **9/2**[2]

0-06 **5** ½ **Axis Mundi (IRE)**[37] 4671 3-8-12 40.................................. TQuinn 7 51
(T J Etherington) *chsd ldr: rdn over 2f out: kpt on same pce* **80/1**

0 **6** *nk* **Mark Of The Fen**[12] 5390 3-9-3 0...................................(e) DaneO'Neill 1 55
(Rae Guest) *s.i.s: bhd: rdn and hdwy on outer wl over 1f out: r.o wl: nt rch ldrs* **33/1**

00 **7** *nk* **Formidable Guest**[119] 2153 3-8-12 0.............................. TPQueally 4 49
(J Pearce) *s.i.s: towards rr: rdn and hdwy over 2f out: no imp fnl f* **25/1**

-005 **8** *1* **Pure Velvet (IRE)**[93] 2951 3-8-12 45.............................. LPKeniry 2 47
(S Kirk) *t.k.h: hld up in midfield on outer: hdwy over 3f out: rdn and hanging rt over 1f out: no imp after* **25/1**

50 **9** *2* **Highest Esteem**[10] 5450 3-9-3 0.............................. FergusSweeney 13 48
(G L Moore) *s.i.s: rdn and sme hdwy on inner over 2f out: no imp fnl f* **9/1**

005 **10** *1* **Hugo Quick**[35] 4707 3-9-0 52.................................. NeilChalmers(3) 6 45
(T M Jones) *w.w in midfield: rdn over 2f out: no hdwy: fin lame* **66/1**

0020 **11** ¾ **Elmasong**[36] 4684 3-8-12 45.................................. SteveDrowne 9 39
(J J Bridger) *chsd ldrs: rdn over 2f out: wknd over 1f out: eased ins fnl f* **20/1**

12 *hd* **Mtoto Girl** 3-8-5 0.. SophieDoyle(7) 10 38
(Ms J S Doyle) *s.i.s: a in rr: n.d* **33/1**

0-4 **13** *hd* **Norman Tradition**[27] 4977 3-8-12 0.............................. MartinDwyer 12 38
(A M Balding) *w.w in midfield: rdn and effrt on inner over 2f out: wknd wl over 1f out* **8/1**

14 *26* **Gracefull Model** 3-8-7 0.. KevinGhunowa(5) 5 —
(Mrs C A Dunnett) *lost pl and dropped to rr wl over 4f out: t.o last 2f* **66/1**

1m 39.58s (-1.22) **Going Correction** -0.25s/f (Stan) **14** Ran SP% **126.5**
Speed ratings (Par 101): **96,93,93,92,92 92,91,90,88,87 87,86,86,60**
CSF £85.03 TOTE £10.90: £2.30, £3.60, £1.10; EX 122.20.
Owner Mrs E Roberts **Bred** Mrs E Roberts **Trained** Patching, W Sussex

FOCUS
This was a much inferior maiden to the opening juvenile race over the same trip, and the winning time was fractionally slower despite a visually impressive winner. The proximity of the fifth and eighth limits the form, which is weak.
Mark Of The Fen Official explanation: trainer said gelding lost a hind shoe
Hugo Quick Official explanation: vet said gelding finished lame

5729 DIGIBET.COM NURSERY 7f (P)
7:20 (7:21) (Class 6) (0-65,65) 2-Y-0 **£2,047** (£604; £302) **Stalls** High

Form RPR

540 **1** **Polar Annie**[38] 4629 2-9-5 **63**.................................. FrancisNorton 6 68+
(M S Saunders) *t.k.h: hld up bhd ldrs: jnd ldrs gng wl over 2f out: led 2f out: r.o strly* **12/1**

5600 **2** 1 ½ **Southwest Star (IRE)**[18] 5216 2-9-4 **62**.............................. LPKeniry 7 63
(J S Moore) *chsd ldrs: rdn and hdwy wl over 2f out: chsd wnr over 1f out: no imp last 100yds* **6/1**

0006 **3** ¾ **Tiger's Rocket (IRE)**[19] 5199 2-9-3 **61**...................... RichardHughes 10 60
(R Hannon) *in tch: rdn over 2f out: kpt on u.p: wnt 3rd ins fnl f: nt pce to rch ldrs* **11/2**[3]

0502 **4** 1 ¾ **Lady Sandicliffe (IRE)**[33] 4783 2-9-2 **60**.......................... DaneO'Neill 13 55
(Miss Jo Crowley) *towards rr on rail: nt clr run and swtchd lft over 2f out: styd on fnl f: nvr able to chal* **6/1**

006 **5** ½ **Vilna (USA)**[16] 5277 2-9-7 **65**.................................. SimonWhitworth 1 58
(N A Callaghan) *s.i.s: hld up towards rr on outer: hdwy wl over 2f out: kpt on u.p fnl f: nt trble ldrs* **12/1**

6000 **6** ¾ **Wooden King (IRE)**[32] 4832 2-9-0 **58**.............................. J-PGuillambert 2 49
(P D Evans) *chsd ldr tl led over 5f out: rdn and hdd 2f out: wknd fnl f* **16/1**

0340 **7** *nk* **Softly Killing Me**[41] 4547 2-9-3 **61**.............................. JimCrowley 11 51
(J Gallagher) *a towards rr: rdn over 2f out: nvr trbld ldrs* **14/1**

0600 **8** *nk* **Bahamian Blue (IRE)**[7] 5529 2-9-6 **64**.............................. EddieAhern 9 54
(H J L Dunlop) *led for over 1f: chsd ldr after: ev ch and rdn over 2f out: wknd jst over 1f out* **33/1**

050 **9** ½ **Lunar Limelight**[33] 4777 2-9-2 **60** SebSanders 3 48
(P J Makin) *s.i.s: bhd: rdn and effrt on outer over 2f out: n.d* **4/1**[1]

040 **10** ½ **Plaka (FR)**[22] 5110 2-9-7 **65** TPQueally 8 52
(J A Osborne) *racd in midfield: rdn wl over 2f out: wknd 2f out* **16/1**

504 **11** *shd* **Elizabeth's Quest**[32] 4823 2-9-0 **65** SophieDoyle(7) 4 52
(R Simpson) *sn chsng ldrs: rdn over 2f out: sn wknd* **16/1**

0605 **12** 1 ¾ **Deckguard**[27] 4963 2-9-2 **60** JohnEgan 12 52+
(J S Moore) *t.k.h: hld up in tch on rail: hdwy and nt clr run fr wl over 1f out: eased fnl f* **5/1**[2]

066 **13** *1* **Siryena**[15] 5309 2-9-3 **61** SteveDrowne 5 41
(E A L Dunlop) *a towards rr: rdn and no hdwy wl over 2f out* **16/1**

050 **14** *50* **Tobago Bay**[16] 5274 2-9-4 **62** TPO'Shea 14 —
(M R Channon) *s.i.s: sn rdn and lost tch: t.o fr 1/2-way: virtually p.u last 2f* **28/1**

1m 26.28s (-0.52) **Going Correction** -0.25s/f (Stan) **14** Ran SP% **132.6**
Speed ratings (Par 93): **92,90,89,87,86 86,85,85,84,84 84,82,80,23**
CSF £90.77 CT £463.80 TOTE £17.90: £4.40, £3.50, £1.80; EX 238.00.
Owner Lockstone Business Services Ltd **Bred** Cobhall Court Stud **Trained** Green Ore, Somerset
■ Stewards' Enquiry : Richard Hughes five-day ban: used whip with excessive frequency without giving colt time to respond (Oct 8-12)

FOCUS
A poor quality, wide-open looking nursery, but a decisive winner. The form is rated around the placed horses.

NOTEBOOK
Polar Annie had been dropped unsuccessfully in distance after a fairly encouraging debut, so connections went the other way distance wise and it worked a treat. Always going well just in behind the leaders, she saw out this trip strongly to get off the mark at the fourth attempt. The Handicapper should not be too harsh on her. (op 14-1)
Southwest Star(IRE) was up in trip but down in grade, and it was a combination that resulted in an improved effort. He made up ground from midfield but was well held by the winner. (op 15-2)
Tiger's Rocket(IRE) looked worth another crack at 7f having been nearest at the finish over 6f here earlier in the month, and he certainly did not contradict that thought, keeping on for third. (op 5-1 tchd 6-1)
Lady Sandicliffe(IRE) looked to have strong chances on the basis of her second place, albeit in a seller, at Thirsk last month, plus a favourable draw, and she ran creditably. (op 9-1)
Lunar Limelight appeared to lose her chance with a slow start on this handicap debut. (op 15-2)
Plaka(FR), who this trip promised to suit, was unable to get competitive from a midfield position. (op 14-1)
Elizabeth's Quest, who had run well on two of her three starts prior to this, looked worth another try at this distance, but she may well be dropped back to 6f next time. (op 14-1)
Deckguard was 10lb better off with Plaka on Lingfield running over 6f last month, but he was trapped on the inner all the way up the straight and was not given a hard time once his chance had gone. Official explanation: jockey said colt was denied a clear run (tchd 11-2)
Siryena looked one of the more likely contenders on her handicap debut, but she was never in the hunt.
Tobago Bay Official explanation: jockey said colt was slowly away

5730 DIGIBET H'CAP 7f (P)
7:50 (7:52) (Class 6) (0-50,51) 3-Y-O+ £2,047 (£604; £302) Stalls High

Form RPR

3030 **1** **Solicitude**[165] 1038 4-9-2 **49** RobertHavlin 8 58
(D Haydn Jones) *racd in midfield: hdwy wl over 1f out: led ins fnl f: rdn out* **11/1**

3000 **2** 1 ¼ **Royal Envoy (IRE)**[12] 5386 4-9-3 **50** GeorgeBaker 9 56+
(D Shaw) *hmpd s: wl bhd: hdwy wl over 1f out: r.o strly fnl f: snatched 2nd on line: nt rch wnr* **16/1**

2444 **3** *shd* **Shunkawakhan (IRE)**[14] 5336 4-9-0 **47** (p) OscarUrbina 5 53
(G C H Chung) *in tch: hdwy to chal over 2f out: led 2f out: rdn over 1f out: hdd ins fnl f: nt qckn* **5/1**[2]

0250 **4** *nk* **Briery Blaze**[16] 5269 4-9-1 **48** SteveDrowne 11 53
(J W Unett) *chsd ldrs: rdn and ev ch 2f out: unable qckn wl ins fnl f* **12/1**

2650 **5** *nk* **Shava**[134] 1753 7-9-2 **49** FergusSweeney 2 53+
(H J Evans) *bhd: hdwy on outer over 2f out: r.o u.p fnl f: nt rch ldrs* **11/1**

6000 **6** *1* **Ganache (IRE)**[21] 5132 5-9-3 **50** JimCrowley 13 51
(P R Chamings) *chsd ldrs: rdn and ev ch 2f out: fdd last 100yds* **8/1**[3]

30-0 **7** *nk* **Palais Polaire**[50] 4257 5-9-3 **50** (p) RichardThomas 10 51
(J A Geake) *taken down early: wnt lft s: sn pushed up into midfield: rdn and hanging rt fr 2f out: no imp fnl f* **8/1**[3]

60P0 **8** 1 ¼ **Grand Palace (IRE)**[27] 4978 4-9-3 **50** (v) DaneO'Neill 6 47
(D Shaw) *racd in midfield: rdn and hdwy over 2f out: no hdwy fnl f* **16/1**

0662 **9** 1 ½ **Laphonic (USA)**[14] 5336 4-9-1 **48** TQuinn 4 41
(T J Etherington) *s.i.s: bhd: hdwy on rail over 2f out: chsd ldrs and rdn over 1f out: wknd 1f out* **7/2**[1]

-000 **10** ½ **Clearing Sky (IRE)**[11] 5425 6-8-8 **48** HarryPoulton(7) 7 40
(J R Boyle) *a bhd: rdn 3f out: n.d* **20/1**

0000 **11** 2 ½ **Tipsy Lad**[12] 5391 5-9-2 **49** (bt) JohnEgan 12 34+
(D J S Ffrench Davis) *sn pushed into ld: hdd 3f out: wknd qckly 2f out: eased ins fnl f: sddle slipped* **16/1**

5000 **12** 1 ¾ **Under Fire (IRE)**[11] 5433 4-9-3 **50** SebSanders 3 30
(A W Carroll) *chsd ldrs tl rdn and wknd qckly wl over 2f out* **16/1**

054 **13** 1 ½ **Silver Hotspur**[11] 5425 3-9-0 **50** FrancisNorton 1 26
(M Wigham) *chsd ldrs: rdn wl over 2f out: sn wknd* **8/1**[3]

0000 **14** *13* **Devonia Plains (IRE)**[42] 4505 5-8-13 **51** ow3 JamesMillman(5) 14 —
(Mrs P N Dutfield) *sn rdn along: racd in midfield tl 3f out: sn wl bhd: t.o* **50/1**

1m 25.58s (-1.22) **Going Correction** -0.25s/f (Stan)
WFA 3 from 4yo+ 3lb **14** Ran SP% **126.8**
Speed ratings (Par 101): **96,94,94,94,93 92,92,90,89,88 85,83,82,67**
CSF £185.01 CT £1010.48 TOTE £15.90: £4.70, £7.40, £2.00; EX 278.60.
Owner David Llewelyn Partnership **Bred** Mrs M L Parry **Trained** Efail Isaf, Rhondda C Taff

FOCUS
A poor handicap, effectively a classified race, with the third looking the best guide to the form.
Palais Polaire Official explanation: jockey said mare hung left leaving stalls
Grand Palace(IRE) Official explanation: jockey said gelding hung left
Laphonic(USA) Official explanation: jockey said gelding was akward on leaving stalls
Tipsy Lad Official explanation: jockey said saddle slipped
Devonia Plains(IRE) Official explanation: jockey said gelding had no more to give

5731 DIGIBET SPORTS BETTING H'CAP 6f (P)
8:20 (8:20) (Class 6) (0-65,65) 3-Y-O+ £2,047 (£604; £302) Stalls High

Form RPR

3602 **1** **Bobby Rose**[31] 4853 4-8-12 **62** JamesO'Reilly(5) 9 77
(D K Ivory) *w.w in midfield: rdn and hdwy over 2f out: rdn to ld 1f out: in command after: rdn out* **8/1**[3]

6034 **2** *1* **Bucharest**[12] 5387 4-9-6 **65** (b[1]) TQuinn 10 77
(M Wigham) *sn led: clr 2f out: hdd 1f out: kpt on* **8/1**[3]

3213 **3** *1* **Glencal**[21] 5136 3-8-13 **60** SteveDrowne 5 69+
(H Morrison) *racd in midfield: rdn 3f out: kpt on u.p over 1f out: wnt 3rd last 100yds: nt rch ldrs* **15/8**[1]

4000 **4** 1 ½ **Bold Argument (IRE)**[69] 3686 4-8-12 **57** RobertHavlin 2 62
(Mrs P N Dutfield) *s.i.s: sn prom: rdn wl over 2f out: kpt on same pce* **50/1**

3300 **5** *shd* **Caustic Wit (IRE)**[20] 5160 9-9-3 **62** RichardHughes 7 66
(M S Saunders) *sn outpcd in rr: styd on fnl f: nt rch ldrs* **14/1**

0043 **6** *1* **Jayanjay**[14] 5340 8-8-13 **58** SebSanders 1 59
(P Mitchell) *racd in midfield on outer: rdn over 3f out: nvr trbld ldrs* **16/1**

6060 **7** *hd* **Supercast (IRE)**[16] 5275 4-9-1 **60** LiamJones 6 61
(W M Brisbourne) *v awkward leaving stalls: wl bhd tl sme late hdwy: n.d* **12/1**

0001 **8** ½ **Anfield Dream**[14] 5340 5-9-2 **61** MickyFenton 11 60
(J R Jenkins) *chsd ldr: rdn over 2f out: wknd qckly fnl f* **10/1**

0624 **9** *shd* **Nautical**[14] 5340 9-9-1 **60** JimCrowley 8 59
(A W Carroll) *bhd: n.m.r wl over 2f out: sn rdn and no hdwy* **11/2**[2]

2331 **10** *2* **Rosie Cross (IRE)**[11] 5420 3-9-4 **65** StephenCarson 12 58
(Eve Johnson Houghton) *chsd ldrs tl 1/2-way: sn wknd* **10/1**

5500 **11** *shd* **Gavarnie Beau (IRE)**[14] 5339 4-8-13 **58** (b) FrancisNorton 3 51
(M Blanshard) *a wl bhd* **25/1**

4162 **12** *nk* **Burford Lass (IRE)**[12] 5386 4-9-1 **60** MartinDwyer 4 52
(D K Ivory) *chsd ldrs: rdn over 2f out: wknd qckly* **20/1**

1m 12.12s (-1.58) **Going Correction** -0.25s/f (Stan)
WFA 3 from 4yo+ 2lb **12** Ran SP% **121.4**
Speed ratings (Par 101): **100,98,97,95,95 93,93,92,92,90 90,89**
CSF £70.89 CT £175.72 TOTE £11.30: £3.60, £3.50, £1.20; EX 113.90.
Owner T G N Burrage **Bred** Mrs L R Burrage **Trained** Radlett, Herts

FOCUS
This modest handicap was the most competitive of the evening and the runner-up, who made the running, sets the standard, although the form does not look that solid.
Gavarnie Beau(IRE) Official explanation: jockey said gelding hung left-handed

5732 TFM NETWORKS H'CAP 1m 4f (P)
8:50 (8:50) (Class 5) (0-75,75) 3-Y-O+ £2,914 (£867; £433; £216) Stalls Low

Form RPR

6-05 **1** **Pinch Of Salt (IRE)**[63] 3854 4-9-4 **69** MartinDwyer 12 83+
(A M Balding) *led tl over 10f out: stdd to chse ldrs: rdn to ld over 1f out: r.o strly* **16/1**

4344 **2** 2 ½ **Turner's Touch**[11] 5422 5-8-8 **66** (b) RossAtkinson(7) 8 74
(G L Moore) *s.i.s: hld up towards rr: hdwy over 2f out: r.o to chse wnr ins fnl f: no imp last 50yds* **14/1**

0030 **3** ¾ **Hope Road**[32] 4815 3-8-8 **70** WilliamBuick(3) 1 76
(J R Fanshawe) *in tch: hdwy to join ldrs over 2f out: led 2f out: sn rdn: hdd over 1f out: one pce* **9/2**[3]

0/0- **4** *hd* **Golano**[623] 88 7-9-5 **70** DaneO'Neill 13 76
(P R Webber) *w.w in midfield: hdwy over 2f out: swtchd rt over 1f out: styd on u.p* **25/1**

4620 **5** *1* **Amwell Brave**[8] 5500 6-8-10 **61** EddieAhern 11 65
(J R Jenkins) *w.w in midfield: hdwy on outer 6f out: rdn over 2f out: no imp over 1f out* **11/2**

3424 **6** *nk* **Chia (IRE)**[26] 5018 4-9-0 **65** RobertHavlin 10 69
(D Haydn Jones) *mounted on crse: in tch: rdn and ev ch 2f out: wknd fnl f* **10/1**

2000 **7** 2 ½ **Street Life (IRE)**[39] 4610 9-9-1 **66** BrettDoyle 3 66
(W J Musson) *stdd s: hld up towards rr: rdn and effrt on outer over 2f out: nvr trbld ldrs* **12/1**

3404 **8** *1* **Baan (USA)**[14] 5334 4-9-5 **70** (b[1]) JohnEgan 6 68
(M Johnston) *sn pushed up to chse ldrs: led over 10f out: rdn wl over 2f out: hdd 2f out: sn wknd* **7/2**[1]

0306 **9** *nk* **Medieval Maiden**[65] 3803 4-9-1 **66** NeilPollard 7 64
(W J Musson) *hld up in last: sme modest late hdwy: nvr on terms* **20/1**

0443 **10** *shd* **Arctic Wings (IRE)**[11] 5432 3-8-9 **68** SebSanders 14 66
(W R Muir) *t.k.h: in tch: rdn 3f out: wknd over 2f out* **4/1**[2]

100 **11** 1 ½ **Pocketwood**[79] 3385 5-9-4 **69** StephenCarson 9 64
(Jean-Rene Auvray) *hld up towards rr: dropped to last and rdn over 3f out: n.d after* **20/1**

5100 **12** *3* **Pothos Way (GR)**[23] 5093 4-8-12 **63** JimCrowley 5 54
(P R Chamings) *prom: chsd ldr 10f out: ev ch and rdn over 2f out: wknd qckly over 1f out* **10/1**

13 *20* **Phone Call**[347] 4-9-7 **75** TravisBlock(3) 2 34
(Mouse Hamilton-Fairley) *chsd ldrs: rdn 3f out: wknd over 2f out: eased fnl f* **40/1**

2m 32.48s (-4.42) **Going Correction** -0.25s/f (Stan)
WFA 3 from 4yo+ 8lb **13** Ran SP% **130.0**
Speed ratings (Par 103): **104,102,101,101,101 100,99,98,98,98 97,95,81**
CSF £230.27 CT £1202.59 TOTE £21.20: £4.90, £3.30, £2.60; EX 88.60.
Owner The Hon Robert Hanson **Bred** The Hon R Hanson **Trained** Kingsclere, Hants

FOCUS
Not quite as much strength in depth here as the previous race could muster, but this modest handicap was competitive enough and the form looks solid.

5733 BARRETTSTOWN STUD H'CAP 1m (P)
9:20 (9:20) (Class 6) (0-65,65) 3-Y-O+ £2,047 (£604; £302) Stalls High

Form RPR

6004 **1** **Henry The Seventh**[14] 5338 3-9-3 **65** TQuinn 12 72
(J W Hills) *pushed along to chse ldr after 1f out: rdn to ld 1f out: hld on wl* **5/1**[2]

4525 **2** *shd* **Pactolos Way**[42] 4504 4-9-5 **63** JimCrowley 5 70
(P R Chamings) *w.w in midfield: hdwy over 2f out: str chal over 1f out: a jst hld* **4/1**[1]

0304 **3** *1* **Scarlet Knight**[16] 5275 4-9-4 **62** IanMongan 10 67
(P Mitchell) *chsd ldrs: rdn and ev ch 2f out: no ex last 100yds* **7/1**

0400 **4** 1 ¾ **Fateful Attraction**[22] 5118 4-9-2 **60** (b) JamesDoyle 11 61
(I A Wood) *t.k.h: hld up in midfield: rdn and effrt over 2f out: kpt on same pce* **20/1**

6000 **5** *hd* **Seneschal**[11] 5424 6-9-6 **64** SamHitchcott 14 64
(A B Haynes) *led: rdn over 1f out: hdd 1f out: wknd ins fnl f* **14/1**

-305 **6** ½ **The Cool Sandpiper**[21] 5136 3-9-2 **64** (p) StephenCarson 3 63
(P Winkworth) *t.k.h: chsd ldr for 1f: chsd ldrs after: rdn over 2f out: wknd over 1f out* **13/2**

0500 **7** *nk* **Where's Broughton**[20] 5178 4-9-4 **62** TPO'Shea 9 60
(W J Musson) *hld up in midfield: rdn and effrt over 1f out: kpt on but nt pce to threaten ldrs* **14/1**

0300 **8** *hd* **Roxie Princess (IRE)**[85] 3176 3-9-3 **65** GeorgeBaker 4 63
(J A R Toller) *hld up in rr: rdn over 2f out: nvr pce to trble ldrs* **20/1**

5560 **9** ½ **Magic Warrior**[56] 4063 7-9-5 **63**........................(b[1]) PatDobbs 1 60
(J C Fox) *s.i.s: bhd: hdwy over 3f out: rdn and no real imp last 2f* **15/2**
0020 **10** *nk* **Shouldntbethere (IRE)**[20] 5166 3-9-3 **65**.................. RobertHavlin 13 61
(Mrs P N Dutfield) *hld up in last: n.d* **16/1**
5640 **11** *nk* **Emily's Place (IRE)**[19] 5189 4-9-3 **61**........................ TPQueally 7 56
(J Pearce) *hld up in rr: nvr pce to trble ldrs* **6/1**[3]
4653 **12** *1* **Saarat**[43] 4470 3-9-2 **64**.. EddieAhern 6 57
(J W Hills) *a bhd* **14/1**

1m 38.48s (-2.32) **Going Correction** -0.25s/f (Stan)
WFA 3 from 4yo+ 4lb **12** Ran SP% **124.0**
Speed ratings (Par 101): **101,100,99,98,97 97,97,96,96,96 95,94**
CSF £26.58 CT £144.69 TOTE £10.80: £2.90, £2.30, £4.00; EX 34.90 Place 6 £147.52, Place 5 £109.14.
Owner The Seventh Pheasant Inn Partnership **Bred** Shortgrove Manor Stud **Trained** Upper Lambourn, Berks

FOCUS
Another modest handicap and a desperate finish, with the form straightforward.
Seneschal Official explanation: jockey said saddle slipped
T/Plt: £233.00 to a £1 stake. Pool: £62,134.50. 194.60 winning tickets. T/Qpdt: £134.90 to a £1 stake. Pool: £5,015.50. 27.50 winning tickets. SP

5483 REDCAR (L-H)

Wednesday, September 26

OFFICIAL GOING: Good (good to soft in places; 7.4) changing to good to soft after race 3 (2.40)
After 6mm rain over the previous 24 hours continuous heavy showers resulted in 'genuine soft ground'.
Wind: Strong half-against Weather: Overcast, windy and heavy showers

5734 E B F / CELEBRATING ELSIE CALVERT'S 100TH BIRTHDAY MAIDEN STKS (DIV I) 7f

1:40 (1:40) (Class 5) 2-Y-O **£2,817** (£838; £418; £209) **Stalls** Centre

Form RPR
6 **1** **Zakhaaref**[66] 3761 2-9-3 0.. GregFairley 8 87+
(M Johnston) *mde all: rdn clr 2f out: easily* **5/2**[2]
2 *7* **Salsa Time** 2-8-12 0.. TomEaves 2 65
(Miss J A Camacho) *dwlt and towards rr: swtchd lft and hdwy on outer wl over 2f out: rdn and edgd rt over 1f out: chsd wnr ent fnl f and sn no imp* **18/1**
622 **3** ¾ **Hamalka (IRE)**[11] 5399 2-8-12 73................................ MichaelHills 7 63
(B W Hills) *a.p: rdn along 2f out: sn drvn and kpt on same pce* **2/1**[1]
4 ½ **Red Tarn** 2-9-3 0.. RoystonFfrench 3 66
(B Smart) *s.i.s and bhd: hdwy 2f out: styd on ins fnl f: nrst fin* **8/1**[3]
5 ½ **Shanafarahan (IRE)** 2-9-3 0..................................... MickyFenton 4 65
(T P Tate) *s.i.s: sn in tch: rdn along over 2f out: keeping on same pce whn n.m.r appr fnl f* **16/1**
6 *nk* **La Fortalesa (IRE)** 2-9-3 0.. NCallan 5 64
(K A Ryan) *trckd ldrs: rdn along 2f out: sn one pce* **10/1**
7 1½ **Benedict Spirit (IRE)** 2-8-12 0............................ PatrickHills[(5)] 1 61+
(M H Tompkins) *in tch: pushed along 1/2-way: rdn and styng on whn hmpd over 1f out: sn wknd* **17/2**
8 *nk* **Points Of View** 2-9-3 0.. JamieMackay 9 60
(Sir Mark Prescott) *s.i.s: bhd tl sme late hdwy* **9/1**
0 **9** *5* **Primer Lugar**[8] 5501 2-8-9 0.............................. AndrewMullen[(3)] 10 42
(W J H Ratcliffe) *midfield: rdn along 1/2-way: n.d* **100/1**
0 **10** 1¼ **Whaston (IRE)**[18] 5227 2-9-3 0..................................... TedDurcan 11 44
(J D Bethell) *chsd ldrs: rdn along 3f out: sn wknd* **50/1**
00 **11** *4* **Mchepple**[33] 4783 2-8-9 0.................................. DominicFox[(3)] 12 29
(W Storey) *prom: rdn along 1/2-way: wknd wl over 2f out* **100/1**

1m 30.23s (5.33) **Going Correction** +0.775s/f (Yiel) **11** Ran SP% **117.7**
Speed ratings (Par 95): **100,92,91,90,90 89,87,87,81,80 75**
CSF £47.11 TOTE £3.20: £1.10, £3.60, £1.30; EX 60.90.
Owner Hamdan Al Maktoum **Bred** Shadwell Estate Company Limited **Trained** Middleham Moor, N Yorks

FOCUS
Marginally the quicker division but overall much the weaker half. The winner has clearly improved a good deal since his debut but the form behind is modest.

NOTEBOOK
Zakhaaref made this a true test and the further he went the further he drew clear. He looks a relentless galloper. (tchd 9-4)
Salsa Time, a March foal is a half-sister to the smart stayer Dancing Bay. A rangy filly, she made her effort on the outer but came off a straight line causing a few problems. Her dam won seven times over hurdles and she will make a better three-year-old. (op 16-1)
Hamalka(IRE), a close-coupled filly, was keen to post. She had no excuse but the ground may well have turned against her. (op 15-8)
Red Tarn, a good-bodied April foal, is a half-brother to the stable's smart sprinter Hellvelyn. After a tardy start he picked up in encouraging fashion late on but looks in need of more time yet. (tchd 15-2)
Shanafarahan(IRE), a March foal, has size and scope. He showed ability on his debut but will not be seen at his best until next year. (op 14-1)
La Fortalesa(IRE), a March foal, is up in the air. Very noisy beforehand, this should have taught him plenty. (op 13-2)
Points Of View, a January foal, was noisy and coltish in the paddock. He was hopelessly inexperienced and will no doubt start his three-year-old handicap career from a suitably modest mark. (op 28-1)

5735 E B F / CELEBRATING ELSIE CALVERT'S 100TH BIRTHDAY MAIDEN STKS (DIV II) 7f

2:10 (2:11) (Class 5) 2-Y-O **£2,817** (£838; £418; £209) **Stalls** Centre

Form RPR
1 **Mazaaya (USA)** 2-8-12 0.. GregFairley 4 77
(M Johnston) *w ldrs: led over 3f out tl over 1f out: styd on wl to ld last stride* **9/1**
2 **2** *shd* **Tiger Dream**[14] 5321 2-9-3 0....................................... NCallan 10 82
(K A Ryan) *w ldrs: hung lft and led over 1f out: hdd post* **4/7**[1]
056 **3** *1* **Jabal Tariq**[26] 5011 2-9-3 80................................... MichaelHills 1 79
(B W Hills) *trckd ldrs: effrt over 2f out: nt qckn ins fnl f* **5/1**[2]
002 **4** *nk* **Andaman Sunset**[16] 5281 2-9-3 72.............................. TedDurcan 6 79+
(G Wragg) *chsd ldrs: shkn up over 2f out: styd on strly ins fnl f: fin wl* **14/1**
2 **5** *5* **Mangham (IRE)**[66] 3761 2-9-3 0.............................. RoystonFfrench 12 66
(B Smart) *w ldrs: t.k.h: wknd over 1f out* **6/1**[3]
04 **6** *shd* **Sergeant Sharpe**[11] 5399 2-8-12 0......................... PatrickHills[(5)] 7 66
(M H Tompkins) *mid-div: outpcd over 2f out: kpt on fnl f* **40/1**
06 **7** *nk* **Jackday (IRE)**[44] 4448 2-9-3 0..................................... DavidAllan 3 65
(T D Easterby) *hld up in mid-div: outpcd over 2f out: styd on fnl f* **100/1**
04 **8** ¾ **Grecian Slave**[40] 4578 2-9-3 0..................................... TomEaves 11 63
(B Smart) *chsd ldrs: outpcd over 2f out: kpt on fnl f* **50/1**
9 *5* **Umverti** 2-8-12 0.. SilvestreDeSousa 8 46
(N Bycroft) *s.s: a in rr* **200/1**
00 **10** *17* **Dawn Whisper**[9] 5483 2-8-12 0.............................. PaulMulrennan 2 —
(M E Sowersby) *led tl over 3f out: sn lost pl and bhd* **200/1**
11 *6* **Ournina** 2-8-9 0.. PJMcDonald[(3)] 9 —
(C R Wilson) *s.s: in rr: bhd fnl 2f* **200/1**

1m 30.26s (5.36) **Going Correction** +0.775s/f (Yiel) **11** Ran SP% **118.2**
Speed ratings (Par 95): **100,99,98,98,92 92,92,91,85,66 59**
CSF £14.93 TOTE £14.80: £2.90, £1.02, £2.20; EX 21.40.
Owner Saif Ali **Bred** Needham/betz Thoroughbreds & Carl Freeman **Trained** Middleham Moor, N Yorks

FOCUS
Much the stronger division overall with the third possibly the best guide to the strength of the form.

NOTEBOOK
Mazaaya(USA), a March foal, is a length filly out of a half-sister to the Breeders' Cup Turf winner Miss Alleged. Long in the back, she knew her job and after being crowded by the winner, she put her head in front right on the line. She looks a potential stayer. (op 17-2 tchd 10-1)
Tiger Dream, a May foal, still looks on the weak side. He always wanted to hang left, crowding the winner who in turn left the third short of room, and was mugged right on the line. He will be seen to much better effect at three. (op 4-6 tchd 8-11)
Jabal Tariq, quite a big type, was just found lacking inside the last. He will appreciate a mile plus. (tchd 9-2 and 11-2)
Andaman Sunset, who showed a scratchy action, is improving with every outing. He stayed on strongly late on under a sympathetic ride, and while he already has a rating of 72, connections have nine days to exploit it in a nursery before his rating shoots up.
Mangham(IRE), withdrawn on his intended second start at Ayr in August after rearing in the stalls and cutting a leg, was much too keen for his own good and simply ran himself to a standstill. He will need to be handled with great care. Official explanation: jockey said colt ran too free in the early stages (op 11-2 tchd 13-2)
Sergeant Sharpe again showed ability and looks a likely type for a mile nursery.
Jackday(IRE), keen to post, picked up in his own time late on and looks a likely nursery type.

5736 CONSTANT SECURITY NURSERY 1m

2:40 (2:49) (Class 6) (0-65,65) 2-Y-O **£1,943** (£578; £288; £144) **Stalls** Centre

Form RPR
0000 **1** **Mganga**[15] 5298 2-9-5 **63**.. ChrisCatlin 13 64
(M R Channon) *trckd ldrs: hdwy over 2f out: led wl over 1f out and sn rdn: drvn and edgd lft ent fnl f: styd on wl towards fin* **16/1**
3602 **2** ¾ **Natural Rhythm (IRE)**[15] 5298 2-9-6 **64**.................. DanielTudhope 2 63
(D W Chapman) *hld up in rr: swtchd rt and hdwy over 2f out: chal wl over 1f out: sn rdn and ev ch tl drvn and no ex last 50yds* **8/1**
0630 **3** ½ **No Nines**[19] 5199 2-9-7 **65**.. MichaelHills 6 63
(B W Hills) *trckd ldrs: hdwy over 2f out and sn ev ch: rdn over 1f out: drvn and one pce ins fnl f* **8/1**
0130 **4** 1½ **Pequeno Dinero (IRE)**[41] 4524 2-8-12 **61**.............. KellyHarrison[(5)] 3 56
(C W Fairhurst) *in rr: hdwy 2f out: sn rdn and styd on appr fnl f: nrst fin* **9/1**
000 **5** 1¼ **Graylyn Ruby (FR)**[13] 5344 2-9-3 **61**........................ JamieSpencer 15 53
(J Jay) *hld up in tch: hdwy on wd outside over 2f out: rdn to chse ldrs over 1f out: sn hung lft and no imp* **7/1**
0002 **6** 1½ **I Certainly May**[11] 5423 2-9-6 **64**.......................... PaulFitzsimons 5 53
(S Dow) *trckd ldrs: effrt and hdwy 3f out: sn rdn and wknd wl over 1f out* **8/1**
6006 **7** *4* **Classical Rhythm (IRE)**[15] 5314 2-9-7 **65**.................. PatCosgrave 10 45
(J R Boyle) *led 1f: prom tl rdn along over 2f out and grad wknd* **11/2**[1]
000 **8** *1* **Mubher**[28] 4946 2-9-3 **61**.. NCallan 9 39
(J L Dunlop) *dwlt: sn in tch: rdn along wl over 2f out and sn wknd* **6/1**[2]
0530 **9** *3* **Bourbon Highball (IRE)**[41] 4524 2-9-5 **63**.................. LeeEnstone 14 34
(P C Haslam) *cl up: led after 1f: rdn along over 2f out: hdd wl over 1f out and sn wknd* **13/2**[3]
000 **10** *9* **Melwood Dreams**[19] 5194 2-9-3 **61**............................... TedDurcan 7 12
(Paul Green) *prom: rdn along wl over 2f oiut and sn wknd* **50/1**
050 **11** ¾ **Spectrana**[62] 3874 2-9-3 **61**..(b[1]) KDarley 11 11
(Mrs A J Perrett) *cl up: rdn along 3f out: sn wknd* **20/1**
000 **U** **Recoil (IRE)**[13] 5343 2-9-7 **65**..................................... PaulEddery 12 —
(Christian Wroe) *stmbld and uns rdr s* **20/1**

1m 46.7s (8.90) **Going Correction** +0.775s/f (Yiel) **12** Ran SP% **116.2**
Speed ratings (Par 93): **86,85,84,83,82 80,76,75,72,63 62,—**
CSF £132.67 CT £1125.61 TOTE £17.80: £4.40, £3.00, £2.90; EX 189.40.
Owner Billy Parish **Bred** Norman Court Stud **Trained** West Ilsley, Berks

FOCUS
A weak nursery rated on the negative side with the runner-up not finding much for pressure.

NOTEBOOK
Mganga, unplaced in four previous starts but stopped in his run at Beverley last time, seemed to rather outbattle the runner-up in the closing stages. (op 11-1)
Natural Rhythm(IRE), who had the winner eight lengths behind him at Beverley, ranged upsides looking to be travelling best but in the end the winner saw it out just the better. (tchd 9-1)
No Nines, gelded before Kempton, appreciated the step up in trip and in the end was only just found wanting. (op 10-1)
Pequeno Dinero(IRE), well supported at long odds, struggled but stayed on in good style in the closing stages. A stiffer track will play to her strengths. (op 14-1 tchd 7-1)
Graylyn Ruby(FR), making his handicap debut, raced towards the far side. He gave his rider problems wanting to hang left. (op 13-2 tchd 15-2)
I Certainly May, much improved at Kempton, seems better suited by Polytrack than soft ground on turf. (op 6-1)
Classical Rhythm(IRE), suprisingly sent off favourite, showed a bit more sparkle this time but in the end he dropped right away. (op 6-1 tchd 5-1)

5737 JOHN SMITH'S REDCAR STRAIGHT-MILE CHAMPIONSHIP QUALIFIER (PREMIER CLAIMING STKS) 1m

3:15 (3:18) (Class 4) 3-Y-O+ **£4,728** (£1,406; £702; £351) **Stalls** Centre

Form RPR
3034 **1** **Boundless Prospect (USA)**[7] 5545 8-9-1 68................ NicolPolli[(5)] 4 81
(Miss Gay Kelleway) *hld up in rr: hdwy and swtchd stands' side over 1f out: hrd rdn and edgd lft: styd on to ld nr fin* **16/1**
3000 **2** ½ **Bustan (IRE)**[26] 5012 8-10-0 86............................... JamieSpencer 3 88
(G C Bravery) *hld up in rr: hdwy over 2f out: led over 1f out: hdd nr fin* **10/3**[2]
0142 **3** *4* **El Coto**[9] 5479 7-9-6 78...(p) NCallan 13 71
(K A Ryan) *chsd ldrs: upsides over 1f out: kpt on same pce* **11/4**[1]

-100 **4** *3* **Mineral Star (IRE)**[32] 4820 5-9-7 73..............................(v[1]) TedDurcan 2 65
(M H Tompkins) *hld up in rr: gd hdwy to ld over 2f out: hdd over 1f out: fdd* **6/1**

0433 **5** *3* **Efidium**[18] 5228 9-8-12 69.. NeilBrown(5) 11 54
(N Bycroft) *in rr-div: hdwy over 2f out: nvr nr ldrs* **11/2**[3]

1125 **6** *1/2* **Gleneagles (IRE)**[5] 5585 3-9-3 80.. LanceBetts(7) 14 64
(N Wilson) *chsd ldrs one pce fnl 2f* **6/1**

400 **7** *1 1/2* **Moonstreaker**[26] 4998 4-9-1 52...................................... PaulMulrennan 10 48
(R M Whitaker) *hld up in rr: hdwy over 2f out: nvr nr ldrs* **66/1**

30-0 **8** *3/4* **Typhoon Ginger (IRE)**[17] 5255 12-8-11 58................. TGMcLaughlin 8 42
(G Woodward) *hld up in rr: hdwy over 2f out: nvr nr ldrs* **33/1**

0-4 **9** *1/2* **Mister Pete (IRE)**[151] 1301 4-8-8 0.................................. DominicFox(3) 9 41
(W Storey) *in rr: sme hdwy over 2f out: nvr a factor* **100/1**

/1-5 **10** *20* **Amorist (IRE)**[113] 2347 5-8-11 74...................................... DanielTudhope 7 —
(D W Chapman) *in tch: rdn and lost pl over 2f out: t.o* **33/1**

-000 **11** *2 1/2* **Hypnotic**[91] 2986 5-9-6 74..................................(vt) AdrianTNicholls 15 —
(D Nicholls) *led taking t.k.h: clr over 3f out: hung lft and hdd over 2f out: sn eased and bhd: t.o* **16/1**

0-00 **12** *1 1/2* **Kaymich Perfecto**[18] 5228 7-9-3 65..................(v[1]) MichaelJStainton(3) 5 —
(R M Whitaker) *prom on far side: rdn over 3f out: sn rdn and lost pl: t.o* **33/1**

5200 **13** *3/4* **Smart Cat (IRE)**[28] 4945 4-8-12 52.............................. AndrewElliott(3) 12 —
(A P Jarvis) *chsd ldr: wknd over 2f out: sn bhd: t.o* **50/1**

3600 **14** *15* **Kudbeme**[31] 4846 5-8-9 55 ow2.................................. JamieMoriarty(3) 1 —
(N Bycroft) *in rr: rdn and detached 3f out: sn t.o: virtually p.u* **33/1**

1m 42.84s (5.04) **Going Correction** +0.775s/f (Yiel)
WFA 3 from 4yo+ 4lb **14** Ran SP% **121.7**
Speed ratings (Par 105): **105,104,100,97,94 94,92,91,91,71 68,67,66,51**
CSF £67.28 TOTE £21.80: £4.20, £2.00, £1.40; EX 126.50.Gleneagles was claimed by T Wall for £23,000.
Owner M M Foulger **Bred** Mrs Edgar Scott Jr & Mrs Lawrence Macelree **Trained** Exning, Suffolk
FOCUS
A premier claimer but the form is tied down by the proximity of the seventh. It has been rated through the placed horses.
Hypnotic Official explanation: jockey said gelding ran too freely and hung left

5738 PERTEMPS PEOPLE DEVELOPMENT GROUP H'CAP 1m 2f
3:50 (3:50) (Class 5) (0-70,70) 3-Y-0+ **£2,817** (£838; £418; £209) **Stalls** Low

Form RPR
5442 **1** **Keisha Kayleigh (IRE)**[6] 5563 4-8-8 **57**.................(v) JamieMoriarty(3) 5 66+
(B Ellison) *hld up in rr: gd hdwy on outer over 2f out: rdn and edgd lft over 1f out: styd on strly ins fnl f to ld nr fin* **7/2**[2]

-331 **2** *1/2* **Teodora Adivina**[15] 5304 3-9-2 **68**.................................... TedDurcan 12 76
(H R A Cecil) *trckd ldng pair: hdwy to ld 2 1/2f out: rdn clr over 1f out: drvn ins fnl f: hdd and no ex towards fin* **4/1**[3]

0643 **3** *nk* **Trouble Mountain (USA)**[4] 5620 10-9-4 **64**.................(t) DaleGibson 10 71+
(M W Easterby) *in rr: hdwy 3f out: rdn along whn n.m.r and swtchd lft over 1f out: swtchd rt and rdn ins fnl f: styd on wl towards fin* **8/1**

041 **4** *1 3/4* **Nutkin**[35] 4707 3-9-3 **69**.. JamieSpencer 7 73
(J R Fanshawe) *trckd ldrs on inner: hdwy over 2f out: swtchd rt and rdn over 1f out: sn drvn and edgd lft ins fnl f: one pce* **2/1**[1]

-410 **5** *1/2* **Lauro**[26] 4998 7-8-9 **62**.. DawnRankin(7) 8 65
(Miss J A Camacho) *hld up in rr: hdwy on inner over 2f out: rdn along to chse ldrs wl over 1f out: kpt on same pce ins fnl f* **16/1**

0-00 **6** *5* **Moorlander (USA)**[20] 5166 3-8-12 **64**...........................(t) DavidAllan 13 57
(Mrs A J Perrett) *trckd ldrs: hdwy to chal over 2f out: sn rdn and grad wknd* **22/1**

0065 **7** *7* **Apsara**[22] 4081 6-8-10 **56** oh1...(p) TomEaves 6 35
(G M Moore) *dwlt: sn cl up: rdn along 3f out and grad wknd* **14/1**

6 **8** *7* **Puy D'Arnac (FR)**[9] 5482 4-9-4 **64**.. NCallan 4 29
(G A Swinbank) *in tch: effrt over 3f out: sn rdn and wknd* **9/1**

600 **9** *6* **Magic Sting**[56] 4081 6-8-10 **56** oh5.............................. PaulMulrennan 14 9
(B S Rothwell) *led: rdn along 3f out: sn hdd & wknd* **66/1**

5600 **10** *10* **Up The Chimney**[30] 4889 3-8-3 **58**........................... AndrewElliott(3) 11 —
(A P Jarvis) *chsd ldrs: rdn along 3f out and sn wknd* **50/1**

2m 11.92s (5.12) **Going Correction** +0.65s/f (Yiel)
WFA 3 from 4yo+ 6lb **10** Ran SP% **117.0**
Speed ratings (Par 103): **105,104,104,102,102 98,92,87,82,74**
CSF £17.79 CT £104.82 TOTE £4.90: £1.50, £1.80, £3.10; EX 23.70.
Owner C E Sherry **Bred** Ronnie Boland **Trained** Norton, N Yorks
FOCUS
A low-grade handicap but sound form rated through the placed horses.

5739 TURFTV BETTING SERVICE (S) STKS 1m 2f
4:25 (4:26) (Class 6) 3-5-Y-O **£2,047** (£604; £302) **Stalls** Low

Form RPR
5006 **1** **Cherri Fosfate**[13] 5367 3-9-1 46.. DavidAllan 12 58
(D Carroll) *mid-div: hdwy over 2f out: led 1f out: jst hld on* **12/1**

0302 **2** *nk* **Dot's Delight**[7] 5542 3-8-4 59.................................(b[1]) RoystonFfrench 11 46
(M H Tompkins) *in rr: sn pushed along: hdwy on outside over 2f out: styd on strly fnl f: jst hld* **9/2**[2]

0040 **3** *hd* **Anything Once (USA)**[6] 5557 4-9-1 51.................(b) StephenDonohoe 5 51
(D Carroll) *stdd s: hdwy over 3f out: styd on wl fnl f* **14/1**

0020 **4** *2 1/2* **Yo Pedro (IRE)**[9] 5479 5-9-1 58......................................(b) NCallan 10 46
(D Carroll) *in rr: hdwy 3f out: nt clr run over 1f out: kpt on same pce* **7/1**

625 **5** *hd* **Prince Noel**[6] 5553 3-8-9 52.. DanielTudhope 9 46
(N Wilson) *sn trcking ldrs: led over 2f out: hdd 1f out: wknd ins fnl f* **3/1**[1]

5204 **6** *nk* **Give Evidence**[8] 5511 3-8-6 48.................................... AndrewElliott(3) 3 45
(A P Jarvis) *led tl 3f out: one pce* **10/1**

4440 **7** *1 3/4* **Hot Property (IRE)**[11] 5422 3-8-9 55.................................. TedDurcan 6 42
(W R Muir) *prom: nt clr run over 2f out: hung lft and wknd over 1f out* **6/1**

0040 **8** *2 1/2* **Playtotheaudience**[9] 5487 4-9-1 50................................ PaulHanagan 7 37
(R A Fahey) *trckd ldrs: led 3f out: sn hdd: hung lft and wknd over 1f out* **11/2**[3]

0500 **9** *4* **Betteras Bertie**[37] 4673 4-9-1 42.. TomEaves 4 29
(M Brittain) *s.s: a in rr* **33/1**

00-0 **10** *2 1/2* **Nell Tupp**[147] 1413 4-9-1 45...(t) TGMcLaughlin 1 24
(G Woodward) *unruly s: sn chsng ldrs: lost pl over 2f out* **80/1**

6400 **11** *nk* **Flaming Cat (IRE)**[6] 5553 4-9-1 50................................ PaulMulrennan 8 23
(F Watson) *trckd ldrs: t.k.h: wknd over 1f out: b.b.v* **28/1**

24-0 **12** *11* **Lansdown**[9] 5487 3-7-12 54 ow1........................... PatrickDonaghy(7) 13 —
(R Johnson) *in rr: bhd fnl 4f* **33/1**

06/0 **13** *5* **Penmon Point (IRE)**[75] 3497 4-8-12 40.................. DuranFentiman(3) 14 —
(R Johnson) *in rr: bhd fnl 3f* **80/1**

2m 13.56s (6.76) **Going Correction** +0.65s/f (Yiel)
WFA 3 from 4yo+ 6lb **13** Ran SP% **120.6**
Speed ratings (Par 101): **98,97,97,95,95 95,93,91,88,86 86,77,73**
CSF £64.11 TOTE £14.50: £4.50, £1.30, £5.00; EX 95.80.There was no bid for the winner. Dot's Delight was claimed by M Kelly for £6,000.
Owner Document Express Ltd **Bred** The Newchange Syndicate **Trained** Sledmere, E Yorks
FOCUS
A weak seller with little solid recent form to work on. Perhaps the third is the best guide to the overall value.
Flaming Cat(IRE) Official explanation: trainer's rep said gelding had bled from the nose

5740 PERTEMPS EMPLOYMENT ALLIANCE H'CAP 5f
5:00 (5:02) (Class 5) (0-70,70) 3-Y-0+ **£2,817** (£838; £418; £209) **Stalls** Centre

Form RPR
6123 **1** **Digital**[6] 5576 10-9-2 **67**...(v) ChrisCatlin 8 79
(M R Channon) *rrd s: in rr tl gd hdwy wl over 1f out: sn rdn and styd on strly ins fnl f to ld last 50yds* **7/2**[1]

0064 **2** *1* **Mr Rooney (IRE)**[8] 5507 4-8-6 **57**.............................. AdrianTNicholls 13 65
(D Nicholls) *chsd clr ldr: rdn wl over 1f out: styd on to ld ins fnl f: drvn: hdd and no ex last 50yds* **15/2**[3]

2100 **3** *2 1/2* **Raccoon (IRE)**[15] 5297 7-9-1 **66**.. NCallan 1 65
(D W Chapman) *sn led and clr on far rail: rdn over 1f out: hdd and one pce ins fnl f* **15/2**[3]

1100 **4** *1 1/2* **Toy Top (USA)**[8] 5507 4-8-7 **63**..................................(b) NeilBrown(5) 12 57+
(M Dods) *chsd ldrs: rdn along wl over 1f out and kpt on same pce* **10/1**

1052 **5** *nk* **Strensall**[9] 5481 10-9-3 **68**... PaulHanagan 7 61
(R E Barr) *chsd ldrs: rdn 2f out: drvn and no imp appr fnl f* **15/2**[3]

-006 **6** *3/4* **Niteowl Lad (IRE)**[8] 5507 5-8-11 **62**....................................... TomEaves 2 52
(J Balding) *in rr tl hdwy wl over 1f out: sn rdn and kpt on ins fnl f: n.d* **8/1**

5353 **7** *3/4* **Galipette**[53] 4186 3-9-2 **68**.. TedDurcan 3 55
(H R A Cecil) *dwlt: in tch: rdn along wl over 1f out and no imp* **4/1**[2]

0000 **8** *3/4* **The Thrifty Bear**[15] 5295 4-8-0 **56** oh11..................(b) KellyHarrison(5) 9 40
(C W Fairhurst) *chsd clr ldr: rdn along 2f out and sn wknd* **80/1**

5410 **9** *1 1/4* **Miacarla**[6] 5565 4-8-8 **62** 6ex....................................... PatrickMathers(3) 4 42
(A Berry) *dwlt: a towards rr* **8/1**

0050 **10** *1/2* **Bond Boy**[6] 5552 10-9-5 **70**...(b) DanielTudhope 11 48
(G R Oldroyd) *chsd ldrs: rdn over 2f out: sn wknd* **15/2**[3]

62.24 secs (3.54) **Going Correction** +0.775s/f (Yiel)
WFA 3 from 4yo+ 1lb **10** Ran SP% **121.8**
Speed ratings (Par 103): **102,100,96,94,93 92,91,89,87,87**
CSF £31.77 CT £196.19 TOTE £4.40: £1.90, £2.50, £3.30; EX 47.60.
Owner W G R Wightman **Bred** W G R Wightman **Trained** West Ilsley, Berks
FOCUS
A run-of-the-mill sprint handicap rated through the first two home and the fourth.

5741 ELKHORN H'CAP 6f
5:35 (5:35) (Class 6) (0-65,65) 3-Y-0+ **£2,047** (£604; £302) **Stalls** Centre

Form RPR
6060 **1** **Paddywack (IRE)**[15] 5297 10-8-13 **58**..................................(b) NCallan 3 67+
(D W Chapman) *trckd ldrs: led over 1f out: r.o strly* **11/1**

2042 **2** *1* **Monda**[40] 4583 5-8-8 **53**... TomEaves 1 59+
(Miss J A Camacho) *led one other far side: kpt on wl fnl f* **6/1**[3]

1000 **3** *3/4* **Kind Of Fizzy**[21] 5130 3-9-1 **62**.. JamieMackay 8 66
(Rae Guest) *in rr-div: hdwy centre over 2f out: edgd rt and styd on fnl f* **28/1**

6306 **4** *3/4* **Choreography**[9] 5476 4-9-1 **60**................................. AdrianTNicholls 14 62
(D Nicholls) *dwlt: trckd other pair stands' side: hdwy over 2f out: styd on fnl f* **13/2**

5220 **5** *1/2* **Prince Rossi (IRE)**[51] 4224 3-8-10 **57**............................(p) TedDurcan 12 57
(J D Bethell) *led centre gp: kpt on same pce appr fnl f* **20/1**

0262 **6** *3/4* **Petite Mac**[9] 5489 7-8-0 **52**.. DanielleMcCreery(7) 11 50
(N Bycroft) *in rr: hdwy over 2f out: kpt on wl fnl f* **15/2**

6543 **7** *hd* **Baybshambles (IRE)**[21] 5139 3-8-7 **54**.............................. PaulHanagan 6 51
(R E Barr) *w ldrs centre: fdd fnl f* **16/1**

0512 **8** *1 3/4* **Inka Dancer (IRE)**[41] 4545 5-9-1 **65**................................... NeilBrown(5) 2 57
(B Palling) *dwlt: sn trcking ldr far side: wknd fnl f* **9/2**[2]

24-0 **9** *2* **Wind Shuffle (GER)**[28] 4932 4-9-1 **60**............................ DanielTudhope 7 46
(J S Goldie) *mid-div: rdn over 2f out: nvr a factor* **14/1**

6-55 **10** *hd* **Edge End**[15] 5315 3-9-1 **62**.. ChrisCatlin 15 47
(R A Farrant) *chsd ldr stands' side: led over 2f out: sn hdd & wknd* **9/1**

4232 **11** *1/2* **Conjecture**[16] 5284 5-8-12 **57**................................... RoystonFfrench 13 41
(R Bastiman) *overall ldr and led gp of 3 on stands' side: hdd 2f out: sn lost pl* **11/4**[1]

0005 **12** *3/4* **Night In (IRE)**[27] 4978 4-8-13 **58**...(t) KimTinkler 10 40
(N Tinkler) *s.s: a in rr* **28/1**

1m 17.28s (5.58) **Going Correction** +0.775s/f (Yiel)
WFA 3 from 4yo+ 2lb **12** Ran SP% **126.8**
Speed ratings (Par 101): **93,91,90,89,89 88,87,85,82,82 81,80**
CSF £79.30 CT £1856.28 TOTE £21.10: £4.10, £2.30, £7.90; EX 99.80 Place 6 £81.56, Place 5 £55.99.
Owner David W Chapman **Bred** C McEvoy **Trained** Stillington, N Yorks
FOCUS
A low-grade sprint handicap but a spirited effort from the evergreen ten-year-old Paddywack who benefited from the change of pilot. The form is modest with the third the best guide.
Conjecture Official explanation: jockey said gelding ran flat
T/Plt: £39.90 to a £1 stake. Pool: £42,095.20. 769.80 winning tickets. T/Qpdt: £20.20 to a £1 stake. Pool: £2,678.70. 97.70 winning tickets. JR

5557 PONTEFRACT (L-H)
Thursday, September 27

OFFICIAL GOING: Good to firm (8.0)
Wind: Moderate, behind Weather: Overcast

5745 EUROPEAN BREEDERS' FUND POPPIN LANE MAIDEN STKS 6f
2:20 (2:21) (Class 4) 2-Y-O **£5,181** (£1,541; £770; £384) **Stalls** Low

Form RPR
53 **1** **Generous Thought**[59] 4014 2-9-3 0................................ JamieSpencer 2 76+
(P Howling) *trckd ldrs: hdwy 2f out: rdn to ld and hung lft over 1f out: edgd lft ins fnl f and kpt on wl* **2/1**[1]

35 **2** *1 1/4* **Royal Applord**[26] 5033 2-9-3 0... NCallan 8 72
(K A Ryan) *wnt lft s: sn prom: rdn along 2f out: drvn over 1f out: kpt on u.p ins fnl f* **16/1**

63 **3** *nk* **Deira Dubai**[22] 5140 2-8-12 0 RHills 3 66
(B W Hills) *t.k.h: trckd ldrs: effrt and nt clr run wl over 1f out: swtchd rt and rdn ent fnl f: kpt on towards fin* **2/1**[1]

50 **4** *½* **Castles In The Air**[68] 3747 2-9-3 0 PaulEddery 14 70
(Pat Eddery) *led to 1/2-way: cl up: rdn 2f out and ev ch whn sltly hmpd over 1f out: drvn and kpt on ins fnl f* **12/1**[3]

50 **5** *¾* **Rio Sands**[26] 5042 2-9-0 0 MichaelJStainton(3) 17 68
(R M Whitaker) *chsd ldrs on outer: rdn along over 2f out: kpt on same pce appr fnl f* **66/1**

6 *hd* **Debonnaire** 2-8-12 0 GregFairley 10 62+
(M Johnston) *midfield: hdwy 2f out: sn rdn and styd on ins fnl f: nrst fin* **9/1**[2]

66 **7** *1 ¼* **Oasis Davis**[30] 4921 2-9-3 0 PatCosgrave 5 63
(K A Ryan) *cl up: led 1/2-way: rdn along 2f out: drvn and hdd over 1f out: grad wknd* **33/1**

656 **8** *2* **Afton View (IRE)**[8] 5521 2-9-3 0 JohnEgan 11 57
(D J Murphy) *in tch: rdn along over 2f out: kpt on same pce* **66/1**

9 *nk* **Rossini's Dancer** 2-9-0 0 JamieMoriarty(3) 9 56+
(R A Fahey) *wnt bdly rt s: bhd tl sme late hdwy* **100/1**

60 **10** *1* **Admiralcollingwood**[8] 5521 2-9-3 0 DanielTudhope 15 53
(J J Quinn) *a outpcd in rr* **66/1**

11 *1 ¾* **Fujin Dancer (FR)** 2-9-3 0 PaulHanagan 12 48
(R A Fahey) *s.i.s: a in rr* **50/1**

6543 **12** *1 ¾* **Misplaced Fortune**[22] 5143 2-8-12 70 EddieAhern 4 38+
(N Tinkler) *midfield whn hmpd and swtchd rt 1/2-way: nvr a factor* **12/1**[3]

35 **13** *½* **Pintano**[33] 4818 2-9-3 0 TomEaves 16 41
(J Howard Johnson) *chsd ldrs: rdn along over 2f out: sn drvn and wknd* **14/1**

50 **14** *2 ½* **Our Joan**[8] 5527 2-8-12 0 FrankieMcDonald 6 29
(P T Midgley) *in tch: rdn along 1/2-way: sn wknd* **150/1**

15 *43* **Que Beauty (IRE)** 2-8-12 0 PaulMulrennan 7 —
(R C Guest) *v.s.a: a wl bhd* **100/1**

0 **P** **Clean Sheet (USA)**[8] 5540 2-8-12 0 LiamJones 1 —
(W J Haggas) *midfield whn lost action 1/2-way and sn p.u* **50/1**

1m 16.52s (-0.88) **Going Correction** -0.225s/f (Firm) **16** Ran SP% **118.6**
Speed ratings (Par 97): **96,94,93,93,92 92,90,87,87,85 83,81,80,77,19** —
CSF £39.70 TOTE £2.80: £1.10, £4.10, £1.50; EX 33.40.
Owner Liam Sheridan **Bred** Aston Mullins Stud **Trained** Newmarket, Suffolk

FOCUS
A fair maiden and solid enough form that could be rated a little higher.

NOTEBOOK
Generous Thought, returning from a two-month break, was happier back on quick ground and made it third-time lucky. He still holds an entry in the Dewhurst and, while that may be flying a bit high, he looks an interesting type for nurseries this autumn. (op 11-4)
Royal Applord, dropping back from 7f, kept on in the closing stages as though he will appreciate returning to that distance. Nurseries are now an option for him as well. (op 20-1)
Deira Dubai, who still holds a Cheveley Park entry, was another dropping back from 7f. She was a bit too keen for her own good but had every chance in the straight if getting a clear run. Unfortunately, she did not, and can be rated better than the bare form. (op 7-4)
Castles In The Air, whose pedigree gave hope that he would improve for this faster surface, certainly put up a better display, especially considering his wide draw. He is another who is now eligible to run in handicaps. (op 16-1)
Rio Sands was another to run with credit from a bad draw. This was probably his best performance so far from three starts and it will be interesting to see what sort of mark he gets, especially as he might improve again for soft ground given that he is by Captain Rio.
Debonnaire, a half-sister to Dramatic Quest, a triple winner between 6f and 1m2f, and Proceed With Care, a dual 6f to 7f winner, was putting in her best work at the finish and, like most from her stable, is likely to improve a good deal for her debut.
Oasis Davis was another having his third run for a rating and handicaps are likely to present him with a better chance of getting off the mark.
Misplaced Fortune Official explanation: jockey said filly suffered interference in running
Pintano Official explanation: jockey said gelding hung left-handed throughout

5746 RACING UK ON CHANNEL 432 FILLIES' NURSERY 1m 4y
2:50 (2:57) (Class 4) (0-85,82) 2-Y-O **£4,533** (£1,348; £674; £336) **Stalls** Low

Form RPR

303 **1** **Jazz Jam**[25] 5061 2-8-11 72 TQuinn 8 75
(P F I Cole) *hld up in tch: hdwy and pushed along over 2f out: rdn to chse ldrs over 1f out: styd on to ld last 100yds* **9/1**

41 **2** *1* **Dona Alba (IRE)**[25] 5063 2-9-7 82 EddieAhern 7 83
(J L Dunlop) *trckd ldrs: swtchd lft and gd hdwy 2f out: led over 1f out: sn rdn and edgd lft ent fnl f: hdd and no ex last 100yds* **7/4**[1]

0251 **3** *1 ½* **Destinys Dream (IRE)**[16] 5298 2-8-12 73 RoystonFfrench 2 71
(Mrs A Duffield) *prom: effrt on inner and ev ch over 1f out: sn rdn and one pce ins fnl f* **7/1**[3]

350 **4** *2 ½* **Threestoneburn (USA)**[33] 4796 2-8-8 69 JamieSpencer 3 61
(P C Haslam) *hld up in tch: hdwy over 2f out: rdn to chse ldrs wl over 1f out: sn one pce* **8/1**

0000 **5** *2* **Kashmina**[16] 5314 2-8-7 68 TPO'Shea 5 55
(M R Channon) *prom: hdwy to chse wnr 3f out: rdn to chal 2f out: sn drvn and wknd wl over 1f out* **16/1**

0002 **6** *3* **Double Attack (FR)**[11] 5443 2-9-0 75 GregFairley 6 55
(M Johnston) *bolted bef s: hld up in rr: hdwy over 2f out: sn rdn and styd on ins fnl f: nrst fin* **9/1**

2104 **7** *¾* **Shepherds Warning (IRE)**[7] 5551 2-7-12 59 oh4 JimmyQuinn 1 38
(N J Vaughan) *led: rdn along 2f out: drvn and hdd over 1f out: wknd* **4/1**[2]

450 **8** *¾* **Pantherii (USA)**[25] 5063 2-8-4 65 NelsonDeSouza 10 42
(P F I Cole) *chsd ldrs on outer: rdn along wl over 2f out and sn wknd* **33/1**

0053 **9** *5* **Danamight (IRE)**[12] 5423 2-8-6 67 PaulHanagan 9 32
(G G Margarson) *a in rr* **12/1**

060 **10** *2 ½* **Blazing Mask (IRE)**[16] 5294 2-7-9 59 oh5 (p) DuranFentiman(3) 4 19
(Mrs A Duffield) *cl up: rdn along 1/2-way and sn wknd* **200/1**

1m 43.76s (-1.94) **Going Correction** -0.225s/f (Firm) **10** Ran SP% **117.0**
Speed ratings (Par 94): **100,99,97,95,93 90,89,88,83,81**
CSF £25.16 CT £123.83 TOTE £11.60: £2.60, £1.30, £2.30; EX 33.20.
Owner Faisal Salman **Bred** Belgrave Bloodstock Ltd **Trained** Whatcombe, Oxon

FOCUS
A fair nursery and solid form rated through the third.

NOTEBOOK
Jazz Jam appreciated every yard of this longer trip on her handicap debut and looks a progressive sort. Softer ground ought not to worry her, being by Pivotal, and she looks set for further success this autumn. (op 10-1 tchd 11-1)
Dona Alba(IRE), winner of her maiden at Folkestone last time out, was another who threatened to improve for this step up in distance, being a half-sister to a 2m winner. She ran well and is another progressive filly who should not mind softer ground. (op 15-8 tchd 2-1 in places)
Destinys Dream(IRE), the most experienced filly in the line-up, ran away with a nursery at Beverley last time and that had resulted in a 9lb rise in the ratings. She ran a solid race off her new mark and is probably the best guide to the level of the form. (tchd 15-2)
Threestoneburn(USA) did not run too well at Beverley last time but she was returning from a two-month break that day and her previous efforts suggested that she was fairly rated on a mark of 69 for her handicap debut. She ran alright in what was a competitive heat. (op 10-1)
Kashmina, who looked as though she was worth a go at this distance when running on late over 7f at Lingfield last time, appeared not to get home. (tchd 20-1)
Double Attack(FR), who unseated her rider and bolted before the start, ran well in the circumstances but she has been keen in her races before and is clearly not the easiest of rides. (op 13-2 tchd 6-1)
Shepherds Warning(IRE) looked well handicapped on her performance at Ayr seven days earlier even though she was 4lb out of the weights, but that effort in novice company came on softish ground and conditions were very different here. She will be more effective when she gets her toe in again, but her mark is already due to go up to 72 in future. (op 9-2)
Danamight(IRE) Official explanation: jockey said filly lost her action

5747 S B HONDA H'CAP 5f
3:20 (3:22) (Class 5) (0-75,75) 3-Y-O+ **£4,533** (£1,348; £674; £336) **Stalls** Low

Form RPR

4332 **1** **Hotham**[7] 5552 4-8-11 67 JimmyQuinn 5 76
(N Wilson) *dwlt: sn in midfield: hdwy 2f out: swtchd rt and rdn over 1f out: styd on strly ins fnl f to ld last 100yds* **7/2**[1]

3221 **2** *½* **Joyeaux**[4] 5667 5-8-8 67 6ex DuranFentiman(3) 14 74
(J Hetherton) *towards rr: hdwy wl over 1f out: rdn ent fnl f and styd on wl towards fin* **9/1**

5000 **3** *nk* **Steelcut**[45] 4452 3-9-3 74 PaulHanagan 8 80
(R A Fahey) *prom: rdn along wl over 1f out: drvn ins fnl f and kpt on* **16/1**

4111 **4** *nk* **Making Music**[16] 5297 4-8-7 63 (b) DavidAllan 9 68
(T D Easterby) *cl up: rdn over 1f out: drvn to ld briefly and hung bdly lft ins fnl f: sn hdd and nt qckn* **7/1**[3]

2233 **5** *¾* **Welcome Approach**[8] 5522 4-9-1 71 PhillipMakin 12 73
(J R Weymes) *midfield: hdwy on outer wl over 1f out: rdn and styd on ins fnl f: nrst fin* **10/1**

3000 **6** *½* **High Reach**[33] 4800 7-8-7 68 ow1 NeilBrown(5) 4 68
(T D Barron) *trckd ldrs: hdwy on inner 2f out: sn rdn and one pce ins fnl f* **18/1**

2060 **7** *shd* **Namir (IRE)**[5] 5648 5-9-5 75 (vt) TPQueally 17 75
(D Shaw) *hld up in rr: hdwy on outer wl over 1f out: sn rdn and kpt on ins fnl f: nrst fin* **14/1**

5200 **8** *1* **Darcy's Pride (IRE)**[15] 5332 3-8-13 70 TonyHamilton 2 70+
(D W Barker) *led: rdn along wl over 1f out: drvn and hdd ins fnl f: wkng whn hmpd last 75yds* **22/1**

1144 **9** *nk* **Back In The Red (IRE)**[14] 5358 3-9-4 75 JohnEgan 6 70
(R A Harris) *chsd ldrs: rdn along 2f out: sn drvn: edgd rt and btn* **10/1**

042 **10** *nk* **Valley Of The Moon (IRE)**[22] 5139 3-8-10 70 JamieMoriarty(3) 13 64
(R A Fahey) *a towards rr* **14/1**

0001 **11** *¾* **Greek Secret**[10] 5489 4-8-2 61 oh11 AndrewMullen(3) 15 53
(J O'Reilly) *dwlt and in rr: hdwy wl over 1f out: sn rdn and kpt on ins fnl f: nt rch ldrs* **33/1**

6600 **12** *hd* **Royal Challenge**[21] 5168 6-9-1 71 NCallan 10 62
(M H Tompkins) *a towards rr* **11/2**[2]

4065 **13** *1* **Bridge It Jo**[9] 5506 3-9-4 75 EddieAhern 11 62
(G G Margarson) *midfield: effrt on outer and in tch whn n.m.r wl over 1f out: sn wknd* **28/1**

2140 **14** *nk* **Never Without Me**[16] 5297 7-8-12 68 ChrisCatlin 7 54
(J F Coupland) *chsd ldrs: rdn along 2f out: wknd over 1f out* **20/1**

5655 **15** *1* **Winthorpe (IRE)**[8] 5522 7-8-6 62 TPO'Shea 16 45
(J J Quinn) *stdd s: hld up and a bhd* **22/1**

-300 **16** *8* **Tender Process (IRE)**[95] 2912 4-9-4 74 J-PGuillambert 1 28
(E S McMahon) *dwlt: sn outpcd and a bhd* **22/1**

62.13 secs (-1.67) **Going Correction** -0.225s/f (Firm)
WFA 3 from 4yo+ 1lb **16** Ran SP% **127.0**
Speed ratings (Par 103): **104,103,102,102,101 100,100,98,98,97 96,96,94,93,92 79**
CSF £32.21 CT £488.42 TOTE £3.90: £1.30, £2.40, £5.00, £2.10; EX 31.50 Trifecta £370.00
Part won. Pool: £521.20 - 0.50 winning tickets..
Owner Paul & Linda Dixon **Bred** Capt J H Wilson **Trained** Flaxton, N Yorks
■ Stewards' Enquiry : Jimmy Quinn one-day ban: careless riding (Oct 12)

FOCUS
There was a good pace on here and the form looks solid rated around the in-form winner and runner-up.
Never Without Me Official explanation: jockey said gelding bled from the nose
Tender Process(IRE) Official explanation: jockey said gelding was unsuited by the good to firm ground

5748 DALBY SCREW-DRIVER H'CAP 1m 2f 6y
3:50 (3:50) (Class 2) (0-100,100) 3-Y-O+
£11,217 (£3,358; £1,679; £840; £419; £210) **Stalls** Low

Form RPR

6021 **1** **Gulf Express (USA)**[20] 5208 3-9-2 92 RyanMoore 2 101+
(Sir Michael Stoute) *trckd ldng pair: hdwy over 2f out: rdn to ld over 1f out: drvn ins fnl f and styd on gamely* **5/4**[1]

0512 **2** *nk* **Many Volumes (USA)**[14] 5351 3-9-10 100 RichardHughes 5 109+
(H R A Cecil) *hld up: gd hdwy 2f out: rdn to chal ins fnl f and ev ch tl drvn and nt qckn nr fin* **5/4**[1]

0210 **3** *1 ¼* **Robustian**[12] 5432 4-8-13 83 (b) StephenCarson 1 89
(Eve Johnson Houghton) *trckd ldrs: hdwy and cl up 2f out: sn rdn and kpt on same pce ins fnl f* **16/1**[3]

1040 **4** *2* **Fort Churchill (IRE)**[36] 4720 6-9-5 89 (bt) TomEaves 3 91
(B Ellison) *chsd ldr: rdn along and outpcd 2f out: styd on u.p fnl f* **16/1**[3]

2000 **5** *shd* **Along The Nile**[15] 5327 5-8-10 80 oh1 (p) TQuinn 7 82
(K G Reveley) *led: rdn along over 2f out: hdd over 1f out: sn drvn and wknd* **20/1**

00-2 **6** *6* **Dancing Lyra**[166] 846 6-8-10 80 PaulHanagan 4 70
(R A Fahey) *hld up: a in rr* **12/1**[2]

2m 14.04s (-0.04) **Going Correction** -0.225s/f (Firm)
WFA 3 from 4yo+ 6lb **6** Ran SP% **113.1**
Speed ratings (Par 109): **91,90,89,88,88 83**
CSF £2.93 TOTE £2.60: £1.50, £1.10; EX 3.40.
Owner Saeed Suhail **Bred** Gracefield And Brad Ray **Trained** Newmarket, Suffolk

FOCUS
An uncompetitive handicap that was steadily run and, as was to be expected, the two three-year-olds fought out the finish. The form is rated through the runner-up.

NOTEBOOK

Gulf Express(USA), a progressive colt who finished well on top when winning at Newbury last time, was up 6lb, but this was effectively a straight match on paper and he got first run on Many Volumes. Almost joined inside the final furlong, he responded well to pressure and kept on strongly, just doing enough to prevail. He will need to improve again to defy a further rise, but that is entirely possible. (tchd 11-8 tchd 6-4 in a place)

Many Volumes(USA), winner of a conditions race at Newmarket two starts back, found only the smart Kirklees too good at Doncaster last time and, although returning to handicaps off a stiff mark, it would have been a surprise had he not gone close. He came to challenge inside the final furlong but the winner, who had got first run, pulled out more and he was made to settle for second. He looks an improved performer, but is likely to be tricky to place from now on. (op 6-4)

Robustian, a narrow winner at Sandown two starts back, disappointed at Warwick next time, but this was better and there was no disgrace in finding a couple of progressive three-year-olds too good. (op 18-1)

Fort Churchill(IRE) has generally struggled off this mark since winning at Goodwood back in the summer and he was always going to find it difficult to match a couple of progressive three-year-olds. (op 14-1)

Along The Nile ran well for a long way and is beginning to ease in the weights again. (op 16-1)

5749 EUROPEAN BREEDERS' FUND FRIER WOOD MAIDEN STKS 1m 4y

4:20 (4:20) (Class 4) 2-Y-O **£5,181** (£1,541; £770; £384) **Stalls** Low

Form RPR

0660 **1** **Prince Desire (IRE)**[18] 5251 2-9-3 69..........(b[1]) MichaelHills 7 77
(B W Hills) *mde all: pushed clr 3f out: rdn along 2f out: styd on strly* **10/1**

02 **2** *4* **Downhiller (IRE)**[14] 5344 2-9-3 0.......... EddieAhern 2 68
(J L Dunlop) *t.k.h: trckd ldrs: hdwy to chse wnr wl over 1f out: sn rdn and hung lft ent fnl f: sn drvn and no imp* **2/1[1]**

00 **3** *2* **Tarbolton (IRE)**[31] 4890 2-9-3 0.......... RyanMoore 9 63
(M Johnston) *hld up: stdy hdwy over 2f out: rdn to chse ldrs wl over 1f out: sn drvn and kpt on same pce* **8/1[3]**

04 **4** *1 1/4* **Bigalo's Magic (UAE)**[30] 4916 2-9-3 0.......... ChrisCatlin 1 60
(E J O'Neill) *chsd wnr: rdn along 2f out: drvn and n.m.r over 1f out: sn one pce* **9/1**

05 **5** *5* **Kabuku**[6] 5599 2-9-3 0.......... JimmyQuinn 3 49
(M H Tompkins) *chsd ldrs: rdn along 3f out: drvn 2f out and sn wknd* **16/1**

043 **6** *nk* **Summon Up Theblood**[14] 5361 2-9-3 81.......... TPO'Shea 6 48
(M R Channon) *a towards rr* **9/4[2]**

34 **7** *nk* **Silk Drum (IRE)**[85] 3199 2-9-3 0.......... TomEaves 8 47
(J Howard Johnson) *hld up: hdwy on outer to chse ldrs over 2f out: sn rdn and btn* **16/1**

0 **8** *nk* **Red Lily (IRE)**[41] 4564 2-8-12 0.......... JamieSpencer 10 42
(J R Fanshawe) *a in rr* **8/1[3]**

00 **9** *nk* **Jetta Joy (IRE)**[6] 5580 2-8-12 0.......... RoystonFfrench 5 41
(Mrs A Duffield) *midfield: rdn along over 3f out and sn wknd* **200/1**

5 **10** *10* **Defies Logic**[19] 5226 2-9-3 0.......... TPQueally 4 23
(J G Given) *chsd ldrs: rdn along 3f out: sn wknd* **40/1**

1m 44.17s (-1.53) **Going Correction** -0.225s/f (Firm) **10** Ran SP% **120.1**
Speed ratings (Par 97): **98,94,92,90,85 85,85,84,84,74**
CSF £31.27 TOTE £11.30: £3.10, £1.10, £1.90; EX 48.30.
Owner De La Warr Racing **Bred** Epona Bloodstock Ltd **Trained** Lambourn, Berks

FOCUS

A modest maiden won readily by the 69-rated Prince Desire and a race with little strength in depth.

NOTEBOOK

Prince Desire(IRE) had looked modest in a handful of previous starts, but he was fitted with the blinkers here and sprang into life. Allowed his own way in front, he received a fine ride from Hills and ran right away with it in the straight. His future prospects very much depend on which way he goes from this, as the headgear is far from garuanteed to have the same effect next time. (tchd 11-1)

Downhiller(IRE), who improved on his initial effort when second over this trip at Chepstow, looked to hold obvious claims and he ran well, but proved no match for the easy winner. He will appreciate trips in excess of this sooner rather than later. (tchd 9-4 in a place)

Tarbolton(IRE) had shown little in two previous starts, but this step back up in trip suited and he kept on well in the straight. Now qualified for nurseries, he should fare better in that sphere, with his trainer's juveniles going particularly well at present.

Bigalo's Magic(UAE) showed improved form for this step up in trip and he is now eligible for handicaps, a sphere he will find easier opportunities in. (op 12-1)

Kabuku, who ran quite well at Newmarket last time, was making a quick reappearance and failed to confirm the promise of that recent effort. He may be the type to do better in low-grade nurseries.

Summon Up Theblood arguably brought the best form into this, but he never got into it following a sluggish start and proved to be most disappointing. He has already shown himself to be much better than this and probably deserves another chance. Official explanation: jockey said colt missed the break (op 5-2)

Silk Drum(IRE) Official explanation: jockey said gelding hung left throughout

5750 BETFAIR.COM APPRENTICE SERIES H'CAP (FINAL ROUND) 1m 2f 6y

4:50 (4:50) (Class 6) (0-65,65) 3-Y-O+ **£3,238** (£963; £481; £240) **Stalls** Low

Form RPR

0021 **1** **Red Current**[14] 5347 3-9-4 63.......... WilliamCarson 5 72
(R A Harris) *trckd ldrs: hdwy on inner to ld over 3f out: rdn wl over 1f out: drvn ins fnl f and styd on gamely* **11/2[2]**

-002 **2** *2* **Boppys Pride**[7] 5557 4-8-13 55.......... JamesRogers[(3)] 10 60
(R A Fahey) *hld up: hdwy 2f out: rdn over 1f out: styd on along inner ins fnl f: nrst fin* **4/1[1]**

0060 **3** *1/2* **Julatten (IRE)**[35] 4741 3-8-5 50 oh5.......... SophieDoyle 14 54
(D J Murphy) *towards rr: hdwy 2f out: swtchd outside and rdn over 1f out: styd on wl towards fin* **100/1**

1005 **4** *nk* **Royal Indulgence**[5] 5636 7-9-10 63.......... WJCafferty 1 66
(W M Brisbourne) *hld up towards rr: hdwy over 2f out: sn rdn and chsd ldrs ent fnl f: kpt on same pce* **10/1**

4204 **5** *nk* **Moment Of Clarity**[7] 5557 5-8-11 50..........(p) GaryBartley 2 52
(R C Guest) *in tch: hdwy 3f out: rdn to chse wnr ent fnl f: sn drvn and kpt on same pce* **11/2[2]**

6215 **6** *1 1/4* **Thornaby Green**[7] 5557 6-9-10 63.......... DeanHeslop 9 63
(T D Barron) *led: rdn along and hdd over 3f out: wknd over 1f out* **8/1[3]**

2450 **7** *1 1/4* **Intavac Boy**[17] 5286 6-9-3 56.......... PatrickDonaghy 4 53
(S P Griffiths) *cl up: rdn along 3f out: drvn 2f out and grad wknd appr fnl f* **14/1**

3021 **8** *1 3/4* **Ruby Legend**[41] 4580 9-9-2 55..........(b) DanielleMcCreery 6 49
(K G Reveley) *hld up and bhd tl styd on fnl 2f* **11/1**

2104 **9** *shd* **Winged Farasi**[42] 4550 3-9-2 61.......... AlanRutter 13 55
(R A Harris) *bhd tl sme late hdwy* **16/1**

-032 **10** *3/4* **River Deuce**[8] 5530 3-9-1 65.......... AshleyMorgan[(5)] 16 57
(M H Tompkins) *chsd ldrs: rdn along over 4f out and sn wknd* **14/1**

6605 **11** *nk* **Newcorp Lad**[27] 5000 7-8-4 50 oh5..........(p) IanCraven[(7)] 3 42
(Mrs G S Rees) *a in rr* **40/1**

6514 **12** *16* **Collette's Choice**[22] 5144 4-9-8 64..........(p) MatthewDavies[(3)] 11 24
(R A Fahey) *chsd ldrs: rdn along 4f out and sn wknd* **10/1**

0123 **13** *3 1/2* **Starcross Maid**[114] 2348 5-9-0 56.......... JosephWalsh[(3)] 7 9
(J F Coupland) *hld up: a in rr* **25/1**

0010 **14** *1 1/2* **Garibaldi (GER)**[2] 5704 5-8-13 55..........(b) LanceBetts[(3)] 8 5
(J O'Reilly) *chsd ldrs: rdn along over 3f out: sn wknd* **10/1**

040- **15** *32* **Genoa Star**[540] 887 4-8-6 50 oh5.......... BradleyRoper[(5)] 15 —
(D J Murphy) *v.s.a: a t.o* **80/1**

2m 11.9s (-2.18) **Going Correction** -0.225s/f (Firm)
WFA 3 from 4yo+ 6lb **15** Ran SP% **125.2**
Speed ratings (Par 101): **99,97,97,96,96 95,94,93,93,92 92,79,76,75,49**
CSF £28.19 CT £2046.75 TOTE £5.40: £2.70, £2.50, £23.00; EX 21.30 Place 6 £11.48, Place 5 £8.71.
Owner Leeway Group Limited **Bred** Wretham Stud **Trained** Earlswood, Monmouths
■ Stewards' Enquiry : W J Cafferty one-day ban: used whip with excessive frequency (Oct 8)

FOCUS

A modest handicap but solid form rated around the runner-up, fourth and fifth.

Genoa Star Official explanation: jockey said filly missed the break

T/Jkpt: Not won. T/Plt: £5.70 to a £1 stake. Pool: £72,041.10. 9,137.40 winning tickets. T/Qpdt: £3.40 to a £1 stake. Pool: £3,341.90. 711.15 winning tickets. JR

5643 WOLVERHAMPTON (A.W) (L-H)

Thursday, September 27

OFFICIAL GOING: Standard

Wind: Fresh, against Weather: Overcast with the odd light shower

5751 LLOYD FRASER DAIRY SERVICE NURSERY 5f 216y(P)

7:00 (7:00) (Class 6) (0-65,63) 2-Y-O **£2,047** (£604; £302) **Stalls** Low

Form RPR

054 **1** **Wee Buns**[39] 4629 2-9-7 63.......... LPKeniry 5 65
(S Kirk) *chsd ldrs: pushed along 1/2-way: rdn to ld ins fnl f: hung rt: jst hld on* **11/2[2]**

0015 **2** *hd* **Loose Caboose (IRE)**[23] 5117 2-8-8 57..........(p) RobbieEgan[(7)] 12 58
(A J McCabe) *hld up: hdwy 1/2-way: rdn over 1f out: edgd lft: r.o* **12/1**

5040 **3** *nk* **Valhillen**[22] 5127 2-9-2 58.......... JamieSpencer 4 58
(M J Wallace) *sn chsng ldrs: rdn to ld over 1f out: hdd ins fnl f: edgd rt: styd on* **6/1[3]**

4330 **4** *3/4* **Mystickhill (IRE)**[152] 1291 2-8-13 60..........(t) JamesO'Reilly[(5)] 10 58
(D J Murphy) *hld up: hdwy over 1f out: nt clr run ins fnl f: r.o* **16/1**

0553 **5** *1/2* **Weet A Surprise**[24] 5096 2-9-7 63.......... FergusSweeney 11 59
(R Hollinshead) *chsd ldr: rdn and ev ch over 1f out: styd on same pce ins fnl f* **9/2[1]**

11 **6** *1/2* **Genethni**[24] 5081 2-9-7 63.......... NCallan 9 58
(K A Ryan) *led: hung rt over 2f out: rdn and hdd over 1f out: styng on same pce whn n.m.r towards fin* **6/1[3]**

0045 **7** *1* **Tommytush (IRE)**[10] 5484 2-9-5 61.......... DavidAllan 8 53
(E J Alston) *prom: rdn over 1f out: styd on same pce fnl f* **16/1**

000 **8** *1* **Futune (IRE)**[23] 5110 2-9-1 57.......... StephenDonohoe 13 46
(B J Meehan) *s.i.s: outpcd: rdn and hung lft over 1f out: nt trble ldrs* **28/1**

6363 **9** *1 1/4* **Myriola**[14] 5365 2-9-5 61.......... RichardKingscote 6 46
(B Palling) *mid-div: hdwy over 1f out: no imp fnl f* **8/1**

025 **10** *1 1/4* **Mister Beano (IRE)**[24] 5096 2-9-1 60..........(p) JerryO'Dwyer[(3)] 1 41+
(V Smith) *hld up: hung lft and nt clr run over 1f out: n.d* **10/1**

4555 **11** *2 1/2* **Varinia (IRE)**[52] 4221 2-9-4 60.......... DaleGibson 3 34
(M Brittain) *s.i.s: a in rr* **16/1**

606 **12** *3 1/2* **Fu Wa (USA)**[14] 5363 2-9-6 62.......... PaulMulrennan 2 25
(M W Easterby) *mid-div: lost pl 4f out: wknd over 2f out* **28/1**

0605 **13** *3/4* **Mandarinka**[8] 5529 2-8-13 60..........(b) TolleyDean[(5)] 7 21
(P Winkworth) *s.i.s: a in rr* **14/1**

1m 16.5s (0.69) **Going Correction** -0.025s/f (Stan) **13** Ran SP% **121.2**
Speed ratings (Par 93): **94,93,93,92,91 91,89,88,86,85 81,77,76**
CSF £71.27 CT £425.24 TOTE £6.20: £3.20, £4.30, £3.20; EX 92.40.
Owner Club ISM & S Kirk **Bred** M J Hills **Trained** Upper Lambourn, Berks

FOCUS

A tight nursery with only 6lb covering the field, and the first six finished in a heap. Moderate form, rated through the placed horses.

NOTEBOOK

Wee Buns, back up to 6f, looked to have been handed a reasonable mark for his nursery debut. Sticking to the inside in the home straight, he proved game under pressure and, after taking a slender lead inside the last, just held the runner-up's late lunge after hanging right near the line. He should not be put up too much for this and there could be a bit more improvement in him. (op 13-2)

Loose Caboose(IRE), successful in a seller on this surface at Lingfield two starts back, had shaped as if a return to this trip would suit following a creditable effort in a nursery over 7f last time. In the event she needed a bit further, as she came home strongly after being switched to the outside and just failed to get up. (op 11-1)

Valhillen was down in trip after seemingly finding 1m too far for him last time. Never far from the pace, he travelled strongly until let down in the straight and showed narrowly ahead, but could not quite hold on. (op 8-1)

Mystickhill(IRE), making her nursery debut after five months off the track, was fitted with a tongue tie for the first time. Upped a furlong in trip, she was inconvenienced when the runner-up was switched going to the final furlong but came home well to snatch fourth. She is entitled to come on for the run.

Weet A Surprise was 2lb lower than when a solid third in a decent nursery here last time. Back up in trip, she was right there in the straight but her stamina looked to fail her in the heat of battle.

Genethni was unbeaten in two starts prior to this, a seller and a claimer, and although she lost her unbeaten record she performed with credit. On her sand debut, she showed bright pace to lead but could not hold on in the straight. Official explanation: jockey said filly was hampered final furlong (op 4-1)

Mister Beano(IRE) Official explanation: jockey said colt hung left throughout

Varinia(IRE) Official explanation: jockey said filly was hampered leaving stalls

Mandarinka Official explanation: jockey said gelding missed the break

5752 LLOYD FRASER CONTRACTS MEDIAN AUCTION MAIDEN STKS 5f 20y(P)

7:30 (7:33) (Class 5) 3-5-Y-O **£2,968** (£876; £438) **Stalls** Low

Form RPR

3062 **1** **Mickleberry (IRE)**[17] 5282 3-8-12 50.......... JimmyQuinn 3 54
(J D Bethell) *chsd ldrs: nt clr run over 1f out: rdn to ld ins fnl f: r.o* **9/4[1]**

0005 **2** *2* **Whats Your Game (IRE)**[17] 5282 3-9-3 45..........(b[1]) StephenDonohoe 7 52
(A Berry) *a.p: rdn and hung lft fr over 1f out: styd on* **16/1**

4235 **3** *1 1/2* **By The Edge (IRE)**[29] 4935 3-8-12 50.......... PhillipMakin 13 42
(T D Barron) *s.s: hdwy 1/2-way: rdn over 1f out: hung lft ins fnl f: r.o* **7/2[3]**

0050 **4** *hd* **Mind That Fox**[15] 2104 5-9-4 40.......... ChrisCatlin 6 46
(T Wall) *led: rdn and edgd rt over 1f out: hdd and no ex ins fnl f* **40/1**

-560 **5** *hd* **Millsini**[83] 3281 3-8-12 52 NCallan 2 46+
(Rae Guest) *wnt lft s: chsd ldrs: rdn and nt clr run over 1f out: continually hmpd fnl f: nvr able to chal* **8/1**

6005 **6** *½* **Esteemed Prince**[21] 5175 3-9-3 47 (e) GeorgeBaker 12 43
(D Shaw) *s.s: outpcd: r.o ins fnl f: nvr nrr* **33/1**

000 **7** *½* **Pathway To Glory**[17] 5270 3-9-3 31 (v[1]) SamHitchcott 5 42
(M Quinn) *sn pushed along in rr: n.d* **50/1**

00 **8** *nk* **Ring Of Charm**[17] 5270 5-8-10 0 TravisBlock[(3)] 1 35
(C J Down) *hmpd s: a in rr* **33/1**

5640 **9** *1* **Jabraan (USA)**[28] 4966 5-9-4 39 (b) DaleGibson 8 37
(D W Chapman) *dwlt: a in rr* **12/1**

00-0 **10** *½* **Earl Compton (IRE)**[9] 5495 3-9-3 61 (t) NelsonDeSouza 9 35
(P F I Cole) *chsd ldrs: rdn over 1f out: wknd fnl f* **10/3**[2]

5-50 **11** *1¼* **Dora's Green**[98] 2798 4-8-10 42 (p) JerryO'Dwyer[(3)] 10 26
(S W Hall) *chsd ldrs: rdn whn hmpd 1f out: sn wknd* **18/1**

62.48 secs (-0.34) **Going Correction** -0.025s/f (Stan)
WFA 3 from 4yo+ 1lb **11** Ran SP% **116.3**
Speed ratings (Par 103): **101,97,95,95,94 93,93,92,91,90 88**
CSF £40.06 TOTE £1.80: £1.60, £4.60, £1.30; EX 24.00.
Owner Clarendon Thoroughbred Racing **Bred** Yeomanstown Stud **Trained** Middleham Moor, N Yorks
■ Stewards' Enquiry : Stephen Donohoe four-day ban: careless riding (Oct 10-13)

FOCUS
A low-grade maiden, little better than selling class. The form seems sound enough.
By The Edge(IRE) Official explanation: jockey said filly missed the break

5753 LLOYD FRASER 20TH ANNIVERSARY H'CAP 5f 216y(P)
7:55 (7:56) (Class 5) (0-75,72) 3-Y-0+ **£2,968** (£876; £438) **Stalls** Low

Form RPR

3044 **1** **Desert Master**[105] 2608 4-9-6 70 GeorgeBaker 8 79
(C F Wall) *led: hdd 4f out: led over 2f out: rdn over 1f out: styd on* **10/1**

1614 **2** *½* **Napoleon Dynamite (IRE)**[19] 5238 3-9-6 72 JamieSpencer 2 79+
(J W Hills) *s.i.s: nt clr run over 2f out: hdwy sn after: nt clr run ent fnl f: r.o* **11/2**

3211 **3** *½* **Ryedane (IRE)**[13] 5387 5-9-0 67 (b) DuranFentiman[(3)] 1 73
(T D Easterby) *w wnr: led 4f out: hdd over 2f out: rdn over 1f out: styd on* **4/1**[2]

0010 **4** *2* **Woqoodd**[31] 4896 3-9-4 70 PaulHanagan 7 70
(R A Fahey) *chsd ldrs: rdn over 2f out: styd on same pce fnl f* **22/1**

1100 **5** *nk* **Mozakhraf (USA)**[7] 5556 5-9-1 65 NCallan 3 64
(K A Ryan) *chsd ldrs: rdn over 1f out: no ex ins fnl f* **9/2**[3]

6054 **6** *1¾* **Rainbow Bay**[5] 5648 4-8-11 66 (v) TolleyDean[(5)] 5 59
(P D Evans) *hld up: hdwy over 2f out: sn rdn: styd on same pce fnl f* **11/2**

2332 **7** *6* **Ebraam (USA)**[13] 5387 4-9-4 68 JimmyQuinn 6 43
(D Shaw) *hld up: racd keenly: hdwy over 2f out: wknd over 1f out* **7/2**[1]

3500 **8** *shd* **Speed Dial Harry (IRE)**[13] 5387 5-9-3 67 (b) LiamJones 4 42
(C R Dore) *s.i.s: outpcd* **33/1**

3206 **9** *nk* **Bluebelle Dancer (IRE)**[19] 5234 3-8-11 63 (p) SaleemGolam 9 37
(W R Muir) *s.s: outpcd* **20/1**

6106 **10** *½* **Mr Loire**[13] 5387 3-8-7 66 MarkCoumbe[(7)] 11 39
(A J Chamberlain) *chsd ldrs over 3f* **50/1**

0-50 **11** *1½* **Wicked Uncle**[13] 5379 8-9-5 69 (v) IanMongan 10 37
(S Gollings) *mid-div: rdn and wknd over 2f out* **50/1**

1m 14.91s (-0.90) **Going Correction** -0.025s/f (Stan)
WFA 3 from 4yo+ 2lb **11** Ran SP% **116.2**
Speed ratings (Par 103): **105,104,103,101,100 98,90,90,89,89 87**
CSF £59.74 CT £263.49 TOTE £13.80: £2.80, £1.30, £2.00; EX 67.70.
Owner S Fustok **Bred** Deerfield Farm **Trained** Newmarket, Suffolk

FOCUS
A modest handicap, but the form is good for the grade. It was steadily run and not many got involved.

5754 LLOYD FRASER SUPPLY CHAIN MAIDEN STKS 1m 5f 194y(P)
8:25 (8:26) (Class 5) 3-Y-0+ **£2,968** (£876; £438) **Stalls** Low

Form RPR

6 **1** **Hareem (IRE)**[14] 5346 3-9-2 0 JamieSpencer 1 71+
(J A Osborne) *hld up: hdwy over 5f out: rdn to chse ldr over 1f out: edgd lft ins fnl f: styd on u.p to ld nr fin* **7/2**[2]

2 **2** *nk* **Vivacita**[14] 5346 3-8-11 0 ChrisCatlin 10 63
(E J O'Neill) *chsd ldrs: hmpd 4f out: led over 2f out: rdn fnl f: hdd nr fin* **4/1**[3]

0 **3** *2½* **Icansingarainbow**[14] 5346 3-8-11 0 RussellKennemore[(5)] 7 64
(R Hollinshead) *hld up: hdwy over 2f out: styd on* **66/1**

6400 **4** *3½* **Tivers Song (USA)**[23] 5111 3-9-2 59 (p) JimCrowley 3 59
(Mrs A J Perrett) *prom: shkn up 1/2-way: rdn over 2f out: wknd over 1f out: hung lft fnl f* **11/4**[1]

0253 **5** *2½* **Sadler's Leap (IRE)**[35] 4738 4-9-7 63 PaulEddery 9 51
(Pat Eddery) *chsd ldrs: swtchd rt 4f out: rdn and wknd over 1f out* **9/2**

6 *1* **Easement**[25] 4-9-12 0 SimonWhitworth 6 54
(C A Cyzer) *s.s: hdwy over 11f out: led wl over 2f out: sn rdn and hdd: wknd over 1f out* **9/1**

7 *1½* **Itsy Bitsy**[223] 5-9-7 0 NeilPollard 4 47
(W J Musson) *s.s: hld up: nvr trbld ldrs* **33/1**

2 **8** *nk* **Optimistic Alfie**[10] 5474 7-9-12 0 (b) GeorgeBaker 11 52
(B G Powell) *reminders after s: sn chsng ldr: led over 4f out: rdn and hdd over 2f out: wknd over 1f out* **12/1**

6- **9** *18* **Grafty Green (IRE)**[264] 6923 4-9-12 0 TGMcLaughlin 12 26
(W M Brisbourne) *s.s: a in rr: wknd over 3f out* **50/1**

6 **10** *½* **Resaass (USA)**[41] 4563 4-9-7 0 JamesO'Reilly[(5)] 13 26
(J O'Reilly) *chsd ldrs: lost pl 10f out: wknd over 3f out* **66/1**

6043 **11** *13* **Miss Invincible**[50] 4292 3-8-11 47 LiamJones 5 —
(Mrs A L M King) *led: hdd over 4f out: wknd over 3f out* **14/1**

3m 6.01s (-1.36) **Going Correction** -0.025s/f (Stan)
WFA 3 from 4yo+ 10lb **11** Ran SP% **119.3**
Speed ratings (Par 103): **102,101,100,98,96 96,95,95,85,84 77**
CSF £18.01 TOTE £4.30: £1.40, £2.20, £15.80; EX 22.90.
Owner Mountgrange Stud **Bred** Bernard Cooke **Trained** Upper Lambourn, Berks
■ Stewards' Enquiry : Paul Eddery two-day ban: careless riding (Oct 8-9)

FOCUS
A modest maiden in which they went just a steady pace. The first three had all made their debuts in the 1m4f Chepstow maiden won by Theta a fortnight ago and the fourth is probably the best guide to the form.

5755 LLOYD FRASER MANAGEMENT SERVICES H'CAP 1m 4f 50y(P)
8:55 (8:55) (Class 6) (0-60,60) 3-Y-0 **£2,047** (£604; £302) **Stalls** Low

Form RPR

0422 **1** **Bond Casino**[13] 5388 3-8-12 54 ChrisCatlin 7 63
(G R Oldroyd) *chsd ldrs: pushed along 5f out: rdn and ev ch whn hmpd ins fnl f: r.o to join wnr on line: fin 1st, dht: awrdd r* **10/1**

0002 **2** *dht* **Heights Of Golan**[5] 5647 3-8-11 53 (v[1]) LPKeniry 2 62
(I A Wood) *hld up in tch: rdn to ld and hung rt ins fnl f: jnd on line: fin 1st, dht: plcd 2nd* **9/4**[1]

4516 **3** *2½* **Hatton Flight**[15] 5333 3-9-4 60 (b) FrancisNorton 11 65
(A M Balding) *chsd ldrs: led 2f out: sn rdn: hdd and no ex ins fnl f* **5/1**[3]

4504 **4** *2½* **Pertemps Power**[14] 5364 3-8-10 52 JimmyQuinn 8 53
(A D Smith) *s.i.s: sn mid-div: hdwy 3f out: rdn over 1f out: styd on same pce* **20/1**

0053 **5** *2½* **Geordie's Pool**[15] 5341 3-9-2 58 JamieSpencer 12 55
(J W Hills) *led: rdn over 3f out: hdd 2f out: wknd fnl f* **9/2**[2]

0634 **6** *6* **Sir Sandicliffe (IRE)**[13] 5388 3-9-2 58 LiamJones 9 45
(W M Brisbourne) *mid-div: hdwy over 5f out: sn rdn: wknd over 2f out* **20/1**

0530 **7** *1¼* **Mounafes**[10] 5482 3-9-3 59 (b) StephenCarson 3 44
(G A Butler) *s.i.s: hld up: hdwy over 4f out: sn rdn and wknd* **33/1**

000 **8** *¾* **Opera Crown (IRE)**[28] 4960 3-8-6 53 TolleyDean[(5)] 10 37
(P F I Cole) *hld up: a in rr* **16/1**

3350 **9** *hd* **Arabiyah**[33] 4821 3-8-12 54 NickyMackay 6 38
(L M Cumani) *chsd ldr 10f out: rdn over 3f out: hung rt and wknd over 2f out* **11/2**

3505 **10** *1* **Snowflight**[10] 5482 3-9-0 56 PaulHanagan 5 38
(R A Fahey) *hld up: racd keenly: rdn over 3f out: sn wknd* **16/1**

2440 **11** *3* **Musical Land (IRE)**[10] 5482 3-9-3 59 DaleGibson 4 36
(J R Weymes) *hld up: rdn over 4f out: sn wknd* **66/1**

0013 **12** *½* **Giddywell**[63] 3871 3-8-9 56 RussellKennemore[(5)] 1 33
(R Hollinshead) *hld up: wknd over 3f out* **18/1**

2m 40.98s (-1.44) **Going Correction** -0.025s/f (Stan) **12** Ran SP% **121.1**
Speed ratings (Par 99): **103,103,101,99,98 94,93,92,92,91 89,89**
CSF £32.18 CT £133.02 TOTE £15.30: £1.50, £2.20, £2.20; EX 30.70.
Owner R C Bond **Bred** Bishopswood Bloodstock And Trickledown Stud **Trained** Brawby, N Yorks
■ Stewards' Enquiry : L P Keniry one-day ban: careless riding (Oct 8)

FOCUS
A moderate handicap in which the majority of the field appeared exposed. It produced a cracking finish with the judge unable to separate Bond Casino and Heights Of Golan, with the former promoted to outright winner following a Stewards' enquiry. Sound form rated around the third and fourth.

5756 LLOYD FRASER DISTRIBUTION H'CAP 1m 1f 103y(P)
9:20 (9:20) (Class 6) (0-50,51) 3-Y-0+ **£2,047** (£604; £302) **Stalls** Low

Form RPR

5445 **1** **Moyoko (IRE)**[17] 5280 4-9-2 48 JimmyQuinn 8 57
(M Blanshard) *hld up in tch: shkn up over 2f out: rdn to ld ins fnl f: r.o* **15/2**

0530 **2** *1* **Alasil (USA)**[14] 5348 7-8-13 50 TolleyDean[(5)] 6 57
(R J Price) *hld up: hdwy u.p over 1f out: r.o* **16/1**

0041 **3** *½* **Private Soldier**[6] 5606 4-9-5 51 6ex SamHitchcott 1 57
(N J Vaughan) *trckd ldr: racd keenly: led 2f out: rdn and edgd lft over 1f out: hdd and no ex ins fnl f* **5/2**[1]

0032 **4** *½* **Domesday (UAE)**[9] 5503 6-8-12 47 DuranFentiman[(3)] 5 52
(W G Harrison) *led: rdn and hdd 2f out: wknd ins fnl f* **6/1**[3]

0002 **4** *dht* **Bobering**[21] 5179 7-8-11 50 SoniaEaton[(7)] 10 55+
(B P J Baugh) *s.i.s: hld up: hdwy over 1f out: edgd lft: nt rch ldrs* **5/1**[2]

0640 **6** *15* **Kathleen Kennet**[29] 4945 7-9-1 47 FergusSweeney 7 20
(C Tinkler) *hld up: rdn over 3f out: wknd over 2f out* **8/1**

2566 **7** *1½* **Showtime Annie**[32] 4846 6-8-11 46 (v[1]) NeilChalmers[(3)] 11 16
(A Bailey) *hld up: hdwy over 3f out: sn rdn and wknd* **20/1**

4003 **8** *1* **Zhitomir**[9] 5503 9-9-3 49 TomEaves 2 17
(M Dods) *chsd ldrs: rdn 4f out: wknd over 2f out* **8/1**

0006 **9** *2½* **Gifted Flame**[8] 5525 8-9-2 48 (p) PhillipMakin 4 11
(T D Barron) *chsd ldrs tl rdn and wknd over 2f out* **9/1**

0-40 **10** *7* **Primeshade Promise**[51] 4259 6-8-12 49 KevinGhunowa[(5)] 13 —
(J L Flint) *hld up: rdn over 3f out: n.d* **20/1**

/06- **11** *8* **Spinning Gold**[292] 6759 4-9-1 47 (t) LiamJones 3 —
(Miss Gay Kelleway) *mid-div: rdn over 6f out: wknd over 3f out* **33/1**

1000 **12** *6* **Steel Grey**[67] 3765 6-9-3 49 DaleGibson 12 —
(M Brittain) *s.i.s: hld up: n.d* **33/1**

000/ **13** *5* **Anna Walhaan (IRE)**[785] 4042 8-9-1 47 ChrisCatlin 9 —
(Ian Williams) *chsd ldrs 6f* **40/1**

2m 2.50s (-0.12) **Going Correction** -0.025s/f (Stan) **13** Ran SP% **127.2**
Speed ratings (Par 101): **99,98,97,97,97 83,82,81,79,73 66,60,56**
CSF £120.08 CT £394.70 TOTE £8.60: £3.30, £4.20, £1.80; EX 113.30 Place 6 £79.94, Place 5 £31.88.
Owner Mrs N L Young **Bred** P F Headon **Trained** Upper Lambourn, Berks

FOCUS
A low-grade handicap. The first five finished a long way clear and the form is sound for the grade.
Private Soldier Official explanation: jockey said gelding ran too freely
Kathleen Kennet Official explanation: jockey said mare hung both ways
T/Plt: £69.80 to a £1 stake. Pool: £90,563.40. 946.70 winning tickets. T/Qpdt: £19.90 to a £1 stake. Pool: £5,358.00. 198.75 winning tickets. CR

5757 - 5760a (Foreign Racing) - See Raceform Interactive

4861
DUNDALK (A.W) (L-H)
Thursday, September 27

OFFICIAL GOING: Standard

5761a BAILEY'S H'CAP 7f
8:45 (8:45) (60-100,98) 3-Y-0+ **£12,096** (£3,548; £1,690; £576)

RPR

1 **Dynamo Dancer (IRE)**[19] 5242 4-10-0 98 JMurtagh 1 105+
(G M Lyons, Ire) *chsd ldrs: 6th ent st: rdn into 4th 1f out: r.o strly to ld cl home* **13/2**[3]

2 1/2 **Miss Gorica (IRE)**[19] 5242 3-9-4 91 .... WMLordan 13 96
(Ms Joanna Morgan, Ire) *chsd ldrs: cl 2nd 1/2-way: rdn to chal 2f out: led 1f out: styd on wl: hdd cl home* **5/1**[1]
3 1 1/2 **Akua'Ba (IRE)**[13] 5398 3-9-2 89 ....(p) KJManning 12 90
(J S Bolger, Ire) *sn led: rdn and chal 2f out: hdd 1f out: no ex: kpt on* **5/1**[1]
4 1/2 **Ireland's Call (IRE)**[8] 5549 6-9-5 89 .... JAHeffernan 10 88
(Peter Casey, Ire) *chsd ldrs: 3rd 1/2-way: rdn 2f out: 3rd 1f out: kpt on* **6/1**[2]
5 hd **Lake Pontchartrain (IRE)**[9] 5517 3-8-12 85 .... FMBerry 9 84
(John Geoghegan, Ire) *towards rr: hdwy into 8th 2f out: 6th under 1f out: kpt on* **10/1**
6 nk **Bomber Command (USA)**[31] 4886 4-9-5 94 ....(b[1]) PatrickHills(5) 8 92
(J W Hills) *chsd ldrs: 7th and rdn ent st: kpt on one pce* **6/1**[2]
7 nk **Orpailleur**[8] 5549 6-9-11 95 .... PShanahan 5 92
(Ms Joanna Morgan, Ire) *prom early: sn chsd ldr: 4th 1/2-way: 5th and no ex over 1f out: kpt on one pce* **5/1**[1]
8 3/4 **Rockie**[6] 5609 4-8-12 82 .... MCHussey 4 77
(T Hogan, Ire) *sn mid-div: sme hdwy into 7th 2f out: 8th and no imp 1f out* **14/1**
9 3/4 **Braydeen (IRE)**[373] 5464 3-9-3 90 .... PJSmullen 3 83
(D K Weld, Ire) *towards rr: sme hdwy into 9th over 1f out: n.d fnl f* **12/1**
10 3 **Regional Counsel**[8] 5549 3-9-3 90 ....(b) DPMcDonogh 11 75
(Kevin Prendergast, Ire) *in rr of mid-div early: sn chsd ldrs: 5th 1/2-way: rdn and no ex ent st* **33/1**
11 3 **Amarula Ridge (IRE)**[115] 2322 6-9-0 84 .... DMGrant 6 60
(Niall Madden, Ire) *a towards rr* **25/1**
12 3 **Out Of The Red (IRE)**[29] 4954 3-8-10 83 .... CDHayes 7 51
(Lester Winters, Ire) *dwlt: a towards rr* **25/1**
13 1 3/4 **Rathgowney Lad (IRE)**[28] 4984 7-8-13 83 .... RPCleary 14 46
(Patrick Martin, Ire) *in rr of mid-div early: sn chsd ldrs on outer: rdn and wknd 1/2-way* **33/1**
14 1 **Holbien (IRE)**[56] 4116 4-8-5 82 .... SFoley(7) 2 42
(Liam Roche, Ire) *sn towards rr and nvr a factor* **14/1**

1m 24.4s (84.40)
WFA 3 from 4yo+ 3lb **14** Ran SP% **135.6**
CSF £42.81 CT £191.78 TOTE £8.00: £3.70, £1.50, £1.70; DF 57.00.
Owner Third Avenue Syndicate **Bred** Victor Stud Bloodstock Ltd **Trained** Dunsany, Co. Meath

NOTEBOOK
Bomber Command(USA), successful in the first-time visor at Ascot back in July, has not done too badly since and he looked interesting here with the first-time blinkers applied. A bit behind turning into the straight, he kept plugging away, but never really threatened and remains considerably higher in the weights on All-Weather than Turf. (op 7/1)

5762 - 5763a (Foreign Racing) - See Raceform Interactive

4372 ASCOT (R-H)
Friday, September 28

OFFICIAL GOING: Straight course - good; round course - good to soft changing to straight course - good to soft; round course soft after race 4 (3.45)
Wind: breezy, strong across Weather: Wet

5764 EBF RATCLIFFES SYNDICATION CLASSIFIED STKS 1m 2f
2:00 (2:04) (Class 3) 3-Y-0+

£11,217 (£3,358; £1,679; £840; £419; £210) **Stalls** High

Form RPR
0233 **1** **King Charles**[21] 5208 3-8-10 89 .... SteveDrowne 4 99
(E A L Dunlop) *led for 3f: prom: led 2f out: forged clr ent fnl f: styd on wl* **20/1**
22-1 **2** 2 **Ajhar (USA)**[133] 1812 3-8-10 89 .... RHills 1 95
(M P Tregoning) *trckd ldrs: rdn to chal 2f out: kpt on but hld by wnr ent fnl f* **15/2**
210 **3** nk **Tears Of A Clown (IRE)**[48] 4388 4-9-2 89 .... TPQueally 3 94+
(J A Osborne) *hld up in last pair but in tch: swtchd out and hdwy 2f out: sn rdn: wnt 3rd over 1f out: styd on fnl f* **13/2**[3]
3213 **4** 1 1/4 **Font**[37] 4720 4-9-2 89 .... JamieSpencer 5 95+
(J R Fanshawe) *lw: hld up last pair but in tch: nt clr run under 2f out: hdwy over 1f out: sn shkn up: styd on to go 4th ins fnl f: nt rch ldrs* **10/3**[2]
3264 **5** 1 3/4 **Ballinteni**[48] 4399 5-9-2 90 ....(t) JohnEgan 6 88
(Miss Gay Kelleway) *cl up: rdn over 2f out: wnt 3rd briefly over 1f out: kpt on same pce* **14/1**
3-12 **6** 3 **Lang Shining (IRE)**[28] 5012 3-8-10 89 .... RyanMoore 8 82
(Sir Michael Stoute) *lw: trckd ldrs: rdn over 2f out: wknd ent fnl f* **6/4**[1]
1512 **7** 1/2 **Padlocked (IRE)**[14] 5382 3-8-10 90 .... EddieAhern 2 81
(D M Simcock) *cl up: effrt 2f out: wknd ent fnl f* **10/1**
-400 **8** 1/2 **Chantaco (USA)**[16] 5326 5-8-13 88 .... WilliamBuick(3) 9 80
(A M Balding) *cl up: rdn over 2f out: wknd over 1f out* **40/1**
310- **9** 4 **Winged Flight (USA)**[402] 4680 3-8-10 90 .... RoystonFfrench 7 72
(M Johnston) *prom: led after 3f: rdn and hdd 2f out: grad fdd* **22/1**

2m 9.77s (1.77) **Going Correction** +0.375s/f (Good)
WFA 3 from 4yo+ 6lb **9** Ran SP% **115.5**
Speed ratings (Par 107): **107,105,105,104,102 100,99,99,96**
CSF £158.28 TOTE £26.70: £4.90, £1.80, £1.90; EX 260.90 Trifecta £872.60 Part won. Pool £1,229.10 - 0.10 winning units..
Owner Khalifa Sultan **Bred** Hunscote House Farm Stud **Trained** Newmarket, Suffolk

FOCUS
Quite a competitive little classified event with just 2lb covering the field on adjusted official ratings. The pace was just fair, but this was a race where it paid to race handily and the front pair were always to the fore. The third and fourth, on the other hand, were held up, so they may well be a bit better than the bare form.

NOTEBOOK
King Charles ◆, whose recent Newbury third had been boosted by the pair that beat him both going in since, was always in the perfect position on the shoulder of the leader. When asked to go and win his race, he found plenty and was well in control over the last furlong or so. He still seems to be improving and there may be even better to come from him next season. (op 25-1)
Ajhar(USA), returning from a four-month break, has already shown that he can go well fresh. He was obliged to race wide of the field from his outside draw in the early stages and was rather keen as a result, but despite that he had every chance and just ran into a better horse on the day. He is yet to finish out of the first two in five starts and probably still has some improvement in him. (op 8-1)
Tears Of A Clown(IRE), about whom there seemed to be some concern at the start, had to be trotted up and down behind the stalls before he was allowed to take part. Switched off last in a race where it was probably an advantage to race handy, he tried to put in an effort down the wide outside in the straight and probably achieved as much as could be expected under the circumstances. There will be other days, especially as the ground eases. (op 11-2)
Font ◆, was not only held up in a race that seemed to suit those that raced prominently, but he also had a problem getting a run through in the home straight and by the time he did it was much too late. It should not be long before he is winning again. (op 4-1 tchd 3-1)
Ballinteni, making his debut for the yard, had the tongue tie on for the first time since his racecourse debut and had every chance. He is on a career-high mark these days and probably needs to drop a few pounds. Official explanation: jockey said horse lost a shoe leaving the stalls and slipped on the first bend (op 20-1)
Lang Shining(IRE), one of the least exposed in the field, was certainly in a good enough position for much of the way, but this was his first attempt at the trip and he performed like a non-stayer. (op 11-8 tchd 13-8, tchd 7-4 in a place)
Padlocked(IRE) did not pick up and once again did not seem to show his form over this trip. (op 11-1)

5765 JEAN BRYANT MEMORIAL H'CAP 6f
2:35 (2:36) (Class 2) (0-100,97) 3-Y-0

£12,464 (£3,732; £1,866; £934; £466; £234) **Stalls** Centre

Form RPR
1212 **1** **Genki (IRE)**[21] 5209 3-9-1 **94** .... SteveDrowne 7 106
(R Charlton) *lw: bmpd s: chsd ldrs: rdn 2f out: led ent fnl f: narrowly hdd fnl 50yds: rallied to ld fnl stride* **7/2**[1]
2220 **2** shd **Sohraab**[56] 4123 3-8-6 **85** ow1 .... JohnEgan 2 97
(H Morrison) *awkward leaving stalls: mid-div: rdn and hdwy over 1f out: pressed wnr ent fnl f: tk narrow advantage fnl 50yds: hdd fnl stride* **14/1**
1212 **3** 2 **Esteem Machine (USA)**[12] 5449 3-8-7 **86** .... KerrinMcEvoy 5 92
(R A Teal) *wnt sltly rt s: led: rdn and hdd ent fnl f: no ex* **9/2**[3]
0301 **4** nk **Everymanforhimself (IRE)**[11] 5473 3-8-9 **88** 6ex ....(b) JimCrowley 6 93
(J G Given) *squeezed up s: towards rr: rdn over 2f out: stdy prog over 1f out: r.o ins fnl f* **14/1**
5523 **5** nk **Majuro (IRE)**[15] 5355 3-9-3 **96** .... TedDurcan 3 100
(M R Channon) *mid-div: rdn 3f out: outpcd 2f out: edgd rt but r.o ins fnl f* **14/1**
2046 **6** 1 1/2 **Mambo Spirit (IRE)**[15] 5356 3-8-4 **86** .... WilliamBuick(3) 9 86
(J G Given) *t.k.h trcking ldr: rdn 2f out: one pce fnl f* **20/1**
2111 **7** nk **Edge Closer**[30] 4950 3-9-4 **97** .... RyanMoore 1 96
(R Hannon) *chsd ldrs: rdn over 2f out: wknd ins fnl f* **4/1**[2]
2020 **8** 1 **Off The Record**[13] 5407 3-9-4 **97** .... TPQueally 4 93
(J G Given) *chsd ldrs: rdn over 2f out: wknd ins fnl f* **12/1**
0064 **9** hd **Heywood**[28] 4990 3-8-8 **87** .... TPO'Shea 8 82
(M R Channon) *hld up towards rr: short lived effrt over 2f out* **25/1**
2411 **10** 8 **Jimmy Styles**[42] 4574 3-8-10 **89** .... EddieAhern 10 60
(C G Cox) *in tch: swtchd to far side and racd alone after 2f: rdn over 2f out: wknd over 1f out* **4/1**[2]

1m 16.08s (1.18) **Going Correction** +0.30s/f (Good) **10** Ran SP% **116.7**
Speed ratings (Par 107): **104,103,101,100,100 98,98,96,96,85**
CSF £53.83 CT £231.18 TOTE £4.90: £1.80, £4.10, £1.90; EX 58.70 Trifecta £333.10 Pool £1,313.74 - 2.80 winning units..
Owner Ms Gillian Khosla **Bred** Rathbarry Stud **Trained** Beckhampton, Wilts
■ Stewards' Enquiry : Steve Drowne one-day ban: used whip with excessive frequency (Oct 9)

FOCUS
A decent little three-year-old sprint in which the bulk of the field came down the centre - which is where the stalls were - whilst one went more towards the far side. It attracted several highly progressive types, but very few got into it. The winner continues his rapid ascent.

NOTEBOOK
Genki(IRE) ◆, back against his own age-group after a cracking effort against his elders at Newbury last time, took a bit of a nudge when Esteem Machine knocked Everymanforhimself into him leaving the stalls. It did not affect him though, as he was brought with his effort at the furlong pole and when it came down to the battle with the runner-up in the closing stages, he wanted it that much more. He has not been out of the first two in eight starts since his racecourse debut and even though he continues to climb the weights the best of him is probably still to be seen. His trainer is looking forward to stepping him up to 7f. (op 10-3 tchd 4-1 in places)
Sohraab had conditions come in his favour and seemed to be suited by the return to this trip. He appeared to have been produced with a race-winning challenge, but ran into a tough rival who would simply not be denied, though there will be those who will point to the 1lb overweight. He has finished runner-up rather too often for comfort, but he has also won twice this year and did not do much wrong here. (op 16-1)
Esteem Machine(USA) had his conditions and ran a good race from the front if unable to cope with the finishing pace of the front pair. He is 8lb higher than for his last win, but has now run two decent races off this mark since then, so can hardly expect much leniency. (op 5-1 tchd 11-2)
Everymanforhimself(IRE), carrying a 6lb penalty for his recent Leicester victory, was rather the meat in the sandwich between Esteem Machine and the winner at the start which left him with quite a bit to make up. He probably did well to eventually finish as close as he did and, even though he is a bit more exposed than a few of these, he should be able to find another sprint handicap or two. (op 25-1)
Majuro(IRE) was tackling a trip this short for only the second time in his career, and for the first time on turf. Because of that it was not the biggest surprise that he had a problem going the pace, but he was staying on at the end of this stiff 6f. He remains on a career-high mark, but will obviously be suited by a return to further. (op 16-1)
Mambo Spirit(IRE) was inclined to throw his head about behind the leaders in the early stages and then found little once off the bridle. (op 25-1)
Edge Closer was up another 8lb in his bid for a four-timer, which meant he was 20lb higher than when the sequence started. He made just about every yard when winning twice over course and distance in July, but could not do the same thing against these better rivals and he failed to get home.
Jimmy Styles, put up 11lb after slamming Esteem Machine at Newbury and 2lb worse off with that colt here, whether by accident or design soon found himself racing alone more towards the far rail, whilst his rivals all came down the centre. It was obvious from some way out that he was well beaten and, although connections thought the easing ground was too blame, this was far too bad to be true. Official explanation: trainer said colt was unsuited by the good ground (op 10-3)

5766 WATERSHIP DOWN STUD SALES RACE (FILLIES) 6f 110y
3:10 (3:13) (Class 2) 2-Y-0

£134,354 (£53,741; £26,870; £13,421; £6,710; £6,710) **Stalls** Centre

Form RPR
2115 **1** **Lady Rangali (IRE)**[48] 4406 2-8-2 68 .... RoystonFfrench 11 81
(Mrs A Duffield) *mid-div: hdwy over 2f out: led ent fnl f: kpt on gamely whn chal: drvn out* **8/1**[3]
022 **2** nk **Izzibizzi**[31] 4916 2-8-2 0 .... JimmyQuinn 3 80
(E A L Dunlop) *s.i.s: towards rr: hdwy over 2f out: rdn wl over 1f out: wnt 3rd ent fnl f: r.o: tk 2nd fnl stride* **20/1**
0116 **3** shd **Sophie's Girl**[16] 5322 2-8-10 76 .... KDarley 8 88
(P W Chapple-Hyam) *trckd ldrs: rdn over 2f out: ev ch thrght fnl f: no ex towards fin* **8/1**[3]
4 3/4 **Insaaf** 2-9-0 0 .... RHills 17 90
(W J Haggas) *w'like: trckd ldrs: rdn 2f out: chal over 1f out: kpt on but no ex* **25/1**

1220 **5** 3 1/2 **Anosti**[16] 5322 2-8-2 0 .... DO'Donohoe 20 68
(K A Ryan) *prom: rdn to ld 2f out: edgd rt and hdd ent fnl f: no ex* **4/1**[1]

1 **6** 1 1/4 **Spell Caster**[32] 4875 2-8-6 0 .... KerrinMcEvoy 10 69
(R M Beckett) *unf: hld up towards rr: hmpd 3f out: rdn 2f out: no imp tl styd on ins fnl f: nrst fin* **9/2**[2]

1 **7** 1/2 **Artistic License (IRE)**[26] 5065 2-8-6 0 .... SteveDrowne 2 68
(M R Channon) *w'like: leggy: hld up towards rr: hdwy over 2f out: sn rdn: styd on fnl f: nvr trbld ldrs* **16/1**

1204 **8** 1 1/2 **Reel Gift**[16] 5324 2-8-8 0 .... RyanMoore 7 65
(R Hannon) *hld up towards rr: hdwy over 2f out: sn rdn: kpt on same pce fnl f* **9/2**[2]

4531 **9** hd **Eastern Romance**[9] 5521 2-8-11 78 .... PaulMulrennan 15 68
(K A Ryan) *led tl over 2f out: sn hung rt and fdd* **20/1**

10 2 1/2 **Mary Montagu (IRE)** 2-8-10 0 .... EddieAhern 19 60
(J W Hills) *w'like: towards rr: rdn and hdwy over 2f out: kpt on same pce fnl f* **80/1**

420 **11** nk **Fifty (IRE)**[22] 5164 2-8-10 0 .... TedDurcan 12 59
(R Hannon) *prom: rdn over 2f out: grad fdd* **20/1**

5000 **12** nk **Talamahana**[6] 5628 2-8-4 0 .... SimonWhitworth 4 52
(S Kirk) *nvr bttr than mid-div* **100/1**

2355 **13** 3/4 **Carnival Dream**[10] 5501 2-7-12 0 .... WilliamBuick 1 44
(A Berry) *prom: rdn 3f out: wknd 2f out* **66/1**

14 1 1/2 **Marfeng** 2-8-0 0 .... LiamJones 5 42
(W M Brisbourne) *leggy: s.i.s: nvr bttr than fin position* **100/1**

00 **15** 3/4 **Our Tallulah (IRE)**[24] 5110 2-8-4 0 .... RichardThomas 13 44
(C G Cox) *mainly towards rr* **100/1**

2103 **16** 1/2 **Meridian Line (IRE)**[4] 5692 2-8-4 0 .... RichardKingscote 9 43
(J G Portman) *a mid-div* **25/1**

0 **17** 1 1/2 **Badoura**[15] 5357 2-8-10 0 .... NickyMackay 21 45
(G A Butler) *leggy: mid-div: rdn 3f out: wknd 2f out* **25/1**

0 **18** 1/2 **Town And Gown**[91] 3055 2-8-12 0 .... JimmyFortune 18 45
(J H M Gosden) *s.i.s: a towards rr* **10/1**

04 **19** 4 **Madam Carwell**[11] 5483 2-8-0 0 .... JamieMackay 14 22
(J G Given) *mid-div tl wknd 2f out* **100/1**

06 **20** 1/2 **Bond Scissorsister (IRE)**[18] 5281 2-7-12 0 .... AdrianMcCarthy 16 19
(G R Oldroyd) *a towards rr* **100/1**

046 **21** nk **Pay Pay Pay**[62] 3977 2-8-0 0 .... DominicFox 6 20
(P D Evans) *a bhd* **100/1**

0 **22** hd **Tea Cake (IRE)**[63] 3895 2-8-8 0 .... JimCrowley 22 27
(H J L Dunlop) *chsd ldrs tl wknd 2f out* **100/1**

1m 23.35s (0.51) **Going Correction** +0.30s/f (Good) **22** Ran SP% **129.0**
Speed ratings (Par 98): **101,100,100,99,95 94,93,91,91,88 88,88,87,85,84 84,82,81,77,76 76,76**
CSF £167.79 TOTE £10.90: £3.40, £5.70, £2.90; EX 414.10 TRIFECTA Not won..
Owner Mrs Sarah E Woodhead **Bred** Mrs C Hartery **Trained** Constable Burton, N Yorks
■ Stewards' Enquiry : D O'Donohoe two-day ban: careless riding (Oct 9-10)

FOCUS
A huge field but, as with many races like this, not as competitive as the numbers or the prizemoney might suggest, with barely a handful of serious contenders on form. Although the field stuck together as one group down the middle of the track early on, the principals were all inclined to edge towards the far rail as the race progressed. The front four pulled well clear of the others and the time was about what one would expect for a race of its type.

NOTEBOOK
Lady Rangali(IRE), who has been running in nurseries and was possibly unlucky at Redcar last time, had landed three of her last four races prior to that so she knew how to win. The easing ground was never going to be problem for her, and once coming through to hit the front, she dug deep under strong pressure to keep her rivals at bay and net this huge pot for her connections. (op 9-1)
Izzibizzi, still a maiden, was dropping slightly in trip and came home in good style after being patiently ridden. The battle-hardened winner was too tough to crack, but she would have been 9lb better off with Lady Rangali in a nursery so deserves plenty of credit. After a run of three consecutive second places, she very much deserves to get off the mark. (op 33-1)
Sophie's Girl arguably could have done without the rain, so she deserves plenty of credit for battling away right to the end and a line through Izzibizzi suggests she ran very close to her current mark.
Insaaf ◆, a 130,000gns half-sister to three winners at up to 7f, including the useful Doctor Brown, faced a stiff introduction under a big weight yet was always up with the pace towards the far side of the field and never stopped trying. She did much the best of the three newcomers and should have little difficulty in finding a maiden. Official explanation: jockey said filly suffered interference in running (op 20-1)
Anosti, rather disappointing in a nursery over this trip at Doncaster last time when adrift of Sophie's Girl, ran better here and was in front at one stage before being done for foot. However, she would have been upwards of 10lb worse off with the front three had this been a nursery, so may not have achieved that much. Official explanation: jockey said filly hung right (op 9-2 tchd 5-1)
Spell Caster ◆, dropping a furlong and a half in trip compared with her successful Chepstow debut, was struggling to go the pace from some way out and faced an even bigger task after getting quite seriously hampered at halfway. Her stamina eventually kicked in though, and she did very well to stay on and reach her final position under the circumstances. She still has a future. (op 4-1)
Artistic License(IRE), whose Folkestone debut victory has not really worked out, plugged on to land some prize money and still has the scope to make her mark back in more modest company. (op 14-1)
Reel Gift fourth over this trip in the St Leger Yearling Stakes at Doncaster, looked as though she might play a part entering the last quarter-mile but her effort amounted to little. She was by far best in of those with an official rating, but ran way below that mark here. (op 4-1 tchd 7-2, tchd 5-1 in places)
Eastern Romance showed up for a long way, but this longer trip on a stiff track against better rivals eventually found her out. (op 22-1 tchd 18-1)
Bond Scissorsister(IRE) Official explanation: trainer said filly was unsuited by the good going

5767 EBF PRICEWATERHOUSECOOPERS HARVEST STKS (LISTED RACE) (F&M) 1m 4f
3:45 (3:45) (Class 1) 3-Y-0+
£17,034 (£6,456; £3,231; £1,611; £807; £405) **Stalls** High

Form RPR

4423 **1** **Brisk Breeze (GER)**[15] 5352 3-8-9 105 .... TedDurcan 7 109
(H R A Cecil) *trckd ldr: rdn to ld 2f out: length up ent fnl f: kpt on wl u.p: drvn out* **7/1**[2]

3232 **2** 1/2 **All My Loving (IRE)**[15] 5352 3-8-9 0 .... MJKinane 1 108
(A P O'Brien, Ire) *sn pushed into ld: rdn and hdd 2f out: length down ent fnl f: rallied gamely: hld nr fin* **4/6**[1]

2345 **3** 1 3/4 **Under The Rainbow**[15] 5352 4-9-3 104 ....(p) JimmyFortune 5 105
(B W Hills) *cl up: rdn over 2f out: chsd ldng pair wl over 1f out: kpt on* **8/1**[3]

4311 **4** 1 1/4 **Maid To Believe**[28] 5006 3-8-9 89 .... EddieAhern 3 103+
(J L Dunlop) *lw: hld up: rdn 3f out: hdwy 2f out: styd on: nvr trbld ldrs* **20/1**

1030 **5** 3 1/2 **Dance Of Light (USA)**[36] 4748 3-8-9 94 .... RyanMoore 4 98
(Sir Michael Stoute) *hld up: rdn over 3f out: hung rt fr 2f out: sme late prog but nvr a danger* **20/1**

1112 **6** 4 **Generous Jem**[10] 5504 4-9-3 81 .... GeorgeBaker 6 91
(G G Margarson) *hld up: rdn 3f out: hdwy 2f out: wknd over 1f out* **50/1**

31-6 **7** 3 **Lake Toya (USA)**[9] 5544 5-9-3 103 .... LDettori 8 86
(Saeed Bin Suroor) *trckd ldng pair: rdn over 3f out: wandered u.p over 2f out: sn wknd* **7/1**[2]

2535 **8** 13 **Mont Etoile (IRE)**[9] 5544 4-9-3 99 .... TPQueally 9 66
(W J Haggas) *cl up: rdn 3f out: wknd 2f out* **20/1**

2m 36.32s (3.32) **Going Correction** +0.575s/f (Yiel)
WFA 3 from 4yo+ 8lb **8** Ran SP% **112.3**
Speed ratings (Par 111): **111,110,109,108,106 103,101,93**
CSF £11.42 TOTE £8.70: £1.70, £1.10, £2.00; EX 15.10 Trifecta £42.30 Pool £1,434.28 - 24.04 winning units..
Owner Ennismore Racing I **Bred** Dr R Wilhelms **Trained** Newmarket, Suffolk

FOCUS
A fair pace for this Listed event and the front pair, who were the best fillies in the race on official ratings, dominated the contest throughout. Ordinary form for the grade, however, and a little muddling too.

NOTEBOOK
Brisk Breeze(GER), a length behind All My Loving in the Park Hill, was probably the better suited of the pair by this shorter trip. Always on the shoulder of her old rival, she forged her way to the front soon after turning in and from then on it was just a case of holding on, which she did bravely. She has kept improving all season and a return to this track for the Group 3 Princess Royal Stakes in two weeks' time would appear the obvious target. (tchd 15-2)
All My Loving(IRE), still without a win since her racecourse debut despite all her placings in top company, was sent straight to the front and set just a fair pace. However, her lack of a change of gear was again evident as she could not respond straight away when her old rival Brisk Breeze went past her soon after turning in. As at Doncaster, she did her level best to try and get back up, but she could never quite do so. Whether she would have been better off setting a more searching pace over this trip is hard to say, but what is true is that a solitary maiden win for a filly of her ability is scant reward. (op 8-11)
Under The Rainbow, fifth in this race last year and still bidding to end a near two-year losing run, does not do anything quickly and merely plodded on to finish about the same distance behind the front pair as she had done in the Park Hill. (op 9-1)
Maid To Believe came into this in fine form and deserved a crack at a race like this, but she had about a stone to find to be competitive with the principals. Her staying-on fourth was probably about as much as could be expected, but she perhaps deserves a bit of extra credit for getting there from off the pace.
Dance Of Light(USA), who is still to totally convince over this trip, never looked like taking a hand and has questions to answer. (op 14-1)
Generous Jem may have been running well in handicaps in recent months, but she had no chance against these rivals on official ratings and so it proved.
Lake Toya(USA) did not step up from her recent return to action and either bounced or did not stay. (op 6-1)

5768 DJP INTERNATIONAL H'CAP 1m (S)
4:20 (4:23) (Class 4) (0-85,84) 3-Y-0 **£6,477** (£1,927; £963; £481) **Stalls** Centre

Form RPR

01 **1** **Bankable (IRE)**[18] 5285 3-8-11 77 .... LDettori 14 94+
(L M Cumani) *w'like: str: scope: lw: hld up bhd on far side: swtchd rt and gd hdwy 3f out: led wl over 1f out: drifted lft: r.o wl: comf* **5/2**[1]

3614 **2** 1 **Oceana Gold**[42] 4566 3-8-10 79 .... WilliamBuick(3) 1 90+
(A M Balding) *overall ldr on stands' side: rdn and hdd wl over 1f out: sn edgd rt: kpt on but a hld by wnr* **13/2**[3]

5045 **3** 1 3/4 **Lazy Darren**[14] 5383 3-8-10 76 .... RyanMoore 11 83
(R Hannon) *t.k.h towards rr on far side: hdwy over 2f out: sn rdn: styd on to go 3rd ins fnl f* **5/1**[2]

4413 **4** 1/2 **Jawaab (IRE)**[4] 5693 3-8-4 70 oh1 .... JimmyQuinn 19 77+
(M A Buckley) *hld up bhd on far side: hdwy and nt clr run briefly over 2f out and again over 1f out: swtchd rt: styd on: nrst fin* **8/1**

3005 **5** 3/4 **Baylini**[9] 5537 3-9-1 81 .... JamesDoyle 13 86
(Ms J S Doyle) *mid-div on far side: rdn and hdwy 2f out: swtchd rt ent fnl f: styd on* **66/1**

0402 **6** 2 1/2 **Okikoki**[15] 5360 3-8-10 76 .... SaleemGolam 15 75
(W R Muir) *chsd ldrs on far side: rdn over 2f out: one pce fnl f* **33/1**

1040 **7** 1 **Buckie Massa**[4] 5684 3-8-10 76 .... LPKeniry 3 72
(S Kirk) *hld up bhd on stands' side: rdn and stdy prog fr 2f out: styd on: nvr trbld ldrs* **33/1**

8 3 **Shabahar (IRE)**[100] 2783 3-9-4 84 .... JohnEgan 12 74
(M J McGrath) *hld up bhd on far side: rdn and hdwy over 2f out: no further imp fr 1f out* **40/1**

-161 **9** 1/2 **Mount Hermon (IRE)**[24] 5122 3-8-12 78 .... SteveDrowne 4 66
(H Morrison) *lw: nvr bttr than mid-div on stands' side* **13/2**[3]

1205 **10** nk **Bajan Pride**[14] 5382 3-9-0 80 .... JimmyFortune 17 68
(R Hannon) *prom on far side: rdn over 2f out: wknd and edgd rt ent fnl f* **16/1**

4200 **11** 3/4 **Curzon Prince (IRE)**[85] 3235 3-9-0 80 .... EddieAhern 7 66
(C F Wall) *led far side gp tl wl over 1f out wknd ent fnl f* **16/1**

052- **12** 9 **Wateera (IRE)**[367] 5596 3-8-8 74 .... RHills 2 39
(J L Dunlop) *trckd ldrs on stands' side: rdn 3f out: wknd 2f out* **20/1**

431- **13** 4 **Hanbrin Bhoy (IRE)**[331] 6290 3-8-6 72 .... RoystonFfrench 16 28
(R Dickin) *nvr bttr than mid-div on far side* **33/1**

610 **14** 2 **Azeema (IRE)**[118] 2243 3-8-11 77 .... OscarUrbina 9 29
(B W Hills) *chsd ldrs on far side: rdn 3f out: sn wknd* **22/1**

2-00 **15** 3 1/2 **Minos (IRE)**[21] 5208 3-8-8 74 .... KDarley 6 17
(R Hannon) *mid-div on stands' side: rdn 3f out: wknd over 1f out* **33/1**

5010 **16** 2 **Elusive Dreams (USA)**[24] 5122 3-8-6 72 .... TedDurcan 18 11
(J H M Gosden) *chsd ldrs on far side for 3f* **16/1**

1-06 **17** 21 **Messiah Garvey**[15] 5360 3-8-5 71 .... PaulDoe 5 —
(M R Channon) *chsd ldrs on far side: rdn 3f out: sn btn* **50/1**

3364 **18** shd **Bateleur**[15] 5360 3-8-9 75 .... TPO'Shea 10 —
(M R Channon) *chsd ldrs on far side tl 3f out* **50/1**

1m 42.98s (1.18) **Going Correction** +0.30s/f (Good) **18** Ran SP% **129.4**
Speed ratings (Par 103): **106,105,103,102,102 99,98,95,95,94 93,84,80,78,75 73,52,52**
CSF £17.10 CT £85.00 TOTE £3.40: £1.40, £2.10, £1.70, £2.10; EX 22.20 Trifecta £33.10 Pool £972.65 - 20.82 winning units..
Owner JMC Breed & Race Limited **Bred** Barronstown Stud And Cobra **Trained** Newmarket, Suffolk

FOCUS
A competitive handicap, albeit one in which progressive types were in somewhat short supply. The field split into two, with a group of 12 racing centre to far side, whilst the smaller group of six came centre to stands' side. The two groups had just about merged reaching the three-furlong pole and with the field eventually finishing well spread out, the form has a solid look to it.

Jawaab(IRE) Official explanation: jockey said gelding suffered interference in running

5769 BOLLINGER CHAMPAGNE CHALLENGE SERIES FINAL H'CAP (FOR GENTLEMAN AMATEUR RIDERS) 1m 4f
4:55 (4:56) (Class 4) (0-80,80) 4-Y-0+

£6,002 (£1,875; £937; £469; £234; £118) **Stalls** High

Form RPR

0511 **1** **Elopement (IRE)**[4] 5676 5-10-5 **66** 6ex.................... MrPCollington(5) 10 85
(W M Brisbourne) *lw: trckd ldrs: jnd ldr 4f out: led over 2f out: drifted rt but sn clr: readily* **13/2**

3013 **2** 6 **Apache Fort**[12] 5454 4-10-7 **66** oh1.................... MrSPearce(3) 9 75
(T Keddy) *t.k.h trcking ldrs: rdn over 2f out: styd on to go 2nd ins fnl f: no ch w wnr* **11/2**[3]

0605 **3** 2 **Cape Greko**[19] 2218 5-10-11 **72**.................... MrCPHuxley(5) 11 78
(B G Powell) *prom: led over 5f out: rdn and hdd over 2f out: sn no ch w wnr: lost 2nd ins fnl f* **16/1**

1440 **4** hd **Sand Repeal (IRE)**[37] 4708 5-10-5 **66** oh1....................(v) MrRBirkett(5) 4 71
(Miss J Feilden) *in tch: rdn 3f out: kpt on same pce fnl 2f* **33/1**

3213 **5** 2½ **Trafalgar Day**[85] 3243 4-10-9 **70**.................... MrBenBrisbourne(5) 2 71
(W M Brisbourne) *t.k.h: mid-div: tk clsr order 5f out: effrt over 2f out: sn one pce* **5/2**[1]

00-5 **6** 1½ **Katies Tuitor**[42] 4572 4-11-2 **72**.................... MrLeeNewnes 7 71
(B W Duke) *lw: chsd ldrs: reminders after 2f: lost position 5f out: rdn to cl on ldrs 4f out: btn over 2f out* **9/1**

0240 **7** 1¾ **Mystic Storm**[28] 5007 4-10-12 **68**.................... MrSWalker 1 64
(Lady Herries) *hld up: hdwy 5f out: rdn over 3f out: wknd 2f out* **9/2**[2]

3013 **8** 10 **Rare Coincidence**[17] 5300 6-10-9 **70**....................(p) MrBMcHugh(5) 12 50
(R F Fisher) *led tl over 5f out: wknd over 2f out* **9/1**

4431 **9** 4 **Salute (IRE)**[13] 5427 8-11-5 **80**.................... MrFFairchild(5) 8 54
(P G Murphy) *mid-div tl 4f out* **16/1**

1452 **10** 6 **Gallego**[6] 5636 5-10-3 **66** oh6.................... MrMPrice(7) 3 30
(R J Price) *s.i.s: a bhd* **14/1**

/2-0 **11** 17 **Turtle Soup (IRE)**[33] 4850 11-10-13 **69**.................... MrSDobson 5 6
(J J Bridger) *a bhd: t.o fr wl over 2f out* **25/1**

2m 39.42s (6.42) **Going Correction** +0.575s/f (Yiel) **11** Ran SP% **120.7**
Speed ratings (Par 105): **101,97,95,95,93 92,91,85,82,78 67**
CSF £43.37 CT £560.42 TOTE £6.40: £2.70, £2.10, £3.20; EX 45.10 Trifecta £497.60 Pool £1,191.50 - 497.60 winning units. Place 6 £275.36, Place 5 £65.23.
Owner Stratford Bards Racing **Bred** Haras Du Mezeray **Trained** Great Ness, Shropshire
■ Charlie Huxley is the Series winner.

FOCUS
Even though the time was over three seconds slower than the fillies' Listed event, this was still run at a good pace considering the type of contest and there were some big margins separating the runners at the line. The winner was in a different league.
Mystic Storm Official explanation: trainer said gelding was unsuited by the soft ground
T/Jkpt: Not won. T/Plt: £169.40 to a £1 stake. Pool: £127,840.50. 550.90 winning tickets. T/Qpdt: £23.70 to a £1 stake. Pool: £8,231.70. 256.00 winning tickets. TM

5328 HAYDOCK (L-H)
Friday, September 28

OFFICIAL GOING: Soft (good to soft in places)
The ground was described as 'dead and tacky' on the straight course, 'soft' in the back straight.
Wind: light 1/2 behind Weather: overcast and cool, light rain later

5770 VALE UK MAIDEN FILLIES' STKS 6f
1:40 (1:41) (Class 5) 2-Y-0 **£2,817** (£838; £418; £209) **Stalls** Centre

Form RPR

44 **1** **No Page (IRE)**[21] 5192 2-9-0 0.................... MichaelHills 8 77
(B W Hills) *trckd ldrs: led over 1f out: hld on towards fin* **4/1**[2]

2 **2** nk **Maimoona (IRE)**[34] 4810 2-9-0 0.................... MartinDwyer 5 77+
(W J Haggas) *sn chsng ldrs: swtchd rt and bumpe dover 1f out: no ex ins fnl f* **8/15**[1]

3 1½ **Jeninsky (USA)** 2-8-10 0.................... FrancisNorton 1 68
(P J McBride) *s.s: bhd and green: hdwy 2f out: styd on wl ins fnl f* **50/1**

0 **4** 1½ **Sylvias Grove**[23] 5143 2-9-0 0.................... StephenDonohoe 6 67
(D Carroll) *led tl over 1f out: kpt on same pce* **18/1**

04 **5** ½ **Glittering Prize (UAE)**[27] 5033 2-9-0 0.................... GregFairley 12 66
(M Johnston) *bmpd s: chsd ldrs: hmpd over 1f out: kpt on same pce* **10/1**[3]

6 3 **Reclamation (IRE)** 2-8-10 0.................... SebSanders 10 53
(Sir Mark Prescott) *sn outpcd and drvn along: kpt on fnl 2f: nvr a factor* **12/1**

060 **7** 1¾ **Holly Golightley**[132] 1848 2-9-0 63.................... NCallan 3 51
(K A Ryan) *chsd ldrs: wknd over 1f out* **22/1**

00 **8** 4 **Swift Acclaim (IRE)**[14] 5393 2-8-7 0.................... DeclanCannon(7) 7 39
(K R Burke) *chsd ldrs: wknd 2f out* **100/1**

06 **9** ¾ **Steph The Ref**[8] 5558 2-8-11 0.................... MichaelJStainton(3) 2 37
(R M Whitaker) *chsd ldrs: edgd lft and lost pl over 1f out* **100/1**

10 5 **Make Acquaintance** 2-8-10 0.................... RichardMullen 11 18
(M Mullineaux) *wnt rt s: chsd ldrs: lost pl 2f out* **100/1**

0 **11** 1¾ **Babilu**[21] 5193 2-9-0 0.................... J-PGuillambert 14 17
(J G Given) *in rr-div: effrt over 2f out: sn wknd* **100/1**

0 **12** 1 **Reel Classy**[9] 5526 2-8-7 0.................... DeanHeslop(7) 13 14
(M A Peill) *missed break sltly and hmpd s: nvr wnt pce* **200/1**

13 10 **Rose De Rita** 2-8-10 0.................... VinceSlattery 4 —
(L P Grassick) *sn outpcd in rr: bhd fnl 3f* **100/1**

1m 15.75s (1.86) **Going Correction** +0.20s/f (Good) **13** Ran SP% **119.0**
Speed ratings (Par 92): **95,94,92,90,89 85,83,78,77,70 68,66,53**
CSF £6.32 TOTE £4.40: £1.60, £1.10, £11.30; EX 8.20.
Owner Philip G Harvey **Bred** Philip Graham Harvey **Trained** Lambourn, Berks

FOCUS
Probably just an ordinary maiden and the second looked the best horse on the day.

NOTEBOOK
No Page(IRE), dropping back in trip, in the end did just enough. (tchd 9-2)
Maimoona(IRE) met traffic problems and was buffeted when coming between horses. Just held in the end, he looked a shade unlucky. (op 8-13 tchd 1-2, tchd 4-6 in places)
Jeninsky(USA), who has a fair amount of size and scope, missed a beat at the start and was then clueless. She was putting in some solid work late on and should be much wiser in future.
Sylvias Grove, who has a big-race entry, showed a lot more than on her debut, taking them along but being comfortably run out of it in the end. (op 16-1 tchd 20-1)
Glittering Prize(UAE) took a bump leaving the stalls. She contributed to some bunching coming to the final furlong and may improve given a little more time. (op 9-1)
Reclamation(IRE), a half-sister to Irish Oaks winner Vintage Tipple and from the family of Vintage Crop, looks paceless and will not come into her own until tackling middle-distances at three.

5771 JMC IT MAIDEN STKS (DIV I) 6f
2:10 (2:11) (Class 5) 2-Y-0 **£2,169** (£645; £322; £161) **Stalls** Centre

Form RPR

334 **1** **Hunt The Bottle (IRE)**[27] 5042 2-9-0 77.................... MichaelHills 2 73
(B W Hills) *hld up in tch: rdn over 1f out: led wl ins fnl f: r.o* **2/1**[1]

6 **2** ½ **Barbary Boy (FR)**[14] 5380 2-9-0 0.................... HayleyTurner 15 72
(M L W Bell) *t.k.h: led over 3f out: rdn over 1f out: edgd lft and hdd wl ins fnl f: kpt on* **6/1**[3]

3 1¼ **Italian Art (IRE)** 2-9-0 0.................... SebSanders 14 68
(R M Beckett) *hld up in tch: rdn and ev ch over 1f out: nt qckn ins fnl f* **9/2**[2]

5 **4** ¾ **Farpedon**[29] 4962 2-9-0 0.................... DaneO'Neill 3 66
(H Candy) *led over 2f: rdn and ev ch over 1f out: nt qckn whn n.m.r wl ins fnl f* **16/1**

5 **5** 2 **Game Park (USA)**[58] 4070 2-9-0 0.................... AdamKirby 9 60
(J R Fanshawe) *s.i.s and n.m.r s: hdwy over 3f out: sn rdn: one pce fnl f* **10/1**

6 hd **Dharori (IRE)** 2-9-0 0.................... PhilipRobinson 1 59
(M A Jarvis) *dwlt: rdn and hdwy over 2f out: wknd over 1f out* **8/1**

7 ¾ **Tito (IRE)** 2-9-0 0.................... PhillipMakin 8 57
(T D Barron) *wnt lft s: hld up in mid-div: no hdwy fnl 2f* **33/1**

56 **8** hd **Gardes (IRE)**[20] 5222 2-9-0 0.................... RichardHughes 5 56
(Jane Chapple-Hyam) *hld up: hdwy over 2f out: nt clr run wl over 1f out: n.d after* **20/1**

00 **9** hd **Rio Sabotini**[98] 2818 2-8-11 0.................... PJMcDonald(3) 6 55
(G A Swinbank) *hld up towards rr: short-lived effrt wl over 1f out* **66/1**

10 ¾ **Horatio Carter** 2-9-0 0.................... NCallan 12 53
(K A Ryan) *wnt lft s: hld up: hdwy over 3f out: wknd over 2f out* **11/1**

040 **11** 1¾ **An Scaribh**[108] 2539 2-9-0 63.................... StephenDonohoe 10 48
(P D Evans) *a bhd* **66/1**

0 **12** 2½ **Rough Sketch (USA)**[10] 5498 2-9-0 0.................... J-PGuillambert 4 40
(Sir Mark Prescott) *hld up in tch: wkng whn n.m.r over 2f out* **100/1**

13 nk **Change Alley (USA)** 2-9-0 0.................... GregFairley 13 40
(M Johnston) *chsd ldrs: rdn over 3f out: wknd wl over 1f out* **11/1**

14 ¾ **Addwaitya** 2-9-0 0.................... IanMongan 11 37
(C F Wall) *s.i.s and hmpd s: outpcd* **50/1**

50 **15** 9 **Sir Joey**[46] 4459 2-8-9 0.................... RussellKennemore(5) 7 10
(J T Stimpson) *prom: rdn over 3f out: wknd over 2f out* **100/1**

1m 15.95s (2.06) **Going Correction** +0.20s/f (Good) **15** Ran SP% **123.2**
Speed ratings (Par 95): **94,93,91,90,88 87,86,86,86,85 82,79,79,78,66**
CSF £13.42 TOTE £2.70: £1.10, £2.10, £2.60; EX 16.00.
Owner Jack Hanson & Sir Alex Ferguson **Bred** Darley **Trained** Lambourn, Berks
■ Stewards' Enquiry : Hayley Turner one-day ban: careless riding (Oct 9); caution: used whip with excessive frequency

FOCUS
This was fractionally slower than the second division with not much previous form to go on.

NOTEBOOK
Hunt The Bottle(IRE) put his previous experience to good use and did not mind the soft ground as his pedigree suggested might be the case. (op 9-4 tchd 5-2 in places)
Barbary Boy(FR) ◆, all the better for his Sandown debut, did not help his chance by drifting left in the closing stages over this extra furlong and his rider was handed a one-day ban. He seems to be going the right way. (op 8-1 tchd 5-1)
Italian Art(IRE) ◆ is a half-brother to six- and seven-furlong winner Smash N'Grab. Making a highly satisfactory debut, normal improvement should see him off the mark. (op 6-1)
Farpedon improved on his Polytrack debut at Lingfield at the end of last month. Rather squeezed out when the second came off a true line in the closing stages, he looked held at the time but this was still a good effort.
Game Park(USA) did not have things go his way at the start and seems to be progressing along the right lines. (op 11-1 tchd 12-1)
Dharori(IRE) is a 300,000 guineas half-brother to the multiple if modest winner Inside Story. Showing signs of ability after missing the break, he should be better for the experience. (op 11-2 tchd 9-1)
An Scaribh Official explanation: jockey said colt hung left-handed throughout
Rough Sketch(USA) Official explanation: jockey said colt was denied a clear run

5772 JMC IT MAIDEN STKS (DIV II) 6f
2:45 (2:50) (Class 5) 2-Y-0 **£2,169** (£645; £322; £161) **Stalls** Centre

Form RPR

5 **1** **Exclamation**[54] 4198 2-9-0 0.................... RichardHughes 2 85+
(B J Meehan) *trckd ldr: led over 1f out: wnt bdly rt: r.o wl* **3/1**[1]

2 3½ **Corrybrough** 2-9-0 0.................... DaneO'Neill 14 74
(H Candy) *in rr: hdwy over 3f out: styd on to go 2nd ins fnl f* **9/2**[3]

0 **3** ½ **Spice Trade**[27] 5042 2-9-0 0.................... MartinDwyer 1 73
(J Noseda) *in rr: hdwy over 2f out: kpt on steadily fnl f* **6/1**

20 **4** 1½ **Effingham (IRE)**[51] 4286 2-9-0 0.................... MichaelHills 7 68
(B W Hills) *in tch: sn pushed along: kpt on fnl 2f: nvr a threat* **4/1**[2]

5 1¾ **Peter's Storm (USA)** 2-9-0 0.................... NCallan 13 63
(K A Ryan) *chsd ldrs: outpcd over 2f out: kpt on fnl f* **16/1**

46 **6** 2½ **Gain Share**[116] 2297 2-9-0 0.................... PaulFessey 11 55
(T D Barron) *led tl over 1f out: hung lft and sn wknd* **40/1**

20 **7** 4 **Bahamian Lad**[21] 5194 2-8-9 0.................... RussellKennemore(5) 6 43
(R Hollinshead) *chsd ldrs: wknd over 1f out* **7/1**

00 **8** 3½ **Cross Fell (USA)**[93] 2991 2-9-0 0.................... GregFairley 12 33
(M Johnston) *chsd ldrs: hung lft and wknd over 2f out* **18/1**

0 **9** ½ **Patthepainter (GER)**[37] 4725 2-8-7 0.................... DeclanCannon(7) 10 31
(K R Burke) *mid-div: lost pl over 3f out* **16/1**

10 2½ **Feeling Lucky (IRE)** 2-9-0 0.................... SebSanders 9 24
(W Jarvis) *a towards rr* **9/1**

00 **11** 7 **Captain Turbot (IRE)**[19] 5252 2-9-0 0.................... TonyHamilton 4 —
(D W Barker) *in rr: bhd fnl 2f* **100/1**

12 shd **Emerald Toffee (IRE)** 2-9-0 0.................... MickyFenton 5 —
(J T Stimpson) *dwlt: a bhd: hung lft fnl 2f* **100/1**

0 **13** 2 **Charlie Oxo**[21] 5192 2-9-0 0.................... TGMcLaughlin 8 —
(B P J Baugh) *dwlt: a bhd* **200/1**

1m 15.82s (1.93) **Going Correction** +0.20s/f (Good) **58** Ran SP% **121.9**
Speed ratings (Par 95): **95,90,89,87,85 82,76,72,71,68 58,58,55**
CSF £16.64 TOTE £4.10: £1.70, £2.40, £2.10; EX 21.10.
Owner Raymond Tooth **Bred** Exors Of The Late Seymour Cohn **Trained** Manton, Wilts

FOCUS
A fair maiden and improvement likely from both the placed horses.

NOTEBOOK
Exclamation, a decent sort, travelled strongly. He veered across the track once in front but kept going well and is clearly useful. (tchd 7-2)

Corrybrough ◆, a grand type, showed his inexperience in the preliminaries. Taking time to pick up, he took second spot inside the last and should improve a fair bit in time. (tchd 5-1)
Spice Trade, happy to amble along in the rear, put in some pleasing late work. He needs another outing to qualify for a handicap mark but looks sure to make his mark in the longer term. (tchd 13-2)
Effingham(IRE), who walks stiff on his near hind, was soon being pushed along in pursuit of the leaders and never threatened to take a real hand. (op 7-2, tchd 9-2 in a place)
Peter's Storm(USA), who stands over plenty of ground, was very inexperienced beforehand. He stuck on after getting tapped for toe and should do a fair bit better in time.
Gain Share, gelded since Carlisle, showed bags of toe to take them along but he still does not look the most straightforward of individuals. This does, however, open up the nursery route for him. (tchd 50-1)

5773 VALE UK NURSERY — 6f
3:20 (3:21) (Class 4) (0-85,84) 2-Y-O — **£4,857** (£1,445; £722; £360) **Stalls** Centre

Form — RPR
0230 **1** — **Westwood**[35] 4755 2-9-2 **79** ... RobertHavlin 5 — 87
(D Haydn Jones) *mde all: rdn over 1f out: r.o wl* **12/1**
6566 **2** 4 **Eager Diva (USA)**[17] 5294 2-8-9 **72** ... NCallan 1 — 68
(K A Ryan) *a.p: chsd wnr over 2f out: rdn over 1f out: no imp fnl f* **10/1**
5103 **3** 3 **Regal Rhythm (IRE)**[35] 4762 2-9-5 **82** ... RichardHughes 7 — 69
(B J Meehan) *racd keenly in tch: rdn and hung lft over 1f out: wknd fnl f* **3/1**[2]
0306 **4** 1 ½ **Legendary Guest**[13] 5400 2-9-1 **78** ... ChrisCatlin 4 — 61
(M R Channon) *mid-div: rdn and sme hdwy over 2f out: edgd rt wl over 1f out: no further prog* **12/1**
0022 **5** ¾ **Silver Wind**[6] 5629 2-9-7 **84** ... (b) StephenDonohoe 8 — 64
(P D Evans) *nvr trbld ldrs* **11/4**[1]
1024 **6** 1 ½ **Artsu**[28] 4995 2-9-5 **82** ... HayleyTurner 10 — 58
(M L W Bell) *hld up in mid-div: swtchd lft wl over 1f out: sn rdn: no rspnse* **4/1**[3]
16 **7** 1 **Danzig Fox**[8] 5551 2-9-1 **78** ... DaneO'Neill 6 — 51
(M Mullineaux) *a bhd* **25/1**
3201 **8** 7 **Our Acquaintance**[22] 5176 2-9-3 **80** ... RichardMullen 2 — 32
(W R Muir) *hd down whn stalls opened and s.s: hdwy over 2f out: wknd over 1f out* **17/2**
0330 **9** 3 **Cordon Bleu (IRE)**[17] 5314 2-8-4 **67** ... GregFairley 9 — 10
(M Johnston) *w wnr: rdn and hung lft 3f out: sn wknd* **12/1**

1m 15.53s (1.64) **Going Correction** +0.20s/f (Good) — **9** Ran SP% **118.2**
Speed ratings (Par 97): **97,91,87,85,84 82,81,72,68**
CSF £127.48 CT £460.42 TOTE £14.40: £3.40, £3.20, £1.80; EX 118.00.
Owner Merry Llewelyn And Runeckles **Bred** D Llewelyn & J Runeckles **Trained** Efail Isaf, Rhondda C Taff

FOCUS
This ordinary nursery did not prove to be as competitive as expected.
NOTEBOOK
Westwood appreciated the give in the ground and put a disappointing display last time behind him by turning the race into a bit of a procession. Official explanation: trainer's rep said, regarding apparent improvement in form, that the gelding was suited by the softer ground
Eager Diva(USA) was clearly second best on this first run on soft ground after probably failing to stay the extended mile at Beverley last time. (op 11-1)
Regal Rhythm(IRE), raised 2lb after his good second at Newbury, again raced rather freely and, after hanging left, failed to get home in the softer ground. (op 9-2)
Legendary Guest was back down to six for his first run with give underfoot. (op 16-1)
Silver Wind, set to go up 3lb in the future, was disappointing having already run well on ground more testing than this. Official explanation: jockey said colt never travelled (tchd 7-2)
Artsu ran a lacklustre race with the going apparently in his favour. (op 3-1 tchd 11-4)
Our Acquaintance Official explanation: jockey said colt mised the break

5774 VALE UK (S) STKS — 1m 2f 120y
3:55 (3:56) (Class 4) 3-4-Y-O — **£5,505** (£1,637; £818; £408) **Stalls** High

Form — RPR
4-30 **1** — **Hall Of Fame**[11] 5472 3-8-11 72 ... VinceSlattery 3 — 67
(C J Mann) *in rr: drvn over 6f out: hdwy on outer over 1f out: styd on to ld nr fin* **33/1**
2402 **2** ½ **Can Can Star**[13] 5432 4-9-8 74 ... SebSanders 8 — 70
(A W Carroll) *hld up in rr: hdwy on ins and nt clr run over 2f out: wnt 2nd over 1f out: led ins fnl f: hdd nr fin* **5/1**
0104 **3** hd **Grethel (IRE)**[8] 5555 3-8-3 56 ... DanielleMcCreery(7) 4 — 65
(A Berry) *t.k.h in midfield: effrt on outer over 3f out: hit on hd by anther rdr's whip over 1f out: kpt on wl ins fnl f* **25/1**
0623 **4** 1 ½ **Sienna Storm (IRE)**[11] 5479 4-9-4 73 ... (b) NCallan 2 — 63
(M H Tompkins) *sn trcking ldrs: led 2f out: wandered and hdd ins fnl f* **3/1**[2]
0312 **5** 1 ¾ **Brastar Jelois (FR)**[8] 5553 4-8-12 59 ... (p) RussellKennemore(5) 1 — 58
(R Hollinshead) *mid-div: hdwy 3f out: kpt on: nvr trbld ldrs* **9/1**
3-05 **6** 9 **Sea Cookie**[34] 4828 3-8-6 48 ... FrankieMcDonald 9 — 37
(W De Best-Turner) *in rr-div: nvr on terms* **100/1**
3300 **7** 1 **Still Dreaming**[48] 4391 3-8-7 60 ow1 ... (b[1]) TomEaves 10 — 36
(M Dods) *trckd ldrs: led over 2f out: sn hdd: lost pl over 1f out* **20/1**
6000 **8** hd **Ful Of Grace (IRE)**[34] 4821 3-8-8 50 ow5 ... JamieMoriarty(3) 12 — 40
(M G Quinlan) *mid-div: rdn over 4f out: sn btn* **40/1**
-435 **9** 1 **Telegonus**[24] 3076 4-9-1 68 ... (b) PJMcDonald(3) 7 — 38
(D McCain Jnr) *chsd ldrs: lost pl over 2f out* **25/1**
0025 **10** ¾ **Old Romney**[28] 4993 3-8-11 78 ... MartinDwyer 6 — 37
(N A Callaghan) *t.k.h: trckd ldrs: wknd 2f out* **9/4**[1]
0622 **11** 13 **Tufton**[11] 5472 4-9-4 77 ... (t) RichardHughes 11 — 12
(Ian Williams) *led tl hdd over 2f out: hung rt lost pl over 1f out: heavily eased* **4/1**[3]

2m 21.38s (5.24) **Going Correction** +0.40s/f (Good)
WFA 3 from 4yo 7lb — **11** Ran SP% **121.3**
Speed ratings (Par 105): **96,95,95,94,93 86,85,85,84,84 74**
CSF £186.46 TOTE £47.40: £6.80, £1.90, £4.10; EX 434.90.There was no bid for the winner.
Owner Colin Gordon And Terry Moyise **Bred** Darley **Trained** Upper Lambourn, Berks

FOCUS
A fair seller but the form held down by the proximity of the lowly-rated third and fifth.
Old Romney Official explanation: trainer had no explanation for the poor form shown
Tufton Official explanation: jockey said colt hung right-handed final 2f

5775 VALE UK H'CAP — 1m 2f 120y
4:30 (4:30) (Class 4) (0-85,82) 3-Y-O+ — **£5,181** (£1,541; £770; £384) **Stalls** High

Form — RPR
6002 **1** — **Best Prospect (IRE)**[8] 5554 5-9-11 **82** ... (t) JamieSpencer 7 — 91+
(M Dods) *hld up and bhd: stdy hdwy over 2f out: rdn over 1f out: led ins fnl f: r.o* **6/5**[1]
0056 **2** 1 **Folio (IRE)**[15] 5362 7-9-9 **80** ... PhilipRobinson 2 — 85
(W J Musson) *a.p: rdn to ld 1f out: hdd ins fnl f: nt qckn* **9/1**
3110 **3** nk **Suits Me**[17] 5296 4-9-5 **76** ... MickyFenton 6 — 80
(T P Tate) *led: hdd 1f out: nt qckn ins fnl f* **9/2**[2]
0033 **4** hd **Stravara**[40] 4631 4-8-6 **68** oh9 ... RussellKennemore(5) 4 — 72?
(R Hollinshead) *stdd s: t.k.h in rr: rdn over 1f out: styd on wl fnl f: nvr nrr* **25/1**
036 **5** 2 **Aegean Prince**[25] 5099 3-9-2 **80** ... (p) RichardMullen 1 — 81
(W R Muir) *hld up and bhd: rdn 2f out: swtchd rt ins fnl f: r.o* **14/1**
0S55 **6** hd **Isidore Bonheur (IRE)**[30] 4932 6-9-8 **79** ... NCallan 3 — 79
(G A Swinbank) *hld up in tch: rdn over 2f out: wknd over 1f out* **7/1**[3]
2342 **7** 2 ½ **Flighty Fellow (IRE)**[21] 5196 7-9-8 **79** ... (b) DavidAllan 8 — 75
(T D Easterby) *prom: rdn and ev ch over 1f out: wknd fnl f* **7/1**[3]
000 **8** 2 **Blue Spinnaker (IRE)**[16] 5327 8-9-0 **78** ... NSLawes(7) 5 — 70
(M W Easterby) *hld up in tch: rdn over 2f out: sn wknd* **14/1**

2m 21.68s (5.54) **Going Correction** +0.40s/f (Good)
WFA 3 from 4yo+ 7lb — **8** Ran SP% **115.8**
Speed ratings (Par 105): **95,94,94,93,92 92,90,89**
CSF £13.42 CT £38.31 TOTE £2.00: £1.20, £2.70, £1.60; EX 11.20.
Owner D Neale **Bred** Farmers Hill Stud **Trained** Denton, Co Durham

FOCUS
A very moderate winning time for a race of its class, 0.3 seconds slower than the seller.

5776 GRIFFITHS & ARMOUR H'CAP — 1m 30y
5:05 (5:05) (Class 3) (0-90,88) 3-Y-O+
£9,348 (£2,799; £1,399; £700; £349; £175) **Stalls** Low

Form — RPR
1260 **1** — **Zaahid (IRE)**[42] 4566 3-9-1 **85** ... MartinDwyer 13 — 99+
(B W Hills) *swtchd lft sfater s: hld up: nt clr run over 2f out tl swtchd outside over 1f out: fin strly to ld last stride* **8/1**
3621 **2** hd **Observatory Star (IRE)**[34] 4820 4-8-8 **74** oh1 ... (p) DavidAllan 12 — 83
(T D Easterby) *hld up towards rr: gd hdwy on outside over 1f out: hung lft and led ins fnl f: hdd post* **8/1**
4055 **3** 1 ¼ **Nevada Desert (IRE)**[6] 5615 7-9-3 **86** ... MichaelJStainton(3) 9 — 92
(R M Whitaker) *chsd ldrs: edgd lft kpt on same pce fnl f* **20/1**
5623 **4** nk **Osteopathic Remedy (IRE)**[7] 5585 3-8-11 **81** ... TomEaves 4 — 86
(M Dods) *t.k.h: trckd ldr: led 3f out tl ins fnl f: n.m.r and no ex* **10/1**
4366 **5** 1 **Full Victory (IRE)**[59] 4049 5-9-1 **81** ... DaneO'Neill 11 — 84
(R A Farrant) *trckd ldrs: t.k.h: effrt on outer over 2f out: kpt on same pce* **12/1**
2210 **6** hd **Blue Monkey (IRE)**[44] 4502 3-8-6 **81** ... LukeMorris(5) 6 — 84
(M L W Bell) *sn chsng ldrs: kpt on same pce fnl 2f* **11/1**
2404 **7** 1 ¼ **Wheels In Motion (IRE)**[21] 5196 3-8-4 **74** ... RichardMullen 10 — 74
(T P Tate) *sn prom: effrt over 2f out: kpt on same pce* **11/1**
3001 **8** 1 **St Andrews (IRE)**[34] 4827 7-9-8 **88** ... PhilipRobinson 8 — 85
(M A Jarvis) *in rr-div: effrt on inner 3f out: sn chsng ldrs: keeping on same pce whn n.m.r ins fnl f* **7/2**[1]
3350 **9** 7 **Granston (IRE)**[20] 5221 6-9-4 **84** ... JamieSpencer 1 — 72
(J D Bethell) *trckd ldrs: chal on inner over 2f out: wknd and eased over 1f out* **6/1**[2]
4100 **10** 1 ¾ **Medici Pearl**[40] 4640 3-8-4 **77** ... DuranFentiman(3) 5 — 54
(T D Easterby) *s.i.s: hdwy on ins over 3f out: lost pl over 2f out* **50/1**
0 **11** 2 **Fan Club**[15] 5355 3-8-5 **82** ... DanielleMcCreery(7) 7 — 55
(D W Chapman) *hld up in mid-div: lost pl over 2f out* **100/1**
4600 **12** ¾ **Kamanda Laugh**[42] 4566 6-9-1 **81** ... NCallan 2 — 52
(K A Ryan) *led tl 3f out: lost pl over 1f out* **12/1**
5315 **13** ½ **Paceman (USA)**[69] 3745 3-9-3 **87** ... RichardHughes 3 — 57
(R Hannon) *trckd ldrs: lost pl over 1f out: lame* **7/1**[3]

1m 47.28s (1.77) **Going Correction** +0.40s/f (Good)
WFA 3 from 4yo+ 4lb — **13** Ran SP% **120.1**
Speed ratings (Par 107): **107,106,105,105,104 104,102,101,94,93 91,90,89**
CSF £70.18 CT £854.24 TOTE £9.90: £3.80, £3.30, £7.20; EX 109.80.
Owner Hamdan Al Maktoum **Bred** Shadwell Estate Company Limited **Trained** Lambourn, Berks
■ Stewards' Enquiry : Michael J Stainton caution: careless riding

FOCUS
Solid form. The first two showed improved form, the third and fourth ran to their pre-race marks.
NOTEBOOK
Zaahid(IRE) ◆, a grand stamp of individual, would have been a most unlucky loser. Worst drawn, he was switched inside at the start and saw no daylight at all from halfway up the straight. Pulled wide coming to the final furlong, he flew to lead right on the line and, in this mood, he can surely find further success. (op 11-1)
Observatory Star(IRE), drawn one off the outside, came flying through to show ahead inside the last. Once in front he hung left and was mugged on the line.
Nevada Desert(IRE), making a quick return, ran right up to his best on ground that suits. He is all heart. (op 16-1)
Osteopathic Remedy(IRE), 3lb higher, would not settle. After taking charge he was edged out in the closing stages. (op 12-1)
Full Victory(IRE), 2lb lower after a two-month break, ran well on ground that he likes. (op 14-1)
Blue Monkey(IRE), 5lb higher than his last win, was returning after a six-week break and bounced back on the type of ground he loves. (op 14-1)
Wheels In Motion(IRE) is learning to settle better and ran with credit. (op 10-1)
St Andrews(IRE), 3lb higher, had the ground he likes but he was going nowhere when tightened up inside the last. (op 10-3 tchd 4-1 in places)
Paceman(USA) Official explanation: trainer's rep said colt finished lame

5777 BRAND NEW ST.HELENS H'CAP — 1m 3f 200y
5:35 (5:35) (Class 5) (0-75,75) 3-Y-O+ — **£2,817** (£838; £418; £209) **Stalls** High

Form — RPR
4426 **1** — **Mae Cigan (FR)**[9] 5531 4-8-12 **58** ... FrancisNorton 13 — 69
(M Blanshard) *hld up towards rr: rdn and hdwy over 2f out: swtchd rt over 1f out: r.o u.p to ld last strides* **6/1**
4311 **2** hd **Rudry World (IRE)**[37] 4717 4-9-1 **68** ... SophieDoyle(7) 12 — 78+
(M Mullineaux) *hld up and bhd: smooth hdwy on outside over 2f out: rdn to ld wl ins fnl f: hdd last strides* **3/1**[2]
4023 **3** nk **Art Professor (IRE)**[28] 5018 3-8-12 **66** ... SebSanders 3 — 76
(J W Hills) *chsd ldr: rdn to ld over 3f out: sn hdd: led over 2f out tl wl ins fnl f: kpt on* **11/2**[3]
031 **4** 1 **The Flying Cowboy (IRE)**[39] 4660 3-8-12 **66** ... TGMcLaughlin 8 — 74
(Jane Chapple-Hyam) *hld up in mid-div: hdwy over 3f out: hrd rdn and ev ch ins fnl f: nt qckn* **11/4**[1]
5324 **5** 1 ¼ **Pretty Demanding (IRE)**[21] 5211 3-9-4 **75** ... JamieMoriarty(3) 4 — 81
(M G Quinlan) *hld up in mid-div: rdn and hdwy on ins 2f out: one pce fnl f* **8/1**
3340 **6** 5 **Topflight Wildbird**[37] 4717 4-8-12 **58** oh2 ... TomEaves 2 — 56
(Mrs G S Rees) *hld up in tch: rdn over 3f out: wknd over 1f out* **16/1**

0104 **7** *8* **Distiller (IRE)**[13] 5405 3-9-3 **71** RichardMullen 11 57
(W R Muir) *nvr nr ldrs* **33/1**

3015 **8** *1* **Bronze Dancer (IRE)**[107] 2567 5-9-12 **72** NCallan 7 56
(G A Swinbank) *hld up towards rr: rdn and hdwy over 2f out: swtchd rt over 1f out: wknd fnl f* **16/1**

560 **9** *shd* **Covert Mission**[14] 5384 4-8-13 **59** StephenDonohoe 14 43
(P D Evans) *prom: led over 3f out: rdn and hdd over 2f out: wknd over 1f out* **20/1**

0350 **10** *5* **Fossgate**[16] 5334 6-9-4 **67** PJMcDonald(3) 9 43
(J D Bethell) *hld up in tch: rdn 4f out: wknd 3f out* **12/1**

6253 **11** *5* **Delta Shuttle (IRE)**[90] 3081 3-8-7 **61** DaleGibson 5 29
(K R Burke) *prom tl wknd over 3f out* **33/1**

6166 **12** *24* **King's Ransom**[23] 5144 4-9-10 **70** MartinDwyer 6 —
(S Gollings) *t.k.h: led: rdn and hdd over 3f out: wknd over 2f out: sn eased* **33/1**

2m 39.63s (4.64) **Going Correction** +0.40s/f (Good)
WFA 3 from 4yo+ 8lb 12 Ran SP% **125.5**
Speed ratings (Par 103): **100,99,99,99,98 94,89,88,88,85 82,66**
CSF £24.91 CT £107.59 TOTE £7.70: £2.20, £1.70, £2.30; EX 26.90 Place 6 £79.23, Place 5 £65.31.
Owner A D Jones **Bred** J Jay **Trained** Upper Lambourn, Berks
■ Stewards' Enquiry : T G McLaughlin two-day ban: used whip with excessive frequency (Oct 9-10)
Seb Sanders caution: used whip with excessive frequency

FOCUS
A modest handicap but the form looks solid with the first five finishing clear.
King's Ransom Official explanation: jockey said gelding ran too free early stages
T/Plt: £79.80 to a £1 stake. Pool: £54,397.85. 497.45 winning tickets. T/Qpdt: £71.30 to a £1 stake. Pool: £3,084.30. 32.00 winning tickets. KH

5751 WOLVERHAMPTON (A.W) (L-H)
Friday, September 28

OFFICIAL GOING: Standard
Wind: Light against Weather: Overcast

5778 LADBROKES THE HOME OF FOOTBALL BETTING H'CAP 5f 216y(P)
7:00 (7:01) (Class 6) (0-55,57) 3-Y-0+ **£2,388** (£705; £352) **Stalls** Low

Form RPR

0022 **1** **Kindallachan**[13] 5425 4-9-4 **54** SebSanders 6 64
(G C Bravery) *chsd ldrs: rdn and nt clr run over 1f out: r.o u.p to ld nr fin* **7/1**

4403 **2** *1/2* **Boreana**[14] 5391 4-9-1 **54** TravisBlock(3) 10 62
(Jedd O'Keeffe) *chsd ldrs: led over 2f out: sn rdn and edgd lft: hdd nr fin* **6/1[3]**

3330 **3** *shd* **Mistral Sky**[28] 5016 8-9-5 **55** (p) MickyFenton 8 63
(Stef Liddiard) *chsd ldr: rdn and ev ch over 2f out: r.o* **8/1**

0506 **4** *1* **Bond Playboy**[28] 5016 7-9-4 **54** (v) JamieSpencer 5 59
(G R Oldroyd) *s.s: hld up: hdwy u.p over 1f out: nt rch ldrs* **4/1[1]**

2500 **5** *nk* **Lady Lafitte (USA)**[65] 3853 3-9-3 **55** AdamKirby 9 59
(M Wellings) *sn pushed along in rr: hdwy and edgd lft over 2f out: rdn over 1f out: r.o* **50/1**

2441 **6** *nk* **Willofcourse**[13] 5425 6-8-12 **55** AmyScott(7) 12 58
(H Candy) *hld up: hdwy whn hit over hd by rivals whip over 1f out: edgd lft: nt rch ldrs* **5/1[2]**

000 **7** *2* **Victory Spirit**[31] 4919 3-9-3 **55** (b) DaneO'Neill 13 52
(H J L Dunlop) *prom: rdn over 1f out: no ex fnl f* **50/1**

5000 **8** *nk* **Gone'N'Dunnett (IRE)**[3] 5711 8-8-11 **52** (v) KirstyMilczarek(5) 7 48
(Mrs C A Dunnett) *prom: racd keenly: rdn over 1f out: styd on same pce* **20/1**

-024 **9** *1* **Berti Bertolini**[80] 3408 4-9-5 **55** ChrisCatlin 1 48
(Rae Guest) *mid-div: lost pl 4f out: nt clr run 1/2-way: n.d after* **15/2**

3144 **10** *1* **Kennington**[8] 5576 7-9-5 **55** DMylonas 3 45
(Mrs C A Dunnett) *chsd ldrs: hmpd over 2f out: wknd over 1f out* **17/2**

554/ **11** *2* **Cost Analysis (IRE)**[331] 6560 5-8-12 **53** HaddenFrost(5) 4 37
(Mrs P Ford) *led: rdn and hdd over 2f out: wknd fnl f* **28/1**

3251 **12** *1* **Dasheena**[6] 5627 4-9-0 **57** 6ex (be) RobbieEgan(7) 11 38
(A J McCabe) *s.s: outpcd* **8/1**

1m 14.78s (-1.03) **Going Correction** -0.20s/f (Stan)
WFA 3 from 4yo+ 2lb 12 Ran SP% **120.1**
Speed ratings (Par 101): **98,97,97,95,95 95,92,92,90,89 86,85**
CSF £47.71 CT £348.00 TOTE £10.50: £2.60, £3.30, £4.20; EX 59.40.
Owner Herts And Hinds Racing Syndicate **Bred** F D Harvey **Trained** Newmarket, Suffolk

FOCUS
A moderate but competitive sprint handicap. The form looks sound.
Bond Playboy Official explanation: jockey said gelding missed the break
Lady Lafitte(USA) Official explanation: jockey said filly hung both ways
Kennington Official explanation: jockey said gelding hung right from halfway

5779 LADBROKES IN WOLVERHAMPTON H'CAP 1m 5f 194y(P)
7:30 (7:30) (Class 5) (0-75,71) 3-Y-0+ **£3,071** (£906; £453) **Stalls** Low

Form RPR

4031 **1** **Bold Adventure**[9] 5533 3-7-13 **52** 6ex AdrianMcCarthy 12 69+
(W J Musson) *hld up: hdwy over 2f out: edgd lft fnl f: shkn up to ld post: comf* **6/1[2]**

1145 **2** *hd* **Champagne Shadow (IRE)**[31] 4915 6-10-0 **71** (p) ChrisCatlin 1 83
(Miss Tor Sturgis) *chsd ldrs: pushed along over 4f out: rdn to ld and edgd lft ins fnl f: hdd post* **14/1**

0611 **3** *1 1/2* **Double Banded (IRE)**[11] 5486 3-8-10 **63** 6ex KerrinMcEvoy 7 73
(J L Dunlop) *dwlt: sn prom: led over 1f out: rdn and hdd ins fnl f: no ex* **11/8[1]**

05-0 **4** *4* **Play Master (IRE)**[12] 4878 6-9-1 **58** RichardThomas 13 62
(C Roberts) *hld up: hdwy over 4f out: rdn and ev ch over 1f out: styd on same pce* **66/1**

4110 **5** *nk* **Mighty Kitchener (USA)**[18] 5283 4-9-9 **66** IanMongan 3 70
(P Howling) *hld up: nt clr run over 2f out: hdwy over 1f out: sn rdn: wknd ins fnl f* **9/1**

6101 **6** *1* **Adage**[15] 5364 4-9-2 **62** (t) NeilChalmers(3) 9 64
(David Pinder) *hld up: hdwy over 3f out: nt clr run over 1f out: styd on same pce* **14/1**

2424 **7** *3* **Red Wine**[10] 5500 8-9-5 **62** SebSanders 8 60
(A J McCabe) *hld up: hdwy over 2f out: rdn and nt clr run over 1f out: sn wknd* **15/2**

6236 **8** *3* **Ha'Penny Beacon**[6] 5647 4-9-5 **62** (v) AdamKirby 6 56
(D Carroll) *chsd ldrs: rdn over 3f out: wknd over 1f out* **20/1**

2345 **9** *nk* **Louviere**[16] 5333 3-9-3 **70** (v[1]) RichardHughes 5 63
(Pat Eddery) *trckd ldr: rdn to ld 2f out: sn hdd & wknd* **12/1**

/00- **10** *12* **Moonshine Beach**[473] 2501 9-9-6 **70** WilliamCarson(7) 2 47
(P W Hiatt) *led: rdn and hdd 2f out: wknd over 1f out* **100/1**

3 **11** *14* **The Chip Chopman (IRE)**[31] 4114 5-9-13 **70** (t) JamieSpencer 11 27
(Seamus G O'Donnell, Ire) *hld up: rdn over 4f out: wknd over 2f out* **7/1[3]**

/00- **12** *27* **Picot De Say**[176] 3270 5-8-11 **54** HayleyTurner 10 —
(C Roberts) *hld up: wknd over 3f out* **100/1**

3m 3.66s (-3.71) **Going Correction** -0.20s/f (Stan)
WFA 3 from 4yo+ 10lb 12 Ran SP% **119.9**
Speed ratings (Par 103): **102,101,101,98,98 98,96,94,94,87 79,64**
CSF £85.89 CT £180.67 TOTE £7.60: £1.50, £6.00, £1.60; EX 171.40.
Owner Mustard Cord Cads **Bred** Bricklow Ltd **Trained** Newmarket, Suffolk
■ Stewards' Enquiry : Chris Catlin two-day ban: used whip with excessive force (Oct 10-11)

FOCUS
Just a modest staying handicap, but a few of these came into this in good order and the form looks reasonable for the level. The winner is value for a bit extra. The pace was just ordinary.
Ha'Penny Beacon Official explanation: jockey said filly became unbalanced
The Chip Chopman(IRE) Official explanation: jockey said gelding never travelled
Picot De Say Official explanation: jockey said gelding had no more to give

5780 LADBROKES SERIOUS ABOUT SERVICE MAIDEN STKS 7f 32y(P)
7:55 (7:56) (Class 5) 2-Y-0 **£2,968** (£876; £438) **Stalls** High

Form RPR

1 **Pearl Dealer (IRE)** 2-9-3 0 KerrinMcEvoy 10 78
(Saeed Bin Suroor) *hld up in tch: rdn and hung lft ins fnl f: r.o to ld nr fin* **7/1[3]**

2 *nk* **James Dean (IRE)** 2-9-3 0 TQuinn 2 77
(P F I Cole) *s.i.s: sn chsng ldr: led over 1f out: rdn and hdd nr fin* **20/1**

2 **3** *nk* **Bullet Man (USA)**[25] 5088 2-9-3 0 JamieSpencer 3 76
(L M Cumani) *s.i.s: sn prom: rdn over 1f out: r.o* **10/11[1]**

03 **4** *2* **Dr Livingstone (IRE)**[28] 5010 2-9-3 0 SteveDrowne 5 71
(C R Egerton) *led: rdn and hdd over 1f out: edgd rt and no ex ins fnl f* **10/3[2]**

030 **5** *1/2* **Spic 'n Span**[12] 5448 2-9-3 0 SimonWhitworth 9 70
(C A Cyzer) *trckd ldrs: rdn over 1f out: no ex fnl f* **25/1**

6 *2 1/2* **Marino Prince (FR)** 2-8-10 0 JackDean(7) 6 64
(W G M Turner) *s.i.s: rdn 1/2-way: hung lft and styd on ins fnl f: nvr trbld ldrs* **100/1**

7 *1* **Mission Control (IRE)** 2-9-3 0 J-PGuillambert 12 61
(M Johnston) *s.s: outpcd: rdn over 4f out: styd on fnl f: nrst fin* **9/1**

0 **8** *1 1/4* **General Ting (IRE)**[10] 5498 2-9-3 0 SebSanders 7 58
(Sir Mark Prescott) *s.i.s: hld up: effrt over 2f out: sn outpcd* **33/1**

35 **9** *2* **Jaconet (USA)**[41] 4611 2-8-12 0 PhillipMakin 4 48
(T D Barron) *chsd ldrs: rdn over 2f out: sn wknd* **16/1**

10 *3/4* **Run From Nun** 2-8-12 0 RichardSmith 8 46
(J A Osborne) *s.i.s: rdn 1/2-way: wknd over 2f out* **66/1**

1m 30.31s (-0.09) **Going Correction** -0.20s/f (Stan) 10 Ran SP% **117.9**
Speed ratings (Par 95): **92,91,91,89,88 85,84,83,80,79**
CSF £133.98 TOTE £10.40: £2.20, £4.40, £1.10; EX 91.30.
Owner Godolphin **Bred** Hadi Al Tajir **Trained** Newmarket, Suffolk

FOCUS
This looked like a decent maiden for the track, with some big stables represented.

NOTEBOOK
Pearl Dealer(IRE), a son of Marju, first foal of a 7f three-year-old winner, overcame greenness to make a winning debut. He drifted to his left when produced with challenge in the straight, but kept responding to pressure and got on top close home. He is not the biggest, but he displayed a likeable attitude and should stay further. (op 8-1 tchd 17-2)
James Dean(IRE), 47,000euros son of Clodovil, half-brother to 1m2f winner Zain, out of a mare who was placed over 5f at two, knew his job and made a pleasing debut. Having shown up well for much of the way, he kept on for pressure in the straight, but was eventually just reeled in. He looks well up to winning a similar event on the sand. (op 10-1)
Bullet Man(USA) did not really build on the form he showed when running second on his debut on the turf at Lingfield. He took an age to pick up in the straight and, on this evidence, he may be happier back on turf. (op Evens tchd 5-6)
Dr Livingstone(IRE) was given some big-race entries earlier in the season and had shown ability on both his previous starts at Sandown, including when third in a decent contest there last time. He failed to show any progression, but this was still not a bad run and he will have more options now he is qualified for a handicap mark. (op 3-1 tchd 9-2)
Spic 'n Span ◆ showed up well for much of the way, but he seemed to race a little freely and could not sustain his effort. He will be of interest when dropped in trip.
Mission Control(IRE) ◆, a Dubai Destination colt, half-brother to smart 6f juvenile Leicester Square, who was later useful over 1m, out of a useful 1m1f-1m4f winner at two and three in France, was never seen with a chance after missing the break. He was under strong pressure some way out, but he gradually got the hang of things and came home well, giving the distinct impression he will be all the better for this experience. (op 10-1 tchd 17-2)

5781 LADBROKES YOUR BEST BET MEDIAN AUCTION MAIDEN STKS 7f 32y(P)
8:25 (8:26) (Class 6) 3-5-Y-0 **£2,388** (£705; £352) **Stalls** High

Form RPR

3-00 **1** **Four Tel**[90] 3079 3-9-3 59 SamHitchcott 5 68
(N J Vaughan) *mde all: rdn clr over 1f out: styd on wl* **25/1[3]**

0060 **2** *3 1/2* **Blue Bird's Dream**[20] 5237 4-9-6 53 GrahamGibbons 6 59
(E J Alston) *chsd wnr: rdn over 2f out: styd on same pce appr fnl f* **50/1**

0-54 **3** *nk* **Far Seeking**[23] 5129 3-9-3 69 RichardHughes 2 58
(Mrs A J Perrett) *trckd ldrs: rdn over 2f out: styd on same pce appr fnl f* **6/1[2]**

2050 **4** *shd* **Just Oscar (GER)**[16] 5330 3-9-3 59 (v[1]) DavidAllan 10 58
(W M Brisbourne) *hld up: hdwy u.p and hung lft fr over 1f out: nrst fin* **28/1**

400 **5** *2* **Johnston's Glory (IRE)**[20] 5231 3-8-12 50 MickyFenton 1 48
(E J Alston) *s.i.s: hld up: rdn 1/2-way: hdwy over 2f out: hung lft over 1f out: no imp* **40/1**

40 **6** *3* **Tumbleweed Di**[18] 5282 3-8-8 0 ow1 SladeO'Hara(5) 4 40
(G R Oldroyd) *chsd ldrs: rdn over 2f out: wknd over 1f out* **80/1**

2-32 **7** *1 1/4* **Gemology (USA)**[14] 5390 3-9-3 77 KerrinMcEvoy 11 41
(Saeed Bin Suroor) *trckd ldrs: racd keenly: rdn: hung lft and wknd over 1f out* **1/5[1]**

0-4 **8** *22* **Artistic Liason**[45] 4470 3-8-13 0 ow1 IanMongan 8 —
(G C H Chung) *sn pushed along in rr: lost tch fnl 3f* **100/1**

40 **9** *1/2* **Champagne Mindy**[25] 5082 3-8-9 0 NeilChalmers(3) 9 —
(Garry Moss) *s.i.s: hdwy over 5f out: wknd 1/2-way* **200/1**

10 25 **Indared** 3-9-3 0 ChrisCatlin 7 —
(M Mullineaux) *s.s: outpcd* **100/1**

1m 29.15s (-1.25) **Going Correction** -0.20s/f (Stan)
WFA 3 from 4yo 3lb 10 Ran SP% **113.0**
Speed ratings (Par 101): **99,95,94,94,92 88,87,62,61,33**
CSF £696.74 TOTE £29.30: £9.00, £33.00, £1.50; EX 636.40.
Owner Owen Promotions Limited **Bred** Owen Promotions Ltd **Trained** Malpas, Cheshire

FOCUS
An uncompetitive maiden, but a real turn up with the odds-on favourite, Gemology, finishing out of the frame. Shaky form, the fourth perhaps the best guide.
Gemology(USA) Official explanation: jockey said colt lost its action

5782 WOLVERHAMPTON-RACECOURSE.CO.UK CLASSIFIED STKS 1m 141y(P)
8:55 (8:55) (Class 7) 3-Y-O+ £1,911 (£564; £282) Stalls Low

Form RPR
4603 1 **Justcallmehandsome**[7] 5606 5-8-10 45 (v) SophieDoyle(7) 10 58
(D J S Ffrench Davis) *hld up: hdwy over 5f out: led over 2f out: clr fnl f* **8/1**
3006 2 3½ **Lightning Queen (USA)**[43] 4531 3-8-12 45 JamieSpencer 13 50
(B W Hills) *s.i.s: hld up: hdwy over 2f out: sn rdn: hung lft ins fnl f: nt rch wnr* **9/2**[2]
0413 3 ½ **Private Soldier**[1] 5756 4-9-9 44 SamHitchcott 6 55
(N J Vaughan) *s.i.s: hld up: hdwy 1/2-way: chsd wnr 2f out: sn rdn and hung lft: no ex fnl f* **15/8**[1]
0006 4 1 **Procrastinate (IRE)**[11] 5479 5-9-3 45 ChrisCatlin 9 47
(R F Fisher) *chsd ldr over 6f out: led 3f out: sn rdn and hdd: no ex fnl f* **22/1**
4034 5 shd **Fantastic Delight**[15] 5366 4-9-3 45 GeorgeBaker 2 46
(B G Powell) *hld up: hdwy 1/2-way: rdn over 2f out: no ex fnl f* **11/2**[3]
516 6 nk **Mountain Climb (IRE)**[37] 3186 5-8-12 45 HaddenFrost(5) 5 50+
(J D Frost) *led: hdd 7f out: chsd ldrs: nt clr run and lost pl over 2f out: rallied over 1f out: hmpd ins fnl f: swtchd rt: styd on wl* **12/1**
3530 7 ¾ **Dexileos (IRE)**[7] 5606 8-9-0 45 NeilChalmers(3) 11 44
(David Pinder) *chsd ldrs: rdn over 2f out: sayed on same pce appr fnl f* **20/1**
-200 8 2½ **Indian Sundance (IRE)**[189] 746 4-9-3 45 PhillipMakin 7 38
(K R Burke) *hld up in tch: lost pl over 3f out: rdn over 2f out: wknd over 1f out* **40/1**
362 9 3 **Jiminor Mack**[67] 3789 4-9-3 45 (p) SebSanders 3 31
(W J H Ratcliffe) *hld up: rdn over 3f out: n.d* **11/2**[3]
5646 10 hd **Beck**[6] 5625 3-8-12 45 TGMcLaughlin 4 31
(W M Brisbourne) *hld up: rdn over 2f out: a in rr* **16/1**
0360 11 nk **Crush On You**[22] 5179 4-9-3 45 GrahamGibbons 8 30
(R Hollinshead) *hld up: sme hdwy wl over 2f out: sn rdn and wknd* **33/1**
0666 12 5 **Nawayea**[8] 5566 4-9-3 45 (t) JimmyQuinn 1 19
(C N Allen) *hld up: rdn and wknd over 2f out* **16/1**
0200 13 3 **Sydneyroughdiamond**[8] 5566 5-9-3 45 (b) DaneO'Neill 12 12
(M Mullineaux) *led 7f out: hdd 3f out: sn rdn and wknd* **66/1**

1m 50.32s (-1.44) **Going Correction** -0.20s/f (Stan)
WFA 3 from 4yo+ 5lb 13 Ran SP% **130.3**
Speed ratings (Par 97): **98,94,94,93,93 93,92,90,87,87 87,82,80**
CSF £45.84 TOTE £13.30: £4.80, £3.30, £1.40; EX 70.80.
Owner Mrs J E Taylor **Bred** Mrs J E Taylor **Trained** Lambourn, Berks

FOCUS
A classified contest for horses rated 0-45, so obviously very moderate form, but not bad for the grade.
Mountain Climb(IRE) Official explanation: jockey said gelding was denied a clear run

5783 LADBROKES IN THE COMMUNITY CHARITABLE TRUST H'CAP 1m 1f 103y(P)
9:20 (9:21) (Class 6) (0-65,65) 3-Y-O £2,388 (£705; £352) Stalls Low

Form RPR
3053 1 **Pivotalia (IRE)**[15] 5367 3-9-3 64 (v[1]) AdamKirby 5 73
(W R Swinburn) *hung lft s: mde all: hrd rdn and hung rt ins fnl f: all out* **7/2**[2]
0356 2 nk **The King And I (IRE)**[50] 4309 3-9-4 65 (v[1]) RichardHughes 9 73
(Miss E C Lavelle) *hld up in tch: chsd wnr over 2f out: rdn over 1f out: nt clr run ins fnl f: hung rt nr fin: styd on* **8/1**
0055 3 4 **Skye But N Ben**[30] 4936 3-8-9 56 (b) PhillipMakin 11 59+
(T D Barron) *s.i.s: hld up: hdwy and hmpd over 2f out: sn rdn: nt rch ldrs* **16/1**
0660 4 ½ **Bold Saxon (IRE)**[9] 5528 3-8-13 60 HayleyTurner 6 59
(M D I Usher) *chsd ldrs: rdn over 2f out: styd on same pce appr fnl f* **16/1**
-642 5 ½ **Auntie Mame**[25] 5102 3-8-13 60 JimmyQuinn 13 58
(D J Coakley) *hld up: nt clr run over 2f out: hdwy over 1f out: sn rdn and no imp* **12/1**
03 6 1 **Antrim Rose**[36] 4742 3-9-1 62 SebSanders 3 58
(E F Vaughan) *hmpd s: hld up: hdwy over 2f out: sn rdn: wknd fnl f* **5/1**[3]
0533 7 3½ **Six Of Hearts**[9] 5528 3-8-13 60 (p) JamieSpencer 2 48
(J A Osborne) *wnt rt s: hld up: rdn and hung lft over 1f out: n.d* **11/4**[1]
050 8 2 **Susanna's Dance**[35] 4765 3-8-13 65 (b[1]) AshleyHamblett(5) 12 49
(M Botti) *hld up: rdn over 2f out: a in rr* **40/1**
0-30 9 1¾ **Halkerston**[111] 2477 3-9-1 62 DaneO'Neill 1 43
(C G Cox) *chsd wnr tl rdn over 3f out: wknd 2f out* **14/1**
6306 10 1¼ **Doyles Lodge**[16] 5339 3-8-11 65 AmyScott(7) 8 43
(H Candy) *hld up: wknd 3f out* **8/1**
3-23 11 13 **My Beautaful**[23] 661 3-8-13 60 JamesDoyle 10 11
(Miss J S Davis) *chsd ldrs: rdn and hung rt 4f out: sn wknd* **20/1**

2m 1.25s (-1.37) **Going Correction** -0.20s/f (Stan) 11 Ran SP% **121.1**
Speed ratings (Par 99): **98,97,94,93,93 92,89,87,85,84 73**
CSF £32.98 CT £406.75 TOTE £5.20: £1.30, £2.60, £6.20; EX 36.50 Place 6 £184.93, Place 5 £56.75.
Owner Precision Partnership **Bred** Kildaragh Stud **Trained** Aldbury, Herts
■ Stewards' Enquiry : Adam Kirby caution: careless riding

FOCUS
A modest three-year-old handicap. The first two finished clear but the form looks less than solid behind.
T/Plt: £323.60 to a £1 stake. Pool: £93,399.70. 210.65 winning tickets. T/Qpdt: £48.30 to a £1 stake. Pool: £5,838.50. 89.30 winning tickets. CR

5784 - 5787a (Foreign Racing) - See Raceform Interactive

5757 DUNDALK (A.W) (L-H)
Friday, September 28

OFFICIAL GOING: Standard

5788a KRITERION CONSERVATION ARCHITECTS H'CAP 1m
8:45 (8:47) (60-80,80) 3-Y-O+ £6,303 (£1,468; £647; £373)

RPR
1 **King Cannavaro (IRE)**[13] 5438 3-9-7 77 JMurtagh 8 85
(Eoin Griffin, Ire) *chsd ldrs: 5th ent st: rdn in 3rd 1f out: styd on wl to ld cl home* **14/1**
2 ½ **Landucci**[20] 5223 6-9-6 77 (p) PatrickHills(5) 10 84
(J W Hills) *chsd ldrs: 3rd ent st: chal 2f out: led over 1f out: hdd cl home* **3/1**[1]
3 1¼ **Carlowsantana (IRE)**[6] 5659 4-9-11 77 JAHeffernan 3 81
(Adrian Sexton, Ire) *chsd ldrs: 3rd ent st: rdn in 4th 1f out: kpt on* **5/1**[2]
4 nk **Keen Look (IRE)**[17] 5318 8-9-10 76 DPMcDonogh 14 79
(Gerard Keane, Ire) *towards rr: hdwy to 5th over 1f out: kpt on* **10/1**
5 nk **Nurenberg (IRE)**[26] 5072 5-9-3 76 PTownend(7) 2 79
(Edward Lynam, Ire) *led: rdn and hdd over 1f out: kpt on one pce* **11/2**[3]
6 1¼ **Mooretown Boy (IRE)**[51] 4303 7-9-12 78 DMGrant 12 78
(M P Cash, Ire) *mid-div: 8th 1/2-way: 6th and rdn over 1f out: kpt on* **12/1**
7 shd **Rockazar**[14] 5398 6-10-0 80 WJSupple 13 80
(G M Lyons, Ire) *in rr of mid-div: sme hdwy to 8th over 1f out: kpt on* **10/1**
8 ½ **Waitingforanalibi**[6] 5658 4-9-11 77 (p) WMLordan 7 75
(T J O'Mara, Ire) *mid-div: rdn 2f out: no ex in 7th over 1f out* **15/2**
9 1½ **Accentuate (IRE)**[12] 5460 3-9-6 76 FMBerry 1 71
(Charles O'Brien, Ire) *dwlt: towards rr: no imp in 10th over 1f out* **7/1**
10 ¾ **Salazaar (IRE)**[17] 5318 3-8-13 76 SFoley(7) 11 69
(Francis Ennis, Ire) *sn chsd ldrs: 5th 1/2-way: rdn bef st: lost pl and kpt on one pce* **10/1**
11 ¾ **Sling Back (IRE)**[22] 5184 6-9-12 78 KJManning 6 70
(Eamon Tyrrell, Ire) *mid-div: rdn 2f out: no ex in 9th over 1f out* **16/1**
12 2½ **Colonial Cross (IRE)**[47] 4439 3-9-6 76 RPCleary 9 62
(M Halford, Ire) *chsd ldr: rdn in 3rd 2f out: sn wknd* **20/1**
13 8 **Aqualung**[22] 5185 6-9-11 77 (t) NPMadden 5 44
(D Broad, Ire) *s.i.s and a towards rr* **25/1**
14 1¾ **Dryandra (IRE)**[57] 4115 4-10-0 80 KFallon 4 43
(John Joseph Murphy, Ire) *dwlt and a towards rr* **20/1**

1m 37.3s (97.30)
WFA 3 from 4yo+ 4lb 14 Ran SP% **142.2**
CSF £64.35 CT £271.53 TOTE £8.00: £3.00, £2.30, £2.10; DF 29.60.
Owner Thomas Radley **Bred** Tom Radley **Trained** Slieverue, Co. Kilkenny
■ Stewards' Enquiry : R P Cleary one-day ban: moved across marker poles (Oct 7)

NOTEBOOK
Landucci has been in decent form, winning at Kempton two starts back, and it was no surprise to see him made favourite on this first start at the track. Never far from the leaders, he looked the winner when going on over a furlong out, but could not repel the winners late challenge. He should find a similar if returning. (op 4/1)

5789 - 5793a (Foreign Racing) - See Raceform Interactive

5764 ASCOT (R-H)
Saturday, September 29

OFFICIAL GOING: Round course - soft (7.0); straight course - good to soft (7.7) (overall 7.3)
Wind: Gentle breeze, across Weather: Dry

5794 SPACE PROPERTY ROSEMARY STKS (H'CAP) (LISTED RACE) (F&M) 1m (R)
2:00 (2:01) (Class 1) (0-110,103) 3-Y-O+
£17,034 (£6,456; £3,231; £1,611; £807; £405) Stalls High

Form RPR
1221 1 **Perfect Star**[23] 5163 3-8-7 89 MJKinane 7 99
(C G Cox) *lw: led after 2f: wnt 2 l clr 2f out: styd on gamely: edgd lft towards fin: rdn out* **4/1**[1]
2003 2 2½ **Lady Gloria**[59] 4060 3-8-10 92 SebSanders 12 97
(J G Given) *s.i.s: towards rr: hdwy 5f out: rdn to chse wnr over 2f out: kpt on but a hld* **5/1**[2]
1520 3 shd **Contentious (USA)**[28] 5058 3-9-1 97 EddieAhern 9 102
(J L Dunlop) *hld up towards rr: hdwy over 3f out: rdn over 2f out: wnt 3rd wl over 1f out: styd on* **20/1**
0006 4 3 **Tiana**[16] 5359 4-8-12 90 (b) JimCrowley 8 88
(Mrs A J Perrett) *mid-div: tk clsr order 3f out: sn rdn: kpt on same pce fnl 2f* **25/1**
1662 5 shd **Gold Hush (USA)**[13] 5445 3-8-7 89 RyanMoore 1 87+
(Sir Michael Stoute) *lw: racd wd and alone but in tch: jnd main gp at rr over 3f out: sn rdn: swtchd lft over 2f out: styd on but nvr trbld ldrs* **4/1**[1]
1221 6 6 **Ventura (USA)**[10] 5537 3-8-7 89 SPasquier 6 75
(Mrs A J Perrett) *lw: s.i.s: sn mid-div: effrt over 2f out: sn one pce* **4/1**[1]
552 7 4 **Apply Dapply**[35] 4814 4-8-7 85 oh4 SteveDrowne 2 62
(H Morrison) *chsd ldrs: rdn 3f out: wknd 2f out* **13/2**[3]
4103 8 nk **Passion Fruit**[16] 5354 6-8-7 85 TedDurcan 13 62
(C W Fairhurst) *s.i.s: a bhd* **16/1**
4054 9 2 **Bicoastal (USA)**[28] 5047 3-9-7 103 (p) LDettori 11 75
(B J Meehan) *s.i.s: sn chsng ldr: rdn 3f out: wknd 2f out* **12/1**
3560 10 1 **Impetious**[20] 5266 3-9-6 102 (b) KJManning 4 72
(Eamon Tyrrell, Ire) *a towards rr* **50/1**
1010 11 13 **Pintle**[28] 5047 7-9-4 96 KerrinMcEvoy 5 39
(J L Spearing) *led for 2f: chsd ldrs tl over 3f out: sn bhd* **20/1**

1m 42.6s (0.50) **Going Correction** +0.275s/f (Good)
WFA 3 from 4yo+ 4lb 11 Ran SP% **118.9**
Speed ratings (Par 111): **108,105,105,102,102 96,92,92,90,89 76**
CSF £22.99 CT £361.93 TOTE £4.30: £1.70, £2.30, £5.10; EX 32.20 Trifecta £716.20 Pool: £1,109.72 - 1.10 winning tickets..
Owner Dr Bridget Drew & E E Dedman **Bred** Mrs A M Jenkins And E D Kessly **Trained** Lambourn, Berks

FOCUS
The way this contest panned out followed the trend of the previous day, in that it paid to race handily. The pace was a decent one too, for they finished very well spread out and the winning time was only 0.15 seconds slower than the QE II, though they may have had the best of the ground in this contest.

NOTEBOOK

Perfect Star ◆, a most progressive filly, adopted the same positive tactics that had proved so effective at Salisbury last time and the extra furlong was never going to be a problem as she saw it out well when winning over the trip at the same track earlier in the season. She was always holding her rivals comfortably in the home straight and, in her current mood, could be capable of finding a Group race confined to her own sex, though in the meantime a race of this stature will still do very nicely. (tchd 9-2 in places)

Lady Gloria, for whom the ground had come right, emerged from the pack to chase the winner up the home straight but could never make any impression on her. Still, she has done remarkably well for a filly that was winning a Class 6 Fibresand maiden back in the bleak midwinter. (op 10-1)

Contentious(USA), back in trip after failing to stay an extended 1m2f at Longchamp last time, did best of those that tried to come from off the pace in the second half of the contest, but although she was staying on all the way down the straight she was not doing it quickly enough. She may need to go back abroad if she is to win at this level. (op 16-1)

Tiana, having her eighth consecutive start in Listed company, had her chance but lacked the speed to get competitive in the home straight. This was arguably her best performance for some time, but does not really convince that she is capable of winning at this level. (tchd 22-1)

Gold Hush(USA), probably on the easiest ground she has faced, was taken the 'Willie Carson' route under the trees on the run up from Swinley Bottom, but found herself stone last after she was taken over to join the main group on the home bend. She did stay on, but was never going to get there and it seemed that the drop in trip did her few favours. (tchd 9-2)

Ventura(USA), raised 4lb for her Sandown victory, failed to run up to that form even though this race may not have been run to suit. The easier ground should not have been a problem to her either as she already has enough form on it. (op 7-2)

5795 JUDDMONTE ROYAL LODGE STKS (GROUP 2) (C&G) 1m (R)

2:35 (2:38) (Class 1) 2-Y-O

£70,975 (£26,900; £13,462; £6,712; £3,362; £1,687) **Stalls** High

Form RPR

12 **1** **City Leader (IRE)**[28] 5048 2-8-12 99 .... KDarley 7 110
(B J Meehan) *trckd ldr: rdn to ld and edgd lft 2f out: sn hrd pressed: kpt on gamely: drvn out* **9/1**

2 *¾* **Achill Island (IRE)**[30] 4986 2-8-12 0 .... JMurtagh 2 108
(A P O'Brien, Ire) *str: hld up: rdn over 2f out: swtchd rt and str run over 1f out: ev ch ins fnl f: hld nr fin* **13/2**[2]

1432 **3** *hd* **Scintillo**[29] 5004 2-8-12 98 .... RyanMoore 5 108
(R Hannon) *hld up: rdn and hdwy 2f out: swtchd to rails and ev ch ins fnl f: kpt on but no ex nr fin* **7/1**[3]

6011 **4** *nk* **Ridge Dance**[11] 5509 2-8-12 80 .... JimmyFortune 8 107
(J H M Gosden) *lw: hld up and bhd: rdn over 2f out: no imp tl r.o strly wl ins fnl f: nrst fin* **8/1**

31 **5** *nk* **Alfathaa**[22] 5206 2-8-12 0 .... RHills 3 107
(W J Haggas) *lw: trckd ldrs: rdn over 2f out: ev ch ent fnl f: kpt on but no ex* **7/1**[3]

213 **6** *nk* **Yahrab (IRE)**[29] 5004 2-8-12 94 .... SebSanders 4 106
(C E Brittain) *trckd ldrs: rdn over 2f out: kpt on but nvr quite able to mount a chal* **33/1**

21 **7** *½* **Emmrooz**[14] 5417 2-8-12 0 .... LDettori 10 105
(Saeed Bin Suroor) *lw: trckd ldrs: rdn and ev ch 2f out: no ex ins fnl f* **9/2**[1]

3415 **8** *shd* **Let Us Prey**[14] 5406 2-8-12 97 .... MJKinane 6 105
(N A Callaghan) *racd keenly: hld up: hdwy 4f out: rdn over 2f out: str chal ent fnl f: no ex* **11/1**

11 **9** *11* **Sharp Nephew**[42] 4598 2-8-12 0 .... RichardHughes 11 80
(B J Meehan) *s.i.s: hld up in mid-div: rdn over 2f out: wknd over 1f out* **9/2**[1]

141 **10** *1 ½* **Campanologist (USA)**[21] 5217 2-8-12 92 .... JamieSpencer 9 77+
(M Johnston) *led: rdn and hdd 2f out: sn wknd* **10/1**

5 **11** *3 ½* **Aussie Battler (IRE)**[63] 3957 2-8-12 0 ....(t) PaulFitzsimons 1 69
(B W Duke) *w'like: s.i.s: mid-div: rdn 3f out: sn btn* **100/1**

1m 43.64s (1.54) **Going Correction** +0.40s/f (Good) **11** Ran SP% **117.2**
Speed ratings (Par 107): **108,107,107,106,106 106,105,105,94,93 89**
CSF £66.20 TOTE £14.10: £3.70, £2.60, £3.10; EX 101.90 Trifecta £1253.70 Pool: £5,120.99 - 2.90 winning tickets..
Owner Sangster Family **Bred** Swettenham Stud **Trained** Manton, Wilts

FOCUS

These was a thrilling contest to watch as a whole host of horses had a chance in the home straight and the result was still very most in doubt well inside the last furlong. However, from a form point of view it looks a sub-standard renewal which is unlikely to produce many stars of the future. The front eight were covered by a little over two lengths and the winning time was 0.34 seconds slower than the Fillies' Mile. The eventual winner again held a prominent position throughout.

NOTEBOOK

City Leader(IRE), trying a mile for the first time, was always up there and deserves a lot of credit for grinding out victory, as he looked sure to be swallowed up as challenger after challenger loomed on both sides at various points in the home straight. Although he is obviously useful and a Group 2 victory is never to be sniffed at, the main significance of his vcitory was that it provided a big boost to Raven's Pass who had beaten him hollow in the Solario. (op 11-1)

Achill Island(IRE), whose stable had won three of the past eight runnings of this event, was produced with his effort in plenty of time and never stopped trying, but he ran into a very dogged rival and could never quite get up. He will no doubt take his chance in the top middle-distance races next season, but is unlikely to be amongst the very best that his powerful stable will have at their disposal. (op 10-1)

Scintillo has just fallen short in Listed company in his last two starts, but he does stay this trip well and it was that which enabled him to put in a spirited late effort against the inside rail and finish a highly-creditable third. His proximity does, however, suggest that this is a little way below genuine Group 2 form. (tchd 11-2)

Ridge Dance, bidding for a hat-trick, was taking a huge step up in class after winning a Yarmouth nursery off 80. With a wall of horses in front of him entering the last couple of furlongs, he was finishing best of all on his first try at this trip and can certainly find other opportunities, but again his proximity does not do a great deal for the strength of the form. (op 13-2)

Alfathaa deserved a crack at this level after his easy Newbury maiden victory, but after holding every chance he had no more to give inside the last furlong. This was only his third start and the best of him will probably be seen next season. (tchd 15-2)

Yahrab(IRE), held by Scintillo on Salisbury running behind McCartney, had every chance on this easier surface and finished a little closer to his old rival without suggesting he is quite up to this class. He will appreciate middle distances next year.

Emmrooz was always in a good position, but after holding every chance he was firmly put in his place in the last furlong or so. He finished no closer to Ridge Dance than when second to him on his racecourse debut at Sandown last month, so perhaps this easier ground was not in his favour. (tchd 11-2)

Sharp Nephew, unbeaten in two starts before this, was a big disappointment, especially as he had finished in front of Scintillo when successful at Newbury last time. Connections blamed the ground. Official explanation: trainer said colt was unsuited by the soft ground (op 4-1, tchd 5-1 in places)

Campanologist(USA) tried to make every yard, but the bell had tolled for him on reaching the home straight.

Aussie Battler(IRE) Official explanation: trainer said colt had a breathing problem

5796 MEON VALLEY STUD FILLIES' MILE (GROUP 1) 1m (R)

3:10 (3:12) (Class 1) 2-Y-O

£123,942 (£46,974; £23,509; £11,721; £5,871; £2,946) **Stalls** High

Form RPR

122 **1** **Listen (IRE)**[27] 5073 2-8-12 0 .... JMurtagh 6 113+
(A P O'Brien, Ire) *w'like: scope: trckd ldrs: led over 1f out: kpt on wl: rdn out* **10/3**[2]

1 **2** *1* **Proviso**[42] 4626 2-8-12 0 .... SPasquier 7 111+
(A Fabre, France) *w'like: scope: cl up whn squeezed out and lost pl over 6f out: rdn and hdwy fr over 2f out: wnt 2nd jst ins fnl f: no ex fnl 75yds* **11/10**[1]

5311 **3** *2 ½* **Saoirse Abu (USA)**[27] 5073 2-8-12 0 ....(v[1]) KJManning 3 105
(J S Bolger, Ire) *w'like: w ldr: rdn to ld briefly jst over 2f out: kpt on same pce fnl f* **5/1**[3]

12 **4** *5* **Kotsi (IRE)**[16] 5353 2-8-12 107 .... LDettori 8 94
(E F Vaughan) *lw: trckd ldrs: rdn and swtchd lft 2f out: sn one pce* **11/2**

5300 **5** *2* **Kay Es Jay (FR)**[17] 5322 2-8-12 100 .... RyanMoore 4 90
(B W Hills) *led: rdn and hdd jst over 2f out: grad wknd* **66/1**

24 **6** *4* **Sugar Mint (IRE)**[16] 5353 2-8-12 0 .... MichaelHills 1 81
(B W Hills) *chsd ldrs: rdn over 2f out: wknd over 1f out* **16/1**

7 *9* **Wadlia (USA)** 2-8-12 0 .... SebSanders 5 61+
(C E Brittain) *w'like: leggy: outpcd in rr: wknd 2f out* **100/1**

1m 43.3s (1.20) **Going Correction** +0.40s/f (Good) **7** Ran SP% **111.1**
Speed ratings (Par 106): **110,109,106,101,99 95,86**
CSF £6.93 TOTE £4.70: £2.30, £1.40; EX 8.40 Trifecta £13.00 Pool: £6,610.31 - 359.29 winning tickets..
Owner D Smith, Mrs J Magnier, M Tabor **Bred** Brittas House Stud **Trained** Ballydoyle, Co Tipperary

FOCUS

With high-class juvenile fillies from Britain, Ireland and France, this looked a genuine Group 1 event. The pace was decent, the front three pulled miles clear of the others, and the winning time was 0.34 seconds quicker than that recorded by City Leader in the Royal Lodge. This was the sort of performance that had been expected of Listen in recent races, and it is debatable if Proviso was unlucky

NOTEBOOK

Listen(IRE) ◆, a length and a half behind Saoirse Abu when odds-on for the Moyglare Stud Stakes, was nonetheless shorter than her in the betting once again and the market got it right. She was always in a good position and, once she had mastered her old rival entering the last quarter-mile, was always holding the French-trained favourite. Provided all goes well during the winter, she is going to have a very big say in next year's 1000 Guineas. (op 9-2 tchd 3-1)

Proviso, an attractive filly unbeaten in two races in France, probably owed her position in the market, both for this race and the 1000 Guineas, to who trains her rather than what she has achieved, as the form of her win in the Prix Du Calvados looks nothing special. To be fair, she encountered plenty of trouble early on here and dropped to the rear, and then when finally asked for her effort had to be brought widest of all. She still had every chance, but the winner proved a tough nut to crack and she could never quite get to her. Whilst she can be rated a little better than the pure form, it is hard to say that she will ever turn things around with Listen should they meet again. (tchd 5-4)

Saoirse Abu(USA), bidding for a Group 1 hat-trick after victories in the Phoenix Stakes and Moyglare Stud Stakes, had a first-time visor replacing the blinkers. She was given every chance and was always up there, but as soon as her old rival Listen was brought through to challenge the writing was on the wall. There is a chance that she did not see out this longer trip as well as the first two, though her trainer was more inclined to blame the 'loose' ground. (op 4-1)

Kotsi(IRE) was the disappointment of the race. Her effort in the May Hill suggested the trip was never going to be a problem and her win had come on an easy surface, but she found precious little off the bridle and finished well adrift of the front trio. This was only her third start though, so it is too early to start writing her off. (op 5-1)

Kay Es Jay(FR), whose only win from six previous starts had come on Polytrack, enjoyed her moment of glory by making much of the running, but once headed she was soon left behind.

Sugar Mint(IRE), yet to win, finished further behind Kotsi than in the May Hill, but neither filly advertised the Doncaster form. (op 22-1)

Wadlia(USA), a $75,000 filly out of a champion two-year-old in Canada, faced an immense task on her debut and was soon struggling.

5797 TOTESPORT.COM CHALLENGE CUP (HERITAGE H'CAP) 7f

3:40 (3:45) (Class 2) 3-Y-O+

£93,480 (£27,990; £13,995; £7,005; £3,495; £1,755) **Stalls** Centre

Form RPR

51-2 **1** **Candidato Roy (ARG)**[33] 4907 6-9-7 **105** .... JMurtagh 1 116
(W J Haggas) *str: racd alone on stands' side: prom: overall ldr 3f out: kpt on wl u.p: drvn out* **50/1**

2111 **2** *¾* **Shevchenko (IRE)**[45] 4509 3-8-9 **96** .... SebSanders 11 106
(J Noseda) *mid-div: hdwy 2f out: rdn to ld main gp jst ins fnl f but overall 2nd: sn edgd lft: hld fnl 50yds* **11/2**[2]

2112 **3** *hd* **Docofthebay (IRE)**[37] 4745 3-8-11 **98** .... LDettori 24 107+
(J A Osborne) *s.i.s: bhd: rdn and hdwy over 1f out: r.o strly ins fnl f: nrst fin* **9/1**

0032 **4** *1 ½* **Presumptive (IRE)**[14] 5413 7-8-11 **95** .... SteveDrowne 3 100
(R Charlton) *lw: patiently rdn: hld up in last: swtchd lft over 1f out: sn rdn: r.o wl: nrst fin* **33/1**

4000 **5** *shd* **Dhaular Dhar (IRE)**[7] 5616 5-8-11 **95** .... CSoumillon 15 100
(J S Goldie) *mid-div: rdn to ld main gp wl over 1f out tl jst ins fnl f: kpt on* **33/1**

1240 **6** *shd* **Wise Dennis**[63] 3941 5-9-6 **104** .... KDarley 9 109
(A P Jarvis) *mid-div: rdn over 2f out: kpt on ins fnl f* **17/2**[3]

1111 **7** *¾* **Lovelace**[25] 5112 3-9-8 **109** .... JamieSpencer 10 112
(M Johnston) *lw: trckd ldrs: rdn 2f out: ev ch over 1f out: no ex* **9/1**

-031 **8** *hd* **Utmost Respect**[8] 5584 3-9-2 **103** .... PaulHanagan 19 105
(R A Fahey) *prom: rdn and ev ch over 1f out: kpt on same pce* **4/1**[1]

0665 **9** *hd* **Fonthill Road (IRE)**[7] 5616 7-8-12 **99** .... JamieMoriarty(3) 28 101
(R A Fahey) *mid-div: rdn and hdwy 2f out: kpt on same pce fnl f* **20/1**

1154 **10** *½* **Mutanaseb (USA)**[48] 4420 3-8-8 **95** ....(b[1]) RHills 18 95
(M A Jarvis) *lw: led tl 3f out: sn rdn: one pce fr over 1f out* **10/1**

1101 **11** *shd* **Danehillsundance (IRE)**[16] 5355 3-8-8 **95** .... RyanMoore 8 95+
(R Hannon) *hld up towards rr: rdn and hdwy over 1f out: kpt on but nvr a danger* **14/1**

1410 **12** *hd* **Giganticus (USA)**[28] 5031 4-9-4 **102** .... MichaelHills 25 102
(B W Hills) *mid-div: hdwy 2f out: sn rdn: one pce fnl f* **20/1**

0102 **13** *1* **Viking Spirit**[33] 4886 5-9-4 **102** .... AdamKirby 7 99
(W R Swinburn) *hld up towards rr: sme late prog: nvr a threat* **33/1**

1340 **14** *shd* **Binanti**[34] 4851 7-8-10 **94** .... PaulDoe 12 91
(P R Chamings) *lw: prom: rdn over 2f out: wknd ins fnl f* **33/1**

3360 **15** *nk* **Partners In Jazz (USA)**[7] 5616 6-8-11 **95** .... PhillipMakin 14 91
(T D Barron) *s.i.s: sn mid-div: effrt over 2f out: wknd ent fnl f* **18/1**

3000 **16** *3 1/2* **Royal Power (IRE)**[16] 5359 4-8-13 **97** .... TPO'Shea 13 84
(M R Channon) *nvr bttr than mid-div* **66/1**

0046 **17** *3/4* **Mine (IRE)**[14] 5412 9-9-7 **105** .... (v) TQuinn 6 90
(J D Bethell) *bmpd s: a towards rr* **25/1**

0251 **18** *10* **Mac Gille Eoin**[13] 5449 3-8-8 **95** .... JimCrowley 23 54
(J Gallagher) *prom: rdn 3f out: wknd over 1f out* **50/1**

4256 **19** *7* **Tony James (IRE)**[35] 4806 5-8-9 **93** .... RichardHughes 26 34
(K O Cunningham-Brown) *a towards rr* **66/1**

0064 **20** *3 1/2* **Areyoutalkingtome**[14] 5416 4-9-6 **104** .... EddieAhern 21 36
(C A Cyzer) *chsd ldrs tl wknd 2f out* **50/1**

6000 **21** *5* **Steenberg (IRE)**[7] 5616 8-8-10 **94** .... JimmyQuinn 2 13
(M H Tompkins) *a towards rr* **50/1**

3-00 **22** *7* **Cupid's Glory**[28] 5031 5-8-11 **95** .... (p) RobertHavlin 5 —
(Mrs L C Jewell) *wnt rt s: sn prom: wknd 2f out* **100/1**

0300 **23** *28* **Minority Report**[14] 5413 7-8-11 **95** .... KerrinMcEvoy 29 —
(L M Cumani) *hld up towards rr: rdn and hdwy over 2f out: sn lost action and heavily eased* **16/1**

1m 28.66s (0.56) **Going Correction** +0.325s/f (Good)
WFA 3 from 4yo+ 3lb **23** Ran SP% **129.8**
Speed ratings (Par 109): **109,108,107,106,106 105,105,104,104,104 103,103,102,102,102 98,97,85,77,73 68,60,28**
CSF £288.91 CT £2826.94 TOTE £53.40: £10.40, £2.10, £2.60, £5.60; EX 435.20 Trifecta £17095.80 Pool: £98,722.42 - 4.10 winning tickets..
Owner Robert Muir & Des Scott **Bred** Vacacion **Trained** Newmarket, Suffolk
■ Stewards' Enquiry : Seb Sanders one-day ban: careless riding (Oct 10)

FOCUS

A fiercely competitive handicap for this big prize, or at least it should have been, but as things turned out the race was won by the only horse to come down the stands' rail, whilst the others all came down the middle as they had done in all the previous races on the straight course at this meeting. The time was good, but obviously the form may not be totally reliable because of the way the race was run.

NOTEBOOK

Candidato Roy(ARG), a Group 1 winner in South Africa before his Dubai win, had run with credit on his British debut at Warwick last month and had obviously benefited from that, but the key to this victory was a shrewd tactical ride. Brought straight over to the stands' rail from his number one draw, whilst all his rivals merged towards the centre, it was clear from some way out that he was right up with the pace, if not leading, and over the last furlong or so it was merely a case of hanging on. He is obviously useful, but the way the race was run does make the form a little suspect and he will need to improve again to follow up this victory.

Shevchenko(IRE), who has been hitting the target more than his namesake in recent months, had beaten the winner of the first race here, Perfect Star, in his last two starts. Raised another 9lb in his bid for a four-timer, he was delivered with his effort in plenty of time and won the separate race down the centre, but unfortunately the winner was racing alone down the stands' rail. He lost nothing in defeat, but he is likely to be hoisted up again for this so things will not get any easier. (op 13-2)

Docofthebay(IRE) ◆, on probably the easiest ground he has faced, and on a career-high mark, does not know how to run a bad race. Given a patient ride early, he finished very strongly down the centre of the track and nearly got up for second, therefore maintaining his record of never finishing outside the first three in 11 outings. He is still in the Cambridgeshire and that race ought to suit him, so he would have to be on anyone's shortlist.

Presumptive(IRE), currently on a career-high mark, has not won on turf since June 2005 though he was off the track for a long time soon after that. He was noted finishing in good style towards the nearside of the main group and on this evidence he has not yet been handicapped out of things.

Dhaular Dhar(IRE), who never had a chance to show his true running in the Ayr Gold Cup, was down to a mark just 1lb higher than for his last win. Finding himself just about in front a furlong out, this was a cracking effort from a horse that stands his busy schedule extremely well, this being his 15th start of the year.

Wise Dennis, 8lb higher than when bolting up in the Victoria Cup here in May, came off the bridle a fair way out but he did keep on trying and was not beaten far at the line. He will need to find improvement to defy this sort of mark, but can never be left out of calculations in these type of races. (op 11-1)

Lovelace, bidding for a five-timer, found himself off an 18lb higher mark than when last in a handicap thanks to his victory in a Group 3 last time. Despite that, he was brought through to hold every chance and might even have held on to fourth had he not had to snatch up when Shevchenko ran across him well inside the last furlong. He will surely be back in Group company before too long. (tchd 8-1)

Utmost Respect, raised 10lb for his Ayr Silver Cup win and trying this trip for the first time, showed up well on the far side of the main group for a long way but he was not doing much in the last furlong or so. The ground would not have been a problem, but it remains to be seen if this is his trip. (op 10-3, tchd 9-2 in places)

Fonthill Road(IRE) ◆ is now getting a little relief from the Handicapper and is just 2lb higher than for his win in last year's Ayr Gold Cup. He stayed on down the far side of the track to finish alongside his stable-companion and may find an opportunity before the season is out on ground he likes.

Mutanaseb(USA), who would have appreciated the trip and ground, may have done a bit too much in the first-time blinkers and did not get home. (op 12-1)

Minority Report Official explanation: trainer said gelding was unsuited by the good to soft ground

5798 QUEEN ELIZABETH II STKS (GROUP 1) 1m (R)

4:20 (4:24) (Class 1) 3-Y-O+

£123,783 (£46,914; £23,479; £11,706; £5,864; £2,943) **Stalls** High

Form RPR

2112 **1** **Ramonti (FR)**[20] 5261 5-9-3 122 .... (t) LDettori 8 125
(Saeed Bin Suroor) *lw: trckd ldr: qcknd up to ld 2f out: 2 l clr ent fnl f: all out* **5/1**[3]

-412 **2** *1/2* **Excellent Art**[59] 4058 3-8-13 0 .... JamieSpencer 1 124+
(A P O'Brien, Ire) *hld up: nt clr run briefly over 1f out: sn rdn: r.o strly: nt quite catch wnr* **15/8**[1]

4242 **3** *1/2* **Duke Of Marmalade (IRE)**[21] 5243 3-8-13 0 .... MJKinane 6 123
(A P O'Brien, Ire) *led: rdn and hdd 2f out: chsd wnr: rallied gamely ins fnl f: kpt on* **13/2**

1512 **4** *hd* **Cesare**[35] 4805 6-9-3 115 .... JMurtagh 4 123
(J R Fanshawe) *hld up in 4th: rdn over 2f out: wnt 3rd over 1f out: kpt on ins fnl f* **6/1**

0315 **5** *4* **Stormy River (FR)**[48] 4445 4-9-3 0 .... TThulliez 9 114
(N Clement, France) *hld up: effrt over 2f out: sn one pce* **18/1**

2136 **6** *shd* **Blue Ksar (FR)**[13] 5451 4-9-3 112 .... (t) KerrinMcEvoy 10 114
(Saeed Bin Suroor) *trckd ldrs: rdn over 2f out: wknd ent fnl f* **25/1**

1311 **7** *shd* **Darjina (FR)**[20] 5261 3-8-10 0 .... CSoumillon 3 111
(A De Royer-Dupre, France) *lw: hld up: rdn over 2f out: no imp* **11/4**[2]

1m 42.45s (0.35) **Going Correction** +0.40s/f (Good)
WFA 3 from 4yo+ 4lb **7** Ran SP% **114.8**
Speed ratings (Par 117): **114,113,113,112,108 108,108**
CSF £14.98 TOTE £4.80: £2.00, £2.30; EX 16.90 Trifecta £30.70 Pool: £10,804.65 - 249.76 winning tickets..
Owner Godolphin **Bred** S P A Siba **Trained** Newmarket, Suffolk
■ Ramonti was gaining his third win of the year in a Group 1, a level at which none of his stablemates has scored at so far.
■ Stewards' Enquiry : Jamie Spencer one-day ban: used whip with excessive frequency (Oct 10)

FOCUS

A fascinating race, even though the likes of George Washington and Cockney Rebel were missing for various reasons. After last year's controversies, Godolphin and Ballydoyle fielding four of the seven runners between them added extra spice. The pace was a fair one, without being breakneck, and the winning time was just 0.15 seconds faster than the earlier fillies' Listed handicap. It was noticeable that the runners shunned the inside rail on the run up from Swinley Bottom. The right horses dominated the finish, but this is not outstanding mile form.

NOTEBOOK

Ramonti(FR), beaten a couple of lengths by Darjina in the Moulin, appeared less inconvenienced by this easier ground as things turned out. He was always in a great position behind Duke Of Marmalade, and when Dettori asked him to go and win his race he was able to take a couple of lengths out of his rivals and crucially got first run on Excellent Art. He was being closed down by the runner-up at the line, but it is worth remembering that he beat the Ballydoyle colt by a similar margin in the Sussex Stakes so he should be considered to have won this purely on merit. If he is seen again this year, it is most likely to be in Hong Kong in December. (op 4-1 tchd 11-2)

Excellent Art, for whom this ground would not have been a problem, was switched off out the back alongside the French pair whilst his stable-companion got on with it out in front. He had a bit to do on turning in, especially as front-runners were being favoured at the meeting, but his biggest problem was that he did not see daylight straight away, for he had to get around and then past Cesare. Once he did so, he finished off very strongly, but he never really looked like overhauling Ramonti. Whilst many will question the tactics and whether the right horse won, that would be unfair on the winner. (tchd 2-1 in places)

Duke Of Marmalade(IRE) set the pace, though whether he was adopting the role of pacemaker in its true sense is hard to say, especially with a horse from Ballydoyle. What is not in doubt is that he gave it his best shot and, even after Ramonti had headed him, he never gave up for an instant and managed to hit the frame at the top level yet again, finishing about the same distance behind Excellent Art as in the St James's Palace. However, as with his stable-companion All My Loving here the previous day, a solitary maiden victory seems modest reward for a horse of his class. (op 7-1 tchd 15-2)

Cesare, who has some soft-ground victories to his name from the dim and distant past, was back at his favourite venue and had every chance but again found himself a little short of what was required at this level. He did at least run almost to the inch with Ramonti on Queen Anne form. (op 8-1)

Stormy River(FR), rather held at this level since winning last year's Prix Jean Prat, was switched off right out the back but did not find a great deal when finally let down. He reportedly retires to stud now. (op 16-1)

Blue Ksar(FR) had the ground in his favour, but that was about all. If he was in this race as a pacemaker it was soon obvious he had not read the script, but in the context of his previous form he did well to finish within around five lengths of the winner. (op 33-1)

Darjina(FR), who had not been at her best on similar ground here at the Royal Meeting, again failed to show her best in the conditions. She never looked that happy out the back and when asked to get closer down the wide outside after turning in, found very little. She is much better than this. Official explanation: trainer said filly was unsuited by the soft ground (op 7-2)

5799 MILES & MORRISON OCTOBER STKS (LISTED RACE) (F&M) 7f

4:55 (4:58) (Class 1) 3-Y-O+

£17,034 (£6,456; £3,231; £1,611; £807; £405) **Stalls** Centre

Form RPR

4222 **1** **Miss Lucifer (FR)**[16] 5355 3-8-10 95 .... MichaelHills 12 102
(B W Hills) *lw: t.k.h bhd ldrs: rdn and edgd lft over 1f out: led jst ins fnl f: r.o: rdn out* **7/2**[2]

1222 **2** *3/4* **Diamond Diva**[14] 5403 3-8-10 93 .... EddieAhern 13 100
(J W Hills) *trckd ldrs: led 2f out: rdn and hdd jst ins fnl f: kpt on* **8/1**

1434 **3** *1/2* **Steam Cuisine**[23] 5163 3-8-10 87 .... TPO'Shea 9 101+
(M G Quinlan) *mid-div: rdn over 2f out: clsng whn nt clr run sn after and lost pl: r.o ins fnl f: wnt 3rd cl home* **16/1**

6321 **4** *1/2* **Fidelia (IRE)**[33] 4901 3-8-10 78 .... SteveDrowne 11 98+
(G Wragg) *hld up: clsng whn nt clr run over 1f out: rdn and r.o ins fnl f* **16/1**

1302 **5** *1/2* **Graduation**[80] 3430 3-8-10 95 .... RyanMoore 8 96
(E A L Dunlop) *lw: hld up: swtchd rt 2f out: rdn and hdwy over 1f out: kpt on same pce fnl f* **5/1**[3]

1466 **6** *1 1/4* **Italian Girl**[28] 5047 3-8-10 100 .... JamieSpencer 3 98+
(A P Jarvis) *t.k.h: mid-div: nt clr run and lost pl 2f out: nt clr run again 1f out: no ch after* **3/1**[1]

1552 **7** *shd* **Our Faye**[16] 5354 4-8-13 87 .... JimmyFortune 14 93
(S Kirk) *hld up: hdwy 2f out: sn rdn: kpt on same pce fnl f* **7/1**

0500 **8** *nk* **Vital Statistics**[16] 5354 3-8-10 101 .... TQuinn 5 91
(D R C Elsworth) *s.i.s: mid-div: rdn to chse ldrs over 2f out: sn hung rt: kpt on same pce* **15/2**

1010 **9** *4* **Ivory Lace**[16] 5359 6-8-13 90 .... JimCrowley 15 82
(S Woodman) *chsd ldrs: rdn over 2f out: wkng whn hmpd over 1f out* **33/1**

2210 **10** *1/2* **Awwal Malika (USA)**[16] 5354 3-8-10 74 .... RichardHughes 1 79?
(C E Brittain) *led: rdn and hdd 2f out: sn wknd* **50/1**

0300 **11** *2 1/2* **Daniella**[16] 5354 5-8-13 80 .... (b) MJKinane 2 74
(Rae Guest) *trckd ldrs: rdn and ev ch 2f out: sn wknd* **33/1**

1m 29.44s (1.34) **Going Correction** +0.325s/f (Good)
WFA 3 from 4yo+ 3lb **11** Ran SP% **118.9**
Speed ratings (Par 111): **105,104,103,103,102 101,100,100,95,95 92**
CSF £31.74 TOTE £4.10: £1.70, £2.00, £4.80; EX 20.20 Trifecta £311.20 Pool: £1,249.37 - 2.85 winning tickets..
Owner Gainsborough **Bred** Gainsborough Stud Management Ltd **Trained** Lambourn, Berks
■ Stewards' Enquiry : T P O'Shea two-day ban: careless riding (Oct 10-11)

FOCUS

A competitive Listed race, despite the four non-runners. The whole field soon decided to come right over to the stands' rail and there were one or two traffic problems, but the winner did it well and the form looks sound overall.

NOTEBOOK

Miss Lucifer(FR) had finished runner-up in five of her last six starts, including behind Perfect Star, winner of the opener at this meeting, two starts back. She never seemed to do much wrong though, and certainly did everything right here, always having the leaders in her sights on the outside of the pack before finding plenty when asked. Both of her wins have been on easy ground and there may be more to come, but whatever happens she has done her value plenty of good with a victory at this level. (tchd 10-3 and 4-1)

Diamond Diva, like the winner, has been suffering from a touch of seconditis. After racing up with the pace throughout, she was sent for home around a quarter of a mile out and only just failed to see it out. She would have been getting 2lb from the winner in a handicap, so has run to form, and she should be winning again before long, possibly over an easier 7f. (tchd 15-2)

Steam Cuisine, over a length behind Miss Lucifer at Salisbury last time and 3lb worse off, got into a scrap with Italian Girl entering the last couple of furlongs and looked like dropping right out, but she then got her second wind and was finishing to some purpose. She had a bit to find at these weights, so this was a good effort, and she looks worth another try over 1m. (op 12-1)

The Form Book, Raceform Ltd, Compton, RG20 6NL

Fidelia(IRE) had a mountain to climb on official ratings, but she may well have finished even closer had she not had to be taken out wide in order to get a run after meeting traffic problems. This was a decent effort under the circmstances, but her prospects now depend on how the Handicapper views this. Official explanation: jockey said filly was denied a clear run (op 20-1)
Graduation, given a short break since her last start and trying an easy surface for the first time, did not have a great deal of room to play with when trying to get closer and rather had to weave her way through, but although she stayed on she never looked like getting there in time. (op 9-2 tchd 6-1)
Italian Girl, who got warm beforehand, had a great chance on official ratings, but was also dropping in trip. However, her race was effectively ended when she got into all sorts of bother when Steam Cuisine came across her over two furlongs from home, losing her ground in the process, and she never saw much daylight after that either. It may be best to ignore this. (op 9-2 tchd 11-4)
Our Faye was held by Miss Lucifer and Steam Cuisine on Salisbury running and could never make much impression. (op 6-1 tchd 11-2, 15-2 and 8-1 in a place)
Vital Statistics, another who got warm in the preliminaries, had the highest rating of these after contesting Group company for most of the season, but although she had her chance she never looked like winning and is likely to continue to be hard to place. (op 10-1 tchd 7-1)

5800 CAPLAN GORDON CARTER STKS (H'CAP) 2m
5:30 (5:30) (Class 2) (0-100,97) 3-Y-0+ **£10,363** (£3,083; £1,540; £769) **Stalls** High

Form RPR
1222 **1** **Samurai Way**[21] 5215 5-10-0 **97** ... JimmyFortune 12 108
(L M Cumani) *trckd ldrs: jnd ldrs 4f out: led over 2f out: sn rdn: styd on wl ins fnl f: gng away towards fin* **5/4**[1]
3 **2** *2 1/2* **Gabier**[105] 2675 4-8-11 **80** ... RyanMoore 5 88
(G L Moore) *hld up and bhd: hdwy 3f out: sn rdn: wnt 2nd ent fnl f: no ex* **12/1**
4051 **3** *1/2* **Gee Dee Nen**[28] 5034 4-8-13 **82** ... JimmyQuinn 10 89
(M H Tompkins) *mid-div: rdn and hdwy over 2f out: styd on ins fnl f* **9/1**[3]
0622 **4** *3* **Kasthari (IRE)**[15] 5375 8-10-0 **97** ... TedDurcan 8 101
(J D Bethell) *s.i.s: sn swtchd lft: trckd ldr after 2f: led over 5f out tl 3f out: sn rdn: kpt on same pce fnl 2f* **16/1**
4222 **5** *hd* **Prince Zafonic**[9] 5573 4-8-5 **79** oh5 ...(t) NicolPolli[(5)] 4 83
(Miss Gay Kelleway) *hld up: hmpd 5f out: hung rt and sme hdwy over 2f out: sn rdn: styd on fnl f* **16/1**
0424 **6** *1 3/4* **Velvet Heights (IRE)**[36] 4779 5-9-3 **86** ... EddieAhern 11 87
(J L Dunlop) *mid-div: hdwy to join ldrs 4f out: led 3f out: sn rdn and hdd: wknd over 1f out* **14/1**
5015 **7** *4* **Odiham**[49] 4375 6-9-7 **90** ...(v) SteveDrowne 1 87
(H Morrison) *led tl over 5f out: chsd ldrs: rdn over 2f out: sn wknd* **9/2**[2]
1006 **8** *1 1/4* **Castle Howard (IRE)**[15] 5375 5-9-9 **92** ... RichardHughes 6 87
(W J Musson) *hld up: rdn over 2f out: no imp whn bmpd over 1f out* **9/2**[2]
65-5 **9** *2 1/2* **Midas Way**[154] 763 7-9-10 **93** ... JimCrowley 7 85
(P R Chamings) *trckd ldrs: rdn 3f out: sn wknd* **25/1**

3m 39.02s (8.86) **Going Correction** +0.40s/f (Good) 9 Ran SP% **120.8**
Speed ratings (Par 109): **93,91,91,90,89 89,87,86,85**
CSF £19.89 CT £105.03 TOTE £2.10: £1.10, £2.90, £2.10; EX 21.80 Trifecta £134.20 Pool: £1,244.28 - 6.58 winning tickets. Place 6 £177.70, Place 5 £65.40.
Owner K Bailey, P Booth, D Boorer **Bred** Darley **Trained** Newmarket, Suffolk
■ Stewards' Enquiry : Nicol Polli three-day ban: careless riding (Oct 10-12)

FOCUS
A decent quality staying event even with the non-runners, but they went no pace and so it was not the test of stamina than it might have been. The form looks sound nevertheless, and there should be more to come from the winner now over similar distances.

NOTEBOOK
Samurai Way, raised 4lb for getting beaten in his most recent start, was trying this trip for the first time but the way the race was run did not put the emphasis on stamina. He was always travelling well and moved to the front easily enough after turning in. Although it looked as though the runner-up might present him with a problem or two he found another gear and pulled away again. He shapes as though he will cope with a truly-run 2m just as well and remains unexposed as a stayer. The Cesarewitch is next, and he will merit the utmost respect. (op 6-4)
Gabier ◆, returning from three months off, was ridden with plenty of patience before arriving with a dangerous-looking effort down the outside in the home straight, but the favourite had another gear left whilst he did not. He could find a staying handicap on the Flat before the season is out, but this will also have set him up nicely for a return to hurdles and he would be of obvious interest if turning out for the big four-year-old event at Chepstow in the middle of October. (op 14-1)
Gee Dee Nen, whose mark was left unchanged after he won a messy race at Chester last time, found himself in another one. Although he was staying on at the line, he was not getting there quickly enough. (op 8-1 tchd 15-2)
Kasthari(IRE), who continues to creep back up the weights despite not winning, had every chance and was bang there approaching the turn for home, but he was always likely to be found wanting for speed in the straight. He has still to score on the level since dead-heating for the 2004 Doncaster Cup. (op 14-1)
Prince Zafonic, still to win after 12 Flat starts and two over hurdles, had been bumped up 7lb for finishing second to an in-form rival at Yarmouth last time and was another 5lb out of the handicap here to boot. Getting into some argy-bargy with Castle Howard on the run up from Swinley bottom merely added to his problems so under the circumstances he did not fare too badly. However, his record obviously does not make him an attractive betting proposition.
Velvet Heights(IRE) had every chance turning for home, but faded rather tamely. It is over three years since his sole turf victory. (op 16-1)
Odiham, 1lb higher than when winning another slowly-run race from the front on similar ground over course and distance in July, attempted the same tactics but he did not see it out anything like as well this time and was not at his best. (op 6-1)
Castle Howard(IRE) had his ground, but he is still to show much over this sort of trip and failed to pick up at all, even in a steadily-run race like this. (op 4-1 tchd 5-1)
T/Jkpt: Not won. T/Plt: £199.20 to a £1 stake. Pool: £201,342.91. 737.75 winning tickets. T/Qpdt: £13.50 to a £1 stake. Pool: £8,437.60. 461.65 winning tickets. TM

5399 CHESTER (L-H)
Saturday, September 29

OFFICIAL GOING: Good (good to soft in places; 8.2)
Wind: Almost nil Weather: Fine

5801 IN OUT CLUB MAIDEN FILLIES' STKS 7f 2y
2:15 (2:15) (Class 5) 2-Y-0 **£4,533** (£1,348; £674; £336) **Stalls** Low

Form RPR
3502 **1** **Honky Tonk Sally**[16] 5357 2-9-0 85 ... NCallan 2 83
(M L W Bell) *mde all: qcknd clr wl over 1f out: edgd rt fnl f: easily* **10/11**[1]
2 *5* **Sayyedati Symphony (USA)** 2-9-0 0 ... JohnEgan 4 71
(C E Brittain) *hld up towards rr: rdn over 3f out: hdwy on ins 2f out: wnt 2nd 1f out: no ch w wnr* **12/1**
5 **3** *2 1/2* **Tiger Spice**[28] 5042 2-9-0 0 ... PaulMulrennan 3 64
(W J Haggas) *hld up in tch: kpt on same pce fnl f* **7/2**[2]
06 **4** *1 1/4* **Madame Rio (IRE)**[51] 4328 2-9-0 0 ... RoystonFfrench 1 61
(K R Burke) *t.k.h early: a.p: rdn to chse wnr 2f out to 1f out: wknd ins fnl f* **25/1**
5 *1 1/4* **Bewdley** 2-9-0 0 ... TGMcLaughlin 6 58
(P D Evans) *s.i.s: sme hdwy on ins over 1f out: n.d* **66/1**
66 **6** *nk* **Lady Zabeen (IRE)**[58] 4094 2-9-0 0 ... RichardMullen 8 57
(D M Simcock) *nvr trbld ldrs* **11/2**[3]
7 *hd* **Chaenomeles (USA)** 2-9-0 0 ... J-PGuillambert 9 57
(M Johnston) *s.i.s: a in rr* **14/1**
5 **8** *11* **Incarnation (IRE)**[17] 5328 2-9-0 0 ... TPQueally 7 29+
(J G Given) *hld up in tch: rdn over 3f out: wknd over 2f out: eased whn no ch ins fnl f* **10/1**
5 **9** *hd* **Brick (IRE)**[7] 5644 2-9-0 0 ... LiamJones 5 29+
(M Mullineaux) *chsd wnr: rdn over 3f out: wknd over 1f out: eased whn no ch ins fnl f* **40/1**

1m 28.34s (-0.13) **Going Correction** +0.125s/f (Good) 9 Ran SP% **121.2**
Speed ratings (Par 92): **105,99,96,95,93 93,93,80,80**
CSF £15.09 TOTE £1.90: £1.20, £3.10, £1.20; EX 16.70.
Owner W J Gredley **Bred** Stetchworth Park Stud Ltd **Trained** Newmarket, Suffolk

FOCUS
Honky Tonk Sally was different class and put up a very smart winning time for what looked an ordinary maiden.

NOTEBOOK
Honky Tonk Sally probably had her easiest task so far and proved far too good for this opposition. She seems suited by the longer trip and had the race sewn up when drifting towards the stands' side from the furlong pole. (op 11-10)
Sayyedati Symphony(USA) is a half-sister to Champagne Stakes winner Alamushahar. She proved no match for the winner but comes from a stable whose newcomers are usually better for a run. (op 11-1 tchd 10-1)
Tiger Spice came in for some support in the ring and did not appear to be inconvenienced by the extra furlong. (op 5-1)
Madame Rio(IRE) failed to get home on this step up in distance after racing freely early on. She was far from disgraced, however, and now qualifies for a mark. (op 33-1)
Brick(IRE) Official explanation: jockey said filly moved poorly throughout

5802 BOODLES DIAMOND NURSERY 5f 16y
2:50 (2:51) (Class 4) (0-85,86) 2-Y-0 **£6,477** (£1,927; £963; £481) **Stalls** Low

Form RPR
450 **1** **Not My Choice (IRE)**[22] 5192 2-8-12 **76** ... JohnEgan 3 85
(D J Murphy) *mde all: rdn over 1f out: r.o wl* **8/1**
5102 **2** *1 3/4* **Thunder Bay**[12] 5480 2-9-8 **86** ... RichardMullen 6 89
(M R Channon) *lost pl after 1f: hdwy on ins over 2f out: swtchd rt and rdn over 1f out: kpt on ins fnl f* **4/1**[2]
0102 **3** *nk* **Baldemar**[4] 5699 2-8-11 **75** ... PaulMulrennan 4 77
(K R Burke) *chsd wnr: rdn over 2f out: kpt on same pce fnl f* **5/2**[1]
2244 **4** *1* **Style Award**[23] 5167 2-8-5 **72** ... AndrewMullen[(3)] 2 70
(W J H Ratcliffe) *chsd ldrs: rdn over 2f out: one pce fnl f* **11/2**[3]
5142 **5** *2 1/2* **Ridge Wood Dani (IRE)**[10] 5534 2-8-4 **68** ... MatthewHenry 11 57+
(E J Alston) *outpcd: nt clr run and swtchd rt 2f out: hdwy on outside 1f out: nvr trbld ldrs* **14/1**
2233 **6** *nk* **Foreign Rhythm (IRE)**[10] 5521 2-8-2 **73** ...(t) DanielleMcCreery[(7)] 12 61
(N Tinkler) *s.s: hld up in rr: nt clr run over 2f out tl swtchd rt over 1f out: r.o ins fnl f: nvr nrr* **33/1**
542 **7** *1 3/4* **Grudge**[31] 4937 2-8-7 **71** ... TonyHamilton 9 53+
(D W Barker) *bmpd s: sn outpcd: hdwy on ins whn n.m.r over 1f out: no imp fnl f* **33/1**
0044 **8** *1/2* **Barraland**[10] 5534 2-8-3 **74** ... MatthewDavies[(7)] 10 54
(M R Channon) *prom: rdn over 2f out: wkng whn hung lft over 1f out* **14/1**
2342 **9** *2* **Magical Speedfit (IRE)**[27] 5065 2-8-11 **75** ... NCallan 7 48+
(G G Margarson) *prom: wkng whn nt clr run over 1f out* **15/2**
1 **10** *3/4* **Ocean Glory (IRE)**[14] 5429 2-8-13 **77** ... LPKeniry 5 47+
(Peter Grayson) *chsd ldrs: rdn and wkng whn edgd lft and bmpd over 1f out* **12/1**
10 **11** *5* **Cheshire Rose**[32] 4921 2-8-11 **75** ... PaulFessey 8 27
(T D Barron) *wnt rt s: prom tl rdn and wknd over 2f out* **10/1**

62.44 secs (0.39) **Going Correction** +0.125s/f (Good) 11 Ran SP% **122.8**
Speed ratings (Par 97): **101,98,97,96,92 91,88,88,84,83 75**
CSF £41.90 CT £105.79 TOTE £11.10: £3.40, £2.00, £1.50; EX 60.20.
Owner David Kilpatrick **Bred** Alan Dargan **Trained** Bawtry, S Yorks

FOCUS
The majority of this field were well exposed, but the form looks solid enough, with the second and fourth setting the standard.

NOTEBOOK
Not My Choice(IRE) ◆ was having only his second outing since running creditably over course and distance in the Lily Agnes at the May meeting. Without the tongue tie he wore on his comeback at Haydock, he dominated throughout from his low draw and may well continue to make up for lost time. (tchd 17-2)
Thunder Bay has kept his form remarkably well since making a winning debut on the Polytrack at Lingfield in early April. This was a very respectable effort under top weight after he lost his early position. (op 9-2)
Baldemar seems better suited to 6f, especially on a course as sharp as this. (op 9-4 tchd 11-4)
Style Award is another who shaped as though she needs a return to six. (op 7-1)
Ridge Wood Dani(IRE) did well to finish so close from a poor draw after meeting traffic problems over a trip that again looked on the short side for him.
Foreign Rhythm(IRE), tried in a tongue tie, also ran better than her finishing position suggests after meeting trouble in running from a wide draw.
Magical Speedfit(IRE) Official explanation: jockey said colt hung right-handed on bend into home straight

5803 AUTUMN MAIDEN FILLIES' STKS 1m 2f 75y
3:25 (3:26) (Class 4) 3-Y-0+ **£5,829** (£1,734; £866; £432) **Stalls** High

Form RPR
4004 **1** **House Maiden (IRE)**[26] 5102 3-8-7 57 ... KirstyMilczarek[(5)] 9 63
(D M Simcock) *mde all: rdn 1f out: r.o* **20/1**
5-42 **2** *1 1/2* **Pearl (IRE)**[17] 5335 3-8-12 68 ... J-PGuillambert 2 60
(W J Haggas) *chsd wnr: rdn over 2f out: hung lft over 1f out: nt qckn ins fnl f* **11/4**[2]
0-5 **3** *2 1/2* **Change Course**[29] 5013 3-8-12 0 ... NCallan 5 55
(Sir Michael Stoute) *hld up in mid-div: hdwy over 3f out: rdn over 1f out: one pce fnl f* **15/8**[1]
-030 **4** *2 1/2* **Verbatim**[24] 5131 3-8-9 65 ... WilliamBuick[(3)] 10 50+
(A M Balding) *hld up and bhd: rdn over 3f out: swtchd rt over 2f out: styd on fr over 1f out on outside: nvr nrr* **10/1**

5 shd **Idun** 3-8-12 0 RichardMullen 6 50
(P W Chapple-Hyam) *hld up in mid-div: rdn and sme hdwy whn swtchd lft wl over 1f out: no further prog* **8/1**

5000 6 shd **Buds Dilemma**[34] 4846 3-8-12 43 DavidAllan 1 50
(W M Brisbourne) *prom tl rdn and wknd over 2f out* **66/1**

4455 7 3½ **Smart Pick**[11] 5503 4-9-4 50 LiamJones 12 43
(Mrs L Williamson) *hld up and bhd: sme hdwy on ins whn nt clr run wl over 1f out: sn swtchd and edgd rt: no imp* **14/1**

0063 8 ¾ **Chicamia**[37] 4736 3-8-5 45 SophieDoyle(7) 11 42
(M Mullineaux) *nvr nr ldrs* **50/1**

0206 9 ½ **Ashwell Rose**[9] 5573 5-9-4 56 (v) JohnEgan 7 41
(J R Jenkins) *hld up and bhd: hdwy over 5f out: rdn and wknd over 3f out* **12/1**

0 10 shd **Storm Lily (USA)**[40] 4666 3-8-12 0 DO'Donohoe 8 40
(Saeed Bin Suroor) *t.k.h: lost pl after 2f: shortlived effrt 3f out* **10/1**

00-5 11 6 **Taran Tregarth**[29] 4989 3-8-12 40 TGMcLaughlin 3 28
(W M Brisbourne) *t.k.h: prom tl rdn and wknd over 3f out* **80/1**

-406 12 1¼ **Balliasta (IRE)**[36] 4760 3-8-12 62 OscarUrbina 4 26
(B W Hills) *hld up in tch: lost pl 5f out: sn bhd* **7/1[3]**

2m 14.05s (0.91) **Going Correction** +0.125s/f (Good)
WFA 3 from 4yo+ 6lb **12 Ran SP% 127.1**
Speed ratings (Par 102): **101,99,97,95,95 95,92,92,91,91 86,85**
CSF £78.90 TOTE £31.10: £4.90, £1.40, £1.40; EX 117.60.
Owner The Metropolitans **Bred** Dahoar Partnership **Trained** Newmarket, Suffolk
■ Stewards' Enquiry : Richard Mullen caution: careless riding

FOCUS
A weak maiden that featured plenty of disappointing types. The 43-rated sixth limits the form.
Balliasta(IRE) Official explanation: trainer had no explanation for the poor form shown

5804 INNOSPEC H'CAP 7f 2y
4:00 (4:01) (Class 3) (0-95,94) 3-Y-0+ **£9,715** (£2,890; £1,444; £721) **Stalls** Low

Form RPR

4512 1 **South Cape**[7] 5641 4-8-9 89 MatthewDavies(7) 6 100
(M R Channon) *hld up in tch: led over 1f out: rdn ins fnl f: r.o* **4/1[1]**

-100 2 ½ **Thabaat**[35] 4811 3-8-2 81 WilliamBuick(3) 10 90
(B W Hills) *hld up in tch: rdn over 1f out: r.o ins fnl f* **9/1**

4344 3 nk **Celtic Sultan (IRE)**[20] 5254 3-9-4 94 MickyFenton 3 102
(T P Tate) *led: rdn and hdd over 1f out: kpt on* **5/1[2]**

3206 4 1¾ **Imperial Echo (USA)**[7] 5617 6-8-10 83 PaulFessey 1 87
(T D Barron) *hld up in mid-div: rdn and hdwy whn swtchd rt over 1f out: nt qckn ins fnl f* **9/1**

5030 5 ¾ **The Kiddykid (IRE)**[22] 5209 7-8-12 85 TGMcLaughlin 2 87
(P D Evans) *a.p: rdn over 1f out: one pce* **15/2[3]**

0000 6 ½ **Phluke**[25] 5115 6-8-3 83 ThomasO'Brien(7) 7 84
(Eve Johnson Houghton) *s.i.s: sn mid-div: rdn and kpt on ins fnl f* **9/1**

5005 7 ½ **H Harrison (IRE)**[11] 5512 7-8-6 84 NataliaGemelova(5) 5 83
(I W McInnes) *chsd ldr tl rdn over 1f out: wknd ins fnl f* **9/1**

0611 8 nk **Inter Vision (USA)**[11] 5505 7-9-0 90 MichaelJStainton(3) 14 89
(A Dickman) *stdd s: sn swtchd lft: hld up in rr: sme late hdwy: n.d* **11/1**

2650 9 ¾ **Obe Gold**[7] 5617 5-8-8 81 JohnEgan 11 78
(M R Channon) *hld up towards rr: nt clr run 2f out: sn rdn: n.d* **14/1**

6305 10 hd **Fiefdom (IRE)**[4] 5712 5-8-5 81 PatrickMathers(3) 13 77
(I W McInnes) *bhd: pushed along over 4f out: shortlived effrt over 3f out* **33/1**

0002 11 hd **Mezuzah**[8] 5585 7-8-9 82 PaulMulrennan 9 77
(M W Easterby) *a bhd* **16/1**

0200 12 ¾ **Sir Xaar (IRE)**[37] 4745 4-9-5 92 (t) RoystonFfrench 4 85
(B Smart) *s.i.s: hld up towards rr: rdn over 4f out: sme hdwy on ins wl over 1f out: wknd ins fnl f* **16/1**

2005 13 2½ **Gallantry**[7] 5638 5-8-10 83 DeanMcKeown 8 70
(D Shaw) *a bhd* **12/1**

-0B0 14 27 **Blades Girl**[29] 4990 4-8-13 86 (p) NCallan 12 —
(K A Ryan) *prom tl wknd over 2f out: eased whn no ch over 1f out* **25/1**

1m 27.81s (-0.66) **Going Correction** +0.125s/f (Good)
WFA 3 from 4yo+ 3lb **14 Ran SP% 129.7**
Speed ratings (Par 107): **108,107,107,105,104 103,103,102,101,101 101,100,97,66**
CSF £43.37 CT £199.82 TOTE £4.80: £2.20, £3.70, £2.40; EX 50.10.
Owner Heart Of The South Racing **Bred** John And Mrs Caroline Penny **Trained** West Ilsley, Berks

FOCUS
This looked a fair handicap, but the form is nothing special. The winner was back to his best and the runner-up improved on his maiden form, but both were helped by their riders' claims.

NOTEBOOK
South Cape, back down to 7f, was by no means hard pressed to register a narrow victory, with his capable young rider taking off a valuable 7lb. He remains in fine form. (op 5-1)
Thabaat ◆, dropped 2lb, showed signs of a return to form and this lightly-raced colt is capable of picking up a similar event. (op 7-1)
Celtic Sultan(IRE) had been kept exclusively to 6f since he ran in the Champagne Stakes just over a year ago. He looked suited by the return to seven and stuck on willingly when collared. (op 8-1)
Imperial Echo(USA), showing no tendency to hang this time, showed that he was none the worse for his outings on consecutive days at Ayr last week. (op 8-1)
The Kiddykid(IRE) had no excuses from a good draw but has yet to win beyond 6f. (op 8-1)
Phluke was ridden from further back than usual after a sluggish start.
Gallantry Official explanation: trainer said gelding was unsuited by the good, good to soft in places ground; vet said gelding finished lame
Blades Girl Official explanation: jockey said filly hung right-handed throughout

5805 DAVID MCLEAN O&T AWARD H'CAP 1m 2f 75y
4:35 (4:35) (Class 2) (0-100,95) 3-Y-0
£21,188 (£6,344; £3,172; £1,587; £792; £397) **Stalls** High

Form RPR

0561 1 **Buccellati**[17] 5327 3-8-10 90 (v) WilliamBuick(3) 11 100+
(A M Balding) *hld up towards rr: hdwy 4f out: edgd lft over 1f out: hrd rdn to ld wl ins fnl f: r.o* **6/1[3]**

4614 2 ½ **Cabinet (IRE)**[35] 4799 3-8-12 89 RichardMullen 14 98
(Sir Michael Stoute) *hld up in tch: led wl over 1f out: sn rdn: hdd wl ins fnl f: nt qckn* **3/1[1]**

2100 3 1¼ **Sahrati**[37] 4749 3-8-12 89 JohnEgan 10 96
(C E Brittain) *a.p: rdn over 2f out: hung lft 1f out: kpt on same pce* **16/1**

3013 4 1 **Philanthropy**[11] 5504 3-9-0 91 NCallan 9 96
(K A Ryan) *a.p: led over 2f out: rdn and hdd wl over 1f out: one pce* **16/1**

0634 5 nk **Smokey Oakey (IRE)**[9] 5554 3-8-9 86 RoystonFfrench 1 92+
(M H Tompkins) *plld hrd in mid-div: rdn and hdwy over 1f out: nt clr run jst ins fnl f: one pce* **5/1[2]**

5500 6 1¾ **Smart Instinct (USA)**[35] 4799 3-9-4 95 (p) TonyHamilton 3 95
(R A Fahey) *sn in tch: rdn over 2f out: wknd over 1f out* **10/1**

-156 7 1 **Overrule (USA)**[79] 3460 3-8-12 89 TPQueally 2 87
(J Noseda) *prom: rdn over 2f out: wknd over 1f out* **8/1**

0250 8 1 **Rosbay (IRE)**[9] 5554 3-8-8 85 DavidAllan 12 81
(T D Easterby) *hld up and bhd: hdwy over 2f out: n.d* **20/1**

3125 9 6 **La Vecchia Scuola (IRE)**[14] 5405 3-7-13 81 oh15 KellyHarrison(5) 5 65
(R Johnson) *led: hdd over 2f out: rdn and wknd wl over 1f out* **50/1**

20 10 2 **Northern Jem**[54] 4228 3-8-8 85 MickyFenton 7 65
(G G Margarson) *a bhd* **8/1**

1210 11 21 **Parisian Dream**[17] 5327 3-8-8 85 OscarUrbina 8 23
(B W Hills) *hld up towards rr: rdn 4f out: sn struggling* **14/1**

0064 12 13 **Regal Parade**[14] 5419 3-8-10 87 J-PGuillambert 4 —
(M Johnston) *in rr: rdn and lost tch 7f out: t.o fnl 3f* **8/1**

2m 12.66s (-0.48) **Going Correction** +0.125s/f (Good) **12 Ran SP% 123.5**
Speed ratings (Par 107): **106,105,104,103,103 102,101,100,95,94 77,66**
CSF £25.35 CT £286.76 TOTE £7.80: £2.60, £1.90, £3.80; EX 20.40.
Owner P C & Mrs J A McMahon **Bred** Burton Agnes Stud Co Ltd **Trained** Kingsclere, Hants

FOCUS
Some very good prize money attracted a decent field for this 86-100 handicap, even though the top weight was only rated 95. The second, third and fourth, who were always prominent, look the best guides to the form.

NOTEBOOK
Buccellati followed up his win at Doncaster and seems to have benefitted from the fitting of a visor. He did well to come from behind on this sharp course and Buick quickly straightened him when he started to edge left. (op 7-1)
Cabinet(IRE) did his best to make amends for an unlucky run at Beverley and lost nothing in defeat. (op 7-2)
Sahrati, who presumably failed to stay 1m6f last time, was back down to a mark only 2lb higher than when winning at Newmarket in July. He could not raise his game sufficiently in the last 200 yards after hanging left. (tchd 20-1)
Philanthropy, a springer in the market, was again 6lb higher than when making all at York last month. He did not cave in when headed and would appreciate a return to 1m4f. (op 33-1)
Smokey Oakey(IRE) did well to finish so close given that he refused to settle and he was done no favours 200 yards from home. Official explanation: jockey said colt was hampered 2f out (op 9-2)
Smart Instinct(USA) had been dropped 2lb but seems to need more respite from the Handicapper. (op 8-1 tchd 15-2)
Regal Parade Official explanation: jockey said gelding was never travelling

5806 SUMMER FINALE H'CAP (SPONSORED BY DAVID WILLIAMS) 5f 16y
5:10 (5:11) (Class 4) (0-85,90) 3-Y-0+ **£6,477** (£1,927; £963; £481) **Stalls** Low

Form RPR

215 1 **Topflightcoolracer**[37] 4740 3-8-10 77 LiamJones 1 88
(Mrs G S Rees) *chsd ldrs: rdn to ld jst over 1f out: r.o* **20/1**

6140 2 nk **River Thames**[57] 4140 4-8-13 79 NCallan 13 89
(K A Ryan) *swtchd lft sn after s: hld up in rr: hdwy over 1f out: r.o ins fnl f* **20/1**

0211 3 ½ **Ishetoo**[11] 5506 3-9-6 90 MichaelJStainton(3) 7 101+
(A Dickman) *a.p: rdn over 1f out: kpt on ins fnl f* **10/1**

0410 4 nk **Circuit Dancer (IRE)**[6] 5667 7-8-9 75 SilvestreDeSousa 8 82
(D Nicholls) *hld up towards rr: nt clr run briefly over 2f out: hdwy over 1f out: hrd rdn and nt qckn ins fnl f* **14/1**

4024 5 1½ **Holbeck Ghyll (IRE)**[13] 5447 5-8-12 78 (p) LPKeniry 4 80
(A M Balding) *chsd ldrs: nt clr run wl over 2f out: nt clr run and lost pl over 1f out: kpt on ins fnl f* **10/1**

0600 6 shd **The Nifty Fox**[15] 5379 3-8-13 80 (b) DavidAllan 5 81
(T D Easterby) *a.p: led 2f out: rdn and rdr dropped whip whn edgd lft over 1f out: sn hdd: no ex ins fnl f* **20/1**

1111 7 1 **Prospect Court**[65] 3886 5-8-10 79 AndrewMullen(5) 3 77
(A C Whillans) *mid-div: rdn and hdwy over 1f out: one pce fnl f* **5/1[2]**

0004 8 ¾ **Dig Deep (IRE)**[11] 5513 5-9-4 84 PaulMulrennan 9 79
(W J Haggas) *hld up towards rr: nt clr run over 2f out: nvr nrr* **15/2[3]**

0004 9 1½ **Highland Warrior**[8] 5581 8-8-11 77 MickyFenton 12 67
(P T Midgley) *s.i.s: in rr: c wd st: n.d* **28/1**

4111 10 1¾ **Malapropism**[3] 5726 7-8-6 79 (v) MatthewDavies(7) 11 62
(M R Channon) *prom tl rdn and wknd over 1f out* **8/1**

2102 11 1 **Coconut Moon**[14] 5401 5-9-0 80 JohnEgan 2 60
(E J Alston) *led: hdd 2f out: sn rdn: wknd 1f out* **2/1[1]**

4403 12 nk **Rasaman (IRE)**[16] 5358 3-8-13 83 WilliamBuick(3) 6 62
(M A Jarvis) *mid-div: rdn and lost pl over 2f out: n.d after* **8/1**

-345 13 1 **Tartatartufata**[217] 554 5-8-11 77 (v) DeanMcKeown 10 52
(D Shaw) *a bhd* **50/1**

0000 14 3½ **Varadouro (BRZ)**[8] 5584 5-8-11 77 AdrianTNicholls 14 39
(D Nicholls) *wnt sltly rt s: sn chsng ldrs: rdn over 2f out: sn wknd* **33/1**

62.26 secs (0.21) **Going Correction** +0.125s/f (Good)
WFA 3 from 4yo+ 1lb **14 Ran SP% 131.5**
Speed ratings (Par 105): **103,102,101,101,98 98,97,95,93,90 89,88,87,81**
CSF £376.18 CT £4334.06 TOTE £27.70: £5.90, £8.60, £4.30; EX 1054.10.
Owner P Bamford **Bred** Dandy's Farm **Trained** Sollom, Lancs

FOCUS
Several of these sprinters came into the race in good form. There is a suspicion the leaders went too fast here, and the winner had the run of the race, chasing that pace from her inside draw.
Coconut Moon Official explanation: jockey said mare was unsuited by the good, good to soft in places ground
Varadouro(BRZ) Official explanation: jockey said gelding lost its action

5807 LEGAT OWEN H'CAP 1m 5f 89y
5:40 (5:42) (Class 4) (0-80,79) 3-Y-0+ **£6,477** (£1,927; £963; £481) **Stalls** Low

Form RPR

0111 1 **Ainama (IRE)**[63] 3964 3-8-7 67 MickyFenton 6 84+
(M Wigham) *hld up in mid-div: smooth hdwy 4f out: led on bit wl over 1f out: sn clr: v easily* **11/4[1]**

3600 2 2 **Kyoto Summit**[20] 5256 4-10-0 79 PaulMulrennan 12 86
(M W Easterby) *hld up in tch: nt clr run wl over 1f out: rdn and wnt 2nd jst over 1f out: no ch w wnr* **12/1**

6553 3 2½ **Hue**[20] 5257 6-9-0 65 (b) J-PGuillambert 7 68
(B Ellison) *hld up and bhd: hdwy on outside 2f out: styd on one pce fnl f* **5/1[2]**

2315 4 ¾ **Prelude**[28] 5034 6-9-6 71 LiamJones 2 73
(W M Brisbourne) *prom: rdn over 4f out: lost pl 3f out: rallied 2f out: one pce fnl f* **11/2[3]**

5 hd **Directa's Digger (IRE)**[147] 3-7-9 62 FrankiePickard(7) 5 64
(M Scudamore) *hld up towards rr: swtchd rt over 1f out: styd on ins fnl f: nvr nrr* **25/1**

6006 6 1¾ **Stretton (IRE)**[21] 5229 9-9-8 73 RoystonFfrench 4 72
(J D Bethell) *hld up in mid-div: sme hdwy whn nt clr run briefly 2f out: sn rdn: no further prog* **7/1**

5206 **7** *shd* **Maneki Neko (IRE)**[12] 5486 5-9-0 **65**.............................. TonyHamilton 9 64
(E W Tuer) *a.p: led over 2f out: rdn and hdd wl over 1f out: wknd ins fnl f* **28/1**

0-46 **8** *1/2* **Merrymaker**[14] 5404 7-8-11 **65**.................................. PatrickMathers(3) 1 63
(W M Brisbourne) *s.i.s: bhd: rdn over 4f out: nvr nr ldrs* **10/1**

2400 **9** *3* **York Cliff**[14] 5404 9-8-9 **60** oh3.. DavidAllan 8 54
(W M Brisbourne) *hld up in mid-div: rdn and hdwy over 3f out: wknd over 1f out* **22/1**

0235 **10** *8* **Red Chairman**[19] 5283 5-8-6 **62**................................. KellyHarrison(5) 14 44
(R Johnson) *led after 1f: rdn and hdd over 2f out: wknd wl over 1f out* **20/1**

5340 **11** *6* **Feeling (IRE)**[64] 3908 3-9-0 **74**..................................(b1) RichardMullen 3 47
(P W Chapple-Hyam) *led 1f: chsd ldr tl over 4f out: wkng whn nt clr run over 2f out* **20/1**

0-52 **12** *20* **Colinette**[47] 4458 4-8-12 **63**... JohnEgan 10 6
(R T Phillips) *rdn over 5f out: a bhd: t.o* **8/1**

04-0 **P** **Lake Wakatipu**[26] 5087 5-8-9 **60** oh4.................................. TPQueally 13 —
(M Mullineaux) *s.i.s: bhd: rdn over 4f out: sn lost tch: eased over 1f out: p.u and dismntd nr fin* **33/1**

2m 57.58s (2.16) **Going Correction** +0.125s/f (Good)
WFA 3 from 4yo+ 9lb **13** Ran SP% **123.2**
Speed ratings (Par 105): **98,96,95,94,94 93,93,93,91,86 82,70,—**
CSF £35.09 CT £165.19 TOTE £3.50: £1.70, £4.20, £2.20; EX 48.00 Place 6 £86.74, Place 5 £66.58.
Owner R Morecombe & D Morrison **Bred** Roundhill Stud And A Stroud **Trained** Newmarket, Suffolk

FOCUS
This turned into a one-horse race in the short home straight and the winner has been rated value for at least a 6-length win.
Colinette Official explanation: jockey said filly was never travelling
Lake Wakatipu Official explanation: jockey said mare hung right
T/Plt: £138.10 to a £1 stake. Pool: £66,027.75. 348.80 winning tickets. T/Qpdt: £66.80 to a £1 stake. Pool: £2,221.25. 24.60 winning tickets. KH

5770 HAYDOCK (L-H)
Saturday, September 29

OFFICIAL GOING: Soft (good to soft in places) (6.8)
Wind: Virtually nil Weather: Dry, sunny periods

5808 TURFTV H'CAP 1m 6f
2:25 (2:25) (Class 3) (0-90,85) 3-Y-0+
£11,217 (£3,358; £1,679; £840; £419; £210) **Stalls** Low

Form RPR

1341 **1** **Broughtons Revival**[66] 3844 5-9-10 **76**........................ PhilipRobinson 8 88+
(W J Musson) *trckd ldrs: hdwy 4f out: led 2 1/2f out: rdn and edgd lft over 1f out: sn drvn and styd on wl* **8/1**

6140 **2** *1 3/4* **Bogside Theatre (IRE)**[37] 4749 3-9-9 **85**.................... DanielTudhope 2 91
(G M Moore) *hld up: gd hdwy 3f out: rdn to chse ldrs whn n.m.r and swtchd rt over 1f out: sn drvn and kpt on ins fnl f* **7/1**

0603 **3** *1/2* **Dr Sharp (IRE)**[77] 3533 7-10-0 **80**....................................... DaneO'Neill 4 85
(T P Tate) *led: rdn along 4f out: hdd 2 1/2f out: sn drvn and kpt on same pce* **15/2**

13 **4** *nk* **Daryal (IRE)**[24] 5145 6-9-13 **79**....................................... HayleyTurner 10 84
(A King) *hld up in rr: pushed along and outpcd over 4f out: sn rdn: gd hdwy 2f out: drvn and kpt on ins fnl f: nrst fin* **13/2**[3]

0-10 **5** *shd* **Alaghiraar (IRE)**[42] 4617 3-9-3 **79**................................. MartinDwyer 3 84
(J L Dunlop) *trckd ldrs: hdwy over 3f out: rdn and hung lft over 1f out: sn one pce* **11/2**[1]

0610 **6** *1 1/4* **Winged D'Argent (IRE)**[63] 3976 6-9-13 **79**...........(b) StephenDonohoe 5 82
(B J Llewellyn) *chsd ldrs on outer: effrt 4f out and sn rdn: drvn over 2f out and sn one pce* **9/1**

4324 **7** *4* **Mighty Moon**[7] 5623 4-9-12 **78**..(t) TomEaves 7 76
(J O'Reilly) *chsd ldr: rdn along 4f out: drvn 3f out and sn wknd* **12/1**

1012 **8** *9* **Dhehdaah**[22] 5204 6-9-7 **73**... MickyFenton 6 58
(Mrs P Sly) *hld up: effrt and sme hdwy over 3f out: sn rdn and btn* **6/1**[2]

4-41 **9** *5* **Rock 'N' Roller (FR)**[128] 1968 3-9-1 **77**........................ FrancisNorton 1 55
(W R Muir) *in tch: pushed along 4f out: sn rdn and wknd* **6/1**[2]

1036 **10** *37* **Multicultural**[22] 5205 4-9-6 **72**... DarryllHolland 9 —
(D M Simcock) *a in rr* **22/1**

3m 9.77s (3.48) **Going Correction** +0.325s/f (Good)
WFA 3 from 4yo+ 10lb **10** Ran SP% **114.7**
Speed ratings (Par 107): **103,102,101,101,101 100,98,93,90,69**
CSF £61.87 CT £438.18 TOTE £9.60: £2.90, £2.90, £2.20; EX 89.20 Trifecta £171.20 Pool: £410.10 - 1.70 winning tickets..
Owner Broughton Thermal Insulation **Bred** Broughton Bloodstock And M Billings **Trained** Newmarket, Suffolk

FOCUS
A fair staying handicap, run at an even gallop. The form is sound enough, rated through the fourth, with a step up from the winner who was value for a bit extra.

NOTEBOOK
Broughtons Revival ◆ defied a 7lb rise in the weights for her recent success over an extended 1m3f at Leicester with a much-improved effort over this longer trip. Having travelled nicely just off the lead, she picked up well when asked to go and win her race in the straight and, always doing enough once in front, she was ultimately a very convincing winner. She did not make her debut until she was four, so she is still relatively lightly raced, and she should have even more to offer. She is well suited by plenty of give underfoot and gives the impression she may stay even further. She is entered in the Cesarewitch and, provided she makes the cut - she is on 7st 9lb but has now picked up a penalty - she should not be underestimated if the ground is on the soft side, even though her stamina for such an extreme test would have to be taken on trust. (op 7-1)
Bogside Theatre(IRE) ◆ travelled well towards the rear for much of the way and was still going well on the turn into straight. She found enough under pressure to move into second, but she struggled to make any real impression on the improving winner. This was just her sixth-career start and she is progressing into a very useful stayer. (op 8-1)
Dr Sharp(IRE) took the field along at an even gallop, but he just struggled against a couple of speedier types under his big weight in the straight. He looks better over further. (op 7-1)
Daryal(IRE), trying his furthest trip to date on the Flat, plugged on in the straight, but he made rather heavy weather of it all. (op 6-1)
Alaghiraar(IRE) hardly ran a bad race, but he failed to show the sort of improvement one might have expected on this step up in trip. It might just be that his yard is not in the best of form right now. (op 6-1)
Winged D'Argent(IRE) appeared to run his best race so far this year. (op 10-1)

Multicultural Official explanation: jockey said gelding hung both ways throughout

5809 AKZO NOBEL PREMIER H'CAP 6f
3:00 (3:01) (Class 2) (0-100,98) 3-Y-0+ **£12,954** (£3,854; £1,926; £962) **Stalls** Centre

Form RPR

3000 **1** **Dabbers Ridge (IRE)**[37] 4747 5-9-6 **98**........................ DarryllHolland 2 109
(B W Hills) *chsd ldrs: pushed along 1/2-way: hdwy 2f out: rdn to ld appr fnl f: styd on wl* **4/1**[2]

0501 **2** *1 1/4* **Commando Scott (IRE)**[7] 5617 6-8-13 **91**........................ GregFairley 6 98
(I W McInnes) *cl up: led wl over 2f out: rdn and hdd over 1f out: sn drvn and kpt on* **10/3**[1]

0155 **3** *shd* **Compton's Eleven**[14] 5413 6-8-7 **85**................................ MartinDwyer 1 92
(M R Channon) *towards rr: gd hdwy 2f out: rdn and styd on wl appr fnl f: nrst fin* **11/1**

-650 **4** *1/2* **Cape**[70] 3746 4-8-7 **85**.. FrancisNorton 9 90
(P Howling) *chsd ldrs: hdwy and ev ch over 1f out: sn rdn and one pce ins fnl f* **16/1**

0500 **5** *1/2* **Burning Incense (IRE)**[20] 5254 4-9-1 **93**...........(b) RichardKingscote 12 97
(R Charlton) *trckd ldrs: swtchd rt and hdwy 2f out: chal and ev ch over 1f out: sn rdn and btn* **6/1**[3]

0106 **6** *2 1/2* **River Falcon**[7] 5616 7-9-6 **98**.. DanielTudhope 3 94
(J S Goldie) *bhd tl styd on fnl 2f: nrst fin* **6/1**[3]

6260 **7** *shd* **Geojimali**[8] 5584 5-8-6 **84** oh3..................................... SaleemGolam 5 80
(J S Goldie) *dwlt and bhd tl styd on fnl 2f* **10/1**

2000 **8** *1 1/4* **Turnkey**[7] 5616 5-8-10 **95**.. AdeleRothery(7) 4 87
(D Nicholls) *sn outpcd and wl bhd tl sme late hdwy* **11/1**

0300 **9** *1/2* **Caribbean Coral**[8] 5584 8-8-12 **90**............................ GrahamGibbons 8 81
(J J Quinn) *cl up: rdn along over 2f out and sn wknd* **14/1**

1065 **10** *5* **Continent**[8] 5584 10-8-7 **88**.. PJMcDonald(3) 10 64
(D Nicholls) *dwlt: hdwy and in tch 1/2-way: rdn over 2f out and sn wknd* **16/1**

00-0 **11** *2* **Sadeek**[16] 5355 3-9-2 **96**... TomEaves 7 66
(B Smart) *led: rdn along and hdd wl over 2f out: sn wknd* **25/1**

1m 14.2s (0.31) **Going Correction** +0.275s/f (Good)
WFA 3 from 4yo+ 2lb **11** Ran SP% **119.7**
Speed ratings (Par 109): **108,106,106,105,104 101,101,99,99,92 89**
CSF £18.10 CT £141.00 TOTE £5.80: £2.00, £1.90, £3.30; EX 29.90 Trifecta £306.70 Part won. Pool: £432.00 - 0.40 winning tickets..
Owner Maurice Mogg **Bred** Franco Castelfranci **Trained** Lambourn, Berks

FOCUS
A good sprint handicap and solid form. They tended to race up the middle of the track.

NOTEBOOK
Dabbers Ridge(IRE) ◆ had not raced over a trip this short since making his debut back in 2004, with all his runs coming over 7f-1m, but he displayed sufficient speed to hold a handy position and ultimately ran out a clear-cut winner for his in-form yard, justifying a significant move in the market. Already proven as a smart type, he will have more options open to him now and he could well progress in the sprint division when the ground is on the easy side. Official explanation: trainer's rep said horse had been suited by the drop in trip to 6f (op 13-2)
Commando Scott(IRE) ran well off a mark 4lb higher than when winning over 7f at Ayr the previous weekend. He would not have minded the drop in trip, but basically just ran into a better-handicapped horse on the day. (op 7-2 tchd 3-1)
Compton's Eleven ◆, dropped back in trip, ran right up to his recent best and can have few excuses. Currently rated 85, he is qualified for lower-grade races and will be hard to beat if dropped to a Class 4 contest. (op 12-1)
Cape, having her first outing since leaving James Fanshawe, ran to a useful level of form in defeat, but she has basically failed to progress since looking unlucky at Goodwood earlier in the season. She is entitled to be sharper next time, though, as this was her first run in over two months. (op 10-1)
Burning Incense(IRE) has not been in much form lately and he again finished up well held. (tchd 11-2)
River Falcon was not at his best and this may have come a little soon following his fine sixth in the Ayr Gold Cup, especially considering he had also contested the Portland the previous week. (tchd 11-2)

5810 LESTER PIGGOTT "START TO FINISH" H'CAP 5f
3:35 (3:36) (Class 2) (0-100,97) 3-Y-0+ **£19,431** (£5,781; £2,889; £1,443) **Stalls** Centre

Form RPR

1-20 **1** **Oldjoesaid**[28] 5050 3-8-13 **92**... DaneO'Neill 10 107
(H Candy) *trckd ldrs gng wl: smooth hdwy to ld over 1f out: pushed out* **7/1**[3]

0201 **2** *2* **Efistorm**[36] 4780 6-8-9 **87**... PhilipRobinson 3 95
(C R Dore) *hld up: hdwy 2f out: rdn to chse wnr ent fnl f: kpt on same pce* **9/2**[1]

5012 **3** *hd* **Bo McGinty (IRE)**[6] 5667 6-8-5 **83** oh2........................(b) HayleyTurner 1 90
(R A Fahey) *a.p: effrt 2f out and ev ch tl rdn over 1f out and kpt on same pce* **9/1**

312- **4** *2* **Chief Editor**[491] 1977 3-8-9 **88**.. TomEaves 4 88
(M J Wallace) *led: rdn along 2f out: drvn and hdd over 1f out: kpt on same pce* **22/1**

0001 **5** *1/2* **Invincible Force (IRE)**[15] 5394 3-9-1 **94**..................(v1) FrancisNorton 9 93
(Paul Green) *wnt lft s: cl up: rdn along 2f out: sn edgd lft and one pce* **12/1**

3000 **6** *shd* **Green Park (IRE)**[8] 5584 4-9-0 **92**................................ DaleGibson 11 90
(R A Fahey) *midfield: hdwy 2f out: sn rdn and no imp ent fnl f* **10/1**

0400 **7** *1/2* **Orientor**[7] 5616 9-8-12 **90**.. DanielTudhope 2 86
(J S Goldie) *towards rr: hdwy wl over 1f out: sn rdn and no imp fnl f* **15/2**

5000 **8** *nk* **Mecca's Mate**[7] 5616 6-9-0 **97**.. NeilBrown(5) 5 92
(D W Barker) *hmpd s: a in rr* **7/1**[3]

0020 **9** *2* **Fantasy Believer**[14] 5407 9-9-2 **94**................................ DarryllHolland 8 82
(J J Quinn) *bdly hmpd s and bhd tl sme late hdwy* **5/1**[2]

0400 **10** *3/4* **Northern Empire (IRE)**[8] 5584 4-8-9 **87**..............(b1) StephenDonohoe 7 73
(K A Ryan) *hmpd s: a in rr* **20/1**

0050 **11** *2 1/2* **Blazing Heights**[8] 5584 4-8-5 **83** oh4............................ SaleemGolam 12 60
(J S Goldie) *in tch: pushed along over 2f out: sn rdn and btn* **14/1**

1210 **12** *15* **Obstructive**[57] 4123 3-8-13 **92**.................................... MartinDwyer 6 17
(Andrew Reid) *hmpd s: a in rr* **12/1**

60.25 secs (0.13) **Going Correction** +0.275s/f (Good)
WFA 3 from 4yo+ 1lb **12** Ran SP% **121.9**
Speed ratings (Par 109): **109,105,105,102,101 101,100,100,96,95 91,67**
CSF £39.65 CT £299.05 TOTE £6.30: £2.10, £2.20, £2.60; EX 38.80 Trifecta £254.60 Pool: £430.40 - 1.20 winning tickets..
Owner J J Byrne **Bred** Mrs R D Peacock **Trained** Kingston Warren, Oxon
■ Stewards' Enquiry : Neil Brown caution: used whip with excessive frequency

FOCUS
Another good sprint handicap. Solid form, the winner up 8lb on his previous best. They raced middle to far side.

NOTEBOOK

Oldjoesaid ◆ did not show much on his return from a break at Sandown, but that run clearly brought him on significantly and he took this in pretty impressive fashion. He looks a smart sprinter in the making. (tchd 15-2)

Efistorm ran well off a 4lb higher mark than when winning at Newmarket on his previous start, but he probably just ran into a smart sprinter in the making. (op 5-1)

Bo McGinty(IRE) has been in fine form lately and this was another solid effort from 2lb out of the handicap. (op 12-1 tchd 8-1)

Chief Editor showed very useful form as a juvenile, winning two of his four starts and finishing second in a six-runner Listed event, but he had been off the track since last May. He did not look on a bad mark for his handicap debut and he made a very pleasing return to action, showing bright early speed before understandably getting tired late on. He can be expected to come on for the run and will be one to respect in the closing weeks of the season, with soft ground very much in his favour.

Invincible Force(IRE) was able to race off the same mark as when winning at the Curragh on his previous start, but this ground was probably softer than he really wants and he could not show his best in a first-time visor. (tchd 11-1)

Green Park(IRE), a stablemate of the third-placed horse, had conditions to suit and could have been expected to run better. (op 8-1)

Obstructive has left Dean Ivory's yard and is now in the care of his owner, Andrew Reid, who has taken out a trainer's licence once again. Already successful twice this season, he looked sure to keep improving, but he had not been seen since running poorly at Goodwood nearly two months ago and this was another disappointing effort. He may have some sort of physical problem, but he basically just looks like a horse low on confidence and perhaps a step up in trip will help, as he will have more chance to get into that giant stride of his without having to be bustled along.

5811 MTB GROUP EBF MAIDEN FILLIES' STKS (DIV I) — 1m 30y

4:10 (4:11) (Class 5) 2-Y-O — **£2,590** (£770; £385; £192) **Stalls** Low

Form — RPR

222 **1** **Badalona**[35] 4796 2-9-0 80 .... HayleyTurner 5 — 79
(M L W Bell) *trckd ldr: hdwy to ld 2f out and sn rdn: drvn ins fnl f and styd on gamely* **3/1**[2]

2 3/4 **Katimont (IRE)** 2-9-0 0 .... DarryllHolland 9 — 77
(B W Hills) *hld up in rr: stdy hdwy 3f out: rdn to chse wnr ent fnl f: edgd lft and no ex towards fin* **7/1**

00 **3** 5 **Zerky (USA)**[43] 4565 2-9-0 0 .... StephenDonohoe 6 — 66
(E A L Dunlop) *prom: effrort and ev ch over 2f out tl rdn and one pce appr fnl f* **33/1**

06 **4** 3/4 **Sparkling Montjeu (IRE)**[26] 5100 2-8-9 0 .... PatrickHills(5) 11 — 65
(J W Hills) *chsds ldrs on outer: effrt and hdwy 3f out: rdn 2f out and kpt on same pce* **66/1**

4 **5** 1 1/4 **Bookish**[18] 5309 2-9-0 0 .... GregFairley 8 — 62
(M Johnston) *led: rdn along 3f out: hdd 2f out: sn drvn and grad wknd* **7/1**

3 **6** hd **Snowy Indian**[23] 5162 2-9-0 0 .... JDSmith 1 — 62
(Sir Michael Stoute) *hld up and bhd: hdwy on inner wl over 2f out: no imp appr fnl f* **7/4**[1]

7 6 **Caffari (GER)** 2-9-0 0 .... TomEaves 10 — 48
(K R Burke) *wnt rt s: hdwy and in tch 1/2-way: rdn aling over 3f out and sn outpcd* **33/1**

002 **8** 1 1/2 **Baraari (USA)**[18] 5301 2-9-0 76 .... MartinDwyer 4 — 45
(J L Dunlop) *trckd ldrs: hdwy 4f out: rdn along 3f out and sn wknd* **7/2**[3]

00 **9** 11 **Miss Bouggy Wouggy**[79] 3446 2-9-0 0 .... DaleGibson 3 — 21
(M Blanshard) *in tch: rdn along 3f out: n.d* **50/1**

0 **10** 7 **Miss Okaloosa**[25] 5116 2-9-0 0 .... RichardKingscote 2 — 5
(D M Simcock) *a in rr* **50/1**

1m 48.89s (3.38) **Going Correction** +0.325s/f (Good) — **10** Ran SP% **119.9**
Speed ratings (Par 92): **96,95,90,89,88 88,82,80,69,62**
CSF £24.08 TOTE £4.10: £1.50, £2.10, £5.50; EX 25.10.

Owner Sheikh Marwan Al Maktoum **Bred** Darley **Trained** Newmarket, Suffolk

FOCUS

Just a fair fillies' maiden. The early pace was just ordinary, but the front two still finished clear. Most of these jockeys were happy to avoid the far rail in the straight. The winning time was 0.44 seconds slower than the second division, but just 0.07 seconds slower than the later colts & geldings maiden over this trip.

NOTEBOOK

Badalona had found one too good on all three of her previous starts, and had been a beaten favourite the last twice, but she made no mistake stepped up to 1m for the first time. She was plenty keen enough in the early stages, but had enough left in the straight to hold off the promising newcomer, Katimont, who had pulled well clear of the remainder. She is going to find things harder now, but is at least progressing and she looks quite a tough sort. (op 5-2)

Katimont(IRE) ◆, a 260,000 euros daughter of Montjeu and half-sister to six winners from the family of Shahrastani, raced in the Maids Causeway colours and made a very pleasing debut. She took a while to pick up in the straight, but came home well when finally getting the message and, although unable to reel in the winner, she pulled well clear of the remainder. She looks potentially smart. (op 12-1)

Zerky(USA), a one-time Fillies' Mile entrant, sported Hamdan Al Maktoum's second colours and ran a respectable race in third. She seems to be progressing with each run and will have more options now she is qualified for a handicap mark.

Sparkling Montjeu(IRE) had shown just moderate form on her two previous starts, but she has a middle-distance pedigree and a testing 1m on a galloping track was always going to suit at this stage of her career. This was her best effort and she is another now qualified for a handicap mark, but she is unlikely to come into her own until sent over further next year. (op 100-1)

Bookish was allowed her own way in front and held a nice advantage at one point, but she could not sustain her challenge and failed to build on the promise she showed over 7f on Polytrack on her debut. (op 9-1)

Snowy Indian, a sister to 2003 Royal Lodge winner Snow Ridge, was unable to confirm the promise she showed when third on her debut over 7f at Salisbury. She was set plenty to do, especially considering the pace was just ordinary through the early stages, and she was also produced with her challenge a lot closer to the far rail than many of her rivals in the straight, but she should still have run better. This ground was probably softer than she would have liked though, and it would probably be unwise to be give up on her just yet. (tchd 2-1, 9-4 in places)

Baraari(USA), Hamdan Al Maktoum's first string, was well below the form she showed when second at Leicester on her previous start and is another who may not have appreciated the testing ground. Official explanation: jockey said filly was unsuited by the soft, good to soft in places ground (op 9-2)

Miss Okaloosa Official explanation: jockey said filly lost her action

5812 MTB GROUP EBF MAIDEN FILLIES' STKS (DIV II) — 1m 30y

4:45 (4:46) (Class 5) 2-Y-O — **£2,590** (£770; £385; £192) **Stalls** Low

Form — RPR

0 **1** **Barawin (IRE)**[50] 4350 2-9-0 0 .... FrancisNorton 7 — 82
(K R Burke) *in tch: pushed along and outpcd 1/2-way: hdwy over 2f out: swtchd lft and rdn ent fnl f: styd on wl to ld last 75yds* **40/1**

2 nk **Miracle Seeker** 2-9-0 0 .... RichardKingscote 10 — 81
(C G Cox) *in tch on outer: hdwy over 2f out: rdn to ld ent fnl f and sn hung lft: hdd and no ex last 75yds* **16/1**

04 **3** 2 1/2 **Armure**[35] 4796 2-9-0 0 .... PhilipRobinson 5 — 76
(M A Jarvis) *cl up: led wl over 2f out: sn rdn and hung lft: hdd over 1f out and kpt on same pce* **8/11**[1]

2 **4** nk **Red Icon**[18] 5308 2-8-11 0 .... PJMcDonald(3) 3 — 75
(R M Beckett) *chsd ldrs: rdn along over 2f out: drvn over 1f out: kpt on same pce* **5/1**[2]

5 hd **Funseeker (UAE)** 2-9-0 0 .... GregFairley 11 — 74
(M Johnston) *hld up in rr: stdy hdwy on inner 3f out: rdn and ch wl over 1f out: sn drvn and one pce* **8/1**[3]

6 1 **Silk Affair (IRE)** 2-8-11 0 .... JerryO'Dwyer(3) 8 — 72
(M G Quinlan) *towards rr: hdwy 3f out: rdn wl over 1f out and kpt on same pce* **20/1**

7 1/2 **Trianon** 2-9-0 0 .... DaneO'Neill 4 — 71
(R Charlton) *chsd ldrs: hdwy 3f out: rdn along 2f out and grad wknd appr fnl f* **16/1**

00 **8** 7 **Khibraat**[35] 4796 2-9-0 0 .... MartinDwyer 9 — 56
(E A L Dunlop) *a towards rr* **25/1**

9 1 1/2 **Kayflaa (IRE)** 2-9-0 0 .... DarryllHolland 6 — 52
(M R Channon) *chsd ldrs: rdn along over 2f out: grad wknd* **8/1**[3]

05 **10** 13 **Warsaw Waltz**[17] 5329 2-9-0 0 .... TomEaves 1 — 24
(J G Given) *led: rdn along 3f out: sn hdd & wknd* **28/1**

1m 48.45s (2.94) **Going Correction** +0.325s/f (Good) — **10** Ran SP% **123.1**
Speed ratings (Par 92): **98,97,95,94,94 93,93,86,84,71**
CSF £568.86 TOTE £43.20: £5.80, £4.30, £1.10; EX 1090.90.

Owner M J Halligan **Bred** Jim Halligan **Trained** Middleham Moor, N Yorks

FOCUS

This fillies' maiden looked to have more strength in depth than the first division and the winning time was 0.44 seconds quicker, although the pace was noticeably stronger. The time was also 0.37 seconds faster than the following colts & geldings maiden run over this distance. Big improvement from the winner, but it was no fluke. Once again the jockeys were keen to avoid the far rail early in the straight.

NOTEBOOK

Barawin(IRE) offered little on her debut over 6f here the previous month, but this trip was much more suitable and she produced an improved effort to get off the mark at the second attempt. A daughter of the brilliant Hawk Wing, she had to be niggled along to stay in touch from some way out, but she kept responding and really found her stride in the straight. She had to be switched left with her challenge and also edged that way under pressure, with the eventual runner-up encouraging her in that direction when hanging left on her outside, but she just did enough. She has a bit of size and very much gives the impression this run will bring her on again. (tchd 33-1)

Miracle Seeker, a daughter of Rainbow Quest and half-sister to top-class juvenile hurdler Katchit, who was also a 1m2f winner on the Flat, out of a dual 1m winner at two and four, made a pleasing debut. She finished well when getting the hang of things in the straight, but hung to her left and was just held by a filly with the benefit of previous experience. She should improve and ought to be up to winning a similar event. (op 12-1)

Armure, who produced an improved effort to take fourth at Beverley on her previous start, looked likely to justify her short odds when sent on over two furlongs from the finish, but it quickly became apparent she had a race on her hands and she could only manage third. If her breeding is anything to go by, she can do better over further next year. (op 11-10 tchd 5-4 and 6-5 in place)

Red Icon ran second in a 7f Polytrack maiden at Lingfield on her debut, but this was tougher. (op 4-1 tchd 7-2 in places)

Funseeker(UAE), a daughter of Halling, closely related to quite useful 7f juvenile winner Finity, out of a quite useful middle-distance scorer, made a respectable debut and is open to improvement. (op 7-1)

Silk Affair(IRE) ◆, an 80,000gns daughter of Barathea, sister to dual 1m3f winner Subtle Affair, out of a winner over 1m6f, shaped nicely and should do well over further next year. (op 16-1)

5813 TOM BUCKLEY 21ST BIRTHDAY E B F MAIDEN STKS (C&G) — 1m 30y

5:20 (5:20) (Class 5) 2-Y-O — **£3,238** (£963; £481; £240) **Stalls** Low

Form — RPR

042 **1** **Ballochroy (IRE)**[17] 5328 2-9-0 76 .... DaneO'Neill 1 — 80
(B W Hills) *trckd ldrs: effrt over 2f out: rdn over 1f out: swtchd lft and drvn ins fnl f: styd on to ld nr line* **10/1**

3 **2** shd **All The Aces (IRE)**[17] 5329 2-9-0 0 .... PhilipRobinson 7 — 80
(M A Jarvis) *cl up: rdn along 3f out: drvn and edgd rt over 1f out: styd on to ld ins fnl f: hdd nr line* **11/2**[3]

2 **3** 1 **Green Wadi**[14] 5417 2-9-0 0 .... DarryllHolland 4 — 78
(M R Channon) *led: rdn along and hdd over 2f out: cl up and ev ch tl drvn and no ex wl ins fnl f* **6/4**[1]

4 nk **Prime Exhibit** 2-9-0 0 .... RichardKingscote 6 — 77
(R Charlton) *t.k.h: chsd ldrs: hdwy after 3f and sn cl up: led gng wl over 2f out: rdn wl over 1f out: hdd ins fnl f: wknd* **5/2**[2]

0 **5** hd **Enroller (IRE)**[50] 4362 2-9-0 0 .... FrancisNorton 9 — 76
(W R Muir) *t.k.h: prom on outer whn bmpd and lost grnd after 3f: hdwy over 2f out: sn rdn and kpt on u.p ins fnl f: nrst fin* **66/1**

03 **6** 3/4 **Blue Citadel (USA)**[8] 5580 2-9-0 0 .... MartinDwyer 3 — 75
(J H M Gosden) *towards rr: stdy hdwy over 2f out: styd on ins fnl f: nrst fin* **7/1**

0 **7** 1/2 **Manor Park (IRE)**[29] 5011 2-8-11 0 .... PJMcDonald(3) 2 — 74
(C G Cox) *towards rr: hdwy over 2f out: sn rdn and kpt on appr fnl f: nrst fin* **25/1**

40 **8** 6 **Rivington Pike (IRE)**[36] 4764 2-9-0 0 .... GrahamGibbons 5 — 61
(J J Quinn) *chsd ldrs: rdn along 3f out: sn wknd* **25/1**

00 **9** 7 **Feeling Fresh (IRE)**[17] 5329 2-9-0 0 .... TomEaves 8 — 45
(Paul Green) *stdd s: a in rr* **100/1**

10 8 **Fly With The Stars (USA)** 2-9-0 0 .... GregFairley 10 — 28
(M Johnston) *dwlt: a towards rr* **16/1**

11 13 **Ministerofinterior** 2-9-0 0 .... HayleyTurner 11 — —
(C F Wall) *t.k.h: chsd ldrs over 2f: sn lost pl and bhd fr 1/2-way* **40/1**

1m 48.82s (3.31) **Going Correction** +0.325s/f (Good) — **11** Ran SP% **124.0**
Speed ratings (Par 95): **96,95,94,94,94 93,93,87,80,72 59**
CSF £65.34 TOTE £12.90: £2.70, £2.20, £1.20; EX 40.00.

Owner The Mystic Mogg Partnership **Bred** Manister House Stud **Trained** Lambourn, Berks

■ Stewards' Enquiry : Dane O'Neill four-day ban: used whip with excessive frequency (Oct 10-13)
Philip Robinson three-day ban: used whip with excessive frequency and without allowing colt time to respond (Oct 10-12)

FOCUS

A decent maiden but the first seven finished in a bit of heap. The winning time was 0.07 seconds quicker than the first division of the fillies' maiden, but 0.37 seconds slower than the second division. They all raced stands' side early in the straight, but a few drifted back towards the centre near the line.

NOTEBOOK
Ballochroy(IRE) benefited from the step up to 1m and improved on his three previous efforts. He looked held around two furlongs from the finish, but he clearly stays well and just got up close home. He already looks in need of further and should make a nice middle-distance or staying type. (op 16-1 tchd 9-1)
All The Aces(IRE)'s debut third came over 7f on quick ground round here, but he was able to confirm that promise under these vastly different conditions. He should win a maiden this year. (tchd 5-1, 6-1 in a place)
Green Wadi was not beaten that far, but he still ran well below the form he showed when second over 1m on quick ground in a good maiden at Goodwood on his debut. This ground may have been a little softer than ideal. (op 11-8 tchd 7-4, 15-8 in places)
Prime Exhibit ◆, a 135,000gns son of Selkirk, out of an unraced half-sister to the useful middle-distance/stayer Moments Of Joy, looked all over the winner when looming large against the stands' rail early in the straight, and he was still apparently travelling strongly when sent to the front, but he found little when let down. He had raced a little keenly through the early stages and probably just got tired in the testing ground late on. A Racing Post Trophy entrant, he looks to possess a serious engine and should make no mistake next time. (tchd 3-1)
Enroller(IRE) showed ability when mid-division on his debut at Newmarket and this was another promising effort. A Racing Post Trophy and Derby entrant, he looks capable of progressing into a useful sort.
Blue Citadel(USA) promised to be suited by the return to 1m, but he struggled to land a telling blow.
Manor Park(IRE) has ability and should come into his own over further next year. (op 40-1)

5814 EUROPEAN BREEDERS' FUND "REPROCOLOR" FILLIES' H'CAP 1m 2f 120y
5:50 (5:50) (Class 3) (0-90,85) 3-Y-0+ £11,658 (£3,468; £1,733; £865) Stalls High

Form RPR
3242 1 **Ronaldsay**[22] 5210 3-9-11 **85** ... FrancisNorton 4 98+
(R Hannon) *hld up in rr: stdy hdwy 3f out: rdn to ld 1f out: styd on strly* 5/2[1]
3024 2 2 **Sunisa (IRE)**[63] 3972 6-9-3 **75** ... NeilBrown(5) 7 84
(J Mackie) *hld up: hdwy 3f out: rdn to ld over 1f out: hdd 1f out and kpt on same pce* 11/2
32 3 2 **Princess Cocoa (IRE)**[42] 4615 4-9-3 **70** ... DaleGibson 8 75
(R A Fahey) *trckd ldrs: hdwy to ld wl over 2f out: rdn and hdd over 1f out: kpt on same pce* 7/1
6124 4 3 1/2 **Tebee**[24] 5131 3-9-6 **80** ... MartinDwyer 1 79
(J H M Gosden) *prom: rdn along 3f out: drvn 2f out and sn one pce* 7/2[2]
1350 5 3 **Tcherina (IRE)**[24] 5145 5-9-8 **78** ... DuranFentiman(3) 3 71
(T D Easterby) *prom: rdn along over 3f out: grad wknd* 10/1
4123 6 3 **Lady Friend**[30] 4976 5-9-10 **77** ... DarryllHolland 5 65
(J W Hills) *hld up in rr: hdwy on outer over 3f out: rdn along over 2f out and sn wknd* 4/1[3]
-100 7 12 **Toccata (IRE)**[95] 2971 3-9-2 **76** ... HayleyTurner 6 42
(D M Simcock) *led: rdn along 3f out: sn hdd & wknd* 12/1

2m 20.76s (4.62) **Going Correction** +0.325s/f (Good)
WFA 3 from 4yo+ 7lb 7 Ran SP% **115.5**
Speed ratings (Par 104): **96,94,93,90,88 86,77**
CSF £17.02 CT £84.80 TOTE £2.90: £1.80, £4.10; EX 25.30 Place 6 £138.49, Place 5 £21.21.
Owner S P Tindall **Bred** Stowell Hill Ltd **Trained** East Everleigh, Wilts

FOCUS
A fair fillies' handicap, and sound form. Despite the early pace looking just ordinary, they finished well strung out. They raced up the middle of the track in the straight.

NOTEBOOK
Ronaldsay, reunited for the first time with the only rider to have won on her, gained compensation for an unlucky defeat at Newbury on her previous start and showed that she does not require the exaggerated waiting tactiucs that have often been employed. This was her first run on ground this soft, but she handled it well and ran out a convincing winner. (op 2-1)
Sunisa(IRE) has been in good order since returning to the level and this was another decent effort. (op 5-1 tchd 6-1)
Princess Cocoa(IRE) ran a respectable race on ground that was probably a little softer than ideal. (op 8-1)
Tebee is another who may have found the ground plenty soft enough, but she looks too high in the weights in any case. (op 4-1 tchd 9-2)
Tcherina(IRE) did not run very well at York on her previous start and this was another below-par effort. (op 8-1)
Lady Friend had conditions to suit but, having had to be pushed along to find her stride almost as soon at the stalls opened, she was never really going. She had looked a handicapper to follow earlier in the season, but this was rather off putting. Official explanation: jockey said mare ran flat and lost her action on the bend turning in (op 11-2 tchd 6-1 in a place)
T/Plt: £81.80 to a £1 stake. Pool: £90,046.85. 803.25 winning tickets. T/Qpdt: £12.30 to a £1 stake. Pool: £3,314.30. 198.90 winning tickets. JR

5727 KEMPTON (A.W) (R-H)
Saturday, September 29

OFFICIAL GOING: Standard
Wind: Slight half-against

5815 JUMP RACING BACK HERE OCTOBER 21ST MAIDEN AUCTION STKS 5f (P)
6:50 (6:52) (Class 6) 2-Y-0 £2,047 (£604; £302) Stalls High

Form RPR
65 1 **Really Really Wish**[116] 2333 2-8-13 0 ... RyanMoore 12 77
(J R Best) *a.p: rdn over 1f out: styd on to ld ins fnl f* 7/4[1]
6200 2 3/4 **Lady Vibeeka**[27] 5065 2-8-4 63 ... PaulHanagan 8 65
(Mrs H Sweeting) *led: hrd rdn appr fnl f: hdd ins fnl f: kpt on* 9/1
2663 3 1 1/4 **Ben**[14] 5429 2-8-10 73 ... (v[1]) RobertHavlin 5 67
(P G Murphy) *trckd ldr: rdn over 1f out: one pce fnl f* 11/4[2]
04 4 1 1/2 **Shakespeare's Son**[26] 5097 2-8-11 0 ... ChrisCatlin 10 62
(H J Evans) *mid-div: hdwy 2f out: hdwy over 1f out: edgd lft: no imp* 7/1
005 5 1/2 **In A Pickle**[24] 5126 2-8-6 57 ... EddieAhern 3 55
(H J L Dunlop) *in rr: rdn and hdwy on outside over 2f out: kpt on one pce* 14/1
04 6 nk **Tournevr (IRE)**[64] 3915 2-8-7 0 ... PaulDoe 7 55
(Jane Chapple-Hyam) *trckd ldrs: rdn 1/2-way: wknd over 1f out* 6/1[3]
2404 7 3/4 **Ronsai (USA)**[19] 5267 2-8-6 66 ... RichardSmith 9 52
(R Hannon) *trckd ldrs: rdn and wknd over 1f out* 8/1
8 3 **Madame Montom (USA)** 2-7-11 0 ... JCorrigan(7) 1 39
(S W Hall) *slowly away and wnt lft s: a bhd* 50/1
0 9 1 **Tiepie**[8] 5587 2-8-10 0 ... StephenCarson 4 41
(J Akehurst) *outpcd: a bhd* 33/1

60.04 secs (-0.36) **Going Correction** -0.35s/f (Stan) 9 Ran SP% **122.5**
Speed ratings (Par 93): **88,86,84,82,81 81,79,75,73**
CSF £20.53 TOTE £2.80: £1.10, £3.40, £1.50; EX 25.70.
Owner Malcolm Ward **Bred** Vincent Howley **Trained** Hucking, Kent

FOCUS
A fair maiden for a time of year, but something of a surprise to see the juvenile course record fall. Really Really Wish is going the right way.

NOTEBOOK
Really Really Wish, who showed plenty of speed before fading late on over this trip at Lingfield last time, had the best of the draw and he held a prominent position. Asked for his effort over a furlong out, he gradually got on top and broke the juvenile course record in the process. He is now likely to head into nurseries and this strong sort should have more to offer. (op 5-2)
Lady Vibeeka has not been progressing, but she showed improved form here and it was only in the final half-furlong she cried enough. This was an improved effort and she may do better in nurseries. (op 8-1 tchd 10-1)
Ben failed to take advantage of several good opportunities earlier in the season and as a result he came into this winless in 11 starts. Sporting a first-time visor, he ran one of his better races back in third, but is likely to remain vulnerable in maidens. He requires a drop in grade. (op 7-2 tchd 9-2)
Shakespeare's Son, who needed this to qualify for a handicap mark, was dropping a furlong in trip and it was no surprise to see him done for speed. He should fare better in nurseries. (op 12-1)
In A Pickle has improved a little with each run and she gave the impression a return to further will suit once contesting nurseries. (op 10-1)

5816 VIRGIN ACTIVE MAIDEN STKS 1m 2f (P)
7:20 (7:23) (Class 5) 3-Y-0+ £2,817 (£838; £418; £209) Stalls High

Form RPR
35 1 **Viva Vettori**[15] 5384 3-9-3 0 ... RichardHughes 2 82+
(D R C Elsworth) *sn led: mde rest: rdn out fnl f* 7/4[1]
-245 2 2 **Comma (USA)**[51] 4338 3-8-12 77 ... RyanMoore 12 73+
(Sir Michael Stoute) *trckd ldrs: rdn 3f out: wnt 2nd over 1f out: no imp on wnr ins fnl f* 11/4[3]
2040 3 1 1/2 **Putra Square**[119] 2231 3-9-3 90 ... TQuinn 10 75
(P F I Cole) *chsd wnr: rdn over 2f out: one pce and lost 2nd over 1f out* 5/2[2]
222- 4 1/2 **Garafena**[444] 3419 4-9-4 81 ... SebSanders 8 69
(Pat Eddery) *mid-div: hdwy 1/2-way: styd on one pce fnl f* 13/2
5 10 **Summerofsixtynine**[103] 4-9-9 0 ... RobertHavlin 9 54
(J G M O'Shea) *s.i.s: mde sme late hdwy but no ch w first 4* 50/1
6 1/2 **Bothar Brugha (IRE)**[486] 2152 3-9-3 0 ... FergusSweeney 6 53
(J G M O'Shea) *s.i.s: sn mid-div: rdn over 3f out: wknd 2f out* 50/1
5 7 2 **Istibian (IRE)**[25] 5113 3-9-3 0 ... GeorgeBaker 5 49
(Mrs H Sweeting) *a towards rr* 25/1
00 8 1/2 **Lady Lorins**[24] 5129 3-8-9 0 ... TravisBlock(3) 3 43
(Andrew Turnell) *chsd ldrs: wknd 3f out* 100/1
000- 9 5 **Premier Cru**[306] 6616 4-9-9 41 ... ChrisCatlin 11 38
(Andrew Turnell) *a bhd* 66/1
10 2 1/2 **Bora Shaamit (IRE)**[102] 5-9-4 0 ... VinceSlattery 1 28
(M Scudamore) *s.i.s: sn in tch: wknd 4f out* 100/1
0634 11 shd **Winforjoe (IRE)**[24] 5137 3-8-12 41 ... FrankieMcDonald 7 28
(J J Bridger) *mid-div: rdn 4f out: sn btn* 100/1
4066 12 1 3/4 **Nothingtodeclaire**[11] 5510 3-8-10 68 ... EddieSemaan(7) 4 29
(G A Huffer) *a bhd* 66/1
0 13 9 **Cumae (USA)**[104] 2693 3-8-12 0 ... JimmyQuinn 13 6
(J Pearce) *mid-div: rdn and wknd 4f out* 100/1

2m 4.46s (-4.54) **Going Correction** -0.35s/f (Stan)
WFA 3 from 4yo+ 6lb 13 Ran SP% **119.6**
Speed ratings (Par 103): **104,102,101,100,92 92,90,90,86,84 84,82,75**
CSF £6.62 TOTE £3.20: £1.30, £1.50, £1.20; EX 10.50.
Owner Mike Watson **Bred** Stanley Estate And Stud Co **Trained** Newmarket, Suffolk

FOCUS
Only a handful of these could be given a chance in what was an uncompetitive maiden.
Istibian(IRE) Official explanation: jockey said gelding would not face the kickback early on
Cumae(USA) Official explanation: jockey said filly had no more to give

5817 DIGIBET.COM H'CAP 7f (P)
7:50 (7:55) (Class 6) (0-50,50) 3-Y-0+ £2,047 (£604; £302) Stalls High

Form RPR
-000 1 **Sarah's Art (IRE)**[153] 1321 4-9-0 **50** ... TolleyDean(5) 1 63
(Stef Liddiard) *mid-div: rdn and hdwy over 2f out: r.o to ld wl ins fnl f* 20/1
0-00 2 1 **Palais Polaire**[3] 5730 5-9-5 **50** ... RichardThomas 2 60
(J A Geake) *in tch: rdn to ld appr fnl f: edgd rt: hdd wl ins fnl f* 15/2[3]
0032 3 1 1/2 **Brave Jack (IRE)**[5] 5688 3-9-2 **50** ... RyanMoore 6 56+
(J R Best) *in rr: rdn and hdwy over 1f out: r.o wl fnl f: nvr nrr* 9/4[1]
0000 4 1 **Tipsy Lad**[3] 5730 5-9-4 **49** ... (t) TQuinn 9 52
(D J S Ffrench Davis) *in rr: rdn and picked up appr fnl f: r.o: nvr nrr* 12/1
3300 5 nk **Simpsons Gamble (IRE)**[142] 1612 4-9-4 **49** ... EddieAhern 8 51
(R A Teal) *t.k.h: in tch: rdn and hdwy 2f out: one pce fnl f* 5/1[2]
0000 6 1 1/4 **Time For Change (IRE)**[26] 5095 3-9-2 **50** ... (v[1]) RobertHavlin 14 49
(P G Murphy) *in tch: rdn 2f out: nt qckn fnl f* 20/1
000 7 3/4 **Pont Wood**[15] 5390 3-9-2 **50** ... JimmyQuinn 3 47
(M Blanshard) *towards rr: styd on fnl f: nvr nr to chal* 33/1
0003 8 1/2 **Gyration (IRE)**[33] 4901 3-9-2 **50** ... (p) SebSanders 7 46
(J G Given) *trckd ldr: led over 2f out: bmpd and hdd over 1f out: wknd fnl f* 8/1
4620 9 2 1/2 **Rubilini**[39] 4684 3-9-2 **50** ... TPO'Shea 10 39
(M R Channon) *chsd ldrs: rdn and wknd 2f out* 15/2[3]
0000 10 1 1/2 **Golden Square**[26] 5094 5-9-0 **50** ... (b) LukeMorris(5) 13 35
(A W Carroll) *a in rr* 9/1
300 11 3/4 **Sun Bian**[89] 3173 5-9-3 **48** ... VinceSlattery 4 31
(L P Grassick) *a bhd* 33/1
3400 12 1/2 **Desert Lover (IRE)**[169] 1027 5-9-5 **50** ... RichardHughes 12 32
(R J Price) *led tl hdd over 2f out: wknd qckly appr fnl f* 8/1
0- 13 9 **Mujobliged (IRE)**[313] 6545 4-9-2 **47** ... (tp) ChrisCatlin 5 4
(Seamus G O'Donnell, Ire) *a bhd: lost tch over 2f out* 10/1

1m 24.97s (-1.83) **Going Correction** -0.35s/f (Stan)
WFA 3 from 4yo+ 3lb 13 Ran SP% **135.4**
Speed ratings (Par 101): **96,94,93,92,91 90,89,88,85,84 83,82,72**
CSF £177.36 CT £488.46 TOTE £29.70: £7.70, £4.50, £1.50; EX 330.60.
Owner ownaracehorse.co.uk (Shefford) **Bred** Newtownbarry House Stud **Trained** Great Shefford, Berks

FOCUS
A poor handicap.

5818 DIGIBET NURSERY 7f (P)
8:20 (8:25) (Class 6) (0-65,64) 2-Y-0 £2,047 (£604; £302) Stalls High

Form RPR
005 1 **It's My Day (IRE)**[19] 5274 2-9-3 **60** ... JimCrowley 14 64+
(Jane Chapple-Hyam) *in rr: rdn and hdwy 2f out: swept through to ld nr fin* 9/2[1]

0602 **2** ¾ **Hurstpierpoint (IRE)**[7] 5644 2-9-3 **60** .... PaulHanagan 10 62
(R A Fahey) *led rdn over 1f out: kpt on but hdd nr fin* **9/2[1]**

1250 **3** 3½ **Llab Nala**[10] 5534 2-8-8 **58** .... ThomasO'Brien(7) 6 51
(M R Channon) *in tch: rdn 3f out: hung rt bef r.o ins fnl f* **8/1**

460 **4** 2 **Lowry's Art**[68] 3796 2-9-7 **64** .... SebSanders 5 52
(R M Beckett) *mid-div: rdn 3f out: kpt on one pce fnl f* **5/1[2]**

5506 **5** nk **Too Grand**[13] 5443 2-8-10 **56** ....(v1) NeilChalmers(3) 3 44
(A M Balding) *slowly away: sn trckd ldrs: wnt 2nd over 2f out: rdn and wknd fnl f* **8/1**

655 **6** 2 **Maiden Miss (IRE)**[44] 4537 2-9-2 **59** .... TPO'Shea 4 42
(M R Channon) *trckd ldr tl rdn over 2f out: sn btn* **6/1[3]**

000 **7** ½ **Peer Pressure**[19] 5274 2-9-5 **62** .... JimmyQuinn 1 43
(P Mitchell) *slowly away: mde sme late hdwy: nvr on terms* **33/1**

006 **8** hd **Colmar Magic (IRE)**[26] 5088 2-9-1 **58** .... RichardHughes 12 39
(R Hannon) *chsd ldrs: short of room over 1f out: one pce after* **8/1**

000 **9** ½ **Riorun (IRE)**[56] 4181 2-9-1 **58** .... EddieAhern 8 38
(J G Portman) *t.k.h in rr: effrt over 2f out: wknd over 1f out* **7/1**

000 **10** nk **Lady Maya**[25] 5110 2-9-0 **57** .... FergusSweeney 9 36
(Dr J R J Naylor) *a in rr* **80/1**

060 **11** ½ **Oronsay**[19] 5267 2-9-3 **60** .... ChrisCatlin 11 38
(B R Millman) *mid-div: hdwy 3f out: rdn and wknd 2f out* **25/1**

0006 **12** 2 **Eastbourne**[14] 5429 2-9-0 **57** .... StephenCarson 2 30
(Eve Johnson Houghton) *in tch tl rdn over 2f out: sn bhd* **25/1**

0500 **13** 3 **Tobago Bay**[3] 5729 2-9-3 **60** ....(v1) SamHitchcott 13 25
(M R Channon) *a bhd* **33/1**

1m 25.85s (-0.95) **Going Correction** -0.35s/f (Stan) **13** Ran SP% **128.0**
Speed ratings (Par 93): **91,90,86,83,83 81,80,80,79,79 78,76,73**
CSF £25.21 CT £171.83 TOTE £8.10: £2.80, £1.70, £3.10; EX 41.30.
Owner Gordon Li **Bred** Keatly Overseas Ltd **Trained** Newmarket, Suffolk

FOCUS
A weak nursery. The first two finished clear and the runner-up sets the standard.

NOTEBOOK
It's My Day(IRE), handed a mark of 60 following three down-the-field runs in maidens, had the best of the draw, but his rider elected to drop him in and he found himself virtually last turning for home. However, he really began to motor in the final quarter mile and ultimately won going away, seeing the juvenile course record being broken for the second time on the day. He is likely to stay further in time and may well have more to offer. (op 11-2 tchd 7-1)
Hurstpierpoint(IRE), runner-up in a seller at Wolverhampton last time, was made plenty of use of on this return to handicaps and looked the winner until It's My Day swept past close home. She should find a race before long. (op 5-1)
Llab Nala, a selling winner earlier in the season, has been falling short off this mark in handicaps and he once again found a couple too good. (op 5-1)
Lowry's Art, handed a mark of 64 following three down-the-field runs in maidens, could not quicken sufficiently to throw down a serious challenge, but she gave the impression there will be better to come under a more positive ride. (op 7-2)
Too Grand ran a bit better in the first-time visor, but it is probably going to take a drop in grade/trip if she is to score. (op 10-1)

5819 DIGIBET SPORTS BETTING H'CAP — 1m (P)
8:50 (8:55) (Class 5) (0-75,75) 3-Y-O — £2,817 (£838; £418; £209) Stalls High

Form RPR

5020 **1** **Touch Of Style (IRE)**[10] 5532 3-8-13 **70** .... RichardHughes 10 81
(J R Boyle) *hld up: hdwy to ld over 1f out: hld on gamely fnl f* **20/1**

0161 **2** hd **Lawyers Choice**[17] 5339 3-9-2 **73** .... PaulEddery 1 83
(Pat Eddery) *mid-div: rdn 2f out: gd hdwy to press wnr ins fnl f* **6/1[2]**

2000 **3** 3½ **Hucking Heat (IRE)**[4] 5708 3-8-7 **64** ....(v1) JimCrowley 3 66
(J R Best) *slowly away: hdwy on ins over 2f out: n.m.r and swtchd rt over 1f out: kpt on fnl f but no ch w first 2* **9/1**

006 **4** shd **Chin Wag (IRE)**[78] 3491 3-9-3 **74** .... FergusSweeney 2 76
(K R Burke) *prom tl lost pl 3f out: r.o fnl f* **14/1**

106 **5** nk **Satyricon**[26] 5092 3-8-12 **74** ....(v) NicolPolli(5) 8 75
(M Botti) *hld up in rr: mde sme late hdwy* **7/1[3]**

054 **6** nk **Garden Party**[23] 5178 3-8-9 **66** ....(b1) RyanMoore 7 66
(Sir Michael Stoute) *trckd ldr: led briefly over 2f out: rdn and one pce after* **9/2[1]**

1000 **7** ¾ **Tasweet (IRE)**[17] 5339 3-8-12 **69** .... SebSanders 5 68
(T G Mills) *in tch tl rdn and wknd wl over 1f out* **9/1**

0336 **8** shd **Le Singe Noir**[26] 5102 3-8-11 **68** ....(b1) JimmyQuinn 14 66
(M Botti) *trckd ldrs: rdn over 1f out: wknd ins fnl f* **16/1**

6600 **9** nk **Proper (IRE)**[11] 5508 3-8-9 **66** .... TPO'Shea 9 64
(M R Channon) *trckd ldr tl rdn over 2f out: wkng whn hmpd ins fnl f* **10/1**

0006 **10** hd **Resplendent Ace (IRE)**[10] 5532 3-9-0 **71** .... PaulHanagan 6 68
(P Howling) *mid-div: rdn over 2f out: sn bhd* **9/2[1]**

4001 **11** hd **Pivotal Truth**[9] 5567 3-9-0 **71** .... TQuinn 12 68
(B W Hills) *led tl hdd over 2f out: wknd over 1f out* **8/1**

6040 **12** 3 **Majestic Cheer**[112] 2444 3-9-1 **72** .... EddieAhern 13 62
(E A L Dunlop) *in rr: tl hdwy on ins over 2f out: wknd ent fnl f* **16/1**

-640 **13** 8 **Divine Love (IRE)**[16] 5347 3-8-8 **65** ....(b) ChrisCatlin 4 37
(E J O'Neill) *a bhd* **33/1**

1m 38.13s (-2.67) **Going Correction** -0.35s/f (Stan) **13** Ran SP% **129.5**
Speed ratings (Par 101): **99,98,95,95,94 94,93,93,93,93 93,90,82**
CSF £146.93 CT £1242.48 TOTE £27.50: £5.60, £1.60, £3.90; EX 202.20.
Owner Inside Track Racing Club **Bred** Yeomanstown Stud **Trained** Epsom, Surrey

FOCUS
A modest handicap.
Majestic Cheer Official explanation: jockey said gelding did not stay

5820 PANORAMIC BAR AND RESTAURANT H'CAP — 2m (P)
9:20 (9:22) (Class 6) (0-65,65) 3-Y-O+ — £2,047 (£604; £302) Stalls High

Form RPR

2031 **1** **Featherlight**[14] 5426 3-9-1 **62** ....(b) RobertHavlin 14 79+
(Jamie Poulton) *towards rr: hdwy over 4f out: n.m.r 3f out: led over 2f out: qcknd clr and eased ins fnl f* **7/2[2]**

0264 **2** 3 **Sovereign Spirit (IRE)**[17] 5341 5-9-10 **59** ....(t) AdamKirby 11 71
(W R Swinburn) *in tch: rdn and 2nd over 2f out: kpt on but sn no ch w wnr* **8/1**

0234 **3** ½ **Capitalise (IRE)**[172] 994 4-9-1 **53** .... JerryO'Dwyer(3) 8 64
(V Smith) *mid-div: hdwy 4f out: outrdn over 2f out: styd on one pce* **15/2**

-342 **4** 10 **Born West (USA)**[7] 5626 3-9-4 **65** .... SebSanders 10 64
(P W Chapple-Hyam) *trckd ldrs: rdn 3f out: wknd 2f out* **15/8[1]**

0300 **5** 1 **Al Moulatham**[77] 3533 8-9-6 **55** ....(bt) SamHitchcott 9 53
(R Ford) *led: rdn over 3f out: hdd & wknd over 2f out* **25/1**

636- **6** 4 **Haatmey**[274] 6979 5-9-9 **58** .... JimCrowley 5 51
(P R Chamings) *in rr and nvr on terms* **10/1**

0604 **7** 3 **Arabian Sun**[14] 5426 3-8-11 **58** .... ChrisCatlin 4 47
(M J Attwater) *trckd ldrs: rdn 1/2-way: wknd 3f out* **16/1**

0-05 **8** hd **Forfeiter (USA)**[35] 148 5-9-3 **52** ....(t) PaulHanagan 2 41
(R Ford) *a bhd* **25/1**

-304 **9** nk **Salym (FR)**[191] 730 6-8-12 **47** .... TQuinn 1 36
(D J S Ffrench Davis) *a in rr* **33/1**

/2-5 **10** 1½ **Jockser (IRE)**[13] 5453 6-10-0 **63** .... EddieAhern 13 50
(J W Mullins) *in tch tl wknd 3f out* **11/2[3]**

0-00 **11** 2½ **Jaufrette**[53] 4253 4-9-1 **50** .... FergusSweeney 6 34
(Dr J R J Naylor) *a bhd* **100/1**

0600 **12** 16 **Merchant Bankes**[19] 5273 4-8-10 **50** .... TolleyDean(5) 12 15
(W G M Turner) *sn chsd ldr: wknd qckly over 2f out: eased fnl f: t.o* **33/1**

3m 25.83s (-5.57) **Going Correction** -0.35s/f (Stan)
WFA 3 from 4yo+ 12lb **12** Ran SP% **124.8**
Speed ratings (Par 101): **99,97,97,92,91 89,88,88,88,87 86,78**
CSF £31.99 CT £207.21 TOTE £5.10: £1.90, £1.90, £2.60; EX 22.40 Place 6 £60.55, Place 5 £46.99.
Owner Jirena Partnership **Bred** Keith Wills **Trained** Whitcombe, Dorset

FOCUS
A modest staying handicap in which yet another course record fell. The first three finished clear.
Jockser(IRE) Official explanation: jockey said gelding ran flat
T/Plt: £59.90 to a £1 stake. Pool: £76,012.00. 926.15 winning tickets. T/Qpdt: £20.80 to a £1 stake. Pool: £4,066.60. 144.50 winning tickets. JS

2706 SAN SIRO (R-H)
Saturday, September 29

OFFICIAL GOING: Heavy

5821a PREMIO FEDERICO TESIO (GROUP 3) — 1m 3f
3:25 (3:31) 3-Y-O+ — **£24,628** (£10,836; £5,911; £2,955)

RPR

1 **Pressing (IRE)**[20] 5264 4-8-12 .... EBotti 12 114
(M A Jarvis) *mde all: r.o strly fr over 1 1/2f out to go clr: easily* **98/100[1]**

2 3½ **Gimmy (IRE)**[104] 3-8-5 .... FBranca 8 108
(B Grizzetti, Italy) *racd in 2nd: drvn to chse ldr 2f out:m kpt on but nt pce of wnr* **105/10**

3 3¼ **Montalegre (IRE)**[146] 1518 5-8-12 .... MDemuro 4 103
(A & G Botti, Italy) *hld up in last: r.o wl fr over 1 1/2f out: nrest at fin* **46/10[2]**

4 1¼ **Sopran Promo (IRE)**[132] 1875 3-8-5 .... DVargiu 9 100
(B Grizzetti, Italy) *mid-div: drvn 2 1/2f out: styd on steadily to take 4th* **62/10**

5 2½ **Proud Boris (GER)**[188] 3-8-5 .... JBojko 2 96
(J Hanacek, Czech Republic) *prom to over 2f out* **153/10**

6 1¾ **Il Cadetto**[27] 3-8-6 .... GMarcelli 7 94
(L Di Dio, Italy) *hld up: nvr in contention* **5/1[3]**

7 ½ **Place In Line**[98] 5-8-12 .... GBietolini 10 92
(Gianluca Bietolini, Italy) *mid-div: n.d* **24/1**

8 3 **Dragon Fly (GER)**[31] 4957 5-8-12 .... AHelfenbein 6 87
(Frau Jutta Mayer, Germany) *mid-div: n.d* **25/1**

9 6 **Speciano**[173] 4-8-12 .... MMonteriso 1 77
(E Borromeo, Italy) *prom: u.p 3f out: wknd* **91/10**

10 ¾ **Inter Mondo (GER)**[29] 4-8-12 .... IRossi 3 76
(P Rau, Germany) *hld up: n.d* **81/1**

11 nk **Quality Son (ITY)**[335] 6-8-12 .... PConvertino 11 75
(V Oriani, Italy) *towards rr on outside: drvn early st: unable qck* **19/1**

2m 20.7s (2.10)
WFA 3 from 4yo+ 7lb **11** Ran SP% **137.7**
(Including 1 Euro stake): WIN 1.98; PL 1.35, 2.31, 1.76; DF 10.46.
Owner Gary A Tanaka **Bred** Azienda Agricola Del Parco **Trained** Newmarket, Suffolk

NOTEBOOK
Pressing(IRE), a good second in a valuable race in Turkey on his previous start, was sent to the front from the outset by Edmondo Botti and never looked in any danger, ultimately running out an impressive winner. He is likely to return to Italy to contest the remaining middle-distance Group 1 races.

5441 BELMONT PARK (L-H)
Saturday, September 29

OFFICIAL GOING: Firm

5822a FLOWER BOWL INVITATIONAL (GRADE 1) (F&M) — 1m 2f (T)
9:40 (9:46) 3-Y-O+
£183,673 (£61,224; £30,612; £15,306; £9,184; £1,531)

RPR

1 **Lahudood**[49] 4413 4-8-7 .... AGarcia 1 115
(K McLaughlin, U.S.A) **212/10**

2 ¾ **Rosinka (IRE)**[26] 4-8-7 .... JRose 7 113
(H G Motion, U.S.A) **179/10**

3 ½ **Wait A While (USA)**[37] 4-8-9 .... GKGomez 6 114
(T Pletcher, U.S.A) **19/20[1]**

4 nk **Hostess (USA)**[26] 4-8-7 .... CHill 2 111
(H J Bond, U.S.A) **81/1**

5 nk **Argentina (IRE)**[63] 5-8-7 .... KDesormeaux 9 111
(R J Frankel, U.S.A) **67/10[3]**

6 2 **Royal Highness (GER)**[49] 4413 5-8-11 .... RRDouglas 8 111
(Christophe Clement, U.S.A) **71/20[2]**

7 1¾ **Alexander Tango (IRE)**[21] 5248 3-8-7 .... SXBridgmohan 4 109
(T Stack, Ire) *held up, closed up to 5th over 4f out, 7th and one pace straight* **114/10**

8 4¼ **My Typhoon (IRE)**[37] 5-8-11 .... ECastro 5 99
(W Mott, U.S.A) **91/10**

9 7¾ **Masseuse (USA)**[69] 5-8-9 .... JCastellano 3 81
(James J Toner, U.S.A) **33/1**

1m 59.05s (-2.24)
WFA 3 from 4yo+ 6lb **9** Ran SP% **118.2**
PARI-MUTUEL (including $2 stakes): WIN 44.40; PL (1-2) 16.40, 14.20; SHOW (1-2-3) 8.20, 7.10, 2.90; SF 565.00.
Owner Shadwell Stable **Bred** Shadwell Estate Company Ltd **Trained** USA

NOTEBOOK
Lahudood did not appear on the original list of nominees for this race, and McLaughlin was thinking of running the Shadwell-owned filly in a second-level allowance race. However, when Makderah, who is also owned by Shadwell, sustained an injury and couldn't run, McLaughlin secured an invitation for this filly. She made the most of her opportunity with a surprise success and is now likely to be supplemented for the Breeders' Cup Filly & Mare Turf at Monmouth Park at a cost of $180,000.
Alexander Tango(IRE) found this tougher than the Grade 1 she landed over 1m1f her on her previous start and she could make little impression. This trip probably just stretches her.

5823a **KELSO H'CAP (GRADE 2)** **1m (T)**
10:12 (10:19) 3-Y-0+
£76,531 (£25,510; £12,755; £6,378; £3,827; £510)

				RPR
1		**Trippi's Storm (USA)**[21] 5250 4-8-3 (S Hough, U.S.A)	JCastellano 6 **53/10**[2]	113
2	½	**After Market (USA)**[34] 4-8-12 (J Shirreffs, U.S.A)	ASolis 5 **27/20**[1]	121
3	1½	**Palace Episode (USA)**[499] 1805 4-8-4 (Saeed Bin Suroor)	J-LSamyn 1 **108/10**	110
4	nk	**Woodlander (USA)**[35] 5-8-2 (G Contessa, U.S.A)	ECastro 10 **34/1**	107
5	nk	**English Colony** 3-8-3 ow2 (A Penna, U.S.A)	(b) CVelasquez 4 **56/10**[3]	111
6	1	**Strike A Deal (USA)**[28] 3-8-3 ow1 (A Goldberg, U.S.A)	RADominguez 7 **17/2**	109
7	¾	**Icy Atlantic (USA)**[28] 6-8-5 (T Pletcher, U.S.A)	JRVelazquez 8 **83/10**	105
8	nse	**Kavafi (IRE)**[34] 4873 5-8-4 (C Laffon-Parias, France)	ECoa 3 **159/10**	104
9	1½	**Jet Propulsion (USA)**[77] 4-8-4 (Daniel C Hurtak, U.S.A)	(b) ENunez 2 **27/1**	101
10	11	**Got The Last Laugh (USA)**[329] 6339 3-8-3 ow3 (W Mott, U.S.A)	KDesormeaux 9 **36/1**	78

1m 32.36s (-2.24)
WFA 3 from 4yo+ 4lb **10** Ran SP% **118.4**
PARI-MUTUEL: WIN 12.60; PL (1-2) 5.10, 3.20; SHOW (1-2-3) 3.90, 2.60,5.50; SF 42.00.
Owner E Paul Robsham Stable LLC **Bred** E Paul Robsham **Trained** USA

NOTEBOOK
Trippi's Storm(USA) recieved 9lb from After Market and took full advantage with a half-length success. He could now head for the Breeders' Cup Mile.
After Market(USA), arguably the best turf performer in the US, finished fast after being forced five wide and this was a fine effort conceding upwards of 7lb all round. He could re-oppose the winner in the Breeders' Cup Mile, but there is an outside chance he could be switched to the Classic.
Palace Episode(USA), the 2005 Racing Post Trophy winner for Kevin Ryan, ran a big race in defeat and looks to have a bright future in the US.

SANTA ANITA (L-H)
Saturday, September 29
OFFICIAL GOING: Dirt course - fast; turf course - firm

5824a **GOODWOOD STKS (GRADE 1) (CUSHION TRACK)** **1m 1f (D)**
12:30 (12:49) 3-Y-0+ **£153,061** (£51,020; £30,612; £15,306; £5,102)

				RPR
1		**Tiago (USA)**[77] 3-8-9 (J Shirreffs, U.S.A)	MESmith 4 **23/10**[2]	118
2	nse	**Awesome Gem (USA)**[41] 4-8-12 (Craig Dollase, U.S.A)	(b) DFlores 6 **37/10**[3]	116
3	1	**Big Booster (USA)**[41] 6-8-12 (M Mitchell, U.S.A)	(b) MCBaze 5 **152/10**	114
4	¾	**Lewis Michael (USA)**[63] 4-8-12 (W Catalano, U.S.A)	(b) EBaird 3 **23/10**[1]	112
5	2¼	**A. P. Xcellent (USA)**[41] 4-8-12 (J Shirreffs, U.S.A)	(b) JValdiviaJr 7 **21/1**	108
6	¾	**Hello Sunday (FR)**[41] 4-8-12 (R J Frankel, U.S.A)	BBlanc 2 **13/1**	106
7	hd	**Arson Squad (USA)**[41] 4-8-12 (B Headley, U.S.A)	VEspinoza 1 **48/10**	106
8	11	**Wanna Runner (CAN)**[26] 4-8-12 (B Baffert, U.S.A)	(b) TBaze 8 **38/1**	83

1m 46.93s (-1.97)
WFA 3 from 4yo+ 5lb **8** Ran SP% **119.5**
PARI-MUTUEL: WIN 6.60; PL (1-2) 3.40, 3.40; SHOW (1-2-3) 2.80, 2.60, 6.00; SF 24.00.
Owner Mr & Mrs Jerome S Moss **Bred** Mr & Mrs Jerome S Moss **Trained** USA

NOTEBOOK
Tiago(USA) goes very well at Santa Anita and, in his first start at the track since winning the Santa Anita Derby on the old dirt track, he ran out a nose winner on the new Cushion Track. A half-brother to 2005 Kentucky Derby winner Giacomo, he may now be aimed at the Breeders' Cup Classic.

5825a **YELLOW RIBBON STKS (GRADE 1) (F&M)** **1m 2f (T)**
9:30 (9:32) 3-Y-0+ **£122,449** (£40,816; £24,490; £12,245; £4,082)

				RPR
1		**Nashoba's Key (USA)**[55] 4-8-11 (Carla Gaines, U.S.A)	JTalamo 2 **17/10**[2]	113
2	¾	**Citronnade (USA)**[49] 4413 4-8-11 (R J Frankel, U.S.A)	DFlores 6 **9/10**[1]	111
3	nse	**Black Mamba (NZ)**[28] 4-8-11 (J W Sadler, U.S.A)	TBaze 5 **108/10**	111
4	3	**Memorette (USA)**[56] 5-8-11 (W Currin, U.S.A)	MESmith 3 **305/10**	105
5	2¼	**Imagine (USA)**[36] 4-8-11 (J Shirreffs, U.S.A)	CNakatani 4 **97/10**	100
6	5½	**Mauralakana (FR)**[26] 4-8-11 (P L Biancone, U.S.A)	VEspinoza 1 **91/10**[3]	89

1m 59.73s (0.45) **6** Ran SP% **120.6**
PARI-MUTUEL: WIN 5.40; PL (1-2) 2.80, 2.40; SHOW (1-2-3) 2.40, 2.10, 2.60; SF 10.00.
Owner Warren B Williamson **Bred** Williamson Racing **Trained** USA

NOTEBOOK
Nashoba's Key(USA) landed her seventh consecutive race in a career that did not begin until January, and she recorded a very good time in the process. Having won her first three races on turf, she then won another three on dirt, and confirmed her versatility back on the grass. She will take her unblemished record into the Breeders' Cup and her trainer has indicated she will probably be aimed at the Filly & Mare Turf, rather than the Distaff on dirt.

5826a **OAK LEAF STKS (GRADE 1) (FILLIES) (CUSHION TRACK)** **1m 110y(D)**
11:30 (11:45) 2-Y-0 **£76,531** (£25,510; £15,306; £7,653; £2,551)

				RPR
1		**Cry And Catch Me (USA)**[34] 2-8-10 (B Baffert, U.S.A)	MESmith 4 **7/5**[1]	110
2	nse	**Izarra (USA)**[26] 2-8-10 (R McAnally, U.S.A)	VEspinoza 8 **57/10**	110
3	1½	**Runforthemoneybaby (USA)** 2-8-10 (Jeff Mullins, U.S.A)	TBaze 5 **37/1**	107
4	1	**Gentle Audrey (USA)**[62] 2-8-10 (Melody Conlon, U.S.A)	(b) JTalamo 6 **55/1**	104
5	hd	**Tasha's Miracle (USA)**[52] 2-8-10 (J W Sadler, U.S.A)	DFlores 9 **38/10**[2]	104
6	1¾	**Sunday Geisha (USA)**[26] 2-8-10 (Martin F Jones, U.S.A)	CNakatani 2 **245/10**	100
7	½	**Set Play (USA)**[26] 2-8-10 (Peter Miller, U.S.A)	BBlanc 1 **53/10**[3]	99
8	nk	**The Golden Noodle (USA)**[91] 2-8-10 (J Van Berg, U.S.A)	CLPotts 3 **126/10**	98
9	2½	**Golden Doc A (USA)**[26] 2-8-10 (B Abrams, U.S.A)	MGarcia 7 **40/1**	93
10	1	**P. S. U. Grad (USA)**[14] 2-8-10 (Craig Dollase, U.S.A)	MCBaze 10 **112/10**	91

1m 42.91s (0.49) **10** Ran SP% **119.6**
PARI-MUTUEL: WIN 4.80; PL (1-2) 3.20, 5.60; SHOW (1-2-3) 2.80, 4.20, 9.00; SF 26.00.
Owner Stetson Land and Cattle LLP **Bred** Hurstland Farm Inc & W Kartozian **Trained** USA

NOTEBOOK
Cry And Catch Me(USA) provided trainer Bob Baffert with his seventh win in theOak Leaf Stakes in the past 11 years with a game effort. Purchased privately after her debut in July, she has progressed well for her new connections and is now likely to be aimed at the Breeders' Cup Juvenile Fillies.

TURFWAY PARK (L-H)
Saturday, September 29
OFFICIAL GOING: Fast

5827a **KENTUCKY CUP CLASSIC (GRADE 2) (POLYTRACK)** **1m 1f**
10:42 (10:48) 3-Y-0+ **£142,857** (£35,714; £17,857; £8,929)

				RPR
1		**Hard Spun (USA)**[35] 3-8-6 (J Larry Jones, U.S.A)	MPino 1 **9/10**[2]	122
2	1¼	**Street Sense (USA)**[35] 4840 3-8-8 (C Nafzger, U.S.A)	CHBorel 3 **4/5**[1]	121+
3	3¼	**Stream Cat (USA)**[49] 4414 4-8-6 (P L Biancone, U.S.A)	(b) JRLeparoux 4 **61/10**[3]	108
4	11¼	**Cat Shaker (USA)**[896] 5-8-6 (C Callis, U.S.A)	CWoods 2 **46/1**	84

1m 48.48s (108.48)
WFA 3 from 4yo+ 5lb **4** Ran SP% **124.4**
PARI-MUTUEL (including $2 stakes): WIN 3.80; PL (1-2) 2.10, 2.10; SF 5.60.
Owner Fox Hill Farms Inc **Bred** Michael Moran & Brushwood Stable **Trained** USA

FOCUS
A key line of form with the Breeders' Cup Classic in mind, although they will not be racing on Polytrack at Monmouth Park.

NOTEBOOK
Hard Spun(USA) had finished behind Street Sense twice this year, firstly when second in the Kentucky Derby and then when third in the Preakness, but he appreciated the Polytrack and was able to reverse form. He showed his liking for this surface when winning the Grade 2 Lanes' End Stakes in March, whereas the runner-up has yet to win on this surface. He will now be pointed at the Breeders' Cup Classic, but could have a job to confirm form with the runner-up.
Street Sense(USA), winner of the Kentucky Derby before running second to Curlin in the Preakness Stakes, came into this off the back of a half-length success Travers Stakes but, unlike Hard Spun, he has yet to win on Polytrack, and he could not confirm earlier form with that rival. Interestingly, he has finished second or third in each of his three attempts over the Polytrack, but his trainer noted that each of this horse's greatest victories - last year's Breeders' Cup Juvenile and this year's Kentucky Derby - came after a Polytrack prep. He will now be aimed at the Breeders' Cup Classic and looks set to go very close.

5794 ASCOT (R-H)
Sunday, September 30
OFFICIAL GOING: Straight course - good (8.7); round course - good to soft (soft in places; 7.9) (overall 8.3)
Wind: Virtually nil Weather: Dry

5828 **SECURITY COMPANY NURSERY** **7f**
2:00 (2:01) (Class 3) 2-Y-0
£7,478 (£2,239; £1,119; £560; £279; £140) **Stalls** Centre

Form					RPR
41	1		**Ibn Khaldun (USA)**[19] 5306 2-9-4 **85** (Saeed Bin Suroor) *w'like: athletic: lw: hld up bhd: smooth hdwy over 2f out: led over 1f out: sn qcknd clr: readily*	LDettori 8 **9/4**[1]	102+
1	2	2	**Hurricane Hymnbook (USA)**[15] 5428 2-9-1 **82** (B J Meehan) *str: hld up towards rr: hdwy 3f out: sn rdn: ev ch wl over 1f out: nt pce of wnr*	NickyMackay 16 **10/1**	88+
41	3	1½	**Kal Barg**[22] 5222 2-8-11 **78** (M A Jarvis) *lw: chsd ldrs: rdn to chal 2f out: kpt on same pce fnl f*	PhilipRobinson 2 **13/2**[2]	80+
0045	4	2½	**Atheer Dubai (IRE)**[30] 4991 2-9-3 **84** (C E Brittain) *chsd ldrs: rdn over 2f out: kpt on fnl f: wnt 4th fnl stride*	JimmyFortune 1 **33/1**	80
41	5	hd	**Seeking Star (IRE)**[113] 2478 2-9-4 **85** (M R Channon) *mid-div: hdwy over 2f out: sn rdn and nt clr run: swtchd rt: kpt on fnl f*	DarryllHolland 6 **14/1**	81+

1 **6** *nk* **Zaskar**[27] 5097 2-8-1 **68** HayleyTurner 13 63
(Tom Dascombe) *mid-div: rdn 3f out: styd on ins fnl f* **14/1**

1630 **7** *nk* **Fathsta (IRE)**[17] 5350 2-8-7 **74** EddieAhern 10 68
(S Kirk) *trckd ldrs: rdn to ld over 2f out: hdd over 1f out: one pce* **12/1**

6133 **8** *2 ½* **Dan Tucket**[9] 5597 2-9-7 **88** TPO'Shea 15 76
(M R Channon) *lw: hld up towards rr: hdwy over 2f out: sn rdn: no further imp fnl f* **16/1**

2301 **9** *¾* **Romany Princess (IRE)**[19] 5309 2-8-10 **77** RyanMoore 5 63+
(R Hannon) *hld up towards rr: swtchd rt over 2f out: sn rdn: sme late prog: nvr a danger* **9/1**[3]

0401 **10** *2* **Indian Days**[29] 5053 2-8-8 **75** TPQueally 9 56
(J G Given) *swtg: trckd ldr: led over 3f out: hdd over 2f out: grad wknd* **16/1**

3332 **11** *1* **Howdigo**[13] 5471 2-8-12 **79** DaneO'Neill 14 57
(J R Best) *mid-div: hdwy and nt clr run over 2f out: sn rdn: wknd over 1f out* **28/1**

052 **12** *5* **Gala Casino Star (IRE)**[25] 5143 2-8-5 **72** PaulHanagan 4 38
(R A Fahey) *mid-div: rdn over 3f out: sn btn* **40/1**

5144 **13** *4* **River Bounty**[23] 5207 2-8-4 **71** RichardMullen 12 27
(A P Jarvis) *mid-div: rdn and hdwy over 3f out: ch briefly over 2f out: sn wknd* **40/1**

01 **14** *3 ½* **Nowaira (IRE)**[19] 5301 2-8-10 **77** RoystonFfrench 3 24
(M Johnston) *led tl over 3f out: sn wknd* **12/1**

0525 **15** *5* **Polygraph (IRE)**[65] 3909 2-8-4 **74** WilliamBuick(3) 7 9
(A M Balding) *mid-div: rdn over 2f out: sn wknd* **12/1**

1m 28.14s (0.04) **Going Correction** 0.0s/f (Good) **15** Ran SP% **122.6**
Speed ratings (Par 99): **99,96,95,92,91 91,91,88,87,85 84,78,73,69,64**
CSF £24.20 CT £136.43 TOTE £2.80: £1.40, £3.10, £2.60; EX 21.80 Trifecta £44.00 Pool £938.21 - 15.13 winning units..
Owner Godolphin **Bred** Darley **Trained** Newmarket, Suffolk

FOCUS
A decent nursery in which the whole field came stands' side. The early pace was not strong but the form looks solid. Ibn Khaldun impressed and looks capable of holding his own in better company.

NOTEBOOK
Ibn Khaldun(USA), who holds entries in the Dewhurst and Racing Post Trophy, looked potentially well treated off a mark of just 85, and he proved that to be just the case with a very fluent success. He travelled well throughout and quickened up in good style to put the race to bed, and he now fully deserves to take his chance at Pattern level. The Horris Hill could come next. (op 2-1 tchd 5-2, tchd 11-4 in a place)
Hurricane Hymnbook(USA), who overcame inexperience to win on his debut, looked sure to benefit from the step up to 7f, and although he had no chance with the easy winner, he saw it out well to beat the rest convincingly. (op 11-1, tchd 12-1 in a place)
Kal Barg, another with a Dewhurst entry, had a good draw the way things turned out, as the whole field congregated on the stands' side. He ran a sound race but shapes as though another furlong will not go amiss. (tchd 7-1 in places)
Atheer Dubai(IRE) did not run too badly at Chester last time when poorly drawn. Down 2lb and better berthed this time, he kept on well for fourth, but he is becoming a bit exposed now. (tchd 40-1)
Seeking Star(IRE), off for 113 days since winning a Windsor maiden back in June, might just have needed this, as he did not find a great deal under pressure in the latter stages. He should strip fitter next time. (op 16-1)
Zaskar, a Polytrack maiden winner on her debut, crept in at the bottom of the weights and ran well up in class despite not settling in the early stages. She was staying on at the finish and a stronger pace would probably have suited her. Official explanation: jockey said filly was denied a clear run (op 12-1)
Fathsta(IRE), the most experienced runner in the line-up, showed good pace but did not get home. The Handicapper knows where he stands with him now.
Dan Tucket, who could have done with a stronger pace, is another on a high enough mark at present. (tchd 14-1)
Romany Princess(IRE) made some late headway down the outside but was never a real threat. However, she might be capable of better back on a quicker surface. (op 14-1)
Polygraph(IRE) Official explanation: trainer said gelding was unsuited by the good ground

5829 SIS FENWOLF STKS (LISTED RACE) 2m
2:35 (2:35) (Class 1) 3-Y-O+

£10,179 (£10,179; £2,800; £1,396; £699; £351) **Stalls** High

Form RPR

-044 **1** **Distinction (IRE)**[16] 5376 8-9-3 111 RyanMoore 1 108
(Sir Michael Stoute) *lw: hld up in last pair: gd hdwy 3f out: led over 2f out: sn drvn and edgd rt: hrd pressed thrght fnl f: jnd on line* **13/8**[1]

2500 **1** *dht* **Solent (IRE)**[29] 5030 5-9-3 100 JimmyFortune 5 108
(R Hannon) *swtg: led: rdn and hdd over 2f out: battled on gamely: chal again ent fnl f: hd to hd and tight for room: dead heated on line* **28/1**

4143 **3** *5* **Sunley Peace**[24] 5165 3-8-6 96 ow1 TQuinn 8 103
(D R C Elsworth) *lw: trckd ldr: rdn and ev ch 3f out: styd on but hld by front two fr 2f out* **6/1**

11-2 **4** *1 ¼* **New Guinea**[15] 5411 4-9-3 103 LDettori 3 101
(Saeed Bin Suroor) *lw: prom: ev ch over 2f out: sn rdn: kpt on same pce* **9/4**[2]

0200 **5** *½* **Baddam**[16] 5376 5-9-3 100 IanMongan 6 100
(M R Channon) *hld up in last trio: effrt 3f out: one pce fnl 2f* **14/1**

3340 **6** *hd* **Land 'n Stars**[16] 5376 7-9-3 98 PaulDoe 4 100
(R A Fahey) *trckd ldrs: lost position over 3f out: nt a danger after* **25/1**

-444 **7** *½* **Hawridge Prince**[36] 4825 7-9-3 106 JimCrowley 7 99
(B R Millman) *hld up last: tk clsr order 5f out: effrt over 2f out: sn one pce* **11/2**[3]

3m 39.72s (9.56) **Going Correction** +0.45s/f (Yiel)
WFA 3 from 4yo+ 12lb **7** Ran SP% **112.5**
Speed ratings (Par 111): **94,94,91,90,90 90,90**
Win: Distinction £1.20, Solent £11.50; Pl: D £1.50, S £4.70. Exacta: D/S £17.10, S/D £25.10; CSF: D/S £22.49, S/D £35.94. TRIFECTA D/S/SP £229.80 (1.25 winning units), S/D/SP £287.30 (0.55 winning units). Pool £809.48..
Owner Highclere Thoroughbred Racing Ltd **Bred** Orpendale And Minch Bloodstock **Trained** Newmarket, Suffolk
Owner Mrs J Wood **Bred** Quay Bloodstock And Samac Ltd **Trained** East Everleigh, Wilts

FOCUS
A slowly-run staying contest which developed into something of a sprint. The winning time was very slow for a Listed contest. There was a stewards' enqury before the result was confirmed. There were doubts over many going into the race, including Distinction, and the form is perhaps best judged through Solent.

NOTEBOOK
Distinction(IRE) has not been at his best this season and, luckily for him, he did not need to be here. He came with what looked a race-winning move turning into the straight, but he hung right under pressure and the long-time leader battled back well next to the rail to force a dead-heat. His current mark of 111 flatters him and it might just be that he will never regain the level of form he showed before his tendon injury. (op 6-4)
Solent(IRE), who has gradually edged up the handicap this season despite not winning, had his stamina to prove over this longer trip, but he was able to dictate a steady early gallop and that may have helped him in the end, as he rallied courageously after being headed and bumped by Distinction. He goes to the sales now and could well be of interest to wealthy jumps owners. (op 6-4)
Sunley Peace has a poor strike-rate so far, but it is only in the second half of this season that he has been campaigned over the sort of trip he clearly needs, and this performance as the lowest rated runner in the field once again confirmed that he needs a proper test to be seen at his best. A strongly-run 2m plus is what he needs and the Cesarewitch looks the obvious race for him. (op 15-2)
New Guinea had every chance turning in but appeared not to get home. That was disappointing considering that the early pace was not strong, meaning that there was less of an emphasis on stamina. (op 5-2 tchd 11-4)
Baddam needs further than this ideally, and so the way this race was run would not have suited him at all. (op 20-1)
Land 'n Stars has had a disappointing time this year.
Hawridge Prince, who won this race last year when in fine form, was running this time in altogether different circumstances, having missed most of the summer due to a leg injury. (op 9-2)

5830 MARCHPOLE H'CAP 1m 4f
3:10 (3:10) (Class 2) (0-105,102) 3-Y-O+

£18,696 (£5,598; £2,799; £1,401; £699; £351) **Stalls** High

Form RPR

5024 **1** **All The Good (IRE)**[18] 5326 4-9-4 **96** EddieAhern 10 107+
(G A Butler) *hld up bhd: smooth hdwy fr 2f out: shkn up to ld fnl 50yds: readily* **8/1**

0303 **2** *nk* **Ladies Best**[18] 5326 3-8-8 **94** RyanMoore 7 104
(Sir Michael Stoute) *lw: hld up in mid-div: rdn and hdwy over 2f out: led over 1f out: no ex whn hdd fnl 50yds* **3/1**[1]

3000 **3** *1 ½* **Dubai Twilight**[36] 4799 3-7-13 **88** WilliamBuick(3) 6 97+
(B W Hills) *trckd ldrs: nt clr run fr over 2f out tl ent fnl f: rdn and styd on* **12/1**

1-06 **4** *½* **Heaven Knows**[18] 5326 4-8-10 **88** oh1 RHills 11 95
(W J Haggas) *hld up towards rr: gd hdwy on inner jst under 3f out: sn rdn: ev ch over 1f out: no ex* **15/2**[3]

12-5 **5** *nk* **Rampallion**[15] 5411 4-9-4 **96** LDettori 12 103
(Saeed Bin Suroor) *lw: led after 1f: rdn over 2f out: hdd over 1f out: kpt on same pce* **11/2**[2]

2242 **6** *1 ¾* **Prince Sabaah (IRE)**[15] 5415 3-8-2 **88** oh2 HayleyTurner 2 92
(R Hannon) *mid-div: rdn 3f out: swtchd lft ent fnl f: styd on* **8/1**

-631 **7** *¾* **Before You Go (IRE)**[44] 4588 4-9-8 **100** MichaelHills 4 103
(T G Mills) *chsd ldrs: rdn wl over 2f out: ev ch over 1f out: wknd ins fnl f* **14/1**

2423 **8** *nk* **Lundy's Lane (IRE)**[15] 5402 7-9-8 **100** SteveDrowne 13 102
(A M Balding) *lw: mid-div: hdwy 3f out: sn rdn: wknd over 1f out* **12/1**

3050 **9** *hd* **Akarem**[40] 4690 6-9-5 **97** PhillipMakin 9 99
(K R Burke) *hld up towards rr: rdn over 2f out: no imp* **20/1**

0206 **10** *2 ½* **Lake Poet (IRE)**[15] 5411 4-9-10 **102** JimmyFortune 5 100
(C E Brittain) *in tch: rdn 3f out: wknd 2f out* **14/1**

0414 **11** *1* **Mustajed**[22] 5225 6-8-10 **88** oh1 JimCrowley 15 84
(B R Millman) *led for 1f: trckd ldr: rdn and ev ch 2f out: wknd over 1f out* **40/1**

-204 **12** *½* **Mikao (IRE)**[29] 5030 6-9-1 **93** JimmyQuinn 8 89
(M H Tompkins) *mid-div: rdn 3f out: nt clr run and eased ent fnl f* **16/1**

2-25 **13** *1* **Millville**[231] 437 7-9-8 **100** PhilipRobinson 1 94
(M A Jarvis) *a towards rr* **16/1**

2m 35.64s (2.64) **Going Correction** +0.45s/f (Yiel)
WFA 3 from 4yo+ 8lb **13** Ran SP% **122.1**
Speed ratings (Par 109): **109,108,107,107,107 106,105,105,105,103 102,102,101**
CSF £32.78 CT £299.19 TOTE £10.20: £2.90, £1.70, £4.30; EX 41.70 Trifecta £662.80 Part won. Pool £933.60 - 0.30 winning units..
Owner Future In Mind Partnership **Bred** Mount Coote Partnership **Trained** Blewbury, Oxon

FOCUS
A decent handicap and solid form which should work out. The first two came from a good handicap at Doncaster, the fourth and fifth were progressive last year, and the sixth ran to his solid recent form.

NOTEBOOK
All The Good(IRE), always travelling well off the pace, came through readily to challenge Ladies Best and went on to win narrowly, but with a fair amount in hand, turning around Doncaster form with the Stoute colt in the process. Being settled in over this longer trip suited him and even after reassessment he will remain of interest. He may even be able to pick up a Listed contest somewhere. However, current plans see him going to the sales.
Ladies Best, who finished in front of All The Good over an extended 1m2f at Doncaster last time, could not confirm the form over this longer distance, and although the margin was narrow he seemed to be beaten quite comfortably in the end. A bit of give in the ground does seem to suit him. (op 7-2)
Dubai Twilight, who racked up three duck eggs on fast ground over the summer, appreciated the bit of cut in the ground that he got here and returned to the spring form that saw him run third to Zaham in a good Newbury handicap. He could be set for a good backend to the campaign. (op 14-1)
Heaven Knows, 1lb wrong at the weights, ran his best race since returning from a year on the sidelines and showed that there is a good handicap to be won with him this autumn. He got the longer trip well. (op 8-1)
Rampallion, as expected, appreciated the easier ground conditions, but he may just have done a bit too much in front on this occasion. (op 9-2)
Prince Sabaah(IRE), 2lb wrong at the weights, is a reliable type and his performance is a good guide to the quality of this handicap. (op 10-1, tchd 11-1 in a place)
Before You Go(IRE) picked up a little conditions event last time out but he remains vulnerable in handicap company off his current mark. Official explanation: jockey said gelding lost its action
Mikao(IRE) was under pressure when getting no run in the straight and being eased down. He too looks high enough in the weights at present.

5831 GROSVENOR CASINOS CUMBERLAND LODGE STKS (GROUP 3) 1m 4f
3:45 (3:45) (Class 1) 3-Y-O+

£28,390 (£10,760; £5,385; £2,685; £1,345; £675) **Stalls** High

Form RPR

24-1 **1** **Ask**[142] 1618 4-9-3 114 RyanMoore 1 125
(Sir Michael Stoute) *hld up bhd: rdn and hdwy over 2f out: str run to ld ent fnl f: styd on wl* **11/4**[2]

1132 **2** *2* **Zaham (USA)**[14] 5451 3-8-6 108 RHills 2 119
(M Johnston) *trckd ldrs: rdn to chal 2f out: ev ch and edgd rt ent fnl f: no ex* **8/1**

123 **3** *¾* **Honolulu (IRE)**[15] 5408 3-8-6 0 DarryllHolland 7 118
(A P O'Brien, Ire) *trckd ldrs: led over 2f out: sn rdn: hdd and edgd lft ent fnl f: no ex* **6/4**[1]

2461 **4** 1 **Hattan (IRE)**[15] 5402 5-9-0 110 JimmyFortune 4 116
(C E Brittain) *lw: hld up bhd: rdn over 2f out: hdwy over 1f out: styd on* **20/1**

2443 **5** 1 1/4 **Laverock (IRE)**[21] 5264 5-9-0 118 LDettori 6 118+
(Saeed Bin Suroor) *hld up: hdwy 2f out: sn rdn: chalng whn squeezed out ent fnl f: nt rcvr* **5/1**[3]

2040 **6** 3 1/2 **Acapulco (IRE)**[15] 5408 3-8-6 0 DavidMcCabe 10 108
(A P O'Brien, Ire) *s.i.s: sn pushed along to ld after 1f and set decent pce: rdn and hdd over 2f out: wknd jst over 1f out* **20/1**

1520 **7** 28 **Classic Punch (IRE)**[15] 5411 4-9-0 110 TQuinn 9 64
(D R C Elsworth) *lw: led for 1f: chsd ldr: rdn and ev ch over 2f out: wknd qckly: eased* **33/1**

131- **8** 6 **Young Mick**[371] 5547 5-9-0 111 (v) GeorgeBaker 8 54
(G G Margarson) *hld up: hdwy on inner to chse ldrs wl over 2f out: sn rdn: hung rt and wknd qckly: virtually p.u* **14/1**

2m 34.47s (1.47) **Going Correction** +0.45s/f (Yiel)
WFA 3 from 4yo+ 8lb **8** Ran SP% **113.6**
Speed ratings (Par 113): **113,111,111,110,109 107,88,84**
CSF £23.67 TOTE £3.50: £1.40, £2.30, £1.20; EX 23.90 Trifecta £41.10 Pool £1,702.56 - 29.39 winning units..
Owner Patrick J Fahey **Bred** Side Hill Stud **Trained** Newmarket, Suffolk

FOCUS
A strong renewal of the Cumberland Lodge Stakes. The pace was good through the early stages, thanks to pacemaker Acapulco, and though it just slowed a touch when that one came back to the field, the winning time was 1.17 seconds quicker than the earlier 91-105 handicap won by the 96-rated All The Good. The form looks good, and it was an excellent effort from Ask under his penalty.

NOTEBOOK
Ask ◆ stepped up significantly on the form he showed during his three-year-old campaign when beating Scorpion by two lengths in the Ormonde Stakes at Chester on his reappearance back in May, but he had been off the track since with a foot injury and was not ready in time to take his chance in the King George. His connections' patience was rewarded with a fine effort on his return to the track, especially considering he was conceding 3lb all round. He took a while to pick up when first coming under pressure, and reportedly felt a little rusty, but he was well on top at the line. He looked a potential Group 1 horse at Chester and this effort surely confirms he is capable of making an impression at the highest level. The Arc de Triomphe will probably come too soon and his connections are now considering the Gran Premio del Jockey Club, a Group 1 in Italy. Fascinatingly, his owner is refusing to rule out sending him over hurdles at some point. (tchd 3-1)
Zaham(USA), trying 1m4f for the first time, had no chance of dominating this time, but he seemed happy enough settled off the pace. He looked a real threat when moving into contention going well early in the straight, and while he ultimately proved no match for the winner he showed improved form for the stiffer test. This tough individual is probably not finished for the season just yet, but he gives the impression he can do even better next year. (op 9-1 tchd 10-1)
Honolulu(IRE), a beaten favourite when apparently unsuited by the way the race was run in the St Leger on his previous start, did not look to have too many excuses this time. He has produced some big performance figures this season, this being another, and he is clearly capable of high-class form, but there is just a nagging doubt about his attitude. (op 7-4, tchd 15-8 in a place)
Hattan(IRE), stepped back up in grade after winning a Listed race at Chester on his previous start, ran right up to form in defeat. He was still last on the turn into the straight, but he responded well when asked for his effort. (op 25-1 tchd 28-1 and 16-1)
Laverock(IRE), third in a valuable race in Turkey on his previous start, was denied a clear run when starting to stay on in the straight and he is better than he was able to show. He may well have been third with a clear run. (op 9-2)
Acapulco(IRE), eighth in the St Leger on his previous start, was basically a pacemaker for his stablemate, Honolulu, and he finished up well held. (op 25-1)
Classic Punch(IRE) ran no sort of race and his form has become very patchy to say the least. (op 20-1)
Young Mick had not been seen since winning this race last year and he showed next to nothing on his return to action. He was apparently as fit his as his trainer could get him without a run, so that makes this performance all the more disappointing, but it is obviously too early to be giving up on him just yet. He could make a quick reappearance in a Listed contest at Newmarket. (op 10-1 tchd 9-1)

5832 JOHN GUEST DIADEM STKS (GROUP 2) 6f
4:20 (4:22) (Class 1) 3-Y-0+

£51,102 (£19,368; £9,693; £4,833; £2,421; £1,215) **Stalls** Centre

Form RPR

-013 **1** **Haatef (USA)**[42] 4648 3-8-12 0 (t) RHills 11 116
(Kevin Prendergast, Ire) *hld up towards rr of centre gp: hdwy 2f out: sn rdn: r.o ins fnl f: led fnl strides* **8/1**

4102 **2** shd **Dark Missile**[50] 4373 4-8-11 102 HayleyTurner 20 113
(A M Balding) *lw: mid-div of centre gp: hdwy 2f out: rdn to be overall ldr over 1f out: ct fnl strides* **25/1**

0503 **3** nk **Assertive**[17] 5359 4-9-0 105 DaneO'Neill 8 115
(R Hannon) *chsd ldrs in centre: rdn 2f out: ev ch ent fnl f: kpt on* **66/1**

4101 **4** 1 1/4 **Zidane**[57] 4150 5-9-0 106 LDettori 18 111
(J R Fanshawe) *lw: hld up bhd centre gp: hdwy 2f out: sn rdn: wnt 4th jst over 1f out: kpt on* **6/1**[3]

021 **5** 3/4 **Al Qasi (IRE)**[49] 4438 4-9-0 113 KerrinMcEvoy 4 109
(P W Chapple-Hyam) *chsd ldrs on stands' side: rdn over 2f out: styd on to ld stands' side gp ent fnl f but a hld by centre gp* **5/1**[2]

1515 **6** 1/2 **Beckermet (IRE)**[9] 5588 5-9-0 109 ChrisCatlin 17 108
(R F Fisher) *overall ldr in centre: rdn over 2f out: hdd over 1f out: kpt on but no ex* **28/1**

0130 **7** nk **Knot In Wood (IRE)**[8] 5616 5-9-0 103 PaulHanagan 12 107
(R A Fahey) *mid-div in centre: rdn over 2f out: styd on fnl f* **25/1**

0634 **8** 1 1/4 **Sonny Red (IRE)**[35] 4869 3-8-12 107 PatDobbs 15 103
(R Hannon) *mid-div in centre gp: rdn over 2f out: kpt on fnl f* **33/1**

2-1 **9** hd **Abraham Lincoln (IRE)**[16] 5392 3-8-12 0 DarryllHolland 2 102
(A P O'Brien, Ire) *w'like: chsd ldr on stands' side: led that gp over 2f out: sn rdn: one pce fnl f* **20/1**

0520 **10** 1/2 **Baltic King**[36] 4798 7-9-0 104 (t) SteveDrowne 3 101
(H Morrison) *hld up towards rr on stands' side: rdn over 2f out: styd on ins fnl f: n.d* **25/1**

2053 **11** 2 **Prime Defender**[15] 5436 3-8-12 110 MichaelHills 10 95
(B W Hills) *lw: a mid-div of centre gp* **12/1**

0135 **12** 1 1/4 **Silver Touch (IRE)**[43] 4600 4-8-11 110 TPO'Shea 7 88
(M R Channon) *mainly towards rr of centre gp* **14/1**

0015 **13** 1 1/2 **Ripples Maid**[15] 5403 4-8-11 100 RoystonFfrench 5 84
(J A Geake) *chsd ldrs on stands' side: rdn over 2f out: wknd fnl f* **80/1**

1623 **14** shd **Balthazaar's Gift (IRE)**[22] 5214 4-9-0 114 JimmyFortune 19 86
(L M Cumani) *a towards rr of centre gp* **9/4**[1]

1-66 **15** 1 **Captain Marvelous (IRE)**[15] 5409 3-8-12 117 WilliamBuick 13 83
(B W Hills) *hung lft thrght: chsd ldr in centre: wknd wl over 1f out* **40/1**

1312 **16** 1 **Galeota (IRE)**[15] 5416 5-9-0 107 RyanMoore 16 80
(R Hannon) *chsd ldrs in centre: rdn over 2f out: wknd over 1f out* **14/1**

0660 **17** 1/2 **Scarlet Runner**[22] 5214 3-8-9 107 PhilipRobinson 1 76
(J L Dunlop) *led stands' side gp tl over 2f out: grad fdd* **50/1**

1m 13.96s (-0.94) **Going Correction** +0.225s/f (Good)
WFA 3 from 4yo+ 2lb **17** Ran SP% **123.7**
Speed ratings (Par 115): **115,114,114,112,111 111,110,109,108,108 105,103,101,101,100 99,98**
CSF £199.70 TOTE £9.30: £3.30, £5.90, £7.30; EX 295.50 TRIFECTA Not won..
Owner Hamdan Al Maktoum **Bred** Shadwell Farm LLC **Trained** Friarstown, Co Kildare

FOCUS
A big field, but there were plenty of exposed types and it looked a very ordinary renewal of the Diadem Stakes. They split into two groups and the larger bunch up the middle of the track had the edge over those on the stands' side. Six of the first eight home were drawn in double-figure stalls.

NOTEBOOK
Haatef(USA) was a one-time Guineas fancy, but he failed to stay 1m at Newmarket in the spring and he could manage only third over that trip in a Group 3 at Leopardstown on his previous start. Very much sprint bred, the return to this trip suited and he proved good enough to record his first Group-race success, albeit very narrowly. He only had a couple behind him in his group down the centre of the track at halfway, but he finished best of all. He basically looks like a 6f-7f horse and gives the impression he can step forward again next year. (op 9-1 tchd 15-2 and 10-1 in a place)
Dark Missile, the winner of the Wokingham here earlier in the season and also second in the Shergar Cup Distaff over this course and distance, once again showed her liking for this track with a blinding effort in defeat. She looked the winner when sent to the front over a furlong from the finish, but she was pegged back literally on the line. She is progressing into a smart sprinter and her form figures at this track now read 1122. Her connections mentioned she could head to Canada at some point. (op 20-1)
Assertive has yet to win outside of Listed company and he rarely makes much impression in Group races, so for all that this was clearly one of his better efforts, his proximity suggests the form is limited for the level. He may now be aimed at the Rous Stakes.
Zidane, the narrow winner of the Stewards' Cup off a mark of 100 on his previous start, found this tougher but still ran a good race in defeat, very much continuing his progression. He remains a sprinter to keep on side. (op 11-2, tchd 13-2 in a place)
Al Qasi(IRE) ◆ has not exactly reached the level one might have expected this season, but he managed to win a Group 3 in Ireland on his previous start, and came home best of the smaller group on the stands' side this time. He appears to be very much back on track now and it would no surprise to see him make an impression in top sprint company next year. (tchd 11-2)
Beckermet(IRE) is another who has yet to win outside of Listed level and he probably went off a little too quickly. (op 25-1)
Knot In Wood(IRE) had a bit to find at this level and he ran about as well as could have been expected. (op 20-1)
Sonny Red(IRE) ran better than when a beaten favourite in a Group 2 in Germany on his previous start, but he was still readily held. (op 40-1)
Abraham Lincoln(IRE) ◆, an attractive type, was stepped up significantly in class following his recent success at the Curragh, but he acquitted himself most creditably, running second in the small group on the stands' side. He looks the type who can improve again next year. (op 25-1)
Baltic King raced on the wrong side and he could make little impression.
Prime Defender had his work cut out at this level, but he was not at his best in any case.
Silver Touch(IRE) promised to be suited by this stiff 6f, but she ran well below her best. (op 12-1)
Balthazaar's Gift(IRE) looked to have plenty going for him beforehand, as some of best efforts have come at this track, and he came into the race in great form having run third in the Group 1 Haydock Sprint Cup on his previous start. He was a major disappointment, and there was no obvious explanation. Official explanation: jockey said colt never travelled (op 5-2 tchd 11-4)

5833 BRUNSWICK H'CAP 1m (S)
4:55 (4:57) (Class 2) (0-100,98) 3-Y-0+

£15,580 (£4,665; £2,332; £1,167; £582; £292) **Stalls** Centre

Form RPR

0305 **1** **Orchard Supreme**[149] 1449 4-8-8 84 TPO'Shea 1 93
(R Hannon) *mde all: rdn and hung rt fr over 2f out: jst hld on* **25/1**

0140 **2** nk **River Tiber**[39] 4720 4-9-8 98 JimmyFortune 4 106+
(L M Cumani) *lw: mid-div: rdn over 2f out: no imp tl r.o strly ent fnl f: jst failed* **9/2**[1]

1113 **3** nk **Samarinda (USA)**[22] 5221 4-8-10 86 MickyFenton 14 93
(Mrs P Sly) *rrd leaving stalls: w wnr: rdn and carried sltly rt fr over 2f out: ev ch ins fnl f: no ex towards fin* **8/1**[2]

2510 **4** 1 1/4 **Annemasse**[38] 4745 3-9-4 98 LDettori 8 102
(M Johnston) *wnt lft s: chsd ldrs: rdn 2f out: wnt 3rd over 1f out: r.o fnl 100yds* **9/2**[1]

1150 **5** 3/4 **Para Siempre**[17] 5354 3-8-10 90 (b) PaulHanagan 13 93
(B Smart) *mid-div: rdn over 2f out: styd on ins fnl f* **50/1**

1000 **6** nk **Seal Point (USA)**[29] 5049 3-8-7 87 RoystonFfrench 6 89
(Christian Wroe) *mid-div: rdn over 3f out: styd on ins fnl f* **50/1**

0004 **7** 1/2 **Prince Of Thebes (IRE)**[15] 5413 6-8-8 84 oh2 PaulDoe 9 85
(J Akehurst) *chsd ldng pair tl over 1f out: kpt on same pce* **14/1**

510- **8** 1 3/4 **Danski**[387] 5150 4-8-8 84 TQuinn 11 81
(P J Makin) *t.k.h towards rr: short of room after 2f: rdn 2f out: sme late prog: nvr a danger* **12/1**

1-50 **9** 1 1/2 **Beauchamp Viceroy**[29] 5031 3-9-1 95 EddieAhern 12 88
(G A Butler) *t.k.h trcking ldrs: rdn over 2f out: wknd ent fnl f* **16/1**

0334 **10** 1 **Pentecost**[14] 5444 8-9-0 93 (p) WilliamBuick(3) 15 84
(A M Balding) *t.k.h early: mid-div: hdwy 3f out: sn rdn: wknd and hung rt over 1f out* **10/1**

0000 **11** 1 1/2 **Plum Pudding (IRE)**[39] 4720 4-9-5 95 RyanMoore 5 83
(R Hannon) *a towards rr* **17/2**[3]

1-02 **12** 2 **Kinsya**[8] 5615 4-8-13 89 JimmyQuinn 2 72
(M H Tompkins) *a towards rr* **9/2**[1]

0060 **13** 1 3/4 **Capable Guest (IRE)**[15] 5419 5-8-13 89 ChrisCatlin 10 68
(M R Channon) *sn pushed along: a towards rr* **11/1**

-000 **14** dist **Zafonical Storm (USA)**[17] 5355 3-8-13 93 TPQueally 7 —
(B W Duke) *squeezed out s: towards rr: lost action over 2f out: immediately eased* **50/1**

1m 42.68s (0.88) **Going Correction** +0.225s/f (Good)
WFA 3 from 4yo+ 4lb **14** Ran SP% **123.6**
Speed ratings (Par 109): **104,103,103,102,101 101,100,98,97,96 94,92,91,—**
CSF £135.91 CT £1037.01 TOTE £42.20: £7.70, £2.30, £2.70; EX 380.90 TRIFECTA Not won.
Place 6 £196.64, Place 5 £117.01..
Owner Brian C Oakley **Bred** Mrs M H Goodrich **Trained** East Everleigh, Wilts

FOCUS
A competitive handicap, but possibly not the most solid of form. They seemed to go an ordinary pace through the first couple of furlongs or so and both Orchard Supreme and Samarinda were able to take a good three or four lengths out of the field when asked to extend around three furlongs from the finish, but they were treading water late on. They raced up the middle of the track.

NOTEBOOK

Orchard Supreme ◆ progressed to a mark of 100 on sand during the All-Weather season, but his turf mark was left untouched and he was able to take full advantage off the back of a 149-day break, his first run since a gelding operation. Both he and Samarinda were kicked into a clear lead in the final three furlongs and, having done enough to win their private battle, he just held off the strong-finishing River Tiber, despite appearing to get very tired. He edged to his right for much of the way in the closing stages, hardly doing the eventual third any favours, but he kept finding enough. He can win again on turf and should also add to his already smart record on sand.

River Tiber ◆, racing off a mark 3lb higher than when winning on the round course here back in July, returned to form with an eye-catching run. He looked to be going nowhere for much of the closing stages, but he eventually responded to his rider's urgings and very nearly got up. This was obviously a smart effort in defeat under top weight, but it would probably be unwise to get too carried away, as the leaders were stopping in front having used up plenty when kicked clear, and his overall profile is not that consistent. That said, his next run could well come in the Cambridgeshire and, on this evidence, he looks made for the 1m1f trip. (tchd 11-2)

Samarinda(USA), like the winner racing off a lower mark than that of his sand rating, in this case 7lb, put up his usual bold showing and was just held. He was done few favours in the closing stages by Orchard Supreme, who continually edged into him. (op 9-1 tchd 10-1)

Annemasse had not been seen for over a month, but this was a creditable effort against his elders. (op 5-1)

Para Siempre, the only filly in the line up, would have found this a little easier than the Listed race she contested at Doncaster on her previous start and she ran well. (op 40-1)

Seal Point(USA) ◆, a maiden winner in Dubai at the start of the year, has dropped to a realistic mark, having started the British season rated 100. He offered some promise. Official explanation: jockey said colt was hampered early (tchd 66-1)

Danski Official explanation: jockey said colt was hampered early

Pentecost was reportedly running his last race. He won eight races, including three good handicaps here, and almost £270,000. (op 9-1)

Kinsya failed to build on his recent second at Ayr. Official explanation: jockey said gelding ran flat (tchd 4-1)

Zafonical Storm(USA) Official explanation: jockey said colt lost its action

T/Jkpt: Not won. T/Plt: £429.30 to a £1 stake. Pool: £165,026.00. 280.60 winning tickets. T/Qpdt: £131.80 to a £1 stake. Pool: £6,875.10. 38.60 winning tickets. TM

5476 MUSSELBURGH (R-H)

Sunday, September 30

OFFICIAL GOING: Good (good to firm in places; 8.3)

Wind: Virtually nil Weather: Dry and sunny

5834 ROYAL SCOTS CUP H'CAP — 5f

2:25 (2:26) (Class 6) (0-65,68) 3-Y-O — **£2,730** (£806; £403) **Stalls** Low

Form — RPR

3423 **1** **Princess Ellis**[15] [5430] 3-8-13 **57** ... SebSanders 3 — 66
(E J Alston) *disp ld tl led 1/2-way: rdn clr appr fnl f: styd on wl* **7/2**[2]

0664 **2** *2* **Rann Na Cille (IRE)**[12] [5507] 3-9-4 **62** ... (b) NCallan 10 — 64
(K A Ryan) *chsd ldrs: hdwy wl over 1f out: sn rdn and styd on ins fnl f* **10/1**

3 *shd* **Copper Dock (IRE)**[17] [5372] 3-8-10 **61** ... AmyKathleenParsons(7) 2 — 62
(T G McCourt, Ire) *trckd ldrs: hdwy to chse wnr ent fnl f: sn rdn and kpt on same pce* **20/1**

5500 **4** *½* **Triple Shadow**[7] [5662] 3-9-0 **58** ... PaulFessey 9 — 58
(T D Barron) *chsd ldrs: hdwy over 1f out: rdn ent fnl f and kpt on same pce towards fin* **7/1**[3]

3033 **5** *1* **Jojesse**[12] [5507] 3-8-9 **53** ... PatCosgrave 6 — 49
(G A Swinbank) *in tch: hdwy wl over 1f out: sn rdn and styd on ins fnl f: nrst fin* **5/2**[1]

0006 **6** *shd* **The Carpet Man**[20] [5270] 3-8-6 **50** ... LiamJones 4 — 46
(A W Carroll) *chsd ldrs: rdn along wl over 1f out: kpt on same pce ent fnl f* **40/1**

4441 **7** *1* **Beechside (IRE)**[20] [5282] 3-8-4 **48** ... DaleGibson 1 — 40
(W A Murphy, Ire) *dwlt and towards rr tl styd on fnl 2f* **11/1**

1000 **8** *½* **Morristown Music (IRE)**[11] [5522] 3-9-2 **60** ... TonyHamilton 14 — 50
(J S Wainwright) *in tch: swtchd rt and effrt to chse ldrs on outer 2f out: sn rdn and wknd appr fnl f* **33/1**

4023 **9** *¾* **The Cube**[20] [5282] 3-8-7 **51** ow1 ... DavidAllan 13 — 39
(J Balding) *a towards rr* **12/1**

1120 **10** *3* **Put It On The Card**[158] [1238] 3-9-1 **62** ... (p) PJMcDonald(3) 5 — 39
(J S Wainwright) *dwlt: a in rr* **33/1**

0230 **11** *nk* **Stir Crazy (IRE)**[5] [5711] 3-9-1 **59** ... TomEaves 12 — 35
(M R Channon) *prom: rdn along wl over 1f out: sn wknd* **9/1**

5404 **12** *1 ¼* **Hawaii Prince**[12] [5506] 3-9-5 **68** ... (p) GaryBartley(5) 8 — 39
(S T Mason) *disp ld to 1/2-way: rdn wl over 1f out: wknd ins fnl f and eased* **12/1**

-000 **13** *1 ¼* **Centreboard (USA)**[12] [5507] 3-9-1 **59** ... PaulMulrennan 11 — 26
(M W Easterby) *prom: rdn along 2f out and sn wknd* **33/1**

14 *nk* **Golden Hope (IRE)**[95] [3004] 3-8-5 **49** ow2 ... (b) GregFairley 7 — 15
(T G McCourt, Ire) *a in rr* **33/1**

59.78 secs (-0.72) **Going Correction** -0.125s/f (Firm) — **14** Ran SP% **125.1**

Speed ratings (Par 99): **100,96,96,95,94 94,92,91,90,85 85,83,81,80**

CSF £37.18 CT £656.99 TOTE £4.20: £1.70, £3.40, £8.60; EX 44.30.

Owner John Jackson **Bred** J E Jackson **Trained** Longton, Lancs

FOCUS

A moderate sprint. Those drawn low were at an advantage and the runner-up sets the level.

The Cube Official explanation: jockey said gelding was denied a clear run

5835 RSP CONSULTING ENGINEERS' (S) STKS — 1m 4f

3:00 (3:00) (Class 6) 3-Y-O+ — **£2,590** (£770; £385; £192) **Stalls** High

Form — RPR

2 **1** **Drizzi (IRE)**[12] [5497] 6-9-10 66 ... (p) SebSanders 12 — 72+
(A W Carroll) *hld up: smooth hdwy 3f out: trckd ldr over 1f out: shkn up to ld ins fnl f and sn clr* **6/4**[1]

0005 **2** *3* **On Every Street**[24] [5158] 6-9-4 40 ... (vt) PatCosgrave 8 — 55
(R Bastiman) *trckd ldrs: hdwy 3f out: rdn and ch 2f out: sn drvn and kpt on same pce* **16/1**

0/66 **3** *1 ½* **Perfect Storm**[15] [5427] 8-8-11 55 ... JackDean(7) 3 — 53
(W G M Turner) *trckd ldrs: hdwy over 3f out: led over 2f out and sn rdn: drvn over 1f out: hdd and one pce ins fnl f* **4/1**[3]

0100 **4** *1 ¾* **Paparaazi (IRE)**[18] [5341] 5-9-10 60 ... DanielTudhope 4 — 56
(I W McInnes) *hld up towards rr: hdwy on outer over 2f out: rdn to chse ldrs over 1f out: sn drvn and no imp* **11/4**[2]

60-0 **5** *1* **Annibale Caro**[36] [3753] 5-9-1 75 ... MarkLawson(3) 2 — 48
(Grant Tuer) *in tch: hdwy to chse ldrs 3f out: rdn along 2f out and kpt on same pce* **12/1**

000/ **6** *½* **Mejhar (IRE)**[707] 7-9-1 64 ... AlanCreighton(3) 14 — 47
(E J Creighton) *trckd ldrs on inner: hdwy 3f out: rdn along over 2f out and kpt on same pce* **33/1**

6500 **7** *5* **Borsch (IRE)**[20] [5283] 5-9-4 42 ... (v1) TonyHamilton 11 — 39
(Miss L A Perratt) *led: rdn along over 3f out: hdd over 2f out and sn wknd* **12/1**

/060 **8** *¾* **Pre Eminance (IRE)**[83] [3381] 6-9-4 42 ... (t) StephenDonohoe 5 — 38
(L R James) *a towards rr* **40/1**

-000 **9** *1 ¼* **Scurra**[47] [4475] 8-9-1 33 ... (p) AndrewMullen(3) 6 — 36
(A C Whillans) *a towards rr* **50/1**

10 *5* **Brook Lass (IRE)**[25] [5146] 3-8-5 0 ... (b1) GregFairley 13 — 23
(T G McCourt, Ire) *s.i.s: a in rr* **40/1**

0000 **11** *1* **Minstrel Flyer (IRE)**[53] [4267] 5-8-8 37 ... (b1) SCreighton(5) 10 — 22
(E J Creighton) *prom: rdn along over 3f out and sn wknd* **100/1**

00 **12** *10* **Roman Fun (IRE)**[39] [4718] 3-8-7 47 ow2 ... (b1) TomEaves 9 — —
(I Semple) *prom: rdn along over 3f out and sn wknd* **33/1**

2m 37.86s (0.96) **Going Correction** -0.025s/f (Good)

WFA 3 from 5yo+ 8lb — **12** Ran SP% **121.6**

Speed ratings (Par 101): **95,93,92,90,90 89,86,86,85,81 81,74**

CSF £29.25 TOTE £2.40: £1.30, £4.00, £1.70; EX 32.40.There was no bid for the winner.

Owner J T Billson **Bred** Azienda Agricola La Vigna **Trained** Cropthorne, Worcs

FOCUS

A typical seller. The easy winner rates velue for further than the winning margin and the form seems sound.

Scurra Official explanation: jockey said gelding never travelled

5836 DRUMMOND MILLER LLP SUPPORTING ST. COLUMBA'S HOSPICE H'CAP — 5f

3:35 (3:36) (Class 6) (0-65,62) 4-Y-O+ — **£2,590** (£770; £385; £192) **Stalls** Low

Form — RPR

60 **1** **Sandwith**[10] [5552] 4-8-13 **57** ... (p) PJMcDonald(3) 2 — 67
(J S Wainwright) *trckd ldrs: hdwy over 1f out: rdn to ld ins fnl f: kpt on* **12/1**

0502 **2** *hd* **No Time (IRE)**[12] [5507] 7-9-0 **55** ... SebSanders 1 — 65+
(A J McCabe) *trckd ldrs: effrt and nt clr run on stands' rail over 1f out: squeezed through ent fnl f and fin strly: jst hld* **11/4**[1]

2052 **3** *1* **Jadan (IRE)**[6] [5672] 6-8-7 **48** ... (b1) GrahamGibbons 3 — 53+
(E J Alston) *s.i.s: t.k.h in rr: hdwy wl over 1f out: swtchd rt and rdn ent fnl f: styd on wl towards fin* **10/3**[2]

0066 **4** *hd* **Niteowl Lad (IRE)**[4] [5740] 5-9-5 **60** ... DavidAllan 11 — 65
(J Balding) *in tch: hdwy wl over 1f out: sn rdn and kpt on ins fnl f: nrst fin* **8/1**[3]

0030 **5** *hd* **Maromito (IRE)**[37] [4773] 10-8-8 **52** ... AndrewMullen(3) 5 — 56
(R Bastiman) *led: rdn over 1f out: drvn and hdd ins fnl f: edgd lft and no ex towards fin* **16/1**

0400 **6** *½* **Henry Hall (IRE)**[12] [5507] 11-8-9 **50** ... KimTinkler 14 — 52
(N Tinkler) *chsd ldrs on outer: rdn along wl over 1f out: kpt on same pce ins fnl f* **16/1**

0-00 **7** *1* **Tornadodancer (IRE)**[14] [5460] 4-9-7 **62** ... NCallan 12 — 61
(T G McCourt, Ire) *cl up: rdn wl over 1f out and grad wknd* **28/1**

4000 **8** *¾* **Strawberry Patch (IRE)**[6] [5672] 8-8-7 **48** ... (p) TomEaves 8 — 44
(J S Goldie) *towards rr: rdn along 2f out: kpt on appr fnl f: n.d* **10/1**

0600 **9** *shd* **Vondova**[6] [5673] 5-8-5 **46** ow1 ... (p) GregFairley 7 — 42
(D A Nolan) *cl up: rdn along 2f out: sn wknd* **33/1**

136- **10** *½* **Art Elegant**[31] [4980] 5-8-0 **48** ... (p) AmyKathleenParsons(7) 9 — 42
(T G McCourt, Ire) *a towards rr* **9/1**

0300 **11** *nk* **Four Kings**[30] [4996] 6-8-6 **47** ... PaulFessey 4 — 40
(Karen McLintock) *a towards rr* **66/1**

0060 **12** *nk* **Steel City Boy (IRE)**[12] [5507] 4-9-7 **62** ... StephenDonohoe 10 — 54
(D Carroll) *cl up: rdn along wl over 1f out: wknd ent fnl f* **12/1**

5000 **13** *3* **Seafield Towers**[6] [5672] 7-8-4 **45** ... (p) DO'Donohoe 13 — 26
(Miss L A Perratt) *towards rr: effrt and sme hdwy 1/2-way: sn rdn and wknd* **33/1**

0006 **14** *nk* **Alexia Rose (IRE)**[30] [4996] 5-7-11 **45** ... (t) DanielleMcCreery(7) 6 — 25
(A Berry) *s.i.s: a bhd* **16/1**

59.86 secs (-0.64) **Going Correction** -0.125s/f (Firm) — **14** Ran SP% **123.8**

Speed ratings (Par 101): **100,99,98,97,97 96,95,93,93,92 92,91,87,86**

CSF £45.11 CT £139.47 TOTE £16.70: £4.00, £1.40, £1.90; EX 67.30.

Owner M Sawers **Bred** R R Whitton **Trained** Kennythorpe, N Yorks

FOCUS

A moderate sprint which saw the lowest three stalls fill the placings. Sound form for the grade.

Sandwith Official explanation: trainer said, regarding apparent improvement in form, that the gelding was better suited by the quicker ground

5837 E.B.F./ROYAL SCOTS CLUB CUP FILLIES' NURSERY — 7f 30y

4:10 (4:10) (Class 3) (0-90,85) 2-Y-O

£7,790 (£2,332; £1,166; £583; £291; £146) **Stalls** High

Form — RPR

0223 **1** **Sourire**[15] [5400] 2-9-7 **85** ... SebSanders 2 — 88
(Sir Mark Prescott) *hld up in tch: gd hdwy on outer 2f out: rdn and edgd rt ent fnl f: styd on to ld last 100yds* **11/4**[3]

5105 **2** *1 ½* **Serena's Storm (IRE)**[18] [5322] 2-9-3 **81** ... GrahamGibbons 5 — 80
(J J Quinn) *cl up: led over 2f out: rdn and hung lft ent fnl f: sn drvn: hdd and nt qckn fnl 100yds* **9/4**[2]

1020 **3** *1 ½* **Willyn (IRE)**[9] [5582] 2-7-10 **65** ... KellyHarrison(5) 1 — 61
(J S Goldie) *hld up in rr: hdwy on inner 2f out: sn swtchd outside and rdn: styd on fnl f: nrst fin* **20/1**

1100 **4** *2* **Johar Jamal (IRE)**[18] [5324] 2-9-6 **84** ... TomEaves 7 — 75
(M R Channon) *chsd ldrs: rdn along over 2f out: drvn over 1f out and one pce* **85/40**[1]

5304 **5** *½* **Fidelias Dance**[33] [4923] 2-8-7 **71** ... GregFairley 3 — 60
(M Johnston) *led: rdn along 3f out: hdd over 2f out: sn drvn and wknd over 1f out* **6/1**

3543 **6** *1 ½* **Prunes**[8] [5644] 2-7-5 **62** oh3 ... DanielleMcCreery(7) 6 — 48
(A Berry) *a towards rr* **33/1**

1065 **7** *nk* **Casino Night**[8] [5624] 2-8-2 **66** ... DO'Donohoe 4 — 51
(J R Weymes) *prom: rdn along 3f out: grad wknd* **28/1**

1m 29.18s (-0.76) **Going Correction** -0.025s/f (Good) — **7** Ran SP% **114.9**

Speed ratings (Par 96): **103,101,99,97,96 95,94**

CSF £9.34 TOTE £3.60: £1.40, £1.60; EX 11.10.

Owner Miss K Rausing **Bred** Miss K Rausing **Trained** Newmarket, Suffolk

FOCUS

A decent winning time for a race like this, due to the decent early pace, and the form looks sound for the grade.

NOTEBOOK

Sourire, placed on four of her five outings since breaking her duck back in July, belatedly made amends and did the job in determined fashion. This success was deserved and she has developed into a hardy filly, but her official mark still looks to have her about right. (op 5-2 tchd 9-4 and 3-1)
Serena's Storm(IRE), back up in trip, was given a positive ride and had every chance. She probably hit the front plenty soon enough, but still finished nicely clear in second and remains open to a bit more improvement at this distance. (op 5-2 tchd 15-8)
Willyn(IRE) was given a patient ride on this return to the extra furlong and finished her race well without threatening the first pair. She will likely go up in the weights for this. (op 22-1 tchd 25-1)
Johar Jamal(IRE), down in grade, failed to raise her game for the extra furlong and was well held. She is probably better off back over 6f for the short term. (op 5-2 tchd 3-1)
Fidelias Dance dropped out when headed and probably went off too fast for her own good. (op 15-2 tchd 8-1)

5838 MUSSELBURGH NEWS CLAIMING STKS — 1m 1f
4:45 (4:45) (Class 6) 4-Y-0+ — **£2,590** (£770; £385; £192) **Stalls High**

Form — RPR
0340 **1** **Oeuf A La Neige**[10] 5552 7-8-12 52 ... DO'Donohoe 8 — 60
(Miss L A Perratt) *towards rr: hdwy on inner over 2f out: rdn and styd on ins fnl f to ld last 100yds* **25/1**
2062 **2** ¾ **Little Jimbob**[19] 5296 6-9-3 73 ... TonyHamilton 10 — 63
(R A Fahey) *set stdy pce: qcknd 3f out: rdn wl over 1f out: edgd lft ent fnl f: hdd and nt qckn last 100yds* **3/1**[2]
1143 **3** ½ **Inside Story (IRE)**[21] 5255 5-9-7 76 ... (b) SebSanders 2 — 66
(M W Easterby) *hld up in rr: gd hdwy on inner over 2f out: n.m.r ent fnl f: sn rdn and styd on wl towards fin* **3/1**[2]
0002 **4** *shd* **Langford**[18] 5338 7-9-4 72 ... PaulMulrennan 3 — 63
(M H Tompkins) *in midfield: smooth hdwy on outer wl over 2f out: rdn to chal over 1f out: drvn and ev ch ins fnl f: no ex last 100yds* **8/1**
1423 **5** *shd* **El Coto**[4] 5737 7-9-5 75 ... (p) NCallan 5 — 64
(K A Ryan) *trckd ldrs: hdwy 2f out: rdn over 1f out: styng on whn hmpd wl ins fnl f* **5/2**[1]
5420 **6** 1 ¼ **Apache Point (IRE)**[11] 5525 10-8-9 50 ... KimTinkler 9 — 51
(N Tinkler) *in tch: pushed along 3f out: rdn along 2f out: kpt on same pce u.p appr fnl f* **40/1**
2- **7** *shd* **Meadow Soprano (IRE)**[30] 2279 5-8-7 0 ... GregFairley 1 — 49
(M P Sunderland, Ire) *hld up in rr: effrt and hdwy over 2f out: sn rdn and kpt on same pce appr fnl f* **66/1**
4024 **8** *nk* **Sarraaf (IRE)**[13] 5479 11-8-13 57 ... TomEaves 7 — 54
(I Semple) *hld up: effrt and hdwy over 2f out: sn rdn and kpt on ins fnl f* **25/1**
2604 **9** ¾ **Tizzy May (FR)**[10] 5553 7-8-10 68 ... (p) JamieMoriarty(3) 4 — 53
(B Ellison) *trckd ldrs: hdwy 3f out: sn rdn along and wknd wl over 1f out* **5/1**[3]
0520 **10** *shd* **Sekula Pata (NZ)**[10] 5569 8-8-8 58 ... (b) SCreighton(5) 6 — 52
(E J Creighton) *cl up: rdn along over 2f out: drvn over 1f out: wknd ent fnl f* **66/1**
0000 **11** 4 **Brace Of Doves**[12] 5503 5-8-10 45 ... PJMcDonald(3) 11 — 44
(D W Whillans) *chsd ldrs: rdn along wl over 2f out and sn wknd* **100/1**

1m 53.73s (-0.13) **Going Correction** -0.025s/f (Good) — **11** Ran SP% **120.5**
Speed ratings (Par 101): **99,98,97,97,97 96,96,96,95,95 91**
CSF £99.16 TOTE £28.50: £4.80, £2.10, £1.70; EX 165.10.
Owner Peter Tsim **Bred** Gainsborough Stud Management Ltd **Trained** Ayr, S Ayrshire

FOCUS
The early pace was only steady. Not a bad claimer, but the winner had no right to beat some of the higher-rated horses at these weights and the form should be treated with some caution.
El Coto Official explanation: jockey said gelding was denied a clear run, and so he had to stop riding shortly before the line
Sarraaf(IRE) Official explanation: jockey said gelding was denied a clear run

5839 DELTA AIR LINES CHALLENGE H'CAP — 1m 6f
5:15 (5:15) (Class 4) (0-80,78) 3-Y-0+
£6,232 (£1,866; £933; £467; £233; £117) **Stalls High**

Form — RPR
3513 **1** **Tonnante**[13] 5478 3-8-11 71 ... SebSanders 8 — 79+
(Sir Mark Prescott) *hld up in rr: gd hdwy on outer wl over 2f out: rdn over 1f out: styd on strly ins fnl f to ld nr fin* **2/1**[1]
0134 **2** *nk* **Sonara (IRE)**[18] 5333 3-8-8 68 ... PaulMulrennan 5 — 75
(M H Tompkins) *trckd ldrs: hdwy over 3f out: led over 2f out: rdn wl over 1f out: drvn ins fnl f: hdd and no ex nr fin* **11/1**
0210 **3** 1 **Hurricane Thomas (IRE)**[18] 5333 3-8-11 71 ... GregFairley 6 — 77
(M Johnston) *trckd ldrs: hdwy over 2f out: rdn to chal over 1f out and ev ch tl drvn and nt qckn ins fnl f* **6/1**[3]
1665 **4** *hd* **Danzatrice**[21] 5257 5-8-10 60 ... TomEaves 2 — 66
(C W Thornton) *hld up in rr: hdwy on inner wl over 2f out: swtchd to wd outside and rdn wl over 1f out: styd on strly ins fnl f: nrst fin* **12/1**
0032 **5** 4 **Spanish Diva**[18] 5333 3-9-2 76 ... NCallan 7 — 76
(S C Williams) *trckd ldrs: hdwy 3f out: rdn along 2f out and sn one pce* **3/1**[2]
150 **6** 1 ¼ **Kyber**[13] 5478 6-8-9 59 ... DanielTudhope 4 — 57
(J S Goldie) *in tch: effrt 3f out: rdn along 2f out and sn no imp* **16/1**
302 **7** *shd* **Boxhall (IRE)**[21] 5257 5-8-9 66 ... LanceBetts(7) 1 — 64
(N Wilson) *led: rdn along 3f out: hdd over 2f out and grad wknd* **7/1**
0361 **8** 3 **Mister Arjay (USA)**[21] 5256 7-10-0 78 ... TonyHamilton 3 — 72
(B Ellison) *chsd ldr: rdn along 3f out: drvn 2f out and sn wknd* **12/1**
15 **9** ½ **Revolving World (IRE)**[45] 4521 4-8-2 59 oh7....(t) DanielleMcCreery(7) 9 — 52
(L R James) *a towards rr* **100/1**

3m 4.10s (-1.60) **Going Correction** -0.025s/f (Good)
WFA 3 from 4yo+ 10lb — **9** Ran SP% **115.7**
Speed ratings (Par 105): **103,102,102,102,99 99,99,97,97**
CSF £25.80 CT £114.76 TOTE £2.90: £1.30, £2.40, £1.90; EX 33.10.
Owner Miss K Rausing **Bred** Miss K Rausing **Trained** Newmarket, Suffolk

FOCUS
A fair staying handicap. The first three are all progressive 3yos and the form looks straightforward enough.

5840 EAST LOTHIAN NEWS H'CAP — 7f 30y
5:45 (5:46) (Class 5) (0-70,70) 3-Y-0+ — **£3,238** (£963; £481; £240) **Stalls High**

Form — RPR
0004 **1** **Dispol Isle (IRE)**[5] 5701 5-9-3 66 ... PaulFessey 12 — 76
(T D Barron) *trckd ldrs: hdwy 2f out: sn rdn and styd on u.p ins fnl f to ld nr fin* **14/1**
4640 **2** *nk* **Champain Sands (IRE)**[10] 5559 8-9-2 65 ... StephenDonohoe 3 — 74
(E J Alston) *hld up in midfield: hdwy over 2f out: swtchd rt and rdn ent fnl f: styd on wl* **25/1**
0606 **3** *nk* **King Harson**[21] 5253 8-9-5 68 ... PatCosgrave 7 — 76
(J D Bethell) *chsd ldr: rdn to chal over 1f out and ev ch tl drvn and nt qckn towards fin* **8/1**[3]
6-6 **4** ½ **Chapelizod (IRE)**[9] 5607 4-8-4 60 ... (p) AmyKathleenParsons(7) 2 — 67
(T G McCourt, Ire) *led: rdn wl over 1f out: drvn ent fnl f: hdd and no ex last 50yds* **14/1**
1321 **5** 1 ¼ **Kirkby's Treasure**[13] 5476 9-9-0 66 ... PJMcDonald(3) 9 — 69
(G A Swinbank) *hld up towards rr: hdwy 2f out: sn rdn and styd on ins fnl f: nrst fin* **5/1**[2]
0121 **6** ¾ **Sands Of Barra (IRE)**[10] 5556 4-9-5 68 ... DanielTudhope 13 — 69
(I W McInnes) *in midfield: hdwy whn nt clr run on inner 2f out: swtchd lft and nt clr run over 1f out: rdn and kpt on ins fnl f* **7/2**[1]
6303 **7** 1 ½ **Attacca**[13] 5476 6-8-7 56 oh1 ... DO'Donohoe 8 — 53
(J R Weymes) *in midfield: hdwy over 2f out: rdn to chse ldrs whn n.m.r ent fnl f: sn one pce* **18/1**
0150 **8** ½ **Cornus**[8] 5642 5-8-13 69 ... (be) RobbieEgan(7) 10 — 65
(A J McCabe) *hld up in midfield: effrt and sme hdwy over 2f out: sn rdn and btn* **18/1**
4114 **9** ¾ **Esoterica (IRE)**[10] 5556 4-9-1 69 ... (b) GaryBartley(5) 4 — 63
(J S Goldie) *hld up: a in rr* **9/1**
0132 **10** *hd* **Dudley Docker (IRE)**[11] 5532 5-9-7 70 ... LiamJones 1 — 63
(C R Dore) *hld up: a in rr* **5/1**[2]
-004 **11** 2 **Elusive Warrior (USA)**[13] 5489 4-8-11 60 ... (p) TonyHamilton 11 — 48
(R A Fahey) *chsd ldrs: rdn along over 2f out: sn drvn and wknd* **16/1**
4140 **12** 1 ¾ **Spiritual Peace (IRE)**[10] 5552 4-9-0 63 ... (p) NCallan 14 — 46
(K A Ryan) *chsd ldrs: rdn along on inner over 2f out: sn wknd* **10/1**
0-U0 **13** 1 ¼ **Stay Active (USA)**[10] 5555 3-8-7 59 oh2 ow3 ... TomEaves 5 — 39
(I Semple) *a in rr* **40/1**
3001 **14** ½ **Grand Diamond (IRE)**[31] 4971 3-8-8 60 ... (p) PaulMulrennan 6 — 39
(J S Goldie) *hld up: a towards rr* **22/1**

1m 28.32s (-1.62) **Going Correction** -0.025s/f (Good)
WFA 3 from 4yo+ 3lb — **14** Ran SP% **126.1**
Speed ratings (Par 103): **108,107,107,106,105 104,102,102,101,101 98,96,95,94**
CSF £340.21 CT £3073.96 TOTE £22.20: £6.70, £7.30, £4.00; EX 496.20 Place 6 £44.21, Place 5 £13.76..
Owner W B Imison **Bred** Mrs I A Balding **Trained** Maunby, N Yorks

FOCUS
A competitive handicap for the class, run at a decent pace. The first four came clear and the form seems sound.
Sands Of Barra(IRE) Official explanation: jockey said gelding was denied a clear run
T/Plt: £11.30 to a £1 stake. Pool: £64,222.35. 4,113.50 winning tickets. T/Qpdt: £6.90 to a £1 stake. Pool: £3,154.00. 337.10 winning tickets. JR

5455 CURRAGH (R-H)
Sunday, September 30

OFFICIAL GOING: Yielding

5841a A.E.S. RECYCLING H'CAP — 5f
2:30 (2:31) (60-100,97) 3-Y-0+ — **£11,436** (£3,355; £1,598; £544)

RPR
1 *shd* **Tournedos (IRE)**[5] 5700 5-9-6 89 ... AdrianTNicholls 2 — 99
(D Nicholls) *trckd ldrs on stands' rail: 6th 1/2-way: impr into 2nd and chal under 1f out: sn hmpd: kpt on wl cl home: jst failed; fin 2nd; plcd 1st* **7/1**[2]
2 **Inourthoughts (IRE)**[16] 5392 3-9-6 93 ... DJMoran(3) 14 — 103
(Francis Ennis, Ire) *prom on outer: led 2f out: sn rdn: strly pressed whn drifted lft ins fnl f: kpt on wl u.p: all out; fin 1st; plcd 2nd* **14/1**
3 2 ½ **Ms Victoria (IRE)**[35] 4861 3-9-1 85 ... (t) RPCleary 5 — 86
(M Halford, Ire) *mid-div on stands' rail: swtchd rt 1f out: kpt on wl cl home* **10/1**
4 *nk* **Mist And Stone (IRE)**[16] 5394 4-9-2 85 ... DPMcDonogh 12 — 85
(G M Lyons, Ire) *prom: 3rd 1/2-way: 4th u.p 1 1/2f out: kpt on same pce fnl f* **5/1**[1]
5 *hd* **Fly By Magic (IRE)**[17] 5372 3-8-1 74 ... SMGorey(3) 1 — 73
(Patrick Carey, Ire) *trckd ldrs on stands' rail: 7th after 1/2-way: 3rd and chalng whn hmpd and checked ins fnl f: kpt on same pce* **20/1**
6 ¾ **Moone Cross (IRE)**[15] 5436 4-10-0 97 ... (b[1]) FMBerry 16 — 94
(Mrs John Harrington, Ire) *s.i.s and hld up towards rr: prog on stands' rail 2f out: nt clr run 1f out: kpt on* **16/1**
7 *nk* **Girl Power (IRE)**[16] 5394 3-8-6 76 ... (t) WMLordan 11 — 71
(Edward Lynam, Ire) *trckd ldrs: prog 2f out: 5th and rdn 1 1/2f out: no ex ins fnl f* **16/1**
8 1 **The Last Laugh**[42] 4643 3-7-8 74 ... (p) JPFahy(10) 19 — 66
(M J Grassick, Ire) *sn towards rr: styd on fr over 1f out* **12/1**
9 ½ **Flash McGahon (IRE)**[16] 5394 3-9-13 97 ... (b) MJKinane 8 — 87
(John M Oxx, Ire) *prom: 2nd bef 1/2-way: 5th 2f out: no ex fr over 1f out* **8/1**[3]
10 *nk* **If Paradise**[16] 5394 6-8-7 83 ... SFoley(7) 4 — 72
(M Halford, Ire) *led: rdn and hdd 2f out: 2nd 1f out: sn wknd* **12/1**
11 ½ **Gower**[12] 5515 3-8-0 77 ... (p) MJLane(7) 6 — 64
(Ms F M Crowley, Ire) *mid-div: rdn and no imp fr under 2f out* **20/1**
12 1 ¾ **Seven Gold Rings (IRE)**[16] 5394 4-8-9 78 ... PJSmullen 10 — 59
(Ms Joanna Morgan, Ire) *mid-div: no imp fr 1 1/2f out* **12/1**
13 ½ **Nanotech (IRE)**[30] 5023 3-9-1 85 ... WJLee 18 — 64
(Jarlath P Fahey, Ire) *towards rr on outer: no imp fr under 2f out* **10/1**
14 *nk* **King Of Swords (IRE)**[30] 5023 3-9-5 89 ... WJSupple 21 — 67
(Tracey Collins, Ire) *towards rr: no imp fr 2f out* **16/1**
15 1 ½ **Murfreesboro**[16] 5392 4-9-11 94 ... JMurtagh 7 — 67
(M Halford, Ire) *hld up towards rr: no imp fr 1 1/2f out* **10/1**
16 ½ **Kid Creole (IRE)**[24] 5182 9-8-1 73 ... (b) PBBeggy(3) 17 — 44
(T M Walsh, Ire) *a bhd* **25/1**
17 *nk* **Derpat (IRE)**[28] 5069 3-7-11 74 ... MHarley(7) 15 — 44
(J S Bolger, Ire) *a bhd* **16/1**
18 2 ½ **Maid Ofiron (IRE)**[13] 5491 3-7-11 74 ... JamesPSullivan(7) 9 — 35
(M O Quigley, Ire) *prom: 3rd 1/2-way: sn rdn: wknd fr under 2f out* **33/1**
19 *hd* **Paris Sue (IRE)**[17] 5372 7-8-4 73 ... MCHussey 13 — 33
(Marcus Callaghan, Ire) *chsd ldrs in centre: rdn 1/2-way: sn wknd* **25/1**

63.60 secs (2.30) **Going Correction** +0.55s/f (Yiel)
WFA 3 from 4yo+ 1lb — **21** Ran SP% **141.0**
Speed ratings: **102,103,98,98,98 96,96,94,93,93 92,89,89,88,86 85,84,80,80**
CSF £108.01 CT £1055.71 TOTE £7.30: £1.90, £4.00, £3.20, £1.50; DF 579.20.
Owner Mike Browne **Bred** Pat Grogan **Trained** Sessay, N Yorks
■ Stewards' Enquiry : D J Moran two-day ban: careless riding (Oct 10-11)

FOCUS
A decent handicap followed by a lengthy stewards' enquiry. The form has been rated through the fifth.

NOTEBOOK
Tournedos(IRE) was awarded the race in the Stewards' room after finishing a short-head second to Inourthoughts. Hampered by Inourthoughts drifting left from over a furlong out, he was closing the gap all the way to the line, and given the narrow margin of defeat, it would be difficult to argue with the decision. Fourth in a conditions event over this trip at Beverley on Tuesday, he was scoring his fifth win and first this season. (op 6/1)
Inourthoughts(IRE), a maiden winner of the trip on fast ground at Tipperary last year, had gone up7lb for her second to Abraham Lincoln in a 6f conditions event here 16 days previously. She had a high draw and raced in the centre of the track to beyond halfway and confirmed her improvement, keeping on to the line after running about under pressure. She was disqualified for hampering Tournedos. (op 12/1)

5842a WATERFORD TESTIMONIAL STKS (LISTED RACE) 6f
3:00 (3:02) 3-Y-O+ **£21,993** (£6,452; £3,074; £1,047)

RPR

1 **US Ranger (USA)**[102] 2752 3-9-4 KFallon 5 122+
(A P O'Brien, Ire) *hld up in tch: 5th and hdwy on outer 2f out: led over 1f out: qcknd clr ins fnl f: v easily* **1/1**[1]

2 3 1/2 **Senor Benny (USA)**[15] 5436 8-9-3 104 PJSmullen 11 107
(M McDonagh, Ire) *s.i.s and hld up in rr: hdwy under 2f out: 2nd and kpt on ins fnl f: no ch w wnr* **20/1**

3 1 1/4 **Benwilt Breeze (IRE)**[8] 5616 5-9-3 102 (t) JAHeffernan 12 103
(G M Lyons, Ire) *towards rr: prog on outer under 2f out: 3rd u.p 1f out: kpt on same pce* **14/1**

4 2 **Snaefell (IRE)**[15] 5436 3-9-4 106 JMurtagh 13 100
(M Halford, Ire) *hld up: kpt on wout threatening fr over 1f out* **14/1**

5 2 **Confuchias (IRE)**[92] 3088 3-9-6 111 FMBerry 14 96
(Francis Ennis, Ire) *hld up towards rr: kpt on wout threatening fr 1 1/2f out* **7/1**[3]

6 hd **Evening Time (IRE)**[22] 5241 3-9-1 108 DPMcDonogh 2 91
(Kevin Prendergast, Ire) *prom: 3rd 1/2-way: 4th u.p over 1f out: sn no ex* **4/1**[2]

7 1/2 **Bravely (IRE)**[162] 1174 3-9-1 KJManning 9 89?
(J S Bolger, Ire) *s.i.s and hld up towards rr: kpt on one pce fr over 1f out* **33/1**

8 3/4 **Liscanna (IRE)**[64] 3982 3-9-3 103 WMLordan 3 89
(David Wachman, Ire) *chsd ldrs: 6th bef 1/2-way: kpt on same pce fr 2f out* **20/1**

9 1 1/2 **Strike Up The Band**[6] 5673 4-9-3 AdrianTNicholls 4 82
(D Nicholls) *led: rdn 1/2-way: strly pressed over 2f out: hdd & wknd fr over 1f out* **12/1**

10 1 **Empirical Power (IRE)**[22] 5242 6-9-3 95 CDHayes 8 79
(Edward Lynam, Ire) *cl 2nd: chal over 2f out: wknd fr 1 1/2f out* **20/1**

11 3/4 **Majestic Times (IRE)**[8] 5616 7-9-3 98 RPCleary 10 77
(Liam McAteer, Ire) *chsd ldrs on outer: rdn 1/2-way: no ex fr under 2f out* **25/1**

12 hd **Gist (IRE)**[12] 5515 4-9-0 86 (b) WJSupple 6 74
(W J Martin, Ire) *chsd ldrs in 5th: wknd after 1/2-way* **50/1**

13 5 **Gunga Din (IRE)**[37] 4790 3-9-1 (b[1]) VRDeSouza 7 62
(A Kinsella, Ire) *prom: 4th 1/2-way: sn rdn and wknd* **25/1**

1m 16.1s (1.60) **Going Correction** +0.55s/f (Yiel)
WFA 3 from 4yo+ 2lb **14** Ran SP% **130.4**
Speed ratings: **111,106,104,102,99 99,98,97,95,94 93,92,86**
CSF £32.88 TOTE £2.00: £1.10, £7.70, £5.10; DF 63.60.
Owner Michael Tabor **Bred** J Allen **Trained** Ballydoyle, Co Tipperary

FOCUS
The form is rated through the third and fourth.

NOTEBOOK
US Ranger(USA) ◆, who was unbeaten in four runs in France before running good races in defeat in the 2,000 Guineas and the Jersey Stakes at Royal Ascot, has always been highly regarded and it was going to be fascinating to see how he reacted to this first try at sprinting on his debut for O'Brien. Expected to be suited by this easier ground, he cruised to the front over a furlong out and pulled right away, winning easily. He looks well worth his place back at Group level and remains an exciting prospect. (op 4/5 tchd 11/10)
Strike Up The Band, back to form when third at Hamilton the other day, found this far too competitive and faded right out of it late on.

5843a C.L.WELD PARK STKS (GROUP 3) (FILLIES) 7f
3:30 (3:31) 2-Y-O **£35,189** (£10,324; £4,918; £1,675)

RPR

1 **Eva's Request (IRE)**[16] 5395 2-8-12 MJKinane 13 100
(M R Channon) *trckd ldrs: 5th travelling wl 2f out: 6th 1 1/2f out: 4th and hdwy over 1f out: led 100yds out: styd on wl* **14/1**

2 1 **Kyniska (IRE)**[55] 4243 2-8-12 WJSupple 7 98
(Tracey Collins, Ire) *hld up: hdwy 2f out: 3rd under 1 1/2f out: led 1f out: hdd 100yds out: kpt on* **12/1**

3 2 **Indiana Gal (IRE)**[13] 5492 2-8-12 91 (p) FMBerry 8 93
(Patrick Martin, Ire) *sn led: rdn and strly pressed fr over 2 1/2f out: hdd 1f out: kpt on same pce u.p* **11/1**

4 hd **Carribean Sunset (IRE)**[16] 5395 2-8-12 93 PJSmullen 4 92
(D K Weld, Ire) *trckd ldrs in 4th: prog 2f out: 2nd and chal under 1 1/2f out: no ex ins fnl f: kpt on* **7/1**

5 1 1/4 **Yarastar**[17] 5370 2-8-12 CDHayes 11 89
(Kevin Prendergast, Ire) *hld up in tch: drvn along 2f out: kpt on fnl f* **20/1**

6 shd **Lady Jane Digby**[17] 5353 2-8-12 JMurtagh 2 89
(M Johnston) *cl 3rd: rdn over 2f out: wknd fr over 1f out* **2/1**[1]

7 shd **Sassy Gal (IRE)**[11] 5548 2-8-12 74 DMGrant 3 88?
(John Joseph Murphy, Ire) *hld up on outer: rdn 3f out: kpt on fnl f* **33/1**

8 2 **Raja (IRE)**[118] 2325 2-8-12 87 DPMcDonogh 1 83
(Kevin Prendergast, Ire) *chsd ldrs: 6th after 1/2-way: 5th and rdn under 2f out: sn no ex* **14/1**

9 1 1/4 **Kitty Matcham (IRE)**[22] 5239 2-8-12 JAHeffernan 10 80
(A P O'Brien, Ire) *trckd ldrs in 6th: lost pl over 2f out: sn no ex* **10/3**[2]

10 3 **Longing To Dance**[15] 5435 2-8-12 KFallon 12 73
(David Wachman, Ire) *a towards rr* **5/1**[3]

11 nk **Solas Na Greine (IRE)**[15] 5435 2-8-12 90 (p) KJManning 6 72
(J S Bolger, Ire) *cl 2nd: rdn to chal 2 1/2f out: wknd fr under 2f out* **11/1**

12 nk **Mystical Lady (IRE)**[22] 5239 2-8-12 SMLevey 5 71
(Joseph Crowley, Ire) *a in rr* **100/1**

1m 30.2s (2.70) **Going Correction** +0.55s/f (Yiel) **13** Ran SP% **132.0**
Speed ratings: **106,104,102,102,100 100,100,98,96,93 93,92**
CSF £187.44 TOTE £22.90: £7.00, £3.10, £4.00; DF 172.30.
Owner Liam Mulryan **Bred** Ballylinch Stud **Trained** West Ilsley, Berks

FOCUS
A number of these produced big steps up in form, including Eva's Request, but the time backs up the level of the form.

NOTEBOOK
Eva's Request(IRE), third behind the potentially high-class Sense Of Joy in the Prestige Stakes at Goodwood on her penultimate start, failed to run near that level when eighth behind Lush Lashes in the Goffs Fillies Million at the course last time, but she bounced back to her best here and ran on strongly under pressure to win going away. Connections are hopeful she can develop into a Guineas contender, but she has a fair way to go yet.
Lady Jane Digby, beaten three lengths behind Spacious in the Group 2 May Hill at Doncaster, was encountering easy ground for the first time and after racing prominently she came under pressure almost three furlongs out and was done with well over 1f out. Official explanation: jockey said filly travelled well early on but tired 3f out (op 9/4)

5845a JUDDMONTE BERESFORD STKS (GROUP 2) 1m
4:30 (4:33) 2-Y-O **£54,898** (£16,047; £7,601; £2,533)

RPR

1 **Curtain Call (FR)**[36] 4833 2-9-1 109 FMBerry 10 112+
(Mrs John Harrington, Ire) *mde all: rdn clr fr over 1f out: styd on wl: easily* **9/2**[2]

2 4 **Domestic Fund (IRE)**[42] 4645 2-9-1 90 PJSmullen 1 103
(D K Weld, Ire) *trckd ldrs: 3rd 1/2-way: rdn st: mod 2nd ins fnl f: kpt on* **9/1**

3 1 1/2 **Going Public (IRE)**[28] 5070 2-9-1 100 MJKinane 8 100
(D K Weld, Ire) *settled 2nd: rdn st: no imp fr under 2f out: 3rd ins fnl f: kpt on* **20/1**

4 hd **Brazilian Star (IRE)**[37] 4789 2-9-1 102 (b[1]) CDHayes 9 100
(Kevin Prendergast, Ire) *dwlt: hld up towards rr: 7th 1/2-way: rdn st: 6th 1f out: styd on cl home* **16/1**

5 nk **Lisvale (IRE)**[16] 5397 2-9-1 104 WMLordan 7 99
(David Wachman, Ire) *trckd ldrs in 4th: 5th and rdn early st: kpt on same pce fr 1 1/2f out* **6/1**[3]

6 1 **Lizard Island (USA)**[14] 5458 2-9-4 113 KFallon 5 100
(A P O'Brien, Ire) *chsd ldrs in 5th: 6th u.p early st: kpt on same pce fr 2f out* **1/1**[1]

7 nk **Capt Chaos (IRE)**[14] 5456 2-9-1 101 JMurtagh 4 96
(Edward Lynam, Ire) *hld up in rr: hdwy on outer early st: 5th over 1f out: sn no ex* **16/1**

8 3/4 **Lucifer Sam (USA)**[15] 5406 2-9-1 97 JAHeffernan 3 94
(A P O'Brien, Ire) *towards rr: no imp st* **10/1**

9 1 1/2 **Via Galilei (IRE)**[14] 5458 2-9-1 KJManning 2 91
(J S Bolger, Ire) *hld up: 6th and prog 1/2-way: 4th into st: sn rdn and wknd* **12/1**

1m 46.7s (4.60) **Going Correction** +0.75s/f (Yiel) **10** Ran SP% **125.8**
Speed ratings: **107,103,101,101,101 100,99,98,97**
CSF £48.77 TOTE £5.70: £1.60, £3.00, £5.40; DF 42.50.
Owner Mrs P K Cooper **Bred** Famille Niarchos **Trained** Moone, Co Kildare

FOCUS
An impressive win from Curtain Call and a further boost to New Approach. There was not much strength in depth.

NOTEBOOK
Curtain Call(FR), still a maiden coming into this, shaped as though a return to this distance would suit when splitting New Approach and Henrythenavigator in the Futurity Stakes and he received a fine ride from Berry to make every yard of the running. He readily came clear in the final furlong, winning easily, and on this evidence it is no surprise he is being trained for next year's Derby. He is now likely to head for the Racing Post Trophy. (op 4/1 tchd 5/1)
Domestic Fund(IRE), off the mark in a 7f maiden at Leopardstown last time, coped well with the rise in grade and kept on best of the rest, but the winner proved in a different league. He will require further in time and remains a smart prospect. (op 7/1)
Going Public(IRE) had previously failed to build on his impressive debut effort, but this first try at 1m brought about an improved effort. He is unlikely to prove up to winning races at this level, but can find a Listed contest.
Lizard Island(USA), shouldering a 3lb penalty, has shown some smart form in defeat behind the likes of Rio De La Plata and New Approach, and the return to this softer ground was expected to suit. However, he seemed unable to quicken when asked for maximum effort and proved most disappointing. (op 11/10 tchd 4/5)

5844 - 5847a (Foreign Racing) - See Raceform Interactive

2705 DORTMUND (R-H)
Sunday, September 30

OFFICIAL GOING: Heavy

5848a PREIS VON DEW21 - BBAG AUKTIONSRENNEN DORTMUND (FILLIES) 6f
2:35 (2:45) 2-Y-O

£16,892 (£7,432; £4,054; £2,703; £1,351; £1,351)

RPR

1 **Lips Arrow (GER)**[36] 4837 2-8-12 (b) ASuborics 3 —
(Andreas Lowe, Germany) **56/10**

2 3 **De La Vista (GER)**[36] 4837 2-8-12 AStarke 8 —
(W Hickst, Germany) **11/5**[1]

3 3/4 **Easy Wonder (GER)**[14] 5462 2-8-13 ow1 THellier 9 —
(I A Wood) *led tl hdd 2f out: one pce* **4/1**

4 1/2 **Sacota**[14] 5462 2-8-12 PVanDeKeere 1 —
(E Kurdu, Germany) **20/1**

5 5 **Traumsternchen (GER)** 2-8-12 ABest 5 —
(P Hirschberger, Germany) **11/1**

6 1 3/4 **My Summer Of Love (FR)**[36] 4837 2-9-2 ADeVries 2 —
(K Woodburn) **32/10**[2]

7 1 **Fly My Dream (GER)**[36] 4837 2-8-12 AHelfenbein 6 —
(Mario Hofer, Germany) **7/2**[3]

8 14 **Bella Ciao (GER)** 2-8-12 ABoschert 7 —
(A Oertel, Germany) **46/1**

9 2 1/2 **Tapisserie (GER)**[14] 5462 2-8-12 (b) EPedroza 4 —
(C Von Der Recke, Germany) **34/1**

1m 18.56s (78.56) **9** Ran SP% **130.5**
(including ten euro stakes): WIN 66; PL 21, 18, 18; SF 224.
Owner Stall Lintec **Bred** Stall Partenaue **Trained** Germany

NOTEBOOK
Easy Wonder(GER) has run well in defeat in similar events in Germany on her last two starts and this was another solid effort in defeat. She tried to make every yard, but had to use up plenty to get across from her wide draw and this ground was probably more testing than she would have liked. She also carried 1lb overweight.

5849a GROSSER PREIS VON DSW21 - 123RD DEUTSCHES ST LEGER (GROUP 3) 1m 6f
4:20 (4:35) 3-Y-0+ **£27,027** (£10,135; £4,054; £2,703)

RPR
1 **El Tango (GER)**[39] 4722 5-9-6 .... AStarke 7 106
(P Schiergen, Germany) *dropped out in last: hdwy to go 4th 2f out: wnt 2nd pressing ldng ins fnl f: hrd rdn to ld cl home* **9/10**[1]
2 ½ **Scatina (IRE)**[42] 4651 3-8-5 .... AHelfenbein 5 100
(Mario Hofer, Germany) *in tch in 5th: hrd rdn and hung rt over 1f out: led 1f out: hdd and no ex cl home* **138/10**
3 2½ **Waldvogel (IRE)**[32] 4957 3-8-9 .... EPedroza 6 101
(A Wohler, Germany) *6th early: 4th 4f out: led 3f out: hdd 1f out: one pce* **5/1**[3]
4 3 **Avanti Polonia (GER)**[7] 5669 3-8-7 ow2 ....(p) ABoschert 3 95
(P Schiergen, Germany) *reluctant to load: 4th early: 3rd st: sn wnt 2nd: disputing 3rd but looked btn whn hmpd over 1f out* **16/1**
5 7 **Peppertree Lane (IRE)**[36] 4830 4-9-6 .... KDarley 2 88
(M Johnston) *led 6f: 2nd whn brought wd to r alone against stands' rails ent st: sn outpcd* **3/1**[2]
6 7 **Rising Cross**[56] 4215 4-9-2 .... J-PGuillambert 1 74
(J R Best) *racd in 3rd tl lost pl ent st: n.d after* **17/2**
7 2 **N'Oubliez Jamais (GER)**[57] 4191 4-9-6 .... ASuborics 4 75
(H Blume, Germany) *racd in 2nd tl led after 6f: hdd 3f out: wknd* **25/2**
R **Jump For You (FR)**[32] 4957 5-9-6 .... THellier 8 —
(W Baltromei, Germany) *ref to r* **13/1**

3m 10.14s (4.64)
WFA 3 from 4yo+ 10lb **8** Ran SP% **132.0**
WIN 19; PL 14, 21, 15; SF 242.
Owner Stall Mydlinghoven **Bred** Gestut Wittekindshof **Trained** Germany
■ El Tango became the first horse to win two German St Legers, following up his 2005 success.

NOTEBOOK
El Tango(GER), a fine sixth at 100/1 in the Ebor on his previous start, relished the testing conditions and followed up his success in this race in 2005.
Peppertree Lane(IRE), three times a winner already this season, raced alone against the stands'-side rail in the straight, but the tactics did not pay off and he was well beaten.
Rising Cross has struggled this season and, only small, she was always going to find such demanding conditions against her.

5266 HANOVER (L-H)
Sunday, September 30
OFFICIAL GOING: Heavy

5850a HTP-CUP (LISTED RACE) (F&M) 6f 110y
3:35 (3:46) 3-Y-0+ **£8,108** (£2,973; £1,622; £811)

RPR
1 **Slade (GER)**[21] 5-9-0 .... FilipMinarik 5 92
(M Trybuhl, Germany) **5/2**[1]
2 nk **Hanover Lady (GER)**[21] 5266 3-8-13 .... DVSmith 11 93
(Frau Lucie Vondrova, Germany) **25/1**
3 nk **Zut Alors (IRE)**[37] 3-9-1 .... J-BHamel 13 94
(Robert Collet, France) **68/10**
4 1¾ **Hashbrown (GER)**[21] 5266 3-9-1 .... J-PCarvalho 6 89
(C Sprengel, Germany) **38/10**[2]
5 nse **Lumiere Noire (FR)**[37] 3-9-1 .... TRicher 9 89
(R Gibson, France) **11/2**
6 1¼ **The Fairy (GER)** 3-8-8 ....(b) NRichter 7 78
(J Hirschberger, Germany) **57/10**
7 3 **Zoom (GER)**[42] 4-9-4 .... APietsch 4 76
(C Von Der Recke, Germany) **72/10**
8 nk **Hunting Girl (GER)**[57] 4-9-0 .... JBojko 15 71
(T Reineke, Germany) **47/1**
9 1 **Pinkabout (IRE)**[98] 2914 3-8-8 .... LPKeniry 3 65
(J S Moore) *disp 2nd or 3rd on ins: lost pl over 2f out: n.d after* **20/1**
10 shd **Mimisel**[85] 3332 3-8-8 .... JamieMackay 1 65
(Rae Guest) *in tch on ins: hdwy to chse ldrs ent st: wknd 1 1/2f out* **9/2**[3]

1m 24.66s (84.66)
WFA 3 from 4yo+ 2lb **10** Ran SP% **133.6**
(including ten euro stakes): WIN 35; PL 23, 34, 24; SF 649.
Owner U Zerrath **Bred** Gestut Schaffauer Hof - Granum Zucht **Trained** Germany

NOTEBOOK
Pinkabout(IRE) has left John Gosden since she was last seen in June and she was well beaten on her debut for new connections. This ground was probably softer than she would have liked, especially considering she had been off the track for three months. She is very well bred and her connections will no doubt be keen to pick up some black type.
Mimisel's maiden win came on soft ground, and she had been running well in defeat in pattern company in the UK in recent starts, so this has to be considered disappointing.

5822 BELMONT PARK (L-H)
Sunday, September 30
OFFICIAL GOING: Dirt course - fast; turf course - firm

5852a VOSBURGH STKS (GRADE 1) 6f (D)
9:10 (9:11) 3-Y-0+ **£122,449** (£40,816; £20,408; £10,204; £6,122; £1,361)

RPR
1 **Fabulous Strike (USA)**[85] 4-8-12 .... RADominguez 1 122
(Todd M Beattie, U.S.A) **46/10**[3]
2 5¾ **Talent Search (USA)**[53] 4-8-12 ....(b) RFogelsonger 8 104
(Mark Shuman, U.S.A) **18/1**
3 nk **Discreet Cat (USA)**[183] 863 4-8-12 .... GKGomez 4 103
(Saeed Bin Suroor) **19/20**[1]
4 nse **Mach Ride (USA)**[50] 4-8-12 ....(b) ETrujillo 6 103
(Steve W Standridge, U.S.A) **111/10**
5 nse **E Z Warrior (USA)**[18] 3-8-10 ....(b) VEspinoza 3 103
(B Baffert, U.S.A) **26/1**
6 ¾ **Park Avenue Ball (USA)**[29] 5-8-12 .... RBejarano 2 101
(James T Ryerson, U.S.A) **283/10**
7 2¾ **First Defence (USA)**[36] 3-8-10 .... JCastellano 5 92
(R J Frankel, U.S.A) **59/20**[2]
8 11½ **Will He Shine (USA)**[88] 5-8-12 ....(b) AGarcia 7 56
(Dale Romans, U.S.A) **216/10**

69.22 secs (0.02)
WFA 3 from 4yo+ 2lb **8** Ran SP% **119.5**
PARI-MUTUEL (including $2 stake): WIN 11.20; PL (1-2) 5.50, 11.80;SHOW (1-23) 3.70, 6.00, 2.70; SF 107.50.
Owner Walter Downey **Bred** Tea Party Stable Inc **Trained** North America

NOTEBOOK
Fabulous Strike(USA) broke well from the inside post and, after duelling with Talent Search through the first half mile, he pulled well clear when asked to run out an impressive winner. He will now be aimed at the Breeders' Cup Sprint and is likely to be thereabouts.
Discreet Cat(USA), having his first run since flopping in the Dubai World Cup back in March, after which it was discovered her was suffering from an aggressive throat abscess, made just a satisfactory return to the track. He should improve plenty for the run and is now likely to be aimed the new Breeders' Cup (Dirt) Mile race, although the Classic has yet to be ruled out.

5853a JOE HIRSCH TURF CLASSIC INVITATIONAL (GRADE 1) (TURF) 1m 4f
9:41 (9:45) 3-Y-0+ **£183,673** (£61,224; £30,612; £15,306; £9,184; £3,061)

RPR
1 **English Channel (USA)**[50] 4415 5-9-0 .... JRVelazquez 1 117
(T Pletcher, U.S.A) **2/5**[1]
2 2¼ **Stream Of Gold (IRE)**[206] 642 6-9-0 .... ECastro 6 113
(K McLaughlin, U.S.A) **83/10**[3]
3 3 **Interpatation (USA)**[15] 5-9-0 .... JLEspinoza 5 108
(Robert Barbara, U.S.A) **192/10**
4 hd **Kiss The Kid (USA)**[56] 4-9-0 ....(b) StewartElliott 4 108
(Amy Tarrant, U.S.A) **145/10**
5 1 **Mission Approved (USA)**[28] 3-8-9 .... ECoa 3 109
(G Contessa, U.S.A) **16/1**
6 hd **Green Girl (FR)**[14] 5-8-11 .... AGarcia 7 103
(J E Hammond, France) **193/10**
7 nk **Mustanfar (USA)**[64] 6-9-0 ....(b) GKGomez 2 105
(K McLaughlin, U.S.A) **59/10**[2]

2m 25.73s (-2.85)
WFA 3 from 4yo+ 8lb **7** Ran SP% **118.9**
PARI-MUTUEL: WIN 2.80; PL (1-2) 2.20, 4.50; SHOW (1-2-3) 2.10, 3.80,4.40; SF 12.80.
Owner James T Scatuorchio **Bred** Keene Ridge Farm **Trained** USA

NOTEBOOK
English Channel(USA), one of the best turf horses in the US, had to force his way through a small gap, but found plenty once in the clear and won in good style. He will now try to win the elusive Breeders' Cup Turf for the first time in three tries.

5854a BELDAME STKS (GRADE 1) (F&M) 1m 1f (D)
10:12 (10:15) 3-Y-0+ **£183,673** (£61,224; £30,612; £15,306; £9,184; £2,041)

RPR
1 **Unbridled Belle (USA)**[37] 4794 4-8-11 ....(b) RADominguez 5 117
(T Pletcher, U.S.A) **67/10**
2 hd **Indian Vale (CAN)**[37] 4794 5-8-11 .... JRVelazquez 3 117
(T Pletcher, U.S.A) **72/10**
3 2¼ **Ginger Punch (USA)**[22] 5249 4-8-11 .... RBejarano 2 112
(R J Frankel, U.S.A) **11/10**[1]
4 4½ **Balance (USA)**[56] 4-8-11 ....(b) VEspinoza 7 104
(D Hofmans, U.S.A) **63/20**[2]
5 4½ **Mo Cuishle (USA)**[162] 4-8-11 .... ECoa 6 95
(B Tagg, U.S.A) **265/10**
6 1½ **Miss Shop (USA)**[22] 5249 4-8-11 .... JCastellano 1 92
(H A Jerkens, U.S.A) **57/10**[3]
7 21 **Ice Cool Kitty (USA)**[77] 4-8-11 .... MLuzzi 4 48
(R Dutrow Jr, U.S.A) **30/1**

1m 48.63s (0.83) **7** Ran SP% **118.7**
PARI-MUTUEL: WIN 15.40; PL (1-2) 6.70, 7.70; SHOW (1-2-3) 3.60, 3.80,2.20; SF 72.00.
Owner Team Valor Stables **Bred** Joe Sutton & Laszlo Makk **Trained** USA

NOTEBOOK
Unbridled Belle(USA) did not enjoy the best of trips and her rider felt she might even clip heels at one point, but she picked up well when in the clear and was still able to get up and deny her stablemate, Indian Vale. She now head for the Breeders' Cup Distaff, along with today's runner-up, and they will also be joined by Todd Pletcher's Octave. Interestingly Pletcher had won this race for the last two years, but both his winners were beaten favourites in the Distaff, although in Fleet Indian's case she had to be pulled up.

5855a JOCKEY CLUB GOLD CUP INVITATIONAL (GRADE 1) 1m 2f (D)
10:45 (10:46) 3-Y-0+ **£229,592** (£76,531; £38,265; £19,133; £11,480; £3,827)

RPR
1 **Curlin (USA)**[56] 3-8-10 .... RAlbarado 5 129
(S Asmussen, U.S.A) **21/10**[2]
2 nk **Lawyer Ron (USA)**[29] 5059 4-9-0 .... VEspinoza 6 126
(T Pletcher, U.S.A) **7/10**[1]
3 4 **Political Force (USA)**[29] 5059 4-9-0 .... CVelasquez 3 118
(H A Jerkens, U.S.A) **11/2**[3]
4 6 **Sun King (USA)**[29] 5059 5-9-0 .... AGarcia 2 107
(N Zito, U.S.A) **112/10**
5 nk **Brother Bobby (USA)**[43] 4-9-0 .... StewartElliott 1 106
(G Forster, U.S.A) **41/1**
6 6½ **Indy Wind (USA)**[43] 5-9-0 .... RBejarano 7 94
(Amy Tarrant, U.S.A) **81/1**
7 3½ **Malibu Moonshine (USA)**[42] 5-9-0 ....(b) CHill 4 87
(G Contessa, U.S.A) **77/1**

2m 1.20s (0.58)
WFA 3 from 4yo+ 6lb **7** Ran SP% **119.5**
PARI-MUTUEL: WIN 6.20; PL (1-2) 3.10, 2.40; SHOW (1-2-3) 2.40, 2.10,2.70; SF 12.40.
Owner Stonestreet, Padua, Midnight Cry Stables, G Bolton **Bred** Fares Farm Inc **Trained** USA

FOCUS
A key Breeders' Cup Classic trial.
NOTEBOOK
Curlin(USA), the Preakness winner, stayed on strongest of all in the straight and just denied Lawyer Ron on his first run against older horses. He had a hard race and his trainer is hoping this has not taken too much out of him ahead of the Breeders' Cup Classic.
Lawyer Ron(USA), a hugely impressive winner of the Woodward Stakes on his previous start, ran a blinder in defeat. His trainer felt he had learned something afterwards and reported this free-going individual will probably be better off being allowed to go on and do what he wants to do in future. He will now be aimed the Breeders' Cup Classic.

5442 BATH (L-H)
Monday, October 1

OFFICIAL GOING: Good to soft
Wind: strong behind Weather: wet and miserable

5856 E.B.F./JOHN SISK MAIDEN STKS — 5f 161y
2:10 (2:13) (Class 5) 2-Y-O — **£3,238** (£963; £481; £240) **Stalls** Centre

Form — RPR
3 **1** **Your Pleasure (USA)**[17] 5380 2-8-12 0 .... FrancisNorton 11 76
(A M Balding) *mde all: kpt on gamely: drvn out* **9/1**
00 **2** ½ **Prime Aspiration (USA)**[19] 5337 2-9-3 0 .... RichardThomas 4 79
(Christian Wroe) *in tch: clsd on ldrs 3f out: sn rdn: hung lft and swtchd rt ent fnl f: r.o* **66/1**
0 **3** ¾ **Miss Poppy**[27] 5110 2-8-12 0 .... JimCrowley 2 72
(P R Chamings) *chsd wnr: rdn over 2f out: no ex ins fnl f: lost 2nd nr fin* **25/1**
0503 **4** *nk* **Tina's Best (IRE)**[17] 5393 2-8-12 76 .... RichardSmith 13 71
(R Hannon) *towards rr: rdn over 2f out: hdwy over 1f out: styd on: nt rch ldrs* **10/1**
5 *1* **Sister Moonshine** 2-8-9 0 .... WilliamBuick(3) 16 67
(W R Muir) *mid-div: rdn and stdy hdwy fr over 2f out: chsd ldrs ent fnl f: no ex* **50/1**
2250 **6** 2½ **Aaim For Applause**[11] 5575 2-9-3 64 .... GeorgeBaker 3 64
(M R Channon) *mid-div: rdn 3f out: hung lft over 1f out: kpt on same pce* **6/1**[3]
533 **7** 1¼ **First Trim (IRE)**[15] 5448 2-9-3 85 .... KDarley 14 60
(B J Meehan) *chsd ldrs: rdn 3f out: wknd fnl f* **6/4**[1]
0 **8** ½ **Todber**[90] 3187 2-8-12 0 .... MartinDwyer 1 53
(M P Tregoning) *s.i.s: towards rr: rdn and stdy prog fr over 2f out: one pce fnl f* **14/1**
3052 **9** ¾ **Pha Mai Blue**[16] 5428 2-9-3 81 .... JimmyQuinn 5 56
(W J Knight) *chsd ldrs: rdn over 2f out: carried sltly lft ent fnl f: wknd* **4/1**[2]
05 **10** *5* **Copperbottomed (IRE)**[12] 5521 2-9-3 0 .... GrahamGibbons 12 39
(R Hollinshead) *mid-div: effrt over 2f out: wknd ent fnl f* **100/1**
11 ¾ **Premier Yank (USA)** 2-9-3 0 .... TPQueally 8 37
(J A Osborne) *s.i.s: hmpd ent fnl f: mainly towards rr* **25/1**
12 3½ **Dubai Petal (IRE)** 2-8-7 0 .... TolleyDean(5) 15 20
(J S Moore) *s.i.s: a towards rr* **16/1**
00 **13** *6* **Defnikov**[46] 4527 2-9-3 0 .... DavidKinsella 7 —
(A B Haynes) *chsd ldrs: rdn 3f out: sn wknd* **100/1**
0 **14** 1½ **Bute Street**[28] 5088 2-8-12 0 .... HaddenFrost(5) 10 —
(R J Hodges) *s.i.s: a towards rr* **100/1**

1m 11.42s (0.22) **Going Correction** +0.05s/f (Good) **14 Ran SP% 120.0**
Speed ratings (Par 95): **100,99,98,97,96 93,91,90,89,83 82,77,69,67**
CSF £512.76 TOTE £11.50: £2.60, £22.60, £5.40; EX 851.50.
Owner George Strawbridge **Bred** George Strawbridge Jr **Trained** Kingsclere, Hants

FOCUS
Plenty of runners, but a few of the form horses failed to run up to their best and this looked just a fair maiden.
NOTEBOOK
Your Pleasure(USA) flashed her tail and showed just modest form when third on her debut at Sandown, but she has clearly gone right the way since then. The bare form looks pretty ordinary, so she should not be too harshly treated by the Handicapper. (op 17-2 tchd 10-1)
Prime Aspiration(USA) finished down the field on his two previous starts, but this was a weak race and he very nearly caused an upset. He is now qualified for a handicap mark and will have more options.
Miss Poppy, a half-sister to Kyllachy, confirmed the ability she showed when mid-division in a reasonable maiden at Goodwood on her debut with a creditable effort in third. (op 20-1)
Tina's Best(IRE) ran to just a modest level of form and she looks flattered by the bare form of her recent third in a valuable race at the Curragh. (op 12-1)
Sister Moonshine, an 80,000gns daughter of Averti, half-sister to seven winners, including top-class juvenile Donna Blini, out of a triple 6f-7f winner at two, showed ability and should improve plenty.
Aaim For Applause was well below his best and he is not progressing. (op 7-1)
First Trim(IRE) had shown plenty of ability on his three previous runs, including when third at Goodwood on his previous start, but this was disappointing. (tchd 13-8)
Todber was not totally without promise on her debut on the Polytrack at Lingfield, but she finished up well held. She might find her level once handicapped. (op 16-1)
Pha Mai Blue, a Dewhurst entry, was well below the pick of his form and the easing in the ground was probably against him. Official explanation: jockey said colt hung left-handed (op 7-2 tchd 10-3)
Premier Yank(USA) Official explanation: jockey said colt suffered interference in running
Bute Street Official explanation: jockey said gelding stumbled and lost its action

5857 BRISTOL UNIVERSITY AND LITERARY CLUB H'CAP — 2m 1f 34y
2:40 (2:41) (Class 5) (0-75,74) 3-Y-O+ — **£2,914** (£867; £433; £216) **Stalls** Low

Form — RPR
2254 **1** **Plane Painter (IRE)**[14] 5478 3-9-5 **74** .... GregFairley 3 78
(M Johnston) *mde all: styd on wl: rdn out* **7/2**[1]
5063 **2** *nk* **Sweetheart**[33] 4951 3-8-12 **67** .... JimCrowley 6 71
(Jamie Poulton) *hld up: swtchd to stands' side 3f out: sn rdn and hdwy: chsd wnr over 1f out: styd on* **17/2**
0663 **3** ¾ **How's Business**[12] 5533 3-8-2 **57** .... FrancisNorton 2 60
(C A Cyzer) *trckd ldrs: rdn 3f out: kpt on but nvr quite able to chal wnr* **7/1**[3]
0621 **4** ¾ **Missoula (IRE)**[16] 5404 4-10-0 **72** .... JimmyQuinn 4 74
(M H Tompkins) *mid-div: rdn and stdy prog fr 3f out: styd on ins fnl f* **6/1**[2]
5032 **5** *4* **My Legal Eagle (IRE)**[16] 5427 13-8-4 **53** oh5 .... TolleyDean(5) 1 51
(E G Bevan) *hld up: hdwy over 3f out: sn rdn: kpt on same pce fnl f* **25/1**
0204 **6** *nk* **Valance (IRE)**[31] 5007 7-9-5 **63** ....(tp) NelsonDeSouza 7 61
(C R Egerton) *racd keenly: trckd wnr: rdn 3f out: wknd ent fnl f* **6/1**[2]
0656 **7** *4* **The Composer**[46] 4544 5-8-11 **55** .... FergusSweeney 9 48
(M Blanshard) *hld up: hdwy over 3f out: sn rdn: wknd over 1f out* **9/1**
40/4 **8** *26* **Red Opera**[28] 5087 5-9-1 **59** .... KDarley 8 24
(D E Pipe) *trckd ldrs tl completely failed to handle bnd 5f out: bhd and nvr gng after* **7/2**[1]

3m 54.83s (5.23) **Going Correction** +0.20s/f (Good)
WFA 3 from 4yo+ 11lb **8 Ran SP% 109.9**
Speed ratings (Par 103): **95,94,94,94,92 92,90,78**
CSF £31.25 CT £180.79 TOTE £5.30: £1.70, £3.50, £2.50; EX 32.30.
Owner Favourites Racing XXIV **Bred** J Cockburn **Trained** Middleham Moor, N Yorks
■ Love Brothers was withdrawn due to unsuitable ground (14/1, deduct 5p in the £ under Rule 4).

FOCUS
A modest staying handicap and the pace was just ordinary. The form seems to make sense but the fifth lends a note of caution from 5lb wrong.
Red Opera Official explanation: jockey said gelding lost its action

5858 THORN BAKER CONSTRUCTION RECRUITMENT MAIDEN STKS — 1m 2f 46y
3:10 (3:13) (Class 5) 2-Y-O — **£2,914** (£867; £433; £216) **Stalls** Low

Form — RPR
03 **1** **Inventor (IRE)**[10] 5599 2-9-3 0 .... MartinDwyer 6 77+
(B J Meehan) *trckd ldrs: jnd ldr over 2f out: led over 1f out: styd on wl: rdn out* **10/11**[1]
2 1¼ **Planetarium** 2-9-3 0 .... GregFairley 8 75+
(M Johnston) *mid-div: rdn and stdy prog fr 3f out: styd on to go 2nd ins fnl f* **12/1**
24 **3** ½ **Synergistic (IRE)**[12] 5526 2-9-3 0 .... KDarley 12 74
(M Johnston) *trckd ldrs: rdn 3f out: styd on fnl f* **7/2**[2]
656 **4** *2* **Al Azy (IRE)**[16] 5417 2-9-3 76 .... RHills 4 71
(J L Dunlop) *led: rdn and hdd over 1f out: sn edgd rt: kpt on same pce* **10/1**[3]
6045 **5** *2* **King Bathwick (IRE)**[16] 5423 2-9-3 62 .... JimCrowley 2 67
(B R Millman) *mid-div: hdwy 3f out: sn rdn: one pce fnl f* **20/1**
500 **6** *7* **Shadows Fall (USA)**[27] 5116 2-9-3 70 .... NelsonDeSouza 10 54
(P F I Cole) *prom: rdn 3f out: wknd wl over 1f out* **66/1**
004 **7** *3* **Dubai Land**[14] 5485 2-9-3 70 .... TPQueally 11 49
(M R Channon) *mid-div: rdn 3f out: wknd 2f out* **12/1**
00 **8** *4* **Balais Folly (FR)**[24] 5186 2-9-3 0 .... DavidKinsella 7 42
(B Palling) *restrained s: a towards rr* **100/1**
0 **9** *nk* **Pay The Grey**[36] 4852 2-8-12 0 .... RichardSmith 13 36
(R Hannon) *a towards rr* **50/1**
060 **10** *2* **Nikolaievich (IRE)**[24] 5200 2-8-12 71 .... TolleyDean(5) 9 38
(P F I Cole) *t.k.h: a towards rr* **14/1**
660 **11** *1* **Champagne Dancer**[49] 4454 2-9-3 55 .... GeorgeBaker 1 36
(D J S Ffrench Davis) *a bhd* **66/1**

2m 13.71s (2.71) **Going Correction** +0.20s/f (Good) **11 Ran SP% 116.4**
Speed ratings (Par 95): **97,96,95,94,92 86,84,81,80,79 78**
CSF £13.20 TOTE £1.70: £1.10, £2.80, £1.20; EX 15.40.
Owner Highclere Thoroughbred Racing (Lake Con) **Bred** B Holland And P Connell **Trained** Manton, Wilts

FOCUS
Quite a test for these juveniles, but still fair form, with the fifth helping with the level. They came stands' side in the straight.
NOTEBOOK
Inventor(IRE) confirmed the promise he showed on his debut at Sandown when third in a 1m maiden at Newmarket on his previous start and he continued his progression with a ready success on this step up in trip. To be winning over this trip at this stage of his career suggests he is very much a stayer in the making. (op 8-11 tchd evens in a place)
Planetarium, a 120,000gns son of Fantastic Light, half-brother to 1m winner Pearl's Girl, and dual 7f scorer Contractor, raced more towards the centre of the track than many of these, but he finished well when getting the hang of things late on. It was a little disconcerting to see him make his debut over such a long trip, but he will have learnt plenty and should prove hard to beat in similar company next time. (op 10-1 tchd 8-1)
Synergistic(IRE), unsuited by the drop back to an extended 7f at Beverley when beaten at odds on last time, looked sure to improve for the step up to this trip, but he ran to just a fair level of form. The easy ground may have been against him. (op 4-1 tchd 9-2 and 3-1)
Al Azy(IRE) probably just found this too much of a test at this stage of his career and he could not build on his earlier efforts. (tchd 9-1 and 12-1)
King Bathwick(IRE) ran a respectable race stepped up in trip and he could find his level once handicapped. (op 22-1 tchd 25-1)
Nikolaievich(IRE) Official explanation: jockey said colt hung right-handed throughout

5859 EUROPEAN BREEDERS' FUND & THATCHER ASSOCIATES MAIDEN FILLIES' STKS — 1m 2f 46y
3:40 (3:42) (Class 5) 3-Y-O+ — **£4,533** (£1,348; £674; £168; £168) **Stalls** Low

Form — RPR
2-2 **1** **Sharp Dresser (USA)**[17] 5384 3-8-12 0 .... JimCrowley 8 69
(Mrs A J Perrett) *trckd ldrs: wnt 2nd over 2f out: led over 1f out: sn drew clr: comf* **9/4**[2]
4205 **2** *6* **Anthea**[43] 4630 3-8-12 57 .... FergusSweeney 1 57
(B R Millman) *led: rdn over 2f out: hdd over 1f out: sn no cnance w wnr: jst hld on for 2nd* **8/1**
3 *nk* **Lady Splodge** 3-8-12 0 .... RichardThomas 6 56
(C G Cox) *s.i.s: sn mid-div: hdwy 3f out: sn rdn to chse ldng pair: kpt on same pce* **50/1**
3622 **4** *hd* **Ashmal (USA)**[25] 5157 3-8-12 65 ....(b) RHills 10 56
(J L Dunlop) *hld up bhd: rdn and hdwy 2f out: styd on same pce* **6/1**[3]
4P04 **4** *dht* **Restless Soul**[27] 5113 3-8-12 51 .... TPQueally 5 56
(C A Cyzer) *hld up towards rr: hdwy into midfield over 3f out: sn rdn: styd on fnl 2f* **25/1**
46-5 **6** *5* **Poyle Kiera**[12] 5530 3-8-12 48 .... FrancisNorton 2 46
(M Blanshard) *trckd ldrs: rdn over 3f out: wknd fnl f* **66/1**
7 *12* **Star Of Pompey** 3-8-12 0 .... DavidKinsella 7 22
(A B Haynes) *dwlt and a bhd* **100/1**
460 **8** 1½ **Miss Habershon**[17] 5384 3-8-12 65 .... MartinDwyer 3 19
(A King) *s.i.s: t.k.h and sn mid-div: wknd 2f out* **20/1**
5 **9** *3* **Bochinche (USA)**[13] 5494 3-8-12 0 .... KDarley 9 13
(Saeed Bin Suroor) *trckd ldr: rdn over 2f out: sn wknd: eased fnl f* **8/1**
6 **10** *16* **Fashion Accessory**[20] 5304 3-8-12 0 .... JimmyQuinn 11 —
(M Appleby) *s.i.s: a bhd* **100/1**
35 **U** **Propaganda (IRE)**[68] 3847 3-8-9 0 .... WilliamBuick(3) 4 —
(L M Cumani) *mid-div: rdn whn stmbld wl over 1f out: uns rdr sn after* **7/4**[1]

2m 12.74s (1.74) **Going Correction** +0.20s/f (Good) **11 Ran SP% 117.7**
Speed ratings (Par 100): **101,96,95,95,95 91,82,81,78,65 —**
CSF £19.44 TOTE £2.90: £1.10, £2.60, £9.20; EX 22.60.
Owner K Abdulla **Bred** Juddmonte Farms Inc **Trained** Pulborough, W Sussex

FOCUS
An uncompetitive fillies' maiden and it is doubtful if the winner had to improve with the likes of the fifth and sixth limiting the form. They raced towards the stands'-side rail in the straight.

Bochinche(USA) Official explanation: jockey said filly lost its action

5860 CLYDESDALE BANK H'CAP 1m 5y
4:10 (4:12) (Class 5) (0-70,70) 3-Y-O **£3,238** (£963; £481; £240) **Stalls** Low

Form RPR
104 **1** **Poppets Sweetlove**[16] 5433 3-8-7 **59**........................... DavidKinsella 11 66
(A B Haynes) *trckd ldr: rdn to chal over 2f out: led over 1f out: kpt on wl* **25/1**
5014 **2** 2 **Magroom**[12] 5528 3-8-4 **56**.................... FrancisNorton 15 58
(R J Hodges) *mid-div: rdn and hdwy 2f out: kpt on to go 2nd ins fnl f but a hld* **13/2**[2]
0-36 **3** 1 1/4 **Alecia (IRE)**[31] 5019 3-8-13 **68**.......................... WilliamBuick(3) 4 67
(A M Balding) *chsd ldrs: rdn over 2f out: kpt on same pce* **14/1**
0013 **4** nk **Feolin**[25] 5166 3-9-1 **70**.............................. TravisBlock(3) 10 68
(H Morrison) *led: rdn over 2f out: hdd over 1f out: edgd lft: no ex* **7/1**[3]
4524 **5** hd **Nicada (IRE)**[27] 5122 3-8-9 **66**..........................(p) TolleyDean(5) 13 64
(J S Moore) *hld up towards rr: rdn and hdwy over 2f out: kpt on same pce fnl f* **6/1**[1]
1040 **6** 1/2 **Winged Farasi**[4] 5750 3-8-9 **61**.......................... NelsonDeSouza 7 58
(R A Harris) *s.i.s: sn pushed into midfield: squeezed out and lost pl 6f out: rdn and hdwy over 2f out: one pce fnl f* **8/1**
2043 **7** 1 3/4 **Astroangel**[11] 5563 3-8-9 **61**........................ JimmyQuinn 2 54
(M H Tompkins) *hld up towards rr: rdn and hdwy over 2f out: one pce fnl f* **13/2**[2]
0500 **8** 1 1/2 **Woodins Way**[38] 4760 3-8-5 **57**.......................... JamieMackay 12 46
(P J Makin) *hld up towards rr: rdn and hdwy 2f out: one pce fnl f* **14/1**
2255 **9** 1 1/4 **Princess Zada**[18] 5360 3-9-0 **66**......................... FergusSweeney 8 52
(B R Millman) *mid-div: rdn over 2f out: sn btn* **8/1**
2140 **10** 3/4 **Bidable**[18] 5347 3-8-10 **62**.............................. GregFairley 1 47
(B Palling) *mid-div: hdwy 4f out: rdn over 2f out: wknd over 1f out* **17/2**
0030 **11** 1 **Apollo Five**[14] 5475 3-8-8 **60**............................ TPQueally 16 42
(D J Coakley) *trckd ldrs: rdn over 2f out: wknd ent fnl f* **11/1**
6006 **12** 2 1/2 **Storm Petrel**[11] 5576 3-8-5 **57**.......................(t) RichardThomas 6 34
(R M Beckett) *s.i.s: sn mid-div: rdn 3f out: wknd 2f out* **16/1**

1m 42.16s (1.06) **Going Correction** +0.20s/f (Good) **12** Ran SP% **117.6**
Speed ratings (Par 101): **102,100,98,98,98 97,96,94,93,92 91,89**
CSF £178.85 CT £2421.41 TOTE £29.20: £5.00, £3.00, £3.40; EX 311.40.
Owner Graham Robinson **Bred** G And Mrs Robinson **Trained** Limpley Stoke, Bath

FOCUS
A moderate handicap, with the winner a surprise improver. They tended to race up the middle of the track in the straight.
Astroangel Official explanation: jockey said filly was hampered at the start

5861 PERTEMPS PEOPLE DEVELOPMENT "HANDS AND HEELS" APPRENTICE H'CAP 5f 161y
4:40 (4:40) (Class 6) (0-58,57) 3-Y-0+ **£1,943** (£578; £288; £144) **Stalls** Centre

Form RPR
5040 **1** **Hello Roberto**[11] 5565 6-9-0 **52**..........................(p) AmyBaker 5 59
(R A Harris) *mde all: kpt on gamely: edgd lft towards fin* **6/1**[2]
0000 **2** 3/4 **Royal Guest**[7] 5688 3-8-6 **50**..........................(v) MatthewDavies(5) 10 55
(M R Channon) *hld up bhd: swtchd lft and hdwy over 1f out: r.o ins fnl f: nt rch wnr* **10/1**
0345 **3** 3/4 **Vogarth**[24] 5190 3-9-1 **57**.............................. AlanRutter(3) 14 59
(B R Millman) *towards rr: hdwy over 2f out: styd on fnl f: wnt 3rd nr fin* **9/2**[1]
2660 **4** nk **Cyfrwys (IRE)**[132] 1921 6-8-5 **48**.......................(p) LanceBetts(5) 1 49
(B Palling) *chsd ldrs: chsd wnr 3f out tl ent fnl f: no ex* **9/1**[3]
6010 **5** 2 **Cerulean Rose**[5] 5726 8-8-12 **55**.......................... MarkCoumbe(5) 2 49
(A W Carroll) *mid-div: swtchd lft and hdwy 2f out: one pce fnl f* **6/1**[2]
0000 **6** 1 1/4 **Banana Belle**[41] 4689 3-8-3 **45**..........................(p) FrankiePickard(3) 11 35
(J Ryan) *chsd ldrs: kpt on same pce fnl 2f* **40/1**
000 **7** 2 **Katie Coniston**[46] 4541 3-7-13 **45**...................... MatthewCosham(7) 7 28
(Dr J R J Naylor) *a mid-div* **40/1**
-030 **8** 1/2 **The Crooked Ring**[35] 4879 5-9-3 **55**.....................(b) HaddenFrost 12 36
(A G Newcombe) *chsd ldrs tl wknd over 1f out* **9/2**[1]
0000 **9** nk **Mostanad**[18] 5368 5-8-2 **47**..........................(p) DavidProbert(7) 8 27
(R A Harris) *prom tl wknd over 1f out* **25/1**
0000 **10** 1 3/4 **Enjoy The Buzz**[18] 5349 8-8-2 **45**......................(p) BarrySavage(5) 9 19
(J M Bradley) *nvr bttr than mid-div* **16/1**
5000 **11** 3 **Exponential (IRE)**[36] 4853 5-8-11 **54**.................(v[1]) PietroRomeo(5) 6 18
(J M Bradley) *chsd ldrs: effrt 2f out: sn wknd* **16/1**
0504 **12** 1 1/4 **Yorke's Folly (USA)**[21] 5282 6-8-2 **45**.................(b) DeclanCannon(5) 15 5
(C W Fairhurst) *mainly towards rr* **11/1**
550 **13** 4 **Half A Tsar (IRE)**[17] 5386 3-8-4 **48**...................(b[1]) SoniaEaton(5) 16 —
(Mark Gillard) *a towards rr* **33/1**
060- **14** 3 **Trace Clip**[436] 3728 9-8-2 **45**.......................... LauraReynolds(5) 17 —
(N I M Rossiter) *dwlt bdly: a wl bhd* **25/1**

1m 12.2s (1.00) **Going Correction** +0.05s/f (Good)
WFA 3 from 5yo+ 1lb **14** Ran SP% **119.6**
Speed ratings (Par 101): **95,94,93,92,89 88,85,84,84,82 78,76,71,67**
CSF £60.80 CT £304.10 TOTE £5.40: £1.90, £4.50, £2.10; EX 85.10 Place 6 £887.93, Place 5 £68.11.
Owner Peter A Price **Bred** I B Barker **Trained** Earlswood, Monmouths

FOCUS
A moderate sprint handicap restricted to riders who, at the start of the turf season, had not ridden more than ten winners. They tended to race middle to stands' side and the form is rated through the first two.
Katie Coniston Official explanation: jockey said filly was hampered at start
Trace Clip Official explanation: jockey said gelding missed the break
T/Jkpt: Not won. T/Plt: £825.30 to a £1 stake. Pool: £75,472.75. 66.75 winning tickets. T/Qpdt: £29.30 to a £1 stake. Pool: £4,829.70. 121.80 winning tickets. TM

5705 BRIGHTON (L-H)
Monday, October 1

OFFICIAL GOING: Good to soft (soft in places)
Wind: Fresh, half against Weather: Rain

5862 HORSEMART.CO.UK APPRENTICE H'CAP 7f 214y
2:20 (2:20) (Class 5) (0-70,70) 3-Y-0+ **£2,914** (£867; £433; £216) **Stalls** Low

Form RPR
2321 **1** **Young Bertie**[11] 5563 4-9-4 **66**..........................(v) LukeMorris 9 78
(H Morrison) *disp ld 3f then pressed ldr: drvn to ld over 1f out: styd on wl and drew clr fnl f* **2/1**[1]
241 **2** 2 1/2 **Rowan Lodge (IRE)**[18] 5345 5-8-12 **63**...................... HarryPoulton(3) 8 69
(J R Boyle) *disp ld: led 5f out tl over 1f out: nt qckn* **8/1**
0462 **3** 6 **Kavachi (IRE)**[31] 5001 4-9-0 **67**.......................... JemmaMarshall(5) 1 59
(G L Moore) *dwlt: sn in midfield: rdn to go 3rd 2f out: nt pce of ldng pair* **5/1**[3]
1000 **4** hd **Mythical Charm**[25] 5166 8-8-8 **56**...............................(t) NicolPolli 4 48
(J J Bridger) *dwlt: towards rr: rdn and sme hdwy 3f out: no imp* **14/1**
1213 **5** hd **Wrighty Almighty (IRE)**[9] 5645 5-9-2 **64**..................... JamesMillman 2 55
(P R Chamings) *s.s: sn chsng ldrs: brought wd towards stands' rail over 2f out: one pce* **4/1**[2]
1432 **6** nk **Ten To The Dozen**[6] 5708 4-8-5 **56** oh2..................... WilliamCarson(3) 5 47
(P W Hiatt) *towards rr: brought wd to centre over 2f out: nt pce to chal* **5/1**[3]
0000 **7** 1 **Putra Laju (IRE)**[16] 5424 3-8-8 **59** oh3 ow3...................(p) PatrickHills 3 47
(J W Hills) *bhd: hdwy 4f out: rdn and btn 2f out* **33/1**
0000 **8** 8 **Happy As Larry (USA)**[7] 5693 5-9-5 **70**..................(t) JamesO'Reilly(3) 6 40
(D J Murphy) *prom over 4f* **33/1**
00-0 **9** 2 1/2 **Lit Et Mixe (FR)**[196] 117 4-9-5 **70**........................ SCreighton(3) 7 34
(Noel T Chance) *s.s: hdwy into midfield after 2f: wknd over 3f out* **50/1**

1m 35.43s (0.39) **Going Correction** +0.10s/f (Good)
WFA 3 from 4yo+ 3lb **9** Ran SP% **112.3**
Speed ratings (Par 103): **102,99,93,93,93 92,91,83,81**
CSF £18.11 CT £69.13 TOTE £3.10: £1.10, £2.20, £1.70; EX 19.00.
Owner M T Bevan **Bred** Red House Stud **Trained** East Ilsley, Berks

FOCUS
A moderate handicap, but two in-form horses came clear.
Ten To The Dozen Official explanation: jockey said gelding ran too free

5863 EUROPEAN BREEDERS' FUND MEDIAN AUCTION MAIDEN STKS 5f 213y
2:50 (2:54) (Class 6) 2-Y-0 **£2,266** (£674; £337; £168) **Stalls** Low

Form RPR
5524 **1** **Replicator**[13] 5496 2-9-3 71............................ PatDobbs 4 71+
(Pat Eddery) *dwlt: sn trcking ldrs: brought v wd st: hung bdly lft 2f out: drvn to ld ins fnl f* **3/1**[2]
0305 **2** 1 3/4 **Spic 'n Span**[3] 5780 2-8-12 75........................ PatrickHills(5) 5 66
(C A Cyzer) *reluctant to go to post: disp ld: led 3f out: styd far side st: hrd rdn and hdd ins fnl f: fnd little* **2/1**[1]
3550 **3** 1 1/4 **We'Re Delighted**[10] 5605 2-9-3 72........................ TPO'Shea 7 62+
(M R Channon) *dwlt: settled in 5th: brought v wd st: hrd rdn and wnt mod 3rd 2f out: styd on fnl f* **2/1**[1]
4 2 1/2 **Autumn Charm** 2-8-12 0............................ SaleemGolam 3 50
(W Jarvis) *s.s: bhd: brought to centre st: rdn 3f out: nvr rchd ldrs* **8/1**[3]
5003 **5** 3 1/2 **Fraamington**[12] 5520 2-9-3 38........................ ChrisCatlin 6 44
(M R Channon) *disp ld 3f: brought to centre st: wknd 2f out* **25/1**
5000 **6** 1 **Tobago Bay**[2] 5818 2-9-3 60............................ SamHitchcott 1 41
(M R Channon) *chsd ldrs: pushed along after 2f: brought to centre st: wknd over 2f out* **20/1**

1m 10.83s (0.73) **Going Correction** +0.10s/f (Good) **6** Ran SP% **111.4**
Speed ratings (Par 93): **99,96,95,91,87 85**
CSF £9.28 TOTE £3.90: £2.00, £1.50; EX 9.40.
Owner Pat Eddery Racing (Cadeaux Genereux) **Bred** R And Mrs Heathcote **Trained** Nether Winchendon, Bucks

FOCUS
A poor maiden in which the front two were the only ones to stay far side. The form has been rated negatively, with the fifth too close for comfort.

NOTEBOOK
Replicator has shown improved form since moving into handicaps and this looked a very winnable opportunity with hot favourite Silver Guest being taken out. One of only two to stay far side, he ran about under pressure, but was well on top close home and could improve further returned to handicaps. (tchd 10-3)
Spic 'n Span has shown glimpses of ability and this looked a golden opportunity. However, having given the winner a nice tow through he was unable to fend him off and found disappointingly little. (op 15-8 tchd 7-4)
We'Re Delighted, a promising third over this trip on debut at Newbury, has been disappointing over further since, but he lacked the pace on this drop in trip and got going all too late towards the centre of the track. (op 5-2)
Autumn Charm, a daughter of Reel Buddy, comes from a yard whose juveniles often need a run to set them straight and she shaped promisingly, running on well late on. An extra furlong will suit in time. (op 13-2)
Fraamington is no better than selling level.
Tobago Bay is not progressing and looks another who will benefit from a drop into selling grade. (op 25-1)

5864 JEAN'S 90TH BIRTHDAY CLAIMING STKS 6f 209y
3:20 (3:21) (Class 6) 4-Y-0+ **£1,943** (£578; £288; £144) **Stalls** Low

Form RPR
0532 **1** **Halfwaytoparadise**[41] 4685 4-8-8 44......................(p) SaleemGolam 7 56
(W G M Turner) *disp ld: led over 1f out: drvn out* **10/1**
0210 **2** 1 **Blue Empire (IRE)**[32] 4978 6-8-4 63......................(p) NeilChalmers(3) 3 52
(C R Dore) *disp ld tl over 1f out: hrd rdn: kpt on* **5/2**[1]
0100 **3** 3/4 **Coup D'Etat**[7] 5693 5-9-7 72..................................(b) PaulDoe 1 64
(R A Harris) *towards rr: gd hdwy towards far side 2f out: rdn to dispute ld 1f out: one pce fnl f* **11/4**[2]
0000 **4** shd **Megalala (IRE)**[75] 3644 6-8-13 45........................ FrankieMcDonald 11 56
(J J Bridger) *mid-div: hrd rdn and r.o fnl 2f: nrst fin* **20/1**
0060 **5** 1 **Royal Tavira Girl (IRE)**[12] 5546 4-8-7 49...............(b[1]) JamieJones(5) 4 52
(M G Quinlan) *hld up in tch: chsd ldrs over 2f out: no ex fnl f* **16/1**
0000 **6** 2 1/2 **Convince (USA)**[24] 5190 6-8-9 52..........................(p) LPKeniry 13 42
(J M Bradley) *towards rr: rdn over 2f out: nvr nrr* **10/1**
4055 **7** hd **Franky'N'Jonny**[19] 5338 4-8-4 42..........................(p) ChrisCatlin 10 37
(M J Attwater) *in rr: rdn over 2f out: nvr rchd ldrs* **25/1**
004 **8** shd **Fire At Will**[41] 4685 5-8-6 42............................ LukeMorris(5) 8 43
(A W Carroll) *s.s: bhd: rdn and hdwy towards far side 2f out: no ex 1f out* **10/1**
3200 **9** 2 **Windy Prospect**[31] 5001 5-8-9 53..........................(p) AmirQuinn 2 36
(Mrs L J Mongan) *chsd ldrs tl hrd rdn and wknd 2f out* **8/1**[3]
0500 **10** 3 1/2 **Cayman Breeze**[24] 5190 7-8-4 45........................ KevinGhunowa(5) 5 27
(J M Bradley) *in tch: steadily lost pl fr 1/2-way: n.d fnl 2f* **14/1**
0000 **11** 1/2 **Pertemps Green**[7] 5690 4-9-3 52.......................... TGMcLaughlin 12 33
(Stef Liddiard) *dwlt: hld up in rr: sme hdwy on stands' rail over 2f out: rdn and no imp over 1f out* **33/1**
0000 **12** 5 **North Fleet**[29] 5062 4-8-11 42............................ AdrianMcCarthy 6 14
(J M Bradley) *plld hrd: prom over 4f: bhd and eased 1f out* **50/1**

0/00 **13** *8* **Danehill Folly (IRE)**[53] 4321 4-8-8 25 ow6............ JemmaMarshall(7) 9 —
(J M Bradley) *chsd ldrs tl hrd rdn and wknd qckly over 2f out: sn bhd*
100/1

1m 23.7s (1.00) **Going Correction** +0.10s/f (Good) **13** Ran SP% **120.7**
Speed ratings (Par 101): **98,96,96,95,94 91,91,91,89,85 84,78,69**
CSF £34.01 TOTE £9.20: £2.50, £1.20, £1.60; EX 47.50.
Owner Mascalls Stud **Bred** Mascalls Stud **Trained** Sigwells, Somerset

FOCUS
Once again it paid to race prominently in this claimer. The form is not solid.

5865 WEATHERBYS BLOODSTOCK INSURANCE H'CAP 1m 1f 209y
3:50 (3:52) (Class 6) (0-65,65) 3-Y-O **£2,266** (£674; £337; £168) **Stalls** High

Form RPR
4506 **1** **Spirit Of Adjisa (IRE)**[18] 5347 3-9-2 **63**..........................(b[1]) PatDobbs 9 81
(Pat Eddery) *prom: led over 1f out: rdn clr: easily* **16/1**
1U13 **2** *7* **Chant De Guerre (USA)**[29] 5068 3-9-3 **64**....................... BrettDoyle 12 68
(P Mitchell) *chsd ldrs: hrd rdn over 2f out: kpt on to take mod 2nd fnl 100yds* **7/1**[3]
0211 **3** *1* **Red Current**[4] 5750 3-9-2 **63**.. LPKeniry 3 65
(R A Harris) *plld hrd: chsd ldrs: hrd rdn over 1f out: nt pce of wnr* **11/4**[1]
0003 **4** *nk* **Stark Contrast (USA)**[21] 5280 3-9-4 **65**...................... J-PGuillambert 8 66
(J Akehurst) *plld hrd: sn led: rdn and hdd over 1f out: no ex* **12/1**
0005 **5** *hd* **Aegis (IRE)**[20] 5307 3-8-11 **65**..................................... WilliamCarson(7) 7 66
(B W Hills) *chsd ldrs: rdn and outpcd fnl 2f* **7/2**[2]
2534 **6** *3 ½* **Cow Girl (IRE)**[11] 5563 3-8-10 **62**....................................... NicolPolli(5) 5 56
(Miss Gay Kelleway) *t.k.h in rr: hdwy towards ins 3f out: hung lft and wknd over 1f out* **7/1**[3]
5405 **7** *1 ½* **Irish Dancer**[18] 5347 3-9-1 **62**..(b) ChrisCatlin 6 53
(J L Dunlop) *towards rr: rdn over 2f out: nvr trbld ldrs* **12/1**
0420 **8** *2* **Doubly Guest**[81] 3469 3-9-4 **65**... PaulDoe 13 52
(G G Margarson) *towards rr: rdn over 2f out: n.d* **28/1**
644 **9** *¾* **Withywood (USA)**[6] 5710 3-8-4 **51** oh5...................... AdrianMcCarthy 2 37
(G L Moore) *towards rr: mod effrt over 2f out: no imp* **25/1**
1654 **10** *6* **Mayireneyrbel**[21] 5279 3-8-3 **55**.................................... LukeMorris(5) 15 29
(J Akehurst) *mid-div: effrt and brought wd to stands' rail 3f out: hrd rdn and wknd 2f out* **14/1**
6456 **11** *8* **Beech Games**[17] 5390 3-8-12 **59**.................................. TGMcLaughlin 4 17
(F Jordan) *a bhd: eased whn no ch fnl f* **33/1**
6064 **12** *2 ½* **Joyful Tears (IRE)**[18] 5347 3-9-3 **64**................................... TPO'Shea 14 17
(M G Quinlan) *hld up in midfield: short-lived effrt over 2f out: eased whn no ch fnl f* **16/1**

2m 4.17s (1.57) **Going Correction** +0.10s/f (Good) **12** Ran SP% **117.9**
Speed ratings (Par 99): **97,91,90,90,90 87,86,84,84,79 72,70**
CSF £120.99 CT £408.43 TOTE £25.20: £4.50, £1.60, £1.50; EX 263.70.
Owner Darr, Johnson, Weston & Whitaker **Bred** C J Haughey J Flynn And E Mulhern **Trained** Nether Winchendon, Bucks

FOCUS
An uncompetitive handicap won easily by first-time blinkered Spirit Of Adjisa who turned around Chepstow form with Red Current. It remains to be seen if the form can be taken at face value.
Red Current Official explanation: trainer said filly was unsuited by the good to soft ground

5866 JACK HARE H'CAP 5f 213y
4:20 (4:20) (Class 6) (0-60,60) 3-Y-O+ **£2,590** (£770; £385; £192) **Stalls** Low

Form RPR
6500 **1** **Memphis Man**[40] 4706 4-8-9 **50** ow1............................ TGMcLaughlin 5 62
(P D Evans) *dwlt: bhd: gd hdwy over 1f out: r.o to ld ins fnl f* **12/1**
3502 **2** *1 ¾* **Musical Script (USA)**[19] 5340 4-9-1 **56**........................(b) ChrisCatlin 10 63
(Mouse Hamilton-Fairley) *prom: hrd rdn over 1f out: nt qckn fnl f* **8/1**
040 **3** *¾* **With Confidence**[31] 5013 3-9-2 **58**...................................... PatDobbs 8 63
(D R C Elsworth) *chsd ldrs: rdn over 2f out: kpt on fnl f* **15/2**[3]
4010 **4** *nk* **Ishibee (IRE)**[36] 4853 3-8-10 **52**................................(p) FrankieMcDonald 7 56
(J J Bridger) *in tch: rdn to chal over 1f out: one pce ins fnl f* **14/1**
4060 **5** *½* **Rhapsilian**[46] 4545 3-8-10 **52**.. PaulDoe 2 54
(J A Geake) *dwlt: sn wl bhd: rdn and styd on wl fnl 2f: nrst fin* **14/1**
106 **6** *1* **Trinculo (IRE)**[7] 5687 10-8-12 **58**..............................(b) LukeMorris(5) 12 57
(R A Harris) *led: brought wd w rest st: hung bdly lft to far rail ins fnl 2f: wknd and hdd ins fnl f* **7/1**[2]
3000 **7** *hd* **Peruvian Style (IRE)**[24] 5191 6-8-3 **49**..................... KevinGhunowa(5) 4 48
(J M Bradley) *hld up in midfield: rdn to press ldrs 2f out: no ex fnl f* **12/1**
4410 **8** *1 ¾* **Limonia (GER)**[11] 5576 5-8-4 **52**............................ JosephWalsh(7) 11 46
(Mike Murphy) *s.s: bhd: rdn and hdwy over 2f out: wknd over 1f out* **17/2**
4003 **9** *shd* **Summer Recluse (USA)**[6] 5711 8-9-5 **60**..........................(t) LPKeniry 1 53
(J M Bradley) *towards rr: sn pushed along: nvr rchd ldrs* **3/1**[1]
6000 **10** *½* **Wainwright (IRE)**[21] 5276 7-7-12 **46** oh1...................... SophieDoyle(7) 9 38
(P A Blockley) *in tch: outpcd 3f out: sn btn* **16/1**
0050 **11** *3* **Campeon (IRE)**[18] 5349 5-8-5 **46** oh1...................... AdrianMcCarthy 16 29
(J M Bradley) *prom tl hrd rdn and wknd 2f out* **25/1**
66-0 **12** *1 ¼* **Noble Mount**[48] 4471 6-8-4 **48** oh1 ow2....................(p) NeilChalmers(3) 3 27
(A B Haynes) *sn wl bhd* **50/1**
060 **13** *19* **Charming Ballet (IRE)**[25] 5174 4-9-2 **57**........................(b) TPO'Shea 14 —
(N P Littmoden) *chsd ldrs 3f: bhd whn eased over 1f out* **9/1**

1m 10.66s (0.56) **Going Correction** +0.10s/f (Good)
WFA 3 from 4yo+ 1lb **13** Ran SP% **121.3**
Speed ratings (Par 101): **100,97,96,96,95 94,94,91,91,90 86,85,59**
CSF £106.45 CT £784.26 TOTE £21.50: £5.70, £2.60, £2.90; EX 180.30.
Owner M D Jones **Bred** R T And Mrs Watson **Trained** Pandy, Monmouths

FOCUS
A moderate sprint handicap but a little more interesting than most of its type and the form looks sound.

5867 FRIDAY-AD.CO.UK H'CAP 5f 59y
4:50 (4:50) (Class 6) (0-65,65) 3-Y-O+ **£2,266** (£674; £337; £168) **Stalls** Low

Form RPR
6021 **1** **Sofinella (IRE)**[11] 5564 4-8-2 **54**..................................... LukeMorris(5) 10 66
(A W Carroll) *mde all: hrd rdn and hld on wl fnl 2f* **8/1**[3]
3245 **2** *1 ½* **Make My Dream**[26] 5130 4-9-1 **62**... TPO'Shea 6 69
(J Gallagher) *sn rdn towards rr: hdwy over 1f out: r.o to take 2nd ins fnl f* **4/1**[1]
0631 **3** *1 ½* **Dancing Mystery**[16] 5430 13-9-1 **62**......................................(b) LPKeniry 9 64
(E A Wheeler) *chsd wnr tl no ex fnl f* **4/1**[1]
4100 **4** *hd* **Jucebabe**[5] 5726 4-8-12 **59**..(p) ChrisCatlin 4 60
(J L Spearing) *chsd ldrs: sn pushed along: kpt on same pce fnl 2f* **5/1**[2]
0436 **5** *1* **Jayanjay**[5] 5731 8-9-4 **65**... PatDobbs 3 63
(P Mitchell) *prom: styd alone on far rail st: wknd fnl f* **4/1**[1]
000 **6** *2 ½* **Piccostar**[24] 5191 4-8-5 **55** ow3..................................(b) NeilChalmers(3) 1 44
(A B Haynes) *rdn over 2f out: nvr trbld ldrs* **20/1**
0000 **7** *1 ¾* **Our Archie**[12] 5535 3-7-13 **51** oh6.....................................(p) NicolPolli(5) 7 34
(M J Attwater) *stdd and hmpd s: bhd: hdwy over 2f out: hung lft and wknd over 1f out* **40/1**
0120 **8** *2* **Briery Lane (IRE)**[25] 5160 6-8-8 **60**............................ KevinGhunowa(5) 8 36
(J M Bradley) *hmpd s: a bhd* **4/1**[1]

62.27 secs (-0.03) **Going Correction** +0.10s/f (Good) **8** Ran SP% **115.0**
Speed ratings (Par 101): **104,101,99,98,97 93,90,87**
CSF £40.21 CT £149.06 TOTE £9.20: £1.90, £1.80, £1.70; EX 46.70 Place 6 £44.34, Place 5 £26.31.
Owner Serafino Agodino **Bred** Dr Paschal Carmody **Trained** Cropthorne, Worcs

FOCUS
A modest but competitive sprint that saw Sofinella record back-to-back wins. Sound form.
Our Archie Official explanation: jockey said gelding hung left
Briery Lane(IRE) Official explanation: jockey said gelding suffered interference at start
T/Plt: £18.20 to a £1 stake. Pool: £55,334.00. 2,210.50 winning tickets. T/Qpdt: £8.70 to a £1 stake. Pool: £2,669.70. 226.10 winning tickets. LM

4823 WINDSOR (R-H)
Monday, October 1

OFFICIAL GOING: Good to soft
Wind: Light, against Weather: Miserable

5868 EUROPEAN BREEDERS' FUND MAIDEN STKS (DIV I) 6f
2:30 (2:35) (Class 5) 2-Y-O **£2,817** (£838; £418; £209) **Stalls** High

Form RPR
03 **1** **Unbreak My Heart (IRE)**[13] 5501 2-9-3 0..................... SteveDrowne 4 83+
(R Charlton) *dwlt: rcvrd and sn prom: led 2f out: stmbld bdly sn after: rdn and styd on wl fnl f: a holding on* **5/2**[1]
2 *¾* **Brave Prospector** 2-9-3 0... JimmyFortune 11 81+
(P W Chapple-Hyam) *racd wd early: chsd ldrs: prog to chal 2f out: stmbld sn after: pressed wnr fnl f: a jst hld* **3/1**[2]
52 **3** *3 ½* **Balata**[14] 5470 2-9-3 0... SimonWhitworth 5 70
(B R Millman) *pressed ldr: upsides 2f out: outpcd fr jst over 1f out* **9/1**
4 *hd* **Fly In Johnny (IRE)** 2-9-3 0... DaneO'Neill 12 70
(R Hannon) *dwlt: in tch: prog on outer to press ldrs 2f out: outpcd over 1f out* **16/1**
0 **5** *1 ¼* **Hawa Khana (IRE)**[12] 5540 2-8-12 0......................... StephenDonohoe 6 61
(N P Littmoden) *in tch in rr: outpcd over 2f out: rdn and styd on fr over 1f out* **66/1**
4 **6** *shd* **Cotton Reel**[10] 5587 2-9-3 0.. TQuinn 13 66+
(P F I Cole) *racd alone nr side to 1/2-way: chsng ldrs whn jnd far side gp: drvn and cl up 2f out: wknd over 1f out* **9/2**[3]
7 *shd* **Miss Phoebe (IRE)** 2-8-12 0... RobertHavlin 7 60
(S Kirk) *in tch: outpcd 2f out: pushed along and styd on steadily fnl f* **33/1**
8 *nk* **Pont Des Soupirs (USA)** 2-9-3 0.................................... EddieAhern 3 65
(Saeed Bin Suroor) *mde most to 2f out: wknd jst over 1f out* **15/2**
9 *4* **So Glamorous** 2-8-12 0... IanMongan 9 48
(C F Wall) *dwlt: trckd ldrs tl wknd 2f out* **33/1**
10 *½* **Dickie Valentine** 2-9-3 0.. AdamKirby 1 51
(M R Bosley) *chsd ldrs: reminder over 2f out: wknd over 1f out* **100/1**
11 *4* **My Flame** 2-9-3 0.. MickyFenton 10 39
(J R Jenkins) *wl bhd in last bef 1/2-way* **100/1**
12 *1 ½* **Queens Mantle** 2-8-12 0... NCallan 8 30
(P J Makin) *reluctant to post: sideways whn stalls opened and v.s.a: sn in tch and hld up: wknd rapidly 2f out* **16/1**

1m 16.58s (2.91) **Going Correction** +0.375s/f (Good) **12** Ran SP% **114.6**
Speed ratings (Par 95): **95,94,89,89,87 87,87,86,81,80 75,73**
CSF £9.28 TOTE £3.50: £1.40, £1.70, £2.50; EX 13.20 Trifecta £62.70 Pool £439.23 - 4.97 winning units..
Owner Mountgrange Stud **Bred** Redpender Stud Ltd **Trained** Beckhampton, Wilts

FOCUS
An average first division of the juvenile maiden which saw the first two come nicely clear. The form should work out. The winner deserves extra credit as he slipped badly when meeting the plastic path which was still in place at the 2f pole from a recent show at the track. There was a course inspection as a result after the race and Fibresand was put on the path to ensure the course was safe to race on.

NOTEBOOK
Unbreak My Heart(IRE) came good at the third attempt and deserves real credit for overcoming a bad stumble shortly on passing the 2f pole - where a false path was still in place having been in use for a recent show at the track. He looked happier on this easing surface and left the impression he is capable of a deal better yet, so rates a nice handicap prospect in the making. This also looks to be his ideal trip at present, but he can be expected to stay a little further next season. (op 3-1 tchd 10-3)
Brave Prospector ◆, a 140,000gns purchase, half-brother to high-class sprinter Welsh Dream and the smart Majestic Times among others, was very well backed ahead of this racecourse bow and the support looked inspired as he threw down a strong challenge to the eventual winner from 2f out. He eventually lacked the resolution of that rival at the business end, and also stumbled slightly after the two pole, but he can be expected to come on a deal for this debut experience and this scopey colt should not remain a maiden for too long. (op 7-2 tchd 11-4)
Balata posted another fair effort in defeat and did not have any real trouble with this softer ground. He now has the option of nurseries. (op 14-1)
Fly In Johnny(IRE), a 29,000gns first foal of a 7f juvenile winner, showed ability on this racecourse bow, despite greenness, and left the impression he will get another furlong before long. He should come on a deal for the experience. (op 14-1)
Cotton Reel, fourth on his debut at Newbury ten days previously, proved very free to post and not surprisingly drifted markedly in the betting ring as a result. He was at a disadvantage in racing alone on the stands' side through the early parts and by the time he merged with the main group at halfway he was already cooked. This effort leaves him with something to prove, but he should be capable of better again as he becomes more streetwise and will be eligible for a nursery mark after his next outing. (op 3-1)

5869 MEUC RACING TO SAVE LIVES (S) STKS 1m 67y
3:00 (3:33) (Class 5) 2-Y-O **£2,817** (£838; £418; £209) **Stalls** High

Form RPR
0603 **1** **Blandys Wood**[11] 5572 2-8-0 60............................ ThomasO'Brien(7) 11 60
(M R Channon) *s.i.s: wl in rr: gd prog on outer over 2f out: edgd lft but drvn to ld over 1f out: sn clr* **9/2**[2]
000 **2** *4* **Aneebee (IRE)**[35] 4875 2-8-7 53.. EddieAhern 7 51
(R Hannon) *trckd ldrs: rdn to ld 2f out: hdd over 1f out: outpcd* **16/1**
404 **3** *1 ½* **The Willowy Wigeon**[20] 5302 2-8-7 57......................... StephenCarson 12 48
(P Winkworth) *hld up towards rr: prog on outer 3f out: hanging lft after: upsides over 1f out: sn btn* **9/2**[2]

6633 **4** 1 1/2 **What's For Tea**[52] 4363 2-8-7 55 HayleyTurner 5 45
(Tom Dascombe) *stdd s: hld up in last pair to 1/2-way: swtchd lft and prog over 2f out: nvr rchd ldrs* **7/2**[1]

00 **5** 1/2 **Racey Rachel (IRE)**[24] 5201 2-8-7 0 LiamJones 8 44
(E F Vaughan) *t.k.h: hld up bhd ldrs: hanging lft fr 3f out: no prog whn bmpd 2f out: one pce after* **16/1**

000 **6** 2 **Tapas Lad (IRE)**[98] 2941 2-8-9 54 JerryO'Dwyer(3) 2 44
(V Smith) *towards rr: sme prog over 2f out: outpcd fr over 1f out* **8/1**[3]

4006 **7** 1/2 **Rubytwosox (IRE)**[27] 5117 2-8-7 58 RichardMullen 1 38
(W R Muir) *pressed ldrs: grabbed far side rail and led 3f out: hdd 2f out: wknd over 1f out* **14/1**

6 **8** 3 1/2 **Caltire (GER)**[9] 5646 2-8-12 0 MickyFenton 10 35
(J A Osborne) *wl in rr: drvn in last pair 1/2-way: sme prog on outer 2f out: n.d* **11/1**

0000 **9** 3 1/2 **American Welcome (IRE)**[11] 5571 2-8-12 58 (b1) StephenDonohoe 6 28
(B J Meehan) *chsd ldrs: rdn and no prog whn squeezed out 2f out: no ch after* **9/1**

0601 **10** 4 **Adam Eterno (IRE)**[11] 5572 2-9-4 54 (t) RichardKingscote 13 25
(Tom Dascombe) *w ldr to over 2f out: wknd: eased over 1f out* **12/1**

0 **11** 1/2 **Alannah (IRE)**[111] 2539 2-8-9 0 ow2 RobertHavlin 9 15
(Mrs P N Dutfield) *hld up in midfield: gng wl enough 3f out: btn whn nudged 2f out: wknd* **100/1**

50 **12** 5 **Just Mossie**[59] 4136 2-8-5 0 JackDean(7) 3 7
(W G M Turner) *t.k.h: mde most to 3f out: wknd 2f out* **100/1**

313 **13** 8 **Pearo (IRE)**[117] 2356 2-8-13 58 JimmyFortune 14 —
(J S Moore) *trckd ldrs tl wknd rapidly over 2f out: sn eased* **16/1**

0 **14** 3/4 **Its Sensational**[51] 4405 2-8-4 0 DuranFentiman(3) 4 —
(K R Burke) *drvn in last pair 1/2-way: a bhd* **100/1**

1m 48.67s (3.97) **Going Correction** +0.375s/f (Good) 14 Ran SP% **123.0**
Speed ratings (Par 95): **95,91,89,88,87 85,85,81,78,74 73,68,60,59**
CSF £76.84 TOTE £4.60: £2.00, £6.10, £2.10; EX 114.40 TRIFECTA Not won..The winner was bought in for 6,200gns.
Owner Nick Quesnel **Bred** N Quesnel **Trained** West Ilsley, Berks

FOCUS
A typically poor event for the class. The winner was back to her modest best and rates full value for her winning margin.

NOTEBOOK
Blandys Wood had to come from behind after blowing the start, but the sound early pace played into her hands and she eventually came through to break her duck in ready fashion. This switch to easier ground evidently proved right up her street and she was full value for her winning margin, so could have a little more to offer still now that she ought to be high on confidence. (op 6-1 tchd 13-2)
Aneebee(IRE) showed her first worthwhile form to date on this drop in grade and appreciated the softer ground. She can build on this and looks to need all of this distance now. (tchd 14-1)
The Willowy Wigeon, popular in the betting ring, had her chance on this step up in trip and posted an improved effort. She did not look to really get stay the distance, however, and a drop back in distance in this class now looks in order for her. (op 13-2)
What's For Tea was given too much to do on this step up in distance and was never a serious player. She appeared to get the trip and ought to be capable of better again when able to race more handily. (tchd 10-3 and 4-1)
Adam Eterno(IRE), penalised for beating today's winner in a selling nursery last time, was racing on 22lb worse terms with that rival and was done with passing the 2f pole. He probably needs quicker ground. Official explanation: trainer said gelding was unsuited by the good to soft ground (op 10-1)

5870 EUROPEAN BREEDERS' FUND H'CAP 1m 2f 7y
3:30 (4:00) (Class 4) (0-85,85) 3-Y-0+ **£7,772** (£2,312; £1,155; £577) **Stalls** Low

Form RPR

6233 **1** **Shela House**[42] 4666 3-8-7 76 OscarUrbina 9 90+
(J R Fanshawe) *hld up towards rr: stdy prog over 2f out: rdn to ld jst over 1f out: sn wl in command: pushed out* **7/1**

4155 **2** 3 1/2 **Nightspot**[15] 5454 6-8-8 72 StephenCarson 5 79
(Eve Johnson Houghton) *led at decent pce: jnd 3f out: hdd jst over 1f out: kpt on but no ch w wnr* **6/1**[3]

6656 **3** 1 1/4 **Woodcraft**[24] 5208 3-8-6 75 RichardMullen 6 80
(B W Hills) *trckd ldr: upsides 3f out to over 1f out: fdd fnl f* **4/1**[1]

-060 **4** 1 **Simba Sun (IRE)**[17] 5385 3-8-9 78 AdamKirby 12 81
(R M Beckett) *slowly away: hmpd and swvd sn after s: rchd midfield 1/2-way: effrt over 2f out: kpt on: nt pce to threaten* **14/1**

00-5 **5** 1/2 **Inchloch**[214] 587 5-9-6 84 TQuinn 11 86
(B G Powell) *plld hrd: hld up in last trio: rdn and sme prog over 2f out: plugged on but no threat over 1f out* **20/1**

0030 **6** 1/2 **The Snatcher (IRE)**[10] 5593 4-9-2 80 RyanMoore 3 81
(R Hannon) *hld up in midfield: effrt 3f out: rdn and no imp on ldrs fr 2f out: plugged on* **9/2**[2]

0025 **7** 3 1/2 **Calculating (IRE)**[24] 5198 3-8-2 71 oh2 HayleyTurner 1 65
(M D I Usher) *hld up in last trio: rdn and hanging lft over 2f out: nvr on terms* **25/1**

0-00 **8** 3/4 **Pagan Crest**[10] 5593 4-8-7 71 oh1 JamesDoyle 8 63
(Mrs A J Perrett) *chsd ldrs: rdn over 3f out: hanging lft and no prog 2f out: fdd* **33/1**

0050 **9** 1 1/2 **Eva Soneva So Fast (IRE)**[45] 4572 5-9-2 80 EddieAhern 4 69
(J L Dunlop) *cl up tl wknd fr over 2f out* **8/1**

0/1- **10** 5 **Ryan's Future (IRE)**[487] 2162 7-9-7 85 SteveDrowne 2 64
(J S Moore) *s.s: a in last trio: shkn up and no prog 3f out* **14/1**

-204 **11** 2 **Bedizen**[94] 3060 4-9-1 79 MickyFenton 7 54
(Mrs P Sly) *prom tl wknd 3f out: sn bhd* **22/1**

2520 **12** 1/2 **I Have Dreamed (IRE)**[24] 5205 5-9-4 82 (b) JimmyFortune 10 56
(T G Mills) *hld up in rr: rdn 3f out: no rspnse: wknd over 2f out* **13/2**

2m 10.59s (2.29) **Going Correction** +0.375s/f (Good)
WFA 3 from 4yo+ 5lb 12 Ran SP% **118.6**
Speed ratings (Par 105): **105,102,101,100,100 99,96,96,95,91 89,89**
CSF £46.19 CT £193.81 TOTE £6.30: £1.80, £2.20, £2.20; EX 46.60 Trifecta £87.80 Part won. Pool £123.71 - 0.10 winning units..
Owner J H Richmond-Watson **Bred** Lawn Stud **Trained** Newmarket, Suffolk

FOCUS
A fair handicap, run at a sound pace. The winner looks progressive and the form looks sound, rated through the runner-up and the third.
Simba Sun(IRE) Official explanation: jockey said gelding missed the break and suffered interference on leaving stalls
Inchloch Official explanation: jockey said gelding was carried right leaving stalls

5871 MORELLI NURSERY 1m 67y
4:00 (4:31) (Class 4) (0-85,82) 2-Y-0 **£3,886** (£1,156; £577; £288) **Stalls** High

Form RPR

512 **1** **Safari Sunup (IRE)**[47] 4501 2-9-6 81 StephenCarson 4 91+
(P Winkworth) *trckd ldrs: shkn up and swtchd to far rail 3f out: led over 2f out: drvn and in command over 1f out: styd on wl* **9/4**[1]

0020 **2** 2 **Doctor Robert**[18] 5350 2-9-0 75 SteveDrowne 6 81+
(R Charlton) *t.k.h: hld up in tch: prog over 2f out: chsd wnr over 1f out: sn clr of rest but no imp fnl f* **9/2**[2]

4403 **3** 5 **Golden Penny**[31] 5002 2-9-0 75 RobertHavlin 1 70
(H Morrison) *hld up towards rr: rdn over 2f out: prog over 1f out: kpt on to take 3rd last 100yds* **8/1**

436 **4** 1 **Sainglend**[18] 5361 2-9-7 82 DaneO'Neill 10 74
(H Candy) *settled in rr: pushed along over 2f out: no prog tl rdn and kpt on fr over 1f out: no ch w ldrs* **8/1**

043 **5** 3/4 **Southern Mistral**[19] 5337 2-8-9 70 (p) LiamJones 13 61
(W J Haggas) *led after 2f to 3f out: outpcd fr 2f out: wknd ins fnl f* **14/1**

0120 **6** 1 1/2 **Tamrai Dancer**[57] 4202 2-8-10 71 JamesDoyle 11 58
(R M Beckett) *trckd ldrs: outpcd fr 2f out: n.d after* **20/1**

013 **7** 2 1/2 **Dancer's Legacy**[11] 5571 2-9-2 77 (t) JimmyFortune 12 59
(E A L Dunlop) *cl up: effrt to join ldrs over 3f out to over 2f out: wknd over 1f out* **8/1**

0561 **8** 1/2 **Dancing Marabout (IRE)**[10] 5601 2-9-2 77 LDettori 5 58
(C R Egerton) *sn detached in last: nvr a factor: pushed along and no ch fnl 2f* **7/1**[3]

005 **9** shd **Sabre Light**[28] 5091 2-8-7 68 RichardMullen 9 49
(G L Moore) *dwlt: hld up in last pair: shuffled along and no prog over 2f out: eased over 1f out: pushed along and one pce fnl f: nvr nr ldrs* **33/1**

0604 **10** 3/4 **Valentino Sky (USA)**[49] 4461 2-8-6 67 RichardKingscote 7 46
(N P Littmoden) *led for 2f: pressed ldr: led 3f out to over 2f out: wknd over 1f out* **16/1**

0205 **11** 1/2 **Her Name Is Rio (IRE)**[13] 5516 2-8-11 72 SimonWhitworth 8 50
(J S Moore) *plld hrd early: cl up tl wknd over 2f out* **50/1**

2203 **12** 1 3/4 **Quick Sands (IRE)**[15] 5443 2-8-11 72 RyanMoore 2 46
(R Hannon) *a in rr: shkn up and no prog over 2f out: eased over 1f out* **12/1**

1m 48.27s (3.57) **Going Correction** +0.375s/f (Good) 12 Ran SP% **124.7**
Speed ratings (Par 97): **97,95,90,89,88 86,84,83,83,82 82,80**
CSF £12.22 CT £73.59 TOTE £3.30: £1.20, £2.00, £3.10; EX 17.30 Trifecta £107.40 Pool £305.73 - 2.02 winning units..
Owner P Winkworth **Bred** Lars Pearson **Trained** Chiddingfold, Surrey

FOCUS
A fair nursery which saw the first two finish clear. The wuinner did it readily and this is strong form for the grade.

NOTEBOOK
Safari Sunup(IRE) got back to winning ways under a strong ride and showed a game attitude when asked to get on top inside the final furlong. He evidently loves some cut in the ground, looked suited by the extra furlong, and it will be little surprise to see him out under a penalty before the Handicapper can react to this. (op 5-2 tchd 11-4 and 3-1 in a place)
Doctor Robert ◆ held every chance, yet ultimately looked to pay for running freely when under restraint in the early stages. This was still a much better effort, however, and he finished nicely clear of the remainder in second. It would be a surprise if he were not to be found a winning opportunity before the season's end. (tchd 5-1)
Golden Penny ran close to his recent level on this return to a softer surface, but was never a serious threat from off the pace. He helps to set the level of this form.
Sainglend looks to have begun life in nuseries off a tough mark on this evidence and he was never in the hunt under top weight. It is still fair to expect better from him as a three-year-old, however, when he can be expected to enjoy a longer trip. (op 11-1)
Southern Mistral, making his nursery debut in first-time cheekpieces, failed to get home on this step up in trip on this more demanding surface. A more patient ride in the future will probably see him back in a better light, as will a return to faster ground. (op 12-1)
Sabre Light Official explanation: jockey said colt was denied a clear run
Quick Sands(IRE) Official explanation: jockey said filly was denied a clear run

5872 EUROPEAN BREEDERS' FUND MAIDEN STKS (DIV II) 6f
4:30 (5:03) (Class 5) 2-Y-0 **£2,817** (£838; £418; £209) **Stalls** High

Form RPR

1 **Seasider** 2-9-3 0 RyanMoore 11 84+
(Sir Michael Stoute) *dwlt: hld up last of main gp: gd prog over 2f out: sustained effrt and pushed along to ld last 150yds* **10/3**[2]

43 **2** 1 1/4 **Kalligal**[18] 5357 2-8-12 0 RobertHavlin 2 75
(R Ingram) *led and sn 2 l clr: rdn over 1f out: kpt on but hdd last 150yds* **7/2**[3]

0 **3** 1 1/2 **Vineyard**[52] 4362 2-9-3 0 LiamJones 12 76+
(W J Haggas) *wl in tch: effrt on outer 2f out: kpt on but nvr able to chal: snatched 3rd last stride* **13/2**

5 **4** shd **Compton Ridge**[114] 2473 2-9-3 0 OscarUrbina 8 75
(Mrs A J Perrett) *hld up: effrt whn hmpd over 2f out: prog over 1f out but no imp on ldrs: 3rd ins fnl f: pushed along and lost pl last stride* **17/2**

5 nk **Melt (IRE)** 2-8-12 0 DaneO'Neill 7 69
(R Hannon) *hld up early: prog to chse ldr 1/2-way: no imp u.p over 1f out: one pce* **20/1**

6 5 **Moksi** 2-9-3 0 JimmyFortune 5 62+
(P W Chapple-Hyam) *s.v.s: detached in last: sme prog fnl 2f: no ch but plugged on* **5/2**[1]

7 1/2 **Caprio (IRE)** 2-9-3 0 RichardKingscote 3 58
(R Charlton) *uns rdr and bolted bef s: prom tl wknd 2f out* **14/1**

0 **8** 3 1/2 **Seductive Witch**[91] 3162 2-8-12 0 HayleyTurner 4 42
(M D I Usher) *in tch tl wknd 2f out* **100/1**

0 **9** 1 1/4 **Listed Art**[109] 2590 2-9-3 0 StephenDonohoe 6 44
(B J Meehan) *prom over 3f: sn wknd* **20/1**

10 2 1/2 **Silky Steps (IRE)** 2-8-12 0 NCallan 1 31
(P J Makin) *s.s: rn green but prom after 2f: wknd rapidly 2f out* **16/1**

0 **11** 6 **Emir Bagatelle**[16] 5428 2-9-3 0 SteveDrowne 10 18
(H Morrison) *t.k.h: prom to 1/2-way: wknd rapidly* **40/1**

1m 16.79s (3.12) **Going Correction** +0.375s/f (Good) 55 Ran SP% **123.2**
Speed ratings (Par 95): **94,92,90,90,89 83,82,77,76,72 64**
CSF £15.73 TOTE £3.60: £1.60, £1.40, £2.30; EX 10.60 Trifecta £36.80 Pool £342.85 - 6.60 winning units..
Owner K Abdulla **Bred** Juddmonte Farms Ltd **Trained** Newmarket, Suffolk

FOCUS
This second divison of the juvenile maiden was the slower of the pair, but that was due to an ordinary early pace and the form has been rated positively. The winner looks capable of better.

NOTEBOOK

Seasider ◆, first foal of a mare who won a 1m 2f maiden for this stable in 2003, got his career off to a perfect start with a taking debut success. He did well to overcome a sluggish start and showed a willing attitude when asked for his effort, not having to be fully extended to get on top at the business end. The easy ground looked in his favour and he left the impression he would enjoy another furlong before too long. Entries in the Group 1 Dewhurst and the Racing Post Trophy indicate that his leading trainer thinks a good deal of him and, on this evidence, he looks to have a very bright future. (op 6-4 tchd 4-1)

Kalligal, third in a fair fillies' maiden over 5f last time, had the run of the race out in front and momentarily looked to have made a decisive move when quickening things up nearing 2f out. She was ultimately a sitting duck for the ready winner, but still finished nicely clear of the remainder in second and is clearly a fair filly in the making. She also now becomes eligible for a nursery mark. (op 4-1 tchd 9-2 and 5-2)

Vineyard, down the field on his debut at Newmarket over 7f in August, was the subject of market support and posted a much more encouraging effort in defeat. He did not prove that suited by the drop back in trip, although a stronger early pace would have helped on that front, and it would not be a surprise to see him fare better once qualified for nurseries after his next assignment. (op 8-1)

Compton Ridge, who made an eye-catching debut at this venue in June, did not get the best of passages from off the pace on this return to action and left the impression he really now wants an extra furlong. (op 11-1 tchd 8-1)

Melt(IRE), who cost just 5,500gns and is bred to come into her own over longer distances in due course, posted a pleasing debut effort under a fairly considerate ride. She ought to learn plenty from this and has a future. (op 25-1)

Moksi, half-brother to a 5f three-year-old winner, was all the rage in the betting ring ahead of this racecourse bow. He effectively lost his chance at the start, however, and proved too green to do himself full justice. This effort leaves him with something to prove, but he is obviously entitled to another chance with this experience under his belt. Official explanation: jockey said colt missed the break (op 6-1 tchd 13-2)

Caprio(IRE), whose trainer/rider combination took the first division with Unbreak My Heart, lost his chance by bolting to post and was not totally disgraced in the circumstances. He is bred to enjoy easy ground and is one to keep an eye on with a view to nurseries in due course. (tchd 12-1)

5873 ROYAL WINDSOR FIREWORKS EXTRAVAGANZA SATURDAY 3RD NOVEMBER MAIDEN STKS — 1m 67y

5:00 (5:31) (Class 5) 3-Y-O+ — **£2,817** (£838; £418; £209) **Stalls** High

Form	Pos	Dist	Horse / details	RPR
62	1		**Zero Cool (USA)**[13] 5499 3-9-3 0 ... JimmyFortune 6 (J H M Gosden) *led for 2f: chsd ldr: rdn over 2f out: looked hld tl drvn and r.o to ld last strides* **2/1**[1]	86+
4302	2	nk	**Axiom**[13] 5494 3-9-3 80 ... EddieAhern 13 (E A L Dunlop) *led after 2f and set str pce: rdn and clr w wnr over 2f out: looked in command tl worn down last strides* **9/2**[2]	85+
	3	9	**Imperial Quest** 3-8-12 0 ... OscarUrbina 8 (J R Fanshawe) *chsd ldrs: awkward bnd over 5f out: rdn and kpt on to take 3rd jst over 1f out: no ch w ldng pair* **20/1**	59
3322	4	1 3/4	**Cassiara**[9] 5625 3-8-12 72 ...(b) NCallan 1 (J Pearce) *towards rr: rdn 3f out: prog on outer 2f out and chal for 3rd 1f out: no ex* **5/1**[3]	55
0	5	nk	**Stalking Tiger (IRE)**[125] 2127 3-9-3 0 ... SteveDrowne 9 (R Charlton) *hld up in midfield: nudged along over 2f out: nvr on terms: do bttr* **6/1**	60
2-	6	1/2	**Las Beatas**[507] 1630 4-9-1 0 ... AdamKirby 7 (W R Swinburn) *hld up off the pce: shkn up 3f out: kpt on but nvr a threat* **14/1**	53
0000	7	1 3/4	**My Spring Rose**[12] 5528 3-8-12 50 ... MickyFenton 2 (J R Jenkins) *prom: steadily lost pl fr 3f out: kpt on again fnl f* **100/1**	49
0	8	shd	**Heavenward**[17] 5384 3-9-3 0 ... RyanMoore 5 (Sir Michael Stoute) *hld up in rr: nvr on terms: no ch whn hmpd wl over 1f out* **9/1**	54
6-	9	3	**Spice Gardens (IRE)**[339] 6200 3-8-12 0 ... LDettori 11 (W Jarvis) *t.k.h: chsd ldng pair: no ch over 2f out: wknd jst over 1f out* **10/1**	42
-64	10	3	**Schoenberg (USA)**[55] 4258 3-9-3 0 ...(p) RobertHavlin 14 (C R Egerton) *chsd ldng pair tl wknd over 2f out* **16/1**	40
0	11	shd	**Interactive (IRE)**[173] 1001 4-9-3 0 ... JerryO'Dwyer(3) 12 (Andrew Turnell) *hld up wl in rr: nvr on terms: no ch fnl 3f* **100/1**	40
00-5	12	5	**Is It Time (IRE)**[175] 973 3-8-12 61 ... PaulEddery 10 (Mrs P N Dutfield) *chsd ldrs: rdn and wknd over 3f out* **66/1**	24
	13	11	**Hoober**[186] 6-9-6 0 ... JamesDoyle 3 (A W Carroll) *a bhd: t.o over 2f out* **100/1**	3
	14	12	**De Port Heights (IRE)** 3-9-0 0 ... MarcHalford(3) 4 (M Madgwick) *dwlt: immediately t.o* **100/1**	—

1m 47.63s (2.93) **Going Correction** +0.375s/f (Good)
WFA 3 from 4yo+ 3lb — **14** Ran SP% **124.3**
Speed ratings (Par 103): **100,99,90,88,88 88,86,86,83,80 80,75,64,52**
CSF £10.77 TOTE £3.10: £1.60, £1.90, £6.90; EX 14.40 Trifecta £213.70 Pool £313.07 - 1.04 winning units..
Owner H R H Princess Haya Of Jordan **Bred** Robert N Clay & River Bend Farm **Trained** Newmarket, Suffolk

FOCUS
A fair maiden, run at an uneven pace. The first two came well clear and the form is not solid behind them.
Spice Gardens(IRE) Official explanation: jockey said filly stopped quickly

5874 COME RACING AGAIN HERE NEXT MONDAY H'CAP — 6f

5:30 (6:00) (Class 5) (0-75,75) 3-Y-O+ — **£2,817** (£838; £418; £209) **Stalls** High

Form	Pos	Dist	Horse / details	RPR
1634	1		**Nouveau (GER)**[13] 5495 3-8-13 70 ... RyanMoore 8 (R Hannon) *settled towards rr: stdy prog on outer fr 2f out: rdn to ld last 150yds: styd on wl* **11/2**[3]	81
1000	2	1 1/4	**Makabul**[18] 5356 4-9-3 73 ... HayleyTurner 2 (B R Millman) *sn prom: pressed ldr 1/2-way: led jst over 1f out to last 150yds: one pce* **8/1**	80
101	3	shd	**Tamino (IRE)**[38] 4767 4-9-0 70 ...(t) SteveDrowne 3 (H Morrison) *w ldrs: led 1/2-way to jst over 1f out: nt qckn fnl f* **5/1**[2]	77
0000	4	3/4	**Adantino**[9] 5648 8-9-0 75 ...(b) JamesMillman(5) 11 (B R Millman) *wl in rr: rdn and prog over 2f out: chsd ldng pair over 1f out: nt qckn fnl f* **14/1**	79
-610	5	1/2	**Social Rhythm**[18] 5360 3-9-1 75 ... MarcHalford(3) 14 (H J Collingridge) *stdd s: wl in rr on wd outside: prog 2f out: styd on same pce fnl f* **25/1**	78
5400	6	1 3/4	**Linda Green**[5] 5722 6-8-8 71 ... ThomasO'Brien(7) 10 (M R Channon) *mostly in last pair: sme prog fr 2f out but nvr rchd ldrs* **10/1**	69
0	7	1	**Kelamon**[33] 4950 3-8-11 75 ... GHannon(7) 13 (M D I Usher) *racd on outer: pressed ldrs: nt qckn 2f out: urged along and one pce after: fdd fnl f* **25/1**	70
1060	8	1 1/2	**Tipsy Prince**[23] 5238 3-8-13 70 ... DaneO'Neill 9 (David Pinder) *dwlt: towards rr: no real imp on ldrs fr over 1f out* **33/1**	60
/224	9	nk	**Rydal (USA)**[5] 5726 6-8-13 69 ... EddieAhern 15 (J A Osborne) *sn wl in rr on outer: effrt 2f out: no real imp on ldrs over 1f out* **4/1**[1]	58
-600	10	nk	**My Learned Friend (IRE)**[18] 5360 3-9-2 73 ... RichardMullen 16 (A M Balding) *racd on outer: in tch: rdn and no prog fr 2f out* **20/1**	61
2360	11	2	**Morse (IRE)**[159] 1252 6-8-9 72 ... RyanRaftery(7) 6 (J A Osborne) *cl up tl wknd jst over 2f out* **50/1**	54
3266	12	nk	**Blue Aura (IRE)**[42] 4664 4-9-3 73 ...(b) AdamKirby 1 (R M Beckett) *wl in tch: trckd ldrs against far rail 2f out: wknd jst over 1f out* **9/1**	55
0600	13	3/4	**His Master's Voice (IRE)**[59] 4134 4-9-2 72 ... JamesDoyle 5 (D W P Arbuthnot) *cl up: rdn over 2f out: wknd rapidly over 1f out* **20/1**	51
0-60	14	3	**Cool Panic (IRE)**[135] 1845 5-9-2 72 ...(v[1]) JimmyFortune 7 (M L W Bell) *led to 1/2-way: sn btn* **11/1**	42

1m 15.92s (2.25) **Going Correction** +0.375s/f (Good)
WFA 3 from 4yo+ 1lb — **14** Ran SP% **119.4**
Speed ratings (Par 103): **100,98,98,97,96 94,92,90,90,90 87,87,86,82**
CSF £43.82 CT £237.68 TOTE £6.30: £2.50, £2.90, £2.10; EX 59.80 Trifecta £55.20 Pool £342.33 - 4.40 winning units. Place 6 £31.03, Place 5 £20.47.
Owner Jenny Powell & Sue Jensen **Bred** W Bischoff **Trained** East Everleigh, Wilts

FOCUS
A fair sprint, featuring plenty of course regulars. Those drawn low were at an advantage. A progressive winner, and solid form.
T/Plt: £25.90 to a £1 stake. Pool: £77,571.30. 2,181.30 winning tickets. T/Qpdt: £6.90 to a £1 stake. Pool: £3,391.40. 361.50 winning tickets. JN

5875 - 5878a (Foreign Racing) - See Raceform Interactive

5427 WARWICK (L-H)

Tuesday, October 2

OFFICIAL GOING: Good to firm (good in places; 8.6)
Wind: Light against Weather: Overcast with a light shower prior to the last

5879 WARWICKRACECOURSE.CO.UK H'CAP — 6f

2:10 (2:11) (Class 6) (0-65,65) 3-Y-O+ — **£2,047** (£604; £302) **Stalls** Centre

Form	Pos	Dist	Horse / details	RPR
0020	1		**Calabaza**[6] 5726 5-8-8 58 ...(p) KirstyMilczarek(5) 6 (J Akehurst) *trckd ldrs towards inner: hdwy 2f out: rdn over 1f out: styd on to ld last 100yds* **7/1**[3]	68
2003	2	nk	**Brandywell Boy (IRE)**[10] 5642 4-9-2 61 ... RichardThomas 14 (D J S Ffrench Davis) *sn chsng ldrs: hdwy on outer over 2f out: rdn to ld over 1f out: drvn ent fnl f: hdd and nt qckn last 100yds* **17/2**	70
0006	3	3/4	**Brigadore**[52] 4390 8-8-13 58 ... SebSanders 2 (J G Given) *towards rr: stdy hdwy on inner wl over 1f out: rdn and styd on to chse ldrs ins fnl f: kpt on* **4/1**[1]	65
6646	4	hd	**Chatshow (USA)**[10] 5648 6-8-10 62 ... MarkCoumbe(7) 17 (A W Carroll) *in tch on outer: wd st: gd hdwy on stands' rail over 1f out: sn rdn and kpt on ins fnl f: nrst fin* **16/1**	68+
0000	5	1/2	**Figaro Flyer (IRE)**[26] 5160 4-9-3 62 ... AmirQuinn 3 (P Howling) *trckd ldr: hdwy 2f out: rdn and ev ch over 1f out: drvn and edgd lft jst ins fnl f: one pce* **8/1**	66
1020	6	1/2	**Support Fund (IRE)**[7] 5711 3-9-3 63 ... StephenCarson 11 (Eve Johnson Houghton) *towards rr: hdwy 2f out: styd on ins fnl f: nrst fin* **25/1**	66+
0305	7	1/2	**Swing On A Star (IRE)**[26] 5174 3-8-12 58 ... AdamKirby 8 (W R Swinburn) *chsd ldrs: hdwy 2f out and sn ev ch: rdn over 1f out and kpt on same pce* **16/1**	59
00-4	8	1 1/4	**Obe Royal**[12] 5565 3-9-1 61 ... TGMcLaughlin 16 (P D Evans) *s.i.s and bhd tl sme late hdwy* **20/1**	58
500	9	1 1/2	**Loves Bidding**[10] 5643 3-8-13 59 ...(v) DaneO'Neill 5 (R Ingram) *midfield: effrt and sme hdwy over 2f out: sn rdn and no imp* **66/1**	51
2565	10	nk	**Roman Quintet (IRE)**[17] 5430 7-9-4 63 ... TQuinn 10 (R J Price) *trckd ldr: effrt over 2f out and sn rdn: wkng whn n.m.r ent fnl f* **11/2**[2]	54
3110	11	1 3/4	**Viewforth**[12] 5576 9-8-13 58 ...(b) RyanMoore 7 (M A Buckley) *led: wd st and rdn 2f out: sn drvn and hdd over 1f out: sn wknd* **8/1**	44
0600	12	2	**Supercast (IRE)**[6] 5731 4-9-1 60 ... DarryllHolland 12 (W M Brisbourne) *a in rr* **16/1**	39
4153	13	6	**Krakatau (FR)**[125] 2150 3-8-13 59 ... VinceSlattery 9 (D J Wintle) *chsd ldrs: rdn along bef 1/2-way: sn lost pl and bhd fnl 2f* **33/1**	19
0000	14	1/2	**Fisberry**[69] 3851 5-9-4 63 ... MickyFenton 4 (M S Saunders) *in tch on inner to 1/2-way: sn lost pl and bhd* **12/1**	22

1m 13.03s (-1.25) **Going Correction** -0.175s/f (Firm)
WFA 3 from 4yo+ 1lb — **14** Ran SP% **119.0**
Speed ratings (Par 101): **101,100,99,99,98 98,97,95,93,93 90,88,80,79**
CSF £62.10 CT £281.10 TOTE £7.40: £2.60, £3.30, £2.00; EX 70.50.
Owner Canisbay Bloodstock **Bred** Canisbay Bloodstock Ltd **Trained** Epsom, Surrey

FOCUS
A very modest event that contained some well-handicapped sorts. Straightforward form for the grade.
Swing On A Star(IRE) Official explanation: jockey said filly slipped on bend
Roman Quintet(IRE) Official explanation: jockey said gelding had no more to give
Viewforth Official explanation: jockey said gelding ran too freely
Supercast(IRE) Official explanation: jockey said gelding hung both ways

5880 BRYANT HOMES MAIDEN STKS (C&G) — 7f 26y

2:40 (2:45) (Class 5) 2-Y-O — **£3,071** (£906; £453) **Stalls** Low

Form	Pos	Dist	Horse / details	RPR
52	1		**Lord Peter Flint (IRE)**[10] 5633 2-9-0 0 ... RichardHughes 2 (B J Meehan) *led 6f out: rdn and edgd lft fnl f: r.o* **8/1**[1]	78+
	2	1 1/2	**Detonator (IRE)** 2-9-0 0 ... RoystonFfrench 7 (M Johnston) *s.i.s and n.m.r s: hld up: hdwy and hung lft fr over 1f out: r.o wl* **33/1**	74+
	3	nk	**Dubai Meydan (IRE)** 2-9-0 0 ... JimmyQuinn 3 (Miss Gay Kelleway) *trckd ldrs: racd keenly: shkn up over 1f out: n.m.r ins fnl f: styd on same pce* **13/2**[3]	74+

4 **4** *1 1/4* **Autumn Blades (IRE)**[20] 5337 2-9-0 0 .... TQuinn 12 70
(J W Hills) *led: hdd 6f out: chsd wnr tl rdn over 1f out: edgd lft: styd on same pce* **9/1**

5 *3* **El Duende (USA)** 2-9-0 0 .... LDettori 14 66+
(W Jarvis) *chsd ldrs: rdn over 1f out: sn edgd lft and wknd* **25/1**

0 **6** *3* **Robbmaa (FR)**[8] 5680 2-9-0 0 .... PhilipRobinson 4 55
(M A Jarvis) *chsd ldrs: rdn over 2f out: wknd over 1f out* **25/1**

0 **7** *1/2* **Points Of View**[6] 5734 2-9-0 0 .... SebSanders 1 54
(Sir Mark Prescott) *hld up in tch: rdn and wknd over 1f out* **22/1**

3 **8** *shd* **Sea Admiral**[29] 5091 2-9-0 0 .... SteveDrowne 5 54
(R Charlton) *mid-div: lost pl 5f out: nt clr run 3f out: nvr nr to chal* **6/1[2]**

9 *nk* **Legion D'Honneur (UAE)** 2-9-0 0 .... GregFairley 9 53
(M Johnston) *chsd ldrs to 1/2-way* **25/1**

0 **10** *nk* **Dual Faith (IRE)**[12] 5575 2-9-0 0 .... RyanMoore 6 52
(B J Meehan) *hld up: nvr nrr* **50/1**

11 *shd* **Ski Sunday** 2-9-0 0 .... MatthewHenry 13 52
(M A Jarvis) *s.i.s: hdwy over 4f out: rdn and wkng whn hmpd over 1f out* **100/1**

12 *2* **Tyfos** 2-9-0 0 .... TGMcLaughlin 8 47
(W M Brisbourne) *s.i.s: outpcd* **100/1**

0 **13** *6* **John Potts**[25] 5193 2-9-0 0 .... J-PGuillambert 11 32
(B P J Baugh) *hld up in tch: plld hrd: wknd over 2f out* **200/1**

14 *3* **Doubloon** 2-9-0 0 .... RichardThomas 10 25
(J Gallagher) *s.i.s: in rr whn hung rt over 2f out: sn wknd* **150/1**

1m 25.43s (1.23) **Going Correction** +0.025s/f (Good) **14** Ran SP% **119.5**
Speed ratings (Par 95): **93,91,90,89,86 82,82,81,81,81 81,78,72,68**
CSF £41.93 TOTE £1.60: £1.10, £9.10, £2.60; EX 32.10.
Owner The Comic Strip Heroes **Bred** M Al Qatami And Hugo Merry **Trained** Manton, Wilts

FOCUS
A fair-looking maiden with a host of promising efforts behind. Lord Peter Flint ran to his latest form in success.

NOTEBOOK
Lord Peter Flint(IRE) was given a positive ride and made his experience tell. He looks a fair prospect in the making if normal progression is maintained. (op 10-11)
Detonator(IRE) ◆, who has already been gelded, looked fit enough for his debut and shaped really well for a horse bred to stay middle distances. He looks more than capable of going one better next time. (op 40-1 tchd 50-1)
Dubai Meydan(IRE) ◆, a massive individual who significantly holds a Dewhurst entry, ran a race full of promise for a backward-looking sort and looks more than capable of landing a maiden, although it must be noted that his head carriage under pressure was fairly high despite being fitted with a noseband. (op 6-1 tchd 7-1)
Autumn Blades(IRE) followed up his debut run with another solid effort. He will be winning races in due course, as he possibly still needed the run. Official explanation: jockey said gelding hung left (op 12-1)
El Duende(USA) ◆ was one of the biggest individuals in the race and should be all the better for the experience, as he tired inside the final furlong. (op 33-1)
Sea Admiral ran really poorly for no obvious reason. The interference he met did not end his chance, but he might be more the sort for handicaps as a three-year-old. (op 9-2 tchd 13-2)
Legion D'Honneur(UAE), who played up in the paddock, did not show a lot of promise but will need to come on mentally for the run. (op 33-1)
Ski Sunday ran better than his final position suggests and may be suited by a drop in trip next time. (op 80-1)
Doubloon Official explanation: jockey said gelding hung right throughout

5881 WEATHERBYS BANK MAIDEN FILLIES' STKS (DIV I) 7f 26y
3:10 (3:12) (Class 5) 2-Y-O **£2,388** (£705; £352) **Stalls** Low

Form RPR

60 **1** **Swanky Lady**[43] 4662 2-9-0 0 .... RichardHughes 4 78
(R Hannon) *trckd ldng pair: hdwy over 1f out and sn rdn: styd on u.p ins fnl f to ld last 50yds* **7/2[2]**

64 **2** *1/2* **Hieroglyph**[14] 5498 2-9-0 0 .... GregFairley 1 77
(M Johnston) *led: rdn and qcknd 2f out: drvn ins fnl f: hdd and no ex last 50yds* **9/2[3]**

0 **3** *3* **Broken Moon**[39] 4774 2-9-0 0 .... JamieSpencer 10 69+
(J R Fanshawe) *trckd ldrs: effrt 2f out: sn rdn and kpt on same pce ent fnl f* **9/2[3]**

0 **4** *hd* **Counterclaim**[17] 5428 2-9-0 0 .... LDettori 12 69
(Saeed Bin Suroor) *trckd ldr: effrt 2f out: sn rdn and one pce appr fnl f* **11/4[1]**

0 **5** *4* **Striving (IRE)**[39] 4774 2-9-0 0 .... RyanMoore 2 59+
(Sir Michael Stoute) *chsd ldrs: pushed along 3f out and kpt on same pce fnl 2f* **6/1**

6 **6** *1 1/4* **Saratee**[13] 5524 2-9-0 0 .... PhilipRobinson 3 56
(C E Brittain) *midfield: pushed along and outpcd 3f out: styd on appr fnl f: nrst fin* **25/1**

7 *1 1/4* **La Coveta (IRE)** 2-9-0 0 .... SteveDrowne 7 53+
(B J Meehan) *s.i.s and bhd tl sme late hdwy* **33/1**

8 *nk* **Berry Baby (IRE)** 2-9-0 0 .... EddieAhern 14 52
(G A Butler) *in tch: rdn along 3f out and sn btn* **50/1**

00 **9** *nk* **Ogre (USA)**[17] 5428 2-9-0 0 .... MartinDwyer 11 51+
(J A Osborne) *s.i.s and bhd: effrt and nt clr run over 1f out: swtchd outside and styd on fnl f: nvr nr ldrs* **50/1**

10 *2* **Silver Diamond** 2-9-0 0 .... DarryllHolland 13 46+
(W Jarvis) *a in rr* **66/1**

0 **11** *1* **Bobal Girl**[21] 5294 2-8-7 0 .... MCGeran(7) 8 44
(E F Vaughan) *a towards rr* **100/1**

0 **12** *2 1/2* **Lady Docker (IRE)**[21] 5313 2-9-0 0 .... MickyFenton 9 37
(H J L Dunlop) *chsd ldrs: rdn along 3f out and sn wknd* **80/1**

13 *8* **Ginger Fountain** 2-9-0 0 .... DaneO'Neill 6 17
(H Candy) *in tch: pushed along 1/2-way: wknd over 2f out* **28/1**

1m 24.28s (0.08) **Going Correction** +0.025s/f (Good) **13** Ran SP% **117.4**
Speed ratings (Par 92): **100,99,96,95,91 89,88,88,87,85 84,81,72**
CSF £18.18 TOTE £4.00: £1.10, £1.90, £2.20; EX 17.80.
Owner William Durkan **Bred** W And R Barnett Ltd **Trained** East Everleigh, Wilts

FOCUS
Only a modest fillies' maiden, which was slightly quicker than the second division. Improvement from the first two, who finished clear.

NOTEBOOK
Swanky Lady got that all-important victory against her name with a battling display. Her previous form was good enough for her to take this race and one would suspect connections will search for some black type for her now. (op 9-2)
Hieroglyph looked to have stolen the race turning into the home straight but was reeled in during the final furlong. She has the option of handicaps now if connections feel she is given a handy mark, but she is fully capable of landing an ordinary maiden. (op 11-2 tchd 6-1)
Broken Moon ◆ looked really green again in the final stages and will have gained a lot of experience for this effort. She should be ready to do the business next time. (op 7-1)
Counterclaim moved well towards the head of affairs but could not pick up when asked to quicken. (op 9-4)
Striving(IRE) is clearly not one of the stable's better fillies and looks a long-term project. (op 4-1)
Saratee kept on from the rear of the field and was noted staying on well in the final furlong. (op 33-1)
La Coveta(IRE) ◆ was given plenty of time to find her feet and caught the eye staying on from the back of the pack.
Ogre(USA) ◆ reared when the stalls opened and was restrained shortly afterwards. After trailing the field for much of the race, she was taken towards the inside rail up the home straight - where she got hampered - before being moved back out again to the middle of the track. It would be a surprise if she is not capable of much better. Official explanation: jockey said, regarding running and riding, his orders were to get some cover early stages, as the trainer was worried that the filly may run too freely, adding that it reared as the stalls opened, losing several lengths, and was then outpaced back straight before running on through beaten horses.

5882 WEATHERBYS BANK MAIDEN FILLIES' STKS (DIV II) 7f 26y
3:40 (3:41) (Class 5) 2-Y-O **£2,388** (£705; £352) **Stalls** Low

Form RPR

24 **1** **Love Of Dubai (USA)**[23] 5252 2-9-0 0 .... PhilipRobinson 11 76
(C E Brittain) *chsd ldr tl led over 1f out: rdn out* **9/2[2]**

0440 **2** *1 1/2* **Miss Emma May (IRE)**[19] 5353 2-9-0 80 .... (v[1]) TQuinn 4 72
(D R C Elsworth) *a.p: rdn to chse wnr and hung lft over 1f out: styd on* **11/4[1]**

0 **3** *3* **Bikini**[98] 2968 2-9-0 0 .... DaneO'Neill 3 65
(H Candy) *chsd ldrs: rdn and edgd lft over 1f out: styd on same pce* **20/1**

4 *1 1/2* **Top Draw (USA)** 2-9-0 0 .... EddieAhern 9 61
(M L W Bell) *hld up: hdwy 3f out: rdn over 1f out: styd on same pce* **12/1**

5 *nk* **Ella Junior (USA)** 2-9-0 0 .... RichardHughes 12 60
(B J Meehan) *s.i.s: hdwy 5f out: rdn over 2f out: styd on same pce appr fnl f* **7/1[3]**

6 *shd* **Astrodonna** 2-9-0 0 .... JimmyQuinn 5 60+
(M H Tompkins) *hld up: hdwy over 1f out: nt trble ldrs* **100/1**

6 **7** *2 1/2* **Bianca Capello**[13] 5541 2-9-0 0 .... JamieSpencer 2 54
(J R Fanshawe) *hld up: rdn over 2f out: n.d* **9/2[2]**

56 **8** *hd* **Keep Your Head (USA)**[6] 5727 2-9-0 0 .... MartinDwyer 7 53
(J A Osborne) *led: rdn: edgd lft and hdd over 1f out: sn wknd* **33/1**

0600 **9** *nk* **Compton Abbess**[13] 5534 2-8-11 62 ow2 .... JamesMillman(5) 1 55
(B R Millman) *hld up in tch: rdn over 2f out: wknd over 1f out* **100/1**

10 *shd* **Colorado Springs** 2-9-0 0 .... DarryllHolland 10 52+
(W Jarvis) *s.s: a in rr* **66/1**

0 **11** *1* **Krisnando**[14] 5498 2-9-0 0 .... PaulHanagan 6 50+
(W J Knight) *s.i.s: a in rr* **17/2**

0303 **12** *3* **Stand In Flames**[13] 5526 2-9-0 60 .... DavidKinsella 8 42
(Pat Eddery) *hld up: rdn over 2f out: a in rr* **14/1**

13 *1 3/4* **Always Attractive (IRE)** 2-9-0 0 .... GregFairley 14 38
(M Johnston) *mid-div: sn pushed along: bhd fnl 3f* **14/1**

1m 24.53s (0.33) **Going Correction** +0.025s/f (Good) **77** Ran SP% **118.3**
Speed ratings (Par 92): **99,97,93,92,91 91,88,88,88,88 87,83,81**
CSF £16.51 TOTE £5.70: £2.10, £1.50, £5.90; EX 15.30.
Owner Mohammed Al Shafar **Bred** M G G Holdings **Trained** Newmarket, Suffolk

FOCUS
This was the slightly slower of the two divisions, but it had plenty of eyecatchers. An improved effort from the winner but the favourite was slightly disappointing.

NOTEBOOK
Love Of Dubai(USA) put her experience to good use and won the race after bursting clear about a furlong from home. She was also helped by a runner-up that looked very ungenuine under pressure. Another furlong will be within her range. (op 4-1 tchd 5-1)
Miss Emma May(IRE), who was wearing a visor for the first time, is not a horse to have on your side in a battle. (op 7-2)
Bikini ◆ ran much better than she did on her debut but still looked green as she hung away from the inside rail in the final furlong. There is definitely more to come from her.
Top Draw(USA) ◆ was given a really kind introduction to racing - she did not appear to be hit with the whip at any stage - and looked like a filly more than capable of landing a maiden event. (op 11-1)
Ella Junior(USA) ran a race full of promise and will be all the better for the experience. (op 8-1)
Astrodonna took a little while to pick up but kept on strongly inside the final furlong. She will stay further and ought to win races once she has found her level. (op 66-1)
Bianca Capello was not completely disgraced and looks the sort to make her mark in handicaps when eligible. (tchd 5-1)
Colorado Springs ◆ caught the eye in a big way in the final furlong, finishing nicely from an unpromising position. She is much better than her effort suggests. (op 50-1 tchd 80-1)
Krisnando Official explanation: jockey said filly missed the break

5883 BRYANT HOMES NURSERY 7f 26y
4:10 (4:13) (Class 5) (0-75,75) 2-Y-O **£3,071** (£906; £453) **Stalls** Low

Form RPR

0540 **1** **Tobogganist**[53] 4364 2-9-2 **70** .... DarryllHolland 5 72
(W Jarvis) *hld up: hdwy 3f out: swtchd lft and rdn to chse ldrs ent fnl f: styd on wl to ld nr fin* **8/1[3]**

0552 **2** *nk* **Shadow Cabinet (IRE)**[21] 5314 2-9-3 **71** .... JamieSpencer 7 72
(M L W Bell) *trckd ldr: effrt 2f out: sn rdn and ev ch: drvn to ld briefly wl ins fnl f: sn hdd and no ex* **7/4[1]**

500 **3** *shd* **Landikhaya (IRE)**[20] 5337 2-9-3 **71** .... RyanMoore 3 72
(R Hannon) *hld up: hdwy 3f out: rdn to chse ldrs over 1f out: drvn and ev ch ins fnl f: no ex nr fin* **8/1[3]**

2352 **4** *1 1/4* **Lady Rochbonne**[11] 5601 2-9-1 **74** .... AshleyHamblett(5) 2 72
(Mrs G S Rees) *led: rdn along 2f out: drvn 1f out: hdd & wknd wl ins fnl f* **8/1[3]**

306 **5** *hd* **Society Venue**[27] 5143 2-9-4 **72** .... PaulHanagan 14 69
(Jedd O'Keeffe) *chsd ldrs on outer: rdn along and outpcd 3f out: hdwy u.p over 1f out: swtchd lft ins fnl f and styd on wl* **20/1**

1 **6** *1/2* **Mistress Eva**[41] 4709 2-9-7 **75** .... StephenCarson 6 71
(P Winkworth) *chsd ldrs: rdn over 2f out: drvn and one pce ent fnl f* **7/1[2]**

002 **7** *nk* **Mahadee (IRE)**[14] 5502 2-9-4 **72** .... SebSanders 9 67
(C E Brittain) *sn outpcd and bhd: rdn and hdwy on inner wl over 1f out: drvn and styd on wl fnl furlng: nrst fin* **25/1**

065 **8** *1* **Athboy Auction**[19] 5357 2-9-2 **70** .... JimmyQuinn 1 63
(H J Collingridge) *prom: rdn along 2f out: drvn appr fnl f and wknd* **7/1[2]**

000 **9** *3 1/2* **Free Fallin**[11] 5596 2-8-11 **72** .... MCGeran(7) 8 56
(P W Chapple-Hyam) *chsd ldrs: rdn along over 2f out: drvn and wknd appr fnl f* **25/1**

005 **10** *1* **Jelly Mo**[45] 4593 2-9-2 **70** .... EddieAhern 11 51
(J W Hills) *a towards rr* **16/1**

006 **11** 3/4 **Morestead (IRE)**21 5306 2-9-2 **70** TQuinn 4 50
(B G Powell) *a in rr* **25/1**
1m 25.14s (0.94) **Going Correction** +0.025s/f (Good) **11** Ran SP% **116.9**
Speed ratings (Par 95): **95,94,94,93,92 92,91,90,86,85 84**
CSF £21.06 CT £115.56 TOTE £10.60: £2.70, £1.40, £2.20; EX 31.10.
Owner The Dark Blue Partnership **Bred** Mrs Sally Roberts **Trained** Newmarket, Suffolk

FOCUS
A fair nursery for the grade likely to produce its share of winners. The principals were close to form.

NOTEBOOK
Tobogganist, a disappointment on his nursery debut, had been dropped 3lb and the way he was supported in the market beforehand suggested a much better run was expected. Ridden under restraint, he started to come with a run inside the final quarter mile and really picked up well in between runners to run down Shadow Cabinet in the final strides. This winning effort pointed towards a step up to 1m suiting and there should be more to come from the son of Tobougg. (op 12-1)
Shadow Cabinet(IRE), narrowly denied off a 4lb lower mark on his recent handicap debut, always held a good position and looked the winner when edging ahead inside the final furlong, but Tobogganist proved too strong in the finish and he was again made to settle for second. He has shown enough to suggest one of these should come his way before long. (op 13-8 tchd 2-1)
Landikhaya(IRE), who qualified for this with three down-the-field runs in maidens, looked to be reasonably weighted off a mark of 71 and it was no surprise to see him take a significant step forward. There should be more to come and he is another who looks capable of winning a nursery. (op 11-1)
Lady Rochbonne, although bred for stamina on the dam's side, is by a speedy sire and not for the first time she failed to get home having showed plenty of early speed. She has yet to run over 6f and looks well worth a go. (tchd 17-2)
Society Venue improved on anything he had done in maidens and can be rated a little better than the bare form, having to use up plenty of early pace to get a good position from his wide draw. He should appreciate 1m and looks one to keep on side. (op 25-1 tchd 16-1)
Mistress Eva, who caused something of a surprise when making a winning debut at Folkestone, looked vulnerable on this handicap debut off a mark of 75 and she came up short. It was only her second start however and she deserves a chance to show she can improve. Official explanation: jockey said filly hung on the bend (op 9-1 tchd 13-2)
Mahadee(IRE) showed greatly improved form when second in a maiden at Thirsk last time and he stayed on well late on to claim a never-nearer seventh. There should be more to come from him over 1m. (op 16-1 tchd 14-1)

5884 WEATHERBYS FINANCE H'CAP — 2m 39y
4:40 (4:41) (Class 4) (0-85,83) 3-Y-O+ **£5,181** (£1,541; £770; £384) **Stalls** Low

Form RPR
4-33 **1** **Aphorism**31 5034 4-8-12 **67** JamieSpencer 10 81+
(J R Fanshawe) *s.i.s: hld up: hdwy over 2f out: led over 1f out: rdn out* **11/8**1
-124 **2** 3/4 **Hawridge King**17 5404 5-9-1 **75** JamesMillman(5) 1 88
(W S Kittow) *hld up in tch: led over 2f out: rdn and hdd over 1f out: styd on* **7/1**3
1151 **3** 3 1/2 **Atlantic Coast (IRE)**12 5573 3-8-9 **75** (v) RoystonFfrench 3 87+
(M Johnston) *chsd ldrs: rdn over 6f out: outpcd over 2f out: sn hung lft: styd on u.p fnl f* **7/2**2
2450 **4** 4 **Kayf Aramis**62 4056 5-9-3 **72** SteveDrowne 2 76
(J L Spearing) *prom: chsd ldr 4f out: rdn and edgd rt over 2f out: wknd over 1f out* **16/1**
6216 **5** 1/2 **Takafu (USA)**49 4483 5-10-0 **83** SebSanders 4 86
(W S Kittow) *prom: rdn over 5f out: sn lost pl: rallied over 2f out: wknd over 1f out* **12/1**
5133 **6** nk **Abstract Folly (IRE)**23 5256 5-8-12 **67** DarryllHolland 6 70
(J D Bethell) *s.i.s: hld up: swtchd rt and hdwy 2f out: sn rdn: edgd lft and wknd* **12/1**
6006 **7** 8 **Nordwind (IRE)**17 5415 6-9-13 **82** AdamKirby 5 75
(W R Swinburn) *hld up: hdwy over 5f out: rdn whn rdr dropped rein over 1f out: sn hung lft and wknd* **11/1**
6325 **8** 9 **Mister Completely (IRE)**17 5404 6-8-2 **64** oh1 (v) SophieDoyle(7) 9 47
(Ms J S Doyle) *chsd ldr 12f: wknd over 2f out* **25/1**
0-00 **9** 21 **Astrobella**53 4365 4-8-9 **64** JimmyQuinn 8 21
(M H Tompkins) *mid-div: rdn and lost pl 1/2-way: bhd fnl 3f* **100/1**
00-0 **10** 1 1/2 **Moonshine Beach**4 5779 9-8-8 **70** WilliamCarson(7) 7 26
(P W Hiatt) *led: rdn and hung rt fr over 4f out: hdd & wknd over 2f out: eased fnl f* **100/1**
3m 31.77s (-0.93) **Going Correction** +0.025s/f (Good)
WFA 3 from 4yo+ 11lb **10** Ran SP% **112.3**
Speed ratings (Par 105): **103,102,100,98,98 98,94,89,79,78**
CSF £10.86 CT £27.34 TOTE £2.20: £1.10, £1.90, £1.30; EX 10.80.
Owner Dr Catherine Wills **Bred** St Clare Hall Stud **Trained** Newmarket, Suffolk

FOCUS
A modest staying handicap. Fair form for the grade, with Aphorism capable of better still.

5885 TURFTV H'CAP — 1m 22y
5:10 (5:12) (Class 5) (0-75,75) 3-Y-O+ **£3,071** (£906; £453) **Stalls** Low

Form RPR
0301 **1** **Russki (IRE)**27 5128 3-8-11 **73** (b) KirstyMilczarek(5) 13 84
(D M Simcock) *racd wd to 1/2-way: a cl up: rdn to ld over 1f out: styd on strly ins fnl f* **18/1**
0050 **2** 1 1/4 **Eager Igor (USA)**13 5539 3-9-4 **75** StephenCarson 15 83
(Eve Johnson Houghton) *racd wd to 1/2-way: cl up: rdn wl over 1f out and ev ch tl drvn and nt qckn wl ins fnl f* **18/1**
1222 **3** nk **Optimus (USA)**18 5383 5-9-7 **75** TQuinn 1 82
(B G Powell) *trckd ldrs: hdwy over 2f out: rdn over 1f out: kpt on ins fnl f* **9/2**1
0563 **4** 1 **Aggravation**12 5559 5-8-13 **70** MarcHalford(3) 17 75
(D R C Elsworth) *racd wd to 1/2-way: in tch: hdwy on outer 2f out: rdn over 1f out: styd on ins fnl f: nrst fin* **12/1**
2030 **5** hd **Sister Act**89 3247 3-9-2 **73** OscarUrbina 2 78
(J R Fanshawe) *in tch on inner: hdwy over 2f out: rdn along over 1f out: kpt on same pce ins fnl f* **11/2**2
1134 **6** 1/2 **Super Frank (IRE)**28 5115 4-9-3 **71** RichardHughes 14 74
(J Akehurst) *racd wd to 1/2-way: led: rdn along wl over 1f out: sn hdd: drvn and wknd ins fnl f* **15/2**
0005 **7** 3/4 **Hula Ballew**12 5559 7-9-3 **71** PhillipMakin 8 73
(M Dods) *in tch: wd st: effrt on outer 2f out: sn rdn and kpt on same pce fnl f* **14/1**
3000 **8** 3/4 **Glenmuir (IRE)**8 5693 4-9-0 **68** DarryllHolland 3 68
(B R Millman) *prom: rdn along on inner over 2f out: drvn over 1f out and grad wknd* **25/1**
6014 **9** 1/2 **Tyzack (IRE)**8 5693 6-9-6 **74** MickyFenton 5 73
(Stef Liddiard) *hld up: a towards* **10/1**
2412 **10** 1 1/4 **Libre**12 5569 7-8-11 **65** JimmyQuinn 16 61
(F Jordan) *racd wd to 1/2-way: in tch: rdn along over 2f out and grad wknd* **20/1**
6303 **11** hd **Waterline Twenty (IRE)**18 5383 4-9-4 **72** TGMcLaughlin 7 67
(P D Evans) *chsd ldrs: rdn along over 2f out and sn btn* **16/1**
0604 **12** hd **Zonta Zitkala**15 5475 3-9-0 **71** SebSanders 9 66
(R M Beckett) *a towards rr* **7/1**3
0031 **13** 5 **Malinsa Blue (IRE)**12 5559 5-8-12 **66** (p) J-PGuillambert 10 50
(B Ellison) *chsd ldrs: rdn along 2f out and sn wknd* **14/1**
6143 **14** 5 **Bid For Gold**46 4581 3-9-3 **74** PaulHanagan 12 46
(Jedd O'Keeffe) *in tch: rdn along over 2f out and sn wknd* **16/1**
1m 39.58s (-0.02) **Going Correction** +0.025s/f (Good)
WFA 3 from 4yo+ 3lb **14** Ran SP% **118.8**
Speed ratings (Par 103): **101,99,99,98,98 97,97,96,95,94 94,94,89,84**
CSF £306.19 CT £1759.27 TOTE £21.30: £5.80, £7.30, £1.70; EX 395.10.
Owner DXB Bloodstock Ltd **Bred** Mark Commins **Trained** Newmarket, Suffolk

FOCUS
A modest handicap in which four of the first six home raced in the group that separated early on, racing wide before merging with the others on the home turn. Ordinary form which has been rated at face value.

5886 DUKE OF BRISSAC CHALLENGE H'CAP (FOR GENTLEMAN AMATEUR RIDERS) — 1m 2f 188y
5:40 (5:41) (Class 6) (0-60,58) 3-Y-O+ **£1,977** (£608; £304) **Stalls** Low

Form RPR
0563 **1** **Terminate (GER)**14 5497 5-11-3 **54** MrDHutchison(3) 1 59
(Ian Williams) *hld up in tch: racd keenly: hmpd over 1f out: rdn to ld and hung rt ins fnl f: jst hld on* **9/2**2
6000 **2** hd **Chapter (IRE)**17 5427 5-10-4 **45** (p) MrOJMurphy(7) 12 49
(Mrs A L M King) *hld up: hdwy and nt clr run over 1f out: sn rdn: r.o* **25/1**
5003 **3** 3/4 **Summer Bounty**19 5345 11-10-12 **46** MrJJDoyle 5 49
(F Jordan) *s.i.s: hld up: hdwy over 3f out: led over 1f out: hdd and unable qck ins fnl f* **11/1**
5-04 **4** shd **Play Master (IRE)**4 5779 6-11-7 **58** MrTWeston(3) 17 61
(C Roberts) *hmpd s: hld up: hdwy and nt clr run over 1f out: rdn and hung rt ins fnl f: hung lft towards fin: r.o* **12/1**
0314 **5** 3/4 **Desert Hawk**8 5676 6-11-8 **56** MrSWalker 3 57
(W M Brisbourne) *hld up: hdwy over 2f out: nt clr run over 1f out: carried rt ins fnl f: r.o* **11/4**1
0400 **6** nk **General Flumpa**7 5704 6-11-3 **56** MrBenBrisbourne(5) 4 57
(Miss Tor Sturgis) *s.i.s: hld up: hdwy and nt clr run over 1f out: r.o* **13/2**3
050 **7** 1/2 **West End Lad**33 4977 4-11-8 **56** MrJ-PBoisgontier 7 56
(S R Bowring) *chsd ldr to 1/2-way: rdn and hung lft over 1f out: no ex ins fnl f* **80/1**
0 **8** hd **Bythehokey (IRE)**17 5427 6-10-6 **45** MrCPHuxley(5) 15 45
(W M Brisbourne) *prom: chsd ldr 1/2-way: led 2f out: rdn: edgd lft and hdd over 1f out: styd on same pce* **25/1**
6000 **9** 1/2 **L'Oiseau De Feu (USA)**24 3405 3-11-4 **58** MrFGuy 11 57
(Mrs K Waldron) *prom: rdn and hung lft 2f out: hung rt over 1f out: swvd lft and no ex wl ins fnl f* **66/1**
0024 **10** nk **Dream Master (IRE)**13 5530 4-10-5 **46** MrDavidMcMinn(7) 14 44
(J Ryan) *chsd ldrs: rdn over 2f out: no ex fnl f* **20/1**
0255 **11** 1 1/2 **Joy In The Guild (IRE)**17 5427 4-10-9 **48** MrDCottin(5) 13 44
(W S Kittow) *chsd ldrs: rdn and lost pl over 3f out: n.d after* **10/1**
00-0 **12** 1/2 **Picot De Say**4 5779 5-11-1 **54** MrBMcHugh(5) 9 49
(C Roberts) *hld up: a in rr* **66/1**
4600 **13** 1 1/4 **King's Account (USA)**13 5525 5-10-13 **47** (b1) MrFPradeau 6 39
(S Gollings) *led: rdn and hdd 2f out: wkng whn n.m.r over 1f out* **20/1**
-060 **14** 16 **Miss Glory Be**25 5187 9-10-6 **45** (p) MrDBurton(5) 10 9
(C J Down) *hld up: hdwy 6f out: wknd over 3f out* **50/1**
600- **15** 2 1/2 **Ocean Valentine**500 1851 4-11-4 **55** MrSPearce(3) 2 14
(J T Stimpson) *hld up in tch: plld hrd: rdn and wknd over 3f out* **28/1**
4500 **16** 4 **Doctor Ned**66 3949 3-10-0 **45** (t) MrAMerriam(5) 8 —
(Miss Sheena West) *s.i.s: a in rr: wknd over 3f out* **33/1**
2002 **R** **Prince Des Neiges (FR)**49 4473 4-11-7 **58** MrMPBrasme(3) 16 —
(A M Hales) *hung rt s: ref to r* **10/1**
2m 25.1s (5.70) **Going Correction** +0.025s/f (Good)
WFA 3 from 4yo+ 6lb **17** Ran SP% **122.2**
Speed ratings (Par 101): **80,79,79,79,78 78,78,77,77,77 76,75,75,63,61 58,—**
CSF £119.03 CT £1190.74 TOTE £6.20: £1.80, £6.40, £2.70, £4.00; EX 172.50 Place 6 £10.13, Place 5 £4.90..
Owner Dr Marwan Koukash **Bred** Gestut Hofgut Mappen **Trained** Portway, Worcs

FOCUS
A poor handicap confined to amateurs. A bunch finish and very modest form.
T/Jkpt: £65,667.50 to a £1 stake. Pool: £92,489.50. 0.50 winning tickets. T/Plt: £21.60 to a £1 stake. Pool: £62,375.30. 2,102.00 winning tickets. T/Qpdt: £4.50 to a £1 stake. Pool: £2,836.90. 456.60 winning tickets. CR

5778 WOLVERHAMPTON (A.W) (L-H)
Tuesday, October 2

OFFICIAL GOING: Standard
Wind: Almost nil Weather: Cloudy

5887 COME EVENING RACING THIS SATURDAY NURSERY — 5f 20y(P)
2:20 (2:20) (Class 6) (0-65,65) 2-Y-O **£2,388** (£705; £352) **Stalls** Low

Form RPR
5535 **1** **Weet A Surprise**5 5751 2-9-5 **63** FergusSweeney 9 67
(R Hollinshead) *hld up in mid-div: swtchd rt wl over 1f out: rdn and str run to ld nr fin* **7/1**2
1133 **2** 1/2 **Fabuleux Cherie**7 5715 2-9-5 **63** KerrinMcEvoy 5 65
(W R Muir) *a.p: rdn over 1f out: led wl ins fnl f: hdd nr fin* **13/8**1
116 **3** nk **Genethni**5 5751 2-9-5 **63** NCallan 1 64
(K A Ryan) *led: rdn over 1f out: hdd wl ins fnl f* **7/1**2
3001 **4** 1 1/4 **Rightcar Ellie (IRE)**7 5715 2-9-1 **64** 6ex (b) RussellKennemore(5) 4 61+
(Peter Grayson) *hld up: nt clr run on ins over 3f out: swtchd rt and hdwy over 1f out: kpt on ins fnl f* **16/1**
2400 **5** 1/2 **Alabama Spirit (USA)**11 5601 2-9-7 **65** DeanMcKeown 6 60
(D Shaw) *hld up in mid-div: hdwy 2f out: rdn and one pce fnl f* **16/1**
6646 **6** 3/4 **Rio Rocket (IRE)**41 4715 2-8-12 **59** PJMcDonald(3) 11 51
(G A Swinbank) *hld up towards rr: c wd st: kpt on and edgd lft ins fnl f: nvr trbld ldrs* **25/1**
6060 **7** 3/4 **Maybe I Wont**13 5534 2-9-7 **65** PaulFitzsimons 13 54
(S Dow) *s.i.s: sn swtchd lft: rdn over 2f out: nvr nr ldrs* **16/1**

The Form Book, Raceform Ltd, Compton, RG20 6NL

4002 **8** ½ **Don't Tell Anna (IRE)**13 5529 2-9-0 **58**........ PatDobbs 2 46
(R Hannon) *prom: rdn over 2f out: wknd ins fnl f* **7/1**2

6304 **9** 1 **Linnet Park**15 5484 2-9-3 **61**........ TomEaves 10 45+
(J G Given) *n.m.r s: hld up towards rr: rdn over 1f out: no ch whn sltly hmpd ins fnl f* **20/1**

3041 **10** ¾ **Rope Bridge (IRE)**33 4970 2-9-1 **59**........(b) DavidAllan 12 40
(T D Easterby) *chsd ldr: ev ch over 2f out: sn rdn: wknd over 1f out: edgd rt ins fnl f* **16/1**

6053 **11** 3 **Hucking Harmony (IRE)**16 5452 2-9-1 **62**........ StephaneBreux(3) 8 32
(J R Best) *prom tl rdn and wknd wl over 1f out* **11/1**3

004 **12** 17 **Little Evie**16 5442 2-9-0 **58**........ FrancisNorton 7 —
(R J Hodges) *sn outpcd: lost tch 2f out* **25/1**

62.62 secs (-0.20) **Going Correction** -0.175s/f (Stan) **12** Ran SP% **119.9**
Speed ratings (Par 93): **94,93,92,90,89 88,87,86,85,83 79,51**
CSF £18.36 CT £85.56 TOTE £7.10: £2.10, £1.10, £2.70; EX 26.90 Trifecta £157.90 Pool £233.53 - 1.05 winning units..
Owner Ed Weetman (haulage & Storage) Ltd **Bred** Longdon Stud Ltd **Trained** Upper Longdon, Staffs
■ Stewards' Enquiry : Pat Dobbs two-day ban: careless riding (Oct 13-14)

FOCUS
The winning time of this modest nursery was 1.88 seconds slower than the later 76-90 handicap on the card. Low-grade but solid form.

NOTEBOOK
Weet A Surprise, back in trip, mowed down her rivals inside the final 100 yards to score, reversing previous course form with the runner-up on these 8lb better terms. This looks to be her ideal trip and she ought to continue to pay her way despite a higher mark. (op 13-2)
Fabuleux Cherie was only reeled in by the winner near the line and ran another solid race in defeat. This consistent filly deserves to go one better again and rates a decent benchmark for this modest form. (op 5-2)
Genethni, ideally drawn, had every chance from the front and only gave way inside the final 150 yards. She ran very close to her official mark and is developing into a likeable filly. (op 9-2)
Rightcar Ellie(IRE), penalised for scoring at Folkestone a week previously, was not asked to get to the front on this return to the sand and ran creditably. She would have been a little closer with a better run nearing the home turn. (op 14-1)

5888 HOTEL & CONFERENCING AT WOLVERHAMPTON RACECOURSE MAIDEN AUCTION STKS 5f 216y(P)
2:50 (2:51) (Class 6) 2-Y-O **£2,388** (£705; £352) **Stalls** Low

Form RPR
32 **1** **Tobar Suil Lady (IRE)**15 5483 2-8-1 0........ AndrewMullen(3) 7 72+
(K A Ryan) *a.p: rdn to ld and edgd lft over 1f out: r.o wl* **11/8**1

3 **2** 1 ¾ **Kyllis**26 5154 2-8-6 0 ow1........ TomEaves 2 67
(B Smart) *led over 1f: w ldr: led over 2f out: rdn and hdd over 1f out: swtchd rt jst ins fnl f: nt qckn* **8/1**3

2240 **3** 1 ¼ **Rub Of The Relic (IRE)**10 5613 2-8-6 72........ KevinGhunowa(5) 9 68
(P A Blockley) *mid-div: rdn and outpcd over 2f out: r.o wl towards fin* **11/4**2

4 1 **Storey Hill (USA)** 2-8-10 0........ DeanMcKeown 6 64
(D Shaw) *sn chsng ldrs: rdn 2f out: btn whn hung lft 1f out* **40/1**

000 **5** 3 **Border Defence (IRE)**38 4823 2-8-10 57........ FrankieMcDonald 12 55
(P A Blockley) *hld up and bhd: rdn and edgd lft over 1f out: kpt on: n.d* **33/1**

00 **6** 2 **Joss Stick**44 4629 2-8-9 0........ NCallan 1 48
(P J Makin) *prom: led over 4f out tl over 2f out: rdn and wknd wl over 1f out* **12/1**

00 **7** 1 ¾ **Last Angel (IRE)**129 2041 2-8-7 0........ NickyMackay 5 41
(M Wigham) *mid-div: rdn over 3f out: short-lived effrt on ins over 2f out* **66/1**

60 **8** nk **Magical Song**15 5470 2-8-9 0........ ChrisCatlin 11 42
(E J O'Neill) *bhd: rdn over 4f out: sn struggling* **16/1**

5500 **9** 3 **Avian Flew**63 4041 2-8-4 55........ FrancisNorton 3 28+
(J A Pickering) *prom: wkng whn n.m.r briefly wl over 2f out* **66/1**

10 shd **Libertytyne** 2-8-7 0........ SimonWhitworth 4 31
(S Kirk) *s.i.s: outpcd* **20/1**

11 ½ **Chunsa** 2-8-10 0........ KerrinMcEvoy 10 32
(W Jarvis) *s.i.s: outpcd* **9/1**

12 40 **Rightcar Lewis** 2-8-13 0 ow5........ BrettDoyle 8 —
(Peter Grayson) *s.i.s: outpcd: t.o* **33/1**

1m 15.87s (0.06) **Going Correction** -0.175s/f (Stan) **12** Ran SP% **119.5**
Speed ratings (Par 93): **92,89,88,86,82 80,77,77,73,73 72,19**
CSF £12.65 TOTE £2.10: £1.10, £2.60, £1.10; EX 7.40 Trifecta £11.70 Pool £147.52 - 8.93 winning units..
Owner Eye Opener Syndicate **Bred** Roland H Alder **Trained** Hambleton, N Yorks

FOCUS
A weak juvenile maiden. The form is limited by the fifth and seventh and the winner just needed to reproduce her earlier form..

NOTEBOOK
Tobar Suil Lady(IRE) deservedly broke her maiden tag at the third time of asking and did the job readily enough. This was her easiest assignment to date, but she left the impression she would do a little better when faced with another furlong now and can make her mark in nurseries. (op 6-4 tchd 10-11)
Kyllis, third on her debut at Redcar 26 days previously, posted another sound effort on this step up of a furlong and finished nicely clear in second. She will be eligible for a nursery mark after her next outing and it should be noted her rider put up 1lb overweight here. (op 9-2)
Rub Of The Relic(IRE) is now fully exposed and, while this was one of his better efforts in defeat, still looks flattered by his official rating at present. (op 5-1)
Storey Hill(USA), a half-brother to high-class juvenile sprinter Lucky Lionel, showed ability on this racecourse debut and should improve for the outing. (op 33-1)

5889 SPONSOR A RACE BY CALLING 0870 220 2442 H'CAP 1m 141y(P)
3:20 (3:20) (Class 4) (0-80,80) 3-Y-O+ **£5,181** (£1,541; £770; £384) **Stalls** Low

Form RPR
3532 **1** **Voliere**13 5543 4-9-5 **75**........ KerrinMcEvoy 3 87
(S C Williams) *hld up: hdwy 2f out: rdn to ld ins fnl f: r.o* **7/1**

5043 **2** 1 **Mafeking (UAE)**36 4889 3-9-3 **77**........ PaulDoe 6 87
(M R Hoad) *prom: wnt 2nd over 6f out: led over 3f out: rdn 2f out: hdd ins fnl f: nt qckn* **13/2**3

4040 **3** 3 **Red Romeo**46 4585 6-9-8 **78**........ DanielTudhope 4 82
(N Wilson) *led early: prom: rdn wl over 1f out: wknd ins fnl f* **25/1**

6055 **4** ¾ **Hoh Wotanite**12 5568 4-9-2 **72**........(p) JimCrowley 5 74
(R Hollinshead) *hld up: rdn over 1f out: styng on whn edgd lft ins fnl f: n.d* **15/2**

0431 **5** 2 ½ **Red Birr (IRE)**12 5568 6-9-6 **76**........ ChrisCatlin 8 73
(P R Webber) *sn led: hdd over 3f out: rdn and wknd over 2f out* **11/2**2

5101 **6** ½ **Hits Only Cash**10 5645 5-8-12 **68**........ DeanMcKeown 1 64
(J Pearce) *hld up and bhd: rdn over 2f out: no rspnse* **11/1**

0112 **7** ¾ **Cnoc Moy (IRE)**57 4234 3-9-6 **80**........ GeorgeBaker 2 74
(C F Wall) *prom tl rdn and wknd wl over 1f out* **6/4**1

3230 **8** 3 **Tous Les Deux**10 5648 4-9-2 **72**........ BrettDoyle 7 60
(Peter Grayson) *a in rr* **14/1**

1m 49.12s (-2.64) **Going Correction** -0.175s/f (Stan)
WFA 3 from 4yo+ 4lb **8** Ran SP% **111.8**
Speed ratings (Par 105): **104,103,100,99,97 97,96,93**
CSF £49.14 CT £1056.06 TOTE £7.90: £2.00, £2.60, £4.50; EX 72.60 Trifecta £265.50 Part won. Pool £374.03 - 0.20 winning units..
Owner J W Parry **Bred** Juddmonte Farms Ltd **Trained** Newmarket, Suffolk

FOCUS
A fair handicap for the class, but it was run at just a sedate early pace. The winning time was 1.21 seconds quicker than the following 46-52. The form is sound despite the disappointing effort of the favourite.
Cnoc Moy(IRE) Official explanation: jockey said gelding lost its action

5890 STAY AT THE WOLVERHAMPTON HOLIDAY INN H'CAP 1m 141y(P)
3:50 (3:50) (Class 6) (0-52,53) 3-Y-O+ **£2,388** (£705; £352) **Stalls** Low

Form RPR
-00 **1** **Ya Late Maite**32 5019 4-8-12 **50**........ GrahamGibbons 3 61
(E S McMahon) *a.p: rdn over 3f out: hrd rdn to ld wl ins fnl f: r.o* **16/1**

5050 **2** ½ **Machinate (USA)**25 5190 5-8-11 **49**........ LiamJones 12 59
(W M Brisbourne) *hld up towards rr: hdwy over 2f out: bmpd jst over 1f out: rdn to ld briefly ins fnl f: kpt on* **5/1**1

6604 **3** 2 **Marmooq**18 5391 4-9-0 **52**........ ChrisCatlin 11 57
(M J Attwater) *a.p: wnt 2nd over 6f out: led over 3f out: rdn and edgd rt jst over 1f out: hdd ins fnl f: no ex* **13/2**2

4050 **4** 3 ½ **Anthemion (IRE)**15 5476 10-8-10 **51**........ AndrewMullen(3) 1 48
(Mrs J C McGregor) *led: rdn and hdd over 3f out: wknd fnl f* **12/1**

0005 **5** ¾ **Musicmaestroplease (IRE)**29 5098 4-9-0 **52**........ DanielTudhope 4 47
(S Parr) *hld up in mid-div: hdwy on ins whn nt clr run over 2f out: rdn and swtchd rt over 1f out: no further prog* **12/1**

3060 **6** hd **Ermine Grey**12 5569 6-8-9 **52**........ LukeMorris(5) 9 47
(A W Carroll) *dwlt: hld up in rr: pushed along over 3f out: rdn and hdwy wl over 1f out: no imp whn edgd lft ins fnl f* **17/2**

0061 **7** 2 ½ **Avontuur (FR)**12 5566 5-8-4 **49**........(b) DanielleMcCreery(7) 7 38
(D W Chapman) *s.i.s: hld up in rr: hdwy on ins wl over 1f out: sn rdn: wknd fnl f* **20/1**

0605 **8** 5 **Summer Gift**10 5625 4-8-10 **53** ow4........ JamesO'Reilly(5) 10 31
(J O'Reilly) *hld up in mid-div: hdwy over 4f out: rdn and wknd over 2f out* **20/1**

0453 **9** 2 ½ **Uhuru Peak**13 5525 6-8-13 **51**........(bt) DaleGibson 13 23
(M W Easterby) *hld up towards rr: rdn over 3f out: sn struggling* **5/1**1

6463 **10** ½ **Miss Sure Bond (IRE)**19 5366 4-8-10 **53** ow1........(p) SladeO'Hara(5) 2 24
(G R Oldroyd) *chsd ldrs tl rdn and wknd over 2f out* **8/1**3

0600 **11** ¾ **Royal Orissa**32 5016 5-8-13 **51**........(b1) BrettDoyle 8 20
(D Haydn Jones) *hld up in mid-div: hung bdly rt over 3f out: sn bhd: rn wd and no ch whn eased wl over 1f out* **10/1**

0330 **12** 3 **Tenancy (IRE)**12 5386 3-8-3 **52**........ RobbieEgan(7) 5 14
(A J McCabe) *plld hrd: prom: rdn and wknd 2f out* **8/1**3

1m 50.33s (-1.43) **Going Correction** -0.175s/f (Stan)
WFA 3 from 4yo+ 4lb **12** Ran SP% **119.3**
Speed ratings (Par 101): **99,98,96,93,93 92,90,86,83,83 82,80**
CSF £94.79 CT £588.94 TOTE £21.70: £6.20, £2.50, £1.90; EX 113.50 TRIFECTA Not won..
Owner Mrs J McMahon **Bred** Exors Of The Late M J Paver **Trained** Lichfield, Staffs

FOCUS
A very moderate handicap and the winning time was 1.21 seconds slower than the previous 66-80. The form is sound, rated through the second and third.
Uhuru Peak Official explanation: jockey said gelding never travelled
Royal Orissa Official explanation: jockey said gelding hung right

5891 WOLVERHAMPTON-RACECOURSE.CO.UK H'CAP 5f 20y(P)
4:20 (4:20) (Class 3) (0-90,90) 3-Y-O+ **£9,715** (£2,890; £1,444; £721) **Stalls** Low

Form RPR
3123 **1** **Matsunosuke**8 5689 5-8-11 **83**........ KerrinMcEvoy 7 104+
(A B Coogan) *hld up and bhd: hdwy wl over 1f out: rdn to ld wl ins fnl f: r.o wl* **7/2**2

1122 **2** 3 **Tamagin (USA)**10 5638 4-9-3 **89**........ NCallan 3 99
(K A Ryan) *chsd ldrs: rdn over 2f out: edgd rt ins fnl f: kpt on* **5/2**1

663 **3** 1 **Tony The Tap**14 5513 6-8-5 **77**........ HayleyTurner 4 83
(W R Muir) *mid-div: hdwy on ins over 2f out: rdn wl over 1f out: kpt on same pce ins fnl f* **13/2**

0000 **4** shd **Gallery Girl (IRE)**18 5379 4-8-7 **79**........ DavidAllan 2 85
(T D Easterby) *a.p: rdn to chse ldr 2f out: no ex towards fin* **16/1**

6110 **5** shd **Inter Vision (USA)**3 5804 7-9-4 **90**........ DanielTudhope 5 96
(A Dickman) *s.i.s: hld up in rr: rdn and hdwy on ins over 1f out: r.o ins fnl f* **6/1**3

1050 **6** ¾ **Bertoliver**10 5632 3-9-2 **88**........ IanMongan 1 91
(D K Ivory) *led: rdn wl over 1f out: hdd wl ins fnl f: fdd* **20/1**

1460 **7** ½ **Bahamian Ballet**18 5379 5-8-10 **82**........ JimCrowley 6 83
(E S McMahon) *hld up in mid-div: rdn and no real prog fnl f* **16/1**

260 **8** ¾ **Desert Dreamer (IRE)**10 5617 6-8-9 **81**........ NickyMackay 9 79
(G A Butler) *s.i.s: nvr nr ldrs* **14/1**

3530 **9** 2 **Jack Rackham**24 5212 3-9-0 **86**........ TomEaves 13 77
(B Smart) *outpcd* **28/1**

0100 **10** 5 **Cashel Mead**9 5666 7-9-1 **87**........ FrancisNorton 10 60
(J L Spearing) *outpcd* **22/1**

32-0 **11** 2 ½ **Stolt (IRE)**7 5700 3-9-3 **89**........ GrahamGibbons 12 53
(N Wilson) *chsd ldrs tl rdn and wknd over 2f out* **66/1**

5603 **12** 2 **Merlin's Dancer**17 5401 7-9-3 **89**........ PaulDoe 8 46
(S Dow) *chsd ldr tl rdn 2f out: sn wknd* **12/1**

60.74 secs (-2.08) **Going Correction** -0.175s/f (Stan) **12** Ran SP% **118.6**
Speed ratings (Par 107): **109,104,102,102,102 101,100,99,95,87 83,80**
CSF £12.04 CT £54.87 TOTE £5.90: £1.30, £1.50, £2.40; EX 12.90 Trifecta £39.60 Pool £265.57 - 4.76 winning units..
Owner A B Coogan **Bred** R Coogan **Trained** Soham, Cambs

FOCUS
A good sprint handicap, and solid form. A career best from Matsunosuke. The pace was strong and the winning time was 1.88 seconds quicker than the earlier 0-65 nursery.

NOTEBOOK
Matsunosuke, six times a winner on turf, including twice this year, had never previously raced on Polytrack, but he handled the surface very well ran out a most convincing winner. This is the highest mark he has ever won off, but he is very much on the up and remains one to keep on side. (tchd 4-1)
Tamagin(USA), an extremely tough sort, has done very well since joining Kevin Ryan and this was a decent effort in defeat off a career-high mark. He was unable to dominate, as he often has done in the past, but he is clearly fully effective chasing the pace. (op 11-4 tchd 3-1)

Tony The Tap could not take advantage of a mark 8lb lower than that of his turf rating and his losing run stretches back to 2004. (op 8-1 tchd 11-2)
Gallery Girl(IRE), having her first start on Polytrack, ran a little better than of late and offered some encouragement.
Inter Vision(USA) was never involved after starting slowly and he looks a better horse on turf.
Official explanation: jockey said gelding was hampered on final bend (op 9-2)
Bertoliver was well held on his only previous start on Polytrack and he again failed to show his best. Official explanation: jockey said colt hung right throughout

5892 HORIZONS RESTAURANT H'CAP 1m 4f 50y(P)
4:50 (4:51) (Class 4) (0-85,85) 3-Y-0+ **£5,181** (£1,541; £770; £384) **Stalls** Low

Form RPR
221 **1** **Tropical Strait (IRE)**[8] 5683 4-9-1 **77** 6ex.................. FergusSweeney 8 91+
(D W P Arbuthnot) *s.i.s: hld up: hdwy over 8f out: led over 5f out: rdn and qcknd clr wl over 1f out: comf* **8/11**[1]
000 **2** *3* **Southern Regent (IND)**[10] 5619 6-9-9 **85**............................ NCallan 2 91
(G A Swinbank) *led 2f: a.p: rdn and chsd wnr over 2f out: no imp* **25/1**
3105 **3** *1 1/4* **Heathyards Pride**[20] 5334 7-9-9 **85**................................ GeorgeBaker 4 89
(R Hollinshead) *hld up: rdn and hdwy 3f out: one pce fnl 2f* **9/1**[3]
4050 **4** *1 3/4* **Active Asset (IRE)**[13] 5543 5-8-13 **75**.............................. ChrisCatlin 5 76
(M Quinn) *prom: rdn and outpcd wl over 3f out: styd on fnl f* **20/1**
0220 **5** *3* **Arsad (IRE)**[60] 4131 4-8-9 **71** oh1................................(b) KerrinMcEvoy 3 67
(C E Brittain) *hld up: hdwy over 8f out: wknd over 3f out* **16/1**
5042 **6** *nk* **Paymaster General (IRE)**[14] 5500 3-8-5 **74**................ FrancisNorton 1 70
(M D I Usher) *plld v hrd: dropped to rr 8f out: rdn and no ch fnl 3f* **14/1**
-231 **7** *2 1/2* **Fisher Bridge (IRE)**[51] 4421 4-9-2 **78**.......................... SaleemGolam 9 70
(W R Swinburn) *sn prom: led after 2f: hdd over 5f out: rdn 4f out: wknd over 2f out* **4/1**[2]
525 **8** *4* **Ravenna**[13] 5523 3-8-7 **76**... HayleyTurner 6 62
(M P Tregoning) *prom tl rdn and wknd over 2f out* **12/1**

2m 39.92s (-2.50) **Going Correction** -0.175s/f (Stan)
WFA 3 from 4yo+ 7lb **8** Ran SP% **116.8**
Speed ratings (Par 105): **101,99,98,97,95 94,93,90**
CSF £24.96 CT £106.63 TOTE £1.70: £1.02, £8.80, £3.10; EX 29.20 Trifecta £274.10 Part won. Pool £386.16 - 0.70 winning units..
Owner Francis Ward and Anthony Ward **Bred** George Ward **Trained** Compton, Berks

FOCUS
Just an ordinary handicap for the grade. Tropical Strait was 8lb well in and did not need to improve.
Paymaster General(IRE) Official explanation: jockey said gelding ran too freely

5893 BOOK TICKETS ONLINE AT WOLVERHAMPTON-RACECOURSE.CO.UK H'CAP 7f 32y(P)
5:20 (5:21) (Class 5) (0-70,69) 3-Y-0+ **£3,412** (£1,007; £504) **Stalls** High

Form RPR
3360 **1** **Another Genepi (USA)**[26] 5155 4-9-0 **63**...........................(b) NCallan 5 74
(K A Ryan) *led after 1f: rdn over 1f out: r.o wl* **5/1**[2]
6P33 **2** *1 1/2* **Towy Girl (IRE)**[13] 5532 3-8-9 **65**.................................. LukeMorris(5) 7 71+
(A W Carroll) *hld up towards rr: hdwy over 2f out: rdn and edgd lft fr jst over 1f out: kpt on: nt trble wnr* **8/1**
0620 **3** *1 1/4* **All You Need (IRE)**[18] 5387 3-8-13 **69**.............. RussellKennemore(5) 1 72
(R Hollinshead) *led 1f: a.p: rdn and edgd lft jst over 1f out: one pce* **7/1**
-103 **4** *1 1/4* **Maysarah (IRE)**[40] 4740 3-9-2 **67**.................................... NickyMackay 6 66
(G A Butler) *s.i.s: sn hld up in tch: hung lft over 2f out: swtchd rt jst over 1f out: one pce* **9/1**
1216 **5** *2 1/2* **Sands Of Barra (IRE)**[2] 5840 4-9-2 **68**................. PatrickMathers(3) 11 61
(I W McInnes) *hld up towards rr: rdn and hdwy on ins over 2f out: wknd 1f out* **13/2**[3]
1300 **6** *1 1/4* **Empire Dancer (IRE)**[13] 5532 4-9-0 **63**............................ FrancisNorton 2 53
(C N Allen) *prom: rdn 2f out: wknd 1f out* **12/1**
-000 **7** *hd* **Smokin Joe**[251] 233 6-9-0 **63**......................................(b) JimCrowley 3 53
(J R Best) *hld up towards rr: nvr nr ldrs* **25/1**
0100 **8** *5* **Meditation**[21] 5303 5-9-4 **67**.. JamesDoyle 10 43
(I A Wood) *hld up in mid-div: rdn over 3f out: sn bhd* **16/1**
5465 **9** *1* **Colchium (IRE)**[32] 5001 3-9-0 **68**.............................. TravisBlock(3) 4 40
(H Morrison) *prom tl rdn and wknd over 2f out* **4/1**[1]
0034 **10** *1 1/4* **Red Contact (USA)**[26] 5177 6-9-6 **69**......................(p) DanielTudhope 12 39
(A Dickman) *hld up in mid-div: short-lived effrt on outside over 3f out* **14/1**
-020 **11** *3 1/2* **Dance Spirit (IRE)**[17] 5424 4-9-0 **63**.............................. KerrinMcEvoy 8 24
(W R Muir) *s.i.s: outpcd* **13/2**[3]
3500 **12** *8* **Multitude (IRE)**[36] 4898 3-8-13 **64**.................................(b) DavidAllan 9 3
(T D Easterby) *outpcd* **66/1**

1m 28.57s (-1.83) **Going Correction** -0.175s/f (Stan)
WFA 3 from 4yo+ 2lb **12** Ran SP% **122.5**
Speed ratings (Par 103): **103,101,99,98,95 94,93,88,87,85 81,72**
CSF £46.54 CT £292.56 TOTE £4.90: £1.80, £2.10, £3.90; EX 36.40 Trifecta £119.90 Part won. Pool £168.94 - 0.35 winning units. Place 6 £23.60, Place 5 £15.74..
Owner Hambleton Racing Ltd I **Bred** Joseph Lacombe Stables Inc **Trained** Hambleton, N Yorks

FOCUS
A modest handicap, the winner back to her April course-and-distance mark, and straightforward form.
Empire Dancer(IRE) Official explanation: jockey said gelding lost its action home straight
Multitude(IRE) Official explanation: jockey said gelding never travelled
T/Plt: £47.20 to a £1 stake. Pool: £55,978.35. 864.40 winning tickets. T/Qpdt: £35.40 to a £1 stake. Pool: £3,099.00. 64.70 winning tickets. KH

5815 KEMPTON (A.W) (R-H)
Wednesday, October 3

OFFICIAL GOING: Standard
Wind: Nil Weather: Fine

5894 PANORAMIC BAR & RESTAURANT CLASSIFIED STKS 1m 2f (P)
6:20 (6:21) (Class 6) 3-Y-0+ **£2,047** (£604; £302) **Stalls** High

Form RPR
-304 **1** **Papradon**[30] 5095 3-9-0 52..(v[1]) DaneO'Neill 9 56
(J R Best) *cl up on inner: drvn to ld over 1f out: kpt on wl u.p* **13/2**[2]
-002 **2** *1* **Ardmaddy (IRE)**[20] 5366 3-8-11 55.............................. WilliamBuick(3) 5 54
(J A R Toller) *settled midfield: rdn and prog on outer over 2f out: chal and w wnr jst over 1f out: nt qckn* **2/1**[1]
4003 **3** *1/2* **Astrolibra**[8] 5710 3-9-0 52.. JimmyQuinn 12 53
(M H Tompkins) *settled midfield: prog on inner 2f out: cl up over 1f out: nt qckn u.p: kpt on* **13/2**[2]
0 **4** *1/2* **Tullythered (IRE)**[26] 5188 3-9-0 47.................................. JamesDoyle 7 52
(K R Burke) *towards rr: rdn and prog on inner wl over 1f out: kpt on fnl f* **16/1**
6-00 **5** *shd* **Botham (USA)**[32] 5037 3-9-0 48.................................. FrancisNorton 14 52
(D J Murphy) *disp ld: narrow advantage 2f out to over 1f out: fdd last 100yds* **11/1**
6 *3/4* **Fairy Festival (IRE)**[136] 1865 3-9-0 50.................................. JohnEgan 2 50
(J S Moore) *chsd ldrs: rdn and prog on wd outside over 2f out: nt qckn over 1f out: one pce after* **13/2**[2]
00-0 **7** *3* **Classic Blue (IRE)**[20] 5347 3-9-0 53........................ StephenDonohoe 11 44
(Ian Williams) *awkward s and stdd: towards rr tl prog on inner 2f out: no imp on ldng gp over 1f out* **33/1**
4-55 **8** *2 1/2* **Mariaverdi**[36] 4918 3-9-0 48.. RobertHavlin 13 39
(B J Meehan) *disp ld to 2f out: wknd over 1f out* **12/1**
0-60 **9** *shd* **Art Gallery**[117] 2425 3-9-0 52.....................................(b) FergusSweeney 6 39
(G L Moore) *t.k.h: hld up bhd ldrs: rdn over 2f out: wknd over 1f out* **10/1**[3]
0000 **10** *1* **Tavares (IRE)**[33] 5020 4-9-5 55...................................... SaleemGolam 10 37
(J Jay) *mostly in last pair: drvn and no prog over 3f out: n.d after* **16/1**
3060 **11** *1 1/2* **County Kerry (UAE)**[49] 4504 3-9-0 54....................(t) FrankieMcDonald 1 34
(Jean-Rene Auvray) *dwlt: wl in rr: rdn over 2f out: no prog* **20/1**
564/ **12** *1 1/2* **Stokesies Boy**[24] 4767 7-9-5 45................................... RichardThomas 3 31
(C Roberts) *a wl in rr: no ch fnl 2f* **33/1**
00-0 **13** *4* **Vettori Dancer**[18] 5421 4-9-5 47.. NeilPollard 4 23
(G G Margarson) *a in last pair: drvn and no prog over 3f out* **66/1**
000- **14** *4* **Stokesies Luck (IRE)**[366] 5728 4-9-5 42............................ ChrisCatlin 8 15
(C Roberts) *prom tl wknd rapidly 3f out* **100/1**

2m 7.28s (-1.72) **Going Correction** -0.25s/f (Stan)
WFA 3 from 4yo+ 5lb **14** Ran SP% **123.3**
Speed ratings (Par 101): **96,95,94,94,94 93,91,89,89,88 87,86,82,79**
CSF £19.52 TOTE £8.40: £2.70, £1.50, £4.30; EX 35.70.
Owner Donna Rooks & Pam Rooks **Bred** B Whitehouse **Trained** Hucking, Kent

FOCUS
A low-grade event in which the field had run a total of 71 times without winning. Muddling form. As has been the case here recently, the winning time was very fast for the class of horse on show.

5895 ABACUS LIGHTING MAIDEN AUCTION STKS 7f (P)
6:50 (6:52) (Class 6) 2-Y-O **£2,047** (£604; £302) **Stalls** High

Form RPR
1 **Avertis** 2-8-13 0.. OscarUrbina 3 71+
(M Botti) *chsd ldrs: shkn up and prog wl over 1f out: rdn to ld jst ins fnl f: styd on wl* **6/1**[3]
05 **2** *nk* **Locum**[14] 5526 2-8-9 0.. JimmyQuinn 13 66
(M H Tompkins) *cl up: effrt 2f out: rdn to ld briefly 1f out: pressed wnr last 150yds but a hld* **10/1**
00 **3** *1 1/4* **Agglestone Rock**[48] 4540 2-8-2 0.................................... JackDean(7) 2 63+
(W G M Turner) *t.k.h: pressed ldng pair: rdn and nt qckn on outer over 2f out: kpt on again fnl f* **66/1**
04 **4** *1/2* **Poppy Dean (IRE)**[110] 2624 2-8-6 0.................................. ChrisCatlin 11 58
(J G Portman) *mde most to 1f out: one pce* **4/1**[2]
0604 **5** *1/2* **Janet's Delight**[12] 5603 2-8-4 61.................................. AdrianMcCarthy 8 55
(S Curran) *in tch at rr of main gp: shkn up over 2f out: styd on fr over 1f out: nrst fin* **12/1**
6 *nk* **Word Games** 2-8-13 0.. FrancisNorton 9 63+
(A M Balding) *in tch: pushed along on inner over 3f out: drvn and prog jst over 2f out: no hdwy fnl f* **20/1**
2400 **7** *1* **I Dont Do Walkin (USA)**[16] 5470 2-8-10 68........(b[1]) StephenDonohoe 4 57
(B J Meehan) *t.k.h: pressed ldr: upsides 3f out: wknd jst over 1f out* **8/1**
8 *1/2* **Candida's Beau** 2-8-13 0.. SebSanders 10 59
(R M Beckett) *chsd ldrs: nt qckn and lost pl over 2f out: no imp after* **15/2**
00 **9** *1/2* **Reel Man**[12] 5591 2-8-13 0.. RichardHughes 14 58
(R Hannon) *trckd ldrs on inner: pushed along over 3f out: stl cl up whn nowhere to go and snatched up jst over 1f out: no ch after* **7/2**[1]
0 **10** *2 1/2* **It's Josr**[102] 2876 2-8-11 0.. RichardThomas 5 49
(I A Wood) *dwlt: a off the pce in last quartet: bhd 1/2-way: hanging and green but plugged on over 1f out* **33/1**
11 *6* **Hucking Harrier (IRE)** 2-8-11 0.. DaneO'Neill 1 33
(J R Best) *dwlt and swvd lft s: rn green and mostly last: bhd fr 1/2-way* **12/1**
00 **12** *nk* **Lord's Bidding**[102] 2876 2-8-11 0.................................. RobertHavlin 7 32
(R Ingram) *sn pushed along in last pair: bhd fr 1/2-way* **66/1**
13 *3* **Ba Dreamflight** 2-8-12 0.. TravisBlock(3) 6 28
(H Morrison) *struggling in last trio over 4f out: bhd after* **10/1**

1m 26.85s (0.05) **Going Correction** -0.25s/f (Stan) **13** Ran SP% **123.6**
Speed ratings (Par 93): **89,88,87,86,86 85,84,84,83,80 73,73,69**
CSF £65.42 TOTE £9.40: £3.10, £3.00, £14.90; EX 103.60.
Owner Dr Ornella Carlini Cozzi **Bred** Mrs Sally Doyle **Trained** Newmarket, Suffolk
■ Stewards' Enquiry : Stephen Donohoe one-day ban: failed to ride to draw (Oct 14)
Oscar Urbina one-day ban: careless riding (Oct 14)

FOCUS
The close proximity of lots of juveniles who already look ordinary holds down this form - as does the winning time given the strong early gallop.

NOTEBOOK
Avertis, whose dam was a smart performer in the USA, impressed on this debut despite the narrow winning margin. A scopey colt, who should be considerably better at three, he showed a pleasing turn of foot when asked to go about his business before seeming to idle once in front. He has more to give, and could end up being a good bit better than those he beat here. (op 15-2)
Locum showed nothing on his first run but a fair bit more on his second, and he was better still again here. This qualifies him for handicaps, and that could be his sphere. (tchd 12-1)
Agglestone Rock is the type to do better at three. Showing much more than in his previous two outings, he travelled quite easily and held his position throughout the race, definitely doing enough to suggest that he is anything but a lost cause.
Poppy Dean(IRE), without the tongue tie for this first run since June, was not disgraced having tried to make all. She is now eligible for handicaps. (op 6-1)
Janet's Delight, back over 7f, ran on late in the race, but it's hard to imagine that she has suddenly found much improvement. (op 14-1)
Word Games, a half-brother to several winners, mainly at sprint distances, shaped encouragingly on his debut. He got bang into the thick of things close to the rail, and is bound to have learnt a lot from the experience. (tchd 18-1)

The Form Book, Raceform Ltd, Compton, RG20 6NL

Reel Man became a little tight for room inside the final furlong, but he was probably beaten at the time and, in all probability, is not very good. (op 10-3)

5896 DIGIBET.COM NURSERY 1m (P)
7:20 (7:21) (Class 6) (0-65,66) 2-Y-O £2,047 (£604; £302) Stalls High

Form RPR

060 **1** **Distant Diamond (IRE)**[21] 5337 2-9-4 **62** SebSanders 9 66
(W R Swinburn) *chsd ldrs: rdn over 2f out: prog over 1f out to chse ldr ins fnl f: styd on to ld last stride* **6/1**[3]

0643 **2** *hd* **Bermacha**[14] 5527 2-9-4 **65** WilliamBuick(3) 2 69
(W R Muir) *prom: effrt to ld jst over 2f out: drvn and kpt on fnl f: hdd last stride* **7/1**

0060 **3** *1* **Race The Moon (IRE)**[47] 4584 2-8-13 **60** (e[1]) JerryO'Dwyer(3) 5 62+
(V Smith) *restrained into last sn after s: prog on inner 2f out: urged along hands and heels and styd on wl: tk 3rd nr fin* **50/1**

3305 **4** *3/4* **Ezthegezza**[15] 5509 2-9-2 **65** TolleyDean(5) 13 65
(J S Moore) *chsd ldrs: rdn over 2f out: disp 2nd u.p 1f out: one pce* **14/1**

5600 **5** *nk* **Xtravaganza (IRE)**[28] 5127 2-9-2 **60** JamesDoyle 10 59
(J W Hills) *pressed ldr: upsides over 2f out: chsd new ldr after tl fdd ins fnl f* **50/1**

0026 **6** *1/2* **I Certainly May**[7] 5736 2-9-6 **64** DaneO'Neill 7 62
(S Dow) *towards rr on outer: drvn over 2f out: prog over 1f out: kpt on fnl f: nrst fin* **8/1**

61 **7** *3/4* **Ten Spot (IRE)**[11] 5644 2-9-4 **62** ChrisCatlin 11 58+
(J A Osborne) *lost pl on inner after 3f: effrt over 2f out: nt clr run and swtchd lft over 1f out: keeping on same pce whn n.m.r last 50yds* **8/1**

000 **8** *1 1/4* **Fernlawn Hope (IRE)**[22] 5309 2-9-2 **60** StephenDonohoe 12 54
(J A Osborne) *towards rr: hrd rdn over 2f out: plugging on but n.d whn no room last 50yds* **50/1**

6303 **9** *1 1/2* **No Nines**[7] 5736 2-9-7 **65** MichaelHills 1 55
(B W Hills) *racd on wd outside: in tch: rdn over 2f out: no prog fnl 2f* **5/1**[2]

4062 **10** *3* **Synge Street**[28] 5127 2-9-7 **65** RichardHughes 14 48
(R Hannon) *led to jst over 2f out: wknd and eased over 1f out* **9/4**[1]

050 **11** *1 3/4* **Rampant Ronnie (USA)**[18] 5428 2-9-7 **65** GeorgeBaker 8 44
(P W D'Arcy) *chsd ldrs: lost pl u.p 3f out: n.d after* **10/1**

0000 **12** *5* **Isander (USA)**[13] 5571 2-9-5 **63** (b[1]) JimCrowley 3 31
(Mrs A J Perrett) *cl up tl rdn and wknd over 2f out* **25/1**

000U **13** *18* **Recoil (IRE)**[7] 5736 2-9-7 **65** (b[1]) SaleemGolam 4 —
(Christian Wroe) *last and reluctant after 3f: sn detached: t.o* **25/1**

1m 39.78s (-1.02) **Going Correction** -0.25s/f (Stan) **13** Ran SP% **125.8**
Speed ratings (Par 93): **95,94,93,93,92 92,91,90,88,85 84,79,61**
CSF £48.39 CT £2011.40 TOTE £6.60: £2.70, £2.10, £17.50; EX 51.30.
Owner Team Premier **Bred** C J Foy **Trained** Aldbury, Herts
■ Stewards' Enquiry : James Doyle one-day ban: careless riding (Oct 14)
William Buick one-day ban: failed to ride to draw (Oct 15)

FOCUS
Amodest nursery, the placed horses helping set the level.

NOTEBOOK
Distant Diamond(IRE), a fair sixth at Newbury on his second outing before enduring touble in running in a maiden here, got up almost on the line to score on his handicap debut, helped by a determined Seb Sanders drive. His attitude is good, and he will improve when upped in trip. (op 8-1)
Bermacha took over about two furlongs out and was unlucky to be caught on the line. She gets every yard of the mile and should gain some compensation before long. (op 8-1 tchd 6-1)
Race The Moon(IRE) was restrained back into the rear early in the race, and so was required to come from a long way back up the straight. Despite having to make up lots of ground, he really motored through the final furlong and might well have won in a few more strides. He must surely take something off his basement rating.
Ezthegezza was not disgraced having been prominent from the start.
Xtravaganza(IRE), dropped 4lb since her nursery debut here, ran her best race to date.
Ten Spot(IRE) completely lost her place when hampered down the back straight, from which point she faced a stiff task. In the circumstances, she did not do badly. (op 5-1 tchd 10-1)
Synge Street, 4lb higher than when scoring over course and distance a month ago, adopted different tactics here and failed to get home. (op 5-2)
Recoil(IRE) Official explanation: jockey said colt did not face the blinkers

5897 DIGIBET CASINO H'CAP 6f (P)
7:50 (7:52) (Class 6) (0-55,54) 3-Y-O+ £2,047 (£604; £302) Stalls High

Form RPR

0104 **1** **Ishibee (IRE)**[2] 5866 3-8-11 **52** (p) SebSanders 1 61
(J J Bridger) *hld up in last: stdy prog on inner over 2f out: led 1f out: drvn and hld on wl* **6/1**[3]

U450 **2** *1/2* **Mister Elegant**[30] 5090 5-8-10 **50** FrancisNorton 9 58
(J L Spearing) *wl in tch: prog 2f out: rdn to chal 1f out: pressed wnr after: a hld* **7/1**

4060 **3** *1 3/4* **Formidable Will (FR)**[85] 3408 5-8-12 **52** (vt) JimmyQuinn 12 54
(D Shaw) *pressed ldr: led jst over 2f out: drvn and hdd 1f out: one pce* **14/1**

5400 **4** *nk* **Monashee Prince (IRE)**[13] 5576 5-9-0 **54** (v) DaneO'Neill 4 59+
(J R Best) *hld up in rr: shkn up over 2f out: trbld run fr wl over 1f out: r.o fnl f: nrst fin* **7/1**

6620 **5** *3/4* **Laphonic (USA)**[7] 5730 4-8-8 **48** (b[1]) SaleemGolam 11 47
(T J Etherington) *cl up: rdn and nt qckn jst over 2f out: kpt on same pce after: nvr able to chal* **11/2**[2]

000 **6** *shd* **Fast Freddie**[18] 5420 3-8-4 **48** WilliamBuick(3) 6 47
(D J Murphy) *mostly midfield: effrt 2f out: chsng ldrs and rdn 1f out: kpt on one pce* **14/1**

0223 **7** *3/4* **Master Malarkey**[18] 5425 4-8-10 **50** (b) ChrisCatlin 8 47
(Mrs C A Dunnett) *led to jst over 2f out: nt qckn u.p: fdd over 1f out* **8/1**

5020 **8** *3/4* **Meikle Barfil**[13] 5564 5-8-9 **49** (tp) RobertHavlin 10 43+
(J M Bradley) *n.m.r s: hld up in rr: effrt whn nt clr run over 1f out: no ch* **20/1**

3202 **9** *nk* **Bens Georgie (IRE)**[19] 5391 5-8-13 **53** JimCrowley 2 46
(D K Ivory) *chsd ldrs on outer: wandered u.p 2f out: fdd* **3/1**[1]

003 **10** *hd* **White's Ruby**[27] 5175 3-8-9 **50** (b[1]) PaulEddery 7 43
(B Smart) *pressed ldrs: edgd lft then rt u.p fr 2f out: wknd fnl f* **14/1**

3405 **11** *11* **Chalentina**[19] 5391 4-8-13 **53** IanMongan 3 13
(P Howling) *pushed along on outer bef 1/2-way: bhd over 2f out: t.o* **10/1**

1m 12.15s (-1.55) **Going Correction** -0.25s/f (Stan)
WFA 3 from 4yo+ 1lb **11** Ran SP% **124.6**
Speed ratings (Par 101): **100,99,97,96,95 95,94,93,93,92 78**
CSF £50.80 CT £590.41 TOTE £5.30: £1.50, £2.30, £6.40; EX 37.30.
Owner Clarke Gammon Wellers I **Bred** Ambersham Stud **Trained** Liphook, Hants

FOCUS
A very moderate handicap, but solid form for the grade.
Monashee Prince(IRE) Official explanation: jockey said gelding was denied a clear run
Meikle Barfil Official explanation: jockey said gelding was denied a clear run

5898 DIGIBET SPORTS BETTING MEDIAN AUCTION MAIDEN STKS 1m 4f (P)
8:20 (8:21) (Class 6) 3-5-Y-O £2,047 (£604; £302) Stalls Centre

Form RPR

4-53 **1** **Top Tiger**[85] 3399 3-9-3 67 JimmyQuinn 6 66
(M H Tompkins) *hld up in rr: prog and sltly hmpd over 3f out: hdwy to chse ldr wl over 1f out: styd on to ld last 150yds: sn clr* **5/2**[2]

5653 **2** *3* **Trump Call (IRE)**[49] 4504 3-9-3 65 SebSanders 5 62
(R M Beckett) *hld up in midfeld: prog over 3f out: led over 2f out: drvn and hdd last 150yds: one pce* **7/4**[1]

335 **3** *5* **Yab Adee**[19] 5390 3-8-10 67 TalibHussain(7) 2 54
(M P Tregoning) *t.k.h: prom on outer: outpcd wl over 2f out: plugged on to take 3rd nr fin* **12/1**

4 *1* **Ramvaswani (IRE)**[6] 4123 4-9-7 0 JerryO'Dwyer(3) 7 52
(N B King) *chsd ldrs: rdn and prog to go 2nd over 4f out: led 3f out to over 2f out: sn btn* **25/1**

0 **5** *6* **Stroppi Poppi**[53] 4392 3-8-12 0 FrankieMcDonald 1 37
(Jean-Rene Auvray) *dwlt: mostly last: rdn over 4f out: passed toiling rivals fr over 2f out* **100/1**

6000 **6** *9* **Versatile**[26] 5204 4-9-10 54 (bt) RobertHavlin 3 28
(G A Ham) *led to 3f out: sn wknd* **100/1**

0-00 **7** *3* **Pearl Of Esteem**[14] 5546 4-8-12 50 JCorrigan(7) 4 18
(Mrs C A Dunnett) *hld up in midfield on inner: nt clr run 3f out: sn u.p and outpcd* **100/1**

03 **8** *2* **Princess Danehill (IRE)**[19] 5390 3-8-12 0 NelsonDeSouza 9 15
(P F I Cole) *in tch tl wknd 3f out* **16/1**

3 **9** *4* **Dart**[14] 5530 3-8-12 0 KerrinMcEvoy 8 9+
(J R Fanshawe) *hld up in last pair: in tch whn hmpd over 3f out: nt rcvr and eased* **13/2**

00-0 **10** *10* **Balfour House**[20] 5345 4-9-10 35 RichardThomas 12 —
(C Roberts) *prom on inner tl wknd over 3f out: t.o* **100/1**

-000 **11** *hd* **Keagles (ITY)**[38] 4859 4-9-0 44 NataliaGemelova(5) 11 —
(J E Long) *t.k.h: trckd ldr to over 4f out: wknd rapidly: t.o* **100/1**

0303 **U** **Driving Miss Suzie**[21] 5342 3-8-9 63 (b) WilliamBuick(3) 10 —
(A M Balding) *sn hld up towards rr: effrt whn stmbld and uns rdr over 3f out* **4/1**[3]

2m 34.18s (-2.72) **Going Correction** -0.25s/f (Stan)
WFA 3 from 4yo 7lb **12** Ran SP% **120.6**
Speed ratings (Par 101): **99,97,93,93,89 83,81,79,77,70 70,—**
CSF £7.36 TOTE £4.80: £1.20, £1.10, £4.70; EX 10.70.
Owner Chris Tremewan **Bred** M P Bowring **Trained** Newmarket, Suffolk

FOCUS
A weak maiden which saw the field come home strung out. The runner-up sets the level.
Dart Official explanation: jockey said filly lost its action

5899 TFM NETWORKS H'CAP 1m 4f (P)
8:50 (8:54) (Class 6) (0-65,68) 3-Y-O £2,047 (£604; £302) Stalls Centre

Form RPR

-506 **1** **Ommadawn (IRE)**[38] 4858 3-9-0 **61** (t) KerrinMcEvoy 3 68
(J R Fanshawe) *hld up in last pair: prog on inner over 2f out: qcknd to ld 1f out: drvn out* **14/1**

5-24 **2** *nk* **Perfect Reward**[21] 5342 3-9-4 **65** JimCrowley 7 72
(Mrs A J Perrett) *hld up in midfield: prog on outer 2f out: led briefly jst over 1f out: hung lft fnl f: styd on* **8/1**

0400 **3** *1/2* **She's So Pretty (IRE)**[21] 5342 3-8-12 **59** (e[1]) ChrisCatlin 8 65
(W R Swinburn) *hld up in rr: rdn fr 4f out: prog u.p after: styd on fr over 1f out on outer: nrst fin* **25/1**

060 **4** *shd* **Bugsy's Boy**[149] 1523 3-8-4 **51** FrancisNorton 2 57
(P W D'Arcy) *hld up wl in rr: outpcd 4f out and wl bhd: prog 3f out: rdn and styd on wl fnl 2f: hopeless task* **12/1**

3600 **5** *shd* **Colonel Flay**[33] 5014 3-9-0 **61** RobertHavlin 12 68+
(Mrs P N Dutfield) *hld up wl in rr: prog whn nt clr run and swtchd lft 2f out: drvn and kpt on: unable to chal* **20/1**

0221 **6** *1* **Little Carmela**[28] 5132 3-9-1 **62** SaleemGolam 6 66+
(S C Williams) *dwlt: rousted along to go prom: rdn over 2f out: kpt on but outpcd fr over 1f out* **11/4**[1]

0000 **7** *1 1/4* **Mystical Moon**[18] 5426 3-8-10 **57** ow1 (b) RichardHughes 9 59+
(Lady Herries) *led after 1f: increased pce fr 4f out: hdd jst over 1f out: folded tamely* **10/1**

6621 **8** *1 1/4* **Chunky's Choice (IRE)**[8] 5709 3-9-7 **68** 6ex DarryllHolland 13 68
(J Noseda) *prom: chsd ldr over 2f out: nt qckn wl over 1f out: steadily lost pl after* **4/1**[2]

4300 **9** *1/2* **Woolfall Rose**[31] 5068 3-9-1 **62** JimmyQuinn 14 61
(G G Margarson) *hld up in midfield on inner: gng strly over 2f out: rdn and effrt sn after: fnd nil over 1f out* **20/1**

0000 **10** *6* **Christalini**[21] 5342 3-8-12 **59** PatDobbs 10 49
(J C Fox) *hld up in last: effrt 3f out: nvr on terms* **25/1**

4151 **11** *13* **Spritza (IRE)**[14] 5531 3-9-3 **64** HayleyTurner 11 33
(M L W Bell) *led 1f: chsd ldr to over 2f out: wknd rapidly over 1f out* **5/1**[3]

0001 **12** *8* **Present**[14] 5542 3-8-6 **53** NelsonDeSouza 5 9
(M J Gingell) *cl up tl wknd over 4f out: t.o* **33/1**

0510 **13** *19* **Sangfroid**[27] 5158 3-8-7 **54** (b[1]) SebSanders 1 —
(Sir Mark Prescott) *prog to dispute 2nd 8f out: rdn 1/2-way: wknd rapidly over 4f out: sn t.o* **15/2**

2m 31.52s (-5.38) **Going Correction** -0.25s/f (Stan) **13** Ran SP% **129.8**
Speed ratings (Par 99): **107,106,106,106,106 105,104,104,103,99 91,85,73**
CSF £123.13 TOTE £20.20: £3.20, £3.10, £7.20; EX 182.40.
Owner Mr & Mrs R Scott **Bred** Barronstown Stud And Orpendale **Trained** Newmarket, Suffolk

FOCUS
A modest handicap which produced a decent winning time for a race like this, 2.66 seconds faster than the preceding maiden, and the form looks sound. The first five all came from off the strong pace.
Ommadawn(IRE) ◆ Official explanation: trainer said, regarding apparent improvement in form, that the filly was up in trip and had a first-time tongue strap

5900 BARRETTSTOWN STUD H'CAP 7f (P)
9:20 (9:23) (Class 6) (0-55,55) 3-Y-O+ £2,047 (£604; £302) Stalls High

Form RPR

3000 **1** **Forced Upon Us**[22] 5299 3-9-0 **55** (b) RichardHughes 12 65
(P J McBride) *cl up gng wl: effrt on inner to ld over 1f out: drvn and pressed after: hld on all out* **13/2**

2056 **2** *nk* **Emma Jean Lad (IRE)**[28] 5134 3-9-0 **55** JohnEgan 5 64
(J S Moore) *prom: reminders over 3f out: drvn to chal over 1f out: pressed wnr fnl f: nt qckn and jst hld* **6/1**[3]

000 **3** ½ **Dancing Duo**[28] 5136 3-9-0 **55**....(v) DaneO'Neill 9 62+
(D Shaw) *s.i.s: hld up in rr: prog on inner fr over 2f out: clsd on ldng pair fnl f: nt quite able to chal* **33/1**

0006 **4** 1¼ **Ganache (IRE)**[7] 5730 5-8-11 **50**.... FrancisNorton 14 54
(P R Chamings) *t.k.h: mde most to over 1f out: one pce* **7/2**[1]

0000 **5** 5 **Sovereignty (JPN)**[21] 5340 5-9-1 **54**.... JimCrowley 13 45
(D K Ivory) *t.k.h: w ldr to 2f out: fdd* **11/2**[2]

0006 **6** hd **Convince (USA)**[2] 5864 6-8-13 **52**....(p) RobertHavlin 10 42
(J M Bradley) *hld up in midfield on inner: rdn over 2f out: outpcd and btn over 1f out* **8/1**

0000 **7** hd **Theatre Royal**[8] 5708 4-8-7 **53**....(b) JamieHamblett(7) 4 42
(Mouse Hamilton-Fairley) *rdn in midfield after 3f: nvr on terms: no ch over 1f out* **16/1**

0002 **8** 1¾ **Wodhill Be**[13] 5566 7-8-4 **48**.... LukeMorris(5) 8 33
(D Morris) *hld up in midfield: cl enough over 2f out: edgd lft and wknd over 1f out* **8/1**

060 **9** ½ **I'm Agenius**[19] 5390 4-8-9 **48**.... TGMcLaughlin 7 31
(C Roberts) *wl in rr: drvn 3f out: no real prog* **100/1**

0020 **10** nk **Wisdom's Kiss**[35] 4931 3-9-0 **55**.... JimmyQuinn 2 38
(J D Bethell) *s.i.s: wl in rr on outer: sme prog 2f out: nvr on terms: wknd fnl f* **16/1**

0300 **11** 1 **Quantum Leap**[9] 5687 10-9-2 **55**....(v) SebSanders 1 35
(S Dow) *racd v wd: a in rr: pushed along and no prog over 2f out* **8/1**

4300 **12** nk **Musical Locket (IRE)**[20] 5366 3-8-9 **50**.... BThomas 11 29
(J C Fox) *detached in last after 2f: nvr a factor* **33/1**

0000 **13** nk **Golden Square**[4] 5817 5-8-6 **50**....(p) KirstyMilczarek(5) 3 28
(A W Carroll) *chsd ldrs on outer tl wknd u.p wl over 2f out* **14/1**

6000 **14** 2 **Fervent**[48] 4529 3-9-0 **55**.... RichardThomas 6 28
(J M Bradley) *trckd ldrs tl wknd rapidly over 2f out* **33/1**

1m 24.96s (-1.84) **Going Correction** -0.25s/f (Stan)
WFA 3 from 4yo+ 2lb **14** Ran SP% **126.8**
Speed ratings (Par 101): **100,99,99,97,91 91,91,89,88,88 87,87,86,84**
CSF £46.89 CT £1267.15 TOTE £10.90: £2.70, £2.10, £7.70; EX 60.50 Place 6 £1,024.44, Place 5 £661.21.
Owner Mrs Julie King **Bred** Lady Fairhaven **Trained** Newmarket, Suffolk

FOCUS
A low-grade handicap which saw the first four finish clear of the remainder. Modest form, but sound enough.
Forced Upon Us Official explanation: trainer said, regarding apparent improvement in form, that the gelding travelled better in blinkers and appreciated the drop back to 7f
Golden Square Official explanation: jockey said gelding hung left
T/Plt: £1,327.10 to a £1 stake. Pool: £61,175.50. 33.65 winning tickets. T/Qpdt: £462.80 to a £1 stake. Pool: £5,754.80. 9.20 winning tickets. JN

5281 NEWCASTLE (L-H)
Wednesday, October 3

OFFICIAL GOING: Good (good to soft in places; 7.4)
The ground was reckoned 'just on the slow side of good'.
Wind: Moderate, half-against Weather: Fine

5901 ACF SPORTS PROMOTIONS MAIDEN AUCTION STKS (DIV I) 7f
2:10 (2:10) (Class 6) 2-Y-O **£1,943** (£578; £288; £144) **Stalls** High

Form RPR

25 **1** **Kiwi Bay**[56] 4279 2-8-12 0.... PhillipMakin 6 76+
(M Dods) *trckd ldrs: led jst ins fnl f: sn clr: easily* **6/4**[1]

00 **2** 2 **Dolly No Hair**[40] 4781 2-8-12 0.... TonyHamilton 9 71
(D W Barker) *led tl hdd jst ins fnl f: no ch w wnr* **100/1**

2603 **3** 5 **Creative (IRE)**[11] 5624 2-8-12 71.... NCallan 1 57
(M H Tompkins) *chsd ldrs: one pce fnl 2f* **9/4**[2]

4 1½ **Montefiore (IRE)** 2-8-12 0....(t) MickyFenton 10 53
(M Botti) *s.i.s: hdwy over 1f out: nvr nr ldrs* **14/1**

3000 **5** ½ **Emef Princess**[33] 5015 2-8-4 45....(b[1]) AndrewMullen(7) 7 47
(K A Ryan) *chsd ldrs: wknd over 1f out* **50/1**

0 **6** nk **Evette**[7] 5727 2-8-4 0.... RoystonFfrench 8 43
(M Johnston) *chsd ldrs: sn drvn along: wknd over 1f out* **16/1**

434 **7** ½ **Moment's Notice**[8] 5707 2-9-1 0.... KDarley 4 52+
(S Kirk) *sn trcking ldrs on outside: eased 2f out* **9/2**[3]

03 **8** 1½ **East Coast Girl (IRE)**[41] 4733 2-8-10 0.... LiamJones 3 43
(S W Hall) *hld up towards rr: effrt over 3f out: edgd lft and wknd over 1f out* **14/1**

0006 **9** 3½ **Howe's Jack (IRE)**[8] 5699 2-8-2 40.... DanielleMcCreery(7) 5 33
(M C Chapman) *dwlt: a towards rr* **100/1**

0000 **10** 9 **Big Slick (IRE)**[13] 5550 2-8-12 46.... DaleGibson 2 12
(M Brittain) *prom: drvn over 3f out: sn lost pl and bhd* **100/1**

11 dist **Maid Of Lamancha** 2-8-4 0.... DO'Donohoe 11 —
(J R Weymes) *slowly away: hung lft thrght: in rr: virtually p.u over 1f out: t.o: lame* **20/1**

1m 27.88s (-0.14) **Going Correction** -0.175s/f (Firm) **11** Ran SP% **117.9**
Speed ratings (Par 93): **93,90,85,83,82 82,81,80,76,65 —**
CSF £213.47 TOTE £3.20: £1.10, £14.10, £1.10; EX 333.20 TRIFECTA Not won..
Owner Kiwi Racing **Bred** Templeton Stud **Trained** Denton, Co Durham
■ Both divisions of this maiden were worth just £1,519 to the winning owner.

FOCUS
Probably just a very ordinary maiden auction race but an easy winner, who only ran to form in success, and a much improved effort from the runner-up. The overall value of the form is limited by the 45-rated fifth.

NOTEBOOK
Kiwi Bay, held back waiting for better ground, travelled strongly and scored with plenty in hand. He has plenty of potential. (op 5-4 tchd 11-10 and 13-8, 7-4 in places)
Dolly No Hair, who had beaten just three horses in two previous starts, seemed to show vastly improved form after a five-week break. He finished clear of a 71-rated animal and cannot expect a lenient nursery mark. (op 80-1)
Creative(IRE), who is not that big, was having his sixth start. (op 3-1)
Montefiore(IRE), a May foal, is narrow and moved short to post. After a tardy start, he picked up in encouraging fashion late on. Official explanation: jockey said colt had a breathing problem (op 16-1)
Emef Princess, tried in blinkers this time, is not progressing and she seemed to find the seventh furlong a bridge too far.
Evette, a cheap buy, is nothing to look at. At least she ran in a straight line this time, tried on turf, but she has plenty to find if she is to make any mark.
Moment's Notice was still in the firing line when heavily eased and he was afterwards reported to have a breathing problem. Official explanation: jockey said gelding had a breathing problem (tchd 5-1)
East Coast Girl(IRE) Official explanation: jockey said filly hung left-handed throughout
Big Slick(IRE) Official explanation: jockey said colt lost its action
Maid Of Lamancha Official explanation: jockey said filly hung left-handed from halfway and finished lame

5902 ACF SPORTS PROMOTIONS MAIDEN AUCTION STKS (DIV II) 7f
2:40 (2:41) (Class 6) 2-Y-O **£1,943** (£578; £288; £144) **Stalls** High

Form RPR

2 **1** **Reel Buddy Star**[40] 4770 2-8-10 0 ow1.... DanielTudhope 6 73
(G M Moore) *hld up in tch: smooth hdwy over 2f out: rdn to ld over 1f out: styd on strly* **4/1**[3]

2 1¼ **Tamasou (IRE)** 2-8-9 0.... DominicFox(3) 9 72
(S Parr) *prom: effrt over 2f out: chsd wnr 1f out: kpt on fin* **50/1**

5454 **3** 5 **Countrywide Comet (IRE)**[22] 5298 2-8-12 59.... NCallan 8 58
(K A Ryan) *cl up: led over 2f out to over 1f out: sn outpcd* **2/1**[1]

4 1¼ **Hawk Mountain (UAE)** 2-8-12 0.... GrahamGibbons 5 55
(J J Quinn) *s.i.s: rn green in rr: kpt on fnl f: nrst fin* **14/1**

54 **5** nk **Geezers Colours**[57] 4247 2-8-12 0.... PatCosgrave 3 54
(K R Burke) *hld up in tch: hdwy on outside and ch over 2f out: wknd over 1f out* **9/4**[2]

0400 **6** 2½ **Lavemill (IRE)**[16] 5477 2-8-4 37.... PaulHanagan 4 39
(R F Fisher) *trckd ldrs tl rdn and wknd fr 2f out* **100/1**

4 **7** 1½ **Lu's Woman**[14] 5521 2-8-4 0.... DaleGibson 2 35
(M W Easterby) *bhd: pushed along over 2f out: nvr able to chal* **7/1**

0605 **8** 7 **Straight (IRE)**[57] 4247 2-8-12 60.... KDarley 10 24
(M Brittain) *led to over 2f out: edgd lft and wknd wl over 1f out* **9/1**

0500 **9** 2 **Caribbean Cruiser**[55] 4328 2-8-9 54.... MarkLawson(3) 7 19
(Garry Moss) *towards rr: drvn 1/2-way: sn struggling* **50/1**

0 **10** 25 **Spooky**[23] 5281 2-8-9 0.... PaulFessey 1 —
(W Storey) *s.s and wnt bdly rt s: t.o thrght* **100/1**

1m 27.62s (-0.40) **Going Correction** -0.175s/f (Firm) **10** Ran SP% **119.2**
Speed ratings (Par 93): **95,93,87,86,86 83,81,73,71,42**
CSF £180.39 TOTE £5.50: £2.00, £9.90, £1.10; EX 234.40 TRIFECTA Not won..
Owner J W Armstrong & M J Howarth **Bred** M Pennell **Trained** Middleham Moor, N Yorks

FOCUS
A very moderate event in which the field raced stands' side and the pace was only fair. The exposed third and sixth ran to form.

NOTEBOOK
Reel Buddy Star, who shaped with a degree of promise in an ordinary claimer on his debut over this course and distance in August, bettered that effort on this first run for new connections. He will have no problems with 1m and may do better in run-of-the-mill handicaps. (op 9-2)
Tamasou(IRE), a half-brother to a winner in Italy, was very easy to back but showed ability on this racecourse debut. This was not much of a race but he may do better over a bit further once handicapped.
Countrywide Comet(IRE), who has shown ability at a modest level, once again underlined his vulnerability in this type of event. The step into modest nursery company or a drop in grade may be required if he is to get off the mark. (op 5-2)
Hawk Mountain(UAE) ♦, a 9,000gns half-brother to fair 1m2f performer Garrulous, took the eye in the paddock as a workmanlike sort with plenty of scope and he caught the eye in the race after being too green to do himself justice. He will be suited by a mile and beyond and appeals as the sort to win a small event in due course. (op 12-1)
Geezers Colours failed to build on the bit of improvement he had shown at Catterick on his previous start but he is now eligible for a handicap mark and may do better in low-grade nursery company. (tchd 5-2 in places)
Lavemill(IRE), exposed as poor, was not totally disgraced in the face of a stiff task but she is always going to look vulnerable in this type of event. Official explanation: jockey said filly hung left throughout
Straight(IRE) Official explanation: jockey said colt hung left throughout
Spooky Official explanation: jockey said gelding missed the break and veered right and hung right-handed throughout

5903 DREAM STARTS HERE/E.B.F. MAIDEN STKS 6f
3:10 (3:17) (Class 4) 2-Y-O **£4,533** (£1,348; £674; £336) **Stalls** High

Form RPR

03 **1** **Resounding Glory (USA)**[13] 5558 2-9-3 0.... PaulHanagan 9 77+
(R A Fahey) *trckd ldrs on inner: nt clr run over 2f out: chal over 1f out: led ins fnl f: drvn out* **7/1**

034 **2** 1¼ **Hamish McGonagall**[13] 5550 2-9-3 83.... KDarley 6 73+
(T D Easterby) *t.k.h on outer: led over 1f out: edgd rt: hdd and no ex ins fnl f* **11/8**[1]

3 6 **Drill Sergeant** 2-9-3 0.... RoystonFfrench 7 55
(M Johnston) *w ldrs: edgd lft over 1f out: sn wl outpcd* **6/1**[3]

0040 **4** 2 **Piccolo Pete**[16] 5484 2-9-3 50.... DanielTudhope 8 49
(J J Quinn) *in tch: rdn over 2f out: kpt on same pce* **80/1**

0 **5** 1 **Island Music (IRE)**[39] 4818 2-8-12 0.... GrahamGibbons 5 41
(J J Quinn) *chsd ldrs: one pce fnl 2f* **12/1**

6 2½ **Capone (IRE)** 2-9-0 0.... DominicFox(3) 1 39+
(S Parr) *s.s: hdwy on wd outside over 2f out: nvr nr ldrs* **100/1**

40 **7** ¾ **Bellas Chicas (IRE)**[36] 4924 2-8-12 0.... MickyFenton 11 31
(P T Midgley) *led tl hdd & wknd over 1f out* **80/1**

0 **8** ½ **Princess Maria (USA)**[12] 5580 2-8-12 0.... TonyHamilton 12 30
(R A Fahey) *s.i.s: kpt on fnl 2f: nvr on terms* **20/1**

9 shd **Power Desert (IRE)** 2-9-3 0.... DeanMcKeown 13 34
(M Johnston) *chsd ldrs: hung lft over 2f out: sn lost pl* **16/1**

0 **10** 1½ **Senora's Best**[14] 5521 2-8-12 0.... DaleGibson 10 25
(M W Easterby) *swvd rt s: in rr and sn drvn along: nvr on terms* **100/1**

3 **11** ½ **Cathedral Walk (USA)**[79] 3582 2-9-3 0.... PatCosgrave 3 28
(K R Burke) *chsd ldrs: rdn over 2f out: wknd over 1f out* **7/2**[2]

0 **12** 9 **Glamoroso (IRE)**[142] 1706 2-9-3 0.... TomEaves 2 —
(D W Barker) *sn outpcd in rr: bhd fnl 2f* **66/1**

1m 14.53s (-0.56) **Going Correction** -0.175s/f (Firm) **12** Ran SP% **115.4**
Speed ratings (Par 97): **96,94,86,83,82 79,78,77,77,75 74,62**
CSF £15.64 TOTE £8.20: £2.50, £1.10, £2.20; EX 22.20 Trifecta £107.80 Pool £287.17 - 1.89 winning units..
Owner M Wynne **Bred** Timothy Byrnes **Trained** Musley Bank, N Yorks
■ Blindspin was withdrawn (12/1, unruly and ref to enter stalls). Deduct 5p in the £ under Rule 4.

FOCUS
The first two finished clear but the overall value of the form is held down by the 50-rated fourth.

NOTEBOOK
Resounding Glory(USA), stepping back up in trip, never left the inside rail but was forced to bide his time. He was right on top at the finish and should give a good account of himself in nursery company. (op 9-1)
Hamish McGonagall, very keen to get on with it, took charge but edged in and in the end was very much second best. He is proving costly to follow. (tchd 13-8)
Drill Sergeant, a March foal, is related to Soldier Of Fortune. He stands over a fair amount of ground but looks on the weak side at present and may not be seen to full advantage until next year. (op 5-1 tchd 9-2)
Piccolo Pete, with the visor left off, seemed to show improved form on his fifth start. (tchd 100-1)
Island Music(IRE) again showed ability and there may be a bit better to come in time. (op 14-1)

Capone(IRE), a rangy newcomer, never turned a hair when having to be re-shod before going to the start. After a slow start he showed that he has a modicum of ability. Official explanation: jockey said colt missed the break (op 66-1)
Bellas Chicas(IRE) Official explanation: jockey said filly hung left-handed throughout
Power Desert(IRE) Official explanation: jockey said gelding hung left-handed from halfway
Cathedral Walk(USA), who has missed a couple of engagements since finishing third on his debut at Ayr in July, was most disappointing for no obvious reason. (op 6-1)

5904 PERSIMMON HOMES PLC/E.B.F. MAIDEN STKS 1m (R)
3:40 (3:43) (Class 4) 2-Y-O **£4,339** (£1,291; £645; £322) **Stalls** Centre

Form RPR
04 **1** **Redford (IRE)**[44] 4656 2-9-3 0 PaulHanagan 14 82+
(M L W Bell) *prom: smooth hdwy to ld over 2f out: shkn up to go clr appr fnl f: readily* **7/4**[2]
0 **2** 2 **Full Speed (GER)**[21] 5321 2-9-0 0 PJMcDonald[(3)] 5 72
(G A Swinbank) *hld up in midfield: smooth hdwy over 2f out: rdn to chse wnr ent fnl f: edgd lft: kpt on: no imp* **11/1**[3]
0F **3** 2 **Laterly (IRE)**[47] 4578 2-9-3 0 MickyFenton 10 68
(T P Tate) *led to over 2f out: sn one pce* **66/1**
50 **4** 2 **Eton Fable (IRE)**[49] 4487 2-9-0 0 AndrewMullen[(3)] 16 63
(W J H Ratcliffe) *midfield: drvn 1/2-way: kpt on fr 2f out: nrst fin* **66/1**
2 **5** 2 1/2 **Oberlin (USA)**[11] 5646 2-9-3 0 RoystonFfrench 8 57
(M Johnston) *midfield: drvn and outpcd 3f out: rallied 2f out: sn n.d* **11/10**[1]
0 **6** 4 **Bouggler**[64] 4037 2-9-3 0 TomEaves 12 48
(Miss J A Camacho) *s.i.s: hld up: rdn 3f out: nvr nr ldrs* **50/1**
3032 **7** nk **Hyper Viper (IRE)**[13] 5572 2-9-3 64 KDarley 13 48
(C Grant) *in tch on outside tl edgd lft and wknd fr 2f out* **14/1**
8 5 **Harrison's Star** 2-9-3 0 DanielTudhope 6 36
(G M Moore) *bhd: drvn and outpcd 1/2-way: n.d* **66/1**
00 **9** hd **Larkfield**[16] 5483 2-8-12 0 (b) LeeEnstone 4 31
(T D Easterby) *trckd ldrs tl rdn and wknd fr 2f out* **125/1**
10 2 1/2 **Moscow Oznick** 2-9-3 0 SamHitchcott 7 30
(N J Vaughan) *in tch tl rdn and wknd over 2f out* **25/1**
6000 **11** shd **Harlequinn Danseur (IRE)**[18] 5423 2-9-3 58 (vt[1]) KimTinkler 11 30
(N Tinkler) *cl up tl wknd fr over 2f out* **100/1**
0 **12** 3/4 **Iron Cross (IRE)**[14] 5541 2-9-3 0 JamieMackay 2 28
(Sir Mark Prescott) *s.i.s: a bhd* **33/1**
04 **13** 6 **Social Spirit (IRE)**[10] 5663 2-8-12 0 DO'Donohoe 3 9
(J R Weymes) *bhd: drvn 1/2-way: nvr on terms* **100/1**
14 2 **Endeavor** 2-9-3 0 PaulFessey 9 9
(P Monteith) *missed break: nvr on terms* **100/1**
15 3/4 **Al Mogeer (IRE)** 2-9-3 0 NCallan 1 8
(K A Ryan) *bhd: drvn and outpcd after 3f: nvr on terms* **14/1**

1m 43.3s (-0.18) **Going Correction** 0.0s/f (Good) **15** Ran SP% **122.6**
Speed ratings (Par 97): **100,98,96,94,91 87,87,82,82,79 79,78,72,70,69**
CSF £21.24 TOTE £2.70: £1.40, £2.70, £17.90; EX 22.30 TRIFECTA Not won..
Owner Highclere T'bred Racing (Housemaster) **Bred** T J Rooney **Trained** Newmarket, Suffolk

FOCUS
Little strength in depth and the favourite disappointed but nonetheless an impressive performance from Redford, who was value for more than the winning margin and is the type to hold his own in stronger company.

NOTEBOOK
Redford(IRE) ◆, who took the eye in the paddock, comes from a race at Leicester that is working out really well and, although his main market rival disappointed, he created a most favourable impression on this first run over 1m. He holds an entry in the Racing Post Trophy and, while he will have to improve a fair bit to land that prize, he does appeal as the sort to hold his own in stronger company. (op 13-8 tchd 2-1)
Full Speed(GER) did not show much on his debut at Doncaster but, while flattered by his proximity to the ready winner, he turned in a much improved effort, despite carrying his head a shade high and edging towards the far rail. He is the type to fare better in handicaps and is one to keep an eye on. (op 12-1 tchd 10-1)
Laterly(IRE), who reared and fell on his second start at this course in August, had the run of the race and bettered the form of his racecourse debut. He is another that is likely to fare better once handicapped. (tchd 80-1)
Eton Fable(IRE) turned in his best effort to date and is likely to be suited by a decent test of stamina once stepping into run-of-the-mill handicap company. (op 80-1 tchd 100-1)
Oberlin(USA), who shaped with a fair bit of promise over this trip on his debut at Wolverhampton, proved a disappointment in a race lacking strength for this first run on turf. However he is in very good hands and is worth another chance in ordinary company, especially if returned to artificial surfaces. (op 11-8)

5905 BETFRED H'CAP 1m 3y(S)
4:10 (4:14) (Class 5) (0-70,70) 3-Y-0+ **£3,562** (£1,059; £529; £264) **Stalls** High

Form RPR
0542 **1** **Crocodile Bay (IRE)**[13] 5556 4-9-7 70 AdrianTNicholls 17 81
(D Nicholls) *hld up in tch stands' side: hdwy to ld that gp over 1f out: styd on wl fnl f* **6/1**[2]
2232 **2** 2 **Mystical Ayr (IRE)**[9] 5674 5-9-2 65 PhillipMakin 13 71
(Miss L A Perratt) *chsd stands' side ldr: rdn over 2f out: kpt on fnl f: 2nd of 8 in gp* **13/2**[3]
1512 **3** 1/2 **Dechiper (IRE)**[23] 5286 5-8-13 62 RoystonFfrench 15 67+
(R Johnson) *hld up stands' side: hdwy over 1f out: kpt on wl fnl f: nrst fin: 3rd of 8 in gp* **9/2**[1]
3203 **4** 1 **White Moss (IRE)**[32] 5036 3-8-8 60 PaulFessey 11 63
(M H Tompkins) *in tch stands' side: effrt over 2f out: hung lft over 1f out: no imp: 4th of 8 in gp* **28/1**
1140 **5** shd **Esoterica (IRE)**[3] 5840 4-9-6 69 (b) DanielTudhope 9 71
(J S Goldie) *bhd stands' side tl styd on over 1f out: nrst fin: 5th of 8 in gp* **12/1**
1303 **6** 1 **Top Jaro (FR)**[13] 5553 4-8-13 62 TonyHamilton 12 62
(D W Barker) *led stands' side tl hung lft and hdd over 1f out: sn btn: 6th of 8 in gp* **12/1**
0331 **7** 1 1/4 **Magical Music**[25] 5221 4-9-0 63 NCallan 10 60
(J Pearce) *prom stands' side: drvn over 2f out: sn no ex: 7th of 8 in gp* **6/1**[2]
0520 **8** 1 3/4 **Kildare Sun (IRE)**[19] 5383 5-9-2 70 NeilBrown[(5)] 4 63
(J Mackie) *bhd far side: hdwy on outside to ld that gp appr fnl f: kpt on: no ch w stands' side: 1st of 7 in gp* **12/1**
-001 **9** 1 1/4 **Four Tel**[5] 5781 3-8-13 65 6ex SamHitchcott 2 55
(N J Vaughan) *prom far side: ev ch that gp over 1f out: kpt on u.p fnl f: 2nd of 7 in gp* **12/1**
0600 **10** 1 1/2 **Valdan (IRE)**[14] 5545 3-9-4 70 DeanMcKeown 6 57
(M A Barnes) *led far side to appr fnl f: no ex: 3rd of 7 in gp* **66/1**
6663 **11** 1/2 **Pianoforte (USA)**[10] 5664 5-8-11 60 MickyFenton 5 50
(E J Alston) *bhd far side: hdwy to chse ldrs that gp over 1f out: no ex ins fnl f: 4th of 7 in gp* **14/1**
2060 **12** 1 **Emperor's Well**[13] 5557 8-8-7 63 NSLawes[(7)] 14 46
(M W Easterby) *t.k.h: prom stands' side tl rdn and wknd over 2f out: last of 8 in gp* **33/1**
0200 **13** 3 **Fair Shake (IRE)**[13] 5556 7-8-10 59 (v) PaulHanagan 7 35
(Karen McLintock) *hld up in tch far side: effrt over 2f out: btn over 1f out: 5th of 7 in gp* **20/1**
2464 **14** shd **Shy Glance (USA)**[10] 5664 5-9-3 69 MarkLawson[(3)] 1 45
(P Monteith) *cl up far side tl rdn and no ex fr over 2f out: 6th of 7 in gp* **25/1**
5342 **15** 1/2 **Titinius (IRE)**[13] 5559 7-9-0 63 KDarley 3 38
(Micky Hammond) *in tch far side tl hung lft and wknd over 2f out: last of 7 in gp* **14/1**

1m 40.76s (-1.14) **Going Correction** -0.175s/f (Firm)
WFA 3 from 4yo+ 3lb **15** Ran SP% **120.7**
Speed ratings (Par 103): **98,96,95,94,94 93,92,90,89,87 87,86,83,83,82**
CSF £41.86 CT £168.31 TOTE £5.10: £2.90, £2.80, £1.90; EX 20.20 Trifecta £48.00 Pool £201.85 - 2.98 winning units..
Owner Ian Bishop **Bred** James And Joe Brannigan **Trained** Sessay, N Yorks

FOCUS
Seven raced on the far side but the first seven home all raced towards the stands' side. Sound form among the high-drawn group. The winner is progressing nicely in his new yard and is still well treated compared to his juvenile mark.
Top Jaro(FR) Official explanation: jockey said gelding hung left-handed throughout

5906 JONJOONEILLRACING.COM H'CAP 2m 19y
4:40 (4:40) (Class 5) (0-70,70) 3-Y-O **£3,238** (£963; £481; £240) **Stalls** Centre

Form RPR
00-2 **1** **Hora**[14] 5533 3-8-3 52 JamieMackay 10 63+
(Sir Mark Prescott) *mde all: qcknd over 3f out: hld on wl towards fin* **3/1**[2]
1120 **2** nk **Toboggan Lady**[53] 4409 3-8-6 55 RoystonFfrench 13 62
(Mrs A Duffield) *chsd ldrs: drvn over 5f out: styd on appr fnl f: no ex wl ins fnl f* **11/2**[3]
0105 **3** 1 1/4 **Blue Jet (USA)**[28] 5144 3-8-7 56 DeanMcKeown 2 62
(R M Whitaker) *prom: stdy hdwy on ins over 2f out: styd on same pce fnl f* **16/1**
2303 **4** 3/4 **Dansimar**[11] 5626 3-9-2 65 PatCosgrave 4 70
(M R Channon) *hld up in rr: hdwy 3f out: rdn over 1f out: kpt on same pce* **10/1**
0-53 **5** 1 1/2 **Group Force (IRE)**[14] 5531 3-8-9 58 ow1 NCallan 3 61
(M H Tompkins) *chsd ldrs: styd on same pce fnl 2f* **14/1**
3211 **6** 5 **Kentucky Boy (IRE)**[45] 4638 3-8-10 59 TonyHamilton 1 56
(Jedd O'Keeffe) *trckd ldrs on inner: effrt over 2f out: wknd over 1f out* **2/1**[1]
6040 **7** nk **Forrest Flyer (IRE)**[33] 5000 3-8-2 51 oh3 DO'Donohoe 5 47
(Miss L A Perratt) *hld up in rr: kpt on fnl 3f: nvr a factor* **33/1**
4460 **8** nk **President Dan**[35] 4943 3-8-3 52 PaulHanagan 12 48
(M R Channon) *in rr: drvn 6f out: kpt on fnl 2f: nvr a factor* **14/1**
3205 **9** 3/4 **Hook Money (IRE)**[11] 5647 3-8-2 51 oh1 (b) DaleGibson 6 46
(A J McCabe) *slowly into stride: in rr and pushed along: kpt on fnl 3f: nvr a factor* **33/1**
0000 **10** 1 3/4 **Currahee**[72] 3792 3-8-0 52 oh5 ow1 AndrewMullen[(3)] 11 45
(Miss J A Camacho) *in rr: drvn 6f out: sme hdwy 3f out: nvr a factor* **33/1**
6006 **11** nk **Troialini**[12] 5604 3-9-7 70 LiamJones 9 63
(S W Hall) *trckd ldrs: wknd over 1f out* **20/1**
12 1 1/4 **Ergo (FR)**[102] 3-9-1 67 (v[1]) PJMcDonald[(3)] 8 58
(James Moffatt) *in rr-div: effrt over 3f out: nvr a factor* **28/1**
0400 **13** 5 **Firestorm (IRE)**[39] 4821 3-8-2 51 oh6 PaulFessey 14 36
(C W Fairhurst) *sn chsng ldrs on outer: drvn over 4f out: lost pl 3f out* **50/1**
0030 **14** 3 **Foxxy**[23] 5283 3-8-4 53 oh6 ow2 AdrianTNicholls 15 35
(J R Norton) *trckd ldrs: drvn over 3f out: lost pl over 2f out* **20/1**
-500 **15** 11 **Starbougg**[16] 5486 3-8-8 57 ow2 TomEaves 7 25
(K G Reveley) *in rr: pushed along 6f out: bhd fnl 2f* **50/1**

3m 35.88s (0.68) **Going Correction** 0.0s/f (Good) **15** Ran SP% **127.7**
Speed ratings (Par 101): **98,97,97,96,96 93,93,93,92,92 91,91,88,87,81**
CSF £19.16 CT £240.21 TOTE £3.60: £3.30, £1.90, £6.40; EX 25.90 TRIFECTA Not won..
Owner Dr Catherine Wills **Bred** St Clare Hall Stud **Trained** Newmarket, Suffolk
■ Stewards' Enquiry : Jamie Mackay caution: used whip without giving filly time to respond.
Royston Ffrench two-day ban: used whip with excessive frequency (Oct 14-15)

FOCUS
Just a steady gallop and the winner was in pole position throughout. Limited but sound form. with more to come from Hora.
Foxxy Official explanation: trainer said filly was in season

5907 LAMBRINI GIRLS WANNA HAVE FUN/E.B.F. FILLIES H'CAP 7f
5:10 (5:11) (Class 5) (0-75,75) 3-Y-0+ **£3,465** (£1,030; £515; £257) **Stalls** High

Form RPR
431 **1** **Goodbye**[68] 3914 3-8-12 72 PJMcDonald[(3)] 3 85+
(G A Swinbank) *overall ldr far side: clr over 1f out: r.o strly* **4/1**[1]
0030 **2** 2 **Regal Quest (IRE)**[11] 5635 3-9-4 75 KDarley 15 83+
(S Kirk) *in tch stands' side: effrt and swtchd lft wl over 1f out: led that gp ins fnl f: nt rch far side wnr* **11/2**[2]
0630 **3** 2 **Indian's Feather (IRE)**[14] 5532 6-9-4 73 TomEaves 4 76
(N Tinkler) *chsd wnr far side: effrt over 2f out: kpt on same pce fnl f* **14/1**
3502 **4** hd **Eternal Legacy (IRE)**[42] 4705 5-8-6 61 oh7 AdrianTNicholls 8 63
(E J Alston) *led stands' side to ins fnl f: no ex* **10/1**
2025 **5** 1 **Tour D'Amour (IRE)**[11] 5627 4-7-13 61 oh2 LanceBetts[(7)] 13 60+
(R Craggs) *bhd stands' side tl hdwy over 1f out: nrst fin* **14/1**
160 **6** 1/2 **Dressed To Dance (IRE)**[21] 5330 3-8-9 66 PhillipMakin 1 64
(N Tinkler) *chsd far side ldrs: drvn over 2f out: one pce appr fnl f* **20/1**
0100 **7** 1 **Karmest**[12] 5602 3-8-1 61 oh4 AndrewMullen[(3)] 5 56
(A D Brown) *prom on outside of stands' side gp: ev ch over 2f out: no ex over 1f out* **40/1**
3450 **8** 3 **Gap Princess (IRE)**[13] 5556 3-8-7 64 PaulHanagan 7 51
(R A Fahey) *in tch stands' side: drvn over 2f out: sn no ex* **8/1**
-336 **9** 1 1/2 **Bussel (USA)**[10] 5662 3-8-13 70 LiamJones 6 53
(W J Haggas) *prom stands' side: rdn over 2f out: wknd wl over 1f out* **9/1**
1550 **10** 6 **Inaminute (IRE)**[47] 4589 4-9-6 75 PatCosgrave 17 42
(K R Burke) *t.k.h: w stands' side ldr tl wknd fr 2f out* **6/1**[3]
-600 **11** hd **Thumpers Dream**[11] 5620 4-9-3 72 RoystonFfrench 9 38
(I W McInnes) *bhd and sn rdn stands' side: nvr on terms* **40/1**
040 **12** 1 **Karma Llama (IRE)**[11] 5643 3-8-4 61 oh2 PaulFessey 12 25
(B Smart) *prom stands' side tl rdn and wknd fr over 2f out* **33/1**

10-0 **13** *shd* **Theoretical**[93] 3168 3-8-7 **64** DO'Donohoe 10 27
(A J McCabe) *hld up stands' side: pushed along 2f out: n.d* **33/1**

4-00 **14** *3/4* **Lansdown**[7] 5739 3-7-13 **61** oh9 (p) KellyHarrison[(5)] 11 22
(R Johnson) *in tch stands' side tl wknd over 2f out* **100/1**

42 **15** *dist* **Fluffy**[62] 4106 4-8-9 **64** NCallan 14 —
(K A Ryan) *towards rr stands' side: rdn over 3f out: wknd over 2f out: virtually p.u fr over 1f out* **6/1**[3]

1m 26.49s (-1.53) **Going Correction** -0.175s/f (Firm)
WFA 3 from 4yo+ 2lb **15** Ran SP% **124.0**
Speed ratings (Par 103): **101,98,96,96,95 94,93,89,88,81 81,79,79,79,—**
CSF £24.17 CT £297.06 TOTE £4.00: £1.40, £2.20, £5.10; EX 28.50 Trifecta £88.30 Pool £243.78 - 1.96 winning units..
Owner Guy Reed **Bred** G Reed **Trained** Melsonby, N Yorks

FOCUS
An ordinary handicap run at a sound pace and one in which the three to race far side finished in the first six, including the winner. Those to take that route could still be better than the bare form. The form is sound amongst the larger stands'-side group.
Inaminute(IRE) Official explanation: jockey said filly hung left-handed throughout
Fluffy Official explanation: vet said filly finished lame on left-fore

5908 CLARKE FAMILY SUPPORT IJF & SIA H'CAP 5f
5:40 (5:40) (Class 6) (0-65,71) 3-Y-0+ **£2,590** (£770; £385; £192) **Stalls** High

Form RPR

5022 **1** **No Time (IRE)**[3] 5836 7-8-8 **55** PatCosgrave 6 68
(A J McCabe) *prom far side: effrt 2f out: led that gp wl ins fnl f: kpt on* **4/1**[1]

0642 **2** *1/2* **Mr Rooney (IRE)**[7] 5740 4-8-8 **55** AdrianTNicholls 7 66
(D Nicholls) *led far side to 1f out: rallied u.p: kpt on towards fin: 2nd of 7 in gp* **11/2**[2]

3166 **3** *shd* **Funfair Wane**[13] 5552 8-8-10 **64** OliveGaule[(7)] 1 75
(D Nicholls) *chsd far side ldrs: rdn to ld 1f out: hdd wl ins fnl f: kpt on: 3rd of 7 in gp* **8/1**

3332 **4** *1* **Miss Daawe**[13] 5576 3-8-6 **53** RoystonFfrench 5 60
(B Ellison) *in tch far side: sn drvn along: hdwy over 1f out: kpt on: 4th of 7 in gp* **6/1**[3]

0204 **5** *1* **Soto**[14] 5522 4-9-1 **62** DaleGibson 14 66+
(M W Easterby) *midfield stands' side: drvn 1/2-way: gd hdwy to ld gp ins fnl f: kpt on: nt rch far side: 1st of 9 in gp* **14/1**

5000 **6** *nk* **Monashee Brave (IRE)**[16] 5476 4-8-11 **58** GrahamGibbons 15 61
(J J Quinn) *prom stands' side: led appr fnl f to ins fnl f: kpt on u.p: 2nd of 9 in gp* **14/1**

4006 **7** *nk* **Henry Hall (IRE)**[3] 5836 11-8-4 **51** oh1 KimTinkler 16 53
(N Tinkler) *in tch stands' side: drvn over 2f out: r.o fnl f: 3rd of 9 in gp* **14/1**

1260 **8** *3/4* **Whozart (IRE)**[72] 3782 4-8-4 **51** oh3 PaulHanagan 8 50
(A Dickman) *dwlt: bhd stands' side: hdwy and hung lft 2f out: no imp fnl f: 4th of 9 in gp* **16/1**

2626 **9** *nk* **Petite Mac**[7] 5741 7-8-1 **55** DanielleMcCreery[(7)] 3 53
(N Bycroft) *bhd and outpcd far side: gd hdwy over 1f out: kpt on: no imp: 5th of 7 in gp* **20/1**

5004 **10** *1/2* **Dazzler Mac**[40] 4768 6-8-4 **51** oh4 (b) PaulFessey 2 47
(N Bycroft) *outpcd and bhd far side tl kpt on fnl f: n.d: 6th of 7 in gp* **28/1**

4404 **11** *shd* **Mulligan's Gold (IRE)**[25] 5232 4-8-11 **58** (p) MickyFenton 17 54
(T D Easterby) *w stands' side ldr: led 1/2-way to appr fnl f: sn no ex: 5th of 9 in gp* **10/1**

1004 **12** *1/2* **Toy Top (USA)**[7] 5740 4-8-10 **62** (b) NeilBrown[(5)] 12 56
(M Dods) *in tch stands' side: drvn 2f out: sn one pce: 6th of 9 in gp* **20/1**

2033 **13** *1 1/4* **Highland Song (IRE)**[30] 5085 4-8-1 **51** oh1 AndrewMullen[(3)] 13 40
(R F Fisher) *sn bhd stands' side: drvn 1/2-way: n.d: 7th of 9 in gp* **25/1**

0150 **14** *2* **Come What May**[18] 5420 3-8-10 **57** (bt) NCallan 4 39
(Rae Guest) *in tch far side: sn drvn along: wknd over 1f out: last of 7 in gp* **25/1**

0041 **15** *2 1/2* **Brut**[9] 5672 5-9-10 **71** 6ex (p) TonyHamilton 9 44
(D W Barker) *led stands' side to 1/2-way: wknd ent fnl f: 8th of 9 in gp* **12/1**

0000 **16** *20* **Signor Panettiere**[14] 5522 6-8-13 **60** TomEaves 11 —
(A D Brown) *prom stands' side tl wknd qckly fr 2f out: t.o: last of 9 in gp* **100/1**

60.49 secs (-1.01) **Going Correction** -0.175s/f (Firm) **16** Ran SP% **125.1**
Speed ratings (Par 101): **101,100,100,98,96 96,95,94,94,93 93,92,90,87,83 51**
CSF £22.88 CT £176.11 TOTE £5.40: £2.00, £1.60, £2.60, £1.40; EX 22.90 Trifecta £115.20 Pool £115.20 - 2.00 winning units. Place 6 £31.91, Place 5 £22.44.
Owner Paul J Dixon **Bred** Tally-Ho Stud **Trained** Babworth, Notts
■ Stewards' Enquiry : Dale Gibson caution: careless riding

FOCUS
A modest but strongly run handicap in which the far side held the clear edge this time, although there was probably no real bias either side and the form has been rated at face value. The form is solid for the grade.
Whozart(IRE) Official explanation: jockey said gelding hung left-handed throughout
T/Jkpt: £19,890.40 to a £1 stake. Pool: £84,044.24. 3.00 winning tickets. T/Plt: £33.70 to a £1 stake. Pool: £58,494.55. 1,266.60 winning tickets. T/Qpdt: £12.70 to a £1 stake. Pool: £3,878.60. 225.80 winning tickets. RY

4481 NOTTINGHAM (L-H)
Wednesday, October 3

OFFICIAL GOING: Good to firm (8.6)
Wind: Almost nil Weather: Overcast

5909 BETFAIR APPRENTICE H'CAP (PART OF THE BETFAIR "APPRENTICE TRAINING RACE" SERIES) 6f 15y
1:50 (1:50) (Class 5) (0-70,69) 3-Y-0+ **£2,914** (£867; £433; £216) **Stalls** High

Form RPR

6021 **1** **Bobby Rose**[7] 5731 4-9-5 **68** 6ex JamesO'Reilly 5 78
(D K Ivory) *prom: cl up 1/2-way: rdn to ld wl over 1f out: kpt on* **13/2**

3064 **2** *nk* **Choreography**[7] 5741 4-8-5 **59** AdeleRothery[(5)] 3 68
(D Nicholls) *sn led: rdn along 2f out: sn hdd: rallied wl u.p ins fnl f: styng on towards fin* **6/1**[3]

0516 **3** *1 1/2* **Plateau**[8] 5711 8-9-3 **66** WilliamCarson 6 71
(C R Dore) *towards rr: hdwy on outer over 2f out: sn rdn and styd on wl fnl f* **5/1**[2]

1500 **4** *shd* **Cornus**[3] 5840 5-9-3 **69** (be) RobbieEgan[(3)] 9 73+
(A J McCabe) *t.k.h: hld up in rr: hdwy and nt clr run 2f out: sn rdn and styd on strly ins fnl f* **9/2**[1]

0010 **5** *1 1/2* **Greek Secret**[6] 5747 4-8-9 **58** MCGeran 7 58
(J O'Reilly) *hld up in rr: effrt over 2f out: swtchd lft and rdn wl over 1f: kpt on fnl f: nrst fin* **14/1**

2400 **6** *2 1/2* **Currency**[28] 5130 10-8-5 **59** BarrySavage[(5)] 11 51
(J M Bradley) *in tch on stands' rail: rdn along and outpcd 1/2-way: bhd and swtchd lft 2f out: styd on u.p appr fnl f: nrst fin* **16/1**

2300 **7** *3/4* **Stir Crazy (IRE)**[3] 5834 3-8-6 **59** MatthewDavies[(3)] 4 49
(M R Channon) *hld up: hdwy to chse ldrs 2f out: sn rdn and btn* **14/1**

4200 **8** *2* **High Ridge**[23] 5272 8-8-10 **64** (p) PietroRomeo[(5)] 8 48
(J M Bradley) *midfield: rdn along over 2f out and sn btn* **28/1**

2336 **9** *1 1/4* **Haroldini (IRE)**[159] 1280 5-8-3 **55** oh8 (p) DeanHeslop[(3)] 10 35
(J Balding) *chsd ldrs: rdn along 1/2-way and sn wknd* **16/1**

2540 **10** *hd* **Joy And Pain**[60] 4180 6-8-2 **54** oh3 ow1 (v) JosephWalsh[(5)] 1 36
(M J Attwater) *sn trcking ldrs: rdn along over 2f out and sn wknd* **16/1**

0305 **11** *nk* **Grey Boy (GER)**[24] 5253 6-8-13 **67** MarkCoumbe[(5)] 2 46
(A W Carroll) *in tch on outer: rdn along 1/2-way and sn wknd* **15/2**

0000 **U** **Puskas (IRE)**[7] 5726 4-8-9 **65** (v[1]) JakePayne[(7)] 13 —
(J M Bradley) *cl up tl sddle slipped and uns rdr over 2f out* **20/1**

1m 13.3s (-1.70) **Going Correction** -0.225s/f (Firm)
WFA 3 from 4yo+ 1lb **12** Ran SP% **113.4**
Speed ratings (Par 103): **102,101,99,99,97 94,93,90,88,88 88,—**
CSF £43.17 CT £210.13 TOTE £5.40: £1.90, £2.10, £2.10; EX 36.30.
Owner T G N Burrage **Bred** Mrs L R Burrage **Trained** Radlett, Herts
■ Stewards' Enquiry : William Carson two-day ban: used whip with excessive frequency (Oct 14-15)
Adele Rothery four-day ban: used whip with excessive frequency and down the shoulder in forehand position (Oct 14-17)

FOCUS
A modest handicap, run at no more than a fair pace. A clear best on turf from winner Bobby Rose.

5910 SARREGO MEMORIAL EBF MAIDEN STKS 6f 15y
2:20 (2:42) (Class 5) 2-Y-0 **£3,886** (£1,156; £577; £288) **Stalls** High

Form RPR

26 **1** **Prohibit**[15] 5498 2-9-3 0 JimmyFortune 6 82
(J H M Gosden) *trckd ldrs: rdn to ld ins fnl f: edgd lft: r.o* **7/2**[2]

4246 **2** *1 1/4* **Mansii**[15] 5496 2-9-3 77 PatDobbs 1 78
(C E Brittain) *chsd ldrs: rdn to ld and edgd rt over 1f out: hdd and unable qck ins fnl f* **33/1**

0 **3** *1* **Mafioso**[136] 1858 2-9-3 0 GregFairley 4 75+
(M Johnston) *in tch: n.m.r and outpcd over 4f out: r.o ins fnl f* **40/1**

3 **4** *nk* **Dunn'o (IRE)**[33] 5003 2-9-3 0 PhilipRobinson 5 74
(C G Cox) *hld up: racd keenly: hdwy over 2f out: styd on same pce ins fnl f* **6/1**

30 **5** *hd* **Sweet Kiss (USA)**[20] 5353 2-8-12 0 IanMongan 9 69
(B J Meehan) *prom: rdn and ev ch over 1f out: no ex ins fnl f* **5/2**[1]

6 **6** *shd* **Lord Sandicliffe (IRE)**[12] 5587 2-9-3 0 TQuinn 14 73
(B W Hills) *chsd ldrs: outpcd 2f out: styd on ins fnl f* **50/1**

42 **7** *1* **Flowing Cape (IRE)**[12] 5587 2-9-3 0 TedDurcan 3 73+
(R Hollinshead) *led: hdd over 4f out: rdn over 2f out: styd on same pce appr fnl f* **4/1**[3]

8 *1 1/2* **Bishopbriggs (USA)** 2-9-3 0 SteveDrowne 11 66+
(D J Murphy) *s.i.s: in rr: styng on whn nt clr run ins fnl f: nvr trbld ldrs* **66/1**

9 *1 1/4* **Slugger O'Toole** 2-9-3 0 SebSanders 12 62
(G A Huffer) *w ldrs: rdn: hung lft and ev ch over 1f out: wknd ins fnl f* **20/1**

23 **10** *2 1/2* **Alsadeek (IRE)**[12] 5587 2-9-3 0 RHills 7 60+
(J L Dunlop) *w ldr: led over 4f out: rdn: edgd lft and hdd over 1f out: sn wknd* **8/1**

0 **11** *nk* **Topazes**[13] 5575 2-9-3 0 HayleyTurner 10 54
(M L W Bell) *sn outpcd* **100/1**

3 **12** *hd* **The Lady Granuaile (USA)**[55] 4328 2-8-12 0 TPO'Shea 13 48
(K A Ryan) *prom over 3f* **16/1**

0 **13** *3* **Reve Vert (FR)**[16] 5470 2-9-3 0 JimCrowley 2 44
(A W Carroll) *s.i.s: sn hung lft and outpcd* **100/1**

0 **14** *32* **Westwood Dawn**[63] 4070 2-9-3 0 TGMcLaughlin 8 —
(Mrs N Macauley) *dwlt: outpcd* **200/1**

1m 14.24s (-0.76) **Going Correction** -0.225s/f (Firm) **14** Ran SP% **118.1**
Speed ratings (Par 95): **96,94,93,92,92 92,90,88,87,83 83,83,79,36**
CSF £122.50 TOTE £5.00: £1.70, £6.80, £8.40; EX 105.50.
Owner K Abdulla **Bred** Juddmonte Farms Ltd **Trained** Newmarket, Suffolk

FOCUS
A fair maiden and the form looks sound enough rated through the runner-up.

NOTEBOOK
Prohibit, making his debut on turf, showed a decent attitude when asked to win his race and got off the mark at the third attempt. The drop in trip played into his hands and he looked suited by the fast ground, so it could be that he has more to offer now as a sprinter. However, his future would appear to lie with the Handicapper. (op 4-1 tchd 10-3)
Mansii was always handy and held every chance, but hung right when put under maximum pressure and does not look that straightforward. With an official rating of 77 he sets the standard of this form and would perhaps now benefit for the application of some headgear. (tchd 40-1)
Mafioso, ninth on his debut back in May, shaped a little better than his finishing position suggests and did enough to suggest he is now ready to tackle a stiffer test. He can build on this. (op 33-1)
Dunn'o(IRE), third on his debut at Salisbury, was held up early on this time and proved too free under restraint. He was not disgraced, but should be seen back in a better light when ridden more positively again and we have yet to see the best of this half-brother to Ashdown Express. He will also have the option of nurseries after his next run. (tchd 5-1)
Sweet Kiss(USA), outclassed in a decent renewal of the May Hill 20 days previously, was given her chance on this drop back in grade and has to rate somewhat disappointing. Perhaps the return to a longer trip is now what she requires. (op 15-8 tchd 11-4)
Lord Sandicliffe(IRE) hit a flat spot before staying on again all too late in the day. This was an improved effort as he reversed debut form with the seventh and a step up to 7f now looks in order. (op 40-1)
Flowing Cape(IRE) was unable to match the level of his latest improved effort at Newbury and failed to confirm form with the sixth. He at least now has the option of nurseries and could be ready for a step up in trip. (op 6-1 tchd 13-2)
Bishopbriggs(USA) Official explanation: jockey said he had steering problems

5911 TURFTV A MATTER OF COURSE H'CAP 2m 9y
2:50 (3:14) (Class 4) (0-85,80) 3-Y-0 **£6,477** (£1,927; £963; £481) **Stalls** Low

Form RPR

212 **1** **Shine And Rise (IRE)**[25] 5224 3-9-4 **77** PhilipRobinson 1 93+
(C G Cox) *t.k.h: hld up in tch: smooth hdwy 3f out: cl up 2f out: led over 1f out and sn clr: edgd lft ins fnl f: eased towards fin* **11/4**[2]

0401 **2** *2 1/2* **Lord Oroko**[23] 5273 3-8-9 **68** VinceSlattery 2 78
(J G M O'Shea) *hld up in rr: hdwy over 3f out: rdn along 2f out: styd on to chse wnr ins fnl f: sn no imp* **20/1**

5011 **3** *1 ½* **Make Haste (IRE)**[38] **4843** 3-9-7 **80** .... SteveDrowne 8 88
(R Charlton) *trckd ldr: niggled along 1/2-way: pushed along 5f out: rdn to chal over 2f out: drvn over 1f out and kpt on same pce* **15/8**[1]

2322 **4** *¾* **Jawaaneb (USA)**[18] **5404** 3-9-4 **77** .... RHills 7 84
(J L Dunlop) *set stdy pce: qcknd over 5f out: pushed along and qcknd over 3f out: rdn along over 2f out: hdd over 1f out and sn wknd* **6/1**

0636 **5** *2 ½* **Love Brothers**[14] **5523** 3-8-12 **71** .... TPO'Shea 6 75
(M R Channon) *hld up: effrt and sme hdwy 3f out: rdn over 2f out and sn no imp* **16/1**

1303 **6** *1 ¼* **Bollin Felix**[11] **5619** 3-9-5 **78** ....(b) DavidAllan 5 81
(T D Easterby) *trckd ldrs: pushed along over 4f out: rdn along over 3f out and sn outpcd* **11/1**

2211 **7** *1 ½* **Strobe**[13] **5561** 3-9-4 **77** .... JimCrowley 3 78
(J A Osborne) *trckd ldng pair: pushed along 4f out: rdn 3f out and sn wknd* **11/2**[3]

3m 29.98s (-3.52) **Going Correction** -0.225s/f (Firm) **7** Ran SP% **110.1**
Speed ratings (Par 103): **99,97,97,96,95 94,94**
CSF £47.65 CT £116.42 TOTE £5.10: £3.00, £5.60; EX 71.90.
Owner Gerald C S Siu **Bred** Freynestown Partners **Trained** Lambourn, Berks

FOCUS
A fair three-year-old staying handicap, run at just an average gallop. Some progressive stayers took part and this is decent form for the grade. The winner is value for around treble his winning margin.

5912 EUROPEAN BREEDERS' FUND MAIDEN FILLIES' STKS (DIV I) 1m 54y
3:20 (3:38) (Class 5) 2-Y-O **£3,238** (£963; £481; £240) **Stalls** Centre

Form RPR

63 **1** **La Rosa Nostra**[9] **5681** 2-9-0 0 .... AdamKirby 5 74
(W R Swinburn) *hld up in tch: r.o u.p to ld nr fin* **7/1**

3 **2** *nk* **Riverscape (IRE)**[22] **5308** 2-9-0 0 .... JimCrowley 7 74
(Mrs A J Perrett) *a.p: chsd ldr over 2f out: rdn to ld wl ins fnl f: hdd nr fin* **5/1**[3]

54 **3** *nk* **Burn The Breeze (IRE)**[22] **5301** 2-9-0 0 .... TedDurcan 2 73
(H R A Cecil) *chsd ldr: led over 6f out: rdn over 1f out: hdd wl ins fnl f* **7/4**[1]

55 **4** *½* **Astania**[83] **3453** 2-9-0 0 .... JimmyFortune 10 72
(P W D'Arcy) *hld up: hdwy over 2f out: rdn over 1f out: styd on* **50/1**

5 *½* **Inchwood (IRE)** 2-9-0 0 .... PhilipRobinson 6 71+
(M A Jarvis) *s.s: outpcd: hdwy and edgd lft over 1f out: nt rch ldrs* **9/1**

0 **6** *2* **Hamsat Elqamar**[12] **5596** 2-9-0 0 .... RHills 9 66+
(J H M Gosden) *s.i.s: hld up: nt clr run over 1f out: swtchd rt: shkn up and styd on ins fnl f: nvr nr to chal* **3/1**[2]

7 *7* **Sarah's First** 2-9-0 0 .... TQuinn 1 50
(E A L Dunlop) *s.i.s: sn pushed along in rr: effrt over 3f out: wknd over 2f out* **25/1**

8 *1 ¼* **Soxy Doxy (IRE)** 2-9-0 0 .... GregFairley 4 47
(M Johnston) *chsd ldrs: rdn 1/2-way: wknd 2f out* **16/1**

00 **9** *2* **Siren Call**[12] **5599** 2-9-0 0 .... SebSanders 3 46+
(W J Haggas) *led: hdd over 6f out: chsd ldr tl rdn over 2f out: wknd over 1f out: eased* **33/1**

00 **10** *2 ½* **Lady Van Gogh**[14] **5538** 2-9-0 0 .... PatDobbs 8 37
(R Hannon) *prom: rdn over 3f out: wknd over 2f out* **150/1**

1m 44.91s (-1.49) **Going Correction** -0.225s/f (Firm) **10** Ran SP% **115.8**
Speed ratings (Par 92): **98,97,97,96,96 94,87,86,84,81**
CSF £40.66 TOTE £10.30: £3.10, £1.80, £1.50; EX 42.50.
Owner The Eternal Optimists **Bred** Mrs Erna Van Doorn **Trained** Aldbury, Herts

FOCUS
A fair juvenile fillies' maiden. The first five were closely covered at the finish.

NOTEBOOK
La Rosa Nostra, making her turf debut, appreciated the step up to this longer trip and just did enough to repel her challengers at the line. She has a likeable attitude, proved suited by this sound surface, and looks a likely nursery sort. She can be expected to stay middle distances next term. (op 13-2)
Riverscape(IRE) ♦, third on her debut at Lingfield, posted another solid effort in defeat and was only just held. While her pedigree suggests a longer trip will be her game next season, this looks as far as she wants to go at present and she can be found an opening before too long. (op 11-2)
Burn The Breeze(IRE) was given a more positive ride this time and can have no excuses. She went down fighting and did nothing wrong in defeat, but she may well be better off now she is eligible to race in nurseries. An official mark in the mid-70s can now be expected. (op 2-1 tchd 9-4 in places)
Astania, stepping up again in trip, came through to run her best race to date and was not beaten far. She clearly gets all of this trip and now becomes eligible for a nursery mark.
Inchwood(IRE) ♦, a 200,000gns purchase, proved very easy to back ahead of this racecourse bow and ultimately proved very green through the race, losing ground with a sluggish start. She still finished her race with some purpose when the penny dropped, however, and it would be a surprise were she not to improve a deal for this debut experience. (op 8-1)
Hamsat Elqamar lost ground with a clumsy start before being short of room when trying to make her challenge and should be rated better than the bare form. She is still clearly very much still learning her trade.
Sarah's First Official explanation: jockey said filly was slowly into stride
Siren Call Official explanation: jockey said filly had no more to give

5913 EUROPEAN BREEDERS' FUND MAIDEN FILLIES' STKS (DIV II) 1m 54y
3:50 (4:07) (Class 5) 2-Y-O **£3,238** (£963; £481; £240) **Stalls** Centre

Form RPR

1 **Classic Legend** 2-9-0 0 .... IanMongan 5 82+
(B J Meehan) *hld up towards rr: swtchd outside and stdy hdwy over 2f out: led wl over 1f out: sn edgd lft and rdn clr ent fnl f* **22/1**

5 **2** *4* **Madame Hoi (IRE)**[12] **5592** 2-9-0 0 .... JimmyFortune 10 72+
(M R Channon) *sn led: rdn along wl over 2f out: hdd wl over 1f out: kpt on same pce appr fnl f* **4/1**[2]

3 *1 ¾* **Almamia** 2-9-0 0 .... SebSanders 6 68
(Sir Mark Prescott) *towards rr: hdwy on outer to chse ldrs over 3f out: rdn and ch over 2f out: sn drvn and kpt on same pce* **8/1**

0 **4** *1* **Italian Goddess**[22] **5301** 2-9-0 0 .... HayleyTurner 2 66
(M L W Bell) *prom on inner: rdn along 3f out and kpt on same pce fnl 2f* **16/1**

22 **5** *nk* **Forsyte Saga**[14] **5524** 2-9-0 0 .... GregFairley 8 65
(M Johnston) *prom: trckd ldr after 2f: cl up 3f out: sn rdn and wknd 2f out* **11/10**[1]

6 **6** *¾* **Secret Gem (IRE)**[27] **5162** 2-9-0 0 .... PhilipRobinson 1 64
(C G Cox) *chsd ldrs on inner: rdn along over 3f out: drvn and wknd over 2f out* **9/2**[3]

7 *½* **Rahaan (USA)** 2-9-0 0 .... JimCrowley 7 62
(C E Brittain) *trckd ldrs: effrt 3f out: sn rdn along and wknd 2f out* **50/1**

8 *9* **Ethereal Flame** 2-9-0 0 .... TedDurcan 9 42
(H R A Cecil) *s.i.s: v green and a wl bhd* **14/1**

1m 45.54s (-0.86) **Going Correction** -0.225s/f (Firm) **8** Ran SP% **115.8**
Speed ratings (Par 92): **95,91,89,88,87 87,86,77**
CSF £109.10 TOTE £19.20: £5.50, £3.00, £1.70; EX 109.30.
Owner Mrs Moira McNamara **Bred** B Walters **Trained** Manton, Wilts

FOCUS
This second division of the maiden looked just an average affair, but the debutante winner did the job in taking style.

NOTEBOOK
Classic Legend ♦, a 140,000gns purchase whose dam won a Group 3 for Mick Channon, was allowed to go off at a massive price for this racecourse debut and was presumably thought to need the run. Nevertheless she defied such market weakness and ran out a very taking winner, having the race sewn up soon after hitting the front. While this was probably just an average maiden, no doubt she will come on again for the experience and she looks a very useful filly in the making. Where she goes from here is not certain, however, and she may have to be put away for the season now as opportunties in a higher grade over this sort of trip are few and far between. (op 14-1)
Madame Hoi(IRE), well backed, had her chance from the front and was made to look one-paced when the eventual winner asserted for home. She must learn to settle a little better, and her Classic entries for next year do look very ambitious at this stage, but she still has ability and ought to find an opening as she becomes more experienced. (op 13-2 tchd 7-1)
Almamia, the fourth foal of Alborada, who was a top-class middle-distance filly for this yard, proved easy to back and ran green through the race. She still looks a little weak and will no doubt benefit for this debut run. (op 9-2)
Italian Goddess did not do a great deal wrong and posted a slight improvement from her debut effort 22 days previously. She will have the option of nurseries after her next assignment. (tchd 18-1)
Forsyte Saga, a runner-up on both her previous outings, was done with before the 2f pole and ran well below her recent level. She has something to prove after this, but now qualifies for a nursery mark and it is far too soon to be writing her off. (op 11-8 tchd 6-4 in a place)
Secret Gem(IRE), up in trip, was not given too hard a time when her chance became apparent and again left the impression she would come on for the run. (op 6-1)

5914 BEST UK RACECOURSES ON TURFTV NURSERY 1m 1f 213y
4:20 (4:32) (Class 5) (0-75,75) 2-Y-O **£2,914** (£867; £433; £216) **Stalls** Low

Form RPR

0332 **1** **La Columbina**[14] **5527** 2-9-5 **73** .... PatDobbs 1 76+
(R Hannon) *chsd ldrs: led over 1f out: rdn out* **11/2**[2]

2425 **2** *½* **Altitude**[11] **5646** 2-9-5 **73** .... SebSanders 5 75+
(Sir Mark Prescott) *hld up: hdwy u.p fr over 2f out: edgd lft over 1f out: r.o* **7/1**

506 **3** *1 ¼* **Warming Up (IRE)**[14] **5526** 2-8-7 **61** .... PhilipRobinson 3 61
(C E Brittain) *s.i.s: sn mid-div: hdwy over 3f out: rdn over 1f out: styd on same pce ins fnl f* **25/1**

0600 **4** *1 ½* **Ovthenight (IRE)**[28] **5127** 2-8-7 **61** .... DavidKinsella 14 58
(Mrs P Sly) *led: hdd over 8f out: chsd ldr: rdn to ld over 2f out: hdd over 1f out: styd on same pce* **40/1**

0001 **5** *¾* **Mganga**[7] **5736** 2-8-8 **69** 6ex .... MatthewDavies(7) 13 64
(M R Channon) *hld up: hdwy and hung lft over 1f out: styd on same pce ins fnl f* **16/1**

2513 **6** *1 ¾* **Destinys Dream (IRE)**[6] **5746** 2-9-2 **73** .... DuranFentiman(3) 6 65
(Mrs A Duffield) *chsd ldrs: rdn over 2f out: wknd ins fnl f* **11/1**

2102 **7** *shd* **Townkab (IRE)**[12] **5600** 2-8-12 **66** .... TGMcLaughlin 4 57
(N P Littmoden) *hld up: hdwy over 3f out: rdn and edgd lft over 2f out: ev ch over 1f out: wknd ins fnl f* **10/1**

6035 **8** *6* **Boomtown**[37] **4892** 2-9-4 **72** .... GregFairley 2 51
(M Johnston) *w ldr: led over 8f out: rdn and hdd over 2f out: wknd over 1f out* **13/2**[3]

0040 **9** *nk* **Dream Bee**[22] **5298** 2-8-10 **64** .... RHills 15 43
(E A L Dunlop) *chsd ldrs: rdn and hmpd over 2f out: wknd over 1f out* **16/1**

0464 **10** *1 ¾* **Smith Esquire (USA)**[28] **5127** 2-8-8 **62** .... AdamKirby 8 37
(W R Swinburn) *hld up: rdn over 3f out: wknd over 1f out* **16/1**

060 **11** *1 ¼* **Redesdale**[12] **5605** 2-8-11 **65** .... JimCrowley 16 38
(P W D'Arcy) *s.i.s: hld up: bhd fnl 4f* **33/1**

641 **12** *shd* **Lanterns Of Gold**[16] **5485** 2-9-5 **73** .... JimmyFortune 10 46
(Mrs A Duffield) *mid-div: rdn 1/2-way: hung lft and wknd over 2f out* **4/1**[1]

204 **13** *1 ¼* **Isent She Rich (IRE)**[73] **3760** 2-9-7 **75** .... TedDurcan 9 45
(M G Quinlan) *hld up: rdn 1/2-way: a in rr* **20/1**

654 **14** *2* **Bozeman Trail**[26] **5186** 2-9-2 **70** .... TQuinn 7 36
(P F I Cole) *prom: rdn over 3f out: n.m.r and wknd over 2f out* **16/1**

6022 **15** *2 ½* **Natural Rhythm (IRE)**[7] **5736** 2-8-10 **64** .... HayleyTurner 12 25
(D W Chapman) *mid-div: hdwy 1/2-way: wknd over 3f out* **16/1**

060 **16** *28* **Valiant Vicar (USA)**[37] **4882** 2-9-0 **68** ....(b[1]) SteveDrowne 11 —
(B J Meehan) *s.i.s: sn outpcd and bhd* **66/1**

2m 8.80s (-0.90) **Going Correction** -0.225s/f (Firm) **16** Ran SP% **123.5**
Speed ratings (Par 95): **94,93,92,91,90 89,89,84,84,82 81,81,80,79,77 54**
CSF £41.99 CT £912.62 TOTE £5.50: £1.90, £2.80, £5.20, £4.90; EX 37.60.
Owner Raymond Tooth **Bred** P And Mrs A G Venner **Trained** East Everleigh, Wilts
■ Stewards' Enquiry : Seb Sanders two-day ban: used whip with excessive frequency (Oct 14-15)

FOCUS
A modest fillies' nursery, which would have respresented a real stamina test, run at an average pace.

NOTEBOOK
La Columbina relished the longer distance, as could have been expected after her latest effort on Polytrack, and got off the mark at the fifth time of asking. She won this in good style and there is little reason why she cannot go in again. (op 7-1 tchd 5-1)
Altitude emerged from off the pace to run an improved race in defeat and the step up to this trip helped. She also went well on the quicker ground. (tchd 15-2)
Warming Up(IRE), making his nursery bow, did not help his cause with a slow start and again had to come from behind. He still posted his best effort to date, however, and got the longer trip without fuss.
Ovthenight(IRE) was given an aggressive ride over this longer distance and was not at all disgraced. He looks very one-paced, but is going the right way now.
Mganga, penalised for his Redcar success a week previously, finished his race well after being set a fair bit to do and reversed Beverley form with the sixth in the process. (op 14-1)
Dream Bee Official explanation: jockey said filly hung left-handed throughout
Lanterns Of Gold tended to hang left when put under pressure and failed to convince she wants this extra furlong, but was still someway below her previous best. (op 9-2)

Bozeman Trail Official explanation: jockey said colt lost its action 2 1/2f out

5915 TURFTV.CO.UK MAIDEN STKS — 1m 54y

4:50 (5:04) (Class 5) 3-Y-O+ — **£3,238** (£963; £481; £240) **Stalls** Centre

Form — RPR

1 **Northern Spy (USA)** 3-9-3 0 .... SteveDrowne 13 — 81+
(Saeed Bin Suroor) *midfield: hdwy 3f out: rdn to chse ldrs wl over 1f out: edgd lft and styd on ins fnl f to ld nr fin* — **6/1**^{3}

2 ½ **Tazeez (USA)** 3-9-3 0 .... RHills 11 — 80
(J H M Gosden) *trckd ldrs: smooth hdwy over 3f out: led wl over 2f out: sn pushed clr: rdn ins fnl f: hdd and no ex towards fin* — **8/1**

2- 3 ¾ **Eco Centrism**^{384} 5321 3-9-3 0 .... SebSanders 12 — 78+
(W J Haggas) *t.k.h: hld up in rr: hdwy whn nt clr run and swtchd rt wl over 2f out: effrt to chse ldrs over 1f out: sn rdn and kpt on ins fnl f* — **15/8**^{1}

4- 4 4 **Drawn Gold**^{362} 5790 3-9-3 0 .... JimCrowley 8 — 69
(R Hollinshead) *midfield: hdwy 3f out: sn rdn along and styd on wl appr fnl f: nrst fin* — **25/1**

0523 5 3 ½ **Timber Treasure (USA)**^{19} 5384 3-9-3 73 ....(v) TedDurcan 15 — 61
(H R A Cecil) *chsd ldrs: rdn along over 2f out: drvn and wkng whn hung rt ent fnl f* — **13/2**

606/ 6 ½ **Grey Gurkha**^{1187} 3512 6-9-6 45 ....(t) GregFairley 16 — 60
(B Ellison) *chsd ldrs: rdn along over 2f out and sn one pce* — **150/1**

7 2 **Ballad Maker (IRE)** 3-9-3 0 .... JimmyFortune 2 — 60+
(J H M Gosden) *trckd ldrs: pushed along 3f out: rdn 2f out: hld whn hmpd ent fnl f* — **11/2**^{2}

323 8 1 ¼ **O Fourlunda**^{15} 5510 3-8-12 60 .... PhilipRobinson 5 — 47
(C E Brittain) *led: rdn along over 3f out: hdd wl over 2f out and sn wknd* — **9/1**

-5 9 3 **Beautiful Dancer (IRE)**^{15} 5499 3-8-12 0 .... NickyMackay 1 — 40
(L M Cumani) *trckd ldrs: hdwy over 3f out: rdn along over 2f out and grad wknd* — **12/1**

0 10 3 **Just Crystal**^{13} 5567 3-8-12 0 .... TGMcLaughlin 9 — 33
(B P J Baugh) *a towards rr* — **150/1**

00 11 1 ¼ **Ivanasbo**^{48} 4530 3-9-3 0 .... TQuinn 10 — 35
(C G Cox) *a towards rr* — **66/1**

0005 12 nk **Arabellas Homer**^{9} 5690 3-8-9 42 .... DuranFentiman$^{(3)}$ 4 — 30
(Mrs N Macauley) *in tch: rdn along 3f out: sn wknd* — **125/1**

0000 13 1 **Perry's Pride**^{41} 4741 3-8-12 43 .... HayleyTurner 7 — 27
(Mrs G S Rees) *in tch to 1/2-way: sn wknd* — **200/1**

2060 14 25 **Cape Of Storms**^{90} 3241 4-9-1 43 ....(p) GaryBartley$^{(5)}$ 14 — —
(R Brotherton) *cl up: rdn along over 3f out and sn wknd* — **150/1**

15 27 **Quorn Master**^{483} 5-9-3 0 .... MarcHalford$^{(3)}$ 17 — —
(Mrs P Ford) *s.i.s: a bhd* — **150/1**

1m 43.44s (-2.96) **Going Correction** -0.225s/f (Firm)
WFA 3 from 4yo+ 3lb — **15** Ran SP% **115.9**
Speed ratings (Par 103): **105,104,103,99,96 95,93,92,89,86 85,84,83,58,31**
CSF £50.76 TOTE £6.50: £3.10, £3.30, £1.10; EX 29.10.
Owner Godolphin **Bred** Gainsborough Farm Llc **Trained** Newmarket, Suffolk

FOCUS
Rather muddling form at face value and little solid behind the first three, but they came clear and could well prove better than the bare form.
Cape Of Storms Official explanation: trainer said gelding ran too freely

5916 AMATEUR JOCKEYS ASSOCIATION H'CAP (FOR GENTLEMAN AMATEUR RIDERS) — 1m 1f 213y

5:20 (5:28) (Class 5) (0-70,69) 3-Y-O+ — **£2,966** (£912; £456) **Stalls** Low

Form — RPR

0432 1 **Prime Number (IRE)**^{22} 5307 5-11-3 67 .... MrJGuerriero$^{(5)}$ 8 — 81
(J Akehurst) *hld up: hdwy over 2f out: rdn over 1f out: styd on to ld wl ins fnl f* — **5/1**^{1}

0066 2 2 **King's Majesty (IRE)**^{22} 5307 5-11-10 69 .... MrJJDoyle 1 — 79
(V R A Dartnall) *hld up in tch: led over 2f out: rdn and hdd wl ins fnl f* — **10/1**

6331 3 2 **Rawdon (IRE)**^{26} 5198 6-11-4 68 ....(v) MrCPHuxley$^{(5)}$ 13 — 74
(M L W Bell) *hld up: hdwy over 3f out: rdn to ld over 2f out: sn hdd: hung lft over 1f out: no ex fnl f* — **15/2**^{3}

1133 4 3 ½ **Snark (IRE)**^{7} 5725 4-11-9 68 .... MrSWalker 2 — 67
(P J Makin) *chsd ldrs: led over 3f out: rdn and hdd over 2f out: wknd fnl f* — **5/1**^{1}

2610 5 2 **Blu Manruna**^{17} 5454 4-10-6 58 ....(b) MrAdamWest$^{(7)}$ 11 — 53
(J Akehurst) *hld up: styd on appr fnl f: nvr nrr* — **28/1**

6603 6 1 **Barbirolli**^{9} 5674 5-10-13 63 .... MrBenBrisbourne$^{(5)}$ 10 — 56
(W M Brisbourne) *hld up: swtchd lft and hdwy over 1f out: nt trble ldrs* — **7/1**^{2}

0551 7 1 ¼ **Lobengula (IRE)**^{8} 5704 5-11-5 64 6ex .... MrSDobson 16 — 55
(I W McInnes) *chsd ldrs over 7f* — **12/1**

0052 8 2 ½ **Mulaazem**^{26} 5198 4-10-13 63 .... MrPCollington$^{(5)}$ 14 — 49
(J Mackie) *mid-div: lost pl 1/2-way: n.d after* — **9/1**

613 9 shd **Ile Michel**^{28} 5132 10-11-1 60 .... MrTGreenall 12 — 45
(Lady Herries) *hld up: hdwy over 3f out: wknd over 2f out* — **14/1**

0526 10 4 **Sol Rojo**^{26} 5198 5-11-3 65 ....(v) MrSPearce$^{(3)}$ 7 — 42
(J Pearce) *s.s: hld up: sme hdwy u.p over 1f out: n.d* — **16/1**

6 11 2 ½ **Little Red Roaster (USA)**^{41} 4736 3-10-0 55 .... RichardEvans$^{(5)}$ 4 — 27
(P D Evans) *hld up: rdn over 3f out: sn wknd* — **50/1**

0403 12 ½ **Lincolneurocruiser**^{14} 5546 5-10-12 60 ....(v) MrDHutchison$^{(3)}$ 3 — 31
(Mrs N Macauley) *prom: rdn over 3f out: wknd 2f out* — **18/1**

2004 13 nk **Fabrian**^{16} 5472 9-11-2 68 .... MrMPrice$^{(7)}$ 6 — 39
(R J Price) *prom over 5f* — **14/1**

0050 14 2 ½ **Sea Frolic (IRE)**^{27} 5159 6-10-7 55 oh10 ....(p) MrOWilliams$^{(3)}$ 9 — 21
(Jennie Candlish) *chsd ldrs: rdn over 4f out: sn wknd* — **100/1**

0-00 15 13 **New Diamond**^{27} 5179 8-10-3 55 oh10 .... MrKFord$^{(7)}$ 15 — —
(Mrs P Ford) *plld hrd and prom: lost pl 8f out: bhd fr 1/2-way* — **150/1**

4020 16 1 ¾ **Surdoue**^{27} 5179 7-10-3 55 oh10 .... MrBMMorris$^{(7)}$ 5 — —
(D Morris) *led: hdd over 3f out: sn wknd* — **40/1**

2m 8.84s (-0.86) **Going Correction** -0.225s/f (Firm)
WFA 3 from 4yo+ 5lb — **16** Ran SP% **118.4**
Speed ratings (Par 103): **94,92,90,88,86 85,84,82,82,79 77,76,76,74,64 62**
CSF £51.68 CT £376.54 TOTE £6.00: £1.50, £4.00, £2.50, £2.20; EX 88.00 Place 6 £395.36, Place 5 £196.57.
Owner A D Spence **Bred** Ballylinch Stud **Trained** Epsom, Surrey

FOCUS
A modest handicap, confined to amateur riders, which saw the field finish fairly strung out. Solid form.
T/Plt: £321.80 to a £1 stake. Pool: £43,340.55. 98.30 winning tickets. T/Qpdt: £64.20 to a £1 stake. Pool: £3,462.90. 39.90 winning tickets. JR

5160 SALISBURY (R-H)

Wednesday, October 3

OFFICIAL GOING: Good to soft
Wind: Almost nil

5917 AXMINSTER CARPETS APPRENTICE H'CAP — 1m

1:30 (1:36) (Class 6) (0-65,65) 3-Y-O+ — **£3,238** (£963; £481; £240) **Stalls** High

Form — RPR

1115 1 **Ellen's Girl (IRE)**^{27} 5166 4-9-4 64 .... HaddenFrost$^{(3)}$ 11 — 80
(R Hannon) *chsd ldrs: drvn to ld ins fnl 2f: styd on to go clr fnl f: comf* — **7/1**^{3}

/-30 2 3 ½ **Call Me Punch**^{37} 4905 6-9-1 58 .... AshleyHamblett 9 — 66
(E S McMahon) *sn chsng ldr: drvn to chal 2f out: chsd wnr sn after but no ch fnl f* — **16/1**

4260 3 2 **The Grey One (IRE)**^{23} 5280 4-9-7 64 ....(p) RussellKennemore 14 — 67
(J M Bradley) *towards rr: hdwy 4f out out: styd on to chse ldrs over 1f out but nvr gng pce of ldng duo* — **12/1**

6105 4 2 **Dancing Storm**^{26} 5189 4-8-3 56 .... TimothyMeadows$^{(10)}$ 10 — 55
(W S Kittow) *led: hdd ins fnl 2f: wknd over 1f out* — **10/1**

0004 5 ½ **Blue Line**^{8} 5708 5-8-5 51 oh4 .... ThomasO'Brien$^{(3)}$ 13 — 49
(M Madgwick) *chsd ldrs: rdn and one pce fnl 2f* — **25/1**

3400 6 2 **The Gaikwar (IRE)**^{9} 5693 8-9-6 63 ....(b) LukeMorris 16 — 56
(R A Harris) *b: mid-div: rdn 3f out: styd on same pce fr over 1f out* — **16/1**

0-02 7 ¾ **Juzilla (IRE)**^{13} 5567 3-8-13 64 .... AlanRutter$^{(5)}$ 12 — 55
(W R Swinburn) *in rr tl mod prog fnl 2f* — **12/1**

3640 8 2 **Gracie's Gift (IRE)**^{27} 5166 5-9-1 58 .... JamesMillman 3 — 45+
(A G Newcombe) *lw: in rr: styd on fr over 2f out: nvr rchd ldrs* — **11/2**^{1}

3065 9 1 ¼ **Parnassian**^{50} 4481 7-9-4 64 ....(v) HarryPoulton$^{(3)}$ 15 — 48+
(J A Geake) *b: lw: mid-div 1/2-way: sn rdn and nvr in contention* — **7/1**^{3}

5600 10 ½ **Binnion Bay (IRE)**^{81} 3525 6-9-7 64 ....(b) TolleyDean 5 — 47
(J J Bridger) *in tch over 5f* — **25/1**

0530 11 4 **Greenwood**^{53} 4395 9-9-1 63 ow6 .... RyanBird$^{(5)}$ 2 — 37
(P G Murphy) *in rr tl mod prog fnl 2f* — **33/1**

-000 12 ½ **Gracechurch (IRE)**^{127} 2107 4-9-2 62 .... KMay$^{(3)}$ 7 — 34
(R J Hodges) *swtg: a towards rr* — **16/1**

3043 13 1 ½ **Scarlet Knight**^{7} 5733 4-8-13 62 ....(p) JackMitchell$^{(6)}$ 6 — 31
(P Mitchell) *chsd ldrs tl over 2f out* — **8/1**

14 1 **Monticelli (GER)**^{172} 7-9-8 65 .... PatrickHills 4 — 32
(J R Gask) *lw: a in rr* — **6/1**^{2}

3050 15 ¾ **Hamilton House**^{22} 5310 3-8-0 54 .... AshleyMorgan$^{(8)}$ 1 — 19
(M H Tompkins) *chsd ldrs over 5f* — **66/1**

5020 16 hd **Dr Synn**^{39} 4807 6-9-8 65 .... KirstyMilczarek 8 — 29
(J Akehurst) *b: chsd ldrs 5f* — **9/1**

1m 44.34s (1.25) **Going Correction** +0.25s/f (Good)
WFA 3 from 4yo+ 3lb — **16** Ran SP% **130.0**
Speed ratings (Par 101): **103,99,97,95,95 93,92,90,89,88 84,84,82,81,80 80**
CSF £118.27 CT £1362.41 TOTE £5.80: £1.80, £5.00, £2.70, £3.20; EX 136.20.
Owner Con Harrington **Bred** Mrs Chris Harrington **Trained** East Everleigh, Wilts
■ Stewards' Enquiry : Ashley Morgan one-day ban: used whip when out of contention (Oct 14)

FOCUS
An ordianary sprint, where high numbers held a big advantage. Solid form, with a big step up from Ellen's Girl.
Dr Synn Official explanation: jockey said gelding ran flat

5918 ALLIED IRISH BANK SOUTHAMPTON EBF MAIDEN STKS (DIV I) — 1m

2:00 (2:06) (Class 4) 2-Y-O — **£4,533** (£1,348; £674; £336) **Stalls** High

Form — RPR

1 **Look Here** 2-8-12 0 .... KerrinMcEvoy 13 — 80
(R M Beckett) *w'like: leggy: racd far side: chsd ldrs: led ins fnl 2f: rdn and styd on strly thrght fnl f* — **16/1**^{3}

2 2 2 ½ **Doctor Fremantle**^{52} 4417 2-9-3 0 .... RyanMoore 15 — 79
(Sir Michael Stoute) *lw: racd fast side: chsd ldrs: rdn to chal over 2f out: rdn and no imp on wnr appr fnl f: kpt on for clr 2nd* — **1/3**^{1}

0 3 1 ¼ **Ragamuffin Man (IRE)**^{14} 5538 2-9-3 0 .... PaulDoe 10 — 76
(W J Knight) *raced far side and overall ldr: hdd ins fnl 2f: one pce appr fnl f* — **16/1**^{3}

00 4 7 **Slip**^{15} 5498 2-9-0 0 .... WilliamBuick$^{(3)}$ 2 — 60
(M P Tregoning) *racd stands' side: chsd ldrs and led that gp ins fnl 3f: kpt on but a wl hld by far side gp* — **66/1**

5 ¾ **Simone Martini (IRE)** 2-9-3 0 .... RichardKingscote 3 — 58
(R Charlton) *w'like: racd stands' side and bhd: kpt on fr over 1f out to take 2nd that grnd but no ch w far side* — **50/1**

0 6 ¾ **Fort Hull (IRE)**^{23} 5274 2-9-3 0 .... GeorgeBaker 6 — 57
(Mrs A J Perrett) *w'like: racd stands' side and rr: styd on fr over 1f out to take 3rd that gp but no ch w* — **100/1**

00 7 1 ¼ **Yathreb (USA)**^{20} 5361 2-9-3 0 .... MartinDwyer 4 — 54
(J L Dunlop) *racd stands' side and led that gp 5f out: nvr gng pce of far side and hdd ins fnl 3f: wknd over 1f out: finsished 4th in gp* — **6/1**^{2}

8 shd **Tara's Garden** 2-8-12 0 .... FergusSweeney 12 — 48
(M Blanshard) *w'like: bit bkwd: racd far side: s.i.s: rr tl styd on fnl 2f: fin 4th in gp* — **100/1**

0 9 shd **Sleepy Hollow**^{20} 5361 2-9-3 0 .... RobertHavlin 14 — 53
(H Morrison) *racd far side: plld hrd and stdd towards rr: styd on fnl f: fin 5th in gp* — **33/1**

00 10 2 ½ **Bravo Bolivar (IRE)**^{43} 4683 2-9-3 0 .... JimmyQuinn 16 — 47
(J L Dunlop) *racd far side and chsd ldrs: wknd 2f out: fin 6th in gp* — **100/1**

5 11 2 **Daddy's Boy**^{26} 5206 2-9-3 0 .... OscarUrbina 7 — 43
(Mrs A J Perrett) *w'like: racd stands' side: sn chsng ldrs: wknd 2f out: fin 5th in gp* — **16/1**^{3}

12 ½ **Desiderio** 2-9-3 0 .... RichardHughes 1 — 42
(R Hannon) *str: bit bkwd: racd stands' side: a in rr: fin 6th in gp* — **25/1**

04 13 3 ½ **Zen Factor**^{60} 4162 2-9-3 0 .... JamesDoyle 8 — 34
(J G Portman) *racd far side: chsd ldrs 5f: fin 6th in gp* — **50/1**

14 1 ¾ **Banquet (IRE)** 2-9-3 0 .... DarryllHolland 5 — 30
(M R Channon) *w'like: scope: lengthy: lw: racd stands' side and sn in ld but nvr quite on terms w far side: hdd 5f out: wknd 3f out: finsished 7th in gp* — **25/1**

0 15 5 **High Dee Jay (IRE)**^{7} 5721 2-9-3 0 .... DaneO'Neill 11 — 18
(R Hannon) *racd far side: a in rr: fin 7th in gp* — **66/1**

16 2 **Promised Gold** 2-9-3 0 .... RichardThomas 9 — 14
(J A Geake) *w'like: bit bkwd: racd far side: s.i.s: a bhd: fin 8th in gp* **100/1**

1m 44.88s (1.79) **Going Correction** +0.25s/f (Good) — **16** Ran SP% **128.5**
Speed ratings (Par 97): **101,98,97,90,89 88,87,87,87,84 82,82,78,77,72 70**
CSF £22.20 TOTE £28.50: £4.90, £1.02, £4.10; EX 44.90.

Owner J H Richmond-Watson **Bred** Lawn Stud **Trained** Whitsbury, Hants

FOCUS

A fair-looking maiden, which is hard to properly assess due to the big draw bias.

NOTEBOOK

Look Here took advantage of a decent draw to beat the boys. She is bred to be a decent filly and it will be interesting to see what sort of path connections choose to take with her now, but the immediate plan was to put her away now until next spring.

Doctor Fremantle, an athletic type, was made a very short price considering the promise he showed on his debut. However, that maiden was a moderate one to say the least and he once again came up short. His attitude was slightly questionable under pressure. (op 1-2 tchd 4-7)

Ragamuffin Man(IRE) ◆ followed up his promising debut run with another good effort. He is one to keep the right side of. (op 14-1 tchd 18-1)

Slip won the race on the stands' side but had absolutely no chance with those drawn high. He had not shown any obvious promise on the Polytrack before this effort. (tchd 80-1)

Simone Martini(IRE), who was badly drawn, shaped really well after being clueless early. He could well be a decent sort in the making. (op 40-1)

Fort Hull(IRE) had no chance of winning coming down the stands' side, but he did stay on quite well for pressure.

Yathreb(USA) did not have any chance of winning from his stalls position but really should have 'won' his race. (op 5-1 tchd 13-2)

Sleepy Hollow ran a bit better than his final position suggests and could make up into a nice staying prospect in time.

Daddy's Boy Official explanation: jockey said gelding hit the rail in running

Banquet(IRE) showed good speed early but dropped out in the latter stages. Much will depend now on how he comes on for the run.

Promised Gold is an athletic type.

5919 ALLIED IRISH BANK SOUTHAMPTON EBF MAIDEN STKS (DIV II) 1m

2:30 (2:36) (Class 4) 2-Y-O **£4,533** (£1,348; £674; £336) **Stalls** High

Form	Pos	Btn	Horse / Details	RPR
4225	1		**Huzzah (IRE)**[19] 5374 2-9-3 76 MichaelHills 15 (B W Hills) *mde all: c clr fr 2f out: unchal* **7/2**[2]	88+
023	2	6	**Meer Kat (IRE)**[25] 5227 2-9-3 80 RyanMoore 7 (R Charlton) *sn mid-div: hdwy 3f out: rdn to chse wnr ins fnl 2f but nvr any ch: kpt on for clr 2nd* **5/6**[1]	74+
	3	2 1/2	**Nemo Spirit (IRE)** 2-9-3 0 RichardMullen 16 (W R Muir) *w'like: scope: s.i.s: sn mid-div: rdn 3f out: styd on to chse ldng duo over 1f out but nvr any ch* **40/1**	68
	4	2	**Driven (IRE)** 2-9-3 0 OscarUrbina 12 (Mrs A J Perrett) *unf: scope: chsd ldrs: rdn over 2f out: wknd fnl f* **33/1**	64
	5	3 1/2	**Manyriverstocross (IRE)** 2-9-3 0 DaneO'Neill 6 (A King) *unf: s.i.s: mid-div and pushed along 1/2-way: kpt on again fr over 1f out but nvr in contention* **50/1**	56
0	6	2	**Daisy Nook**[27] 5162 2-8-12 0 JDSmith 2 (S Kirk) *rr: drvn along over 3f out: mod prog fr over 1f out* **66/1**	46
06	7	4	**Seventh Hill**[11] 5633 2-9-3 0 FergusSweeney 4 (M Blanshard) *mind-div: hdwy to trck ldrs 3f out: wknd qckly appr fnl 2f* **25/1**	42
0	8	shd	**Mazara (IRE)**[11] 5628 2-9-3 0 MartinDwyer 14 (J L Dunlop) *rr: mod late prog* **40/1**	42
	9	2	**Whitcombe Spirit** 2-9-3 0 PaulDoe 1 (Jamie Poulton) *w'like: rr: effrt over 3f out: sn wknd* **80/1**	37
	10	nk	**Sarah's Boy** 2-9-3 0 JimmyQuinn 11 (S Dow) *w'like: s.i.s: a in rr* **40/1**	36
0	11	1/2	**Cape Rock**[11] 5628 2-9-3 0 SimonWhitworth 8 (C A Horgan) *w'like: chsd ldrs to 1/2-way* **50/1**	35
	12	nk	**Mista Rossa** 2-9-3 0 RobertHavlin 3 (H Morrison) *str: bit bkwd: a in rr* **33/1**	35
325	13	6	**Aboriginie (USA)**[14] 5538 2-9-3 79 KerrinMcEvoy 9 (J H M Gosden) *lw: chsd wnr tl wknd qckly ins fnl 2f* **7/2**[2]	21
0	14	6	**Karate Queen**[27] 5162 2-8-12 0 LPKeniry 13 (A M Balding) *chsd ldrs tl wknd qckly wl over 2f out* **25/1**	—
	15	3	**Fiume** 2-9-3 0 RichardHughes 10 (R Hannon) *w'like: a in rr* **16/1**[3]	—
0	16	10	**Veras Joy**[44] 4662 2-8-12 0 JamesDoyle 5 (T D McCarthy) *leggy: chsd ldrs* **100/1**	—

1m 44.69s (1.60) **Going Correction** +0.25s/f (Good) **16** Ran SP% **133.4**

Speed ratings (Par 97): **102,96,93,91,88 86,82,81,79,79 79,78,72,66,63 53**

CSF £6.84 TOTE £4.00: £1.60, £1.30, £13.20; EX 8.70.

Owner J Gale,J Finch,D Cole,R Dollar,D Powell **Bred** S And S Hubbard Rodwell **Trained** Lambourn, Berks

FOCUS

A maiden full of staying types completely blown apart by the winner Huzzah, who had already been given a few chances. He enjoyed plenty of advantages and capitalised on them.

NOTEBOOK

Huzzah(IRE) made use of his experience and highly-favourable draw to win with plenty in hand. However, it would be unwise to go too overboard about this victory considering all of the advantages he enjoyed. (op 4-1 tchd 10-3)

Meer Kat(IRE), who is officially rated 4lb higher than the winner, was not well placed to make his challenge after his rival had flown. He is worth another chance. (op 6-4 tchd 13-8)

Nemo Spirit(IRE), who looks almost white already, will presumably be a better horse with time and extra distance. This was a fair debut effort to build from. (tchd 50-1)

Driven(IRE) had every chance and kept battling away for pressure. He looks sure to benefit from further - one of his half-brothers, Copernican, stays well. (op 25-1)

Manyriverstocross(IRE) looks a backward sort who took his time to get involved. He was staying on at the one pace throughout the final furlong. (op 66-1)

Daisy Nook kept on steadily from the rear of the pack, suggesting she will be capable of going close with more experience behind her. (tchd 100-1)

Aboriginie(USA) probably paid for chasing the leader early in the race. That said, it was a disappointing effort to be beaten so far. Official explanation: jockey said colt hung left-handed and felt wrong behind (op 3-1)

5920 UPTON MCGOUGAN CONSULTING ENGINEERS EBF NOVICE STKS 6f 212y

3:00 (3:04) (Class 4) 2-Y-O **£5,181** (£1,541; £770; £384) **Stalls** High

Form	Pos	Btn	Horse / Details	RPR
21	1		**Fifteen Love (USA)**[67] 3957 2-9-5 90 RichardHughes 5 (R Charlton) *lw: mde all: shkn up and c clr fr over 1f out: comf* **4/6**[1]	99
	2	1 1/4	**Collection (IRE)** 2-8-8 0 KerrinMcEvoy 2 (W J Haggas) *w'like: disp 2nd to 3f out: shkn up and chsd wnr 2f out: kpt on wel fnl f but a readily hld* **9/4**[2]	85
024	3	6	**House**[17] 5448 2-8-12 80 DarryllHolland 3 (M R Channon) *disp 2nd tl rdn to chse wnr 3f out: wknd fr 2f out* **11/2**[3]	73
	4	9	**Yakama (IRE)** 2-8-8 0 LPKeniry 1 (D J S Ffrench Davis) *a in 4th: rdn and effrt 3f out: hung rt and wknd 2f out* **66/1**	45

1m 31.32s (2.26) **Going Correction** +0.25s/f (Good) **4** Ran SP% **107.6**

Speed ratings (Par 97): **97,95,88,78**

CSF £2.40 TOTE £1.50; EX 2.30.

Owner K Abdulla **Bred** Juddmonte Farms Inc **Trained** Beckhampton, Wilts

FOCUS

Probably an uninformative event. The winner is classy and open to improvement at a slightly higher level, while the runner-up is well regarded and sure to progress from the run.

NOTEBOOK

Fifteen Love(USA) had shown plenty already on the track already and managed to concede 11lb to the well-regarded runner-up with a bit in hand. He has a couple of nice entries this season and connections are swaying towards the Horris Hill at Newbury later this month. (op 4-5 after 6-5 in places and 10-11 in a place)

Collection(IRE), am attractive sort who holds some Group 1 entries, ran a really nice race on his debut and, although getting plenty of weight, he showed that a maiden is well within his capabilites. He will be a lot wiser for the run. (op 2-1 tchd 5-2)

House had a bit to find at the weights with the winner on official figures and never posed a serious threat despite having every chance. (tchd 5-1 and 13-2)

Yakama(IRE), a lean sort, faced a stiff task on his debut and was, unsurprisingly, put in his place. No firm conclusions can be taken about him from this effort. (op 50-1 tchd 80-1)

5921 POSHCHATEAUX.COM CLAIMING STKS 1m 1f 198y

3:30 (3:30) (Class 5) 3-4-Y-O **£3,238** (£963; £481; £240) **Stalls** High

Form	Pos	Btn	Horse / Details	RPR
-516	1		**Secret Liaison**[91] 3201 4-9-7 85 RyanMoore 4 (Sir Mark Prescott) *in rr: rdn and stl plenty to do 3f out: styd on strly fr 2f out to ld 1f out: drvn out* **9/4**[1]	80
3565	2	1 3/4	**Best Selection**[28] 5131 3-8-11 67 RichardHughes 6 (A P Jarvis) *hld up in rr: stl plenty to do 3f out and sn pushed along: hdwy fr 2f out: styd on wl fnl f and tk 2nd cl home but a hld by wnr* **13/2**	71
0001	3	3/4	**Castara Bay**[16] 5472 3-8-11 75 HaddenFrost(5) 8 (R Hannon) *in rr: rdn 4f out: hdwy over 2f out: styd on wl fnl f to take 3rd cl home but a readily hld by wnr* **3/1**[2]	75
010	4	nk	**Drawback (IRE)**[37] 4909 4-9-2 72 (p) LukeMorris(5) 7 (R A Harris) *chsd ldrs: rdn to chal over 1f out and wnt 2nd ins fnl f: no imp on wnr and outpcd into 4th cl home* **7/2**[3]	74
3005	5	3 1/2	**Surrey Spinner**[8] 5718 3-9-5 83 (b) OscarUrbina 1 (Mrs A J Perrett) *lw: led after 1f: rdn 3f out: hdd 1f out: sn wknd* **10/1**	70
524-	6	1	**Art Man**[456] 3162 4-9-5 74 GeorgeBaker 3 (G L Moore) *b: led 1f: styd chsng ldr tl over 1f out: sn wknd* **20/1**	63
1050	7	14	**History Boy**[12] 5594 3-9-5 80 DaneO'Neill 2 (D J Coakley) *chsd ldrs: rdn 3f out: wknd 2f out* **8/1**	40

2m 11.25s (2.79) **Going Correction** +0.25s/f (Good)

WFA 3 from 4yo 5lb **7** Ran SP% **116.3**

Speed ratings (Par 103): **98,96,96,95,92 92,80**

CSF £18.10 TOTE £2.90: £1.90, £3.30; EX 16.90.The winner was claimed by S Parr for £24,000.

Owner W E Sturt - Osborne House **Bred** Cheveley Park Stud Ltd **Trained** Newmarket, Suffolk

FOCUS

Probably a fair claimer in terms of quality with three of the seven runners officially rated 80 or higher, but it appeared as though the leaders went off too quick as the first three home were all detached from the leading quartet passing the half-mile pole. The form seems to make sense.

5922 SMITH & WILLIAMSON CONDITIONS STKS 6f

4:00 (4:02) (Class 2) 2-Y-O

£11,217 (£3,358; £1,679; £840; £419; £210) **Stalls** High

Form	Pos	Btn	Horse / Details	RPR
0100	1		**Major Eazy (IRE)**[64] 4046 2-9-1 94 RichardHughes 2 (B J Meehan) *racd towards centre: trckd ldrs and chal fr 3f out tl def advantage 1f out: sn rdn and in command whn rdr dropped reins fnl 50yds* **12/1**	103
4143	2	1	**Berbice (IRE)**[11] 5630 2-9-1 106 RyanMoore 3 (R Hannon) *lw: chsd ldr: chal fr 3f out tl slt ld ins fnl 2f: hdd 1f out: nt qckn u.p* **6/5**[1]	100
3126	3	1/2	**Oasis Wind**[21] 5324 2-9-1 91 KerrinMcEvoy 1 (P F I Cole) *lw: racd towards centre of crse and trckd wnr: rdn and effrt over 1f out: kpt on same pce ins fnl f* **15/8**[2]	99
1400	4	2	**Aide Memoir (IRE)**[64] 4046 2-8-7 97 LPKeniry 7 (S Kirk) *in tch: rdn and effrt 2f out: wknd ins fnl f* **9/1**[3]	85
3213	5	1	**Gross Prophet**[9] 5691 2-8-12 86 RichardKingscote 4 (Tom Dascombe) *wnt rt s: led: rdn 3f out: hdd ins fnl 2f: wknd fnl f* **12/1**	87
0403	6	nk	**Carleton**[12] 5583 2-9-4 96 DarryllHolland 5 (M R Channon) *bmpd s: sn rcvrd: rdn and effrt over 2f out: no imp: wknd appr fnl f* **11/1**	92

1m 16.64s (1.66) **Going Correction** +0.25s/f (Good) **6** Ran SP% **114.0**

Speed ratings (Par 101): **98,96,96,93,92 91**

CSF £27.81 TOTE £12.80: £5.00, £1.10; EX 39.50.

Owner The Comic Strip Heroes **Bred** Swettenham Stud **Trained** Manton, Wilts

FOCUS

A decent little conditions event in which a group of four stayed close to the fair rail whilst the other pair, comprising of the eventual winner and third, raced wider. The pace was only ordinary. Muddling form on the face of things, with Major Eazy producing big improvement, but he shaped as good as this a couple of times earlier in the year.

NOTEBOOK

Major Eazy(IRE), who has tackled Group company in his last two outings, was kept noticeably wider than the main bulk of the field throughout. This was his first attempt at the trip and he saw it out well, and not even his rider losing his reins made any difference to his superiority. He had quite a bit to find with a couple of these at the weights, so this was a good effort, but it remains to be seen whether he is truly up to Pattern class. (op 11-1 tchd 10-1)

Berbice(IRE), another taking a drop in class after finishing third in the Mill Reef, had every chance over towards the far side of the track but could not match the winner for foot. He would have been 12lb worse off with him in a handicap and probably needs further now, whilst it is impossible to say whether the winner was racing on the faster strip. (op 10-11 tchd 5-4 and 11-8 in places)

Oasis Wind, well backed, kept the winner company down the middle of the track and was far from disgraced considering he had a bit to find with most of his rivals at these weights. (op 3-1)

Aide Memoir(IRE), who appears to have been losing her way in Group company recently, tried to put in a bid over on the far side entering the last couple of furlongs but it came to little. It may be that she needs genuinely fast ground to show her best, but she may not be the easiest to place in any case. (op 8-1 tchd 10-1)

Gross Prophet, worst in at the weights, made much of the running but was unable to hold on against these rivals. (op 14-1 tchd 16-1)

Carleton would probably have preferred even softer ground than this and was comfortably held late on. He looks totally exposed now. (op 9-1 tchd 12-1)

5923 WOOD BMW H'CAP 6f
4:30 (4:32) (Class 4) (0-85,85) 3-Y-0+ £6,477 (£1,927; £722; £722) Stalls High

Form RPR

1200 **1** **Masai Moon**[11] 5635 3-8-11 **83** .... JamesMillman(5) 15 92
(B R Millman) *chsd ldrs: drvn to ld ins fnl f: rdn out* **20/1**

030 **2** 1/2 **Rainbow Mirage (IRE)**[11] 5635 3-9-1 **82** .... J-PGuillambert 16 89
(E S McMahon) *chsd ldrs: rdn to chal ins fnl f: no ex cl home* **16/1**

0021 **3** 3/4 **Don Pele (IRE)**[7] 5722 5-9-5 **85** 6ex........(p) RyanMoore 10 90+
(R A Harris) *b: lw: in rr: hdwy towards centre crse 2f out: styd on fnl f to press for 3rd cl home but nt pce to rch ldng duo* **13/2**[2]

205 **3** dht **Idle Power (IRE)**[39] 4816 9-9-2 **82** .... AmirQuinn 18 87
(J R Boyle) *chsd ldrs: drvn to chal over 1f out: nt qckn ins fnl f* **14/1**

1263 **5** 1 1/2 **Bel Cantor**[20] 5356 4-8-11 **77** ....(p) RichardKingscote 11 78
(W J H Ratcliffe) *led: rdn 2f out: hdd ins fnl f: wknd nr fin* **8/1**

4036 **6** shd **Swinbrook (USA)**[22] 5312 6-8-12 **78** ....(v) LPKeniry 13 78
(J A R Toller) *lw: hmpd s: in rr: hdwy 2f out: styd on fnl f: nt rch ldrs* **8/1**

6060 **7** nk **Cape Of Luck (IRE)**[8] 5712 4-9-5 **85** .... GeorgeBaker 4 84+
(P Mitchell) *racd stands' side: rr that gp: hdwy fr 2f out: styd on to ld that gp last strides but nvr any ch w far side* **25/1**

062 **8** nk **Transcend**[39] 4811 3-9-0 **81** ....(p) RobertHavlin 1 79+
(J H M Gosden) *racd stands' side: led that gp and sn clr but a hld by far side: rdn over 2f out: hdd that gp last strides* **6/1**[1]

2250 **9** 2 1/2 **China Cherub**[39] 4806 4-9-5 **85** ....(b) RichardHughes 17 76
(R Hannon) *in rr: chsd ldrs: rdn 2f out: wknd ins fnl f: eased cl home* **14/1**

300 **10** 2 **Abwaab**[39] 4816 4-8-11 **77** ....(v[1]) JimmyQuinn 6 62
(Eve Johnson Houghton) *racd stands' side: nvr gng pce to be competitive but kpt on fnl f: fin 3rd that gp* **50/1**

315 **11** hd **Impromptu**[37] 4885 3-8-13 **80** .... MartinDwyer 9 64
(R M Beckett) *chsd ldrs: rdn 2f out: wknd fnl f* **16/1**

0062 **12** nk **Mujood**[8] 5712 4-9-1 **81** ....(b) StephenCarson 2 64
(Eve Johnson Houghton) *racd stands' side: outpcd tl styd on fnl f to fin 4th that gp* **12/1**

1553 **13** 1 3/4 **Compton's Eleven**[4] 5809 6-9-5 **85** .... DarryllHolland 14 63
(M R Channon) *t.k.h: racd in mid-div: rdn and no imp fnl 2f* **7/1**[3]

1030 **14** shd **Mason Ette**[7] 5722 3-8-13 **80** .... KerrinMcEvoy 7 58
(C G Cox) *chsd ldrs: rdn 1/2-way: wknd fnl f* **20/1**

2004 **15** 1/2 **Go On Be A Tiger (USA)**[26] 5209 3-9-3 **84** .... RichardMullen 12 60
(M R Channon) *outpcd fr 1/2-way* **10/1**

0450 **16** nk **Stamford Blue**[27] 5168 6-8-11 **82** ....(b) LukeMorris(5) 5 57
(R A Harris) *racd centre crse: outpcd fr 1/2-way* **14/1**

2266 **17** 1/2 **Who's Winning (IRE)**[11] 5638 6-8-5 **78** .... KylieManser(7) 3 52
(B G Powell) *racd stands' side: outpcd fr 1/2-way and fin 5th that gp* **33/1**

5-00 **18** 3 **Loyal Royal (IRE)**[117] 2427 4-8-11 **82** .... KevinGhunowa(5) 8 47
(J M Bradley) *chsd ldrs 4f* **33/1**

1m 16.28s (1.30) **Going Correction** +0.25s/f (Good)
WFA 3 from 4yo+ 1lb **18 Ran SP% 132.1**
Speed ratings (Par 105): **101,100,99,99,97 97,96,96,93,90 90,89,87,87,86 86,85,81**
PL: Don Pele £2.30, Idle Power £4.60; TR: Masai Moon/Rainbow Mirage/DP £1,171.48, MM/RM/IP £1,264.76 CSF £311.02 TOTE £22.80: £4.40, £5.30; EX 584.40.
Owner C Roper **Bred** Mrs B A Matthews **Trained** Kentisbeare, Devon

FOCUS
A competitive handicap though the final time was ordinary and it took a while for the shape of this contest to develop. They eventuallty split into two groups with the larger group of 13 going far side and the other five came stands' side. The first six home all raced over on the far side. Improved efforts from the first two.
Impromptu Official explanation: jockey said gelding was lame
Compton's Eleven Official explanation: jockey said gelding suffered interference in running

5924 TORI TUCKER MEMORIAL "HAMMER OUT" BRAIN TUMOURS H'CAP 1m 6f 21y
5:00 (5:00) (Class 5) (0-75,75) 3-Y-0+ £3,886 (£1,156; £577; £288)

Form RPR

0125 **1** **Rehearsed (IRE)**[50] 4483 4-9-8 **69** .... KerrinMcEvoy 13 77
(H Morrison) *stdd towards rr: stdy hdwy 3f out: str run to ld 1f out: drvn out* **7/2**[2]

3120 **2** 3/4 **Synonymy**[14] 5533 4-8-10 **57** ....(b) LPKeniry 4 64
(M Blanshard) *chsd ldrs: rdn and effrt whn bmpd wl over 1f out: styd on ins fnl f but a hld by wnr* **14/1**

3264 **3** 3/4 **Lapina (IRE)**[14] 5533 3-8-9 **65** ....(b) RichardMullen 6 71
(Pat Eddery) *in rr: hdwy fr 5f out: styng on whn bmpd wl over 1f out: kpt on ins fnl f* **8/1**[3]

2110 **4** hd **Squadron**[49] 4511 3-9-3 **73** .... RyanMoore 10 79
(Mrs A J Perrett) *chsd ldrs: led 3f out: sn rdn: hdd 1f out: one pce* **3/1**[1]

452- **5** 5 **Rio De Janeiro (IRE)**[235] 3256 6-9-11 **75** .... LiamTreadwell(3) 5 74
(Miss E C Lavelle) *chsd ldrs: rdn 3f out: wknd 2f out* **12/1**

0040 **6** 3/4 **Brief Goodbye**[14] 5539 7-9-11 **72** .... DarryllHolland 2 70
(John Berry) *in rr: rdn and sme hdwy fr 3f out: nvr gng pce to rch ldrs* **14/1**

310- **7** 11 **Spinning Coin**[181] 6202 5-10-0 **75** ....(p) GeorgeBaker 9 57
(J G Portman) *sn led: hdd 3f out: hung rt and wknd 2f out* **16/1**

0200 **8** 3 **Debord (FR)**[83] 3467 4-8-10 **57** .... PaulDoe 1 35
(Jamie Poulton) *chsd ldrs to 3f out: wknd 2f out* **16/1**

4-24 **9** 26 **Cantabilly (IRE)**[161] 1253 4-9-9 **75** .... HaddenFrost(5) 3 17
(R J Hodges) *a in rr* **8/1**[3]

4020 **10** 29 **Love Always**[15] 5514 5-9-8 **69** .... RichardHughes 14 —
(S Dow) *a in rr* **12/1**

3m 8.81s (1.81) **Going Correction** +0.25s/f (Good)
WFA 3 from 4yo+ 9lb **10 Ran SP% 109.9**
Speed ratings (Par 103): **104,103,103,103,100 99,93,91,76,60**
CSF £44.20 CT £272.87 TOTE £4.20: £1.70, £4.90, £2.30; EX 67.10 Place 6 £24.64, Place 5 £5.22.
Owner Mrs G C Maxwell & J D N Tillyard **Bred** J C Condon **Trained** East Ilsley, Berks
■ Abounding was withdrawn on vet's advice (8/1, deduct 10p in the £ under Rule 4).

FOCUS
An ordinary staying handicap, but at least the pace was sound thanks to Spinning Coin. The majority of the field were inclined to race wide of the inside rail up the home straight and those that came widest did appear to be on the quicker strip in the closing stages. Sound form.
Rehearsed(IRE) Official explanation: trainer said, regarding apparent improvement in form, he had no explanation for the poor form shown previous outing
T/Plt: £14.70 to a £1 stake. Pool: £52,513.75. 2,606.70 winning tickets. T/Qpdt: £3.70 to a £1 stake. Pool: £2,711.20. 533.80 winning tickets. ST

5925 - 5928a (Foreign Racing) - See Raceform Interactive

HOPPEGARTEN (R-H)
Wednesday, October 3

OFFICIAL GOING: Soft

5929a PREIS DER DEUTSCHEN EINHEIT (GROUP 3) 1m 2f
3:35 (3:50) 3-Y-0+ £21,622 (£6,757; £3,378; £2,027)

RPR

1 **Waleria (GER)**[10] 4-9-0 .... VSchulepov 11 106
(H J Groschel, Germany) *dropped out in last: hdwy on ins 2f out: swtchd off rail over 1f out: swtchd bk to rail and wnt through on ins to ld cl home* **213/10**

2 3/4 **Axxos (GER)**[31] 5077 3-8-11 .... AStarke 3 106
(P Schiergen, Germany) *cl up: 4th st: hrd rdn to dispute ld under 2f out: led 1f out: hdd and no ex cl home* **1/2**[1]

3 1 1/2 **Davidoff (GER)**[35] 4958 3-8-11 .... TMundry 8 103
(P Schiergen, Germany) *in tch: 3rd st on outside: disp ld under 2f out to 1f out: one pce* **15/2**[3]

4 1 1/2 **Simple Exchange (IRE)**[10] 5670 6-9-4 .... HGrewe 4 102
(A Savujev, Czech Republic) *in tch on outside: styd on steadily u.p fnl f* **43/1**

5 4 **Auvano (GER)** 3-8-11 .... APietsch 10 92
(R Dzubasz, Germany) *led to under 2f out: one pce* **43/1**

6 1 1/4 **White Lightning (GER)**[164] 5-9-4 .... JBojko 6 92
(U Stech, Norway) *hld up towards rr: rdn and one pce fnl 2f* **36/1**

7 2 1/2 **Fighting Johan (GER)**[17] 5464 3-8-11 ....(b) J-PCarvalho 5 85
(H Blume, Germany) *prom: 2nd st: wknd 2f out* **43/1**

8 3/4 **Simonas (IRE)**[39] 4838 8-9-4 .... EPedroza 9 85
(A Wohler, Germany) *nvr a factor* **135/10**

9 1/2 **Andorn (GER)**[38] 3-8-11 .... TPQueally 2 82
(J Hirschberger, Germany) *trckd ldr in 3rd or 4th: outpcd fr over 2f out* **81/10**

10 2 **San Moritz (POL)** 3-8-11 .... AReznikov 7 78
(A Walicki, Germany) *a in rr* **67/10**[2]

U **Sommersturm (GER)**[66] 4013 3-8-11 .... JiriPalik 1 —
(J Hirschberger, Germany) *uns rdr leaving stalls* **20/1**

2m 7.60s (0.90)
WFA 3 from 4yo+ 5lb **11 Ran SP% 128.1**
(Including 10 Euro stake): WIN 223; PL 27, 12, 19; SF 566.
Owner Frau Dr C Otto **Bred** Frau Dr C Otto **Trained** Germany

5613 AYR (L-H)
Thursday, October 4

OFFICIAL GOING: Good to soft (soft in places on straight course)
Wind: Virtually nil

5930 WEDDINGS AT WESTERN HOUSE HOTEL LINFERN H'CAP 5f
2:10 (2:11) (Class 6) (0-58,54) 3-Y-0+ £2,730 (£806; £403) Stalls Centre

Form RPR

0523 **1** **Jadan (IRE)**[4] 5836 6-8-10 **48** ....(b) DavidAllan 12 60
(E J Alston) *sn prom centre: rdn to ld ins fnl f: kpt on wl* **3/1**[1]

000 **2** 1/2 **Mint**[16] 5507 4-8-7 **45** .... TonyHamilton 14 55
(D W Barker) *w ldr: led 1/2-way to ins fnl f: edgd lft: hld nr fin* **100/1**

1654 **3** 1 3/4 **Throw The Dice**[10] 5672 5-8-13 **54** ....(v) PatrickMathers(3) 1 57
(A Berry) *led far side gp: rdn 2f out: kpt on fnl f: nt rch first two in centre* **9/1**[3]

3600 **4** 1 **Legal Set (IRE)**[43] 4719 11-8-10 **53** ....(b) AnnStokell(5) 9 53
(Miss A Stokell) *prom centre: effrt over 2f out: kpt on u.p fnl f* **33/1**

6536 **5** 1/2 **Dunn Deal (IRE)**[48] 4583 7-8-7 **45** .... PaulMulrennan 15 43
(J Balding) *hld up in tch centre: effrt over 1f out: kpt on fnl f: no imp* **9/1**[3]

6502 **6** nk **Valiant Romeo**[23] 5295 7-8-10 **48** .... PatCosgrave 7 45
(R Bastiman) *prom far side: rdn over 2f out: one pce appr fnl f* **12/1**

0060 **7** hd **Alexia Rose (IRE)**[4] 5836 5-8-4 **45** ....(t) AndrewMullen(3) 2 41
(A Berry) *dwlt: bhd far side tl hdwy over 1f out: n.d* **33/1**

0000 **8** 1/2 **The Thrifty Bear**[8] 5740 4-8-2 **45** ....(b) KellyHarrison(5) 13 39
(C W Fairhurst) *led to 1/2-way: edgd lft and no ex over 1f out* **25/1**

0450 **9** hd **Indian Spark**[24] 5284 13-8-6 **49** .... GaryBartley(5) 20 43
(J S Goldie) *chsd stands' side ldrs: rdn and outpcd 1/2-way: kpt on fnl f: no imp* **12/1**

4410 **10** 2 **Beechside (IRE)**[4] 5834 3-8-10 **48** .... DaleGibson 3 34
(W A Murphy, Ire) *chsd far side ldrs: drvn over 2f out: one pce over 1f out* **18/1**

0000 **11** 1/2 **Compton Lad**[10] 5672 4-8-8 **49** ow4........(t) PJMcDonald(3) 5 34
(D A Nolan) *cl up far side tl rdn and no ex fnl f* **100/1**

4600 **12** 1 **Spinning Game**[23] 5295 3-8-0 **45** ....(p) DanielleMcCreery(7) 18 26
(D W Chapman) *dwlt: bhd and outpcd stands' side: nvr rchd ldrs* **20/1**

5100 **13** shd **Fern House (IRE)**[36] 4942 5-9-2 **54** .... PaulHanagan 4 35
(Garry Moss) *prom far side tl rdn and wknd over 1f out* **16/1**

3100 **14** shd **Dodaa (USA)**[10] 5672 4-8-0 **45** .... LanceBetts(7) 17 25
(N Wilson) *spd stands' side tl rdn and wknd over 1f out* **25/1**

0435 **15** hd **Newkeylets**[34] 4996 4-8-11 **49** ....(p) TomEaves 8 29
(I Semple) *in tch centre: rdn 1/2-way: sn outpcd* **16/1**

600 **16** 1 **Regal Cheer**[64] 4066 3-8-12 **50** .... RichardMullen 21 26
(C F Wall) *cl up stands' side tl wknd fr 2f out* **16/1**

5331 **17** 3/4 **She's Our Beauty (IRE)**[71] 3837 4-8-4 **45** ....(p) DuranFentiman(3) 16 18
(S T Mason) *prom centre tl edgd lft and wknd fr 2f out* **5/1**[2]

62.25 secs (1.81) **Going Correction** +0.40s/f (Good) **17 Ran SP% 120.3**
Speed ratings (Par 101): **101,100,97,95,95 94,94,93,93,89 89,87,87,87,86 85,84**
CSF £401.13 CT £2554.10 TOTE £4.30: £1.40, £5.80, £2.20, £10.00; EX 193.10.
Owner Derrick Mossop **Bred** Michael Rourke **Trained** Longton, Lancs
■ Stewards' Enquiry : Lance Betts one-day ban: failed to ride to draw (Oct 15)

FOCUS
A modest event in which the pace was sound and the field fanned across the whole track.
Alexia Rose(IRE) Official explanation: jockey said mare missed the break

Spinning Game Official explanation: jockey said filly missed the break

5931 EARLY DISCOUNTS FOR 2008 CORAL SGN MEDIAN AUCTION MAIDEN STKS 6f

2:45 (2:46) (Class 5) 2-Y-O **£2,914** (£867; £433; £216) **Stalls** Centre

Form RPR

3200 **1** **Quest For Success (IRE)**[22] 5324 2-9-3 82 PaulHanagan 1 85+
(R A Fahey) *trckd ldrs gng wl: led 2f out: shkn up and edgd lft: wnt clr* **6/5**[1]

3 **2** *5* **Safebreaker**[10] 5675 2-9-3 0 RoystonFfrench 5 70
(M Johnston) *led 1f: chsd ldrs: drvn 3f out: styd on: no ch w wnr* **6/1**

5000 **3** *1 ¼* **Andrasta**[27] 5199 2-8-9 65 PatrickMathers(3) 4 61
(A Berry) *in tch: sn pushed along: styd on appr fnl f* **66/1**

225 **4** *¾* **Nickel Silver**[57] 4286 2-9-3 77 TomEaves 3 64
(B Smart) *hld up in rr: effrt over 2f out: kpt on same pce* **4/1**[3]

4222 **5** *11* **Tugalu (IRE)**[25] 5252 2-9-3 76 DO'Donohoe 2 31
(K A Ryan) *t.k.h: w ldrs: rdn and edgd lft over 1f out: sn lost pl* **11/4**[2]

06 **6** *¾* **Lunar Lass**[28] 5154 2-8-12 0 RichardMullen 7 24
(G Woodward) *swvd rt s: led after 1f: hdd 2f out: sn wknd* **100/1**

0 **7** *19* **Ugly Betty**[22] 5328 2-8-12 0 PaulMulrennan 6 —
(Garry Moss) *chsd ldrs: drvn 3f out: sn lost pl and bhd* **250/1**

1m 15.29s (1.62) **Going Correction** +0.40s/f (Good) **7** Ran SP% **109.3**
Speed ratings (Par 95): **105,98,96,95,81 80,54**
CSF £8.31 TOTE £1.80: £1.20, £2.00; EX 8.60.
Owner Rob Lloyd Racing Limited **Bred** D Monahan **Trained** Musley Bank, N Yorks

FOCUS
A very smart winning time for a race of its type, 1.43 seconds faster than the following nursery. The winner impressed and was entitled to score with something in hand, but the 65-rated third limits the form.

NOTEBOOK
Quest For Success(IRE), back at a more realistic level, travelled supremely well and despite drifting towards the far rail he sprinted clear. A late foal, he should make a very useful sprinter at three. (op 6-4 tchd 13-8 in places)
Safebreaker was soon making hard work of it but to his credit he stuck to his guns and will be much better suited by seven furlongs or even a mile. (op 7-2)
Andrasta, who has changed stables, had the cheekpieces left off. Soon struggling to keep up, she will be better suited by 7f in nursery company. (tchd 80-1)
Nickel Silver, absent for eight weeks, should be sharper as a result. (op 9-2)
Tugalu(IRE) would not settle and drifted towards the far side before dropping right away. The soft ground was not solely to blame for this poor effort. (op 5-2 tchd 9-4)

5932 BEN NURSERY 6f

3:20 (3:20) (Class 5) (0-75,73) 2-Y-O **£3,238** (£963; £481; £240) **Stalls** Centre

Form RPR

5451 **1** **Carrickmacross (IRE)**[31] 5089 2-9-3 69 RichardMullen 7 73
(E S McMahon) *pressed ldr: rdn and led over 1f out: hld on wl fnl f* **7/2**[2]

1202 **2** *½* **Lady Benjamin**[11] 5665 2-9-7 73 KDarley 13 75
(P C Haslam) *prom: rdn over 2f out: effrt over 1f out: edgd lft and chsd wnr ins fnl f: r.o* **5/2**[1]

6205 **3** *2 ½* **Angle Of Attack (IRE)**[35] 4975 2-9-0 66 PaulHanagan 8 61
(R A Fahey) *led to over 1f out: kpt on same pce ins fnl f* **7/1**[3]

5436 **4** *1 ¼* **Prunes**[4] 5837 2-8-4 59 PatrickMathers(3) 6 50
(A Berry) *chsd ldrs: effrt and ev ch over 1f out: no ex ins fnl f* **25/1**

0400 **5** *2* **Zaplamation (IRE)**[23] 5298 2-7-13 51 RoystonFfrench 15 36
(D W Barker) *midfield: drvn along 1/2-way: rallied over 1f out: kpt on: nrst fin* **28/1**

4000 **6** *3* **Fitolini**[35] 4975 2-9-0 66 J-PGuillambert 4 42
(Mrs G S Rees) *hld up: smooth hdwy to press ldrs over 1f out: sn rdn and wknd* **10/1**

5000 **7** *nk* **Lord Of The Wing**[49] 4527 2-8-3 55 PaulFessey 10 30
(P T Midgley) *wnt rt s: chsd ldrs: outpcd over 2f out: n.d after* **66/1**

3365 **8** *nk* **Woodford Regen**[25] 5251 2-8-7 59 PaulMulrennan 9 33
(M W Easterby) *in tch: drvn along 1/2-way: sn no imp* **8/1**

000 **9** *3* **James's Lass (IRE)**[14] 5558 2-7-12 50 PaulQuinn 5 15
(R A Fahey) *bhd: drvn 1/2-way: sme hdwy over 1f out: nvr on terms* **66/1**

045 **10** *1 ¾* **Scruffy Skip (IRE)**[41] 4769 2-9-1 67 DaleGibson 14 27
(M Dods) *bhd: rdn 1/2-way: n.d* **8/1**

0400 **11** *4* **Powys Lad**[23] 5298 2-8-0 55 AndrewMullen(3) 2 3
(K R Burke) *midfield: drvn and prom over 2f out: wknd over 1f out* **33/1**

5016 **12** *9* **Mac Dalia**[18] 5452 2-9-7 73 PatCosgrave 16 —
(M G Quinlan) *t.k.h: chsd ldrs tl edgd lft and wknd fr 2f out* **16/1**

0500 **13** *3 ½* **Tenth Night (IRE)**[55] 4363 2-7-13 54 DuranFentiman(3) 18 —
(P T Midgley) *midfield: drvn 1/2-way: btn over 1f out* **40/1**

420 **14** *5* **Lambrini Lace (IRE)**[37] 4924 2-8-13 65 TonyHamilton 12 —
(Mrs L Williamson) *sn bhd: struggling 1/2-way: nvr on terms* **20/1**

1m 16.72s (3.05) **Going Correction** +0.40s/f (Good) **14** Ran SP% **120.9**
Speed ratings (Par 95): **95,94,91,89,86 82,82,81,77,75 70,58,53,46**
CSF £11.78 CT £58.92 TOTE £3.70: £2.00, £1.40, £2.80; EX 14.00.
Owner J C Fretwell **Bred** Vincent Dunne **Trained** Lichfield, Staffs

FOCUS
A run-of-the-mill nursery in which the field raced in the centre. The pace was sound but those up with the pace held the edge and, although there was not much strength in depth, the form is sound rated through the third.

NOTEBOOK
Carrickmacross(IRE) ◆, who showed improved form to win at Lingfield last time, had the run of the race and turned in his best effort yet. He showed a good attitude, should have no problems with 7f and appeals as the sort to win more races. (op 4-1)
Lady Benjamin is exposed but is a reliable yardstick who seemed to give it her best shot and she looks a good guide to the worth of this form. While vulnerable to the more progressive sorts, she should continue to go well over this trip. (tchd 11-4)
Angle Of Attack(IRE) has yet to win a race but he had the run of the race and ran creditably back on turf. He is in good hands and is capable of picking up a small event away from progressive sorts. (op 8-1)
Prunes, having her second run for Alan Berry, ran creditably returned to this trip and showed enough to suggest a modest event over this trip or over 7f can be found. (tchd 33-1)
Zaplamation(IRE), back on easy ground, fared the best of those to come from just off the pace and, although his record so far has been one of inconsistency, he shaped as though the return to 7f would be in his favour. (op 25-1 tchd 33-1)
Fitolini travelled strongly for much of the way but did not seem to get home in the conditions and, although she has been a bit disappointing since her maiden win, the return to a quicker surface or Polytrack could enable her to return to winning ways. (op 16-1)
Scruffy Skip(IRE) Official explanation: trainer had no explanation for the poor form shown

Mac Dalia Official explanation: jockey said filly had run too free early

5933 CHRISTMAS PARTIES AT PR SUITE H'CAP 1m 5f 13y

3:55 (3:55) (Class 3) (0-90,86) 3-Y-O+ **£7,124** (£2,119; £1,059; £529) **Stalls** Low

Form RPR

3-66 **1** **St Savarin (FR)**[12] 5619 6-9-13 85 PaulHanagan 1 93+
(R A Fahey) *trckd ldng pair: t.k.h: smooth hdwy over 2f out: led over 1f out: pushed out: readily* **4/1**[2]

0604 **2** *1 ¼* **Lets Roll**[12] 5619 6-9-6 81 PJMcDonald(3) 4 86
(C W Thornton) *chsd ldrs: effrt over 3f out: styd on to take 2nd ins fnl f: no imp* **11/4**[1]

6/2- **3** *1 ½* **First Look (FR)**[162] 1502 7-8-12 70 PatCosgrave 2 73
(P Monteith) *in tch: effrt over 3f out: sn chsng ldrs: kpt on same pce appr fnl f* **17/2**

5000 **4** *½* **La Estrella (USA)**[46] 4637 4-9-9 81 J-PGuillambert 9 83
(J G Given) *chsd ldr: kpt on same pce appr fnl f* **10/1**

1044 **5** *shd* **Nero West (FR)**[13] 5586 6-8-11 69 (b) TomEaves 8 71
(I Semple) *soft ld: qcknd over 3f out: hdd over 1f out: kpt on one pce* **11/2**[3]

0 **6** *1 ¾* **Los Nadis (GER)**[10] 5677 3-8-11 77 PaulFessey 7 76
(P Monteith) *dwlt: hld up in rr: hdwy 7f out: edgd lft 2f out: sn wknd* **16/1**

003- **7** *7* **Idarah (USA)**[160] 6051 4-10-0 86 PhillipMakin 6 75
(L Lungo) *hld up in rr: effrt over 3f out: lost pl 2f out* **12/1**

4006 **8** *1 ¾* **Clueless**[16] 5504 5-9-9 81 PaulMulrennan 5 67
(N G Richards) *t.k.h in rr: drvn over 4f out: bhd fnl 3f* **25/1**

4406 **9** *2* **Monolith**[69] 3898 9-9-12 84 RoystonFfrench 3 67
(L Lungo) *mid-div: drvn 7f out: lost pl 3f out* **6/1**

3m 1.19s (4.58) **Going Correction** +0.15s/f (Good)
WFA 3 from 4yo+ 8lb **9** Ran SP% **113.4**
Speed ratings (Par 107): **91,90,89,89,88 87,83,82,81**
CSF £15.09 CT £86.30 TOTE £5.30: £2.00, £1.40, £2.40; EX 13.20.
Owner J H Tattersall **Bred** F W Holtkotter **Trained** Musley Bank, N Yorks

FOCUS
A tactical affair resulting in a very moderate winning time for the class. The winner was having only his third start this time and scored in good style but overall the form is anything but solid.

NOTEBOOK
St Savarin(FR), still quite fresh, came there travelling supremely well and in the end had only to be pushed out. He might well follow up. (op 7-2)
Lets Roll, ahead of the winner here two weeks ago, could have done with a much stronger gallop. It was a laboured effort to secure second spot. (op 9-4)
First Look(FR), better known as a jumper, was having his first outing since April. He ran with real credit and no doubt will soon be facing obstacles once again. (op 10-1)
La Estrella(USA), back after a six-week break and with the blinkers discarded, had to settle for a lead. He kept on willing fashion and has clearly returned in a better frame of mind. (op 16-1)
Nero West(FR), out of sorts on his last three starts, was allowed to set his own pace. He wound it up off the home turn but over this trip was never going to be quick enough to hold on. (op 8-1)
Los Nadis(GER) showed a lot more than on his first outing here and is no doubt being primed for a hurdling campaign.

5934 SUBSCRIBE ONLINE@RACINGUK.TV H'CAP 6f

4:30 (4:32) (Class 5) (0-70,70) 3-Y-O+ **£3,238** (£963; £481; £240) **Stalls** Centre

Form RPR

-030 **1** **Double Carpet (IRE)**[61] 4177 4-8-5 56 oh3 PaulFessey 8 65
(G Woodward) *cl up: led and edgd lft over 1f out: hld on wl fnl f* **25/1**

6000 **2** *½* **Rothesay Dancer**[13] 5581 4-8-7 63 KellyHarrison(5) 10 71+
(J S Goldie) *hld up in tch: hdwy over 1f out: kpt on fnl f* **16/1**

1226 **3** *¾* **Lake Chini (IRE)**[15] 5522 5-9-5 70 (b) DaleGibson 6 75
(M W Easterby) *cl up: effrt and ev ch over 1f out: no ex ins fnl f* **15/2**

5600 **4** *3* **Dorn Dancer (IRE)**[14] 5556 5-8-9 60 PatCosgrave 2 56+
(D W Barker) *chsd ldr centre: effrt over 2f out: kpt on fnl f: no imp* **6/1**[3]

5524 **5** *nk* **Angel Voices (IRE)**[39] 4855 4-8-5 56 RoystonFfrench 3 51+
(K R Burke) *showed up wl in centre tl no ex fr over 1f out* **7/2**[1]

5133 **6** *1 ½* **Howards Tipple**[14] 5552 3-9-2 68 (p) TomEaves 5 59
(I Semple) *hld up: hdwy over 2f out: sn rdn: btn over 1f out* **4/1**[2]

6642 **7** *1* **Rann Na Cille (IRE)**[4] 5834 3-8-7 62 (b) AndrewMullen(3) 9 50
(K A Ryan) *prom: drvn 1/2-way: no ex over 1f out* **12/1**

0000 **8** *½* **Campo Bueno (FR)**[14] 5556 5-8-2 56 oh1 (b) PatrickMathers(3) 11 42
(A Berry) *bhd and sn drvn along: sme late hdwy: nvr rchd ldrs* **28/1**

0006 **9** *3* **High Reach**[7] 5747 7-8-9 67 DeanHeslop(7) 12 44
(T D Barron) *led to over 1f out: sn wknd* **10/1**

0350 **10** *6* **Stellite**[113] 2566 7-9-2 67 DanielTudhope 4 26
(J S Goldie) *in tch tl rdn and wknd fr over 2f out* **13/2**

00-0 **11** *10* **Johnston's Diamond (IRE)**[132] 1999 9-8-13 69 GaryBartley(5) 7 —
(E J Alston) *bhd: drvn 1/2-way: sn struggling* **22/1**

0030 **P** **Aye Aye Definitely (IRE)**[12] 5648 3-8-8 60 PaulHanagan 1 —
(R A Fahey) *racd centre: sn struggling: p.u 1/2-way* **18/1**

1m 16.21s (2.54) **Going Correction** +0.40s/f (Good)
WFA 3 from 4yo+ 1lb **12** Ran SP% **121.2**
Speed ratings (Par 103): **99,98,97,93,92 90,89,88,84,76 63,—**
CSF £378.62 CT £3290.82 TOTE £38.50: £8.00, £6.90, £2.30; EX 542.40.
Owner R W Empson **Bred** Dr John Waldron **Trained** Maltby, S Yorks

FOCUS
Another ordinary sprint in which the larger group raced stands' side. The form is sound enough rated around the placed horses, but ordinary.
Double Carpet(IRE) Official explanation: trainer said, regarding the apparent improvement in form, gelding had appreciated the return to 6f and easier ground
Johnston's Diamond(IRE) Official explanation: jockey said gelding lost its action
Aye Aye Definitely(IRE) Official explanation: jockey said filly pulled up lame but subsequently returned sound

5935 DAWN GROUP H'CAP 6f

5:05 (5:05) (Class 6) (0-60,60) 3-Y-O+ **£2,730** (£806; £403) **Stalls** Centre

Form RPR

5032 **1** **Dendor**[73] 3786 3-8-7 49 TonyHamilton 6 63+
(D W Barker) *mde all: clr over 1f out: hld on wl* **10/1**

0100 **2** *2* **Strabinios King**[59] 4223 3-9-2 58 KDarley 13 63
(P C Haslam) *in tch: hdwy to chse wnr over 1f out: kpt on fnl f: no imp* **14/1**

0000 **3** *1 ¼* **Mis Chicaf (IRE)**[9] 5701 6-8-7 48 oh1 ow2 DavidAllan 1 49
(D Carroll) *sn drvn towards rr: hdwy over 1f out: nrst fin* **20/1**

0033 **4** *hd* **Obe One**[14] 5566 7-8-3 47 (b) PatrickMathers(3) 8 48
(A Berry) *hld up: hdwy over 1f out: kpt on fnl f: no imp* **14/1**

0000 **5** *1 ½* **Ulysees (IRE)**[10] 5676 8-8-9 50 RoystonFfrench 10 46
(J Barclay) *sn drvn in rr: hdwy whn bdly hmpd twice over 1f out: kpt on strly fnl f: nrst fin* **25/1**

30/0 **6** *1 ¾* **Nok Twice (IRE)**[64] 4075 6-9-5 **60** PaulFessey 19 51
(D Carroll) *hld up: edgd lft and hdwy over 1f out: nvr rchd ldrs* **66/1**

3400 **7** *hd* **Nevinstown (IRE)**[59] 4223 7-8-7 **48** PaulMulrennan 2 38
(C Grant) *in tch tl rdn and wknd over 1f out* **28/1**

3163 **8** *1 ¼* **The Salwick Flyer (IRE)**[10] 5672 4-8-12 **53** TomEaves 17 40
(I Semple) *chsd ldrs tl rdn and wknd over 1f out* **9/2**[1]

1051 **9** *¾* **Quicks The Word**[24] 5284 7-8-11 **57** KellyHarrison(5) 18 41
(T A K Cuthbert) *chsd wnr: rdn over 2f out: wknd appr fnl f* **9/2**[1]

2200 **10** *½* **Five Wishes**[36] 4931 3-9-1 **57** (e[1]) PhillipMakin 12 40
(M Dods) *in tch: outpcd whn edgd rt wl over 1f out: sn no room and btn* **9/1**

6600 **11** *¾* **Hit's Only Money (IRE)**[24] 5284 7-8-4 **48** DuranFentiman(3) 9 29
(J S Goldie) *bhd: pushed along 1/2-way: n.d* **16/1**

0006 **12** *hd* **Only A Grand**[59] 4224 3-8-1 **46** oh1 (b) AndrewMullen(3) 5 26
(R Bastiman) *prom tl rdn and wknd fr 2f out* **40/1**

0-03 **13** *2* **Toberogan (IRE)**[48] 4583 6-8-7 **48** DaleGibson 4 22
(W A Murphy, Ire) *bhd: rdn 1/2-way: sn btn* **13/2**[2]

4106 **14** *1 ¼* **Missus Molly Brown**[12] 5627 3-8-8 **50** (p) PaulHanagan 16 20
(R A Fahey) *in tch tl rdn and wknd wl over 1f out* **12/1**

-000 **15** *3* **Wolf Pack**[31] 5083 5-8-8 **52** oh1 ow6 (t) PJMcDonald(3) 3 13
(D A Nolan) *s.i.s: a bhd* **200/1**

-001 **16** *16* **Tequila Sheila (IRE)**[47] 4595 5-8-10 **51** PatCosgrave 15 —
(K R Burke) *chsd ldrs: drvn over 2f out: sn wknd: eased whn no ch fnl f* **7/1**[3]

1m 16.03s (2.36) **Going Correction** +0.40s/f (Good)
WFA 3 from 4yo+ 1lb **16** Ran SP% **124.7**
Speed ratings (Par 101): **100,97,95,95,93 91,90,89,88,87 86,86,83,81,77 56**
CSF £137.63 CT £2868.46 TOTE £11.70: £3.10, £3.10, £4.50, £3.70; EX 250.30.
Owner D G Clayton **Bred** D G Clayton **Trained** Scorton, N Yorks
■ Stewards' Enquiry : Phillip Makin one-day ban: careless riding (Oct 15)

FOCUS
Modest stuff but a good pace and the winner may be a bit better than the bare form suggests.
Quicks The Word Official explanation: jockey said gelding was unsuited by the (good to soft, soft in places) ground
Five Wishes Official explanation: jockey said filly was denied a clear run
Toberogan(IRE) Official explanation: jockey said gelding never travelled
Tequila Sheila(IRE) Official explanation: trainer had no explanation for the poor form shown

5936 BOOK NOW FOR CHRISTMAS H'CAP 1m 1f 20y
5:40 (5:40) (Class 6) (0-65,66) 3-Y-O **£2,730** (£806; £403) **Stalls** Low

Form RPR

0501 **1** **Moheebb (IRE)**[9] 5703 3-9-6 **66** 6ex PJMcDonald(3) 5 78
(D W Chapman) *hld up in mid-div: stdy hdwy over 2f out: led over 1f out: styd on strly* **9/4**[1]

2150 **2** *2 ½* **Zain (IRE)**[22] 5342 3-8-12 **55** (t) RoystonFfrench 3 62
(J G Given) *trckd ldrs: led over 2f out: hdd over 1f out: kpt on same pce* **7/2**[2]

1043 **3** *6* **Grethel (IRE)**[6] 5774 3-8-8 **58** DanielleMcCreery(7) 9 52
(A Berry) *hld up in midfield: hdwy on outer 3f out: edgd lft and styd on same pce fnl f* **5/1**

3105 **4** *1 ¼* **Chasing Memories (IRE)**[48] 4579 3-8-11 **59** NeilBrown(5) 1 51
(B Smart) *s.i.s: bhd: drvn over 5f out: hdwy over 2f out: kpt on same pce fnl f* **9/2**[3]

0230 **5** *¾* **Beaumont Boy**[59] 4224 3-8-13 **56** PaulHanagan 11 46
(A G Foster) *trckd ldrs: effrt over 2f out: one pce* **12/1**

1540 **6** *8* **Mangano**[23] 5299 3-8-5 **55** ow2 AdamCarter(7) 2 28
(A Berry) *s.i.s: sme hdwy on inner 3f out: wknd 2f out* **20/1**

0606 **7** *3 ½* **Chookie Hamilton**[36] 4936 3-9-4 **61** (b[1]) TomEaves 7 27
(I Semple) *trckd ldrs: effrt over 2f out: sn wknd* **12/1**

6000 **8** *1* **Just Dust**[14] 5563 3-9-2 **59** DaleGibson 12 23
(M W Easterby) *led: hdd over 2f out: sn wknd* **16/1**

6000 **9** *11* **Seteem (USA)**[133] 1964 3-9-3 **60** KimTinkler 8 —
(N Tinkler) *t.k.h in midfield: lost pl over 2f out: sn bhd* **50/1**

3-00 **10** *12* **Bert's Memory**[51] 4480 3-9-0 **57** (p) PatCosgrave 4 —
(K A Ryan) *trckd ldrs: chal over 3f out: lost pl 2f out: sn bhd* **20/1**

2m 1.41s (1.41) **Going Correction** +0.15s/f (Good) **10** Ran SP% **120.6**
Speed ratings (Par 99): **99,96,91,90,89 82,79,78,68,58**
CSF £10.17 CT £37.60 TOTE £2.70: £1.30, £1.50, £2.20; EX 12.70 Place 6 £281.39, Place 5 £102.31.
Owner Michael Hill **Bred** Hascombe & Valiant Studs **Trained** Stillington, N Yorks

FOCUS
Just a steady gallop for this low-grade handicap but a most decisive and fast-improving winner.
Just Dust Official explanation: trainer said gelding was found to be distressed after the race
T/Plt: £173.20 to a £1 stake. Pool: £54,098.20. 227.95 winning tickets. T/Qpdt: £41.80 to a £1 stake. Pool: £2,527.50. 44.70 winning tickets. RY

5720 GOODWOOD (R-H)
Thursday, October 4

OFFICIAL GOING: Soft
Wind: Almost nil

5937 EUROPEAN BREEDERS' FUND JOHN KENT MEDIAN AUCTION MAIDEN STKS 7f
2:20 (2:20) (Class 4) 2-Y-O **£3,238** (£963; £481; £240) **Stalls** High

Form RPR

4250 **1** **Blues Minor (IRE)**[27] 5207 2-9-3 72 PatDobbs 11 80
(R Hannon) *mde all: shkn up 1f out: rdn ins fnl f: jst hld on* **8/1**

2253 **2** *shd* **Bailey (IRE)**[30] 5109 2-9-3 78 RobertHavlin 8 80
(B J Meehan) *trckd ldrs: hdwy and squeezed through to chse wnr ins fnl f: fin strly: nt quite get up* **6/4**[1]

002 **3** *1 ¼* **Connor's Choice**[21] 5343 2-9-3 78 ChrisCatlin 10 77
(Andrew Turnell) *chsd wnr: rdn over 1f out: lost 2nd ins fnl f and kpt on same pce* **11/2**[3]

4 *2 ½* **Spin Again (IRE)** 2-9-3 0 GeorgeBaker 3 70
(R M Beckett) *chsd ldrs: pushed along 2f out: wknd ins fnl f* **12/1**

06 **5** *1 ½* **Addikt (IRE)**[21] 5344 2-9-3 0 SimonWhitworth 1 67
(S Kirk) *sn chasing ldrs: pushed along over 2f out: wknd ins fnl f* **9/1**

6 *½* **Rakeekah** 2-8-12 0 MartinDwyer 6 60+
(J H M Gosden) *slow to gather stride: green early and bhd: effrt whn n.m.r 2f out: r.o ins fnl f but nvr in contention* **5/1**[2]

0 **7** *½* **Clear Daylight**[13] 5595 2-9-3 0 JohnEgan 7 64
(J R Best) *in tch 1/2-way: outpcd over 2f out: kpt on again ins fnl f* **18/1**

0 **8** *½* **Io (IRE)**[13] 5592 2-8-12 0 DaneO'Neill 4 58
(J L Dunlop) *in rr: hdwy over 3f out: nvr in contention and nt a danger fnl 2f* **50/1**

9 *hd* **Hepburn Bell (IRE)** 2-8-12 0 OscarUrbina 5 57+
(J R Fanshawe) *s.i.s: in rr: effrt whn nt clr run 2f out: nvr in conention* **25/1**

10 *6* **Bainisteoir** 2-9-3 0 JDSmith 9 47
(S Kirk) *sn in tch: rdn over 3f out: sn btn* **50/1**

00 **11** *shd* **Pinnacle Point**[21] 5361 2-9-3 0 JimCrowley 2 47
(G L Moore) *a in rr* **66/1**

1m 31.05s (3.01) **Going Correction** +0.50s/f (Yiel) **11** Ran SP% **115.4**
Speed ratings (Par 97): **102,101,100,97,95 95,94,94,93,87 86**
CSF £19.59 TOTE £8.90: £2.30, £1.10, £1.80; EX 18.10.
Owner Michael Pescod **Bred** Liam Queally **Trained** East Everleigh, Wilts

FOCUS
An average juvenile maiden in which it paid to race prominently. The form looks straightforward enough.

NOTEBOOK
Blues Minor(IRE), below par on his nursery bow last time, showed his true colours and made all with a gritty display from the front. He was ideally drawn to grab the early lead, and was no doubt at an advantage in racing on the pace, eventually doing just enough to edge it in the bobbing finish. His official mark looks to have him about right at present, but he does look happiest on this sort of ground and could have a little more to offer yet. (op 7-1 tchd 6-1)
Bailey(IRE), very well backed, settled better on this drop back a furlong yet did not enjoy the run of the race like the eventual winner and just missed out by the smallest of margins. With a clearer passage nearing the final furlong he would have probably opened his account and he does deserve to go one better now, but this may well have been his golden opportunity all the same. (op 15-8)
Connor's Choice proved too free for his own good through the first furlong or so and paid the price at the business end. This effort still confirmed him to be an improving juvenile, however, and he went without fuss on this softer ground. (op 6-1 tchd 13-2)
Spin Again(IRE), a 25,000gns half-brother to fair sprinter Radiator Rooney, posted a pleasing debut effort and travelled well until appearing to run out of stamina inside the final furlong. He should learn from this and a drop back a furlong could yield success. (op 14-1)
Addikt(IRE) was not disgraced, but was firmly put in his place nearing the final furlong. He now qualifies for a nursery mark. (tchd 10-1)
Rakeekah ◆, a half-sister to her stable's former 1000 Guineas heroine Lahan, proved easy to back and accordingly ran too green too do herself full justice after making a sluggish start. She shaped a bit better than the bare form, as it was not easy to come from behind in this race, and looks one to take from the race with the future in mind. (op 4-1 tchd 6-1)

5938 GOODWOOD RACEHORSE OWNERS' GROUP MAIDEN STKS 1m 6f
2:55 (2:55) (Class 5) 3-Y-O+ **£4,210** (£1,252; £625; £312) **Stalls** Low

Form RPR

3 **1** **Whenever**[30] 5113 3-9-1 0 JohnEgan 13 79
(R T Phillips) *in rr: hdwy over 4f out: rdn and str run fr 3f out: styd on to ld jst ins fnl f: drvn out* **20/1**

646 **2** *2 ½* **Bukit Tinggi (IRE)**[10] 5683 3-9-1 0 MartinDwyer 9 75
(M A Jarvis) *in rr: stl plenty to do over 3f out: rdn and r.o wl fnl 2f: kpt on to go 2nd cl home but nvr any ch of rching wnr* **14/1**

4005 **3** *1 ¼* **Crimson Monarch (USA)**[89] 3300 3-9-1 64 (b) DarryllHolland 1 73
(Mrs A J Perrett) *sn trcking ldr: chal gng wl fr over 3f out: stl upsides and rdn ins fnl 2f: outpcd insde fnl f: ct for 2nd cl home* **20/1**

-224 **4** *1 ¾* **Ned Ludd (IRE)**[103] 2860 4-9-10 83 TPQueally 2 71
(J G Portman) *led: rdn and styd on wl whn chal fr over 2f out: hdd jst ins fnl f: wknd fnl 100yds* **11/8**[1]

0030 **5** *1 ¾* **Sister Agnes (IRE)**[87] 3367 3-8-10 70 (b[1]) LiamJones 4 63
(Jane Chapple-Hyam) *chsd ldrs: rdn over 3f out: sn one pce: no ch w ldrs fnl 2f* **33/1**

0420 **6** *6* **Lady Dedlock**[21] 5352 3-8-10 55 SimonWhitworth 8 55
(C A Cyzer) *mid-div: hdwy 5f out: nvr gng pce to trble ldrs: wknd over 2f out* **14/1**

33-0 **7** *1 ½* **Altenburg (FR)**[46] 4630 5-9-10 75 GeorgeBaker 14 58
(Mrs N Smith) *sn in mid-div: hdwy over 4f out: chsd ldrs 3f out: wknd ins fnl 2f* **8/1**

-040 **8** *½* **Elusory**[34] 5005 3-9-1 59 DaneO'Neill 11 57
(J L Dunlop) *in rr: hdwy 5f out: nvr gng pce to trble ldrs: wknd over 2f out* **33/1**

0 **9** *nk* **Tweed River (USA)**[87] 3366 3-9-1 0 PatDobbs 5 57
(Miss E C Lavelle) *chsd ldrs: rdn 4f out: wknd over 2f out* **66/1**

5360 **10** *1 ¾* **Pugnacious Lady**[20] 5388 3-8-10 64 JamesDoyle 7 49
(J W Hills) *mid-div: rdn 5f out: nvr in contention* **28/1**

20 **11** *6* **Optimistic Alfie**[7] 5754 7-9-10 0 AdamKirby 6 46
(B G Powell) *in rr whn rdn 6f out: nvr in contention after* **66/1**

6463 **12** *2 ½* **Hesivorthedriver (GER)**[10] 5683 3-9-1 78 JimCrowley 12 42
(Mrs A J Perrett) *in rr: brief effrt over 4f out: sn wknd* **7/1**[3]

0-0 **13** *6* **Burntoakboy**[130] 1300 9-9-10 70 GregFairley 10 34
(Dr R D P Newland) *chsd ldrs: rdn over 3f out: sn btn* **5/1**[2]

14 *30* **Come Bye (IRE)**[164] 11-9-10 0 (t) ChrisCatlin 3 —
(Miss A M Newton-Smith) *slowly away: a in rr* **66/1**

3m 11.4s (7.43) **Going Correction** +0.50s/f (Yiel)
WFA 3 from 4yo+ 9lb **14** Ran SP% **119.0**
Speed ratings (Par 103): **98,96,95,94,93 90,89,89,89,88 84,83,79,62**
CSF £255.39 TOTE £16.30: £3.70, £3.50, £4.20; EX 410.20.
Owner Mr & Mrs W J Williams **Bred** D J And Mrs Deer **Trained** Adlestrop, Gloucs

FOCUS
A modest staying maiden in which the market leaders were below their best. They came over to the stands' side in the straight. The form is assessed through the 64-rated third, with winner Whatever a big improver.
Lady Dedlock Official explanation: jockey said filly lost a hind shoe
Tweed River(USA) Official explanation: trainer said colt returned lame

5939 RACING UK ON SKY 432 NURSERY 6f
3:30 (3:31) (Class 4) (0-80,82) 2-Y-O **£4,857** (£1,445; £722; £360) **Stalls** Low

Form RPR

4056 **1** **Leading Edge (IRE)**[15] 5529 2-8-2 **60** ChrisCatlin 5 63
(M R Channon) *chsd ldrs: rdn 2f out: styd on strly u.p fnl f to ld fnl 50yds* **16/1**

040 **2** *¾* **Thunder Gorge (USA)**[31] 5088 2-8-12 **73** NeilChalmers(3) 4 74
(Mouse Hamilton-Fairley) *s.i.s: sn rcvrd: in rr but in tch: hdwy and hd high fr 2f out: sn hanging rt: styd on strly but stl hanging fnl f: tk 2nd last strides* **20/1**

060 **3** *½* **Minwir (IRE)**[19] 5428 2-8-10 **68** MartinDwyer 13 68
(M A Jarvis) *in rr: hdwy fr 2f out: styd on wl fnl f: nvr quite gng pce to press ldrs* **13/2**[3]

2105 **4** *nk* **Luscious Lips**[40] 4823 2-9-4 **76** PatDobbs 14 75
(R Hannon) *in rr: hdwy 1/2-way: drvn to ld jst ins fnl f: hdd and outpcd fnl 50yds* **8/1**

0440 **5** ½ **Caradoc Place**[18] 5452 2-8-12 **70** DaneO'Neill 11 67
(M P Tregoning) *in rr: rdn 2f out: rapid hdwy ins fnl f: fin wl: nt rch ldrs* **14/1**

4501 **6** 1¼ **Not My Choice (IRE)**[5] 5802 2-9-10 **82** 6ex JohnEgan 6 75
(D J Murphy) *led: rdn over 1f out: hdd jst ins fnl f: wknd nr fin* **7/2**[1]

5100 **7** 3 **Shamrock Lady (IRE)**[28] 5164 2-9-7 **79** JimCrowley 9 63
(Pat Eddery) *chsd ldrs: rdn 1f out: sn outpcd* **7/1**

6000 **8** ½ **Ava Gee**[21] 5357 2-8-7 **65** DavidKinsella 7 48
(B De Haan) *chsd ldr: rdn 1/2-way: wknd fnl f* **20/1**

566 **9** 1½ **Silca Destination**[41] 4756 2-8-2 **60** TPO'Shea 8 38
(M R Channon) *in rr: rdn 1/2-way: sme prog fr 2f out but nvr gng pce to be competitive* **11/1**

0000 **10** 3 **Follow The Band**[19] 5417 2-8-7 **65** RichardSmith 10 34
(R Hannon) *outpcd* **33/1**

002 **11** *hd* **Smokey Rye**[57] 4265 2-7-12 **63** RossAtkinson(7) 1 32
(G L Moore) *spd over 3f* **8/1**

4031 **12** 8 **Sawpit Sunshine (IRE)**[71] 3841 2-8-10 **68** LiamJones 3 13
(J L Spearing) *chsd ldrs: rdn over 2f out: n.m.r over 1f out and wknd qckly* **11/2**[2]

1m 15.18s (2.33) **Going Correction** +0.35s/f (Good) **12** Ran SP% **119.0**
Speed ratings (Par 97): **98,97,96,95,95 93,89,88,86,82 82,72**
CSF £303.57 CT £2326.45 TOTE £18.10: £5.50, £7.50, £2.10; EX 529.00.

Owner Wood Street Syndicate II **Bred** Rathasker Stud **Trained** West Ilsley, Berks

FOCUS
A poor nursery by Goodwood standards. The first five were fairly closely covered at the finish, and this is not form to be too positive about.

NOTEBOOK
Leading Edge(IRE) came good at the ninth time of asking and ran out a determined winner, showing the benefit of a 4lb drop in the weights. This softer ground was evidently more to her liking and she ought to continue to pay her despite going back up in the weights.

Thunder Gorge(USA), having his first run in a nursery, had to come from behind after a slow start and was doing all of his best work towards the finish. He was not beaten far and has the talent to defy his current mark, but he left the impression that he may not be a straightforward ride. (tchd 25-1)

Minwir(IRE), making his nursery debut, still looks to be learning his trade and appeared a little one paced on this softer ground. He still ran his best race to date, however, and seems to have begun life in this sphere on a fair mark so a move to 7f could bring about further improvement. (op 7-1 tchd 15-2 and 6-1)

Luscious Lips showed improved form on this switch to easier ground and was produced to have every chance. On this evidence, however, she looks in need of a drop back to the mimimum trip. (op 7-1)

Caradoc Place looked a threat passing two out on this step back up in trip, but he failed to raise his game when it really mattered and could be ready to tackle 7f now. Nevertheless this was still a much more encouraging display. (op 16-1)

Not My Choice(IRE), penalised for getting off the mark on his nursery bow five days previously, was given a positive ride over the extra furlong yet simply looked a non-stayer. He is also probably a lot happier on quicker ground. Official explanation: jockey said colt was unsuited by the soft ground (op 10-3 tchd 4-1)

5940 JOHN WOOTON FILLIES' AND MARES' H'CAP 1m 4f
4:05 (4:05) (Class 3) (0-95,92) 3-Y-0+ **£7,772** (£2,312; £1,155; £577) **Stalls** Low

Form RPR

-333 **1** **Candle**[48] 4572 4-8-13 **82** DaneO'Neill 2 91
(H Candy) *trckd ldrs: qcknd 2f out and led jst ins fnl f: drvn clr fnl 100yds* **6/1**[3]

1212 **2** 2 **Pivotal Answer (IRE)**[10] 5686 3-8-9 **85** TPQueally 1 91
(J Noseda) *sn trcking ldr: led wl over 2f out: rdn sn after: hdd jst ins fnl f: styd on same pce* **5/4**[1]

1100 **3** 2 **Intiquilla (IRE)**[63] 4113 3-8-2 **78** oh2 TPO'Shea 6 81
(Mrs A J Perrett) *in rr but in tch: rdn over 3f out and styd on to press ldrs fr 2f out: upsides u.p over 1f out: wknd ins fnl f* **14/1**

266 **4** 5 **Oh Glory Be (USA)**[10] 5686 4-9-9 **92** PatDobbs 8 87
(R Hannon) *in rr: pushed along 2f oit: r.o ins fnl f: nvr in contention* **20/1**

3114 **5** 1¼ **Opal Haze (USA)**[12] 5619 3-8-12 **88** RobertHavlin 4 81
(J H M Gosden) *led: rdn and hdd wl over 2f out: sn btn* **15/2**

4032 **6** 10 **Lisathedaddy**[13] 5593 5-8-13 **82** AdamKirby 3 59
(B G Powell) *in rr: rdn and hdwy 3f out: nvr rchd ldrs and sn wknd* **12/1**

11/2 **7** *hd* **Desert D'Argent (IRE)**[26] 5225 4-8-13 **82** MartinDwyer 5 58
(H Morrison) *chsd ldrs: lost position 4f out: rallied 3f out: sn wknd* **7/2**[2]

2m 42.71s (3.79) **Going Correction** +0.50s/f (Yiel)
WFA 3 from 4yo+ 7lb **7** Ran SP% **111.8**
Speed ratings (Par 104): **107,105,104,101,100 93,93**
CSF £13.34 CT £97.41 TOTE £7.40: £3.40, £1.20; EX 16.80.

Owner Mrs David Blackburn **Bred** Mrs M J Blackburn **Trained** Kingston Warren, Oxon

FOCUS
A good fillies' and mares' handicap for the class, run at a sound pace. The field finished fairly strung out and the form is straightforward rated around the winner and third.

NOTEBOOK
Candle, third on each of her three previous outings this term, showed her true colours on this return to softer ground and eventually did the job comfortably. She was always going best of all behind the leaders and responded kindly when asked for her effort on the stands' side nearing the final furlong, winning with something to spare. This is clearly her ground and, while she may not be the most straightforward, it would not be a surprise to see her go in again now her confidence will have been enhanced. (op 7-1)

Pivotal Answer(IRE), officially 8lb ahead of the Handicapper after her latest second at Kempton ten days previously, had every chance if good enough on this return to turf yet could not cope with the winner when it mattered. She did not run up to her best, but it may be that she now requires a sound surface to shine and she should not be written off yet, despite having to race from a higher mark now. (tchd 11-8 and 11-10)

Intiquilla(IRE), 2lb out of the handicap and down in trip, came through from off the pace to run an improved race on ground she clearly enjoys. She can find easier assignments, despite the likelihood of going back up a pound or two again for this. (tchd 12-1)

Oh Glory Be(USA), well beaten by the runner-up at Kempton last time, did not appear that happy on this softer surface and was never in the hunt under top weight. (op 16-1 tchd 25-1)

Opal Haze(USA), 2lb lower, set out to make all and went off at a sound pace. She proved a sitting duck when the race became serious, however, and is now starting to look exposed. (op 7-1 tchd 6-1)

Lisathedaddy seems better on a sound surface.

Desert D'Argent(IRE), just denied by the runner-up on her return from a layoff at Kempton 26 days previously, was in trouble soon after turning for home and ran well below form. She can have no excuses with the ground, as she won on heavy as a two-year-old, and has something to prove now, but it is also possible that she "bounced" here. Official explanation: jockey said filly had no more to give (op 4-1 tchd 9-2)

5941 TURFTV IN YOUR BETTING SHOP H'CAP 1m 3f
4:40 (4:40) (Class 4) (0-80,77) 3-Y-0 **£5,505** (£1,637; £818; £408) **Stalls** Low

Form RPR

12 **1** **Dustoori**[10] 5677 3-9-3 **76** MartinDwyer 9 84
(Saeed Bin Suroor) *hld up in rr: hdwy and rdn over 2f out: c to stands' rail and styd on u.p to ld fnl 50yds: r.o wl* **4/6**[1]

0110 **2** 1¼ **Gib (IRE)**[27] 5210 3-9-0 **73** ChrisCatlin 3 79
(B W Hills) *led: rdn and r.o gamely whn strly chal fr 2f out: hdd and no ex fnl 50yds* **16/1**

3215 **3** ½ **Hibiki (IRE)**[13] 5594 3-8-9 **73** TolleyDean(5) 1 78
(J S Moore) *chsd ldrs: rdn over 2f out: str chal fr 2f out and upsides fr over 1f out tl no ex fnl 50yds* **14/1**

001 **4** *hd* **Give Me A Break**[30] 5113 3-9-3 **76** DarryllHolland 8 81
(P W Chapple-Hyam) *chsd ldrs: lost position 4f out: drvn and hdwy to press ldrs fr 2f out: upsides u.p insfnl ft: one pce fnl 50yds* **4/1**[2]

1351 **5** 5 **Rustic Gold**[66] 4015 3-8-9 **68** DaneO'Neill 6 64
(J R Best) *s.i.s: in rr: hdwy fr 3f out: nvr gng pce to rch ldrs and styd on same pce* **14/1**

-522 **6** 1¼ **Unreachable Star**[18] 5450 3-9-2 **75** JimCrowley 5 69
(Mrs A J Perrett) *in tch: hdwy to dispute 2nd over 3f out: sn rdn: wknd fr 2f out* **16/1**

100 **7** 7 **Seleet (IRE)**[85] 3416 3-9-4 **77** RobertHavlin 7 59
(M A Jarvis) *t.k.h: chsd ldr to 3f out: sn btn* **50/1**

1646 **8** 7 **Rock Anthem (IRE)**[34] 5014 3-9-3 **76** TPQueally 4 46
(J L Dunlop) *in rr: sme hdwy 3f out: nvr rchd ldrs and sn dropped to rr* **12/1**[3]

2m 32.02s (4.81) **Going Correction** +0.50s/f (Yiel) **8** Ran SP% **114.7**
Speed ratings (Par 103): **102,101,100,100,96 96,90,85**
CSF £14.15 CT £86.34 TOTE £1.60: £1.10, £3.00, £2.80; EX 17.70.

Owner Godolphin **Bred** Shadwell Estate Company Limited **Trained** Newmarket, Suffolk

FOCUS
A fair handicap that was run at a sound pace and the form is sound enough rated around those in the frame behind the winner, each of whom raced in the centre of the track in the home straight.
Rock Anthem(IRE) Official explanation: jockey said colt was unsuited by the soft ground

5942 TURFTV FOR BETTING SHOPS APPRENTICE H'CAP 5f
5:15 (5:15) (Class 5) (0-70,73) 3-Y-0+ **£3,562** (£1,059; £529; £264) **Stalls** Low

Form RPR

4300 **1** **Hereford Boy**[12] 5642 3-8-11 **67** JamesO'Reilly(5) 10 77
(D K Ivory) *sn trcking ldrs: led over 1f out: drvn out* **25/1**

3005 **2** 1 **Caustic Wit (IRE)**[8] 5731 9-8-8 **62** TolleyDean(3) 8 68
(M S Saunders) *chsd ldrs: rdn to go 2nd fnl f: kpt on but nvr gng pce of wnr* **6/1**[3]

1231 **3** 1½ **Digital**[8] 5740 10-9-3 **73** 6ex (v) ThomasO'Brien(5) 2 74
(M R Channon) *in rr and outpcd: rdn 1/2-way: swtchd rt over 1f out and r.o ins fnl f but nvr gng pce to ldng duo* **13/2**

1422 **4** 1¾ **Dixieland Boy (IRE)**[8] 5722 4-9-5 **70** GregFairley 1 65+
(P J Makin) *outpcd and rdn along after 2f: styd on fr over 1f out but nvr in contention* **15/8**[1]

0240 **5** 1¼ **Bookiesindex Boy**[29] 5139 3-9-3 **68** LiamJones 4 58
(J R Jenkins) *in rr: rdn and hdwy 2f out: nvr gng pce to press ldrs and sn outpcd* **20/1**

0613 **6** *hd* **Contented (IRE)**[31] 5090 5-8-1 **57** ow1 (p) SCreighton(5) 5 46
(Mrs L C Jewell) *chsd ldrs: rdn 1/2-way: wknd over 1f out* **9/2**[2]

2105 **7** 1 **Our Fugitive (IRE)**[14] 5565 5-8-10 **64** LukeMorris(3) 7 50
(A W Carroll) *pressed ldr: led over 2f out: hdd over 1f out and sn wknd* **9/2**[2]

6500 **8** ¾ **Matterofact (IRE)**[8] 5726 4-8-9 **63** ow1 HaddenFrost(3) 9 46
(M S Saunders) *led tl hdd over 2f out: wknd over 1f out* **25/1**

0005 **9** ½ **Lindbergh**[15] 5535 5-9-0 **65** (p) AlanCreighton 6 46
(A J Lidderdale) *chsd ldrs to 1/2-way* **33/1**

60.33 secs (1.28) **Going Correction** +0.35s/f (Good) **9** Ran SP% **114.2**
Speed ratings (Par 103): **103,101,99,96,94 93,92,91,90**
CSF £158.94 CT £1111.20 TOTE £46.80: £5.40, £2.00, £1.60; EX 372.80 Place 6 £1,233.44, Place 5 £856.93.

Owner T G N Burrage **Bred** Mrs L R Burrage **Trained** Radlett, Herts

FOCUS
A modest sprint handicap, run at a strong early pace and sound enough rated through the runner-up to his recent marks.
Bookiesindex Boy Official explanation: jockey said colt hung left

T/Plt: £742.80 to a £1 stake. Pool: £55,814.55. 54.85 winning tickets. T/Qpdt: £17.50 to a £1 stake. Pool: £3,934.60. 165.90 winning tickets. ST

5894 KEMPTON (A.W) (R-H)
Thursday, October 4

OFFICIAL GOING: Standard
Wind: Light, against Weather: Fine

5943 DAY TIME, NIGHT TIME, GREAT TIME H'CAP 1m 2f (P)
6:50 (6:53) (Class 5) (0-75,74) 3-Y-0 **£3,238** (£963; £481; £240) **Stalls** High

Form RPR

3445 **1** **Going To Work (IRE)**[8] 5725 3-9-3 **73** IanMongan 9 85
(D R C Elsworth) *trckd ldrs: led on inner wl over 2f out and sn kicked 2l clr: rdn and maintained advantage fnl 2f* **6/1**[3]

6201 **2** 1½ **Candy Mountain**[12] 5636 3-9-4 **74** GeorgeBaker 7 83
(L M Cumani) *hld up in midfield: prog on inner to chse wnr jst over 2f out: hanging over 1f out: kpt on but no real imp* **7/2**[1]

1604 **3** 2½ **Silca Key**[19] 5424 3-8-10 **66** TPO'Shea 3 70+
(M R Channon) *settled in rr: rdn and prog on inner over 2f out: chsd ldng pair over 1f out: one pce and no imp* **11/2**[2]

1-63 **4** 2 **Golan Way**[19] 5405 3-8-9 **72** HarryPoulton(7) 5 72
(I A Wood) *trckd ldrs: outpcd over 2f out: disp 3rd wl over 1f out: one pce* **13/2**

0200 **5** ½ **Shouldntbethere (IRE)**[8] 5733 3-8-9 **65** AdrianMcCarthy 6 64
(Mrs P N Dutfield) *stdd s: hld up in last: gd prog over 2f out: v wd bnd sn after and lost all ch: one pce* **33/1**

2140 **6** ½ **Yes One (IRE)**[67] 3993 3-9-3 **73** ChrisCatlin 1 71
(J W Hills) *in tch: outpcd and rdn over 2f out: n.d after* **12/1**

5-14 **7** *4* **Red Blooded Woman (USA)**[23] 5303 3-8-12 **68**............... TPQueally 2 58
(J Noseda) *t.k.h: trckd ldrs and racd wd: lost pl wl over 2f out: no ch after* **7/2**[1]

640 **8** *nk* **Professor Twinkle**[18] 5454 3-9-2 **72**..................................(v) PaulDoe 10 61
(W J Knight) *led: hanging lft fr 4f out: hdd wl over 2f out: c wd bnd sn after and wknd* **16/1**

3606 **9** *2* **Blackberry Pie (USA)**[17] 5475 3-8-9 **65**.............. OscarUrbina 4 50
(R Charlton) *slipped s: prom: rdn and wknd over 2f out* **10/1**

-006 **10** *12* **Moorlander (USA)**[8] 5738 3-8-10 **66** ow2...................(t) DarryllHolland 8 27
(Mrs A J Perrett) *mostly trckd ldr to 3f out: losing pl rapidly whn squeezed out over 2f out: t.o* **20/1**

2m 5.76s (-3.24) **Going Correction** -0.275s/f (Stan) **10** Ran SP% **117.8**
Speed ratings (Par 101): **101,99,97,96,95 95,92,91,90,80**
CSF £27.61 CT £124.12 TOTE £6.70: £2.40, £1.30, £1.70; EX 33.20.
Owner Matthew Green **Bred** Glending Bloodstock **Trained** Newmarket, Suffolk

FOCUS
A modest handicap run as just a fair pace and a couple did not enjoy the smoothest of runs due to some trouble on the home turn. The third is the best guide to the form.
Red Blooded Woman(USA) Official explanation: jockey said filly was hampered on final bend
Professor Twinkle Official explanation: jockey said colt hung left on final bend

5944 PANORAMIC RESTAURANT LOYALTY AND REWARD SCHEME MEDIAN AUCTION MAIDEN FILLIES' STKS 1m (P)

7:20 (7:22) (Class 6) 2-Y-O **£2,047** (£604; £302) **Stalls** High

Form RPR

32 **1** **Lady Sorcerer**[13] 5580 2-9-0 0.. SebSanders 7 76
(A P Jarvis) *chsd ldng trio: rdn over 2f out: prog to go 2nd 1f out: led last 100yds: jst hld on* **4/5**[1]

4 **2** *shd* **Spiritofthestorm (USA)**[15] 5527 2-9-0 0.......................... ChrisCatlin 9 76
(R A Teal) *trckd ldrs: pushed along whn nt clr run briefly 3f out: swtchd lft over 2f out: drvn and r.o fr over 1f out: jst failed* **15/2**

3 *1/2* **Leamington (USA)** 2-9-0 0.. GregFairley 3 75
(M Johnston) *led: kicked on over 2f out: collared last 100yds: kpt on* **6/1**[3]

5 **4** *1 1/4* **Vallani (IRE)**[23] 5308 2-9-0 0.. AdamKirby 13 72
(W R Swinburn) *wl in tch: prog on inner 3f out: chsd ldrs 2f out: kpt on but nvr able to chal* **9/2**[2]

63 **5** *1 1/2* **Oceana Blue**[13] 5605 2-8-11 0..................... WilliamBuick(3) 12 68
(A M Balding) *trckd ldng pair: wnt 2nd 3f out to 1f out: wknd* **14/1**

005 **6** *2* **Lella Beya**[10] 5682 2-9-0 0.. DaneO'Neill 10 64
(S Kirk) *s.i.s: sn in midfield: rdn over 2f out: outpcd and no ch fnl 2f* **25/1**

0 **7** *3/4* **Appointment**[13] 5596 2-9-0 0...................................... DarryllHolland 11 62
(Mrs A J Perrett) *wl in rr: pushed along and rn green over 2f out: kpt on fr over 1f out: n.d* **25/1**

04 **8** *shd* **Cherished Song**[19] 5429 2-8-9 0.......................... KirstyMilczarek(5) 6 62
(N A Callaghan) *t.k.h: hld up in midfield: rdn over 2f out: sn outpcd and btn* **50/1**

0 **9** *3/4* **Crimsonwing (IRE)**[10] 5681 2-8-9 0.......................... PatrickHills(5) 2 60
(A M Hales) *in tch on outer: rdn and outpcd over 2f out: no ch after* **66/1**

00 **10** *nk* **Teadancer (IRE)**[23] 5309 2-9-0 0.. TPQueally 14 59
(J G Portman) *settled wl in rr: pushed along 3f out: outpcd sn after: sme hdwy 2f out: no ch* **100/1**

11 *1 1/2* **Flower** 2-9-0 0.. SimonWhitworth 4 56
(C A Cyzer) *rel to r and detached in last: pushed along and kpt on fnl 2f: no ch* **66/1**

05 **12** *shd* **Amie Magnificent (IRE)**[15] 5527 2-9-0 0.......................... IanMongan 8 56
(P Winkworth) *chsd ldr to 3f out: sn wknd* **50/1**

03 **13** *4* **Xaravella (IRE)**[33] 5038 2-9-0 0.. RobertHavlin 1 46
(J G M O'Shea) *pushed along in rr 1/2-way: wknd over 2f out* **66/1**

1m 40.3s (-0.50) **Going Correction** -0.275s/f (Stan) **13** Ran SP% **123.5**
Speed ratings (Par 90): **91,90,90,89,87 85,84,84,84,83 82,82,78**
CSF £7.60 TOTE £1.90: £1.10, £2.20, £2.40; EX 6.30.
Owner The Aston Partnership **Bred** David J Brown And Mrs J Berry **Trained** Twyford, Bucks
■ Stewards' Enquiry : Seb Sanders caution: used whip with excessive frequency

FOCUS
This did not look a great maiden and not that many got into it. There was little to get excited about outside the front five.

NOTEBOOK
Lady Sorcerer, up another furlong, probably only needed to repeat the form of her first two starts to win this, but she made hard work of it. She had to fight very hard in order to get to the front in the first place, and then only managed to hold off the runner-up by the skin of her teeth. It may be that she is better suited to turf, but she will still need to improve on this in order to be competitive in better company. (op 10-11 tchd Evens)
Spiritofthestorm(USA) ◆, whose debut fourth over this course and distance is working out alright, rather found herself locked away in traffic starting up the home straight and had to be brought out wide to make her effort. To her credit she finished in great style and would have nailed the favourite in another stride. She should not take long in getting off the mark. (op 9-1)
Leamington(USA), out of a winning half-sister to Fahal, was able to set her own pace and it looked as though she would take some catching at one stage, but she hung over to the inside rail after the intersection and was just run out of it by two fillies with previous experience. She may be nothing special, but should be able to find an ordinary maiden with this under her belt. (op 15-2)
Vallani(IRE) ◆, up a furlong from her debut, was always in a good position on the inside but although she kept on, she lacked the speed to get in an effective blow. She should continue to progress with racing and as she goes up in trip.
Oceana Blue was given another prominent ride, but after having every chance did not seem to see out the trip so well this time. She now qualifies for nurseries and that may be her best option.

5945 DIGIBET.COM H'CAP 1m (P)

7:50 (7:54) (Class 6) (0-52,52) 3-Y-O **£2,047** (£604; £302) **Stalls** High

Form RPR

1040 **1** **Smash N'Grab (IRE)**[10] 5688 3-8-13 **51**.......................... LiamJones 9 58
(J R Jenkins) *chsd ldrs: rdn to cl fr over 2f out: led jst over 1f out: hung lft fnl f: jst hld on* **12/1**

0050 **2** *shd* **Brouhaha**[39] 4856 3-8-12 **50**..............................(tp) OscarUrbina 14 57
(Miss Diana Weeden) *dwlt: hld up wl in rr and off the pce: nt clr run over 3f out: prog wl over 2f out: taken to outer and clsd over 1f out: pressed wnr fnl f: jst failed* **12/1**

0000 **3** *3 1/2* **Tokyo Jo (IRE)**[47] 4596 3-8-12 **50**...........................(p) TGMcLaughlin 12 49
(T T Clement) *chsd ldrs: drvn on inner to ld over 2f out: hdd jst over 1f out: wknd ins fnl f* **33/1**

4500 **4** *shd* **Nou Camp**[44] 4685 3-8-7 **50**.......................... KirstyMilczarek(5) 1 48
(N A Callaghan) *s.s: plld hrd and hld up in last trio: prog on outer 3f out: looked dangerous over 1f out: fnd nil* **12/1**

4060 **5** *nk* **Palanoverre (IRE)**[21] 5347 3-8-13 **51**......................(tp) RichardThomas 4 49
(D J S Ffrench Davis) *wl bhd in last pair after 3f: drvn and prog on inner fr 3f out: kpt on but nvr rchd ldrs* **11/1**

0405 **6** *nk* **Beresford Lady**[46] 4641 3-8-12 **50**.......................... SilvestreDeSousa 10 47
(A D Brown) *dwlt: pushed along and prom after 2f: chsd ldr over 4f out: tried to cl over 2f out but wandering: wknd fnl f* **16/1**

2005 **7** *1/2* **Path To Glory**[15] 5528 3-8-13 **51**.......................... AdrianMcCarthy 13 47
(Miss Z C Davison) *towards rr and wl off the pce: drvn 3f out: plugged on fnl 2f: nrst fin but n.d* **13/2**[3]

0503 **8** *1 1/2* **Ravenhill Ralph (IRE)**[21] 5347 3-8-13 **51**.......................... SebSanders 7 44
(J G M O'Shea) *prom in fast run r: rdn 3f out: tried to cl 2f out: wknd and lost pls fnl f* **9/2**[1]

5360 **9** *nk* **Silent Beauty (IRE)**[12] 5647 3-8-12 **50**.......................... ChrisCatlin 11 42
(S C Williams) *sn rdn in rr: nvr on terms: plugged on fnl 2f: no ch* **9/1**

0006 **10** *1 1/4* **Time For Change (IRE)**[5] 5817 3-8-12 **50**...................(v) RobertHavlin 8 39
(P G Murphy) *blasted off in ld at furious pce: rdn and hdd over 2f out: wknd jst over 1f out* **15/2**

0340 **11** *13* **Meadfoot**[24] 5269 3-8-13 **51**.......................... DarryllHolland 3 10
(B R Millman) *nvr on terms: u.p and bhd fnl 3f* **12/1**

0000 **12** *13* **Quite A Splash (USA)**[26] 2796 3-9-0 **52**.......................... PaulDoe 6 —
(S Curran) *wl bhd in last pair after 3f: t.o* **25/1**

046 **13** *2* **Welsh Auction**[22] 5338 3-8-9 **50**.......................... EmmettStack(3) 5 —
(K J Burke) *chsd ldrs to 1/2-way: wknd over 3f out: t.o* **12/1**

0645 **14** *dist* **Glenridding**[21] 5366 3-8-12 **50**..(b) TPQueally 2 —
(J G Given) *pressed ldr: wknd rapidly over 4f out: sn t.o* **5/1**[2]

1m 39.79s (-1.01) **Going Correction** -0.275s/f (Stan) **14** Ran SP% **129.4**
Speed ratings (Par 99): **94,93,90,90,90 89,89,87,87,86 73,60,58,—**
CSF £159.67 CT £4639.25 TOTE £17.00: £5.10, £6.10, £9.60; EX 224.60.
Owner Bookmakers Index Ltd **Bred** Paul Kavanagh **Trained** Royston, Herts

FOCUS
They went off far too fast in this handicap. Those that helped force it all eventually fell in heap and set the race up for the closers. Just how much the pace collapsed is reflected by a modest winning time and the form is far from solid.
Meadfoot Official explanation: jockey said filly hung right in straight
Glenridding Official explanation: vet said gelding returned distressed

5946 DIGIBET CASINO H'CAP 7f (P)

8:20 (8:22) (Class 6) (0-52,53) 3-Y-O+ **£2,047** (£604; £302) **Stalls** High

Form RPR

2415 **1** **The Jailer**[21] 5368 4-8-5 **50**.......................... MCGeran(7) 12 59
(J G M O'Shea) *mde all: kicked on at least 2l clr over 2f out: all out fnl f: jst hld on* **14/1**

3200 **2** *shd* **Siesta (IRE)**[56] 4336 3-8-8 **48**..........................(e) OscarUrbina 2 57
(J R Fanshawe) *settled in rr: prog on wd outside over 2f out: r.o fnl f to press wnr nr fin: jst failed* **12/1**

0041 **3** *hd* **Jools**[22] 5336 9-8-9 **52**.......................... PatrickHills(5) 13 60
(D K Ivory) *prom: rdn to chse wnr 2f out: clsd fnl f: nt quite get up and lost 2nd last strides* **5/1**[2]

0323 **4** *1 1/2* **Brave Jack (IRE)**[5] 5817 3-8-10 **50**.......................... SteveDrowne 10 54
(J R Best) *settled in midfield: prog over 2f out: chsd ldrs over 1f out: nt qckn and no imp fnl f* **5/2**[1]

6006 **5** *1/2* **Reveur**[49] 4533 4-8-8 **46**.......................... TPQueally 9 49+
(M Mullineaux) *mostly midfield on inner: rdn and styd on fr 2f out: nvr quite rchd ldrs* **7/1**

2305 **6** *5* **Lost All Alone**[14] 5576 3-8-3 **48**.......................... KirstyMilczarek(5) 5 38
(D M Simcock) *chsd ldrs: rdn and no imp wl over 2f out: wknd over 1f out* **10/1**

6606 **7** *hd* **Feelin Irie (IRE)**[15] 5546 4-8-8 **53** ow1...................(p) HarryPoulton(7) 6 42
(J R Boyle) *chsd wnr to 2f out: bmpd along and wknd* **10/1**

0405 **8** *2 1/2* **Minnie Mill**[20] 5386 3-8-9 **49**.......................... PaulEddery 8 31
(B P J Baugh) *dwlt: mostly wl in rr: outpcd over 2f out: no ch after* **66/1**

0446 **9** *1* **Sir Loin**[61] 4180 6-9-0 **52**.......................... LPKeniry 7 32
(P Burgoyne) *a towards rr: outpcd over 2f out: no ch after* **25/1**

3005 **10** *shd* **Xalted**[10] 5688 3-8-2 **49**.......................... WilliamCarson(7) 3 28
(S C Williams) *racd wd: chsd ldrs: hanging and nt qckn over 2f out: sn btn* **12/1**

5040 **11** *hd* **Wodhill Schnaps**[20] 5391 6-9-0 **52**.......................... AdrianMcCarthy 1 31
(D Morris) *sn pushed along in last trio: nvr a factor* **14/1**

6505 **12** *1 1/4* **Shava**[8] 5730 7-8-11 **49**.......................... FergusSweeney 4 24
(H J Evans) *racd wd in midfield: u.p and struggling wl over 2f out: wknd* **11/2**[3]

2204 **13** *3/4* **Miss Taboo (IRE)**[12] 5625 3-8-9 **49**.......................... MickyFenton 14 22
(P T Midgley) *prom: rdn whn hmpd 3f out and again over 2f out: nt rcvr and bhd after* **16/1**

1m 25.46s (-1.34) **Going Correction** -0.275s/f (Stan)
WFA 3 from 4yo+ 2lb **13** Ran SP% **131.2**
Speed ratings (Par 101): **96,95,95,93,93 87,87,84,83,83 83,81,80**
CSF £188.55 CT £1008.25 TOTE £23.80: £6.60, £3.60, £2.40; EX 366.60.
Owner N M Lowe **Bred** D R Tucker **Trained** Elton, Gloucs

FOCUS
With Smash N'Grab winning the previous contest it seems appropriate that The Jailer should win this. Another strongly-run handicap, but this time the one that set it benefited the most, albeit it narrowly. Very few ever got competitive and the front five pulled miles clear suggesting the form is solid.

5947 DIGIBET SPORTS BETTING H'CAP 6f (P)

8:50 (8:52) (Class 6) (0-52,52) 3-Y-O+ **£2,047** (£604; £302) **Stalls** High

Form RPR

0035 **1** **Stormburst (IRE)**[59] 4224 3-8-4 **50**.......................... WilliamCarson(7) 12 61+
(S C Williams) *chsd ldr: rdn to ld over 1f out: pushed out and wl in command fnl f* **8/1**

450 **2** *1 1/4* **Littledodayno (IRE)**[24] 5284 4-9-0 **52**.......................... NickyMackay 1 59
(M Wigham) *settled in rr and sn wl off the pce: prog 2f out: styd on to take 2nd nr fin: no ch w wnr* **5/1**[2]

0005 **3** *1/2* **One Way Ticket**[21] 5349 7-8-12 **50**..............................(b[1]) HayleyTurner 4 55
(J M Bradley) *led at str pce: gng strly over 2f out: hdd and no ex over 1f out: lost 2nd nr fin* **9/2**[1]

0000 **4** *3 1/2* **King Egbert (FR)**[10] 5687 6-8-9 **52**..............................(p) TolleyDean(5) 8 46
(R J Price) *hld up bhd ldng trio: rdn over 2f out: nt qckn and no imp after* **12/1**

0215 **5** *1/2* **Knead The Dough**[9] 5716 6-8-7 **50**.......................... NataliaGemelova(5) 2 43
(A E Price) *chsd ldrs: rdn wl over 2f out: one pce and no imp* **6/1**[3]

0006 **6** *2* **Piccostar**[3] 5867 4-9-0 **52**..............................(v) SamHitchcott 9 38
(A B Haynes) *sn rdn in midfield: nvr on terms: n.d fnl 2f: plugged on* **15/2**

0053 **7** *1* **Davids Mark**[125] 2221 7-9-0 **52**.......................... MickyFenton 3 35
(J R Jenkins) *hld up in rr: c wd bnd 3f out: shkn up and no prog over 2f out* **6/1**[3]

0000 **8** *nk* **Peruvian Style (IRE)**[3] 5866 6-8-11 **49**.......................... SteveDrowne 7 31
(J M Bradley) *rdn in midfield over 3f out: no imp over 2f out: wknd* **5/1**[2]

5500 **9** *6* **Half A Tsar (IRE)**[3] 5861 3-8-2 48 JackDean(7) 6 11
(Mark Gillard) *bmpd s: nvr beyond midfield: wknd over 2f out* **50/1**
5000 **10** *4* **Almora Guru**[33] 5041 3-8-13 52 LiamJones 5 2
(W M Brisbourne) *hanging and racd on wd outside: wnt v wd bnd 3f out: bhd after* **20/1**
1m 11.79s (-1.91) **Going Correction** -0.275s/f (Stan)
WFA 3 from 4yo+ 1lb **10** Ran SP% **117.4**
Speed ratings (Par 101): **101,99,98,94,93 90,89,88,80,75**
CSF £48.11 CT £208.52 TOTE £9.40: £2.90, £2.20, £2.20; EX 59.60.
Owner bellhouseracing.com **Bred** Ralph And Helen O'Brien **Trained** Newmarket, Suffolk
■ Majestical (13/1, spread a plate) was withdrawn. R4, deduct 10p in the £.
FOCUS
Another race run at a decent pace and they finished very well spread out for a sprint handicap. Very few ever looked like getting involved but the form is rated positively and should work out.
Almora Guru Official explanation: jockey said filly hung left

5948 AFTERNOON RACING HERE SATURDAY H'CAP 2m (P)
9:20 (9:21) (Class 6) (0-65,65) 3-Y-O+ **£2,047** (£604; £302) **Stalls** High

Form RPR
0301 **1** **Go Amwell**[18] 5453 4-8-11 48 LiamJones 6 59
(J R Jenkins) *hld up in last pair: prog on wd outside wl over 2f out: rdn to ld ent fnl f: styd on wl whn pressed* **15/2**[3]
0416 **2** *nk* **Susie May**[9] 5709 3-8-10 58 SebSanders 8 69
(C A Cyzer) *hld up towards rr: prog on outer 3f out: clsd on ldrs over 1f out: drvn to chal ent fnl f: jst hld last 75yds* **15/2**[3]
2343 **3** *1* **Capitalise (IRE)**[5] 5820 4-8-13 53 JerryO'Dwyer(3) 3 62
(V Smith) *hld up in rr: prog gng wl on outer 4f out: wd st: rdn to ld wl over 1f out: hdd and nt qckn ent fnl f* **3/1**[2]
6040 **4** *3 ½* **Arabian Sun**[5] 5820 3-8-10 58 (v[1]) ChrisCatlin 13 63
(M J Attwater) *prom on inner: effrt 3f out: rdn to chal and upsides 2f out: sn outpcd* **33/1**
2003 **5** *3* **Teorban (POL)**[27] 5204 8-9-8 59 StephenDonohoe 5 61
(Mrs N S Evans) *wl in rr: rdn 4f out: sn struggling: styd on fr 2f out on inner: n.d* **12/1**
5050 **6** *¾* **Watchmaker**[16] 5500 4-9-11 62 FergusSweeney 2 63
(Miss Tor Sturgis) *hld up in midfield: prog on outer over 3f out: rdn to chal 2f out: wknd over 1f out* **20/1**
0042 **7** *¾* **Composing (IRE)**[19] 5426 3-8-10 58 (t) SteveDrowne 7 58
(H Morrison) *prom: rdn to chse ldr over 3f out: nt qckn 2f out: steadily wknd* **2/1**[1]
0000 **8** *½* **Tromp**[16] 5500 6-10-0 65 DaneO'Neill 4 64
(D J Coakley) *hld up in rr: gng strly 4f out: prog to chse ldrs 2f out: sn rdn: wknd jst over 1f out* **14/1**
26-0 **9** *nk* **Dubai Ace (USA)**[133] 1959 6-9-10 64 (p) NeilChalmers(3) 12 63
(Miss Sheena West) *chsd ldrs: rdn wl over 2f out: no imp after: fdd over 1f out* **16/1**
2060 **10** *shd* **Spinal Tap (IRE)**[15] 5533 3-8-11 59 (p) RobertHavlin 1 58
(C R Egerton) *w ldr: led 4f out: hdd & wknd wl over 1f out* **20/1**
6/0 **11** *1* **Menelaus**[33] 4531 6-9-5 56 (p) JamesDoyle 9 54
(K A Morgan) *prom: rdn and lost pl over 3f out: no hdwy or imp fnl 2f* **33/1**
4000 **12** *4* **Ronsard (IRE)**[34] 5007 5-9-5 56 TGMcLaughlin 14 49
(P D Evans) *mostly in midfield on inner: rdn wl over 2f out: wknd over 1f out* **20/1**
20 **13** *11* **Sun Lane**[10] 5683 3-9-3 65 (e[1]) AdamKirby 11 45
(W R Swinburn) *mde most to 4f out: wknd rapidly over 3f out* **20/1**
6/00 **14** *nk* **Revelino (IRE)**[19] 5426 8-9-1 57 RussellKennemore(5) 10 36
(Mrs N S Evans) *dwlt: hld up in last: rdn over 4f out: sn btn* **100/1**
3m 27.3s (-4.10) **Going Correction** -0.275s/f (Stan)
WFA 3 from 4yo+ 11lb **14** Ran SP% **128.0**
Speed ratings (Par 101): **99,98,98,96,95 94,94,94,93,93 93,91,85,85**
CSF £61.20 CT £214.03 TOTE £11.40: £3.20, £2.40, £1.50; EX 82.70 Place 6 £331.97, Place 5 £181.66.
Owner Robin Stevens **Bred** Michael Ng **Trained** Royston, Herts
FOCUS
Quite a competitive staying event, though the pace was ordinary. Even so the principals all came from well off the pace and it may be significant that the first three home were the trio that came widest up the home straight. The form looks solid and reliable.
T/Plt: £270.60 to a £1 stake. Pool: £69,873.80. 188.45 winning tickets. T/Qpdt: £112.10 to a £1 stake. Pool: £4,290.70. 28.30 winning tickets. JN

5636
NEWMARKET (ROWLEY) (R-H)
Thursday, October 4

OFFICIAL GOING: Good (7.9)
Wind: Light, half-behind Weather: Cloudy with sunny spells

5949 E B F GRAND PRIX WHITE TURF ST MORITZ MAIDEN FILLIES' STKS 6f
2:00 (2:01) (Class 3) 2-Y-O **£6,477** (£1,927; £963; £481) **Stalls** Low

Form RPR
2 **1** **Shabiba (USA)**[18] 5448 2-9-0 0 RHills 12 82
(M P Tregoning) *w ldrs: led over 1f out: sn rdn and edgd lft: r.o* **5/2**[1]
22 **2** *½* **Elizabeth Swann**[14] 5550 2-9-0 0 RyanMoore 11 81
(R Hannon) *lw: w ldr: led over 2f out: rdn and hdd over 1f out: styd on* **7/2**[2]
320 **3** *hd* **Spinning Lucy (IRE)**[20] 5395 2-9-0 0 MichaelHills 10 80
(B W Hills) *hld up in tch: rdn and ev ch over 1f out: styd on* **5/1**[3]
4 *shd* **Provence** 2-9-0 0 PhilipRobinson 6 80+
(B W Hills) *str: cl cpld: dwlt: hld up: hdwy over 2f out: nt clr run over 1f out: r.o* **25/1**
3 **5** *2* **Just Like A Woman**[21] 5363 2-9-0 0 HayleyTurner 3 74
(M L W Bell) *chsd ldrs: rdn over 1f out: styd on same pce* **22/1**
5 **6** *1* **Meydan Princess (IRE)**[15] 5540 2-9-0 0 LDettori 4 71
(J Noseda) *w'like: chsd ldrs: rdn over 1f out: no ex fnl f* **13/2**
7 *1 ½* **Storyland (USA)** 2-9-0 0 KerrinMcEvoy 1 66
(W J Haggas) *leggy: bit bkwd: hld up: shkn up over 1f out: r.o ins fnl f: nvr nrr* **33/1**
8 *shd* **Jennie Jerome (IRE)** 2-9-0 0 RichardHughes 16 66
(B J Meehan) *leggy: b.hind: s.s: hld up: hdwy over 1f out: no imp ins fnl f* **7/1**
6 **9** *1 ½* **Garland**[12] 5628 2-9-0 0 TedDurcan 7 61
(R Hannon) *str: scope: prom: rdn and hung rt over 2f out: wknd over 1f out* **33/1**
2 **10** *shd* **Toasted Special (USA)**[18] 5442 2-9-0 0 SteveDrowne 13 61
(B J Meehan) *lw: w'like: leggy: chsd ldrs: rdn over 2f out: sn lost pl* **28/1**
0000 **11** *½* **Ile Royale**[15] 5534 2-9-0 56 JimmyQuinn 14 60
(C N Allen) *w'like: swtg: hld up: hdwy over 1f out: wknd fnl f* **200/1**
12 *¾* **Coloratura (IRE)** 2-9-0 0 JimmyFortune 8 57
(E A L Dunlop) *leggy: bit bkwd: s.i.s: sn prom: lost pl 1/2-way* **66/1**
05 **13** *hd* **Arcetri (IRE)**[24] 5281 2-9-0 0 NCallan 5 57
(K A Ryan) *w'like: bit bkwd: led over 3f: wknd over 1f out* **100/1**
5 **14** *1 ¼* **Gaabal (IRE)**[28] 5162 2-9-0 0 SebSanders 2 53
(C E Brittain) *unf: scope: lengthy: hld up: hdwy 1/2-way: rdn and wknd over 1f out* **10/1**
15 *1 ¾* **Jamaali (USA)** 2-8-11 0 WilliamBuick(3) 9 48
(M P Tregoning) *lengthy: scope: s.s: outpcd* **33/1**
1m 11.86s (-1.24) **Going Correction** -0.30s/f (Firm) **15** Ran SP% **125.8**
Speed ratings (Par 96): **96,95,95,94,92 90,88,88,86,86 86,85,84,83,80**
CSF £10.48 TOTE £3.50: £1.50, £1.50, £2.20; EX 13.30.
Owner Hamdan Al Maktoum **Bred** Shadwell Farm LLC **Trained** Lambourn, Berks
■ Stewards' Enquiry : Richard Hughes £75 fine: entered wrong stall
FOCUS
Just a reasonable maiden in which the first four finished in a heap. The form seems sound enough.
NOTEBOOK
Shabiba(USA), runner-up taking on colts on her debut over this trip at Goodwood, went one better against her own sex. Never far from the pace, she took up the running going to the final furlong and held on well. This could well prove her optimum trip although she may get another furlong. (op 11-4 tchd 3-1)
Elizabeth Swann finished second on both her first two starts and again was forced to settle for the runner-up spot. She did nothing wrong and her attitude does not appear to be in question, so her turn will surely come. (op 4-1 tchd 9-2 in a place)
Spinning Lucy(IRE), out of her depth in a valuable sales race at the Curragh, ran better back in maiden company. She was staying on at the end and another try over 7f looks worthwhile. (op 11-2)
Provence ◆, a stablemate of the filly in third, made a very promising debut, running on well at the end after things had not really gone her way through the race. She looks a ready-made winner of a similar event.
Just Like A Woman, who ran well on her debut in a maiden auction event on the Polytrack at Wolverhampton, confirmed that she handles turf too and should be able to win in ordinary company. (op 20-1)
Meydan Princess(IRE), fifth on her debut at Yarmouth last month, ran respectably again but did not see out the trip as well on this stiffer track. Official explanation: jockey said filly ran too free early (op 10-1)
Storyland(USA) ◆, who was sold this year for 47,000gns at the breeze-ups, is out of an unraced half-sister to the smart Strategic Prince and former smart stayer/hurdler Yorkshire. She looks sure to improve for this debut experience and there should be races to be won with her. (op 40-1)

5950 NEWMARKETRACECOURSES.CO.UK H'CAP 1m
2:35 (2:35) (Class 3) (0-95,95) 3-Y-O+
£9,348 (£2,799; £1,399; £700; £349; £175) **Stalls** Low

Form RPR
1321 **1** **Blackat Blackitten (IRE)**[10] 5685 3-8-5 85 6ex WilliamBuick(3) 9 104+
(G A Butler) *lw: hld up: hdwy to ld over 1f out: edgd lft: pushed clr fnl f: eased nr fin* **10/3**[1]
322 **2** *4* **Heroes**[12] 5617 3-8-11 88 SebSanders 14 95
(G A Huffer) *mid-div: hdwy over 2f out: sn rdn: styd on same pce fnl f* **17/2**
121 **3** *shd* **Kasumi**[57] 4268 4-8-7 81 SteveDrowne 12 88
(H Morrison) *chsd ldrs: led over 1f out: sn rdn and hdd: no ex fnl f* **13/2**[3]
5502 **4** *¾* **Ekhtiaar**[48] 4566 3-9-4 95 RHills 5 100+
(J H M Gosden) *lw: dwlt: hld up: swtchd rt over 2f out: hdwy over 1f out: nt rch ldrs* **4/1**[2]
0206 **5** *¾* **Rain Stops Play (IRE)**[48] 4587 5-8-7 81 oh8 FrancisNorton 4 84
(M Quinn) *led: rdn and hdd over 1f out: hung rt: styd on same pce* **25/1**
4400 **6** *1* **Cross The Line (IRE)**[13] 5585 5-8-7 81 oh2 JimmyQuinn 6 82
(A P Jarvis) *chsd ldrs: rdn over 3f out: styd on same pce appr fnl f* **25/1**
011 **7** *¾* **Persian Express (USA)**[12] 5641 4-8-13 87 MichaelHills 8 86
(B W Hills) *lw: prom: rdn over 2f out: wknd ins fnl f* **10/1**
3100 **8** *¾* **Robema**[13] 5585 4-8-7 81 oh1 GrahamGibbons 3 79
(J J Quinn) *mid-div: rdn over 3f out: n.d* **33/1**
2341 **9** *½* **Tender The Great (IRE)**[15] 5532 4-8-8 82 TQuinn 7 78
(B G Powell) *mid-div: hdwy over 3f out: rdn and wknd over 1f out* **40/1**
0000 **10** *hd* **Plum Pudding (IRE)**[4] 5833 4-9-7 95 RyanMoore 2 91
(R Hannon) *chsd ldrs: rdn over 2f out: wknd over 1f out* **7/1**
002 **11** *½* **Formax (FR)**[19] 5419 5-8-13 87 RichardHughes 10 82
(M P Tregoning) *s.i.s: hld up: a in rr* **12/1**
0-10 **12** *3* **Trafalgar Square**[106] 2755 5-9-1 89 PaulDoe 11 77
(J Akehurst) *swtg: chsd ldr tl rdn over 2f out: wknd over 1f out* **16/1**
5401 **13** *hd* **Orpen Wide (IRE)**[20] 5196 5-8-8 87 (b) RussellKennemore(5) 1 74
(M C Chapman) *broke wl: chsd ldrs: rdn 1/2-way: wknd over 2f out* **33/1**
-500 **14** *29* **Safe Investment (USA)**[135] 1929 3-8-5 82 HayleyTurner 13 3
(B N Pollock) *s.i.s: a in rr: wknd 3f out* **100/1**
1m 34.99s (-4.38) **Going Correction** -0.30s/f (Firm)
WFA 3 from 4yo+ 3lb **14** Ran SP% **119.1**
Speed ratings (Par 107): **109,105,104,104,103 102,101,100,100,100 99,96,96,67**
CSF £29.47 CT £178.58 TOTE £3.90: £1.70, £2.90, £2.70; EX 40.40.
Owner Beetle N Wedge Partnership **Bred** Conor Murphy **Trained** Blewbury, Oxon
FOCUS
A decent handicap, run at a good pace. The form is solid other than a slight doubt over the proximity of the fifth.
NOTEBOOK
Blackat Blackitten(IRE) ◆, who looked a horse to follow when winning at Kempton, readily defied the penalty for that victory. He scored in similar style, sweeping past his rivals on the outside and coming away for a comfortable success. On the upgrade, he might not run again this year but further progress can be expected of him next season, when the Cambridgeshire could be a suitable target. (op 7-2)
Heroes, back up to a mile, stuck on willingly to snatch second close home but the favourite was much too strong. He is running well, but is edging back up the weights in the process. (op 11-1)
Kasumi, raised 4lb for her win last time out at Brighton in August, ran well off this career-high mark and was only denied second spot on the line. (tchd 6-1 and 7-1)
Ekhtiaar, runner-up off a 4lb lower mark when last in action at Doncaster in August, missed the kick and was left with plenty to do but was running on nicely at the end. Official explanation: jockey said gelding reared in stalls (op 9-2)
Rain Stops Play(IRE), racing from 8lb out of the handicap, likes it here and ran his usual bold race from the front. He looks on the way back to his best and some ease in the ground will suit him in the remainder of the season. Official explanation: jockey said gelding hung right-handed
Cross The Line(IRE) is well capable of winning on turf, but this frustrating sort has been a little below his best lately. (op 20-1)
Persian Express(USA), aiming for a hat-trick, was 4lb higher than when scoring over course and distance last time and seemed to have no real excuses. (op 8-1)
Plum Pudding(IRE), who won this event last year from a 3lb lower mark, has been a bit disappointing of late but might have found this coming a bit soon. (op 13-2 tchd 6-1)

Formax(FR) Official explanation: jockey said gelding was unsuited by the good ground

5951 VOUTE SALES MAIDEN STKS (C&G) 1m

3:10 (3:13) (Class 3) 2-Y-O **£6,477** (£1,927; £963; £481) **Stalls** Low

Form RPR

1 **Twice Over** 2-9-0 0 RichardHughes 15 93
(H R A Cecil) *w'like: scope: lw: w ldrs: led over 2f out: pushed out* **4/1**[2]

4 2 2 **Austintatious (USA)**[47] 4593 2-9-0 0 LDettori 12 89
(B J Meehan) *lw: mde most over 5f: rdn and ev ch over 1f out: styd on same pce ins fnl f* **4/1**[2]

3 1 1/4 **Made To Ransom** 2-9-0 0 JimmyFortune 16 86
(J H M Gosden) *str: medium-sized: bit bkwd: w ldrs: rdn and ev ch over 1f out: no ex ins fnl f* **10/3**[1]

4 2 **Savarain** 2-9-0 0 SebSanders 14 81
(L M Cumani) *tall: scope: lengthy: bit bkwd: chsd ldrs: rdn over 2f out: styd on same pce appr fnl f* **12/1**

5 3/4 **French Art** 2-9-0 0 TQuinn 17 80
(D R C Elsworth) *w'like: medium-sized: leggy: hld up: hdwy over 3f out: rdn over 1f out: no ex* **22/1**

6 1 1/2 **First Avenue** 2-9-0 0 PhilipRobinson 3 77
(M A Jarvis) *w'like: bit bkwd: chsd ldrs: shkn up over 2f out: edgd rt and wknd over 1f out* **7/1**[3]

00 7 nk **Jack Got Even (USA)**[26] 5217 2-9-0 0 (b[1]) StephenDonohoe 7 76
(B J Meehan) *lw: chsd ldrs: rdn over 2f out: wknd over 1f out* **66/1**

05 8 1 1/2 **Averoo**[10] 5679 2-9-0 0 TedDurcan 6 73
(E A L Dunlop) *prom: rdn and wknd over 1f out* **33/1**

9 3 1/2 **Majeen** 2-9-0 0 MichaelHills 2 65
(W J Haggas) *w'like: leggy: hld up: hdwy over 3f out: hung rt and wknd over 1f out* **11/1**

0 10 3/4 **Rory Boy (USA)**[79] 3625 2-9-0 0 TGMcLaughlin 10 63
(E A L Dunlop) *lw: mid-div: rdn over 3f out: wknd over 2f out* **100/1**

11 2 **Black Rain** 2-9-0 0 (t) FrancisNorton 1 59
(P J McBride) *unf: s.s: bhd and bucked for the first f: nvr nrr* **66/1**

0 12 1 1/4 **Tasheba**[21] 5361 2-9-0 0 KerrinMcEvoy 4 56
(P W Chapple-Hyam) *hld up: wknd 3f out* **40/1**

0 13 1 1/4 **Jaser**[13] 5598 2-9-0 0 RyanMoore 13 53+
(P W Chapple-Hyam) *chsd ldrs: edgd rt and wknd over 1f out: eased fnl f* **8/1**

14 1 1/4 **Mezzanisi (IRE)** 2-9-0 0 HayleyTurner 9 51
(M L W Bell) *w'like: bit bkwd: hld up: rdn and wknd over 3f out* **50/1**

15 7 **Augmentation** 2-9-0 0 MickyFenton 8 35
(P W D'Arcy) *rangy: bit bkwd: s.s: a bhd* **28/1**

0 16 2 1/2 **Rock Me (IRE)**[36] 4947 2-9-0 0 (b[1]) SteveDrowne 11 30
(N A Callaghan) *hld up in tch: rdn and wknd over 3f out* **100/1**

17 shd **Hotel Felix** 2-9-0 0 NCallan 5 29
(Miss Gay Kelleway) *w'like: leggy: bit bkwd: s.s: hung lft: outpcd* **50/1**

1m 36.72s (-2.65) **Going Correction** -0.30s/f (Firm) **17** Ran SP% **124.8**
Speed ratings (Par 99): **101,99,97,95,95 93,93,91,88,87 85,84,82,81,74 72,72**
CSF £19.43 TOTE £5.70: £2.10, £1.50, £1.80; EX 18.40.
Owner K Abdulla **Bred** Juddmonte Farms Ltd **Trained** Newmarket, Suffolk

FOCUS
Probably a decent maiden and Twice Over certainly looks a nice prospect. The principals were all drawn high.

NOTEBOOK
Twice Over ◆, the first foal of a mare who won a three-runner Lingfield Oaks Trial, is Cecil's first winning 2yo debutant this season. Getting on top inside the last and coming away in good style without his rider needing to use his stick, he looks a nice prospect for next season, when he should stay 1m2f. (op 6-1)
Austintatious(USA), who made his debut over 6f at Lingfield in August, was always up with the pace and stuck on to secure second, suggesting he stayed this longer trip well enough. He probably came up against a useful opponent and is well up to winning a maiden. (op 3-1)
Made To Ransom comes from a yard which had won two of the last three runnings of this event, with Pevensey and Asperity. Racing on the outside of the pack, he had every chance and was not knocked about when held inside the last. (op 7-2)
Savarain, a scopey colt who looked in need of the run, made a taking debut. Keeping on steadily at the end, this Derby entry looks a nice prospect over middle distances next year. (op 16-1)
French Art, bred for middle distances and another to hold a Derby entry, shaped with promise and should come into his own next season. (op 25-1 tchd 28-1)
First Avenue, whose dam was unplaced in a couple of runs at two, was sold for 100,000gns as a yearling. After chasing the leaders towards the outer, he faded inside the final furlong but should come on plenty for the run. (op 4-1)
Majeen, the subject of support ahead of this debut, is a half-brother to several winners notably useful miler Mawsoof and middle-distance performer Murzim. He can step up on this effort with the experience under his belt. (op 33-1 tchd 40-1)
Jaser Official explanation: jockey said colt hung right

5952 GROVE FARM STUD NOEL MURLESS STKS (LISTED RACE) 1m 6f

3:45 (3:50) (Class 1) 3-Y-O

£15,330 (£5,810; £2,907; £1,449; £726; £364) **Stalls** Centre

Form RPR

1453 1 **Lion Sands**[26] 5220 3-9-0 109 RyanMoore 1 114
(L M Cumani) *hld up: hdwy and nt clr run over 2f out: swtchd lft over 1f out: rdn to ld and edgd rt ins fnl f: styd on wl* **6/4**[1]

3156 2 2 1/2 **Spanish Hidalgo (IRE)**[42] 4749 3-9-0 103 KerrinMcEvoy 2 111
(J L Dunlop) *lw: a.p: rdn and ev ch ins fnl f: styd on same pce* **13/2**[3]

6514 3 hd **Veenwouden**[31] 5101 3-8-9 80 SteveDrowne 6 105
(E F Vaughan) *hld up: hdwy over 1f out: styd on: nrst fin* **100/1**

1001 4 nk **Tranquil Tiger**[28] 5165 3-9-3 113 RichardHughes 3 113
(H R A Cecil) *hld up in tch: led over 1f out: sn rdn and hung lft: edgd rt: hdd and no ex ins fnl f* **11/4**[2]

0251 5 3 **Dansant**[20] 5375 3-9-0 98 WilliamBuick 7 106
(G A Butler) *lw: chsd ldr tl led 3f out: rdn and hdd over 1f: wknd ins fnl f* **15/2**

6433 6 4 **Metaphoric (IRE)**[14] 5574 3-9-0 100 (vt[1]) JimmyFortune 5 100
(M L W Bell) *bustled along early: chsd ldrs: rdn and ev ch over 2f out: wknd over 1f out* **8/1**

2203 7 3 1/2 **Shawhill**[68] 3973 3-8-9 89 RichardKingscote 8 90
(Tom Dascombe) *led: rdn and hdd 3f out: wknd over 1f out* **40/1**

1130 8 1 **Sagredo (USA)**[26] 5215 3-9-0 100 SebSanders 4 94
(Sir Mark Prescott) *hld up: rdn: hung lft and wknd over 2f out* **16/1**

2m 54.45s (-5.68) **Going Correction** -0.30s/f (Firm) **8** Ran SP% **112.2**
Speed ratings (Par 109): **104,102,102,102,100 98,96,95**
CSF £11.51 TOTE £2.40: £1.20, £2.10, £7.70; EX 14.60.
Owner Stronach Stables **Bred** Fittocks Stud **Trained** Newmarket, Suffolk

FOCUS
The winning time was modest for a race of its type. This is essentially ordinary Listed form, but Lion Sands can rate higher and the form makes sense.

NOTEBOOK
Lion Sands, tackling his longest trip so far, was down in grade after contesting a trio of Group races since winning his maiden at Haydock. He was denied a clear run going to the two pole and then caught a bit flat-footed, but stayed on for pressure to lead inside the last and was well on top at the line. He will get further and should make a nice four-year-old. (tchd 11-8 and 13-8 in places)
Spanish Hidalgo(IRE), who raced in about fifth place before closing in the long straight, stuck on for second and reversed Melrose Handicap form with Dansant and Metaphoric on these more favourable terms. (op 7-1 tchd 15-2 and 8-1 in a place)
Veenwouden faced a very stiff task at these weights, but the step up to this trip suited her and she stayed on most determinedly to secure some valuable black type. (op 66-1)
Tranquil Tiger, successful at Salisbury on his latest start, carried a 3lb penalty for his win in the Bahrain Trophy at the July festival here. After getting to the front, he could not hold on inside the final furlong and was run out of the places. (op 5-2)
Dansant put up a smart performance to win the Mallard Handicap at Doncaster but was found out by this rise in grade. (op 9-1)
Metaphoric(IRE), equipped with a first-time visor, was sooon in a prominent position but was unable to quicken up when required. He does not look straightforward.

5953 G4S ROUS STKS (LISTED RACE) 5f

4:20 (4:20) (Class 1) 3-Y-O+

£15,330 (£5,810; £2,907; £1,449; £726; £364) **Stalls** Low

Form RPR

6203 1 **Judd Street**[12] 5632 5-8-12 105 (v[1]) StephenCarson 12 113
(Eve Johnson Houghton) *lw: chsd ldrs: rdn to ld 1f out: r.o* **11/2**[2]

1331 2 nk **Rowe Park**[12] 5632 4-9-4 110 LPKeniry 10 118
(Mrs L C Jewell) *chsd ldrs: rdn and ev ch ins fnl f: r.o* **8/1**[3]

0231 3 1/2 **Tax Free (IRE)**[18] 5468 5-9-4 110 AdrianTNicholls 3 116
(D Nicholls) *hld up: hdwy u.p over 1f out: r.o* **9/4**[1]

-000 4 1 **Tawaassol (USA)**[30] 5112 4-8-12 103 (v[1]) RHills 13 107
(Sir Michael Stoute) *chsd ldrs: led over 1f out: sn rdn and hdd: styd on same pce ins fnl f* **10/1**

1046 5 hd **Green Manalishi**[19] 5407 6-9-1 102 NCallan 5 109
(K A Ryan) *lw: prom: rdn over 1f out: styd on same pce ins fnl f* **20/1**

4303 6 nk **Hoh Hoh Hoh**[9] 5700 5-8-12 94 SebSanders 11 105
(R J Price) *chsd ldrs: rdn over 1f out: styd on same pce ins fnl f* **14/1**

6062 7 nk **Pivotal's Princess (IRE)**[11] 5666 5-8-7 98 TQuinn 6 99
(E S McMahon) *s.i.s: rdn over 1f out: r.o ins fnl f: nrst fin* **14/1**

4620 8 nk **The Jobber (IRE)**[12] 5632 6-8-12 98 TedDurcan 4 103
(M Blanshard) *hld up: rdn ins fnl f: nvr trbld ldrs* **25/1**

4411 9 nk **Loch Verdi**[11] 5666 4-8-10 90 FrancisNorton 8 100
(A M Balding) *lw: led: rdn and hdd over 1f out: edgd lft and no ex ins fnl f* **8/1**[3]

0042 10 2 **Bond City (IRE)**[9] 5700 5-8-12 98 (p) RichardHughes 14 94
(G R Oldroyd) *chsd ldrs: rdn over 1f out: wknd ins fnl f* **22/1**

5053 11 1/2 **Conquest (IRE)**[22] 5325 3-8-12 104 (t) JimmyFortune 7 93
(W J Haggas) *s.i.s: hld up: effrt over 1f out: no ch whn hmpd ins fnl f* **11/1**

43-5 12 1 3/4 **Fyodor (IRE)**[194] 762 6-8-12 100 SteveDrowne 15 86
(W J Haggas) *hld up: a in rr* **33/1**

3001 13 1 1/2 **Stoneacre Lad (IRE)**[67] 3990 4-8-12 96 (b) KerrinMcEvoy 1 81
(Peter Grayson) *racd alone stands' side: sn outpcd* **25/1**

57.56 secs (-2.91) **Going Correction** -0.30s/f (Firm) **13** Ran SP% **118.9**
Speed ratings (Par 111): **111,110,109,108,107 107,106,106,105,102 101,99,96**
CSF £44.84 TOTE £5.20: £2.40, £2.80, £1.30; EX 52.30.
Owner R F Johnson Houghton **Bred** R F Johnson Houghton **Trained** Blewbury, Oxon

FOCUS
A decent race of its type, and sound form with Judd Strret and Rowe Park close to their Newbury marks.

NOTEBOOK
Judd Street, equipped with a first-time visor, reversed Newbury form with Rowe Park on these 6lb better terms to post his first win in this grade. He has had a fine season, especially considering he was seriously ill with a stomach disorder earlier in the year, and there could be further improvement in him.
Rowe Park, a surprise winner of a Newbury Group 3 last time, could not quite confirm the form with Judd Street on 6lb worse terms but this was still a fine performance. He is a credit to his trainer. (op 7-1)
Tax Free(IRE), who has enjoyed a fruitful season, could not quite get to the leading pair after being held up but this was still a decent effort under his Group 3 penalty. (op 5-2 tchd 11-4 in a place)
Tawaassol(USA) wore a first-time visor but the tongue strap was dispensed with. He did not stay 7f at Glorious Goodwood but ran a big race on this drop back in trip, just lacking a change of gear late on. (op 12-1)
Green Manalishi, penalised for his win in this grade over 6f at Chester, ran creditably with no excuses.
Hoh Hoh Hoh has had a successful season despite having only the one win to show for his efforts. This was a fine run on his first crack at Listed company. (op 16-1 tchd 18-1)
Loch Verdi could not quite confirm Hamilton superiority over Pivotal's Princess, but despite finishing ninth she was far from disgraced, showing fine pace to lead and only fading up the final hill to be beaten only around three lengths. (op 13-2)

5954 EUROPEAN BREEDERS' FUND FILLIES' H'CAP 6f

4:55 (4:55) (Class 2) (0-100,96) 3-Y-O+

£12,464 (£3,732; £1,866; £934; £466; £234) **Stalls** Low

Form RPR

0052 1 **Angus Newz**[16] 5513 4-8-8 **85** (v) FrancisNorton 8 93
(M Quinn) *w ldr: led over 3f out: rdn over 1f out: r.o* **12/1**

3212 2 1 1/4 **Plucky**[39] 4848 3-8-6 **84** KerrinMcEvoy 3 88
(J H M Gosden) *lw: hld up: hdwy over 2f out: rdn and edgd rt over 1f out: r.o* **9/2**[1]

0135 3 1 1/4 **Misphire**[73] 3784 4-8-5 **82** oh6 (b) SaleemGolam 12 82
(M Dods) *lw: a.p: rdn over 1f out: styd on same pce ins fnl f* **33/1**

0023 4 1/2 **Mango Music**[8] 5722 4-8-0 **84** MatthewDavies(7) 1 82
(M R Channon) *chsd ldrs: outpcd over 2f out: r.o ins fnl f* **15/2**[3]

5006 5 1/2 **Leopoldine**[54] 4373 4-8-12 **89** SteveDrowne 11 86
(H Morrison) *sn led: hdd over 3f out: rdn over 1f out: no ex ins fnl f* **10/1**

213 6 nk **Fleuret**[23] 5303 3-8-4 **82** oh14 HayleyTurner 5 78
(Eve Johnson Houghton) *lw: sn outpcd: r.o ins fnl f: nrst fin* **50/1**

6115 7 hd **Medicea Sidera**[21] 5355 3-8-8 **86** NCallan 2 81
(E F Vaughan) *s.i.s: outpcd: r.o ins fnl f: nvr trble ldrs* **8/1**

2520 8 2 **Special Day**[26] 5212 3-8-13 **91** MichaelHills 9 80
(B W Hills) *b.hind: chsd ldrs: chsd ldrs: rdn over 1f out: edgd lft and wknd ins fnl f* **15/2**[3]

1504 9 hd **Shes Minnie**[10] 5673 4-8-7 **84** FergusSweeney 16 72
(J G M O'Shea) *s.i.s: hld up: n.d* **25/1**

4101 10 nk **Lady Lily (IRE)**[14] 5560 3-8-11 **89** TedDurcan 10 76
(H R A Cecil) *lw: s.i.s: sn chsng ldrs: rdn over 1f out: sn wknd* **7/1**[2]

0004 **11** ¾ **Pretty Majestic (IRE)**[12] 5638 3-8-4 **82** oh4.................. JimmyQuinn 13 67
(M R Channon) *chsd ldrs: rdn over 2f out: wknd over 1f out* **18/1**

0030 **12** *nk* **Titian Saga (IRE)**[121] 2343 4-8-5 **82** oh37..............(bt) NelsonDeSouza 4 66?
(C N Allen) *broke wl: plld hrd: stdd and lost pl 5f out: n.d after* **125/1**

-000 **13** *hd* **El Soprano (IRE)**[68] 3940 3-8-7 **85**..(b) TQuinn 6 68
(K A Ryan) *chsd ldrs: rdn over 2f out: wkng whn hmpd ins fnl f* **66/1**

2510 **14** *1* **Diane's Choice**[18] 5449 4-8-10 **87**.................................. NickyMackay 14 67
(J Akehurst) *s.i.s: hld up: hdwy 1/2-way: rdn and wknd over 1f out* **20/1**

0334 **15** *hd* **Riotous Applause**[11] 5666 4-9-5 **96**.................................. RyanMoore 15 75
(J R Fanshawe) *hld up: hdwy over 1f out: wknd ins fnl f* **9/2**[1]

1m 10.78s (-2.32) **Going Correction** -0.30s/f (Firm)
WFA 3 from 4yo 1lb **15** Ran SP% **121.3**
Speed ratings (Par 96): **103,101,99,99,98 97,97,95,94,94 93,92,92,91,91**
CSF £62.13 CT £1814.13 TOTE £14.70: £4.40, £1.90, £8.20; EX 81.40 Trifecta £598.40 Part won. Pool £842.90 - 0.50 winning units..
Owner M J Quinn **Bred** Henry And Mrs Rosemary Moszkowicz **Trained** Newmarket, Suffolk
■ Stewards' Enquiry : Matthew Davies one-day ban: failed to keep straight from the stalls (Oct 15)

FOCUS
There are doubts over how solid this form is, with the third and sixth both out of the weights. The winner was close to this year's best.

NOTEBOOK
Angus Newz, who showed clear signs of a return to form at Yarmouth, was just 2lb higher here. Making virtually all on a day when front-running tactics were favoured, she was always going to last home. (tchd 10-1)
Plucky, whose four previous runs were all over 7f, came through for second inside the final furlong but could not get to the winner. She loses nothing in defeat. (op 7-2 tchd 5-1 in a place)
Misphire, who did not enjoy the rub of the green at Ayr, plugged on well for third. This was a good effort from 6lb out of the handicap.
Mango Music ran a respectable race off this 5lb higher mark, still 2lb higher than when last successful over a year ago. (op 8-1 tchd 9-1 and 7-1)
Leopoldine set a good pace, if anything just shading the eventual winner for a couple of furlongs, but could not hold on inside the last. She has been officially rated 89 for the past year now and, one poor run at Ascot apart, has been too consistent for that to change much. (op 12-1)
Fleuret, racing from a stone out of the weights, was doing her best work in the latter stages. A return to 7f might suit her. (op 66-1)
Medicea Sidera, dropped in trip, was unable to take up her favoured role at the head of affairs after missing the break but was running on at the end from off the pace. (op 9-1)
El Soprano(IRE) Official explanation: jockey said filly suffered interference
Riotous Applause, back up in trip and contesting a handicap for the first time, was conceding 6lb and more to her rivals and was rather disappointing. Official explanation: jockey said filly stopped very quickly (tchd 5-1 in a place)

5955 TURFTV H'CAP (IN MEMORY OF REG DAY) 1m 6f
5:30 (5:30) (Class 4) (0-85,85) 3-Y-O **£6,477** (£1,927; £963; £481) **Stalls** Low

Form RPR

3-11 **1** **Kahara**[19] 5415 3-8-12 **76**.................................. SebSanders 6 91+
(L M Cumani) *s.i.s and hmpd s: hld up: hdwy over 3f out: rdn over 1f out: styd on ld wl ins fnl f* **4/1**[3]

1125 **2** 1½ **Duty Free (IRE)**[34] 5006 3-9-0 **78**.................................. SteveDrowne 13 91+
(H Morrison) *chsd ldrs: led 2f out: sn rdn and hdd: styd on same pce fnl f* **15/2**

6143 **3** *hd* **Hot Diamond**[12] 5640 3-8-12 **76**.................................. TQuinn 11 89
(D R C Elsworth) *hld up: hdwy over 4f out: led over 1f out: sn rdn: hdd wl ins fnl f* **25/1**

3443 **4** *8* **Fretwork**[34] 5006 3-9-4 **82**.................................. RichardHughes 3 84
(R Hannon) *hld up: hdwy over 3f out: nt clr run and lost pl over 2f out: n.d after* **20/1**

1111 **5** 1½ **Ainama (IRE)**[5] 5807 3-8-9 **73** 6ex.................................. MickyFenton 8 72
(M Wigham) *hld up: hdwy over 3f out: wknd over 1f out* **15/8**[1]

0565 **6** 2½ **Cavalry Twill (IRE)**[22] 5342 3-8-2 **66** oh2..............(b) NelsonDeSouza 14 62
(P F I Cole) *led: rdn and hdd 2f out: wknd fnl f* **66/1**

-241 **7** *1* **Grand Heights (IRE)**[17] 5474 3-9-2 **80**.................................. TedDurcan 5 75
(J L Dunlop) *hld up: hdwy over 3f out: wknd 2f out* **25/1**

2112 **8** 3½ **Irish Quest (IRE)**[14] 5574 3-9-3 **81**.................................. PhilipRobinson 9 71
(M A Jarvis) *chsd ldr: rdn over 2f out: wknd over 1f out* **7/2**[2]

3210 **9** *5* **Ancient Culture**[42] 4749 3-9-6 **84**..................................(v) RyanMoore 12 67
(Sir Michael Stoute) *chsd ldrs: rdn over 2f out: sn hung rt and wknd* **8/1**

-210 **10** *11* **Starry Messenger**[34] 5006 3-8-11 **75**.................................. NCallan 7 42
(M P Tregoning) *edgd lft s: hld up: rdn and wknd over 3f out* **50/1**

1016 **11** *hd* **Horseford Hill**[29] 5141 3-9-5 **83**.................................. MichaelHills 1 50
(D R C Elsworth) *hld up: rdn over 3f out: sn wknd* **33/1**

-105 **12** *11* **Starparty (USA)**[49] 4542 3-8-7 **71**.................................. FrancisNorton 15 23
(Mrs A J Perrett) *prom: rdn and wknd over 3f out* **66/1**

6210 **13** *22* **Natural Action**[36] 4951 3-8-8 **72**.................................. KerrinMcEvoy 10 —
(W Jarvis) *hld up: rdn and wknd over 3f out* **50/1**

2m 55.62s (-4.51) **Going Correction** -0.30s/f (Firm) **13** Ran SP% **122.2**
Speed ratings (Par 103): **100,99,99,94,93 92,91,89,86,80 80,74,61**
CSF £32.02 CT £677.30 TOTE £5.10: £2.00, £2.50, £6.00; EX 47.80 Place 6 £13.82, Place 5 £10.83.
Owner Fittocks Stud & Mrs John Magnier **Bred** Fittocks Stud **Trained** Newmarket, Suffolk

FOCUS
An interesting handicap containing some progressive types. The first three finished clear and the form looks solid.
Natural Action Official explanation: jockey said colt was unsuited by the good ground
T/Jkpt: Not won. T/Plt: £19.20 to a £1 stake. Pool: £87,417.50. 3,319.90 winning tickets. T/Qpdt: £11.00 to a £1 stake. Pool: £4,825.60. 323.10 winning tickets. CR

5956 - 5963a (Foreign Racing) - See Raceform Interactive

5834 MUSSELBURGH (R-H)
Friday, October 5

OFFICIAL GOING: Good (good to firm in places)
Wind: Slight, across Weather: Sunny

5964 CORNHILL BUILDING SERVICES APPRENTICE H'CAP 1m
2:20 (2:20) (Class 6) (0-65,64) 4-Y-0+ **£2,590** (£770; £385; £192) **Stalls** Low

Form RPR

5200 **1** **Mandarin Rocket (IRE)**[11] 5674 4-7-11 **50**.............. DeclanCannon(7) 5 58
(Miss L A Perratt) *cl up: effrt to ld wl over 1f out: sn rdn: kpt on wl u.p ins fnl f* **20/1**

3230 **2** ¾ **Apache Nation (IRE)**[74] 3789 4-8-13 **59**.................................. PJMcDonald 14 65
(M Dods) *dwlt: sn trcking ldrs on inner: hdwy 2f out: rdn to chal ent fnl f and ev ch tl no ex towards fin* **5/1**[3]

3401 **3** 1¼ **Oeuf A La Neige**[5] 5838 7-8-9 **58** 6ex................. RussellKennemore(3) 6 61
(Miss L A Perratt) *trckd ldrs: hdwy 3f out: rdn over 1f out: kpt on ins fnl f* **9/2**[2]

031 **4** *1* **Grandad Bill (IRE)**[17] 5503 4-8-1 **52**.................................. KellyHarrison(5) 3 53+
(J S Goldie) *hld up in rr: hdwy over 2f out: rdn over 1f out: kpt on ins fnl f: nrst fin* **4/1**[1]

0000 **5** *nk* **Rigat**[20] 5433 4-8-7 **56** ow1.................................. NeilBrown(3) 12 56
(T D Barron) *in tch on inner: rdn along over 2f out: sn swtchd lft and drvn: kpt on ins fnl f* **9/2**[2]

1500 **6** ½ **Whittinghamvillage**[25] 5286 6-8-0 **53** ow2.................... LanceBetts(7) 13 52
(J P L Ewart) *led: rdn along over 2f out: hdd wl over 1f out: wknd appr fnl f* **16/1**

0-00 **7** ½ **Just Intersky (USA)**[39] 4891 4-9-4 **64**...................... MichaelJStainton 2 62
(R M Whitaker) *prom: rdn along over 2f out: grad wknd* **20/1**

2040 **8** *shd* **Maison Dieu**[20] 5433 4-8-8 **59** ow3.................................. GaryBartley(5) 10 57
(E J Alston) *in tch: rdn along over 2f out and sn one pce* **8/1**

0420 **9** *5* **General Feeling (IRE)**[21] 5391 6-8-7 **53**.................(tp) DuranFentiman 4 39
(S T Mason) *chsd ldrs: rdn along 3f out: drvn and wknd 2f out* **12/1**

0000 **10** *4* **Ignition**[11] 5674 5-8-6 **57**..................................(p) DeanHeslop(5) 9 34
(W M Brisbourne) *hld up: hdwy on wd outside 3f out: rdn 2f out and sn btn* **20/1**

0000 **11** ½ **Foreign Edition (IRE)**[10] 5701 5-8-13 **59**..................(b) AndrewMullen 8 35
(Miss J A Camacho) *v s.i.s: a in rr* **40/1**

4000 **12** *2* **Cadogen Square**[13] 5627 5-8-0 **51**...................... DanielleMcCreery(5) 7 22
(D W Chapman) *a in rr* **28/1**

1m 40.74s (-1.76) **Going Correction** -0.10s/f (Good) **12** Ran SP% **117.9**
Speed ratings (Par 101): **104,103,102,101,100 100,99,99,94,90 90,88**
CSF £109.97 CT £549.44 TOTE £25.10: £5.50, £2.10, £1.80; EX 224.50.
Owner Mrs F Mitchell **Bred** Brides Well Stud **Trained** Ayr, S Ayrshire

FOCUS
A moderate apprentice handicap and very few came into this in any sort of form. Sound form.
Mandarin Rocket(IRE) Official explanation: trainer had no explanation for the apparent improvement in form
Foreign Edition(IRE) Official explanation: jockey said gelding missed the break

5965 TAY FIRTH LAMINATES/E.B.F. MAIDEN STKS 7f 30y
2:55 (2:56) (Class 5) 2-Y-O **£3,238** (£963; £481; £240) **Stalls** Low

Form RPR

222 **1** **Bonny Rose**[11] 5675 2-8-12 0.................................. RoystonFfrench 5 70+
(M Johnston) *cl up on inner: led after 2f: rdn 2f out: drvn and styd on wl fnl f* **8/11**[1]

00 **2** *2* **Fandangerina**[11] 5682 2-8-12 0.................................. SebSanders 3 65
(Sir Mark Prescott) *led 2f: cl up: rdn and ev ch 2f out tl drvn and one pce ent fnl f* **11/2**[3]

25 **3** 1¾ **Mangham (IRE)**[9] 5735 2-9-3 0.................................. PaulMulrennan 1 66
(B Smart) *plld hrd: chsd ldrs: rdn along 2f out and kpt on same pce* **11/4**[2]

0000 **4** *3* **Jafra (IRE)**[24] 5298 2-9-3 53.................................. DeanMcKeown 4 58
(R M Whitaker) *in tch: effrt and hdwy over 2f out: sn rdn and no imp appr fnl f* **25/1**

0 **5** *3* **Chanteuse De Rue (IRE)**[15] 5550 2-8-12 0................ J-PGuillambert 2 46+
(M Johnston) *s.i.s and bhd: hdwy and rdn along 3f out: drvn and kpt on fnl 2f: nt rch ldrs* **25/1**

0003 **6** *5* **Eternal Optimist (IRE)**[17] 5502 2-8-12 63.................... DanielTudhope 7 33
(C W Thornton) *chsd ldrs: rdn along 3f out and sn btn* **40/1**

0030 **7** *15* **La Guancha**[18] 5480 2-8-9 48..................................(tp) PJMcDonald(3) 6 —
(D A Nolan) *s.i.s: a towards rr* **150/1**

1m 29.5s (-0.44) **Going Correction** -0.10s/f (Good) **7** Ran SP% **110.7**
Speed ratings (Par 95): **98,95,93,90,86 81,64**
CSF £4.80 TOTE £1.60: £1.20, £2.00; EX 4.90.
Owner Greenland Park Stud **Bred** Greenland Park Ltd **Trained** Middleham Moor, N Yorks

FOCUS
Just an ordinary maiden dominated by those at the head of the market but run just 0.35sec slower than the following handicap. A rather messy affair and the principals were below form.

NOTEBOOK
Bonny Rose, with a fair amount in hand on those with official ratings, looked to have more to fear from the less-exposed contenders and so it proved. However, given a forceful ride, she established a clear advantage inside the quarter-mile point and never looked likely to be reeled in. After finishing runner-up in her first three starts this should help her confidence, and she is unlikely to go up much from her current mark for this. (tchd 8-13, 5-6 in a place)
Fandangerina put up her best effort so far on this third start, finding a second wind in the final furlong after looking well held. She will probably come into her own in handicaps over further next season, despite being related to a couple of sprinters. (op 13-2 tchd 7-1)
Mangham(IRE), who failed to build on his promising debut when too keen last time, again refused to settle in the early stages and after looking a threat halfway up the straight his effort rather petered out. He clearly has ability but will struggle to fulfil his potential until he becomes more amenable. (tchd 10-3)
Jafra(IRE), on the heels of the leaders early in the straight, was eventually well held, although running as well as he was entitled on his official rating. Official explanation: jockey said gelding hung right-handed throughout (tchd 22-1 and 28-1)
Chanteuse De Rue(IRE), a stable companion of the winner, missed the break but was staying on at the finish and, with her pedigree, may do better in handicaps on sand after one more run. (op 16-1)

5966 DM HALL H'CAP 7f 30y
3:30 (3:30) (Class 6) (0-65,65) 3-Y-O+ **£2,590** (£770; £385; £192) **Stalls** Low

Form RPR

5200 **1** **Spinning**[18] 5476 4-9-1 **58**..................................(b) PaulFessey 3 65
(T D Barron) *hld up in rr: hdwy on outer over 2f out: sn rdn and str run ins fnl f to ld nr line* **20/1**

0055 **2** *shd* **Cabourg (IRE)**[49] 4583 4-8-6 **52**.................................. PJMcDonald(3) 13 59
(R Bastiman) *in tch: n.m.r on inner bnd after 2f: trckd ldrs over 2f out: effrt and nt clr run over 1f out: squeezed through ins fnl f and rdn to ld briefly last 50yds: hdd nr line* **11/1**

4-00 **3** ½ **Wind Shuffle (GER)**[9] 5741 4-9-3 **60**.................................. DanielTudhope 9 65
(J S Goldie) *trckd ldng pair: hdwy over 2f out: rdn to ld jst ins fnl f: sn drvn and edgd rt: hdd and nt qckn last 50yds* **33/1**

4650 **4** ¾ **Nufoudh (IRE)**[26] 5253 3-8-11 **56**.................................. RoystonFfrench 12 59
(Miss Tracy Waggott) *in tch: n.m.r after 2f: chsd ldrs over 2f out: rdn and nt clr run over 1f out: styd on ins fnl f* **16/1**

0224 **5** *shd* **Terry Molloy (IRE)**[50] 4526 3-8-11 **56**....................(v) PaulMulrennan 14 59
(K R Burke) *s.i.s: hdwy on inner to ld after 2f: rdn along over 2f out: hdd wl over 1f out: kpt on wl u.p ins fnl f* **15/2**[3]

0601 **6** *shd* **Border Artist**[16] 5546 8-9-1 **58**.................................. PatCosgrave 4 61+
(J Pearce) *stdd s: hld up and bhd: hdwy 3f out: n.m.r and swtchd lft over 1f out: rdn and styd on wl fnl f* **9/2**[1]

0210 **7** *1* **No Grouse**[26] 5253 7-9-1 **58**.................................. SebSanders 5 58
(E J Alston) *hld up in rr: pushed along 3f out: hdwy 2f out: sn rdn and styd on ins fnl f: nrst fin* **9/2**[1]

263 **8** *shd* **Ducal Pip Squeak**^{15} 5555 3-9-6 **65**................................ PhillipMakin 10 65
(M Dods) *led 2f cl up tl rdn to ld again wl over 1f out: drvn and hdd jst ins fnl f: kpt on same pce* **8/1**

0240 **9** *½* **Sarraaf (IRE)**^{5} 5838 11-9-0 **57**.................................... TonyHamilton 1 55
(I Semple) *hld up in rr: hdwy 3f out: rdn 2f out and kpt on same pce fnl f* **20/1**

3030 **10** *shd* **Attacca**^{5} 5840 6-8-12 **55**.. DavidAllan 6 53+
(J R Weymes) *midfield: hdwy on inner 2f out: effrt and nt clr run over 1f out: nt rcvr* **11/1**

0000 **11** *1 ½* **Fairy Monarch (IRE)**^{17} 5503 8-8-3 **49** oh2...........(b) DuranFentiman$^{(3)}$ 7 43
(P T Midgley) *a in rr* **50/1**

1310 **12** *¾* **Mister Jingles**^{15} 5563 4-9-2 **62**.........................(v) MichaelJStainton$^{(3)}$ 11 54
(R M Whitaker) *trckd ldng pair: effrt and n.m.r over 2f out tl hmpd and nt rcvr appr fnl f* **6/1**^{2}

0006 **13** *1* **Falmassim**^{25} 5284 4-8-4 **50**.....................................(p) AndrewMullen$^{(3)}$ 2 39
(Miss J A Camacho) *a towards rr* **14/1**

6000 **14** *7* **Bold Haze**^{25} 5284 5-8-9 **52**..(v) AdrianTNicholls 8 23
(Miss S E Hall) *midfield: hdwy on outer to chse ldrs wl over 2f out: sn rdn and wknd* **20/1**

1m 29.15s (-0.79) **Going Correction** -0.10s/f (Good)
WFA 3 from 4yo+ 2lb **14** Ran SP% **121.9**
Speed ratings (Par 101): **100,99,99,98,98 98,97,96,96,96 94,93,92,84**
CSF £215.82 CT £7225.21 TOTE £29.30: £5.90, £3.80, £7.60; EX 290.20.
Owner Mrs J Hazell **Bred** Cheveley Park Stud **Trained** Maunby, N Yorks
■ Stewards' Enquiry : Pat Cosgrave one-day ban: careless riding (Oct 16)

FOCUS
A moderate contest and run only 0.35secs faster than the preceding maiden. Spinning did well to win from off the pace but was still 5lb off this year's best.
Attacca Official explanation: jockey said gelding was denied a clear run
Falmassim Official explanation: trainer's rep said gelding failed to stay the 7f
Bold Haze Official explanation: jockey said gelding had no more to give

5967 BRODIES SOLICITORS (S) STKS 1m 1f
4:05 (4:06) (Class 6) 3-Y-O **£2,590** (£770; £385; £192) **Stalls** Low

Form RPR

6255 **1** **Prince Noel**^{9} 5739 3-9-0 52.. SebSanders 6 57
(N Wilson) *trckd ldrs on outer: bmpd home turn: hdwy 2f out: rdn to chal over 1f out: sn drvn and edgd rt ent fnl f: hrd rdn and kpt on to ld nr line* **3/1**^{1}

0200 **2** *nk* **Kings Art (IRE)**^{10} 5710 3-9-0 52... DavidAllan 1 56
(W M Brisbourne) *sn led: rdn along over 2f out: drvn over 1f out: edgd rt ins fnl f: hdd and nt qckn nr fin* **33/1**

0005 **3** *1 ¼* **Falimar**^{18} 5487 3-8-9 53..(v) RoystonFfrench 3 50+
(Miss J A Camacho) *in tch: chsd ldrs whn bmpd home bnd: hdwy 2f out: rdn and swtchd rt ent fnl f: styng on whn nt clr run on inner last 100yds* **6/1**^{3}

05 **4** *¾* **Soul Angel**^{11} 5678 3-9-0 0... PaulMulrennan 13 52
(Miss S E Forster) *chsd ldrs on inner: n.m.r and hung lft home bnd: rdn along and sltly outpcd over 2f out: styd on wl u.p ins fnl f* **33/1**

0553 **5** *hd* **Skye But N Ben**^{7} 5783 3-9-0 56..................................(b) NeilBrown$^{(5)}$ 10 56
(T D Barron) *trckd ldng pair: effrt 3f out: rdn to chal 2f out and ev ch tl drvn and hld whn n.m.r ins fnl f* **7/2**^{2}

3000 **6** *½* **Still Dreaming**^{7} 5774 3-8-9 60.......................................(b) PhillipMakin 7 45+
(M Dods) *bhd: hdwy 2f out: sn rdn and styd on strly ins fnl f: nrst fin* **8/1**

0660 **7** *2 ½* **Heaven's Gates**^{37} 4936 3-8-11 49...........................(p) AndrewMullen$^{(3)}$ 4 45
(K A Ryan) *cl up: rdn along over 2f out and grad wknd* **12/1**

045 **8** *1* **Papa's Princess**^{24} 5299 3-8-11 53 ow2.................. DanielTudhope 8 39
(J S Goldie) *hld up towards rr: effrt and sme hdwy on wd outside wl over 2f out: sn rdn and no imp* **7/1**

0040 **9** *1* **Sangreal**^{50} 4526 3-8-9 50.. J-PGuillambert 5 35
(K R Burke) *a towards rr* **22/1**

-000 **10** *hd* **Bold Nevison (IRE)**^{24} 5299 3-8-11 45................... MarkLawson$^{(3)}$ 2 40
(B Smart) *midfield: rdn along over 3f out and sn wknd* **33/1**

0506 **11** *6* **Blue Madeira**^{62} 4155 3-8-11 65...............................(p) PJMcDonald$^{(3)}$ 14 27
(Mrs L Stubbs) *s.i.s: a in rr* **10/1**

0000 **12** *4* **Simba's Pride**^{24} 5299 3-9-0 40.. TonyHamilton 11 18
(Miss L A Perratt) *a in rr* **100/1**

1m 54.75s (0.89) **Going Correction** -0.10s/f (Good) **12** Ran SP% **116.1**
Speed ratings (Par 99): **92,91,90,89,89 89,87,86,85,85 79,76**
CSF £114.16 TOTE £3.10: £1.10, £6.60, £2.80; EX 53.20.There was no bid for the winner.
Owner The Giggle Factor Partnership **Bred** P And Mrs A G Venner **Trained** Flaxton, N Yorks
■ Stewards' Enquiry : Neil Brown four-day ban: failed to ride out for best possible placing (Oct 16-19)

FOCUS
A modest seller but despite it being a non-handicap the majority of the field were quite closely matched judged on their official marks.

5968 EDINBURGH EVENING NEWS H'CAP 1m 4f
4:40 (4:40) (Class 5) (0-75,73) 3-Y-O+ **£3,886** (£1,156; £577; £288) **Stalls** High

Form RPR

5111 **1** **Elopement (IRE)**^{7} 5769 5-9-1 **70** 6ex........................ DeanHeslop$^{(7)}$ 7 84+
(W M Brisbourne) *cl up: led 1/2-way: rdn over 2f out: styd on strly fnl f* **2/1**^{2}

1-00 **2** *2 ½* **Dollar Chick (IRE)**^{34} 5043 3-9-4 **73**........................... RoystonFfrench 2 78
(M Johnston) *hld up in rr: hdwy 3f out: rdn 2f out: kpt on u.p ins fnl f* **12/1**

0530 **3** *nk* **Campli (IRE)**^{26} 5257 5-9-1 **63**...................................... PaulMulrennan 3 68
(Micky Hammond) *hld up: hdwy 3f out: rdn along over 2f out: kpt on u.p ins fnl f: nrst fin* **14/1**

4040 **4** *nk* **Nelsons Column (IRE)**^{18} 5478 4-9-9 **71**..................... DanielTudhope 6 75
(G M Moore) *led to 1/2-way: rdn over 2f out and ev ch tl drvn and wknd appr fnl f* **11/2**^{3}

03-6 **5** *6* **Calatagan (IRE)**^{14} 5586 8-9-0 **65**.............................. PJMcDonald$^{(3)}$ 5 59
(J M Jefferson) *chsd ldng pair: rdn along over 3f out and sn one pce* **11/1**

4102 **6** *2 ½* **View From The Top**^{10} 5709 3-8-7 **62** ow2.................... SebSanders 1 52
(Sir Mark Prescott) *hld up in rr: effrt and sme hdwy 3f out: sn rdn and btn* **7/4**^{1}

0600 **7** *9* **Run Free**^{15} 5555 3-8-7 **62**... PatCosgrave 4 38
(N Wilson) *chsd ldrs: rdn along over 3f out and sn btn* **25/1**

2m 35.75s (-1.15) **Going Correction** -0.10s/f (Good)
WFA 3 from 4yo+ 7lb **7** Ran SP% **111.6**
Speed ratings (Par 103): **99,97,97,96,92 91,85**
CSF £24.24 TOTE £2.50: £1.40, £4.10; EX 16.10.
Owner Stratford Bards Racing **Bred** Haras Du Mezeray **Trained** Great Ness, Shropshire

FOCUS
A modest handicap but it was truly run and produced a clear-cut winner in Elopement, although she was 5lb off her Ascot figure. Solid form.

5969 TILNEY PRIVATE WEALTH MANAGEMENT CLAIMING STKS 5f
5:10 (5:10) (Class 6) 3-Y-O+ **£2,590** (£770; £385; £192) **Stalls** Low

Form RPR

6103 **1** **Compton Classic**^{14} 5581 5-9-0 77................................ GaryBartley$^{(5)}$ 4 64
(J S Goldie) *in tch: pushed along and hdwy 2f out: rdn ent fnl f: styd on strly to ld on line* **4/1**^{2}

0324 **2** *shd* **Harry Up**^{21} 5379 6-9-4 84..(b^{1}) AndrewMullen$^{(3)}$ 2 66
(K A Ryan) *led after 1f: pushed clr over 1f out: shkn up cl home: nt qckn and hdd on line* **1/2**^{1}

0000 **3** *hd* **Navigation (IRE)**^{37} 4939 5-8-5 43............................(v) PJMcDonald$^{(3)}$ 5 52
(T J Etherington) *in tch: hdwy 2f out: rdn and styd on strly ins fnl f* **33/1**

006 **4** *¾* **Ashes (IRE)**^{12} 5667 5-8-9 57... PhillipMakin 6 50
(K R Burke) *led 1f: cl up tl rdn over 1f out and kpt on same pce* **9/1**^{3}

6543 **5** *nk* **Throw The Dice**^{1} 5930 5-8-9 54..............................(v) PatrickMathers$^{(3)}$ 3 52
(A Berry) *in tch: pushed along 2f out: sn rdn and kpt on ins fnl f* **9/1**^{3}

0060 **6** *2 ½* **The Brat**^{60} 4226 3-8-3 43.......................................(p) RoystonFfrench 11 34
(Miss Tracy Waggott) *chsd ldrs to 1/2-way: sn rdn along and wknd* **80/1**

0000 **7** *15* **Mister Marmaduke**^{73} 3814 6-8-9 38 ow3.............(p) MarkLawson$^{(3)}$ 10 —
(D A Nolan) *s.i.s: a in rr* **200/1**

60.84 secs (0.34) **Going Correction** -0.025s/f (Good) **7** Ran SP% **111.3**
Speed ratings (Par 101): **96,95,95,94,93 89,65**
CSF £6.04 TOTE £4.10: £2.50, £1.10; EX 7.60.The winner was claimed by Mustafa Khan for £15,000. Harry Up was subject to a friendly claim.
Owner Jim Goldie Racing Club **Bred** James Thom And Sons And Peter Orr **Trained** Uplawmoor, E Renfrews

FOCUS
An uncompetitive claimer that produced a desperate finish but the time was slower than the closing three-year-old handicap. The front pair are well above average for the grade but the lack of pace and proximity of the third hold the form down.

5970 PREMIER PROPERTY GROUP INAUGURAL H'CAP 5f
5:40 (5:40) (Class 6) (0-65,65) 3-Y-O **£2,590** (£770; £385; £192) **Stalls** Low

Form RPR

4231 **1** **Princess Ellis**^{5} 5834 3-9-5 **63** 6ex..................................... SebSanders 9 75
(E J Alston) *cl up: led wl over 1f out: rdn clr ins fnl f* **11/10**^{1}

2353 **2** *4* **By The Edge (IRE)**^{8} 5752 3-8-6 **50**.................................. PaulFessey 4 48
(T D Barron) *led: rdn along 2f out and sn hdd: drvn and kpt on same pce fnl f* **6/1**^{2}

5650 **3** *¾* **Violet's Pride**^{24} 5295 3-8-2 **46** oh1...................................... KimTinkler 8 41
(N Tinkler) *in tch: hdwy to chse wnr appr fnl f: sn rdn and kpt on same pce* **14/1**

6300 **4** *½* **Kilvickeon (IRE)**^{10} 5716 3-8-3 **50** oh1 ow4.............. PatrickMathers$^{(3)}$ 7 44
(Peter Grayson) *towards rr: hdwy wl over 1f out: sn rdn and styd on ins fnl f* **33/1**

2345 **5** *½* **Silly Gilly (IRE)**^{43} 4734 3-9-1 **59**.. PhillipMakin 1 51
(K R Burke) *in tch: effrt 2f out: sn rdn and kpt on ins fnl f* **17/2**

0052 **6** *½* **Whats Your Game (IRE)**^{8} 5752 3-8-2 **46** oh1........(b) RoystonFfrench 2 36
(A Berry) *chsd ldrs: n.m.r 2f out tl over 1f out: sn rdn and one pce* **7/1**^{3}

5605 **7** *1* **Millsini**^{8} 5752 3-8-8 **52**.. DavidAllan 10 38
(Rae Guest) *cl up: rdn along 2f out and grad wknd* **16/1**

0000 **8** *3 ½* **Senora Lenorah**^{36} 4971 3-8-6 **53** oh1 ow7................. PJMcDonald$^{(3)}$ 5 27
(D A Nolan) *a in rr* **150/1**

-060 **9** *1 ½* **Now Look Out**^{60} 4233 3-9-7 **65**.................................... J-PGuillambert 6 33
(E S McMahon) *cl up: rdn along 2f out and sn wknd* **9/1**

0540 **10** *2 ½* **Silver Hotspur**^{9} 5730 3-9-2 **60**...................................... AdrianTNicholls 3 19
(M Wigham) *a in rr* **14/1**

59.79 secs (-0.71) **Going Correction** -0.025s/f (Good) **10** Ran SP% **117.8**
Speed ratings (Par 99): **104,97,96,95,94 94,92,86,84,80**
CSF £8.01 CT £63.39 TOTE £1.90: £1.10, £1.90, £4.90; EX 8.80 Place 6 £220.07, Place 5 £83.72.
Owner John Jackson **Bred** J E Jackson **Trained** Longton, Lancs

FOCUS
A very modest handicap but still run 1.05sec faster than the preceding claimer. Improved form from winner Princess Ellis.
Whats Your Game(IRE) Official explanation: jockey said gelding was denied a clear run
Silver Hotspur Official explanation: jockey said gelding anticipated the start and hit its head on the stalls
T/Plt: £295.10 to a £1 stake. Pool: £47,041.60. 116.35 winning tickets. T/Qpdt: £85.10 to a £1 stake. Pool: £2,888.40. 25.10 winning tickets. JR

5949 NEWMARKET (ROWLEY) (R-H)
Friday, October 5

OFFICIAL GOING: Good (good to firm in places; 8.5)
Wind: Light, half-against Weather: Cloudy with sunny spells becoming overcast from race 2 onwards

5971 NGK SPARK PLUGS EBF MAIDEN STKS (DIV I) 7f
1:05 (1:06) (Class 3) 2-Y-O **£5,829** (£1,734; £866; £432) **Stalls** High

Form RPR

6 **1** **Fireside**^{21} 5397 2-9-3 0... RyanMoore 3 90+
(P W Chapple-Hyam) *lengthy: scope: unf: lw: racd centre: chsd ldr tl overall ldr over 1f out: rdn out: edgd lft nr fin* **5/6**^{1}

52 **2** *shd* **Slam**^{28} 5206 2-9-3 0.. RichardHughes 16 90+
(B W Hills) *lw: racd far side: led overall 3f: rdn and ev ch fr over 1f out: r.o: edgd lft nr fin* **5/2**^{2}

0 **3** *2 ½* **Deo Valente (IRE)**^{14} 5598 2-9-3 0.......................... StephenDonohoe 15 84
(B J Meehan) *lw: racd far side: chsd ldrs: rdn over 1f out: styd on* **66/1**

4 *nk* **Whitcombe Minister (USA)** 2-9-3 0.................................. JohnEgan 4 83
(Jamie Poulton) *leggy: racd centre: hld up: hdwy over 2f out: rdn and edgd rt over 1f out: styd on* **66/1**

5 *1 ¾* **Lazy Days** 2-9-3 0... TQuinn 13 79+
(D R C Elsworth) *tall: rangy: lw: racd far side: s.i.s: hld up: swtchd rt and hdwy over 1f out: nt trble ldrs* **50/1**

6 *½* **Speedy Dollar (USA)** 2-9-3 0.................................. PhilipRobinson 12 77
(M A Jarvis) *athletic: scope: lw: racd far side: chsd ldr: rdn over 2f out: wknd fnl f* **25/1**

0 **7** *nk* **Tharawaat (IRE)**^{48} 4598 2-9-3 0.. RHills 11 77
(B W Hills) *racd far side: hld up in tch: rdn: edgd rt and wknd over 1f out* **25/1**

8 1 ½ **Cadre (IRE)** 2-9-3 0 .... JimmyFortune 14 73+
(J H M Gosden) *w'like: cl cpld: s.i.s: racd far side: hld up: r.o ins fnl f: nvr nrr* **16/1**

30 9 ¾ **Accused (IRE)**[21] 5397 2-9-3 0 .... LDettori 1 71
(J Noseda) *w'like: lw: led centre trio: overall ldr 4f out: rdn: edgd rt and hdd over 1f out: wknd fnl f* **11/1**[3]

05 10 2 **Red Merlin (IRE)**[51] 4508 2-9-3 0 .... AdamKirby 9 66
(C G Cox) *racd far side: chsd ldrs: rdn over 2f out: wknd over 1f out* **50/1**

0 11 *shd* **Sun**[56] 4362 2-9-3 0 .... (t) MartinDwyer 5 66+
(P W Chapple-Hyam) *w'like: racd far side: mid-div: hdwy 1/2-way: rdn and wknd over 1f out* **80/1**

12 1 ¾ **Falcativ** 2-9-3 0 .... JamieSpencer 10 61+
(L M Cumani) *w'like: scope: bit bkwd: s.i.s: hld up: rdn over 2f out: sn wknd* **16/1**

13 1 ¼ **Chinese Profit** 2-9-3 0 .... OscarUrbina 7 58
(G C Bravery) *lengthy: bit bkwd: hld up: a in rr* **100/1**

14 ½ **Hellzapoppin** 2-9-3 0 .... NCallan 8 57
(B W Hills) *w'like: racd far side: prom: stdd and lost pl after 1f: rdn and wknd over 2f out* **33/1**

1m 25.85s (-0.65) **Going Correction** +0.025s/f (Good) **14** Ran SP% **123.0**
Speed ratings (Par 99): **104,103,101,100,98 98,97,96,95,92 92,90,89,88**
CSF £2.65 TOTE £2.00: £1.10, £1.30, £10.80; EX 4.10.
Owner Highclere Thoroughbred Racing (VCI) **Bred** Brick Kiln Farming **Trained** Newmarket, Suffolk

FOCUS
This looked a very strong maiden even by Newmarket standards. The winning time was 0.36 seconds faster than the second division and only 0.14 seconds slower than the Group 3 that followed. The main bulk of the field raced against the far rail which is where the stalls were positioned, but three raced noticeably wider and that did not do them much harm as they included the eventual winner and fourth. Several of these are likely to go on to much better things.

NOTEBOOK
Fireside ◆, who ran so well in the face of a stiff task on his racecourse debut in the Goffs Million, was one of the three that raced wider than the main bulk of the field. Once asked to go and win his race, he showed a decent attitude to just get the better of the runner-up after a protracted duel. He should have little difficulty getting a mile at least on pedigree, though his trainer believes this will always be his sort of trip, and he should go on to better things. (op Evens tchd 11-10 in places)
Slam was allowed to stride on against the far rail and appeared to settle much better as a result. Edging left to join his main rival on reaching the rising ground, the pair were engaged in a right battle to the line and he only lost out on the nod. He will win races, whether it be this season or next. (tchd 3-1)
Deo Valente(IRE), stepped up considerably from his debut here last month, as many from his yard do, and was staying on as well as any at the line. He should have little difficulty in winning his maiden.
Whitcombe Minister(USA) ◆, who fetched $50,000 as a yearling and 15,000gns as a two-year-old, like the winner was happy to take a lead down the middle of the track and stayed on to fare best of the newcomers. His dam was a winning sprinter in the US, but she was a half-sister to the high-class middle-distance performer Muhtarram and this performance suggests he will get a bit further than this. Obviously held in high regard, it will be fascintaing to see if he can build on this most promising debut.
Lazy Days ◆, a 32,000gns half-brother to two winners including Diamond Diva, was another noted doing some good late work on the far side of the track. His other winning half-brother and his dam both won over 1m2f and the way he performed here suggests he too will appreciate stepping up in trip. There are races to be won with him.
Speedy Dollar(USA), a $70,000 yearling and 60,000gns two year-old, showed up for a long way in the far-side group until lack of a run started to tell. He should come on for it and his American pedigree could make him especially interesting if tried on sand. (tchd 22-1)
Tharawaat(IRE), who finished a mile behind Slam on his racecourse debut in the Washington Singer, performed better here. Although he never looked like winning, at least this was a step in the right direction.
Cadre(IRE), who was green in the paddock, was never in contention but showed definite ability and should come on plenty for the experience. Official explanation: jockey said colt missed the break and ran green (op 14-1)
Accused(IRE), who had little chance with Fireside on their running in the Goffs Million, led the trio that raced more towards the centre of the track but did not get home. He does not seem to be progressing. (tchd 10-1)
Sun (op 66-1)

5972 SOMERVILLE TATTERSALL STKS (GROUP 3) (C&G) 7f
1:35 (1:37) (Class 1) 2-Y-O

£34,068 (£12,912; £6,462; £3,222; £1,614; £810) **Stalls** High

Form RPR

120 1 **River Proud (USA)**[20] 5406 2-8-12 110 .... TQuinn 4 108
(P F I Cole) *lw: hld up in tch: rdn to ld and edgd rt over 1f out: r.o* **11/4**[2]

21 2 ¾ **Iguazu Falls (USA)**[23] 5337 2-8-12 92 .... LDettori 1 106+
(Saeed Bin Suroor) *lw: trckd ldrs: racd keenly: led over 5f out: rdn: edgd rt and hdd over 1f out: ev ch ins fnl f: unable qck towards fin* **9/4**[1]

1 3 *nk* **Yankadi (USA)**[42] 4777 2-8-12 0 .... RichardHughes 3 105
(B W Hills) *leggy: athletic: s.i.s: hld up: hdwy over 2f out: rdn and hung rt over 1f out: r.o* **10/3**[3]

03 4 1 **Bazergan (IRE)**[23] 5323 2-8-12 0 .... KerrinMcEvoy 7 103
(C E Brittain) *lw: hld up: outpcd 1/2-way: hdwy over 1f out: edgd rt ins fnl f: r.o* **40/1**

6341 5 3 ½ **Fool's Wildcat (USA)**[13] 5628 2-8-12 89 .... (b) JimmyFortune 8 94
(B J Meehan) *led: hdd over 5f out: rdn over 1f out: no ex* **11/1**

6160 6 *nk* **Paveroc**[23] 5324 2-8-12 93 .... JohnEgan 10 93
(J S Moore) *hld up: effrt over 2f out: styd on same pce appr fnl f* **66/1**

2221 7 2 **Bellomi (IRE)**[20] 5399 2-8-12 88 .... DarryllHolland 6 88
(M R Channon) *trckd ldrs: rdn over 2f out: wknd over 1f out* **25/1**

41 8 4 **Tasdeer (USA)**[16] 5541 2-8-12 90 .... RHills 9 78
(M A Jarvis) *lw: chsd ldrs: rdn over 2f out: wknd over 1f out* **9/2**

1m 25.71s (-0.79) **Going Correction** +0.025s/f (Good) **8** Ran SP% **114.8**
Speed ratings (Par 105): **105,104,103,102,98 98,96,91**
CSF £9.31 TOTE £4.40: £1.50, £1.40, £1.40; EX 9.20 Trifecta £31.80 Pool: £560.22 - 12.50 winning tickets..
Owner Mrs Michael Spencer **Bred** Brereton C Jones And B Ned Jones **Trained** Whatcombe, Oxon

FOCUS
The early pace was modest for this Group 3 until the favourite took over after a couple of furlongs. The field threatened to split into two groups of four early, but they soon merged and all eight runners were inclined to spurn the far rail, though they did edge back over there late on. The front quartet pulled clear of the others and the winning time was quicker than both divisions of the maiden, as it should have been. Sound form.

NOTEBOOK
River Proud(USA), who apparently had excuses for his moderate effort in the Champagne Stakes at Doncaster after his big run in the July Stakes, was back to his best here. The most pleasing aspect to this victory was the way he refused to give in when it appeared that the favourite was holding him and his perseverance eventually paid off. He is in the Dewhurst and Racing Post Trophy and would be worth his place in either. (op 5-2 tchd 7-2)
Iguazu Falls(USA), taking a big step up in class after his breeze in a Kempton Polytrack maiden, was allowed to stride on after a couple of furlongs and attempted to make every yard. It looked for a long time as though he would see it out, but the winner was like a terrier and eventually managed to worry him out of it. He is probably not yet the finished article and still has a future at a high level next season. (tchd 5-2 in places)
Yankadi(USA) ◆, winner of a maiden on the July Course in August that has already produced a few winners and representing the same connections that were successful in this last year, was given a patient ride. He tried to put in an effort over the last couple of furlongs, but still showed a few signs of greenness as he tried to get on terms with the front pair, which is probably understandable in only his second outing. This was still a very promising effort and he should be up to winning some decent races next year. (op 7-2 tchd 4-1 in places)
Bazergan(IRE) ran a similar race to here last time, staying on very nicely after getting outpaced. His smart relatives all came into their own when stepped up in trip at three and it should be no different for him. It would not be the biggest surprise to see him line up for one of the Derby trials next spring. (tchd 33-1)
Fool's Wildcat(USA), with the blinkers retained, ran well for a long way but probably found this much stiffer company too hot rather than the headgear not having the same effect. (op 14-1)
Paveroc, by far the most exposed in the field, never looked like taking a hand.
Bellomi(IRE), upped in class, was inclined to take a grip until the pace quickened after a couple of furlongs, but was still beaten fair and square. Official explanation: jockey said gelding anticipated start and ran too free (op 28-1 tchd 33-1)
Tasdeer(USA) may have been taking on much better company, but was still disappointing in the way he dropped out after looking so promising when winning his Yarmouth maiden. (op 5-1 after 13-2 in a place 6-1 in a place and 11-2 in a place, tchd 7-2)

5973 SKYBET.COM CHEVELEY PARK STKS (GROUP 1) (FILLIES) 6f
2:05 (2:09) (Class 1) 2-Y-O

£102,601 (£38,886; £19,461; £9,703; £4,860; £2,439) **Stalls** High

Form RPR

112 1 **Natagora (FR)**[47] 4653 2-8-12 0 .... C-PLemaire 11 117+
(P Bary, France) *w'like: mde virtually all: rdn out* **7/2**[2]

1131 2 *nk* **Fleeting Spirit (IRE)**[21] 5377 2-8-12 109 .... LDettori 8 116
(J Noseda) *a.p: rdn to chse wnr fnl f: r.o* **7/2**[2]

1025 3 4 **Festoso (IRE)**[43] 4744 2-8-12 105 .... EddieAhern 13 104
(H J L Dunlop) *hld up: rdn over 2f out: r.o ins fnl f: nt rch ldrs* **33/1**

2 4 1 **Perfect Polly**[33] 5070 2-8-12 0 .... TedDurcan 6 101
(Andrew Oliver, Ire) *chsd ldrs: rdn over 1f out: no ex fnl f* **20/1**

21 5 *shd* **Missit (IRE)**[24] 5313 2-8-12 0 .... DarryllHolland 9 101
(M R Channon) *lw: chsd ldrs: rdn over 1f out: styd on same pce* **12/1**

133 6 ¾ **Elletelle (IRE)**[54] 4437 2-8-12 0 .... JMurtagh 7 99
(G M Lyons, Ire) *s.i.s: hld up: racd keenly: styd on ins fnl f: nvr nrr* **6/1**[3]

3103 7 ½ **Lady Aquitaine (USA)**[27] 5219 2-8-12 99 .... KDarley 1 97
(B J Meehan) *chsd ldrs: rdn over 1f out: no ex fnl f* **25/1**

212 8 *nk* **Visit**[43] 4744 2-8-12 109 .... RyanMoore 5 96
(Sir Michael Stoute) *hld up: hdwy over 2f out: no ex fnl f* **11/4**[1]

1341 9 *hd* **Unilateral (IRE)**[13] 5614 2-8-12 106 .... TomEaves 12 96
(B Smart) *chsd ldrs: rdn over 1f out: sn outpcd* **20/1**

141 10 ½ **Dubai Princess (IRE)**[10] 5713 2-8-12 87 .... TPQueally 3 94+
(J A Osborne) *hld up in tch: racd keenly: effrt and swtchd rt over 1f out: styng on same pce whn nt clr run ins fnl f* **20/1**

1010 11 *nk* **Polar Circle (USA)**[68] 3988 2-8-12 99 .... JimmyFortune 4 93
(P W Chapple-Hyam) *s.i.s: hld up: rdn over 2f out: a in rr* **50/1**

2160 12 1 **Gone Fast (USA)**[13] 5614 2-8-12 92 .... OscarUrbina 14 90
(J R Fanshawe) *chsd ldrs: rdn over 2f out: wknd fnl f* **100/1**

1206 13 1 ½ **Lady Avenger (IRE)**[13] 5614 2-8-12 96 .... KerrinMcEvoy 2 86
(J M P Eustace) *hld up: rdn over 2f out: a in rr* **66/1**

61 14 2 **Falcolnry (IRE)**[49] 4565 2-8-12 80 .... JamieSpencer 10 80
(J R Fanshawe) *chsd ldrs over 4f* **22/1**

1m 11.55s (-1.55) **Going Correction** +0.025s/f (Good) **14** Ran SP% **123.0**
Speed ratings (Par 106): **111,110,105,103,103 102,102,101,101,100 100,99,97,94**
CSF £14.44 TOTE £4.90: £1.80, £1.90, £9.30; EX 23.30 Trifecta £717.20 Part won. Pool: £1,010.24 - 0.60 winning tickets..
Owner Stefan Friborg **Bred** Bertrand Gouin & Georges Duca **Trained** Chantilly, France
■ A first winner in Britain for trainer Pascal Bary.
■ Stewards' Enquiry : C-P Lemaire caution: used whip in the incorrect place

FOCUS
This looked a cracking renewal of the Cheveley Park, at least in the way that two top-class fillies pulled miles clear of a talented field. The winning time was very smart too, 0.53 seconds faster than the Middle Park and 1.08 seconds faster than the October Auction Stakes. The winner, who was the first since 1999 to win this having not been successful in her most recent start, set a very solid pace and made this a proper test.

NOTEBOOK
Natagora(FR) ◆, a good-bodied filly who ran a blinder against the boys in the Prix Morny, probably appreciated this better ground. Although making the running was apparently not the plan, she soon took herself to the front and did it the hard way. She travelled very strongly throughout and even though the runner-up got very close throughout the last furlong, she never really looked like being passed and was well on top at the line. Afterwards her rider was of the opinion that she may not stay a mile next season, even though her pedigree suggests she might, as she possesses so much speed, so if connections decide to have a crack at a Guineas she may be better off staying at home for the French version, which is usually more of a test of speed than at Newmarket. (op 9-2 tchd 5-1 in places)
Fleeting Spirit(IRE), whose only defeat until now had come in her only previous try over this trip in the Lowther, put to bed any doubts over her stamina. She was awkward leaving the stalls, but it did not appear to affect her as she travelled well in the pack for most of the way. Once asked for her effort, she quickened up very nicely to sweep clear of the bulk of the field and in most cases that would have been enough to win a race like this, but she ran into a very smart filly on the day and as hard as she tried she could never quite get to her. There is a little bit of stamina on the dam's side of her pedigree, but rather like the winner she has shown so much speed on the track that it is hard to imagine her as a Guineas filly. Provided she trains on, her future is likely to be as a top-class sprinter. (op 10-3 tchd 4-1)
Festoso(IRE) was settled out the back for most of the way, but stayed on late up the hill to win the separate race for third. She reversed the Lowther form with both Visit and Unilateral, but finished much further behind Fleeting Spirit than she had at York so it is hard to know what she has achieved. What is certain is that she has every chance of staying a mile at least next season, and whilst she may not be out of the top drawer she may be able to win a Pattern race or two over further in due course.
Perfect Polly had every chance and showed that her effort in the Round Tower was no fluke. She never stopped trying and there should be some nice races to be won with her, espcially with some cut in the ground.
Missit(IRE) ◆, easy winner of a Lingfield maiden, faced a very stiff task on this debut at Pattern level, but after having raced close to the pace throughout, stayed on to finish a very respectable fifth. This should have given her trainer some idea of where he stands with Nahoodh, who accounted for four of these in the Lowther, but as far as this filly is concerned she should more than pay her way next term as she came into this as one of the least experienced in the line-up. (op 10-1)

Elletelle(IRE), not for the first time, was last to break from the stalls but the ground she lost was by no means fatal and certainly did not affect her chances of making the frame. She finished a bit further behind Festoso than she did in the Cherry Hinton despite being 3lb better off, but should still win her share of decent races over sprint trips next season. (op 7-1 tchd 11-2)
Lady Aquitaine(USA), who was free to post and had plenty to find with a couple of these on Princess Margaret running, saw a lot of daylight on the wide outside which was not ideal, but she still managed to reverse the Ascot form with the pair on this better ground. (op 33-1)
Visit, who it transpired had ACP in her system when runner-up in the Lowther, had three of these rivals behind her that day. She never looked entirely happy though and a brief effort after halfway amounted to little. The fact that two of her York victims finished well ahead of her here shows how far below form she performed. (tchd 3-1 in places)
Dubai Princess(IRE) did not go unsupported, but she did her chances little good by taking a keen grip. Scratchy to post, she would not have made the frame, but would have finished a little closer had she not run out of room when trying to stay on between Festoso and Perfect Polly. (op 33-1)

5974 £250000 TATTERSALLS OCTOBER AUCTION STKS 6f
2:40 (2:42) (Class 2) 2-Y-O

£189,390 (£75,756; £37,839; £22,726; £15,112; £7,575) **Stalls** High

Form RPR
51 **1** **Exclamation**[7] 5772 2-8-13 0 JamieSpencer 13 98
(B J Meehan) *lw: chsd ldrs far side: sustained run fr over 1f out: edgd rt: drvn ahd fnl 50yds: gamely* **13/2**[2]
2205 **2** *nk* **Anosti**[7] 5766 2-8-2 0 DO'Donohoe 30 86
(K A Ryan) *led or disp far side: overall ldr 1/2-way: hrd rdn and hdd 50yds out: kpt on wl* **12/1**
4513 **3** *1 1/4* **Copywriter**[23] 5324 2-8-13 0 JimmyFortune 24 93
(J H M Gosden) *lw: chsd ldrs far side: rdn and effrt over 1f out: no imp and a hld fnl 100yds* **10/3**[1]
02 **4** *1/2* **Terry's Tip (IRE)**[16] 5521 2-8-7 0 TomEaves 26 86
(Mrs L Stubbs) *prom far side: rdn over 1f out: r.o but unable qck w ldng pair* **100/1**
12 **5** *nk* **Perfect Act**[21] 5374 2-8-4 0 MartinDwyer 29 82
(C G Cox) *pressed ldrs far side: no imp ins fnl f* **8/1**[3]
1103 **6** *shd* **Gaspar Van Wittel (USA)**[34] 5048 2-9-1 101 DaneO'Neill 9 93+
(N A Callaghan) *centre gp: gd prog over 1f out: fin stoutly despite veering rt* **8/1**[3]
0052 **7** *3/4* **Fanatical**[35] 4992 2-8-4 0 RichardKingscote 5 79+
(E F Vaughan) *t.k.h: prom stands' side gp of six: led that gp fnl strides but n.d to far side bunch after 1/2-way* **8/1**[3]
2212 **8** *shd* **Eastern Gift**[20] 5414 2-9-1 0 RyanMoore 2 90+
(R Hannon) *prom stands' side: led that gp of 6 over 1f tl nr fin but nvr any hope of rching far side protagonists* **11/1**
4130 **9** *1/2* **Bosun Breese**[45] 4695 2-8-9 79 LPKeniry 10 83
(P W D'Arcy) *led centre bunch over 2f out: drvn and nt trble far side gp fnl 2f* **40/1**
1452 **10** *hd* **Archived (IRE)**[42] 4769 2-8-7 85 EddieAhern 25 80
(M G Quinlan) *missed break: sn chsng ldrs far side: no ex over 1f out* **40/1**
4351 **11** *3/4* **Cat Whistle**[55] 4406 2-8-8 73 PaulHanagan 18 79
(R A Fahey) *pressed ldrs in centre tl one pce wl over 1f out* **20/1**
6120 **12** *shd* **Wise Son**[36] 4975 2-8-11 0 KerrinMcEvoy 17 81
(W J Haggas) *led centre gp tl over 2f out: sn lost pl* **66/1**
0006 **13** *nk* **Jebel Tara**[13] 5630 2-8-7 88 (t) HayleyTurner 4 77+
(C E Brittain) *a bhd on stands' side* **25/1**
2635 **14** *shd* **Ellemujie**[14] 5597 2-8-8 79 ow1 PatDobbs 23 77
(D K Ivory) *chsd ldrs far side over 4f* **33/1**
033 **15** *shd* **Loyal Knight (IRE)**[28] 5186 2-8-7 0 FrancisNorton 11 76
(S Kirk) *struggling in centre 1/2-way* **80/1**
321 **16** *1/2* **Rash Judgement**[41] 4823 2-8-11 0 FergusSweeney 3 78+
(W S Kittow) *led gp of 6 on stands' side tl over 1f out* **20/1**
21 **17** *1/2* **Errigal Lad**[28] 5194 2-9-1 0 NCallan 19 81
(K A Ryan) *sn drvn along in centre gp: n.d fr 1/2-way* **25/1**
2002 **18** *hd* **Thought Is Free**[24] 5309 2-8-8 92 JohnEgan 14 73
(J S Moore) *rdn and struggling in rr of centre gp at 1/2-way* **22/1**
44 **19** *1/2* **Another Decree**[55] 4378 2-8-11 0 PhilipRobinson 1 75+
(M Dods) *dwlt: bhd on stands' side: btn 1/2-way* **100/1**
6601 **20** *3/4* **Prince Desire (IRE)**[8] 5749 2-9-1 0 (b) MichaelHills 12 77
(B W Hills) *struggling in centre gp after 1/2-way* **33/1**
0010 **21** *1 1/2* **Geoffdaw**[13] 5629 2-8-7 75 ChrisCatlin 16 64
(M J Wallace) *centre gp: handy tl drvn 1/2-way: sn btn* **100/1**
105 **22** *nk* **Dry Speedfit (IRE)**[60] 4225 2-8-11 0 TQuinn 20 67
(G G Margarson) *lw: n.d in centre gp fr 1/2-way* **50/1**
5030 **23** *nk* **Cracking (IRE)**[41] 4812 2-9-3 93 RichardHughes 27 72
(R Hannon) *lw: w far side ldr 3f* **40/1**
6031 **24** *1 1/2* **Maximus Aurelius (IRE)**[13] 5624 2-9-1 0 LukeMorris 22 66
(J Jay) *lw: racd far side: handy tl 1/2-way* **100/1**
3420 **25** *shd* **Magical Speedfit (IRE)**[6] 5802 2-8-11 82 TPQueally 21 62
(G G Margarson) *cl up in centre tl 1/2-way* **100/1**
320 **26** *hd* **Dhhamaan (IRE)**[42] 4784 2-8-5 0 PaulDoe 8 55+
(C E Brittain) *missed break: bhd in stands' side gp* **100/1**
0006 **27** *2* **Feeling Proud (USA)**[67] 4022 2-8-6 80 TPO'Shea 7 50
(Jane Chapple-Hyam) *centre gp: bhd fr 1/2-way* **100/1**
2321 **28** *2* **Graceful Descent (FR)**[15] 5551 2-8-4 0 DaleGibson 28 42
(R A Fahey) *upset in stalls: slowly away and lagging thrght on far side* **66/1**

1m 12.63s (-0.47) **Going Correction** +0.025s/f (Good) **28** Ran SP% **133.6**
Speed ratings (Par 101): **104,103,101,101,100 100,99,99,98,98 97,97,97,97,96 96,95,95,94,93 91,91,90,88,88 88,85,83**
CSF £71.22 TOTE £7.60: £2.90, £5.30, £2.50; EX 161.10 Trifecta £1073.00 Part won. Pool: £1,511.40 - 0.80 winning tickets..
Owner Raymond Tooth **Bred** Exors Of The Late Seymour Cohn **Trained** Manton, Wilts

FOCUS
The usual cavalry charge for this type of event and the field split into three. Nine went far side, six came stands' side whilst the largest group of 13 raced down the middle. It was the far-side group that had the advantage, even though the winner raced in the centre group until edging towards the far side late on. The winning time was 1.08 seconds slower than the Cheveley Park and 0.55 seconds slower than the Middle Park, but given the difference in class the time was still very acceptable. The form looks rock solid.

NOTEBOOK
Exclamation ◆, who only broke his maiden seven days earlier, raced in the centre group for most of the way. Although he edged towards the far side entering the last furlong, it was not to the same degree as when winning at Haydock and he maintained his effort to get up near the line. There is no reason why he should not continue to progress and should be capable of winning in Listed company at least. (op 7-1 tchd 6-1)
Anosti had a great chance at the weights, but still had a few questions to answer after a couple of ordinary efforts including at Ascot the previous week. However, she was drawn on the right side as things turned out and ran a fine race under a positive ride, only losing out well inside the last furlong. This was much more like it. (op 10-1)
Copywriter, who had run well in a similar type of event at Doncaster, was trying his shortest trip to date. Never far away in the far-side group, he kept on right to the line but just lacked finishing pace where it mattered. (op 4-1)
Terry's Tip(IRE), one of the least experienced in the line-up, was favoured by the draw but still posted a cracking effort in this much hotter company. A maiden victory should be a formality now.
Perfect Act, another unexposed sort who was going in her coat, had run over 7f in both of her previous outings. Her stamina was an advantage in a race like this on a stiff track and she ran a fine race having been up there the whole way in the favoured far-side group. (op 7-1)
Gaspar Van Wittel(USA), who had contested Group races in his last two starts and was starting to go in his coat, emerges with credit ad he stayed on to fare best of the group that raced down the middle throughout. (op 15-2)
Fanatical stayed on late to eventually finish best of the small group that came up the stands' side, but she never had a hope of getting to those on the other flank. (op 10-1)
Eastern Gift, who was dull in his coat and dropping back from 1m, raced to the fore in the stands' side group throughout, but was always fighting a losing battle with the other two groups and failed to hang on to the advantage on his flank. (op 12-1)
Dry Speedfit(IRE) Official explanation: jockey said colt was squeezed out at start

5975 SHADWELL MIDDLE PARK STKS (GROUP 1) (ENTIRE COLTS) 6f
3:15 (3:16) (Class 1) 2-Y-O

£102,601 (£38,886; £19,461; £9,703; £4,860; £2,439) **Stalls** High

Form RPR
4101 **1** **Dark Angel (IRE)**[13] 5630 2-8-12 105 MichaelHills 1 114
(B W Hills) *led: hdd 5f out: led over 3f out: rdn and hung rt fr over 1f out: r.o* **8/1**
3102 **2** *1/2* **Strike The Deal (USA)**[13] 5630 2-8-12 107 EddieAhern 10 112+
(J Noseda) *hld up: hdwy over 2f out: rdn over 1f out: n.m.r ins fnl f: r.o* **9/1**
14 **3** *nk* **Tajdeef (USA)**[20] 5406 2-8-12 0 RHills 5 111
(B W Hills) *hld up: hdwy over 2f out: rdn to chse wnr over 1f out: hmpd ins fnl f: styd on* **9/2**[2]
3122 **4** *1 1/2* **Red Alert Day**[27] 5219 2-8-12 103 LDettori 7 107
(N A Callaghan) *lw: chsd ldrs: rdn over 1f out: styng on same pce whn hmpd ins fnl f* **9/1**
1402 **5** *1 1/4* **Achilles Of Troy (IRE)**[23] 5324 2-8-12 0 JMurtagh 2 103
(A P O'Brien, Ire) *lw: chsd ldrs: rdn over 1f out: edgd rt: no ex ins fnl f* **7/1**[3]
6331 **6** *shd* **Dream Eater (IRE)**[23] 5324 2-8-12 99 FrancisNorton 8 103
(A M Balding) *hld up: rdn and hung rt over 1f out: styd on ins fnl f: nt trble ldrs* **7/1**[3]
1 **7** *3 1/2* **Rock Of Rochelle (USA)**[19] 5456 2-8-12 0 (t) VRDeSouza 9 92
(A Kinsella, Ire) *awkward leaving stalls: chsd ldrs: rdn over 2f out: wknd fnl f* **14/1**
141 **8** *3* **Sir Gerry (USA)**[44] 4721 2-8-12 111 JamieSpencer 4 92+
(J R Fanshawe) *dwlt: hld up: rdn over 1f out: sn wknd and eased* **2/1**[1]
4 **9** *3* **Proud Linus (USA)**[44] 4724 2-8-12 0 StephenDonohoe 6 74
(D Carroll) *racd freely: led 5 out to over 3f out: wknd 2f out* **25/1**

1m 12.08s (-1.02) **Going Correction** +0.025s/f (Good) **9** Ran SP% **118.1**
Speed ratings (Par 109): **107,106,105,103,102 102,97,93,89**
CSF £79.02 TOTE £10.70: £3.20, £2.70, £1.80; EX 73.00 Trifecta £203.90 Pool: £1,120.31 - 3.90 winning tickets..
Owner The Hon Mrs J M Corbett & C Wright **Bred** Yeomanstown Stud **Trained** Lambourn, Berks
■ Stewards' Enquiry : Michael Hills two-day ban: careless riding (Oct 16-17)
V R De Souza three-day ban: used whip with excessive frequency and when out of contention (Oct 16-18)

FOCUS
A decent race despite the absence of Winker Watson and a boost to the form of the Mill Reef with the front pair from Newbury filling those places again, but whether this is genuine Group 1 form remains to be seen, especially as the winning time was 0.53 seconds slower than the fillies in the Cheveley Park. The field threatened to split into two in the early stages, with five staying far side early and the other four in indian file more towards the centre, but they had basically merged in one group away from the far rail by halfway.

NOTEBOOK
Dark Angel(IRE) adopted the same positive tactics that proved successful in the Mill Reef and despite hanging to his right up the final climb, was always holding his old rival from Newbury. His enthusiasm for racing cannot be questioned and his future will be as a sprinter provided he trains on, but he has already achieved so much in his first season that he owes nothing to anyone. (op 12-1)
Strike The Deal(USA) put in a strong finish up the inside rail and he and his old rival Dark Angel provided almost an action replay of their finish in the Mill Reef. At least he does already have a Group 2 win to his name, because as consistent as he is he may not be the easiest to place next season. (tchd 10-1)
Tajdeef(USA) ◆, who was starting to go in his coat, was dropped in trip after a solid run over an extra furlong in Doncaster's Champagne Stakes, came through to hold every chance up the final climb, but although he did not have much room to play with between the front pair in the closing stages it would be hard to say it cost him his chance. He is much less exposed than the front pair and may emerge as the best of them in the longer term. (op 11-2)
Red Alert Day, who did not go unbacked, is a very consistent sort but has not always had the best of luck in his races and was a bit unfortunate again here, as he was still in there pitching when squeezed right out around half a furlong from home. He does not possess much in the way of scope, but if he trains on has the ability to pick up a Pattern race enxt season. (op 14-1 tchd 16-1 in places)
Achilles Of Troy(IRE) had every chance, but was making no impression on the leaders in the last furlong. He is not the best that Ballydoyle have to offer, but will give his connections a good guide to the value of this form. (op 6-1)
Dream Eater(IRE) never managed to get involved and failed to confirm Doncaster running withe Achilles Of Troy on 4lb worse terms. He probably needs the extra furlong now. (op 8-1)
Rock Of Rochelle(USA) showed up for a while, but appeared to find this step up in grade too much. (tchd 12-1 and 16-1 in a place)
Sir Gerry(USA), not seen since his dramatic win in the Gimcrack, did not break at all well and it was obvious from some way out that he was struggling. His rider was looking down before easing him off and perhaps some reason will eventually surface for this poor effort. Official explanation: jockey said colt never travelled (op 7-4 tchd 9-4, 13-8 in a place and 5-2 in a place)

5976 NEWMARKET EQUINE SECURITY GODOLPHIN STKS (LISTED RACE) 1m 4f
3:50 (3:50) (Class 1) 3-Y-O+

£15,330 (£5,810; £2,907; £1,449; £726; £364) **Stalls** Centre

Form RPR
5211 **1** **Galactic Star**[20] 5411 4-9-0 106 RyanMoore 3 115+
(Sir Michael Stoute) *lw: hld up: hdwy over 3f out: led and hung rt over 1f out: rdn out* **11/8**[1]

1302 **2** *hd* **Munsef**[29] 5165 5-9-0 105 RHills 4 115+
(J L Dunlop) *hld up in tch: lost pl over 3f out: hdwy and swtchd lft over 1f out: r.o wl* **14/1**

15-2 **3** *1* **Soapy Danger**[14] 5589 4-9-0 118 KDarley 8 113
(M Johnston) *led: rdn and hdd over 1f out: styd on same pce ins fnl f* **2/1**[2]

-411 **4** *¾* **Crime Scene (IRE)**[211] 648 4-9-0 110 LDettori 7 112
(Saeed Bin Suroor) *chsd ldr: rdn and ev ch over 1f out: no ex ins fnl f* **6/1**[3]

5602 **5** *1 ¾* **Foxhaven**[20] 5402 5-9-0 108 (v) JimCrowley 5 109
(P R Chamings) *chsd ldrs: rdn and ev ch over 1f out: wknd ins fnl f* **16/1**

2105 **6** *2 ½* **Book Of Music (IRE)**[20] 5402 4-9-0 112 (v) KerrinMcEvoy 1 105
(Saeed Bin Suroor) *hld up: effrt over 1f out: no imp* **20/1**

/606 **7** *nk* **Kong (IRE)**[91] 3271 5-9-0 93 EddieAhern 2 105?
(J L Dunlop) *hld up: shkn up over 1f out: nvr nr to chal* **66/1**

31-0 **8** *2 ½* **Young Mick**[5] 5831 5-9-0 111 TQuinn 6 101
(G G Margarson) *chsd ldrs: rdn over 2f out: wknd over 1f out* **14/1**

2m 34.49s (0.99) **Going Correction** +0.025s/f (Good) **8** Ran SP% **115.2**
Speed ratings (Par 111): **97,96,96,95,94 92,92,91**
CSF £23.11 TOTE £2.20: £1.20, £3.00, £1.20; EX 20.90.
Owner Saeed Suhail **Bred** Hascombe And Valiant Studs **Trained** Newmarket, Suffolk

FOCUS
This was notable for a very modest early pace and it developed into something of a sprint. Despite that, the front pair came from off the pace and may have achieved even more than it appears because of that. The winning time was very modest for a Listed race as a result.

NOTEBOOK
Galactic Star ◆, tackling Pattern company for the first time in his hat-trick bid, had a bit to find with a few of these on official ratings despite starting a short-priced favourite. The race may not have been run to suit him either, as he had to come from a detached last in a steadily-run race and had to circle the entire field in order to get to the front. He did not have much to spare on the runner-up at the line, but given how the race worked out he can probably be given some extra credit and there may be even better to come from him. The Group 3 St Simon Stakes at Newbury at the end of this month looks an obvious option. (op 6-4)
Munsef, a consistent performer at his level, was still buried away in the pack as the favourite rather got first run on him and although he was closing him down after being switched, he ran out of time. He looks happier without the blinkers these days and provides a solid benchmark to the form. (op 16-1)
Soapy Danger was returning to the track soon enough following his recent reappearance from a long absence, but did not run like a horse suffering from the bounce. Allowed to set his own pace, he predictably proved hard to pass and ran right to the line even after getting headed. Provided he remains sound, he could do well in staying Group races next season. (op 15-8 tchd 9-4 in places)
Crime Scene(IRE), not seen since winning in Dubai in March, had every chance but lacked a turn of foot where it mattered. He should come on for this if another opportunity can be found. (tchd 13-2)
Foxhaven, with the visor retained, held a prominent position throughout, but had little more to offer over the last furlong or so. He does seem happier on a sharper track. (op 22-1)
Book Of Music(IRE), held by Foxhaven on recent Chester running, never got competitive and did not really step forward from that return to action. (op 25-1)
Kong(IRE) was never in the hunt and looks a shadow of his former self.
Young Mick was inclined to race rather keenly behind the leaders, but even so he was rather easily seen off and is still to show much of his old spark. (op 12-1)

5977 NGK SPARK PLUGS EBF MAIDEN STKS (DIV II) 7f
4:25 (4:25) (Class 3) 2-Y-O **£5,829** (£1,734; £866; £432) **Stalls** High

Form RPR

1 **Almajd (IRE)** 2-9-3 0 RHills 14 85+
(Sir Michael Stoute) *athletic: scope: chsd ldrs: led over 1f out: sn hdd: rdn to ld ins fnl f: r.o wl* **11/4**[2]

2 **2** *1 ¼* **Virtual**[14] 5598 2-9-3 0 JimmyFortune 1 82
(J H M Gosden) *lw: chsd ldrs: led over 1f out: rdn and hdd ins fnl f: styd on same pce* **2/1**[1]

3 *2* **Porthole (USA)** 2-9-3 0 RichardHughes 8 77
(B W Hills) *w'like: leggy: dwlt: hld up: hdwy over 2f out: rdn over 1f out: styd on* **9/2**[3]

4 *hd* **Roaring Forte (IRE)** 2-9-3 0 JMurtagh 12 79+
(W J Haggas) *str: w'like: s.i.s: hld up: rdn over 2f out: hung lft fr over 1f out: r.o wl ins fnl f: will improve* **25/1**

5 *1* **Foolin Myself** 2-9-3 0 NCallan 10 74+
(B W Hills) *unf: s.i.s: hdwy over 4f out: rdn over 2f out: sn outpcd: styd on ins fnl f* **40/1**

53 **6** *½* **King's Wonder**[24] 5306 2-9-3 0 RichardMullen 5 73
(W R Muir) *hld up in tch: rdn over 2f out: styd on same pce fnl f* **14/1**

7 *½* **Resurge (IRE)** 2-9-3 0 TPQueally 9 72
(J Noseda) *athletic: bit bkwd: chsd ldrs: rdn and ev ch over 1f out: wknd ins fnl f* **14/1**

5 **8** *½* **Kinnego Bay (IRE)**[63] 4132 2-9-3 0 MichaelHills 7 70
(B W Hills) *w'like: str: chsd ldrs: rdn and ev ch over 1f out: wknd ins fnl f* **12/1**

9 *nk* **Whistledownwind** 2-9-3 0 RyanMoore 13 70
(P W Chapple-Hyam) *w'like: scope: bit bkwd: sn pushed along in rr: n.d* **12/1**

06 **10** *1* **Conquisto**[65] 4070 2-9-3 0 PhilipRobinson 15 67
(C G Cox) *led: rdn and hdd over 1f out: sn wknd* **33/1**

11 *½* **Cossack Prince** 2-9-3 0 TedDurcan 2 66
(B J Meehan) *str: scope: prom: rdn and hung rt over 2f out: sn wknd* **25/1**

6 **12** *shd* **Blue Admiral**[14] 5598 2-9-3 0 JimmyQuinn 11 66
(M H Tompkins) *mid-div: wknd over 1f out* **40/1**

13 *1* **Arabian Spirit** 2-9-3 0 JamieSpencer 6 63+
(E A L Dunlop) *w'like: cl cpld: s.s: a in rr* **20/1**

14 *7* **Might Be Magic** 2-9-3 0 MartinDwyer 4 46+
(P W Chapple-Hyam) *str: hld up: a in rr* **50/1**

15 *20* **Lady Florence** 2-8-12 0 KerrinMcEvoy 3 —
(A B Coogan) *w'like: bit bkwd: sn outpcd* **66/1**

1m 26.21s (-0.29) **Going Correction** +0.025s/f (Good) **15** Ran SP% **130.6**
Speed ratings (Par 99): **102,100,98,98,96 96,95,95,94,93 93,93,91,83,61**
CSF £8.63 TOTE £4.30: £1.60, £1.70, £2.10; EX 12.00.
Owner Hamdan Al Maktoum **Bred** Shadwell Estate Company Limited **Trained** Newmarket, Suffolk

FOCUS
The winning time was 0.36 seconds slower than the first division, but there were still some eye-catching performances and the form looks solid even though the race was ultimately dominated by the two market leaders. This time the whole field came right away from the far rail and raced down the centre.

NOTEBOOK
Almajd(IRE) ◆ has a very classy pedigree, being a half-brother to seven winners including the top-class Alhaarth. He was expected to run a big race on this debut according to the market and duly did so, always holding a handy position on the far side of the field and battling on really well in what became a dual between him and the favourite. His pedigree suggests he will stay further and looks a very nice prospect for next season. (op 5-2 tchd 10-3 and 7-2 in places)
Virtual ◆, a well-supported favourite following his promising debut over course and distance last month, was always there or thereabouts and did nothing wrong, but he bumped into a very smart newcomer who made his effort on the opposite flank of the field. He deserves to go one better before long. (tchd 15-8 and 9-4 in places)
Porthole(USA) ◆, a half-brother to two winners, was very well backed and came from well back to chase home the two market leaders. This was a very promising debut and he should stay much further than this. (op 12-1)
Roaring Forte(IRE) ◆, a 25,000gns half-brother to two winning sprinters, looked very green but was noted finishing very well after being given just one crack with the whip. He should come on a lot for this and looks a surefire future winner. Official explanation: jockey said colt hung left
Foolin Myself ◆, out of an unraced half-sister to User Friendly, was doing some solid late work without being given at all a hard time. He should really come into his own when stepped up to middle distances next year. (op 33-1)
King's Wonder had his chance and stayed on to the line to record another creditable effort, even though he had the edge in experience on those ahead of him. He should win races at the right level and now qualifies for a mark.
Resurge(IRE) ◆, a 290,000gns half-brother to two winners including the top-class Araafa, ran well for a long way and should have learnt from this. (op 33-1)
Kinnego Bay(IRE) showed up for a long way, but did not appear to see out the extra furlong. (op 10-1)

5978 GREENE KING IPA H'CAP 1m 2f
5:00 (5:00) (Class 2) (0-100,94) 3-Y-O
£12,464 (£3,732; £1,866; £934; £466; £234) **Stalls** High

Form RPR

0334 **1** **Habalwatan (IRE)**[17] 5504 3-8-10 86 KerrinMcEvoy 7 96
(C E Brittain) *chsd ldrs: rdn over 1f out: styd on to ld wl ins fnl f* **9/1**

0113 **2** *hd* **Free Offer**[19] 5445 3-8-7 83 DaneO'Neill 9 92
(J L Dunlop) *hld up: plld hrd: hdwy 3f out: led over 1f out: hdd wl ins fnl f: no ex* **12/1**

1 **3** *1 ½* **Gold Sovereign (IRE)**[17] 5494 3-9-0 90 LDettori 4 96+
(Saeed Bin Suroor) *hld up: plld hrd: hdwy over 6f out: rdn and edgd rt over 1f out: styd on* **9/4**[1]

0006 **4** *shd* **Eradicate (IRE)**[13] 5631 3-9-4 94 GregFairley 5 100
(M Johnston) *chsd ldrs: led over 3f out: rdn and hdd over 1f out: styd on same pce ins fnl f* **9/1**

0233 **5** *1* **Snaafy (USA)**[21] 5385 3-8-9 85 RHills 6 89
(B W Hills) *led 1f: chsd ldr: rdn and ev ch over 1f out: styng on same pce whn nt clr run ins fnl f* **15/2**

102 **6** *2* **Urban Spirit**[13] 5639 3-8-12 88 RichardHughes 2 88
(B W Hills) *hld up: plld hrd: hdwy over 2f out: rdn over 1f out: no ex* **7/2**[2]

2041 **7** *6* **Gyroscope**[16] 5543 3-8-12 88 RyanMoore 3 76
(Sir Michael Stoute) *hld up: outpcd over 3f out: n.d after* **11/2**[3]

1043 **8** *5* **First Buddy**[21] 5382 3-8-4 80 PaulHanagan 8 58
(W J Haggas) *led 9f out: hdd over 3f out: rdn and wknd over 2f out* **16/1**

2062 **9** *11* **Noticeable (IRE)**[10] 5717 3-8-4 80 oh2 TPO'Shea 1 36
(M R Channon) *lw: hld up: rdn and wknd over 2f out* **20/1**

2m 5.04s (-0.67) **Going Correction** +0.025s/f (Good) **9** Ran SP% **118.5**
Speed ratings (Par 107): **103,102,101,101,100 99,94,90,81**
CSF £112.82 CT £328.69 TOTE £12.20: £2.80, £2.50, £1.40; EX 143.30.
Owner Mohammed Rashid **Bred** Darley **Trained** Newmarket, Suffolk

FOCUS
A fair handicap in which the field split early, but had merged by halfway and tended to race centre to far side. The early pace was not that strong, which resulted in a couple taking a grip, and the winning time was ordinary. Something of a bunch finish, but the form makes sense at face value.

NOTEBOOK
Habalwatan(IRE), who never got into the race over an extra couple of furlongs at Thirsk last time, would not have necessarily been suited by the ordinary gallop here, but this stiff track would have suited and, with the far rail to help him, battled on for a dour victory. He should not go up much for this and should remain competitive provided the race is run to suit. (op 10-1)
Free Offer, still 5lb higher than for her last win, was one of several to race keenly thanks to the modest early gallop but she still had every chance and was only just outbattled. She would have appreciated even quicker ground than this and remains in good form, but it becoming ever less likely that she will get her ideal conditions again this term. (op 16-1)
Gold Sovereign(IRE), having only his second outing and his first on turf, did himself no favours at all by taking a fierce grip and under the circumstances probably did well to get into contention and finish as close as he did. He should be given another chance to prove whether he is currently on a good mark or not. Official explanation: jockey said colt ran too free (op 5-2 tchd 11-4 and 3-1 in places)
Eradicate(IRE) was always up there and kept on trying, but lacked the speed of the principals over the last furlong. He is more exposed than most in this field, but this was a fair effort and he is dropping back to a more feasible mark. (op 8-1)
Snaafy(USA) was given a positive ride and had every chance, but again looked short of pace when it mattered. (op 8-1)
Urban Spirit, up 2lb after running well here last month, was again inclined to take a grip out the back thanks to the modest early pace. He tried to get involved approaching the last quarter-mile, but the damage had been done and he is surely capable of much better given a stronger gallop. (op 4-1 tchd 9-2 in a place)
Gyroscope raised 4lb for her Yarmouth victory, got left behind as the tempo increased and was very disappointing. (op 9-2 tchd 4-1)

5979 NEWMARKET CHALLENGE WHIP (H'CAP) 1m 2f
5:30 (5:31) (Class 6) (0-85,83) 3-Y-0+ **£0Stalls** High

Form RPR

1532 **1** **Sister Maria (USA)**[36] 4976 3-8-7 76 DaneO'Neill 2 82
(E A L Dunlop) *led: hdd over 1f out: drvn and battled on: regained advantage fnl 50yds* **3/1**[3]

1056 **2** *½* **Royal Fantasy (IRE)**[28] 5210 4-8-8 72 JamieSpencer 5 77
(J R Fanshawe) *hld up: effrt to ld over 1f out: sn rdn: fnd little: repassed and no ex last 50yds* **3/1**[3]

0044 **3** *1 ¼* **Opera Music**[21] 5385 3-9-0 83 RichardHughes 3 85
(S Kirk) *prom: rdn wl over 2f out: kpt hanging lft after: one pce ins fnl f* **5/2**[2]

1631 **4** *5* **Sumner (IRE)**[15] 5557 3-8-7 76 JimmyQuinn 4 68
(M H Tompkins) *hld up in tch: rdn 3f out: sn outpcd and plodded on* **9/4**[1]

006 **5** *6* **Kitebrook**[43] 4738 6-7-12 62 oh17 DavidKinsella 1 42?
(Mrs Mary Hambro) *t.k.h: prom tl rdn 3f out: immediately struggling and continued in detached last* **50/1**

2m 6.66s (0.95) **Going Correction** +0.025s/f (Good)
WFA 3 from 4yo+ 5lb **5** Ran SP% **111.3**
Speed ratings (Par 101): **97,96,95,91,86**
CSF £12.38 TOTE £3.70: £2.00, £2.00; EX 11.00 Place 6 £18.95, Place 5 £15.27.
Owner Cliveden Stud **Bred** Cliveden Stud **Trained** Newmarket, Suffolk

FOCUS
A steady pace in this traditional contest, which had previously been run at the Houghton meeting, produced a decent finish. The form is dubious.

T/Jkpt: Not won. T/Plt: £23.10 to a £1 stake. Pool: £110,571.45. 3,489.90 winning tickets. T/Qpdt: £23.40 to a £1 stake. Pool: £5,548.20. 175.10 winning tickets. CR

5887 WOLVERHAMPTON (A.W) (L-H)

Friday, October 5

OFFICIAL GOING: Standard

Wind: Nil Weather: Fine

5980 MACE RACING AT WOLVERHAMPTON APPRENTICE H'CAP 1m 5f 194y(P)

7:00 (7:01) (Class 6) (0-65,65) 3-Y-O £2,047 (£604; £302) Stalls Low

Form RPR

5002 1 **Diamond Key (IRE)**[11] 5690 3-8-11 55 ow8..........(b) JamesO'Reilly(3) 9 68
(M G Quinlan) *hld up in mid-div: hdwy over 3f out: rdn to ld 1f out: drvn out* **25/1**

2215 2 nk **Right Option (IRE)**[16] 5533 3-9-0 55.............................. HaddenFrost 12 67
(J L Flint) *s.i.s: hld up towards rr: hdwy over 4f out: rdn and ev ch 1f out: styd on* **9/2**[2]

-632 3 6 **Fire In Cairo (IRE)**[77] 3722 3-8-5 51.................. PatrickDonaghy(5) 10 55
(P C Haslam) *t.k.h early: sn chsng ldr: rdn over 2f out: hung lft and wknd 1f out* **10/1**

5424 4 1 **Golden Wave (IRE)**[27] 5224 3-9-7 65...................... KirstyMilczarek(3) 3 68
(D M Simcock) *led: rdn and hdd 1f out: wknd ins fnl f* **3/1**[1]

5512 5 2 ½ **Jocheski (IRE)**[42] 4757 3-9-10 65................................ JamesMillman 11 64
(A G Newcombe) *hld up towards rr: reminder 4f out: rdn over 2f out: styd on fr over 1f out: n.d* **7/1**[3]

0040 6 3 **The Diamond Bond**[29] 5158 3-8-4 48...................... WilliamCarson(3) 1 43
(G R Oldroyd) *hld up and bhd: rdn and hdwy wl over 1f out: no further prog* **33/1**

0050 7 1 **Kingsmead (USA)**[13] 5647 3-8-3 47..............................(vt) AmyBaker(3) 4 41
(Miss J Feilden) *prom: rdn over 3f out: wknd 2f out* **17/2**

5050 8 1 ¾ **Always Best**[22] 5364 3-8-4 48....................................(p) JackMitchell(3) 6 39
(M Johnston) *prom tl rdn and wknd over 2f out* **8/1**

6346 9 3 **Sir Sandicliffe (IRE)**[8] 5755 3-9-3 58.................................. PatrickHills 5 45
(W M Brisbourne) *hld up in mid-div: rdn over 4f out: wknd over 3f out* **14/1**

0603 10 nk **Julatten (IRE)**[8] 5750 3-8-0 46 oh1............................... SophieDoyle(5) 2 32
(D J Murphy) *t.k.h: a in rr* **10/1**

0653 11 9 **Regal Ovation**[13] 5622 3-8-8 49....................................... TolleyDean 7 23
(W R Muir) *hld up in mid-div: rdn 4f out: bhd fnl 3f* **12/1**

060- 12 ¾ **Gorgeous Girl**[449] 3435 3-8-11 52.. LukeMorris 13 25
(P W D'Arcy) *rdn over 4f out: a in rr* **33/1**

3m 4.61s (-2.76) **Going Correction** -0.10s/f (Stan) 12 Ran SP% **119.6**

Speed ratings (Par 99): **103,102,99,98,97 95,95,94,92,92 87,86**

CSF £133.71 CT £1227.40 TOTE £23.20: £9.00, £1.20, £5.10; EX 113.60.

Owner Mrs J Quinlan **Bred** Michael Dalton **Trained** Newmarket, Suffolk

■ Stewards' Enquiry : James O'Reilly one-day ban: used whip with excessive frequency (Oct 16)

FOCUS

A poor handicap, but the time was decent and the form has been rated slightly positively. An improved effort from Diamond Key.

Gorgeous Girl Official explanation: jockey said filly hung left

5981 CALL WOLVERHAMPTON RACECOURSE ON 0870 220 2442 CLAIMING STKS 5f 216y(P)

7:30 (7:31) (Class 6) 3-Y-O+ £2,047 (£604; £302) Stalls Low

Form RPR

1554 1 **Mafaheem**[69] 3965 5-8-9 68.. TGMcLaughlin 4 73
(P D Evans) *hld up and bhd: nt clr run briefly over 2f out: rdn and hdwy on ins to ld jst over 1f out: drvn clr* **15/2**[3]

2240 2 3 ½ **Rydal (USA)**[4] 5874 6-9-9 77.. MickyFenton 10 76
(J A Osborne) *towards rr: c wd st: rdn and hdwy on outside over 1f out: r.o ins fnl f: nt trble wnr* **4/1**[1]

4004 3 shd **Millfields Dreams**[16] 5535 8-9-1 62.................................. IanMongan 6 67
(M G Quinlan) *chsd ldrs: lost pl over 4f out: rallied over 1f out: kpt on ins fnl f* **8/1**

3502 4 ¾ **Green Pirate**[13] 5643 5-8-13 58......................................(p) LiamJones 7 63
(W M Brisbourne) *hld up and bhd: rdn and hdwy 1f out: nt qckn towards fin* **13/2**[2]

0406 5 2 **Ocean Gift**[27] 5233 5-8-11 58.. JohnEgan 8 55
(N Tinkler) *bhd: rdn 3f out: kpt on towards fin: nvr nrr* **8/1**

1620 6 hd **Burford Lass (IRE)**[9] 5731 4-8-4 60............................ AdrianMcCarthy 2 47
(D K Ivory) *mid-div: rdn over 3f out: hdwy over 2f out: wknd ins fnl f* **8/1**

4400 7 hd **Larky's Lob**[15] 5576 8-8-10 62.................................... JamesO'Reilly(5) 1 57
(J O'Reilly) *led after 1f: rdn and hdd jst over 1f out: wknd ins fnl f* **12/1**

0405 8 2 **Regal Raider (IRE)**[27] 5233 4-8-13 67...............................(p) TomEaves 9 49
(I Semple) *led 1f: w ldr: rdn over 1f out: wknd ins fnl f* **9/1**

503 9 ¾ **The Fisio**[15] 5565 7-9-9 63.......................................(v) ChrisCatlin 12 57
(S Gollings) *chsd ldrs: rdn over 3f out: wknd over 2f out* **20/1**

0060 10 ½ **Charlie Delta**[25] 5275 4-9-5 59....................................(v) LPKeniry 11 51
(J M Bradley) *chsd ldrs: rdn over 2f out: wknd wl over 1f out* **50/1**

00 11 1 ½ **Ten Shun**[49] 4561 4-8-6 60.. TolleyDean(5) 3 38
(P D Evans) *hld up and bhd: rdn 3f out: short-lived effrt on ins wl over 1f out* **16/1**

1155 12 9 **Came Back (IRE)**[136] 1935 4-9-9 76...................................... TPQueally 13 21
(J Mackie) *w ldrs tl rdn over 2f out: sn wknd* **11/1**

0R0 13 6 **Florentine Lady**[15] 5567 4-8-1 0.................................... DominicFox(3) 5 —
(D Shaw) *rel to r: a wl in rr* **200/1**

1m 14.75s (-1.06) **Going Correction** -0.10s/f (Stan) 13 Ran SP% **117.6**

Speed ratings (Par 101): **103,98,98,97,94 94,94,91,90,89 87,75,67**

CSF £36.44 TOTE £8.30: £2.50, £2.10, £2.80; EX 49.20.

Owner W Clifford **Bred** J H And J M Wall **Trained** Pandy, Monmouths

FOCUS

The first three came from off the pace in this strongly-run sprint claimer. Not a bad race of its type, rated through the third and fourth.

5982 RINGSIDE SUITE THEATRE STYLE CONFERENCING CLASSIFIED STKS 5f 216y(P)

7:55 (7:55) (Class 6) 3-Y-O+ £2,047 (£604; £302) Stalls Low

Form RPR

0000 1 **Vintage (IRE)**[20] 5420 3-8-12 55....................................(t) IanMongan 6 65+
(P Mitchell) *a gng wl: rdn to ld jst over 1f out: sn clr: r.o wl* **28/1**

0400 2 3 ½ **Mineral Rights (USA)**[18] 5476 3-8-12 55.................................. TomEaves 8 54
(I Semple) *led early: hld up in tch: rdn over 1f out: kpt on ins fnl f: no ch w wnr* **7/1**

220 3 ¾ **Alto Vertigo**[27] 5231 4-8-13 50.. LeeEnstone 7 52
(P C Haslam) *prom: rdn over 3f out: nt clr run wl over 1f out: edgd lft and kpt on ins fnl f* **13/2**[3]

-064 4 nk **Piccolo Diamante (USA)**[10] 5716 3-8-12 45....................(t) JohnEgan 4 51
(D J Murphy) *led after 1f: rdn and hdd jst over 1f out: no ex ins fnl f* **10/1**

4464 5 1 **Bonnet O'Bonnie**[21] 5386 3-8-9 50.............................. DominicFox(3) 13 47
(J Mackie) *hld up and bhd: swtchd rt wl over 1f out: sn rdn: kpt on fnl f* **20/1**

5005 6 1 ¾ **Lady Lafitte (USA)**[7] 5778 3-8-12 55.................................. LiamJones 11 42
(M Wellings) *broke wl: sn mid-div: rdn and hdwy on ins over 1f out: wknd ins fnl f* **9/1**

254 7 hd **Sweetsformysweet (USA)**[48] 4616 3-8-12 55................... TPQueally 12 41
(J Noseda) *s.i.s: plld hrd: sn mid-div: hdwy over 2f out: rdn over 1f out: wknd ins fnl f* **9/4**[1]

-050 8 1 ¾ **Lauder**[13] 5625 3-8-12 34.. MickyFenton 2 36
(J Balding) *outpcd: c wd st: nvr nr ldrs* **100/1**

0000 9 1 ¾ **Imperial Gain (USA)**[28] 5190 4-8-13 55............................(v) LPKeniry 10 30
(J M Bradley) *bhd fnl 2f* **9/1**

0000 10 5 **Diksie Dancer**[29] 5175 3-8-12 55..................................(b[1]) ChrisCatlin 5 14
(K A Ryan) *sn led: hdd after 1f: w ldr tl rdn 2f out: sn wknd* **7/2**[2]

0000 11 5 **Miss Wolf**[36] 4961 7-8-13 30.. VinceSlattery 9 —
(G H Jones) *outpcd* **150/1**

1m 15.42s (-0.39) **Going Correction** -0.10s/f (Stan)

WFA 3 from 4yo+ 1lb 11 Ran SP% **117.8**

Speed ratings (Par 101): **98,93,92,91,90 88,88,85,83,76 70**

CSF £209.88 TOTE £37.20: £9.30, £4.70, £2.60; EX 312.90.

Owner Sheldon Homes Ltd **Bred** Mountarmstrong Stud **Trained** Epsom, Surrey

FOCUS

A weak contest, but sound form with an improved effort from Vintage.

5983 JOIN WBX.COM FOR FREE FOOTBALL SHIRT H'CAP 1m 1f 103y(P)

8:25 (8:25) (Class 5) (0-70,70) 3-Y-O+ £2,914 (£867; £433; £216) Stalls Low

Form RPR

53 1 **Our Kes (IRE)**[28] 5188 5-8-13 63.. IanMongan 3 73+
(P Howling) *hld up and bhd: rdn 3f out: nt clr run wl over 1f out: sn swtchd lft and hdwy on ins: swtchd rt wl ins fnl f: r.o wl to ld last strides* **12/1**

6400 2 shd **Emily's Place (IRE)**[9] 5733 4-8-11 61.................................. TPQueally 5 70
(J Pearce) *hld up towards rr: c wd st: rdn and hdwy on outside over 1f out: r.o wl ins fnl f* **20/1**

0021 3 ¾ **Kansas Gold**[15] 5569 4-8-12 62.. KDarley 12 69
(J Mackie) *sn chsng ldr: rdn to ld over 2f out: hdd last strides* **4/1**[2]

3562 4 shd **The King And I (IRE)**[7] 5783 3-8-11 65...........................(v) ChrisCatlin 6 72
(Miss E C Lavelle) *hld up in tch: wnt 2nd 2f out: hrd rdn over 1f out: kpt on ins fnl f* **6/1**[3]

1024 5 1 **Alberts Story (USA)**[10] 5704 3-8-3 57............................... PaulHanagan 1 62
(R A Fahey) *hld up in mid-div: rdn over 2f out: hdwy over 1f out: styng on whn stmbld last strides* **15/2**

601 6 1 ¾ **Abbondanza (IRE)**[37] 4932 4-9-6 70..............................(p) TomEaves 11 71+
(I Semple) *hld up and bhd: bdly hmpd wl over 1f out: swtchd rt ent fnl f: r.o ins fnl f: nt rch ldrs* **16/1**

0506 7 2 ½ **Siena Star (IRE)**[13] 5636 9-9-1 65.................................. MickyFenton 2 61
(Stef Liddiard) *led 1f: prom: rdn over 3f out: wknd over 1f out* **20/1**

0500 8 ¾ **Floodlight Fantasy**[44] 4717 4-8-6 56..........................(b) DaleGibson 8 50
(Jedd O'Keeffe) *n.m.r s: in rr: rdn over 3f out: nvr nr ldrs* **66/1**

0060 9 shd **Dream Catcher (SWE)**[15] 5568 4-9-2 66.........................(t) LPKeniry 7 60
(R A Kvisla) *t.k.h towards rr: c wd st: n.d* **16/1**

5303 10 4 **Lunar River (FR)**[15] 5569 4-8-12 62........................(t) FergusSweeney 4 47
(David Pinder) *hld up in mid-div: hdwy 3f out: rdn and wknd over 1f out* **14/1**

2223 11 ½ **Billy One Punch**[17] 5514 5-9-1 65.. JohnEgan 13 49
(G G Margarson) *t.k.h in mid-div: hdwy 3f out: rdn and wknd over 1f out* **7/2**[1]

0124 12 3 ½ **Moves Goodenough**[74] 3799 4-9-3 67..............(b) RichardKingscote 10 43
(Andrew Turnell) *t.k.h: led after 1f: rdn and hdd over 2f out: wknd wl over 1f out* **8/1**

-060 13 25 **Bay Of Light**[34] 5046 3-8-9 63.................................. AdrianMcCarthy 9 —
(P W Chapple-Hyam) *hld up in mid-div: rdn over 3f out: sn bhd: eased fnl f* **25/1**

2m 1.31s (-1.31) **Going Correction** -0.10s/f (Stan)

WFA 3 from 4yo+ 4lb 13 Ran SP% **120.4**

Speed ratings (Par 103): **101,100,100,100,99 97,95,94,94,91 90,87,65**

CSF £237.02 CT £1139.82 TOTE £10.70: £3.70, £4.00, £2.50; EX 262.40.

Owner S J Hammond **Bred** Yeomanstown Stud **Trained** Newmarket, Suffolk

FOCUS

This competitive if modest handicap was run at a strong pace and the first two came from the back. Sound form overall.

Abbondanza(IRE) Official explanation: jockey said gelding was denied a clear run

Billy One Punch Official explanation: jockey pulled a muscle and eased gelding

Moves Goodenough Official explanation: jockey said gelding ran too freely

5984 SPONSOR A RACE BY CALLING 0870 220 2442 MAIDEN AUCTION STKS 1m 141y(P)

8:55 (8:55) (Class 6) 2-Y-O £2,047 (£604; £302) Stalls Low

Form RPR

5 1 **Bushy Dell (IRE)**[28] 5202 2-8-0 0.................................. AmyBaker(7) 1 65
(Miss J Feilden) *led early: a.p: rdn over 1f out: r.o to ld post* **4/1**[2]

025 2 shd **No To Trident**[14] 5605 2-8-9 72................................. TGMcLaughlin 4 67
(P D Evans) *a.p: led 2f out: rdn and edgd lft over 1f out: swvd rt ins fnl f: hdd post* **9/2**[3]

0 3 2 **Express Princess (IRE)**[9] 5727 2-8-6 0.................................. URispoli 3 60
(M Botti) *hld up in mid-div: hdwy over 3f out: ev ch 2f out: rdn over 1f out: carried rt ins fnl f: nt qckn* **14/1**

6334 4 1 ¼ **What's For Tea**[4] 5869 2-8-6 55.......................... RichardKingscote 6 57
(Tom Dascombe) *hld up in mid-div: hdwy on ins over 2f out: rdn over 1f out: one pce fnl f* **7/1**

500 5 1 ¾ **Lady Jinks**[42] 4761 2-7-11 52.................................. FrankiePickard(7) 9 52
(M D I Usher) *s.i.s: hld up towards rr: hdwy 3f out: rdn over 1f out: one pce* **100/1**

300 6 3 **Coral Shores**[31] 5110 2-8-7 62.................................. AdrianMcCarthy 10 48
(P W Chapple-Hyam) *hld up in mid-div: hdwy over 2f out: rdn over 1f out: wknd ins fnl f* **20/1**

7 1 **Crimson Mitre** 2-8-4 0.. LukeMorris(5) 7 48
(J Jay) *s.i.s: bhd tl sme hdwy over 1f out: hung rt to stands' rail ins fnl f: n.d* **33/1**

8 6 **Rsmiya** 2-8-5 0.. DaleGibson 13 32
(C E Brittain) *s.i.s: outpcd: nvr nr ldrs* **25/1**

0446 **9** *2 1/2* **Always Brave**[18] 5470 2-8-11 73 .... GregFairley 11 32
(M Johnston) *prom: led over 6f out to 2f out: rdn and wknd over 1f out* **13/8**[1]

10 *1 1/2* **Tobouggornotobougg** 2-8-11 0 .... TPQueally 8 29
(D Shaw) *a towards rr* **50/1**

0000 **11** *5* **Saturday Boy**[14] 5605 2-8-10 63 .... TomEaves 12 18
(Paul Green) *prom tl rdn and wknd over 3f out* **40/1**

00 **12** *36* **Stellar Rose (USA)**[32] 5097 2-8-7 0 ow2 .... KDarley 2 —
(B J Meehan) *sn led: hdd over 6f out: w ldr tl rdn and wknd over 2f out: eased wl over 1f out* **14/1**

0460 **13** *3* **Friction**[28] 5186 2-8-4 46 .... ChrisCatlin 5 —
(J G Portman) *a bhd: t.o fnl 4f* **66/1**

1m 51.8s (0.04) **Going Correction** -0.10s/f (Stan) **13** Ran SP% **120.5**
Speed ratings (Par 93): **95,94,93,92,90 87,86,81,79,78 73,41,38**
CSF £21.32 TOTE £5.20: £1.70, £2.20, £3.60; EX 30.00.
Owner R J Creese **Bred** Don Commins **Trained** Exning, Suffolk

FOCUS
A very ordinary maiden, the fourth and fifth helping to set the level.

NOTEBOOK
Bushy Dell(IRE) duly appreciated the longer trip but would not have won had the runner-up kept straight. (op 6-1 tchd 13-2)
No To Trident threw the race away when swerving right in the closing stages after he had originally been inclined to go the other way. (op 4-1 tchd 5-1)
Express Princess(IRE) improved on her recent debut at Kempton. Done no favours by the runner-up, she did look third best on merit. (op 22-1)
What's For Tea was switching to sand after being beaten in seller on each of her last three starts. (op 10-1)
Lady Jinks was stepping up in distance for her first start on the All-Weather.
Coral Shores appeared to get found out by the longer trip on her first try on sand. (op 11-1)
Always Brave was back up to 1m on his sand debut and folded up tamely after having plenty of use made of him. (op 15-8 tchd 2-1, 6-4 and 9-4 in places)
Stellar Rose(USA) Official explanation: jockey said filly lost its action

5985 WBX.COM £25 FOR NEW ACCOUNTS H'CAP 1m 141y(P)

9:20 (9:20) (Class 5) (0-75,75) 3-Y-0+ **£2,914** (£867; £433; £216) **Stalls** Low

Form RPR

-006 **1** **Strawberry Lolly**[28] 5203 4-9-4 73 .... GregFairley 10 81
(M Botti) *hld up in tch: rdn wl over 1f out: led ins fnl f: r.o* **14/1**

3642 **2** *1 1/4* **Trifti**[20] 5424 6-8-7 67 .... PatrickHills(5) 11 72
(C A Cyzer) *hld up in tch: wnt 2nd 4f out: led 2f out: rdn over 1f out: hdd and nt qckn ins fnl f* **7/2**[1]

1000 **3** *shd* **Meditation**[3] 5893 5-8-12 67 .... JamesDoyle 9 72
(I A Wood) *led: hdd 2f out: rdn over 1f out: styd on towards fin* **16/1**

5664 **4** *3/4* **Call My Bluff (FR)**[32] 5099 4-9-2 71 .... ChrisCatlin 6 74
(Rae Guest) *hld up in mid-div: hdwy on ins 4f out: rdn wl over 1f out: nt qckn ins fnl f* **5/1**[3]

0044 **5** *3/4* **Postsprofit (IRE)**[17] 5508 3-8-2 61 oh1 .... RichardThomas 2 63
(N A Callaghan) *bhd: rdr dropped reins over 1f out: r.o ins fnl f: nvr nrr* **12/1**

0600 **6** *3/4* **Bold Diktator**[21] 5383 5-9-1 75 .... TolleyDean(5) 3 75
(Tom Dascombe) *chsd ldr to 4f out: rdn over 2f out: wknd over 1f out* **4/1**[2]

1234 **7** *nk* **Casablanca Minx (IRE)**[15] 5569 4-8-10 65 ....(v) TGMcLaughlin 1 64
(P D Evans) *hld up towards rr: hdwy over 3f out: wkng whn edgd lft over 1f out* **11/2**

0000 **8** *shd* **Gaelic Princess**[29] 5163 7-9-2 71 .... FergusSweeney 8 70
(A G Newcombe) *hld up and bhd: rdn whn swtchd lft wl over 1f out: nvr trbld ldrs* **9/1**

6000 **9** *1 3/4* **Riley Boys (IRE)**[24] 5296 6-9-6 75 .... TomEaves 4 70
(J G Given) *bhd fnl 3f* **16/1**

5000 **10** *2 1/2* **Rabbit Fighter (IRE)**[15] 5568 3-8-4 63 .... PaulHanagan 7 53
(D Shaw) *a in rr* **20/1**

1m 52.47s (0.71) **Going Correction** -0.10s/f (Stan)
WFA 3 from 4yo+ 4lb **10** Ran SP% **115.2**
Speed ratings (Par 103): **92,90,90,90,89 88,88,88,86,84**
CSF £61.89 CT £623.95 TOTE £9.20: £2.70, £2.00, £5.80; EX 68.00 Place 6 £ 589.16, Place 5 £ 160.69.
Owner Mrs R J Jacobs **Bred** Newsells Park Stud Limited **Trained** Newmarket, Suffolk

FOCUS
This slowly-run affair was 0.67 seconds slower than the preceeding juvenile maiden. There was a bunch finish and the bare form is not up to much.
T/Plt: £397.00 to a £1 stake. Pool: £84,901.85. 156.10 winning tickets. T/Qpdt: £97.60 to a £1 stake. Pool: £5,676.40. 43.00 winning tickets. KH

5996 - 5997a (Foreign Racing) - See Raceform Interactive

5956 GOWRAN PARK (R-H)

Friday, October 5

OFFICIAL GOING: Good (good to yielding in places)

5998a DENNY CORDELL & LANWADES STUD FILLIES STKS (GROUP 3) 1m 1f 100y

5:05 (5:05) 3-Y-0+ **£43,918** (£12,837; £6,081; £2,027)

RPR

1 **Timarwa (IRE)**[33] 5071 3-8-12 109 .... MJKinane 4 106
(John M Oxx, Ire) *a.p: 2nd 1/2-way: led 2f out: strly pressed fr over 1f out: kpt on wl u.p* **2/1**[1]

2 *1/2* **Many Colours**[33] 5071 3-8-12 103 .... KJManning 8 105
(J S Bolger, Ire) *hld up towards rr: hdwy on outer early st: 2nd and chal fr over 1f out: ev ch: no ex cl home* **9/2**[2]

3 *2* **Uimhir A Haon (IRE)**[13] 5654 3-8-12 104 .... JAHeffernan 7 101
(A P O'Brien, Ire) *hld up in tch: 5th and prog early st: 4th over 1f out: kpt on u.p* **10/1**

4 *1/2* **Jalmira (IRE)**[13] 5654 6-9-2 96 .... DJCondon 2 100
(C F Swan, Ire) *hld up towards rr: smooth hdwy on outer ent st: 3rd and rdn 1 1/2f out: 4th and kpt on ins fnl f* **14/1**

5 *nk* **She's Our Mark**[27] 5241 3-9-1 106 .... DMGrant 11 103
(Patrick J Flynn, Ire) *trckd ldrs on inner: 6th 1/2-way: nt clr run and lost pl 3f out: 10th whn swtchd to outer 2f out: styd on wl fr over 1f out* **6/1**[3]

6 *7* **Queen Of France (USA)**[33] 5071 3-8-12 94 .... KFallon 6 86
(David Wachman, Ire) *chsd ldrs: 5th 1/2-way: kpt on same pce st* **12/1**

7 *3/4* **Truly Mine (IRE)**[27] 5240 3-8-12 103 .... PJSmullen 3 85
(D K Weld, Ire) *chsd ldrs: 4th 1/2-way: 3rd briefly appr st: sn no ex* **10/1**

8 *1* **Mango Mischief (IRE)**[21] 5396 6-9-2 .... DPMcDonogh 5 83
(M R Channon) *led: rdn and hdd 2f out: sn no ex and wknd* **10/1**

9 *2* **Magic Carpet (IRE)**[33] 5071 3-8-12 102 .... WMLordan 9 79
(David Wachman, Ire) *2nd early: 3rd 1/2-way: rdn and wknd fr 3f out: lame* **6/1**[3]

10 *shd* **Bold Bibi (IRE)**[33] 5071 3-8-12 94 .... RPCleary 10 79
(M Halford, Ire) *a towards rr* **20/1**

2m 2.70s (-4.30)
WFA 3 from 6yo 4lb **11** Ran SP% **126.5**
CSF £11.91 TOTE £2.60: £1.70, £1.40, £2.50; DF 13.60.
Owner H H Aga Khan **Bred** His Highness The Aga Khan's Stud S C **Trained** Currabeg, Co Kildare

FOCUS
A quality Group 3 contest with seven of the 10 runners holding an official rating in excess of 100.

NOTEBOOK
Timarwa(IRE) had a lot going for her on overall form and seemed to have conditions very much in her favour. She put a disappointing effort behind her and got to the front still travelling passing the two-furlong pole and did enough to hold off her nearest challenger. Whether she stays in trainign next season is doubtful. (op 7/2)
Many Colours had Timarawa behind in fourth last time at the Curragh. She proved the only serious threat after racing in last place approaching the straight, but she could not get there and was not helped by hanging under pressure. (op 4/1 tchd 5/1)
Uimhir A Haon(IRE) had run a reasonable race in a Fairyhouse Listed race previously and she plugged on looking in need of further. (op 12/1)
Jalmira(IRE) had a bit to do on official figures. She was travelling sweetly turning for home but the distress signals soon went out. (op 16/1)
She's Our Mark has been going the right way all season but may be feeling the effects of a busy campaign. (op 11/1)
Mango Mischief(IRE) had scored five times in contrasting ground and on her 106 mark was entitled to every chance here if putting her best foot forward. After making the running, she was another to weaken in the straight.
Magic Carpet(IRE) Official explanation: vet said filly finished lame

5999 - 6000a (Foreign Racing) - See Raceform Interactive

5943 KEMPTON (A.W) (R-H)

Saturday, October 6

OFFICIAL GOING: Standard

Wind: Moderate, half behind Weather: Fine

6001 BET WITH BETTER ON 08000 89 88 87 CONDITIONS STKS 1m (P)

2:05 (2:07) (Class 3) 2-Y-0
£7,478 (£2,239; £1,119; £560; £279; £140) **Stalls** High

Form RPR

216 **1** **Art Master**[36] 5004 2-9-0 92 .... FrancisNorton 2 101
(S Kirk) *hld up in last: rdn and prog on wd outside 2f out: led jst ins fnl f: styd on strly* **9/2**[2]

3215 **2** *2* **Al Muheer (IRE)**[21] 5410 2-8-11 94 ....(t) DaneO'Neill 7 94
(C E Brittain) *s.i.s: t.k.h and hld up: prog 2f out to ld over 1f out: hdd and outpcd jst ins fnl f* **5/2**[1]

140 **3** *1 1/4* **Ghetto**[23] 5350 2-9-0 82 .... PatDobbs 4 94
(R Hannon) *fractious bef r: trckd ldrs: rdn and nt qckn 2f out: one pce after* **16/1**

2135 **4** *1* **Donegal (USA)**[36] 5004 2-9-0 100 ....(v[1]) LPKeniry 6 92
(A M Balding) *cl up: rdn to chal and upsides over 1f out: fdd over 1f out* **5/2**[1]

0105 **5** *1/2* **Ernie Owl (USA)**[23] 5350 2-9-0 86 ....(b[1]) MartinDwyer 3 91
(B J Meehan) *t.k.h: mde most to over 1f out: fdd* **12/1**

3115 **6** *nk* **Solent Ridge (IRE)**[17] 5536 2-8-6 88 .... TolleyDean(5) 1 87
(J S Moore) *racd on outer in rr: rdn over 2f out: sn outpcd* **11/1**

4515 **7** *6* **Abolition (USA)**[15] 5590 2-8-11 89 .... KDarley 5 73
(M Johnston) *cl up: jnd ldr 4f out: wknd 2f out* **6/1**[3]

1m 38.22s (-2.58) **Going Correction** -0.30s/f (Stan) **7** Ran SP% **111.5**
Speed ratings (Par 99): **100,98,96,95,95 94,88**
CSF £15.34 TOTE £5.90: £3.10, £1.90; EX 17.10.
Owner Lady Davis **Bred** A G Antoniades **Trained** Upper Lambourn, Berks

FOCUS
A decent little conditions event, in which only two had raced on sand before, and the seven horses were virtually in a line across the track entering the last quarter-mile. The pace was fair, but it still favoured those that were held up as the front pair both came from well off the pace. Course record have been falling like autumn leaves here recently, and Art Master took 0.34 seconds off the existing two-year-old best time.

NOTEBOOK
Art Master, making his sand debut, was settled right off the pace but, having been brought widest down the home straight, produced a telling turn of foot to score. He had a bit to find with a few of these on official ratings so this was no mean effort, and although he was held in Listed company on turf last time it could be a different story on this surface. (op 4-1)
Al Muheer(IRE), trying his longest trip so far on this sand debut, also had the assistance of a first-time tongue tie. He gave his rivals a start, but he was soon back on terms without expending too much energy and came through between horses to hold every chance. He would have been 5lb worse off with the winner in a handicap and is more exposed than most of these, so is not going to be easy to place. (op 10-3)
Ghetto, another making his sand debut, was up to 18lb badly in with these rivals compared with a handicap. He gave himself every chance though, and despite not being able to match the finishing pace of the front pair still emerged with credit. Provided he has not ruined his handicap mark, there should be races to be won with him on this surface or back on easy ground on turf.
Donegal(USA), best in at the weights and visored for the first time on this sand debut, was not ridden so positively this time but did not see out the trip and failed to confirm recent Salisbury form with Art Master on the same terms. (op 2-1 tchd 11-4)
Ernie Owl(USA) was given a positive ride in the first-time blinkers on this switch to sand, but he was easily picked off and failed to confirm recent Doncaster running with Ghetto despite being 4lb better off.
Solent Ridge(IRE), a winner on the Lingfield Polytrack, was up a furlong but was the most exposed in the field and failed to make much impression. (op 9-1)
Abolition(USA), easy winner over a couple of previous scorers in a four-runner Wolverhampton auction event in his only previous try on sand, showed up for a long way but dropped out very tamely and this was too bad to be true. (op 15-2)

6002 £25 FREE BET AT BETTERBET.COM H'CAP 1m (P)

2:35 (2:37) (Class 3) (0-90,90) 3-Y-0
£9,348 (£2,799; £1,399; £700; £349; £175) **Stalls** High

Form RPR

1105 **1** **Kay Gee Be (IRE)**[115] 2578 3-9-2 88 .... DaneO'Neill 14 100
(M J Wallace) *trckd ldng trio: pushed along 3f out: prog to ld over 1f out: drvn and styd on wl* **10/1**[3]

4111 **2** *1/2* **Amarna (USA)**[22] 5382 3-9-4 90 .... MartinDwyer 6 101
(Saeed Bin Suroor) *dwlt: hld up towards rr: prog over 2f out: pressed wnr jst over 1f out: styd on but a hld fnl 150yds* **1/1**[1]

263 **3** *1 1/2* **World's Heroine (IRE)**[17] 5537 3-8-9 **81** .... NickyMackay 5 89
(G A Butler) *hld up in rr: prog on outer over 2f out: chsd ldng pair 1f out: kpt on but no imp* **16/1**

0600 **4** *1 1/4* **Cesc**[22] 5382 3-9-4 **90** .... KDarley 4 95
(P J Makin) *racd wd towards rr: rdn over 2f out: styd on fr over 1f out: nrst fin* **16/1**

66 **5** *1 3/4* **Cool Box (USA)**[15] 5593 3-8-9 **81** .... JimCrowley 10 82
(Mrs A J Perrett) *settled midfield: rdn over 2f out: kpt on same pce: nvr able to chal* **14/1**

3465 **6** *1/2* **Rudry Dragon (IRE)**[35] 5043 3-8-1 **78** oh5 ow2..(b[1]) KevinGhunowa[(5)] 7 78
(P A Blockley) *plld hrd early: pressed ldng pair: led wl over 2f out to over 1f out: wknd* **22/1**

330 **7** *nk* **Spirit Of The Mist (IRE)**[143] 1773 3-8-8 **85** ow2....... JamesO'Reilly[(5)] 2 84
(D J Murphy) *s.s: wl in rr: drvn wl over 2f out: plugged on: n.d* **25/1**

0111 **8** *1* **Mountain Cat (IRE)**[23] 5367 3-8-5 **77** .... FrancisNorton 8 74
(W J Musson) *pressed ldr: upsides over 2f out to over 1f out: wknd* **10/3**[2]

316 **9** *nk* **Jaleela (USA)**[122] 2369 3-8-11 **83** .... LiamJones 3 79
(W J Haggas) *chsd ldrs: u.p and no prog over 2f out: sn btn* **16/1**

0000 **10** *1* **Fantasy Parkes**[40] 4898 3-8-8 **80** .... SamHitchcott 13 79+
(K A Ryan) *snatched up after 1f and dropped to rr: nvr on terms after: eased whn no ch fnl 100yds* **66/1**

4336 **11** *2 1/2* **Sunoverregun**[64] 4127 3-8-6 **78** .... SaleemGolam 12 66
(J R Boyle) *settled in midfield on inner: rdn 3f out: no prog after: wknd over 1f out* **33/1**

4140 **12** *1* **Thunderousapplause**[48] 4639 3-8-11 **83** .... LPKeniry 11 68+
(K A Ryan) *bdly hmpd after 1f and dropped to last: nvr rcvrd: hanging fnl 2f* **33/1**

2210 **13** *1 1/2* **Spriggan**[32] 5114 3-8-5 **77** .... RichardThomas 9 59
(C G Cox) *led to wl over 2f out: wknd rapidly sn after* **33/1**

1m 37.63s (-3.17) **Going Correction** -0.30s/f (Stan) **13** Ran SP% **125.0**
Speed ratings (Par 105): **103,102,101,99,98 97,97,96,95,94 92,91,89**
CSF £20.07 CT £188.45 TOTE £18.50: £3.80, £1.10, £4.10; EX 31.30.
Owner Par Jeu Partnership **Bred** Pursuit Of Truth Syndicate **Trained** Newmarket, Suffolk
■ Stewards' Enquiry : Sam Hitchcott jockey said filly suffered interference after a furlong and was denied a clear run final furlong
L P Keniry jockey said filly suffered interference

FOCUS
A competitive handicap run at a solid pace, though a rough race with a couple getting badly hampered halfway down the back straight. The form looks sound nonetheless, and worth taking a positive view on.

NOTEBOOK
Kay Gee Be(IRE), winner of his only previous start on sand, was reappearing after four months off but he has won after a much longer layoff in the past so there were few worries on that score. Always up with the pace, he faced a serious challenge from the favourite over the last furlong or so but always appeared to be holding him. Given his fine record fresh, he is one to keep in mind if given a break before returning next spring. (op 8-1 tchd 14-1 in a place)
Amarna(USA), a winner twice over this course and distance in his only two previous starts on sand and off a 6lb higher mark in his bid for a four-timer, was ridden with a lot of confidence and was brought with his effort in plenty of time had he been good enough, but he just ran into a more determined rival on the day. (op 5-4 tchd 10-11)
World's Heroine(IRE), on sand for the first time, held every chance on the stands' side coming to the last furlong, but just lacked the required foot to trouble the front pair. She should be up to winning a race like this on Polytrack with this experience under her belt. (op 12-1)
Cesc, slightly disappointing on turf this year having shown some very smart form on this surface last winter, had finished over seven lengths behind Amarna at Sandown last time and was just 3lb better off. He stayed on over the last couple of furlongs, but even though he was not doing it anything like quickly enough this effort did back up the opinion that he is a much better horse on Polytrack.
Cool Box(USA), 3lb lower than when last on sand, lacked the pace to land a blow and may be worth another try over further.
Rudry Dragon(IRE), dropping back in trip after a couple of tries over further, pulled like a train in the first-time blinkers so may have done well to last for as long as he did. (op 20-1 tchd 25-1)
Mountain Cat(IRE), up another 4lb in his bid for a Polytrack four-timer, showed up for a long way but eventually found this company too hot. (op 7-2 tchd 3-1)
Fantasy Parkes may have had little chance anyway, but was unable to show her form after getting badly hampered midway down the back straight. Official explanation: jockey said filly suffered interference 1f after start and was denied a clear run in final furlong
Thunderousapplause was badly hampered by Fantasy Parkes when that filly got squeezed out halfway down the back straight. Official explanation: jockey said filly suffered interference

6003 BETTER FASTEST GROWING BOOKMAKER IN LONDON H'CAP 6f (P)
3:10 (3:11) (Class 2) (0-100,100) 3-Y-0+
£24,928 (£7,464; £3,732; £1,868; £932; £468) **Stalls** High

Form RPR

06 **1** **Bonus (IRE)**[41] 4864 7-9-4 **99** .... NickyMackay 5 109
(G A Butler) *trckd ldrs: prog to ld over 1f out: drvn and styd on wl* **12/1**

5214 **2** *1/2* **Beaver Patrol (IRE)**[14] 5616 5-9-5 **100** ....(v) StephenCarson 11 108
(Eve Johnson Houghton) *mde most to over 1f out: rallied ent fnl f: styd on but hld last 100yds* **5/2**[1]

0600 **3** *1 1/2* **Qadar (IRE)**[21] 5407 5-8-11 **97** ....(b) PatrickHills[(5)] 8 101
(N P Littmoden) *towards rr: rdn wl over 2f out and struggling: prog on outer over 1f out: snatched 3rd nr fin* **16/1**

5416 **4** *hd* **Siren's Gift**[14] 5632 3-9-0 **96** .... LPKeniry 1 99
(A M Balding) *trckd ldrs: rdn and effrt 2f out: nt qckn over 1f out: kpt on* **16/1**

004 **5** *shd* **Orpsie Boy (IRE)**[21] 5407 4-8-7 **93** .... LukeMorris[(5)] 6 96+
(N P Littmoden) *hmpd and hit rail after 1f: midfield: drvn on inner and kpt on fnl 2f: nvr able to chal* **7/1**[3]

1046 **6** *hd* **Border Music**[12] 5689 6-9-5 **100** ....(b) FrancisNorton 10 102
(A M Balding) *trckd ldrs: gng easily 2f out: shkn up over 1f out: no rspnse* **9/2**[2]

4000 **7** *1 1/4* **Mastership (IRE)**[49] 4607 3-8-13 **95** ....(b) DaneO'Neill 3 93
(C E Brittain) *dwlt: hld up in rr: prog over 2f out: chsd ldrs over 1f out: fdd* **15/2**

0500 **8** *1/2* **Dazed And Amazed**[35] 5050 3-9-3 **99** .... PatDobbs 2 96
(R Hannon) *a midfield: rdn and no imp on ldrs over 2f out* **20/1**

5235 **9** *3/4* **Majuro (IRE)**[8] 5765 3-8-13 **95** .... KDarley 7 90
(M R Channon) *outpcd and detached in last: kpt on fnl 2f: no ch* **7/1**[3]

2560 **10** *nk* **Tony James (IRE)**[7] 5797 5-8-13 **94** .... LiamJones 12 88
(K O Cunningham-Brown) *w ldr to over 1f out: wknd* **12/1**

-040 **11** *hd* **Murfreesboro**[6] 5841 4-8-13 **94** .... JimCrowley 9 87
(K J Burke) *mostly in last pair: rdn and struggling over 2f out* **50/1**

0010 **12** *nk* **One More Round (USA)**[21] 5407 9-8-12 **93** ....(b) JamesDoyle 4 85
(N P Littmoden) *towards rr: rdn over 2f out: sn btn* **20/1**

1m 11.31s (-2.39) **Going Correction** -0.30s/f (Stan)
WFA 3 from 4yo+ 1lb **12** Ran SP% **122.2**
Speed ratings (Par 109): **103,102,100,100,99 99,98,97,96,95 95,95**
CSF £42.46 CT £515.11 TOTE £14.30: £4.40, £1.40, £4.80; EX 52.00.
Owner The Bonus Partnership **Bred** A Stroud & J Hanly **Trained** Blewbury, Oxon

FOCUS
A hot handicap and yet another course record with Bonus taking 0.18 seconds off the existing best time. Despite that, the winning time was nothing out of the ordinary when compared to other times on the day and the front pair were always handy. Straightforward form.

NOTEBOOK
Bonus(IRE), possibly a bit unlucky on the Dundalk Polytrack last time, returned to winning form with a convincing success off a 3lb higher mark than he has previously been successful off. Never far away, he showed a willing attitude to get the better of the favourite and, having gone very close in Listed company on Polytrack in the spring, will no doubt be given the chance to go one better at some stage. (op 9-1)
Beaver Patrol(IRE), back on Polytrack after his cracking effort in the Ayr Gold Cup, tried to make just about all and did nothing wrong but just found one too good. His limited appearances on Polytrack before this have been creditable without quite matching his better turf efforts and this has to rank as the best so far, but he is on a career-high mark now so things will not get any easier for the time being. (op 10-3)
Qadar(IRE), back on his favourite surface after four modest efforts on turf, had the race run to suit and, as he often does, was doing all his best work late. He was kept very busy on sand last winter and that will no doubt be the case again, but he is not the easiest of rides as his effort needs timing just right. (op 20-1)
Siren's Gift had it to do from the outside stall on this sand debut especially as her best form has been over the minimum trip, but she gave herself every chance and went down fighting. She is well worth another try on this surface. (op 14-1)
Orpsie Boy(IRE), thanks to some decent form in the meantime, was 16lb higher than when successful on his last try on Polytrack at Lingfield in April. This very creditable staying-on effort suggests he may not be handicapped out of things on this surface just yet, especially as he collided with the rails when the eventual winner crossed in front of him exiting the back straight. (op 11-2)
Border Music, back on a more feasible mark for this return to sand, travelled like a dream and looked sure to take a hand in the finish, but he did not find as much off the bridle as had looked likely. (op 4-1)
Mastership(IRE), who can look very good when things go his way, was another that seemed to be travelling supremely well crossing the intersection, but found nothing at all off the bridle. (op 8-1)

6004 ALEXANDER FORBES NURSERY 5f (P)
3:45 (3:46) (Class 5) (0-85,85) 2-Y-O **£3,238** (£963; £481; £240) **Stalls** High

Form RPR

0301 **1** **Hadaf (IRE)**[63] 4173 2-9-1 **79** .... MartinDwyer 11 87+
(M P Tregoning) *hld up in midfield: prog 2f out: led 1f out: sn clr: decisively* **4/1**[1]

4301 **2** *1 3/4* **Piscean (USA)**[20] 5452 2-8-12 **76** ....(b) NickyMackay 5 78
(T Keddy) *s.s: wl in rr: prog over 1f out: r.o to chse wnr ins fnl f: nvr able to chal* **4/1**[1]

210 **3** *3/4* **Mister Fips (IRE)**[21] 5410 2-9-1 **84** .... PatrickHills[(5)] 7 83
(Jane Chapple-Hyam) *chsd ldrs: rdn and cl enough over 1f out: disp 2nd ins fnl f: kpt on* **8/1**

0165 **4** *hd* **Hobson**[17] 5534 2-8-10 **74** ....(b[1]) StephenCarson 10 73
(Eve Johnson Houghton) *mde most to 1f out: sn btn* **7/1**[3]

045 **5** *2 1/2* **Wild Bill Tracey**[34] 5065 2-8-11 **75** .... DaneO'Neill 12 65
(M J Wallace) *outpcd in last trio: styd on fr over 1f out: nrst fin* **14/1**

4000 **6** *3/4* **Ten Down**[58] 4315 2-9-0 **78** ....(b[1]) PatDobbs 3 65
(J A Osborne) *t.k.h: w ldr to jst over 1f out: wknd rapidly* **28/1**

0400 **7** *nk* **Enodoc**[19] 5480 2-9-2 **80** ....(t) SaleemGolam 8 66
(W R Muir) *nvr beyond midfield on inner: no imp over 1f out* **66/1**

2210 **8** *1 1/4* **Nawaaff**[29] 5207 2-9-6 **84** .... FrancisNorton 9 65
(M R Channon) *outpcd in last trio: nvr a factor* **13/2**[2]

5016 **9** *nk* **Not My Choice (IRE)**[2] 5939 2-9-0 **83** .... JamesO'Reilly[(5)] 2 63
(D J Murphy) *racd wd in midfield: lost grnd on bnd over 2f out: nt gng wl and btn over 1f out* **7/1**[3]

6100 **10** *1/2* **Little Knickers**[59] 4274 2-9-2 **80** .... JimCrowley 1 58
(Andrew Reid) *dwlt: struggling in last trio: nvr on terms* **14/1**

5330 **11** *1 1/4* **First Trim (IRE)**[5] 5856 2-9-7 **85** .... KDarley 4 59
(B J Meehan) *prom early but racd awkwardly rnd bnd: struggling in rr fnl 2f* **7/1**[3]

10 **12** *1 1/4* **Ocean Glory (IRE)**[7] 5802 2-8-13 **77** .... LPKeniry 6 46
(Peter Grayson) *chsd ldrs tl wknd rapidly over 1f out* **25/1**

59.11 secs (-1.29) **Going Correction** -0.30s/f (Stan) **12** Ran SP% **124.1**
Speed ratings (Par 95): **98,95,94,93,89 88,88,86,85,84 82,80**
CSF £19.44 CT £129.37 TOTE £5.00: £1.90, £2.40, £3.50; EX 21.00.
Owner Hamdan Al Maktoum **Bred** Shadwell Estate Company Limited **Trained** Lambourn, Berks
■ Stewards' Enquiry : Stephen Carson jockey said colt hung left on bend
James O'Reilly jockey said colt hung badly left in home straight

FOCUS
A hot nursery run at a rapid pace and the front four pulled right away from the others. Not only did Hadaf take 0.93 seconds off the juvenile course record, he also shaved 0.17 seconds off the all-aged record.

NOTEBOOK
Hadaf(IRE) ◆, making his sand and nursery debuts, was always travelling well off the pace from his decent draw and produced a smart turn of foot to destroy this field. He looks progressive and must have every chance of netting the hat-trick. (op 9-2)
Piscean(USA) ◆, raised 6lb for his victory in the first-time blinkers despite badly missing the break at Goodwood, gave away a significant amount of ground at the start once again which is usually fatal over this sharp 5f. The fact that he stayed on through the field to finish very much second best earns him a huge amount of credit and if he can learn to break better, there are plenty more races to be won with him. He looks worth another try over 6f. (op 6-1 tchd 13-2)
Mister Fips(IRE) was never far away on this return to the minimum trip for his sand debut, but could not match the finishing pace of the front pair. A stiffer track or a return to 6f probably suits him better. (op 9-1)
Hobson, yet another making his sand debut, showed decent pace from the start from his good draw even though he was inclined to throw his head about in the first-time blinkers rounding the bend, but he may have done a bit too much and was eventually picked off. Official explanation: jockey said colt hung left on bend (op 8-1)
Wild Bill Tracey ◆, making his nursery and sand debuts after three runs in turf maidens, had the best of the draw but that became academic when he found himself unable to lay up, so he probably did well to plug on and finish where he did under the circumstances. He was less exposed than the majority of these and may be of interest if stepped up a furlong.
Ten Down, rather disappointing since showing promise in his early starts, is dropping down the weights but did himself few favours by taking a strong hold around the outside in the first-time blinkers rounding the bend and, after showing up for a long way, folded once in line for home. (op 20-1)

Not My Choice(IRE), back over probably his best trip, had it to do from his draw and he gave away ground by racing too wide around the bend, so perhaps he should not be judged too harshly for this. Official explanation: jockey said colt hung badly left in home straight

First Trim(IRE) faced a stiff task on this nursery and sand debut, but was unable to show his true ability as he was very awkward around the bend. (op 11-2)

6005 BETTERPOKER.COM MAIDEN STKS 1m 2f (P)

4:20 (4:23) (Class 5) 3-Y-O **£4,533** (£1,348; £674; £336) **Stalls** High

Form RPR

4 **1** **Prairie Tiger (GER)**[25] 5304 3-9-3 0 SamHitchcott 4 74+
(N J Vaughan) *dwlt: hld up in last trio: prog 2f out: str run fnl f to ld nr fin* **9/1**

352 **2** ½ **Abydos**[16] 5562 3-9-3 79 MartinDwyer 6 73+
(Saeed Bin Suroor) *trckd ldrs: prog to go 2nd over 3f out: led 2f out: rdn 2 l clr ins fnl f: styd on but hdd nr fin* **11/10**[1]

3 3 **Speed Ticket** 3-9-3 0 NickyMackay 1 67+
(L M Cumani) *dwlt: hld up in last trio: reminder over 1f out: styd on wl to take 3rd ins fnl f: do bttr* **9/1**

034 **4** 1 ½ **Emperor Court (IRE)**[86] 3454 3-9-3 75 KDarley 2 64
(P J Makin) *hld up: plld way through to ld over 6f out: hdd 2f out: wknd fnl f* **10/1**

6406 **5** nk **Spice Bar**[36] 5001 3-9-3 59 (p) FrancisNorton 10 63
(A M Balding) *led to over 6f out: styd cl up tl outpcd over 1f out* **16/1**

2 **6** shd **Srikuantan (IRE)**[12] 5683 3-9-3 0 NelsonDeSouza 9 63
(P F I Cole) *trckd ldrs: t.k.h 1/2-way: outpcd over 1f out: plugged on* **9/2**[2]

6- **7** 1 ¾ **Wyeth**[346] 6173 3-9-3 0 DaneO'Neill 3 59+
(J R Fanshawe) *chsd ldrs and racd wd: outpcd fr 2f out: n.d after* **9/1**

0 **8** 2 ½ **Emily's Rainbow (IRE)**[24] 5335 3-8-12 0 LiamJones 8 49
(W J Haggas) *chsd ldrs: outpcd fr 2f out: wknd fnl f* **50/1**

3450 **9** shd **Louviere**[8] 5779 3-8-12 68 (v) PatDobbs 11 49
(Pat Eddery) *w ldr to over 6f out: wl in tch tl wknd rapidly 1f out* **17/2**[3]

0 **10** 8 **Instantly (IRE)**[120] 2429 3-8-12 0 LPKeniry 7 33
(W Jarvis) *in tch tl wknd over 2f out* **33/1**

0 **11** 22 **Mtoto Girl**[10] 5728 3-8-5 0 SophieDoyle(7) 5 —
(Ms J S Doyle) *lost tch 4f out: t.o* **100/1**

2m 6.54s (-2.46) **Going Correction** -0.30s/f (Stan) 11 Ran SP% **127.2**

Speed ratings (Par 101): **97,96,94,93,92 92,91,89,89,82 65**

CSF £20.80 TOTE £14.10: £3.50, £1.10, £2.70; EX 36.60.

Owner Owen Promotions Limited **Bred** Gestut Etzean **Trained** Malpas, Cheshire

■ Stewards' Enquiry : K Darley jockey said colt ran too free

Sophie Doyle jockey said filly hung left

FOCUS

This did not look a great maiden with the fifth horse rated 59 and the pace was ordinary. A couple did catch the eye, but there was not much to get excited about outside the placed horses, who are all capable of better than the bare form.

Emperor Court(IRE) Official explanation: jockey said colt ran too free

Mtoto Girl Official explanation: jockey said filly hung left

6006 BETTER BETTING ON 08000 89 88 87 H'CAP 7f (P)

4:55 (4:56) (Class 4) (0-80,85) 3-Y-O+ **£5,181** (£1,541; £770; £384) **Stalls** High

Form RPR

6560 **1** **Shustraya**[14] 5635 3-9-3 79 MartinDwyer 10 93
(P J Makin) *dwlt: sn in midfield on inner: eased out fr over 2f out: r.o to ld jst ins fnl f: drvn out* **16/1**

0033 **2** hd **Abunai**[14] 5635 3-9-2 78 RichardKingscote 7 91
(R Charlton) *hld up in rr: prog jst over 2f out: styd on strly to take 2nd ins fnl f: clsng on wnr fin* **7/1**[3]

605 **3** 2 **Sailor King (IRE)**[28] 5223 5-9-3 77 JimCrowley 6 85
(D K Ivory) *trckd ldrs: effrt to ld 2f out: hdd and one pce jst ins fnl f* **9/1**

3001 **4** 1 **Alfresco**[28] 5223 3-9-5 81 (b) PatDobbs 1 86
(Pat Eddery) *dwlt: hld up in last trio: stdy prog over 2f out: chsd ldrs over 1f out: kpt on but nt pce to chal* **8/1**

4331 **5** 1 ½ **Giant Slalom**[28] 5238 3-9-3 79 LiamJones 11 80+
(W J Haggas) *t.k.h: w ldrs: narrow ld 4f out to 2f out: wknd fnl f* **9/2**[1]

0615 **6** nk **Viva Volta**[40] 4895 4-9-4 78 (b) NickyMackay 3 78
(T D Easterby) *mostly in midfield: drvn on outer 2f out: kpt on but no imp on ldrs* **14/1**

0006 **7** shd **Phluke**[7] 5804 6-9-4 78 StephenCarson 4 78
(Eve Johnson Houghton) *pushed along in last 4f out: struggling after: styd on u.p over 1f out* **9/1**

4002 **8** nk **Russian Symphony (USA)**[25] 5312 6-9-6 80 NelsonDeSouza 13 79
(C R Egerton) *disp ld for 3f: styd cl up on inner tl fdd fr over 1f out* **9/1**

0446 **9** nk **Mandarin Spirit (IRE)**[22] 5381 7-9-4 78 (b) SaleemGolam 2 76
(G C H Chung) *hld up in rr: n.m.r on inner over 3f out: effrt over 2f out: no prog over 1f out* **16/1**

4434 **10** 1 ¼ **Goodbye Cash (IRE)**[12] 5684 3-8-12 79 TolleyDean(5) 5 74
(P D Evans) *pushed along towards rr by 1/2-way: struggling over 2f out* **16/1**

3510 **11** 5 **Jacaranda Ridge**[50] 4589 3-9-4 80 KDarley 12 61
(M A Jarvis) *disp ld for 3f: pressed ldr to 2f out: wknd and eased fnl f* **12/1**

1502 **12** 1 ¾ **Nobilissima (IRE)**[42] 4816 3-9-0 79 MarcHalford(3) 8 56
(J L Spearing) *w ldrs early: struggling in rr over 2f out* **14/1**

241 **13** 2 ½ **Crystal Gazer (FR)**[12] 5684 3-9-9 85 FrancisNorton 9 55
(R Hannon) *hld up in rr: pushed along and no prog 2f out: eased fnl f* **11/2**[2]

1m 24.12s (-2.68) **Going Correction** -0.30s/f (Stan)

WFA 3 from 4yo+ 2lb 13 Ran SP% **125.9**

Speed ratings (Par 105): **103,102,100,99,97 97,97,96,96,95 89,87,84**

CSF £130.54 CT £1101.13 TOTE £24.20: £6.90, £3.00, £3.80; EX 167.70.

Owner Four Leaf Clover **Bred** Millsec Limited **Trained** Ogbourne Maisey, Wilts

■ Stewards' Enquiry : Francis Norton trainer had no explanation for the poor form shown

FOCUS

A competitive handicap run at a decent pace and three of the first four home came from well back. Decent form for the grade.

Crystal Gazer(FR) Official explanation: trainer had no explanation for the poor form shown

6007 20 SHOPS, ONE YEAR, THAT'S BETTER! APPRENTICE DERBY H'CAP 1m 4f (P)

5:30 (5:31) (Class 4) (0-80,79) 3-Y-O+ **£5,181** (£1,541; £770; £384) **Stalls** Centre

Form RPR

1400 **1** **Muhannak (IRE)**[10] 5725 3-9-2 76 (b[1]) RichardKingscote 7 87+
(G A Butler) *hld up in last pair: stdy prog wl over 2f out: rdn to ld over 1f out: drew clr fnl f* **11/2**[2]

001 **2** 3 **Kaateb (IRE)**[22] 5384 4-9-12 79 LiamJones 5 85+
(W J Haggas) *hld up towards rr: prog over 3f out: led jst over 2f out: drvn and hdd over 1f out: sn outpcd* **6/1**[3]

1621 **3** 1 ½ **Jack Rolfe**[15] 5594 5-9-5 77 WilliamCarson(5) 6 81
(G L Moore) *trckd ldrs: prog to 2nd over 3f out: hanging but rdn to ld wl over 2f out: hdd jst over 2f out: one pce* **3/1**[1]

6454 **4** nk **Spiderback (IRE)**[11] 5718 3-9-1 78 (b) HaddenFrost(3) 2 82
(R Hannon) *hld up in last pair: rdn and prog over 2f out: kpt on to take 3rd ins fnl f: nt pce to chal* **11/2**[2]

4023 **5** ¾ **Vallemeldee (IRE)**[24] 5333 3-8-11 74 LukeMorris(3) 1 76
(P W D'Arcy) *sn towards rr on outer: rdn over 3f out: plugged on fnl 2f: n.d* **10/1**

114- **6** 1 ¼ **Bedouin Blue (IRE)**[49] 4612 4-8-13 71 PatrickDonaghy(5) 8 71
(P C Haslam) *hld up in midfield: prog on inner 3f out: chsd ldrs 2f out: wknd fnl f* **12/1**

0360 **7** 6 **Multicultural**[7] 5808 4-8-12 70 KirstyMilczarek(5) 10 61
(D M Simcock) *cl up: racd wd fr 4f out: veered rt over 2f out and hung lft sn after: wknd* **9/1**

0000 **8** 10 **Mahmjra**[29] 5205 5-9-3 75 (t) SCreighton(5) 3 50
(C N Allen) *trckd ldrs: rdn in midfield over 3f out: sn wknd* **33/1**

1540 **9** nk **Transvestite (IRE)**[15] 5593 5-9-8 78 (v) PatrickHills(3) 11 52
(J W Hills) *w ldr for 4f: stdd: effrt to ld over 4f out: hdd wl over 2f out: sn wknd and eased* **6/1**[3]

0255 **10** 10 **Precept**[25] 5311 3-8-12 72 TravisBlock 9 30
(H Candy) *prom tl wknd over 4f out: t.o* **25/1**

4600 **11** 8 **Poseidon's Secret (IRE)**[61] 4231 4-9-0 72 (b) KMay(5) 4 17
(Pat Eddery) *mde most to over 4f out: wknd rapidly: t.o* **16/1**

2m 31.6s (-5.30) **Going Correction** -0.30s/f (Stan)

WFA 3 from 4yo+ 7lb 11 Ran SP% **123.8**

Speed ratings (Par 105): **105,103,102,101,101 100,96,89,89,82 77**

CSF £40.77 CT £121.13 TOTE £7.40: £2.50, £2.60, £1.50; EX 51.30 Place 6 £59.71, Place 5 £30.58..

Owner Fawzi Abdulla Nass **Bred** Mount Coote Stud **Trained** Blewbury, Oxon

■ Stewards' Enquiry : Kirsty Milczarek jockey said gelding hung both ways

FOCUS

They went a good early pace in this, but the pair that helped force it eventually finished in the last three, so they probably did too much. The winner scored nicely though and the form looks solid enough.

Multicultural Official explanation: jockey said gelding hung both ways

T/Plt: £215.80 to a £1 stake. Pool: £56,931.05. 192.50 winning tickets. T/Qpdt: £88.50 to a £1 stake. Pool: £2,523.80. 21.10 winning tickets. JN

5971 NEWMARKET (ROWLEY) (R-H)

Saturday, October 6

OFFICIAL GOING: Good to firm (8.9)

Wind: Light, half-against Weather: Overcast

6008 FINNFOREST OH SO SHARP STKS (GROUP 3) (FILLIES) 7f

2:10 (2:10) (Class 1) 2-Y-O

£22,712 (£8,608; £4,308; £2,148; £1,076; £540) **Stalls** High

Form RPR

133 **1** **Raymi Coya (CAN)**[30] 5164 2-8-12 95 KerrinMcEvoy 8 97
(M Botti) *trckd ldrs: racd keenly: swtchd lft over 1f out: r.o to ld wl ins fnl f* **15/2**

116 **2** ½ **Step Softly**[23] 5353 2-8-12 92 JimmyFortune 5 96
(R Hannon) *chsd ldr: rdn over 1f out: led ins fnl f: sn hdd: styd on* **9/1**

21 **3** hd **Annie Skates (USA)**[29] 5202 2-8-12 84 JohnEgan 3 95
(Jane Chapple-Hyam) *hld up in tch: edgd lft and outpcd over 1f out: r.o ins fnl f* **13/2**[3]

5211 **4** nk **Royal Confidence**[24] 5322 2-8-12 91 RHills 4 94
(B W Hills) *hld up: rdn over 1f out: r.o ins fnl f: nrst fin* **10/3**[2]

11 **5** hd **Rosa Grace**[15] 5592 2-8-12 86 PhilipRobinson 1 94
(Rae Guest) *s.i.s: hld up: rdn over 1f out: r.o ins fnl f* **13/2**[3]

12 **6** shd **Dream Day**[15] 5592 2-8-12 88 RyanMoore 6 94
(R Hannon) *hld up: rdn over 2f out: r.o wl ins fnl f: nt rch ldrs* **17/2**

01 **7** ½ **Joffe's Run (USA)**[30] 5162 2-8-12 93 RichardHughes 7 92
(B J Meehan) *lw: sn led: qcknd over 2f out: rdn over 1f out: hdd and no ex ins fnl f* **11/4**[1]

0412 **8** 6 **Then 'n Now**[18] 5496 2-8-12 72 SimonWhitworth 2 77
(C A Cyzer) *chsd ldrs: rdn over 2f out: wknd fnl f* **100/1**

1m 27.51s (1.01) **Going Correction** +0.05s/f (Good) 8 Ran SP% **109.7**

Speed ratings (Par 102): **96,95,95,94,94 94,93,87**

CSF £65.93 TOTE £9.60: £2.40, £2.60, £2.10; EX 81.60 TRIFECTA Not won..

Owner C Pizarro **Bred** Anderson Farms Ont Inc & Marrette Farrell **Trained** Newmarket, Suffolk

FOCUS

A decent renewal of this fillies' contest, being run as a Group 3 for the first time. The early pace was steady, and as a result the time was 0.89sec slower than the later nursery and the field finished closely bunched.

NOTEBOOK

Raymi Coya(CAN) stepping up in both trip and grade, having been placed in Listed company last time, had the highest official rating coming into this. She is clearly progressing and, after being switched to get the room to make her challenge, picked up well up the hill to score narrowly. She looks capable of going on from this and, with her connections, could be aimed at the Italian Guineas next season, although the Nell Gwyn back here could be first on the agenda. (op 8-1)

Step Softly, who beat the winner at Haydock earlier in the season, was close to the pace throughout and made a bold bid, only getting caught close home. This looks her level as she had been well held in the May Hill last time. (op 10-1)

Annie Skates(USA) ◆, who looked dull in her coat, took a real step forward on this first encounter with faster ground, having made her debut on soft ground and then got off the mark on Polytrack. She ran on really well having been held up in a steadily-run race, and she finished strongly. She looks capable of winning Group races and could be the one to take from the race. (op 6-1)

Royal Confidence, who had the beating of the winner on a line through Fashion Rocks and had won her last two races, including a valuable fillies' nursery last time, was another to finish well having been held up and is continuing to progress with racing. She can be placed to gain black type on this evidence as she only just missed out on it here. (tchd 7-2)

Rosa Grace, who was starting to go in her coat, beat Dream Day at Newbury recently. She missed the break and was quite keen under restraint before getting tapped for toe when the pace quickened. Her sire is an influence for stamina and she looks as though she will get 1m, but she may be best ridden more positively in future. (op 6-1 tchd 11-2)

Dream Day, held up off the pace, was one of several to make good late ground and looks capable of further progress over another furlong. (op 8-1)

Joffe's Run(USA) set a very steady pace and tried to step it up from the top of the hill, but she could not shake off her rivals and eventually got run out of it up the hill. This was still a decent effort and she may have been better setting a more even gallop. (tchd 3-1)

6009 COUNTRYWIDE STEEL AND TUBES JOEL STKS (GROUP 3) 1m
2:45 (2:45) (Class 1) 3-Y-O+

£28,390 (£10,760; £5,385; £2,685; £1,345; £675) **Stalls** High

Form RPR

1226 **1** **Creachadoir (IRE)**[109] 2734 3-9-0 118 .... KerrinMcEvoy 2 118+
(Saeed Bin Suroor) *lw: trckd ldrs: led over 1f out: hung rt: r.o wl* **11/4**[1]

601 **2** *3* **Tell**[20] 5444 4-9-0 102 .... (b) EddieAhern 8 108
(J L Dunlop) *led: hdd over 6f out: rdn and ev ch over 1f out: styd on same pce* **66/1**

2362 **3** *1 ¼* **Heaven Sent**[35] 5047 4-8-11 106 .... RyanMoore 11 102
(Sir Michael Stoute) *lw: hld up: hdwy over 2f out: rdn over 1f out: no ex ins fnl f* **11/2**[2]

1531 **4** *nk* **Tobosa**[22] 5378 3-8-11 111 .... JimmyFortune 9 105
(W Jarvis) *lw: hld up: rdn over 2f out: hdwy over 1f out: hung rt ins fnl f: nt rch ldrs* **11/4**[1]

2031 **5** *½* **King Of Argos**[41] 4851 4-9-0 104 .... SteveDrowne 10 103
(E A L Dunlop) *lw: hld up: hdwy over 1f out: styd on same pce ins fnl f* **11/1**

0242 **6** *2* **Metropolitan Man**[21] 5412 4-9-0 108 .... GeorgeBaker 5 99
(D M Simcock) *hld up: hdwy and hung rt over 1f out: no imp fnl f* **20/1**

1011 **7** *3* **Jumbajukiba**[20] 5459 4-9-3 0 .... (b) FMBerry 4 95
(Mrs John Harrington, Ire) *chsd ldr: led over 4f out: rdn and hdd over 1f out: wknd ins fnl f* **6/1**[3]

2004 **8** *3 ½* **Ferneley (IRE)**[14] 5654 3-8-11 0 .... (b[1]) JMurtagh 7 84
(Francis Ennis, Ire) *dwlt: hld up: rdn over 2f out: sn wknd* **20/1**

342 **9** *2 ½* **Dunelight (IRE)**[32] 5112 4-9-0 109 .... (v) PhilipRobinson 1 78
(C G Cox) *racd alone centre: in rr fr 1/2-way* **9/1**

5363 **10** *15* **Olympian Odyssey**[14] 5634 4-9-0 106 .... (v) RHills 6 44
(Saeed Bin Suroor) *led over 6f out: hdd over 4f out: wknd wl over 1f out* **25/1**

1m 36.68s (-2.69) **Going Correction** +0.05s/f (Good)
WFA 3 from 4yo 3lb **10** Ran SP% **116.2**
Speed ratings (Par 113): **115,112,110,110,109 107,104,101,98,83**
CSF £242.79 TOTE £3.40: £1.40, £7.60, £1.80; EX 111.60 Trifecta £556.40 Part won. Pool £783.80 - 0.10 winning units..
Owner Godolphin **Bred** Frank Dunne **Trained** Newmarket, Suffolk

FOCUS
Not the strongest renewal of this Group 3 with several upgraded handicappers and Listed performers taking on the Group-class three-year-olds. The runner-up holds the form down for now, otherwise the winner could be rated close to the top milers.

NOTEBOOK
Creachadoir(IRE) ◆ was clear best on official ratings, following a successful time for Jim Bolger, which included second places in the French and Irish Guineas. Making his debut for Godolphin, he won this in the style of one who is a cut above his rivals and he looks capable of winning at the top level before too long. (op 5-2 tchd 3-1)
Tell, improved for the re-application of blinkers last time, adopted forcing tactics once again and ran on well, despite having no chance with the winner. He may have more to offer and can win at this level next season if maintaining the improvement, although he could return for the Darley Stakes at the next meeting here.
Heaven Sent, the only filly in nthe line-up, came through with the winner but could not match that rival's pace from the dip, despite keeping on well enough. (tchd 5-1)
Tobosa, another who was held up, ran on from over a furlong out but the winner had already gone beyond recall. He goes well on the Newmarket tracks but otherwise his best efforts have been on flatter courses. (op 7-2 tchd 4-1 and 9-2 in a place)
King Of Argos, an improving handicapper, ran a big race, staying on well in the closing stages. He may be able to establish himself at this level next season. (op 12-1 tchd 10-1)
Metropolitan Man, really struggles in handicaps of his current mark and is having trouble bridging the gap to Group races. However, this was more encouraging and on this evidence he is certainly capable of scoring in Listed company.
Jumbajukiba, who was edgy before the race and a market drifter, likes to lead and has been in good form this term, but he was taken on up front and gave way on the run into the dip. (op 4-1 tchd 13-2)
Ferneley(IRE) Official explanation: jockey said colt hung left throughout and moved poorly
Dunelight(IRE), another who is best from the front, was restrained and kept wide of his rivals throughout. He never really got competitive and finished up well beaten. (op 10-1)
Olympian Odyssey Official explanation: jockey said colt ran too freely

6010 KINGDOM OF BAHRAIN SUN CHARIOT STKS (GROUP 1) (F&M) 1m
3:20 (3:23) (Class 1) 3-Y-O+

£105,043 (£39,812; £19,924; £9,934; £4,976; £2,497) **Stalls** High

Form RPR

2054 **1** **Majestic Roi (USA)**[23] 5354 3-8-13 108 .... DarryllHolland 7 115
(M R Channon) *hld up: hdwy over 3f out: rdn and swtchd lft over 1f out: r.o to ld wl ins fnl f* **16/1**

3140 **2** *¾* **Nannina**[63] 4149 4-9-2 115 .... JimmyFortune 3 113
(J H M Gosden) *chsd ldrs: led over 2f out: rdn and edgd rt over 1f out: hdd wl ins fnl f* **5/1**[3]

5611 **3** *1* **Echelon**[28] 5241 5-9-2 116 .... RyanMoore 6 111
(Sir Michael Stoute) *chsd ldrs: rdn and nt clr run over 1f out: styd on same pce* **11/8**[1]

3613 **4** *nk* **Simply Perfect**[69] 4010 3-8-13 116 .... JMurtagh 4 110
(J Noseda) *chsd ldr: led over 3f out: hdd over 2f out: sn rdn: kpt on* **7/2**[2]

1501 **5** *nk* **Harvest Queen (IRE)**[28] 5213 4-9-2 106 .... EddieAhern 2 109
(P J Makin) *lw: hld up: hdwy over 3f out: outpcd over 1f out: styd on ins fnl f* **16/1**

2400 **6** *2* **Barshiba (IRE)**[28] 5241 3-8-13 106 .... TQuinn 1 105
(D R C Elsworth) *hld up: outpcd over 2f out: rdn and edgd rt over 1f out: nt trble ldrs* **40/1**

2026 **7** *6* **Speciosa (IRE)**[63] 4149 4-9-2 114 .... MickyFenton 9 91
(Mrs P Sly) *swtg: led: hung lft thrght: hdd over 3f out: wknd wl over 1f out* **15/2**

0166 **8** *3* **Darrfonah (IRE)**[22] 5396 3-8-13 99 .... (t) RichardHughes 5 84
(C E Brittain) *hld up: rdn over 3f out: wknd over 2f out* **66/1**

4143 **9** *hd* **Wake Up Maggie (IRE)**[21] 5409 4-9-2 115 .... GeorgeBaker 8 84
(C F Wall) *hld up in tch: wknd over 2f out* **14/1**

1m 37.83s (-1.54) **Going Correction** +0.05s/f (Good)
WFA 3 from 4yo+ 3lb **9** Ran SP% **115.1**
Speed ratings (Par 117): **109,108,107,106,106 104,98,95,95**
CSF £93.66 TOTE £23.20: £4.60, £2.00, £1.20; EX 127.50 Trifecta £688.50 Pool £5,043.04 - 5.20 winning units..
Owner Jaber Abdullah **Bred** Gaines-Gentry Thoroughbreds **Trained** West Ilsley, Berks
■ Stewards' Enquiry : Jimmy Fortune one-day ban; careless riding (Oct 17)

FOCUS
This promised to be a good renewal of this Group 1 but despite what looked a strong early gallop the time was 1.15secs slower than the preceding Group 3 and for the second season in a row there was a somewhat surprising result. Tricky form to assess, but the winner has been rated up 12lb on this year's form.

NOTEBOOK
Majestic Roi(USA), warm beforehand, beat no lesser rival than Indian Ink when winning the Group 3 that was formerly the Fred Darling on her seasonal debut. She had not really had things go her way since, but she appreciated the return to 1m and stayed on well to collar the Cheveley Park pair up the hill, seemingly showing much improved form. She stays in training next season and may only now be coming to herself.
Nannina, a top-class filly on fast ground, has not looked quite as good this season, apart from a good win at Royal Ascot. However, back on the track where she won the Fillies' Mile in 2005 and with the ground to suit, she made a bold bid from the front, only to be worn down on the climb to the line. She will now retire to stud. (op 7-2)
Echelon, who has progressed steadily throughout her career and gained her first Group 1 in the Matron Stakes last time, was well backed to follow up. She made her ground with Nannina but that filly got the better of her and then did her no favours by cutting across when edging towards the rail. She stayed on again up the hill but was held in slightly by the winner and never looked likely to get back up. Like Nannina she retires to stud now after a career that has produced nine successses, eight of them at Listed level and above. (op 15-8 tchd 2-1 in places)
Simply Perfect, a filly whose only disappointing effort was when she failed to stay the Oaks trip, ran her race again. She was led early on by Speciosa but once getting to the head of affairs was soon taken on by the runner-up and could not respond immediately. That said, she did stay on again up the hill and was not beaten far, giving the imprression that 1m2f may not be beyond her next year if she is kept in training. (op 10-3 tchd 4-1)
Harvest Queen(IRE) is a good filly at Listed level but connections presumably decided to to give this Group 1 race a try before the filly retires to stud. She ran with credit and did about as well as could be expected, without ever looking likely to be involved in the finish.
Barshiba(IRE) had disappointed since finishing one place behind Simply Perfect in the Prix d'Astarte at Deauville, but the return to a straight track seemed to help. However, she never got near the principals. Official explanation: jockey said filly hung left
Speciosa(IRE), as she likes to do, set off in front but tended to drift left, another trait she has displayed before. On ground that was probably on the fast side for her, she was headed a good way from home and dropped away tamely. This is likely to have been her swan-song, but while she has not scored since taking the 1000 Guineas last season, she has done her connections proud and been runner-up to both Manduro and Peeping Fawn this year. (op 9-1 tchd 10-1)

6011 TOTESPORT.COM CAMBRIDGESHIRE (HERITAGE H'CAP) 1m 1f
3:55 (4:01) (Class 2) 3-Y-O+

£99,712 (£29,856; £14,928; £7,472; £3,728; £1,872) **Stalls** High

Form RPR

1141 **1** **Pipedreamer**[65] 4092 3-8-12 102 .... JimmyFortune 11 116+
(J H M Gosden) *lw: hld up far side: smooth hdwy wl over 2f out: led 2f out: sn clr and in command: pushed out* **5/1**[1]

1123 **2** *1* **Docofthebay (IRE)**[7] 5797 3-8-8 98 .... RichardHughes 20 110+
(J A Osborne) *s.i.s: wl bhd on far side: hdwy 2f out: hmpd and swtchd rt over 1f out: r.o wl to chse wnr last 100yds* **8/1**[3]

011 **3** *1 ½* **Teslin (IRE)**[14] 5639 3-8-11 101 4ex .... J-PGuillambert 5 109+
(B Ellison) *lw: hld up bhd on stands' side: hdwy over 2f out: swtchd rt over 1f out: r.o to ld that gp last 100yds: no ch w far side* **12/1**

0426 **4** *hd* **Yarqus**[17] 5543 4-8-3 89 .... (t) HayleyTurner 17 97
(C E Brittain) *midfield on far side: hdwy 3f out: rdn and ev ch 2f out: kpt on but no ch w wnr* **33/1**

4111 **5** *hd* **The Illies (IRE)**[21] 5412 3-8-9 99 4ex .... DarryllHolland 23 107
(B W Hills) *swtg: hld up far side: hdwy over 2f out: rdn and hung lft over 1f out: kpt on: nt pce to rch ldrs* **12/1**

1221 **6** *1* **Monte Alto (IRE)**[14] 5631 3-8-9 99 4ex ow3 .... JMurtagh 35 104+
(L M Cumani) *hld up in midfield on far side: hdwy 3f out: rdn and hung rt over 1f out: one pce* **7/1**[2]

1541 **7** *shd* **Fremen (USA)**[14] 5615 7-8-7 93 4ex .... AdrianTNicholls 33 98+
(D Nicholls) *t.k.h: hld up bhd on far side: hdwy wl over 2f out: chsd ldrs jst over 1f out: sn outpcd but kpt on* **14/1**

0204 **8** *½* **Humungous (IRE)**[21] 5412 4-9-2 102 .... FMBerry 2 106
(C R Egerton) *awkward leaving stalls: hld up stands' side: hdwy over 2f out: rdn to ld that gp over 1f out tl ins fnl f: no ch far side* **66/1**

1402 **9** *1* **River Tiber**[6] 5833 4-8-12 98 .... PhilipRobinson 10 100
(L M Cumani) *lw: hld up in midfield on far side: rdn 2f out: kpt on fnl f: nvr trbld ldrs* **20/1**

5104 **10** *¾* **Annemasse**[6] 5833 3-8-8 98 .... GregFairley 16 98
(M Johnston) *lw: chsd ldrs far side: jnd ldr 3f out: rdn 2f out: kpt on same pce* **50/1**

0000 **11** *¾* **My Paris**[14] 5615 6-8-4 93 .... AndrewMullen(3) 19 92
(K A Ryan) *led far side and overall ldr: rdn and hdd 2f out: sn outpcd* **80/1**

45-4 **12** *½* **Raptor (GER)**[189] 848 4-9-2 102 .... FergusSweeney 7 99
(K R Burke) *swtg: hld up stands' side: rdn and effrt over 2f out: sn no imp* **40/1**

0600 **13** *nk* **Capable Guest (IRE)**[6] 5833 5-8-5 91 .... (v) TPO'Shea 22 88
(M R Channon) *racd in mid-div on far side: nvr trbld ldrs* **80/1**

-361 **14** *½* **Seabow (USA)**[23] 5362 4-8-7 93 4ex .... (t) KerrinMcEvoy 18 89
(Saeed Bin Suroor) *hld up far side: n.d* **20/1**

361 **15** *½* **Escape Route (USA)**[21] 5419 3-8-5 95 4ex .... RobertHavlin 34 90
(J H M Gosden) *lw: hld up bhd on far side: nvr a threat* **14/1**

1240 **16** *nk* **Pinpoint (IRE)**[64] 4119 5-9-11 111 .... AdamKirby 4 105
(W R Swinburn) *chsd ldrs stands' side: rdn over 2f out: sn struggling* **33/1**

0010 **17** *1 ½* **Impeller (IRE)**[14] 5631 8-8-11 97 .... JohnEgan 3 88
(J S Moore) *hld up in tch stands' side: hdwy over 2f out: wknd over 1f out* **66/1**

1650 **18** *hd* **Benandonner (USA)**[14] 5631 4-7-12 91 .... MatthewDavies(7) 6 81
(R A Fahey) *led stands' side tl wl over 1f out: sn wknd* **100/1**

1236 **19** *shd* **Ace Of Hearts**[21] 5419 8-8-2 95 .... JackMitchell(7) 29 85
(C F Wall) *prom far side tl wknd 2f out* **66/1**

4513 **20** *3 ½* **Greek Well (IRE)**[14] 5631 4-8-7 93 ow2 .... (v) RyanMoore 21 75
(Sir Michael Stoute) *swtg: hld up in rr far side: nvr on terms* **8/1**[3]

1366 **21** *1 ¾* **Unshakable (IRE)**[28] 5221 8-8-5 91 .... PaulEddery 32 69
(Bob Jones) *b: in tch on far side: effrt to chse ldrs 2f out: sn wknd* **50/1**

1603 **22** *¾* **Very Wise**[16] 5554 5-8-9 95 .... PaulMulrennan 13 72
(W J Haggas) *trckd ldrs on far side: rdn over 2f out: wknd wl over 1f out* **33/1**

4420 **23** *shd* **Snoqualmie Boy**[41] 4874 4-9-4 104 .... TQuinn 26 81
(D R C Elsworth) *lw: prom far side: rdn over 2f out: sn wknd* **33/1**

1030 **24** *1 ¾* **Rio Riva**[21] 5412 5-8-13 102 .... JamieMoriarty(3) 15 75
(Miss J A Camacho) *hld up in mid-div on far side: n.d* **66/1**

0100 **25** *1 ¼* **Star Of Light**[24] 5326 6-8-9 95 .... SteveDrowne 25 65
(B J Meehan) *in tch on far side: rdn and btn 2f out* **50/1**

0404 **26** *1½* **Fort Churchill (IRE)**[9] 5748 6-8-3 **89** (bt) CDHayes 27 56
(B Ellison) *s.i.s: t.k.h and hld up in rr: n.d* **100/1**

2141 **27** *4* **Night Cru**[42] 4814 4-8-10 **96** WJSupple 31 54
(C F Wall) *lw: in tch on far side: rdn to chse ldrs over 2f out: wknd over 1f out* **20/1**

-140 **28** *1½* **Supaseus**[64] 4119 4-8-12 **98** JimmyQuinn 14 53
(H Morrison) *prom far side tl wknd 2f out* **16/1**

-030 **29** *hd* **Night Crescendo (USA)**[67] 4043 4-8-4 **90** DaleGibson 28 44
(Mrs A J Perrett) *chsd ldrs on far side tl wknd over 2f out* **33/1**

00 **30** *1* **Bazart**[127] 2209 5-8-9 **95** LeeEnstone 9 47
(K R Burke) *chsd ldrs stands' side: rdn 4f out: no ch and eased fnl 2f* **100/1**

2040 **31** *1½* **Moody Tunes**[14] 5615 4-8-2 **88** DavidKinsella 1 37
(K R Burke) *chsd ldrs stands' side: rdn 4f out: no ch and eased over 1f out* **100/1**

3200 **32** *4* **Babodana**[44] 4745 7-8-12 **98** EddieAhern 30 38
(M H Tompkins) *prom far side tl wknd qckly 2f out: eased fnl f* **80/1**

2645 **33** *2½* **Ballinteni**[8] 5764 5-8-4 **90** (t) SilvestreDeSousa 8 24
(Miss Gay Kelleway) *swtg: chsd ldrs stands' side: rdn over 4f out: sn wl bhd* **66/1**

50 **P** **Zero Tolerance (IRE)**[67] 4043 7-8-7 **94** MickyFenton 24 —
(T D Barron) *prom far side tl lost pl qckly and p.u over 4f out* **66/1**

1m 49.81s (-2.14) **Going Correction** +0.05s/f (Good)
WFA 3 from 4yo+ 4lb **35** Ran SP% **139.9**
Speed ratings (Par 109): **111,110,108,108,108 107,107,107,106,105 104,104,104,103,103 102,101,101,101,98 96,95,95,94,93**
CSF £36.34 CT £492.07 TOTE £7.10: £2.80, £2.90, £3.30, £6.40; EX 78.00 Trifecta £1015.40 Pool £22,455.05 - 15.70 winning units..
Owner Cheveley Park Stud **Bred** Cheveley Park Stud Ltd **Trained** Newmarket, Suffolk

FOCUS
A strong renewal of this ultra-competitive handicap that was totally dominated by the favourite, with fellow progresive three-year-olds second and third. The right horses finished close up and the form looks rock-solid.

NOTEBOOK
Pipedreamer ◆ has been favourite for this race virtually since winning at Goodwood in August but his participation was only confirmed after his trainer walked the course in the morning. He had looked a Group horse in the making and duly confirmed it with a hugely impressive display, cruising throughout and then sweeping effortlessly to the front to establish a clear lead before scoring cosily with his rider barely having to move. He looks to have a big future and may come back here for a Group 3 at the Houghton meeting, but he will need decent ground next season when Group races will be on the agenda. (op 6-1)
Docofthebay(IRE) ◆ is a terrifically consistent and progressive colt and caught a tartar here, otherwise would a have been a good winner of this race. He missed the break and was held up just a length or so behind the eventual winner, but while his rival swept down the outside he tried to weave through the pack and got crossed by The Illies and had to switch before running on really well up the hill. He was unlucky, but the winner was never off the bit so it is arguable as to whether he would have given that rival a race with a clear passage. However, this hugely consistent colt has now been in the first three in all 12 of his starts and deserves to pick up a big race, with Listed races at least likely to be on the agenda next term. (op 10-1 tchd 11-1 in places)
Teslin(IRE), has done well since bought out of Mark Johnston's yard and gelded, and signalled a big run in this race was likely when scoring at the last meeting here. He was unfortunate to be drawn in the smaller stands'-side group and, although he came through to head that group and finish well, the principals up the centre held the advantage. He is in good form at present and connections may look for another decent handicap before the season is out, providing the ground does not go against him. (op 10-1 tchd 14-1 in a place)
Yargus seems to like these big-field handicaps and ran with plenty of credit to make the frame, admittedly getting weight from the three younger horses ahead of him. It will be no surprise if he is put away now with a view to returning to Nad Al Sheba for the carnival in the New Year.
The Illies(IRE), who has struck up a good partnership with William Buick this season, resulting in a hat-trick of valuable handicaps, was unable to continue that run with his rider suspended. He was 8lb worse off with today's runner-up compared with York and ran pretty close to that form despite hanging and hampering his old rival in the dip. He still looks to be progressing on that evidence but may be most effective at a mile. (op 11-1 tchd 14-1 in a place)
Monte Alto(IRE), who won a valuable Newbury handicap that in the past has been a good trial for this race, had a 4lb penalty to carry plus 3lb of overweight and in the circumstances did well to finish on the heels of the placed horses over a trip that looks the bare minimum for him. (op 13-2)
Fremen(USA), who has really been in good form of late, ran another fine race and helps back up the York form with the runner-up and fifth. (op 16-1 tchd 18-1 in a place)
Humungous(IRE), another to race on the stands' side, ran his race and ran close to Doncaster form with The Illies on 4lb better terms.
River Tiber has been running well since joining Luca Cumani this season and this was another good effort that ties in with Annemasse from their recent meeting at Ascot.
Greek Well(IRE) was the only well-backed horse to not finish near the front of the field as he should have finished close to Monte Alto on Newbury form, but perhaps this shorter trip found him out after a series of decent efforts. (op 11-1 tchd 16-1 in a place and 12-1 in a place)
Supaseus Official explanation: jockey said gelding stopped very quickly
Zero Tolerance(IRE) Official explanation: jockey said gelding felt wrong

6012 EUROPEAN BREEDERS' FUND JERSEY LILY FILLIES' NURSERY 7f
4:30 (4:33) (Class 2) 2-Y-O

£18,696 (£5,598; £2,799; £1,401; £699; £351) **Stalls** High

Form RPR

2330 **1** **Talk Of Saafend (IRE)**[23] 5350 2-8-3 **75** DavidKinsella 10 79
(R Hannon) *chsd ldrs: rdn to ld nr fin: hung lft on line* **15/2**

3402 **2** *hd* **Dalkey Girl (IRE)**[15] 5597 2-8-5 **84** AshleyMorgan(7) 12 88
(V Smith) *hld up in tch: outpcd 2f out: r.o wl ins fnl f: hmpd on line* **20/1**

3201 **3** *1* **Feisty Royale**[12] 5692 2-8-5 **77** GregFairley 3 78
(M Johnston) *led: hdd 4f out: rdn and ev ch ins fnl f: styng on same pce whn nt clr run nr fin* **16/1**

5240 **4** *shd* **Geestring (IRE)**[24] 5322 2-8-1 **73** JimmyQuinn 7 74
(R Hannon) *trckd ldrs: rdn to ld ins fnl f: sn hdd: hld whn hmpd nr fin* **10/1**

001 **5** *1* **Blue Rhapsody**[25] 5308 2-8-3 **75** (t) HayleyTurner 1 73
(L M Cumani) *hld up: rdn and hung lft fr over 1f out: r.o: nrr fin* **14/1**

050 **6** *1¼* **Infinite Patience**[65] 4094 2-7-12 **70** oh2 AdrianMcCarthy 8 65
(J S Moore) *hld up: hdwy over 1f out: rdn and edgd lft ins fnl f: styd on same pce* **22/1**

414 **7** *¾* **Rosaleen (IRE)**[42] 4804 2-9-7 **93** SteveDrowne 6 86
(B J Meehan) *hld up: rdn whn bmpd over 1f out: nt trble ldrs* **13/2**[3]

024 **8** *1* **Binfield (IRE)**[80] 3643 2-7-13 **71** ow1 DaleGibson 13 61
(B G Powell) *chsd ldrs: rdn over 2f out: wknd ins fnl f* **50/1**

214 **9** *hd* **Winter Bloom (USA)**[22] 5374 2-8-8 **80** RichardHughes 9 70
(H R A Cecil) *lw: chsd ldr: led 4f out: rdn and edgd lft fr over 1f out: hdd & wknd ins fnl f* **5/2**[1]

0504 **10** *½* **Jennifers Joy (IRE)**[14] 5624 2-8-3 **75** TPO'Shea 4 64
(M R Channon) *s.s: hld up: hdwy over 1f out: wknd ins fnl f* **20/1**

021 **11** *nk* **Presbyterian Nun (IRE)**[34] 5061 2-9-1 **87** RyanMoore 2 75
(J L Dunlop) *hld up: hdwy 1/2-way: rdn 2f out: wknd over 1f out* **11/4**[2]

016 **12** *nk* **Marchpane**[15] 5592 2-8-7 **79** KerrinMcEvoy 14 66
(R M Beckett) *in rr whn pushed along over 5f out: reminders 4f out: a in rr* **28/1**

1m 26.62s (0.12) **Going Correction** +0.05s/f (Good) **12** Ran SP% **121.3**
Speed ratings (Par 98): **101,100,99,99,98 96,96,94,94,94 93,93**
CSF £154.47 CT £2376.21 TOTE £8.10: £2.90, £6.50, £3.70; EX 140.40.
Owner J B R Leisure Ltd **Bred** Michael Dalton **Trained** East Everleigh, Wilts
■ Stewards' Enquiry : David Kinsella three-day ban: careless riding (Oct 17-19)

FOCUS
A decent fillies' nursery, run 0.89sec faster than the opening Group 3 and producing a close finish.

NOTEBOOK
Talk Of Saafend(IRE) finally got her deserved reward following a series of consistent efforts in similar events. She got a good lead and a clear run near the rail and really picked up on the climb to the line to score, although she dived left near the finish and banged into the runner-up crossing the line, a manoeuvre that cost her rider a three-day ban. (op 9-1 tchd 10-1 in a place)
Dalkey Girl(IRE) ◆ was closely matched with the winner from a valuable nursery on the July course and they ran virtually to the pound. She goes well for her young rider and picked up really well on the climb to the line, although the winner was fractionally quicker. She received a hefty bump from her old rival virtually on the line but it made no difference to the result. She deserves her day in the limelight before the season is out, and her ability to handle easy ground may enable her to get it.
Feisty Royale, who got off the mark in a similar but lower-grade contest last time, ran with plenty of credit off a 5lb higher mark and was only run out of it by two tough, consistent fillies. She looks on the upgrade. (op 20-1)
Geestring(IRE) ran arguably her best race since returning from a midsummer break, travelling well and only getting run out of things in the final half-furlong. She might prefer a little more cut in the ground and could get it in the coming weeks. (op 12-1)
Blue Rhapsody, who put up an improved effort to win her maiden on Polytrack, had a tough task against more experienced rivals and did not help her rider by tending to hang. She ran on at the finish and the experience should benefit her in future. (op 10-1)
Infinite Patience, making her handicap debut after three unplaced efforts, was pitched in at the deep end here from 2lb out of the handicap and deserves credit for getting so close. (op 33-1 tchd 20-1)
Rosaleen(IRE), who brought Group-race form into this, having finished fourth to Sense Of Joy at Goodwood, did not appear to be making much headway when her chance was ended by a receiving a bump in the dip. (op 6-1 tchd 11-2)
Binfield(IRE), making her handicap debut following a break, faded out of contention in the closing stages and may be better at shorter on easier ground. (op 40-1)
Winter Bloom(USA), who finished behind the subsequent sales-race winner Dubai Dynamo at Doncaster last time, tried to dictate the pace but was taken on and probably did too much too early as she dropped away under pressure up the hill. (op 11-4 tchd 3-1 in places)
Presbyterian Nun(IRE), who was another to have form with Sense Of Joy, appeared to see too much daylight on the outside of her field and failed to respond when the pressure was applied. Official explanation: jockey said filly ran flat (tchd 3-1)
Dixey

6013 TOTESPORT 0800 221 221 H'CAP 7f
5:05 (5:11) (Class 2) (0-100,99) 3-Y-O+

£12,464 (£3,732; £1,866; £934; £466; £234) **Stalls** High

Form RPR

3443 **1** **Celtic Sultan (IRE)**[7] 5804 3-9-0 **95** MickyFenton 24 105
(T P Tate) *mde all: sn clr: rdn over 1f out: edgd lft fnl f: hld on wl* **10/1**

2000 **2** *1* **Sir Xaar (IRE)**[7] 5804 4-8-11 **90** (bt[1]) PaulMulrenan 17 97
(B Smart) *lw: chsd wnr for 2f and again 3f out: clsd u.p over 1f out: kpt on same pce last 100yds* **16/1**

3000 **3** *¾* **Daniella**[7] 5799 5-8-6 **85** oh6 (b) PhilipRobinson 9 90
(Rae Guest) *lw: stdd s: hld up bhd: hdwy 2f out: styd on u.p fnl f: wnt 3rd towards fin: nt rch wnr* **33/1**

1624 **4** *½* **Vitznau (IRE)**[41] 4851 3-8-13 **94** RichardHughes 18 98+
(R Hannon) *lw: hld up in midfield: hdwy over 2f out: chsd ldrs over 1f out: kpt on u.p: nt rch wnr* **6/1**[3]

1303 **5** *shd* **Purus (IRE)**[11] 5712 5-8-6 **85** oh2 AdrianTNicholls 10 88
(R A Teal) *in tch in main gp: rdn and hdwy over 2f out: kpt on same pce fnl f* **25/1**

0100 **6** *hd* **Damika (IRE)**[15] 5584 4-8-11 **90** FMBerry 4 93+
(R M Whitaker) *stdd s: hld up wl bhd: hdwy 2f out: swtchd rt over 1f out: nt clr run 1f out tl wl ins fnl f: r.o wl: nt rch ldrs* **28/1**

0321 **7** *shd* **Salient**[23] 5360 3-8-6 **87** PaulDoe 14 90
(J Akehurst) *sn prom in main gp: rdn and outpcd 2f out: plugged on u.p ins fnl f* **12/1**

1- **8** *½* **Kafuu (IRE)**[365] 5790 3-8-4 **85** oh3 EddieAhern 1 86+
(J Noseda) *lw: h.d.w: hld up wl bhd: stl gng wl over 2f out: hdwy 2f out: kpt on ins fnl f: nvr pce to rch ldrs* **9/2**[1]

0603 **9** *1¼* **Jedburgh**[21] 5413 6-9-0 **93** (b) JimmyFortune 3 91
(J L Dunlop) *lw: sn bhd and niggled along: hdwy 3f out: kpt on u.p ins fnl f: n.d* **15/2**

040- **10** *hd* **Johannes (IRE)**[378] 5535 4-8-8 **87** TPO'Shea 19 84
(E J O'Neill) *b.hind: awkwd s: sn prom in main gp: chsd wnr 5f out tl 3f out: wknd 2f out* **28/1**

1100 **11** *½* **Guilded Warrior**[21] 5413 4-8-9 **88** FergusSweeney 8 84
(W S Kittow) *prom in main gp: rdn over 2f out: wknd over 1f out* **25/1**

4430 **12** *¾* **Farleigh House (USA)**[107] 2788 3-8-7 **88** JimmyQuinn 23 82
(M H Tompkins) *stmbld s and v.s.a: nvr trbld ldrs* **12/1**

5121 **13** *2½* **South Cape**[7] 5804 4-8-7 **93** MatthewDavies(7) 2 80
(M R Channon) *held up in tch: rdn over 2f out: sn outpcd* **15/2**

0101 **14** *¾* **Capricorn Run (USA)**[14] 5638 4-8-10 **89** (p) AdamKirby 6 74
(A J McCabe) *racd in midfield of main gp: rdn 3f out: n.d* **10/1**

0000 **15** *nk* **Bahiano (IRE)**[56] 4401 6-8-6 **85** oh3 HayleyTurner 16 69
(C E Brittain) *in tch in main gp: rdn over 3f out: wknd 2f out* **22/1**

43-0 **16** *13* **Kompete**[171] 1096 3-8-9 **90** ow1 DarryllHolland 22 39
(V Smith) *hld up in tch in main gp: lost pl 3f out: no ch after: eased fnl f* **20/1**

10-3 **17** *shd* **Paper Talk (USA)**[240] 394 5-9-6 **99** KerrinMcEvoy 15 48
(Saeed Bin Suroor) *chsd ldrs in main gp: rdn 3f out: wknd 2f out: no ch and eased fnl f* **5/1**[2]

1m 24.67s (-1.83) **Going Correction** +0.05s/f (Good)
WFA 3 from 4yo+ 2lb **17** Ran SP% **138.8**
Speed ratings (Par 109): **112,110,110,109,109 109,108,108,106,106 106,105,102,101,101 86,86**
CSF £166.80 CT £5283.35 TOTE £16.70: £2.80, £4.10, £6.00, £2.10; EX 201.90.
Owner Mrs Sylvia Clegg and Louise Worthington **Bred** Miss C Lyons **Trained** Tadcaster, N Yorks

FOCUS
A competitive handicap on paper and the figures look solid, even though the first two held those positions throughout.

NOTEBOOK

Celtic Sultan(IRE) has been running consistently well all season without getting his head in front, but put up a particularly game effort to record his first success since his maiden win. He went off like a scalded cat and established a clear lead, but when the pack closed in on the run into the dip he looked sure to be swallowed up, only for him to find extra reserves on meeting the rising ground. He was placed in Listed company as a juvenile, and may in time develop into a successor to his owner's redoubtable performer Welsh Emperor. (op 16-1)

Sir Xaar(IRE), fitted with blinkers for the first time along with the tongue tie, ran his best race for a while and finished closer to the winner than he had at Chester last time. He chased his old rival throughout and stuck to his guns really well without ever looking likely to reel him in. If the headgear works as well next time he may be able to recerd his first win since his juvenile days. (op 25-1 tchd 28-1 in a place)

Daniella, who has been struggling in Listed company of late, had a stiff task from 6lb out of the handicap and ran her best race ever, doing good work late on.

Vitznau(IRE) ◆ has done all his winning when there has been cut in the ground, but did not have the likes of Docofthebay and King Of Argos to contend with this time and ran on really well in the closing stages. He looks one to watch out for between now and the end of the year. (op 5-1)

Purus(IRE), whose wins have all been on turning tracks, was another racing from out of the handicap and put up a decent effort on his second run back from a break. He will no doubt be returning to Polytrack before long.

Damika(IRE) ◆ has won at this trip but seems most effective at 6f. He came from well back and did not get the clearest of passages, so can be given credit for finishing as close as he did. He has been a little in-and-out this season but is useful when on song. (op 33-1)

Salient has run some fine races this season and did not do badly off a 7lb higher mark for his recent win. (op 14-1 tchd 11-1)

Kafuu(IRE) ◆, an expensive colt who won well on his sole start exactly a year ago, was made favourite despite eacing from out of the handicap against more battle-hardened rivals. Held up well out the back, he ran on late and will know a lot more next time. (op 11-2)

Paper Talk(USA), having his first run for Godolphin and first since Dubai in February, dropped out of contention some way from home. (op 6-1 tchd 9-2)

6014 SUFFOLK INSULATION AND RENOVATION SERVICES H'CAP — 1m 4f

5:40 (5:44) (Class 3) (0-95,95) 3-Y-0+

£9,348 (£2,799; £1,399; £700; £349; £175) **Stalls** Centre

Form				RPR
1140	**1**		**Malt Or Mash (USA)**[44] 4749 3-9-2 **91** ... RyanMoore 5 (R Hannon) *lw: hld up in rr: hdwy over 3f out: rdn to ld 2f out: hld on wl last 100yds* **9/4**[1]	105+
4412	**2**	½	**Sanbuch**[31] 5141 3-9-6 **95** ... JimmyFortune 1 (L M Cumani) *lw: stdd s and dropped in bhd: plld out and hdwy over 3f out: chsd wnr 1f out: unable qckn last 100yds* **4/1**[2]	108+
0040	**3**	1 ¾	**Bandama (IRE)**[14] 5631 4-9-7 **89** ... JMurtagh 14 (Mrs A J Perrett) *lw: chsd ldng pair: rdn 2f out: chsd ldng pair ins fnl f: kpt on same pce* **8/1**[3]	99+
21/4	**4**	3 ½	**Cutting Crew (USA)**[50] 4572 6-9-8 **90** ... AdamKirby 2 (W R Swinburn) *chsd ldr: rdn 3f out: lost 2nd 2f out: wknd fnl f* **9/1**	95
0265	**5**	hd	**Zaif (IRE)**[15] 5593 4-8-12 **80** ... TQuinn 11 (D R C Elsworth) *lw: hld up towards rr: swtchd lft over 2f out: plugged on u.p fnl f: nvr trbld ldrs* **25/1**	84
0113	**6**	1 ½	**Esthlos (FR)**[167] 1180 4-8-12 **80** ... HayleyTurner 9 (J Jay) *hld up towards rr: hdwy 4f out: chsd ldrs and rdn over 2f out: sn wknd* **33/1**	82
1414	**7**	2 ½	**Soul Mountain (IRE)**[20] 5445 3-8-6 **81** ... PhilipRobinson 12 (B W Hills) *hld up in midfield: hdwy 4f out: rdn and btn over 2f out* **14/1**	79
5440	**8**	nk	**Hernando Royal**[46] 4690 4-9-6 **88** ... SteveDrowne 3 (H Morrison) *chsd ldrs: rdn 3f out: wknd wl over 1f out* **9/1**	86
1035	**9**	1	**Invasian (IRE)**[14] 5631 6-9-4 **86** ... (e) RobertHavlin 10 (P W D'Arcy) *led: rdn and hdd 2f out: sn wknd* **16/1**	82
0012	**10**	13	**Realism (FR)**[14] 5623 7-9-9 **91** ... PaulMulrennan 4 (M W Easterby) *b: hld up towards rr: hdwy 6f out: rdn and wkng whn short of room over 2f out* **20/1**	66
1	**11**	½	**Bold Glance**[16] 5562 3-8-9 **84** ... KerrinMcEvoy 15 (Saeed Bin Suroor) *hld up in midfield: rdn 3f out: sn btn: no ch last 2f* **9/1**	58
2040	**12**	4	**Mikao (IRE)**[6] 5830 6-9-11 **93** ... GeorgeBaker 6 (M H Tompkins) *lw: w.w in midfield: rdn 3f out: sn wknd: t.o* **18/1**	61
0464	**13**	18	**Quince (IRE)**[98] 3112 4-9-1 **83** ... RichardHughes 7 (J Pearce) *stdd s and dropped in bhd: rdn and brief effrt over 2f out: sn btn and eased* **25/1**	22
-066	**14**	2	**Cresta Gold**[21] 5402 4-8-13 **88** ... JackMitchell(7) 13 (A Bailey) *in tch tl rdn and lost pl 4f out: sn wl bhd: t.o* **40/1**	24
00/0	**15**	nk	**Inchpast**[16] 5574 6-8-11 **79** oh4 ... (b) EddieAhern 8 (M H Tompkins) *racd in midfield: reminder over 6f out: bhd and rdn 4f out: no ch last 2f: t.o* **66/1**	15

2m 29.66s (-3.84) **Going Correction** +0.05s/f (Good)

WFA 3 from 4yo+ 7lb — **15** Ran SP% **129.0**

Speed ratings (Par 107): **114,113,112,110,110 109,107,107,106,97 97,94,82,81,81**

CSF £10.34 CT £67.53 TOTE £3.40: £1.70, £2.20, £3.40; EX 14.40 Place 6 £718.68, Place 5 £167.99.

Owner A P Patey **Bred** Delahanty Stock Farm **Trained** East Everleigh, Wilts

■ Stewards' Enquiry : Hayley Turner three-day ban: careless riding (Oct 17-19)

FOCUS

Another competitive handicap run at a strong gallop, and the first two were at the back of the field half a mile from home. The two principals are progressive, and the third can be rated a bit better than the bare result. Solid form.

NOTEBOOK

Malt Or Mash(USA) was better behaved beforehand this time, and better suited by this drop back in trip too, for having swept down the outside to lead going into the dip he was always finding enough to resist the runner-up on the climb to the line. He gives the impression he has the scope to make up into a really decent performer over this trip next season. (op 7-2 tchd 4-1 in places)

Sanbuch, held up alongside the winner at the rear, came through in his walk to deliver a challenge on meeting the rising ground, but was always being held. He seems progressive but the blinkers may need to be re-applied if he is to add to his Goodwood success. (tchd 9-2)

Bandama(IRE), without the headgear he wore last time, was never far away and stayed on after the principals up the hill, doing well to pull clear of the rest. Although still 4lb higher than when he last scored in June 2006 he has slipped back to a fair mark, and this was better. (op 7-1)

Cutting Crew(USA), a promising three-year-old in 2004, was having only his second outing since July of that year. As on his return in August, since when he has been given plenty of time to recover, he showed the ability is still there, keeping going having been prominent throughout. He might now be given a little leeway by the Handicapper, and if that is the case can pick up a similar race. (op 10-1)

Zaif(IRE), having a rare try over this trip as he usually races over 1m2f, was noted doing his best work late on but he never really threatened.

Esthlos(FR), better known as an All-Weather performer but with a decent record on his rare outings on turf, may have found the surface faster than he likes on his first try at this trip. He may have found the extra quarter mile too far, but this was his first run since April so he was entitled to need it. He should pay his way again this winter.

Bold Glance, winner of a Pontefract maiden on his belated debut, was settled off the pace but never got into contention. McEvoy looked down at one stage as though not happy with him, so he may have some sort of physical problem. (op 11-2)

Cresta Gold Official explanation: jockey said filly had a breathing problem

Inchpast Official explanation: jockey said gelding had no more to give

T/Jkpt: Not won. T/Plt: £2,280.70 to a £1 stake. Pool: £173,715.41. 55.60 winning tickets. T/Qpdt: £226.70 to a £1 stake. Pool: £8,594.20. 28.05 winning tickets. CR

5734 REDCAR (L-H)

Saturday, October 6

OFFICIAL GOING: Good (9.3)

After 12mm rain over the previous eight days the ground was reckoned to be riding 'on the dead side of good'.

Wind: Almost nil Weather: Fine and sunny

6015 EUROPEAN BREEDERS' FUND MAIDEN FILLIES' STKS — 7f

2:25 (2:26) (Class 4) 2-Y-0

£5,375 (£1,599; £799; £399) **Stalls** Centre

Form				RPR
0025	**1**		**Coachhouse Lady (USA)**[42] 4796 2-9-0 73 ... NCallan 7 (K A Ryan) *mde all: qcknd 3f out: rdn and edgd rt 1f out: hld on wl* **15/2**	76
4	**2**	¾	**Tathkaar**[14] 5633 2-9-0 0 ... RichardMullen 5 (C E Brittain) *chsd ldrs: rdn over 2f out: styd on to go 2nd ins fnl f: no ex* **5/1**[2]	74
0	**3**	2	**Gingham**[43] 4774 2-9-0 0 ... TPQueally 3 (L M Cumani) *hld up in midfield: outpcd 3f out: hdwy and edgd rt over 1f out: kpt on wl ins fnl f* **14/1**	69
3	**4**	shd	**Aromatherapy**[15] 5598 2-9-0 0 ... TedDurcan 9 (H R A Cecil) *sn trcking ldrs: effrt over 2f out: wnt 2nd over 1f out: kpt on same pce* **4/6**[1]	69
6	**5**	hd	**Debonnaire**[9] 5745 2-9-0 0 ... RoystonFfrench 2 (M Johnston) *w wnr: drvn 3f out: hung lft over 1f out: kpt on same pce* **6/1**[3]	68
	6	7	**Lady In Chief** 2-9-0 0 ... TonyHamilton 1 (Miss J A Camacho) *dwlt: sn in rr and pushed along: nvr a factor* **66/1**	51
053	**7**	1 ¾	**Strictly Elsie (IRE)**[43] 4781 2-9-0 63 ... PaddyAspell 10 (J R Norton) *chsd ldrs: rdn and lost pl 3f out* **66/1**	47
	8	7	**Reel Cool** 2-9-0 0 ... TomEaves 11 (B Smart) *dwlt: sn outpcd and pushed along: bhd fnl 2f* **66/1**	29
	9	2	**Super Starlet (IRE)** 2-9-0 0 ... DO'Donohoe 4 (M Botti) *s.i.s: sn drvn along and outpcd: bhd fnl 3f* **50/1**	24

1m 25.06s (0.16) **Going Correction** +0.175s/f (Good) — **9** Ran SP% **115.8**

Speed ratings (Par 94): **106,105,102,102,102 94,92,84,82**

CSF £44.25 TOTE £7.20: £2.20, £1.80, £3.70; EX 46.60.

Owner Iona Equine **Bred** B P Walden Et Al **Trained** Hambleton, N Yorks

FOCUS

A fair maiden lacking any strength in depth but the form should prove solid.

NOTEBOOK

Coachhouse Lady(USA), a fluent mover, had a big reputation prior to her debut but she finally broke her duck here at the fifth attempt. Rated just 73 she almost certainly ran above that mark here. (tchd 7-1)

Tathkaar, a tall, narrow filly, is out of a stayer who herself is a daughter of the Ascot Gold Cup winner Indian Queen. One of the first to come under pressure, she stuck on to push the winner hard in the end. A May foal, she should come into her own over middle distances at three. (tchd 11-2)

Gingham, a big, strong filly, has a pronounced round action. She stuck on strongly in the closing stages despite edging right-handed and she is just the type her trainer does so well with in handicap company at three. (op 12-1 tchd 10-1)

Aromatherapy, who continually swished her tail beforehand, did not improve on her debut effort two weeks earlier. She will be seen to much better advantage on fast ground next year. (op 4-5 tchd 5-6, 10-11 in places)

Debonnaire matched strides with the winner but was always tending to hang left-handed. Still very inexperienced, there ought to be better to come. (op 7-1)

6016 JOHN SMITH'S REDCAR STRAIGHT-MILE CHAMPIONSHIP FINAL (H'CAP) — 1m

3:00 (3:00) (Class 2) 3-Y-0+

£18,696 (£5,598; £2,799; £1,401; £699; £351) **Stalls** Centre

Form				RPR
422	**1**		**Fragrancy (IRE)**[17] 5537 3-9-4 **86** ... NCallan 2 (M A Jarvis) *trckd ldrs: smooth hdwy to ld 2f out: rdn over 1f out: styd on strly ins fnl f* **10/1**	96
6212	**2**	1 ¼	**Observatory Star (IRE)**[8] 5776 4-8-12 **77** ... (p) DavidAllan 16 (T D Easterby) *hld up: gd hdwy over 2f out: trckd ldrs and n.m.r over 1f out: effrt and nt clr run jst ins fnl f: sn rdn and fin wl* **11/2**[2]	84
1200	**3**	shd	**Karoo Blue (IRE)**[28] 5221 3-9-5 **87** ... TedDurcan 18 (C E Brittain) *in tch on outer: hdwy over 2f out: rdn wl over 1f out: kpt on u.p ins fnl f* **14/1**	94
2135	**4**	nk	**Soccerjackpot (USA)**[85] 3503 3-9-0 **82** ... DeanMcKeown 4 (G A Swinbank) *midfield: gd hdwy 3f out: rdn wl over 1f out: drvn and kpt on ins fnl f* **5/1**[1]	88
0341	**5**	shd	**Boundless Prospect (USA)**[10] 5737 8-8-8 **78** ... NicolPolli(5) 5 (Miss Gay Kelleway) *hld up: swtchd lft and hdwy 2f out: sn rdn and styd on wl fnl f: nrst fin* **16/1**	84
4550	**6**	shd	**Nanton (USA)**[16] 5554 5-9-4 **83** ... DanielTudhope 8 (N Wilson) *in rr and rdn along 1/2-way: hdwy over 2f out: styd on wl u.p ins fnl f: nrst fin* **6/1**[3]	89
013	**7**	nk	**Monkey Glas (IRE)**[58] 4331 3-8-8 **76** ... RoystonFfrench 15 (K R Burke) *prom: effrt 2f out and ev ch tl rdn and wknd ins fnl f* **25/1**	81
1200	**8**	½	**Il Castagno (IRE)**[63] 4176 4-9-1 **80** ... TomEaves 14 (B Smart) *led: rdn along and hdd 2f out: drvn over 1f out: wknd ins fnl f* **14/1**	84
4126	**9**	¾	**Motafarred (IRE)**[25] 5296 5-8-5 **70** ... PaulHanagan 10 (Micky Hammond) *chsd ldr: rdn along over 2f out and grad wknd* **16/1**	72
6630	**10**	¾	**Pianoforte (USA)**[3] 5905 5-7-12 **63** oh1 ... PaulQuinn 1 (E J Alston) *hld up towards rr: hdwy 2f out: sn rdn and kpt on same pce ins fnl f* **25/1**	63
0002	**11**	1 ¾	**Bustan (IRE)**[10] 5737 8-9-6 **85** ... SebSanders 19 (G C Bravery) *midfield: effrt over 2f out: sn rdn and no hdwy* **9/1**	81
0-00	**12**	1 ¼	**Typhoon Ginger (IRE)**[10] 5737 12-7-7 **63** oh8 ... NataliaGemelova(5) 7 (G Woodward) *in rr: rdn along over 2f out: sme late hdwy* **33/1**	56
0506	**13**	½	**Exit Smiling**[16] 5559 5-8-7 **72** ... FrankieMcDonald 13 (P T Midgley) *chsd ldrs: rdn along wl over 2f out and sn wknd* **25/1**	64

0200 **14** ½ **Hartshead**[39] 4922 8-9-7 **89** .... PJMcDonald(3) 3 80
(G A Swinbank) *nvr bttr than midfield* **25/1**

611 **15** *nk* **Middlemarch (IRE)**[50] 4581 7-8-11 **81** .... (v) GaryBartley(5) 20 71
(J S Goldie) *midfield: rdn along over 2f out and sn btn* **10/1**

4335 **16** 1½ **Efidium**[10] 5737 9-7-10 **68** .... DanielleMcCreery(7) 6 55
(N Bycroft) *rrd s: a towards rr* **20/1**

5300 **17** *nk* **Darfour**[42] 4811 3-8-4 **72** .... JamieMackay 12 58
(J S Goldie) *dwlt: a in rr* **50/1**

6005 **18** *nk* **Will He Wish**[12] 5685 11-8-11 **76** .... IanMongan 9 62
(S Gollings) *in tch: rdn along wl over 2f out and sn wknd* **33/1**

4120 **19** 6 **Borodinsky**[42] 4820 6-7-9 **63** oh1 .... DuranFentiman(3) 17 35
(R E Barr) *midfield: rdn along 3f out and sn wknd* **66/1**

1m 37.48s (-0.32) **Going Correction** +0.175s/f (Good)
WFA 3 from 4yo+ 3lb **19** Ran SP% **129.1**
Speed ratings (Par 109): **108,106,106,106,106 106,105,105,104,103 102,100,100,99,99 98,97,97,91**
CSF £59.32 CT £821.68 TOTE £12.00: £3.00, £1.80, £3.80, £1.60; EX 44.40 Trifecta £222.40 Part won. Pool £313.30 - 0.20 winning units..
Owner Mohammed Al Nabouda **Bred** Darley **Trained** Newmarket, Suffolk

FOCUS
A competitive Final and the form looks rock solid at this level.

NOTEBOOK
Fragrancy(IRE) has edged up the weights since winning off a 10lb lower mark at Windsor in June. Happy to accept a lead, she travelled strongly and took this with the minimum of fuss. (op 11-1)
Observatory Star(IRE) is in very good form at present and with better luck would have given the winner a fraction more to do. (op 6-1)
Karoo Blue(IRE), a winner from a 7lb lower mark here in August, was attempting to make it three wins from three starts at this track. He made his effort bang on the inside and to his credit was coming back for more at the line. (op 16-1)
Soccerjackpot(USA), easily the least experienced in the line-up, stuck on in willing fashion inside the last and he looks the type to prosper at four. (op 11-2)
Boundless Prospect(USA), banged up 10lb after his victory in a claimer here ten days earlier, finished best of all and is clearly right at the top of his game at present.
Nanton(USA), who took this a year ago from a 1lb lower mark, put a poor effort on soft ground last time behind him, finishing strongly from an unpromising position. (op 7-1 tchd 11-2)
Monkey Glas(IRE), absent for two months, is a free-going sort and 7f might suit him better. (op 33-1)
Il Castagno(IRE), 5lb higher than when striking here in June, was back in action at his favourite track after two months on the sidelines.

6017 TOTESCOOP6 TWO-YEAR-OLD TROPHY (LISTED RACE) 6f
3:35 (3:39) (Class 1) 2-Y-O
£125,285 (£47,483; £23,764; £11,848; £5,935; £2,978) **Stalls** Centre

Form RPR

0351 **1** **Dubai Dynamo**[22] 5374 2-9-2 75 .... DeanMcKeown 14 95
(J S Moore) *mde all: hrd rdn fnl f: hld on towards fin* **40/1**

04P6 **2** ½ **Vhujon (IRE)**[14] 5629 2-9-0 86 .... TGMcLaughlin 7 91
(P D Evans) *fly-jmpd s: in rr: hdwy and n.m.r over 2f out: swtchd rt over 1f out: fin wl* **66/1**

3100 **3** ¾ **Pelican Prince**[28] 5216 2-8-9 85 .... PhillipMakin 16 84
(K R Burke) *w ldrs: styd on same pce ins fnl f* **50/1**

1105 **4** *hd* **Easy Target (FR)**[14] 5630 2-9-2 99 .... TomEaves 3 90
(B Smart) *hld up in rr: hdwy on outer over 2f out: hung rt and styd on wl fnl f* **20/1**

0350 **5** *hd* **Mister Hardy**[24] 5324 2-9-2 91 .... TonyHamilton 10 90
(R A Fahey) *chsd ldrs: kpt on same pce fnl f* **25/1**

3311 **6** 1 **Craggy Cat (IRE)**[24] 5331 2-9-0 78 .... SebSanders 12 85
(L M Cumani) *prom: sn pushed along: hrd rdn over 1f out: kpt on same pce* **7/2**[1]

3111 **7** *nk* **Mr Keppel (IRE)**[14] 5629 2-9-2 80 .... TPQueally 2 86+
(J A Osborne) *sn trcking ldrs on outer: kpt on same pce whn n.m.r ins fnl f* **15/2**

1041 **8** ¾ **Spitfire**[21] 5410 2-8-6 87 .... RoystonFfrench 4 74
(J R Jenkins) *prom on outer: rdn over 2f out: kpt on: nvr a threat* **6/1**[3]

2606 **9** ½ **New Jersey (IRE)**[15] 5583 2-9-0 97 .... NCallan 13 80
(K A Ryan) *chsd ldrs: one pce fnl 2f* **40/1**

2442 **10** ½ **Broken Applause (IRE)**[14] 5614 2-8-9 85 .... (b[1]) PaulHanagan 5 74
(R A Fahey) *chsd ldrs on outer: rdn 2f out: one pce* **11/2**[2]

2300 **11** *nk* **Kersaint (IRE)**[22] 5374 2-8-6 85 .... (b[1]) DO'Donohoe 11 70
(K A Ryan) *s.i.s: sme hdwy over 2f out: nvr on terms* **40/1**

41 **12** *shd* **C'Mon You Irons (IRE)**[12] 5675 2-8-9 0 .... RichardMullen 6 72
(B Smart) *mid-div on outer: drvn 3f out: nvr a threat* **40/1**

1335 **13** 1¼ **Cristal Clear (IRE)**[14] 5614 2-8-9 86 .... DavidAllan 23 69
(T D Easterby) *in rr stands' side: nvr on terms* **14/1**

612 **14** 1¾ **Vive Les Rouges**[30] 5164 2-8-9 97 .... IanMongan 20 63
(C F Wall) *trckd ldrs on inner: fdd over 1f out* **6/1**[3]

0505 **15** 1¾ **Lindoro**[24] 5324 2-9-2 83 .... (t) TedDurcan 19 65
(W R Swinburn) *hld up in mid-div: drvn over 2f out: nvr a threat* **20/1**

6300 **16** 1¾ **Fathsta (IRE)**[6] 5828 2-8-9 74 .... JDSmith 21 53
(S Kirk) *racd stands' side: hld up in mid-div: rdn over 2f out: n.d* **100/1**

1250 **17** *nk* **Art Advisor (IRE)**[45] 4721 2-9-0 101 .... (b[1]) DanielTudhope 17 57+
(J Howard Johnson) *trckd ldrs on inner: wkng whn hmpd over 1f out* **18/1**

4035 **18** 1½ **Kinout (IRE)**[15] 5582 2-9-2 76 .... StephenDonohoe 1 55
(K A Ryan) *trckd ldrs on outer: wknd over 1f out* **150/1**

5024 **19** ½ **Russian Reel**[19] 5480 2-8-6 85 .... PatCosgrave 18 43+
(K A Ryan) *trckd ldrs on ins: t.k.h: wkng whn hmpd over 1f out* **18/1**

610 **20** 1½ **Captain Macarry (IRE)**[21] 5410 2-8-12 77 .... PJMcDonald 9 45
(B Smart) *chsd ldrs on outer: lost pl 2f out* **150/1**

2231 **21** 2 **Non Sucre (USA)**[51] 4527 2-8-3 74 .... (b) FrankieMcDonald 15 30
(P A Blockley) *s.i.s: bhd fnl 3f* **80/1**

6633 **22** 7 **Ben**[7] 5815 2-8-12 74 .... (v) JamieMackay 8 18
(P G Murphy) *s.s: in rr: bhd fnl 2f* **150/1**

2104 **23** 1¼ **Sinead Of Aglish (IRE)**[11] 5713 2-8-7 79 .... DuranFentiman 22 9
(A B Haynes) *sn bhd on inner* **200/1**

1m 11.99s (0.29) **Going Correction** +0.175s/f (Good) **23** Ran SP% **126.4**
Speed ratings (Par 103): **105,104,103,103,102 101,101,100,99,98 98,98,96,94,91 89,89,87,86,84 81,72,70**
CSF £1659.90 TOTE £67.30: £9.90, £20.10, £18.70; EX 2516.90 TRIFECTA Not won..
Owner Mrs Fitri Hay **Bred** T K And Mrs P A Knox **Trained** Upper Lambourn, Berks
■ Dean McKeown's third success in this valuable Listed prize, first run in 1989.
■ Stewards' Enquiry : Dean McKeown three-day ban; using whip with excessive frequency (Oct 17-19)

FOCUS
Not a strong renewal by any means. The enterprisingly ridden winner stole first run and proved very brave. There was not a lot to choose between the first dozen at the line and it is hard to be positive about the form.

NOTEBOOK
Dubai Dynamo, successful in a nursery over seven at Doncaster last month, made the most of his proven stamina and never flinched. He is tough and progressive.
Vhujon(IRE), who lacks size and substance, was probably unlucky. Exiting the stalls in awkward fashion and having to make his way to the stands'-side rail from a low draw to find room to deliver his finishing effort, he was fast catching the winner at the line.
Pelican Prince ran out of his skin especially considering he really prefers quicker ground than he encountered here. (op 66-1)
Easy Target(FR), fifth to Dark Angel in the Mill Reef, was taken very quietly to post. Drawn on the outside, he tended to hang left and leant on Mr Keppel in the final furlong. Official explanation: jockey said colt hung right-handed
Mister Hardy is not that big but he is very tough. He had run well in the big sales races at York and Doncaster and again gave a very good account of himself.
Craggy Cat(IRE), the biggest in the line-up and easily the paddock pick, had plenty to find on official ratings. Soon pushed along, he stuck to his task without ever really threatening. Seven furlongs will suit him a lot better. (op 9-2)
Mr Keppel(IRE) is improving fast and looked a picture of health. He was drawn wide and was not helped when Easy Target started leaning on him. (op 8-1 tchd 9-1)
Spitfire, drawn towards the outside, was making hard work of it some way from home and, though he stuck to his task, he never really entered the argument. (op 9-2)
Broken Applause(IRE), tried in blinkers, had the best chance on official ratings but she was not at her best and probebly needs much softer ground. (op 6-1)
Vive Les Rouges, who ran so well in Listed company at Salisbury, did not reproduce that effort here. (op 11-2 tchd 5-1)

6018 WEATHERBYS PRINTING GUISBOROUGH STKS (LISTED RACE) 7f
4:10 (4:11) (Class 1) 3-Y-O+
£14,762 (£5,595; £2,800; £1,396; £699; £351) **Stalls** Centre

Form RPR

2050 **1** **Appalachian Trail (IRE)**[14] 5616 6-9-0 104 .... (b) TomEaves 2 113
(I Semple) *hld up towards rr: swtchd lft and hdwy over 1f out: str run ins fnl f to ld last 75yds* **20/1**

3055 **2** *nk* **Rahiyah (USA)**[23] 5354 3-8-7 111 .... TedDurcan 6 107
(J Noseda) *wnt rt s: t.k.h: hld up: hdwy over 2f out: rdn over 1f out: edgd lft and styd on wl fnl f* **10/1**

3-04 **3** ¾ **Caradak (IRE)**[27] 5265 6-9-0 111 .... SebSanders 1 110
(Saeed Bin Suroor) *trckd ldrs: hdwy to ld wl over 1f out: sn rdn: hdd and nt qckn wl ins fnl f* **2/1**[1]

0201 **4** ¾ **Advanced**[14] 5616 4-9-0 114 .... NCallan 8 108
(K A Ryan) *chsd ldr: rdn wl over 1f out: edgd lft and one pce ins fnl f* **11/4**[2]

201 **5** 1 **Jack Sullivan (USA)**[40] 4907 6-9-0 106 .... (b) PaulHanagan 5 105
(G A Butler) *trckd ldrs: effrt 2f out: sn rdn and kpt on same pce appr fnl f* **8/1**

2304 **6** *shd* **Racer Forever (USA)**[23] 5359 4-9-0 108 .... (b) RichardMullen 3 105
(J H M Gosden) *trckd ldng pair: effrt 2f out: sn rdn and bmpd 1f out: one pce* **9/2**[3]

13-2 **7** ½ **Kilworth (IRE)**[20] 5444 4-9-0 105 .... DO'Donohoe 7 104
(Saeed Bin Suroor) *hmpd s: t.k.h and sn led: rdn along over 2f out: hdd wl over 1f out: sn edgd lft and grad wknd* **16/1**

4060 **8** 1¼ **Rising Shadow (IRE)**[14] 5616 6-9-3 103 .... RoystonFfrench 4 103
(T D Barron) *s.i.s: a in rr* **25/1**

1030 **9** 1¼ **Passion Fruit**[7] 5794 6-8-9 85 .... DeanMcKeown 9 92
(C W Fairhurst) *hld up in rr: effrt and sme hdwy over 2f out: sn rdn and btn* **33/1**

1m 24.31s (-0.59) **Going Correction** +0.175s/f (Good)
WFA 3 from 4yo+ 2lb **9** Ran SP% **115.8**
Speed ratings (Par 111): **110,109,108,107,106 106,106,104,103**
CSF £200.28 TOTE £27.10: £5.00, £3.70, £1.10; EX 238.60.
Owner G L S Partnership **Bred** Swettenham Stud **Trained** Carluke, S Lanarks

FOCUS
Rather a messy Listed race and the exposed winner had plenty to find. The form may not prove too solid.

NOTEBOOK
Appalachian Trail(IRE), who had something to find with Advanced on Ayr Gold Cup running, swept to the front near the line to record his best ever effort. (tchd 22-1)
Rahiyah(USA), third in the French 1,000 Guineas, has been hit and miss since but this marked a return to form. She does not look entirely straightfoward though. (tchd 9-1)
Caradak(IRE), who took the Group 1 Prix de la Foret on this day a year ago, had no penalty. He went on and looked the likely winner only to miss out in the end. (op 15-8 tchd 7-4 and 9-4)
Advanced, his confidence bolstered by his big-race win at Ayr, is happier over six and with a stronger pace assured. (tchd 5-2 and 3-1)
Jack Sullivan(USA), in blinkers rather than cheekpieces, is better over a bit further on the All-Weather surfaces. (op 9-1)
Racer Forever(USA) keeps running well at a high level but he is proving very hard to win with. (op 11-2)
Kilworth(IRE), having his second outing for Godolphin, soon pulled his way to the front. Considering he stays much further it was disappointing to see him beat a retreat in the final furlong.

6019 REDCARRACING.CO.UK SUPER (S) STKS 1m 2f
4:45 (4:45) (Class 5) 3-5-Y-O **£3,886** (£1,156; £577; £288) **Stalls** High

Form RPR

0511 **1** **Birkside**[12] 5690 4-9-6 64 .... DavidAllan 12 65
(D Carroll) *hld up in rr: hdwy on outside to go 2nd 3f out: led over 1f out: hung lft: drvn rt out* **10/3**[2]

0400 **2** 1 **Playtotheaudience**[10] 5739 4-9-0 46 .... (b) PaulHanagan 15 57
(R A Fahey) *led tl over 1f out: keeping on same pce whn n.m.r and swtchd rt ins fnl f* **12/1**

4000 **3** 2 **Ming Vase**[16] 5563 5-9-0 47 .... FrankieMcDonald 7 53
(P T Midgley) *chsd ldr: styd on same pce fnl 2f* **20/1**

0100 **4** ½ **Garibaldi (GER)**[9] 5750 5-9-1 54 .... (b) GaryBartley(5) 4 58
(J O'Reilly) *hld up in tch: effrt on inner 3f out: styd on same pce* **25/1**

6234 **5** *shd* **Sienna Storm (IRE)**[8] 5774 4-9-0 68 .... (b) NCallan 10 52
(M H Tompkins) *hld up in rr: hdwy 3f out: nvr rchd ldrs* **6/5**[1]

0403 **6** ½ **Anything Once (USA)**[10] 5739 4-9-0 50 .... (b) StephenDonohoe 8 51
(D Carroll) *in rr: effrt over 3f out: kpt on fnl f* **16/1**

4400 **7** ¾ **Musical Land (IRE)**[9] 5755 3-8-9 55 .... (b[1]) PhillipMakin 2 49
(J R Weymes) *chsd ldrs: one pce fnl 3f* **33/1**

5535 **8** 5 **Skye But N Ben**[1] 5967 3-8-10 55 .... (b) NeilBrown(5) 13 45
(T D Barron) *trckd ldrs: effrt 3f out: wknd over 1f out* **7/1**[3]

9 3 **Lady In The Bath** 3-8-4 0 .... RoystonFfrench 6 28
(P C Haslam) *mid-div: drvn over 5f out: lost pl over 2f out* **33/1**

0440 **10** 7 **Roman History (IRE)**[19] 5479 4-9-0 52 .... (p) PatCosgrave 3 19
(Miss Tracy Waggott) *chsd ldrs: lost pl 3f out* **16/1**

6000 **11** *2* **Kudbeme**[10] 5737 5-8-12 53 PJMcDonald(3) 1 16
(N Bycroft) *s.v.s: nvr on terms* **33/1**

2m 8.30s (1.50) **Going Correction** +0.175s/f (Good)
WFA 3 from 4yo+ 5lb 11 Ran SP% **117.9**
Speed ratings (Par 103): **101,100,98,98,98 97,97,93,90,85 83**
CSF £39.36 TOTE £4.00: £1.20, £3.40, £3.90; EX 48.40.The winner was bought in for 7,000gns.
Owner Document Express Ltd **Bred** Pendley Farm **Trained** Sledmere, E Yorks
■ Stewards' Enquiry : Paul Hanagan five-day ban: used whip with excessive frequency (Oct 17-21)

FOCUS
A run-of-the-mill seller but the winner is useful at this level. The form makes sense.

6020 SHEPHERD CONSTRUCTION H'CAP 5f
5:20 (5:22) (Class 5) (0-75,75) 3-Y-0+ **£2,817** (£838; £418; £209) **Stalls** Centre

Form RPR

4015 **1** **Ocean Blaze**[14] 5642 3-9-1 72 BrettDoyle 8 79
(B R Millman) *mde most: rdn wl over 1f out: styd on strly ins fnl f* **9/2**[1]

0600 **2** *1 1/4* **Steel City Boy (IRE)**[6] 5836 4-8-5 62 RoystonFfrench 14 63
(D Carroll) *in tch: hdwy wl over 1f out: sn rdn and styd on wl fnl f* **14/1**

-000 **3** *hd* **Kerry's Dream**[13] 5662 3-8-12 69 DavidAllan 7 70
(T D Easterby) *in tch: hdwy to chse ldrs 2f out: sn rdn and kpt on ins fnl f* **33/1**

0026 **4** *shd* **Guto**[18] 5505 4-8-9 73 MCGeran(7) 9 73
(W J H Ratcliffe) *prom: hdwy tpo chse wnr 2f out: sn rdn and one pce ins fnl f* **7/1**

1030 **5** *3/4* **Methaaly (IRE)**[14] 5648 4-8-12 69 RichardMullen 3 66
(M Mullineaux) *towards rr: hdwy 2f out: snr idden and styd on ins fnl f: nrst fin* **12/1**

2340 **6** *shd* **Stonecrabstomorrow (IRE)**[28] 5223 4-9-1 72 TonyHamilton 6 69
(R A Fahey) *towards rr: rdn along 1/2-way: styd on u.p appr fnl f* **17/2**

1520 **7** *hd* **Dark Champion**[59] 4289 7-8-1 61 (v) DuranFentiman(3) 4 57
(R E Barr) *chsd ldrs: rdn along over 2f out: sn drvn: edgd lft and wknd appr fnl f* **33/1**

1003 **8** *nk* **Raccoon (IRE)**[10] 5740 7-8-5 65 PJMcDonald(3) 2 60
(D W Chapman) *racd alone far side: prom tl rdn along wl over 1f out and grad wknd* **5/1**[2]

6650 **9** *1/2* **Ingleby Princess**[28] 5232 3-8-8 70 NeilBrown(5) 1 64
(T D Barron) *sn outpcd and bhd tl styd on fnl f* **20/1**

4200 **10** *nk* **Windjammer**[19] 5481 3-8-13 70 TedDurcan 13 63
(T D Easterby) *in tch: rdn along over 2f out: sn btn* **16/1**

2335 **11** *3/4* **Welcome Approach**[9] 5747 4-9-1 72 PhillipMakin 10 62
(J R Weymes) *in tch: rdn along over 2f out and sn btn* **8/1**

4150 **12** *3/4* **Strathmore (IRE)**[105] 2892 3-8-12 69 PaulHanagan 12 57
(R A Fahey) *a towards rr* **12/1**

3410 **13** *1/2* **Desert Opal**[42] 4800 7-9-4 75 (p) NCallan 15 60
(C R Dore) *a towards rr* **13/2**[3]

1200 **14** *1 3/4* **Almaty Express**[140] 1854 5-9-1 72 (b) DO'Donohoe 5 51
(J R Weymes) *nvr nr ldrs* **33/1**

0525 **15** *1 1/4* **Strensall**[10] 5740 10-8-13 70 TomEaves 11 44
(R E Barr) *chsd ldrs: rdn along over 2f out and sn btn* **20/1**

58.90 secs (0.20) **Going Correction** +0.175s/f (Good) 15 Ran SP% **128.6**
Speed ratings (Par 103): **105,103,102,102,101 101,100,100,99,99 97,96,95,93,91**
CSF £67.99 CT £1930.11 TOTE £4.60: £2.00, £6.20, £5.80; EX 149.40.
Owner Ocean View Properties International Ltd **Bred** Longdon Stud And Robin Lawson **Trained** Kentisbeare, Devon
■ Stewards' Enquiry : Brett Doyle six-day ban: careless riding (Oct 17-22)

FOCUS
A fair handicap. They finished in a heap behind the progressive winner and the form may not prove very strong.

6021 CHRISTMAS PARTIES AT REDCAR H'CAP 1m 2f
5:50 (5:53) (Class 5) (0-75,77) 3-Y-0+ **£2,817** (£838; £418; £209) **Stalls** High

Form RPR

5640 **1** **King Of The Moors (USA)**[47] 4672 4-9-2 68 PhillipMakin 3 81+
(T D Barron) *soft ld: qcknd 4f out: clr over 2f out: unchal: eased towards fin* **14/1**

4421 **2** *3 1/2* **Keisha Kayleigh (IRE)**[10] 5738 4-8-9 61 (v) TonyHamilton 12 65
(B Ellison) *hld up in mid-div: hdwy on outside 3f out: wnt 2nd over 1f out: no ch w wnr* **9/2**[2]

2102 **3** *nk* **Four Miracles**[37] 4960 3-9-2 73 NCallan 6 76
(M H Tompkins) *chsd ldrs: kpt on same pce fnl 2f* **9/1**

6433 **4** *1 3/4* **Trouble Mountain (USA)**[10] 5738 10-8-7 66 (t) NSLawes(7) 9 66+
(M W Easterby) *mid-div: hdwy over 3f out: kpt on same pce fnl 2f* **8/1**[3]

-531 **5** *shd* **King Of Rhythm (IRE)**[38] 4933 4-9-6 72 StephenDonohoe 10 72
(D Carroll) *chsd ldrs: wnt 2nd over 2f out: styd on same pce* **12/1**

3422 **6** *2* **Violent Velocity (IRE)**[45] 4704 4-9-3 69 PatCosgrave 13 65
(J J Quinn) *t.k.h in rr: effrt 4f out: kpt on: nvr nr ldrs* **14/1**

3312 **7** *1* **Teodora Adivina**[10] 5738 3-8-13 70 TedDurcan 4 64+
(H R A Cecil) *sat down in stalls: hld up in last: nt clr run over 2f out and over 1f out: nt rcvr* **5/2**[1]

1000 **8** *nk* **Wasalat (USA)**[16] 5559 5-9-2 68 PaulHanagan 5 61
(D W Barker) *chsd ldrs: wnt 2nd over 3f out: one pce* **16/1**

0164 **9** *hd* **Sforzando**[29] 5197 6-8-9 68 KristinStubbs(7) 7 61
(Mrs L Stubbs) *t.k.h towards rr: effrt 3f out: hung lft: nvr on terms* **28/1**

0402 **10** *hd* **Dark Energy**[16] 5555 3-8-9 66 TomEaves 15 58
(B Smart) *hld up in rr: effrt over 3f out: nvr nr ldrs* **14/1**

3215 **11** *shd* **Kirkby's Treasure**[6] 5840 9-8-11 66 PJMcDonald(3) 14 58
(G A Swinbank) *hld up in rr: effrt over 3f out: nvr a factor* **12/1**

0140 **12** *1* **Frank Crow**[35] 5035 4-9-2 73 GaryBartley(5) 8 63
(J S Goldie) *t.k.h in rr: nvr a factor* **33/1**

4340 **13** *nk* **Onatopp (IRE)**[16] 5555 3-8-10 67 DavidAllan 11 57
(T D Easterby) *s.s: drvn 4f out: nvr on terms* **33/1**

4465 **14** *nk* **Cripsey Brook**[14] 5623 9-9-6 77 ow2 (t) JamesReveley(5) 1 66
(K G Reveley) *trckd ldrs: effrt over 3f out: lost pl 2f out* **16/1**

4356 **15** *7* **Deadline (UAE)**[11] 5703 3-8-8 70 ow2 NeilBrown(5) 2 45
(P T Midgley) *chsd ldrs: effrt on inner 3f out: lost pl over 1f out: eased ins fnl f* **16/1**

2m 10.04s (3.24) **Going Correction** +0.175s/f (Good)
WFA 3 from 4yo+ 5lb 15 Ran SP% **130.2**
Speed ratings (Par 103): **94,91,90,89,89 87,87,86,86,86 86,85,85,85,79**
CSF £80.29 CT £627.35 TOTE £19.80: £4.80, £1.90, £3.00; EX 134.80 Place 6 £6,668.02, Place 5 £1,652.31.
Owner Dave Scott **Bred** F Brown, Hedberg Hall & Keith Hernandez **Trained** Maunby, N Yorks

FOCUS
A modest handicap. The winner was gifted a soft lead and his rider deserves full marks. The runner-up did well from off the pace, while everything went wrong for Teodora Adivina.
Teodora Adivina Official explanation: jockey said filly missed the break

T/Plt: £49,436.30 to a £1 stake. Pool: £81,265.20. 1.20 winning tickets. T/Qpdt: £1,687.10 to a £1 stake. Pool: £3,875.80. 1.70 winning tickets. WG

5980 WOLVERHAMPTON (A.W) (L-H)
Saturday, October 6

OFFICIAL GOING: Standard
Wind: Nil Weather: Fine

6022 WBX.COM 0% COMMISSION ON BIG RACES MEDIAN AUCTION MAIDEN STKS 5f 216y(P)
7:00 (7:00) (Class 5) 2-Y-0 **£2,968** (£876; £438) **Stalls** Low

Form RPR

6 **1** **Concealment (IRE)**[15] 5603 2-8-12 0 SebSanders 3 68+
(R M Beckett) *mde all: clr run: rdn over 1f out: eased cl home* **3/1**[2]

0 **2** *3* **Gunner Fly (IRE)**[31] 5143 2-9-0 0 JamieMoriarty(3) 10 61
(R A Fahey) *s.i.s: hmpd over 4f out: hdwy on ins over 2f out: rdn and swtchd lft ins fnl f: r.o: no ch w wnr* **12/1**

556 **3** *1/2* **Howards Hope**[38] 4930 2-9-3 59 (b[1]) DaneO'Neill 2 59
(I Semple) *s.s: swtchd rt and n.m.r over 4f out: rdn and hdwy over 1f out: edgd lft ins fnl f: nrst fin* **9/1**

4 **4** *2* **Socceroo**[161] 1285 2-8-12 0 JohnEgan 7 48
(D J Murphy) *plld hrd: w wnr 4f: sn rdn: wknd fnl f* **11/10**[1]

00 **5** *1 1/4* **General Ting (IRE)**[8] 5780 2-9-3 0 JamieMackay 9 49
(Sir Mark Prescott) *hld up towards rr: c wd bnd over 2f out: nvr nr ldrs* **50/1**

0 **6** *1 1/4* **Fantasy Fighter (IRE)**[16] 5558 2-9-3 0 J-PGuillambert 1 46
(J J Quinn) *prom tl rdn and wknd 2f out* **33/1**

450 **7** *8* **Weet By Far**[15] 5603 2-8-9 65 PatrickMathers(3) 8 17
(R Hollinshead) *prom: rdn 3f out: sn wknd* **6/1**[3]

8 *13* **Stoneacre Baby (USA)** 2-8-12 0 LPKeniry 6 —
(Peter Grayson) *s.s: a in rr* **20/1**

4006 **9** *33* **Erin Thomas (IRE)**[33] 5096 2-8-12 55 (p) TPQueally 4 —
(M G Quinlan) *hld up in tch: 4th whn sddle slipped and virtually p.u over 2f out* **33/1**

1m 15.89s (0.08) **Going Correction** -0.10s/f (Stan) 9 Ran SP% **117.2**
Speed ratings (Par 95): **95,91,90,87,86 84,73,56,12**
CSF £36.42 TOTE £3.80: £1.60, £4.00, £2.80; EX 26.60.
Owner Mrs Ralph Beckett **Bred** Patrick Kennedy **Trained** Whitsbury, Hants

FOCUS
A moderate maiden with little strength in depth, but Concealment did it well and was value for extra.

NOTEBOOK
Concealment(IRE) ◆, sharpened by her debut over course and distance last month, was a convincing winner from the front and there should be more improvement to come. (op 11-4)
Gunner Fly(IRE) stepped up on his York debut but is a shade flattered by his proximity to the winner. A longer trip may help. (tchd 16-1)
Howards Hope was tried in blinkers after having his first three outings at Ayr. Supported in the market, he showed why he had been tried over 7f when a 100/1 shot last time. (op 16-1)
Socceroo had not been seen since showing promise on her Haydock debut towards the end of April. She ran much too freely over this extra furlong and failed to get home. (op 13-8 tchd 7-4 in places)
General Ting(IRE) ◆, rejected by Seb Sanders in favour of the winner, would not have been suited by the drop back from 7f being a brother to dual 1m4f winner King's Ransom and half-brother to the high-class Hattan. Now qualified for handicaps, it would come as no surprise to see him leave this form behind over further in due course. (op 40-1)
Erin Thomas(IRE) Official explanation: jockey said saddle slipped

6023 WBX.COM 0% COMMISSION ON BIG FOOTBALL MATCHES (S) STKS 5f 20y(P)
7:30 (7:30) (Class 6) 2-Y-0 **£2,047** (£604; £302) **Stalls** Low

Form RPR

0062 **1** **Golden Dane (IRE)**[11] 5706 2-8-11 62 SebSanders 1 68
(I A Wood) *mde all: clr over 1f out: rdn out* **6/4**[1]

3000 **2** *1 1/2* **Structura (USA)**[26] 5267 2-8-6 61 (p) JamesDoyle 4 58
(J S Moore) *a.p: rdn to chse wnr wl over 1f out: r.o one pce fnl f* **12/1**

4500 **3** *1 1/4* **Diademas (USA)**[23] 5365 2-9-2 68 (b) TPQueally 5 63
(J A Osborne) *t.k.h in tch: rdn and hung lft over 1f out: kpt on same pce fnl f* **9/4**[2]

0423 **4** *1 3/4* **Liani (IRE)**[11] 5706 2-7-13 58 SophieDoyle(7) 7 47
(P D Evans) *chsd ldrs: hung lft over 1f out: one pce* **11/2**[3]

000 **5** *3* **Joint Agency (IRE)**[17] 5521 2-7-13 50 LanceBetts(7) 9 36
(N Wilson) *in rr: sme hdwy on ins wl over 1f out: nvr trbld ldrs* **33/1**

6 *shd* **Bahia Palace** 2-8-6 0 JamieMackay 12 36
(M D I Usher) *s.i.s: in rr: pushed along over 3f out: sme late hdwy: n.d* **20/1**

00 **7** *4* **Ruby's Rainbow (IRE)**[18] 5501 2-8-4 0 ow1 PatrickMathers(3) 6 22
(J Balding) *chsd ldrs: rdn 3f out: wknd 2f out* **66/1**

0050 **8** *1 3/4* **Frizzini**[23] 5365 2-8-11 60 IanMongan 2 20
(N Tinkler) *t.k.h: chsd wnr: rdn over 2f out: wknd over 1f out* **8/1**

0 **9** *8* **Phoenix Bay**[17] 5521 2-8-7 0 ow1 LPKeniry 3 —
(J J Quinn) *s.i.s: outpcd* **66/1**

62.35 secs (-0.47) **Going Correction** -0.10s/f (Stan) 9 Ran SP% **115.6**
Speed ratings (Par 93): **99,96,94,91,87 86,80,77,64**
CSF £20.53 TOTE £2.70: £1.10, £3.50, £1.30; EX 29.90.The winner was bought in for 6,500gns.
Owner Neardown Stables **Bred** Tally-Ho Stud **Trained** Upper Lambourn, Berks

FOCUS
This looks good selling form and this was possibly one of the strongest races of its type so far this season.

NOTEBOOK
Golden Dane(IRE), second in similar company at Brighton last time, dominated throughout from the inside draw under a positive ride. (op 9-4)
Structura(USA), tried in cheekpieces for this drop into a seller, stuck to her task without really troubling the winner. (op 17-2)
Diademas(USA) could not take advantage of a drop in grade and failed to help his cause by hanging. His sole win came on Fibresand and it may be unfortunate for him that Southwell is out of action at the moment. (op 11-4)
Liani(IRE), a drifter in the ring, had finished a length and three-quarters behind the winner on identical terms at Brighton. (op 100-30 tchd 6-1)
Joint Agency(IRE) was down in grade on her All-Weather debut.

Bahia Palace is a half-sister to three winning sprinters including one who scored over this trip on Polytrack. (op 16-1)

6024 WBX.COM 0% COMMISSION ON BIG RACES CLAIMING STKS 7f 32y(P)
7:55 (7:55) (Class 5) 3-Y-0+ £2,968 (£876; £438) Stalls High

Form RPR

2213 **1** **Samuel Charles**[21] 5424 9-9-0 69........................(p) JohnEgan 6 75
(C R Dore) *led early: chsd ldr: led over 2f out: rdn out* **3/1**[2]

0400 **2** *nk* **Councellor (FR)**[17] 5545 5-9-12 81........................(t) JamieSpencer 3 86
(Stef Liddiard) *a.p: rdn to chse wnr wl over 1f out: r.o ins fnl f* **11/4**[1]

4600 **3** *1/2* **Teasing**[70] 3960 3-8-11 68........................ J-PGuillambert 7 72
(J Pearce) *s.i.s: nt clr run on ins wl over 1f out: sn swtchd rt and hdwy: r.o ins fnl f* **28/1**

0000 **4** *shd* **Ninth House (USA)**[31] 5128 5-9-4 73........................(t) IanMongan 12 77
(N P Littmoden) *swtchd lft sn after s: hld up in rr: rdn and hdwy wl over 1f out: r.o ins fnl f* **15/2**

1004 **5** *1* **Mineral Star (IRE)**[10] 5737 5-9-4 72........................(v) SebSanders 2 74
(M H Tompkins) *hld up in mid-div: hdwy and swtchd rt over 1f out: nt qckn ins fnl f* **11/2**[3]

2000 **6** *3* **Local Poet**[28] 5233 6-8-11 64........................(b) JamieMoriarty(3) 1 62
(I Semple) *hld up towards rr: hdwy on ins 2f out: rdn over 1f out: wknd ins fnl f* **16/1**

-606 **7** *3/4* **Middleton Grey**[25] 5303 9-9-0 68........................(b) LPKeniry 5 60
(A G Newcombe) *t.k.h early: sn mid-div: rdn over 1f out: no hdwy fnl f* **18/1**

-350 **8** *shd* **Tobago Reef**[184] 935 3-8-10 70........................(p) DaneO'Neill 9 58
(Mrs L Stubbs) *sn led: hdd over 2f out: wknd ins fnl f* **14/1**

9 *4* **Frankalbert (IRE)**[48] 3-9-10 0........................(t) SLobina 11 61
(E Pellegrino, Italy) *c wd st: a towards rr* **11/1**

1600 **10** *1/2* **Copper King**[21] 5424 3-9-10 65........................ JamesDoyle 10 60
(J W Hills) *hld up in mid-div: hdwy 3f out: sn rdn: wknd over 1f out* **33/1**

1003 **11** *1 1/2* **Coup D'Etat**[5] 5864 5-9-8 72........................(b) TPQueally 4 52
(R A Harris) *prom tl wknd wl over 1f out* **9/1**

1m 30.26s (-0.14) **Going Correction** -0.10s/f (Stan)
WFA 3 from 5yo+ 2lb 11 Ran SP% **121.4**
Speed ratings (Par 103): **96,95,95,94,93 90,89,89,84,84 82**
CSF £12.13 TOTE £3.20: £1.10, £2.40, £8.40; EX 9.60.
Owner Chris Marsh **Bred** Sheikh Mohammed Obaid Al Maktoum **Trained** West Pinchbeck, Lincs

FOCUS
A competitive, fair claimer. Decent form for the grade, the fourth perhaps the best guide.
Copper King Official explanation: jockey said gelding had no more to give

6025 MALTHOUSE ENGINEERING 60TH ANNIVERSARY H'CAP 1m 141y(P)
8:25 (8:25) (Class 5) (0-75,75) 3-Y-0+ £2,968 (£876; £438) Stalls Low

Form RPR

3102 **1** **Trivia (IRE)**[17] 5545 3-9-1 **72**........................ JamieSpencer 4 81
(N A Callaghan) *a.p: rdn over 1f out: led wl ins fnl f: r.o* **7/2**[2]

0000 **2** *nk* **Gaelic Princess**[1] 5985 7-9-4 **71**........................ DaneO'Neill 1 79
(A G Newcombe) *hld up towards rr: hdwy on ins wl over 1f out: sn rdn: r.o ins fnl f* **5/1**[3]

0105 **3** *hd* **Bold Indian (IRE)**[16] 5555 3-8-6 **63**........................ PaulMulrennan 7 71
(I Semple) *stdd s: plld hrd: hdwy to chse ldr over 6f out: rdn to ld over 1f out: hdd wl ins fnl f* **12/1**

6006 **4** *5* **Bold Diktator**[1] 5985 5-9-3 **75**........................ TolleyDean(5) 3 71
(Tom Dascombe) *led: rdn over 2f out: hdd over 1f out: wknd wl ins fnl f* **7/1**

0505 **5** *3/4* **King's Bastion (IRE)**[19] 5473 3-8-10 **72**........................ LukeMorris(5) 2 66
(M L W Bell) *hld up in rr: rdn wl over 1f out: n.d* **13/2**

3132 **6** *5* **Le Chiffre (IRE)**[29] 5203 5-9-5 **72**........................(p) SebSanders 8 55
(S Curran) *hld up towards rr: rdn wl over 1f out: no imp whn sltly hmpd ent fnl f* **3/1**[1]

0000 **7** *nk* **Linda's Colin (IRE)**[29] 5189 5-8-8 **61** oh1........................ JohnEgan 5 43
(R A Harris) *t.k.h: prom: wknd and hung lft fr wl over 1f out* **20/1**

1102 **8** *2 1/2* **Joshua's Gold (IRE)**[11] 5701 6-9-3 **70**........................(v) TPQueally 6 46
(D Carroll) *prom: lost pl over 4f out: rdn and wknd over 2f out* **7/1**

1m 50.4s (-1.36) **Going Correction** -0.10s/f (Stan)
WFA 3 from 5yo+ 4lb 8 Ran SP% **114.7**
Speed ratings (Par 103): **102,101,101,97,96 92,91,89**
CSF £21.44 CT £188.20 TOTE £3.70: £1.70, £1.60, £3.20; EX 26.90.
Owner Michael Tabor **Bred** Mrs Jean O'Brien **Trained** Newmarket, Suffolk

FOCUS
The first three eventually came clear in a race run at a modest pace and the form might not be that solid.
Linda's Colin(IRE) Official explanation: jockey said gelding hung badly left

6026 JOIN WBX.COM FOR FREE FOOTBALL SHIRT H'CAP 1m 1f 103y(P)
8:55 (8:56) (Class 6) (0-55,55) 3-Y-0 £2,047 (£604; £302) Stalls Low

Form RPR

000- **1** **Alonso De Guzman (IRE)**[354] 6025 3-8-8 **54**........................ LukeMorris(5) 7 62
(J R Boyle) *hld up in mid-div: stdy hdwy on outside over 4f out: rdn over 1f out: led wl ins fnl f: r.o* **6/1**[3]

0533 **2** *shd* **Cap St Jean (IRE)**[25] 5299 3-9-0 **55**........................ JamieSpencer 12 63
(R Hollinshead) *stdd s: sn swtchd lft: hld up in rr: hdwy wl over 1f out: rdn and swtchd rt 1f out: ev ch wl ins fnl f: r.o* **7/2**[1]

0305 **3** *1 1/2* **Pegasus Prince (USA)**[33] 5084 3-8-7 **48**........................ PaulMulrennan 5 53
(Miss J A Camacho) *t.k.h: w ldr: led over 3f out: rdn wl over 1f out: hdd and nt qckn wl ins fnl f* **10/1**

0600 **4** *2* **Officer Material (IRE)**[66] 4073 3-8-11 **52**........................(b[1]) AdamKirby 4 53
(C G Cox) *prom: rdn over 3f out: hung rt 1f out: one pce* **20/1**

005 **5** *1 1/4* **Botham (USA)**[3] 5894 3-8-7 **48**........................(b) JohnEgan 9 46
(D J Murphy) *hld up in mid-div: nt clr run over 2f out: rdn whn nt clr run briefly 1f out: edgd lft ins fnl f: one pce* **13/2**

2442 **6** *1 1/4* **Slavonic Lake**[15] 5606 3-8-6 **47**........................(t) JamesDoyle 3 42
(I A Wood) *prom: rdn over 1f out: wknd ins fnl f* **9/2**[2]

0030 **7** *1 3/4* **Gallows Hill (USA)**[17] 5525 3-8-6 **47**........................(b) DaleGibson 6 39
(R A Fahey) *t.k.h: sn mid-div: rdn over 3f out: hdwy over 2f out: wknd over 1f out* **16/1**

0002 **8** *shd* **Monsieur Dumas (IRE)**[25] 5299 3-9-0 **55**........................ SebSanders 10 47
(R Bastiman) *hld up towards rr: c wd st: sn rdn: nvr nr ldrs* **7/2**[1]

003 **9** *2* **Pagan Rose (IRE)**[19] 5474 3-8-9 **50**........................ DaneO'Neill 11 37
(J A R Toller) *hld up towards rr: hdwy on outside over 2f out: wknd wl over 1f out* **40/1**

0003 **10** *1/2* **Autograph Hunter**[28] 5233 3-9-0 **55**........................ LPKeniry 13 41
(Peter Grayson) *stdd s: sn swtchd lft: a bhd* **14/1**

0006 **11** *8* **Buds Dilemma**[7] 5803 3-8-9 **50**........................ TGMcLaughlin 8 19
(W M Brisbourne) *t.k.h: prom: rdn over 3f out: wknd 2f out* **40/1**

4040 **12** *17* **Allaire**[23] 5348 3-8-12 **53**........................ J-PGuillambert 1 —
(M Johnston) *led: hdd over 3f out: sn wknd* **20/1**

2m 0.94s (-1.68) **Going Correction** -0.10s/f (Stan) 12 Ran SP% **126.3**
Speed ratings (Par 99): **103,102,101,99,98 97,96,95,94,93 86,71**
CSF £28.04 CT £215.99 TOTE £7.00: £3.50, £2.40, £1.10; EX 52.00.
Owner M Khan X2 **Bred** G And Mrs Middlebrook **Trained** Epsom, Surrey

FOCUS
A closely-knit, low grade handicap. The form is best rated through the runner-up and looks less than solid.
Botham(USA) Official explanation: jockey said colt suffered interference in running

6027 WBX.COM #25 BET FOR NEW ACCOUNTS H'CAP 1m 4f 50y(P)
9:20 (9:20) (Class 5) (0-70,69) 3-Y-0+ £2,968 (£876; £438) Stalls Low

Form RPR

3311 **1** **Boz**[14] 5647 3-9-1 **66**........................ JamieSpencer 1 79+
(L M Cumani) *a.p: rdn wl over 1f out: r.o to ld nr fin* **10/11**[1]

2201 **2** *nk* **Potentiale (IRE)**[24] 5342 3-9-2 **67**........................(p) SebSanders 3 77
(J W Hills) *hld up: hdwy on ins over 2f out: rdn over 1f out: led ins fnl f: hdd nr fin* **4/1**[2]

1666 **3** *2 1/2* **Princely Ted (IRE)**[16] 5569 6-8-12 **56**........................ DaneO'Neill 4 62
(D Burchell) *set stdy pce: rdn over 2f out: hdd and no ex ins fnl f* **28/1**

4000 **4** *nk* **Desert Leader (IRE)**[28] 5225 6-9-11 **69**........................ JamieMackay 2 75
(R W Price) *hld up in tch: rdn and one pce fnl 2f* **10/1**

0021 **5** *1* **Heights Of Golan**[9] 5755 3-8-7 **58** ow1........................(v) LPKeniry 7 62+
(I A Wood) *hld up towards rr: c wd st: sn rdn: nvr able to chal* **9/2**[3]

016 **6** *4* **Global Traffic**[37] 4976 3-9-3 **68**........................ TGMcLaughlin 6 66
(P D Evans) *chsd ldr: rdn and ev ch 2f out: wknd 1f out* **18/1**

3400 **7** *4* **Thorny Mandate**[23] 5364 5-9-4 **62**........................ JohnEgan 5 53
(W M Brisbourne) *s.i.s: hld up in rr: rdn over 2f out: no rspnse* **16/1**

2m 41.19s (-1.23) **Going Correction** -0.10s/f (Stan)
WFA 3 from 5yo+ 7lb 7 Ran SP% **114.2**
Speed ratings (Par 103): **100,99,98,97,97 94,91**
CSF £4.81 TOTE £1.80: £1.40, £2.50; EX 4.80 Place 6 £36.26, Place 5 £8.96..
Owner Aston House Stud **Bred** Aston House Stud **Trained** Newmarket, Suffolk

FOCUS
A slowly-run tactical affair. The third sets the standard and the first two are progressive.
T/Plt: £49.40 to a £1 stake. Pool: £69,496.50. 1,025.00 winning tickets. T/Qpdt: £13.10 to a £1 stake. Pool: £4,693.80. 264.60 winning tickets. KH

5660 LONGCHAMP (R-H)
Saturday, October 6

OFFICIAL GOING: Soft

6028a PRIX CHAUDENAY CASINO BARRIERE DE MENTON (GROUP 2) 1m 7f
1:15 (1:15) 3-Y-0 £50,068 (£19,324; £9,223; £6,149; £3,074)

RPR

1 **Coastal Path**[29] 5258 3-9-2........................ SPasquier 5 112+
(A Fabre, France) *hld up disputing 4th or 5th: cl 4th st: led 150yds out: pushed out* **4/9**[1]

2 *3/4* **Noble Prince (GER)**[29] 5258 3-9-2........................ KFallon 3 111
(A Fabre, France) *hld up in rr: last st: hdwy on rail 2f out: hrd rdn over 1f out: hrd rdn to take 2nd last strides*

3 *hd* **Royal And Regal (IRE)**[29] 5258 3-9-2........................ OPeslier 1 111
(A Fabre, France) *trckd ldr: led over 8f out to over 2f out: led again 1 1/2f out to 150yds out: one pce* **12/1**[3]

4 *2* **Friston Forest (IRE)**[34] 5080 3-9-2........................ JVictoire 4 108
(A Fabre, France) *led to over 8f out: 2nd st: tk narrow ld 2f out to 1 1/2f out: one pce* **16/1**

5 *1* **Harbore (FR)**[55] 4446 3-9-2........................ C-PLemaire 2 107
(E Lellouche, France) *disp 3rd: 3rd st: wknd fr dist* **40/1**

6 *snk* **Mores Wells**[21] 5437 3-9-2........................ DPMcDonogh 7 107
(Kevin Prendergast, Ire) *hld up: 6th st: rdn wl over 1f out: nvr able to chal* **4/1**[2]

7 *10* **Gat (FR)**[29] 5258 3-9-2........................ CNora 6 95
(Mme C Dufreche, France) *disp 3rd to 3f out: cl 5th st: sn rdn and btn* **50/1**

3m 17.8s (-0.60) **Going Correction** +0.05s/f (Good) 7 Ran SP% **113.9**
Speed ratings: **103,102,102,101,100 100,95**
PARI-MUTUEL: WIN 1.40; PL 1.10, 3.50; SF 15.40 (Industry CSF £8.68).
Owner K Abdulla **Bred** Juddmonte Farms Ltd **Trained** Chantilly, France
■ Andre Fabre was responsible for the first four.
■

NOTEBOOK
Coastal Path is a top-class horse in the making. He is still a little immature, but he won this Group 2 event with something in reserve. On this occasion he did not take the advantage until inside the final furlong and stayed on well to keep his unbeaten record. He is unlikely to be seen out again this year and will be aimed at top-class races over a mile and a half in 2008.
Noble Prince(GER) was not seen until the latter part of this event. He found a nice gap at the furlong marker and finished best of all, and a Group 3 is certainly within his grasp.
Royal And Regal(IRE), always close up, helped set the pace. He hugged the rail throughout the straight and stayed on bravely, but at only the same pace and only lost second place in the final few strides.
Friston Forest(IRE), the long-time leader, still held the advantage one and a half furlongs out, but was one paced throughout the final furlong. This distance was probably just beyond his best.

6029a PRIX DE LA FORET CASINO BARRIERE DE BIARRITZ (GROUP 1) 7f
2:25 (2:26) 3-Y-0+ £96,520 (£38,615; £19,307; £9,645; £4,831)

RPR

1 **Toylsome**[13] 8-9-2........................ SPasquier 13 123
(J Hirschberger, Germany) *broke fast fr outside draw: mde all: clr fnl 2f: drvn out* **100/1**

2 *2 1/2* **Welsh Emperor (IRE)**[12] 5673 8-9-2........................ IMendizabal 9 116
(T P Tate) *trckd wnr thrght: r.o same pce fnl 2f* **33/1**

3 *3/4* **Marchand D'Or (FR)**[28] 5214 4-9-2........................ DBonilla 4 114
(F Head, France) *plld v hrd first 2f: 6th st: hdwy 2f out: 3rd over 1f out: r.o same pce* **5/1**[3]

4 *nse* **US Ranger (USA)**[6] 5842 3-9-0........................ KFallon 11 114
(A P O'Brien, Ire) *in tch: 5th on outside st: hrd rdn and disp 3rd fr 2f out: r.o same pce* **4/1**[2]

5 1 ½ **Tariq**^{67} 4045 3-9-0 .... LDettori 3 110
(P W Chapple-Hyam) *hld up: 11th st: styd on fnl 2f: nvr nr to chal* **7/2**^{1}

6 2 ½ **Dutch Art**^{62} 4214 3-9-0 .... TThulliez 10 103
(P W Chapple-Hyam) *hld up: 12th st: hdwy on outside fr 2f out: nvr nrr* **7/1**

7 ½ **Jeremy (USA)**^{66} 4058 4-9-2 .... JVictoire 5 102
(Sir Michael Stoute) *7th st: rdn over 2f out: no hdwy fr over 1f out* **9/1**

8 snk **Garnica (FR)**^{41} 4871 4-9-2 .... C-PLemaire 1 101
(J-C Rouget, France) *4th st: disp 3rd 2f out: sn wknd* **28/1**

9 3 **Linngari (IRE)**^{27} 5261 5-9-2 .... CSoumillon 12 93
(A De Royer-Dupre, France) *racd in 3rd: rdn over 2f out: wknd wl over 1f out* **10/1**

10 1 **Red Evie (IRE)**^{28} 5241 4-8-13 .... JamieSpencer 8 87
(M L W Bell) *hld up: last st: nvr a factor* **10/1**

11 **Impressionnante**^{27} 5259 4-8-13 .... OPeslier 6 87
(C Laffon-Parias, France) *10th st: nvr a factor* **81/1**

12 **Vital Equine (IRE)**^{133} 2051 3-9-0 .... ChrisCatlin 2 90
(E J O'Neill) *midfield: 8th st: wknd over 2f out* **26/1**

13 **Red Clubs (IRE)**^{28} 5214 4-9-2 .... MichaelHills 7 90
(B W Hills) *9th st: wknd 2f out* **24/1**

1m 22.5s (0.10) **Going Correction** +0.20s/f (Good)
WFA 3 from 4yo+ 2lb **13 Ran SP% 115.9**
Speed ratings: **107,104,103,103,101 98,98,97,94,93 93,93,93**
PARI-MUTUEL: WIN 51.30; PL 8.80, 11.70, 1.90; DF 545.80 (Industry CSF £2,010.28, TC £17,972.13).
Owner Baron G Von Ullmann **Bred** Serpentine Bloodstock Et Al **Trained** Germany

FOCUS
An extraordinary result to what looked an exceptionally strong renewal of a race that is traditionally among the very best of the year over this intermediate distance, with eight-year-olds first and second. However, the result needs treating with extreme caution as the first two were first and second throughout and the hold-up horses were clearly at a major disadvantage.

NOTEBOOK
Toylsome gained a magnificent victory and has been totally underestimated, having been used as a pacemaker for Manduro in the Prix Jacques le Marois at Deauville where he still managed to finish fourth. Quickly into his stride from a wide draw, he was soon in control. Still with a big advantage coming into the straight, he kept up the gallop to the line and most of the other jockeys probably thought that he would have come back to them in the final furlong. There are no plans at the moment, but he is a favourite of the owner so he could be kept in training next year, even though he is still an entire.
Welsh Emperor(IRE) is a grand old campaigner who particularly likes a little cut in the ground. He was given an intelligent ride as he was one of the few who did not want the winner to build up too big an advantage. He tried to get on terms early in the straight, but never really threatened, though did well to finish runner-up in this for the second year in succession.
Marchand D'Or(FR) was not particularly lucky as he ran a little free and was hampered early on. He came with a promising run from over a furlong out, but never looked like threatening the front pair. He is now likely to be prepared for a race in Hong Kong in early December.
US Ranger(USA) was running just six days after his previous run in Ireland and was not really seen until the latter part of the race. He came with a run from one and a half furlongs out and just failed to take third place.
Tariq was a disappointing favourite and had an enormous amount to do coming into the straight. He was extricated from the rail halfway up the straight and finished well, but never looked like finishing in the frame. The soft ground was considered not to have suited him. Official explanation: jockey said colt was unsuited by soft ground
Dutch Art had an enormous amount to do at the entrance to the straight, but did run on up the centre of the track in the final stages. This certainly was not his true form and his trainer felt he might have been beaten by the draw, but the winner was drawn widest. Official explanation: trainer said colt was beaten by its draw
Jeremy(USA) was never really seen with a big chance. He started his run from two furlongs out, but never showed his normal speed inside the final furlong. He should have handled the ground and a longer trip would have certainly been an advantage
Red Evie(IRE) was disappointing and she never looked likely to take a place in the frame. She was extricated to challenge in the straight, but made very little late progress.
Vital Equine(IRE) surprisingly lacked the early speed to get a prominent position and he was among the first under pressure. This was very disappointing and he may have found these conditions too testing after a five-month absence.
Red Clubs(IRE) was hampered in the early stages and never really got into a challenging position. He was another who was not at home on the soft ground. Official explanation: jockey said colt was unsuited by tacky, soft ground

6030a PRIX DE ROYALLIEU HOTEL HERMITAGE BARRIERE (GROUP 2) (FILLIES) 1m 4f 110y

2:55 (2:59) 3-Y-0+ **£50,068** (£19,324; £9,223; £6,149; £3,074)

RPR

1 **Anna Pavlova**^{14} 5618 4-9-1 .... LDettori 3 111+
(R A Fahey) *hld up: 8th st: hdwy on outside over 2f out: led over 1f out: pushed out: r.o strly* **11/4**^{1}

2 2 ½ **Princesse Dansante (IRE)**^{41} 4872 4-9-1 .... TThulliez 4 107
(F Doumen, France) *a cl up on ins: 6th st: wnt 2nd over 2f out: kpt on at one pce fnl f* **66/1**

3 ¾ **Darsha (FR)**^{18} 5519 3-8-7 .... CSoumillon 9 106
(A De Royer-Dupre, France) *hld up: 7th st: swtchd out and hdwy over 2f out: disp 3rd wl over 1f out: one pce* **6/1**

4 ¾ **Synopsis (IRE)**^{23} 5352 3-8-7 .... SPasquier 1 105
(A Fabre, France) *prom: 4th st: drvn to ld over 2f out: hdd over 1f out: one pce* **5/1**^{3}

5 4 **Doe Ray Me**^{31} 5150 3-8-7 .... DBoeuf 2 99
(H-A Pantall, France) *a.p: 5th st: disp 3rd 2f out: one pce* **25/1**

6 3 **Baldoria (IRE)**^{27} 4-9-1 .... JHorcajada 7 94
(M Delcher-Sanchez, Spain) *s.s: rdn along and 6l bhd: last st: styd on fnl 2f: nrst fin* **66/1**

7 2 **Kaloura (IRE)**^{18} 5519 3-8-7 .... JVictoire 6 91
(A Fabre, France) *trckd ldr: 2nd st: wknd over 2f out* **8/1**

8 6 **Ioannina**^{13} 5671 4-9-1 .... OPeslier 10 82
(J Hirschberger, Germany) *led to over 2f out* **11/1**

9 8 **All My Loving (IRE)**^{8} 5767 3-8-7 ....(v^{1}) KFallon 5 70
(A P O'Brien, Ire) *a in tch: 3rd st wknd over 2f out* **3/1**^{2}

10 10 **Pearl Sky (FR)**^{41} 4872 4-9-1 .... ACrastus 8 55
(Y De Nicolay, France) *9th st: sn rdn and btn: eased* **11/1**

2m 41.3s (-3.30) **Going Correction** +0.05s/f (Good)
WFA 3 from 4yo 7lb **10 Ran SP% 117.2**
Speed ratings: **112,110,110,109,107 105,104,100,95,89**
PARI-MUTUEL: WIN 4.40; PL 2.50, 6.90, 3.20; DF 94.50 (Industry CSF £191.21, TC £1,020.37).
Owner Galaxy Racing **Bred** Raymond Cowie **Trained** Musley Bank, N Yorks

FOCUS
A clear-cut win in this high-class fillies' contest that was run at a sound gallop.

NOTEBOOK
Anna Pavlova came with a storming late run up the centre of the track. She was last but one and had an enormous task at the beginning of the straight, but she quickened one and a half furlongs out and mowed down her rivals. This was an impressive performance and she has now been marked down for the Premio Lydio Tesio in Rome on October 28th.
Princesse Dansante(IRE), held up in the early stages, was putting in her best work as the race came to an end. She took second place a furlong out, but never looked like pegging back the winner and there are no plans for her at present.
Darsha(FR) put up a much better performance having been slowly away and unsuited by a moderate pace in her last race. She was another who had plenty to do early in the straight, but she finished very well to take third place inside the final furlong.
Synopsis(IRE) was well up there throughout and was at the head of affairs at the entrance to the straight. She began to shorten her stride at the furlong marker, but did stay on at one pace.

6031a PRIX DANIEL WILDENSTEIN CASTEL MARIE-LOUISE DE LA BAULE (GROUP 2) 1m

3:30 (3:32) 3-Y-0 **£50,068** (£19,324; £9,223; £6,149; £3,074)

RPR

1 **Spirito Del Vento (FR)**^{41} 4873 4-9-1 .... OPeslier 7 120
(J-M Beguigne, France) *hld up: last st: hdwy on outside fr 2f out: drvn to ld ins fnl f: r.o wl* **9/1**

2 2 **Racinger (FR)**^{84} 3523 4-9-3 .... DBonilla 6 118
(F Head, France) *led to 1/2-way: 2nd st: led 1 1/2f out to ins fnl f: one pce* **9/1**

3 1 ½ **Blythe Knight (IRE)**^{14} 5618 7-9-1 .... GrahamGibbons 4 113
(J J Quinn) *hld up: 9th st: hdwy fr 2f out: hrd rdn over 1f out: r.o to take 3rd wl ins fnl f* **28/1**

4 1 ½ **Bertranicus (FR)**^{27} 5259 4-9-1 .... CSoumillon 3 110
(L Urbano-Grajales, France) *hld up: 10th st: hdwy on outside fr 2f out: 3rd over 1f out: one pce* **20/1**

5 3 **Echo Of Light**^{31} 5142 5-9-1 .... LDettori 9 104
(Saeed Bin Suroor) *sn trckd ldr: led 1/2-way to 1 1/2f out: sn wknd* **5/4**^{1}

6 1 **Gloria De Campeao (BRZ)**^{48} 4-9-3 .... IMendizabal 5 104
(P Bary, France) *led 1f: 4th st: rdn wl over 1f out: grad wknd* **25/1**

7 4 **Pride Of Nation (IRE)**^{51} 4543 5-9-1 .... JamieSpencer 1 94
(L M Cumani) *midfield: 7th st: in rr whn nt clr run ins fnl 2f: no rspnse whn swtchd* **11/2**^{3}

8 ¾ **Decado (IRE)**^{20} 5459 4-9-1 .... DPMcDonogh 11 93
(Kevin Prendergast, Ire) *prom: 4th on outside and pushed along st: wknd wl over 1f out* **20/1**

9 ½ **Holocene (USA)**^{27} 5261 3-8-11 .... C-PLemaire 8 91
(P Bary, France) *hld up: 8th st: nvr a factor* **9/2**^{2}

10 3 **Kilometre Neuf (FR)**^{41} 4873 4-9-1 .... SPasquier 2 86
(F Doumen, France) *hdwy and 3rd st: rdn and btn 2f out* **40/1**

11 **Smart Enough**^{28} 5213 4-9-1 .... KFallon 10 86
(M A Magnusson) *s.i.s: hdwy after 2f: 6th st: wknd wl over 1f out* **37/1**

1m 40.9s (-1.50) **Going Correction** +0.05s/f (Good)
WFA 3 from 4yo+ 3lb **11 Ran SP% 119.9**
Speed ratings: **109,107,105,104,101 100,96,95,94,91 91**
PARI-MUTUEL: WIN 7.80 (coupled with Racinger); PL 3.20, 6.60, 9.00; DF 55.50 (Industry CSF £79.10, TC £2,199.84).
Owner L Ciampi **Bred** Haras Des Sablonnets **Trained** France

FOCUS
A decent renewal of this Group 2 producing a decisive winner.

NOTEBOOK
Spirito Del Vento(FR) is a top-class performer when on form. As usual he was held up for a long time before being brought with a spectacular late run up the centre of the track. He surged past his rivals and had the race sewn up just inside the final furlong. His trainer hopes he will receive an invitation for the Hong Kong Mile.
Racinger(FR), considering he had not been out for some time, put up an excellent performance. He broke well from the stalls and was in a perfect place to challenge halfway up the straight. He took the lead a furlong out, but had nothing in hand when the winner unleashed his final challenge.
Blythe Knight(IRE) was equipped with cheekpieces and his connections decided on a waiting race for him. He was not really seen until the straight and although not having the pace of the winner, ran on well to take third.
Bertranicus(FR) still had plenty to do at the entrance to the straight. He made his run at the same time as the winner, but was not able to make his presence felt towards the end.
Echo Of Light, last year's winner, wore cheekpieces on this occasion. Quickly into his stride, he took the advantage before the descent into the straight, but could not respond when the winner made his challenge. Official explanation: jockey said horse hated the soft ground and was always making hard work of it
Pride Of Nation(IRE) was unlucky as he was hampered halfway up the straight. He then stayed on up the far rail, but never looked like troubling the leaders.
Smart Enough, ridden less positively than usual after a ponderous start, moved into a challenging position rounding the final turn, but was a spent force in the straight.

6032a PRIX DOLLAR CASINO BARRIERE DE MONTREUX (GROUP 2) 1m 1f 165y

4:00 (4:00) 3-Y-0+ **£50,068** (£19,324; £9,223; £6,149; £3,074)

RPR

1 **Musical Way (FR)**^{11} 5719 5-8-10 .... RonanThomas 7 111
(P Van De Poele, France) *trckd ldr tl led wl over 1f out: rdn and edgd lft ins fnl f: drvn out* **9/1**

2 nk **Loup Breton (IRE)**^{49} 4627 3-8-9 .... C-PLemaire 9 115
(E Lellouche, France) *7th st: hdwy on outside wl over 1f out: disp 2nd ins fnl f: r.o one pce: fin 3rd, 1l, nk: plcd 2nd* **14/1**

3 nk **Boris De Deauville (IRE)**^{160} 1340 4-9-4 .... TThulliez 3 118
(S Wattel, France) *4th st: kpt on same pce fnl 2f: fin 4th: plcd 3rd* **8/1**

4 3 **Sageburg (IRE)**^{20} 5466 3-8-9 .... CSoumillon 5 108
(A Fabre, France) *hld up: 8th st: hdwy 2f out: 4th over 1f out: styng on u.p whn bmpd and hmpd ins fnl f: fin 5th: plcd 4th* **5/2**^{2}

5 1 **Rhenus**^{31} 5151 4-8-13 .... SPasquier 6 113
(A Fabre, France) *racd in 3rd to st: wnt 2nd over 1f out: hung lft ins fnl f: r.o same pce: fin 2nd, 1l: disq: plcd 5th* **20/1**

6 nk **Runaway**^{27} 5264 5-8-13 .... DBonilla 8 105
(R Pritchard-Gordon, France) *set gd pce: hdd wl over 1f out: grad wknd* **40/1**

7 nk **Stage Gift (IRE)**^{70} 3974 4-9-4 .... LDettori 2 109
(Saeed Bin Suroor) *5th st: rdn 2f out: one pce* **6/4**^{1}

8 8 **Troque (FR)**^{50} 4590 3-8-9 .... OPeslier 4 89
(F Doumen, France) *last st: a bhd* **40/1**

9 4 **Touch Of Land (FR)**^{31} 5151 7-8-13 .... JVictoire 1 80
(H-A Pantall, France) *hld up: 6th st: btn over 2f out* **15/2**^{3}

2m 4.20s (-0.20) **Going Correction** +0.05s/f (Good)
WFA 3 from 4yo+ 5lb **9 Ran SP% 117.8**
Speed ratings: **102,100,100,98,101 98,97,91,88**
PARI-MUTUEL: WIN 10.90; PL 2.60, 2.90, 3.50; DF 32.00 (Industry CSF £122.91, TC £1,049.88).

Owner S Constantinidis **Bred** Sarl Haras Du Tallis **Trained** France
■ Stewards' Enquiry : S Pasquier two-day ban; careless riding (Oct 15-16)

NOTEBOOK
Musical Way(FR) has really blossomed during the past month as she has won a Listed, a Group 3 and now a Group 2. She settled behind the pacemaker early on and took control halfway up the straight. She quickened clear and was never really in danger of losing her advantage. She now has many options as she could go for the Premio Lydia Tesio, the E. P. Taylor Stakes, and also to Hong Kong later in the season.
Loup Breton(IRE) started to make a challenge up the centre of the track from one and a half furlongs out and was putting his best work in at the finish. He was promoted to second place after a Stewards' enquiry.
Boris De Deauville(IRE), dropped out early on, came with a late run up the far rail. He had to wait a little bit before finding a gap and finished really well. This was his first outing for several months and this Group 2 winner is now likely to be aimed at the Premio Roma in early November.
Sageburg(IRE), who was supplemented for this race, as usual sweated up in the paddock. He had plenty to do coming into the straight and was then hampered half a furlong out. He was eventually promoted to fourth.
Rhenus had every chance and ran on at the same pace, but was eventually demoted for causing interference to Sageburg.
Stage Gift(IRE), who was in good form in the summer, was disappointing on ground he should have handled. Fourth coming into the straight, he was going nowhere by the furlong-and-a-half marker.

FLEMINGTON (L-H)
Saturday, October 6

OFFICIAL GOING: Good to soft

6033a BART CUMMINGS STKS (LISTED RACE) 1m 4f 133y
4:45 (4:45) 3-Y-O+ **£37,097** (£25,845; £12,923; £6,461)

				RPR
1		**Dolphin Jo (AUS)**[14] 5-8-5 (Terry & Karina O'Sullivan, Australia)	SebastianMurphy	111
2	2 1/2	**The Fuzz (NZ)** 5-8-5 (D Hayes, Australia)	CraigAWilliams	107
3	shd	**Light Vision (NZ)** 4-8-5 (R Smerdon, Australia)	CoreyBrown	107
4	1 1/2	**Sentire (NZ)**[364] 5817 6-8-5 (R Laing, Australia)	(b) BMelham	105
5	3	**Desert Master (AUS)**[175] 6-8-5 (B Jenkins, New Zealand)	DwayneDunn	100
6	hd	**Cefalu (CHI)**[336] 6346 6-8-10 (Lee Freedman, Australia)	WHernan	105
7	shd	**Bay Story (USA)**[278] 15 5-8-5 (B Ellison) 133/10[1]	MZahra	100
8	1 3/4	**Black Tom (AUS)**[278] 15 7-9-2 (F Maynard, Australia)	PHall	108
9	3	**Dicktator (NZ)** 7-8-5 (R Laing, Australia)	VDuric	92
10	1 1/4	**Shuaily (PER)**[294] 5-8-5 (Lee Freedman, Australia)	DMoor	90
11	4	**Derringer (AUS)**[481] 8-8-5 (J Salantri, Australia)	SSeamer	84
12	1 1/2	**Mont Fay (NZ)** 5-8-5 (Danny O'Brien, Australia)	JWinks	81
13	nk	**Bugatti Royale (USA)**[333] 6391 7-8-5 (Peter Morgan, Australia)	BShinn	81
14	3/4	**Red Lord (AUS)**[49] 4-8-5 (A Cummings, Australia)	CNewitt	87
15	1/2	**Special Scene (AUS)**[333] 6391 9-8-5 (Dan O'Sullivan, New Zealand)	LCurrie	79
16	20	**Utility (NZ)** 6-8-5 (P Carey, Australia)	MRodd	47

2m 39.06s (159.06) **16** Ran SP% **7.0**
WIN 5.10; PL 2.00, 2.70, 1.90; DF 25.00; SF 40.90.
Owner G N & Mrs L D Herrmann **Bred** Mrs G N Herrmann **Trained** Australia

6034 - 6035a (Foreign Racing) - See Raceform Interactive

5369 TIPPERARY (L-H)
Sunday, October 7

OFFICIAL GOING: Good (good to yielding in places on flat course)

6036a ABERGWAUN STKS (LISTED RACE) 5f
2:15 (2:16) 3-Y-O+ **£21,993** (£6,452; £3,074; £1,047)

				RPR
1		**Senor Benny (USA)**[7] 5842 8-9-1 104 (M McDonagh, Ire) *a.p: 3rd and rdn to chal after 1/2-way: led 1 1/2f out: sn drew clr: styd on wl ins fnl f* **3/1**[2]	DPMcDonogh 2	111
2	2 1/2	**City Of Tribes (IRE)**[88] 3431 3-9-1 103 (G M Lyons, Ire) *cl 2nd: led briefly under 2f out: 2nd and kpt on fr 1 1/2f out* **8/1**[3]	WJLee 4	102
3	shd	**Benwilt Breeze (IRE)**[7] 5842 5-9-1 102 (G M Lyons, Ire) *hld up in tch: 6th 1/2-way: 3rd over 1f out: kpt on u.p* **9/4**[1]	(t) MJKinane 11	102
4	2	**Empirical Power (IRE)**[7] 5842 6-9-2 95 ow1 (Edward Lynam, Ire) *led: hdd under 2f out: mod 4th and no imp fr over 1f out* **12/1**	DJCondon 7	95
5	nk	**Girl Power (IRE)**[7] 5841 3-8-12 76 (Edward Lynam, Ire) *hld up: prog under 2f out: 5th under 1 1/2f out: kpt on* **40/1**	(t) SMGorey 6	90
6	nk	**Canadian Danehill (IRE)**[19] 5513 5-9-1 (R M H Cowell) *chsd ldrs: 4th 1/2-way: wknd fr under 2f out* **8/1**[3]	(p) JAHeffernan 8	92
7	hd	**Majestic Times (IRE)**[7] 5842 7-9-1 98 (Liam McAteer, Ire) *chsd ldrs: 4th 1/2-way: sn rdn: no ex fr 1 1/2f out* **20/1**	(b) PatCosgrave 3	92
8	nk	**Moone Cross (IRE)**[7] 5841 4-8-12 97 (Mrs John Harrington, Ire) *hld up: nt clr run under 2f out: swtchd lft: kpt on same pce fnl f* **12/1**	(b) TPO'Shea 9	87
9	hd	**Speed Dream (IRE)**[42] 4861 3-9-1 100 (David Wachman, Ire) *a towards rr* **8/1**[3]	WMLordan 10	90
10	2 1/2	**Wildwish (IRE)**[37] 5023 3-8-12 81 (Enda Kelly, Ire) *towards rr: rdn and no imp fr over 2f out* **25/1**	CDHayes 5	78
11	4 1/2	**Bravely (IRE)**[7] 5842 3-9-1 90 (J S Bolger, Ire) *s.i.s and nvr a factor: bhd whn eased fnl f* **25/1**	DJMoran 1	65

58.66 secs (-0.34) **11** Ran SP% **119.4**
CSF £26.39 TOTE £4.30: £1.70, £2.90, £1.60; DF 30.90.
Owner M McDonagh **Bred** Landon Knight **Trained** Turloughmore, Co Galway
■ Stewards' Enquiry : D P McDonogh caution: used whip with excessive frequency and unnecessarily in the closing stages

NOTEBOOK
Senor Benny(USA), runner-up to US Ranger over 6f at the Curragh on his previous start, he had performed creditably behind Prix de L'Abbaye victor Benbaun in two Group 3 events at the Curragh last month, and he ran out an easy winner, stretching clear inside the final furlong having raced prominently. He may now be aimed at a Group 3 race in France and is to remain in training next year. (op 3/1 tchd 7/2)
City Of Tribes(IRE), back from a break, would have preferred faster ground. He raced in the front rank and got to the front under two furlongs out. Unable to match the winner, he kept on in the closing stages and just shaded the verdict for second place.
Benwilt Breeze(IRE) has been kept busy and, following his narrow defeat in the Ayr Gold Cup, he had finished one and a quarter lengths behind Senor Benny at the Curragh on his previous start. (op 9/4 tchd 2/1)
Empirical Power(IRE), dropping down in distance and with a bit to do at the weights, broke smartly and led for over three furlongs. Unable to make any impression over a furlong out, he kept on in the closing stages.
Girl Power(IRE) had a lot on her plate at the weights, and produced her best effort to date, chasing the leaders and keeping on inside the final furlong.
Canadian Danehill(IRE), who was gaining his sixth success of the year when winning off a mark of 83 at Yarmouth on his previous start, ran well upped in class.

6038a COOLMORE STUD HOME OF CHAMPIONS CONCORDE STKS (GROUP 3) 7f 100y
3:55 (3:56) 3-Y-O+ **£35,135** (£10,270; £4,864; £1,621)

				RPR
1		**Eastern Appeal (IRE)**[29] 5241 4-9-3 112 (M Halford, Ire) *settled 4th: prog ent st: 2nd and chal 1 1/2f out: led 1f out: kpt on wl* **5/2**[1]	MJKinane 7	109
2	nk	**Excelerate (IRE)**[29] 5242 4-9-3 99 (Edward Lynam, Ire) *s.i.s and bhd: last and rdn st: hdwy on outer under 1 1/2f out: 5th wl ins fnl f: r.o strly: nrest at fin* **9/1**	CDHayes 9	108
3	hd	**King Jock (USA)**[22] 5409 6-9-3 107 (R J Osborne, Ire) *trckd ldrs in 5th: prog into 3rd 1 1/2f out: kpt on u.p ins fnl f* **10/1**	TPO'Shea 5	108
4	hd	**Anna's Rock (IRE)**[38] 4985 3-8-12 103 (J S Bolger, Ire) *settled 2nd: rdn over 3f out: led under 2f out: hdd 1f out: no ex cl home* **6/1**[3]	DJMoran 4	104
5	1 1/4	**Hard Rock City (USA)**[63] 4211 7-9-3 112 (M J Grassick, Ire) *trckd ldrs in 3rd: 4th and rdn 1 1/2f out: no imp: kpt on same pce* **7/2**[2]	JAHeffernan 3	105
6	1/2	**Liscanna (IRE)**[7] 5842 3-9-1 103 (David Wachman, Ire) *hld up in tch: 8th 1/2-way: kpt on same pce st* **10/1**	WMLordan 8	104
7	nk	**Crooked Throw (IRE)**[16] 5609 8-9-3 97 (C F Swan, Ire) *dwlt: hld up in tch: 7th 1/2-way: rdn and no imp st* **16/1**	WJLee 1	103
8	2 1/2	**Brave Tin Soldier (USA)**[15] 5654 3-9-1 104 (A P O'Brien, Ire) *hld up in tch: rdn and no imp st* **12/1**	SMLevey 6	97
9	1 1/4	**Dynamo Dancer (IRE)**[10] 5761 4-9-3 104 (G M Lyons, Ire) *chsd ldrs in 6th: wknd ent st* **10/1**	WJSupple 10	95
10	1/2	**An Tadh (IRE)**[29] 5242 4-9-3 106 (G M Lyons, Ire) *led: rdn and hdd under 2f out: sn wknd* **9/1**	DPMcDonogh 2	94

1m 35.49s (95.49)
WFA 3 from 4yo+ 2lb **11** Ran SP% **125.9**
CSF £28.68 TOTE £2.20: £1.50, £4.00, £2.00; DF 31.00.
Owner Fair Is Fair Syndicate **Bred** Glashare House Stud **Trained** the Curragh, Co Kildare
■ Stewards' Enquiry : D J Moran caution: used whip with excessive frequency

NOTEBOOK
Eastern Appeal(IRE) produced a career-best effort to finish third in the Group 1 Matron Stakes (subsequently demoted to fourth) on her previous start. Always close up, she hit the front entering the final furlong and ran on well under pressure to prevail in a four-way photo finish. Her connections are toying with the idea of sending her to California on a Grade 1 mission. (op 5/2 tchd 9/4)
Excelerate(IRE), a three-time winner at this trip, had no easy task at the weights, and after being slowly into his stride and being well adrift of the rest early on, he came with a strong run on the outside in the straight and finished well. (op 8/1)
King Jock(USA) has performed quite well this season without managing to get his head in front, and he produced another good effort, keeping on well under pressure in the closing stages having been fifth into the straight.
Anna's Rock(IRE) had more to do here than when making all over the same course and trip last month, but she acquitted herself well, racing prominently and going to the front early in the straight. Headed under pressure about a furlong out, she kept on well to the line. (op 11/2)
Hard Rock City(USA), another consistent performer, was returning from a break following his big handicap win at Galway early in August. He tracked the leaders and had every chance before failing to raise his effort sufficiently inside the final furlong. (op 3/1)

6037 - 6038a (Foreign Racing) - See Raceform Interactive

6028 LONGCHAMP (R-H)
Sunday, October 7

OFFICIAL GOING: Good to soft

6039a PRIX DE L'ABBAYE DE LONGCHAMP MAJESTIC BARRIERE DE CANNES (GROUP 1) 5f (S)
1:15 (1:18) 2-Y-O+ **£96,520** (£38,615; £19,307; £9,645; £4,831)

				RPR
1		**Benbaun (IRE)**[22] 5436 6-9-11 (M J Wallace) *trckd ldrs: hdwy 1/2-way: led over 1f out: drvn out* **13/2**[3]	(v) PJSmullen 8	125
2	2	**Kingsgate Native (IRE)**[45] 4746 2-8-7 (J R Best) *trckd ldrs: hdwy wl over 1f out: rchd 2nd ins fnl f: r.o same pce* **5/2**[1]	JimmyQuinn 9	113
3	2	**Desert Lord**[15] 5632 7-9-11 (K A Ryan) *disp ld: led after 2f to wl over 1f out: kpt on u.p* **15/2**	(b) NCallan 10	111
4	shd	**Moss Vale (IRE)**[22] 5436 6-9-11 (D Nicholls) *prssed ldrs on outside: led briefly wl over 1f out: one pce* **12/1**	KFallon 17	111+

5 *nk* **Patavellian (IRE)**[15] 5616 9-9-11 ....(b) SteveDrowne 3 110
(R Charlton) *outpcd early: rdn and hdwy fr 2f out: nrest at fin* **40/1**

6 *nk* **Tiza (SAF)**[42] 4871 5-9-11 .... CSoumillon 14 108+
(A De Royer-Dupre, France) *towards rr tl hdwy fr wl over 1f out: nrst at fin* **40/1**

7 *3/4* **Derison (USA)**[21] 5468 5-9-11 ....(b) TJarnet 7 106
(P Van De Poele, France) *mid-div: hdwy over 2f out: 6th 1f out: one pce* **50/1**

8 *1* **Strike Up The Band**[7] 5842 4-9-11 .... LDettori 6 102
(D Nicholls) *disp ld on rails to over 2f out: one pce* **50/1**

9 *nk* **New Girlfriend (IRE)**[42] 4869 4-9-8 .... OPeslier 12 98
(Robert Collet, France) *nvr nrr than mid-div* **50/1**

10 *3/4* **Dandy Man (IRE)**[35] 5075 4-9-11 .... PShanahan 11 98
(Tracey Collins, Ire) *disp ld: cl 3rd whn hmpd and lost pl wl over 1f out: nt rcvr* **6/1**[2]

11 *hd* **Kocooning (IRE)**[21] 5468 4-9-8 .... C-PLemaire 2 95
(Robert Collet, France) *a towards rr* **150/1**

12 *hd* **Peace Offering (IRE)**[25] 5325 7-9-11 .... AdrianTNicholls 1 97
(D Nicholls) *nvr nrr than mid-div* **12/1**

13 *1* **Tycoon's Hill (IRE)**[44] 8-9-11 .... J-BHamel 5 93
(Robert Collet, France) *a outpcd* **150/1**

13 *dht* **Hoh Mike (IRE)**[45] 4746 3-9-11 .... JamieSpencer 13 93
(M L W Bell) *outpcd: last after 1f: sme prog fr over 1f out* **8/1**

15 *1 1/2* **Sonny Red (IRE)**[7] 5832 3-9-11 .... RyanMoore 15 88
(R Hannon) *a outpcd* **33/1**

16 *3* **Beauty Is Truth (IRE)**[45] 4746 3-9-8 ....(b) TThulliez 4 74
(Robert Collet, France) *stmbd start: a towards rr* **9/1**

17 *2* **Hogmaneigh (IRE)**[25] 5325 4-9-11 .... JimmyFortune 16 70
(S C Williams) *a outpcd* **25/1**

56.70 secs (-2.10) **Going Correction** -0.05s/f (Good) **17** Ran SP% **123.3**
Speed ratings: **114,110,107,107,106 106,105,103,103,102 101,101,99,99,97 92,89**
PARI-MUTUEL: WIN 6.80; PL 2.50, 1.80, 4.30; DF 8.80 (Industry CSF £21.87, TC £130.87).
Owner Ransley, Birks, Hillen **Bred** Dr T A Ryan **Trained** Newmarket, Suffolk

FOCUS
While this was fiercely competitive in terms of sheer numbers, it is hard to escape the conclusion that quality wise it was another pretty ordinary renewal. As usual, British-trained runners outnumbered the domestic sprinters, and they were overwhelmingly dominant at the finish. Benbaun was a clear-cut winner, appearing to show career-best form.

NOTEBOOK
Benbaun(IRE) is remarkably consistent by sprinting standards and had run up five Group wins at the Curragh since graduating from the handicap ranks. However, they were all Group 3s, and on the rare occasions he had been tried at this level, including in this race two years ago, he had been found wanting. He may well be better than ever at the age of six though, for he won this well after racing handily behind the fast pace from the start, but he is no champion. He will now have another go at the Hong Kong Sprint, in which he was beaten five lengths into third last year, and then next year his programme will revolve around the Global Sprint Challenge and so start with a trip to Australia.
Kingsgate Native(IRE), the Nunthorpe winner, was bidding to become the first juvenile winner since Sigy in 1978, but the weight-for-age allowance was not quite so generous as at York and he was encountering much softer ground. He ran a blinder in defeat, never far away from Benbaun and chasing him hard through the final furlong, but under the prevailing conditions and at the revised weights he was beaten fair and square. Connections did not blame the going, but they reckon he is better on fast ground and believe it will be a different story next year. Opportunities are few and far between for three-year-olds with Group 1 penalties in the first half of the season however, and one wonders how much advantage he has been enjoying this year as a highly-mature juvenile getting a massive weight concession.
Desert Lord, last year's winner, is another who would have preferred quicker conditions - the winning time was very nearly two seconds slower than in 2006 - so he did well to finish third, showing bags of speed as usual but finishing a place behind Kingsgate Native, just as he had at York. He could reoppose the winner in Hong Kong, but while he ought to get his ground there, the race is over 6f and he finished last in it in 2006.
Moss Vale(IRE) was a close third here last year and just missed out on the same position again. He had his chance and looked just for a moment or two as if he might win, but there were no excuses.
Patavellian(IRE), who has been handicapping lately but was the winner of this race back in 2003, came fast and late after being held up among the backmarkers. He is a veteran now, and while it was a cracking effort he will have enjoyed this ground more than most.
Tiza(SAF), a former South African-trained sprinter, did just the best of the locally-trained runners. He also came from well back and finished even better than Patavellian.
Strike Up The Band, who had helped force it up the rail, faded out of contention in the closing stages.
Dandy Man(IRE)'s luckless run continues. He would not have won, but he would have been considerably closer but for being badly squeezed out approaching the furlong pole. This relatively easy 5f should have suited him, but the ground had not dried out enough.
Peace Offering(IRE), a course-and-distance scorer in May, has never won at higher than Group 3 level.
Hoh Mike(IRE) wants a stiffer track. This one does not play to his strengths at all, and having made some late headway from the back of the field, the situation was accepted in the closing stages and he was eased down.
Sonny Red(IRE) was running over the minimum trip for the first time this season.
Hogmaneigh(IRE) was running in a Group race for the first time.

6040a PRIX MARCEL BOUSSAC ROYAL BARRIERE DE DEAUVILLE (GROUP 1) (FILLIES) 1m
1:50 (2:01) 2-Y-O **£115,824** (£46,338; £23,169; £11,574; £5,797)

RPR

1 **Zarkava (IRE)**[28] 2-8-11 .... CSoumillon 3 119+
(A De Royer-Dupre, France) *held up in tch: 7th st: hdwy on ins over 1 1/2f out: rdn and qcknd 1f out: rapid hdwy to ld cl home: readily* **6/1**

2 *2 1/2* **Conference Call**[34] 2-8-11 .... SPasquier 8 111
(P Bary, France) *led: rdn and r.o 1 1/2f out: hdd cl home* **9/2**[2]

3 *1 1/2* **Mad About You (IRE)**[35] 5073 2-8-11 .... PJSmullen 4 108
(D K Weld, Ire) *sn 2nd: rdn to press ldr 1 1/2f out: styd on at one pce* **11/2**[3]

4 *2 1/2* **Savethisdanceforme (IRE)**[10] 5757 2-8-11 .... KFallon 2 102
(A P O'Brien, Ire) *prom: 3rd st: drvn over 1 1/2f out: styd on at one pce to line* **28/1**

5 *1* **Don't Forget Faith (USA)**[24] 5353 2-8-11 .... PhilipRobinson 5 100
(C G Cox) *in tch: 4th st: sn rdn: styd on to line but nvr threatened ldr* **25/1**

6 *shd* **Peace Royale (GER)**[21] 5462 2-8-11 .... EPedroza 10 100
(A Wohler, Germany) *hld up in last: effrt and hdwy in centre fr over 1 1/2f out: nrest at fin* **20/1**

7 *nse* **Queen Of Naples**[16] 5596 2-8-11 .... JimmyFortune 9 99
(J H M Gosden) *hld up: pushed along st: rdn and no ex fr 1 1/2f out* **11/1**

8 *snk* **Laureldean Gale (USA)**[50] 4626 2-8-11 .... LDettori 11 99
(Saeed Bin Suroor) *midfield: 6th st: rdn to chse ldrs over 1f out: one pce* **6/5**[1]

9 *shd* **Belle Allure (IRE)**[20] 5493 2-8-11 .... DBonilla 1 99
(R Pritchard-Gordon, France) *prom: 5th and pushed along st: rdn and no ex fr 1 1/2f out* **100/1**

10 *1 1/2* **Gagnoa (IRE)**[21] 2-8-11 .... OPeslier 6 95
(Y De Nicolay, France) *towards rr: 8th st: n.d* **20/1**

1m 37.0s (-5.40) **Going Correction** -0.40s/f (Firm) **10** Ran SP% **119.4**
Speed ratings: **111,108,107,104,103 103,103,103,103,101**
PARI-MUTUEL: WIN 5.50; PL 1.80, 1.90, 2.20; DF 7.10 (Industry CSF £31.69).
Owner H H Aga Khan **Bred** His Highness The Aga Khan's Studs S C **Trained** Chantilly, France
■ Gipson Dessert (8/1) was withdrawn (broke out of stalls). R4, deduct 10p in the £.

FOCUS
After a period in the doldrums, this race looks to have turned the corner, with the likes of Finsceal Beo, Divine Proportions and Six Perfections figuring among the last five winners. Whether any of the ten fillies who took their chance in this latest renewal match the subsequent achievements of that sparkling trio remains to be seen, but Zarkava impressed and looks better than the bare facts. The third helps set the standard.

NOTEBOOK
Zarkava(IRE), a visually impressive winner, now figures prominently in the betting for the 1000 Guineas and Oaks. The winner of a maiden over this course and distance last month on her only previous public outing, she was supplemented for the race having pleased connections at home. She looked to have plenty on her plate when she was still towards the rear as they straightened up, and when she was snatched up 2f out it looked as if her chance may have gone. However, when seeing daylight, she quickened up nicely to win this by a comfortable two and a half lengths. She clearly has gears, but both the way she has finished her races, and her breeding, suggest she will have no trouble with middle distances next year. She is as short as 7-1 for next season's 1000 Guineas, and 8-1 for the Oaks, a race which at this stage would look the more likely target for her should she head across the Channel next year, although connections at this stage are favouring staying on their own shores.
Conference Call, whose trainer has a fantastic record in the race, made the running and it looked as if she might add to his tally. Having been shaken up 2f from home, she was not headed until the winner swept by inside the final half-furlong. This was the first time she had tasted defeat in three starts, and she looks a nice prospect for next year when the French 1000 Guineas will be her big early-season target.
Mad About You(IRE), the Moyglare Stud Stakes third, again filled the bronze medal position. She is another who looks like she will have no problems with middle distances (her dam won the Ribblesdale) and an opening quote of 20-1 for the Epsom Classic looks to be plenty fair enough.
Savethisdanceforme(IRE) was making a huge step-up in class. It took her four goes to lose her maiden tag and, while her trainer has more likely candidates for next year's Classics, it would be dangerous to suggest that she would not figure in the big races, particularly as the stable's star three-year-old filly of this season - Peeping Fawn - took the same number of starts to get off the mark.
Don't Forget Faith(USA), who disappointed in the May Hill last time, ran much better and got the verdict in the four-way battle for fifth. She looked to be slightly inconvenienced but it did not cost her and she looks a nice prospect for next year.
Peace Royale(GER) had done all her previous racing over 7f in her native Germany. It was probably the step-up in company rather than the longer trip which resulted in her finishing out of the frame for the first time.
Queen Of Naples looked up against it here having just the one run, a second in a Newmarket maiden, under her belt. She acquitted herself as well as could have been expected and will no doubt be winning soon.
Laureldean Gale(USA), runner-up to Proviso in the Prix du Calvados, was the big disappointment of the race after failing to find anything at all when asked. It is unusual for her connections to run one of their two-year-old purchases in their juvenile days, so she must have been showing plenty at home and it would be no surprise if it comes to light that something was amiss on this occasion.

6041a PRIX JEAN-LUC LAGARDERE (GRAND CRITERIUM) (GROUP 1) (C&F) 7f
2:25 (2:30) 2-Y-O **£135,128** (£54,061; £27,030; £13,503; £6,764)

RPR

1 **Rio De La Plata (USA)**[21] 5458 2-9-0 .... LDettori 2 119+
(Saeed Bin Suroor) *trckd ldr in 2nd or 3rd: smooth hdwy on ins to ld wl over 1f out: r.o strly* **8/13**[1]

2 *2 1/2* **Declaration Of War (IRE)**[86] 3504 2-9-0 .... RyanMoore 4 112
(P W Chapple-Hyam) *disp 2nd on outside: rdn to dispute ld briefly 1 1/2f out: sn hdd: styd on u.p* **16/1**

3 *shd* **Shediak (FR)**[28] 5260 2-9-0 .... CSoumillon 3 112
(A Fabre, France) *racd in 4th: pulling hrd early: stl keen and 5th st: swtchd ins to trck wnr over 1 1/2f out: kpt on* **5/1**[2]

4 *1* **Hatta Fort**[86] 3504 2-9-0 .... DarryllHolland 8 109
(M R Channon) *midfield: 4th st on outside: styd on at one pce u.p fr over 1 1/2f out* **20/1**

5 *1 1/2* **Young Pretender (FR)**[28] 5260 2-9-0 .... JimmyFortune 7 105
(J H M Gosden) *hld up in rr: 7th st: kpt on fnl 2f but nvr a factor* **5/1**[2]

6 *snk* **Greatwallofchina (USA)**[21] 5455 2-9-0 .... KFallon 1 105
(A P O'Brien, Ire) *led to wl over 1f out: wknd* **159/10**[3]

7 *2 1/2* **Manassas (IRE)**[17] 5575 2-9-0 .... RichardHughes 6 99
(B J Meehan) *last st: a in rr* **50/1**

8 *1/2* **Minneapolis**[10] 5760 2-9-0 .... JMurtagh 5 97
(A P O'Brien, Ire) *hld up: 6th st: outpcd fnl 2f* **33/1**

1m 21.5s (-0.90) **Going Correction** +0.10s/f (Good) **8** Ran SP% **116.7**
Speed ratings: **109,106,106,104,103 103,100,99**
PARI-MUTUEL 1.80; PL 1.40, 2.60, 1.40; DF 16.60 (Industry CSF £13.21).
Owner Godolphin **Bred** J De Camargo, Robert N Clay Et Al **Trained** Newmarket, Suffolk

FOCUS
This did not look a particularly strong renewal of the Grand Criterium, and there were fewer runners than usual. The winning time here was up to standard.

NOTEBOOK
Rio De La Plata(USA) set the standard, having won the Vintage Stakes and finished runner-up to New Approach in the National Stakes. None of his opponents had even run in a Group 1 before, so it was not surprising to see him start hot favourite and he justified that support in comfortable fashion. The last three winners of this - Oratorio, Horatio Nelson and Holy Roman Emperor - all subsequently finished runner-up in the Dewhurst and whether that contest will come too soon is something connections will decide next week, although they pointed out that he takes his racing well, suggesting he may be given the chance to turn out again at Newmarket. They believe that next season 1m2f will be within his compass, and that the Derby trip of 1m4f might also be within range. His National Stakes conqueror New Approach still heads the Guineas market but on this evidence he could give that rival more of a fight next time.
Declaration Of War(IRE), like the winner, was always quite prominent and kept on well, suggesting a mile will be no problem. He had been beaten a neck by Hatta Fort in a Group 2 at Newmarket the time before, but finished just over a length in front of him this time, suggesting he is progressing.

Shediak(FR) deserves plenty of credit for finishing third, seeing that he pulled hard virtually throughout. He had finished half a length behind Young Pretender in a Group 3 over this course and distance previously, but two and a half in front of that rival here, suggesting he is progressing.

Hatta Fort, having his first run since July, basically was never much better or worse than his finishing position, and has been a model of consistency.

Young Pretender(FR) ran on, having been ridden from off the pace. His dam was a winner over 1m2f and he may need further.

Greatwallofchina(USA) set the pace but was left well behind in the end.

Manassas(IRE) was well beaten, but was closer to Young Pretender than he had been at Newmarket on his debut.

6042a PRIX DE L'OPERA CASINO BARRIERE D'ENGHIEN (GROUP 1) (FILLIES) 1m 2f

3:00 (3:01) 3-Y-0+ **£96,250** (£38,615; £19,307; £9,645; £4,831)

RPR

1 **Satwa Queen (FR)**[49] 4652 5-9-2 .... TThulliez 7 116
(J De Roualle, France) *hld up: 8th st: hdwy trcking 2nd fr 2f out: drvn 1f out: r.o to ld last strides* **3/1**[2]

2 *hd* **Promising Lead**[53] 4503 3-8-12 .... RyanMoore 4 116
(Sir Michael Stoute) *hld up: 7th st: hdwy over 2f out: led over 1f out tl ct last strides* **12/1**

3 *hd* **Legerete (USA)**[21] 5465 3-8-12 .... OPeslier 9 116
(A Fabre, France) *hld up: last st: hdwy on outside 2f out: rdn 1 1/2f out: drvn and ev ch ins fnl f: unable qck cl home* **11/1**

4 *1 1/2* **Mystic Lips (GER)**[49] 4654 3-8-12 .... SPasquier 1 113
(Andreas Lowe, Germany) *set gd pce: led to over 1f out: r.o* **12/1**

5 *3/4* **Finsceal Beo (IRE)**[29] 5243 3-8-12 .... KJManning 8 112
(J S Bolger, Ire) *9th st: hdwy over 2f out: 5th over 1f out: r.o same pce* **8/1**

6 *1/2* **Light Shift (USA)**[64] 4149 3-8-12 .... TedDurcan 5 111
(H R A Cecil) *trckd ldrs: 5th st: rdn 2f out: one pce* **11/4**[1]

7 *3/4* **Diyakalanie (FR)**[21] 5465 3-8-12 .... TJarnet 3 109
(J Boisnard, France) *trckd ldrs: 2nd st: rdn and 4th on rail 1f out: grad wknd* **20/1**

8 *3* **Dominante (GER)**[70] 4013 3-8-12 .... EPedroza 6 103
(A Wohler, Germany) *6th st: sn btn* **20/1**

9 *6* **Vadapolina (FR)**[21] 5465 3-8-12 .... CSoumillon 11 91
(A Fabre, France) *10th st: a bhd* **4/1**[3]

10 *6* **Majounes Song**[49] 4651 3-8-12 .... KDarley 10 79
(M Johnston) *trckd ldr: 3rd st: rdn and btn 2f out* **40/1**

11 *3* **Mahara (USA)**[15] 3-8-12 .... LDettori 2 73
(J E Hammond, France) *hdwy and 4th on ins: wknd wl over 1f out: eased* **40/1**

2m 3.80s (-4.20) **Going Correction** -0.05s/f (Good)
WFA 3 from 5yo 5lb 11 Ran SP% **120.9**
Speed ratings: **114,113,113,112,111 111,110,108,103,98 96**
PARI-MUTUEL: WIN 4.00; PL 1.50, 4.20, 3.30; DF 37.30 (Industry CSF £38.10).
Owner S Lamprell **Bred** Ste Sogir **Trained** France

FOCUS

Not quite the quality of last year's outstanding renewal, but it still featured two Classic winners as well as last year's second and a couple of others with realistic claims. However, while three fillies fought out one of the finishes of the meeting, the two best fillies were below their best and the form does not look particularly strong by Group 1 standards.

NOTEBOOK

Satwa Queen(FR), who was racing exclusively against three-year-olds, had run the race of her life when second to Mandesha in this race last year, and she lined up again on the back of a similarly light campaign, with a last-time-out win at Deauville under her belt. The bare form at Deauville looked well short of Group 1 level, but she had been prepared especially for this and came from off the pace to collar Promising Lead in the last strides and record her first success at this level. In December she will go back to Hong Kong, where she was only sixth last year after running first at the Breeders' Cup.

Promising Lead had gained her Salisbury win at only Listed level, but is from a stable with a good record in this event. She was travelling well into the straight still under restraint, and she picked up in such style when asked to improve that she went to the front looking the likely winner. A good-looking filly from a superb family, she was only just worn down and clearly has a Group win in her if time does not run out.

Legerete(USA) raced in last until coming with a strong run up the outside which failed only narrowly. She is suited by further and might have won if she had been closer to the pace.

Mystic Lips(GER) enjoyed an easy lead, but was outpaced by quicker fillies in the straight. She looks to want further.

Finsceal Beo(IRE) was trying 1m2f again, having finished last in the Irish Champion on her only previous try. This was not her form, but it did not look as if it was the trip that beat her. She has been on the go a long time and seemed a bit flat, so she is probably finished for the season now. She stays in training with one of the big prizes in Dubai in March as her early target.

Light Shift(USA) was perfectly poised as they straightened for home, but it was soon clear that the change of pace she showed at Epsom was not going to be forthcoming this time. She might well stay in training next season.

Diyakalanie(FR), who has yet to win, raced handily on the inside and finished clear of the rest.

Vadapolina(FR), an enigmatic filly, was especially disappointing.

Majounes Song, a winner of a German Group 3 last time, faced a stiff task in this company and down in trip.

6043a PRIX DE L'ARC DE TRIOMPHE LUCIEN BARRIERE (GROUP 1) (C&F) 1m 4f

3:40 (3:40) 3-Y-0+ **£772,162** (£308,919; £154,459; £77,162; £38,649)

RPR

1 **Dylan Thomas (IRE)**[29] 5243 4-9-5 .... KFallon 6 127
(A P O'Brien, Ire) *hld up: disputing 9th st: sn pushed along and hdwy: wnt rt and crossed Zambesi Sun 1 1/2f out: r.o to ld appr fnl f: drvn out* **11/2**[3]

2 *hd* **Youmzain (IRE)**[35] 5077 4-9-5 .... RichardHughes 4 126
(M R Channon) *hld up in 7th: hdwy 2f out: drvn and hdwy to press ldrs over 1f out: fin strly and ev ch fnl 100yds* **66/1**

3 *1 1/2* **Sagara (USA)**[21] 5466 3-8-11 .... TGillet 11 123
(J E Pease, France) *hld up: disputing 9th st: fin wl through field fr 1 1/2f out: tk 3rd cl home* **33/1**

4 *shd* **Getaway (GER)**[21] 5469 4-9-5 .... OPeslier 10 124
(A Fabre, France) *hld up: 11th st: rdn and r.o over 2f out: styd on steadily down outside fr 1 1/2f out* **50/1**

5 *1/2* **Soldier Of Fortune (IRE)**[21] 5466 3-8-11 .... JMurtagh 5 124+
(A P O'Brien, Ire) *prom: disputing 3rd 1/2-way: led over 2f out: rdn over 1 1/2f out: u.p and hdd appr fnl f: one pce* **10/3**[2]

6 *4* **Saddex**[56] 4442 4-9-5 .... TMundry 2 117
(P Rau, Germany) *in tch: disputing 4th st: rdn and r.o to dispute 2nd 2f out: no ex fnl f* **25/1**

7 *3/4* **Mandesha (FR)**[21] 5467 4-9-2 .... (p) CSoumillon 3 112
(A De Royer-Dupre, France) *mid-div: 8th st: rdn 2f out: styd on u.p fnl f: nrest at fin* **12/1**

8 *2 1/2* **Zambezi Sun**[21] 5466 3-8-11 .... SPasquier 8 115+
(P Bary, France) *mid-div: disputing 4th on outside st: running on fr 2f out: crossed by wnr and snatched up 1 1/2f out: nt rcvr* **11/2**[3]

9 *1 1/2* **Dragon Dancer**[21] 5467 4-9-5 .... DarryllHolland 1 109
(G Wragg) *led 1f: disputing 3rd 1/2-way: disputing 4th st: drvn to keep pl over 2f out: wknd over 1f out* **150/1**

10 *snk* **Authorized (IRE)**[47] 4693 3-8-11 .... LDettori 12 108
(P W Chapple-Hyam) *settled in last: drvn on outside st: sn u.p: unable qck* **11/10**[1]

11 *15* **Yellowstone (IRE)**[29] 5250 3-8-11 .... PJSmullen 9 84
(A P O'Brien, Ire) *sn prom: 2nd 1/2-way: drvn and disputing ld st: sn hdd and one pce* **150/1**

12 *15* **Song Of Hiawatha**[21] 5466 3-8-11 .... DavidMcCabe 7 60
(A P O'Brien, Ire) *led after 1f: hrd rdn appr st: hdd over 2f out: sn eased* **150/1**

2m 28.5s (-6.50) **Going Correction** -0.05s/f (Good)
WFA 3 from 4yo 7lb 12 Ran SP% **121.4**
Speed ratings: **119,118,117,117,117 114,114,112,111,111 101,91**
PARI-MUTUEL: WIN 3.50 (coupled with Soldier of Fortune, Yellowstone & Song of Hiawatha); PL 2.70, 13.20, 5.80; DF 119.00 (Industry CSF £318.64).
Owner Mrs John Magnier **Bred** Tower Bloodstock **Trained** Ballydoyle, Co Tipperary

FOCUS

Although the field was half as big again as when Rail Link got the better of his seven rivals a year ago, this was still among the smallest Arc fields of recent times, with only one other renewal in the last 20 years - when Sinndar triumphed in 2000 - contested by fewer runners. The enforced absence of Manduro took the shine off the race slightly, and this renewal has been rated inferior to all but Sagamix's year in the last decade, with Dylan Thomas 4lb off his best in victory. It was still a high-class field for Europe's premier all-age race, and it culminated in enthralling fashion, the result only being confirmed after a painfully long stewards' inquiry.

NOTEBOOK

Dylan Thomas(IRE) was having his eighth race of the season, seven of which have been at the highest level, and five of which he has now won, while he finished runner-up on the other three occasions. With the ground softer than ideal, he was settled towards the rear and was always travelling sweetly before making headway over 2f out. He took up the running over 1f from home, before drifting right when he came under pressure, an incident which looked to inconvenience Soldier Of Fortune and Zambezi Sun and led to a nail-biting enquiry before the result was confirmed. This was only the fourth time he has raced over this trip and he was full of running at the end, having enough left in reserve to see off the challenge of the gallant runner-up. While future plans for him have yet to be confirmed, a trip to the Breeders' Cup Turf is a possibility. If we have seen the last of him, it will be fitting that he goes out on a high, and his name looks a worthy addition to the roll-call of great winners of this race.

Youmzain(IRE) put up a superb performance, running another excellent race in defeat, but whether he would have finished in such a prominent position if all his rivals had enjoyed a trouble-free passage is open to some debate. After tracking Dylan Thomas for much of the race, he was really motoring in the closing stages, getting much closer to him than when the pair finished first and second in the King George. He stays in training next year.

Sagara(USA), on whom the hold-up tactics worked well in the Prix Niel last time out, found them working again as he fared best of the six three-year-olds in the field. He was another to come from well off the pace and was again doing his best work late on. He proved that latest effort was no fluke, and could well be an interesting prospect for next season with connections revealing he will remain in training.

Getaway(GER) was always going to find it tough as a replacement for Manduro, but his connections must have been delighted with what they saw from their super-sub. Dropping back in trip and stepping up in grade, the stayer ran a cracker, particularly as he looked to suffer when Mandesha hung to the left 1f from home. He could prove to be a big player in the top Group races over this distance next year.

Soldier Of Fortune(IRE) had been campaigned with this race in mind for him some time. His jockey got first run on them at the top of the straight, although it looked unlikely that he would add to the fantastic record of Prix Niel winners in this race even before the scrimmaging. The race may have come a bit too quick for him, and he is another who will remain in training as a four-year-old.

Saddex was another who looked to have been aimed at this for some time having had just the three starts before this in 2007. He was up against a different class of rival here, and although he looked a little outpaced in the closing stages, connections were satisfied with this run. He will be off to either Japan or Hong Kong for his next start.

Mandesha(FR), who wore cheekpieces, came here off the back of a second in her trial, the Prix Foy three weeks earlier. This was the first time she had finished out of the first two since her debut in April of last year, and supporters of the normally consistent filly were aware of their fate a long way from home, as she never looked happy. She now retires to the paddocks.

Zambezi Sun went into plenty of notebooks after finishing third in the Niel, when not given too hard a time. He looked to be bang in contention before coming off by far the worst of those squeezed up in the incident a furlong from home. He stays in training at four.

Dragon Dancer looked to be lacking a change of gears when it mattered.

Authorized(IRE), a fine Derby winner who went on to beat Dylan Thomas in the International Stakes at York, had apparently been working well in the build-up to the Arc but was most disappointing. Drawn on the outside, he was none too well away and always in the rear. On the wide outside and still among the backmarkers into the straight, he failed to pick up when he came under pressure and could only beat the winner's two pacemakers, Frankie Dettori reporting afterwards he was never happy. It had been intended he should be ridden much handier, but the tactics employed were not to blame and Peter Chapple-Hyam later conceded the colt might have been overcooked. Already bought privately by Sheikh Mohammed, he now retires to stud.

Song Of Hiawatha, a supplementary entry, shared pacemaking duties with Yellowstone.

6044a PRIX DU CADRAN CASINO-THEATRE BARRIERE DE TOULOUSE (GROUP 1) 2m 4f

4:25 (4:50) 4-Y-0+ **£96,520** (£38,615; £19,307; £9,645; £4,831)

RPR

1 **Le Miracle (GER)**[21] 5469 6-9-2 .... DBoeuf 2 114
(W Baltromei, Germany) *settled in 5th: moved up to ld after 9f: rdn and r.o fr 2f out: styd on gamely fnl f: rdn out* **7/1**[2]

2 *shd* **Varevees**[21] 5469 4-8-13 .... TJarnet 7 111
(J Boisnard, France) *2nd early: disputing 3rd 1/2-way: 4th st: drvn and r.o to go 2nd 2f out: fin strly last 100yds: ev ch cl home: jst failed* **9/1**[3]

3 *3* **Yeats (IRE)**[22] 5437 6-9-2 .... KFallon 4 111
(A P O'Brien, Ire) *settled in 4th: 5th 1/2-way: pushed along on outside st: rdn over 2f out: wnt 3rd 1 1/2f out: nvr threatened ldng pair* **30/100**[1]

4 *1 1/2* **Balkan Knight**[23] 5376 7-9-2 .... JimmyFortune 5 110
(D R C Elsworth) *hld up in last: hdwy 1 1/2f out: disputing 3rd fnl f: kpt on* **12/1**

5 *2 1/2* **Juniper Girl (IRE)**[47] 4691 4-8-13 .... JamieSpencer 6 104
(M L W Bell) *led 9f: 2nd st: drvn 2f out: sn rdn and one pce* **20/1**

6 20 **Belle Epine (FR)**[16] 5-8-13 .... ACrastus 1 84?
(J J Chavarrias, Spain) *3rd: disputing 3rd 1/2-way: 3rd st: sn wknd* **200/1**
4m 29.8s (6.00) **Going Correction** -0.05s/f (Good) **6** Ran SP% **112.4**
Speed ratings: **86,85,84,84,83 75**
PARI-MUTUEL: WIN 7.70; PL 3.20, 3.00; SF 18.30 (Industry CSF £62.96).
Owner Rennstall Gestut Hachtsee **Bred** Comtesse B Von Norman **Trained** Germany

FOCUS
This looked a superb opportunity for Yeats to stretch his unbeaten record this year to five, but the form did not turn out as might have been expected in a race run at a very slow pace.

NOTEBOOK
Le Miracle(GER), whose rider was not happy with the moderate early pace, opted to kick on and increase the tempo with a mile and a half a mile left to go. It only proved to be a temporary injection of pace, however, and in what must be described as a brilliant tactical ride, Boeuf kept just enough up his sleeve to repel Varevees in what developed into a sprint finish. He had finished five lengths behind Yeats in the Gold Cup at Ascot, but that had been on ground more favourable to the latter. The last 11 different winners of this race to run again the same season all headed back here for the Prix Royal-Oak, which is apparently the plan for him, but only Westerner in 2003 and 2004 went on to victory there.
Varevees, receiving 3lb from the winner, only just failed to get up. He had beaten Arc fourth Getaway by a neck in a Group 3 here last month with Le Miracle five lengths back in third, conceding 8lb. That rather muddies the waters as far as the form is concerned, and it is no certainty these placings would be confirmed in the Royal Oak, especially if Le Miracle is not allowed a similarly soft lead.
Yeats(IRE) was well beaten, not looking at home on the ground, and perhaps not being ridden close enough to the pace. He may also have been unsuited by this course, so whether his campaign next year will be aimed towards Longchamp again must be debatable. He is unlikely to go for the Melbourne Cup now.
Balkan Knight has scored only at Listed level and was contesting his first Group 1. Given those facts, this was a fair effort. As a gelding, assuming he shows no sign of deteriorating over the winter, he's liable to be back next year.
Juniper Girl(IRE), who was also contesting her first race at this level, set a very slow pace and gradually faded after being headed after a mile.
Belle Epine(FR) was a 200-1 shot and ran like a 200-1 shot.

5462 DUSSELDORF (R-H)
Sunday, October 7

OFFICIAL GOING: Soft

6045a GROSSER PREIS DER LANDESHAUPTSTADT DUSSELDORF (GROUP 3) — 1m 110y
3:50 (4:00) 3-Y-O+ **£21,622** (£8,784; £4,392; £2,365)

RPR
1 **Mharadono (GER)**[99] 3122 4-9-1 .... WPanov 2 108
(P Hirschberger, Germany) *mde all: hrd rdn and hld on gamely whn strly pressed fr over 1f out* **403/10**
2 hd **Dubai's Touch**[28] 5265 3-8-9 .... RoystonFfrench 1 105
(M Johnston) *trckd ldr in 3rd: swtchd off rail and wnt 2nd over 2f out: sn hrd rdn: r.o gamely u.str driving: jst hld* **139/10**
3 6 **Santiago (GER)**[14] 5670 5-9-1 .... AStarke 7 95
(H Blume, Germany) *racd in 2nd: outpcd by first two fr 2f out: kpt on for 3rd* **2/1**[2]
4 1 **Wiesenpfad (FR)**[21] 5464 4-9-3 .... ADeVries 5 95
(W Hickst, Germany) *racd in 4th or 5th: wnt 4th over 2f out: sn rdn and nt qckn* **3/5**[1]
5 3/4 **Itzmo (GER)**[14] 5-9-1 .... HGrewe 3 91
(G Sybrecht, Germany) *a mid-div* **171/10**
6 2 1/2 **Lord Areion (GER)**[35] 5-9-1 .... THellier 4 86
(C Sprengel, Germany) *hld up in last: nvr a factor* **114/10**
7 18 **Mohandas (FR)**[7] 5851 6-9-1 .... ABoschert 6 48
(W Hefter, Germany) *racd in 4th or 5th: 4th st: sn wknd: eased* **19/1**
8 9 **Idealist (GER)**[14] 5670 5-9-1 .... TPQueally 8 29
(J Hirschberger, Germany) *a in rr: eased 2f out* **89/10**[3]
1m 46.45s (-1.13)
WFA 3 from 4yo+ 3lb **8** Ran SP% **133.7**
(Including 10 Euro stake): WIN 413; PL 57, 39, 18; SF 3,952.
Owner Stall Sonnenschein **Bred** Ralf Paulick **Trained** Germany

NOTEBOOK
Dubai's Touch none the worse for his recent trip to Turkey, put up a game effort in an attempt to win his first Group 3. He battled all the way to the line on ground that was on the soft side for him, but the front-running outsider did just enough to hold on.

5464 FRANKFURT (L-H)
Sunday, October 7

OFFICIAL GOING: Soft

6046a FRANKFURTER STUTENPREIS (GROUP 3) (F&M) — 1m 2f 165y
2:45 (2:52) 3-Y-O+ **£21,622** (£8,784; £4,392; £2,365)

RPR
1 **La Dancia (IRE)**[32] 5151 4-9-4 .... NRichter 2 102
(P Rau, Germany) *prom: led 1/2-way: rdn over 1f out: styd on to line: drvn out* **54/10**
2 3/4 **Fair Breeze (GER)**[43] 4838 4-9-4 .... AHelfenbein 11 101
(Mario Hofer, Germany) *prom: 2nd 1/2-way: pushed along appr st: rdn to chal on outside 1 1/2f out: ev ch over 1f out: styd on* **32/10**[1]
3 4 1/2 **Foreign Music (FR)**[35] 3-8-10 .... ABest 10 90
(H J Groschel, Germany) *hld up: hdwy 2f out: styd on to take 3rd 50yds out* **81/10**
4 4 **Go East (GER)**[35] 3-8-10 .... FilipMinarik 8 83
(P Schiergen, Germany) *in tch: styd on at one pce st: tk 4th nr fin* **36/10**[2]
5 1 1/4 **Highness (GER)**[84] 3-8-10 .... ASuborics 9 80
(W Baltromei, Germany) *led to 1/2-way: styd in tch tl one pce ins fnl f* **25/2**
6 1 **Nizza (GER)**[35] 3-8-10 .... AlxiBadel 1 79
(P Schiergen, Germany) *mid-div: 3rd 1/2-way: drvn early st: kpt on at one pce u.p tl wknd fnl f* **13/2**
7 1 **Vinea Federspiel (IRE)**[53] 3-8-10 ....(b) DPorcu 3 77
(Werner Glanz, Germany) *mid-div: shkn up 1 1/2f out: no imp* **9/2**[3]
8 1 1/2 **Red Diva**[35] 3-8-10 .... FrancisNorton 6 74
(Mario Hofer, Germany) *towards rr: n.d* **9/2**[3]
9 9 **Rabbit Montjeu (IRE)** 3-8-10 .... MSrnec 7 57
(V Luka Jr, Czech Republic) *towards rr: nvr a factor* **37/1**
2m 17.39s (137.39)
WFA 3 from 4yo+ 6lb **9** Ran SP% **131.9**
(Including 10 Euros stake): WIN 64; PL 24, 18, 28; SF 273.
Owner Gestut Brummerhof **Bred** Gestut Brummerhof **Trained** Germany

5821 SAN SIRO (R-H)
Sunday, October 7

OFFICIAL GOING: Good

6047a PREMIO DORMELLO (GROUP 3) (FILLIES) — 1m
3:10 (12:00) 2-Y-O **£38,767** (£17,057; £9,304; £4,652)

RPR
1 **Celtic Slipper (IRE)**[24] 5353 2-8-11 .... SebSanders 7 106+
(R M Beckett) *hld up: 9th st: n.m.r over 2f out: hdwy between rivals to ld 1 1/2f out: pushed out: easily* **5/4**[1]
2 5 1/2 **Short Affair**[35] 2-8-11 .... NMurru 11 95
(M Gasparini, Italy) *hld up in last: styd on down outside fr over 2f out to take 2nd on line* **104/10**
3 hd **Mia Diletta**[21] 2-8-11 .... DVargiu 5 95
(B Grizzetti, Italy) *prom: 3rd st: wnt 2nd 1 12/f out: kpt on but outpcd by wnr: lost 2nd on line* **43/10**[3]
4 2 1/2 **Mystic Lipstick (IRE)**[21] 2-8-11 .... EBotti 8 89
(J Heloury, Italy) *hld up in rr: 12th st: hdwy 3rd out: tk 4th ins fnl f* **25/1**
5 1 1/4 **Manipura (GER)**[43] 4837 2-8-11 .... URispoli 4 86
(A Wohler, Germany) *in tch: 6th st: ev ch 1 1/2f out: 3rd over 1f out: one pce* **2/1**[2]
6 1 3/4 **Belle Isnarde (IRE)** 2-8-11 .... LManiezzi 9 82
(V Caruso, Italy) *hld up: styd on at same pce fnl 3f* **68/1**
7 shd **Yacht Woman (USA)**[20] 5493 2-8-11 .... ASanna 13 82
(E Borromeo, Italy) *racd in 2nd: ev ch 1 1/2f out: wknd* **151/10**
8 snk **Radhakunda** 2-8-11 .... LSorrentino 14 82
(S Billeri, France) *hld up: rdn and nt qckn over 2f out* **119/1**
9 1 1/2 **Riblad (ITY)**[35] 2-8-11 .... MEsposito 10 79
(A Renzoni, Italy) *in tch: hdwy on outside to go 4th st: wknd over 2f out* **152/10**
10 2 **Lady Peanut (IRE)** 2-8-11 .... SMulas 6 74
(D Gambarota, Italy) *nvr a factor* **130/1**
11 1 1/4 **Luna Nel Pozzo**[35] 2-8-11 .... MDemuro 1 71
(L Riccardi, Italy) *racd in 3rd or 4th on ins: 5th st: ev ch on ins 1 1/2f out: wknd: eased fnl f* **137/10**
12 snk **Tremoto** 2-8-11 .... PConvertino 12 71
(F & L Camici, Italy) *midfield: wknd over 1 1/2f out* **23/1**
13 1/2 **Sopran Wolina (IRE)**[49] 2-8-11 .... GArena 2 70
(B Grizzetti, Italy) *led to 1 1/2f out: wknd qckly* **79/1**
14 15 **Sensazione World (IRE)** 2-8-11 .... FBranca 3 37
(B Grizzetti, Italy) *in tch tl wknd suddenly and eased 2f out* **43/10**[3]
1m 39.2s (-2.90) **14** Ran SP% **155.8**
(including 1 Euro stake): WIN 2.23; PL 1.37, 2.35, 2.03; DF 15.28.
Owner P D Savill **Bred** Peter Savill **Trained** Whitsbury, Hants

NOTEBOOK
Celtic Slipper(IRE), who finished third in the May Hill last time after chasing home Sense Of Joy at Goodwood, rewarded connections' enterprise by picking up this valuable Group 3 in straightforward fashion. She handled the ease in the ground well enough and came right away, and may stay in Italy for the Gran Criterium next weekend.

5745 PONTEFRACT (L-H)
Monday, October 8

OFFICIAL GOING: Good (good to firm in places; 8.4)
Wind: Virtually nil Weather: Overcast

6051 EBF SATURDAY RACING AT SANTA ROSA MAIDEN STKS — 1m 2f 6y
2:10 (2:10) (Class 4) 2-Y-O **£5,181** (£1,541; £770; £384) **Stalls** Low

Form RPR
2 1 **Planetarium**[7] 5858 2-9-3 0 .... GregFairley 1 90
(M Johnston) *mde virtually all: jnd and rdn 2f out: drvn ent fnl f and styd on wl* **7/4**[1]
34 2 1 1/2 **Mushtaaq (USA)**[18] 5570 2-9-3 0 .... RHills 6 87
(M A Jarvis) *trckd wnr: effrt 2f out: sn chal and ev ch tl rdn and one pce ins fnl f* **15/8**[2]
05 3 9 **Hada Men (USA)**[23] 5417 2-9-3 0 .... TedDurcan 4 71
(M P Tregoning) *in tch: hdwy to chse ldrs over 3f out: sn rdn along and kpt on same pce fnl 2f* **15/2**[3]
53 4 1/2 **Bite The Boss**[21] 5485 2-9-3 0 .... JamieSpencer 8 70
(E J O'Neill) *towards rr: pushed along 1/2-way: rdn 3f out: swtchd rt and hdwy u.p over 1f out: edgd lft ins fnl f: nrst fin* **14/1**
05 5 1 1/4 **House Of Tudor**[12] 5721 2-9-3 0 ....(v[1]) RobertHavlin 2 68
(J H M Gosden) *in tch: effrt and hdwy over 3f out: sn rdn along and no imp* **18/1**
642 6 1 1/2 **Elk Trail (IRE)**[21] 5485 2-9-3 75 .... MickyFenton 9 65
(T P Tate) *trckd ldrs: puswhed along 4f out: sn rdn and wknd 2f out* **14/1**
0 7 5 **Generous Boy**[69] 4037 2-9-3 0 .... DavidAllan 10 56
(T D Easterby) *a in rr* **100/1**
6 8 6 **Mashrai (IRE)**[31] 5206 2-9-3 0 .... TomEaves 5 45
(M R Channon) *chsd ldrs: rdn along over 3f out and sn wknd* **12/1**
9 4 **Bulas Boy** 2-9-3 0 .... PaulMulrennan 7 38
(E W Tuer) *s.i.s: a bhd* **100/1**
060 10 7 **Don Picolo**[61] 4293 2-9-0 46 .... PatrickMathers(3) 3 26
(P A Blockley) *chsd ldrs: rdn along on inner over 3f out: sn wknd* **100/1**
0000 U **Mister Cafnex (IRE)**[28] 5268 2-9-3 44 .... WandersonD'Avila 11 —
(B W Duke) *towards rr whn stmbld and uns rdr after 4f* **200/1**
2m 10.56s (-3.52) **Going Correction** -0.225s/f (Firm) **11** Ran SP% **112.7**
Speed ratings (Par 97): **105,103,96,96,95 94,90,85,82,76** —
CSF £4.94 TOTE £2.90: £1.20, £1.30, £2.40; EX 5.30.
Owner Sheikh Mohammed **Bred** Goldford Stud And P E Clinton **Trained** Middleham Moor, N Yorks

FOCUS
A staying maiden in which the front pair drew well clear and posted very good form. The winning time was smart.

NOTEBOOK

Planetarium, the one to beat on the evidence of his recent debut second over this trip at Bath, had clearly learned a great deal from that and Fairley soon had him in front. He looked vulnerable when joined by Mushtaaq turning into the straight, but in a fashion typical of his trainer's horses, found extra when strongly pressed and was nicely in top at the line. He is clearly going to appreciate trips in excess of this next season, but first it would not surprise to see him take his chance in the Zetland Stakes at Newmarket. (tchd 13-8, 15-8 in places)

Mushtaaq(USA), a highly promising third behind the smart Alfathaa on his debut at Newbury, failed to build on that when only fourth at Yarmouth last time, and although running better on this rise in distance, in the end he was no match for the winner. He was clear of the third though and a similar contest should come his way eventually. (tchd 2-1 in places)

Hada Men(USA) seems to be progressing a little with every run, but he was left trailing by the front pair in the final quarter mile and may prove best at 1m for the time being. He is now qualified for a handicap mark and should fare better in that sphere. (op 7-1 tchd 8-1)

Bite The Boss improved significantly on his debut effort when third over 1m1f at Redcar last time, keeping on as though this extra furlong would suit, but he got a bit too far back early on and, although making some late headway, he was never anywhere near the front two. He is another now qualified for handicaps.

House Of Tudor travelled well in the first-time visor, but he was readily left trailing in the straight and looks a horse of limited ability. (tchd 20-1)

6052 SOCA WARRIORS NURSERY — 6f

2:40 (2:41) (Class 5) (0-85,83) 2-Y-O — **£3,886** (£1,156; £577; £288) **Stalls** Low

Form — RPR

6406 **1** **Merchant Navy**[39] 4964 2-8-10 **72** .... TPQueally 3 — 75
(E A L Dunlop) *towards rr: hdwy 1/2-way: swtchd rt and rdn ent fnl f: styd on strly to ld last 50yds* **25/1**

2310 **2** *1/2* **Ramatni**[31] 5207 2-9-3 **79** .... RoystonFfrench 9 — 80
(M Johnston) *led: rdn 2f out: drvn and hung bdly lft ins fnl f: hdd last 50yds* **25/1**

2240 **3** *nk* **Natmana**[17] 5582 2-8-10 **72** .... TomEaves 12 — 72
(M R Channon) *cl up: rdn and ev ch 2f out tl drvn and one pce ins fnl f* **22/1**

2010 **4** *3/4* **Irving Place**[26] 5331 2-9-2 **78** .... HayleyTurner 4 — 76
(M L W Bell) *chsd ldrs: rdn along 2f out: kpt on u.p appr fnl f* **22/1**

5140 **5** *1* **Maddy**[56] 4453 2-7-13 **66** .... LukeMorris(5) 2 — 61
(R M Beckett) *in rr: hdwy over 2f out: rdn over 1f out: styd on wl fnl f: nrst fin* **12/1**

0561 **6** *1/2* **Leading Edge (IRE)**[4] 5939 2-8-4 **66** 6ex .... GregFairley 1 — 59
(M R Channon) *trckd ldrs on inner: rdn along 2f out: edgd lft and drvn ent fnl f and kpt on same pce* **10/1**

1600 **7** *3/4* **Dark Tara**[17] 5582 2-8-11 **73** .... (p) TonyHamilton 5 — 64
(R A Fahey) *towards rr: rdn along over 2f out: styd on u.p appr fnl f* **16/1**

0040 **8** *2* **Ski School (IRE)**[18] 5571 2-8-6 **68** .... PaulMulrennan 13 — 53
(W J Haggas) *s.i.s: a in rr* **25/1**

1 **9** *1 1/4* **Keep Discovering (IRE)**[28] 5277 2-9-7 **83** .... LDettori 8 — 64
(Saeed Bin Suroor) *trckd ldrs: rdn along 1/2-way: sn wknd* **7/4**[1]

403 **10** *1* **Birkintastic**[31] 5194 2-9-2 **78** .... KDarley 6 — 56
(B J Meehan) *a in rr* **8/1**[3]

1000 **11** *1 1/2* **Just Sort It**[44] 4812 2-9-2 **78** .... TedDurcan 7 — 52
(W Jarvis) *s.i.s: a in rr* **16/1**

2435 **12** *2 1/2* **Mission Impossible**[75] 3838 2-9-0 **76** .... LeeEnstone 10 — 42
(P C Haslam) *in tch: rdn along over 2f out and sn wknd* **16/1**

441 **13** *5* **No Page (IRE)**[10] 5770 2-9-1 **77** .... JamieSpencer 11 — 28
(B W Hills) *midfield on outer: pushed along 1/2-way: rdn 2f out: sn wknd and heavily eased ent fnl f* **9/2**[2]

1m 16.31s (-1.09) **Going Correction** -0.225s/f (Firm) — **13** Ran SP% **120.3**
Speed ratings (Par 95): **98,97,96,95,94 93,92,90,88,87 85,81,75**
CSF £522.73 CT £13593.91 TOTE £39.80: £7.70, £6.50, £7.50; EX 1190.60.
Owner Gainsborough **Bred** Gainsborough Stud Management Ltd **Trained** Newmarket, Suffolk

FOCUS

A modest but competitive enough nursery and a clean sweep for outsiders. Solid form for the grade.

NOTEBOOK

Merchant Navy, who ran well for a long way before failing to last the 7f trip at Lingfield last time, was down 3lb and managed to overcome trouble in running to run out a deserved winner, getting well on top close home from the wayward Ramatni. A soundly-run 6f clearly suits best and there may well be more to come from the son of Green Desert.

Ramatni, a tough filly who failed to run her race when last of 11 at Newbury a month ago, bounced right back to her best under an aggressive ride and may well have won had she not hung across towards the stands' rail. Her task is only going to get tougher, but she is the type who will continue to give a good account of herself. (op 22-1 tchd 20-1)

Natmana remains a maiden, but he ran above himself back in third and showed his recent disappointment in soft ground at Ayr to be all wrong. He is likely to remain vulnerable to improvers but a small race, possibly back in maidens, is bound to come his way eventually.

Irving Place, narrow winner off a mark of 75 two starts back, bounced back from a poor effort at Haydock last time, keeping on well in fourth, but he is likely to remain vulnerable to less exposed sorts. (op 25-1 tchd 20-1)

Maddy, never involved when getting going too late at Windsor last time, again left it too late before coming with her challenge and it may be worth employing more positive tactics on her in future. (op 16-1)

Keep Discovering(IRE), a 550,000gns buy who did not impress with his winning debut at Folkestone, had been handed a stiff-looking mark of 83 and he never threatened to justify favouritism, dropping away tamely. He is never going to live up to his price tag and has a fair bit to prove now. (op 2-1)

No Page(IRE) Official explanation: jockey said filly was unsuited by the good to firm (firm in places) ground

6053 TRINIDAD & TOBAGO H'CAP — 1m 4y

3:10 (3:17) (Class 3) (0-95,95) 3-Y-O

£9,348 (£2,799; £1,399; £700; £349; £175) **Stalls** Low

Form — RPR

5312 **1** **Dream Lodge (IRE)**[49] 4672 3-8-8 **85** .... TPQueally 6 — 97
(J G Given) *led: qcknd 2f out and sn clr: rdn over 1f out and styd on strly: edgd rt towards fin* **14/1**

1111 **2** *1 3/4* **Ella Woodcock (IRE)**[15] 5664 3-8-6 **83** ow2 .... DavidAllan 1 — 91
(E J Alston) *trckd ldrs on inner: hdwy wl over 1f out: rdn to chse wnr ent fnl f: kpt on* **10/1**

3011 **3** *3/4* **Russki (IRE)**[6] 5885 3-7-13 **79** 6ex .... (b) KirstyMilczarek(5) 7 — 87
(D M Simcock) *chsd ldrs on outer: effrt 2f out and sn rdn: drvn and edgd lft ins fnl f: kpt on same pce* **15/2**

1010 **4** *1* **Danehillsundance (IRE)**[9] 5797 3-9-4 **95** .... KDarley 5 — 99
(R Hannon) *hld up in rr: effrt and pushed along over 2f out: sn rdn and styd on appr fnl f: nrst fin* **9/4**[2]

3222 **5** *1 3/4* **Heroes**[4] 5950 3-8-12 **89** .... JamieSpencer 2 — 89
(G A Huffer) *t.k.h: cl up: pushed along over 2f out: sn rdn: wandered and wknd ent fnl f* **85/40**[1]

130 **6** *6* **Monkey Glas (IRE)**[2] 6016 3-8-4 **81** oh5 .... RoystonFfrench 3 — 67
(K R Burke) *chsd ldrs: rdn along wl over 2f out and sn wknd* **14/1**

5333 **7** *4* **Millestan (IRE)**[30] 5230 3-8-7 **84** .... TedDurcan 4 — 61
(H R A Cecil) *in tch: rdn along 1/2-way: sn lost pl and bhd* **13/2**[3]

1m 42.92s (-2.78) **Going Correction** -0.225s/f (Firm) — **7** Ran SP% **110.3**
Speed ratings (Par 105): **104,102,101,100,98 92,88**
CSF £129.22 TOTE £13.50: £4.40, £3.80; EX 79.80.
Owner The G-Guck Group **Bred** C H Wacker Iii **Trained** Willoughton, Lincs

FOCUS

A fair handicap dominated by three progressive sorts. The winner set only a moderate pace and the form has been rated at face value through the third.

NOTEBOOK

Dream Lodge(IRE), successful off a mark of 77 at Wolverhampton on his penultimate start, did little wrong in defeat back there next time and he seemed to benefit from this return to turf, showing improved form to defy a mark of 85. He is progressing extremely well and there should be more to come. (op 12-1 tchd 10-1)

Ella Woodcock(IRE), in search of a five-timer following back-to-back wins in claimers, was 13lb higher than when last winning a handicap and he arguably ran a personal best in defeat. It is likely he will be nudged up a few pounds for this, but he should continue to give a good account. (op 7-1)

Russki(IRE), another progressive sort in search of a hat-trick, was 6lb higher under his penalty, but it did not prevent him giving a bold showing back in third. He will need to improve further to win off this mark, but that is entirely possible. (op 11-1 tchd 7-1)

Danehillsundance(IRE), a progressive colt who just found things a bit too competitive in a big-field handicap at Ascot the other day, should have been suited by this step back up to 1m, but he got going too late having been held up and would have benefited from a more positive ride. (op 5-2)

Heroes has been running consistently well in defeat, but he has crept up the handicap as a result and this was a rare poor showing, failing to last home having taken a keen grip early. (op 9-4)

6054 PHIL BULL TROPHY CONDITIONS STKS — 2m 1f 216y

3:40 (3:40) (Class 3) 3-Y-O+

£7,478 (£2,239; £1,119; £560; £279; £140) **Stalls** Low

Form — RPR

6365 **1** **Love Brothers**[5] 5911 3-8-6 72 ow1 .... DavidAllan 1 — 73+
(M R Channon) *set stdy pce: pushed along and qcknd over 2f out: sn rdn clr: styd on wl* **20/1**[3]

2252 **2** *5* **Geordieland (FR)**[24] 5376 6-9-3 114 .... JamieSpencer 7 — 64
(J A Osborne) *hld up in rr: hdwy on wd outside 4f out: shkn up to chse wnr 2f out: sn rdn: drvn and edgd rt ent fnl f: sn no imp* **1/4**[1]

2005 **3** *1/2* **Baddam**[8] 5829 5-9-3 100 .... IanMongan 5 — 63
(M R Channon) *hld up in rr: hdwy on wd outside 4f out: rdn along 3f out and sn outpcd: styd on u.p fnl f* **4/1**[2]

6633 **4** *hd* **How's Business**[7] 5857 3-8-0 57 .... RoystonFfrench 6 — 59
(C A Cyzer) *chsd ldng pair: rdn along 3f out: drvn over 2f out and kpt on same pce* **50/1**

1300 **5** *1 1/2* **Victory Quest (IRE)**[146] 1752 7-9-3 59 .... (v) TomEaves 2 — 61
(Mrs S Lamyman) *chsd wnr: rdn along over 3f out and sn one pce* **150/1**

3325 **6** *3 1/2* **True (IRE)**[108] 2839 6-8-12 48 .... PaulMulrennan 3 — 53
(Mrs S Lamyman) *chsd ldrs: rdn along 4f out: wknd over 3f out* **200/1**

6 **7** *18* **Easement**[11] 5754 4-9-3 0 .... SimonWhitworth 4 — 38
(C A Cyzer) *in tch: hdwy to chse ldrs 6f out: rdn along 3f out and sn wknd* **200/1**

4m 3.89s (0.89) **Going Correction** -0.225s/f (Firm)
WFA 3 from 4yo+ 12lb — **7** Ran SP% **108.4**
Speed ratings (Par 107): **89,86,86,86,85 84,76**
CSF £24.15 TOTE £17.60: £7.30, £1.02; EX 34.40.
Owner Exors Of The Late Graeme Love **Bred** The Kingwood Partnership **Trained** West Ilsley, Berks

FOCUS

A slowly-run affair and clearly not form to take literally. Geordieland once again failed to live up to expectations and the winner did not need to improve.

NOTEBOOK

Love Brothers, officially rated some 42lb lower than favourite Geordieland on official ratings, managed to get the run of the race, with the 'big' two being restrained well in rear, and it was clear from the turn into the straight that he had it won. This was not a true test at the distance though and only a fool would take the form with Geordieland literally, so his future very much depends on what the Handicapper does now. (tchd 18-1)

Geordieland(FR) is one of the biggest underachievers around and cannot be backed on this evidence. Often a strong traveller in his races, he usually finds little under pressure and that was once again the case when runner-up toYeats in this year's Ascot Gold Cup. Without a win since coming from France, this looked the best opportunity he would find for a much needed confidence booster, but having been restrained well in rear he again failed to find under pressure and the winner pulled right away from him. He was reported to have finished distressed and will not run again this season, with a switch to hurdling also ruled out. (tchd 3-10 in places)

Baddam has been performing below his best for a while now and he was ridden all wrong. A winner over 2m6f at Royal Ascot last season, he was left woefully outpaced having tracked Geordieland through and failed to run his race.

How's Business, a 57-rated filly, had no right to finish as close as she did and connections must now hope the Handicapper does nothing silly.

6055 BUCCOO REEF "PREMIER" CLAIMING STKS — 1m 4y

4:10 (4:10) (Class 4) 3-Y-O — **£5,181** (£1,541; £770; £384) **Stalls** Low

Form — RPR

0020 **1** **Snow Dancer (IRE)**[13] 5703 3-8-4 68 .... PatrickMathers(3) 5 — 72
(A Berry) *hld up in rr: stdy hdwy 3f out: effrt to chse ldrs and n.m.r 2f out: rdn to chse ldr ent fnl f: sn edgd lft: styd on to ld last 75yds* **14/1**

0254 **2** *1* **Shotley Mac**[13] 5703 3-8-1 59 .... (b) AndrewMullen(3) 8 — 67
(N Bycroft) *led: rdn and qcknd clr wl over 1f out: drvn ins fnl f: hdd and no ex last 75yds* **14/1**

0453 **3** *1* **Lazy Darren**[10] 5768 3-9-0 76 .... TedDurcan 1 — 74
(R Hannon) *hld up and bhd: stdy hdwy 3f out: rdn over 1f out: styd on u.p ins fnl f: nrst fin* **8/13**[1]

6000 **4** *3/4* **Proper (IRE)**[9] 5819 3-8-9 70 .... TomEaves 4 — 68
(M R Channon) *in tch: hdwy to chse ldrs 3f out: rdn wl over 1f out: drvn and one pce ins fnl f* **16/1**

064 **5** *1 1/2* **Chin Wag (IRE)**[9] 5819 3-8-4 73 .... DaleGibson 7 — 59
(K R Burke) *t.k.h: chsd ldr: rdn along over 2f out: drvn wl over 1f out and grad wknd* **8/1**[2]

2165 **6** *2* **Demolition**[12] 5724 3-9-10 76 .... SimonWhitworth 10 — 75
(C A Cyzer) *trckd ldrs: effrt 3f out: sn rdn and wknd wl over 1f out* **9/1**[3]

0433 **7** *5* **Grethel (IRE)**[4] 5936 3-7-11 60 .... DanielleMcCreery(7) 3 — 43
(A Berry) *tk keen hld up towards rr: hdwy on inner: 1/2-way: rdn along 3f out and sn btn* **12/1**

1400 **8** 3 1/2 **Oscarshall (IRE)**[19] 5532 3-8-6 70 .... RoystonFfrench 6 37
(M H Tompkins) *midfield: rdn along 4f out: sn btn* **14/1**
6000 **9** 1/2 **Feeling Peckish (USA)**[73] 3908 3-7-11 38 ....(t) SophieDoyle(7) 2 34
(M C Chapman) *in tch: rdn along 4f out: sn wknd* **150/1**
0 **10** 9 **Mister Castlefield (IRE)**[38] 5026 3-9-5 47 .... AO'Shea(5) 9 33
(Mrs A M O'Shea, Ire) *chsd ldrs: rdn along over 3f out: sn wknd* **200/1**
1m 43.75s (-1.95) **Going Correction** -0.225s/f (Firm) **10** Ran SP% **117.8**
Speed ratings (Par 103): **100,99,98,97,95 93,88,85,84,75**
CSF £195.03 TOTE £13.40: £3.10, £2.60, £1.10; EX 127.40.
Owner Anthony Hanlon & Linda Wohlers **Bred** Liam Queally **Trained** Cockerham, Lancs
FOCUS
A modest claimer. The favourite disappointed but the front pair ran to form.
Snow Dancer(IRE) Official explanation: trainer had no explanation for the apparent improvement in form

6056 DEM WINDOW SOLUTIONS H'CAP 1m 4f 8y
4:40 (4:40) (Class 6) (0-60,60) 3-Y-0+ **£3,238** (£963; £481; £240) **Stalls** Low

Form RPR
3124 **1** **Compton Dragon (USA)**[87] 3496 8-9-2 58 .... KirstyMilczarek(5) 13 67
(W M Brisbourne) *towards rr: pushed along 3f out: gd hdwy over 2f out: chsd ldrs whn n.m.r and swtchd lft over 1f out: rdn to ld ent fnl f and styd on wl* **16/1**
3440 **2** 1 1/2 **Star Of Angels**[14] 5676 3-8-13 57 .... GregFairley 8 64
(M Johnston) *chsd ldrs on inner: hdwy over 3f out: rdn and ev ch over 1f out: drvn and one pce ins fnl f* **11/1**
0035 **3** 3/4 **Fenners (USA)**[27] 5300 4-9-6 57 .... DaleGibson 6 63
(M W Easterby) *in tch: hdwy over 3f out: rdn wl over 1f out and ev ch ent fnl f: sn drvn and kpt on same pce* **16/1**
5020 **4** 1 **Mabel (IRE)**[18] 5573 4-9-9 60 .... RoystonFfrench 11 64
(S C Williams) *s.i.s and hebind: pushed along and hdwy wl over 2f out: rdn and styng on whn n.m.r over 1f out: swtchd rt and r.o strly ins fnl f: nrst fin* **20/1**
435 **5** 1 3/4 **Fantasy Ride**[16] 5640 5-9-8 59 .... TPQueally 5 60
(J Pearce) *in tch: hdwy on outer to chse ldrs over 2f out: sn rdn and hung lft jst over 1f out: drvn and kpt on same pce ins fnl f* **17/2**[3]
4500 **6** 1/2 **Intavac Boy**[11] 5750 6-8-10 54 .... PatrickDonaghy(7) 4 55
(S P Griffiths) *in tch: hdwy to chse ldrs 1/2-way: rdn and ch whn edgd lft over 1f out: sn drvn and wknd ins fnl f* **20/1**
0021 **7** 3 **Mister Fizzbomb (IRE)**[13] 5698 4-9-4 55 ....(v) DanielTudhope 14 51
(J S Wainwright) *chsd ldng pair: hdwy to ld 3f out: rdn wl over 1f out: drvn and hdd ent fnl f: wknd* **10/1**
0010 **8** 6 **Hermanita**[19] 5531 3-9-2 60 .... TedDurcan 3 46
(G Wragg) *midfield: effrt 3f out: sn rdn and no imp* **14/1**
0622 **9** nk **Dance Sauvage**[35] 5087 4-8-10 50 .... PJMcDonald(3) 1 36
(C W Thornton) *towards rr: effrt and sme hdwy over 4f out: sn rdn along and nvr a factor* **8/1**[2]
4330 **10** 3 **Hugs Destiny (IRE)**[29] 5257 6-8-13 57 ....(t) SophieDoyle(7) 7 38
(M A Barnes) *led: rdn along 4f out: hdd 3f out and grad wknd fnl 2f* **20/1**
1004 **11** 1 3/4 **Paparaazi (IRE)**[8] 5835 5-9-9 60 .... TonyHamilton 2 38
(I W McInnes) *midfield: effrt 3f out: sn rdn and nvr a factor* **33/1**
0204 **12** 30 **Dreams Jewel**[15] 4463 7-9-2 53 .... RobertHavlin 17 —
(C Roberts) *dwlt: hdwy on wd outside and in tch 1/2-way: sn rdn and wknd* **50/1**
00-1 **13** 12 **Me Fein**[41] 4914 3-9-0 58 .... JamieSpencer 9 —
(B J Curley) *trckd ldrs: effrt and hdwy over 3f out: rdn ov er 2f out and sn wknd* **6/5**[1]
-600 **14** 6 **Vehari**[31] 5188 4-8-9 53 .... DanielleMcCreery(7) 10 —
(G F Bridgwater) *dwlt: a in rr* **100/1**
600 **15** dist **El Alamein (IRE)**[29] 5257 4-9-9 60 .... PaulMulrennan 12 —
(Sir Mark Prescott) *chsd ldr: rdn along over 5f out: sn wknd and bhd* **16/1**
2m 36.86s (-3.44) **Going Correction** -0.225s/f (Firm)
WFA 3 from 4yo+ 7lb **15** Ran SP% **129.0**
Speed ratings (Par 101): **102,101,100,99,98 98,96,92,92,90 88,68,60,56,—**
CSF £179.51 CT £2898.66 TOTE £21.80: £5.10, £3.40, £4.30; EX 277.30.
Owner John Connor **Bred** Orpendale & Partners **Trained** Great Ness, Shropshire
FOCUS
A moderate handicap run at a good pace. Solid form, the winner rated to his 2005 level.
Me Fein Official explanation: trainer had no explanation for the poor form shown

6057 MARACAS BAY MAIDEN STKS 1m 4y
5:10 (5:10) (Class 5) 3-Y-0 **£3,238** (£963; £481; £240) **Stalls** Low

Form RPR
6223 **1** **Handset (USA)**[12] 5728 3-8-12 66 .... TedDurcan 1 72
(H R A Cecil) *trckd ldrs: hdwy on inner to ld 2f out: rdn clr over 1f out: styd on wl fnl f* **5/1**[3]
5203 **2** 1 3/4 **Sonning Star (IRE)**[13] 5703 3-9-3 72 .... IanMongan 9 73
(D R C Elsworth) *dwlt: trckd ldrs on inner: hdwy 3f out: rdn to chse wnr wl over 1f out: drvn ins fnl f and kpt on same* **15/8**[2]
3532 **3** 6 **Paradise Dancer (IRE)**[18] 5568 3-8-12 70 .... JamieSpencer 8 54
(Pat Eddery) *hld up in tch: hdwy 3f out: rdn to chse ldng pair 2f out: sn drvn and btn* **7/4**[1]
0640 **4** 6 **Joyful Tears (IRE)**[7] 5865 3-8-12 64 .... GregFairley 6 40
(M G Quinlan) *trckd leaders: rdn along over 3f out: wknd over 2f out* **16/1**
6634 **5** 9 **First Valentini**[21] 5488 3-8-9 45 .... DuranFentiman(3) 3 20
(N Bycroft) *prom: lft in ld after 2f: rdn along over 2f out: sn hdd & wknd* **100/1**
3-3 **6** 5 **Namibian Pink (IRE)**[53] 4541 3-8-9 0 .... PJMcDonald(3) 7 8
(R M Beckett) *chsd ldrs: rdn along 3f out and sn wknd* **8/1**
0-6 **7** 7 **Still Calm**[26] 5335 3-9-3 0 .... PaulMulrennan 2 —
(N J Vaughan) *hung rt thrght: led tl rn wd bnd after 2f: prom tl rdn along and wkng whn rn v wd home turn and sn bhd* **14/1**
056 **8** 8 **Betterlatethanever (IRE)**[37] 5045 3-9-3 41 .... TomEaves 5 —
(C J Teague) *prom: wd bnd after 2f: rdn along 1/2-way: sn lost pl and bhd* **100/1**
1m 44.33s (-1.37) **Going Correction** -0.225s/f (Firm) **8** Ran SP% **113.5**
Speed ratings (Par 101): **97,95,89,83,74 69,62,54**
CSF £14.55 TOTE £5.90: £1.70, £1.30, £1.30; EX 12.50 Place 6 £9,290.92, Place 5 £8,058.68.
Owner K Abdulla **Bred** Juddmonte Farms Inc **Trained** Newmarket, Suffolk
FOCUS
A modest maiden in which two drew clear. Most of these looked exposed and the form has not been rated too positively.
Paradise Dancer(IRE) Official explanation: jockey said filly hung right throughout
Still Calm Official explanation: jockey said gelding hung right throughout
T/Plt: £708.90 to a £1 stake. Pool: £50,936.75. 52.45 winning tickets. T/Qpdt: £56.00 to a £1 stake. Pool: £4,345.30. 57.40 winning tickets. JR

5868 WINDSOR (R-H)
Monday, October 8
OFFICIAL GOING: Good (good to soft in places)
Wind: Almost nil Weather: Overcast

6058 EUROPEAN BREEDERS' FUND MAIDEN STKS 1m 67y
2:30 (2:32) (Class 4) 2-Y-O **£4,533** (£1,348; £674; £336) **Stalls** High

Form RPR
233 **1** **Rochefort (IRE)**[14] 5679 2-9-3 83 .... JimmyFortune 7 73+
(J H M Gosden) *mde all: drew clr over 2f out: abt 4 l clr 1f out: eased* **15/8**[2]
2 **2** 1 **City Stable (IRE)**[19] 5541 2-9-3 0 .... KerrinMcEvoy 4 71+
(Sir Michael Stoute) *hld up in midfield: plenty to do 3f out: pushed along and prog over 2f out: rdn and r.o to take 2nd ins fnl f: no ch of chalng wnr* **1/1**[1]
6043 **3** 3/4 **Hit The Roof**[14] 5680 2-9-3 75 .... PatDobbs 10 69
(R Hannon) *prom: chsd wnr over 4f out: rdn and carried hd high over 2f out: no imp tl passed for 2nd and r.o ins fnl f* **16/1**
06 **4** 5 **Oxbridge**[26] 5329 2-9-3 0 .... SteveDrowne 12 59
(B J Meehan) *chsd wnr to over 4f out: outpcd over 2f out: n.d after* **50/1**
5 1 1/2 **Clovis** 2-9-3 0 .... J-PGuillambert 5 55
(M Johnston) *s.i.s: rn green in rr: shkn up 1/2-way: no real prog tl styd on fr over 1f out* **25/1**
05 **6** shd **Looter (FR)**[27] 5306 2-9-3 0 .... DaneO'Neill 11 55
(J L Dunlop) *chsd ldrs: rdn over 2f out: grad wknd* **50/1**
000 **7** 2 1/2 **Ice Choice (IRE)**[17] 5592 2-8-6 51 ow1 .... JackDean(7) 8 46
(Mark Gillard) *chsd ldrs: rdn over 3f out: wandering 2f out: wknd* **100/1**
60 **8** 1 **Hadron Collider (FR)**[42] 4876 2-9-3 0 .... DarryllHolland 13 48
(R Hannon) *chsd ldrs: rdn over 3f out: wknd 2f out* **28/1**
9 shd **Special Feature (IRE)** 2-9-3 0 .... RichardMullen 2 48
(C R Egerton) *v green in last pair: nvr a factor: modest late prog* **66/1**
00 **10** 3 **Oli James (USA)**[20] 5498 2-9-3 0 .... NelsonDeSouza 1 41
(P F I Cole) *a wl in rr: rdn and no prog 4f out* **33/1**
204 **11** 1 1/4 **Effingham (IRE)**[10] 5772 2-9-3 78 .... MichaelHills 6 39
(B W Hills) *chsd ldrs: u.p and struggling wl over 3f out: wknd 2f out* **8/1**[3]
00 **12** 3/4 **All Lit Up**[34] 5116 2-9-3 0 .... FergusSweeney 3 37
(A King) *a in last trio: rdn over 3f out: no prog* **100/1**
1m 45.92s (1.22) **Going Correction** +0.05s/f (Good) **12** Ran SP% **119.4**
Speed ratings (Par 97): **95,94,93,88,86 86,84,83,83,80 78,78**
CSF £3.86 TOTE £2.60: £1.10, £1.10, £4.20; EX 5.20 Trifecta £29.00 Pool £300.17 - 7.33 winning units..
Owner H R H Princess Haya Of Jordan **Bred** John Fielding **Trained** Newmarket, Suffolk
FOCUS
Just an ordinary maiden and, with Rochefort allowed the run of the race in front, few of these got involved from off the pace. The likes of the seventh home govern the merit, and the first two can do better.
NOTEBOOK
Rochefort(IRE) had been a beaten favourite on all three of his career starts, including when turned over at 1/2 on the Polytrack at Kempton on his previous start, but he was allowed the run of the race this time and made no mistake. This was a good effort, but everything fell kindly for him and he is likely to find things tougher next time. (op 9-4)
City Stable(IRE), a four-length second on his debut over 7f at Yarmouth, again found one too good. He just took too long to pick up and was unable to reel in Rochefort, who had enjoyed a soft lead. (tchd 10-11 and 11-10)
Hit The Roof finished well clear of the remainder and ran about as well as could have been expected. He might find his level once switched to nursery company. (tchd 20-1)
Oxbridge ran a respectable race in fourth and will have more options now he is qualified for a handicap mark.
Clovis, a Kingmambo colt, brother to 6f juvenile winner Catherine Howard, out of a quite useful dual 6f-7f winner, ran green and looked in need of the experience. He should know a lot more next time and can show improved form. (op 16-1)
Looter(FR) is another now qualified for a handicap mark and he could be one to keep on the right side of.

6059 GOLDRINGSECURITY.COM NURSERY 5f 10y
3:00 (3:01) (Class 4) (0-95,95) 2-Y-O **£3,886** (£1,156; £577; £288) **Stalls** High

Form RPR
0125 **1** **Mesmerize Me**[17] 5583 2-8-13 87 .... RichardMullen 2 89
(E S McMahon) *bmpd s: gd spd and rcvrd to chse ldr over 3f out: rdn to ld over 1f out: hld on wl u.p* **8/1**
14 **2** 1/2 **Ancien Regime (IRE)**[23] 5410 2-9-5 93 .... PhilipRobinson 5 93
(M A Jarvis) *t.k.h: hld up in rr: prog 2f out: sltly impeded and swtchd lft 1f out: pressed wnr last 150yds: nt qckn* **6/4**[1]
6506 **3** 1/2 **Master Chef (IRE)**[17] 5597 2-9-7 95 ....(b) JimmyFortune 7 93
(J H M Gosden) *slowly away: hld up in rr: prog on wd outside 2f out: drvn to press ldrs fnl f: a hld* **7/1**
0440 **4** 1 **Barraland**[9] 5802 2-8-0 74 .... AdrianMcCarthy 3 69
(M R Channon) *led to over 1f out: one pce u.p* **10/1**
1022 **5** 3/4 **Thunder Bay**[9] 5802 2-9-0 88 .... DarryllHolland 1 80
(M R Channon) *chsd ldrs: shkn up and nt qckn wl over 1f out: one pce after* **5/1**[2]
1166 **6** 1 1/4 **Concertmaster**[24] 5393 2-8-5 79 ow1 .... KerrinMcEvoy 8 67
(R M Beckett) *chsd ldr to over 3f out: lost pl 1/2-way: no prog over 1f out* **6/1**[3]
2010 **7** 1 **Our Acquaintance**[10] 5773 2-8-3 77 .... LiamJones 9 61
(W R Muir) *a towards rr: rdn and no imp wl over 1f out* **25/1**
6223 **8** 3 1/2 **Rathmolyon**[32] 5176 2-8-0 74 .... DavidKinsella 4 45
(D Haydn Jones) *plld hrd: hld up: stl taking t.k.h 2f out: wknd tamely jst over 1f out* **16/1**
60.17 secs (-0.93) **Going Correction** -0.25s/f (Firm) **8** Ran SP% **113.4**
Speed ratings (Par 97): **97,96,95,93,92 90,89,83**
CSF £20.11 CT £90.16 TOTE £8.90: £1.90, £1.10, £2.00; EX 36.70 Trifecta £139.60 Pool £273.35 - 1.39 winning units..
Owner J C Fretwell **Bred** Mrs R Pease **Trained** Lichfield, Staffs
FOCUS
A good, competitive nursery and solid form.
NOTEBOOK
Mesmerize Me struggled in Listed company at Ayr on his previous start, but he was able to take advantage of the drop in class. He was a touch slow to find his stride and was bumped slightly by Barraland, but he soon recovered and picked up best of all when it mattered. He may be off to the sales at some point, but should make a nice sprinter for somebody next year. (op 15-2 tchd 9-1)
Ancien Regime(IRE), a beaten favourite in a conditions contest over 6f at Doncaster on his previous start, had to switch round the eventual winner ever so slightly in the closing stages, but he was not unlucky. This was still a very useful effort in defeat. (op 11-8 tchd 11-10)

Master Chef(IRE) ran right up to his best under top weight, but he just gave the impression he might be capable of even better back over 6f. (op 5-1)
Barraland took them along at a strong pace from the outset, trying to make the most of his light weight, but he was gradually reeled in. Similar tactics could pay off in a lesser contest. Official explanation: jockey said gelding jumped awkwardly on leaving stalls (op 14-1)
Thunder Bay did not seem to do much wrong, but he basically just looks plenty high enough in the weights. (op 13-2 tchd 7-1)
Concertmaster, carrying 1lb overweight, struggled to make any real impression and was not at his best. Official explanation: jockey said colt hung left first 3f (op 8-1)

6060 ARENA LEISURE CATERING (S) STKS 1m 2f 7y
3:30 (3:31) (Class 5) 3-Y-O **£2,817** (£838; £418; £209) **Stalls** Centre

Form RPR
0002 **1** **Almahaza (IRE)**[35] 5095 3-9-0 55....................(b) PatDobbs 11 55
(Mrs A J Perrett) *trckd ldrs: rdn and prog over 2f out: led 1f out: hung bdly lft but sn wl in command* **4/1**[1]
0050 **2** *2* **Doonigan (IRE)**[23] 5421 3-9-0 45.................... DarryllHolland 9 51
(A M Balding) *led to 6f out: pressed ldr: led 3f out to 1f out: kpt on but no real ch w wnr* **14/1**
5230 **3** *½* **Dr Dream (IRE)**[30] 5235 3-9-0 50....................(b[1]) FergusSweeney 8 50
(J G M O'Shea) *w ldr: led 6f out to 3f out: upsides jst over 1f out: nt qckn* **14/1**
660- **4** *½* **Fasuby (IRE)**[398] 5084 3-8-9 53.................... TGMcLaughlin 15 44
(P D Evans) *towards rr: outpcd over 3f out: kpt on u.p fr 2f out: nrst fin* **33/1**
-503 **5** *hd* **Persian Fox (IRE)**[20] 5511 3-9-0 55.................... SteveDrowne 1 49+
(G A Huffer) *t.k.h early: hld up: last over 4f out: shkn up and r.o fr over 2f out: gng on at fin but no ch* **7/1**
4600 **6** *shd* **Miss Habershon**[7] 5859 3-8-9 65.................... DaneO'Neill 4 43
(A King) *chsd ldrs: rdn and outpcd 3f out: tried to rally on wd outside 2f out: kpt on one pce* **11/2**[2]
-056 **7** *nk* **Sea Cookie**[10] 5774 3-8-6 45.................... TravisBlock(3) 14 43
(W De Best-Turner) *towards rr: outpcd over 3f out: kpt on u.p fnl 2f: n.d* **14/1**
0 **8** *1 ½* **Go Dude**[26] 5342 3-8-11 59....................(b[1]) MarcHalford(3) 12 45
(J Ryan) *rousted along to go prom: drvn over 3f out: wknd 2f out* **11/1**
0006 **9** *hd* **Ten Black**[25] 5345 3-9-0 40.................... LiamJones 5 44
(R Brotherton) *rousted along early: rchd midfield after 4f: rdn over 3f out: sn outpcd: n.d after* **50/1**
3054 **10** *1* **Party Palace**[159] 1397 3-8-9 47.................... AdrianMcCarthy 10 37
(H S Howe) *trckd ldrs: outpcd 3f out: rdn and brief effrt 2f out: sn wknd* **20/1**
6540 **11** *1* **Mayireneyrbel**[7] 5865 3-9-1 55.................... J-PGuillambert 16 41
(J Akehurst) *nvr bttr than midfield: rdn over 3f out: sn btn* **9/1**
2046 **12** *5* **Give Evidence**[12] 5739 3-9-0 46.................... NelsonDeSouza 13 30
(A P Jarvis) *t.k.h early: hld up in rr: struggling fr 4f out: bhd after* **6/1**[3]
00-0 **13** *3 ½* **Bronco's Filly (IRE)**[103] 2978 3-8-2 40.................... MCGeran(7) 3 18
(J G M O'Shea) *a wl in rr: rdn and struggling over 3f out* **100/1**
4400 **14** *12* **Hot Property (IRE)**[12] 5739 3-9-0 53....................(b[1]) RichardMullen 7 —
(W R Muir) *wnt lft s: drvn to press ldrs: wknd u.p 3f out: t.o: lame* **14/1**
0400 **15** *7* **Bertrada (IRE)**[46] 4742 3-8-9 48....................(v[1]) SaleemGolam 6 —
(G P Enright) *rousted along early: a wl in rr: t.o* **66/1**
00- **16** *6* **Break 'N' Dish**[357] 6016 3-9-0 0.................... RichardSmith 2 —
(B R Johnson) *w ldrs for 4f: sn btn: t.o* **50/1**

2m 9.35s (1.05) **Going Correction** +0.05s/f (Good) **16** Ran SP% **121.3**
Speed ratings (Par 101): **97,95,95,94,94 94,94,92,92,91 91,87,84,74,69 64**
CSF £58.77 TOTE £5.30: £2.20, £4.20, £4.00; EX 80.70 TRIFECTA Not won..The winner was bought by S Heffernan for £5,000. Persian Fox was claimed by A G Juckes for £6,000.
Owner Winterfields Farm Ltd And Miss A Nagle **Bred** Castletown And Associates **Trained** Pulborough, W Sussex

FOCUS
A very ordinary seller, but the winner was a cut above these. Prominent runners were favoured.
Persian Fox(IRE) Official explanation: jockey said gelding was hanging badly left on bends, making it impossible to steer and losing many lengths
Hot Property(IRE) Official explanation: jockey said gelding lost its action in straight; vet said gelding was lame in front

6061 ARENA LEISURE H'CAP 1m 3f 135y
4:00 (4:02) (Class 4) (0-85,85) 3-Y-O **£4,728** (£1,406; £702; £351) **Stalls** Centre

Form RPR
203 **1** **Russian Invader (IRE)**[26] 5335 3-8-7 **74** ow2.......... FergusSweeney 5 84+
(A King) *w.w in last trio: prog over 3f out: rdn to ld over 1f out: wandered but hld on wl* **14/1**
1 **2** *nk* **Watchful (IRE)**[22] 5450 3-9-0 **81**.................... DarryllHolland 7 91+
(L M Cumani) *t.k.h early: trckd ldrs: plld out and effrt 2f out: drvn to press wnr ins fnl f and edgd lft: jst hld* **4/1**[2]
1040 **3** *½* **Mandragola**[12] 5725 3-8-9 **76**.................... MichaelHills 6 85
(B W Hills) *hld up in last trio: effrt 3f out: drvn on outer and styd on fnl 2f: a hld* **6/1**[3]
-101 **4** *nk* **Venerable**[24] 5385 3-9-4 **85**.................... JimmyFortune 3 94
(J H M Gosden) *led to over 3f out: led over 2f out and drvn: hdd over 1f out: nt qckn* **5/4**[1]
-403 **5** *6* **Wait For The Light**[13] 5718 3-9-0 **81**....................(p) KerrinMcEvoy 4 80
(E A L Dunlop) *trckd ldrs: effrt over 3f out: nt qckn and btn whn n.m.r wl over 1f out* **17/2**
2423 **6** *3* **Know The Law**[18] 5562 3-8-6 **76**.................... MarcHalford(3) 8 70
(D R C Elsworth) *t.k.h: pressed ldr: led over 3f out to over 2f out: sn wknd and eased* **8/1**
300 **7** *10* **Master Halling**[126] 2320 3-8-9 **76**.................... SteveDrowne 2 54
(R Charlton) *a last: wknd over 3f out* **18/1**

2m 27.91s (-2.19) **Going Correction** +0.05s/f (Good) **7** Ran SP% **112.3**
Speed ratings (Par 103): **109,108,108,108,104 102,95**
CSF £66.18 CT £376.06 TOTE £16.10: £4.80, £2.40; EX 75.20 Trifecta £358.20 Part won. Pool £504.59 - 0.99 winning units..
Owner Nigel Bunter **Bred** Gestut Gorlsdorf **Trained** Barbury Castle, Wilts

FOCUS
Quite a hot little handicap and, although the first four home finished in a bit of a bunch, the winning time was decent. Solid form, with more to come from the first two in particular.
Know The Law Official explanation: jockey said gelding ran too free

6062 AT THE RACES MAIDEN STKS 6f
4:30 (4:33) (Class 5) 3-Y-O+ **£2,817** (£838; £418; £209) **Stalls** High

Form RPR
4405 **1** **High 'n Dry (IRE)**[52] 4575 3-8-12 69.................... J-PGuillambert 12 57
(C A Cyzer) *prom: chsd ldr 2f out: drvn to ld last 100yds: jst hld on* **8/1**
2 *nk* **Sintenis Mac (GER)** 4-9-4 0.................... DarryllHolland 4 61+
(P J O'Gorman) *awkward s: rn green and hld up: last after 2f: swtchd to wd outside 1/2-way: rapid prog over 1f out: r.o fnl f: jst failed* **12/1**
043 **3** *nk* **Hawridge Miss**[14] 5688 3-8-12 43.................... RichardKingscote 3 56
(B R Millman) *dwlt: wl in rr on outer: prog fr 1/2-way: clsd on ldrs over 1f out: upsides fnl f: nt qckn* **25/1**
5203 **4** *shd* **Al Badeya (IRE)**[18] 5567 3-8-12 69.................... KerrinMcEvoy 16 55
(Sir Michael Stoute) *mde most against nr side rail: def advantage over 1f out: hdd and no ex last 100yds* **4/1**[2]
00 **5** *¾* **Barbar**[27] 5315 4-9-4 0.................... StephenCarson 7 58
(Eve Johnson Houghton) *chsd ldng gp: rdn over 2f out: kpt on fr over 1f out: nrst fin* **66/1**
000 **6** *1 ½* **Detonate**[38] 5009 5-9-4 42.................... RichardMullen 10 53
(I A Wood) *awkward s: hld up wl in rr: rdn 2f out: styd on fnl f: nrst fin* **100/1**
3453 **7** *nk* **Vogarth**[7] 5861 3-8-12 57.................... JamesMillman(5) 8 52
(B R Millman) *chsd ldrs: rdn over 2f out: kpt on same pce: nvr able to chal* **5/1**[3]
56 **8** *nk* **Compulsion**[33] 5129 4-8-13 0.................... DaneO'Neill 1 46+
(Pat Eddery) *dwlt: t.k.h and hld up wl in rr: nudged along and stdy prog fnl 2f: nvr on terms: do bttr* **20/1**
5000 **9** *4* **Woodins Way**[7] 5860 3-9-3 57....................(b[1]) SteveDrowne 2 38
(P J Makin) *dwlt: racd on outer and sn in tch: rdn and no prog 2f out: wknd over 1f out* **14/1**
4000 **10** *shd* **Pajada**[106] 2916 3-8-12 40....................(v) RichardSmith 13 33
(M D I Usher) *cl up: losing pl and btn whn hmpd over 1f out* **100/1**
3022 **11** *¾* **Hazytoo**[13] 5714 3-9-3 70.................... JimmyFortune 15 36
(N A Callaghan) *w ldr to over 2f out: wknd and hanging after* **7/2**[1]
12 *5* **Crimson Fern (IRE)** 3-8-12 0.................... TGMcLaughlin 14 15
(M S Saunders) *s.s: hld up wl in rr: a bhd* **66/1**
400 **13** *3 ½* **Batchworth Fleur**[35] 5090 4-8-13 48.................... AdamKirby 9 —
(E A Wheeler) *nvr bttr than midfield: rdn and no prog 2f out* **50/1**
00 **14** *½* **Terandeil**[133] 2077 3-8-12 0.................... FergusSweeney 11 —
(J G M O'Shea) *dwlt: a wl in rr* **100/1**
032- **15** *hd* **Mumaathel (IRE)**[358] 5988 4-9-4 78.................... PatDobbs 6 6
(M A Buckley) *t.k.h: hld up towards rr: wknd 2f out* **7/2**[1]
-006 **16** *20* **Danjoe**[53] 4530 3-9-3 43.................... LiamJones 5 —
(R Brotherton) *stmbld bdly s: a wl in rr: t.o* **100/1**

1m 13.81s (0.14) **Going Correction** -0.25s/f (Firm)
WFA 3 from 4yo+ 1lb **16** Ran SP% **124.1**
Speed ratings (Par 103): **89,88,88,88,87 85,84,84,78,78 77,71,66,65,65 38**
CSF £97.23 TOTE £10.60: £2.70, £4.40, £5.30; EX 227.90 TRIFECTA Not won..
Owner Mrs Charles Cyzer **Bred** Darley **Trained** Maplehurst, W Sussex

FOCUS
A weak maiden and the winning time was moderate. The form is not up to much and the winner was a stone off this year's best, with the third anchoring the form.
Hazytoo Official explanation: jockey said colt hung right
Danjoe Official explanation: jockey said gelding stumbled coming out of stalls

6063 ROYAL WINDSOR FIREWORKS EXTRAVAGANZA 3RD NOVEMBER H'CAP 1m 67y
5:00 (5:00) (Class 5) (0-70,70) 3-Y-O+ **£2,817** (£838; £418; £209) **Stalls** High

Form RPR
3211 **1** **Young Bertie**[7] 5862 4-9-2 **68**....................(v) TravisBlock(3) 10 78
(H Morrison) *t.k.h: cl up on inner: lost pl 3f out and sn shkn up: effrt and led over 1f out: drvn out* **11/8**[1]
4005 **2** *½* **Roodolph**[35] 5092 3-9-4 **70**....................(b[1]) StephenCarson 4 79
(Eve Johnson Houghton) *hld up in midfield: clsd on ldrs over 2f out: hanging and nt qckn tl styd on fnl f to press wnr nr fin* **20/1**
5634 **3** *¾* **Aggravation**[6] 5885 5-9-4 **70**.................... MarcHalford(3) 3 77
(D R C Elsworth) *hld up in last pair: prog 3f out: got through over 1f out: styd on fnl f: nt rch ldng pair* **9/2**[2]
5040 **4** *2* **Pirouetting**[23] 5424 4-9-3 **66**.................... MichaelHills 9 68
(B W Hills) *mde most to over 1f out: nt qckn* **14/1**
0115 **5** *¾* **Im Ova Ere Dad (IRE)**[26] 5339 4-9-6 **69**.................... JimmyFortune 12 70
(D E Cantillon) *hld up in rr: prog on outer over 2f out: pressed ldrs 1f out: wknd last 100yds* **7/1**[3]
4301 **6** *½* **Desert Island Miss**[23] 5424 4-9-4 **67**.................... AdamKirby 5 67
(W R Swinburn) *cl up: outpcd over 2f out and rdn: kpt on fnl f: n.d* **9/1**
5000 **7** *1 ½* **Daniel Thomas (IRE)**[31] 5198 5-9-3 **66**.................... LiamJones 11 62
(Mrs A L M King) *dwlt: hld up tl prog to press ldrs over 3f out: wknd jst over 1f out* **20/1**
1504 **8** *shd* **Very Well Red**[98] 3156 4-8-11 **67**.................... WilliamCarson(7) 14 63
(P W Hiatt) *hld up in midfield: prog and cl up over 3f out: wknd over 1f out* **20/1**
005 **9** *shd* **Quaglino Way (GR)**[49] 4666 3-9-3 **69**.................... SteveDrowne 7 65
(P R Chamings) *dwlt: sn trckd ldrs: lost pl and rdn 3f out: struggling after* **12/1**
0050 **10** *hd* **Small Stakes (IRE)**[42] 4879 5-8-13 **62**.................... DarryllHolland 6 57
(P J Makin) *hld up in last: off the pce over 3f out: nvr a factor after* **28/1**
-000 **11** *1 ¼* **Minos (IRE)**[10] 5768 3-9-2 **68**.................... PatDobbs 2 60
(R Hannon) *chsd ldr to over 2f out: wknd* **25/1**

1m 44.02s (-0.68) **Going Correction** +0.05s/f (Good)
WFA 3 from 4yo+ 3lb **11** Ran SP% **118.7**
Speed ratings (Par 103): **105,104,103,101,101 100,99,98,98,98 97**
CSF £39.07 CT £108.58 TOTE £2.10: £1.10, £3.90, £2.10; EX 44.00 TRIFECTA Pool £300.35 - 1.09 winning units. Place 6 £239.75, Place 5 £211.30.
Owner M T Bevan **Bred** Red House Stud **Trained** East Ilsley, Berks

FOCUS
A modest handicap, but the form looks solid with Young Bertie, who was 4lb well in, landing the hat-trick.
Im Ova Ere Dad(IRE) Official explanation: jockey said gelding ran too free
T/Jkpt: Not won. T/Plt: £362.40 to a £1 stake. Pool: £72,678.75. 146.40 winning tickets. T/Qpdt: £221.50 to a £1 stake. Pool: £5,029.30. 16.80 winning tickets. JN

6022 WOLVERHAMPTON (A.W) (L-H)

Monday, October 8

OFFICIAL GOING: Standard

Wind: Virtually nil Weather: Fine

6064 COME RACING AT WOLVERHAMPTON APPRENTICE H'CAP 5f 216y(P)

2:20 (2:21) (Class 6) (0-65,64) 3-Y-O+ £2,900 (£856; £428) Stalls Low

Form RPR

5064 1 **Bond Playboy**[10] 5778 7-9-1 **54**....(p) SladeO'Hara 5 68+
(G R Oldroyd) *s.i.s: sn prom: wnt 2nd jst over 2f out: n.m.r on ins over 1f out tl swtchd rt wl ins fnl f: r.o to ld nr fin* **6/1**[1]

2510 2 ½ **Jilly Why (IRE)**[22] 5460 6-8-13 **55**....(b) FrankiePickard(3) 3 67
(Paul Green) *a.p: led over 3f out: rdn and edgd lft over 1f out: hdd nr fin* **6/1**[1]

6240 3 3½ **Nautical**[12] 5731 9-9-0 **58**.... MarkCoumbe(5) 8 59
(A W Carroll) *hld up in mid-div: swtchd rt and hdwy wl over 1f out: sn rdn and edgd lft: kpt on same pce fnl f* **7/1**[2]

000 4 ½ **Canina**[101] 3064 4-8-8 **52**.... AndrewHeffernan(5) 9 51+
(Paul Green) *hld up towards rr: rdn and hdwy over 1f out: kpt on ins fnl f* **40/1**

0060 5 1¼ **Snow Bunting**[37] 5037 9-8-7 **46**.... JamesO'Reilly 1 47+
(Jedd O'Keeffe) *hld up towards rr: rdn whn nt clr run on ins wl over 1f out: r.o fnl f: nvr nrr* **9/1**

1005 6 nk **Mozakhraf (USA)**[11] 5753 5-9-11 **64**.... JamieJones 11 58
(K A Ryan) *hld up in mid-div: hdwy whn swtchd lft and squeezed through over 1f out: rdn and one pce fnl f* **6/1**[1]

0650 7 1 **Guildenstern (IRE)**[16] 5642 5-9-9 **62**.... JackMitchell 7 53
(P Howling) *prom: rdn over 3f out: wkng whn n.m.r 2f out* **8/1**[3]

52 8 ¾ **Diamond Hurricane (IRE)**[37] 5041 3-8-12 **57**.... AshleyMorgan(5) 13 46
(M Wellings) *s.i.s: in rr: c v wd st: n.d* **22/1**

0610 9 shd **Avontuur (FR)**[6] 5890 5-8-10 **49**....(b) JamieHamblett 4 37
(D W Chapman) *s.s: hdwy on outside 3f out: rdn wl over 1f out: wknd ins fnl f* **17/2**

3050 10 ¾ **Aggbag**[14] 5688 3-8-9 **54**.... SoniaEaton(5) 2 40
(B P J Baugh) *hld up in mid-div: hdwy on ins whn hmpd over 1f out: sn wknd* **50/1**

4460 11 1 **Buzzin'Boyzee (IRE)**[31] 5190 4-8-0 **46**.... RossAtkinson(7) 10 29
(P D Evans) *s.i.s: c wd st: hung lft over 1f out: a in rr* **16/1**

0550 12 ½ **Seesawmilu (IRE)**[65] 4180 4-8-4 **48**.... DeclanCannon(5) 6 29
(E J Alston) *chsd ldr: ev ch over 2f out: rdn and wknd wl over 1f out* **12/1**

401 13 2½ **Hello Roberto**[7] 5861 6-9-5 **58** 6ex....(p) AmyBaker 12 31
(R A Harris) *led: hdd over 3f out: rdn over 2f out: wknd wl over 1f out* **11/1**

1m 15.21s (-0.60) **Going Correction** -0.15s/f (Stan)
WFA 3 from 4yo+ 1lb **13** Ran SP% **117.7**
Speed ratings (Par 101): **98,97,92,92,90 89,88,87,87,86 85,84,81**
CSF £39.30 CT £260.50 TOTE £7.20: £1.70, £2.40, £3.80; EX 29.70.
Owner R C Bond **Bred** P A Mason **Trained** Brawby, N Yorks
■ Stewards' Enquiry : Jamie Jones two-day ban: careless riding (Oct 19,21)

FOCUS

A modest handicap, but a strong early pace with three horses battling for the lead from the start and not many got into it. Solid form for the grade.

6065 DINE IN HORIZONS RESTAURANT MEDIAN AUCTION MAIDEN STKS 5f 216y(P)

2:50 (2:50) (Class 6) 2-Y-O £2,730 (£806; £403) Stalls Low

Form RPR

6300 1 **Spinning Ridge (IRE)**[34] 5117 2-8-12 59.... KevinGhunowa(5) 3 69
(R A Harris) *a.p: rdn to ld and edgd lft ins fnl f: r.o wl* **12/1**[3]

0055 2 2½ **In A Pickle**[9] 5815 2-8-12 59.... FrancisNorton 9 57
(H J L Dunlop) *led early: chsd ldr: rdn over 1f out: nt qckn ins fnl f* **22/1**

2403 3 nk **Rub Of The Relic (IRE)**[6] 5888 2-9-3 72.... JohnEgan 2 61
(P A Blockley) *a.p: rdn wl over 1f out: kpt on one pce fnl f* **4/1**[2]

55 4 1 **Blitzen (IRE)**[21] 5470 2-9-3 0.... GrahamGibbons 7 58
(E S McMahon) *chsd ldrs: hung rt bnd over 2f out: c wd st: rdn and one pce fnl f* **9/4**[1]

5 1½ **World View (IRE)** 2-8-12 0.... PaulFitzsimons 5 48
(M P Tregoning) *s.i.s: sn mid-div: rdn over 2f out: swtchd lft wl over 1f out: no imp fnl f* **14/1**

60 6 hd **Lyrical Symphony**[20] 5498 2-8-12 0.... PaulDoe 1 48
(W J Knight) *sn led: rdn wl over 1f out: hdd & wknd ins fnl f* **25/1**

5 7 ½ **Laureldean Breeze (USA)**[18] 5558 2-8-12 0.... PaulHanagan 6 46
(R A Fahey) *prom tl rdn and wknd over 3f out* **14/1**

00 8 ¾ **Sweet Mind**[18] 5550 2-8-9 0.... JamieMoriarty(3) 10 44
(R A Fahey) *outpcd* **33/1**

9 5 **Regal Tradition (IRE)** 2-9-3 0.... GeorgeBaker 11 34
(P A Blockley) *outpcd* **25/1**

10 6 **Admirals Way** 2-8-12 0.... RussellKennemore(5) 4 16
(C N Kellett) *s.i.s: sn outpcd* **66/1**

6 P **Dharori (IRE)**[10] 5771 2-9-3 0.... NCallan 8 —
(M A Jarvis) *s.i.s: bhd whn p.u lame over 3f out* **9/4**[1]

1m 16.15s (0.34) **Going Correction** -0.15s/f (Stan) **11** Ran SP% **119.0**
Speed ratings (Par 93): **91,87,87,85,83 83,83,82,75,67** —
CSF £249.48 TOTE £15.60: £3.10, £4.80, £1.50; EX 364.70.
Owner Leeway Group Limited **Bred** Eddie O'Leary **Trained** Earlswood, Monmouths

FOCUS

A very modest maiden with only three of the 11 runners starting at less than 14-1 and made even less competitive when one of the joint favourites broke down at halfway. The time ordinary too and the form looks weak.

NOTEBOOK

Spinning Ridge(IRE), who had only beaten one horse in his last two outings, returned to the sort of form he was showing at this track prior to that. He saw it out well and even though the form looks very weak, his trainer has a knack of finding the right opportunities with horses like him. (op 16-1)

In A Pickle, suited by the step back up trip, was up there the whole way and kept on going pretty well but could not withstand the finishing pace of the winner. She may be worth a try in a modest nursery off her current mark. (op 16-1)

Rub Of The Relic(IRE), weak in the market, had every chance but could only plod on to finish in the first three for the eighth time in 11 career outings. It is again obvious that he did not run to anything like his current mark and either needs it to go down considerably or dropping in class. (op 11-4)

Blitzen(IRE) was again well supported in the market on this switch to sand, but he was very awkward rounding the home bend and never had a hope of making up the ground he lost as a result. (op 9-2)

World View(IRE), a half-sister to five winners including the useful pair Side Saddle and Greek Renaissance, looked to need the experience especially after missing the break. She should come on for it, but this was such a weak race that she will need to. (op 11-1 tchd 10-1)

Sweet Mind Official explanation: jockey said filly suffered interference in running

Regal Tradition(IRE) Official explanation: jockey said colt would not face the kickback

6066 WOLVERHAMPTON-RACECOURSE.CO.UK NURSERY 7f 32y(P)

3:20 (3:21) (Class 6) (0-65,65) 2-Y-O £2,900 (£856; £428) Stalls High

Form RPR

000 1 **Cross Fell (USA)**[10] 5772 2-8-12 **56**.... DeanMcKeown 2 70+
(M Johnston) *mde all: clr over 1f out: pushed out* **15/2**

4056 2 6 **Elusive Deal (USA)**[23] 5423 2-9-2 **60**....(p) PaulHanagan 1 59
(R A Fahey) *chsd ldrs: rdn and sltly outpcd over 3f out: swtchd rt over 1f out: r.o to take 2nd cl home: no ch w wnr* **6/1**[3]

435 3 ½ **One Called Alice**[17] 5603 2-9-3 **61**.... GeorgeBaker 5 59
(J R Holt) *chsd wnr: ev ch over 2f out: rdn wl over 1f out: sn btn* **15/2**

0050 4 2½ **Weetfromthechaff**[41] 4923 2-9-1 **59**.... VinceSlattery 9 51
(R Hollinshead) *t.k.h: sn in tch: rdn 2f out: fdd fnl f* **14/1**

2503 5 1½ **Llab Nala**[9] 5818 2-8-12 **56**.... FrancisNorton 3 44
(M R Channon) *hld up towards rr: nt clr run on ins bnd after 1f: rdn over 2f out: swtchd rt ent st: rdn and sme hdwy over 1f out: n.d* **7/2**[1]

4300 6 shd **Observatory Ridge**[39] 4964 2-8-8 **59**.... FrankiePickard(7) 7 47
(M D I Usher) *in rr: rdn over 2f out: sme hdwy on ins wl over 1f out: swtchd rt 1f out: nvr nr ldrs* **16/1**

0000 7 ¾ **Melwood Dreams**[12] 5736 2-8-9 **58**.... RussellKennemore(5) 8 44
(Paul Green) *hld up towards rr: rdn over 2f out: no rspnse* **100/1**

0036 8 nk **Eternal Optimist (IRE)**[3] 5965 2-8-12 **63**.... DeanHeslop(7) 12 48
(C W Thornton) *a bhd* **33/1**

000 9 1¼ **Feeling Fresh (IRE)**[9] 5813 2-9-4 **65**.... NeilChalmers(3) 10 47
(Paul Green) *s.i.s: a bhd* **33/1**

526 10 5 **Redbrick Girl**[165] 1255 2-9-5 **63**.... NCallan 11 32
(K A Ryan) *prom tl rdn and wknd over 2f out* **16/1**

3014 11 9 **Bahamarama (IRE)**[25] 5365 2-9-6 **64**.... JohnEgan 4 11
(R A Harris) *prom: rdn over 2f out: wknd and eased wl over 1f out* **6/1**[3]

0400 12 4 **Red Skipper (IRE)**[17] 5582 2-9-4 **62**.... GrahamGibbons 6 —
(N Wilson) *rdn 4f out: a bhd* **9/2**[2]

1m 30.39s (-0.01) **Going Correction** -0.15s/f (Stan) **12** Ran SP% **117.8**
Speed ratings (Par 93): **94,87,86,83,82 81,81,80,79,73 63,58**
CSF £51.21 CT £354.08 TOTE £10.50: £2.50, £2.00, £2.40; EX 65.40.
Owner Sheikh Mohammed **Bred** Darley **Trained** Middleham Moor, N Yorks

FOCUS

What had looked to be a competitive nursery beforehand was turned into an embarrassingly one-sided contest. Despite the winner looking so impressive, posting big improvement in the process, the time was only fair so the likelihood is that the form of the beaten horses is very moderate.

NOTEBOOK

Cross Fell(USA), making his nursery debut after apparently not seeing out his races in three starts in maiden company, was a completely different proposition here. He basically won the race at the start, bouncing out of the gates from his low draw and soon establishing a significant advantage. He just went further and further clear as the race progressed and came home in splendid isolation, but the Handicapper will hit him very hard and, with his rivals not looking up to much, he may be best off turning out again quickly under a penalty. (op 8-1)

Elusive Deal(USA), tried in cheekpieces, stayed on late over this shorter trip to finish a remote second, though in truth in this race there was no second. Her best chance of breaking her duck is back over further. (op 11-2 tchd 5-1)

One Called Alice, making her nursery debut after three outings in 6f maidens here, was always in hopeless pursuit of the winner and her efforts to do so may eventually have lost her second. (op 8-1)

Weetfromthechaff, down 6lb on this switch to sand, was keen enough behind the leaders but proved woefully one-paced when eventually let down. Official explanation: jockey said colt hung left (op 12-1)

Llab Nala was well supported in the market, but never got into the race and is by far the most exposed of these. (tchd 9-2)

Feeling Fresh(IRE) Official explanation: jockey said colt missed the break

Redbrick Girl Official explanation: jockey said filly hung right throughout

Bahamarama(IRE) showed up prominently for a long way, but this was her first try at the trip and she failed to see it out. Official explanation: jockey said filly lost its action (tchd 5-1)

Red Skipper(IRE) was very well supported in the market, but never gave his supporters any hope. Official explanation: jockey said gelding lost its action (op 15-2)

6067 WOLVERHAMPTON-RACECOURSE.CO.UK H'CAP 1m 141y(P)

3:50 (3:50) (Class 4) (0-85,85) 3-Y-O+ £5,181 (£1,541; £770; £384) Stalls Low

Form RPR

3103 1 **Just Bond (IRE)**[31] 5196 5-9-1 **83**.... SladeO'Hara(5) 6 93+
(G R Oldroyd) *hld up in rr: hdwy over 2f out: rdn to ld ins fnl f: sn edgd rt: r.o* **8/1**

3665 2 ½ **Full Victory (IRE)**[10] 5776 5-9-2 **79**.... NCallan 7 85
(R A Farrant) *hld up in tch: rdn over 2f out: r.o ins fnl f: nt clr run last strides* **7/1**[3]

6320 3 nk **Lord Theo**[13] 5703 3-8-7 **74**.... JamesDoyle 9 79
(N P Littmoden) *hld up and bhd: rdn over 1f out: hdwy fnl f: r.o* **16/1**

-015 4 1¼ **Habshan (USA)**[19] 5545 7-9-8 **85**.... GeorgeBaker 10 87
(C F Wall) *hld up towards rr: hdwy over 3f out: chsd ldr over 2f out tl rdn jst over 1f out: one pce* **8/1**

1450 5 nk **Apex**[17] 5593 6-8-13 **81**.... HaddenFrost(5) 1 83+
(M Hill) *prom: nt clr run on ins and lost pl 3f out: sn swtchd rt: rdn over 1f out: kpt on ins fnl f* **16/1**

5113 6 nk **Officer**[19] 5545 3-8-5 **79**....(v) JamieHamblett(7) 5 80+
(Sir Michael Stoute) *prom: led 3f out: rdn clr 2f out: hdd and no ex ins fnl f* **11/4**[1]

5004 7 8 **Dragon Slayer (IRE)**[19] 5539 5-9-2 **79**....(p) JohnEgan 4 61
(P A Blockley) *t.k.h: prom: led 5f out to 3f out: rdn and wknd 2f out* **4/1**[2]

00 8 2 **Fan Club**[10] 5776 3-8-1 **75**.... FrankiePickard(7) 2 53
(D W Chapman) *bhd fnl 3f* **100/1**

3604 9 9 **Daaweitza**[16] 5641 4-8-13 **79**....(p) JamieMoriarty(3) 3 36
(B Ellison) *led: hdd 5f out: nt clr run on ins 3f out: sn wknd* **7/1**[3]

0212 10 ½ **New World Order (IRE)**[15] 5664 3-8-12 **79**....(t) PhillipMakin 8 35
(K R Burke) *hld up in tch: rdn 4f out: wknd over 2f out* **8/1**

1m 49.94s (-1.82) **Going Correction** -0.15s/f (Stan)
WFA 3 from 4yo+ 4lb **10** Ran SP% **117.8**
Speed ratings (Par 105): **102,101,101,100,99 99,92,90,82,82**
CSF £63.59 CT £882.79 TOTE £6.00: £2.20, £2.60, £3.50; EX 65.10.
Owner R C Bond **Bred** Schwindibode Ag **Trained** Brawby, N Yorks
■ Just Bond completed a 62-1 double for owner Reg Bond, trainer Geoff Oldroyd and jockey Slade O'Hara.

The Form Book, Raceform Ltd, Compton, RG20 6NL

FOCUS
A reasonably competitive handicap, but even though the early gallop did not appear that strong the principals all came from off the pace. Another career best from track specialist Just Bond who is rated a bit better than the bare form.

Dragon Slayer(IRE) Official explanation: jockey said gelding ran too free

6068 SPONSOR A RACE BY CALLING 0870 220 2442 H'CAP 1m 4f 50y(P)
4:20 (4:20) (Class 6) (0-65,63) 3-Y-0+ £2,900 (£856; £428) Stalls Low

Form RPR
-220 1 **Stagecoach Emerald**[84] 3598 5-9-7 **61**..........(p) NCallan 8 70
(R W Price) *a.p: rdn and wnt 2nd over 3f out: led over 1f out: sn edgd lft: r.o wl* **16/1**

400- 2 *2* **Gamesters Lady**[428] 4173 4-9-4 **58**.......... GrahamGibbons 6 64
(W M Brisbourne) *led 1f: chsd ldr: led over 4f out: rdn over 2f out: hdd over 1f out: one pce* **33/1**

5420 3 *3/4* **Sir Haydn**[19] 5531 7-9-5 **59**..........(v) JohnEgan 12 64+
(J R Jenkins) *stdd s: sn swtchd lft: hld up in rr: rdn and hdwy over 2f out: styd on one pce fnl f* **13/2**[2]

0543 4 *shd* **Sopran Gath (ITY)**[13] 5709 4-9-4 **58**.......... JamesDoyle 1 62
(J W Hills) *hld up in mid-div: hdwy over 3f out: rdn 2f out: one pce fnl f* **15/2**[3]

4006 5 *2 1/2* **Cortesia (IRE)**[20] 5514 4-9-9 **63**.......... PaulHanagan 11 63
(P W Chapple-Hyam) *hld up in rr: rdn and sme hdwy on ins wl over 1f out: nvr trbld ldrs* **8/1**

0-10 6 *nk* **Royal Melbourne (IRE)**[16] 5647 7-9-4 **58**.......... SilvestreDeSousa 4 58
(A D Brown) *t.k.h in tch: rdn and wknd over 2f out* **13/2**[2]

0065 7 *2 1/2* **Zabeel House**[16] 5645 4-9-1 **60**.......... PatrickHills(5) 10 56
(J A R Toller) *hld up in rr: rdn wl over 1f out: nvr nr ldrs* **14/1**

4000 8 *nk* **Thorny Mandate**[2] 6027 5-9-3 **62**.......... RussellKennemore(5) 5 57
(W M Brisbourne) *hld up in mid-div: lost pl and nt clr run on ins over 3f out: sn bhd* **12/1**

0364 9 *1/2* **Zalkani (IRE)**[19] 5531 7-9-5 **59**.......... GeorgeBaker 7 54
(J Pearce) *hld up towards rr: hdwy over 3f out: rdn over 2f out: sn wknd: eased whn btn wl ins fnl f* **7/2**[1]

5302 10 *5* **Alasil (USA)**[11] 5756 7-8-6 **51**.......... TolleyDean(5) 2 38
(R J Price) *t.k.h in tch: rdn and wknd over 3f out* **9/1**

5045 11 *3/4* **Blue Hedges**[70] 4031 5-8-11 **54**.......... JerryO'Dwyer(3) 9 39
(H J Collingridge) *a towards rr* **16/1**

0400 12 *10* **Dark Planet**[157] 1451 4-8-12 **57**..........(v[1]) HaddenFrost(5) 3 26
(D Burchell) *led after 1f: hdd over 4f out: wknd over 3f out* **14/1**

2m 40.06s (-2.36) **Going Correction** -0.15s/f (Stan) **12** Ran SP% **117.5**
Speed ratings (Par 101): **101,99,99,99,97 97,95,95,95,91 91,84**
CSF £448.04 CT £3740.81 TOTE £16.30: £2.80, £12.20, £2.10; EX 484.60.
Owner Dhafi Al Marri **Bred** T R G Vestey **Trained** Newmarket, Suffolk

FOCUS
Thanks to the free-running Dark Planet, the early pace was strong and the field were well spread out, but things were much steadier late on and the final time was about right for the grade. Ordinary form.

Thorny Mandate Official explanation: jockey said gelding was denied a clear run
Dark Planet Official explanation: jockey said gelding ran too free

6069 BOOK NOW FOR CHRISTMAS H'CAP 1m 5f 194y(P)
4:50 (4:52) (Class 6) (0-65,65) 3-Y-0+ £2,900 (£856; £428) Stalls Low

Form RPR
0215 1 **Heights Of Golan**[2] 6027 3-8-11 **57**..........(v) NCallan 9 65
(I A Wood) *hld up in mid-div: smooth hdwy over 4f out: rdn over 1f out: led ins fnl f: styd on wl* **11/4**[1]

3034 2 *1 1/2* **Dansimar**[5] 5906 3-9-2 **62**.......... FrancisNorton 4 68
(M R Channon) *hld up in tch: led over 2f out: rdn wl over 1f out: hdd and nt qckn ins fnl f* **3/1**[2]

4000 3 *3* **York Cliff**[9] 5807 9-9-5 **56**.......... GeorgeBaker 3 58
(W M Brisbourne) *hld up in rr: rdn and hdwy wl over 1f out: styd on same pce fnl f* **17/2**

2000 4 *1 1/2* **Little Richard (IRE)**[198] 767 8-9-3 **57**..........(p) NeilChalmers(3) 6 57
(M Wellings) *hld up towards rr: hdwy over 3f out: rdn wl over 1f out: one pce* **25/1**

555/ 5 *3* **Mister Troubridge**[843] 2651 5-8-10 **47**.......... RichardThomas 5 43
(J A Geake) *hld up in rr: rdn over 2f out: styd on fnl f: nvr nr ldrs* **50/1**

5000 6 *2* **Zaville**[32] 5158 5-8-7 **49** oh1 ow3..........(b) JamesO'Reilly(5) 7 42
(J O'Reilly) *chsd ldr: led over 5f out: rdn and hdd over 2f out: wknd wl over 1f out* **12/1**

004 7 *1* **Spinaimanwin (IRE)**[40] 4951 3-7-11 **46**.......... DominicFox(3) 2 37
(Ian Williams) *prom: n.m.r over 3f out: wknd over 2f out* **18/1**

0006 8 *nk* **Maria Antonia (IRE)**[33] 5132 4-8-8 **50**.......... KevinGhunowa(5) 1 41
(P A Blockley) *plld hrd in mid-div: rdn and hdwy on ins over 2f out: wknd fnl f* **20/1**

6605 9 *nk* **Qaasi (USA)**[16] 5626 5-8-11 **48**..........(t) GrahamGibbons 13 38
(M Brittain) *s.i.s: hld up and bhd: rdn and sme hdwy on ins over 2f out: wknd over 1f out* **12/1**

1105 10 *1 1/2* **Mighty Kitchener (USA)**[10] 5779 4-10-0 **65**.......... AmirQuinn 11 53
(P Howling) *hld up in mid-div: rdn over 3f out: hdwy over 2f out: wknd over 1f out* **9/2**[3]

2200 11 *2 1/2* **Bulberry Hill**[103] 2996 6-9-3 **54**.......... JamesDoyle 8 39
(R W Price) *t.k.h in mid-div: rdn and hdwy over 3f out: wknd over 2f out* **25/1**

4465 12 *5* **Treasure Isle**[24] 5388 3-8-2 **48**.......... PaulHanagan 10 26
(R A Fahey) *hld up towards rr: rdn over 4f out: short-lived effrt over 3f out* **16/1**

0006 13 *16* **Slip Silver**[24] 5388 3-8-0 **46** oh1..........(p) JamieMackay 12 1
(P J Makin) *led: hdd over 5f out: wkng whn n.m.r on ins over 3f out* **40/1**

3m 4.64s (-2.73) **Going Correction** -0.15s/f (Stan)
WFA 3 from 4yo+ 9lb **13** Ran SP% **123.8**
Speed ratings (Par 101): **101,100,98,97,95 94,94,93,93,92 91,88,79**
CSF £10.67 CT £65.11 TOTE £3.60: £1.60, £1.40, £3.10; EX 13.80.
Owner C S Tateson **Bred** Minster Enterprises Ltd **Trained** Upper Lambourn, Berks

FOCUS
A modest event, but they went a fair pace and this was a reasonable test of stamina. Ordinary but sound form, with the winner on the up.

Mister Troubridge Official explanation: jockey said gelding was denied a clear run

Mighty Kitchener(USA) Official explanation: trainer had no explanation for the poor form shown

6070 ARENA LEISURE MEDIAN AUCTION MAIDEN STKS 1m 4f 50y(P)
5:20 (5:20) (Class 6) 3-4-Y-0 £2,559 (£755; £378) Stalls Low

Form RPR
-222 1 **Gordonsville**[27] 5311 4-9-10 72.......... FrancisNorton 8 81
(A M Balding) *s.i.s: sn rcvrd: chsd ldr after 1f: led over 5f out: rdn over 1f out: drew clr fnl f: easily* **6/4**[1]

2423 2 *5* **Sweet Request**[28] 5271 3-8-12 66.......... NCallan 7 68
(R M Beckett) *a.p: chsd wnr wl over 2f out: sn rdn: one pce fnl f* **7/4**[2]

0406 3 *16* **The Diamond Bond**[3] 5980 3-8-12 48.......... SladeO'Hara(5) 5 47+
(G R Oldroyd) *hld up and bhd: rdn 4f out: struggling whn nt clr run on ins 3f out: swtchd rt over 2f out: wnt poor 3rd 1f out* **12/1**

0 4 *5* **Camerooney**[18] 5562 4-9-10 0.......... SilvestreDeSousa 9 39
(A D Brown) *led: hdd over 5f out: rdn over 3f out: wknd over 2f out* **20/1**

06 5 *12* **Mark Of The Fen**[12] 5728 3-8-12 0..........(e) PatrickHills(5) 3 20
(Rae Guest) *hld up: hdwy on outside over 5f out: rdn and wknd over 3f out* **17/2**

050- 6 *hd* **Salawat**[398] 5098 4-9-5 22.......... DeanMcKeown 1 15
(T T Clement) *a in rr* **66/1**

6050 7 *5* **Winning Show**[13] 5714 3-9-3 58.......... JohnEgan 6 12
(R A Harris) *plld hrd: hdwy after 3f: wknd 4f out* **7/1**[3]

0 8 *18* **Indared**[10] 5781 3-9-3 0.......... GeorgeBaker 2 —
(M Mullineaux) *bhd fnl 4f: t.o* **66/1**

2m 38.74s (-3.68) **Going Correction** -0.15s/f (Stan)
WFA 3 from 4yo 7lb **8** Ran SP% **114.8**
Speed ratings (Par 101): **106,102,92,88,80 80,77,65**
CSF £4.30 TOTE £2.30: £1.02, £1.10, £4.00; EX 4.30.
Owner George Strawbridge **Bred** George Strawbridge **Trained** Kingsclere, Hants

FOCUS
An uncompetitive maiden and the result that the market and official ratings would have predicted, but the winning time was 1.32 seconds faster than the earlier 51-63 handicap over the same trip. The form seems to make sense around the third and fourth.

Mark Of The Fen Official explanation: jockey said gelding hung right throughout
Winning Show Official explanation: jockey said gelding ran too free
T/Plt: £448.60 to a £1 stake. Pool: £51,968.65. 84.55 winning tickets. T/Qpdt: £162.20 to a £1 stake. Pool: £3,354.30. 15.30 winning tickets. KH

5963 CHANTILLY (R-H)
Monday, October 8

OFFICIAL GOING: Good to soft

6071a PRIX DE BONNEVAL (LISTED RACE) 5f 110y
2:35 (2:35) 3-Y-0+ £17,568 (£7,027; £5,270; £3,514; £1,757)

RPR
1 **Loda (FR)**[29] 5259 4-8-8.......... SPasquier 9 98
(C Baillet, France)

2 *nk* **Mariol (FR)**[4] 4-8-11.......... DBoeuf 11 100
(Robert Collet, France)

3 *hd* **Zut Alors (IRE)**[8] 5850 3-8-8.......... J-BHamel 8 97
(Robert Collet, France)

4 *3/4* **Biniou (IRE)**[44] 4813 4-8-11.......... TThulliez 12 97
(R M H Cowell) *in tch in stands' side gp: styd on against ins rail fr over 1f out* **17/1**[3]

5 *hd* **Objecto De Arte (BRZ)** 4-8-11.......... C-PLemaire 10 96
(P Bary, France)

6 *nk* **Kourka (FR)**[22] 5468 5-8-12.......... RonanThomas 13 96
(J-M Beguigne, France)

7 *1/2* **Rakiza (IRE)**[65] 4190 3-8-8.......... DBonilla 7 92
(F Head, France)

8 *shd* **Aahayson**[57] 4438 3-8-11.......... PatCosgrave 6 94
(K R Burke) *overall ldr in centre gp tl hdd under 2f out: one pce* **87/10**[1]

9 *nk* **Place Vendome (FR)**[22] 5468 3-8-8.......... TJarnet 14 90
(Mlle S-V Tarrou, France)

10 *hd* **Sacho (GER)**[22] 9-9-2.......... ABadel 5 97
(W Kujath, Germany)

11 **Prince Fasliyev**[21] 3-8-11.......... OPeslier 4 93
(H-A Pantall, France)

12 **Masta Plasta (IRE)**[16] 5616 4-8-11.......... AdrianTNicholls 2 92
(D Nicholls) *prom racing wdst of all: rdn 2f out: sn one pce* **14/1**[2]

13 **Manzila (FR)**[89] 3445 4-8-12.......... CSoumillon 1 93
(F Head, France)

14 **Miyasaki (CHI)**[17] 5588 5-8-11..........(b) JJohansen 3 92
(Rune Haugen, Norway)

65.00 secs (-1.20) **14** Ran SP% **22.5**
PARI-MUTUEL: WIN 24.10; PL 6.10, 2.00, 5.50; DF 247.40.
Owner B Vaitilingon **Bred** Jean-Pierre Dubois **Trained** France

NOTEBOOK
Biniou(IRE) had hinted at a return to form when third in a Listed race at Newmarket last time, and this was a solid effort. Two wins from 24 starts is not a great return, though, and he remains difficult to place.
Aahayson showed good early speed but could not sustain it.
Masta Plasta(IRE), another who is difficult to place, was done no favours by his draw in stall two.

5621 CATTERICK (L-H)
Tuesday, October 9

OFFICIAL GOING: Good (good to soft in places; 8.2)
There was 9mm rain before the start of racing and more was to come resulting in 'genuine soft ground', yet the official misleading version was never changed.
Wind: Light, half-against Weather: persistent rain 1st 5 races

6072 20TH OCTOBER IS TOTESPORT SATURDAY MAIDEN STKS (DIV I) 5f
2:00 (2:01) (Class 5) 2-Y-0 £2,266 (£674; £337; £168) Stalls Low

Form RPR
20 1 **Princess Rhianna (IRE)**[42] 4924 2-8-12 0.......... PaulHanagan 6 67
(Mrs G S Rees) *swvd rt s: mid-div: hdwy 2f out: styd on to ld towards fin* **11/2**[3]

3302 2 nk **Paddy Jack**[19] 5558 2-9-3 69 SebSanders 10 71
(J R Weymes) *hmpd s: sn chsng ldrs on outside: styd on to ld ins fnl f: hdd and no ex towards fin* **2/1**[1]
0500 3 1 1/2 **Swindon Town Flyer (IRE)**[14] 5707 2-9-3 69 (b[1]) LPKeniry 8 66
(A B Haynes) *swvd rt s: sn chsng ldrs: kpt on same pce ins fnl f* **11/1**
0000 4 3/4 **Mr Funshine**[20] 5529 2-9-3 54 GregFairley 1 63
(Mrs P N Dutfield) *led: edgd rt and hdd ins fnl f: wknd towards fin* **25/1**
4 5 1/2 **Bourbon Balistic**[19] 5558 2-9-3 0 RoystonFfrench 3 62
(Mrs A Duffield) *s.i.s: sn chsng ldrs: kpt on same pce fnl 2f* **6/1**
402 6 2 1/2 **Atephobia**[36] 5081 2-9-3 66 PatCosgrave 7 53
(K R Burke) *bmpd s: hld up towards rr: hdwy over 2f out: nvr nr ldrs* **3/1**[2]
60 7 2 1/2 **Smarterthanuthink (USA)**[20] 5521 2-9-0 0 JamieMoriarty(3) 9 44
(R A Fahey) *hmpd s: sn outpcd and in rr: nvr a factor* **8/1**
000 8 5 **Captain Turbot (IRE)**[11] 5772 2-9-3 35 (p) TonyHamilton 2 26
(D W Barker) *chsd ldrs: wknd 2f out* **28/1**
0000 9 6 **Magnushomestwo (IRE)**[19] 5550 2-9-0 38 PatrickMathers(3) 4 4
(A Berry) *sn outpcd and in rr: bhd fnl 2f* **125/1**

63.24 secs (2.64) **Going Correction** +0.50s/f (Yiel) 9 Ran SP% **115.5**
Speed ratings (Par 95): **98,97,95,93,93 89,85,77,67**
CSF £16.72 TOTE £5.90: £2.00, £1.10, £2.90; EX 17.90.
Owner U N Syndicate & Douglas McMahon **Bred** Rathasker Stud **Trained** Sollom, Lancs

FOCUS
A modest maiden but the form looks fairly solid rated through the runner-up.

NOTEBOOK
Princess Rhianna(IRE), only with this trainer for a couple of weeks, stuck on to nail the runner-up near the line. The soft ground, much more testing than the misleading official version, was not a problem. (op 9-2 tchd 4-1)
Paddy Jack had the worst of the draw and was knocked over leaving the stalls. He worked hard to get his head in front only to be mugged on the line. (op 15-8 tchd 5-2)
Swindon Town Flyer(IRE), down in trip and fitted with blinkers, went sideways leaving the traps. This was his eighth start and he looks to be going nowhere. (tchd 10-1 and 12-1)
Mr Funshine, unplaced in four previous starts, was down in trip. He took them along but his stride shortened significantly near the line. (op 16-1)
Bourbon Balistic, who looks weak at present, missed a beat at the start and only stuck on in his own time. (op 11-2 tchd 9-2)
Atephobia, beaten in a 6f claimer last time, took a bump at the start and never really figured. (op 9-2)

6073 20TH OCTOBER IS TOTESPORT SATURDAY MAIDEN STKS (DIV II) 5f
2:30 (2:31) (Class 5) 2-Y-O **£2,266** (£674; £337; £168) **Stalls** Low

Form RPR
6025 1 **Miesko (USA)**[14] 5705 2-9-3 75 GregFairley 10 75
(M Johnston) *overall ldr stands' side: clr that trio over 1f out: jst hld on* **11/4**[1]
6 2 shd **President Elect (IRE)**[66] 4173 2-9-3 0 PhillipMakin 6 75
(T D Barron) *racd far side: chsd ldrs: led that gp over 1f out: styd on wl: jst hld* **8/1**[3]
4 3 3 1/2 **Klarity**[20] 5540 2-8-12 0 SebSanders 1 57
(J Pearce) *sn chsng ldrs: kpt on fnl f: nvr a threat* **11/4**[1]
026 4 1 1/4 **Mandelieu (IRE)**[19] 5575 2-9-3 76 LiamJones 2 58
(W J Haggas) *led far side gp tl over 1f out: wknd ins fnl f* **3/1**[2]
000 5 3/4 **Swift Acclaim (IRE)**[11] 5770 2-8-5 0 DeclanCannon(7) 5 50
(K R Burke) *chsd ldrs: outpcd over 1f out* **80/1**
005 6 2 1/2 **Sistos Fascination**[25] 5380 2-9-3 70 (p) NickyMackay 8 46
(M Botti) *racd far side: chsd ldrs: outpcd over 1f out: wknd ins fnl f* **16/1**
50 7 3 **Curio**[119] 2526 2-8-12 0 DeanMcKeown 3 30
(R M Whitaker) *chsd ldrs: sn drvn along: lost pl over 1f out* **20/1**
8 3 1/2 **Aerialist** 2-8-9 0 PatrickMathers(3) 4 17
(A Berry) *dwlt: racd towards far side: a outpcd and bhd* **66/1**
000 9 3 1/2 **Kyzer Chief**[21] 5501 2-9-3 49 TomEaves 9 10
(R E Barr) *racd stands' side: chsd wnr: wknd over 1f out* **80/1**
5 10 6 **Climaxtackledotcom**[101] 3092 2-9-3 0 PaulMulrennan 7 —
(M W Easterby) *s.i.s: racd stands' side: sn wl bhd* **10/1**

63.15 secs (2.55) **Going Correction** +0.50s/f (Yiel) 10 Ran SP% **113.1**
Speed ratings (Par 95): **99,98,93,91,90 86,81,75,70,60**
CSF £24.03 TOTE £3.50: £1.40, £2.70, £1.60; EX 24.90.
Owner Sheikh Mohammed **Bred** Darley **Trained** Middleham Moor, N Yorks

FOCUS
An almost identical time to division one and the winner, who raced alone down the favoured stands' side, sets the standard.

NOTEBOOK
Miesko(USA), who is only small, had the outside draw and raced alone down the stands' side. The post came just in time. (op 10-3 tchd 7-2)
President Elect(IRE), a grand type, was easily the paddock pick. He took charge on the far side coming to the final furlong and in the end only just missed out. (tchd 9-1)
Klarity, taken to post early, never threatened to land a blow and the soft ground was possibly against her. (op 7-2)
Mandelieu(IRE), having his second outing since being gelded, was dropping back in trip and was another taken down early. He took them along on the far side but in the soft ground did not get home. (op 9-4)
Swift Acclaim(IRE), who is only small, had shown little in three previous starts. (op 66-1)
Sistos Fascination, with the cheekpieces retained, did not run up to his improved Sandown form which was on fast ground. (op 14-1)

6074 SUBSCRIBE TO RACING UK ON 08700 506947 NURSERY (H'CAP) 5f 212y
3:00 (3:01) (Class 6) (0-65,65) 2-Y-O **£2,730** (£806; £403) **Stalls** Low

Form RPR
0003 1 **Andrasta**[5] 5931 2-9-4 65 PatrickMathers(3) 9 71
(A Berry) *chsd ldrs: led over 1f out: styd on wl ins fnl f* **12/1**
0152 2 2 **Loose Caboose (IRE)**[12] 5751 2-9-2 60 (p) SebSanders 12 60
(A J McCabe) *chsd ldrs: effrt on ins and chsd wnr 1f out: no ex* **7/2**[1]
0410 3 1 3/4 **Rope Bridge (IRE)**[7] 5887 2-8-12 59 (b) DuranFentiman(3) 6 54
(T D Easterby) *w ldrs: styd on same pce appr fnl f* **14/1**
3425 4 1/2 **Upstanding**[30] 5252 2-9-5 63 TomEaves 4 56
(M Brittain) *led tl over 1f out: kpt on same pce* **8/1**
3004 5 1 **Thomas Malory (IRE)**[14] 5715 2-8-10 59 LukeMorris(5) 1 49
(Miss V Haigh) *sn chsng ldrs: kpt on same pce fnl 2f* **5/1**[2]
2051 6 3/4 **Prigsnov Dancer (IRE)**[20] 5520 2-9-2 65 (p) JamesO'Reilly(5) 8 53
(J O'Reilly) *hld up in mid-div: hdwy towards centre over 2f out: fdd ins fnl f* **7/1**[3]
0014 7 1/2 **Rightcar Ellie (IRE)**[7] 5887 2-9-4 62 (b) LPKeniry 7 49
(Peter Grayson) *mid-div: styd far side and racd alone in home st: nvr trbld ldrs* **8/1**
2030 8 1 1/4 **Stormy Journey**[33] 5167 2-9-3 64 PJMcDonald(3) 11 47
(Mrs K Walton) *mid-div: effrt over 2f out: nvr trbld ldrs* **14/1**
3060 9 1 **She's Our Dream**[16] 5665 2-9-1 59 PaulMulrennan 10 39
(R C Guest) *hld up towards rr: nvr a threat* **18/1**
006 10 1 3/4 **Bathwick Icon (IRE)**[29] 5267 2-9-0 58 PaulHanagan 5 33
(A B Haynes) *chsd ldrs: drvn over 3f out: lost pl 2f out* **10/1**
0000 11 nk **Galley Slave (IRE)**[20] 5541 2-8-7 58 CharlotteKerton(7) 2 32
(M C Chapman) *in rr: drvn 3f out: nvr a factor* **28/1**
065 12 1/2 **Viscaya (IRE)**[17] 5621 2-9-2 60 (p) RoystonFfrench 3 32
(Mrs A Duffield) *s.i.s: a in rr* **14/1**

1m 17.68s (3.68) **Going Correction** +0.50s/f (Yiel) 12 Ran SP% **119.1**
Speed ratings (Par 93): **95,92,90,89,88 87,86,84,83,81 80,79**
CSF £53.95 CT £621.37 TOTE £20.80: £5.30, £1.60, £5.10; EX 92.80.
Owner A B Parr **Bred** Peter Barclay **Trained** Cockerham, Lancs

FOCUS
A modest nursery rated through the runner-up.

NOTEBOOK
Andrasta, having her second outing for this stable, seems to have turned over a new leaf and in the end won going away. (op 10-1)
Loose Caboose(IRE), drawn wide, went in pursuit of the winner but was in the end very much second best. Despite fears beforehand the soft ground did not seem to be a problem. (op 9-2)
Rope Bridge(IRE) is ending his season in better form and seemed suited by both the sixth furlong and the soft ground. (op 12-1)
Upstanding, having her tenth start, took them along but did not improve for the step up to 6f. (tchd 17-2)
Thomas Malory(IRE), having his 14th start, is very tough and holding his form remarkably well. (tchd 11-2)
Prigsnov Dancer(IRE), 5lb higher, was having his first outing for his new connections. The sixth furlong in this testing ground seemed to overstretch him. (op 11-1)

6075 TURFTV.CO.UK FILLIES' NURSERY (H'CAP) 7f
3:30 (3:31) (Class 4) (0-85,84) 2-Y-O **£4,210** (£1,252; £625; £312) **Stalls** Low

Form RPR
03 1 **Geordie Girl**[30] 5251 2-7-11 63 ow1 DuranFentiman(3) 2 66
(R C Guest) *mde all: 4 l clr 1f out: jst hld on* **9/1**
0005 2 hd **Kashmina**[12] 5746 2-8-2 65 NickyMackay 13 67
(M R Channon) *chsd ldrs on outer: lost pl bnd over 4f out: hdwy over 1f out: wnt 2nd jst ins fnl f: styd on strly: jst hld* **15/2**[3]
000 3 3 **True Time**[37] 5061 2-8-3 66 PaulHanagan 8 61
(E A L Dunlop) *chsd ldrs: kpt on same pce appr fnl f* **9/1**
030 4 1 **Khandala (IRE)**[18] 5595 2-7-13 67 LukeMorris(5) 12 59
(M L W Bell) *chsd ldrs: outpcd 3f out: styd on fnl f* **8/1**
3524 5 2 **Lady Rochbonne**[7] 5883 2-8-4 72 AshleyHamblett(5) 5 59
(Mrs G S Rees) *chsd wnr: wknd fnl f* **9/2**[1]
634 6 1 1/4 **On Instinct (IRE)**[29] 5281 2-8-3 66 RoystonFfrench 7 50
(B Smart) *chsd ldrs: hung rt and wknd over 1f out* **13/2**[2]
1020 7 2 **La Chicaluna**[27] 5322 2-9-4 81 TomEaves 11 60
(J G Given) *chsd ldrs on outside: lost pl over 4f out: sme hdwy over 2f out: nvr a threat* **9/2**[1]
4364 8 1/2 **Prunes**[5] 5932 2-7-5 61 oh2 DanielleMcCreery(7) 9 39
(A Berry) *s.i.s: hdwy towards centre over 2f out: nvr a factor* **11/1**
041 9 1 1/4 **Veronicas Way**[31] 5226 2-7-12 64 AndrewMullen(3) 6 39
(G M Moore) *hld up: sn in tch: effrt over 2f out: sn btn* **15/2**[3]
005 10 14 **Honeycott (IRE)**[22] 5483 2-7-12 61 oh7 LiamJones 1 1
(J D Bethell) *s.i.s: drvn along and sn chsng ldrs: lost pl over 2f out: sn bhd* **40/1**
4040 11 5 **Alexander Monarchy (IRE)**[39] 5015 2-7-12 61 oh5 PaulQuinn 14 —
(D W Barker) *s.i.s: in rr: bhd fnl 2f* **33/1**

1m 30.82s (3.46) **Going Correction** +0.50s/f (Yiel) 11 Ran SP% **118.1**
Speed ratings (Par 94): **100,99,96,95,92 91,89,88,87,71 65**
CSF £75.22 CT £643.63 TOTE £9.00: £3.60, £2.50, £2.50; EX 102.60.
Owner James S Kennerley & Miss Jenny Hall **Bred** Wyck Hall Stud **Trained** Carburton, Notts

FOCUS
No strength in depth in this fillies' nursery but overall the form looks fairly solid rated through the third and fourth.

NOTEBOOK
Geordie Girl had an inside draw. She looked likely to score by a comfortable margin at one stage but in the end she was crying out for the line. (op 12-1)
Kashmina, 3lb lower and dropped back in trip, had an outside draw. She dropped right back starting the home turn but finished with a rattle. A return to a mile should see her getting off the mark. (op 11-1 tchd 7-1)
True Time, who is not that big, ran with credit on her first try in nursery company. (op 5-1)
Khandala(IRE), making her nursery bow, had an outside draw to overcome and will be better suited by a mile. (op 9-1)
Lady Rochbonne, unable to dominate, did not see it out in the rain-soaked ground. (op 5-1)
On Instinct(IRE), tending to hang right-handed, did not improve for the step up in trip on her handicap bow but the testing conditions may not have been in her favour. Official explanation: jockey said filly hung right-handed throughout (op 7-1 tchd 15-2)
La Chicaluna, drawn in double figures, lost her place starting the home turn. She is better than the bare form. (op 13-2)

6076 SKYRAM H'CAP 1m 7f 177y
4:00 (4:00) (Class 6) (0-60,60) 3-Y-O+ **£2,730** (£806; £403) **Stalls** Low

Form RPR
0630 1 **Pagan Starprincess**[68] 4104 3-8-1 52 (p) MatthewDavies(7) 1 61
(G M Moore) *sn chsng ldrs: outpcd and lost pl over 4f out: hdwy over 2f out: edgd rt and led nr fin: dived rt, hit rail and uns rdr sn after line* **11/1**
5121 2 nk **Let It Be**[17] 5626 6-9-13 60 PhillipMakin 4 69
(K G Reveley) *trckd ldrs: styd on to go 2nd over 1f out: no ex nr fin: bdly hmpd and uns rdr sn after line* **4/1**[1]
2060 3 nk **Squirtle (IRE)**[20] 5533 4-9-3 50 LiamJones 13 58
(W M Brisbourne) *s.i.s: hdwy 8f out: sn drvn and chsng ldrs: led 2f out: hdd wl ins fnl f: hmpd line* **11/1**
3234 4 6 **Mr Mischief**[10] 5300 7-9-8 55 SebSanders 2 56
(M C Chapman) *s.i.s: sn chsng ldrs: edgd rt and one pce fnl 2f* **9/2**[2]
1064 5 3 **Jenny Soba**[17] 5626 4-8-8 46 LukeMorris(5) 3 43
(Lucinda Featherstone) *chsd ldrs: wknd fnl 2f* **14/1**
2540 6 3 1/2 **Mcqueen (IRE)**[24] 5426 7-9-9 56 PatCosgrave 9 49
(J T Stimpson) *trckd ldr: led over 5f out tl 2f out: sn wknd* **10/1**
2260 7 19 **Just Waz (USA)**[67] 4124 5-9-8 58 MichaelJStainton(3) 11 28
(R M Whitaker) *hld up in mid-div: lost pl over 4f out* **9/1**[3]
1204 8 1 1/2 **Silver Mont (IRE)**[57] 4451 4-9-8 55 (b) GregFairley 15 24
(S R Bowring) *hld up in midfield: hdwy to join ldrs over 6f out: wknd 2f out* **10/1**
3460 9 1 **Vice Admiral**[17] 5626 4-8-12 52 NSLawes(7) 7 19
(M W Easterby) *hld up in rr: sme hdwy over 5f out: wknd 3f out* **11/1**
4442 10 2 **Moyne Pleasure (IRE)**[76] 3840 9-8-10 46 oh1 (p) DuranFentiman(3) 6 11
(R Johnson) *hld up in rr: sme hdwy over 4f out: wknd 3f out* **12/1**

11 30 **Relix (FR)**[86] 7-9-5 **52**.....................(t) TomEaves 10 —
(A M Crow) *s.i.s: rn in snatches in rr: bhd fnl 5f: t.o* **66/1**

5501 12 18 **Mystified (IRE)**[45] 4246 4-9-11 **58**.....................(b) PaulHanagan 5 —
(R F Fisher) *led tl hdd over 5f out: sn lost pl and bhd: t.o* **14/1**

000/ 13 25 **Beamish Prince**[157] 5663 8-8-11 **47**..................... PJMcDonald(3) 12 —
(Mrs S A Watt) *chsd ldrs: reminders and lost pl 6f out: t.o 4f out* **20/1**

3m 42.67s (11.27) **Going Correction** +0.50s/f (Yiel)
WFA 3 from 4yo+ 11lb **13 Ran SP% 118.6**
Speed ratings (Par 101): **91,90,90,87,86 84,74,74,73,72 57,48,36**
CSF £54.14 CT £508.50 TOTE £17.30: £5.40, £2.40, £6.30; EX 76.30.
Owner Richard Phizacklea **Bred** Richard J Phizacklea **Trained** Middleham Moor, N Yorks
■ Stewards' Enquiry : Matthew Davies caution: careless riding

FOCUS
A low-grade handicap run at a sound pace. The runner-up looks the best guide to the overall value of the form.
Mystified(IRE) Official explanation: jockey said gelding was unsuited by the good (good to soft places) ground

6077 BOOK ON-LINE AT CATTERICKBRIDGE.CO.UK H'CAP 1m 3f 214y
4:30 (4:31) (Class 5) (0-75,72) 3-Y-0+ **£2,914** (£867; £433; £216) **Stalls** High

Form RPR

-136 1 **Ballet Boy (IRE)**[92] 3379 3-9-2 **69**..................... SebSanders 5 85+
(Sir Mark Prescott) *trckd ldrs: led over 2f out: rdn and styd on strly fnl 2f: readily* **11/4**[1]

-460 2 4 **Merrymaker**[10] 5807 7-8-13 **62**..................... PatrickMathers(3) 6 69
(W M Brisbourne) *s.i.s: rn in snatches in last: hdwy over 3f out: styd on to go 2nd 1f out: no imp* **10/1**

0400 3 2 **Frosty Night (IRE)**[25] 5385 3-8-12 **65**.....................(b[1]) GregFairley 3 69
(M Johnston) *led 2f: chsd ldr: led over 3f out tl over 2f out: one pce* **12/1**

1053 4 1 **Its Moon (IRE)**[20] 5523 3-9-5 **72**..................... GrahamGibbons 1 74
(T D Walford) *chsd ldrs: drvn 5f out: one pce fnl 2f* **7/2**[2]

6001 5 4 **Contemplation**[22] 5487 4-9-0 **60**..................... PatCosgrave 4 56
(G A Swinbank) *hld up in tch: effrt over 2f out: rdn and wknd appr fnl f* **11/1**

5533 6 2 **Hue**[10] 5807 6-9-3 **63**.....................(b) TomEaves 8 56
(B Ellison) *hld up in tch: effrt over 2f out: sn rdn and hung lft: lost pl over 1f out* **4/1**[3]

0603 7 4 **Wulimaster (USA)**[15] 5676 4-8-12 **58**..................... TonyHamilton 7 44
(D W Barker) *chsd ldrs: rdn and lost pl over 2f out* **9/1**

0130 8 3 **Rare Coincidence**[11] 5769 6-9-6 **69**.....................(p) PaulHanagan 2 50
(R F Fisher) *w ldr: led after 2f: hdd over 3f out: wkng whn styd far side to r alone over 3f out* **15/2**

2m 46.46s (7.46) **Going Correction** +0.50s/f (Yiel)
WFA 3 from 4yo+ 7lb **8 Ran SP% 115.8**
Speed ratings (Par 103): **95,92,91,90,87 86,83,81**
CSF £31.51 CT £284.96 TOTE £3.30: £1.20, £3.10, £3.60; EX 33.00.
Owner Syndicate 2005 **Bred** Knocklong House Stud **Trained** Newmarket, Suffolk

FOCUS
A sound gallop and in the end a most decisive winner who looks sure to better the bare form. The time confirmed that the official going report was wildly misleading.

6078 GO RACING AT YORK THIS FRIDAY APPRENTICE H'CAP 5f
5:00 (5:01) (Class 6) (0-55,61) 3-Y-0+ **£2,730** (£806; £403) **Stalls** Low

Form RPR

5430 1 **Baybshambles (IRE)**[13] 5741 3-8-13 **52**..................... DuranFentiman 1 63
(R E Barr) *racd far side: hld up: hdwy over 1f out: styd on wl towards centre to ld last 100yds* **10/1**

5000 2 1 **Spirit Of Coniston**[40] 4973 4-8-2 **48**..................... AdeleRothery(7) 5 56
(D Nicholls) *racd far side: overall ldr: hung lft intersection over 3f out: hdd and no ex ins fnl f* **8/1**

-000 3 ½ **Two Acres (IRE)**[20] 5535 4-8-11 **50**..................... MarkLawson 3 56
(A G Newcombe) *racd far side: w ldrs: kpt on same pce ins fnl f* **25/1**

0002 4 2 **Royal Guest**[8] 5861 3-8-8 **47**.....................(v) LiamJones 13 46+
(M R Channon) *s.s: racd stands' side: hdwy 2f out: styd on to ld that gp ins fnl f* **5/1**[2]

5026 5 2½ **Valiant Romeo**[5] 5930 7-8-9 **48**..................... PJMcDonald 4 38
(R Bastiman) *racd stands' side: chsd ldrs: led that gp and edgd lft over 1f out: kpt on same pce* **8/1**

0221 6 nk **No Time (IRE)**[6] 5908 7-9-3 **61** 6ex..................... MCGeran(5) 2 50
(A J McCabe) *racd far side: chsd ldrs: wknd fnl f* **3/1**[1]

000 7 ¾ **Sharp Hat**[19] 5566 13-8-7 **46** oh1..................... GregFairley 9 32
(D W Chapman) *rrd s: racd stands' side: hdwy to chse ldrs over 3f out: kpt on same pce over 1f out* **11/1**

3500 8 2½ **The Geester**[24] 5420 3-8-4 **46** oh1.....................(b) LukeMorris(3) 10 23
(S R Bowring) *dwlt and sltly hmpd sn after s: racd stands' side: nvr trbld ldrs* **33/1**

5004 9 ½ **Axis Shield (IRE)**[56] 4485 4-8-0 **46** oh1..................... SoniaEaton(7) 6 21
(M C Chapman) *racd far side: w ldrs: wknd appr fnl f* **40/1**

6004 10 ½ **Legal Set (IRE)**[5] 5930 11-8-9 **53**.....................(b) JamesO'Reilly(5) 12 26
(Miss A Stokell) *led stands' side tl hdd & wknd over 1f out* **6/1**[3]

660 11 4 **Safranine (IRE)**[17] 5627 10-8-11 **50**..................... MichaelJStainton 15 9
(Miss A Stokell) *racd stands' side: w ldrs: lost pl 2f out* **22/1**

305 12 2½ **Maromito (IRE)**[9] 5836 10-8-13 **52**..................... AndrewMullen 7 2
(R Bastiman) *racd stands' side: w ldrs: lost pl over 1f out* **9/1**

0-00 13 9 **Golband**[28] 5297 5-8-4 **46** oh1.....................(b[1]) NicolPolli(3) 11 —
(J O'Reilly) *racd far side: chsd ldrs: hung rt and lost pl 2f out* **50/1**

63.38 secs (2.78) **Going Correction** +0.50s/f (Yiel) **13 Ran SP% 121.1**
Speed ratings (Par 101): **97,95,94,91,87 86,85,81,80,80 73,69,55**
CSF £84.35 CT £1286.70 TOTE £11.70: £2.20, £2.60, £9.10; EX 103.70 Place 6 £191.89, Place 5 £106.89.
Owner Miss S Haykin **Bred** Mrs H F Mahr **Trained** Seamer, N Yorks

FOCUS
Five raced towards the far side, including the first three home. The form seems sound enough and the decisive winner should improve again at four. The soft ground was blamed by three of the unplaced riders but it was never changed during a very wet afternoon. The off-course punters can rightly feel let down by officialdom.
Royal Guest Official explanation: jockey said gelding missed the break
Valiant Romeo Official explanation: jockey said gelding was unsuited by the good (good to soft places) ground
No Time(IRE) Official explanation: jockey said horse was unsuited by the good (good to soft places) ground
Sharp Hat Official explanation: jockey said gelding reared as the stalls opened
Maromito(IRE) Official explanation: jockey said gelding was unsuited by the good (good to soft places) ground
T/Jkpt: Not won. T/Plt: £209.40 to a £1 stake. Pool: £55,936.00. 195.00 winning tickets. T/Qpdt: £151.70 to a £1 stake. Pool: £3,054.80. 14.90 winning tickets. WG

5712 FOLKESTONE (R-H)
Tuesday, October 9

OFFICIAL GOING: Soft changing to heavy after race 2 (2.20) (meeting abandoned after race 5 (3.50) on grounds of safety)
The official report was that 20mm of rain had fallen by the fifth race and there was lying water in the dip after a furlong.
Wind: Moderate becoming strong, half-behind Weather: Heavy rain

6079 P A GRANT ELECTRICAL MAIDEN STKS (DIV I) 7f (S)
1:50 (1:53) (Class 5) 2-Y-O **£2,266** (£674; £337; £168) **Stalls** Low

Form RPR

00 1 **Desert Thistle (IRE)**[17] 5633 2-9-3 0..................... IanMongan 6 76
(H J L Dunlop) *w.w in rr: shkn up and prog against nr side rail 2f out: sustained effrt to ld last 75yds: won gng away* **33/1**

045 2 1 **Glittering Prize (UAE)**[11] 5770 2-8-12 67..................... DarryllHolland 5 69
(M Johnston) *led: shkn up 2f out: hdd and no ex last 75yds* **11/4**[2]

3 2 **Street Devil (USA)** 2-9-3 0..................... GeorgeBaker 11 69
(P A Blockley) *dwlt: hld up in rr: smooth prog on outer 3f out: rdn over 1f out: one pce after* **11/1**

54 4 nk **Compton Ridge**[8] 5872 2-9-3 0..................... OscarUrbina 8 68
(Mrs A J Perrett) *prom: chsd ldr 2f out to 1f out: wknd* **2/1**[1]

5 1¼ **Spiritonthemount (USA)** 2-9-3 0..................... MichaelHills 7 65
(B W Hills) *s.s: v green and sn t.o: prog on wd outside fr 3f out: kpt on: n.d: bttr for experience* **8/1**

0 6 shd **Muharjam**[20] 5541 2-9-3 0..................... KerrinMcEvoy 3 64
(C E Brittain) *settled in rr: outpcd 2f out: pushed along on outer and kpt on fnl f* **16/1**

0 7 4 **My Flame**[8] 5868 2-9-3 0..................... PaulDoe 9 54
(J R Jenkins) *mostly chsd ldr to 2f out: hanging lft and wknd* **100/1**

0 8 1¼ **Romford Car Two**[31] 5222 2-9-0 0..................... JerryO'Dwyer(3) 2 51
(Miss J Feilden) *cl up against nr side rail: reminder after 3f: wknd wl over 1f out* **20/1**

6 9 1¾ **Redarsene**[15] 5679 2-8-12 0..................... JamieJones(5) 1 47
(M G Quinlan) *chsd ldrs: shkn up and no prog 2f out: wknd sn after* **4/1**[3]

0000 10 5 **Jermajesty (IRE)**[54] 4547 2-8-10 50.....................(v[1]) HarryPoulton(7) 10 34
(J R Boyle) *in tch on outer: wknd rapidly and floundering over 1f out* **100/1**

05 11 5 **Ryan's Rock**[41] 4946 2-9-3 0..................... RobertHavlin 4 22
(T D McCarthy) *dwlt: in tch tl wknd over 2f out: sn bhd* **66/1**

1m 30.86s (2.96) **Going Correction** +0.325s/f (Good) **11 Ran SP% 116.5**
Speed ratings (Par 95): **96,94,92,92,90 90,86,84,82,76 71**
CSF £119.92 TOTE £39.90: £8.10, £1.70, £3.40; EX 169.90.
Owner Harry Dunlop Racing Partnership **Bred** Allan A Brown **Trained** Lambourn, Berks

FOCUS
An ordinary juvenile maiden which saw the field finish fairly strung out on the testing surface. The winner, who had the advantage of the stands' rail in the final 2f, was much improved but it was no fluke.

NOTEBOOK
Desert Thistle(IRE), who had shown just moderate form in two previous outings, proved a totally different proposition on this switch to softer ground and got off the mark with a ready display. He took time to wind up, but he appreciated being taken to the stands' rail around 2f out and finished his race in good style. The step up to 1m promises to suit him even better now and he can expect an official mark in the mid 60s for this. (op 50-1)
Glittering Prize(UAE) enjoyed the switch to a more positive ride and again showed a liking for this sort of ground, but she failed to see out the extra furlong as well as the winner. She will look better off when switching to nurseries and has a small race within her compass. (tchd 5-2)
Street Devil(USA), a 40,000gns half-brother to dual 1m-1m2f winner Art Sale, took time to warm up and was noted doing his best work inside the final 2f. He should improve a deal for this debut experience, will stay further in time, and may appreciate a sounder surface in due course. (tchd 10-1 and 12-1)
Compton Ridge ran below his recent level and failed to see out the longer trip on this more testing surface. He now has the option of nurseries and is capable of better in that sphere. (op 15-8)
Spiritonthemount(USA), a 60,000gns Derby entrant, proved easy to back for this racecourse bow and proved too green to do himself full justice. He got the hang of things when the race was effectively over, however, and should learn plenty from this run. (op 7-1)
Redarsene, again the subject of market support, failed to raise his game on this switch to the turf and never seriously threatened over this shorter trip. He needs one more run to qualify for a handicap mark. (op 7-1)

6080 P A GRANT ELECTRICAL MAIDEN STKS (DIV II) 7f (S)
2:20 (2:23) (Class 5) 2-Y-O **£2,266** (£674; £337; £168) **Stalls** Low

Form RPR

52 1 **Quam Celerrime**[15] 5680 2-9-3 0..................... JamieSpencer 1 76
(P A Blockley) *s.s: in tch against nr side rail: prog over 2f out: chal over 1f out: led ins fnl f: hld on* **4/1**[2]

5 2 hd **Funseeker (UAE)**[10] 5812 2-8-12 0..................... DarryllHolland 3 71
(M Johnston) *w nr side ldrs: led 3f out: rdr dropped whip wl over 1f out: hdd ins fnl f: battled on wl* **13/2**

0 3 2½ **Skycruiser (IRE)**[20] 5541 2-9-3 0..................... KerrinMcEvoy 4 69
(Saeed Bin Suroor) *hld up in rr nr side: prog on outer over 2f out: pressed ldrs 1f out: wknd last 100yds* **9/1**

45 4 1 **Mcconnell (USA)**[18] 5595 2-9-3 0..................... JohnEgan 7 67
(J R Best) *t.k.h: hld up bhd ldrs: rdn 2f out: chsd ldng trio 1f out: nudged along and no imp* **6/1**[3]

62 5 3 **Shanzu**[13] 5720 2-8-12 0..................... DaneO'Neill 8 54
(H Candy) *w nr side ldrs to 2f out: grad fdd* **9/4**[1]

06 6 1¾ **Hawk House**[76] 3850 2-9-3 0..................... MichaelHills 2 55
(B W Hills) *restless in stalls: chsd nr side ldrs: one pce and no imp 2f out: fdd fnl f* **8/1**

0 7 ½ **Last Of The Line**[18] 5587 2-9-3 0..................... RobertHavlin 11 54
(H J L Dunlop) *led far side quartet: clr of others 3f out: hung bdly lft fnl 2f and nt on terms* **33/1**

8 7 **Serious Choice (IRE)** 2-9-3 0..................... IanMongan 5 36
(J R Boyle) *s.s: racd nr side: a wl bhd* **40/1**

05 9 ½ **Aim**[19] 5570 2-9-3 0..................... PaulDoe 6 35
(J R Jenkins) *mde most nr side to 3f out: wknd 2f out* **100/1**

0 10 5 **Trudder (USA)**[18] 5599 2-9-3 0..................... AdrianMcCarthy 10 22
(P W Chapple-Hyam) *chsd far side ldr to 1/2-way but nvr on terms: hung lft over 2f out* **25/1**

11 11 **Floral Guest** 2-8-12 0..................... TQuinn 12 —
(G G Margarson) *s.s: sn rdn in last on far side: t.o* **40/1**

12 20 **Fungible** 2-9-3 0 .... PhilipRobinson 9 —
(E A L Dunlop) *chsd far side ldr to 1/2-way: wknd and sn t.o* **20/1**

1m 31.29s (3.39) **Going Correction** +0.325s/f (Good) **12** Ran SP% **116.9**
Speed ratings (Par 95): **93,92,89,88,85 83,82,74,74,68 55,33**
CSF £27.50 TOTE £5.40: £2.20, £1.40, £3.30; EX 29.40.
Owner Mrs Jacqueline Connolly **Bred** Mrs C Regalado-Gonzalez **Trained** Lambourn, Berks

FOCUS
This second division of the maiden was another modest affair in deteriorating ground. All bar four of the runners kept to the near side. The first pair came clear and set the standard.

NOTEBOOK
Quam Celerrime again took time to hit full stride, but the taxing surface on this switch to turf played into his hands on that front and he eventually just did enough to open his account at the third attempt. The return to 1m ought to be more in his favour again now and it will be interesting to see what official mark he is now given. (op 7-2)
Funseeker(UAE) ◆, dropping down a furlong, proved game under maximum pressure and only just failed. She handled the deep surface without fuss and, nicely clear of the remainder at the finish, should not be long in going one better. Official explanation: jockey said whip was knocked from his hand closing stages (op 4-1 tchd 7-1)
Skycruiser(IRE) was given a patient ride and came through to have his chance, before running out of steam on this more demanding surface. This was a step in the right direction and he can build on this again, but he does look like proving a very expensive acquisition. (op 11-1)
Mcconnell(USA) proved too free for his own good on this step up in trip and was never really in the hunt. He should learn from his run and is worth chancing again over this distance when reverting to a sounder surface. He also now qualifies for nurseries. Official explanation: jockey said colt was unsuited by the soft ground (op 4-1)
Shanzu, well backed, dropped out disappointingly when push came to shove and looked to find this ground too soft for her liking. She is now eligible for a nursery mark and it is too soon to write her off. (op 7-2)
Last Of The Line Official explanation: jockey said colt hung left
Trudder(USA) Official explanation: trainer's rep said colt finished lame

6081 SANDOM ROBINSON H'CAP 7f (S)
2:50 (2:53) (Class 5) (0-75,75) 3-Y-0+ **£2,914** (£867; £433; £216) **Stalls** Low

Form RPR
0120 **1** **The Fifth Member (IRE)**[35] 5122 3-8-12 **71** .... IanMongan 3 89
(J R Boyle) *trckd nr side ldrs: rdn to ld over 1f out: drew clr fnl f* **6/1**[3]
4001 **2** 5 **Red Somerset (USA)**[15] 5693 4-9-3 **74** .... JamieSpencer 4 79
(R J Hodges) *s.i.s: hld up bhd nr side ldrs: effrt and nt clr run over 1f out: wnt 2nd ins fnl f: no ch w wnr* **3/1**[1]
3343 **3** 1 ¼ **Best One**[37] 5064 3-8-13 **72** .... (t) JohnEgan 2 74
(C E Brittain) *pressed nr side ldr: led 3f out to over 1f out: one pce u.p* **12/1**
3334 **4** *hd* **Alpes Maritimes**[29] 5285 3-9-2 **75** .... DarryllHolland 9 76
(G Wragg) *led nr side to 3f out: cl up tl fdd 1f out* **5/1**[2]
103 **5** 1 ¼ **Perfect Treasure (IRE)**[19] 5560 4-9-4 **75** .... RobertHavlin 12 73
(J A R Toller) *led far side pair: nt on terms w nr side over 1f out* **15/2**
5130 **6** 5 **Finsbury**[39] 4999 4-8-12 **69** .... DaneO'Neill 7 54
(J M Bradley) *outpcd in last on nr side: effrt over 2f out: nt rch ldrs over 1f out: wknd* **11/1**
4240 **7** 16 **Highland Harvest**[17] 5620 3-9-1 **74** .... TQuinn 11 18
(D R C Elsworth) *jnd far side ldr after 1f: wknd over 2f out: eased over 1f out: t.o* **9/1**
3506 **8** 2 ½ **Averticus**[17] 5635 3-9-1 **74** .... (b) MichaelHills 5 11
(B W Hills) *trckd nr side ldrs tl wknd over 2f out: eased: t.o* **9/1**
6005 **9** 13 **Grizedale (IRE)**[35] 5115 8-8-13 **70** .... (t) PaulDoe 10 —
(J Akehurst) *chsd nr side ldrs 3f: sn wknd: t.o* **10/1**
0100 **10** 1 ¼ **Glencalvie (IRE)**[14] 5712 6-9-4 **75** .... (p) GeorgeBaker 6 —
(J Akehurst) *bhd fr 1/2-way: t.o* **16/1**

1m 30.05s (2.15) **Going Correction** +0.525s/f (Yiel)
WFA 3 from 4yo+ 2lb **10** Ran SP% **118.7**
Speed ratings (Par 103): **108,102,100,100,99 93,75,72,57,56**
CSF £24.81 CT £188.98 TOTE £8.10: £2.70, £1.20, £3.40; EX 35.10.
Owner Chris Simpson, Miss Elizabeth Ross **Bred** Ms Amy Mulligan **Trained** Epsom, Surrey

FOCUS
The ground was officially changed to heavy prior to this race. A modest handicap and the winner rates full value for his winning margin.
Grizedale(IRE) Official explanation: jockey said gelding was unsuited by the heavy ground
Glencalvie(IRE) Official explanation: jockey said gelding was unsuited by the heavy ground

6082 REACTIVE UK MAIDEN FILLIES' STKS 6f
3:20 (3:24) (Class 5) 2-Y-0 **£2,914** (£867; £433; £216) **Stalls** Low

Form RPR
3 **1** **Danseuse Volante (IRE)**[18] 5591 2-9-0 0 .... TQuinn 1 69
(J W Hills) *racd against nr side rail: mde virtually all: drvn and pressed over 1f out: kpt on wl* **2/1**[1]
06 **2** 1 **Luminous Gold**[13] 5720 2-9-0 0 .... DarryllHolland 9 66
(C F Wall) *pressed ldng pair: wnt 2nd wl over 1f out and sn jnd wnr: no ex last 100yds* **4/1**[2]
0 **3** 2 ½ **Santa Clara**[24] 5428 2-9-0 0 .... JamieSpencer 5 59
(Jane Chapple-Hyam) *w wnr to 2f out: sn outpcd: plugged on again fnl f* **5/1**[3]
4 *shd* **Indian Diva (IRE)** 2-9-0 0 .... (b[1]) JohnEgan 3 58
(P A Blockley) *sn trckd ldrs: shkn up and nt qckn wl over 1f out: one pce after* **12/1**
6 **5** 12 **Rowan Dancer**[32] 5202 2-9-0 0 .... MichaelHills 7 22+
(J R Boyle) *sn bhd: t.o* **5/1**[3]
36 **6** *nk* **Lady Of The Park (IRE)**[40] 4968 2-9-0 0 .... FrankieMcDonald 12 21
(P A Blockley) *wl in tch on outer tl wknd rapidly 2f out: t.o* **16/1**
7 3 **Redchete** 2-9-0 0 .... DaneO'Neill 2 12
(C E Brittain) *sn wl bhd: t.o* **15/2**

1m 18.3s (4.70) **Going Correction** +0.525s/f (Yiel) **7** Ran SP% **112.0**
Speed ratings (Par 92): **89,87,84,84,68 67,63**
CSF £9.63 TOTE £2.70: £1.10, £3.10; EX 11.40.
Owner Mrs F Hills **Bred** Churchtown Bloodstock **Trained** Upper Lambourn, Berks

FOCUS
An uncompetitive fillies' maiden run on what by this stage was really bad ground. They all raced stands' side and the winner ran close to her debut form.

NOTEBOOK
Danseuse Volante(IRE) handled the testing ground and confirmed the promise she showed when third on her debut at Newbury, but she was made to work very hard. This was not a very competitive maiden, and she may want a bit of time to recover, but she looks a nice prospect. (tchd 9-4)
Luminous Gold ◆, dropped back to 6f for the first time, ensured the favourite had a proper race and finished nicely clear of the remainder. She will have more options now she is qualified for a handicap mark and she is in the right hands to pick up a race or two. (op 7-2 tchd 9-2)
Santa Clara improved on the form she showed on her debut on much quicker ground at Warwick, but she was still well held. (tchd 4-1 and 11-2)
Indian Diva(IRE), a 40,000euros daughter of Indian Danehill, half-sister to among others multiple 5f winner Straffan, was fitted with blinkers on her racecourse debut. She showed ability and is entitled to come on for the experience. (tchd 14-1)
Rowan Dancer should do much better when stepped up in trip and it might be worth noting her yard recently landed a big gamble with a handicap debutant. (op 6-1)

6083 PENTINS H'CAP 6f
3:50 (3:52) (Class 6) (0-65,65) 3-Y-0+ **£2,388** (£705; £352) **Stalls** Low

Form RPR
0020 **1** **Proud Killer**[46] 4767 4-8-11 **61** .... JerryO'Dwyer(3) 8 73
(J R Jenkins) *racd against nr side rail: pressed ldr: rdn to ld over 1f out: clr ins fnl f* **6/1**
1060 **2** 2 ½ **Looks Could Kill (USA)**[57] 4462 5-9-1 **62** .... RobertHavlin 1 67
(A B Haynes) *chsd ldrs: rdn 2f out: kpt on to take 2nd ins fnl f: no threat to wnr* **4/1**[2]
0036 **3** 1 ¼ **Our Ruby**[59] 4395 3-9-2 **64** .... (b) AdrianMcCarthy 4 65
(P W Chapple-Hyam) *sn rdn in last and struggling: kpt on fnl 2f against nr side rail: nvr able to chal* **7/1**
1000 **4** 1 ½ **Castano**[22] 5473 3-9-3 **65** .... DarryllHolland 11 61
(B R Millman) *led to over 1f out: wknd* **5/1**[3]
4200 **5** 2 **Goose Green (IRE)**[15] 5687 3-9-1 **63** .... GeorgeBaker 6 53
(R J Hodges) *trckd ldrs tl wknd wl over 1f out* **6/1**
5400 **6** 5 **Silver Hotspur**[4] 5970 3-8-12 **60** .... TQuinn 9 35
(M Wigham) *cl up tl wknd 2f out* **20/1**
5163 **7** ¾ **Plateau**[6] 5909 8-9-4 **65** .... JohnEgan 10 38
(C R Dore) *awkward s: settled in rr on outer: reminder and no prog over 2f out: no ch whn eased fnl f* **5/2**[1]

1m 16.59s (2.99) **Going Correction** +0.525s/f (Yiel)
WFA 3 from 4yo+ 1lb **7** Ran SP% **111.1**
Speed ratings (Par 101): **101,97,96,94,91 84,83**
CSF £28.26 CT £164.43 TOTE £7.30: £3.10, £2.90; EX 29.70 Place 6 £59.98, Place 5 £22.16.
Owner Nolan's Bar Racing Syndicate **Bred** Grove Stud Farm **Trained** Royston, Herts

FOCUS
A modest sprint handicap run in bad ground. They stayed stands' side and the winner, rated back to his maiden win, had the advantage of racing against the rail.

6084 PARKER STEEL H'CAP 6f
() (Class 4) (0-80,) 3-Y-0+ £

6085 COLOUR DECOR H'CAP 5f
() (Class 5) (0-70,) 3-Y-0+ £

6086 NASONS OF CANTERBURY LTD H'CAP 1m 4f
() (Class 5) (0-75,) 3-Y-0+ £

T/Plt: £129.70 to a £1 stake. Pool: £53,562.35. 301.45 winning tickets. T/Qpdt: £17.10 to a £1 stake. Pool: £3,673.40. 158.20 winning tickets. JN

5687 LEICESTER (R-H)
Tuesday, October 9

OFFICIAL GOING: Soft (good to soft in places)
Wind: Light, across Weather: Overcast, but getting brighter as the afternoon went on

6087 EBF LADBROKES.COM MAIDEN FILLIES' STKS (DIV I) 7f 9y
2:10 (2:15) (Class 4) 2-Y-0 **£4,210** (£1,252; £625; £312) **Stalls** Centre

Form RPR
1 **Laughter (IRE)** 2-9-0 0 .... JimmyFortune 9 86+
(Sir Michael Stoute) *prom: shkn up over 2f out: rdn to ld ins fnl f: edgd lft: r.o* **4/1**[2]
2 ½ **Full Marks** 2-9-0 0 .... KDarley 8 85+
(J Noseda) *led: rdn over 1f out: hdd and nt clr run ins fnl f: styd on* **12/1**
3 1 ¼ **Desert Chill (USA)** 2-9-0 0 .... LDettori 4 82
(Saeed Bin Suroor) *chsd ldrs: rdn and ev ch over 1f out: styd on same pce ins fnl f* **15/8**[1]
4 3 **Diamond Royal (IRE)** 2-9-0 0 .... TPQueally 7 74
(E A L Dunlop) *hld up: hdwy over 2f out: rdn over 1f out: styd on same pce* **20/1**
5 3 ½ **Syvilla** 2-9-0 0 .... MickyFenton 3 65
(Rae Guest) *s.i.s: hld up: hdwy over 1f out: edgd rt: nt trble ldrs* **66/1**
6 3 **Alseraaj (USA)** 2-9-0 0 .... RHills 13 58
(Sir Michael Stoute) *s.i.s: hld up: hdwy 1/2-way: wknd fnl f* **7/1**
7 *nk* **Pretty Orchid** 2-9-0 0 .... SaleemGolam 12 57
(G C H Chung) *hld up: hdwy over 4f out: rdn and wknd over 1f out* **100/1**
8 1 ¾ **Tahajjum** 2-9-0 0 .... J-PGuillambert 14 53
(C E Brittain) *chsd ldrs: rdn 1/2-way: wknd over 2f out* **33/1**
9 *nk* **Madame Bountiful** 2-9-0 0 .... FergusSweeney 15 52
(A King) *sn chsng ldrs: rdn over 2f out: sn hung lft and wknd* **50/1**
10 2 ½ **Sterope (FR)** 2-9-0 0 .... TedDurcan 6 46
(H R A Cecil) *prom: rdn: hung rt and wknd 1/2-way* **5/1**[3]
11 ½ **Centenerola (USA)** 2-9-0 0 .... JimCrowley 1 45
(B W Hills) *sn outpcd* **28/1**
12 4 **Alabama Mama (IRE)** 2-9-0 0 .... FrancisNorton 10 35
(H J L Dunlop) *chsd ldrs over 4f* **25/1**
13 1 ½ **Marraasi (USA)** 2-9-0 0 .... DaleGibson 11 31
(M P Tregoning) *chsd ldrs: rdn over 2f out: wknd over 1f out* **16/1**
0 **14** 8 **Que Beauty (IRE)**[12] 5745 2-9-0 0 .... DanielTudhope 5 11
(R C Guest) *dwlt: in rr: rdn 1/2-way: sn lost tch* **150/1**

1m 28.16s (2.06) **Going Correction** +0.30s/f (Good) **14** Ran SP% **117.6**
Speed ratings (Par 94): **100,99,98,94,90 87,86,84,84,81 81,76,74,65**
CSF £46.06 TOTE £4.50: £1.60, £3.50, £1.70; EX 38.80 Trifecta £157.00 Part won. Pool: £221.24 - 0.44 winning tickets..
Owner Highclere Thoroughbred Racing(Petrushka) **Bred** Quay Bloodstock **Trained** Newmarket, Suffolk

FOCUS
Probably a fair maiden, and the quicker of the two divisions by 0.93sec.

NOTEBOOK
Laughter(IRE), who cost 185,000gns, is a half-sister to a winner over 7f plus in the US. She relished the soft ground, being a daughter of Sadler's Wells, and looks a useful middle-distance prospect for next year. (op 11-2)
Full Marks, whose dam won over 1m at two and was later quite useful over 1m4f at three, made much of the running and battled on well to the line. She is entitled to improve for the outing but will not be seen at her best until next year.

Desert Chill(USA), whose dam won the Breeders' Cup Juvenile Fillies and was US champion two-year-old, is a half-sister to Another Storm, a two-year-old winner on turf in the US, and to a US winner at 1m plus. The ground, which had softened considerably from the forecast good to firm, was probably not in her favour, so she did not run badly in the circumstances. She can do better on quicker ground. (op 6-4 tchd 2-1)

Diamond Royal(IRE), a half-sister to Chantilly Tiffany, a dual 1m winner at three, and Turner, a 2m winner at four, was staying on at the finish and is going to appreciate a good deal further next season.

Syvilla, a half-sister to smart La Martina, a multiple 7f winner in Italy and the US, Icing, a 7f winner at two, and Kinball, a multiple 1m winner in Italy, is by Nayef and another bred to want a good deal further in time. She was staying on nicely after a slow start. (op 50-1)

Alseraaj(USA), whose dam was a 6f winner on her only start at two and was later quite useful over 1m3f at three, was the lesser fancied of the Stoute pair, but she did not shape too badly until tiring in the soft ground. (tchd 13-2)

Sterope(FR), a half-sister to high-class Multidimensional, was a bit disappointning on her debut but should be capable of better in time. (op 6-1 tchd 13-2)

6088 LADBROKES.COM APPRENTICE H'CAP 7f 9y

2:40 (2:41) (Class 5) (0-70,70) 3-Y-0+ **£2,914** (£867; £433; £216) **Stalls** Centre

Form RPR

6260 **1** **Rydal Mount (IRE)**[31] 5223 4-8-13 **69** TimothyMeadows[(7)] 4 76
(W S Kittow) *chsd ldrs: led ins fnl f: r.o* **11/1**

0603 **2** *¾* **Crow's Nest Lad**[14] 5701 3-8-9 **63** GaryBartley[(3)] 3 68
(T D Easterby) *a.p: rdn and hung rt over 1f out: styd on* **12/1**

310 **3** *1* **One Giant Leap (IRE)**[43] 4880 3-8-13 **69** ow5 RyanBird[(5)] 13 71
(H Morrison) *mid-div: hdwy over 2f out: rdn over 1f out: no ex ins fnl f* **12/1**

0200 **4** *nk* **Regal Dream (IRE)**[24] 5433 5-8-5 **57** JackMitchell[(3)] 14 59
(J W Unett) *chsd ldrs: led over 4f out: rdn over 1f out: hdd and no ex ins fnl f* **16/1**

3143 **5** *hd* **Pelham Crescent (IRE)**[14] 5708 4-8-6 **60** LanceBetts[(5)] 7 61
(B Palling) *mid-div: rdn over 2f out: sn outpcd: styd on ins fnl f* **11/2**[2]

0000 **6** *hd* **Tempsford Flyer (IRE)**[19] 5568 4-9-6 **69** PatrickHills 10 70
(J W Hills) *chsd ldrs: rdn 1/2-way: edgd lft over 1f out: styd on same pce* **9/1**

0200 **7** *¾* **Certain Justice (USA)**[17] 5638 9-9-7 **70** TolleyDean 12 69
(Stef Liddiard) *mid-div: rdn over 2f out: styd on* **5/1**[1]

-000 **8** *nk* **Queen's Composer (IRE)**[67] 4137 4-9-5 **68** NeilBrown 5 66
(B Smart) *s.i.s: hld up: rdn: hung rt and r.o ins fnl f: nvr nrr* **12/1**

300 **9** *nk* **Kassuta**[36] 5098 3-8-4 **60** oh11 ow4 (p) MarkCoumbe[(5)] 15 57
(John A Harris) *s.i.s: hld up: hdwy u.p over 2f out: no ex fnl f* **50/1**

5003 **10** *¾* **Kingscross**[15] 5687 9-8-7 **61** LauraReynolds[(5)] 8 56
(M Blanshard) *s.i.s: in rr: rdn over 1f out: n.d* **7/1**[3]

3050 **11** *hd* **Spy Gun (USA)**[74] 3906 7-8-0 **56** oh11 Julie-AnneCumine[(7)] 9 51
(T Wall) *chsd ldrs: lost pl over 5f out: n.d after* **50/1**

134 **12** *12* **Goodenough Mover**[14] 5711 11-9-1 **67** (b) ThomasO'Brien[(3)] 1 30
(Andrew Turnell) *led: hdd over 5f out: rdn over 2f out: sn wknd* **8/1**

6445 **13** *50* **Pride Of Northcare (IRE)**[20] 5546 3-8-6 **60** JamieHamblett[(3)] 11 —
(G A Huffer) *plld hrd: led over 5f out: hdd over 4f out: wknd over 2f out* **8/1**

1m 28.21s (2.11) **Going Correction** +0.30s/f (Good)
WFA 3 from 4yo+ 2lb **13** Ran SP% **118.0**
Speed ratings (Par 103): **99,98,97,96,96 96,95,95,94,93 93,79,22**
CSF £134.86 CT £1660.68 TOTE £14.60: £5.50, £3.20, £2.30; EX 173.20 TRIFECTA Not won..
Owner Reg Gifford **Bred** D R Tucker **Trained** Blackborough, Devon

■ A first winner for apprentice Timothy Meadows.

■ Stewards' Enquiry : Gary Bartley two-day ban: used whip with excessive frequency (Oct 21-22)

FOCUS
A modest handicap restricted to apprentices who had not ridden more than 50 winners. Something of a bunch finish and rather muddling form.

Pride Of Northcare(IRE) Official explanation: jockey said gelding finished lame

6089 LADBROKESCASINO.COM FILLIES' H'CAP 5f 218y

3:10 (3:11) (Class 5) (0-70,70) 3-Y-0+ **£2,914** (£867; £433; £216) **Stalls** Low

Form RPR

5300 **1** **Scarlet Oak**[34] 5136 3-8-8 **60** RichardThomas 4 73
(D J S Ffrench Davis) *chsd ldrs: rdn to ld 1f out: edgd lft: styd on* **16/1**

3004 **2** *¾* **Overwing (IRE)**[17] 5642 4-8-11 **62** LDettori 2 72
(R M H Cowell) *led: rdn and hdd over 1f out: styd on* **9/2**[2]

5100 **3** *1 ¼* **Metal Guru**[46] 4759 3-8-9 **66** RussellKennemore[(5)] 3 73
(R Hollinshead) *hld up in tch: rdn and ev ch ins fnl f: styd on same pce* **14/1**

2510 **4** *1* **Dasheena**[11] 5778 4-7-12 **56** (be) SophieDoyle[(7)] 8 60
(A J McCabe) *chsd ldrs: rdn over 1f out: no ex ins fnl f* **16/1**

2401 **5** *hd* **Feelin Foxy**[16] 5662 3-9-4 **70** TPQueally 10 73
(J G Given) *trckd ldr: led over 1f out: sn rdn and hdd: no ex* **11/1**

5052 **6** *¾* **Poppy's Rose**[16] 5662 3-8-13 **65** DanielTudhope 6 66
(I W McInnes) *hld up: hdwy u.p over 1f out: nt trble ldrs* **13/2**[3]

4006 **7** *nk* **Linda Green**[8] 5874 6-9-4 **69** DavidAllan 1 69
(M R Channon) *chsd ldrs: n.m.r and lost pl 5f out: sn rdn: hung rt fr 1/2-way: n.d after* **4/1**[1]

1515 **8** *3 ½* **Pragmatist**[34] 5134 3-8-10 **62** JimCrowley 11 51
(P Winkworth) *hld up: hdwy over 2f out: rdn: edgd lft and wknd over 1f out* **13/2**[3]

5232 **9** *hd* **Tilsworth Charlie**[17] 5627 4-8-8 **59** (b) StephenCarson 7 48
(J R Jenkins) *hld up: rdn over 1f out: a in rr* **7/1**

4100 **10** *6* **Limonia (GER)**[8] 5866 5-8-0 **58** oh4 ow2 JosephWalsh[(7)] 13 29
(Mike Murphy) *trckd ldrs: rdn 1/2-way: wknd 2f out* **16/1**

3504 **11** *3 ½* **Appleby**[21] 5510 3-8-12 **64** JimmyFortune 15 24
(J H M Gosden) *wnt rt s: hld up: rdn over 2f out: sn wknd* **16/1**

1m 13.88s (0.68) **Going Correction** +0.30s/f (Good)
WFA 3 from 4yo+ 1lb **11** Ran SP% **115.9**
Speed ratings (Par 100): **107,106,104,103,102 101,101,96,96,88 83**
CSF £85.41 CT £767.35 TOTE £23.10: £5.00, £1.80, £4.60; EX 173.10 TRIFECTA Not won..
Owner Miss A Jones **Bred** Juddmonte Farms Ltd **Trained** Lambourn, Berks

FOCUS
Modest handicap form, rated at face value through the runner-up and fifth.

Appleby Official explanation: jockey said filly moved badly and felt slightly lame on pulling up

6090 LADBROKES.COM STOAT (S) STKS 1m 1f 218y

3:40 (3:41) (Class 6) 3-Y-0 **£2,590** (£770; £385; £192) **Stalls** High

Form RPR

03 **1** **Everyman**[14] 5698 3-8-11 45 (b) JimCrowley 5 56
(A W Carroll) *hld up: hdwy over 3f out: led 2f out: sn rdn clr and hung rt: styd on* **11/2**[3]

4L0 **2** *3 ½* **Hester Brook (IRE)**[34] 3394 3-8-6 49 AdrianTNicholls 2 44
(J G M O'Shea) *hld up: hdwy over 2f out: styd on u.p: no ch w wnr* **16/1**

4402 **3** *3 ½* **Leprechaun's Gold (IRE)**[14] 5698 3-8-11 47 FrancisNorton 6 42
(B J Llewellyn) *hld up: hdwy over 3f out: rdn over 1f out: styd on same pce* **10/3**[2]

0061 **4** *nk* **Cherri Fosfate**[13] 5739 3-9-2 57 DavidAllan 9 46
(D Carroll) *hld up: hdwy over 2f out: rdn over 1f out: one pce* **15/8**[1]

0000 **5** *4* **Snake Hips**[26] 5345 3-8-11 42 DavidKinsella 11 33
(B Palling) *chsd ldrs: rdn over 2f out: wknd over 1f out* **15/2**

0- **6** *¾* **Hawk Gold (IRE)**[35] 5124 3-8-11 47 JamieMackay 1 32
(M D I Usher) *led 9f out: hdd over 7f out: chsd ldr: ev ch over 2f out: wknd over 1f out* **20/1**

0000 **7** *1* **Tenterhooks (IRE)**[38] 5041 3-7-13 37 (be) SophieDoyle[(7)] 7 25
(A J McCabe) *hld up: rdn over 2f out: sn wknd* **12/1**

0000 **8** *10* **Hard As Iron**[46] 4763 3-8-11 41 (b[1]) FergusSweeney 3 10
(M Blanshard) *led 1f: chsd ldrs: led over 3f out: rdn and hdd 2f out: sn wknd* **20/1**

60 **9** *1 ½* **Fashion Accessory**[8] 5859 3-8-6 0 SimonWhitworth 10 2
(M Appleby) *hld up: rdn and wknd over 2f out* **100/1**

0000 **10** *43* **Valeesha**[21] 5511 3-8-6 39 SaleemGolam 12 —
(W G M Turner) *s.i.s: plld hrd: hdwy to ld over 7f out: hdd & wknd over 3f out* **25/1**

2m 12.2s (3.90) **Going Correction** +0.40s/f (Good) **10** Ran SP% **112.9**
Speed ratings (Par 99): **100,97,94,94,90 90,89,81,80,45**
CSF £79.39 TOTE £5.30: £1.90, £4.20, £1.40; EX 106.20 Trifecta £222.30 Part won. Pool: £313.20 - 0.10 winning tickets..There was no bid for the winner.
Owner M Woodall **Bred** Natton House Thoroughbreds & Mark Woodall **Trained** Cropthorne, Worcs

FOCUS
A very modest seller, no better than a banded race. The form is not solid.

6091 LADBROKES.COM QUORN H'CAP 1m 3f 183y

4:10 (4:10) (Class 2) (0-100,90) 3-Y-0
£9,971 (£2,985; £1,492; £747; £372; £187) **Stalls** High

Form RPR

11 **1** **Pippa Greene**[52] 4603 3-9-4 **90** LDettori 2 101+
(P F I Cole) *hld up: racd wd and hdwy 8f out: led over 1f out: rdn clr fnl f: edgd rt: jst hld on* **7/4**[1]

3311 **2** *nk* **Harry Tricker**[13] 5724 3-9-1 **87** JimCrowley 4 97+
(Mrs A J Perrett) *hld up: hdwy over 2f out: rdn to chse wnr and edgd lft over 1f out: hung rt ins fnl f: styd on* **10/3**[2]

-312 **3** *4* **Sugar Ray (IRE)**[39] 5014 3-8-13 **85** JimmyFortune 3 88
(Sir Michael Stoute) *led after 1f: rdn and hdd over 1f out: styd on same pce* **7/2**[3]

0530 **4** *shd* **Always Fruitful**[34] 5141 3-9-0 **86** J-PGuillambert 6 89
(M Johnston) *chsd ldrs: rdn over 2f out: sn outpcd: styd on u.p ins fnl f* **16/1**

2426 **5** *8* **Prince Sabaah (IRE)**[9] 5830 3-9-1 **87** TedDurcan 5 77
(R Hannon) *trckd ldrs: rdn over 2f out: sn wknd* **5/1**

1431 **6** *hd* **Music Review**[20] 5523 3-8-6 **78** DaleGibson 1 68
(R A Fahey) *chsd ldr: rdn over 2f out: wknd over 1f out* **20/1**

2m 37.08s (2.58) **Going Correction** +0.40s/f (Good) **6** Ran SP% **109.0**
Speed ratings (Par 107): **107,106,104,104,98 98**
CSF £7.28 TOTE £2.50: £1.10, £2.90; EX 4.90.
Owner R A H Evans **Bred** D And Mrs V Fleet **Trained** Whatcombe, Oxon

FOCUS
A decent little handicap, in which the first two, both progressive and chasing hat-tricks, came nicely clear. Good form, with the fourth the best guide.

NOTEBOOK
Pippa Greene defied an 8lb higher mark to remain unbeaten in three starts. He has clearly not been the easiest to train but has plenty of ability, and it will not be a surprise if he makes the grade at Pattern level next year. (op 13-8 tchd 15-8)

Harry Tricker, another 6lb higher, has progressed significantly since moving into handicap company, and he was only narrowly denied a hat-trick of successes by a lightly-raced, unbeaten rival. He finished well clear of the third, will get further in time, and may well win again before the season is out. (op 7-2)

Sugar Ray(IRE) looked likely to be suited by the step up from 1m2f, but he was put in his place by the first two. He has been a bit disappointing to date but remains lightly raced and open to improvement as a four-year-old. (op 3-1 tchd 4-1)

Always Fruitful ran poorly at York last time and these softer conditions did not bring about a turnaround in form. He looks likely to continue to struggle.

Prince Sabaah(IRE) should have run better than this even allowing for the fact that he is handicapped up to the hilt. Official explanation: jockey said colt had no more to give (op 6-1 tchd 9-2)

6092 LADBROKES.COM SQUIRREL CONDITIONS STKS 1m 1f 218y

4:40 (4:41) (Class 3) 2-Y-0 **£6,919** (£2,116; £1,090; £577) **Stalls** High

Form RPR

31 **1** **Tomintoul Flyer**[18] 5599 2-9-1 85 TedDurcan 5 81
(H R A Cecil) *trckd ldr: rdn whn hmpd over 1f out: hung rt and styd on to ld wl ins fnl f* **5/6**[1]

0414 **2** *1 ¼* **Palmerin**[31] 5222 2-9-1 79 JimmyFortune 1 79
(R Hannon) *led: hrd rdn and hung lft over 1f out: hdd wl ins fnl f* **7/1**

633 **3** *4* **Judgethemoment (USA)**[18] 5590 2-8-11 81 JimCrowley 4 68
(Jane Chapple-Hyam) *chsd ldrs: rdn over 2f out: styd on same pce appr fnl f* **3/1**[2]

01 **4** *5* **Flying Time**[28] 5294 2-8-6 70 FrancisNorton 3 54
(M R Channon) *hld up in tch: rdn over 2f out: edgd rt and wknd over 1f out* **13/2**[3]

0 **U** **Amouretta**[32] 5202 2-8-6 0 SaleemGolam 2 —
(T T Clement) *s.s: uns rdr sn after s* **100/1**

2m 16.95s (8.65) **Going Correction** +0.40s/f (Good) **5** Ran SP% **106.4**
Speed ratings (Par 99): **81,80,76,72,—**
CSF £6.69 TOTE £1.90: £1.10, £4.70; EX 5.40.
Owner Angus Dundee Distillers plc **Bred** Whitsbury Manor Stud **Trained** Newmarket, Suffolk

FOCUS
There was a slow pace to this conditions event and the form is probably not entirely reliable.

NOTEBOOK
Tomintoul Flyer, sent off a short-priced favourite, got the job done in what was a messy race that did not see him to best effect. A stronger pace would have suited him, he will get further next year and looks just the type to improve from two to three. (op 4-6)

Palmerin was probably aided by the fact that he was allowed to set a slow pace in front as there were doubts about him on the stamina front beforehand. He got the trip well enough this time but it might be different in a stronger-run race. (op 8-1)

Judgethemoment(USA) had looked to be crying out for this sort of trip at Newbury last time and so he was probably inconvenienced more than most by the lack of early pace. Whether he was entirely at home on this ground is open to question, as his American breeding suggests otherwise. (op 11-4 tchd 5-2)

Flying Time, who had a bit to find with the principals on what we knew beforehand, also had stamina question marks next to her name, especially on this ground. (op 8-1)

6093 EBF LADBROKES.COM MAIDEN FILLIES' STKS (DIV II) 7f 9y

5:10 (5:11) (Class 4) 2-Y-O **£4,210** (£1,252; £625; £312) **Stalls** Centre

Form RPR

05 1 **Brave Mave**[48] 4709 2-9-0 0 .... J-PGuillambert 9 74
(W Jarvis) *chsd ldr: led over 4f out: rdn and hdd over 1f out: rallied to ld nr fin* **8/1**

2 *nk* **Siyabona (USA)** 2-9-0 0 .... LDettori 8 73
(Saeed Bin Suroor) *s.s: hdwy over 1f out: rdn to ld ins fnl f: hdd nr fin* **10/3**[2]

3 *nk* **Portodora (USA)** 2-9-0 0 .... TedDurcan 2 73
(H R A Cecil) *s.i.s: sn chsng ldrs: led over 1f out: sn rdn and hdd: styd on* **6/1**

4 *1 1/4* **Paradise Island (IRE)** 2-9-0 0 .... JimCrowley 7 69
(E A L Dunlop) *hld up: hdwy to ld 1f out: hdd and no ex ins fnl f* **12/1**

5 *1* **Pinewood Lulu** 2-8-7 0 .... MarkCoumbe(7) 5 67
(R C Guest) *trckd ldrs: rdn over 1f out: edgd rt and styd on* **100/1**

3 6 *2 1/2* **Sayedati Elhasna (IRE)**[105] 2969 2-9-0 0 .... RHills 13 61
(J L Dunlop) *chsd ldrs: rdn and ev ch over 1f out: wknd ins fnl f* **3/1**[1]

7 *3/4* **Lambda (USA)** 2-9-0 0 .... JimmyFortune 6 59
(Sir Michael Stoute) *mid-div: hdwy over 2f out: wknd fnl f* **4/1**[3]

0 8 *1* **Dark Camellia**[17] 5628 2-9-0 0 .... FrancisNorton 12 56
(H J L Dunlop) *prom: rdn over 2f out: wknd fnl f* **40/1**

9 *hd* **Broughtons Flight (IRE)** 2-9-0 0 .... NeilPollard 14 56
(W J Musson) *s.i.s: sn prom: wknd over 1f out* **66/1**

0 10 *hd* **Corking (IRE)**[15] 5681 2-9-0 0 .... StephenCarson 4 55
(Eve Johnson Houghton) *led: hdd over 4f out: sn rdn: wknd over 1f out* **33/1**

11 *1 3/4* **Flower Song** 2-9-0 0 .... FergusSweeney 3 51
(A King) *s.i.s: rdn over 2f out: a in rr* **16/1**

F6 12 *20* **Emma's Secrets**[133] 2109 2-9-0 0 .... AdamKirby 1 —
(Miss M E Rowland) *hld up: wknd over 2f out* **100/1**

1m 29.09s (2.99) **Going Correction** +0.30s/f (Good) **12 Ran SP% 115.9**
Speed ratings (Par 94): **94,93,93,91,90 87,87,85,85,85 83,60**
CSF £33.55 TOTE £8.70: £2.00, £2.00, £2.70; EX 36.90 TRIFECTA Not won..
Owner J W Munroe Construction Ltd **Bred** Genesis Green Stud Ltd **Trained** Newmarket, Suffolk
■ Stewards' Enquiry : J-P Guillambert two-day ban: used whip with excessive frequency (Oct 21-22)

FOCUS
The slower of the two divisions by 0.93sec and probably not such strong form.

NOTEBOOK
Brave Mave had not achieved much in two previous starts but she had an excuse last time as she finished lame after suffering interference early on. She improved on those efforts here following a 49-day break, rallying to get the better of two well-bred newcomers from big stables, and her future now lies in the hands of the Handicapper. (op 9-1 tchd 15-2)
Siyabona(USA), whose dam was quite a useful 1m2f winner at three in a light career, holds an entry in next year's Derby so is clearly well regarded. Slowly away, she ran on well to lead inside the final furlong, only to succumb to the more experienced Brave Mave close home. She will improve for this and has the makings of a useful sort. (op 3-1 tchd 7-2)
Portodora(USA), who is a half-sister to Heather Moor, who won over a mile at three, out of a mare who is a half-sister to Oaks winner Reams Of Verse and Eclipse/Irish Champion Stakes winner Elmaamul, is going to improve with time and this was a promising debut on ground that would have been plenty soft enough. (op 9-2 tchd 13-2)
Paradise Island(IRE) is a sister to multiple winning sprinter Desert Commander so obviously there were worries about her stamina over this trip and especially in this ground. She did not quite see it out, but it was still a good effort, and on better ground she might well be up to winning over this distance. (op 16-1)
Pinewood Lulu, a half-sister to Fenomena, a dual 1m winner in Italy, and to Penny Glitters, a 7f winner at three, changed hands cheaply at the sales and was unsurprisingly a big price for her debut. She ran quite well in the circumstances. (op 80-1)
Sayedati Elhasna(IRE) was a bit disappointing, failing to build on her promising debut at Newbury. (tchd 11-4)
Lambda(USA), whose dam won over 6f on her only start at two and is a half-sister to top-class juvenile Gay Gallanta, may well appreciate quicker ground than this. (tchd 9-2)

6094 LADBROKES.COM DORMOUSE MAIDEN STKS 7f 9y

5:40 (5:43) (Class 5) 3-Y-O **£2,914** (£867; £433; £216) **Stalls** Centre

Form RPR

3022 1 **Axiom**[8] 5873 3-9-3 80 .... JimmyFortune 7 75
(E A L Dunlop) *mde all: pushed clr fnl f* **4/11**[1]

-4 2 *3 1/2* **Cinnamon Hill**[28] 5315 3-8-12 0 .... StephenCarson 8 61
(Eve Johnson Houghton) *trckd wnr: plld hrd: rdn over 1f out: sn outpcd* **12/1**[3]

3223 3 *nk* **Laura's Best (IRE)**[21] 5494 3-8-12 68 .... TPQueally 4 60
(W J Haggas) *trckd ldrs: rdn over 1f out: styd on same pce* **5/1**[2]

4 *1* **Naledi** 3-9-3 0 .... (b[1]) PaddyAspell 3 63
(J R Norton) *s.i.s: hld up: rdn over 2f out: n.d* **100/1**

5- 5 *1* **Samahir (USA)**[505] 1896 3-8-12 0 .... AdamKirby 9 55
(T T Clement) *hld up: racd keenly: hdwy over 2f out: wknd fnl f* **16/1**

0000 6 *7* **Katie Coniston**[8] 5861 3-8-5 45 .... MatthewCosham(7) 1 37
(Dr J R J Naylor) *prom 5f* **125/1**

00- 7 *4* **Arthur's Edge**[388] 5371 3-9-3 0 .... DavidKinsella 2 32
(B Palling) *chsd ldrs over 4f* **125/1**

8 *6* **Vigo Bridge** 3-8-12 0 .... FergusSweeney 6 11
(B R Millman) *chsd ldrs over 4f* **40/1**

1m 28.31s (2.21) **Going Correction** +0.30s/f (Good) **8 Ran SP% 108.6**
Speed ratings (Par 101): **99,95,94,93,92 84,79,72**
CSF £5.04 TOTE £1.30: £1.02, £1.90, £1.30; EX 4.80 Trifecta £8.80 Pool: £418.53 - 33.61 winning tickets. Place 6 £193.31, Place 5 £130.74.
Owner Cheveley Park Stud **Bred** Cheveley Park Stud Ltd **Trained** Newmarket, Suffolk

FOCUS
An uncompetitive maiden and easy for the winner. The form has been rated through the placed horses.
Arthur's Edge Official explanation: jockey said, regarding running and riding, that his orders were to jump out, get the gelding travelling and do his best, adding that he was unable to carry them out as he had to take a pull from halfway, when horses were carrying him in from the outside towards Katy Coniston, which had moved up his inside on the rail, having broken the gelding's stride, he was anxious to avoid causing interference when extricating himself, once clear, he felt he would not have finished closer for more vigorous riding
T/Plt: £285.00 to a £1 stake. Pool: £63,329.85. 162.20 winning tickets. T/Qpdt: £30.40 to a £1 stake. Pool: £3,540.30. 86.10 winning tickets. CR

LYON PARILLY (R-H)

Tuesday, October 9

OFFICIAL GOING: Soft

6095a PRIX ANDRE BABOIN (GRAND PRIX DES PROVINCES) (GROUP 3) 1m 2f

2:35 (2:36) 3-Y-O+ **£27,027** (£10,811; £8,108; £5,405; £2,703)

RPR

1 **Bal De La Rose (IRE)**[54] 4556 3-8-4 .... SPasquier 4 104
(F Rohaut, France) *led after 1f to over 2f out: drvn 1 1/2f out: r.o to ld again 100yds out: drvn out* **82/10**

2 *1* **Elasos (FR)**[55] 4520 5-9-1 .... DBonilla 1 108
(D Sepulchre, France) *racd in 3rd: wnt cl 2nd on ins st: led over 2f out: hrd rdn fnl f: hdd 100yds out: one pce* **46/10**[2]

3 *3/4* **Criticism**[13] 5744 3-8-4 .... JVictoire 7 101
(H-A Pantall, France) *hld up in rr: hdwy 3f out to go 4th on ins st: hrd rdn 1 1/2f out: ev ch 1f out: one pce* **1/1**[1]

4 *3 1/2* **Kiton (GER)**[34] 5151 6-9-1 .... OPeslier 3 100
(P Rau, Germany) *racd in 5th: 6th st: rdn 2f out: nvr nr to chal* **9/1**

5 *1* **Musketier (GER)**[55] 4520 5-8-12 .... C-PLemaire 2 95
(P Bary, France) *led 1f: trckd ldr: cl 3rd on outside st: btn wl over 1f out* **73/10**

6 *3/4* **Willywell (FR)**[55] 4520 5-9-1 .... IMendizabal 6 96
(J-P Gauvin, France) *racd in 6th: last st: nvr a factor* **72/10**[3]

7 *8* **Michikabu (IRE)**[55] 4-8-8 .... TThulliez 5 73
(R Gibson, France) *disp 3rd to 1/2-way: 5th st: sn btn* **22/1**

2m 13.63s (133.63)
WFA 3 from 4yo+ 5lb **7 Ran SP% 117.3**
PARI-MUTUEL (including one euro stakes): WIN 9.20; PL 5.00, 2.70; SF54.50.
Owner B Van Dalfsen **Bred** B Van Dalfsen **Trained** Sauvagnon, France

NOTEBOOK
Bal De La Rose(IRE), already a Listed winner in the provinces, added a Group 3 victory to her laurels in good style. She made virtually all the running and still had plenty in hand to fend off all challenges in the straight. She may well be allowed to take her chance in the Prix de Flore of Prix Fille de l'Air at Saint-Cloud.
Elasos(FR) was always following the winner but could never get on terms.
Criticism was slowly into her stride and she did not appear to completely go through with her challenge.
Kiton(GER), mid-division for much of this race, fought well to hold fourth position inside the final furlong.

6001 KEMPTON (A.W) (R-H)

Wednesday, October 10

OFFICIAL GOING: Standard
Wind: Virtually nil Weather: overcast

6096 ALADDIN H'CAP 1m 2f (P)

6:20 (6:21) (Class 6) (0-52,52) 3-Y-O+ **£2,047** (£604; £302) **Stalls** High

Form RPR

0000 1 **Theatre Royal**[7] 5900 4-8-11 50 .... (b) NeilChalmers(3) 4 58+
(Mouse Hamilton-Fairley) *w.w in midfield: hdwy to trck ldrs gng wl 2f out: rdn to ld last 100yds: r.o wl* **25/1**

6512 2 *3/4* **Charlottebutterfly**[27] 5368 7-9-1 51 .... IanMongan 6 57
(P J McBride) *hld up in tch: rdn and hdwy over 2f out: drvn to ld over 1f out: hdd and no ex last 100yds* **9/1**

0406 3 *hd* **Roman Boy (ARG)**[15] 5708 8-8-9 50 .... TolleyDean(5) 8 56
(Stef Liddiard) *hld up in last: hdwy 2f out: sn swtchd rt: r.o strly: wnt 3rd towards fin: nt rch ldrs* **7/1**

4554 4 *1/2* **Magic Amigo**[25] 5421 6-8-11 47 .... (v) AdamKirby 3 52
(J R Jenkins) *hld up towards rr: hdwy over 3f out: rdn 2f out: kpt on u.p fnl f* **6/1**[2]

-000 5 *hd* **Fortune Point (IRE)**[31] 3616 9-8-11 47 .... JimCrowley 1 51
(A W Carroll) *hld up towards rr: hdwy over 2f out: swtched lft over 1f out: r.o u.p: nt rch ldrs* **25/1**

0000 6 *hd* **Don Pasquale**[20] 5569 5-8-8 49 .... (v) JamesO'Reilly(5) 5 55+
(J T Stimpson) *stdd s: hld up bhd: hdwy over 2f out: effrt on rail whn hmpd over 1f out: r.o wl ins fnl f: nt rch ldrs* **25/1**

4451 7 *1* **Moyoko (IRE)**[13] 5756 4-9-2 52 .... LPKeniry 13 54
(M Blanshard) *trckd ldrs: nt clr run and swtchd lft over 1f out: nt clr run tl jst ins fnl f: one pce* **9/2**[1]

0200 8 *nk* **Surdoue**[7] 5916 7-9-0 50 .... SaleemGolam 12 51
(D Morris) *chsd ldr: rdn 3f out: ev ch over 2f out tl wknd jst ins fnl f* **14/1**

00-0 9 *2 1/2* **Henry Holmes**[21] 5530 4-9-0 50 .... AlanDaly 10 46
(Mrs L Richards) *in tch: rdn 3f out: wknd 1f out* **66/1**

5160 10 *hd* **Fantasy Crusader**[18] 5636 8-9-0 50 .... J-PGuillambert 2 46
(R M H Cowell) *t.k.h: chsd ldrs: rdn on outer over 2f out: wknd wl over 1f out* **13/2**[3]

2002 11 *3* **Kings Art (IRE)**[5] 5967 3-8-11 52 .... MartinDwyer 14 42
(W M Brisbourne) *led tl rdn and hdd over 1f out: sn wknd* **9/1**

4200 12 *hd* **Miss Porcia**[29] 5310 6-8-7 48 .... KevinGhunowa(5) 9 37
(P A Blockley) *sn rdn along in midfield: drvn over 2f out: sn outpcd* **20/1**

0000 13 *5* **Quite A Splash (USA)**[6] 5945 3-8-11 52 .... (b[1]) PaulDoe 11 31
(S Curran) *s.i.s: rdn and effrt on outer wl over 2f out: wl btn 2f out* **66/1**

1203 14 *24* **Saucy**[25] 5440 6-9-0 50 .... FrancisNorton 7 —
(Daniel Mark Loughnane, Ire) *t.k.h: chsd ldrs: rdn 4f out: lost pl over 3f out: virtually p.u fnl f: t.o* **9/2**[1]

2m 6.64s (-2.36) **Going Correction** -0.20s/f (Stan)
WFA 3 from 4yo+ 5lb **14 Ran SP% 122.4**
Speed ratings (Par 101): **101,100,100,99,99 99,98,98,96,96 93,93,89,70**
CSF £226.88 CT £1768.38 TOTE £22.50: £7.50, £3.20, £3.20; EX 409.30.
Owner Mrs Richard Plummer & Partners **Bred** Mrs A Plummer **Trained** Bramshill, Hants

FOCUS
Moderate form however one looks at it, best assessed through the second and fourth.
Don Pasquale Official explanation: jockey said gelding was denied a clear run
Moyoko(IRE) Official explanation: jockey said filly was denied a clear run
Surdoue Official explanation: jockey said gelding lost a shoe
Kings Art(IRE) Official explanation: trainer said gelding had a breathing problem

Saucy Official explanation: vet said mare scoped dirty

6097 SUMMER NEVER ENDS AT KEMPTON MEDIAN AUCTION MAIDEN STKS — 1m (P)

6:50 (6:53) (Class 6) 3-5-Y-O — £2,047 (£604; £302) Stalls High

Form	Pos	Dist	Horse / Trainer / Comment	Jockey / Odds	RPR
0305	1		**Sister Act**[8] 5885 3-8-12 73 (J R Fanshawe) *mde all: rdn 2f out: styd on wl*	OscarUrbina 10 — 9/4[1]	75
204-	2	1 1/4	**Multakka (IRE)**[433] 4083 4-9-6 83 (M P Tregoning) *hld up in midfield: hmpd over 5f out: hdwy to chse ldng pair over 3f out: drvn to chse wnr 1f out: no imp last 100yds*	MartinDwyer 6 — 9/4[1]	77
0	3	3	**Ballad Maker (IRE)**[7] 5915 3-9-3 0 (J H M Gosden) *mostly chsng wnr: rdn over 2f out: lost 2nd 1f out: one pce*	JimmyFortune 11 — 11/4[2]	70
5	4	6	**Thea Di Bisanzio (IRE)**[44] 4908 3-8-12 0 (G A Butler) *prom: rdn over 3f out: wknd over 2f out: no ch after*	FrancisNorton 4 — 9/1[3]	51
0044	5	shd	**Split The Wind (USA)**[14] 5728 3-8-12 57 (Eve Johnson Houghton) *bhd: rdn and struggling 1/2-way: n.d after*	StephenCarson 5 — 12/1	51
0050	6	1 1/4	**Pure Velvet (IRE)**[14] 5728 3-8-12 45 (S Kirk) *a towards rr: rdn 3f out: sn struggling*	LPKeniry 3 — 66/1	48
0-00	7	1/2	**Diamond World**[28] 5336 4-9-1 44 (C A Horgan) *hld up bhd: swtchd lft over 5f out: effrt to chse ldng trio over 2f out: sn wl outpcd: fdd fnl f*	SimonWhitworth 1 — 66/1	47
50	8	17	**Ka'u Mauna Kea**[54] 4575 3-8-12 0 (J A Geake) *in tch: rdn over 3f out: wl bhd last 2f: eased fnl f: t.o*	RobertHavlin 9 — 50/1	8
-006	9	1	**Bright**[51] 4663 4-9-3 32 (W K Goldsworthy) *chsd ldrs to 1/2-way: sn struggling: t.o fnl f*	(v[1]) NeilChalmers(3) 7 — 80/1	11
	U		**North South Divide (IRE)** 3-9-3 0 (P Mitchell) *v s.i.s: last but in tch whn stmbld and uns rdr 5f out*	JimCrowley 2 — 20/1	—

1m 38.17s (-2.63) **Going Correction** -0.20s/f (Stan)
WFA 3 from 4yo 3lb — **10** Ran SP% **116.8**
Speed ratings (Par 101): **105,103,100,94,94 93,92,75,74,—**
CSF £7.29 TOTE £3.50: £1.40, £1.30, £1.50; EX 8.70.
Owner Elite Racing Club **Bred** Elite Racing Club **Trained** Newmarket, Suffolk

FOCUS
No great strength in depth to this maiden but the first three came clear. The form is limited by the performances of the fifth and sixth.

6098 DIGIBET.COM NURSERY — 6f (P)

7:20 (7:23) (Class 6) (0-65,65) 2-Y-O — £2,047 (£604; £302) Stalls High

Form	Pos	Dist	Horse / Trainer / Comment	Jockey / Odds	RPR
0064	1		**Gipsy Prince**[29] 5314 2-9-7 **65** (M G Quinlan) *hld up bhd: rdn over 2f out: grad swtchd lft: str run over 1f out: led ins fnl f: sn clr*	GregFairley 5 — 6/1[3]	74
6002	2	2 1/2	**Southwest Star (IRE)**[14] 5729 2-9-6 **64** (J S Moore) *hld up in tch: hdwy over 2f out: rdn to ld jst over 1f out: hdd ins fnl f: nt pce of wnr*	LPKeniry 4 — 7/2[1]	65
5240	3	1 3/4	**Attribution**[24] 5452 2-9-7 **65** (A B Haynes) *hld up in midfield: effrt on rail over 2f out ev ch jst over 1f out: kpt on same pce*	DavidKinsella 11 — 10/1	61
6526	4	nk	**Richardthesecond (IRE)**[27] 5365 2-9-4 **62** (R M Beckett) *chsd ldrs: rdn 3f out: kpt on same pce u.p over 1f out*	MartinDwyer 8 — 4/1[2]	57
4005	5	1	**Alabama Spirit (USA)**[8] 5887 2-9-7 **65** (D Shaw) *dropped in bhd sn after s: hdwy 2f out: kpt on past btn horses fnl f: n.d*	DeanMcKeown 3 — 20/1	57
0403	6	3/4	**Valhillen**[13] 5751 2-9-2 **60** (M J Wallace) *chsd ldrs: rdn over 3f out: outpcd over 2f out: plugged on*	J-PGuillambert 9 — 6/1[3]	50
3300	7	3/4	**Sandy Par**[44] 4903 2-9-7 **65** (P Winkworth) *led: rdn over 2f out: hdd jst over 1f out: sn wknd*	StephenCarson 10 — 12/1	52
2355	8	1/2	**Betty Burke**[19] 5601 2-9-7 **65** (H J L Dunlop) *chsd ldr: rdn over 2f out: wknd over 1f out*	RobertHavlin 12 — 8/1	51
044	9	1/2	**Shakespeare's Son**[11] 5815 2-9-2 **65** (H J Evans) *t.k.h: hld up in midfield: rdn 3f out: nt pce to trble ldrs after*	TolleyDean(5) 7 — 12/1	49
6000	10	1/2	**Compton Abbess**[8] 5882 2-8-13 **62** (B R Millman) *wnt lft s: sn rdn in rr: nvr on terms*	JamesMillman(5) 2 — 12/1	45
4300	11	1/2	**Zahwah**[122] 2488 2-9-0 **61** (J G Portman) *a towards rr: rdn over 2f out: no hdwy*	NeilChalmers(3) 6 — 20/1	42

1m 12.69s (-1.01) **Going Correction** -0.20s/f (Stan) — **11** Ran SP% **118.8**
Speed ratings (Par 93): **98,94,92,91,90 89,88,87,87,86 85**
CSF £26.85 CT £214.64 TOTE £6.50: £2.80, £2.00, £3.10; EX 36.00.
Owner O'Connor Racing **Bred** Mrs Joan M Langmead **Trained** Newmarket, Suffolk

FOCUS
A modest nursery run at a good pace.

NOTEBOOK
Gipsy Prince, dropping back a furlong in distance on his Polytrack debut, came with a sweeping run down the centre of the track and won going away. He will merit plenty of interest if turned out under a penalty back over this course and distance on 17 October as he looks very much an improving type. (tchd 11-2)

Southwest Star(IRE), who showed improved form on his last start here, had no chance with the easy winner but he beat the rest well enough. He can probably win a similar event if the Handicapper does not put him up too much. (op 4-1)

Attribution, a beaten favourite on his last two starts, hung left off the inside rail in the closing stages but held on for third. He lost his action last time at Goodwood, but apart from that effort his form has a consistent look about it.

Richardthesecond(IRE), back up to his best distance, ran a solid race, but he is going to have to find a little improvement to win off this mark. (tchd 9-2)

Alabama Spirit(USA) hinted at a return to form last time out and this was another fair effort from off the pace. (op 16-1)

Valhillen failed to run up to the form he showed at Wolverhampton last time despite looking to have conditions to suit.

Sandy Par, who set a decent pace up front, may need to drop a few pounds before he becomes of interest. (op 16-1 tchd 20-1)

6099 DIGIBET CASINO CLAIMING STKS — 7f (P)

7:50 (7:50) (Class 6) 2-Y-O — £2,047 (£604; £302) Stalls High

Form	Pos	Dist	Horse / Trainer / Comment	Jockey / Odds	RPR
3344	1		**What's For Tea**[5] 5984 2-8-7 55 (Tom Dascombe) *mde all: rdn over 2f out: styd on gamely u.p*	RichardKingscote 14 — 4/1[2]	56
6050	2	1 1/2	**Deckguard**[14] 5729 2-9-2 60 (J S Moore) *in tch: chsd ldng pair and drvn wl over 1f out: wnt 2nd wl ins fnl f: nt threaten wnr*	LPKeniry 10 — 3/1[1]	61
1050	3	nk	**Ramblin Bob**[34] 5167 2-9-2 65 (R M Beckett) *chsd wnr: rdn and ev ch over 2f out: no ex fnl f*	(b[1]) MartinDwyer 8 — 15/2	60
3010	4	1	**Lord Deevert**[22] 5496 2-8-7 71 (W G M Turner) *in tch: rdn 3f out: kpt on u.p fnl f: nt trble wnr*	JackDean(7) 4 — 7/1[3]	56
060	5	shd	**Khana Ras (IRE)**[27] 5343 2-8-12 66 (E J O'Neill) *chsd ldrs: rdn over 3f out: outpcd wl over 2f out: styd on u.p wl ins fnl f*	JamesDoyle 5 — 12/1	53
4000	6	shd	**Rosy Dawn**[14] 5727 2-8-4 56 (H J L Dunlop) *chsd ldrs: rdn wl over 2f out: kpt on same pce*	(v) PaulDoe 2 — 12/1	45
04	7	1 1/4	**Dusk Ballet**[18] 5644 2-8-5 0 (S C Williams) *hld up in midfield: hdwy over 3f out: chsd ldrs and rdn 2f out: wknd over 1f out*	SaleemGolam 6 — 16/1	43
0306	8	1/2	**Ochenvay**[20] 5572 2-7-13 54 (M Quinn) *wl bhd: hdwy whn hung rt briefly over 2f out: r.o fnl f: n.d*	KirstyMilczarek(5) 9 — 20/1	41
062	9	1 1/4	**Magnol**[110] 2838 2-8-4 57 (J G M O'Shea) *s.i.s: wl bhd: styd on fnl f: n.d*	ThomasO'Brien(7) 7 — 16/1	44
4000	10	nk	**Powys Lad**[6] 5932 2-9-5 55 (K R Burke) *racd in midfield: rdn and struggling 3f out: n.d after*	J-PGuillambert 11 — 25/1	53+
0000	11	1/2	**Riorun (IRE)**[11] 5818 2-8-13 55 (J G Portman) *s.i.s: sn midfield on outer: hdwy over 3f out: rdn and hanging rt over 2f out: sn btn*	NeilChalmers(3) 3 — 66/1	47
00	12	2	**No No Ninette**[58] 4454 2-8-9 0 (C R Egerton) *a bhd*	(p) NelsonDeSouza 12 — 50/1	35
6	13	3/4	**Word Games**[7] 5895 2-9-0 0 (A M Balding) *racd in midfield tl lost pl 1/2-way: n.d after*	FrancisNorton 13 — 8/1	38

1m 26.98s (0.18) **Going Correction** -0.20s/f (Stan) — **13** Ran SP% **119.6**
Speed ratings (Par 93): **90,88,87,86,86 86,85,84,83,82 82,79,79**
CSF £15.78 TOTE £5.90: £1.90, £1.50, £2.20; EX 15.70.
Owner Alan Solomon **Bred** Helshaw Grange Farms Ltd **Trained** Lambourn, Berks

FOCUS
A moderate juvenile claimer and not many ever got into it. Weak, but solid form.

NOTEBOOK
What's For Tea, who has been running with credit over 1m of late, had a decent chance on adjusted official ratings. Her rider immediately made sure that this was going to be run at a proper pace and she was soon in front from the rails draw. She did not seem to be travelling as well as some on the turn for home, but she kept on pulling out more and saw it out in game style.

Deckguard went off favourite despite having failed to make the frame in five previous starts and also had up to 13lb to find with some of these on adjusted official ratings. To be fair, he was always up with the pace and kept going right to the line, but could never get on terms with the winner. (op 10-3 tchd 11-4)

Ramblin Bob, back up to 7f for this sand debut, had the blinkers on for the first time on this drop in class and was soon in a handy position. He seemed to be travelling much better than the winner on the home turn, but when let down could never make any impression on her. (op 8-1)

Lord Deevert, already the winner of a seller and a claimer on Polytrack and best in at these weights, raced wide the whole way and had his chance but could not find the required turn of foot. This was his first try at the trip in his tenth outing, but lack of stamina did not seem to be an issue. (op 6-1 tchd 15-2 in a place)

Khana Ras(IRE), making his sand debut after finishing unplaced in three turf maidens, had a problem laying up on this surface in the middle part of the contest, but was doing some solid late work up the inside rail. He may be able to find a modest race on this surface over an extra furlong. Official explanation: jockey said colt hung right (op 16-1)

Rosy Dawn, who ran too freely in the first-time visor here last time, raced handily over this shorter trip but still settled better. The problem was that she was always having to race very wide from her low draw and then had little left at the business end.

Powys Lad Official explanation: jockey said colt was denied a clear run

6100 DIGIBET SPORTS BETTING CLASSIFIED STKS — 7f (P)

8:20 (8:26) (Class 6) 3-Y-O+ — £2,047 (£604; £302) Stalls High

Form	Pos	Dist	Horse / Trainer / Comment	Jockey / Odds	RPR
0562	1		**Emma Jean Lad (IRE)**[7] 5900 3-9-0 55 (J S Moore) *in tch: rdn and hdwy over 2f out: led 1f out: drvn and hld on wl fnl f*	JohnEgan 6 — 11/4[1]	60
0064	2	1/2	**Ganache (IRE)**[7] 5900 5-9-2 48 (P R Chamings) *t.k.h: chsd ldr: rdn to ld 2f out: hdd 1f out: rallied u.p: hld last 100yds*	FrancisNorton 2 — 7/1[2]	59
-534	3	3/4	**Hills Place**[164] 1320 3-9-0 54 (J R Best) *t.k.h: chsd ldrs for 1f: sn stdd into midfield: drvn and effrt 2f out: styd on to go 3rd last 100yds*	GeorgeBaker 10 — 10/1[3]	57
00	4	1	**Raise Again (IRE)**[51] 4660 4-8-9 54 (Mrs P N Dutfield) *chsd ldrs: rdn over 2f out: kpt on same pce: lost 3rd last 100yds*	NBazeley(7) 1 — 50/1	54
0001	5	shd	**Vintage (IRE)**[5] 5982 3-9-6 55 (P Mitchell) *plld hrd: trckd ldrs: rdn and effrt over 2f out: kpt on same pce*	(t) IanMongan 7 — 11/4[1]	60
0502	6	1 1/4	**Machinate (USA)**[8] 5890 5-9-2 49 (W M Brisbourne) *bhd: rdn over 3f out: styd on u.p over 1f out: nvr able to chal*	LiamJones 11 — 7/1[2]	50
-350	7	1 1/2	**The Slider**[21] 5528 3-9-0 48 (Mrs L C Jewell) *in tch: drvn over 3f out: nvr pce to trble ldrs after*	(p) LPKeniry 4 — 33/1	46
06/6	8	nk	**Grey Gurkha**[7] 5915 6-9-2 45 (B Ellison) *rn wout declared tongue strap: t.k.h: sn led: hdd 2f out: wknd qckly 1f out*	J-PGuillambert 14 — 11/1	45
6600	9	3/4	**Lordswood (IRE)**[47] 4760 3-9-0 47 (J J Bridger) *bhd: rdn and effrt on inner over 2f out: n.d*	FrankieMcDonald 9 — 66/1	43
00-5	10	nk	**Torver**[19] 5602 3-9-0 53 (Dr J D Scargill) *s.i.s: a bhd: rdn and little rspnse over 2f out*	MickyFenton 5 — 33/1	43
0000	11	nk	**Fervent**[7] 5900 3-9-0 55 (J M Bradley) *in tch in midfield: rdn and wknd wl over 2f out*	RichardKingscote 3 — 66/1	42
-304	12	1	**Call Me Rosy (IRE)**[34] 5175 3-9-0 55 (C F Wall) *bdly hmpd sn after s: a bhd*	MartinDwyer 8 — 12/1	39
1300	13	1 1/4	**Pearl Farm**[60] 4395 6-9-2 54 (C A Horgan) *in tch on inner: rdn and effrt over 2f out: fnd nil and sn btn*	StephenCarson 13 — 12/1	36

1m 26.21s (-0.59) **Going Correction** -0.20s/f (Stan)
WFA 3 from 4yo+ 2lb — **13** Ran SP% **122.0**
Speed ratings (Par 101): **95,94,93,92,92 90,89,88,87,87 87,86,84**
CSF £21.57 TOTE £3.40: £1.50, £2.50, £3.60; EX 31.60.
Owner Roger Ambrose William Reilly Stan Moore **Bred** Mrs H D McCalmont **Trained** Upper Lambourn, Berks

FOCUS
Not a bad race for the grade, but it was run at no more than an ordinary pace and the winning time was modest. Two horses were very well supported in the market and they finished first and second. Sound form among the placed horses.

Grey Gurkha Official explanation: jockey said horse had a breathing problem

6101 JUMP RACING HERE 21ST OCTOBER H'CAP — 6f (P)

8:50 (8:53) (Class 6) (0-60,60) 3-Y-0+ — **£2,047** (£604; £302) **Stalls** High

Form — RPR

3303 **1** **Mistral Sky**[12] 5778 8-9-3 **58**........(v) MickyFenton 11 — 67
(Stef Liddiard) *mde all: rdn wl over 1f out: r.o wl* **9/2[1]**

340- **2** 1 1/4 **Herb Paris (FR)**[52] 4643 3-9-4 **60**........ IanMongan 12 — 65
(M Phelan, Ire) *trckd ldrs: rdn and effrt over 2f out: chsd wnr over 1f out: kpt on same pce* **12/1**

6030 **3** 1 1/4 **Strut The Stage (IRE)**[17] 5118 3-9-4 **60**........ WandersonD'Avila 9 — 61
(B W Duke) *hld up in midfield on rail: hdwy over 2f out: styd on u.p to chse ldng pair 1f out: no imp after* **33/1**

600 **4** 1/2 **Siraj**[26] 5387 8-8-13 **57**........(p) MarcHalford(3) 5 — 57+
(J Ryan) *s.i.s: bhd: rdn 3f out: hdwy u.p 2f out: kpt on but nvr rchd ldrs* **9/1**

3050 **5** 1 3/4 **Swing On A Star (IRE)**[8] 5879 3-9-2 **58**........ AdamKirby 1 — 53
(W R Swinburn) *bhd on outer: rdn and hdwy over 2f out: no imp ins fnl f* **8/1**

0221 **6** 1 1/2 **Kindallachan**[12] 5778 4-9-4 **59**........ J-PGuillambert 4 — 49
(G C Bravery) *chsd ldrs: rdn 3f out: sn outpcd: kpt on one pce after* **5/1[2]**

1041 **7** 3/4 **Ishibee (IRE)**[7] 5897 3-9-2 **58** 6ex........(p) FrankieMcDonald 3 — 56+
(J J Bridger) *dropped in bhd after s: hld up in last: nt clr run on rail over 2f out: tl swtchd lft and rdn over 1f out: keeping on same pce whn nt clr run ins fnl f* **8/1**

0010 **8** 1 1/4 **Anfield Dream**[14] 5731 5-9-5 **60**........ LiamJones 6 — 44
(J R Jenkins) *chsd ldrs: ev ch over 2f out: sn rdn and hanging rt: wknd qckly fnl f* **11/2[3]**

5000 **9** 1 1/4 **Loves Bidding**[8] 5879 3-9-3 **59**........ RobertHavlin 8 — 39
(R Ingram) *a bhd: nvr on terms* **20/1**

-550 **10** nk **Edge End**[14] 5741 3-9-4 **60**........ PaulDoe 7 — 39
(R A Farrant) *sn chsng ldr: rdn and ev ch 2f out: sn wknd* **13/2**

600 **11** 2 **Lithaam (IRE)**[34] 5177 3-9-3 **59**........ LPKeniry 10 — 32
(J M Bradley) *s.i.s: sn chsng ldrs: rdn and wknd 3f out* **20/1**

1m 12.62s (-1.08) **Going Correction** -0.20s/f (Stan)
WFA 3 from 4yo+ 1lb — **11** Ran SP% **115.9**
Speed ratings (Par 101): **99,97,95,95,92 90,89,88,86,85 83**
CSF £56.12 CT £1127.69 TOTE £5.10: £2.10, £4.60, £7.30; EX 41.00.
Owner Shefford Valley Stud **Bred** Peter Nelson **Trained** Great Shefford, Berks

FOCUS
A moderate sprint handicap in which a high draw was an advantage. The winner had slipped to a good mark and made all.
Ishibee(IRE) Official explanation: jockey said filly was denied a clear run

6102 THE PANORAMIC RESTAURANT LOYALTY AND REWARD SCHEME H'CAP — 1m 4f (P)

9:20 (9:24) (Class 6) (0-65,69) 3-Y-0+ — **£2,047** (£604; £302) **Stalls** Low

Form — RPR

5061 **1** **Spirit Of Adjisa (IRE)**[9] 5865 3-9-9 **69** 6ex........(b) PatDobbs 12 — 77
(Pat Eddery) *hld up wl in tch: hdwy to ld over 2f out: sn rdn clr: pushed out last 100yds: jst lasted* **9/2[2]**

2241 **2** nk **Bridgewater Boys**[51] 4663 6-9-0 **53**........ GeorgeBaker 5 — 61
(G L Moore) *hld up in last trio: rdn and effrt over 2f out: hdwy over 1f out: r.o fnl f: jst hld* **8/1**

054/ **3** 3/4 **Master At Arms**[49] 4729 4-9-3 **59**........ JerryO'Dwyer(3) 14 — 66
(Daniel Mark Loughnane, Ire) *hld up in last: swtchd rt and gd hdwy over 2f out: kpt on fnl f: nt rch wnr* **33/1**

-331 **4** 3/4 **Constant Cheers (IRE)**[58] 4458 4-9-11 **64**........(p) AdamKirby 11 — 70
(W R Swinburn) *t.k.h: led for 1f: trckd ldrs: rdn to chse wnr over 2f out: sn outpcd by wnr: kpt on same pce* **9/1**

4261 **5** 3/4 **Mae Cigan (FR)**[12] 5777 4-9-8 **61**........ GregFairley 9 — 65
(M Blanshard) *w.w in midfield: rdn and effrt over 2f out: kpt on fnl f but nt pce to trble wnr* **6/1[3]**

6060 **6** nk **Hatch A Plan (IRE)**[58] 4458 6-8-13 **55**........ NeilChalmers(3) 13 — 59
(Mouse Hamilton-Fairley) *t.k.h: hld up in midfield: hdwy 3f out: rdn and ev ch of 2nd over 1f out: one pce* **25/1**

05-4 **7** 1 1/2 **Ruse**[282] 1 4-9-2 **55**........ MartinDwyer 2 — 57
(J R Fanshawe) *t.k.h: hld up towards rr: rdn wl over 2f out: plugged on fnl f: nt pce to trble ldrs* **16/1**

5163 **8** shd **Hatton Flight**[13] 5755 3-9-0 **60**........ FrancisNorton 3 — 61
(A M Balding) *t.k.h: hld up in midfield: drvn and outpcd wl over 2f out: kpt on u.p fnl f* **7/2[1]**

00-0 **9** hd **Safari Sundowner (IRE)**[38] 2079 3-9-2 **62**........ StephenCarson 7 — 63
(P Winkworth) *hld up in rr: effrt and nt clr run wl over 2f out: rdn and hdwy 2f out: no hdwy 1f out* **50/1**

10 1 **Jago (SWI)**[115] 4-9-10 **63**........ LPKeniry 10 — 62
(A M Hales) *t.k.h: chsd ldrs: rdn over 2f out: wknd 2f out* **33/1**

0054 **11** 3 **Royal Premier (IRE)**[22] 5514 4-9-8 **61**........(v) MickyFenton 4 — 56
(H J Collingridge) *chsd ldr after 2f: jnd ldr 7f out: rdn 3f out: bmpd 2f out: wknd over 1f out: eased fnl f* **14/1**

6205 **12** 1 1/4 **Amwell Brave**[14] 5732 6-9-7 **60**........ LiamJones 8 — 53
(J R Jenkins) *hld up in rr: plld out and rdn wl over 2f out: no hdwy* **13/2**

0/ **13** 5 **Royal Shakespeare (FR)**[167] 6195 8-9-7 **60**........ IanMongan 6 — 45
(S Gollings) *s.i.s: t.k.h: hld up towards rr: hdwy on outer over 3f out: rdn and btn 3f out* **12/1**

3060 **14** 1 1/4 **Doyles Lodge**[12] 5783 3-9-2 **62**........ FergusSweeney 1 — 45
(H Candy) *led after 1f: rdn and hdd over 2f out: sn wknd and eased* **20/1**

2m 34.58s (-2.32) **Going Correction** -0.20s/f (Stan)
WFA 3 from 4yo+ 7lb — **14** Ran SP% **125.8**
Speed ratings (Par 101): **99,98,98,97,97 97,96,96,95,95 93,92,89,88**
CSF £40.09 CT £1098.94 TOTE £5.10: £2.20, £1.70, £13.70; EX 43.90 Place 6 £98.46, Place 5 £13.42.
Owner Darr, Johnson, Weston & Whitaker **Bred** C J Haughey J Flynn And E Mulhern **Trained** Nether Winchendon, Bucks

FOCUS
A moderate middle-distance handicap. Solid form, the winner not needing to improve under his penalty.
Royal Premier(IRE) Official explanation: jockey said gelding suffered interference on dropping back

T/Plt: £254.40 to a £1 stake. Pool: £74,316.40. 213.25 winning tickets. T/Qpdt: £37.10 to a £1 stake. Pool: £6,783.40. 135.00 winning tickets. SP

5909 NOTTINGHAM (L-H)

Wednesday, October 10

OFFICIAL GOING: Good to soft (soft in places; 7.1)
After 10mm rain the previous day the ground was reckoned 'genuine soft'. There were 16 non-runners due to the change in conditions.
Wind: Light, half-behind Weather: overcast

6103 JOHN SMITH'S H'CAP — 6f 15y

1:40 (1:41) (Class 5) (0-70,70) 3-Y-0+ — **£2,914** (£867; £433; £216) **Stalls** High

Form — RPR

5004 **1** **Cornus**[7] 5909 5-9-4 **69**........(be) JamesDoyle 10 — 80
(A J McCabe) *hld up towards rr: hdwy over 2f out: effrt and n.m.r over 1f out: rdn and squeezed through ins fnl f: bmpd and led last 50yds: r.o* **11/2[2]**

0000 **2** 3/4 **Steel Blue**[32] 5232 7-9-3 **68**........ HayleyTurner 16 — 77
(R M Whitaker) *t.k.h: cl up: led 2f out and sn rdn: drvn ins fnl f: hung lft: hdd and no ex last 50yds* **5/1[1]**

3405 **3** 1 1/4 **After The Show**[26] 5387 6-9-1 **66**........ NCallan 1 — 71
(Rae Guest) *hld up towards rr: stdy hdwy over 2f out: effrt over 1f out: rdn and ev ch ins fnl f tl no ex last 100yds* **13/2[3]**

1000 **4** nk **Equuleus Pictor**[17] 5662 3-9-1 **67**........ FrancisNorton 13 — 71
(J L Spearing) *trckd ldrs: smooth hdwy over 2f out: rdn to chal ent fnl f and ev ch tl wknd last 100yds* **10/1**

4160 **5** 1 **Dualagi**[25] 5418 3-9-2 **68**........ LPKeniry 12 — 69
(J S Moore) *hld up in rr: hdwy over 2f out: swtchd lft and rdn over 1f out: styd on ins fnl f: nrst fin* **14/1**

0600 **6** 2 1/2 **Tipsy Prince**[9] 5874 3-9-4 **70**........ FergusSweeney 4 — 64
(David Pinder) *in rr: pushed along 1/2-way: rdn 2f out: styd on appr fnl f: nrst fin* **12/1**

0010 **7** 2 1/2 **Hollow Jo**[26] 5387 7-9-2 **67**........ MickyFenton 11 — 53
(J R Jenkins) *chsd ldrs: rdn along over 2f out: grad wknd* **22/1**

044 **8** nk **Farefield Lodge (IRE)**[17] 5662 3-9-4 **70**........(b[1]) KDarley 6 — 55
(C G Cox) *chsd ldrs on outer: rdn along wl over 2f out and grad wknd* **13/2[3]**

5600 **9** hd **Russian Rocket (IRE)**[77] 3852 5-8-9 **65**........ KirstyMilczarek(5) 8 — 50+
(Mrs C A Dunnett) *midfield: hdwy on outer to chse ldrs 2f out: sn rdn and wknd over 1f out* **11/1**

5500 **10** shd **Gilded Cove**[34] 5177 7-8-10 **66**........ RussellKennemore(5) 5 — 50+
(R Hollinshead) *midfield: hdwy on outer to chse ldrs over 2f out: sn rdn and wknd wl over 1f out* **11/1**

0-00 **11** 3 1/2 **Johnston's Diamond (IRE)**[6] 5934 9-9-4 **69**........(p) DavidAllan 17 — 43
(E J Alston) *led: rdn along 3f out: hdd 2f out and sn wknd* **16/1**

4050 **12** 2 1/2 **Romany Nights (IRE)**[14] 5722 7-9-5 **70**........(bt) JohnEgan 2 — 36
(Miss Gay Kelleway) *a in rr* **16/1**

1m 13.91s (-1.09) **Going Correction** -0.10s/f (Good)
WFA 3 from 5yo+ 1lb — **12** Ran SP% **114.9**
Speed ratings (Par 103): **103,102,100,99,98 95,91,91,91,91 86,83**
CSF £32.02 CT £185.24 TOTE £5.60: £1.90, £2.20, £2.60; EX 16.70.
Owner Club ROA **Bred** G Russell **Trained** Babworth, Notts

FOCUS
A modest but competitive sprint handicap. Solid form. They raced towards the near-side rail and those taken towards the middle of the track with their efforts could make little impressions.
Tipsy Prince Official explanation: jockey said gelding missed the break
Romany Nights(IRE) Official explanation: jockey said gelding moved poorly throughout

6104 E.B.F./ WBX.COM £25 BET FOR NEW ACCOUNTS MAIDEN STKS (DIV I) — 5f 13y

2:10 (2:18) (Class 4) 2-Y-0 — **£3,238** (£963; £481; £240) **Stalls** High

Form — RPR

1 **Blue Jack** 2-9-3 0........ RichardMullen 8 — 71
(W R Muir) *dwlt: sn chsng ldrs: hung lft and styd on to ld ins fnl f* **11/1**

5530 **2** 1 **Faber Hall Flyer**[23] 5470 2-9-3 77........ HayleyTurner 11 — 67
(Mrs C A Dunnett) *trckd ldrs: hrd rdn and edgd lft over 1f out: kpt on to take 2nd towards fin* **11/2[3]**

6302 **3** shd **Ever Hopeful**[25] 5429 2-8-12 69........ FrancisNorton 4 — 62
(H J L Dunlop) *w ldrs: kpt on same pce fnl f* **4/1[2]**

40 **4** 1 1/2 **Casla Beag (IRE)**[116] 2651 2-8-12 0........ SteveDrowne 2 — 57
(B Palling) *swvd rt s: led tl hdd & wknd ins fnl f* **9/1**

06 **5** 1/2 **Operachy**[19] 5591 2-9-3 0........ FergusSweeney 12 — 60
(B R Millman) *hld up in mid-div: outpcd over 2f out: kpt on wl fnl f* **6/1**

6 3 **Mayview** 2-8-12 0........ JamieMackay 3 — 44
(Rae Guest) *sn outpcd and in rr: kpt on fnl f* **9/1**

634 **7** 2 1/2 **Mayaar (USA)**[26] 5380 2-8-12 71........ RyanMoore 1 — 35
(P W Chapple-Hyam) *hit hd on stalls: chsd ldrs: outpcd 2f out: sn wknd* **15/8[1]**

00 **8** 6 **Captain Crooner (IRE)**[27] 5363 2-9-3 0........ DeanMcKeown 5 — 18
(D Shaw) *sn outpcd and in rr: bhd fnl 2f* **50/1**

0 **9** 2 1/2 **Rose De Rita**[12] 5770 2-8-12 0........ VinceSlattery 9 — 4
(L P Grassick) *chsd ldrs: rdn and lost pl over 2f out: sn bhd* **125/1**

61.01 secs (-0.79) **Going Correction** -0.10s/f (Good) — **9** Ran SP% **115.5**
Speed ratings (Par 97): **102,100,100,97,97 92,88,78,74**
CSF £70.27 TOTE £12.70: £3.50, £1.60, £1.90; EX 74.60.
Owner Martin P Graham **Bred** Miss S N Ralphs **Trained** Lambourn, Berks

FOCUS
This was a fairly weak maiden and it is probably worth noting there was a false start, which was obviously far from ideal for these inexperienced two-year-olds, all of whom ran for between one and four furlongs before being recalled. The winning time was 0.19 seconds quicker than the second division but this does not look a race to be with.

NOTEBOOK
Blue Jack, a 30,000gns son of Cadeaux Genereux, half-brother to high-class multiple sprint winner Just James, out of a 6f juvenile winner, was nibbled at in the market and proved good enough to make a successful debut. The bare form looks modest, but he displayed a good attitude under pressure having travelled nicely and should go on from this. (op 14-1)
Faber Hall Flyer, dropped in trip with the tongue-tie left off for the first time, did not appear to run up to his official mark of 77, but this was hardly a bad performance. (op 7-2)
Ever Hopeful showed bright early speed and did not look to have too many excuses. (op 5-1)
Casla Beag(IRE) is now qualified for a handicap mark and she should find her level in low-grade events. (op 17-2)
Operachy is another who will have more options now he is qualified for a handicap mark. (op 11-1)

The Form Book, Raceform Ltd, Compton, RG20 6NL

Mayaar(USA) is only modest, but she was still some way below the form she had shown on her three previous starts. Official explanation: jockey said filly hit head on the starting stalls (op 7-4 tchd 2-1)

6105 E.B.F./ WBX.COM £25 BET FOR NEW ACCOUNTS MAIDEN STKS (DIV II) 5f 13y

2:40 (2:42) (Class 4) 2-Y-O **£3,238** (£963; £481; £240) **Stalls** High

Form RPR

1 **Quiet Elegance** 2-8-12 0 KDarley 4 75+
(E J Alston) *dwlt: sn trcking ldrs on outer: hdwy 2f out: rdn to chal over 1f out: led ent fnl f and kpt on wl* **11/1**

3 2 1 1/4 **Recent Times**[47] 4782 2-8-12 0 DavidAllan 9 70+
(T D Easterby) *led: rdn along and jnd over 1f out: drvn: edgd lft and hdd ent fnl f: kpt on same pce* **5/2**[1]

3 3 **Filligree (IRE)** 2-8-12 0 JamieMackay 5 59
(Rae Guest) *hld up towards rr and green: hdwy 2f out: styd on ins fnl f: nrst fin* **16/1**

4 4 1/2 **Tittle**[15] 5699 2-8-12 0 FergusSweeney 8 57
(H Candy) *chsd ldrs: rdn along wl over 1f out: kpt on same pce ins fnl f* **4/1**[3]

5 shd **Lullaby Lady** 2-8-12 0 MichaelHills 10 57
(B W Hills) *s.i.s and sn detached: hdwy 2f out: swtchd lft to outer over 1f out: styd on wl fnl f: nrst fin* **6/1**

6 1/2 **Another Socket** 2-8-12 0 GrahamGibbons 6 55
(E S McMahon) *trckd ldrs: effrt 2f out: sn rdn and wknd* **7/2**[2]

7 hd **My Mate Pete (IRE)** 2-9-3 0 GeorgeBaker 1 60
(R M Beckett) *wnt lft s: sn cl up: effrt and ev ch 2f out: sn rdn and wknd* **7/1**

00 8 7 **Emir Bagatelle**[9] 5872 2-9-3 0 MickyFenton 11 34
(H Morrison) *pushed along to chse ldrs: rdn after 2f: sn lost pl and bhd* **50/1**

00 9 2 **Charlie Oxo**[12] 5772 2-9-3 0 J-PGuillambert 3 27
(B P J Baugh) *dwlt: sn cl up: pushed along 1/2-way: sn lost pl and bhd* **150/1**

61.20 secs (-0.60) **Going Correction** -0.10s/f (Good) **9** Ran SP% **114.4**
Speed ratings (Par 97): **100,98,93,92,92 91,91,79,76**
CSF £38.40 TOTE £14.00: £4.40, £1.10, £6.00; EX 45.00.

Owner Mr & Mrs G Middlebrook **Bred** G And Mrs Middlebrook **Trained** Longton, Lancs

FOCUS
The bare form of this maiden looks just fair at best, but there were some nicely bred types on show and a few of these are open to improvement. The winning time was 0.19 seconds slower than the first division.

NOTEBOOK
Quiet Elegance, a daughter of Fantastic Light, half-sister to the stable's top-class sprinter Reverence, out of a high-class 5f winner at two, who was later a useful sprinter, made a very pleasing racecourse debut. She was forced to make her move on the outside of the main group, but she picked up nicely and was well on top at the line. The bare form looks just fair at best, but she is extremely well bred and could be very useful in time. (op 9-1)
Recent Times, a fair third on her debut over 6f at Thirsk, showed good early speed and can have few excuses. (op 11-4)
Filligree(IRE) ◆, a Kyllachy half-sister to among others 7f juvenile winner Porcelain, out of a multiple 6f winner at two and three, made an eye-catching debut. She ran green and was not given a hard time at all, but was still able to get up for third. She should be able to show considerable improvement next time. Official explanation: jockey said, regarding the running and riding, his orders were to have the filly handy and get her to travel as well as possible, adding that the filly ran in snatches and was outpaced 2 1/2f out and idled when asked to go for a gap towards the rails; once sure he could go into the gap the filly ran on well to finish second
Tittle improved on the form she showed on her debut at Beverley and is going the right way. (tchd 7-2, tchd 9-2 in places)
Lullaby Lady, a 60,000gns daughter of Piccolo, half-sister to among others 6f juvenile winner Mameyuki, out of a 7f-1m2f winner, showed real signs of inexperience and was last through the early stages, but she gradually got the hang of things. She is another who can be expected to come on a fair bit for the experience.
Another Socket, a daughter of Overbury, half-sister to among others quite useful triple sprint juvenile winner Socket Set, failed to justify strong market support. She has presumably been showing something at home and is worth another chance. (op 4-1, tchd 9-2 in places)

6106 WBX.COM 0% COMMISSION ON DAY'S BIG MAIDEN STKS (DIV I) 1m 54y

3:10 (3:10) (Class 5) 2-Y-O **£2,590** (£770; £385; £192) **Stalls** Centre

Form RPR

1 **Tajaaweed (USA)** 2-9-3 0 RHills 9 85+
(Sir Michael Stoute) *trckd ldrs: led over 1f out: pushed clr: v readily* **3/1**[2]

40 2 5 **Hyde Lea Flyer**[55] 4547 2-9-3 0 DarryllHolland 12 74
(E S McMahon) *trckd ldrs: led 3f out tl over 1f out: kpt on: no ch w wnr* **11/2**[3]

0 3 1 1/2 **Legion D'Honneur (UAE)**[8] 5880 2-9-3 0 GregFairley 3 71
(M Johnston) *led: hdd 3f out: hung lft over 1f out: styd on same pce* **8/1**

03 4 shd **Spice Trade**[12] 5772 2-9-3 0 KDarley 2 70
(J Noseda) *sn chsng ldrs: drvn over 4f out: styd on same pce fnl 2f* **15/8**[1]

06 5 4 **General Tufto**[19] 5599 2-9-3 0 SteveDrowne 7 62
(R Charlton) *chsd ldrs: drvn 4f out: wknd over 1f out* **17/2**

3400 6 nk **Softly Killing Me**[14] 5729 2-8-12 59 FergusSweeney 6 56
(J Gallagher) *t.k.h: in tch: effrt over 2f out: wknd 2f out* **33/1**

7 2 **Good Return** 2-9-3 0 JohnEgan 13 57
(Jane Chapple-Hyam) *s.s: in rr: kpt on fnl 2f: nvr on terms* **50/1**

8 1/2 **Paint The Town Red** 2-9-3 0 MickyFenton 11 56
(H J Collingridge) *in rr: sme hdwy on inner 4f out: nvr nr ldrs* **50/1**

00 9 2 **Kalokairi (IRE)**[19] 5596 2-8-12 0 TedDurcan 1 46
(J L Dunlop) *chsd ldrs: lost pl 3f out* **20/1**

0 10 shd **Mount Lavinia (IRE)**[34] 5162 2-8-12 0 JamesDoyle 8 46
(R M Beckett) *chsd ldrs: lost pl 3f out: sn bhd* **12/1**

00 11 6 **Rock Me (IRE)**[6] 5951 2-9-3 0 (b) SimonWhitworth 5 38
(N A Callaghan) *mid-div: lost pl over 3f out: sn bhd* **125/1**

12 21 **Lets Go Jo** 2-9-3 0 TomEaves 4 —
(Mrs L Stubbs) *slowly away: wl bhd fnl 2f* **66/1**

1m 45.82s (-0.58) **Going Correction** 0.0s/f (Good) **12** Ran SP% **118.4**
Speed ratings (Par 95): **102,97,95,95,91 91,89,88,86,86 80,59**
CSF £18.95 TOTE £4.20: £1.50, £1.70, £3.80; EX 30.60.

Owner Hamdan Al Maktoum **Bred** Herman Sarkowsky **Trained** Newmarket, Suffolk

FOCUS
Just an ordinary maiden, but an impressive winner and the time was 3.16 seconds quicker than the second division. The form seems sound, rated through the runner-up.

NOTEBOOK
Tajaaweed(USA) ◆, a $400,000 son of Dynaformer, half-brother to Manosh, a multiple 6f-1m winner in the US, and dual 7f-1m juvenile winner Kingfield, has been given an entry in the Racing Post Trophy and was an impressive winner on his racecourse debut. Always travelling noticeably strongly, he bounded clear when asked for his effort and recorded a much faster time than the second division in the process. It remains to be seen what the plans are, but he looks a smart colt in the making. (tchd 11-4)
Hyde Lea Flyer did not show much at Sandown last time, but he had previously shown plenty of ability on his debut at Newmarket and he confirmed that earlier promise with a distant second behind the potentially smart winner. He is now qualified for a handicap mark and will have more options. (op 13-2 tchd 7-1)
Legion D'Honneur(UAE) was given a positive ride and improved on the form he showed on his debut over 7f at Warwick.
Spice Trade failed to really build on the promise of his two runs over 6f on this significant step up in trip. He is, though, now qualified for a handicap mark and will have more options. (tchd 2-1)
General Tufto ◆ had shown promise in good maidens on his two previous starts and he again hinted at ability. He should do better when he grows up and ought to make his mark over a little further in handicaps next year. (op 8-1 tchd 10-1)

6107 WBX.COM 0% COMMISSION ON DAY'S BIG MAIDEN STKS (DIV II) 1m 54y

3:40 (3:42) (Class 5) 2-Y-O **£2,590** (£770; £385; £192) **Stalls** Centre

Form RPR

6 1 **Patkai (IRE)**[21] 5538 2-9-3 0 RyanMoore 9 73+
(Sir Michael Stoute) *towards rr and sn pushed along: hdwy whn n.m.r and hmpd 5f out: rdn along and n.m.r over 2f out: swtchd outside and hdwy wl over 1f out: str run ins fnl f to ld last 100yds* **11/10**[1]

2 1 1/4 **Etruscan (IRE)** 2-9-3 0 LDettori 13 70+
(Saeed Bin Suroor) *t.k.h and led on outer after 1f tl 5f out: cl up tl rdn to ld again over 1f out and sn wandered: hung rt ins fnl f: hdd and no ex last 100yds* **3/1**[2]

3 1 1/4 **Just Rob** 2-8-12 0 RussellKennemore(5) 5 68+
(R Hollinshead) *t.k.h: trckd ldrs: n.m.r 5f out: hdwy over 2f out: rdn and styng on whn hmpd ins fnl f: kpt on* **66/1**

04 4 2 **Langham House**[30] 5274 2-9-3 0 JohnEgan 11 63
(J R Jenkins) *chsd ldrs: effrt on outer and rdn along over 2f out: ev ch whn edgd lft over 1f out: one pce ins fnl f* **16/1**

0 5 nk **Chaenomeles (USA)**[11] 5801 2-8-12 0 GregFairley 10 57
(M Johnston) *prom: led over 3f out: rdn along and hdd over 1f out: drvn and hung lft ins fnl f: sn wknd* **14/1**

00 6 1 1/4 **Red Lily (IRE)**[13] 5749 2-8-12 0 TPQueally 4 55
(J R Fanshawe) *in rr: hdwy wl over 2f out: sn rdn along and styd on appr fnl f: nrst fin* **25/1**

7 1/2 **High Stepping (USA)** 2-9-3 0 SteveDrowne 1 59
(E A L Dunlop) *dwlt: towards rr: hdwy on inner over 2f out: styd on appr fnl f: nrst fin* **25/1**

000 8 4 **Love Dancer (IRE)**[53] 4593 2-9-3 50 HayleyTurner 7 50
(M L W Bell) *led 1f: cl up tl led again 5f out: rdn along and hdd over 3f out: sn wknd* **66/1**

0 9 hd **Hits Only Time**[19] 5595 2-9-3 0 DeanMcKeown 8 49
(J Pearce) *plld hrd: hld up: a towards rr* **66/1**

33 10 shd **Mon Plaisir (USA)**[30] 5274 2-9-3 0 TedDurcan 6 49
(J L Dunlop) *trckd ldrs: n.m.r 5f out: rdn along 3f out: sn drvn and wknd over 2f out* **7/2**[3]

11 1/2 **River Kent** 2-9-3 0 RoystonFfrench 12 48
(Mrs A Duffield) *a towards rr* **50/1**

12 14 **Northgate Maisie** 2-8-12 0 PaulMulrennan 2 12
(Jedd O'Keeffe) *chsd ldrs on inner: n.m.r and lost pl qckly after 1f: sn in rr* **100/1**

1m 48.98s (2.58) **Going Correction** 0.0s/f (Good) **12** Ran SP% **122.5**
Speed ratings (Par 95): **87,85,84,82,82 80,80,76,76,76 75,61**
CSF £4.44 TOTE £2.00: £1.10, £1.70, £8.80; EX 6.10.

Owner Ballymacoll Stud **Bred** Ballymacoll Stud Farm Ltd **Trained** Newmarket, Suffolk

FOCUS
The early pace was very ordinary and even though things quickened up considerably in the straight, the winning time was still very moderate, 3.16 seconds slower than the first division. A couple did show promise for the future though, and are likely to improve quite a bit from this, although the bare form of the race is nothing special.

NOTEBOOK
Patkai(IRE) ◆ still looked green and took an age to get into top gear. The long straight was a big help to him, however, and once switched out wide he gradually reeled in the leaders and in the end won with a degree of comfort. His pedigree suggested he would enjoy the easier ground, and despite the winning time doing little for the form his breeding also suggests he will appreciate stepping up in trip next term. (op 13-8)
Etruscan(IRE) ◆, a 190,000gns half-brother to 1m6f winner Meryaat, like the winner was bred to appreciate the easy ground being by Selkirk. Greenness was a bit of a problem though, as he wandered about a few times during the course of the race, but he was always up with the pace and had every chance until the favourite cut him down late on. This may not have been the strongest of maidens, but even so he should know more next time. (tchd 7-2)
Just Rob, related to the useful Restrained on the dam's side, ran a blinder on this debut and would have finished even closer had he not been squeezed out between Etruscan and Chaenomeles over a furlong from home. There is nothing flashy about his pedigree and the winning time does not suggest the form is anything special, but he obviously has ability and should be able to pick up a race or due in due course. Official explanation: jockey said colt hung right-handed in home straight
Langham House had every chance and was one of five in a line across the track passing the furlong pole, but lacked speed towards the end. He now qualifies for nurseries, but he was inclined to carry his head at an awkward angle down the home straight and was more experienced than those that beat him, so it would be wrong to get too carried away. (op 14-1)
Chaenomeles(USA) was much sharper than on her debut and showed up for a long way until getting tired late on. She may not be anything special, but this was an improvement and her American pedigree could maker her interesting if tried on sand. (op 10-1)
Red Lily(IRE) ◆ stayed on without offering a threat, but did show a bit more on this easier ground. Bred to stay, she now qualifies for a handicap and could be of some interest in that sphere given a stamina test. (op 18-1)
High Stepping(USA) ◆, a $140,000 half-brother to six winners in the US, never looked like winning but neither did he ever give up and he is likely to come on a lot for this. His breeding suggests he could be of special interest if tried on sand. (op 16-1)

Mon Plaisir(USA) failed to see out the extra furlong on this easier ground and disappointed once again. Official explanation: jockey said colt was unsuited by the good to soft (soft in places) ground (op 4-1 tchd 5-1)

6108 JOHN SMITH'S (S) H'CAP — 1m 1f 213y
4:10 (4:11) (Class 6) (0-55,54) 3-Y-O — £2,047 (£604; £302) Stalls Low

Form — RPR

0106 **1** **Vietnam**[17] 5128 3-9-0 **54** ....(b) SteveDrowne 8 — 63
(G A Huffer) *hld up in rr: hdwy on wd outside over 3f out: led over 1f out: edgd lft: drvn out* **17/2**

0606 **2** *2* **Etoile D'Or (IRE)**[18] 5640 3-8-11 **51** .... TedDurcan 2 — 56
(M H Tompkins) *led tl over 1f out: eased whn wl hld nr fin* **9/2**[3]

0006 **3** *2 1/2* **Still Dreaming**[5] 5967 3-8-10 **50** ....(b) PhillipMakin 1 — 50
(M Dods) *chsd ldrs: effrt over 4f out: kpt on same pce fnl 2f* **11/4**[1]

6200 **4** *4* **Rubilini**[11] 5817 3-8-6 **46** ow1 .... JohnEgan 10 — 38
(M R Channon) *chsd ldrs: one pce fnl 2f* **7/2**[2]

3400 **5** *shd* **Meadfoot**[6] 5945 3-8-7 **47** .... RichardKingscote 5 — 39
(B R Millman) *trckd ldrs: t.k.h: rdn over 3f out: wknd over 1f out* **14/1**

2550 **6** *3* **Roxy Singer**[43] 4914 3-8-5 **45** ....(v) HayleyTurner 7 — 31
(W J Musson) *trckd ldrs: wknd over 2f out* **13/2**

-044 **7** *1 1/4* **Zilli**[198] 791 3-8-4 **47** .... LukeMorris(3) 3 — 30
(N P Littmoden) *s.i.s: mid-div: effrt over 3f out: nvr trbld ldrs* **10/1**

4000 **8** *7* **Sahara Dawn (IRE)**[11] 5228 3-8-7 **47** ow2 ....(v[1]) DavidAllan 13 — 16
(D Carroll) *chsd ldrs: rdn over 4f out: lost pl over 3f out* **16/1**

3060 **9** *6* **Flamestone**[22] 5508 3-8-5 **45** .... LiamJones 6 — 2
(A E Price) *hld up in rr: hdwy on ins 4f out: lost pl 2f out* **22/1**

0006 **10** *24* **First Frost**[197] 794 3-8-2 **45** .... DuranFentiman(3) 12 — —
(M J Gingell) *hld up detached in last: rdn over 5f out: lost pl over 3f out: sn bhd: t.o* **100/1**

2m 11.25s (1.55) **Going Correction** +0.325s/f (Good) — **10** Ran SP% **117.9**
Speed ratings (Par 99): **106,104,102,99,99 96,95,90,85,66**
CSF £47.15 CT £134.94 TOTE £9.90: £2.70, £1.90, £1.30; EX 49.50.The winner was bought in for 5,800gns.
Owner Fran O'Brien **Bred** D R Tucker **Trained** Newmarket, Suffolk

FOCUS
A modest seller and probably just ordinary form for the grade, but this was run at a very decent pace thanks to the runner-up. As a result they recorded a smart winning time for a race like this and the fastest of the three races over the trip at the meeting. The field finished well spread out and the front pair came up the middle of the track in the straight which seemed to be an advantage.

6109 WBX.COM FREE FOOTBALL SHIRT FOR NEW ACCOUNT MAIDEN STKS — 1m 1f 213y
4:40 (4:40) (Class 5) 3-Y-O+ — £3,238 (£963; £481; £240) Stalls Low

Form — RPR

1 **Envisage (IRE)** 3-9-3 0 .... LDettori 7 — 78+
(Saeed Bin Suroor) *cl up: led 1/2-way: rdn along 2f out: drvn ins fnl f and styd on* **6/4**[1]

00 **2** *2 1/2* **Heavenward**[9] 5873 3-9-3 0 .... RyanMoore 9 — 67+
(Sir Michael Stoute) *in tch: hdwy to chse ldrs 3f out: rdn over 1f out: ch ins fnl f: sn drvn and one pce* **8/1**[3]

22-4 **3** *nk* **Garafena**[11] 5816 4-9-3 79 .... PatDobbs 4 — 61
(Pat Eddery) *trckd ldrs: lost pl over 4f out: hdwy to chse ldng pair over 1f out: kpt on same pce* **7/2**[2]

0-4 **4** *5* **Wraith**[20] 5562 3-9-3 0 .... TedDurcan 12 — 56
(H R A Cecil) *trckd ldrs: hdwy and cl up 1/2-way: effrt and ev ch 3f out: rdn over 2f out: drvn and wknd wl over 1f out* **7/2**[2]

6-0 **5** *1* **Grafty Green (IRE)**[13] 5754 4-9-8 0 .... LiamJones 10 — 54?
(W M Brisbourne) *in tch: hdwy on outer to chse ldrs over 4f out: rdn along 3f out: drvn and wknd wl over 1f out* **200/1**

6 **6** *3/4* **Lady Killer Queen**[20] 5562 3-8-12 0 .... DavidAllan 1 — 48?
(D Carroll) *s.i.s and bhd: rdn along and hdwy 3f out: styd on u.p appr fnl f: nrst fin* **100/1**

6-3R **7** *3/4* **Moral Code (IRE)**[46] 4815 3-9-3 0 .... RichardMullen 14 — 51
(E J O'Neill) *s.i.s and bhd tl styd on fnl 2f: nvr a factor* **10/1**

0662 **8** *2* **Djalalabad (FR)**[15] 5710 3-8-12 57 .... JohnEgan 13 — 42
(Mrs C A Dunnett) *plld hrd early: hld up towards rr: hdwy on outer to trck ldrs over 4f out: rdn along over 2f out: edgd lft and wknd over 1f out* **25/1**

5000 **9** *nk* **Cat Six (USA)**[33] 5188 3-8-12 57 .... DarryllHolland 5 — 41
(T Wall) *led to 1/2-way: sn rdn along and grad wknd* **66/1**

60 **10** *hd* **Resaass (USA)**[13] 5754 4-9-8 0 .... TomEaves 8 — 46
(J O'Reilly) *s.i.s: a in rr* **200/1**

00 **11** *1* **Pheidias (IRE)**[219] 611 3-9-3 0 .... MickyFenton 11 — 44
(Mrs P Sly) *hld up: a towards rr* **66/1**

0 **12** *1* **Royal Rainbow**[49] 4707 3-9-0 0 .... TravisBlock(3) 6 — 42
(P W Hiatt) *in tch: rdn along 4f out: sn wknd* **125/1**

03 **13** *nk* **Icansingarainbow**[13] 5754 3-8-12 0 .... RussellKennemore(5) 3 — 41
(R Hollinshead) *chsd ldrs: rdn along over 4f out: sn wknd* **33/1**

60 **14** *10* **Winter Lane**[173] 1129 3-9-3 0 .... PaddyAspell 2 — 21
(J R Norton) *a towards rr* **125/1**

2m 13.1s (3.40) **Going Correction** +0.325s/f (Good)
WFA 3 from 4yo 5lb — **14** Ran SP% **118.0**
Speed ratings (Par 103): **99,97,96,92,91 91,90,89,88,88 87,87,86,78**
CSF £14.50 TOTE £2.50: £1.10, £3.20, £2.00; EX 15.80.
Owner Godolphin **Bred** Kilfrush Stud **Trained** Newmarket, Suffolk

FOCUS
Not a strong maiden, certainly not as strong as the numbers would suggest as less than half the field had any realistic chance. The principals were always handy and the front three pulled a long way clear, but a modest early pace meant that the winning time was the slowest of the three races over the trip, including being 1.85 seconds slower than the preceding seller. Because of the slow pace the form cannot be taken seriously.
Djalalabad(FR) Official explanation: jockey said filly had no more to give

6110 WBX.COM 0% COMMISSION ON DAY'S BIG H'CAP — 1m 1f 213y
5:10 (5:10) (Class 4) (0-85,84) 3-Y-O+ — £5,181 (£1,541; £770; £384) Stalls Low

Form — RPR

4000 **1** **Chantaco (USA)**[12] 5764 5-9-7 **84** .... SteveDrowne 7 — 96
(A M Balding) *led after 1f: set modest pce: qcknd over 3f out: hld on wl* **14/1**

-100 **2** *1 1/2* **Forroger (CAN)**[131] 2209 4-9-6 **83** .... NCallan 15 — 92+
(M A Jarvis) *hld up in rr: smooth hdwy 3f out: rdn over 1f out: no real imp* **5/1**[3]

2331 **3** *1* **Shela House**[9] 5870 3-9-0 **82** 6ex .... RyanMoore 14 — 89+
(J R Fanshawe) *hld up in rr: effrt 3f out: styd on fnl f: nrst fin* **15/8**[1]

560- **4** *nk* **Shogun Prince (IRE)**[387] 5428 4-8-13 **76** .... FergusSweeney 8 — 82
(A King) *chsd ldrs: styd on same pce fnl 2f* **50/1**

0310 **5** *3* **New Star (UAE)**[25] 5432 3-8-9 **77** .... GrahamGibbons 11 — 77
(W M Brisbourne) *chsd ldrs: one pce fnl 2f* **66/1**

003 **6** *nk* **Master Pegasus**[37] 5099 4-9-4 **81** .... GeorgeBaker 6 — 81
(C F Wall) *trckd ldrs: effrt 3f out: one pce* **25/1**

365 **7** *1/2* **Aegean Prince**[12] 5775 3-8-10 **78** ....(b[1]) RichardMullen 9 — 77
(W R Muir) *mid-div: effrt over 3f out: nvr rchd ldrs* **25/1**

-004 **8** *1/2* **Tommy Toogood (IRE)**[33] 5205 4-9-1 **78** .... MichaelHills 4 — 76
(B W Hills) *mid-div: effrt on ins 3f out: fdd appr fnl f* **14/1**

5-00 **9** *1/2* **First Mate (IRE)**[15] 5703 3-7-13 **70** .... AndrewMullen(3) 3 — 67
(M Johnston) *led 1f: chsd ldrs: drvn over 3f out: wknd over 1f out* **18/1**

2154 **10** *2* **Le Soleil (GER)**[21] 5543 6-8-13 **76** .... TPQueally 12 — 69
(B J Curley) *hld up in midfield: effrt on outer 3f out: edgd lft: nvr nr ldrs* **14/1**

0562 **11** *1 1/4* **Folio (IRE)**[12] 5775 7-9-4 **81** .... DarryllHolland 5 — 71
(W J Musson) *hld up in rr: effrt on wd outside over 3f out: nvr on terms* **13/2**

2212 **12** *4* **Celtic Change (IRE)**[53] 4608 3-8-10 **78** .... TedDurcan 2 — 60
(M Dods) *hld up towards rr: effrt 4f out: nvr a factor: wknd 2f out* **9/2**[2]

2m 11.53s (1.83) **Going Correction** +0.325s/f (Good)
WFA 3 from 4yo+ 5lb — **12** Ran SP% **119.4**
Speed ratings (Par 105): **105,103,103,102,100 100,99,99,98,97 96,93**
CSF £81.07 CT £196.43 TOTE £17.80: £4.00, £2.20, £1.50; EX 100.60 Trifecta £266.40 Pool: £450.30 - 1.20 winning tickets. Place 6 £50.24, Place 5 £27.38.
Owner The Pink Hat Racing Partnership **Bred** London Thoroughbred Services **Trained** Kingsclere, Hants

FOCUS
A decent handicap and reasonable form for the grade. The early pace threatened to be modest, but quickened up a bit when the eventual winner was sent to the front after a furlong. The winning time was faster than the maiden, but slower than the seller and was probably about what you would expect for the grade. It was noticeable that the jockeys wanted to give the inside rail a wide berth turning into the straight and came down the middle.
T/Jkpt: Not won. T/Plt: £51.50 to a £1 stake. Pool: £44,852.05. 635.40 winning tickets. T/Qpdt: £9.30 to a £1 stake. Pool: £3,027.00. 240.30 winning tickets. JR

6096 KEMPTON (A.W) (R-H)
Thursday, October 11

OFFICIAL GOING: Standard
Wind: nil Weather: dry, cooling down after a pleasent day

6119 ONLINE GROUP MEDIAN AUCTION MAIDEN STKS — 7f (P)
6:50 (6:50) (Class 6) 2-Y-O — £2,047 (£604; £302) Stalls High

Form — RPR

1 **Harlem Shuffle (UAE)** 2-8-12 0 .... GregFairley 9 — 74+
(M Johnston) *w'like: leggy: pressed ldr and clr of remainder: rdn to ld 3f out: forged clr fnl f: r.o wl* **8/1**

5 **2** *1 3/4* **Duty Doctor**[65] 4254 2-8-12 0 .... LPKeniry 10 — 70+
(S Kirk) *leggy: racd in midfield: hdwy over 2f out: chsd ldng pair 2f out: kpt on u.p to chse wnr ins fnl f: nt trble wnr* **33/1**

3 *1* **Transfer** 2-9-0 0 .... NeilChalmers(3) 12 — 72
(A M Balding) *sn led: clr w wnr: hdd 3f out: rdn over 2f out: ev ch tl fdd last 100yds* **33/1**

5 **4** *1 1/2* **Morocchius (USA)**[15] 5720 2-9-3 0 .... SebSanders 5 — 68
(R M Beckett) *t.k.h: hld up in midfield: rdn and hdwy over 2f out: chsd ldng trio wl over 1f out: kpt on: nvr able to chal* **11/4**[2]

0 **5** *shd* **Miss Phoebe (IRE)**[10] 5868 2-8-12 0 .... SimonWhitworth 3 — 63
(S Kirk) *wl bhd: stayed on fnl f: nvr nr ldrs* **20/1**

0 **6** *shd* **Where's Susie**[17] 5681 2-8-12 0 .... RobertHavlin 2 — 63
(D K Ivory) *racd wd: wl bhd tl styd on fnl f: nvr nr ldrs* **33/1**

7 *1/2* **Rowaad** 2-9-3 0 .... RHills 11 — 67
(M P Tregoning) *w'like: wl bhd: pushed along and hdwy wl over 1f out: kpt on: n.d* **9/1**

8 *hd* **Jasoora** 2-8-12 0 .... MartinDwyer 4 — 61
(M P Tregoning) *w'like: s.i.s: wl bhd: sme late hdwy: nvr on terms* **16/1**

54 **9** *nk* **Silk Hall (UAE)**[17] 5679 2-9-3 0 .... JamesDoyle 8 — 65
(D W P Arbuthnot) *rring in stalls: sn hand in main gp: rdn 3f out: no hdwy: no ch last 2f* **15/2**[3]

6 **10** *1/2* **Marino Prince (FR)**[13] 5780 2-8-10 0 .... JackDean(7) 13 — 64
(W G M Turner) *leggy: racd in midfield: drvn 4f out: n.d* **20/1**

00 **11** *2 1/2* **Dual Faith (IRE)**[9] 5880 2-9-3 0 .... RyanMoore 7 — 58
(B J Meehan) *promnent in main gp tl 4f out: sn lost pl: no ch last 2f* **33/1**

04 **12** *2 1/2* **Tepee**[17] 5682 2-8-12 0 .... JamieSpencer 14 — 47
(L M Cumani) *w'like: leggy: lw: chsd clr ldng pair: rdn wl over 2f out: hld hd awkwardly and sn no imp: eased fnl f* **7/4**[1]

0 **13** *2* **Addwaitya**[13] 5771 2-9-3 0 .... GeorgeBaker 6 — 47+
(C F Wall) *s.i.s: a bhd* **80/1**

1m 25.87s (-0.93) **Going Correction** -0.30s/f (Stan) — **13** Ran SP% **124.3**
Speed ratings (Par 93): **93,91,89,88,88 87,87,87,86,86 83,80,78**
CSF £255.48 TOTE £12.70: £3.20, £5.00, £6.90; EX 188.70.
Owner Sheikh Mohammed **Bred** Darley **Trained** Middleham Moor, N Yorks

FOCUS
Probably not the most competitive of maidens, especially with the favourite running no sort of race, although the form looks solid rated around those close up behind the winner. The winner and third set a strong early pace and were well clear by halfway, and very few ever got into it. A few of these are entitled to improve.

NOTEBOOK
Harlem Shuffle(UAE) ◆, out of a half-sister to three sprint winners in the US, certainly knew her job and deserves credit for this winning debut as she and Transfer went off at a rate of knots, yet she still had enough in reserve to run out a clear-cut winner. There should be more races to be won with her. (op 7-1)
Duty Doctor ◆, stepping up two furlongs from her turf debut, did much the best of those that raced in the main group adrift of the two pace-setters and finished in decent style. She should get another furlong and ought to win a race before too long.
Transfer, a brother to Trans Sonic and half-brother to Oceancookie, is bred to be suited by this sort of trip. He helped set a rapid pace alongside the eventual winner and the pair were well clear of the rest by halfway. He did not see his race out quite as well as the winner, but this was still an encouraging debut effort.
Morocchius(USA), ridden more patiently than on his Goodwood debut, stayed on from off the pace up the home straight without ever quite managing to land a blow, but this was a step in the right direction. (op 7-2)
Miss Phoebe(IRE), a stable-companion of the runner-up who seemed to find 6f far too sharp on her debut, never looked like winning but was staying on well down the centre of the track and shaped as though she could do with going up in trip again.
Where's Susie, who failed to get home when ridden more prominently over course and distance on her debut, ran the complete opposite this time and her finishing position was as close as she got. She may be one for nurseries after one more run.

Rowaad, a 45,000gns half-brother to Even Bolder, was messed about at the start and soon had plenty to do. He did make a little late progress and is entitled to come on for it. (op 8-1)
Jasoora, out of a half-sister to Ameerat, made some late progress from off the pace without being given a hard time. She looks capable of better.
Silk Hall(UAE) played up in the stalls and was also probably not helped by the drop in trip. He now qualifies for nurseries and that is probably where his future lies. (tchd 8-1)
Tepee, an unlucky fourth here last time, was in a good position at the front of the main group for much of the way, but she looked very awkward soon after turning for home, carrying her head to one side and looking very reluctant under pressure. Unless an obvious reason comes to light soon, she now has plenty of questions to answer. Official explanation: jockey said filly hung right throughout (op 6-4)
Addwaitya Official explanation: jockey said colt did not face the kickback

6120 TTL NURSERY 1m (P)
7:20 (7:21) (Class 5) (0-85,85) 2-Y-O **£2,817** (£838; £418; £209) **Stalls** High

Form RPR
01 **1** **Bronze Cannon (USA)**[17] 5680 2-9-2 **80** .... JimmyFortune 2 87
(J H M Gosden) *lw: bhd and bustled along early: stl last wl over 2f out: plld wd and str run over 1f out: led last strides* **11/2**
4016 **2** *hd* **Palm Court**[21] 5571 2-9-3 **81** .... SteveDrowne 4 88
(R Charlton) *lw: in tch: rdn to chse ldr 2f out: led wl ins fnl f: hdd last strides* **10/1**
2251 **3** *1/2* **Huzzah (IRE)**[8] 5919 2-9-4 **82** 6ex...................... MichaelHills 5 87
(B W Hills) *lw: led: rdn over 2f out: hdd wl ins fnl f: kpt on same pce* **4/1**[2]
6516 **4** *1* **Keenes Day (FR)**[25] 5463 2-9-2 **80** .... GregFairley 9 83
(M Johnston) *s.i.s: wl bhd: rdn and hdwy over 2f out: r.o fnl f: nt rch ldrs* **20/1**
0621 **5** *1 1/4* **Noble Citizen (USA)**[20] 5597 2-9-4 **82** .... MartinDwyer 13 82
(D M Simcock) *chsd ldr tl 4f out: styd handy: rdn and effrt over 2f out: kpt on same pce* **9/2**[3]
16 **6** *3/4* **Spell Caster**[13] 5766 2-9-4 **82** .... SebSanders 7 80
(R M Beckett) *racd in midfield: rdn 3f out: effrt to chse ldrs 2f out: kpt on same pce* **7/2**[1]
5610 **7** *1* **Dancing Marabout (IRE)**[10] 5871 2-8-13 **77** .... RobertHavlin 10 73
(C R Egerton) *lw: hld up towards rr on rail: rdn and hdwy over 2f out: kpt on u.p but nt pce to rch ldrs* **80/1**
6050 **8** *2* **Dome Rock (IRE)**[33] 5216 2-8-11 **75** .... JamieSpencer 11 67
(L M Cumani) *lw: hld up towards rr: rdn and effrt wl over 2f out: no imp* **14/1**
2422 **9** *nk* **Always Ready**[21] 5571 2-9-5 **83** .... KerrinMcEvoy 6 74
(C E Brittain) *hld up towards rr: nvr nr ldrs* **11/1**
0510 **10** *1 1/4* **Night Skier (IRE)**[62] 4364 2-9-2 **80** .... EddieAhern 14 68
(J L Dunlop) *hld up in midfield on rail: rdn over 2f out: sn outpcd* **25/1**
1050 **11** *1 1/2* **Flight Plan**[29] 5323 2-9-7 **85** .... J-PGuillambert 8 70
(C A Cyzer) *t.k.h: chsd ldrs: wnt 2nd 4f out tl 2f out: sn wknd* **20/1**
6440 **12** *1 3/4* **Higgy's Boy (IRE)**[27] 5374 2-8-10 **74** .... PatDobbs 1 55
(R Hannon) *racd in midfield on outer: rdn 3f out: sn btn* **66/1**
1650 **13** *hd* **Barbarossa**[19] 5629 2-8-10 **74** .... RyanMoore 3 54
(R Hannon) *s.i.s: a bhd* **10/1**
133 **14** *5* **Semah Harold**[33] 5236 2-9-2 **80** .... RichardMullen 12 49
(E S McMahon) *in tch: rdn and lost pl 3f out: no ch last 2f* **33/1**

1m 38.57s (-2.23) **Going Correction** -0.30s/f (Stan) **14** Ran SP% **128.0**
Speed ratings (Par 95): **99,98,98,97,96 95,94,92,92,90 89,87,87,82**
CSF £59.05 CT £215.46 TOTE £7.60: £1.90, £5.20, £1.80; EX 78.80.
Owner A E Oppenheimer **Bred** Hascombe And Valiant Studs **Trained** Newmarket, Suffolk

FOCUS
A very competitive nursery run at a strong pace from the outset thanks to Huzzah, and the form looks rock-solid.

NOTEBOOK
Bronze Cannon(USA) ◆, making his nursery debut after winning his maiden over course and distance, looked an unlikely winner for much of the way as he was out the back and struggling to go the pace, but one thing he does possess is stamina and, under a hard drive, he came with a wet sail down the centre of the track to snatch the race near the line. He is still improving and there should be more to come, especially over a bit further.
Palm Court, 10lb higher than when winning a similar event on his only previous try on sand at Wolverhampton in July, did nothing wrong and having managed to get the better of the clear leader in the closing stages, had the race snatched from him near the line. This effort shows that he is not handicapped out of things just yet, though he may go up again for this. (op 14-1)
Huzzah(IRE), carrying a 6lb penalty for his easy Salisbury maiden victory when possibly aided by a track bias, made sure there was no messing about and set a very decent pace. He tried to get away from his rivals crossing the intersection and although he was ultimately unable to hold off the finishing efforts of the front pair, he never gave in and lost nothing in defeat. However, he is due to go up another 7lb so life is about to get that much harder. (op 7-2 tchd 9-2)
Keenes Day(FR), well beaten in Listed company at Dusseldorf in his most recent outing, was trying sand for the first time. He soon had plenty to make up and was doing all his best work late, but as his victory came over the stiff extended 1m at Beverley, he probably needs a stiffer test than this. (op 16-1)
Noble Citizen(USA), raised 7lb for his Newmarket victory, was never too far off the pace and, although he kept on right to the line, he could not match the finishing pace of the principals. The longer trip did not seem to be a problem. (op 6-1)
Spell Caster, back over her winning trip on this switch to sand, was being ridden along from a long way out and it was only her stamina that enabled her to plug on for sixth. She needs a stiffer test than this. (tchd 4-1)
Flight Plan Official explanation: jockey said gelding ran too freely

6121 TRANSPORTER ENGINEERING MACMILLAN CLAIMING STKS 1m (P)
7:50 (7:50) (Class 6) 3-5-Y-0 **£2,047** (£604; £302) **Stalls** High

Form RPR
0536 **1** **Gazboolou**[48] 4785 3-9-7 74 .... FergusSweeney 6 78
(K R Burke) *chsd ldrs: rdn to chse ldr 3f out: led over 2f out: jst hld on* **12/1**
6- **2** *shd* **Forbidden (IRE)**[50] 4728 4-8-8 0 ow1 .... (t) JerryO'Dwyer(3) 10 65
(Daniel Mark Loughnane, Ire) *hld up bhd: gd hdwy on inner over 2f out: wnt 2nd ins fnl f: jst failed* **33/1**
4002 **3** *1/2* **Councellor (FR)**[5] 6024 5-9-4 81 .... (t) JamieSpencer 14 71
(Stef Liddiard) *w.w in midfield: hdwy 3f out: drvn to chse ldrs wl over 1f out: nt qckn* **2/1**[1]
0041 **4** *nk* **Henry The Seventh**[15] 5733 3-9-2 68 .... EddieAhern 12 71
(J W Hills) *chsd ldr tl 3f out: styd chsng ldrs: rdn wl over 2f out: unable qck fnl f* **8/1**
1433 **5** *shd* **Inside Story (IRE)**[11] 5838 5-9-10 76 .... (b) SebSanders 9 76
(M W Easterby) *hld up towards rr: hdwy and rdn over 2f out: nt clr run and grad swtchd lft 1f out: r.o: nt rch ldrs* **4/1**[2]
0662 **6** *1 1/4* **Rubenstar (IRE)**[17] 5693 4-9-4 74 .... GeorgeBaker 5 67
(M H Tompkins) *hld up in last: hdwy over 3f out: chsd ldrs and rdn wl over 1f out: no imp* **4/1**[2]
0000 **7** *4* **Tasweet (IRE)**[12] 5819 3-8-13 66 .... (b[1]) JohnEgan 13 56
(T G Mills) *led tl hdd over 2f out: wknd qckly wl over 1f out* **11/1**
0013 **8** *5* **Castara Bay**[8] 5921 3-9-5 75 .... RyanMoore 11 50
(R Hannon) *a bhd: rdn and no rspnse over 3f out* **6/1**[3]
5305 **9** *4* **Grand Symphony**[23] 5508 3-9-2 64 .... LiamJones 1 38
(W Jarvis) *racd in midfield: rdn and effrt 3f out: wknd qckly 2f out* **20/1**
0060 **10** *5* **Time For Change (IRE)**[7] 5945 3-8-11 48 .... (v) SteveDrowne 8 22
(P G Murphy) *in tch: rdn over 2f out: sn btn* **66/1**
0/ **11** *13* **Pippins Corner**[782] 4575 5-8-7 0 .... (t) PaulDoe 4 —
(M A Allen) *b.hind: a bhd: t.o last 2f* **100/1**

1m 38.33s (-2.47) **Going Correction** -0.30s/f (Stan)
WFA 3 from 4yo+ 3lb **11** Ran SP% **124.9**
Speed ratings (Par 101): **100,99,99,99,99 97,93,88,84,79 66**
CSF £361.73 TOTE £19.80: £6.30, £10.40, £1.60; EX 715.60.The winner was claimed by A Pinder for £20,000. Forbidden was subject to a friendly claim.
Owner Mrs Maura Gittins **Bred** Cheveley Park Stud Ltd **Trained** Middleham Moor, N Yorks

FOCUS
A routine claimer with less than a length covering the first five, though the pace seemed solid enough. The fourth is the best guide to the level.

6122 DAWSON RENTALS MACMILLAN H'CAP 6f (P)
8:20 (8:20) (Class 5) (0-75,74) 3-Y-0+ **£2,817** (£838; £418; £209) **Stalls** High

Form RPR
4150 **1** **Cativo Cavallino**[15] 5722 4-8-11 **71** .... NataliaGemelova(5) 7 84
(J E Long) *chsd ldr tl led wl over 1f out: clr 1f out: r.o strly* **7/1**
-202 **2** *2 1/2* **Prince Of Delphi**[23] 5510 4-9-0 **69** .... SebSanders 8 74
(R M Beckett) *hld up bhd: rdn over 2f out: rn wl fnl f: wnt 2nd nr fin: no ch w wnr* **11/2**
5052 **3** *hd* **Dvinsky (USA)**[19] 5648 6-9-2 **71** .... IanMongan 11 75
(P Howling) *led tl rdn and hdd wl over 1f out: kpt on but no ch w wnr: lost 2nd nr fin* **9/2**[2]
6000 **4** *hd* **Royal Challenge**[14] 5747 6-8-13 **68** .... NCallan 10 71
(M H Tompkins) *hld up in midfield: hdwy and rdn wl over 2f out: chsd ldrs over 1f out: kpt on* **8/1**
05 **5** *hd* **Jacquart (NZ)**[22] 5532 5-9-5 **74** .... (p) AdamKirby 12 77
(C G Cox) *chsd ldrs: rdn over 2f out: kpt on same pce u.p* **10/1**
6142 **6** *1 3/4* **Napoleon Dynamite (IRE)**[14] 5753 3-9-4 **74** .... EddieAhern 6 71
(J W Hills) *racd in midfield: rdn over 2f out: sn no imp* **7/2**[1]
0400 **7** *hd* **Majestic Cheer**[12] 5819 3-9-0 **70** .... RyanMoore 9 67
(E A L Dunlop) *hld up towards rr on inner: drvn and effrt over 2f out: nvr trbld ldrs* **16/1**
0422 **8** *1 1/2* **Hucking Hill (IRE)**[17] 5684 3-9-0 **73** .... (b) StephaneBreux(3) 3 65
(J R Best) *bhd: rdn and lost tch 3f out: no ch after* **5/1**[3]
3000 **9** *2* **Abwaab**[8] 5923 4-9-5 **74** .... (b) StephenCarson 4 59
(Eve Johnson Houghton) *prom tl 3f out: sn rdn and wknd* **20/1**
1440 **10** *1* **Back In The Red (IRE)**[14] 5747 3-8-13 **74** .... KevinGhunowa(5) 2 56
(R A Harris) *ldrs: rdn and outpcd wl over 2f out: no ch after* **25/1**
0650 **11** *1* **Bridge It Jo**[14] 5747 3-9-2 **72** .... TPQueally 5 51
(G G Margarson) *stdd s: t.k.h and hld up in rr: n.d* **33/1**

1m 11.72s (-1.98) **Going Correction** -0.30s/f (Stan)
WFA 3 from 4yo+ 1lb **11** Ran SP% **122.6**
Speed ratings (Par 103): **101,97,97,97,96 94,94,92,89,88 86**
CSF £46.28 CT £198.27 TOTE £9.20: £3.20, £2.20, £2.00; EX 107.00.
Owner P Saxon **Bred** Miss A M Rees **Trained** Caterham, Surrey

FOCUS
A modest handicap, though the early pace was decent and the first and third were always at the sharp end. The form is somewhat fluid and could go higher or lower.

6123 DHL FORD LLP H'CAP 7f (P)
8:50 (8:50) (Class 6) (0-60,60) 3-Y-0+ **£2,047** (£604; £302) **Stalls** High

Form RPR
0000 **1** **Linda's Colin (IRE)**[5] 6025 5-9-0 **60** .... KevinGhunowa(5) 10 71
(R A Harris) *b. chsd ldrs: rdn 3f out: hdwy 2f out: led jst over 1f out: edgd lft ins fnl f: hld on wl* **25/1**
4062 **2** *1/2* **Grand Lucre**[22] 5528 3-9-3 **60** .... FrancisNorton 8 69
(G A Butler) *lw: led to s: v awkward leaving stalls: bhd: plld out and rdn over 2f out: gd hdwy 2f out: chal ins fnl f: hld last 100yds* **9/1**
0151 **3** *2* **Blue Quiver (IRE)**[38] 5094 7-9-3 **58** .... SimonWhitworth 11 62
(C A Horgan) *taken down early: racd in midfield: rdn over 2f out: styd on wl fnl f: wnt 3rd nr fin: nt rch ldrs* **9/1**
2520 **4** *nk* **Carlitos Spirit (IRE)**[24] 5475 3-9-3 **60** .... TPQueally 4 66+
(B R Millman) *hld up in tch: shkn up whn nt clr run and snatched up over 1f out: r.o strly fnl f: nt rch ldrs* **14/1**
0005 **5** *nk* **Swiper Hill (IRE)**[19] 5643 4-9-4 **59** .... (t) TomEaves 12 61
(B Ellison) *b. hld up bhd on inner: rdn and hdwy over 2f out: n.m.r ins fnl f: swtchd lft and r.o nr fin* **15/2**
4531 **6** *1/2* **Metropolitan Chief**[20] 5602 3-8-12 **60** .... (b) KirstyMilczarek(5) 6 61
(D M Simcock) *led: rdn and hdd over 1f out: sn btn* **3/1**[1]
053- **7** *nk* **Sorrel Point**[416] 4666 4-9-2 **60** .... JerryO'Dwyer(3) 9 60
(H J Collingridge) *lw: wnt lft s: bhd: rdn over 2f out: styd on fnl f: nvr able to chal* **50/1**
2133 **8** *hd* **Glencal**[15] 5731 3-9-3 **60** .... SteveDrowne 1 59
(H Morrison) *sn prom: rdn and ev ch over 2f out: wknd ins fnl f* **11/2**[2]
6016 **9** *1/2* **Border Artist**[6] 5966 8-9-3 **58** .... SebSanders 13 56
(J Pearce) *t.k.h: hld up towards rr: rdn and hdwy over 2f out: chsd ldrs 1f out: hanging rt and no imp after* **7/1**[3]
1200 **10** *6* **Millfield (IRE)**[26] 5433 4-9-4 **59** .... GeorgeBaker 3 41
(P R Chamings) *chsd ldrs: rdn and wknd over 2f out: wl btn whn hmpd 2f out* **16/1**
3051 **11** *hd* **Inquisitress**[22] 5528 3-9-3 **60** .... EddieAhern 5 41
(J J Bridger) *chsd ldrs: rdn and ev ch over 2f out: wknd qckly 2f out* **10/1**
1653 **12** *3* **Granakey (IRE)**[206] 712 4-9-3 **58** .... PaulDoe 7 31
(M Wigham) *swtg: taken down early: a bhd* **16/1**
0043 **13** *3/4* **Punching**[16] 5714 3-9-2 **59** .... StephenCarson 14 30
(Eve Johnson Houghton) *chsd ldr tl over 2f out: wknd qckly over 1f out* **28/1**
0400 **14** *nk* **Take To The Skies (IRE)**[45] 4884 3-9-3 **60** .... NCallan 2 30
(A P Jarvis) *racd in midfield: rdn 3f out: sn wknd* **33/1**

1m 25.41s (-1.39) **Going Correction** -0.30s/f (Stan)
WFA 3 from 4yo+ 2lb **14** Ran SP% **124.4**
Speed ratings (Par 101): **95,94,92,91,91 90,90,90,89,82 82,79,78,78**
CSF £237.51 CT £2214.16 TOTE £28.10: £5.90, £4.00, £5.20; EX 264.40.
Owner Drag Star On Swan **Bred** Saud Bin Saad **Trained** Earlswood, Monmouths

FOCUS
A poor race run in a modest time and one or two did not enjoy the best of runs. The form makes sense but the pace may have been too strong early, allowing the placed horses to come from off the pace, in contrast to earlier races.

Carlitos Spirit(IRE) ◆ Official explanation: jockey said gelding was denied a clear run

6124 COBELFRET MACMILLAN H'CAP 1m 3f (P)
9:20 (9:20) (Class 5) (0-75,75) 3-Y-0+ **£2,817** (£838; £418; £209) **Stalls** High

Form RPR

-051 **1** **Pinch Of Salt (IRE)**[15] 5732 4-9-10 **75**.................... MartinDwyer 2 91+
(A M Balding) *lw: a gng wl: in tch: led on bit over 2f out: sn pushed wl clr: eased towards fin* **2/1**[1]

2362 **2** *3* **Maslak (IRE)**[20] 5604 3-9-1 **75**.................... TravisBlock(3) 5 79
(P W Hiatt) *chsd ldrs: rdn over 2f out: chsd wnr over 1f out: no ch w wnr* **11/2**[3]

4441 **3** *¾* **Lord Of Dreams (IRE)**[23] 5497 5-8-8 **64**.................... JamieJones(5) 6 67
(G L Moore) *hld up towards rr: hdwy over 3f out: drvn to dispute 2nd 1f out: no ch w wnr* **11/2**[3]

1660 **4** *2* **Ocean Avenue (IRE)**[33] 5225 8-9-6 **71**.................... SimonWhitworth 4 70
(C A Horgan) *hld up in last pair: rdn and hdwy over 2f out: plugged on: n.d* **12/1**

0303 **5** *shd* **Hope Road**[15] 5732 3-8-13 **70**.................... RyanMoore 1 69
(J R Fanshawe) *lw: chsd ldr: rdn and ev ch over 2f out: sn hanging rt and btn* **5/2**[2]

3060 **6** *4* **Medieval Maiden**[15] 5732 4-8-13 **64**.................... NeilPollard 9 56
(W J Musson) *hld up in last: rdn and racd awkwardly 3f out: nvr on terms* **25/1**

0550 **7** *4* **Spring Goddess (IRE)**[71] 4060 6-9-6 **71**.................... SebSanders 3 57
(A P Jarvis) *lw: hld up in midfield: rdn and effrt on outer 3f out: no ch last 2f* **10/1**

001/ **8** *2½* **Devolution (IRE)**[639] 3699 9-9-5 **70**.................... VinceSlattery 7 51
(Miss C Dyson) *bit bkwd: s.i.s: sn in midfield: rdn and wknd wl over 2f out* **50/1**

1000 **9** *4* **Border Edge**[35] 5166 9-8-10 **61** oh2....................(b) NCallan 8 36
(J J Bridger) *t.k.h: led and clr tl 4f out: hdd over 2f out: sn wknd* **20/1**

2m 19.81s (-2.87) **Going Correction** -0.30s/f (Stan)
WFA 3 from 4yo+ 6lb **9** Ran SP% **120.0**
Speed ratings (Par 103): **98,95,95,93,93 90,87,86,83**
CSF £13.95 CT £54.38 TOTE £3.30: £1.30, £2.30, £2.40; EX 20.30.
Owner The Hon Robert Hanson **Bred** The Hon R Hanson **Trained** Kingsclere, Hants

FOCUS
A furious early pace thanks to the free-running Border Edge, but things became much slower in the second half of the contest and the final time was ordinary. This looked a fairly competitive handicap beforehand, but it turned into a rout, and the runner-up is the best guide to the level.
Border Edge Official explanation: jockey said gelding ran too free early on
T/Plt: £1,163.10 to a £1 stake. Pool: £84,846.75. 53.25 winning tickets. T/Qpdt: £34.70 to a £1 stake. Pool: £8,896.30. 189.40 winning tickets. SP

5628 NEWBURY (L-H)
Thursday, October 11

OFFICIAL GOING: Good to soft
Jockeys felt the ground was riding nearer soft than the official good to soft.
Wind: Virtually nil

6125 NEWVOICEMEDIA E B F MAIDEN STKS (DIV I) 6f 110y
1:10 (1:14) (Class 4) 2-Y-0 **£5,829** (£1,734; £866; £432) **Stalls** Centre

Form RPR

1 **Fateh Field (USA)** 2-9-3 0.................... LDettori 1 85+
(Saeed Bin Suroor) *trckd ldrs: qcknd to ld appr fnl f: comf* **10/3**[2]

4 **2** *3½* **Thannaan (USA)**[20] 5591 2-9-3 0.................... RHills 11 75
(B W Hills) *in tch: hdwy fr 2f out to chse wnr ins fnl f: kpt on but nvr any ch* **5/2**[1]

3 *1* **Brazilian Brush (IRE)** 2-9-3 0.................... SteveDrowne 4 72
(H Morrison) *in tch: hdwy 2f out: chsd ldrs over 1f out and kpt on ins fnl f but nvr gng pce to trble wnr* **14/1**

4 **4** *1¼* **Fly In Johnny (IRE)**[10] 5868 2-9-3 0.................... RyanMoore 6 69
(R Hannon) *led tl hdd appr fnl f: wknd fnl 100yds* **7/2**[3]

5 *¾* **Annes Rocket (IRE)**[161] 1441 2-9-3 0.................... PatDobbs 10 67
(J C Fox) *s.i.s: in rr: hdwy 1/2-way: qcknd to chse ldrs jst ins fnl f but sn one pce* **80/1**

0 **6** *shd* **Bainisteoir**[7] 5937 2-9-3 0.................... LPKeniry 13 66
(S Kirk) *s.i.s: in rr: hdwy over 1f out: styd on ins fnl f but nvr in contention* **100/1**

7 *¾* **Carmela Maria** 2-8-12 0.................... IanMongan 5 59
(C F Wall) *chsd ldrs: rdn over 2f out: wknd fnl f* **33/1**

64 **8** *¾* **Trumpet Lily**[17] 5681 2-8-12 0.................... JamesDoyle 7 57
(J G Portman) *pressed ldr and upsides fr 3f out to 2f out: wknd over 1f out* **15/2**

9 *2* **Saranome (IRE)** 2-9-3 0.................... RichardKingscote 2 57
(R Charlton) *mid-div 1/2-way: sn pushed along and nvr gng pce to be competitive* **22/1**

5 **10** *5* **Bombardier Wells**[20] 5591 2-9-3 0.................... StephenCarson 3 43
(Eve Johnson Houghton) *chsd ldrs tl wknd over 1f out* **14/1**

11 *1* **Timber Creek** 2-9-3 0.................... FergusSweeney 8 40
(H Candy) *s.i.s: a outpcd* **20/1**

12 *nk* **Rocketry** 2-9-0 0.................... EmmettStack(3) 9 40
(T Keddy) *chsd ldrs over 3f* **80/1**

1m 23.01s (2.71) **Going Correction** +0.40s/f (Good) **12** Ran SP% **114.5**
Speed ratings (Par 97): **100,96,94,93,92 92,91,90,88,82 81,81**
CSF £10.88 TOTE £4.10: £1.60, £1.30, £4.10; EX 12.70.
Owner Godolphin **Bred** WinStar Farm LLC **Trained** Newmarket, Suffolk

FOCUS
The first division of a maiden run over a relatively new distance for the course and Fateh Field won in the style of a smart performer. The form behind is somewhat fluid with the sixth dictating the level.

NOTEBOOK
Fateh Field(USA), a $500,000 Derby entrant, has a fair bit of speed in his pedigree and that showed as he sprinted clear off the slow pace inside the final furlong, after travelling strongly towards the far side. Many of the Godolphin juveniles have needed their initial outing this term, including Rio De La Plata, but Fateh Field was an exception and he looks well worth his place in Pattern company now. (op 3-1 tchd 7-2 in places)
Thannaan(USA), who ran well following a slow start when fourth over course and distance on debut, ahead of Bombardier Wells, had slower ground to contend with here and he simply found the winner too pacey. The way he was keeping on in second suggests he will be suited by 7f and a standard maiden should come his way. (op 3-1)
Brazilian Brush(IRE) comes from a yard whose juveniles often improve for a run and he started to get outpaced from over 3f out. It was pleasing to see him come home strongly and a truer-run race at this distance should see him in a better light. (op 20-1)
Fly In Johnny(IRE), always outpaced following a sluggish start on debut at Windsor, was tackling an extra half-furlong here and showed plenty of early pace, but was left for dead when the winner kicked for home and may be more of a nursery type. (op 3-1)
Annes Rocket(IRE), who could make no impact following a slow start for Kevin Prendergast at Tipperary on his debut in May, was returning from a lengthy absence, but shaped most promisingly, outperforming his 80/1 odds, and will be qualified for nurseries following another outing. (op 66-1)
Bainisteoir improved significantly on his initial effort and is another who will not be seen at his best until contesting nurseries, for which he will be qualified after one more run. The Stewards' enquired into his running and riding, but opted to take no further action. Official explanation: jockey said, regarding running and riding, his orders were to drop the gelding in, get some cover and finish as close as possible, adding that this he was able to do and that he asked for an effort after switching left for a run a furlong out, further adding that in his view it needed further and ran on through beaten horses (op 66-1)
Carmela Maria hails from a yard whose juveniles often benefit from a run and as a result this can go down as a reasonable effort.
Trumpet Lily, although by speedy first-season sire Acclamation, shaped as though in need of further when fourth over 7f at Kempton last time and she was unable to make much of an impact. Now qualified for nurseries, she can be expected to fare better in that sphere. (op 7-1 tchd 8-1)
Bombardier Wells, although behind Thannaan on debut, shaped with plenty of promise there following a sluggish start and it was interesting that connections were seemingly happy to reoppose. He failed to race on with the principals, though, having not been far off the gallop early, and proved quite disappointing. (op 16-1)

6126 NEWVOICEMEDIA E B F MAIDEN STKS (DIV II) 6f 110y
1:40 (1:43) (Class 4) 2-Y-0 **£5,829** (£1,734; £866; £432) **Stalls** Centre

Form RPR

2 **1** **Beacon Lodge (IRE)**[34] 5193 2-9-3 0.................... AdamKirby 7 92+
(C G Cox) *hld up: hdwy over 2f out: led and hung lft over 1f out: sn rdn: r.o: eased nr fin* **3/1**[2]

3 **2** *1¼* **Drill Sergeant**[8] 5903 2-9-3 0.................... GregFairley 4 89
(M Johnston) *led 1f: led 3f out: rdn and hdd over 1f out: styd on same pce ins fnl f* **7/1**

24 **3** *4* **Dubai Power**[35] 5164 2-8-12 0.................... KerrinMcEvoy 2 73
(C E Brittain) *chsd ldrs: rdn over 2f out: outpcd fr over 1f out* **9/4**[1]

0 **4** *shd* **Dubai Petal (IRE)**[10] 5856 2-8-12 0.................... JohnEgan 1 72
(J S Moore) *hld up: outpcd 1/2-way: styd on u.p fr over 1f out: nvr trbld ldrs* **40/1**

24 **5** *5* **Copperwood**[29] 5329 2-9-3 0.................... SebSanders 10 64
(M Blanshard) *hld up: hdwy over 2f out: rdn and wknd over 1f out* **6/1**[3]

0 **6** *1½* **High Plains (FR)**[74] 3991 2-9-3 0.................... RyanMoore 3 59
(R Hannon) *hld up: rdn 1/2-way: n.d* **8/1**

0 **7** *1¾* **Wave Hill (IRE)**[124] 2443 2-9-3 0.................... RobertHavlin 12 55
(B J Meehan) *led over 5f out: hdd 3f out: edgd lft and wknd over 1f out* **20/1**

0 **8** *3½* **Valento**[15] 5720 2-9-3 0.................... StephenCarson 5 45
(Eve Johnson Houghton) *prom over 4f* **66/1**

0 **9** *2½* **Bairag (USA)**[21] 5575 2-9-3 0.................... NCallan 6 38
(Mrs C A Dunnett) *chsd ldrs: rdn over 2f out: sn wknd* **22/1**

10 *hd* **Segal (IRE)** 2-9-3 0.................... TPQueally 11 38
(J Noseda) *hld up: a in rr: wknd over 2f out* **14/1**

0 **11** *1* **Holden Caulfield (IRE)**[56] 4539 2-9-0 0.................... NeilChalmers(3) 9 35
(Mouse Hamilton-Fairley) *hld up: a in rr: wknd over 2f out* **100/1**

1m 22.02s (1.72) **Going Correction** +0.40s/f (Good) **11** Ran SP% **114.4**
Speed ratings (Par 97): **106,104,100,99,94 92,90,86,83,83 82**
CSF £22.22 TOTE £4.20: £1.50, £2.00, £1.30; EX 25.50.
Owner Mr & Mrs P Hargreaves **Bred** Mrs Bill O'Neill **Trained** Lambourn, Berks

FOCUS
The stronger of the two divisions, on paper at least, and it was certainly run at a better pace, with the time being almost a second quicker. The first two were clear but the third is rated below the level of his previous outing.

NOTEBOOK
Beacon Lodge(IRE), who cost 150,000gns, may well have made a winning debut at Haydock had he run straight under pressure. He again hung on this occasion, but was in a different class to the opposition and was good value for the win. A son of Clodovil, he is going to benefit from a bit further in time and looks one to keep on-side. (op 4-1)
Drill Sergeant is a well-related son of Rock Of Gibraltar, but shaped with only limited promise when third over 6f on debut at Newcastle, ending up being comfortably beaten. However, it is no secret his trainer's juveniles often benefit greatly from a run and he gave a much better account of himself here, sticking on once headed to finished clear of the favourite. An ordinary maiden should come his way before long. (op 13-2 tchd 15-2)
Dubai Power confirmed the promise of her debut second when filling fourth spot behind Fashion Rocks in a decent 6f Listed contest at Salisbury (third Raymi Coya subsequently winning the Oh So Sharp Stakes) and it had to be significant she took up this engagement ahead of the Listed Rockingham Stakes at York on Saturday. However, having raced towards the far side, she could make only limited headway and perhaps this slower surface led to her below-par effort. (op 5-2)
Dubai Petal(IRE), always toiling following a slow start on debut at Bath, was up a furlong in trip and has clearly learned greatly from that initial experience. It is likely her future lies in handicaps and she will be qualified for a mark following one more run. (op 28-1)
Copperwood had run well on each of his two previous starts in 7f maidens, but this was a bit too hot for him. He is now qualified for a handicap mark and should be more at home in that sphere. (op 5-1 tchd 7-1)
High Plains(FR) had been off since disappointing on his debut at Ascot back in July and he looked a bit rusty on this return, keeping on late having been outpaced from an early stage. His dam was a useful sprinter in America, but it may be that he has inherited his King George-winning sire's stamina requirements. (op 7-1)
Wave Hill(IRE) raced freely on this first start since June and does not look the most straightforward. (op 18-1)
Valento, a half-brother to a 1m winner and a scorer over hurdles, had no buyer at the yearling sales and is probably going to need further than this in time. (op 40-1)

6127 FAIRFAX PROPERTIES MAIDEN STKS (DIV I) 1m (S)
2:10 (2:13) (Class 4) 2-Y-0 **£5,829** (£1,734; £866; £432) **Stalls** Centre

Form RPR

36 **1** **Strategic Mission (IRE)**[92] 3435 2-9-3 0.................... TQuinn 10 82+
(P F I Cole) *mde virtually all: shkn up whn chal fr over 2f out: drvn to assert ins fnl f: readily* **10/3**[2]

3 **2** *1¾* **Saleima (IRE)**[20] 5596 2-8-12 0.................... LDettori 6 73
(J Noseda) *in tch: hdwy over 2f out and sn ev ch: chsd wnr fnl f but a readily hld* **6/4**[1]

3 *1¼* **Changing Skies (IRE)** 2-8-12 0.................... JimmyFortune 2 70
(B J Meehan) *chsd ldrs: rdn and ev ch 2f out: one pce ins fnl f* **11/2**[3]

4 *nk* **Clowance** 2-8-12 0.................... SteveDrowne 14 70
(R Charlton) *s.i.s: in rr: hdwy over 2f out: pushed along and styd on wl fnl f but nvr gng pce to be competitive* **14/1**

33 **5** 1 ½ **Monashee Rock (IRE)**[19] 5633 2-8-12 0.................. SimonWhitworth 8 66
(M Salaman) *chsd ldrs: rdn and effrt 2f out: sn upsides: wknd ins fnl f* **9/1**

6 3 **Red Twist** 2-9-3 0.. RobertHavlin 7 65
(H Morrison) *chsd ldrs: pushed along 3f out: wknd over 1f out* **25/1**

7 ½ **Contrada** 2-9-3 0.. RichardKingscote 9 64+
(R Charlton) *in rr: pushed along fr 3f out: styd on ins fnl f: gng on cl home but nvr in contention* **25/1**

6 **8** 1 ½ **Leitmotif (USA)**[38] 5091 2-9-3 0.. SebSanders 1 60
(J L Dunlop) *w wnr: rdn and ev ch 2f out: wknd appr fnl f* **16/1**

9 nk **Longevity** 2-9-3 0.. KerrinMcEvoy 3 60
(W Jarvis) *chsd ldrs: drvn along 3f out: wknd ins fnl 2f* **18/1**

10 5 **Hawkstar Express (IRE)** 2-9-3 0................................ PatCosgrave 11 49
(J R Boyle) *s.i.s: in rr tl sme prog over 3f out: nvr in contention and bhd fnl 2f* **66/1**

00 **11** 1 ½ **High Dee Jay (IRE)**[8] 5918 2-9-3 0..................................... PatDobbs 13 45
(R Hannon) *chsd ldrs: rdn 3f out: wknd 2f out* **100/1**

0 **12** shd **Desiderio**[8] 5918 2-9-3 0.. RyanMoore 4 45
(R Hannon) *rdn and bhd fr 1/2-way* **20/1**

13 1 ½ **Rettorical Lad** 2-9-3 0.. JohnEgan 5 42
(Jamie Poulton) *s.i.s: hdwy to trck ldrs 1/2-way: fdd fr ins fnl 3f* **50/1**

1m 44.97s (4.35) **Going Correction** +0.40s/f (Good) **13** Ran SP% **123.2**
Speed ratings (Par 97): **94,92,91,90,89 86,85,84,83,78 77,77,75**
CSF £8.42 TOTE £4.70: £1.60, £1.40, £2.10; EX 11.40.
Owner H R H Sultan Ahmad Shah **Bred** Ruskerne Ltd **Trained** Whatcombe, Oxon

FOCUS
A fair maiden likely to produce winners, especially next season, with the winner returning from a break and likely to go on from this.

NOTEBOOK
Strategic Mission(IRE) was given the perfect ride in the underfoot conditions. Absent since the middle of July, he had plenty of decent form to make his mark in this sort of company. His last run at Newmarket was in a maiden that could not have worked out any better - every horse that finished in front of him and has raced since has won at least one race. Indeed, he did not have everything in his favour that day and could have finished a bit closer to Rio De La Plata with a bit more luck. This is probably mission accomplished for this season now and he should be one to follow next year. (op 4-1 tchd 9-2 in places)
Saleima(IRE) was unfancied on her debut but ran fairly well on quick ground - Queen Of Naples, who finished one place in front of her, was thought good enough to take her place in the Prix Marcel Boussac last weekend. An Irish Oaks entrant, she was settled in midfield early before being produced about 2f from home. She did well to close the gap considering the ease in the ground and should have little trouble winning a maiden, especially if found one against her own sex. (tchd 15-8 and 2-1 in places)
Changing Skies(IRE), a sister to Percussionist and Playful Act, must have pleased connections with a sound first effort. Much like the runner-up, she should be placed to do better next time. (op 7-1)
Clowance , who looked the stable's first string on jockey bookings, got outpaced when the tempo increased but stayed on in taking style throughout the final furlong. This filly looks bred to appreciate middle distances next season, being by Montjeu out of a dam that stayed well. (op 16-1)
Monashee Rock(IRE) would not have enjoyed the way the race was run and will be better suited by a stronger gallop. She could be the sort for a race on the All-Weather, where she should get a decent pace to chase. (tchd 11-1)
Red Twist is a half-brother to a couple of very useful sorts, especially Necklace, who won the Moyglare Stud Stakes as a two-year-old before holding her own in top-class company at three. He was green to post and shaped well in the circumstances. The experience alone will have done him good. (op 28-1)
Contrada, a 160,000gns half-brother to a couple of fair performers, he was slowly away and going nowhere quickly at the halfway point. However, he stayed on quite well when getting the hang of things and suggested races will be won with him.
Rettorical Lad Official explanation: trainer said colt had a breathing problem

6128 SIR GERALD WHENT MEMORIAL NURSERY 6f 8y
2:40 (2:43) (Class 4) (0-85,85) 2-Y-O **£6,477** (£1,927; £963; £481) **Stalls** Centre

Form RPR

2013 **1** **Feisty Royale**[5] 6012 2-8-13 **77**.. GregFairley 12 80
(M Johnston) *hld up: swtchd rt and hdwy over 1f out: rdn to ld wl ins fnl f: edgd lft nr fin* **9/1**

1230 **2** nk **Perfect Flight**[19] 5629 2-8-13 **77**...................................... PaulHanagan 7 79
(M Blanshard) *trckd ldrs: rdn: hung lft and ev ch fr over 1f out: hung rt ins fnl f: styd on* **20/1**

1505 **3** ½ **Tadalavil**[26] 5400 2-9-5 **83**... JimmyFortune 15 84
(M R Channon) *hld up in tch: racd keenly: led over 1f out: sn rdn: hdd wl ins fnl f* **16/1**

1500 **4** 1 ½ **Sofia's Star**[40] 5053 2-9-6 **84**... StephenCarson 8 80
(P Winkworth) *hld up: swtchd lft and hdwy over 1f out: styd on* **40/1**

3064 **5** 2 **Legendary Guest**[13] 5773 2-8-10 **74**............................(v[1]) DarryllHolland 3 64
(M R Channon) *hld up: hdwy over 2f out: sn rdn: wknd ins fnl f* **22/1**

0205 **6** 1 **Albaqaa**[57] 4501 2-8-10 **74**.. RHills 14 61
(E A L Dunlop) *trckd ldrs: rdn and ev ch over 1f out: wknd ins fnl f* **8/1**[3]

5034 **7** 1 ½ **Tina's Best (IRE)**[10] 5856 2-8-12 **76**................................... RyanMoore 9 59
(R Hannon) *hld up: swtchd rt over 2f out: sn rdn: nt trble ldrs* **16/1**

0354 **8** 1 ¾ **Superduper**[20] 5595 2-8-9 **73**.. EddieAhern 13 50
(R Hannon) *chsd ldrs over 4f* **33/1**

2254 **9** ¾ **Blue Zenith (IRE)**[19] 5629 2-8-5 **69** ow1.............................. JohnEgan 16 44
(J S Moore) *led: rdn and hdd over 1f out: wknd ins fnl f* **12/1**

3341 **10** ½ **Hunt The Bottle (IRE)**[13] 5771 2-8-13 **77**........................ MichaelHills 5 51
(B W Hills) *s.s: hld up: effrt over 2f out: bmpd sn after: rdn and wknd over 1f out* **7/1**[2]

0402 **11** ¾ **Thunder Gorge (USA)**[7] 5939 2-8-6 **73**.................... NeilChalmers[(3)] 10 44
(Mouse Hamilton-Fairley) *s.s: hld up: rdn over 2f out: n.d* **12/1**

1211 **12** 2 **Edge Of Gold**[48] 4775 2-9-1 **79**.. SteveDrowne 2 44
(B Palling) *chsd ldrs: rdn and ev ch over 1f out: sn wknd* **9/2**[1]

5103 **13** 1 **Farsighted**[23] 5509 2-8-9 **73**... DaleGibson 4 35
(J M P Eustace) *chsd ldrs over 3f* **33/1**

1 **14** 3 ½ **Candela Bay (IRE)**[21] 5558 2-8-4 **68**.................................. LiamJones 11 20
(W J Haggas) *prom: lost pl over 3f out: wknd over 2f out* **9/2**[1]

1033 **15** 7 **Regal Rhythm (IRE)**[13] 5773 2-9-4 **82**......................... JamieSpencer 17 13
(B J Meehan) *stdd s: hld up: effrt over 2f out: sn wknd* **16/1**

1m 16.19s (1.87) **Going Correction** +0.40s/f (Good) **15** Ran SP% **120.4**
Speed ratings (Par 97): **103,102,101,99,97 95,93,91,90,89 88,86,84,80,70**
CSF £184.79 CT £2892.70 TOTE £12.80: £3.70, £7.60, £7.20; EX 269.80 TRIFECTA Not won..
Owner T T Bloodstocks **Bred** Aston Mullins Stud **Trained** Middleham Moor, N Yorks
■ Stewards' Enquiry : Greg Fairley one-day ban: careless riding (Oct 22)

FOCUS
A most competitive nursery, but only a handful of these could be classed as either progressive or unexposed. The principals ran close totheir pre-race marks.

NOTEBOOK
Feisty Royale made up for a slightly unlucky effort at Newmarket last time. Racing off a 5lb higher mark than when winning at Leicester on her penultimate outing, she handled the ease in the ground surprisingly well for a daughter of Royal Applause and came home under a strong ride to edge out Perfect Flight. She has already proven her ability to stay 7f and may be given another outing before the season is out. (tchd 10-1)
Perfect Flight has been running well in defeat since winning at Haydock earlier in the season and she was travelling particularly well behind runners over 2f out, but tended to wander under pressure and the winner proved too strong. Official explanation: jockey said saddle slipped (op 16-1)
Tadalavil, winner of a Ripon maiden earlier in the season, has been struggling of late, but this was a much more creditable effort and perhaps the ease in the ground was to his liking. (op 22-1)
Sofia's Star had previously made little impact in handicaps and the blinkers did little to improve him at Sandown last time. This was a much better effort, but he is likely to continue to find a few too good off his current mark.
Legendary Guest has not really gone on from his course debut when chasing home Winker Watson, but he had been dropped 4lb following his recent Haydock effort and the application of a first-time visor enabled him to show improved form. Official explanation: jockey said colt hung right (op 25-1)
Albaqaa, who shaped really well in soft ground when second at Newmarket earlier in the season, has since disappointed and looked well worth another try at this trip. Soon prominent, he had his chance, but could not race on with the principals and does not look to be progressing. (op 9-1)
Tina's Best(IRE), who showed improved form to finish third in a minor sales race at the Curragh, has disappointed either side of that and this effort suggested she is going to remain vulnerable to less-exposed sorts.
Superduper showed only modest form in maidens and she did little here to suggest she will be winning any time soon. (tchd 28-1)
Blue Zenith(IRE) has been running well in defeat off similar marks, but she found this a bit too competitive and dropped out having been responsible for the early pace. Official explanation: jockey said filly was unsuited by the good to soft ground (op 14-1)
Hunt The Bottle(IRE), off the mark in 6f soft ground maiden at Haydock last time, fluffed the start and was always struggling to get involved thereafter. (tchd 13-2)
Thunder Gorge(USA) Official explanation: jockey said colt missed the break
Edge Of Gold, first past the post in three of her four previous starts, took a valuable Newmarket sales race in soft ground last time and looked fairly treated off a mark of 79 for this nursery debut. However, having held every chance, she could find no more and looked to perform some way below her best. Official explanation: jockey said filly had no more to give (tchd 5-1)
Candela Bay(IRE), ready winner of a modest 5f maiden on debut at Pontefract, handled the firm ground surprisingly well that day considering she is a daughter of the soft-ground loving Captain Rio, and it was not hard to see why she was fancied for this nursery debut off a mark of 68. She showed early pace, but it was clear from well over 2f out she was not going to be supplementing that victory and she has a bit to prove now. Official explanation: jockey said filly was unsuited by the good to soft ground (op 7-2)
Regal Rhythm(IRE) Official explanation: jockey said gelding ran too free

6129 ELECTROLUX PROFESSIONAL FILLIES' H'CAP 1m 2f 6y
3:15 (3:16) (Class 4) (0-85,85) 3-Y-O+ **£4,857** (£1,445; £722; £360) **Stalls** Centre

Form RPR

6043 **1** **Silca Key**[7] 5943 3-8-6 **75**.. FrancisNorton 6 86
(M R Channon) *t.k.h early: in rr tl stdy hdwy 3f out: drvn to ld over 1f out: styd on strly ins fnl f* **9/1**

4451 **2** 3 **Going To Work (IRE)**[7] 5943 3-8-11 **80** 6ex..................... SebSanders 11 85
(D R C Elsworth) *chsd ldrs: led over 2f out: rdn and hdd over 1f out: sn one pce* **11/2**

5520 **3** hd **Apply Dapply**[12] 5794 4-9-3 **81**.. SteveDrowne 8 86
(H Morrison) *hld up towards rr: hdwy over 2f oit: drvn to chse ldrs fnl f: styd on to press for 2nd but nvr gng pce to rch wnr* **4/1**[3]

0242 **4** 8 **Sunisa (IRE)**[12] 5814 6-8-7 **76** ow1................................. NeilBrown[(5)] 12 65
(J Mackie) *in tch: hdwy to trck ldrs over 2f out: rdn and c to stands' side over 1f out and sn wknd* **7/2**[2]

52-0 **5** 4 **Wateera (IRE)**[13] 5768 3-8-4 **73** ow1................................. MartinDwyer 7 54
(J L Dunlop) *in rr tl hdwy 3f out: sn chsng ldrs: wknd qckly over 1f out* **10/1**

1502 **6** 4 **Magic Echo**[19] 5620 3-8-8 **77**.. JamieSpencer 13 50
(M Dods) *chsd ldrs: rdn to ld 3f out: hdd over 2f out: sn btn* **11/4**[1]

0120 **7** 1 ½ **Uig**[40] 5052 6-8-7 **71** oh1.. AdrianMcCarthy 4 41
(H S Howe) *chsd ldrs: rdn 3f out: sn wknd* **16/1**

10-0 **8** 5 **Looker**[220] 620 4-8-7 **71** oh7.. JamesDoyle 2 31
(J Gallagher) *led tl hdd 4f out: wknd fr 3f out* **40/1**

0041 **9** 9 **House Maiden (IRE)**[12] 5803 3-7-12 **72** oh4 ow1.... KirstyMilczarek[(5)] 9 14
(D M Simcock) *pressed ldr 7f out: led 4f out: hdd 3f out: sn wknd* **12/1**

2m 11.98s (3.27) **Going Correction** +0.40s/f (Good)
WFA 3 from 4yo+ 5lb **9** Ran SP% **119.4**
Speed ratings (Par 102): **102,99,99,93,89 86,85,81,74**
CSF £59.75 CT £234.25 TOTE £10.30: £1.90, £2.10, £1.80; EX 60.10.
Owner Aldridge Racing Partnership **Bred** Genesis Green Stud Ltd **Trained** West Ilsley, Berks
■ Stewards' Enquiry : Francis Norton two-day ban: used whip with excessive frequency (Oct 22-23)

FOCUS
A somewhat depleted fillies' handicap with six of the original 15 being withdrawn, and it turned into a messy affair with runners gradually edging into the centre of the track down the straight. The form is rated around the placed horses.
Uig Official explanation: jockey said mare never travelled

6130 FAIRFAX PROPERTIES MAIDEN STKS (DIV II) 1m (S)
3:50 (3:50) (Class 4) 2-Y-O **£5,829** (£1,734; £866; £432) **Stalls** Centre

Form RPR

2 **1** **Robby Bobby**[21] 5570 2-9-3 0.. GregFairley 1 83
(M Johnston) *mde all: rdn clr and hung rt fr over 1f out: styd on wl* **2/1**[1]

04 **2** 3 **Brexca (IRE)**[22] 5538 2-9-3 0.. AdamKirby 7 76
(C G Cox) *chsd ldrs: rdn over 2f out: styd on same pce appr fnl f* **7/1**[3]

2 **3** shd **Sayyedati Symphony (USA)**[12] 5801 2-8-12 0.......................... JohnEgan 2 71
(C E Brittain) *prom: rdn over 2f out: styd on same pce appr fnl f* **7/1**[3]

05 **4** ¾ **Enroller (IRE)**[12] 5813 2-9-3 0.. RichardMullen 11 75
(W R Muir) *hld up: hdwy 5f out: rdn over 2f out: sn outpcd: styd on ins fnl f* **7/1**[3]

5 4 **Double Duty (IRE)** 2-8-12 0.. TedDurcan 12 61+
(B J Meehan) *s.s: hld up: rdn over 2f out: n.d* **14/1**

6 1 **Touch Of Pep (IRE)** 2-9-3 0.. IanMongan 6 64
(Jamie Poulton) *hld up in tch: rdn over 2f out: wknd over 1f out* **40/1**

7 ½ **King's Alchemist** 2-9-3 0... RichardSmith 4 62
(M D I Usher) *hld up: rdn over 2f out: n.d* **66/1**

8 ¾ **Grand Strategy (IRE)** 2-9-3 0.. NCallan 9 61
(M A Jarvis) *s.s: sn prom: chsd wnr 3f out tl rdn and wknd over 1f out* **11/2**[2]

9 *nk* **Royal Straight** 2-9-3 0 FrancisNorton 8 60
(A M Balding) *hld up in tch: rdn and wknd over 2f out* **20/1**

0 10 ½ **Mista Rossa**[8] 5919 2-9-3 0 RobertHavlin 13 59
(H Morrison) *chsd ldrs: rdn over 2f out: wknd over 1f out* **100/1**

11 3½ **Martyr** 2-9-3 0 RyanMoore 14 51
(R Hannon) *chsd ldrs over 5f* **10/1**

12 6 **Kiribati King (IRE)** 2-9-3 0 DarryllHolland 10 38
(M R Channon) *sn pushed along in rr: bhd fr 1/2-way* **20/1**

13 9 **Teen Spirit (IRE)** 2-9-3 0 EddieAhern 3 18
(J W Hills) *hld up: bhd fr 1/2-way* **50/1**

1m 45.08s (4.46) **Going Correction** +0.40s/f (Good) **13** Ran SP% **118.4**
Speed ratings (Par 97): **93,90,89,89,85 84,83,82,82,82 78,72,63**
CSF £14.76 TOTE £3.00: £1.20, £3.10, £2.30; EX 21.70.
Owner C M , B J & R F Batterham Ii **Bred** Highclere Stud **Trained** Middleham Moor, N Yorks

FOCUS
A slightly slower time than the first division, but it was hard not to be impressed with Robby Bobby's winning performance. Those in the frame behind the winner were close to their marks and they were clear of the rest, suggesting the form is sound.

NOTEBOOK
Robby Bobby ◆, a half-brother to a couple of middle-distance soft-ground performers, including the smart Foxhaven, was caught out by inexperience when narrowly denied on his debut at Yarmouth and again showed signs of greenness here in drifting right across to the stands' rail under pressure, but was so far clear it made little difference. This was a taking performance from the son of Selkirk, who certainly enjoyed the cut in the ground, and he deserves to take his chance in something a bit better now. It would not be a surprise to see him develop into a good middle-distance handicapper next term. (op 5-2 tchd 11-4 in places)
Brexca(IRE) had shown reasonable form in a couple of Sandown maidens, latterly over this distance, and this represented another step forward. He will now have the option of handicaps and should find a race before the season is out. (op 8-1 tchd 13-2)
Sayyedati Symphony(USA), a half-sister to Champagne Stakes winner Almushahar, shaped well when second over 7f on her debut at Chester and confirmed the promise of that run with a sound effort in defeat here. The ground may have been slower than ideal and she can find an ordinary maiden. (op 4-1)
Enroller(IRE), who holds an entry in the Racing Post Trophy, had run well under similar conditions at Haydock last time and he was again doing his best work late. His trainer had a juvenile winner earlier in the week and this one should find a small race before long. (tchd 11-2)
Double Duty(IRE) could be an interesting one for next time as she travelled strongly but had to wait for a run and was then allowed to come home under a far from stern ride. (tchd 16-1)
Touch Of Pep(IRE), a brother to high-class middle-distance performer Touch Of Land, comes from a yard that is hardly renowned for success with juveniles, but he shaped nicely enough to suggest he could go close in an ordinary maiden before the season is out. He should do better next year. (tchd 50-1)
King's Alchemist, a half-brother to the useful Royal Alchemist, who made her name with this yard, was unable to follow her in winning first time up, but showed enough to suggest he is not devoid of ability. (op 50-1)
Grand Strategy(IRE) showed up well for a long way before dropping out and can be expected to improve on this initial experience. Official explanation: jockey said colt had no more to give (op 6-1 tchd 5-1)

6131 TILNEY PRIVATE WEALTH MANAGEMENT H'CAP — 2m
4:25 (4:25) (Class 5) (0-75,75) 3-Y-O+ **£3,238** (£963; £481; £240) **Stalls** High

Form RPR

0133 **1** **Highland Legacy**[112] 2808 3-9-0 **72** NCallan 13 88+
(M L W Bell) *hld up in rr: stdy hdwy over 3f out: led ins fnl 2f: hung bdly rt ins fnl f but sn wl clr* **12/1**

3250 **2** 6 **Mister Completely (IRE)**[9] 5884 6-9-2 **63** (v) JamesDoyle 8 69
(Ms J S Doyle) *hld up in rr: hdwy over 3f out: styd on u.p fr over 1f out: tk 2nd wl ins fnl f but nvr any ch w wnr* **50/1**

1104 **3** ½ **Squadron**[8] 5924 3-9-1 **73** RyanMoore 11 78
(Mrs A J Perrett) *hld up in rr: hdwy and n.m.r over 2f out: rdn and styd on to press for 2nd fnl f but nvr any ch w wnr* **6/1**[2]

5606 **4** *nk* **Mind How You Go (FR)**[32] 5256 9-9-10 **71** TedDurcan 15 76
(J R Best) *led: rdn and narrowly hdd 3f out: styd pressing ldrs and disp 2nd ins fnl f: nvr any ch w wnr and one pce* **16/1**

4040 **5** 1 **Baan (USA)**[15] 5732 4-9-7 **68** GregFairley 1 72
(M Johnston) *chsd ldr: slt ld 3f out tl hdd ins fnl 2f: outpcd ins fnl f* **14/1**

2123 **6** ½ **Last Flight (IRE)**[21] 5561 3-9-1 **73** (v[1]) KerrinMcEvoy 7 76
(J L Dunlop) *chsd ldrs: rdn to disp 2nd over 1f out but nvr any ch w wnr and outpcd ins fnl f* **6/1**[2]

0632 **7** 1 **Sweetheart**[10] 5857 3-8-9 **67** JohnEgan 2 69
(Jamie Poulton) *chsd ldrs: rdn 3f out: wknd fnl f* **9/1**

4244 **8** 7 **Sa Nau**[31] 5283 4-8-9 **56** oh1 NickyMackay 16 49
(T Keddy) *chsd ldrs: rdn 3f out: wknd fnl f* **10/1**

00/- **9** 4 **Isle De Maurice**[139] 6356 5-9-2 **63** (b) SamHitchcott 10 52
(D M Grissell) *in rr and rdn along fr 1/2-way: nvr rchd ldrs* **66/1**

21-4 **10** *nk* **Esprit De Corps**[71] 4056 5-9-12 **73** JamieSpencer 14 61
(P J Hobbs) *hld up: hdwy 4f out: n.m.r whn rdn over 2f out: nvr in contention and eased whn no ch wl ins fnl f* **11/4**[1]

1242 **11** 1¼ **Hawridge King**[9] 5884 5-9-9 **75** JamesMillman[(5)] 3 62
(W S Kittow) *in tch: rdn to chse ldrs over 3f out: wknd fr 2f out* **8/1**[3]

-410 **12** ¾ **Rock 'N' Roller (FR)**[12] 5808 3-9-3 **75** RichardMullen 5 61
(W R Muir) *chsd ldrs: rdn 3f out: wknd fr ins fnl 2f* **25/1**

1202 **13** 17 **Synonymy**[8] 5924 4-8-10 **57** (b) LPKeniry 18 22
(M Blanshard) *chsd ldrs: rdn 3f out: wknd 2f out* **16/1**

020/ **14** 5 **Historic Place (USA)**[566] 6133 7-9-9 **70** SteveDrowne 4 29
(J A Geake) *a towards rr* **50/1**

066- **15** 3½ **River City (IRE)**[166] 6735 10-9-4 **65** VinceSlattery 12 20
(Noel T Chance) *rdn 1/2-way: a in rr* **28/1**

0000 **16** 8 **Tavares (IRE)**[8] 5894 4-8-9 **56** oh1 SaleemGolam 9 2
(J Jay) *a towards rr* **80/1**

3m 39.94s (5.08) **Going Correction** +0.40s/f (Good)
WFA 3 from 4yo+ 11lb **16** Ran SP% **125.5**
Speed ratings (Par 103): **103,100,99,99,99 98,98,94,92,92 92,91,83,80,78 74**
CSF £546.27 CT £3940.99 TOTE £14.90: £2.90, £9.10, £1.90, £5.30; EX 1122.60.
Owner B J Warren **Bred** Deerfield Farm **Trained** Newmarket, Suffolk

FOCUS
Nothing happened quickly in this 2m handicap and it proved a proper test in the ground. The placed horses are the best guides to the form.
Hawridge King Official explanation: jockey said gelding had no more to give

6132 FFI THE COFFEE PEOPLE APPRENTICE H'CAP — 1m 3f 5y
4:55 (4:55) (Class 5) (0-75,74) 3-Y-O+ **£3,238** (£963; £481; £240) **Stalls** Centre

Form RPR

326/ **1** **Crete (IRE)**[784] 4514 5-9-9 **72** LiamJones 16 80
(W J Haggas) *hld up: hdwy over 4f out: rdn to ld and edgd rt ins fnl f: r.o* **8/1**[3]

5015 **2** 1 **Up In Arms (IRE)**[31] 5279 3-8-5 **63** LukeMorris[(3)] 6 69
(P Winkworth) *chsd ldrs: rdn over 3f out: styd on* **14/1**

2210 **3** ½ **Selkirk Grace**[23] 5500 7-8-8 **62** (p) AmyBaker[(5)] 15 67+
(K A Morgan) *hld up: hdwy over 4f out: rdn to ld over 1f out: hdd and unable qck ins fnl f* **14/1**

0424 **4** 1½ **Adorabella (IRE)**[31] 5271 4-9-1 **64** TravisBlock 17 67+
(A King) *hld up: hdwy u.p over 2f out: styd on* **11/2**[2]

0360 **5** ½ **Effigy**[37] 5122 3-8-11 **66** RichardKingscote 7 68
(H Candy) *chsd ldrs: rdn and ev ch over 1f out: nt clr run ins fnl f: no ex* **11/1**

1-06 **6** ½ **Grande Caiman (IRE)**[15] 5724 3-9-2 **74** HaddenFrost[(3)] 12 75
(R Hannon) *led: hdd over 8f out: chsd ldrs: rdn over 3f out: styd on same pce appr fnl f* **16/1**

3515 **7** 3 **Rustic Gold**[7] 5941 3-8-13 **68** StephaneBreux 3 64
(J R Best) *hld up: hdwy u.p over 2f out: wknd ins fnl f* **9/1**

-050 **8** 1½ **Kingdom Of Dreams (IRE)**[117] 2660 5-9-4 **70** NeilBrown[(3)] 5 63
(J Mackie) *hld up: rdn over 3f out: hung rt over 1f out: wknd ins fnl f* **20/1**

0032 **9** 1¼ **Cat De Mille (USA)**[49] 4735 3-8-12 **72** MCGeran[(5)] 18 63
(P W Chapple-Hyam) *chsd ldrs: lost pl over 4f out: n.d after* **11/1**

3160 **10** 2 **Darghan (IRE)**[23] 5514 7-8-7 **63** DebraEngland[(7)] 9 51
(W J Musson) *hld up: shkn up and nt clr run over 1f out: sn wknd* **16/1**

11 1¼ **Manhattan Boy (GER)**[307] 5-9-6 **74** HarryPoulton[(5)] 13 60
(P J Hobbs) *sn chsng ldrs: led over 7f out: clr 5f out: hung rt fr over 3f out: hdd & wknd over 1f out* **3/1**[1]

4001 **12** 6 **Duelling Banjos**[107] 2967 8-8-6 **60** JackMitchell[(5)] 1 35
(J Akehurst) *chsd ldr: led over 8f out: hdd over 7f out: rdn and wknd over 1f out* **8/1**[3]

0 **13** 5 **Phone Call**[15] 5732 4-9-2 **70** JamieHamblett[(5)] 4 37
(Mouse Hamilton-Fairley) *s.i.s: a in rr: bhd whn hung lft fnl f* **66/1**

2m 30.34s (8.07) **Going Correction** +0.40s/f (Good)
WFA 3 from 4yo+ 6lb **13** Ran SP% **120.6**
Speed ratings (Par 103): **86,85,84,83,83 83,80,79,78,77 76,72,68**
CSF £116.22 CT £1555.79 TOTE £8.50: £3.30, £5.00, £4.80; EX 202.80 Place 6 £63.55, Place 5 £44.11.
Owner Highclere Thoroughbred Racing (Crete) **Bred** Scuderia Siba S P A **Trained** Newmarket, Suffolk

FOCUS
A modest apprentices' handicap run at just a steady gallop and best rated around the principals with the runner-up to his recent level.
Darghan(IRE) Official explanation: jockey said gelding was unsuited by the good to soft ground
T/Jkpt: Not won. T/Plt: £68.30 to a £1 stake. Pool: £67,719.65. 723.40 winning tickets. T/Qpdt: £25.20 to a £1 stake. Pool: £3,708.30. 108.70 winning tickets. ST

6133 - 6135a (Foreign Racing) - See Raceform Interactive

6071 CHANTILLY (R-H)
Thursday, October 11

OFFICIAL GOING: Very soft

6136a PRIX ECLIPSE (GROUP 3) — 6f
1:50 (1:51) 2-Y-O **£27,027** (£10,811; £8,108; £5,405; £2,703)

RPR

1 **Domingues**[25] 5456 2-8-11 DPMcDonogh 4 106
(Edward Lynam, Ire) *s.i.s: bustled up to press ldr after 1f: led over 3f out: drvn out* **68/10**[3]

2 ¾ **Salut L'Africain (FR)**[32] 5260 2-8-11 CSoumillon 3 104
(Robert Collet, France) *racd in 3rd: styd on fr over 1f out: nvr rchd wnr* **76/10**

3 1 **War Officer (USA)**[20] 2-8-11 C-PLemaire 5 101
(J-C Rouget, France) *racd in 5th: wnt 3rd over 1f out: styd on same pce* **7/5**[1]

4 3 **Surething (FR)**[13] 5791 2-8-11 OPeslier 1 92
(M Rolland, France) *disp 3rd: btn wl over 1f out* **26/1**

5 1 **Galaktea (IRE)**[28] 5373 2-8-8 MBlancpain 6 86
(C Laffon-Parias, France) *a outpcd*

6 *nk* **Stern Opinion (USA)**[32] 5260 2-8-11 SPasquier 2 88
(P Bary, France) *led to over 3f out: wknd wl over 1f out* **8/5**[2]

1m 13.4s (0.60) **6** Ran SP% **117.4**
PARI-MUTUEL: WIN 7.80; PL 4.10, 4.00; SF 54.70.
Owner Lady O'Reilly **Bred** R F & Mrs Knipe **Trained** Dunshaughlin, Co Meath

FOCUS
Solid Group 3 form.

NOTEBOOK
Domingues, smartly into his stride, was always well placed and, having built up a lead of several lengths inside the final three furlongs, he stuck to his task bravely in the closing stages. This was his first Group-race success and he could go back to France for the Criterium de Maisons-Laffitte.
Salut L'Africain(FR), a very consistent and much raced colt, once again put in a fine performance. He chased the winner from three out and was closing fast at the finish, suggesting he may benefit from a longer trip.
War Officer(USA), held up early on, made a forward move from one and a half out, but never looked like getting there and basically got going too late. He may appreciate better ground.
Surething(FR) showed early speed, but he was well held when it mattered.

6137a PRIX SCARAMOUCHE (LISTED RACE) — 1m 7f
2:50 (2:50) 3-Y-O+ **£17,568** (£7,027; £5,270; £3,514; £1,757)

RPR

1 **Latin Mood (FR)**[25] 5469 4-9-4 CSoumillon 6 101
(P Demercastel, France)

2 3 **Sureyya (GER)**[36] 5150 4-9-1 GFaucon 4 94
(E Lellouche, France)

3 *nk* **Distalino (FR)**[45] 4-9-4 SPasquier 1 97
(F Doumen, France)

4 *shd* **Zibimix (IRE)**[47] 4839 3-8-8 OPeslier 3 97
(F Head, France)

5 3 **Dance The Classics (IRE)**[36] 5150 3-8-5 (b) IMendizabal 2 91
(J L Dunlop) *w ldrs and t.k.h early: led over 12f out to 2f out: one pce* **12/1**[1]

6 5 **Risk (IRE)**[67] 4-9-4 TGillet 7 88
(J E Hammond, France)

7 *nk* **Queen Of Stars (FR)**[20] 4-9-1 SMaillot 9 85
(M Delzangles, France)

8 3 **Dilshaan's Prize (IRE)**[34] 5258 3-8-8 (b) DBonilla 8 84
(R Pritchard-Gordon, France)

The Form Book, Raceform Ltd, Compton, RG20 6NL

9 *15* **Mick Jerome (IRE)**[25] 4218 6-9-4 .... J-MBreux 5 68
(Rune Haugen, Norway)

3m 17.7s (1.30)
WFA 3 from 4yo+ 10lb 9 Ran SP% **7.7**
PARI-MUTUEL: WIN 5.70; PL 1.90, 1.60, 1.60; DF 14.60.
Owner Naji Pharaon **Bred** N Pharaon **Trained** France

NOTEBOOK
Dance The Classics(IRE) attempted to make all but her stride began to shorten halfway in the straight and in the end she was well held. She should get this trip at the right level, though.

5494 LINGFIELD (L-H)
Friday, October 12

OFFICIAL GOING: Standard
Wind: Almost nil Weather: Overcast becoming fine

6138 NORMAN HILL MEMORIAL MAIDEN STKS (DIV I) 7f (P)
1:50 (1:50) (Class 5) 2-Y-O £2,590 (£770; £385; £192) Stalls Low

Form RPR

1 **Storm Force (IRE)** 2-9-3 0 .... KerrinMcEvoy 9 86+
(Saeed Bin Suroor) *leggy: w'like: trckd ldr after 1f: led over 1f out: sn clr: v comf* **10/1**

522 2 *3 ½* **Hold The Gold (IRE)**[61] 4431 2-9-3 84 .... ChrisCatlin 3 75
(E J O'Neill) *plld hrd early: trckd ldrs: effrt 2f out: wnt 2nd ins fnl f: no ch w wnr* **9/2**[2]

3 *1 ¼* **Turn Left (IRE)** 2-9-3 0 .... GeorgeBaker 5 72
(R M Beckett) *w'like: hld up in last trio: taken wd bnd 2f out: shuffled along and r.o fnl f: tk 3rd last stride* **40/1**

4 *shd* **Asfurah's Dream (IRE)** 2-8-12 0 .... MartinDwyer 11 67
(M P Tregoning) *unf: angular: leggy: dwlt: plld hrd and trckd ldng pair after 2f: outpcd over 1f out: one pce after* **15/2**[3]

05 5 *½* **Penchesco (IRE)**[20] 5628 2-9-3 0 .... PaulEddery 7 71
(Pat Eddery) *hld up bhd ldrs: outpcd wl over 1f out: kpt on one pce after* **50/1**

52 6 *nk* **Greylami (IRE)**[18] 5679 2-9-3 0 .... JohnEgan 1 70+
(T G Mills) *hld up in midfield on inner: shuffled along and kpt on fr over 1f out: nvr nr ldrs* **9/2**[2]

2 7 *nk* **Storm Sir (USA)**[21] 5591 2-9-3 0 .... SebSanders 4 69
(J Noseda) *unf: scope: lw: hld up towards rr: n.m.r 2f out: nt qckn and no prog over 1f out* **13/8**[1]

00 8 *2 ½* **Points Of View**[10] 5880 2-9-3 0 .... JamieMackay 8 63
(Sir Mark Prescott) *str: swtg: dwlt: hld up in last and racd on outer: outpcd and no ch wl over 1f out: kpt on* **80/1**

0 9 *1* **Change Alley (USA)**[14] 5771 2-9-3 0 .... RoystonFfrench 12 60
(M Johnston) *w'like: lengthy: led after 100yds to over 1f out: wknd* **16/1**

0 10 *8* **Pretty Officer (USA)**[37] 5126 2-8-12 0 .... RichardMullen 2 35
(Rae Guest) *angular: a in rr: wknd 2f out* **100/1**

5 11 *3 ½* **Ella Junior (USA)**[10] 5882 2-8-12 0 .... JamieSpencer 6 27
(B J Meehan) *b: b.hind: leggy: led for 100yds: prom tl wknd rapidly 2f out* **12/1**

00 12 *2 ½* **Up The Wycombe**[65] 4273 2-9-3 0 .... TQuinn 10 25
(S Dow) *racd wd towards rr: wknd over 2f out* **100/1**

1m 26.47s (0.58) **Going Correction** 0.0s/f (Stan) 12 Ran SP% **116.5**
Speed ratings (Par 95): **96,92,90,90,89 89,89,86,85,76 72,69**
CSF £53.30 TOTE £14.40: £3.70, £1.70, £9.90; EX 68.90 TRIFECTA Not won..
Owner Godolphin **Bred** Gerrardstown House Stud **Trained** Newmarket, Suffolk

FOCUS
A decent maiden likely to produce its share of winners.

NOTEBOOK
Storm Force(IRE), a close relation of high-class but quirky sprinter Conquest, comes from a stable who have really hit top stride now and he ran out a most impressive winner, clearing right away inside the final furlong. This was just an ordinary race and it would be unwise to get carried away, but he is clearly a potentially smart sort and looks well worth his place in something a bit better now. (op 9-1 tchd 11-1)
Hold The Gold(IRE), twice run out of it in the closing stages in maidens, not for the first time hindered his chances by pulling, but it made no difference to the outcome as the winner proved in a different league. A race will come his way eventually. (tchd 5-1)
Turn Left(IRE), a half-brother to a useful performer in Hong Kong, comes from a stable who are more than capable of readying one to win first time up and he shaped with an abundance of promise back in third. Not given a hard time inside the final quarter mile, he can be expected to improve for this initial experience and should find a similar race his for the taking. (op 33-1)
Asfurah's Dream(IRE), withdrawn because of soft ground at Newbury the previous day, is a daughter of top-class middle-distance performer Nayef, who did so well for the yard, and she shaped extremely well over a trip that will prove short of her best. She failed to settle early, but really saw her race out and is another likely maiden winner before the year is out. (op 10-1)
Penchesco(IRE) has improved a little with each run and again gave the impression that trips in excess of this will suit once handicapping. He is now qualified for a mark and should find a race in that sphere.
Greylami(IRE), who found only the one too good when outpaced late on over 1m at Kempton last time, was never going to be suite by this drop to 7f and lacked the pace to get involved, but on the plus side he is now qualified for handicaps, a sphere he should do well in. (op 7-2)
Storm Sir(USA), the one to beat on the evidence of his debut second at Newbury, found himself in a tricky position as they began the turn into the straight and never really had a chance to show what he can do. He has already shown himself to be better than this and deserves another chance. (op 2-1 tchd 5-2)
Up The Wycombe Official explanation: jockey said colt hung left-handed

6139 NORMAN HILL MEMORIAL MAIDEN STKS (DIV II) 7f (P)
2:20 (2:20) (Class 5) 2-Y-O £2,590 (£770; £385; £192) Stalls Low

Form RPR

2 1 **The Which Doctor**[63] 4362 2-9-3 0 .... TPQueally 9 76+
(J Noseda) *w'like: t.k.h: cl up: wnt 2nd over 2f out: led over 1f out: in n.d after: pushed out* **10/11**[1]

0425 2 *1 ½* **City Hustler (USA)**[31] 5294 2-9-3 68 .... JohnEgan 10 72
(J S Moore) *hld up at rr of main gp: prog 2f out: shkn up to dispute 2nd 1f out: styd on but no imp on wnr* **6/1**[2]

0 3 *½* **Amhooj**[71] 4094 2-8-12 0 .... MartinDwyer 4 66
(M P Tregoning) *dwlt: sn in midfield: effrt 2f out: disp 2nd 1f out: styd on but no ch w wnr* **6/1**[2]

0532 4 *5* **Straight And Level (CAN)**[101] 3174 2-9-3 72 .... ChrisCatlin 11 59
(Miss Jo Crowley) *hld up at rr of main gp: rdn 3f out: outpcd wl over 1f out: kpt on fnl f* **12/1**[3]

5 *shd* **Commander Cave (USA)** 2-9-3 0 .... PatDobbs 3 58
(R Hannon) *chsd ldrs: outpcd over 2f out: no ch after: plugged on* **20/1**

6 *½* **Persistent (IRE)** 2-9-3 0 .... RoystonFfrench 7 57
(M Johnston) *w'like: scope: bit bkwd: pressed ldr: led wl over 2f out to over 1f out: hrd rdn and wknd* **6/1**[2]

00 7 *2* **Rough Sketch (USA)**[14] 5771 2-9-3 0 .... SebSanders 8 52
(Sir Mark Prescott) *in tch: rdn over 2f out: outpcd wl over 1f out: no ch after* **40/1**

8 *3 ½* **Tenraninthemist (IRE)** 2-8-12 0 .... RobertHavlin 5 38
(T D McCarthy) *leggy: bit bkwd: s.i.s: sn detached in last and rn green: nvr a factor* **80/1**

0 9 *nk* **Better In Heaven**[30] 5329 2-9-3 0 .... SteveDrowne 1 43
(H J L Dunlop) *led to wl over 2f out: wknd rapidly wl over 1f out* **33/1**

1m 26.72s (0.83) **Going Correction** 0.0s/f (Stan) 71 Ran SP% **114.3**
Speed ratings (Par 95): **95,93,92,87,86 86,84,80,79**
CSF £6.36 TOTE £1.70: £1.20, £1.90, £1.90; EX 7.10 Trifecta £25.50 Pool: £467.54 - 12.97 winning tickets..
Owner G C Stevens **Bred** Limestone And Tara Studs **Trained** Newmarket, Suffolk

FOCUS
Easily the lesser of the two divisions. Sound form though, with the winner marginally below his previous best and the first three clear.

NOTEBOOK
The Which Doctor, narrowly denied on his debut at Newmarket, found himself in the weaker of the two divisions and he did what was required to get the job done, being kept up to his work in front. He ought to get 1m in time, but he seems to have a tendency to race keenly and will need to learn to settle better before he can fulfil his potential. (op 6-5)
City Hustler(USA), exposed as a modest maiden, appeared to run an improved race in second, keeping on well down the outside having been given plenty to do, and it is surely time now that he took his chance in a handicap. He should find a small race before long. (tchd 11-2 and 13-2)
Amhooj, green and never involved in a decent maiden behind Celtic Slipper on her debut at Goodwood, had been given a break from that and returned with an improved effort, if lacking the pace of the winner. She is clearly nothing special, but was clear of the remainder. (op 15-2)
Straight And Level(CAN), beaten in a claimer earlier in the season, was always going to be vulnerable to improvers and he will find easier opportunities back down in grade. (op 14-1)
Commander Cave(USA), whose dam was a sprinter, is an athletic type but made nothing more than a satisfactory debut and gave the impression he will be struggling to win a maiden. Low-grade handicaps are more likely to be his thing next season. (op 16-1)
Persistent(IRE), whose stable's juvenile often benefit from a run, appeared to know his job and showed up well to a point, but stopped disappointingly quickly under pressure and ended up being well beaten. He will need to step up markedly on this. (op 4-1)

6140 LADBROKES.COM FOR THE BEST BET IN PLAY MAIDEN FILLIES' STKS 1m (P)
2:50 (2:55) (Class 5) 2-Y-O £3,238 (£963; £481; £240) Stalls High

Form RPR

1 **Comeback Queen** 2-9-0 0 .... LPKeniry 2 74+
(S Kirk) *unf: scope: dwlt: sn trckd ldrs: sltly outpcd over 2f out: prog over 1f out: r.o to ld last 100yds: sn clr* **20/1**

4 2 *1 ¾* **Heritage Coast (USA)**[56] 4565 2-9-0 0 .... JamieSpencer 11 70
(Sir Michael Stoute) *bit bkwd: prom: trckd ldr 1/2-way: rdn over 2f out: clsd fnl f but sn outpcd by wnr* **5/2**[1]

5 3 *1 ¼* **Edie Superstar (USA)**[167] 1285 2-9-0 0 .... (t) AdamKirby 4 67
(M A Magnusson) *w'like: fractious preliminaries: mde most: kicked on over 2f out: hdd & wknd last 100yds* **12/1**

2 4 *½* **Freedom Song**[18] 5681 2-9-0 0 .... SteveDrowne 10 66
(R Charlton) *w'like: b.hind: trckd ldrs: rdn over 2f out: kpt on fnl f but nvr pce to threaten* **5/2**[1]

5 *nk* **Elysee Palace (IRE)** 2-9-0 0 .... MatthewHenry 7 66
(M A Jarvis) *leggy: scope: b: b.hind: bit bkwd: dwlt: hld up: prog to trck ldrs 1/2-way: outpcd over 2f out: kpt on fnl f* **20/1**

6 6 *1 ¾* **Reclamation (IRE)**[14] 5770 2-9-0 0 .... SebSanders 6 62
(Sir Mark Prescott) *settled in rr: outpcd over 2f out: pushed along and plugged on steadily* **8/1**

0 7 *1* **Flower**[8] 5944 2-9-0 0 .... SimonWhitworth 9 60+
(C A Cyzer) *bit bkwd: plld hrd: hld up in midfield: outpcd over 2f out: no imp after* **66/1**

8 *½* **Dove (IRE)** 2-9-0 0 .... KerrinMcEvoy 5 58
(Saeed Bin Suroor) *lw: dwlt: hld up and last after 2f: nudged along over 2f out: reminder over 1f out: modest late prog* **7/1**[3]

43 9 *3* **Especially (IRE)**[16] 5720 2-9-0 0 .... RoystonFfrench 3 52
(M Johnston) *w ldr to 1/2-way: sn lost pl and struggling* **5/1**[2]

10 *1 ½* **Amandalini** 2-9-0 0 .... RobertHavlin 12 49
(B J Meehan) *unf: s.s: hld up towards rr: rdn 3f out: sn outpcd and struggling* **33/1**

0 11 *4* **Recast (IRE)**[23] 5527 2-9-0 0 .... PatDobbs 1 40
(R Hannon) *a in rr: bhd over 2f out* **66/1**

1m 41.41s (1.98) **Going Correction** 0.0s/f (Stan) 11 Ran SP% **120.6**
Speed ratings (Par 92): **90,88,87,86,86 84,83,82,79,78 74**
CSF £69.20 TOTE £23.40: £4.20, £1.60, £3.20; EX 88.00 TRIFECTA Not won..
Owner Mr & Mrs Christopher Wright **Bred** Stratford Place Stud **Trained** Upper Lambourn, Berks

FOCUS
Probably just a fair fillies' maiden. The form could have been rated higher but the likes of the seventh temper enthusiasm.

NOTEBOOK
Comeback Queen, whose half-sister Worldly won over this distance as a juvenile, was nibbled at in the market to provide her trainer with a rare debut winner and she came with a sweeping run from over a furlong out to win going away despite having been on her toes beforehand. This was a taking performance from the daughter of Nayef, who is already making a good impression as a sire, and it will be interesting to see whether she is allowed to take her chance again before the season is out. (op 25-1 tchd 16-1)
Heritage Coast(USA), a one-paced fourth in a decent maiden on her debut at Doncaster, was up in trip and it was no surprise to see her improve on that initial effort, just finding the winner's late charge too much. She is evidently nothing special, but is in good hands and can find a similar race. (op 10-3 tchd 7-2)
Edie Superstar(USA), who made a pleasing debut over 5f at Haydock back in April, has evidently had a problem and she had a tongue tie on for this reappearance. Stepping up three furlongs in trip, she really pressed on under a positive ride, but her stamina limitations were exposed in the end. A drop back to either 6f or 7f will give her more of a chance, but it may be that connections decide to wait for handicaps with her. (op 16-1)
Freedom Song, entitled to go close on the evidence of her debut second over an inadequate 7f at Kempton, is a half-sister to the yard's formerly smart Luvah Girl and it was a bit disappointing she could not do better, considering she held a good position. (op 11-4 tchd 3-1)
Elysee Palace(IRE), a sister to the high-class Notability, was evidently not fancied to make much of an impact on this debut, but she demonstrated a fair level of ability in finishing fifth and natural progression should see her going close in a similar contest.
Reclamation(IRE), always outpaced over 6f on her debut at Haydock, was up two furlongs in trip and expected to go well, but she was never really in a threatening position and could only make limited headway down the straight. She will be qualified for a handicap mark after one more run. (tchd 9-1)

Dove(IRE), a half-sister to the yard's formerly smart Naheef, interestingly holds a Derby entry, but she never left the rear following a sluggish start and made only limited headway in the straight. She is going to benefit for a switch to turf, but needs to improve dramatically. (op 8-1)
Especially(IRE) came into this having shown a fair level of form over 7f at Goodwood last time, but having disputed it to just past halfway, she began to struggle and dropped right out. (op 4-1 tchd 11-2)

6141 LADBROKES.COM FOR THE BEST ONLINE BINGO H'CAP 5f (P)

3:25 (3:26) (Class 4) (0-85,91) 3-Y-0+ **£5,362** (£1,604; £802; £401; £199) **Stalls** High

Form				RPR
1231	**1**		**Matsunosuke**[10] 5891 5-9-10 **91** 6ex ...... KerrinMcEvoy 3 *(A B Coogan) settled in last pair: prog wl over 1f out: wl-timed chal to ld last 75yds: decisively* **3/1**[1]	104+
113	**2**	1	**Osiris Way**[91] 3489 5-8-13 **80** ...... JimCrowley 2 *(P R Chamings) trckd ldrs: rdn 2f out: effrt to chal and upsides 1f out: styd on same pce* **13/2**[2]	89
0230	**3**	½	**Texas Gold**[18] 5689 9-8-13 **80** ...... MartinDwyer 5 *(W R Muir) trckd ldrs: prog on inner wl over 1f out: led ent fnl f: hdd and nt qckn last 75yds* **3/1**[1]	87
1653	**4**	½	**Safari Mischief**[28] 5381 4-8-6 **80** ...... JackMitchell(7) 9 *(P Winkworth) in tch in midfield: rdn 2f out: nt qckn over 1f out: styd on ins fnl f* **12/1**	85
0245	**5**	nk	**Holbeck Ghyll (IRE)**[13] 5806 5-8-10 **77** ...... FrancisNorton 1 *(A M Balding) led: hung rt fr over 1f out: hdd and nt qckn ent fnl f* **15/2**[3]	81
6633	**6**	hd	**Tony The Tap**[10] 5891 6-8-10 **77** ...... RichardMullen 8 *(W R Muir) pushed along in rr 3f out: struggling after: wd in st but styd on fnl f* **9/1**	81
3345	**7**	shd	**Fromsong (IRE)**[28] 5379 9-8-13 **80** ...... SebSanders 10 *(D K Ivory) swtg: trckd ldng pair: nt qckn over 1f out: one pce after* **11/1**	83
0466	**8**	nk	**Mambo Spirit (IRE)**[14] 5765 3-9-3 **84** ...... TPQueally 6 *(J G Given) dwlt: last and outpcd 1/2-way: wd bnd 2f out: styd on fnl f* **14/1**	86
4050	**9**	½	**Misaro (GER)**[16] 5722 6-8-11 **83** ...... (b) KevinGhunowa(5) 7 *(R A Harris) b.hind: chsd ldr to over 1f out: fdd* **20/1**	83
2660	**10**	5	**Who's Winning (IRE)**[9] 5923 6-8-11 **78** ...... TQuinn 4 *(B G Powell) b: a towards rr: wknd over 1f out* **33/1**	60

58.58 secs (-1.20) **Going Correction** 0.0s/f (Stan) **10** Ran SP% **115.5**
Speed ratings (Par 105): **109,107,106,105,105 105,104,104,103,95**
CSF £22.39 CT £62.81 TOTE £3.30: £1.50, £2.10, £1.50; EX 19.80 Trifecta £36.70 Pool: £626.68 - 12.11 winning tickets..
Owner A B Coogan **Bred** R Coogan **Trained** Soham, Cambs

FOCUS
A decent sprint handicap won by the in-form and progressive Matsunosuke who is developing into a smart sprinter. Solid form.
Holbeck Ghyll(IRE) Official explanation: jockey said gelding hung right-handed
Mambo Spirit(IRE) Official explanation: jockey said gelding missed the break

6142 LADBROKES FREEPHONE BETTING ON 0800 777 888 H'CAP 6f (P)

4:00 (4:00) (Class 3) (0-90,90) 3-Y-0+

£8,101 (£2,425; £1,212; £607; £302; £152) **Stalls** Low

Form				RPR
2016	**1**		**Barney McGrew (IRE)**[35] 5209 4-9-2 **87** ...... OscarUrbina 2 *(J A R Toller) trckd ldrs: effrt towards inner wl over 1f out: shkn up and led 150yds out: readily* **15/2**	101+
1010	**2**	½	**Capricorn Run (USA)**[6] 6013 4-9-4 **89** ...... (v) SebSanders 1 *(A J McCabe) dwlt: drvn to rcvr on ins but only rchd midfield: effrt 2f out: r.o fnl f to take 2nd nr fin: nt rch wnr* **15/2**	96
0506	**3**	nk	**Bertoliver**[10] 5891 3-9-2 **88** ...... KerrinMcEvoy 11 *(D K Ivory) trckd ldrs on outer: prog to ld over 1f out gng strly: hdd 150yds out: fin weakly* **16/1**	94
0044	**4**	hd	**Dingaan (IRE)**[26] 5449 4-9-3 **88** ...... FrancisNorton 12 *(A M Balding) dwlt: hld up in rr: prog on outer over 1f out: r.o ins fnl f: nrst fin* **15/2**	93
2012	**5**	2 ½	**Efistorm**[13] 5810 6-9-3 **88** ...... GeorgeBaker 3 *(C R Dore) settled in last trio: rdn 2f out: no prog tl styd on wl last 150yds: no ch* **6/1**[2]	85
1010	**6**	shd	**Lady Lily (IRE)**[8] 5954 3-9-3 **89** ...... TPQueally 10 *(H R A Cecil) prom: trckd ldr 3f out: led 2f out: hdd over 1f out: wknd rapidly ins fnl f* **9/1**	86
2500	**7**	1	**China Cherub**[9] 5923 4-9-0 **85** ...... (b) PatDobbs 7 *(R Hannon) drvn in last pair after 1f: nvr a factor: kpt on fnl f* **16/1**	79
3000	**8**	hd	**Sand Cat**[70] 4122 4-9-0 **85** ...... RoystonFfrench 5 *(G L Moore) snatched up after 1f: nvr on terms w ldrs: no imp over 1f out* **50/1**	78
6-33	**9**	½	**Grand Show**[16] 5722 5-9-0 **85** ...... AdamKirby 9 *(W R Swinburn) chsd ldrs: rdn 2f out: no imp: wknd fnl f* **4/1**[1]	77
5-P0	**10**	1 ¾	**Mr Lambros**[24] 5513 6-9-5 **90** ...... (t) JohnEgan 8 *(Miss Gay Kelleway) w ldr: led 4f out to 2f out: wknd rapidly jst over 1f out* **16/1**	76
1522	**11**	hd	**Buy On The Red**[17] 5711 6-9-2 **87** ...... (p) MartinDwyer 6 *(W R Muir) led for 2f: u.p and losing pl sn after 1/2-way: eased whn no ch fnl f* **7/1**[3]	72
4246	**12**	4	**Moonlight Man**[46] 4886 6-9-0 **85** ...... MatthewHenry 4 *(C R Dore) outpcd and a in last pair* **20/1**	58

1m 11.37s (-1.44) **Going Correction** 0.0s/f (Stan)
WFA 3 from 4yo+ 1lb **12** Ran SP% **116.4**
Speed ratings (Par 107): **109,108,107,107,104 104,102,102,101,99 99,94**
CSF £61.63 CT £887.97 TOTE £8.90: £3.30, £2.80, £5.30; EX 83.80 TRIFECTA Not won..
Owner M A Whelton **Bred** Mrs H B Raw **Trained** Newmarket, Suffolk

FOCUS
A typically competitive sprint handicap for the course. The winner was value for a bit extra and the next three close to form.

NOTEBOOK
Barney McGrew(IRE), 3lb higher than when winning at Newmarket on his penultimate outing, came up short in a hot handicap at Newbury last time, but this was easier and he came through under a well-timed ride to win readily. He has generally been in decent form, but will need to progress again if he is to defy a further rise. (op 7-1 tchd 17-2)
Capricorn Run(USA), put up 7lb for winning at Newmarket last month, was unable to cope with that rise when down the field in a competitive 7f handicap back there next time, but this return to sprinting brought about a much better effort and it is possible the first-time visor also contributed. (op 9-1 tchd 7-1)
Bertoliver, a dual 5f winner earlier in the season, has been struggling to make an impact off this sort of mark, but he ran well for a long way here and certainly shaped as though a return to 5f would suit. (tchd 20-1)
Dingaan(IRE) has been running well in defeat and he was noted putting in some good late work, but it is unlikely he will prove up to winning off this mark. (op 8-1)
Efistorm is rarely seen over this trip, but he has been in decent form at 5f and in hindsight his rider would have made a bit more use of him as he got going all too late. Official explanation: jockey said gelding was denied a clear run (op 5-1)
Lady Lily(IRE) stopped disappointingly quickly in the straight and has not yet built on September's Pontefract win. Official explanation: jockey said filly had no more to give (op 8-1)
Grand Show failed to run his race and his rider reported he got upset in the stalls. Official explanation: jockey said gelding got upset in the stalls (tchd 9-2)
Buy On The Red Official explanation: jockey said gelding ran too keenly

6143 LADBROKES.COM LEADS THE WAY H'CAP 1m (P)

4:35 (4:36) (Class 3) (0-95,94) 3-Y-0+

£8,101 (£2,425; £1,212; £607; £302; £152) **Stalls** High

Form				RPR
4000	**1**		**Troubadour (IRE)**[22] 5554 6-8-13 **88** ...... SteveDrowne 5 *(W Jarvis) hld up towards rr: gng strly but only 9th wl over 1f out: gd prog to chse ldr fnl f: edgd rt but r.o to ld last stride* **25/1**	99
6-21	**2**	hd	**Jalil (USA)**[128] 2376 3-8-9 **87** ...... KerrinMcEvoy 12 *(Saeed Bin Suroor) lw: trckd ldr: led over 2f out and kicked on: edgd rt fr over 1f out: hdd last stride* **7/2**[2]	98
4230	**3**	1 ¾	**Hazzard County (USA)**[49] 4785 3-8-9 **87** ...... JohnEgan 8 *(D M Simcock) hld up in last trio: pushed along on wd outside 2f out: prog over 1f out: styd on wl to take 3rd ins fnl f: nvr able to chal* **16/1**	94+
0450	**4**	¾	**Wavertree Warrior (IRE)**[20] 5615 5-8-11 **86** ...... (b) JamesDoyle 11 *(N P Littmoden) hld up in last pair: drvn and prog over 1f out: styd on fnl f: nt rch ldrs* **25/1**	91
0306	**5**	½	**The Snatcher (IRE)**[11] 5870 4-8-5 **80** ...... FrancisNorton 10 *(R Hannon) racd wd in midfield: rdn 2f out: styd on fnl f: n.d* **14/1**	84+
00-0	**6**	hd	**Basra (IRE)**[103] 3143 4-8-3 **83** ...... KevinGhunowa(5) 6 *(Miss Jo Crowley) mostly in midfield: rdn and no prog wl over 1f out: styd on fnl f* **100/1**	86
4500	**7**	nk	**Manchurian**[20] 5635 3-8-13 **91** ...... TPQueally 3 *(M J Wallace) trckd ldrs: drvn to chse ldr briefly jst over 1f out: sn wknd* **25/1**	94
2656	**8**	¾	**Bomber Command (USA)**[15] 5761 4-9-5 **94** ...... TQuinn 9 *(J W Hills) prom: drvn to chse ldr 2f out: wknd 1f out* **16/1**	95
-213	**9**	2 ½	**Al Khaleej (IRE)**[76] 3940 3-8-13 **91** ...... SebSanders 1 *(E A L Dunlop) prom: rdn over 2f out: nt qckn: wknd over 1f out* **11/8**[1]	86
3000	**10**	shd	**Killena Boy (IRE)**[34] 5221 5-8-13 **88** ...... PaulDoe 4 *(W Jarvis) hld up towards rr: n.m.r on inner 2f out: sn drvn and no prog* **25/1**	83
1026	**11**	¾	**Dichoh**[18] 5685 4-8-9 **84** ...... MartinDwyer 7 *(M A Jarvis) hld up in last trio: rdn and no prog 2f out* **16/1**	77
1133	**12**	10	**Samarinda (USA)**[12] 5833 4-9-4 **93** ...... MickyFenton 2 *(Mrs P Sly) awkward s: rousted along to ld: hdd over 2f out: sn wknd: heavily eased fnl f* **13/2**[3]	63

1m 37.68s (-1.75) **Going Correction** 0.0s/f (Stan)
WFA 3 from 4yo+ 3lb **12** Ran SP% **118.3**
Speed ratings (Par 107): **108,107,106,105,104 104,104,103,101,100 100,90**
CSF £106.45 CT £1505.40 TOTE £42.00: £7.20, £1.60, £3.70; EX 173.40 TRIFECTA Not won..
Owner Dr J Walker **Bred** Swettenham Stud **Trained** Newmarket, Suffolk

FOCUS
A shock result to this decent 1m handicap. Hold-up horses seemed advantaged even though the pace did not look to be that fast. The runner-up did best of those to race prominently.

NOTEBOOK
Troubadour(IRE) had not done much of note since returning from Hong Kong where he managed to win three times, including on dirt, but he had been dropped a total of 7lb by the Handicapper and the return to this surface sparked him back to life. Well in rear early, he was noted travelling particularly well as they turned into the straight and, once getting his run, he finished strongly to get up close home. He is capable of winning off higher marks than this on old form and is one to take seriously on this surface over the winter.
Jalil(USA) was always unlikely to live up to his $9.7m price tag and he made hard enough work of winning a modest maiden at Ripon in June. The Handicapper had taken no chances in putting him on a mark of 87, but this switch to Polytrack was always going to suit the son of Storm Cat and he showed a marked improvement in form. Ridden positively on this drop in trip, he looked all over the winner when kicking off the home bend, but in the end the formerly classy winner proved too strong. He remains capable of better, but will always be known as the $9.7m failure. (op 9-2 tchd 10-3)
Hazzard County(USA) has gone up 8lb in the weights since going handicapping, despite having not won one, but this effort again suggested he is capable and he could be worth a try at 1m2f now. (tchd 20-1)
Wavertree Warrior(IRE) was going on well close home having been a bit too far back and showed his recent running at Ayr to be no wrong. He has not won since February, but is 2lb lower now and his turn may not be far away. (op 16-1)
The Snatcher(IRE) has not won since the summer of 2006 and, although he finds himself on a considerably lower mark, he remains below a winning level.
Basra(IRE), readily dismissed in the market on this first start in England, was arguably unlucky not to get a bit closer as he did not have much room to operate in and in the end got going too late. He could be of interest for something similar if the Handicapper eases him a little. Official explanation: jockey said gelding was denied a clear run
Bomber Command(USA) Official explanation: jockey said gelding lost its action
Al Khaleej(IRE), a progressive three-year-old returning from a break, looked the one they all had to beat having shown some smart form back in the summer, but he failed to reproduce anything like his best and dropped away disappointingly in the straight. He had already won on Polytrack at Wolverhampton, so the surface cannot be used as an excuse, but he deserves another chance to show his true form. (op 13-8 tchd 7-4 in places)
Samarinda(USA) got warm beforehand and dropped out very tamely. Official explanation: jockey said gelding ran flat (op 9-2)

6144 LADBROKES.COM FOR THE BEST ONLINE POKER H'CAP 1m 4f (P)

5:05 (5:05) (Class 4) (0-85,85) 3-Y-0+ **£5,362** (£1,604; £802; £401; £199) **Stalls** Low

Form				RPR
5500	**1**		**Polish Power (GER)**[34] 5225 7-9-9 **80** ...... JohnEgan 7 *(J S Moore) lw: hld up towards rr: pushed along and prog fr 4f out: rdn 2f out: clsd to ld ins fnl f: kpt on wl* **14/1**	89
150	**2**	½	**First To Call**[16] 5724 3-9-2 **80** ...... AmirQuinn 10 *(P J Makin) lw: t.k.h: trckd ldng pair: wnt 2nd over 3f out: led wl over 2f out and kicked 3 l clr: idled and edgd rt: hdd ins fnl f: kpt on* **66/1**	88
4001	**3**	hd	**Muhannak (IRE)**[6] 6007 3-8-12 **76** ...... (b) RichardKingscote 1 *(G A Butler) hld up in midfield: prog over 3f out: tried to cl on ldng pair on inner over 1f out: kpt on but a hld* **5/2**[1]	84
5140	**4**	2 ½	**Doctor Scott**[18] 5677 4-9-3 **74** ...... RoystonFfrench 6 *(M Johnston) s.s: drvn in rr early: nvr gng wl: bhd over 3f out: styd on u.p fnl 2f* **16/1**	78
4600	**5**	nk	**Solo Flight**[55] 4597 10-9-8 **79** ...... SteveDrowne 8 *(H Morrison) hld up towards rr: prog over 3f out: outpcd over 2f out: kpt on* **33/1**	82

1331 **6** *shd* **Kingscape (IRE)**[16] 5725 4-9-9 **80** KerrinMcEvoy 4 83
(J R Fanshawe) *hld up in rr: pushed along and effrt over 3f out: outpcd over 2f out: hanging but kpt on fnl f: nt pce to threaten ldrs* **3/1**[2]
0005 **7** *3/4* **Shimoni**[18] 5686 3-9-1 **79** (v[1]) PaulDoe 9 81
(W J Knight) *dwlt: hld up in rr: rdn 5f out: effrt 3f out: kpt on but n.d* **50/1**
1010 **8** *1* **Chord**[35] 5205 3-9-7 **85** (v) TPQueally 11 85
(Sir Michael Stoute) *lw: trckd ldr: led over 4f out: hdd wl over 2f out: wknd over 1f out* **7/1**
661 **9** *3* **Wise Little Girl**[27] 5405 3-9-3 **81** RobertHavlin 2 76
(M A Jarvis) *lw: prom: rdn 3f out: wknd tamely 2f out* **16/1**
0426 **10** *5* **Paymaster General (IRE)**[10] 5892 3-8-10 **74** AdamKirby 13 61
(M D I Usher) *plld hrd: hld up tl wnt prom after 4f: wknd rapidly over 2f out: eased fnl f* **25/1**
5040 **11** *14* **Captain General**[24] 5500 5-8-11 **68** oh2 MartinDwyer 12 33
(J A R Toller) *in tch on outer tl wknd 4f out: sn bhd* **20/1**
5215 **12** *30* **Dar Es Salaam**[58] 4510 3-9-0 **78** SebSanders 3 —
(E A L Dunlop) *dwlt: sn led: reminders bnd over 9f out: drvn and hdd over 4f out: dropped out rapidly: t.o* **9/2**[3]
14-5 **13** *1* **Altilhar (USA)**[174] 593 4-9-11 **82** GeorgeBaker 5 —
(G L Moore) *hld up in last pair: rdn and wknd 5f out: t.o* **16/1**

2m 33.84s (-0.55) **Going Correction** 0.0s/f (Stan)
WFA 3 from 4yo+ 7lb **13** Ran SP% **123.6**
Speed ratings (Par 105): **101,100,100,98,98 98,98,97,95,92 82,62,62**
CSF £755.71 CT £3066.62 TOTE £21.40: £5.00, £19.10, £1.20; EX 639.10 TRIFECTA Not won..
Owner Mrs Fitri Hay **Bred** Gestut Hofgut Mappen **Trained** Upper Lambourn, Berks

FOCUS
A fair handicap. Slightly muddling form, with a big-priced runner-up, but the winner had slipped to a good mark and the third was well in.
Polish Power(GER) Official explanation: trainer's rep said, regarding apparent improvement in form, that the horse had benefited from a five-week break
Altilhar(USA) Official explanation: jockey said gelding had no more to give

6145 LADBROKES.COM FOR THE BEST ONLINE CASINO H'CAP 1m 2f (P)
5:35 (5:35) (Class 4) (0-80,80) 3-Y-O+ **£5,362** (£1,604; £802; £401; £199) **Stalls** Low

Form RPR
2143 **1** **Risque Heights**[42] 5014 3-9-1 **78** SteveDrowne 1 93+
(G A Butler) *stdd s: hld up in last pair: smooth prog on outer fr 3f out: shkn up to ld jst ins fnl f: kpt on* **6/1**[3]
1400 **2** *3/4* **Sign Of The Cross**[18] 5685 3-8-13 **76** OscarUrbina 6 89
(J R Fanshawe) *settled in midfield: prog 3f out: drvn to chal 1f out: styd on fnl f but a hld* **16/1**
0432 **3** *1/2* **Mafeking (UAE)**[10] 5889 3-9-0 **77** PaulDoe 5 89
(M R Hoad) *trckd ldrs: prog to ld 3f out: drvn over 1f out: hdd jst ins fnl f: kpt on* **11/2**[2]
1600 **4** *5* **Coeur Courageux (FR)**[18] 5685 5-9-5 **77** (t) GeorgeBaker 12 79
(G L Moore) *rrd s: hld up: prog on outer over 3f out: drvn 2f out: cl enough over 1f out: wknd* **14/1**
6422 **5** *1/2* **Trifti**[7] 5985 6-8-4 **67** PatrickHills(5) 11 68
(C A Cyzer) *trckd ldrs: wnt 2nd wl over 2f out tl wknd over 1f out* **11/1**
-021 **6** *3/4* **Rhyming Slang (USA)**[24] 5499 3-9-3 **80** SebSanders 8 80
(J Noseda) *hld up in midfield: urged along over 4f out: one pce u.p fr over 2f out* **15/8**[1]
2210 **7** *hd* **Veiled Applause**[27] 5432 4-9-7 **79** KerrinMcEvoy 3 78
(R M Beckett) *led for 2f: trckd ldrs: outpcd 3f out: n.d after* **17/2**
S556 **8** *1* **Isidore Bonheur (IRE)**[14] 5775 6-9-2 **77** PJMcDonald(3) 2 74
(G A Swinbank) *in tch tl dropped to rr u.p over 3f out: no ch after* **16/1**
3025 **9** *3/4* **Don Pietro**[23] 5539 4-9-3 **75** TPQueally 7 71
(D J Coakley) *hld up: gng wl but in last pair 3f out: pushed along over 2f out: reminder and no real prog over 1f out: nvr nr ldrs* **12/1**
1531 **10** *hd* **Queen Noverre (IRE)**[23] 5539 3-9-1 **78** (p) TQuinn 9 73
(J W Hills) *pressed ldr: upsides 3f out: wknd on inner wl over 1f out* **16/1**
6060 **11** *1 3/4* **Prime Contender**[140] 2003 5-9-0 **72** AdamKirby 4 64
(G L Moore) *hld up in rr: rdn and lost tch over 3f out: no ch after* **66/1**
4430 **12** *15* **Arctic Wings (IRE)**[16] 5732 3-8-4 **67** (b[1]) MartinDwyer 10 29
(W R Muir) *t.k.h: led after 2f to 3f out: wknd rapidly: t.o* **33/1**

2m 6.63s (-1.16) **Going Correction** 0.0s/f (Stan)
WFA 3 from 4yo+ 5lb **12** Ran SP% **119.8**
Speed ratings (Par 105): **104,103,103,99,98 98,97,97,96,96 94,82**
CSF £99.10 CT £565.15 TOTE £7.80: £2.60, £4.70, £2.20; EX 109.90 TRIFECTA Not won. Place 6 £238.65, Place 5 £60.04.
Owner Serendipity Syndicate 2006 **Bred** R Charles **Trained** Blewbury, Oxon

FOCUS
The front three drew clear in what was a very decent handicap for the grade. The winner and third are both progressive and the form seems pretty sound.
Rhyming Slang(USA) Official explanation: jockey said he had no explanation for the poor form shown
Arctic Wings(IRE) Official explanation: jockey said colt ran too free
T/Plt: £316.30 to a £1 stake. Pool: £53,261.20. 122.90 winning tickets. T/Qpdt: £90.60 to a £1 stake. Pool: £4,412.40. 36.00 winning tickets. JN

6064 WOLVERHAMPTON (A.W) (L-H)
Friday, October 12

OFFICIAL GOING: Standard
The Clerk of the Course thought the going was probably a shade on the slow side.
Wind: Nil Weather: Fine

6146 MACE RACING AT WOLVERHAMPTON H'CAP 1m 1f 103y(P)
6:30 (6:30) (Class 5) (0-70,70) 3-Y-O+ **£2,968** (£876; £438) **Stalls** Low

Form RPR
0213 **1** **Kansas Gold**[7] 5983 4-8-12 **62** PatCosgrave 10 72
(J Mackie) *a.p: wnt 2nd 7f out: led 2f out: rdn over 1f out: edgd lft wl ins fnl f: drvn out* **4/1**[1]
4002 **2** *1/2* **Emily's Place (IRE)**[7] 5983 4-8-8 **58** J-PGuillambert 5 67
(J Pearce) *hld up in tch: rdn over 3f out: r.o to take 2nd cl home* **5/1**[2]
1040 **3** *1 1/4* **Distiller (IRE)**[14] 5777 3-9-2 **70** FergusSweeney 6 76
(W R Muir) *hld up towards rr: rdn and hdwy wl over 1f out: r.o ins fnl f* **11/1**
016 **4** *shd* **Abbondanza (IRE)**[7] 5983 4-9-6 **70** (p) TomEaves 3 76
(I Semple) *t.k.h: led after 1f: hdd 2f out: rdn over 1f out: no ex towards fin* **4/1**[1]
531 **5** *2 1/2* **Our Kes (IRE)**[7] 5983 5-9-5 **69** 6ex IanMongan 9 70+
(P Howling) *hld up in mid-div: nt clr run over 2f out: r.o fnl f: nt trble ldrs* **6/1**[3]
1-00 **6** *3/4* **Alekhine (IRE)**[67] 4231 6-9-2 **66** GrahamGibbons 1 65
(J W Unett) *hld up in mid-div: rdn and hdwy on ins wl over 1f out: no imp fnl f* **40/1**
0132 **7** *1 1/2* **Corrib (IRE)**[29] 5348 4-9-1 **65** HayleyTurner 2 61
(B Palling) *led 1f: prom: rdn over 2f out: wknd over 1f out* **14/1**
6063 **8** *3/4* **Ella Y Rossa**[45] 4918 3-8-8 **62** TGMcLaughlin 11 57
(P D Evans) *a bhd* **16/1**
0500 **9** *1* **Tanforan**[20] 5645 5-8-7 **57** (p) TPO'Shea 4 49
(B P J Baugh) *s.i.s: a bhd* **16/1**
0330 **10** *7* **Climate (IRE)**[202] 768 8-8-6 **61** RussellKennemore(5) 8 39
(R Hollinshead) *plld hrd in tch: rdn 3f out: wknd wl over 1f out* **22/1**
1656 **11** *1 1/4* **Vesuvio**[22] 5555 3-8-4 **58** ChrisCatlin 7 33
(C W Thornton) *a bhd* **13/2**

2m 3.55s (0.93) **Going Correction** -0.05s/f (Stan)
WFA 3 from 4yo+ 4lb **11** Ran SP% **117.8**
Speed ratings (Par 103): **93,92,91,91,89 88,87,86,85,79 78**
CSF £23.64 CT £205.74 TOTE £6.40: £2.20, £1.20, £4.90; EX 31.40.
Owner A J Winterton **Bred** Coln Valley Stud **Trained** Church Broughton , Derbys

FOCUS
The pace was steady for much of the way, resulting in a time 1.01 seconds slower than the later 0-45 classified contest, and the form wants treating with a bit of caution. The winner, second and fourth were always up with the pace.

6147 RINGSIDE SUITE 700 THEATRE STYLE CONFERENCE CLASSIFIED STKS 1m 4f 50y(P)
7:00 (7:01) (Class 6) 3-Y-O **£2,047** (£604; £302) **Stalls** Low

Form RPR
5634 **1** **Sir Duke (IRE)**[22] 5573 3-8-12 54 (e[1]) LiamJones 4 64
(P W D'Arcy) *a.p: led 5f out tl over 3f out: led over 2f out: rdn over 1f out: edgd lft ins fnl f: drvn out* **15/8**[1]
0022 **2** *1 3/4* **Ardmaddy (IRE)**[9] 5894 3-8-12 55 TPO'Shea 2 61
(J A R Toller) *hld up towards rr: hdwy on outside over 2f out: rdn wl over 1f out: wnt 2nd and hung lft ins fnl f: nt qckn* **4/1**[3]
0400 **3** *3* **Soldier Field**[34] 5237 3-8-9 55 NeilChalmers(3) 1 56
(A M Balding) *prom 2f: hld up in mid-div: hdwy over 3f out: rdn over 1f out: wknd wl ins fnl f* **7/2**[2]
2303 **4** *2* **Black Mogul**[27] 5427 3-8-12 52 (b) RichardMullen 8 53
(W R Muir) *a.p: led over 3f out tl over 2f out: sn rdn: wknd fnl f* **17/2**
0064 **5** *3* **Lawyer To World**[20] 5640 3-8-12 55 HayleyTurner 6 48
(Mrs C A Dunnett) *t.k.h in tch: rdn over 3f out: wkng whn hung lft wl over 1f out* **12/1**
-U00 **6** *4* **Stay Active (USA)**[12] 5840 3-8-12 54 TomEaves 7 42
(I Semple) *hld up in tch: rdn and wknd over 3f out* **25/1**
0052 **7** *3/4* **Beckenham's Secret**[35] 5187 3-8-12 52 FergusSweeney 5 41
(A W Carroll) *stdd s: a bhd* **8/1**
60 **8** *4* **Little Red Roaster (USA)**[9] 5916 3-8-12 55 TGMcLaughlin 10 34
(P D Evans) *hld up towards rr: hdwy over 5f out: wknd over 3f out* **33/1**
-000 **9** *9* **Iceni Princess**[62] 4392 3-8-12 36 LPKeniry 3 20
(P Howling) *s.i.s: rdn over 3f out: a bhd* **50/1**
-230 **10** *44* **My Beautaful**[14] 5783 3-8-12 55 AdrianMcCarthy 9 —
(Miss J S Davis) *led: hdd 5f out: rdn and wknd 4f out: t.o fnl 3f* **28/1**
0U00 **11** *8* **Come On Nellie (IRE)**[29] 5347 3-8-12 44 ChrisCatlin 11 —
(J G M O'Shea) *s.i.s: a in rr: t.o fnl 5f* **66/1**

2m 41.8s (-0.62) **Going Correction** -0.05s/f (Stan) **11** Ran SP% **120.0**
Speed ratings (Par 99): **100,98,96,95,93 90,90,87,81,52 47**
CSF £9.16 TOTE £3.30: £1.60, £1.50, £1.30; EX 11.10.
Owner Mrs Jan Harris **Bred** Southern Bloodstock **Trained** Newmarket, Suffolk
■ Stewards' Enquiry : Liam Jones one-day ban: used whip with excessive force (Oct 23)

FOCUS
A weak classified event, but sound for the grade, with the winner back to form and the second running to his recent level.
My Beautaful Official explanation: jockey said filly was hanging in closing stages

6148 JOIN WBX.COM FOR FREE FOOTBALL SHIRT H'CAP 7f 32y(P)
7:30 (7:30) (Class 6) (0-65,64) 3-Y-O+ **£2,047** (£604; £302) **Stalls** High

Form RPR
0020 **1** **Sedge (USA)**[17] 5701 7-9-5 **63** (b) HayleyTurner 2 77+
(P T Midgley) *a gng wl: led on bit 1f out: sn rdn: r.o wl* **4/1**[1]
0500 **2** *3* **Northern Boy (USA)**[89] 3571 4-9-2 **60** PaulMulrennan 1 66
(M W Easterby) *w ldr: led over 2f out: rdn and hdd 1f out: one pce* **6/1**[2]
1216 **3** *1/2* **Bold Cross (IRE)**[20] 5645 4-9-5 **63** PaulFitzsimons 11 68+
(E G Bevan) *s.i.s: towards rr: rdn over 3f out: hdwy on outside over 2f out: r.o ins fnl f* **9/1**
0030 **4** *nk* **Summer Recluse (USA)**[11] 5866 8-9-3 **61** (t) LPKeniry 6 65
(J M Bradley) *hld up and bhd: swtchd rt over 1f out: sn edgd lft: hdwy fnl f: nrst fin* **25/1**
0004 **5** *nk* **Proper (IRE)**[4] 6055 3-9-3 **63** DarryllHolland 10 66
(M R Channon) *hld up in mid-div: hdwy 4f out: rdn over 2f out: one pce fnl f* **6/1**[2]
0662 **6** *1 1/4* **Airman (IRE)**[27] 5433 4-9-4 **62** JamieSpencer 3 62
(W M Brisbourne) *sn outpcd and bhd: nt clr run on ins over 2f out: hdwy over 1f out: one pce fnl f* **4/1**[1]
3400 **7** *1 1/2* **Benny The Bus**[20] 5643 5-9-2 **60** GrahamGibbons 5 56
(Mrs G S Rees) *prom: rdn over 2f out: wknd ins fnl f* **8/1**[3]
3360 **8** *2* **Haroldini (IRE)**[9] 5909 5-8-10 **59** (p) TolleyDean(5) 8 49
(J Balding) *hld up in tch: rdn over 4f out: wknd wl over 1f out* **16/1**
0000 **9** *3/4* **Sir Orpen (IRE)**[62] 4407 4-9-4 **62** TomEaves 9 50
(T D Barron) *s.i.s: hld up and bhd: rdn over 3f out: nvr nr ldrs* **16/1**
1060 **10** *3 1/2* **Mr Loire**[15] 5753 3-8-9 **62** (b) MarkCoumbe(7) 7 41
(A J Chamberlain) *a towards rr* **66/1**
5650 **11** *2 1/2* **Roman Quintet (IRE)**[10] 5879 7-9-5 **63** TGMcLaughlin 4 35
(R J Price) *hld up in mid-div: nt clr run on ins over 2f out: rdn over 1f out: wknd fnl f* **9/1**
/040 **12** *2* **Pivotal Era**[111] 2877 4-9-6 **64** (p) RichardThomas 12 31
(Jim Best) *led: rdn and hdd over 2f out: wknd over 1f out* **33/1**

1m 29.99s (-0.41) **Going Correction** -0.05s/f (Stan)
WFA 3 from 4yo+ 2lb **12** Ran SP% **119.7**
Speed ratings (Par 101): **100,96,96,95,95 93,92,89,89,85 82,79**
CSF £27.39 CT £210.07 TOTE £6.00: £1.50, £2.00, £2.60; EX 44.20.
Owner Colin Alton **Bred** Twin Creeks Farm **Trained** Westow, N Yorks

FOCUS
A modest handicap. The winner impressed for the grade and the third looks perhaps the best guide.

6149 WBX.COM £25 FOR NEW ACCOUNTS H'CAP 5f 216y(P)
7:55 (7:56) (Class 6) (0-55,61) 3-Y-O+ **£2,047** (£604; £302) **Stalls** Low

Form | | | | RPR
5102 **1** **Jilly Why (IRE)**[4] 6064 6-9-0 **55** ....(b) JamieSpencer 5 70+
(Paul Green) *hld up and bhd: nt clr run over 2f out: swtchd rt ent st: rdn and hdwy over 1f out: led wl ins fnl f: r.o wl* **13/2**[3]
0641 **2** *2 ½* **Bond Playboy**[4] 6064 7-8-8 **54** ....(p) SladeO'Hara(5) 13 61
(G R Oldroyd) *s.i.s: sn prom: rdn to ld wl over 1f out: sn edgd lft: hdd and nt qckn wl ins fnl f* **4/1**[1]
036 **3** *½* **Perlachy**[40] 5066 3-8-11 **53** ....(v) DanielTudhope 7 58
(Mrs N Macauley) *hld up and bhd: hdwy on wd outside over 2f out: rdn over 1f out: kpt on ins fnl f* **33/1**
0602 **4** *1 ¼* **Blue Bird's Dream**[14] 5781 4-9-0 **55** .... SebSanders 10 56
(E J Alston) *a.p: rdn over 3f out: one pce fnl 2f* **9/2**[2]
0050 **5** *¾* **Night In (IRE)**[16] 5741 4-8-13 **54** ....(vt[1]) KimTinkler 1 53
(N Tinkler) *s.i.s: in rr: rdn over 1f out: kpt on ins fnl f: nt rch ldrs* **10/1**
0422 **6** *¾* **Monda**[16] 5741 5-8-9 **50** .... TomEaves 4 47
(Miss J A Camacho) *chsd ldrs: rdn over 3f out: wknd wl ins fnl f* **4/1**[1]
0000 **7** *1 ¼* **Blythe Spirit**[85] 3674 8-8-9 **50** ....(v) LiamJones 2 43
(Mrs L Williamson) *chsd ldrs: lost pl after 2f: n.d after* **25/1**
0-00 **8** *shd* **Almondillo (IRE)**[168] 1282 3-8-11 **53** .... DarryllHolland 11 45
(C F Wall) *prom: hmpd over 3f out: sn lost pl* **14/1**
0053 **9** *nk* **One Way Ticket**[8] 5947 7-8-9 **50** ....(b) HayleyTurner 6 41
(J M Bradley) *led: rdn and hdd wl over 1f out: wknd ins fnl f* **13/2**[3]
3300 **10** *6* **Tenancy (IRE)**[10] 5890 3-8-3 **52** ....(be[1]) RobbieEgan(7) 8 24
(A J McCabe) *t.k.h: sn mid-div: rdn and wknd wl over 1f out: eased ins fnl f* **25/1**
0000 **11** *1 ½* **Exponential (IRE)**[11] 5861 5-8-13 **54** ....(b) LPKeniry 9 21
(J M Bradley) *w ldr tl rdn over 2f out: wknd wl over 1f out* **40/1**

1m 15.75s (-0.06) **Going Correction** -0.05s/f (Stan)
WFA 3 from 4yo+ 1lb **11 Ran SP% 113.7**
Speed ratings (Par 101): **98,94,94,92,91 90,88,88,88,80 78**
CSF £30.24 CT £805.22 TOTE £7.10: £1.40, £2.30, £6.50; EX 16.00.
Owner Paul Green (Oaklea) **Bred** K & Mrs Cullen **Trained** Lydiate, Merseyside

FOCUS
A moderate sprint handicap in which the first two reversed C/D placings from earlier in the week. Fairly sound form.
Almondillo(IRE) Official explanation: jockey said gelding lost its place on the bend

6150 AIR TECHNOLOGY SYSTEMS QUINDECENNIAL ANNIVERSARY NURSERY 1m 141y(P)
8:25 (8:26) (Class 6) (0-65,65) 2-Y-O **£2,047** (£604; £302) **Stalls** Low

Form | | | | RPR
0603 **1** **Race The Moon (IRE)**[9] 5896 2-8-13 **60** ....(e) JerryO'Dwyer(3) 12 69
(V Smith) *stdd s: hld up in rr: hdwy on ins wl over 1f out: rdn to ld ins fnl f: r.o wl* **9/1**
6432 **2** *2* **Bermacha**[9] 5896 2-9-7 **65** .... RichardMullen 10 70
(W R Muir) *hld up in tch: led over 3f out: rdn over 2f out: hdd and nt qckn ins fnl f* **5/1**[2]
5063 **3** *2 ½* **Warming Up (IRE)**[9] 5914 2-9-3 **61** .... SebSanders 6 61
(C E Brittain) *bhd: rdn 7f out: hdwy on outside over 3f out: one pce fnl f* **4/1**[1]
0110 **4** *2 ½* **Marmite (IRE)**[37] 5127 2-9-6 **64** ....(b) LPKeniry 13 58
(E F Vaughan) *bhd: rdn and hdwy 1f out: sn hung lft: nvr trbld ldrs* **20/1**
0560 **5** *2* **Ras Laffan**[27] 5423 2-9-5 **63** .... GrahamGibbons 2 53+
(E S McMahon) *led over 1f: prom: rdn over 3f out: nt clr run briefly on ins 2f out: sn wknd* **10/1**
4500 **6** *2* **Weet By Far**[6] 6022 2-9-7 **65** .... FergusSweeney 11 51
(R Hollinshead) *hld up and bhd: rdn and hdwy over 2f out: wknd over 1f out* **66/1**
4543 **7** *½* **Countrywide Comet (IRE)**[9] 5902 2-9-1 **59** ....(p) DO'Donohoe 9 44
(K A Ryan) *prom: rdn over 2f out: wknd 1f out* **16/1**
056 **8** *5* **Cryptonite Diamond (USA)**[17] 5707 2-9-2 **60** .... HayleyTurner 4 34
(W R Swinburn) *wnt lft s: prom: lost pl over 4f out: n.d after* **7/1**[3]
0210 **9** *3 ½* **Never Sold Out (IRE)**[38] 5117 2-9-1 **59** .... PaulEddery 7 26
(J G M O'Shea) *bhd fnl 3f* **66/1**
3400 **10** *1 ¾* **Heavenly Saint**[16] 5727 2-9-0 **58** .... DarryllHolland 1 21
(M R Channon) *led 7f out: rdn and hdd over 3f out: wknd wl over 1f out* **20/1**
006 **11** *6* **Lenouska (IRE)**[35] 5186 2-9-2 **60** .... ChrisCatlin 3 11
(B De Haan) *n.m.r s: a in rr* **20/1**
0064 **12** *3* **Johnny Friendly**[33] 5251 2-9-1 **59** .... JamieSpencer 5 3+
(K R Burke) *prom: w ldr 6f out tl rdn and wknd wl over 2f out: eased whn no ch over 1f out* **10/1**
6022 **13** *9* **Hurstpierpoint (IRE)**[13] 5818 2-9-6 **64** .... PaulHanagan 8 —
(R A Fahey) *prom: hmpd and lost pl after 1f: rdn 3f out: sn bhd* **5/1**[2]

1m 52.21s (0.45) **Going Correction** -0.05s/f (Stan) **13 Ran SP% 117.2**
Speed ratings (Par 93): **96,94,92,89,88 86,85,81,78,76 71,68,60**
CSF £49.21 CT £218.22 TOTE £8.40: £6.20, £1.90, £2.20; EX 33.40.
Owner Stephen Dartnell **Bred** Tally-Ho Stud **Trained** Exning, Suffolk

FOCUS
A modest nursery run at a good pace. Solid form with the first two clear, Race The Moon reversing Kempton form with Bertacha.

NOTEBOOK
Race The Moon(IRE) was ridden with tremendous confidence by Jerry O'Dwyer, who held his mount up at least ten lengths off the lead early in the back straight having dropped in from his wide draw, and he then had the audacity to stick to the inside rail on the turn for home. The winner is clearly progressing, although he does seem reliant on a strong pace. (op 15-2 tchd 11-1)
Bermacha ran her race and took care of all bar the patiently ridden winner, who looks a step ahead of the Handicapper. She is holding her form well and looks capable of winning a similar event. (op 9-2 tchd 11-2)
Warming Up(IRE) was in trouble a long way out and he appeared unsuited by the drop in trip. He is very much a stayer in the making. (op 9-2 tchd 3-1)
Marmite(IRE) was well placed to win a couple of sellers in the summer, but she was not quite up to this. (op 18-1 tchd 22-1)
Ras Laffan finished up well held and will need to improve to win off his current mark. (op 16-1)
Johnny Friendly Official explanation: jockey said colt ran too freely early
Hurstpierpoint(IRE) was squeezed out on the first bend and looked beaten down the back straight. Official explanation: jockey said filly suffered interference in running (tchd 9-2)

6151 STAY AT THE WOLVERHAMPTON HOLIDAY INN CLAIMING STKS 5f 216y(P)
8:55 (8:56) (Class 6) 2-Y-O **£2,047** (£604; £302) **Stalls** Low

Form | | | | RPR
1006 **1** **What Katie Did (IRE)**[21] 5601 2-9-5 74 .... JamieSpencer 10 68
(J A Osborne) *w ldr: rdn over 1f out: led ins fnl f: r.o* **5/4**[1]
4000 **2** *½* **I Dont Do Walkin (USA)**[9] 5895 2-9-0 68 ....(b) DarryllHolland 3 61
(B J Meehan) *led: rdn over 1f out: hdd ins fnl f: kpt on* **14/1**
0 **3** *1 ½* **Young Ivanhoe**[22] 5575 2-9-2 0 ....(t) SebSanders 5 59
(P J McBride) *hld up in mid-div: rdn over 1f out: swtchd rt jst ins fnl f: r.o* **4/1**[2]
2100 **4** *nk* **Brixworth Scribe**[30] 5331 2-9-5 71 .... PaulEddery 6 61
(B Smart) *s.i.s: sn mid-div: rdn wl over 1f out: edgd lft ins fnl f: kpt on* **20/1**
050 **5** *hd* **Copperbottomed (IRE)**[11] 5856 2-9-2 0 .... GrahamGibbons 2 57
(R Hollinshead) *hld up: hdwy on ins over 2f out: rdn over 1f out: one pce ins fnl f* **28/1**
2665 **6** *nk* **Tenjack Queen (IRE)**[37] 5133 2-8-4 61 .... ChrisCatlin 1 44
(Miss Tor Sturgis) *prom: rdn wl over 1f out: no ex ins fnl f* **6/1**[3]
00 **7** *hd* **Listed Art**[11] 5872 2-9-0 0 .... TPO'Shea 9 54
(B J Meehan) *sn prom: rdn wl over 1f out: no ex ins fnl f* **20/1**
0104 **8** *¾* **Lord Deevert**[2] 6099 2-8-7 71 .... JackDean(7) 8 51
(W G M Turner) *sn prom: rdn wl over 1f out: fdd ins fnl f* **14/1**
6 **9** *hd* **Bahia Palace**[6] 6023 2-8-4 0 .... HayleyTurner 13 41
(M D I Usher) *in rr: hdwy on ins wl over 1f out: one pce whn nt clr run wl ins fnl f* **28/1**
00 **10** *9* **April Reigns**[31] 5302 2-8-4 0 .... RichardThomas 4 14
(D Burchell) *prom: rdn over 2f out: wknd wl over 1f out* **100/1**
1163 **11** *2 ½* **Genethni**[10] 5887 2-8-11 62 .... DO'Donohoe 12 13
(K A Ryan) *hung rt thrght: prom: rn wd ent st: sn wknd: drifted to stands' rail ins fnl f* **7/1**
00 **12** *1 ½* **Muga (SPA)**[20] 5644 2-8-1 0 .... SCreighton(5) 11 4
(E J Creighton) *prom: lost pl after 2f: bhd fnl 3f* **100/1**

1m 16.25s (0.44) **Going Correction** -0.05s/f (Stan) **12 Ran SP% 123.0**
Speed ratings (Par 93): **95,94,92,91,91 91,91,90,89,77 74,72**
CSF £21.31 TOTE £1.80: £1.30, £3.30, £2.20; EX 20.80.
Owner Mountgrange Stud **Bred** Brian Williamson **Trained** Upper Lambourn, Berks

FOCUS
A reasonable claimer on paper, but the time was pretty ordinary and the first two home were in the first two throughout. The likes of the fifth help set the level.

NOTEBOOK
What Katie Did(IRE) has not progressed since winning a couple of Polytrack nurseries back in August, but the drop in grade did the trick. He was able to dispute the lead with the eventual runner-up at a sensible pace and stayed on best of all in the straight. (op 7-4 tchd 11-10)
I Dont Do Walkin(USA), dropped in grade, was always well positioned considering the lack of pace and she ran well in second. (op 8-1)
Young Ivanhoe showed ability on his debut at Yarmouth and this was another respectable effort. He fared best of those to race off the moderate pace and gives the impression he can progress again, although the need for a tongue-tie is a bit of a concern. (op 6-1)
Brixworth Scribe ran a respectable race dropped in class and he should be able to find a similar event. (op 16-1)
Copperbottomed(IRE) hinted at ability at Beverley two starts back and this was a respectable effort. (op 25-1 tchd 33-1)
Tenjack Queen(IRE) was backed in from 16/1, but she failed to land the gamble. (op 14-1 tchd 16-1)
Bahia Palace Official explanation: jockey said filly was denied a clear run
Genethni Official explanation: jockey said filly hung badly right-handed

6152 WOLVERHAMPTON-RACECOURSE.CO.UK CLASSIFIED STKS 1m 1f 103y(P)
9:20 (9:20) (Class 7) 3-Y-O+ **£1,911** (£564; £282) **Stalls** Low

Form | | | | RPR
0-00 **1** **Pindar (GER)**[269] 152 3-8-12 45 .... JamieSpencer 7 58
(B J Curley) *t.k.h in rr: hdwy on outside over 2f out: sn rdn: led wl ins fnl f: r.o* **2/1**[1]
0345 **2** *1 ¾* **Fantastic Delight**[14] 5782 4-9-2 45 .... SebSanders 2 54
(B G Powell) *hld up in mid-div: hdwy over 3f out: rdn to ld wl over 1f out: edgd rt and hdd wl ins fnl f: nt qckn* **4/1**[3]
5166 **3** *3 ½* **Mountain Climb (IRE)**[14] 5782 5-8-11 45 .... HaddenFrost(5) 10 47
(J D Frost) *t.k.h: led after 1f: hdd over 6f out: one pce fnl f* **10/3**[2]
000 **4** *1 ¾* **Mighty Mover (IRE)**[17] 5709 5-9-2 45 .... HayleyTurner 8 43
(B Palling) *a.p: led wl over 2f out: rdn and hdd wl over 1f out: wknd ins fnl f* **66/1**
0060 **5** *shd* **Gifted Flame**[15] 5756 8-9-2 45 ....(p) TomEaves 1 43
(T D Barron) *s.i.s: hld up in rr: c wd st: rdn over 1f out: one pce fnl f* **17/2**
0040 **6** *3* **Shadow Jumper (IRE)**[21] 5606 6-8-11 44 ....(v) RussellKennemore(5) 6 36
(J T Stimpson) *led 1f: prom: lost pl over 4f out: rdn over 3f out: wknd ins fnl f* **16/1**
0000 **7** *¾* **Fairy Monarch (IRE)**[7] 5966 8-9-2 44 ....(b) MickyFenton 9 35
(P T Midgley) *hld up towards rr: rdn 3f out: nt clr run and swtchd rt over 1f out: n.d* **20/1**
0000 **8** *2* **Alisar (IRE)**[248] 372 7-8-13 45 ....(t) AlanCreighton(3) 5 31
(E J Creighton) *prom: rdn and ev ch over 2f out: wknd wl over 1f out* **33/1**
0050 **9** *1 ¾* **Arabellas Homer**[9] 5915 3-8-12 45 .... DanielTudhope 4 27
(Mrs N Macauley) *hld up in tch: rdn over 2f out: wknd wl over 1f out* **50/1**
00-0 **10** *1 ¾* **Scene Three**[139] 2032 3-8-12 45 .... GrahamGibbons 13 23
(J J Quinn) *stdd s: sn swtchd lft: rdn over 4f out: a in rr* **28/1**
0000 **11** *1* **Goodwood Spirit**[35] 5189 5-9-2 45 ....(v) LPKeniry 3 21
(J M Bradley) *hld up towards rr: stdy hdwy over 3f out: wknd wl over 1f out* **16/1**
3000 **12** *7* **Richtee (IRE)**[10] 4031 6-9-2 45 ....(b[1]) RoystonFfrench 11 7
(I W McInnes) *s.s after rdr slow to remove blindfold: hdwy to ld over 6f out: rdn and hdd wl over 2f out: sn wknd* **12/1**
0300 **13** *13* **Show Me The Lolly (FR)**[36] 5179 7-9-2 44 ....(t) RichardMullen 12 —
(S W Hall) *s.i.s: sn carried lft: a in rr* **20/1**

2m 2.54s (-0.08) **Going Correction** -0.05s/f (Stan)
WFA 3 from 4yo+ 4lb **13 Ran SP% 125.8**
Speed ratings (Par 97): **98,96,93,91,91 89,88,86,85,83 82,76,64**
CSF £9.63 TOTE £3.20: £1.40, £1.70, £1.80; EX 18.70 Place 6 £17.64, Place 5 £8.68.
Owner Curley Leisure **Bred** Gestut Schlenderhan **Trained** Newmarket, Suffolk

FOCUS
A reasonable event for the lowly grade, won by the unexposed Pindar from a consistent runner-up. The winning time was 1.01 seconds quicker than the earlier 56-70 handicap, although that race was slowly run and direct comparisons will be misleading.
T/Plt: £26.20 to a £1 stake. Pool: £82,635.05. 2,297.75 winning tickets. T/Qpdt: £7.80 to a £1 stake. Pool: £6,164.90. 578.40 winning tickets. KH

[5251]YORK (L-H)

Friday, October 12

OFFICIAL GOING: Good (good to soft in places; 6.9)

Wind: Moderate, across Weather: Warm, sunny periods

6153 GARBUTT & ELLIOTT STKS (CONDITIONS RACE) 1m 2f 88y

2:10 (2:11) (Class 3) 3-Y-0+

£9,348 (£2,799; £1,399; £700; £349; £175) **Stalls** Low

Form RPR

1332 **1** **Fairmile**[30] 5326 5-9-2 **107** TedDurcan 3 114+
(Saeed Bin Suroor) *hld up: hdwy on bit 4f out: trckd ldrs 3f out: cl up 2f out: sn led: rdn clr ent fnl f: kpt on wl* **7/2**[3]

3045 **2** *3* **Sunshine Kid (USA)**[20] 5618 3-8-11 **107** JimmyFortune 2 108
(J H M Gosden) *trckd ldrs on inner: hdwy to chse wnr 3f out: rdn along over 2f out: drvn and kpt on ins fnl f* **8/1**

1-60 **3** *1* **Best Alibi (IRE)**[195] 861 4-9-2 **114** LDettori 7 106
(Saeed Bin Suroor) *led: pushed along over 3f out: rdn 2f out: hdd wl over 1f out: sn drvn and kpt on same pce* **5/2**[1]

1 **4** *hd* **Arqaam**[36] 5157 3-8-13 **0** RHills 4 108
(Saeed Bin Suroor) *s.i.s and bhd: stdy hdwy 1/2-way: chsd ldrs over 2f out: rdn to chse wnr ent fnl f: sn drvn and one pce* **16/1**

4160 **5** *nk* **Charlie Tokyo (IRE)**[20] 5618 4-9-2 **105** (b) PaulHanagan 8 105
(R A Fahey) *hld up in tch: hdwy 3f out: rdn 2f out: styd on ins fnl f: nrst fin* **14/1**

1- **6** *1 1/2* **Spanish Moon (USA)**[349] 6220 3-8-11 **96** RyanMoore 5 102
(Sir Michael Stoute) *trckd ldrs: effrt 4f out: rdn along 3f out: wknd 2f out* **3/1**[2]

0- **7** *22* **Ursis (FR)**[170] 6336 6-9-2 **92** DarryllHolland 1 61
(S Gollings) *a bhd* **100/1**

3022 **8** *1 1/2* **Dunaskin (IRE)**[20] 5618 7-9-2 **107** KDarley 9 58
(Karen McLintock) *s.i.s: sn chsng ldrs: rdn along over 4f out and wknd qckly: sn bhd* **7/1**

3-0 **9** *25* **Britannic**[27] 5411 4-9-2 **99** NCallan 6 10
(T P Tate) *prom: rdn along 4f out: wknd over 3f out and sn eased* **80/1**

2m 10.97s (-1.53) **Going Correction** +0.20s/f (Good)
WFA 3 from 4yo+ 5lb **9** Ran SP% **114.2**
Speed ratings (Par 107): **114,111,110,110,110 109,91,90,70**
CSF £31.21 TOTE £4.40: £1.60, £2.40, £1.50; EX 36.40.
Owner Godolphin **Bred** Pendley Farm **Trained** Newmarket, Suffolk

FOCUS
A good-quality contest considering the status of the race and strong form for the grade. Fairmile did not quite have to match his latest improved run, and the second and fifth ran to form.

NOTEBOOK
Fairmile, runner-up in a good handicap at Doncaster on his return from a break last time out, had clearly come on for that and was strong in the market beforehand despite carrying the second colours of Godolphin. He travelled well into contention and came clear in good style, albeit while flashing his tail under pressure. He deserves to take his chance in Pattern company now. (op 4-1)
Sunshine Kid(USA), fifth in a Listed race last time out, kept on under pressure to beat the rest for second place. He likes a bit of dig in the ground and seemed to run to his best, but he looks like one of those hard-to-place types. (op 11-1)
Best Alibi(IRE) had the highest official rating in the race and wore the first colours of Godolphin, but he had not been seen since disappointing in the desert back in the spring and, while he won a Group 2 race over this course and distance last year for Sir Michael Stoute, he had yet to show that level of form for his current connections. He made most of the running, but his stablemate had too much toe for him in the closing stages and this has to go down as a bit of a disappointing effort. (tchd 11-4 and 3-1 in a place)
Arqaam, the stable's third string on jockey bookings, had only won a modest maiden at Redcar 36 days earlier, but he is well bred and this represented a marked step up on that form. He can only improve for this and, while it is probably the last of his connections' concerns, it has blown what would have been a very favourable handicap mark. Official explanation: jockey said colt missed the break (tchd 14-1)
Charlie Tokyo(IRE), who has graduated out of handicap company but threatens to become something of a twilight horse now, was staying on nicely enough at the finish. (op 16-1 tchd 11-1)
Spanish Moon(USA) had at one stage been considered a Derby prospect but he had been absent for almost a year since winning a soft-ground Newmarket maiden and he was a bit disappointing here considering conditions appeared to be in his favour and the betting suggested he was fit and ready. (op 11-4 tchd 5-2)
Dunaskin(IRE) is at his best when allowed an uncontested lead. Official explanation: jockey said gelding lost its action (op 8-1)
Britannic Official explanation: jockey said gelding moved poorly throughout

6154 ACORN WEB OFFSET STKS (NURSERY) 6f

2:40 (2:40) (Class 3) 2-Y-0 **£7,124** (£2,119; £1,059; £529) **Stalls** Centre

Form RPR

031 **1** **Floristry**[26] 5442 2-9-7 **89** RyanMoore 10 97
(Sir Michael Stoute) *hld up: gd hdwy towards stands' side over 2f out: rdn to ld 1f out: hld on wl towards fin* **8/1**

51 **2** *nk* **Striking Spirit**[35] 5193 2-9-3 **85** MichaelHills 2 92
(B W Hills) *trckd ldrs: hdwy on wd outside 1/2-way: cl up 2f out: rdn to ld wl over 1f out: hdd 1f out: drvn: edgd rt and kpt on fnl f* **4/1**[1]

41 **3** *1 3/4* **Excitement (IRE)**[33] 5252 2-8-12 **80** PaulHanagan 4 82
(R A Fahey) *t.k.h: in tch: hdwy 2f out: sn rdn to chse ldrs: styd on ins fnl f* **13/2**[2]

0013 **4** *3/4* **Upton Grey (IRE)**[21] 5582 2-9-6 **88** JimmyFortune 7 88
(J H M Gosden) *prom: rdn 2f out and ev ch tl drvn ent fnl f and kpt on same pce* **8/1**

6013 **5** *3/4* **Aye Aye Digby (IRE)**[23] 5536 2-9-5 **87** FergusSweeney 9 84
(H Candy) *chsd ldrs: rdn along wl over 1f out: drvn and kpt on same pce fnl f* **12/1**

1 **6** *nk* **Mazaaya (USA)**[16] 5735 2-8-11 **79** GregFairley 1 75
(M Johnston) *cl up: led 1/2-way: rdn along 2f out: sn hdd and grad wknd appr fnl f* **15/2**[3]

2146 **7** *1/2* **Guertino (IRE)**[34] 5216 2-9-7 **89** TomEaves 6 84
(B Smart) *hld up in rr: hdwy and nt clr run over 2f out: swtchd rt over 1f out: sn rdn and kpt on same pce ins fnl f* **8/1**

01 **8** *nk* **Love Valentine (IRE)**[23] 5527 2-7-13 **67** LiamJones 12 61
(M Johnston) *chsd ldrs: rdn along 2f out: sn no imp* **22/1**

0005 **9** *2* **Border Defence (IRE)**[10] 5888 2-7-13 **67** oh9 ow1(v[1]) FrankieMcDonald 3 55
(P A Blockley) *led to 1/2-way: cl up tl rdn along 2f out and sn wknd* **100/1**

51 **10** *3/4* **Writingonthewall (IRE)**[24] 5501 2-8-10 **78** DarryllHolland 5 64
(M L W Bell) *t.k.h: chsd ldrs: rdn along over 2f out: wknd over 1f out* **13/2**[2]

1060 **11** *3/4* **Lieutenant Pigeon**[69] 4175 2-7-10 **67** DuranFentiman(3) 8 51
(T D Easterby) *prom: rdn along 2f out and grad wknd* **66/1**

10 **12** *nk* **Artistic License (IRE)**[14] 5766 2-8-5 **73** TPO'Shea 13 56
(M R Channon) *hld up: a towards rr* **16/1**

5202 **13** *8* **Rubirosa (IRE)**[21] 5582 2-9-4 **86** PhillipMakin 11 45
(M Dods) *in tch: rdn along over 2f out: sn wknd* **9/1**

1m 13.67s (1.11) **Going Correction** +0.20s/f (Good) **13** Ran SP% **122.2**
Speed ratings (Par 99): **100,99,97,96,95 94,94,93,91,90 89,88,78**
CSF £40.53 CT £235.29 TOTE £8.70: £3.10, £2.20, £2.30; EX 31.20.
Owner Gainsborough **Bred** Gainsborough Stud Management Ltd **Trained** Newmarket, Suffolk
■ Stewards' Enquiry : Tom Eaves one-day ban: careless riding (Oct 23)

FOCUS
A strong nursery, but there was not a great deal of early pace on. The first two look progressive and the form seems solid.

NOTEBOOK
Floristry, who won a weak race at Bath last time, picked up well towards the stands' side and held off Striking Spirit, who challenged more towards the centre, by a comfy neck. She is clearly progressive, has the size to develop into a nice three-year-old, and is one to keep on side. (op 15-2 tchd 7-1)
Striking Spirit challenged more towards the centre of the track and duelled with the eventual winner inside the last. He only went down narrowly, although the winner appeared to hold him a shade comfortably, and the pair finished nicely clear of the rest, and on this evidence he should be able to win a similar race. (op 9-2 tchd 5-1)
Excitement(IRE), who won her maiden over 5f here last month, looked fairly handicapped on that form off a mark of 80. She ran well, especially as the early pace was not as fast as she would have liked and resulted in her racing a touch keenly, and she was probably just unlucky to run into a pair of even better handicapped rivals. (op 5-1)
Upton Grey(IRE), who was not beaten far off 85 last time out, had 3lb more to carry this time and probably ran to a similar level. His pedigree suggests he should appreciate a good deal further than this in time. (op 9-1)
Aye Aye Digby(IRE), dropping back a furlong in distance, could have done with a stronger pace and was not disgraced in the circumstances. (op 10-1)
Mazaaya(USA), another dropping back in trip having won over 7f on her debut, did not have the pace of one or two of her rivals in the closing stages. (op 8-1 tchd 7-1)
Guertino(IRE) did not get the best of runs having been held up at the back of the field off a steady early pace, but the overall impression is that he is high enough in the handicap at present. (op 9-1 tchd 10-1)
Writingonthewall(IRE) ruined his chance by pulling for his head in the early stages. (op 7-1 tchd 6-1)

6155 TSG STKS (H'CAP) 1m

3:15 (3:16) (Class 2) (0-100,98) 3-Y-0+ **£11,658** (£3,468; £1,733; £865) **Stalls** Low

Form RPR

1112 **1** **Amarna (USA)**[6] 6002 3-8-10 **90** LDettori 14 100+
(Saeed Bin Suroor) *trckd ldrs on outer: wd st: swtchd lft and effrt over 2f out: sn rdn: styd on u.p fr over 1f out to ld last 100yds* **5/2**[1]

0040 **2** *1/2* **Prince Of Thebes (IRE)**[12] 5833 6-8-2 **84** oh2 KirstyMilczarek(5) 11 93
(J Akehurst) *swtg: prom: effrt and cl up 3f out: sn rdn: drvn and styd on to ld ent fnl f: hdd and nt qckn last 100yds* **33/1**

2601 **3** *nk* **Zaahid (IRE)**[14] 5776 3-8-10 **90** RHills 7 98+
(B W Hills) *hld up in rr: smooth hdwy centre over 2f out: rdn to chal over 1f out and ev ch: drvn and edgd rt ins fnl f: no ex towards fin* **11/4**[2]

4010 **4** *1* **Orpen Wide (IRE)**[8] 5950 5-8-10 **87** (b) RyanMoore 5 93
(M C Chapman) *prom: wd st to stands' rail: hdwy to ld 3f out: rdn 2f out: drvn and hdd ent fnl f: one pce* **33/1**

-020 **5** *1 1/4* **Kinsya**[12] 5833 4-8-5 **89** AshleyMorgan(7) 6 92
(M H Tompkins) *midfield: hdwy centre wl over 2f out: rdn and edgd rt wl over 1f out: kpt on same pce* **16/1**

3R00 **6** *shd* **Skhilling Spirit**[20] 5616 4-8-13 **95** NeilBrown(5) 4 98+
(T D Barron) *hld up: hdwy 3f out: rdn to chse ldrs wl over 1f out: kpt on ins fnl f* **20/1**

0400 **7** *hd* **Moody Tunes**[6] 6011 4-8-10 **87** KDarley 3 89
(K R Burke) *midfield: hdwy centre 3f out: rdn to chse ldrs 2f out: sn drvn and one pce appr fnl f* **40/1**

0553 **8** *hd* **Nevada Desert (IRE)**[14] 5776 7-8-6 **86** MichaelJStainton(3) 10 88
(R M Whitaker) *led: rdn along and hdd 3f out: drvn and grad wknd fnl 2f* **18/1**

161 **9** *3 1/2* **Gongidas**[49] 4785 3-8-13 **93** (v) TedDurcan 13 87
(Saeed Bin Suroor) *midfield: wd st: effrt and sme hdwy over 2f out: sn rdn and no imp* **9/1**[3]

-210 **10** *1/2* **Bid For Glory**[92] 3460 3-9-0 **94** DarryllHolland 9 87
(H J Collingridge) *chsd ldrs: wd st: rdn along wl over 2f out: grad wknd* **16/1**

3600 **11** *2 1/2* **Partners In Jazz (USA)**[13] 5797 6-9-3 **94** PhillipMakin 8 81
(T D Barron) *hld up in rr: wd st: sme hdwy over 2f out: sn rdn and no imp* **16/1**

1110 **12** *1/2* **Gentleman's Deal (IRE)**[195] 848 6-8-12 **89** PaulMulrennan 15 75
(M W Easterby) *a towards rr* **16/1**

10-0 **13** *2* **Winged Flight (USA)**[14] 5764 3-8-6 **86** GregFairley 1 67
(M Johnston) *cl up: rdn along 3f out: wknd 2f out* **25/1**

0401 **14** *2 1/2* **Wigwam Willie (IRE)**[21] 5585 5-8-9 **86** (p) NCallan 2 62
(K A Ryan) *in tch: wd st: effrt and hdwy over 2f out: sn rdn and btn* **12/1**

3000 **15** *8* **Flipando (IRE)**[20] 5631 6-9-7 **98** JimmyFortune 12 55
(T D Barron) *hld up: a in rr* **16/1**

1m 39.85s (0.35) **Going Correction** +0.20s/f (Good)
WFA 3 from 4yo+ 3lb **15** Ran SP% **124.5**
Speed ratings (Par 109): **106,105,105,104,102 102,102,102,98,98 95,95,93,90,82**
CSF £103.33 CT £262.22 TOTE £3.20: £1.50, £9.70, £1.60; EX 105.80.
Owner Godolphin **Bred** Darley **Trained** Newmarket, Suffolk

FOCUS
The market suggested that this warm handicap was not as competitive as the numbers suggested, and it was proved correct. The winner and third are progressive types, but the second and fourth lend a note of caution.

NOTEBOOK
Amarna(USA) has been steadily progressive this year and, as one of only a limited number of such horses in this line-up, he was unsurprisingly quite short in the betting. He stayed on well up the stands'-side rail to record another win for his in-form stable. (op 11-4 tchd 3-1)
Prince Of Thebes(IRE) is well handicapped on last year's form but he had not hit those heights previously this season. This was a return to form and he clearly handles a bit of cut, despite all four of his career wins coming on good to firm ground. (op 28-1)
Zaahid(IRE), who has shown a liking for a bit of give, has improved again this autumn after a mid-season lull on fast ground. He ran a solid race and could well win again before the season is out, providing conditions allow. Longer term, he looks the type to improve further as a four-year-old. (op 10-3)
Orpen Wide(IRE) ran well off a career-high mark but it is difficult seeing him winning a race off this sort of perch unless he is gifted an uncontested lead.

Kinsya, who also likes cut in the ground, is not the most consistent and is another who looks high enough in the weights at present. (tchd 14-1)
Skhilling Spirit was better behaved this time but never really threatened the principals from off the pace. (op 22-1)
Gongidas, 4lb higher for his narrow Thirsk win, wore the second colours of Godolphin and never really threatened. (op 10-1)
Gentleman's Deal(IRE) was entitled to need this first run since March, and his return to the All-Weather is eagerly awaited. (tchd 14-1)

6156 IG INDEX EBF MAIDEN STKS 6f
3:50 (3:50) (Class 3) 2-Y-O **£6,606** (£1,965; £982; £490) **Stalls** Centre

Form RPR
1 **Calming Influence (IRE)** 2-9-3 0 .... LDettori 15 93+
(Saeed Bin Suroor) *dwlt: sn trcking ldrs: led on bit over 1f out: shkn up and wnt clr ins fnl f: impressive* **1/1**[1]
0342 2 5 **Hamish McGonagall**[9] 5903 2-9-3 83 .... DavidAllan 14 78
(T D Easterby) *trckd ldrs: led over 2f out: hdd over 1f out: fdd ins fnl f* **9/2**[2]
2424 3 ½ **Harrison George (IRE)**[28] 5393 2-9-3 80 .... PaulHanagan 13 76
(R A Fahey) *trckd ldrs: led 3f out: sn hdd: kpt on same pce* **6/1**[3]
0 4 ½ **Horatio Carter**[14] 5771 2-9-3 0 .... NCallan 8 75
(K A Ryan) *chsd ldrs: kpt on same pce fnl 2f* **25/1**
5 ¾ **Pavershooz** 2-9-3 0 .... EddieAhern 12 72
(N Wilson) *s.s: mid-div: kpt on wl fnl 2f* **100/1**
6 6 1 ¼ **Always Certain (USA)**[29] 5343 2-9-3 0 .... GregFairley 11 69
(M Johnston) *chsd ldrs: outpcd 2f out: kpt on fnl f* **7/1**
7 ½ **Ninefineirishmen (IRE)** 2-9-3 0 .... PhillipMakin 1 67
(K R Burke) *dwlt: sn chsng ldrs: rdn and edgd rt 2f out: sn wknd* **100/1**
8 3 **Spirit Of A Nation (IRE)** 2-9-3 0 .... RyanMoore 3 58
(D J Murphy) *s.s: swtchd rt after s: n.m.r on inner over 1f out: nvr on terms* **20/1**
04 9 1 ¼ **Sylvias Grove**[14] 5770 2-8-12 0 .... DO'Donohoe 2 49
(D Carroll) *chsd ldrs: wknd 2f out* **25/1**
505 10 1 ¼ **Rio Sands**[15] 5745 2-9-0 73 .... MichaelJStainton(3) 9 51
(R M Whitaker) *led tl 3f out: lost pl over 1f out* **33/1**
0 11 hd **Umverti**[16] 5735 2-8-12 0 .... TonyHamilton 4 45
(N Bycroft) *chsd ldrs: wknd over 1f out* **100/1**
12 5 **Petite Music (IRE)** 2-8-9 0 .... DuranFentiman(3) 5 30
(T D Easterby) *s.i.s: a outpcd and bhd* **100/1**
13 13 **Fools Gold** 2-9-3 0 .... TedDurcan 10 —
(T D Easterby) *prom: lost pl over 2f out: sn bhd* **33/1**
14 10 **Littonfountain (IRE)** 2-9-3 0 .... KDarley 6 —
(K R Burke) *dwlt: in rr: wl bhd fnl 2f* **100/1**

1m 13.74s (1.18) **Going Correction** +0.20s/f (Good) **14** Ran SP% **118.3**
Speed ratings (Par 99): **100,93,92,92,91 89,88,84,83,81 81,74,57,43**
CSF £4.76 TOTE £1.90: £1.10, £1.80, £1.70; EX 6.40.
Owner Godolphin **Bred** Mrs Helen Lyons **Trained** Newmarket, Suffolk

FOCUS
A fair maiden and the performances of the placed horses, who both have ratings in the 80s, suggest that winner Calming Influence could be very useful. He looks destined for better things.

NOTEBOOK
Calming Influence(IRE) is a half-brother to Steel Light, a dual 5-7f winner at two and later high-class 6f winner at four in Canada, and Marajel, a 6f winner at three. His dam won over 7f at three and is from the family of Twilight Agenda, Refuse To Bend and Media Puzzle. Sent off a short price on his debut for his in-form stable, he made an impressive debut, beating a couple of fair rivals with ratings in the 80s with ease. He looks a very useful prospect and it was no surprise that he was given quotes of 33-1 for the Guineas and the Derby on the back of this. The former looks the more realisitc as his pedigree would suggest he will be a miler next year. (op 5-6 tchd 11-10 in a place)
Hamish McGonagall, who is a solid enough yardstick, won the separate race for second but had no chance with the easy winner, who looked different class. He has done enough to suggest he can win a minor maiden when lucky enough to avoid a hotpot. (op 6-1)
Harrison George(IRE), who also had a bank of form behind him which gave him a solid each-way chance, ran a fair race, but in this sort of contest he remains vulnerable to something a little less exposed with more improvement in it. (tchd 13-2)
Horatio Carter, a half-brother to winning miler Pirouetting, did not show a great deal on his debut but this was a better effort and he will be eligible for handicaps after one more outing. (tchd 20-1)
Pavershooz, a half-brother to five winners at a modest level, ran a promising race, staying on without threatening, and he looks the type to follow in the family tradition and make his mark in handicap company next term. (op 50-1)
Always Certain(USA) was expected to appreciate the drop back in distance but he got outpaced when the leaders quickened before keeping on late. (op 13-2)
Littonfountain(IRE) Official explanation: jockey said colt moved poorly throughout

6157 PERSIMMON HOMES STKS (H'CAP) 5f
4:25 (4:25) (Class 5) (0-75,75) 3-Y-O+ **£5,181** (£1,541; £770; £384) **Stalls** Centre

Form RPR
2311 1 **Princess Ellis**[7] 5970 3-8-12 69 12ex .... KDarley 20 77+
(E J Alston) *led: hdd over 2f out: rdn to ld again over 1f out: drvn and edgd lft ins fnl f: jst hld on* **5/1**[1]
420 2 shd **Valley Of The Moon (IRE)**[15] 5747 3-8-12 69 .... PaulHanagan 6 77
(R A Fahey) *in tch: hdwy 2f out: rdn over 1f out: chal ins fnl f and ev ch: jst hld* **20/1**
4441 3 hd **Charles Parnell (IRE)**[22] 5552 4-9-3 74 .... PhillipMakin 7 81+
(M Dods) *hld up: hdwy over 1f out: rdn and str run ins fnl f: nt qckn nr fin* **8/1**[2]
1663 4 nk **Funfair Wane**[9] 5908 8-8-7 64 .... AdrianTNicholls 13 70
(D Nicholls) *cl up: led over 2f out: rdn and hdd over 1f out: drvn and ev ch ins fnl f: hmpd nr line* **8/1**[2]
6002 5 ¾ **Steel City Boy (IRE)**[6] 6020 4-8-5 62 .... DO'Donohoe 10 65
(D Carroll) *chsd ldng pair: rdn along 2f out: drvn and wknd ins fnl f* **14/1**
6600 6 shd **Paris Bell**[41] 5044 5-9-2 73 .... PaulQuinn 11 76
(T D Easterby) *in tch: hdwy 2f out: sn rdn and kpt on same pce ins fnl f* **25/1**
0002 7 ¾ **Rothesay Dancer**[8] 5934 4-7-13 63 .... LanceBetts(7) 18 63+
(J S Goldie) *in rr: hdwy 2f out: sn rdn and styd on ins fnl f: nrst fin* **20/1**
0201 8 ½ **Calabaza**[10] 5879 5-8-1 63 6ex .... (p) KirstyMilczarek(5) 16 61
(J Akehurst) *prom: rdn along 2f out: sn drvn and wknd appr fnl f* **16/1**
-450 9 hd **Sea Salt**[76] 3954 4-9-2 73 ....[1] TonyHamilton 15 70
(R A Fahey) *in rr: hdwy 2f out: sn rdn and kpt on ins fnl f: nt rch ldrs* **22/1**
0305 10 nk **Methaaly (IRE)**[6] 6020 4-8-5 69 .... SophieDoyle(7) 12 65
(M Mullineaux) *midfield: effrt over 2f out: sn rdn and no imp* **20/1**
0035 11 nk **Colorus (IRE)**[48] 4800 4-8-12 69 .... DaleGibson 19 64
(M W Easterby) *chsd ldrs: rdn along over 2f out: sn hung lft and wknd* **25/1**
2313 12 ½ **Digital**[8] 5942 10-9-3 74 .... (v) DarryllHolland 17 67
(M R Channon) *hld up: a towards rr* **8/1**[2]
-054 13 1 ¼ **Argentine (IRE)**[19] 5667 3-8-13 75 .... GaryBartley(5) 1 64
(L Lungo) *led far side gp to 1/2-way: sn rdn and wknd* **20/1**
3001 14 shd **Hereford Boy**[8] 5942 3-8-5 67 .... JamesO'Reilly(5) 5 56
(D K Ivory) *racd towards far side: bhd fr 1/2-way* **11/1**[3]
3450 15 shd **Tartatartufata**[13] 5806 5-9-4 75 .... (v) DeanMcKeown 8 63
(D Shaw) *a in rr* **50/1**
0040 16 1 **Highland Warrior**[13] 5806 8-9-1 75 .... JamieMoriarty(3) 9 60
(P T Midgley) *s.i.s: a in rr* **12/1**
0006 17 3 **Coseadrom (IRE)**[27] 5430 5-8-9 66 .... NCallan 3 40
(M F Harris) *racd far side: in rr fr 1/2-way* **11/1**[3]
2212 18 1 ½ **Joyeaux**[15] 5747 5-8-10 70 .... DuranFentiman(3) 4 38
(J Hetherton) *racd towards far side: in rr fr 1/2-way* **12/1**
0003 19 3 ½ **Kerry's Dream**[6] 6020 3-8-12 69 .... DavidAllan 2 25
(T D Easterby) *racd towards far side: in rr fr 1/2-way* **22/1**

60.41 secs (1.09) **Going Correction** +0.20s/f (Good) **19** Ran SP% **132.0**
Speed ratings (Par 103): **99,98,98,98,96 96,95,94,94,93 93,92,90,90,90 88,83,81,75**
CSF £113.74 CT £844.58 TOTE £5.50: £1.70, £5.80, £2.40, £2.30; EX 233.80.
Owner John Jackson **Bred** J E Jackson **Trained** Longton, Lancs
■ Stewards' Enquiry : K Darley two-day ban: careless riding (Oct 23-24)

FOCUS
A typically competitive sprint handicap. Five went far side but were well beaten. Straightforward form, with further improvement from Princess Ellis.
Calabaza Official explanation: jockey said gelding was unsuited by the good to soft (soft in places) ground
Coseadrom(IRE) Official explanation: jockey said gelding hung right-handed throughout

6158 BETFAIR APPRENTICE TRAINING SERIES FINALE STKS (H'CAP) 1m 4f
4:55 (4:55) (Class 4) (0-85,85) 3-Y-O+ **£5,829** (£1,734; £866; £432) **Stalls** Centre

Form RPR
1136 1 **Esthlos (FR)**[6] 6014 4-9-7 80 .... LukeMorris 5 94+
(J Jay) *hld up in midfield: hdwy over 3f out: swtchd rt and rdn to chse ldr over 1f out: styd on u.p to ld last 100yds* **6/1**[3]
2251 2 2 **Sporting Gesture**[37] 5145 10-8-12 71 .... NeilBrown 11 78
(M W Easterby) *led after 2f: pushed clr over 2f out: rdn over 1f out: hdd and no ex last 100yds* **14/1**
003- 3 2 **According To Pete**[230] 5770 6-8-9 75 .... PaulPickard(7) 2 79
(J M Jefferson) *trckd ldrs: hdwy to chse ldr 4f out: rdn along over 2f out: kpt on same pce appr fnl f* **20/1**
3112 4 hd **Rudry World (IRE)**[14] 5777 4-8-9 71 oh1 .... SophieDoyle(3) 1 74+
(M Mullineaux) *hld up towards rr: hdwy over 2f out: rdn over 1f out: kpt on ins fnl f: nrst fin* **11/2**[2]
6002 5 2 **Kyoto Summit**[13] 5807 4-9-2 80 .... NSLawes(5) 4 80
(M W Easterby) *trckd ldrs on inner: effrt 3f out: rdn 2f and one pce appr fnl f* **13/2**
4650 6 1 **Cripsey Brook**[6] 6021 9-9-2 75 .... (t) DanielleMcCreery 6 74
(K G Reveley) *hld up in rr: hdwy 3f out: sn rdn and styd on appr fnl f: nt rch ldrs* **40/1**
3505 7 ½ **Tcherina (IRE)**[13] 5814 5-9-2 75 .... MCGeran 7 73
(T D Easterby) *trckd ldrs: effrt over 2f out: sn rdn and btn* **11/1**
1060 8 1 ¾ **High Treason (USA)**[52] 4690 5-9-9 85 .... AlanRutter(3) 10 80
(W J Musson) *hld up in rr: sme hdwy over 2f out: sn rdn and no imp* **9/2**[1]
064 9 ½ **Rationale (IRE)**[61] 4419 4-9-8 81 .... WilliamCarson 9 75
(S C Williams) *hld up: hdwy and in tch over 4f out: rdn along 3f out: wknd fnl 2f* **9/1**
3300 10 3 ½ **Moonwalking**[34] 5229 3-8-5 71 .... KirstyMilczarek 3 60
(Jedd O'Keeffe) *led 2f: prom tl rdn along 3f out and grad wknd* **22/1**
-531 11 3 **Top Tiger**[9] 5898 3-8-3 74 6ex ow1 .... AshleyMorgan(5) 8 58
(M H Tompkins) *in tch: rdn along 3f out and sn wknd* **6/1**[3]
155- 12 6 **Swains Bridge (USA)**[425] 4392 5-9-5 78 .... GaryBartley 13 52
(Micky Hammond) *hld up in rr: swtchd wd and effrt over 3f out: sn rdn and nvr a factor* **100/1**
1131 13 2 ½ **Turn Of Phrase (IRE)**[76] 3978 8-8-12 76 .... (b) LanceBetts(5) 12 46
(N Wilson) *chsd ldrs: wd st: rdn along 3f out and sn wknd* **10/1**

2m 35.9s (1.30) **Going Correction** +0.20s/f (Good)
WFA 3 from 4yo+ 7lb **13** Ran SP% **122.1**
Speed ratings (Par 105): **103,101,100,100,98 98,97,96,96,94 92,88,86**
CSF £85.73 CT £1600.47 TOTE £8.00: £2.80, £3.00, £6.50; EX 152.80 Place 6 £50.31, Place 5 £30.80.
Owner Ms Medina Jessop **Bred** J Jay **Trained** Newmarket, Suffolk
■ Kirsty Milczarek is the series winner.

FOCUS
A fair handicap but the pace was not that strong. Neil Brown tried to nick it from the front on Sporting Gesture and the winner had to quicken up well to score. The form is not entirely convincing but the winner is progressive and better than this bare form.
High Treason(USA) Official explanation: trainer had no explanation for the poor form shown
Moonwalking Official explanation: jockey said gelding hung left
T/Jkpt: £4,982.50 to a £1 stake. Pool: £31,579.50. 4.50 winning tickets. T/Plt: £23.80 to a £1 stake. Pool: £105,399.90. 3,225.45 winning tickets. T/Qpdt: £14.30 to a £1 stake. Pool: £4,819.10. 247.90 winning tickets. JR

6159 - 6160a (Foreign Racing) - See Raceform Interactive

5986 DUNDALK (A.W) (L-H)
Friday, October 12

OFFICIAL GOING: Standard

6161a IRISH STALLION FARMS EUROPEAN BREEDERS FUND STAR APPEAL STKS (LISTED RACE) 7f
7:45 (7:54) 2-Y-O **£30,790** (£9,033; £4,304; £1,466)

RPR
1 **Great War Eagle (USA)**[40] 5076 2-9-1 .... (t) JMurtagh 1 100+
(David Wachman, Ire) *chsd ldrs: 4th ent st: swtchd 2f out: 3rd and rdn 1f out: kpt on strly cl home to ld on line* **9/4**[1]
2 hd **Going Public (IRE)**[12] 5845 2-9-1 105 .... PJSmullen 6 100
(D K Weld, Ire) *chsd ldrs: disp ld ent st: edgd ahd 1f out: kpt on wl: hdd on line* **5/1**[3]
3 hd **Billyford (IRE)**[15] 5758 2-9-1 96 .... FMBerry 4 99
(Liam Roche, Ire) *chsd ldr: impr to ld ent st and strly pressed: jst hdd 1f out: kpt on wl* **6/1**
4 1 ¾ **Minneapolis**[5] 6041 2-9-1 104 .... JAHeffernan 7 95
(A P O'Brien, Ire) *s.i.s: sn mid-div: 7th ent st: 5th 2f out: kpt on into 4th under 1f out: no imp on ldrs* **7/2**[2]
5 1 ¼ **Brazilian Star (IRE)**[12] 5845 2-9-1 105 .... (b) CDHayes 5 92
(Kevin Prendergast, Ire) *mid-div: 7th 1/2-way: rdn in 6th 2f out: kpt on same pce* **9/1**

6 3/4 **Solent Ridge (IRE)**[6] 6001 2-9-1 .... MJKinane 3 90
(J S Moore) *led: rdn and hdd ent st: no ex in 4th over 1f out: wknd fnl f* **14/1**

7 *shd* **Queen Jock (USA)**[40] 5073 2-8-12 89 .... PShanahan 2 86
(Tracey Collins, Ire) *mid-div: 6th 1/2-way: rdn and lost pl ent st: kpt on same pce* **40/1**

8 *1* **Northgate (IRE)**[15] 5759 2-9-1 88 .... (b) WJSupple 9 87
(Joseph G Murphy, Ire) *dwlt: towards rr: mod 9th and no imp over 1f out* **20/1**

9 *hd* **Rock Moss (IRE)**[15] 5760 2-9-1 95 .... KJManning 8 86
(J S Bolger, Ire) *in rr of mid-div: mod 8th and no imp over 1f out* **14/1**

10 1/2 **Deal Breaker**[26] 5456 2-9-1 98 .... (t) DPMcDonogh 11 85
(Edward Lynam, Ire) *a towards rr* **9/1**

11 4 1/2 **Contingency Plan (IRE)**[14] 5785 2-8-12 .... DMGrant 10 71
(Patrick Tallis, Ire) *chsd ldrs: 5th 1/2-way: rdn in 6th ent st: wknd 2f out* **100/1**

1m 26.1s (86.10) **11** Ran SP% **125.5**
CSF £14.60 TOTE £3.30: £2.20, £2.10, £2.30; DF 11.80.
Owner Michael Tabor **Bred** Orpendale **Trained** Goolds Cross, Co Tipperary
■ Stewards' Enquiry : J Murtagh caution (reduced from one-day ban on appeal): careless riding

FOCUS
A cracking 2yo race for the sand, and solid form.

NOTEBOOK
Great War Eagle(USA) was having his first run out of maiden company and only the second run of his life, so it was a fair performance to get up to win. Taking a keen grip on the inside rail early on, Johnny Murtagh getting some cover appeared to be key. He pulled him off the rail two furlongs out, and while he could not quicken immediately with the eventual runner-up, he ran on strongly inside the final furlong to get up on the line. He will have no problem getting a mile this season and should be a nice horse up to around 1m2f next year. (op 2/1 tchd 5/2)
Solent Ridge(IRE) led early and disputed turning in but just was not good enough.

6162 - 6166a (Foreign Racing) - See Raceform Interactive

5828 ASCOT (R-H)
Saturday, October 13

OFFICIAL GOING: Good to soft (soft in places on round course)
Wind: Virtually nil Weather: Bright, partly cloudy

6167 WILLMOTT DIXON CORNWALLIS STKS (GROUP 3) 5f
1:10 (1:11) (Class 1) 2-Y-O

£22,712 (£8,608; £4,308; £2,148; £1,076; £540) **Stalls** Low

Form RPR

3141 **1** **Captain Gerrard (IRE)**[22] 5583 2-9-0 108 .... TomEaves 12 110
(B Smart) *mde all: rdn wl over 1f out: styd on strly fnl f* **9/4**[1]

4123 **2** 1 1/2 **Cute Ass (IRE)**[29] 5377 2-8-11 105 .... TedDurcan 13 102
(K R Burke) *prom: chsd wnr 1/2-way: rdn wl over 1f out: one pce and no imp on wnr last 100yds* **8/1**

0120 **3** *shd* **Cake (IRE)**[29] 5377 2-8-11 100 .... LDettori 6 102
(R Hannon) *hld up towards rr: plld out and rdn over 1f out: r.o wl fnl f: nrly snatched 2nd but nvr trbld wnr* **14/1**

4321 **4** 3/4 **Hammadi (IRE)**[21] 5621 2-9-0 93 .... DO'Donohoe 2 102
(K A Ryan) *hld up in tch: rdn and hdwy 2f out: disputing 2nd 1f out: no ex last 100yds* **16/1**

4132 **5** *nk* **Hitchens (IRE)**[29] 5397 2-9-0 99 .... GeorgeBaker 5 101
(G L Moore) *hld up in tch: hdwy 2f out: sn hung rt: kpt on same pce fnl f* **6/1**[3]

1410 **6** 1/2 **Dubai Princess (IRE)**[8] 5973 2-8-11 87 .... JamieSpencer 8 96
(J A Osborne) *hld up: rdn and effrt 2f out: no imp fnl f* **16/1**

6150 **7** 1 1/4 **Littlemisssunshine (IRE)**[57] 4573 2-8-11 98 .... (p) JohnEgan 11 92
(J S Moore) *chsd wnr for 1f: styd prom: rdn wl over 1f out: fdd jst ins fnl f* **33/1**

0225 **8** *4* **Thunder Bay**[5] 6059 2-9-0 88 .... TPO'Shea 4 80
(M R Channon) *sn bhd: rdn 3f out: nvr on terms* **50/1**

4036 **9** *nk* **Carleton**[10] 5922 2-9-0 96 .... DarryllHolland 3 79
(M R Channon) *sn wl outpcd in rr: nvr on terms* **25/1**

2040 **10** *1* **Reel Gift**[15] 5766 2-8-11 97 .... RyanMoore 7 72
(R Hannon) *prom: chsd wnr after 1f tl 1/2-way: rdn 2f out: wkng whn sltly hmpd over 1f out* **12/1**

3062 **11** 2 1/2 **Spirit Of Sharjah (IRE)**[29] 5377 2-9-0 110 .... KerrinMcEvoy 9 66+
(P W Chapple-Hyam) *missed break and squeezed out sn after s: pushed along and hdwy into midfield after 1f: rdn and wknd qckly 2f out* **5/2**[2]

5050 **12** *18* **Lindoro**[7] 6017 2-9-0 89 .... (vt[1]) SebSanders 10 2+
(W R Swinburn) *taken down early: chsd ldrs tl wknd rapidly 2f out: virtually p.u ins fnl f: dismntd after fin: t.o: sddle slipped* **33/1**

60.81 secs (-0.59) **Going Correction** +0.125s/f (Good) **12** Ran SP% **122.6**
Speed ratings (Par 105): **109,106,106,105,104 103,101,95,95,93 89,60**
CSF £21.22 TOTE £3.00: £1.50, £2.00, £2.90; EX 20.20 Trifecta £254.10 Pool: £912.69 - 2.55 winning units..
Owner R C Bond **Bred** Alan Dargan **Trained** Hambleton, N Yorks

FOCUS
The last three winners of the Cornwallis have so far failed to register a subsequent success, but this looked a reasonable renewal with the placed horses close to pre-race levels and it will be a surprise if Captain Gerrard cannot buck that trend. The time was good, 0.82 seconds quicker than the closing older-horse 71-85 handicap. They raced up the middle of the track.

NOTEBOOK
Captain Gerrard(IRE) followed up his recent success in a Listed contest at Ayr in similarly convincing fashion to record his first Group-race victory. Quickly into his stride as usual, he set a strong enough pace out in front, but had plenty left for the business end and never looked like being caught. He had finished behind both Spirit Of Sharjah and Cute Ass in the Flying Childers the previous month, but the ground was considered too fast for him that day and his record clearly shows he is at his best with a bit of give underfoot, with his form figures over 5f on ground good or softer now reading 113111. He has been kept very busy this season, but he seems the type who thrives on his racing and physically he looks as though he should train on. His connections want to try him over 6f next year and an early target could be the Duke of York Stakes. (op 11-4 tchd 3-1 and 10-3 in places)
Cute Ass(IRE) could not confirm recent Flying Childers form with Captain Gerrard, with that one improving for the switch to easier ground, but she confirmed herself a most progressive filly with another good effort in defeat. Provided she trains on she should do well against her own sex next year. (tchd 7-1)
Cake(IRE) possibly lacked the pace of the front two at a crucial stage, but she really found her stride late on and this was an improvement on the form she showed when last of eight in the Flying Childers on her previous start. (op 16-1)
Hammadi(IRE) took four runs to get off the mark, but he looked very useful when scoring by ten lengths over 6f at Catterick on his previous start and he confirmed himself a decent sort with a solid effort in defeat.
Hitchens(IRE), second to Luck Money in the Goffs Million over 7f at the Curragh on his previous start, was not quite at his best dropped back to the minimum trip for the first time since his racecourse debut back in July. His pedigree is not short of speed but, having travelled well enough, he just seemed to lack the pace to get seriously competitive and may be happier back over a little further. (op 5-1)
Dubai Princess(IRE) looked a little better than her finishing position suggested in the Cheveley Park on her previous start, but she never landed a blow, dropped both in trip and grade. (op 14-1)
Spirit Of Sharjah(IRE) had the first three home from today's field behind him when second in the Flying Childers on his previous start, so this was a big disappointment, and it would be hard to use the slight trouble he had the start as an excuse. At the time of writing Peter Chapple-Hyam had saddled just one winner from 23 runners in October, and had sent out four beaten favourites in that period, so there has to be a question mark over the form of his stable. Official explanation: jockey said colt suffered interference leaving stalls (op 3-1 tchd 10-3 in places)
Lindoro Official explanation: jockey said saddle slipped

6168 PRINCESS ROYAL WILLMOTT DIXON STKS (GROUP 3) (F&M) 1m 4f
1:45 (1:52) (Class 1) 3-Y-O+

£27,254 (£10,329; £5,169; £2,577; £1,291; £648) **Stalls** High

Form RPR

0330 **1** **Trick Or Treat**[30] 5352 4-9-0 101 .... TPQueally 3 108
(J G Given) *lw: mde all: rdn wl over 2f out: clr 2f out: edgd lft but battled on gamely fnl f* **14/1**

2112 **2** 1/2 **Queen's Best**[29] 5396 4-9-3 109 .... RyanMoore 7 110
(Sir Michael Stoute) *swtg: hld up towards rr: hdwy over 4f out: rdn and effrt on inner 3f out: chsd wnr 2f out: ev ch 1f out: unable qck and hld by wnr last 100yds* **3/1**[2]

2011 **3** 1 1/4 **Samira Gold (FR)**[24] 5544 3-8-7 106 .... JamieSpencer 12 105
(L M Cumani) *swtg: s.i.s: hld up in tch: rdn and outpcd 3f out: 7th over 1f out: styd on wl fnl f: wnt 3rd nr fin* **4/1**[3]

4231 **4** 1/2 **Brisk Breeze (GER)**[15] 5767 3-8-7 108 .... TedDurcan 9 104
(H R A Cecil) *chsd ldrs: hit rail 3f out: sn rdn to chse wnr: no imp: lost 2nd 2f out: one pce* **11/4**[1]

115 **5** 1 1/4 **Winter Sunrise**[51] 4748 3-8-7 98 .... KerrinMcEvoy 4 102
(Sir Michael Stoute) *chsd ldrs: rdn and unable qck 2f out: plugged on same pce after* **9/1**

616 **6** *shd* **Dash To The Front**[94] 3434 4-9-0 97 .... OscarUrbina 5 102
(J R Fanshawe) *hld up towards rr: hdwy 3f out: rdn to chse ldrs 2f out: sn no imp and btn* **20/1**

-421 **7** 2 1/2 **Loulwa (IRE)**[86] 3678 3-8-7 82 .... (t) DarryllHolland 1 98
(J Noseda) *lw: t.k.h: hld up bhd: lost tch 3f out: styd on over 1f out: n.d* **33/1**

0006 **8** *1* **Rising Cross**[13] 5849 4-9-0 105 .... GeorgeBaker 11 97
(J R Best) *chsd ldr tl 3f out: sn rdn: wknd 2f out* **20/1**

-106 **9** *3* **Kayah**[30] 5352 3-8-7 100 .... SebSanders 6 92
(R M Beckett) *m in snatches in rr: rdn over 3f out: nvr trbld ldrs* **8/1**

2200 **10** *11* **Athenian Way (IRE)**[24] 5544 3-8-7 97 .... SteveDrowne 10 74
(J R Fanshawe) *a bhd: lost tch 4f out* **50/1**

-200 **11** *9* **Party (IRE)**[74] 4055 3-8-7 100 .... RHills 8 60
(R Hannon) *prom tl stdd into midfield after 1f out: rdn 8f out: hrd rdn and lost pl 4f out: no ch after: t.o* **16/1**

5000 **12** 3/4 **Satulagi (USA)**[42] 5047 3-8-7 94 .... JohnEgan 2 59
(J S Moore) *stdd and dropped in after s rdn and no hdwy over 3f out: t.o* **66/1**

2m 36.93s (3.93) **Going Correction** +0.625s/f (Yiel)
WFA 3 from 4yo 7lb **12** Ran SP% **121.2**
Speed ratings (Par 113): **111,110,109,109,108 108,106,106,104,96 90,90**
CSF £54.53 TOTE £20.20: £4.00, £1.50, £1.90; EX 90.30 Trifecta £232.30 Pool: £1,599.97 - 4.89 winning units..
Owner Peter Onslow & Ian Henderson **Bred** P Onslow **Trained** Willoughton, Lincs

FOCUS
A fair renewal of this Group 3 contest. The pace seemed good - a winning time 0.82 seconds quicker than the following 0-105 confirms they were not hanging around - but Trick Or Treat managed to get a breather in and caught out a few of her rivals when kicking for home rounding the final bend. The form is rated at face value around the runner-up, fifth and sixth.

NOTEBOOK
Trick Or Treat had struggled a touch since winning a Listed race at Haydock on her seasonal reappearance, including when well behind both Brisk Breeze and Kayah in the Park Hill at Doncaster on her previous start, but she returned to her very best under a fine front-running ride from Queally. She was forced to set a fair enough pace from the outset, but Queally managed to get a good breather in just before the turn into the straight and she caught several of her rivals flat-footed when quickening from the front on the final bend. She looked vulnerable when Queen's Best loomed large around a furlong out, but found reserves and was a most game winner. This was a deserved first Group-race victory, but her connections are undecided as to whether she stays in training. (op 16-1 tchd 12-1)
Queen's Best has been much improved this year, winning in Listed and Group 3 company and only just failing to complete the hat-trick in a Group 2 at the Curragh on her most recent start, but she was just found out under her 3lb penalty. (op 5-2)
Samira Gold(FR), on her toes beforehand, was well worth her place in this line-up following a couple of wins in Listed company, but she tends to hit a flat spot in her races and she was caught out when Trick Or Treat kicked for home off the final bend. She stayed on well for a place, securing some Group-race black type, but she had no chance with the front two. (op 10-3 tchd 3-1)
Brisk Breeze(GER) landed a Listed race over course and distance on her previous start, but she was not quite at her best this time. She hit the rail on the turn for home, but that did not seem to cost her any momentum and it might just be that a busy season is beginning to catch up with her, as this was her tenth outing of the year. (tchd 3-1)
Winter Sunrise, a beaten favourite in a Listed contest at York when last seen nearly two months previously, was well held upped in class and does not look quite ready for this level just yet. She was well positioned for much of the way, but was left behind when the eventual winner kicked for home off the bend. (op 12-1)
Dash To The Front, who had to be replated at the start, was just beginning to creep into contention when Trick Or Treat increased the tempo rounding the final bend and her effort soon flattened out. (op 25-1)
Party(IRE) Official explanation: trainer said filly never travelled
Satulagi(USA) Official explanation: jockey said filly was unsuited by the good to soft ground

6169 LADBROKES.COM STKS (HERITAGE H'CAP) 1m 4f
2:20 (2:25) (Class 2) (0-105,102) 3-Y-O+

£46,740 (£13,995; £6,997; £3,502; £1,747; £877) **Stalls** High

Form RPR

5611 **1** **Buccellati**[14] 5805 3-8-12 96 .... (v) KerrinMcEvoy 1 105
(A M Balding) *hld up towards rr: plld out and hdwy wl over 2f out: styd on wl u.p fnl f: led on post* **10/1**

-661 **2** *shd* **St Savarin (FR)**[9] 5933 6-9-1 92 .... TonyHamilton 11 101
(R A Fahey) *lw: t.k.h: trckd ldrs: rdn 3f out: lft 2nd and hmpd 2f out: kpt on u.p to ld last 50yds: hdd on post* **20/1**

0610 **3** *nk* **Players Please (USA)**[21] 5631 3-8-11 **95** .... GregFairley 9 103
(M Johnston) *prom tl led 10f out: clr wl over 5f out: rdn and hrd pressed whn lft clr 2f out: hdd and no ex last 50yds* **25/1**

0003 **4** *1 1/4* **Dubai Twilight**[13] 5830 3-8-5 **89** .... JohnEgan 13 95
(B W Hills) *t.k.h: trckd ldrs: hdwy over 3f out: rdn whn lft 3rd 2f out: unable qck fnl f* **9/1**[3]

1-11 **5** *nk* **Red Gala**[31] 5326 4-9-10 **101** .... RyanMoore 5 109+
(Sir Michael Stoute) *lw: stdd after s and hld up wl in rr: stl wl bhd over 2f out: rdn and hdwy sn after: styd on steadily but nvr threatened ldrs* **11/4**[1]

2655 **6** *1/2* **Zaif (IRE)**[7] 6014 4-8-2 **79** .... LiamJones 10 84
(D R C Elsworth) *towards rr: rdn 4f out: c wd over 2f out: styd on u.p: nvr trbld ldrs* **33/1**

1000 **7** *1/2* **Nosferatu (IRE)**[52] 4722 4-8-12 **89** .... JamieSpencer 14 93
(Mrs A J Perrett) *led for 2f: styd prom: rdn over 3f out: lft 4th 2f out: one pce fnl f* **16/1**

-002 **8** *3* **Leslingtaylor (IRE)**[14] 5334 5-8-0 **77** .... FrancisNorton 2 76
(J J Quinn) *towards rr: rdn and struggling whn sltly hmpd 3f out: sme late hdwy: n.d* **9/1**[3]

0500 **9** *1/2* **Akarem**[13] 5830 6-9-3 **94** .... SebSanders 8 93
(K R Burke) *racd in midfield: wl in tch: rdn and effrt wl over 2f out: sn no imp* **33/1**

1005 **10** *1/2* **Pevensey (IRE)**[23] 5554 5-9-4 **95** .... GrahamGibbons 16 93
(J J Quinn) *s.i.s: nvr bttr than midfield: rdn and no imp whn hmpd 2f out* **10/1**

0060 **11** *1/2* **Castle Howard (IRE)**[14] 5800 5-8-13 **90** .... TPQueally 3 87
(W J Musson) *hld up bhd: c wd and rdn bnd over 2f out: nvr on terms* **16/1**

3320 **12** *nk* **Peruvian Prince (USA)**[21] 5631 5-8-10 **90** .... JamieMoriarty(3) 7 87
(R A Fahey) *lw: hld up wl bhd: rdn 3f out: no ch whn hmpd and swtchd lft 2f out* **33/1**

1205 **13** *2* **Crossbow Creek**[35] 5225 9-8-4 **84** .... LukeMorris(3) 12 77
(M G Rimell) *t.k.h: hld up in tch: rdn over 2f out: sn outpcd* **50/1**

3032 **14** *3* **Ladies Best**[13] 5830 3-8-13 **97** .... TedDurcan 19 86
(Sir Michael Stoute) *hld up in tch: chsng ldrs and rdn whn bdly hmpd 2f out: no ch after: eased fnl f* **13/2**[2]

2134 **15** *1* **Font**[15] 5764 4-8-12 **89** .... DarryllHolland 6 76
(J R Fanshawe) *lw: hld up in rr: effrt on inner 3f out: wl btn whn hmpd 2f out* **9/1**[3]

-250 **16** *7* **Millville**[13] 5830 7-9-4 **95** .... RHills 4 71
(M A Jarvis) *s.i.s: a bhd: no ch whn c v wd bnd over 2f out* **40/1**

1-10 **P** **Mariotto (USA)**[73] 4059 3-9-4 **102** .... (t) LDettori 18 —
(Saeed Bin Suroor) *lw: w ldrs: chsd ldr 10f out: effrt and chalng whn broke down and p.u jst over 2f out* **14/1**

2m 37.75s (4.75) **Going Correction** +0.625s/f (Yiel)
WFA 3 from 4yo+ 7lb **17** Ran SP% **128.4**
Speed ratings (Par 109): **109,108,108,107,107 107,107,105,104,104 104,103,102,100,99 95,—**
CSF £207.31 CT £4845.42 TOTE £14.70: £2.70, £6.30, £8.20, £3.30; EX 364.80 Trifecta £6910.40 Pool: £12,652.98 - 1.30 winning units..
Owner P C & Mrs J A McMahon **Bred** Burton Agnes Stud Co Ltd **Trained** Kingsclere, Hants
■ Stewards' Enquiry : Tony Hamilton two-day ban: used whip with excessive force (Oct 24-25)

FOCUS
A very good, seriously competitive handicap. The winning time was 0.82 seconds slower than the previous fillies & mares' Group 3 contest. The first and third are progressive sorts, and it was a personal best from the second. The fourth has been rated to his recent course-and-distance form.

NOTEBOOK
Buccellati had never previously raced over a trip this far, but as it turned out he needed every yard of it to get on top and he was narrowly able to defy a 6lb rise in the weights for his recent Chester success to complete the hat-trick. He had a good three or four lengths to make up on Players Please at the furlong pole, but he found a late surge and forced his head in front on the line. He has Australian connections and the long-term target could be the 2008 Melbourne Cup. (op 12-1)
St Savarin(FR) only just failed to defy a 7lb rise in the weights for his recent Ayr success and this must rate as a career-best effort. It would be no surprise to see him try and improve on last year's eighth in the November Handicap. (op 16-1)
Players Please(USA) beat just one home at Newbury on his previous start, but he returned to his best under a positive ride, faring best of the three-year-olds in the process. He handled the ease in the ground well and appears on the up. (tchd 20-1)
Dubai Twilight returned to form when getting his favoured easy ground over course and distance on his previous start and this was another respectable effort. He is one to have on-side when there is some give underfoot.
Red Gala had it all to do under top weight, having been raised 8lb for his recent Doncaster success, but he ran a big race in defeat and can be rated even better than the bare form, as he was much further back than was probably ideal at the top of the straight. His two wins this season were gained over 1m2f, but he stays this longer trip well and he looks capable of progressing into a smart sort next year. (op 7-2)
Zaif(IRE) has dropped to a mark 1lb lower than when last winning and this was a creditable effort. (op 40-1)
Peruvian Prince(USA) Official explanation: jockey said gelding hung right
Ladies Best was badly hampered two furlongs out when Mariotto was being pulled up and he is better than was able to show. (op 7-1)
Font was also hampered two furlongs out and is better than his finishing position suggests. (op 10-1)
Mariotto(USA) was in with every chance and just beginning to challenge Players Please for the lead when sadly breaking down badly just over two furlongs from the finish. (op 12-1)

6170 DELOITTE AUTUMN STKS (GROUP 3) 1m (R)
3:00 (3:00) (Class 1) 2-Y-O

£21,008 (£7,962; £3,984; £1,986; £995; £499) **Stalls** High

Form RPR

411 **1** **Ibn Khaldun (USA)**[13] 5828 2-9-0 85 .... LDettori 4 110+
(Saeed Bin Suroor) *hld up in last: hdwy and swtchd rt over 2f out: swtchd lft and shkn up over 1f out: pushed into ld ins fnl f: comf* **4/7**[1]

210 **2** *1* **Redolent (IRE)**[29] 5397 2-9-0 92 .... RyanMoore 7 106
(R Hannon) *chsd ldr tl led 6f out tl wl over 3f out: rdn to ld again 2f out: hdd ins fnl f: one pce* **16/1**

2136 **3** *1 1/2* **Yahrab (IRE)**[14] 5795 2-9-0 103 .... KerrinMcEvoy 8 103
(C E Brittain) *racd alone on inner tl 1/2-way: led wl over 3f out: rdn and narrowly hdd wl over 1f out: wknd ins fnl f* **5/1**[2]

2145 **4** *1 1/2* **Naomh Geileis (USA)**[35] 5219 2-8-11 94 .... GregFairley 2 96
(M Johnston) *trckd ldrs: rdn over 2f out: kpt on same pce* **14/1**

5215 **5** *1* **Jedediah**[35] 5217 2-9-0 92 .... FrancisNorton 1 97
(A M Balding) *in tch: rdn and outpcd over 3f out: rallied u.p 2f out: no imp over 1f out* **16/1**

3011 **6** *1* **Meeriss (IRE)**[28] 5414 2-9-0 101 .... DarryllHolland 5 95
(M R Channon) *led for 2f out: styd handy: rdn wl over 2f out: btn whn short of room over 1f out* **10/1**[3]

1606 **7** *5* **Paveroc**[8] 5972 2-9-0 93 .... JohnEgan 3 84
(J S Moore) *steadied s: hld up bhd: rdn and effrt 3f out: wl btn last 2f* **33/1**

461U **8** *1/2* **Ramona Chase**[22] 5590 2-9-0 95 .... DPMcDonogh 6 83
(S Kirk) *plld hrd: stdd s: plld way up to join ldrs after 3f: wknd over 2f out* **11/1**

1m 44.24s (2.14) **Going Correction** +0.40s/f (Good) **8** Ran SP% **119.1**
Speed ratings (Par 105): **105,104,102,101,100 99,94,93**
CSF £13.36 TOTE £1.60: £1.10, £4.20, £1.40; EX 19.90 Trifecta £132.80 Pool: £1,650.56 - 8.82 winning units..
Owner Godolphin **Bred** Darley **Trained** Newmarket, Suffolk

FOCUS
A fairly weak renewal of this Group 3, but the progressive winner was a cut above this and scored in a decent time. All bar Yahrab were taken to race under the trees soon after the start.

NOTEBOOK
Ibn Khaldun(USA) ◆ looked a smart sort in the making when bolting up in a 7f nursery round here off a mark of 85 on his previous start and he took the step up in class in his stride, albeit in what was an ordinary race for a Group 3. He was still last at the top of the straight, but he was travelling noticeably strongly and, once switched to the inside, he readily moved into third. He then had to be switched back towards the outside, but he was always going to pick up both Redolent and Yahrab and his rider never had to go for the whip. Although the bare form is nothing special, he was in a different league to this lot and is progressing into a very smart colt. His improvement has apparently taken his connections a little by surprise, but there should be even more to come and he could now be aimed at the Racing Post Trophy at Doncaster. He will apparently also be given an entry in the Breeders' Cup Juvenile Turf. (op 4-6 tchd 8-11 in places)
Redolent(IRE) was well held in the Goffs Million on his previous start, but the step up to 1m suited and he produced an improved effort behind the classy winner. He is clearly smart and there could be more to come over this trip. (op 14-1)
Yahrab(IRE), sixth in the Royal Lodge on his previous start, found this less competitive and ran well in third. He raced alone through the early stages, close to the inside rail, rather than following all the others under the trees, but it is impossible to know whether or not he was at an advantage. He should come into this own over middle-distances and possibly even staying trips next year. (tchd 11-2)
Naomh Geileis(USA), stepping up from 6f, struggled to make any real impression and will probably be better off against her own sex. (tchd 16-1)
Jedediah did not run a bad race, but this company was probably just a little too hot. (tchd 14-1 and 20-1 in a place)
Meeriss(IRE), chasing the hat-trick, ran some way below the form he showed when winning a Listed race at Goodwood on his previous start and this ground was probably a little softer than he would have liked. (op 12-1)
Paveroc Official explanation: jockey said colt had no more to give

6171 ASCOT ANNUAL BADGEHOLDERS' HYPERION CONDITIONS STKS 7f
3:35 (3:36) (Class 2) 2-Y-O

£7,478 (£2,239; £1,119; £560; £279; £140) **Stalls** Low

Form RPR

2 **1** **Confront**[21] 5628 2-9-0 0 .... RyanMoore 7 105+
(Sir Michael Stoute) *lw: trckd ldrs: led 2f out: edgd rt fnl f: styd on wl* **2/1**[1]

1 **2** *1* **Stimulation (IRE)**[22] 5587 2-9-0 0 .... SteveDrowne 3 103+
(H Morrison) *s.i.s: hld up wl in tch in last: swtchd rt and hdwy wl over 1f out: sn chsng wnr: kpt on same pce ins fnl f* **3/1**[2]

21 **3** *9* **Sam's Cross (IRE)**[27] 5448 2-9-0 90 .... KerrinMcEvoy 1 80
(W R Swinburn) *led: pushed along 3f out: hdd 2f out: outpcd by ldng pair over 1f out* **7/1**

2120 **4** *1/2* **Eastern Gift**[8] 5974 2-9-0 100 .... JamieSpencer 2 79
(R Hannon) *t.k.h: trckd ldrs: ev ch and rdn over 2f out: outpcd by ldng pair over 1f out: no ch after* **9/2**[3]

2135 **5** *nk* **Gross Prophet**[10] 5922 2-9-0 87 .... HayleyTurner 5 78
(Tom Dascombe) *chsd ldr: rdn over 2f out: outpcd over 1f out: no ch after* **25/1**

4233 **6** *1 1/4* **Major Willy**[29] 5397 2-9-0 97 .... TPQueally 6 75
(W Jarvis) *s.i.s: t.k.h: hld up in tch: effrt over 2f out: sn outpcd* **5/1**

1m 28.77s (0.67) **Going Correction** +0.125s/f (Good) **6** Ran SP% **109.5**
Speed ratings (Par 101): **101,99,89,89,88 87**
CSF £7.75 TOTE £3.10: £1.90, £2.00; EX 8.10 Trifecta £29.00 Pool: £806.64 - 19.74 winning units..
Owner K Abdulla **Bred** Juddmonte Farms Ltd **Trained** Newmarket, Suffolk

FOCUS
This looked like a decent conditions event and the first two home, in pulling so far clear, marked themselves down as very smart colts in the making, with the time backing that up. They raced stands' side, but the front two ended up more towards the middle of the track.

NOTEBOOK
Confront ◆'s debut second in a fast-ground 7f maiden at Newbury represented just fair form, but this was a much-improved effort, with the easy surface clearly posing him no problems. He continually edged to his right under pressure, but was always holding Stimulation after getting first run and the pair pulled a huge nine lengths clear of the remainder. He looks sure to develop into a Group horse and, now likely to be aimed at either the Horris Hill or the Racing Post Trophy, it could take a good one to stop him. (op 5-2)
Stimulation(IRE) ◆, the well-backed winner of a 6f maiden on his debut at Newbury, is an athletic type and improved considerably on the bare form of that effort with a fine run in defeat. Having been held up through the early stages, he was forced to switch out towards the centre of the track to get into the clear, by which time Confront had kicked for home. He was carried right by the winner in the closing stages, but was always just being held and was not unlucky. Being by Choisir, he was not an obvious type to be stepped up in distance so soon, but there is stamina on his dam's side and he had no problems with the trip. It is interesting to note Sakhee's Secret was beaten in this race last year and Hughie Morrison looks to have another smart colt on his hands. (op 5-2)
Sam's Cross(IRE), officially rated 90 off the back of his success in a 6f Goodwood maiden, found this a lot tougher and probably ran into a couple of very useful colts. (op 8-1)
Eastern Gift has some very useful form to his name, but there is no way he ran up to his official mark of 100 this time and he has to be considered a little disappointing. (op 6-1 tchd 13-2 in places)
Gross Prophet had a bit to find in this company and he looks better over 6f in any case. (op 28-1)
Major Willy raced keenly and he was well below the form he showed when third in the Goffs Million. (op 7-2)

6172 DAVID & TONI EYLES H'CAP 1m 2f
4:10 (4:10) (Class 2) (0-105,104) 3-Y-O+

£9,971 (£2,985; £1,492; £747; £372; £187) **Stalls** High

Form RPR

0300 **1** **Night Crescendo (USA)**[7] 6011 4-8-7 **90** oh2 .... TedDurcan 6 103
(Mrs A J Perrett) *t.k.h: hld up in midfield: hdwy on inner over 2f out: led ins fnl f: rdn out* **20/1**

1114 **2** *1* **Mutajarred**[21] 5615 3-8-10 **98** .... RHills 11 109
(W J Haggas) *lw: trckd ldrs: rdn to ld over 1f out: hdd and no ex ins fnl f* **7/2**[2]

0420 **3** *3 1/2* **Mr Aviator (USA)**[21] 5631 3-8-3 **91** .... FrancisNorton 9 95
(R Hannon) *in tch: rdn and plld out over 2f out: kpt on but nt pce to trble ldng pair* **11/2**

1-15 **4** *2 1/2* **Perfectperformance (USA)**[71] 4117 5-9-7 **104** .... LDettori 1 103
(Saeed Bin Suroor) *hld up bhd: hdwy 3f out: chsd ldrs and swtchd rt over 1f out: sn no imp* **10/3**[1]

1421 **5** *3/4* **Press The Button (GER)**[18] 5717 4-8-7 **90** oh2 .... KerrinMcEvoy 8 87
(J R Boyle) *led: rdn over 2f out: hdd over 1f out: wknd fnl f* **11/1**

50P **6** *2 1/2* **Zero Tolerance (IRE)**[7] 6011 7-8-9 **92** .... RyanMoore 2 84
(T D Barron) *pressed ldr: rdn and ev ch over 2f out: wknd fnl f* **7/1**

0060 **7** *2 1/2* **Corriolanus (GER)**[34] 5255 7-8-10 **93** .... (p) SteveDrowne 5 80
(A M Balding) *hld up towards rr: rdn and effrt 3f out:* **40/1**

6103 **8** *1/2* **Lady Stardust**[78] 3897 4-8-7 **90** .... OscarUrbina 10 76
(J R Fanshawe) *hld up towards: rdn and struggling 3f out: no ch last 2f* **14/1**

0402 **9** *3* **Speedy Sam**[21] 5631 4-8-9 **92** .... SebSanders 7 72
(K R Burke) *pushed along early: sn chsng ldrs: rdn 3f out: sn wknd* **5/1**[3]

3-60 **10** *20* **Ofaraby**[52] 4720 7-8-13 **96** .... DarryllHolland 4 36
(M A Jarvis) *hld up in last: nvr on terms: virtually p.u fnl f: t.o* **16/1**

2m 11.97s (3.97) **Going Correction** +0.625s/f (Yiel)
WFA 3 from 4yo+ 5lb **10** Ran SP% **117.9**
Speed ratings (Par 109): **109,108,105,103,102 100,98,98,96,80**
CSF £90.13 CT £453.80 TOTE £30.50: £7.30, £1.80, £2.30; EX 201.80 Trifecta £939.80 Part won. Pool: £1,323.72 - 0.35 winning units..
Owner John Connolly **Bred** Audley Farm Inc **Trained** Pulborough, W Sussex

FOCUS
A good handicap run at a fair pace. The first two pulled clear and the form is rated around the next three home.

NOTEBOOK
Night Crescendo(USA) did not put up much of a show in the Cambridgeshire on his previous start, and he had also failed to beat a rival at Goodwood the time before, but he bounced right back to his best with a most decisive success from 2lb out of the handicap. He was unproven over a trip this far, but he saw his race out very well and will have more options now he has proven his stamina. Official explanation: trainer said, regarding apparent improvement in form, that the gelding was better suited by the good to soft (soft in places) ground (op 16-1 tchd 22-1)
Mutajarred, trying 1m2f for the first time, had the ground to suit and ran close to his best in second. Like the winner, he will have more options now he has proven his stamina. (tchd 3-1)
Mr Aviator(USA) is plenty high enough in the weights, but he would have appreciated the ease in the ground and this was respectable effort. (op 13-2)
Perfectperformance(USA) had not been seen for over two months and he was not at his best. He looked very smart when winning the 2004 Royal Lodge, but has been lightly raced since and has not gone on as might have been hoped. (op 7-2 tchd 4-1)
Press The Button(GER) found this tougher than the Folkestone handicap he won on his previous start and he could not defy a 5lb higher mark (including being 2lb out of the handicap). (op 12-1)
Zero Tolerance(IRE), who pulled up in the Cambridgeshire, showed himself none the worse, but he was still well held. (tchd 8-1 and 9-1 in a place)
Speedy Sam, 4lb higher than when second at Newbury on his previous start, was never really going and he was well below form.

6173 GOODING GROUP APPRENTICE H'CAP 5f
4:40 (4:43) (Class 4) (0-85,85) 3-Y-O+
£6,232 (£1,866; £933; £467; £233; £117) **Stalls** Low

Form RPR

2-00 **1** **Godfrey Street**[22] 5581 4-8-11 **77** .... (b[1]) AndrewMullen 7 88
(K A Ryan) *racd in centre: mde all: rdn wl over 1f out: edgd lft 1f out: r.o strly* **20/1**

0660 **2** *1 3/4* **Brunelleschi**[49] 4816 4-8-5 **74** .... (b) TolleyDean(3) 1 79
(M G Quinlan) *racd stands' side: trckd ldrs: rdn over 1f out: hung rt but r.o fnl f: wnt 2nd nr fin: nt trble wnr* **25/1**

0123 **3** *1/2* **Bo McGinty (IRE)**[14] 5810 6-9-4 **84** .... (b) JamieMoriarty 10 87
(R A Fahey) *taken down early: racd in centre: prom: rdn and disputing 2nd 2f out: kpt on same pce* **10/1**

1406 **4** *1/2* **Tilly's Dream**[79] 3886 4-8-2 **73** .... RobbieEgan(5) 4 74
(G C Bravery) *racd stands' side: hld in tch: rdn and effrt 2f out: led stands' side gp 1f out: kpt on same pce* **33/1**

1206 **5** *1/2* **Rebel Duke (IRE)**[99] 3278 3-8-6 **77** .... JamieJones(5) 18 76
(M G Quinlan) *racd in centre: chsd ldrs: rdn and disputing 2nd over 1f out: wknd ins fnl f* **33/1**

0213 **6** *3/4* **Don Pele (IRE)**[10] 5923 5-9-2 **85** .... (p) LukeMorris(3) 14 82
(R A Harris) *racd in centre: bhd and rdn after 2f out: sme late hdwy: nvr trbld ldrs* **8/1**[2]

2043 **7** *3/4* **Elkhorn**[20] 5667 5-8-13 **82** .... (b) PatrickHills(3) 17 76
(Miss J A Camacho) *racd in centre: chsd ldrs: rdn over 2f out: edgd lft over 1f out: sn wknd* **8/1**[2]

1110 **8** *1/2* **Malapropism**[14] 5806 7-8-13 **84** .... (v) ThomasO'Brien(5) 3 76
(M R Channon) *racd stands' side: led that gp tl 1f out: fdd* **16/1**

0040 **9** *1/2* **Dig Deep (IRE)**[14] 5806 5-9-2 **82** .... LiamJones 2 72
(W J Haggas) *taken down early: racd stands' side: chsd ldr rdn 2f out: wknd over 1f out* **7/2**[1]

151 **10** *1/2* **Topflightcoolracer**[14] 5806 3-8-13 **82** .... NeilBrown(3) 11 71
(Mrs G S Rees) *racd in centre: midfield tl rdn and struggling 1/2-way: n.d after* **10/1**

0320 **11** *nk* **Yungaburra (IRE)**[22] 5581 3-9-2 **85** .... (t) JamesMillman(3) 20 73
(D J Murphy) *racd in centre: s.i.s: nvr nr ldrs* **16/1**

1105 **12** *2 1/2* **Diminuto**[19] 5684 3-8-5 **76** .... FrankiePickard(5) 12 55
(M D I Usher) *taken down early: racd centre: bhd and rdn 1/2-way: n.d* **33/1**

5260 **13** *1 1/4* **Cuppacocoa**[30] 5358 3-8-6 **72** .... TravisBlock 8 46
(C G Cox) *racd centre: awkward s: bhd and rdn wl over 2f out: nvr on terms* **20/1**

0055 **14** *1 3/4* **Corridor Creeper (FR)**[25] 5513 10-9-3 **83** .... (p) DuranFentiman 5 51
(J M Bradley) *racd in centre: chsd ldrs tl 1/2-way: sn rdn and struggling* **14/1**

1031 **15** *shd* **Compton Classic**[8] 5969 5-8-6 **77** .... HarryPoulton(5) 6 44
(J R Boyle) *racd stands' side: a bhd* **14/1**

1060 **16** *1/2* **Bold Minstrel (IRE)**[31] 5332 5-8-5 **76** .... MCGeran(5) 16 42
(M Quinn) *racd in centre: chsd ldrs for 2f: sn dropped out* **40/1**

1300 **17** *3/4* **Black Moma (IRE)**[54] 4664 3-8-6 **75** .... HaddenFrost(3) 13 38
(R Hannon) *racd in centre: rdn and bhd after 2f* **20/1**

4316 **18** *1 1/4* **Glasshoughton**[22] 5581 4-9-4 **84** .... GregFairley 19 42
(M Dods) *w wnr for 2f: sn drvn and lost pl: no ch last 2f* **9/1**[3]

61.63 secs (0.23) **Going Correction** +0.125s/f (Good) **18** Ran SP% **127.1**
Speed ratings (Par 105): **103,100,99,98,97 96,95,94,93,93 92,88,86,83,83 82,81,79**
CSF £408.32 CT £4653.80 TOTE £26.20: £5.30, £6.60, £1.90, £4.10; EX 1016.40 TRIFECTA Not won. Place 6 £76.91, Place 5 £37.67.
Owner Club ISM **Bred** Miss S N Ralphs **Trained** Hambleton, N Yorks
■ Digital was withdrawn (16/1, unruly in stalls.) R4, deduct 5p in the £.

FOCUS
Just a fair sprint handicap, restricted to apprentices. The winning time was 0.82 seconds slower than the Cornwallis. The majority raced down the middle of the track, and that's where the winner raced, but the five on the stands' side were at no disadvantage. The third, running to his recent form, is the best guide to the level.
Black Moma(IRE) Official explanation: jockey said filly had no more to give
T/Plt: £123.90 to a £1 stake. Pool: £102,466.50. 603.70 winning tickets. T/Qpdt: £46.30 to a £1 stake. Pool: £4,871.20. 77.70 winning tickets. SP

[6119]KEMPTON (A.W) (R-H)
Saturday, October 13

OFFICIAL GOING: Standard
Wind: Light across, becoming fresher from race 2 onwards Weather: Overcast

6174 CARIBBEAN PARTY NIGHT HERE OCTOBER 24TH H'CAP 5f (P)
6:50 (6:51) (Class 6) (0-65,65) 3-Y-O+ **£2,047** (£604; £302) **Stalls** High

Form RPR

006 **1** **Stoneacre Boy (IRE)**[23] 5565 4-8-10 **57** .... LPKeniry 9 70
(Peter Grayson) *chsd ldrs: rdn to ld ins fnl f: r.o* **8/1**[3]

5022 **2** *1* **Musical Script (USA)**[12] 5866 4-8-10 **57** .... (b) SebSanders 3 66
(Mouse Hamilton-Fairley) *sn pushed along in rr: hdwy 1/2-way: rdn and edgd rt 1f out: r.o* **4/1**[1]

0010 **3** *3/4* **Multahab**[21] 5642 8-9-4 **65** .... (t) JamieSpencer 12 71
(M Wigham) *led: rdn over 1f out: hdd and unable qck ins fnl f* **4/1**[1]

4365 **4** *hd* **Jayanjay**[12] 5867 8-8-8 **55** .... TQuinn 11 61
(P Mitchell) *prom: nt clr run over 1f out: r.o wl towards fin* **6/1**[2]

6064 **5** *3/4* **Minnow**[28] 5420 3-8-2 **56** .... (v) WilliamCarson(7) 10 59
(S C Williams) *s.i.s: outpcd: hdwy over 1f out: nt rch ldrs* **12/1**

3310 **6** *3/4* **Rosie Cross (IRE)**[17] 5731 3-8-13 **65** .... PatrickHills(5) 2 65
(Eve Johnson Houghton) *mid-div: pushed along 1/2-way: nt pce to chal* **10/1**

0610 **7** *1 1/4* **Blessed Place**[37] 5174 7-8-3 **55** .... (t) AshleyHamblett(5) 8 51
(D J S Ffrench Davis) *chsd ldr over 3f: wknd ins fnl f* **6/1**[2]

6433 **8** *3/4* **Talcen Gwyn (IRE)**[17] 5726 5-8-5 **59** .... (v) JosephWalsh(7) 5 52
(M F Harris) *s.i.s and hmpd s: outpcd* **10/1**

2450 **9** *shd* **Scarlett Heart (IRE)**[45] 4944 3-9-4 **65** .... GregFairley 6 58
(J Gallagher) *hmpd s: a in rr* **33/1**

0-06 **10** *1 3/4* **Pamir (IRE)**[201] 787 5-9-3 **64** .... (b) GeorgeBaker 1 50
(P R Chamings) *chsd ldrs: rdn over 1f out: wknd fnl f* **11/1**

1-00 **11** *2 1/2* **Juncea**[51] 4740 3-9-4 **65** .... SteveDrowne 4 42
(H Morrison) *sn outpcd* **20/1**

0000 **12** *13* **Winning Spirit (IRE)**[76] 4001 3-8-10 **57** .... AdrianMcCarthy 7 —
(Miss Z C Davison) *wnt lft s: sn chsng ldrs: wknd wl over 1f out* **66/1**

59.37 secs (-1.03) **Going Correction** -0.20s/f (Stan) **12** Ran SP% **123.1**
Speed ratings (Par 101): **100,98,97,96,95 94,92,91,91,88 84,63**
CSF £40.98 CT £154.53 TOTE £10.20: £5.20, £1.60, £1.90; EX 44.60.
Owner Richard Teatum **Bred** Michael Dalton **Trained** Formby, Lancs

FOCUS
An ordinary handicap but pretty competitive nonetheless and sound form rated around the placed horses.
Talcen Gwyn(IRE) Official explanation: jockey said gelding hung right throughout

6175 DIGIBET SPORTS BETTING CLAIMING STKS 1m 2f (P)
7:20 (7:23) (Class 6) 3-Y-O+ **£2,047** (£604; £302) **Stalls** High

Form RPR

0024 **1** **Langford**[13] 5838 7-9-3 66 .... GeorgeBaker 3 71
(M H Tompkins) *hld up: hdwy over 2f out: styd on to ld wl ins fnl f* **13/2**

5652 **2** *hd* **Best Selection**[10] 5921 3-8-12 69 .... RichardMullen 13 71
(A P Jarvis) *a.p: rdn to ld ins fnl f: sn hdd: kpt on* **14/1**

0004 **3** *1 1/2* **Art Modern (IRE)**[20] 5454 5-9-13 82 .... (b) RyanMoore 4 78
(G L Moore) *hld up: slipped wl over 3f out: hdwy over 1f out: nt rch ldrs* **9/2**[3]

6220 **4** *3/4* **Tufton**[15] 5774 4-9-13 81 .... (t) OscarUrbina 6 77
(Ian Williams) *led: rdn over 1f out: edgd lft and hdd ins fnl f: styd on same pce* **14/1**

4553 **5** *1 3/4* **Laugh 'n Cry**[105] 3083 6-8-9 50 .... (p) LPKeniry 1 55
(Eoin Doyle, Ire) *prom: chsd ldr 1/2-way: rdn over 2f out: no ex fnl f* **33/1**

000 **6** *nk* **General Knowledge (USA)**[11] 3672 4-9-11 77 .... (t) TQuinn 7 70
(B G Powell) *racd keenly: trckd ldr to 1/2-way: rdn over 2f out: no ex fnl f* **20/1**

21 **7** *1 1/4* **Drizzi (IRE)**[13] 5835 6-9-5 66 .... (p) SebSanders 5 62
(A W Carroll) *hld up: rdn over 2f out: n.d* **10/3**[2]

0000 **8** *1/2* **Compton Express**[28] 5422 4-8-10 40 .... (v[1]) JohnEgan 8 52
(Jamie Poulton) *hld up: rdn over 1f out: n.d* **100/1**

/000 **9** *nk* **Top Gear**[6] 3943 5-9-5 72 .... (b[1]) IanMongan 11 60
(Mrs L J Mongan) *hld up: rdn over 2f out: n.d* **40/1**

-600 **10** *5* **Mr Belvedere**[30] 5368 6-9-3 42 .... (p) JamesDoyle 10 48
(A J Lidderdale) *prom: rdn over 3f out: wknd 2f out* **50/1**

0000 **11** *7* **Always A Story**[116] 2745 5-8-11 43 .... (p) PaulEddery 2 28
(Miss D Mountain) *hld up: wknd over 2f out* **100/1**

12- **12** *dist* **Petrovich (USA)**[478] 2775 4-9-8 109 .... JamieSpencer 12 —
(B J Curley) *s.i.s: sn prom: rdn over 3f out: wknd and eased over 2f out* **11/8**[1]

2m 6.49s (-2.51) **Going Correction** -0.20s/f (Stan)
WFA 3 from 4yo+ 5lb **12** Ran SP% **124.1**
Speed ratings (Par 101): **102,101,100,100,98 98,97,97,96,92 87,—**
CSF £90.94 TOTE £7.70: £2.30, £2.60, £1.60; EX 73.20.Best Selection was claimed by Mrs L. J. Mongan for £15,000. Petrovich (USA) was claimed by Ms Jane Chapple-Hyam for £15,000
Owner Marlborough Electronics **Bred** Summertree Stud **Trained** Newmarket, Suffolk

FOCUS
Not a bad claimer, the talking point of which was the performance of the highly-rated but long-time absent Petrovich. The pace was not that strong and the form does not look solid despite most of the first five running close to their marks.

Petrovich(USA) Official explanation: jockey said colt was hanging badly on final bend

6176 DIGIBET MEDIAN AUCTION MAIDEN STKS 7f (P)
7:50 (7:56) (Class 5) 3-5-Y-0 **£2,047** (£604; £302) **Stalls** High

Form RPR
3360 **1** **Le Singe Noir**[14] 5819 3-9-3 65...(b) GregFairley 1 66
(M Botti) *hld up: hdwy over 2f out: styd on u.p to ld wl ins fnl f* **12/1**
6-04 **2** *1 1/4* **Sophia Gardens**[19] 5687 3-8-12 65.................................. SebSanders 3 57
(D W P Arbuthnot) *chsd ldr: rdn and hung lft fr over 1f out: led ins fnl f: sn hdd and no ex* **7/2**[2]
42 **3** *1 1/4* **Cape Cobra**[123] 2541 3-9-3 0...(b[1]) RyanMoore 7 59
(J H M Gosden) *s.i.s: hld up: rdn over 2f out: hdwy on outside fr over 1f out: nt rch ldrs* **3/1**[1]
6305 **4** *1/2* **Foreland Sands (IRE)**[22] 5606 3-9-3 42.....................(v[1]) RobertHavlin 4 58
(J R Best) *led: rdn and hung lft fr over 1f out: hdd and no ex ins fnl f* **25/1**
2005 **5** *4* **The Jay Factor (IRE)**[18] 5714 3-9-3 62...................... JamieSpencer 10 47
(Pat Eddery) *prom: rdn and ev ch over 1f out: wknd fnl f* **10/1**[3]
00 **6** *3/4* **Wattys The Craic**[29] 5390 3-9-3 0....................................... LiamJones 9 45
(G Prodromou) *chsd ldrs: rdn over 4f out: wknd over 2f out* **50/1**
00 **7** *3 1/2* **Beau Bramble**[25] 5494 3-9-3 0.. GeorgeBaker 2 35
(C F Wall) *chsd ldrs: rdn over 2f out: wknd over 1f out* **100/1**
8 *1 1/4* **Tagula Sands (IRE)** 3-9-3 0.. RichardSmith 6 32
(J C Fox) *s.i.s: hld up: effrt over 2f out: wknd over 1f out* **100/1**

1m 26.08s (-0.72) **Going Correction** -0.20s/f (Stan) **8** Ran SP% **71.8**
Speed ratings (Par 103): **96,94,93,92,88 87,83,81**
CSF £19.08 TOTE £9.10: £2.40, £1.10, £1.10; EX 17.10.
Owner Jaber Ramadhan **Bred** Poulton Farm Stud **Trained** Newmarket, Suffolk
■ L'Hirondelle (11/10F) & Artistic Liaison (100/1) were withdrawn after refusing to enter the stalls. R4, deduct 45p in the £.

FOCUS
A poor maiden in the absence of the Godolphin newcomer L'Hirondelle. who refused to go into the stalls. The time was moderate and the form looks weak and somewhat dubious.

6177 DIGIBET.COM MAIDEN AUCTION STKS 6f (P)
8:20 (8:23) (Class 5) 2-Y-0 **£2,817** (£838; £418; £209) **Stalls** High

Form RPR
3 **1** **Jeninsky (USA)**[15] 5770 2-8-9 0.................................... FrancisNorton 5 83+
(P J McBride) *chsd ldrs: rdn to ld over 1f out: sn clr: eased nr fin* **3/1**[3]
00 **2** *5* **Bobal Girl**[11] 5881 2-7-11 0.. MCGeran[(7)] 10 57
(E F Vaughan) *s.i.s: outpcd: r.o ins fnl f: nrst fin* **66/1**
5 **3** *hd* **Heron (IRE)**[40] 5097 2-8-13 0... SebSanders 8 65
(N P Littmoden) *chsd ldr: rdn and ev ch over 1f out: styd on same pce* **8/1**
34 **4** *3/4* **Solo River**[26] 5470 2-8-4 0... JamieMackay 4 54
(P J Makin) *hld up: rdn over 2f out: hdwy over 1f out: nvr nrr* **16/1**
432 **5** *1 3/4* **Kalligal**[12] 5872 2-8-6 79.. RobertHavlin 9 51
(R Ingram) *led: rdn and hdd over 1f out: wknd ins fnl f* **2/1**[1]
5320 **6** *1/2* **River Gleam (IRE)**[22] 5582 2-8-5 70............................ RichardMullen 3 48
(A P Jarvis) *edgd lft s: sn chsng ldrs: rdn 1/2-way: wknd over 1f out* **8/1**
0 **7** *1 3/4* **Libertytyne**[11] 5888 2-8-7 0.................................... SimonWhitworth 2 45+
(S Kirk) *s.i.s and hmpd s: a in rr* **40/1**
8 *4* **Traitor's Gate** 2-9-1 0.. GregFairley 7 41
(M Johnston) *mid-div: sn drvn along: wknd wl over 1f out* **11/4**[2]
0 **9** *27* **Rightcar Lewis**[11] 5888 2-8-8 0.. LPKeniry 1 —
(Peter Grayson) *bhd fnl 4f* **100/1**

1m 13.03s (-0.67) **Going Correction** -0.20s/f (Stan) **9** Ran SP% **118.0**
Speed ratings (Par 95): **96,89,89,88,85 85,82,77,41**
CSF £174.11 TOTE £4.10: £1.40, £18.00, £2.00; EX 376.50.
Owner J M Beever **Bred** Dr R And Mrs Smiser West & And Mrs M **Trained** Newmarket, Suffolk

FOCUS
An ordinary maiden but a taking performance from the winner, who was value for further than the winning margin of five lengths although she did not beat a great deal.

NOTEBOOK
Jeninsky(USA), who shaped with promise despite running green when a good third on her debut at Haydock, knew her job better this time and was always well placed behind the pace, before kicking clear a furlong out to run out a decisive winner. Evidently at home on this surface, she could be interesting in a nursery as long as the Handicapper does not go mad. (op 7-2)
Bobal Girl, a sister to Amanda Carter, a dual winner at up to 1m2f, and a half-sister to seven other winners, ran her best race to date on her third start. She is bred to want further than this and ran as such, and it will be interesting to see what sort of mark she gets. (op 100-1)
Heron(IRE), who chased the leader for much of the race, was firmly put in his place when the winner kicked clear. Narrowly beaten for second place, this was nevertheless a solid effort, and after one more outing he will be eligible for handicaps. (op 9-1)
Solo River probably did not improve on her previous couple of efforts, but she has now had the requisite three runs for a mark and will have better opportunities in the handicapping sphere. (op 14-1)
Kalligal looked the one to beat on her second to a Stoute colt at Windsor last time, but she failed to translate that form to the Polytrack. She set a good pace but dropped out tamely when tackled.
Traitor's Gate, a brother to Morning Pride, a high-class triple 5f winner at two, and a half-brother to three three-year-old winners over 1m plus, was too green to do himself justice and paddock inspection suggested that he could be got fitter. He should come on for the experience. (op 9-4)

6178 BOOK YOUR TICKETS ON 01372 47 00 47 H'CAP 1m 4f (P)
8:50 (8:50) (Class 6) (0-60,60) 3-Y-0 **£2,047** (£604; £302) **Stalls** Low

Form RPR
6043 **1** **Polyquest (IRE)**[40] 5095 3-8-12 54.................................. NickyMackay 1 64+
(G A Butler) *hld up: hdwy over 2f out: led over 1f out: drvn out* **6/1**[3]
000- **2** *3/4* **Spanish Conquest**[381] 5608 3-8-4 46.......................... JamieMackay 12 54+
(Sir Mark Prescott) *chsd ldr tl led over 2f out: rdn and hdd over 1f out: styd on u.p* **3/1**[1]
4003 **3** *4* **She's So Pretty (IRE)**[10] 5899 3-9-4 60.........................(e) SebSanders 9 62
(W R Swinburn) *s.i.s: hld up: nt clr run over 2f out: styd on ins fnl f: nrst fin* **5/1**[2]
0033 **4** *hd* **Astrolibra**[10] 5894 3-8-4 51.. PatrickHills[(5)] 2 53
(M H Tompkins) *hld up: hdwy over 2f out: rdn over 1f out: no ex fnl f* **12/1**
0245 **5** *1/2* **Alberts Story (USA)**[8] 5983 3-8-12 57..................... JamieMoriarty[(3)] 7 58
(R A Fahey) *hld up: rdn over 2f out: styd on ins fnl f: nrst fin* **15/2**
3041 **6** *nk* **Papradon**[10] 5894 3-9-0 56.......................................(v) RobertHavlin 11 56
(J R Best) *prom: rdn over 2f out: no ex fnl f* **10/1**
0604 **7** *shd* **Bugsy's Boy**[10] 5899 3-8-11 53.. JohnEgan 10 53
(P W D'Arcy) *hld up in tch: rdn over 2f out: no ex fnl f* **6/1**[3]
4065 **8** *7* **Spice Bar**[7] 6005 3-9-3 59...(p) FrancisNorton 6 48
(A M Balding) *chsd ldrs: rdn over 2f out: wknd over 1f out* **10/1**
0000 **9** *9* **Opera Crown (IRE)**[16] 5755 3-8-8 50.....................................(b) TQuinn 4 25
(P F I Cole) *led: rdn and hdd over 2f out: sn wknd* **12/1**
0405 **10** *10* **Kyloe Belle (USA)**[18] 5710 3-8-12 54............................(vt[1]) OscarUrbina 3 13
(Mrs A J Perrett) *s.s: a in rr: wknd 3f out* **33/1**
0050 **11** *11* **Path To Glory**[9] 5945 3-8-7 49.................................. AdrianMcCarthy 5 —
(Miss Z C Davison) *prom: rdn over 4f out: wknd wl over 2f out* **25/1**

2m 33.15s (-3.75) **Going Correction** -0.20s/f (Stan) **11** Ran SP% **122.4**
Speed ratings (Par 99): **104,103,100,100,100 100,100,95,89,82 75**
CSF £25.36 CT £100.71 TOTE £7.20: £2.00, £2.10, £2.10; EX 55.20.
Owner The Fairy Story Partnership **Bred** Deepwood Farm Stud **Trained** Blewbury, Oxon

FOCUS
A moderate contest but a decent gallop and solid form for the grade. It is likely to throw up a winner or two at the right level.
Bugsy's Boy Official explanation: jockey said gelding hung left in home straight

6179 HALLOWE'EN PARTY HERE OCTOBER 31ST H'CAP 1m (P)
9:20 (9:20) (Class 6) (0-55,55) 3-Y-0+ **£2,817** (£838; £418; £209) **Stalls** High

Form RPR
6031 **1** **Justcallmehandsome**[15] 5782 5-8-6 52....................(v) SophieDoyle[(7)] 4 62
(D J S Ffrench Davis) *chsd ldrs: led over 1f out: styd on* **11/2**[2]
2400 **2** *1 1/4* **Postmaster**[24] 5546 5-9-1 54.. SteveDrowne 12 61
(R Ingram) *hld up: hdwy over 2f out: rdn over 1f out: styd on* **8/1**
0413 **3** *1 1/4* **Jools**[9] 5946 9-9-1 54.. SebSanders 3 58
(D K Ivory) *hld up: hdwy over 1f out: nt rch ldrs* **11/2**[2]
6043 **4** *1/2* **Marmooq**[11] 5890 4-8-13 52..(p) TQuinn 10 55
(M J Attwater) *led: hdd over 4f out: led again over 2f out: rdn and hdd over 1f out: no ex ins fnl f* **8/1**
0000 **5** *1/2* **Play Up Pompey**[72] 4108 5-9-2 55.................................. OscarUrbina 9 57
(J J Bridger) *hld up: r.o ins fnl f: nvr nrr* **33/1**
5122 **6** *3/4* **Charlottebutterfly**[3] 6096 7-8-11 50................................... IanMongan 5 50
(P J McBride) *hld up: hdwy over 2f out: rdn over 1f out: styd on same pce* **7/2**[1]
1455 **7** *1/2* **Azreme**[28] 5424 7-9-2 55.. AmirQuinn 11 54
(P Howling) *s.i.s: hld up: hdwy over 1f out: nt rch ldrs* **8/1**
010- **8** *1 1/4* **Take It There**[288] 6641 5-9-1 54.. JamesDoyle 6 50
(A J Lidderdale) *s.i.s: nt clr run over 1f out: n.d* **50/1**
0301 **9** *shd* **Solicitude**[17] 5730 4-9-0 53.. RobertHavlin 7 49
(D Haydn Jones) *mid-div: hdwy over 3f out: rdn and wknd over 1f out* **15/2**[3]
1046 **10** *1 1/2* **Trevian**[36] 5188 6-9-2 55... LPKeniry 8 47
(J M Bradley) *hld up: nt clr run over 2f out: n.d* **16/1**
004 **11** *1 3/4* **George's Flyer (IRE)**[35] 5237 4-9-0 53.....................(b) TonyHamilton 1 41
(R A Fahey) *chsd ldrs: rdn over 2f out: wknd over 1f out* **12/1**
0066 **12** *2* **Convince (USA)**[10] 5900 6-8-10 49..............................(v[1]) GregFairley 2 33
(J M Bradley) *chsd ldrs over 5f* **40/1**
3160 **13** *9* **Moonlight Fantasy (IRE)**[18] 5704 4-8-12 54........... NeilChalmers[(3)] 13 17
(Lucinda Featherstone) *chsd ldr tl led over 4f out: hdd over 2f out: wknd over 1f out* **40/1**

1m 39.22s (-1.58) **Going Correction** -0.20s/f (Stan) **13** Ran SP% **121.4**
Speed ratings (Par 101): **99,97,96,96,95 94,94,93,92,91 89,87,78**
CSF £48.86 CT £266.84 TOTE £9.50: £2.60, £2.40, £2.10; EX 113.10 Place 6 £ 73.68, Place 5 £ 43.03.
Owner Mrs J E Taylor **Bred** Mrs J E Taylor **Trained** Lambourn, Berks

FOCUS
Moderate handicap form but straightforward form and solid enough for the level rated around the placed horses.
Take It There Official explanation: jockey said mare was denied a clear run
Moonlight Fantasy(IRE) Official explanation: jockey said gelding ran too free
T/Plt: £239.10 to a £1 stake. Pool: £65,016.50. 198.45 winning tickets. T/Qpdt: £18.50 to a £1 stake. Pool: £5,149.10. 205.40 winning tickets. CR

6153 YORK (L-H)
Saturday, October 13

OFFICIAL GOING: Good to soft (good in places; 6.7)
No significant rain yet the ground was reckoned a good deal more testing, tackier and stickier than the previous day.
Wind: light, half behind Weather: Overcast, light drizzle

6180 WOODFORD RESERVE BOURBON STKS (H'CAP) 1m 208y
2:10 (2:10) (Class 4) (0-85,85) 3-Y-0+ **£7,772** (£2,312; £1,155; £577) **Stalls** Low

Form RPR
2020 **1** **Jewelled Dagger (IRE)**[54] 4672 3-8-9 78.......................(b) LeeEnstone 1 92
(I Semple) *mde all: stvd far side in home st: clr 4f out: styd on strly* **33/1**
2114 **2** *3* **Ahlawy (IRE)**[32] 5296 4-9-0 79...................................... PaulMulrennan 2 86
(M W Easterby) *chsd ldrs: styd far side and chsd wnr 4f out: kpt on: no imp* **16/1**
0000 **3** *3* **Vicious Warrior**[22] 5585 8-9-4 83................................. DeanMcKeown 7 84
(R M Whitaker) *w ldrs: c wd and led stands' side gp in st: kpt on wl fnl 2f* **25/1**
2112 **4** *1 3/4* **Montrachet**[59] 4497 3-8-8 77.. MartinDwyer 6 74
(M L W Bell) *hld up in mid-div: effrt over 3f out: kpt on same pce fnl 2f* **15/2**[2]
1103 **5** *nk* **Suits Me**[15] 5775 4-8-11 76.. MickyFenton 19 72
(T P Tate) *chsd ldrs: kpt on same pce fnl 2f* **12/1**
0-26 **6** *1 1/4* **Dancing Lyra**[16] 5748 6-9-0 79... PaulHanagan 17 73+
(R A Fahey) *dwlt: styd on fnl 2f: nvr nr ldrs* **14/1**
3420 **7** *1 1/2* **Flighty Fellow (IRE)**[15] 5775 7-9-0 79.............................(b) DavidAllan 14 69
(T D Easterby) *in rr: hdwy wl outside over 2f out: kpt on wl fnl f* **20/1**
6451 **8** *hd* **She's Our Lass (IRE)**[21] 5620 6-8-9 74........................ RoystonFfrench 9 64
(D Carroll) *hld up in mid-div: styd on fnl 2f: nt rch ldrs* **11/1**
0050 **9** *3/4* **Lucayan Dancer**[31] 5327 7-9-2 81............................... AdrianTNicholls 5 69
(D Nicholls) *in rr and pushed along: styd on fnl 2f: nvr a factor* **28/1**
5315 **10** *3/4* **King Of Rhythm (IRE)**[7] 6021 4-8-7 72................................ JimmyQuinn 8 59
(D Carroll) *prom: one pce fnl 3f* **40/1**
6-14 **11** *7* **Noisy Silence (IRE)**[43] 4993 3-9-0 83.................................. NCallan 11 54
(E F Vaughan) *chsd ldrs: lost pl over 2f out* **9/1**[3]
4555 **12** *1* **Goodbye Mr Bond**[21] 5641 7-9-6 85...................................... KDarley 16 54
(E J Alston) *hld up in rr: hdwy towards far side 4f out: edgd rt: wknd over 1f out* **6/1**[1]
0000 **13** *hd* **Blue Spinnaker (IRE)**[15] 5775 8-8-3 75 ow1................. NSLawes[(7)] 13 43
(M W Easterby) *in rr: nvr on terms* **16/1**
1-3 **14** *2* **Sumi Girl (IRE)**[178] 1089 3-8-10 79...................................... DaleGibson 4 43
(R A Fahey) *dwlt: hdwy and chsd other 2 far side 4f out: sn wknd* **12/1**
-340 **15** *1* **Instructor**[34] 3989 6-8-9 81.. JamesRogers[(7)] 3 43
(R A Fahey) *chsd ldrs: lost pl over 2f out: heavily eased ins fnl f* **16/1**

6010 **16** *1* **Malyana**[43] 5014 3-8-11 80 PhilipRobinson 10 40
(M A Jarvis) *chsd ldrs: drvn over 3f out: lost pl over 2f out* **11/1**

6652 **17** *14* **Full Victory (IRE)**[5] 6067 5-9-0 79 EddieAhern 12 8
(R A Farrant) *mid-div: rdn and lost pl over 3f out: virtually p.u ins fnl f* **9/1**[3]

3125 **18** *6* **Cool Ebony**[19] 5693 4-8-8 73 PhillipMakin 15 —
(M Dods) *mid-div: drvn on outer to chse ldrs over 4f out: sn lost pl: bhd whn virtually p.u ins fnial f* **33/1**

1m 51.87s (0.88) **Going Correction** +0.20s/f (Good)
WFA 3 from 4yo+ 4lb **18** Ran SP% **122.8**
Speed ratings (Par 105): **104,101,98,97,96 95,94,94,93,92 86,85,85,83,82 82,69,64**
CSF £466.44 CT £12664.68 TOTE £53.60: £10.00, £6.20, £5.80, £1.90; EX 1044.60 TRIFECTA Not won..
Owner A R M Galbraith **Bred** Ballyhane Stud **Trained** Carluke, S Lanarks

FOCUS
The first two stuck to the far side in the home straight, which subsequent events proved was the place to be on the round course. Vicious Warrior, who led the charge of the wide brigade, was six lengths adrift of the winner at the line and the form, rated through the runner-up, has a dubious look about it. He and the others in the main group could all be 7lb or 8lb better than their bare form.
Full Victory(IRE) Official explanation: trainer had no explanation for the poor form shown

6181 SHEPHERD GROUP STKS (H'CAP) 2m 2f
2:40 (2:40) (Class 3) (0-95,91) 3-Y-0+ **£8,096** (£2,408; £1,203; £601) **Stalls** Low

Form RPR

6214 **1** **Missoula (IRE)**[12] 5857 4-8-10 73 oh2 JimmyQuinn 3 90
(M H Tompkins) *trckd ldrs: hdwy 5f out: led 4f out: rdn clr 2f out: unchal* **8/1**

4504 **2** *13* **Kayf Aramis**[11] 5884 5-8-10 73 oh2 (p) ChrisCatlin 1 76
(J L Spearing) *led: jinked rt and hdd briefly 10f out: sn led again: rdn along and hdd 4f out: sn drvn and kpt on fnl 2f: no ch w wnr* **6/1**[3]

2225 **3** *1 1/2* **Prince Zafonic**[14] 5800 4-8-13 76 (t) NCallan 2 77
(Miss Gay Kelleway) *hld up in rr: hdwy 5f out: rdn along to chse ldrs 3f out: drvn and kpt on same pce fnl 2f* **6/1**[3]

1513 **4** *1 3/4* **Atlantic Coast (IRE)**[11] 5884 3-8-0 75 RoystonFfrench 6 74
(M Johnston) *trckd ldrs: pushed along 5f out: rdn to chse wnr over 2f out: sn drvn and wknd over 1f out* **9/4**[1]

301 **5** *6* **Mirjan (IRE)**[47] 4893 11-10-0 91 (b) PaulHanagan 4 84
(L Lungo) *in tch: rdn along over 4f out and sn outpcd* **9/1**

011 **6** *2 1/2* **Gallileo Figaro (USA)**[77] 3976 4-8-7 73 JerryO'Dwyer(3) 7 63
(N B King) *hld up in rr: effrt and sme hdwy over 4f out: sn rdn and btn* **10/3**[2]

4060 **7** *21* **Monolith**[9] 5933 9-9-1 83 GaryBartley(5) 5 50
(L Lungo) *cl up: led briefly 1f out: sn hdd: rdn along 5f out and sn wknd* **16/1**

3m 56.61s (-1.69) **Going Correction** +0.20s/f (Good)
WFA 3 from 4yo+ 12lb **7** Ran SP% **109.4**
Speed ratings (Par 107): **111,105,104,103,101 100,90**
CSF £49.56 TOTE £10.20: £4.10, £2.90; EX 59.70.
Owner Pollards Bloodstock **Bred** Pollards Stables **Trained** Newmarket, Suffolk

FOCUS
This turned out to be a very one-sided stayers' handicap. The form has been taken at face value for now but whether the winner is this good only time will tell. It could be that she is a bit flattered.

NOTEBOOK
Missoula(IRE), suited by going left-handed, travelled strongly and came right away. Her rating will shoot up as a result and she is unlikely to make the cut in the Cesarewitch. (op 9-1)
Kayf Aramis, effectively 3lb higher than his course-and-distance success in May, had the cheekepieces back on. He gave his rider a scare passing the stable crossing but in the end had but a distant view of the winner. (op 13-2)
Prince Zafonic, a big sort, has been in good form but as a result he keeps creeping up the ratings. (tchd 11-2)
Atlantic Coast(IRE), without any headgear, is a tricky ride and, after going in pursuit of the winner, in the end he seemed to give in rather tamely. For some reason this track does not bring out the best in him. (tchd 5-2 in places)
Mirjan(IRE) is still 3lb above his last winning mark and, in his twelfth year, is an unlikely improver. (op 6-1)
Gallileo Figaro(USA), 3lb higher than when scoring on her latest outing here in July, was in trouble once in line for home. (op 7-2)

6182 STOWE FAMILY LAW LLP SILVER JUBILEE ROCKINGHAM STKS (LISTED RACE) 6f
3:10 (3:11) (Class 1) 2-Y-O **£14,817** (£5,602; £2,800; £1,400) **Stalls** Centre

Form RPR

13 **1** **Max One Two Three (IRE)**[22] 5592 2-8-9 82 RichardKingscote 8 99
(Tom Dascombe) *hld up in stands' side: swtchd lft and gd hdwy 2f out: rdn over 1f out: styd on wl to ld last 100yds* **12/1**

1160 **2** *2* **Maze (IRE)**[28] 5406 2-9-3 96 RoystonFfrench 5 101
(B Smart) *trckd ldrs far side: hdwy over 2f out: led over 1f out: rdn and veered sharply lft jst ins fnl f: sn drvn: hdd and nt qckn last 100yds* **14/1**

2242 **3** *nk* **Look Busy (IRE)**[22] 5583 2-8-9 93 PhilipRobinson 13 92
(A Berry) *in tch stands' side: hdwy 2f out: rdn to chse ldrs over 1f out: kpt on ins fnl f* **12/1**

5310 **4** *1/2* **Eastern Romance**[15] 5766 2-8-9 81 PaulMulrennan 4 91
(K A Ryan) *prom far side: hdwy and overall ldr over 2f out: rdn and hdd over 1f out: sn drvn and kpt on same pce ins fnl f* **100/1**

10 **5** *2 1/2* **Lytton**[35] 5219 2-9-0 94 AdamKirby 10 88
(W R Swinburn) *trckd ldrs stands' side: effrt 2f out and n.m.r: sn rdn and kpt on same pce ins fnl f* **9/1**

2140 **6** *nk* **Mey Blossom**[31] 5322 2-8-9 85 DeanMcKeown 15 82
(R M Whitaker) *prom stands' side: rdn along 2f out: sn drvn and kpt on same pce appr fnl f* **100/1**

3505 **7** *1/2* **Mister Hardy**[7] 6017 2-9-0 91 PaulHanagan 12 86
(R A Fahey) *chsd ldrs stands' side: rdn and sltly outpcd 2f out: kpt on u.p ins fnl f* **10/1**

0440 **8** *shd* **Loch Jipp (USA)**[21] 5614 2-8-12 101 KDarley 14 83
(J S Wainwright) *led stands' side gp: ev ch over 2f out: sn rdn and hung lft: wezakened appr fnl f* **12/1**

616 **9** *1* **Sudden Impact (IRE)**[28] 5435 2-8-9 97 EddieAhern 9 77
(Paul Green) *cl up stands' side: rdn along 2f out: sn edgd lft and wknd over 1f out* **8/1**[3]

3012 **10** *3/4* **Piscean (USA)**[7] 6004 2-9-0 76 (b) MickyFenton 11 80
(T Keddy) *hld up stands' side: gd hdwy on stands rail 2f out: sn rdn and wknd appr fnl f* **40/1**

4P62 **11** *1* **Vhujon (IRE)**[7] 6017 2-9-0 85 TGMcLaughlin 1 77
(P D Evans) *towards rr far side: swtchd rt and sme hdwy over 2f out: sn rdn and no imp* **14/1**

1001 **12** *nk* **Major Eazy (IRE)**[10] 5922 2-9-0 94 RichardHughes 6 76
(B J Meehan) *overall ldr far side: rdn along and hdd over 2f out: sn wknd* **4/1**[2]

1606 **13** *8* **Mazzanti**[28] 5410 2-9-0 87 NCallan 7 52
(K A Ryan) *always in rr far side* **16/1**

14 *1* **Shining Armour (IRE)**[21] 5649 2-9-0 0 (b) PJSmullen 3 49
(D K Weld, Ire) *chsd ldrs far side whn edgd lft after 1f: rdn along 1/2-way: nvr a factor* **7/2**[1]

1003 **15** *2 1/2* **Burnwynd Boy**[20] 5665 2-9-0 89 (v[1]) PhillipMakin 2 42
(I Semple) *chsd ldrs far side: bmpd after 1f: sn lost pl and bhd fr 1/2-way* **20/1**

1m 13.08s (0.52) **Going Correction** +0.20s/f (Good) **15** Ran SP% **123.9**
Speed ratings (Par 103): **104,101,100,100,96 96,95,95,94,93 92,91,81,79,76**
CSF £170.39 TOTE £22.00: £5.20, £4.60, £2.50; EX 404.50 Trifecta £480.30 Part won. Pool: £676.59 - 0.50 winning units..
Owner 123 Racing Partnership **Bred** P J Towell **Trained** Lambourn, Berks
■ A first Listed-race success for trainer Tom Dascombe and jockey Richard Kingscote.

FOCUS
A sub-standard renewal of this Listed event, the form held down by the proximity of the 81-rated fourth.

NOTEBOOK
Max One Two Three(IRE), given a much more patient ride, was handed the lead when the runner-up threw it away, but the impression was that she was the winner on merit. This was much improved form, but she has always been well regarded. (tchd 14-1 in a place)
Maze(IRE), taken down early and awash with sweat beforehand, was dropping back in trip after running too keen at Sandown and Doncaster. He took it up coming to the final furlong but threw away his chance when diving badly left inside the last. He is his own worst enemy at present. (tchd 16-1)
Look Busy(IRE), runner-up to Captain Gerrard at Ayr after a slow break, has done nothing but improve and here, in probably her final start this time, she probably ran her best race to date. (op 14-1)
Eastern Romance, having her eighth start, is looking fully exposed and had something to find. She ran out of her skin and gained some valuable black type. (op 40-1)
Lytton, done no favours by the draw at Kempton, is a most attractive colt. He should make a smart sprinter at three. (op 8-1)
Mey Blossom, highly rated by her trainer, belied her long odds and ran as if the sixth furlong was very much needed. (op 66-1)
Mister Hardy again gave a good account of himself but opportunities here will be thin on the ground at three. (op 11-1)
Major Eazy(IRE), taken to post early, took them along racing towards the far side but he was in trouble at the halfway mark and soon dropped right out. This was too bad to be true. Official explanation: jockey said colt ran flat (tchd 9-2 and 5-1 in a place)
Shining Armour(IRE), a well-made individual who got off the mark at Fairyhouse last time, was in trouble at halfway and probably wants much quicker ground than he encountered here. Official explanation: jockey said colt was unsuited by the good to soft (good in places) ground (op 9-2)

6183 PADDYPOWER.COM SPRINT TROPHY (H'CAP) 6f
3:45 (3:46) (Class 2) (0-105,105) 3-Y-0+**£22,669** (£6,744; £3,370; £1,683) **Stalls** Centre

Form RPR

6650 **1** **Fonthill Road (IRE)**[14] 5797 7-8-12 98 PaulHanagan 4 109
(R A Fahey) *in rr and sn pushed along: hdwy over 2f out: styd on wl to ld towards fin* **13/2**[2]

3036 **2** *nk* **Hoh Hoh Hoh**[9] 5953 5-9-0 100 J-PGuillambert 11 111
(R J Price) *led: rdr dropped whip ins fnl f: hdd nr fin* **20/1**

5012 **3** *1 1/2* **Commando Scott (IRE)**[14] 5809 6-8-6 92 RoystonFfrench 2 98
(I W McInnes) *mid-div: hdwy over 2f out: kpt on same pce f* **10/1**[3]

1066 **4** *1 1/2* **River Falcon**[14] 5809 7-8-11 97 DanielTudhope 8 99
(J S Goldie) *in rr: hdwy on outer over 2f out: styd on fnl f* **16/1**

0000 **5** *1/2* **King Orchisios (IRE)**[21] 5616 4-8-9 95 (p) NCallan 1 95
(K A Ryan) *prom: styd on same pce appr fnl f* **33/1**

0001 **6** *nk* **Dabbers Ridge (IRE)**[14] 5809 5-9-2 102 MichaelHills 15 101
(B W Hills) *mid-div: effrt on inner over 2f out: kpt on: nvr rchd ldrs* **4/1**[1]

1020 **7** *1/2* **Viking Spirit**[14] 5797 5-9-2 102 (v[1]) AdamKirby 7 100
(W R Swinburn) *trckd ldrs: effrt 2f out: edgd rt and kpt on same pce* **16/1**

0000 **8** *hd* **Turnkey**[14] 5809 5-8-7 93 SilvestreDeSousa 3 90
(D Nicholls) *in rr: hdwy 2f out: kpt on: nvr rchd ldrs* **20/1**

0160 **9** *1/2* **Zomerlust**[21] 5616 5-8-11 97 (v) PatCosgrave 10 93
(J J Quinn) *prom: drvn over 2f out: kpt on same pce* **14/1**

0020 **10** *3/4* **Obe Brave**[21] 5616 4-9-3 103 ChrisCatlin 12 96
(M R Channon) *chsd ldr: kpt on same pce appr fnl f* **20/1**

0015 **11** *nk* **Invincible Force (IRE)**[14] 5810 3-8-10 97 EddieAhern 6 89
(Paul Green) *mid-div: effrt over 2f out: nvr a threat* **50/1**

-600 **12** *nk* **Somnus**[35] 5214 7-9-5 105 (t) KDarley 14 96
(T D Easterby) *in rr: hdwy over 1f out: nvr on terms* **25/1**

1100 **13** *hd* **Golden Dixie (USA)**[28] 5407 8-8-5 96 KevinGhunowa(5) 13 87
(R A Harris) *pronient: rdn over 2f out: sn outpcd* **33/1**

0600 **14** *1 1/4* **Rising Shadow (IRE)**[7] 6018 6-9-3 103 JimmyQuinn 9 90
(T D Barron) *in rr: sme hdwy 2f out: nvr a factor* **14/1**

0530 **15** *2 1/2* **Conquest (IRE)**[9] 5953 3-8-13 100 RichardHughes 16 80
(W J Haggas) *hld up in rr: hdwy over 2f out: n.m.r 1f out: sn wknd and eased* **14/1**

0005 **16** *3/4* **Dhaular Dhar (IRE)**[14] 5797 5-8-6 97 ow1 GaryBartley(5) 17 74
(J S Goldie) *a towards rr* **12/1**

0042 **17** *1/2* **Tournedos (IRE)**[13] 5841 5-8-10 96 AdrianTNicholls 5 72
(D Nicholls) *a towards rr* **25/1**

401 **18** *hd* **Philharmonic**[18] 5700 6-8-12 98 DaleGibson 18 73
(R A Fahey) *a in rr* **12/1**

0004 **19** *3* **Tawaassol (USA)**[9] 5953 4-9-2 102 (v) MartinDwyer 19 68
(Sir Michael Stoute) *a in rr* **12/1**

4255 **20** *11* **Chicken Soup**[129] 2368 5-9-0 100 DavidAllan 20 33
(D J Murphy) *chsd ldrs: lost pl over 2f out: sn bhd: eased* **33/1**

1m 12.14s (-0.42) **Going Correction** +0.20s/f (Good)
WFA 3 from 4yo+ 1lb **20** Ran SP% **130.0**
Speed ratings (Par 109): **110,109,107,105,104 104,103,103,102,101 101,101,100,99,95 94,94,93,89,75**
CSF £140.65 CT £1352.76 TOTE £7.10: £2.40, £2.70, £2.40, £4.60; EX 163.10 Trifecta £1275.80 Part won. Pool: £1,796.99 - 0.90 winning units..
Owner Mrs Una Towell **Bred** D N Wallace **Trained** Musley Bank, N Yorks

FOCUS
A very strong renewal but a suspicion that the best horse on the day had to settle for second spot. Eight of the runners had lined up for the Ayr Gold Cup and the winner had done best of them there, finishing fifth overall. The form looks pretty solid, with the third a sound guide.

NOTEBOOK
Fonthill Road(IRE), just 1lb higher than when taking the 2006 Ayr Gold Cup, had the slow ground he likes and came from almost last to first to put his head in front almost on the line. (op 6-1)

Hoh Hoh Hoh, 18lb higher than for his last win, has been a revelation for this yard this year. He hit the traps running and looked to be holding the upper hand when his rider dropped his stick inside the last. It might well have made the difference between victory and defeat. (op 22-1)
Commando Scott(IRE), the last to make the cut, is in the form of his life. Though fully effective over six, he is better suited by seven. (tchd 11-1)
River Falcon, having his fourteenth start here, was racing from a mark 5lb higher than his success over 5f at the August meeting when he defeated Hoh Hoh Hoh a length.
King Orchisios(IRE), dropped 5lb, looked at his very best and ran his best race for some time. His last three wins have been on the All-Weather tracks. (op 50-1)
Dabbers Ridge(IRE), who readily accounted for Commando Scott at Haydock, was racing from a 4lb higher mark. He seems happier over 7f. (op 11-2)
Turnkey ran a lot better than on his last four starts. (op 25-1)
Conquest(IRE) Official explanation: jockey said gelding ran flat

6184 COLLINGWOOD TEAM SERVICE E.B.F MAIDEN STKS — 1m
4:20 (4:21) (Class 3) 2-Y-O — **£7,124** (£2,119; £1,059; £529) **Stalls** Low

Form — RPR
1 — **Bright Falcon** 2-9-3 0 — RichardHughes 3 — 81
(D J Murphy) *mde most: pushed along over 2f out: rdn clr appr last and styd on strly* — **11/1**
0252 2 3 — **No To Trident**[8] 5984 2-9-3 75 — TGMcLaughlin 9 — 74
(P D Evans) *hld up: hdwy over 3f out: swtchd rt and rdn wl over 1f out: styd on ins fnl f: nrst fin* — **14/1**
2 3 ½ — **Mystery Star (IRE)**[22] 5599 2-9-3 0 — JimmyQuinn 6 — 73
(M H Tompkins) *in tch: heawday 4f out: rdn to chse wnr over 1f out: drvn and one pce ins fnl f* — **11/4**[2]
6 4 1 — **La Fortalesa (IRE)**[17] 5734 2-9-3 0 — NCallan 8 — 71
(K A Ryan) *cl up: rdn along 3f out: drvn wl over 1f out and grad wknd* — **12/1**
5 shd — **Top Man Dan (IRE)** 2-9-3 0 — RoystonFfrench 2 — 70
(D Carroll) *chsd ldrs: rdn along 3f out: kpt on same pce fnl 2f* — **14/1**
6 1 ½ — **Tighnabruaich (IRE)** 2-9-3 0 — PhilipRobinson 10 — 67
(M A Jarvis) *trckd ldrs: effrt 3f out: sn rdn along: edgd lft 2f out and sn btn* — **2/1**[1]
5 7 1 — **Pondapie (IRE)**[23] 5551 2-9-0 0 — MichaelJStainton(3) 1 — 65
(R M Whitaker) *dwlt: a towards rr* — **20/1**
8 hd — **Blimey O'Riley (IRE)** 2-9-3 0 — PaulMulrennan 5 — 65
(M H Tompkins) *a in rr* — **20/1**
9 ½ — **Ghizlaan (USA)** 2-8-12 0 — MartinDwyer 4 — 58
(M Johnston) *in tch on inner: rdn along 3f out: sn wknd* — **4/1**[3]
0 10 22 — **Royal Musketeer (IRE)**[116] 2739 2-9-3 0 — DavidAllan 7 — 15
(T D Easterby) *dwlt: a towards rr* — **33/1**

1m 42.75s (3.25) **Going Correction** +0.20s/f (Good) — **10** Ran SP% **121.8**
Speed ratings (Par 99): **91,88,87,86,86 84,83,83,83,61**
CSF £154.54 TOTE £15.00: £3.70, £4.10, £1.40; EX 189.60.
Owner J David Abell & Willie McKay **Bred** A J Coleing **Trained** Bawtry, S Yorks

FOCUS
Just an ordinary maiden race with the exposed runner-up rated just 75. However, the winner has the potential to go on to much better things.

NOTEBOOK
Bright Falcon, a half-brother to Treat who took the Fillies' Mile at Ascot and finished fourth in the 1000 Guineas, is a well-made March foal. Racing on the favoured inside, he came right away and looks a fair long-term prospect. (op 12-1 tchd 10-1)
No To Trident, who threw away a winning opportunity at Wolverhampton, stuck on to claim second spot but the winner was different gear. He is starting to look fully exposed. (op 16-1)
Mystery Star(IRE), who split two subsequent winners when runner-up on his debut at Newmarket last month, went in pursuit of the winner but could never get on terms. (op 9-4)
La Fortalesa(IRE), free to post, didn't see it out and will need to learn to settle better. (op 14-1)
Top Man Dan(IRE) made a satisfactory debut but he looks the type who will improve given a little more time. (op 50-1)
Tighnabruaich(IRE) ♦, a grand type with a powerful action, proved very inexperienced and wanted to do nothing but hang left-handed. He will leave this debut effort a long way behind in time. Official explanation: jockey said colt hung left-handed in straight (op 9-4 tchd 5-2 in a place)
Pondapie(IRE) showed a fair bit more than on his debut and should improve again. (op 18-1 tchd 16-1)
Ghizlaan(USA), on the leg and narrow, cost a handy $600,000 as a yearling. Soon pushed along, she has a lot to prove after this rather inept debut. (op 7-2 tchd 9-2)

6185 PARSONAGE COUNTRY HOUSE HOTEL STKS (H'CAP) — 1m 2f 88y
4:50 (4:50) (Class 3) (0-95,93) 3-Y-O+ — **£7,772** (£2,312; £1,155; £577) **Stalls** Low

Form — RPR
4600 1 — **Flying Clarets (IRE)**[21] 5631 4-9-2 88 — (p) PaulHanagan 1 — 99
(R A Fahey) *trckd ldrs: led over 8f out: qcknd over 4f out: hld on gamely* — **8/1**
1631 2 nk — **The Grey Berry**[23] 5554 3-9-1 92 — KDarley 3 — 102
(T D Walford) *s.i.s: shkn up and sn t.k.h in rr: effrt 4f out: n.m.r over 2f out: chal 1f out: no ex towards fin* — **2/1**[1]
0021 3 2 — **Best Prospect (IRE)**[15] 5775 5-9-0 86 — (t) PhillipMakin 2 — 93
(M Dods) *hld up in rr: smooth hdwy and nt clr run over 2f out: effrt 1f out: sn rdn and kpt on same pce* — **6/1**[2]
4130 4 2 ½ — **Yossi (IRE)**[21] 5619 3-8-3 80 — (b) JimmyQuinn 5 — 82
(M H Tompkins) *sn trcking ldrs: n.m.r on inner over 2f out: fdd appr fnl f* — **16/1**
6260 5 5 — **Red Lancer**[51] 4732 6-8-9 81 — SilvestreDeSousa 4 — 73
(D Nicholls) *mid-div: one pce fnl 3f* — **16/1**
-606 6 1 — **Hollow Ridge**[59] 4503 3-8-12 89 — RichardHughes 6 — 79
(B W Hills) *t.k.h: led after 1f: hdd 8f out: wknd over 1f out* — **14/1**
15/ 7 2 ½ — **Extreme Measures**[766] 5046 4-9-7 93 — EddieAhern 8 — 79
(Saeed Bin Suroor) *hld up in rr: drvn 4f out: nvr a threat* — **15/2**[3]
6056 8 3 ½ — **Hassaad**[31] 5327 4-8-12 84 — (b) MartinDwyer 7 — 63
(W J Haggas) *prom: drvn 4f out: wknd 2f out* — **11/1**
0605 9 4 — **Wind Star**[24] 5543 4-8-8 83 — PJMcDonald(3) 12 — 54
(G A Swinbank) *prom on outer over 3f out: wknd 2f out* — **10/1**
5253 10 8 — **Go Tech**[22] 5593 7-8-8 80 — DavidAllan 11 — 36
(T D Easterby) *led 1f: chsd ldrs: lost pl over 3f out* — **16/1**
3250 11 4 — **Bailieborough (IRE)**[91] 3558 8-8-8 87 — LanceBetts(7) 10 — 36
(N Wilson) *hld up in rr: hdwy on wd outside 4f out: lost pl over 2f out* **25/1**
0300 12 21 — **Golden Dagger (IRE)**[93] 3460 3-8-6 83 — PaulMulrennan 13 — —
(K A Ryan) *prom: drvn 4f out: sn lost pl: bhd and eased ins fnl f* — **25/1**

2m 11.93s (-0.57) **Going Correction** +0.20s/f (Good)
WFA 3 from 4yo+ 5lb — **12** Ran SP% **119.9**
Speed ratings (Par 107): **110,109,108,106,102 101,99,96,93,86 83,66**
CSF £24.49 CT £105.44 TOTE £8.50: £1.90, £1.60, £2.20; EX 23.30.
Owner The Matthewman Partnership **Bred** Gabriel Bell **Trained** Musley Bank, N Yorks

FOCUS
Flying Clarets had the benefit of racing against the far-side running rail. She simply would not accept defeat and the runner-up deserves plenty of credit. Straightforward form with the winner running to the same mark as in the John Smith's Cup.

NOTEBOOK
Flying Clarets(IRE), on the same mark as when runner-up in the John Smith's Cup here in July, had the cheekpieces re-applied. She set sail for home turning in and, with the rail to help, she would not be denied. (op 9-1)
The Grey Berry, 6lb higher, missed a beat at the start and then took a fierce grip. Left short of room when trying to mount a challenge, in the end he came off second best after going head-to-head. He looks a very marketable commodity now. (op 9-4 tchd 5-2)
Best Prospect(IRE) as usual travelled smoothly but when asked to tackle the first two he declined politely. He must be a nightmare for in-running punters. (op 11-2)
Yossi(IRE), tried in blinkers again, is a weak finisher and one to have reservations about. (op 18-1)
Red Lancer seems to have forgotten how to win. (op 18-1 tchd 20-1)
Hollow Ridge, absent for two months, pulled her way to the front and had nothing left at the business end. (op 12-1)
Extreme Measures, winner of the first of his two starts at two, looked as fit as a flea on his first start for over two years. He was in trouble once in line for home and never figured. (op 8-1 tchd 7-1)

6186 COLDSTREAM GUARDS ASSOCIATION STKS (H'CAP) — 1m 6f
5:20 (5:20) (Class 4) (0-85,88) 3-Y-O+ — **£6,477** (£1,927; £963; £481) **Stalls** Low

Form — RPR
1421 1 — **Market Forces**[77] 3963 3-9-12 88 — RichardHughes 14 — 102+
(H R A Cecil) *trckd ldrs: effrt on inner 4f out: led over 2f out: shkn up and forged clr over 1f out: v readily* — **7/4**[1]
3415 2 4 — **Casual Affair**[26] 5486 4-8-10 63 — JimmyQuinn 1 — 71+
(J D Bethell) *s.i.s: t.k.h in rr: hdwy and nt clr run 3f out: styd on to take 2nd nr fin* — **10/1**
601/ 3 nk — **Traprain (IRE)**[17] 5698 5-9-9 76 — DavidAllan 12 — 82
(D Carroll) *s.i.s: effrt and swtchd outside over 2f out: styd on to take 2nd jst ins fnl f: kpt on same pce* — **25/1**
3240 4 2 — **Mighty Moon**[14] 5808 4-9-3 75 — (tp) JamesO'Reilly(5) 4 — 78
(J O'Reilly) *led after 1f: qcknd over 4f out: hdd over 2f out: one pce* **14/1**
0604 5 3 — **Galianna (IRE)**[22] 5594 3-9-0 76 — KDarley 10 — 75
(Pat Eddery) *led 1f: chsd ldrs: fdd appr fnl f* — **10/1**
0132 6 5 — **Apache Fort**[15] 5769 4-9-0 67 — DaleGibson 5 — 59
(T Keddy) *mid-div: effrt over 3f out: outpcd fnl 2f* — **9/1**[3]
0004 7 2 — **La Estrella (USA)**[9] 5933 4-10-0 81 — J-PGuillambert 2 — 70
(J G Given) *mid-div: effrt over 3f out: wknd 2f out* — **14/1**
5 8 2 ½ — **Marsam (IRE)**[18] 5717 4-9-12 79 — NCallan 7 — 65
(M G Quinlan) *hld up in rr: effrt over 3f out: nvr nr ldrs* — **20/1**
4316 9 1 ½ — **Treason Trial**[39] 5111 6-8-9 62 oh6 — MickyFenton 9 — 45
(Stef Liddiard) *hld up in rr: hdwy over 5f out: wknd 3f out* — **10/1**
3134 10 shd — **Trance (IRE)**[50] 4786 7-9-13 80 — PhillipMakin 6 — 63
(T D Barron) *in rr: drvn over 4f out: nvr on terms* — **12/1**
/23- 11 nk — **Hernando's Boy**[526] 1457 6-9-0 67 — PaulHanagan 15 — 50
(K G Reveley) *chsd ldrs: lost pl over 2f out* — **25/1**
-105 12 1 ¼ — **Alaghiraar (IRE)**[14] 5808 3-9-3 79 — (b[1]) MartinDwyer 11 — 60
(J L Dunlop) *trckd ldrs: effrt and nt clr run 3f out: wknd fnl 2f* — **8/1**[2]
6-05 13 7 — **Riodan (IRE)**[134] 2204 5-8-11 64 — DanielTudhope 13 — 35
(J J Quinn) *mid-div: hdwy over 6f out: lost pl 3f out* — **33/1**
1436 14 7 — **Go But Go**[46] 4917 3-8-11 73 — ChrisCatlin 16 — 34
(E J O'Neill) *sn chsng ldrs: lost pl 3f out* — **33/1**
0-00 15 6 — **One To Follow**[17] 5724 3-9-0 76 — PhilipRobinson 3 — 29
(C G Cox) *trckd ldrs: t.k.h: wknd 3f out: sn bhd* — **25/1**

3m 3.99s (4.49) **Going Correction** +0.20s/f (Good)
WFA 3 from 4yo+ 9lb — **15** Ran SP% **128.0**
Speed ratings (Par 105): **95,92,92,91,89 86,85,84,83,83 83,82,78,74,71**
CSF £18.84 CT £354.46 TOTE £2.80: £1.50, £2.70, £9.70; EX 33.50 Place 6 £3,364.27, Place 5 £582.18.
Owner K Abdulla **Bred** Juddmonte Farms Ltd **Trained** Newmarket, Suffolk

FOCUS
Just a steady pace but in the end a very ready and unexposed winner. The race had a bit of an end-of-season feel to it but a fairly positive view has been taken of the form.
T/Jkpt: Not won. T/Plt: £2,082.00 to a £1 stake. Pool: £135,478.66. 47.50 winning tickets. T/Qpdt: £31.00 to a £1 stake. Pool: £6,070.20. 144.70 winning tickets. WG

5791 SAINT-CLOUD (L-H)
Saturday, October 13

OFFICIAL GOING: Soft

6187a PRIX THOMAS BRYON (GROUP 3) — 1m
3:00 (2:59) 2-Y-O — **£27,027** (£10,811; £8,108; £5,405; £2,703)

RPR
1 — **Thewayyouare (USA)**[22] 5612 2-8-11 — SPasquier 3 — 107+
(A Fabre, France) *hld up: 5th 1/2-way: last on outside st: pushed along to chal 2f out: led gng easily over 1f out: wnt clr fnl f: impressive* — **13/10**[1]
2 2 ½ — **Centennial (IRE)**[22] 5590 2-8-11 — JimmyFortune 4 — 100
(J H M Gosden) *racd in 4th on outside: drvn and disputing ld 2f out: led narrowly to over 1f out: hld 2nd easily but no ch w wnr* — **18/10**[2]
3 4 — **Macellya (FR)**[43] 2-8-8 — CSoumillon 1 — 88
(X Nakkachdji, France) *racd in last: 5th st: rdn to go 3rd 1 1/2f out: styd on* — **44/10**[3]
4 2 ½ — **Chirango (FR)**[63] 2-8-11 — ACrastus 5 — 86
(P Demercastel, France) *racd in 2nd: disputing 2nd st: sn drvn and u.p: outpcd* — **12/1**
5 nse — **Without Precedent (FR)**[22] 5612 2-8-8 — TThulliez 2 — 83
(Y De Nicolay, France) *settled in tch: 3rd 1/2-way: disputing 2nd st: disputing ld 2f out: no ex fnl 1 1/2f* — **15/1**
6 8 — **Sagamihara (FR)**[5] 2-8-8 — JVictoire 6 — 65
(R Chotard, France) *led: pushed along st: hdd 2f out: qckly wknd* — **16/1**

1m 44.9s (-2.60) — **6** Ran SP% **117.5**
PARI-MUTUEL: WIN 2.30; PL 1.40, 1.60; SF 4.80.
Owner S Mulryan **Bred** Barnett Enterprises **Trained** Chantilly, France

NOTEBOOK
Thewayyouare(USA), a winner of a Listed race last time, took this Group 3 contest in the style of a real Classic prospect. The most outstanding aspect was the way he accelerated in the straight and he proved far too good for his five rivals. Having been waited with through the early stages, he quickened to take control one and a half furlongs from the finish and nothing could live with him. It will be no surprise to see him back over course and distance for the Criterium International next month.

Centennial(IRE), never far from the leaders, raced in third place early on and took the advantage for a short time coming into the final two furlongs, but he could find nothing when tackled by the winner, who was in a class of his own.
Macellya(FR) was dropped out last early on and was still at the tail of the field at the entrance to the straight. She did make some late progress but never looked like getting on terms with the winner and runner-up.
Chirango(FR), handy from the start, had nothing in reserve when things quickened in the straight and he battled gamely to hold fourth place by inches.

6192 - 6193a (Foreign Racing) - See Raceform Interactive

5856 BATH (L-H)
Sunday, October 14

OFFICIAL GOING: Good to firm (good in places; 8.7)
Wind: Virtually nil

6194 TOTEPLACEPOT NOVICE STKS — 1m 5y
2:00 (2:00) (Class 5) 2-Y-O — **£3,886** (£1,156; £577; £288) **Stalls** Low

Form — RPR
0232 **1** — **Meer Kat (IRE)**[11] 5919 2-8-12 79 — MartinDwyer 6 — 85+
(R Charlton) *in tch: chsd ldrs 3f out: chal 2f out: led ins fnl f: rdn out* **4/1**[3]
61 **2** 1 1/4 **Zakhaaref**[18] 5734 2-9-5 92 — RHills 3 — 89
(M Johnston) *led tl hdd over 4f out: led again over 2f out: rdn and hdd ins fnl f: styd on same pce* **11/10**[1]
23 **3** 1 **Green Wadi**[15] 5813 2-8-12 0 — DarryllHolland 7 — 80
(M R Channon) *hld up in tch: hdwy to chse ldrs over 3f out: rdn 2f out: hung lft and one pce ins fnl f* **5/2**[2]
5210 **4** 3 **Joinedupwriting**[22] 5613 2-9-2 75 — DeanMcKeown 2 — 77
(R M Whitaker) *chsd ldrs: rdn 3f out: wknd fnl f* **25/1**
051 **5** 1/2 **Black Jacari (IRE)**[31] 5344 2-9-2 78 — FergusSweeney 1 — 76
(A King) *t.k.h: chsd ldr tl led over 4f out: hdd over 2f out: sn btn* **11/1**
0000 **6** 19 **Ephesian (IRE)**[44] 5017 2-8-3 55 ow3 — JackDean(7) 4 — 26
(C L Popham) *a in rr: lost tch fnl 3f* **200/1**

1m 40.3s (-0.80) **Going Correction** -0.10s/f (Good) — **6** Ran SP% **108.9**
Speed ratings (Par 95): **100,98,97,94,94 75**
CSF £8.29 TOTE £5.00: £1.90, £1.50; EX 9.60.
Owner Mountgrange Stud **Bred** Darley **Trained** Beckhampton, Wilts

FOCUS
A decent little novice event. The winner and the fourth govern the merit of the form, which looks sound.

NOTEBOOK
Meer Kat(IRE) showed his true colours under a more positive ride and readily lost his maiden tag at the fifth attempt. He also seemed better suited by this quicker ground and, while a hike in the ratings is now likely, he rates a nice handicap prospect for next season.
Zakhaaref, rated 92 after easily getting off the mark at Redcar 18 days previously, failed to see out the extra furlong as well as the winner. It should be noted he was conceding 7lb to that rival and he still remains open to further improvement. However, on this evidence he has been too highly rated by the Handicapper. (op Evens)
Green Wadi, well backed, was under the pump at the top of the home straight and then wanted to hang left when entering the final furlong. This was still an improvement on his Haydock form, but he has not yet confirmed the promise of his Goodwood debut effort and his future now lies with the Handicapper. (op 3-1)
Joinedupwriting enjoyed the faster ground, but failed to convince he gets this trip at present. (op 20-1)
Black Jacari(IRE) ran too freely for his own good and not surprisingly paid the price when taken on for the lead nearing the 2f pole. (op 12-1 tchd 9-1)

6195 TOTESPORTCASINO.COM NURSERY — 5f 11y
2:35 (2:36) (Class 4) (0-85,85) 2-Y-O — **£4,857** (£1,445; £722; £360) **Stalls** Centre

Form — RPR
0251 **1** — **Miesko (USA)**[5] 6073 2-9-3 81 6ex — RHills 11 — 86
(M Johnston) *trckd ldrs: led 1f out: sn drvn and in control: readily* **4/1**[1]
1300 **2** 1 1/4 **Bosun Breese**[9] 5974 2-9-7 85 — LPKeniry 4 — 86
(P W D'Arcy) *slt ld tl narrowly hdd ins fnl 2f: styd upsides and kpt on gamely for 2nd but a hld by wnr ins fnl f* **7/1**
2140 **3** hd **Zippi Jazzman (USA)**[22] 5629 2-8-13 77 — MartinDwyer 13 — 77+
(R M Beckett) *s.i.s: in rr: plenty to do 2f out: rdn and gd hdwy on outside over 1f out: fin wl but nt rch ldng pair* **6/1**[3]
5310 **4** nk **Good Gorsoon (USA)**[37] 5207 2-9-6 84 — MichaelHills 1 — 87+
(B W Hills) *plld hrd in rr: n.m.r on rails over 2f out: eased rt to outside over 1f out and rapid hdwy ins fnl f: fin strly but nt pce to rch wnr* **9/2**[2]
4404 **5** nk **Barraland**[6] 6059 2-8-10 74 — DarryllHolland 10 — 72
(M R Channon) *pressed ldr tl slt ld ins fnl 2f: hdd 1f out: kpt on same pce ins fnl f* **7/1**
4200 **6** 1 1/4 **Splash The Cash**[28] 5452 2-8-3 67 — LiamJones 12 — 60
(P Winkworth) *in tch: hdwy on outside to chse ldrs over 2f out: sn rdn: wknd ins fnl f* **50/1**
1054 **7** shd **Luscious Lips**[10] 5939 2-8-13 77 — TedDurcan 9 — 70
(R Hannon) *in rr: hdwy fr 2f out: nvr quite gng pce to press ldrs: wknd wl ins fnl f* **8/1**
200 **8** shd **Bahamian Lad**[16] 5772 2-8-8 72 — DeanMcKeown 5 — 64
(R Hollinshead) *chsd ldrs: lost pl and n.m.r over 2f out: kpt on again ins fnl f but nvr in contention* **16/1**
515 **9** 1/2 **The Game**[67] 4274 2-9-0 78 — PatCosgrave 6 — 69+
(J R Boyle) *slowly away: plld hrd and hmpd 3f out: styd on fr over 1f out and gng on cl home but nvr in contention* **12/1**
1002 **10** nk **Cocabana**[28] 5452 2-8-4 68 — NelsonDeSouza 7 — 58
(J G Portman) *chsd ldrs: rdn fr 3f out: wknd ins fnl f* **9/1**
4000 **11** 4 **Only In Jest**[31] 5365 2-8-2 73 — JackDean(7) 2 — 48
(W G M Turner) *chsd ldrs: rdn 1/2-way: sn wknd* **66/1**
3140 **12** 6 **The Real Guru**[32] 5331 2-8-10 74 — MickyFenton 3 — 28
(Mrs A Duffield) *chsd ldrs 3f* **25/1**

61.87 secs (-0.63) **Going Correction** -0.10s/f (Good) — **12** Ran SP% **119.5**
Speed ratings (Par 97): **101,99,98,98,97 95,95,95,94,94 87,78**
CSF £31.94 CT £171.73 TOTE £5.70: £2.00, £2.10, £2.50; EX 41.60 Trifecta £84.30 Pool: £157.92 - 1.33 winning units..
Owner Sheikh Mohammed **Bred** Darley **Trained** Middleham Moor, N Yorks
■ Stewards' Enquiry : Pat Cosgrave caution: used whip with arm above shoulder height

FOCUS
This was a bit messy and several weren't seen to advantage, but it was a fair race and it went to a progressive colt.

NOTEBOOK
Miesko(USA) ◆ confirmed himself a progressive juvenile and followed up his Catterick maiden success in taking fashion under his penalty. He has really found his stride since being dropped to the minimum distance the last twice and, while the Handicapper will now have his say, further improvement cannot be ruled out yet. (op 5-1)
Bosun Breese, back in trip, showed good early speed and posted a brave effort in defeat under top weight. He looks worth keeping to the trip for now and helps to set the standard of this form. (op 6-1)
Zippi Jazzman(USA) had to come from a fair way back after blowing the start and has to rate somewhat unlucky, as he finished fastest of all. He is better than the bare form, but looks worth another try over 6f now. (op 13-2)
Good Gorsoon(USA) ◆, another dropping in trip, proved most keen under restraint through the early stages and then met trouble when trying to make up his ground on the inner in the home straight. By the time he was in the clear it was much too late, but he was flying at the finish and may have been unlucky. He is much better than the bare form and, while he will have to learn to settle, he certainly has another race in him over this trip when things go more his way. Official explanation: jockey said colt was denied a clear run (op 4-1 tchd 5-1)
Barraland did nothing wrong in defeat and ran another fair race. He is a sound benchmark. (op 9-1)
Bahamian Lad Official explanation: jockey said colt was denied a clear run
The Game was not seen to advantage here one way or another. (op 14-1 tchd 16-1)

6196 TOTEQUADPOT H'CAP — 1m 2f 46y
3:10 (3:12) (Class 6) (0-65,65) 3-Y-O+ — **£2,590** (£770; £385; £192) **Stalls** Low

Form — RPR
4520 **1** — **Gallego**[16] 5769 5-9-6 62 — HayleyTurner 17 — 71
(R J Price) *hld up in rr: stdy hdwy fr 3f out: edgd lft 2f out: chsd ldrs over 1f out: rdn to ld ins fnl f: styd on u.p* **7/1**[2]
5060 **2** 3/4 **Siena Star (IRE)**[9] 5983 9-9-7 63 — MickyFenton 2 — 70
(Stef Liddiard) *in rr: hdwy fr 3f out: pressing ldrs whn edgd lft over 1f out: chsd wnr ins fnl f but a hld* **17/2**[3]
6105 **3** hd **Blu Manruna**[11] 5916 4-9-0 56 — (b) PaulDoe 16 — 63
(J Akehurst) *led tl hdd 7f out: styd w ldr tl rdn to ld again ins fnl 2f: edgd rt over 1f out: hdd and one pce ins fnl f* **12/1**
5631 **4** 1/2 **Terminate (GER)**[12] 5886 5-8-9 56 — HaddenFrost(5) 5 — 62
(Ian Williams) *t.k.h: in tch: hdwy to chal 2f out: sn rdn: kpt on same pce ins fnl f* **6/1**[1]
3500 **5** 1/2 **Barry Island**[26] 5514 8-9-1 60 — MarcHalford(3) 14 — 65
(D R C Elsworth) *in rr: rdn and hdwy over 2f out: styd on fnl f but nvr quite gng pce to rch ldrs* **14/1**
0000 **6** 3 1/2 **Gracechurch (IRE)**[11] 5917 4-9-1 57 — RichardThomas 9 — 55
(R J Hodges) *in rr: hdwy and rdn fr 3f out: styd on fnl f but nvr gng pce to rch ldrs* **20/1**
4315 **7** 1/2 **Spunger**[24] 5569 4-9-7 63 — (v) MartinDwyer 1 — 60
(H J L Dunlop) *chsd ldrs: rdn and effrt whn hmpd over 1f out: nt rcvr* **6/1**[1]
5033 **8** 1/2 **Jackie Kiely**[24] 5557 6-9-9 65 — (t) DarryllHolland 15 — 61+
(R Brotherton) *hld up in rr: hdwy on rails whn hmpd and stmbld 2f out: styd on fnl f but nvr in contention* **7/1**[2]
2603 **9** nk **The Grey One (IRE)**[11] 5917 4-9-2 63 — (p) KevinGhunowa(5) 12 — 58
(J M Bradley) *in rr: hdwy and c wd bnd 3f out: kpt on but nvr in contention* **14/1**
6036 **10** 1/2 **Barbirolli**[11] 5916 5-9-5 61 — LiamJones 6 — 55
(W M Brisbourne) *chsd ldrs: rdn 3f out: wknd ins fnl 2f* **6/1**[1]
5600 **11** 1 1/4 **Covert Mission**[16] 5777 4-9-1 57 — LPKeniry 4 — 49
(P D Evans) *t.k.h: chsd ldrs 1/2-way: wknd 2f out* **25/1**
6663 **12** nk **Princely Ted (IRE)**[8] 6027 6-9-0 56 — VinceSlattery 10 — 47
(D Burchell) *chsd ldrs: led 7f out: hdd & wknd ins fnl 2f* **20/1**
0366 **13** 6 **Little Miss Tara (IRE)**[28] 5454 3-9-4 65 — DavidKinsella 3 — 44
(A B Haynes) *chsd ldrs: rdn 3f out: wknd over 2f out* **25/1**
6550 **14** 8 **Odessa Star (USA)**[24] 5569 4-9-8 64 — TedDurcan 13 — 27
(J G Portman) *chsd ldrs: rdn 4f out: sn wknd* **40/1**
004 **15** 36 **Smash Hit (IRE)**[24] 5567 4-9-7 63 — FergusSweeney 11 — —
(David Pinder) *chsd ldrs: wd into st 3f out and sn wknd: t.o fnl 2f* **22/1**

2m 9.86s (-1.14) **Going Correction** -0.10s/f (Good)
WFA 3 from 4yo+ 5lb — **15** Ran SP% **123.4**
Speed ratings (Par 101): **100,99,99,98,98 95,95,94,94,94 93,92,88,81,52**
CSF £59.73 CT £719.85 TOTE £9.00: £3.00, £3.90, £5.00; EX 100.60 TRIFECTA Not won..
Owner My Left Foot Racing Syndicate **Bred** Mrs C C Regalado-Gonzalez **Trained** Ullingswick, H'fords
■ Stewards' Enquiry : Hayley Turner three-day ban: careless riding (Oct 25,26,29)

FOCUS
A modest handicap full of exposed performers, but the form is solid enough of its type. The first two have good records here, and the third ran to form from the front. The fourth was to his recent best.
The Grey One(IRE) Official explanation: jockey said gelding hung right-handed
Smash Hit(IRE) Official explanation: jockey said gelding hung right-handed

6197 TOTESPORT.COM H'CAP — 5f 11y
3:45 (3:51) (Class 3) (0-95,95) 3-Y-O — **£7,570** (£2,265; £1,132; £566; £282) **Stalls** Centre

Form — RPR
001 **1** — **Kay Two (IRE)**[20] 5689 5-8-7 84 — (p) HayleyTurner 12 — 91
(R J Price) *chsd ldrs: rdn to ld ins fnl f: hld on all out* **5/1**[2]
1210 **2** shd **Little Edward**[20] 5689 9-8-11 88 — MickyFenton 13 — 95
(R J Hodges) *chsd ldrs: rdn over 1f out: str run ins fnl f: fin strly: jst failed* **8/1**
6003 **3** nk **Qadar (IRE)**[8] 6003 5-8-8 90 — (b) PatrickHills(5) 8 — 96
(N P Littmoden) *in rr: hdwy on outside over 1f out: str run ins fnl f: fin fast but nt quite pce to get up* **7/1**[3]
0005 **4** shd **Roman Maze**[35] 5254 7-8-10 87 — TedDurcan 14 — 93+
(W M Brisbourne) *stdd s: in rr: str run on outside fnl f: fin wl but a jst hld* **12/1**
3113 **5** 1/2 **Zahour Al Yasmeen**[29] 5418 3-8-7 84 — DarryllHolland 7 — 88
(M R Channon) *led tl hdd ins fnl f: wknd cl home* **12/1**
5000 **6** 1/2 **Dazed And Amazed**[8] 6003 3-8-11 93 — HaddenFrost(5) 5 — 95
(R Hannon) *chsd ldrs: rdn 2f out: outpcd ins fnl f* **12/1**
1005 **7** shd **Maker's Mark (IRE)**[20] 5689 3-8-6 83 ow1 — FergusSweeney 6 — 85
(H Candy) *in tch: rdn 2f out: styd on ins fnl f but nvr gng pce to be competitive* **7/2**[1]
16/0 **8** 3/4 **Playful**[130] 2352 4-8-10 87 — MartinDwyer 4 — 86
(M R Beckett) *plld hrd: chsd ldrs: rdn fnl f and wknd nr fin* **20/1**
5050 **9** 1/2 **The Tatling (IRE)**[28] 5449 10-9-4 95 — LPKeniry 10 — 92
(J M Bradley) *towards rr but in tch: rdn 1/2-way: sme prog ins fnl f but nvr in contention* **8/1**
1500 **10** 3/4 **Ishi Adiva**[20] 5689 3-8-9 86 — RichardThomas 3 — 80
(Tom Dascombe) *in tch: rdn and n.m.r over 1f out: nvr gng pce to be competitive* **16/1**
0052 **11** shd **Cape Royal**[20] 5689 7-8-10 92 — (bt) KevinGhunowa(5) 2 — 86
(J M Bradley) *in tch: rdn over 2f out: wknd ins fnl f* **11/1**
0000 **12** hd **Spanish Ace**[18] 5722 6-8-4 81 oh6 — LiamJones 9 — 74
(J M Bradley) *chsd ldrs: rdn 2f out: wknd fnl f* **40/1**

-460 **13** *5* **Cav Okay (IRE)**[130] 2352 3-8-12 **89** MichaelHills 1 64
(R Hannon) *plld hrd: hmpd on rails after 1f: a in rr* **25/1**

61.65 secs (-0.85) **Going Correction** -0.10s/f (Good) **13** Ran SP% **122.0**

Speed ratings (Par 107): **102,101,101,101,100 99,99,98,97,96 96,95,87**

CSF £44.82 CT £287.67 TOTE £7.70: £2.30, £2.90, £2.60; EX 62.30 Trifecta £191.70 Part won. Pool: £270.03 - 0.35 winning units..

Owner H McGahon, D McCarthy & B Llewellyn **Bred** Roger A Ryan **Trained** Ullingswick, H'fords

FOCUS

A bunch finish and almost certainly ordinary form.

NOTEBOOK

Kay Two(IRE), 4lb higher, just did enough to repel his challengers at the business end and register back-to-back successes. The recent application of cheekpieces has had the desired effect and he is versatile as regards underfoot conditions. He should now make a bold bid for the hat-trick. (tchd 11-2)

Little Edward, behind the winner last time, failed to reverse form by the smallest of margins on this return to quicker ground. He does go well at this venue and continues in good heart.

Qadar(IRE) was motoring inside the final furlong, but found the line coming a stride too soon. He is well handicapped on turf in relation to the sand, as he is yet to win a race on grass, but he is very hard to actually win with these days. (op 9-1)

Roman Maze, back in trip, was another doing all of his best work towards the finish and was not beaten at all far. He is still high enough in the weights, but deserves a change of fortune. A more positive ride over this trip on a stiff track could see him in the winners' enclosure again. (tchd 14-1)

Zahour Al Yasmeen, another 2lb higher, proved game from the front and was far from disgraced in this first race against older horses. (op 11-1)

Dazed And Amazed ran respectably, back in trip, returning to turf and also benefiting from a 6lb drop in the weights. (op 14-1 tchd 10-1)

Maker's Mark(IRE), well backed, never seriously looked like reversing form with the winner on this stiffer track yet still ran creditably enough. (op 9-2)

6198 TOTESPORT 0800 221 221 CONDITIONS STKS 1m 5y

4:20 (4:21) (Class 3) 3-Y-0+ **£7,570** (£2,265; £1,132; £566; £282) **Stalls** Low

Form RPR

-020 **1** **Smart Enough**[8] 6031 4-9-1 105 FergusSweeney 2 108
(M A Magnusson) *trckd ldr: rdn to ld appr fnl 2f: styd on strly u.p fnl f* **5/1**[3]

21-0 **2** *1 1/2* **Dijeerr (USA)**[154] 1703 3-8-12 107 TedDurcan 6 104
(Saeed Bin Suroor) *in tch and rdn 5f out and again 3f out: hdwy over 2f out: styd on u.p to chse wnr fnl f but no imp* **15/8**[1]

3000 **3** *1 1/4* **Minority Report**[15] 5797 7-9-1 94 MichaelHills 4 101+
(L M Cumani) *in rr but in tch: hdwy 2f out: n.m.r wl over 1f out: styd on ins fnl f to take 3rd nr fin but nvr gng pce to rch ldng duo* **8/1**

-402 **4** *1/2* **Tucker**[94] 3468 5-9-1 102 (p) AdamKirby 3 100
(W R Swinburn) *in tch: rdn 3f out: styd on fnl 2f but nvr gng pce to rch ldrs* **12/1**

015 **5** *1* **Jack Sullivan (USA)**[8] 6018 6-9-5 106 (p) StephenCarson 5 102
(G A Butler) *hld up in rr: rdn 3f out: sme prog u.p fnl f but nvr in contention* **11/2**

3035 **6** *hd* **Mesbaah (IRE)**[29] 5419 3-8-12 96 RHills 8 97
(M A Jarvis) *in rr: rdn 3f out: sme prog fnl f but nvr in contention* **9/2**[2]

2504 **7** *1* **Gravitas**[31] 5351 4-9-1 108 DarryllHolland 7 95
(Saeed Bin Suroor) *chsd ldrs: rdn over 2f out: wknd ins fnl f* **9/1**

0400 **8** *3 1/2* **Murfreesboro**[8] 6003 4-9-1 93 DeanMcKeown 1 87
(K J Burke) *drvn into ld: hdd & wknd appr fnl 2f* **66/1**

1m 39.03s (-2.07) **Going Correction** -0.10s/f (Good)

WFA 3 from 4yo+ 3lb **8** Ran SP% **115.3**

Speed ratings (Par 107): **106,104,103,102,101 101,100,97**

CSF £14.95 TOTE £6.30: £1.90, £1.40, £2.50; EX 16.80 Trifecta £97.50 Pool: £499.86 - 3.64 winning units..

Owner East Wind Racing Ltd **Bred** Whitsbury Manor Stud And Mrs M E Slade **Trained** Upper Lambourn, Berks

FOCUS

A quality conditions event for the class and track, run at a sound pace, but the proximity of the fourth, who had little solid recent form, casts a bit of a doubt over it.

NOTEBOOK

Smart Enough, last of 11 in a Group 2 in France eight days previously, was ridden more positively again and ran out a ready winner, opening his account for the season at the fourth attempt. The drop into this class was a big help, as was the sounder surface, and there was a lot to like about the manner in which he settled the issue this time. It is still unlikely that we have seen the best of this son of Cadeaux Genereux, and he has options at home and abroad before the end of the season. (op 3-1)

Dijeerr(USA), last seen running below par in the French 2,000 Guineas, was always playing second fiddle to the winner yet still made a respectable return to action. He is really happier on easier ground and can build on this now. (op 9-4 tchd 7-4)

Minority Report ran a big race in defeat according to official figures, but again managed to find trouble in running and can be rated a little better than the bare form. This is his ground, but he really is a frustrating horse to follow and a hike in the ratings is now inevitable. (op 13-2)

Tucker, returning from a 94-day break, left the impression he would come on for the run and may prefer easier ground these days. He is on a long losing run. (tchd 14-1)

Jack Sullivan(USA), with the cheekpieces back on, failed to raise his game on this return to the extra furlong and posted a laboured effort. (op 6-1 tchd 5-1)

Mesbaah(IRE), well backed, had a fairly stiff task at these weights and was unable to land a serious blow from off the pace. (op 9-1)

Gravitas, down in trip, is one of Godolphin's lesser lights and is going to prove very hard to place successfully again from this sort of rating. (tchd 10-1)

6199 TOTEEXACTA H'CAP 1m 5y

4:55 (4:55) (Class 5) (0-70,70) 3-Y-0+ **£3,886** (£1,156; £577; £288) **Stalls** Low

Form RPR

0142 **1** **Magroom**[13] 5860 3-8-5 57 MartinDwyer 4 64
(R J Hodges) *in rr: hdwy and rdn 3f out: styd on u.p to ld fnl 50yds: drvn out* **13/2**[3]

3511 **2** *1* **Myfrenchconnection (IRE)**[25] 5525 3-8-7 59 MickyFenton 11 64
(P T Midgley) *trckd ldr: chal fr 2f out tl def advantage jst ins fnl f: hdd and no ex fnl 50yds* **11/4**[1]

3114 **3** *nk* **Palmetto Point**[24] 5559 3-9-1 70 (p) TravisBlock(3) 14 74
(H Morrison) *in tch: chsd ldrs 3f out: rdn and hung lft but styd on ins fnl f: kpt on cl home but nt rch wnr* **9/2**[2]

041 **4** *nk* **Poppets Sweetlove**[13] 5860 3-8-13 65 DavidKinsella 2 68
(A B Haynes) *chsd ldrs: rdn fr 3f out: outpcd ins fnl f* **10/1**

4151 **5** *1* **The Jailer**[10] 5946 4-8-0 56 oh3 (p) MCGeran(7) 12 57
(J G M O'Shea) *led: rdn over 2f out: hdd jst ins fnl f: wknd fnl 50yds* **12/1**

0320 **6** *1/2* **Cape Velvet (IRE)**[22] 5645 3-9-0 66 RHills 10 66
(J W Hills) *chsd ldrs: rdn 3f out: wknd fnl 100yds* **14/1**

0260 **7** *3/4* **Valley Observer (FR)**[72] 4129 3-9-1 67 AdamKirby 9 65
(W R Swinburn) *in rr: hdwy 4f out: drvn and styd on fr 2f out but nvr gng pce to rch ldrs* **8/1**

0000 **8** *1 3/4* **Glenmuir (IRE)**[12] 5885 4-9-2 65 (b) HayleyTurner 3 59
(B R Millman) *chsd ldrs: rdn 3f out: wknd fnl f* **14/1**

0060 **9** *1 3/4* **Huxley (IRE)**[37] 5189 8-8-7 56 oh11 FergusSweeney 7 46
(D J Wintle) *in rr: sme prog 3f out: no imp on ldrs fnl 2f* **66/1**

0650 **10** *2 1/2* **Norwegian**[125] 2521 6-8-7 56 oh3 RichardThomas 6 40
(Ian Williams) *chsd ldrs: rdn 3f out: wknd fr 2f out* **33/1**

1530 **11** *2 1/2* **Sky Quest (IRE)**[30] 5383 9-9-7 70 PatCosgrave 15 49
(J R Boyle) *t.k.h: stdd in rr after 2f: rdn 3f out but nvr in contention* **16/1**

2110 **12** *1* **Bethanys Boy (IRE)**[24] 5569 6-8-12 61 VinceSlattery 1 37
(M Wigham) *nvr bttr than mid-div: bhd fnl 3f* **16/1**

1000 **13** *1 1/2* **Outer Hebrides**[20] 5687 6-9-3 66 (v) LPKeniry 13 39
(J M Bradley) *mid-div: rdn 3f out: sn btn* **25/1**

5-60 **14** *17* **Coleridge (AUS)**[95] 3420 8-9-5 68 BThomas 5 2
(J C Fox) *unruly in stalls: chsd ldrs 4f: sn wl bhd* **28/1**

4000 **15** *2 1/2* **Nordic Affair**[104] 3165 3-9-0 66 (b[1]) DarryllHolland 16 —
(D R C Elsworth) *a in rr* **16/1**

0000 **16** *nk* **Enjoy The Buzz**[13] 5861 8-8-7 56 oh11 (p) LiamJones 8 —
(J M Bradley) *bhd fr 1/2-way* **50/1**

1m 40.3s (-0.80) **Going Correction** -0.10s/f (Good)

WFA 3 from 4yo+ 3lb **16** Ran SP% **130.7**

Speed ratings (Par 103): **100,99,98,98,97 96,96,94,92,90 87,86,85,68,65 65**

CSF £25.39 CT £99.67 TOTE £8.70: £1.80, £1.20, £1.70, £2.80; EX 31.90 Trifecta £75.10 Pool: £190.62 - 1.80 winning units. Place 6 £66.49, Place 5 £48.57..

Owner Mrs A Hart Mrs A Hodges Mrs C Penny **Bred** Mrs M Chaworth-Musters **Trained** Charlton Mackrell, Somerset

FOCUS

A modest handicap, dominated by the three-year-olds. The form looks sound.

T/Jkpt: Not won. T/Plt: £109.30 to a £1 stake. Pool: £64,417.85. 429.90 winning units. T/Qpdt: £34.80 to a £1 stake. Pool: £3,885.80. 82.40 winning units. ST

5937 GOODWOOD (R-H)

Sunday, October 14

OFFICIAL GOING: Soft (good to soft in places; 7.2)

Wind: Almost nil Weather: Fine

6200 UCELLO II AND UBU III TROPHY STKS (H'CAP) (FOR NATIONAL HUNT JOCKEYS) 2m

2:20 (2:20) (Class 5) (0-70,67) 4-Y-0+ **£3,238** (£963; £481; £240) **Stalls** Low

Form RPR

0/0 **1** **Estate**[58] 4582 5-11-1 56 TimmyMurphy 4 66+
(E J O'Neill) *hld up: dropped to last trio 1/2-way: stealthy prog over 3f out: pushed into ld ins fnl f: shkn up and sn asserted* **9/1**

05-2 **2** *1/2* **To Arms**[108] 3033 5-11-3 58 TonyEvans 6 67
(K J Burke) *hld up in midfield: prog 5f out: led gng easily over 2f out: drvn and hdd ins fnl f: kpt on but no match for wnr* **7/2**[1]

3011 **3** *1 1/4* **Go Amwell**[10] 5948 4-10-12 53 AndrewTinkler 8 61
(J R Jenkins) *lw: s.s: hld up in last trio: prog 1/2-way: led gng wl 3f out: sn hdd: pressed ldr and n.m.r on inner over 1f out: one pce fnl f* **4/1**[2]

0-00 **4** *17* **Moonshine Beach**[12] 5884 9-11-9 64 JAMcCarthy 7 51
(P W Hiatt) *mde most to 3f out: wknd* **33/1**

4404 **5** *3* **Sand Repeal (IRE)**[16] 5769 5-11-10 65 (v) OwynNelmes 1 49
(Miss J Feilden) *lw: trckd ldng pair: wnt 2nd over 5f out: upsides over 3f out: sn wknd u.p* **7/1**[3]

0325 **6** *5* **My Legal Eagle (IRE)**[13] 5857 13-10-7 48 TJO'Brien 9 26
(E G Bevan) *hld up in midfield: rdn and no prog 4f out: sn wknd* **8/1**

5030 **7** *10* **Cavallini (USA)**[36] 5225 5-11-12 67 JamieMoore 10 33
(G L Moore) *b: dwlt: hld up in last trio: rdn and wknd 4f out: t.o* **15/2**

36-6 **8** *8* **Haatmey**[15] 5820 5-11-0 55 (v) JamesDavies 5 11
(P R Chamings) *trckd ldng pair tl wknd over 4f out: t.o* **14/1**

055 **9** *2 1/2* **Beaver (AUS)**[20] 5676 8-11-5 60 PCO'Neill 3 13
(J G M O'Shea) *a in last trio: wknd 4f out: t.o* **7/1**[3]

3000 **10** *26* **Harcourt (USA)**[52] 4534 7-10-9 50 SEDurack 2 —
(M Madgwick) *w ldr tl wknd u.p over 5f out: t.o* **18/1**

3m 40.58s (9.79) **Going Correction** +0.575s/f (Yiel) **10** Ran SP% **115.0**

Speed ratings (Par 103): **98,97,97,88,87 84,79,75,74,61**

CSF £39.98 CT £147.79 TOTE £11.40: £3.60, £1.80, £1.70; EX 86.30.

Owner R S Brookhouse **Bred** Stratford Place Stud & Watership Down Stud **Trained** Averham Park, Notts

FOCUS

A moderate handicap in which the runners were all ridden by jump jockeys. The front three pulled well clear.

Beaver(AUS) Official explanation: jockey said gelding was unsuited by the soft (good to soft places) ground

6201 EUROPEAN BREEDERS' FUND "FINALE" NURSERY 7f

2:55 (2:56) (Class 4) (0-85,84) 2-Y-O **£5,505** (£1,637; £818; £408) **Stalls** High

Form RPR

031 **1** **Unbreak My Heart (IRE)**[13] 5868 2-9-6 83 JimmyFortune 9 88+
(R Charlton) *dwlt: settled in midfield: prog on outer 3f out: led 2f out: drvn and styd on wl fr over 1f out* **10/3**[1]

0154 **2** *1 1/2* **Harry Gee**[29] 5400 2-9-1 78 (b) RichardMullen 11 79
(W R Muir) *chsd ldrs: drvn over 2f out: prog over 1f out: styd on to take 2nd nr fin* **33/1**

410 **3** *nk* **Blue Sky Basin**[31] 5350 2-8-13 76 FrancisNorton 15 76
(A M Balding) *w ldrs: upsides 3f out to wl over 1f out: chsd wnr after: no imp and lost 2nd nr fin* **9/2**[3]

004 **4** *3/4* **Grand Cuvee**[18] 5720 2-8-7 70 ow2 JohnEgan 5 68
(D M Simcock) *mostly in midfield: rdn over 2f out: swtchd sharply rt over 1f out: styd on: nvr able to chal* **16/1**

6540 **5** *1 1/2* **Jasmines Hero (USA)**[45] 4964 2-7-8 64 SophieDoyle(7) 7 58
(J S Moore) *dwlt: hld up in detached last: shkn up 3f out: prog on outer fr 2f out: hanging rt but kpt on* **20/1**

1100 **6** *3/4* **Distant Charm (IRE)**[60] 4501 2-9-1 78 RichardHughes 2 70
(R Hannon) *wl in rr: rdn over 3f out: swtchd rt and sme prog u.p 2f out: hanging after: wknd fnl f* **16/1**

010 **7** *1/2* **Giant Love (USA)**[25] 5536 2-9-6 83 GregFairley 10 74
(M Johnston) *w ldr: upsides 2f out: nt qckn wl over 1f out: wknd ins fnl f* **7/1**

5333 **8** *nk* **Fervent Prince**[19] 5705 2-8-10 73 (p) RobertHavlin 3 63
(H Morrison) *stmbld s: mde most to 2f out: wknd over 1f out* **16/1**

534 **9** *2* **Karky Schultz (GER)**[108] 3024 2-8-10 76 LukeMorris(3) 13 61
(J M P Eustace) *cl up: chal and upsides over 2f out: wkng whn bmpd over 1f out* **25/1**

The Form Book, Raceform Ltd, Compton, RG20 6NL

6402 **10** *nk* **Greystoke Prince**[40] 5117 2-8-4 **67** .... SaleemGolam 6 52
(W R Swinburn) *nvr on terms: struggling u.p over 3f out* **8/1**

4100 **11** *5* **Close To Paradise (IRE)**[20] 5692 2-8-13 **76** .... TPQueally 12 48
(E A L Dunlop) *hld up in rr: brief effrt u.p 2f out: sn wknd* **25/1**

1 **12** *7* **Pearl Dealer (IRE)**[16] 5780 2-9-5 **82** .... KerrinMcEvoy 14 37+
(Saeed Bin Suroor) *swtg: s.s: hld up in rr: c wdst of all in st: wknd over 2f out: t.o* **4/1**[2]

1m 31.76s (3.72) **Going Correction** +0.575s/f (Yiel) **12** Ran SP% **117.9**
Speed ratings (Par 97): **101,99,98,97,96 95,94,94,92,91 86,78**
CSF £127.33 CT £514.25 TOTE £4.50: £1.70, £5.90, £2.00; EX 108.80.

Owner Mountgrange Stud **Bred** Redpender Stud Ltd **Trained** Beckhampton, Wilts

■ Stewards' Enquiry : Sophie Doyle one-day ban: careless riding (Oct 25)
John Egan caution: careless riding

FOCUS
A fair nursery, likely to produce its share of winners. A few may have been unsuited by the ground, but the form looks solid through the placed horses.

NOTEBOOK
Unbreak My Heart(IRE) has progressed with each run and got off the mark at the third attempt when running out a workmanlike winner at Windsor last time. Up in trip for this nursery debut, he looked on a reasonable mark and again handled the cut in the ground well, running on strongly under pressure to win with a bit in hand. He should get a bit further in time and rates as a bright three-year-old handicap prospect. (op 7-2, tchd 3-1)

Harry Gee showed improved form in the blinkers when fourth at Chester last time and stepped up again on that effort with a keeping-on second, handling the soft ground better than anticipated. He should find a similar race if continuing to hold his form.

Blue Sky Basin, who failed to last out the 1m when disappointing on his nursery debut at Doncaster, ran better on this return to 7f, but again did not see it out as well as one would have liked, possibly finding the soft ground against him. His half-brother Gordonsville stays middle-distances well and maybe he is worth another chance back on a sound surface. (op 5-1)

Grand Cuvee got a little better with each start in maidens and he looked a little unfortunate not to finish closer on this nursery debut, getting going a little too late having had to be switched for a run. He should find easier opportunities as a slightly lower level. (op 20-1)

Jasmines Hero(USA) improved on his Lingfield effort, keeping on late having been a bit behind, and he is another for whom easier opportunities should arise. (op 28-1)

Pearl Dealer(IRE), who took his time to get on top on debut at Wolverhampton, comes from a yard who are really firing at present, but he was unable to build on that initial effort and the way he ran suggested something may have been amiss. He got very warm beforehand though and could be worth giving another chance to. Official explanation: jockey said colt ran too keenly (op 3-1)

6202 EUROPEAN BREEDERS' FUND TURFTV MAIDEN STKS 1m 1f

3:30 (3:33) (Class 5) 2-Y-O **£4,533** (£1,348; £674; £336) **Stalls** High

Form RPR

30 **1** **Cool Judgement (IRE)**[71] 4151 2-9-3 0 .... PhilipRobinson 6 79
(M A Jarvis) *awkward s: hld up towards rr: prog over 3f out: rdn to chse ldng pair over 1f out: styd on wl fnl f: led last stride* **9/2**[3]

22 **2** *shd* **Rattan (USA)**[31] 5361 2-9-3 0 .... RichardHughes 3 78
(H R A Cecil) *lw: trckd ldng pair: led over 3f out and grabbed nr side rail: 2 l clr over 1f out: rdn ins fnl f: hung rt nr fin: hdd last stride* **7/4**[1]

036 **3** *hd* **Blue Citadel (USA)**[15] 5813 2-9-3 75 .... JimmyFortune 7 78
(J H M Gosden) *settled in midfield: prog 3f out: chsd ldr 2f out: hrd rdn and clsd fnl f: lost 2nd nr fin and jst hld* **3/1**[2]

030 **4** *11* **Little Toto**[34] 5274 2-9-3 71 .... TQuinn 5 56
(C G Cox) *trckd ldr: led over 4f out to over 3f out: chsd ldr to 2f out: wknd over 1f out* **33/1**

5 **5** *1 1/2* **Highly Regal (IRE)**[20] 5680 2-9-3 0 .... EddieAhern 8 53
(R A Teal) *chsd ldrs: cl enough over 2f out: wknd over 1f out* **25/1**

00 **6** *nk* **Bobby Darling (IRE)**[18] 5721 2-8-12 0 .... TPO'Shea 13 47
(M R Channon) *mostly in midfield: rdn to chse ldrs over 2f out: wknd over 1f out* **50/1**

3 **7** *2 1/2* **Leamington (USA)**[10] 5944 2-8-12 0 .... GregFairley 9 42
(M Johnston) *trckd ldrs: rdn over 2f out: wknd over 1f out* **9/2**[3]

5460 **8** *15* **Insomnitas**[59] 4524 2-9-3 56 .... RichardMullen 2 17
(M G Quinlan) *chsd ldrs: rdn and in tch over 2f out: sn wknd* **80/1**

06 **9** *hd* **Fort Hull (IRE)**[11] 5918 2-9-3 0 .... JimCrowley 12 17
(Mrs A J Perrett) *dwlt: sn pushed along in rr: wknd 3f out* **22/1**

00 **10** *3/4* **Imperial Mark (IRE)**[33] 5313 2-9-3 0 .... FrancisNorton 1 16
(P J O'Gorman) *racd freely: led: c wd and hdd over 4f out: sn wknd* **100/1**

11 *29* **Dancing Ellie** 2-8-12 0 .... IanMongan 10 —
(P M Phelan) *leggy: s.s: a bhd: t.o 3f out* **66/1**

12 *nk* **Border Owl (IRE)** 2-9-3 0 .... TPQueally 11 —
(R Hannon) *rangy: scope: bit bkwd: s.s: a bhd: t.o fnl 3f* **20/1**

00 **P** **Valentine Blue**[18] 5720 2-9-3 0 .... SamHitchcott 4 —
(A B Haynes) *dwlt: a in rr: t.o whn p.u over 2f out: dismntd* **40/1**

2m 2.81s (5.95) **Going Correction** +0.575s/f (Yiel) **13** Ran SP% **121.7**
Speed ratings (Par 95): **96,95,95,85,84 84,82,68,68,67 42,41,—**
CSF £12.02 TOTE £6.40: £1.70, £1.20, £1.50; EX 16.10.

Owner H R H Sultan Ahmad Shah **Bred** Crone Stud Farms Ltd **Trained** Newmarket, Suffolk

■ Stewards' Enquiry : Richard Hughes one-day ban: careless riding (Oct 25)

FOCUS
A modest maiden in which the front three drew well clear.

NOTEBOOK
Cool Judgement(IRE), who made a promising debut in soft ground at Newmarket, failed to improve on that when faced with fast ground at this course last time, but this rise in distance was expected to suit and the ground had also come in his favour. Well in rear early, he was running on whilst looking held inside the final furlong, but really found his stride as they raced for the line and just managed to get there. He could be of interest in a nursery with the ground having come in his favour, and he rates as a promising handicapper for next year. (op 11-2)

Rattan(USA) had shown useful form in defeat in two Sandown maidens, latterly over 1m, and it looked to be his turn as he held a two-length lead with 100 yards to go. However, he curled up in the dying strides and was nailed by Cool Judgement. A race will come his way eventually, but he somewhat grabbed defeat from the jaws of victory here and is clearly not one to take a short price about. (op 15-8, tchd 2-1 in places)

Blue Citadel(USA) is not really progressing as expected, but it was hard to knock this effort as he did little wrong and finished a long way clear of the remainder. He is another who will win a race before long and may prefer a return to a sounder surface. (op 10-3, tchd 7-2)

Little Toto ran a little better than his finishing position suggests, failing to last home in the conditions, and he will be of interest once sent handicapping. (op 20-1)

Leamington(USA), made plenty of use of when third over 1m on debut at Kempton, is an athletic type but looked far from certain to be suited by this extra furlong, especially in the ground, and she failed to last home. (op 4-1)

Imperial Mark(IRE) Official explanation: jockey said colt ran too free

Valentine Blue Official explanation: jockey said gelding lost its action

6203 CEDARS OF LEBANON 250TH ANNIVERSARY H'CAP 1m

4:05 (4:07) (Class 4) (0-85,87) 3-Y-0+ **£7,124** (£2,119; £1,059; £529) **Stalls** High

Form RPR

6315 **1** **Don't Panic (IRE)**[22] 5635 3-9-2 **83** .... KerrinMcEvoy 4 101
(P W Chapple-Hyam) *b.hind: hld up wl in rr: gd prog on outer over 3f out: led jst over 2f out: sn rdn wl clr* **11/2**[1]

5421 **2** *4* **Crocodile Bay (IRE)**[11] 5905 4-8-13 **77** .... AdrianTNicholls 15 85+
(D Nicholls) *lw: hld up in midfield: effrt whn nt clr run 2f out: drvn and styd on to take 2nd ins fnl f: no ch w wnr* **6/1**[2]

0600 **3** *1 3/4* **St Petersburg**[33] 5312 7-9-4 **82** .... IanMongan 14 86
(J R Boyle) *wl in rr: rdn over 3f out: eased to outer over 2f out: drvn and styd on: nrst fin* **16/1**

1303 **4** *1 1/2* **Vainglory (USA)**[22] 5615 3-9-2 **83** .... RichardMullen 1 84+
(D M Simcock) *swtg: trckd ldrs: rdn wl over 2f out: outpcd wl over 1f out: plugged on* **9/1**[3]

3051 **5** *4* **Orchard Supreme**[14] 5833 4-9-9 **87** .... RichardHughes 12 79
(R Hannon) *trckd ldrs: upsides gng strly jst over 2f out: chsd wnr after: wknd ins fnl f: eased* **9/1**[3]

5350 **6** *2* **Tudor Prince (IRE)**[65] 4360 3-8-7 **77** .... LukeMorris[(3)] 2 64
(A W Carroll) *prom: chal and upsides over 2f out: wknd over 1f out* **50/1**

3013 **7** *6* **Titan Triumph**[40] 5114 3-8-9 **76** ....(t) TPQueally 17 49
(W J Knight) *cl up tl wknd u.p fr 2f out* **6/1**[2]

0 **8** *2* **Shabahar (IRE)**[16] 5768 3-8-13 **80** .... JohnEgan 13 49
(M J McGrath) *awkward s: wl in rr: no ch fr 2f out: plugged on fnl f* **25/1**

0050 **9** *1 1/2* **Grizedale (IRE)**[5] 6081 8-8-2 **71** oh1 ....(t) KirstyMilczarek[(5)] 16 36
(J Akehurst) *nvr a factor: no ch over 2f out: passed wkng rivals fnl f* **25/1**

5301 **10** *nk* **Blue Java**[19] 5712 6-8-10 **74** .... RobertHavlin 9 39
(H Morrison) *nodded s: sn chsd ldrs: wknd wl over 1f out* **12/1**

0056 **11** *3* **Kingsholm**[21] 5664 5-8-11 **75** .... FrancisNorton 7 33
(A M Balding) *b.hind: pressed ldr: led 5f out to jst over 2f out: wknd* **12/1**

2210 **12** *shd* **Indian Edge**[55] 4657 6-8-8 **72** .... GregFairley 10 30
(B Palling) *dwlt: a wl in rr: struggling in last trio 3f out* **18/1**

4010 **13** *1 1/4* **Namid Reprobate (IRE)**[20] 5685 4-8-12 **81** .... TolleyDean[(5)] 5 36
(P F I Cole) *a wl in rr: u.p and no prog over 3f out* **16/1**

0100 **14** *5* **Archiestown (USA)**[50] 4814 4-8-11 **75** .... TQuinn 8 18
(J L Dunlop) *rdn in rr after 2f: a struggling* **20/1**

2050 **15** *19* **Bajan Pride**[16] 5768 3-8-11 **78** .... EddieAhern 6 —
(R Hannon) *lw: led to 5f out: wknd rapidly 3f out: eased: t.o* **20/1**

10-0 **16** *110* **Danski**[14] 5833 4-9-4 **82** .... JimmyFortune 3 —
(P J Makin) *racd on outer in midfield: rdn over 3f out: sn wknd: virtually p.u over 1f out* **10/1**

1m 43.31s (3.04) **Going Correction** +0.575s/f (Yiel)
WFA 3 from 4yo+ 3lb **16** Ran SP% **124.6**
Speed ratings (Par 105): **107,103,101,99,95 93,87,85,84,83 80,80,79,74,55 —**
CSF £35.29 CT £534.41 TOTE £6.00: £1.60, £2.00, £3.90, £2.90; EX 22.30.

Owner A B S Webb **Bred** Bernard Colclough **Trained** Newmarket, Suffolk

FOCUS
A competitive handicap won by a clear margin by Don't Panic. It's hard to know how literally to take the form, but they were strung out behind him and the first two could both have been underestimated.

Blue Java Official explanation: jockey said gelding was unsuited by the soft (good to soft places) ground

Bajan Pride Official explanation: jockey said gelding was unsuited by the soft (good to soft places) ground

Danski Official explanation: jockey said colt lost its action but returned sound

6204 TURFTV FOR BETTING SHOPS MEDIAN AUCTION MAIDEN STKS 1m 1f 192y

4:40 (4:43) (Class 5) 3-4-Y-O **£3,886** (£1,156; £577; £288) **Stalls** High

Form RPR

2423 **1** **Fringe**[26] 5500 4-9-3 80 .... JohnEgan 2 74
(Jane Chapple-Hyam) *hld up in tch: rdn to chse clr ldr over 2f out: clsd to ld over 1f out: drew clr fnl f* **10/11**[1]

4 **2** *5* **Accusation (IRE)**[20] 5678 3-8-12 0 .... JimmyFortune 4 64
(L M Cumani) *w'like: scope: led: kicked at least 3 l clr 3f out: hdd over 1f out: wknd fnl f* **10/3**[2]

46 **3** *2 1/2* **Kokkokila**[28] 5450 3-8-7 0 .... KirstyMilczarek[(5)] 7 59
(Lady Herries) *cl up: chsd ldr 3f out to over 2f out: sn outpcd* **14/1**

405 **4** *3 1/2* **Meon Mix**[31] 5346 3-8-12 58 .... KerrinMcEvoy 1 52
(J R Fanshawe) *mostly chsd ldr to 3f out: steadily wknd* **9/1**

64 **5** *1 3/4* **Fixation**[26] 5499 3-9-3 0 .... RichardHughes 5 54
(Mrs A J Perrett) *str: hld up in tch: rdn and hanging 4f out: struggling after* **11/2**[3]

0 **6** *2* **Star Of Pompey**[13] 5859 3-8-12 0 .... SamHitchcott 6 45
(A B Haynes) *leggy: dwlt: rdn in last over 5f out: n.d after* **50/1**

0036 **7** *3/4* **New Light**[25] 5530 3-8-12 48 .... EddieAhern 3 43
(Eve Johnson Houghton) *hld up: prog on outer 4f out: wknd over 2f out* **25/1**

2m 14.57s (6.82) **Going Correction** +0.575s/f (Yiel)
WFA 3 from 4yo 5lb **7** Ran SP% **113.3**
Speed ratings (Par 103): **95,91,89,86,84 83,82**
CSF £4.03 TOTE £1.70: £1.30, £1.90; EX 4.60.

Owner Franconson Partners **Bred** Nawara Stud Co Ltd **Trained** Newmarket, Suffolk

FOCUS
A weak maiden in which the winner did not need to be at her best.

Fixation Official explanation: jockey said gelding hung left

6205 RACING UK ON SKY 432 STKS (H'CAP) 6f

5:15 (5:16) (Class 3) (0-95,95) 3-Y-0+ **£7,124** (£2,119; £1,059; £529) **Stalls** Low

Form RPR

6500 **1** **Obe Gold**[15] 5804 5-8-6 **82** oh1 ow1 ....(v) JohnEgan 17 93
(M R Channon) *hld up in centre: prog 2f out: drvn to ld ins fnl f: styd on wl* **16/1**

2222 **2** *1 1/4* **Chjimes (IRE)**[51] 4778 3-8-1 **81** oh4 .... LukeMorris[(3)] 15 88
(K R Burke) *bmpd s: sn pressed ldrs in centre: led over 2f out: hdd and hung lft over 1f out: kpt on again fnl f* **20/1**

3014 **3** *1 1/4* **Everymanforhimself (IRE)**[16] 5765 3-8-11 **88** ....(b) TPQueally 16 91
(J G Given) *lw: bmpd s: pressed ldrs in centre: drvn to ld overall over 1f out: hdd and fdd ins fnl f* **16/1**

5005 **4** *1 1/4* **Burning Incense (IRE)**[15] 5809 4-9-2 **92** ....(p) JimmyFortune 11 91
(R Charlton) *b.hind: lw: hld up in rr of centre gp: effrt 2f out: kpt on one pce: nvr able to chal* **11/2**[2]

0550 **5** *1* **Gift Horse**[23] 5584 7-9-2 **92** ....(v) RichardHughes 1 88+
(D Nicholls) *lw: hld up last of nr side gp: rdn and prog 2f out: kpt on to ld his gp nr fin: nvr on terms* **4/1**[1]

0460 **6** *nk* **Kyle (IRE)**[22] 5635 3-8-4 **81** oh1 .... RichardMullen 7 76+
(R Hannon) *hld up nr side: drvn over 2f out: kpt on fnl f: nvr on terms* **33/1**

0100 **7** *1/2* **Phantom Whisper**[20] 5689 4-9-1 **91** .... JimCrowley 8 84+
(B R Millman) *w nr side ldrs: nvr on terms: one pce fnl f* **20/1**

053 **8** *nk* **Idle Power (IRE)**[11] 5923 9-8-6 **82** .... KerrinMcEvoy 13 74
(J R Boyle) *overall ldr in centre to over 2f out: wkng whn squeezed out over 1f out* **6/1**[3]

40-0 **9** *hd* **Johannes (IRE)**[8] 6013 4-8-9 **85** .... GregFairley 9 77+
(E J O'Neill) *taken down early: dwlt: rcvrd and sn prom nr side: led gp 1/2-way: drifted towards centre 2f out: nvr on terms: fdd ins fnl f* **18/1**

1353 **10** *nk* **Misphire**[10] 5954 4-8-5 **81** oh3 .... (b) SaleemGolam 14 72
(M Dods) *bmpd s: chsd ldrs in centre: wknd u.p 2f out* **20/1**

6504 **11** *1/2* **Cape**[15] 5809 4-8-9 **85** .... PhilipRobinson 4 74+
(P Howling) *hld up nr side: drvn over 2f out: no prog over 1f out* **7/1**

0234 **12** *1 3/4* **Mango Music**[10] 5954 4-8-6 **82** .... TPO'Shea 12 65
(M R Channon) *prom in centre 2f: lost pl and struggling over 2f out* **12/1**

2123 **13** *1/2* **Esteem Machine (USA)**[16] 5765 3-8-11 **88** .... EddieAhern 6 70+
(R A Teal) *lw: w nr side ldrs tl wknd u.p over 1f out* **13/2**

5530 **14** *4* **Compton's Eleven**[11] 5923 6-8-10 **86** .... SamHitchcott 2 55
(M R Channon) *hld up in rr nr side: nvr a factor* **25/1**

1000 **15** *15* **Cashel Mead**[12] 5891 7-8-9 **85** .... FrancisNorton 3 6
(J L Spearing) *nvr on terms nr side: wknd 2f out: t.o* **22/1**

4100 **16** *3 1/2* **Maltese Falcon**[119] 2688 7-9-5 **95** .... (t) TQuinn 10 5
(P F I Cole) *lw: led nr side gp to 1/2-way: wknd rapidly: t.o* **28/1**

1m 13.73s (0.88) **Going Correction** +0.325s/f (Good)
WFA 3 from 4yo+ 1lb **16** Ran SP% **129.1**
Speed ratings (Par 107): **107,105,103,102,100 100,99,99,98,98 97,95,94,89,69 64**
CSF £314.68 CT £2872.17 TOTE £25.00: £4.40, £3.70, £3.00, £2.10; EX 641.00 Place 6 £ 31.45, Place 5 £ 17.42.
Owner BDR Partnership 1 **Bred** Mrs M Mason **Trained** West Ilsley, Berks

FOCUS
The field split in two and the group that went centre to far side held a significant advantage over the stands'-side group at the finish. Tricky form to assess with confidence.

NOTEBOOK
Obe Gold carried a pound overweight and was a pound wrong at the weights. However, he still came out best in what on paper looked a competitive affair, but in effect concerned only the seven that raced centre to far side. He appreciated the drop back to sprinting and finally came back to form following a barren spell going back to February 2006. (op 18-1 tchd 20-1)
Chjimes(IRE), runner-up in a claimer last time out, took his run of second places to five. While this was his best effort in a while from 4lb out of the handicap, he is proving frustrating to follow. (op 25-1)
Everymanforhimself(IRE) hung under pressure after getting to the front, which did him no good, but he continued his run of decent form and helps set the level.
Burning Incense(IRE), with cheekpieces replacing blinkers, is another who has proved expensive to follow this term. He effectively finished fourth of seven, considering the advantage he had racing in the centre-to-far-side group. (op 6-1)
Gift Horse, second on the wrong side in the Ayr Silver Cup last time out, deserves plenty of credit once again as he came home first on the unfavoured stands' side this time. He is clearly in the form to win when the cards fall right. (tchd 9-2)
Kyle(IRE), back over his best trip, finished second on the unfavoured stands' side from 1lb out of the handicap and should not be written off in similar company. (op 40-1)
Phantom Whisper showed good speed but was another disadvantaged by racing on the stands' side. (op 16-1)
Idle Power(IRE) led them up the centre of the track but was not at his best and simply set it up for his companions that side. (op 7-1)
Compton's Eleven Official explanation: jockey said gelding was unsuited by the soft (good to soft places) ground
Cashel Mead Official explanation: jockey said mare never travelled
T/Plt: £27.90 to a £1 stake. Pool: £68,869.95. 1,801.20 winning tickets. T/Qpdt: £11.20 to a £1 stake. Pool: £4,142.10. 272.70 winning tickets. JN

6138 LINGFIELD (L-H)

Sunday, October 14

OFFICIAL GOING: Standard
Wind: modest behind Weather: overcast but mild

6206 CORAL.CO.UK APPRENTICE H'CAP 1m 2f (P)

2:10 (2:11) (Class 6) (0-60,60) 3-Y-O **£2,730** (£806; £403) **Stalls** Low

Form RPR

3510 **1** **Picky**[25] 5531 3-9-2 **57** .... (v) JamesO'Reilly 4 59
(C Tinkler) *t.k.h: chsd ldrs: rdn wl over 1f out: led ins fnl f: all out* **9/4**[1]

0-00 **2** *nk* **My Monna**[19] 5709 3-8-2 **48** .... JosephWalsh(5) 5 50
(Miss Sheena West) *chsd ldrs: drvn 3f out: chsd wnr ins fnl f: clsng towards fin* **33/1**

6530 **3** *1* **Saaratt**[18] 5733 3-9-5 **60** .... JamieJones 1 60
(J W Hills) *stdd s: t.k.h: hld up in rr: hdwy wl over 2f out: rdn wl over 1f out: chsd ldng pair ins fnl f: no imp last 100yds* **16/1**

-000 **4** *1 1/2* **Full Of Promise (USA)**[44] 5013 3-9-3 **58** .... KMay 7 55
(Mrs A J Perrett) *led at slow pce for 2f: sn settled in midfield: rdn and unable qck over 2f out: styd on u.p ins fnl f* **20/1**

6 **5** *nk* **Fairy Festival (IRE)**[11] 5894 3-8-6 **50** .... RobbieEgan(3) 9 46
(J S Moore) *w ldr tl led 8f out: sn hdd: chsd ldrs: rdn wl over 2f out: kpt on same pce* **9/1**

6000 **6** *shd* **Lordswood (IRE)**[4] 6100 3-8-6 **47** .... ThomasO'Brien 10 43
(J J Bridger) *hld up in midfield: hdwy wl over 2f out: kpt on same pce over 1f out* **16/1**

0501 **7** *hd* **Blue Mistral (IRE)**[19] 5710 3-9-5 **60** .... (vt) JackMitchell 11 55+
(W J Knight) *stdd s: hld up in last whn carried v wd after 2f and lost many l: clsd and in tch 6f out: drvn and effrt on outer over 2f out: no imp after* **7/1**

0000 **8** *1 1/4* **Pajada**[6] 6062 3-8-2 **46** oh1 .... (v) FrankiePickard(3) 12 39
(M D I Usher) *in tch: chsd ldr wl over 7f out: led wl over 1f out: hdd ins fnl f: wknd qckly* **50/1**

0050 **9** *1* **Xalted**[10] 5946 3-8-3 **47** .... DeanHeslop(3) 2 38
(S C Williams) *hld up in rr: rdn and struggling over 4f out: n.d after* **6/1**[3]

3-46 **10** *8* **Fowey (USA)**[267] 193 3-9-3 **58** .... GaryBartley 6 33
(Sir Mark Prescott) *prom tl led wl over 7f out: rdn over 2f out: hdd wl over 1f out: sn btn* **3/1**[2]

000 **11** *4* **Tia Jade**[165] 1409 3-8-2 **48** .... LanceBetts(5) 3 15
(G Prodromou) *hld up in midfield: rdn and wknd 3f out* **33/1**

50 **P** **Istibian (IRE)**[15] 5816 3-8-11 **55** .... KylieManser(3) 8 —
(Mrs H Sweeting) *s.i.s: bhd whn tried to run out after 2f: reluctant and t.o after: plld himself up 2f out* **16/1**

2m 11.23s (3.44) **Going Correction** +0.05s/f (Slow) **12** Ran SP% **122.8**
Speed ratings (Par 99): **88,87,86,85,85 85,85,84,83,77 73,—**
CSF £95.60 CT £1017.07 TOTE £4.20: £1.80, £10.80, £7.20; EX 104.60.
Owner Colin Tinkler **Bred** T C Ellis **Trained** Compton, Berks
■ Stewards' Enquiry : James O'Reilly caution: used whip with excessive frequency

FOCUS
A very moderate apprentices' handicap run at a very steady gallop. Poor form, and Picky did not need to improve on the form of his C/D classified stakes win
Blue Mistral(IRE) Official explanation: jockey said filly was carried wide on the bend
Istibian(IRE) Official explanation: jockey said gelding was reluctant to race

6207 CORAL - OVER 1550 BETTING SHOPS NATIONWIDE CLAIMING STKS 1m (P)

2:45 (2:46) (Class 6) 2-Y-O **£2,047** (£604; £302) **Stalls** High

Form RPR

60 **1** **Caltire (GER)**[13] 5869 2-8-5 0 .... (b[1]) NickyMackay 12 48
(J A Osborne) *s.i.s: bhd: hdwy into midfield 5f out: rdn over 3f out: 6th and hrd rdn wl over 1f out: str run fnl f to ld last strides* **33/1**

500 **2** *1/2* **Seconds Out (IRE)**[31] 5343 2-9-5 55 .... (b[1]) PaulMulrennan 6 61
(Sir Mark Prescott) *w ldr tl led 5f out: clr and rdn wl over 1f out: wknd ins fnl f and ct last strides* **25/1**

0000 **3** *shd* **Isander (USA)**[11] 5896 2-9-1 56 .... SteveDrowne 7 57
(Mrs A J Perrett) *hld up in midfield tl gd hdwy to join ldr 5f out: rdn and outpcd 2f out: styd on u.p ins fnl f* **16/1**

22 **4** *2 1/2* **Bollywood Style**[39] 5133 2-8-10 0 .... DaneO'Neill 5 47
(J R Best) *t.k.h: chsd ldrs tl settled in midfield over 4f out: rdn over 2f out: kpt on ins fnl f: nvr pce to rch ldrs* **9/1**[3]

0203 **5** *shd* **Bencorr (USA)**[23] 5601 2-9-5 71 .... JamieSpencer 9 55
(M J Wallace) *hld up bhd: hdwy 5f out: chsd ldrs and hrd rdn over 2f out: kpt on at one pce* **1/1**[1]

3006 **6** *hd* **Observatory Ridge**[6] 6066 2-8-10 59 .... JimmyQuinn 10 46
(M D I Usher) *racd in midfield: hdwy to chse ldrs 3f out: sn rdn: no hdwy last 2f* **12/1**

6010 **7** *1* **Adam Eterno (IRE)**[13] 5869 2-8-2 54 ow2 .... PNolan(7) 2 43
(A B Haynes) *flyleaped leaving stalls: hld up bhd: swtchd to outer over 4f out: sme modest late hdwy: n.d* **33/1**

0002 **8** *1/2* **Aneebee (IRE)**[13] 5869 2-8-8 59 .... RichardSmith 8 41
(R Hannon) *hld up towards rr: hmpd and lost pl 5f out: sn rdn: styd on fnl f: n.d* **10/1**

610 **9** *1 1/2* **Ten Spot (IRE)**[11] 5896 2-8-7 62 .... (b) RobbieEgan(7) 1 43
(J A Osborne) *chsd ldrs: rdn and lost pl over 4f out: n.d after* **6/1**[2]

5050 **10** *1* **Abfabfong (IRE)**[44] 5002 2-9-1 52 .... NCallan 4 42
(P F I Cole) *t.k.h: hld up in tch: bmpd and lost pl 5f out: rdn and no hdwy over 2f out: eased ins fnl f* **10/1**

00 **11** *3 1/2* **Avril Valley**[18] 5727 2-8-2 0 .... AdrianMcCarthy 3 21
(D J S Ffrench Davis) *led tl 5f out: rdn 3f out: wknd 2f out and sn bhd* **100/1**

1m 42.84s (3.41) **Going Correction** +0.05s/f (Slow) **11** Ran SP% **116.8**
Speed ratings (Par 93): **84,83,83,80,80 80,79,79,77,76 73**
CSF £651.16 TOTE £31.60: £4.80, £7.60, £4.40; EX 364.50.The winner was claimed by M. Quinlan for £5,000
Owner Elaine and Martyn Booth **Bred** L & K Zimmermann **Trained** Upper Lambourn, Berks

FOCUS
A very moderate claimer and winner Caltire only ran to 47, 7lb below his previous best.

NOTEBOOK
Caltire(GER) failed to beat a rival on his debut and he was only mid-division in a seller on the turf at Windsor last time, but he improved for the fitting of blinkers. He played up before the start, but was fine in the race itself and finished strongly in the straight to get up close home. He was claimed for £5,000 by Mick Quinlan. (tchd 28-1)
Seconds Out(IRE) did not show much in three runs over 7f in maiden company but, like the winner, he was fitted with blinkers for the first time and produced an improved run over this longer trip under a positive ride. He should be able to find a similar race. (op 14-1)
Isander(USA), without the blinkers on this drop into claiming company, finished clear of the remainder in third. He is another who is probably up to winning a weak race.
Bollywood Style, runner-up in a couple of 6f sellers round here on her first two starts, ran a respectable race upped to 1m on her debut for new connections. (op 17-2)
Bencorr(USA) ran nowhere near his official rating on this drop into claiming company and was a bitter disappointment. He has something to prove now. (op 11-8 tchd 6-4)

6208 CORAL BET BY FREEPHONE 0800 242 232 FILLIES' H'CAP 1m (P)

3:20 (3:21) (Class 4) (0-85,85) 3-Y-O+ **£4,857** (£1,445; £722; £360) **Stalls** High

Form RPR

1432 **1** **World Spirit**[50] 4828 3-8-9 **76** .... ChrisCatlin 11 89
(Rae Guest) *sn last and pushed along: drvn and hdwy 3f out: stl 8th over 2f out: str run on outer fnl f: edgd lft: led last 50yds* **16/1**

3410 **2** *1 1/4* **Tender The Great (IRE)**[10] 5950 4-9-4 **82** .... GeorgeBaker 10 92
(B G Powell) *hld up in rr: gd hdwy 3f out: jnd ldrs 2f out: rdn and ev ch 2f out: led 1f out: flashed tail ins fnl f: hdd last 50yds* **12/1**

5321 **3** *1 1/2* **Voliere**[12] 5889 4-9-2 **80** .... JamieSpencer 7 87
(S C Williams) *hld up in midfield: hdwy to trck ldrs gng wl 2f out: chsd ldr and rdn 1f out: fnd little and one pce whn short of room ins fnl f* **11/4**[1]

1213 **4** *3/4* **Kasumi**[10] 5950 4-9-4 **82** .... SteveDrowne 2 87
(H Morrison) *chsd ldrs tl wnt 2nd 4f out: ev ch and rdn over 2f out: led over 1f out: sn hdd: wknd ins fnl f* **7/2**[2]

3310 **5** *2 1/2* **Magical Music**[11] 5905 4-9-7 **85** .... JimmyQuinn 9 85
(J Pearce) *hld up bhd: hdwy wl over 4f out rdn over 2f out: no imp over 1f out* **8/1**

0141 **6** *3* **Hessian (IRE)**[33] 5312 3-8-4 **71** .... AdrianMcCarthy 4 64
(P Howling) *chsd ldrs: rdn over 2f out: led narrowly 2f out: hdd & wknd qckly over 1f out* **12/1**

633 **7** *7* **World's Heroine (IRE)**[8] 6002 3-9-0 **81** .... NickyMackay 6 58
(G A Butler) *in tch: rdn and struggling 3f out: no ch after* **11/2**[3]

1550 **8** *2* **Furbeseta**[25] 5545 3-8-10 **77** .... PaulMulrennan 8 49
(L M Cumani) *hld up in rr: rdn and effrt wl over 2f out: n.d* **17/2**

0046 **9** *2 1/2* **Rakata (USA)**[36] 5230 5-9-5 **83** .... NCallan 5 49
(P F I Cole) *led at fast pce: rdn and hdd 2f out: sn wknd* **14/1**

0510 **10** *5* **Tara Too (IRE)**[40] 5115 4-8-10 **74** .... (b) DaneO'Neill 1 29
(J G Portman) *s.i.s: sn drvn up to chse ldr: lost pl 4f out: sn rdn and dropped out* **40/1**

1303 **11** 3/4 **Baltic Belle (IRE)**[55] 4665 3-8-8 **75** .... RichardSmith 3 28
(R Hannon) *s.i.s: sn pushed along: a bhd* **25/1**

1m 37.2s (-2.23) **Going Correction** +0.05s/f (Slow)
WFA 3 from 4yo+ 3lb **11** Ran SP% **120.1**
Speed ratings (Par 102): **113,111,110,109,107 104,97,95,92,87 86**
CSF £198.32 CT £697.16 TOTE £18.60: £3.20, £4.40, £2.50; EX 219.60.
Owner R J Searle **Bred** Chippenham Lodge Stud Ltd **Trained** Newmarket, Suffolk
■ Stewards' Enquiry : Chris Catlin one-day ban: careless riding (Oct 25)

FOCUS
There was a good pace to this handicap and the first three came from off the pace. Sound form which should prove reliable.

6209 CORAL COMMENTARIES 0871 2 000 000 H'CAP 7f (P)
3:55 (3:55) (Class 4) (0-85,84) 3-Y-O+ **£4,857** (£1,445; £722; £360) **Stalls** Low

Form RPR
0305 **1** **The Kiddykid (IRE)**[15] 5804 7-9-6 **84** .... TGMcLaughlin 13 94
(P D Evans) *broke wl: settled in midfield on outer: hdwy over 2f out: rdn to chal 1f out: r.o wl to ld nr fin* **25/1**

0046 **2** *hd* **Bobski (IRE)**[37] 5196 5-9-4 **82** ....(p) NCallan 11 91
(G A Huffer) *hld up towards rr: stdy hdwy on bit over 3f out: shkn up and effrt jst over 1f out: rdn to ld ins fnl f: hdd nr fin* **7/1**[3]

6010 **3** 1 1/4 **Carnivore**[78] 3943 5-9-2 **80** .... ChrisCatlin 10 86
(T D Barron) *sn rdn and outpcd in rr on outer: hdwy over 1f out: r.o strly fnl f: wnt 3rd last strides: nt rch ldrs* **10/1**

4103 **4** *nk* **Golden Desert (IRE)**[20] 5684 3-9-1 **84** .... DuranFentiman(3) 9 89
(T G Mills) *t.k.h: in tch: rdn to ld 2f out: hdd ins fnl f: no ex last 100yds* **25/1**

3050 **5** *hd* **Fiefdom (IRE)**[15] 5804 5-9-2 **80** .... DanielTudhope 6 85
(I W McInnes) *racd in midfield tl lost pl wl over 4f out: bhd and rdn over 2f out: r.o fnl f: nt rch ldrs* **33/1**

2600 **6** 1 3/4 **Desert Dreamer (IRE)**[12] 5891 6-9-1 **79** .... NickyMackay 14 79+
(G A Butler) *stdd after s: hld up in rr: nt clr run and stmbld 2f out: pushed along and r.o fnl f: nvr nr ldrs* **12/1**

0122 **7** *nk* **Landucci**[16] 5788 6-9-1 **79** ....(p) JimmyQuinn 5 78
(J W Hills) *chsd ldrs: hdwy over 2f out: rdn and ev ch 2f out tl wknd jst ins fnl f* **10/1**

0520 **8** 1 **Trimlestown (IRE)**[40] 5115 4-9-1 **79** ....(b[1]) DaneO'Neill 1 76
(H Candy) *s.i.s: sn in midfield: rdn 2f out: wknd over 1f out* **12/1**

3021 **9** 1 1/2 **Piper's Song (IRE)**[20] 5687 4-8-6 **77** ....(v) AmyScott(7) 7 69
(H Candy) *chsd ldrs: wnt 2nd over 3f out: led over 2f out: sn hdd: wknd over 1f out* **12/1**

0003 **10** 1 3/4 **Yaroslav (USA)**[33] 5312 3-9-1 **81** ....(b) SteveDrowne 2 69
(R Charlton) *in tch in midfield on inner: rdn and struggling 3f out: no ch last 2f out* **3/1**[1]

3340 **11** 3 1/2 **Princess Valerina**[49] 4848 3-8-9 **82** .... KMay(7) 8 60
(B W Hills) *hld up bhd: hdwy on rail and gng wl whn hmpd 2f out: no ch after* **33/1**

0050 **12** 1/2 **H Harrison (IRE)**[15] 5804 7-8-8 **77** .... NataliaGemelova(5) 4 54
(I W McInnes) *led tl 4f out sn rdn: wknd 3f out: sn bhd* **20/1**

1353 **13** 1 1/4 **Flying Goose (IRE)**[27] 5473 3-9-0 **80** .... PaulMulrennan 12 54
(L M Cumani) *stdd s: hld up in last: hmpd 5f out: n.d* **12/1**

1 **14** 16 **Step In Line (USA)**[27] 5488 3-9-1 **81** .... JamieSpencer 3 11
(Saeed Bin Suroor) *chsd ldr tl led 4f out: hung lft and hdd over 2f out: sn btn and eased: t.o* **5/1**[2]

1m 24.9s (-0.99) **Going Correction** +0.05s/f (Slow)
WFA 3 from 4yo+ 2lb **14** Ran SP% **121.5**
Speed ratings (Par 105): **107,106,105,105,104 102,102,101,99,97 93,93,91,73**
CSF £183.93 CT £1250.89 TOTE £29.90: £6.80, £3.80, £3.40; EX 200.10.
Owner Mrs Claire Massey **Bred** Knocklong House Stud **Trained** Pandy, Monmouths
■ Stewards' Enquiry : Nicky Mackay two-day ban: careless riding (Oct 25-26)

FOCUS
A good handicap run at a strong pace. The Kiddykid took advantage of a slide in the weights and the second was a length off his sand best.
Landucci Official explanation: jockey said gelding lost a near-fore shoe
Step In Line(USA) Official explanation: jockey said colt hung left throughout and lost its action on final bend

6210 CORAL ON CH4 TELETEXT PAGE 611 H'CAP 6f (P)
4:30 (4:31) (Class 6) (0-60,60) 3-Y-O+ **£2,730** (£806; £403) **Stalls** Low

Form RPR
4004 **1** **Monashee Prince (IRE)**[11] 5897 5-8-13 **53** ....(v) JimmyQuinn 2 68
(J R Best) *in tch: hdwy 2f out: rdn to chse ldr jst over 1f out: led ins fnl f: r.o strly* **7/1**

0001 **2** 1 3/4 **Forced Upon Us**[11] 5900 3-9-4 **59** ....(b) NCallan 7 68
(P J McBride) *chsd ldrs on outer: rdn to chse ldr 2f out: led over 1f out: hdd ins fnl f: nt pce of wnr* **6/1**[3]

6000 **3** 2 **Ever Cheerful**[54] 4689 6-9-2 **56** ....(p) SteveDrowne 11 59
(A B Haynes) *sn bhd and pushed along: rdn 3f out: wl bhd tl r.o wl fnl f: wnt 3rd on post* **14/1**

4121 **4** *shd* **Shaded Edge**[39] 5136 3-9-5 **60** .... DaneO'Neill 1 62
(D W P Arbuthnot) *in tch: edgd out and rdn over 2f out: kpt on same pce over 1f out* **4/1**[1]

046 **5** 1/2 **Tibinta**[37] 5190 3-8-4 **45** .... SimonWhitworth 10 46
(P D Evans) *rrd in stalls and v.s.a: detached in last tl rdn and gd hdwy over 2f out: chsd ldrs jst over 1f out: no ex after* **25/1**

0133 **6** 3/4 **Razzano (IRE)**[22] 5627 3-8-13 **54** .... JamieSpencer 3 52
(A M Hales) *chsd ldr tl led over 2f out: sn rdn: hdd over 1f out: wknd ins fnl f* **9/1**

0035 **7** 3/4 **Nikki Bea (IRE)**[40] 5118 4-8-12 **59** .... HarryPoulton(7) 6 55+
(Jamie Poulton) *racd in midfield tl lost pl bnd jst over 2f out: kpt on u.p fnl f: nvr trbld ldrs* **8/1**

0300 **8** *nk* **Titian Saga (IRE)**[10] 5954 4-8-10 **50** ....(bt) TGMcLaughlin 9 45
(C N Allen) *plld hrd: hld up towards rr on inner: swtchd lft and rdn over 1f out: no imp* **18/1**

0105 **9** 2 **Greek Secret**[11] 5909 4-8-12 **57** .... JamesO'Reilly(5) 12 46
(J O'Reilly) *hld up in rr: n.d* **14/1**

-000 **10** 1 3/4 **Diamond Josh**[29] 5430 5-8-5 **45** .... AdrianMcCarthy 5 28
(M Mullineaux) *wnt rt s: led tl rdn and hdd over 2f out: wknd qckly over 1f out* **50/1**

4416 **11** 1 1/4 **Willofcourse**[16] 5778 6-8-8 **55** .... AmyScott(7) 4 34
(H Candy) *hld up towards rr: rdn 2f out: no prog* **6/1**[3]

6136 **12** 2 **Contented (IRE)**[10] 5942 5-9-1 **55** ....(p) ChrisCatlin 8 28
(Mrs L C Jewell) *chsd ldrs: rdn jst over 2f out: wknd qckly wl over 1f out* **5/1**[2]

1m 12.63s (-0.18) **Going Correction** +0.05s/f (Slow)
WFA 3 from 4yo+ 1lb **12** Ran SP% **123.3**
Speed ratings (Par 101): **103,100,98,97,97 96,95,94,92,89 88,85**
CSF £50.75 CT £597.20 TOTE £9.80: £2.90, £3.00, £5.10; EX 84.60.
Owner Michael Hurd, Ray Rooks, Paul Rooks **Bred** Mrs Dolores Gleeson **Trained** Hucking, Kent

FOCUS
A moderate sprint handicap. Sound form, the winner running to last winter's level and the second producing a slight step up.
Tibinta Official explanation: jockey said filly reared on leaving stalls
Diamond Josh Official explanation: jockey said gelding was awkward leaving stalls

6211 CORAL SHOPS NOW OPEN AT 8.30AM MEDIAN AUCTION MAIDEN STKS 1m 4f (P)
5:05 (5:05) (Class 6) 3-5-Y-O **£2,730** (£806; £403) **Stalls** Low

Form RPR
0320 **1** **River Deuce**[17] 5750 3-9-3 65 .... JimmyQuinn 7 76
(M H Tompkins) *hld up in tch: hdwy to trck ldng pair wl over 3f out: rdn to ld jst over 1f out: rdn clr fnl f* **6/1**

0403 **2** 3 **Putra Square**[15] 5816 3-9-3 82 ....(b[1]) JamieSpencer 5 71
(P F I Cole) *str reminders sn after s: sn led: hrd drvn and hdd 2f out: one pce* **2/1**[1]

26 **3** 6 **Srikuantan (IRE)**[8] 6005 3-9-3 0 .... NCallan 4 61
(P F I Cole) *chsd ldrs: wnt 2nd over 4f out: sn rdn: hrd rdn to ld 2f out: hdd jst over 1f out: flashed tail and wknd rapidly fnl f* **5/1**

5 **4** 1 1/4 **Summerofsixtynine**[15] 5816 4-9-5 0 .... RussellKennemore(5) 1 59
(J G M O'Shea) *rn in snatches: towards rr: hrd rdn and lost tch over 4f out: chsd ldng trio over 2f out: no real imp* **14/1**

5 **5** 20 **Idun**[15] 5803 3-8-12 0 .... SteveDrowne 6 22
(P W Chapple-Hyam) *t.k.h early: chsd ldr tl over 4f out: sn rdn and wl bhd: t.o last 3f* **4/1**[3]

6 **6** 8 **Bothar Brugha (IRE)**[15] 5816 3-9-3 0 .... DaneO'Neill 8 15
(J G M O'Shea) *hld up in last pair: hdwy 5f out: sn rdn and lost tch: t.o last 3f* **50/1**

22 **7** 5 **Vivacita**[17] 5754 3-8-12 0 .... ChrisCatlin 2 —
(E J O'Neill) *t.k.h: chsd ldrs tl rdn and dropped to rr 5f out: no ch after: t.o last 3f* **11/4**[2]

-000 **8** 20 **Pearl Of Esteem**[11] 5898 4-9-5 45 .... TGMcLaughlin 3 —
(Mrs C A Dunnett) *s.i.s: a bhd: rdn and lost tch: over 4f out: t.o last 3f* **66/1**

2m 32.89s (-1.50) **Going Correction** +0.05s/f (Slow)
WFA 3 from 4yo 7lb **8** Ran SP% **121.1**
Speed ratings (Par 101): **107,105,101,100,86 81,78,64**
CSF £19.64 TOTE £6.80: £2.00, £1.20, £2.00; EX 23.20.
Owner Robert Levitt **Bred** Dullingham Park **Trained** Newmarket, Suffolk

FOCUS
A weak and uncompetitive maiden. The winner was up 5lb but the runner-up is regressing.

6212 PLAY POKER IN ALL CORAL SHOPS CLASSIFIED STKS 1m 2f (P)
5:35 (5:36) (Class 7) 3-Y-O+ **£2,047** (£604; £302) **Stalls** Low

Form RPR
0400 **1** **Dawson Creek (IRE)**[133] 2273 3-8-12 44 .... NCallan 12 52
(B Gubby) *t.k.h: chsd ldrs: rdn to ld 2f out: hld on wl last 100yds* **12/1**

000/ **2** 1/2 **Smokey The Bear**[527] 5819 5-9-0 45 .... NeilChalmers(3) 1 51
(Miss Sheena West) *stdd after s: t.k.h: hld up in rr on inner: hdwy on rail 2f out: rdn over 1f out: chsd wnr ins fnl f: hld last 100yds* **33/1**

3452 **3** 3/4 **Fantastic Delight**[2] 6152 4-9-3 45 .... JamieSpencer 2 49
(B G Powell) *hld up in midfield: hdwy to chse ldrs over 2f out: wnt 2nd jst over 1f out: sn rdn and nt run on* **11/4**[1]

-460 **4** 2 **Abbeygate**[29] 5421 6-9-0 44 .... EmmettStack(3) 4 45
(T Keddy) *t.k.h: in tch: rdn and effrt to chse ldrs 2f out: kpt on same pce* **13/2**[3]

5200 **5** *shd* **Lady Ambitious**[30] 5389 4-8-12 45 .... JamesO'Reilly(5) 13 45
(D K Ivory) *racd in midfield tl hdwy to trck ldrs over 5f out: rdn 2f out: wknd 1f out* **14/1**

-606 **6** *hd* **Future Deal**[29] 5421 6-9-3 45 .... SimonWhitworth 5 44
(C A Horgan) *t.k.h: hld up in midfield: hdwy 4f out: rdn to chse wnr 2f out: wknd jst ins fnl f* **8/1**

0004 **7** 3 **Megalala (IRE)**[13] 5864 6-9-3 45 .... FrankieMcDonald 3 38
(J J Bridger) *hld up in rr: rdn and struggling 4f out: sme modest late hdwy: n.d* **7/1**

6000 **8** 2 1/2 **Oasis Sun (IRE)**[52] 4739 4-9-3 45 ....(v) DaneO'Neill 10 33
(J R Best) *t.k.h: chsd ldr after 2f: led 3f out: sn rdn: hdd 2f out: sn wknd* **5/1**[2]

0520 **9** *nk* **Bollywood (IRE)**[44] 5001 4-9-3 44 .... SteveDrowne 6 33
(J J Bridger) *hld up towards rr: rdn 4f out: sn struggling* **8/1**

0543 **10** *nk* **Cool Isle**[25] 5542 4-9-3 45 ....(b) JimmyQuinn 14 32
(P Howling) *chsd ldr over 8f out tl led wl over 7f out: rdn and hdd 3f out: sn dropped out* **17/2**

056- **11** 1 3/4 **Rainbow Prince**[405] 5060 4-8-12 44 .... RussellKennemore(5) 11 29
(M J Gingell) *stdd after s: t.k.h: hld up in rr: rdn and effrt on outer over 3f out: wknd over 2f out* **50/1**

6005 **12** *nk* **Littlemissdynamite**[52] 4736 4-9-3 44 .... TGMcLaughlin 9 28
(S W Hall) *s.i.s: a bhd: no ch last 2f* **33/1**

5060 **13** 17 **Myrtle Bay (IRE)**[120] 2656 4-9-3 44 .... ChrisCatlin 7 —
(J C Tuck) *led tl wl over 7f out: chsd ldrs tl rdn and wknd over 3f out: t.o and eased fnl f* **11/1**

2m 9.94s (2.15) **Going Correction** +0.05s/f (Slow)
WFA 3 from 4yo+ 5lb **13** Ran SP% **132.5**
Speed ratings (Par 97): **93,92,92,90,90 90,87,85,85,85 83,83,70**
CSF £384.47 TOTE £11.60: £5.10, £8.50, £1.80; EX 1068.00 Place 6 £6252.61, Place 5 £2213.07.
Owner Brian Gubby **Bred** Eastersnow Stud **Trained** Bagshot, Surrey

FOCUS
An ordinary race for the lowly grade. The winner confirmed his maiden form and the fifth helps with the standard.
Megalala(IRE) Official explanation: jockey said gelding ran too free
T/Plt: £13,457.80 to a £1 stake. Pool: £57,149.60. 3.10 winning tickets. T/Qpdt: £145.90 to a £1 stake. Pool: £4,634.00. 23.50 winning tickets. SP

6213 - 6215a (Foreign Racing) - See Raceform Interactive

4241 NAAS (L-H)
Sunday, October 14

OFFICIAL GOING: Good

6216a CASTLEMARTIN STUD EUROPEAN BREEDERS FUND GARNET STKS (LISTED RACE) (FILLIES) 1m
5:00 (5:00) 3-Y-0+ **£32,989** (£9,679; £4,611; £1,570)

RPR

1 **Cheyenne Star (IRE)**[130] 2381 4-9-6 108........................ JAHeffernan 12 100+
(Ms F M Crowley, Ire) *trckd ldrs: 7th appr st: lost pl briefly 2f out: 8th over 1f out: r.o wl u.p to ld cl home* **4/1**[1]

2 *nk* **Thoughtless Moment (IRE)**[28] 5459 3-8-12 99................ PJSmullen 3 93
(D K Weld, Ire) *trckd ldrs in 5th: chal early st: led under 2f out: kpt on wl u.p: hdd cl home* **5/1**[2]

3 *hd* **Baby Blue Eyes (IRE)**[42] 5071 4-9-4 105............................ DMGrant 2 96
(Patrick J Flynn, Ire) *mid-div: prog on inner early st: 3rd 2f out: cl 2nd and chal fnl f: no ex cl home* **6/1**[3]

4 *nk* **Dimenticata (IRE)**[22] 5654 3-8-12 109.............................. CDHayes 13 92
(Kevin Prendergast, Ire) *towards rr: hdwy on outer early st: 5th under 1 1/2f out: kpt on ins fnl f* **8/1**

5 *hd* **Crossing**[22] 5654 6-9-1 103... DJMoran 15 91
(William J Fitzpatrick, Ire) *prom: 3rd 1/2-way: chal early st: kpt on u.p fr over 1f out* **10/1**

6 *hd* **Akua'Ba (IRE)**[17] 5761 3-8-12 90...................................(p) KJManning 10 91
(J S Bolger, Ire) *prom: 4th 1/2-way: lost pl early st: 5th over 1f out: kpt on u.p* **8/1**

7 *nk* **In Safe Hands (IRE)**[43] 5047 3-8-12 .... WJSupple 6 90
(C G Cox) *cl up: dispiuted ld 1/2-way: led enteirng st: hdd under 2f out: no ex whn short of room and checked cl home* **16/1**

8 *nk* **Deauville Vision (IRE)**[51] 4790 4-9-4 107......................... JMurtagh 1 93
(M Halford, Ire) *towards rr: prog on inner early st: 7th over 1f out: kpt on same pce* **7/1**

9 *nk* **Mooretown Lady (IRE)**[14] 5846 4-9-1 84........................ PShanahan 16 89
(H Rogers, Ire) *towards rr: kpt on wout threatening fr over 2f out* **14/1**

10 *1* **Impetious**[15] 5794 3-9-1 100...(b) WJLee 7 90
(Eamon Tyrrell, Ire) *chsd ldrs: 8th 1/2-way: rdn st: no imp fr under 2f out* **33/1**

11 *1/2* **Lee Applause**[22] 5654 5-8-10 72..................................... PBBeggy(5) 14 85
(Edward P Harty, Ire) *towards rr: effrt on inner early st: no imp fr under 2f out* **50/1**

12 *1/2* **Sandtime (IRE)**[14] 5846 3-8-12 85.................................... MCHussey 4 84
(John M Oxx, Ire) *towards rr: rdn and no imp st* **25/1**

13 *1* **Divine Night (IRE)**[45] 4985 3-8-12 98..............................(p) WMLordan 5 82
(David Wachman, Ire) *hld up: no imp st* **20/1**

14 *1 1/4* **Dressmaker (USA)**[69] 4237 3-8-12 90............................... MJKinane 11 79
(John M Oxx, Ire) *led: jnd 1/2-way: hdd ent st: sn wknd* **10/1**

15 *1/2* **Bush Maiden (IRE)**[14] 5846 7-9-1 95................................. DJCondon 17 78
(Mrs Seamus Hayes, Ire) *s.i.s: hld up towards rr: no imp st* **33/1**

16 *1 3/4* **Nell Gwyn (IRE)**[135] 2211 3-8-12 100.............................. DavidMcCabe 9 74
(A P O'Brien, Ire) *a bhd* **12/1**

17 *1 3/4* **Regalline (IRE)**[10] 5958 3-8-12 75................................. DPMcDonogh 8 70
(Kevin Prendergast, Ire) *chsd ldrs on outer: 6th 1/2-way: wknd early st* **25/1**

1m 39.8s (-0.20)
WFA 3 from 4yo+ 3lb **17** Ran SP% **144.4**
CSF £25.84 TOTE £4.90: £1.90, £2.00, £1.90, £2.00; DF 17.40.
Owner Mrs Jacqueline Alder **Bred** Roland H Alder **Trained** Curragh, Co Kildare

FOCUS
A large handkerchief would have covered the majority of these and it has been rated through the seventh and 12th to their recent best.

NOTEBOOK
Cheyenne Star(IRE) had to be patient and wait for a gap to appear, but when it did she seized the opportunity and ran on strongly inside the last half-furlong to prevail by a neck. This was her first run since June, since when she had been sick with mastitis, so it was a fair performance for a filly whose next stop may be a Listed race at Dundalk in a few weeks' time. (op 7/2)
In Safe Hands(IRE) was in front early in the straight, but could not sustain her effort from there.

6217 - 6218a (Foreign Racing) - See Raceform Interactive

5669 COLOGNE (R-H)
Sunday, October 14

OFFICIAL GOING: Good to soft

6219a CHRISTLACKE-PREIS DES WINTERFAVORITEN (GROUP 3) 1m
4:20 (4:24) 2-Y-O
£57,432 (£20,946; £13,851; £6,959; £3,716; £1,824)

RPR

1 **Precious Boy (GER)**[35] 2-9-2 .... ADeVries 8 —
(W Hickst, Germany) *slowly away: in rr tl pushed along and hdwy 1/2-way: 6th st: r.o u.p fr over 2f out: led last 100yds: rdn out* **24/10**[2]

2 *1/2* **Liang Kay (GER)** 2-9-2 .... ABoschert 4 —
(U Ostmann, Germany) *pressed ldr tl led over 2f out: rdn and strly pressed 1f out tl hdd last 100yds: no ex* **27/10**[3]

3 *5* **Abbashiva (GER)** 2-9-2 .... TMundry 7 —
(P Rau, Germany) *in tch: 4th st: wnt 2nd briefly over 1f out: one pce* **131/10**

4 *1 3/4* **Konig Concorde (GER)** 2-9-2 .... THellier 5 —
(C Sprengel, Germany) *unruly bef s: hld up in 7th: 5th st: one pce fnl 2f* **18/1**

5 *5* **Santero (GER)** 2-9-2 .... J-LSilverio 6 —
(N Sauer, Germany) *7th st: a in rr* **113/10**

5 *5* **Sahara Boy (GER)** 2-9-2 .... EPedroza 1 —
(A Wohler, Germany) *set str pce tl hdd over 2f out: wknd steadily* **2/1**[1]

7 *2 1/2* **Mercator (GER)** 2-9-2 .... AHelfenbein 9 —
(K Woodburn) *8th st: nvr a factor* **34/1**

8 *8* **Illimani (GER)** 2-9-2 .... JiriPalik 2 —
(A Trybuhl, Germany) *trckd ldr in 3rd: wknd qckly fr over 2f out* **56/1**

9 *40* **Diacaro**[44] 5028 2-9-2 .... J-PCarvalho 3 —
(H Blume, Germany) *cl up early: last and btn ent st: eased* **52/10**

1m 37.78s (-0.61) **9** Ran SP% **131.0**
WIN 34; PL 14, 13, 18; SF 58.
Owner Gestut Park Wiedingen **Bred** Gestut Park Wiedingen **Trained** Germany

4013 MUNICH (L-H)
Sunday, October 14

OFFICIAL GOING: Good

6220a NEREIDE-RENNEN (LISTED RACE) (F&M) 1m 2f
3:25 (3:28) 3-Y-O+ **£8,108** (£2,973; £1,622; £811)

RPR

1 **Beiramar (IRE)**[60] 4-8-13 .... PHeugl 5 97
(W Hickst, Germany) **116/10**[3]

2 *1/2* **Carolines Secret**[60] 3-8-6 .... ASchikora 12 87
(Mario Hofer, Germany)

3 *3* **Wonderful Day (GER)**[126] 5-9-3 .... MKolb 11 95
(Frau C Brandstatter, Germany) **148/10**

4 *1/2* **Lemonette (USA)**[21] 5669 4-9-1 .... WMongil 1 92
(J W Hills) *trckd ldr in 3rd on ins: swtchd off rail 2f out: wnt 2nd appr fnl f: lost 2nd clsng stages* **3/1**[2]

5 *1/2* **Soft Morning**[32] 5327 3-8-11 .... JamieMackay 9 91
(Sir Mark Prescott) *broke fast: set gd pce tl hdd over 1 1/2f out: one pce* **22/10**[1]

6 *hd* **Aramina (GER)**[14] 4-8-13 .... FilipMinarik 4 88
(P Schiergen, Germany)

7 *1 1/2* **Lavana (GER)**[21] 4-8-13 .... BClos 7 85
(Werner Glanz, Germany)

8 *2* **Sun Valley (GER)** 4-8-13 ....(b) VSchulepov 13 81
(Frau E Mader, Germany)

9 *3* **Macuna** 4-8-13 .... WPanov 16 75
(C Sprengel, Germany)

10 *1/2* **Pearl Island (GER)**[812] 3791 5-8-13 .... PKrowicki 10 74
(Frau J Meyer, Germany)

11 *1 1/4* **Manda Honor (GER)**[35] 5266 4-8-13 ....(b) JBojko 14 71
(A Wohler, Germany)

12 *1/2* **Sun Moon Orpen (IRE)**[21] 4-8-13 .... RPiechulek 3 70
(U Stoltefuss, Germany)

13 *2* **Shades Of Beige (UAE)**[19] 5719 5-9-3 .... CCzachary 8 70
(Frau E Mader, Germany)

14 *1 1/4* **Loa Loa (GER)**[133] 2294 3-8-6 ....(b) EFrank 2 62
(A Wohler, Germany)

2m 10.89s (1.92) **12** Ran SP% **70.5**
(including ten euro stakes); WIN 126; PL 42, 29, 17; SF 1700.
Owner C Berglar **Bred** Gestut Schlenderhan **Trained** Germany

NOTEBOOK
Lemonette(USA), third at a similar level over 1m4f last time, gained some more black type with another solid effort. She appreciated the decent pace.
Soft Morning, who has an official rating of 85, set a decent pace and tried to burn them all off. It did not come off but she probably ran to her best in defeat.

6047 SAN SIRO (R-H)
Sunday, October 14

OFFICIAL GOING: Good

6221a PREMIO SERGIO CUMANI (GROUP 3) (FILLIES) 1m
2:00 (2:04) 3-Y-O+ **£24,628** (£10,836; £5,911; £2,955)

RPR

1 **Whazzis**[49] 4873 3-8-9 ....(v) RyanMoore 102
(W J Haggas) *hld up in rr tl hdwy fr wl over 2f out: led over 1 1/2f out: rdn out (correct SP 54/100)* **1/2**[1]

2 *1 1/2* **Mimetico (IRE)**[14] 3-8-9 .... DVargiu 99
(B Grizzetti, Italy) *led to over 1 1/2f out: rallied to regain 2nd last strides* **79/10**[3]

3 *nk* **Donoma (IRE)**[15] 3-8-9 .... EBotti 98
(A & G Botti, Italy) *racd in 3rd: wnt 2nd ent st: ev ch over 1 1/2f out: kpt on at one pce: lost 2nd last strides* **5/2**[2]

4 *1/2* **Prianca (GER)**[36] 3-8-9 .... AStarke 97
(Mario Hofer, Germany) *racd in 5th to st: outpcd 2f out: styd on again fnl f* **10/1**

5 *shd* **Mia Kross (IRE)**[120] 4-8-12 .... MDemuro 97
(B Grizzetti, Italy) *disp 5th: 6th st: on ins tl swtchd lft jst over 1f out: styd on fnl f* **119/10**

6 *3 1/2* **Fresh Bread (USA)**[15] 4-8-12 .... LManiezzi 89
(Maria Rita Salvioni, Italy) *racd in 4th to st: btn 2f out* **27/1**

7 *shd* **Mrs Snow**[35] 5266 4-8-12 .... KDarley 89
(Mario Hofer, Germany) *trckd ldr: 3rd st: wknd wl over 1f out* **20/1**

1m 39.6s (-2.50)
WFA 3 from 4yo 3lb **7** Ran SP% **131.7**
(including 1 Euro stake): WIN 1.54; PL 1.42, 2.36; DF 4.98.
Owner W Gredley & The Hon Mrs Peter Stanley **Bred** Eurostrait Ltd **Trained** Newmarket, Suffolk

NOTEBOOK
Whazzis, not beaten far in a French Group 3 last time, found this opposition weaker and landed the odds fairly comfortably.

6222a GRAN CRITERIUM (GROUP 1) (C&F) 1m
3:00 (3:25) 2-Y-O **£72,973** (£32,108; £17,514; £8,757)

RPR

1 **Scintillo**[15] 5795 2-8-12 .... RyanMoore 2 110
(R Hannon) *hld up: 6th st: hdwy 3f out: led 2f out: drvn out* **24/10**[1]

2 *1/2* **Gladiatorus (USA)**[14] 2-8-12 .... LDettori 5 109
(Maria Rita Salvioni, Italy) *led over 6f out: 4 l clr st: hdd 2f out: r.o one pce* **39/10**

3 *1 3/4* **Farrel (IRE)**[21] 2-8-12 .... DVargiu 6 105
(B Grizzetti, Italy) *reluctant to load: hld up: 7th st: r.o fr 2f out on outside: nrst at fin* **5/2**[2]

4 *hd* **Pomellato (GER)**[44] 5028 2-8-12 .... AStarke 3 105
(P Schiergen, Germany) *racd in 3rd: one pce fr over 2f out* **36/10**

5 *3/4* **Celtic Slipper (IRE)**[7] 6047 2-8-8 .... KDarley 9 99
(R M Beckett) *racd in 5th: wnt 4th st: outpcd over 2f out: hrd rdn over 1f out: styd on at one pce* **3/1**[3]

6 1 1/2 **Eldest (IRE)**[21] 2-8-12 .... MDemuro 7 100
(V Caruso, Italy) *reshod bef s: trckd ldr to st: stl 3rd 1f out: wknd qckly* **29/1**

7 8 **Silver Arrow (ITY)** 2-8-12 .... LManiezzi 1 82
(Maria Rita Salvioni, Italy) *led over 1f: 5th st: wknd over 2f out* **39/10**

8 2 1/2 **Glentire (GER)**[49] 2-8-12 .... ASuborics 8 77
(H J Groschel, Germany) *last st: a in rr* **26/1**

9 7 1/2 **Cima On Fly (IRE)**[14] 2-8-12 .... FBranca 4 60
(B Grizzetti, Italy) *8th st: bhd fr 3f out* **68/1**

1m 38.2s (-3.90) 9 Ran SP% **154.0**
WIN 3.36; PL 1.41, 1.68, 1.37; DF 11.35.
Owner White Beech Farm **Bred** Woodcote Stud Ltd **Trained** East Everleigh, Wilts
■ The race was off 25 minutes late after Eldest spread a plate and Farrel was reluctant to enter the stalls.

FOCUS
An early boost for the Royal Lodge form. Those in behind Scintillo appear to have a bit of quality about them and the level of this form seems sound.

NOTEBOOK
Scintillo, third in the Royal Lodge last time, took it up two furlongs out and ran out a half-length winner of this Group 1 event. His rider reported that he was a bit lazy when hitting the front and perhaps he is the type who needs delivering late. He should get 1m2f next year without much problem.
Celtic Slipper(IRE), who ran away with a fillies' Group 3 over this course and distance last time out, may have found the ground a bit quicker than ideal, but it was still a solid effort against the colts.

6223a GRAN PREMIO DEL JOCKEY CLUB (GROUP 1) 1m 4f
4:05 (4:57) 3-Y-0+ **£72,973** (£32,108; £17,514; £8,757)

RPR

1 **Schiaparelli (GER)**[21] 5671 4-9-5 .... AStarke 7 116
(P Schiergen, Germany) *mde all: pushed out: r.o strly* **14/10**[1]

2 1 3/4 **Champs Elysees**[49] 4872 4-9-5 .... SPasquier 6 113
(A Fabre, France) *4th st: 5th over 1f out: r.o fnl f to take 2nd cl home* **24/10**[2]

3 1 1/4 **Laverock (IRE)**[14] 5831 5-9-5 .... LDettori 2 111
(Saeed Bin Suroor) *hld up: 7th st: hdwy on outside over 2f out: tk 2nd appr fnl f: no ex and lost 2nd cl home* **38/10**

4 1 3/4 **Bussoni (GER)**[35] 5264 6-9-5 .... ASuborics 5 108
(H Blume, Germany) *trckd ldr: 2nd st: one pce fr over 1f out* **28/10**[3]

5 3/4 **Gimmy (IRE)**[15] 5821 3-8-13 .... DVargiu 4 108
(B Grizzetti, Italy) *3rd st: hrd rdn and disp 2nd over 1f out: one pce* **32/1**

6 2 **Sopran Promo (IRE)**[15] 5821 3-8-13 .... FBranca 8 105
(B Grizzetti, Italy) *6th st: nvr a factor* **55/1**

7 2 **Estejo (GER)**[119] 3-8-13 .... DPorcu 3 102
(R Rohne, Germany) *5th st: btn over 2f out* **47/1**

8 2 3/4 **Distant Way (USA)**[28] 5467 6-9-5 .... MDemuro 1 96
(L Brogi, Italy) *last st: a bhd* **118/10**

2m 28.5s (-3.00)
WFA 3 from 4yo+ 7lb 8 Ran SP% **132.9**
TOTE: WIN 2.40; PL 1.21, 1.32, 1.51; DF 3.86.
Owner Stall Blankenese **Bred** Gestut Karlshof **Trained** Germany
■ The race was off 52 minutes late.

NOTEBOOK
Schiaparelli(GER) made every yard to complete a hat-trick of Group 1 wins. It is yet to be decided if he stays in training.
Champs Elysees ran well but is not quite up to this level.
Laverock(IRE), who won this race last year, was a bit below his best and could probably have done with softer ground.

6224a PREMIO OMENONI (GROUP 3) 5f
5:10 (6:04) 3-Y-0+ **£24,628** (£10,836; £5,911; £2,955)

RPR

1 **Le Cadre Noir (IRE)**[49] 4871 3-8-13 .... MDemuro 111
(A Renzoni, Italy) *hdwy on outside 1/2-way: led over 1f out: pushed clr: easily* **9/20**[1]

2 1 3/4 **Sakhee's Song (IRE)**[28] 3-8-10 .... PConvertino 102
(B Grizzetti, Italy) *led to over 1f out: kpt on same pce* **19/1**

3 shd **Velvet Revolver (IRE)**[28] 4-8-10 .... GMarcelli 102
(L Riccardi, Italy) *pressed ldr: ev ch over 1f out: one pce* **135/10**

4 1 **Docksil**[95] 3445 3-8-13 .... DVargiu 101
(B Grizzetti, Italy) *chsd ldrs: one pce fr over 1f out* **63/10**[3]

5 1 1/4 **Mood Music**[28] 3-8-13 .... EBotti 97
(Mario Hofer, Germany) *disp 4th on rails: nvr able to chal* **51/10**[2]

6 1 **Polar Wind (ITY)**[166] 3-8-13 .... IRossi 93
(Maria Rita Salvioni, Italy) *a towards rr* **28/1**

7 shd **Etoile Nocturne (FR)**[51] 3-8-10 .... DBoeuf 90
(F Rohaut, France) *a outpcd* **17/2**

8 2 1/2 **Krisman (IRE)**[28] 8-8-13 .... LManiezzi 84
(M Ciciarelli, Italy) *a outpcd* **103/10**

57.40 secs (-1.80) 8 Ran SP% **133.8**
WIN 1.45; PL 1.22, 3.13, 2.41; DF 14.40.
Owner Scuderia Jerome **Bred** Azienda Agricola Al Deni **Trained** Italy

6206 LINGFIELD (L-H)
Monday, October 15

OFFICIAL GOING: Standard
Wind: Medium half-behind Weather: overcast

6225 BOOK YOUR CHRISTMAS PARTY HERE MAIDEN FILLIES' STKS (DIV I) 6f (P)
1:40 (1:41) (Class 5) 2-Y-0 **£2,590** (£770; £385; £192) **Stalls Low**

Form RPR

042 1 **Naughty Frida (IRE)**[25] 5575 2-9-0 77 .... PaulHanagan 9 75
(E A L Dunlop) *t.k.h: chsd ldrs: wnt 2nd 1/2-way: rdn to ld over 1f out: clr ins fnl f: a holding on* **3/1**[2]

2 1/2 **Messias Da Silva (USA)** 2-9-0 0 .... TedDurcan 10 73
(J Noseda) *bhd: rdn and hdwy on outer wl over 2f out: chsd ldng trio over 1f out: r.o to go 2nd nr fin: nt quite rch wnr* **5/1**[3]

605 3 nk **Acquifer**[35] 5277 2-9-0 75 .... EddieAhern 8 73
(J L Dunlop) *wnt lft s: chsd ldrs: rdn to take 3rd wl over 1f out: kpt on: wnt 2nd ins fnl f: lost 2nd nr fin* **11/4**[1]

4 1 1/2 **Fastella (IRE)** 2-9-0 0 .... StephenCarson 5 68+
(G A Butler) *s.i.s: bhd: effrt whn nt clr run and swtchd rt wl over 1f out: r.o wl fnl f: nt rch ldrs* **12/1**

5 nk **Arthur's Girl** 2-9-0 0 .... RobertHavlin 6 67+
(G Wragg) *s.i.s: bhd: rdn and hdwy on outer over 1f out: r.o wl fnl f: nt rch ldrs* **16/1**

03 6 nk **Miss Poppy**[14] 5856 2-9-0 0 .... PaulDoe 11 66
(P R Chamings) *sn led and clr: rdn and hdd over 1f out: wknd ins fnl f* **17/2**

5 7 2 **Sister Moonshine**[14] 5856 2-9-0 0 .... RichardMullen 1 60
(W R Muir) *chsd ldrs: rdn wl over 2f out: sn outpcd* **7/1**

05 8 3 **Hawa Khana (IRE)**[14] 5868 2-9-0 0 .... HayleyTurner 7 51
(N P Littmoden) *t.k.h: hld up in midfield: rdn over 2f out: wknd wl over 1f out* **14/1**

0 9 1 3/4 **Queens Mantle**[14] 5868 2-9-0 0 .... MartinDwyer 3 46
(P J Makin) *a towards rr: rdn wl over 2f out: n.d* **20/1**

0060 10 4 **Erin Thomas (IRE)**[9] 6022 2-9-0 50 .... (p) TPO'Shea 4 34
(M G Quinlan) *chsd ldr tl 1/2-way: sn rdn: wknd wl over 1f out* **66/1**

0 11 22 **Stoneacre Baby (USA)**[9] 6022 2-9-0 0 .... LPKeniry 2 —
(Peter Grayson) *sn drvn along in midfield: dropped to last over 2f out: t.o and eased fnl f* **100/1**

1m 13.66s (0.85) **Going Correction** +0.025s/f (Slow) 11 Ran SP% **118.8**
Speed ratings (Par 92): **95,94,93,91,91 91,88,84,82,76 47**
CSF £18.53 TOTE £3.80: £1.20, £2.60, £1.10; EX 26.10.
Owner P H Lassen **Bred** J Hanly **Trained** Newmarket, Suffolk

FOCUS
An ordinary maiden run at a fair pace though the winning time was 0.15 seconds slower than the second division and the form looks fairly reliable. Very few ever got into it, but a some of these are likely to improve from their efforts here.

NOTEBOOK
Naughty Frida(IRE) pulled like the proverbial train early and was undoubtedly helped by getting a lead from the tearaway leader. She picked her off nicely once in line for home and though her previous efforts suggest she is nothing special, she is improving and should make her mark in nurseries. (op 11-4 tchd 10-3)
Messias Da Silva(USA) ◆, a $700,000 two-year-old and half-sister to a winning sprinter in the US, took a while to realise what was required but finished in good style and was closing down the winner at the line. She is sure to come on for this and is very likely to turn out the best of these. (op 4-1)
Acquifer was very well backed to improve on her three previous efforts even though she already has an official mark of 75 and had the option of nurseries. She was certainly close enough if good enough turning in but lacked the speed to take advantage. She will remain vulnerable to more progressive types in races like these. (op 6-1)
Fastella(IRE) ◆, a 35,000gns daughter of the high-class middle-distance performer Ela Athena, was staying on when done no favours by the hanging Hawa Khana turning for home, but kept on again in promising style afterwards. There should be better to come from her and she will stay further. (op 11-1)
Arthur's Girl, a half-sister to Messiah Garvey, was another that was doing her best work late and, as with most fillies from the yard, is likely to improve a good deal at three. (tchd 14-1)
Miss Poppy, switched to sand after showing some ability in two starts on turf, did far too much early from her wide draw and was soon in a clear lead. However, a combination of her earlier exertions telling and sticking tight to the inside rail saw her fold dramatically in the home straight. (op 8-1 tchd 9-1)

6226 GOLF AND RACING APPRENTICE H'CAP 1m (P)
2:10 (2:10) (Class 6) (0-65,65) 3-Y-0+ **£3,071** (£906; £453) **Stalls High**

Form RPR

0005 1 **Seneschal**[19] 5733 6-9-1 63 .... PNolan(5) 2 68+
(A B Haynes) *dwlt: sn pushed up to ld: mde rest: drew clr over 3f out: 4l ahd over 2f out: pushed along over 1f out: kpt on* **12/1**

0000 2 1 3/4 **Putra Laju (IRE)**[14] 5862 3-9-2 62 .... (p) RyanBird 6 63
(J W Hills) *stdd after s: hld up in rr: hdwy over 3f out: rdn and kpt on over 1f out: wnt 2nd on post: no ch w wnr* **20/1**

-000 3 shd **Bonne D'Argent (IRE)**[26] 5532 3-9-5 65 .... MarkCoumbe 5 66
(J R Boyle) *in tch: rdn and effrt wl over 2f out: chsd wnr over 1f out: plugged on: lost 2nd on line* **16/1**

5000 4 1 1/4 **Royal Amnesty**[30] 5422 4-9-1 58 .... AshleyMorgan 3 56+
(G C H Chung) *hld up in tch on rail: nt clr run 2f out: swtchd rt over 1f out: kpt on: nvr threatened wnr* **10/1**

5300 5 shd **Greenwood**[12] 5917 9-9-0 57 .... LauraReynolds 9 55
(P G Murphy) *plld hrd: in tch on outer: pushed along and short of room over 2f out: kpt on fnl f: nvr threatened wnr* **12/1**

0510 6 1 1/4 **Inquisitress**[4] 6123 3-9-0 60 .... ThomasBubb 10 55
(J J Bridger) *hld up in rr: rdn and hdwy over 1f out: nr nr ldrs* **17/2**[3]

0463 7 3/4 **Isphahan**[32] 5348 4-8-11 59 .... (p) DavidProbert(5) 4 52
(A M Balding) *in tch: rdn and lost pl over 3f out: n.d after* **13/2**[2]

0421 8 2 1/2 **King After**[41] 5118 5-8-8 56 .... (v) KierenFox(5) 8 44
(J R Best) *plld hrd: chsd ldrs: chsd wnr 2f out tl over 1f out: sn wknd* **7/2**[1]

0400 9 1/2 **James Street (IRE)**[25] 5565 4-8-7 55 .... RyanHill(5) 7 41
(Peter Grayson) *in tch on outer: rdn 3f out: n.d after* **17/2**[3]

412 10 2 1/2 **Rowan Lodge (IRE)**[14] 5862 5-9-7 64 .... BarrySavage 1 45
(J R Boyle) *chsd wnr tl 2f out: sn btn* **7/2**[1]

1m 40.12s (0.69) **Going Correction** +0.025s/f (Slow)
WFA 3 from 4yo+ 3lb 10 Ran SP% **114.0**
Speed ratings (Par 101): **97,95,95,93,93 92,91,89,88,86**
CSF £219.92 CT £3784.96 TOTE £10.40: £3.20, £6.50, £4.00; EX 253.30.
Owner P Cook **Bred** Michael E Broughton **Trained** Limpley Stoke, Bath
■ Paul Nolan's first winner.
■ Stewards' Enquiry : Mark Coumbe one-day ban: careless riding (Oct 26)

FOCUS
A very moderate handicap but a race that came down to tactics and the winner had this prize in the bag from a long way out. The form may not be totally reliable as a result and looks weak.

6227 LINGFIELDPARK.CO.UK NURSERY 5f (P)
2:40 (2:40) (Class 6) (0-65,65) 2-Y-0 **£2,730** (£806; £403) **Stalls High**

Form RPR

2053 1 **Angle Of Attack (IRE)**[11] 5932 2-9-7 65 .... PaulHanagan 8 74
(R A Fahey) *chsd ldrs: wnt 2nd wl over 2f out: led jst over 2f out: styd on wl fnl f* **3/1**[1]

1332 2 1 1/4 **Fabuleux Cherie**[13] 5887 2-9-7 65 .... RichardMullen 4 70
(W R Muir) *racd in midfield: hdwy on outer 3f out: wnt 3rd over 2f out: chsd wnr over 1f out: kpt on same pce fnl f* **4/1**[2]

0140 3 1 1/2 **Rightcar Ellie (IRE)**[6] 6074 2-9-4 62 .... (b) LPKeniry 2 61
(Peter Grayson) *led: rdn and hdd 3f out: rallied u.p to chse ldng pair jst over 1f out: kpt on same pce* **9/1**

0600 **4** ¾ **Maybe I Wont**[13] 5887 2-9-5 **63** .... PaulFitzsimons 1 59
(S Dow) *chsd ldrs: rdn and lost pl over 2f out: rallied u.p over 1f out: kpt on fnl f* **12/1**

0000 **5** ¾ **Wynberg (IRE)**[30] 5428 2-8-8 **57** .... KirstyMilczarek(5) 9 51+
(N A Callaghan) *t.k.h: hld up in rr: hdwy whn nt clr run and stmbld wl over 1f out: sn swtchd lft and gd hdwy: no imp fnl f* **20/1**

0002 **6** nk **New Balls Please (IRE)**[20] 5715 2-8-9 **60** ....(b[1]) JackMitchell(7) 10 53
(P M Phelan) *towards rr on outer: rdn and effrt on outer over 2f out: nvr able to chal* **14/1**

6050 **7** hd **Mandarinka**[18] 5751 2-9-0 **58** .... StephenCarson 3 50
(P Winkworth) *in tch in midfield: rdn wl over 2f out: no hdwy* **9/1**

0000 **8** 1 **Ile Royale**[11] 5949 2-8-12 **56** .... MartinDwyer 7 44
(C N Allen) *hld up bhd: rdn and bmpd wl over 1f out: no prog* **14/1**

2403 **9** 2½ **Attribution**[5] 6098 2-9-7 **65** .... DavidKinsella 6 44+
(A B Haynes) *in tch: rdn and outpcd over 2f out: bmpd and lost action wl over 1f out: sn btn: eased ins fnl f* **11/2**[3]

0002 **10** 1¼ **Structura (USA)**[9] 6023 2-9-1 **59** ....(p) RichardHughes 5 34+
(J S Moore) *chsd ldrs tl led 3f out: rdn and hdd jst over 2f out: wknd qckly over 1f out: eased wl ins fnl f* **10/1**

59.38 secs (-0.40) **Going Correction** +0.025s/f (Slow) **10** Ran SP% **115.3**
Speed ratings (Par 93): **104,102,99,98,97 96,96,94,90,88**
CSF £14.43 CT £97.68 TOTE £3.10: £1.50, £1.60, £2.60; EX 11.30.
Owner Eddie Tynan **Bred** Travel Spot Girl Partnership **Trained** Musley Bank, N Yorks
■ Stewards' Enquiry : Kirsty Milczarek caution: careless riding

FOCUS
A modest nursery on paper, but they went a very decent pace and the winning time was smart. The form looks solid enough although somewhat limited.

NOTEBOOK
Angle Of Attack(IRE) ◆, who ran better than his finishing position would suggest on his sand debut two starts back, had no such problem this time. He was always in a good position and saw his race out well when asked to get off the mark at the ninth attempt. He ought to be able to win again on this surface. (op 10-3)
Fabuleux Cherie, up another 2lb despite getting beaten last time, came through to hold every chance in the straight but despite giving it everything, ran into a very determined winner. She is very consistent and there will be other days. (op 3-1 tchd 11-4)
Rightcar Ellie(IRE), just behind Fabuleux Cherie at Wolverhampton earlier this month and 4lb better off, seemed likely to drop away at halfway after showing early speed, but to her great credit she stayed on again to make the frame and finished marginally closer to her old rival. (tchd 8-1)
Maybe I Wont is sliding down the weights and plugged on late to reach his final position. He is still a maiden after 12 attempts and looks exposed, but shapes as though he will appreciate a return to 6f. (op 9-1)
Wynberg(IRE) ◆, making his sand and nursery debuts after showing nothing in four starts on turf, was backed at fancy prices and showed a little bit more. He can be given a little extra credit as he was forced to switch and make his effort closer to the inside rail than is probably ideal and the market support suggests he is not totally without ability. Official explanation: jockey said gelding was denied a clear run (op 33-1 tchd 40-1 in a place)
Attribution, well backed, was beaten rounding the home bend and not for the first time appeared to lose his action. (op 8-1)

6228 BOOK YOUR CHRISTMAS PARTY HERE MAIDEN FILLIES' STKS (DIV II) 6f (P)
3:10 (3:10) (Class 5) 2-Y-O £2,590 (£770; £385; £192) Stalls Low

Form RPR

56 **1** **Meydan Princess (IRE)**[11] 5949 2-9-0 0 .... TedDurcan 6 77+
(J Noseda) *in tch: rdn and c wd bnd 2f out: str run 1f out: led wl ins fnl f: readily* **5/2**[2]

00 **2** 1½ **Town And Gown**[17] 5766 2-9-0 0 .... RobertHavlin 7 73
(J H M Gosden) *t.k.h: prom: chsd ldr 4f out: led 2f out: riddn wl over 1f out: kep ton tl hdd wl ins fnl f: nt pce of wnr* **7/1**

6 **3** 1½ **Doric Lady**[24] 5595 2-9-0 0 .... OscarUrbina 2 68
(J A R Toller) *racd in midfield: pushed along 3f out: hdwy 2f out: kpt on same pce u.p fnl f* **8/1**

4200 **4** ½ **Fifty (IRE)**[17] 5766 2-9-0 80 .... RichardHughes 3 67
(R Hannon) *led for 1f: chsd ldrs: rdn over 2f out: wknd ins fnl f* **9/4**[1]

4424 **5** 1¾ **Gower Belle**[24] 5601 2-9-0 69 ....(b[1]) RichardMullen 8 61
(W R Muir) *chsd ldrs on outer: rdn over 2f out: wknd jst ins fnl f* **15/2**

00 **6** nk **Tea Cake (IRE)**[17] 5766 2-9-0 0 .... HayleyTurner 1 60
(H J L Dunlop) *stdd s: t.k.h: hld up in last: wl bhd 2f out: hdwy over 1f out: kpt on: nvr nr ldrs* **33/1**

5 **7** ¾ **Danvers**[38] 5201 2-9-0 0 .... EddieAhern 9 58
(J L Dunlop) *racd freely: led after 1f: rdn and hdd 2f out: wknd qckly over 1f out* **13/2**[3]

0 **8** 5 **Run From Nun**[17] 5780 2-9-0 0 .... RichardSmith 10 43
(J A Osborne) *rrd s: a towards rr: rdn and lost tch over 2f out: hung rt over 1f out* **50/1**

0 **9** ¾ **Silky Steps (IRE)**[14] 5872 2-9-0 0 .... MartinDwyer 4 41
(P J Makin) *s.i.s: a bhd:* **40/1**

10 1¼ **Where's Killoran** 2-9-0 0 .... LPKeniry 5 37
(Peter Grayson) *s.i.s: racd in midfield tl lost pl over 3f out: no ch whn hung lft over 1f out* **66/1**

1m 13.51s (0.70) **Going Correction** +0.025s/f (Slow) **10** Ran SP% **116.9**
Speed ratings (Par 92): **96,94,92,91,89 88,87,80,79,78**
CSF £20.08 TOTE £3.40: £1.60, £2.20, £2.10; EX 24.70.
Owner Franconson Partners **Bred** J Costello **Trained** Newmarket, Suffolk

FOCUS
Like the first division, this looked an ordinary maiden though the winning time was 0.15 seconds quicker. A couple of these are entitled to improve though and the fifth sets the level.

NOTEBOOK
Meydan Princess(IRE), who had shown some ability in two starts over this trip on turf, took to this surface well and showed a decent turn of foot to cut down the runner-up. She is bred to stay a little bit further and should be able to find another race on Polytrack. (op 9-4)
Town And Gown, well beaten in two starts on turf though she faced a very stiff task last time, ran much better on this switch to sand and led the field into the straight, but had no answer to the winner's turn of foot. She may be nothing special, but should find a race on this surface. (op 8-1)
Doric Lady, who showed a bit of promise on her Newmarket debut, improved on that and stayed on well after being produced between horses. Although by a top-class sprinter, there is a bit more stamina on the dam's side and this performance suggests she will appreciate another furlong. (tchd 15-2)
Fifty(IRE), down in class after contesting a very valuable sales race at Ascot last time where she finished well ahead of Town And Gown, had every chance but did not get home and probably did not run to her official mark. (tchd 5-2)
Gower Belle, blinkered for the first time on this drop back down in trip, was close enough starting up the home straight but did not see her race out. On the face of it she performed well in finishing so close to a rival rated 11lb above her, but that is probably misleading and she looks exposed. (op 9-1)
Where's Killoran Official explanation: jockey said filly hung left

6229 ARENA LEISURE PLC MEDIAN AUCTION MAIDEN STKS 1m (P)
3:40 (3:41) (Class 5) 3-5-Y-O £3,071 (£906; £453) Stalls High

Form RPR

02 **1** **Oat Cuisine**[19] 5728 3-8-12 0 .... HayleyTurner 6 62
(M L W Bell) *hld up in tch: hdwy to trck ldrs over 2f out: rdn to ld jst ins fnl f: jst hld on* **7/2**[2]

306 **2** hd **Rolexa**[59] 4575 3-8-12 70 .... MartinDwyer 10 62
(C F Wall) *hld up towards rr: reminders over 4f out: drvn and hdwy over 2f out: swtchd rt 1f out: str run last 100yds: jst hld* **10/3**[1]

0050 **3** 1¼ **Quaglino Way (GR)**[7] 6063 3-9-3 69 .... PaulDoe 5 64
(P R Chamings) *chsd ldr tl led over 3f out: rdn over 2f out: hdd jst ins fnl f: one pce* **9/2**[3]

4 **4** ½ **Fair Sailing (IRE)**[31] 5390 3-8-12 0 .... EddieAhern 1 58
(J W Hills) *awkward leaving stalls: sn chsng ldrs: chsd ldr 3f out: rdn and ev ch 2f out: one pce fnl f* **7/1**

0240 **5** 3 **Batchworth Blaise**[38] 5189 4-9-6 49 .... StephenCarson 4 56
(E A Wheeler) *stdd s: bhd: rdn 4f out: hdwy on outer 3f out: chsd ldng pair briefly 2f out: wknd over 1f out* **12/1**

046 **6** 10 **Witchingham**[159] 1587 3-9-3 65 .... RichardSmith 8 33
(R Hannon) *bhd: rdn 5f out: wl bhd last 3f* **25/1**

0- **7** 2 **She Knows Too Much**[338] 6433 3-8-12 0 .... LPKeniry 7 23
(A M Hales) *in tch in midfield: rdn 3f out: wl bhd last 2f* **50/1**

3 **8** 7 **Foxy Diplomat**[97] 3394 3-9-3 0 .... PaulFitzsimons 3 12
(Miss J R Tooth) *t.k.h: led tl over 3f out: sn rdn and wknd: t.o* **16/1**

9 nk **Vistaria (USA)** 3-8-12 0 .... RichardHughes 2 7
(J H M Gosden) *t.k.h: chsd ldrs tl rdn over 2f out: sn btn: eased fnl f: t.o* **7/2**[2]

1m 40.33s (0.90) **Going Correction** +0.025s/f (Slow)
WFA 3 from 4yo 3lb **9** Ran SP% **117.6**
Speed ratings (Par 103): **96,95,94,94,91 81,79,72,71**
CSF £15.96 TOTE £4.00: £2.00, £1.70, £1.30; EX 18.20.
Owner Mrs G Rowland-Clark **Bred** Glebe Stud & J F Dean **Trained** Newmarket, Suffolk

FOCUS
A modest event, as maidens for older horses at this stage of the season tend to be, and the form, although sound enough, is limited by the proximity of the fifth.
Vistaria(USA) Official explanation: jockey said filly lost its action

6230 LINGFIELD PARK FOR WEDDINGS H'CAP 1m 4f (P)
4:10 (4:10) (Class 3) (0-90,90) 3-Y-O+
£9,348 (£2,799; £1,399; £700; £349; £175) Stalls Low

Form RPR

0500 **1** **Eva Soneva So Fast (IRE)**[14] 5870 5-9-4 **85** .... EddieAhern 3 91
(J L Dunlop) *in tch: hdwy to join ldrs and rdn 2f out: led ins fnl f: hld on* **9/2**[3]

3045 **2** nk **Torrens (IRE)**[22] 5664 5-8-10 **77** .... PaulHanagan 7 82
(R A Fahey) *hld up in tch: hdwy to trck ldrs over 2f out: plld out and rdn over 1f out: r.o strly ins fnl f: wnt 2nd last strides* **12/1**

2311 **3** nk **Double Doors**[33] 5334 3-8-9 **83** ....(v[1]) RichardHughes 1 88
(J H M Gosden) *trckd ldrs: hdwy on inner to ld narrowly over 2f out: sn hrd rdn: hdd and edgd rt ins fnl f: no ex nr fin* **7/2**[2]

4632 **4** ½ **Chocolate Caramel (USA)**[19] 5725 5-9-4 **85** .... TedDurcan 8 89
(Mrs A J Perrett) *trckd ldr: upsides and gng wl 2f out: rdn over 1f out: fnd little: n.m.r briefly ins fnl f* **11/4**[1]

0101 **5** 8 **Nobelix (IRE)**[23] 5640 5-9-1 **87** .... JamesMillman(5) 5 78
(J R Gask) *hld up towards rr: hdwy over 3f out: rdn and wknd 2f out* **14/1**

025 **6** 5 **Cape Secret (IRE)**[37] 5215 4-9-6 **87** .... GeorgeBaker 4 70
(R M Beckett) *led: rdn over 3f out: hdd over 2f out: sn wknd* **11/2**

040- **7** 3½ **Honduras (SWI)**[311] 6744 6-8-11 **85** .... JemmaMarshall(7) 6 63
(G L Moore) *rrd stalls: a bhd in last pair: no ch last 3f* **25/1**

002- **8** 16 **Cold Turkey**[331] 6515 7-9-9 **90** .... SimonWhitworth 2 42
(G L Moore) *stdd s: hld up wl bhd in last pair: nudged along 3f out: sn lost tch* **8/1**

2m 33.19s (-1.20) **Going Correction** +0.025s/f (Slow)
WFA 3 from 4yo+ 7lb **8** Ran SP% **111.8**
Speed ratings (Par 107): **105,104,104,104,98 95,93,82**
CSF £53.23 CT £205.65 TOTE £5.40: £1.40, £2.90, £1.60; EX 56.80.
Owner Eurostrait Ltd **Bred** John O'Connor **Trained** Arundel, W Sussex

FOCUS
A decent handicap run at a good pace and, although the front four finished in a heap, they pulled a long way clear of the rest. The form looks very solid for the grade and has been rated positively.

NOTEBOOK
Eva Soneva So Fast(IRE), 7lb lower than when last in a handicap on sand and back on his last winning mark, was extremely consistent at this track last winter. He travelled well throughout and eventually came out best in a four-horse war over the last furlong or so. He will no doubt be kept busy here during the winter. (op 11-2)
Torrens(IRE), 5lb higher than when last on sand having won twice on turf in the meantime, produced a strong late effort down the wide outside and was eating into the winner's advantage at the line. Although not obviously well handicapped, this track does at least suit his style of running. (op 14-1)
Double Doors, up another 5lb in his hat-trick bid, had the visor on for the first time. Travelling well behind the leaders racing towards the final bend, his rider decided to dive for a gap that presented itself on the inside in order to get to the front, but that meant he found himself on the slower ground. He proved very willing in the straight, but was just outstayed. (op 3-1 tchd 11-4)
Chocolate Caramel(USA), proven under these conditions, travelled well up with the pace and had every chance turning in, but once under pressure he could only stay on at the one pace. (op 3-1 tchd 10-3)
Nobelix(IRE), 11lb higher than when last on sand which was when finishing third behind Chocolate Caramel over course and distance in June of last year, was making his debut for the yard having been claimed after winning at Newmarket last time. He never got into the race this time though, and seems to have two distinctly opposite ways of running at present. (op 11-1)
Cape Secret(IRE) tried to make every yard, but those tactics are very hard over the longer distances here and the writing was on the wall racing down the false straight. Official explanation: trainer said gelding did not handle the track (op 6-1)
Honduras(SWI) never got into the race after playing up badly in the stalls.
Cold Turkey, returning from 11 months off, was completely left behind from the home bend and even allowing for the layoff this was way below his best. (op 13-2)

6231 LINGFIELD PARK GOLF COURSE H'CAP 6f (P)
4:40 (4:40) (Class 4) (0-85,85) 3-Y-O+ £5,181 (£1,541; £770; £384) Stalls Low

Form RPR

0045 **1** **Ajigolo**[29] 5449 4-9-4 **84** .... TPO'Shea 2 93+
(M R Channon) *hld up in tch: rdn 2f out: r.o wl to ld last 50yds* **11/2**[3]

3000 **2** ½ **George The Second**[46] 4965 4-8-7 **73** .... PaulHanagan 7 80
(Mrs H Sweeting) *chsd ldr: rdn to ld 2f out: battled on wl tl hdd and no ex last 50yds* **14/1**

3250 **3** *hd* **Forest Dane**[73] 4122 7-8-9 **82** .... SophieDoyle(7) 1 88+
(Mrs N Smith) *hld up in rr: stl plenty to do 2f out: hdwy over 1f out: rdn ins fnl f: r.o wl* **14/1**

436 **4** *hd* **Buxton**[39] 5168 3-8-11 **78** .... RobertHavlin 9 84
(R Ingram) *hld up in midfield: hdwy to chse ldrs and rdn 2f out: ev ch ins fnl f: unable qckn nr fin* **8/1**

6336 **5** ¾ **Tony The Tap**[3] 6141 6-8-9 **75** .... HayleyTurner 3 78
(W R Muir) *stdd s: hld up bhd: rdn wl over 2f out: styd on over 1f out: nt rch ldrs* **7/1**

0020 **6** *1* **Teen Ager (FR)**[46] 4965 3-8-10 **77** .... LPKeniry 8 77
(J S Moore) *t.k.h: chsd ldrs: rdn and hdwy wl over 2f out: ev ch over 1f out: wknd last 100yds* **9/1**

3211 **7** *3* **Wolf River (USA)**[27] 5495 3-8-6 **78** .... KirstyMilczarek(5) 6 69
(D M Simcock) *restless in stalls: s.i.s: a towards rr on outer: rdn 3f out: nvr nr ldrs* **9/2[2]**

2303 **8** *shd* **Texas Gold**[3] 6141 9-9-0 **80** .... RichardMullen 11 70
(W R Muir) *dropped in bhd after s: hld up in rr on rail: swtchd rt and rdn wl over 1f out: no hdwy* **7/2[1]**

-006 **9** *shd* **Estimator**[21] 5684 3-8-10 **77** .... TedDurcan 4 67
(Pat Eddery) *chsd ldrs: rdn 3f out: wknd 2f out* **12/1**

6030 **10** *5* **Merlin's Dancer**[13] 5891 7-8-12 **85** .... JackMitchell(7) 5 59
(S Dow) *taken down early: led tl hdd 2f out: sn rdn: wknd qckly jst over 1f out* **25/1**

1m 11.75s (-1.06) **Going Correction** +0.025s/f (Slow)
WFA 3 from 4yo+ 1lb **10** Ran SP% **114.3**
Speed ratings (Par 105): **108,107,107,106,105 104,100,100,100,93**
CSF £77.59 CT £1040.19 TOTE £5.20: £2.40, £4.30, £5.40; EX 105.30.
Owner Timberhill Racing Partnership **Bred** Timber Hill Racing Partnership **Trained** West Ilsley, Berks

FOCUS
A decent sprint handicap and Merlin's Dancer made sure there was no hanging about. Even though only a little over a length separated the front five at the line, the form looks solid rated around the placed horses and backed up by the fourth and sixth.
Wolf River(USA) Official explanation: jockey said colt banged its head in the stalls

6232 BOOK ONLINE FOR DISCOUNTED PRICES H'CAP 7f (P)
5:10 (5:10) (Class 5) (0-75,75) 3-Y-0+ **£3,562** (£1,059; £529; £264) **Stalls** Low

Form RPR

6003 **1** **Teasing**[9] 6024 3-8-11 **68** .... RobertHavlin 3 78+
(J Pearce) *stdd s: hld up: stdy hdwy on bit over 2f out: shkn up and hdwy 1f out: r.o to ld last stride* **20/1**

4013 **2** *shd* **Minaash (USA)**[23] 5648 3-8-12 **74** .... KirstyMilczarek(5) 8 81
(D M Simcock) *t.k.h: chsd ldr tl led narrowly 2f out: kpt on u.p tl hdd last stride* **10/1**

03 **3** *nk* **Angaric (IRE)**[73] 4140 4-9-3 **72** .... TomEaves 11 78
(B Smart) *trckd ldrs: rdn and ev ch 2f out: unable qckn wl ins fnl f* **9/2[1]**

6341 **4** ½ **Nouveau (GER)**[14] 5874 3-9-3 **74** .... RichardHughes 9 79
(R Hannon) *hld up in tch: hdwy to chse ldrs and rdn 2f out: kpt on same pce ins fnl f* **5/1[2]**

2350 **5** ½ **Corlough Mountain**[86] 3752 3-8-11 **68** .... PaulHanagan 2 71
(N A Callaghan) *chsd ldrs on rail: switched rt and rdn wl over 1f out: kpt on u.p* **16/1**

0100 **6** ½ **Pagan Belief**[32] 5360 3-8-11 **68** .... OscarUrbina 10 70
(J A R Toller) *taken down early: hld up bhd: hdwy 3f out: rdn and unable qckn 2f out: kpt on u.p fnl f* **12/1**

5621 **7** ½ **Excessive**[23] 5643 3-8-9 **66** .... TedDurcan 1 67
(W Jarvis) *hld up in midfield on rail: effrt and rdn 2f out: kpt on same pce* **10/1**

0344 **8** ½ **Carmenero (GER)**[26] 5532 4-9-6 **75** .... RichardMullen 6 74
(W R Muir) *hld up wl bhd: rdn and hdwy wl over 1f out: styd on but nvr able to chal* **7/1[3]**

5323 **9** ½ **Paradise Dancer (IRE)**[7] 6057 3-8-13 **70** .... MartinDwyer 12 68
(Pat Eddery) *in tch: rdn and effrt on outer bnd 2f out: no hdwy over 1f out* **8/1**

4220 **10** *shd* **Hucking Hill (IRE)**[4] 6122 3-8-13 **73** ....(b) StephaneBreux(3) 4 71
(J R Best) *t.k.h: hld up wl in tch: rdn to chse ldrs over 1f out: wknd last 100yds* **16/1**

0003 **11** 1¾ **Meditation**[10] 5985 5-8-6 **68** .... SophieDoyle(7) 5 61
(I A Wood) *led tl 2f out: wknd over 1f out* **16/1**

6303 **12** *3* **Indian's Feather (IRE)**[12] 5907 6-9-3 **72** .... IanMongan 7 57
(N Tinkler) *hld up bhd: pushed along wl over 4f out: drvn and no hdwy over 2f out* **12/1**

6000 **13** *2* **His Master's Voice (IRE)**[14] 5874 4-9-5 **74** .... EddieAhern 13 53
(D W P Arbuthnot) *in tch: rdn 2f out: wknd qckly over 1f out* **12/1**

5000 **14** *9* **Safe Investment (USA)**[11] 5950 3-9-4 **75** .... VinceSlattery 14 30
(B N Pollock) *chsd ldrs on outer: rdn and wknd 3f out: wl bhd last 2f* **33/1**

1m 25.55s (-0.34) **Going Correction** +0.025s/f (Slow)
WFA 3 from 4yo+ 2lb **14** Ran SP% **123.3**
Speed ratings (Par 103): **102,101,101,100,100 99,99,98,98,98 96,92,90,80**
CSF £212.74 CT £1108.29 TOTE £25.80: £8.20, £4.40, £1.80; EX 235.80 Place 6 £212.02, Place 5 £161.30.
Owner D Leech **Bred** Chippenham Lodge Stud Ltd **Trained** Newmarket, Suffolk

FOCUS
A modest race, but extremely competitive and the front ten finished in a heap. The form looks reasonable with hte runner-up to recent form and the third and fifth to their All-Weather marks.
T/Plt: £658.00 to a £1 stake. Pool: £50,256.05. 55.75 winning tickets. T/Qpdt: £18.40 to a £1 stake. Pool: £4,176.30. 167.80 winning tickets. SP

6058 WINDSOR (R-H)
Monday, October 15

OFFICIAL GOING: Soft (good to soft in places; 7.6)
Wind: Moderate behind

6233 AT THE RACES NURSERY 1m 67y
2:30 (2:30) (Class 5) (0-75,75) 2-Y-0 **£2,817** (£838; £418; £209) **Stalls** High

Form RPR

2043 **1** **Suzi Spends (IRE)**[28] 5471 2-9-1 **69** .... GregFairley 6 72
(M Johnston) *rn off bnd 6f out and bhd: rdn and c stands' side fr 3f out: hdd sole opponent that side 2f out but jst hld by far side gp tl styd on gamely to ld fnl strides* **8/1[3]**

055 **2** *shd* **Bavarian Nordic (USA)**[61] 4487 2-9-6 **74** .... JimmyFortune 13 77
(E A L Dunlop) *chsd ldrs: rdn along 3f out: styd on to press ldr ins fnl f: carried rt and upsides fnl 50yds: led cl home: hdd last strides* **13/2[2]**

5522 **3** ½ **Shadow Cabinet (IRE)**[13] 5883 2-9-4 **72** .... JamieSpencer 2 74
(M L W Bell) *sn led: rdn over 2f out: edgd rt u.p and hdd cl home* **4/1[1]**

5003 **4** *2* **Landikhaya (IRE)**[13] 5883 2-9-4 **72** .... RyanMoore 12 70
(R Hannon) *chsd ldrs: rdn fr 3f out: styd on same pce ins fnl f* **9/1**

500 **5** *2* **Dusk**[24] 5599 2-9-1 **69** .... JimmyQuinn 1 63
(J L Dunlop) *chsd ldrs: rdn 3f out: wknd fnl f* **33/1**

0645 **6** *nk* **Spent**[25] 5571 2-9-5 **73** .... JimCrowley 3 66
(R M Beckett) *chsd ldrs: lost position 5f out: sn rcvrd: drvn and effrt over 3f out: nvr quite gng pce to chal and wknd fnl f* **8/1[3]**

5401 **7** *shd* **Tobogganist**[13] 5883 2-9-4 **72** .... DarryllHolland 10 65
(W Jarvis) *chsd ldrs: c stands' side and hdd by sole opponent that side over 2f out: styd on same pce fnl f* **17/2**

2030 **8** *shd* **Quick Sands (IRE)**[14] 5871 2-9-4 **72** .... PatDobbs 11 65
(R Hannon) *pressed ldrs 2f: styd front rnk: rdn 3f out: wknd fnl f* **33/1**

0114 **9** 1½ **Tuanku (IRE)**[27] 5509 2-9-1 **69** .... ChrisCatlin 7 58
(M R Channon) *in rr: hdwy 3f out: rdn to chse ldrs 2f out: no imp and sn one pce* **11/1**

064 **10** *nk* **Musashi (IRE)**[23] 5628 2-9-7 **75** .... JohnEgan 8 64
(J S Moore) *a towards rr* **16/1**

042 **11** *2* **Miss Jolyon (USA)**[21] 5682 2-9-4 **72** .... PhilipRobinson 4 57
(M A Jarvis) *rn off bnd and in rr after 2f: hdwy on rails 3f out: n.m.r ins fnl 2f: n.d after* **14/1**

500 **12** *hd* **Double On Red**[21] 5682 2-9-7 **75** .... TQuinn 14 59
(J M P Eustace) *nt handle bnd after 2f: rdn and hdwy 3f out: wknd fr 2f out* **8/1[3]**

2040 **13** *3* **Isent She Rich (IRE)**[12] 5914 2-9-4 **72** .... SteveDrowne 5 50
(M G Quinlan) *chsd ldrs over 5f* **50/1**

0310 **14** *hd* **Maximus Aurelius (IRE)**[10] 5974 2-9-7 **75** .... DaneO'Neill 9 52
(J Jay) *rn off bnd after 2f out: in rr: sme prog 3f out: sn btn* **25/1**

1m 46.67s (1.97) **Going Correction** +0.15s/f (Good) **14** Ran SP% **119.8**
Speed ratings (Par 95): **96,95,95,93,91 91,91,90,89,89 87,86,83,83**
CSF £57.08 CT £249.40 TOTE £11.80: £4.00, £2.00, £1.70; EX 115.90 Trifecta £128.70 Part won. Pool £181.33 - 0.45 winning units..
Owner Greenstead Hall Racing **Bred** G Callanan **Trained** Middleham Moor, N Yorks

FOCUS
Plenty of interesting runners and this looked a fair nursery with the form best rated around the winner and third. The pace was good early on but, as is usually the case at Windsor, it slowed significantly on the bend. The majority of these raced middle to far side in the straight, but the winner was one of just two horses who stayed stands' side.

NOTEBOOK
Suzi Spends(IRE) proved suited by the step up to 1m and narrowly gained her first success at the sixth attempt. She began to head towards the middle of the track with most of the others, but was switched sharply right towards the stands'-side rail and is probably a little better than the bare form suggests. She handled the cut in the ground well and could win again. (op 11-1)
Bavarian Nordic(USA) improved for the step up to 1m on his nursery debut and, having been taken middle to far side in the straight, he was just denied by a rival on the stands' side. He should be able to find a similar race. (op 7-1)
Shadow Cabinet(IRE), trying 1m for the first time, had plenty of use made of him, so his connections clearly had no worries on the stamina front, and he ran well to take a close third. Official explanation: jockey said colt hung right-handed (op 9-2 tchd 7-2)
Landikhaya(IRE) promised to be suited by this step up in trip and this was a respectable effort. He gives the impression he can do even better on a more galloping track. (op 8-1 tchd 10-1)
Dusk did not have as much improvement to come as some of these having already raced over this trip in maiden company, but he acquitted himself with credit. He should come into his own over middle-distances and staying trips next year and beyond. (op 25-1)
Double On Red Official explanation: jockey said filly failed to handle the bend and lost its action closing stages

6234 EUROPEAN BREEDERS' FUND MAIDEN STKS (DIV I) 6f
3:00 (3:00) (Class 5) 2-Y-0 **£2,817** (£838; £418; £209) **Stalls** High

Form RPR

2 **1** **Corrybrough**[17] 5772 2-9-3 0 .... DaneO'Neill 9 92+
(H Candy) *trckd ldrs: led ins fnl 2f: pushed clr fnl f: easily* **11/10[1]**

2 *3* **Barnaby Rudge (IRE)** 2-9-3 0 .... JohnEgan 7 81+
(Jane Chapple-Hyam) *bmpd s: sn in tch: hdwy: hung lft and green 2f out: styd on wl to chse wnr ins fnl f but nvr any ch* **33/1**

50 **3** 1¾ **Kinnego Bay (IRE)**[10] 5977 2-9-3 0 .... MichaelHills 2 76
(B W Hills) *pressed ldrs tl slt advantage over 3f out: sn rdn: hdd ins fnl 2f: wknd ins fnl f* **8/1[3]**

002 **4** *3* **Prime Aspiration (USA)**[14] 5856 2-9-3 85 .... RichardThomas 1 67
(Christian Wroe) *pressed ldrs: rdn and hung lft 2f out: wknd fnl f* **8/1[3]**

5 *2* **Lady Carollina** 2-8-12 0 .... JimCrowley 3 56+
(C F Wall) *s.i.s: in rr tl styd on ins fnl 2f: nvr in contention* **66/1**

03 **6** ½ **Vineyard**[14] 5872 2-9-3 0 .... LiamJones 5 59
(W J Haggas) *wnt lft s: sn in tch: rdn 3f out: no ch w ldrs fnl 2f* **9/2[2]**

4 **7** ¾ **Sir Ike (IRE)**[94] 3478 2-9-3 0 .... FergusSweeney 13 57
(W S Kittow) *chsd ldrs: rdn 3f out: wknd fr 2f out* **9/1**

6500 **8** *2* **Eye Catching**[26] 5529 2-8-12 57 .... DarryllHolland 10 46
(J R Jenkins) *led tl hdd over 3f out: wknd 2f out* **80/1**

9 *1* **Yamanmickmccann** 2-9-3 0 .... PatDobbs 6 48
(R Hannon) *wnt rt s: sn rdn and bhd* **33/1**

0 **10** *8* **Emperors Jade**[25] 5550 2-9-3 0 .... TQuinn 11 24
(A P Jarvis) *chsd ldrs over 3f* **14/1**

11 1¼ **Adeje (IRE)** 2-9-3 0 .... PhilipRobinson 4 20+
(C G Cox) *bmpd s: in rr: no ch whn stmbld 1f out* **22/1**

00 **12** *1* **Veras Joy**[12] 5919 2-8-12 0 .... ChrisCatlin 12 12
(T D McCarthy) *spd 3f* **150/1**

13 *48* **Dome Blonde** 2-8-12 0 .... NeilPollard 8 —
(W J Musson) *bmpd s: continually flashed tail and t.o after 1f* **100/1**

1m 13.05s (-0.62) **Going Correction** -0.075s/f (Good) **13** Ran SP% **119.3**
Speed ratings (Par 95): **101,97,94,90,88 87,86,83,82,71 70,68,4**
CSF £56.55 TOTE £1.80: £1.10, £6.10, £2.70; EX 38.10 Trifecta £140.30 Pool £332.00 - 1.68 winning units..
Owner Thurloe Thoroughbreds XXI **Bred** Mrs Sheila Oakes **Trained** Kingston Warren, Oxon

FOCUS
This did not look too bad a maiden and the winner was most impressive. The winning time was 0.98 seconds quicker than the second division and the third helps set the level, although the ground would have been cutting up as the meeting progressed and direct comparisons are misleading. They all headed towards the far side.

NOTEBOOK

Corrybrough ◆ ran very green when an encouraging second on his debut under similar conditions at Haydock and he improved on that form to get off the mark in impressive fashion. A big, very imposing individual, he will not run again this season and a winter over his back should see him develop into an awesome three-year-old. Henry Candy, who trained this one's sire, Kyllachy, to win the 2002 Nunthorpe in the same colours, said "I hope he'll make a Group sprinter". (op 5-4 tchd 11-8 in places)

Barnaby Rudge(IRE), a 20,000euros son of Danetime out of a winner over 1m4f, made a very encouraging debut. He briefly looked a threat to Corrybrough inside the final third, but had no answer when that one really extended. He is entitled to come on for this. (op 25-1)

Kinnego Bay(IRE) ◆ had shown ability in a couple of Newmarket maidens and this was another reasonable effort. He can be expected to do better over further in handicaps next year. (op 13-2)

Prime Aspiration(USA) showed up well for much of the way, but he was eventually put in his place and the Handicapper looks to have been very harsh in giving him a mark of 85.

Lady Carollina, a Bertolini, first foal of a mare who was placed over 1m2f, offered encouragement on her racecourse debut. She is with a very capable trainer and appeals as one to keep an eye on.

Vineyard ◆ was never really going the pace and he could not build on his recent course-and-distance third. This Derby entry is going to be suited by further and is one to keep on-side now he is qualified for a handicap mark. (op 13-2 tchd 7-1)

Emperors Jade Official explanation: jockey said colt was unsuited by the soft (good to soft places) ground

Dome Blonde Official explanation: jockey said filly was reluctant to race

6235 PETER WICKENS CEDAR BAR PROMOTIONS H'CAP 1m 3f 135y

3:30 (3:32) (Class 5) (0-70,70) 3-Y-0 £2,817 (£838; £418; £209) Stalls Centre

Form RPR

-242 **1** **Perfect Reward**[12] 5899 3-9-1 **67** JimCrowley 13 76+
(Mrs A J Perrett) *in tch: hdwy over 3f out: chal fr 2f out tl led over 1f out: rdn and hung rt and lft ins fnl f: styd on strly* **9/2**[2]

6056 **2** 2 **Dan Tucker**[40] 5131 3-9-2 **68** JamieSpencer 7 74+
(B J Meehan) *in rr tl: hdwy 3f out: rdn over 2f out: styd on to chse wnr fnl f but no imp* **8/1**

U132 **3** shd **Chant De Guerre (USA)**[14] 5865 3-8-12 **64** JimmyQuinn 11 70
(P Mitchell) *hmpd s: in rr tl hdwy over 2f out: styd on wl to chse ldrs ins fnl f but nvr gng pce of wnr* **10/1**

0065 **4** 2 **Iceman George**[24] 5604 3-8-12 **64** (v) LiamJones 1 67
(D Morris) *chsd ldrs: chal ins fnl 3f: led ins fnl 2f: hdd over 1f out: wknd ins fnl f* **25/1**

4200 **5** 1 ½ **Doubly Guest**[14] 5865 3-8-11 **63** (p) TQuinn 6 63
(G G Margarson) *in rr: rdn 3f out: hdwy fr 2f out but nt rch ldrs* **50/1**

0031 **6** nk **Sweet World**[25] 5553 3-8-10 **65** TravisBlock(3) 16 65
(A P Jarvis) *chsd ldrs: led over 3f out: hdd ins fnl 2f: sn btn* **11/1**

2216 **7** shd **Little Carmela**[12] 5899 3-8-10 **62** SaleemGolam 9 62
(S C Williams) *in rr: rdn over 3f out: kpt on fnl 2f but nvr in contention* **13/2**[3]

2662 **8** 4 **I Predict A Riot (IRE)**[23] 5637 3-9-2 **68** (p) RyanMoore 3 61
(J W Hills) *chsd ldrs: rdn 3f out: wknd ins fnl 2f* **7/1**

4 **9** 8 **Power Shared (IRE)**[21] 5683 3-9-4 **70** SteveDrowne 15 51
(P G Murphy) *in rr tl sme hdwy fnl 2f: nvr in contention* **28/1**

31-0 **10** shd **Hanbrin Bhoy (IRE)**[17] 5768 3-9-4 **70** MickyFenton 14 50
(R Dickin) *chsd ldrs: hung lft and wknd ins fnl 3f* **66/1**

3300 **11** 1 ¼ **Lemon Silk (IRE)**[33] 5342 3-8-10 **62** (p) GregFairley 10 40
(K J Burke) *led tl hdd over 3f out: sn btn* **33/1**

1400 **12** 8 **Down The Brick (IRE)**[33] 5333 3-9-2 **68** (b) FergusSweeney 2 34
(B R Millman) *chsd ldrs: rdn 3f out and sn wknd* **14/1**

314 **13** 2 ½ **The Flying Cowboy (IRE)**[17] 5777 3-9-0 **66** JohnEgan 4 28
(Jane Chapple-Hyam) *in rr: hdwy 4f out: pressed ldrs fr 2f out tl wknd over 1f out: eased whn no ch ins fnl f* **4/1**[1]

0034 **14** 2 **Stark Contrast (USA)**[14] 5865 3-8-12 **64** ChrisCatlin 5 22
(J Akehurst) *bmpd s: in rr whn hmpd ins fnl 3f* **16/1**

3400 **15** 4 **Feeling (IRE)**[16] 5807 3-9-4 **70** (b) AdrianMcCarthy 12 22
(P W Chapple-Hyam) *wnt lft s: t.k.h and chsd ldr to 4f out: sn wknd* **66/1**

2m 29.86s (-0.24) **Going Correction** +0.15s/f (Good) **15** Ran SP% **120.3**

Speed ratings (Par 101): **106,104,104,103,102 102,102,99,94,93 93,87,86,84,82**

CSF £37.92 CT £346.95 TOTE £4.80: £1.80, £3.00, £3.00; EX 37.00 TRIFECTA Not won..

Owner Nicholas Cooper **Bred** Normandie Stud Ltd **Trained** Pulborough, W Sussex

FOCUS

A modest middle-distance handicap run a fair pace considering the conditions. The winning time was decent for the grade and the form looks pretty sound rated around the placed horses. They raced up the middle of the track in the straight.

The Flying Cowboy(IRE) Official explanation: jockey said gelding never travelled

Feeling(IRE) Official explanation: jockey said colt hung left-handed

6236 BANK OF SCOTLAND H'CAP 1m 2f 7y

4:00 (4:01) (Class 4) (0-85,85) 3-Y-0 £4,728 (£1,406; £702; £351) Stalls Centre

Form RPR

3132 **1** **Duchess Royale (IRE)**[56] 4665 3-9-0 **81** RyanMoore 7 90
(Sir Michael Stoute) *hld up in rr: drvn and hdwy over 2f out: rdn and hung lft ins fnl f: led fnl 75yds: drvn out* **4/1**[2]

4656 **2** ¾ **Rudry Dragon (IRE)**[9] 6002 3-8-9 **76** JamieSpencer 9 83
(P A Blockley) *t.k.h: stdd in tch: hdwy over 2f out: drvn to ld ins fnl f: hdd and no ex fnl 75yds* **9/1**

621 **3** ¾ **Zero Cool (USA)**[14] 5873 3-9-0 **81** JimmyFortune 1 87
(J H M Gosden) *led tl hdd over 4f out: led again and hrd drvn over 2f out: hdd ins fnl f: styd on same pce u.p* **11/4**[1]

-416 **4** 1 ½ **Just Two Numbers**[88] 3689 3-8-11 **78** DarryllHolland 3 81
(W Jarvis) *in rr: styd on fnl 2f: gng on ins fnl f: nvr in contention* **20/1**

3142 **5** 1 **Shadow The Wind (IRE)**[29] 5454 3-8-9 **76** KerrinMcEvoy 6 77
(E F Vaughan) *hld up in rr but in tch: pushed along and hdwy over 2f out but nvr quite gng pce to rch ldrs* **9/2**[3]

1102 **6** 1 ¾ **Gib (IRE)**[11] 5941 3-8-7 **74** MichaelHills 8 71
(B W Hills) *chsd ldr tl led over 4f out: hdd over 2f out: wknd over 1f out* **5/1**

2043 **7** ¾ **Oakley Heffert (IRE)**[61] 4510 3-8-9 **76** PatDobbs 10 72
(R Hannon) *chsd ldrs: rdn 3f out: wknd fr 2f out* **12/1**

6100 **8** 4 **Murrin (IRE)**[41] 5114 3-8-10 **77** SteveDrowne 2 65
(T G Mills) *in tch: rdn and effrt over 3f out: n.d and wknd fr 2f out* **18/1**

2300 **9** nk **Leptis Magna**[26] 5545 3-8-7 **74** TQuinn 4 61
(D R C Elsworth) *in rr: rdn over 3f out: nvr in contention* **25/1**

0006 **10** 2 **Seal Point (USA)**[15] 5833 3-9-4 **85** PaulEddery 5 68
(Christian Wroe) *chsd ldrs: rdn and wknd 3f out* **40/1**

2m 9.21s (0.91) **Going Correction** +0.15s/f (Good) **10** Ran SP% **115.5**

Speed ratings (Par 103): **102,101,100,99,98 97,96,93,93,91**

CSF £38.33 CT £114.74 TOTE £5.30: £1.90, £2.90, £1.40; EX 53.20 Trifecta £224.20 Pool £691.66 - 2.19 winning units..

Owner Mrs Elizabeth Moran **Bred** Mrs E Moran **Trained** Newmarket, Suffolk

■ Stewards' Enquiry : Paul Eddery caution: used whip when out of contention

FOCUS

A fair handicap and pretty straightforward form rated around the runner-up backed up by the fourth. They raced towards the far side of the track in the straight.

6237 EUROPEAN BREEDERS' FUND MAIDEN STKS (DIV II) 6f

4:30 (4:32) (Class 5) 2-Y-O £2,817 (£838; £418; £209) Stalls High

Form RPR

565 **1** **Moral Duty (USA)**[30] 5428 2-9-3 75 PaulEddery 3 75
(Pat Eddery) *chsd ldrs: rdn 2f out: led ins fnl f: drvn out* **3/1**[1]

636 **2** 1 **Sakhacity**[45] 5003 2-8-12 68 JohnEgan 5 67
(J R Jenkins) *led: rdn and hung lft fnl f and sn hdd: styd on same pce* **10/3**[2]

0 **3** 2 **Educated Risk**[51] 4810 2-9-3 0 LiamJones 4 66
(W J Haggas) *s.i.s: in rr: shkn up and styd on fr over 1f out to take 3rd fnl f but nvr in contention w ldng duo* **13/2**[3]

0000 **4** ¾ **Peer Pressure**[16] 5818 2-9-3 58 JimmyQuinn 6 64
(P Mitchell) *t.k.h: in tch: chsd ldrs 1/2-way: styd on same pce fnl f* **18/1**

0 **5** 2 ½ **Caprio (IRE)**[14] 5872 2-9-3 0 RichardKingscote 7 56
(R Charlton) *uns rdr bef s and rn loose 1f: hld up in rr: hdwy to trck ldrs over 2f out: sn pushed along: wknd fnl f* **3/1**[1]

6 ¾ **Croeso Cusan** 2-8-12 0 SteveDrowne 1 49
(J L Spearing) *pressed ldrs: ev ch 2f out: wknd over 1f out* **11/1**

000 **7** 1 ½ **Berties Goodenough**[72] 4181 2-9-0 52 EmmettStack(3) 12 50
(Andrew Turnell) *chsd ldrs: rdn 1/2-way: wknd fr 2f out* **100/1**

00 **8** 2 **Sunshine Lady (IRE)**[32] 5363 2-8-12 0 MickyFenton 10 39
(D Haydn Jones) *early spd: sn rdn and dropped to rr: nvr a factor after* **40/1**

9 nk **Spate River** 2-9-3 0 JimCrowley 2 43
(C F Wall) *in rr: rdn and no imp on ldrs fr 1/2-way* **16/1**

0 **10** 1 ½ **Dickie Valentine**[14] 5868 2-9-3 0 ChrisCatlin 9 38
(M R Bosley) *sn outpcd* **66/1**

11 8 **Duneen Dream (USA)** 2-9-3 0 NeilPollard 11 14
(W J Musson) *chsd ldrs to 1/2-way* **16/1**

1m 14.03s (0.36) **Going Correction** -0.075s/f (Good) **11** Ran SP% **116.7**

Speed ratings (Par 95): **94,92,90,89,85 84,82,80,79,77 66**

CSF £12.88 TOTE £3.20: £1.20, £1.40, £2.90; EX 10.00 Trifecta £11.90 Pool £255.54 - 15.24 winning units..

Owner K Abdulla **Bred** Juddmonte Farms Inc **Trained** Nether Winchendon, Bucks

FOCUS

An ordinary maiden limited by the proximity of the fourth. The winning time was 0.98 seconds slower than the first division, but the ground would have deteriorated as the meeting progressed and comparisons are probably misleading. They ended up towards the far side at the line.

NOTEBOOK

Moral Duty(USA) probably did not have to improve a great deal on his previous efforts to get off the mark at the fourth attempt. He is likely to find things tougher from now on, but could improve for a step up in trip. (tchd 10-3)

Sakhacity ran right up to her best in second, but she came into this rated just 68 and her proximity suggests the form is limited. She also has the option of going for nurseries. (op 11-4)

Educated Risk did not show much on his debut at Newmarket, but this was better and he gave the impression he can step forward again. He could win a maiden, but one suspects he will come into his own once handicapped. (op 7-1 tchd 15-2)

Peer Pressure ran well dropped in trip and returned to turf although, like the second, his proximity does not do much for the overall form of the race. He is likely to find things easier in nursery company. (op 25-1)

Caprio(IRE), just as he did on his debut over course and distance, got rid of his rider and ran loose, although he was caught quickly enough. He may be one for handicaps in time, but will need to curb his errant ways. (op 7-2 tchd 4-1 in a place)

Sunshine Lady(IRE) Official explanation: jockey said filly hung left-handed

6238 WINDSOR FIREWORKS EXTRAVAGANZA SATURDAY 3RD NOVEMBER MAIDEN STKS 1m 67y

5:00 (5:03) (Class 5) 3-Y-0+ £2,817 (£838; £418; £209) Stalls High

Form RPR

1 **Shadowy Figure** 3-9-3 0 KerrinMcEvoy 5 81+
(Saeed Bin Suroor) *hld up towards rr: hdwy 2f out: drvn and str run fnl f to ld fnl 50yds: won gng away* **7/4**[1]

2423 **2** ½ **Red Blossom**[34] 5315 3-8-12 64 (b[1]) RyanMoore 6 68
(Sir Mark Prescott) *chsd ldrs: led over 1f out: sn rdn and hd high: hdd and no ex fnl 50yds* **13/2**

05 **3** 3 **Stalking Tiger (IRE)**[14] 5873 3-9-3 0 SteveDrowne 8 66
(R Charlton) *led: rdn and hdd over 1f out: sn one pce* **5/1**[3]

4 2 ½ **Rum Jungle** 3-9-3 0 DaneO'Neill 9 60+
(H Candy) *in rr: hdwy 3f out: chsd ldrs over 1f out: styd on but nvr gng pce to be competitive* **12/1**

00 **5** 3 **Emily's Rainbow (IRE)**[9] 6005 3-8-12 0 LiamJones 4 48
(W J Haggas) *chsd ldrs: rdn 2f out: wknd fnl f* **66/1**

-030 **6** 1 **Ernmoor**[38] 5188 5-9-3 47 JerryO'Dwyer(3) 13 51
(J R Jenkins) *chsd ldr to 2f out: wknd over 1f out* **100/1**

7 1 **Accolation** 3-9-3 0 PatDobbs 11 49
(Pat Eddery) *t.k.h: sn chsng ldrs: wknd fr 2f out* **66/1**

8 1 **Clear Reef** 3-9-3 0 JimCrowley 3 46
(Jane Chapple-Hyam) *slowly away: rn off bnd 6f out: drvn and green over 3f out: styd on fnl f but nvr in contention* **40/1**

50 **9** 1 **Valassini**[32] 5345 7-8-8 0 KylieManser(7) 10 39
(B G Powell) *s.i.s: in rr whn hmpd 3f out: hung lft and sme prog over 2f out: nvr in contention* **100/1**

0/0- **10** 1 ½ **Club Captain (USA)**[538] 1212 4-9-6 0 FergusSweeney 12 41
(T D McCarthy) *chsd ldrs over 5f* **100/1**

3 **11** 2 **Imperial Quest**[14] 5873 3-8-12 0 JamieSpencer 1 31
(J R Fanshawe) *in tch: rdn to chse ldrs ins fnl 3f: hung lft 2f out and sn wknd* **10/3**[2]

12 ½ **Celestial Sphere (USA)** 3-9-3 0 JimmyFortune 7 35
(J H M Gosden) *a towards rr* **8/1**

55 **13** 2 **Legend Erry (IRE)**[97] 3399 3-9-3 0 JohnEgan 2 30
(Jane Chapple-Hyam) *chsd ldrs tl wknd fr 3f out* **20/1**

1m 45.67s (0.97) **Going Correction** +0.15s/f (Good)

WFA 3 from 4yo+ 3lb **13** Ran SP% **121.4**

Speed ratings (Par 103): **101,100,97,95,92 91,90,89,88,86 84,84,82**

CSF £13.78 TOTE £2.80: £1.50, £1.30, £2.10; EX 14.70 Trifecta £38.60 Pool £360.39 - 6.62 winning units..

Owner Godolphin **Bred** Dermot Cantillon And Fiona Craig **Trained** Newmarket, Suffolk

FOCUS

A modest and uncompetitive maiden limited by the proximity of the sixth. They raced towards the stands' side in the straight.

Imperial Quest Official explanation: jockey said filly failed to handle the bend and hung left-handed

6239 ARENA LEISURE H'CAP 6f
5:30 (5:33) (Class 5) (0-70,70) 3-Y-0+ **£2,817** (£838; £418; £209) **Stalls** High

Form RPR
31-0 **1** **Efisio Princess**[152] [1766] 4-8-5 **55** oh1 RichardThomas 13 66
(J E Long) *mde all: rdn 2f out: styd on strly fnl f* **20/1**
6005 **2** 1 1/2 **Roman Quest**[19] [5722] 4-9-0 **64** SteveDrowne 1 70
(H Morrison) *s.i.s: sn rcvrd: drvn to chse ldrs over 2f out: chsd wnr fnl f but a hld* **13/2**[1]
5000 **3** 1 **Capricho (IRE)**[50] [4853] 10-8-0 **55** oh1 (b) NataliaGemelova[(5)] 10 58
(J Akehurst) *chsd ldrs: rdn 3f out: styd on same pce ins fnl f* **20/1**
0003 **4** 3/4 **Kind Of Fizzy**[19] [5741] 3-8-9 **60** DarryllHolland 7 61
(Rae Guest) *in rr: hdwy 2f out: rdn and styd on fnl f: kpt on cl home* **12/1**
0060 **5** shd **Linda Green**[6] [6089] 6-9-5 **69** ChrisCatlin 12 69
(M R Channon) *in rr: rdn over 2f out: hdwy over 1f out: styd on ins fnl f: nt rch ldrs* **10/1**
3366 **6** 1 1/4 **Endless Summer**[19] [5726] 10-8-6 **56** SaleemGolam 2 53
(A W Carroll) *in rr: rdn over 2f out: hdwy over 1f out: styd on ins fnl f but nvr in contention* **9/1**
6006 **7** nk **Tipsy Prince**[5] [6103] 3-9-3 **68** FergusSweeney 3 64
(David Pinder) *chsd ldrs: rdn to chal 2f out: wknd ins fnl f* **16/1**
6500 **8** 3/4 **Guildenstern (IRE)**[7] [6064] 5-8-12 **62** JamieSpencer 8 56
(P Howling) *in rr: sme prog fnl f: kpt on cl home* **7/1**[2]
0201 **9** shd **Proud Killer**[6] [6083] 4-9-0 **67** 6ex JerryO'Dwyer[(3)] 4 60
(J R Jenkins) *chsd ldrs: rdn over 2f out: wknd fnl f* **13/2**[1]
1605 **10** 1 3/4 **Dualagi**[5] [6103] 3-9-3 **68** JohnEgan 6 56
(J S Moore) *chsd ldrs: rdn over 2f out: wknd fnl f* **16/1**
0533 **11** 1 1/4 **Game Lady**[81] [3870] 3-9-5 **70** RyanMoore 15 54
(I A Wood) *broke wl: stdd in rr: rdn and soem hdwy 2f out: nvr in contention* **16/1**
0301 **12** 3/4 **Double Carpet (IRE)**[11] [5934] 4-8-10 **60** JimmyQuinn 9 42
(G Woodward) *chsd ldrs tl wknd over 1f out* **9/1**
0052 **13** shd **Caustic Wit (IRE)**[11] [5942] 9-8-8 **63** (p) TolleyDean[(5)] 11 45
(M S Saunders) *chsd ldrs 4f* **8/1**[3]
120 **14** 7 **Inka Dancer (IRE)**[19] [5741] 5-9-0 **64** GregFairley 5 25
(B Palling) *sn outpcd* **22/1**
030 **15** 1 3/4 **The Fisio**[10] [5981] 7-8-13 **63** (v) TQuinn 16 18
(S Gollings) *sn outpcd* **25/1**
0-50 **16** nk **Is It Time (IRE)**[14] [5873] 3-8-8 **59** PaulEddery 14 14
(Mrs P N Dutfield) *chsd ldrs over 3f* **100/1**

1m 12.95s (-0.72) **Going Correction** -0.075s/f (Good)
WFA 3 from 4yo+ 1lb **16** Ran SP% **123.4**
Speed ratings (Par 103): **101,99,97,96,96 94,94,93,93,91 89,88,88,78,76 76**
CSF £139.29 CT £2783.22 TOTE £23.40: £5.30, £2.00, £5.10, £2.30; EX 247.30 TRIFECTA Not won. Place 6 £18.94, Place 5 £10.05..
Owner Miss M B Fernandes **Bred** Mrs A Yearley **Trained** Caterham, Surrey

FOCUS
A moderate sprint handicap with the placed horses regressive which tends to limit the form. They raced towards the stands' side.
Guildenstern(IRE) Official explanation: jockey said gelding hung left-handed
Double Carpet(IRE) Official explanation: jockey said gelding stopped quickly
T/Jkpt: £11,490.20 to a £1 stake. Pool: £16,183.50. 0.50 winning tickets. T/Plt: £19.80 to a £1 stake. Pool: £76,894.45. 2,821.00 winning tickets. T/Qpdt: £7.00 to a £1 stake. Pool: £4,269.80. 449.40 winning tickets. ST

6146 WOLVERHAMPTON (A.W) (L-H)
Monday, October 15

OFFICIAL GOING: Standard
Wind: Moderate behind Weather: Fine

6240 LADBROKES IN WOLVERHAMPTON MEDIAN AUCTION MAIDEN STKS 5f 216y(P)
2:20 (2:22) (Class 6) 3-Y-0 **£2,047** (£604; £302) **Stalls** Low

Form RPR
0005 **1** **Damhsoir (IRE)**[25] [5566] 3-8-7 44 HaddenFrost[(5)] 12 52
(H S Howe) *a.p: rdn to ld ins fnl f: drvn out* **40/1**
4040 **2** 1/2 **Lawdy Miss Clawdy**[20] [5716] 3-8-12 44 JamesDoyle 5 50
(D W P Arbuthnot) *hld up in mid-div: rdn and hdwy 1f out: r.o ins fnl f* **66/1**
0 **3** shd **Crimson Fern (IRE)**[7] [6062] 3-8-12 0 TGMcLaughlin 9 50+
(M S Saunders) *hld up in rr: hdwy on ins over 2f out: nt clr run over 1f out: swtchd rt ins fnl f: r.o* **200/1**
0230 **4** 3/4 **The Cube**[15] [5834] 3-9-3 50 DavidAllan 8 53
(J Balding) *chsd ldr: rdn and ev ch wl over 1f out: nt qckn ins fnl f* **20/1**
P332 **5** 1 1/2 **Towy Girl (IRE)**[13] [5893] 3-8-9 66 LukeMorris[(3)] 1 43
(A W Carroll) *s.i.s: sn chsng ldrs: led wl over 1f out: rdn and hdd ins fnl f: no ex* **5/2**[2]
60 **6** 2 **North Stars (IRE)**[28] [5488] 3-8-12 0 (p) JamesO'Reilly[(5)] 4 41
(J O'Reilly) *s.i.s: sn chsng ldrs: rdn and wknd wl over 1f out* **150/1**
2 **7** nk **Distant Drama (USA)**[51] [4808] 3-8-12 0 TPQueally 6 36
(J Noseda) *sn outpcd: rdn and swtchd rt wl over 1f out: no rspnse* **8/15**[1]
6050 **8** 2 **Millsini**[10] [5970] 3-8-12 49 J-PGuillambert 10 29
(Rae Guest) *hld up in mid-div: rdn over 2f out: sn wknd* **25/1**
-060 **9** 1 **Saint Remus (IRE)**[32] [5368] 3-9-3 42 (b[1]) AdamKirby 3 31
(Peter Grayson) *led: rdn over 2f out: hdd wl over 1f out: wknd ent fnl f* **150/1**
10 1 **Night Rider** 3-8-10 0 AmyBaker[(7)] 11 28
(Miss J Feilden) *outpcd: swtchd lft 4f out: sn struggling* **100/1**
300 **11** 3 **Vadinka**[99] [3342] 3-9-3 54 (t) KimTinkler 7 18
(N Tinkler) *prom tl wknd over 3f out* **16/1**[3]
0000 **12** 3 1/2 **Pathway To Glory**[18] [5752] 3-9-3 43 (v) SamHitchcott 13 7
(M Quinn) *towards rr: rdn and short-lived effrt on outside 3f out* **200/1**

1m 16.09s (0.28) **Going Correction** 0.0s/f (Stan) **12** Ran SP% **115.5**
Speed ratings (Par 99): **98,97,97,96,94 91,91,88,87,85 81,77**
CSF £1411.17 TOTE £48.90: £8.00, £11.40, £33.40; EX 1623.20.
Owner Roly Roper **Bred** Irish National Stud **Trained** Oakford, Devon

FOCUS
A very weak maiden and the form looks dubious with the form horses well below par.

Distant Drama(USA) Official explanation: jockey said filly missed the break

6241 LADBROKES HOME OF FOOTBALL BETTING H'CAP 1m 5f 194y(P)
2:50 (2:50) (Class 5) (0-70,75) 3-Y-0+ **£2,968** (£876; £438) **Stalls** Low

Form RPR
316 **1** **Noora (IRE)**[26] [5533] 6-9-8 **64** (v) AdamKirby 2 75
(C G Cox) *hld up: rdn and hdwy wl over 1f out: led ins fnl f: styd on wl* **16/1**
1361 **2** 4 **Ballet Boy (IRE)**[6] [6077] 3-9-10 **75** 6ex JamieMackay 4 80
(Sir Mark Prescott) *led early: hld up in tch: led over 3f out: rdn wl over 1f out: hdd ins fnl f: one pce* **7/4**[1]
/0-4 **3** shd **Golano**[19] [5732] 7-10-0 **70** J-PGuillambert 3 75
(P R Webber) *hld up towards rr: rdn and hdwy on outside over 1f out: edgd lft ins fnl f: styd on* **17/2**
4330 **4** 2 1/2 **Abounding**[33] [5333] 3-9-2 **67** JamesDoyle 1 69
(R M Beckett) *a.p: rdn over 3f out: one pce fnl 2f* **15/2**[3]
2151 **5** 1 1/2 **Heights Of Golan**[7] [6069] 3-8-12 **63** 6ex (v) PaulMulrennan 6 62
(I A Wood) *hld up: stdy hdwy over 4f out: rdn and wnt 2nd over 2f out: wknd jst over 1f out* **5/2**[2]
230 **6** 1 **Ross Moor**[30] [5415] 5-9-9 **68** PJMcDonald[(3)] 5 66
(Mike Murphy) *hld up in rr: hdwy over 3f out: rdn over 2f out: wknd wl over 1f out* **16/1**
4406 **7** 5 **Red Sun**[10] [5561] 10-8-9 **51** oh2 (t) DaleGibson 8 42
(R C Guest) *a in rr* **33/1**
0313 **8** 7 **Critical Stage (IRE)**[30] [5426] 8-9-4 **65** HaddenFrost[(5)] 9 46
(J D Frost) *sn chsng ldr: led over 4f out tl over 3f out: wknd over 2f out* **8/1**
0006 **9** 5 **Zaville**[7] [6069] 5-8-7 **54** oh6 ow3 (p) JamesO'Reilly[(5)] 7 28
(J O'Reilly) *sn led: hdd over 4f out: rdn and wknd over 3f out* **25/1**

3m 6.02s (-1.35) **Going Correction** 0.0s/f (Stan)
WFA 3 from 5yo+ 9lb **9** Ran SP% **116.9**
Speed ratings (Par 103): **103,100,100,99,98 97,94,90,88**
CSF £44.99 CT £269.11 TOTE £16.40: £4.80, £1.10, £2.30; EX 73.80.
Owner P G Jacobs & Partners **Bred** Shadwell Estate Company Limited **Trained** Lambourn, Berks

FOCUS
A modest handicap rated through the third to his latest mark.
Red Sun Official explanation: jockey said gelding hung right-handed throughout

6242 WOLVERHAMPTON-RACECOURSE.CO.UK (S) STKS 7f 32y(P)
3:20 (3:21) (Class 6) 2-Y-0 **£2,047** (£604; £302) **Stalls** High

Form RPR
6014 **1** **Ambrose Princess (IRE)**[30] [5423] 2-8-12 58 J-PGuillambert 9 60
(J S Moore) *s.i.s: hld up towards rr: rdn over 2f out: c wd st: hdwy over 1f out: sn edgd lft: r.o to ld cl home* **7/2**[1]
45 **2** nk **Wiseman's Diamond (USA)**[30] [5429] 2-8-6 0 (p) PaulMulrennan 11 53
(K A Ryan) *a.p: rdn and wnt 2nd jst over 2f out: led jst over 1f out: hdd cl home* **9/2**[2]
0000 **3** shd **Melwood Dreams**[7] [6066] 2-8-6 58 RussellKennemore[(5)] 12 58
(Paul Green) *s.i.s: in rr: rdn over 2f out: c wd and hdwy wl over 1f out: ev ch wl ins fnl f: r.o* **66/1**
0030 **4** 3 1/2 **Polish Priory (IRE)**[21] [5692] 2-8-8 58 ow2 TGMcLaughlin 2 46
(P D Evans) *led early: chsd ldrs: rdn over 2f out: edgd lft jst over 1f out: one pce* **8/1**
4234 **5** 1/2 **Liani (IRE)**[9] [6023] 2-8-3 56 LukeMorris[(3)] 4 45+
(P D Evans) *hld up towards rr: rdn over 2f out: hdwy wl over 1f out: n.m.r on ins ins fnl f: nt qckn* **6/1**[3]
0060 **6** 3/4 **Rubytwosox (IRE)**[14] [5869] 2-8-3 57 AndrewMullen[(3)] 7 41
(W R Muir) *led over 5f out: rdn 3f out: hdd jst over 1f out: wknd ins fnl f* **16/1**
0506 **7** 1 1/4 **Iamagrey (IRE)**[20] [5706] 2-8-6 62 DeanMcKeown 10 38
(J S Moore) *prom: rdn over 2f out: wkng whn nt clr run ent st* **9/1**
0 **8** 1/2 **Spoilt Madame**[142] [2039] 2-8-6 0 JamesDoyle 8 37+
(P D Evans) *sn outpcd: sme hdwy wl over 1f out: n.d* **100/1**
0055 **9** 5 **Son Of Spartacus (IRE)**[26] [5520] 2-8-11 55 (p) DavidAllan 6 30+
(Mrs L Stubbs) *prom: n.m.r sn after s: nt clr run and lost pl over 5f out: rdn and bhd fnl 3f* **25/1**
1500 **10** 3 **Smokeyourpipe (IRE)**[26] [5529] 2-8-12 55 SladeO'Hara[(5)] 3 28
(C Tinkler) *mid-div: rdn 3f out: sn bhd* **20/1**
6 **11** 2 1/2 **Casa Mia (IRE)**[27] [5501] 2-8-7 0 ow1 TonyHamilton 1 12
(R A Fahey) *led early: prom tl rdn and wknd over 2f out* **8/1**
0 **12** 1 **Mandalay King (IRE)**[110] [2991] 2-8-11 0 TPQueally 5 14
(Jane Chapple-Hyam) *sn led: hdd over 5f out: w ldr tl rdn over 2f out: wknd wl over 1f out* **6/1**[3]

1m 31.88s (1.48) **Going Correction** 0.0s/f (Stan) **12** Ran SP% **118.2**
Speed ratings (Par 93): **91,90,90,86,85 85,83,83,77,73 71,69**
CSF £18.14 TOTE £4.30: £1.60, £2.00, £11.60; EX 22.20.The winner was sold to R Harris for 6,000gns.
Owner R S S Ambrose, H Wilson & J Wells **Bred** Tally-Ho Stud **Trained** Upper Lambourn, Berks

FOCUS
This turned out to be a competitive seller and is rated positively through the runner-up.

NOTEBOOK
Ambrose Princess(IRE) had finished a good fourth in a mile nursery at Kempton last time after winning a similar race to this at Ripon. She came through to snatch it after missing the break and was subsequently sold to Ron Harris for 6,000 guineas. (op 4-1 tchd 9-2)
Wiseman's Diamond(USA) was fitted with cheekpieces over this longer trip. She did not lose ground at the start this time and certainly ran her race on this drop into selling company. (op 4-1 tchd 11-4 and 5-1)
Melwood Dreams, down in both distance and grade, did not get the best of breaks from the outside draw and gave a good account of himself.
Polish Priory(IRE) was trying an extra furlong in this easier company with her rider putting up 2lb overweight on her sand debut. (tchd 17-2)
Liani(IRE), back up to 7f, showed no tendency to hang left this time although she was on the rail in the home straight. She may have finished a little closer with a trouble-free run. (op 8-1)
Rubytwosox(IRE) had also failed to get home over a mile when dropped into a seller on soft ground at Windsor last time.

6243 LADBROKES SERIOUS ABOUT SERVICE H'CAP 7f 32y(P)
3:50 (3:50) (Class 4) (0-85,85) 3-Y-0+ **£4,857** (£1,445; £722; £360) **Stalls** High

Form RPR
1254 **1** **Gunfighter (IRE)**[24] [5585] 4-8-6 **74** PJMcDonald[(3)] 2 82+
(J S Wainwright) *hld up towards rr: swtchd rt over 1f out: str run to ld nr fin* **7/1**
0403 **2** 1/2 **Red Romeo**[13] [5889] 6-8-11 **76** DaleGibson 3 82
(N Wilson) *t.k.h: prom: chsd ldr 5f out: led 1f out: sn rdn and hung lft: hdd nr fin* **11/1**

6364 **3** *nk* **Bonnie Prince Blue**[37] 5223 4-8-11 **76**........................ DeanMcKeown 6 81
(B W Hills) *hld up in mid-div: rdn and hdwy over 1f out: r.o ins fnl f* **6/1**[2]
00 **4** *2* **Kelamon**[14] 5874 3-8-4 **74**.. LukeMorris(3) 1 74
(M D I Usher) *led early: a.p: rdn wl over 1f out: one pce fnl f* **33/1**
1-16 **5** *hd* **Braddock (IRE)**[94] 3489 4-8-13 **78**............................ GrahamGibbons 10 77
(T D Barron) *sn led: rdn and hdd 1f out: no ex ins fnl f* **13/2**[3]
0620 **6** *nk* **Grimes Faith**[23] 5617 4-8-6 **74**............................. AndrewMullen(3) 9 73
(K A Ryan) *t.k.h towards rr: c wd st: rdn and hdwy over 1f out: one pce fnl f* **16/1**
2600 **7** *nk* **Geojimali**[16] 5809 5-9-1 **80**.. DanielTudhope 4 82+
(J S Goldie) *s.i.s: hld up and bhd: rdn whn nt clr run over 1f out: n.d* **11/2**[1]
0000 **8** *hd* **Desert Commander (IRE)**[36] 5254 5-9-6 **85**..............(p) PatCosgrave 7 82
(K A Ryan) *hld up in mid-div: rdn and sme hdwy whn edgd lft over 1f out: no imp fnl f* **12/1**
0213 **9** *¾* **Barons Spy (IRE)**[23] 5638 6-8-9 **79**.................... RussellKennemore(5) 5 84+
(R J Price) *hld up in mid-div: rdn and hdwy on ins wl over 1f out: styng on whn nt clr run ins fnl f: nt rcvr* **15/2**
1010 **10** *2½* **Rhuepunzel**[37] 5230 3-8-13 **80**....................................... NickyMackay 11 69
(G A Butler) *s.i.s: a bhd* **11/1**
2050 **11** *1¾* **Briannsta (IRE)**[93] 3549 5-8-12 **77**.............................. PaulMulrennan 12 61
(B Smart) *prom: rdn over 2f out: wkng whn n.m.r over 1f out* **20/1**
5641 **12** *5* **Yorkshire Blue**[42] 5083 8-8-8 **73**.............................. J-PGuillambert 8 43
(J S Goldie) *rdn over 3f out: a in rr* **11/1**

1m 29.84s (-0.56) **Going Correction** 0.0s/f (Stan)
WFA 3 from 4yo+ 2lb **12** Ran SP% **113.5**
Speed ratings (Par 105): **103,102,102,99,99 99,98,98,97,94 92,87**
CSF £78.13 CT £487.36 TOTE £7.00: £1.90, £2.80, £2.20; EX 70.50.
Owner M Sawers **Bred** Round Hill Stud **Trained** Kennythorpe, N Yorks
■ Stewards' Enquiry : P J McDonald one-day ban: careless riding (Oct 26)

FOCUS
A wide-open handicap that could be better than rated with the placed horses setting the standard.
Barons Spy(IRE) Official explanation: jockey said gelding was denied a clear run

6244 LADBROKES IN THE COMMUNITY CHARITABLE TRUST H'CAP 5f 20y(P)
4:20 (4:20) (Class 6) (0-62,63) 3-Y-0+ **£2,047** (£604; £302) **Stalls** Low

Form RPR
01 **1** **Sandwith**[15] 5836 4-8-5 **55**..(p) PJMcDonald(3) 2 66
(J S Wainwright) *hld up towards rr: hdwy on ins wl over 1f out: rdn to ld wl ins fnl f: r.o* **4/1**[1]
4000 **2** *1¼* **Larky's Lob**[10] 5981 8-8-10 **62**................................... JamesO'Reilly(5) 5 69
(J O'Reilly) *chsd ldrs: rdn to ld ins fnl f: sn hdd: nt qckn* **12/1**
6420 **3** *½* **Rann Na Cille (IRE)**[11] 5934 3-8-12 **62**.................(b) AndrewMullen(3) 9 67
(K A Ryan) *hld up towards rr: c wd st: rdn and hdwy over 1f out: edgd lft ins fnl f: kpt on* **10/1**[3]
-610 **4** *1½* **Divalini**[128] 2459 3-8-13 **60**.. NickyMackay 10 60
(J Akehurst) *s.i.s: sn swtchd lft: hld up in rr: rdn and hdwy 1f out: no ex ins fnl f* **16/1**
0002 **5** *1* **Triskaidekaphobia**[25] 5565 4-8-8 **55**..........................(t) JamesDoyle 6 51
(Miss J R Tooth) *w ldrs: led over 2f out: rdn wl over 1f out: hdd ins fnl f: fdd towards fin* **4/1**[1]
5000 **6** *1¼* **Matterofact (IRE)**[11] 5942 4-8-7 **59**.............................. HaddenFrost(5) 11 51
(M S Saunders) *led over 1f: w ldrs: rdn over 1f out: wknd ins fnl f* **22/1**
3334 **7** *¾* **Gifted Lass**[182] 1067 5-9-1 **62**...................................... DavidAllan 7 51
(J Balding) *chsd ldrs: rdn over 2f out: wknd wl over 1f out* **15/2**[2]
0600 **8** *1½* **Now Look Out**[10] 5970 3-8-13 **60**...........................(t) GrahamGibbons 8 43
(E S McMahon) *hld up in mid-div: rdn wl over 1f out: wknd ins fnl f* **16/1**
6212 **9** *3½* **Thoughtsofstardom**[114] 2879 4-8-13 **60**...............(be) TGMcLaughlin 4 31
(G C Bravery) *s.i.s: a in rr* **15/2**[2]
0211 **10** *2½* **Sofinella (IRE)**[14] 5867 4-8-10 **60**................................ LukeMorris(3) 1 22
(A W Carroll) *w ldr: led over 3f out tl over 2f out: rdn wl over 1f out: sn wknd* **4/1**[1]

62.45 secs (-0.37) **Going Correction** 0.0s/f (Stan) **10** Ran SP% **116.4**
Speed ratings (Par 101): **102,100,99,96,95 93,92,89,84,80**
CSF £55.13 CT £461.97 TOTE £6.20: £1.70, £5.10, £3.00; EX 61.70.
Owner M Sawers **Bred** R R Whitton **Trained** Kennythorpe, N Yorks

FOCUS
A closely-knit minor sprint handicap and the form looks pretty solid with those in the frame behind the winner setting the level.
Sofinella(IRE) Official explanation: trainer had no explanation for the poor form shown

6245 LADBROKES - YOUR BEST BET H'CAP 1m 1f 103y(P)
4:50 (4:52) (Class 5) (0-70,70) 3-Y-0 **£2,968** (£876; £438) **Stalls** Low

Form RPR
0403 **1** **Distiller (IRE)**[3] 6146 3-9-4 **70**.. FrancisNorton 8 76
(W R Muir) *uns rdr and galloped loose bef s: hld up in rr: swtchd lft sn after s: hdwy on outside 2f out: sn rdn and edgd lft: led 1f out: rdn out* **10/3**[2]
0250 **2** *1* **Tri Chara (IRE)**[20] 5703 3-8-8 **60**................................... GrahamGibbons 2 64
(R Hollinshead) *hld up: n.m.r on ins bnd 7f out: hdwy on ins wl over 1f out: hrd rdn and ev ch ins fnl f: nt qckn* **8/1**
6000 **3** *shd* **Run Free**[10] 5968 3-8-8 **60**.. PatCosgrave 3 64
(N Wilson) *led: rdn and hdd 1f out: kpt on same pce* **16/1**
010 **4** *shd* **Grand Diamond (IRE)**[15] 5840 3-8-5 **60**........................ PJMcDonald(3) 4 65+
(J S Goldie) *hld up: hdwy on ins wl over 1f out: sn nt clr run: swtchd rt ins fnl f: r.o* **6/1**
6604 **5** *3½* **Bold Saxon (IRE)**[17] 5783 3-8-6 **58**.............................. JamieMackay 1 54
(M D I Usher) *a.p: rdn over 1f out: wknd ins fnl f* **6/1**
6 *1* **Satindra (IRE)**[103] 3219 3-8-9 **61**................................... PaulMulrennan 6 55
(John A Harris) *prom: lost pl ent st: n.d after* **40/1**
2414 **7** *4* **Magdalene**[24] 5604 3-9-3 **69**.. DeanMcKeown 5 55
(Rae Guest) *hld up: hdwy over 5f out: rdn 3f out: wknd wl over 1f out* **11/4**[1]
2113 **8** *¾* **Red Current**[14] 5865 3-8-11 **68**................................. KevinGhunowa(5) 7 52
(R A Harris) *t.k.h: sn chsng ldr: rdn and ev ch over 2f out: wknd wl over 1f out* **5/1**[3]

2m 2.07s (-0.55) **Going Correction** 0.0s/f (Stan) **8** Ran SP% **114.4**
Speed ratings (Par 101): **102,101,101,100,97 96,93,92**
CSF £29.96 CT £370.61 TOTE £5.10: £1.40, £2.50, £4.60; EX 33.30 Place 6 £3,649.01, Place 5 £107.32.
Owner D G Clarke & C L A Edginton **Bred** Mount Coote Stud **Trained** Lambourn, Berks
■ Stewards' Enquiry : Graham Gibbons one-day ban: used whip with excessive frequency without giving colt time to respond (Oct 26)

FOCUS
They went a steady pace in this moderate affair and the form is not solid with the runner-up the best guide for now.
Magdalene Official explanation: trainer had no explanation for the poor form shown
Red Current Official explanation: jockey said filly ran too free
T/Plt: £31,101.60 to a £1 stake. Pool: £53,256.30. 1.25 winning tickets. T/Qpdt: £77.00 to a £1 stake. Pool: £5,322.30. 51.10 winning tickets. KH

6087 LEICESTER (R-H)
Tuesday, October 16

OFFICIAL GOING: Good to soft (good in places) (7.3)
Wind: Light behind Weather: Overcast, turning showery after race 3

6246 EBF REFERENCE POINT MAIDEN STKS (C&G) (DIV I) 7f 9y
2:10 (2:10) (Class 4) 2-Y-0 **£4,210** (£1,252; £625; £312) **Stalls** Centre

Form RPR
0 **1** **Port Quin**[67] 4362 2-9-0 0... TedDurcan 12 75
(G Wragg) *s.i.s: hdwy 1/2-way: rdn and edgd lft over 1f out: styd on to ld wl ins fnl f* **16/1**
0 **2** *½* **Majeen**[12] 5951 2-9-0 0.. RHills 8 74
(W J Haggas) *trckd ldrs: rdn to ld over 1f out: hdd wl ins fnl f* **3/1**[1]
3 *1½* **Barricado (FR)** 2-9-0 0.. SteveDrowne 6 70
(R Charlton) *trckd ldrs: shkn up over 1f out: styd on* **9/1**
0 **4** *2* **Arabian Spirit**[11] 5977 2-9-0 0.................................... JimmyFortune 1 65
(E A L Dunlop) *hld up: hdwy over 2f out: rdn and hung rt fr over 1f out: no ex ins fnl f* **7/2**[3]
55 **5** *nk* **Govenor Eliott (IRE)**[28] 5502 2-9-0 0............................. GregFairley 11 64
(M Johnston) *chsd ldrs: led over 2f out: rdn and hdd over 1f out: styd on same pce* **10/3**[2]
6 *3½* **Hellfire Bay** 2-9-0 0.. NCallan 7 55
(K A Ryan) *s.i.s: sn prom: outpcd over 2f out: n.d after* **14/1**
00 **7** *¾* **Drumhallagh (IRE)**[25] 5591 2-9-0 0.......................... RichardKingscote 4 53
(Tom Dascombe) *hld up: rdn over 2f out: nvr trbld ldrs* **14/1**
00 **8** *nk* **Follow Your Spirit**[20] 5720 2-9-0 0.................................. DavidKinsella 9 53
(B Palling) *led over 4f: hung lft and wknd over 1f out* **200/1**
9 *3* **Elemental Hero (FR)** 2-9-0 0... JohnEgan 3 45
(Jane Chapple-Hyam) *prom: racd keenly: lost pl 3f out: sn wknd* **12/1**
10 *nk* **Animator** 2-9-0 0.. TQuinn 10 44
(P F I Cole) *prom to 1/2-way* **14/1**
00 **11** *4* **Reve Vert (FR)**[13] 5910 2-9-0 0.. JimCrowley 2 34
(A W Carroll) *s.i.s: hld up: rdn 1/2-way: sn wknd* **100/1**

1m 26.47s (0.37) **Going Correction** +0.125s/f (Good) **11** Ran SP% **115.4**
Speed ratings (Par 97): **102,101,99,97,97 93,92,91,88,88 83**
CSF £62.50 TOTE £21.20: £5.70, £1.40, £3.30; EX 78.90 TRIFECTA Not won..
Owner Mollers Racing **Bred** Equibreed S R L **Trained** Newmarket, Suffolk

FOCUS
An ordinary maiden but run in a fair time for a race like this, 1.8 seconds faster than the second division, although the ground did soften through the card. Not easy to assess the level, but the likes of the eighth do hold down the form.

NOTEBOOK
Port Quin, last of 20 in a Newmarket maiden on his debut, did not go without support on this second start and made use of his stamina in this easier ground to outstay the favourite. He could make up into a fairly useful middle-distance handicapper next season. (op 18-1 tchd 20-1)
Majeen, who ran with promise on his debut at HQ, was up there throughout and had every chance. He just found the winner staying on too strongly for him in the closing stages, but this was still a solid effort and he should be able to find an opening soon, either on turf or on the All-Weather. (tchd 100-30)
Barricado(FR), a half-brother to Spring Is Here and Domani, who both won over a mile in France, and Aubade d'Irlande, a 1m2f winner in France, did best of the newcomers and should benefit from the experience. (op 10-1 tchd 12-1)
Arabian Spirit, whose dam won over 1m2f, is a half-brother to First Fought, who was placed over 1m and was also a winner over hurdles. He showed little on his debut and went off a surprisingly short price considering that, but ran a lot better and he will be interesting for handicaps after one more run. (tchd 100-30 and 4-1)
Govenor Eliott(IRE) has let his supporters down somewhat in his three runs to date, but at least handicaps are an option for him now. (op 7-2)
Hellfire Bay, a half-brother to Ephesus, a triple 1m to 1m2f winner, showed signs of inexperience on his debut and should know more next time. (op 12-1)

6247 WHISSENDINE (S) H'CAP 7f 9y
2:40 (2:40) (Class 6) (0-60,60) 3-4-Y-0 **£2,590** (£770; £385; £192) **Stalls** Centre

Form RPR
-000 **1** **Bert's Memory**[12] 5936 3-8-10 **50**....................................(p) NCallan 12 59
(K A Ryan) *chsd ldrs: led over 2f out: rdr dropped whip over 1f out: pushed out* **25/1**
4000 **2** *1* **Moonstreaker**[20] 5737 4-9-0 **52**.................................. DeanMcKeown 1 58
(R M Whitaker) *dwlt: hdwy over 2f out: r.o* **11/1**[3]
6000 **3** *shd* **Al Rayanah**[65] 4416 4-8-10 **48**.. LiamJones 9 54
(G Prodromou) *s.i.s: plld hrd and hdwy over 4f out: rdn and ev ch over 1f out: styd on same pce ins fnl f* **14/1**
5001 **4** *1* **Memphis Man**[15] 5866 4-9-5 **57**...................................... TGMcLaughlin 10 60
(P D Evans) *hld up: hdwy over 1f out: styd on* **8/1**[2]
5500 **5** *nk* **Seesawmilu (IRE)**[8] 6064 4-8-10 **48**............................ AdrianTNicholls 2 51
(E J Alston) *hld up: hdwy over 2f out: rdn and hung rt fr over 1f out: no ex ins fnl f* **20/1**
4600 **6** *2* **Buzzin'Boyzee (IRE)**[8] 6064 4-8-8 **46**.............................. JohnEgan 18 43+
(P D Evans) *hld up: nt clr run fr over 2f out tl r.o ins fnl f: nvr nrr* **14/1**
2324 **7** *shd* **Calloff The Search**[22] 5688 3-9-1 **55**........................(v) SaleemGolam 17 52
(W G M Turner) *hmpd s: hld up in tch: outpcd over 2f out: styd on ins fnl f* **8/1**[2]
2030 **8** *¾* **Fistral**[43] 5084 3-8-2 **47**.. KirstyMilczarek(5) 14 42+
(J Hetherton) *hld up: hmpd over 2f out: styd on ins fnl f: n.d* **14/1**
2000 **9** *hd* **Smart Cat (IRE)**[20] 5737 4-8-12 **50**............................... LeeEnstone 4 44
(A P Jarvis) *chsd ldrs: rdn over 2f out: wknd fnl f* **20/1**
6601 **10** *nk* **Montemayorprincess (IRE)**[22] 5688 3-8-9 **49**..............(p) TedDurcan 5 42
(D Haydn Jones) *s.i.s: hld up: rdn 1/2-way: hdwy over 2f out: no ex fnl f* **15/2**[1]
5035 **11** *3½* **Persian Fox (IRE)**[8] 6060 3-9-1 **55**.............................. AdamKirby 15 39
(A G Juckes) *s.i.s: hdwy 1/2-way: rdn over 1f out: wknd ins fnl f* **12/1**
0303 **12** *1* **Strut The Stage (IRE)**[6] 6101 3-9-6 **60**.................. WandersonD'Avila 7 41
(B W Duke) *chsd ldrs over 5f* **16/1**
2566 **13** *nk* **Acapulco Bay**[81] 3914 3-8-7 **50**.............................. JamieMoriarty(3) 16 31
(Miss J A Camacho) *chsd ldrs: rdn over 2f out: wknd over 1f out* **16/1**
2600 **14** *3½* **Danawi (IRE)**[63] 4469 4-8-13 **51**....................................... ChrisCatlin 6 22
(M R Hoad) *led: hung rt 4f out: hdd over 2f out: sn rdn and wknd* **16/1**
6024 **15** *2½* **Blue Bird's Dream**[4] 6149 4-9-3 **55**............................ DarryllHolland 8 19
(E J Alston) *mid-div: rdn over 2f out: wkg whn hmpd sn after* **8/1**[2]

2504 **16** 1/2 **Briery Blaze**[20] 5730 4-8-10 **48**........ SteveDrowne 3 11
(J W Unett) *chsd ldrs 5f* **11/1**[3]

0000 **17** 8 **Musical Parkes**[57] 4661 3-8-1 **48**........ LanceBetts(7) 11 —
(W J H Ratcliffe) *prom rdn 1/2-way: sn wknd* **100/1**

3300 **18** 14 **Crafty Fox**[34] 5338 4-9-1 **53**........(v) StephenDonohoe 13 —
(John A Harris) *s.i.s: outpcd* **50/1**

1m 26.45s (0.35) **Going Correction** +0.125s/f (Good)
WFA 3 from 4yo 2lb **18** Ran SP% **123.4**
Speed ratings (Par 101): **103,101,101,100,100 97,97,97,96,96 92,91,90,86,84 83,74,58**
CSF £268.58 CT £4108.77 TOTE £31.20: £5.30, £3.10, £4.10, £2.00; EX 389.10 TRIFECTA Not won..The winner was bought in for 7,000gns.
Owner D Fower & N J Titterton **Bred** D Fower And N J Titterton **Trained** Hambleton, N Yorks

FOCUS
An ordinary seller but sound form for the grade. The winner was close to her 2yo level with the third, fourth and fifth all close to their recent marks.
Montemayorprincess(IRE) Official explanation: jockey said filly had no more to give closing stages
Persian Fox(IRE) Official explanation: jockey said gelding had steering problems
Danawi(IRE) Official explanation: jockey said gelding hung right-handed
Crafty Fox Official explanation: jockey said gelding lost its action

6248 EBF SOAR MAIDEN STKS 1m 60y
3:10 (3:11) (Class 4) 2-Y-O **£4,857** (£1,445; £722; £360) **Stalls** High

Form RPR

35 **1** **Mountain Pride (IRE)**[24] 5633 2-9-3 0........ LDettori 14 82+
(J L Dunlop) *chsd ldrs: rdn to ld wl ins fnl f: sn clr* **6/4**[1]

2 2 1/2 **Cuban Missile** 2-9-3 0........ SteveDrowne 5 76+
(R Charlton) *hld up: pushed along over 4f out: swtchd lft and hdwy over 1f out: edgd rt ins fnl f: r.o wl* **20/1**

3 **3** 1/2 **Top Ticket (IRE)**[26] 5570 2-9-3 0........ RichardMullen 13 75
(D M Simcock) *chsd ldrs: rdn over 2f out: styd on* **17/2**

4 shd **Last Three Minutes (IRE)** 2-9-3 0........ JimmyFortune 6 74
(E A L Dunlop) *hld up in tch: rdn and hung rt fr over 2f out: led over 1f out: hdd and no ex wl ins fnl f* **16/1**

5 shd **Unleashed (IRE)** 2-9-3 0........ TedDurcan 2 74+
(H R A Cecil) *hld up: hdwy over 2f out: edgd rt fr over 1f out: styd on* **8/1**[3]

5 **6** 1 3/4 **Clovis**[8] 6058 2-9-3 0........ GregFairley 1 71
(M Johnston) *dwlt: sn rcvrd to ld: rdn and hdd over 1f out: wknd ins fnl f* **11/2**[2]

7 3/4 **Art Value** 2-9-3 0........ AdrianMcCarthy 9 69
(P W Chapple-Hyam) *mid-div: hdwy over 3f out: sn rdn: styd on same pce appr fnl f* **20/1**

8 6 **Black Tor Figarro (IRE)** 2-9-3 0........ WandersonD'Avila 10 56
(B W Duke) *hld up: hdwy over 3f out: rdn and wknd over 1f out* **100/1**

9 1/2 **Mardood** 2-9-3 0........ RHills 12 55
(W J Haggas) *s.i.s: rn green: outpcd* **16/1**

10 hd **Pacifism (UAE)** 2-9-3 0........ PhilipRobinson 11 55
(M A Jarvis) *chsd ldr tl rdn over 2f out: wknd over 1f out* **12/1**

6 **11** 1/2 **Koraleva Tectona (IRE)**[22] 5681 2-8-12 0........ PaulEddery 7 49
(Pat Eddery) *chsd ldrs over 6f* **33/1**

12 4 **Allied Powers (IRE)** 2-9-3 0........ NCallan 8 46
(M L W Bell) *hld up: rdn over 3f out: wknd over 2f out* **33/1**

13 1 1/2 **Rockjumper** 2-9-3 0........ RobertHavlin 3 42
(H Morrison) *in rr whn hmpd over 6f out: n.d* **40/1**

14 16 **Great Future** 2-8-12 0........ TPQueally 4 —
(H R A Cecil) *sn outpcd and bhd* **25/1**

1m 46.09s (0.79) **Going Correction** +0.125s/f (Good) **14** Ran SP% **119.2**
Speed ratings (Par 97): **101,98,98,97,97 96,95,89,88,88 88,84,82,66**
CSF £40.09 TOTE £1.90: £1.10, £6.70, £2.60; EX 37.30 Trifecta £139.80 Part won. Pool £197.00 - 0.35 winning units..
Owner Ian Cameron **Bred** Raymond P Doyle **Trained** Arundel, W Sussex

FOCUS
A fair maiden, rated through the winner. The third comes from a Yarmouth race that is working out well.

NOTEBOOK
Mountain Pride(IRE) took a while to hit top gear but in the end the extra furlong and easier ground played to his strengths and he stayed on best of all to win readily in the end. Although entered in the Derby and Irish Derby, he looks more likely to develop into a useful handicapper next year, when middle distances will of course suit him. (op 7-4 tchd 15-8)
Cuban Missile, whose dam won over 1m4f in France, also looked held when the leaders kicked on, but he really got a move on late in the race and ran on well for second. He should come on for this debut and looks a nice prospect for handicaps next season.
Top Ticket(IRE), who ran with promise on his debut at Yarmouth in a race that is working out quite well, gave a boost to that form himself with a solid effort. He needs one more run for a mark but could well win a maiden beforehand. (op 15-2 tchd 9-1)
Last Three Minutes(IRE) ◆, a half-brother to six winners, travelled up strongly inside the final two furlongs looking all over the winner, but he might have got there too soon as the closers finished well to rob him of even a place by the time they crossed the line. He certainly looks capable of winning a similar race and, being by Val Royal, one would expect a sounder surface to suit him. Official explanation: jockey said colt hung right (tchd 14-1)
Unleashed(IRE), whose dam was a high-class multiple winner over middle distances in Germany and the US, shaped well enough and looks the type who will be very much suited by a proper test at three.
Clovis was strangely taken on by his owner's other runner in the race, Pacifism, at the head of affairs. That did neither of them any good. (op 15-2 tchd 5-1)
Art Value, a brother to Barathea Blazer, a smart, multiple winner at up to 1m7f, and Barathea Blue, a 1m2f winner at three, was weak in the market on his debut. He finished clear of the rest, though, and can only improve with experience. (op 14-1)

6249 EUROPEAN BREEDERS' FUND WREAKE FILLIES' CONDITIONS STKS 1m 60y
3:40 (3:40) (Class 4) 3-Y-O **£7,570** (£2,265; £1,132; £566; £282) **Stalls** High

Form RPR

2540 **1** **Sudoor**[27] 5544 3-8-12 98........ RHills 8 94
(J L Dunlop) *chsd ldrs: rdn to ld over 1f out: edgd lft: styd on wl* **5/2**[2]

0032 **2** 1/2 **Lady Gloria**[17] 5794 3-8-12 92........ TPQueally 3 93
(J G Given) *trckd ldr: rdn and ev ch over 1f out: styd on* **10/11**[1]

6420 **3** 1 **Marzelline (IRE)**[27] 5544 3-9-1 95........(v[1]) AdamKirby 2 94
(W R Swinburn) *chsd ldrs: rdn and outpcd over 2f out: styd on ins fnl f* **15/2**[3]

6600 **4** 2 1/2 **Chantilly Tiffany**[33] 5354 3-9-4 90........ JimmyFortune 1 91
(E A L Dunlop) *led: rdn and hdd over 1f out: wknd ins fnl f* **12/1**

01 **5** 12 **Turban Heights (IRE)**[57] 4659 3-8-12 76........ ChrisCatlin 7 58
(E J O'Neill) *swvd lft s: bhd: plld hrd and hdwy 6f out: rdn: hung lft and wknd over 2f out* **11/1**

0003 **6** 4 **Tokyo Jo (IRE)**[12] 5945 3-8-12 49........(p) TGMcLaughlin 6 48?
(T T Clement) *hld up in tch: rdn and wknd over 2f out* **200/1**

0344 **7** 23 **Little Darlin**[32] 5378 3-8-12 0........ AdrianMcCarthy 4 —
(G J Smith) *hld up: rdn and wknd over 3f out* **400/1**

1m 45.87s (0.57) **Going Correction** +0.125s/f (Good) **7** Ran SP% **109.5**
Speed ratings (Par 100): **102,101,100,98,86 82,59**
CSF £4.62 TOTE £3.20: £1.70, £1.30; EX 5.00 Trifecta £22.10 Pool £608.08 - 19.51 winning units..
Owner Hamdan Al Maktoum **Bred** Shadwell Estate Company Limited **Trained** Arundel, W Sussex

FOCUS
A race full of useful fillies who have been hard to place this season. It was steadily run and the form may not prove solid.

6250 FOSSE WAY CLAIMING STKS 1m 3f 183y
4:10 (4:11) (Class 6) 3-4-Y-O **£2,590** (£770; £385; £192) **Stalls** High

Form RPR

0060 **1** **Troialini**[13] 5906 3-9-2 66........ LiamJones 8 69
(S W Hall) *a.p: led over 4f out: rdn clr fr over 1f out: hung lft ins fnl f: styd on* **11/2**[2]

0060 **2** 3 1/2 **Maria Antonia (IRE)**[8] 6069 4-9-2 50........ TPO'Shea 14 56
(P A Blockley) *hld up: plld hrd: hdwy over 4f out: rdn to chse wnr 2f out: no imp* **11/1**

4036 **3** 2 **Anything Once (USA)**[10] 6019 4-9-3 48........(b) StephenDonohoe 1 54
(D Carroll) *hld up: hdwy over 3f out: nt rch ldrs* **16/1**

031 **4** 1 **Everyman**[7] 6090 3-9-0 45........(v) JimCrowley 11 57
(A W Carroll) *hld up: hdwy over 3f out: rdn over 2f out: styd on same pce* **11/2**[2]

2550 **5** 3/4 **Joy In The Guild (IRE)**[14] 5886 4-8-13 46........ FergusSweeney 16 47
(W S Kittow) *hld up: hdwy u.p over 2f out: styd on same pce appr fnl f* **12/1**

2050 **6** nk **Hook Money (IRE)**[13] 5906 3-8-12 49........(b) JamesDoyle 12 53
(A J McCabe) *led after 1f: sn hdd: chsd ldrs: rdn over 2f out: sn hung rt: no ex* **20/1**

5030 **7** shd **Mardi**[24] 5640 3-9-5 70........ RHills 10 60
(W J Haggas) *mid-div: rdn over 3f out: nvr trbld ldrs* **5/1**[1]

620 **8** 7 **Jiminor Mack**[18] 5782 4-8-6 45........(p) LanceBetts(7) 7 36
(W J H Ratcliffe) *hld up in tch: outpcd over 3f out: no ch whn hung rt fnl f* **33/1**

0040 **9** 1 1/2 **Long Gone**[51] 4859 4-8-11 31........(p) AdrianMcCarthy 15 31
(John A Harris) *led over 10f out: hdd over 4f: rdn and wknd over 1f out* **100/1**

66-5 **10** 1 3/4 **Bamboo Banks (IRE)**[29] 5472 4-9-7 53........ TedDurcan 4 38
(J L Dunlop) *prom: rdn and hung rt fr over 3f out: wknd over 2f out* **9/1**

0050 **11** 1 3/4 **Sterling Moll**[42] 5120 4-9-0 46........ FrankieMcDonald 2 29
(W De Best-Turner) *s.i.s: hld up: a in rr* **100/1**

2530 **12** shd **Delta Shuttle (IRE)**[18] 5777 3-8-11 58........ LeeEnstone 6 32
(K R Burke) *chsd ldrs over 9f* **11/1**

4023 **13** 2 1/2 **Leprechaun's Gold (IRE)**[7] 6090 3-8-3 47........ DavidProbert(7) 13 27
(B J Llewellyn) *prom over 9f* **16/1**

0000 **14** 9 **Wizby**[103] 3241 4-8-12 40........ TGMcLaughlin 17 8
(P D Evans) *chsd ldrs: lost pl 1/2-way: wknd over 3f out* **100/1**

2002 **15** 24 **Raise The Heights (IRE)**[132] 2355 4-9-4 60........(t) RobertHavlin 5 —
(B J Llewellyn) *hld up: in rr whn rdn over 4f out: sn wknd* **8/1**[3]

6-56 **16** 39 **Poyle Kiera**[15] 5859 3-8-10 50 ow1........ NCallan 9 —
(M Blanshard) *led early: chsd ldrs tl rdn and wknd over 3f out* **25/1**

0 **P** **Go Dude**[8] 6060 3-9-0 59........(b) AdamKirby 3 —
(J Ryan) *hld up: rdn over 3f out: in rr whn p.u and dismntd ins fnl f* **33/1**

2m 36.16s (1.66) **Going Correction** +0.125s/f (Good)
WFA 3 from 4yo 7lb **17** Ran SP% **122.1**
Speed ratings (Par 101): **99,96,95,94,94 93,93,89,88,87 85,85,84,78,62 36,—**
CSF £61.17 TOTE £6.50: £2.60, £3.90, £5.10; EX 84.10 TRIFECTA Not won..Troialini was claimed by D. Pipe for £12,000.
Owner Mrs C Casserly **Bred** Mrs A M Varey **Trained** Claydon, Suffolk

FOCUS
A weakish claimer run at an ordinary pace, though quite a competitive one due to the size of the field. The level is pretty sound but the winner only had to run to his recent form.

6251 WYMESWOLD CONDITIONS STKS 7f 9y
4:40 (4:41) (Class 4) 2-Y-O **£4,533** (£1,348; £674; £336) **Stalls** Centre

Form RPR

415 **1** **Seeking Star (IRE)**[16] 5828 2-9-2 84........ TPO'Shea 4 91+
(M R Channon) *trckd ldrs: rdn to ld over 1f out: hung rt ins fnl f: r.o* **9/4**[1]

100 **2** 1 1/2 **Shaker (IRE)**[32] 5395 2-8-11 84........ RobertHavlin 7 81
(M L W Bell) *a.p: rdn and ev ch over 1f out: styd on same pce ins fnl f* **7/2**[2]

3361 **3** 1 **Golan Knight (IRE)**[46] 4991 2-9-2 87........ NCallan 1 84
(K A Ryan) *led: rdn and hdd over 1f out: nt clr run ins fnl f: no ex* **9/4**[1]

U162 **4** hd **Ocean Transit (IRE)**[22] 5692 2-8-3 82........ TolleyDean(5) 6 75
(W G M Turner) *w ldr tl rdn over 2f out: styd on same pce fnl f* **11/1**

1350 **5** 6 **Soopacal (IRE)**[24] 5624 2-9-2 85........ RichardMullen 5 68
(B Smart) *trckd ldrs: plld hrd: rdn over 2f out: hung rt and wknd over 1f out* **14/1**

5 **6** 4 **El Duende (USA)**[14] 5880 2-8-13 0........ LDettori 3 55
(W Jarvis) *s.i.s: hld up: pushed along 4f out: rdn and wknd over 2f out* **8/1**[3]

1m 27.49s (1.39) **Going Correction** +0.125s/f (Good) **6** Ran SP% **109.9**
Speed ratings (Par 97): **97,95,94,93,87 82**
CSF £9.90 TOTE £2.70: £1.50, £2.30; EX 11.70.
Owner Jaber Abdullah **Bred** Pier House Stud **Trained** West Ilsley, Berks

FOCUS
The pace was nothing special in this, but the conditions seemed to take their toll on these youngsters as a couple tended to roll about under pressure. The sextet all came down the centre of the track. An improved effort from Seeking Star and the form could have rated 4-5lb higher.

NOTEBOOK
Seeking Star(IRE), all the better for his return from a short break in an Ascot nursery last month - form that was boosted by the winner landing a Group 3 since - was badly in at these weights with all of his rivals apart from El Duende who does not yet have a mark. After getting a nice lead from Golan Knight and Ocean Transit, once pulled out for his effort he quickened up well in the ground and saw it out nicely despite hanging to his right late on. He still has a bit of scope and could be up to winning something better, especially in conditions like these. (op 3-1)
Shaker(IRE), who has been found out in a Sandown Listed contest and the Goffs Fillies Million since winning on soft ground on her Yarmouth debut, was produced to hold every chance over on the far side of the field and finished very much second best. She likes these conditions, but it seems she is not up to Pattern class so may not be the easiest to place. (tchd 4-1)
Golan Knight(IRE), proven in these conditions, tried to make every yard once again but did not get home this time and was already beaten when the winner hung across him. (op 2-1)

Ocean Transit(IRE) was best in at the weights, but was also the most exposed in the field. Trying this trip for the first time, she helped force the pace for much of the way but did not see it out and hung as she got tired in the latter stages. (op 17-2)
Soopacal(IRE), who has struggled since winning a heavy-ground maiden on his debut, should have appreciated the conditions but he expended too much energy by refusing to settle early. As soon as he was hit with the whip passing the two-furlong pole, he started to hang and that was the beginning of the end. (op 12-1 tchd 16-1)
El Duende(USA) on much easier ground than on his debut, was also taking on much better company and was struggling from a long way out. (op 15-2 tchd 7-1)

6252 EBF REFERENCE POINT MAIDEN STKS (C&G) (DIV II) 7f 9y
5:10 (5:10) (Class 4) 2-Y-O £4,210 (£1,252; £625; £312) Stalls Centre

Form RPR
4 **1** **Prime Exhibit**[17] 5813 2-9-0 0 SteveDrowne 7 80+
(R Charlton) *hld up in tch: plld hrd: led over 1f out: shkn up and r.o wl* **4/6**[1]
2 *1 1/2* **Endless Luck (USA)** 2-9-0 0 GregFairley 1 73+
(M Johnston) *wnt lft s: sn prom: led over 5f out: rdn and hdd over 1f out: styd on* **12/1**[3]
0 **3** *2 1/2* **Monterrico**[74] 4132 2-9-0 0 TedDurcan 3 67
(G Wragg) *chsd ldrs: rdn over 2f out: edgd rt and styd on same pce fnl f* **50/1**
4 *1 1/4* **Regal Best (IRE)** 2-9-0 0 JimCrowley 10 64
(Mrs A J Perrett) *hld up in tch: effrt over 2f out: no ex fnl f* **50/1**
4 **5** *1 1/2* **Red Leaves**[40] 5161 2-9-0 0 TQuinn 4 60
(P F I Cole) *led: hdd over 5f out: rdn over 2f out: wknd ins fnl f* **50/1**
50 **6** *2* **Charmel's Lad**[34] 5337 2-9-0 0 (t) AdamKirby 6 55
(W R Swinburn) *stdd s: hld up: shkn up over 1f out: sn wknd* **250/1**
0 **7** *1* **Buddy Holly**[46] 5003 2-9-0 0 RichardMullen 8 53
(Pat Eddery) *hld up in tch: racd keenly: rdn over 2f out: sn outpcd* **200/1**
8 *1* **Nordic Commander (IRE)** 2-9-0 0 JimmyFortune 5 50
(E A L Dunlop) *hld up: rdn and wknd over 1f out* **33/1**
9 *3 1/2* **Plavius (USA)** 2-9-0 0 LDettori 11 41
(Saeed Bin Suroor) *chsd ldrs over 5f* **9/4**[2]
560 **10** *3* **Gardes (IRE)**[18] 5771 2-9-0 66 JohnEgan 12 34
(Jane Chapple-Hyam) *plld hrd and prom: rdn and wknd wl over 1f out* **40/1**

1m 28.27s (2.17) **Going Correction** +0.125s/f (Good) **10** Ran SP% **110.6**
Speed ratings (Par 97): **92,90,87,86,84 82,80,79,75,72**
CSF £9.67 TOTE £1.90: £1.02, £2.90, £5.90; EX 13.00 Trifecta £83.80 Pool £369.84 - 3.13 winning units..
Owner Mountgrange Stud **Bred** Matthews Breeding And Racing Ltd **Trained** Beckhampton, Wilts

FOCUS
This did not look the strongest of maidens and the winning time was 1.8 seconds slower than the first division, but the front pair look nice types who may be capable of better. The winner only needed to repeat his debut form.

NOTEBOOK
Prime Exhibit ◆, down a furlong from his Haydock debut, duly confirmed the promise of that effort despite again racing a bit keenly early on. There was nothing wrong with the way he came home though and he looks a nice type for next season, especially when put over further. (tchd 4-7 and 8-11 in places)
Endless Luck(USA) ◆, an 80,000gns two-year-old and half-brother to a mutiple winner in the US, looked green early especially when he shot out of the stalls sideways, but he ran a very promising debut having been up with the pace throughout and only the more experienced winner had the legs of him late on. It should not be long before he goes one better. (op 11-1 tchd 14-1)
Monterrico, stepping up a furlong from his debut and on much easier ground, lasted much longer this time and as his useful half-sisters Monnavanna and Monturani both really came into their own at three, it is likely to be a similar story with him. (op 66-1 tchd 40-1)
Regal Best(IRE), a 45,000gns half-brother to three winners, showed enough on this debut to suggest he has a future especially as the stable's youngters tend to improve with racing. Two of his siblings scored over 1m4f so he is likely to appreciate further himself in time. (op 66-1)
Red Leaves, beaten out of sight in a novice event on his debut, was down a furlong and on easier ground. He showed up for a long way before getting tired in the ground and may still just have needed it. (op 80-1 tchd 100-1)
Charmel's Lad Official explanation: jockey said colt ran too freely
Plavius(USA), a $9,200,000 brother to Dijeerr and half-brother to Sharp Writer, showed up for a long way before dropping out. He may not have liked this ground, but he will need to be totally transformed by a quicker surface if he is to start justifying that purchase price. (tchd 11-4)

6253 STEWARDS H'CAP 1m 1f 218y
5:40 (5:40) (Class 5) (0-75,75) 3-Y-0+ £3,238 (£963; £481; £240) Stalls High

Form RPR
3120 **1** **Teodora Adivina**[10] 6021 3-9-0 70 TedDurcan 12 79+
(H R A Cecil) *chsd ldrs: led 2f out: rdn out* **4/1**[1]
4134 **2** *1* **Jawaab (IRE)**[18] 5768 3-9-0 70 RichardMullen 15 77
(M A Buckley) *hld up: hdwy over 3f out: rdn to chse wnr over 1f out: r.o* **6/1**[2]
3313 **3** *shd* **Rawdon (IRE)**[13] 5916 6-9-3 68 (v) JimmyFortune 4 75
(M L W Bell) *hld up: hdwy over 2f out: rdn and edgd rt over 1f out: r.o* **13/2**[3]
4305 **4** *nk* **Dove Cottage (IRE)**[50] 4909 5-9-2 67 FergusSweeney 2 73
(W S Kittow) *led: hdd over 8f out: chsd ldrs tl led over 2f out: sn hdd: r.o* **14/1**
5600 **5** *hd* **Davenport (IRE)**[151] 1819 5-9-3 73 JamesMillman(5) 5 79+
(B R Millman) *hld up: nt clr run over 2f out: hdwy over 1f out: r.o* **16/1**
0000 **6** *nk* **Street Life (IRE)**[20] 5732 9-8-6 64 DebraEngland(7) 11 69
(W J Musson) *hld up: hdwy over 1f out: r.o: nt rch ldrs* **20/1**
2140 **7** *2* **Norman The Great**[50] 4909 3-9-5 75 JohnEgan 6 76
(Jane Chapple-Hyam) *hld up: swtchd lft over 3f out: hdwy over 2f out: styd on* **16/1**
-026 **8** *2* **Trans Sonic**[131] 2403 4-9-2 67 LeeEnstone 3 64
(A P Jarvis) *trckd ldrs: racd keenly: led 7f out: rdn and hdd over 2f out: wknd fnl f* **28/1**
1044 **9** *5* **Snowed Under**[31] 5432 6-9-9 74 DarryllHolland 1 61
(J D Bethell) *chsd ldrs: rdn over 2f out: hung rt and wknd over 1f out* **9/1**
0500 **10** *3* **Kingdom Of Dreams (IRE)**[5] 6132 5-9-5 70 (t) AdrianTNicholls 7 51
(J Mackie) *hld up: effrt over 2f out: n.d* **25/1**
210 **11** *3 1/2* **Drizzi (IRE)**[3] 6175 6-9-1 66 (p) AdamKirby 14 40
(A W Carroll) *hld up: racd keenly: hdwy over 3f out: wknd over 2f out* **20/1**
-000 **12** *2* **Typhoon Ginger (IRE)**[10] 6016 12-8-9 60 oh5 RichardKingscote 9 30
(G Woodward) *hld up: rdn over 4f out: a in rr* **100/1**
-000 **13** *shd* **Pagan Crest**[15] 5870 4-9-4 69 JimCrowley 8 39
(Mrs A J Perrett) *prom over 7f* **20/1**
0-42 **14** *10* **Given A Choice (IRE)**[14] 3955 5-9-8 73 TPQueally 10 23
(J G Given) *led over 8f out: hdd 7f out: rdn and wknd over 2f out* **12/1**
0250 **15** *3 1/2* **Old Romney**[18] 5774 3-8-12 75 NSLawes(7) 13 18
(M W Easterby) *hld up: bhd fnl 4f* **40/1**
4235 **16** *shd* **El Coto**[16] 5838 7-9-6 71 (p) NCallan 17 14
(K A Ryan) *prom: rdn over 3f out: wknd over 2f out* **8/1**

2m 10.44s (2.14) **Going Correction** +0.125s/f (Good)
WFA 3 from 4yo+ 5lb **16** Ran SP% **119.9**
Speed ratings (Par 103): **96,95,95,94,94 94,92,91,87,84 82,80,80,72,69 69**
CSF £23.15 CT £156.05 TOTE £5.40: £1.70, £1.80, £2.50, £3.70; EX 35.40 Trifecta £162.10 Pool £475.09 - 2.08 winning units. Place 6 £117.80, Place 5 £49.30..
Owner Felipe Hinojosa **Bred** Chevington Stud **Trained** Newmarket, Suffolk

FOCUS
An ordinary handicap run in a modest time, but quite competitive and the front six were separated by less than two lengths at the line. The bare form, rated around the third amd fourth, is only ordinary, but the first pair are progressive and could prove a bit better.
T/Plt: £106.30 to a £1 stake. Pool: £56,176.10. 385.45 winning tickets. T/Qpdt: £12.50 to a £1 stake. Pool: £3,846.70. 226.80 winning tickets. CR

5901 NEWCASTLE (L-H)
Tuesday, October 16

OFFICIAL GOING: Good to soft (soft in places) (6.5)
Wind: Fresh, half against Weather: Cloudy

6254 WEATHERBYS BANK/E.B.F. MAIDEN FILLIES' STKS 7f
2:20 (2:20) (Class 5) 2-Y-O £4,210 (£1,252; £625; £312) Stalls Low

Form RPR
1 **Hallingdal (UAE)** 2-9-0 0 RoystonFfrench 4 77+
(M Johnston) *dwlt: in tch: rn green and lost pl 1/2-way: rallied and swtchd rt over 2f out: led 1f out: edgd lft: styd on strly* **7/4**[1]
0000 **2** *3 1/2* **Ice Choice (IRE)**[8] 6058 2-9-0 51 EddieAhern 3 68
(Mark Gillard) *led to 1f out: kpt on same pce* **25/1**
5430 **3** *2 1/2* **Misplaced Fortune**[19] 5745 2-9-0 67 KDarley 8 62
(N Tinkler) *hld up in tch: smooth hdwy over 2f out: rdn over 1f out: sn one pce* **11/4**[2]
4 *1/2* **African Flight** 2-9-0 0 HayleyTurner 1 61
(M L W Bell) *cl up tl rdn and outpcd over 1f out* **5/1**[3]
40 **5** *3 1/2* **Lu's Woman**[13] 5902 2-9-0 0 DaleGibson 6 52
(M W Easterby) *hld up ins: hdwy and prom 2f out: sn rdn and wknd* **20/1**
0 **6** *2 1/2* **Caffari (GER)**[17] 5811 2-8-7 0 DeclanCannon(7) 9 46
(K R Burke) *in tch: hdwy over 2f out: wknd wl over 1f out* **15/2**
0 **7** *4* **Floral Guest**[7] 6080 2-9-0 0 JimmyQuinn 10 36
(G G Margarson) *s.i.s: bhd and sn pushed along: nvr on terms* **25/1**
000 **8** *4* **Mchepple**[20] 5734 2-8-11 43 DominicFox(3) 2 26
(W Storey) *t.k.h: cl up tl wknd 2f out* **125/1**
06 **9** *3 1/2* **Snickers First**[28] 5502 2-9-0 0 PaulMulrennan 7 17
(M W Easterby) *cl up tl wknd fr 3f out* **33/1**
0 **10** *shd* **Reel Cool**[10] 6015 2-9-0 0 TomEaves 5 17
(B Smart) *plld hrd: hld up: pushed along over 2f out: sn btn* **16/1**

1m 33.32s (5.30) **Going Correction** +0.55s/f (Yiel) **10** Ran SP% **113.5**
Speed ratings (Par 92): **91,87,84,83,79 76,72,67,63,63**
CSF £54.98 TOTE £2.20: £1.10, £4.30, £1.30; EX 40.30.
Owner Sheikh Mohammed **Bred** Darley **Trained** Middleham Moor, N Yorks

FOCUS
A weak juvenile maiden, run at an average pace. The debutante winner could rate higher but did not beat too much.

NOTEBOOK
Hallingdal(UAE), half-sister to a 7f three-year-old winner, took time to find her stride yet eventually ran out a taking debut winner, justifying market support in the process. This was only a weak affair, but there should be plenty of improvement in her for this experience and she ought to get further next season. (op 2-1 tchd 13-8)
Ice Choice(IRE) showed her best form to date on this switch to easier ground and finished nicely clear of the remainder. She would have to be of interest if found an opportunity in a nursery before the Handicapper can reassess her, but it should be noted that with an official rating of 51 she does put this form into perspective. (op 28-1)
Misplaced Fortune, up in trip, found only the same pace when asked for maximum effort and ran below her official rating in defeat. It remains to be seen which way she is going at present. (op 3-1)
African Flight, a 65,000gns first foal of a useful three-year-old 6f winner, knew her job and showed up well until becoming outpaced nearing the final furlong. She looks in need of further experience and ought to come on for this run, but looks just modest on this evidence. (op 4-1 tchd 11-2)

6255 PERSIMMON HOMES MAIDEN STKS (C&G) 7f
2:50 (2:53) (Class 5) 2-Y-O £3,886 (£1,156; £577; £288) Stalls Low

Form RPR
2 **1** **Collection (IRE)**[13] 5920 2-9-0 0 SebSanders 7 85+
(W J Haggas) *chsd ldrs: led over 2f out: rdn and edgd lft fr over 1f out: kpt on wl* **4/9**[1]
2 *3 1/2* **Solar Spirit (IRE)** 2-8-11 0 PJMcDonald(3) 1 74
(G A Swinbank) *chsd ldrs: effrt and ev ch 2f out: one pce fnl f* **22/1**
3 *2 1/2* **Roman Legion (IRE)** 2-9-0 0 GrahamGibbons 5 68
(P A Blockley) *in tch: rdn and outpcd 1/2-way: rallied 2f out: kpt on: nt rch first two* **100/1**
30 **4** *nk* **Manuka Bee**[25] 5580 2-9-0 0 PaulMulrennan 13 67
(J Howard Johnson) *bhd tl hdwy over 2f out: kpt on fnl f: nrst fin* **40/1**
4 **5** *2 1/2* **Red Tarn**[20] 5734 2-9-0 0 TomEaves 12 61
(B Smart) *dwlt: bhd and pushed along: hdwy 2f out: edgd lft: n.d* **10/1**[3]
000 **6** *3* **Paint Stripper**[79] 3995 2-8-11 55 DominicFox(3) 11 53
(W Storey) *hld up: hdwy over 2f out: rdn and wknd over 1f out* **150/1**
7 *1/2* **Hampton Court** 2-9-0 0 RoystonFfrench 8 52
(M Johnston) *in tch: drvn 1/2-way: wknd over 2f out* **8/1**[2]
3640 **8** *3/4* **Lekin Sedona (IRE)**[40] 5167 2-9-0 50 TonyHamilton 10 50
(J M Saville) *led to over 2f out: rdn and wknd over 1f out* **100/1**
00 **9** *nk* **Patthepainter (GER)**[18] 5772 2-8-7 0 DeclanCannon(7) 2 49
(K R Burke) *t.k.h: prom tl wknd over 2f out* **100/1**
352 **10** *4* **Royal Applord**[19] 5745 2-9-0 77 DO'Donohoe 4 39
(K A Ryan) *chsd ldrs tl edgd lft and wknd over 2f out* **8/1**[2]
5 **11** *1 1/2* **Shanafarahan (IRE)**[20] 5734 2-9-0 0 MickyFenton 3 35
(T P Tate) *midfield: rdn 1/2-way: wknd over 2f out* **14/1**
12 *28* **Cashmere Jack** 2-9-0 0 PhillipMakin 6 —
(K G Reveley) *missed break: bhd and sn drvn along: lost tch fr 1/2-way* **100/1**

1m 33.04s (5.02) **Going Correction** +0.55s/f (Yiel) **12** Ran SP% **118.6**
Speed ratings (Par 95): **93,89,86,85,82 79,78,78,77,73 71,39**
CSF £18.50 TOTE £1.40: £1.02, £5.90, £24.60; EX 15.40.
Owner Highclere Thoroughbred Racing (Brunel) **Bred** P D Savill **Trained** Newmarket, Suffolk

The Form Book, Raceform Ltd, Compton, RG20 6NL

FOCUS
An average juvenile maiden which saw the field finish fairly strung out. Collection did it well enough but did not have a great deal to beat.

NOTEBOOK
Collection(IRE) confirmed the promise of his Salisbury debut second and duly got off the mark with a fairly straightforward display. He looked better the further he went here, as he was still quite green, and still looks to be very much learning his trade. No doubt he will make up into a better three-year-old and he should have little trouble in staying beyond 1m in time, with his Group 1 entries next year indictating his connections think a good deal of him. (op 8-15 tchd 8-13 and 4-6 in places)

Solar Spirit(IRE) ◆, the first foal of a 1m2f three-year-old winner, posted a very pleasing debut effort and finished nicely clear of the remainder in second. He travelled sweetly on the far rail for most of the way, and looked a brief threat to the winner nearing the 2f pole, but he lacked the finishing speed of that rival when it mattered. With improvement looking assured for this debut experience, he ought to be placed to advantage before the season's end, and looks a nice handicap prospect in the making. (op 20-1 tchd 25-1)

Roman Legion(IRE), the eighth foal of a dam who was a 1m6f winner at four, and whose only winning sibling so far has been over hurdles, defied his odds of 100/1 with a fair effort in defeat and was noted doing all of his best work towards the finish. He already looks in need of an extra furlong and can build on this with some experience now under his belt.

Manuka Bee was another doing all of his best work inside the final furlong and posted his most encouraging effort to date. He now has the option of nurseries and should enjoy a step up in trip. (tchd 33-1)

Red Tarn, as was the case on his debut, lost ground with a sluggish start and was never in the hunt. He needs one more run to qualify for a nursery mark and clearly needs some further experience. (op 8-1)

Hampton Court, a 100,000gns half-brother to his yard's decent three-year-old miler Colorado Rapid, failed to shine on this racecourse bow and is going to need to come on a lot for the experience in order to justify his price tag. (op 11-1)

Royal Applord ran disappointingly on this step back up in trip and probably failed to act on this softer ground. He has a little to prove now. (op 9-1)

Shanafarahan(IRE) Official explanation: trainer said colt was unsuited by the good to soft (soft in places) ground

6256 LYCETTS H'CAP 6f
3:20 (3:21) (Class 5) (0-70,70) 3-Y-O £4,210 (£1,252; £625; £312) Stalls Low

Form RPR
0403 1 **Umpa Loompa (IRE)**[24] 5625 3-8-4 56 oh1..........(v) SilvestreDeSousa 3 65
(D Nicholls) *t.k.h: mde all: clr 1f out: hld on wl* **8/1**
0-40 2 *hd* **Obe Royal**[14] 5879 3-8-8 60.......................................(p) J-PGuillambert 10 68
(P D Evans) *hld up in tch: hdwy to chse wnr ent fnl f: kpt on wl: jst hld* **7/1**
2145 3 *4* **Rainbow Fox**[23] 5662 3-9-4 70....................................... PaulHanagan 11 66+
(R A Fahey) *hld up: hdwy 2f out: kpt on fnl f: no imp* **11/2**[2]
1336 4 *1/2* **Howards Tipple**[12] 5934 3-9-2 68.......................................(p) TomEaves 6 63
(I Semple) *hld up in tch: effrt over 2f out: kpt on same pce fnl f* **13/2**[3]
0010 5 *1* **Vivi Belle**[89] 3686 3-8-5 57.. HayleyTurner 7 49
(M L W Bell) *prom: effrt over 2f out: no ex over 1f out* **8/1**
0210 6 *nk* **Orotund**[29] 5489 3-8-2 57 .... DuranFentiman(3) 4 48
(T D Easterby) *chsd wnr tl rdn and wknd ent fnl f* **11/1**
2000 7 *1 1/2* **Windjammer**[10] 6020 3-9-1 67... DavidAllan 13 61+
(T D Easterby) *towards rr: drvn 1/2-way: nvr rchd ldrs* **14/1**
1606 8 *1 1/4* **Dressed To Dance (IRE)**[13] 5907 3-8-13 65.................. SebSanders 2 48
(N Tinkler) *chsd ldrs tl rdn and wknd over 1f out* **5/1**[1]
1200 9 *1 1/4* **Put It On The Card**[16] 5834 3-8-8 60........................(v) TonyHamilton 12 39
(J S Wainwright) *t.k.h: hld up: rdn over 2f out: sn btn* **33/1**
-000 10 *7* **Lansdown**[13] 5907 3-7-12 57 oh6 ow1..................(p) PatrickDonaghy(7) 5 15
(R Johnson) *towards rr: drvn 1/2-way: sn struggling* **50/1**

1m 17.68s (2.59) **Going Correction** +0.55s/f (Yiel) **10** Ran SP% **100.0**
Speed ratings (Par 101): **104,103,98,97,96 96,94,92,90,81**
CSF £47.90 CT £232.52 TOTE £7.60: £2.20, £2.60, £1.80; EX 52.30.
Owner Chocolate Factory **Bred** Bold Fashion Partnership **Trained** Sessay, N Yorks
■ Staked A Claim was withdrawn (7/1, bolted to post). R4 applies, deduct 10p in the £.

FOCUS
A modest handicap which saw the first pair come clear. Tricky to assess, with the winner posting improvement, but the form makes sense overall.
Windjammer Official explanation: jockey said gelding was denied a clear run

6257 WEATHERBYS FINANCE MEDIAN AUCTION MAIDEN STKS 1m 4f 93y
3:50 (3:51) (Class 6) 3-4-Y-O £2,914 (£867; £433; £216) Stalls Centre

Form RPR
3442 1 **Snake's Head**[36] 5271 3-8-12 69... SebSanders 5 64
(J L Dunlop) *set modest pce: pushed along over 2f out: hld on wl fnl f* **15/8**[1]
30 2 *1/2* **Dart**[13] 5898 3-8-9 0 .... WilliamBuick(3) 3 68+
(J R Fanshawe) *hld up: rdn and swtchd rt wl over 1f out: kpt on wl fnl f: a hld* **14/1**
402 3 *1 1/2* **Lochiel**[89] 3678 3-9-3 66.. PaulMulrennan 7 65
(Mrs S C Bradburne) *in tch: effrt and chse wnr wl over 1f out: no ex ins fnl f* **8/1**
4402 4 *3/4* **Star Of Angels**[8] 6056 3-9-3 57.. RoystonFfrench 4 64
(M Johnston) *prom: drvn and outpcd over 4f out: rallied over 2f out: kpt on: no imp* **7/2**[2]
-030 5 *7* **Golden Folly**[31] 5426 3-9-3 49...(b[1]) DaleGibson 2 53
(Lady Herries) *chsd wnr to wl over 1f out: sn no ex* **25/1**
6 *1 1/4* **Masra**[149] 4-9-7 0 .... PJMcDonald(3) 8 51
(G A Swinbank) *hld up: stdy hdwy over 2f out: rdn and hung lft wl over 1f out: sn btn* **8/1**
7 *1 1/2* **Lyon's Hill** 3-9-3 0 .... TomEaves 1 49
(M Mullineaux) *racd wd: hld up: struggling over 5f out: sn btn* **50/1**
0535 8 *1/2* **Geordie's Pool**[19] 5755 3-9-3 57.....................................(p) EddieAhern 9 48
(J W Hills) *hld up in tch: rdn over 2f out: sn btn* **13/2**[3]
9 *2* **Etxalar (FR)**[503] 4-9-10 0 .... PaddyAspell 6 45
(Miss Lucinda V Russell) *chsd ldrs: rdn over 3f out: wknd over 2f out* **66/1**
3040 10 *11* **Ja Myford**[34] 5341 3-9-3 54..(p) MickyFenton 10 27
(P T Midgley) *prom: rdn 4f out: wknd 3f out: t.o* **8/1**

2m 49.02s (5.47) **Going Correction** +0.55s/f (Yiel)
WFA 3 from 4yo 7lb **10** Ran SP% **117.6**
Speed ratings (Par 101): **103,102,101,101,96 95,94,94,93,85**
CSF £31.23 TOTE £2.40: £1.10, £3.50, £2.50; EX 29.70.
Owner Nicholas Jones **Bred** Coln Valley Stud **Trained** Arundel, W Sussex

FOCUS
A very moderate maiden. Sound but limited form, with the winner 9lb off his best.

6258 BET365 CALL 08000 322 365 H'CAP 1m 2f 32y
4:20 (4:23) (Class 5) (0-70,70) 3-Y-O+ £3,886 (£1,156; £577; £288) Stalls Centre

Form RPR
4020 1 **Dark Energy**[10] 6021 3-9-1 65... TomEaves 5 77
(B Smart) *hld up: hdwy whn n.m.r over 2f out: rdn to ld ins fnl f: styd on wl* **18/1**
060 2 *1 3/4* **Sedgwick**[60] 4582 5-9-6 65 .... J-PGuillambert 16 73
(J G Given) *hld up outside: hdwy to ld over 1f out: hdd ins fnl f: kpt on* **16/1**
1640 3 *1 1/4* **Sforzando**[10] 6021 6-9-7 66.. SebSanders 13 72
(Mrs L Stubbs) *hld up outside: hdwy to chse ldrs 2f out: sn rdn: one pce fnl f* **20/1**
4334 4 *hd* **Trouble Mountain (USA)**[10] 6021 10-9-6 65................(t) DaleGibson 15 70
(M W Easterby) *hld up: hdwy over 2f out: r.o fnl f: nrst fin* **12/1**
0005 5 *shd* **Rigat**[11] 5964 4-8-9 54 .... PaulMulrennan 14 59
(T D Barron) *hld up: rdn over 2f out: styd on wl fr over 1f out: nrst fin* **20/1**
5123 6 *hd* **Dechiper (IRE)**[13] 5905 5-8-11 63 .... PatrickDonaghy(7) 11 68
(R Johnson) *hld up: hdwy and prom appr fnl f: no ex ins fnl f* **7/1**[3]
401 7 *1/2* **Neil's Legacy (IRE)**[22] 5674 5-9-4 68............................. GaryBartley(5) 2 72
(Miss L A Perratt) *prom: effrt and ev ch over 1f out: no ex ins fnl f* **9/1**
2302 8 *5* **Apache Nation (IRE)**[11] 5964 4-9-1 60............................... PhillipMakin 12 54
(M Dods) *hld up: drvn 3f out: sme hdwy over 1f out: n.d* **12/1**
0022 9 *3/4* **Boppys Pride**[19] 5750 4-8-11 56 .... PaulHanagan 3 48
(R A Fahey) *midfield: effrt whn nt clr run over 2f out: rdn whn hmpd wl over 1f out: nt rcvr* **3/1**[1]
4226 10 *1 1/2* **Violent Velocity (IRE)**[10] 6021 4-9-9 68 .... GrahamGibbons 4 57
(J J Quinn) *chsd ldrs: drvn 3f out: wknd over 1f out* **20/1**
2156 11 *3 1/2* **Thornaby Green**[19] 5750 6-8-10 62................................ DeanHeslop(7) 6 44
(T D Barron) *led tl hdd over 1f out: sn btn* **16/1**
3406 12 *shd* **Topflight Wildbird**[18] 5777 4-8-7 55 .... WilliamBuick(3) 10 37
(Mrs G S Rees) *chsd ldrs tl rdn and wknd fr 2f out* **12/1**
3650 13 *3/4* **News Of The Day (IRE)**[48] 4936 3-8-7 60.................... PJMcDonald(3) 8 40
(P Monteith) *prom tl rdn and wknd over 2f out* **66/1**
301 14 *14* **Monsoon Wedding**[22] 5678 3-9-6 70.......................... RoystonFfrench 9 22
(M Johnston) *cl up: rdn 3f out: wknd over 1f out* **13/2**[2]
06-6 15 *3 1/2* **Little Bob**[146] 1944 6-9-0 59..(b) JimmyQuinn 1 4
(J D Bethell) *midfield: drvn over 3f out: sn btn* **33/1**
0210 U **Ruby Legend**[19] 5750 9-8-10 55 ....(b) TonyHamilton 17 —
(K G Reveley) *stmbld and uns rdr s* **25/1**

2m 15.64s (3.84) **Going Correction** +0.55s/f (Yiel)
WFA 3 from 4yo+ 5lb **16** Ran SP% **123.5**
Speed ratings (Par 103): **106,104,103,103,103 103,102,98,98,97 94,94,93,82,79** —
CSF £258.90 CT £5725.91 TOTE £24.80: £4.50, £4.90, £4.60, £2.80; EX 484.50.
Owner Pinnacle Observatory Partnership **Bred** Bearstone Stud **Trained** Hambleton, N Yorks

FOCUS
An ordinary handicap for the grade, run at a decent early pace. The form looks sound.
Boppys Pride Official explanation: jockey said colt was denied a clear run
Monsoon Wedding Official explanation: jockey said filly had no more to give

6259 ENVIRONMENT AGENCY DUMP-IT AND LEG-IT AMATEUR JOCKEYS H'CAP (FOR AMATEUR RIDERS) 1m 4f 93y
4:50 (4:51) (Class 6) (0-65,62) 3-Y-O+ £2,307 (£709; £354) Stalls Centre

Form RPR
3632 1 **Harry The Hawk**[21] 5704 3-10-12 60 .... MrSWalker 14 71+
(T D Walford) *midfield: effrt over 2f out: led over 1f out: rdn out fnl f* **7/2**[1]
2152 2 *1 3/4* **Right Option (IRE)**[11] 5980 3-10-5 60........................ MrRPFlint(7) 15 66
(J L Flint) *in tch: hdwy to ld over 2f out: hdd over 1f out: kpt on fnl f* **6/1**[2]
61-0 3 *1 1/4* **Aston Lad**[154] 1745 6-10-2 48 oh1 .... MrsGHogg(5) 17 52
(Micky Hammond) *s.s: bhd tl gd hdwy fr 2f out: kpt on wl fnl f: nt rch first two* **11/1**
5 4 *1/2* **Directa's Digger (IRE)**[17] 5807 3-10-8 61.................. MrJMahot(5) 4 64
(M Scudamore) *prom: drvn over 2f out: one pce over 1f out* **12/1**
0166 5 *1/2* **Global Traffic**[10] 6027 3-10-13 61 .... MissEFolkes 3 63
(P D Evans) *hld up: hdwy 2f out: kpt on fnl f: nrst fin* **10/1**
6654 6 *6* **Danzatrice**[16] 5839 5-11-6 61.. MissLEllison 13 54
(C W Thornton) *missed break: bhd tl hdwy 2f out: nvr rchd ldrs* **8/1**[3]
3050 7 *1/2* **Bijou Dan**[68] 4333 6-11-0 62...(p) MrGRSmith(7) 11 54
(D W Thompson) *racd wd in midfield: stdy hdwy 3f out: rdn 2f out: sn btn* **20/1**
054 8 *1/2* **Soul Angel**[11] 5967 3-10-3 51 .... MrCStorey 2 42
(Miss S E Forster) *chsd ldrs tl rdn and wknd over 2fout* **40/1**
1620 9 *2* **English Archer**[47] 4972 4-10-3 49.......................... MrBenBrisbourne(5) 16 37
(W M Brisbourne) *t.k.h: led to over 2f out: wknd over 1f out* **10/1**
0002 10 *3/4* **Chapter (IRE)**[14] 5886 5-10-0 48 oh2............................(p) MrOJMurphy(7) 7 35
(Mrs A L M King) *dwlt: bhd: rdn over 3f out: n.d* **16/1**
2661 11 *1 1/4* **Dispol Peto**[11] 3840 7-10-4 50...................................(vt) MrAMerriam(5) 12 35
(R Johnson) *chsd ldrs: blkd after 3f: rdn and wknd over 2f out* **16/1**
-430 12 *11* **Hunting Haze**[36] 5286 4-10-7 55 .... MrsDWilkinson(7) 6 22
(Miss S E Hall) *in tch tl wknd fr 3f out* **25/1**
4-0P 13 *1 1/2* **Lake Wakatipu**[17] 5807 5-10-10 56 .... MissMMullineaux(5) 1 21
(M Mullineaux) *bhd: pushed along over 4f out: nvr on terms* **50/1**
4621 14 *5* **Lady Pickpocket**[24] 5622 3-10-1 49 .... MissADeniel 5 6
(F P Murtagh) *missed break: a bhd* **16/1**
466- 15 *3* **Champion Lion (IRE)**[525] 1562 8-10-10 51 .... MissRDavidson 10 3
(R Allan) *midfield: rdn over 3f out: sn wknd* **25/1**
02-0 16 *29* **Mutamaasek (USA)**[27] 5531 5-11-4 59 .... MrTGreenall 9 —
(Lady Herries) *in tch tl rdn and wknd fr 3f out* **9/1**
055 U **Mysterious World (IRE)**[26] 5562 3-10-7 60 .... MrCPHuxley(5) 8 —
(Mrs K Walton) *cl up: edgd rt and uns rdr after 3f* **80/1**

2m 53.58s (10.03) **Going Correction** +0.55s/f (Yiel)
WFA 3 from 4yo+ 7lb **17** Ran SP% **127.6**
Speed ratings (Par 101): **88,86,86,85,85 81,81,80,79,78 78,70,69,66,64 45**,—
CSF £22.00 CT £222.61 TOTE £4.30: £1.60, £2.30, £2.80, £3.10; EX 17.20 Place 6 £86.87, Place 5 £59.49..
Owner David Dickson **Bred** Robe Farm Stud **Trained** Sheriff Hutton, N Yorks
■ Stewards' Enquiry : Mr Ben Brisbourne seven-day ban: careless riding (Nov 12,21,27, Dec 3-4,10, Jan 4)

FOCUS
A moderate handicap, confirmed to amateur riders, and run at an ordinary pace. The form looks sound at face value, with the winner capable of better.
T/Jkpt: Not won. T/Plt: £115.20 to a £1 stake. Pool: £61,685.75. 390.65 winning tickets. T/Qpdt: £58.90 to a £1 stake. Pool: £3,678.90. 46.20 winning tickets. RY

6174 **KEMPTON (A.W)** (R-H)

Wednesday, October 17

OFFICIAL GOING: Standard

Wind: Moderate, half-against

6260 TFM NETWORKS H'CAP 1m 2f (P)

6:20 (6:20) (Class 6) (0-60,60) 3-Y-0+ **£2,047** (£604; £302) **Stalls High**

Form RPR

4114 1 **Majehar**[36] 5307 5-9-2 **58** TravisBlock(3) 9 67
(A G Newcombe) *in rr: rdn and hdwy 2f out: swtchd lft ent fnl f: styd on to ld post* **9/2**[1]

0000 2 *hd* **Smokin Joe**[15] 5893 6-9-7 **60** (b) GeorgeBaker 7 69
(J R Best) *in rr: hdwy over 2f out: r.o fnl f: jst failed* **16/1**

0061 3 *shd* **Alfie Tupper (IRE)**[34] 5366 4-9-3 **56** SimonWhitworth 3 64
(S Kirk) *in rr: hdwy on outside over 1f out: r.o fnl f: nvr nrr* **8/1**[3]

4004 4 *shd* **Fateful Attraction**[21] 5733 4-9-6 **59** (b) JamesDoyle 6 67
(I A Wood) *in tch: rdn over 1f out: led ins fnl f: ct by first 3 cl home* **20/1**

0544 5 *1 1/2* **Wee Charlie Castle (IRE)**[63] 4517 4-9-3 **56** (b) OscarUrbina 2 61
(G C H Chung) *in tch: hdwy over 4f out: rdn over 1f out: one pce fnl f* **10/1**

4203 6 *hd* **Sir Haydn**[9] 6068 7-9-6 **59** (v) MickyFenton 13 64
(J R Jenkins) *hld up: t.k.h: effrt 2f out: kpt on fnl f* **9/1**

0230 7 *shd* **Revolve**[126] 2572 7-9-6 **59** (b) IanMongan 12 64
(Mrs L J Mongan) *trckd ldrs: led 2f out: rdn and hdd ins fnl f: no ex* **16/1**

0333 8 *hd* **And Again (USA)**[69] 4327 4-9-4 **57** EddieAhern 8 61
(R A Teal) *sn trckd ldr: led 4f out: rdn and hdd 2f out: wknd ins fnl f* **8/1**[3]

0005 9 *1* **Play Up Pompey**[4] 6179 5-9-2 **55** JimCrowley 4 57+
(J J Bridger) *rrd up s and slowly away: bhd: mde sme late hdwy* **16/1**

130 10 *1 1/2* **Ile Michel**[14] 5916 10-9-4 **60** WilliamBuick(3) 11 59
(Lady Herries) *in tch: rdn over 2f out: wknd over 1f out* **8/1**[3]

000/ 11 *shd* **Leighton (IRE)**[1022] 7000 7-9-7 **60** FergusSweeney 5 59
(M S Saunders) *a towards rr* **50/1**

0303 12 *3 1/2* **Mr Napoleon (IRE)**[36] 5310 5-9-5 **58** JamieSpencer 1 50
(G Prodromou) *hld up: nvr on terms* **7/1**[2]

4003 13 *5* **Greenmeadow**[44] 5094 5-9-2 **55** FrancisNorton 14 37
(S Kirk) *chsd ldrs tl rdn and wknd 3f out* **9/1**

-460 14 *24* **El Dottore**[52] 4858 3-9-2 **60** TQuinn 10 —
(M L W Bell) *led tl rdn and hdd 4f out: sn wknd: t.o* **25/1**

2m 7.47s (-1.53) **Going Correction** -0.125s/f (Stan)
WFA 3 from 4yo+ 5lb **14** Ran SP% **121.3**
Speed ratings (Par 101): **101,100,100,100,99 99,99,99,98,97 97,94,90,71**
CSF £79.14 CT £572.08 TOTE £4.60: £1.50, £4.00, £3.10; EX 65.40.
Owner J R Salter **Bred** Darley **Trained** Yarnscombe, Devon
■ Stewards' Enquiry : Travis Block caution: careless riding

FOCUS
This was not a good event – quality wise – as one of the joint top weights had not been seen since the end of December 2004. However, the race was competitive enough for the grade and the form should work out, despite the first four finishing so close together.
Greenmeadow Official explanation: jockey said mare suffered interference in running

6261 REUTERS FIRST FOR NEWS CLAIMING STKS 1m 3f (P)

6:50 (6:50) (Class 6) 3-Y-0+ **£2,047** (£604; £302) **Stalls High**

Form RPR

5111 1 **Birkside**[11] 6019 4-9-9 70 DavidAllan 2 71
(D Carroll) *hld up in tch: hdwy on outside over 3f out: rdn to ld over 1f out: kpt up to work* **7/2**[2]

3406 2 *1* **Magic Mountain (IRE)**[32] 5422 3-8-12 62 HaddenFrost(5) 11 69
(R Hannon) *led tl rdn and hdd over 1f out: no imp ins fnl f* **15/2**

3442 3 *1/2* **Turner's Touch**[21] 5732 5-9-6 67 (b) RossAtkinson(7) 5 72
(G L Moore) *slowly away: wl in rr tl rdn and hdwy over 2f out: r.o fnl f to go 3rd post* **9/2**[3]

5535 4 *shd* **Laugh 'n Cry**[4] 6175 6-8-8 50 (p) LPKeniry 8 53
(Eoin Doyle, Ire) *t.k.h: in tch: rdn over 1f out: lost 3rd post* **12/1**

1501 5 *3* **Atlantic Gamble (IRE)**[32] 5422 7-9-9 63 (p) FergusSweeney 10 63
(K R Burke) *trckd ldr early: rdn 2f out: fdd appr fnl f* **11/4**[1]

3004 6 *1* **Our Herbie**[23] 5690 3-8-13 58 RichardHughes 7 57
(J W Hills) *t.k.h: in tch tl rdn & outpcd 3f out: styd on one pce fnl f* **8/1**

0540 7 *1 1/2* **Party Palace**[9] 6060 3-8-0 42 AdrianMcCarthy 6 42
(H S Howe) *t.k.h: chsd ldrs: rdn and wknd over 1f out* **50/1**

0000 8 *2 1/2* **Fairy Monarch (IRE)**[5] 6152 8-8-9 42 (p) MickyFenton 1 41
(P T Midgley) *towards rr: rdn 4f out: nvr on terms* **25/1**

3000 9 *1* **Wind Chime (IRE)**[71] 4259 10-8-8 46 TravisBlock(3) 4 41
(A G Newcombe) *t.k.h: chsd ldr after 4f: rdn and wknd over 2f out* **16/1**

002/ 10 *1/2* **Strength 'n Honour**[786] 4639 7-9-10 75 JerryO'Dwyer(3) 9 56
(Karen George) *mid-div: plld hrd: wknd over 2f out* **16/1**

11 *2 1/2* **Forest Emerald (IRE)**[11] 5-9-0 0 JamesDoyle 3 39
(J W Mullins) *in tch tl wknd over 2f out* **80/1**

2m 24.1s (1.42) **Going Correction** -0.125s/f (Stan)
WFA 3 from 4yo+ 6lb **11** Ran SP% **116.4**
Speed ratings (Par 101): **89,88,87,87,85 84,83,82,81,80 79**
CSF £29.38 TOTE £4.10: £1.10, £4.00, £2.00; EX 48.90.
Owner Document Express Ltd **Bred** Pendley Farm **Trained** Sledmere, E Yorks

FOCUS
Not many of these could be seriously fancied on recent evidence and the early gallop was noticeably slow. It only really quickened up as the field turned into the home straight.

6262 DIGIBET.COM MEDIAN AUCTION MAIDEN STKS 1m (P)

7:20 (7:21) (Class 6) 2-Y-O **£2,047** (£604; £302) **Stalls High**

Form RPR

5 1 **King Columbo (IRE)**[39] 5222 2-9-0 0 JerryO'Dwyer(3) 6 70
(Miss J Feilden) *w ldrs: rdn wl over 1f out: drvn to ld cl home* **12/1**

00 2 *1/2* **Ablaan (USA)**[35] 5321 2-9-3 0 JamieSpencer 5 69
(M F De Kock, South Africa) *s.i.s: sn in tch: hdwy over 2f out: rdn to go 2nd post* **5/1**[2]

52 3 *shd* **Funseeker (UAE)**[8] 6080 2-8-12 0 GregFairley 1 64
(M Johnston) *chsd ldrs: rdn over 2f out: r.o fnl f* **11/8**[1]

00 4 *hd* **Appointment**[13] 5944 2-8-12 0 JimCrowley 7 64
(Mrs A J Perrett) *a.p: rdn to ld 2f out: hdd wl ins fnl f: no ex nr fin* **16/1**

5 *shd* **Rondeau (GR)** 2-9-3 0 PaulDoe 10 68
(P R Chamings) *v.s.a: in rr: hdwy and swtchd rt to outside over 1f out: fin wl: nvr nrr* **33/1**

5 6 *1 3/4* **Bluebell Ridge (IRE)**[21] 5727 2-8-12 0 JamesDoyle 14 59
(D W P Arbuthnot) *led tl hung lft and hdd 2f out: one pce after* **16/1**

7 *nk* **Fair Gale** 2-9-3 0 RichardHughes 12 64+
(S Kirk) *slowly away: sn mid-div: hdwy 2f out: eased whn hld ins fnl f: sddle slipped* **13/2**

00 8 *hd* **It's Josr**[14] 5895 2-9-3 0 AdamKirby 4 63
(I A Wood) *in rr tl hdwy over 2f out: fdd ins fnl f* **66/1**

0 9 *1 1/4* **Sendefaa (IRE)**[36] 5301 2-8-12 0 OscarUrbina 11 56
(M Botti) *trckd ldrs: wkng whn hmpd ins fnl f* **6/1**[3]

0 10 *2 1/2* **Lady Charlemagne**[130] 2457 2-8-12 0 StephenDonohoe 3 50
(N P Littmoden) *in tch: rdn 3f out: sn btn* **100/1**

11 *hd* **Oriental Girl** 2-8-12 0 RichardThomas 9 50
(J A Geake) *s.i.s and sn outpcd* **50/1**

0 12 *3 1/2* **Ba Dreamflight**[14] 5895 2-9-0 0 TravisBlock(3) 2 47
(H Morrison) *sn rdn: a bhd* **25/1**

00 13 *2 1/2* **Faraami (IRE)**[32] 5428 2-8-12 0 PatDobbs 13 37
(Pat Eddery) *mid-div: rdn 1/2-way: wknd over 2f out* **66/1**

14 *1 1/2* **Amicus** 2-8-12 0 TQuinn 8 33
(D K Ivory) *rdn 1/2-way: a bhd* **33/1**

1m 41.34s (0.54) **Going Correction** -0.125s/f (Stan) **14** Ran SP% **121.5**
Speed ratings (Par 93): **92,91,91,91,91 89,89,88,87,85 84,81,78,77**
CSF £69.30 TOTE £13.90: £3.80, £2.20, £1.10; EX 55.70.
Owner Columbian Kings **Bred** Don Commins **Trained** Exning, Suffolk

FOCUS
As they hit the final furlong pole, it seemed unlikely that Appointment would be caught. However, she wavered in the latter stages and got caught by three rivals close to the line. Not an easy race to assess, but in all likelihood a pretty ordinary affair.

NOTEBOOK
King Columbo(IRE), fifth over 7f on his debut here, just outstayed his rivals once hitting full stride. He looks like a horse that will stay well next season.
Ablaan(USA) had only shown a bit of promise on the track before and came very close to breaking his maiden tag. A similar event is within his grasp. (op 13-2)
Funseeker(UAE) was not going anywhere quickly rounding the home bend, but she kept on well once straightened out and was staying on passing the line. (tchd 5-4)
Appointment, who travelled well during the race, should be capable of going even closer next time with more exaggerated waiting tactics.
Rondeau(GR), who started very slowly, absolutely flew home after being anchored towards the rear early. He ought to come on for the experience. Official explanation: jockey said gelding missed the break
Bluebell Ridge(IRE) was the early leader but looked most reluctant when placed under pressure. Official explanation: jockey said filly hung left-handed
Fair Gale hinted at ability and was not beaten far. Official explanation: jockey said saddle slipped (op 7-1)
It's Josr made good headway up the home straight after being towards the back of the field early. He can be found a race now he is qualified for a handicap.
Sendefaa(IRE) had every chance but still looked green when asked to quicken. (op 4-1)
Oriental Girl ran better than her final position suggests. (op 66-1)

6263 DIGIBET CASINO NURSERY 6f (P)

7:50 (7:50) (Class 6) (0-65,71) 2-Y-O **£2,047** (£604; £302) **Stalls High**

Form RPR

0005 1 **High Standing (USA)**[28] 5541 2-9-2 **60** JamieSpencer 12 77+
(N A Callaghan) *a in tch and gng wl: led on bit over 1f out: qcknd clr: easily* **3/1**[2]

0022 2 *3 1/2* **Southwest Star (IRE)**[7] 6098 2-9-6 **64** LPKeniry 7 66
(J S Moore) *in tch: led briefly wl over 1f out: hung lft and no ch w wnr fnl f* **6/1**[3]

6040 3 *1 1/2* **Valentino Sky (USA)**[16] 5871 2-9-7 **65** (b[1]) JamesDoyle 10 63
(N P Littmoden) *hmpd leaving stalls: towards rr: hdwy over 1f out: kpt on fnl f* **14/1**

0641 4 *2 1/2* **Gipsy Prince**[7] 6098 2-9-13 **71** 6ex JimmyQuinn 2 61
(M G Quinlan) *bmpd s: sn mid-div: kpt on one pce ins fnl f* **2/1**[1]

3001 5 *3/4* **Spinning Ridge (IRE)**[9] 6065 2-9-2 **65** 6ex KevinGhunowa(5) 8 53+
(R A Harris) *outpcd: mde sme late hdwy* **10/1**

0055 6 *nk* **Alabama Spirit (USA)**[7] 6098 2-9-4 **62** GeorgeBaker 3 49
(D Shaw) *wnt lft s: towards rr tl mde sme late hdwy* **14/1**

006 7 *3* **Joss Stick**[15] 5888 2-8-13 **57** EddieAhern 9 35
(P J Makin) *prom tl hung lft and wknd over 1f out* **25/1**

3300 8 *1/2* **Cordon Bleu (IRE)**[19] 5773 2-9-4 **62** GregFairley 4 38
(M Johnston) *led tl rdn and hdd wl over 1f out: sn btn* **12/1**

0020 9 *2* **Don't Tell Anna (IRE)**[15] 5887 2-9-0 **58** RichardHughes 11 28
(R Hannon) *wnt lft leaving stalls: a bhd* **16/1**

0000 10 *nk* **Battlecruiser (IRE)**[41] 5153 2-8-12 **56** RoystonFfrench 5 25
(M Johnston) *outpcd: a bhd* **16/1**

0060 11 *hd* **Eastbourne**[18] 5818 2-8-11 **55** StephenCarson 6 24
(Eve Johnson Houghton) *in tch tl wknd 2f out* **80/1**

064 12 *3* **Madame Rio (IRE)**[18] 5801 2-9-7 **65** SebSanders 1 25
(K R Burke) *mid-div: rdn and wknd over 2f out* **33/1**

1m 12.71s (-0.99) **Going Correction** -0.125s/f (Stan) **12** Ran SP% **122.5**
Speed ratings (Par 93): **101,96,94,91,90 89,85,84,82,81 81,77**
CSF £22.10 CT £229.50 TOTE £5.30: £1.90, £2.90, £5.40; EX 35.90.
Owner SP Racing Investments S A **Bred** Dr Melinda Blue **Trained** Newmarket, Suffolk

FOCUS
The contest was effectively over a furlong from home as High Standing raced clear of his rivals. He was value for more than the winning distance. The placed horses set a fair standard and the form looks solid.

NOTEBOOK
High Standing(USA) ◆, raised from an official mark of 38 to 60 after his effort last time in maiden company, looks to be improving quickly and would be difficult to beat next time. The winning time was very good, which makes the form look reasonably sound for the grade. (op 11-4 tchd 5-2)
Southwest Star(IRE) has picked up a nasty habit of finishing second but, to be fair, he did little wrong and had no chance against an easy winner. (op 9-1)
Valentino Sky(USA), wearing blinkers for the first time, was held up in rear and kept on at the one pace up the home straight. Seven furlongs will probably be his trip. Official explanation: jockey said colt was hampered at the start (tchd 16-1)
Gipsy Prince, who finished in front of tonight's runner-up when winning here last week, looked anchored by his big weight and could not quicken when asked a serious question. (tchd 9-4)
Spinning Ridge(IRE) is just an ordinary sort and merely kept plugging away for pressure. (op 8-1)
Alabama Spirit(USA) was well weighted with Gipsy Prince on their running last week but failed to make any impact from off the pace.
Battlecruiser(IRE) Official explanation: jockey said colt was never travelling

6264 DIGIBET SPORTS BETTING H'CAP 6f (P)

8:20 (8:20) (Class 6) (0-52,52) 3-Y-O+ **£2,047** (£604; £302) **Stalls High**

Form RPR

0-03 1 **Ruman (IRE)**[123] 2664 5-9-0 **52** IanMongan 8 69+
(M J Attwater) *in tch: led over 1f out: sn clr: easily* **5/1**[3]

0530 **2** 3 1/2 **Davids Mark**13 5947 7-8-9 **50** WilliamBuick(3) 12 55
(J R Jenkins) *hmpd after 1f: hdwy on ins over 2f out: rdn and chsd wnr fnl f* **7/1**

4502 **3** 1 1/2 **Mister Elegant**14 5897 5-9-0 **52** FrancisNorton 5 52
(J L Spearing) *in rr: rdn over 2f out: r.o fnl f: nvr nrr* **7/2**1

50 **4** 1/2 **Majestical (IRE)**47 5016 5-9-0 **52** (p) JamieSpencer 9 51
(V Smith) *slowly away: hdwy over 1f out: styd on: nvr nrr* **4/1**2

0000 **5** 1/2 **Land Ahoy**42 5134 3-8-13 **52** FergusSweeney 4 49
(D W P Arbuthnot) *bhd: rdn 1/2-way: mde sme late hdwy* **50/1**

0005 **6** 1 **Sovereignty (JPN)**14 5900 5-9-0 **52** JimCrowley 3 46
(D K Ivory) *prom tl rdn and wknd wl over 1f out* **7/1**

3000 **7** 1/2 **Titian Saga (IRE)**3 6210 4-8-12 **50** (bt) TGMcLaughlin 7 43
(C N Allen) *chsd ldrs tl hung bdly lft 2f out* **16/1**

1000 **8** 1 1/2 **Limonia (GER)**8 6089 5-8-7 **50** KevinGhunowa(5) 11 38
(Mike Murphy) *chsd ldrs tl rdn and wknd 2f out* **10/1**

0003 **9** 3 **Navigation (IRE)**12 5969 5-8-9 **50** (b) PJMcDonald(3) 10 29
(T J Etherington) *broke wl: hmpd after 1f: styd prom on ins tl wknd 2f out* **14/1**

0004 **10** 6 **King Egbert (FR)**13 5947 6-8-7 **50** (p) TolleyDean(5) 1 11
(R J Price) *prom on outside tl rdn and wknd 2f out* **20/1**

4460 **11** 4 **Sir Loin**13 5946 6-8-12 **50** (v) TQuinn 6 —
(P Burgoyne) *led tl rdn and hdd over 1f out: wknd qckly* **20/1**

1m 12.43s (-1.27) **Going Correction** -0.125s/f (Stan)
WFA 3 from 4yo+ 1lb **11** Ran SP% **117.0**
Speed ratings (Par 101): **103,98,96,95,95 93,93,91,87,79 73**
CSF £38.71 CT £141.27 TOTE £8.40: £3.10, £2.30, £1.80; EX 41.40.
Owner The Attwater Partnership **Bred** Noel And Michael Buckley **Trained** Epsom, Surrey
■ Stewards' Enquiry : T Quinn three-day ban: careless riding (Oct 29-31)

FOCUS
Quite a few of these did not look badly treated on their best efforts, so the form should be quite reliable for the lowly grade. The time was under standard once again.
Majestical(IRE) Official explanation: jockey said gelding missed the break
Sir Loin Official explanation: jockey said gelding had been hanging right; trainer said gelding was found to be dehydrated after the race

6265 REUTERS FIRST FOR NEWS H'CAP — 1m 4f (P)
8:50 (8:50) (Class 6) (0-55,60) 3-Y-0+ — **£2,047** (£604; £302) **Stalls** Low

Form RPR

0431 **1** **Polyquest (IRE)**4 6178 3-9-1 **60** 6ex WilliamBuick(3) 12 71+
(G A Butler) *hld up: hdwy 2f out: led 1f out: pushed out* **2/1**1

2412 **2** 3/4 **Bridgewater Boys**7 6102 6-9-4 **53** (b) GeorgeBaker 11 61
(G L Moore) *hld up in tch: led 2f out: edgd lft and hdd 1f out: kpt on one pce* **11/4**2

5304 **3** 1 1/4 **Recalcitrant**25 5636 4-9-6 **55** SebSanders 7 61
(S Dow) *trckd ldrs: rdn and ev ch appr fnl f: one pce after* **8/1**3

6640 **4** shd **Andorran (GER)**26 5586 4-8-9 **47** (b) NeilChalmers(3) 6 53
(A Bailey) *hld up: t.k.h: hdwy 2f out: styd on one pce: nvr nrr* **25/1**

0030 **5** hd **Autograph Hunter**11 6026 3-8-11 **53** LPKeniry 10 58
(Peter Grayson) *hld up in rr: mde late hdwy* **33/1**

0005 **6** shd **Lord Laing (USA)**35 5341 4-8-11 **46** PatDobbs 9 51
(H J Collingridge) *mid-div: styd on ins fnl 2f* **16/1**

0363 **7** 1 1/2 **Anything Once (USA)**1 6250 4-8-13 **48** (b) StephenDonohoe 13 51
(D Carroll) *mid-div: effrt on ins over 1f out: fdd ins fnl f* **10/1**

0060 **8** 1 **Tabulate**28 5531 4-9-1 **50** JimmyQuinn 2 51
(P Howling) *slowly away: t.k.h: in rr tl sme late hdwy* **50/1**

060- **9** 7 **Meantime (USA)**346 5770 4-8-10 **52** (p) CharlotteKerton(7) 14 42
(G Prodromou) *a in rr* **100/1**

6205 **10** 1/2 **Missie Baileys**32 5421 5-8-11 **46** (p) IanMongan 5 35
(Mrs L J Mongan) *mid-div: rdn 3f out: wknd over 2f out* **16/1**

0200 **11** 1/2 **Ardent Prince**34 5364 4-9-4 **53** GrahamGibbons 3 41
(Heather Dalton) *plld hrd: led for 1f: in tch tl wknd over 1f out* **50/1**

0003 **12** 2 1/2 **Divine River**23 5690 4-9-6 **55** TPO'Shea 8 39
(J G Portman) *in rr tl hdwy to ld over 4f out: hung lft and hdd 2f out: sn btn* **33/1**

2005 **13** 12 **Key Partners (IRE)**32 5422 6-9-6 **55** JimCrowley 4 20
(P A Blockley) *led after 4f: hdd over 4f out: rdn 3f out: wknd 2f out: eased* **20/1**

4002 **14** 7 **Playtotheaudience**11 6019 4-9-1 **50** (b) TonyHamilton 1 4
(R A Fahey) *led after 1f: hdd after 4f: wknd over 2f out: eased* **10/1**

2m 34.15s (-2.75) **Going Correction** -0.125s/f (Stan)
WFA 3 from 4yo+ 7lb **14** Ran SP% **120.5**
Speed ratings (Par 101): **104,103,102,102,102 102,101,100,96,95 95,93,85,81**
CSF £6.63 CT £36.75 TOTE £2.60: £1.60, £1.40, £2.00; EX 6.30.
Owner The Fairy Story Partnership **Bred** Deepwood Farm Stud **Trained** Blewbury, Oxon

FOCUS
Plenty of these were long-standing maidens or without a win for some considerable amount of time, but the winning time was good again. The form seems solid and should work out.

6266 BARRETTSTOWN STUD CLASSIFIED STKS — 1m (P)
9:20 (9:20) (Class 6) 3-Y-0+ — **£2,047** (£604; £302) **Stalls** High

Form RPR

5002 **1** **Ours (IRE)**28 5525 4-9-3 53 SebSanders 7 60
(John A Harris) *t.k.h: a.p: led 2f out: hung lft ins fnl f: hld on* **4/1**1

0002 **2** 1/2 **Royal Envoy (IRE)**21 5730 4-9-3 50 GeorgeBaker 5 59+
(D Shaw) *in rr: rdn and hdwy appr fnl f: r.o to go 2nd nr fin* **6/1**3

4443 **3** nk **Shunkawakhan (IRE)**21 5730 4-9-3 47 (p) OscarUrbina 13 58
(G C H Chung) *chsd ldrs: styd on ins fnl f* **8/1**

5343 **4** hd **Hills Place**7 6100 3-9-0 54 JamieSpencer 6 58
(J R Best) *hld up in rr: hdwy on outside 2f out: r.o fnl f* **9/2**2

3234 **5** hd **Brave Jack (IRE)**13 5946 3-8-11 49 WilliamBuick(3) 4 57
(J R Best) *in tch: ev ch whn bmpd ins fnl f: no ex after* **6/1**3

4063 **6** 1 1/4 **Roman Boy (ARG)**7 6096 8-8-12 50 TolleyDean(5) 8 54+
(Stef Liddiard) *in rr: rdn and hdwy over 1f out: nvr nr to chal* **4/1**1

0653 **7** 1/2 **Golden Brown (IRE)**26 5602 3-9-0 55 FergusSweeney 3 53
(David Pinder) *trckd ldrs: rdn over 1f out: wknd ins fnl f* **18/1**

4000 **8** 2 **James Street (IRE)**2 6226 4-9-3 55 LPKeniry 14 48
(Peter Grayson) *trckd ldrs tl rdn and wknd 2f out* **16/1**

6205 **9** nk **Laphonic (USA)**14 5897 4-9-3 47 (b) GregFairley 9 48
(T J Etherington) *mid-div: rdn over 2f out: sn btn* **16/1**

-065 **10** 3/4 **Axis Mundi (IRE)**21 5728 3-8-11 47 PJMcDonald(3) 10 46
(T J Etherington) *w ldrs tl rdn and wknd wl over 1f out* **50/1**

3000 **11** nk **Winds Of Kildare (IRE)**35 5336 4-9-3 45 (t) StephenDonohoe 11 45
(C N Allen) *mid-div: rdn over 2f out: sn wknd* **80/1**

2000 **12** 1 **Indian Sundance (IRE)**19 5782 4-9-3 44 (t) JimCrowley 1 43
(K R Burke) *led tl hdd 2f out: wknd ent fnl f* **50/1**

0000 **13** 7 **Keagles (ITY)**14 5898 4-8-12 40 NataliaGemelova(5) 12 27
(J E Long) *a in rr* **40/1**

1m 40.64s (-0.16) **Going Correction** -0.125s/f (Stan)
WFA 3 from 4yo+ 3lb **13** Ran SP% **122.5**
Speed ratings (Par 101): **95,94,94,94,93 92,92,90,89,89 88,87,80**
CSF £28.48 TOTE £4.10: £2.10, £1.90, £2.90; EX 28.80 Place 6 £29.37, Place 5 £11.17..
Owner D A Spencer **Bred** David John Brown **Trained** Eastwell, Leics

FOCUS
A moderate race that was steadily run, but probably fair form for the grade.
Hills Place Official explanation: jockey said gelding hung left-handed
T/Plt: £21.90 to a £1 stake. Pool: £64,535.85. 2,145.55 winning tickets. T/Qpdt: £6.20 to a £1 stake. Pool: £5,133.30. 611.00 winning tickets. JS

6225 LINGFIELD (L-H)
Wednesday, October 17

OFFICIAL GOING: Standard
Wind: fresh against Weather: bright partly cloudy

6267 DAWSON NEWS E B F MAIDEN STKS — 7f (P)
2:20 (2:21) (Class 5) 2-Y-O — **£3,465** (£1,030; £515; £257) **Stalls** Low

Form RPR

1 **Whispered Dreams (GER)** 2-8-12 0 LDettori 3 75+
(Saeed Bin Suroor) *racd keenly: led for 2f: w ldr after tl shkn up to ld 1f out: sn in command: readily* **10/11**1

020 **2** 2 **Our Chairman (IRE)**21 5720 2-9-3 76 RyanMoore 1 73
(R Hannon) *dwlt: sn pushed up to chse ldr: led after 2f: rdn 2f out: hdd 1f out: kpt on but no ch w wnr* **6/1**2

053 **3** 1/2 **Sweet Hope (USA)**25 5628 2-8-12 78 NCallan 4 67
(K A Ryan) *in tch: hdwy to chse ldng pair: sn rdn and hung rt: kpt on but nvr pce to trble ldrs* **8/1**3

4 1/2 **Southpaw Lad** 2-9-3 0 DaneO'Neill 8 70+
(J R Best) *s.i.s: t.k.h: hld up in rr: hdwy on outer 2f out: plld out wl over 1f out: r.o wl: nt rch ldrs* **66/1**

55 **5** 1 3/4 **Game Park (USA)**19 5771 2-9-3 0 OscarUrbina 5 66+
(J R Fanshawe) *hld up in midfield: rdn wl over 1f out: kpt on but nt pce to trble ldrs* **16/1**

6 **6** 1 1/2 **Wannabe Free**28 5540 2-8-12 0 TPQueally 6 57+
(J Noseda) *hld up towards rr: effrt and n.m.r wl over 1f out: kpt on but nvr nr ldrs* **10/1**

3200 **7** nk **Dhhamaan (IRE)**12 5974 2-9-3 83 RichardHughes 10 61
(C E Brittain) *in tch: rdn 3f out: wknd wl over 1f out* **12/1**

8 1 3/4 **Hla Tun (USA)** 2-9-3 0 AdamKirby 13 57
(W R Swinburn) *s.i.s: hld up bhd: hdwy on rail wl over 1f out: sme late hdwy: n.d* **25/1**

9 nk **Solemn** 2-9-3 0 SebSanders 9 56
(Sir Mark Prescott) *chsd ldrs: rdn over 4f out: wknd 2f out* **16/1**

0 **10** 2 **Ski Sunday**15 5880 2-9-3 0 PhilipRobinson 12 51
(M A Jarvis) *t.k.h: chsd ldrs on outer: rdn and wknd over 2f out* **25/1**

20 **11** nk **Toasted Special (USA)**13 5949 2-8-12 0 StephenDonohoe 7 45
(B J Meehan) *s.i.s: a last trio: rdn 3f out: no prog* **25/1**

12 1 **Hennessy Island (USA)** 2-9-3 0 SteveDrowne 2 47
(T G Mills) *s.i.s: sn in midfield: rdn and wknd over 2f out* **20/1**

1m 26.24s (0.35) **Going Correction** -0.075s/f (Stan) **12** Ran SP% **124.1**
Speed ratings (Par 95): **95,92,92,91,89 87,87,85,85,82 82,81**
CSF £6.27 TOTE £1.80: £1.20, £2.30, £2.10; EX 9.10 Trifecta £33.90 Pool £336.39 - 7.04 winning units..
Owner Godolphin **Bred** Gestut Romerhof **Trained** Newmarket, Suffolk

FOCUS
An ordinary maiden in which a couple had some placed form against their names. Very few ever got into it and the winning time was nothing to get excited about, but a couple of these are entitled to improve.

NOTEBOOK
Whispered Dreams(GER), a 110,000euros sister to a high-class winner in Italy, was up there all the way alongside the runner-up and was in the better position on the outside of the pair. She picked up really well when asked in the home straight and with improvement likely, should go on to better things. She should have no problem getting an extra furlong. (op 11-10 tchd 5-4)
Our Chairman(IRE), very disappointing when stepped up to this trip at Goodwood, was not ridden as though he was regarded a non-stayer but he was always racing against the inside rail and that would not have been a help to him in the home straight. He was probably up against an above-average newcomer in any case, and he was not beaten because he did not stay. (tchd 7-1)
Sweet Hope(USA) stayed on over the last couple of furlongs, but was never getting there in time. On a line through the runner-up she did not quite run up to her mark, but she shapes as though she would appreciate going up in trip again. (tchd 15-2)
Southpaw Lad ◆, out of a half-sister to five winners including Missile and Anyhow, took a while to realise what was required but was noted finishing in great style down the outside. The market did not suggest that he was expected at the first time of asking and with the stable's record at the track, he should be placed to advantage before long.
Game Park(USA), taking another step up in trip on this switch to sand, could not get to the principals but now qualifies for a mark so it would not be a surprise to see him step up in that sphere.
Wannabe Free was again going her best work late without looking like figuring in the finish. Her half-brother King Of Argos scored at up to 1m2f and she shapes as though she will appreciate a bit further than this too. (op 8-1)
Hennessy Island(USA) Official explanation: jockey said colt had no more to give

6268 PAUL RAYMOND PUBLICATIONS CLAIMING STKS — 7f (P)
2:50 (2:50) (Class 6) 3-Y-0+ — **£2,047** (£604; £302) **Stalls** Low

Form RPR

2131 **1** **Samuel Charles**11 6024 9-9-0 70 (p) JohnEgan 11 70
(C R Dore) *in tch: hdwy to chse ldr over 2f out: rdn to ld ins fnl f: in command after: pushed out* **6/4**1

5604 **2** 3/4 **Katiypour (IRE)**35 5339 10-8-12 66 TQuinn 9 66
(P Mitchell) *racd in midfield: hdwy on outer over 2f out: r.o over 1f out: wnt 2nd ins fnl f: nt rch wnr* **10/3**2

4050 **3** 1 1/4 **Chalentina**14 5897 4-8-1 49 JimmyQuinn 4 52
(P Howling) *led for 1f: chsd ldr tl led over 2f out: sn rdn: hdd ins fnl f: sn outpcd by wnr* **25/1**

0045 **4** hd **Mineral Star (IRE)**11 6024 5-9-2 72 (v) SebSanders 12 66
(M H Tompkins) *racd in midfield: rdn and hdwy on outer 2f out: styd on fnl f: nvr able to chal* **9/2**3

0450 **5** 3/4 **Izabela Hannah**26 5602 3-8-1 56 (b) FrancisNorton 14 51
(R M Beckett) *chsd ldrs: rdn 3f out: kpt on same pce 'ast 2f* **20/1**

0056 **6** ½ **Mozakhraf (USA)**[9] 6064 5-9-6 64 NCallan 2 67
(K A Ryan) *taken down early: t.k.h: chsd ldrs: rdn and wknd over 1f out* **8/1**

0400 **7** ¾ **Pivotal Era**[5] 6148 4-9-0 64 RichardThomas 13 59
(Jim Best) *stdd s: hld up bhd: rdn and effrt over 1f out: no imp fnl f* **25/1**

2000 **8** 1 ¾ **Windy Prospect**[16] 5864 5-8-8 55 (p) PaulDoe 8 48
(Mrs L J Mongan) *bhd: early reminders: sme hdwy u.p on outer over 2f out: sn no imp* **25/1**

0600 **9** 2 ½ **Rafferty (IRE)**[88] 3730 8-8-2 48 ow3 ThomasBubb[(7)] 7 42
(S Dow) *s.i.s: nvr nr ldrs* **33/1**

0004 **10** 5 **Tipsy Lad**[18] 5817 5-8-6 48 (vt) ChrisCatlin 3 26
(D J S Ffrench Davis) *bhd and rdn over 4f out: nvr on terms* **25/1**

0-0 **11** 1 ¾ **Mujobliged (IRE)**[18] 5817 4-8-13 47 (t) JerryO'Dwyer[(3)] 5 31
(Seamus G O'Donnell, Ire) *chsd ldrs tl rdn 3f out: sn wknd* **33/1**

03-0 **12** 3 **Captain Darling (IRE)**[112] 2990 7-8-10 57 SamHitchcott 10 17
(R W Price) *racd in midfield on outer: rdn over 4f out: wknd 3f out* **50/1**

0000 **13** 1 **Da Schadenfreude (USA)**[20] 1561 3-8-4 50 RichardMullen 1 10
(W G M Turner) *led after 1f: rdn and hdd over 2f out: sn wknd* **66/1**

1m 25.62s (-0.27) **Going Correction** -0.075s/f (Stan)
WFA 3 from 4yo+ 2lb **13** Ran SP% **121.9**
Speed ratings (Par 101): **98,97,95,95,94 94,93,91,88,82 80,77,76**
CSF £5.52 TOTE £2.50: £1.10, £1.70, £7.90; EX 7.90 Trifecta £102.20 Pool £295.12 - 2.05 winning units..Chalentina was claimed by T H Bambridge for £5,000.
Owner Chris Marsh **Bred** Sheikh Mohammed Obaid Al Maktoum **Trained** West Pinchbeck, Lincs

FOCUS
A routine Polytrack claimer contested by the usual suspects and the result was very much in line with adjusted official ratings. The form looks sound enough but is unlikely to mean much outside this level.
Captain Darling(IRE) Official explanation: vet said gelding finished lame

6269 MENZIES DISTRIBUTION H'CAP 1m (P)
3:25 (3:26) (Class 5) (0-75,75) 3-Y-0+ **£2,817** (£838; £418; £209) **Stalls** High

Form RPR

266 **1** **Pendulum Star**[131] 2428 3-9-3 71 AdamKirby 2 86+
(W R Swinburn) *hld in midfield: swtchd off rail over 3f out: hdwy over 2f out: rdn over 1f out: rn to ld ins fnl f: readily* **13/2**[3]

2102 **2** 1 ¼ **Reeling N' Rocking (IRE)**[35] 5339 4-9-1 69 WilliamBuick[(3)] 6 78
(B W Hills) *hld up towards rr: hdwy on outer 3f out: rdn to ld and edgd lft over 1f out: hdd ins fnl f: nt pce of wnr* **9/2**[1]

3060 **3** ¾ **Scarlet Flyer (USA)**[22] 5712 4-9-6 71 RyanMoore 12 78
(G L Moore) *hld up in last: hdwy wl over 2f out: chsd ldrs 2f out: swtchd rt over 1f out: styd on to chse ldng pair ins fnl f: kpt on* **8/1**

1660 **4** 2 ½ **King's Ransom**[19] 5777 4-9-2 67 IanMongan 7 69
(S Gollings) *chsd ldrs: wnt 2nd over 2f out: ev ch and hung rt bnd 2f out: short of room briefly over 1f out: wknd ins fnl f* **33/1**

6620 **5** hd **Reballo (IRE)**[35] 5339 4-9-3 68 NCallan 8 69
(J R Fanshawe) *bhd early hdwy into midfield after 2f: rdn and effrt on outer over 2f out: kpt on same pce fnl f* **11/2**[2]

2400 **6** ½ **Highland Harvest**[8] 6081 3-9-6 74 TQuinn 5 74
(D R C Elsworth) *trckd ldrs: rdn wl over 1f out: wknd 1f out* **12/1**

633 **7** 1 **Tom Paris**[30] 5475 3-9-4 72 RichardMullen 10 70
(W R Muir) *hld up bhd: effrt on inner 2f out: wknd 1f out* **8/1**

0030 **8** 2 **Meditation**[2] 6232 5-9-3 68 JamesDoyle 9 61
(I A Wood) *led for 2f: led again over 3f out: rdn over 2f out: hdd over 1f out: sn wknd* **16/1**

5336 **9** 1 ½ **Practicallyperfect (IRE)**[52] 4847 3-9-7 75 (v[1]) SebSanders 11 65
(P D Evans) *chsd ldrs on outer: rdn 3f out: wknd over 2f out* **8/1**

5040 **10** 1 ¼ **Very Well Red**[9] 6063 4-9-2 67 ChrisCatlin 4 54
(P W Hiatt) *in tch: rdn over 3f out: wl bhd last 2f* **20/1**

0000 **11** nk **Minos (IRE)**[9] 6063 3-9-0 68 RichardHughes 1 54
(R Hannon) *sn rdn up to chse ldrs: rdn over 3f out: sn lost pl: no ch last 2f* **12/1**

4-10 **12** 31 **Atraas (IRE)**[125] 2598 3-9-7 75 RHills 3 —
(M P Tregoning) *chsd ldr tl led after 2f: hdd over 3f out: wknd qckly over 2f out: virtually p.u fnl f* **7/1**

1m 38.24s (-1.19) **Going Correction** -0.075s/f (Stan)
WFA 3 from 4yo+ 3lb **12** Ran SP% **121.7**
Speed ratings (Par 103): **102,100,100,97,97 96,95,93,92,91 90,59**
CSF £36.84 CT £248.13 TOTE £8.00: £2.30, £1.90, £3.40; EX 33.20 Trifecta £250.90 Part won. Pool £353.44..
Owner Spirit Of Racing **Bred** Mrs F Denniff **Trained** Aldbury, Herts
■ Stewards' Enquiry : William Buick caution: careless riding
Richard Hughes one-day ban: used whip when out of contention (Oct 29)

FOCUS
A modest handicap, though fairly competitive. The pace was solid enough and the front three all came from off the pace. Sound form.
Atraas(IRE) Official explanation: jockey said gelding had breathing problems

6270 NEWS INTERNATIONAL E B F CONDITIONS STKS 6f (P)
3:55 (3:55) (Class 4) 2-Y-0 **£4,533** (£1,348; £674; £336) **Stalls** Low

Form RPR

5350 **1** **Kylayne**[26] 5583 2-8-13 89 JohnEgan 6 85
(P W D'Arcy) *wnt lft s: sn chsng ldrs: led over 2f out: edgd rt fnl f but r.o wl* **7/1**

1055 **2** ½ **Ernie Owl (USA)**[11] 6001 2-9-4 91 (b) SteveDrowne 8 89
(B J Meehan) *t.k.h: chsd ldrs on outer: rdn 2f out: chsd wnr ins fnl f: a hld* **5/2**[2]

4004 **3** 1 ¼ **Aide Memoir (IRE)**[14] 5922 2-8-9 93 RyanMoore 4 76
(S Kirk) *mostly chsd ldr: chsd wnr and rdn jst over 2f out: one pce and lost 2nd ins fnl f* **9/4**[1]

10 **4** 2 **Swallow Star**[95] 3550 2-8-9 77 JamesDoyle 5 70
(R M Beckett) *short of room s: in tch: rdn and outpcd 2f out: kpt on* **16/1**

1000 **5** nk **Little Knickers**[11] 6004 2-8-13 75 JimCrowley 7 73
(Andrew Reid) *bhd: rdn wl over 2f out: kpt on fnl f: nvr trbld ldrs* **33/1**

5561 **6** 3 ½ **Sharps Gold**[42] 5133 2-8-6 51 (t) LukeMorris[(3)] 9 58
(P J McBride) *stdd s: t.k.h: hld up in last: rdn and effrt wl over 1f out: no hdwy* **50/1**

3041 **7** 1 **May Day Queen (IRE)**[91] 3648 2-8-13 83 DaneO'Neill 1 59
(R Hannon) *in tch in midfield: hanging bdly lft over 3f out: n.d after* **4/1**[3]

0520 **8** 2 ½ **Pha Mai Blue**[16] 5856 2-8-11 81 TQuinn 3 50
(W J Knight) *led tl over 2f out: wknd wl over 1f out* **9/1**

1m 13.33s (0.52) **Going Correction** -0.075s/f (Stan) **8** Ran SP% **112.6**
Speed ratings (Par 97): **93,92,90,88,87 82,81,78**
CSF £24.12 TOTE £8.90: £1.50, £1.80, £1.40; EX 20.70 Trifecta £81.70 Pool £366.35 - 3.18 winning unit..
Owner Mrs Jan Harris **Bred** D P And Mrs J A Martin **Trained** Newmarket, Suffolk

FOCUS
A race dominated by the three runners best in at the weights. The form looks best rated through the fourth, fifth and sixth.

NOTEBOOK
Kylayne, running on the All-Weather for the first time, was taking a drop in class having contested Listed races on her previous two starts. Kicked for home off the final bend, she was always holding Ernie Owl's late challenge and probably did not have to be at her very best to win this. She now goes to the sales. (tchd 8-1)
Ernie Owl(USA), dropping back in distance having not got home over a mile last time, was again a bit too keen in the blinkers, but he had every chance in the straight and sprinting looks the way to go with him. (tchd 3-1)
Aide Memoir(IRE), officially best in at the weights, was another making her All-Weather debut. She was not helped by racing next to the inside rail the whole way up the straight and in the circumstances she ran a fair race. Her rating probably flatters her on this evidence, though. (op 15-8 tchd 5-2 in a place)
Swallow Star, not seen since July, ran quite well on this step up in class considering that she was the least experienced runner in the line-up. She should not go up in the weights for this, though, as she finished just under four lengths in front of a rival rated just 51.
Little Knickers arguably ran her best race to date on the All-Weather, but she was never a threat to the principals.
May Day Queen(IRE), who beat subsequent Listed race winner Fashion Rocks in a maiden here back in July, had been absent since and this was a very disappointing comeback run as she hung badly left for much of the race. Official explanation: jockey said filly hung left (op 7-2)
Pha Mai Blue, who made the running, was stuck on the deeper stuff near the inside rail throughout. (op 10-1)

6271 HIGGS INTERNATIONAL H'CAP 2m (P)
4:30 (4:30) (Class 6) (0-65,63) 3-Y-0+ **£2,047** (£604; £302) **Stalls** Low

Form RPR

0021 **1** **Diamond Key (IRE)**[12] 5980 3-8-12 61 (b) JamesO'Reilly[(5)] 7 71
(M G Quinlan) *hld up in tch: grad edgd out rt 3f out: trckd ldrs gng wl 2f out: rdn to ld ins fnl f: sn clr: comf* **10/1**

6-00 **2** 2 **Dubai Ace (USA)**[13] 5948 6-9-11 62 (p) NeilChalmers[(3)] 5 70
(Miss Sheena West) *in tch: rdn to chse ldr over 2f out: led jst over 1f out: hdd ins fnl f: no ch w wnr* **14/1**

2642 **3** 2 ½ **Sovereign Spirit (IRE)**[18] 5820 5-10-0 62 (t) AdamKirby 13 67
(W R Swinburn) *chsd ldr tl led over 3f out: rdn over 2f out: hdd jst over 1f out: sn wknd* **4/1**[2]

4162 **4** 1 **Susie May**[13] 5948 3-9-0 58 SebSanders 6 61
(C A Cyzer) *in tch in midfield: hdwy 3f out: chsd ldng pair and rdn over 2f out: wknd 1f out* **9/4**[1]

6005 **5** ½ **Colonel Flay**[14] 5899 3-9-5 63 RobertHavlin 12 66
(Mrs P N Dutfield) *s.i.s: hld up in rr: hdwy and rdn 3f out: no real imp tl styd on u.p fnl f* **8/1**[3]

1016 **6** 3 ½ **Adage**[19] 5779 4-9-13 61 (t) FergusSweeney 14 60
(David Pinder) *hld up towards rr: rdn over 4f out: hdwy over 3f out: kpt on same pce last 2f* **12/1**

0000 **7** shd **Into Action**[11] 4809 3-9-1 59 RyanMoore 8 57
(R Hannon) *hld up in rr: nt clr run over 2f out: sn rdn: plugged on but nvr nr ldrs* **14/1**

200 **8** 3 ½ **Optimistic Alfie**[13] 5938 7-9-10 58 (b) GeorgeBaker 4 52
(B G Powell) *in tch: hdwy to chse ldrs 7f out: rdn 4f out: wknd over 2f out* **33/1**

4206 **9** 10 **Lady Dedlock**[13] 5938 3-8-10 54 FrancisNorton 2 36
(C A Cyzer) *chsd ldrs: rdn wl over 3f out: wknd 3f out: t.o* **10/1**

0000 **10** 10 **Ronsard (IRE)**[13] 5948 5-9-5 53 TGMcLaughlin 11 23
(P D Evans) *stdd s and dropped in bhd: effrt and sme hdwy on outer over 3f out: sn wl btn: t.o* **20/1**

6530 **11** 1 **Regal Ovation**[12] 5980 3-8-4 48 (b[1]) RichardMullen 9 17
(W R Muir) *led: clr 10f out tl 5f out: hdd over 3f out: sn wknd: t.o* **25/1**

6/20 **12** nk **Beliar (GER)**[21] 5742 4-9-11 59 (p) LPKeniry 10 28
(Eoin Doyle, Ire) *chsd ldrs tl rdn and wknd over 3f out: t.o* **25/1**

4600 **13** 11 **President Dan**[14] 5906 3-8-4 48 ChrisCatlin 3 —
(M R Channon) *in tch tl drvn and lost pl over 4f out: t.o last 2f* **12/1**

0000 **14** 20 **Ridgeway Star**[32] 5421 3-8-4 48 RichardThomas 1 —
(R Ingram) *in tch in midfield tl lost pl and rdn 6f out: t.o last 3f* **66/1**

3m 25.92s (-2.87) **Going Correction** -0.075s/f (Stan)
WFA 3 from 4yo+ 10lb **14** Ran SP% **125.7**
Speed ratings (Par 101): **104,103,101,101,101 99,99,97,92,87 86,86,81,71**
CSF £139.86 CT £667.35 TOTE £10.30: £2.30, £4.20, £2.20; EX 208.80 TRIFECTA Not won..
Owner Mrs J Quinlan **Bred** Michael Dalton **Trained** Newmarket, Suffolk

FOCUS
A moderate staying handicap, but it was truly-run and this looks solid form.

6272 DAILY MAIL H'CAP 1m 2f (P)
5:00 (5:01) (Class 5) (0-70,70) 3-Y-0 **£2,817** (£838; £418; £209) **Stalls** Low

Form RPR

504 **1** **Dream Of Fortune (IRE)**[29] 5494 3-8-13 65 SebSanders 4 72
(J Noseda) *racd in midfield on outer: hdwy to chse ldr wl over 2f out: drvn to ld over 1f out: drvn out* **13/8**[1]

0060 **2** ½ **Resplendent Ace (IRE)**[18] 5819 3-9-2 68 JimmyQuinn 2 74
(P Howling) *hld up towards rr: hdwy 4f out: chsd ldng pair 2f out: kpt on u.p: wnt 2nd ins fnl f* **9/1**

0126 **3** 1 ½ **Kindlelight Blue (IRE)**[27] 5557 3-9-2 68 JamesDoyle 11 71
(N P Littmoden) *chsd ldrs: wnt 2nd 8f out: led and hung lft 3f out: rdn 2f out: hdd over 1f out: no ex ins fnl f* **4/1**[2]

0630 **4** 1 ¼ **Ella Y Rossa**[5] 6146 3-8-10 62 TGMcLaughlin 10 63
(P D Evans) *s.i.s: hld up bhd: hdwy to chse ldng trio 2f out: kpt on but nvr pce to chal* **14/1**

-634 **5** 1 ¾ **Golan Way**[13] 5943 3-9-4 70 NCallan 8 67
(I A Wood) *chsd ldr for 2f: styd prom: drvn and struggling 4f out: kpt on same pce after* **4/1**[2]

5245 **6** nk **Nicada (IRE)**[16] 5860 3-8-13 70 (p) TolleyDean[(5)] 6 66
(J S Moore) *chsd ldrs: rdn wl over 3f out: kpt on same pce last 2f* **8/1**[3]

140 **7** 10 **Coppergirl (IRE)**[29] 5514 3-8-13 65 ChrisCatlin 9 41
(G A Huffer) *hld up towards rr: effrt on outer 3f out: wl btn last 2f* **16/1**

0040 **8** 1 ½ **Sea Willow (IRE)**[28] 5546 3-8-4 56 oh6 LiamJones 1 29
(D R C Elsworth) *a bhd: rdn over 5f out: wl bhd last 3f* **25/1**

0000 **9** ½ **Hannahbecc**[22] 5710 3-8-5 57 SaleemGolam 7 29
(S C Williams) *led tl rdn and hdd 3f out: sn wknd* **25/1**

3000 **10** 2 ½ **Roxie Princess (IRE)**[21] 5733 3-8-11 63 TPO'Shea 5 30
(J A R Toller) *a bhd: rdn 4f out: no ch last 3f* **25/1**

2m 6.31s (-1.48) **Going Correction** -0.075s/f (Stan) **10** Ran SP% **123.3**
Speed ratings (Par 101): **102,101,100,99,98 97,89,88,88,86**
CSF £18.71 CT £51.38 TOTE £2.10: £1.20, £1.90, £1.80; EX 20.80 Trifecta £105.50 Pool £323.97 - 2.18 winning units..
Owner Mrs J Magnier, D Smith & M Tabor **Bred** Newborough Stud **Trained** Newmarket, Suffolk

The Form Book, Raceform Ltd, Compton, RG20 6NL

FOCUS
A fair handicap run at a reasonable pace, but the winner may prove a bit better than this grade. Ordinary form, but solid enough.
Kindlelight Blue(IRE) Official explanation: jockey said gelding hung left throughout
Golan Way Official explanation: jockey said gelding was never travelling
Coppergirl(IRE) Official explanation: jockey said filly hung right throughout
Roxie Princess(IRE) Official explanation: jockey said filly had no more to give

6273 HBLB H'CAP 6f (P)
5:30 (5:30) (Class 4) (0-80,80) 3-Y-0+ **£4,728** (£1,406; £702; £351) **Stalls** Low

Form RPR
1211 **1** **For Life (IRE)**[22] 5711 5-8-6 72 NataliaGemelova[(5)] 3 79
(J E Long) *mde all: rdn over 1f out: styd on wl* **10/3**[1]
6-50 **2** *3/4* **Bertie Southstreet**[22] 5712 4-8-12 73 JimmyQuinn 5 78
(J R Best) *t.k.h: hld up bhd: hdwy and rdn 2f out: nt clr run and swtchd lft over 1f out: r.o wl to go 2nd nr fin* **8/1**
4364 **3** *shd* **Buxton**[2] 6231 3-9-2 78 RobertHavlin 7 83
(R Ingram) *racd in midfield: rdn and hdwy jst over 2f out: kpt on u.p: nt rch wnr* **4/1**[2]
0523 **4** *nk* **Dvinsky (USA)**[6] 6122 6-8-10 71 RichardHughes 11 75
(P Howling) *chsd wnr: rdn 2f out: kpt on same pce fnl f* **15/2**
0600 **5** *1 1/2* **Cape Of Luck (IRE)**[14] 5923 4-8-9 77 JackMitchell[(7)] 1 76
(P Mitchell) *s.i.s: bhd: rdn over 2f out: hanging lft over 1f out: kpt on fnl f: n.d* **8/1**
3450 **6** *1/2* **Fromsong (IRE)**[5] 6141 9-9-0 80 PatrickHills[(5)] 6 77
(D K Ivory) *in tch: rdn to chse ldng pair over 1f out: wknd ins fnl f* **11/2**
1200 **7** *1/2* **Ken's Girl**[75] 4127 3-8-6 68 TPO'Shea 8 64
(W S Kittow) *chsd ldrs: rdn over 2f out: wknd wl over 1f out* **25/1**
0002 **8** *1 3/4* **Makabul**[16] 5874 4-8-12 73 SebSanders 2 63
(B R Millman) *chsd ldrs on inner: rdn over 2f out: wknd over 1f out* **9/2**[3]
3410 **9** *5* **Nusoor (IRE)**[25] 5648 4-8-6 67 (b) LPKeniry 9 41
(Peter Grayson) *racd wd: t.k.h: chsd ldrs tl hung rt bnd over 2f out: no ch after* **20/1**
3400 **10** *2* **Silent Storm**[43] 5119 7-8-5 73 RyanHill[(7)] 4 41
(Peter Grayson) *a towards rr: rdn over 3f out: sn bhd* **33/1**

1m 11.76s (-1.05) **Going Correction** -0.075s/f (Stan)
WFA 3 from 4yo+ 1lb **10 Ran SP% 122.2**
Speed ratings (Par 105): **104,103,102,102,100 99,99,96,90,87**
CSF £31.59 CT £113.87 TOTE £2.80: £1.10, £4.00, £2.30; EX 50.50 TRIFECTA Not won. Place 6 £14.59, Place 5 £12.25..
Owner T H Bambridge **Bred** R N Auld **Trained** Caterham, Surrey

FOCUS
A fair handicap and another win for the revitalised For Life. The form is rated through the third and fourth.
Cape Of Luck(IRE) Official explanation: jockey said gelding hung left
Nusoor(IRE) Official explanation: jockey said gelding hung right
T/Jkpt: Not won. T/Plt: £17.00 to a £1 stake. Pool: £61,003.55. 2,612.00 winning tickets. T/Qpdt: £14.30 to a £1 stake. Pool: £3,032.10. 156.70 winning tickets. SP

5862 BRIGHTON (L-H)
Thursday, October 18

OFFICIAL GOING: Good to soft (8.3)
Wind: Moderate, half behind

6274 EBF MATTHEW CLARKE MEDIAN AUCTION MAIDEN STKS 7f 214y
2:30 (2:31) (Class 5) 2-Y-0 **£2,849** (£847; £423; £211) **Stalls** Low

Form RPR
1 **Captain Webb** 2-9-0 0 J-PGuillambert 8 73
(M Johnston) *mde all: rdn over 1f out: kpt on u.p fnl f* **13/2**[3]
0500 **2** *2* **Spectrana**[22] 5736 2-8-9 54 JimCrowley 12 64
(Mrs A J Perrett) *towards rr: rdn 1/2-way: r.o strly to go 2nd ins fnl f* **33/1**
0225 **3** *3/4* **Soggy Dollar**[26] 5613 2-9-0 77 JimmyQuinn 5 67
(M H Tompkins) *prom: chsd wnr fr 1/2-way: no ex ins fnl f* **11/4**[2]
0202 **4** *1* **Doctor Robert**[17] 5871 2-9-0 78 ChrisCatlin 4 65
(R Charlton) *towards rr: hdwy to trck ldrs 1/2-way: one pce fnl f* **4/6**[1]
00 **5** *hd* **Crimsonwing (IRE)**[14] 5944 2-8-9 0 EddieAhern 6 59
(A M Hales) *a in tch: rdn and nt qckn fnl f* **66/1**
06 **6** *hd* **Reel Star**[27] 5605 2-9-0 0 SimonWhitworth 9 64
(S Kirk) *towards rr: mde sme late hdwy* **33/1**
0 **7** *hd* **Crimson Mitre**[13] 5984 2-8-11 0 LukeMorris[(3)] 7 63
(J Jay) *towards rr: racd alone centre 3f out: c over to stands' side fnl f* **66/1**
00 **8** *3 1/2* **Okafranca (IRE)**[55] 4764 2-9-0 0 SaleemGolam 3 56
(W R Muir) *mid-div: wknd over 1f out* **66/1**
4 **9** *9* **Yakama (IRE)**[15] 5920 2-8-8 0 ow1 KylieManser[(7)] 10 37
(D J S Ffrench Davis) *towards rr: rdn over 3f out: hung lft fnl 2f* **20/1**
000 **10** *7* **Jay Gee Wigmo**[66] 4454 2-8-11 40 WilliamBuick[(3)] 11 21
(A W Carroll) *nvr bttr than mid-div: c alone over to stands' side 3f out and nvr on terms* **100/1**
0000 **11** *5* **Amwell House**[37] 5306 2-9-0 42 TPO'Shea 1 10
(J R Jenkins) *t.k.h: trckd wnr to 1/2-way: sn wknd* **100/1**

1m 37.1s (2.06) **Going Correction** +0.175s/f (Good) **11 Ran SP% 117.1**
Speed ratings (Par 95): **96,94,93,92,92 91,91,88,79,72 67**
CSF £176.71 TOTE £7.80: £2.10, £6.80, £1.20; EX 102.90 Trifecta £258.40 Part won. Pool: £364.07 - 0.35 winning units..
Owner Gainsborough **Bred** Gainsborough Stud Management Ltd **Trained** Middleham Moor, N Yorks

FOCUS
A weak juvenile maiden, run at an average pace. the fourth was below form and the runner-up and sixth set the level.

NOTEBOOK
Captain Webb, whose dam was a useful 7f juvenile winner, defied market weakness and made all in ready fashion. He has the scope to improve with a winter over his back, proved suited by this easy surface, and can be expected to stay further next season. (op 5-1)
Spectrana, with the blinkers abandoned, took an age to pick up from off the pace yet was motoring at the finish and this rates her most encouraging effort to date. She seemed to appreciate this softer surface, and clearly got all of the trip, but is no doubt tricky so would not be certain to build on this much-improved effort. A rise in the ratings can also now be expected. (op 25-1)
Soggy Dollar was given a positive ride and held every chance on this return to maiden company. This could be deemed as somewhat disappointing, but he did little wrong in defeat. (op 3-1 tchd 7-2)
Doctor Robert, second from a mark of 75 in Windsor nursery last time out, can have no excuses and simply proved very one-paced when push came to shove. He has it to prove after this, but it may be that he can do better again when returning to a more conventional track. (tchd 8-11 in places)
Crimsonwing(IRE), who had shown little in two previous outings at Kempton, posted a greatly-improved display on this switch to the turf. Her proximity at the finish does hold down the form, but she is worth a chance to prove she is going the right way and she now has the option of nurseries.
Reel Star got himself behind early on and was staying on all too late in the day. He is another who needed this for a nursery mark. (op 28-1)

6275 MAKING SPORT MORE EXCITING - "BETLIVE" @WILLIAMHILL.COM MAIDEN STKS 1m 3f 196y
3:00 (3:01) (Class 5) 3-Y-0+ **£2,849** (£847; £423; £211) **Stalls** High

Form RPR
0053 **1** **Crimson Monarch (USA)**[14] 5938 3-9-3 67 (b) JimCrowley 4 76
(Mrs A J Perrett) *hld up in rr: hdwy and swtchd rt over 2f out: led jst ins fnl f: styd on wl* **7/2**[2]
0- **2** *1 3/4* **Saloon (USA)**[419] 4768 3-9-0 0 WilliamBuick[(3)] 8 73
(Sir Michael Stoute) *hld up: hdwy on outside over 3f out: led 2f out: rdn and hdd jst ins fnl f: styd on one pce* **4/1**[3]
35U **3** *1 1/2* **Propaganda (IRE)**[17] 5859 3-8-12 0 EddieAhern 7 66
(L M Cumani) *hld up: hung lft fr over 2f out tl styd on fnl f: nvr nrr* **6/1**
4630 **4** *9* **Hesivorthedriver (GER)**[14] 5938 3-9-3 73 PatDobbs 1 56
(Mrs A J Perrett) *trckd ldr to 2f out: rdn and wknd over 1f out* **10/1**
2042 **5** *1/2* **Tafiya**[30] 5514 4-9-5 65 ChrisCatlin 2 51
(J W Hills) *led tl hdd 2f out: rdn and wknd appr fnl f* **11/2**
303 **6** *13* **Compton Falcon**[101] 3366 3-9-3 76 NickyMackay 5 35
(G A Butler) *trckd ldrs: hit rail over 2f out: eased whn btn over 3f out* **5/2**[1]
6340 **7** *dist* **Winforjoe (IRE)**[19] 5816 3-8-12 41 FrankieMcDonald 6 —
(J J Bridger) *a bhd: t.o fnl 4f* **100/1**

2m 33.02s (0.82) **Going Correction** +0.175s/f (Good)
WFA 3 from 4yo 7lb **7 Ran SP% 110.5**
Speed ratings (Par 103): **104,102,101,95,95 86,—**
CSF £16.59 TOTE £3.60: £1.90, £2.70; EX 18.30 Trifecta £105.10 Pool: £361.38 - 2.44 winning units..
Owner John Connolly **Bred** Sun Valley Farm & Vinery Llc **Trained** Pulborough, W Sussex
■ Stewards' Enquiry : Eddie Ahern three-day ban: careless riding (Oct 29-31)

FOCUS
A modest maiden run at a good pace which saw the first three come clear. The third sets the standard.
Compton Falcon Official explanation: jockey said gelding hung left
Winforjoe(IRE) Official explanation: jockey said filly never travelled

6276 TACKLE THE RUGBY ODDS - "BETLIVE" @WILLIAMHILL.COM H'CAP 1m 3f 196y
3:30 (3:32) (Class 5) (0-75,73) 3-Y-0+ **£3,238** (£963; £481; £240) **Stalls** High

Form RPR
6210 **1** **Chunky's Choice (IRE)**[15] 5899 3-8-11 68 WilliamBuick[(3)] 7 73+
(J Noseda) *a.p: rdn to ld over 1f out: drvn out* **11/4**[1]
1023 **2** *1 1/2* **Four Miracles**[12] 6021 3-9-5 73 JimmyQuinn 5 76
(M H Tompkins) *hld up: rdn and hdwy fr over 1f out: r.o to go 2nd ins fnl f* **7/2**[3]
4260 **3** *1/2* **Esclarmonde (IRE)**[28] 5573 3-8-13 67 (v[1]) EddieAhern 3 69
(L M Cumani) *led tl hdd appr 2f out: rdn: kpt on one pce and lost 2nd ins fnl f* **10/1**
2316 **4** *1 3/4* **Burgundy**[77] 4108 10-9-2 70 (b) JackMitchell[(7)] 9 69
(P Mitchell) *hld up in rr: reminders 1/2-way: r.o fnl f: nvr nr to chal* **28/1**
2255 **5** *1 1/2* **Bienheureux**[23] 5709 6-9-1 62 (t) MickyFenton 8 59
(Miss Gay Kelleway) *hld up in tch: hung rt over 3f out: one pce ins fnl 2f* **8/1**
1340 **6** *nk* **Rickety Bridge (IRE)**[96] 3554 4-9-4 65 JimCrowley 4 62
(P R Chamings) *prom: rdn to ld appr 2f out: hung lft and hdd over 1f out: wknd* **20/1**
616 **7** *3/4* **Global Strategy**[122] 2715 4-9-5 66 ChrisCatlin 1 61
(Rae Guest) *mid-div: pushed along 4f out: outpcd fnl 2f* **17/2**
60 **8** *hd* **Matarazzo (IRE)**[29] 5531 5-8-9 56 oh6 FergusSweeney 6 51
(G L Moore) *hld up: a bhd* **40/1**
1323 **9** *2 1/2* **Chant De Guerre (USA)**[3] 6235 3-8-10 64 NickyMackay 2 55
(P Mitchell) *prom: ev ch over 2f out: wknd over 1f out* **3/1**[2]

2m 37.99s (5.79) **Going Correction** +0.175s/f (Good)
WFA 3 from 4yo+ 7lb **9 Ran SP% 115.3**
Speed ratings (Par 103): **87,86,85,84,83 83,82,82,81**
CSF £12.29 CT £82.15 TOTE £3.20: £1.40, £1.70, £3.00; EX 11.70 Trifecta £117.80 Pool: £589.06 - 3.55 winning units..
Owner C Fox & J Wright **Bred** John Davison **Trained** Newmarket, Suffolk

FOCUS
A modest handicap, run at a sedate early pace. The winning time was nearly 5secs slower than the preceding maiden with the placed horses to form but limited by the eighth.
Chant De Guerre(USA) Official explanation: jockey said filly had no more to give

6277 EVERY MINUTE, EVERY MATCH "BETLIVE" @WILLIAMHILL.COM H'CAP 7f 214y
4:00 (4:00) (Class 6) (0-60,60) 3-Y-0 **£2,266** (£674; £337; £168) **Stalls** Low

Form RPR
006 **1** **Surprise Act**[101] 3365 3-9-1 57 PaulDoe 16 69
(P R Chamings) *a.p: led over 4f out: clr over 1f out: rdn out: comf* **10/1**
000 **2** *4* **Kassuta**[9] 6088 3-8-3 52 oh1 ow6 (p) MarkCoumbe[(7)] 10 55
(John A Harris) *hld up in rr: hdwy on outside 2f out: r.o to go 2nd ins fnl f: no ch w wnr* **12/1**
2004 **3** *2* **Rubilini**[8] 6108 3-8-4 46 oh1 ChrisCatlin 14 44
(M R Channon) *a.p: rdn 3f out: chsd wnr fr over 1f out tl ins fnl f* **7/1**[3]
0000 **4** *2* **Pajada**[4] 6206 3-7-11 46 oh1 (v) FrankiePickard[(7)] 11 39
(M D I Usher) *a.p: rdn 2f out: kpt on one pce after* **33/1**
5004 **5** *shd* **Nou Camp**[14] 5945 3-7-13 46 oh1 KirstyMilczarek[(5)] 3 39
(N A Callaghan) *plld hrd: sn prom: rdn 2f out: one pce after* **8/1**
2060 **6** *hd* **Bluebelle Dancer (IRE)**[21] 5753 3-9-4 60 SaleemGolam 4 53
(W R Muir) *slowly away: hdwy on outside over 2f out: one pce fr over 1f out* **9/2**[2]
0036 **7** *1 1/4* **Tokyo Jo (IRE)**[2] 6249 3-8-0 49 (p) AmyBaker[(7)] 12 42+
(T T Clement) *in tch: hung lft fr 2f out: hmpd jst ins fnl f* **12/1**
0000 **8** *hd* **Whipchord (IRE)**[113] 3000 3-9-1 57 PatDobbs 6 46
(R Hannon) *hld up in rr: nvr on terms* **20/1**
2034 **9** *2 1/2* **White Moss (IRE)**[15] 5905 3-9-3 59 JimmyQuinn 5 43+
(M H Tompkins) *prom: hld whn hung lft and bdly hmpd over 1f out: n.d after* **7/2**[1]
0401 **10** *1* **Smash N'Grab (IRE)**[14] 5945 3-8-12 54 EddieAhern 1 35
(J R Jenkins) *t.k.h in mid-div: rdn whn hmpd jst ins fnl f* **15/2**
0600 **11** *1 1/2* **Holyfield Warrior (IRE)**[45] 5095 3-8-8 50 JimCrowley 2 28
(I A Wood) *led tl hdd over 4f out: wknd over 1f out* **20/1**

0-6 **12** *21* **Hawk Gold (IRE)**[9] 6090 3-8-2 47................................. WilliamBuick(3) 7 —
(M D I Usher) *a bhd: t.o 3f out: eased fnl f* **20/1**

1m 36.58s (1.54) **Going Correction** +0.175s/f (Good) **12** Ran SP% **117.5**
Speed ratings (Par 99): **99,95,93,91,90 90,89,89,86,85 84,63**
CSF £115.44 CT £901.10 TOTE £12.00: £3.10, £4.30, £2.70; EX 220.40 TRIFECTA Not won..

Owner Act Surprised Partnership **Bred** Wheelersland Stud **Trained** Baughurst, Hants

■ Stewards' Enquiry : Amy Baker one-day ban: careless riding (Oct 29)

FOCUS

A poor handicap that saw a decisive winner who looks progressive. The third sets the standard but along with the fourth also limits things.

Bluebelle Dancer(IRE) Official explanation: jockey said filly hung left

Hawk Gold(IRE) Official explanation: jockey said gelding moved poorly throughout

6278 "BETLIVE" ON THE GRAND PRIX @WILLIAMHILL.COM H'CAP 6f 209y

4:30 (4:30) (Class 5) (0-70,70) 3-Y-0+ **£3,238** (£963; £481; £240) **Stalls** Low

Form RPR

0206 **1** **Support Fund (IRE)**[16] 5879 3-8-9 61........................ StephenCarson 12 69
(Eve Johnson Houghton) *mid-div: rdn over 2f out: led appr fnl f: drvn out* **6/1**[2]

2000 **2** *½* **Certain Justice (USA)**[9] 6088 9-9-6 70........................ MickyFenton 13 76
(Stef Liddiard) *mid-div on outside: hdwy over 1f out: r.o to go 2nd nr fin* **8/1**

2060 **3** *½* **Masterofthecourt (USA)**[24] 5685 4-9-3 70........................ TravisBlock(3) 1 75
(H Morrison) *s.i.s: sn led: rdn 2f out: hdd over 1f out: kpt on ins fnl f* **13/2**[3]

0000 **4** *½* **Border Edge**[7] 6124 9-8-9 59...(v) TPO'Shea 5 63
(J J Bridger) *mid-div: rdn 3f out: kpt on ins fnl f* **16/1**

5346 **5** *1* **Cow Girl (IRE)**[17] 5865 3-8-6 61........................ WilliamBuick(3) 8 62
(Miss Gay Kelleway) *mid-div: rdn to ld briefly over 1f out: fdd ins fnl f* **11/2**[1]

3100 **6** *nk* **Lordship (IRE)**[23] 5703 3-8-11 66................................ LukeMorris(3) 15 66
(A W Carroll) *in rr: hdwy over 1f out: styd on ins fnl f: nvr nrr* **6/1**[2]

0605 **7** *¾* **Rhapsilian**[17] 5866 3-8-0 57 oh6 ow1........................ KirstyMilczarek(5) 3 55
(J A Geake) *trckd ldrs on outside: rdn 2f out: one pce whn hmpd ins fnl f* **12/1**

0004 **8** *nk* **Mythical Charm**[17] 5862 8-8-6 56..................................(t) EddieAhern 14 53
(J J Bridger) *hld up in rr: mde sme late hdwy* **10/1**

010 **9** *1 ½* **Torquemada (IRE)**[24] 5687 6-9-5 69.. PaulDoe 7 62
(J Akehurst) *s.i.s: in rr tl hdwy on ins 2f out: wknd fnl f* **12/1**

0-00 **10** *1* **Start Of Authority**[61] 4595 6-8-6 56 oh11........................ JimmyQuinn 2 47
(J Gallagher) *plld hrd: trckd ldr to 2f out: sn wknd* **50/1**

4540 **11** *¾* **Comrade Cotton**[107] 3178 3-8-11 63................................ PatDobbs 10 52
(N A Callaghan) *a towards rr* **12/1**

4-05 **12** *shd* **Regal Curtsy**[63] 4549 3-8-13 65.. JimCrowley 9 53
(P R Chamings) *in tch: rdn over 2f out: sn wknd* **20/1**

-060 **13** *5* **Messiah Garvey**[20] 5768 3-9-0 66.. ChrisCatlin 6 41
(M R Channon) *prom tl wknd 2f out* **12/1**

1m 23.3s (0.60) **Going Correction** +0.175s/f (Good)
WFA 3 from 4yo+ 2lb **13** Ran SP% **120.9**
Speed ratings (Par 103): **103,102,101,101,100 99,98,98,96,95 94,94,89**
CSF £54.17 CT £338.99 TOTE £5.70: £1.90, £3.10, £2.50; EX 59.30 Trifecta £208.70 Part won. Pool: £294.02 - 0.30 winning units..

Owner Fighttheban Partnership II **Bred** W Maxwell Ervine **Trained** Blewbury, Oxon

■ Stewards' Enquiry : Micky Fenton one-day ban: careless riding (Oct 29)

FOCUS

A moderate handicap that saw the first four fairly closely covered at the finish. The form is not entirely solid with the runner-up the best guide for now.

Masterofthecourt(USA) Official explanation: jockey said gelding hung right

Rhapsilian Official explanation: jockey said filly suffered interference final half furlong

6279 COME PLAY WITH US @WILLIAMHILLCASINO.COM H'CAP 5f 59y

5:00 (5:00) (Class 5) (0-70,68) 3-Y-0+ **£3,238** (£963; £481; £240) **Stalls** Low

Form RPR

2010 **1** **Calabaza**[6] 6157 5-8-12 62...(p) PaulDoe 1 71
(J Akehurst) *hld up: rdn and hdwy 2f out: led over 1f out: drvn out: fnl f* **9/1**

6313 **2** *¾* **Dancing Mystery**[17] 5867 13-8-12 62......................(b) StephenCarson 10 68
(E A Wheeler) *prom: c over to stands' side over 2f out: r.o wl fnl f to go 2nd nr fin* **8/1**

0410 **3** *shd* **Ishibee (IRE)**[8] 6101 3-8-7 57...(p) MickyFenton 7 63
(J J Bridger) *in tch: rdn 1/2-way: chsd wnr fnl f: lost 2nd nr fin* **20/1**

2452 **4** *½* **Make My Dream**[17] 5867 4-8-10 63........................ WilliamBuick(3) 3 67
(J Gallagher) *a in tch: rdn and styd on ins fnl f* **4/1**[1]

1532 **5** *hd* **Twosheetstothewind**[63] 4546 3-9-4 68........................ EddieAhern 12 71
(C R Dore) *hld up in tch on outside: kpt on fnl f* **5/1**[2]

3654 **6** *nk* **Jayanjay**[5] 6174 8-8-12 62.. PatDobbs 11 64
(P Mitchell) *hld up: hdwy 2f out: one pce fnl f* **6/1**[3]

6100 **7** *1 ½* **Blessed Place**[5] 6174 7-8-11 66............................(t) AshleyHamblett(5) 9 63
(D J S Ffrench Davis) *led tl rdn and hdd over 1f out: wknd ins fnl f* **8/1**

5425 **8** *¾* **Hythe Bay**[46] 5066 3-9-2 66.. JimmyQuinn 5 60
(J R Best) *prom on outside: rdn 3f out: wknd over 1f out* **12/1**

-060 **9** *hd* **Pamir (IRE)**[5] 6174 5-9-0 64..(b) JimCrowley 2 57
(P R Chamings) *chsd ldrs: rdn 2f out: wknd appr fnl f* **11/1**

0024 **10** *2* **Royal Guest**[9] 6078 3-8-4 54 oh2.......................................(v) TPO'Shea 4 40
(M R Channon) *slowly away: a bhd* **5/1**[2]

63.12 secs (0.82) **Going Correction** +0.175s/f (Good) **10** Ran SP% **120.6**
Speed ratings (Par 103): **100,98,98,97,97 97,94,93,93,89**
CSF £81.69 CT £1445.19 TOTE £12.60: £3.10, £2.60, £4.90; EX 85.70 TRIFECTA Not won. Place 6 £630.53, Place 5 £245.38.

Owner Canisbay Bloodstock **Bred** Canisbay Bloodstock Ltd **Trained** Epsom, Surrey

FOCUS

A typically modest but open sprint handicap for the track and sound enough for rated around the placed horses and the fifth. Those racing down the middle of the home straight seemed at an advantage.

Royal Guest Official explanation: jockey said gelding missed the break

T/Jkpt: Not won. T/Plt: £2,860.00 to a £1 stake. Pool: £57,983.90. 14.80 winning tickets. T/Qpdt: £250.90 to a £1 stake. Pool: £4,747.20. 14.00 winning tickets. JS

6103 NOTTINGHAM (L-H)

Thursday, October 18

OFFICIAL GOING: Soft (good to soft in places; 6.5)

13mm rain two days beforehand resulted in 'genuine soft ground'.

Wind: Almost nil Weather: Fine and sunny

6281 TURFTV.CO.UK MAIDEN AUCTION STKS 6f 15y

2:10 (2:11) (Class 5) 2-Y-O **£3,071** (£906; £453) **Stalls** High

Form RPR

3 **1** **Italian Art (IRE)**[20] 5771 2-9-1 0.. SebSanders 7 85
(R M Beckett) *trckd ldrs: swtchd rt 2f out: effrt wl over 1f out: rdn to ld ins fnl f: styd on* **11/4**[2]

66 **2** *1 ¼* **Lord Sandicliffe (IRE)**[15] 5910 2-9-1 0........................ MichaelHills 13 81
(B W Hills) *cl up: led 1/2-way: rdn over 1f out: hdd and nt qckn ins fnl f* **14/1**

024 **3** *¾* **Terry's Tip (IRE)**[13] 5974 2-8-11 90.. TomEaves 2 75
(Mrs L Stubbs) *in tch on outer: hdwy over 2f out and sn ev ch: rdn over 1f out and one pce ins fnl f* **2/1**[1]

6 **4** *1 ¼* **Capone (IRE)**[15] 5903 2-8-7 0.. DominicFox(3) 14 70
(S Parr) *dwlt: sn chsng ldrs: effrt and ev ch over 1f out: sn rdn and kpt on same pce* **33/1**

4 **5** *2* **Incomparable**[118] 2832 2-8-13 0.. NCallan 6 67+
(A J McCabe) *hld up towards rr: effrt and nt clr run 2f out: styd on appr fnl f: nrst fin* **6/1**[3]

5 **6** *¾* **Melt (IRE)**[17] 5872 2-8-5 0.. FrancisNorton 5 57
(R Hannon) *outpcd and bhd: hdwy over 2f out: kpt on appr fnl f: nrst fin* **14/1**

0 **7** *hd* **Bluejain**[43] 5143 2-8-10 0.. JohnEgan 1 61
(Miss Gay Kelleway) *towards rr: hdwy on outer over 2f out: sn rdn and kpt on ins fnl f: nrst fin* **20/1**

200 **8** *nk* **Lambrini Lace (IRE)**[14] 5932 2-8-3 65........................ TolleyDean(5) 10 59
(Mrs L Williamson) *led to 1/2-way: cl up tl rdn: edgd lft and wknd over 1f out* **100/1**

0 **9** *½* **Fujin Dancer (FR)**[21] 5745 2-8-10 0........................ JamieMoriarty(3) 11 62
(R A Fahey) *s.i.s and bhd: swtchd outside and sme hdwy over 2f out: swtchd rt and rdn over 1f out: kpt on ins fnl f* **125/1**

0 **10** *¾* **Expediter**[48] 5003 2-8-8 0 ow1.. DaneO'Neill 9 55
(H Candy) *prom: rdn along over 2f out: sn wknd* **25/1**

30 **11** *3* **Boot Strap Bill**[26] 5628 2-8-10 0.. JamesDoyle 3 48
(Miss J R Tooth) *sn outpcd and a in rr* **66/1**

02 **12** *nk* **Actabou**[30] 5501 2-8-10 0.. JamieSpencer 4 47
(M Dods) *chsd ldrs: rdn along over 2f out: drvn and wknd wl over 1f out* **8/1**

0000 **13** *hd* **Bold Diva**[32] 5443 2-8-4 40.. LiamJones 8 40
(A W Carroll) *midfield: rdn along 1/2-way: wkng whn hmpd 2f out* **200/1**

14 *7* **To Bubbles** 2-8-8 0.. PhillipMakin 12 23
(T D Barron) *a towards rr* **50/1**

1m 15.19s (0.19) **Going Correction** +0.05s/f (Good) **14** Ran SP% **116.0**
Speed ratings (Par 95): **100,98,97,95,93 92,91,91,90,89 85,85,85,75**
CSF £36.74 TOTE £3.30: £1.40, £3.20, £1.10; EX 36.10.

Owner Matthew Green **Bred** Paul Kavanagh **Trained** Whitsbury, Hants

■ Stewards' Enquiry : Seb Sanders two-day ban: careless riding (Oct 29-30)

FOCUS

A better-than-average median auction maiden run 1.17sec faster than the following nursery and 0.46sec than the older-horse handicap over the same trip. The form has been rated positvely, with a much improved effort from winner Italian Art.

NOTEBOOK

Italian Art(IRE), who showed plenty of promise on similar ground on his debut, built on that to get off the mark in decisive fashion. He should make up into a decent handicapper next season. (tchd 3-1)

Lord Sandicliffe(IRE), who improved on his debut over course and distance last time, stepped up again and made good use of his high draw. He now qualifies for handicaps and should make his mark in that grade. (op 16-1)

Terry's Tip(IRE), who earned an official mark of 90 after running fourth in a Newmarket sales race last time, went off favourite but had to race on the outside of his field and a combination of that and the soft going may have found him out. He should win his maiden on better ground, but his handicap mark could flatter him and may be a problem once he contests handicaps.

Capone(IRE) was another to step up considerably on his debut, possibly helped by the rail draw. He stuck on having been on the heels of the leaders throughout, and if this can be taken at face value, he should not be too long in winning. (tchd 40-1)

Incomparable ◆, who made his debut in a Newmarket maiden in June and finished just half a length behind Rio De La Plata on that occasion, had not been seen since. A big, scopey sort, he was held up and did not get the best of runs, being hampered by the winner when making ground, but finished well and can be expected to step up a fair amount on this next time. (tchd 11-2 and 13-2)

Melt(IRE), a half-sister to the stayer Numero Due, showed some promise on her debut earlier in the month and did so again, unsurprisingly looking as if she needs further. Handicaps over a mile plus, once qualified, should prove her forte. (tchd 16-1)

Bluejain Official explanation: jockey said colt lost its action

Lambrini Lace(IRE), rated 65 and with plenty of experience, set the pace and ran her race, so helps set the standard. Official explanation: jockey said filly hung left-handed throughout

Actabou Official explanation: jockey said colt was unsuited by the soft ground

6282 NOTTINGHAMSHIRE COUNTY CRICKET CLUB NURSERY 6f 15y

2:40 (2:40) (Class 5) (0-75,75) 2-Y-O **£3,238** (£963; £481; £240) **Stalls** High

Form RPR

3201 **1** **We Have A Dream**[29] 5529 2-8-13 **67**.. DaneO'Neill 4 70
(W R Muir) *w ldrs: led over 1f out: hld on wl towards fin* **8/1**[3]

0452 **2** *hd* **Glittering Prize (UAE)**[9] 6079 2-8-13 **67**........................ GregFairley 8 69
(M Johnston) *dwlt: hdwy over 2f out: chal ins fnl f: no ex nr fin* **9/2**[2]

4461 **3** *hd* **Kaldoun Kingdom (IRE)**[23] 5705 2-9-4 **72**........................ RyanMoore 11 76+
(E A L Dunlop) *hmpd s: bhd: hmpd over 4f out: hdwy whn sltly hmpd 2f out: chal ins fnl f: no ex* **4/1**[1]

2050 **4** *½* **Her Name Is Rio (IRE)**[17] 5871 2-9-1 **69**........................ LPKeniry 7 69
(J S Moore) *w ldrs: led appr 2f out tl over 1f out: no ex ins fnl f* **40/1**

0645 **5** *2* **Legendary Guest**[7] 6128 2-9-6 **74**.....................(v) DarryllHolland 9 68
(M R Channon) *swvd rt s: hmpd over 4f out: hdwy over 2f out: kpt on: nvr trbld ldrs* **11/1**

4405 **6** *¾* **Caradoc Place**[14] 5939 2-9-2 **70**.. MartinDwyer 16 62
(M P Tregoning) *chsd ldrs: kpt on same pce fnl 2f* **17/2**

0031 **7** *¾* **Andrasta**[9] 6074 2-9-2 **73** 6ex........................ PatrickMathers(3) 1 63
(A Berry) *edgd rt after s: sn chsng ldrs: one pce fnl 2f* **25/1**

0065 **8** 1 3/4 **Stage Acclaim (IRE)**[30] 5496 2-8-12 **71**..............(b[1]) JamesMillman(5) 2 56
(B R Millman) *bmpd sn after s: sn chsng ldrs: lost pl over 2f out* **12/1**

100 **9** 3 1/2 **Cheshire Rose**[19] 5802 2-9-2 **70**.............................. PhillipMakin 17 44
(T D Barron) *t.k.h towards rr: nvr a factor* **20/1**

6130 **10** 3/4 **Bohobe (IRE)**[36] 5322 2-9-5 **73**.............................. TPQueally 15 45
(J G Given) *chsd ldrs: lost pl over 2f out* **10/1**

2336 **11** 1 3/4 **Foreign Rhythm (IRE)**[19] 5802 2-9-2 **70**..............................(t) KDarley 12 37
(N Tinkler) *hmpd s: mid-div on outer: effrt over 2f out: sn wknd* **12/1**

4650 **12** 3 **Charlotti Carlotti (IRE)**[42] 5153 2-9-1 **69**.............................. TomEaves 13 27+
(D W Chapman) *in rr: hmpd after 1f: nvr on terms* **22/1**

0160 **13** hd **Rough Rock (IRE)**[38] 5277 2-9-7 **75**..............................(bt) JohnEgan 14 32
(Miss Gay Kelleway) *led tl hdd & wknd over 2f out* **16/1**

0200 **14** 14 **Penrice Castle**[29] 5534 2-9-2 **70**.............................. RichardHughes 5 —
(R Hannon) *chsd ldrs: lost pl over 2f out: heavily eased ins fnl f* **18/1**

1m 16.46s (1.46) **Going Correction** +0.05s/f (Good) **14** Ran SP% **119.2**
Speed ratings (Par 95): **92,91,91,90,88 87,86,83,79,78 75,71,71,52**
CSF £41.22 CT £169.16 TOTE £8.20: £2.50, £1.80, £1.40.
Owner The Dreaming Squires **Bred** Whitsbury Manor Stud **Trained** Lambourn, Berks

FOCUS
A modest but competitive nursery run 1.17sec slower than the opening maiden. Solid but limited form, the runner-up as good a guide as any.

NOTEBOOK
We Have A Dream, who had won on soft ground and came into this off the back of a win in similar company on Polytrack, was well backed and showed a good attitude to hold on once getting to the front over a furlong out. Another rise in the weights will not make things easy but he is improving. (op 12-1)
Glittering Prize(UAE) was held up off the pace but made good headway to challenge inside the last furlong only to find the battle-hardened winner too determined. She looks capable of winning a similar contest, possibly back over 7f. (op 7-2)
Kaldoun Kingdom(IRE) ◆, raised 4lb for a narrow win at Brighton, was the unlucky horse of the race. He was totally squeezed out at the start and given a bump over half a mile from home which left him on the wide outside. He did well to get into a challenging position inside the final furlong, but could not find anything extra close home. He deserves compensation. (op 9-2 tchd 7-2)
Her Name Is Rio(IRE), the outsider of the field, is nevertheless by a sire whose progeny tend to handle soft ground and ran arguably her best race yet. She did get a good position near the rail but kept on pretty well and has the ability to win a similar race on this ground. (tchd 50-1)
Legendary Guest, who was involved in the incident at the start that affected the chance of the third, ran on late from well back but was never near the leaders. (op 16-1)
Caradoc Place tracked the leaders near the rail and did at least keep going under strong pressure. (op 15-2)
Foreign Rhythm(IRE) Official explanation: jockey said filly suffered interference at start

6283 OVAL H'CAP 6f 15y
3:10 (3:13) (Class 5) (0-70,75) 3-Y-O+ **£3,238** (£963; £481; £240) **Stalls** High

Form RPR

0041 **1** **Cornus**[8] 6103 5-9-10 **75** 6ex..............................(be) JamesDoyle 14 87
(A J McCabe) *trckd ldrs: hdwy on stands' rails wl over 1f out: rdn and qcknd to ld jst ins fnl f: styd on wl* **17/2**[3]

0460 **2** 1 1/2 **Mr Cellophane**[46] 5064 4-9-1 **66**.............................. JamieSpencer 11 73
(J R Jenkins) *plld hrd: hld up in rr: hdwy on stands' rails 1/2-way: nt clr run wl over 1f out: swtchd lft and rdn: styd on strly ins fnl f* **11/1**

0002 **3** hd **Steel Blue**[8] 6103 7-9-3 **68**.............................. SebSanders 13 74
(R M Whitaker) *trckd ldrs: hdwy 2f out: swtchd lft and rdn over 1f out: n.m.r ins fnl f: kpt on* **4/1**[1]

4053 **4** nk **After The Show**[8] 6103 6-9-1 **66**.............................. NCallan 1 71+
(Rae Guest) *trckd ldrs: hdwy 2f out: rdn to chse ldrs over 1f out: kpt on same pce ins fnl f* **12/1**

6634 **5** 1 3/4 **Funfair Wane**[6] 6157 8-9-2 **67**.............................. AdrianTNicholls 16 67
(D Nicholls) *led: rdn along and hdd 2f out: led again over 1f out and sn drvn: edgd lft and hdd jst ins fnl f: wknd* **11/2**[2]

0052 **6** 3/4 **Roman Quest**[3] 6239 4-8-13 **64**.............................. SteveDrowne 5 61+
(H Morrison) *midfield: pushed along and outpcd 1/2-way: hdwy on outer over 2f out: sn rdn and kpt on appr fnl f: nrst fin* **4/1**[1]

6203 **7** 1 1/2 **All You Need (IRE)**[16] 5893 3-9-2 **68**..............................(p) GrahamGibbons 10 61
(R Hollinshead) *midfield: pushed along and hdwy over 2f out: sn rdn: drvn over 1f out: nt rch ldrs* **28/1**

2263 **8** hd **Lake Chini (IRE)**[14] 5934 5-9-5 **70**..............................(b) DaleGibson 3 62
(M W Easterby) *chsd ldrs on outer: rdn along 2f out: grad wknd* **14/1**

1003 **9** nk **Metal Guru**[9] 6089 3-8-9 **66**.............................. RussellKennemore(5) 12 57
(R Hollinshead) *chsd ldrs: rdn along 2f out: grad wknd* **22/1**

3001 **10** 1 1/4 **Scarlet Oak**[9] 6089 3-9-0 **66** 6ex.............................. RichardThomas 8 53
(D J S Ffrench Davis) *a in rr* **12/1**

1500 **11** 1/2 **Strathmore (IRE)**[12] 6020 3-9-0 **66**.............................. TonyHamilton 2 51
(R A Fahey) *a in rr* **66/1**

0060 **12** 2 **High Reach**[14] 5934 7-9-0 **65**..............................(b[1]) PhillipMakin 9 44
(T D Barron) *cl up: led 2f out: sn rdn: hdd over 1f out and wknd qckly* **22/1**

3600 **13** 5 **Morse (IRE)**[17] 5874 6-9-5 **70**.............................. RyanMoore 6 33
(J A Osborne) *cl up: rdn along over 2f out and sn wknd* **12/1**

50-0 **14** 3 **Patavium Prince (IRE)**[110] 3101 4-8-12 **63**.............................. DaneO'Neill 7 16
(J R Best) *a in rr* **66/1**

1m 15.65s (0.65) **Going Correction** +0.05s/f (Good)
WFA 3 from 4yo+ 1lb **14** Ran SP% **119.1**
Speed ratings (Par 103): **97,95,94,94,92 91,89,88,88,86 86,83,76,72**
CSF £92.45 CT £344.90 TOTE £9.10: £2.90, £3.80, £1.70; EX 149.60.
Owner Club ROA **Bred** G Russell **Trained** Babworth, Notts

FOCUS
An ordinary sprint handicap full of exposed horses run 0.46sec slower than the opening juvenile maiden. High draws were favoured, but this was still improvement from Cornus, who beat the third and fourth further than he had over C/D last time.
Funfair Wane Official explanation: jockey said gelding hung left-handed

6284 SAVILLS H'CAP 2m 9y
3:40 (3:40) (Class 3) (0-95,94) 3-Y-O+ **£7,124** (£2,119; £1,059; £529) **Stalls** Low

Form RPR

1331 **1** **Highland Legacy**[7] 6131 3-8-6 **79** 6ex ow1.............................. JamieSpencer 5 95+
(M L W Bell) *trckd ldr: chal 6f out: led over 2f out: edgd rt and clr over 1f out: readily* **13/8**[2]

4211 **2** 3 **Market Forces**[5] 6186 3-9-7 **94** 6ex.............................. RichardHughes 6 105
(H R A Cecil) *led tl 3f out: styd on to take 2nd ins fnl f: no ch w wnr* **5/4**[1]

-331 **3** 1 3/4 **Aphorism**[16] 5884 4-8-10 **73**.............................. TPQueally 4 82
(J R Fanshawe) *hld up in last: hdwy over 5f out: to trck ldrs over 5f out: challnged over 2f out: hung lft and wandered: lost 2nd ins fnl f* **15/2**[3]

6106 **4** 5 **Winged D'Argent (IRE)**[19] 5808 6-9-1 **78**..............(b) StephenDonohoe 3 81
(B J Llewellyn) *in tch: sn pushed along: hrd drvn 7f out: outpcd and lost pl over 5f out: kpt on fnl 2f* **22/1**

0123 **5** 5 **Sphinx (FR)**[24] 5677 9-9-13 **90**..............................(b) JohnEgan 7 87
(Jamie Poulton) *trckd ldrs: t.k.h: lost pl 3f out: eased ins fnl f* **9/1**

3m 36.6s (3.10) **Going Correction** +0.25s/f (Good)
WFA 3 from 4yo+ 10lb **5** Ran SP% **108.7**
Speed ratings (Par 107): **102,100,99,97,94**
CSF £3.89 TOTE £2.40: £1.30, £1.20; EX 3.90.
Owner B J Warren **Bred** Deerfield Farm **Trained** Newmarket, Suffolk
■ No surprise that there was a small field for this £11,000, 76-95 2m handicap just two days before the Cesarewitch.

FOCUS
A small field for this staying handicap and a race dominated by the younger contingent. Decent and solid form, with the progressive first three finishing clear.

NOTEBOOK
Highland Legacy has looked an improved performer since being stepped up to 2m and, despite being effectively 7lb higher, won in similar style to when scoring at Newbury last time and looks one to keep on the right side. He again tended to wander about once in front, suggesting he is either still immature or slightly quirky, but galloped on strongly and should make a high-grade handicapper next season providing he is not snapped up by a jumping trainer in the meantime. (op 6-4)
Market Forces, another carrying a penalty, was stepping up 2f in search of the hat-trick. She set the pace but was taken on turning for home by the winner and could not pick up in response to that rival. She kept galloping however, and time may prove that she was attempting the near impossible in trying to give 16lb to the winner. (op 11-8 tchd 6-4 in a place)
Aphorism, held up at the back, moved up early in the straight looking a big threat to her younger rivals but the effort petered out. She is a fair sort and looks a reasonable guide to the form of this contest. (op 13-2)
Winged D'Argent(IRE), who has made the running in the past, was settled in on this occasion. He was outpaced when the pace picked up turning for home, and although he ran on was never really a factor. (op 25-1 tchd 28-1)
Sphinx(FR), who was unbeaten in three runs here prior to this, was stepping up in trip. He tracked the leaders and was a little keen but was the first beaten and that was before stamina became an issue. (op 10-1)

6285 SHOWSEC INTERNATIONAL LTD MAIDEN STKS 1m 54y
4:10 (4:11) (Class 5) 2-Y-O **£3,071** (£906; £453) **Stalls** Centre

Form RPR

00 **1** **Sleepy Hollow**[15] 5918 2-9-3 0.............................. RyanMoore 5 70
(H Morrison) *hld up in rr: hdwy on outer 3f out: rdn to chal ent fnl f and sn led: drvn and styd on wl towards fin* **10/3**[2]

2 3/4 **Cuban Rhythm (USA)** 2-8-12 0.............................. SteveDrowne 12 63
(R Charlton) *trckd ldrs: smooth hdwy 3f out: led wl over 1f out: rdn and hdd jst ins fnl f: drvn and ev ch tl no ex towards fin* **3/1**[1]

0 **3** 1 1/4 **Mezzanisi (IRE)**[14] 5951 2-9-3 0.............................. NCallan 1 66
(M L W Bell) *hld up: hdwy 3f out: swtchd rt and rdn over 1f out: kpt on ins fnl f: nrst fin* **13/2**

00 **4** 3 **Captain Mainwaring**[27] 5599 2-9-3 0.............................. JamesDoyle 10 59
(N P Littmoden) *cl up: led wl over 2f out: sn rdn and hdd wl over 1f out: kpt on same pce* **80/1**

0 **5** 2 1/2 **Fly With The Stars (USA)**[19] 5813 2-9-3 0.............................. GregFairley 7 54
(M Johnston) *led: rdn along and hdd wl over 2f out: grad wknd* **8/1**

6 1 **Dark Prospect** 2-9-3 0.............................. PhilipRobinson 2 51
(M A Jarvis) *trckd ldrs on inner: pushed along over 3f out: rdn wl over 2f out and sn btn* **9/2**[3]

0 **7** 3 1/2 **Augmentation**[14] 5951 2-9-3 0.............................. JohnEgan 4 44
(P W D'Arcy) *in tch: effrt on outer over 3f out: sn rdn along and wknd fnl 2f* **12/1**

0 **8** 6 **Timber Creek**[7] 6125 2-9-3 0.............................. DaneO'Neill 13 30
(H Candy) *t.k.h: prom on outer: rdn along over 3f out: rdn and wknd over 2f out* **17/2**

00 **9** 3 1/2 **Casual Garcia**[24] 5680 2-9-3 0.............................. SebSanders 3 23
(Sir Mark Prescott) *a in rr* **20/1**

0 **10** 4 **Emerald Toffee (IRE)**[20] 5772 2-8-12 0.............. RussellKennemore(5) 8 14
(J T Stimpson) *chsd ldrs: rdn along 1/2-way: sn wknd* **100/1**

1m 49.22s (2.82) **Going Correction** +0.25s/f (Good) **10** Ran SP% **115.9**
Speed ratings (Par 95): **95,94,93,90,87 86,83,77,73,69**
CSF £13.53 TOTE £3.60: £1.50, £1.40, £2.60; EX 13.70.
Owner Lady Blyth **Bred** Stowell Hill Ltd **Trained** East Ilsley, Berks

FOCUS
An interesting maiden full of relatively unexposed sorts, but the bare form is pretty weak.

NOTEBOOK
Sleepy Hollow, related to winners at all sorts of distances including several juveniles, was well backed on this third start and came through from off the pace to wear down the inexperienced runner-up. He should appreciate middle distances next season. (op 13-2)
Cuban Rhythm(USA) ◆, a $170,000 daughter of a mile juvenile winner, was sent off favourite on this debut and ran really well, only getting worn down by a more experienced colt late on. She should not be too long in gaining compensation. (op 10-3 tchd 4-1)
Mezzanisi(IRE) ◆, a half-brother to The Kiddykid, has clearly inherited stamina from his sire. He stayed on nicely from off the pace under a considerate ride to hunt up the principals and looks more than capable of winning races. (op 8-1)
Captain Mainwaring, a big, scopey colt, stepped up on his two previous efforts, seemingly helped by the easier ground. He was no match for the first three but he now qualifies for a mark and should pay his way in handicaps in due course. (op 66-1)
Fly With The Stars(USA) set the pace but, when the race began in earnest, he was unable to find another gear. His pedigree suggests he will appreciate a little more time. (op 13-2 tchd 11-2)
Dark Prospect, the first foal of a dual 6f juvenile winner, is clearly not as precocious as his dam but showed a fair amount of promise racing on the unfavoured far rail and should have learned a fair amount from this experience. (op 10-3)
Timber Creek, a half-brother to Free Offer, showed up until dropping away in the last quarter-mile. He gives the impression he can do better than this, but will need to step up a fair amount on what he has done so far before he is winning. (op 9-1 tchd 10-1)
Emerald Toffee(IRE) Official explanation: jockey said colt hung left-handed

6286 POWER ON CONNECTIONS MAIDEN STKS 1m 1f 213y
4:40 (4:42) (Class 5) 3-Y-O **£3,238** (£963; £481; £240) **Stalls** Low

Form RPR

3522 **1** **Abydos**[12] 6005 3-9-3 **77**..............................(p) LDettori 12 83+
(Saeed Bin Suroor) *mde all: shkn up over 2f out: rdn and edgd lft: styd on strly: eased towards fin* **2/1**[1]

2-3 **2** 2 1/2 **Eco Centrism**[15] 5915 3-9-3 0.............................. NCallan 13 77
(W J Haggas) *trckd ldrs: wnt 2nd 3f out: rdn over 1f out: no imp* **2/1**[1]

6 **3** 3/4 **Mythical Story (IRE)**[34] 5384 3-8-12 0.............................. OscarUrbina 3 71
(J R Fanshawe) *sn trcking ldrs: effrt over 2f out: kpt on ins fnl f* **40/1**

4-4 **4** 7 **Drawn Gold**[15] 5915 3-9-3 0.............................. GrahamGibbons 10 62
(R Hollinshead) *chsd ldrs: effrt and outpcd over 3f out: kpt on fnl f* **25/1**

6 **5** 1¼ **Kissing**[30] 5499 3-8-12 0 SebSanders 11 54
(Sir Mark Prescott) *sn chsng ldrs: drvn over 3f out: wknd over 1f out* **11/2**[3]

6 5 **Aladdins Cave** 3-9-3 0 RyanMoore 2 49
(Sir Michael Stoute) *s.s: in rr: sme hdwy over 3f out: nvr on terms* **9/2**[2]

0-44 **7** 9 **Wraith**[8] 6109 3-9-3 0 TedDurcan 9 31
(H R A Cecil) *mid-div: effrt over 3f out: sn lost pl* **10/1**

6-0 **8** 6 **Wyeth**[12] 6005 3-9-3 0 JamieSpencer 1 19
(J R Fanshawe) *in rr: reminders over 6f out: rdn 4f out: no rspnse* **25/1**

00 **9** 3½ **Elegans**[56] 4738 3-8-12 0 JohnEgan 14 7
(Mrs C A Dunnett) *chsd ldrs: lost pl over 3f out* **200/1**

0 **10** 10 **Shady Bay**[31] 5488 3-8-5 0 DanielleMcCreery(7) 4 —
(D W Chapman) *s.i.s: tk fierce hold in rr: lost pl over 4f out: sn bhd* **200/1**

11 3 **Troys Steps** 3-8-12 0 DavidAllan 6 —
(E J Alston) *s.s: in rr: bhd fnl 4f* **100/1**

12 8 **Overbay** 3-8-12 0 AdrianTNicholls 8 —
(E J Alston) *unruly and uns rdr s: in rr: bhd fnl 3f* **125/1**

2m 11.79s (2.09) **Going Correction** +0.25s/f (Good) **12** Ran SP% **122.2**
Speed ratings (Par 101): **101,99,98,92,91 87,80,75,73,65 62,56**
CSF £5.78 TOTE £2.90: £1.20, £1.20, £8.00; EX 8.30.
Owner Godolphin **Bred** Darley **Trained** Newmarket, Suffolk

FOCUS
A late-season three-year-old maiden featuring a number of lightly-raced but a few well-bred sorts. The field came up the centre of the track in the straight and the first three were clear. The form is very ordinary, with the winner a slight improver.

6287 COLWICK PARK H'CAP 5f 13y
5:10 (5:12) (Class 6) (0-65,65) 3-Y-0+ **£2,047** (£604; £302) **Stalls** High

Form RPR

2106 **1** **El Potro**[52] 4881 5-8-9 **56** SteveDrowne 16 66
(J R Holt) *mde most stands' rail: rdn wl over 1f out: drvn ins fnl f and styd on gamely towards fin* **11/2**[2]

0006 **2** 1 **Monashee Brave (IRE)**[15] 5908 4-8-10 **57** (t) GrahamGibbons 14 63
(J J Quinn) *prom towards stands' side: ev ch 2f out: sn rdn along and kpt on u.p ins fnl f* **8/1**

0664 **3** nk **Niteowl Lad (IRE)**[18] 5836 5-8-13 **60** DavidAllan 11 65
(J Balding) *cl up stands' side: rdn and ev ch wl over 1f out: drvn ins fnl f and no ex towards fin* **10/1**

1200 **4** ½ **Briery Lane (IRE)**[17] 5867 6-8-11 **58** StephenDonohoe 15 61
(J M Bradley) *hld up stands' rail: hdwy wl over 1f out: swtchd lft and rdn ins fnl f: fin wl* **20/1**

0000 **5** nk **Morristown Music (IRE)**[18] 5834 3-8-10 **57** TonyHamilton 17 59
(J S Wainwright) *chsd ldrs stands' rail: rdn along 1/2-way: kpt on u.p ins fnl f* **14/1**

2210 **6** 1¾ **Polar Force**[78] 4083 7-8-12 **62** MarcHalford(3) 12 58+
(Mrs C A Dunnett) *chsd ldrs centre: rdn along wl over 1f out: kpt on same pce ins fnl f* **12/1**

6422 **7** 1¾ **Mr Rooney (IRE)**[15] 5908 4-8-13 **60** AdrianTNicholls 5 49+
(D Nicholls) *prom centre: rdn along 2f out: wknd ins fnl f* **6/1**[3]

000U **8** ½ **Puskas (IRE)**[15] 5909 4-9-1 **62** (v) DaneO'Neill 8 50
(J M Bradley) *bmpd s and bhd: hdwy 2f out: styd on ins fnl f* **20/1**

000 **9** nk **Green Lagonda (AUS)**[100] 3408 5-8-11 **58** TPQueally 2 45
(J G Given) *chsd ldrs centre: effrt 2f out and ev ch tl rdn and wknd appr fnl f* **14/1**

1004 **10** nk **Jucebabe**[17] 5867 4-8-11 **58** (p) FrancisNorton 10 43
(J L Spearing) *in tch: rdn along 2f out: no imp* **14/1**

0032 **11** nk **Brandywell Boy (IRE)**[16] 5879 4-9-3 **64** RichardThomas 7 48
(D J S Ffrench Davis) *in tch: rdn along over 2f out: sn wknd* **14/1**

0042 **12** ¾ **Overwing (IRE)**[9] 6089 4-9-1 **62** LDettori 1 44
(R M H Cowell) *prom centre: rdn along 2f out and sn wknd* **11/4**[1]

0601 **13** nk **Paddywack (IRE)**[22] 5741 10-8-8 **62** (b) DanielleMcCreery(7) 6 43
(D W Chapman) *s.i.s: a in rr* **12/1**

4 **14** 5 **Bungie**[285] 54 3-8-13 **65** RussellKennemore(5) 9 28
(Paul Green) *prom centre: rdn along over 2f out and sn wknd* **66/1**

4104 **15** 4 **Billy Red**[47] 5051 3-9-4 **65** (b) JohnEgan 4 13
(J R Jenkins) *chsd ldrs centre: rdn along over 2f out: sn wknd* **50/1**

4100 **16** 5 **Miacarla**[22] 5740 4-8-8 **58** PatrickMathers(3) 3 —
(A Berry) *s.i.s: a in rr* **33/1**

61.51 secs (-0.29) **Going Correction** +0.05s/f (Good) **16** Ran SP% **134.5**
Speed ratings (Par 101): **104,102,101,101,100 97,95,94,93,93 92,91,91,83,76 68**
CSF £51.97 CT £342.90 TOTE £8.20: £2.00, £2.30, £3.50, £4.70; EX 56.90 Place 6 £6.49, Place 5 £4.71.
Owner David J Facer-Harrison **Bred** L A C Ashby **Trained** Peckleton, Leics
■ Stewards' Enquiry : David Allan caution: used whip down shoulder in forehand position
Graham Gibbons one-day ban: used whip with excessive frequency (Oct 29)

FOCUS
A moderate but tightly-knit sprint handicap in which the field split into two groups, with those racing near the stands' rail having a clear advantage. The form makes sense among the principals.
Overwing(IRE) Official explanation: trainer had no explanation the filly's poor run
T/Plt: £5.60 to a £1 stake. Pool: £59,094.30. 7,639.90 winning tickets. T/Qpdt: £3.40 to a £1 stake. Pool: £2,748.10. 581.10 winning tickets. JR

6240 WOLVERHAMPTON (A.W) (L-H)
Thursday, October 18

OFFICIAL GOING: Standard
Wind: Almost nil Weather: Cloudy

6288 BOOK YOUR CHRISTMAS PARTY NOW CLAIMING STKS 5f 216y(P)
6:50 (6:51) (Class 6) 3-Y-0+ **£2,047** (£604; £302) **Stalls** Low

Form RPR

1500 **1** **Whitbarrow (IRE)**[29] 5535 8-9-4 80 (b) JamesMillman(5) 3 82
(B R Millman) *led 5f out: rdn over 1f out: jst hld on* **13/2**

0003 **2** shd **Magic Glade**[77] 4095 8-9-9 89 RichardKingscote 13 81
(Tom Dascombe) *hld up: swtchd lft sn after s: hdwy over 1f out: r.o wl towards fin* **7/2**[3]

4050 **3** 1 **Regal Raider (IRE)**[13] 5981 4-8-9 64 (p) TomEaves 5 64
(I Semple) *hld up: hdwy over 1f out: styd on u.p* **14/1**

0000 **4** 2½ **Swing The Ring (IRE)**[30] 5505 4-9-9 75 RobertHavlin 11 70
(A Berry) *sn outpcd: r.o ins fnl f: nrst fin* **28/1**

0004 **5** hd **Royal Challenge**[7] 6122 6-9-5 68 GeorgeBaker 2 65
(M H Tompkins) *stmbld s: sn prom: rdn and edgd lft over 1f out: styd on same pce* **10/3**[2]

4500 **6** shd **Phinerine**[96] 3535 4-8-7 48 (b) TolleyDean(5) 1 58
(Miss J E Foster) *s.i.s: sn prom: rdn over 1f out: no ex fnl f* **66/1**

4645 **7** nk **Bonnet O'Bonnie**[13] 5982 3-8-2 49 DominicFox(3) 6 51
(J Mackie) *s.i.s: hld up: hdwy over 2f out: sn rdn: styd on same pce fnl f* **66/1**

1550 **8** ¾ **Came Back (IRE)**[13] 5981 4-9-3 70 RoystonFfrench 12 60
(J Mackie) *hld up: effrt over 1f out: nt clr run ins fnl f: nvr trbld ldrs* **20/1**

2402 **9** ¾ **Rydal (USA)**[13] 5981 6-9-1 77 JamieSpencer 7 55
(J A Osborne) *prom: stdd and lost pl 5f out: effrt and nt clr run over 1f out: n.d* **5/2**[1]

0043 **10** hd **Millfields Dreams**[13] 5981 8-8-13 65 GregFairley 8 53
(M G Quinlan) *chsd ldrs: rdn 1/2-way: sn lost pl* **8/1**

0400 **11** 4 **Maison Dieu**[13] 5964 4-9-3 56 DanielTudhope 10 44
(E J Alston) *mid-div: hdwy over 2f out: rdn and wknd over 1f out* **33/1**

0000 **12** 6 **Blythe Spirit**[6] 6149 8-8-11 50 (v) LiamJones 4 19
(Mrs L Williamson) *chsd ldrs over 4f* **66/1**

0 **13** 2½ **Miss Spirit (IRE)**[104] 3288 4-9-1 52 CDHayes 9 15
(Michael Mulvany, Ire) *led: hdd 5f out: wknd over 2f out: hmpd over 1f out* **33/1**

1m 14.62s (-1.19) **Going Correction** -0.15s/f (Stan)
WFA 3 from 4yo+ 1lb **13** Ran SP% **123.6**
Speed ratings (Par 101): **101,100,99,96,95 95,95,94,93,93 87,79,76**
CSF £29.06 TOTE £8.60: £3.60, £1.50, £7.00; EX 31.40.Regal Raider was claimed by A. M. Hales for £4,000.
Owner Mrs H Brain **Bred** James Burns And A Moynan **Trained** Kentisbeare, Devon

FOCUS
A routine Polytrack claimer run at no more than a fair pace and those that came out best were amongst those most favoured by the weights, so the form is probably reliable for the grade, although the proximity of the sixth and seventh raises doubts.
Royal Challenge Official explanation: jockey said gelding hung right-handed
Rydal(USA) Official explanation: jockey said gelding hung right-handed

6289 HORIZONS RESTAURANT MEDIAN AUCTION MAIDEN STKS 7f 32y(P)
7:20 (7:22) (Class 6) 2-Y-0 **£2,047** (£604; £302) **Stalls** High

Form RPR

0330 **1** **Loyal Knight (IRE)**[13] 5974 2-9-3 79 JamieSpencer 10 72
(S Kirk) *led 6f out: shkn up and edgd lft over 1f out: r.o* **4/5**[1]

32 **2** hd **Safebreaker**[14] 5931 2-9-3 0 GregFairley 7 72
(M Johnston) *led: hdd 6f out: chsd wnr: rdn and n.m.r fr over 1f out: r.o* **2/1**[2]

0 **3** 3½ **Regal Tradition (IRE)**[10] 6065 2-9-3 0 FrankieMcDonald 3 63
(P A Blockley) *prom: rdn over 1f out: styd on same pce* **66/1**

0 **4** 1 **Artistic Light**[26] 5633 2-8-12 0 SteveDrowne 6 55
(W R Muir) *chsd ldrs: rdn over 2f out: styd on same pce appr fnl f* **25/1**

000 **5** 2½ **Miss Bouggy Wouggy**[19] 5811 2-8-12 46 DaneO'Neill 2 49
(M Blanshard) *s.i.s: hld up: rdn 1/2-way: swtchd rt over 1f out: n.d* **80/1**

000 **6** 3½ **Jimmy Dean**[67] 4417 2-9-0 34 (b[1]) NeilChalmers(3) 4 45
(M Wellings) *chsd ldrs: rdn 1/2-way: wknd wl over 1f out* **100/1**

4 **7** 2½ **My Shadow**[23] 5702 2-9-3 0 RichardMullen 9 39
(E S McMahon) *hld up: effrt 1/2-way: wknd 2f out* **10/1**[3]

0 **8** 1¾ **Marfeng**[20] 5766 2-8-12 0 LiamJones 1 30
(W M Brisbourne) *prom: n.m.r and lost pl over 6f out: rdn over 4f out: n.d after* **16/1**

9 1¾ **Poppy Red** 2-8-12 0 PaulFitzsimons 5 25
(Miss J R Tooth) *s.i.s: outpcd* **66/1**

5 **10** ½ **Bewdley**[19] 5801 2-8-12 0 RobertHavlin 8 24
(P D Evans) *chsd ldrs: rdn 1/2-way: wknd 2f out* **25/1**

1m 30.51s (0.11) **Going Correction** -0.15s/f (Stan) **10** Ran SP% **116.8**
Speed ratings (Par 93): **93,92,88,87,84 80,77,75,73,73**
CSF £2.39 TOTE £2.30: £1.02, £1.10, £11.40; EX 3.50.
Owner Pillar To Post Racing (IV) **Bred** Fergus Cousins **Trained** Upper Lambourn, Berks
■ Stewards' Enquiry : Greg Fairley one-day ban: used whip down shoulder in forehand position (Oct 29)

FOCUS
No strength in depth here and the two market leaders duly played out a tight finish with the winner not needing to be at his best to score.

NOTEBOOK
Loyal Knight(IRE), making his All-Weather debut, got an aggressive ride over this extra furlong and just did enough to open his account at the fifth attempt. This looks to be his optimum trip at present, and a sound surface looks key to him, but he can expected to stay further as a three-year-old despite his sire's speed influence. He rates a useful handicap prospect. (op Evens)
Safebreaker, another having his first run on an artificial surface, proved easy to back in relation to the eventual winner yet still went down all guns blazing. He had no trouble with the extra furlong, now qualifies for a nursery mark, and deserves to go one better after this. (op 6-4)
Regal Tradition(IRE) showed the benefit of his debut at this track over a shorter trip earlier in the month and posted a much-improved effort. He got the distance without fuss and is going the right way, but should really be of greater interest when qualiying for nurseries after his next outing. (op 50-1)
Artistic Light stepped up on the level of her Newbury debut last month and left the impression she will improve again for the experience. She needs another run to qualify for a handicap mark and can be expected to relish a longer trip as a three-year-old. (op 20-1)

6290 NAME A RACE TO ENHANCE YOUR BRAND H'CAP 7f 32y(P)
7:50 (7:50) (Class 6) (0-60,60) 3-Y-0+ **£2,047** (£604; £302) **Stalls** High

Form RPR

0000 **1** **Vanadium**[48] 5009 5-9-5 **60** GeorgeBaker 6 70
(G L Moore) *mde all: drvn out* **5/2**[2]

4531 **2** ¾ **The City Kid (IRE)**[34] 5391 4-9-3 **58** JamieSpencer 3 66
(S C Williams) *trckd ldrs: rdn to chse wnr over 1f out: styd on* **9/4**[1]

0002 **3** 1¾ **Richelieu**[48] 5023 5-9-3 **58** CDHayes 1 61
(J J Lambe, Ire) *hld up in tch: hrd rdn fr over 1f out: styd on same pce ins fnl f* **8/1**[3]

0040 **4** ½ **Elusive Warrior (USA)**[18] 5840 4-9-2 **57** (p) TonyHamilton 10 59
(R A Fahey) *chsd wnr tl rdn over 1f out: styd on same pce* **33/1**

505- **5** nk **Hits Only Jude (IRE)**[345] 6390 4-9-3 **58** J-PGuillambert 4 59
(J Pearce) *hld up: r.o ins fnl f: nrst fin* **20/1**

036 **6** 1¼ **Antrim Rose**[20] 5783 3-9-3 **60** (p) TedDurcan 5 58
(E F Vaughan) *chsd ldrs: rdn over 2f out: no ex fnl f* **14/1**

0434 **7** hd **Task Complete**[43] 5129 4-9-2 **57** SebSanders 2 54
(Jean-Rene Auvray) *hld up: racd keenly: nt clr run over 1f out: nvr trbld ldrs* **12/1**

2100 **8** 1¼ **No Grouse**[13] 5966 7-9-2 **57** DavidAllan 9 51
(E J Alston) *hld up: nvr nrr* **9/1**

0304 **9** ½ **Summer Recluse (USA)**[6] 6148 8-9-5 **60** (t) LPKeniry 11 52
(J M Bradley) *hld up: effrt over 2f out: wknd over 1f out* **16/1**

4032 **10** 1 **Boreana**[20] 5778 4-9-2 **57** DaneO'Neill 7 47
(Jedd O'Keeffe) *prom: rdn over 2f out: wknd fnl f* **8/1**[3]

The Form Book, Raceform Ltd, Compton, RG20 6NL

4065 **11** *shd* **Ocean Gift**^{13} 5981 5-9-3 58 .... KimTinkler 8 48
(N Tinkler) *hld up: plld hrd: hdwy over 2f out: wknd over 1f out* **20/1**

1m 30.63s (0.23) **Going Correction** -0.15s/f (Stan)
WFA 3 from 4yo+ 2lb **11** Ran SP% **124.3**
Speed ratings (Par 101): **92,91,89,88,88 86,86,85,84,83 83**
CSF £8.88 CT £41.97 TOTE £3.20: £1.90, £1.60, £2.70; EX 10.40.

Owner A V Racing **Bred** Bolton Grange **Trained** Woodingdean, E Sussex

FOCUS
This moderate handicap was run at a crawl early and the winning time was 0.12 seconds slower than the preceding two-year-old maiden. Not surprisingly that helped those that raced prominently no end and the principals were always handy.

6291 WOLVERHAMPTON-RACECOURSE.CO.UK NURSERY 1m 141y(P)
8:20 (8:20) (Class 3) (0-95,85) 2-Y-O £6,477 (£1,927; £963; £481) **Stalls** Low

Form RPR

3106 **1** **Menadha (USA)**^{42} 5153 2-9-2 80 .... DarryllHolland 3 85
(M R Channon) *s.i.s: hld up: hdwy to chse ldr over 1f out: rdn to ld and hung lft ins fnl f: r.o* **12/1**

051 **2** *1 1/4* **Step This Way (USA)**^{45} 5100 2-9-2 80 .... GregFairley 6 82
(M Johnston) *led: rdn over 1f out: hdd and unable qckn ins fnl f* **3/1**^{3}

6350 **3** *1 3/4* **Ellemujie**^{13} 5974 2-9-7 85 .... JamieSpencer 1 83
(D K Ivory) *chsd ldrs: rdn: n.m.r and lost pl over 2f out: rallied over 1f out: styd on same pce fnl f* **13/2**

1534 **4** *hd* **The Betchworth Kid**^{35} 5350 2-9-6 84 ....(v^{1}) TedDurcan 2 82
(M L W Bell) *reminders in rr sn after s: hld up: rdn over 3f out: hdwy over 2f out: edgd lft over 1f out: styd on same pce* **15/8**^{1}

040 **5** *1 1/2* **Grecian Slave**^{22} 5735 2-8-2 66 .... RoystonFfrench 4 61
(B Smart) *chsd ldr tl rdn over 1f out: styd on same pce* **28/1**

0162 **6** *5* **Palm Court**^{7} 6120 2-9-3 81 .... SteveDrowne 5 65
(R Charlton) *trckd ldrs: rdn to go 2nd 2f out: wknd fnl f* **2/1**^{2}

1m 50.37s (-1.39) **Going Correction** -0.15s/f (Stan) **6** Ran SP% **117.6**
Speed ratings (Par 99): **100,98,97,97,95 91**
CSF £50.08 TOTE £11.20: £3.60, £1.80; EX 41.30.

Owner Sheikh Ahmed Al Maktoum **Bred** Calumet Farm **Trained** West Ilsley, Berks

FOCUS
Only a small field, but this looked a decent nursery as the pace set by the runner-up was solid throughout. There are doubts about the form with a couple running below their marks.

NOTEBOOK
Menadha(USA), trying this trip for the first time, was switched off right out the back in order to help him get it. He did not have much room to play with when trying to manoeuvre his way through on the home turn, but once there he produced a bright turn of foot to cut down the leader and stamina was not a problem at all. (op 16-1)

Step This Way(USA), making her nursery debut after easily winning her maiden over course and distance last month, tried the same forcing tactics and made a good fist of it, but she had no answer to the winner's turn of foot. This effort suggests the Handicapper has got her about right. (op 11-4 tchd 5-2 and 4-1)

Ellemujie, on a career-high mark for this return to sand, was struggling on the home bend and though he plugged on for third he was never a threat to the front pair. He is more exposed than most in this field and looks on a stiff mark now. (op 6-1 tchd 15-2)

The Betchworth Kid, trying sand for the first time, did not appear to take to the first-time visor at all and was under the cosh soon after leaving the stalls. He did eventually give himself every chance, but had little left down the home straight though he did finish a bit closer to Ellemujie than he did at Doncaster on 1lb better terms. (op 7-2)

Grecian Slave, making his nursery and Polytrack debuts after showing a little ability in three turf maidens, was getting lumps of weight from his five rivals and showed up for a long way. He may be up to winning a race on this surface at a slightly more modest level. (op 16-1)

Palm Court, a winner on his only previous visit to this track, seemed to travel well enough behind the leaders for most of the way, but he faded very disappointingly in the home straight and this was too bad to be true. (op 15-8 tchd 9-4)

6292 RINGSIDE SUITE CONFERENCE SUITE CLASSIFIED STKS 1m 4f 50y(P)
8:50 (8:51) (Class 7) 3-Y-0+ £1,911 (£564; £282) **Stalls** Low

Form RPR

604- **1** **Ndola**^{84} 6551 8-9-5 45 ....(v) JamieSpencer 3 57
(B J Curley) *hld up in tch: chsd ldr 2f out: rdn to ld over 1f out: hung lft: styd on* **5/2**^{1}

0025 **2** *1 1/2* **Cragganmore Creek**^{34} 5389 4-9-2 45 ....(v) LukeMorris$^{(3)}$ 7 54
(D Morris) *hld up: hdwy to ld over 2f out: rdn and hdd over 1f out: styd on same pce* **4/1**

0240 **3** *4* **Dream Master (IRE)**^{16} 5886 4-9-5 45 .... AdamKirby 6 48
(J Ryan) *dwlt: hld up: hdwy over 2f out: rdn over 1f out: styd on same pce* **14/1**

314 **4** *3 1/2* **Everyman**^{2} 6250 3-9-4 45 .... GregFairley 10 48
(A W Carroll) *hld up: hdwy and edgd lft over 2f out: sn rdn: wknd over 1f out* **11/4**^{2}

5430 **5** *3/4* **Cool Isle**^{4} 6212 4-9-5 45 ....(b) J-PGuillambert 5 41
(P Howling) *hld up: rdn over 3f out: nt trble ldrs* **20/1**

0000 **6** *1* **Croft (IRE)**^{26} 5647 4-9-5 45 .... DaneO'Neill 8 40
(M S Saunders) *chsd ldrs: led over 2f out: sn rdn and hdd: hung lft and wknd over 1f out* **25/1**

000- **7** *1/2* **Valeureux**^{375} 5836 9-9-5 45 .... DaleGibson 1 39
(J Hetherton) *chsd ldrs: rdn over 2f out: sn wknd* **33/1**

2005 **8** *3/4* **Lady Ambitious**^{4} 6212 4-9-0 45 .... JamesO'Reilly$^{(5)}$ 4 38
(D K Ivory) *hld up: rdn and nt clr run over 2f out: n.d* **16/1**

6000 **9** *3* **Boppys Dancer**^{53} 4843 4-9-2 45 ....(p) JamieMoriarty$^{(3)}$ 9 33
(P T Midgley) *hld up: rdn over 2f out: a in rr* **33/1**

0000 **10** *13* **Alisar (IRE)**^{6} 6152 7-9-2 45 ....(t) AlanCreighton$^{(3)}$ 12 12
(E J Creighton) *chsd ldr 9f out: led over 3f out: rdn: hdd & wknd over 2f out* **66/1**

0000 **11** *11* **Richtee (IRE)**^{6} 6152 6-9-5 45 .... RoystonFfrench 2 —
(I W McInnes) *led: rdn and hdd over 3f out: wknd over 2f out* **33/1**

0062 **12** *3* **Lightning Queen (USA)**^{20} 5782 3-8-12 45 .... SebSanders 11 —
(B W Hills) *hld up in tch: rdn and wkng whn hmpd over 2f out* **7/2**^{3}

2m 41.04s (-1.38) **Going Correction** -0.15s/f (Stan)
WFA 3 from 4yo+ 7lb **12** Ran SP% **128.9**
Speed ratings (Par 97): **98,97,94,92,91 90,90,90,88,79 72,70**
CSF £13.26 TOTE £3.30: £2.50, £2.90, £3.00; EX 19.30.

Owner Curley Leisure **Bred** Loan And Development Corporation **Trained** Newmarket, Suffolk

FOCUS
A poor race though the pace was fair. The front pair pulled right away, but the form, although solid enough, is unlikely to mean much outside of this grade.

6293 SPONSOR A RACE BY CALLING 0870 200 2442 H'CAP 1m 1f 103y(P)
9:20 (9:20) (Class 5) (0-75,73) 3-Y-0+ £2,817 (£838; £418; £209) **Stalls** Low

Form RPR

0002 **1** **Gaelic Princess**^{12} 6025 7-9-7 73 .... DaneO'Neill 3 83
(A G Newcombe) *hld up in tch: rdn over 1f out: r.o to ld post* **12/1**

2133 **2** *hd* **Kalasam**^{26} 5636 3-9-2 72 .... RichardMullen 5 82
(W R Muir) *chsd ldrs: rdn to ld over 1f out: hdd post* **11/2**^{3}

4246 **3** *2 1/2* **Chia (IRE)**^{22} 5732 4-8-11 63 ....(p) RobertHavlin 4 67
(D Haydn Jones) *chsd ldrs: rdn over 1f out: no ex ins fnl f* **7/1**

0554 **4** *1 1/4* **Hoh Wotanite**^{16} 5889 4-9-4 70 ....(p) JamieSpencer 10 72
(R Hollinshead) *hld up: rdn over 1f out: r.o ins fnl f: nvr nrr* **5/1**^{2}

6644 **5** *3/4* **Call My Bluff (FR)**^{13} 5985 4-9-4 70 .... TedDurcan 7 70
(Rae Guest) *hld up: hdwy over 1f out: rdn and hung lft ins fnl f: styd on same pce* **8/1**

0000 **6** *3/4* **Art Market (CAN)**^{11} 4234 4-9-3 69 .... GeorgeBaker 1 68
(G L Moore) *trckd ldrs: rdn over 3f out: no ex fnl f* **20/1**

200 **7** *1 1/4* **Passing Hour (USA)**^{74} 4205 3-9-3 73 ....(b^{1}) NickyMackay 6 69
(G A Butler) *mde most tl rdn and hdd over 1f out: wknd ins fnl f* **14/1**

5200 **8** *1/2* **Kildare Sun (IRE)**^{15} 5905 5-9-6 72 .... RoystonFfrench 8 67
(J Mackie) *hld up in tch: rdn over 2f out: no ex fnl f* **9/2**^{1}

1016 **9** *shd* **Hits Only Cash**^{16} 5889 5-9-2 68 .... J-PGuillambert 11 63
(J Pearce) *hld up: rdn over 1f out: n.d* **14/1**

10 *2* **Dushstorm (IRE)**^{102} 6-9-2 68 ....(p) SebSanders 12 58
(M Botti) *hld up: effrt and edgd lft over 1f out: wknd fnl f* **6/1**

1326 **11** *1* **Le Chiffre (IRE)**^{12} 6025 5-8-12 71 ....(p) WilliamCarson$^{(7)}$ 9 59
(S Curran) *chsd ldrs: rdn and ev ch over 1f out: wknd fnl f* **12/1**

12 *1 1/2* **Winter Cruise (IRE)**^{459} 3577 3-8-4 60 .... RichardThomas 2 45
(Ian Williams) *prom: rdn over 4f out: wknd over 2f out* **40/1**

2m 0.97s (-1.65) **Going Correction** -0.15s/f (Stan)
WFA 3 from 4yo+ 4lb **12** Ran SP% **124.0**
Speed ratings (Par 103): **101,100,98,97,96 96,95,94,94,92 91,90**
CSF £80.33 CT £514.95 TOTE £13.60: £4.50, £2.50, £1.70; EX 46.70 Place 6 £110.67, Place 5 £41.57.

Owner M K F Seymour **Bred** Mrs N Quinn **Trained** Yarnscombe, Devon

FOCUS
A routine handicap for the track in which the pace was solid enough and the front two came clear. the third and fourth are the best guides to the level.
T/Plt: £55.70 to a £1 stake. Pool: £86,011.95. 1,126.40 winning tickets. T/Qpdt: £25.50 to a £1 stake. Pool: £5,972.70. 172.90 winning tickets. CR

6008 NEWMARKET (ROWLEY) (R-H)
Friday, October 19

OFFICIAL GOING: Soft (good to soft in places; 6.7)

6294 ANGLO HIBERNIAN BLOODSTOCK INSURANCE EBF MAIDEN STKS (DIV I) 1m
1:00 (1:01) (Class 3) 2-Y-O £5,829 (£1,734; £866; £432) **Stalls** Low

Form RPR

1 **General Eliott (IRE)** 2-9-3 0 .... TQuinn 11 83+
(P F I Cole) *mde all: rdn over 1f out: r.o: eased towards fin* **6/1**^{3}

2 *nk* **Sortita (GER)** 2-8-12 0 .... RHills 10 77+
(M A Jarvis) *hld up: hdwy over 3f out: outpcd over 1f out: edgd lft and r.o wl ins fnl f* **15/2**

2 **3** *2 1/2* **Polmaily**^{77} 4132 2-9-3 0 .... RichardHughes 8 77
(B J Meehan) *chsd ldrs: rdn over 1f out: styd on same pce ins fnl f* **8/13**^{1}

4 *2* **Wine 'n Dine** 2-9-3 0 .... J-PGuillambert 1 72
(C A Cyzer) *chsd wnr tl rdn over 1f out: styd on same pce* **80/1**

5 *3/4* **Manalito** 2-9-3 0 .... DarryllHolland 5 71+
(M R Channon) *dwlt: hld up: hdwy over 2f out: rdn to chse wnr over 1f out: wknd ins fnl f* **11/2**^{2}

6 *1/2* **Amanjena** 2-8-12 0 .... FrancisNorton 9 65+
(A M Balding) *s.i.s: sn prom: outpcd over 2f out: styd on ins fnl f* **33/1**

7 *1 1/2* **Indian Skipper (IRE)** 2-9-3 0 .... JimmyQuinn 6 66+
(M H Tompkins) *hld up: hdwy over 1f out: wknd fnl f* **50/1**

0 **8** *2* **Hellzapoppin**^{14} 5971 2-9-3 0 .... NCallan 7 62
(B W Hills) *hld up: hdwy over 1f out: wknd fnl f* **50/1**

0 **9** *4* **Serious Choice (IRE)**^{10} 6080 2-9-3 0 .... FergusSweeney 4 53
(J R Boyle) *mid-div: rdn and wknd over 2f out* **100/1**

0 **10** *8* **Sarah's Boy**^{16} 5919 2-9-3 0 .... JohnEgan 3 36
(S Dow) *hld up in tch: plld hrd: wknd over 2f out* **100/1**

0 **11** *3/4* **Hotel Felix**^{15} 5951 2-8-10 0 .... StephenCooper$^{(7)}$ 2 34
(Miss Gay Kelleway) *chsd ldrs over 5f* **100/1**

1m 41.48s (2.11) **Going Correction** +0.25s/f (Good) **11** Ran SP% **114.4**
Speed ratings (Par 99): **99,98,96,94,93 92,91,89,85,77 76**
CSF £47.19 TOTE £7.60: £1.70, £2.10, £1.10; EX 34.30.

Owner Sir George Meyrick **Bred** Maddenstown Equine Enterprise Ltd **Trained** Whatcombe, Oxon

FOCUS
A typical backend maiden in which they bet 33/1 bar four and the slowest of the three juvenile races over the trip. A nice debut from General Eliott and several others shaped with promise too.

NOTEBOOK
General Eliott(IRE), a half-brother to Shanghai Lily and Eden Rock, was a bit excitable went he first came into the paddock but settled down and in the race was thoroughly professional. He set off in front and, clear running into the dip, galloped on well to score with something in hand of the runner-up. He has the scope to go on from this. (op 7-1 tchd 8-1)

Sortita(GER) ◆, a 750,000euros sister to the top-class German performers Schiaparelli and Samum, wore a cross noseband and was quite keen going to post. She was settled off the pace and really picked up well when asked, closing down on the winner all the way to the line, although flattered by the official margin. Hopefully the experience will help her settle and she could develop into a decent middle-distance filly next year. (op 9-2)

Polmaily, the first foal of a 6f winner, had shown plenty of promise on his debut on the July course and was sent off odds on. He got a good lead from the winner but the response when asked for an effort was limited and he just kept on at the one pace up the hill. (op 4-6 tchd 8-11 and 4-7)

Wine 'n Dine, a half-brother to several winning middle-distance performers for the same connections, showed plenty of promise on this debut and kept going up the hill. He will come into his own over further next year. (op 66-1)

Manalito, a 200,000gns half-brother to a couple of winners including the useful Kassiopeia, missed the break but made a good forward move before fading up the hill. He looks the type to come on a good deal for the experience. (op 13-2)

Amanjena, a half-sister to Presto Vento, missed the break but tracked the leaders until getting outpaced down the hill. She did run on again and this was a promising effort considering she is from a yard whose juveniles are rarely fully wound up for their debuts.

Indian Skipper(IRE), a half-brother to the sprinter Loyal Tycoon, was held up at the back and did make some headway around the halfway mark, but his effort flattened out in the latter stages. He should do better given time. (op 66-1)

6295 FEDERATION OF BLOODSTOCK AGENTS EBF MAIDEN STKS 6f

1:30 (1:31) (Class 3) 2-Y-O £6,477 (£1,927; £963; £481) **Stalls** Low

Form RPR

4 **1** **Insaaf**[21] 5766 2-8-12 0 .... RHills 7 90+
(W J Haggas) *chsd ldr: led over 2f out: hdd over 1f out: rallied to ld ins fnl f: r.o* **9/4**[1]

2 ¾ **Tawaash (USA)** 2-9-3 0 .... MartinDwyer 13 93
(M A Jarvis) *chsd ldrs: led over 1f out: rdn and hdd ins fnl f: styd on* **33/1**

4 **3** ½ **Provence**[15] 5949 2-8-12 0 .... MichaelHills 10 86
(B W Hills) *hld up: hdwy 1/2-way: rdn and ev ch over 1f out: edgd lft and styd on same pce ins fnl f* **3/1**[3]

2 **4** *hd* **Brave Prospector**[18] 5868 2-9-3 0 .... JimmyFortune 1 91
(P W Chapple-Hyam) *a.p: rdn over 1f out: styd on* **11/4**[2]

5 ½ **Film Maker (IRE)** 2-9-3 0 .... StephenDonohoe 5 89+
(B J Meehan) *hld up: hdwy over 1f out: r.o wl* **14/1**

3 **6** *4* **Danish Art (IRE)**[29] 5575 2-9-0 0 .... WilliamBuick(3) 11 77
(J A R Toller) *sn led: hdd over 2f out: wknd over 1f out* **25/1**

7 *1 ½* **Etosha (IRE)** 2-9-3 0 .... LDettori 15 73
(Saeed Bin Suroor) *s.i.s: hld up: hdwy over 2f out: wknd over 1f out* **7/1**

8 *2 ½* **Minus Fifteen (IRE)** 2-9-3 0 .... NCallan 6 65
(K A Ryan) *prom over 3f* **20/1**

9 *2* **Chartist** 2-9-3 0 .... RichardHughes 9 59+
(R Hannon) *chsd ldrs over 4f* **66/1**

00 **10** *nk* **Saafend Geezer**[23] 5720 2-9-3 0 .... TedDurcan 12 58
(B J Meehan) *chsd ldrs 4f* **100/1**

00 **11** *1 ¼* **Hits Only Time**[9] 6107 2-9-3 0 .... J-PGuillambert 3 55
(J Pearce) *s.i.s: a in rr* **150/1**

12 *2 ½* **Human Touch** 2-8-12 0 .... SteveDrowne 8 42+
(E A L Dunlop) *s.i.s: hdwy over 2f out: wknd over 1f out* **100/1**

13 *hd* **Diamond Seeker** 2-8-5 0 .... AshleyMorgan(7) 4 41
(V Smith) *hld up: wknd over 2f out* **150/1**

0 **14** *9* **Racie Gracie**[28] 5595 2-8-12 0 .... AdrianMcCarthy 2 14
(John Berry) *mid-div: plld hrd: wknd over 2f out* **150/1**

1m 14.08s (0.98) **Going Correction** +0.25s/f (Good) **14** Ran SP% **118.6**
Speed ratings (Par 99): **103,102,101,101,100 95,93,89,87,86 85,81,81,69**
CSF £89.63 TOTE £3.80: £1.60, £4.10, £1.40; EX 47.90.
Owner Hamdan Al Maktoum **Bred** Lostford Manor Stud **Trained** Newmarket, Suffolk

FOCUS

A strong maiden in which they bet 20/1 bar five and the first five finished clear. A nice win from Insaaf, with the runner-up and fifth particularly making promising debuts.

NOTEBOOK

Insaaf ◆, who made such an eyecatching debut in a sales race at Ascot, looked in trouble in the dip but rallied well to assert inside the final furlong. She may not get much further than this, but could make up into a Pattern-race performer in time. (tchd 5-2)

Tawaash(USA) ◆, a $1.55m son of a multiple winner in the USA, showed plenty of promise on this debut. Going on running down into the dip, he kept galloping but could not hold the more experienced runner-up. He has a long way to go to repay his purchase price, but he should come on a good deal for the experience and can win his share of races.

Provence, who made a promising debut here earlier in the month, raced on the outside of her field but had every chance and could not find another gear up the hill. (op 10-3 tchd 7-2 in a place)

Brave Prospector, runner-up to a subsequent winner on his debut at Windsor, was always close up towards the stands' side but could only stay on at the one pace. He helps set the standard for the form. (op 5-2 tchd 3-1 in places)

Film Maker(IRE), a 75,000gns first foal, was backed beforehand and caught the eye on this debut having been held up in the rear. He looked green when making his effort but galloped on to good effect up the hill and looks sure to benefit a great deal from the experience. (op 20-1)

Danish Art(IRE), on very different ground to his debut, set the pace but was left behind when the principals began to race in earnest. He will do better in handicaps in time. Official explanation: jockey said colt became unbalanced 2f out

Etosha(IRE), a 340,000gns half-brother to two winners from the family for Gossamer and Barathea, is a long-striding sort but got rather stranded on the outside of his field and failed to pick up in the last quarter-mile. He will do better in time. (op 6-1 tchd 15-2)

Chartist, a speedily-bred half-brother to a dual 5f winner, not surprisingly showed good pace early before fading and is likely to be seen to better effect on a sound surface.

6296 ANGLO HIBERNIAN BLOODSTOCK INSURANCE EBF MAIDEN STKS (DIV II) 1m

2:00 (2:01) (Class 3) 2-Y-O £5,829 (£1,734; £866; £432) **Stalls** Low

Form RPR

1 **Mukhber** 2-9-3 0 .... RHills 3 88+
(J H M Gosden) *hld up: hdwy 3f out: edgd rt and outpcd wl over 1f out: swtchd lft 1f out: r.o to ld wl ins fnl f* **7/2**[2]

03 **2** *nk* **Irish Mayhem (USA)**[30] 5538 2-9-3 0 .... TedDurcan 7 85
(B J Meehan) *led 6f: rallied to ld ins fnl f: sn hdd: styd on* **7/2**[2]

0 **3** *1 ¼* **Black Rain**[15] 5951 2-9-3 0 .... (t) FrancisNorton 6 83
(P J McBride) *chsd ldr: rdn to ld 1f out: sn edgd lft and hdd: styd on same pce* **16/1**

2 **4** *2 ½* **Katimont (IRE)**[20] 5811 2-8-12 0 .... MichaelHills 1 72
(B W Hills) *chsd ldrs: led 2f out: sn rdn: edgd lft and hdd 1f out: no ex* **7/4**[1]

0 **5** *2 ½* **Sarah's First**[16] 5912 2-8-12 0 .... StephenDonohoe 9 67
(E A L Dunlop) *prom: rdn over 2f out: sn hung lft and outpcd: styd on ins fnl f* **40/1**

6 *2* **Stow** 2-9-3 0 .... SteveDrowne 4 67
(H Morrison) *s.s: rn green in rr: nvr nrr* **12/1**

7 *3* **Kuriyama (IRE)** 2-9-3 0 .... GeorgeBaker 11 61
(M H Tompkins) *hld up: wknd over 2f out* **33/1**

8 *1 ¾* **No Rules** 2-9-3 0 .... JimmyQuinn 10 57
(M H Tompkins) *hld up: wknd over 2f out* **20/1**

0 **9** *nk* **Hawkstar Express (IRE)**[8] 6127 2-9-3 0 .... FergusSweeney 5 56
(J R Boyle) *chsd ldrs over 5f* **100/1**

10 *12* **Special Reserve (IRE)** 2-9-3 0 .... RichardHughes 8 30
(R Hannon) *dwlt: sn chsng ldrs: wknd over 2f out* **8/1**[3]

1m 41.05s (1.68) **Going Correction** +0.25s/f (Good) **10** Ran SP% **116.6**
Speed ratings (Par 99): **101,100,99,96,94 92,89,87,87,75**
CSF £15.70 TOTE £4.30: £1.70, £1.40, £3.90; EX 22.40.
Owner Hamdan Al Maktoum **Bred** Shadwell Estate Company Limited **Trained** Newmarket, Suffolk

FOCUS

The second division of this maiden was run 0.43sec faster than the first division and fortunes changed several times in the last 2f. There is much better to come from Mukhber, with improved efforts from the next four.

NOTEBOOK

Mukhber ◆, the first foal of a half-sister to the 1000 Guineas winner Lahan, is already gelded but was representing a trainer with an outstanding record in this race. He travelled well enough, but looked in trouble running into the dip before staying on strongly up the hill to snatch the race in the last 50yds. This should bring him on significantly and he looks a decent prospect. (op 10-3 tchd 4-1)

Irish Mayhem(USA) has gradually improved with racing and put up a fine effort from the front, repelling a couple of challenges before being collared near the line. He now qualifies for a handicap mark and can win races in that sphere. (op 9-2)

Black Rain, who looked a a difficult ride on his debut, had clearly settled down for the experience and showed up throughout. He looked likely to score at a about the furlong pole before his effort faltered up the hill and he should be up to winning a race, possibly on an easier track. (op 20-1)

Katimont(IRE), a 260,000gns half-sister to six winners from the family of Shahrastani, finished clear of the rest when making an encouraging debut at Haydock and looked likely to build on that when making her challenge running into the dip.However, she could not sustain her effort and the colts drew away from her on the climb to the line. (op 13-8 tchd 6-4 and 15-8 tchd 2-1 in a place)

Sarah's First, on very different ground from her debut, showed ability but will probably be seen to better effect next season once handicapped. (op 33-1)

Stow, related to the handicappers Bajan Pride and Serramanna and from the family of Slip Anchor, looked badly in need of the experience but was getting the hang of things late on.

Special Reserve(IRE), a Derby entry and a full-brother to The Great Gatsby, who was runner-up in that event, raced close enough to the pace early but was one of the first to come under pressure and dropped right away as his rider accepted the situation. (op 9-1)

6297 PETER STONE MEMORIAL HOUGHTON CONDITIONS STKS 1m

2:35 (2:37) (Class 2) 2-Y-O

£9,348 (£2,799; £1,399; £700; £349; £175) **Stalls** Low

Form RPR

21 **1** **Kandahar Run**[37] 5321 2-9-3 90 .... TedDurcan 3 103+
(H R A Cecil) *chsd ldrs: led 2f out: sn rdn and hung rt: styd on wl* **9/4**[2]

403 **2** *3 ½* **Ghetto**[13] 6001 2-9-3 85 .... RichardHughes 2 95
(R Hannon) *led 6f: sn rdn: styd on same pce* **10/1**

210 **3** *1 ¼* **Emmrooz**[20] 5795 2-9-3 102 .... LDettori 6 92
(Saeed Bin Suroor) *hld up in tch: rdn over 1f out: wknd ins fnl f* **5/4**[1]

321 **4** *3 ½* **Lady Sorcerer**[15] 5944 2-8-7 79 .... KDarley 5 75
(A P Jarvis) *chsd ldr tl rdn: hung rt and wknd over 2f out* **20/1**

1 **5** *3 ½* **Autocue**[83] 3958 2-9-3 0 .... RyanMoore 1 77
(Sir Michael Stoute) *dwlt: sn pushed along and prom: rdn and wknd over 2f out* **9/2**[3]

0301 **6** *nk* **Cordell (IRE)**[25] 5679 2-9-3 82 .... PatDobbs 7 76
(R Hannon) *hld up in tch: rdn and wknd over 2f out* **50/1**

0U **7** *10* **Amouretta**[10] 6092 2-8-10 0 ow3 .... (v[1]) StephenDonohoe 4 47
(T T Clement) *s.s: a in rr: wknd 3f out* **250/1**

1m 39.99s (0.62) **Going Correction** +0.25s/f (Good) **7** Ran SP% **109.6**
Speed ratings (Par 101): **106,102,101,97,94 93,83**
CSF £21.48 TOTE £3.10: £1.80, £2.70; EX 18.80.
Owner Gestut Ammerland **Bred** Britton House Stud **Trained** Newmarket, Suffolk

FOCUS

A conditions race that often throws up a decent performer, run 1.06sec faster than the quickest of the two divisions of the maiden over the same trip. Winner Kandahar Run looks a nice prospect for next year.

NOTEBOOK

Kandahar Run, whose win at Doncaster was on much faster ground, had shown on his debut that he handles cut and won this decent contest in the style of a progressive performer. He had 12lb to find with the favourite judged on official ratings but the pair made their challenges simultaneously and it was soon clear he was travelling the stronger. He drew away up the hill despite wandering into the middle of the track and his style of racing suggests that he will get 1m2f at least next season. (op 15-8 tchd 5-2 in a place)

Ghetto, who had 5lb to find with the winner judged on official ratings, was nevertheless well backed at double-figure odds and justified the support with a fine effort from the front. He was no match for the winner but resisted the challenge of the favourite and the return to soft ground, on which he gained his maiden win, clearly suited. (op 16-1)

Emmrooz, who had a clear advantage judged on official ratings, not surprisingly went off favourite having been a close-up seventh in the Royal Lodge on his most recent outing. He travelled well enough into the race but when asked to deliver his challenge the response was distinctly limited and, as at Ascot, he may not have been suited by the soft ground. (op 11-8 tchd 6-4)

Lady Sorcerer, who scrambled home in a Polytrack maiden last time, had previously looked better than that on her only previous outing on soft turf. She was beaten a fair distance in the end, but showed up for a long way and helps to set the level of the form.

Autocue, who dead-heated for a maiden on the July Course on his debut, had been absent since. After missing the break, he was being pushed along from an early stage and was never travelling on this much softer ground. (op 7-2)

6298 GEORGIA HOUSE STUD DARLEY STKS (GROUP 3) 1m 1f

3:10 (3:10) (Class 1) 3-Y-O+

£26,686 (£10,114; £5,061; £2,523; £1,264; £634) **Stalls** Low

Form RPR

42-3 **1** **Windsor Knot (IRE)**[23] 5723 5-9-3 111 .... TedDurcan 6 117
(Saeed Bin Suroor) *chsd ldrs: led 2f out: rdn and edgd rt ins fnl f: styd on* **7/1**[3]

2300 **2** ¾ **Mashaahed**[83] 3974 4-9-3 112 .... MartinDwyer 11 115
(B W Hills) *hld up: hdwy over 2f out: rdn and hung lft over 1f out: styd on* **14/1**

1366 **3** *shd* **Blue Ksar (FR)**[20] 5798 4-9-3 111 .... (t) LDettori 3 115
(Saeed Bin Suroor) *s.i.s: hld up: hdwy over 2f out: rdn over 1f out: hung rt ins fnl f: eased last strides* **3/1**[1]

6012 **4** ½ **Tell**[13] 6009 4-9-3 109 .... (b) EddieAhern 10 114
(J L Dunlop) *chsd ldr tl led 1/2-way: hdd 2f out: sn rdn: nt clr run ins fnl f: styd on* **28/1**

252 **5** *3 ½* **Ordnance Row**[23] 5723 4-9-3 107 .... RyanMoore 1 107
(R Hannon) *hld up in tch: rdn over 2f out: wknd ins fnl f* **8/1**

1232 **6** *1 ¾* **Docofthebay (IRE)**[13] 6011 3-8-13 103 .... RichardHughes 7 103+
(J A Osborne) *s.i.s: hld up: swtchd lft over 2f out: rdn and hung rt over 1f out: nvr trbld ldrs* **5/1**[2]

1043 **7** ½ **Blythe Knight (IRE)**[13] 6031 7-9-7 110 .... GrahamGibbons 9 106
(J J Quinn) *prom: racd keenly: rdn and wknd over 1f out* **11/1**

4535 **8** *4* **Grand Passion (IRE)**[41] 5220 7-9-3 104 .... SteveDrowne 2 93
(G Wragg) *hld up: n.d* **66/1**

012 **9** ½ **Al Tharib (USA)**[41] 5220 3-8-13 106 .... RHills 13 92
(Sir Michael Stoute) *led to 1/2-way: rdn and wknd over 1f out* **16/1**

-202 **10** *1 1/2* **Jack Junior (USA)**[100] 3436 3-8-13 109 .... MichaelHills 12 89
(B J Meehan) *chsd ldrs: rdn over 2f out: wknd over 1f out* **25/1**

2406 **11** *nk* **Wise Dennis**[20] 5797 5-9-3 105 .... KDarley 4 89
(A P Jarvis) *hld up: rdn over 3f out: wknd 2f out* **14/1**

5625 **12** *10* **Bahia Breeze**[35] 5396 5-9-0 110 .... JimmyFortune 8 65
(Rae Guest) *chsd ldrs: rdn over 2f out: sn wknd* **9/1**

4214 **13** *2 1/2* **Illustrious Blue**[23] 5723 4-9-3 109 .... PaulDoe 5 62
(W J Knight) *s.i.s: hdwy over 4f out: rdn and wknd over 2f out* **10/1**

1m 52.38s (0.43) **Going Correction** +0.25s/f (Good)
WFA 3 from 4yo+ 4lb **13** Ran SP% **120.7**
Speed ratings (Par 113): **108,107,107,106,103 102,101,98,97,96 96,87,84**
CSF £100.52 TOTE £8.60: £3.00, £4.30, £1.60; EX 151.90.
Owner Godolphin **Bred** Tally-Ho Stud **Trained** Newmarket, Suffolk
■ Stewards' Enquiry : L Dettori seven-day ban: failed to ride out for second place (Oct 30-Nov 5)

FOCUS
A competitive-looking renewal of this Group 3, which had previously been part of the Champions' Day programme, producing a close finish. Fair form for the grade, rated through the second and third.

NOTEBOOK
Windsor Knot(IRE), who was beaten a head in this contest in 2006, gained compensation on only his second outing since. Clearly a fragile sort, this was only his 11th outing in four seasons, but he is genuine and consistent and battled on well up the hill to hold his stable companion. He clearly handles soft ground well, so connections may look for another race at a slightly higher level before the end of the season. (op 11-2)
Mashaahed, dropping in trip and grade having been held in a couple of Group 2s, had the highest official rating in the race. He was held up off the pace before being produced with a sustained challenge from the dip and saw his race out well enough, finishing closer to the winner than he did when fourth in this race last season. (op 16-1)
Blue Ksar(FR), who ran no sort of race when the stable's second string in the Queen Elizabeth II Stakes at Ascot, was Dettori's choice over the winner and went off favourite despite having never won at this level. He travelled well enough into a challenging position, but his rider soon had to get serious with him and, although he stuck to his task, his stable companion refused to let him by. As his rider accepted defeat close home and eased his mount, he lost second place which resulted in a seven-day ban. Ironically three of his four wins have been with Durcan aboard. (op 9-2)
Tell, who has looked an improved performer since being fitted with blinkers and ridden from the front, adopted the same tactics despite the longer trip and softer ground and ran a fine race once again. He was short of room once headed but stuck on again up the hill and was not beaten that far in the end. (op 25-1, 40-1 in a place)
Ordnance Row, who has plenty of form on easy ground, had finished ahead of today's winner at Goodwood recently. However, on this occasion he was being urged along some way from home and, although sticking to his task, was never really in contention and may now be feeling the effects of an arduous season. (op 15-2)
Docofthebay(IRE), who has been running well all season in handicaps, culminating in a strong-finishing second in the Cambridgeshire last time, was stepping up in grade and had the lowest official rating in the race. He never got competitive on this occasion, finishing out of the first three for the first time in his career, and maybe the soft ground at the end of a long season was a factor. (op 9-2 and 11-2 in places)
Blythe Knight(IRE), who had a 4lb penalty for beating Blue Ksar at Epsom earlier in the season, was somewhat keen early and did not get home.
Al Tharib(USA) Official explanation: vet said colt returned lame
Bahia Breeze, who had divided today's winner and third in this race last season, had been generally consistent since without winning. She failed to really figure on this occasion. (op 8-1)
Illustrious Blue Official explanation: jockey said colt ran flat

6299 LANWADES STUD SEVERALS STKS (LISTED RACE) (F&M) 1m 2f
3:45 (3:47) (Class 1) 3-Y-O+
£15,330 (£5,810; £2,907; £1,449; £726; £364) **Stalls** Low

Form RPR

261- **1** **Short Skirt**[363] 6103 4-9-2 110 .... LDettori 15 101
(Saeed Bin Suroor) *led over 6f: rdn to ld over 1f out: styd on* **11/8**[1]

2421 **2** *1/2* **Ronaldsay**[20] 5814 3-8-11 89 .... FrancisNorton 13 100+
(R Hannon) *hld up: rdn over 2f out: hdwy and edgd lft over 1f out: r.o wl* **16/1**

4615 **3** *nk* **Sweet Lilly**[41] 5241 3-9-0 111 .... DarryllHolland 12 102
(M R Channon) *trckd ldrs: plld hrd: rdn and ev ch ins fnl f: unable qck towards fin* **13/2**[2]

1224 **4** *hd* **Sell Out**[30] 5544 3-8-11 98 .... SteveDrowne 14 99
(G Wragg) *hld up: hdwy over 3f out: rdn over 1f out: styd on* **10/1**[3]

-030 **5** *1 1/2* **Mussoorie (FR)**[36] 5352 4-9-2 100 .... JimmyFortune 2 96
(J H M Gosden) *chsd ldr: led over 3f out: rdn and hdd over 1f out: no ex ins fnl f* **16/1**

5-00 **6** *3/4* **Guilia**[36] 5352 4-9-2 96 .... NCallan 10 95
(Rae Guest) *hld up: hdwy over 2f out: rdn over 1f out: styd on same pce ins fnl f* **20/1**

0431 **7** *2 1/2* **Silca Key**[8] 6129 3-8-11 73 .... TPO'Shea 16 90
(M R Channon) *hld up: styd on fr over 1f out: nt trble ldrs* **33/1**

5203 **8** *1 1/4* **Contentious (USA)**[20] 5794 3-8-11 97 .... EddieAhern 5 87
(J L Dunlop) *mid-div: hdwy 1/2-way: wknd over 1f out* **14/1**

P044 **9** *1* **Restless Soul**[18] 5859 3-8-11 55 .... J-PGuillambert 11 85?
(C A Cyzer) *hld up: rdn over 1f out: nvr nrr* **200/1**

1-43 **10** *nk* **Wagtail**[61] 4633 4-9-2 95 ....(t) StephenDonohoe 1 84
(E A L Dunlop) *chsd ldrs: rdn over 2f out: wknd over 1f out* **20/1**

3000 **11** *3/4* **Tanzanite (IRE)**[155] 1789 5-9-2 88 .... FergusSweeney 9 83
(D W P Arbuthnot) *s.i.s: hld up: hdwy over 2f out: rdn: hung rt and wknd over 1f out* **100/1**

4042 **12** *3* **Shorthand**[30] 5544 3-8-11 99 .... RyanMoore 8 77
(Sir Michael Stoute) *mid-div: n.m.r and lost pl over 3f out: wknd over 2f out* **13/2**[2]

6625 **13** *3* **Gold Hush (USA)**[20] 5794 3-8-11 89 .... TedDurcan 3 71
(Sir Michael Stoute) *chsd ldrs 8f* **16/1**

4666 **14** *2* **Italian Girl**[20] 5799 3-8-11 100 .... RichardMullen 7 67
(A P Jarvis) *hld up: plld hrd: rdn and wknd over 2f out* **25/1**

4542 **15** *1 1/4* **Vale De Lobo**[47] 5067 5-9-2 75 .... DaneO'Neill 4 64
(B R Millman) *hld up: hdwy over 3f out: wknd wl over 1f out* **100/1**

0503 **16** *hd* **Dont Dili Dali**[33] 5444 4-9-2 105 ....(p) MartinDwyer 6 64
(J S Moore) *hld up: rdn and wknd over 2f out* **33/1**

2m 7.35s (1.64) **Going Correction** +0.25s/f (Good)
WFA 3 from 4yo+ 5lb **16** Ran SP% **123.9**
Speed ratings (Par 111): **103,102,102,102,101 100,98,97,96,96 95,93,90,89,88 88**
CSF £24.79 TOTE £2.20: £1.40, £4.30, £2.30; EX 28.20.
Owner Godolphin **Bred** J M Greetham **Trained** Newmarket, Suffolk

FOCUS
A fairly uncompetitive renewal of this Listed contest with the winner and third standing out on official ratings. They went a very steady pace and this is muddling form, with the second and ninth flattered greatly and the winner a stone off her best.

NOTEBOOK
Short Skirt, who won the Musidora and St Simon Stakes for Sir Michael Stoute last season, was making her first start for Godolphin on her first appearance for almost a year and looked to have been found a good opportunity in this grade. She had no problems with the trip and ground and was ridden positively, showing plenty of resolution to hold off a number of challenges in the last quarter mile. She could got for the Group 1 Premio Lydia Tesio next weekend if she recovers from this race in time. (op 13-8, tchd 7-4 in a place)
Ronaldsay has been progressing steadily in handicaps this season and came through to earn black type in the style of a progressive filly. This performance may mean that ordinary handicaps are out of the question for her now. (op 14-1)
Sweet Lilly, who had the highest official rating in the race, did not help her chance by refusing to settle in the early stages. In the circumstances she did well to finish so close and, although she stays this longer trip, she may be best suited by returning to a mile. (tchd 7-1)
Sell Out is a consistent sort who has gradually progressed from handicapping. She again ran her race but just lacks a change of gear in this company and, although she generally runs well when held up, with that in mind it may be worth adopting more positive tactics at some stage. (op 12-1)
Mussoorie(FR), who failed to stay in the Park Hill last time, was taking a big drop in trip and was sensibly ridden up with the pace. She stuck on well but without being able to quicken and a return to 1m4f may be connections' best option.
Guilia has not really built on her early promise but this was her best effort of the season and she handled the soft ground much better than on her previous encounter with it.
Shorthand, a younger sister of the winner, is clearly not as good as her sibling and, after being held up, never figured. (op 6-1, tchd 8-1 in a place)

6300 EBF NATIONAL STUD BOADICEA FILLIES' STKS (LISTED RACE) 6f
4:20 (4:20) (Class 1) 3-Y-O+
£17,601 (£6,671; £3,338; £1,664; £833; £418) **Stalls** Low

Form RPR

1030 **1** **Lady Grace (IRE)**[77] 4118 3-8-12 101 .... MichaelHills 16 97+
(W J Haggas) *hld up on outside of centre gp: hdwy over 2f out: drifted lft to stands' side ins fnl f: kpt on wl to ld towards fin* **5/1**[2]

0-00 **2** *1/2* **Wid (USA)**[36] 5354 3-8-12 95 .... RHills 6 95
(J L Dunlop) *cl up on stands' side: led ent fnl f: hdd and no ex towards fin* **20/1**

0521 **3** *3/4* **Angus Newz**[15] 5954 4-8-13 89 ....(v) FrancisNorton 10 93
(M Quinn) *overall ldr centre: hung lft over 1f out: hdd ent fnl f: no ex nr fin* **10/1**

5040 **4** *nk* **Cape**[5] 6205 4-8-13 85 .... KDarley 4 92
(P Howling) *in tch on stands' side: rdn over 2f out: kpt on ins fnl f* **16/1**

5000 **5** *3/4* **Vital Statistics**[20] 5799 3-8-12 95 .... TQuinn 13 90
(D R C Elsworth) *towards rr in centre: drvn over 2f out: no imp tl kpt on wl fnl f: nrst fin* **16/1**

2122 **6** *1/2* **Plucky**[15] 5954 3-8-12 84 .... JimmyFortune 17 88+
(J H M Gosden) *in tch in centre: effrt over 2f out: edgd lft over 1f out: kpt on same pce fnl f* **6/1**[3]

0150 **7** *2* **Ripples Maid**[19] 5832 4-9-2 98 .... LDettori 11 85
(J A Geake) *hld up in midfield in centre: effrt over 1f out: nt pce to chal* **6/1**[3]

3062 **8** *nk* **Paradise Isle**[34] 5407 6-8-13 104 .... RichardHughes 1 81
(C F Wall) *trckd stands' side ldrs: effrt and swtchd rt over 1f out: no ex ins fnl f* **4/1**[1]

3025 **9** *hd* **Graduation**[20] 5799 3-8-12 94 .... RyanMoore 15 81
(E A L Dunlop) *hld up in centre: effrt 2f out: kpt on: nvr able to chal* **9/1**

-451 **10** *shd* **Salsa Steps (USA)**[24] 5714 3-8-12 80 ....(t) SteveDrowne 9 80
(H Morrison) *hld up in centre: drvn and outpcd over 2f out: kpt on fnl f: n.d* **14/1**

0003 **11** *hd* **Daniella**[13] 6013 5-8-13 85 ....(b) DarryllHolland 5 80
(Rae Guest) *s.i.s: bhd on stands' side tl kpt on fnl f: nrst fin* **50/1**

-303 **12** *3* **Blue Rocket (IRE)**[26] 5666 3-8-12 95 .... JohnEgan 7 71
(D J Murphy) *prom on stands' side: pushed along 1/2-way: wknd over 1f out* **14/1**

4051 **13** *3/4* **High 'n Dry (IRE)**[11] 6062 3-8-12 69 .... J-PGuillambert 3 69
(C A Cyzer) *in tch on stands' side: hung rt and outpcd over 2f out: sn btn* **125/1**

0666 **14** *2* **Katie Boo (IRE)**[26] 5666 5-8-13 85 .... TedDurcan 14 63
(A Berry) *chsd centre ldrs tl rdn and wknd fr over 2f out* **66/1**

-350 **15** *2* **Pinkabout (IRE)**[19] 5850 3-8-12 83 .... MartinDwyer 18 57
(J S Moore) *racd on outside of centre gp: rdn and hung rt 2f out: sn btn* **66/1**

1400 **16** *1/2* **Thunderousapplause**[13] 6002 3-8-12 83 .... NCallan 12 55
(K A Ryan) *prom in centre tl rdn and wknd fr 2f out* **66/1**

1125 **17** *4* **Day By Day**[26] 5666 3-8-12 90 ....(b) RobertHavlin 8 43
(B J Meehan) *in tch in centre tl wknd over 2f out* **50/1**

1m 13.39s (0.29) **Going Correction** +0.25s/f (Good)
WFA 3 from 4yo+ 1lb **17** Ran SP% **123.4**
Speed ratings (Par 108): **108,107,106,105,104 104,101,101,100,100 100,96,95,92,90 89,84**
CSF £109.86 TOTE £7.10: £2.80, £6.90, £3.90; EX 201.00.
Owner F C T Wilson **Bred** Frank Barry **Trained** Newmarket, Suffolk
■ Stewards' Enquiry : Michael Hills caution: careless riding

FOCUS
An ordinary renewal of this Listed contest with only two rated above 100, but a close finish. The runners raced in three groups across the track early but mostly converged towards the stands' rail at the finish. The form is best rated through the third and sixth but is a bit muddling.

NOTEBOOK
Lady Grace(IRE), who likes soft ground and stays as far as a mile, put her stamina to good use to wear down her rivals in the closing stages. She deserves extra credit as she started her run in the far-side group and drifted right across the track under pressure. (op 11-2 tchd 6-1)
Wid(USA), having only her third run of the season, showed that she retained some ability at Doncaster last time and built on that on this drop back to 6f, sticking on really well having been close up throughout. If kept in training she should find suitable opportunities at this level next year. (op 18-1)
Angus Newz has been a terrific standard-bearer for her stable and put up another fine effort from the front on ground that she handles well. She was just run out of things late on but ran virtually to the pound with Plucky compared with their form over course and distance earlier in the month. Official explanation: jockey said filly hung left
Cape had been struggling a little in handicaps and had plenty to find on official ratings, but she had won on her only previous race on this track and showed her liking for it by staying on good style to finish on the heels of the principals. She may yet be able to add to her tally. (op 20-1, tchd in 33-1 in a place)
Vital Statistics, who beat today's runner-up in a Listed race at Salisbury last season, had found things difficult in Pattern company over longer trips this year and the drop in trip saw clear signs of a revival. She came from well off the pace and was closing down on her rivals at the finish, so may have more to offer if connections persevere with her. Official explanation: jockey said filly hung left (tchd 14-1)
Plucky, relatively inexperienced and making her debut at this level, ran right up to recent form on a line through Angus Newz and helps set the standard. (op 13-2)

Ripples Maid, who appreciates some cut in the ground, had a penalty to carry and never really got in a blow. (op 13-2)
Paradise Isle, top on official ratings and with a good record on this track, broke smartly but was settled just off the pace. She was unable to respond when asked and, unless connections take another trip to Dubai this winter, it may be that she is off to stud now. (op 7-2 tchd 9-2)
Day By Day Official explanation: jockey said filly was unsuited by the soft (good to soft places) ground

6301 TURFTV H'CAP 7f
4:55 (4:55) (Class 2) (0-100,98) 3-Y-0+

£12,464 (£3,732; £1,866; £934; £466; £234) **Stalls** Low

Form RPR
1006 **1** **Damika (IRE)**[13] 6013 4-9-0 **90** ... TedDurcan 20 99
(R M Whitaker) *hld up: hdwy to ld over 1f out: sn rdn: r.o* **50/1**
6244 **2** ½ **Vitznau (IRE)**[13] 6013 3-9-2 **94** ... RichardHughes 16 101+
(R Hannon) *hld up: swtchd lft over 2f out: hdwy over 1f out: r.o* **8/1**[2]
6000 **3** ½ **Capable Guest (IRE)**[13] 6011 5-8-10 **86** ...(v) ChrisCatlin 18 92
(M R Channon) *hld up: hdwy over 1f out: r.o* **25/1**
2001 **4** ¾ **Masai Moon**[16] 5923 3-8-9 **87** ... JimCrowley 25 91
(B R Millman) *hld up: hdwy over 2f out: rdn and ev ch over 1f out: edgd lft: styd on same pce ins fnl f* **33/1**
3035 **5** ½ **Purus (IRE)**[13] 6013 5-8-5 **84** ... LukeMorris(3) 4 87
(R A Teal) *hld up: hdwy and nt clr run over 1f out: nrst fin* **33/1**
1210 **6** ½ **Starlight Gazer**[83] 3943 4-8-6 **82** ... RichardThomas 23 83
(J A Geake) *prom: rdn over 2f out: styd on same pce fnl f* **33/1**
-306 **7** *nk* **Evens And Odds (IRE)**[36] 5355 3-9-4 **96** ... NCallan 22 97+
(K A Ryan) *chsd ldrs: led over 1f out: sn hung lft and hdd: no ex ins fnl f* **33/1**
2202 **8** *nk* **Sohraab**[21] 5765 3-8-11 **89** ... SteveDrowne 26 89
(H Morrison) *hld up: hdwy over 1f out: nt rch ldrs* **20/1**
0402 **9** ½ **Prince Of Thebes (IRE)**[7] 6155 6-8-6 **82** oh1 ... JimmyQuinn 14 81+
(J Akehurst) *chsd ldrs: hmpd and lost pl over 1f out: styd on ins fnl f* **12/1**
0123 **10** 1 ½ **Commando Scott (IRE)**[6] 6183 6-9-2 **92** ... GregFairley 9 87
(I W McInnes) *chsd ldrs: rdn over 2f out: edgd rt over 1f out: no ex fnl f* **8/1**[2]
0000 **11** *shd* **Royal Power (IRE)**[20] 5797 4-9-5 **95** ... DarryllHolland 13 89
(M R Channon) *chsd ldrs: rdn over 2f out: no ex fnl f* **66/1**
0104 **12** ¾ **Danehillsundance (IRE)**[11] 6053 3-9-3 **95** ... RyanMoore 11 87
(R Hannon) *s.i.s: hld up: hdwy over 1f out: nvr nrr* **22/1**
2225 **13** 1 ½ **Heroes**[11] 6053 3-8-8 **89** ... WilliamBuick(3) 8 78
(G A Huffer) *mid-div: rdn 1/2-way: n.d* **18/1**
2064 **14** *hd* **Imperial Echo (USA)**[20] 5804 6-8-6 **82** ... RichardMullen 17 70
(T D Barron) *hld up: rdn over 2f out: n.d* **33/1**
0000 **15** *nk* **King's Caprice**[34] 5413 6-9-2 **92** ...(vt) StephenCarson 15 79
(J A Geake) *led: rdn and hdd over 1f out: wknd ins fnl f* **25/1**
1002 **16** ½ **Thabaat**[20] 5804 3-8-5 **83** ... MartinDwyer 7 69
(B W Hills) *chsd ldrs over 4f* **16/1**
1424 **17** *shd* **Artimino**[69] 4401 3-9-6 **98** ...(t) OscarUrbina 19 84
(J R Fanshawe) *hld up: rdn and wknd over 1f out* **17/2**[3]
3210 **18** *nk* **Salient**[13] 6013 3-8-8 **86** ... PaulDoe 1 71
(J Akehurst) *chsd ldrs: rdn 1/2-way: wknd over 1f out* **50/1**
1210 **19** ¾ **South Cape**[13] 6013 4-9-3 **93** ... TPO'Shea 10 76
(M R Channon) *sn pushed along in rr: effrt 1/2-way: n.d* **28/1**
6030 **20** 1 **Jedburgh**[13] 6013 6-9-2 **92** ...(b) JimmyFortune 6 72
(J L Dunlop) *hld up: sme hdwy whn bmpd over 1f out: n.d* **22/1**
1540 **21** *nk* **Mutanaseb (USA)**[20] 5797 3-9-2 **94** ...(p) RHills 24 74
(M A Jarvis) *prom: rdn 1/2-way: wknd over 1f out* **12/1**
3-00 **22** 2 **Kompete**[13] 6013 3-8-1 **86** ow1 ... AMorgan(7) 12 60
(V Smith) *prom over 4f* **50/1**
4230 **23** 2 ½ **Lone Wolfe**[28] 5588 3-9-5 **97** ... JohnEgan 2 65
(Jane Chapple-Hyam) *chsd ldrs: rdn over 2f out: wknd over 1f out* **100/1**
1505 **24** ½ **Para Siempre**[19] 5833 3-8-11 **89** ...(b) PaulMulrennan 21 56
(B Smart) *chsd ldrs over 5f* **100/1**
1-0 **25** *shd* **Kafuu (IRE)**[13] 6013 3-8-6 **84** ... EddieAhern 3 50
(J Noseda) *prom: lost pl over 5f out: rdn over 2f out: sn wknd* **3/1**[1]
0140 **26** 1 ¾ **Jamieson Gold (IRE)**[49] 4990 4-8-11 **87** ... MichaelHills 5 49
(B W Hills) *chsd ldrs: lost pl over 3f out: wknd over 2f out* **50/1**

1m 26.57s (0.07) **Going Correction** +0.25s/f (Good)
WFA 3 from 4yo+ 2lb **26** Ran SP% **134.9**
Speed ratings (Par 109): **109,108,107,107,106 105,105,105,104,102 102,101,100,99,99 99,98,98,97,96 96,93,91,90,90 88**
CSF £376.93 CT £9991.17 TOTE £75.50: £11.40, £2.80, £5.40, £4.60; EX 433.10.
Owner G B Bedford **Bred** Patrick J Monahan **Trained** Scarcroft, W Yorks

FOCUS
A good, competitive handicap run at a strong early gallop in which the runners were spread across the entire width of the course. Sound form.

NOTEBOOK
Damika(IRE), who had looked somewhat unlucky in a similar race at the Cambridgeshire meeting, came through towards the far side of the course to reverse placings with the runner-up and fifth, who had finished ahead of him on that occasion. He handled the ground well enough and is clearly in good heart at present.
Vitznau(IRE) ◆ is a very consistent individual and looked somewhat unfortunate once again as he travelled well and made what looked like a winning effort towards the centre of the track, only to find the winner on the far side had established too much of an advantage. He really deserves to pick up one of these good handicaps before long. (tchd 17-2)
Capable Guest(IRE) ◆ was dropping in trip having been running over a mile and nine furlongs for most of the season. He had also dropped back to his last winning mark and finished to good effect in the wake of the runner-up. He handles most ground so should have a choice of options next, with a return to Polytrack also possible.
Masai Moon, who recently returned to winning form following a summer break, like the winner raced towards the far side and deserves plenty of credit for another decent effort off his highest-ever mark. He looks progressive and should make a decent four-year-old.
Purus(IRE) put up another good effort following his fifth, ahead of today's winner, here a fortnight previously. He is clearly in good heart and could pick up a similar contest, especially on a turning track.
Starlight Gazer, a progressive performer earlier in the season, was returning from a 12-week break. He ran a fine race and, given similar ground, could well pick up another race before the end of the season.
Evens And Odds(IRE), only recently returned to action after finishing out the back in the 2000 Guineas, showed up well throughout and, leading briefly in the dip, did not drop away once headed. This was a fine effort on his first try on this sort of ground.
Sohraab, who has been generally consistent over sprint trips this season, was given a waiting ride on this first try at 7f and never got into contention.
Prince Of Thebes(IRE), racing from just out of the handicap, was hampered at a vital stage before running on again. He is another who has found some form of late and could be one to keep in mind. (op 14-1)
Commando Scott(IRE) has run well on several occasions over course and distance but his only success here was over a furlong shorter. He appeared to have his chance but could not produce the extra gears in the last furlong. (op 7-1)
Kafuu(IRE), who was a big eyecatcher when running on late to finish a half-length behind today's winner here at the Cambridgeshire meeting on his first outing for a year, was not surprisingly all the rage to reverse placings. However, it appeared that he suffered from the dreaded 'bounce' as he dropped out of contention at the top of the hill and finished out the back. He can be given another chance but may need a fair while to recover. (op 7-2)

6302 THOROUGHBRED OWNER AND BREEDER MAGAZINE H'CAP 1m 4f
5:30 (5:30) (Class 2) (0-100,96) 3-Y-0+

£12,464 (£3,732; £1,866; £934; £466; £234) **Stalls** Low

Form RPR
-120 **1** **Greek Envoy**[59] 4690 3-9-7 **96** ... TedDurcan 1 109+
(T P Tate) *hld up: smooth hdwy over 2f out: rdn to ld and edgd rt over 1f out: hld on wl u.p* **8/1**
1/44 **2** *nk* **Cutting Crew (USA)**[13] 6014 6-9-7 **89** ... AdamKirby 6 102
(W R Swinburn) *led: rdn over 2f out: edgd lft and hdd over 1f out: rallied u.p: hld towards fin* **7/2**[3]
1361 **3** 5 **Esthlos (FR)**[7] 6158 4-8-8 **79** ... LukeMorris(3) 3 84
(J Jay) *hld up: rdn and outpcd over 2f out: rallied over 1f out: kpt on: no ch w first 2* **15/8**[1]
664 **4** ¾ **Oh Glory Be (USA)**[15] 5940 4-9-7 **89** ... RichardHughes 5 93
(R Hannon) *pressed ldr: effrt over 2f out: no ex over 1f out* **20/1**
4246 **5** *hd* **Velvet Heights (IRE)**[20] 5800 5-9-3 **85** ... EddieAhern 9 88
(J L Dunlop) *hld up: drvn and outpcd over 3f out: rallied fnl f: no imp* **14/1**
000 **6** 2 **Kings Quay**[90] 2859 5-9-6 **88** ...(t) GrahamGibbons 8 88
(J J Quinn) *prom: drvn along 3f out: wknd over 1f out* **25/1**
0034 **7** 1 ¼ **Dubai Twilight**[6] 6169 3-9-0 **89** ... MichaelHills 7 87
(B W Hills) *t.k.h: chsd ldrs: effrt and rdn over 2f out: wknd over 1f out* **11/4**[2]
0400 **8** ¾ **Mikao (IRE)**[13] 6014 6-9-9 **91** ... GeorgeBaker 2 88
(M H Tompkins) *hld up in tch: drvn over 2f out: sn btn* **20/1**

2m 34.07s (0.57) **Going Correction** +0.25s/f (Good)
WFA 3 from 4yo+ 7lb **8** Ran SP% **114.8**
Speed ratings (Par 109): **108,107,104,103,103 102,101,101**
CSF £35.19 CT £74.62 TOTE £7.90: £2.00, £1.70, £1.30; EX 32.70 Place 6 £ 34.83, Place 5 £ 29.37.
Owner T P Tate **Bred** Worksop Manor Stud **Trained** Tadcaster, N Yorks
■ An 11,933/1 four-timer for Ted Durcan, his first in Britain.
■ Stewards' Enquiry : Ted Durcan caution: careless riding; one-day ban: used whip with excessive frequency down shoulder in forehand position (Oct 30)

FOCUS
A good handicap run at a sound gallop and the first two drew clear. The form has been taken at face value.

NOTEBOOK
Greek Envoy, having his second try at this trip and back on his favoured soft ground, travelled well and looked sure to pull away when delivering his challenge, but possibly his stamina began to ebb and his in-form rider had to be at his strongest to resist the renewed effort of the runner-up. This was only his seventh race and he looks a progressive sort, and with plenty of size about him his owner/trainer can expect to get offers for him from the jumping boys, although he is more than capable in that sphere himself. (op 7-1)
Cutting Crew(USA) ◆, who has come back really well following three years off the track due to injury, is a really likeable, enthusiastic individual and, having made the running, fought back tigerishly despite being dwarfed and intimidated by the winner in the closing stages. He deserves to pick up a decent handicap at around this trip. (op 4-1 tchd 9-2)
Esthlos(FR), winner of an apprentice handicap at York the previous week following a decent effort here, was unpenalised for that and was sent off favourite. However, he was up in grade and was unable to pick up enough to deliver a meaningful challenge, so may need to drop back in grade to score again. (op 9-4)
Oh Glory Be(USA) has generally been taking on decent company since winning in the early summer and, although this was a better effort than of late, she seems better at Salisbury than anywhere else. (op 25-1)
Velvet Heights(IRE) the majority of whose wins have been on the All-Weather, was also dropping back in trip and ran as if he needs longer trips, being outpaced before staying on well up the climb to the line. (op 11-1 tchd 10-1)
Kings Quay, who has taken really well to hurdles but is still a capable performer on the Flat, was having his first outing for nearly three months. Presumably this will have primed him for a return to jumping, with something like the Greatwood Hurdle at Cheltenham next month likely to be on the agenda. (op 16-1)
Dubai Twilight, who has run well in a couple of even more competitive handicaps at Ascot of late, was too keen early on and not surprisingly failed to get home. (op 3-1 tchd 5-2)
T/Plt: £60.90 to a £1 stake. Pool: £57,467.30. 688.60 winning tickets. T/Qpdt: £23.30 to a £1 stake. Pool: £3,395.30. 107.55 winning tickets. CR

6015 REDCAR (L-H)
Friday, October 19

OFFICIAL GOING: Good (good to firm in places; 9.8)
The ground was reckoned to be riding just on the easy side of good.
Wind: light 1/2 behind Weather: Overcast and cool

6303 TRANSMORE VAN HIRE MEDIAN AUCTION MAIDEN STKS (DIV I) 1m
1:40 (1:42) (Class 6) 2-Y-0 **£1,365** (£403; £201) **Stalls** Centre

Form RPR
4462 **1** **Celtic Strand (IRE)**[30] 5526 2-9-3 74 ... MickyFenton 9 72
(T P Tate) *mde all: pushed clr 3f out: rdn wl over 1f out: drvn and edgd lft ins fnl f: hld on wl* **7/2**[2]
02 **2** *hd* **Long Distance (FR)**[24] 5702 2-9-3 0 ... JamieSpencer 7 72
(J R Fanshawe) *prom: trckd wnr fr over 2f out: rdn to chal ins fnl f: sn drvn and ev ch tl no ex nr fin* **8/11**[1]
0 **3** 1 ¼ **Bishopbriggs (USA)**[16] 5910 2-8-12 0 ... JamesO'Reilly(5) 8 69
(D J Murphy) *stdd s: t.k.h and hld up in rr: stdy hdwy 3f out: chsd ldrs 2f out: ev ch ent fnl f: sn rdn and kpt on same pce* **11/2**[3]
0 **4** 3 ½ **Ibrox (IRE)**[29] 5551 2-9-0 0 ... MichaelJStainton(3) 5 61
(R M Whitaker) *towards rr: hdwy on outer 1/2-way: rdn to chse ldrs 2f out: kpt on u.p ins fnl f* **28/1**
00 **5** 3 **Umverti**[7] 6156 2-8-12 0 ... SilvestreDeSousa 2 50
(N Bycroft) *chsd ldrs: rdn along over 2f out and kpt on same pce* **33/1**
0 **6** 3 ½ **Harrison's Star**[16] 5904 2-9-3 0 ... PhillipMakin 10 47
(G M Moore) *towards rr: pushed along 1/2-way: styd on u.p fnl 2f: nvr nr ldrs* **40/1**
0 **7** 1 **Northgate Maisie**[9] 6107 2-8-12 0 ... TonyHamilton 11 40
(Jedd O'Keeffe) *chsd ldrs: rdn along 1/2-way: grad wknd* **150/1**

The Form Book, Raceform Ltd, Compton, RG20 6NL

06 **8** *shd* **Evette**[16] 5901 2-8-12 0 RoystonFfrench 4 40
(M Johnston) *chsd ldrs: rdn along 3f out and sn wknd* **16/1**
9 *nk* **Orkney (IRE)** 2-9-3 0 TomEaves 3 44
(Miss J A Camacho) *s.i.s: a towards rr* **50/1**
06 **10** *5* **Wimoweh (IRE)**[32] 5485 2-9-3 0 (t) DavidAllan 6 33
(T D Easterby) *in tch: rdn along 1/2-way and grad wknd* **66/1**
11 *10* **Dancing Maite** 2-9-3 0 PaulEddery 12 11
(S R Bowring) *hung rt and a towards rr* **100/1**

1m 39.47s (1.67) **Going Correction** -0.025s/f (Good) 11 Ran SP% **115.3**
Speed ratings (Par 93): **90,89,88,85,82 78,77,77,77,72 62**
CSF £6.04 TOTE £3.70: £1.30, £1.02, £2.00; EX 7.20.
Owner Mrs Louise Worthington **Bred** P D Savill **Trained** Tadcaster, N Yorks

FOCUS
The first division of this maiden lacked strength in depth and was run at just a modest gallop until the tempo increased from halfway. The winner is rated as having improved slightly.

NOTEBOOK
Celtic Strand(IRE), who made all the running, lobbed along in front with his ears pricked for much of the race. Edging to his right under pressure, he looked to be staring defeat in the face when the runner-up loomed large, but he battled on gamely. (op 3-1)
Long Distance(FR) travelled smoothly through the race and looked sure to overhaul the winner when asked to go about his business, but he failed to find as much as he had promised for pressure and the winner was just holding him to the finish. (op 4-5 tchd 4-6)
Bishopbriggs(USA) clearly has a fair level of ability, for he ran well here despite failing to settle through the early stages. Once he relaxes a little more, he should begin to progress. (op 5-1 tchd 6-1)
Ibrox(IRE), a half-brother to five winners, shaped better than on his debut and shapes as though he will get a bit further. (op 40-1)
Umverti will have better prospects now that she qualifies for a handicap mark.
Dancing Maite Official explanation: jockey said colt hung right-handed and lost its action

6304 SAWFISH SOFTWARE LADIES' H'CAP (FOR LADY AMATEUR RIDERS) 1m 2f
2:10 (2:12) (Class 6) (0-60,60) 3-Y-0+ **£1,977** (£608; £304) **Stalls** Low

Form RPR
3366 **1** **Gala Sunday (USA)**[24] 5704 7-10-1 **54** (bt) MissSBrotherton 8 63
(M W Easterby) *trckd ldrs: hdwy on inner to ld appr fnl f: drvn out* **5/1**[1]
3360 **2** *1 1/4* **Waterloo Corner**[39] 5286 5-9-13 **52** MissFayeBramley 12 58
(R Craggs) *in tch: effrt over 2f out: styd on to go 2nd jst ins fnl f: no ex* **17/2**[3]
0345 **3** *1 3/4* **Zabeel Tower**[32] 5476 4-9-9 **53** MissAWallace(5) 6 56
(R Allan) *chsd ldr: styd on same pce appr fnl f* **11/1**
0-40 **4** *1 1/2* **Mister Pete (IRE)**[23] 5737 4-9-10 **52** MissGDGracey-Davison(3) 4 52
(W Storey) *in tch: effrt 3f out: kpt on fnl f* **18/1**
6030 **5** *1/2* **Wulimaster (USA)**[10] 6077 4-10-5 **58** MissADeniel 5 57
(D W Barker) *in rr: effrt 3f out: swtchd rt and styd on wl fnl f* **10/1**
0015 **6** *nk* **Contemplation**[10] 6077 4-10-7 **60** MissLEllison 3 58
(G A Swinbank) *hld up in rr: effrt on outer over 2f out: kpt on fnl f: nvr trbld ldrs* **6/1**[2]
0020 **7** *3/4* **Playtotheaudience**[2] 6265 4-9-4 **50** (b) MissLEBurke(7) 14 46
(R A Fahey) *t.k.h: led after 1f: clr over 5f out: wknd and hdd appr fnl f* **11/1**
314 **8** *1/2* **Grandad Bill (IRE)**[14] 5964 4-9-12 **51** MrsCBartley 11 46
(J S Goldie) *hld up in mid-div: effrt over 3f out: sn btn* **6/1**[2]
1054 **9** *1/2* **Chasing Memories (IRE)**[15] 5936 3-9-11 **58** MissARyan(3) 10 52
(B Smart) *mid-div: effrt over 3f out: nvr a threat* **14/1**
6300 **10** *5* **Pianoforte (USA)**[13] 6016 5-10-0 **60** MissSESiddall(7) 2 44
(E J Alston) *hld up in rr: sme hdwy over 2f out: sn wknd* **11/1**
1004 **11** *2* **Garibaldi (GER)**[13] 6019 5-9-7 **53** (b) MissACollev(7) 7 33
(J O'Reilly) *s.s: hdwy on outer 7f out: hrd rdn and hung lft over 1f out: sn wknd* **25/1**
0050 **12** *2* **Scotty's Future (IRE)**[24] 5704 9-9-8 **52** MissMMullineaux(5) 15 28
(A Berry) *s.s: swtchd lft after s: sn wl bhd: nvr on terms* **40/1**
4215 **13** *1/2* **Catherines Cafe (IRE)**[103] 3343 4-9-8 **52** MissHCuthbert(5) 1 27
(A C Whillans) *hld up towards rr: effrt 3f out: sn wknd* **12/1**
3000 **14** *2* **Magnum Opus (IRE)**[24] 5704 5-9-6 **52** MissKECooper(7) 9 23
(D J Murphy) *led 1f: chsd ldrs: lost pl over 2f out* **20/1**
0500 **15** *8* **West End Lad**[17] 5886 4-10-2 **55** MrsMMorris 13 10
(S R Bowring) *in rr: hung rt and bhd fnl 3f* **40/1**

2m 9.58s (2.78) **Going Correction** -0.025s/f (Good)
WFA 3 from 4yo+ 5lb 15 Ran SP% **123.0**
Speed ratings (Par 101): **87,86,84,83,83 82,82,81,81,77 75,74,73,72,65**
CSF £45.39 CT £455.55 TOTE £5.90: £2.20, £2.80, £3.50; EX 64.10.
Owner Steve Hull **Bred** Juddmonte Farms Inc **Trained** Sheriff Hutton, N Yorks

FOCUS
A weak lady riders' handicap. The winner had run to this mark previously this year but overall the form is a shade dubious.
Contemplation Official explanation: jockey said gelding had a breathing problem
Garibaldi(GER) Official explanation: jockey said gelding hung left in straight
West End Lad Official explanation: jockey said gelding hung right throughout

6305 CLAIRE & KENNY GOT MARRIED IN VEGAS CLAIMING STKS 7f
2:45 (2:48) (Class 6) 2-Y-0 **£2,047** (£604; £302) **Stalls** Centre

Form RPR
5430 **1** **Countrywide Comet (IRE)**[7] 6150 2-8-13 59 (b1) JamieSpencer 5 61
(K A Ryan) *trckd ldng pair: hdwy 2f out: rdn to ld over 1f out: kpt on* **2/1**[1]
0000 **2** *1 1/4* **Bonny's Babe**[27] 5644 2-8-8 50 (t) PaulEddery 10 53
(B Smart) *in tch: hdwy over 2f out: rdn to chse wnr ent fnl f: sn edgd lft and one pce* **12/1**
3640 **3** *1 3/4* **Prunes**[10] 6075 2-8-5 57 PatrickMathers(3) 11 49
(A Berry) *in tch: hdwy over 2f out: sn rdn: styd on u.p ins fnl f: nrst fin* **13/2**[3]
5000 **4** *1/2* **Tenth Night (IRE)**[15] 5932 2-8-7 48 MickyFenton 12 46
(P T Midgley) *sn outpcd and bhd: hdwy over 2f out: styd on wl appr fnl f: nrst fin* **25/1**
0050 **5** *shd* **Scientific**[32] 5477 2-8-3 50 DaleGibson 7 42
(R A Fahey) *towards rr: hdwy over 2f out: sn rdn: kpt on u.p ins fnl f* **22/1**
5002 **6** *6* **Seconds Out (IRE)**[5] 6207 2-9-0 55 (b) TravisBlock(3) 9 41
(Sir Mark Prescott) *led: rdn along 2f out: drvn and hdd over 1f out: wknd ins fnl f* **11/4**[2]
0000 **7** *1 1/4* **Powys Lad**[9] 6099 2-9-3 49 (v1) TPQueally 8 38
(K R Burke) *chsd ldr: rdn along and hd high 2f out: sn edgd lft and wknd over 1f out* **14/1**
0305 **8** *1 3/4* **Buju**[29] 5572 2-8-5 55 DO'Donohoe 13 22
(N Tinkler) *midfield: effrt and rdn along over 2f out: sn hung lft and no imp* **14/1**
0660 **9** *1 1/4* **Abbey Express**[46] 5081 2-8-9 56 PhillipMakin 2 22
(M Dods) *chsd ldrs: rdn along 3f out: sn wknd* **20/1**
0065 **10** *shd* **Eboracum Dream**[32] 5477 2-8-8 52 (b) DavidAllan 6 21
(T D Easterby) *nvr nr ldrs* **14/1**
0550 **11** *4* **Son Of Spartacus (IRE)**[4] 6242 2-8-13 55 (b) TomEaves 1 16
(Mrs L Stubbs) *nvr nr ldrs* **25/1**
0 **12** *3* **Call Of Ktulu (IRE)**[56] 4784 2-9-0 0 (p) PJMcDonald(3) 3 13
(J S Wainwright) *a in rr* **100/1**
0000 **13** *6* **Premier Class (IRE)**[29] 5572 2-9-3 50 TonyHamilton 15 —
(J S Wainwright) *bhd fr 1/2-way* **33/1**
0 **14** *12* **Ournina**[23] 5735 2-8-2 0 RoystonFfrench 14 —
(C R Wilson) *s.i.s: a bhd* **100/1**

1m 25.88s (0.98) **Going Correction** -0.025s/f (Good) 14 Ran SP% **122.7**
Speed ratings (Par 93): **93,91,89,89,88 82,80,78,77,77 72,69,62,48**
CSF £26.35 TOTE £3.00: £1.40, £4.00, £2.30; EX 36.10.
Owner Countrywide Racing **Bred** Mrs R Leonard **Trained** Hambleton, N Yorks

FOCUS
An ordinary contest and the form, rated through the winner, probably means little outside this level.

NOTEBOOK
Countrywide Comet(IRE), who had some respectable bits of form to his credit, seemed to appreciate this drop back in distance and this drop down in grade. Always travelling comfortably in first-time blinkers, he threatened to hang fire when asked to go about his job, but Spencer made up his mind for him and he did what was required. (op 11-4 tchd 3-1)
Bonny's Babe, with a tongue-tie fitted, was produced to have every chance but did not get home quite as well as the winner. (op 14-1)
Prunes, dropped down in grade, ran a respectable race in third even though she was comfortably held by the first two. (op 6-1 tchd 11-2)
Tenth Night(IRE), who is rated only 48, was next home, and his close proximity puts the overall standard of this contest into some sort of perspective. (op 33-1)
Scientific was not beaten that far, but probably achieved little. (op 25-1)
Seconds Out(IRE) did not do so well in the headgear this time on this return to turf and did not get home despite the shorter trip. (tchd 9-4)

6306 EBF CHRISTMAS PARTIES AT REDCAR MAIDEN FILLIES' STKS 6f
3:20 (3:23) (Class 5) 2-Y-0 **£3,465** (£1,030; £515; £257) **Stalls** Centre

Form RPR
3203 **1** **Spinning Lucy (IRE)**[15] 5949 2-9-0 82 SebSanders 3 83+
(B W Hills) *mde all: qckly clr over 1f out: pushed out* **4/5**[1]
5306 **2** *5* **Hasty Lady**[27] 5624 2-9-0 68 DO'Donohoe 2 68
(K A Ryan) *chsd ldrs: styd on to go 2nd ins fnl f: no ch w wnr* **20/1**
05 **3** *1/2* **Island Music (IRE)**[16] 5903 2-9-0 0 PatCosgrave 7 67
(J J Quinn) *prom: kpt on wl fnl f* **28/1**
4 *1 1/2* **Anne Of Kiev (IRE)** 2-9-0 0 DaleGibson 9 62+
(J H M Gosden) *s.i.s: sn midfield: effrt 3f out: hung lft: kpt on wl fnl f* **12/1**[3]
6 **5** *1/2* **Seta Pura**[37] 5328 2-9-0 0 RoystonFfrench 12 61
(Mrs A Duffield) *chsd wnr: edgd rt and one pce fnl 2f* **14/1**
060 **6** *1* **Steph The Ref**[21] 5770 2-8-11 44 MichaelJStainton(3) 11 58
(R M Whitaker) *mid-div: kpt on fnl 2f: nvr trbld ldrs* **125/1**
5 **7** *3* **Piverina (IRE)**[29] 5550 2-9-0 0 PhillipMakin 4 49
(T D Barron) *dwlt: sn drvn along to chse ldrs: outpcd over 2f out: no threat after* **14/1**
0000 **8** *1 3/4* **Miss Sunshine**[32] 5484 2-8-9 51 GaryBartley(5) 6 43
(J S Goldie) *t.k.h in mid-div: effrt over 2f out: nvr nr ldrs* **125/1**
0 **9** *nk* **Cealtra Star (IRE)**[57] 4733 2-8-11 0 AndrewMullen(3) 14 42
(K A Ryan) *chsd ldrs: wknd over 1f out* **33/1**
0 **10** *nk* **Petidium**[31] 5501 2-8-7 0 DanielleMcCreery(7) 15 41
(N Bycroft) *chsd ldrs: edgd lft and lost pl over 1f out* **125/1**
00 **11** *2* **Princess Maria (USA)**[16] 5903 2-9-0 0 TonyHamilton 5 35
(R A Fahey) *sn outpcd in rr: nvr on terms* **100/1**
0 **12** *nk* **Petite Music (IRE)**[7] 6156 2-9-0 0 DavidAllan 8 35
(T D Easterby) *s.s: a in rr* **100/1**
13 *6* **Ibis (USA)** 2-9-0 0 JamieSpencer 1 17+
(Saeed Bin Suroor) *rrd over and uns rdr bef s: dwlt: sn in tch on outer: lost pl and eased over 1f out* **5/2**[2]
14 *2* **Tendulkar's Diva (IRE)** 2-8-11 0 PatrickMathers(3) 10 11
(A Berry) *s.s: a bhd* **125/1**
15 *nk* **Mathool (IRE)** 2-9-0 0 TomEaves 13 10
(C W Thornton) *s.s: a bhd* **80/1**

1m 11.5s (-0.20) **Going Correction** -0.025s/f (Good) 15 Ran SP% **122.7**
Speed ratings (Par 92): **100,93,92,90,90 88,84,82,81,81 78,78,70,67,67**
CSF £26.19 TOTE £1.70: £1.10, £4.00, £5.50; EX 23.30.
Owner Steve Jenkins **Bred** Patrick Cummins **Trained** Lambourn, Berks

FOCUS
An ordinary maiden with the exposed runner-up rated just 68 and the guide to the level, and the sixth only 44. The 82-rated winner was fully entitled to score in good style.

NOTEBOOK
Spinning Lucy(IRE), who really stretches out and covers the ground, forged clear coming to the final furlong to score in most convincing fashion. (op 11-10 tchd 6-5)
Hasty Lady, having her sixth start, found the drop back to six no problem but the winner was much too good. (tchd 18-1)
Island Music(IRE) ran her best race on her third start and this sets her up for modest handicaps at three. (op 33-1)
Anne Of Kiev(IRE), third foal and half-sister to two winners, cost 250,000gns. A medium-sized, good-bodied filly, she was fairly clueless but stayed on in encouraging fashion late in the day. She will not be seen at her best until next year.
Seta Pura, who showed ability on her debut over further on her debut, is not very big but very robust. Connections will be hoping she comes good over middle distances in handicap company at three. (op 12-1)
Steph The Ref, who had shown little in three previous starts, is rated just 44. (op 100-1)
Ibis(USA), a narrow type, was fitted with a rope halter and wore a blanket for stalls entry. However, she reared over at the start and proved awkward to load. After a tardy start she never got competitive and in the end her rider threw in the towel. With her it is all in the mind. Official explanation: jockey said filly had no more to give having become upset in stalls (op 2-1)

6307 TRANSMORE VAN HIRE MEDIAN AUCTION MAIDEN STKS (DIV II) 1m
3:55 (3:57) (Class 6) 2-Y-0 **£1,365** (£403; £201) **Stalls** Centre

Form RPR
3352 **1** **Benhavis**[23] 5721 2-9-3 80 (t) SebSanders 9 75+
(J L Dunlop) *mde all: rdn wl over 1f out: hung lft ent fnl f: styd on wl* **2/1**[1]
435 **2** *1 1/4* **Carnival Queen**[38] 5313 2-8-12 67 JamieSpencer 11 67
(J R Fanshawe) *hld up in rr: smooth hdwy wl over 2f out: rdn to chse wnr over 1f out: sn drvn and one pce* **5/1**
0F3 **3** *3/4* **Laterly (IRE)**[16] 5904 2-9-3 0 MickyFenton 2 71
(T P Tate) *a.p: effrt over 2f out: sn rdn and ev ch tl drvn and one pce ent fnl f* **9/2**[3]

2 **4** 3 **Tamasou (IRE)**[16] 5902 2-9-0 0 DominicFox(3) 5 64
(S Parr) *chsd ldrs: rdn along over 2f out: sn drvn and kpt on same pce* **8/1**

02 **5** ½ **Full Speed (GER)**[16] 5904 2-9-0 0 PJMcDonald(3) 12 63
(G A Swinbank) *in tch on wd outside: hdwy 3f out: rdn along to chse ldrs wl over 1f out: kpt on same pce* **11/4**[2]

06 **6** 6 **Bouggler**[16] 5904 2-9-3 0 TomEaves 3 50
(Miss J A Camacho) *dwlt: sn trcking ldrs: effrt over 2f out: sn rdn and wknd* **40/1**

0600 **7** nk **Carlton Mac**[30] 5520 2-9-3 34 SilvestreDeSousa 8 49
(N Bycroft) *chsd ldrs: rdn along over 3f out and sn wknd* **200/1**

0600 **8** 4 **Viscount Monty**[30] 5526 2-9-3 40 (v) PhillipMakin 1 40
(N Tinkler) *prom: rdn along 3f out: grad wknd* **200/1**

9 nk **Three Gold Leaves** 2-9-3 0 TPQueally 4 40
(J G Given) *in tch: rdn along wl over 2f out and grad wknd* **25/1**

10 2½ **Jontobel** 2-9-0 0 TravisBlock(3) 7 34
(Jedd O'Keeffe) *a in rr* **50/1**

0004 **11** 4 **Flashy Max**[48] 5038 2-9-3 45 TonyHamilton 10 25
(Jedd O'Keeffe) *chsd ldrs to 1/2-way: sn wknd* **100/1**

1m 38.19s (0.39) **Going Correction** -0.025s/f (Good) **11** Ran SP% **116.2**
Speed ratings (Par 93): **97,95,95,92,91 85,85,81,80,78 74**
CSF £12.11 TOTE £2.70: £1.30, £2.30, £1.90; EX 13.00.
Owner Mrs J M Khan **Bred** Elsdon Farms **Trained** Arundel, W Sussex

FOCUS
The second division of this maiden and comfortably the fastest leg. The runner-up sets the standard.

NOTEBOOK
Benhavis is only small, but he plainly has a decent engine and, having earned himself an 80-rating on previous efforts, he finally got his head in front here with a workmanlike effort to keep the 67-rated runner-up at bay, as he was entitled to do. (op 9-4 tchd 5-2)
Carnival Queen, who travelled well, failed to find much extra for pressure, but at these weights she clearly ran a creditable race. (op 7-2)
Laterly(IRE), always in the front rank, ran a sound race in third, keeping on again to the finish. (op 11-2 tchd 13-2)
Tamasou(IRE), despite finishing well adrift of the front three, ran a decent race just as he did on his debut. (tchd 9-1)
Full Speed(GER), having finished ahead of Laterly last time at Newcastle, was unable to confirm that form here but was far from disgraced. Handicaps will serve him better in due course. (op 3-1)

6308 SAM HALL MEMORIAL H'CAP 1m 6f 19y
4:30 (4:30) (Class 5) (0-75,75) 3-Y-0+ **£2,817** (£838; £418; £209) **Stalls** Low

Form RPR

6113 **1** **Double Banded (IRE)**[21] 5779 3-8-10 66 SebSanders 2 80+
(J L Dunlop) *sn trcking ldrs: led over 1f out: rdn and styd on strly: readily* **9/4**[1]

0500 **2** 1½ **Dium Mac**[114] 2987 6-9-10 74 AndrewMullen(3) 11 83
(N Bycroft) *stdd s: t.k.h in rr: hdwy on outside over 3f out: led over 2f out tl over 1f out: kpt on same pce ins fnl f* **25/1**

6462 **3** 2½ **Bukit Tinggi (IRE)**[15] 5938 3-9-0 70 PhilipRobinson 6 76
(M A Jarvis) *hld up in midfield: effrt and n.m.r over 2f out: styd on same pce* **9/2**[2]

6220 **4** 2½ **Dance Sauvage**[11] 6056 4-8-9 56 oh6 DavidAllan 9 58
(C W Thornton) *in rr: hdwy over 2f out: styd on fnl f* **16/1**

0003 **5** hd **Zefooha (FR)**[32] 5486 3-8-5 66 KellyHarrison(5) 3 68
(T D Walford) *chsd ldrs: chal over 3f out: one pce fnl 2f* **16/1**

5-44 **6** 1¼ **Categorical**[23] 5486 4-9-7 68 TonyHamilton 12 68
(K G Reveley) *in rr: effrt over 4f out: kpt on: nvr nr ldrs* **20/1**

0235 **7** ½ **Vallemeldee (IRE)**[13] 6007 3-8-6 62 RoystonFfrench 8 61
(P W D'Arcy) *sn prom: one pce fnl 3f* **7/1**

6546 **8** ½ **Danzatrice**[3] 6259 5-9-0 61 TomEaves 5 60
(C W Thornton) *hld up in rr: hdwy on ins over 3f out: hung lft: nvr nr ldrs* **9/1**

1212 **9** 3½ **Let It Be**[10] 6076 6-8-13 60 PhillipMakin 7 54
(K G Reveley) *mid-div: hdwy to chal over 2f out: wknd over 1f out* **5/1**[3]

0-00 **10** 5 **You Live And Learn**[45] 5120 4-8-6 56 oh3 TravisBlock(3) 1 43
(H Morrison) *led 1f: chsd ldrs: drvn over 4f out: lost pl over 2f out* **20/1**

2600 **11** nk **Just Waz (USA)**[10] 6076 5-8-8 58 MichaelJStainton(3) 4 44
(R M Whitaker) *mid-div: lost pl over 3f out* **50/1**

0600 **12** 1¾ **Pre Eminance (IRE)**[19] 5835 6-8-2 56 oh11 (tp) DanielleMcCreery(7) 13 40
(L R James) *led after 1f tl over 3f out: lost pl over 2f out* **150/1**

0364 **13** 1½ **Cecina Marina**[24] 5698 4-8-8 58 oh11 ow2 PJMcDonald(3) 14 40
(C W Thornton) *sn trcking ldrs: wnt 2nd 6f out: led over 3f out tl over 2f out: sn wknd* **100/1**

3m 3.61s (-1.41) **Going Correction** -0.025s/f (Good)
WFA 3 from 4yo+ 9lb **13** Ran SP% **116.9**
Speed ratings (Par 103): **103,102,100,99,99 98,98,97,95,93 92,91,91**
CSF £73.16 CT £240.79 TOTE £2.40: £1.50, £9.90, £1.70; EX 107.40.
Owner Sir Thomas Pilkington **Bred** Sir Thomas Pilkington **Trained** Arundel, W Sussex

FOCUS
A sound gallop and in the end a ready winner. The form has a sound look about it overall rated through the fifth and backed up by the fourth.

6309 REDCARRACING.CO.UK MAIDEN STKS 6f
5:05 (5:07) (Class 5) 3-Y-0+ **£2,817** (£838; £418; £209) **Stalls** Centre

Form RPR

423 **1** **Cape Cobra**[6] 6176 3-9-3 0 (b) SebSanders 3 69
(J H M Gosden) *mde most: rdn and edgd lft ent fnl f: drvn out* **15/8**[2]

0620 **2** 1¾ **Navene (IRE)**[93] 3647 3-8-5 56 JamieHamblett(7) 2 59
(C F Wall) *trckd ldrs: hdwy 1/2-way: rdn to chse wnr wl over 1f out: drvn and one pce ins fnl f* **12/1**

6-0 **3** nk **Spice Gardens (IRE)**[18] 5873 3-8-12 0 PatCosgrave 7 58
(W Jarvis) *midfield: hdwy wl over 2f out: rdn to chse ldrs over 1f out: kpt on same pce* **20/1**

344- **4** 3 **Until When (USA)**[335] 6525 3-9-3 74 TomEaves 10 54
(B Smart) *towards rr: hdwy over 2f out: sn rdn and kpt on ins fnl f: nrst fin* **8/1**[3]

-545 **5** 1¼ **Land's End (IRE)**[31] 5510 3-9-3 65 TPQueally 9 50
(J Noseda) *chsd ldrs: cl up over 2f out: sn rdn and grad wknd* **8/1**[3]

2420 **6** 3 **Trees Of Green (USA)**[29] 5567 3-9-3 75 JamieSpencer 13 41
(Saeed Bin Suroor) *in tch: rdn along wl over 2f out and sn btn* **13/8**[1]

06P0 **7** ¾ **Cape Dancer (IRE)**[38] 5299 3-8-9 48 (p) PJMcDonald(3) 14 34
(J S Wainwright) *towards rr tl sme late hdwy* **50/1**

0035 **8** ¾ **Boppys Dream**[32] 5488 5-8-13 45 (p) PhillipMakin 15 32
(P T Midgley) *chsd ldrs: rdn along wl over 2f out: sn one pce* **40/1**

020 **9** 2½ **Cumberland Road**[41] 5231 4-8-11 45 (v) SophieDoyle(7) 4 29
(C A Mulhall) *chsd ldrs: rdn along over 3f out and sn wknd* **80/1**

10 1 **Boppys Diamond** 3-8-12 0 MickyFenton 12 21
(P T Midgley) *dwlt: a towards rr* **100/1**

11 1¾ **Music Box Express** 3-8-12 0 JamesO'Reilly(5) 6 21
(D J Murphy) *s.i.s: a bhd* **33/1**

60/ **12** 3½ **Bellalini**[785] 4696 4-8-13 0 DavidAllan 5 6
(E J Alston) *dwlt: a in rr* **66/1**

0 **13** 4 **Josama**[55] 4795 3-8-12 0 RoystonFfrench 1 —
(R Bastiman) *bhd fr 1/2-way* **100/1**

56 **14** hd **The Blue Stacks (USA)**[182] 1135 3-9-3 0 TonyHamilton 11 —
(K A Ryan) *prom: rdn along 1/2-way and sn wknd* **40/1**

1m 11.27s (-0.43) **Going Correction** -0.025s/f (Good)
WFA 3 from 4yo+ 1lb **14** Ran SP% **122.0**
Speed ratings (Par 103): **101,98,98,94,92 88,87,86,83,81 79,74,69,69**
CSF £23.47 TOTE £2.70: £1.10, £2.30, £5.40; EX 28.00.
Owner H R H Princess Haya Of Jordan **Bred** Templeton Stud **Trained** Newmarket, Suffolk
■ A four-timer for championship-chasing Seb Sanders.
■ Stewards' Enquiry : Tony Hamilton one-day ban: used whip with excessive force (Oct 30)

FOCUS
A weak maiden and a race that took little winning but the time was not bad and the form has been rated slightly positively as a result.
Music Box Express Official explanation: jockey said colt missed the break

6310 THANKS & SEE YOU NEXT SEASON H'CAP 7f
5:40 (5:40) (Class 5) (0-70,69) 3-Y-0 **£2,817** (£838; £418; £209) **Stalls** Centre

Form RPR

5055 **1** **King's Bastion (IRE)**[13] 6025 3-9-4 69 TPQueally 8 77
(M L W Bell) *s.i.s: hld up: hdwy on ins over 2f out: hrd rdn over 1f out: edgd lft and styd on wl to ld post* **6/1**[2]

2542 **2** shd **Shotley Mac**[11] 6055 3-8-5 59 (b) AndrewMullen(3) 12 67
(N Bycroft) *led: edgd lft fnl f: hdd post* **8/1**

3503 **3** ½ **Aussie Blue (IRE)**[40] 5253 3-8-5 61 NataliaGemelova(5) 6 68
(R M Whitaker) *mid-div: hdwy over 2f out: keeping on same pce whn n.m.r towards fin* **15/2**

3103 **4** 1¼ **One Giant Leap (IRE)**[10] 6088 3-8-10 64 TravisBlock(3) 9 67
(H Morrison) *mid-div: hdwy on outer 2f out: kpt on wl ins fnl f* **6/1**[2]

601 **5** nk **Singleb (IRE)**[27] 5625 3-8-10 61 SebSanders 10 63
(T D Barron) *chsd ldrs: rdn and hung lft over 1f out: kpt on same pce* **3/1**[1]

400 **6** 2½ **Karma Llama (IRE)**[16] 5907 3-8-4 55 (p) RoystonFfrench 15 51
(B Smart) *mid-div: drvn over 4f out: sn outpcd: edgd lft 2f out: kpt on* **33/1**

5000 **7** ¾ **Multitude (IRE)**[17] 5893 3-8-9 60 TomEaves 11 54
(T D Easterby) *w ldrs: wknd over 1f out* **66/1**

3130 **8** shd **Rebel Pearl (IRE)**[98] 3490 3-8-11 65 JerryO'Dwyer(3) 4 58
(M G Quinlan) *s.i.s: in rr: styd on fnl 2f: nvr on terms* **25/1**

6032 **9** 1¼ **Crow's Nest Lad**[10] 6088 3-8-12 63 DavidAllan 7 53
(T D Easterby) *w ldrs: wknd over 1f out* **7/1**[3]

4464 **10** hd **Pietersen (IRE)**[112] 3066 3-9-2 67 PhillipMakin 14 57
(T D Barron) *in rr: drvn 4f out: nvr a factor* **14/1**

0065 **11** 1¼ **Tracer**[24] 5701 3-8-12 63 DaleGibson 5 49
(M W Easterby) *chsd ldrs on outer: lost pl 2f out* **16/1**

0000 **12** nk **Spume (IRE)**[24] 5701 3-8-13 69 (t) JamesO'Reilly(5) 13 54
(D J Murphy) *hld up in tch: wkng whn hmpd over 2f out* **16/1**

5006 **13** shd **Amber Isle**[28] 5602 3-8-4 55 oh2 DO'Donohoe 3 40
(D Carroll) *chsd ldrs on outside: lost pl over 1f out* **25/1**

2030 **14** 4 **Ghafeer (USA)**[27] 5625 3-9-3 68 (b) TonyHamilton 1 42
(B Ellison) *sn chsng ldrs on outer: lost pl over 1f out: sn bhd* **25/1**

1m 24.84s (-0.06) **Going Correction** -0.025s/f (Good) **14** Ran SP% **123.4**
Speed ratings (Par 101): **99,98,98,96,96 93,92,92,91,91 89,89,89,84**
CSF £51.85 CT £387.32 TOTE £8.50: £2.90, £2.30, £2.90; EX 68.80 Place 6 £ 9.88, Place 5 £ 9.45.
Owner Edward J Ware **Bred** Floors Farming And Dominic Burke **Trained** Newmarket, Suffolk

FOCUS
A modest handicap and ordinary form but sound at this level rated through the runner-up to his mark.
Rebel Pearl(IRE) Official explanation: jockey said filly missed the break
Amber Isle Official explanation: jockey said gelding had no more to give
T/Plt: £13.70 to a £1 stake. Pool: £38,147.75. 2,025.95 winning tickets. T/Qpdt: £4.10 to a £1 stake. Pool: £2,681.60. 477.50 winning tickets. JR

6288 WOLVERHAMPTON (A.W) (L-H)
Friday, October 19

OFFICIAL GOING: Standard
Wind: Nil Weather: Fine and becoming a little misty

6311 MACE RACING AT WOLVERHAMPTON APPRENTICE CLASSIFIED STKS 7f 32y(P)
7:00 (7:00) (Class 7) 3-Y-0+ **£1,911** (£564; £282) **Stalls** High

Form RPR

0-60 **1** **Ceris Star (IRE)**[36] 5347 3-8-6 45 RichardKingscote 2 54
(B R Millman) *hld up in rr: rdn and hdwy whn swtchd rt over 1f out: r.o wl to ld post* **6/1**[3]

5321 **2** shd **Halfwaytoparadise**[18] 5864 4-8-5 45 (p) TolleyDean(3) 6 54
(W G M Turner) *led over 1f: chsd ldr: rdn over 2f out: led 1f out: hdd post* **7/1**

0003 **3** 1¾ **Mis Chicaf (IRE)**[15] 5935 6-8-8 45 DuranFentiman 5 49
(D Carroll) *chsd ldrs: rdn over 4f out: kpt on same pce ins fnl f* **7/1**

3021 **4** hd **Sion Hill (IRE)**[36] 5368 6-8-8 45 (p) StephenDonohoe 10 48
(John A Harris) *sn chsng ldr: led over 5f out: rdn 2f out: hdd 1f out: one pce* **9/2**[2]

0000 **5** nk **Hornpipe**[125] 2652 5-8-8 45 ow3 HaddenFrost(3) 12 51
(M Hill) *t.k.h in tch: hdwy over 2f out: rdn and one pce fnl f* **20/1**

000 **6** ½ **Ivanasbo**[16] 5915 3-8-1 45 DeanHeslop(5) 7 46
(C G Cox) *a.p: rdn 2f out: carried hd high and edgd lft fnl f: one pce* **16/1**

5000 **7** nk **Divine White**[36] 5348 4-8-4 45 ow1 RobbieEgan(5) 1 46
(P Bowen) *broke wl: sn lost pl: rdn over 2f out: hdwy over 1f out: swtchd rt ins fnl f: kpt on* **16/1**

46 **8** shd **Van Ruymbeke (IRE)**[41] 5231 3-8-6 45 (t) LiamJones 4 45
(D J Murphy) *towards rr: rdn and hdwy wl over 1f out: nvr nrr* **4/1**[1]

4000 **9** 2½ **Nevinstown (IRE)**[15] 5935 7-8-8 45 JamieMoriarty 3 38
(C Grant) *hld up in rr: rdn over 1f out: nvr nr ldrs* **8/1**

4050 **10** nk **Minnie Mill**[15] 5946 3-7-13 45 (p) SoniaEaton(7) 9 38
(B P J Baugh) *a towards rr* **40/1**

060- **11** 10 **Harrington Bates**[353] 6274 6-8-8 45 MarkLawson 11 11
(J J Lambe, Ire) *a towards rr* **20/1**

The Form Book, Raceform Ltd, Compton, RG20 6NL

0000 **12** *39* **Golden Square**[16] 5900 5-8-5 45..........................(v[1]) KirstyMilczarek(3) 8 —
(A W Carroll) *a in rr: eased whn no ch fnl f* **12/1**

1m 29.85s (-0.55) **Going Correction** -0.20s/f (Stan)
WFA 3 from 4yo+ 2lb **12** Ran SP% **120.0**
Speed ratings (Par 97): **95,94,92,92,92 91,91,91,88,88 76,32**
CSF £47.08 TOTE £8.20: £2.50, £1.90, £3.00; EX 39.80.
Owner Mrs S A J Kinsella-Hurley **Bred** Peter Harms **Trained** Kentisbeare, Devon

FOCUS
A poor contest rated at face value through the third but the form is not surprisingly weak.
Golden Square Official explanation: jockey said gelding never travelled

6312 SPONSOR A RACE BY CALLING 0870 220 2442 MAIDEN AUCTION STKS 5f 216y(P)
7:30 (7:36) (Class 6) 2-Y-O **£2,218** (£654; £327) **Stalls** Low

Form RPR
3520 **1** **Elijah Pepper (USA)**[76] 4175 2-8-12 70.......................... JamieSpencer 9 74
(T D Barron) *mde all: rdn over 1f out: rdn out* **7/2**[3]
545 **2** *1 ¾* **Geezers Colours**[16] 5902 2-8-11 67.......................... FergusSweeney 7 68
(K R Burke) *t.k.h in tch: rdn over 1f out: kpt on ins fnl f* **9/4**[2]
3304 **3** *¾* **Mystickhill (IRE)**[22] 5751 2-8-5 61..........................(t) JamesDoyle 10 60
(D J Murphy) *a.p: wnt 2nd over 3f out: ev ch 2f out: rdn and nt qckn fnl f* **11/2**
5245 **4** *1 ½* **Lady Rochbonne**[10] 6075 2-7-13 71.......................... KirstyMilczarek(5) 8 54
(Mrs G S Rees) *chsd wnr over 2f: rdn and ev ch over 1f out: wknd ins fnl f* **2/1**[1]
6300 **5** *3* **Night Robe**[73] 4255 2-8-4 55.......................... FrancisNorton 6 45
(P D Evans) *sn outpcd: hdwy on outside over 2f out: c wd st: wknd wl over 1f out* **33/1**
0600 **6** *1 ½* **Erin Thomas (IRE)**[4] 6225 2-7-12 50..........................(p) MCGeran(7) 5 42
(M G Quinlan) *uns rdr and got loose bef s: hld up in tch: rdn over 2f out: sn wknd* **40/1**
7 *1 ¼* **Sweet Andromeda** 2-8-4 0.......................... LiamJones 11 37
(T J Fitzgerald) *outpcd* **80/1**
0206 **8** *5* **Kaystar Ridge**[43] 5176 2-8-9 69.......................... AdrianMcCarthy 4 27
(D K Ivory) *s.i.s: sn chsng ldrs: rdn over 2f out: wknd wl over 1f out* **20/1**
9 *1 ½* **Offshore Star (IRE)** 2-8-10 0.......................... FrankieMcDonald 3 23
(P A Blockley) *s.i.s: outpcd* **20/1**
4 **10** *1 ½* **Ridgeway Jazz**[189] 1029 2-8-4 0.......................... SaleemGolam 1 13
(M D I Usher) *s.i.s: outpcd* **40/1**

1m 15.03s (-0.78) **Going Correction** -0.20s/f (Stan) **10** Ran SP% **120.3**
Speed ratings (Par 93): **97,94,93,91,87 85,84,77,75,73**
CSF £11.43 TOTE £5.30: £2.20, £1.60, £2.30; EX 16.50.
Owner Harrowgate Bloodstock Ltd **Bred** Liberation Farm & Oratis Thoroughbreds **Trained** Maunby, N Yorks

FOCUS
This modest affair may not have taken much winning, but the form looks reasonable rated around the placed horses.

NOTEBOOK
Elijah Pepper(USA) had no problem with a step up from the minimum distance on this switch to sand but the form does not seem to amount to much. (tchd 9-2)
Geezers Colours was reverting back to 6f for his sand debut and stuck to his task after racing rather freely. (op 4-1 tchd 15-8)
Mystickhill(IRE) had no excuses after possibly getting her head in front for a stride or two at the quarter-mile marker. (op 7-1)
Lady Rochbonne had the best form coming into the race. She rather surprisingly did not appear to quite get home having previously been exclusively campaigned over 7f. (op 15-8 tchd 5-2)
Night Robe did not find a switch to sand the answer. (op 25-1)
Erin Thomas(IRE) did not exert himself enough when getting loose to warrant being withdrawn. (op 33-1)
Offshore Star(IRE) Official explanation: jockey said colt missed the break

6313 JOIN WBX.COM FOR FREE FOOTBALL SHIRT H'CAP 5f 216y(P)
7:55 (8:00) (Class 5) (0-75,75) 3-Y-O+ **£3,238** (£963; £481; £240) **Stalls** Low

Form RPR
031 **1** **Carcinetto (IRE)**[27] 5648 5-9-0 **70**.......................... TGMcLaughlin 4 81
(P D Evans) *led 1f: prom: rdn over 2f out: led wl ins fnl f: r.o* **13/2**[3]
0000 **2** *1* **First Order**[35] 5379 6-9-5 **75**..........................(v) DaneO'Neill 9 83
(I Semple) *led after 1f: rdn over 2f out: hdd wl ins fnl f: nt qckn* **6/1**[2]
3050 **3** *1 ½* **Methaaly (IRE)**[7] 6157 4-8-12 **68**.......................... JamieSpencer 7 71+
(M Mullineaux) *n.m.r and lost pl sn after s: hld up in rr: rdn and hdwy 1f out: fin wl* **5/1**[1]
2120 **4** *¾* **Joyeaux**[7] 6157 5-9-0 **70**.......................... PaulMulrennan 3 71
(J Hetherton) *prom: outpcd over 3f out: rallied over 1f out: kpt on ins fnl f* **12/1**
0211 **5** *nk* **Bobby Rose**[16] 5909 4-9-2 **72**.......................... RobertHavlin 6 72
(D K Ivory) *a.p: hrd rdn and no ex ins fnl f* **13/2**[3]
0000 **6** *1* **River Kirov (IRE)**[23] 5722 4-9-3 **73**.......................... FrancisNorton 2 70
(M Wigham) *s.s: hld up in rr: late hdwy: nrst fin* **25/1**
6105 **7** *nk* **Social Rhythm**[18] 5874 3-9-0 **74**.......................... MarcHalford(3) 12 70
(H J Collingridge) *hld up in tch: rdn over 2f out: fdd ins fnl f* **16/1**
3406 **8** *1* **Stonecrabstomorrow (IRE)**[13] 6020 4-8-7 **70**.......... JamesRogers(7) 5 63
(R A Fahey) *in rr: rdn 3f out: nvr nr ldrs* **5/1**[1]
2113 **9** *½* **Ryedane (IRE)**[22] 5753 5-8-9 **68**..........................(b) DuranFentiman(3) 11 59
(T D Easterby) *hld up in tch: rdn over 2f out: sn wknd* **17/2**
0104 **10** *3* **Woqoodd**[22] 5753 3-8-8 **68**.......................... JamieMoriarty(3) 13 49
(R A Fahey) *a bhd* **33/1**
1310 **11** *shd* **John Keats**[28] 5581 4-9-2 **72**.......................... DanielTudhope 8 53
(J S Goldie) *a bhd* **9/1**
1540 **12** *14* **Yerevan**[58] 4710 3-9-4 **75**.......................... FergusSweeney 10 11
(R T Phillips) *prom tl rdn and wknd over 2f out* **33/1**

1m 13.87s (-1.94) **Going Correction** -0.20s/f (Stan)
WFA 3 from 4yo+ 1lb **12** Ran SP% **118.1**
Speed ratings (Par 103): **104,102,100,99,99 97,97,96,95,91 91,72**
CSF £44.26 CT £215.00 TOTE £9.20: £2.10, £2.20, £3.00; EX 60.00.
Owner Mrs Sally Edwards **Bred** M A Doyle **Trained** Pandy, Monmouths

FOCUS
This wide-open sprint handicap looked a fair race for the grade and the form looks pretty sound.
River Kirov(IRE) ◆ Official explanation: jockey said gelding missed the break
John Keats Official explanation: jockey said gelding lost its action
Yerevan Official explanation: jockey said filly had no more to give

6314 WBX.COM £25 BET FOR NEW ACCOUNTS H'CAP 1m 4f 50y(P)
8:25 (8:26) (Class 5) (0-70,70) 3-Y-O+ **£2,914** (£867; £433; £216) **Stalls** Low

Form RPR
41-2 **1** **Bank On Benny**[286] 48 5-9-9 **69**.......................... FrancisNorton 3 79+
(P W D'Arcy) *a.p: wnt 2nd over 3f out: led 2f out: sn rdn: r.o wl* **10/3**[1]
0-54 **2** *1 ¾* **Evita**[160] 1685 3-8-13 **66**.......................... JamieSpencer 2 72
(L M Cumani) *hld up in rr: hdwy whn swtchd rt over 2f out: rdn and hung lft wl over 1f out: hung lft towards fin: tk 2nd post* **10/3**[1]
4221 **3** *shd* **Bond Casino**[22] 5755 3-8-6 **59**.......................... ChrisCatlin 8 65
(G R Oldroyd) *chsd ldr tl over 3f out: rdn over 2f out: wnt 2nd again wl over 1f out: no imp fnl f* **7/1**[3]
-520 **4** *2* **Colinette**[20] 5807 4-9-3 **63**.......................... RobertHavlin 1 66
(R T Phillips) *hld up: rdn over 4f out: hdwy 3f out: wknd over 1f out* **20/1**
6-43 **5** *5* **Strong Survivor (USA)**[97] 3554 4-9-5 **65**.......................... DaneO'Neill 5 60
(P R Webber) *hld up in tch: rdn over 3f out: wknd over 2f out* **9/2**[2]
1406 **6** *½* **Yes One (IRE)**[15] 5943 3-9-2 **69**.......................... JamesDoyle 4 63
(J W Hills) *a bhd* **8/1**
6000 **7** *5* **El Dececy (USA)**[24] 5703 3-9-3 **70**..........................(b) RichardHughes 7 56
(D J Murphy) *led: rdn and hdd 2f out: wknd over 1f out* **8/1**
0004 **8** *19* **Desert Leader (IRE)**[13] 6027 6-9-2 **69**.......................... StephenCooper(7) 6 25
(R W Price) *hld up: hdwy over 5f out: wknd over 3f out* **8/1**

2m 39.69s (-2.73) **Going Correction** -0.20s/f (Stan)
WFA 3 from 4yo+ 7lb **8** Ran SP% **114.9**
Speed ratings (Par 103): **101,99,99,98,95 94,91,78**
CSF £14.41 CT £71.83 TOTE £3.80: £1.40, £1.40, £1.80; EX 16.50.
Owner The Golf Oil Partnership **Bred** Gilridge Bloodstock Ltd **Trained** Newmarket, Suffolk

FOCUS
A modest little handicap but the form looks reasonable.

6315 PARADE RESTAURANT CLASSIFIED STKS 1m 1f 103y(P)
8:55 (8:55) (Class 6) 3-Y-O+ **£2,047** (£604; £302) **Stalls** Low

Form RPR
2551 **1** **Prince Noel**[14] 5967 3-8-12 54.......................... DanielTudhope 7 55
(N Wilson) *hld up towards rr: hdwy on outside 3f out: rdn and edgd lft jst over 1f out: led ins fnl f: drvn out* **8/1**
004 **2** *1 ¼* **Mighty Mover (IRE)**[7] 6152 5-9-2 45.......................... ChrisCatlin 1 52
(B Palling) *led: hdd 3f out: rdn wl over 1f out: rallied wl ins fnl f* **50/1**
6641 **3** *½* **Lilac Moon (GER)**[74] 4220 3-8-12 55.......................... RichardKingscote 13 51
(N J Vaughan) *a.p: rdn and wnt 2nd wl over 1f out: kpt on same pce ins fnl f* **10/3**[1]
5200 **4** *nk* **Sekula Pata (NZ)**[19] 5838 8-8-11 52..........................(v[1]) SCreighton(5) 3 50
(E J Creighton) *a.p: rdn and rdr lost whip over 1f out: kpt on ins fnl f* **12/1**
65 **5** *shd* **Fairy Festival (IRE)**[5] 6206 3-8-12 50.......................... LPKeniry 12 50
(J S Moore) *w ldr: led 3f out: rdn clr wl over 1f out: hdd and no ex ins fnl f* **14/1**
4056 **6** *2* **Beresford Lady**[15] 5945 3-8-12 48..........................(p) DaneO'Neill 2 46
(A D Brown) *hld up in mid-div: hdwy over 2f out: rdn over 1f out: one pce* **40/1**
00-0 **7** *1 ¾* **Ocean Valentine**[17] 5886 4-8-11 51.................. RussellKennemore(5) 10 43
(J T Stimpson) *stdd s: hld up in rr: rdn 3f out: sme hdwy on ins wl over 1f out: no further prog* **100/1**
3500 **8** *3 ½* **Arabiyah**[22] 5755 3-8-12 52.......................... JamieSpencer 9 36
(L M Cumani) *hld up towards rr: rdn over 2f out: no rspnse* **4/1**[3]
055 **9** *½* **Botham (USA)**[13] 6026 3-8-12 50..........................(b) RichardHughes 4 35
(D J Murphy) *prom: rdn over 2f out: sn wknd* **7/2**[2]
0645 **10** *2 ½* **Lawyer To World**[7] 6147 3-8-12 55..........................(p) TGMcLaughlin 6 30
(Mrs C A Dunnett) *a in rr* **25/1**
230 **11** *¾* **Credential**[37] 5341 5-9-2 55.......................... StephenDonohoe 8 28
(John A Harris) *hld up in mid-div: rdn and wknd over 2f out* **9/2**
4000 **12** *4* **Musical Land (IRE)**[13] 6019 3-8-9 52..........................(b) JamieMoriarty(3) 5 20
(J R Weymes) *reminders sn after s: a towards rr* **40/1**
0006 **13** *21* **Scruffy (IRE)**[69] 4411 3-8-12 39.......................... FrankieMcDonald 11 —
(C J Teague) *plld hrd: prom: lost pl over 6f out: rdn and struggling 4f out: t.o fnl 2f* **100/1**

2m 1.57s (-1.05) **Going Correction** -0.20s/f (Stan)
WFA 3 from 4yo+ 4lb **13** Ran SP% **121.6**
Speed ratings (Par 101): **96,94,94,94,94 92,90,87,87,84 84,80,62**
CSF £372.05 TOTE £9.50: £2.80, £5.60, £2.00; EX 275.00.
Owner The Giggle Factor Partnership **Bred** P And Mrs A G Venner **Trained** Flaxton, N Yorks

FOCUS
A weak event but sound enough form rated around those just outside the frame.

6316 HORIZONS RESTAURANT H'CAP 1m 141y(P)
9:20 (9:22) (Class 6) (0-60,60) 3-Y-O+ **£2,388** (£705; £352) **Stalls** Low

Form RPR
1435 **1** **Pelham Crescent (IRE)**[10] 6088 4-9-8 **60**.......... RichardKingscote 4 70
(B Palling) *hld up towards rr: c wd st: rdn and hdwy 1f out: r.o to ld wl ins fnl f* **11/2**[3]
0/06 **2** *1* **Nok Twice (IRE)**[15] 5935 6-9-6 **58**.......................... StephenDonohoe 6 66
(D Carroll) *hld up in tch: nt clr run wl over 1f out: sn swtchd rt: rdn and ev ch ins fnl f: r.o* **25/1**
4200 **3** *nk* **General Feeling (IRE)**[14] 5964 6-8-9 **50**..........(t) DuranFentiman(3) 2 57
(S T Mason) *hld up towards rr: c v wd st: rdn and hdwy 1f out: r.o ins fnl f* **16/1**
0311 **4** *nk* **Justcallmehandsome**[6] 6179 5-8-13 **58** 6ex..........(v) SophieDoyle(7) 10 64
(D J S Ffrench Davis) *a.p: led gng wl 1f out: hdd wl ins fnl f: nt qckn* **7/2**[2]
1513 **5** *1 ¾* **Blue Quiver (IRE)**[8] 6123 7-9-6 **58**.......................... SimonWhitworth 5 60
(C A Horgan) *dwlt: hld up towards rr: rdn and hdwy on ins wl over 1f out: nt qckn ins fnl f* **8/1**
5016 **6** *1* **Pitbull**[29] 5568 4-9-4 **56**..........................(p) LiamJones 7 56
(Mrs G S Rees) *hld up towards rr: hdwy over 3f out: rdn over 2f out: wknd ins fnl f* **9/1**
0000 **7** *shd* **Sir Bond (IRE)**[97] 3534 6-8-13 **56**..........................(t) SladeO'Hara(5) 12 56
(G R Oldroyd) *s.i.s: sn rcvrd: led over 6f out: rdn and hdd 1f out: wknd wl ins fnl f* **12/1**
50-0 **8** *1 ¼* **Compton Eclipse**[95] 3600 7-9-3 **55**.......................... PaulMulrennan 3 52
(J J Lambe, Ire) *led early: prom: rdn over 2f out: wknd ins fnl f* **33/1**
3065 **9** *½* **First Friend (IRE)**[131] 2492 6-9-2 **59**.......................... HaddenFrost(5) 8 55
(M Hill) *sn led: hdd over 6f out: w ldr: ev ch wl over 1f out: wknd ins fnl f* **12/1**
4312 **10** *½* **Weet Yer Tern (IRE)**[34] 5421 5-9-1 **53**.......................... JamieSpencer 13 56+
(W M Brisbourne) *stdd s: sn swtchd lft: hld up in rr: rdn wl over 1f out: no real prog whn nt clr run and eased ins fnl f* **3/1**[1]
0055 **11** *nk* **Musicmaestroplease (IRE)**[17] 5890 4-8-12 **50**.......... DanielTudhope 1 44
(S Parr) *hld up in mid-div: rdn wl over 1f out: wknd fnl f* **20/1**
0030 **12** *½* **Wodhill Gold**[29] 5568 6-9-2 **54**..........................(v) AdrianMcCarthy 11 47
(D Morris) *prom: lost pl 4f out: sn rdn and bhd* **33/1**

1m 50.09s (-1.67) **Going Correction** -0.20s/f (Stan) **12** Ran SP% **119.5**
Speed ratings (Par 101): **99,98,97,97,96 95,95,93,93,93 92,92**
CSF £142.17 CT £2062.56 TOTE £6.10: £1.80, £10.90, £9.70; EX 190.80 Place 6 £ 191.63, Place 5 £ 63.20.
Owner Flying Eight Partnership **Bred** Cathal M Ryan **Trained** Tredodridge, Vale Of Glamorgan

FOCUS
There was something of a bunch finish to this low-key handicap but the form looks fair enough rated through the third.
Weet Yer Tern(IRE) Official explanation: jockey said gelding was denied a clear run

5077 BADEN-BADEN (L-H)
Friday, October 19

OFFICIAL GOING: Good

6324a **FERDINAND LEISTEN-MEMORIAL (BBAG AUKTIONSRENNEN IFFEZHEIM)** **7f**
3:35 (3:54) 2-Y-O
£54,054 (£20,270; £13,514; £6,757; £4,054; £2,703)

RPR
1 **Schutzenjunker (GER)** 2-9-2 .... ABoschert 15 85
(U Ostmann, Germany)
2 *1* **Four Dancers (GER)** 2-8-12 .... JiriPalik 9 79
(Frau E Mader, Germany)
3 *hd* **Let's Rock (GER)**[54] 2-9-0 .... TMundry 11 80
(P Rau, Germany)
4 *nk* **Aiakos (GER)** 2-9-0 .... AStarke 6 80
(P Schiergen, Germany)
5 *hd* **Mister Minister (GER)**[16] 2-9-0 .... RPiechulek 12 79
(C Von Der Recke, Germany)
6 *1 1/4* **De La Vista (GER)**[19] 5848 2-8-12 .... EPedroza 14 74
(W Hickst, Germany)
7 *2 1/2* **Easy Wonder (GER)**[19] 5848 2-8-7 .... FilipMinarik 5 63
(I A Wood) *pressed ldr in 2nd: led briefly over 1 1/2f out: sn hdd and one pce* **123/10**[1]
8 *1 3/4* **Event Open (GER)** 2-8-12 .... J-PCarvalho 1 63
(W Hefter, Germany)
9 *4* **Earl Of Fire (GER)**[16] 2-8-12 .... ASuborics 8 53
(W Baltromei, Germany)
10 *nk* **Delacroix (GER)** 2-8-12 .... JBojko 13 53
(W Kujath, Germany)
11 *2* **Arboraetas (GER)** 2-8-12 .... AHelfenbein 3 48
(W Figge, Germany)
12 *2 1/2* **The Storm (GER)** 2-8-12 .... THellier 7 41
(Z Koplik, France)
13 *nse* **Pionero (GER)** 2-8-12 .... PVanDeKeere 10 41
(E Kurdu, Germany)
14 *3/4* **Traumsternchen (GER)**[19] 5848 2-8-7 .... ABest 2 34
(P Hirschberger, Germany)

1m 26.07s (2.17) **14 Ran** SP% **7.5**
(Including 10 Euros stake): WIN 52; PL 24, 32, 45; SF 384.
Owner W Busch **Bred** W Busch **Trained** Germany

NOTEBOOK
Easy Wonder(GER) was given positive ride on this step back up in trip and failed to see out it out.

6072 CATTERICK (L-H)
Saturday, October 20

OFFICIAL GOING: Good (8.1)
Two wet days in the last eleven resulted in 'perfect ground'.
Wind: Light 1/2 behind Weather: Fine and sunny

6325 **TOTEPLACEPOT APPRENTICE CLAIMING STKS** **1m 3f 214y**
1:55 (1:55) (Class 6) 3-Y-O+ **£2,730** (£806; £403) **Stalls** High

Form RPR
0210 1 **Mister Fizzbomb (IRE)**[12] 6056 4-8-12 54 ....(v) SladeO'Hara(5) 11 59
(J S Wainwright) *trckd ldr: led after 3f: qckned clr over 2f out: hld on wl* **12/1**
0150 2 *3/4* **Bronze Dancer (IRE)**[22] 5777 5-9-9 70 .... PJMcDonald 8 64
(G A Swinbank) *led 3f: chsd wnr: hung lft and kpt on wl fnl f* **5/1**[2]
6506 3 *1 1/4* **Cripsey Brook**[8] 6158 9-9-4 73 ....(t) DanielleMcCreery(5) 10 62
(K G Reveley) *sn trcking ldrs: t.k.h: effrt over 2f out: styd on same pce fnl f* **9/1**[3]
0003 4 *nk* **York Cliff**[12] 6069 9-8-8 55 .... DeanHeslop(5) 7 52
(W M Brisbourne) *hld up in rr: hdwy to trck ldrs 7f out: kpt on same pce fnl 2f* **12/1**
0452 5 *shd* **Torrens (IRE)**[5] 6230 5-9-5 77 .... JamieMoriarty 6 59+
(R A Fahey) *hld up in midfield: nt clr run on inner over 2f out: swtchd rt over 1f out: kpt on: nt rch ldrs* **4/5**[1]
00-5 6 *3 1/2* **Dimashq**[74] 4246 5-8-8 41 ow3 .... JamesO'Reilly(3) 4 44
(J O'Reilly) *hld up in rr: effrt over 3f out: nvr a factor* **100/1**
0040 7 *1 1/2* **Paparaazi (IRE)**[12] 6056 5-8-13 57 ....(p) GregFairley 1 44
(I W McInnes) *s.i.s: sn w ldrs: wknd over 1f out* **12/1**
04 8 *1* **Camerooney**[12] 6070 4-9-6 0 .... AndrewMullen 2 49?
(A D Brown) *t.k.h in rr: lost pl and bhd 6f out: sme hdwy 2f out: nvr on terms* **125/1**
5000 9 *nk* **The Mighty Ogmore**[26] 5674 3-7-12 49 ow4 ....(p) SophieDoyle(5) 3 39
(R C Guest) *trckd ldrs: lost pl over 6f out* **50/1**
1230 10 *3/4* **Starcross Maid**[23] 5750 5-8-9 52 ow2 .... RussellKennemore(3) 9 39
(J F Coupland) *hld up in rr: effrt over 3f out: nvr a factor* **33/1**
0506 11 *4* **Hook Money (IRE)**[4] 6250 3-8-1 49 ....(b) RobbieEgan(5) 5 34
(A J McCabe) *reminders after s: in rr: hdwy to chse ldrs over 7f out: rdn 3f out: hung lft and sn wknd* **28/1**

2m 40.7s (1.70) **Going Correction** -0.075s/f (Good)
WFA 3 from 4yo+ 7lb **11 Ran** SP% **115.4**
Speed ratings (Par 101): **91,90,89,89,89 87,86,85,85,84 82**
CSF £68.08 TOTE £19.30: £4.00, £2.20, £2.20; EX 77.00.Torrens was claimed by Diamond Racing Ltd for £14,000. Mister Fizzbomb was the subject of a friendly claim.
Owner S Enwright **Bred** Remora Bloodstock Ltd **Trained** Kennythorpe, N Yorks
■ Five of the seven winners on the card made virtually all the running and it clearly paid to race up with the pace.
■ Stewards' Enquiry : Dean Heslop caution: used whip with excessive frequency

FOCUS
A very steady gallop and the enterprisingly ridden winner stole a march. The form looks dubious.

Torrens(IRE) Official explanation: jockey said gelding was unsuited by the slow early pace

6326 **TOTESCOURSE TO COURSE EBF NOVICE STKS** **5f**
2:30 (2:45) (Class 5) 2-Y-O **£3,886** (£1,156; £577; £288) **Stalls** Low

Form RPR
6106 1 **Firenza Bond**[67] 4476 2-8-11 75 .... SladeO'Hara(5) 1 80
(G R Oldroyd) *mde all: drvn out* **20/1**
0516 2 *1 3/4* **Prigsnov Dancer (IRE)**[11] 6074 2-8-9 65 ....(p) JamesO'Reilly(5) 7 72
(J O'Reilly) *chsd ldrs: styd on to take 2nd nr line* **16/1**
62 3 *hd* **President Elect (IRE)**[11] 6073 2-8-12 0 .... PhillipMakin 14 69
(T D Barron) *gd spd centre to chse wnr: swtchd lft over 2f out: kpt on same pce fnl f* **11/4**[1]
2000 4 *2 1/2* **Fast Feet**[58] 4743 2-8-12 81 .... PaulMulrennan 6 60
(K A Ryan) *chsd ldrs: wknd fnl f* **11/2**[3]
3101 5 *2 1/2* **Speedy Senorita (IRE)**[25] 5706 2-8-11 68 .... LeeEnstone 5 50+
(K R Burke) *sat down whn stalls opened: sn chsng ldrs: one pce fnl 2f* **6/1**
0160 6 *1* **Not My Choice (IRE)**[14] 6004 2-9-5 83 .... GregFairley 4 55
(D J Murphy) *stmbld s: in rr: styd on fnl f* **3/1**[2]
7 *hd* **Royal Acclamation (IRE)** 2-8-9 0 .... SilvestreDeSousa 8 44
(G A Harker) *in rr: swtchd lft after 1f to r far side: kpt on fnl 2f* **33/1**
5351 8 *3/4* **Weet A Surprise**[18] 5887 2-8-13 67 .... DaneO'Neill 13 45
(R Hollinshead) *mid-div: swtchd lft to r far side after 1f: sn outpcd* **10/1**
5050 9 *shd* **Rio Sands**[8] 6156 2-8-9 71 .... MichaelJStainton(3) 12 44
(R M Whitaker) *racd stands' side: detached in rr: kpt on fnl 2f* **12/1**
6001 10 *nk* **Handsinthemist (IRE)**[33] 5484 2-8-9 55 ....(p) TomEaves 3 40
(P T Midgley) *mid-div: outpcd over 2f out* **33/1**
5202 11 *2* **Tanley**[59] 4715 2-8-12 56 .... DavidAllan 10 36
(J F Coupland) *in rr: swtchd lft to r stands' side after 1f: nvr on terms* **25/1**
0000 12 *2 1/2* **Lord Of The Wing**[16] 5932 2-8-9 48 .... JamieMoriarty(3) 11 27
(P T Midgley) *racd stands' side: sn detached in rr* **100/1**

60.21 secs (-0.39) **Going Correction** -0.075s/f (Good) **12 Ran** SP% **119.5**
Speed ratings (Par 95): **100,97,96,92,88 87,86,85,85,85 81,77**
CSF £293.86 TOTE £28.80: £5.70, £3.50, £1.90; EX 242.70.
Owner R C Bond **Bred** R C Bond **Trained** Brawby, N Yorks
■ The Real Guru (28/1, crashed through rails and uns rdr going to s) & Ursus (100/1, ref to ent stalls) were withdrawn. No Rule 4.

FOCUS
A slightly messy race and improvement from both the well-drawn winner and the runner-up. The form may not prove totally reliable.

NOTEBOOK
Firenza Bond, who lives on his nerves, had the best of the draw and dominated throughout. (op 16-1)
Prigsnov Dancer(IRE), who had something to find, seems to be thriving in his new stable. (op 33-1)
President Elect(IRE), drawn widest of all, went to race towards the stands' side but his rider changed his mind at the halfway stage. Still inexperienced, he should certainly lose his maiden tag. (op 10-3 tchd 7-2)
Fast Feet, who had finished last on his two most recent starts, is not very big and looks regressive. His official rating of 81 is hard to justify now. (op 5-1 tchd 9-2)
Speedy Senorita(IRE) was sat down on her hind quarters when the stalls opened. Official explanation: jockey said filly slipped on leaving the stalls (op 11-2 tchd 5-1)
Not My Choice(IRE), who had 5lb in hand of the winner on official ratings, slipped leaving the traps and with that mishap his chance had gone. Official explanation: jockey said colt slipped on leaving the stalls (op 11-4)

6327 **TOTESPORT.COM CATTERICK DASH (H'CAP)** **5f**
3:05 (3:06) (Class 2) (0-100,100) 3-Y-O+ **£10,363** (£3,083; £1,540; £769) **Stalls** Low

Form RPR
0005 1 **King Orchisios (IRE)**[7] 6183 4-8-11 93 ....(p) DO'Donohoe 4 103
(K A Ryan) *chsd ldr: led jst ins fnl f: hld on towards fin* **9/2**[2]
-201 2 *nk* **Oldjoesaid**[21] 5810 3-9-4 100 .... DaneO'Neill 1 109
(H Candy) *chsd ldrs: upsides 1f out: no ex nr fin* **9/4**[1]
2110 3 *3/4* **How's She Cuttin' (IRE)**[96] 3586 4-8-1 86 .... AndrewMullen(3) 14 92
(T D Barron) *racd centre: swtchd rt to r stands' side over 2f out: led one other that side jst ins fnl f: fin wl* **20/1**
1233 4 *1/2* **Bo McGinty (IRE)**[7] 6173 6-8-4 86 oh2 ....(b) DaleGibson 13 90
(R A Fahey) *racd stands' side: hung lft over 3f out: kpt on wl fnl f* **16/1**
0300 5 *hd* **Strike Up The Band**[13] 6039 4-9-4 100 .... AdrianTNicholls 7 103
(D Nicholls) *led: hrd rdn end edgd rt over 1f out: hdd jst ins fnl f: fdd* **9/1**
2311 6 *1* **Matsunosuke**[8] 6141 5-9-1 97 .... TPQueally 8 97
(A B Coogan) *s.i.s: styd on fnl 2f: nt rch ldrs* **11/2**[3]
0150 7 *shd* **Invincible Force (IRE)**[7] 6183 3-8-13 95 .... PhillipMakin 2 94
(Paul Green) *mid-div: hdwy over 2f out: kpt on same pce* **14/1**
6006 8 *1 1/2* **The Nifty Fox**[21] 5806 3-7-13 86 oh7 ....(b) KellyHarrison(5) 3 80
(T D Easterby) *chsd ldrs: fdd appr fnl f* **66/1**
0420 9 *1 1/4* **Bond City (IRE)**[16] 5953 5-8-9 96 ....(p) SladeO'Hara(5) 6 85
(G R Oldroyd) *mid-div: effrt over 1f out: fdd over 1f out* **9/1**
3200 10 *3* **Yungaburra (IRE)**[7] 6173 3-7-11 86 oh4 ....(t) SophieDoyle(7) 10 65
(D J Murphy) *sn outpcd and towards rr* **33/1**
2102 11 *2* **Little Edward**[6] 6197 9-8-6 88 .... GregFairley 9 59
(R J Hodges) *a in rr* **11/1**
3000 12 *6* **Caribbean Coral**[21] 5809 8-8-7 89 ow1 .... GrahamGibbons 11 39
(J J Quinn) *in rr: swtchd lft after 1f to r far side: nvr on terms* **14/1**

59.20 secs (-1.40) **Going Correction** -0.075s/f (Good) **12 Ran** SP% **121.1**
Speed ratings (Par 109): **108,107,106,105,105 103,103,101,99,94 91,81**
CSF £15.05 CT £192.55 TOTE £4.90: £2.30, £1.40, £6.30; EX 21.50.
Owner Mr & Mrs Julian And Rosie Richer **Bred** Rathbarry Stud **Trained** Hambleton, N Yorks
■ Stewards' Enquiry : D O'Donohoe one-day ban: used whip with excessive frequency (Oct 31)

FOCUS
A good-class handicap but a bit messy with the third and fourth electing to race stands' side. The winner and fourth set the level.

NOTEBOOK
King Orchisios(IRE), suited by this better ground, answered his rider's every call to gain the upper hand near the line. (op 5-1)
Oldjoesaid, 8lb higher, had the inside draw. He looked the likely winner a furlong out only to miss out near the line. Highly progressive, he should make his mark in Listed company at four. (tchd 5-2 in a place)
How's She Cuttin'(IRE), out of sorts after finishing down the field at Ayr in July, was racing from a mark 6lb higher than her last success. One of two to race down the stands' side, she was reeling in the first two at the line. She won two of her final three starts last backend and a repeat might well be on the cards. (op 16-1)
Bo McGinty(IRE), 2lb out of the handicap, was drawn one off the stands'-side rail. He has a tendency to hang left and he tested his rider's skills to the limit.
Strike Up The Band, far from disgraced in the L'Abbaye, showed bags of toe to take this competitive field along but he tended to edge towards the middle and was edged out over the final 200 yards.

Matsunosuke, 6lb higher, missed a beat at the start and on this downhill track, they were never coming back to him quickly enough. He is clearly right at the top of his game at present. (tchd 5-1)

6328 TOTEPOOL NURSERY 7f
3:40 (3:42) (Class 4) (0-85,81) 2-Y-O **£4,533** (£1,348; £674; £336) **Stalls** Low

Form RPR

0001 **1** **Cross Fell (USA)**[12] 6066 2-8-9 **69** GregFairley 7 79+
(M Johnston) *mde all: shkn up and qcknd over 2f out: clr over 1f out: readily* **7/1**[3]

21 **2** *3* **Reel Buddy Star**[17] 5902 2-8-9 **72** AndrewMullen[(3)] 10 75
(G M Moore) *prom: drvn and outpcd over 3f out: styd on fnl 2f: tk 2nd ins fnl f: no ch w wnr* **8/1**

4061 **3** *1 1/4* **Merchant Navy**[12] 6052 2-9-3 **77** TPQueally 6 76
(E A L Dunlop) *trckd ldrs: styd on same pce fnl 2f* **7/1**[3]

0454 **4** *1 1/4* **Atheer Dubai (IRE)**[20] 5828 2-9-7 **81** SilvestreDeSousa 2 77
(C E Brittain) *prom: effrt on inner over 2f out: kpt on: nvr trbld ldrs* **3/1**[1]

0202 **5** *shd* **Our Chairman (IRE)**[3] 6267 2-9-2 **76** DaneO'Neill 8 72
(R Hannon) *chsd ldrs: kpt on same pce fnl 2f* **11/2**[2]

1 **6** *1 1/4* **Brasingaman Hifive**[38] 5329 2-9-5 **79** GrahamGibbons 9 72
(Mrs G S Rees) *trckd ldrs: kpt on same pce fnl 2f* **16/1**

203 **7** *nk* **Willyn (IRE)**[20] 5837 2-7-13 **64** KellyHarrison[(5)] 11 56+
(J S Goldie) *in rr: hdwy and n.m.r over 2f out: styd on fnl f* **16/1**

4350 **8** *4* **Mission Impossible**[12] 6052 2-8-4 **71** PatrickDonaghy[(7)] 4 53
(P C Haslam) *mid-div: outpcd and lost pl over 2f out* **25/1**

0310 **9** *nk* **Andrasta**[2] 6282 2-8-9 **72** PatrickMathers[(3)] 13 53
(A Berry) *w wnr: t.k.h: wknd over 1f out* **20/1**

0052 **10** *1 1/2* **Kashmina**[11] 6075 2-8-9 **69** TomEaves 12 47
(M R Channon) *in rr: bhd fnl 2f* **9/1**

060 **11** *1 1/2* **Jackday (IRE)**[24] 5735 2-8-7 **67** DavidAllan 3 41
(T D Easterby) *s.i.s: a in rr* **33/1**

031 **12** *hd* **Geordie Girl**[11] 6075 2-8-9 **69** PaulMulrennan 14 42
(R C Guest) *in rr: bhd fnl 2f* **10/1**

1m 26.45s (-0.91) **Going Correction** -0.075s/f (Good) **12** Ran SP% **118.9**
Speed ratings (Par 97): **102,98,97,95,95 94,93,89,88,87 85,85**
CSF £60.70 CT £412.38 TOTE £8.60: £2.70, £2.80, £2.20; EX 46.20.
Owner Sheikh Mohammed **Bred** Darley **Trained** Middleham Moor, N Yorks

FOCUS
What looked a tight-knit nursery beforehand was turned into a procession by the highly-progressive winner. The form looks rock solid.

NOTEBOOK
Cross Fell(USA), hoisted 13lb, made every yard. He wound it up with intent once in line for home and soon had it in the bag. Highly regarded earlier in the year, he has at last come good. (op 8-1)
Reel Buddy Star, having just his third start and drawn in double figures, stayed on to snatch second spot and will be better suited by a mile.
Merchant Navy, 5lb higher, found the extra furlong no problem but this may be as good as he is. (op 15-2)
Atheer Dubai(IRE), drawn on the inner, found this an insufficient test and though sticking to his task, he never looked like seriously entering the argument. (op 7-2 tchd 11-4)
Our Chairman(IRE), having his second outing in four days, again gave a good account of himself. A modest maiden might be a better option. (op 5-1 tchd 9-2)
Brasingaman Hifive, winner of her only previous start, gave a good account of herself and the experience will not be lost on her. (tchd 14-1)
Willyn(IRE) stayed on in her own time after being tightened up at a crucial stage and she is well worth a try over a mile. (op 14-1)

6329 TOTESPORT 0800 221221 MEDIAN AUCTION MAIDEN STKS 7f
4:15 (4:16) (Class 6) 2-Y-O **£2,730** (£806; £403) **Stalls** Low

Form RPR

35 **1** **Just Like A Woman**[16] 5949 2-8-9 0 AndrewElliott[(3)] 6 72+
(M L W Bell) *in rr: sn drvn along: hdwy and n.m.r 2f out: styd on to ld towards fin* **5/4**[1]

050 **2** *nk* **Averoo**[16] 5951 2-9-3 71 TPQueally 9 77
(E A L Dunlop) *s.i.s: hdwy on wd outside over 2f out: led over 1f out: hdd nr fin* **9/2**[3]

6340 **3** *2 1/2* **Parliamentary (JPN)**[28] 5613 2-9-3 73 GregFairley 4 70
(M Johnston) *led 1f: chsd ldrs: chal over 1f out: kpt on same pce* **5/1**

2205 **4** *1 1/2* **Redsensor**[29] 5587 2-9-3 78 DaneO'Neill 10 67+
(R Hannon) *chsd ldrs: drvn 4f out: kpt on same pce fnl 2f: eased whn wl hld ins fnl f* **4/1**[2]

0302 **5** *5* **Little Bones**[54] 4897 2-8-12 56 AdrianTNicholls 12 49
(J F Coupland) *in rr: sme hdwy 2f out: swtchd rt ins fnl f: nvr nrr* **25/1**

005 **6** *nk* **Northwest**[26] 5675 2-9-0 24 PatrickMathers[(3)] 2 53
(A Berry) *sn chsng ldrs: wknd over 1f out* **100/1**

5600 **7** *1 3/4* **Frammenti**[29] 5601 2-8-12 52 (p) StephenDonohoe 1 44
(A J McCabe) *w ldr: led after 1f tl 4f out: hung rt and lost pl 2f out* **50/1**

00 **8** *hd* **Royal Musketeer (IRE)**[7] 6184 2-9-3 0 DavidAllan 11 48
(T D Easterby) *s.i.s: hdwy to ld 4f out: hdd & wknd over 1f out* **50/1**

00 **9** *1 1/2* **Spooky**[17] 5902 2-8-12 0 RussellKennemore[(5)] 3 45
(W Storey) *s.s: bhd tl sme hdwy fnl 2f* **150/1**

5000 **10** *1 1/4* **Caribbean Cruiser**[17] 5902 2-9-0 47 (b[1]) MarkLawson[(3)] 5 42
(Garry Moss) *chsd ldrs: lost pl over 1f out* **100/1**

0450 **11** *8* **Scruffy Skip (IRE)**[16] 5932 2-9-3 67 (p) DaleGibson 7 22
(M Dods) *in tch: drvn and lost pl over 3f out* **25/1**

00 **12** *6* **Validity**[145] 2086 2-8-5 0 RobbieEgan[(7)] 13 2
(A J McCabe) *sn bhd* **80/1**

1m 27.87s (0.51) **Going Correction** -0.075s/f (Good) **12** Ran SP% **114.8**
Speed ratings (Par 93): **94,93,90,89,83 83,81,80,79,77 68,61**
CSF £6.47 TOTE £1.90: £1.20, £1.60, £1.60; EX 8.20.
Owner Mascalls Stud **Bred** Mascalls Stud **Trained** Newmarket, Suffolk

FOCUS
A modest maiden. The winner did well to win from an unpromising position but the runner-up is rated just 71 and the sixth a lowly 24, so the form is limited.

NOTEBOOK
Just Like A Woman, the only winner all day to come from off the pace, was soon making hard work of it. Tightened up at a crucial stage, she worked hard to show ahead near the line. The tight track did not look in her favour. (op 11-10)
Averoo, rated just 71, was dropping back in trip. After missing a beat at the start, he moved up down the hare rail to show ahead only to miss out near the line. (tchd 5-1 in a place)
Parliamentary(JPN), who carries condition, put a poor effort last time behind him and there may still be time for him to make his mark in nursery company. (op 6-1)
Redsensor, drawn in double figures, was under pressure starting the home turn. He never really threatened and in the end his rider gave up. His official rating, 78, flatters him. (op 9-2)
Little Bones, who changed hands after finishing runner-up in a seller at Ripon, will be suited by a mile in a low-grade nursery. (op 20-1)
Northwest, beaten out of sight in three previous outings, is rated just 24.

6330 TOTEEXACTA H'CAP 1m 5f 175y
4:50 (4:50) (Class 6) (0-60,60) 3-Y-O+ **£2,590** (£770; £385; £192) **Stalls** Low

Form RPR

5406 **1** **Mcqueen (IRE)**[11] 6076 7-9-0 **54** RussellKennemore[(5)] 13 60
(J T Stimpson) *drvn along to ld: clr over 2f out: hld on towards fin* **12/1**

2360 **2** *1* **Ha'Penny Beacon**[22] 5779 4-9-7 **56** (v) StephenDonohoe 4 61
(D Carroll) *mid-div: hdwy on outside over 2f out: wnt 2nd 1f out: fin strly* **16/1**

-535 **3** *3 1/2* **Group Force (IRE)**[17] 5906 3-8-12 **56** TomEaves 6 56
(M H Tompkins) *rr-div: hdwy 4f out: styd on fnl 2f: nvr a threat* **10/1**

4 *1/2* **Amaryllis (GER)**[9] 6135 5-9-8 **57** (t) GregFairley 10 56
(T Hogan, Ire) *mid-div: hdwy to chse ldrs 7f out: styd on same pce fnl 3f* **5/1**[1]

-106 **5** *shd* **Royal Melbourne (IRE)**[12] 6068 7-9-8 **57** DavidAllan 15 56
(A D Brown) *sn chsng ldrs: one pce fnl 3f* **14/1**

430 **6** *hd* **Devilfishpoker Com**[78] 2096 3-8-8 **52** (b) GrahamGibbons 5 51
(R C Guest) *chsd ldrs: outpcd over 3f out: kpt on fnl f* **40/1**

7 *1 1/2* **Runs Riot (IRE)**[54] 4913 3-8-1 **48** ow1 AndrewElliott[(3)] 2 45
(Andrew Oliver, Ire) *trckd ldrs: t.k.h: drvn 4f out: one pce* **14/1**

0204 **8** *2* **Mabel (IRE)**[12] 6056 4-9-11 **60** DaleGibson 7 54
(S C Williams) *in rr: kpt on fnl 3f: nvr a factor* **17/2**[3]

0-05 **9** *1 1/2* **Annibale Caro**[20] 5835 5-9-3 **55** MarkLawson[(3)] 1 47
(Grant Tuer) *mid-div: effrt 4f out: nvr nr ldrs* **20/1**

3256 **10** *nk* **True (IRE)**[12] 6054 6-8-13 **48** PaulMulrennan 11 39
(Mrs S Lamyman) *hld up in rr: sme hdwy 4f out: nvr on terms* **16/1**

5006 **11** *3* **Intavac Boy**[12] 6056 6-8-10 **52** PatrickDonaghy[(7)] 12 39
(S P Griffiths) *in tch: effrt 4f out: wknd over 1f out* **9/1**

1053 **12** *3/4* **Blue Jet (USA)**[17] 5906 3-8-13 **57** DeanMcKeown 3 43
(R M Whitaker) *chsd ldrs: drvn 4f out: lost pl over 2f out* **5/1**[1]

4100 **13** *4* **Parchment (IRE)**[25] 5704 5-9-8 **57** (b) PatCosgrave 14 38
(A J Lockwood) *in rr: rdn 4f out: nvr on terms* **14/1**

0033 **14** *1 1/4* **She's So Pretty (IRE)**[7] 6178 3-9-2 **60** (e) TPQueally 8 39
(W R Swinburn) *in rr: drvn 8f out: nvr a factor* **6/1**[2]

3-00 **15** *32* **Ice And Fire**[243] 389 8-8-9 **49** (b) AshleyHamblett[(5)] 9 —
(J T Stimpson) *a in rr: bhd and eased 2f out: t.o* **80/1**

3m 4.83s (0.33) **Going Correction** -0.075s/f (Good)
WFA 3 from 4yo+ 9lb **15** Ran SP% **125.1**
Speed ratings (Par 101): **96,95,93,93,93 92,92,90,90,89 88,87,85,84,66**
CSF £194.47 CT £2013.06 TOTE £18.20: £5.30, £6.90, £3.90; EX 190.60.
Owner Moorland Racing **Bred** Philip Newton **Trained** Newcastle-Under-Lyme, Staffs

FOCUS
A low-grade handicap run at a sound pace and another all-the-way winner. Weak form rated through the fourth.
Blue Jet(USA) Official explanation: trainer had no explanation for the poor form shown
She's So Pretty(IRE) Official explanation: jockey said filly was never travelling

6331 TOTESPORTGAMES.COM H'CAP 7f
5:25 (5:25) (Class 5) (0-75,75) 3-Y-O+ **£3,238** (£963; £481; £240) **Stalls** Low

Form RPR

5501 **1** **Nuit Sombre (IRE)**[25] 5701 7-9-6 **75** (p) SilvestreDeSousa 13 82
(G A Harker) *mde all: hrd rdn fnl f: hld on towards fin* **25/1**

6063 **2** *nk* **King Harson**[20] 5840 8-9-0 **69** PatCosgrave 8 75
(J D Bethell) *chsd wnr: kpt on fnl f: no ex wl ins fnl f* **15/2**[2]

33 **3** *shd* **Angaric (IRE)**[5] 6232 4-9-0 **72** MarkLawson[(3)] 7 78
(B Smart) *chsd ldrs: kpt on fnl 2f: no ex ins fnl f* **3/1**[1]

2413 **4** *1* **Distant Sun (USA)**[27] 5662 3-9-3 **74** TomEaves 9 77
(I Semple) *trckd ldrs: t.k.h: swtchd lft ins fnl f: no ex* **16/1**

01 **5** *1/2* **Chicken George (IRE)**[49] 5036 3-9-3 **74** AdrianTNicholls 5 76+
(D Nicholls) *hld up in rr: hdwy on ins over 2f out: kpt on: nvr rchd ldrs* **9/1**[3]

1320 **6** *nk* **Cha Cha Cha**[27] 5662 3-8-12 **72** AndrewMullen[(3)] 1 73
(K A Ryan) *s.i.s: sn mid-div: styd on fnl 2f: nvr a threat* **14/1**

5302 **7** *shd* **Flying Valentino**[52] 4940 3-8-12 **72** PJMcDonald[(3)] 2 73
(G A Swinbank) *mid-div: effrt on outer 2f out: kpt on: nvr trbld ldrs* **12/1**

3220 **8** *1 1/2* **Guest Connections**[29] 5581 4-8-13 **75** AdeleRothery[(7)] 6 72
(D Nicholls) *in rr: kpt on fnl 2f: nvr a factor* **9/1**[3]

0020 **9** *hd* **Kenmore**[52] 4932 5-9-6 **75** TPQueally 4 71
(J G Given) *chsd ldrs: drvn 3f out: sn outpcd* **14/1**

1020 **10** *1/2* **Joshua's Gold (IRE)**[14] 6025 6-9-1 **70** (v) StephenDonohoe 11 65
(D Carroll) *in rr: kpt on fnl 2f: nvr a factor* **16/1**

0041 **11** *3/4* **Dispol Isle (IRE)**[20] 5840 5-8-9 **69** NeilBrown[(5)] 12 62
(T D Barron) *prom on outer: brought to r alone stands' side 3f out: nvr a threat after* **12/1**

0500 **12** *1* **Stoic Leader (IRE)**[50] 4999 7-9-6 **75** PaulMulrennan 10 65
(R F Fisher) *in rr: kpt on fnl 2f: nvr a factor* **12/1**

3335 **13** *3 1/2* **The Osteopath (IRE)**[79] 4107 4-9-1 **73** (p) MichaelJStainton[(3)] 14 54
(M Dods) *s.s: in rr: wnt rt 2f out: nvr on terms* **9/1**[3]

2300 **14** *17* **Top Bid**[56] 4811 3-9-3 **74** (b[1]) DavidAllan 15 9
(T D Easterby) *mid-div: lost pl over 2f out: sn wl bhd* **18/1**

1m 26.94s (-0.42) **Going Correction** -0.075s/f (Good)
WFA 3 from 4yo+ 2lb **14** Ran SP% **124.0**
Speed ratings (Par 103): **99,98,98,97,96 96,96,94,94,93 93,91,87,68**
CSF £208.82 CT £767.46 TOTE £31.30: £8.10, £3.40, £1.50; EX 471.80 Place 6 £346.19, Place 5 £112.54.
Owner P I Harker **Bred** M P B Bloodstock Ltd **Trained** Thirkleby, N Yorks

■ Stewards' Enquiry : Silvestre De Sousa two-day ban: used whip with excessive frequency (Oct 31-Nov 1)

FOCUS
Another low-grade handicap and another all-the-way winner. The placed horses ran to their pre-race marks.

T/Plt: £280.80 to a £1 stake. Pool: £52,197.10. 135.65 winning tickets. T/Qpdt: £40.40 to a £1 stake. Pool: £2,997.60. 54.90 winning tickets. WG

6294 **NEWMARKET (ROWLEY)** (R-H)

Saturday, October 20

OFFICIAL GOING: Good to soft (soft in places; 6.9)

Wind: Nil

6332 VC BET CHALLENGE STKS (GROUP 2) 7f

2:05 (2:06) (Class 1) 3-Y-O+

£54,963 (£20,831; £10,425; £5,198; £2,603; £1,306) **Stalls** Low

Form RPR

2221 **1** **Miss Lucifer (FR)**[21] 5799 3-8-12 95 MichaelHills 4 118
(B W Hills) *hw: hld up in tch: swtchd rt over 2f out: rdn to ld 1f out: r.o* **20/1**

215 **2** 1 1/4 **Al Qasi (IRE)**[20] 5832 4-9-3 113 TedDurcan 3 117+
(P W Chapple-Hyam) *chsd ldrs: rdn over 1f out: hmpd ins fnl f: styd on* **9/1**

/241 **3** 2 **Toylsome**[14] 6029 8-9-7 0 SPasquier 2 116
(J Hirschberger, Germany) *chsd ldrs: led over 2f out: rdn and hdd 1f out: styd on same pce* **6/1**[2]

6230 **4** 1 1/2 **Balthazaar's Gift (IRE)**[20] 5832 4-9-3 114 JimmyFortune 9 108
(L M Cumani) *hld up: hdwy and swtchd rt over 1f out: nt rch ldrs* **10/1**

6262 **5** nk **Asset (IRE)**[29] 5588 4-9-3 111 (b) RyanMoore 10 107
(R Hannon) *chsd ldrs: rdn and ev ch wl over 1f out: hmpd sn after: no ex* **10/1**

1351 **6** 3/4 **Arabian Gleam**[35] 5409 3-9-5 115 JMurtagh 14 109+
(J Noseda) *hld up: rdn 1/2-way: swtchd rt and hdwy over 1f out: nrst fin* **8/1**[3]

1-21 **7** 1/2 **Candidato Roy (ARG)**[21] 5797 6-9-3 105 LDettori 8 104
(W J Haggas) *swtg: chsd ldrs: rdn over 2f out: hmpd over 1f out: sn wknd* **10/1**

-660 **8** 1/2 **Captain Marvelous (IRE)**[20] 5832 3-9-1 112 DarryllHolland 1 102
(B W Hills) *swtg: hld up: hung rt and hdwy over 1f out: n.d* **66/1**

4312 **9** nk **Duff (IRE)**[35] 5409 4-9-3 0 DPMcDonogh 12 102
(Edward Lynam, Ire) *led over 4f: wknd fnl f* **16/1**

1041 **10** 1 1/2 **Eisteddfod**[37] 5359 6-9-3 106 NelsonDeSouza 15 98
(P F I Cole) *chsd ldr tl rdn over 2f out: wknd over 1f out* **25/1**

1110 **11** 1/2 **Lovelace**[21] 5797 3-9-1 109 RoystonFfrench 5 96
(M Johnston) *prom: rdn over 2f out: hung rt and wknd over 1f out* **16/1**

430 **12** 1/2 **Caldra (IRE)**[28] 5618 3-9-1 104 KJManning 13 95
(S Kirk) *s.i.s: hld up: rdn over 3f out: a in rr* **33/1**

4110 **13** 10 **Pride Of Nation (IRE)**[14] 6031 5-9-3 110 C-PLemaire 7 68
(L M Cumani) *swtg: hld up: rdn and wknd over 2f out* **9/1**

6645 **14** 4 **Mac Love**[35] 5409 6-9-3 106 EddieAhern 6 57
(J Noseda) *hld up: hdwy over 4f out: rdn and wknd over 2f out* **66/1**

5124 **15** 3/4 **Cesare**[21] 5798 6-9-7 115 JamieSpencer 11 59
(J R Fanshawe) *hld up in tch: rdn and wknd over 2f out* **11/4**[1]

1m 25.56s (-0.94) **Going Correction** +0.225s/f (Good)
WFA 3 from 4yo+ 2lb **15** Ran SP% **125.6**
Speed ratings (Par 115): **114,112,110,108,108 107,106,106,105,104 103,103,91,87,86**
CSF £190.50 TOTE £25.90: £5.00, £3.80, £2.40; EX 361.50 Trifecta £868.80 Part won. Pool £1,223.76 - 0.50 winning units..
Owner Gainsborough **Bred** Gainsborough Stud Management Ltd **Trained** Lambourn, Berks

FOCUS
An interesting renewal of this Group 2 but a surprise result. The time was slightly slower than the Dewhurst that followed but still respectable for the grade. The form has been rated slightly negatively with doubts over a number of the runners, but Miss Lucifer was still up a stone on her previous best.

NOTEBOOK
Miss Lucifer(FR), who has been consistent all season but stepped up on previous efforts when winning a Listed race last time, had been supplemented for this for £7,500 and justified connections' faith with a decisive victory. Her trainer has an excellent record in this race and she handled the step up in grade well, with the easy ground appearing to be the key to her recent improvement. She is apparently due to join Godolphin now, and could be a very useful addition for them next season, when races like the Prix Maurice de Gheest and Prix de la Foret could be on the agenda. (op 25-1)
Al Qasi(IRE) ◆, a progressive sort last season, has moved up into Group company this year and ran close to his best despite being done few favours by the winner when trying to deliver his challenge. He has not been over-raced and there could be more to come.
Toylsome, a surprise winner of the Prix de la Foret last time, carried his Group 1 penalty with distinction, being up with the pace from the start. However, he was unable to shake off his rivals as he did at Longchamp and was outpaced by the principals up the hill. (tchd 13-2 in a place)
Balthazaar's Gift(IRE), stepping back up to this trip for the first time since the spring, was held up as usual and ran on from well back but never got into a challenging position. (op 11-1)
Asset(IRE) has not really gone on from his Abernant win here in the spring, despite running several good races in the top sprints. This was another fair effort and he had a chance when suffering interference in the dip. The jury is still out on him but if the key can be found he is capable of scoring at this level. (op 11-1)
Arabian Gleam has been progressive on a fast surface but was encountering easy ground for the first time. He never really figured but improved on his recent form with Duff despite being worse off at the weights. (op 10-1)
Candidato Roy(ARG), who made all to win a hot handicap at Ascot last time on only his second start in Britain, should have handled the ground but the step up in grade seemed to find him out. (op 11-1)
Pride Of Nation(IRE), whose wins have all been at a mile, was unable to get competitive and a combination of the higher grade and shorter trip seemed to find him out, although this was a performance of a horse that has gone over the top. (op 10-1)
Cesare has been highly consistent all season but never figured having been held up and his rider let him come home in his own time. He is another who may have had enough for the season.
Official explanation: trainer's rep said gelding may have gone over the top at the end of a long season (early 4-1 7-2 tchd 10-3 and 3-1 in places)

6333 DARLEY DEWHURST STKS (GROUP 1) (C&F) 7f

2:40 (2:41) (Class 1) 2-Y-O

£149,558 (£56,683; £28,368; £14,144; £7,085; £3,555) **Stalls** Low

Form RPR

111 **1** **New Approach (IRE)**[34] 5458 2-9-1 0 KJManning 5 125
(J S Bolger, Ire) *gd sort: str: lw: awkward leaving stalls: sn chsng ldrs: shkn up 4f out: rdn fr over 2f out: led ins fnl f: r.o u.p* **6/4**[1]

11 **2** 1/2 **Fast Company (IRE)**[60] 4694 2-9-1 0 TedDurcan 3 124
(B J Meehan) *sn pushed along in rr: hdwy over 1f out: r.o* **14/1**

111 **3** 2 1/2 **Raven's Pass (USA)**[49] 5048 2-9-1 114 JimmyFortune 4 118
(J H M Gosden) *lw: trckd ldrs: racd keenly: led over 2f out: rdn and edgd rt over 1f out: hdd and no ex ins fnl f* **3/1**[2]

1121 **4** 2 1/2 **Rio De La Plata (USA)**[13] 6041 2-9-1 120 LDettori 9 111+
(Saeed Bin Suroor) *lw: hld up: hdwy 2f out: nt clr run and swtchd lft over 1f out: wknd ins fnl f* **9/2**[3]

131 **5** 1 3/4 **Luck Money (IRE)**[36] 5397 2-9-1 108 TQuinn 6 107
(P F I Cole) *lw: w ldr: rdn and ev ch over 2f out: wknd over 1f out* **14/1**

1314 **6** hd **Hatta Fort**[13] 6041 2-9-1 102 DarryllHolland 1 106
(M R Channon) *trckd ldrs: plld hrd: wknd over 1f out* **50/1**

3111 **7** nk **McCartney (GER)**[35] 5406 2-9-1 115 RyanMoore 8 106
(M Johnston) *lw: mid-div: hdwy over 2f out: sn rdn: wknd fnl f* **15/2**

06 **8** 2 1/2 **Greatwallofchina (USA)**[13] 6041 2-9-1 0 JMurtagh 10 99
(A P O'Brien, Ire) *dwlt: sn pushed along in rr: rdn 1/2-way: n.d* **100/1**

1011 **9** 1/2 **Dark Angel (IRE)**[15] 5975 2-9-1 109 MichaelHills 7 98+
(B W Hills) *led over 4f: wkng whn n.m.r over 1f out* **25/1**

3 **10** 17 **Dubai Meydan (IRE)**[18] 5880 2-9-1 0 JimmyQuinn 2 56
(Miss Gay Kelleway) *str: hld up: wknd over 2f out* **100/1**

1m 25.29s (-1.21) **Going Correction** +0.225s/f (Good) **10** Ran SP% **116.1**
Speed ratings (Par 109): **115,114,111,108,106 106,106,103,102,83**
CSF £25.17 TOTE £2.50: £1.10, £3.80, £1.50; EX 27.40 Trifecta £133.60 Pool £1,844.60 - 9.80 winning units..
Owner Mrs J S Bolger **Bred** Lodge Park Stud **Trained** Coolcullen, Co Carlow
■ Stewards' Enquiry : K J Manning five-day ban: used whip with excessive frequency (Oct 31-Nov 4)

FOCUS
A hot renewal of this traditional juvenile championship event with most of the recent two-year-old Group-race winners taking their chance. The time was exceptional, being 0.27sec faster than the preceding Group 2 for older horses and 1.72sec faster than the Rockfel and the form looks rock-solid. New Approach looks a worthy champion juvenile, with Fast Company posting a big step up on his York form.

NOTEBOOK
New Approach(IRE) ◆, whose trainer has been teaching him to settle with next season in mind, found it working too well. Taken down early with a hack for company, he was sluggish from the stalls and had to be really rousted to make his challenge, earning his rider a five-day ban for excessive use of the whip. However, the colt responded really well and had enough in hand to hold the late challenge of the runner-up. He goes into the winter as favourite for both the 2000 Guineas and the Derby with connections hoping he avoids the injury problems that befell Teofilo, whose career path he has emulated to the letter so far. (op 13-8 tchd 7-4 in places)
Fast Company(IRE) ◆, who looked impressive when winning the Acomb Stakes at York, put up a terrific performance having come from well off the pace and briefly looked as if he might catch the winner on the climb to the line. He is entitled to renew rivalry with the winner in the 2000 Guineas and with his pedigree that seems a more likely target than the Derby. Also, being less experienced he is possibly open to more improvement than the winner. (op 12-1)
Raven's Pass(USA), another who came into this unbeaten, has had his Solario Stakes win boosted by the subsequent success of the runner-up in the Royal Lodge. He looked a major player going into the dip but the winner powered by and he could not respond, but this was his first encounter with easy ground and it may be that he will be more effective back on a fast surface. (op 5-2 tchd 10-3 in places)
Rio De La Plata(USA), who was runner-up to New Approach in the National Stakes, has since been an impressive winner of the Group 1 Prix Jean-Luc Lagardere at the Arc meeting on similar going to this. Connections took a long time before deciding whether to run him in this race, but he took his chance and travelled well enough, before not getting the clearest of runs in the dip and failing to pick up from that point. He can be said to have run below par in relation to the winner, and may be best avoiding that rival in the big races next season. (tchd 4-1 and 5-1)
Luck Money(IRE), who followed his third in the Coventry Stakes by picking up a huge pot in a sales race at the Curragh, was stepping up in grade and racing on easy ground for the first time. He was ridden positively and ran pretty well, despite being well held in the end, and looks capable of winning at Group level next season. (op 20-1)
Hatta Fort, who finished fourth behind Rio De La Plata in France, was a couple of lengths closer to him here, which confirms that colt to have run below par. He can win decent races next season if avoiding the top-notchers.
McCartney(GER), who was impressive when completing a hat-trick in the Champagne Stakes at Doncaster, was ridden a little more patiently on this easier ground but came to have every chance at the top of the hill before fading quite quickly in the closing stages - unusual for one from this yard - so he may have had excuses and can be given another chance. (op 9-1 tchd 10-1 in a place)
Dark Angel(IRE) has been a real money-spinner for the yard this season and reached new heights when winning the Middle Park. However, he ran much too freely on this step up to 7f and it was no surprise to see him drop right out in the closing stages.

6334 EMIRATES AIRLINE CHAMPION STKS (GROUP 1) 1m 2f

3:15 (3:17) (Class 1) 3-Y-O+

£222,350 (£84,272; £42,175; £21,028; £10,534; £5,286) **Stalls** Low

Form RPR

1211 **1** **Literato (FR)**[28] 5661 3-8-12 0 C-PLemaire 5 124
(J-C Rouget, France) *gd sort: neat: lw: hld up: hdwy over 2f out: rdn to ld ins fnl f: r.o* **7/2**[2]

3U21 **2** shd **Eagle Mountain**[69] 4435 3-8-12 0 JMurtagh 10 124
(A P O'Brien, Ire) *chsd ldrs: led and edgd lft over 2f out: rdn and hdd ins fnl f: r.o* **5/1**[3]

3331 **3** 3 **Doctor Dino (FR)**[42] 5250 5-9-3 0 OPeslier 8 118
(R Gibson, France) *lw: hld up: hdwy and hmpd over 1f out: sn rdn: no imp ins fnl f* **12/1**

2261 **4** 3 **Creachadoir (IRE)**[14] 6009 3-8-12 118 LDettori 7 112
(Saeed Bin Suroor) *lw: hld up: hdwy over 2f out: rdn over 1f out: wknd ins fnl f* **9/1**

01-1 **5** 1/2 **Multidimensional (IRE)**[28] 5634 4-9-3 111 TedDurcan 1 115+
(H R A Cecil) *lw: hld up: hdwy and hmpd over 1f out: nvr able to chal* **7/1**

1313 **6** 2 1/2 **Notnowcato**[60] 4693 5-9-3 123 RyanMoore 9 106
(Sir Michael Stoute) *prom: rdn over 2f out: wknd fnl f* **9/4**[1]

0260 **7** 1/2 **Speciosa (IRE)**[14] 6010 4-9-0 114 MickyFenton 4 102
(Mrs P Sly) *led over 6f: rdn: swtchd rt and hmpd over 1f out: sn wknd* **22/1**

2353 **8** hd **Mullins Bay**[34] 5451 6-9-3 0 (t) JamieSpencer 11 105
(M F De Kock, South Africa) *b: prom: jnd ldr 6f out: led over 3f out: hdd over 2f out: wknd over 1f out* **25/1**

1460 **9** 7 **Championship Point (IRE)**[28] 5618 4-9-3 113 DarryllHolland 3 91
(M R Channon) *hld up: rdn over 2f out: sn wknd* **50/1**

3135 **10** 7 **Maraahel (IRE)**[42] 5243 6-9-3 118 (b) RHills 6 77
(Sir Michael Stoute) *dwlt: hdwy 1/2-way: wknd over 2f out* **16/1**

1- **11** 16 **Mount Nelson**[356] 6249 3-8-12 0 JimmyFortune 12 45
(A P O'Brien, Ire) *chsd ldrs: rdn over 3f out: wknd over 2f out* **16/1**

34/ **12** 45 **Pinot Noir (GER)**[537] 4-9-3 0 MDemuro 2 —
(L Ottofulling, Germany) *chsd ldrs over 6f* **100/1**

2m 4.24s (-1.47) **Going Correction** +0.225s/f (Good)
WFA 3 from 4yo+ 5lb **12** Ran SP% **122.8**
Speed ratings (Par 117): **114,113,111,109,108 106,106,106,100,94 82,46**
CSF £21.68 TOTE £4.60: £1.20, £2.10, £3.10; EX 31.40 Trifecta £304.70 Pool £5,407.64 - 12.60 winning units..

Owner H Morin **Bred** Bsh Of Administrativa **Trained** Pau, France
■ Jean-Claude Rouget's first winner in Britain.

FOCUS
Not a strong renewal of this high-class event, the form weakened by Notnowcato's poor showing. The finish was dominated by three-year-olds. Literato was up 7lb on his wins in lesser grade and Eagle Mountain improved by 3lb on his Derby second.

NOTEBOOK
Literato(FR) ◆, an admirably consistent performer who has taken Group races at Deauville and Longchamp since finishing runner-up in the Prix du Jockey-Club, is developing into a specialist at this distance and, given a fine ride by Lemaire, who was winning this race for the second successive year, came through to collar the runner-up on the climb to the line and win slightly more comfortably than the margin suggests. He might be retired to stud, but it is to be hoped he is kept in training next season as there are plenty of good 1m2f races for him, starting off with the Prix Ganay. (op 4-1 tchd 9-2 in places)
Eagle Mountain has been placed in both the Epsom and Irish Derbies this season but is arguably most effective at this trip. He was ridden positively, going on at the top of the hill in an attempt to draw the sting out of the finishers and running on bravely, but the winner had a little too much pace. He has apparently been sold and will race for Mike de Kock in future, presumably starting in Dubai in the New Year. (op 11-2)
Doctor Dino(FR), a globetrotter who won the Man o'War Stakes last time, was held up at the back and was making his run when clashing with Multidimensional running into the dip, an incident that knocked him sideways. Nevertheless, he kept going but never got in a blow at the principals. He may be off on his travels again soon, with connections targeting the Hong Kong meeting in December.
Creachadoir(IRE), an impressive winner on his debut for Godolphin at the last meeting here, was supplemented for this but was stepping back up in trip and grade. He appeared to have every chance but did not get home, and will presumably be dropped back to a mile next time. (op 8-1)
Multidimensional(IRE), one of the least experienced in the field, was held up at the rear on this step up to this level and failed to get a clear run on more than one occasion. He was going for a gap when clashing with the third, which lost him impetus, and in the circumstances he did well to finish as close as he did. He can win more Group races next season, by which time he should be fully mature. (op 11-2)
Notnowcato, an admirably consistent performer having his final start before retiring to stud, had run his only disappointing race in the last two years in this race last season and repeated that. Sent off favourite, he appeared to have every chance but was never going that well and was a spent force at the top of the hill. This should not detract from his record which includes three Group 1 wins at this distance. (op 3-1 tchd 10-3 in places)
Speciosa(IRE), another having her final outing before retirement, was back on her favourite course, appeared to have conditions in her favour and got the lead with a rail on her left. Sadly she was unable to show the fire she displayed earlier in her career and was in trouble three furlongs from home. (op 20-1)
Mullins Bay took on Speciosa for the lead and switched to race wide of his field after halfway. He was left behind when the race began in earnest but probably ran as well as he was entitled to on recent form. Official explanation: jockey said horse ran too free (op 33-1 tchd 40-1 in a place)
Mount Nelson, whose season has been blighted by niggling problems, looked big and well for this belated return to action yet was a little edgy. He showed he was on good terms with himself in bowling along up with the pace, before getting tired and being allowed to come home in his own time. Connections are looking forward to a clear year with him in 2008. Official explanation: jockey said colt ran too free (op 14-1)

6335 £2.5 MILLION TOTESCOOP6 CESAREWITCH (HERITAGE H'CAP) 2m 2f
3:55 (4:00) (Class 2) 3-Y-O+

£99,712 (£29,856; £14,928; £7,472; £3,728; £1,872) **Stalls** High

Form — RPR

/401 **1** **Leg Spinner (IRE)**^{27} [4375] 6-8-11 **92**........ JMurtagh 23 109
(A J Martin, Ire) *hld up towards rr: stdy hdwy 8f out: trckd ldrs over 2f out: rdn to ld over 1f out: styd on wl fnl f* **14/1**

-321 **2** *3/4* **Caracciola (GER)**^{34} [5446] 10-8-11 **92** 4ex........ EddieAhern 28 108
(N J Henderson) *chsd ldrs: led 2f out: hdd and rdn over 1f out: kpt on same pce* **33/1**

14-2 **3** *3/4* **Fair Along (GER)**^{164} [1582] 5-8-7 **88**........ JamieSpencer 26 103
(P J Hobbs) *lw: hld up towards rr: hmpd appr bnd 11f out: stdy hdwy over 5f out: rdn to chse ldng pair over 1f out: kpt on but nt pce to chal* **6/1**^{1}

43/4 **4** *4* **Al Eile (IRE)**^{90} [3090] 7-9-1 **96**........ KJManning 1 107+
(John Queally, Ire) *hld up bhd: rdn and effrt 3f out: swtchd rt 2f out: styd on u.p to chse ldng trio ins fnl f: nvr able to chal* **25/1**

0130 **5** *6* **Inchnadamph**^{42} [5215] 7-8-4 **85**........(t) RichardMullen 14 89
(T J Fitzgerald) *hld up in midfield: hdwy over 3f out: ev ch and rdn 2f out: sn wknd* **20/1**

6224 **6** *1* **Kasthari (IRE)**^{21} [5800] 8-9-0 **95**........ TedDurcan 34 98
(J D Bethell) *chsd ldrs: rdn over 3f out: kpt on same pce: no ch w ldrs over 1f out* **50/1**

1433 **7** *1 3/4* **Sunley Peace**^{20} [5829] 3-8-1 **93**........ HayleyTurner 25 94
(D R C Elsworth) *lw: racd in midfield: rdn and outpcd 6f out: plugged on u.p last 2f: no ch w ldrs* **10/1**^{3}

0150 **8** *nk* **Odiham**^{21} [5800] 6-8-9 **90**........(v) SteveDrowne 13 91
(H Morrison) *w.w in midfield: rdn over 3f out: no hdwy* **80/1**

-062 **9** *shd* **Afrad (FR)**^{80} [4056] 6-8-11 **92**........ MichaelHills 24 93
(N J Henderson) *hld up in midfield: hdwy travelling wl 4f out: chsd ldrs and rdn jst over 2f out: sn btn* **16/1**

6033 **10** *nk* **Dr Sharp (IRE)**^{21} [5808] 7-7-10 **80**........ WilliamBuick$^{(3)}$ 31 80
(T P Tate) *lw: led: rdn 3f out: hdd 2f out: sn wknd* **7/1**^{2}

3400 **11** *1/2* **Golden Quest**^{36} [5375] 6-9-0 **95**........ RoystonFfrench 32 95
(M Johnston) *chsd ldrs: rdn over 4f out: wknd wl over 2f out* **50/1**

2165 **12** *3* **Takafu (USA)**^{18} [5884] 5-8-2 **83**........ FrankieMcDonald 11 79
(W S Kittow) *hld up in midfield: hdwy on outer 7f out: rdn over 2f out: sn wknd* **100/1**

0513 **13** *1/2* **Gee Dee Nen**^{21} [5800] 4-8-1 **82**........ JimmyQuinn 27 78
(M H Tompkins) *in tch: rdn wl over 3f out: wknd over 2f out* **33/1**

3650 **14** *nk* **Great As Gold (IRE)**^{41} [5256] 8-7-9 **79** oh1........ LukeMorris$^{(3)}$ 29 74
(B Ellison) *a towards rr: rdn over 4f out: n.d* **100/1**

4201 **15** *1/2* **Desert Sea (IRE)**^{64} [4569] 4-8-5 **86** ow1........ FergusSweeney 3 81
(D W P Arbuthnot) *hld up towards rr: grad swtchd lft over 4f out: sme hdwy on outer u.p 3f out: nvr nr ldrs* **66/1**

1340 **16** *1* **Trance (IRE)**^{7} [6186] 7-7-13 **80**........(p) JamieMackay 5 74
(T D Barron) *wl bhd: lost tch 5f out: sme modest late hdwy: n.d* **66/1**

3503 **17** *nk* **Som Tala**^{54} [4893] 4-8-9 **90**........ TPO'Shea 15 83
(M R Channon) *uns rdr and loose bef s: hld up in rr: nvr on terms* **16/1**

2244 **18** *hd* **Ned Ludd (IRE)**^{16} [5938] 4-8-2 **83**........ NickyMackay 33 76
(J G Portman) *swtg: chsd ldr tl 9f out and again 7f out: ev ch and rdn 3f out: wknd qckly 2f out* **40/1**

6413 **19** *5* **Secret Ploy**^{34} [5446] 7-7-12 **79** oh1........ DavidKinsella 18 67
(H Morrison) *chsd ldrs: wnt 2nd 9f out tl 7f out: sn rdn: wknd over 3f out* **28/1**

0104 **20** *2 1/2* **Enjoy The Moment**^{64} [4569] 4-9-5 **100**........ RyanMoore 6 85
(J A Osborne) *hld up wl bhd: hdwy 6f out: rdn 4f out: chsd ldrs over 2f out: sn wknd* **10/1**^{3}

3505 **21** *2 1/2* **Mudawin (IRE)**^{34} [5469] 6-8-12 **93**........ JohnEgan 19 75
(Jane Chapple-Hyam) *hld up towards rr: hdwy 6f out: rdn and btn over 3f out* **50/1**

1120 **22** *2* **Olimpo (FR)**^{43} [5197] 6-8-2 **83**........ ChrisCatlin 9 63
(B R Millman) *t.k.h: hld up bhd: rdn and effrt 4f out: n.d* **100/1**

11-0 **23** *2* **Raslan**^{123} [2736] 4-8-5 **86**........(v^{1}) MartinDwyer 17 64
(D E Pipe) *chsd ldrs tl drvn and wknd over 3f out* **20/1**

2221 **24** *14* **Samurai Way**^{21} [5800] 5-9-2 **97** 4ex........ JimmyFortune 2 59
(L M Cumani) *hld up in rr: grad swtchd to outer fr 10f out: nvr nr ldrs: wl bhd last 2f: eased: t.o* **6/1**^{1}

0004 **25** *3/4* **Greenwich Meantime**^{36} [5375] 7-9-2 **97**........ DPMcDonogh 10 59
(R A Fahey) *swtg: hld up towards rr: rdn and struggling over 4f out: t.o and eased over 1f out* **50/1**

110 **26** *2* **Full House (IRE)**^{80} [4056] 8-8-9 **90**........ LDettori 7 49
(P R Webber) *lw: stdd s hld up in last: hdwy 8f out: rdn and btn 4f out: t.o and eased over 1f out* **33/1**

4021 **27** *1 1/4* **Indonesia**^{30} [5561] 5-7-9 **78** 4ex........ DuranFentiman$^{(3)}$ 30 37
(T D Walford) *racd in midfield: hmpd appr bnd 11f out: no ch last 4f: t.o: eased* **66/1**

520- **28** *1/2* **Lightning Strike (GER)**^{191} [5963] 4-8-13 **94**........ FrancisNorton 21 52
(Miss Venetia Williams) *in tch: rdn and wkng whn short of room over 3f out: eased fnl f: t.o* **50/1**

3406 **29** *3/4* **Land 'n Stars**^{20} [5829] 7-9-7 **102**........ PaulDoe 16 59
(R A Fahey) *chsd ldrs: rdn 6f out: sn wknd: t.o and eased last 2f* **100/1**

0053 **30** *27* **Baddam**^{12} [6054] 5-9-10 **105**........ DarryllHolland 12 32
(M R Channon) *a bhd: lost tch 5f out: t.o and eased last 2f* **100/1**

0-00 **31** *3 1/2* **Savannah Bay**^{26} [5677] 8-8-7 **88** ow2........ TonyHamilton 8 11
(B Ellison) *b: bhd: rdn and brief effrt 5f out: t.o and eased last 2f* **100/1**

50-0 **32** *11* **Diego Cao (IRE)**^{149} [1959] 6-7-12 **79** oh2........(b^{1}) LiamJones 22 —
(N J Gifford) *a bhd: lost tch over 4f out: t.o last 3f* **40/1**

6224 **33** *48* **Macorville (USA)**^{35} [5437] 4-9-0 **95**........ KDarley 20 —
(G M Moore) *t.k.h: chsd ldrs tl rdn 5f out: sn wknd: virtually p.u last 2f: t.o* **7/1**^{2}

3m 54.13s (-0.67) **Going Correction** +0.225s/f (Good)
WFA 3 from 4yo+ 11lb **34** Ran SP% **142.2**
Speed ratings (Par 109): **110,109,109,107,104 104,103,103,103,103 103,101,101,101,101 100,100,100,98,97 96,95,94,88,87**
CSF £448.35 CT £3103.17 TOTE £16.50: £3.90, £7.90, £3.30, £5.60; EX 617.40 Trifecta £7168.70 Pool £21,203.46 - 2.10 winning units..
Owner W A Moffett **Bred** Steven Nolan **Trained** Summerhill, Co. Meath

FOCUS
A typically large field for this long-distance handicap and the finish was dominated by horses better known as jumpers, with the first three clear. This looked a good renewal with Leg Spinner progressive on the Flat and the form looking pretty sound.

NOTEBOOK
Leg Spinner(IRE), who stays really well and mixes hurdling with Flat racing, had shown in the past that he handles cut and that these big-field staying races hold no fears for him and, with a big-handicap specialist for a trainer and a big-race jockey aboard, it was surprising he was not shorter in the betting. Travelling well throughout, he moved steadily into contention and outstayed his closest rivals up the hill. He is always to be feared in this sort of race, either on the Flat or over hurdles. (tchd 12-1 and 14-1 in a place)
Caracciola(GER), who is better known as a hurdler and chaser, has been successfully campaigned on the Flat this summer and is with a trainer who has won this in the past with a useful hurdler. He travelled well and cruised to the front running into the dip, but was outstayed by the winner up the hill. Nevertheless, he ran virtually to form with the winner compared with their meeting at Ascot in August, and possibly the penalty he picked up for winning at Bath in the meantime made the difference between victory and defeat.
Fair Along(GER), generally a front-runner over fences and hurdles, was having his first outing since finishing second in the Chester Cup in the spring but was well backed. He was settled off the pace but got into a tangle with Great As Gold on the turn into the long straight. That did not seem to affect him as he moved up smoothly into contention, and he was on the winner's tail over 2f out. However he had to switch to get a run and could make no further impression in the last furlong and a half. This should put him right for a return to jumping. (op 11-2)
Al Eile(IRE), in the frame in the Northumberland Plate in the summer, is yet another best known for his jumping exploits. He was held up well off the pace before staying on well in the last quarter mile without getting near enough to deliver a challenge. This was a fine effort from his draw.
Inchnadamph, who had been placed in this race in each of the two previous years, travelled into the race going noticeably well but when asked to go and win the response was limited and he surprisingly faded. His tongue was hanging out in the race so maybe the tongue tie had worked loose and his breathing was affected.
Kasthari(IRE), yet another from the jumping field but quite busy this season on the Flat, was close to the pace throughout and ran his race without being able to quicken.
Sunley Peace, only a three-year-old, is developing into a strong stayer and is the sort who could make up into a major contender for this in a year's time. (op 11-1)
Odiham, unplaced in this in both of the last two seasons, ran a similar race to last year, staying on from the back in the closing stages having been held up.
Afrad(FR), yet another hurdler/chaser, went off a well-backed favourite for this two years ago but was well beaten. He again moved up threateningly but found very little when asked and he seems to be found out by the peculiar stamina demands of this race. (op 22-1)
Dr Sharp(IRE), made the running when third in this last season and adopted similar tactics from his good draw. However, he was under pressure before being headed at the quarter-mile pole and could not respond. (op 10-1 tchd 12-1 in a place)
Secret Ploy Official explanation: jockey said gelding hung right
Samurai Way, who had the profile of an improver and looked the type to be suited by this race, unfortunately had an outside draw which necessitated him being settled at the back. He never figured at any stage and this was well below par, as on a line through Kasthari and Odiham from his Ascot win, he should have been close to making the frame at least. (op 7-1 tchd 15-2)
Macorville(USA), a resolute stayer who appreciates really testing conditions, was quite keen early on the outside of his field but he was under pressure to hold his place a long way from home and eventually dropped right out to finish tailed off. This was clearly not his true running. Official explanation: jockey said gelding became tired

6336 SERIOUSQUITTERS.CO.UK ROCKFEL STKS (GROUP 2) (FILLIES) 7f
4:30 (4:34) (Class 1) 2-Y-O

£39,746 (£15,064; £7,539; £3,759; £1,883; £945) **Stalls** Low

Form — RPR

0 **1** **Kitty Matcham (IRE)**^{6} [6214] 2-8-12 0........ JMurtagh 5 105
(A P O'Brien, Ire) *hld up in tch: rdn over 2f out: styd on u.p to ld wl ins fnl f* **10/1**

215 **2** *nk* **Missit (IRE)**^{15} [5973] 2-8-12 105........ DarryllHolland 8 104
(M R Channon) *lw: chsd ldrs: rdn to ld over 1f out: hdd wl ins fnl f* **4/1**^{2}

2114 **3** ¾ **Royal Confidence**[14] 6008 2-8-12 95 .... MichaelHills 9 102
(B W Hills) *b.hind: hld up: hdwy over 2f out: rdn and ev ch fr over 1f out: unable qckn towards fin* **9/1**[3]

115 **4** 1 ¾ **Rosa Grace**[14] 6008 2-8-12 94 .... PhilipRobinson 3 98
(Rae Guest) *trckd ldrs: nt clr run over 2f out: sn outpcd: hung rt and styd on ins fnl f* **10/1**

3005 **5** *nk* **Kay Es Jay (FR)**[21] 5796 2-8-12 99 .... RyanMoore 4 97
(B W Hills) *chsd ldrs: rdn over 1f out: no ex ins fnl f* **11/1**

241 **6** ¾ **Love Of Dubai (USA)**[18] 5882 2-8-12 83 .... JimmyFortune 1 95
(C E Brittain) *led: rdn and hdd over 1f out: styd on same pce* **28/1**

1 **7** *hd* **Makaaseb (USA)**[29] 5596 2-8-12 0 .... RHills 2 95
(M A Jarvis) *lw: trckd ldr: rdn over 2f out: styd on same pce appr fnl f* **11/8**[1]

4022 **8** 1 ¼ **Dalkey Girl (IRE)**[14] 6012 2-8-12 87 .... JamieSpencer 6 92
(V Smith) *hld up: rdn 1/2-way: n.d* **20/1**

0 **9** 1 ¼ **Cassablanca**[29] 5598 2-8-12 0 .... NCallan 7 88
(M L W Bell) *hld up: hdwy 1/2-way: wknd over 2f out* **33/1**

32 **10** *shd* **Applauded (IRE)**[31] 5540 2-8-12 0 .... LDettori 10 88
(B J Meehan) *b.hind: lw: mid-div: hdwy and hung rt over 2f out: wknd fnl f* **9/1**[3]

1m 27.01s (0.51) **Going Correction** +0.225s/f (Good) **10** Ran SP% **119.8**
Speed ratings (Par 104): **106,105,104,102,102 101,101,99,98,98**
CSF £50.18 TOTE £13.80: £3.20, £1.90, £2.70; EX 73.70.
Owner Mrs David Nagle & Mrs John Magnier **Bred** Barronstown Stud & Tower Blood **Trained** Ballydoyle, Co Tipperary

FOCUS
This looked no better than a fair renewal of this usually informative Group 2 with only one filly officially rated above 100. They finished rather compressed too and it remaind to be seen if the form works out.

NOTEBOOK
Kitty Matcham(IRE) is beautifully bred, being by a 2000 Guineas winner out of an Oaks winner, both of whom represented this filly's trainer. She had previously failed to show similar ability to her parents, having narrowly won a 6f Naas maiden last time when officially rated just 86, but she seems to be progressing quickly now and ran on well to beat a filly who finished fifth in the Cheveley Park on her previous run. If she continues to improve from this she could make up into a Classic contender next year, but she still seems to have some way to go on the evidence so far. (op 12-1 tchd 14-1 in a place)
Missit(IRE), who finished fifth in the Cheveley Park on her previous outing, is clearly a little way below the top of the juvenile tree and her trainer also has the likes of Nahoodh and Nijoom Dubai. However, she ran a fine race in defeat and looks the sort who can win at Group level next season. (op 7-2 tchd 4-1 in a place)
Royal Confidence, fourth in the Oh So Sharp Stakes over course and distance last time, had her chance but on this easier ground could not find an extra gear up the hill. She did, however, finish further ahead of Rosa Grace than in that race a fortnight ago. (op 12-1)
Rosa Grace, a close fifth in the Oh So Sharp Stakes a fortnight earlier, did not get the clearest passage and finished a length and a half further behind today's third. She seems to just lack a change of gear at this level. (op 12-1)
Kay Es Jay(FR), a well-beaten fifth in the Fillies' Mile, is another who by her proximity suggests this form is below par. She did finish closer to her stable companion than at Ascot previously, but was a lot better off at the weights this time.
Love Of Dubai(USA), rated just 83, made the running and, although left behind in the closing stages, did finish close enough to add to the doubts over the form.
Makaaseb(USA), an imposing filly who won her maiden here last month, had already started growing her winter coat and was trace clipped. Nevertheless she was a strong favourite, but failed to pick up having travelled well enough up with the pace. The impression was that we may see a different filly back on fast ground next season. Official explanation: jockey said filly was unsuited by the good to soft (soft in places) ground (op 6-4 tchd 13-8)
Dalkey Girl(IRE) is a consistent handicapper but not up to this level and she was always out the back. (op 25-1)
Cassablanca was taking a big step up in grade having been soundly beaten in a maiden here on her debut. She put up an improved effort but was ultimately well held.
Applauded(IRE), who had shown plenty of promise in a couple of 6f maidens, was forced to race wide from her draw and dropped out in the last quarter-mile Official explanation: jockey said filly hung right (op 10-1)

6337 JOCKEY CLUB CUP (GROUP 3) 2m
5:05 (5:08) (Class 1) 3-Y-O+

£28,390 (£10,760; £5,385; £2,685; £1,345; £675) **Stalls** High

Form RPR

2033 **1** **Royal And Regal (IRE)**[14] 6028 3-8-4 0 .... SPasquier 10 114+
(A Fabre, France) *w'like: chsd clr ldr tl led over 2f out: rdn and edgd lft ins fnl f: r.o* **2/1**[1]

4264 **2** 1 ¼ **Balkan Knight**[13] 6044 7-9-0 111 .... JimmyFortune 7 112
(D R C Elsworth) *b.hind: hld up: hdwy over over 2f out: rdn to chse wnr fnl f: sn ev ch: styd on same pce* **3/1**[3]

5143 **3** 1 **Veenwouden**[16] 5952 3-8-1 101 .... FrancisNorton 4 108
(E F Vaughan) *swtg: hld up: hdwy over 2f out: rdn over 1f out: styd on* **14/1**

0441 **4** 2 **Distinction (IRE)**[20] 5829 8-9-0 111 ....(v[1]) RyanMoore 8 108
(Sir Michael Stoute) *lw: chsd ldrs: rdn over 2f out: no ex fnl f* **11/4**[2]

3453 **5** 12 **Under The Rainbow**[22] 5767 4-8-11 104 .... NCallan 3 91
(B W Hills) *chsd ldrs: rdn over 2f out: sn wknd* **13/2**

4440 **6** 1 **Hawridge Prince**[20] 5829 7-9-0 102 .... JimCrowley 9 93
(B R Millman) *dwlt: hld up: effrt over 4f out: wknd over 2f out* **16/1**

0350 **7** ½ **Invasian (IRE)**[14] 6014 6-9-0 85 ....(e) RobertHavlin 6 92
(P W D'Arcy) *led and sn clr: hdd over 2f out: wknd over 1f out* **33/1**

8 84 **Tobaro (GER)** 6-9-0 0 .... SaleemGolam 1 —
(T T Clement) *dwlt: outpcd* **100/1**

3m 30.52s (3.60) **Going Correction** +0.225s/f (Good)
WFA 3 from 4yo+ 10lb **8** Ran SP% **114.8**
Speed ratings (Par 113): **100,99,98,97,91 91,91,49**
CSF £8.27 TOTE £2.90: £1.40, £1.40, £2.30; EX 8.70.
Owner P D Savill **Bred** P D Savill **Trained** Chantilly, France

FOCUS
Another event that looked a little below the standard of previous renewals and the time was very modest for the grade. Another step up from the French-trained winner.

NOTEBOOK
Royal And Regal(IRE), a relatively lightly-raced three-year-old, has progressed since being upped to this sort of trip and produced a good staying performance to see off the runner-up and record his first Group win. Chasing the clear leader, he gradually reeled that rival in and then made the best of his way home. He looked likely to be caught a furlong out, but he found a little extra and scored cosily in the end. He should pay his way in similar races in France next year, but seems to need the ground on the soft side so is unlikely to be back for the Gold Cup unless we have rain. (tchd 9-4 in places)
Balkan Knight is a generally consistent stayer but has never won above Listed level. He ran his race and looked briefly as if he was coming to take the race, but the winner found more when challenged. There appeared no excuses. (op 7-2)
Veenwouden, who has looked improved since switching to Ed Vaughan and being stepped up in trip, has now been placed in a Listed race and a Group 3 and ran on well having been held up in the rear. It will be interesting to see if connections keep her in training next year in an attempt to win a race at this level. (tchd 12-1)
Distinction(IRE), who would have hacked up in this in his prime, has not looked the same horse since returning from 15 months off this season and the application of a visor failed to improve matters. He had his chance but faded out of things in the closing stages. (op 5-2)
Under The Rainbow, who stays this trip but has been campaigned mainly at middle distances since the spring, had the cheekpieces left off and put up a lacklustre show. Connections may feel it is time to draw stumps with her. (op 8-1 tchd 6-1)
Hawridge Prince, the winner of this race in 2006 when he was completing a hat-trick, has run nowhere near that level this season and connections must be scratching their heads. (op 12-1)
Invasian(IRE) better known as a front-running middle-distance handicapper, established a clear lead before halfway but was reeled in easily by the main contenders and clearly did not stay.

6338 IGLOOS BENTINCK STKS (GROUP 3) 6f
5:40 (5:41) (Class 1) 3-Y-O+

£26,686 (£10,114; £5,061; £2,523; £1,264; £634) **Stalls** Low

Form RPR

1301 **1** **Greek Renaissance (IRE)**[32] 5512 4-9-1 107 .... TedDurcan 11 119
(Saeed Bin Suroor) *racd in midfield on far side: rdn and hdwy wl over 1f out: led 1f out: drvn clr* **12/1**

5156 **2** 2 **Beckermet (IRE)**[20] 5832 5-9-1 109 .... ChrisCatlin 14 113
(R F Fisher) *led far side: rdn wl over 1f out: hdd 1f out: kpt on but nt pce of wnr* **20/1**

3120 **3** ½ **Galeota (IRE)**[20] 5832 5-9-1 106 .... JimmyFortune 17 112
(R Hannon) *lw: racd in midfield on far side: rdn and effrt 2f out: kpt on u.p fnl f: wnt 3rd nr fin* **25/1**

0220 **4** ½ **Borderlescott**[28] 5616 5-9-1 112 .... RoystonFfrench 15 110
(R Bastiman) *t.k.h: chsd ldrs on far side: rdn wl over 1f out: kpt on same pce fnl f* **7/1**[3]

2014 **5** ¾ **Advanced**[14] 6018 4-9-1 114 .... NCallan 6 108+
(K A Ryan) *bhd on far side: rdn and effrt 2f out: kpt on u.p fnl f: nvr able to chal* **9/2**[2]

1300 **6** *nk* **Knot In Wood (IRE)**[20] 5832 5-9-1 102 .... TonyHamilton 18 107
(R A Fahey) *chsd ldrs on far side: rdn wl over 1f out: fdd ins fnl f* **16/1**

0035 **7** *nk* **Patavellian (IRE)**[13] 6039 9-9-1 100 ....(b) SteveDrowne 8 106
(R Charlton) *b: taken down early: racd in midfield on far side: rdn wl over 2f out: kpt on u.p fnl f: nvr able to chal* **14/1**

0362 **8** ¾ **Hoh Hoh Hoh**[7] 6183 5-9-1 100 .... J-PGuillambert 13 104
(R J Price) *chsd ldr on far side: ev ch and rdn 2f out: wknd ins fnl f* **11/1**

315 **9** 1 ½ **Kapil (SAF)**[174] 5-9-1 0 .... C-PLemaire 10 99
(M F De Kock, South Africa) *a bhd on far side: n.d* **16/1**

5033 **10** *nk* **Assertive**[20] 5832 4-9-1 109 .... RichardHughes 4 98+
(R Hannon) *lw: led stands' side gp: clr of that gp and rdn wl over 1f out: no ch w far side: 1st of 6 in gp* **14/1**

1014 **11** 1 ¾ **Zidane**[20] 5832 5-9-1 106 .... JamieSpencer 1 93+
(J R Fanshawe) *b: hld up in rr on stands' side: swtchd rt and hdwy over 1f out: sn rdn: styd on to chse stands' side ldr ins fnl f: no ch: 2nd of 6 in gp* **3/1**[1]

0030 **12** *nk* **Grantley Adams**[28] 5616 4-9-1 98 .... DarryllHolland 16 92
(M R Channon) *taken down early: stdd s: a bhd on far side: no ch fr 1/2-way* **40/1**

015 **13** *nk* **Confuchias (IRE)**[20] 5842 3-9-4 0 .... PhilipRobinson 2 95+
(Francis Ennis, Ire) *in tch on stands' side: chsd ldr that gp over 2f out: sn rdn and no imp: no ch w far side: 3rd of 6 in gp* **16/1**

-541 **14** 4 **Opera Cape**[26] 5673 4-9-1 102 ....(t) LDettori 9 79
(Saeed Bin Suroor) *lw: s.i.s: bhd on far side: rdn 1/2-way: sn wl btn: eased ins fnl f* **8/1**

0010 **15** 3 ½ **Fullandby (IRE)**[28] 5616 5-9-1 101 .... TQuinn 3 69
(T J Etherington) *lw: bhd on stands' side: rdn over 2f out: sn no ch: 4th of 6 in gp* **25/1**

5200 **16** 1 ½ **Baltic King**[20] 5832 7-9-1 102 ....(t) KDarley 7 64
(H Morrison) *stdd s: hld up in rr of stands' side gp: n.d: 5th of 6 in gp* **33/1**

0200 **17** 4 **Obe Brave**[7] 6183 4-9-1 103 .... TPO'Shea 5 52
(M R Channon) *chsd ldrs on stands' side tl over 2f out: sn wknd: eased ins fnl f: 6th of 6 gp* **80/1**

1m 12.21s (-0.89) **Going Correction** +0.225s/f (Good)
WFA 3 from 4yo+ 1lb **17** Ran SP% **132.9**
Speed ratings (Par 113): **114,111,110,110,109 108,108,107,105,104 102,102,101,96,91 89,84**
CSF £251.79 TOTE £17.60: £4.10, £7.80, £8.60; EX 597.70 Place 6 £157.63, Place 5 £42.89..
Owner Godolphin **Bred** Ballymacoll Stud Farm Ltd **Trained** Newmarket, Suffolk

FOCUS
Plenty of runners, but not a strong sprint by Group-race standards, with most of the field having been running in high-class handicaps rather than Group races, and it was unsatisfactory in that they split into two groups and those that stayed near the stands' rail were never on terms. The time, however, was up to standard for the grade, and the form is sound, rated around the second and third. It was career best from Greek Renaissance.

NOTEBOOK
Greek Renaissance(IRE) had been highly progressive last year and he was a winner in Dubai for Godolphin before returning from a break to land a conditions race at Yarmouth last month. This was his first run in a Group race but he won most convincingly, making his effort on the wide outside and coming away up the hill for a clear-cut success. He could have more to offer next season, although presumably he will be back off to Dubai again this winter.
Beckermet(IRE) has been in great form recently, picking up a couple of Listed races, and ran another fine race from the front, being close to his best and helping to set the standard. (tchd 22-1)
Galeota(IRE), another who likes to lead, was settled in this time with plenty of competition for that role. He kept on pretty well in the closing stages and ran within a pound or two of last month's Goodwood form with the runner-up.
Borderlescott, caught close home in this race last year, has looked just as good this year, but has been unlucky not to get his head in front, having been beaten half a length or less on four occasions. He was always handy and gave his all as usual, but it was not quite enough once again. He is thoroughly genuine and deserves to win a Pattern race so possibly connections may opt to try cheekpieces or something similar to squeeze that little extra out of him. (op 15-2)
Advanced, back at 6f after a fruitless try over further, had the highest official rating, but although he kept on for a respectable fifth he never looked like winning. (op 5-1)
Knot In Wood(IRE) ran pretty well but may be better off in Listed company, although he is in danger of becoming a 'twilight' horse.
Patavellian(IRE), who has shown a revival in form in recent races, was somewhat isolated in the far-side group but towards the middle of the track and could never land a blow. (op 12-1)
Assertive led throughout in the stands'-side group and finished clear, but he never had a hope of getting on terms with the main group. He deserves credit for this and is running really well at present.

Zidane, who was held up in the stands'-side group, never seriously troubled Assertive, let alone the principals in the main group. (op 4-1)
T/Plt: £176.00 to a £1 stake. Pool: £170,264.65. 706.20 winning tickets. T/Qpdt: £44.50 to a £1 stake. Pool: £7,161.60. 119.05 winning tickets. CR

6311 WOLVERHAMPTON (A.W) (L-H)

Saturday, October 20

OFFICIAL GOING: Standard
Wind: Nil Weather: Fine and becoming misty

6339 WBX.COM 0% COMMISSION ON BIG FOOTBALL MATCHES MAIDEN STKS 5f 20y(P)

7:00 (7:00) (Class 5) 3-Y-0+ **£2,968** (£876; £438) **Stalls** Low

Form RPR
3532 **1** **By The Edge (IRE)**[15] 5970 3-8-12 50 PhillipMakin 4 56
(T D Barron) *led 1f: chsd ldr: rdn over 2f out: led wl ins fnl f: r.o* **11/2**[2]
0363 **2** ¾ **Perlachy**[8] 6149 3-9-0 53 (v) StephaneBreux(3) 5 58
(Mrs N Macauley) *mid-div: rdn and sltly outpcd over 2f out: swtchd rt jst ins fnl f: fin wl* **16/1**
2034 **3** ¾ **Al Badeya (IRE)**[12] 6062 3-8-12 64 (v[1]) SebSanders 10 51
(Sir Michael Stoute) *led after 1f: rdn over 1f out: hdd and no ex wl ins fnl f* **6/4**[1]
4 1 **Brave Falcon (IRE)**[82] 4034 3-9-0 0 (bt) JerryO'Dwyer(3) 1 52
(Leo J Temple, Ire) *hld up in tch: rdn wl over 1f out: nt qckn ins fnl f* **16/1**
0430 **5** hd **Punching**[9] 6123 3-9-3 54 StephenCarson 11 51
(Eve Johnson Houghton) *hld up towards rr: rdn over 2f out: r.o ins fnl f: nrst fin* **33/1**
2540 **6** 1 ¾ **Sweetsformysweet (USA)**[15] 5982 3-8-12 52 JimmyQuinn 9 40
(J Noseda) *t.k.h in tch: rdn over 1f out: wknd ins fnl f* **13/2**[3]
54 **7** 2 ½ **Thea Di Bisanzio (IRE)**[10] 6097 3-8-12 0 NickyMackay 6 31
(G A Butler) *mid-div: rdn over 2f out: sn struggling: eased whn btn wl ins fnl f* **8/1**
030 **8** nk **Epidaurian King (IRE)**[173] 1350 4-9-3 54 AdamKirby 2 35
(D Shaw) *a towards rr* **25/1**
9 1 ½ **Elizabeth Spirit (IRE)** 3-8-9 0 JamieMoriarty(3) 8 25
(E S McMahon) *n.m.r sn after s: a in rr* **66/1**
0526 **10** shd **Whats Your Game (IRE)**[15] 5970 3-9-3 48 (b) FergusSweeney 12 29
(A Berry) *prom: rdn over 2f out: wknd over 1f out* **50/1**
2206 **11** 1 ½ **Spiffing (IRE)**[84] 3968 3-9-3 66 (b[1]) GeorgeBaker 7 24
(R M Beckett) *a in rr* **7/1**
12 3 ½ **Flashin Amber** 3-9-3 0 LPKeniry 3 11
(Peter Grayson) *s.i.s: a in rr* **80/1**
62.77 secs (-0.05) **Going Correction** -0.075s/f (Stan) **12** Ran SP% **115.6**
Speed ratings (Par 103): **97,95,94,93,92 89,85,85,83,82 80,74**
CSF £82.84 TOTE £7.80: £1.70, £3.80, £1.10; EX 112.20.
Owner Chris McHale **Bred** A M Burke **Trained** Maunby, N Yorks

FOCUS
Most of these were fully exposed in this weak maiden. The form is rated through the runner-up, with winner By The Edge back to his turf best.
Epidaurian King(IRE) Official explanation: jockey said gelding never travelled
Whats Your Game(IRE) Official explanation: jockey said gelding hung left-handed up the straight
Spiffing(IRE) Official explanation: jockey said colt ran green in first-time blinkers

6340 WBX.COM £25 BET FOR NEW ACCOUNTS CLAIMING STKS 5f 20y(P)

7:30 (7:30) (Class 6) 3-Y-0+ **£2,047** (£604; £302) **Stalls** Low

Form RPR
4100 **1** **Desert Opal**[14] 6020 7-9-5 74 (b) LiamJones 4 79
(C R Dore) *mde all: rdn wl over 1f out: r.o* **11/4**[1]
6000 **2** ½ **Macademy Royal (USA)**[85] 3906 4-8-5 60 (t) JimmyQuinn 11 63
(H Morrison) *bhd: swtchd lft after 1f: hdwy on ins over 2f out: rdn over 1f out: ev ch wl ins fnl f: nt qckn* **8/1**[3]
2065 **3** 2 ½ **Rebel Duke (IRE)**[7] 6173 3-9-0 75 JamieJones(5) 3 68
(M G Quinlan) *a.p: rdn over 1f out: one pce* **11/4**[1]
4002 **4** 3 **Dysonic (USA)**[110] 3169 5-8-8 49 (v) TolleyDean(5) 8 51
(J Balding) *mid-div: rdn and hdwy wl over 1f out: wknd fnl f* **9/1**
60-0 **5** ¾ **Harrington Bates**[1] 6311 6-8-9 0 PhillipMakin 2 45
(J J Lambe, Ire) *bhd: rdn over 3f out: hdwy over 1f out: n.d* **50/1**
5460 **6** 3 ½ **Time Share (IRE)**[35] 5420 3-8-3 50 (be) KevinGhunowa(5) 1 31
(G C Bravery) *outpcd* **40/1**
064 **7** ½ **Ashes (IRE)**[15] 5969 5-8-10 69 SebSanders 9 31
(K R Burke) *led to post: mid-div: rdn over 2f out: sn wknd* **9/2**[2]
0032 **8** 1 **Twinned (IRE)**[30] 5564 4-8-9 50 FergusSweeney 7 27
(M J Wilkinson) *prom tl rdn and wknd wl over 1f out* **8/1**[3]
4500 **9** 4 **Scarlett Heart (IRE)**[7] 6174 3-7-13 60 LukeMorris(3) 12 5
(J Gallagher) *s.s: swtchd lft sn after s: rdn over 2f out: c wd st: a in rr* **12/1**
454 **10** 3 **Royal Becky (IRE)**[10] 6111 3-8-7 0 (p) WilliamBuick(3) 5 3
(Patrick Morris, Ire) *w wnr tl rdn 2f out: sn wknd* **20/1**
62.48 secs (-0.34) **Going Correction** -0.075s/f (Stan) **10** Ran SP% **116.5**
Speed ratings (Par 101): **99,98,94,89,88 82,81,80,73,69**
CSF £25.44 TOTE £4.30: £1.50, £3.60, £1.70; EX 33.00.
Owner Page, Ward, Marsh **Bred** Juddmonte Farms **Trained** West Pinchbeck, Lincs

FOCUS
This looked a shade above-average claimer. The form could have been rated higher but it is likely that the second and third were not at their best rather than that the winner improved.
Twinned(IRE) Official explanation: jockey said gelding hung right-handed

6341 WBX.COM FOR FREE FOOTBALL SHIRT H'CAP 2m 119y(P)

7:55 (7:56) (Class 6) (0-65,66) 3-Y-0+ **£2,047** (£604; £302) **Stalls** Low

Form RPR
0/01 **1** **Estate**[6] 6200 5-9-11 62 6ex JamesDoyle 7 75+
(E J O'Neill) *hld up towards rr: stdy hdwy over 4f out: wnt 2nd over 2f out: led on bit jst ins fnl f: cleverly* **4/1**[2]
0404 **2** nk **Arabian Sun**[16] 5948 3-8-8 55 (v) MickyFenton 3 68
(M J Attwater) *led early: hld up in mid-div: hdwy over 5f out: led over 4f out: rdn over 1f out: hdd jst ins fnl f: no ch w wnr* **10/1**
0342 **3** 14 **Dansimar**[12] 6069 3-9-4 65 JimmyQuinn 2 61
(M R Channon) *hld up in tch: wnt 2nd over 3f out: rdn and wknd over 2f out* **7/1**[3]
0000 **4** 1 ¾ **Ronsard (IRE)**[3] 6271 5-9-2 53 TGMcLaughlin 5 47
(P D Evans) *s.i.s: hld up towards rr: hdwy 4f out: rdn and wknd over 2f out* **33/1**
2201 **5** 2 **Stagecoach Emerald**[12] 6068 5-9-12 66 (p) WilliamBuick(3) 11 58
(R W Price) *hld up in tch: pushed along over 6f out: rdn and wknd wl over 2f out* **9/1**
006- **6** ¾ **Snowberry Hill (USA)**[386] 5650 4-9-4 55 LiamJones 4 46
(Lucinda Featherstone) *sn chsng ldr: wknd 4f out* **66/1**
4602 **7** 2 ½ **Merrymaker**[11] 6077 7-9-11 65 PatrickMathers(3) 1 53
(W M Brisbourne) *s.i.s: rn in snatches in rr: styd on fnl 2f: nvr nr ldrs* **16/1**
0065 **8** 10 **Kitebrook**[15] 5979 6-8-9 46 oh1 VinceSlattery 6 22
(Mrs Mary Hambro) *hld up in mid-div: rdn over 4f out: sn wknd* **100/1**
0-21 **9** ¾ **Hora**[17] 5906 3-8-9 56 SebSanders 13 31
(Sir Mark Prescott) *prom: led over 5f out tl over 4f out: rdn over 3f out: wknd and eased over 2f out* **5/4**[1]
4060 **10** 9 **Red Sun**[5] 6241 10-8-12 49 (t) PhillipMakin 8 13
(R C Guest) *hld up in mid-div: rdn over 6f out: sn bhd* **33/1**
0645 **11** 3 ½ **Jenny Soba**[11] 6076 4-8-6 46 oh1 NeilChalmers(3) 9 6
(Lucinda Featherstone) *a towards rr* **66/1**
00/0 **12** 7 **My Portfolio (IRE)**[8] 3677 5-8-10 50 JamieMoriarty(3) 10 2
(J J Lambe, Ire) *a in rr* **40/1**
3005 **13** 5 **Al Moulatham**[21] 5820 8-9-1 52 (bt) JimCrowley 12 —
(R Ford) *sn led: hdd over 5f out: wknd qckly* **33/1**
3m 40.5s (-2.63) **Going Correction** -0.075s/f (Stan)
WFA 3 from 4yo+ 10lb **38** Ran SP% **117.2**
Speed ratings (Par 101): **103,102,96,95,94 94,92,88,87,83 82,78,76**
CSF £40.76 CT £274.00 TOTE £5.50: £1.20, £2.80, £1.70; EX 66.80.
Owner R S Brookhouse **Bred** Stratford Place Stud & Watership Down Stud **Trained** Averham Park, Notts

FOCUS
They went a decent pace in what turned out to be a fairly uncompetitive low-grade stayers' handicap with the warm favourite a flop. That said the first two finished clear and a fairly positive view has been taken of the form, with the winner rated value for 4l.
Hora Official explanation: trainer said filly lost its action

6342 TOWN & COUNTRY SCAFFOLDING NORTH WEST LTD H'CAP 1m 1f 103y(P)

8:25 (8:25) (Class 6) (0-65,66) 3-Y-0+ **£2,047** (£604; £302) **Stalls** Low

Form RPR
1000 **1** **Pothos Way (GR)**[24] 5732 4-9-4 61 JimCrowley 8 68+
(P R Chamings) *a.p: rdn over 2f out: nt clr run over 1f out: hrd rdn to ld nr fin* **8/1**[3]
0022 **2** nk **Emily's Place (IRE)**[8] 6146 4-9-5 62 JimmyQuinn 13 67
(J Pearce) *hld up towards rr: hdwy over 2f out: hrd rdn and edgd rt ins fnl f: r.o* **9/1**
5510 **3** shd **Lobengula (IRE)**[17] 5916 5-9-1 58 SebSanders 12 63
(I W McInnes) *led after 1f: rdn over 1f out: hdd nr fin* **12/1**
3120 **4** 2 **Weet Yer Tern (IRE)**[1] 6316 5-8-10 53 FergusSweeney 3 54
(W M Brisbourne) *hld up in mid-div: hdwy over 2f out: rdn over 1f out: kpt on ins fnl f* **4/1**[2]
-604 **5** ¾ **Semi Detached (IRE)**[229] 611 4-9-3 60 AdamKirby 5 59
(J W Unett) *led 1f: chsd ldr tl rdn wl over 1f out: one pce fnl f* **16/1**
0602 **6** 1 ¾ **Siena Star (IRE)**[6] 6196 9-9-6 63 MickyFenton 9 59
(Stef Liddiard) *hld up in rr: c v wd st: styd on fnl f: nvr nrr* **9/1**
0-00 **7** 1 **Compton Eclipse**[1] 6316 7-8-9 55 JamieMoriarty(3) 2 48
(J J Lambe, Ire) *hld up in tch: rdn over 1f out: wknd ins fnl f* **50/1**
3145 **8** ½ **Desert Hawk**[18] 5886 6-8-8 56 PatrickHills(5) 1 48
(W M Brisbourne) *hld up in mid-div: rdn over 3f out: no rspnse* **8/1**[3]
/0-0 **9** ¾ **Safin (GER)**[219] 685 7-9-3 60 LPKeniry 6 51
(F Jordan) *a towards rr* **66/1**
2131 **10** 2 **Kansas Gold**[8] 6146 4-9-9 66 RoystonFfrench 10 53
(J Mackie) *s.i.s: in rr: rdn and short-lived effrt over 2f out* **7/2**[1]
6500 **11** 9 **Norwegian**[6] 6199 6-9-2 62 (p) WilliamBuick(3) 7 30
(Ian Williams) *hld up towards rr: stdy hdwy on outside over 4f out: rdn and wknd 3f out* **9/1**
4120 **12** 1 ¼ **Libre**[18] 5885 7-9-8 65 TGMcLaughlin 4 30
(F Jordan) *hld up in mid-div: rdn 3f out: sn bhd* **12/1**
2m 1.69s (-0.93) **Going Correction** -0.075s/f (Stan)
WFA 3 from 4yo+ 4lb **12** Ran SP% **119.2**
Speed ratings (Par 101): **101,100,100,98,98 96,95,95,94,92 84,83**
CSF £78.59 CT £869.53 TOTE £12.50: £4.20, £1.60, £3.60; EX 83.70.
Owner Mrs Alexandra J Chandris **Bred** Ippotour Stud **Trained** Baughurst, Hants

FOCUS
A modest handicap run at an ordinary pace. The third looks the best guide.
Kansas Gold Official explanation: jockey said gelding missed the break

6343 WBX.COM 0% COMMISSION ON BIG RACES FILLIES' H'CAP 1m 141y(P)

8:55 (8:55) (Class 5) (0-70,70) 3-Y-0+ **£2,968** (£876; £438) **Stalls** Low

Form RPR
23 **1** **Princess Cocoa (IRE)**[21] 5814 4-9-5 70 JamieMoriarty(3) 4 79
(R A Fahey) *hld up in mid-div: hdwy over 2f out: led ins fnl f: rdn and r.o* **7/2**[1]
6006 **2** 1 ¼ **Daring Affair**[30] 5553 6-9-6 68 (p) PhillipMakin 10 74
(K R Burke) *hld up in tch: rdn to ld over 1f out: hdd ins fnl f: nt qckn* **8/1**
2340 **3** ½ **Casablanca Minx (IRE)**[15] 5985 4-9-0 62 (v) TGMcLaughlin 3 67
(P D Evans) *stdd s: hld up in rr: hdwy over 2f out: rdn and hung lft fr over 1f out: kpt on* **6/1**[2]
0330 **4** 2 **Fealeview Lady (USA)**[25] 5703 3-9-0 69 TravisBlock(3) 13 70
(H Morrison) *hld up in rr: rdn and hdwy over 1f out: hung lft and one pce fnl f* **6/1**[2]
1550 **5** ½ **Keidas (FR)**[77] 4170 3-8-11 70 JamieHamblett(7) 1 70
(C F Wall) *led early: prom: rdn wl over 1f out: wknd ins fnl f* **10/1**
0220 **6** 4 **My Michelle**[50] 5020 6-9-0 62 FergusSweeney 5 53
(B Palling) *led 7f out: rdn and hdd over 1f out: wknd fnl f* **11/1**
0-00 **7** nk **Classic Blue (IRE)**[17] 5894 3-8-1 56 oh7 WilliamBuick(3) 11 46
(Ian Williams) *hld up in rr: rdn over 3f out: sme hdwy whn hung lft over 1f out: n.d* **40/1**
0000 **8** 5 **Wasalat (USA)**[14] 6021 5-9-4 66 RoystonFfrench 7 45
(D W Barker) *s.i.s: a bhd* **9/1**
4330 **9** 1 **Grethel (IRE)**[12] 6055 3-7-12 57 DanielleMcCreery(7) 9 34
(A Berry) *hld up in mid-div: wknd over 3f out* **25/1**
0622 **10** 7 **Grand Lucre**[9] 6123 3-8-11 63 StephenCarson 8 24
(G A Butler) *sn led: hdd 7f out: rdn and ev ch over 2f out: wknd wl over 1f out* **15/2**[3]
2233 **11** 2 ½ **Laura's Best (IRE)**[11] 6094 3-9-1 67 (b[1]) SebSanders 2 23
(W J Haggas) *hld up in mid-div: rdn 3f out: wknd 2f out* **15/2**[3]
1m 50.14s (-1.62) **Going Correction** -0.075s/f (Stan)
WFA 3 from 4yo+ 4lb **11** Ran SP% **119.1**
Speed ratings (Par 100): **104,102,102,100,100 96,96,91,91,84 82**
CSF £32.17 CT £168.73 TOTE £5.20: £2.50, £3.50, £1.80; EX 50.70.
Owner P Ashton **Bred** Corduff Stud **Trained** Musley Bank, N Yorks

FOCUS
A pretty weak fillies' handicap. The winner is rated in line with this year's best.

Wasalat(USA) Official explanation: jockey said mare missed the break

6344 WBX.COM £25 BET FOR NEW ACCOUNTS H'CAP — 1m 141y(P)
9:20 (9:20) (Class 6) (0-65,65) 3-Y-0+ — £2,047 (£604; £302) Stalls Low

Form — RPR

4-50 **1** **Robert The Brave**[175] 1289 3-8-11 **63** — TolleyDean[(5)] 11 — 71+
(P R Webber) *hld up in rr: rdn over 3f out: hdwy on ins wl over 1f out: r.o u.p to ld cl home* **16/1**

4250 **2** ½ **Zelos (IRE)**[30] 5559 3-9-2 **63** — (b) LPKeniry 9 — 70
(D J S Ffrench Davis) *hld up in tch: rdn to ld wl over 1f out: hdd cl home* **10/1**

6626 **3** ½ **Airman (IRE)**[8] 6148 4-9-5 **62** — SebSanders 8 — 68
(W M Brisbourne) *hld up in mid-div: hdwy over 2f out: sn rdn: r.o ins fnl f* **7/1**[3]

3300 **4** ½ **Climate (IRE)**[8] 6146 8-8-11 **59** — RussellKennemore[(5)] 4 — 64
(R Hollinshead) *hld up towards rr: rdn and hdwy 2f out: kpt on ins fnl f* **16/1**

1053 **5** 3 **Bold Indian (IRE)**[14] 6025 3-9-4 **65** — TomEaves 6 — 63
(I Semple) *s.i.s: hld up towards rr: rdn over 3f out: styd on fnl f: nvr trbld ldrs* **4/1**[1]

0023 **6** ½ **Richelieu**[2] 6290 5-9-1 **58** — PhillipMakin 3 — 55
(J J Lambe, Ire) *hld up in mid-div: nt clr run over 2f out: rdn wl over 1f out: no real prog fnl f* **15/2**

3020 **7** hd **Radiator Rooney (IRE)**[37] 5372 4-9-3 **63** — (p) WilliamBuick[(3)] 5 — 60
(Patrick Morris, Ire) *w ldr: led over 2f out: rdn and hdd wl over 1f out: wknd ins fnl f* **25/1**

5252 **8** 2½ **Pactolos Way**[24] 5733 4-9-8 **65** — JimCrowley 7 — 56
(P R Chamings) *prom: rdn over 2f out: wknd fnl f* **9/2**[2]

0-00 **9** 3½ **Mulligans Pursuit (IRE)**[115] 2995 3-8-10 **60** — JerryO'Dwyer[(3)] 12 — 43
(M D I Usher) *stdd sn after s: hld up in rr: rdn over 2f out: swtchd lft and short-lived effrt on ins over 1f out* **66/1**

6045 **10** 3 **Bold Saxon (IRE)**[5] 6245 3-8-6 **58** — PatrickHills[(5)] 10 — 35
(M D I Usher) *hld up in mid-div: hdwy over 4f out: rdn over 3f out: wknd over 2f out* **16/1**

40/0 **11** nk **New Wave**[13] 5636 5-8-11 **59** — (p) KirstyMilczarek[(5)] 13 — 35
(R Lee) *a towards rr* **33/1**

2403 **12** 5 **Nautical**[12] 6064 9-8-10 **56** — LukeMorris[(3)] 2 — 21
(A W Carroll) *led: rdn and hdd over 2f out: sn wknd* **7/1**[3]

1230 **13** 50 **Bolton Hall (IRE)**[43] 5198 5-9-3 **63** — JamieMoriarty[(3)] 1 — —
(R A Fahey) *v rel to r: a t.o* **8/1**

1m 50.89s (-0.87) **Going Correction** -0.075s/f (Stan)
WFA 3 from 4yo+ 4lb — **13** Ran SP% **121.1**
Speed ratings (Par 101): **100,99,99,98,96 95,95,93,90,87 87,82,38**
CSF £167.41 CT £1240.06 TOTE £16.80: £7.00, £8.50, £2.30; EX 246.90 Place 6 £176.79, Place 5 £116.84..
Owner T R Pearson **Bred** Alan Gibson **Trained** Mollington, Oxon

FOCUS
A slower pace meant this modest affair was 0.69 seconds slower than the previous fillies' handicap. The winner is unexposed and the form is rated through the placed horses.
T/Plt: £452.10 to a £1 stake. Pool: £72,661.10. 117.30 winning tickets. T/Qpdt: £175.30 to a £1 stake. Pool: £4,739.20. 20.00 winning tickets. KH

6345 - 6352a (Foreign Racing) - See Raceform Interactive

6324 BADEN-BADEN (L-H)
Saturday, October 20

OFFICIAL GOING: Soft

6353a HEEL - BADEN-WURTTEMBERG-TROPHY (GROUP 3) — 1m 3f
3:40 (3:43) 3-Y-0+ — £20,270 (£8,446; £3,378; £1,689)

RPR

1 **Egerton (GER)**[27] 5671 6-9-4 — TMundry 9 — 111
(P Rau, Germany) *racd in 3rd bhd clr ldrs: clsd up gng wl 3f out: led 2f out: drvn out* **6/5**[1]

2 ½ **Belmundo (GER)**[133] 3-8-7 — FilipMinarik 6 — 105
(P Schiergen, Germany) *racd in 5th: wnt 2nd ins fnl f: hld by wnr clsng stages* **7/2**[3]

3 3 **Dickens (GER)**[27] 5671 4-9-2 — ASuborics 7 — 103
(H Blume, Germany) *hld up in last: hdwy 3f out: wnt 3rd cl home* **97/10**

4 ½ **Prince Flori (GER)**[48] 5077 4-9-6 — HGrewe 8 — 106
(S Smrczek, Germany) *hld up: 6th st: hrd rdn on outside over 1f out: kpt on at one pce* **47/10**

5 ¾ **Pont Des Arts (FR)**[132] 2503 3-8-9 — OPlacais 4 — 100
(K Schafflutzel, Switzerland) *pressed ldr clr of remainder: led 3f out: hdd 2f out: one pce* **25/1**

6 1¼ **Poseidon Adventure (IRE)**[27] 5671 4-9-2 — (b) ADeVries 2 — 99
(W Figge, Germany) *hld up: last st: no room over 1f out: styd on fnl f* **34/10**[2]

7 1½ **White Lightning (GER)**[17] 5929 5-9-0 — JBojko 5 — 95
(U Stech, Norway) *racd in 4th: one pce fnl 2f* **28/1**

8 nse **Equip Hill (SWE)**[41] 5263 5-9-4 — P-AGraberg 1 — 99
(B Bo, Sweden) *midfield: 7th st: sn one pce* **27/1**

9 13 **Art Attack (GER)**[13] 4-9-2 — EPedroza 3 — 76
(Rune Haugen, Norway) *set str pce clr w one other: hdd 3f out: wknd 2f out* **39/1**

2m 17.89s (-1.38)
WFA 3 from 4yo+ 6lb — **9** Ran SP% **130.7**
(including 10 Euro stake): WIN 22; PL 11, 13, 18; SF 121.
Owner Stall Reckendorf **Bred** Gestut Rottgen **Trained** Germany

6189 CAULFIELD (R-H)
Saturday, October 20

OFFICIAL GOING: Good

6354a BMW CAULFIELD CUP (GROUP 1) (H'CAP) — 1m 4f
7:00 (12:00) 3-Y-0+
£622,581 (£151,210; £80,645; £44,355; £36,290; £30,242)

RPR

1 **Master O'Reilly (NZ)**[7] 6191 5-8-0 — VDuric 4 — 117
(Danny O'Brien, Australia)

2 2¼ **Douro Valley (AUS)**[14] 6034 6-8-2 — (b) JWinks 3 — 114
(Danny O'Brien, Australia)

3 1¼ **Princess Coup (AUS)**[14] 4-8-1 — (b) GBoss 15 — 111
(M Walker, New Zealand)

4 2 **Blue Monday**[14] 6034 6-8-11 — NashRawiller 7 — 118
(D Hayes, Australia)

5 ¾ **Tawqeet (USA)**[14] 6034 5-9-0 — DwayneDunn 13 — 120
(D Hayes, Australia)

6 nk **Purple Moon (IRE)**[59] 4722 4-8-6 — KerrinMcEvoy 11 — 111
(L M Cumani) *racd in 13th on outside: 14th st: nt clr run over 1f out: styd on wl clsng stages* **20/1**[1]

7 1¼ **Blutigeroo (AUS)**[14] 6034 6-8-10 — DMOliver 10 — 113
(C Little, Australia)

8 hd **Annenkov (IRE)**[7] 6189 5-8-3 — LNolen 8 — 106
(P Moody, Australia)

9 snk **Maybe Better (AUS)**[7] 6189 5-8-7 — CoreyBrown 5 — 110
(B Mayfield-Smith, Australia)

10 1¼ **Scenic Shot (AUS)**[14] 6034 5-8-4 — SKatsidis 14 — 105
(D Morton, Australia)

11 ¾ **Mandela (NZ)**[14] 6-8-4 — DNikolic 6 — 103
(R Yuill, New Zealand)

12 hd **Sirmione (AUS)**[28] 4-8-2 — SebastianMurphy 9 — 101
(J B Cummings, Australia)

13 ½ **Black Tom (AUS)**[14] 6033 7-8-6 — PHall 12 — 104
(F Maynard, Australia)

14 shd **Railings (AUS)**[14] 6-8-10 — GChilds 16 — 108
(Roger James, New Zealand)

15 shd **Anamato (AUS)**[7] 6189 4-8-2 — (b) SDye 1 — 100
(D Hayes, Australia)

16 ¾ **Cinque Cento (AUS)**[14] 6034 6-8-4 — (b) SSeamer 2 — 101
(P Moody, Australia)

2m 26.15s (146.15) — **16** Ran SP% **4.8**
S.P.: 17/2, 11/1, 16/1, 70/1 (Maldivian and Eskimo Queen were both withdrawn at the start on vet's advice; local bookmakers deducted 48 cents in the dollar).
Owner W F Sutcliffe, Mrs D Sutcliffe, Miss J F Mawer **Bred** D B & Mrs M P Jones **Trained** Australia

FOCUS
This was the third-fastest running of a race that usually is the best pointer for the Melbourne Cup. The race lost some of its interest when the favourite Maldivian was withdrawn at the start, along with the well-supported Eskimo Queen.

NOTEBOOK
Master O'Reilly(NZ), who won a Group 2 the weekend before, showed a very good attitude under pressure and won going away. Eleven horses have completed the Caulfield Cup-Melbourne Cup double, and even with roughly a 3lb penalty, he looks the one to beat at Flemington.
Douro Valley(AUS) has been running consistently well through the spring in Australia's big handicaps and led them into the final stages after going past Annenkov. However, Master O'Reilly swept past him soon after and he was quickly beaten.
Princess Coup(AUS), who won New Zealand's richest race last time, was always well placed during the race and kept on strongly up the reasonably short straight. She will probably contest the Mackinnon Stakes at Flemington next, three days before the Melbourne Cup.
Blue Monday has shown mixed form in Australia since moving out there but, arguably, ran his best race in this event. A Group 1 performer in England, he may be hitting his peak at just the right time and his jockey believes he will relish the extra distance at Flemington.
Tawqeet(USA) ran his best race for some time and was closing on the leaders in the final furlong. It is easy to forget that he started a well-backed favourite for the Melbourne Cup last year.
Purple Moon(IRE), having his first start since winning the Ebor two months ago, was always towards the rear and wide for most of the race before making his effort up the home straight. He was not given a hard time after meeting some interference and connections were delighted with the run. The prime target has always been the Melbourne Cup and he heads there with a leading chance, although he will need to improve significantly to get the better of Master O'Reilly.
Blutigeroo(AUS) often makes a late charge and was finishing really well in the latter stages. His season looks to be building towards the Melbourne Cup and he will be a very lively outsider in November, as he looks sure to stay the 2m trip well.
Annenkov(IRE) tried to get away from his rivals rounding the final bend but was soon caught. The jockey thought he was not up to this class at the trip.
Maybe Better(AUS) had every chance but failed to pick up when asked to quicken.

6339 WOLVERHAMPTON (A.W) (L-H)
Sunday, October 21

OFFICIAL GOING: Standard
Wind: Moderate, behind

6355 SPONSOR A RACE BY CALLING 0870 220 2442 H'CAP — 5f 216y(P)
2:10 (2:10) (Class 4) (0-85,90) 3-Y-0+ — £4,857 (£1,445; £722; £360) Stalls Low

Form — RPR

0451 **1** **Ajigolo**[6] 6231 4-9-10 **90** 6ex — TPO'Shea 4 — 100
(M R Channon) *trckd ldr: led appr fnl f: rdn out* **5/2**[1]

2204 **2** 1¼ **Sir Nod**[34] 5481 5-9-0 **80** — PaulMulrennan 11 — 86+
(Miss J A Camacho) *t.k.h: hld up in tch: hdwy 1/2-way: r.o to go 2nd ins fnl f* **16/1**

302 **3** ½ **Rainbow Mirage (IRE)**[18] 5923 3-9-3 **84** — SebSanders 1 — 88
(E S McMahon) *chsd ldrs: rdn 1/2-way: kpt on fnl f* **5/1**[2]

1346 **4** 1¼ **Super Frank (IRE)**[19] 5885 4-8-10 **76** — TPQueally 3 — 76
(J Akehurst) *led tl rdn and hdd appr fnl f: no ex ins fnl f* **6/1**[3]

0000 **5** nk **Coleorton Dancer**[30] 5584 5-8-13 **79** — TedDurcan 10 — 78+
(K A Ryan) *hld up in tch: rdn 2f out: one pce after* **17/2**

004 **6** shd **Kelamon**[6] 6243 3-8-4 **74** — LukeMorris[(3)] 2 — 73
(M D I Usher) *nvr bttr than mid-div* **20/1**

0240 **7** ½ **Curtail (IRE)**[30] 5584 4-9-5 **85** — (v) TomEaves 7 — 83
(I Semple) *s.i.s: sn prom: outpcd 2f out: nvr on terms after* **10/1**

-000 **8** 2½ **Loyal Royal (IRE)**[18] 5923 4-8-5 **78** — PietroRomeo[(7)] 13 — 68
(J M Bradley) *a towards rr on outside: nvr on terms* **100/1**

6006 **9** ½ **Desert Dreamer (IRE)**[7] 6209 6-8-13 **79** — (b[1]) NickyMackay 8 — 67
(G A Butler) *chsd ldrs: rdn 1/2-way: wknd wl over 1f out* **8/1**

150- **10** 2½ **Frontline In Focus (IRE)**[398] 5434 3-9-2 **83** — FergusSweeney 5 — 63
(K R Burke) *in rr and lost tch fr 1/2-way* **50/1**

4500 **11** 3 **Tartatartufata**[9] 6157 5-8-6 **72** — DeanMcKeown 12 — 42
(D Shaw) *a bhd* **50/1**

0640 **12** 2½ **Baltimore Jack (IRE)**[38] 5356 3-8-13 **80** — DaleGibson 9 — 42
(M W Easterby) *racd wd in mid-div: wknd over 2f out* **40/1**

311- **13** 3 1/2 **Crimson King (IRE)**[542] 1258 6-8-11 **77**.......................... AdamKirby 6 28
(R W Price) *mid-div: rdn 1/2-way: sn btn* **9/1**
1m 14.42s (-1.39) **Going Correction** -0.15s/f (Stan)
WFA 3 from 4yo+ 1lb **13** Ran SP% **118.2**
Speed ratings (Par 105): **103,101,100,99,98 98,97,94,93,90 86,83,78**
CSF £45.22 CT £198.04 TOTE £3.50: £1.20, £4.80, £2.00; EX 55.10 Trifecta £169.20 Pool £314.65 - 1.32 winning units..
Owner Timberhill Racing Partnership **Bred** Timber Hill Racing Partnership **Trained** West Ilsley, Berks

FOCUS
Ordinary handicap form best rated through the placed horses and solid enough.
Desert Dreamer(IRE) Official explanation: jockey said gelding had no more to give

6356 WOLVERHAMPTON HOLIDAY INN H'CAP 1m 5f 194y(P)
2:40 (2:40) (Class 4) (0-85,81) 3-Y-O+ **£4,857** (£1,445; £722; £360) **Stalls** Low

Form RPR
4434 **1** **Fretwork**[17] 5955 3-9-8 **81**.......................... PatDobbs 6 94+
(R Hannon) *trckd ldr: a gng wl: led wl over 2f out: clr whn kpt up to work ins fnl f* **13/2**
4310 **2** 4 **Salute (IRE)**[23] 5769 8-9-13 **77**.......................... RobertHavlin 2 84
(P G Murphy) *in tch: rdn to chse wnr 2f out: no imp fr over 1f out* **11/2**
2502 **3** 4 **Mister Completely (IRE)**[10] 6131 6-9-7 **71**..................(v) JamesDoyle 4 72
(Ms J S Doyle) *in rr tl rdn and hdwy 3f out: styd on to go 3rd ins fnl f* **10/1**
1404 **4** 1 1/2 **Doctor Scott**[9] 6144 4-9-9 **73**.......................... GregFairley 5 72
(M Johnston) *led tl rdn and hdd wl over 2f out: wknd over 1f out* **5/1**[3]
5131 **5** 1 **Tonnante**[21] 5839 3-9-2 **75**.......................... SebSanders 3 73
(Sir Mark Prescott) *hld up in rr: rdn 3f out: nvr got into r* **15/8**[1]
1452 **6** 1 1/2 **Champagne Shadow (IRE)**[23] 5779 6-9-12 **76**.......(p) FergusSweeney 1 72
(Miss Tor Sturgis) *trckd ldrs: pushed along 6f out: wknd over 4f out* **4/1**[2]
3m 2.69s (-4.68) **Going Correction** -0.15s/f (Stan)
WFA 3 from 4yo+ 9lb **6** Ran SP% **109.3**
Speed ratings (Par 105): **107,104,102,101,101 100**
CSF £38.36 TOTE £8.00: £4.00, £2.10; EX 45.60.
Owner The Queen **Bred** The Queen **Trained** East Everleigh, Wilts

FOCUS
A competitive handicap on paper but Fretwork won it easily in the end. the form is not that solid with the placed horses rated a little below par.

6357 ED WEETMAN (NORTH WEST) LTD H'CAP 1m 4f 50y(P)
3:15 (3:15) (Class 4) (0-85,84) 3-Y-O+ **£4,857** (£1,445; £722; £360) **Stalls** Low

Form RPR
0040 **1** **La Estrella (USA)**[8] 6186 4-9-4 **79**.......................... TPQueally 3 92
(J G Given) *trckd ldr after 3f: led over 4f out: edgd rt appr fnl f: rdn out* **9/2**[3]
0403 **2** 3/4 **Mandragola**[13] 6061 3-8-8 **76**.......................... MichaelHills 5 88
(B W Hills) *in tch: chsd ldrs 6f out: wnt 2nd 4f out: rdn over 1f out: no imp ins fnl f* **9/4**[1]
1431 **3** 5 **Risque Heights**[9] 6145 3-9-2 **84**.......................... SteveDrowne 1 88
(G A Butler) *bhd: rdn and hdwy on outside over 2f out: wnt 3rd over 1f out: nvr nr to chal* **5/2**[2]
1053 **4** 1 **Heathyards Pride**[19] 5892 7-9-9 **84**.......................... TedDurcan 4 86
(R Hollinshead) *towards rr: hdwy to chse ldrs over 3f out: wknd over 1f out* **7/1**
0504 **5** 11 **Active Asset (IRE)**[19] 5892 5-8-12 **73**.......................... ChrisCatlin 6 58
(M Quinn) *in rr: rdn 3f out: no hdwy after* **14/1**
2505 **6** 30 **Luna Landing**[33] 5504 4-8-11 **72**.......................... PaulMulrennan 2 9
(Jedd O'Keeffe) *led for 2f: rdn over 5f out: sn lost tch* **16/1**
4035 **7** 10 **Wait For The Light**[13] 6061 3-8-12 **80**..........................(b[1]) SebSanders 7 1
(E A L Dunlop) *s.i.s: rdn to ld after 2f: rdn and hdd over 4f out: sn wknd* **10/1**
2m 38.89s (-3.53) **Going Correction** -0.15s/f (Stan)
WFA 3 from 4yo+ 7lb **7** Ran SP% **111.7**
Speed ratings (Par 105): **105,104,101,100,93 73,66**
CSF £14.33 TOTE £5.70: £2.40, £1.30; EX 18.20.
Owner The G-Guck Group **Bred** Five Horses Ltd And Theatrical Syndicate **Trained** Willoughton, Lincs

FOCUS
A fair handicap and worth taking at face value with the fourth a track specialist.

6358 EUROPEAN BREEDERS' FUND MAIDEN STKS 7f 32y(P)
3:50 (3:50) (Class 5) 2-Y-O **£3,465** (£1,030; £515; £257) **Stalls** High

Form RPR
1 **Staying On (IRE)** 2-9-3 0.......................... AdamKirby 5 80+
(W R Swinburn) *trckd ldr: led over 1f out: pushed out* **13/2**
04 **2** 2 **Counterclaim**[19] 5881 2-8-12 0.......................... TedDurcan 4 70+
(Saeed Bin Suroor) *trckd ldrs: rdn to chse wnr fnl f* **9/2**[3]
642 **3** 2 **Hieroglyph**[19] 5881 2-8-12 78.......................... GregFairley 11 65
(M Johnston) *led tl rdn and hdd over 1f out: one pce fnl f* **15/8**[1]
53 **4** 1 1/4 **Tiger Spice**[22] 5801 2-8-12 0.......................... LiamJones 12 62
(W J Haggas) *trckd ldrs: rdn and one pce ins fnl 2f* **17/2**
5 3 1/2 **Tantris (IRE)** 2-9-3 0.......................... TPQueally 2 58
(J A Osborne) *mid-div: rdn 3f out: no hdwy after* **20/1**
00 **6** 3 1/2 **Run From Nun**[6] 6228 2-8-12 0.......................... RichardSmith 9 44
(J A Osborne) *mid-div: rdn 3f out: kpt on one pce after* **100/1**
00 **7** 3 1/2 **Whaston (IRE)**[25] 5734 2-9-3 0.......................... SteveDrowne 8 41
(J D Bethell) *a towards rr* **100/1**
0 **8** nk **Didntcomeback**[83] 4014 2-9-3 0.......................... FergusSweeney 7 40
(M S Saunders) *s.i.s: rdn 3f out: sn btn* **66/1**
00 **9** hd **John Potts**[19] 5880 2-9-3 0.......................... DeanMcKeown 1 39
(B P J Baugh) *a bhd* **200/1**
10 8 **Aleatricis** 2-9-3 0.......................... JamieMackay 10 19
(Sir Mark Prescott) *slowly away: a bhd* **33/1**
11 3/4 **Yippyiayippyio** 2-8-12 0.......................... ChrisCatlin 6 13
(Mrs C A Dunnett) *in tch to 1/2-way: sn bhd* **100/1**
12 12 **Tucker's Town (IRE)** 2-9-3 0.......................... SebSanders 3 —
(Sir Michael Stoute) *mid-div: rdn over 3f out: c wd into st: eased fnl f* **11/4**[2]
1m 29.87s (-0.53) **Going Correction** -0.15s/f (Stan) **12** Ran SP% **116.2**
Speed ratings (Par 95): **97,94,92,91,87 83,79,78,78,69 68,54**
CSF £34.25 TOTE £8.30: £2.00, £1.50, £1.20; EX 46.50 Trifecta £170.30 Pool £316.65 - 1.32 winning units..
Owner M H Dixon **Bred** M H Dixon **Trained** Aldbury, Herts

FOCUS
A fair maiden and the level looks solid through the runner-up with the field fairly well strung out.

NOTEBOOK
Staying On(IRE), who is a half-brother to winning hurdler Inchlaggan, is out of a mare who placed over middle distances, but his sire is an influence for speed. While not looking an obvious choice on this debut, he actually won nicely without being given a hard time, and on this evidence he should make up into a useful handicapper next year. (op 4-1 tchd 7-1)
Counterclaim appears to be progressing slowly with each run but is a long way from justifying her 250,000gns purchase price. (tchd 5-1)
Hieroglyph appeared to set a fair standard on her form to date, and she tried to make every yard, but she was cooked with a furlong to run. (op 2-1)
Tiger Spice, as a half-sister to UAE Oaks winner Tamarillo, could be expected to improve for this surface, but it is questionable whether she did. Handicaps are now an option for her. (op 9-1 tchd 8-1)
Tantris(IRE), a half-brother to Miss Emerald, a triple winner at up to 1m2f in Italy, is bred for middle distances next season and looks the type to do better once handicapped.
Tucker's Town(IRE), a half-brother to Red Ash, who won over this trip at two, was well backed on his debut but proved very disappointing. He is surely better than this. (op 7-2)

6359 ED WEETMAN (HAULAGE & STORAGE) LTD. H'CAP 1m 141y(P)
4:25 (4:25) (Class 3) (0-95,90) 3-Y-O+ **£7,448** (£2,216; £1,107; £553) **Stalls** Low

Form RPR
0113 **1** **Russki (IRE)**[13] 6053 3-8-6 **80**..........................(b) KirstyMilczarek(5) 3 91
(D M Simcock) *led after 1f: mde rest: drvn out fnl f* **6/1**
3121 **2** 1 1/4 **Dream Lodge (IRE)**[13] 6053 3-9-7 **90**.......................... TPQueally 4 98
(J G Given) *led for 1f: trckd wnr after: kpt on but no imp fnl f* **4/1**[1]
4505 **3** 2 **Apex**[13] 6067 6-8-10 **80**.......................... HaddenFrost(5) 6 84
(M Hill) *trckd ldrs: rdn over 2f out: kpt on but no imp on first 2 after* **14/1**
0000 **4** 1 **Happy As Larry (USA)**[20] 5862 5-9-2 **81**..........................(t) GregFairley 7 83
(D J Murphy) *in rr: hdwy on ins over 1f out: nvr nr to chal* **25/1**
5544 **5** 3/4 **Hoh Wotanite**[3] 6293 4-8-5 **73** oh3..........................(p) WilliamBuick(3) 5 73
(R Hollinshead) *towards rr: rdn 2f out: mde sme late hdwy* **8/1**
5506 **6** 1/2 **Nanton (USA)**[15] 6016 5-9-1 **80**.......................... DanielTudhope 9 79
(N Wilson) *racd on outside: rdn over 3f out: no hdwy after* **6/1**
1031 **7** 1 3/4 **Just Bond (IRE)**[13] 6067 5-9-3 **87**.......................... SladeO'Hara(5) 1 82
(G R Oldroyd) *a struggling in rr* **11/2**[3]
1001 **8** 1/2 **Stargazer Jim (FR)**[80] 4107 5-9-2 **81**.......................... LiamJones 2 75
(W J Haggas) *prom tl rdn and wknd wl over 2f out* **5/1**[2]
5142 **9** 13 **Guacamole**[36] 5431 3-9-2 **85**.......................... MichaelHills 8 51
(B W Hills) *chsd ldrs: rdn over 3f out: sn wknd: eased over 1f out* **7/1**
1m 48.91s (-2.85) **Going Correction** -0.15s/f (Stan)
WFA 3 from 4yo+ 4lb **9** Ran SP% **114.7**
Speed ratings (Par 107): **106,104,103,102,101 101,99,99,87**
CSF £30.02 CT £321.92 TOTE £9.10: £2.50, £1.70, £3.60; EX 43.70 Trifecta £338.10 Part won. Pool £476.22 - 0.97 winning units..
Owner DXB Bloodstock Ltd **Bred** Mark Commins **Trained** Newmarket, Suffolk

FOCUS
A competitive handicap in which, like in races earlier on the card, it proved difficult to make up ground from off the pace. The form looks reasonable with the winner up slightly and the third to recent form.

NOTEBOOK
Russki(IRE) looks to be improving and, given a positive ride on a day when prominent racers appeared to have an edge, reversed recent form with Dream Lodge on 4lb better terms. (op 9-1)
Dream Lodge(IRE) could not confirm recent turf form with Russki on 4lb worse terms, but he still ran well in defeat, albeit in a race and on a night where prominent racers appeared to be favoured. He is now on a pretty stiff mark. (op 9-2)
Apex is another who remains high enough in the weights. He is fairly consistent, though, and his performance is probably a good guide to the level of the form. (op 11-1)
Happy As Larry(USA), a better horse on this surface than on turf, is another who could do with a little help from the Handicapper. This was quite a promising run, though, as he stayed on from off the pace on a day when that proved difficult to do. (op 20-1)
Hoh Wotanite, running from 3lb out of the handicap, is another who helps set the level of the form as he generally runs to his mark. (tchd 9-1)
Nanton(USA) has dropped to a fair mark but the track was not riding in his favour on this occasion. (op 8-1)
Just Bond(IRE), a winner of seven of his previous 14 starts at this track, never got competitive on a day when hold-up horses generally struggled. (op 7-2)

6360 HOTEL & CONFERENCING AT WOLVERHAMPTON H'CAP 5f 20y(P)
4:55 (4:55) (Class 5) (0-70,70) 3-Y-O+ **£3,071** (£906; £453) **Stalls** Low

Form RPR
3320 **1** **Ebraam (USA)**[24] 5753 4-9-2 **68**.......................... DeanMcKeown 5 87+
(D Shaw) *hld up: gd hdwy 2f out: led 1f out: sn clr* **4/1**[1]
2210 **2** 3 **Silver Prelude**[29] 5642 6-9-1 **67**.......................... TedDurcan 2 72
(D K Ivory) *led tl rdn and hdd 1f out: kpt on but nt pce of wnr* **5/1**[2]
3250 **3** nk **Monte Major (IRE)**[80] 4103 6-8-8 **65**.......................... PatrickHills(5) 4 69+
(D Shaw) *trckd ldrs: rdn wl over 1f out: kpt on* **17/2**
2636 **4** 1 **Charlotte Grey**[70] 4432 3-8-12 **64**.......................... NickyMackay 3 64
(C N Allen) *in rr: hdwy over 1f out: r.o: nvr nrr* **20/1**
2000 **5** nk **Almaty Express**[15] 6020 5-9-4 **70**..........................(b) TomEaves 7 69
(J R Weymes) *trckd ldr: rdn 2f out: kpt on one pce after* **12/1**
3005 **6** 1/2 **Azygous**[25] 5726 4-8-13 **65**.......................... TPQueally 11 62
(J Akehurst) *prom: rdn 2f out: one pce after* **7/1**
0103 **7** 1 **Multahab**[8] 6174 8-8-10 **65**..........................(t) WilliamBuick(3) 13 59+
(M Wigham) *racd wd: rdn fr 1/2-way: no hdwy fr over 1f out* **8/1**
00 **8** 1/2 **Peopleton Brook**[39] 5332 5-9-3 **69**.......................... GregFairley 9 61
(J M Bradley) *s.i.s: sn in tch: no hdwy fr over 1f out* **12/1**
360 **9** hd **Calypso King**[64] 4606 4-9-1 **67**.......................... AdamKirby 12 58
(Peter Grayson) *in tch on outside: rdn over 2f out: sn wknd* **16/1**
2216 **10** 3/4 **No Time (IRE)**[12] 6078 7-8-10 **62**.......................... SebSanders 1 51
(A J McCabe) *chsd ldrs tl rdn and wknd 1/2-way* **6/1**[3]
6000 **11** nk **Russian Rocket (IRE)**[11] 6103 5-8-5 **62**.......................... KirstyMilczarek(5) 10 50
(Mrs C A Dunnett) *prom tl rdn 1/2-way: sn wknd* **20/1**
5335 **12** 1 **Fish Called Johnny**[79] 4127 3-8-10 **69**.......................... RyanHill(7) 8 53
(Peter Grayson) *slowly away: a bhd* **28/1**
61.89 secs (-0.93) **Going Correction** -0.15s/f (Stan) **12** Ran SP% **119.3**
Speed ratings (Par 103): **101,96,95,94,93 92,91,90,90,88 88,86**
CSF £22.72 CT £164.24 TOTE £6.00: £2.20, £1.50, £4.20; EX 25.50 Trifecta £77.30 Part won. Pool £108.93 - 0.10 winning units..
Owner The Circle Bloodstock I Limited **Bred** Shadwell Farm LLC **Trained** Danethorpe, Notts

FOCUS
A competitive handicap on paper that was run at a good clip. The runner-up sets the standard.

Ebraam(USA) ◆ Official explanation: trainer said, regarding apparent improvement in form, gelding probably appreciated the drop down to 5f

6361 RINGSIDE SUITE MEDIAN AUCTION MAIDEN STKS 7f 32y(P)
5:25 (5:25) (Class 6) 3-5-Y-0 **£2,388** (£705; £352) **Stalls** High

Form RPR

03 **1** **Crimson Fern (IRE)**[6] 6240 3-8-12 0 FergusSweeney 3 56
(M S Saunders) *t.k.h: trckd ldr: led wl over 2f out: clr over 1f out: pushed out* **10/1**

6660 **2** *3* **Nawayea**[23] 5782 4-8-9 42 (t) KirstyMilczarek(5) 9 48
(C N Allen) *in rr: hdwy on ins wl over 1f out: r.o to go 2nd ins fnl f* **25/1**

0050 **3** *1/2* **Jessica Wigmo**[31] 5566 4-8-11 43 LukeMorris(3) 7 47
(A W Carroll) *hld up: hdwy over 2f out: rdn to go 2nd 1f out: lost 2nd ins fnl f* **40/1**

5040 **4** *1* **Briery Blaze**[5] 6247 4-9-0 48 AdamKirby 4 44
(J W Unett) *trckd ldr for 3f: rdn over 1f out: styd prom: one pce fnl f* **10/1**

0506 **5** *1 1/4* **Pure Velvet (IRE)**[11] 6097 3-8-12 45 PatDobbs 1 41
(S Kirk) *in rr: mde sme late hdwy* **25/1**

0504 **6** *1/2* **Just Oscar (GER)**[23] 5781 3-9-3 57 SebSanders 2 45
(W M Brisbourne) *mid-div: wnt briefly 2nd over 1f out: sn btn* **11/4**[2]

4450 **7** *1/2* **Derricks Dotty**[84] 3999 3-9-3 66 SamHitchcott 10 43+
(N J Vaughan) *hld up in rr: rdn over 2f out: nvr on terms* **5/1**[3]

0550 **8** *1 3/4* **Franky'N'Jonny**[20] 5864 4-9-0 42 (v) PaulFitzsimons 5 34
(M J Attwater) *in rr: effrt whn hmpd over 1f out: nt rcvr* **20/1**

3 **9** *nk* **Bernabeu (IRE)**[54] 4914 5-9-0 43 MGCleary(5) 8 38
(S Curran) *chsd ldrs on outside: rdn and wknd 2f out* **9/1**

2630 **10** *1/2* **Ducal Pip Squeak**[16] 5966 3-8-12 64 PhillipMakin 11 38+
(M Dods) *in tch: effrt whn n.m.r over 1f out: nt rcvr* **9/4**[1]

U-00 **11** *5* **Commander Wish**[21] 4925 4-9-2 45 (p) NeilChalmers(3) 6 23
(Lucinda Featherstone) *led tl rdn and hdd wl over 2f out: wknd qckly* **100/1**

1m 29.85s (-0.55) **Going Correction** -0.15s/f (Stan)
WFA 3 from 4yo+ 2lb 11 Ran SP% **118.2**
Speed ratings (Par 101): **97,93,93,91,90 89,89,87,86,86 80**
CSF £236.42 TOTE £6.20: £1.90, £8.20, £10.70; EX 222.30 TRIFECTA Not won. Place 6 £97.16, Place 5 £52.85..
Owner M S Saunders **Bred** David Brickley **Trained** Green Ore, Somerset
■ Stewards' Enquiry : Kirsty Milczarek three-day ban: careless riding (Nov 1-3)
Luke Morris one-day ban: careless riding (Nov 1)

FOCUS
Very poor maiden form but sound enough rated around the placed horses.
Briery Blaze Official explanation: jockey said filly hung left-handed
T/Plt: £299.30 to a £1 stake. Pool: £58,619.45. 142.95 winning tickets. T/Qpdt: £12.50 to a £1 stake. Pool: £4,008.20. 236.80 winning tickets. JS

6362 - (Foreign Racing) - See Raceform Interactive

5841 CURRAGH (R-H)
Sunday, October 21

OFFICIAL GOING: Good to yielding (yielding in straight)

6363a WWW.HACKETTS.IE JOE MCGRATH EUROPEAN BREEDERS FUND H'CAP (PREMIER HANDICAP) 6f
2:25 (2:29) 3-Y-0+ **£29,910** (£8,775; £4,181; £1,424)

RPR

1 **Fonthill Road (IRE)**[8] 6183 7-9-9 103 JamieMoriarty(3) 6 110
(R A Fahey) *hld up towards rr: hdwy on outer 2f out: led under 1f out: styd on wl* **6/1**[1]

2 *1/2* **Mooretown Lady (IRE)**[7] 6216 4-8-9 86 DMGrant 5 91
(H Rogers, Ire) *in rr of mid-div: nt clr run under 2f out: hdwy into 5th 1f out: r.o wl* **14/1**

3 *3/4* **Alone He Stands (IRE)**[63] 4646 7-8-8 85 WMLordan 4 88
(J C Hayden, Ire) *towards rr: rdn over 2f out: hdwy on outer over 1f out: styd on wl* **20/1**

4 *hd* **Teachers Choice (IRE)**[16] 5994 4-7-11 81 SFoley(7) 20 83
(Adrian McGuinness, Ire) *in rr of mid-div: rdn bef 1/2-way: hdwy whn edgd lft over 1f out: 2nd ins fnl f: no ex cl home* **16/1**

5 *1/2* **Mist And Stone (IRE)**[9] 6160 4-8-8 85 EddieAhern 18 86
(G M Lyons, Ire) *mid-div: nt clr run fr under 2f out: r.o ins fnl f* **11/1**[3]

6 *1/2* **Ms Victoria (IRE)**[21] 5841 3-8-7 85 (t) WJSupple 9 84
(M Halford, Ire) *towards rr: rdn and kpt on fr under 2f out* **12/1**

7 *1 1/4* **Dawla**[33] 5517 3-8-10 88 CDHayes 2 83
(Kevin Prendergast, Ire) *towards rr: swtchd to outer 2f out: kpt on fnl f* **25/1**

8 *hd* **Zhukhov (IRE)**[35] 5460 4-7-11 81 AmyKathleenParsons(7) 11 76
(T G McCourt, Ire) *prom: led 2f out: sn strly pressed: hdd under 1f out: no ex* **25/1**

9 *2 1/2* **Nastrelli (IRE)**[9] 6160 4-8-13 90 (b) RPCleary 14 77
(M Halford, Ire) *trckd ldrs: 4th after 1/2-way: chal over 1f out: sn no ex* **12/1**

10 *nk* **Flash McGahon (IRE)**[21] 5841 3-9-5 97 (b) FMBerry 12 83
(John M Oxx, Ire) *prom: 2nd 1/2-way: chal 2f out: wknd ins fnl f* **20/1**

11 *shd* **Nanotech (IRE)**[9] 6160 3-8-9 85 ow2 WJLee 17 71
(Jarlath P Fahey, Ire) *chsd ldrs on outer: no imp fr 1 1/2f out* **20/1**

12 *1 1/2* **Toberogan (IRE)**[17] 5935 6-8-1 81 DJMoran(3) 13 63
(W A Murphy, Ire) *towards rr: kpt on same pce fr 1 1/2f out* **100/1**

13 *nk* **Senor Benny (USA)**[14] 6036 8-10-2 107 DPMcDonogh 15 88
(M McDonagh, Ire) *hld up in tch: no ex fr under 2f out: eased fnl f* **10/1**[2]

14 *1/2* **Prospect Court**[22] 5806 5-8-1 81 AndrewMullen(3) 21 60
(A C Whillans) *nvr bttr than mid-div* **14/1**

15 *3/4* **Newgate Lodge (IRE)**[33] 5517 3-8-12 90 (b[1]) JAHeffernan 16 67
(M Halford, Ire) *dwlt: sn trckd ldrs: nt clr run 2f out: hmpd over 1f out: no ex* **20/1**

16 *4* **Masta Plasta (IRE)**[13] 6071 4-9-6 97 AdrianTNicholls 19 62
(D Nicholls) *in rr of mid-div: no ex fr 1 1/2f out* **12/1**

17 *1/2* **Benwilt Breeze (IRE)**[14] 6036 5-9-11 102 (t) KJManning 8 65
(G M Lyons, Ire) *prom: 4th early: 6th 1/2-way: no ex 1 1/2f out: eased ins fnl f* **10/1**[2]

17 *dht* **Rainbow Rising (IRE)**[56] 4864 5-9-9 100 PJSmullen 1 63
(Adrian McGuinness, Ire) *mid-div on stands' rail: nt clr run under 2f out: hmpd over 1f out: no ex* **6/1**[1]

19 *1/2* **If Paradise**[21] 5841 6-8-6 83 (p) JohnEgan 10 45
(M Halford, Ire) *cl up: led 1/2-way: hdd 2f out: bdly hmpd over 1f out: no ex* **33/1**

20 *2* **Loughsider (IRE)**[2] 6319 3-8-4 82 (p) MCHussey 3 38
(H Rogers, Ire) *mid-div: rdn after 1/2-way: no ex fr 2f out* **33/1**

21 *1/2* **Tajneed (IRE)**[43] 5242 4-8-7 87 (bt) SMGorey(3) 7 41
(D K Weld, Ire) *led on stands' rail: rdn and hdd 1/2-way: sn wknd* **14/1**

1m 16.59s (2.09) **Going Correction** +0.575s/f (Yiel)
WFA 3 from 4yo+ 1lb 21 Ran SP% **137.7**
Speed ratings: **109,108,107,107,106 105,104,103,100,100 99,97,97,96,95 90,89,89,89,86 85**
CSF £86.34 CT £1056.60 TOTE £7.30: £2.20, £5.30, £4.20, £2.90; DF 211.70.
Owner Mrs Una Towell **Bred** D N Wallace **Trained** Musley Bank, N Yorks
■ Stewards' Enquiry : S Foley three-day ban: careless riding (Nov 3,4,9)
S M Gorey one-day ban: failed to keep straight from stalls (Nov 3)

NOTEBOOK
Fonthill Road(IRE), one of three British raiders, recorded his tenth career win. The seven-year-old, successful in last season's Ayr Gold Cup on marginally better ground, had resumed winning ways earlier this month at York over this journey. Ridden similarly here, he was brought from off the pace to take up the running inside the final furlong and stayed on well. He is a tough sort who has suffered from back trouble, but on this ground he can certainly hold his own. (op 5/1)
Prospect Court never got in a blow. (op 12/1)
Masta Plasta(IRE) failed to trouble the principals. (op 10/1)

6366a HACKETTS BOOKMAKERS IRISH CESAREWITCH (PREMIER H'CAP) 2m
4:00 (4:02) 3-Y-0+ **£35,189** (£10,324; £4,918; £1,675) **Stalls** Far side

RPR

1 **Sandymount Earl (IRE)**[70] 4441 4-9-3 83 JAHeffernan 22 93+
(Mrs John Harrington, Ire) *mid-div: 9th and rdn ent st: 4th 1 1/2f out: 2nd and chal ins fnl f: sn led: styd on wl* **12/1**

2 *3 1/2* **Orbit O'Gold (USA)**[7] 6217 5-9-6 86 (p) NPMadden 17 92
(Noel Meade, Ire) *trckd ldrs in 5th: 3rd travelling easily 4f out: led over 2f out: sn clr: strly pressed ins fnl f: sn hdd and no ex* **10/1**

3 *1 3/4* **Jawad (IRE)**[15] 5439 6-8-0 73 (p) AmyKathleenParsons(7) 10 77
(Ms Joanna Morgan, Ire) *hld up towards rr: hdwy 4f out: 5th whn sltly hmpd under 2f out: 3rd 1f out: kpt on* **20/1**

4 *5 1/2* **Man On The Nile (IRE)**[15] 4730 7-9-0 80 KJManning 23 78
(W P Mullins, Ire) *mid-div: 9th 6f out: rdn st: styd on fnl f* **14/1**

5 *1/2* **Mrs Gillow (IRE)**[21] 5847 6-9-7 87 (b) EddieAhern 7 84
(Eoin Griffin, Ire) *in rr of mid-div: rdn and prog on outer early st: styd on fnl f* **25/1**

6 *1/2* **Do The Trick (AUS)**[21] 5847 6-9-3 83 RPCleary 14 80
(M Halford, Ire) *mid-div: prog into 6th 6f out: 5th and rdn ent st: kpt on same pce* **14/1**

7 *nk* **Daramas (IRE)**[14] 5181 5-8-7 76 SMGorey(3) 6 73
(Rodger Sweeney, Ire) *cl 2nd: led appr st: hdd over 2f out: kpt on same pce* **25/1**

8 *2* **Munnings (IRE)**[148] 2048 4-9-6 86 RichardHughes 3 80
(A J Martin, Ire) *towards rr: last appr st: styd on wout threatening fr over 2f out* **5/1**[1]

9 *1/2* **Duty (IRE)**[178] 5325 4-9-13 93 (p) WJSupple 21 87
(K F O'Brien, Ire) *chsd ldrs in 6th: rdn st: no imp fr over 2f out: kpt on same pce* **25/1**

10 *1 1/2* **Sadler's Kingdom (IRE)**[27] 5677 3-8-10 86 TonyHamilton 20 78
(R A Fahey) *towards rr: kpt on one pce fr over 2f out* **7/1**[3]

11 *3/4* **Hardy Eustace (IRE)**[177] 6115 10-8-1 70 (b) PBBeggy(3) 5 61
(D T Hughes, Ire) *led: hdd appr st: sn no ex* **12/1**

12 *nk* **King Rama (USA)**[36] 5439 6-9-6 93 (t) PTownend(7) 2 84
(John E Kiely, Ire) *in rr of mid-div: 10th 6f out: no imp fr 4f out* **20/1**

13 *nk* **Athlumney Lad (IRE)**[15] 5439 8-9-0 80 (p) JohnEgan 16 71
(Noel Meade, Ire) *towards rr: hdwy 4f out: 7th into st: no ex fr 1 1/2f out* **25/1**

14 *2 1/2* **Classic Croco (GER)**[7] 5579 6-8-4 70 (tp) DMGrant 19 58
(T Hogan, Ire) *towards rr: rdn and no imp st* **25/1**

15 *nk* **Taralaya (IRE)**[21] 5847 3-9-8 98 (b) FMBerry 4 86
(John M Oxx, Ire) *trckd ldrs: 8th early: 6th and hdwy 5f out: 4th bef st: rdn and no imp fr over 2f out: eased fnl f* **6/1**[2]

16 *2 1/2* **Rosaker (USA)**[195] 6504 10-8-8 74 DPMcDonogh 11 59
(Noel Meade, Ire) *trckd ldrs in 4th: lost pl over 4f out: sn no ex and wknd* **12/1**

17 *3/4* **Majestic Concorde (IRE)**[29] 5656 4-9-7 87 (b[1]) PJSmullen 13 71
(D K Weld, Ire) *in rr of mid-div: no ex fr early st* **6/1**[2]

18 *11* **Dancesowell (IRE)**[21] 5847 3-7-11 80 BACurtis(7) 9 52
(John Joseph Murphy, Ire) *a bhd* **50/1**

19 *1/2* **Eagle's Pass (IRE)**[31] 5439 5-9-7 94 SFoley(7) 1 65
(T J O'Mara, Ire) *in rr of mid-div: prog 6f out: 7th over 4f out: wknd early st: eased fr 1 1/2f out* **25/1**

20 *23* **Pepperwood (IRE)**[31] 4487 7-8-9 85 EJMcNamara(10) 15 31
(Noel Meade, Ire) *mid-div on outer: 8th 6f out: wknd appr st: t.o* **25/1**

21 *29* **Akshar (IRE)**[16] 5992 8-8-12 78 PShanahan 8 —
(P M Quinlan, Ire) *sn prom: 3rd 1/2-way: wknd 5f out: eased st: completely t.o* **66/1**

3m 35.4s (8.20) **Going Correction** +0.425s/f (Yiel)
WFA 3 from 4yo+ 10lb 23 Ran SP% **143.1**
Speed ratings: **96,94,93,90,90 90,89,88,88,87 87,87,87,86,85 84,84,78,78,67 52**
CSF £126.01 CT £2470.76 TOTE £11.90: £2.80, £2.50, £5.20, £3.60; DF 159.70.
Owner R Wood **Bred** R Wood **Trained** Moone, Co Kildare

NOTEBOOK
Sadler's Kingdom(IRE) had his stamina to prove over this longer trip and was racing off a career-high mark, but he had ground conditions to suit and came into the race on the back of a personal best run at Hamilton. He never really got into the race from the back of the field, though and was a bit disappointing. (op 8/1 tchd 9/1)

6367a RATHBARRY STUD'S BARATHEA FINALE STKS (LISTED RACE) 1m 4f
4:30 (4:31) 3-Y-0+ **£24,192** (£7,097; £3,381; £1,152)

RPR

1 **Ezima (IRE)**[41] 5289 3-8-11 101 KJManning 10 106+
(J S Bolger, Ire) *hld up in tch: smooth hdwy 4f out: led 2 1/2f out: sn clr: styd on wl: eased cl home* **7/1**[3]

2 *4* **Attercliffe (IRE)**[57] 4830 4-9-7 99 NPMadden 1 102
(Noel Meade, Ire) *trckd ldrs in 5th: 4th st: no imp fr 2f out: kpt on ins fnl f* **14/1**

3 *1/2* **All My Loving (IRE)**[15] 6030 3-8-11 113 JAHeffernan 6 98
(A P O'Brien, Ire) *settled 2nd: led 5f out: hdd 2 1/2f out: sn outpcd: kpt on u.p fr 2f out* **5/2**[1]

4 1 3/4 **Saga Celebre (FR)**[29] 5655 3-8-11 95 FMBerry 9 95
(John M Oxx, Ire) *towards rr: 6th and hdwy ent st: 3rd 2f out: rdn and no imp: 4th and no ex ins fnl f* **7/1**[3]

5 5 1/2 **Galistic (IRE)**[36] 5437 4-9-7 100 DMGrant 3 90
(Patrick J Flynn, Ire) *hld up towards rr: prog over 4f out: 5th st: no ex fr under 2f out* **9/1**

6 3/4 **Baron De'L (IRE)**[16] 5992 4-9-7 96 (b) RPCleary 11 88
(Edward P Harty, Ire) *hld up in tch: 7th 5f out: mod 6th under 2f out: sn no ex* **20/1**

7 2 1/2 **Catch Me (GER)**[177] 1106 5-9-7 95 JohnEgan 2 84
(E J O'Grady, Ire) *towards rr: kpt on one pce st* **10/1**

8 3 **Downtown (IRE)**[76] 4238 3-9-2 103 WMLordan 4 82
(David Wachman, Ire) *chsd ldrs: 3rd 1/2-way: rdn under 5f out: no ex st* **5/1**[2]

9 5 **Uimhir A Haon (IRE)**[16] 5998 3-8-11 103 DPMcDonogh 12 69
(A P O'Brien, Ire) *hld up in tch: 7th and effrt ent st: sn no ex* **7/1**[3]

10 13 **Glitter Baby (IRE)**[32] 5544 4-9-4 MCHussey 8 48
(M G Quinlan) *3rd early: 4th 1/2-way: rdn and wknd fr 4f out: eased fnl f* **25/1**

11 nk **My Dolly Madison**[17] 5960 3-8-11 77 WJSupple 7 47
(A Kinsella, Ire) *chsd ldrs to 1/2-way: sn dropped towards rr: no ex whn eased fnl f* **33/1**

12 22 **Vision Of Grandeur (IRE)**[36] 5439 3-9-0 104 (b) PJSmullen 5 15
(D K Weld, Ire) *led: hdd 5f out: wknd bef st: eased fr 1 1/2f out* **7/1**[3]

2m 40.44s (1.54) **Going Correction** +0.425s/f (Yiel)
WFA 3 from 4yo+ 7lb **12** Ran SP% **132.5**
Speed ratings: **111,108,108,106,103 102,101,99,95,87 86,72**
CSF £110.44 TOTE £7.80: £2.60, £3.20, £1.50; DF 156.80.
Owner Mrs Mary McDonald **Bred** Keatly Overseas Ltd **Trained** Coolcullen, Co Carlow

FOCUS
Average Listed race form rated through the fourth to her previous best.

NOTEBOOK
Ezima(IRE), second in a Listed event over this distance at Galway last month, stepped up another notch here and the contest was as good as over once she swept to the front well over two furlongs out. She was soon clear and won eased down.Trainer Jim Bolger is keen to find a Pattern race opportunity for her before the end of the year but she will remain in training next season.
Attercliffe(IRE), winner of both his starts last season - over 1m2f and on testing ground - was having only his third run of the year. Reportedly slow to come to hand this season, he will be worth watching when he goes hurdling in the coming months. Fourth into the straight, he was unable to raise his game over two furlongs out, but he stayed on quite well without troubling the winner.
All My Loving(IRE) has failed to win since her maiden victory at Leopardstown early in ths season, but she has performed well at a much higher level than this earlier in the campaign. Sent to the front five furlongs out, she failed to raise her game when the winner quickened past her early in the straight, but she did stay on under pressure. She could be feeling the effects of a busy season. (op 5/2 tchd 7/2)
Saga Celebre(FR), successful in a 1m2f maiden at Fairyhouse last month when making a belated reappearance, performed creditably here in this higher league. She made progress from the back of the field before the straight but could make little impression from over a furlong out. (op 8/1)
Galistic(IRE), a Listed winner over 1m6f, was dropping down in trip after two runs over the longer distance. Held up at the back of the field, she went fifth into the straight but could make little or no impression over the last two furlongs. (op 8/1)
Catch Me(GER) Official explanation: jockey said gelding did not travel well in the early stages
Glitter Baby(IRE) weakened out of it once the principals stepped on the gas. (op 20/1)
Vision Of Grandeur(IRE) Official explanation: jockey said colt ran too free early on and tired badly in the straight

6368a DERRINSTOWN STUD APPRENTICE H'CAP FINAL 1m 4f
5:00 (5:03) (60-90,90) 3-Y-0+ **£8,797** (£2,581; £1,229; £418)

RPR

1 **Rockys Choice (IRE)**[25] 5743 4-7-11 66 (b) KarenKenny(7) 4 75+
(Peter Casey, Ire) *sn 2nd: led after 1/2-way: strly pressed st: styd on wl fr over 1f out* **16/1**

2 2 1/2 **Jaamid**[179] 876 5-7-12 67 EJMcNamara(7) 16 72
(Noel Meade, Ire) *settled 3rd: cl 2nd travelling easily 4f out: chal and ev ch st: no ex ins fnl f* **7/2**[1]

3 1 3/4 **Belle Of The Lodge (IRE)**[11] 6117 3-8-12 88 (b) JPFahy(7) 15 90
(John M Oxx, Ire) *towards rr: 14th whn swtchd lft 2f out: styd on wl fr over 1f out: nvr nrr* **8/1**[3]

4 hd **Pretty Demanding (IRE)**[23] 5777 3-8-1 74.. AmyKathleenParsons(4) 20 76
(M G Quinlan) *towards rr: hdwy 4f out: 5th early st: 4th over 1f out: kpt on* **12/1**

5 2 1/2 **Maal (IRE)**[18] 5928 4-8-11 73 (t) WJLee 10 71
(David Marnane, Ire) *hld up: prog over 4f out: 6th bef st: mod 3rd 1 1/2f out: kpt on same pce* **20/1**

6 1 3/4 **Malande (IRE)**[48] 5106 3-8-4 73 (p) DJMoran 17 68
(J S Bolger, Ire) *chsd ldrs: 5th appr 1/2-way: rdn 4f out: kpt on same pce st* **12/1**

7 hd **Deputy Consort (USA)**[33] 6114 4-8-2 71 ow1 NiamhMurphy(7) 1 66
(M J P O'Brien, Ire) *trckd ldrs: 6th bef 1/2-way: 8th early st: kpt on same pce* **12/1**

8 1/2 **Head Of The River (IRE)**[30] 5608 3-9-1 84 CPGeoghegan 3 78
(Charles O'Brien, Ire) *hld up towards rr: kpt on wout threatening st* **16/1**

9 hd **Passarelle (USA)**[23] 5790 3-8-6 75 SMGorey 9 69
(M J Grassick, Ire) *hld up: kpt on one pce fr over 2f out* **7/1**[2]

10 3/4 **Magnet For Money (USA)**[20] 876 5-8-7 69 PBBeggy 5 62
(A J Martin, Ire) *mid-div: 8th appr 1/2-way: no imp st* **7/1**[2]

11 3 1/2 **Road Home**[31] 5578 4-8-7 73 (p) SFoley(4) 6 60
(Mrs John Harrington, Ire) *hld up: hdwy on outer 1/2-way: 3rd over 4f out: wknd st* **14/1**

12 1/2 **Golden Hare (IRE)**[11] 6113 6-8-0 66 MJLane(4) 11 52
(Aidan Anthony Howard, Ire) *hld up early: hdwy into 2nd 1/2-way: wknd fr under 4f out* **20/1**

13 2 1/2 **Imperial Hills (IRE)**[31] 5578 3-8-6 79 PTownend(4) 14 61
(W P Mullins, Ire) *hld up: hdwy into 4th appr st: wknd 2f out* **20/1**

14 2 1/2 **Our Jaffa (IRE)**[35] 5461 6-8-10 72 CDHayes 12 50
(H Rogers, Ire) *a towards rr* **25/1**

15 3 1/2 **Define (IRE)**[17] 5959 4-8-10 76 (tp) CO'Farrell(4) 7 49
(J Motherway, Ire) *sn trckd ldrs: impr into 4th 1/2-way: wknd appr st* **12/1**

16 3 **Masamiyr (IRE)**[51] 5027 6-8-5 74 GFCarroll(7) 13 42
(M Halford, Ire) *a towards rr* **20/1**

17 12 **Sunny'n Smart (USA)**[11] 6118 3-8-13 82 RPCleary 18 31
(Francis Ennis, Ire) *drvn along early: settled towards rr: rdn and no imp st: eased fnl f* **12/1**

18 1 1/4 **Jack Frost Nipping (USA)**[20] 5878 4-8-6 75 (t) IGGrant(7) 2 22
(Seamus Fahey, Ire) *hld up: 10th 1/2-way: wknd fr 4f out* **50/1**

19 5 1/2 **Grafton Street (IRE)**[112] 3143 4-9-10 90 SMLevey(4) 19 28
(A P O'Brien, Ire) *a towards rr: rdn and no imp st: eased over 1f out* **12/1**

20 9 **Dash Of Grey (IRE)**[9] 6164 8-8-3 69 (b) BACurtis(4) 8 —
(Ruaidhri Joseph Tierney, Ire) *sn led: hdd after 1/2-way: sn wknd: eased early st* **33/1**

2m 43.06s (4.16) **Going Correction** +0.425s/f (Yiel)
WFA 3 from 4yo+ 7lb **20** Ran SP% **150.7**
Speed ratings: **103,101,100,100,98 97,97,96,96,96 93,93,91,90,87 85,77,76,73,67**
CSF £79.03 CT £536.64 TOTE £40.40: £7.40, £1.80, £2.00, £2.40; DF 205.80.
Owner J Bowe **Bred** James Nally **Trained** Stamullen, Co Meath

NOTEBOOK
Pretty Demanding(IRE), twice a winner over 1m3f in England this year, made progress from behind before the straight and kept on steadily without ever getting into serious contention.

6369 - (Foreign Racing) - See Raceform Interactive

[6353] BADEN-BADEN (L-H)
Sunday, October 21

OFFICIAL GOING: Soft

6370a BADENER SPRINT-CUP (GROUP 3) 7f
2:25 (2:40) 3-Y-0+ **£20,270** (£8,446; £3,378; £1,689)

RPR

1 **Ricine (IRE)**[56] 4873 5-8-10 (b) F-XBertras 1 106
(F Rohaut, France) *a cl up: 5th st: led 1f out: rdn out* **32/10**[2]

2 hd **Alaska River (GER)**[56] 3-8-9 FilipMinarik 9 106
(P Schiergen, Germany) *mid-div: hdwy over 2f out: led over 1f out to 1f out: hrd rdn and ev ch cl home: jst failed* **118/10**

3 1 1/2 **Smokejumper (GER)**[42] 3-8-9 JiriPalik 6 102
(Frau E Mader, Germany) *mid-div: hdwy and swtchd rt wl over 1f out: r.o fnl f: nrest at fin* **135/10**

4 1 **Key To Pleasure (GER)**[56] 4869 7-9-3 ADeVries 11 105
(Mario Hofer, Germany) *mid-div: brought over to stands' rails in st: kpt on u.p* **84/10**

5 3/4 **Itzmo (GER)**[14] 6045 5-9-1 HGrewe 15 101
(G Sybrecht, Germany) *last to 1/2-way: hdwy over 1f out: nrest at fin* **26/1**

6 2 **Florado (GER)**[28] 4-8-12 THellier 7 93
(H Hesse, Germany) *a.p: 4th st: one pce fr over 1f out* **69/10**

7 nk **Vanderlin**[50] 5031 8-9-1 LPKeniry 4 95
(A M Balding) *prom: 5th st: one pce* **37/10**[3]

8 1 3/4 **Gainsbury (GER)**[95] 3666 3-8-9 J-PCarvalho 12 86
(P Vovcenko, Germany) *a mid-div* **36/1**

9 2 **King Quantas (IRE)**[42] 5262 9-8-12 TMundry 2 82
(B Bo, Sweden) *nvr a factor* **46/1**

10 1 1/2 **Muskateer Steel (IRE)**[42] 5262 6-8-12 P-AGraberg 8 78
(B Bo, Sweden) *led after 1f: c wd st: hdd & wknd over 1f out* **73/1**

11 nk **Molly Max (GER)**[168] 1516 3-8-11 EPedroza 10 78
(Frau K Haustein, Germany) *3rd st: wknd qckly over 1f out* **31/10**[1]

12 shd **Shinko's Best (IRE)**[28] 6-8-12 ASuborics 13 77
(A Kleinkorres, Germany) *dwlt s: a bhd* **154/10**

13 8 **Miyasaki (CHI)**[13] 6071 5-8-12 (b) JJohansen 14 55
(Rune Haugen, Norway) *a outpcd* **29/1**

14 3/4 **Saldario (GER)**[95] 3666 5-8-12 ABest 3 53
(P Vovcenko, Germany) *led 1f: cl 2nd st: wknd wl over 1f out* **55/1**

15 1 **Berri Chis (ARG)**[42] 5262 5-8-12 ABoschert 5 50
(Vanja Sandrup, Sweden) *a outpcd* **48/1**

1m 24.82s (0.92)
WFA 3 from 4yo+ 2lb **15** Ran SP% **130.6**
(Including 10 Euros stake): WIN 42; PL 24, 33, 59; SF 637.
Owner 6c Racing Ltd **Bred** San Gabriel Investments **Trained** Sauvagnon, France

NOTEBOOK
Vanderlin, last seen winning a competitive handicap at Chester in September, would have found this ground plenty soft enough for him and could not raise his game at the business end on this rise in grade.

6371a PREIS DER WINTERKONIGIN (GROUP 3) (FILLIES) 1m
3:45 (3:55) 2-Y-0
£40,541 (£15,541; £7,432; £4,054; £2,027; £1,351)

RPR

1 **Love Academy (GER)** 2-9-0 THellier 9 101
(P Schiergen, Germany) *mid-div: 5th st: led 1f out: r.o wl* **6/4**[1]

2 1 1/2 **Diamantgottin (GER)** 2-9-0 NRichter 7 98
(P Rau, Germany) *led after 1 1/2f: hdd 1f out: r.o one pce* **156/10**

3 1 1/4 **Briseida**[18] 2-9-0 WMongil 5 95
(P Schiergen, Germany) *racd in 3rd: 2nd st: ev ch over 1f out: one pce* **114/10**

4 3/4 **Goose Bay (GER)**[51] 5028 2-9-0 FilipMinarik 3 93
(P Schiergen, Germany) *6th st: kpt on one pce fr over 1f out* **68/10**[3]

5 1 1/4 **Sina (GER)**[35] 5462 2-9-0 ADeVries 2 91
(W Hickst, Germany) *a in tch: 7th st: kpt on one pce* **68/10**[3]

6 3/4 **Every Day (GER)**[51] 5028 2-9-0 ABoschert 6 89
(Mario Hofer, Germany) *trckd ldrs: 4th st: ev ch wl over 1f out: one pce* **22/1**

7 1/2 **Zaya (GER)** 2-9-0 EPedroza 4 88
(A Wohler, Germany) *prom to 3f out* **66/10**[2]

8 3/4 **Time To Beat (GER)**[35] 5462 2-9-0 ASuborics 8 87
(W Baltromei, Germany) *nvr nrr than mid-div* **17/1**

9 nk **Larella (GER)**[35] 5463 2-9-0 TMundry 12 86
(P Rau, Germany) *led over 1f: 3rd st: btn over 1f out* **10/1**

10 1 1/2 **Nujoma (GER)** 2-9-0 F-XBertras 11 83
(C Von Der Recke, Germany) *a outpcd* **31/1**

11 nk **Isily (GER)** 2-9-0 JiriPalik 10 82
(Andreas Lowe, Germany) *a towards rr* **21/1**

1m 41.87s (2.76) **11** Ran SP% **119.6**
WIN 25; PL 17, 35, 32; SF 506.
Owner Gestut Ittlingen **Bred** Gestut Hof Ittlingen **Trained** Germany

6221 SAN SIRO (R-H)

Sunday, October 21

OFFICIAL GOING: Good

6372a PREMIO VITTORIO DI CAPUA (GROUP 1) 1m

3:40 (3:46) 3-Y-O+ **£72,973** (£32,108; £17,514; £8,757)

RPR

1 **Linngari (IRE)**[15] 6029 5-8-12 .... JimmyFortune 1 119
(A De Royer-Dupre, France) *mid-div: 4th st: pushed along 3 1/2f out to ld 2 1/2f out: drvn and r.o over 1f out: drvn out (exact SP 1.03/1)* **26/25**[1]

2 ¾ **Golden Titus (IRE)**[42] 5261 3-8-10 .... DVargiu 7 118
(A Renzoni, Italy) *mid-div: 5th st: hdwy 2f out to chal appr fnl f: kpt on u.p to line* **61/10**

3 4 ½ **Echo Of Light**[15] 6031 5-8-12 ....(b) LDettori 4 107
(Saeed Bin Suroor) *racd in 2nd: led gng easily 3 1/2f out to 2 1/2f out: no ex whn sltly crossed by wnr over 1f out* **9/5**[2]

4 ½ **Dubai's Touch**[14] 6045 3-8-10 .... RoystonFfrench 2 107
(M Johnston) *racd in 3rd: drvn to press ldr st: hld on for 4th but outpcd fr over 1f out* **24/1**

5 snk **Aspectus (IRE)**[42] 5265 4-8-12 .... MDemuro 3 105
(H Blume, Germany) *hld up in 6th: rdn on ins 2f out: nvr able to chal* **15/1**

6 1 ¾ **Miles Gloriosus (USA)**[35] 4-8-12 .... LManiezzi 5 101
(Maria Rita Salvioni, Italy) *led to 3 1/2f out: one pce fnl 2f* **50/1**

7 2 ½ **Apollo Star (GER)**[28] 5670 5-8-12 .... AHelfenbein 6 95
(Mario Hofer, Germany) *racd in last: n.d* **6/1**[3]

1m 37.5s (-4.60)
WFA 3 from 4yo+ 3lb **7** Ran SP% **125.3**
(including one euro stakes): WIN 1.03; PL 1.44, 2.07; SF 6.54.
Owner Peter Walichnowski **Bred** His Highness The Aga Khan's Studs S C **Trained** Chantilly, France

NOTEBOOK
Linngari(IRE), who has had several trainers in and has been well travelled, gained his first Group 1 success and will be off to Dubai in the new year, having won at the carnival for the last two seasons.
Echo Of Light was unable to lead as he likes and, although he had a brief moment in front early in the straight, was already held when the winner drifted across him approaching the furlong pole. Sensibly, Dettori was not hard on him thereafter.
Dubai's Touch was one of four in line disputing the lead with over three furlongs to run but could only plug on at the same pace.

5293 WOODBINE (R-H)

Sunday, October 21

OFFICIAL GOING: Firm

6373a E P TAYLOR STKS (GRADE 1) (F&M) 1m 2f (T)

7:59 (7:59) 3-Y-O+
£263,158 (£92,105; £48,246; £27,632; £13,815; £175)

RPR

1 **Mrs Lindsay (USA)**[35] 5465 3-8-6 .... JMurtagh 4 113
(F Rohaut, France) *raced in 3rd to straight, ridden well over 1f out, driven to lead well inside final f, ran on well* **7/5**[1]

2 ½ **Sealy Hill (CAN)**[35] 3-8-6 ....(b) PHusbands 3 112
(M Casse, Canada) *mid-division, 5th straight, strong run to lead distance, soon ridden, headed & unable to quicken well inside final f* **41/10**[2]

3 1 ½ **Barancella (FR)**[28] 6-8-11 .... JCastellano 10 109
(R J Frankel, U.S.A) *well behind til headway from 3f out, 8th straight, stayed on down outside under pressure to take 3rd 100yds out, one pace* **6/1**

4 nk **The Niagara Queen (CAN)**[28] 4-8-11 ....(b) EmmaJayneWilson 2 108
(Michael J Doyle, U.S.A) *raced in 4th to straight, kept on same pace* **41/1**

5 1 ¼ **Sans Souci Island (CAN)**[15] 3-8-6 .... MESmith 6 106
(R L Attfield, Canada) *well back most of way, last straight, ridden 2f out, kept on to take 5th last strides* **51/1**

6 nk **Essential Edge (CAN)**[35] 4-8-11 .... JonoJones 8 105
(E Coatrieux, Canada) *led after 1f, 3 lengths clear at half-way, headed distance, weakened gradually* **142/10**

7 ½ **Hostess (USA)**[22] 5822 4-8-11 .... CHill 9 104
(H J Bond, U.S.A) *well behind for 7f, 9th straight, never a factor* **108/10**

8 1 ¼ **Four Sins (GER)**[37] 5396 3-8-6 .... MJKinane 5 102
(John M Oxx, Ire) *first to show, tracked leader, 2nd straight, soon weakened* **57/10**[3]

9 4 **Safari Queen (ARG)**[48] 5-8-11 ....(b) JRVelazquez 7 94
(T Pletcher, U.S.A) *mid-division, 6th straight on inside, ridden & beaten 1 1/2f out* **114/10**

10 3 ¾ **Elle Runaway (USA)**[35] 5-8-11 .... ECastro 1 86
(M Pierce, Canada) *mid-division, 7th straight, last & beaten well over 1f out* **36/1**

2m 0.68s (-3.34)
WFA 3 from 4yo+ 5lb **10** Ran SP% **120.6**
PARI-MUTUEL (including $CAN2 stakes): WIN 4.80; PL (1-2) 2.90, 4.70; SHOW (1-2-3) 2.50, 3.20, 3.20; SF 23.40.
Owner Mme B Jenney **Bred** Derry Meeting Farm **Trained** Sauvagnon, France

FOCUS
The going was very fast, which explains how a new course record was set in this race.

NOTEBOOK
Mrs Lindsay(USA), who reversed Prix de Diane form with West Wind when winning the Prix Vermeille at the Arc meeting, coped with the drop back in trip under an inspired ride from Murtagh, breaking the track record in the process. She is expected to remain in training next season.
Four Sins(GER) raced prominently but was backpedalling early in the straight.

6374a PATTISON CANADIAN INTERNATIONAL (GRADE 1) 1m 4f (T)

9:05 (9:07) 3-Y-O+
£526,316 (£175,439; £96,491; £52,632; £26,316; £175)

RPR

1 **Cloudy's Knight (USA)**[28] 7-9-0 .... RZimmerman 8 121
(Frank J Kirby, U.S.A) *raced in 3rd to straight, led 1 1/2f out, all out* **183/10**

2 nse **Ask**[21] 5831 4-9-0 .... RyanMoore 9 121
(Sir Michael Stoute) *hld up, 9th straight, hdwy on outside 2f out, rdn & hung lft 1 1/2f out, ran on wl under strong pressure fnl f, jst failed* **53/20**[1]

3 1 **Quijano (GER)**[49] 5077 5-9-0 .... AStarke 12 119
(P Schiergen, Germany) *held up, 11th straight, headway on outside 2f out, driven 1 1/2f out, took 3rd 1f out, ran on* **39/10**[2]

4 nk **Stream Of Gold (IRE)**[21] 5853 6-9-0 .... ECastro 5 119
(K McLaughlin, U.S.A) *mid-division, 8th straight, edged right & not clear run 1 1/2f out, ran on to dispute 3rd 1f out, kept on same pace* **33/2**

5 ½ **Oracle West (SAF)**[29] 5634 6-9-0 .... JMurtagh 2 118
(M F De Kock, South Africa) *mid-division, 6th straight on inside, kept on one pace* **147/10**

6 ¾ **Sunriver (USA)**[43] 5250 4-9-0 .... GKGomez 11 117
(T Pletcher, U.S.A) *first to show, pressed leader to straight, led over 2f out to 1 1/2f out, soon weakened* **72/10**

7 nk **Sky Conqueror (CAN)**[35] 5-9-0 .... JCastellano 4 117
(Darwin D Banach, Canada) *10th straight on inside, switched outside 2f out, ran on from 1 1/2f out, never nearer* **5/1**[3]

8 1 **Honolulu (IRE)**[21] 5831 3-8-7 .... MJKinane 7 115
(A P O'Brien, Ire) *slowly into stride & pushed along, last to straight, never a factor* **9/1**

9 nse **Windward Islands (USA)**[28] 3-8-7 ....(b) TKabel 3 115
(M Frostad, Canada) *prominent, 4th straight, weakened over 1f out* **38/1**

10 1 ¼ **Irish Wells (FR)**[56] 4872 4-9-0 .... OPeslier 6 113
(F Rohaut, France) *mid-division, headway on outside over 3f out, 7th straight, beaten over 1f out* **98/10**

11 1 ¾ **Linda's Lad**[28] 4-9-0 .... JRVelazquez 10 110
(E Kenneally, U.S.A) *in touch, 5th straight, weakened well over 1f out* **34/1**

12 3 ¾ **Marsh Side (USA)**[28] 4-9-0 .... EmmaJayneWilson 1 104
(M Dickinson, U.S.A) *led to over 2f out, behind from over 1f out* **45/1**

2m 27.71s (-1.89)
WFA 3 from 4yo+ 7lb **12** Ran SP% **120.8**
PARI-MUTUEL: WIN 38.70; PL (1-2) 11.50, 5.40; SHOW (1-2-3) 7.60, 3.40, 4.50; SF 213.80.
Owner S J Stables LLC **Bred** Jerrold Schwartz **Trained** USA

NOTEBOOK
Ask was sent off favourite and ran a terrific race, gradually closing down on the winner but narrowly failing to get there. Moore reported that the ground was too fast for him, indicated by the fact that he hung under pressure, and he would have preferred a stronger gallop.
Quijano(GER) stayed on strongly to pass seven rivals in the straight but was not able to reel in the first two.
Honolulu(IRE) was in last place for much of the time after a slow start and never got into the race.

6375a NEARCTIC STKS (GRADE 2) 6f

10:05 (10:08) 3-Y-O+
£131,579 (£43,860; £24,123; £13,158; £6,579; £175)

RPR

1 **Heros Reward (USA)**[48] 5-8-5 .... JCastellano 8 110
(D Capuano, U.S.A) *disputed lead, led 2f out, tiring last 100yds, driven out* **67/10**[3]

2 ¾ **Quietly Mine (USA)**[331] 3-8-4 ....(b) GKGomez 2 107
(Christophe Clement, U.S.A) *outpaced to half-way, 7th straight, switched out over 1f out, ran on well under strong pressure final f* **67/10**[3]

3 ¾ **Smart Enough (USA)**[48] 4-8-7 .... CDeCarlo 4 107
(J R S Fisher, U.S.A) *led to 2f out, kept on one pace* **13/10**[1]

4 1 ¾ **Moth Ball**[46] 5-8-5 .... MESmith 1 100
(J Cassidy, U.S.A) *pressed early pace, 5th on inside straight, kept on one pace under pressure* **77/10**

5 1 ½ **Dead Red (USA)**[35] 4-8-5 ....(b) ECastro 7 95
(G-E Mikhalides, U.S.A) *chased leaders, close 4th straight on outside, beaten over 1f out* **22/1**

6 1 ¼ **Ecclesiastic (USA)**[29] 6-8-7 ....(b) JValdiviaJr 5 94
(M D Wolfson, U.S.A) *6th straight, never a factor* **23/2**

7 1 ¾ **Dark Missile**[21] 5832 4-8-2 .... MartinDwyer 6 83
(A M Balding) *disputed 3rd, 3rd straight, weakened approaching final f* **34/10**[2]

8 1 **Castle Heights (CAN)** 6-8-5 .... ERamsammy 3 83
(M Mesic, Canada) *last straight, always outpaced* **178/10**

68.04 secs (68.04)
WFA 3 from 4yo+ 1lb **8** Ran SP% **121.3**
PARI-MUTUEL: WIN 15.40; PL (1-2) 6.80, 8.30; SHOW (1-2-3) 3.70, 4.40, 2.40; SF 104.30.
Owner Rob Ry Farm and Marie Jayne Slysz **Bred** Gretchen B Mobberley **Trained** USA

NOTEBOOK
Dark Missile, runner-up in the Diadem at Ascot last month, was unable to build on that despite being close enough turning in. He found little when asked and was possibly feeling the ground.

6039 LONGCHAMP (R-H)

Sunday, October 21

OFFICIAL GOING: Soft changing to good to soft after race 6 (3:50)

6376a PRIX DU CONSEIL DE PARIS (GROUP 2) 1m 4f

2:20 (2:23) 3-Y-O+ **£50,068** (£19,324; £9,223; £6,149; £3,074)

RPR

1 **Montare (IRE)**[35] 5465 5-8-13 .... C-PLemaire 4 114
(J E Pease, France) *hld up mid-div: 5th & pushed along st: hdwy 2f out & wnt 2nd 1 1/2f out: rdn to chal fnl f: led narrowly 50yds out: drvn out* **43/10**[3]

2 nse **Arch Rebel (USA)**[29] 5654 6-9-2 .... IMendizabal 2 117
(Noel Meade, Ire) *missed break & racd in last: 8th st: pushed along & hdwy in centre over 2f out: rdn to chal 1f out: ev ch ins fnl f: jst failed* **17/2**

3 1 **Kocab**[26] 5719 5-9-2 .... SPasquier 6 116
(A Fabre, France) *in tch: disputing 4th 1/2-way: 4th st: r.o to ld 1 1/2f out: rdn fnl f: hdd 50yds out: styd on* **29/10**[1]

4 6 **Anabaa's Creation (IRE)**[29] 5661 3-8-7 ow1........ CSoumillon 7 105
(A De Royer-Dupre, France) *prom: 2nd 1/2-way: 3rd st: effrt on rail 2f out: styd on u.p to take 4th over 1f out* **33/10**[2]

5 1 ½ **Miss Salvador (FR)**[26] 5719 4-8-13 .... TJarnet 5 101
(S Wattel, France) *mid-div on rail: disputing 6th st: nvr able to chal* **30/1**

6 2 ½ **Appel Au Maitre (FR)**[42] 5263 3-8-12 .... FJohansson 9 104
(Wido Neuroth, Norway) *mid-div: disputing 6th st: n.d* **11/2**

7 10 **Kankakee (USA)**[46] 5150 4-8-13 .... DBonilla 1 83
(J E Pease, France) *led early: hdd bef 1/2-way: 2nd and pushed along st: wknd over 1 1/2f out* **43/10**[3]

8 1 1/2 **Dancing Lady (FR)**[44] 5258 3-8-6 .... RonanThomas 3 80
(J-M Beguigne, France) *led bef 1/2-way: pushed along st: hdd over 1 1/2f out: one pce* **43/10**[3]

9 20 **El Comodin (IRE)**[64] 4627 3-8-9 .... TThulliez 8 53
(A Fabre, France) *hld up in 8th: dropped to last and detached st: sn btn* **69/10**

2m 29.4s (-5.60) **Going Correction** -0.075s/f (Good)
WFA 3 from 4yo+ 7lb **9** Ran SP% **147.3**
Speed ratings: **115,114,114,110,109 107,100,99,86**
PARI-MUTUEL: WIN 5.30 (coupled with Kankakee); PL 1.80, 2.20, 1.60; DF 29.70.
Owner George Strawbridge **Bred** George Strawbridge **Trained** Chantilly, France

NOTEBOOK
Montare(IRE) was equipped with the usual sheepskin noseband and cheekpieces ensemble, and is very difficult to win with these days but had the cards fall perfectly in her favour to register the narrowest of wins. Pushed along early in the straight, she was ridden to challenge Kocab with half a furlong to run, then had Arch Rebel draw level on her outside at the ideal time to stop her from downing tools. She could go for the Hong Kong Vase.
Arch Rebel(USA) was a bit unlucky to be inched out, although he contributed to his own misfortune with a slow start and by travelling sluggishly throughout. He came with one long run down the outside from over two furlongs out and only lost out on the nod.
Kocab looked all over the winner when skipping two lengths clear with a furlong and a half to run but failed to sustain his effort.
Anabaa's Creation(IRE) found herself in a pocket against the rail behind the weakening leader approaching the furlong marker but her lack of speed once extricating herself suggested that her slightly troubled passage made no difference to the result, albeit she would have been a bit closer.

6377a PRIX DE CONDE (GROUP 3) 1m 1f
2:50 (2:50) 2-Y-O **£27,027** (£10,811; £8,108; £5,405; £2,703)

RPR

1 **High Rock (IRE)**[33] 2-8-11 .... C-PLemaire 4 103
(J-C Rouget, France) *racd in 2nd: pushed along to ld over 1 1/2f out: rdn over 1f out: drvn out* **61/10**

2 1 **Hannouma (IRE)**[26] 2-8-11 .... DBoeuf 5 101
(D Smaga, France) *racd in 4th: 5th st: drvn out and styd on on outside over 1f out: rdn to take 2nd fnl strides* **5/2**[2]

3 1/2 **Sanjida (IRE)**[33] 2-8-8 .... CSoumillon 1 97
(A De Royer-Dupre, France) *racd in 4th: rdn to chse ldr and wnt 2nd over 1f out: styd on at one pce: lost pl fnl strides* **19/10**[1]

4 8 **Corconte (FR)**[56] 2-8-11 .... PSogorb 3 84
(R Avial Lopez, Spain) *led to over 1 1/2f out: rdn and one pce fnl f* **4/1**[3]

5 1 1/2 **Salsalavie (FR)**[29] 5660 2-8-11 .... SPasquier 2 81
(P Demercastel, France) *racd in last: hdwy 4f out: 3rd and drvn st: rdn and no ex 1 1/2f out* **53/10**

6 20 **Markmanship (FR)**[30] 2-8-11 .... JVictoire 6 41
(C Gourdain, France) *racd in 5th: last st: n.d* **20/1**

1m 51.6s (-7.30) **6** Ran SP% **117.8**
PARI-MUTUEL: WIN 7.10; PL 3.00, 1.90; SF 21.10.
Owner R Bousquet **Bred** Ecurie Skymarc Farm **Trained** Pau, France

NOTEBOOK
High Rock(IRE) got a good lead from Corconte to a furlong and a half out and was always doing enough to hold on quite comfortably. He will not run again until next year when the Prix du Jockey-Club will be his main aim.
Hannouma(IRE) took a long time to make much headway in the straight and only stayed on dourly past Danjida in the last 50 yards.
Sanjida(IRE) went in chase of the winner with over a furlong to run, but never made any real impression and lost second close home.
Corconte(FR) came here on the back of four easy wins in Bordeaux and Spain but found this a very different kettle of fish and, having cut out the pace, was swamped with over a furlong and a half to run.

6051 PONTEFRACT (L-H)
Monday, October 22

OFFICIAL GOING: Good (good to firm in places; 7.7)
Wind: Virtually nil Weather: Overcast

6379 TOTEPLACEPOT NURSERY 1m 4y
2:10 (2:12) (Class 5) (0-75,74) 2-Y-O **£3,886** (£1,156; £577; £288) **Stalls** Low

Form RPR

046 1 **Resplendent Light**[68] 4508 2-9-6 **73** .... NCallan 8 81+
(W R Muir) *trckd ldrs: hdwy 2f out: rdn over 1f out: styd on to ld ins fnl f: edgd lft and kpt on wl* **11/1**

4400 2 1 3/4 **Higgy's Boy (IRE)**[11] 6120 2-9-4 **71** .... DaneO'Neill 5 75
(R Hannon) *a.p: rdn along 2f out: drvn over 1f out: kpt on wl u.p fnl f* **33/1**

0300 3 1/2 **Home**[31] 5601 2-9-1 **68** .... JimmyFortune 2 71+
(E A L Dunlop) *in tch: hdwy to trck ldrs 1/2-way: effrt on inner and n.m.r wl over 1f out: swtchd rt: rdn and nt clr run jst ins fnl f: styd on wl towards fin* **8/1**

2260 4 1 1/4 **Harbour Blues**[41] 5314 2-9-3 **70** .... SebSanders 1 70
(C E Brittain) *led: rdn along 2f out: drvn over 1f out: hdd ins fnl f and kpt on same pce* **16/1**

4033 5 1 1/4 **Golden Penny**[21] 5871 2-9-7 **74** .... RobertHavlin 4 71
(H Morrison) *a.p: effrt to chal 2f out: sn rdn and one pce ent fnl f* **6/1**[3]

0220 6 1 3/4 **Natural Rhythm (IRE)**[19] 5914 2-8-13 **66** .... DanielTudhope 9 60
(D W Chapman) *bhd: hdwy on outer over 2f out: rdn wl over 1f out: styd on ins fnl f: nrst fin* **28/1**

504 7 nk **Eton Fable (IRE)**[19] 5904 2-8-12 **68** .... AndrewMullen(3) 17 61
(W J H Ratcliffe) *towards rr: hdwy over 2f out: sn rdn and styd on appr fnl f: nrst fin* **33/1**

6031 8 1 1/4 **Blandys Wood**[21] 5869 2-8-6 **66** .... ThomasO'Brien(7) 10 56
(M R Channon) *s.i.s and bhd: swtchd rt and hdwy wl over 1f out: kpt on ins fnl f: nrst fin* **16/1**

010 9 2 1/2 **Love Valentine (IRE)**[10] 6154 2-9-0 **67** .... RoystonFfrench 16 52
(M Johnston) *chsd ldrs on outer: rdn along 3f out: grad wknd* **5/1**[1]

0506 10 1 1/4 **Infinite Patience**[16] 6012 2-9-0 **67** .... JohnEgan 15 49
(J S Moore) *hld up in rr: effrt over 2f out: sn rdn and n.d* **15/2**

0266 11 3 1/2 **Elegant Step**[31] 5600 2-9-0 **67** .... LeeEnstone 6 41
(A P Jarvis) *t.k.h: prom: rdn along over 2f out and sn wknd* **25/1**

106 12 1 1/4 **Little Firecracker**[28] 5692 2-8-12 **65** .... NickyMackay 13 36
(L M Cumani) *a in midfield* **12/1**

4000 13 1/2 **Red Skipper (IRE)**[14] 6066 2-8-9 **62** .... JimmyQuinn 11 32
(N Wilson) *towards rr fr 1/2-way* **28/1**

3054 14 1 1/4 **Ezthegezza**[19] 5896 2-8-12 **65** ....(p) SimonWhitworth 3 33
(J S Moore) *t.k.h: chsd ldrs: rdn along wl over 2f out and sn wknd* **16/1**

0320 15 1 1/2 **Hyper Viper (IRE)**[19] 5904 2-8-11 **64** ....(b) KDarley 14 28
(C Grant) *dwlt: a in rr* **22/1**

3432 16 6 **Daring Dream (GER)**[30] 5613 2-9-7 **74** .... DavidAllan 7 25
(T D Easterby) *a towards rr* **11/2**[2]

1m 46.51s (0.81) **Going Correction** +0.05s/f (Good) **16** Ran SP% **123.9**
Speed ratings (Par 95): **97,95,94,93,92 90,90,88,86,85 81,80,79,78,77 71**
CSF £351.63 CT £3053.51 TOTE £12.80: £2.40, £8.50, £2.80, £3.80; EX 369.90.
Owner Middleham Park Racing XLIX **Bred** Usk Valley Stud **Trained** Lambourn, Berks

FOCUS
A fair nursery with a decisive winner and the form rated around the runner-up and fourth.

NOTEBOOK
Resplendent Light had been handed a reasonable mark following three unplaced efforts in 7f maidens and this step up to 1m was always going to suit the son of Fantastic Light. Keen early on, he was still travelling well before the turn into the straight and found plenty under pressure to win going away. He is in the Derby, but that is unrealistic although he should continue to progress in handicaps. (tchd 12-1)
Higgy's Boy(IRE) had previously failed to make an impact in handicaps, but his mark had slipped as a result and this marked an improved effort. He seemed to stay this distance well enough, but the son of Choisir should prove just as effective back at 7f.
Home did not get the clearest of runs when down the field at Wolverhampton last time and he once again met trouble, getting squeezed for room on the inner. He can be rated a little better than the bare form and should find a nursery before long. Official explanation: jockey said colt was denied a clear run (op 10-1)
Harbour Blues had lost his form somewhat following a promising start to his career, but this was a step back in the right direction and he kept plugging away once headed.
Golden Penny has been running well without suggesting he is up to winning, but once again his lack of basic speed proved his undoing. (op 13-2 tchd 7-1)
Love Valentine(IRE), narrow winner of a 1m maiden at Kempton last month, was always outpaced back at 6f last time and, although better was expected on this step back up in trip, her wide draw prevented her from getting involved. Official explanation: jockey said filly hung right-handed throughout (op 4-1)
Infinite Patience Official explanation: jockey said filly had no more to give

6380 TOTECOURSE TO COURSE H'CAP 1m 2f 6y
2:40 (2:46) (Class 5) (0-70,67) 3-Y-O+ **£3,886** (£1,156; £577; £288) **Stalls** Low

Form RPR

0166 1 **Pitbull**[3] 6316 4-8-10 **56** ....(p) JimmyQuinn 5 65
(Mrs G S Rees) *s.i.s and bhd: gd hdwy 2f out: rdn to ld and hung bdly lft ins fnl f: styd on* **10/1**

0330 2 1 1/2 **Jackie Kiely**[8] 6196 6-9-5 **65** ....(t) NCallan 2 73+
(R Brotherton) *hld up in midfield: hdwy on outer over 2f out: rdn to chal over 1f out: ev ch whn bdly hmpd ins fnl f: rallied towards fin* **9/1**[3]

3605 3 3/4 **Effigy**[11] 6132 3-8-13 **64** .... DaneO'Neill 15 69
(H Candy) *prom: effrt 3f out: rdn to ld 2f out: drvn and hdd ins fnl f: kpt on same pce* **10/1**

3420 4 nk **Titinius (IRE)**[19] 5905 7-9-3 **63** .... KDarley 3 67
(Micky Hammond) *hld up: hdwy and nt clr run 2f out: sn swtchd rt and rdn: hung lft and kpt on ins fnl f: nrst fin* **16/1**

2045 5 nk **Moment Of Clarity**[25] 5750 5-8-7 **53** oh1 ....(p) PaulEddery 8 57+
(R C Guest) *chsd ldrs: rdn along and sltly outpcd over 2f out: swtchd lft and drvn appr fnl f: styng on whn n.m.r wl ins fnl f* **12/1**

4212 6 2 1/2 **Keisha Kayleigh (IRE)**[16] 6021 4-9-1 **61** ....(v) TPQueally 9 62+
(B Ellison) *hld up: stdy hdwy on outer 4f out: chsd ldrs 2f out: sn rdn and one pce appr fnl f* **3/1**[1]

0120 7 hd **Holiday Cocktail**[17] 4023 5-9-1 **61** .... GrahamGibbons 6 59
(J J Quinn) *hld up: stdy hdwy on inner 2f out: styng on whn hmpd ent fnl f: kpt on* **5/1**[2]

1600 8 1 **Darghan (IRE)**[11] 6132 7-8-8 **61** .... DebraEngland(7) 1 57
(W J Musson) *towards rr tl styd on fnl 2f: nvr nrr* **25/1**

4206 9 1/2 **Apache Point (IRE)**[22] 5838 10-8-7 **53** oh3 .... KimTinkler 7 48
(N Tinkler) *nvr bttr than midfield* **50/1**

5002 10 1 3/4 **Sunnyside Tom (IRE)**[27] 5703 3-9-2 **67** .... TonyHamilton 16 58
(R A Fahey) *cl up: led 3f out and sn rdn: hedaed 2f out: drvn and wknd appr fnl f* **10/1**

2533 11 3/4 **Bret Maverick (IRE)**[60] 4735 3-8-3 **54** ....(p) HayleyTurner 4 44
(B P J Baugh) *led: rdn along and hdd 3f out: sn wknd* **33/1**

0/ 12 shd **Munching Mike (IRE)**[124] 2781 4-8-10 **56** .... SebSanders 17 46
(K M Prendergast) *chsd ldrs: rdn along 2f out: wkng whn n.m.r ent fnl f* **11/1**

4003 13 1 1/4 **Frosty Night (IRE)**[13] 6077 3-8-12 **63** ....(b) RoystonFfrench 12 50
(M Johnston) *in tch: rdn along 3f out: sn wknd* **11/1**

6000 14 3/4 **Thumpers Dream**[19] 5907 4-9-7 **67** ....(b[1]) DanielTudhope 10 53
(I W McInnes) *cl up: rdn along over 3f out and sn wknd* **50/1**

0500 15 6 **Scotty's Future (IRE)**[3] 6304 9-8-0 **53** oh1 .... DanielleMcCreery(7) 11 27
(A Berry) *s.i.s: a bhd* **50/1**

2m 13.47s (-0.61) **Going Correction** +0.05s/f (Good)
WFA 3 from 4yo+ 5lb **15** Ran SP% **121.9**
Speed ratings (Par 103): **104,102,102,101,101 99,99,98,98,96 96,96,95,94,89**
CSF £94.16 CT £932.03 TOTE £12.50: £4.40, £3.20, £3.80; EX 134.60.
Owner Mrs G S Rees **Bred** J Gittins And Capt J H Wilson **Trained** Sollom, Lancs
■ Stewards' Enquiry : Jimmy Quinn two-day ban: careless riding (Nov 2-3)

FOCUS
A moderate handicap but sound enough with the front five close to their marks.

6381 TOTESPORT 0800 221 221 H'CAP 5f
3:10 (3:15) (Class 4) (0-85,85) 3-Y-O+ **£5,181** (£1,541; £770; £384) **Stalls** Low

Form RPR

0400 1 **Dig Deep (IRE)**[9] 6173 5-8-12 **79** .... TPQueally 7 91
(W J Haggas) *hld up towards rr: gd hdwy 2f out: rdn over 1f out: str run ins fnl f to ld last 75yds* **15/2**[1]

5601 2 3/4 **Westport**[114] 3108 4-8-9 **76** .... PaulMulrennan 11 85
(K A Ryan) *hld up in tch: hdwy 2f out: rdn to ld ent fnl f: hdd and nt qckn last 75yds* **20/1**

4600 3 1 3/4 **Bahamian Ballet**[20] 5891 5-8-13 **80** .... StephenDonohoe 6 83+
(E S McMahon) *s.i.s and bhd: hdwy and nt clr run wl over 1f out: swtchd rt and rdn 1f out: styd on strly towards fin* **10/1**

1100 4 hd **Malapropism**[9] 6173 7-8-9 **83** ....(v) MatthewDavies(7) 14 85
(M R Channon) *hld up: hdwy on outer 2f out: rdn and edgd lft over 1f out: kpt on u.p ins fnl f* **16/1**

0060 5 nk **The Nifty Fox**[2] 6327 3-8-12 **79** ....(b) DavidAllan 17 80
(T D Easterby) *hld up in rr: hdwy on wd outside over 1f out: sn rdn and styd on ins fnl f: nrst fin* **25/1**

0050 **6** ½ **Maker's Mark (IRE)**[8] 6197 3-9-1 **82** (v[1]) FergusSweeney 9 81
(H Candy) *chsd ldrs: hdwy wl over 1f out: sn rdn and one pce ins fnl f* **10/1**

3114 **7** shd **Millisecond**[37] 5418 3-8-11 **78** PhilipRobinson 12 77
(M A Jarvis) *cl up: rdn wl over 1f out and ev ch tl drvn and one pce ins fnl f* **10/1**

2635 **8** 1½ **Bel Cantor**[19] 5923 4-8-3 **77** (p) LanceBetts[(7)] 1 70
(W J H Ratcliffe) *led: rdn along 2f out: drvn over 1f out: hdd & wknd ent fnl f* **8/1**[2]

-001 **9** shd **Godfrey Street**[9] 6173 4-9-1 **85** (b) AndrewMullen[(3)] 15 78
(K A Ryan) *prom: effrt to chal wl over 1f out and ev ch tl rdn and wknd ent fnl f* **9/1**[3]

5020 **10** shd **Avertuoso**[34] 5505 3-8-13 **83** MarkLawson[(3)] 2 76
(B Smart) *chsd ldrs whn bmpd after 1f: in tch: rdn 2f out and wknd appr fnl f* **16/1**

4104 **11** hd **Circuit Dancer (IRE)**[23] 5806 7-8-10 **77** SilvestreDeSousa 13 69
(D Nicholls) *dwlt: a towards rr* **14/1**

2150 **12** 1¼ **Melalchrist**[28] 5689 5-9-3 **84** (b) PatCosgrave 16 71
(K A Ryan) *chsd ldrs towards outer: rdn along 2f out: wkng whn bmpd over 1f out* **16/1**

0430 **13** shd **Elkhorn**[9] 6173 5-9-0 **81** (b) TonyHamilton 10 68+
(Miss J A Camacho) *s.i.s and bhd: hdwy on inner whn n.m.r over 1f out: no prog after* **12/1**

4304 **14** ½ **Prince Namid**[73] 4367 5-8-12 **79** RoystonFfrench 5 64+
(Mrs A Duffield) *chsd ldrs whn bmpd after 1f: sn rdn along and bhd after* **15/2**[1]

2-00 **15** 1¾ **Stolt (IRE)**[20] 5891 3-9-4 **85** GrahamGibbons 8 64
(N Wilson) *prom: edgd lft after 1f: rdn along 2f out and sn wknd* **100/1**

0005 **16** 2 **Distinctly Game**[31] 5581 5-8-10 **77** NCallan 3 49+
(K A Ryan) *chsd ldrs on inner: rdn along 2f out and sn wknd* **8/1**[2]

63.25 secs (-0.55) **Going Correction** +0.05s/f (Good) **16** Ran SP% **124.6**
Speed ratings (Par 105): **106,104,102,101,101 100,100,97,97,97 97,95,95,94,91 88**
CSF £158.98 CT £1530.67 TOTE £6.30: £1.90, £7.00, £2.80, £4.30; EX 301.60.
Owner G Roberts/F Green/Tessona Racing **Bred** Sir Eric Parker **Trained** Newmarket, Suffolk

FOCUS
A competitive sprint handicap run at a good gallop and, although the winner did not need to be at his best to score, the runner-up ran to form and sets the standard.
Circuit Dancer(IRE) Official explanation: jockey said gelding hung left throughout
Elkhorn Official explanation: jockey said gelding was denied a clear run
Distinctly Game Official explanation: jockey said gelding suffered interference in running

6382 TOTESPORT.COM SILVER TANKARD STKS (LISTED RACE) 1m 4y
3:40 (3:42) (Class 1) 2-Y-O
£19,873 (£7,532; £3,769; £1,879; £941; £472) **Stalls** Low

Form RPR

3110 **1** **Siberian Tiger (IRE)**[39] 5350 2-9-2 86 TPO'Shea 3 99
(M R Channon) *hld up: hdwy wl over 1f out: swtchd rt and rdn ent fnl f: styd on to ld last 50yds* **12/1**

12 **2** ¾ **Latin Lad**[65] 4598 2-9-2 0 DaneO'Neill 1 97
(R Hannon) *trckd ldr: effrt 2f out: rdn to chal over 1f out: drvn to ld ins fnl f: sn edgd lft: hdd and no ex last 50yds* **9/4**[1]

6122 **3** 1¼ **Alan Devonshire**[37] 5400 2-9-2 89 JimmyQuinn 7 94
(M H Tompkins) *hld up in rr: hdwy on inner over 1f out: rdn: bmpd and squeezed through wl ins fnl f: kpt on* **9/1**

220 **4** shd **Bold Choice (IRE)**[38] 5397 2-9-2 0 PhilipRobinson 6 94
(M A Jarvis) *led: rdn along and edgd rt wl over 1f out: drvn: edgd lft and hdd ins fnl f: kpt on same pce towards fin* **8/1**

034 **5** 1½ **Bazergan (IRE)**[17] 5972 2-9-2 105 SebSanders 5 91
(C E Brittain) *trckd ldng pair: effrt 2f out: sn rdn and ev ch tl wknd ent fnl f* **11/4**[2]

4150 **6** 2 **Let Us Prey**[23] 5795 2-9-2 103 JimmyFortune 2 86
(N A Callaghan) *trckd ldrs: effrt 2f out and ev ch tl rdn and wknd appr fnl f* **3/1**[3]

1m 46.77s (1.07) **Going Correction** +0.05s/f (Good) **6** Ran SP% **111.2**
Speed ratings (Par 103): **96,95,94,93,92 90**
CSF £38.55 TOTE £12.00: £3.50, £1.50; EX 55.20.
Owner Ridgeway Downs Racing **Bred** Ashley Guest And Mrs John Guest **Trained** West Ilsley, Berks

FOCUS
A weak race by Listed standards and somewhat messy, with the third the best guide.

NOTEBOOK
Siberian Tiger(IRE), a winner off a mark of 78 at Salisbury back in August, could make no impression in a better handicap at Doncaster last time, but he proved good enough to score in what was a weak Listed contest. In rear early, he really got going once switched for his run and ultimately won with a bit in hand. He will go up quite a bit in the ratings for this though and will not be easy to place from now on. (op 16-1)
Latin Lad set a good standard on the form of his Newbury second to Sharp Nephew and there was every chance that this step up to 1m was going to muster further improvement. However, having come to hold every chance he began to look vulnerable and in the end the winner proved too strong. (op 2-1 tchd 15-8)
Alan Devonshire has run well in defeat in a couple of 7f handicaps at Chester, but he was always likely to come up short here unless improving and he ran pretty much as well as could have been expected. He will stay 1m2f in time and remains capable of better. (op 10-1)
Bold Choice(IRE), well down the field in a valuable sales race at the Curragh latest, had previously performed well in a couple of maidens and he ran about as well as could have been expected. He should find a race before long. (tchd 9-1)
Bazergan(IRE), not far behind River Proud in a Group 3 at Newmarket latest, failed to confirm the promise of that effort and failed to see out the extra furlong. He is related to several smart middle-distance horses though and should be capable of better in time. (op 3-1 tchd 10-3)
Let Us Prey, not beaten far in last months Royal Lodge, failed to reproduce that effort and dropped out disappointingly having come to have every chance. (tchd 10-3)

6383 TOTEEXACTA BLUFF COVE H'CAP 2m 1f 216y
4:10 (4:12) (Class 5) (0-75,73) 3-Y-0+ **£3,886** (£1,156; £577; £288) **Stalls** Low

Form RPR

1202 **1** **Toboggan Lady**[19] 5906 3-8-1 **57** RoystonFfrench 8 66
(Mrs A Duffield) *in tch: hdwy 4f out: rdn to ld over 1f out: drvn and hdd ins fnl f: rallied wl to ld last 50yds* **10/3**[1]

3433 **2** nk **Capitalise (IRE)**[18] 5948 4-8-7 **55** JerryO'Dwyer[(3)] 6 64
(V Smith) *hld up towards rr: stdy hdwy over 3f out: rdn to chal over 1f out: drvn to ld ins fnl f: hdd and no ex last 50yds* **5/1**[3]

0/00 **3** 12 **Inchpast**[16] 6014 6-9-7 **73** (b) AshleyMorgan[(7)] 12 69
(M H Tompkins) *hld up in rr: stdy hdwy over 4f out: rdn to chse ldrs and hung lft wl over 1f out: sn drvn and kpt on same pce* **22/1**

004 **4** 4 **Moonshine Beach**[8] 6200 9-9-5 **64** StephenDonohoe 4 55
(P W Hiatt) *chsd ldng pair: hdwy 4f out: rdn to ld 2f out: sn drvn and hdd over 1f out: wknd* **14/1**

020 **5** 3½ **Boxhall (IRE)**[22] 5839 5-9-4 **63** DanielTudhope 5 51
(N Wilson) *chsd ldr: led 12f out: rdn along over 3f out: hdd 2f out: sn drvn and wknd* **6/1**

0630 **6** 12 **Sweet Lavinia**[55] 4925 4-8-9 **54** oh9 JimmyQuinn 1 28
(J D Bethell) *hld up in midfield: pushed along over 4f out: sn rdn and wknd* **40/1**

0035 **7** nk **Matinee Idol**[22] 5561 4-8-9 **54** oh5 PaulMulrennan 7 28
(Mrs S Lamyman) *chsd ldrs: rdn along over 4f out: sn wknd* **50/1**

3352 **8** 13 **Noddies Way**[36] 5453 4-9-3 **62** SebSanders 10 22
(J F Panvert) *in tch: hdwy on outer to chse ldrs over 4f out: sn rdn along and wknd 3f out* **10/3**[1]

3651 **9** 29 **Love Brothers**[14] 6054 3-9-0 **70** DavidAllan 9 —
(M R Channon) *led: hdd 12f out: effrt to chal 3f out: sn rdn along: drvn 2f out and sn wknd* **7/2**[2]

000R **10** 166 **Glad Star (GER)**[58] 4817 4-8-2 **54** oh9 DanielleMcCreery[(7)] 2 —
(D W Chapman) *s.i.s: a in rr* **100/1**

3m 59.08s (-3.92) **Going Correction** +0.05s/f (Good)
WFA 3 from 4yo+ 11lb **10** Ran SP% **115.7**
Speed ratings (Par 103): **110,109,104,102,101 95,95,89,77,—**
CSF £19.70 CT £314.00 TOTE £4.20: £1.40, £2.00, £4.40; EX 20.40.
Owner T P McMahon and D McMahon **Bred** Blenheim Bloodstock **Trained** Constable Burton, N Yorks

FOCUS
They went a decent pace throughout in what was a moderate staying handicap but the proximity of the third and fourth limit things somewhat and the runner-up is the best guide.

6384 TOTESPORTGAMES.COM MAIDEN AUCTION STKS 6f
4:40 (4:43) (Class 5) 2-Y-O **£3,886** (£1,156; £577; £288) **Stalls** Low

Form RPR

1 **Kashimin (IRE)** 2-8-8 0 PJMcDonald[(3)] 4 77+
(G A Swinbank) *trckd ldrs: hdwy on bit to ld over 1f out: qcknd clr ins fnl f: easily* **12/1**

0 **2** 3 **Tito (IRE)**[24] 5771 2-9-0 0 SebSanders 8 68
(T D Barron) *led: rdn along and hung rt over 1f out: sn hdd: drvn and one pce ins fnl f* **7/2**[2]

3 1½ **Warners Bay (IRE)** 2-8-11 0 PatCosgrave 12 60
(R Bastiman) *bmpd s: sn chsng ldrs on outer: rdn along 2f out: kpt on u.p ins fnl f* **40/1**

5 **4** ½ **Pinewood Lulu**[13] 6093 2-8-5 0 JimmyQuinn 5 53
(R C Guest) *chsd ldrs: rdn along wl over 1f out: kpt on same pce appr fnl f* **5/1**[3]

0 **5** nk **Aerialist**[13] 6073 2-7-11 0 SophieDoyle[(7)] 2 51
(A Berry) *in tch: hdwy to chse ldrs wl over 1f out: sn rdn and kpt on same pce* **150/1**

5662 **6** ¾ **Eager Diva (USA)**[24] 5773 2-8-8 75 NCallan 6 53
(K A Ryan) *chsd ldrs: rdn along 2f out: sn drvn and wknd* **9/4**[1]

0450 **7** ½ **Tommytush (IRE)**[25] 5751 2-8-11 56 DavidAllan 9 54
(E J Alston) *cl up: rdn along 2f out: sn drvn and wknd over 1f out* **14/1**

0 **8** ½ **Star Grazer**[31] 5595 2-8-6 0 HayleyTurner 7 48
(C F Wall) *s.i.s: pushed along and hdwy over 2f out: sn rdn and kpt on same pce appr fnl f* **33/1**

4 **9** 5 **Hawk Mountain (UAE)**[19] 5902 2-8-10 0 GrahamGibbons 1 37
(J J Quinn) *a towards rr* **8/1**

0 **10** shd **Mythical Fosroc (USA)**[39] 5357 2-8-8 0 JohnEgan 10 34
(J S Moore) *dwlt: pushed along 1/2-way: a towards rr* **25/1**

11 shd **Graze On And On** 2-8-4 0 TPO'Shea 11 30
(J J Quinn) *bmpd s: sn outpcd and a in rr* **22/1**

00 **12** 2 **Que Beauty (IRE)**[13] 6087 2-8-6 0 PaulEddery 13 26
(R C Guest) *stdd and swtchd lft s: a in rr* **125/1**

45 **13** ½ **Bourbon Balistic**[13] 6072 2-8-12 0 RoystonFfrench 3 30
(Mrs A Duffield) *in tch on inner: rdn along 2f out: sn wknd* **8/1**

1m 19.27s (1.87) **Going Correction** +0.05s/f (Good) **13** Ran SP% **121.3**
Speed ratings (Par 95): **89,85,83,82,81 80,80,79,72,72 72,70,69**
CSF £52.39 TOTE £15.70: £4.40, £1.60, £12.10; EX 65.00 Place 6 ££1068.46, Place 5 £226.16..
Owner Mrs Anna Noble **Bred** Crandon Park Stud **Trained** Melsonby, N Yorks

FOCUS
This was nothing more than a modest maiden, but it was hard not to be impressed with Kashimin's performance. The seventh sets the level and also limits to some extent.

NOTEBOOK
Kashimin(IRE), an 11,000gns son of Kyllachy, ran out quite an impressive winner on this racecourse debut, coming away with ease inside the final furlong. It was not a great race, but he could hardly have done it any better and rates a decent sprinting prospect. (op 10-1)
Tito(IRE), who shaped quite pleasingly on debut at Haydock, appreciated this better ground and only found the useful-looking winner too good. He shows plenty of speed and should have no trouble finding a small maiden. (op 9-2 tchd 5-1)
Warners Bay(IRE) comes from a yard whose juveniles often benefit from a run or two and he shaped quite pleasingly back in third, running on late following an awkward start. (op 33-1)
Pinewood Lulu was always unlikely to be suited by this drop in trip, having shaped well over 7f on debut at Leicester on debut, and he could be of more interest once handicapping. (tchd 13-2)
Aerialist showed little on debut at Catterick, but stepped up markedly on that effort and seemed to appreciate the extra furlong. She is another for whom low-grade handicaps will present better chances. (op 100-1)
Eager Diva(USA), runner-up off a mark of 72 at Haydock last time, failed to giver her running on this return to maiden company and looks one to have reservations over now. (op 5-2 tchd 11-4 in a place)

T/Jkpt: Not won. T/Plt: £3,037.70 to a £1 stake. Pool: £72,614.00. 17.45 winning tickets. T/Qpdt: £66.20 to a £1 stake. Pool: £4,976.30. 55.60 winning tickets. JR

6355 WOLVERHAMPTON (A.W) (L-H)
Monday, October 22

OFFICIAL GOING: Standard
Wind: Almost nil Weather: Overcast

6385 BETANGEL.COM CLAIMING STKS 7f 32y(P)
2:30 (2:30) (Class 6) 3-Y-0+ **£2,047** (£604; £302) **Stalls** High

Form RPR

0023 **1** **Councellor (FR)**[11] 6121 5-9-3 80 (t) JamieSpencer 5 83
(Stef Liddiard) *broke wl: led early: chsd ldr: led over 2f out: pushed out* **13/8**[1]

0004 **2** *nk* **Ninth House (USA)**[16] 6024 5-9-0 73..............................(t) IanMongan 12 79
(N P Littmoden) *hld up towards rr: hdwy over 2f out: rdn over 1f out: r.o ins fnl f* **12/1**

6204 **3** *2* **Ochre Bay**[70] 4462 4-8-11 71.............................. RussellKennemore(5) 4 76
(R Hollinshead) *hld up in tch: rdn over 2f out: nt qckn ins fnl f* **8/1**[3]

3-00 **4** *nk* **Onenightinlisbon (IRE)**[44] 5223 3-8-9 72........................ PhillipMakin 3 70
(K R Burke) *hld up in tch: n.m.r briefly over 2f out: rdn over 1f out: no ex ins fnl f* **10/1**

0366 **5** *2* **Swinbrook (USA)**[19] 5923 6-9-4 76..............................(v) EddieAhern 10 71
(J A R Toller) *hld up in tch: c wd st: sn rdn: one pce fnl f* **5/2**[2]

0006 **6** *nk* **Local Poet**[16] 6024 6-8-9 62..(b) TomEaves 6 62
(I Semple) *prom: rdn and wnt 2nd briefly 2f out: wknd fnl f* **16/1**

0004 **7** *1 ¾* **Swing The Ring (IRE)**[4] 6288 4-9-8 75.......................... SteveDrowne 8 70
(A Berry) *hld up in mid-div: c wd st: rdn and edgd lft over 1f out: no hdwy* **10/1**

0 **8** *3 ½* **Quorn Master**[19] 5915 5-8-4 0.. TolleyDean(5) 9 47
(Mrs P Ford) *s.i.s: mid-div: rdn over 4f out: bhd fnl 3f* **100/1**

0000 **9** *hd* **King's Spear (IRE)**[45] 5188 4-8-9 57............................. JamesDoyle 11 47
(Miss J R Tooth) *hld up towards rr: rdn over 3f out: no rspnse* **40/1**

00 **10** *¾* **Just Crystal**[19] 5915 3-8-9 0.. TGMcLaughlin 2 47
(B P J Baugh) *s.i.s: a in rr* **100/1**

5030 **11** *hd* **On The Map**[57] 4853 3-8-12 59....................................(v) RichardMullen 1 49
(A P Jarvis) *sn led: rdn and hdd over 2f out: wknd over 1f out* **33/1**

00 **12** *14* **Mays Louise**[213] 745 3-8-7 0....................................... DeanMcKeown 7 7
(B P J Baugh) *s.i.s: a in rr: lost tch 2f out* **80/1**

1m 28.99s (-1.41) **Going Correction** -0.15s/f (Stan)
WFA 3 from 4yo+ 2lb 12 Ran SP% **118.1**
Speed ratings (Par 101): **102,101,99,99,96 96,94,90,90,89 89,73**
CSF £22.95 TOTE £1.90: £1.10, £3.10, £3.00; EX 17.00 Trifecta £64.20 Pool £249.02 - 2.75 winning units..
Owner D Gilbert **Bred** Janus Bloodstock & Pontchartrain Stud **Trained** Great Shefford, Berks

FOCUS
A good claimer but not easy to rate with the current form of some of these questionable and assessed around the principals.
Swinbrook(USA) Official explanation: trainer's rep said gelding spread a plate and finished sore
Swing The Ring(IRE) Official explanation: jockey said colt was hampered on the first bend

6386 BE A BOOKIE WITH BETANGEL MEDIAN AUCTION MAIDEN STKS 5f 20y(P)
3:00 (3:00) (Class 6) 2-Y-O **£2,047** (£604; £302) **Stalls** Low

Form RPR

5 **1** **Peter's Storm (USA)**[24] 5772 2-9-3 0............................. JamieSpencer 1 80
(K A Ryan) *hld up in tch: led wl over 1f out: hung rt fnl f: drvn out* **2/1**[1]

6 **2** *nk* **Another Socket**[12] 6105 2-8-12 0.................................. DarryllHolland 8 74
(E S McMahon) *s.s: hdwy and c wd ent st: ev ch ins fnl f: nt qckn* **11/1**

3300 **3** *3 ½* **A Wish For You**[56] 4903 2-8-7 65.............................. JamesO'Reilly(5) 3 61
(D K Ivory) *w ldrs: rdn wl over 1f out: hung lft and wknd ins fnl f* **12/1**

2540 **4** *nk* **Blue Zenith (IRE)**[11] 6128 2-8-12 68.. LPKeniry 9 60
(J S Moore) *led: hdd wl over 1f out: sn rdn and hung lft: wknd ins fnl f* **9/2**[3]

0552 **5** *¾* **In A Pickle**[14] 6065 2-8-12 62.. EddieAhern 4 57
(H J L Dunlop) *hld up in mid-div: rdn and hdwy over 1f out: wknd ins fnl f* **12/1**

0 **6** *½* **Rossini's Dancer**[25] 5745 2-9-3 0.................................. PaulHanagan 11 60
(R A Fahey) *in rr: sltly hmpd over 3f out: rdn and hdwy over 1f out: no ex ins fnl f* **11/1**

4 **7** *½* **Storey Hill (USA)**[20] 5888 2-9-3 0.............................. DeanMcKeown 12 59
(D Shaw) *prom: wkng whn hung lft wl over 1f out* **20/1**

036 **8** *½* **Miss Poppy**[7] 6225 2-8-12 0.. JimCrowley 10 52
(P R Chamings) *s.i.s: hdwy on ins wl over 1f out: squeezed through ent fnl f: n.d* **4/1**[2]

9 *nk* **Blakeshall Diamond** 2-8-5 0...................................... MarkCoumbe(7) 7 51
(A J Chamberlain) *s.i.s: outpcd: nt clr run and swtchd rt wl ins fnl f: nvr nrr* **66/1**

0004 **10** *1 ½* **Mr Funshine**[13] 6072 2-8-12 60.................................. JamesMillman(5) 6 50
(Mrs P N Dutfield) *chsd ldrs: lost pl over 3f out: n.d after* **40/1**

0000 **11** *shd* **Magnushomestwo (IRE)**[13] 6072 2-9-0 32.........(b[1]) PatrickMathers(3) 2 50
(A Berry) *w ldr: ev ch 2f out: wknd qckly 1f out* **200/1**

4022 **12** *hd* **Lavande**[46] 5176 2-8-12 67.. NeilPollard 5 44
(M J Wallace) *w ldrs tl rdn and wknd 2f out* **12/1**

63.00 secs (0.18) **Going Correction** -0.15s/f (Stan) 12 Ran SP% **120.4**
Speed ratings (Par 93): **92,91,85,85,84 83,82,81,81,78 78,78**
CSF £26.21 TOTE £2.70: £1.40, £5.00, £5.60; EX 26.50 Trifecta £117.50 Pool £173.85 - 1.05 winning units..
Owner Peter & Richard Foden Racing Partnership **Bred** Mr & Mrs Hugh G King **Trained** Hambleton, N Yorks

FOCUS
A weak maiden but fairly decent form rated around the third and fifth.

NOTEBOOK
Peter's Storm(USA) improved on the form he showed on his debut at Haydock to get off the mark at the second attempt. He did not help his chance by hanging right in the straight, but he was always going to hold on. (op 11-4)
Another Socket did not show much on her debut at Nottingham, but she was well backed that day, suggesting she had been showing something at home, and this was a lot better. She was well off the pace for much of the way after missing the kick, but she raced enthusiastically and finished well, despite coming extremely wide into the straight. Official explanation: jockey said filly missed the break (op 8-1)
A Wish For You is only modest but she ran right up to her best and probably sets the standard. Official explanation: jockey said filly hung left (op 8-1)
Blue Zenith(IRE) showed plenty of early speed, but she was eventually put in her place.
In A Pickle did not run a bad race but she will probably be better off in nursery company.
Storey Hill(USA) ◆, fourth over 6f round here on his debut, showed good speed early on, but was forced to do all of his racing out wide. He is better than this and could be one to look out for once handicapped. (tchd 22-1)
Miss Poppy was far from ideally drawn in ten and she was never involved. (op 9-2 tchd 11-2)
Mr Funshine Official explanation: jockey said colt finished sore

6387 WIN WHATEVER THE RESULT WITH BETANGEL H'CAP 1m 1f 103y(P)
3:30 (3:30) (Class 6) (0-65,69) 3-Y-O **£2,047** (£604; £302) **Stalls** Low

Form RPR

-501 **1** **Robert The Brave**[2] 6344 3-9-3 69 6ex.......................... TolleyDean(5) 4 79+
(P R Webber) *hld up in mid-div: nt clr run over 3f out: nt clr run on ins over 2f out: hdwy and edgd lft over 1f out: hrd rdn to ld cl home* **7/2**[2]

2005 **2** *nk* **Goose Green (IRE)**[13] 6083 3-8-13 60.......................... SteveDrowne 8 65
(R J Hodges) *hld up in tch: wnt 2nd over 2f out: rdn to ld over 1f out: hdd cl home* **16/1**

5332 **3** *hd* **Cap St Jean (IRE)**[16] 6026 3-8-10 57.......................(p) JamieSpencer 13 62
(R Hollinshead) *s.i.s: sn swtchd lft: hld up in rr: rdn and hdwy whn hung lft wl over 1f out: r.o ins fnl f* **5/2**[1]

3020 **4** *nk* **Intensifier (IRE)**[74] 4339 3-8-6 53 ow1...........................(b) EddieAhern 9 57+
(P A Blockley) *hld up in mid-div: pushed along over 3f out: rdn and hdwy over 1f out: kpt on ins fnl f* **8/1**[3]

1436 **5** *2* **Cavendish**[88] 3876 3-8-13 60..(b) DaleGibson 10 60
(J M P Eustace) *prom: chsd ldr over 6f out tl over 2f out: rdn and hung lft over 1f out: no ex ins fnl f* **9/1**

003 **6** *shd* **King Zeal (IRE)**[51] 5045 3-9-4 65.. DO'Donohoe 6 65
(M Wigham) *hmpd s: hld up towards rr: hdwy over 2f out: rdn and c wd st: one pce fnl f* **12/1**

6004 **7** *1 ½* **Officer Material (IRE)**[16] 6026 3-8-4 51..................(b) RichardThomas 7 47
(C G Cox) *wnt lft s: sn led: rdn 3f out: hdd over 1f out: wknd ins fnl f* **25/1**

2005 **8** *hd* **Shouldntbethere (IRE)**[18] 5943 3-8-11 63............ JamesMillman(5) 11 59
(Mrs P N Dutfield) *stdd s: sn swtchd lft: hld up in rr: short-lived effrt on outside over 2f out* **16/1**

3335 **9** *¾* **Ochre (IRE)**[154] 1903 3-9-2 63.. PaulHanagan 12 57
(R A Fahey) *hld up in mid-div: rdn and hdwy over 3f out: edgd lft over 1f out: wknd fnl f* **9/1**

-000 **10** *1 ½* **Classic Blue (IRE)**[2] 6343 3-8-4 51 oh2............................. ChrisCatlin 1 42
(Ian Williams) *led early: hld up in tch: wknd over 2f out* **28/1**

6304 **11** *3* **Ella Y Rossa**[5] 6272 3-8-13 60...................................... TGMcLaughlin 3 45
(P D Evans) *s.i.s: hld up towards rr: rdn over 4f out: no rspnse* **8/1**[3]

466 **12** *7* **Witchingham**[7] 6229 3-9-4 65... PatDobbs 5 35
(R Hannon) *prom tl rdn and wknd over 3f out* **50/1**

2m 1.58s (-1.04) **Going Correction** -0.15s/f (Stan) 12 Ran SP% **121.7**
Speed ratings (Par 99): **98,97,97,97,95 95,94,93,93,91 89,83**
CSF £59.26 CT £168.25 TOTE £4.30: £1.90, £4.80, £1.80; EX 67.40 Trifecta £164.20 Part won. Pool £231.35 - 0.55 winning units..
Owner T R Pearson **Bred** Alan Gibson **Trained** Mollington, Oxon
■ Stewards' Enquiry : Tolley Dean caution: used whip with excessive frequency

FOCUS
A modest handicap rated around the runner-up and fourth and sound enough.

6388 JOE TATE "LIFETIME IN RACING" NURSERY 5f 216y(P)
4:00 (4:01) (Class 6) (0-65,66) 2-Y-O **£2,047** (£604; £302) **Stalls** Low

Form RPR

0051 **1** **High Standing (USA)**[5] 6263 2-9-8 66 6ex................. JamieSpencer 11 79+
(N A Callaghan) *hld up in rr: rdn and hdwy wl over 1f out: sn edgd lft: r.o wl to ld wl ins fnl f* **4/6**[1]

3043 **2** *2* **Mystickhill (IRE)**[3] 6312 2-8-12 61..........................(t) JamesO'Reilly(5) 10 65
(D J Murphy) *sn chsng ldr: led over 3f out: rdn clr wl over 1f out: ct wl ins fnl f* **14/1**

6400 **3** *1 ½* **Lekin Sedona (IRE)**[6] 6255 2-8-3 50......................... WilliamBuick(3) 2 50
(J M Saville) *sn led: hdd over 3f out: rdn wl over 1f out: sn edgd lft: kpt on one pce fnl f* **25/1**

1522 **4** *½* **Loose Caboose (IRE)**[13] 6074 2-8-11 62...................(p) RobbieEgan(7) 1 60+
(A J McCabe) *s.i.s: hld up and bhd: hdwy on ins whn nt clr run 3f out: sn swtchd rt: hung lft over 1f out: kpt on ins fnl f* **8/1**[2]

0505 **5** *shd* **Copperbottomed (IRE)**[10] 6151 2-9-4 62.......................... JimCrowley 7 60
(R Hollinshead) *hld up towards rr: hdwy on ins 2f out: rdn and kpt on same pce fnl f* **40/1**

201 **6** *1 ¼* **Princess Rhianna (IRE)**[13] 6072 2-9-7 65..................... PaulHanagan 4 59
(Mrs G S Rees) *prom tl rdn and wknd over 1f out* **8/1**[2]

5563 **7** *½* **Howards Hope**[16] 6022 2-9-7 65...............................(v[1]) TomEaves 8 57
(I Semple) *s.i.s: in rr: rdn 3f out: hung lft wl over 1f out: late hdwy: nrst fin* **16/1**

0545 **8** *hd* **Gulf Coast**[41] 5298 2-9-4 62..(v) DeanMcKeown 13 54
(M Johnston) *broke wl: sn mid-div: btn whn hung lft fr over 1f out* **10/1**[3]

0003 **9** *1 ½* **Mairead's Boy (IRE)**[47] 5133 2-8-4 53........................(b) TolleyDean(5) 3 40
(J S Moore) *sn chsng ldrs: rdn 2f out: wknd fnl f* **33/1**

5660 **10** *½* **Silca Destination**[18] 5939 2-8-12 56..............................(v[1]) ChrisCatlin 5 42
(M R Channon) *rdn wl over 2f out: a towards rr* **16/1**

0050 **11** *6* **Border Defence (IRE)**[10] 6154 2-9-0 58.................(v) FrankieMcDonald 9 26
(P A Blockley) *prom tl rdn and wknd over 2f out* **33/1**

0640 **12** *3 ½* **Madame Rio (IRE)**[5] 6263 2-9-7 65.................................. PhillipMakin 6 22
(K R Burke) *hld up in mid-div: bdly hmpd and lost pl over 2f out: n.d after* **80/1**

3630 **13** *2 ½* **Myriola**[25] 5751 2-9-2 60... SteveDrowne 12 10
(B Palling) *led early: prom: hung rt over 3f out: sn rn wd and lost pl: eased wl over 1f out* **20/1**

1m 15.27s (-0.54) **Going Correction** -0.15s/f (Stan) 13 Ran SP% **127.9**
Speed ratings (Par 93): **97,94,92,91,91 89,89,88,86,86 78,73,70**
CSF £12.27 CT £169.68 TOTE £1.70: £1.10, £3.70, £10.40; EX 16.00 Trifecta £291.20 Part won. Pool £410.17 - 0.70 winning units..
Owner SP Racing Investments S A **Bred** Dr Melinda Blue **Trained** Newmarket, Suffolk
■ Stewards' Enquiry : Robbie Egan three-day ban: careless riding (Nov 2-4)

FOCUS
Just a modest nursery, but the winner is better than this level.

NOTEBOOK
High Standing(USA) was an easy winner of a similar race at Kempton on his previous start and a 6lb penalty was nowhere near enough to stop him following up. He was left with plenty to do after taking time to find his stride, but that was probably by design considering his wide draw and he ran on well in the straight to easily reel in the positively-ridden Mystickhill. He is much better than this level and could well defy higher marks. (op 8-13 tchd 8-11)
Mystickhill(IRE) looked like she would take a bit of catching when kicked clear early in the straight, but the winner was too good. She was unlucky to run into such a well-handicapped rival. (op 12-1)
Lekin Sedona(IRE), dropped in trip and switched to Polytrack for the first time, ran one of his best races yet and make be able to land a small race off his lowly mark eventually.
Loose Caboose(IRE), back on Polytrack, she blew the start but responded to pressure in the straight. (op 7-1)
Copperbottomed(IRE) was beaten in a claimer over course and distance on his previous start, but this was not a bad effort.
Myriola Official explanation: jockey said filly hung throughout

6389 WIN BEFORE THE OFF WITH BETANGEL H'CAP 1m 4f 50y(P)
4:30 (4:30) (Class 3) (0-90,89) 3-Y-O **£7,124** (£2,119; £1,059; £529) **Stalls** Low

Form RPR

4130 **1** **Furmigadelagiusta**[30] 5619 3-9-4 89.............................. JamieSpencer 4 95
(L M Cumani) *led early: chsd ldr: rdn and hung lft over 1f out: r.o to ld last strides* **3/1**[1]

4316 **2** *hd* **Music Review**[13] 6091 3-8-5 76.. PaulHanagan 6 82
(R A Fahey) *sn led: rdn over 2f out: hdd last strides* **7/2**[2]

4544 **3** *hd* **Spiderback (IRE)**[16] 6007 3-8-6 **77**........................(b) EddieAhern 5 83
(R Hannon) *reminders sn after s: hld up in tch: swtchd rt 1f out: sn rdn: r.o towards fin* **4/1**[3]
4140 **4** *2* **Soul Mountain (IRE)**[16] 6014 3-8-6 **80**.................. WilliamBuick(3) 1 82
(B W Hills) *hld up in tch: rdn over 2f out: one pce fnl f* **4/1**[3]
6060 **5** *4* **Chookie Hamilton**[18] 5936 3-8-9 **80**....................(v[1]) TomEaves 7 76
(I Semple) *dwlt: hld up: rdn over 2f out: no rspnse* **14/1**
0620 **6** *1* **Noticeable (IRE)**[17] 5978 3-8-8 **79**.................. DarryllHolland 2 73
(M R Channon) *hld up in rr: rdn and edgd lft over 1f out: no rspnse* **6/1**

2m 40.71s (-1.71) **Going Correction** -0.15s/f (Stan) **6** Ran SP% **108.2**
Speed ratings (Par 105): **99,98,98,97,94 94**
CSF £12.62 TOTE £3.20: £1.90, £2.70; EX 7.20.
Owner Scuderia Rencati Srl **Bred** Azienda Agricola Francesca **Trained** Newmarket, Suffolk

FOCUS
A good, competitive handicap, despite the small field, but the pace was just ordinary and the front three finished in a bunch. The third sets the standard.

NOTEBOOK
Furmigadelagiusta ran no sort of race at Ayr on his previous start, but this was much more like it and he showed a good attitude to come out on top in a three-way battle. He should stay further and can do even better in a more strongly-run race. (op 7-2)
Music Review was not at her best at Leicester on her previous start, but she proved well suited by the return to Polytrack and bounced back to form with a career-best effort in defeat. (tchd 4-1)
Spiderback(IRE) required reminders through the early stages, but he responded well enough and was not beaten far. He has won just once from 17 starts. (op 7-2 tchd 9-2)
Soul Mountain(IRE) was not at her best switched to Polytrack for the first time and she probably would have preferred a stronger pace. (op 3-1)
Chookie Hamilton had won four of his last five starts on sand, including three times round here, but he had not been in much form on turf lately and was well held returned to Polytrack with a visor replacing blinkers. (op 12-1)

6390 BOOK YOUR CHRISTMAS PARTY NOW CLASSIFIED STKS 5f 216y(P)
5:00 (5:00) (Class 7) 3-Y-O+ **£1,911** (£564; £282) **Stalls** Low

Form RPR
0605 **1** **Snow Bunting**[14] 6064 9-8-13 45.................. PaulHanagan 8 56+
(Jedd O'Keeffe) *hld up towards rr: nt clr run fr over 1f out tl jst ins fnl f: rdn and r.o wl to ld cl home* **3/1**[1]
6000 **2** *3/4* **Muktasb (USA)**[63] 4668 6-8-13 45....................(v) AdamKirby 13 52
(D Shaw) *stdd s: sn swtchd lft: hdwy on ins 2f out: rdn over 1f out: ev ch ins fnl f: kpt on* **7/1**[2]
500- **3** *hd* **Rapid Flow**[437] 4324 5-8-13 45.................. TGMcLaughlin 2 51
(J W Unett) *a.p: led wl over 1f out: sn rdn: hdd cl home* **14/1**
5005 **4** *1 1/4* **Seesawmilu (IRE)**[6] 6247 4-8-13 45.................. DaleGibson 11 48
(E J Alston) *hld up in rr: hdwy fnl f: nrst fin* **8/1**[3]
3630 **5** *nk* **Boisdale (IRE)**[123] 2791 9-8-13 45.................. RichardThomas 5 47
(P S Felgate) *hld up in tch: rdn over 1f out: nt qckn ins fnl f* **22/1**
053- **6** *1 1/2* **Whos Counting**[322] 6695 3-8-12 45.................. SteveDrowne 1 42
(R J Hodges) *hld up in mid-div: nt clr run jst over 1f out: rdn and one pce ins fnl f* **12/1**
1000 **7** *1/2* **Dodaa (USA)**[18] 5930 4-8-13 45.................. EddieAhern 3 41
(N Wilson) *w ldr: led over 3f out: rdn and hdd wl over 1f out: wknd ins fnl f* **9/1**
0003 **8** *1 1/4* **Smart Cassie**[27] 5716 4-8-6 45....................(b) RobbieEgan(7) 9 37
(H J Evans) *hld up in tch: hung rt bnd over 2f out: rdn over 1f out: hung rt and wknd ins fnl f* **20/1**
-000 **9** *nk* **Bahamian Bay**[123] 2791 5-8-13 45.................. TomEaves 4 36
(M Brittain) *led over 2f: w ldr: rdn wl over 1f out: wknd ins fnl f* **33/1**
500 **10** *5* **Dotty's Daughter**[54] 4935 3-8-12 45....................(p) SaleemGolam 12 21
(Mrs A Duffield) *rdn 3f out: a towards rr* **66/1**
0024 **11** *1/2* **Miss Mujahid Times**[32] 5566 4-8-13 45....................(b) JamieSpencer 7 20
(A D Brown) *hld up in tch: c wd st: wknd over 1f out* **3/1**[1]
0600 **12** *1 1/2* **King Of Charm (IRE)**[131] 2555 4-8-13 45....................(b) JimCrowley 10 15
(G L Moore) *rdn 3f out: a towards rr* **12/1**
006 **13** *5* **Detonate**[14] 6062 5-8-13 45.................. RichardMullen 6 —
(I A Wood) *s.i.s: a in rr* **8/1**[3]

1m 15.84s (0.03) **Going Correction** -0.15s/f (Stan)
WFA 3 from 4yo+ 1lb **13** Ran SP% **130.3**
Speed ratings (Par 97): **93,92,91,90,89 87,87,85,84,78 77,75,68**
CSF £25.82 TOTE £6.50: £2.00, £3.00, £8.10; EX 37.80 TRIFECTA Not won..
Owner W R B Racing 49 (wrbracing.com) **Bred** The Queen **Trained** Middleham Moor, N Yorks

FOCUS
A very moderate classified contest and ordinary form with the winner close to this year's best mark.

6391 TRY BETANGEL AT TRY.BETANGEL.COM H'CAP 7f 32y(P)
5:30 (5:30) (Class 4) (0-85,85) 3-Y-O+ **£4,728** (£1,406; £702; £351) **Stalls** High

Form RPR
0050 **1** **Gallantry**[23] 5804 5-9-2 **81**.................. DeanMcKeown 9 93
(D Shaw) *s.i.s: sn swtchd lft: hld up in mid-div: hdwy over 2f out: rdn to ld ins fnl f: edgd rt nr fin: r.o* **13/2**[3]
4102 **2** *1* **Tender The Great (IRE)**[8] 6208 4-9-3 **82**.................. TQuinn 12 91
(B G Powell) *hld up in tch: nt clr run fr over 2f out tl wl over 1f out: sn rdn and hdwy: edgd lft ins fnl f: r.o* **5/1**[2]
3530 **3** *1* **Flying Goose (IRE)**[8] 6209 3-8-13 **80**.................. ChrisCatlin 10 86
(L M Cumani) *s.i.s: hld up and bhd: c wd st: rdn and hdwy 1f out: edgd lft ins fnl f: kpt on* **10/1**
6156 **4** *hd* **Viva Volta**[16] 6006 4-8-9 **77**....................(b) DuranFentiman(3) 11 83
(T D Easterby) *sn chsng ldr: led over 2f out: rdn and hdd ins fnl f: no ex* **25/1**
1150 **5** *1/2* **Medicea Sidera**[18] 5954 3-9-4 **85**.................. SteveDrowne 7 89
(E F Vaughan) *a.p: rdn wl over 1f out: one pce fnl f* **8/1**
4460 **6** *1/2* **Mandarin Spirit (IRE)**[16] 6006 7-8-12 **77**....................(b) IanMongan 3 80
(G C H Chung) *hld up in tch: chsd ldr 2f out tl over 1f out: wknd ins fnl f* **14/1**
6053 **7** *2* **Sailor King (IRE)**[16] 6006 5-8-12 **77**.................. JimCrowley 5 75
(D K Ivory) *led early: hld up in mid-div: hdwy over 2f out: rdn over 1f out: wknd fnl f* **13/2**[3]
2460 **8** *1* **Moonlight Man**[10] 6142 6-9-3 **82**.................. LiamJones 2 77
(C R Dore) *nvr nr ldrs* **20/1**
5601 **9** *2 1/2* **Shustraya**[16] 6006 3-9-3 **84**.................. EddieAhern 1 72
(P J Makin) *prom: nt clr run on ins over 2f out: sn lost pl: rdn over 1f out: sn struggling* **9/2**[1]
-P00 **10** *11* **Mr Lambros**[10] 6142 6-9-3 **85**....................(vt[1]) WilliamBuick(3) 4 44
(Miss Gay Kelleway) *sn led: rdn and hdd over 2f out: wknd wl over 1f out* **25/1**
-165 **11** *5* **Braddock (IRE)**[7] 6243 4-8-13 **78**.................. PhillipMakin 8 23
(T D Barron) *hld up in tch: rdn and wknd over 3f out: eased whn no ch wl over 1f out* **5/1**[2]

1m 28.2s (-2.20) **Going Correction** -0.15s/f (Stan)
WFA 3 from 4yo+ 2lb **11** Ran SP% **117.5**
Speed ratings (Par 105): **106,104,103,103,102 102,100,98,96,83 77**
CSF £37.91 CT £259.43 TOTE £6.10: £1.70, £2.20, £3.00; EX 42.10 Trifecta £188.60 Part won. Pool £265.75 - 0.35 winning units. Place 6 £17.93, Place 5 £10.08..
Owner The Circle Bloodstock I Limited **Bred** Cheveley Park Stud Ltd **Trained** Danethorpe, Notts

FOCUS
A fair handicap run at an even gallop and the form looks pretty solid and should wotrk out.
Moonlight Man Official explanation: jockey said gelding resented the kickback
Shustraya Official explanation: jockey said filly was denied a clear run
T/Plt: £39.50 to a £1 stake. Pool: £52,367.35. 966.05 winning tickets. T/Qpdt: £13.50 to a £1 stake. Pool: £3,487.30. 190.30 winning tickets. KH

6362 CURRAGH (R-H)
Monday, October 22

OFFICIAL GOING: Soft

6392a CARMEL KEATLEY MEMORIAL RACE 5f
1:15 (1:15) 2-Y-O **£9,017** (£2,645; £1,260; £429)

RPR
1 **Age Of Chivalry (IRE)**[37] 5434 2-9-0.................. MJKinane 10 86+
(John M Oxx, Ire) *a.p: 2nd 1/2-way: impr to ld over 1f out: r.o wl: comf* **5/4**[1]
2 *1 1/2* **La Sylvia (IRE)**[25] 5757 2-8-9.................. DPMcDonogh 6 76
(Desmond McDonogh, Ire) *led: rdn and hdd over 1f out: kpt on same pce* **8/1**
3 *1 1/4* **Toberanthawn (IRE)**[38] 5395 2-8-10 ow1....................(b[1]) WJLee 12 72
(K J Condon, Ire) *trckd ldrs on outer: 5th after 1/2-way: 3rd and kpt on fnl f* **20/1**
4 *1 1/2* **Coach And Four (USA)** 2-9-0.................. JAHeffernan 11 71
(A P O'Brien, Ire) *hld up: 6th and hdwy 1 1/2f out: kpt on ins fnl f* **5/1**[3]
5 *2* **Littlemisssunshine (IRE)**[9] 6167 2-9-0....................(p) PShanahan 8 64
(J S Moore) *trckd ldrs: 4th 1/2-way: 3rd and rdn whn rdr dropped whip over 1f out: no ex* **5/2**[2]
6 *nk* **Inzone (IRE)**[24] 5784 2-8-11 82.................. PBBeggy(3) 9 62
(K J Condon, Ire) *chsd ldrs: 5th 1/2-way: no ex fr over 1f out* **14/1**
7 *1 1/4* **Bringbackmeboots**[10] 6159 2-9-0.................. CDHayes 2 58
(Liam Roche, Ire) *hld up in tch: no imp fr 1 1/2f out* **66/1**
8 *1 1/4* **Turklord (IRE)**[18] 5957 2-9-0.................. PJSmullen 7 53
(D K Weld, Ire) *hld up towards rr: 8th over 1f out: no ex* **16/1**
9 *2 1/2* **Alannahbeckaaoibhe (IRE)**[8] 6214 2-8-9.................. DMGrant 4 39
(Patrick J Flynn, Ire) *a towards rr* **66/1**
10 *1 3/4* **Elas Child (IRE)**[17] 5987 2-8-9.................. RPCleary 3 33
(M Halford, Ire) *a bhd* **66/1**
11 *7* **Katelynstar (IRE)** 2-8-6.................. DJMoran(3) 1 8
(Liam Roche, Ire) *prom: 2nd early: 3rd u.p 1/2-way: sn wknd* **66/1**

64.66 secs (3.36) **Going Correction** +0.725s/f (Yiel) **12** Ran SP% **124.1**
Speed ratings: **102,99,97,95,92 91,89,87,83,80 69**
CSF £13.33 TOTE £2.50: £1.10, £2.80, £10.40; DF 11.50.
Owner Plantation Stud **Bred** Perle O'Rourke **Trained** Currabeg, Co Kildare

NOTEBOOK
Littlemisssunshine(IRE) showed up handily enough but was unable to improve her position in the last furlong and a half.

4870 DEAUVILLE (R-H)
Monday, October 22

OFFICIAL GOING: Turf course - good to soft; all-weather - standard

6400a PRIX VULCAIN (LISTED RACE) 1m 4f 110y
2:35 (2:37) 3-Y-O **£17,568** (£7,027; £5,270; £3,514; £1,757)

RPR
1 **Cristobal (USA)**[75] 3-8-11....................(b) C-PLemaire 6 104
(J-C Rouget, France)
2 *3* **Longville (GER)**[55] 3-8-11.................. DBoeuf 3 99
(Mario Hofer, Germany)
3 *3/4* **Shujoon**[50] 5080 3-9-4.................. JVictoire 2 105
(A Fabre, France)
4 *1/2* **Not Just Swing (IRE)**[30] 5661 3-9-2.................. SPasquier 4 102
(A Fabre, France)
5 *1 1/2* **Bella Ida (FR)**[34] 5519 3-8-8.................. DBonilla 8 92
(J E Hammond, France)
6 *1/2* **Sagredo (USA)**[18] 5952 3-8-11.................. J-BEyquem 5 94
(Sir Mark Prescott) *hld up: hdwy and 6th st on ins: one pce fr 1 1/2f out*
7 *3* **Meshugah (IRE)**[64] 4655 3-9-2.................. OPeslier 7 95
(R Gibson, France)
8 *3/4* **Wutzeline (GER)**[29] 5669 3-8-8.................. TJarnet 10 86
(A Trybuhl, Germany)
9 *nse* **Berenice Pancrisia (FR)**[34] 3-8-8.................. AlxiBadel 9 86
(Mme M Bollack-Badel, France)
10 *shd* **Topka (FR)**[34] 5519 3-8-11.................. TThulliez 1 88
(F Doumen, France)

2m 43.5s (-3.20) **10** Ran
PARI-MUTUEL: WIN 5.80; PL 1.50, 1.50, 1.20; DF 18.00.
Owner E Gann **Bred** Abbot Properties **Trained** Pau, France

NOTEBOOK
Sagredo(USA) likes a bit of cut in the ground but has run poorly on each occasion he has gone right-handed.

The Form Book, Raceform Ltd, Compton, RG20 6NL

6267 LINGFIELD (L-H)

Tuesday, October 23

OFFICIAL GOING: Standard

Wind: Light, against Weather: Fine

6401 DIRECTORYOFTHETURF.COM MAIDEN AUCTION STKS (DIV I) 7f (P)

1:50 (1:52) (Class 5) 2-Y-O £2,169 (£645; £322; £161) Stalls Low

Form RPR

03 1 **Hucking Hero (IRE)**[85] 4028 2-8-11 0 .... DaneO'Neill 7 67+
(J R Best) *t.k.h early: hld up bhd ldng gp: rdn and effrt 2f out: prog on outer over 1f out: r.o to ld last 150yds: edgd lft but sn clr* **7/2**[1]

3050 2 3 **Towy Boy (IRE)**[46] 5199 2-9-1 65 .... NCallan 6 63
(I A Wood) *chsd ldrs: rdn over 2f out: clsd to chal 1f out: outpcd by wnr ins fnl f: kpt on* **9/2**[2]

3 1/2 **Pharaohs Queen (IRE)** 2-8-8 0 .... TPQueally 10 55
(E A L Dunlop) *s.s: hld up in last pair: effrt on outer over 1f out: r.o fnl f to snatch 3rd on line* **9/2**[2]

00 4 shd **Karate Queen**[20] 5919 2-8-10 0 .... LPKeniry 2 57
(A M Balding) *led: rdn 2f out: hdd and outpcd last 150yds* **9/1**

4 5 nk **Autumn Charm**[22] 5863 2-8-4 0 .... MartinDwyer 8 50
(W Jarvis) *chsd ldrs and racd wd: rdn 2f out: sn outpcd: kpt on fnl f* **15/2**

003 6 1 3/4 **Agglestone Rock**[20] 5895 2-8-2 68 .... JackDean(7) 4 50
(W G M Turner) *t.k.h: pressed ldr: stl pressing over 1f out: wknd ins fnl f* **15/2**

7 shd **Bertbrand**[34] 2-8-11 0 .... EddieAhern 5 55+
(M Botti) *trckd ldrs: gng wl 2f out: effrt on inner and chalng 1f out: pushed along and hld whn snatched up last 100yds* **13/2**[3]

6000 8 1 1/4 **Charlie Be (IRE)**[43] 5268 2-8-9 54 .... RobertHavlin 11 47
(Mrs P N Dutfield) *hld up in last trio: cl enough 2f out: sn outpcd* **25/1**

0 9 1 1/2 **Wogan's Sister**[79] 4198 2-8-8 0 .... JamesDoyle 3 42
(I A Wood) *trckd ldrs on inner: wknd over 1f out* **50/1**

10 10 **Whenineedyou** 2-8-4 0 .... GregFairley 9 12
(I A Wood) *v s.i.s: sn drvn and a last: t.o* **16/1**

1m 25.68s (-0.21) **Going Correction** -0.125s/f (Stan) **10** Ran SP% **117.1**

Speed ratings (Par 95): **96,92,92,91,91 89,89,88,86,74**

CSF £19.14 TOTE £5.90: £2.10, £1.70, £1.70; EX 20.10.

Owner Hucking Horses **Bred** Mrs A Hughes **Trained** Hucking, Kent

■ Stewards' Enquiry : L P Keniry two-day ban: careless riding (Nov 3-4)

FOCUS

Just a modest maiden. The winning time was 0.09 seconds quicker than the second division.

NOTEBOOK

Hucking Hero(IRE) improved on his Yarmouth third to get off the mark in convincing fashion. He has progressed with every run so far and will be worthy of respect when going down the handicap route. (op 5-1)

Towy Boy(IRE) had shown a bit of ability on turf and had not enjoyed the clearest of runs in a Kempton nursery last time. He ran creditably enough here, having raced close to the pace from the off, and seemed to see out the longer trip well enough. His official rating of 65 provides a benchmark to the form. (op 4-1)

Pharaohs Queen(IRE) stayed on well in the latter stages, having been slow to break from the stalls, and did much the best of the newcomers. There is plenty of stamina on the dam's side and she will improve as she goes up in trip.

Karate Queen helped force the pace and showed a lot more than in two starts on turf. (op 11-1)

Autumn Charm's debut fourth at Brighton did not amount to much. (op 11-2)

Bertbrand was hampered inside the final furlong by Karate Queen. (op 8-1 tchd 17-2)

6402 LINGFIELDPARK.CO.UK (S) STKS 6f (P)

2:20 (2:20) (Class 6) 3-Y-O £2,047 (£604; £302) Stalls Low

Form RPR

5000 1 **Scarlett Heart (IRE)**[3] 6340 3-9-0 60 .... ChrisCatlin 8 55
(J Gallagher) *dwlt: hld up in last pair: plenty to do 2f out: rapid prog on outer over 1f out: r.o to ld last 50yds* **5/1**[2]

3054 2 3/4 **Foreland Sands (IRE)**[10] 6176 3-9-0 55 ....(v) DaneO'Neill 5 52
(J R Best) *sn pressed ldr: led 4f out: kicked 3 l clr over 1f out: wknd and hdd last 50yds* **4/1**[1]

3240 3 3/4 **Calloff The Search**[7] 6247 3-8-9 55 ....(v) TolleyDean(5) 11 50
(W G M Turner) *rrd s: wl in rr: rdn over 2f out: prog on outer over 1f out: styd on wl fnl f* **4/1**[1]

5R04 4 1 1/4 **Sherjawy (IRE)**[64] 4661 3-9-0 47 ....(b) AdamKirby 2 46
(Miss Z C Davison) *prom: outpcd fr 2f out: styd on fnl f: unable to chal* **33/1**

-000 5 1/2 **Almondillo (IRE)**[11] 6149 3-9-0 50 .... SebSanders 12 44
(C F Wall) *mostly in midfield: outpcd 2f out: effrt but hanging bdly lft over 1f out: kpt on fnl f* **13/2**[3]

0400 6 nk **Davaye**[29] 5688 3-8-9 54 .... FergusSweeney 4 38
(K R Burke) *cl up: effrt to dispute 2nd over 2f out: no imp on ldr over 1f out: wknd ins fnl f* **7/1**

2040 7 1 **Eastern Princess**[78] 4226 3-8-6 45 ....(v) WilliamBuick(3) 9 35
(G H Yardley) *sn prom: rdn to dispute 2nd over 2f out: no imp on ldr over 1f out: wknd fnl f* **25/1**

0500 8 1 1/4 **Xalted**[9] 6206 3-9-0 47 .... J-PGuillambert 1 36
(S C Williams) *dwlt: rousted along on inner and towards rr: struggling over 2f out: kpt on* **9/1**

0006 9 shd **Tang**[28] 5716 3-8-2 44 .... JackDean(7) 10 31
(W G M Turner) *a in rr: pushed along and no prog 2f out* **18/1**

1062 10 4 **Savanagh Forest (IRE)**[28] 5716 3-9-0 45 .... RobertHavlin 3 23
(M Quinn) *led for 2f: chsd ldrs tl wknd wl over 1f out* **16/1**

11 14 **Mango Piccle** 3-9-0 0 .... SamHitchcott 7 —
(L Wells) *rrd s: rn green and a bhd: t.o* **50/1**

0-10 12 1/2 **Inkjet (IRE)**[275] 202 3-9-0 55 .... NCallan 6 —
(P D Evans) *chsd ldrs to 1/2-way: wknd rapidly: t.o* **16/1**

1m 12.8s (-0.01) **Going Correction** -0.125s/f (Stan) 12 Ran SP% **118.3**

Speed ratings (Par 99): **95,94,93,91,90 90,88,87,87,81 63,62**

CSF £24.81 TOTE £4.80: £1.80, £2.00, £1.70; EX 34.70.There was no bid for the winner.

Owner M C S D Racing Partnership **Bred** Mrs P J Makin **Trained** Moreton-in-Marsh, Gloucs

FOCUS

A poor seller and the form will mean little outside this level. The winner did not need to improve on his recent unplaced handicap runs.

Mango Piccle Official explanation: jockey said gelding ran very green

Inkjet(IRE) Official explanation: jockey said filly had no more to give

6403 LINGFIELD PARK FOR WEDDINGS MEDIAN AUCTION MAIDEN STKS 6f (P)

2:50 (2:51) (Class 6) 2-Y-O £2,266 (£674; £337; £168) Stalls Low

Form RPR

4 1 **Indian Diva (IRE)**[14] 6082 2-8-12 0 ....(b) NCallan 12 76+
(P A Blockley) *prom: trckd ldng pair 1/2-way: plld out 1f out: pushed into ld last 100yds: sn clr* **7/1**

2 1 1/2 **Haybrook** 2-9-3 0 .... ChrisCatlin 10 76
(E J O'Neill) *pressed ldr: rdn to ld narrowly over 1f out: hdd and outpcd last 100yds* **10/1**

4 3 1 **Classic Descent**[46] 5193 2-9-3 0 .... SebSanders 7 73
(P J Makin) *mde most: drvn and jnd over 2f out: narrowly hdd over 1f out: nt qckn* **5/2**[2]

4243 4 1 1/2 **Harrison George (IRE)**[11] 6156 2-9-3 80 .... PaulHanagan 5 69+
(R A Fahey) *nt wl plcd towards rr: shkn up and no prog over 2f out: drvn and r.o fr over 1f out: nrst fin but no ch* **2/1**[1]

5 nk **Al Aqabah (IRE)** 2-8-12 0 .... GregFairley 8 63
(B Gubby) *s.s: wl in rr: sme prog on inner 2f out: r.o fnl f: nrst fin* **50/1**

0 6 3 1/2 **Alabama Mama (IRE)**[14] 6087 2-8-12 0 .... MartinDwyer 3 52
(H J L Dunlop) *chsd ldng pair to 1/2-way: lft bhd fnl 2f* **50/1**

0 7 2 **Madame Bountiful**[14] 6087 2-8-12 0 .... FergusSweeney 2 46
(A King) *nvr beyond midfield: outpcd fr over 2f out* **25/1**

0 8 nk **Epsom Salts**[27] 5720 2-9-3 0 .... IanMongan 1 50
(P M Phelan) *dwlt: detached in last and drvn: nvr a factor: passed wkng rivals fnl f* **33/1**

0 9 1/2 **Yamanmickmccann**[8] 6234 2-9-3 0 .... DaneO'Neill 9 49
(R Hannon) *a wl in rr: bhd fnl 2f* **20/1**

10 1 1/4 **Coole Dodger (IRE)** 2-9-3 0 .... TQuinn 4 45
(B G Powell) *sn midfield: losing pl whn edgd rt 2f out: wknd* **50/1**

44 11 1 1/2 **Petit Parc**[136] 2457 2-8-12 0 .... EddieAhern 11 35
(R A Teal) *chsd ldrs: outpcd over 2f out: hanging bdly over 1f out: wknd* **5/1**[3]

00 12 1 3/4 **Lady Docker (IRE)**[21] 5881 2-8-12 0 .... RobertHavlin 6 30
(H J L Dunlop) *dwlt: hld up wl in rr: pushed along and no prog whn snatched up wl over 1f out* **66/1**

1m 12.29s (-0.52) **Going Correction** -0.125s/f (Stan) 12 Ran SP% **119.1**

Speed ratings (Par 93): **98,96,94,92,92 87,84,84,83,82 80,77**

CSF £69.83 TOTE £10.20: £2.50, £3.30, £1.50; EX 64.70.

Owner H Downs **Bred** Mountarmstrong Stud **Trained** Lambourn, Berks

FOCUS

An ordinary race which few ever got into, but the winning time was just over half a second faster than the preceding three-year-old seller. Just fair form.

NOTEBOOK

Indian Diva(IRE) was always handy and showed a fair turn of foot to pick off her two nearest rivals. She seemed to appreciate this surface better than the heavy ground on her Folkestone debut and should be up to winning another race or two on this surface if kept on the go. (op 8-1)

Haybrook, who fetched 38,000gns as a two-year-old, was also handy and showed plenty of ability to fare best of the newcomers. Out of a winning half-sister to two winners from the family of Mr Brooks, she should be able to go one better on this surface before too long. (op 11-1 tchd 9-1)

Classic Descent made much of the running and kept plugging away, showing enough to suggest his turn cannot be too far away. (op 2-1 tchd 11-4)

Harrison George(IRE) was messed about a little in the early stages, but whether it was enough to affect his chance is debatable. By far the most exposed in the field and already rated 80, he may not be easy to place from now on. (tchd 15-8 and 9-4)

Al Aqabah(IRE), a £50,000 two-year-old, ran an encouraging first race, especially as her stable is not renowned for winning debutantes.

6404 DIRECTORYOFTHETURF.COM MAIDEN AUCTION STKS (DIV II) 7f (P)

3:20 (3:21) (Class 5) 2-Y-O £2,169 (£645; £322; £161) Stalls Low

Form RPR

1 **King Hafhafah** 2-8-11 0 .... NCallan 4 72
(I A Wood) *trckd ldrs: effrt 2f out: pushed through gap 1f out to ld ins fnl f: a holding on* **25/1**

00 2 hd **Randama Bay (IRE)**[79] 4201 2-8-11 0 .... RichardThomas 2 71
(I A Wood) *mde most: drvn over 1f out: hdd ins fnl f: kpt on: a hld* **66/1**

4 3 nk **Southpaw Lad**[6] 6267 2-8-9 0 .... DaneO'Neill 10 68
(J R Best) *t.k.h early: in tch and racd wd: nt qckn wl over 1f out: styd on fnl f: gaining at fin* **3/1**[1]

4252 4 3/4 **City Hustler (USA)**[11] 6139 2-8-11 73 .... JohnEgan 9 68
(J S Moore) *chsd ldrs: rdn 2f out: tried to cl 1f out but could only stay on same pce: unable to chal* **3/1**[1]

0340 5 1 1/4 **Tina's Best (IRE)**[12] 6128 2-8-10 76 .... PatDobbs 1 64
(R Hannon) *pressed ldr: stl upsides on inner 1f out: wknd last 100yds* **9/2**[3]

4 6 1 3/4 **Nice Wee Girl (IRE)**[99] 3596 2-8-10 0 .... LPKeniry 8 60
(S Kirk) *in tch towards rr: shkn up 2f out: no prog and btn over 1f out* **8/1**

02 7 1/2 **Samurai Warrior**[32] 5605 2-8-11 0 .... SebSanders 3 59
(P J Makin) *chsd ldrs: no imp 2f out: wknd ins fnl f* **7/2**[2]

5000 8 shd **La Varrosa**[31] 5644 2-8-4 50 .... GregFairley 6 52
(Mrs P N Dutfield) *plld hrd early: lost pl over 5f out: in rr after: no prog 2f out: fdd* **80/1**

00 9 1 1/4 **Clear Daylight**[19] 5937 2-8-8 0 .... StephaneBreux(3) 7 56
(J R Best) *s.i.s: detached in last: reminder over 2f out and over 1f out: kpt on: nvr a factor* **20/1**

10 3 1/2 **Jalons Bridewell** 2-8-9 0 .... ChrisCatlin 5 45
(M Quinn) *hld up: effrt on outer over 4f out: wknd 2f out* **50/1**

1m 25.77s (-0.12) **Going Correction** -0.125s/f (Stan) **10** Ran SP% **114.8**

Speed ratings (Par 95): **95,94,94,93,92 90,89,89,88,84**

CSF £1033.68 TOTE £36.10: £5.80, £16.30, £1.50; EX 1580.40.

Owner Neardown Stables **Bred** J A Beckitt **Trained** Upper Lambourn, Berks

■ A big-priced 1-2 for trainer Ian Wood.

FOCUS

Another modest maiden but the form should prove reliable enough. The fourth and eighth dictate the level. The winning time was 0.09 seconds slower than the second division.

NOTEBOOK

King Hafhafah, a half-brother to two winners in Italy and one in Greece, showed a willing attitude in a tight finish and, as the stable is not renowned for debut winners, this was an encouraging start. (op 28-1 tchd 33-1)

Randama Bay(IRE) had the benefit of previous experience, though he had shown little in two starts on turf. After making much of the running, he battled on gamely all the way to the line and this was a major improvement. He now qualifies for a handicap mark.

Southpaw Lad, a major eyecatcher on his debut here last week, finished well down the outside again without ever quite being able to get to the Wood pair. There are still races to be won with him. (tchd 7-2)

City Hustler(USA) had every chance, but was more exposed than most in this and may be worth trying in a nursery. (op 7-2)
Tina's Best(IRE) disputed the lead for much of the way and found herself against the dreaded inside rail in the home straight, but nonetheless she looks very exposed now. (op 5-1)
Samurai Warrior was unsuited by the drop in trip, but he is now qualified for a handicap mark and is not one to give up on just yet. (op 3-1)

6405 WEATHERBYS BANK H'CAP 5f (P)
3:50 (3:51) (Class 5) (0-75,75) 3-Y-O+ £2,817 (£838; £418; £209) **Stalls** High

Form RPR
0010 1 **Hereford Boy**[11] 6157 3-9-1 **72** .... RobertHavlin 3 82+
(D K Ivory) *pushed along early in midfield: effrt over 1f out: urged along and r.o to ld ins fnl f: kpt on* **12/1**
0155 2 ½ **Desperate Dan**[31] 5648 6-9-2 **73** .... SebSanders 10 81
(A B Haynes) *wl in rr: rdn in last pair wl over 1f out: no prog tl r.o fnl f: clsng on wnr at fin* **11/2**[2]
0206 3 1 ½ **Bluebok**[41] 5332 6-9-4 **75** .... (t) DaneO'Neill 2 78
(J M Bradley) *led: rdn over 1f out: hdd and outpcd ins fnl f* **7/1**[3]
0002 4 1 ¼ **George The Second**[8] 6231 4-9-2 **73** .... GeorgeBaker 5 71
(Mrs H Sweeting) *chsd ldrs: rdn and nt qckn over 1f out: one pce after* **10/3**[1]
2300 5 shd **Tous Les Deux**[21] 5889 4-8-13 **70** .... LPKeniry 6 68
(Peter Grayson) *dwlt: settled in rr but in tch: gng wl enough over 1f out: rdn and nt qckn fnl f* **15/2**
3000 6 ¾ **Black Moma (IRE)**[10] 6173 3-9-1 **72** .... PatDobbs 4 67
(R Hannon) *trckd ldrs: effrt on inner and cl enough over 1f out: wknd ins fnl f* **12/1**
3132 7 shd **Dancing Mystery**[5] 6279 13-9-4 **75** .... (b) StephenCarson 7 70
(E A Wheeler) *pressed ldr to jst over 1f out: fdd* **8/1**
4134 8 2 ½ **Pic Up Sticks**[39] 5381 8-9-2 **73** .... TQuinn 8 59
(B G Powell) *racd on outer: trckd ldrs: rdn and nt qckn over 1f out: fdd* **11/2**[2]
4500 9 3 ½ **Egyptian Lord**[61] 4734 4-9-1 **72** .... AdamKirby 1 45
(Peter Grayson) *broke wl but sn lost pl: struggling in rr 2f out* **20/1**
0600 10 hd **Bold Minstrel (IRE)**[10] 6173 5-9-2 **73** .... ChrisCatlin 9 45
(M Quinn) *in tch: rdn and wknd wl over 1f out* **14/1**

59.40 secs (-0.38) **Going Correction** -0.125s/f (Stan) 10 Ran SP% **116.0**
Speed ratings (Par 103): **98,97,94,92,92 91,91,87,81,81**
CSF £76.30 CT £518.05 TOTE £16.30: £3.90, £1.20, £3.10; EX 107.00.
Owner T G N Burrage **Bred** Mrs L R Burrage **Trained** Radlett, Herts

FOCUS
A fair sprint handicap, although a couple had questions to answer. The runner-up is probably the best guide to the form.

6406 DIRECTORYOFTHETURF.COM H'CAP 6f (P)
4:20 (4:21) (Class 5) (0-70,70) 3-Y-O+ £2,817 (£838; £418; £209) **Stalls** Low

Form RPR
6304 1 **New York Oscar (IRE)**[72] 4432 3-8-12 **70** .... (p) RobbieEgan(7) 4 79
(A J McCabe) *chsd ldr's fast pce: effrt to ld jst over 2f out: hung rt over 1f out: kpt on wl fnl f* **12/1**
3000 2 ½ **Mine Behind**[81] 4122 7-9-5 **69** .... GeorgeBaker 5 77
(J R Best) *settled midfield: prog wl over 1f out: wnt 2nd ent fnl f and looked dangerous: kpt on same pce* **13/2**[3]
1034 3 shd **Maysarah (IRE)**[21] 5893 3-8-12 **66** .... WilliamBuick(3) 9 74
(G A Butler) *taken down early: t.k.h and hld up in last: prog wl over 1f out: r.o fnl f: gaining at fin* **5/1**[1]
0036 4 1 ½ **Sparkling Eyes**[40] 5358 3-9-3 **68** .... SebSanders 8 71
(C E Brittain) *dwlt: hld up wl in rr and off the pce: sme prog on inner over 1f out: kpt on: no ch* **8/1**
650 5 nk **Sun Catcher (IRE)**[42] 5312 4-9-0 **69** .... (b) HaddenFrost(5) 10 71
(R Hannon) *sn outpcd: pushed along wl over 3f out: no prog tl styd on fnl f: nrst fin* **11/2**[2]
1140 6 1 **Halsion Chancer**[130] 2631 3-9-3 **68** .... DaneO'Neill 3 67
(J R Best) *chsd ldng pair: wnt 2nd on inner over 1f out tl ent fnl f: wknd* **12/1**
2000 7 hd **High Ridge**[20] 5909 8-8-12 **62** .... (b[1]) LPKeniry 6 60
(J M Bradley) *mostly in midfield: drvn and struggling over 2f out: no ch after: kpt on ins fnl f* **20/1**
0402 8 2 ½ **Ede's Dot Com (IRE)**[35] 5495 3-8-12 **63** .... IanMongan 7 53
(P M Phelan) *chsd ldng trio: no imp 2f out: wknd over 1f out* **7/1**
0342 9 1 ¾ **Bucharest**[27] 5731 4-9-3 **67** .... (b) TQuinn 12 51
(M Wigham) *led at furious pce to jst over 2f out: wknd over 1f out* **5/1**[1]
0100 10 nk **Hollow Jo**[13] 6103 7-9-3 **67** .... NCallan 11 50
(J R Jenkins) *hld up and racd wd: outpcd fr 4f out: n.d after: eased ins fnl f* **10/1**
00-4 11 12 **Racing Stripes (IRE)**[180] 1270 3-9-5 **70** .... PatDobbs 1 15
(K O Cunningham-Brown) *in tch to 1/2-way: sn wknd: t.o* **25/1**

1m 11.6s (-1.21) **Going Correction** -0.125s/f (Stan)
WFA 3 from 4yo+ 1lb 11 Ran SP% **118.7**
Speed ratings (Par 103): **103,102,102,100,99 98,98,94,92,92 76**
CSF £88.85 CT £456.67 TOTE £20.10: £4.60, £2.20, £2.50; EX 137.30.
Owner Paul J Dixon and James Kennerley **Bred** Corduff Stud And J Judd **Trained** Babworth, Notts

FOCUS
Another fair handicap, although the majority did not come into the race in the greatest of form. The time was good and the race has been viewed fairly positively with the winner up 7lb.
Maysarah(IRE) Official explanation: jockey said filly was denied a clear run
Hollow Jo Official explanation: jockey said gelding hung left throughout

6407 ARENALEISUREPLC.COM H'CAP 1m 4f (P)
4:50 (4:50) (Class 6) (0-60,60) 3-Y-O+ £2,047 (£604; £302) **Stalls** Low

Form RPR
00-2 1 **Spanish Conquest**[10] 6178 3-8-8 **52** .... SebSanders 1 62+
(Sir Mark Prescott) *led 2f: trckd ldr: rdn to ld again over 3f out: styd on u.str.p fnl 2f* **4/5**[1]
3640 2 1 ¼ **Zalkani (IRE)**[15] 6068 7-9-7 **58** .... GeorgeBaker 6 66
(J Pearce) *hld up wl in rr: prog on inner 2f out: rdn and styd on fnl f: tk 2nd last 50yds: no threat to wnr* **8/1**[3]
5434 3 ½ **Sopran Gath (ITY)**[15] 6068 4-9-7 **58** .... EddieAhern 11 65
(J W Hills) *trckd ldrs: wnt 2nd gng easily over 2f out: rdn over 1f out: no rspnse: lost 2nd last 50yds* **7/1**[2]
0000 4 nk **Mid Valley**[55] 4945 4-8-9 **46** oh1 .... J-PGuillambert 12 53
(J R Jenkins) *t.k.h: hld up wl in rr: prog on outer wl over 2f out: nt qckn wl over 1f out: kpt on* **33/1**
0033 5 ½ **Summer Bounty**[21] 5886 11-8-9 **46** oh1 .... LPKeniry 8 52
(F Jordan) *stdd s: hld up wl in rr: sme prog on outer over 2f out: nt qckn over 1f out: kpt on fnl f* **20/1**
0004 6 nk **Little Richard (IRE)**[15] 6069 8-9-3 **57** .... (p) NeilChalmers(3) 14 62+
(M Wellings) *chsd ldrs: lost pl 3f out: nt qckn after: plld wd 1f out: r.o last 100yds: n.d* **16/1**
0620 7 shd **War Of The Roses (IRE)**[39] 5389 4-9-2 **53** .... ChrisCatlin 5 58
(R Brotherton) *chsd ldrs: rdn over 2f out: one pce and n.m.r after: kpt on fnl f* **17/2**
00/6 8 1 ½ **Mejhar (IRE)**[12] 5835 7-9-4 **58** .... AlanCreighton(3) 9 61
(E J Creighton) *mostly midfield: effrt over 2f out: one pce whn n.m.r 1f out* **66/1**
0-00 9 1 ½ **Safari Sundowner (IRE)**[13] 6102 3-9-2 **60** .... StephenCarson 13 60
(P Winkworth) *hld up in midfield: prog 4f out: chsd wnr 3f out to over 2f out: wkng whn n.m.r 1f out* **25/1**
0460 10 8 **Trevian**[10] 6179 6-9-3 **54** .... GregFairley 3 41
(J M Bradley) *led after 2f to over 3f out: sn wknd* **16/1**
0004 11 shd **Full Of Promise (USA)**[9] 6206 3-9-0 **58** .... PatDobbs 10 45
(Mrs A J Perrett) *prom: wkng whn n.m.r over 2f out* **11/1**
0500 12 7 **Hey Presto**[54] 4959 7-8-2 **46** oh1 .... RichardRowe(7) 4 22
(R Rowe) *dwlt: hld up in last: rapid prog on wd outside fr 6f out to dispute 2nd over 2f out: sn wknd rapidly* **66/1**
062- 13 13 **Coastal Breeze**[626] 291 4-9-4 **55** .... VinceSlattery 7 10
(A J Chamberlain) *a in rr: rdn and lost tch 5f out: t.o* **66/1**

2m 32.16s (-2.23) **Going Correction** -0.125s/f (Stan)
WFA 3 from 4yo+ 7lb 13 Ran SP% **125.8**
Speed ratings (Par 101): **102,101,100,100,100 100,100,99,98,92 92,87,79**
CSF £7.79 CT £32.46 TOTE £1.40: £1.30, £2.30, £1.80; EX 9.30 Place 6 £123.38, Place 5 £84.20.
Owner Neil Greig - Osborne House Ii **Bred** Miss K Rausing **Trained** Newmarket, Suffolk
■ Stewards' Enquiry : Richard Rowe caution: allowed gelding to coast home, losing two places

FOCUS
Unusually for races over middle distances here, they seemed to go a decent pace thanks to Trevian. However, front-runners have an abysmal record over this trip and he eventually faded right out of it. The time was decent and the form has been rated fairly positively, with the unexposed winner capable of better.
T/Plt: £194.20 to a £1 stake. Pool: £45,698.30. 171.70 winning tickets. T/Qpdt: £80.80 to a £1 stake. Pool: £3,243.70. 29.70 winning tickets. JN

5570 YARMOUTH (L-H)
Tuesday, October 23

OFFICIAL GOING: Soft (good to soft in places in straight; straight 6.9, back straight 6.3)
Wind: Fresh, across

6408 NORFOLK NELSON MUSEUM (S) STKS 1m 3f 101y
2:00 (2:00) (Class 6) 3-Y-O £1,943 (£578; £288; £144) **Stalls** Low

Form RPR
6062 1 **Etoile D'Or (IRE)**[13] 6108 3-8-7 51 .... JimmyQuinn 1 61+
(M H Tompkins) *mde all: sn clr: eased fnl f: unchal* **5/4**[1]
0000 2 14 **Ful Of Grace (IRE)**[25] 5774 3-8-7 50 ow5 .... (b[1]) JamieJones(5) 5 40
(M G Quinlan) *prom: rdn over 3f out: wknd over 2f out* **16/1**
0- 3 nk **Lap Of The Gods**[17] 6867 3-8-12 0 .... (p) AdrianMcCarthy 4 39
(Miss Z C Davison) *chsd wnr tl rdn and wknd over 2f out* **150/1**
60-4 4 3 ½ **Fasuby (IRE)**[15] 6060 3-8-8 50 ow1 .... TGMcLaughlin 6 30
(P D Evans) *hld up: rdn 1/2-way: wknd 4f out* **17/2**[3]
1061 5 3 ½ **Vietnam**[13] 6108 3-9-5 58 .... (b) JamieSpencer 7 35
(G A Huffer) *stdd s: hld up: hdwy over 3f out: rdn to go remote 2nd over 2f out: sn wknd* **11/8**[2]
0060 6 8 **First Frost**[13] 6108 3-8-11 39 ow4 .... StephenDonohoe 3 13
(M J Gingell) *hld up: hdwy over 7f out: rdn over 4f out: sn wknd* **150/1**
0260 7 72 **Iron Dancer (IRE)**[34] 5528 3-8-12 45 .... (b[1]) TPO'Shea 2 —
(P A Blockley) *chsd ldrs: rdn and wknd over 4f out: eased* **18/1**

2m 34.38s (6.88) **Going Correction** +0.625s/f (Yiel) 7 Ran SP% **109.5**
Speed ratings (Par 99): **99,88,88,86,83 77,25**
CSF £20.20 TOTE £1.90: £1.40, £4.30; EX 20.20.The winner was bought in for 12,000gns by M Gingell. Vietnam was claimed by V. Smith for £5,000.
Owner John Brenchley And Partners **Bred** T J Hurley And Simon And Mrs S Marriot **Trained** Newmarket, Suffolk

FOCUS
Only one horse mattered in what was a seriously uncompetitive seller, especially with Vietnam below par. The winner was up 5lb on this year's form.
Vietnam Official explanation: trainer was unable to explain the poor form shown

6409 EBF/MEDINA HOLE BIRTHDAY MAIDEN STKS 6f 3y
2:30 (2:38) (Class 5) 2-Y-O £3,562 (£1,059; £529; £264) **Stalls** High

Form RPR
1 **Wingbeat (USA)** 2-9-3 0 .... LDettori 16 87+
(Saeed Bin Suroor) *t.k.h: hld up wl in tch: hdwy to chse ldr wl over 1f out: rdn to ld ins fnl f: sn in command: readily* **11/4**[2]
62 2 2 ½ **Barbary Boy (FR)**[25] 5771 2-9-3 0 .... JamieSpencer 12 80+
(M L W Bell) *led stands' side and chsd overall ldr tl led wl over 1f out: rdn and hdd ins fnl f: no ch w wnr: eased nr fin* **5/2**[1]
5302 3 3 ½ **Faber Hall Flyer**[13] 6104 2-9-3 74 .... TGMcLaughlin 17 69
(Mrs C A Dunnett) *t.k.h: sn chsng ldrs: rdn 2f out: outpcd jst over 1f out: kpt on* **9/1**
4 ½ **Credit Swap** 2-9-3 0 .... JimmyFortune 9 68+
(L M Cumani) *s.i.s: t.k.h and sn chsng ldrs: rdn 2f out: outpcd by ldng pair 1f out: lost 3rd nr fin* **25/1**
60 5 nk **Hold That Call (USA)**[76] 4274 2-9-3 66 .... RichardMullen 8 67
(R Hannon) *plld hrd: hld up in tch: hdwy over 2f out: rdn wl over 1f out: outpcd fnl f* **25/1**
6 hd **Romantic Verse** 2-8-12 0 .... MichaelHills 2 61
(W J Haggas) *chsd ldrs: rdn 2f out: kpt on same pce fnl f* **20/1**
7 2 **Welsh Opera** 2-8-12 0 .... JimCrowley 10 55+
(Mrs A J Perrett) *s.i.s: bhd: kpt on steadily fnl f: nvr nr ldrs* **20/1**
8 shd **Parisian Gift (IRE)** 2-9-3 0 .... RichardKingscote 14 60+
(Tom Dascombe) *s.i.s: wl bhd: pushed along over 2f out: kpt on fnl f: nvr nr ldrs* **9/1**
9 ¾ **Too Hot To Handle (IRE)** 2-8-12 0 .... HayleyTurner 11 52
(J M P Eustace) *s.i.s: racd in midfield: rdn 1/2-way: sn struggling* **33/1**
10 1 **Laa Baas (IRE)** 2-8-12 0 .... PhilipRobinson 3 49+
(M A Jarvis) *racd alone in centre: overall ldr tl wl over 1f out: sn wknd* **20/1**
11 ½ **Valatrix (IRE)** 2-8-12 0 .... TedDurcan 6 48
(C F Wall) *s.i.s: sn chsng ldrs: rdn 2f out: sn wknd* **40/1**

The Form Book, Raceform Ltd, Compton, RG20 6NL

43 **12** *2* **Klarity**[14] 6073 2-8-12 0 JimmyQuinn 13 42
(J Pearce) *taken down early: plld v hrd: chsd ldr on stands' side tl wl over 1f out: sn wknd* **8/1**[3]

0 **13** *nk* **Admirals Way**[15] 6065 2-9-3 0 StephenDonohoe 7 46
(C N Kellett) *stdd after s: t.k.h: hld up in tch: rdn 2f out: sn wknd* **200/1**

14 *7* **Hula Hula** 2-8-12 0 SteveDrowne 5 20
(E A L Dunlop) *s.i.s: a bhd* **22/1**

15 *1* **Police Officer** 2-9-3 0 NeilPollard 15 22
(W J Musson) *chsd ldrs tl lost pl over 3f out: no ch last 2f* **125/1**

1m 15.74s (2.04) **Going Correction** +0.325s/f (Good) **15** Ran SP% **119.3**
Speed ratings (Par 95): **99,95,91,90,89 89,87,86,85,84 83,81,80,71,70**
CSF £8.38 TOTE £3.20: £1.70, £1.60, £2.50; EX 9.50 Trifecta £18.30 Pool: £251.25 - 9.71 winning units..
Owner Godolphin **Bred** Darley **Trained** Newmarket, Suffolk

FOCUS

Some powerful stables were represented, and there were no doubt some nice types for the future, but the bare form looks just fair behind the winner, who can go on to better things.

NOTEBOOK

Wingbeat(USA), a son of Elusive Quality, half-brother to 6f winner Vainglory, out of a high-class triple 6f-1m winner at two and three on turf and dirt, ran out a convincing winner on his racecourse debut. The bare form is probably just ordinary, but there was a lot to like about this performance and he looks a very useful performer in the making. It remains to be seen whether he will run again this year, but he is set to winter in Dubai. (op 3-1 tchd 100-30)
Barbary Boy(FR), runner-up over 6f at Haydock on his previous start, was produced to have every chance but just found the Godolphin newcomer too good. He spread a plate beforehand, but it didn't seem to affect him. (op 9-4)
Faber Hall Flyer has fair bits of form to his name and this was a respectable effort. He has an official rating of 74 and probably helps set the standard. (tchd 10-1)
Credit Swap, a 12,000gns son of Diktat, half-brother to 6f winner Vive Belle, out of a fair 5f winner at two, made a pleasing enough introduction on ground that his breeding suggests would suit. (op 20-1)
Hold That Call(USA), gelded since he was last seen, was too keen for his own good off the back of a near three-month break and this should have taken the freshness out of him. (op 33-1)
Romantic Verse, a daughter of Kyllachy, sister to Fervent, unplaced over 6-7f at three, made a pleasing enough debut and ought to improve.
Parisian Gift(IRE), a 60,000euros son of Statue Of Liberty, half-brother to quite useful 1m2f winner Sues Surprise, and dual 1m1f scorer Kova Hall, was well backed on his racecourse debut and was noted keeping on in the closing stages. (op 11-1)
Klarity Official explanation: jockey said filly ran too freely

6410 TOTESPORT.COM NURSERY 1m 3y

3:00 (3:07) (Class 5) (0-75,75) 2-Y-O **£3,562** (£1,059; £529; £264) **Stalls** High

Form RPR

16 **1** **Zaskar**[23] 5828 2-8-13 **67** RichardKingscote 12 75+
(Tom Dascombe) *s.s: hld up: plld hrd: racd centre: swtchd lft and hdwy over 1f out: r.o u.p to ld nr fin* **5/1**[2]

0552 **2** *nk* **Bavarian Nordic (USA)**[8] 6233 2-9-6 **74** SteveDrowne 16 78
(E A L Dunlop) *racd centre: chsd ldrs: rdn to ld over 1f out: hdd nr fin* **4/1**[1]

0652 **3** *1½* **Space Pirate**[35] 5509 2-8-3 **57** HayleyTurner 1 58+
(M L W Bell) *swtchd to r centre: hld up: hdwy and nt clr run over 2f out: swtchd rt over 1f out: sn rdn: styd on same pce ins fnl f* **12/1**

0363 **4** *nk* **Blue Citadel (USA)**[9] 6202 2-9-7 **75** JimmyFortune 10 75
(J H M Gosden) *racd centre: disp ld 6f: sn rdn: styd on same pce fnl f* **4/1**[1]

01 **5** *hd* **Mwindaji**[42] 5302 2-8-10 **64** MickyFenton 9 64
(Mrs P Sly) *racd centre: disp ld tl led over 2f out: rdn and hdd over 1f out: styd on same pce ins fnl f* **20/1**

06 **6** *¾* **Irish Artist (FR)**[53] 5010 2-9-3 **71** RyanMoore 15 69
(R Hannon) *racd centre: hld up: hdwy over 2f out: rdn over 1f out: styd on same pce* **15/2**[3]

0063 **7** *1* **Tiger's Rocket (IRE)**[27] 5729 2-8-7 **61** RichardMullen 17 57
(R Hannon) *racd centre: hld up: rdn over 2f out: no imp fnl f* **20/1**

000 **8** *nk* **Talon (IRE)**[40] 5343 2-8-2 **56** NickyMackay 14 52
(W J Haggas) *racd centre: chsd ldrs: rdn over 2f out: wknd ins fnl f* **14/1**

0015 **9** *1½* **Blue Rhapsody**[17] 6012 2-9-7 **75** JamieSpencer 8 68
(L M Cumani) *racd centre: hld up: hdwy over 2f out: sn rdn: wknd ins fnl f* **11/1**

0104 **10** *hd* **Imperial Decree**[33] 5571 2-9-7 **75** DarryllHolland 13 67
(John Berry) *racd centre: hld up: racd keenly: effrt and swtchd lft over 1f out: nt trble ldrs* **20/1**

023 **11** *2½* **Priceless Speedfit**[45] 5226 2-8-7 **61** ow1 PhilipRobinson 7 48
(G G Margarson) *racd centre: chsd ldrs: rdn over 2f out: wknd fnl f* **28/1**

0460 **12** *nk* **Pay Pay Pay**[25] 5766 2-7-13 **56** LukeMorris(3) 11 42
(P D Evans) *racd centre: chsd ldrs: rdn over 2f out: wknd over 1f out* **100/1**

0020 **13** *4* **Mahadee (IRE)**[21] 5883 2-9-4 **72** TedDurcan 5 50
(C E Brittain) *racd centre: prom: rdn over 3f out: wknd over 1f out* **33/1**

055 **14** *nk* **Kabuku**[26] 5749 2-9-0 **68** JimmyQuinn 3 45
(M H Tompkins) *led far side duo and up w centre gp tl wknd over 2f out: in rr whn hung rt over 1f out* **33/1**

064 **15** *hd* **Oxbridge**[15] 6058 2-8-11 **65** StephenDonohoe 2 42
(B J Meehan) *chsd ldr far side tl rdn over 2f out: wkng whn edgd rt sn after* **20/1**

1m 43.7s (3.80) **Going Correction** +0.325s/f (Good) **15** Ran SP% **120.5**
Speed ratings (Par 95): **94,93,92,91,91 90,89,89,88,87 85,85,81,80,80**
CSF £21.98 CT £238.87 TOTE £6.60: £2.70, £2.20, £2.90; EX 30.50 Trifecta £345.10 Pool: £510.41 - 1.05 winning units.
Owner P A Deal & M J Silver **Bred** Darley **Trained** Lambourn, Berks

FOCUS

A fair nursery won in decent style by Zaskar. Solid form. The winning time was 0.72 seconds slower than the first division of the maiden, and 0.38 seconds off the time recorded in the second division.

NOTEBOOK

Zaskar, a winner on her debut over 6f at Wolverhampton before running a creditable sixth in a hot 7f nursery at Ascot, improved for the step up to 1m and gained a narrow victory. She is said to have her share of temperament, but she is clearly pretty talented as well and, expected to make a nice three-year-old, she may well be put away for the year now. (op 11-2 tchd 9-2)
Bavarian Nordic(USA) ran to the same sort of form he showed when beaten just a short-head at Windsor on his previous start and can have few excuses. (tchd 9-2)
Space Pirate was racing off the same mark as when a distant second over 7f here on his previous start and this was a creditable run in defeat. (op 16-1)
Blue Citadel(USA) has some fair form to his name and this was another reasonable effort, but he gives the impression he can do even better on a quicker surface. (tchd 7-2)
Mwindaji, bought out of Mick Channon's yard after winning a 7f seller on fast ground at Leicester on his previous start, would have found this tougher and he ran with credit under these vastly different conditions.
Irish Artist(FR) looked a nursery type in the making when showing ability in three runs in maiden company and this was a respectable effort. (op 7-1 tchd 6-1)
Blue Rhapsody Official explanation: jockey said filly ran too freely
Imperial Decree Official explanation: trainer said filly was unsuited by the soft ground

6411 TOTESPORT 0800 221 221 MAIDEN FILLIES' STKS (DIV I) 1m 3y

3:30 (3:37) (Class 5) 2-Y-O **£2,266** (£674; £337; £168) **Stalls** High

Form RPR

4402 **1** **Miss Emma May (IRE)**[21] 5882 2-9-0 80 (v) JimmyFortune 2 80
(D R C Elsworth) *s.i.s: t.k.h and sn trcking ldrs: led over 1f out: drvn and forged clr fnl f* **8/1**

2 **2** *3* **Siyabona (USA)**[14] 6093 2-9-0 0 LDettori 11 74
(Saeed Bin Suroor) *rring in stalls: hld up in midfield: hdwy 3f out: ev ch ent fnl f: sn rdn and fnd little: jst hld 2nd* **7/2**[2]

3 *shd* **Wood Chorus** 2-9-0 0 JamieSpencer 5 73+
(M L W Bell) *hld up wl bhd: grad edgd rt wl over 1f out: r.o wl fnl f: nrly snatched 2nd* **20/1**

2 **4** *nk* **Quotation**[67] 4564 2-9-0 0 RyanMoore 9 75+
(Sir Michael Stoute) *hld up midfield: hdwy 3f out: rdn & chsng ldrs whn short of room & stmbld over 1f out: swtchd rt & styd on fnl f: nt rch ldrs* **5/4**[1]

32 **5** *½* **Riverscape (IRE)**[20] 5912 2-9-0 0 JimCrowley 14 72
(Mrs A J Perrett) *chsd ldrs: rdn and ev ch over 1f out: no ex fnl f* **12/1**

6 **6** *3½* **Rakeekah**[19] 5937 2-9-0 0 RHills 10 64
(J H M Gosden) *chsd ldrs: led over 2f out: sn rdn: hdd over 1f out: edgd lft and sn wknd* **11/2**[3]

0 **7** *shd* **Ethereal Flame**[20] 5913 2-9-0 0 TedDurcan 4 64
(H R A Cecil) *chsd ldr tl over 2f out: wkng whn bmpd over 1f out* **33/1**

0 **8** *4* **Broughtons Flight (IRE)**[14] 6093 2-9-0 0 NeilPollard 6 56
(W J Musson) *t.k.h: hld up in tch: nt clr run briefly over 2f out: sn rdn: wknd wl over 1f out* **125/1**

0 **9** *2½* **Kayflaa (IRE)**[24] 5812 2-9-0 0 DarryllHolland 3 51
(M R Channon) *led tl over 2f out: steadily wknd* **50/1**

10 *1½* **Turfani (IRE)** 2-9-0 0 PaulDoe 7 47
(W J Knight) *s.i.s: sn rdn along: a wl bhd* **100/1**

06 **11** *1¼* **Charlevoix (IRE)**[48] 5126 2-9-0 0 HayleyTurner 1 45
(C F Wall) *t.k.h: hld up in midfield: rdn and struggling 1/2-way: no ch after* **100/1**

12 *5* **Raaqia** 2-9-0 0 SteveDrowne 13 34
(B J Meehan) *v.s.a: a wl bhd* **33/1**

0 **13** *2½* **Where To Now**[33] 5570 2-9-0 0 TGMcLaughlin 12 29
(Mrs C A Dunnett) *taken down early: hld up in rr: rdn 3f out: sn struggling: no ch last 2f* **250/1**

1m 42.98s (3.08) **Going Correction** +0.325s/f (Good) **13** Ran SP% **116.6**
Speed ratings (Par 92): **97,94,93,93,93 89,89,85,83,81 80,75,72**
CSF £34.05 TOTE £8.70: £2.40, £1.60, £4.00; EX 39.30 Trifecta £489.80 Pool: £724.37 - 1.05 winning units.
Owner G B Partnership **Bred** Airlie Stud **Trained** Newmarket, Suffolk

FOCUS

A fair maiden in run in a time 0.72sec faster than the nursery, and 0.34sec quicker than the second division. The winner was right back to form and did it decisively.

NOTEBOOK

Miss Emma May(IRE) has an official rating of 80 so deserved respect in this grade, but she has disappointed before in maiden company and was allowed to drift out to 8-1. She ran out an authoritative winner in the end, though, and there could be better to come next year when she should get further than a mile. (op 6-1 tchd 11-2)
Siyabona(USA) travelled well for a long way and looked to hold every chance but inside the final furlong the winner left her behind. It would not be a surprise if she proves suited by quicker ground. (tchd 100-30 and 4-1)
Wood Chorus, a half-sister to Franklins Gardens, a high-class, multiple winner at up to 1m6f, and Polar Ben, a high-class multiple winner between 7f and a mile, ran well on her debut considering that she hails from a stable whose juveniles invariably improve for their debuts and she is bred to excel over middle distances next season. (op 16-1)
Quotation took time to pick up and then got badly hampered approaching the furlong marker. That dropped her back and then she struggled to get back into it. She would have undoubtedly been closer had she enjoyed a clear run. (op 11-8 tchd 6-4)
Riverscape(IRE), who got run out of third close home, is now eligible for handicaps, and the likelihood is that she will be put away for the year now. Middle distances should suit next season. (op 11-1)
Rakeekah had learnt plenty from her debut and showed up well for a long way this time. She might just have found the trip in this ground stretching her at this stage of her career, though. (op 8-1)

6412 JUNE, KAREN AND PAULA ARE HAPPY CLAIMING STKS 1m 3y

4:00 (4:07) (Class 6) 3-Y-O+ **£2,072** (£616; £308; £153) **Stalls** High

Form RPR

3415 **1** **Boundless Prospect (USA)**[17] 6016 8-9-8 78 NicolPolli(5) 6 81
(Miss Gay Kelleway) *hld up: racd centre: hdwy over 3f out: led over 2f out: sn edgd rt: rdn out* **2/1**[1]

0003 **2** *3* **Al Rayanah**[7] 6247 4-8-6 48 SaleemGolam 16 53
(G Prodromou) *s.i.s: swtchd to r centre: hdwy over 5f out: rdn to chse wnr over 1f out: edgd lft: styd on same pce* **14/1**

0 **3** *2* **Sibo Baggins (IRE)**[130] 2625 3-8-9 0 NataliaGemelova(5) 4 59
(J S Moore) *racd centre: s.i.s: hdwy over 2f out: sn rdn and edgd rt: no ex fnl f* **40/1**

6425 **4** *3½* **Split Briefs (IRE)**[50] 5102 3-8-5 63 TPO'Shea 15 42
(C A Dwyer) *racd stands' side: chsd ldrs: rdn over 2f out: wknd fnl f* **14/1**

0006 **5** *¾* **Tempsford Flyer (IRE)**[14] 6088 4-9-8 68 PatrickHills(5) 5 60
(J W Hills) *racd centre: hld up: hdwy over 3f out: rdn over 1f out: sn wknd* **8/1**

4120 **6** *3* **Rowan Lodge (IRE)**[8] 6226 5-8-8 64 HarryPoulton(7) 9 41
(J R Boyle) *racd centre: chsd ldr: led over 2f out: sn rdn and hdd: wknd over 1f out* **9/2**[3]

4500 **7** *1¾* **Music Celebre (IRE)**[41] 5338 7-9-1 55 (e1) PaulDoe 17 37
(S Curran) *racd stands' side: sn pushed along in rr: sme hdwy over 2f out: sn rdn and wknd* **25/1**

0454 **8** *2½* **Mineral Star (IRE)**[6] 6268 5-9-3 72 (b1) JimmyQuinn 7 33
(M H Tompkins) *racd centre: chsd ldrs: rdn and ev ch over 2f out: wknd over 1f out* **4/1**[2]

5400 **9** *5* **Joy And Pain**[20] 5909 6-8-6 50 (v) KevinGhunowa(5) 12 15
(M J Attwater) *racd stands' side tl swtchd centre over 5f out: mid-div: hdwy 1/2-way: rdn and wknd wl over 1f out* **16/1**

0-00 **10** *1* **Only Hope**[31] 5636 3-8-5 55 (p) PaulEddery 2 10
(Miss Diana Weeden) *racd centre: bhd fr 1/2-way* **100/1**

2000 **11** *shd* **Surdoue**[13] 6096 7-8-9 44 AdrianMcCarthy 11 11
(D Morris) *racd stands' side: led those to 1/2-way: rdn over 2f out: sn wknd* **28/1**

0600 **12** *nk* **Joint Expectations (IRE)**[41] 5338 3-8-7 48 ow1.......(b) MickyFenton 10 11
(Mrs C A Dunnett) *led centre over 5f: wkng whn hmpd sn after* **50/1**

0040 **13** *1* **Government (IRE)**[64] 4668 6-8-8 48.................... RussellKennemore(5) 1 12
(M C Chapman) *racd centre: chsd ldrs to 1/2-way* **80/1**

0-04 **14** *3/4* **Swallow Senora (IRE)**[55] 4938 5-8-3 40....................(t) DominicFox(3) 13 3
(M C Chapman) *s.i.s: racd centre: a in rr* **100/1**

0006 **15** *1 1/4* **She's Dunnett**[28] 5714 4-8-4 40......................................(t) HayleyTurner 3 —
(Mrs C A Dunnett) *racd centre: chsd ldrs over 4f* **80/1**

0 **16** *20* **Gracefull Model**[27] 5728 3-8-8 0 ow3............................ TGMcLaughlin 8 —
(Mrs C A Dunnett) *racd centre: sn outpcd* **125/1**

1m 43.87s (3.97) **Going Correction** +0.325s/f (Good)
WFA 3 from 4yo+ 3lb **16** Ran SP% **118.8**
Speed ratings (Par 101): **93,90,88,84,83 80,79,76,71,70 70,70,69,68,67 47**
CSF £31.13 TOTE £2.90: £1.40, £3.20, £17.60; EX 36.80 TRIFECTA Not won..
Owner M M Foulger **Bred** Mrs Edgar Scott Jr & Mrs Lawrence Macelree **Trained** Exning, Suffolk
■ Sawwaah was withdrawn (6/1, injured in paddock). R4 applies, deduct 10p in the £.

FOCUS
An ordinary claimer containing a mixed bag of abilities. The form seems to make sense.
Joint Expectations(IRE) Official explanation: trainer said gelding had been struck into

6413 BANHAM POULTRY H'CAP 7f 3y
4:30 (4:37) (Class 6) (0-65,65) 3-Y-0+ **£3,238** (£963; £481; £240) **Stalls** High

Form RPR

0051 **1** **Seneschal**[8] 6226 6-9-4 **61**.. JamieSpencer 9 71
(A B Haynes) *chsd ldr in centre: led 2f out: rdn over 1f out: styd on wl* **6/1**[2]

1304 **2** *1 1/4* **Encores**[31] 5645 3-9-5 **64**.. JimmyFortune 11 71
(N A Callaghan) *chsd ldrs in centre: hdwy to chse wnr 2f out: kpt on same pce u.p* **9/1**

-402 **3** *3/4* **Obe Royal**[7] 6256 3-9-1 **60**..(p) TGMcLaughlin 14 65
(P D Evans) *racd stands' side: rdn over 2f out: kpt on u.p fnl f: nt rch ldrs* **11/2**[1]

510 **4** *1/2* **Mick Is Back**[58] 4858 3-9-2 **61**...(p) RyanMoore 12 65
(G G Margarson) *hld up towards rr in centre: hdwy and rdn over 2f out: kpt on u.p: nt rch ldrs* **8/1**[3]

0200 **5** *1/2* **Dr Synn**[20] 5917 6-9-0 **62**... KirstyMilczarek(5) 6 64
(J Akehurst) *chsd ldrs in centre: rdn wl over 2f out: kpt on same pce* **20/1**

0100 **6** *3* **Life's A Whirl**[34] 5546 5-9-0 **57**.......................................(p) MickyFenton 7 51
(Mrs C A Dunnett) *t.k.h: hld up towards rr in centre: rdn and effrt wl over 1f out: plugged on but nvr threatened ldrs* **22/1**

0160 **7** *shd* **Border Artist**[12] 6123 8-9-1 **58**... JimmyQuinn 2 52
(J Pearce) *stdd and dropped in bhd in centre after s: hdwy 2f out: no imp over 1f out* **8/1**[3]

2320 **8** *shd* **Tilsworth Charlie**[14] 6089 4-9-1 **58**.................................(b) TedDurcan 15 52
(J R Jenkins) *racd stands' side: wl bhd: drvn 2f out: sme modest late hdwy: nvr on terms* **10/1**

53-0 **9** *nk* **Sorrel Point**[12] 6123 4-8-12 **58**.................................... JerryO'Dwyer(3) 10 51
(H J Collingridge) *hld up in midfield in centre: rdn over 2f out: sn no imp* **16/1**

3006 **10** *5* **Empire Dancer (IRE)**[21] 5893 4-9-5 **62**...................... RichardMullen 16 42
(C N Allen) *led stands' side gp tl over 1f out: sn wknd* **20/1**

0003 **11** *1/2* **Bonne D'Argent (IRE)**[8] 6226 3-9-6 **65**............................... JimCrowley 4 44
(J R Boyle) *in tch in centre: rdn over 2f out: sn no hdwy* **14/1**

0445 **12** *2 1/2* **Postsprofit (IRE)**[18] 5985 3-9-1 **60**........................... StephenDonohoe 1 32
(N A Callaghan) *racd alone on far side: prom tl led overall over 4f out: hdd 2f out: sn wknd* **16/1**

0004 **13** *1/2* **Smokin Beau**[55] 4944 10-9-1 **63**..................................... PatrickHills(5) 5 34
(N P Littmoden) *led in centre and overall tl over 4f out: rdn over 3f out: wknd 2f out: eased ins fnl f* **25/1**

4-60 **14** *1 3/4* **Royal Choir**[28] 5714 3-9-6 **65**.. HayleyTurner 3 31
(C E Brittain) *in tch in centre: rdn wl over 2f out: sn btn* **50/1**

1040 **15** *1 1/4* **Billy Red**[5] 6287 3-9-6 **65**.. TPO'Shea 13 28
(J R Jenkins) *t.k.h: hld up towards rr in centre: rdn over 2f out: sn wl bhd* **50/1**

0363 **16** *3/4* **Our Ruby**[14] 6083 3-9-3 **62**.......................................(b) AdrianMcCarthy 8 23
(P W Chapple-Hyam) *racd in centre: early reminders: bhd and drvn over 4f out: nvr on terms* **14/1**

6200 **17** *3 1/2* **Convallaria (FR)**[35] 5494 4-9-1 **58**................................ SteveDrowne 17 10
(G Wragg) *bhd on stands' side: drvn over 2f out: no hdwy* **16/1**

1m 29.04s (2.44) **Going Correction** +0.325s/f (Good)
WFA 3 from 4yo+ 2lb **17** Ran SP% **123.6**
Speed ratings (Par 101): **99,97,96,96,95 92,92,91,91,85 85,82,81,79,78 77,73**
CSF £54.10 CT £320.97 TOTE £5.50: £1.70, £2.30, £2.00, £2.20; EX 77.00 Trifecta £193.70 Part won. Pool: £272.90 - 0.45 winning units..
Owner P Cook **Bred** Michael E Broughton **Trained** Limpley Stoke, Bath

FOCUS
Modest handicap form but sound enough for the grade. The winner did not nned to improve on this year's form.
Billy Red Official explanation: jockey said gelding ran too freely

6414 TOTESPORT 0800 221 221 MAIDEN FILLIES' STKS (DIV II) 1m 3y
5:00 (5:05) (Class 5) 2-Y-O **£2,266** (£674; £337; £168) **Stalls** High

Form RPR

1 **Michita (USA)** 2-9-0 0.. JimmyFortune 2 82+
(J H M Gosden) *hld up in tch: chsd ldr over 1f out: styd on to ld wl ins fnl f* **11/1**

0 **2** *1/2* **Dove (IRE)**[11] 6140 2-9-0 0.. LDettori 8 81+
(Saeed Bin Suroor) *led: rdn over 1f out: hdd wl ins fnl f* **6/1**[3]

3 *1 3/4* **Dancing Abbie (USA)** 2-9-0 0.. JamieSpencer 9 77+
(M L W Bell) *hld up: hdwy 1/2-way: edgd lft over 2f out: sn rdn: styd on same pce fnl f* **17/2**

4 *4* **Montbretia** 2-9-0 0.. TedDurcan 5 69
(H R A Cecil) *trckd ldrs: shkn up over 2f out: wknd over 1f out* **7/2**[1]

5 **5** *3* **Inchwood (IRE)**[20] 5912 2-9-0 0.................................. PhilipRobinson 4 63
(M A Jarvis) *chsd ldrs: rdn over 2f out: sn wknd* **5/1**[2]

54 **6** *2 1/2* **Tomorrow's World (IRE)**[73] 4393 2-9-0 0........................ RyanMoore 1 57
(Sir Michael Stoute) *chsd ldr: rdn and ev ch over 2f out: wknd over 1f out* **7/2**[1]

7 *5* **Light Sea (IRE)** 2-9-0 0... DarryllHolland 6 47
(M R Channon) *sn pushed along in rr: bhd 1/2-way: nvr nrr* **18/1**

66 **8** *3/4* **Reclamation (IRE)**[11] 6140 2-9-0 0............................. JamieMackay 11 45
(Sir Mark Prescott) *hld up: n.d* **25/1**

00 **9** *hd* **Krisnando**[21] 5882 2-9-0 0... PaulDoe 10 45
(W J Knight) *hld up: hdwy over 5f out: rdn and wknd over 1f out* **33/1**

10 *3/4* **Princess Gee** 2-9-0 0.. AdrianMcCarthy 3 43
(B J McMath) *hld up: rdn over 3f out: sn wknd* **100/1**

0 **11** *1* **Stones Of Venice (IRE)**[46] 5202 2-9-0 0........................ OscarUrbina 13 41
(J R Fanshawe) *hld up: effrt over 3f out: wknd over 2f out* **33/1**

0 **12** *3/4* **Coloratura (IRE)**[19] 5949 2-9-0 0................................ TGMcLaughlin 7 40
(E A L Dunlop) *hld up: sme hdwy over 2f out: sn wknd* **16/1**

5000 **13** *10* **Eye Catching**[8] 6234 2-9-0 57.. TPO'Shea 12 19
(J R Jenkins) *chsd ldrs over 5f* **100/1**

1m 43.32s (3.42) **Going Correction** +0.325s/f (Good) **13** Ran SP% **117.1**
Speed ratings (Par 92): **95,94,92,88,85 83,78,77,77,76 75,74,64**
CSF £71.85 TOTE £14.60: £4.30, £2.00, £3.00; EX 97.60 Trifecta £229.60 Part won. Pool: £323.42 - 0.35 winning units..
Owner Stoneside Stable Llc **Bred** Stoneside Stable **Trained** Newmarket, Suffolk

FOCUS
A fair maiden on paper and the race should work out as the first three came nicely clear. The winning time was 0.34sec slower than the first division, but 0.38 sec quicker than the nursery.

NOTEBOOK
Michita(USA), a half-sister to among others Thunder Mission, a multiple winner at around 6f to 1m1f in the US, scored a pleasing debut success and looks the type to improve next year as she has plenty of scope. She should get middle distances next season and looks a useful prospect. (op 14-1)
Dove(IRE) did not show a great deal on her debut on Polytrack but racing on soft turf was always going to suit this daughter of Sadler's Wells better, and she improved a ton on that debut effort. Another middle-distance prospect for next year, she might well find a maiden under similar conditions before the turf season is finished. (op 8-1)
Dancing Abbie(USA), a half-sister to Jupiter Knight, a dual winner on turf in the US at four, out of a Del Mar Oaks winner, travelled well on her debut but could not quite live with the first two late on. She is entitled to improve for the run and for better ground. (op 12-1)
Montbretia, a half-sister to Portland, a 7f winner at three, and Art Work, a 1m winner at three, kept on for fourth without threatening the leaders. She is bred to want 1m4f next year and this was a perfectly acceptable debut effort. (op 9-2)
Inchwood(IRE), whose dam was a smart middle-distance performer, may not have been ideally suited by the softer ground, and perhaps that was factored into the betting as she drifted badly beforehand. (op 5-2)
Tomorrow's World(IRE) is another who was probably not at home in the soft ground. On the plus side, she is now eligible for a handicap mark. (tchd 3-1)
Light Sea(IRE), a half-sister to a number of winners, including Hurricane Alan, a high-class multiple winner over 6f to 1m, seemed to be getting the hang of things late in the day and should improve for the experience. (op 14-1 tchd 20-1)

6415 NORFOLK CHAMBER OF COMMERCE H'CAP 6f 3y
5:30 (5:32) (Class 6) (0-60,60) 3-Y-0+ **£2,914** (£867; £433; £216) **Stalls** High

Form RPR

014 **1** **Memphis Man**[7] 6247 4-9-3 **57**.. TGMcLaughlin 17 70
(P D Evans) *s.i.s: wl bhd: drvn over 2f out: str run 1f out: led last 50yds* **9/1**[3]

002 **2** *1 3/4* **Mugeba**[34] 5546 6-8-9 **54**..(t) NicolPolli(5) 7 62
(Miss Gay Kelleway) *s.i.s: wl bhd: rdn 3f out: grad edgd to stands' rail: r.o strly fnl f: wnt 2nd last strides* **6/1**[2]

2020 **3** *hd* **Bens Georgie (IRE)**[20] 5897 5-8-13 **53**............................ TedDurcan 15 60
(D K Ivory) *towards rr: rdn and struggling wl over 2f out: styd on u.p fnl f: wnt 3rd nr fin* **12/1**

1440 **4** *1/2* **Kennington**[25] 5778 7-9-0 **54**... NeilPollard 6 59
(Mrs C A Dunnett) *led: hrd pressed and rdn wl over 1f out: hdd and no ex last 50yds* **22/1**

0041 **5** *1/2* **Monashee Prince (IRE)**[9] 6210 5-9-5 **59** 6ex...............(v) JimmyQuinn 4 63
(J R Best) *in tch: hdwy over 2f out: rdn to chal ent fnl f: no ex last 75yds* **10/1**

0351 **6** *1* **Stormburst (IRE)**[19] 5947 3-8-8 **56**........................ WilliamCarson(7) 13 57
(S C Williams) *chsd ldrs: rdn and ev ch wl over 1f out: fdd last 100yds* **9/1**[3]

04 **7** *2* **Majestical (IRE)**[6] 6264 5-8-12 **52**.....................................(p) DarryllHolland 5 46
(V Smith) *wl bhd: rdn wl over 2f out: kpt on fnl f: nvr nr ldrs* **10/1**

0434 **8** *1 1/4* **Marmooq**[10] 6179 4-8-7 **52**...(v) KevinGhunowa(5) 3 42
(M J Attwater) *chsd ldrs: rdn 1/2-way: wknd wl over 1f out* **12/1**

5320 **9** *3/4* **Norcroft**[33] 5576 5-8-12 **57**.......................................(p) KirstyMilczarek(5) 10 45
(Mrs C A Dunnett) *chsd ldrs: rdn wl over 2f out: sn struggling* **14/1**

3230 **10** *shd* **O Fourlunda**[20] 5915 3-9-5 **60**.. HayleyTurner 12 47
(C E Brittain) *racd in midfield: rdn and n.m.r over 2f out: n.d* **20/1**

3040 **11** *3/4* **Registrar**[41] 5340 5-8-13 **53**.. StephenDonohoe 9 38
(Mrs C A Dunnett) *hld up in midfield: rdn and effrt over 2f out: sn edgd lft and no imp* **10/1**

0012 **12** *2 1/2* **Forced Upon Us**[9] 6210 3-8-13 **54**.................................(b) JamieSpencer 1 31
(P J McBride) *hld up bhd: rdn and effrt 2f out: nvr on terms* **7/2**[1]

0000 **13** *1 1/2* **Loves Bidding**[13] 6101 3-9-0 **55**.. DavidKinsella 2 27
(R Ingram) *racd in midfield: rdn over 2f out: sltly hmpd 2f out: no hdwy after* **66/1**

0600 **14** *10* **Charming Ballet (IRE)**[22] 5866 4-8-8 **53**.......................... PatrickHills(5) 11 —
(N P Littmoden) *chsd ldrs tl rdn and wknd jst over 2f out: t.o fnl f* **33/1**

006 **15** *5* **Wattys The Craic**[10] 6176 3-8-12 **53**.................................. SaleemGolam 8 —
(G Prodromou) *sn outpcd in last: t.o over 1f out* **100/1**

0100 **16** *15* **Anfield Dream**[13] 6101 5-9-4 **58**... MickyFenton 16 —
(J R Jenkins) *racd alone on stands' side: prom tl wknd rapidly 2f out: t.o* **33/1**

1m 15.53s (1.83) **Going Correction** +0.325s/f (Good)
WFA 3 from 4yo+ 1lb **16** Ran SP% **123.3**
Speed ratings (Par 101): **100,97,97,96,96 94,92,90,89,89 88,84,82,69,62 42**
CSF £58.96 CT £695.32 TOTE £10.30: £2.40, £2.30, £2.50, £6.20; EX 67.80 TRIFECTA Not won. Place 6 £48.46, Place 5 £23.98..
Owner M D Jones **Bred** R T And Mrs Watson **Trained** Pandy, Monmouths

FOCUS
An ordinary handicap but the leaders went quick and the form looks solid enough rated through the third and fourth.
Marmooq Official explanation: jockey said gelding hung right and left
Norcroft Official explanation: jockey said gelding was unsuited by the soft, good to soft in places going
Forced Upon Us Official explanation: jockey said gelding was unsuited by the soft, good to soft in places going
Wattys The Craic Official explanation: jockey said colt hung right
Anfield Dream Official explanation: jockey said gelding stopped quickly
T/Jkpt: £13,152.40 to a £1 stake. Pool: £287,131.88. 15.50 winning tickets. T/Plt: £43.80 to a £1 stake. Pool: £72,207.65. 1,202.85 winning tickets. T/Qpdt: £18.70 to a £1 stake. Pool: £4,405.30. 174.30 winning tickets. SP

6400 DEAUVILLE (R-H)

Tuesday, October 23

OFFICIAL GOING: Turf course - good to soft; all-weather - standard

6416a PRIX DES RESEVOIRS (GROUP 3) (FILLIES) 1m (R)

1:50 (1:49) 2-Y-O **£27,027** (£10,811; £8,108; £5,405; £2,703)

RPR

1 **Gagnoa (IRE)**[16] 6040 2-8-9 .... CSoumillon 7 102
(Y De Nicolay, France) *broke w ldr: sn settled bhd ldr: led ent st: drvn out* **13/1**

2 *1 1/2* **Gipson Dessert (USA)**[66] 4625 2-8-9 .... C-PLemaire 5 99
(J-C Rouget, France) *hld up: wnt 5th st: hdwy wl over 1f out: 2nd 1f out: r.o but nvr rchd wnr* **1/2**[1]

3 *nse* **African Rose**[36] 5493 2-8-9 .... SPasquier 6 99
(Mme C Head-Maarek, France) *s.i.s: sn in tch: last st: swtchd outside wl over 1f out: hdwy to dispute 2nd ins fnl f: r.o* **52/10**[2]

4 *1 1/2* **Seal Bay (IRE)**[15] 2-8-9 .... DBoeuf 2 95
(D Smaga, France) *racd in 5th: 6th st: styd on fr dist: nvr in position to chal* **10/1**

5 *1* **Blue Ciel**[25] 2-8-9 .... TThulliez 3 93
(P Bary, France) *trckd ldrs: 3rd st: disp 2nd at dist: one pce* **9/1**[3]

6 *2* **Luna Royale (IRE)**[32] 5612 2-8-9 .... JVictoire 4 89+
(H-A Pantall, France) *cl up: 4th st: disp 2nd at dist: btn whn sltly hmpd by 4th ins fnl f* **9/1**[3]

7 *4* **Fleurina (FR)**[17] 2-8-9 .... J-BHamel 8 80
(Robert Collet, France) *7th st: a in rr* **27/1**

8 *nk* **Lady Jane Digby**[23] 5843 2-8-9 .... J-BEyquem 1 79
(M Johnston) *led to st: wknd over 1f out* **22/1**

1m 45.3s (3.00) 8 Ran SP% **126.9**

PARI-MUTUEL: WIN 14.00; PL 1.40, 1.10, 1.20; DF 9.40.

Owner Aleyrion Bloodstock Ltd **Bred** Quay Bloodstock **Trained** France

FOCUS

An improved effort from the winner, with the runner-up to form.

NOTEBOOK

Gagnoa(IRE) got a good tow from Lady Jane Digby then kicked clear off the home bend and was driven right out. Her trainer, who blames himself for messing up her preparation for the Marcel Boussac, will now put her away and aim her at the Prix de Diane which, as a daughter of Sadler's Wells from the family of High Accolade and Awaasif, is no forlorn target.

Gipson Dessert(USA) suffered her first defeat and was beaten fair and square, making ground through the final quarter mile but never looking like reeling in the winner and only just getting up for second.

African Rose recovered from a slow start but was last rounding the final turn. Coming with a a strong run down the outside, she only just lost out in a good battle for second throughout the last furlong.

Seal Bay(IRE) plugged on from sixth place turning in without ever suggesting she would be involved in the finish.

Lady Jane Digby was allowed her own way in front but does not appear to be up to this level.

6194 BATH (L-H)

Wednesday, October 24

OFFICIAL GOING: Good (good to soft in places in back straight)

Wind: Moderate behind Weather: Overcast

6417 HADEN YOUNG MAIDEN STKS (DIV I) 1m 5y

2:00 (2:02) (Class 5) 2-Y-O **£2,266** (£674; £337; £168) **Stalls Low**

Form RPR

0 1 **Colony (IRE)**[54] 5010 2-9-3 0 .... RyanMoore 4 74+
(Sir Michael Stoute) *chsd ldrs: rdn to ld ins fnl f: r.o* **15/8**[1]

3 2 *2* **Roman Legion (IRE)**[8] 6255 2-9-3 0 .... JamieSpencer 8 70
(P A Blockley) *chsd ldr tl led over 2f out: rdn and hdd ins fnl f: styd on same pce* **13/2**[3]

0 3 *1* **World Of Choice (USA)**[41] 5361 2-9-3 0 .... TedDurcan 9 68
(Saeed Bin Suroor) *chsd ldrs: rdn over 2f out: styd on same pce fnl f* **5/1**[2]

0 4 *1* **Cossack Prince**[19] 5977 2-9-3 0 .... RichardHughes 1 66
(B J Meehan) *led: hdd over 2f out: rdn and edgd lft over 1f out: no ex ins fnl f* **12/1**

0 5 *nk* **Royal Straight**[13] 6130 2-9-0 0 .... WilliamBuick(3) 3 65+
(A M Balding) *mid-div: hdwy over 3f out: sn rdn: styd on same pce appr fnl f* **20/1**

5 6 *nk* **Spiritonthemount (USA)**[15] 6079 2-9-3 0 .... JimmyFortune 5 64+
(B W Hills) *s.i.s: hld up: nt clr run over 4f out: hdwy u.p over 1f out: nrst fin* **15/2**

00 7 *1 1/4* **Mista Rossa**[13] 6130 2-9-0 0 .... TravisBlock(3) 6 62+
(H Morrison) *mid-div: effrt over 2f out: no imp* **50/1**

0 8 *1* **River N' Blues (IRE)**[61] 4761 2-8-7 0 .... KevinGhunowa(5) 13 54
(Dr J R J Naylor) *mid-div: hdwy 1/2-way: rdn over 2f out: wknd fnl f* **100/1**

0 9 *hd* **Promised Gold**[21] 5918 2-9-3 0 .... DavidKinsella 11 59+
(J A Geake) *prom: rdn over 2f out: wknd fnl f* **100/1**

10 *3* **Toll Gate (IRE)** 2-8-12 0 .... RichardKingscote 12 47+
(R Charlton) *hld up: shkn up over 2f out: nvr trbld ldrs* **33/1**

0 11 *nk* **Special Feature (IRE)**[16] 6058 2-9-3 0 .... RobertHavlin 2 52
(C R Egerton) *dwlt: sn prom: rdn and wknd over 2f out* **50/1**

60 12 *nk* **Gunnadoit (USA)**[28] 5720 2-9-3 0 .... (b[1]) RichardThomas 7 51
(C G Cox) *s.i.s: hld up: rdn over 3f out: a in rr* **66/1**

13 *shd* **Elliwan** 2-9-3 0 .... GregFairley 10 51
(M Johnston) *sn pushed along: a in rr* **8/1**

60 14 *1 1/4* **Berrynarbor**[83] 4094 2-8-12 0 .... LPKeniry 14 43
(A G Newcombe) *hld up: a in rr: bhd whn nt clr run over 1f out* **28/1**

1m 43.76s (2.66) **Going Correction** +0.075s/f (Good) 14 Ran SP% **113.9**

Speed ratings (Par 95): **89,87,86,85,84 84,83,82,81,78 78,78,78,77**

CSF £11.98 TOTE £2.40: £1.10, £1.90, £2.00; EX 13.20 Trifecta £19.50 Pool £134.09. - 4.87 winning units..

Owner Highclere Thoroughbred Racing (Delilah) **Bred** Barronstown Stud And Orpendale **Trained** Newmarket, Suffolk

FOCUS

A fair-looking maiden in which the jockeys all came to the stands' side down the straight, but the winning time was 1.33 seconds slower than the second division. The winner did not need to find much improvement and several othes including the runner-up were close to their pre-race marks.

NOTEBOOK

Colony(IRE) ◆ got going fairly late to win going away. A fine-looking sort and the most expensive yearling colt sold from his sire's first crop, he was one of many in the field who seem sure to make their mark next year. (op 13-8 tchd 2-1 in a place)

Roman Legion(IRE) was kept close to the pace throughout and looked to be going the best turning in. However, although he stayed on well for pressure, he could not resist the challenge of the winner and was beaten by a better horse on the day. His turn will undoubtedly come. (op 6-1 tchd 7-1)

World Of Choice(USA) held nice entries early but has seemingly taken time to come to hand. This was an improved effort and he is at least heading in the right direction. (op 9-2 tchd 4-1)

Cossack Prince set the fairly sedate gallop early and had the run of the race. It was certainly an improvement on his debut performance at Newmarket. (tchd 10-1)

Royal Straight was never far away and kept on well in the latter stages. He will be better in time. (op 22-1)

Spiritonthemount(USA) ◆ took time to get organised early, much like on his debut, but stayed on strongly in the closing stages. He looks capable of more mental progress and is one to keep an eye on. (tchd 8-1)

Mista Rossa is a nice-looking horse and one to keep an eye on when sent handicapping.

River N' Blues(IRE) shaped quite nicely for her small stable and can find opportunties once found her level.

Elliwan is a grand sort and was one of the nicest in the paddock. He has plenty of size about him and looks sure to improve with time. (op 10-1)

6418 HADEN YOUNG MAIDEN STKS (DIV II) 1m 5y

2:30 (2:30) (Class 5) 2-Y-O **£2,266** (£674; £337; £168) **Stalls Low**

Form RPR

03 1 **Ragamuffin Man (IRE)**[21] 5918 2-9-3 0 .... PaulDoe 13 74
(W J Knight) *led: c wd ent st and hdd over 3f out: rdn over 2f out: hung lft over 1f out: hung lft and led cl home: jst hld on* **11/4**[2]

2 *shd* **Celtic Dragon** 2-9-3 0 .... JimCrowley 7 74+
(Mrs A J Perrett) *hld up in rr: rdn and hdwy whn swtchd rt over 1f out: r.o wl ins fnl f: jst failed* **25/1**

04 3 *nk* **Jollyhockeysticks**[28] 5721 2-8-12 0 .... SamHitchcott 6 68
(M R Channon) *hld up in tch: rdn over 3f out: swtchd lft over 1f out: led ent fnl f: hdd cl home* **12/1**

0 4 *1 1/2* **Criterion**[88] 3957 2-9-3 0 .... (v[1]) RyanMoore 5 72+
(Sir Michael Stoute) *a.p: rdn over 2f out: ev ch fr over 1f out: hmpd towards fin: nt rcvr* **14/1**

5 *1/2* **Prairie Storm** 2-9-3 0 .... LPKeniry 10 69+
(A M Balding) *hld up and bhd: rdn and hdwy over 2f out: r.o ins fnl f* **66/1**

6 *shd* **Kiho** 2-9-3 0 .... StephenCarson 1 69
(Eve Johnson Houghton) *s.i.s: hld up in rr: rdn and hdwy over 1f out: r.o ins fnl f* **50/1**

54 7 *1/2* **Craigstown**[58] 4890 2-9-3 0 .... TedDurcan 8 68+
(Saeed Bin Suroor) *a.p: rdn over 2f out: ev ch over 1f out: nt qckn whn hmpd and eased wl ins fnl f* **1/1**[1]

0 8 *3/4* **Shaftesbury (IRE)**[28] 5721 2-9-3 0 .... GregFairley 2 66
(M Johnston) *sn chsng ldr: styd far side and led over 3f out: rdn over 2f out: hdd ent fnl f: wknd towards fin* **16/1**

0000 9 *3/4* **Just Jimmy (IRE)**[44] 5268 2-9-3 54 .... TGMcLaughlin 9 64
(P D Evans) *s.i.s: hld up in rr: rdn and hdwy over 1f out: no ex ins fnl f* **100/1**

0 10 *1/2* **Flower Song**[15] 6093 2-8-12 0 .... FergusSweeney 3 58
(A King) *hld up in mid-div: rdn and wknd over 2f out* **66/1**

11 *3* **Starlight Prince** 2-8-12 0 .... RussellKennemore(5) 11 56
(R Hollinshead) *s.i.s: in rr: styd far side and rdn over 3f out: n.d* **100/1**

12 *3* **Wing Play (IRE)** 2-9-0 0 .... TravisBlock(3) 14 50
(H Morrison) *s.i.s: a in rr* **40/1**

30 13 *1 1/4* **Sea Admiral**[22] 5880 2-9-3 0 .... RichardKingscote 4 47
(R Charlton) *a towards rr* **9/1**[3]

0000 14 *18* **Lady Maya**[25] 5818 2-8-7 51 .... KevinGhunowa(5) 12 2
(Dr J R J Naylor) *mid-div: sn pushed along: rdn and wknd over 2f out: eased whn no ch jst over 1f out* **100/1**

1m 42.43s (1.33) **Going Correction** +0.075s/f (Good) 14 Ran SP% **121.1**

Speed ratings (Par 95): **96,95,95,94,93 93,93,92,91,91 88,85,83,65**

CSF £78.09 TOTE £3.50: £1.10, £5.20, £2.30; EX 75.20 TRIFECTA Not won..

Owner Hardisty, Hutton & Spiers **Bred** D G Hardisty Bloodstock **Trained** Patching, W Sussex

■ Stewards' Enquiry : Paul Doe four-day ban: careless riding (Nov 4-7)

FOCUS

A messy affair with horses headed in all directions off the home turn. However, the winning time was 1.33 seconds quicker than the first division. The presence of the ninth tempers enthusiasm for the form.

NOTEBOOK

Ragamuffin Man(IRE) came back after giving up the lead when brought wide turning for home. He did not prove the easiest of rides and Doe was given a four-day ban after he hampered two rivals when hanging left for a second time near the finish. He is bred to require middle distances next year. (op 7-2 tchd 4-1)

Celtic Dragon ◆ is an 80,000gns half-brother to the very useful three-year-old Spice Route. Apparently unfancied on his debut, he very nearly sprang a surprise and seems to have a bright future. (op 20-1)

Jollyhockeysticks could not quite hold on after being one of the first under pressure and he continues to progress along the right lines. (tchd 11-1)

Criterion, a half-brother to 1m4f winner Rainbow's Edge, had a visor fitted after being apprentice ridden on his debut at Newmarket in July. He had not given way but may have been just held when the winner took his ground at the death. (op 9-1)

Prairie Storm ◆ is a half-brother to 7f Polytrack scorer Cherie's Dream and three winners in France including one who was quite useful. He showed some promise for the future despite being friendless in the betting and may do better over further.

Kiho ◆ is a half-brother to 1m4f scorer Karlu and a couple of winners abroad. He was another big outsider on his debut who should do better when stepped up in distance. (op 40-1)

Craigstown was just beginning to look beaten when done no favours by the winner. (op 5-4 tchd 11-8 in places)

6419 MITIE ENGINEERING MAIDEN STKS 5f 11y

3:00 (3:01) (Class 5) 2-Y-O **£2,914** (£867; £433; £216) **Stalls Centre**

Form RPR

1 **Masada (IRE)** 2-8-12 0 .... RyanMoore 4 78+
(B J Meehan) *mid-div: hdwy 1/2-way: led and edgd rt ins fnl f: r.o* **8/1**

34 2 *1* **Dunn'o (IRE)**[21] 5910 2-9-3 0 .... JamieSpencer 8 79
(C G Cox) *led 1f: chsd ldr: rdn over 1f out: hung lft ins fnl f: r.o* **3/1**[1]

03 3 *1* **Capefly**[29] 5713 2-8-12 0 .... NCallan 3 70
(P F I Cole) *led 4f out: rdn over 1f out: hdd and unable qck ins fnl f* **14/1**

0 4 *1 3/4* **Saranome (IRE)**[13] 6125 2-9-3 0 .... RichardKingscote 5 70+
(R Charlton) *s.i.s: hld up: hdwy over 1f out: nt rch ldrs* **25/1**

523 5 *1/2* **Balata**[23] 5868 2-9-3 73 .... SimonWhitworth 10 67
(B R Millman) *prom: rdn 1/2-way: no ex fnl f* **8/1**

5003 **6** *nk* **Swindon Town Flyer (IRE)**[15] 6072 2-9-3 66 .... SamHitchcott 6 66
(A B Haynes) *chsd ldrs: rdn 1/2-way: outpcd 2f out: rallied over 1f out: rdr dropped whip ins fnl f: no ex* **33/1**

50 **7** *½* **Au Pair (IRE)**[60] 4832 2-8-12 0 .... TedDurcan 17 59
(P W Chapple-Hyam) *s.i.s: swished tail in rr: effrt over 1f out: n.d* **5/1**[3]

8 *1 ¾* **Little Lovely (IRE)** 2-8-12 0 .... LPKeniry 11 53
(A G Newcombe) *prom: rdn 1/2-way: wknd over 1f out* **80/1**

00 **9** *1* **Wave Hill (IRE)**[13] 6126 2-9-3 0 .... StephenDonohoe 15 55
(B J Meehan) *chsd ldrs over 3f* **20/1**

3023 **10** *nk* **Ever Hopeful**[14] 6104 2-8-12 67 .... JimmyQuinn 1 48+
(H J L Dunlop) *chsd ldrs: rdn 1/2-way: edgd rt and wknd over 1f out* **14/1**

11 *5* **Careless Freedom** 2-8-12 0 .... JimmyFortune 14 54+
(B J Meehan) *hld up: swished tail: stmbld wl over 1f out: no ch whn nt clr run and eased ins fnl f* **16/1**

44 **12** *2 ½* **Fly In Johnny (IRE)**[13] 6125 2-9-3 0 .... RichardHughes 13 26+
(R Hannon) *prom over 3f* **9/2**[2]

0000 **13** *shd* **Victoria Valentine**[48] 5167 2-8-9 70 .... WilliamBuick(3) 16 21
(B W Hills) *prom: lost pl over 3f out: bhd fr 1/2-way* **28/1**

0000 **14** *1 ¾* **Berties Goodenough**[9] 6237 2-9-0 52 .... EmmettStack(3) 7 20
(Andrew Turnell) *chsd ldrs over 3f* **100/1**

15 *6* **Love And Glory (FR)** 2-9-3 0 .... GeorgeBaker 9 —
(G L Moore) *s.s: outpcd* **66/1**

16 *3* **Joshua** 2-8-12 0 .... JamesMillman(5) 2 —
(J R Gask) *s.s: outpcd* **80/1**

62.30 secs (-0.20) **Going Correction** -0.025s/f (Good) **16 Ran SP% 121.2**
Speed ratings (Par 95): **100,98,96,94,93 92,91,89,87,87 79,75,74,72,62 57**
CSF £29.95 TOTE £11.40: £4.30, £1.50, £3.90; EX 45.10 Trifecta £133.40 Pool £187.94. - 1.00 winning unit..

Owner Ballymacoll Stud **Bred** Ballymacoll Stud Farm Ltd **Trained** Manton, Wilts

FOCUS
This looked a reasonable juvenile maiden for the course, the time was creditable, and the race should produce winners. The sixth is the best anchor for the form. They raced towards the stands' side in the straight.

NOTEBOOK
Masada(IRE) ◆, a daughter of Key Of Luck and half-sister to 6f juvenile winner Roshanak, proved good enough to make a winning debut. Having broken well enough, she was given time to find her stride by Ryan Moore and had more in front than behind at halfway, but she was always going well within herself and displayed a willing attitude when asked to pick up. She idled once in front and looks even better than the bare form suggests. Brian Meehan is enjoying a fine year with his two-year-olds and the subsequent exploits of those he has saddled to win first time out suggests this one must be kept on side. (op 6-1)

Dunn'o(IRE), dropped back from 6f, showed plenty of early pace, but he seemed to hit a bit of a flat spot when first asked for his challenge and could not peg back Masada. He very much gave the impression he is still learning and there should be better to come next year. (op 10-3 tchd 5-2)

Capefly showed blistering early speed to hold a clear lead from the off, but found just a couple too strong late on. She is now qualified for a handicap mark and could be able to find a race when the emphasis is firmly on speed. (op 16-1)

Saranome(IRE), down the field on his debut at Newbury, produced an improved performance in fourth and there was a lot to like about this effort. He was noted doing some good late work having struggled to lay up early and he looks to be coming along nicely. He might be up to winning a maiden, but he needs just one more run for a handicap mark.

Balata did not appear to do a great deal wrong, but he will probably be better off in nursery company. (op 10-1)

Swindon Town Flyer(IRE), without the blinkers this time, ran a respectable race and, rated 66, he probably helps give a guide to the strength of the form.

Au Pair(IRE) showed ability after a two-month break and is now qualified for a handicap mark, although she was noted to have flashed her tail. (tchd 11-2)

Ever Hopeful Official explanation: jockey said filly hung right-handed

Careless Freedom ◆ had a bit of a nightmare on her racecourse debut. Having raced enthusiastically in behind the pace, she stumbled badly when switched out with her effort and then continually met trouble in the closing stages. She clearly has plenty of ability, but may just be the type who wants to do everything in a hurry and it remains to be seen which way she will go from this. Official explanation: jockey said filly stumbled 2f out (op 12-1 tchd 11-1)

Fly In Johnny(IRE) was well beaten, but he is at least now qualified for a handicap mark. (op 7-1 tchd 4-1)

6420 WORKPLACE SOLUTIONS CATERING MAIDEN FILLIES' STKS 1m 2f 46y
3:30 (3:32) (Class 5) 3-Y-0+ **£2,849** (£847; £423; £211) **Stalls Low**

Form RPR

-422 **1** **Pearl (IRE)**[25] 5803 3-8-12 66 .... LiamJones 12 70
(W J Haggas) *led over 1f: chsd ldr: led 3f out: sn rdn: hld on wl* **6/1**[3]

6224 **2** *nk* **Ashmal (USA)**[23] 5859 3-8-12 63 ....(b) NCallan 16 69
(J L Dunlop) *hld up in mid-div: hdwy over 2f out: r.o ins fnl f* **16/1**

42 **3** *shd* **Demisemiquaver**[54] 4989 3-8-9 72 .... WilliamBuick(3) 15 69
(J Noseda) *a.p: rdn over 4f out: ev ch whn hung lft jst ins fnl f: kpt on* **11/1**

5226 **4** *1* **Unreachable Star**[20] 5941 3-8-12 75 .... JimCrowley 2 67
(Mrs A J Perrett) *a.p: rdn over 1f out: nt qckn ins fnl f* **11/2**[2]

3062 **5** *3 ½* **Rolexa**[9] 6229 3-8-12 70 .... RichardHughes 9 60
(C F Wall) *prom early: hld up in mid-div: rdn 4f out: hdwy over 2f out: one pce fnl f* **18/1**

0440 **6** *3* **Restless Soul**[5] 6299 3-8-12 55 .... J-PGuillambert 1 54
(C A Cyzer) *a.p: rdn over 1f out: wknd fnl f* **14/1**

3 **7** *nk* **Lady Splodge**[23] 5859 3-8-12 0 .... RichardThomas 14 54
(C G Cox) *hld up in tch: rdn over 2f out: wknd over 1f out* **25/1**

2452 **8** *½* **Comma (USA)**[25] 5816 3-8-12 67 .... RyanMoore 10 53
(Sir Michael Stoute) *hld up towards rr: rdn and hdwy over 2f out: wknd fnl f* **4/1**[1]

0 **9** *3* **Refinement (IRE)**[42] 5335 8-9-3 0 .... GeorgeBaker 8 47
(Jonjo O'Neill) *nvr nr ldrs* **25/1**

56 **10** *1* **Act Three**[91] 3847 3-8-9 0 .... NeilChalmers(3) 11 45
(Mouse Hamilton-Fairley) *t.k.h: prom tl rdn and wknd wl over 1f out* **66/1**

2052 **11** *5* **Anthea**[23] 5859 3-8-12 60 .... FergusSweeney 5 35
(B R Millman) *led over 8f out to 3f out: wknd over 2f out* **25/1**

12 *4* **Sweet Mischief (IRE)** 3-8-12 0 .... JimmyFortune 13 27
(J H M Gosden) *s.i.s: a in rr* **12/1**

13 *7* **True Vision (IRE)** 3-8-12 0 .... TedDurcan 7 13
(Saeed Bin Suroor) *mid-div: rdn over 3f out: sn struggling* **4/1**[1]

14 *10* **Muscovado (USA)** 3-8-12 0 .... JamieSpencer 6 —
(L M Cumani) *s.i.s: a in rr: eased whn no ch over 1f out* **10/1**

-006 **15** *nk* **Hill Of Clare (IRE)**[80] 4200 5-9-0 41 .... DominicFox(3) 3 —
(G H Jones) *a in rr* **150/1**

0600 **P** **I'm Agenius**[21] 5900 4-9-3 45 .... TGMcLaughlin 4 —
(C Roberts) *a in rr: t.o 4f out: p.u over 2f out* **150/1**

2m 10.41s (-0.59) **Going Correction** +0.075s/f (Good)
WFA 3 from 4yo+ 5lb **16 Ran SP% 127.0**
Speed ratings (Par 100): **105,104,104,103,101 98,98,98,95,94 90,87,82,74,73 —**
CSF £97.93 TOTE £9.30: £3.40, £4.30, £3.90; EX 134.10 Trifecta £56.30 Part won. Pool £79.37. - 0.10 winning units..

Owner Mr & Mrs G Middlebrook **Bred** G And Mrs Middlebrook **Trained** Newmarket, Suffolk

FOCUS
A competitive if moderate maiden run in a fair time. Sound form, but the principals are fairly exposed.

Muscovado(USA) Official explanation: jockey said filly moved poorly
I'm Agenius Official explanation: jockey said he was unable to steer the filly

6421 WEATHERBYS PRINTING H'CAP 2m 1f 34y
4:00 (4:03) (Class 5) (0-75,72) 3-Y-0 **£3,238** (£722; £722; £240) **Stalls Low**

Form RPR

2005 **1** **Doubly Guest**[9] 6235 3-8-12 63 ....(p) NCallan 2 71+
(G G Margarson) *hld up in tch: led 2f out: styd on wl: eased nr fin* **16/1**

1236 **2** *2 ½* **Last Flight (IRE)**[13] 6131 3-9-7 72 ....(v) TedDurcan 3 75
(J L Dunlop) *chsd ldrs: rdn to ld over 2f out: sn hdd: hung rt over 1f out: styd on same pce* **3/1**[1]

4012 **2** *dht* **Lord Oroko**[21] 5911 3-9-5 70 .... VinceSlattery 4 73
(J G M O'Shea) *s.i.s: hld up: hdwy 5f out: rdn and ev ch over 2f out: styd on same pce fnl f* **5/1**[2]

2060 **4** *nk* **Lady Dedlock**[7] 6271 3-8-3 54 .... DavidKinsella 1 57
(C A Cyzer) *hld up: rdn over 4f out: hdwy over 2f out: sn edgd rt: no ex fnl f* **9/1**

5125 **5** *8* **Jocheski (IRE)**[19] 5980 3-8-13 64 .... FergusSweeney 10 57
(A G Newcombe) *trckd ldrs: pushed along 1/2-way: rdn and ev ch over 2f out: wknd over 1f out* **12/1**

0420 **6** *½* **Composing (IRE)**[20] 5948 3-8-3 57 ....(t) LukeMorris(3) 9 49
(H Morrison) *hld up in tch: rdn over 4f out: hung lft and wknd 2f out* **13/2**[3]

5300 **7** *3* **Mounafes**[27] 5755 3-8-1 55 ....(b) WilliamBuick(3) 7 44
(G A Butler) *hld up: sme hdwy over 4f out: rdn and wknd over 3f out* **14/1**

-000 **8** *21* **One To Follow**[11] 6186 3-9-7 72 .... JamieSpencer 5 36
(C G Cox) *led over 6f: chsd ldrs: led 3f out: sn hdd: wknd over 1f out* **14/1**

1342 **9** *17* **Sonara (IRE)**[24] 5839 3-9-5 70 .... JimmyQuinn 8 13
(M H Tompkins) *trckd ldr: racd keenly: led over 10f out: rdn and hdd 3f out: sn wknd: eased over 1f out* **3/1**[1]

0-60 **P** **Decision Day**[104] 3447 3-8-7 61 .... TravisBlock(3) 6 —
(J A Geake) *s.i.s: a in rr: hung rt on bnd 13f out: bhd fr 1/2-way: t.o whn p.u over 4f out* **50/1**

3m 49.37s (-0.23) **Going Correction** +0.075s/f (Good) **10 Ran SP% 118.9**
Speed ratings (Par 101): **103,101,101,101,97 97,96,86,78,—**
PL Last Flight 1.90, Lord Oroko 1.70; Ex DG-LF 57.10, DG-LO 50.80; CSF DG-LF 32.52, DG-LO 47.99; TC DG-LF-LO 143.38, DG-LO-LF 156.95 TOTE £18.70: £3.90 TRIFECTA DG-LF-LO 85.50; DG-LO-LF 117.20. Part won. Pool £330.30. - 0.40 winning units..

Owner John Guest **Bred** John Guest Mbe M Univ **Trained** Newmarket, Suffolk

FOCUS
Only a few of these had experience over this sort of trip, and earlier races suggested you needed a horse who stayed well. The pace looked fair for the distance. Ordinary form for the grade.

One To Follow Official explanation: jockey said gelding hung right-handed throughout
Decision Day Official explanation: jockey said filly hung badly right-handed throughout

6422 GEWEFA PRECISION TOOLHOLDING H'CAP 1m 3f 144y
4:30 (4:32) (Class 4) (0-80,79) 3-Y-0+ **£4,857** (£1,445; £722; £360) **Stalls Low**

Form RPR

2153 **1** **Hibiki (IRE)**[20] 5941 3-8-5 73 .... TolleyDean(5) 13 82
(J S Moore) *hld up in mid-div: hdwy 3f out: led over 1f out: rdn and edgd lft ins fnl f: r.o* **10/3**[2]

0050 **2** *¾* **Shimoni**[12] 6144 3-9-0 77 ....(v) PaulDoe 10 85
(W J Knight) *hld up: hdwy 6f out: led wl over 3f out: rdn and hdd over 1f out: ev ch whn edgd lft ins fnl f: kpt on* **28/1**

1350 **3** *1* **Inchinata (IRE)**[39] 5415 3-8-12 75 .... TedDurcan 11 81
(B W Hills) *led: hdd over 8f out: prom: rdn over 3f out: ev ch over 2f out: edgd lft ins fnl f: nt qckn* **28/1**

60-4 **4** *½* **Shogun Prince (IRE)**[14] 6110 4-9-6 76 .... FergusSweeney 2 82
(A King) *hld up in tch: rdn and ev ch over 2f out: kpt on same pce fnl f* **9/1**

2550 **5** *¾* **Venir Rouge**[33] 5594 3-8-10 76 ....(b[1]) WilliamBuick(3) 3 80
(M Salaman) *prom: led over 8f out tl wl over 3f out: rdn and one pce fnl 2f* **16/1**

2615 **6** *shd* **Mae Cigan (FR)**[14] 6102 4-8-9 65 oh4 .... GregFairley 1 69
(M Blanshard) *hld up towards rr: hdwy 2f out: edgd lft ins fnl f: one pce* **17/2**

0430 **7** *1 ½* **Oakley Heffert (IRE)**[9] 6236 3-8-13 76 .... RyanMoore 6 78
(R Hannon) *hld up in tch: rdn over 2f out: btn over 1f out* **8/1**[3]

5116 **8** *7* **Grand Art (IRE)**[39] 5405 3-8-11 74 .... JimmyQuinn 5 65
(M H Tompkins) *hld up in mid-div: rdn 3f out: sn wknd* **9/1**

4510 **9** *shd* **She's Our Lass (IRE)**[11] 6180 6-9-4 74 .... StephenDonohoe 4 64
(D Carroll) *hld up towards rr: rdn 3f out: sn struggling* **14/1**

1050 **10** *1* **Starparty (USA)**[20] 5955 3-8-6 69 ....(p) JimCrowley 12 58
(Mrs A J Perrett) *hld up in tch: rdn and wknd over 2f out* **33/1**

/110 **11** *19* **Mickmacmagoole (IRE)**[64] 4691 5-9-9 79 .... JamieSpencer 9 37
(Seamus G O'Donnell, Ire) *hld up in mid-div: lost pl over 4f out: shortlived effrt on stands' side over 2f out* **9/4**[1]

0600 **12** *8* **Prime Contender**[12] 6145 5-8-13 69 .... JimmyFortune 8 15
(G L Moore) *a towards rr: lost tch 4f out* **50/1**

2m 31.98s (1.68) **Going Correction** +0.075s/f (Good)
WFA 3 from 4yo+ 7lb **12 Ran SP% 119.8**
Speed ratings (Par 105): **97,96,95,95,95 94,93,89,89,88 75,70**
CSF £102.09 CT £2267.83 TOTE £4.60: £1.60, £5.80, £6.80; EX 123.90 TRIFECTA Not won..

Owner Albert Conneally **Bred** Albert Conneally **Trained** Upper Lambourn, Berks

FOCUS
There were question marks hanging over many of these in this ordinary handicap and the winning time was modest. The form looks sound at face value.

Mickmacmagoole(IRE) Official explanation: trainer's representative had no explanation for the poor form shown
Prime Contender Official explanation: jockey said gelding moved poorly throughout

6423 BET365.COM H'CAP 1m 5y
5:00 (5:02) (Class 5) (0-75,74) 3-Y-0+ **£3,238** (£963; £481; £240) **Stalls Low**

Form RPR

0400 **1** **Very Well Red**[7] 6269 4-8-12 65 .... JimCrowley 1 74
(P W Hiatt) *a.p: rdn to ld ins fnl f: r.o* **40/1**

0012 **2** *shd* **Red Somerset (USA)**[15] 6081 4-9-7 **74**........................ RyanMoore 15 83
(R J Hodges) *hld up: hdwy over 2f out: led and hung rt over 1f out: rdn: hung lft and hdd ins fnl f: r.o* **11/2**[3]

3030 **3** *1 1/4* **Waterline Twenty (IRE)**[22] 5885 4-9-3 **70**.................. TGMcLaughlin 9 76
(P D Evans) *hld up: hdwy over 2f out: rdn over 1f out: styd on same pce ins fnl f* **25/1**

0404 **4** *2* **Pirouetting**[16] 6063 4-8-11 **64**.. TedDurcan 3 65
(B W Hills) *hld up: hdwy over 2f out: rdn over 1f out: no ex ins fnl f* **14/1**

1151 **5** *nk* **Ellen's Girl (IRE)**[21] 5917 4-9-4 **71**......................... RichardHughes 16 72
(R Hannon) *hld up: hdwy over 2f out: rdn over 1f out: edgd lft and styd on same pce fnl f* **7/2**[2]

2111 **6** *1* **Young Bertie**[16] 6063 4-9-2 **72**.................................(v) TravisBlock(3) 5 70
(H Morrison) *chsd ldr: led 3f out: rdn and hdd over 1f out: wknd ins fnl f* **3/1**[1]

0010 **7** *2* **Scarlet Oak**[6] 6283 3-8-9 **65**.................................... RichardThomas 4 59
(D J S Ffrench Davis) *chsd ldrs: rdn over 2f out: wknd fnl f* **40/1**

0140 **8** *3/4* **Tyzack (IRE)**[22] 5885 6-9-7 **74**................................... MickyFenton 12 66
(Stef Liddiard) *hld up: racd keenly: nvr trbld ldrs* **16/1**

4550 **9** *3* **Azreme**[11] 6179 7-9-2 **69**... PaulDoe 6 54
(P Howling) *hld up: hdwy 2f out: wknd fnl f* **14/1**

-363 **10** *1/2* **Alecia (IRE)**[23] 5860 3-8-8 **67**.............................. WilliamBuick(3) 10 51
(A M Balding) *led 7f out: hdd 3f out: wknd over 1f out* **16/1**

1440 **11** *1/2* **Street Warrior (IRE)**[66] 4631 4-9-7 **74**........................ VinceSlattery 8 57
(G H Yardley) *hld up: sme hdwy u.p over 2f out: sn wknd* **66/1**

053 **12** *1 1/4* **Passing True (IRE)**[48] 5157 3-8-7 **63**............................. GregFairley 7 43
(M Johnston) *hld up in tch: rdn whn hmpd over 3f out: wknd 2f out* **20/1**

0200 **13** *nk* **Joshua's Gold (IRE)**[4] 6331 6-9-3 **70**...............(v) StephenDonohoe 14 49
(D Carroll) *hld up: hdwy over 3f out: wknd over 1f out* **25/1**

0030 **14** *1* **Hannicean**[32] 5620 3-9-3 **73**.. NCallan 2 50
(M A Jarvis) *hld up: rdn over 2f out: sn wknd* **12/1**

1240 **15** *hd* **Moves Goodenough**[19] 5983 4-8-10 **66**.................. EmmettStack(3) 11 42
(Andrew Turnell) *chsd ldrs: rdn and ev ch 2f out: sn wknd* **25/1**

2100 **16** *9* **Indian Edge**[10] 6203 6-9-5 **72**...................................... FergusSweeney 13 28
(B Palling) *led 1f: chsd ldrs: rdn over 3f out: wknd 2f out* **20/1**

1m 40.42s (-0.68) **Going Correction** +0.075s/f (Good)
WFA 3 from 4yo+ 3lb **16** Ran SP% **122.8**
Speed ratings (Par 103): **106,105,104,102,102 101,99,98,95,95 94,93,93,92,91 82**
CSF £232.65 CT £5836.71 TOTE £81.10: £9.50, £2.10, £6.30, £3.00; EX 502.10 TRIFECTA Not won..
Owner Phil Kelly **Bred** Butts Enterprises Limited **Trained** Hook Norton, Oxon

FOCUS
A modest but competitive handicap run at an even pace. They were well spread out in the straight, but most of them finished up the middle of the track. Solid, straightforward form despite the big-priced winner.
Indian Edge Official explanation: jockey said gelding had no more to give

6424 SHONE BUILDING APPRENTICE H'CAP 5f 161y
5:30 (5:33) (Class 6) (0-58,61) 3-Y-0+ **£1,943** (£578; £288; £144) **Stalls** Centre

Form RPR

0433 **1** **Hawridge Miss**[16] 6062 3-8-11 **55**................................ AlanRutter(3) 14 71+
(B R Millman) *wnt lft s: hld up in mid-div: hdwy over 2f out: led and edgd lft wl over 1f out: r.o wl* **10/1**

3666 **2** *1 3/4* **Endless Summer**[9] 6239 10-9-2 **56**............................... KellyHarrison 9 61+
(A W Carroll) *hld up in rr: swtchd rt 2f out: hdwy over 1f out: r.o ins fnl f: tk 2nd post* **11/2**[2]

2004 **3** *hd* **Briery Lane (IRE)**[6] 6287 6-9-4 **58**................................... MCGeran 11 62
(J M Bradley) *hld up towards rr: rdn over 2f out: hdwy over 1f out: rdn and edgd lft ins fnl f: r.o* **11/1**

0040 **4** *1* **Jucebabe**[6] 6287 4-9-4 **58**... SophieDoyle 5 59
(J L Spearing) *hld up in tch: sltly outpcd over 2f out: kpt on ins fnl f* **16/1**

0003 **5** *1* **Two Acres (IRE)**[15] 6078 4-8-12 **52**.................................. JackDean 3 50
(A G Newcombe) *s.s: sn mid-div: hdwy on ins 3f out: rdn 2f out: one pce fnl f* **16/1**

2000 **6** *nk* **Willhewiz**[44] 5272 7-9-4 **58**... JamieJones 7 55
(M S Saunders) *a.p: rdn 2f out: one pce fnl f* **20/1**

304 **7** *2 1/2* **Inwaan (IRE)**[130] 2664 4-9-2 **56**........................(t) JamieHamblett 6 44
(P R Webber) *s.i.s: sn mid-div: rdn and no hdwy fnl 2f* **7/1**[3]

25-6 **8** *hd* **The Tyke**[34] 5567 4-8-12 **55**.. DeanHeslop(3) 2 42
(C G Cox) *t.k.h: chsd ldrs: rdn 3f out: wknd 2f out* **25/1**

10 **9** *hd* **Hello Roberto**[16] 6064 6-8-10 **57**......................(p) DavidProbert(7) 15 44
(R A Harris) *chsd ldrs: rdn over 2f out: wknd ins fnl f* **20/1**

066 **10** *3/4* **Trinculo (IRE)**[23] 5866 10-9-1 **55**................................(b) SladeO'Hara 4 39
(R A Harris) *led: hdd wl over 1f out: sn rdn and wknd* **16/1**

0105 **11** *hd* **Cerulean Rose**[23] 5861 8-8-13 **53**........................ DanielleMcCreery 16 36
(A W Carroll) *s.i.s: nvr nrr* **14/1**

000 **12** *2 1/2* **Stir Crazy (IRE)**[21] 5909 3-8-12 **56**...................... MatthewDavies(3) 10 31
(M R Channon) *a towards rr* **16/1**

1566 **13** *1 3/4* **Mr Forthright**[61] 4759 3-8-10 **56**.............................. BarrySavage(5) 17 25
(J M Bradley) *a in rr* **33/1**

0056 **14** *1* **Lady Lafitte (USA)**[19] 5982 3-8-8 **54**.................... AshleyMorgan(5) 8 20
(M Wellings) *stdd s: hld up towards rr: rdn wl over 1f out: no rspnse* **40/1**

0600 **15** *1 1/4* **Mr Loire**[12] 6148 3-8-12 **58**.................................(b) MarkCoumbe(5) 13 19
(A J Chamberlain) *hmpd s: a in rr* **40/1**

4031 **16** *2 1/2* **Umpa Loompa (IRE)**[8] 6256 3-9-6 **61** 6ex.....................(v) GaryBartley 1 14
(D Nicholls) *chsd ldr: rdn over 2f out: edgd rt and wknd wl over 1f out* **3/1**[1]

4330 **17** *9* **Talcen Gwyn (IRE)**[11] 6174 5-8-12 **57**....................(v) JosephWalsh(5) 12 —
(M F Harris) *stmbld s: a in rr: eased whn no ch over 1f out* **11/1**

1m 11.55s (0.35) **Going Correction** -0.025s/f (Good)
WFA 3 from 4yo+ 1lb **17** Ran SP% **130.0**
Speed ratings (Par 101): **96,93,93,92,90 90,87,86,86,85 85,81,79,78,76 73,61**
CSF £62.66 CT £642.04 TOTE £16.90: £2.70, £1.90, £3.30, £4.90; EX 113.10 TRIFECTA Not won. Place 6 £214.74, Place 5 £170.33.
Owner Eric Gadsden **Bred** Mrs M Fairbairn And E Gadsden **Trained** Kentisbeare, Devon

FOCUS
This low-grade apprentice sprint handicap was the only race of the day where the runners more or less stuck to the inside part of the course. Solid form. The winning time was modest for the grade.
Two Acres(IRE) Official explanation: jockey said gelding missed the break
Umpa Loompa(IRE) Official explanation: jockey said gelding hung right-handed
Talcen Gwyn(IRE) Official explanation: jockey said gelding finished lame
T/Plt: £184.70 to a £1 stake. Pool: £47,356.30. 187.10 winning tickets. T/Qpdt: £27.40 to a £1 stake. Pool: £3,502.10. 94.30 winning tickets. KH

6260 KEMPTON (A.W) (R-H)
Wednesday, October 24

OFFICIAL GOING: Standard
Wind: Moderate, across Weather: Overcast

6425 JOHN SMITH'S MAIDEN AUCTION FILLIES' STKS 5f (P)
6:20 (6:23) (Class 6) 2-Y-O **£2,047** (£604; £302) **Stalls** High

Form RPR

5404 **1** **Blue Zenith (IRE)**[2] 6386 2-7-13 68...................... NataliaGemelova(5) 10 65+
(J S Moore) *mde all: drew clr wl over 1f out: unchal* **11/4**[2]

56 **2** *4* **Melt (IRE)**[6] 6281 2-8-6 0... TPO'Shea 8 53
(R Hannon) *chsd ldrs: rdn and hanging on inner over 1f out: kpt on to take 2nd last 100yds: no ch w wnr* **7/1**

002P **3** *1/2* **Ely Une (IRE)**[75] 4359 2-7-13 50.......................... FrankiePickard(7) 2 51
(J S Moore) *sn outpcd in last trio: gd prog jst over 1f out: styd on wl to take 3rd nr fin* **20/1**

4325 **4** *nk* **Kalligal**[11] 6177 2-8-10 72.. RobertHavlin 3 54
(R Ingram) *prom: rdn to chse wnr 2f out: no imp: edgd rt and lost 2nd last 100yds* **5/2**[1]

00 **5** *1/2* **Seductive Witch**[23] 5872 2-8-8 0...................................... RichardSmith 1 50
(M D I Usher) *chsd ldrs: effrt 2f out: kpt on same pce: n.d* **100/1**

00 **6** *1 3/4* **Queens Mantle**[9] 6225 2-8-7 0...................................... NeilChalmers(3) 9 46+
(P J Makin) *chsd ldrs: stmbld over 3f out: one pce and no prog fnl 2f* **25/1**

344 **7** *1 1/2* **Solo River**[11] 6177 2-8-4 65.. MartinDwyer 4 34
(P J Makin) *swtchd lft after 1f: chsd ldrs: struggling fr 2f out: fdd* **8/1**

2002 **8** *shd* **Lady Vibeeka**[25] 5815 2-8-4 65.. LiamJones 6 34
(Mrs H Sweeting) *chsd wnr to 2f out: wl hld whn hmpd last 75yds and eased* **5/1**[3]

6 **9** *3* **Mayview**[14] 6104 2-8-10 0... JamieMackay 7 29
(Rae Guest) *a outpcd in last pair* **14/1**

10 *3* **Forever Changes** 2-8-8 0... LPKeniry 5 16
(L Montague Hall) *s.s: a outpcd in last* **33/1**

59.80 secs (-0.60) **Going Correction** -0.275s/f (Stan) **10** Ran SP% **114.7**
Speed ratings (Par 90): **93,86,85,85,84 81,79,79,74,69**
CSF £21.00 TOTE £3.20: £1.80, £2.80, £6.90; EX 27.10.
Owner Miss K Theobald & J S Moore **Bred** Miss Karen Theobald **Trained** Upper Lambourn, Berks
■ Stewards' Enquiry : Richard Smith two-day ban: careless riding (Nov 4-5)

FOCUS
Weak form, to be expected for a race of this nature at this time of the year. The clear-cut winner was exposed and looks the best guide.

NOTEBOOK
Blue Zenith(IRE), who made her Polytrack debut at Wolverhampton just two days earlier, got off the mark with a clear-cut win. Smartly away to lead from her inside draw, she railed well and, ridden approaching the final furlong, steadily drew away. (op 7-2)
Melt(IRE) was down in trip for this sand bow after two runs in 6f maidens on turf. She had no chance with the winner up the straight but plugged on up the inside to secure second, and looks to need a return to further. (op 7-2)
Ely Une(IRE), a stablemate of the winner, had been off the track since losing her action at Lingfield in August. She had just two behind her turning into the straight but finished well to grab third.
Kalligal, back down in trip, could never get to the front but chased the winner in vain in the straight. She was battling for second when she edged right inside the last, hampering Lady Vibeeka and losing a bit of momentum herself. (op 7-2)
Seductive Witch, making her debut on an artificial surface, turned into the home straight in seventh place but stayed on steadily in the latter stages. She is now eligible for handicaps.
Queens Mantle Official explanation: jockey said filly didn't handle the bend
Lady Vibeeka, 2lb higher than when second over course-and-distance last time, ran better than her finishing position suggests as she was in fourth place when being hampered and immediately eased inside the last. (tchd 9-2 and 11-2)

6426 FIREWORK PARTY NIGHT HERE NOVEMBER 3RD NURSERY 5f (P)
6:50 (7:02) (Class 6) (0-60,60) 2-Y-O **£2,047** (£604; £302) **Stalls** High

Form RPR

5065 **1** **Too Grand**[25] 5818 2-8-11 **53**.................................(v) NeilChalmers(3) 1 63+
(A M Balding) *trckd ldrs gng strly: prog over 1f out: rdn to ld last 100yds: won gng away* **12/1**

5264 **2** *1 1/4* **Richardthesecond (IRE)**[14] 6098 2-9-6 **59**................(b[1]) SebSanders 8 64
(R M Beckett) *mde most: drvn over 1f out: hdd and outpcd last 100yds* **9/4**[1]

0060 **3** *1/2* **Joss Stick**[7] 6263 2-9-3 **56**.. TPQueally 2 59
(P J Makin) *chsd ldrs: hanging bdly lft over 2f out to over 1f out: stl cl up 1f out: fnd nil* **17/2**

0000 **4** *2* **Ile Royale**[9] 6227 2-9-3 **56**.................................(be[1]) MartinDwyer 5 52
(C N Allen) *snatched up sn after s: in tch in midfield: rdn 2f out: kpt on fnl f: nvr able to chal* **33/1**

0250 **5** *shd* **Mister Beano (IRE)**[27] 5751 2-8-13 **55**...................(v[1]) JerryO'Dwyer(3) 6 51
(V Smith) *reluctant to enter stalls: chsd ldrs: nt qckn over 1f out: kpt on* **12/1**

5605 **6** *1* **Biased Opinion (IRE)**[29] 5715 2-9-3 **56**.......................(b[1]) DaneO'Neill 3 48
(H J L Dunlop) *dwlt: outpcd in last trio and wl off the pce: styd on fr over 1f out: nrst fin* **8/1**[3]

6466 **7** *shd* **Rio Rocket (IRE)**[22] 5887 2-9-0 **56**............................ PJMcDonald(3) 9 48
(G A Swinbank) *nvr bttr than midfield: outpcd wl over 1f out: kpt on ins fnl f* **9/2**[2]

0006 **8** *3/4* **Honest Value (IRE)**[29] 5715 2-9-2 **55**................................... LPKeniry 10 44
(Mrs L C Jewell) *w ldr to jst over 1f out: wknd ins fnl f* **25/1**

0026 **9** *1 1/2* **New Balls Please (IRE)**[9] 6227 2-9-7 **60**.......................(b) IanMongan 7 44
(P M Phelan) *sn outpcd and wl bhd: nvr a factor* **14/1**

606 **10** *hd* **Lyrical Symphony**[16] 6065 2-9-5 **58**................................... TPO'Shea 11 41
(W J Knight) *lost pl bdly on inner fr 4f out to 2f out: bhd after* **8/1**[3]

0500 **11** *1* **Mandarinka**[9] 6227 2-8-12 **58**...............................(b) JackMitchell(7) 12 37+
(P Winkworth) *s.v.s: drvn to try to rcvr whn hung bdly lft bnd 2f out: no ch* **16/1**

6656 **12** *3/4* **Tenjack Queen (IRE)**[12] 6151 2-9-4 **57**....................(b[1]) GeorgeBaker 4 34
(Miss Tor Sturgis) *ldrs: shkn up 2f out: sn wknd* **14/1**

59.84 secs (-0.56) **Going Correction** -0.275s/f (Stan) **12** Ran SP% **123.1**
Speed ratings (Par 93): **93,91,90,87,86 85,85,83,81,81 79,78**
CSF £40.60 CT £262.15 TOTE £17.50: £5.80, £1.30, £3.00; EX 42.30.
Owner High Maintenance Partnership **Bred** Miss J Chaplin **Trained** Kingsclere, Hants

FOCUS
A moderate maiden in which the first two both looked exposed.

NOTEBOOK

Too Grand had previously shaped as if in need of further and was down at the minimum trip for the first time since her debut. Soon going well on the outside from her wide draw, she was switched towards the inner in the home straight and ran on well to score a shade readily. There may be a bit more to come from her. (op 11-1)

Richardthesecond(IRE) was blinkered for the first time on this drop back in trip. He tried to make all but wandered about a little in the latter stages and was cut down in the final half-furlong. (op 2-1)

Joss Stick, reverting to 5f, again hung to his left when the pressure was on but despite that was closing on the two in front of him. He does not look straightforward. Official explanation: jockey said gelding jumped right leaving stalls (op 10-1 tchd 8-1)

Ile Royale ran a slightly improved race in the first-time headgear but is clearly only moderate.

Mister Beano(IRE), in a visor this time on this drop back in trip, ran his best race so far on sand but looks a tricky individual. (op 18-1 tchd 20-1)

Biased Opinion(IRE), with blinkers replacing the visor, stayed on down the outside once in line for home. He has yet to make the frame in eight attempts now. (op 11-1)

Rio Rocket(IRE), another 3lb lower, could never get into the action. (tchd 11-2)

6427 DIGIBET.COM NURSERY 1m 2f (P)

7:20 (7:30) (Class 6) (0-65,62) 2-Y-O **£2,047** (£604; £302) **Stalls High**

Form RPR

000 **1** **Any Given Day (IRE)**^{35} 5541 2-9-4 **59** TGMcLaughlin 4 63+
(D M Simcock) *wl in rr: pushed along 1/2-way: sme prog u.p but plenty to do 2f out: hung lft but rapid prog over 1f out: led last 75yds: hung lft but stdy on* **9/4**[1]

0065 **2** 3/4 **Vilna (USA)**^{28} 5729 2-9-7 **62** GeorgeBaker 11 65
(N A Callaghan) *chsd ldrs: rdn and effrt 3f out: prog wl over 1f out: hanging lft but jnd ldr ins fnl f: hung lft and nt qckn* **3/1**[2]

5000 **3** 2 **Titfer (IRE)**^{49} 5127 2-9-2 **57** SebSanders 7 56
(A W Carroll) *led at decent pce: kicked on over 3f out and had rest at full stretch: hdd & wknd last 75yds* **16/1**

0600 **4** 2 **Redesdale**^{21} 5914 2-9-5 **60** LiamJones 10 56
(P W D'Arcy) *chsd ldng pair: rdn to go 2nd over 2f out: no imp over 1f out: lost 2 pls fnl f* **16/1**

1104 **5** hd **Marmite (IRE)**^{12} 6150 2-9-7 **62** (b) LPKeniry 6 57
(E F Vaughan) *chsd ldng trio: rdn 4f out: outpcd 2f out: kpt on u.p* **12/1**

3060 **6** 3/4 **Ochenvay**^{14} 6099 2-8-13 **54** RobertHavlin 8 48
(M Quinn) *towards rr: rdn and prog fr 4f out: chsng ldrs over 1f out: one pce and no hdwy after* **33/1**

6005 **7** shd **Xtravaganza (IRE)**^{21} 5896 2-8-13 **59** PatrickHills(5) 9 53
(J W Hills) *mostly midfield: u.p 4f out: modest effrt 3f out: sn outpcd: styd on fnl f* **20/1**

0000 **8** shd **Anabaa's Secret (IRE)**^{39} 5423 2-9-3 **58** TPQueally 1 52
(J A Osborne) *chsd ldr to over 2f out: wknd over 1f out* **50/1**

5024 **9** 1 1/2 **Lady Sandicliffe (IRE)**^{28} 5729 2-9-3 **58** DaneO'Neill 12 49
(Miss Jo Crowley) *chsd ldrs: rdn over 3f out: no prog: wknd over 1f out* **7/1**[3]

6004 **10** 3 1/2 **Ovthenight (IRE)**^{21} 5914 2-9-5 **60** MickyFenton 5 45
(Mrs P Sly) *chsd ldrs: rdn wl over 3f out: wknd wl over 1f out* **7/1**[3]

5005 **11** hd **Lady Jinks**^{19} 5984 2-8-8 **56** FrankiePickard(7) 2 40
(M D I Usher) *s.s: mostly in last trio: nvr a factor* **66/1**

0020 **12** 3 **Aneebee (IRE)**^{10} 6207 2-9-4 **59** EddieAhern 3 38
(R Hannon) *settled wl in rr: last over 4f out: shuffled along and no prog* **25/1**

0060 **13** 1/2 **Colmar Magic (IRE)**^{25} 5818 2-8-13 **54** PatDobbs 14 32
(R Hannon) *chsd ldrs: lost pl u.p over 3f out: sn btn* **50/1**

000 **14** hd **Balais Folly (FR)**^{23} 5858 2-9-6 **61** DavidKinsella 13 39
(B Palling) *s.s: limited prog fr last pair 6f out: u.p and btn over 3f out* **66/1**

2m 7.65s (-1.35) **Going Correction** -0.275s/f (Stan) 14 Ran SP% **118.7**
Speed ratings (Par 93): **94,93,91,90,90 89,89,89,88,85 85,82,82,82**
CSF £7.90 CT £85.40 TOTE £3.60: £1.10, £2.40, £5.40; EX 13.70.
Owner Malcolm Martin Partnership **Bred** Ralph And Helen O'Brien **Trained** Newmarket, Suffolk

FOCUS

A modest-looking nursery run at a fair pace. The winner was unexposed and impressive.

NOTEBOOK

Any Given Day(IRE) ◆, making his handicap debut, looked to have a mountain to climb up the home straight but, despite hanging late on, got up to win. A fine-looking sort, he seems sure to win again, although connections have suggested that he could be put away now. (tchd 5-2 and 11-4 in a place)

Vilna(USA) came to have every chance but does not look completely straightforward, as he ran on again once the winner joined him. Races will be won with him but he may not be one to trust completely. (op 9-4 tchd 2-1)

Titfer(IRE) did plenty of the donkey work in front and kept on well once joined. He deserves to get a win.

Redesdale had every chance off the final bend but did not quite get home as strongly as those in front of him. Official explanation: jockey said gelding hung right (op 20-1)

Marmite(IRE) came home really strongly inside the final furlong after being outpaced off the final bend. The Handicapper seems to have her measure for now.

Xtravaganza(IRE) is a fairly consistent sort and was one of only a few that finished nicely from off the pace. She seems to going the right way.

6428 DIGIBET.COM H'CAP 5f (P)

7:50 (7:58) (Class 6) (0-60,60) 3-Y-O+ **£2,047** (£604; £302) **Stalls High**

Form RPR

0000 **1** **Green Lagonda (AUS)**^{6} 6287 5-9-2 **58** HayleyTurner 6 67+
(J G Given) *trckd ldrs: prog on inner over 1f out: rdn to ld last 100yds: edgd lft but sn in command* **10/1**[3]

0645 **2** 1 **Minnow**^{11} 6174 3-8-6 **55** (e[1]) WilliamCarson(7) 11 60
(S C Williams) *chsd ldr tl ent fnl f: hrd rdn and kpt on to snatch 2nd last stride* **10/1**[3]

0025 **3** shd **Triskaidekaphobia**^{9} 6244 4-8-13 **55** (t) PaulFitzsimons 5 60
(Miss J R Tooth) *led: drvn over 1f out: hdd last 100yds: lost 2nd fnl stride* **12/1**

0222 **4** 1 **Musical Script (USA)**^{11} 6174 4-9-3 **59** (b) SebSanders 7 60
(Mouse Hamilton-Fairley) *settled in midfield: effrt on outer and hanging over 1f out: prog to chse ldng trio fnl f: no imp after* **7/4**[1]

4010 **5** 1 1/2 **Desert Light (IRE)**^{106} 3408 6-9-4 **60** DaneO'Neill 10 61+
(D Shaw) *hld up wl in rr: rdn 1/2-way: nt clr run wl over 1f out: prog ent fnl f: nt rch ldrs* **11/1**

0050 **6** 1/2 **Lindbergh**^{20} 5942 5-9-4 **60** (p) JamesDoyle 2 54
(A J Lidderdale) *dropped in fr wd draw and hld up in last pair: nt clr run briefly wl over 1f out: styd on fnl f: n.d* **33/1**

0600 **7** 1/2 **Pamir (IRE)**^{6} 6279 5-9-4 **60** (b) JimCrowley 8 52
(P R Chamings) *n.m.r s: wl in rr: prog wl over 1f out: no imp on ldrs ent fnl f: fdd* **16/1**

6104 **8** hd **Divalini**^{9} 6244 3-9-4 **60** TPQueally 4 51
(J Akehurst) *mostly chsd ldng pair to 2f out: sn lost pl u.p* **11/1**

20-0 **9** 1/2 **Nistaki (USA)**^{254} 442 6-9-3 **59** GeorgeBaker 1 49+
(D Shaw) *restrained fr wdst draw and hld up in last: prog on inner whn nt clr run over 1f out: no ch after* **16/1**

6546 **10** nk **Jayanjay**^{6} 6279 8-8-6 **55** JackMitchell(7) 3 43
(P Mitchell) *chsd ldrs: losing pl and btn whn squeezed out 1f out* **13/2**[2]

0-00 **11** 2 1/2 **Patavium Prince (IRE)**^{6} 6283 4-8-13 **55** (v[1]) JimmyQuinn 12 34
(J R Best) *chsd ldrs: lost pl u.p over 2f out: btn after* **14/1**

65-0 **12** 1 1/2 **Galaxy Of Stars**^{275} 219 3-8-10 **57** (v) PatrickHills(5) 9 31
(D Shaw) *chsd ldrs tl wknd 2f out* **33/1**

59.20 secs (-1.20) **Going Correction** -0.275s/f (Stan) 12 Ran SP% **116.6**
Speed ratings (Par 101): **98,96,96,94,92 91,90,90,89,89 85,82**
CSF £104.39 CT £1229.89 TOTE £12.10: £3.20, £3.10, £2.80; EX 193.70.
Owner P J & Mrs Y Brain & R S G Jones **Bred** P J Brain **Trained** Willoughton, Lincs

FOCUS

A modest contest full of well-known handicappers. The first four were nicely clear of the staying-on pack at the end of a strongly-run contest.

Nistaki(USA) Official explanation: jockey said gelding was denied a clear run

6429 DIGIBET CASINO CLAIMING STKS 7f (P)

8:20 (8:22) (Class 6) 3-4-Y-O **£2,047** (£604; £302) **Stalls High**

Form RPR

645 **1** **Chin Wag (IRE)**^{16} 6055 3-9-8 **72** (p) FergusSweeney 3 72
(K R Burke) *mde virtually all: drvn and jnd fnl f: hld on wl* **7/2**[2]

1666 **2** nk **Double Valentine**^{39} 5425 4-8-3 **46** ow1 JackMitchell(7) 12 57
(R Ingram) *dwlt: sn in midfield: prog fr 3f out: drvn on inner to join wnr fnl f: nt qckn and hld nr fin* **16/1**

2000 **3** 1/2 **Millfield (IRE)**^{13} 6123 4-9-2 **57** JimCrowley 11 62
(P R Chamings) *t.k.h early: hld up bhd ldrs: effrt over 2f out: drvn to press ldng pair over 1f out: nt qckn fnl f* **13/2**[3]

0000 **4** 3 1/2 **Smart Cat (IRE)**^{8} 6247 4-8-8 **45** (v) AndrewElliott(3) 13 47
(A P Jarvis) *rousted along to rch midfield sn after s: effrt u.p 3f out: kpt on fr over 1f out: n.d* **11/1**

0000 **5** shd **Mannello**^{29} 5716 4-8-7 **44** RichardThomas 10 43
(Jim Best) *chsd wnr: drvn and no imp 2f out: lost 2nd and fdd over 1f out* **16/1**

2400 **6** 1/2 **Jack Oliver**^{61} 4778 3-9-8 **68** IanMongan 4 59
(B J Meehan) *awkward s: wl in rr and off the pce: sme prog but hanging over 2f out: kpt on: n.d* **7/1**

6200 **7** 3 **Ficoma**^{35} 5537 3-8-9 **72** AdamKirby 14 37
(C G Cox) *disp 2nd to over 2f out: wknd over 1f out* **13/8**[1]

8 4 **Ocean Waves (IRE)**^{33} 5607 4-9-1 **42** ChrisCatlin 2 31
(Miss Tor Sturgis) *trckd ldrs: rdn and struggling to go pce 1/2-way: steadily fdd* **33/1**

0006 **9** shd **Katie Coniston**^{15} 6094 3-7-12 **44** MatthewCosham(7) 8 22
(Dr J R J Naylor) *dwlt: wl in rr: prog on inner into midfield over 2f out: wknd wl over 1f out* **50/1**

0030 **10** nk **Hayley's Flower (IRE)**^{33} 5602 3-8-5 **54** (b) RichardSmith 1 22
(J C Fox) *wl in rr: wd bnd 3f out: no prog* **20/1**

0200 **11** 3 **Elmasong**^{28} 5728 3-8-7 **44** TPO'Shea 9 16
(J J Bridger) *chsd ldrs for 3f: sn struggling* **40/1**

00 **12** 15 **Mtoto Girl**^{18} 6005 3-8-9 **0** JamesDoyle 7 —
(Ms J S Doyle) *outpcd in last 1/2-way: t.o* **80/1**

1m 24.87s (-1.93) **Going Correction** -0.275s/f (Stan)
WFA 3 from 4yo 2lb 12 Ran SP% **119.6**
Speed ratings (Par 101): **100,99,99,95,94 94,90,86,86,85 82,65**
CSF £55.40 TOTE £5.80: £1.70, £3.40, £2.20; EX 93.80.
Owner Mrs Maura Gittins **Bred** R N Auld **Trained** Middleham Moor, N Yorks

FOCUS

An uncompetitive claimer and taken at face value with the runner-up to last year's best although not that solid.

Mtoto Girl Official explanation: jockey said filly hung left

6430 HALLOWE'EN RACE NIGHT NEXT WEDNESDAY MEDIAN AUCTION MAIDEN STKS 1m 4f (P)

8:50 (8:50) (Class 6) 3-5-Y-O **£2,047** (£604; £302) **Stalls Low**

Form RPR

2-43 **1** **Garafena**^{14} 6109 4-9-5 **77** PatDobbs 2 56
(Pat Eddery) *led after 1f: mde rest: jnd and drvn 2f out: kpt on to assert fnl f* **1/1**[1]

06 **2** 1 **Star Of Pompey**^{10} 6204 3-8-12 **0** SamHitchcott 5 55
(A B Haynes) *sn in last pair and rn in snatches: drvn 3f out: styd on fr over 1f out to take 2nd last stride* **33/1**

3600 **3** shd **Pugnacious Lady**^{20} 5938 3-8-12 **59** JamesDoyle 3 55
(J W Hills) *in tch: drvn wl over 2f out: kpt on to dispute 2nd nr fin: no real ch w wnr* **12/1**

303U **4** 1/2 **Driving Miss Suzie**^{21} 5898 3-8-9 **63** (b) WilliamBuick(3) 4 54
(A M Balding) *t.k.h: hld up in tch: cruised up to join wnr 2f out: hanging after and ref to go by: gave up ins fnl f* **4/1**[3]

54 **5** 1 3/4 **Summerofsixtynine**^{10} 6211 4-9-10 **0** RobertHavlin 7 56
(J G M O'Shea) *led 1f: styd prom: shkn up 5f out: stl cl up 2f out: one pce* **12/1**

5350 **6** 5 **Geordie's Pool**^{8} 6257 3-9-3 **57** SebSanders 6 48
(J W Hills) *trckd wnr after 2f tl over 2f out: wknd* **7/2**[2]

0/0- **7** 17 **True Ruby**^{450} 4004 4-8-12 **0** MatthewCosham(7) 1 16
(Dr J R J Naylor) *in tch tl wd and wknd over 3f out: t.o* **66/1**

2m 35.41s (-1.49) **Going Correction** -0.275s/f (Stan)
WFA 3 from 4yo 7lb 7 Ran SP% **112.0**
Speed ratings (Par 101): **93,92,92,91,90 87,76**
CSF £37.84 TOTE £2.00: £1.10, £10.00; EX 30.10.
Owner Baker, Eddery, Smith & Thorp **Bred** Patrick Eddery Ltd **Trained** Nether Winchendon, Bucks
■ Stewards' Enquiry : William Buick three-day ban (includes two deferred days): careless riding (Nov 4-6)

FOCUS

A modest maiden run at a steady gallop with the winner not having to run to her mark to score.

6431 BARLOW ROBBINS LLP H'CAP 1m (P)

9:20 (9:20) (Class 6) (0-55,55) 3-Y-O+ **£2,047** (£604; £302) **Stalls High**

Form RPR

6530 **1** **Golden Brown (IRE)**^{7} 6266 3-8-12 **55** NeilChalmers(3) 12 63
(David Pinder) *hld up towards rr: rdn and prog over 2f out: sustained effrt to ld jst ins fnl f: kpt on wl* **25/1**

4420 **2** 1/2 **Beneking**^{130} 2656 7-9-3 **54** ChrisCatlin 6 60
(D Burchell) *t.k.h: hld up in midfield: prog over 2f out: rdn to chal and upsides 1f out: nt qckn last 100yds* **9/1**

The Form Book, Raceform Ltd, Compton, RG20 6NL

2245 **3** *1 1/4* **Terry Molloy (IRE)**[19] 5966 3-9-1 **55**........................(v) FergusSweeney 5 59
(K R Burke) *led to 2f out: nt qckn: kpt on wl again fnl f* **7/1**

0040 **4** *shd* **Mythical Charm**[6] 6278 8-9-3 **54**........................(t) SebSanders 9 57
(J J Bridger) *t.k.h: hld up in midfield: rdn and nt qckn over 2f out: styd on ins fnl f* **7/1**

-002 **5** *1* **Palais Polaire**[25] 5817 5-8-12 **52**........................ WilliamBuick(3) 10 53
(J A Geake) *cl up on inner: shkn up to ld 2f out: idled and hanging in front: hdd and fnd nil jst ins fnl f* **5/1**[1]

3434 **6** *shd* **Hills Place**[7] 6266 3-9-0 **54**........................ DaneO'Neill 13 55
(J R Best) *chsd ldrs: rdn and nt qckn over 2f out: styd on again ins fnl f: unable to chal* **5/1**[1]

4133 **7** *1/2* **Jools**[11] 6179 9-8-12 **54**........................ PatrickHills(5) 1 54
(D K Ivory) *chsd ldrs on outer: drvn and nt qckn over 2f out: kpt on same pce after* **13/2**[3]

44-3 **8** *hd* **Royal Embrace**[292] 42 4-9-3 **54**........................(v) GeorgeBaker 3 53
(D Shaw) *wl in rr: shkn up 2f out: kpt on steadily: nvr nr ldrs* **20/1**

5000 **9** *nk* **Tanforan**[12] 6146 5-9-3 **54**........................ TGMcLaughlin 11 52
(B P J Baugh) *s.s: mostly in last trio: effrt on inner over 2f out: one pce and nvr rchd ldrs* **16/1**

4002 **10** *hd* **Postmaster**[11] 6179 5-9-4 **55**........................ RobertHavlin 14 56+
(R Ingram) *hld up in rr: prog on inner 3f out: cl up and ch whn hmpd 1f out: nt rcvr* **6/1**[2]

0000 **11** *nk* **James Street (IRE)**[7] 6266 4-9-4 **55**........................(v1) LPKeniry 2 52
(Peter Grayson) *pressed ldr: rdn 3f out: stl cl up jst over 1f out: wknd fnl f* **25/1**

0000 **12** *3* **Windy Prospect**[7] 6268 5-9-4 **55**........................(b) IanMongan 8 45
(Mrs L J Mongan) *chsd ldrs: hanging and wd over 2f out: sn btn* **20/1**

001- **13** *3* **Princess Of Aeneas (IRE)**[132] 5837 4-9-1 **52**........................ AdamKirby 4 36
(Peter Grayson) *s.i.s: nvr gng wl: a in rr* **25/1**

1m 38.85s (-1.95) **Going Correction** -0.275s/f (Stan)
WFA 3 from 4yo+ 3lb **13 Ran SP% 122.9**
Speed ratings (Par 101): **98,97,96,96,95 95,94,94,94,93 93,90,87**
CSF £226.98 CT £1808.95 TOTE £26.60: £12.40, £2.90, £3.20; EX 396.20 Place 6 £123.37, Place 5 £44.06.
Owner Miss A Jones **Bred** M G Marenchic Md **Trained** Kingston Lisle, Oxon

FOCUS
A moderate handicap and ordinary form for the grade, although sound enough behind the surprise winner.
Postmaster ◆ Official explanation: jockey said gelding was denied a clear run
Princess Of Aeneas(IRE) Official explanation: jockey said filly was never travelling
T/Plt: £156.10 to a £1 stake. Pool: £61,966.20. 289.60 winning tickets. T/Qpdt: £70.00 to a £1 stake. Pool: £5,612.50. 59.30 winning tickets. JN

6401 LINGFIELD (L-H)
Wednesday, October 24

OFFICIAL GOING: Standard
Wind: Moderate, against Weather: Dull

6432 RACING AHEAD WEEKEND EVERY SATURDAY MAIDEN FILLIES' STKS (DIV I) 7f (P)
1:40 (1:41) (Class 5) 2-Y-O **£2,202** (£655; £327; £163) **Stalls** Low

Form RPR

1 **Malibu Girl (USA)** 2-9-0 0........................ TPQueally 8 78+
(E A L Dunlop) *s.s: hld up towards rr: hdwy gng wl 2f out: qcknd to ld fnl 75yds: smoothly* **8/1**

234 **2** *1 3/4* **Divine Power**[41] 5357 2-9-0 78........................ SebSanders 1 73
(R M Beckett) *led: hrd rdn fnl f: hdd and outpcd by wnr fnl 75yds* **7/2**[1]

5 **3** *nk* **Lullaby Lady**[14] 6105 2-9-0 0........................ MichaelHills 11 72
(B W Hills) *chsd ldrs: effrt over 2f out: nt qckn ins fnl f* **7/1**

05 **4** *nk* **Chaenomeles (USA)**[14] 6107 2-9-0 0........................ RoystonFfrench 12 71
(M Johnston) *prom on outside: rdn to chal over 2f out: one pce ins fnl f* **15/2**

0 **5** *1 1/2* **Mary Montagu (IRE)**[26] 5766 2-9-0 0........................ EddieAhern 6 68
(J W Hills) *s.s: hdwy 4f out: hrd rdn 2f out: styd on same pce fnl f* **13/2**[3]

0 **6** *1* **Marraasi (USA)**[15] 6087 2-9-0 0........................ RHills 4 65
(M P Tregoning) *prom: hrd rdn over 1f out: no ex ins fnl f* **14/1**

04 **7** *1/2* **Dubai Petal (IRE)**[13] 6126 2-9-0 0........................ JamesDoyle 2 64
(J S Moore) *chsd ldrs: pushed along and lost pl 1/2-way: kpt on again fnl f* **5/1**[2]

65 **8** *1/2* **Street Diva (USA)**[30] 5681 2-9-0 0........................ TPO'Shea 9 62
(P A Blockley) *t.k.h: chsd ldrs tl wknd 1f out* **8/1**

4430 **9** *1/2* **Freudian Slip**[33] 5603 2-8-7 69........................ WilliamCarson(7) 13 61
(S Curran) *towards rr: rdn and hung lft fnl 2f: nt trble ldrs* **20/1**

10 *shd* **Lady Petrus** 2-9-0 0........................ ChrisCatlin 3 61+
(H J L Dunlop) *in tch tl dropped to rr after 2f: sme hdwy whn nt clr run on rail wl over 1f out: n.d* **40/1**

000 **11** *nk* **Jemiliah**[69] 4539 2-8-7 49........................(b1) KMay(7) 14 60
(B J Meehan) *dwlt and swtchd lft fr outside draw: bhd: rdn 3f out: nvr nr ldrs* **100/1**

00 **12** *4* **Payne Relief (IRE)**[35] 5540 2-9-0 0........................ HayleyTurner 5 50
(M L W Bell) *chsd ldrs over 4f* **66/1**

0 **13** *3 1/2* **Ginger Fountain**[22] 5881 2-9-0 0........................ DaneO'Neill 10 41
(H Candy) *t.k.h towards rr: effrt on outside 3f out: rdn and wknd 2f out* **66/1**

1m 25.79s (-0.10) **Going Correction** -0.175s/f (Stan) **13 Ran SP% 116.6**
Speed ratings (Par 92): **93,91,90,90,88 87,86,86,85,85 85,80,76**
CSF £34.17 TOTE £10.80: £2.80, £1.70, £1.90; EX 45.30.
Owner Hesmonds Stud **Bred** David E Hager Ii **Trained** Newmarket, Suffolk

FOCUS
Although a couple had already made the frame on turf, this looked a modest maiden and the race went to one of the two newcomers. The winning time was nearly a second slower than the second division and the form looks modest outside the winner with the runner-up the best guide.

NOTEBOOK
Malibu Girl(USA) ◆, a $170,000 half-sister to five winners in the US, was bred to go on the surface though she did not look the likeliest winner for most of the contest. Still only sixth entering the last furlong, a beautiful gap appeared amongst the wilting leaders and she swept through it without having to come under maximum pressure. The form is ordinary, but she won this in taking style so she is likely to have a future. (op 9-1)
Divine Power, making her sand debut in her fourth outing and trying this trip for the first time, was given a positive ride from her in-form jockey and it was noticeable that he kept the filly well away from the inside rail even when he had the opportunity to move across. The tactic almost certainly helped her hold off most of her rivals and she was just unfortunate to bump into an unexposed rival who is likely to prove a class or two above her. Her official rating of 78 provides a useful benchmark to the form. (op 3-1)
Lullaby Lady, stepping up two furlongs from her turf debut, was likely to appreciate this longer trip on the dam's side of her pedigree. Always up there, she kept plugging away and she should be up to winning a race, especially once handicapped.
Chaenomeles(USA), down a furlong for this sand debut, raced up with the pace throughout but was always being forced to race wider than was probably ideal from her high stall and she lacked the necessary pace in the home straight. She now qualifies for a mark and looks the sort for handicaps back over a bit further. (op 8-1)
Mary Montagu(IRE), whose only previous outing was when in mid-division of a valuable sales race at Ascot, came through to hold every chance in the home straight but lacked a change of gear. There is plenty of stamina on the dam's side of her pedigree and she looks one for handicaps over further after one more run. Official explanation: jockey said filly hung left under pressure (op 7-1)
Marraasi(USA), well beaten on her Leicester debut, lasted longer this time though she found herself closer to the inside rail than the other principals in the home straight and she had nothing more to offer. A couple of her siblings won over much further than this and it may be that she will eventually come into her own over a longer trip, especially once handicapped. (op 12-1)

6433 RACING AHEAD WEEKEND NEWSPAPER CLAIMING STKS 1m 2f (P)
2:10 (2:12) (Class 6) 2-Y-O **£2,047** (£604; £302) **Stalls** Low

Form RPR

0006 **1** **Rosy Dawn**[14] 6099 2-8-3 56........................(v) FrancisNorton 8 51
(H J L Dunlop) *led after 1f: hld on wl whn chal fnl 2f* **9/1**

060 **2** *1* **Bookiebasher Babe (IRE)**[73] 4428 2-8-10 54........................ MartinDwyer 3 56
(M Quinn) *pressed ldr: rdn to dispute ld 2f out: nt qckn fnl f* **25/1**

224 **3** *hd* **Bollywood Style**[10] 6207 2-8-8 0........................ DaneO'Neill 9 54
(J R Best) *in tch: effrt over 2f out: hrd rdn over 1f out: styd on* **7/1**[3]

0066 **4** *3/4* **Observatory Ridge**[10] 6207 2-8-6 55........................ HayleyTurner 10 50
(M D I Usher) *bhd: rdn 3f out: styd on wl fnl 2f: nrst fin* **12/1**

000 **5** *shd* **Dual Faith (IRE)**[13] 6119 2-8-13 65........................(b1) TQuinn 2 57
(B J Meehan) *led 1f: stdd to trck ldrs: hrd rdn and one pce appr fnl f* **16/1**

0003 **6** *1/2* **Isander (USA)**[10] 6207 2-9-4 56........................ SteveDrowne 6 61
(Mrs A J Perrett) *chsd ldrs: hrd rdn 2f out: one pce* **11/2**[1]

0605 **7** *2 1/2* **Khana Ras (IRE)**[14] 6099 2-8-13 63........................ ChrisCatlin 13 52+
(E J O'Neill) *towards rr: rdn 3f out: styd on appr fnl f* **6/1**[2]

4600 **8** *1 1/4* **Insomnitas**[10] 6202 2-9-0 56........................ RichardMullen 1 51
(M G Quinlan) *hld up in tch on rail: rdn over 2f out: sn outpcd* **12/1**

000 **9** *3/4* **Got Green (FR)**[41] 5344 2-8-12 58........................ EddieAhern 11 47
(R Hannon) *mid-div: rdn over 3f out: sn btn* **12/1**

00 **10** *2 1/2* **Lady Charlemagne**[7] 6262 2-9-0 0........................ JamesDoyle 7 45
(N P Littmoden) *mid-div tl wknd 3f out* **66/1**

0620 **11** *1/2* **Magnol**[14] 6099 2-8-2 57 ow2........................ ThomasO'Brien(7) 12 39
(J G M O'Shea) *dwlt: rdn 3f out: a bhd* **16/1**

5006 **12** *9* **Shadows Fall (USA)**[23] 5858 2-9-7 67........................ SebSanders 5 35
(P F I Cole) *hld up towards rr: rdn 3f out: no rspnse* **6/1**[2]

13 *1* **City Of Dreams (IRE)** 2-9-4 0........................ TPO'Shea 14 30
(J S Moore) *s.i.s: drvn along most of way: a bhd* **10/1**

0100 **14** *13* **Adam Eterno (IRE)**[10] 6207 2-8-3 54........................ PNolan(7) 4 —
(A B Haynes) *chsd ldrs: rdn 1/2-way: outpcd 3f out: btn in midfield whn eased over 1f out: sddle slipped* **25/1**

2m 8.87s (1.08) **Going Correction** -0.175s/f (Stan) **14 Ran SP% 119.6**
Speed ratings (Par 93): **88,87,87,86,86 85,83,82,82,80 79,72,71,61**
CSF £219.39 TOTE £8.50: £3.10, £8.40, £2.40; EX 447.90.Rosy Dawn was claimed by Ms J. S. Doyle for £5,000.
Owner Be Hopeful Partnership **Bred** Overbury Stallions Ltd **Trained** Lambourn, Berks

FOCUS
This was a long way for juveniles, especially not very good ones, and very few ever got into it. The first two home held those positions virtually throughout and the early pace was not that strong, hence the modest winning time and not a race to be with.

NOTEBOOK
Rosy Dawn, marginally best in on adjusted official ratings, was soon taken to the front and, because she was not taken on, was crucially able to settle at the head of affairs which would have been a big help to her for the latter stages of the contest. She faced a stern challenge from the runner-up over the last couple of furlongs, but she dug very deep and hanging away from the dreaded inside rail in the closing stages was no bad thing either. She was subsequently claimed by Jacqueline Doyle for £5,000.
Bookiebasher Babe(IRE), stepping up three furlongs in trip, was not ridden as though stamina was thought to be an issue as she raced closest to the winner for the vast majority of the contest. The pair were engaged in a protracted duel over the last couple of furlongs and she may even have poked her head in front for a stride or two, but her rival was in no mood to give in and bullied her out of it. She would have been 9lb better off with the winner in a handicap, but the likelihood is that her proximity drags the form down. (tchd 33-1)
Bollywood Style, taking another step up in trip, was never that far away and was closing the front pair down at the line though she never looked like winning. She seemed to stay well enough, but is already exposed at this sort of level. (op 6-1)
Observatory Ridge made up a lot of ground over the last couple of furlongs and did best of those held up, but she is exposed and finished a little further behind Bollywood Style than here last time despite being 2lb better off, so she did not achieve that much.
Dual Faith(IRE), second best-in at the weights, despite having been well beaten in all three of his starts, and blinkered for the first time, was another to benefit from racing handily in a race dominated by those that took a prominent position early. He was probably not helped by sticking to the inside in the home straight, but it did not cost him the race.
Isander(USA) started favourite despite being worst in at the weights. In front of both Bollywood Style and Observatory Ridge here last time, he had every chance but did not see the longer trip out as well as that pair. (op 6-1)
Got Green(FR) Official explanation: jockey said filly hung left
Adam Eterno(IRE) Official explanation: jockey said saddle slipped

6434 RACING AHEAD WEEKEND EVERY SATURDAY MAIDEN FILLIES' STKS (DIV II) 7f (P)
2:40 (2:42) (Class 5) 2-Y-O **£2,202** (£655; £327; £163) **Stalls** Low

Form RPR

5 **1** **Elysee Palace (IRE)**[12] 6140 2-9-0 0........................ PhilipRobinson 3 75
(M A Jarvis) *pressed ldr: led jst over 1f out: rdn and r.o wl: readily* **7/1**[3]

633 **2** *1 3/4* **Deira Dubai**[27] 5745 2-9-0 73........................ RHills 1 70
(B W Hills) *led: hrd rdn and hdd jst over 1f out: nt pce of wnr fnl f* **11/4**[1]

3045 **3** *1* **Fidelias Dance**[24] 5837 2-9-0 71........................ RoystonFfrench 9 67
(M Johnston) *s.s: sn chsng ldrs: rdn over 2f out: kpt on fnl f* **7/1**[3]

4 **4** *1 1/2* **Top Draw (USA)**[22] 5882 2-9-0 0........................ EddieAhern 6 64
(M L W Bell) *prom: hrd rdn over 1f out: no ex* **8/1**

5 *shd* **Lekita** 2-9-0 0........................ AdamKirby 4 63+
(W R Swinburn) *mid-div: rdn 3f out: styd on fnl f* **7/2**[2]

0 **6** *1/2* **Horticulture (USA)**[52] 5061 2-9-0 0........................ SteveDrowne 12 62+
(R Charlton) *t.k.h: in tch: effrt 2f out: no imp* **16/1**

7 *1 1/4* **Cinerama (IRE)** 2-9-0 0........................ PatDobbs 13 59+
(M P Tregoning) *hld up towards rr: rdn 2f out: sme late hdwy* **25/1**

0 **8** ½ **Contessina (IRE)**[84] 4061 2-9-0 0 .... TQuinn 2 57
(P F I Cole) *hld up in midfield: pushed along and no hdwy fnl 3f* **20/1**
9 1 **Sinaaf** 2-9-0 0 .... MartinDwyer 5 55
(M P Tregoning) *towards rr: rdn over 2f out: n.d* **10/1**
03 **10** 2½ **Santa Clara**[15] 6082 2-9-0 0 .... ChrisCatlin 8 48
(Jane Chapple-Hyam) *in tch: rdn over 2f out: wknd over 1f out* **16/1**
11 nk **Bosamcliff (IRE)** 2-9-0 0 .... DaneO'Neill 11 48
(A B Haynes) *s.s: rdn over 2f out: a bhd* **66/1**
04 **12** ½ **Italian Goddess**[21] 5913 2-9-0 0 .... HayleyTurner 10 46
(M L W Bell) *rdn 3f out: a bhd* **14/1**
13 6 **Mellifluous (IRE)** 2-9-0 0 .... MichaelHills 14 31
(J W Hills) *a towards rr: rdn and bhd fnl 3f* **50/1**

1m 24.84s (-1.05) **Going Correction** -0.175s/f (Stan) 13 Ran SP% **124.6**
Speed ratings (Par 92): **99,97,95,94,94 93,92,91,90,87 87,86,79**
CSF £26.84 TOTE £6.40: £2.60, £1.40, £3.40; EX 22.90.
Owner Sheikh Mohammed **Bred** Darley **Trained** Newmarket, Suffolk

FOCUS
Another race dominated by those that raced handily and this looked stronger than the first division, especially as the winning time was nearly a second quicker. The placed horses set the standard and the form looks pretty solid.

NOTEBOOK
Elysee Palace(IRE), who showed distinct promise on her debut here two week earlier, was given a much more prominent ride this time which helped compensate for the furlong-shorter trip. Always on the outside of the favourite, that would have been a help to her in the battle to the line and she took full advantage. She ought to continue to improve. (op 6-1)
Deira Dubai, who has already shown a fair degree of form on turf, was given a positive ride and did not do a lot wrong, but the winner was in the better position on the outside of her in the home straight and proved much the better. She probably ran to form judged on the official rating of the third and has the ability to win a maiden on this surface, but she also looks worth a try in a nursery. (op 4-1)
Fidelias Dance looks exposed now, but her best previous effort had come on this track and she kept plugging away to finish a respectable third. She has already been beaten three times in nurseries though, so she does not have that many options left. (tchd 13-2)
Top Draw(USA) was ridden more positively than on her debut, but could only plug on at one pace once in line for home. She may be better suited to turf and looks the type to do better once handicapped in any case. (op 9-1)
Lekita ◆, a half-sister to eight winners including Tucker, had been withdrawn from her intended debut here last month after refusing to enter the stalls. She consented to go in this time and was the eye-catcher of the race, finishing in fine style with her rider only giving her one light tap with the whip and faring best of the newcomers. There are races to be won with her in due course. (tchd 10-3 and 4-1)
Horticulture(USA) showed a bit more than on her debut and is likely to come into her own in handicaps over further in time. (op 14-1)

6435 RACING AHEAD WEEKEND ONLY £1 H'CAP 1m (P)
3:10 (3:11) (Class 4) (0-85,85) 3-Y-0+ **£4,857** (£1,445; £722; £360) **Stalls** High

Form RPR
1405 **1** **Manaal (USA)**[108] 3350 3-9-1 **79** .... RHills 6 89
(Sir Michael Stoute) *pressed ldr: led 1f out: rdn out* **7/1**[3]
0505 **2** 1 **Fiefdom (IRE)**[10] 6209 5-9-5 **80** .... DanielTudhope 2 88
(I W McInnes) *chsd ldrs: rdn 2f out: r.o to take 2nd fnl 75yds* **14/1**
0462 **3** 1 **Bobski (IRE)**[10] 6209 5-9-7 **82** .... (p) AdamKirby 4 88
(G A Huffer) *s.s: sn in midfield on rail: promising hdwy 2f out: hrd rdn and nt qckn fnl f* **7/2**[1]
0-00 **4** shd **Danski**[10] 6203 4-9-7 **82** .... SebSanders 5 87+
(P J Makin) *bhd: effrt and nt clr run early st: r.o wl fr over 1f out: nrst fin* **10/1**
665 **5** nk **Cool Box (USA)**[18] 6002 3-9-0 **78** .... (b[1]) JamesDoyle 9 83
(Mrs A J Perrett) *prom: rdn 2f out: one pce fnl f* **12/1**
0103 **6** nk **Carnivore**[10] 6209 5-9-5 **80** .... ChrisCatlin 3 85+
(T D Barron) *towards rr: effrt and nt clr run st: nvr able to chal* **9/2**[2]
3065 **7** shd **The Snatcher (IRE)**[12] 6143 4-9-2 **77** .... FrancisNorton 11 81
(R Hannon) *led: hrd rdn and hdd 1f out: no ex* **7/1**[3]
3643 **8** ¾ **Bonnie Prince Blue**[9] 6243 4-9-1 **76** .... MichaelHills 10 78
(B W Hills) *wd: towards rr: rdn and unable to chal fnl 2f* **8/1**
0060 **9** shd **Seal Point (USA)**[9] 6236 3-9-7 **85** .... (p) RoystonFfrench 8 87
(Christian Wroe) *t.k.h: chsd ldrs: rdn 3f out: wknd over 1f out* **33/1**
6626 **10** shd **Rubenstar (IRE)**[13] 6121 4-8-12 **73** .... EddieAhern 12 75
(M H Tompkins) *towards rr: hdwy to chse ldrs ent st: wknd over 1f out* **12/1**
4026 **11** 2 **Okikoki**[26] 5768 3-8-11 **75** .... RichardMullen 7 72
(W R Muir) *hld up in midfield: effrt 2f out: sn wknd* **12/1**
1460 **12** 3½ **Radical Views**[67] 4603 3-9-6 **84** .... DaneO'Neill 1 73
(B W Hills) *s.s: sn prom: wknd wl over 1f out: eased whn no ch fnl f* **20/1**

1m 37.57s (-1.86) **Going Correction** -0.175s/f (Stan)
WFA 3 from 4yo+ 3lb 12 Ran SP% **123.1**
Speed ratings (Par 105): **102,101,100,99,99 99,99,98,98,98 96,92**
CSF £104.96 CT £408.90 TOTE £11.40: £1.60, £5.50, £1.60; EX 171.00.
Owner Hamdan Al Maktoum **Bred** Shadwell Farm LLC **Trained** Newmarket, Suffolk

FOCUS
A typically tight Lingfield handicap, run at no more than an ordinary pace, in which a couple did not enjoy the clearest of runs in the straight. The winner had no such problems though and the runner-up sets the standard.

6436 RACING AHEAD WEEKEND AT ALL NEWSAGENTS MAIDEN STKS (C&G) 7f (P)
3:40 (3:43) (Class 5) 2-Y-0 **£2,849** (£847; £423; £211) **Stalls** Low

Form RPR
1 **Forgotten Voice (IRE)** 2-9-0 0 .... TPQueally 8 75+
(J Noseda) *t.k.h towards rr: gd hdwy over 1f out: r.o strly to ld nr fin* **4/1**[2]
633 **2** ½ **Formation (USA)**[29] 5702 2-9-0 77 .... SteveDrowne 10 74+
(E A L Dunlop) *prom: drvn to ld over 1f out: hdd and nt qckn ins fnl f* **3/1**[1]
3 nk **Nasaq (USA)** 2-9-0 0 .... RHills 13 73+
(M P Tregoning) *wd: hld up in midfield: hdwy 2f out: rdn to narrow ld ins fnl f: hdd and no ex nr fin* **15/2**
0 **4** 3½ **Grand Strategy (IRE)**[13] 6130 2-9-0 0 .... PhilipRobinson 9 65
(M A Jarvis) *hld up in tch: rdn 2f out: styd on same pce* **6/1**
00 **5** ½ **Cape Rock**[21] 5919 2-9-0 0 .... TQuinn 6 63+
(C A Horgan) *plld hrd in midfield: swtchd wd and effrt 2f out: styng on at fin* **66/1**
03 **6** ½ **Skycruiser (IRE)**[15] 6080 2-9-0 0 .... MartinDwyer 4 62
(Saeed Bin Suroor) *prom: led over 2f out tl over 1f out: wknd fnl f* **9/2**[3]
54 **7** nk **Morocchius (USA)**[13] 6119 2-9-0 0 .... SebSanders 2 61+
(R M Beckett) *chsd ldrs tl wknd over 1f out* **13/2**
0 **8** nk **Rosentraub**[51] 5091 2-9-0 0 .... EddieAhern 12 61
(H J L Dunlop) *hld up towards rr: gd hdwy on rail over 1f out: 5th and hld whn hmpd ins fnl f* **33/1**
5 **9** ½ **Commander Cave (USA)**[12] 6139 2-9-0 0 .... PatDobbs 5 59
(R Hannon) *prom: led over 3f out tl over 2f out: wknd 1f out* **66/1**
00 **10** hd **Last Of The Line**[15] 6080 2-9-0 0 .... FrancisNorton 11 63+
(H J L Dunlop) *hld up towards rr: effrt and nt clr run st: nvr able to chal* **33/1**
06 **11** 1½ **Wabbraan (USA)**[47] 5200 2-9-0 0 .... RichardMullen 3 55
(D M Simcock) *chsd ldrs 4f* **28/1**
5 **12** 1¼ **Jerry Hamilton (USA)**[123] 2863 2-9-0 0 .... RoystonFfrench 1 52
(M Johnston) *led tl wknd over 3f out* **20/1**
13 1¼ **Benedetto** 2-9-0 0 .... DaneO'Neill 7 49
(Mrs A J Perrett) *dwlt: t.k.h: sn in tch: rdn and wknd 3f out* **50/1**
14 8 **Valtat** 2-9-0 0 .... RichardSmith 14 29
(B R Johnson) *s.s: a bhd: jockey looking down and no ch fnl 3f* **100/1**

1m 25.17s (-0.72) **Going Correction** -0.175s/f (Stan) 14 Ran SP% **122.6**
Speed ratings (Par 95): **97,96,96,92,91 90,90,90,89,89 87,86,84,75**
CSF £15.68 TOTE £6.70: £2.90, £1.60, £2.30; EX 18.80.
Owner Mrs Susan Roy **Bred** Swettenham Stud And Ben Sangster **Trained** Newmarket, Suffolk

FOCUS
Probably a fair maiden with the runner-up bringing solid form to the table. The winner should prove better than this in time.

NOTEBOOK
Forgotten Voice(IRE), a 230,000gns half-brother to four winners out of a half-sister to Breeders' Cup Classic winner Arcangues, made a successful debut, running on late to take the spoils close home. He looks a useful prospect for next year and has plenty of scope to improve. (op 3-1)
Formation(USA), whose best performance prior to this arguably came on his previous start on Polytrack at Kempton, has an official rating of 77 and set a decent standard. He did nothing wrong, only finding a promising newcomer too strong at the finish, and he certainly has the ability to win a similar contest. (op 7-2)
Nasaq(USA), whose dam was a lightly raced 1m winner at three, shaped with promise on his debut. However, having momentarily hit the front inside the last, he was not only passed by the winner but soon outbattled by Formation as well. He can improve for this and should have no trouble getting off the mark. (op 12-1)
Grand Strategy(IRE), a half-brother to five winners, most notably Sobieski, a high-class multiple 1m2f winner in France, was representing a stable that is not firing on all cylinders at present. He finished adrift of the first three and looks more a handicap type after one more run, when a longer trip will suit. (tchd 13-2)
Cape Rock, a half-brother to four winners out of Ayr Gold Cup winner Wildwood Flower, ran his best race to date on his third start. Despite having pulled in the early stages, he was keeping on well at the finish and options will be greater for him now that handicaps are an option. Official explanation: jockey said colt ran too free
Skycruiser(IRE), who is out of an unraced half-sister to top-class middle distance performers Luso, Warrsan, Needle Gun and Cloud Castle, has shown only modest ability in three starts so far. (tchd 5-1)
Morocchius(USA) is another now eligible for a mark. (op 7-1)
Rosentraub had to be snatched up when going for a run next to the unfavoured far rail in the straight, and he can be rated a bit better than the bare form suggests. Out of a mare who won twice over middle distances at three, he is bred to want further than this in time.
Last Of The Line ◆ finished full of running having enjoyed a luckless run up the straight. A gap never came for him and he can be rated better than his finishing position suggests. Having had no chance on the wrong side at Folkestone last time and no chance here through lack of a clear run he is now eligible for handicaps, and he will of course be of significant interest in that sphere. Official explanation: jockey said colt was denied a clear run
Valtat Official explanation: jockey said gelding hung badly right

6437 RACING AHEAD WEEKEND TIME ORDER RACECARDS H'CAP 7f (P)
4:10 (4:12) (Class 3) (0-95,94) 3-Y-0+
£7,166 (£2,145; £1,072; £537; £267; £134) **Stalls** Low

Form RPR
0102 **1** **Capricorn Run (USA)**[12] 6142 4-9-2 **90** .... (v) SebSanders 14 103+
(A J McCabe) *wd: hld up in midfield: gd hdwy over 1f out: drvn to ld ins fnl f: sn clr* **7/1**[3]
2503 **2** 2 **Forest Dane**[9] 6231 7-8-8 **82** .... RoystonFfrench 8 88
(Mrs N Smith) *towards rr: rdn and hdwy over 1f out: styd on wl to take 2nd nr fin* **12/1**
0023 **3** hd **Ceremonial Jade (UAE)**[47] 5209 4-9-6 **94** .... (tp) OscarUrbina 12 103+
(M Botti) *hld up in tch: nt clr run and lost pl early st: swtchd rt over 1f out: rallied and r.o* **11/2**[1]
0444 **4** 1 **Dingaan (IRE)**[12] 6142 4-9-0 **88** .... (p) FrancisNorton 1 91
(A M Balding) *led: hrd rdn and hdd ins fnl f: no ex* **8/1**
2350 **5** nk **Majuro (IRE)**[18] 6003 3-9-4 **94** .... TPO'Shea 2 96
(M R Channon) *chsd ldrs: rdn and hung lft over 1f out: one pce fnl f* **14/1**
0100 **6** nk **Ivory Lace**[25] 5799 6-8-13 **87** .... TPQueally 6 88
(S Woodman) *hld up in rr: rdn and r.o appr fnl f: nrst fin* **25/1**
5220 **7** shd **Buy On The Red**[12] 6142 6-8-11 **85** .... (p) RichardMullen 11 86
(W R Muir) *hld up in rr: rdn and r.o appr fnl f: nvr nrr* **33/1**
6004 **8** nk **Cesc**[18] 6002 3-8-13 **89** .... EddieAhern 5 89
(P J Makin) *prom tl wknd 1f out* **13/2**[2]
0054 **9** nk **Roman Maze**[10] 6197 7-8-13 **87** .... MartinDwyer 9 86+
(W M Brisbourne) *hld up towards rr: nt clr run over 1f out: nvr able to chal* **16/1**
110 **10** hd **Persian Express (USA)**[20] 5950 4-9-1 **89** .... MichaelHills 13 88
(B W Hills) *chsd ldrs: chal 2f out: wknd 1f out* **12/1**
0000 **11** ½ **Mastership (IRE)**[18] 6003 3-9-3 **93** .... (b) RHills 3 96+
(C E Brittain) *dwlt: hld up in midfield: promising effrt on rail whn n.m.r fr over 1f out tl ins fnl f: eased* **8/1**
4006 **12** hd **Cross The Line (IRE)**[20] 5950 5-8-11 **88** .... AndrewElliott[(3)] 10 85
(A P Jarvis) *prom tl outpcd and n.m.r jst over 1f out* **12/1**
-100 **13** nk **Sandrey (IRE)**[105] 3431 3-8-11 **87** .... SteveDrowne 7 83
(P W Chapple-Hyam) *hld up in midfield: rdn to chse ldrs ent st: wknd fnl f* **17/2**
3400 **14** ¾ **Binanti**[25] 5797 7-9-3 **91** .... ChrisCatlin 4 85
(P R Chamings) *sn towards rr: effrt on rail whn n.m.r over 1f out: wknd fnl f* **14/1**

1m 23.41s (-2.48) **Going Correction** -0.175s/f (Stan)
WFA 3 from 4yo+ 2lb 14 Ran SP% **123.0**
Speed ratings (Par 107): **107,104,104,103,103 102,102,102,101,101 101,100,100,99**
CSF £90.56 CT £518.37 TOTE £6.60: £2.20, £4.10, £2.30; EX 143.10.
Owner Paul J Dixon And Placida Racing **Bred** Santa Rosa Partners **Trained** Babworth, Notts

FOCUS
A competitive handicap and solid enough form for the grade rated through the runner-up.

NOTEBOOK

Capricorn Run(USA), who ran well here over 6f last time when taken to the inner to challenge, was drawn more favourably this time and raced wide throughout before running on strongly down the centre of the track for a clear-cut success. He did not go unbacked and remains progressive, but things will be tougher once he is reassessed for this win. (op 8-1)

Forest Dane is probably more effective over sprint trips but this was still a fine effort. He had no chance with the clear-cut winner but hung on well for second and should remain competitive off this sort of mark. (tchd 14-1)

Ceremonial Jade(UAE) had conditions to suit and cheekpieces on for the first time, but he had to delay his challenge as the winner made his move down the outside, and ultimately he was chasing only second place. He lost out in that battle with Forest Dane, who had the stronger jockey, but had he been on the outside of the two it might have gone the other way. (op 5-1)

Dingaan(IRE) had cheekpieces back on for the first time in a long while and he ran really well under different riding tactics. Normally held up, he made the running this time and, considering he went for home plenty early enough and raced quite near the far-side rail, he deserves rating better than the bare form suggests. (tchd 9-1)

Majuro(IRE) ran a better race back over his favoured distance, but he raced close to the inside rail throughout from his low draw and he was always going to struggle as a result.

Ivory Lace ran on late down the centre of the track but was never a real threat. She was running off a 14lb higher mark than when last seen on sand as a result of a successful summer on turf.

Mastership(IRE) was denied a clear run towards the inside for the length of the straight and crossed the line having not been asked for an effort. It is difficult to forget how impressive he was in a handicap here over 6f in February, and it would not be a surprise to see him pop up in a similar race at some stage. Official explanation: jockey said colt was denied a clear run (op 9-1)

Binanti for some reason went for a run up the unfavoured inside rail from the back of the field. He should be suited to this track, being a horse who tends to finish late from off the pace, but the place to do that is wide, down the centre, where the surface rides faster. (op 12-1)

6438 RACING AHEAD WEEKEND THE PUNTERS' PAPER CLAIMING STKS — 6f (P)

4:40 (4:40) (Class 6) 2-Y-O — **£2,047** (£604; £302) **Stalls** Low

Form — RPR

6004 **1** **Maybe I Wont**[9] 6227 2-8-11 63 — SebSanders 11 — 69
(S Dow) *wd: hld up towards rr: hdwy on outside 2f out: r.o to ld ins fnl f: rdn clr* **7/2**[1]

0500 **2** *1 1/2* **Dome Rock (IRE)**[13] 6120 2-9-5 73 — EddieAhern 4 — 72
(L M Cumani) *chsd ldrs: effrt ent st: kpt on to take 2nd ins fnl f* **4/1**[2]

2006 **3** *1/2* **Splash The Cash**[10] 6195 2-8-5 67 — SaleemGolam 3 — 58+
(P Winkworth) *chsd ldrs: cl 3rd whn hmpd and swtchd lft ins fnl f: one pce* **7/1**

0620 **4** *1/2* **Synge Street**[21] 5896 2-8-11 65 — PatDobbs 5 — 61
(R Hannon) *led: hrd rdn and hdd ins fnl f: no ex* **11/2**[3]

0002 **5** *1/2* **I Dont Do Walkin (USA)**[12] 6151 2-7-9 67 — (b) KMay(7) 8 — 51
(B J Meehan) *plld hrd: w ldr: hrd rdn over 1f out: no ex ins fnl f* **4/1**[2]

0060 **6** *1/2* **Pretty Bonnie**[29] 5706 2-8-6 53 — JamesDoyle 7 — 53
(J G Portman) *towards rr: hdwy and hrd rdn over 1f out: nt rch ldrs* **25/1**

3000 **7** *3/4* **Zahwah**[14] 6098 2-8-6 55 — HayleyTurner 12 — 51
(J G Portman) *hld up in midfield: rdn over 1f out: no imp* **33/1**

3000 **8** *2 1/2* **Black Duke**[29] 5715 2-9-5 55 — RichardMullen 6 — 56
(M G Quinlan) *mid-div: effrt over 2f out: wknd over 1f out* **20/1**

0 **9** *1 1/4* **Chunsa**[22] 5888 2-8-7 0 — RoystonFfrench 9 — 41
(W Jarvis) *dwlt: bhd: rdn 3f out: sme late hdwy* **33/1**

0304 **10** *1 1/2* **Polish Priory (IRE)**[9] 6242 2-8-2 58 — (v[1]) FrancisNorton 2 — 31
(P D Evans) *a towards rr: n.d fr 1/2-way* **8/1**

0 **11** *3 1/2* **Madame Montom (USA)**[25] 5815 2-8-10 0 — NelsonDeSouza 1 — 29
(S W Hall) *mid-div: dropped to rr over 3f out: no ch fnl 2f* **66/1**

3130 **12** *3/4* **Pearo (IRE)**[23] 5869 2-8-2 57 — ChrisCatlin 10 — 18
(J S Moore) *prom 4f* **16/1**

1m 12.54s (-0.27) **Going Correction** -0.175s/f (Stan) **12** Ran SP% **123.1**
Speed ratings (Par 93): **94,92,91,90,90 89,88,85,83,81 76,75**
CSF £17.20 TOTE £5.40: £1.50, £2.10, £4.10; EX 20.70.Splash The Cash was claimed by K. A. Ryan for £5,000.
Owner J R May **Bred** Wheelersland Stud **Trained** Epsom, Surrey

FOCUS
An ordinary claimer but solid enough rated through the second, sixth and eighth.

NOTEBOOK

Maybe I Wont, who was dropping into a claimer for the first time, travelled well out wide throughout and, once asked to pick up the leaders, did so easily. He appreciated the step up to 6f. (op 9-2 tchd 5-1 in a place)

Dome Rock(IRE), another dropping in grade, had run over a mile last time and he shaped as though finding this trip on the sharp side. (op 7-2)

Splash The Cash, stepping up in distance on this drop in grade, did not get the clearest of runs when trying to make up ground next to the unfavoured far rail and did not shape at all badly in the circumstances. He should be capable of winning a similar race on this evidence. (tchd 13-2)

Synge Street was another dropping back in distance having run over 1m on his last two starts. Given a positive ride, he was there to be shot at inside the final furlong. (op 15-2)

I Dont Do Walkin(USA), runner-up in a similar event at Wolverhampton last time, failed to settle in the early stages and as a result she had nothing left for the finish. (op 9-2 tchd 5-1)

Pretty Bonnie had a bit to find with the majority of these at the weights. (op 22-1)

6439 RACING AHEAD WEEKEND NEWSPAPER H'CAP — 1m 2f (P)

5:10 (5:10) (Class 4) (0-85,84) 3-Y-O+ — **£4,857** (£1,445; £722; £360) **Stalls** Low

Form — RPR

0012 **1** **Kaateb (IRE)**[18] 6007 4-9-5 80 — RHills 8 — 89+
(W J Haggas) *prom: led over 1f out: drvn out* **2/1**[1]

0040 **2** *3/4* **Tommy Toogood (IRE)**[14] 6110 4-9-9 84 — MichaelHills 3 — 92
(B W Hills) *t.k.h: in tch: effrt over 2f out: chsd wnr over 1f out: kpt on* **5/1**[2]

5500 **3** *nk* **Pagan Sword**[32] 5631 5-9-7 82 — (p) SebSanders 2 — 89
(Mrs A J Perrett) *s.i.s: towards rr: rdn and hdwy 2f out: styd on fnl f* **5/1**[2]

24-6 **4** *1/2* **Art Man**[21] 5921 4-8-9 70 — RichardMullen 5 — 76
(G L Moore) *hld up towards rr: effrt whn hmpd and swtchd lft over 1f out: r.o promisingly fnl f* **28/1**

6005 **5** *3/4* **Solo Flight**[12] 6144 10-9-3 78 — SteveDrowne 10 — 83
(H Morrison) *hld up towards rr: effrt on outside 2f out: styd on fnl f* **14/1**

1505 **6** *1* **Hunting Tower**[40] 5385 3-9-3 83 — PatDobbs 1 — 86
(R Hannon) *chsd ldrs: effrt 2f out: no ex fnl f* **14/1**

315- **7** *2* **Celtic Step**[368] 6106 3-9-2 82 — RoystonFfrench 9 — 81
(M Johnston) *pressed ldr: led 3f out tl over 1f out: wknd fnl f* **9/1**[3]

1400 **8** *hd* **Norman The Great**[8] 6253 3-8-12 78 — ChrisCatlin 6 — 76
(Jane Chapple-Hyam) *mid-div: outpcd over 2f out: kpt on again fnl f* **12/1**

11-6 **9** *nk* **Circus Polka (USA)**[269] 275 3-8-11 77 — NelsonDeSouza 12 — 75
(P F I Cole) *bhd: shkn up 2f out: sme late hdwy* **25/1**

3310 **10** *1/2* **Sonny Parkin**[35] 5545 5-8-11 72 — (v) AdamKirby 7 — 69
(G A Huffer) *dwlt: bhd: hrd rdn over 1f out: nvr trbld ldrs* **12/1**

0-0R **11** *1 3/4* **Willhego**[35] 5539 6-9-3 78 — DaneO'Neill 11 — 71
(J R Best) *chsd ldrs tl hrd rdn and wknd over 1f out* **14/1**

0340 **12** *3 1/2* **Two Timer (IRE)**[32] 5637 3-9-0 80 — TQuinn 4 — 66
(D R C Elsworth) *plld hrd: led and restrained in front: hdd 3f out: wknd 2f out* **33/1**

2m 5.37s (-2.42) **Going Correction** -0.175s/f (Stan)
WFA 3 from 4yo+ 5lb **12** Ran SP% **122.3**
Speed ratings (Par 105): **102,101,101,100,100 99,97,97,97,96 95,92**
CSF £11.46 CT £46.43 TOTE £2.50: £1.40, £2.40, £2.80; EX 18.00 Place 6 £114.41, Place 5 £49.80..
Owner Hamdan Al Maktoum **Bred** Shadwell Estate Company Limited **Trained** Newmarket, Suffolk
■ Sonny Parkin was 2000 Guineas-winning trainer Geoff Huffer's last runner before retiring.
■ Stewards' Enquiry : Seb Sanders one-day ban: careless riding (Nov 4)

FOCUS
Not a strongly-run handicap and ordinary form for the grade, but the winner is progressive and open to further improvement.
T/Jkpt: Not won. T/Plt: £41.90 to a £1 stake. Pool: £47,889.50. 833.20 winning tickets. T/Qpdt: £6.40 to a £1 stake. Pool: £3,642.90. 418.10 winning tickets. LM

6440 - 6442a (Foreign Racing) - See Raceform Interactive

6111 NAVAN (L-H)

Wednesday, October 24

OFFICIAL GOING: Firm (good to firm in places)

6443a EQUI-ADS IRELAND - IRELAND'S NEW EQUESTRIAN MAGAZINE MAIDEN — 1m

4:05 (4:05) 2-Y-O — **£5,836** (£1,359; £599; £346)

RPR

1 **Kingdom Of Naples (USA)** 2-9-3 — JAHeffernan 3 — 90+
(A P O'Brien, Ire) *trckd ldrs: 3rd 1/2-way: hdwy over 2f out: led 1 1/2f out: clr fnl f: comf* **5/1**[2]

2 *3* **Masiyma (IRE)** 2-8-12 — FMBerry 7 — 78+
(John M Oxx, Ire) *towards rr: 13th appr st: hdwy on outer over 2f out: mod 3rd 1 1/2f out: kpt on wl* **7/1**[3]

3 *1/2* **Veidhleadoir (USA)**[3] 6365 2-8-12 — KJManning 8 — 77
(J S Bolger, Ire) *cl 2nd: led early st: hdd 1 1/2f out: no ex fnl f* **9/4**[1]

4 *3 1/2* **Almolahek (IRE)** 2-9-3 — PJSmullen 13 — 74
(D K Weld, Ire) *chsd ldrs in 6th: lost pl ent st: kpt on one pce u.p fr 2f out* **8/1**

5 *3 1/2* **Amaranda (IRE)** 2-8-12 — WMLordan 15 — 61
(David Wachman, Ire) *hld up: hdwy on outer ent st: 4th over 2f out: no imp fr 1 1/2f out* **14/1**

6 *1/2* **Beyond Compare (IRE)** 2-8-12 — DPMcDonogh 6 — 60
(J S Bolger, Ire) *towards rr: styd on fr 1 1/2f out* **16/1**

7 *1 3/4* **Beach Bunny (IRE)**[19] 5989 2-8-12 — CDHayes 5 — 56
(Kevin Prendergast, Ire) *chsd ldrs: 5th 1/2-way: lost pl appr st: no imp fr 2f out* **8/1**

8 *1/2* **Marching Sandy (IRE)** 2-9-0 — SMGorey(3) 2 — 60
(Edward Lynam, Ire) *dwlt: sn trckd ldrs on inner: 5th early st: no ex fr 2f out* **16/1**

9 *shd* **Hindu Kush (IRE)** 2-8-10 — SMLevey(7) 10 — 59
(A P O'Brien, Ire) *towards rr: kpt on one pce st* **9/1**

10 *1* **Flight Of The Hawk (IRE)**[19] 5997 2-9-3 73 — DMGrant 1 — 57
(Miss Martina Anne Doran, Ire) *led: hdd early st: wknd fr 2f out* **12/1**

11 *hd* **No One Tells Me**[44] 5290 2-8-12 — RPCleary 14 — 52
(Mrs John Harrington, Ire) *a towards rr* **12/1**

12 *2 1/2* **San Roque (USA)**[23] 5876 2-9-3 — WJSupple 9 — 51
(Ms F M Crowley, Ire) *prom: 3rd early: 4th 1/2-way: wknd st* **33/1**

13 *nk* **Jokipur**[14] 6115 2-8-10 — PTownend(7) 11 — 50
(Patrick Cody, Ire) *towards rr: rdn ent st: no ex fr over 2f out* **33/1**

14 *4* **The Best Dub**[23] 5876 2-9-3 — PShanahan 12 — 41
(Eamon Tyrrell, Ire) *sn trckd ldrs on outer: 5th appr st: sn wknd* **20/1**

1m 43.2s (-3.10) **15** Ran SP% **136.6**
CSF £45.17 TOTE £5.80: £1.80, £3.60, £1.70; DF 35.90.
Owner Michael Tabor **Bred** Tower Bloodstock **Trained** Ballydoyle, Co Tipperary

Hindu Kush(IRE) Official explanation: jockey said colt ran very green throughout

6444 - 6446a (Foreign Racing) - See Raceform Interactive

6274 BRIGHTON (L-H)

Thursday, October 25

OFFICIAL GOING: Good (good to firm in places; 9.0)

The middle of the track looked the place to be, and it also proved hard to make up significant amounts of ground from off the pace.

Wind: Fresh, behind Weather: Overcast

6447 VISIT BETTER ON QUEENS ROAD, BRIGHTON H'CAP — 7f 214y

2:00 (2:00) (Class 6) (0-63,67) 3-Y-O+ — **£2,483** (£739; £369; £184) **Stalls** Low

Form — RPR

0006 **1** **Sagunt (GER)**[40] 5433 4-8-13 57 — PaulDoe 13 — 66
(S Curran) *mid-div: rdn and hdwy over 2f out: drvn on to ld ins fnl f: styd on wl* **5/1**[3]

5112 **2** *1 1/2* **Myfrenchconnection (IRE)**[11] 6199 3-8-12 59 — MickyFenton 10 — 65
(P T Midgley) *chsd ldrs: led 2f out tl ins fnl f: nt qckn* **9/2**[2]

3640 **3** *shd* **Haasem (USA)**[40] 5424 4-9-5 63 — JimCrowley 2 — 68
(J R Jenkins) *towards rr: swtchd outside and hdwy over 2f out: hrd rdn and hung lft: r.o to snatch 3rd on line* **66/1**

0004 **4** *shd* **Border Edge**[7] 6278 9-8-12 56 — (v) SebSanders 14 — 61
(J J Bridger) *w ldrs: led over 3f out tl 2f out: one pce fnl f* **6/1**

2061 **5** *1 3/4* **Support Fund (IRE)**[7] 6278 3-9-6 67 6ex — StephenCarson 6 — 68
(Eve Johnson Houghton) *bhd: drvn along and hdwy 2f out: nrst fin* **12/1**

0511 **6** *nk* **Seneschal**[2] 6413 6-9-9 67 6ex — RyanMoore 11 — 67
(A B Haynes) *towards rr: rdn and hdwy 2f out: nt rch ldrs* **3/1**[1]

4326 **7** *2 1/2* **Ten To The Dozen**[24] 5862 4-8-9 56 — TravisBlock(3) 3 — 51
(P W Hiatt) *w ldrs on rail tl wknd 1f out* **9/1**

6030 **8** *2* **The Grey One (IRE)**[11] 6196 4-9-0 63 — (p) KevinGhunowa(5) 4 — 53
(J M Bradley) *chsd ldrs: outpcd 3f out: sn btn* **20/1**

430 **9** *nk* **Crown Office (USA)**[146] 2219 3-9-1 62 — SteveDrowne 5 — 51+
(H Morrison) *led tl over 3f out: hrd rdn and wknd over 1f out* **16/1**

3330 **10** *3 1/2* **And Again (USA)**[8] 6260 4-8-13 57 — EddieAhern 7 — 38
(R A Teal) *unsettled in stalls: mid-div on rail: rdn over 2f out: no imp* **9/1**

6620 **11** *2* **Djalalabad (FR)**[15] 6109 3-8-11 58 — TPQueally 9 — 35
(Mrs C A Dunnett) *s.s: a bhd* **33/1**

4500 **12** *1¾* **Wells Of Badr (IRE)**[35] 5563 3-8-13 **60**.................(b[1]) AdrianMcCarthy 1 33
(P W Chapple-Hyam) *chsd ldrs over 5f: eased whn no ch fnl f* **100/1**

2300 **13** *5* **Revolve**[8] 6260 7-9-1 **59**..(b) IanMongan 15 20
(Mrs L J Mongan) *chsd ldrs tl wknd 2f out: b.b.v* **33/1**

5000 **14** *6* **Speed Dial Harry (IRE)**[28] 5753 5-9-5 **63**........................(b) JohnEgan 8 10
(C R Dore) *bhd and sn rdn along: eased whn no ch fnl 2f* **16/1**

1m 33.67s (-1.37) **Going Correction** -0.20s/f (Firm)
WFA 3 from 4yo+ 3lb **14** Ran SP% **126.7**
Speed ratings (Par 101): **98,96,96,96,94 94,91,89,89,85 83,82,77,71**
CSF £28.29 CT £1414.18 TOTE £7.50: £2.30, £1.80, £11.70; EX 77.20 TRIFECTA Not won..
Owner Miss N Henton **Bred** Gestut Schlenderhan **Trained** Faringdon, Oxon

FOCUS
A modest but competitive handicap run at an even gallop and fairly sound rated around the fourth and fifth. They raced middle-to-far side and it was those up middle who had the call.
Revolve Official explanation: trainer said gelding beld from the nose
Speed Dial Harry(IRE) Official explanation: jockey said gelding was unsuited by the track

6448 JERRY HINDS CELEBRATION MEDIAN AUCTION MAIDEN STKS 6f 209y
2:30 (2:30) (Class 5) 2-Y-O **£2,849** (£847; £423; £211) **Stalls** Low

Form RPR

064 **1** **Maxwil**[36] 5536 2-9-0 82.. RyanMoore 5 78
(G L Moore) *in tch: rdn and hung bdly lft fr 2f out: chsd wnr wl over 1f out: drvn to ld fnl strides* **4/9**[1]

0023 **2** *hd* **Connor's Choice**[21] 5937 2-9-0 77.................................... SebSanders 4 78
(Andrew Turnell) *led: qcknd 3 l ahd over 2f out and stl gng wl: hrd rdn fnl f: ct fnl strides* **10/3**[2]

4033 **3** *6* **Rub Of The Relic (IRE)**[17] 6065 2-9-0 70.....................(b[1]) EddieAhern 7 62
(P A Blockley) *chsd ldr: outpcd over 2f out: lost 2nd pl wl over 1f out: wl hld after* **10/1**[3]

00 **4** *¾* **Flower**[13] 6140 2-8-9 0... GregFairley 2 55
(C A Cyzer) *plld hrd and fly-jumping in rr early: rdn over 2f out: styd on fnl f* **33/1**

0 **5** *10* **Rsmiya**[20] 5984 2-8-9 0.. JohnEgan 1 39+
(C E Brittain) *chsd ldrs 5f: eased whn no ch over 1f out* **33/1**

00 **6** *1½* **Holden Caulfield (IRE)**[14] 6126 2-8-11 0.................. NeilChalmers(3) 6 30
(Mouse Hamilton-Fairley) *stdd s: t.k.h in rr: rdn over 2f out: sn bhd* **100/1**

1m 21.55s (-1.15) **Going Correction** -0.20s/f (Firm) **6** Ran SP% **108.3**
Speed ratings (Par 95): **98,97,90,90,78 76**
CSF £1.93 TOTE £1.50: £1.02, £2.80; EX 2.30.
Owner H R Hunt **Bred** Langton Stud And G E M Wates **Trained** Woodingdean, E Sussex

FOCUS
An uncompetitive maiden, although the winning time was 0.40 seconds quicker than the following nursery. The form looks reliable with the first two clear.

NOTEBOOK
Maxwil ◆ was a real eyecatcher when a running-on fourth in good company at Sandown on his latest start, but he was given an official mark of 82, hardly making the handicap route an attractive proposition at this stage of his career. This looked something of a penalty kick, as the betting suggested, but he failed to handle the track and very nearly threw it away by continually hanging to his left under pressure. Quite a big type, his trainer thinks he is still quite weak and will benefit from a winter over his back, so he will be put away now. He should make a useful handicapper next year and it would be no surprise to see him land a decent prize. (op 4-7 tchd 8-13 in a place)
Connor's Choice, in contrast to the winner, seemed at home on this undulating track and only just failed under a positive ride. He is probably a touch flattered to get so close to Maxwil, but he is still a fair type in his own right and should be placed to advantage at some point. (op 3-1 tchd 7-2)
Rub Of The Relic(IRE) failed to improve for the first-time blinkers and is not progressing. (op 7-1)
Flower ◆ had not shown much in two starts on Polytrack but, switched to turf, she was noted doing some good late work, despite having pulled very hard through the opening stages. She is now qualified for a handicap mark and appeals as one to keep an eye on. (op 25-1)

6449 REGIS RECRUITMENT NURSERY 6f 209y
3:05 (3:05) (Class 5) (0-75,75) 2-Y-O **£2,914** (£867; £433; £216) **Stalls** Low

Form RPR

1344 **1** **Relinquished**[34] 5600 2-9-1 **72**.. WilliamBuick(3) 6 74
(J Noseda) *mde all: hrd rdn 2f out: r.o gamely fnl f: jst hld on* **5/1**[1]

002 **2** *shd* **Fandangerina**[20] 5965 2-9-3 **71**.. SebSanders 14 73+
(Sir Mark Prescott) *chsd ldrs: hrd rdn 2f out: clsd on wnr fnl f: jst failed* **15/2**

0000 **3** *2* **Futune (IRE)**[28] 5751 2-8-0 **54**.. JamieMackay 12 51
(B J Meehan) *prom: hrd rdn 2f out: one pce fnl f* **66/1**

0400 **4** *½* **Ski School (IRE)**[17] 6052 2-8-11 **65**..............................(v[1]) EddieAhern 4 60
(W J Haggas) *plld hrd: trckd ldrs: rdn and sltly outpcd 2f out: styd on fnl f* **8/1**

550 **5** *nk* **Greek Theatre (USA)**[29] 5720 2-9-0 **68**........................(e[1]) JimCrowley 2 62
(Mrs A J Perrett) *mid-div: hrd rdn over 2f out: hdwy over 1f out: nrst fin* **20/1**

2056 **6** *½* **Albaqaa**[14] 6128 2-9-6 **74**..(v[1]) MartinDwyer 1 67
(E A L Dunlop) *t.k.h: chsd ldrs: briefly wnt 2nd 2f out: no ex over 1f out* **13/2**

0003 **7** *1¼* **Ledgerwood**[30] 5707 2-8-13 **67**.. TQuinn 7 57
(J W Hills) *chsd wnr 5f: sn outpcd* **25/1**

060 **8** *½* **Maybe I Will (IRE)**[44] 5314 2-8-13 **67**.............................. DaneO'Neill 15 56
(R Hannon) *wd: in tch: effrt over 2f out: no ex over 1f out* **22/1**

0034 **9** *nk* **Landikhaya (IRE)**[10] 6233 2-9-4 **72**................................... RyanMoore 9 60
(R Hannon) *hld up in rr: rdn and hdwy over 1f out: no further prog* **6/1**[3]

6040 **10** *nk* **Cosmea**[55] 4991 2-9-1 **69**.. FergusSweeney 13 56
(A King) *dwlt: sn in midfield: effrt over 2f out: sn btn* **66/1**

304 **11** *nk* **Park Royal (UAE)**[40] 5428 2-9-7 **75**................................... GregFairley 3 61+
(M Johnston) *hmpd s: bhd: effrt wd of others on ins rail over 2f out: hrd rdn and no imp over 1f out* **11/2**[2]

3553 **12** *1* **Choisky (IRE)**[30] 5705 2-8-7 **61**.. JimmyQuinn 10 45
(J Akehurst) *in tch tl wknd 2f out* **8/1**

5035 **13** *1½* **Llab Nala**[17] 6066 2-8-2 **56** ow1.. TPO'Shea 8 36
(M R Channon) *towards rr: rdn 4f out: swtchd wd and hung lft 2f out: n.d* **20/1**

0020 **14** *4* **Smokey Rye**[21] 5939 2-8-9 **63**... SteveDrowne 5 32
(G L Moore) *mid-div tl wknd 2f out* **20/1**

0050 **15** *1¾* **Sabre Light**[24] 5871 2-8-11 **65**...................................... StephenCarson 11 30
(G L Moore) *a bhd* **33/1**

1m 21.95s (-0.75) **Going Correction** -0.20s/f (Firm) **15** Ran SP% **122.1**
Speed ratings (Par 95): **96,95,93,93,92 92,90,90,89,89 89,87,86,81,79**
CSF £37.59 CT £2277.39 TOTE £5.80: £2.40, £2.50, £12.00; EX 26.90 TRIFECTA Not won..
Owner Mrs Joya Burns **Bred** Cornerstone Bloodstock Ltd **Trained** Newmarket, Suffolk

FOCUS
An open nursery, with a case to be made for any number of these beforehand, and the form looks fair but limited by the proximity of the third. The winner made virtually every yard and appeared to set just an even gallop. As in the first race, the middle of the track proved the place to be. The winning time was 0.40 seconds slower than the previous maiden.

NOTEBOOK
Relinquished was soon in a good rhythm up front and Buick got the fractions spot on, as the filly had just enough left to hold off the fast-finishing Fandangerina. She has had plenty of racing this season and could make little impression when fourth over 1m1f at Newmarket on her previous start, but the shorter trip clearly suited and this also represented a drop in class. A rise in the weights will obviously makes things tougher, but at least she has the right attitude. (tchd 9-2)
Fandangerina had shown just modest form in three runs over 6f-7f in maiden company, but her recent Musselburgh second was promising enough and she produced an improved effort on her nursery debut. She only just failed to get up and very much gave the impression she will benefit from a step up to 1m plus in time. She should win her share of races. (tchd 8-1)
Futune(IRE) seemed to appreciate the step back up in trip and ran her most encouraging race yet. She is clearly limited, but she gives the impression a more galloping track will suit better and there could be a small race in her. (op 50-1)
Ski School(IRE), fitted with a visor for the first time on this step back up in trip, was keen through the early stages, but he was was noted travelling quite well early in the straight and is not without ability. (op 9-1 tchd 10-1)
Greek Theatre(USA), who bolted to post last time, offered some promise on his handicap debut, fitted with an eye-shield for the first time. He ended up racing against the far rail, which may not have been the place to be and there could be better to come. (op 16-1)
Albaqaa was a little keen in the first-time visor and did not see his race out. (op 7-1 tchd 6-1)
Landikhaya(IRE) ◆ struggled to land a blow from off the pace and again gave the impression he will benefit from a return to a more galloping track. He has ability and is not one to give up on just yet. (op 8-1)
Park Royal(UAE) ◆ can be rated better than the bare form, as she was always struggling after being hampered at the start and then tried to make her move against the far rail in the straight, which was probably not the place to be. (tchd 5-1)

6450 SPORTINGINDEX.COM/RACING H'CAP 5f 213y
3:35 (3:36) (Class 4) (0-85,86) 3-Y-O+ **£6,309** (£1,888; £944; £472; £235) **Stalls** Low

Form RPR

620 **1** **Transcend**[22] 5923 3-9-1 **81**..(p) RyanMoore 3 97+
(J H M Gosden) *chsd ldrs: eased outside over 2f out: r.o to ld ins fnl f: rdn out* **11/4**[1]

13 **2** *1½* **Tamino (IRE)**[24] 5874 4-8-5 **70**......................................(t) JimmyQuinn 13 81+
(H Morrison) *prom: led wl over 1f out tl ins fnl f: nt qckn* **7/1**[3]

1050 **3** *2* **Social Rhythm**[6] 6313 3-8-5 **74**.................................... MarcHalford(3) 2 79
(H J Collingridge) *mid-div: hdwy over 2f out: squeezed through on rail to press ldrs over 1f out: no ex fnl f* **22/1**

1132 **4** *¾* **Cosmic Destiny (IRE)**[29] 5726 5-8-6 **71**............................ LPKeniry 12 74
(E F Vaughan) *plld hrd in rr: rdn and hdwy over 2f out: styd on fnl f* **12/1**

6600 **5** *shd* **Who's Winning (IRE)**[13] 6141 6-8-7 **72**................................... TQuinn 7 74
(B G Powell) *in tch: outpcd and hrd rdn over 2f out: styd on fnl f* **20/1**

5001 **6** *1¼* **Obe Gold**[11] 6205 5-9-7 **86** 6ex..(v) JohnEgan 11 85
(M R Channon) *bhd: rdn 3f out: styd on fnl 2f: nrst fin* **7/1**[3]

0620 **7** *nk* **Mujood**[22] 5923 4-9-5 **84**..(b) StephenCarson 8 82
(Eve Johnson Houghton) *dwlt: sn in midfield: rdn and lost pl over 2f out: styd on fnl f* **9/1**

0101 **8** *¾* **Calabaza**[7] 6279 5-8-5 **68** 6ex..(p) PaulDoe 1 66
(J Akehurst) *mid-div: effrt over 2f out: hrd rdn and no imp wl over 1f out* **12/1**

0202 **9** *¾* **Sacre Coeur**[38] 5473 3-8-12 **78**.. EddieAhern 6 71
(J L Dunlop) *prom: led over 2f out tl wl over 1f out: wknd fnl f* **16/1**

1054 **10** *shd* **Peter Island (FR)**[40] 5401 4-8-11 **76**..............................(b) JimCrowley 9 69
(J Gallagher) *led and set str pce tl over 2f out: wknd jst over 1f out* **20/1**

0411 **11** *shd* **Cornus**[7] 6283 5-9-0 **79** 6ex..(be) JamesDoyle 4 81+
(A J McCabe) *hld up in midfield: effrt over 2f out: nt pce to chal: eased whn hld fnl f* **13/2**[2]

1035 **12** *¾* **Perfect Treasure (IRE)**[16] 6081 4-8-9 **74**....................... RobertHavlin 5 64
(J A R Toller) *s.s: a bhd* **11/1**

0600 **13** *1* **Lucayos**[73] 4456 4-8-10 **82**... KylieManser(7) 10 69
(Mrs H Sweeting) *towards rr: rdn 3f out: n.d fnl 2f* **66/1**

67.97 secs (-2.13) **Going Correction** -0.20s/f (Firm)
WFA 3 from 4yo+ 1lb **13** Ran SP% **120.0**
Speed ratings (Par 105): **106,104,101,100,100 98,98,97,96,96 95,94,93**
CSF £20.03 CT £371.60 TOTE £3.60: £1.70, £2.90, £11.40; EX 30.60 TRIFECTA Not won..
Owner H R H Princess Haya Of Jordan **Bred** Keith Freeman **Trained** Newmarket, Suffolk
■ Stewards' Enquiry : James Doyle caution: allowed gelding to coast home with no assistance

FOCUS
A good, competitive sprint handicap and the pace was furious throughout. The main action once again took place down the centre of the track. The winning time was not that far off the track record.

6451 EBF JOHN HUNTER - FOLLOW YOUR INSTINCT MAIDEN STKS 7f 214y
4:10 (4:10) (Class 4) 2-Y-O **£5,181** (£1,541; £577; £577) **Stalls** Low

Form RPR

022 **1** **Yaddree**[36] 5538 2-9-3 80.. PhilipRobinson 1 81
(M A Jarvis) *pressed ldr: drvn level fnl f: jst got up* **2/1**[2]

022 **2** *shd* **Downhiller (IRE)**[28] 5749 2-9-3 76.................................... EddieAhern 8 81
(J L Dunlop) *led: hrd rdn and kpt on wl whn chal fnl f: jst tched off* **16/1**

22 **3** *2½* **City Stable (IRE)**[17] 6058 2-9-3 0....................................... RyanMoore 9 75
(Sir Michael Stoute) *towards rr and sn niggled along: swtchd wd and hdwy 2f out: hrd rdn and hung lft over 1f out: styd on* **1/1**[1]

4 **3** *dht* **Dandy Erin (IRE)**[31] 5680 2-9-3 0....................................... TPQueally 2 75
(J A Osborne) *mid-div: hrd rdn and hdwy over 1f out: no imp fnl f* **12/1**

6022 **5** *1¼* **Ten Pole Tudor**[30] 5707 2-9-3 69... JohnEgan 11 73
(R A Harris) *chsd ldrs: hrd rdn 2f out: one pce* **33/1**

25 **6** *6* **Oberlin (USA)**[22] 5904 2-9-3 0.. GregFairley 5 59
(M Johnston) *prom tl hrd rdn and wknd 2f out* **10/1**[3]

4 **7** *½* **Driven (IRE)**[22] 5919 2-9-3 0... JimCrowley 4 58
(Mrs A J Perrett) *t.k.h: in tch tl wknd 2f out* **14/1**

55 **8** *6* **Highly Regal (IRE)**[11] 6202 2-9-3 0.................................. GeorgeBaker 7 45+
(R A Teal) *a bhd: n.d fnl 3f* **50/1**

00 **9** *1¾* **Dance Easily**[29] 5720 2-8-12 0.. PaulDoe 10 36
(J L Dunlop) *stdd s: wd: hld up in midfield: rdn over 2f out: sn wknd* **100/1**

00 **10** *2* **Iron Cross (IRE)**[22] 5904 2-9-3 0.................................... JamieMackay 6 37
(Sir Mark Prescott) *s.s: a wl bhd* **80/1**

06 **P** **Muharjam**[16] 6079 2-9-3 0..(b[1]) SebSanders 3 —
(C E Brittain) *sn bhd: eased 3f out: sn t.o: p.u and dismntd nr fin* **40/1**

1m 33.38s (-1.66) **Going Correction** -0.20s/f (Firm) **11** Ran SP% **122.2**
Speed ratings (Par 97): **100,99,97,97,96 90,89,83,81,79** —
PL: City Stable £0.60, Dandy Erin £1.30; TRI: Yaddree/Downhiller/CS £21.50, Yaddree/Downhiller/DE £63.30 CSF £34.47 TOTE £3.20: £1.40, £2.40; EX 32.70 TRIFECTA Pool £578.39 - 9.52 winning units..
Owner Sheikh Ahmed Al Maktoum **Bred** Darley **Trained** Newmarket, Suffolk

FOCUS
Just an ordinary maiden, but some powerful stables were represented and the winner is the best guide to the level. The principals tended to race up the middle of the track in the straight and very few got involved from off the pace.

NOTEBOOK
Yaddree had shown plenty of ability on all three of his previous starts, most notably when runner-up on the Polytrack at Kempton and on then on turf in a reasonable race at Sandown, and this was a deserved first success. Having raced on the pace from the outset, he was made to work hard by Downhiller in the closing stages, but he responded gamely to his rider's urgings. He is likely to be put away for the year now and should strengthen up over the winter. (op 5-2)
Downhiller(IRE) came into this with a similar profile to the winner, having run second on his last two starts, but he was rated 6lb inferior to Yaddree and just missed out. Like the winner, he looks a really game sort and deserves to win a race. He also has the option of going for nurseries.
City Stable(IRE) showed a distinct lack of tactical speed when second at Windsor on his previous start and he once again struggled to get himself into a challenging position. He was in trouble a fair way from the finish and, although trying his hardest, he did not look at home on the track. He is pretty limited, but can do better over a lot further next year, and a more galloping track should also help. (op 5-4 tchd 11-8 in a place)
Dandy Erin(IRE) showed ability when fourth on his debut at Kempton and this was another respectable effort. It would be no surprise to see him placed to advantage on the sand at some point and he needs one more run for a handicap mark. (op 5-4 tchd 11-8 in a place)
Ten Pole Tudor, claimed out of Jamie Osborne's yard after running second in a seller at Leicester two starts back, ran well on his debut for this yard round here last time and this was another creditable effort. He should find things easier in nursery company. (tchd 40-1)
Oberlin(USA) will have more options now he is qualified for a nursery mark. (tchd 14-1)
Driven(IRE) was too keen for his own good. (op 12-1 tchd 16-1)
Highly Regal(IRE) ◆ was well held this time, but he had shown plenty of ability on his two previous starts and will be one to watch when sent handicapping. Official explanation: trainer said colt was unsuited by the track (op 40-1)
Iron Cross(IRE) was well beaten, but he can be expected to improve when sent down the handicap route in time. (op 100-1)
Muharjam Official explanation: jockey said colt lost its action

6452 BOB DALEY MEMORIAL (S) H'CAP 1m 1f 209y
4:45 (4:45) (Class 6) (0-60,60) 3-Y-O+ £2,047 (£604; £302) Stalls High

Form RPR
4122 1 **Bridgewater Boys**[8] 6265 6-9-9 60..........(b) RyanMoore 10 71
(G L Moore) *dwlt: hld up in tch gng wl: led over 2f out: c towards stands' rail: rdn clr fnl f* **6/4**[1]
0040 2 3½ **Megalala (IRE)**[11] 6212 6-8-13 50..........TPQueally 5 54
(J J Bridger) *bhd: gd hdwy on far rail 2f out: wnt 2nd over 1f out: nt pce of wnr fnl f* **7/1**[3]
-024 3 hd **Granary Girl**[69] 4558 5-9-1 52..........JimmyQuinn 7 56
(J Pearce) *towards rr: hrd rdn and styd on fnl 2f: nrst fin* **11/2**[2]
1-00 4 2½ **Guadiana (GER)**[34] 5606 5-8-9 46 oh1..........JamesDoyle 8 45
(A W Carroll) *bhd: swtchd wd and hdwy 3f out: hrd rdn 2f out: styd on same pce* **20/1**
0660 5 ¾ **Rock Haven (IRE)**[47] 5235 5-9-2 53..........IanMongan 4 50
(G H Yardley) *t.k.h: chsd ldrs: n.m.r and lost pl over 4f out: hmpd and swtchd lft 2f out: rallied over 1f out: one pce* **12/1**
0605 6 1¼ **Salvestro**[18] 5345 4-8-6 46 oh1..........LukeMorris(3) 2 41
(A W Carroll) *s.s: bhd: swtchd wd over 2f out: styd on u.p: nvr nrr* **16/1**
3030 7 shd **Mr Napoleon (IRE)**[8] 6260 5-9-7 58..........(p) OscarUrbina 11 52
(G Prodromou) *mid-div: effrt over 2f out: hrd rdn and no imp over 1f out* **12/1**
2050 8 hd **Missie Baileys**[8] 6265 5-8-9 46..........(p) LPKeniry 1 40
(Mrs L J Mongan) *prom: hrd rdn 2f out: sn wknd* **12/1**
4000 9 1¾ **Dark Planet**[17] 6068 4-8-12 54..........(v) HaddenFrost(5) 3 45
(D Burchell) *stmbld s: t.k.h towards rr: rdn over 2f out: nt rch ldrs* **14/1**
0006 10 5 **Moving Story**[38] 5487 4-8-9 46 oh1..........MickyFenton 9 27
(P T Midgley) *led tl over 3f out: wknd qckly over 1f out* **20/1**
L02 11 2 **Hester Brook (IRE)**[16] 6090 3-8-4 46 oh1..........PaulEddery 12 23
(J G M O'Shea) *prom tl wknd wl over 1f out: eased whn btn* **20/1**
0050 12 hd **Yenaled**[42] 5345 10-8-2 46 oh1..........PietroRomeo(7) 13 22
(J M Bradley) *chsd ldrs: led over 3f out tl over 2f out: sn wknd* **50/1**
5400 13 31 **Mayireneyrbel**[17] 6060 3-8-10 52..........SebSanders 6 —
(J Akehurst) *in tch tl wknd 3f out: eased whn no ch over 1f out: b.b.v* **16/1**

2m 2.99s (0.39) **Going Correction** -0.20s/f (Firm)
WFA 3 from 4yo+ 5lb 13 Ran SP% 125.6
Speed ratings (Par 101): **90,87,87,85,84 83,83,83,81,77 76,76,51**
CSF £11.85 CT £51.58 TOTE £2.00: £1.20, £2.70, £2.10; EX 15.70 Trifecta £37.60 Pool £621.64 - 11.72 winning units..The winner was bought in for 3,800gns. Mr Napoleon was claimed by G L Moore for £6,000.
Owner Matthew Green & Richard Green **Bred** Southill Stud **Trained** Woodingdean, E Sussex

FOCUS
A standard selling handicap and weak form rated through the third. The early gallop did not look very strong and the winning time was moderate, even for a seller. The winner ended up against the stands'-side rail.
Mayireneyrbel Official explanation: trainer said filly bled from the nose

6453 BRIGHTON BETTING JUST GOT BETTER APPRENTICE H'CAP 1m 3f 196y
5:15 (5:15) (Class 6) (0-55,55) 3-Y-O+ £1,943 (£578; £288; £144) Stalls High

Form RPR
-000 1 **Mixing**[94] 3799 5-8-12 46 oh1..........PatrickHills 1 60+
(J Akehurst) *hld up in midfield: smooth hdwy 3f out: led 2f out: rdn clr fnl f: readily* **10/1**
5560 2 4 **Bob's Your Uncle**[40] 5426 4-9-4 55..........JackDean(3) 5 63
(J G Portman) *mid-div: effrt 3f out: styd on to go 2nd over 1f out: no ch w wnr* **9/2**[1]
0602 3 3½ **Maria Antonia (IRE)**[9] 6250 4-8-10 47..........KellyHarrison(3) 4 49
(P A Blockley) *s.s: hld up in rr: hdwy 4f out: chsd ldrs over 2f out: one pce appr fnl f* **11/2**[3]
0500 4 1¼ **Always Best**[20] 5980 3-8-2 46..........JackMitchell(3) 3 46
(M Johnston) *chsd ldrs: led 3f out tl 2f out: wknd 1f out* **5/1**[2]
4000 5 1 **Mud Monkey**[26] 2259 3-8-8 54..........KylieManser(5) 10 53
(B G Powell) *t.k.h: prom: drvn along and outpcd over 2f out: sn btn* **9/2**[1]
0520 6 1¾ **Beckenham's Secret**[13] 6147 3-8-4 50..........MarkCoumbe(5) 8 46
(A W Carroll) *bhd: c wd and mod effrt over 2f out: hrd rdn: no imp* **12/1**
0000 7 10 **Mahmjra**[19] 6007 5-8-13 50..........SCreighton(3) 12 30
(C N Allen) *led tl 3f out: wknd 2f out* **12/1**
6200 8 6 **English Archer**[9] 6259 4-8-10 49..........DeanHeslop(5) 7 19
(W M Brisbourne) *towards rr: rdn 3f out: n.d whn hung bdly lft 2f out* **15/2**
600 9 7 **Silent Beauty (IRE)**[21] 5945 3-8-2 46 oh1..........WilliamCarson(3) 11 5
(S C Williams) *prom tl hrd rdn and wknd 2f out: no ch whn eased fnl 50yds* **14/1**
0000 10 3 **My Spring Rose**[24] 5873 3-8-4 50..........MatthewDavies(5) 6 4
(J R Jenkins) *in tch to 1/2-way: no ch fnl 4f* **16/1**
60-0 11 8 **Meantime (USA)**[8] 6265 4-9-7 55..........(p) JamesMillman 9 —
(G Prodromou) *mid-div on outside tl wknd qckly over 3f out* **66/1**
0-00 12 4 **Vettori Dancer**[22] 5894 4-8-7 46 oh1..........(b[1]) AshleyMorgan(5) 2 —
(G G Margarson) *in tch: hrd rdn and lost pl 5f out: sn bhd: eased whn no ch fnl 2f* **50/1**

2m 30.95s (-1.25) **Going Correction** -0.20s/f (Firm)
WFA 3 from 4yo+ 7lb 12 Ran SP% 120.7
Speed ratings (Par 101): **96,93,91,90,89 88,81,77,73,71 65,63**
CSF £55.57 CT £281.12 TOTE £11.20: £3.50, £2.10, £2.00; EX 62.30 Trifecta £291.30 Pool £410.37 - 0.45 winning units. Place 6 £17.74, Place 5 £4.88..
Owner Canisbay Bloodstock **Bred** Juddmonte Farms **Trained** Epsom, Surrey

FOCUS
A very moderate middle-distance handicap restricted to apprentices who had not ridden more than 50 winners. The form is weak but sound enough for the grade.
T/Plt: £27.70 to a £1 stake. Pool: £67,730.85. 1,782.10 winning tickets. T/Qpdt: £8.30 to a £1 stake. Pool: £4,421.50. 390.70 winning tickets. LM

6385 WOLVERHAMPTON (A.W) (L-H)
Thursday, October 25

OFFICIAL GOING: Standard
Wind: Light against Weather: Overcast

6454 BOOK ONLINE AT WOLVERHAMPTON-RACECOURSE.CO.UK CLAIMING STKS 7f 32y(P)
6:50 (6:51) (Class 6) 2-Y-O £2,388 (£705; £352) Stalls High

Form RPR
0061 1 **What Katie Did (IRE)**[13] 6151 2-9-3 74..........JamieSpencer 4 73
(J A Osborne) *a.p: chsd ldr 2f out: rdn to ld ins fnl f: styd on* **7/4**[1]
3441 2 nk **What's For Tea**[15] 6099 2-8-6 61..........RichardKingscote 5 61
(Tom Dascombe) *sn led: rdn and edgd rt over 1f out: hdd ins fnl f: styd on* **9/4**[2]
1 3 5 **Stevie Thunder**[38] 5477 2-9-7 67..........NCallan 8 64
(G A Swinbank) *prom: rdn and hung rt over 1f out: styd on same pce* **11/2**[3]
5006 4 1¾ **Weet By Far**[13] 6150 2-8-8 59..........GrahamGibbons 3 47
(R Hollinshead) *chsd ldrs: rdn over 1f out: wknd fnl f* **20/1**
0502 5 1½ **Deckguard**[15] 6099 2-8-6 66..........(p) TolleyDean(5) 1 46
(J S Moore) *prom: rdn over 2f out: wknd over 1f out* **8/1**
0005 6 ½ **Emef Princess**[22] 5901 2-8-1 53..........(b) AndrewMullen(3) 7 38
(K A Ryan) *chsd ldr 6f out: rdn over 2f out: wknd over 1f out* **40/1**
000 7 1½ **Oli James (USA)**[17] 6058 2-8-11 64..........TomEaves 2 41
(P F I Cole) *sn pushed along in rr: rdn 4f out: sme hdwy and hung lft over 1f out: n.d* **10/1**
0 8 shd **Duneen Dream (USA)**[10] 6237 2-8-13 0..........NeilPollard 12 43
(W J Musson) *hld up: rdn 1/2-way: hung lft over 1f out: n.d* **66/1**
0045 9 2½ **Thomas Malory (IRE)**[16] 6074 2-9-2 59..........(v[1]) KirstyMilczarek(5) 9 45
(Miss V Haigh) *s.s: rdn and hung rt over 2f out: a bhd* **28/1**
60 10 2 **Bahia Palace**[13] 6151 2-7-9 0..........FrankiePickard(7) 6 21
(M D I Usher) *hld up: rdn 1/2-way: n.d* **33/1**
00 11 24 **Spoilt Madame**[10] 6242 2-8-4 0..........FrancisNorton 10 —
(P D Evans) *s.i.s: a in rr* **66/1**

1m 30.21s (-0.19) **Going Correction** -0.15s/f (Stan) 11 Ran SP% 119.3
Speed ratings (Par 93): **95,94,88,86,85 84,82,82,79,77 50**
CSF £5.47 TOTE £2.10: £1.02, £1.90, £1.80; EX 7.60.The winner was claimed by P Cole for £16,000.
Owner Mountgrange Stud **Bred** Brian Williamson **Trained** Upper Lambourn, Berks

FOCUS
An ordinary claimer and solid enough form for the grade rated through the winner to form.

NOTEBOOK
What Katie Did(IRE), a winner of a similar race over 6f here last time, travelled well in behind the leader and it seemed a question of how far once he was switched to challenge, but in the end he had to be kept right up to his work to score. It was probably more a case of him not finding a great deal in front rather than him struggling with the extra furlong. (op 11-8 tchd 5-4)
What's For Tea, who made all to win in similar company at Kempton last time, attempted to repeat those tactics and expose any chinks in the favourite's stamina. In the end she was not able to hold him off but she made a brave fist of it, and pulled nicely clear of the third. (op 9-2)
Stevie Thunder, winner of a Musselburgh seller on his debut, had a bit to find at the ratings giving weight away to the majority of the field, so this was a fair effort. (op 9-2 tchd 6-1)
Weet By Far is a half-sister to a 1m4f winner but her sire is an influence for speed. She ran alright, but her best trip remains a mystery. (op 16-1)
Deckguard, wearing cheekpieces for the first time, finished a length and a half behind What's For Tea at Kempton on his last start but was 4lb better off at the weights here. That gave him a chance of reversing the form, but in the end he was beaten even further. (tchd 9-1)
Emef Princess tried to take on What's For Tea at the head of affairs and paid the price. (op 33-1)
Thomas Malory(IRE) Official explanation: jockey said colt hung right-handed throughout

6455 SPONSOR A RACE BY CALLING 0870 220 2442 H'CAP 7f 32y(P)
7:20 (7:20) (Class 6) (0-65,65) 3-Y-O £2,047 (£604; £302) Stalls High

Form RPR
6051 1 **Wadnagin (IRE)**[35] 5576 3-8-11 58..........JamieSpencer 10 67
(I A Wood) *hld up: nt clr run over 2f out: swtchd rt and hdwy over 1f out: rdn to ld and edgd lft wl ins fnl f* **8/1**
0045 2 ½ **Proper (IRE)**[13] 6148 3-9-0 61..........FrancisNorton 4 69
(M R Channon) *chsd ldrs: rdn to ld ins fnl f: sn hdd: kpt on* **4/1**[2]
5316 3 3½ **Metropolitan Chief**[14] 6123 3-8-8 60..........(b) KirstyMilczarek(5) 5 59
(D M Simcock) *chsd ldrs: led over 1f out: sn rdn and hung lft: hdd and no ex ins fnl f* **3/1**[1]
5400 4 1¼ **Comrade Cotton**[7] 6278 3-9-2 63..........(b[1]) PatDobbs 11 58
(N A Callaghan) *hld up: hdwy u.p over 1f out: wknd ins fnl f* **25/1**
0-40 5 4 **Toucantini**[267] 312 3-9-4 65..........JimmyFortune 1 49
(R Charlton) *chsd ldrs: rdn over 1f out: sn wknd* **12/1**
001 6 1¼ **Memphis Marie**[56] 4977 3-8-12 59..........StephenDonohoe 7 40
(C N Allen) *prom: chsd ldr 5f out: led over 2f out: rdn and hdd over 1f out: sn hung lft and wknd* **16/1**
6002 7 ¾ **Anthill**[117] 3087 3-9-2 63..........RichardThomas 9 42
(I A Wood) *led: rdn and hdd over 2f out: wkng whn hmpd ins fnl f* **14/1**
40 8 1¼ **Exit Strategy (IRE)**[30] 5711 3-8-13 65..........(p) KevinGhunowa(5) 2 41
(R A Harris) *hld up: hdwy 2f out: wkng whn hmpd ins fnl f* **20/1**
0000 9 5 **Rabbit Fighter (IRE)**[20] 5985 3-8-13 60..........TomEaves 6 22
(D Shaw) *s.i.s: hdwy over 4f out: wknd over 2f out* **7/1**

-042 **10** 1 1/2 **Sophia Gardens**[12] 6176 3-9-1 **62**.. NCallan 8 20
(D W P Arbuthnot) *chsd ldrs: rdn 1/2-way: hung rt and wknd over 1f out* **9/2**[3]

1m 29.65s (-0.75) **Going Correction** -0.15s/f (Stan) **10** Ran SP% **115.6**
Speed ratings (Par 99): **98,97,93,92,87 86,85,83,78,76**
CSF £39.70 CT £121.41 TOTE £7.50: £3.80, £1.20, £1.10; EX 36.60.
Owner Jim Browne **Bred** Kilnamoragh Stud **Trained** Upper Lambourn, Berks
■ Stewards' Enquiry : Stephen Donohoe two-day ban: careless riding (Nov 5,6)

FOCUS
A moderate handicap run at a decent pace but not that solid and best rated through the runner-up.
Exit Strategy(IRE) Official explanation: jockey said gelding was hampered in the final furlong
Sophia Gardens Official explanation: jockey said filly had no more to give

6456 HOTEL & CONFERENCING AT WOLVERHAMPTON RACECOURSE MEDIAN AUCTION MAIDEN STKS 1m 141y(P)
7:50 (7:50) (Class 5) 2-Y-O **£2,817** (£838; £418; £209) **Stalls** Low

Form RPR
4322 **1** **Bermacha**[13] 6150 2-8-12 70.. JamieSpencer 2 74+
(W R Muir) *chsd ldrs: led wl over 1f out: sn clr and hung rt: styd on wl* **5/4**[1]
0 **2** 7 **Fair Gale**[8] 6262 2-9-3 0.. JimmyFortune 1 64+
(S Kirk) *mid-div: sn pushed along: rdn over 3f out: hdwy to chse wnr and hung lft over 1f out: no imp* **11/8**[2]
0 **3** 6 **Grapes Of Wrath (UAE)**[31] 5679 2-8-9 0................ AndrewMullen(3) 8 47
(M Johnston) *chsd clr ldr tl rdn over 2f out: wknd over 1f out* **9/1**
0 **4** 3 1/2 **Jasoora**[14] 6119 2-8-12 0.. PatDobbs 9 39
(M P Tregoning) *s.i.s: nvr nrr* **7/1**[3]
0000 **5** 6 **Transcendent (IRE)**[58] 4923 2-9-3 51.. NCallan 5 32
(J D Bethell) *hld up: plld hrd: rdn and wknd wl over 2f out* **40/1**
6 nk **No Nukes** 2-9-3 0.. TGMcLaughlin 4 31
(P D Evans) *s.i.s: a bhd: lost tch 1/2-way* **66/1**
0000 **7** 3/4 **Feeling Fresh (IRE)**[17] 6066 2-8-12 60.............. RussellKennemore(5) 7 30
(Paul Green) *sn led: set suicidal pce and clr 7f out: wknd and hdd wl over 1f out* **33/1**

1m 50.98s (-0.78) **Going Correction** -0.15s/f (Stan) 7 Ran SP% **115.9**
Speed ratings (Par 95): **97,90,85,82,77 76,76**
CSF £3.33 TOTE £2.00: £1.20, £1.30; EX 5.00.
Owner Essex Racing Club **Bred** B Root **Trained** Lambourn, Berks

FOCUS
Ordinary maiden form but it was run at a good pace thanks to the trailblazing Feeling Fresh and the race might eventually rate higher.

NOTEBOOK
Bermacha, who boasts an official rating of 70, has been running well in nurseries lately and deserved to get off the mark. She hung right in the straight but kept on well to run out a clear winner, although she did not need to improve to take this prize. (op 6-4)
Fair Gale was under pressure from a long way out but, in fairness, kept responding. A half-brother to Burning Moon, a 1m2f winner at three, Titan Triumph, a 7f winner at three, and to a hurdles winner, he is bred to be a middle-distance performer next year. He needs one more run for a mark. (op 13-8 tchd 7-4)
Grapes Of Wrath(UAE), a sister to Maelstrom, a 1m4f winner at three in France, and Stromstrad, a dual winner over hurdles, led the chasing group for most of the way but lacked the pace to be a threat at the business end. She is another bred to come into her own over much further next year and also requires one more outing for a handicap mark. (op 8-1 tchd 11-1)
Jasoora shaped with a little promise on her debut but failed to land a blow in this weaker affair. (op 11-2 tchd 8-1)
Transcendent(IRE) pulled too hard over this longer trip having done all his previous racing over sprint distances.
Feeling Fresh(IRE) led at a million miles an hour and it was no surprise to anyone when he fell in a heap rounding the turn into the straight. (op 50-1 tchd 66-1)

6457 HORIZONS RESTAURANT MEDIAN AUCTION MAIDEN STKS 1m 141y(P)
8:20 (8:20) (Class 6) 3-4-Y-O **£2,047** (£604; £302) **Stalls** Low

Form RPR
0503 **1** **Quaglino Way (GR)**[10] 6229 3-9-3 65.. JamieSpencer 2 64
(P R Chamings) *mde virtually all: rdn over 2f out: styd on* **9/2**[3]
200 **2** 1 1/4 **Alexander Guru**[100] 3621 3-9-3 70.. FrancisNorton 3 61
(M Blanshard) *trckd wnr: plld hrd: rdn and edgd lft fr over 1f out: styd on* **16/1**
03 **3** 3/4 **Ballad Maker (IRE)**[15] 6097 3-9-3 0.. JimmyFortune 9 59
(J H M Gosden) *chsd ldrs: lost pl 7f out: hdwy over 4f out: hrd rdn fr over 1f out: styd on* **10/11**[1]
046 **4** 3 1/2 **Massams Lane**[172] 1501 3-9-3 58.. NCallan 1 51
(G C Bravery) *trckd ldrs: rdn over 2f out: styd on same pce appr fnl f* **7/2**[2]
6045 **5** 10 **Semi Detached (IRE)**[5] 6342 4-9-7 60.. AdamKirby 7 28
(J W Unett) *chsd ldrs tl rdn and wknd over 2f out* **10/1**
000- **6** 3/4 **Silvabella (IRE)**[477] 3195 4-9-2 39.. LiamJones 5 22
(D Haydn Jones) *prom: rdn 1/2-way: wknd 3f out* **150/1**
30 **7** 1 **Foxy Diplomat**[10] 6229 3-8-12 0.. KevinGhunowa(5) 8 24
(Miss J R Tooth) *hld up: rdn over 3f out: wknd over 2f out* **66/1**
8 16 **Raihanah** 3-8-12 0.. DeanMcKeown 6 —
(D Shaw) *s.s: a in rr: wknd over 3f out* **33/1**

1m 51.42s (-0.34) **Going Correction** -0.15s/f (Stan)
WFA 3 from 4yo 4lb 8 Ran SP% **112.9**
Speed ratings (Par 101): **95,93,93,90,81 80,79,65**
CSF £66.27 TOTE £3.20: £2.10, £5.70, £1.02; EX 63.90.
Owner Mrs Alexandra J Chandris **Bred** Ippotour Stud **Trained** Baughurst, Hants
■ Quaglino Way completed a 305-1 four-timer for jockey Jamie Spencer.

FOCUS
A very moderate older-horse maiden and the order hardly changed throughout the contest. The form looks weak for the grade.
Foxy Diplomat Official explanation: jockey said gelding ran too freely

6458 WOLVERHAMPTON HOLIDAY INN H'CAP 1m 1f 103y(P)
8:50 (8:50) (Class 6) (0-60,60) 3-Y-O+ **£2,047** (£604; £302) **Stalls** Low

Form RPR
5103 **1** **Lobengula (IRE)**[5] 6342 5-9-6 58.. DanielTudhope 5 74
(I W McInnes) *mde all: rdn clr over 2f out: eased nr fin* **3/1**[2]
0613 **2** 3 1/2 **Alfie Tupper (IRE)**[8] 6260 4-9-4 56.. JamieSpencer 13 71+
(S Kirk) *s.i.s: hld up: hdwy over 1f out: wnt 2nd and edgd lft fnl f: no ch w wnr* **11/8**[1]
1204 **3** 5 **Weet Yer Tern (IRE)**[5] 6342 5-9-1 53.. NCallan 11 52
(W M Brisbourne) *hld up: racd keenly: hdwy over 2f out: nt clr run over 1f out: wknd ins fnl f* **10/1**
0065 **4** 1/2 **Reveur**[21] 5946 4-8-8 46 oh1.. RichardMullen 7 43
(M Mullineaux) *chsd ldrs: rdn over 2f out: edgd lft over 1f out: sn wknd* **16/1**
0200 **5** 1/2 **Rainbow Flame**[46] 4915 3-9-4 60........................(v) RichardKingscote 8 56
(Tom Dascombe) *s.i.s: hld up: styd on fnl f: nvr nrr* **14/1**
5303 **6** shd **Saaratt**[11] 6206 3-9-4 60.. FrancisNorton 4 56
(J W Hills) *hld up: plld hrd: swtchd lft over 1f out: styd on: nvr nrr* **20/1**
0044 **7** 1/2 **Fateful Attraction**[8] 6260 4-9-7 59........................(b) AdamKirby 1 54
(I A Wood) *chsd ldrs: rdn over 2f out: wknd over 1f out* **10/1**
4604 **8** shd **Abbeygate**[11] 6212 6-8-8 46 oh1.. TGMcLaughlin 9 41
(T Keddy) *hld up: rdn over 3f out: sme hdwy over 2f out: sn wknd* **14/1**
065 **9** 1/2 **Mark Of The Fen**[17] 6070 3-8-8 50........................(e) DeanMcKeown 2 44
(Rae Guest) *hld up in tch: plld hrd: rdn over 2f out: wknd over 1f out* **20/1**
6314 **10** 1/2 **Terminate (GER)**[11] 6196 5-9-4 56.. StephenDonohoe 10 49
(Ian Williams) *chsd ldrs: rdn over 2f out: wknd over 1f out* **17/2**
0500 **11** 1 1/2 **Band**[40] 5421 7-8-10 48.. GrahamGibbons 3 38
(E S McMahon) *chsd wnr: rdn over 2f out: wknd over 1f out* **8/1**[3]
6-05 **12** 21 **Grafty Green (IRE)**[15] 6109 4-9-8 60.. LiamJones 6 6
(W M Brisbourne) *hld up: hdwy over 5f out: rdn over 3f out: sn wknd* **40/1**

2m 0.49s (-2.13) **Going Correction** -0.15s/f (Stan)
WFA 3 from 4yo+ 4lb 12 Ran SP% **138.1**
Speed ratings (Par 101): **103,99,95,95,94 94,94,93,93,93 91,73**
CSF £8.74 CT £43.99 TOTE £3.80: £1.80, £1.50, £1.70; EX 11.70.
Owner Colin G R Booth **Bred** A S O'Brien And Lars Pearson **Trained** Catwick, E Yorks

FOCUS
Not as competitive as the numbers would suggest as very few ever got into it, but at least the pace was decent thanks to the winner. The form is good for the grade with the runner-up rated to this year's best.

6459 WOLVERHAMPTON-RACECOURSE.CO.UK H'CAP 1m 5f 194y(P)
9:20 (9:21) (Class 5) (0-70,70) 3-Y-O+ **£3,238** (£963; £481; £240) **Stalls** Low

Form RPR
0311 **1** **Bold Adventure**[27] 5779 3-8-8 59.. NeilPollard 2 73+
(W J Musson) *hld up: hdwy over 3f out: chsd ldr over 1f out: rdn to ld and edgd lft ins fnl f: styd on wl* **6/4**[1]
0416 **2** 2 1/2 **Papradon**[12] 6178 3-8-4 55..(v) LiamJones 6 61
(J R Best) *chsd ldr 2f: remained handy: chsd ldr 6f out: led 3f out: rdn over 1f out: hdd and no ex ins fnl f* **11/1**
0-43 **3** 3 **Golano**[10] 6241 7-10-0 70.. RichardMullen 5 72+
(P R Webber) *chsd ldrs: shkn up over 4f out: outpcd over 2f out: rallied over 1f out: hung lft ins fnl f: styd on* **5/1**[3]
3515 **4** 1 1/4 **Theflyingscottie**[100] 3630 5-8-9 51.. DeanMcKeown 8 51
(D Shaw) *hld up: hdwy over 3f out: rdn over 1f out: wknd ins fnl f* **25/1**
3034 **5** 1 1/2 **Black Mogul**[13] 6147 3-8-1 52 oh1 ow1........................(b) FrancisNorton 1 50
(W R Muir) *led: hdd 12f out: led again over 8f out: rdn and hdd 3f out: wknd fnl f* **9/1**
1-30 **6** 2 **Scutch Mill (IRE)**[25] 2201 5-9-2 65........................(t) PatrickDonaghy(7) 10 60
(P C Haslam) *s.s: hld up: hdwy over 2f out: rdn and wknd over 1f out* **8/1**
1306 **7** 2 **Three Boars**[124] 2887 5-9-12 68..(b) JamieSpencer 9 61
(S Gollings) *hld up: hdwy 5f out: rdn and wknd wl over 1f out* **5/2**[2]
1050 **8** 3 **Mighty Kitchener (USA)**[17] 6069 4-9-8 64.. TomEaves 3 52
(P Howling) *hld up: rdn over 4f out: a in rr* **20/1**
3353 **9** 3 **Yab Adee**[22] 5898 3-8-7 65.. TalibHussain(7) 7 49
(M P Tregoning) *chsd ldrs: led 11f out: hdd over 8f out: rdn and wknd over 2f out* **14/1**
-000 **10** 22 **New Diamond**[22] 5916 8-8-4 51 oh6.. TolleyDean(5) 4 4
(Mrs P Ford) *prom: racd keenly: rdn and wknd over 3f out* **100/1**

3m 5.86s (-1.51) **Going Correction** -0.15s/f (Stan)
WFA 3 from 4yo+ 9lb 10 Ran SP% **130.9**
Speed ratings (Par 103): **98,96,94,94,93 92,91,89,87,75**
CSF £23.33 CT £78.85 TOTE £3.00: £1.30, £4.90, £1.30; EX 25.60.
Owner Mustard Cord Cads **Bred** Bricklow Ltd **Trained** Newmarket, Suffolk
■ A very welcome 'spare' for jockey Neil Pollard whose first winner this was after 804 days and 202 rides.

FOCUS
A modest handicap and the pace was modest which resulted in a couple pulling their chances away. The runner-up and fourth sets the level.
Three Boars Official explanation: jockey said gelding stopped very quickly
New Diamond Official explanation: jockey said gelding hung right
T/Plt: £3.60 to a £1 stake. Pool: £88,088.00. 17,411.70 winning tickets. T/Qpdt: £1.80 to a £1 stake. Pool: £5,412.70. 2,112.50 winning tickets. CR

6187 SAINT-CLOUD (L-H)
Thursday, October 25

OFFICIAL GOING: Good

6460a PRIX DE FLORE (GROUP 3) (F&M) 1m 2f 110y
1:20 (1:26) 3-Y-O+ **£27,027** (£10,811; £8,108; £5,405; £2,703)

RPR
1 **La Boum (GER)**[20] 6035 4-8-11.. CSoumillon 1 103
(Robert Collet, France) *mid-div: 6th into st on ins: swtchd out wl over 1f out: rdn and hdwy to ld 100yds out: drvn out* **9/2**[3]
2 1 1/2 **Concentric**[21] 5963 3-8-7.. SPasquier 2 102
(A Fabre, France) *led 1f: hld up bhd ldrs: 3rd into st: hdwy on ins to ld 1 1/2f out: hdd 100yds out: one pce* **13/10**[1]
3 2 **Noble Ginger (FR)**[37] 5519 3-8-7.. C-PLemaire 11 98
(J E Pease, France) *a.p: 2nd into st: ev ch 1 1/2f out: one pce* **38/1**
4 1/2 **Hapsburg (FR)**[54] 5058 3-8-7.. TJarnet 8 97
(E Libaud, France) *a in tch: 5th into st: kpt on one pce* **97/10**
5 nk **Penkinella (FR)**[28] 4-8-11.. AClement 9 94
(A Couetil, France) *7th into st on outside: styd on one pce u.p* **76/1**
6 3/4 **La Dancia (IRE)**[18] 6046 4-9-1.. WMongil 3 97
(P Rau, Germany) *led after 1f: hdd 1 1/2f out: wknd fnl f* **18/1**
7 snk **Tashelka (FR)**[39] 5465 3-8-10.. JAuge 12 98
(A Fabre, France) *drawn on wd outside: dwlt s: 11th and rdn into st: sme late prog* **38/10**[2]
8 nk **Utrecht**[88] 4010 3-8-10.. JVictoire 4 97
(A Fabre, France) *8th into st: nvr a factor* **38/10**[2]
9 2 **Singapore Creek (FR)**[67] 3-8-7.. SMaillot 6 90
(Robert Collet, France) *cl up for 7f: 9th into st: sn bhd* **85/1**
10 hd **Belle Famille (IRE)**[37] 5519 3-8-7.. GFaucon 7 90
(E Lellouche, France) *10th into st: a bhd* **41/1**
11 **Wysiwyg Lucky (FR)**[18] 4-8-11.. RonanThomas 5 88
(J-L Gay, France) *last into st: a bhd* **23/1**

The Form Book, Raceform Ltd, Compton, RG20 6NL

12 **Fontcia (FR)**[30] 5719 3-8-7 .... TThulliez 10 90
(D Sepulchre, France) *prom: 4th into st: rdn and btn wl over 1f out* **11/1**

2m 15.8s (-3.80)
WFA 3 from 4yo 5lb **12** Ran SP% **137.8**
PARI-MUTUEL: WIN 5.50; PL 1.80, 1.20, 5.50; DF 4.80.
Owner E Trussardi **Bred** Gestut Karlshof **Trained** Chantilly, France

NOTEBOOK
La Boum(GER) is stoutly bred and, taken to the outside, hit the front half a furlong out and was not stopping at the line. She stays in training and, since she was unraced until this year, further progress is likely.
Concentric was always prominent but, having moved into the lead a furlong and a half out, had no answer to the winner's late burst.
Noble Ginger(FR) in the front rank throughout, kept on steadily in the home straight to suggest that a return to a longer trip would be in order.
Hapsburg(FR) held a decent enough position on the home turn but was unable to find the required burst of speed in the closing stages.

5930 AYR (L-H)

Friday, October 26

OFFICIAL GOING: Soft changing to soft (heavy in places) after race 5 (4.20)
Wind: Fairly strong, half against Weather: Overcast

6461 EBF DAILY RECORD MAIDEN FILLIES' STKS 1m
2:10 (2:11) (Class 4) 2-Y-O **£4,533** (£1,348; £674; £336) **Stalls** Low

Form RPR
6 1 **Silk Affair (IRE)**[27] 5812 2-9-0 0 .... PaulHanagan 2 72
(M G Quinlan) *prom: effrt over 2f out: chsd ldr over 1f out: styd on wl to ld post* **5/1**[1]
52 2 *shd* **Madame Hoi (IRE)**[23] 5913 2-9-0 0 .... DarryllHolland 5 72
(M R Channon) *led 1f: cl up: led again over 3f out: kpt on u.p fnl f: ct post* **7/2**[2]
3 3 *3½* **Almamia**[23] 5913 2-9-0 0 .... PaulMulrennan 1 65
(Sir Mark Prescott) *dwlt: led after 1f to over 3f out: rallied: one pce appr fnl f* **7/2**[2]
0520 4 *9* **Crying Aloud (USA)**[41] 5435 2-9-0 81 .... JamieSpencer 3 46
(P A Blockley) *dwlt: sn prom: effrt and rdn over 1f out: sn wknd* **5/1**[1]
5 *1½* **Orpen Bid (IRE)** 2-9-0 0 .... AdrianTNicholls 7 43
(A M Crow) *hld up in tch: drvn 3f out: wknd wl over 1f out* **100/1**
05 6 *6* **Chanteuse De Rue (IRE)**[21] 5965 2-9-0 0 .... GregFairley 4 30
(M Johnston) *in tch on outside: drvn over 3f out: sn wknd* **10/1**[3]
0 7 *1¾* **Mathool (IRE)**[7] 6306 2-9-0 0 .... DeanMcKeown 8 26
(C W Thornton) *s.i.s: hld up: rdn 3f out: sn wknd* **100/1**
8 *20* **Parisienne Gem** 2-9-0 0 .... TonyHamilton 6 —
(Miss L A Perratt) *s.i.s: bhd: rdn and lost tch fr 1/2-way* **100/1**

1m 47.05s (3.56) **Going Correction** +0.35s/f (Good) **8** Ran SP% **113.6**
Speed ratings (Par 94): **96,95,92,83,81 75,74,54**
CSF £11.49 TOTE £3.60: £1.30, £1.50, £1.60; EX 19.10.
Owner L Mulryan & M C Fahy **Bred** M Fahy **Trained** Newmarket, Suffolk

FOCUS
A fair maiden run in deteriorating conditions. The pace seemed fair and the runner-up is the best guide to the form.

NOTEBOOK
Silk Affair(IRE), who shaped with promise on her debut, attracted support and turned in an improved effort. She showed a good attitude, should stay a bit further and may be capable of further progress next term. (op 3-1 tchd 10-3)
Madame Hoi(IRE) has improved with every start and finished further in front of the third than at Haydock on her previous start. She had the run of the race on this first start in soft ground but is sure to pick up a similar event. (op 10-3 tchd 4-1)
Almamia, closely matched with Madame Hoi on debut form at Nottingham, finished a bit further behind that rival in these much softer conditions. She is in very good hands and, although unlikely to be anywhere near as good as her illustrious parents, she will stay 1m2f and is sure to win a race in ordinary handicap company in due course. (op 10-3 tchd 4-1 in places)
Crying Aloud(USA) had the form to go close in this company but found a combination of this trip in testing ground far too much of a test of stamina. The return to 7f and switch back to a sound surface should suit and she is capable of winning in ordinary maiden company. (op 9-4)
Orpen Bid(IRE), a half-sister to a multiple winner up to middle distances in Italy, hinted at ability on this racecourse debut but is likely to remain vulnerable in this type of event. (op 66-1)
Chanteuse De Rue(IRE) had a bit to find on form but she seemed to flounder in the conditions over a trip that should have suited. She may do better in ordinary handicaps on turf or All-Weather in due course. (op 16-1)

6462 WBX.COM NURSERY 6f
2:40 (2:43) (Class 5) (0-75,75) 2-Y-O **£3,238** (£963; £481; £240) **Stalls** Centre

Form RPR
4613 1 **Kaldoun Kingdom (IRE)**[8] 6282 2-9-4 72 .... JamieSpencer 6 90+
(E A L Dunlop) *dwlt: hld up: smooth hdwy to ld over 1f out: sn rdn clr* **6/5**[1]
0006 2 *7* **Paint Stripper**[10] 6255 2-7-12 55 .... DominicFox(3) 13 52
(W Storey) *hld up: hdwy over 2f out: chsd wnr ins fnl f: no imp* **20/1**
4356 3 *½* **Chivola (IRE)**[49] 5192 2-9-7 75 .... PaulMulrennan 14 71
(B Smart) *mde most to over 1f out: edgd lft and sn no ex* **10/1**[3]
000 4 *4* **Rio Sabotini**[28] 5771 2-8-6 63 .... AndrewElliott(3) 11 47
(G A Swinbank) *in tch: effrt over 2f out: sn one pce* **16/1**
600 5 *nk* **Admiralcollingwood**[29] 5745 2-8-7 61 .... SilvestreDeSousa 2 44
(J J Quinn) *in tch: effrt 2f out: no imp fnl f* **10/1**[3]
6000 6 *½* **Dark Tara**[18] 6052 2-9-2 70 .... (p) TonyHamilton 3 51
(R A Fahey) *w ldrs tl rdn and no ex wl over 1f out* **11/1**
3040 7 *2½* **Polish Priory (IRE)**[2] 6438 2-8-4 58 .... (v) DaleGibson 12 32
(P D Evans) *bhd tl hdwy over 1f out: nvr rchd ldrs* **28/1**
000 8 *1* **Killer Class**[39] 5483 2-7-11 54 .... DuranFentiman(3) 10 25
(J S Goldie) *bhd tl styd on fr 2f out: nvr on terms* **50/1**
030 9 *2½* **Willyn (IRE)**[6] 6328 2-8-10 64 .... DanielTudhope 1 27
(J S Goldie) *hung lft thrght: bhd: rdn 1/2-way: n.d* **14/1**
4005 10 *3* **Zaplamation (IRE)**[22] 5932 2-7-12 52 oh4 .... PaulHanagan 4 6
(D W Barker) *w ldrs tl wknd fr 2f out* **20/1**
6300 11 *½* **Jazz Stick (IRE)**[39] 5477 2-8-4 61 ow9 .... (t) PatrickMathers(3) 8 14
(D A Nolan) *towards rr: drvn after 2f: nvr on terms* **100/1**
5616 12 *½* **Leading Edge (IRE)**[18] 6052 2-8-11 65 .... DarryllHolland 5 16
(M R Channon) *w ldrs tl wknd fr 2f out* **12/1**
1000 13 *7* **Cheshire Rose**[8] 6282 2-9-2 70 .... PhillipMakin 9 —
(T D Barron) *w ldrs to 2f out: sn btn* **28/1**
5010 14 *12* **Gin Genereux**[50] 5167 2-9-4 72 .... GregFairley 7 —
(M Johnston) *prom 2f: sn wknd* **8/1**[2]

1m 15.4s (1.73) **Going Correction** +0.20s/f (Good) **14** Ran SP% **122.7**
Speed ratings (Par 95): **96,86,86,80,80 79,76,74,71,67 66,66,56,40**
CSF £36.05 CT £194.69 TOTE £1.80: £1.10, £7.80, £3.90; EX 44.90.
Owner Mohammed Jaber **Bred** Gainsborough Stud Management Ltd **Trained** Newmarket, Suffolk

FOCUS
Mainly exposed performers but a good gallop and a much improved effort from the winner, who relished the ground, with the second setting the level. The field raced in the centre of the track.

NOTEBOOK
Kaldoun Kingdom(IRE) ◆, an unlucky loser on his previous start, was ridden with plenty of confidence in this truly-run race and looked good when surging clear as those that made the running floundered. This is his ground and this was a useful effort but life is going to be tougher after reassessment. (op 11-10 tchd 5-4 tchd 11-8 in places)
Paint Stripper, making his handicap debut, ran his best race and left the impression that the return to 7f would be in his favour. He may be able to pick up a modest handicap away from progressive sorts.
Chivola(IRE), back up in distance for this handicap debut, ran creditably and may be a bit better than the bare form as he forced the strong gallop. The return to this trip suited but he has little margin for error from this mark. (op 17-2)
Rio Sabotini travelled well for a long way on this handicap debut and was not disgraced. While coping with the conditions, he should stay a bit further and is worth another chance in ordinary company.
Admiralcollingwood was not totally disgraced on this handicap but left the impression that the step up to 7f would be more to his liking. He is in good hands and is not one to be writing off just yet. (op 14-1)
Dark Tara, back in testing ground, was not at her best having raced up with the decent gallop. She has not really built on her maiden win at York in July and will have to fare better before she is worth a bet. (tchd 12-1)
Gin Genereux Official explanation: jockey said colt never travelled

6463 WBX.COM £25 FREE BET FOR NEW ACCOUNTS H'CAP 7f 50y
3:15 (3:15) (Class 5) (0-70,68) 3-Y-0+ **£3,238** (£963; £481; £240) **Stalls** Low

Form RPR
2001 1 **Spinning**[21] 5966 4-8-13 61 .... (b) JamieSpencer 5 74
(T D Barron) *dwlt: pushed along in rr 1/2-way: gd hdwy on stands' side to ld ins fnl f: sn clr* **17/2**
4023 2 *3* **Obe Royal**[3] 6413 3-8-10 60 .... (p) TGMcLaughlin 9 65
(P D Evans) *in tch: hdwy to ld over 1f out: hdd ins fnl f: no ch w wnr* **4/1**[1]
4013 3 *nk* **Oeuf A La Neige**[21] 5964 7-8-9 57 .... PhillipMakin 3 61
(Miss L A Perratt) *hld up: hdwy over 2f out: ev ch ins fnl f: kpt on same pce* **10/1**
1405 4 *3* **Esoterica (IRE)**[23] 5905 4-9-1 68 .... (b) GaryBartley(5) 8 64
(J S Goldie) *bhd tl hdwy over 2f out: kpt on fnl f: no imp* **12/1**
4041 5 *1¼* **Megalo Maniac**[48] 5233 4-8-11 59 .... PaulHanagan 4 52
(R A Fahey) *chsd ldrs: effrt and ev ch over 1f out: sn no ex* **7/1**[3]
0000 6 *½* **Queen's Composer (IRE)**[17] 6088 4-9-4 66 .... PaulMulrennan 1 58
(B Smart) *hld up: hdwy and prom over 2f out: no ex over 1f out* **14/1**
-003 7 *1¾* **Wind Shuffle (GER)**[21] 5966 4-8-13 61 .... DanielTudhope 2 48
(J S Goldie) *in tch: effrt over 2f out: wknd over 1f out* **12/1**
3500 8 *nk* **Stellite**[22] 5934 7-8-11 64 .... KellyHarrison(5) 10 50
(J S Goldie) *hld up: pushed along over 2f out: nvr rchd ldrs* **14/1**
3100 9 *4* **Mister Jingles**[21] 5966 4-9-0 62 .... (v) DeanMcKeown 7 38
(R M Whitaker) *prom tl hung lft and wknd over 2f out* **16/1**
1300 10 *shd* **Rebel Pearl (IRE)**[7] 6310 3-9-1 65 .... GregFairley 14 41
(M G Quinlan) *pressed ldr tl rdn and wknd over 2f out* **16/1**
000 11 *2* **Fan Club**[18] 6067 3-9-4 68 .... DaleGibson 11 38
(D W Chapman) *racd wd: hld up: rdn 3f out: sn btn* **66/1**
1000 12 *1½* **Wahoo Sam (USA)**[36] 5556 7-9-2 64 .... (p) TonyHamilton 6 31
(D W Barker) *set decent gallop to over 1f out: sn wknd* **25/1**
2165 13 *5* **Sands Of Barra (IRE)**[24] 5893 4-9-3 68 .... AndrewElliott(3) 12 22
(I W McInnes) *prom: rdn 3f out: sn wknd* **9/2**[2]
-101 14 *10* **Carefree**[241] 577 3-8-7 57 .... AdrianTNicholls 13 —
(G A Swinbank) *bhd: drvn over 3f out: sn struggling* **14/1**

1m 36.54s (3.82) **Going Correction** +0.60s/f (Yiel)
WFA 3 from 4yo+ 2lb **14** Ran SP% **122.8**
Speed ratings (Par 103): **102,98,98,94,93 92,90,90,85,85 83,81,76,64**
CSF £43.16 CT £367.56 TOTE £7.40: £2.60, £1.90, £3.20; EX 38.10.
Owner Mrs J Hazell **Bred** Cheveley Park Stud **Trained** Maunby, N Yorks

FOCUS
An ordinary handicap but one in which the pace was sound throughout. The placed horses set the level for the form.
Sands Of Barra(IRE) Official explanation: trainer had no explanation for the poor form shown

6464 WBX.COM 0% COMMISSION ON DAY'S BIG MATCH CLAIMING STKS 1m 1f 20y
3:45 (3:47) (Class 5) 3-Y-O **£2,914** (£867; £433; £216) **Stalls** Low

Form RPR
3300 1 **Grethel (IRE)**[6] 6343 3-8-9 57 .... PatrickMathers(3) 2 61
(A Berry) *prom: effrt over 2f out: led ent fnl f: styd on wl* **8/1**[3]
U006 2 *nk* **Stay Active (USA)**[14] 6147 3-8-7 46 .... (v[1]) TonyHamilton 1 55
(I Semple) *led to ent fnl f: rallied: hld nr fin* **33/1**
0002 3 *5* **Kassuta**[8] 6277 3-8-2 50 .... (p) PaulHanagan 6 40
(John A Harris) *midfield: effrt over 2f out: one pce fnl f* **11/4**[2]
5660 4 *nk* **Acapulco Bay**[10] 6247 3-8-9 50 .... PhillipMakin 10 47
(Miss J A Camacho) *bhd tl styd on fr 2f out: n.d* **11/1**
6025 5 *2½* **Caviar Heights (IRE)**[55] 5040 3-8-7 50 .... (b) GaryBartley(5) 9 45
(Miss L A Perratt) *bhd: pushed along 4f out: sme hdwy over 1f out: n.d* **9/1**
0540 6 *½* **Soul Angel**[10] 6259 3-9-0 51 .... (p) PaulMulrennan 7 46
(Miss S E Forster) *prom tl rdn and wknd fr over 2f out* **16/1**
0634 7 *nk* **Fun In The Sun**[38] 5497 3-8-9 45 .... (v) TGMcLaughlin 12 40
(P D Evans) *s.i.s: effrt on outside over 2f out: sn btn* **14/1**
4005 8 *12* **Johnston's Glory (IRE)**[28] 5781 3-8-9 48 .... DeanMcKeown 4 16
(E J Alston) *prom tl wknd over 2f out* **20/1**
5030 9 *10* **Jane Of Arc (FR)**[9] 5286 3-8-7 55 .... GregFairley 11 —
(J S Goldie) *chsd ldrs tl wknd over 2f out* **8/1**[3]
6630 10 *4* **Superjain**[87] 4042 3-8-0 43 ow3 .... PaulPickard(7) 8 —
(J M Jefferson) *in tch tl wknd over 3f out* **50/1**
00 11 *15* **Shady Bay**[8] 6286 3-7-13 0 .... DuranFentiman(3) 5 —
(D W Chapman) *bhd: drvn 1/2-way: nvr on terms* **100/1**
0001 12 *2½* **Bert's Memory**[10] 6247 3-8-7 50 ow2 .... (p) JamieSpencer 3 —
(K A Ryan) *prom: effrt over 2f out: wknd qckly* **5/2**[1]

2m 7.49s (7.49) **Going Correction** +0.85s/f (Soft) **12** Ran SP% **119.0**
Speed ratings (Par 101): **100,99,95,95,92 92,92,81,72,68 55,53**
CSF £252.70 TOTE £11.80: £2.80, £7.90, £1.80; EX 233.80.
Owner Mrs Linda White **Bred** Liam Queally **Trained** Cockerham, Lancs

■ Stewards' Enquiry : Patrick Mathers two-day ban: used whip with excessive frequency (Nov 6-7)

FOCUS
A modest event but one in which the pace was sound and the winner sets the level backed up by the fourth. The field raced centre to stands' side in the straight.
Bert's Memory Official explanation: jockey said filly was unsuited by the soft ground

6465 WBX.COM 0% COMMISSION ON DAY'S BIG RACE H'CAP 1m 1f 20y
4:20 (4:20) (Class 4) (0-85,85) 3-Y-O+ **£5,181** (£1,541; £770; £384) **Stalls** Low

Form RPR
0003 1 **Vicious Warrior**[13] 6180 8-9-8 **83**................................ DeanMcKeown 9 91
(R M Whitaker) *chsd ldr: rdn and led over 1f out: hld on wl fnl f* **9/1**
6562 2 *shd* **Rudry Dragon (IRE)**[11] 6236 3-8-11 **76**.................... JamieSpencer 6 84
(P A Blockley) *hld up: hdwy 2f out: r.o wl fnl f: jst hld* **7/1**[3]
4311 3 *1/2* **Goodbye**[23] 5907 3-8-13 **78**................................ PatCosgrave 1 85
(G A Swinbank) *prom: effrt and ev ch over 1f out: kpt on fnl f: hld cl home* **13/2**[2]
1100 4 *6* **Future's Dream**[147] 2208 4-9-2 **80**................................ AndrewElliott(3) 2 75
(K R Burke) *led: styd alone centre in st: hdd over 1f out: kpt on same pce* **12/1**
6401 5 *hd* **King Of The Moors (USA)**[20] 6021 4-9-0 **75**.................. PhillipMakin 7 69
(T D Barron) *prom: effrt over 2f out: no ex over 1f out* **16/1**
010 6 *3/4* **Neil's Legacy (IRE)**[10] 6258 5-8-8 **69** oh1.................. PaulHanagan 3 62
(Miss L A Perratt) *chsd ldrs: effrt and ev ch 2f out: sn no ex* **10/1**
0021 7 *1/2* **Bay Boy**[79] 4303 5-8-13 **74**.................................... GregFairley 8 66
(Andrew Oliver, Ire) *midfield: drvn over 3f out: sn no imp* **16/1**
1166 8 *hd* **Hawkit (USA)**[32] 5674 6-8-11 **72**............................ DaleGibson 13 64
(P Monteith) *hld up: drvn 3f out: nvr able to chal* **20/1**
2322 9 *1/2* **Mystical Ayr (IRE)**[23] 5905 5-8-8 **69** oh2..................... TonyHamilton 10 60
(Miss L A Perratt) *hld up: rdn over 2f out: no imp* **15/2**
1 10 *2 1/2* **Northern Spy (USA)**[23] 5915 3-9-6 **85**...................... DarryllHolland 12 71
(Saeed Bin Suroor) *hld up: pushed along over 2f out: nvr on terms* **5/1**[1]
5011 11 *1/2* **Moheebb (IRE)**[22] 5936 3-8-4 **72**............................ DuranFentiman(3) 4 57
(D W Chapman) *hld up in midfield: drvn and outpcd over 3f out: sn n.d* **5/1**[1]
0000 12 *1* **Blue Spinnaker (IRE)**[13] 6180 8-8-4 **72**........................ NSLawes(7) 5 55
(M W Easterby) *bhd: rdn over 3f out: sn btn* **25/1**
221 13 *13* **Ansells Pride (IRE)**[243] 559 4-8-9 **70**...................... PaulMulrennan 11 27
(B Smart) *bhd: struggling over 3f out: sn btn* **28/1**

2m 7.50s (7.50) **Going Correction** +0.85s/f (Soft)
WFA 3 from 4yo+ 4lb **13** Ran SP% **121.5**
Speed ratings (Par 105): **100,99,99,94,93 93,92,92,92,90 89,88,77**
CSF £70.24 CT £447.83 TOTE £12.00: £3.40, £2.80, £2.40; EX 83.60.
Owner James Marshall & Mrs Susan Marshall **Bred** Hellwood Stud Farm **Trained** Scarcroft, W Yorks

FOCUS
A fair handicap in which the pace was ordinary in the conditions. The form looks sound enough considering, with the first three close to form.
Northern Spy(USA) Official explanation: jockey said colt was unsuited by the soft ground
Moheebb(IRE) Official explanation: jockey said gelding never travelled

6466 WBX.COM WORLD BET EXCHANGE H'CAP 5f
4:55 (4:56) (Class 5) (0-70,67) 3-Y-O **£3,238** (£963; £481; £240) **Stalls** Centre

Form RPR
0005 1 **Morristown Music (IRE)**[8] 6287 3-8-8 **57**..................... TonyHamilton 8 67
(J S Wainwright) *t.k.h: cl up: rdn to ld over 1f out: r.o strly* **13/8**[1]
165 2 *2 1/2* **Rue Soleil**[89] 4001 3-8-9 **58**................................ PhillipMakin 7 59
(J R Weymes) *cl up: rdn and ev ch over 1f out: kpt on same pce ins fnl f* **9/1**
4100 3 *1 1/4* **Beechside (IRE)**[22] 5930 3-8-0 **56** oh5 ow3.................. LanceBetts(7) 5 53
(W A Murphy, Ire) *chsd ldng gp: rdn and effrt over 1f out: r.o fnl f* **12/1**
5321 4 *1 1/4* **By The Edge (IRE)**[6] 6339 3-8-8 **57** 6ex ow1................ JamieSpencer 4 49
(T D Barron) *led after 1f to over 1f out: no ex ins fnl f* **5/2**[2]
0240 5 *5* **Royal Guest**[8] 6279 3-8-4 **53** oh3..............................(v) GregFairley 6 27
(M R Channon) *dwlt: sn prom: rdn and wknd over 2f out* **13/2**[3]
4000 6 *hd* **Opal Noir**[36] 5556 3-9-4 **67**...(p) PaulHanagan 1 40
(I Semple) *led 1f: cl up tl wknd fr 2f out* **8/1**

63.99 secs (3.55) **Going Correction** +0.70s/f (Yiel) **6** Ran SP% **108.8**
Speed ratings (Par 101): **99,95,93,91,83 82**
CSF £15.59 CT £113.41 TOTE £2.60: £1.60, £3.20; EX 12.80.
Owner Hurn Racing Club **Bred** J S Wainwright **Trained** Kennythorpe, N Yorks

FOCUS
A modest handicap but a fair pace in the conditions. The form is modest with the winner not needing to run to her best to score and the third close up from out of the handicap.
Royal Guest Official explanation: jockey said gelding was unsuited by the soft ground and lost a hind shoe

6467 WBX.COM FREE FOOTBALL SHIRT FOR NEW ACCOUNTS H'CAP 6f
5:25 (5:27) (Class 6) (0-65,65) 3-Y-O+ **£2,266** (£674; £337; £168) **Stalls** Centre

Form RPR
141 1 **Memphis Man**[3] 6415 4-9-3 **63** 6ex.............................. TGMcLaughlin 10 75
(P D Evans) *midfield on stands' side: hdwy to ld over 1f out: edgd rt ins fnl f: pushed out* **10/3**[1]
0642 2 *1 3/4* **Choreography**[23] 5909 4-9-2 **62**................................ AdrianTNicholls 18 69
(D Nicholls) *in tch on stands' side: hdwy to chse wnr ins fnl f: kpt on* **15/2**[2]
6004 3 *3* **Dorn Dancer (IRE)**[22] 5934 5-8-13 **59**.......................... PatCosgrave 17 57
(D W Barker) *bhd on stands' side tl hdwy over 1f out: kpt on: nt rch first 2* **8/1**[3]
1630 4 *1 1/2* **The Salwick Flyer (IRE)**[22] 5935 4-8-6 **52**................. PaulHanagan 14 46
(I Semple) *cl up on stands' side: effrt and ev ch 2f out: sn rdn and one pce* **11/1**
2045 5 *1 1/2* **Soto**[23] 5908 4-9-1 **61**.................................... PaulMulrennan 11 50
(M W Easterby) *cl up on stands' side: led briefly 2f out: no ex fnl f* **14/1**
444 6 *1 1/2* **Staked A Claim (IRE)**[62] 4795 3-8-8 **55**..................... PhillipMakin 5 40
(T D Barron) *led far side trio: kpt on fnl f: no ch w stands' side* **14/1**
0020 7 *1 1/2* **Rothesay Dancer**[14] 6157 4-9-0 **65**........................ KellyHarrison(5) 2 45
(J S Goldie) *chsd far side ldrs: wnt 2nd that trio ins fnl f: no imp* **33/1**
4226 8 *1 1/2* **Monda**[14] 6149 5-8-8 **54**.................................... SilvestreDeSousa 20 30
(Miss J A Camacho) *midfield on stands' side: drvn 1/2-way: no imp fnl 2f* **12/1**
0000 9 *3/4* **Cadogen Square**[21] 5964 5-7-12 **51** oh6............... DanielleMcCreery(7) 1 24
(D W Chapman) *chsd far side ldr to ins fnl f: no ex* **66/1**
0334 10 *hd* **Obe One**[22] 5935 7-8-2 **51** oh4..............................(b) PatrickMathers(3) 3 24
(A Berry) *dwlt: bhd stands' side: rdn 1/2-way: nvr rchd ldrs* **33/1**
1000 11 *3/4* **Karmest**[23] 5907 3-8-6 **56**.................................... DuranFentiman(3) 15 26
(A D Brown) *dwlt: sn in midfield on stands' side: rdn over 2f out: sn btn* **22/1**
5024 12 *1/2* **Eternal Legacy (IRE)**[23] 5907 5-8-11 **57**.................. DeanMcKeown 8 26
(E J Alston) *led stands' side to 2f out: sn wknd* **12/1**
6550 13 *1* **Winthorpe (IRE)**[29] 5747 7-8-13 **59**............................ DanielTudhope 4 25
(J J Quinn) *cl up on stands' side tl wknd fr 2f out* **40/1**
0000 14 *1 1/4* **Perry's Pride**[23] 5915 3-8-4 **51** oh6.................................... DaleGibson 9 13
(Mrs G S Rees) *cl up on stands' side tl wknd over 2f out* **100/1**
0025 15 *3/4* **Steel City Boy (IRE)**[14] 6157 4-8-11 **62**..................... SladeO'Hara(5) 19 22
(D Carroll) *towards rr: drvn 1/2-way: nvr on terms* **9/1**
0000 16 *1/2* **Imperial Sword**[60] 4895 4-9-0 **65**.................................... NeilBrown(5) 13 23
(T D Barron) *bhd and sn rdn along on stands' side: no ch fr 1/2-way* **20/1**
4500 17 *1* **Indian Spark**[22] 5930 13-8-5 **51** oh3.................................... GregFairley 16 6
(J S Goldie) *sn rdn in rr on stands' side: nvr on terms* **20/1**
0063 18 *3* **Brigadore**[24] 5879 8-8-12 **58**.................................... TonyHamilton 7 4
(J G Given) *in tch on stands' side tl wknd over 2f out* **14/1**
0000 19 *4* **Campo Bueno (FR)**[22] 5934 5-8-0 **53** ow1..................(b) LanceBetts(7) 6 —
(A Berry) *midfield on stands' side: drvn 1/2-way: sn wknd* **25/1**

1m 17.54s (3.87) **Going Correction** +0.70s/f (Yiel)
WFA 3 from 4yo+ 1lb **19** Ran SP% **128.2**
Speed ratings (Par 101): **102,99,95,93,91 89,87,85,84,84 83,82,81,79,78 78,76,72,67**
CSF £23.80 CT £202.51 TOTE £3.60: £1.50, £2.20, £2.90, £3.70; EX 23.20 Place 6 £ 68.22, Place 5 £ 46.93.
Owner M D Jones **Bred** R T And Mrs Watson **Trained** Pandy, Monmouths

FOCUS
A modest handicap in which the larger stands'-side group held the edge over the three to race far side. The runner-up is the best guide to the level.
T/Plt: £57.00 to a £1 stake. Pool: £54,849.25. 701.60 winning tickets. T/Qpdt: £21.20 to a £1 stake. Pool: £3,451.70. 120.00 winning tickets. RY

5406 DONCASTER (L-H)
Friday, October 26

OFFICIAL GOING: Good (good to firm in places; 7.9)
After two dry weeks the ground was described as 'just on the quick side of good'.
Wind: light 1/2 against Weather: overcast

6468 WESTSIDE MAGAZINE EBF MAIDEN STKS (C&G) (DIV I) 7f
1:20 (1:22) (Class 5) 2-Y-O **£3,562** (£1,059; £529; £264) **Stalls** High

Form RPR
6 1 **Speedy Dollar (USA)**[21] 5971 2-9-0 0.......................... PhilipRobinson 6 85+
(M A Jarvis) *trckd ldrs: hdwy over 2f out: rdn to chal over 1f out: led ins fnl f: kpt on wl* **9/1**
22 2 *nk* **Tiger Dream**[30] 5735 2-9-0 0.................................... NCallan 13 84
(K A Ryan) *lw: trckd ldrs: hdwy on inner 2f out: rdn ent fnl f and sn ev ch: kpt on* **10/3**[2]
522 3 *1* **Slam**[21] 5971 2-9-0 **94**.................................... RichardHughes 12 82
(B W Hills) *lw: sn led: rdn along 2f out: drvn and hdd ins fnl f: one pce* **6/4**[1]
4 *1* **King Kenny** 2-9-0 0.................................... TPQueally 10 79+
(D J Murphy) *t.k.h: trckd ldrs: swtchd lft and hdwy 2f out: rn green and wandered over 1f out: hung rt ins fnl f: one pce* **33/1**
5 *1/2* **Colorado Blue (IRE)** 2-9-0 0.................................... SteveDrowne 14 78
(R Charlton) *strong: towards rr: pushed along and hdwy over 2f out: styd on ins fnl f: hmpd nr fin* **33/1**
6 *1/2* **Institute** 2-9-0 0.................................... RyanMoore 4 77
(Sir Michael Stoute) *bit bkwd: leggy: towards rr: hdwy over 2f out: styd on ins fnl f: hmpd nr fin* **10/1**
32 7 *1 1/2* **Drill Sergeant**[15] 6126 2-9-0 0.................................... SebSanders 8 73
(M Johnston) *cl up: rdn along 2f out and grad wknd* **11/2**[3]
8 *shd* **West With The Wind** 2-9-0 0.................................... MickyFenton 11 73
(T P Tate) *unf: scope: bit bkwd: towards rr: hdwy over 2f out: kpt on ins fnl f: nrst fin* **66/1**
9 *1* **Daraahem (IRE)** 2-9-0 0.................................... RHills 9 70
(B W Hills) *w'like: leggy: s.i.s and bhd: swtchd to stands' rail 1/2-way: hdwy over 2f out: shkn up and edgd lft ent fnl f: kpt on: nrst fin* **16/1**
0 10 *3 1/2* **Martyr**[15] 6130 2-9-0 0.................................... JimmyFortune 5 61
(R Hannon) *unf: bit bkwd: in tch: rdn along over 2f out and sn wknd* **80/1**
0 11 *1 1/2* **Longevity**[15] 6127 2-9-0 0.................................... TedDurcan 7 58
(W Jarvis) *lw: chsd ldrs: rdn along over 2f out and sn wknd* **66/1**
12 *shd* **Holden Eagle** 2-9-0 0.................................... RichardMullen 2 57
(A G Newcombe) *strong: a in rr* **100/1**
13 *3 1/2* **Nortune (USA)** 2-9-0 0.................................... TomEaves 1 49
(B Smart) *neat: bit bkwd: in tch on outer: rdn along over 2f out and sn wknd: fin lame* **66/1**
14 *12* **Monte Cassino (IRE)** 2-8-10 0 ow1.......................... JamesO'Reilly(5) 3 20
(J O'Reilly) *w'like: prom on outer: rdn along 3f out: sn wknd* **100/1**

1m 26.6s (-1.17) **Going Correction** -0.275s/f (Firm) **14** Ran SP% **117.0**
Speed ratings (Par 95): **95,94,93,92,91 91,89,89,88,84 82,82,78,64**
CSF £37.16 TOTE £12.00: £2.40, £1.60, £1.20; EX 47.30 Trifecta £189.00 Pool: £332.91, 1.25 winning units.
Owner Stephen Dartnell **Bred** Diamond A Racing Corp **Trained** Newmarket, Suffolk

FOCUS
The winning time was 2.45 seconds faster than the second division, but still only around par for the grade. It was almost certainly much the stronger half, rated round the placed horses.

NOTEBOOK
Speedy Dollar(USA), five lengths behind Slam at Newmarket, is a rangy, well-made individual. He proved very game and in the end did just enough. He should make an even better three-year-old. (op 8-1)
Tiger Dream put a modest effort at Redcar last time behind him. Throwing down a strong challenge racing hard against the running rail, in the end he was just held at bay. He looks sure to win races in time. (op 7-2 tchd 3-1)
Slam took them along and travelled strongly but in the end was run out of it. He too will be stronger with another winter over his head. (op 13-8 tchd 7-4 in a place)
King Kenny, a medium-sized newcomer, took a fierce grip. He went left and right, showing his inexperience, but was sticking on at the end. He obviously has potential providing he goes the right way.
Colorado Blue(IRE), a tall newcomer, showed his inexperience in the paddock. Soon making hard work of it, he finished with quite a flourish before being left short of room near the line. He should improve a fair bit from two to three.
Institute, a lengthy, leggy newcomer, made ground from the rear and was staying on when running out of racing room near the line. He will be much more the finished article at three. (op 8-1)
Drill Sergeant was making quite hard work of this some way out and in the end dropped out in disappointing fashion. (op 5-1)

West With The Wind, a laid-back newcomer, was staying on steadily in the closing stages and he will be seen to much better advantage next year.
Daraahem(IRE), a tall newcomer, displayed a fair level of ability despite showing his inexperience. He is another who will show his true worth at three.
Nortune(USA) Official explanation: vet said on return colt was found to be lame left-fore

6469 WESTSIDE MAGAZINE EBF MAIDEN STKS (C&G) (DIV II) 7f
1:50 (1:53) (Class 5) 2-Y-O **£3,562** (£1,059; £529; £264) **Stalls** High

Form RPR
1 **Naval Review (USA)** 2-9-0 0 (t) RyanMoore 14 74+
(Sir Michael Stoute) *w'like: scope: bit bkwd: dwlt: hld up in rr: hdwy over 2f out: led 1f out: idled: drvn rt out towards fin* **11/4**[1]
2 *nk* **Louis Seffens (USA)** 2-9-0 0 TedDurcan 9 73+
(G A Swinbank) *w'like: scope: bit bkwd: mid-div: effrt over 2f out: sn chsng ldrs: styd on wl towards fin: jst hld* **10/1**
0 3 *nk* **Tourist**[34] 5628 2-9-0 0 RichardHughes 1 73
(B W Hills) *lw: unruly in stalls: swvd lft s: sn w ldrs: no ex ins fnl f* **11/4**[1]
06 4 *hd* **High Plains (FR)**[15] 6126 2-9-0 0 JimmyFortune 11 72
(R Hannon) *lw: led tl hdd 1f out: hrd rdn and kpt on same pce* **8/1**[3]
50 5 *2* **Shanafarahan (IRE)**[10] 6255 2-9-0 0 MickyFenton 10 67+
(T P Tate) *leggy: scope: dwlt: tk fierce hold: sn trcking ldrs: nt clr run over 2f out: styd on wl fnl f* **20/1**
00 6 *1 3/4* **Addwaitya**[15] 6119 2-9-0 0 JimCrowley 4 63
(C F Wall) *w'like: leggy: sn chsng ldrs on outer: effrt over 2f out: fdd fnl f* **150/1**
7 *hd* **Riqaab (IRE)** 2-9-0 0 RHills 2 62
(E A L Dunlop) *bit bkwd: sn trcking ldrs on outer: fdd fnl f* **15/2**[2]
0 8 *2* **Supporting Role (IRE)**[35] 5580 2-9-0 0 RichardMullen 13 57
(E S McMahon) *strong: bit bkwd: in rr: drvn over 3f out: edgd lft and hdwy over 1f out: nvr trbld ldrs* **20/1**
00 9 *2 1/2* **Love Cat (USA)**[44] 5329 2-9-0 0 NCallan 5 51
(K A Ryan) *unf: bit bkwd: chsd ldrs: drvn over 3f out: wknd over 2f out* **25/1**
10 *4* **Jumpin Johnnie** 2-9-0 0 SteveDrowne 7 41
(R T Phillips) *strong: bit bkwd: s.i.s: hdwy on outer over 2f out: sn wknd* **14/1**
11 *nk* **Super Tuscan (IRE)** 2-9-0 0 TPQueally 8 40
(J G Given) *w'like: leggy: b.hind: sn w ldrs: lost pl over 1f out* **50/1**
0 12 *39* **Kavinsky**[48] 5226 2-9-0 0 SebSanders 12 —
(M Johnston) *w'like: prom: sn pushed along: lost pl over 2f out: sn bhd and virtually p.u: t.o* **9/1**

1m 29.05s (1.28) **Going Correction** -0.275s/f (Firm) **57** Ran SP% **118.0**
Speed ratings (Par 95): **81,80,80,80,77 75,75,73,70,65 65,20**
CSF £30.71 TOTE £3.20: £1.60, £2.70, £1.60; EX 33.60 Trifecta £152.90 Pool: £226.19, 1.05 winning units.
Owner The Queen **Bred** The Queen **Trained** Newmarket, Suffolk

FOCUS
A very moderate winning time, 2.45 seconds slower than the first division. The weaker half but the first two will progress at three. The proximity of the sixth holds down the overall level of the form.

NOTEBOOK
Naval Review(USA), a lengthy newcomer, moved very scratchily to post. Warming to his task after missing a beat at the start, he idled in front and had to be kept right up to his work. He has a fair amount of potential. (tchd 3-1)
Louis Seffens(USA), who stands over plenty of ground, moved up on the outer and was cutting the idling winner down at the line. He looks sure to improve and make his mark at three. (op 12-1)
Tourist, edgy in the paddock, became badly upset in the stalls. After going sideways exiting them, he was soon in the firing line and in the end was only just found lacking. (tchd 10-3)
High Plains(FR), a weak type, took them along and was only just found lacking in the closing stages. He will be a much stronger with another year over his head.
Shanafarahan(IRE), rousted along after missing a beat at the start, was set alight. He was picking up nicely at the finish and is the type to thrive in handicap company at three. Official explanation: jockey said colt ran too keen early
Addwaitya, having his third start, is a short-backed leggy individual. This sets him up for a handicap campaign at three, (op 100-1)
Riqaab(IRE), a May foal, is short in the back. He travelled strongly on the outer until tiring in the closing stages and will be a different proposition next year. (op 8-1)

6470 SERIOUSQUITTERS.CO.UK EBF MAIDEN FILLIES' STKS 1m (R)
2:20 (2:25) (Class 5) 2-Y-O **£3,886** (£1,156; £577; £288) **Stalls** Low

Form RPR
1 **Cruel Sea (USA)** 2-9-0 0 RichardHughes 7 85
(B W Hills) *w'like: leggy: scope: dwlt: sn in midfield: hdwy and in tch 3f out: swtchd rt and rdn over 1f out: styd on strly to ld ins fnl f* **9/2**[2]
3 2 *1 1/4* **Desert Chill (USA)**[17] 6087 2-9-0 0 TedDurcan 4 82
(Saeed Bin Suroor) *w'like: scope: lw: trckd ldr gng wl: swtchd rt and effrt wl over 1f out: rdn to chal ent fnl f and ev ch tl nt qckn fnl 100yds* **11/10**[1]
2 3 *1/2* **Miracle Seeker**[27] 5812 2-9-0 0 KDarley 16 81
(C G Cox) *leggy: scope: a.p: effrt 2f out: sn rdn and ev ch tl drvn and one pce ins fnl f* **11/2**[3]
4 *1 1/2* **Red Dune (IRE)** 2-9-0 0 PhilipRobinson 12 78
(M A Jarvis) *w'like: led: rdn along 2f out: drvn over 1f out: hdd and one pce ins fnl f* **12/1**
04 5 *nk* **Calypso Charms**[37] 5541 2-9-0 0 EddieAhern 17 77
(M L W Bell) *chsd ldrs: effrt over 2f out: sn rdn and kpt on same pce fnl f* **50/1**
5 6 *1* **Flam**[35] 5596 2-9-0 0 OscarUrbina 18 75
(J R Fanshawe) *in tch: effrt on outer whn sltly hmpd wl over 1f out: sn rdn and kpt on same pce* **16/1**
0 7 *1/2* **Houri (IRE)**[35] 5596 2-9-0 0 JamesDoyle 19 74
(R M Beckett) *chsd ldrs: rdn along over 2f out: sn drvn and kpt on same pce* **50/1**
8 *2 1/2* **Dedicate** 2-9-0 0 SteveDrowne 9 68
(R Charlton) *towards rr: hdwy over 2f out: kpt on ins fnl f: nrst fin* **33/1**
4 9 *1 1/2* **African Flight**[10] 6254 2-9-0 0 RyanMoore 13 65
(M L W Bell) *w'like: midfield: hdwy on outer 3f out: rdn along over 2f out and sn btn* **25/1**
10 *nk* **Bet Noir (IRE)** 2-9-0 0 AdamKirby 10 64
(W R Swinburn) *leggy: s.i.s and bhd tl sme late hdwy* **66/1**
11 *nk* **Zia Zabel (IRE)** 2-9-0 0 SebSanders 15 64
(J L Dunlop) *w'like: bit bkwd: a in rr* **25/1**
12 *3 1/2* **Montreal (GER)** 2-9-0 0 TPQueally 11 56
(H R A Cecil) *w'like: nvr bttr than midfield* **28/1**
0 13 *2* **Amandalini**[14] 6140 2-9-0 0 RobertHavlin 8 51
(B J Meehan) *chsd ldrs: rdn along over 2f out: sn wknd* **100/1**
6 14 *1 1/2* **Lady In Chief**[20] 6015 2-9-0 0 TomEaves 1 48
(Miss J A Camacho) *w'like: leggy: a towards rr* **100/1**
0 15 *shd* **Great Future**[10] 6248 2-9-0 0 JimmyQuinn 6 48
(H R A Cecil) *lengthy: towards rr fr 1/2-way* **100/1**
00 16 *nk* **Fleur De Montjeu (IRE)**[54] 5063 2-9-0 0 ChrisCatlin 14 47
(W R Swinburn) *a in rr* **100/1**
17 *1* **Molly Ann (IRE)** 2-9-0 0 DavidAllan 3 45
(T D Easterby) *unf: scope: bit bkwd: s.i.s: a bhd* **100/1**

1m 39.46s (-1.15) **Going Correction** -0.15s/f (Firm) **17** Ran SP% **119.2**
Speed ratings (Par 92): **99,97,97,95,95 94,93,91,89,89 89,85,83,82,82 81,80**
CSF £8.70 TOTE £5.50: £1.90, £1.40, £1.70; EX 13.40 Trifecta £29.50 Pool: £321.58, 7.73 winning units.
Owner K Abdulla **Bred** Juddmonte Farms Inc **Trained** Lambourn, Berks
■ La Troupe was withdrawn on vet's advice (12/1, deduct 5p in the £ under Rule 4).

FOCUS
A decent winning time for a race of its type. The runner-up and third set a fair standard and the race should throw up plenty of winners next year.

NOTEBOOK
Cruel Sea(USA), a rangy newcomer, had to pull wide for a run. She stayed on in very willing fashion to master the favourite and looks a good prospect for next year (op 5-1 tchd 4-1)
Desert Chill(USA) travelled supremely well but after being upsides was very much second best at the line. (op 5-4)
Miracle Seeker again showed ability in the thick of things and was only found wanting in the closing stages. She looks sure to make her mark. (tchd 13-2)
Red Dune(IRE) ◆ a leggy newcomer, travelled very strongly in front only to be edged out inside the last. She looks a fine prospect.
Calypso Charms, a May foal, lacks a little size and scope. She made a pleasing debut and hopefully there will be better to come at three.
Flam, a rather delicate type, was closing when left short of racing room coming to the final furlong. By no means knocked about, she will be stronger and more mature next year. (op 14-1)
Houri(IRE) improved on her debut effort and there ought to be even better in the pipeline at three.
African Flight Official explanation: jockey said filly lost its action
Bet Noir(IRE) Official explanation: jockey said filly ran too free early

6471 RACING POST NURSERY 1m (R)
2:50 (2:57) (Class 3) 2-Y-O **£9,715** (£2,890; £1,444; £360; £360) **Stalls** Low

Form RPR
5041 1 **Jack Dawkins (USA)**[43] 5350 2-8-13 **82** TedDurcan 16 97+
(H R A Cecil) *lw: hld up in rr: smooth hdwy on outer over 2f out: led 1f out: styd on strly: readily* **7/2**[1]
5616 2 *1 1/2* **Determind Stand (USA)**[43] 5350 2-8-7 **76** RyanMoore 7 86
(Sir Michael Stoute) *hld up in tch: effrt over 2f out: chal 1f out: styd on same pce* **7/1**[2]
5344 3 *3/4* **The Betchworth Kid**[8] 6291 2-9-1 **84** JimmyFortune 14 92
(M L W Bell) *prom: effrt over 2f out: styd on fnl f* **10/1**
3503 4 *1 1/2* **Ellemujie**[8] 6291 2-9-2 **85** TQuinn 15 90
(D K Ivory) *hld up towards rr: hdwy on outside over 2f out: kpt on wl fnl f* **16/1**
16 4 *dht* **Mazaaya (USA)**[14] 6154 2-8-10 **79** RoystonFfrench 5 84
(M Johnston) *trckd ldrs: led over 1f out: hdd 1f out: no ex* **10/1**
041 6 *1/2* **Silver Regent (USA)**[43] 5361 2-9-0 **83** JimCrowley 3 87
(Mrs A J Perrett) *in tch: effrt over 2f out: hit on hd by rival's whip appr fnl f: kpt on same pce* **7/1**[2]
1006 7 *hd* **Distant Charm (IRE)**[12] 6201 2-8-9 **78** (b[1]) RichardHughes 13 81
(R Hannon) *hld up in mid-div: effrt over 2f out: edgd rt and kpt on fnl f* **40/1**
4010 8 *hd* **Indian Days**[26] 5828 2-8-7 **76** ow1 TomEaves 11 79
(J G Given) *hld up in rr: nt clr run on ins over 2f out: hung rt and styd on fnl f* **25/1**
346 9 *nk* **Black Dahlia**[45] 5301 2-7-12 **70** WilliamBuick(3) 9 72
(A J McCabe) *hmpd after s: in rr: hdwy on wd outside over 2f out: kpt on: nvr nr ldrs* **11/1**
5121 10 *1 3/4* **Safari Sunup (IRE)**[25] 5871 2-9-0 **90** JackMitchell(7) 6 88
(P Winkworth) *lw: sn chsng ldrs: wknd appr fnl f* **9/1**[3]
01 11 *nk* **Barawin (IRE)**[27] 5812 2-8-12 **81** FrancisNorton 10 79+
(K R Burke) *lw: n.m.r sn after s: hld up in rr: effrt over 2f out: hung rt and kpt on ins fnl f* **25/1**
0421 12 *nk* **Ballochroy (IRE)**[27] 5813 2-8-12 **81** MichaelHills 2 78
(B W Hills) *chsd ldrs: wknd appr fnl f* **14/1**
1540 13 *1/2* **Mahusay (IRE)**[91] 3909 2-8-11 **80** SebSanders 4 76
(L M Cumani) *trckd ldrs: wknd jst ins fnl f* **20/1**
225 14 *3* **Forsyte Saga**[23] 5913 2-8-7 **76** J-PGuillambert 1 65
(M Johnston) *led 1f: cl up tl lost pl over 1f out* **33/1**
4030 15 *11* **Birkintastic**[18] 6052 2-8-9 **78** KDarley 12 43
(B J Meehan) *in rr: bhd fnl 2f* **66/1**
000 16 *3/4* **Jack Got Even (USA)**[22] 5951 2-8-4 **73** (b) JimmyQuinn 8 36
(B J Meehan) *lw: wnt rt after s: t.k.h: led after 1f: hdd over 2f out: wknd qckly* **12/1**

1m 38.45s (-2.16) **Going Correction** -0.15s/f (Firm) **16** Ran SP% **123.3**
Speed ratings (Par 99): **104,102,101,100,100 99,99,99,99,97 97,96,96,93,82 81**
4th place Ellemujie 2.20, Mazaaya 1.40 CSF £24.39 CT £242.09 TOTE £4.00: £1.50, £2.00, £2.70; EX 25.70 Trifecta £151.30 Pool: £568.18, 2.75 winning units.
Owner Mark & Sue Harniman **Bred** Clovelly Farms **Trained** Newmarket, Suffolk

FOCUS
A decent contest run at a strong pace and a very ready winner rated through the fourth's effort behind the same horse here at the St Leger meeting.

NOTEBOOK
Jack Dawkins(USA) ◆, who really took the eye in the paddock, defied a 7lb hike in the ratings in smart style. Happy to sit off the pace, he came cruising down the outside and was right on top at the finish. He will make his mark in much stronger company at three. (tchd 4-1)
Determind Stand(USA), on his toes in the paddock, worked hard to get upsides entering the final furlong but the winner skipped past him in a couple of strides. (tchd 15-2)
The Betchworth Kid, with the visor left off, ran right up to his best but he looks weighted to the very limit. (op 11-1)
Ellemujie, left with a lot to do from his outside draw, stuck on strongly down the outside and was putting in all his best work at the finish. (op 12-1)
Mazaaya(USA), who made little appeal beforehand, ran a lot better and, after taking a narrow advantage, was only found wanting inside the last. (op 12-1)
Barawin(IRE) Official explanation: jockey said filly hung right-handed closing stages
Jack Got Even(USA) Official explanation: jockey said colt ran too free

6472 RECTANGLE GROUP H'CAP 6f
3:25 (3:28) (Class 2) (0-100,98) 3-Y-O+ **£15,544** (£4,624; £2,311; £1,154) **Stalls** High

Form RPR
1222 1 **Tamagin (USA)**[24] 5891 4-8-10 **89** TedDurcan 21 102
(K A Ryan) *lw: mde all: qcknd clr over 1f out: styd on strly* **7/1**[2]

1230 **2** *2* **Commando Scott (IRE)**[7] 6301 6-8-13 **92**................ RoystonFfrench 2 99
(I W McInnes) *in tch on outer: hdwy over 2f out: rdn to chse wnr and hung rt ent fnl f: kpt on u.p* **20/1**

0043 **3** *1* **Wyatt Earp (IRE)**[47] 5254 6-8-6 **88**........................ JamieMoriarty(3) 3 91
(R A Fahey) *hld up towards rr: hdwy over 2f out: swtchd outside and rdn over 1f out: kpt on ins fnl f* **16/1**

1241 **4** *1* **Tombi (USA)**[60] 4898 3-8-12 **92**.......................... EddieAhern 9 92
(J Howard Johnson) *lw: in tch: hdwy to chse ldrs over 1f out: sn rdn and sltly hmpd ent fnl f: kpt on* **12/1**

0016 **5** *nk* **Obe Gold**[1] 6450 5-8-7 **86** 6ex........................(v) ChrisCatlin 14 85
(M R Channon) *hld up towards rr: hdwy over 2f out: swtchd lft and rdn over 1f out: kpt on ins fnl f* **14/1**

0000 **6** *hd* **King's Caprice**[7] 6301 6-8-10 **92**....................(t) TravisBlock(3) 22 91
(J A Geake) *trckd ldrs on inner: rdn along 2f out: sn drvn and one pce* **25/1**

0125 **7** *nk* **Efistorm**[14] 6142 6-8-9 **88**.................................. TPQueally 15 86+
(C R Dore) *trckd ldrs: effrt and nt clr run over 1f out: styng on whn hmpd ent fnl f: nt rcvr* **20/1**

0014 **8** *1/2* **Masai Moon**[7] 6301 3-8-7 **87**............................ JimCrowley 18 83
(B R Millman) *chsd ldrs: rdn along 2f out: sn wknd* **11/1**

1000 **9** *hd* **Golden Dixie (USA)**[13] 6183 8-9-1 **94**.................... RyanMoore 6 89
(R A Harris) *hld up in rr: hdwy over 2f out: swtchd lft over 1f out: sn rdn and kpt on ins fnl f: nrst fin* **33/1**

4110 **10** *nk* **Jimmy Styles**[28] 5765 3-8-9 **89**........................ PhilipRobinson 4 83
(C G Cox) *lw: prom: rdn along 2f out: sn drvn and wknd appr fnl f* **10/1**[3]

0200 **11** *3/4* **Fantasy Believer**[27] 5810 9-8-13 **92**.................... JimmyFortune 12 84+
(J J Quinn) *stdd s: hld up and bhd: swtchd to stands' rail 1/2-way: hdwy over 1f out: styng on whn nt clr run ins fnl f: no ch after* **14/1**

0161 **12** *1/2* **Barney McGrew (IRE)**[14] 6142 4-8-13 **92**................ OscarUrbina 20 82+
(J A R Toller) *lw: trckd ldrs on inner: effrt and nt clr run wl over 1f out: swtchd lft and nt clr run appr fnl f: nt rcvr* **13/2**[1]

5430 **13** *3/4* **Greenslades**[49] 5209 8-8-13 **92**........................ SebSanders 13 80
(P J Makin) *chsd ldrs: rdn along and wkng whn n.m.r wl over 1f out* **25/1**

5505 **14** *1/2* **Gift Horse**[12] 6205 7-8-13 **92**....................(v) StephenDonohoe 1 78
(D Nicholls) *hld up on outer: effrt and sme hdwy over 2f out: sn rdn and wknd* **12/1**

1340 **15** *hd* **High Curragh**[35] 5584 4-8-6 **88**................(b) AndrewMullen(3) 16 74
(K A Ryan) *prom: rdn along 2f out: grad wknd appr fnl f* **33/1**

0664 **16** *hd* **River Falcon**[13] 6183 7-9-3 **96**............................ TQuinn 19 81
(J S Goldie) *a in midfield* **14/1**

3030 **17** *nk* **Blue Rocket (IRE)**[7] 6300 3-9-1 **95**........................ JohnEgan 8 79
(D J Murphy) *chsd ldrs: rdn along over 2f out: sn wknd* **33/1**

0006 **18** *shd* **Mutamared (USA)**[42] 5392 7-9-5 **98**........................ NCallan 5 82
(K A Ryan) *hld up in rr: hdwy 2f out: swtchd lft and nt clr run over 1f out: no ch after* **20/1**

1600 **19** *3/4* **Zomerlust**[13] 6183 5-9-2 **95**........................(v) JimmyQuinn 10 76
(J J Quinn) *hld up: a in rr* **25/1**

0-00 **20** *1/2* **Sadeek**[27] 5809 3-8-10 **90**................................ TomEaves 7 70
(B Smart) *dwlt: a in rr* **100/1**

0000 **21** *9* **Out After Dark**[35] 5584 6-8-11 **90**....................(p) AdamKirby 17 41
(C G Cox) *hld up: a in rr* **12/1**

1420 **22** *3* **Malcheek (IRE)**[49] 5195 5-8-11 **90**........................ DavidAllan 11 31
(T D Easterby) *prom: rdn along over 2f out: sn wknd: b.b.v* **50/1**

1m 11.75s (-2.55) **Going Correction** -0.275s/f (Firm)
WFA 3 from 4yo+ 1lb **22** Ran SP% **129.8**
Speed ratings (Par 109): **106,103,102,100,100 100,99,98,98,98 97,96,95,94,94 94,94,93,92,92 80,76**
CSF £147.75 CT £2239.32 TOTE £8.40: £2.50, £5.30, £3.20, £2.70; EX 214.30 Trifecta £562.20 Part won. Pool: £791.97, 0.40 winning units..
Owner Tariq Al Nisf **Bred** Stonehaven Farm LLC **Trained** Hambleton, N Yorks

FOCUS
A good handicap but with plenty of traffic problems in behind but overall solid sprint handicap form with further improvement from the winner.

NOTEBOOK
Tamagin(USA) has been a revelation since switching to this yard. Drawn one off the stands' side rail he made every yard and scored in tremendous fashion. (op 10-1)
Commando Scott(IRE), drawn one off the outside, had to make his effort wide. He stayed on to secure second spot and continues in great heart. (op 16-1)
Wyatt Earp(IRE), drawn one from the outside, had to make his way towards the centre to find racing room. He stuck on in willing fashion to claim third spot and is now back on his last winning mark.
Tombi(USA), 7lb higher than when successful on his last start at Ripon two months earlier, ran right up to his best. This was only his fifth outing this year.
Obe Gold, having his second start in two days, stayed on after having to wait for an opening.
King's Caprice, with the visor dispensed with, had the best of the draw but lacked the sharpness to take full benefit of it.
Efistorm, who is arguably better over the minimum trip, never saw daylight at any stage. (op 18-1)
Golden Dixie(USA) Official explanation: jockey said gelding was denied a clear run
Fantasy Believer had no luck at all. It is over a year since he last won but much of the old ability is still there. Official explanation: jockey said gelding was denied a clear run
Barney McGrew(IRE) was another to have a nightmare run. Official explanation: jockey said gelding was denied a clear run (tchd 6-1)
High Curragh Official explanation: jockey said gelding hung right-handed throughout
River Falcon Official explanation: jockey said gelding was denied a clear run
Mutamared(USA) Official explanation: jockey said gelding was denied a clear run
Out After Dark Official explanation: jockey said gelding lost its action
Malcheek(IRE) Official explanation: jockey said gelding bled from the nose

6473 BETTING SHOP MANAGER OF THE YEAR H'CAP — 1m 6f 132y
3:55 (3:59) (Class 4) (0-85,86) 3-Y-0+ **£6,477** (£1,927; £963; £481) **Stalls** Low

Form RPR
31 **1** **Whenever**[22] 5938 3-8-10 **74**................................ JohnEgan 18 85
(R T Phillips) *hld up in rr: hdwy on wd outside over 3f out: led 1f out: edgd lft: styd on wl* **20/1**

-111 **2** *1 1/4* **Kahara**[22] 5955 3-9-6 **84**................................ SebSanders 14 93
(L M Cumani) *lw: hld up in mid-div: effrt over 3f out: led over 1f out: sn hdd and no ex* **11/8**[1]

1433 **3** *shd* **Hot Diamond**[22] 5955 3-9-2 **80**................................ TQuinn 20 89
(D R C Elsworth) *lw: hld up in rr: hdwy on outside 3f out: styng on same pce whn hit on hd by rival's whip appr fnl f* **12/1**

6042 **4** *3/4* **Lets Roll**[22] 5933 6-10-0 **83**................................ NCallan 15 91
(C W Thornton) *hld up in rr: hdwy on outside over 3f out: styd on fnl f* **25/1**

1115 **5** *1* **Ainama (IRE)**[22] 5955 3-8-13 **77**........................ OscarUrbina 1 84
(M Wigham) *trckd ldrs: t.k.h: effrt 3f out: kpt on same pce appr fnl f* **11/1**

4265 **6** *shd* **Prince Sabaah (IRE)**[17] 6091 3-9-8 **86**.................... RichardHughes 12 93
(R Hannon) *led 1f: chsd ldrs: hung rt and styd on same pce appr fnl f* **16/1**

01/3 **7** *shd* **Traprain (IRE)**[13] 6186 5-9-7 **76**............................ DavidAllan 17 82
(D Carroll) *hld up in rr: styd on fnl 3f: nt rch ldrs* **16/1**

/011 **8** *shd* **Estate**[6] 6341 5-8-13 **68** 12ex............................ ChrisCatlin 5 74
(E J O'Neill) *mid-div: hdwy 4f out: kpt on same pce fnl 2f* **7/1**[2]

5023 **9** *1* **Mister Completely (IRE)**[5] 6356 6-8-9 **64**................(v) JamesDoyle 8 69
(Ms J S Doyle) *in rr: hdwy on outer 3f out: styd on fnl f* **50/1**

5002 **10** *1* **Dium Mac**[7] 6308 6-9-2 **74**........................ AndrewMullen(3) 4 80+
(N Bycroft) *mid-div: hdwy over 2f out: styng on same pce whn hmpd jst ins fnl f* **16/1**

4152 **11** *5* **Casual Affair**[13] 6186 4-8-10 **65**........................ JimmyQuinn 6 62
(J D Bethell) *hld up in rr: hdwy on ins over 3f out: nt clr run over 1f out: sn lost pl* **10/1**[3]

3610 **12** *3* **Mister Arjay (USA)**[26] 5839 7-9-8 **77**.................... J-PGuillambert 16 70
(B Ellison) *chsd ldr: led after 1f tl 9f out: chsd ldr: lost pl 2f out* **66/1**

03-3 **13** *hd* **According To Pete**[14] 6158 6-9-5 **74**........................ TomEaves 7 67
(J M Jefferson) *chsd ldrs: lost pl over 2f out* **16/1**

4-50 **14** *hd* **Altilhar (USA)**[14] 6144 4-9-11 **80**....................(b) RyanMoore 11 73
(G L Moore) *mid-div: effrt 4f out: lost pl over 2f out* **33/1**

404 **15** *nk* **Mighty Moon**[13] 6186 4-8-12 **72**................(tp) JamesO'Reilly(5) 3 64
(J O'Reilly) *chsd ldrs: led after 3f: sn wl clr: wknd and hdd over f out* **33/1**

0120 **16** *3/4* **Dhehdaah**[27] 5808 6-9-1 **70**............................ MickyFenton 13 61
(Mrs P Sly) *mid-div: effrt over 3f out: lost pl over 2f out* **33/1**

20/0 **17** *8* **Historic Place (USA)**[15] 6131 7-8-12 **67**................ SteveDrowne 19 48
(J A Geake) *chsd ldrs: lost pl 4f out: sn bhd* **100/1**

3400 **18** *shd* **Trance (IRE)**[6] 6335 7-9-8 **77**....................(p) PaulFessey 2 58
(T D Barron) *s.i.s: in rr: rdn 6f out: nt run on* **40/1**

4-10 **19** *1/2* **Linden Lime**[254] 457 5-9-2 **71**........................ RobertHavlin 9 51
(Jamie Poulton) *in rr: bhd fnl 3f* **40/1**

3m 7.36s (-2.38) **Going Correction** -0.15s/f (Firm)
WFA 3 from 4yo+ 9lb **19** Ran SP% **130.0**
Speed ratings (Par 105): **100,99,99,98,98 98,98,98,97,97 94,92,92,92,92 92,87,87,87**
CSF £46.94 CT £398.84 TOTE £24.70: £3.30, £1.30, £3.40, £4.60; EX 74.90 Trifecta £336.70 Pool: £616.61, 1.30 winning units.
Owner Mr & Mrs W J Williams **Bred** D J And Mrs Deer **Trained** Adlestrop, Gloucs

FOCUS
A competitive handicap and the early pace looked strong with Mighty Moon going off at a rate of knots, but things slowed down over the last half-mile or so as the final time was ordinary. The way the race was run suited those that were held up but the form looks solid.
Prince Sabaah(IRE) Official explanation: jockey said colt hung right-handed
Dium Mac Official explanation: jockey said gelding was denied a clear run

6474 WEATHERBYS BANK H'CAP — 1m 2f 60y
4:30 (4:30) (Class 4) (0-85,85) 3-Y-O **£6,477** (£1,927; £963; £481) **Stalls** Low

Form RPR
1 **1** **Milne Graden**[72] 4492 3-8-11 **78**............................ TPQueally 4 95+
(J Noseda) *w'like: lw: trckd ldrs on inner: effrt and nt clr run over 1f out: swtchd rt and squeezed through ins fnl f: rdn and qcknd wl to ld nr fin* **6/1**[2]

1112 **2** *nk* **Ella Woodcock (IRE)**[18] 6053 3-9-2 **83**.................... MickyFenton 8 92
(E J Alston) *trckd ldrs and hmpd after 1f: in tch: smooth hdwy 3f out: swtchd rt and rdn to ld over 1f out: drvn ins fnl f: hdd and nt qckn nr fin* **13/2**[3]

0055 **3** *1 1/2* **Surrey Spinner**[23] 5921 3-8-10 **77**........................ JimCrowley 12 83
(Mrs A J Perrett) *trckd ldrs: hdwy over 2f out: rdn to chal wl over 1f out and ev ch tl drvn ent fnl f and one pce* **33/1**

4002 **4** *hd* **Sign Of The Cross**[14] 6145 3-8-12 **79**.................... OscarUrbina 10 85
(J R Fanshawe) *trckd ldrs: effrt 2f out: sn rdn and ch tl n.m.r ent fnl f and sn one pce* **8/1**

2012 **5** *1* **Candy Mountain**[22] 5943 3-8-9 **76**........................ SebSanders 15 80
(L M Cumani) *lw: hld up towards rr: hdwy 3f out: rdn wl over 1f out: kpt on same pce* **13/2**[3]

41 **6** *1/2* **Prairie Tiger (GER)**[20] 6005 3-8-13 **80**.................... SamHitchcott 2 83+
(N J Vaughan) *s.i.s: sn in tch: rdn along and outpcd over 2f out: hdwy and nt clr run on inner over 1f out: swtchd rt and kpt on u.p ins fnl f* **15/2**

3360 **7** *2 1/2* **Milliegait**[41] 5405 3-8-6 **73**................................ KDarley 1 71
(T D Easterby) *trckd ldr: chal over 2f out: rdn to ld briefly over 1f out: sn hdd & wknd* **66/1**

5100 **8** *1 3/4* **Ascalon**[83] 4147 3-9-4 **85**................................ PaulEddery 6 79
(Pat Eddery) *lw: in rr tl sme late hdwy* **14/1**

3105 **9** *nk* **New Star (UAE)**[16] 6110 3-8-9 **76**........................ RichardMullen 13 70
(W M Brisbourne) *towards rr: effrt and sme hdwy on outer 3f out: sn rdn and wknd* **40/1**

1000 **10** *1 1/4* **Medici Pearl**[28] 5776 3-8-7 **74**........................ DavidAllan 11 65
(T D Easterby) *hld up: sme hdwy on outer 3f out: sn rdn along and wknd* **40/1**

5202 **11** *shd* **Hurlingham**[48] 5218 3-9-0 **81**............................ JimmyQuinn 9 72
(M W Easterby) *in tch: hdwy on outer to chse ldrs 3f out: sn rdn and wknd 2f out* **15/2**

1201 **12** *hd* **Teodora Adivina**[10] 6253 3-8-9 **76** 6ex.................... TedDurcan 3 66
(H R A Cecil) *set stdy pce: qcknd 3f out: rdn 2f out: drvn and hdd over 1f out: sn wknd* **11/2**[1]

002 **13** *7* **Heavenward**[16] 6109 3-8-13 **80**............................ RyanMoore 7 56
(Sir Michael Stoute) *lw: in rr: pushed along 1/2-way: nvr a factor: lame* **8/1**

2m 10.75s (-1.08) **Going Correction** -0.15s/f (Firm) **13** Ran SP% **118.1**
Speed ratings (Par 103): **98,97,96,96,95 95,93,91,91,90 90,90,84**
CSF £43.27 CT £1195.70 TOTE £7.90: £2.40, £2.80, £10.20; EX 53.10 TRIFECTA Not won..
Owner Mrs Susan Roy **Bred** Newsells Park Stud Limited **Trained** Newmarket, Suffolk

FOCUS
A fair handicap, but the pace set by the favourite Teodora Adivina was not strong and this developed into something of a sprint. The winning time was modest, 1.75 seconds slower than the following handicap for lady riders and although the runner-up represents solid form the race does not look strong overall.
Ascalon Official explanation: jockey said colt was unsuited by the good (good to firm places) ground
Heavenward Official explanation: jockey said colt slipped on leaving stalls and moved poorly throughout; vet said colt finished lame on right hind

6475 SAWFISH SOFTWARE LADY RIDERS' H'CAP — 1m 2f 60y
5:05 (5:05) (Class 4) (0-80,80) 3-Y-0+ **£6,246** (£1,937; £968; £484) **Stalls** Low

Form RPR
1035 **1** **Suits Me**[13] 6180 4-9-13 **75**............................ MissJAKidd(3) 9 84
(T P Tate) *mde all: hld on towards fin* **4/1**[1]

The Form Book, Raceform Ltd, Compton, RG20 6NL

5620 **2** *hd* **Prince Samos (IRE)**[35] 5585 5-9-10 **72** MissARyan(3) 13 81
(D Nicholls) *swtchd lft after s: hdwy over 2f out: wnt 2nd over 1f out: styd on wl ins fnl f: jst hld* **12/1**

1-13 **3** *1* **Hazelnut**[71] 4542 4-9-7 **66** oh2 MissRDavidson 15 73
(J R Fanshawe) *lw: hld up in rr: hdwy over 2f out: edgd lft: styd on wl fnl f* **4/1**[1]

3622 **4** *5* **Maslak (IRE)**[15] 6124 3-9-8 **75** MrsMarieKing(3) 7 72
(P W Hiatt) *w wnr: one pce appr fnl f* **9/1**[3]

31 **5** *½* **Princess Cocoa (IRE)**[6] 6343 4-10-3 **76** 6ex MissSBrotherton 3 72
(R A Fahey) *chsd ldrs: chal 2f out: one pce* **9/2**[2]

0000 **6** *nk* **El Dececy (USA)**[7] 6314 3-9-6 **70** (b) MsKWalsh 1 66
(D J Murphy) *rn wout declared tongue-strap: sn trcking ldrs: t.k.h: kpt on same pce fnl 2f* **16/1**

00 **7** *¾* **Beau Sancy**[53] 5099 3-9-11 **75** MissFayeBramley 10 69
(R A Harris) *in rr-div: hdwy 3f out: styd on fnl f* **28/1**

0050 **8** *1 ½* **Boo**[61] 4867 5-9-12 **76** (v) MissKellyBurke(5) 2 67
(K R Burke) *mid-div: effrt over 2f out: nvr nr to chal* **16/1**

5000 **9** *¾* **Kingdom Of Dreams (IRE)**[10] 6253 5-9-9 **68** MissEJJones 11 58
(J Mackie) *sn chsng ldrs: hung lft over 1f out: sn wknd* **28/1**

0060 **10** *3* **Clueless**[22] 5933 5-10-0 **80** MissJRRichards(7) 6 64
(N G Richards) *hld up in rr: bhd and rdn 4f out: kpt on fnl 2f: nvr on terms* **22/1**

0003 **11** *nk* **Bed Fellow (IRE)**[38] 5508 3-8-13 **70** MissLEBurke(7) 12 54
(A P Jarvis) *chsd ldrs: edgd lft over 1f out: sn wknd* **16/1**

104 **12** *1 ½* **Drawback (IRE)**[23] 5921 4-9-13 **72** (p) MissLEllison 4 53
(R A Harris) *chsd ldrs: wknd over 2f out* **20/1**

006- **13** *3 ½* **Salute The General**[475] 3292 4-10-2 **80** MrsGHogg(5) 14 54
(Micky Hammond) *mid-div: effrt 3f out: sn wknd* **22/1**

0040 **14** *3* **Dragon Slayer (IRE)**[18] 6067 5-10-5 **78** MrsCBartley 8 47
(P A Blockley) *s.s: sme hdwy on outside over 3f out: sn wknd* **9/1**[3]

4/00 **15** *4* **High Window (IRE)**[9] 5231 7-9-12 **74** oh21 ow8 MissJCoward(3) 5 35
(G P Kelly) *chsd ldrs: lost pl 3f out* **200/1**

2m 9.00s (-2.83) **Going Correction** -0.15s/f (Firm)
WFA 3 from 4yo+ 5lb **15** Ran SP% **124.4**
Speed ratings (Par 105): **105,104,104,100,99 99,98,97,97,94 94,93,90,87,84**
CSF £49.59 CT £211.84 TOTE £4.90: £1.50, £4.80, £1.90; EX 65.20 Trifecta £276.30 Part won. Pool: £389.26 - 0.40 winning units. Place 6 £16.59, Place 5 £12.65.
Owner D E Cook **Bred** R S A Urquhart **Trained** Tadcaster, N Yorks

FOCUS
A decent pace for this lady riders' contest and the winning time was 1.75 seconds faster than the preceding three-year-old handicap. The front three pulled a long way clear of the rest and the form looks sound for a race of its type.
T/Jkpt: Not won. T/Plt: £10.50 to a £1 stake. Pool: £73,412.05. 5,089.45 winning tickets. T/Qpdt: £7.10 to a £1 stake. Pool: £4,495.80. 465.80 winning tickets. JR

6454 WOLVERHAMPTON (A.W) (L-H)
Friday, October 26

OFFICIAL GOING: Standard
Wind: Light half-behind becoming fresher from race 3 onwards Weather: Overcast

6476 MACE RACING AT WOLVERHAMPTON H'CAP 7f 32y(P)
7:00 (7:01) (Class 6) (0-60,64) 3-Y-0+ **£2,047** (£604; £302) **Stalls** High

Form RPR

5312 **1** **The City Kid (IRE)**[8] 6290 4-9-4 **58** SaleemGolam 8 66
(S C Williams) *chsd ldrs: led over 2f out: edgd lft fnl f: rdn out* **10/3**[2]

5002 **2** *1* **Northern Boy (USA)**[14] 6148 4-9-6 **60** SebSanders 2 66
(M W Easterby) *s.i.s: hld up: hdwy over 1f out: sn rdn: r.o* **9/4**[1]

300 **3** *nk* **Spanish Needle**[199] 996 3-9-4 **60** ChrisCatlin 7 65
(P R Webber) *chsd ldr to 1/2-way: rdn over 2f out: edgd lft fnl f: styd on* **20/1**

5024 **4** *¾* **Green Pirate**[21] 5981 5-9-6 **60** (v[1]) LiamJones 4 63
(W M Brisbourne) *s.i.s: hld up: swtchd rt and hdwy over 1f out: hung lft ins fnl f: styd on* **13/2**[3]

200 **5** *1* **Inka Dancer (IRE)**[11] 6239 5-9-6 **60** MartinDwyer 3 60
(B Palling) *chsd ldrs: rdn over 1f out: no ex ins fnl f* **20/1**

3600 **6** *¾* **Haroldini (IRE)**[14] 6148 5-8-12 **57** (p) TolleyDean(5) 5 55
(J Balding) *hld up in tch: rdn and edgd lft over 1f out: styd on same pce* **8/1**

1002 **7** *6* **Strabinios King**[22] 5935 3-9-2 **58** LeeEnstone 11 40
(P C Haslam) *sn led: hdd over 2f out: rdn and hung lft over 1f out: sn wknd* **8/1**

6640 **8** *3* **Imperium**[31] 5711 6-9-6 **60** (p) DaneO'Neill 12 34
(Jean-Rene Auvray) *s.i.s: hld up: rdn and wknd over 2f out* **16/1**

3004 **9** *1* **Climate (IRE)**[6] 6344 8-9-0 **59** (b) RussellKennemore(5) 10 30
(R Hollinshead) *prom over 4f* **14/1**

6010 **10** *2* **Paddywack (IRE)**[8] 6287 10-9-6 **60** (b) TomEaves 9 26
(D W Chapman) *s.s: outpcd* **33/1**

1m 29.33s (-1.07) **Going Correction** -0.075s/f (Stan)
WFA 3 from 4yo+ 2lb **10** Ran SP% **114.4**
Speed ratings (Par 101): **103,101,101,100,99 98,91,88,87,84**
CSF £10.64 CT £128.04 TOTE £3.40: £1.10, £1.80, £3.50; EX 5.60.
Owner Luke McGarrigle **Bred** T B And Mrs T B Russell **Trained** Newmarket, Suffolk

FOCUS
Just 3lb separated the whole field on official figures in this moderate handicap, which was run at a decent gallop. The form looks solid for the grade rated around the first two.

6477 JOIN WBX.COM FOR FREE FOOTBALL SHIRT MAIDEN STKS 5f 216y(P)
7:30 (7:32) (Class 5) 2-Y-0 **£2,914** (£867; £433; £216) **Stalls** Low

Form RPR

20 **1** **Lille Ida**[86] 4061 2-8-12 0 MartinDwyer 4 72+
(M P Tregoning) *hld up in tch: shkn up to ld over 1f out: r.o wl: eased nr fin* **10/11**[1]

00 **2** *4* **Change Alley (USA)**[14] 6138 2-9-3 0 J-PGuillambert 1 65
(M Johnston) *w ldr tl led over 4f out: rdn: hung lft and hdd over 1f out: styd on same pce* **14/1**

0 **3** *1 ½* **Solemn**[9] 6267 2-9-3 0 SebSanders 6 61
(Sir Mark Prescott) *chsd ldrs: rdn over 2f out: hung lft fr over 1f out: styd on same pce* **13/2**[3]

02 **4** *1 ½* **Gunner Fly (IRE)**[20] 6022 2-9-0 0 JamieMoriarty(3) 8 56+
(R A Fahey) *s.i.s: hld up: swtchd lft and styd on fnl f: nvr nr to chal* **9/1**

660 **5** *2 ½* **Oasis Davis**[29] 5745 2-9-0 72 AndrewMullen(3) 5 49
(K A Ryan) *chsd ldrs: rdn over 2f out: wknd fnl f* **7/1**

32 **6** *10* **Kyllis**[24] 5888 2-8-12 0 TomEaves 3 14
(B Smart) *led: hdd over 4f out: chsd ldr tl rdn over 2f out: sn wknd* **9/2**[2]

00 **7** *6* **Westwood Dawn**[23] 5910 2-9-3 0 (v[1]) LeeEnstone 2 —
(Mrs N Macauley) *s.i.s: hung lft thrght: sme hdwy over 3f out: wknd over 2f out* **150/1**

8 *10* **Stoneacre Ma** 2-8-12 0 LPKeniry 7 —
(Peter Grayson) *s.i.s: a in rr: wknd over 2f out* **40/1**

1m 15.41s (-0.40) **Going Correction** -0.075s/f (Stan) **8** Ran SP% **116.2**
Speed ratings (Par 95): **99,93,91,89,86 73,65,51**
CSF £16.79 TOTE £1.50: £1.30, £3.00, £2.00; EX 19.30.
Owner Mrs Mette Campbell-Andenaes **Bred** Mrs M Campbell-Andenaes **Trained** Lambourn, Berks

FOCUS
A fair race of its type, but difficult to accurately assess as, while the winner was impressive, the pre-race form on offer was weak.

NOTEBOOK
Lille Ida ◆ ran out a taking winner on her return to sand. An eyecatching runner-up on her debut at Lingfield before disappointing at Glorious Goodwood, where she paid for racing up with the pace, she was held up this time and, produced to lead going to the final furlong, showed a nice turn of foot to score. She should be able to step up on this. (op 6-5)
Change Alley(USA), down a furlong in trip, again showed decent pace but, after hanging early in the home straight, he had no answer to the filly's challenge. He is now eligible for handicaps. (op 11-1)
Solemn ran with credit but the drop in trip from his debut did not seem to suit and he lacked a change of pace at the business end. He looks a handicap type. (op 9-1)
Gunner Fly(IRE) ◆ caught the eye staying on steadily again after losing his pitch towards the end of the back straight. He now qualifies for handicaps and is one to watch for in that sphere. (tchd 11-1)
Oasis Davis, making his nursery debut, was below par and might not have handled the Polytrack. (op 9-1)
Kyllis found only Tobar Suil Lady too good here on her previous start but faded rather disappointingly after racing prominently. (op 10-3 tchd 5-1)
Stoneacre Ma Official explanation: jockey said filly hung left-handed

6478 PLAY MONOPOLY AT SKYBETVEGAS.COM CASINO NURSERY 1m 141y(P)
7:55 (7:56) (Class 6) (0-65,65) 2-Y-0 **£2,218** (£654; £327) **Stalls** Low

Form RPR

0304 **1** **Khandala (IRE)**[17] 6075 2-9-7 **65** JamieSpencer 7 68
(M L W Bell) *hld up: hdwy 2f out: rdn to ld and hung lft ins fnl f: r.o* **9/4**[1]

0040 **2** *nk* **Imaginemysurprise**[45] 5298 2-8-7 **56** HaddenFrost(5) 6 59
(J A Geake) *chsd ldrs: rdn and ev ch ins fnl f: r.o* **25/1**

0500 **3** *1 ½* **Rampant Ronnie (USA)**[23] 5896 2-9-4 **62** LiamJones 5 62
(P W D'Arcy) *w ldrs: led over 6f out: rdn over 2f out: hdd and unable qck ins fnl f* **9/1**

0562 **4** *¾* **Elusive Deal (USA)**[18] 6066 2-9-0 **61** (p) JamieMoriarty(3) 12 59
(R A Fahey) *hld up: hdwy over 2f out: rdn and hung lft fr over 1f out: kpt on* **9/2**[3]

0360 **5** *1 ¼* **Eternal Optimist (IRE)**[18] 6066 2-8-9 **60** AndrewHeffernan(7) 2 55+
(C W Thornton) *chsd ldrs: hmpd 1/2-way: rdn whn nt clr run and lost pl 2f out: styd on ins fnl f* **66/1**

044 **6** *nk* **Poppy Dean (IRE)**[23] 5895 2-9-6 **64** ChrisCatlin 13 59
(J G Portman) *chsd ldrs: rdn over 2f out: no ex fnl f* **12/1**

0000 **7** *1 ½* **Just Jimmy (IRE)**[2] 6418 2-8-10 **54** J-PGuillambert 9 46
(P D Evans) *sn pushed along in rr: hdwy over 6f out: rdn over 2f out: wknd fnl f* **3/1**[2]

0141 **8** *½* **Ambrose Princess (IRE)**[11] 6242 2-9-1 **64** 6ex KevinGhunowa(5) 4 55
(R A Harris) *led: hdd over 6f out: rdn 1/2-way: wknd fnl f* **7/1**

0620 **9** *2 ½* **Twilight Belle (IRE)**[60] 4892 2-9-7 **65** (p) LeeEnstone 8 50+
(K R Burke) *hld up in tch: rdn whn hmpd 2f out: swtchd rt and wknd fnl f* **14/1**

0000 **10** *6* **Follow The Band**[22] 5939 2-9-4 **62** DaneO'Neill 11 35
(R Hannon) *sn pushed along in rr: rdn over 3f out: sme hdwy over 2f out: sn wknd* **20/1**

1m 53.0s (1.24) **Going Correction** -0.075s/f (Stan) **10** Ran SP% **120.9**
Speed ratings (Par 93): **91,90,89,88,87 87,86,85,83,78**
CSF £68.33 CT £448.84 TOTE £2.60: £1.70, £7.20, £2.30; EX 81.10.
Owner Howard Global Insurance Services **Bred** Mrs S Lloyd And Dr M Klay **Trained** Newmarket, Suffolk
■ Stewards' Enquiry : Jamie Spencer two-day ban: used whip with excessive force (Nov 6-7)

FOCUS
A modest nursery run at an ordinary pace. The form is solid enough.

NOTEBOOK
Khandala(IRE) could never get into the action over Catterick's sharp 7f on her nursery debut but the return to a longer trip suited and she got off the mark on her All-Weather bow. Settled in rear by Spencer and still just about last on straightening up, she cut through her field to edge ahead but there was nothing to spare at the end. (op 2-1)
Imaginemysurprise beat just two home on her nursery debut but this longer trip and return to Polytrack showed her in a much more favourable light and she went down fighting. (op 22-1)
Rampant Ronnie(USA) ran a solid race, soon showing in front and sticking on bravely in the straight, if unable to hold on. (tchd 17-2)
Elusive Deal(USA), up in trip, was held up at the back in company with the winner. She made good progress down the outside on the home turn and stayed on, without looking all that co-operative. Official explanation: jockey said filly hung right-handed (op 4-1)
Eternal Optimist(IRE) ran creditably considering she encountered traffic problems.
Poppy Dean(IRE), tackling her longest trip to date on this nursery debut, faded after racing prominently from her wide draw. (op 11-1)

6479 PLAY ROULETTE AT SKYBETVEGAS.COM CASINO H'CAP 1m 141y(P)
8:25 (8:26) (Class 6) (0-55,55) 3-Y-0+ **£2,047** (£604; £302) **Stalls** Low

Form RPR

6054 **1** **Time To Regret**[38] 5503 7-8-10 **48** (p) RoystonFfrench 11 63
(I W McInnes) *chsd ldr: led over 2f out: rdn over 1f out: styd on wl* **11/2**[3]

5026 **2** *3 ½* **Machinate (USA)**[16] 6100 5-9-0 **52** LiamJones 10 59
(W M Brisbourne) *hld up: hdwy 1/2-way: rdn to chse wnr fnl f: edgd lft: styd on same pce* **7/1**

3453 **3** *2 ½* **Zabeel Tower**[7] 6304 4-9-1 **53** (p) ChrisCatlin 5 55
(R Allan) *hld up: hdwy over 5f out: rdn to chse wnr 2f out: wknd ins fnl f* **9/2**[2]

0040 **4** *¾* **Tipsy Lad**[9] 6268 5-8-10 **48** (bt) FergusSweeney 6 48
(D J S Ffrench Davis) *hld up: hdwy over 3f out: rdn over 2f out: styd on same pce appr fnl f* **33/1**

0504 **5** *2* **Anthemion (IRE)**[24] 5890 10-8-8 **49** AndrewMullen(3) 8 44
(Mrs J C McGregor) *led: rdn and hdd over 2f out: wknd over 1f out* **14/1**

3020 **6** *hd* **Alasil (USA)**[18] 6068 7-8-7 **50** TolleyDean(5) 9 45
(R J Price) *hld up: rdn over 2f out: nvr trbld ldrs* **10/1**

4000 **7** *hd* **Desert Lover (IRE)**[27] 5817 5-8-10 **48** J-PGuillambert 13 43
(R J Price) *chsd ldrs: hung lft over 3f out: rdn and wknd over 1f out* **25/1**

0400 **8** *1* **Wodhill Schnaps**[22] 5946 6-8-13 **51** (v) AdrianMcCarthy 3 43
(D Morris) *dwlt: hdwy over 3f out: sn rdn: wknd 2f out* **16/1**

4530 **9** *shd* **Uhuru Peak**[24] 5890 6-8-12 **50**..(t) SebSanders 4 42
(M W Easterby) *hld up: nt clr run over 1f out: n.d* **8/1**
2400 **10** *¾* **Sarraaf (IRE)**[21] 5966 11-9-3 **55**.. TomEaves 7 46
(I Semple) *hld up: rdn over 2f out: n.d* **14/1**
041 **11** *15* **Lytham (IRE)**[115] 3186 6-8-13 **51**.. VinceSlattery 12 9
(D J Wintle) *hld up: rdn and wknd over 2f out* **10/1**
3330 **12** *57* **Beamsley Beacon**[9] 5525 6-8-10 **48**.. JamieSpencer 1 —
(S T Mason) *chsd ldrs: pushed along over 6f out: lost pl over 4f out: sn wknd and eased* **7/2**[1]

1m 49.36s (-2.40) **Going Correction** -0.075s/f (Stan) **12** Ran SP% **123.6**
Speed ratings (Par 101): **107,103,101,101,99 99,98,97,97,97 83,33**
CSF £45.92 CT £195.76 TOTE £6.60: £1.10, £3.00, £2.20; EX 35.70.
Owner Horses 4 Courses **Bred** Speedlith Group **Trained** Catwick, E Yorks

FOCUS
A low-grade handicap, run in a decent winning time for a race of its class. The placed horses set the standard.
Uhuru Peak Official explanation: jockey said gelding was denied a clear run
Beamsley Beacon Official explanation: jockey said gelding never travelled

6480 WBX.COM £25 BET FOR NEW ACCOUNTS MEDIAN AUCTION MAIDEN STKS 1m 1f 103y(P)

8:55 (8:59) (Class 6) 3-5-Y-0 **£2,047** (£604; £302) **Stalls** Low

Form RPR
00-0 **1** **Kirstys Lad**[44] 5330 5-9-7 41.. GeorgeBaker 8 60
(M Mullineaux) *led: hdd over 7f out: chsd ldr to over 3f out: rdn to ld over 1f out: styd on* **100/1**
524 **2** *1½* **Power Player**[45] 5311 3-9-3 70.. JamieSpencer 7 57
(D J Coakley) *hld up: hdwy over 2f out: rdn to chse wnr and hung lft fnl f: styd on* **2/1**[2]
4550 **3** *2* **Smart Pick**[27] 5803 4-9-2 50.. LiamJones 10 47
(Mrs L Williamson) *chsd ldrs: led over 2f out: rdn and hdd over 1f out: no ex* **16/1**
660 **4** *2* **Witchingham**[4] 6387 3-9-3 65.. DaneO'Neill 2 48
(R Hannon) *chsd ldrs: rdn over 2f out: hung lft and no ex fnl f* **16/1**
2303 **5** *5* **Dr Dream (IRE)**[18] 6060 3-9-3 55..(v) FergusSweeney 3 37
(J G M O'Shea) *chsd ldr tl led over 7f out: hdd over 2f out: rdn and wknd over 1f out* **10/1**[3]
-230 **6** *2* **Cooperstown**[65] 4716 4-9-7 72.. TomEaves 5 33
(I Semple) *hld up in tch: rdn over 2f out: sn hung lft and wknd* **7/4**[1]
46 **7** *15* **Rusty Roof**[271] 272 4-9-2 0.. VinceSlattery 9 —
(Rae Guest) *hld up: rdn and wknd 3f out* **66/1**

2m 2.54s (-0.08) **Going Correction** -0.075s/f (Stan)
WFA 3 from 4yo+ 4lb **7** Ran SP% **93.0**
Speed ratings (Par 101): **97,95,93,92,87 85,72**
CSF £188.61 TOTE £79.10: £19.60, £1.50; EX 278.50.
Owner S A Pritchard **Bred** T S And Mrs Wallace **Trained** Alpraham, Cheshire
■ Blue Eyed Eloise (6/1, ref to enter stalls) & Tweed River (9/1, burst out of stalls) were withdrawn. R4, deduct 20p in the £.

FOCUS
A shock result to this very weak maiden in which the runners were held in the stalls for several minutes before the off. The pace was only steady and the form is not solid with the runner-up the best guide.
Power Player Official explanation: jockey said gelfing hung left-handed

6481 SKYBETVEGAS.COM CASINO H'CAP 1m 4f 50y(P)

9:20 (9:22) (Class 5) (0-75,72) 3-Y-0+ **£3,238** (£963; £481; £240) **Stalls** Low

Form RPR
3111 **1** **Boz**[20] 6027 3-9-5 **71**.. JamieSpencer 1 84+
(L M Cumani) *trckd ldrs: rdn to ld over 1f out: styd on wl* **10/11**[1]
1332 **2** *nk* **Kalasam**[8] 6293 3-9-6 **72**.. MartinDwyer 3 82
(W R Muir) *hld up: hdwy over 2f out: rdn and hung lft over 1f out: styd on* **3/1**[2]
5656 **3** *2* **Cavalry Twill (IRE)**[22] 5955 3-8-10 **62**..(b) SebSanders 2 69
(P F I Cole) *stmbld s: led: hdd over 10f out: chsd ldr: led over 2f out: rdn and hdd over 1f out: styd on same pce fnl f* **13/2**[3]
1124 **4** *3* **Rudry World (IRE)**[14] 6158 4-9-11 **70**.. GeorgeBaker 6 72
(M Mullineaux) *hld up: hdwy over 3f out: rdn over 2f out: hung lft and wknd over 1f out: hung rt ins fnl f* **13/2**[3]
5204 **5** *½* **Colinette**[7] 6314 4-9-4 **63**..(b[1]) FergusSweeney 4 64
(R T Phillips) *hld up: n.m.r 4f out: sn rdn: n.d* **14/1**
0425 **6** *8* **Tafiya**[8] 6275 4-9-6 **65**.. ChrisCatlin 5 54
(J W Hills) *led over 10f out: rdn and hdd over 2f out: wknd over 1f out* **33/1**

2m 41.67s (-0.75) **Going Correction** -0.075s/f (Stan)
WFA 3 from 4yo 7lb **6** Ran SP% **113.7**
Speed ratings (Par 103): **99,98,97,95,95 89**
CSF £3.95 TOTE £2.00: £1.30, £2.50; EX 5.90 Place 6 £ 31.30, Place 5 £ 19.66.
Owner Aston House Stud **Bred** Aston House Stud **Trained** Newmarket, Suffolk

FOCUS
They went a steady pace in this fair handicap and the form is not entirely solid with the placed horses setting the level.
T/Plt: £39.80 to a £1 stake. Pool: £87,534.45. 1,604.05 winning tickets. T/Qpdt: £10.20 to a £1 stake. Pool: £5,196.10. 374.50 winning tickets. CR

MONMOUTH PARK (L-H)

Friday, October 26

OFFICIAL GOING: Turf course - yielding; dirt course - sloppy
Heavy rain ensured the turf course was pretty testing, especially for juveniles, and the dirt course was sloppy; far from ideal for championship racing.

6482a EPITOME BREEDERS' CUP STKS (LISTED RACE) (FILLIES) (TURF) 1m (T)

8:15 (8:15) 2-Y-O **£76,531** (£25,510; £14,031; £7,653; £3,827)

RPR
1 **Sea Chanter (USA)** 2-8-7.. JRVelazquez 2 101
(T Pletcher, U.S.A) **82/10**
2 *¾* **Annie Skates (USA)**[20] 6008 2-8-7.. GKGomez 8 99
(Jane Chapple-Hyam) *held up in rear to straight, switched out, good headway from 1f out, finished well* **37/10**[2]
3 *1¼* **Grace And Power (USA)** 2-8-10.. ECastro 1 99
(Steven B Klesaris, U.S.A) **189/10**
4 *nk* **Bsharpsonata (USA)**[54] 2-8-10.. ECamacho 6 99
(Timothy E Salzman, U.S.A) **362/10**
5 *2* **Namaste's Wish (USA)** 2-8-10.. KDesormeaux 4 94
(W Mott, U.S.A) **23/10**[1]
6 *hd* **Life Is Sweet (USA)** 2-8-7.. ASolis 5 91
(W Mott, U.S.A) **9/2**[3]
7 *¾* **Sales Tax (USA)** 2-8-10.. RMaragh 12 92
(H A Smith, U.S.A) **181/10**
8 *nk* **Cato Major (USA)**[34] 2-8-7.. RBejarano 7 88
(J Kimmel, U.S.A) **114/10**
9 *1¾* **Sammy Van Ammy (USA)**[34] 2-8-7.. CVelasquez 9 85
(R Dutrow Jr, U.S.A) **241/10**
10 *1½* **Joffe's Run (USA)**[20] 6008 2-8-7.. LDettori 11 81
(B J Meehan) *led or disputed lead to straight, weakened final f* **53/10**

1m 39.21s (-38.79) **10** Ran SP% **121.5**
PARI-MUTUEL (including $2 stakes): WIN 18.40; PL (1-2) 8.40, 5.20; SHOW (1-2-3) 6.00, 3.80, 9.60; SF 98.80.
Owner Stoneside Stable **Bred** Stoneside Stable **Trained** USA

NOTEBOOK
Annie Skates(USA), third in a Newmarket Group 3 on her last start, finished strongly, just as she had done at HQ. This was a good effort and the time of the race compared very favourably with the Breeders' Cup Juvenile Turf later on the card, although there was incessant rain in the two hours between the races.
Joffe's Run(USA) probably wants quicker ground and could have done with being allowed an uncontested lead.

6483a BREEDERS' CUP FILLY & MARE SPRINT (F&M) (DIRT) 6f

9:25 (9:28) 3-Y-0+ **£309,949** (£114,796; £57,398; £29,273; £14,349)

RPR
1 **Maryfield (CAN)**[61] 6-8-11..(b) ETrujillo 4 113
(Doug O'Neill, U.S.A) *mid-division, headway on outside & 6th straight, led distance, driven out* **12/1**
2 *½* **Miraculous Miss (USA)**[27] 4-8-11.. JRose 2 111
(Steven B Klesaris, U.S.A) *s.i.s & bhd early, 7th on ins str, gd hdwy on rails over 1f out, every chance ins final f, unable to quicken close home* **40/1**
3 *1½* **Miss Macy Sue (USA)**[41] 4-8-11.. ERazoJr 1 107
(Kelly Von Hemel, U.S.A) *slowly into stride, soon in mid-division, 4th straight, soon ridden & stayed on same pace* **7/1**[3]
4 *2* **Baroness Thatcher (USA)**[20] 3-8-8.. KDesormeaux 10 99
(F Parisel, U.S.A) *broke well on outside, soon outpcd, 8th & angled in str, stayed on up rails from 1f out to take 4th closing stages* **14/1**
5 *1* **Dream Rush (USA)**[83] 3-8-8.. ECoa 3 96
(R Violette Jr, U.S.A) *led to distance, tired* **3/1**[2]
6 *2* **La Traviata (USA)**[62] 3-8-8.. JRLeparoux 7 90
(F Parisel, U.S.A) *chased leader to half-way, 3rd straight, one pace from over 1f out* **2/1**[1]
7 *1¾* **Shaggy Mane (USA)**[41] 4-8-11.. CVelasquez 9 86
(D Chatlos Jr, U.S.A) *chased leaders, 5th straight, soon beaten* **20/1**
8 *1* **Oprah Winney (USA)**[47] 4-8-11.. GKGomez 6 83
(R Dutrow Jr, U.S.A) *prominent, went 2nd 3f out, 2nd straight, ridden & beaten over 1f out* **7/1**[3]
9 *¾* **Wild Gams (USA)**[20] 4-8-11.. RADominguez 8 81
(B Perkins Jr, U.S.A) *broke well, soon outpaced, 9th & beaten straight* **12/1**
10 *3½* **Jazzy (ARG)**[34] 5-8-11.. DFlores 5 71
(M Hennig, U.S.A) *always outpaced, last straight* **11/1**

69.85 secs (69.85)
WFA 3 from 4yo+ 1lb **10** Ran SP% **120.9**
PARI-MUTUEL: WIN 18.00; PL (1-2) 9.00, 37.40; SHOW (1-2-3) 6.00, 17.20, 4.60; SF 374.80 (GB: CSF £400.14, TC £3,593.60).
Owner Mark Gorman Nick J Mestrandrea Jim Perry **Bred** Mike C Carroll & John C Harvey Jr **Trained** USA
■ The first running of this event, one of three new races as the Breeders' Cup is extended to two days.

FOCUS
A strongly-run race which suited those that there were held up early.

NOTEBOOK
Maryfield(CAN) gets further than this and the way the race panned out suited her down to the ground. Swinging widest of all into the straight, she finished with a flourish to edge out the rail runner Miraculous Miss.
Miraculous Miss(USA), who has struggled to go the early pace in the past before finishing well, enjoyed the way this race was run and was seen to best effect. She got a clean run through next to the inside rail rounding the turn into the straight and had every chance.
Miss Macy Sue(USA), another at her best off a strong pace, was never that far off the gallop in the chasing pack and perhaps she could have done with being ridden a touch more patiently. This was a solid effort. (tchd 13/2)
Baroness Thatcher(USA), another who is happier over a longer trip than this, stayed on well late in the day to pick up fourth place from the tiring front-runner Dream Rush.
Dream Rush(USA), whose quality is early speed, had too much use made of her this time. She set a fast pace in front and paid the price in the straight, hitting a brick wall inside the distance. (op 11/4)
La Traviata(USA), unbeaten in her three previous starts, ruined her chance by trying to mix it with the leader, who set suicidal fractions. (op 9/4)

6484a BREEDERS' CUP JUVENILE TURF 1m (T)

10:00 (10:04) 2-Y-O **£275,510** (£102,041; £51,020; £26,020; £12,755)

RPR
1 **Nownownow (USA)**[19] 2-8-10.. JRLeparoux 7 109
(F Parisel, U.S.A) *held up, last straight, came wide, strong run from over 1f out to lead inside final f, ran on well* **11/1**
2 *½* **Achill Island (IRE)**[27] 5795 2-8-10.. JMurtagh 8 108
(A P O'Brien, Ire) *hld up in rr tl closing up on outside fr 3f out, 8th str, driven to ld briefly ent fnl f, ev ch tl no ex wl ins fnl f* **7/2**[1]
3 *1¾* **Cannonball (USA)**[35] 2-8-10.. ETrujillo 2 104
(W Ward, U.S.A) *chased leaders, 4th straight, kept on steadily final f* **28/1**
4 *nse* **Strike The Deal (USA)**[21] 5975 2-8-10.. LDettori 5 104
(J Noseda) *always in touch, 5th straight, went to rails, slipped through on inside to have every chance 1f out, one pace* **6/1**[3]
5 *1* **Domestic Fund (IRE)**[26] 5845 2-8-10..(b) PJSmullen 12 102+
(D K Weld, Ire) *always prominent, disputed 2nd half-way, close 3rd on outside straight, every chance 1f out, one pace* **15/2**
6 *nse* **Texas Fever (USA)**[27] 2-8-10.. GKGomez 11 102
(M Stidham, U.S.A) *mid-division racing wide, 7th straight, stayed on under pressure, never nearer* **20/1**

7 ½ **The Leopard (USA)**[27] 2-8-10 .... JRVelazquez 3 101
(T Pletcher, U.S.A) *first to show, tracked leader, close 2nd straight, every chance approaching final f, one pace* **8/1**

8 hd **Gio Ponti (USA)**[19] 2-8-10 .... RADominguez 6 100
(Christophe Clement, U.S.A) *behind, 9th straight, headway over 1f out, not clear run 1f out, no chance after* **8/1**

9 ¾ **Your Round (USA)**[19] 2-8-10 .... ECastro 1 99
(M Hubley, U.S.A) *rear early, headway to mid-division half-way, not much room on rails & lost place 3f out, 11th straight, never a factor* **33/1**

10 ½ **Prussian (USA)**[40] 2-8-10 .... KDesormeaux 9 97
(W Mott, U.S.A) *led, hard ridden over 1f out, headed & weakened 1f out* **4/1**[2]

11 4½ **Cherokee Triangle (USA)**[34] 2-8-10 ....(b) RAlbarado 4 88
(Michael J Maker, U.S.A) *mid-division, 6th on inside straight, soon beaten* **15/2**

12 3½ **Preachin Man (USA)**[27] 2-8-10 ....(b) CVelasquez 10 80
(R Werner, U.S.A) *prominent, 4th half-way, lost place 3f out, 8th & beaten straight* **40/1**

1m 40.48s (-37.52) **12** Ran SP% **124.2**
PARI-MUTUEL: WIN 27.20; PL (1-2) 8.60, 5.20; SHOW (1-2-3) 6.00, 4.20, 7.80; SF 180.00 (GB: CSF £50.00, TC £1,096.01).
Owner Fab Oak Stable **Bred** Fab Oak Stable **Trained** USA

FOCUS
The inaugural running of the Breeders' Cup Juvenile Turf attracted a good field, although the very best American juveniles usually race on the dirt. There was plenty of European interest, too, but again they were not the very best that their respective countries have to offer. Plenty of rain had got into the track and the ground was riding on the soft side of good, which one would have expected to favour the European challengers, particularly as two of them were sired by Sadler's Wells. The pace did not look frantic, but it was still fair considering the conditions and the early leaders failed to sustain their challenges. The first two home came from well off the pace - indeed the winner was last at the top of the straight, and the runner-up is a good guide to the level of the form.

NOTEBOOK
Nownownow(USA) was beaten on his first three starts on dirt, but he improved for the switch to turf when winning at Saratoga in August and stepped up on that form again when an unlucky second to Gio Ponti at Keeneland. The soft ground was an unknown but his breeding suggested it would suit - his half-brother, Marche De Paix, won twice on heavy in France - and he duly relished the conditions. He was forced to come widest of all with his challenge, but the leaders fell away and he stayed on in terrific style, ultimately winning a shade cosily. He is unlikely to get these conditions too often in the future.
Achill Island(IRE) had to go close judged on the form of his second in the Group 2 Royal Lodge, especially with the ground to suit, and he duly ran a fine race. Like the winner, he was held up well out the back, but he committed for home a touch sooner than Nownownow and always looked like being picked off when that one began his surge. (op 5/1)
Cannonball(USA) had only won a maiden restricted to New York-breds, but that came over 6f and he produced a much-improved effort stepped up in trip. (op 40/1)
Strike The Deal(USA), the Mill Reef and Middle Park runner-up, had to prove his stamina, especially considering he was well beaten on his only previous start beyond 6f, and the easing in the ground cannot have been in his favour. He ran a blinder in defeat, though. Having raced just off the pace, he had to wait for a gap early in the straight, but he stayed on well once switched to far rail and just missed out on third.
Domestic Fund(IRE) finished a four-length second to Curtain Call in the Group 2 Beresford Stakes on a yielding surface, and his brother Refuse To Bend won the Eclipse on good to soft. Fitted with first-time blinkers, he tried to negate his wide draw by rushing up and helping force the early speed, but he was kept a little wider than ideal for much of the way and probably ended up doing too much. Still, he fared best of those to race on the pace. (op 7/1)

6485a BREEDERS' CUP DIRT MILE (DIRT) 1m 70y
10:35 (10:41) 3-Y-0+ **£275,510** (£102,041; £51,020; £26,020; £12,755)

RPR

1 **Corinthian (USA)**[55] 5059 4-9-0 .... KDesormeaux 8 122
(J Jerkens, U.S.A) *a cl up, disp 3rd on rail after 3f, qcknd through on ins to go 2nd over 2f out, led ent str, sn clear, driven out* **9/2**[2]

2 6½ **Gottcha Gold (USA)**[69] 4-9-0 ....(b) CCLopez 6 110
(E Plesa Jr, U.S.A) *led after 1 1/2f til headed entering straight, soon one pace* **5/1**[3]

3 8¼ **Discreet Cat (USA)**[26] 5852 4-9-0 .... GKGomez 1 95
(Saeed Bin Suroor) *broke well, disputed 3rd on outside, 4th straight, soon beaten but stayed on to gain 3rd close home* **7/4**[1]

4 hd **Wanderin Boy (USA)**[55] 5059 6-9-0 .... JCastellano 3 95
(N Zito, U.S.A) *led 1 1/2f, 3rd straight, soon beaten, lost 3rd close home* **15/2**

5 10¾ **Lewis Michael (USA)**[27] 5824 4-9-0 ....(b) JTalamo 2 76
(W Catalano, U.S.A) *chased leader, 5th half-way, pushed along 3f out, 5th & beaten straight* **7/1**

6 8½ **Xchanger (USA)**[21] 3-8-10 ....(b) RADominguez 9 59
(Mark Shuman, U.S.A) *6th straight, always in rear* **10/1**

7 3½ **Park Avenue Ball (USA)**[26] 5852 5-9-0 .... JBravo 7 54
(James T Ryerson, U.S.A) *last much of way, 7th & ridden straight, tailed off from over 1f out* **20/1**

8 12 **High Finance (USA)**[55] 4-9-0 ....(b) JRVelazquez 5 33
(R Violette, U.S.A) *in touch, disputed 5th half-way, weakened over 3f out, last straight, soon taile doff* **12/1**

1m 39.06s (99.06)
WFA 3 from 4yo+ 3lb **8** Ran SP% **117.0**
PARI-MUTUEL: WIN 9.40; PL (1-2) 4.40, 6.20; SHOW (1-2-3) 3.00, 3.40, 2.60; SF 60.20 (GB: CSF £27.54, TC £53.43).
Owner Centennial Farms **Bred** Gracefield Equine & Hargus Sexton **Trained** USA

FOCUS
The first-ever running of the Breeders' Cup Dirt Mile lacked real strength in depth, and very few of these would have been at home on the extremely wet track. Such is the importance of the Breeders' Cup Classic to all concerned with dirt racing in the US and beyond, this race needed something special if it was going to capture the imagination, and it most certainly got that in the form of Corinthian, who looked top class in routing his seven rivals.

NOTEBOOK
Corinthian(USA) was settled well off the pace through the early stages and the strong gallop played into his hands as he crept into contention, tight against the inside rail, down the back straight, surprisingly missing a lot of the kickback in the process. He got a perfect split and had the race won once mastering the long-time leader. He was considered a Classic contender for much of the year, but was re-routed to the Mile after failing to see out 1m1f on his previous start. Add this success to his victory in the Grade 1 Metropolitan Mile earlier in the season and there can be few better, if any, in the world over this trip on dirt. He is now likely to be retired, just as it seems he was beginning to fulfil his potential. (op 5/1)
Gottcha Gold(USA), a course-specialist who had won Grade 3 contests round here on his last two starts, was soon setting a scorching pace in a clear lead. He had no answer when Corinthian swept by, but ran a big race in defeat.
Discreet Cat(USA), for the third race in succession, failed to produce his brilliant best. Having been off the track for six months following the discovery of an aggressive throat abscess after his disappointing run in the Dubai World Cup in March, he did not impress on his comeback over 6f in the Vosburgh Stakes. A fast workout, possibly even a little faster than was ideal, in the build-up to this race suggested he had come on for that outing, but he once again failed to fire. He broke sharply, but his rider seemed reluctant to go to the front and restrained his mount just in behind the pace. On the turn out to the back straight, Gomez switched Discreet Cat wide. It looked quite dramatic, but the horse ended up with a lovely position wide of any trouble just off the lead. For whatever reason, though, he failed to pick up when asked. (op 13/8)

6468 DONCASTER (L-H)
Saturday, October 27

OFFICIAL GOING: Good (good to firm in places; 7.9)
The ground had quickened up slightly since the previous day and was described as 'generally good to firm'.
Wind: Moderate, half-against Weather: becoming overcast, shower after race 4

6486 UNISON "ALL FOR ONE" TRADE UNION NURSERY 7f
2:00 (2:01) (Class 2) 2-Y-0 **£12,954** (£3,854; £1,926; £962) **Stalls** High

Form RPR

413 **1** **Kal Barg**[27] 5828 2-8-10 **78** .... PhilipRobinson 8 91+
(M A Jarvis) *trckd ldrs in centre: smooth hdwy over 2f out: led wl over 1f out: rdn ent fnl f and styd on wl* **7/4**[1]

420 **2** 1¾ **Flowing Cape (IRE)**[24] 5910 2-9-0 **82** .... KerrinMcEvoy 9 89
(R Hollinshead) *trckd ldrs in centre: hdwy to chse wnr over 1f out: sn rdn and no imp ins fnl f* **28/1**

0134 **3** 2 **Upton Grey (IRE)**[15] 6154 2-9-5 **87** .... JimmyFortune 7 89
(J H M Gosden) *dwlt: hld up towards rr in centre: hdwy over 2f out: sn rdn and kpt on ins fnl f* **8/1**[2]

2513 **4** 3 **Huzzah (IRE)**[16] 6120 2-9-7 **89** .... MichaelHills 6 84
(B W Hills) *chsd ldr in centre: hdwy and overall ldr briefly 2f out: sn rdn and hdd: grad wknd* **12/1**

4310 **5** ½ **Lodi (IRE)**[35] 5629 2-8-10 **78** .... KDarley 12 75+
(B J Meehan) *dwlt: hld up stands' side: hdwy over 2f out: sn rdn: edgd lft and styd on appr fnl f: nt rch ldrs* **25/1**

251 **6** ½ **Kiwi Bay**[24] 5901 2-9-1 **83** .... JamieSpencer 4 75
(M Dods) *hld up towards rr in centre: hdwy over 2f out: sn rdn and no imp* **10/1**

044 **7** 1½ **Bigalo's Magic (UAE)**[30] 5749 2-8-2 **70** .... ChrisCatlin 1 58
(E J O'Neill) *overall ldr in centre: rdn along over 2f out: sn hdd & wknd* **33/1**

5340 **8** ¾ **Karky Schultz (GER)**[13] 6201 2-8-3 **74** .... LukeMorris(3) 5 60
(J M P Eustace) *a towards rr in centre* **50/1**

031 **9** nk **Resounding Glory (USA)**[24] 5903 2-9-2 **84** .... PaulHanagan 16 74
(R A Fahey) *hld up stands' side: a towards rr* **9/1**[3]

6160 **10** 1 **Captain Royale (IRE)**[64] 4762 2-9-4 **86** ....(v[1]) NCallan 2 69
(J Noseda) *t.k.h: chsd ldrs in centre: rdn along wl over 2f out and sn wknd: lame* **16/1**

0131 **11** 8 **Feisty Royale**[16] 6128 2-9-0 **82** .... GregFairley 15 49
(M Johnston) *s.i.s and towards rr stands' side: hdwy over 2f out: sn rdn along: edgd lft and n.d* **10/1**

1330 **12** ½ **Dan Tucket**[27] 5828 2-8-13 **88** .... MatthewDavies(7) 13 54
(M R Channon) *trckd ldrs stands' side: hdwy to ld that gp over 2f out: sn rdn and wknd wl over 1f out* **20/1**

5053 **13** 2½ **Tadalavil**[16] 6128 2-9-3 **85** .... TomEaves 14 45
(M R Channon) *led stands' side gp: pushed along 1/2-way: rdn and hdd wl over 2f out and sn wknd* **33/1**

1542 **14** 4 **Harry Gee**[13] 6201 2-8-12 **80** ....(b) RichardMullen 10 30
(W R Muir) *racd stands' side: in rr fr 1/2-way* **25/1**

2221 **15** 6 **Bonny Rose**[22] 5965 2-8-8 **76** .... RoystonFfrench 11 11
(M Johnston) *cl up stands' side: rdn along wl over 2f out and sn wknd* **14/1**

1m 25.88s (-1.89) **Going Correction** -0.275s/f (Firm) **15** Ran SP% **119.6**
Speed ratings (Par 101): **99,97,94,91,90 90,88,87,87,86 76,76,73,68,62**
CSF £66.28 CT £332.98 TOTE £2.60: £1.50, £7.50, £3.30; EX 80.90 Trifecta £129.90 Part won. Pool: £183.00 - 0.80 winning tickets..
Owner Sheikh Ahmed Al Maktoum **Bred** Mrs C G Gardiner **Trained** Newmarket, Suffolk

FOCUS
Strong nursery form, although devalued slightly by the field splitting. The action was all up the middle, and the closing stages were dominated by Kal Barg, who had been third behind the subsequent Racing Post Trophy winner in a similar race at Ascot. The third is the most reliable guide to the overall value of the form.

NOTEBOOK
Kal Barg ◆, a close-coupled individual, really took the eye in the paddock. He came there full of running and had only to be shaken up to make sure. He is a lot better than the 78 he was able to run off here. (op 15-8)
Flowing Cape(IRE), making his nursery bow, did well and stuck on to finish clear second best.
Upton Grey(IRE), a May foal, is not that big. He seemed to appreciate the return to 7f. (op 10-1)
Huzzah(IRE), dropping back in trip, went to post at a million miles an hour. After taking a narrow overall advantage it was no surprise to see him run out of petrol. (op 10-1)
Lodi(IRE) ◆, back after a five-week break, did best of the stands' side group. He looks a likely type for a Polytrack nursery.
Kiwi Bay, quite a big type, was far from disgraced on ground plenty quick enough for him. He should enjoy further success at three. (op 11-1)
Captain Royale(IRE) Official explanation: vet said colt returned lame
Harry Gee Official explanation: trainer's rep said colt ran flat
Bonny Rose Official explanation: trainer's rep had no explanation for the poor form shown

6487 RACINGPOST.CO.UK H'CAP 5f
2:30 (2:30) (Class 2) (0-100,99) 3-Y-0+
£12,464 (£3,732; £1,866; £934; £466; £234) **Stalls** High

Form RPR

0134 **1** **Sunrise Safari (IRE)**[36] 5584 4-8-7 **88** ....(v) TomEaves 15 104
(I Semple) *racd stands' side: hld up: hdwy and swtchd lft 2f out: str run to ld last 75yds: clr winner in gp* **11/1**

1024 **2** 1¼ **Aegean Dancer**[33] 5689 5-8-7 **88** .... RoystonFfrench 7 99
(B Smart) *racd far side: trckd ldrs: styd on to chal 75yds out: no ex: 1st of 8 that gp* **12/1**

2113 **3** ¾ **Ishetoo**[28] 5806 3-8-8 **92** .... MichaelJStainton(3) 8 100
(A Dickman) *racd far side: overall ldr: hdd fnl 50yds: 2nd of 8 that gp* **14/1**

3116 **4** *shd* **Matsunosuke**[7] 6327 5-9-1 **96**.. KerrinMcEvoy 4 104
(A B Coogan) *racd far side: trckd ldrs: styd on to chal last 75yds: no ex: 3rd of 8 that gp* **11/1**

3-50 **5** *1 1/2* **Fyodor (IRE)**[23] 5953 6-9-3 **98**.. JimmyFortune 10 101
(W J Haggas) *racd far side: hld up: stdy hdwy over 1f out: styng on whn eased nr fin: 4th of 8 that gp* **20/1**

5063 **6** *1/2* **Bertoliver**[15] 6142 3-8-7 **88**.. KDarley 2 89
(D K Ivory) *racd far side: w ldrs: kpt on same pce fnl f: 5th of 8 that gp* **20/1**

0520 **7** *1/2* **Cape Royal**[13] 6197 7-8-7 **93** ow2........................(bt) KevinGhunowa(5) 18 92
(J M Bradley) *led stands' side gp tl 1f out: no ex* **16/1**

1103 **8** *nk* **How's She Cuttin' (IRE)**[7] 6327 4-8-2 **86**............... AndrewMullen(3) 19 84
(T D Barron) *s.i.s: racd stands' side: hdwy over 2f out: kpt on fnl f* **13/2**[2]

2334 **9** *hd* **Bo McGinty (IRE)**[7] 6327 6-8-4 **85**..................(b) PaulHanagan 16 82
(R A Fahey) *racd stands' side: in tch: kpt on wl fnl f* **12/1**

1660 **10** *nk* **Final Dynasty**[34] 5666 3-9-0 **95**.................................... GrahamGibbons 6 91
(Mrs G S Rees) *racd far side: w ldrs: kpt on same pce appr fnl f* **33/1**

3111 **11** *nk* **Princess Ellis**[15] 6157 3-7-13 **85** oh10....................... KellyHarrison(5) 17 80
(E J Alston) *racd stands' side: w ldrs: edgd lft and wknd appr fnl f* **20/1**

006 **12** *1* **Luscivious**[59] 4950 3-8-4 **85** oh2..................................(b) GregFairley 1 76
(A J McCabe) *racd far side: w ldrs on wd outside: wknd appr fnl f: 7th of 8 that gp* **40/1**

0500 **13** *3/4* **The Tatling (IRE)**[13] 6197 10-8-5 **93**........................ PietroRomeo(7) 12 82
(J M Bradley) *racd centre: nvr nr ldrs* **14/1**

0051 **14** *2* **King Orchisios (IRE)**[7] 6327 4-9-1 **96**..........................(p) NCallan 13 77
(K A Ryan) *racd stands' side: chsd ldrs: lost pl over 1f out* **4/1**[1]

3005 **15** *3/4* **Strike Up The Band**[7] 6327 4-9-4 **99**........................ AdrianTNicholls 11 78
(D Nicholls) *chsd ldrs stands' side: wknd appr fnl f* **16/1**

0000 **16** *3 1/2* **Caribbean Coral**[7] 6327 8-7-12 **86**........................ KeithMcDonnell(7) 9 52
(J J Quinn) *s.i.s: racd far side: hdwy and edgd lft over 2f out: sn lost pl: last of 8 that gp* **28/1**

0011 **U** **Kay Two (IRE)**[13] 6197 5-8-5 **86**..................................(p) JimmyQuinn 14 —
(R J Price) *stmbld and uns rdr s* **8/1**[3]

58.84 secs (-2.58) **Going Correction** -0.275s/f (Firm) **17** Ran SP% **124.7**
Speed ratings (Par 109): **109,107,105,105,103 102,101,101,100,100 99,98,97,93,92 87,—**
CSF £125.96 CT £1946.52 TOTE £12.00: £3.30, £3.70, £2.10, £3.30; EX 193.80 Trifecta £3838.70 Pool: £17,842.17 - 3.30 winning tickets..
Owner Mrs J Penman **Bred** Mervyn Stewkesbury **Trained** Carluke, S Lanarks

FOCUS
They set off in two separate groups but converged into one by the line. The winner is capable of even better and the form looks very sound, for this was a strongly run handicap.

NOTEBOOK
Sunrise Safari(IRE) ◆, in no hurry to join issue, burst through on the stands side to win going away. The next to finish from his group was only seventh overall, which makes his performance all the more meritorious. His stable is ending the year on a high. (op 12-1)
Aegean Dancer has run well all year and he was only outspeeded in the closing stages. (op 14-1)
Ishetoo has risen two and a half stone in the handicap this year. He is all speed and was only edged out near the line. He is a fine advert for his yard. (tchd 12-1)
Matsunosuke, reunited with Kerrin McEvoy, returned to his very best and was only found wanting in the closing stages. (op 12-1)
Fyodor(IRE), having only his third start this year, was on his toes beforehand. He was sticking on in good style when his rider accepted defeat near the line. Most of his wins have been on the all weather, and while suitable opportunities may be hard to find he will merit plenty of respect when reverting to an artificial surface.
Bertoliver, 5lb higher than his last win, was drawn one from the far side and was unable to dominate.
Cape Royal, who looked very wintry beforehand, showed all his old speed to take them along against the stands' side rail but these days he prefers more cut in the ground.
How's She Cuttin'(IRE), who tends to hang right, had a favourable draw, but after missing a beat at the start she never really figured. (op 6-1)
King Orchisios(IRE), raised just 3lb, looked at his best and had the ground to suit but ran a most disappointing race. He will no doubt bounce back on the all weather. Official explanation: trainer had no explanation for the poor form shown (op 9-2)

6488 CORAL TROPHY STKS (REGISTERED AS THE DONCASTER STAKES) (LISTED RACE) 6f
3:05 (3:06) (Class 1) 2-Y-O **£16,595** (£6,274; £3,136; £1,568) **Stalls** High

Form RPR

0311 **1** **Floristry**[15] 6154 2-8-10 **95**.. JamieSpencer 8 104+
(Sir Michael Stoute) *hld up in rr: hdwy 2f out: swtchd outside over 1f out: qcknd wl to ld ins fnl f: comf* **6/4**[1]

1 **2** *1 1/2* **Fateh Field (USA)**[16] 6125 2-9-1 0.. KerrinMcEvoy 4 102
(Saeed Bin Suroor) *prom: led wl over 2f out: rdn over 1f out: hung bdly rt and hdd ins fnl f: kpt on same pce* **3/1**[2]

2530 **3** *1 1/4* **Nacho Libre**[45] 5324 2-9-1 **98**.. MichaelHills 1 98
(B W Hills) *trckd ldrs: hdwy on outer over 2f out and ev ch tl rdn and one pce ent fnl f* **25/1**

0410 **4** *3/4* **Spitfire**[21] 6017 2-9-1 **98**.. PaulHanagan 3 96
(J R Jenkins) *in tch: hdwy over 2f out: rdn and ev ch over 1f out: kpt on same pce ent fnl f* **14/1**

2423 **5** *1 1/2* **Look Busy (IRE)**[14] 6182 2-8-10 **93**........................ PhilipRobinson 12 92+
(A Berry) *led duo on stands' rail: prom: rdn along wl over 1f out: hld whn hmpd and swtchd lft ins fnl f: kpt on* **12/1**

5063 **6** *3/4* **Master Chef (IRE)**[19] 6059 2-9-1 **96**........................(b) JimmyFortune 10 89
(J H M Gosden) *led centre: pushed along 1/2-way: sn rdn and hdd: drvn and wknd over 1f out* **11/1**

1602 **7** *1* **Maze (IRE)**[14] 6182 2-9-4 **102**.. RoystonFfrench 6 89
(B Smart) *bdly hmpd s: t.k.h: hdwy and in tch over 2f out: rdn wl over 1f out and sn btn* **8/1**[3]

213 **8** *1* **Sam's Cross (IRE)**[14] 6171 2-9-1 **88**.. TomEaves 7 83
(W R Swinburn) *wnt lft s: chsd ldrs: rdn along wl over 2f out: grad wknd* **25/1**

P620 **9** *shd* **Vhujon (IRE)**[14] 6182 2-9-1 **93**.. TGMcLaughlin 9 87+
(P D Evans) *s.i.s: towards rr stands' rail: hdwy 2f out: sn rdn: edgd lft and btn* **20/1**

0552 **10** *3* **Ernie Owl (USA)**[10] 6270 2-9-1 **86**..................................(p) MartinDwyer 5 74
(B J Meehan) *wnt rt s: chsd ldrs: rdn along 2f out and sn wknd* **40/1**

1440 **11** *shd* **Nikindi (IRE)**[45] 5324 2-9-1 **89**.. LPKeniry 11 73
(J S Moore) *in tch: rdn along wl over 2f out and sn wknd* **66/1**

2301 **12** *1* **Westwood**[29] 5773 2-9-1 **91**.. RobertHavlin 2 70
(D Haydn Jones) *prom: rdn along over 2f out and sn wknd* **33/1**

1m 12.41s (-1.89) **Going Correction** -0.275s/f (Firm) **12** Ran SP% **118.1**
Speed ratings (Par 103): **101,99,97,96,94 93,92,90,90,86 86,85**
CSF £5.09 TOTE £2.60: £1.70, £1.40, £6.10; EX 7.80 Trifecta £215.70 Pool: £683.59 - 2.25 winning tickets..
Owner Gainsborough **Bred** Gainsborough Stud Management Ltd **Trained** Newmarket, Suffolk
■ Stewards' Enquiry : Kerrin McEvoy one-day ban: careless riding (Nov 7)

FOCUS
Decent form for the grade and the right horses were to the fore at the finish. The winner goes from strength to strength, and the form should prove at least as good as it has been rated.

NOTEBOOK
Floristry ◆ has improved by leaps and bounds. Ridden with bags of confidence, she swept to the front and was back on the bridle at the line. If the improvement is maintained over the winter there is no telling how far she might progress for the master trainer. (op 7-4)
Fateh Field(USA), a rather delicate individual, gave his rider real problems and in the end was no match whatsoever for the winner. (op 11-4 tchd 7-2)
Nacho Libre put two below-par efforts behind him but this is probably as good as he is. (op 28-1)
Spitfire bounced back after failing to fire at Redcar. (op 16-1)
Look Busy(IRE), on her toes beforehend, led one other on the stands' side rail. She ended up more towards the centre and has made great strides in the second half of her first season. (tchd 11-1)
Master Chef(IRE), who had two handlers in the paddock, was loaded with the help of a rug. He took them along in the centre but in the end came up well short. (op 20-1)
Maze(IRE), left very short of room at the start, wouldn't settle. He will have to learn to accept restraint better if he is to come up to scratch at three. Official explanation: jockey said colt suffered interference at start (op 7-1)

6489 RACING POST TROPHY (GROUP 1) (ENTIRE COLTS & FILLIES) 1m (S)
3:40 (3:43) (Class 1) 2-Y-O
£113,560 (£43,040; £21,540; £10,740; £5,380; £2,700) **Stalls** High

Form RPR

4111 **1** **Ibn Khaldun (USA)**[14] 6170 2-9-0 96.. KerrinMcEvoy 6 120+
(Saeed Bin Suroor) *sltly hmpd s: sn trcking ldrs: led over 1f out: edgd rt: styd on strly* **11/4**[1]

121 **2** *3* **City Leader (IRE)**[28] 5795 2-9-0 107.. KDarley 9 113
(B J Meehan) *w ldr: led 2f out: sn hdd: hung lft and sltly hmpd 1f out: styd on same pce* **8/1**

1360 **3** *shd* **Feared In Flight (IRE)**[43] 5397 2-9-0 95..................... PhilipRobinson 11 113
(B W Hills) *chsd ldrs: edgd lft and kpt on same pce fnl f* **66/1**

2161 **4** *2* **Art Master**[21] 6001 2-9-0 101.. FrancisNorton 4 108
(S Kirk) *hld up towards rr: hdwy over 2f out: styd on same pce fnl f* **66/1**

21 **5** *2 1/2* **Curtain Call (FR)**[27] 5845 2-9-0 0.. FMBerry 5 103
(Mrs John Harrington, Ire) *swvd rt s: sn chsng ldrs: effrt over 2f out: hung lft over 1f out: sn wknd* **4/1**[2]

1022 **6** *1 1/2* **Declaration Of War (IRE)**[20] 6041 2-9-0 103.................. RobertHavlin 2 99
(P W Chapple-Hyam) *chsd ldrs: hrd rdn 2f out: sn btn* **14/1**

1201 **7** *shd* **River Proud (USA)**[22] 5972 2-9-0 110.. TQuinn 7 99
(P F I Cole) *led: shkn up and qcknd 3f out: hdd 2f out: sn wknd* **10/1**

8 *1 1/4* **Frozen Fire (GER)**[80] 4299 2-9-0 0.. JamieSpencer 12 96
(A P O'Brien, Ire) *in rr: drvn over 3f out: kpt on: nvr a factor* **5/1**[3]

20 **9** *1/2* **Internationaldebut (IRE)**[36] 5580 2-9-0 0.. NCallan 3 95
(D J Murphy) *hld up in rr: effrt over 2f out: nvr nr ldrs* **100/1**

1 **10** *hd* **Tajaaweed (USA)**[17] 6106 2-9-0 0.. MartinDwyer 10 94
(Sir Michael Stoute) *hld up in rr: hdwy over 2f out: edgd lft over 1f out: sn lost pl* **10/1**

11 *nk* **King Of Rome (IRE)**[20] 6037 2-9-0 0.. JAHeffernan 8 94
(A P O'Brien, Ire) *hld up in rr: hdwy over 3f out: rdn over 2f out: nvr a factor* **9/1**

0114 **12** *8* **Ridge Dance**[28] 5795 2-9-0 104.. JimmyFortune 1 75
(J H M Gosden) *mid-div: drvn 4f out: sme hdwy and edgd lft over 2f out: sn wknd: bhd whn eased ins fnl f* **14/1**

1m 37.62s (-3.89) **Going Correction** -0.275s/f (Firm) **12** Ran SP% **119.9**
Speed ratings (Par 109): **108,105,104,102,100 98,98,97,97,96 96,88**
CSF £25.80 TOTE £3.40: £1.90, £3.00, £8.20; EX 14.40 Trifecta £1592.50 Part won. Pool: £2,243.05 - 0.75 winning tickets..
Owner Godolphin **Bred** Darley **Trained** Newmarket, Suffolk

FOCUS
The winning time was about what you would expect for a race of its stature, the final domestic Group 1 prize of the year and the season's second best two-year-old test, behind only the Dewhurst. Authorized took it 12 months earlier, when it was run at Newbury, and the last six runnings have produced two other Derby winners, a St Leger winner and a French 2,000 Guineas winner. The third is a bit of a worry but Ibn Khaldun could hardly have been more impressive and it looks well worth chancing that he is as good as he has been rated.

NOTEBOOK
Ibn Khaldun(USA) is not that big but is very well made. He travelled supremely well and took this with the minimum of fuss. He may well prove to have more speed than stamina and attracted plenty of ante-post interest afterwards for the 2000 Guineas, in which Godolphin have a decent hand. How much he progresses from two to three remains to be seen, but he has improved at a rate of knots and could hardly have ended the season on a higher note. (op 7-2)
City Leader(IRE), who still looks on the immature side, hung in front and the winner went across his bows entering the final furlong. This still looks career-best form, and he should make further progress at three.
Feared In Flight(IRE), fresh after a six week break, ran out of his skin on ground plenty firm enough for him. Considering his conformation he has done remarkably well.
Art Master stayed on in his own time on ground plenty quick enough for him. He will be suited by a 1m2f and more at three.
Curtain Call(FR), a good-topped colt, looked quite hard trained. Encountering quick ground for the first time he was unable to dominate and he hung and dropped away coming to the final furlong. This was not his form, but he should bounce back at three. Official explanation: trainer's rep said colt ran flat (op 7-2 tchd 9-2)
Declaration Of War(IRE), third behind Rio De La Plata at Longchamp, ran as if that effort had taken its toll. (op 18-1)
River Proud(USA) took them along and wound up the pace soon after halfway. He stopped too far out for stamina to have been an issue. (op 8-1)
Frozen Fire(GER), winner of a maiden at Gowran Park in August on his only previous start, was never going yet was putting in his best work at the line. He will prove his true worth next year. (op 8-1)
Internationaldebut(IRE), still a maiden and well below form at Ayr, shaped much better and can surely make his mark in leser company next year, probably over further.
Tajaaweed(USA), the biggest in the line-up, came into this on the back of a maiden win at Nottingham. He was not up to the task but looks sure to prove very useful at three. (tchd 11-1)
King Of Rome(IRE), winner of a Tipperary maiden on his second start three weeks earlier, is a grand type, but having been anchored at the back he never figured. No doubt he will prove a good deal better than he showed here over longer distances with another year over his head. (tchd 8-1)

6490 TRADE UNION UNISON "YOUR FRIEND AT WORK" H'CAP 1m 4f
4:15 (4:15) (Class 3) (0-95,93) 3-Y-O+ **£11,658** (£3,468; £1,733; £865) **Stalls** Low

Form RPR

3524 **1** **Night Hour (IRE)**[33] 5686 5-9-2 **86**.. JimmyFortune 2 100+
(J H M Gosden) *dwlt: sn in tch: hdwy on inner to trck ldrs 1/2-way: swtchd lft over 1f out: rdn to ld and hung lft ent fnl f: styd on* **11/2**

The Form Book, Raceform Ltd, Compton, RG20 6NL

0403 **2** 3 **Bandama (IRE)**[21] 6014 4-9-6 **90** .... JamieSpencer 6 97
(Mrs A J Perrett) *trckd ldng pair: effrt 2f out: rdn to ld over 1f out: drvn and hdd ent fnl f and n.m.r: kpt on same pce* **7/2**[2]

5000 **3** ½ **Akarem**[14] 6169 6-9-7 **91** .... KDarley 13 97
(K R Burke) *trckd ldrs: hdwy 4f out: rdn along to chal 2f out and sn ev ch: drvn and one pce ins fnl f* **16/1**

0-55 **4** *hd* **Inchloch**[26] 5870 5-8-13 **83** .... TQuinn 5 89
(B G Powell) *midfield: hdwy over 2f out: rdn to chse ldrs over 1f out: kpt on u.p ins fnl f* **25/1**

020 **5** 1½ **John Terry (IRE)**[56] 5030 4-9-9 **93** .... TPQueally 1 96
(Mrs A J Perrett) *led: pushed clr 1/2-way: rdn along over 2f out: drvn and hdd over 1f out: sn wknd* **16/1**

1 **6** *hd* **Envisage (IRE)**[17] 6109 3-8-11 **88** .... KerrinMcEvoy 14 91
(Saeed Bin Suroor) *in tch on outer: rdn along over 2f out: sn drvn and kpt on same pce* **9/2**[3]

-266 **7** ½ **Dancing Lyra**[14] 6180 6-8-9 **79** oh2 .... PaulHanagan 12 81
(R A Fahey) *hld up towards rr: swtchd outside and hdwy 3f out: rdn along wl over 1f out: sn no imp* **16/1**

000 **8** 1 **Bazart**[21] 6011 5-9-5 **92** .... AndrewElliott(3) 4 93
(K R Burke) *chsd ldrs: rdn along over 2f out: grad wknd* **100/1**

121 **9** ½ **Dustoori**[23] 5941 3-8-4 **81** .... MartinDwyer 3 81
(Saeed Bin Suroor) *trckd ldr: hdwy over 2f out: sn rdn and edgd lft: wknd over 1f out* **2/1**[1]

/1-0 **10** *hd* **Ryan's Future (IRE)**[26] 5870 7-8-11 **81** .... LPKeniry 11 80
(J S Moore) *dwlt: hld up: a towards rr* **25/1**

000- **11** 2½ **Day To Remember**[305] 6097 6-9-1 **85** .... (t) GrahamGibbons 9 80
(J J Quinn) *a towards rr* **50/1**

40-0 **12** 2½ **Honduras (SWI)**[12] 6230 6-8-12 **82** .... RichardMullen 10 73
(G L Moore) *a in rr* **50/1**

4640 **13** 1 **Quince (IRE)**[21] 6014 4-8-11 **81** .... (v) NCallan 7 71
(J Pearce) *s.i.s: a in rr* **33/1**

2m 31.16s (-4.37) **Going Correction** -0.175s/f (Firm)
WFA 3 from 4yo+ 7lb **13** Ran SP% **122.3**
Speed ratings (Par 107): **107,105,104,104,103 103,103,102,102,101 100,98,97**
CSF £24.44 CT £300.69 TOTE £5.60: £2.10, £1.90, £3.30; EX 26.50 Trifecta £364.80 Pool: £693.72 - 1.35 winning tickets..
Owner Charles H Wacker III **Bred** C H Wacker Iii **Trained** Newmarket, Suffolk
■ Stewards' Enquiry : Jimmy Fortune two-day ban: careless riding (Nov 7-8)

FOCUS
Solid handicap form and an improved effort from the winner.

NOTEBOOK
Night Hour(IRE) travelled as sweet as a nut. Pulled wide for his run, he swept to the front for an impressive win. Depending on how he fares when he goes through the ring at Newmarket Sales, he could return for the November Handicap, where the likely easier ground will suit him even better. (op 6-1)
Bandama(IRE), with Jamie Spencer a rare jockey booking for this stable, worked hard to get his head in front, but he had no answer when the winner swept by on his outside. (tchd 4-1)
Akarem has slipped down the ratings and staged a revival after some poor efforts of late. (op 12-1)
Inchloch, having just his third start this time, showed that he retains his ability and will no doubt be back over hurdles sonner rather than later. (op 20-1)
John Terry(IRE), hard to predict, tried to steal a march but in the end he was readily cut down to size.
Envisage(IRE), running from a mark that looked plenty high following his debut win in a Nottingham maiden, stuck to his task without ever threatening to reach the front line. This was improved form, and the experience will not be lost on him. Official explanation: jockey said colt was unsuited by the good (good to firm in places) ground (op 13-2)
Dancing Lyra stayed on when it was all over, and this sets him up for a return to hurdling. (op 14-1)
Dustoori, 5lb higher, was encountering fast ground for the first time and it did not seem to suit him, for he was very disappointing. (op 5-2)

6491 UNISON TRADE UNION "POSITIVELY PUBLIC" CONDITIONS STKS 7f

4:45 (4:48) (Class 3) 3-Y-O+

£9,036 (£2,705; £1,352; £677; £337; £169) **Stalls** High

Form RPR

0501 **1** **Appalachian Trail (IRE)**[21] 6018 6-9-6 110 .... (b) TomEaves 8 116
(I Semple) *hld up: hdwy on ins over 2f out: led jst ins fnl f: drvn out* **15/2**

1-02 **2** ½ **Dijeerr (USA)**[13] 6198 3-8-9 107 .... KerrinMcEvoy 1 106
(Saeed Bin Suroor) *trckd ldrs: effrt 2f out: no ex wl ins fnl f* **7/2**[1]

2040 **3** ½ **Humungous (IRE)**[21] 6011 4-8-11 100 .... (p) FMBerry 4 104+
(C R Egerton) *s.i.s: last and pushed along: hdwy over 2f out: styd on wl fnl f* **13/2**[3]

4431 **4** ½ **Celtic Sultan (IRE)**[21] 6013 3-8-9 100 .... MickyFenton 7 103
(T P Tate) *led: clr after 2f: hdd jst ins fnl f: wknd towards fin* **7/2**[1]

6000 **5** *hd* **Somnus**[14] 6183 7-8-11 100 .... (t) KDarley 2 102
(T D Easterby) *hld up towards rr: hdwy over 2f out: kpt on same pce fnl f* **14/1**

0300 **6** 2½ **Grantley Adams**[7] 6338 4-8-11 98 .... ChrisCatlin 10 96
(M R Channon) *trckd ldrs: effrt over 2f out: wknd 1f out* **14/1**

2200 **7** 1¼ **Excusez Moi (USA)**[119] 3088 5-8-11 102 .... NCallan 6 92
(C E Brittain) *trckd ldrs: effrt over 2f out: wknd fnl f* **16/1**

0003 **8** *hd* **Minority Report**[13] 6198 7-8-11 94 .... JamieSpencer 3 92
(L M Cumani) *t.k.h in rr: hdwy over 2f out: sn wknd* **10/1**

0016 **9** 9 **Dabbers Ridge (IRE)**[14] 6183 5-8-11 102 .... MichaelHills 9 67
(B W Hills) *chsd ldr: lost pl over 1f out: sn bhd* **9/2**[2]

1m 25.11s (-2.66) **Going Correction** -0.275s/f (Firm)
WFA 3 from 4yo+ 2lb **9** Ran SP% **116.0**
Speed ratings (Par 107): **104,103,102,102,102 99,97,97,87**
CSF £34.12 TOTE £8.20: £2.30, £1.90, £2.40; EX 24.00 Trifecta £213.10 Pool: £870.78 - 2.90 winning tickets..
Owner G L S Partnership **Bred** Swettenham Stud **Trained** Carluke, S Lanarks

FOCUS
This race has been taken at face value and rated through the runner-up, but the form is not entirely convincing. Seemingly a better-than-ever effort from the tough winner.

NOTEBOOK
Appalachian Trail(IRE), effectively under a 9lb penalty, faced a mixed bunch but proved himself better than ever, quickening through on the inner under a well judged ride. (op 6-1)
Dijeerr(USA), drawn on the wide outside, was having just his third start this time. He went down fighting and there should be more races to be won with him at this level. (tchd 4-1)
Humungous(IRE), tried in cheekpieces this time, finds this trip his bare minimum. By no means straightforward, he was fast closing down the first two at the line. (tchd 7-1)
Celtic Sultan(IRE), stepping up in grade, soon showed in a clear lead. After looking likely to be swallowed up, he stuck on all the way to the line. He should make an even better four-year-old. (op 9-2)
Somnus, again fitted with a tongue tie, showed he is no has been, but he has declined from his peak in 2004.
Grantley Adams put two below-par efforts behind him and looks set to ply his trade in Dubai again this winter.
Minority Report Official explanation: jockey said gelding was unsuited by the good (good to firm in places) ground
Dabbers Ridge(IRE) tried to keep tabs on the clear leader but in the end dropped right away. This looked one trip to the well too many this time. (op 4-1 tchd 7-2)

6492 PERTEMPS PEOPLE DEVELOPMENT "HANDS AND HEELS" APPRENTICE SERIES FINAL H'CAP 7f

5:15 (5:19) (Class 4) (0-85,82) 3-Y-O **£6,477** (£1,927; £963; £481) **Stalls** High

Form RPR

3315 **1** **Giant Slalom**[21] 6006 3-8-13 77 .... GaryBartley 5 88
(W J Haggas) *led centre gp: styd on to ld overall jst ins fnl f: edgd rt and hld on towards fin* **13/2**

2000 **2** *nk* **Curzon Prince (IRE)**[29] 5768 3-9-0 78 .... RobbieEgan 6 88+
(C F Wall) *hld up in mid-div: hdwy over 2f out: styd on ins fnl f: no ex cl home* **14/1**

2222 **3** 1¼ **Chjimes (IRE)**[13] 6205 3-9-1 82 .... DeclanCannon(3) 14 88
(K R Burke) *overall ldr on stands' side: edgd lft over 1f out: hdd jst ins fnl f: no ex* **7/1**

015 **4** 2 **Chicken George (IRE)**[7] 6331 3-8-7 74 .... AdeleRothery(3) 1 75
(D Nicholls) *trckd ldrs: effrt 2f out: kpt on same pce* **6/1**[3]

0055 **5** ½ **Baylini**[29] 5768 3-9-0 78 .... SophieDoyle 3 78
(Ms J S Doyle) *in rr: hdwy and n.m.r over 2f out: kpt on: nt rch ldrs* **16/1**

1006 **6** 3 **Lordship (IRE)**[9] 6278 3-8-1 68 oh3 .... MarkCoumbe(3) 2 60
(A W Carroll) *in rr: hdwy on wd outside over 2f out: nvr nr ldrs* **25/1**

6234 **7** 2½ **Osteopathic Remedy (IRE)**[29] 5776 3-9-2 80 .... WilliamCarson 11 65
(M Dods) *chsd ldrs: wknd 2f out* **9/2**[1]

0206 **8** *hd* **Teen Ager (FR)**[12] 6231 3-8-3 70 .... LauraReynolds(3) 13 54
(J S Moore) *dwlt: out of tch w ldr on stands' side: kpt on fnl 2f: nvr on terms* **18/1**

4235 **9** 1 **Barkass (UAE)**[63] 4797 3-8-10 74 .... HaddenFrost 10 56
(B Ellison) *mid-div: effrt over 2f out: nvr a factor* **5/1**[2]

4060 **10** ½ **Flores Sea (USA)**[99] 3707 3-8-10 74 .... DeanHeslop 8 54
(T D Barron) *mid-div: drvn and lost pl over 2f out* **25/1**

5000 **11** *shd* **Soviet Palace (IRE)**[35] 5635 3-8-13 77 .... JackMitchell 4 57
(K A Ryan) *fly-jmpd s: sn w ldrs: edgd rt and lost pl 2f out* **28/1**

3643 **12** *shd* **Buxton**[10] 6273 3-8-9 73 .... HarryPoulton 12 53
(R Ingram) *in rr: sn pushed along: nvr on terms* **8/1**

132 **13** ½ **Getrah**[39] 5508 3-8-7 74 .... LanceBetts(3) 7 52
(N Wilson) *in rr: bhd fnl 3f* **20/1**

1m 26.03s (-1.74) **Going Correction** -0.275s/f (Firm) **13** Ran SP% **119.8**
Speed ratings (Par 103): **98,97,96,93,93 89,87,86,85,85 85,84,84**
CSF £89.19 CT £683.00 TOTE £8.50: £3.10, £5.20, £2.40; EX 150.00 TRIFECTA Not won. Place 6 £102.70, Place 5 £60.33. .
Owner B Smith,A Duke,J Netherthorpe,G Goddard **Bred** Old Mill Farm **Trained** Newmarket, Suffolk
■ William Carson is the series winner.

FOCUS
Ordinary handicap form for the final of this series, rated through the luckless third.
Baylini Official explanation: jockey said filly was denied a clear run
Barkass(UAE) Official explanation: jockey said gelding never travelled
T/Jkpt: Not won. T/Plt: £178.00 to a £1 stake. Pool: £116,609.45. 478.05 winning tickets. T/Qpdt: £17.10 to a £1 stake. Pool: £5,500.90. 237.10 winning tickets. JR

6125 NEWBURY (L-H)

Saturday, October 27

OFFICIAL GOING: Soft
Wind: Moderate, half against Weather: Overcast

6493 RELYON CLEANING NEWBURY EBF MAIDEN STKS (DIV I) 1m (S)

1:15 (1:17) (Class 4) 2-Y-O **£6,153** (£1,830; £914; £456) **Stalls** Centre

Form RPR

0 **1** **Whistledownwind**[22] 5977 2-9-3 0 .... TedDurcan 1 88+
(P W Chapple-Hyam) *h.d.w: lw: s.s: hld up in last and grad trckd across to nr side: gd prog 3f out: led over 1f out: drvn out and styd on stoutly* **11/1**

0024 **2** 1¾ **Andaman Sunset**[31] 5735 2-9-3 80 .... DarrylHolland 4 84
(G Wragg) *w ldrs: rdn to ld 2f out to over 1f out: styd on but readily hld by wnr* **5/1**[2]

3 1¼ **Scuffle** 2-8-12 0 .... RichardHughes 11 76
(R Charlton) *w'like: scope: t.k.h: hld up in rr: stdy prog 3f out: chsng ldrs 2f out: rn green and edgd rt: kpt on wl* **7/1**

4 **4** 1¼ **Savarain**[23] 5951 2-9-3 0 .... SebSanders 3 79
(L M Cumani) *pressed ldrs: pushed along 3f out: upsides 2f out: one pce after* **13/8**[1]

3 **5** 4 **Pragmatism**[67] 4683 2-9-3 0 .... RHills 12 70
(M Johnston) *leggy: lw: mde most to 2f out: wknd fnl f* **6/1**[3]

00 **6** 1½ **Dancing Dik**[105] 3552 2-9-3 0 .... JimCrowley 15 66
(Mrs A J Perrett) *stdd s: hld up in rr: prog to chse ldrs 3f out: outpcd and reminder 2f out: kpt on steadily fnl f* **50/1**

4 **7** *nk* **King's Kazeem**[36] 5592 2-8-12 0 .... JohnEgan 13 61
(B W Hills) *hld up bhd ldrs: shkn up over 2f out: sn outpcd and btn* **11/1**

0 **8** *shd* **Fiume**[24] 5919 2-9-3 0 .... DaneO'Neill 16 66
(R Hannon) *lw: w ldrs: shkn up 3f out: steadily wknd fnl 2f* **80/1**

0 **9** 6 **Askar Tau (FR)**[36] 5590 2-9-3 0 .... SteveDrowne 6 52+
(M P Tregoning) *dwlt: wl in rr: rdn and struggling over 3f out: no ch after* **25/1**

0 **10** ½ **Black Tor Figarro (IRE)**[11] 6248 2-9-3 0 .... WandersonD'Avila 5 51
(B W Duke) *leggy: nvr on terms w ldrs: struggling wl over 2f out: wknd* **100/1**

11 *shd* **Eddie Dowling** 2-9-3 0 .... TPO'Shea 14 51
(M R Channon) *leggy: scope: nvr bttr than midfield: wknd over 2f out* **50/1**

12 3½ **Emerald Crystal (IRE)** 2-9-3 0 .... StephenDonohoe 9 43
(B J Meehan) *w'like: a in rr: struggling fr 1/2-way* **25/1**

13 ¾ **The Twelve Steps** 2-9-3 0 .... NelsonDeSouza 8 42
(P F I Cole) *w'like: scope: t.k.h early: trckd ldrs: wknd rapidly 2f out* **40/1**

00 **14** 1¼ **Desiderio**[16] 6127 2-9-3 0 .... PatDobbs 10 39
(R Hannon) *chsd ldrs tl wknd wl over 2f out* **66/1**

15 1¾ **King Of Pentacles** 2-9-3 0 .... EddieAhern 7 41+
(H Morrison) *leggy: w ldr for 5f: wknd rapidly* **50/1**

1m 43.54s (2.92) **Going Correction** +0.45s/f (Yiel) **15** Ran SP% **117.9**
Speed ratings (Par 97): **103,101,100,98,94 93,92,92,86,86 86,82,82,80,79**
CSF £59.93 TOTE £13.90: £3.80, £2.00, £3.50; EX 99.70.
Owner Mrs Susan Roy **Bred** Paramount Bloodstock **Trained** Newmarket, Suffolk

FOCUS
Probably an above-average maiden. The winning time was decent for a race like this and 1.52 seconds quicker than the second division. A race that should work out.

NOTEBOOK
Whistledownwind ◆, a 75,000gns Danehill Dancer colt, has winners in the family up to 1m2f, and benefited from the extra furlong, having made a his debut over 7f. His rider made an audacious move - after missing the break from the lowest stall - to bring him with a smart run up the stands' rail to win readily. Connections were surprised he was forward enough to win this, and expect him to do even better next season. (op 10-1)
Andaman Sunset continues to run well without managing to win. He got the mile well, only to find the winner too good and - if unable to find a maiden - should be well at home in handicaps next season. (op 5-1 tchd 11-2 and 6-1 in a place)
Scuffle ◆, a daughter of Daylami out of a 7f specialist, has winners in the family up to 1m2f, and this trip was ideal for a first racecourse appearance. She should have no problem with an extra 2f next season, and looks sure to improve and win races. (op 13-2)
Savarain, made favourite off the back of a promising debut, was a bit disappointing, but should do better at 1m2f and beyond next season. (op 6-4 tchd 7-4)
Pragmatism gave the impression on his debut that 1m would suit, but in the event the extra furlong proved beyond him in the soft ground. He should stay better next year, but looks a handicapper more than anything better. (tchd 13-2)
Dancing Dik, gelded since his last run, is now ready to take his chance in handicaps and should pick up a race or two judged on his efforts to date. (op 40-1)
King's Kazeem ran straighter this time, and was not knocked about when beaten. She should make a handicapper after one more run. (op 10-1)
Fiume, a son of Medicean, is closely related to some speedy sorts, so he may not stay as far as his sire, and on this occasion 6f was as far as he wanted to go. However, it was his best run to date, and 7f should suit in due course. (op 66-1)

6494 RELYON CLEANING NEWBURY E B F MAIDEN STKS (DIV II) 1m (S)
1:45 (1:53) (Class 4) 2-Y-O £6,153 (£1,830; £914; £456) Stalls Centre

Form RPR
0 1 **Trianon**[28] 6812 2-8-12 0 SteveDrowne 7 75
(R Charlton) *unf: scope: settled towards rr: rdn and prog on outer fr over 2f out: sustained effrt to ld jst ins fnl f: all out to hold on last 75yds* **5/1**[1]
3 2 hd **Nemo Spirit (IRE)**[24] 5919 2-9-3 0 SebSanders 9 80
(W R Muir) *lw: settled midfield: prog against nr side 3f out: rdn to chal 1f out: chsd wnr ins fnl f: clsng at fin* **5/1**[1]
3 1 1/4 **Foresight** 2-9-3 0 RichardHughes 14 77+
(Mrs A J Perrett) *w'like: strong: trckd ldrs: effrt over 2f out: cl enough 1f out: hld whn n.m.r nr fin* **14/1**
5 4 2 1/2 **Simone Martini (IRE)**[24] 5918 2-9-3 0 RichardKingscote 3 72+
(R Charlton) *lw: dwlt: hld up wl in rr: pushed along over 2f out: styd on wl fr over 1f out: nrst fin* **10/1**
0 5 1/2 **Border Owl (IRE)**[13] 6202 2-9-3 0 DaneO'Neill 10 70
(R Hannon) *lw: pressed ldr: led 3f out: drvn and hdd jst ins fnl f: wknd* **50/1**
6 1 **Forget It** 2-9-3 0 PatDobbs 11 68+
(R Hannon) *w'like: scope: hld up wl in rr: pushed along over 2f out: styd on steadily fr wl over 1f out: nrst fin* **25/1**
7 3/4 **Ballisodare** 2-9-3 0 TedDurcan 12 67
(P W Chapple-Hyam) *w'like: dwlt: hld up towards rr: pushed along over 2f out: styd on steadily fr over 1f out* **17/2**[3]
8 1/2 **Empire Seeker (USA)** 2-9-3 0 StephenDonohoe 5 65
(B J Meehan) *unf: scope: bit bkwd: wl in rr: rdn 1/2-way: plugged on fr over 1f out: n.d* **25/1**
6 9 3/4 **Red Twist**[16] 6127 2-9-3 0 JohnEgan 6 64
(H Morrison) *wl in rr: rdn 1/2-way: struggling after: kpt on over 1f out* **11/2**[2]
0 10 1 1/4 **Tara's Garden**[24] 5918 2-8-12 0 FergusSweeney 4 56
(M Blanshard) *led to 3f out: wknd 2f out* **33/1**
00 11 1 1/2 **Io (IRE)**[23] 5937 2-8-12 0 EddieAhern 8 53
(J L Dunlop) *cl up tl wknd wl over 1f out* **25/1**
0 12 hd **Stealth Project**[32] 5702 2-9-3 0 HayleyTurner 1 57
(A M Hales) *w'like: trckd ldrs tl wknd 2f out* **100/1**
13 3/4 **Bugaku** 2-9-3 0 RyanMoore 13 56
(Sir Michael Stoute) *w'like: dwlt: nvr on terms w ldrs: pushed along and no prog over 2f out* **5/1**[1]
0 14 3 **Hampton Court**[11] 6255 2-9-3 0 RHills 15 49+
(M Johnston) *unf: prom tl wknd over 2f out* **9/1**
0 15 2 **Banquet (IRE)**[24] 5918 2-9-3 0 DarryllHolland 2 45
(M R Channon) *dwlt: rcvrd into midfield: wknd over 2f out* **25/1**

1m 45.06s (4.44) **Going Correction** +0.45s/f (Yiel) 15 Ran SP% **122.9**
Speed ratings (Par 97): **95,94,93,91,90 89,88,88,87,86 84,84,83,80,78**
CSF £27.72 TOTE £7.30: £2.40, £1.80, £5.20; EX 37.20.
Owner The Queen **Bred** The Queen **Trained** Beckhampton, Wilts

FOCUS
Probably the lesser of the two divisions, with the winning time 1.52 seconds slower than the first, but there should be future winners in the line-up.

NOTEBOOK
Trianon, a Nayef filly, is closely related to some good winners at 1m2f and beyond. Though getting a bit tired in front, she ought to stay much farther next season, and looks the sort to make up into a decent middle-distance three-year-old. (op 11-2 tchd 9-2)
Nemo Spirit(IRE) stepped up on his recent debut, and made the winner go all the way with a sterling effort against the stands' rail. He is bred to excel over middle distances and should have a good time of it next season. (tchd 11-2)
Foresight ◆, an Observatory colt, is a first foal of a juvenile winner, but has winners in the family up to 1m2f. The two in front of him at the finish had the benefit of a previous run, so he did more than enough on this debut to suggest he will win races at this trip and maybe slightly beyond next year. (op 16-1)
Simone Martini(IRE) has done well in his two races to date and is good enough to win a maiden, but he should make up into a useful handicapper next season, with 1m2f likely to suit. (op 9-1)
Border Owl(IRE), a Selkirk gelding out of a 5f-7f winner, should stay this trip better next year. However, he showed much more speed than he did on his debut, and clearly has far more ability than he showed then. (op 40-1)
Forget It, a 75,000euro Galileo colt, is bred to come into his own over middle distances next season, so this was an encouraging debut. He made up a deal of ground in the closing stages, and looks likely to do better. (op 33-1)
Ballisodare, a 60,000gns son of American dirt and turf performer Elusive Quality, has plenty of winners in the family. His dam stayed 1m4f, so he should stay a bit a farther next season, and this was a satisfactory start from which he should improve. (op 8-1 tchd 9-1)
Empire Seeker(USA), a $50,000 son of top-class American dirt performer Seeking The Gold, should stay at least 1m2f next season. (op 20-1)
Red Twist looks like a 1m2f handicapper in the making after one more run. (op 8-1)
Bugaku, a Montjeu colt, immediately had it to do after missing the break, and was in trouble fully three furlongs from home, but he is bred to stay middle distances and will do better at 1m2f and beyond next season (op 9-2)
Hampton Court, a 100,000gns son of King's Best out of the 1m4f performer Darshaan, ran well for a long way, and should step up on this in due course, with longer trips an option next year. (op 8-1)

6495 MOUNTGRANGE STUD STKS (REGISTERED AS THE HORRIS HILL STAKES) (GROUP 3) (C&G) 7f (S)
2:15 (2:24) (Class 1) 2-Y-O
£21,008 (£7,962; £3,984; £1,986; £995; £499) Stalls Centre

Form RPR
21 1 **Beacon Lodge (IRE)**[16] 6126 2-8-12 92 AdamKirby 4 102
(C G Cox) *trckd ldng pair in centre: wl plcd whn gps merged 1/2-way: prog to ld over 1f out: drvn over length clr fnl f: pushed along and jst hld on* **14/1**
12 2 hd **Stimulation (IRE)**[14] 6171 2-8-12 105 SteveDrowne 13 105+
(H Morrison) *lw: t.k.h early: hld up nr side: trapped against rail whn gps merged: eased out over 1f out: r.o wl fnl f: needed one more stride* **5/1**[3]
212 3 nk **Iguazu Falls (USA)**[22] 5972 2-8-12 108 TedDurcan 7 101
(Saeed Bin Suroor) *lw: trckd ldr nr side: chsng whn gps merged 1/2-way: rdn 2f out: styd on wl fnl f: a hld* **4/1**[2]
24 4 2 **Brave Prospector**[8] 6295 2-8-12 0 SebSanders 3 96
(P W Chapple-Hyam) *trckd ldr in centre: stl 2nd whn gps merged 1/2-way: rdn to ld 2f out: hdd over 1f out: wknd last 100yds* **20/1**
1 5 1/2 **Almajd (IRE)**[22] 5977 2-8-12 0 RHills 10 95+
(Sir Michael Stoute) *trckd nr side ldrs: effrt and taken to outer over 2f out: nt qckn over 1f out: one pce after* **15/8**[1]
3511 6 1 1/2 **Dubai Dynamo**[21] 6017 2-8-12 96 JohnEgan 2 91
(J S Moore) *led quartet in centre: overall ldr whn gps merged 1/2-way: hdd 2f out: fdd* **14/1**
4520 7 1 1/2 **Archived (IRE)**[22] 5974 2-8-12 84 PatDobbs 9 87
(M G Quinlan) *towards rr nr side: drvn over 2f out: in tch over 1f out: no imp after* **80/1**
4151 8 3 **Seeking Star (IRE)**[11] 6251 2-8-12 84 DarryllHolland 12 80
(M R Channon) *plld hrd early: hld up bhd nr side ldrs: in tch 2f out: wknd over 1f out* **12/1**
9 9 **Natal Lad (IRE)**[20] 2-8-12 0 (t) TPO'Shea 8 57
(M G Quinlan) *a towards rr: wknd over 2f out* **100/1**
61U0 10 5 **Ramona Chase**[14] 6170 2-8-12 95 JimCrowley 5 45
(S Kirk) *dwlt: last of centre quartet: struggling u.p over 2f out: sn wknd* **40/1**
211 11 3 **Fifteen Love (USA)**[24] 5920 2-8-12 95 RichardHughes 11 37+
(R Charlton) *lw: led nr side gp: chsng ldrs whn gps merged 1/2-way: wknd rapidly 2f out* **11/2**

1m 29.27s (2.27) **Going Correction** +0.45s/f (Yiel) 11 Ran SP% **117.3**
Speed ratings (Par 105): **105,104,104,102,101 99,98,94,84,78 75**
CSF £80.82 TOTE £18.90: £3.10, £1.90, £1.70; EX 76.90.
Owner Mr & Mrs P Hargreaves **Bred** Mrs Bill O'Neill **Trained** Lambourn, Berks
■ A first Group winner for trainer Clive Cox.

FOCUS
The winning time was around par for a race like this allowing for the conditions, but it was a messy event, with the field spitting early on and then merging. The form is limited by the proximity of the seventh and is nothing special by Group 3 standards.

NOTEBOOK
Beacon Lodge(IRE) is progressing well, and stepped up considerably on his recent maiden win here to take this Group 3. However, he has plenty of pace, and in this soft ground 7f was as far as he wanted to go at present, for he only just held on after holding a clear lead inside the final furlong. He could well stay 1m next year, but that is likely to be his limit. (op 16-1)
Stimulation(IRE) ◆ may well have been an unlucky loser, for he had to be switched off the stands' rail to launch a desperate late bid that only just failed. If he trains on, he should make a decent Group performer next year. (op 4-1)
Iguazu Falls(USA) was never quite going to get there, but saw it out well and might have been second in a few more strides. He is very much at home at Group 3 level, and should stay 1m next season. (op 9-2)
Brave Prospector was trying an extra furlong, and would probably have got it on better ground. Though found wanting late in the day, he did enough to suggest he will belatedly find the winning trail next season. (op 25-1)
Almajd(IRE) looked to have plenty of potential on his debut, so this was rather disappointing. While it was a step up in class, the softer ground may have been an issue, and he deserves another chance back on faster conditions. Official explanation: jockey said colt was unsuited by the soft ground (op 13-8 tchd 2-1)
Dubai Dynamo has lots of speed, and again tried to put it to good use, but in better company and on this softer ground, he ran himself into the ground. 6f is his trip. (op 12-1)
Archived(IRE) had a stiff task and finished a bit close for comfort. (op 66-1)
Seeking Star(IRE) Official explanation: jockey said colt ran too free
Fifteen Love(USA) won last time over this trip on easy ground, but it was softer this time, which may help account for what was a very disappointing effort, even allowing for the better quality of opponent. Official explanation: jockey said colt stopped quickly (op 13-2 tchd 7-1)

6496 WEATHERBYS ST SIMON STKS (GROUP 3) 1m 4f 5y
2:50 (2:50) (Class 1) 3-Y-O+
£26,686 (£10,114; £5,061; £2,523; £1,264; £634) Stalls High

Form RPR
4114 1 **Crime Scene (IRE)**[22] 5976 4-9-3 107 TedDurcan 6 115
(Saeed Bin Suroor) *mde all: kicked on 3f out: drvn and hung rt across the trck fr 2f out: ended up on nr side rail but styd on wl* **8/1**
1543 2 1 3/4 **Ivy Creek (USA)**[35] 5618 4-9-3 111 SteveDrowne 4 112
(G Wragg) *lw: hld up: prog to trck wnr over 2f out: carried rt fr 2f out: checked and swtchd rt ins fnl f: kpt on but no imp* **9/2**[3]
0253 3 nk **Regime (IRE)**[49] 5240 3-8-13 112 RichardHughes 3 115
(M L W Bell) *lw: sn hld up in tch: effrt 2f out: hung rt following ldng pair fr over 1f out: kpt on but nvr able to chal* **11/2**
2111 4 9 **Galactic Star**[22] 5976 4-9-3 110 RyanMoore 2 99
(Sir Michael Stoute) *swtg: hld up in last pair: effrt over 3f out: wknd rapidly 2f out* **11/8**[1]
-115 5 3/4 **Red Gala**[14] 6169 4-9-3 102 SebSanders 5 97
(Sir Michael Stoute) *lw: chsd wnr after 3f to over 2f out: wknd* **4/1**[2]
166 6 4 **Dash To The Front**[14] 6168 4-9-0 100 OscarUrbina 8 88
(J R Fanshawe) *chsd wnr for 3f: wknd wl over 2f out* **20/1**

2m 42.21s (6.22) **Going Correction** +0.575s/f (Yiel)
WFA 3 from 4yo 7lb 6 Ran SP% **111.5**
Speed ratings (Par 113): **102,100,100,94,94 91**
CSF £42.14 TOTE £9.50: £3.70, £2.60; EX 48.20.
Owner Godolphin **Bred** Gainsborough Stud Management Ltd **Trained** Newmarket, Suffolk
■ Linas Selection (8/1) was withdrawn on vet's advice. Deduct 10p in the £ under Rule 4.
■ Stewards' Enquiry : Ted Durcan one-day ban: careless riding (Nov 7)

FOCUS
An uninspiring turnout and moderate pace, and the winning time was very modest for a Group 3, even allowing for the conditions.
NOTEBOOK
Crime Scene(IRE), allowed to dictate a modest pace, was always in charge after quickening the tempo 3f from home, despite wandering all the way over to the stands' rail. This was a well-deserved first win in Pattern company, but the form is nothing special at this level. (old market op 10-1 new market op 15-2)
Ivy Creek(USA) would have been suited by a better pace, so this was a good effort which suggests he can yet win at Group 3 level next year granted a more solid gallop. He was done no favours in being carried across the track by the winner, but he had no chance of getting the race in the stewards' room. (old market op 11-2 new market op 5-1)
Regime(IRE), who made up his own mind to follow the leading pair across the track, proved he gets 1m4f after all, and that gives him extra options at this level from now on. (old market op 15-2 tchd 7-1 and 8-1 in a place new market op 13-2 tchd 5-1)
Galactic Star, who got warm beforehand and looked to have gone in his coat, scored off a modest gallop last time but, being a confirmed hold-up performer, would ideally have appreciated a better pace than he experienced either then or on this occasion. That said, it does not explain why he folded up so weakly in the last 2f - and neither does the soft going, since he won in similar ground a year ago. However, he can be forgiven this, as he simply did not look right, and he will be worth another chance under faster conditions next year. (new market op 5-4)
Red Gala was up in grade, but still ought to have done much better than this, since 1m4f with a bit of cut seemed to suit him last time. (old market op 9-2)
Dash To The Front looks a bit out of her depth in Group 3 company. (old market op 25-1)

6497 EUROPEAN BREEDERS' FUND FILLIES' H'CAP 7f (S)
3:25 (3:26) (Class 3) (0-95,89) 3-Y-O+ **£9,715** (£2,890; £1,444; £721) **Stalls** Centre

Form RPR
4343 **1** **Steam Cuisine**[28] 5799 3-9-5 **88**.......................... TPO'Shea 9 98+
(M G Quinlan) *hld up in tch: effrt jst over 1f out: drvn and r.o wl to ld last 75yds: won gng away* **5/2**[1]
2216 **2** *1 1/4* **Ventura (USA)**[28] 5794 3-9-6 **89**.......................... RichardHughes 16 96
(Mrs A J Perrett) *wl plcd: effrt 2f out: drvn to ld 1f out: hdd and outpcd last 75yds* **9/1**
3044 **3** *3/4* **Froissee**[38] 5537 3-8-8 **77**.......................... DaneO'Neill 10 82
(N A Callaghan) *dwlt: hld up in last trio: stdy prog 2f out: chsd ldrs and rdn 1f out: styd on: unable to chal* **20/1**
5100 **4** *1/2* **Jacaranda Ridge**[21] 6006 3-8-5 **77**.......................... WilliamBuick(3) 14 81
(M A Jarvis) *t.k.h early: pressed ldrs: led over 1f out to 1f out: one pce* **14/1**
1124 **5** *1/2* **Montrachet**[14] 6180 3-8-8 **77**.......................... HayleyTurner 6 79
(M L W Bell) *cl up: rdn over 2f out: outpcd over 1f out: kpt on ins fnl f* **9/1**
1226 **6** *1/2* **Plucky**[8] 6300 3-9-2 **85**.......................... TedDurcan 8 86
(J H M Gosden) *lw: trckd ldrs: swtchd to outer and effrt 2f out: cl up 1f out: fdd* **9/2**[2]
4214 **7** *1 1/4* **Safwa (IRE)**[43] 5382 3-8-11 **80**.......................... RHills 15 78
(Sir Michael Stoute) *hld up towards rr but wl in tch: rdn over 1f out: no rspnse: one pce after* **11/2**[3]
3400 **8** *hd* **Princess Valerina**[13] 6209 3-8-11 **80**.......................... DarryllHolland 13 77
(B W Hills) *mde most to over 1f out: sn wknd u.p* **14/1**
0620 **9** *3 1/2* **Folly Lodge**[44] 5355 3-9-4 **87**.......................... SebSanders 12 75
(B W Hills) *plld hrd early: hld up in last trio: brief effrt u.p 2f out: sn btn* **13/2**
3613 **10** *3 1/2* **Nelly's Glen**[92] 3904 3-7-11 **73** oh7.......................... KMay(7) 5 52
(R Hannon) *pressed ldr to over 2f out: steadily wknd* **50/1**
0004 **11** *5* **Pajada**[9] 6277 3-7-11 **73** oh28..........................(v) FrankiePickard(7) 4 39
(M D I Usher) *in tch in rr: wknd 2f out* **100/1**
0100 **12** *4* **Rhuepunzel**[12] 6243 3-8-10 **79**.......................... NickyMackay 3 35
(G A Butler) *racd on outer: in tch: rdn and effrt over 2f out: wknd rapidly over 1f out* **16/1**
1m 29.1s (2.10) **Going Correction** +0.45s/f (Yiel)
WFA 3 from 4yo 2lb **12** Ran SP% **122.4**
Speed ratings (Par 104): **106,104,103,103,102 102,100,100,96,92 86,82**
CSF £26.78 CT £391.92 TOTE £3.60: £1.60, £2.80, £4.70; EX 36.20.
Owner Burns Farm Racing **Bred** Burns Farm Stud **Trained** Newmarket, Suffolk
FOCUS
A decent line-up and the form looks sound overall. The winner is still on the upgrade.
NOTEBOOK
Steam Cuisine has been in good form of late and was well in if the form of her recent Listed third could be trusted. In winning this off an 11 lb higher mark than her two previous handicap victories she confirmed she is much improved. The further she went, the better she looked, and there is more to come at this trip or 1m. (op 11-4 tchd 3-1 in places)
Ventura(USA) bounced back after a below-par effort last time, and was simply beaten by a progressive performer who looked best at the weights. (op 12-1)
Froissee goes well with a bit of cut, and continues to do well off a rating 10lb above her highest winning mark. This trip is a minimum for her these days, so it was no surprise to see her staying on in the last 2f. (op 33-1)
Jacaranda Ridge has been dropped a few pounds and that, combined with the return to turf, produced an improved performance. She goes well with a bit of cut, having won her maiden on good to soft.
Montrachet acts well on softish ground, but this 7f looked too sharp, so a return to 1m or 1m1f should see her to better effect. (op 10-1)
Plucky threatened for a moment when switched wide to make her run, but gave the impression that the extra furlong was not ideal in this ground. (op 4-1)
Safwa(IRE) needs a stiffer test, having put in her best efforts over a mile on softish ground. (op 13-2)

6498 HEATHERWOLD STUD STKS (REGISTERED AS THE RADLEY STAKES) (LISTED RACE) (FILLIES) 7f (S)
4:00 (4:01) (Class 1) 2-Y-O
£12,207 (£4,626; £2,315; £1,154; £578; £290) **Stalls** Centre

Form RPR
2324 **1** **Lady Deauville (FR)**[35] 5614 2-8-12 97.......................... EddieAhern 5 99
(P A Blockley) *hld up bhd ldrs: prog over 2f out: drvn to ld over 1f out: hrd pressed after: hld on wl* **7/1**[3]
2152 **2** *1/2* **Missit (IRE)**[7] 6336 2-8-12 105.......................... DarryllHolland 4 98
(M R Channon) *hld up bhd ldrs: prog over 2f out: pressed wnr over 1f out: sustained chal but a jst hld* **6/5**[1]
41 **3** *1 1/2* **Maramba (USA)**[40] 5483 2-8-12 84.......................... RyanMoore 8 94
(Sir Michael Stoute) *w'like: lw: hld up in last pair: prog over 2f out: drvn and cl up 1f out: styd on same pce* **8/1**
125 **4** *3* **Perfect Act**[22] 5974 2-8-12 85.......................... AdamKirby 7 87
(C G Cox) *lw: wl in tch: prog to ld over 2f out: hdd over 1f out: wknd ins fnl f* **8/1**
3500 **5** *3/4* **Miss Bootylishes**[36] 5597 2-8-12 82.......................... SteveDrowne 11 85
(A B Haynes) *pressed ldr to 3f out: sn outpcd: one pce fr over 1f out* **40/1**
21 **6** *3/4* **Shamayel**[33] 5681 2-8-12 85.......................... RHills 9 83
(B W Hills) *b.hind: dwlt: hld up in last pair: effrt over 2f out: rdn and no imp over 1f out* **5/1**[2]
1052 **7** *3/4* **Serena's Storm (IRE)**[27] 5837 2-8-12 82.......................... PatCosgrave 3 81
(J J Quinn) *hld up in rr but in tch: effrt over 2f out: sn no prog and btn* **25/1**
3510 **8** *9* **Clifton Dancer**[35] 5629 2-8-12 77.......................... RichardKingscote 1 59
(Tom Dascombe) *racd alone far side tl jnd main gp in midfield jst over 2f out: sn wknd* **33/1**
1001 **9** *5* **Tamara Moon (IRE)**[41] 5443 2-8-12 76.......................... TPO'Shea 6 46
(M R Channon) *led to over 2f out: wknd rapidly* **33/1**
132 **10** *6* **Hobby**[38] 5536 2-8-12 95.......................... SebSanders 2 31
(R M Beckett) *edgy: pressed ldrs tl wknd wl over 2f out: eased* **10/1**
1m 29.8s (2.80) **Going Correction** +0.45s/f (Yiel) **10** Ran SP% **118.1**
Speed ratings (Par 100): **102,101,99,96,95 94,93,83,77,70**
CSF £15.56 TOTE £9.40: £2.50, £1.10, £2.50; EX 22.50.
Owner P J Hughes Developments Ltd **Bred** Aerial Bloodstock Et Al **Trained** Lambourn, Berks
FOCUS
Not a strong Listed race, but the first three home are useful enough.
NOTEBOOK
Lady Deauville(FR) was, amazingly, beaten in a Folkestone maiden two outings ago, but her form at Listed and Group 3 level is very solid, and she deservedly got off the mark at the sixth attempt. Battling well to hold the short-priced favourite, she looks a tough sort, and that will stand her in good stead for the future. (op 8-1)
Missit(IRE) ran below the form she showed when second in an admittedly shaky Rockel at Newmarket, but it would be unfair to mark her down too much just because her price was so short. She has done well in five races to date and, if she trains on, will have plenty more to offer next season. (op 5-4 tchd 11-8 in places)
Maramba(USA) put in a creditable effort on much softer ground than when winning her maiden, stepping up from maiden company to chase home two proven Group performers. She should stay 1m next season, and has decent prospects. (op 15-2)
Perfect Act put in a solid effort on ground softer than she had met beforehand, but looks just short of Listed class at present. (op 9-1)
Miss Bootylishes is not quite up to winning in Listed class at present, but this well-built sort goes well on soft ground and ran one of her best races. She should train on and make a handicapper next season when conditions are favourable. Official explanation: jockey said filly hung left (op 66-1)
Shamayel never really got going, and needs another chance to show what she can do in less-testing conditions or back on Polytrack. Official explanation: jockey said filly was unsuited by the soft ground (tchd 9-2)
Hobby Official explanation: jockey said filly never travelled

6499 DAVID WILSON HOMES H'CAP 1m 2f 6y
4:30 (4:31) (Class 2) (0-100,95) 3-Y-O+
£11,217 (£3,358; £1,679; £840; £419; £210) **Stalls** High

Form RPR
-064 **1** **Heaven Knows**[27] 5830 4-9-0 **88**.......................... RHills 12 103+
(W J Haggas) *hld up wl in rr: stdy prog fr over 2f out: rdn over 1f out: r.o to ld last 100yds and edgd rt: styd on wl* **10/3**[1]
2-12 **2** *1 1/4* **Ajhar (USA)**[29] 5764 3-8-10 **89**.......................... SebSanders 4 102+
(M P Tregoning) *cl up: effrt to ld over 2f out: drvn and kpt on over 1f out: hdd and outpcd last 100yds* **5/1**[2]
3213 **3** *2 1/2* **King's Event (USA)**[35] 5641 3-8-7 **86**.......................... RyanMoore 11 94+
(Sir Michael Stoute) *lw: trckd ldrs: prog to chal and w ldr 2f out: hld over 1f out: one pce* **10/3**[1]
6334 **4** *nk* **Resonate (IRE)**[45] 5327 9-8-11 **85**.......................... FergusSweeney 5 92
(A G Newcombe) *chsd ldrs: rdn and cl enough over 2f out: sn nt qckn and outpcd: kpt on fnl f* **25/1**
6450 **5** *2* **Ballinteni**[21] 6011 5-9-0 **88**.......................... JohnEgan 13 91
(Miss Gay Kelleway) *hld up towards rr: prog over 2f out: chsd ldrs over 1f out: fdd fnl f* **33/1**
3001 **6** *2 1/2* **Night Crescendo (USA)**[14] 6172 4-9-6 **94**.......................... JimCrowley 6 92
(Mrs A J Perrett) *lw: trckd ldrs: rdn and cl enough 2f out: sn fdd* **8/1**[3]
4215 **7** *3 1/2* **Press The Button (GER)**[14] 6172 4-8-13 **87**.......................... EddieAhern 10 78
(J R Boyle) *sn restrained into midfield: rdn and struggling over 2f out: plugged on fnl f* **50/1**
0213 **8** *hd* **Best Prospect (IRE)**[14] 6185 5-8-12 **86**..........................(t) PhillipMakin 1 77
(M Dods) *t.k.h: hld up in rr: smooth prog over 2f out: chsd ldrs over 1f out but nt on terms: wknd fnl f* **10/1**
6001 **9** *5* **Flying Clarets (IRE)**[14] 6185 4-9-2 **93**.......................... JamieMoriarty(3) 2 74
(R A Fahey) *led: styd alone far side in st: lost ld over 3f out: btn after* **20/1**
0001 **10** *1/2* **Chantaco (USA)**[17] 6110 5-9-2 **90**.......................... SteveDrowne 3 70
(A M Balding) *b.hind: trckd ldr: led main gp in st: hdd over 2f out: wknd and eased* **16/1**
4203 **11** *2* **Mr Aviator (USA)**[14] 6172 3-8-12 **91**.......................... RichardHughes 15 67
(R Hannon) *dropped in fr wd draw and hld up in rr: brief effrt 3f out: wl btn 2f out* **12/1**
3610 **12** *3 1/2* **Seabow (USA)**[21] 6011 4-9-7 **95**..........................(t) TedDurcan 7 64
(Saeed Bin Suroor) *hld up in last: shkn up and no prog over 2f out: sn bhd* **10/1**
0000 **13** *3* **Plum Pudding (IRE)**[23] 5950 4-9-4 **92**.......................... PatDobbs 9 55
(R Hannon) *hld up in last trio: hrd rdn and no prog 3f out: wknd* **50/1**
1142 **14** *10* **Ahlawy (IRE)**[14] 6180 4-8-8 **82**.......................... PaulMulrennan 8 25
(M W Easterby) *a in rr: wknd 3f out: t.o* **33/1**
2m 12.19s (3.48) **Going Correction** +0.575s/f (Yiel)
WFA 3 from 4yo+ 5lb **14** Ran SP% **124.1**
Speed ratings (Par 109): **109,108,106,105,104 102,99,99,95,94 93,90,88,80**
CSF £18.70 CT £61.63 TOTE £5.00: £2.20, £2.10, £1.50; EX 26.90.
Owner Hamdan Al Maktoum **Bred** Southcourt Stud **Trained** Newmarket, Suffolk
FOCUS
A good handicap which featured some lightly-raced improversand was run at an honest gallop in the conditions. The first three all have progressive profiles, and the fourth, though exposed and in the veteran stage now, is able enough and was unlucky in this race last year.
NOTEBOOK
Heaven Knows, who had already shown that soft ground suits, had been running steadily into form in a quiet campaign, and this was quite impressive. If he can maintain this level of performance, he could have a much more lucrative season next year. (op 4-1)
Ajhar(USA) has now finished second in five of his six races but, since he won the other one, there is nothing wrong with his overall profile. This was a good first effort in handicap company, and he should prove useful in similar races next year. (op 6-1)
King's Event(USA) was trying a longer trip, and stayed it alright, if not showing much in the way of turn of foot. He is lightly-raced and not overburdened at present, so looks capable of finding a similar contest as he gains experience. (op 5-2)
Resonate(IRE) has been battling against the Handicapper of late, and continues to run with extreme credit in the face of some tough tasks. (tchd 28-1)
Ballinteni, still 7lb above his winning mark, and taking on a combination of decent and unexposed sorts here, ran a fair race in the circumstances. (op 66-1)

Night Crescendo(USA) was said to have been suited by the soft ground when winning last time but, even allowing for a 4lb rise in the weights, he did not reproduce that effort here. (tchd 9-1)

6500 BATHWICK TYRES LADY JOCKEYS' CHAMPIONSHIP H'CAP 1m 4f 5y
5:05 (5:05) (Class 5) (0-75,75) 4-Y-0+ **£3,747** (£1,162; £580; £290) **Stalls** High

Form RPR

1251 **1** **Rehearsed (IRE)**[24] 5924 4-9-13 **72** MissVCartmel(5) 4 83
(H Morrison) *hld up wl in rr: wl adrift over 3f out: drvn over 2f out: gd prog wl over 1f out: styd on to chal last 100yds: led on post* **9/2**[1]

3020 **2** *shd* **Pocket Too**[66] 4056 4-9-0 **61** oh1 (p) MissLauraGray(7) 11 72
(M Salaman) *hld up wl off the pce: prog fr over 2f out: pushed into ld jst ins fnl f: sn pressed: hdd on post* **13/2**[3]

5001 **3** *2 ½* **Polish Power (GER)**[15] 6144 7-10-7 **75** MrsSMoore 7 82
(J S Moore) *hld up wl in rr: stdy prog fr 4f out: styd on to ld on outer jst over 1f out: hdd and one pce jst ins fnl f* **7/1**

2103 **4** *2 ½* **Selkirk Grace**[16] 6132 7-9-9 **63** (p) MissFayeBramley 16 66
(K A Morgan) *b. prom in chsng pack: wnt 3rd 5f out: clsd to ld over 2f out: hdd jst over 1f out: fdd* **10/1**

3150 **5** *shd* **Spunger**[13] 6196 4-9-5 **62** (v) MissMSowerby(3) 5 65
(H J L Dunlop) *hld up wl in rr: prog against far rail fr over 2f out: kpt on but nvr rchd ldrs* **14/1**

000 **6** *1* **Pocketwood**[31] 5732 5-9-12 **71** MissKellyBurke(5) 9 72
(Jean-Rene Auvray) *chsd clr ldng pair to 5f out: lost pl: plugged on same pce fnl 2f* **12/1**

6560 **7** *nk* **The Composer**[26] 5857 5-9-3 **62** oh8 ow1 MissCAllen(5) 1 63
(M Blanshard) *prom in chsng gp: no prog 3f out: plugged on one pce* **20/1**

8 *7* **Painted Sky**[250] 4-10-4 **75** MissARyan(3) 6 65
(R A Fahey) *hld up off the pce: effrt over 3f out: no prog over 2f out: sn wknd* **33/1**

6000 **9** *3 ½* **Poseidon's Secret (IRE)**[21] 6007 4-9-4 **65** MissJessicaLodge(7) 8 49
(Pat Eddery) *a in rr: rdn and no prog 4f out: btn after* **33/1**

1241 **10** *½* **Compton Dragon (USA)**[19] 6056 8-9-8 **62** MissEJJones 14 45
(W M Brisbourne) *hld up off the pce: effrt over 3f out: no prog over 2f out: wknd* **10/1**

2512 **11** *½* **Sporting Gesture**[15] 6158 10-10-5 **73** MissSBrotherton 10 55
(M W Easterby) *pressed ldr and clr of rest after 4f: led over 3f out to over 2f out: wknd rapidly* **8/1**

5201 **12** *1 ¼* **Gallego**[13] 6196 5-9-6 **65** MissABevan(5) 12 45
(R J Price) *dwlt: hld up in last: wl bhd fnl 4f* **10/1**

1552 **13** *3* **Nightspot**[26] 5870 6-10-4 **72** MrsCBartley 13 48
(Eve Johnson Houghton) *led: clr w one chalr after 4f: hdd over 3f out: wknd* **5/1**[2]

2m 45.28s (9.29) **Going Correction** +0.575s/f (Yiel) 13 Ran SP% **124.1**
Speed ratings (Par 103): **92,91,90,88,88 87,87,83,80,80 80,79,77**
CSF £34.01 CT £207.33 TOTE £5.40: £2.30, £3.30, £2.20; EX 54.40 Place 6 £223.27, Place 5 £75.65..
Owner Mrs G C Maxwell & J D N Tillyard **Bred** J C Condon **Trained** East Ilsley, Berks

FOCUS
A fair line-up for the type of race, but Nightspot and Sporting Gesture went off far too fast, allowing the well-ridden Rehearsed to come with a late run from a long way off the pace.
T/Plt: £287.50 to a £1 stake. Pool: £82,606.50. 209.70 winning tickets. T/Qpdt: £22.40 to a £1 stake. Pool: £5,495.60. 181.45 winning tickets. JN

6476 WOLVERHAMPTON (A.W) (L-H)
Saturday, October 27

OFFICIAL GOING: Standard
Wind: Fresh, behind

6501 LADBROKES THE HOME OF FOOTBALL BETTING APPRENTICE CLAIMING STKS 1m 4f 50y(P)
7:00 (7:00) (Class 6) 3-Y-0+ **£2,047** (£604; £302) **Stalls** Low

Form RPR

350 **1** **Nawamees (IRE)**[11] 5415 9-9-10 79 (p) JemmaMarshall 12 81
(G L Moore) *mde virtually all: def advantage 5f out: rdn whn chal 2f out: in command ins fnl f* **3/1**[2]

4525 **2** *1 ½* **Torrens (IRE)**[7] 6325 5-9-9 78 PatrickDonaghy 2 78
(J Hetherton) *trckd ldrs: wnt 2nd over 4f out: pressed wnr 2f out: no imp ins fnl f* **6/4**[1]

2100 **3** *5* **Drizzi (IRE)**[11] 6253 6-9-1 62 (p) NSLawes(3) 7 65
(A W Carroll) *in tch in mid-div: hdwy to go 3rd wl over 2f out: kpt on but no ch w first two* **9/1**

4000 **4** *6* **Oscarshall (IRE)**[19] 6055 3-8-12 58 AshleyMorgan(3) 6 59
(M H Tompkins) *slowly away: rdn and sme hdwy over 3f out: nvr nr to chal* **14/1**

0-50 **5** *3* **Taran Tregarth**[28] 5803 3-7-13 38 Julie-AnneCumine(3) 11 42
(W M Brisbourne) *t.k.h in mid-div: one pce fnl 3f* **100/1**

0 **6** *3* **Itsy Bitsy**[30] 5754 5-8-7 0 DebraEngland(3) 10 38
(W J Musson) *slowly away: nvr on terms* **40/1**

6-43 **7** *1 ¼* **Escoffier**[74] 767 5-8-10 57 (t) JosephWalsh(3) 8 39
(M Appleby) *disp ld tl rdn 5f out: sn wknd* **16/1**

0500 **8** *shd* **History Boy**[24] 5921 3-9-5 77 MatthewDavies 1 52
(D J Coakley) *a struggling in rr* **9/2**[3]

0040 **9** *½* **Star Berry**[20] 4128 4-8-10 47 FrankiePickard 5 35
(T Wall) *mid-div tl wknd over 3f out* **66/1**

4250 **10** *6* **Zaffeu**[253] 481 6-8-11 53 SoniaEaton(3) 4 29
(A G Juckes) *a bhd* **25/1**

200- **11** *13* **Gateland**[421] 4981 4-8-12 52 DavidProbert(3) 9 9
(B J Llewellyn) *t.k.h: trckd ldrs tl wknd qckly 4f out* **40/1**

2m 41.87s (-0.55) **Going Correction** -0.075s/f (Stan) 11 Ran SP% **116.9**
WFA 3 from 4yo+ 7lb
Speed ratings (Par 101): **98,97,93,89,87 85,84,84,84,80 71**
CSF £7.56 TOTE £3.60: £1.30, £1.40, £2.40; EX 9.10.
Owner Paul Stamp **Bred** Kilfrush Stud Ltd **Trained** Woodingdean, E Sussex

FOCUS
An uncompetitive apprentice claimer dominated by the two market leaders who were also joint best-in at the weights who did not run to their best. The early pace was very slow, but quickened up appreciably after halfway.

6502 CATHERINE BIRCH 40TH BIRTHDAY CELEBRATION NURSERY 5f 216y(P)
7:30 (7:32) (Class 5) (0-75,75) 2-Y-0 **£3,071** (£906; £453) **Stalls** Low

Form RPR

41 **1** **Raiding Party (IRE)**[44] 5363 2-9-4 **72** SebSanders 2 78+
(J W Hills) *a in tch and gng wl: rdn to ld jst ins fnl f: readily* **6/4**[1]

2403 **2** *1 ½* **Natmana**[19] 6052 2-9-6 **74** DarryllHolland 12 75
(M R Channon) *sn led: rdn and hdd jst ins fnl f: nt pce of wnr* **5/1**[2]

3623 **3** *1 ¼* **Lake Sabina**[99] 3712 2-9-7 **75** GrahamGibbons 5 72
(E S McMahon) *mid-div: rdn and r.o wl fnl f* **16/1**

2000 **4** *shd* **Bahamian Lad**[13] 6195 2-9-0 **68** JamieSpencer 13 64
(R Hollinshead) *racd wd: rdn and hdwy 2f out: r.o fnl f* **8/1**[3]

0420 **5** *¾* **Wreningham**[32] 5705 2-8-13 **67** TGMcLaughlin 4 61
(T Keddy) *t.k.h: trckd ldr: ev ch appr fnl f: wknd ins fnl f* **12/1**

300 **6** *2* **Honey Monster (IRE)**[34] 5665 2-9-4 **75** AndrewElliott(3) 8 63
(Miss V Haigh) *trckd ldrs: rdn 2f out: wknd fnl f* **33/1**

0056 **7** *½* **Sistos Fascination**[18] 6073 2-9-0 **68** (p) GregFairley 3 55
(M Botti) *s.i.s: in rr tl mde sme late hdwy* **33/1**

0650 **8** *½* **Athboy Auction**[25] 5883 2-8-13 **67** RichardMullen 1 52
(H J Collingridge) *s.i.s: sn mid-div: rdn 2f out: wknd appr fnl f* **14/1**

0014 **9** *1 ½* **Asian Power (IRE)**[40] 5471 2-9-3 **71** OscarUrbina 7 52
(P J O'Gorman) *mid-div tl rdn and wknd over 1f out* **8/1**[3]

1004 **10** *nk* **Brixworth Scribe**[15] 6151 2-9-0 **68** PaulEddery 10 48
(B Smart) *slowly away: a bhd* **33/1**

0541 **11** *2* **Wee Buns**[30] 5751 2-8-11 **68** WilliamBuick(3) 6 42
(S Kirk) *in tch early: losing pl whn hmpd over 3f out* **5/1**[2]

100 **12** *3* **Ocean Glory (IRE)**[21] 6004 2-9-4 **72** LPKeniry 9 37
(Peter Grayson) *in tch on outside tl rdn and wknd wl over 1f out* **66/1**

1m 15.92s (0.11) **Going Correction** -0.075s/f (Stan) 12 Ran SP% **126.1**
Speed ratings (Par 95): **96,94,92,92,91 88,87,87,85,84 82,78**
CSF £9.35 CT £96.99 TOTE £2.10: £1.02, £2.60, £5.80; EX 13.90.
Owner Donald M Kerr **Bred** Airlie Stud **Trained** Upper Lambourn, Berks

FOCUS
An ordinary nursery in which it paid to be handy, but the favourite did it nicely. The form look sound enough with the placed horses to their pre-race marks.

NOTEBOOK
Raiding Party(IRE), winner of a maiden over course and distance last month which has already been boosted by the pair that followed her home, was always in a handy position and quickened up well when switched out for her effort. She is improving all the time and may not have stopped winning yet. (op 7-4 tchd 15-8)
Natmana, who attracted market support, showed good early pace but had to do a fair bit of running in order to get across from his wide draw in front, so he probably did well to keep all bar the favourite at bay. He is yet to score after nine attempts, but has the ability to win a race like this on Polytrack. (op 7-1)
Lake Sabina, making her nursery debut, stayed on towards the inside of the track to snatch the minor berth and may benefit from another furlong.
Bahamian Lad, making his sand debut, had it all to do from the outside draw and was very wide turning for home, but he stayed on very nicely down the centre of the track and ought to get another furlong. (tchd 15-2)
Wreningham was keen enough behind the leaders on the inside, but after holding every chance he did not get home. He may be worth dropping to the minimum trip. (op 11-1)
Asian Power(IRE) Official explanation: jockey said gelding lost its action
Wee Buns, raised 5lb for his recent victory in a similar contest over course and distance, ran no sort of race and was under the cosh in a detached last at halfway. This was too bad to be true. (op 6-1 tchd 13-2 and 9-2)

6503 LADBROKES IN WOLVERHAMPTON MAIDEN AUCTION STKS 7f 32y(P)
7:55 (7:58) (Class 6) 2-Y-0 **£2,047** (£604; £302) **Stalls** Low

Form RPR

1 **Orpen Fire (IRE)** 2-8-6 0 GrahamGibbons 10 68
(E S McMahon) *sn chsd ldrs: edgd lft and led over 1f out: r.o ins fnl f* **33/1**

3633 **2** *¾* **Elusive Lady (IRE)**[40] 5477 2-8-2 56 WilliamBuick(3) 9 65
(J R Weymes) *racd on outside: hdwy 2f out: rdn and r.o to chse wnr fnl f* **10/1**

03 **3** *2 ½* **Regal Tradition (IRE)**[9] 6289 2-8-12 0 JamieSpencer 11 66+
(P A Blockley) *s.i.s: in rr tl hdwy over 1f out: r.o fnl f: nvr nrr* **15/2**

0 **4** *hd* **Nordic Commander (IRE)**[11] 6252 2-8-12 0 SebSanders 5 65
(E A L Dunlop) *chsd ldrs thrght: rdn and nt qckn fnl f* **7/1**

0222 **5** *½* **Southwest Star (IRE)**[10] 6263 2-8-11 67 LPKeniry 2 63
(J S Moore) *trckd ldr: led 2f out: hdd over 1f out: one pce fnl f* **11/4**[1]

6045 **6** *½* **Janet's Delight**[24] 5895 2-8-4 61 AdrianMcCarthy 7 55
(S Curran) *mid-div: rdn over 1f out: mde sme late hdwy* **20/1**

05 **7** *2* **Miss Phoebe (IRE)**[16] 6119 2-8-5 0 SimonWhitworth 6 51
(S Kirk) *chsd ldrs tl wknd wl over 1f out* **9/2**[3]

60 **8** *nk* **Marino Prince (FR)**[16] 6119 2-8-4 0 ow1 JackDean(7) 1 56
(W G M Turner) *led tl hdd 2f out: rdn and wknd appr fnl f* **28/1**

5452 **9** *nk* **Geezers Colours**[8] 6312 2-8-8 69 AndrewElliott(3) 8 55
(K R Burke) *trckd ldrs: 2nd whn hung rt 2f out: sn btn* **10/3**[2]

10 *5* **Black Or Red (IRE)** 2-8-13 0 RichardMullen 12 45
(I A Wood) *slowly away: outpcd thrght* **40/1**

00 **11** *¾* **Regal Veil**[50] 5201 2-8-8 0 SaleemGolam 4 38
(S C Williams) *in tch tl rdn and wknd wl over 1f out* **40/1**

0 **12** *1* **Jimmy Falabella (IRE)**[91] 3962 2-8-6 0 KirstyMilczarek(5) 3 38
(N A Callaghan) *a bhd* **25/1**

1m 30.19s (-0.21) **Going Correction** -0.075s/f (Stan) 12 Ran SP% **121.2**
Speed ratings (Par 93): **98,97,94,94,93 92,90,90,89,84 83,82**
CSF £318.39 TOTE £29.20: £7.10, £2.20, £2.80; EX 353.20.
Owner Facts & Figures **Bred** S Couldrige **Trained** Lichfield, Staffs

FOCUS
This looked a moderate maiden, especially with the market leaders ultimately disappointing, but the time was reasonable so it may be worth taking a more positive view of the form.

NOTEBOOK
Orpen Fire(IRE) ◆, an 11,000euros filly out of a half-sister to a winner in the US, was always travelling well behind the leaders and, despite hanging over to the inside rail once in front, she was always doing enough. The market did not suggest this was expected, so she is probably capable of quite a bit more. (op 20-1)
Elusive Lady(IRE), who has already made the frame a few times in selling and claiming company on turf, had to come the long way round on the home bend in order to get into contention so she did well to get so close. Her official rating of 56 could be seen as holding the form down, but this was her first try on sand so she may well have improved for it and she could be interest in a Polytrack nursery off this mark. (op 14-1 tchd 16-1)

Regal Tradition(IRE) ◆ raced lazily early and needed to be rousted along, but he made up a lot of ground over the last couple of furlongs to snatch third on the line. He now qualifies for nurseries and is one to keep an eye on in that sphere. (op 5-1)
Nordic Commander(IRE), well beaten on his turf debut, seemed to be travelling well behind the leaders for a long way, but did not find as much off the bridle as had looked likely. He is bred to get further and may be one for modest handicaps in time. (tchd 6-1)
Southwest Star(IRE), runner-up in his last three starts, was trying this trip for the first time and, after racing up with the pace for a long way, patently failed to stay. He is looking very exposed now. (op 7-2 tchd 4-1 in places)
Geezers Colours, who had run well on his sand debut over 6f here last time, had appeared to get this trip well enough on turf prior to that, but having been bang there on the outside of the leaders at halfway, he looked rather awkward on the crown of the home bend and dropped tamely away. Official explanation: jockey said colt hung right (op 4-1)

6504 LADBROKES - SERIOUS ABOUT SERVICE H'CAP 1m 141y(P)
8:25 (8:25) (Class 5) (0-75,75) 3-Y-O+ £2,914 (£867; £433; £216) Stalls Low

Form RPR
1000 1 **One Night In Paris (IRE)**[49] 5223 4-9-1 **70** JamieSpencer 3 78
(M J Wallace) *a in tch: rdn appr fnl f: r.o wl fnl f to ld nr fin* 9/2[2]
3-54 2 *nk* **Robinzal**[35] 5643 5-8-3 **61** oh2 LukeMorris(3) 7 68
(A W Carroll) *a.p: rdn 3f out: wnt 2nd 2f out: led over 1f out: kpt on: hdd nr fin* 14/1
3403 3 *1* **Casablanca Minx (IRE)**[7] 6343 4-8-7 **62** (v) JamesDoyle 9 68+
(P D Evans) *hld up in rr: hdwy over 1f out: r.o fnl f: nvr nrr* 8/1
0400 4 *nk* **Buckie Massa**[29] 5768 3-9-1 **74** SimonWhitworth 8 78
(S Kirk) *hld up: hdwy over 1f out: kpt on one pce fnl f* 16/1
2340 5 *nk* **Pab Special (IRE)**[145] 2311 4-8-11 **69** AndrewElliott(3) 4 73
(K R Burke) *led tl rdn and hdd over 1f out: kpt on but nt qckn fnl f* 6/1
0405 6 *nk* **Baan (USA)**[16] 6131 4-8-12 **67** (b) GregFairley 2 70
(M Johnston) *trckd ldrs: rdn over 1f out: one pce fnl f* 11/2[3]
6004 7 *4* **Coeur Courageux (FR)**[15] 6145 5-9-6 **75** (t) GeorgeBaker 1 69
(G L Moore) *hld up: hdwy over 1f out: wknd fnl f* 11/4[1]
4000 8 *7* **Silent Storm**[10] 6273 7-9-1 **70** LPKeniry 10 48
(Peter Grayson) *mid-div on outside: rdn over 2f out: sn btn* 33/1
4031 9 *½* **Distiller (IRE)**[12] 6245 3-9-1 **74** RichardMullen 11 50
(W R Muir) *a towards rr* 8/1
006 10 *¾* **General Knowledge (USA)**[14] 6175 4-9-6 **75** (t) SebSanders 6 50
(B G Powell) *trckd ldr to 2f out: wknd qckly* 14/1
1m 49.93s (-1.83) **Going Correction** -0.075s/f (Stan)
WFA 3 from 4yo+ 4lb 10 Ran SP% **118.9**
Speed ratings (Par 103): **105,104,103,103,103 103,99,93,92,92**
CSF £66.92 CT £505.62 TOTE £5.00: £2.20, £5.70, £1.70; EX 111.00.
Owner D Teevan **Bred** Ken Carroll **Trained** Newmarket, Suffolk
FOCUS
An ordinary handicap, but one run at a solid pace throughout despite the front six finishing rather in a heap. The form looks fair for the grade rated around the placed horses.
Distiller(IRE) Official explanation: jockey said gelding ran flat

6505 LADBROKES IN THE COMMUNITY CHARITABLE TRUST CLASSIFIED STKS 1m 1f 103y(P)
8:55 (8:55) (Class 7) 3-Y-O+ £1,911 (£564; £282) Stalls Low

Form RPR
0654 1 **Reveur**[2] 6458 4-9-0 45 RichardMullen 8 54
(M Mullineaux) *a in tch: rdn to ld ins fnl f: kpt on* 6/1
4001 2 *¾* **Dawson Creek (IRE)**[13] 6212 3-9-0 49 JamieSpencer 4 56
(B Gubby) *led tl edgd rt and hdd ins fnl f: no ex nr fin* 7/2[1]
4523 3 *1 ¼* **Fantastic Delight**[13] 6212 4-9-0 45 SebSanders 12 49
(B G Powell) *racd wd: rdn and ev ch 1f out: hung rt and no imp fnl 100yds* 5/1[3]
5220 4 *2* **High Five Society**[47] 5284 3-8-10 45 (b) PaulEddery 5 45
(S R Bowring) *t.k.h: trckd ldr tl one pce appr fnl f* 8/1
6340 5 *2* **Fun In The Sun**[1] 6464 3-8-10 45 (v) TGMcLaughlin 11 41
(P D Evans) *a.p: ev ch 2f out: rdn and one pce fnl f* 12/1
-601 6 *hd* **Ceris Star (IRE)**[8] 6311 3-9-1 50 RichardKingscote 2 46
(B R Millman) *t.k.h: in tch tl wknd appr fnl f* 4/1[2]
0300 7 *hd* **Drink To Me Only**[38] 5525 4-9-0 45 (t) PaulMulrennan 7 40
(J R Weymes) *slowly away: hld up in rr: mde mod late hdwy* 20/1
0300 8 *1 ¼* **Strathaird (IRE)**[35] 5622 3-8-3 45 PatrickDonaghy(7) 10 38
(P C Haslam) *s.i.s: nvr bttr than mid-div* 33/1
000 9 *shd* **Silent Beauty (IRE)**[2] 6453 3-8-10 45 SaleemGolam 3 37
(S C Williams) *trckd ldrs: rdn 3f out: sn btn* 12/1
0500 10 *shd* **Spy Gun (USA)**[18] 6088 7-8-11 44 NeilChalmers(3) 6 37
(T Wall) *hld up: a in rr* 16/1
5065 11 *7* **Pure Velvet (IRE)**[6] 6361 3-8-10 45 LPKeniry 9 22
(S Kirk) *in tch: hrd rdn over 2f out: wknd qckly* 20/1
000- 12 *9* **Find It Out (USA)**[215] 5082 4-8-7 45 (p) DavidProbert(7) 1 3
(B J Llewellyn) *a bhd* 50/1
2m 3.04s (0.42) **Going Correction** -0.075s/f (Stan)
WFA 3 from 4yo+ 4lb 12 Ran SP% **120.0**
Speed ratings (Par 97): **95,94,93,91,89 89,89,88,88,88 81,73**
CSF £26.40 TOTE £8.70: £2.00, £2.20, £1.70; EX 38.40.
Owner A Jones **Bred** Bishopswood Bloodstock & Trickledown Stud **Trained** Alpraham, Cheshire
FOCUS
A very modest contest as expected and the form, although reasonable enough, will not mean much outside this grade.
Dawson Creek(IRE) Official explanation: jockey said gelding hung both ways in straight
Drink To Me Only Official explanation: jockey said gelding missed the break

6506 LADBROKES YOUR BEST BET H'CAP 1m 4f 50y(P)
9:20 (9:21) (Class 5) (0-70,70) 3-Y-O £2,914 (£867; £433; £216) Stalls Low

Form RPR
1522 1 **Right Option (IRE)**[11] 6259 3-8-4 **61** KevinGhunowa(5) 1 69
(J L Flint) *led for 2f: styd prom: rdn to ld over 1f out: all out* 10/3[2]
0211 2 *hd* **Diamond Key (IRE)**[10] 6271 3-8-12 **69** (b) JamesO'Reilly(5) 5 77+
(M G Quinlan) *a in tch: rdn to press wnr thrght fnl f* 11/2
3304 3 *5* **Abounding**[12] 6241 3-9-0 **66** SebSanders 10 66
(R M Beckett) *trckd ldrs: led over 6f out: hdd 3f out: rdn and wknd fnl f* 9/2[3]
1263 4 *nk* **Kindlelight Blue (IRE)**[10] 6272 3-9-2 **68** JamesDoyle 7 67
(N P Littmoden) *led after 2f to over 6f out: led 3f out to over 1f out: wknd fnl f* 7/1
0204 5 *shd* **Intensifier (IRE)**[5] 6387 3-8-4 **56** oh4 (b) FrankieMcDonald 6 55
(P A Blockley) *t.k.h: hld up: styd on one pce ins fnl 2f* 16/1
44-0 6 *2 ½* **Bantry Bere (IRE)**[140] 2445 3-8-13 **65** LPKeniry 4 60
(J R Best) *t.k.h: prom tl wknd over 1f out* 16/1
-542 7 *nk* **Evita**[8] 6314 3-9-4 **70** JamieSpencer 8 65
(L M Cumani) *mid-div: rdn and hung lft over 1f out: sn btn* 5/2[1]
5150 8 *nk* **Mandalay Prince**[80] 4277 3-8-6 **58** NeilPollard 2 52
(W J Musson) *a bhd* 9/1
0000 9 *8* **Cat Six (USA)**[17] 6109 3-8-2 **60** WilliamBuick(3) 3 38
(T Wall) *in tch tl wknd over 3f out* 33/1
2m 41.8s (-0.62) **Going Correction** -0.075s/f (Stan) 9 Ran SP% **122.4**
Speed ratings (Par 101): **99,98,95,95,95 93,93,93,87**
CSF £23.69 CT £86.19 TOTE £4.10: £1.60, £1.90, £2.00; EX 33.30 Place 6 £192.33, Place 5 £144.47.
Owner Roy Mathias **Bred** Paul Monaghan, R Berns And P Sexton **Trained** Kenfig Hill, Bridgend
FOCUS
An ordinary middle-distance handicap and the pace was not at all strong, which was probably not a help to the guaranteed stayers. The first two came right away although and set the level.
T/Plt: £82.20 to a £1 stake. Pool: £72,101.25. 639.90 winning tickets. T/Qpdt: £34.10 to a £1 stake. Pool: £4,245.20. 92.00 winning tickets. JS

6482 MONMOUTH PARK (L-H)
Saturday, October 27

OFFICIAL GOING: Dirt course - sloppy changing to muddy before last race (10:35); turf course - soft
As on Friday, heavy rain ensured the turf track took plenty of getting. On the dirt course, the weather had taken its toll and base was exposed in places.

6507a GREY GOOSE BREEDERS' CUP JUVENILE FILLIES (GRADE 1) (FILLIES) (DIRT) 1m 110y
5:30 (5:34) 2-Y-O £551,020 (£204,082; £102,041; £52,041; £25,510)

RPR
1 **Indian Blessing (USA)**[21] 2-8-7 (b) GKGomez 4 114
(B Baffert, U.S.A) *mde all: 6 l clr wl over 1f out: tired fnl 100yds: drvn out* 9/4[1]
2 *3 ½* **Proud Spell (USA)**[42] 2-8-7 GSaez 10 107
(J Larry Jones, U.S.A) *disp 2nd first turn: 5th 1/2-way: hdwy to go 2nd jst over 2f out: no imp on wnr tl clsd fnl 100yds* 13/2[3]
3 *½* **Backseat Rhythm (USA)**[21] 2-8-7 JCastellano 7 106
(Patrick L Reynolds, U.S.A) *missed break: last early: in rr tl hdwy on outside 4f out: swtchd ins 3f out: 3rd st: kpt on at same pce* 20/1
4 *4* **Tasha's Miracle (USA)**[28] 5826 2-8-7 (b) DFlores 3 97
(J W Sadler, U.S.A) *midfield: hdwy on outside to go 3rd 2f out: 4th st: one pce* 12/1
5 *2 ¼* **Smarty Deb (USA)**[28] 2-8-7 RFrazier 9 92
(Doris Harwood, U.S.A) *disputing 2nd whn n.m.r on first turn: 3rd 1/2-way: one pce fnl 2f: jst hld on for 5th* 10/1
6 *hd* **Clearly Foxy (USA)**[48] 5293 2-8-7 PHusbands 2 92
(M Casse, Canada) *in rr: last 3f out: styd on steadily fnl 2f* 25/1
7 *7 ¾* **Grace Anatomy (USA)**[22] 2-8-7 LDettori 12 76
(Doug O'Neill, U.S.A) *hld up: 10th 1/2-way: pushed along 3f out: nvr a factor* 10/1
8 *4 ½* **Zee Zee (USA)**[35] 2-8-7 RAlbarado 11 66
(W Mott, U.S.A) *nvr bttr than midfield* 25/1
9 *2* **A To The Croft (USA)**[22] 2-8-7 (b) KDesormeaux 14 62
(K McPeek, U.S.A) *pressed ldr early: settled in 2nd bef 1/2-way: lost 2nd jst over 2f out: wknd* 10/1
10 *1 ¾* **Izarra (USA)**[28] 5826 2-8-7 VEspinoza 8 58
(R McAnally, U.S.A) *8th early: nvr a factor* 11/2[2]
11 *1* **Set Play (USA)**[28] 5826 2-8-7 BBlanc 6 56
(Peter Miller, U.S.A) *a in rr* 20/1
12 *21* **Irish Smoke (USA)**[22] 2-8-7 JRLeparoux 5 12
(F Parisel, U.S.A) *7th early: nvr a factor* 10/1
13 *4* **Phantom Income (USA)**[28] 2-8-7 ECoa 1 —
(R Violette, U.S.A) *disp 2nd early on ins: 4th 1/2-way: wknd over 2f out* 33/1
1m 44.73s (104.73) 13 Ran SP% **123.7**
PARI-MUTUEL (Including $2 stake): WIN 5.40; PL (1-2) 4.80, 8.80, SHOW(1-2-3) 3.20, 5.80, 9.60; SF 54.20.
Owner Hal J Earnhardt III **Bred** Hal & Patti Earnhardt **Trained** USA
FOCUS
Unpleasant conditions and a slow time in relation to the Juvenile later on the card, but a clear-cut success for Frizette Stakes winner Indian Blessing.
NOTEBOOK
Indian Blessing(USA), winner of the Grade 1 Frizette Stakes on her last start, used her early speed to get to the front, but once there her rider was able to settle her and go a sensible pace. She made every yard and was able to draw clear rounding the turn into the straight, and while she got tired in the closing stages, she was always in command.
Proud Spell(USA) looked likely to appreciate this longer trip when winning the Grade 2 Matron Stakes last time out, and she certainly got the distance well. Unfortunately for her, while she stayed on well in the straight, the winner had already gone beyond recall.
Backseat Rhythm(USA), who came into the race with just a turf maiden win to her name, was beaten a similar distance by Indian Blessing when runner-up in the Frizette Stakes, so the form of that race was well and truly upheld.
Tasha's Miracle(USA) got the trip better than some expected, but she was losing ground on the second and third as they approached the line and this looks the very limit of her stamina.
Smarty Deb(USA), unbeaten in her four previous starts, albeit at a minor track called Emerald Downs, was well supported on course. She lost a good early position as a result of bunching at the first bend and struggled to get involved afterwards, but this was still a fair effort considering the steep rise in class.
Clearly Foxy(USA) came into the race unbeaten in two previous starts, but those wins came on turf. Out the back early, she kept on late for an honourable sixth on her dirt debut.

6508a BESSEMER TRUST BREEDERS' CUP JUVENILE (GRADE 1) (C&G) (DIRT) 1m 110y
6:10 (6:13) 2-Y-O £551,020 (£204,082; £102,041; £52,041; £25,510)

RPR
1 **War Pass (USA)**[21] 2-8-10 CVelasquez 2 123+
(N Zito, U.S.A) *mde all: 5 l clr 3f out: unchal* 2/1[1]
2 *4 ¾* **Pyro (USA)**[21] 2-8-10 SXBridgmohan 7 113
(S Asmussen, U.S.A) *hld up: hdwy 3f out: wnt 2nd st: styd on but no imp on wnr* 4/1[2]
3 *12* **Kodiak Kowboy (USA)**[42] 2-8-10 JRVelazquez 3 88
(S Asmussen, U.S.A) *in tch: 3rd 1/2-way: wnt 2nd over 2f out: no ex st but hld on for 3rd* 10/1

			RPR
4	¾	**Tale Of Ekati (USA)**[42] 2-8-10 ECoa 10 (B Tagg, U.S.A) *racd in 3rd: 5th 1/2-way: 4th st: one pce fr over 1f out* **5/1**[3]	86
5	1 ¾	**Z Humor (USA)**[21] 2-8-10 (b) KDesormeaux 1 (W Mott, U.S.A) *mid-div: 5th and hdwy st: nrst fin* **14/1**	83
6	hd	**Old Man Buck (USA)**[21] 2-8-10 (b) RBejarano 9 (K McPeek, U.S.A) *nvr bttr than mid-div* **16/1**	82
7	2 ¼	**Overextended (USA)**[21] 2-8-10 LDettori 6 (Doug O'Neill, U.S.A) *bhd: nvr a factor* **33/1**	78
8	4 ½	**Shore Do (USA)**[27] 2-8-10 (b) MESmith 5 (Chuck Peery, U.S.A) *bhd: n.d* **18/1**	68
9	7 ½	**Salute The Sarge (USA)**[27] 2-8-10 DFlores 12 (Eric J Guillot, U.S.A) *prom: 4th 1/2-way: drvn 2f out: wknd* **16/1**	52
10	7 ½	**Wicked Style (USA)**[21] 2-8-10 RAlbarado 13 (George R Arnold II, U.S.A) *pushed along to r in tch on rail fr wd draw tl wknd 4f out* **7/1**	37
11	28	**Globalization (USA)**[27] 2-8-10 JCastellano 8 (R Violette Jr, U.S.A) *sn racing in 2nd: pushed along 3f out: wknd over 2f out* **25/1**	—

1m 42.76s (102.76) **11** Ran SP% **122.1**
WIN 6.40; PL (1-2) 3.80, 4.60; SHOW (1-2-3) 2.80, 3.60, 6.40; SF 25.20.
Owner Robert V LaPenta **Bred** Cherry Valley Farm LLC **Trained** USA

FOCUS
This too was run in appalling conditions, but it was a good renewal, run in a time almost 2sec quicker than the Juvenile Fillies earlier on the card. The Champagne Stakes form from Belmont was upheld in no uncertain terms, but hard to be dogmatic about the precise level to set it at owing to the conditions.

NOTEBOOK
War Pass(USA), unbeaten in three previous starts and the winner of the Grade 1 Champagne Stakes at Belmont last time, set out to make all and settled well in front. Never troubled at the head of affairs, he had plenty in hand turning into the straight and, while Pyro cut down his winning distance, the margin to the rest lengthened. This was a top-class performance which will no doubt now earn him the title of top juvenile in the US. While winners of this race are naturally aimed at the Kentucky Derby, he would not appear to be a natural candidate as he has plenty of speed and his pedigree suggests he will struggle to get the extra furlong and a half next spring. Connections will no doubt still aim him at the race, though.
Pyro(USA), runner-up to War Pass in the Champagne Stakes, was fancied by many to reverse the form over this half-furlong longer trip in a race which is often run at a frantic gallop. However, the winner was not hassled on the front end and got the run of things, and while he made up plenty of ground in the straight, he was never going to win. There was a long gap back to the third, which suggests the first two are smart colts, and this son of Pulpit may be the better long-term prospect as he looks sure to appreciate a step up in distance next year. It will be a surprise if he does not reverse the form in the Kentucky Derby.
Kodiak Kowboy(USA) was far from sure to appreciate this longer distance on paper but in the end he just managed to reverse Futurity Stakes form with Tale Of Ekati.
Tale Of Ekati(USA), who could not confirm form with Kodiak Kowboy from the Grade 2 Futurity Stakes last time, also came into the race with question marks hanging over his stamina.
Z Humor(USA), third in the Champagne Stakes, got outpaced down the far side but stayed on again in the straight. His performance was another boost for the form of the Belmont race.

6509a EMIRATES AIRLINE BREEDERS' CUP FILLY & MARE TURF (GRADE 1) 1m 3f
6:55 (6:57) 3-Y-0+ **£586,837** (£217,347; £108,673; £55,423; £27,168)

			RPR
1		**Lahudood**[28] 5822 4-8-11 AGarcia 6 (K McLaughlin, U.S.A) *a cl up: jnd ldr 3f out: led 2f out: drvn out* **10/1**	116
2	¾	**Honey Ryder (USA)**[77] 4413 6-8-11 JRVelazquez 2 (T Pletcher, U.S.A) *hld up: a in tch: 5th st: drvn over 1f out: r.o to take 2nd cl home* **11/2**[3]	114
3	nk	**Passage Of Time**[41] 5465 3-8-6 RADominguez 4 (H R A Cecil) *a cl up: w ldrs on outside over 3f out: 3rd st: chsd wnr fr over 1f out: no ex and lost 2nd cl home* **11/4**[1]	115
4	1	**Nashoba's Key (USA)**[28] 5825 4-8-11 JTalamo 3 (Carla Gaines, U.S.A) *a cl up: 4th on ins st: one pce fr over 1f out* **4/1**[2]	112
5	½	**All My Loving (IRE)**[6] 6367 3-8-6 (v) PJSmullen 1 (A P O'Brien, Ire) *hld up: hdwy and 7th st: styd on fr over 1f out: nvr nr to chal* **16/1**	113
6	3 ¼	**Timarwa (IRE)**[22] 5998 3-8-6 MJKinane 8 (John M Oxx, Ire) *a in tch: cl 6th st: one pce* **12/1**	107
7	2 ¼	**Arravale (USA)**[21] 4-8-11 JValdivia 10 (M Benson, Canada) *prom whn carried wd stands' turns over 7f out: rejnd field in rr in bk st: no ch after and 9th st* **33/1**	103
8	3 ¼	**Precious Kitten (USA)**[21] 4-8-11 RBejarano 12 (R J Frankel, U.S.A) *led over 2f: trcking ldr on outside whn carried wd on stands turn and into bk st: rejnd field in rr but no ch after* **16/1**	98
9	2	**Argentina (IRE)**[28] 5822 5-8-11 KDesormeaux 7 (R J Frankel, U.S.A) *trckd ldrs: lft in ld 7f out: hdd 2f out: 2nd st: sn wknd* **10/1**	94
10	1 ¾	**Danzon (USA)**[28] 4-8-11 JRLeparoux 9 (F Parisel, U.S.A) *hld up in rr: in tch to wl over 2f out: 8th and btn st* **14/1**	92
P		**Simply Perfect**[21] 6010 3-8-6 JMurtagh 11 (J Noseda) *hld up: last early: plld hrd after 2f and wnt up fast to ld on first turn: rn wd stands' turn 7f out and p.u in bk st* **12/1**	—

2m 22.75s (142.75)
WFA 3 from 4yo+ 6lb **11** Ran SP% **117.0**
PARI-MUTUEL: WIN 25.40; PL (1-2) 11.40, 6.60; SHOW (1-2-3) 6.40, 4.60,3.40; SF 167.60.
Owner Shadwell Stable **Bred** Shadwell Estate Company Ltd **Trained** USA

FOCUS
An ordinary renewal and the gallop was noticeably steady for much of the way, even allowing for the conditions. The race was weakened further when Simply Perfect, who had pulled her way to the front, veered off the course racing down the back straight for the final time, badly impeding both Arravale and Precious Kitten in the process.

NOTEBOOK
Lahudood was always well placed and, having avoided much of the trouble, stayed on strongest of all in the short straight. She had to be supplemented at a cost of $180,000, having been a surprise winner of the Flower Bowl Invitational on her previous start, a race her connections had been targeting for Makderah until that one picked up an injury. The decision to pay the money was clearly a wise one and this ex-French trained filly, relishing the easy ground, ran out a decisive winner, despite appearing to idle once in front.
Honey Ryder(USA) stayed on from well off the pace and was closing fast in second. An ultra-consistent mare, she had run third to Ouija Board in this race last year and this represented another terrific effort, especially considering she would probably have benefited from a stronger gallop.
Passage Of Time, with the ground in her favour, was well supported and fared best of the European challengers with a respectable third. Always well placed, she looked a real danger on the turn into the straight, but she just lacked a decisive finishing kick.
Nashoba's Key(USA), previously unbeaten, had to wait for a gap early in the straight, but she was not unlucky. She probably wants quicker ground and a stronger-run race.
All My Loving(IRE) had plenty to do at the top of the straight and kept on without being able to get to the leaders. She has not won since making a successful debut earlier in the year, but she has run several big races in defeat, and this was another.
Timarwa(IRE) lost her place when short of room on the turn into the straight. She had a bit to find in this company and the easing in the ground was probably against her, but this was a creditable effort in the circumstances.
Simply Perfect should not have had any problems with the track so it is difficult to explain her antics, but whatever the case this dual Group 1 winner remains a fine broodmare prospect.

6510a TVG BREEDERS' CUP SPRINT (GRADE 1) (DIRT) 6f
7:35 (7:38) 3-Y-0+ **£551,020** (£204,082; £102,041; £52,041; £25,510)

			RPR
1		**Midnight Lute (USA)**[56] 4-9-0 (b) GKGomez 2 (B Baffert, U.S.A) *slowest away: racd in 9th: 7th whn angled out 2f out: wnt 3rd 1f out: r.o strly down wd outside to ld 100yds out* **11/4**[1]	126
2	4 ¾	**Idiot Proof (USA)**[20] 6050 3-8-11 DFlores 7 (Clifford Sise Jr, U.S.A) *disp 2nd on outside: led 1 1/2f out: hung lft 1f out: hdd 100yds out: no ex* **7/1**	110
3	1 ¾	**Talent Search (USA)**[27] 5852 4-9-0 (b) RFogelsonger 4 (Mark Shuman, U.S.A) *led tl hdd 1 1/2f out: one pce* **12/1**	107
4	2 ½	**Benny The Bull (USA)**[56] 4-9-0 MGuidry 8 (R Dutrow Jr, U.S.A) *in rr: last over 2f out: 7th st: styd on wl down outside to take 4th fnl 50yds* **8/1**	100
5	1 ½	**Kelly's Landing (USA)**[210] 860 6-9-0 LDettori 5 (E Kenneally, U.S.A) *racd in 4th: pushed along and hdwy on outside wl over 2f out: 3rd st: one pce: lost 4th last 50yds* **10/1**	95
6	2	**Bordonaro (USA)**[20] 6050 6-9-0 RMigliore 9 (B Spawr, U.S.A) *racd in 8th: nvr a factor* **33/1**	90
7	hd	**Commentator (USA)**[91] 6-9-0 JBravo 6 (N Zito, U.S.A) *disputing 2nd tl cl up bhd ldr: wknd over 1 1/2f out* **12/1**	89
8	4	**Greg's Gold (USA)**[20] 6050 6-9-0 VEspinoza 10 (D Hofmans, U.S.A) *racd in 7th: a in rr* **6/1**[3]	77
9	18	**Smokey Stover (USA)**[56] 4-9-0 AGryder 1 (Greg Gilchrist, U.S.A) *disp 4th to over 2f out: wknd* **10/3**[2]	25
10	11	**Forefathers (USA)**[20] 3-8-11 KDesormeaux 11 (W Mott, U.S.A) *disp 4th to 2f out: wknd: eased* **40/1**	—

69.18 secs (69.18)
WFA 3 from 4yo+ 1lb **10** Ran SP% **117.5**
PARI-MUTUEL: WIN 7.00; PL (1-2) 4.00, 6.60; SHOW (1-2-3) 3.00, 4.60, 8.60; SF 49.80.
Owner Watson & Weitman Performances & Pegram **Bred** Tom Evans, Macon Wilmil Equines & Marjac Farms **Trained** USA

FOCUS
Plenty of pace on here and that suited the winner, who has form over further, but it would be unwise to assume that he was flattered as two of the three who forced the gallop kept on well enough to fill the places.

NOTEBOOK
Midnight Lute(USA), impressive in winning the Grade 1 Forego Stakes over 7f at Saratoga last time, was always going to be suited by a strongly-run race over this shorter distance and that is what he got. He sprouted wings as they straightened up for home, bridging a seven-length gap to the first two in no time at all before sweeping clear to win by almost five lengths at the line. This was a seriously impressive performance and he is clearly a very smart colt indeed.
Idiot Proof(USA), one of only two three-year-olds in the race, showed pace from the off and gave the leader plenty to think about. He took his measure early in the straight, but when the winner came out of the clouds he was only ever going to be chasing second place. This was still a very good effort, though, and he promises to be even better next year.
Talent Search(USA), a confirmed front-runner, set a brisk pace out in front and was harried by Idiot Proof and Commentator. In the end he paid for his efforts, but the dirt track had been largely favouring pace horses so one could not say that his rider did too much wrong.
Benny The Bull(USA), runner-up to Midnight Lute in the Forego Stakes, is the type who stays on late from the back of the field, so the quicker they go the better it is for him. He ran on well late but had nowhere near the pace of the winner.
Kelly's Landing(USA), not seen out since winning the Golden Shaheen in Dubai back in March, would not have been ideally suited by this tight track.
Smokey Stover(USA) did not have the early pace to take advantage of his draw in stall one and looked far from happy getting a load of sloppy dirt kicked in his face. He is a lot better than this.

6511a NETJETS BREEDERS' CUP MILE (GRADE 1) (TURF) 1m (T)
8:20 (8:24) 3-Y-0+ **£724,490** (£268,367; £134,184; £68,434; £33,546)

			RPR
1		**Kip Deville (USA)**[41] 4-9-0 (b) CVelasquez 8 (R Dutrow Jr, U.S.A) *trckd ldr on ins in 4th: 3rd st: edgd off rail and hdwy 1 1/2f out: led jst ins fnl f: r.o wl* **15/2**	122
2	1	**Excellent Art**[28] 5798 3-8-10 JMurtagh 13 (A P O'Brien, Ire) *racd in 12th tl hdwy on outside 3f out: 6th st: styd on steadily u.p on outside to take 2nd 100yds out: r.o* **2/1**[1]	119
3	1	**Cosmonaut (USA)**[21] 5-9-0 JRLeparoux 7 (F Parisel, U.S.A) *led tl hdd jst ins fnl f: one pce* **16/1**	118
4	nk	**Nobiz Like Shobiz (USA)**[21] 3-8-10 JRVelazquez 9 (B Tagg, U.S.A) *towards rr tl hdwy on outside over 3f out: 4th st: one pce fnl 1 1/2f* **4/1**[2]	116
5	½	**Host (CHI)**[41] 7-9-0 GKGomez 4 (T Pletcher, U.S.A) *hld up and bhd: 5 l last 1/2-way: 12th st: styd on down outside fnl 1 1/2f: nrst fin* **28/1**	116
6	¾	**Trippi's Storm (USA)**[28] 5823 4-9-0 JCastellano 6 (S Hough, U.S.A) *towards rr: 8th st: one pce last 1 1/2f* **9/1**	115
7	3 ½	**Remarkable News (VEN)**[41] 5-9-0 RADominguez 14 (A Penna Jr, U.S.A) *pressed ldr in 3rd on outside: 2nd st: wknd* **16/1**	107
8	nk	**Rebellion**[21] 4-9-0 ECoa 1 (H G Motion, U.S.A) *midfield: 10th st: nvr a factor* **40/1**	107
9	1 ¾	**Icy Atlantic (USA)**[28] 5823 6-9-0 CDeCarlo 2 (T Pletcher, U.S.A) *hld up: 11th st: nerver a factor* **40/1**	103
10	1	**Jeremy (USA)**[21] 6029 4-9-0 LDettori 5 (Sir Michael Stoute) *missed break: pushed up to r midfield on ins: 5th st on ins: sn wknd* **6/1**[3]	101
11	1 ½	**Purim (USA)**[21] 5-9-0 JTheriot 12 (T Proctor, U.S.A) *racd in 6th on outside: 7th st: sn wknd* **16/1**	98
12	6	**Silent Name (JPN)**[112] 5-9-0 KDesormeaux 11 (R J Frankel, U.S.A) *covered up in 5th: lost pl and shuffled bk to 9th st: n.d after* **33/1**	85
13	3 ¾	**My Typhoon (IRE)**[28] 5822 5-8-11 ECastro 10 (W Mott, U.S.A) *racd in 2nd tl wknd over 2f out* **22/1**	74

1m 39.78s (-38.22)
WFA 3 from 4yo+ 3lb **13** Ran SP% **122.6**
PARI-MUTUEL: WIN 18.40; PL (1-2) 7.20, 4.20; SHOW (1-2-3) 5.20, 3.00, 6.60; SF 70.80.
Owner IEAH Stables et al **Bred** Center Hills Farm **Trained** USA

FOCUS

A good renewal of Breeders' Cup Mile and, as usual, very competitive. The pace seemed reasonable in the conditions.

NOTEBOOK

Kip Deville(USA), supplemented at a cost of $300,000, enjoyed a dream trip and took full advantage to deny the slightly unlucky Excellent Art. The winner, who warmed up for this with a good second in the Grade 1 Woodbine Mile, held a lovely position just in behind the leaders throughout, tight against the inside rail, and very much got first run on the eventual runner-up when switching round the tiring Cosmonaut at the top of the straight.

Excellent Art came into this with some of the best 1m form in Europe to his name, but he had it all to do from his wide draw. Dropped in well off the pace soon after the start, he struggled to make up much ground down the back straight and was forced to come wide with his challenge on the turn for home. He found plenty for pressure, but the winner had very much got first run and he never looked like pegging that one back. This was an admirable effort in defeat and he may even have won with a little more luck. His connections will now consider the Hong Kong Mile.

Cosmonaut(USA) showed he handles soft turf when winning a Grade 3 at Arlington last year and this was a big run in third. However, he was allowed an easy lead and looks flattered by the bare form.

Nobiz Like Shobiz(USA), a Kentucky Derby also ran, has been a revelation since switched to turf, winning his last three starts. The soft ground was an unknown, but this was a big run in defeat and he can be considered even better than the bare form considering he made his move wide of horses leaving the back straight.

Host(CHI) was detached in last for much of the way, but he flew home in the straight.

Trippi's Storm(USA) could find only the one pace and may have been unsuited by the easy ground.

Jeremy(USA) tracked the eventual winner for much of the way, but he was left behind in the straight and was not at his best. He looked a little short of room against the inside rail on the turn for home, but he was not unlucky and this ground was just softer than he wants.

6512a EMIRATES AIRLINE BREEDERS' CUP DISTAFF (GRADE 1) (F&M) (DIRT) 1m 1f

9:05 (9:07) 3-Y-O+ **£622,653** (£230,612; £115,306; £58,806; £28,827)

RPR

1 **Ginger Punch (USA)**[27] 5854 4-8-11 .... RBejarano 4 117
(R J Frankel, U.S.A) *4th on rail early: 3rd 1/2-way: disputing ld 3f out: narrowly hdd 1f out: rallied u.p to ld again nr fin* **11/2**[2]

2 *nk* **Hystericalady (USA)**[20] 6049 4-8-11 .... ECastro 12 116
(J Hollendorfer, U.S.A) *racd in 2nd: disputing ld 3f out: tk narrow ld 1f out: hdd nr fin* **9/1**

3 *nk* **Octave (USA)**[35] 3-8-7 .... GKGomez 8 115
(T Pletcher, U.S.A) *towards rr: gd hdwy 2 1/2f out on rail: 4th st: sn wnt 3rd: r.o u.p: nrst fin* **10/1**

4 *4 1/4* **Lady Joanne (USA)**[20] 6048 3-8-7 .... CHBorel 5 107
(C Nafzger, U.S.A) *prom: 4th 1/2-way: 3rd and 4 l off ldng pair st: styd on at one pce u.p* **6/1**[3]

5 *2* **Unbridled Belle (USA)**[27] 5854 4-8-11 ....(b) RADominguez 11 104
(T Pletcher, U.S.A) *midfield: effrt to go 4th 4f out: 5th st: styd on at one pce* **11/2**[2]

6 *7 3/4* **Balance (USA)**[27] 5854 4-8-11 ....(b) VEspinoza 1 89
(D Hofmans, U.S.A) *towards rr early: clsd and 6th 1/2-way: outpcd 3f out: n.d after* **20/1**

7 *2 1/4* **Tough Tiz's Sis (USA)**[20] 6049 3-8-7 ....(b) MESmith 3 85
(B Baffert, U.S.A) *in rr: last 1/2-way: nvr a threat* **14/1**

8 *4* **Bear Now (USA)**[35] 3-8-7 .... JBaird 6 77
(Reade Baker, Canada) *led to 3f out: 6th and btn st* **14/1**

9 *1 3/4* **Indian Vale (CAN)**[27] 5854 5-8-11 .... JRVelazquez 10 74
(T Pletcher, U.S.A) *towards rr: 8th st: n.d* **6/1**[3]

10 *1/2* **Lear's Princess (USA)**[42] 5441 3-8-7 ....(b) ECoa 7 73
(K McLaughlin, U.S.A) *towards rr on ins: n.d* **5/1**[1]

11 *25* **Teammate (USA)**[20] 6048 4-8-11 .... CVelasquez 9 25
(H A Jerkens, U.S.A) *bhd: nvr a factor* **25/1**

12 *4 1/4* **Prop Me Up (USA)**[42] 5-8-11 ....(b) JBravo 2 17
(G Sacco, U.S.A) *bhd: nvr a factor* **40/1**

1m 50.11s (110.11)

WFA 3 from 4yo+ 4lb **12** Ran SP% **119.5**

PARI-MUTUEL: WIN 11.00; PL (1-2) 6.20, 9.60; SHOW (1-2-3) 4.40, 7.20, 5.00; SF 141.60.

Owner Stronach Stables **Bred** Adena Springs **Trained** USA

FOCUS

A very competitive renewal of the Distaff on paper and so not a great surprise that it resulted in a tight finish. Surprisingly, the pace was not that strong early.

NOTEBOOK

Ginger Punch(USA), third behind Unbridled Belle in the Grade 1 Beldame Stakes last time, enjoyed a good trip on the rail until being headed by Hystericalady on her outside early in the straight. At that point she looked as though she would drop out of contention, but to her great credit she rallied bravely, overcoming interference bordering on the dangerous at times to get back up and lead near the line.

Hystericalady(USA) looked to have taken Ginger Punch's measure early in the straight but despite all her rider's efforts to deny her rival the opportunity to rally next to the rail, which included leaning in on the eventual winner at one stage, she succumbed close home and was narrowly denied. Justice was done as had the result gone the other way the Stewards would have had no option but to reverse the placings.

Octave(USA) made good headway from off the pace to look a danger at the top of the straight but, while she made relentless progress towards catching the front two, she was never quite going to get there. It was still a good effort from a filly better suited to a more galloping track than this tight circuit.

Lady Joanne(USA) was unable to take advantage of racing fairly handily, like the winner, in a race run at a relatively ordinary gallop.

Unbridled Belle(USA) had Ginger Punch behind her when winning the Beldame Stakes last time, but being drawn out wide on this sharp track in a field this big was always going to be a worry and in the end she failed to show her best. A stronger pace would have helped as unlike many in the field she stays further than this.

Indian Vale(CAN), narrowly beaten in the Beldame Stakes last time, was very disappointing as she was always towards the back of the field.

Lear's Princess(USA), winner of the Grade 1 Gazelle Stakes at Belmont last time, also failed to land a blow.

6513a JOHN DEERE BREEDERS' CUP TURF (GRADE 1) 1m 4f

9:50 (9:54) 3-Y-O+ **£826,531** (£306,122; £153,061; £78,061; £38,265)

RPR

1 **English Channel (USA)**[27] 5853 5-9-0 .... JRVelazquez 6 124
(T Pletcher, U.S.A) *settled in close 3rd, led 2f out, quickened clear straight, readily* **4/1**[2]

2 *7* **Shamdinan (FR)**[21] 3-8-9 .... JRLeparoux 4 115
(A Penna Jr, U.S.A) *led 3f, 2nd half-way, pushed along to chase winner straight, no impression* **16/1**

3 *3/4* **Red Rocks (IRE)**[49] 5243 4-9-0 .... LDettori 2 112
(B J Meehan) *racd in 4th, 5th halfway, drvn on outside to chase ldrs 3f out, rdn & disp 4th str, stayed on for 3rd, nvr able to chal* **4/1**[2]

4 *3/4* **Better Talk Now (USA)**[112] 8-9-0 ....(b) RADominguez 3 111
(H G Motion, U.S.A) *towards rear, 7th half-way, stayed on in straight but never dangerous* **15/2**[3]

5 *hd* **Dylan Thomas (IRE)**[20] 6043 4-9-0 .... JMurtagh 7 110
(A P O'Brien, Ire) *settled in tch, 6th halfway, pushed along to chase ldrs 4f out, under pressure 2f out, rdn whn disp 4th str, sn no extra* **6/5**[1]

6 *1 1/4* **Grand Couturier**[49] 5250 4-9-0 .... CHBorel 5 109
(R Ribaudo, U.S.A) *held up in last, never a factor* **10/1**

7 *1 1/4* **Fri Guy (USA)**[35] 4-9-0 .... KDesormeaux 1 107
(Dale Romans, U.S.A) *raced in 2nd, led after 3f, headed 2f out, 3rd straight, soon beaten* **50/1**

8 *24* **Transduction Gold (USA)**[22] 4-9-0 .... JDGraham 8 71
(J Glenney, U.S.A) *mid-division, 4th half-way, 7th and weakening straight* **66/1**

2m 36.96s (156.96)

WFA 3 from 4yo+ 7lb **8** Ran SP% **115.6**

PARI-MUTUEL: WIN 8.00; PL (1-2) 4.40, 17.60; SHOW (1-2-3) 3.00, 9.40, 4.60; SF 152.00.

Owner James T Scatuorchio **Bred** Keene Ridge Farm **Trained** USA

FOCUS

This looked like a decent renewal of the Breeders' Cup Turf beforehand, but both Dylan Thomas and last year's winner Red Rocks failed to run up to their best, and the form looks relatively weak. As was the theme on the turf track, they went a sensible pace.

NOTEBOOK

English Channel(USA) deserves plenty of credit for what was a magnificent performance on the night, but it is worth remembering he could manage only fifth in this race in 2005, and third last year, and it may be unwise to take the bare form too literally. His record does show, however, that he excels on tight tracks – he won the Grade 1 United Nations Stakes round here both this year and last – and he was in a league of his own. Always in a good position, he travelled well throughout and fairly bounded clear of his seven rivals when asked to go on in the straight.

Shamdinan(FR), who was third in the French Derby earlier in the year, had lost his form since winning a Grade 1 on his US debut. The easy ground was in his favour and this was better than his recent efforts, but he was still beaten a fair way.

Red Rocks(IRE) looked set for a big year when winning a Group 3 at Sandown on his return to the UK earlier in the campaign, but he has struggled a little in top company in recent starts and he never really looked like repeating last season's victory. The pace was frantic when he won this last year, but he was never going to get the race run to suit in these conditions and the steady gallop on such a tight track was totally against him.

Better Talk Now(USA) won this race in 2004 and was second to Red Rocks last year, but he is eight now and had little chance against some of these.

Dylan Thomas(IRE) has enjoyed a magnificent season, winning four Group 1s, including the King George and most recently the Arc, but he was nowhere near his best this time. He got away with an easy surface in France on his previous start, but this surface was totally unsuitable for a horse who excels on quick ground, and the tight track was also against him. Interestingly enough, he was slowly away from the stalls and had to be niggled to find his stride, suggesting his busy season was just beginning to catch up with him as well. This performance does not detract from a wonderful career and he will head to stud the winner of six Group 1 races between 1m2f and 1m4f.

6514a BREEDERS' CUP CLASSIC - POWERED BY DODGE (GRADE 1) (DIRT) 1m 2f

10:35 (10:44) 3-Y-O+ **£1,377,551** (£510,204; £255,102; £130,102; £63,776)

RPR

1 **Curlin (USA)**[27] 5855 3-8-9 .... RAlbarado 4 131
(S Asmussen, U.S.A) *held up in 6th, 10 lengths off lead after 4f, hdwy over 4f out, went 2nd well over 2f out, led 1 1/2f out, driven clr fnl f* **9/2**[3]

2 *4 1/2* **Hard Spun (USA)**[28] 5827 3-8-9 .... MPino 8 122
(J Larry Jones, U.S.A) *led to 1 1/2f out, one pace final f* **8/1**

3 *4 3/4* **Awesome Gem (USA)**[28] 5824 4-9-0 ....(b) DFlores 6 113
(Craig Dollase, U.S.A) *hld up in 8th, 15 lengths off ld after 4f, hdwy on ins to take 4th ent str, kept on to take 3rd close home, nvr nr ldrs* **33/1**

4 *1* **Street Sense (USA)**[28] 5827 3-8-9 .... CHBorel 2 111
(C Nafzger, U.S.A) *racd in 7th, over 10 lengths off ld after 4f, hdwy over 4f out, rdn in cl 3rd 1 1/2f out, sn btn, lost 3rd cl home* **7/2**[1]

5 *8 1/4* **Tiago (USA)**[28] 5824 3-8-9 .... MESmith 9 94
(J Shirreffs, U.S.A) *last and soon 20 lengths off lead, never a factor* **16/1**

6 *10* **Any Given Saturday (USA)**[35] 3-8-9 .... GKGomez 3 74
(T Pletcher, U.S.A) *raced in 4th, 3rd over 3f out, weakened well over 2f out* **4/1**[2]

7 *hd* **Lawyer Ron (USA)**[27] 5855 4-9-0 .... JRVelazquez 1 74
(T Pletcher, U.S.A) *raced in 2nd til weakened well over 2f out* **4/1**[2]

8 *8 1/4* **Diamond Stripes (USA)**[22] 4-9-0 ....(b) CVelasquez 7 57
(R Dutrow Jr, U.S.A) *close 3rd til weakened over 3 1/2f out* **40/1**

P **George Washington (IRE)**[48] 5261 4-9-0 .... MJKinane 5 —
(A P O'Brien, Ire) *raced in 5th, pushed along halfway, weakened over 3 1/2f out, tailed off when broke leg & p.u 1f out, dead* **6/1**

2m 0.59s (120.59)

WFA 3 from 4yo 5lb **9** Ran SP% **117.1**

PARI-MUTUEL: WIN 10.80; PL (1-2) 5.20, 7.60; SHOW (1-2-3) 4.20, 5.80, 9.40; SF 70.80.

Owner StoneStreet & Padua & G Bolton **Bred** Fares Farm Inc **Trained** USA

FOCUS

As ever the Breeders' Cup Classic was eagerly anticipated, and it looked like a quality renewal beforehand, but the race was marred by the tragic death of George Washington. The winning time was just outside the track record set in 1962, but that surely had much to do with the condition of the sloppy track after so much rain.

NOTEBOOK

Curlin(USA) only won his maiden in February, but made quick progress, placing in both the Kentucky Derby and the Belmont Stakes, and winning the Preakness in between. He came here off the back of a narrow victory in the Jockey Club Gold Cup and produced another top-class performance, staking a major claim for 'Horse of the Year' honours. Having been held up off the pace through the early stages, he made good ground down the back straight and stayed on strongly to readily account for the long-time leader Hard Spun.

Hard Spun(USA) finished well clear of the remainder and ran a terrific race in defeat considering he set a searching gallop from the outset. There had not been that much between him and Curlin earlier in the season, but he had to give best this time.

Awesome Gem(USA) fared best of the older horses, but he was never seen with a chance, having been held up well off the pace, and he only claimed third on the line. He looks flattered by the bare form.

Street Sense(USA), last year's Juvenile winner and this year's Kentucky Derby hero, made his move from well off the pace at the same time as Curlin, and he looked equally as threatening, but his run flattened out in the straight.

Tiago(USA) had plenty to prove in this company and was well beaten.

George Washington(IRE) had to be put down after suffering an open fracture of the cannon bone in his off-fore fetlock joint and also fracturing both sesamoids. He was sharply away from the stalls, but found himself in behind the leaders rounding the first bend and never looked happy facing the kickback. He was taken wide down the back straight, but was never really going anywhere before sadly coming to grief in the straight. Last year's 2000 Guineas winner would not have been racing this season but for suffering fertility problems at stud and he had yet to recapture his very best form, but he was a brilliant racehorse on his day and will be remembered as one of the best turf milers of recent times.

6516 - 6517a (Foreign Racing) - See Raceform Interactive

[6372] SAN SIRO (R-H)

Saturday, October 27

OFFICIAL GOING: Soft

6518a ST LEGER ITALIANO (LISTED RACE) 1m 6f

2:50 (3:06) 3-Y-0+ **£18,919** (£8,324; £4,541; £2,270)

			RPR
1		**Spanish Hidalgo (IRE)**[23] 5952 3-8-9 MDemuro 5 (J L Dunlop) *mde all: r.o st: pushed out SP 82-100F*	104
2	1 ¾	**Ryan (IRE)**[216] 4-9-3 JBojko 3 (J Hanacek, Czech Republic)	100
3	hd	**Montalegre (IRE)**[28] 5821 5-9-5 DVargiu 7 (A & G Botti, Italy)	102
4	3 ½	**El Tango (GER)**[27] 5849 5-9-9 AStarke 2 (P Schiergen, Germany)	101
5	1 ¾	**Italian Stallion (IRE)**[376] 6018 3-8-9 BClos 1 (E Schweigert, Germany)	94
6	2	**Quality Son (ITY)**[28] 5821 6-9-3 PConvertino 6 (V Oriani, Italy)	91

3m 15.6s (195.60)
WFA 3 from 4yo+ 9lb **6** Ran
(Including 1 Euro stake): WIN 1.82; PL 1.64, 4.68; SF 12.20.
Owner Windflower Overseas Holdings Inc **Bred** Windflower Overseas Holdings Inc **Trained** Arundel, W Sussex

NOTEBOOK
Spanish Hidalgo(IRE) was given a well-judged front-running ride. Allowed to set a very steady early pace, Demuro wound it up throughout the last three-quarters of a mile and did not resort to the whip when two chasers threatened briefly approaching the furlong pole. Stretching clear in the closing stages, he had probably worked harder some mornings on the Arundel gallops.

6519a PREMIO GIOVANNI FALCK (LISTED RACE) (F&M) 1m 4f

3:50 (4:08) 3-Y-0+ **£18,919** (£8,324; £4,541; £2,270)

			RPR
1		**Go East (GER)**[20] 6046 3-8-11 AStarke 7 (P Schiergen, Germany)	98
2	½	**Silver Mitzva (IRE)**[38] 5523 3-8-9 (b) MMonteriso 6 (M Botti) *mid-div: hdwy and 3rd appr st: led 150yds out: hdd fnl strides SP 8.11-1* **81/10**[1]	95
3	snk	**Cockayne (IRE)**[146] 2296 4-9-1 CColombi 5 (V Valiani, Italy)	94
4	2 ¼	**Belle Hernando (GER)**[130] 4-9-1 PConvertino 8 (Dr A Bolte, Germany)	91
5	1	**Gambara (IRE)**[153] 2070 3-8-9 DVargiu 2 (B Grizzetti, Italy)	90
6	shd	**Soul Of Magic (IRE)**[59] 4957 8-9-1 TCastanheira 11 (Karin Suter, Switzerland)	89
7	3 ½	**Sopran Slam (IRE)**[28] 3-8-9 GArena 9 (B Grizzetti, Italy)	85
8	2	**Athlone (IRE)**[72] 4557 3-8-11 DPorcu 12 (A & G Botti, Italy)	84
9	3	**Rinconada (GER)**[34] 5669 6-9-1 MEsposito 3 (Dr A Bolte, Germany)	76
10	2	**Hopsider (IRE)** 4-9-1 LManiezzi 1 (M Gasparini, Italy)	73
11	8	**Icicariba (IRE)**[214] 3-8-9 MDemuro 4 (F Losani, Italy)	62
12	6	**Wickwing**[27] 4-9-5 EBotti 10 (A & G Botti, Italy)	56

2m 33.9s (2.40)
WFA 3 from 4yo+ 7lb **12** Ran SP% **11.0**
WIN 4.43; PL 1.89, 2.95, 3.90; DF 25.80.
Owner Gestut Ebbesloh **Bred** Gestut Ebbesloh **Trained** Germany

NOTEBOOK
Silver Mitzva(IRE) moved up to track the leader rounding the home turn and was shaken up to lead passing the quarter-mile pole. Ridden along soon after, she was always just holding Cockayne but was mugged by Go East, who swooped down the outside, in the final 50 yards.

[1873] CAPANNELLE (R-H)

Sunday, October 28

OFFICIAL GOING: Very soft

6523a PREMIO GUIDO BERARDELLI (GROUP 3) 1m 1f

2:40 (12:00) 2-Y-0 **£27,365** (£12,041; £6,568; £3,284)

			RPR
1		**Fathayer (USA)** 2-8-11 GForte 7 (P Paciello, Italy) *in tch: 3rd st: led jst over 2f out: drvn out to maintain narrow advantage thrght fnl 2f* **22/10**[1]	—
2	hd	**Magico Marco** 2-8-11 MPasquale 1 (B Grizzetti, Italy) *racd in 2nd: reminder 1/2-way: rdn to chal 2f out: a jst hld* **87/10**	—
3	½	**Permesso** 2-8-11 MDemuro 3 (L Camici, Italy) *hld up in rr: last st: swtchd to stands' side and hdwy 2f out: tk 3rd cl home: fin strly* **28/10**[2]	—
4	½	**Parfaite (IRE)** 2-8-11 MMonteriso 9 (A & G Botti, Italy) *hld up in rr: hdwy between rivals to go 3rd over 1 1/2f out: kpt on: lost 3rd cl home* **44/10**	—
5	2	**Once More Dubai (USA)** 2-8-11 GBietolini 10 (Gianluca Bietolini, Italy) *hld up: swtchd outside and hdwy over 2f out: disp 3rd over 1f out to ins fnl f: wknd* **26/1**	—
6	1 ½	**Sa Kin (IRE)**[105] 2-8-11 SLandi 2 (A Renzoni, Italy) *in tch: 6th st: one pce fnl 2f* **94/10**	—
7	6	**Silver Arrow (ITY)**[14] 6222 2-8-11 CFiocchi 11 (Maria Rita Salvioni, Italy) *cl up: 4th st on outside: wknd over 1 1/2f out* **153/10**	—
8	5	**Fancy Groom** 2-8-11 DVargiu 8 (B Grizzetti, Italy) *in tch tl wknd 2f out* **3/1**[3]	—
9	2	**Aube Claire (IRE)**[28] 2-8-11 (b) FBranca 6 (L Brogi, Italy) *in tch: 5th st: wknd 2f out* **149/10**	—
10	¾	**Deuteronomio (IRE)** 2-8-11 GMarcelli 5 (Maria Rita Salvioni, Italy) *set gd pce to jst over 2f out: wknd qckly* **153/10**	—
11	2	**Imperial Forum**[119] 2-8-11 PAragoni 4 (A Peraino, Italy) *a bhd* **74/1**	—

1m 52.8s (-1.90) **11** Ran SP% **144.6**
(including 1 Euro stake): WIN 3.22; PL 1.74, 2.27, 1.58; DF 20.38.
Owner Scuderia Chemin De Fer **Bred** Majestic Farms Llc **Trained** Italy

6524a PREMIO LYDIA TESIO SHADWELL (GROUP 1) (F&M) 1m 2f

3:40 (3:57) 3-Y-0+ **£72,973** (£32,108; £17,514; £8,757)

			RPR
1		**Turfrose (GER)**[28] 3-8-11 MSanna 10 (P Giannotti, Italy) *in tch: 5th st: rdn to ld narrowly jst over 2f out: hld on gamely u.p* **138/10**	109
2	snk	**Fair Breeze (GER)**[21] 6046 4-9-0 AHelfenbein 5 (Mario Hofer, Germany) *hld up: 8th st: hdwy towards stands side 3f out: wnt 3rd 1 1/2f out: tk 2nd u.str.p last 100yds: fin wl* **37/1**	107
3	¾	**Musical Way (FR)**[22] 6032 5-9-0 RonanThomas 2 (P Van De Poele, France) *racd in 6th: wnt 2nd pressing wnr 1 1/2f out: on pce ins fnl f: lost 2nd last 100yds* **16/10**[1]	105
4	2	**Alamanni (USA)**[32] 3-8-11 FBranca 4 (E Borromeo, Italy) *hld up: 10th st: hdwy towards stands rail over 2f out: wnt 4th wl ins fnl f: kpt on: nrst fin* **102/1**	103
5	¾	**Mystic Lips (GER)**[21] 6042 3-8-11 GBietolini 12 (Andreas Lowe, Germany) *led to jst over 2f out: one pce* **32/10**[3]	102
6	nse	**Les Fazzani (IRE)**[94] 3889 3-8-11 EddieAhern 6 (M J Wallace) *midfield: 7th st: kpt on at one pce u.p fnl 2f* **70/1**	101
7	2 ½	**Short Skirt**[9] 6299 4-9-0 LDettori 1 (Saeed Bin Suroor) *cl up: 4th st: remained prom tl wknd 2f out* **2/1**[2]	94
8	½	**Mara Spectrum (IRE)**[29] 4-9-0 DVargiu 3 (B Grizzetti, Italy) *hld up in rr: last st: kpt on steadily towards far side fr over 2f out* **30/1**	93
9	2	**Mimetico (IRE)**[14] 6221 3-8-11 (b) MDemuro 7 (B Grizzetti, Italy) *prom: 3rd st: racd alone on far rail fnl 4f: btn wl over 2f out* **46/1**	91
10	½	**Whazzis**[14] 6221 3-8-11 (v) TPQueally 11 (W J Haggas) *hld up in rr: 13th st: nvr a factor* **182/10**	90
11		**Fashion Statement**[133] 2707 3-8-11 NCallan 9 (M A Jarvis) *cl up: hdwy to go 2nd ent st: rdn 3f out: sn wknd* **53/10**	90
12		**Miss Annaleo (IRE)**[28] 3-8-11 MMonteriso 8 (I Bugattella, Italy) *hld up: 9th st: a in rr* **32/1**	90

2m 2.60s (-0.70)
WFA 3 from 4yo+ 5lb **12** Ran SP% **136.8**
WIN 14.81; PL 2.99, 5.14, 1.62; DF 225.90.
Owner P Giannotti **Bred** Gestut Auenquelle **Trained** Italy

NOTEBOOK
Les Fazzani(IRE) was almost taken out beforehand, as her trainer felt that the ground was on the fast side, but, in a race where outsiders dominated, ran a cracker, going down by less than four lengths and finishing in front of a number of proven Pattern Race performers.
Short Skirt failed to justify Dettori's dash back from the Breeders' Cup and surely found this coming too soon after her belated seasonal reappearance.
Whazzis was dropped out at the rear to try to preserve her questionable stamina but to no avail.
Fashion Statement was returning from a 19-week absence and ran nowhere near her best, as she had beaten the winner on her previous racecourse appearance.

[6376] LONGCHAMP (R-H)

Sunday, October 28

OFFICIAL GOING: Good

6525a CRITERIUM DE VITESSE (LISTED RACE) 5f (S)

2:15 (2:14) 2-Y-0 **£17,568** (£7,027; £5,270; £3,514; £1,757)

			RPR
1		**Eastern Romance**[15] 6182 2-8-13 SPasquier 8 (K A Ryan) *mde all: rdn out (61/10)*	107
2	5	**Garden City (FR)**[30] 5791 2-8-13 CSoumillon 7 (Y De Nicolay, France)	89
3	2	**Jane Blue (FR)**[37] 2-9-2 J-BEyquem 6 (B Halley Des Fontaines, France)	85
4	hd	**Pull The Plug (USA)**[48] 2-8-13 TGillet 10 (Rod Collet, France)	81
5	1 ½	**Surething (FR)**[17] 6136 2-9-2 MBlancpain 4 (M Rolland, France)	79
6	¾	**Naughty Frida (IRE)**[13] 6225 2-8-13 RyanMoore 5 (E A L Dunlop) *sn pushed along in 5th: nvr a factor (13/2)*	73
7	2	**Bid Again**[20] 2-8-13 TJarnet 2 (R Pritchard-Gordon, France)	66
8	½	**Niska (USA)**[65] 2-8-13 JVictoire 9 (A Fabre, France)	64
9	8	**La Madonetta (IRE)**[12] 2-8-13 J-BHamel 1 (Robert Collet, France)	35

56.20 secs (-2.60) **Going Correction** -0.425s/f (Firm) **9** Ran
Speed ratings: **103,95,91,91,89 87,84,83,71**
PARI-MUTUEL: WIN 7.10; PL 2.60, 1.80, 2.40; DF 13.80.
Owner T G & Mrs M E Holdcroft **Bred** Bearstone Stud **Trained** Hambleton, N Yorks

NOTEBOOK
Eastern Romance put up a smart performance, leading throughout for an easy victory. Smartly away, she took control of the race early on and the rest of the field were beaten by the half way marker. She coasted past the post and is not finished for this year.

The Form Book, Raceform Ltd, Compton, RG20 6NL

Naughty Frida(IRE) never really got into the event. She looked rather one paced and just stayed on at the end.

6526a PRIX ROYAL-OAK PRINCIPAUTE DE MONACO (GROUP 1) 1m 7f 110y

2:45 (2:45) 3-Y-0+ £96,520 (£38,615; £19,307; £9,645; £4,831)

RPR

1 **Allegretto (IRE)**[44] 5376 4-9-1 .... RyanMoore 7 113
(Sir Michael Stoute) *hld up in 10th: 9th st: styd on down outside to ld fnl 70yds: drvn out* **52/10**[3]

2 *snk* **Macleya (GER)**[42] 5465 5-9-1 .... SPasquier 3 113
(A Fabre, France) *hld up in 6th: 7th st: hdwy to ld 150yds out: hdd 70yds out: r.o* **10/1**

3 *1* **Ponte Tresa (FR)**[70] 4655 4-9-1 .... CSoumillon 9 112
(Y De Nicolay, France) *hld up in 7th: cl 6th st on outside: led 2f out: hdd 150yds out: one pce* **11/1**

4 *hd* **Le Miracle (GER)**[21] 6044 6-9-4 .... DBoeuf 11 115
(W Baltromei, Germany) *hld up in 8th: styd on u.p fnl 1 1/2f but nvr threatened ldrs* **54/10**

5 *nk* **Brisant (GER)**[28] 5851 5-9-4 .... WMongil 6 114
(M Trybuhl, Germany) *hld up in rr: 10th st: kpt on towards ins fnl 1 1/2f: nrst fin* **48/1**

6 *1/2* **Anna Pavlova**[22] 6030 4-9-1 .... PaulHanagan 8 111
(R A Fahey) *last tl rdn and hdwy 1 1/2f out: kpt on fnl f: nvr nrr* **66/10**

7 *1 1/2* **Varevees**[21] 6044 4-9-1 .... TJarnet 1 109
(J Boisnard, France) *cl up on ins: 4th st: one pce fr over 1f out* **7/2**[1]

8 *3/4* **Soapy Danger**[23] 5976 4-9-4 .... KDarley 10 111
(M Johnston) *hld up in 5th: hdwy on outside 5f out: rdn along 3 1/2f out: disp ld 2 1/2f out to 2f out: one pce* **11/1**

9 *10* **Latin Mood (FR)**[17] 6137 4-9-4 .... TThulliez 2 100
(P Demercastel, France) *racd in 4th: 5th st: wknd over 1 1/2f out* **33/1**

10 *4* **Lord Du Sud (FR)**[70] 4655 6-9-4 .... C-PLemaire 4 96
(J-C Rouget, France) *set str pce: jnd 2 1/2f out: hdd 2f out: wknd 1 1/2f out* **41/10**[2]

11 **Loup De Mer (GER)**[28] 5851 5-9-4 .... JVictoire 5 96
(W Baltromei, Germany) *racd in 2nd: 3rd st: wknd 2f out* **54/10**

3m 15.5s (-11.10) **Going Correction** -0.225s/f (Firm) **11** Ran SP% **133.1**
Speed ratings: **118,117,117,117,117 116,116,115,110,108 108**
PARI-MUTUEL: WIN 6.20; PL 3.10, 4.00, 3.80; DF 29.00.
Owner Cheveley Park Stud **Bred** Miss K Rausing And Airlie Stud **Trained** Newmarket, Suffolk

FOCUS
A hugely competitive renewal in which tough and progressive filly Allegretto edged the narrow verdict.

NOTEBOOK
Allegretto(IRE) is an amazingly consistent filly and has kept her form throughout the season. This was the cherry on the cake as she had previously won a couple of Group 2 events. Given a highly professional ride, she was allowed to bowl along at the tail of the field early on. Extracted one and a half out, she quickened impressively and then held off the runner-up on the far rail. She apparently stays in training next year and will no doubt make her presence felt again in cup events.
Macleya(GER) never runs a bad race and has been a great credit to her trainer all season. Settled in mid division early on, she came with a run up the far rail and looked the possible winner with 50 yards left to run. She stayed on but could not quite get her nose in front.
Ponte Tresa(FR) raced just behind the leading group, this grey filly went to the head of affairs one and a half furlongs out but could not quicken in the same way as the winner and runner up. She never runs a bad race and may well be around again next season.
Le Miracle(GER) did not quite run up to expectations following his win in the Cadran. He was towards the tail early on and came with a late run in the straight. He stayed on but failed to quicken in the last half furlong. He has had quite a long season and had a fairly hard race in the Cadran.
Anna Pavlova as usual she was dropped out in the early stages before coming with a late run up the centre of the track. The filly did not really fire on this occasion and her trainer stated that he nearly withdrew her because he felt the ground was on the firm side. She remains in training next season.
Soapy Danger, heavily backed before the race, was given every chance but was a little disappointing. Always well up the colt was challenging for the lead early in the straight and then one paced to the line. Connections were left scratching their heads a little and there are no firm plans for him at the moment.

6518 SAN SIRO (R-H)

Sunday, October 28

OFFICIAL GOING: Good

6527a PREMIO RODERO (MAIDEN) 6f

3:20 (12:00) 2-Y-0 £6,757 (£2,973; £1,622; £811)

RPR

1 **Shishangaan (IRE)** 2-8-13 .... URispoli —
(M Rulec, Germany)

2 *3* **L'Unico Erede** 2-8-13 .... GArena 5 —
(B Grizzetti, Italy)

3 *8 1/2* **Negramaro (IRE)** 2-9-2 .... EBotti 11 —
(A & G Botti, Italy)

4 *2 1/2* **Lady Lella (ITY)** 2-8-13 .... GSanna 3 —
(B Grizzetti, Italy)

5 *3/4* **Mon Image (IRE)** 2-8-9 .... SMereu 4 —
(F Turner, Italy)

6 *4 1/2* **Aleph (IRE)** 2-8-13 .... LManiezzi 8 —
(P Paciello, Italy)

7 *10* **Cerbiatta (ITY)** 2-8-9 .... PConvertino 10 —
(M G Quinlan) *cl up on outside: 4th whn rdn 1/2-way: sn wknd (119/10)*

8 *nk* **Magnifico Rettore (IRE)** 2-9-2 .... LSorrentino 2 —
(J Heloury, Italy)

9 *1/2* **Karine Girl (IRE)** 2-8-13 .... SUrru 1 —
(Nicola De Chirico, Italy)

10 *3/4* **Bibi Leon (IRE)** 2-8-13 .... DPorcu 7 —
(R Feligioni, Italy)

11 *11* **Faruffini (ITY)** 2-8-13 .... DDettori 9 —
(L Ledda, Italy)

1m 12.1s (0.30) **11** Ran
PARI-MUTUEL: (including 1 Euro stake): WIN 4.42; PL 1.52, 1.67, 1.30;DF 15.45.
Owner A Schneider **Bred** A Schneider **Trained** Germany

NOTEBOOK
Cerbiatta(ITY) showed speed on the outside before beginning to weaken at halfway.

6425 KEMPTON (A.W) (R-H)

Monday, October 29

OFFICIAL GOING: Standard

Wind: fresh, half against Weather: bright some fluffy white clouds

6528 BETFAIR BET ON SPORTS CASINO POKER H'CAP 5f (P)

1:10 (1:14) (Class 6) (0-55,55) 3-Y-0+ £2,047 (£604; £302) Stalls High

Form RPR

0002 1 **Spirit Of Coniston**[20] 6078 4-8-9 **50** .... JamieSpencer 2 68+
(D Nicholls) *mde all: sn crossed to rail: rdn over 1f out: sn clr: readily* **5/2**[1]

-600 2 *3 1/2* **Fastrac Boy**[33] 5726 4-8-11 **52** .... JohnEgan 11 57
(J R Best) *chsd ldrs on rail: rdn over 1f out: kpt on: wnt 2nd nr fin: no ch w wnr* **10/1**

4600 3 *1/2* **Sir Loin**[12] 6264 6-8-9 **50** .... (v) MartinDwyer 3 53
(P Burgoyne) *t.k.h: pressed wnr: ev ch and rdn 2f out: outpcd fnl f* **25/1**

4100 4 *1* **Tajjree**[167] 1748 4-8-12 **53** .... (t) AdamKirby 12 53
(H J Collingridge) *led to s: s.i.s: bhd on rail: swtchd lft and hdwy over 1f out: kpt on: nvr nr wnr* **25/1**

0000 5 *3/4* **Titian Saga (IRE)**[12] 6264 4-8-7 **48** .... (be) NelsonDeSouza 1 45
(C N Allen) *chsd ldng pair: rdn 1/2-way: wknd over 1f out* **25/1**

0051 6 *nk* **Damhsoir (IRE)**[14] 6240 3-8-8 **49** .... TPO'Shea 10 45
(H S Howe) *in tch tl short of room and lost pl after 1f out: sme late hdwy: n.d* **12/1**

6452 7 *1/2* **Minnow**[5] 6428 3-8-7 **55** .... (e) WilliamCarson(7) 4 49
(S C Williams) *s.i.s: racd on outer: rdn 1/2-way: nvr on terms* **4/1**[2]

0040 8 *shd* **King Egbert (FR)**[12] 6264 6-8-7 **48** .... (p) TomEaves 6 42
(R J Price) *t.k.h: hld up in last: n.d* **20/1**

2230 9 *1 3/4* **Master Malarkey**[26] 5897 4-8-7 **48** .... (b) ChrisCatlin 7 35
(Mrs C A Dunnett) *in tch in midfield: rdn 1/2-way: wknd 2f out* **8/1**[3]

0000 10 *4* **Winning Spirit (IRE)**[16] 6174 3-8-8 **49** .... (p) AdrianMcCarthy 9 22
(Miss Z C Davison) *s.i.s: hdwy into midfield 1/2-way: rdn over 2f out: sn wknd* **100/1**

59.51 secs (-0.89) **Going Correction** -0.075s/f (Stan) **10** Ran SP% **93.8**
Speed ratings (Par 101): **104,98,97,96,94 94,93,93,90,84**
CSF £15.15 CT £211.61 TOTE £2.20: £1.10, £3.20, £5.10; EX 18.40.
Owner Richardson Kelly O'Gara Partnership **Bred** Green Square Racing **Trained** Sessay, N Yorks

FOCUS
A moderate handicap especially after the late withdrawal of the second-favourite Drumming Party, but the pace was strong and not many got into it. The form looks weak and, although the winner has shown a revival,the next three home have been out of form of late.
Damhsoir(IRE) Official explanation: jockey said filly suffered interference in running

6529 BETFAIR MOBILE H'CAP 1m 2f (P)

1:40 (1:42) (Class 6) (0-52,52) 3-Y-0+ £2,047 (£604; £302) Stalls High

Form RPR

2004 1 **Sekula Pata (NZ)**[10] 6315 8-8-12 **50** .... (v) SCreighton(5) 11 57
(E J Creighton) *s.i.s: sn chsng ldr: rdn to ld 2f out: clr fnl f: rdn out* **8/1**

000- 2 *2* **Montana Sky (IRE)**[355] 6398 4-8-9 **47** .... KevinGhunowa(5) 12 50
(R A Harris) *chsd ldrs: rdn wl over 2f out: plld out wl over 1f out: kpt on to chse wnr ins fnl f: unable to chal* **50/1**

0-01 3 *nk* **Faraday (IRE)**[70] 4673 4-9-1 **48** .... JamieSpencer 14 50+
(B J Curley) *t.k.h: hld up towards rr: hdwy and rdn 3f out: chsd ldrs wl over 2f out: kpt on but nvr threatened wnr* **6/4**[1]

0006 4 *shd* **Don Pasquale**[19] 6096 5-9-2 **49** .... (v) ChrisCatlin 6 51+
(J T Stimpson) *stdd s: hld up in last: hdwy on outer 2f out: r.o fnl f: nt rch wnr* **14/1**

0000 5 *1/2* **Surdoue**[6] 6412 7-9-3 **50** .... AdrianMcCarthy 7 51
(D Morris) *led: rdn over 2f out: hdd 2f out: outpcd by wnr fnl f: lost 3 pls ins fnl f* **25/1**

-345 6 *3/4* **Dinner Date**[81] 4340 5-9-5 **52** .... J-PGuillambert 2 51+
(T Keddy) *stdd s: t.k.h: hld up in rr: hdwy and rdn jst over 2f out: kpt on: nvr able to chal* **7/1**[3]

6450 7 *shd* **Bowl Of Cherries**[45] 5389 4-8-13 **46** .... (b) LeeEnstone 8 45
(I A Wood) *t.k.h: hld up in midfield: hdwy jst over 3f out: rdn over 2f out: kpt on same pce* **8/1**

-020 8 *1* **Storm Path (IRE)**[112] 3366 3-9-0 **52** .... LPKeniry 9 49
(D R C Elsworth) *in tch: hdwy over 3f out: sn rdn: wknd 2f out* **16/1**

0334 9 *1/2* **Astrolibra**[16] 6178 3-8-13 **51** .... TomEaves 13 47
(M H Tompkins) *in tch: rdn 4f out: outpcd 3f out: n.d after* **11/1**

4510 10 *2* **Moyoko (IRE)**[19] 6096 4-9-5 **52** .... FrancisNorton 3 44
(M Blanshard) *t.k.h: hld up in rr: n.d* **6/1**[2]

-002 11 *1/2* **My Monna**[15] 6206 3-8-5 **50** .... JosephWalsh(7) 5 41
(Miss Sheena West) *hld up towards rr: bhd and rdn over 2f out* **20/1**

0005 12 *1 1/2* **Fortune Point (IRE)**[19] 6096 9-9-0 **47** .... JamesDoyle 4 35
(A W Carroll) *racd in midfield: rdn 4f out: sn bhd* **20/1**

0050 13 *15* **Cove Mountain (IRE)**[111] 3405 5-9-1 **48** .... JohnEgan 10 6
(M G Rimell) *chsd ldrs: rdn 4f out: sn wknd: eased fnl f* **14/1**

2m 8.22s (-0.78) **Going Correction** -0.075s/f (Stan)
WFA 3 from 4yo+ 5lb **13** Ran SP% **131.9**
Speed ratings (Par 101): **100,98,98,98,97 97,97,96,95,94 93,92,80**
CSF £391.47 CT £943.16 TOTE £10.70: £3.70, £14.80, £1.40; EX 869.80.
Owner The Vixens **Bred** T O Harrison **Trained** East Garston, Berks

FOCUS
A very moderate handicap, little better than classified class, and again not many got into it with the first two home handy throughout. The form looks pretty weak with the runner-up especially raising doubts.
Fortune Point(IRE) Official explanation: jockey said gelding suffered interference in running
Cove Mountain(IRE) Official explanation: jockey said mare had no more to give

6530 BETFAIR BETTING AS IT SHOULD BE EBF MAIDEN STKS 7f (P)

2:10 (2:12) (Class 5) 2-Y-0 £3,238 (£963; £481; £240) Stalls High

Form RPR

2 1 **Adversity**[41] 5498 2-9-3 0 .... RyanMoore 6 74+
(Sir Michael Stoute) *chsd ldr: shkn up to ld 2f out: in command after: pushed out* **1/3**[1]

03 2 *1 1/2* **Mafioso**[26] 5910 2-9-3 0 .... J-PGuillambert 4 70+
(M Johnston) *led tl rdn and hdd 2f out: kpt on same pce* **9/1**[3]

04 3 *1 1/4* **Arabian Spirit**[13] 6246 2-9-3 0 .... FergusSweeney 9 67
(E A L Dunlop) *hmpd s: hld up bhd: gd hdwy on inner over 2f out: kpt on fnl f: wnt 3rd ins fnl f: nt rch ldrs* **10/1**

0 **4** ½ **Rowaad**[18] 6119 2-9-3 0 MartinDwyer 11 66
(M P Tregoning) *in tch: hdwy to chse ldng pair over 2f out: rdn 2f out: kpt on same pce* **14/1**

5 **5** shd **Dan Chillingworth (IRE)**[39] 5575 2-9-3 0 JamieSpencer 7 66+
(J R Fanshawe) *t.k.h: in tch: effrt over 2f out: sn rdn: kpt on same pce* **7/1**[2]

6 3 **Media Stars** 2-9-3 0 ChrisCatlin 10 58+
(J A Osborne) *wnt lft s: bhd: rdn wl over 2f out: kpt on steadily: nvr trbld ldrs* **20/1**

00 **7** 2 **Balletic (IRE)**[35] 5681 2-8-12 0 LPKeniry 12 48
(S Kirk) *t.k.h: hld up in midfield: rdn over 2f out: wknd over 1f out* **66/1**

000 **8** hd **Hits Only Time**[10] 6295 2-9-3 59 FrancisNorton 5 53
(J Pearce) *chsd ldrs: rdn over 2f out: wknd over 1f out* **66/1**

40 **9** 7 **Yakama (IRE)**[11] 6274 2-9-3 0 RichardThomas 8 35
(D J S Ffrench Davis) *a bhd: rdn 3f out: sn lost tch* **100/1**

0 **10** ¾ **Amicus**[12] 6262 2-8-12 0 JohnEgan 3 28
(D K Ivory) *hld up in midfield: rdn wl over 2f out: wknd jst over 2f out* **66/1**

0 **11** ½ **Festival Dreams**[63] 4876 2-9-3 0 AdrianMcCarthy 2 32
(Miss J S Davis) *restless in stalls: s.i.s: sn rdn along inrr: no ch last 3f* **100/1**

0 **12** ½ **Aleatricis**[8] 6358 2-9-3 0 JamieMackay 1 31
(Sir Mark Prescott) *s.i.s: dropped in bhd: rdn 3f out: sn lost tch* **66/1**

1m 26.81s (0.01) **Going Correction** -0.075s/f (Stan) 12 Ran SP% **126.0**
Speed ratings (Par 95): **96,94,92,92,92 88,86,86,78,77 76,76**
CSF £4.86 TOTE £1.50: £1.02, £2.40, £2.50; EX 5.80.
Owner Sir Alex Ferguson **Bred** Branston Stud Ltd **Trained** Newmarket, Suffolk

FOCUS
An ordinary and uncompetitive maiden and another race dominated by those that raced handy. This proved very straightforward for the hot-favourite and the front five pulled well clear of the rest. The third and fourth set the level and several are likely to do better next year.

NOTEBOOK
Adversity, runner-up in a Lingfield maiden on his debut that has produced a subsequent winner without looking anything special, probably only needed reproduce that performance in order to beat this lot, but he stretched out well when asked to go and win his race. Things will be tougher now, and he looks more of a decent handicapping prospect rather than anything better. (op 1-2)
Mafioso, up a furlong in his third outing, tried to make every yard but the favourite had far too much finishing pace for him. He now qualifies for a mark. (op 7-1)
Arabian Spirit ◆ might be one to take from the race, as not only did he fare best of those held up in a contest otherwise dominated by prominent racers, but he also tried to make his effort tight against the inside rail which is not always easy in races around the outer loop here. Bred to get a bit further, he now qualifies for handicaps and could be of interest in that sphere.
Rowaad, ridden much more prominently than on his debut, ran much better and looks one for handicaps after one more run, though his breeding suggests this would be right on the limit of his stamina. (op 12-1)
Dan Chillingworth(IRE) ◆, up a furlong from his turf debut, was in a good position throughout but his rider never picked up his whip and there is almost certainly a great deal more to come from him, especially once handicapped.

6531 BETFAIR PREMIUM BROKERAGE SERVICE CLAIMING STKS 6f (P)
2:40 (2:40) (Class 6) 3-Y-0+ **£2,047** (£604; £302) **Stalls** High

Form RPR
0032 **1** **Magic Glade**[11] 6288 8-9-8 87 RichardKingscote 10 72+
(Tom Dascombe) *t.k.h: prom tl stdd into midfield after 1f: pushed along and hdwy over 1f out: led ins fnl f: comf* **4/7**[1]

4020 **2** 1¾ **Rydal (USA)**[11] 6288 6-9-3 69 JamieSpencer 11 61
(J A Osborne) *led tl over 3f out: rdn to ld over 1f out: hdd ins fnl f: nt pce of wnr* **4/1**[2]

0045 **3** nk **Royal Challenge**[11] 6288 6-8-12 68 (b[1]) AshleyMorgan(7) 4 62
(M H Tompkins) *t.k.h: chsd ldrs tl led over 3f out: clr 3f out: rdn and hdd over 1f out: kpt on same pce* **10/1**[3]

0060 **4** shd **Detonate**[7] 6390 5-8-10 45 RichardThomas 7 53
(I A Wood) *dwlt: t.k.h: sn in tch on inner: rdn and effrt 2f out: kpt on same pce ins fnl f* **33/1**

0503 **5** 1¼ **Regal Raider (IRE)**[11] 6288 4-9-0 64 (p) JohnEgan 9 53
(A M Hales) *t.k.h: prom: rdn over 2f out: kpt on same pce* **10/1**[3]

0500 **6** 4 **Briannsta (IRE)**[14] 6243 5-9-5 75 TomEaves 3 45
(B Smart) *prom on outer: rdn wl over 2f out: sn struggling* **10/1**[3]

2003 **7** 1 **Luloah**[60] 4974 4-8-8 48 PaulEddery 6 31
(J G M O'Shea) *w ldrs tl bdly hmpd over 4f out: bhd after: rdn and no hdwy wl over 2f out* **40/1**

0600 **8** ¾ **Time For Change (IRE)**[18] 6121 3-9-2 44 (b[1]) DavidKinsella 2 38
(P G Murphy) *in tch on outer: rdn over 3f out: no ch fnl 2f* **80/1**

0506 **9** shd **Lindbergh**[5] 6428 5-9-3 60 (p) FrancisNorton 1 37
(A J Lidderdale) *a bhd* **20/1**

1m 13.66s (-0.04) **Going Correction** -0.075s/f (Stan)
WFA 3 from 4yo+ 1lb 9 Ran SP% **122.3**
Speed ratings (Par 101): **97,94,94,94,92 87,85,84,84**
CSF £3.32 TOTE £1.60: £1.10, £1.20, £2.40; EX 3.80.
Owner Alan Solomon **Bred** Juddmonte Farms **Trained** Lambourn, Berks

FOCUS
A moderate and uncompetitive claimer in which the favourite did not need to be anything like at his best to score. The form is far from solid with the fourth finishing close up despite having a stiff task at the weights.
Luloah Official explanation: jockey said filly suffered interference in running

6532 BETFAIR POKER CLASSIFIED STKS 1m (P)
3:10 (3:13) (Class 7) 3-Y-0+ **£1,365** (£403; £201) **Stalls** High

Form RPR
6310 **1** **Kinsman (IRE)**[128] 2875 10-9-3 45 (p) JohnEgan 10 52
(T D McCarthy) *w.w off the pce in midfield: rdn and hdwy over 3f out: drvn to ld ins fnl f: styd on* **14/1**

-400 **2** 1½ **Primeshade Promise**[32] 5756 6-8-12 45 KevinGhunowa(5) 3 49
(J L Flint) *chsd ldrs: rdn and hdwy on outer over 3f out: chsd ldr 2f out: led over 1f out: hdd and no ex ins fnl f* **8/1**

6406 **3** nk **Kathleen Kennet**[32] 5756 7-9-3 45 ChrisCatlin 11 48
(C Tinkler) *wl bhd: c wd and rdn 3f out: hung lft fr over 2f out: r.o u.p: nt rch ldrs* **9/2**[2]

6066 **4** nk **Future Deal**[15] 6212 6-9-3 45 SimonWhitworth 8 47
(C A Horgan) *s.i.s: wl bhd: hdwy over 3f out: rdn wl over 2f out: styd on to chse ldrs 1f out: no ex fnl f* **16/1**

5230 **5** hd **Height Of Spirits**[64] 4850 5-9-3 45 AdamKirby 12 47
(T D McCarthy) *hld up wl in rr: rdn and hdwy wl over 2f out: chsd ldrs 1f out: no imp ins fnl f* **7/1**

6000 **6** ½ **Holyfield Warrior (IRE)**[11] 6277 3-9-0 45 (p) LeeEnstone 5 46
(I A Wood) *chsd ldrs: rdn over 4f out: kpt on u.p tl no ex last 100yds* **40/1**

5000 **7** 2 **Xalted**[6] 6402 3-8-7 45 WilliamCarson(7) 14 42+
(S C Williams) *sn clr w ldr: led over 4f out: rdn 2f out: hdd over 1f out: eased whn btn last 100yds* **25/1**

4-66 **8** 2 **Ponte Vecchio (IRE)**[62] 4918 3-9-0 45 MartinDwyer 6 40+
(J R Boyle) *chsd ldrs: rdn wl over 3f out: keeping on same pce whn hmpd 1f out: eased last 100yds* **11/2**[3]

53-6 **9** ½ **Whos Counting**[7] 6390 3-9-0 45 FrancisNorton 9 35
(R J Hodges) *sn wl bhd: styd on last 2f: n.d* **20/1**

3000 **10** ¾ **Drink To Me Only**[2] 6505 4-9-3 45 (t) TomEaves 13 33
(J R Weymes) *racd in midfield: rdn and outpcd 4f out: n.d after* **8/1**

064 **11** 2 **Natco**[63] 4901 3-9-0 45 J-PGuillambert 1 29
(M Johnston) *sn rdn along in rr: nvr on terms* **12/1**

3000 **12** 3 **Musical Locket (IRE)**[26] 5900 3-9-0 45 BThomas 4 22
(J C Fox) *a bhd: no ch last 3f* **50/1**

0214 **13** 3½ **Sion Hill (IRE)**[10] 6311 6-9-3 45 (p) JamieSpencer 2 14
(John A Harris) *hung rt thrght: led tl over 4f out: chsd ldr tl eased over 2f out: virtually p.u ins fnl f* **15/8**[1]

1m 41.32s (0.52) **Going Correction** -0.075s/f (Stan)
WFA 3 from 4yo+ 3lb 13 Ran SP% **136.3**
Speed ratings (Par 97): **94,92,92,91,91 91,89,87,86,85 83,80,77**
CSF £134.54 TOTE £18.20: £5.90, £4.10, £2.50; EX 287.50.
Owner Exors of the late W Weeding **Bred** Elsdon Farms **Trained** Godstone, Surrey
■ Stewards' Enquiry : B Thomas one-day ban: used whip when out of contention (Nov 9)

FOCUS
A bad race, even for a contest like this, and the time was modest though with the winner getting just £1,365 shows how moderate the quality of the contest was. The form will mean nothing outside this level.
Kathleen Kennet Official explanation: jockey said mare hung left
Height Of Spirits Official explanation: jockey said gelding hung both ways
Sion Hill(IRE) Official explanation: jockey said gelding was unsteerable

6533 BETFAIR RADIO H'CAP 7f (P)
3:40 (3:42) (Class 6) (0-65,65) 3-Y-0+ **£2,047** (£604; £302) **Stalls** High

Form RPR
3042 **1** **Encores**[6] 6413 3-8-13 60 JamieSpencer 6 76+
(N A Callaghan) *hld up in rr: swtchd ins and gd hdwy over 2f out: led jst over 1f out: r.o strly* **5/2**[1]

5621 **2** 2 **Emma Jean Lad (IRE)**[19] 6100 3-8-11 58 JohnEgan 7 65
(J S Moore) *chsd ldrs: rdn and hdwy jst over 2f out: edgd rt over 1f out: chsd wnr 1f out: kpt on but nt pce of wnr* **7/2**[2]

2163 **3** 1¼ **Bold Cross (IRE)**[17] 6148 4-9-4 63 PaulFitzsimons 11 67
(E G Bevan) *t.k.h: chsd ldrs: rdn 2f out: kpt on same pce fnl f* **5/1**[3]

0005 **4** nk **Figaro Flyer (IRE)**[27] 5879 4-9-2 61 SimonWhitworth 4 64+
(P Howling) *t.k.h: hld up towards rr: nt clr run 2f out: shkn up and kpt on fnl f: nt trble ldrs* **12/1**

050 **5** 1 **Blue Bamboo**[48] 5303 3-9-4 65 MartinDwyer 10 65
(Mrs A J Perrett) *led after 1f: rdn over 2f out: hdd jst over 1f out: kpt on same pce fnl f* **9/1**

6006 **6** nk **Buzzin'Boyzee (IRE)**[13] 6247 4-8-6 51 oh6 FrancisNorton 13 53+
(P D Evans) *hld up in midfield: rdn wl over 1f out: keeping same pce whn nt clr run jst ins fnl f: nt pushed after* **14/1**

05-5 **7** nk **Hits Only Jude (IRE)**[11] 6290 4-8-12 57 DeanMcKeown 1 56
(J Pearce) *bhd on outer: rdn over 2f out: kpt on but nvr threatened ldrs* **12/1**

0030 **8** shd **Kingscross**[20] 6088 9-9-0 59 FergusSweeney 3 58
(M Blanshard) *bhd: kpt on u.p fnl 2f: nvr nr ldrs* **20/1**

0650 **9** nk **Zabeel House**[21] 6068 4-8-13 58 (v[1]) TPO'Shea 2 56
(J A R Toller) *chsd ldrs: rdn wl over 2f out: sltly hmpd and swtchd lft over 1f out: no imp after* **16/1**

0300 **10** shd **Attacca**[24] 5966 6-8-9 54 TomEaves 12 52
(J R Weymes) *led from 1f: chsd ldrs after: rdn over 2f out: fdd ins fnl f* **12/1**

40-2 **11** 1¼ **Herb Paris (FR)**[19] 6101 3-8-13 60 IanMongan 5 54
(P M Phelan) *chsd ldr after 1f: ev ch and rdn wl over 2f out: wknd over 1f out* **12/1**

1m 25.87s (-0.93) **Going Correction** -0.075s/f (Stan)
WFA 3 from 4yo+ 2lb 11 Ran SP% **125.5**
Speed ratings (Par 101): **102,99,98,97,96 96,96,96,95,95 94**
CSF £11.81 CT £43.45 TOTE £3.60: £1.60, £1.80, £1.80; EX 12.50.
Owner G C Hartigan **Bred** Chippenham Lodge Stud Ltd **Trained** Newmarket, Suffolk

FOCUS
An ordinary sprint handicap in which the early pace was modest and a couple took too strong a hold as a result. Despite that, the winning time was acceptable, the form looks sound enough rated around the placed horses, and the winner did it well.
Buzzin'Boyzee(IRE) Official explanation: jockey said filly was denied a clear run

6534 BETFAIR CASINO H'CAP 1m 4f (P)
4:10 (4:12) (Class 6) (0-60,60) 3-Y-O **£2,047** (£604; £302) **Stalls** Centre

Form RPR
1630 **1** **Hatton Flight**[19] 6102 3-9-3 59 (b) FrancisNorton 14 68
(A M Balding) *t.k.h: in tch: swtchd rt and hdwy 2f out: rdn to ld over 1f out: styd on wl* **3/1**[2]

2045 **2** nk **Intensifier (IRE)**[2] 6506 3-8-10 52 (b) J-PGuillambert 3 61+
(P A Blockley) *in tch: lost pl over 3f out: shkn up and gd hdwy over 2f out: chsd wnr ins fnl f: kpt on u.p* **7/1**

302 **3** 1½ **Dart**[13] 6257 3-9-4 60 JamieSpencer 9 69+
(J R Fanshawe) *hld up in midfield on inner: n.m.r over 2f out: rdn and hdwy over 1f out: chsd ldrs ins fnl f: keeping on same pce whn short of room nr fin* **6/4**[1]

500 **4** ¾ **Highest Esteem**[33] 5728 3-8-13 55 (p) RyanMoore 11 60
(G L Moore) *s.i.s: n.m.r on rail 2f out: swtchd lft and rdn wl over 1f out: r.o ins fnl f: wnt 4th nr fin* **6/1**

0305 **5** hd **Autograph Hunter**[12] 6265 3-8-11 53 LPKeniry 4 58
(Peter Grayson) *hld up in rr: rdn and effrt on outer 3f out: edgd rt over 1f out: styd on on fnl f: nt rch ldrs* **10/1**

5400 **6** hd **Party Palace**[12] 6261 3-8-4 46 oh1 DavidKinsella 13 51
(H S Howe) *led for 1f: chsd ldr after tl rdn to ld again over 2f out: hdd over 1f out: fdd ins fnl f* **50/1**

0305 **7** 2½ **Golden Folly**[13] 6257 3-8-7 49 (b) RichardKingscote 10 50
(Lady Herries) *s.i.s: bhd: hdwy on outer over 5f out: disp 2nd and rdn wl over 2f out: wknd over 1f out* **16/1**

3460 **8** ½ **Sir Sandicliffe (IRE)**[24] 5980 3-8-13 55 JohnEgan 12 55
(W M Brisbourne) *hld up bhd: rdn and effrt over 2f out: n.m.r over 1f out: nvr trbld ldrs* **33/1**

0060 **9** 1¼ **Slip Silver**[21] 6069 3-8-4 46 oh1 (p) ChrisCatlin 5 44
(P J Makin) *led: tl rdn and hdd over 2f out: wknd 2f out* **50/1**

0005 **10** ¾ **Silver Surprise**[43] 5450 3-8-4 **46** oh1 NelsonDeSouza 7 43
(J J Bridger) *hld up in midfield: rdn and hdwy over 3f out: wknd 2f out* **66/1**

0222 **11** 3½ **Ardmaddy (IRE)**[17] 6147 3-8-12 **54** TPO'Shea 8 45
(J A R Toller) *hld up: rdn and hdwy on outer over 3f out: wknd wl over 1f out: eased ins fnl f* **5/1**[3]

-300 **12** 2 **Halkerston**[31] 5783 3-9-3 **59** AdamKirby 6 47
(C G Cox) *awkward leaving stalls: r in midfield: rdn 6f out: nvr trbld ldrs* **33/1**

5010 **13** 2 **Blue Mistral (IRE)**[15] 6206 3-9-4 **60** (vt) MartinDwyer 2 45
(W J Knight) *v.s.a: a bhd* **20/1**

6001 **14** ¾ **Correy**[16] 4528 3-8-6 **48** AdrianMcCarthy 1 31
(Miss J S Davis) *chsd ldrs: rdn 3f out: sn dropped out* **33/1**

2m 35.56s (-1.34) **Going Correction** -0.075s/f (Stan) **14 Ran SP% 142.4**
Speed ratings (Par 99): **101,100,99,99,99 99,97,97,96,95 93,92,90,90**
CSF £28.54 CT £48.58 TOTE £4.60: £1.50, £2.50, £1.40; EX 35.70 Place 6 £18.27, Place 5 8.55.
Owner David Brownlow **Bred** Fittocks Stud Ltd **Trained** Kingsclere, Hants

FOCUS
No more than an ordinary middle-distance handicap and the pace was only fair. There was not a great deal separating the front six at the line and the form looks modest rated around the fifth, sixth and ninth.

T/Plt: £43.90 to a £1 stake. Pool: £43,146.75. 716.40 winning tickets. T/Qpdt: £12.20 to a £1 stake. Pool: £2,903.80. 175.60 winning tickets. SP

6246 LEICESTER (R-H)

Monday, October 29

OFFICIAL GOING: Good to soft (6.9)
Wind: Light behind Weather: Fine and sunny

6535 HOBY MEDIAN AUCTION MAIDEN FILLIES' STKS 5f 218y
1:20 (1:21) (Class 6) 2-Y-O **£2,590** (£770; £385; £192) **Stalls Low**

Form RPR

34 **1** **Minshar**[95] 3884 2-9-0 0 NickyMackay 1 84
(L M Cumani) *hld up: hdwy 1/2-way: rdn and edgd rt over 1f out: styd on to ld wl ins fnl f* **6/1**[2]

43 **2** nk **Provence**[10] 6295 2-9-0 0 MichaelHills 14 84
(B W Hills) *chsd ldrs: led over 2f out: rdn over 1f out: edgd lft and hdd wl ins fnl f* **8/15**[1]

335 **3** 2½ **Monashee Rock (IRE)**[18] 6127 2-9-0 77 StephenDonohoe 8 76
(M Salaman) *hld up: hdwy over 2f out: rdn over 1f out: styd on same pce ins fnl f* **10/1**[3]

0530 **4** 2 **Red Amaryllis**[34] 5707 2-9-0 73 PhilipRobinson 13 70
(H J L Dunlop) *led over 4f: sn rdn: styd on same pce appr fnl f* **20/1**

0 **5** 2 **Centenerola (USA)**[20] 6087 2-9-0 0 RHills 11 64+
(B W Hills) *s.i.s: sn pushed along in rr: styd on appr fnl f: nvr nrr* **66/1**

6 ½ **Never Catcher (IRE)** 2-9-0 0 FrankieMcDonald 9 63+
(P A Blockley) *dwlt: in rr: r.o ins fnl f: nvr nrr* **50/1**

7 ½ **Didana (IRE)** 2-9-0 0 JimmyQuinn 16 61
(M G Quinlan) *s.i.s: hld up: hung rt and styd on fr over 1f out: nrst fin* **33/1**

52 **8** 1¼ **Duty Doctor**[18] 6119 2-9-0 0 DaneO'Neill 2 57+
(S Kirk) *chsd ldrs: rdn 1/2-way: edgd rt and wknd over 1f out* **10/1**[3]

0600 **9** shd **Holly Golightley**[31] 5770 2-9-0 60 NCallan 4 57
(K A Ryan) *chsd ldr: rdn and ev ch over 2f out: wknd over 1f out* **50/1**

10 nk **Felicia** 2-9-0 0 JimCrowley 10 59+
(S C Williams) *s.s: outpcd: effrt and nt clr run over 1f out: n.d* **66/1**

11 1½ **Rosie Says No** 2-9-0 0 BrettDoyle 5 52
(R M H Cowell) *s.i.s: in rr: effrt and hung rt over 1f out: n.d* **50/1**

00 **12** 3½ **Pretty Officer (USA)**[17] 6138 2-9-0 0 RichardMullen 15 41
(Rae Guest) *mid-div: rdn 1/2-way: wknd over 2f out* **100/1**

00 **13** hd **Cealtra Star (IRE)**[10] 6306 2-8-11 0 AndrewMullen(3) 12 40
(K A Ryan) *wnt lft s: chsd ldrs: rdn 1/2-way: wknd 2f out* **100/1**

14 2½ **Princess Augusta (USA)** 2-8-11 0 NeilChalmers(3) 6 33
(A M Balding) *s.i.s: a in rr: bhd fr 1/2-way* **80/1**

00 **15** ½ **Madame Bountiful**[6] 6403 2-9-0 0 PatCosgrave 7 31
(A King) *mid-div: rdn 1/2-way: sn wknd* **80/1**

1m 14.58s (1.38) **Going Correction** +0.275s/f (Good) **15 Ran SP% 119.2**
Speed ratings (Par 90): **101,100,97,94,91 91,90,88,88,88 86,81,81,78,77**
CSF £8.87 TOTE £5.70: £1.90, £1.02, £2.50; EX 10.90 Trifecta £53.80 Pool: £149.44, 1.97 winning units.
Owner Jaber Abdullah **Bred** Century Farms **Trained** Newmarket, Suffolk
■ Stewards' Enquiry : Nicky Mackay one-day ban: used whip with excessive frequency (Nov 9)

FOCUS
A very decent winning time for the type of race and 0.61 seconds faster than the colts' equivalent later on the card. The first pair came clear in a driving finish and the level is set by the fourth.

NOTEBOOK
Minshar showed a likeable attitude to hold off the runner-up near the line and get off the mark at the third attempt on this first outing for 95 days. This showed her previous flop at York to be all wrong and she has evidently done well for her break, plus this easy ground was in her favour. She ought to get further as a three-year-old and this has now enhanced her all-important potential paddock value. (op 5-1)
Provence ◆ did nothing wrong in defeat and only just lost out, but did not look as suited by this easier ground. She should not be ignored when reverting to a suitably faster surface. (op 8-13 tchd 4-6 in places)
Monashee Rock(IRE), given an official rating of 77 after her three previous runs, got going too late to ever seriously trouble the first pair yet again ran respectably. She has one of these in her when ridden more positively and helps to set the level. (tchd 11-1)
Red Amaryllis was given a positive ride on this drop in trip and, despite putting an a more encouraging display, is probably somewhat flattered by her official rating at present.
Centenerola(USA) blew the start and again ran too green to do herself justice. She needs more time and will be eligible for a handicap mark after her next assignment.
Felicia Official explanation: jockey said filly was denied a clear run

6536 HAYMARKET NURSERY 7f 9y
1:50 (1:51) (Class 6) (0-65,65) 2-Y-O **£2,590** (£770; £385; £192) **Stalls Low**

Form RPR

452 **1** **Wiseman's Diamond (USA)**[14] 6242 2-8-11 **55** (p) NCallan 9 61
(K A Ryan) *hld up: hdwy 1/2-way: chsd ldr over 1f out: styd on u.p to ld wl ins fnl f* **7/2**[1]

0000 **2** ½ **Chrystal Venture (IRE)**[38] 5601 2-9-5 **63** (p) StephenDonohoe 14 68
(A J McCabe) *s.i.s: sn prom: led over 5f out: rdn over 1f out: hdd wl ins fnl f* **33/1**

0006 **3** 1¾ **Tapas Lad (IRE)**[28] 5869 2-8-10 **54** ow1 (v[1]) PatCosgrave 8 54
(V Smith) *dwlt: sn pushed along in rr: hdwy u.p over 2f out: hung rt ins fnl f: styd on* **14/1**

6600 **4** 3½ **Silca Destination**[7] 6388 2-8-12 **56** RichardMullen 11 48
(M R Channon) *mid-div: outpcd over 2f out: rallied over 1f out: no imp fnl f* **16/1**

3006 **5** nk **Coral Shores**[24] 5984 2-8-8 **59** MCGeran(7) 16 50
(P W Chapple-Hyam) *prom: rdn over 2f out: hung lft over 1f out: styd on same pce* **10/1**[3]

0403 **6** 1¼ **Valentino Sky (USA)**[12] 6263 2-9-6 **64** (b) PaulMulrennan 4 52
(N P Littmoden) *trckd ldrs: plld hrd: rdn over 1f out: wknd fnl f* **9/1**[2]

0600 **7** 1¾ **The Hoofer (IRE)**[42] 5471 2-9-3 **61** TedDurcan 5 44
(J L Dunlop) *stdd s: hld up: rdn over 2f out: sme hdwy and hung rt over 1f out: n.d* **12/1**

4353 **8** 1 **One Called Alice**[21] 6066 2-9-3 **61** JimCrowley 15 42
(J R Holt) *s.i.s: hld up: hdwy over 1f out: n.d* **9/1**[2]

0410 **9** 2½ **Veronicas Way**[20] 6075 2-9-1 **62** AndrewMullen(3) 17 37
(G M Moore) *chsd ldrs: rdn 1/2-way: wknd over 1f out* **9/1**[2]

000 **10** 1 **Potemkin (USA)**[47] 5328 2-9-3 **61** DaneO'Neill 2 33
(A King) *mid-div: rdn 1/2-way: sn hung rt: sn btn* **14/1**

3005 **11** 1 **Night Robe**[10] 6312 2-8-8 **52** TGMcLaughlin 3 22
(P D Evans) *sn pushed along in rr: n.d* **22/1**

0000 **12** 7 **Galley Slave (IRE)**[20] 6074 2-8-6 **55** RussellKennemore(5) 6 7
(M C Chapman) *led: hdd over 5f out: rdn 1/2-way: wknd 2f out* **25/1**

0004 **13** 5 **Peer Pressure**[14] 6237 2-9-7 **65** JimmyQuinn 7 5
(P Mitchell) *hld up in tch: rdn 1/2-way: wknd wl over 1f out* **16/1**

4566 **14** 7 **Berrymead**[60] 4975 2-9-4 **62** DaleGibson 12 —
(M W Easterby) *chsd ldrs to 1/2-way* **12/1**

0230 **15** 3 **Priceless Speedfit**[6] 6410 2-9-2 **60** (p) PhilipRobinson 10 —
(G G Margarson) *prom: lost pl over 4f out: sn bhd* **12/1**

040 **16** 3½ **Lord Of Esteem**[38] 5599 2-9-1 **59** BrettDoyle 13 —
(J Ryan) *dwlt: a bhd* **25/1**

5616 **17** 13 **Sharps Gold**[12] 6270 2-9-0 **61** (t) LukeMorris(3) 1 —
(P J McBride) *dwlt: in rr: rdn and hung rt 1/2-way: sn lost tch* **22/1**

1m 28.43s (2.33) **Going Correction** +0.275s/f (Good) **17 Ran SP% 128.8**
Speed ratings (Par 93): **97,96,94,90,90 88,86,85,82,81 80,72,66,58,55 51,36**
CSF £152.41 CT £1516.88 TOTE £4.60: £1.60, £6.80, £4.90, £4.20; EX 223.20 TRIFECTA Not won..
Owner Wright, Hillen and Hatta **Bred** Hatta Bloodstock International **Trained** Hambleton, N Yorks
■ Stewards' Enquiry : N Callan one-day ban: used whip with excessive frequency (Nov 9)

FOCUS
A moderate nursery, run at a fair pace but the form is weak.

NOTEBOOK
Wiseman's Diamond(USA), well backed for this nursery bow, was given a typically strong ride by Callan and rewarded her supporters with a game display. The fact she was second in an All-Weather seller last time puts this form into perspective, but a big run was obviously expected by her connections and she is clearly now going the right way. (op 9-2 tchd 5-1)
Chrystal Venture(IRE) overcame a sluggish start to adopt a handy position and was soon then in the lead. She kept to her task bravely thereafter under pressure and this rates a much-improved effort in first-time cheekpieces.
Tapas Lad(IRE), despite the application of a first-time visor, again looked distinctly tricky. This was still an improved effort on his handicap bow and he could find a weak race if kept on the go during the winter, providing connections can harness his ability. (op 16-1)
Silca Destination, with the visor abandoned for this step up a furlong, showed improved form on this return to the turf and left the impression she is now ready to tackle even further.
Priceless Speedfit Official explanation: jockey said filly had no more to give
Sharps Gold Official explanation: jockey said filly was unsuited by the good to soft ground

6537 TWENTY TWENTY CLAIMING STKS 7f 9y
2:20 (2:20) (Class 5) 3-4-Y-O **£3,238** (£963; £361; £361) **Stalls Low**

Form RPR

3260 **1** **Ten To The Dozen**[4] 6447 4-8-11 56 DaneO'Neill 15 59
(P W Hiatt) *chsd ldrs: nt clr run and lost pl over 2f out: swtchd lft and hdwy over 1f out: r.o to ld wl ins fnl f: comf* **4/1**[1]

0060 **2** 1¼ **Only A Grand**[25] 5935 3-8-0 44 ow5 (b) AndrewMullen(3) 1 50
(R Bastiman) *racd alone on stands' side: w ldrs: rdn over 1f out: styd on* **25/1**

0-00 **3** 1½ **Dado Mush**[101] 3705 4-8-13 44 (p) TGMcLaughlin 16 54
(T T Clement) *hld up: hdwy 1/2-way: led over 1f out: hdd and no ex wl ins fnl f* **50/1**

500 **3** dht **Sparky Vixen**[37] 5627 3-7-9 50 DuranFentiman(3) 6 41
(G A Swinbank) *hld up: hdwy over 2f out: sn rdn: styd on* **14/1**

0300 **5** 1 **Fistral**[13] 6247 3-8-1 47 ow1 AndrewElliott(3) 13 44
(J Hetherton) *mid-div: swtchd rt and hdwy over 2f out: no ex fnl f* **12/1**

0010 **6** hd **Bert's Memory**[3] 6464 3-7-13 54 (p) NataliaGemelova(5) 2 43
(K A Ryan) *chsd ldr: led over 2f out: rdn and hdd over 1f out: no ex* **13/2**[3]

00-0 **7** 3 **Premier Cru**[30] 5816 4-8-0 41 NicolPolli(5) 12 34
(Andrew Turnell) *sn pushed along in rr: rdn fr 1/2-way: nvr nrr* **50/1**

3212 **8** 3 **Halfwaytoparadise**[10] 6311 4-8-6 49 (p) SaleemGolam 14 27
(W G M Turner) *led over 4f: wknd over 1f out* **5/1**[2]

-560 **9** 1 **Lipizza (IRE)**[37] 5638 4-8-12 69 StephenDonohoe 7 30
(N A Callaghan) *s.i.s: hld up: hdwy over 2f out: wknd fnl f* **4/1**[1]

3504 **10** 3 **Ruffie (IRE)**[93] 3966 4-8-6 51 JimmyQuinn 4 16
(Miss Gay Kelleway) *hld up: rdn 1/2-way: n.d* **7/1**

0060 **11** 5 **Fancy You (IRE)**[35] 5690 4-8-4 38 NickyMackay 18 1
(A W Carroll) *chsd ldrs: rdn and ev ch over 2f out: wknd over 1f out* **100/1**

6P00 **12** 6 **Cape Dancer (IRE)**[10] 6309 3-9-0 45 (p) TonyHamilton 11 —
(J S Wainwright) *edgd lft s: chsd ldrs: rdn and wknd over 2f out* **33/1**

-240 **13** hd **Dragon Flame (IRE)**[121] 3102 4-8-13 56 TedDurcan 17 —
(M Quinn) *sn outpcd* **14/1**

5000 **14** ¾ **Kissi Kissi**[81] 4324 4-8-4 43 DaleGibson 9 —
(M J Attwater) *s.i.s and hmpd s: a in rr* **100/1**

000 **15** 12 **Kastan**[48] 5310 3-8-3 41 AdrianTNicholls 8 —
(B Palling) *chsd ldrs over 4f* **50/1**

00P- **16** 30 **Lady Kintyre**[353] 6427 3-8-7 0 ow1 PaulMulrennan 10 —
(M W Easterby) *s.i.s and wnt lft s: outpcd* **100/1**

1m 28.5s (2.40) **Going Correction** +0.275s/f (Good) **16 Ran SP% 119.2**
WFA 3 from 4yo 2lb
Speed ratings (Par 103): **97,95,93,93,92 92,89,85,84,81 75,68,68,67,53 19**
3rd pl DM 7.10; SV 2.10. CSF £110.66 TOTE £5.60: £2.00, £5.70; EX 105.20 TRIFECTA Not won..

Owner Clive Roberts Vince Walsh **Bred** S J Mear **Trained** Hook Norton, Oxon

FOCUS
A very weak claimer and the form looks shaky with the placed horses having no form this year.
Dragon Flame(IRE) Official explanation: jockey said colt lost a shoe

Kastan Official explanation: jockey said gelding had no more to give

6538 SIR GORDON RICHARDS CONDITIONS STKS 1m 3f 183y
2:50 (2:52) (Class 4) 3-Y-0+ **£5,678** (£1,699; £849; £424; £211) **Stalls** High

Form RPR
1-24 **1** **New Guinea**[29] 5829 4-9-2 103 TedDurcan 6 106
(Saeed Bin Suroor) *mde all: rdn and edgd lft over 1f out: hung rt ins fnl f: styd on* **11/10**[1]
1-00 **2** 3/4 **Young Mick**[24] 5976 5-9-8 103 (v) NCallan 3 111
(G G Margarson) *hld up: rdn over 3f out: hung rt fr over 1f out: styd on: nt rch wnr* **9/1**
5206 **3** 3 1/2 **Futun**[39] 5574 4-9-2 96 NickyMackay 7 99
(L M Cumani) *a.p: chsd wnr over 2f out: rdn and hung rt over 1f out: wknd ins fnl f* **9/2**[3]
6025 **4** 2 **Foxhaven**[24] 5976 5-9-8 107 (v) JimCrowley 5 102
(P R Chamings) *chsd wnr tl rdn over 2f out: wknd fnl f* **5/2**[2]
2500 **5** 15 **Millville**[16] 6169 7-9-2 91 PhilipRobinson 2 72
(M A Jarvis) *prom: rdn over 3f out: wknd 2f out* **16/1**
0/00 **6** 22 **Black Wadi**[116] 3244 5-8-11 37 (t) JimmyQuinn 4 32
(T Keddy) *hld up: lost tch fnl 4f* **250/1**
3440 **7** 50 **Little Darlin**[13] 6249 3-8-4 0 AdrianTNicholls 1 —
(G J Smith) *prom: racd keenly: lost pl 7f out: wknd 5f out* **500/1**

2m 36.39s (1.89) **Going Correction** +0.375s/f (Good)
WFA 3 from 4yo+ 7lb 7 Ran SP% **110.9**
Speed ratings (Par 105): **108,107,105,103,93 79,45**
CSF £11.69 TOTE £1.80: £1.10, £2.40; EX 6.90.
Owner Godolphin **Bred** Milton Park Stud Partnership **Trained** Newmarket, Suffolk

FOCUS
A good conditions event that was run at an uneven pace. The form is not that solid despite the first two coming clear.

6539 LEICESTER RACECOURSE CONFERENCE CENTRE H'CAP 1m 60y
3:20 (3:20) (Class 3) (0-90,88) 3-Y-0+
£7,790 (£2,332; £1,166; £583; £291; £146) **Stalls** High

Form RPR
0205 **1** **Kinsya**[17] 6155 4-9-6 **87** JimmyQuinn 2 97+
(M H Tompkins) *hld up: hdwy over 2f out: rdn to ld and edgd rt ins fnl f: r.o* **7/2**[1]
0104 **2** 1 3/4 **Orpen Wide (IRE)**[17] 6155 5-9-6 **87** (b) JimCrowley 8 93
(M C Chapman) *chsd ldrs: led 2f out: sn rdn: hdd and unable qckn ins fnl f* **20/1**
0010 **3** nk **St Andrews (IRE)**[31] 5776 7-9-7 **88** PhilipRobinson 3 93
(M A Jarvis) *hld up: hdwy and edgd rt over 1f out: styd on* **11/2**[2]
6520 **4** shd **Full Victory (IRE)**[16] 6180 5-8-13 **80** NCallan 7 85
(R A Farrant) *prom: rdn over 2f out: styd on* **8/1**
2122 **5** 1 1/4 **Observatory Star (IRE)**[23] 6016 4-8-11 **78** (p) DavidAllan 6 82+
(T D Easterby) *hld up: nt clr run over 1f out: r.o ins fnl f: nt trble ldrs* **7/2**[1]
0020 **6** 1 **Mezuzah**[30] 5804 7-8-13 **80** PaulMulrennan 11 80
(M W Easterby) *prom: rdn over 2f out: nt clr run over 1f out: no ex ins fnl f* **14/1**
2130 **7** 3/4 **Barons Spy (IRE)**[14] 6243 6-8-7 **79** RussellKennemore[(5)] 5 77
(R J Price) *hld up: nt clr run wl over 1f out: swtchd rt and hdwy sn after: rdn and wknd ins fnl f* **18/1**
2065 **8** 2 1/2 **Rain Stops Play (IRE)**[25] 5950 5-8-11 **78** TGMcLaughlin 4 70
(M Quinn) *led: rdn and hdd 2f out: wknd fnl f* **14/1**
5530 **9** 8 **Nevada Desert (IRE)**[17] 6155 7-9-1 **85** MichaelJStainton[(3)] 9 59
(R M Whitaker) *trckd ldrs: rdn over 2f out: wknd over 1f out* **15/2**[3]
0203 **10** 1 1/2 **Shot To Fame (USA)**[37] 5617 8-8-12 **79** (t) AdrianTNicholls 10 50
(D Nicholls) *chsd ldr: rdn over 2f out: wknd over 1f out* **11/1**

1m 47.42s (2.12) **Going Correction** +0.375s/f (Good)
WFA 3 from 4yo+ 3lb 10 Ran SP% **114.4**
Speed ratings (Par 107): **104,102,101,101,100 99,98,96,88,86**
CSF £77.13 CT £387.73 TOTE £5.00: £1.60, £4.40, £2.40; EX 66.10 Trifecta £263.70 Part won. Pool: £371.54, 0.20 winning units..
Owner Roalco Limited **Bred** Whitsbury Manor Stud & Clarendon Farms **Trained** Newmarket, Suffolk

FOCUS
A competitive enough handicap and the form makes sense with the placed horses to form.

NOTEBOOK
Kinsya has been a bit in-and-out since returning this season and was racing here off a 3lb higher mark than when last winning back in October of last year. However, he managed to return right back to his best and really ran on strongly under pressure to reverse York form with Orpen Wide. This was a welcome return to winning form, but it is doubtful whether he can follow-up off a higher mark. (op 4-1)
Orpen Wide(IRE), who managed to finish ahead of Kinsya at York last time, ran a bold race in defeat but was unable to confirm the placings. He kept on well once headed, just hanging on for second, but may be nudged up a pound or two for this and will not be doing much improving at the age of eight. (op 12-1)
St Andrews(IRE), a narrow winner at Windsor back in August, ran reasonably off this mark when fifth at Haydock last time, but this was a better effort and, although just held for second, he should remain competitive off this sort of mark. (op 5-1)
Full Victory(IRE) ran as though something was amiss when virtually pulled up at York last time, but he had earlier run well to finish second off a 1lb lower mark at Wolverhampton and this was much more like his true form. (op 12-1)
Observatory Star(IRE) has been in good form, winning at Redcar back in August, but he was having to compete here off a 10lb higher mark than when last winning and fell short. It was not a bad effort though as he may have been a bit closer with a clear run through. (tchd 4-1)
Shot To Fame(USA) Official explanation: jockey said gelding had no more to give

6540 EBF FOSSE WAY MAIDEN STKS 5f 218y
3:50 (3:52) (Class 4) 2-Y-0 **£4,857** (£1,445; £722; £360) **Stalls** Low

Form RPR
662 **1** **Lord Sandicliffe (IRE)**[11] 6281 2-9-3 82 MichaelHills 1 80
(B W Hills) *chsd ldr: rdn to ld over 2f out: edgd rt over 1f out: r.o* **7/4**[2]
62 **2** nk **Alwaabel**[137] 2596 2-9-3 0 RHills 9 79
(J L Dunlop) *chsd ldrs: ev ch fr over 2f out: rdn over 1f out: r.o* **5/6**[1]
6 **3** 8 **Hellfire Bay**[13] 6246 2-9-3 0 NCallan 3 55
(K A Ryan) *prom: rdn over 2f out: wknd over 1f out* **12/1**[3]
4 1 1/4 **Bad Moon Rising** 2-9-3 0 JimmyQuinn 6 51
(J Akehurst) *chsd ldrs: rdn and hung rt over 2f out: sn wknd* **40/1**
5 1 1/4 **Ricci De Mare** 2-8-12 0 StephenDonohoe 4 43
(Sir Mark Prescott) *in rr: rdn 1/2-way: wknd over 2f out* **25/1**
6 nk **Billberry** 2-9-3 0 SaleemGolam 2 47
(S C Williams) *dwlt: a bhd* **14/1**
00 **7** shd **My Flame**[20] 6079 2-9-3 0 JimCrowley 5 46
(J R Jenkins) *led over 3f: wknd over 1f out* **200/1**

1m 15.19s (1.99) **Going Correction** +0.275s/f (Good) 7 Ran SP% **112.1**
Speed ratings (Par 97): **97,96,85,84,82 82,82**
CSF £3.34 TOTE £2.90: £1.70, £1.40; EX 3.90 Trifecta £16.30 Pool: £617.04, 26.83 winning units.
Owner Henry Barton **Bred** J L Hassett **Trained** Lambourn, Berks

FOCUS
The 'big' two pulled clear in what was an uncompetitive maiden and the form is rated around the first three.

NOTEBOOK
Lord Sandicliffe(IRE), who ran his best race to date when finishing second in similar conditions at Nottingham the other day, had one advantage over the favourite in that he had already proven himself in the ground and he got on top close home. The pair finished eight lengths clear and he looks the type to develop into a smart handicapper next season. (op 15-8 after 2-1 in places)
Alwaabel brought the best form into the contest, but there was a doubt about him in the ground and he lost out in a tight finish. He and the winner were locked in battle throughout the final furlong and a half, but they managed to come clear and he undoubtedly has the ability to win a small maiden. (op 4-5 tchd Evens)
Hellfire Bay, who shaped as though in need of all the 7f when sixth at the course on debut, was unable to cope with the drop in distance and may prove to be more of a handicap sort. He will be qualified after one more run. (op 9-1)
Bad Moon Rising, related to a couple of poor maidens, cost little and he shaped with only a limited amount of promise on this racecourse debut.
Ricci De Mare never got into it, but comes from a yard whose juvenile often need a run or two and she may be more of a sort for low-grade handicaps next season. (op 20-1)

6541 COPLOW CONDITIONS STKS 7f 9y
4:20 (4:21) (Class 4) 3-Y-0+ **£5,678** (£1,699; £849; £424; £211) **Stalls** Low

Form RPR
4262 **1** **Welsh Emperor (IRE)**[23] 6029 8-9-0 113 TedDurcan 5 104+
(T P Tate) *mde all: rdn and hung rt fr over 1f out: styd on* **8/11**[1]
2000 **2** 3/4 **Babodana**[23] 6011 7-9-0 96 NCallan 4 102
(M H Tompkins) *chsd wnr to 1/2-way: rdn over 2f out: edgd rt and r.o ins fnl f* **12/1**
5-40 **3** hd **Raptor (GER)**[23] 6011 4-9-0 100 PhillipMakin 6 101
(K R Burke) *a.p: chsd wnr 1/2-way: rdn over 1f out: styd on* **11/2**[3]
3230 **4** 2 1/2 **Fajr (IRE)**[108] 3505 5-9-0 107 JimmyQuinn 2 95
(Miss Gay Kelleway) *hld up in tch: plld hrd: rdn over 1f out: no ex ins fnl f* **3/1**[2]
0000 **5** 1 1/2 **Penny Glitters**[46] 5368 4-8-6 41 (b) DominicFox[(3)] 8 86?
(S Parr) *hld up: racd keenly: rdn and edgd rt over 1f out: nt trble ldrs* **250/1**
5000 **6** 4 **Elhamri**[51] 5212 3-8-12 92 JimCrowley 7 80
(S Kirk) *hld up in tch: plld hrd: hung rt over 2f out: sn rdn: wknd fnl f* **33/1**

1m 27.72s (1.62) **Going Correction** +0.275s/f (Good)
WFA 3 from 4yo+ 2lb 6 Ran SP% **109.3**
Speed ratings (Par 105): **101,100,99,97,95 90**
CSF £10.45 TOTE £1.70: £1.20, £4.10; EX 10.10 Trifecta £30.60 Pool: £468.29, 10.85 winning units. Place 6 £21.57, Place 5 £19.16.
Owner Mrs Sylvia Clegg **Bred** Times Of Wigan Ltd **Trained** Tadcaster, N Yorks

FOCUS
The fastest of the three races over the trip at the meeting, but not by the margin that might have been expected given the standard of the horses taking part. The form is somewhat muddling with the fifth far closer than expected and the runner-up is the best guide.
T/Jkpt: £4,045.20 to a £1 stake. Pool: £19,941.25. 3.50 winning tickets. T/Plt: £44.80 to a £1 stake. Pool: £50,219.35. 817.05 winning tickets. T/Qpdt: £9.80 to a £1 stake. Pool: £3,684.60. 276.10 winning tickets. CR

6432 LINGFIELD (L-H)
Monday, October 29

OFFICIAL GOING: Standard
Wind: Fresh, half against Weather: Sunny spells

6542 BOOK ONLINE FOR DISCOUNTED PRICES APPRENTICE H'CAP 6f (P)
1:30 (1:30) (Class 6) (0-53,53) 3-Y-0+ **£2,047** (£604; £302) **Stalls** Low

Form RPR
6050 **1** **Rhapsilian**[11] 6278 3-8-12 **52** KMay 12 61+
(J A Geake) *hit side of stall and missed break: hld up in midfield: hdwy and nt clr run early st: qcknd to ld nr fin* **16/1**
0035 **2** 1 **Two Acres (IRE)**[5] 6424 4-8-13 **52** JackDean 7 58
(A G Newcombe) *in tch: drvn along 1/2-way: chsd ldr over 1f out: kpt on: nt pce of wnr nr fin* **4/1**[2]
1000 **3** shd **Blessed Place**[11] 6279 7-8-6 **52** (t) BillyCray[(7)] 8 58
(D J S Ffrench Davis) *led: rdn 3l ahd home turn: hdd and no ex nr fin* **15/2**[3]
502 **4** 1 1/4 **Littledodayno (IRE)**[25] 5947 4-9-0 **53** JackMitchell 1 55+
(M Wigham) *bmpd and hit rail bnd after 1f: towards rr and sn rdn along: hdwy over 1f out: nrst fin* **5/2**[1]
1336 **5** 1 1/2 **Razzano (IRE)**[15] 6210 3-8-13 **53** JamieJones 3 50
(A M Hales) *bhd: hmpd bnd after 1f: rdn 3f out: styd on fnl 2f: nvr nrr* **8/1**
6000 **6** 3/4 **King Of Charm (IRE)**[7] 6390 4-8-0 46 oh1 (b) RossAtkinson[(7)] 6 41
(G L Moore) *chsd ldrs: wd bnd into st: no ex appr fnl f* **25/1**
0000 **7** 1/2 **Gone'N'Dunnett (IRE)**[31] 5778 8-8-11 **50** (p) KellyHarrison 11 44
(Mrs C A Dunnett) *mid-div: drvn along over 3f out: nt pce to chal* **14/1**
6000 **8** 1 **Shantina's Dream (USA)**[56] 5098 3-8-10 **50** HarryPoulton 2 41
(J R Boyle) *prom tl hrd rdn and wknd over 1f out* **50/1**
650 **9** 1 3/4 **Duke Of Milan (IRE)**[39] 5564 4-8-7 **49** (b[1]) RobbieEgan[(3)] 10 34
(G C Bravery) *chsd ldr tl wknd over 1f out* **15/2**[3]
06-0 **10** 1/2 **Sir Mikeale**[47] 5336 4-8-3 **47** LanceBetts[(5)] 9 31
(G Prodromou) *hld up towards rr: shkn up over 2f out: nvr nr ldrs* **50/1**
0000 **11** 1 1/2 **Campbeltown (IRE)**[148] 2273 4-8-2 46 oh1 PNolan[(5)] 5 25
(A B Haynes) *a bhd* **8/1**
000 **12** 1 3/4 **Beau Bramble**[16] 6176 3-8-8 **48** SladeO'Hara 4 22
(C F Wall) *in tch tl 1/2-way* **25/1**

1m 12.22s (-0.59) **Going Correction** -0.075s/f (Stan)
WFA 3 from 4yo+ 1lb 12 Ran SP% **118.5**
Speed ratings (Par 101): **100,98,98,96,94 93,93,91,89,88 86,84**
CSF £76.90 CT £540.41 TOTE £23.10: £2.50, £1.80, £3.50; EX 85.80.
Owner Rex Mead & David Mead **Bred** Compton Down Stud **Trained** Kimpton, Hants

The Form Book, Raceform Ltd, Compton, RG20 6NL

FOCUS
A moderate sprint handicap restricted to apprentices who had not ridden more than 25 winners. The early pace was strong and the form is modest.

6543 COME JUMPING HERE ON NOVEMBER 14TH MEDIAN AUCTION MAIDEN STKS 1m (P)
2:00 (2:01) (Class 5) 2-Y-O **£2,817** (£838; £418; £209) **Stalls** High

Form RPR

1 **Hilbre Court (USA)** 2-9-3 0 IanMongan 6 69
(B J Meehan) *hld up towards rr: hdwy on outside 3f out: led 1f out: drvn out* **14/1**[3]

0 2 3/4 **Colorado Springs**[27] 5882 2-8-12 0 TPQueally 4 62
(W Jarvis) *s.s: hld up in 6th: effrt and nt clr run 2f out: swtchd outside and rdn: styd on wl to take 2nd on line* **33/1**

5324 3 shd **Straight And Level (CAN)**[17] 6139 2-9-3 72 GeorgeBaker 2 67
(Miss Jo Crowley) *hld up and bhd: rdn over 2f out: swtchd outside and hdwy over 1f out: styd on wl fnl 100yds* **20/1**

2 4 nk **Full Marks**[20] 6087 2-8-12 0 KDarley 5 61
(J Noseda) *prom: drvn to chal jst ins fnl f: nt qckn fnl 100yds* **2/7**[1]

523 5 2 **Funseeker (UAE)**[12] 6262 2-8-12 70 DarryllHolland 7 57
(M Johnston) *led: hrd rdn and hdd 1f out: no ex ins fnl f* **9/2**[2]

040 6 3/4 **Tepee**[18] 6119 2-8-7 72 AshleyHamblett(5) 3 55
(L M Cumani) *t.k.h: trckd ldr: hmpd on rail ent st: n.m.r jst ins fnl f: no ex* **14/1**[3]

00 7 5 **Ba Dreamflight**[12] 6262 2-9-0 0 TravisBlock(3) 8 49
(H Morrison) *towards rr: sn drvn along: sme hdwy 4f out: wknd over 2f out* **40/1**

8 3 1/2 **Regulus Way (GR)** 2-9-3 0 PaulDoe 1 42
(P R Chamings) *v.s.a: plld hrd: rapid hdwy 6f out: jnd ldr 4f out: wknd 2f out* **33/1**

1m 39.52s (0.09) **Going Correction** -0.075s/f (Stan) **8** Ran SP% **122.4**
Speed ratings (Par 95): **96,95,95,94,92 92,87,83**
CSF £362.75 TOTE £15.60: £3.90, £15.30, £4.90; EX 343.20.
Owner E H Jones (paints) Ltd **Bred** Richard Nip & Omar Trevino **Trained** Manton, Wilts

FOCUS
They finished in a bit of a bunch and the form wants treating with caution with the third, whose official rating looks high, limiting the form.

NOTEBOOK
Hilbre Court(USA), a 23,000gns son of a 1m1f Grade 2 winner in the US and closely related to smart dual 7f winner Croisiere, was travelling noticeably strongly when switched out wide before the turn into the straight and he responded well to pressure when asked to go on. The bare form is probably not worth a great deal, but it has paid to follow the two-year-olds Brian Meehan has saddled to win first time out this season, and this one looks capable of improving. (op 12-1 tchd 16-1)
Colorado Springs improved significantly on the form she showed when down the field on her debut at Warwick with a close second. She was outpaced on the turn into the straight, but found her stride in the straight and came home well. She might be able to find a similarly weak maiden, but will also have the option of handicaps after one more run. (op 40-1 tchd 50-1)
Straight And Level(CAN), trying 1m for the first time, saw his race and out well and was not beaten far into third. He has the ability to pick up a modest race. (tchd 40-1)
Full Marks ran nowhere near the form she showed when second in a good maiden over 7f on soft ground at Leicester on her debut and was a bitter disappointment. It is too early to give up on her just yet, but it will probably be best to avoid too short a price next time. (op 4-11, tchd 2-5 in places)
Funseeker(UAE) did not find as much as one might have hoped in front and she may be better off in modest nursery company. (op 4-1 tchd 5-1)
Tepee hardly helped her chance by racing keenly for much of the way and was she was hampered when trying to stay on in the straight, so she can be rated better than the bare form. (tchd 16-1)
Regulus Way(GR) Official explanation: jockey said colt missed the break

6544 ARENALEISUREPLC.COM NOVICE STKS 6f (P)
2:30 (2:30) (Class 4) 2-Y-O **£3,886** (£1,156; £577; £288) **Stalls** Low

Form RPR

2 1 **Messias Da Silva (USA)**[14] 6225 2-8-7 0 KDarley 4 82+
(J Noseda) *hld up in 4th: effrt over 1f out: led ins fnl f: drvn out* **6/4**[1]

3102 2 1 1/2 **Ramatni**[21] 6052 2-8-11 82 DarryllHolland 7 82
(M Johnston) *w ldr: led 2f out tl ins fnl f: nt qckn* **11/2**

3104 3 2 **Good Gorsoon (USA)**[15] 6195 2-8-13 84 WilliamBuick(3) 2 81
(B W Hills) *hld up in rr: effrt on outside ent st: nt pce to chal: tk 3rd on line* **5/2**[2]

0024 4 shd **Prime Aspiration (USA)**[14] 6234 2-8-9 77 TravisBlock(3) 5 76
(Christian Wroe) *chsd ldng pair: rdn over 2f out: one pce appr fnl f* **12/1**

20 5 2 1/2 **Crystal Reign (IRE)**[121] 3095 2-8-12 0 JimmyFortune 6 70+
(P W Chapple-Hyam) *sn rdn to ld: hdd 2f out: wknd over 1f out* **4/1**[3]

1m 11.74s (-1.07) **Going Correction** -0.075s/f (Stan) **5** Ran SP% **111.6**
Speed ratings (Par 97): **104,102,99,99,95**
CSF £10.26 TOTE £1.90: £1.10, £2.60; EX 7.90.
Owner Sir Robert Ogden **Bred** Sondra Bender & Howard M Bender **Trained** Newmarket, Suffolk

FOCUS
Just the five runners, but a reasonable novice event rated through the runner-up and the winning time was decent for the level, 0.48 seconds faster than the earlier handicap over the same trip.

NOTEBOOK
Messias Da Silva(USA) ◆ confirmed the promise she showed when second over course and distance on her debut with a ready success. It remains to be seen where she will go next, but she looks a very useful filly in the making. (op 15-8)
Ramatni, trying Polytrack for the first time, helped force the pace and kept on well when headed by the potentially decent winner. (op 5-1 tchd 9-2)
Good Gorsoon(USA), switched to Polytrack for the first time, failed to convince stepped back up to 6f for the first time. (op 2-1, tchd 11-4 in a place)
Prime Aspiration(USA), returned to Polytrack, seemed to have every chance and he can have few excuses.
Crystal Reign(IRE), returning from a four-month break, helped set the pace with the eventual runner-up, but he was well held when it mattered. (op 5-1)

6545 LINGFIELDPARK.CO.UK H'CAP 1m 4f (P)
3:00 (3:00) (Class 4) (0-85,85) 3-Y-O+ **£4,857** (£1,445; £722; £360) **Stalls** Low

Form RPR

4236 1 **Know The Law**[21] 6061 3-8-3 75 (b[1]) MarcHalford(3) 5 85
(D R C Elsworth) *hld up in 4th: hdwy to ld jst over 1f out: rdn clr: readily* **11/1**

034 2 3 **Del Mar Sunset**[38] 5593 8-9-0 76 LiamJones 4 81
(W J Haggas) *dwlt: hld up in rr: hdwy on rail to go 2nd 1f out: nt pce of wnr fnl f* **6/1**[3]

1015 3 2 1/2 **Nobelix (IRE)**[14] 6230 5-9-6 85 WilliamBuick(3) 6 86
(J R Gask) *chsd ldr: rdn to chal on outside 2f out: hung lft in st: one pce* **9/1**

6324 4 1 3/4 **Chocolate Caramel (USA)**[14] 6230 5-9-9 85 JimmyFortune 3 83
(Mrs A J Perrett) *led: rdn over 3f out: hdd & wknd jst over 1f out* **11/10**[1]

3340 5 1 1/4 **Dundry**[39] 5574 6-9-2 78 (p) GeorgeBaker 1 74
(G L Moore) *chsd ldng pair: rdn over 2f out: wknd wl over 1f out* **9/4**[2]

2m 32.96s (-1.43) **Going Correction** -0.075s/f (Stan)
WFA 3 from 5yo+ 7lb **5** Ran SP% **111.0**
Speed ratings (Par 105): **101,99,97,96,95**
CSF £68.36 TOTE £9.80: £2.90, £2.10; EX 48.90.
Owner Raymond Tooth And Steve Gilbey **Bred** Mountgrange Stud Ltd **Trained** Newmarket, Suffolk

FOCUS
A decent handicap but only five runners and the form looks ordinary for the grade with the runner-up setting the level. The pace was just modest through the early stages.

6546 LINGFIELD PARK FOR WEDDINGS MAIDEN STKS 7f (P)
3:30 (3:33) (Class 5) 3-Y-O+ **£2,817** (£838; £418; £209) **Stalls** Low

Form RPR

1 **Swop (IRE)** 4-9-0 0 AshleyHamblett(5) 8 81+
(L M Cumani) *t.k.h towards rr: hdwy over 2f out: wd and bmpd ent st: led ins fnl f: drvn out* **14/1**

3344 2 1 **Alpes Maritimes**[20] 6081 3-9-3 74 DarryllHolland 13 70
(G Wragg) *sn stdd towards rr: effrt and wd st: r.o to take 2nd nr fin* **9/4**[1]

020 3 1 **Mini Mosa**[59] 5013 3-8-12 70 RobertHavlin 9 65+
(J H M Gosden) *chsd ldrs: rdn 2f out: kpt on fnl f* **6/1**

00 4 shd **Interactive (IRE)**[28] 5873 4-9-0 0 KirstyMilczarek(5) 10 67
(Andrew Turnell) *pressed ldr tl ins fnl f: hrd rdn: one pce* **40/1**

-42 5 hd **Cinnamon Hill**[20] 6094 3-8-12 0 KDarley 1 61
(Eve Johnson Houghton) *led tl ins fnl f: no ex* **13/2**

040 6 hd **Labor Day (IRE)**[124] 2998 3-8-12 70 JimmyFortune 5 61+
(J H M Gosden) *plld hrd: in tch: lost pl 4f out: swtchd rt over 2f out: rallied over 1f out: no imp fnl f* **7/2**[2]

U 7 1 1/2 **North South Divide (IRE)**[19] 6097 3-9-3 0 GeorgeBaker 6 62
(P Mitchell) *dwlt: plld hrd in rr: gd hdwy to chse ldrs over 1f out: no ex fnl f* **25/1**

36 8 5 **He's My Best (USA)**[151] 2173 3-9-3 0 TPQueally 4 48
(J Noseda) *in tch: rdn to chse ldrs ent st: wknd qckly over 1f out* **4/1**[3]

9 3 1/2 **Irish Cape** 4-9-0 0 JamesDoyle 11 34
(Mrs N Smith) *plld hrd: towards rr tl hdwy to join ldrs over 4f out: wknd qckly over 1f out* **25/1**

000 10 1 1/4 **Lady Lorins**[30] 5816 3-8-9 50 TravisBlock(3) 2 30
(Andrew Turnell) *in tch: drvn along over 3f out: wknd over 2f out* **66/1**

0-0 11 4 **She Knows Too Much**[14] 6229 3-8-12 0 OscarUrbina 3 19
(A M Hales) *prom 5f* **66/1**

005 12 10 **Broad Town Girl**[217] 788 4-9-0 30 LiamJones 12 —
(Mrs H Sweeting) *s.i.s: wd: hdwy and in tch 5f out: wknd 3f out: eased whn no ch fnl f* **66/1**

0 13 3 1/2 **De Port Heights (IRE)**[28] 5873 3-9-0 0 MarcHalford(3) 7 —
(M Madgwick) *dwlt: sn rdn along: a bhd: no ch fnl 3f* **66/1**

1m 25.53s (-0.36) **Going Correction** -0.075s/f (Stan)
WFA 3 from 4yo 2lb **13** Ran SP% **123.4**
Speed ratings (Par 103): **99,97,96,96,96 94,94,88,84,83 78,67,63**
CSF £45.79 TOTE £19.70: £5.20, £1.30, £2.30; EX 65.90.
Owner Mrs Angie Silver **Bred** Rathbarry Stud **Trained** Newmarket, Suffolk
■ Stewards' Enquiry : Ashley Hamblett two-day ban: careless riding (Nov 9-10)

FOCUS
An ordinary maiden and although a decent start by the winner, there are doubts about the placed horses and a couple of others close up make the form somewhat dubious.
Irish Cape Official explanation: jockey said filly ran too freely
Broad Town Girl Official explanation: jockey said filly hung right

6547 LINGFIELD PARK GOLF CLUB H'CAP 1m (P)
4:00 (4:01) (Class 5) (0-70,70) 3-Y-O+ **£2,817** (£838; £418; £209) **Stalls** High

Form RPR

1155 1 **Im Ova Ere Dad (IRE)**[21] 6063 4-9-7 70 TPQueally 3 81+
(D E Cantillon) *hld up towards rr: smooth hdwy 2f out: led over 1f out: hrd rdn and edgd rt ins fnl f: all out* **5/1**[2]

0100 2 shd **Torquemada (IRE)**[11] 6278 6-8-13 67 KirstyMilczarek(5) 6 78+
(J Akehurst) *hld up in rr: gd hdwy over 1f out: str chal fnl f: jst hld* **16/1**

-500 3 1 1/2 **Naughty Thoughts (IRE)**[139] 2534 3-8-8 65 AshleyHamblett(5) 9 72
(Andrew Turnell) *in tch: rdn to chse ldrs whn n.m.r ent st: kpt on u.p fnl f* **40/1**

1520 4 2 **Tremelo Pointe (IRE)**[39] 5555 3-8-12 67 TravisBlock(3) 12 70
(H Morrison) *wd: towards rr: effrt 2f out: styd on fnl f* **13/2**[3]

0002 5 nk **Smokin Joe**[12] 6260 6-8-13 62 (b) RobertHavlin 11 64+
(J R Best) *t.k.h towards rr: wd and effrt st: nrst fin* **8/1**

6343 6 shd **Aggravation**[21] 6063 5-9-7 70 GeorgeBaker 7 72
(D R C Elsworth) *s.s: bhd: gd hdwy on rail to chse ldrs over 1f out: hrd rdn and no imp fnl f* **7/2**[1]

6604 7 nk **King's Ransom**[12] 6269 4-9-2 65 (p) DarryllHolland 1 66
(S Gollings) *led after 1f tl over 1f out: no ex fnl f* **10/1**

4440 8 1 1/2 **Satin Braid**[42] 5475 3-8-9 64 MarcHalford(3) 5 63+
(D R C Elsworth) *chsd ldrs: rdn over 2f out: 5th and hld whn nt clr run ins fnl f: eased* **16/1**

6400 9 2 1/2 **Professor Twinkle**[25] 5943 3-9-3 69 (v) PaulDoe 4 61
(W J Knight) *chsd ldr tl wknd over 1f out* **14/1**

0300 10 nk **Meditation**[12] 6269 5-9-3 66 (p) JamesDoyle 10 57
(I A Wood) *led 1f: prom tl hrd rdn and wknd over 1f out* **16/1**

0414 11 5 **Henry The Seventh**[18] 6121 3-9-2 68 JimmyFortune 2 48
(J W Hills) *prom on rail: rdn over 3f out: sn wknd* **13/2**[3]

0000 12 3 **Tasweet (IRE)**[18] 6121 3-8-13 65 (b) KDarley 8 38
(T G Mills) *in tch: rdn 3f out: wknd 2f out* **10/1**

1m 37.27s (-2.16) **Going Correction** -0.075s/f (Stan)
WFA 3 from 4yo+ 3lb **12** Ran SP% **121.6**
Speed ratings (Par 103): **107,106,105,103,103 103,102,101,98,98 93,90**
CSF £84.75 CT £2938.10 TOTE £4.60: £1.50, £5.70, £11.20; EX 99.30 Place 6 £5,478.95, Place 5 £1,989.38.
Owner Allan Milton **Bred** Golden Vale Stud **Trained** Newmarket, Suffolk
■ Stewards' Enquiry : T P Queally one-day ban: careless riding (Nov 9)

FOCUS
A fair handicap run at a strong pace and solid form that should work out.
Satin Braid Official explanation: jockey said filly was denied a clear run
T/Plt: £13,628.70 to a £1 stake. Pool: £43,873.50. 2.35 winning tickets. T/Qpdt: £55.50 to a £1 stake. Pool: £4,455.00. 59.30 winning tickets. LM

6548 - (Foreign Racing) - See Raceform Interactive

[5239]LEOPARDSTOWN (L-H)

Monday, October 29

OFFICIAL GOING: Good to firm

6549a KILLAVULLAN STKS (GROUP 3) 7f

1:25 (1:30) 2-Y-O **£30,790** (£9,033; £4,304; £1,466)

RPR

1 **Jupiter Pluvius (USA)**[8] 6362 2-9-1 .... JAHeffernan 8 103
(A P O'Brien, Ire) *trckd ldrs: rdn and prog to ld under 1f out: styd on wl* **6/4**[1]

2 ¾ **Famous Name**[43] 5458 2-9-1 .... PJSmullen 15 101
(D K Weld, Ire) *dwlt sltly and hld up: prog fr 1/2-way: rdn on outer ent st: 4th 1f out: kpt on wl fnl f* **4/1**[2]

3 ½ **Billyford (IRE)**[17] 6161 2-9-1 100.............................. FMBerry 11 100
(Liam Roche, Ire) *prom: led over 2f out: rdn and hdd 1f out: sn no ex* **16/1**

4 ¾ **Great War Eagle (USA)**[17] 6161 2-9-1 ....(t) WMLordan 1 98
(David Wachman, Ire) *hld up: prog fr 2f out: 6th over 1f out: kpt on wl wout threatening cl home* **6/1**[3]

5 shd **Linsalata (IRE)**[9] 6346 2-8-12 91.............................. KJManning 10 95
(J S Bolger, Ire) *mid-div: 6th 3f out: rdn to ld briefly 1f out: sn hdd and no ex* **16/1**

6 shd **Mr Medici (IRE)**[24] 5996 2-9-1 92.............................. DPMcDonogh 12 98
(Kevin Prendergast, Ire) *prom: rdn in 3rd 2f out: no ex fnl f* **14/1**

7 1 ¾ **Capt Chaos (IRE)**[15] 6215 2-9-1 101.............................. JMurtagh 6 93
(Edward Lynam, Ire) *hld up in rr: rdn and no imp fr 2f out* **16/1**

8 hd **Windsor Palace (IRE)**[10] 6321 2-9-1 85.............................. SMLevey 4 93
(A P O'Brien, Ire) *dwlt sltly and in rr: rdn and no imp fr 2f out* **33/1**

9 nk **Great Rumpuscat (USA)**[15] 6213 2-9-1 .... DavidMcCabe 7 92
(A P O'Brien, Ire) *in rr of mid-div: rdn and no imp fr 2f out* **10/1**

10 2 ½ **Pencil Hill (IRE)**[132] 2732 2-9-1 106.............................. PShanahan 9 86
(Tracey Collins, Ire) *mid-div: no imp fr 2f out* **13/2**

11 ½ **Yali (IRE)**[8] 6365 2-8-12 83.............................. RPCleary 14 82
(Francis Ennis, Ire) *mid-div: rdn and wknd fr 2f out* **33/1**

12 ¾ **Northgate (IRE)**[17] 6161 2-9-1 90..............................(b) CDHayes 13 83
(Joseph G Murphy, Ire) *mid-div: rdn and wknd fr 2f out* **50/1**

13 dist **Divinitus**[29] 5844 2-9-1 .... MJKinane 3 —
(M J Grassick, Ire) *mid-div: pushed along whn hmpd 2f out: immediately virtually p.u: t.o* **20/1**

R **Amended**[40] 5548 2-8-12 .... SMGorey 5 —
(D K Weld, Ire) *sn led: hdd over 2f out: wkng whn rn out through rail 2f out* **100/1**

1m 29.19s (-3.01) **Going Correction** -0.25s/f (Firm) **15** Ran SP% **134.6**
Speed ratings: **107,106,105,104,104 104,102,102,101,99 98,97,—,—**
CSF £7.80 TOTE £2.20: £1.40, £1.80, £4.20; DF 9.10.
Owner Mrs John Magnier **Bred** H Smooth Fahlgren **Trained** Ballydoyle, Co Tipperary

FOCUS
Traditionally a decent Group 3 prize, run at a solid pace. The first six were fairly closely covered at the finish and the form can be rated through the third and fourth. Jupiter Pluvius goes into the winter now as short as 12/1 in some ante-post lists for next year's 2,000 Guineas.

NOTEBOOK
Jupiter Pluvius(USA) ◆, a belated debut winner over 6f at the Curragh eight days previously, had been the subject of ante-post support for the 2000 Guineas prior to his racecourse bow and the fact he was reappearing again quickly here - in an event his connections sent out Footstepsinthesand to win in 2004 before going on to Classic success at Newmarket - is an indication of just how highly he is regarded. He was always to the fore, travelling kindly, and showed a most willing attitude when pulled out for his effort nearing the final furlong. Always just doing enough, he relished the extra furlong, and is clearly versatile as regards underfoot conditions. He was later promoted further in the ante-post betting for the 2000 Guineas and, while he has only won a maiden and a Group 3, it would be no surprise to see him emerge as Ballydoyle's leading candidate for that event next year. (op 2/1)
Famous Name, beaten around nine lengths by New Approach in the Group 1 National Stakes last time, was given a patient ride on this drop in grade and emerged to join the leaders turning for home. He ultimately had every chance, but his early exertions from his outside stall eventually told and he was always being held by the winner at the business end. Like that rival he rates a decent prospect for next year where an extra furlong ought to prove in his favour, but whether he will get further than 1m is not certain. (op 4/1 tchd 9/2)
Billyford(IRE), who posted a career-best effort when just denied by Great War Eagle in Listed company at Dundalk 17 days previously, ran a solid race in defeat under a positive ride and reversed form with that rival on this return to the turf. He has had a great year, progressing from nursery success, and it is hoped he can maintain his improvement with a winter over his back to be an even better three-year-old. A sound benchmark for this form. (op 14/1)
Great War Eagle(USA), narrowly off the mark in Listed company at Dundalk last time, had to wait for his challenge on this return to turf and step up in class. He stayed on well towards the finish and just failed to confirm Dundalk form with the third, but this still rates another decent effort and he looks sure to enjoy a stiffer test as a three-year-old. (op 5/1)
Linsalata(IRE), who won her maiden over course and distance in July, stepped up on her facile success at Cork nine days previously and came there with every chance on this return to 7f. She was not beaten at all far and, a typically progressive filly from her stable, this was her best effort to date in defeat.
Mr Medici(IRE), off the mark at the fifth attempt over 1m at Gowran last time, posted another improved display in defeat and was another not beaten far. He just lacked the pace where it mattered on this drop back to 7f and should resume winning ways when stepping back up in trip.
Pencil Hill(IRE), last seen finishing fourth in the Coventry Stakes at Royal Ascot, has presumably been given time since that effort and was somewhat of a surprise inclusion. He never really figured and it is hard to know whether he got the extra furlong as he was beaten too far out. This was unsatisfactory, but he still rates a Group-race prospect for next year, most likely over sprint distances. (op 5/1)

6553a J.R.A. H'CAP 1m

3:25 (3:31) (50-80,80) 3-Y-0+ **£5,836** (£1,359; £599; £346)

RPR

1 **Poppyfield (GER)**[5] 6445 6-9-9 75..............................(b) PJSmullen 2 78
(H Rogers, Ire) *trckd ldrs: rdn 2f out: rdn to ld ins fnl f: kpt on wl* **14/1**

2 ¾ **Reload (IRE)**[24] 5994 4-9-8 74.............................. JMurtagh 8 75
(Thomas Mullins, Ire) *trckd ldrs on inner: rdn in 7th 2f out: styd on wl fnl f: wnt 2nd cl home* **4/1**[1]

3 shd **Drifting Snow**[9] 6350 3-8-13 78.............................. EJMcNamara[(10)] 1 79
(D K Weld, Ire) *sn led: rdn and strly pressed fr 2f out: hdd ins fnl f: kpt on same pce* **13/2**[2]

4 1 ¼ **Kilmannin (IRE)**[1] 6521 7-8-8 70..............................(bt) SMMcGuinness[(10)] 7 68
(H Rogers, Ire) *hld up in rr: prog on outer fr 1/2-way: 6th 2f out: kpt on wout threatening fnl f* **12/1**

5 shd **Regaleya (IRE)**[1] 6521 4-9-7 73..............................(t) WJSupple 15 71
(H Rogers, Ire) *mid-div: prog into 5th 2f out: rdn and kpt on one pce* **20/1**

6 1 **Silly Dancer (IRE)**[7] 6396 4-9-4 80.............................. GPGriffin[(10)] 10 76
(Adrian McGuinness, Ire) *s.i.s: sn mid-div: rdn in 8th 2f out: kpt on one pce* **10/1**

7 nk **Araschan (FR)**[10] 6323 4-9-8 74.............................. FMBerry 9 69
(H Rogers, Ire) *s.i.s: in rr to 2f out: r.o strly fnl f* **12/1**

8 shd **Talihoya (IRE)**[24] 5995 4-9-11 77..............................(p) RPCleary 5 72
(M Halford, Ire) *in rr of mid-div: rdn and sme prog fr 2f out: 9th 1f out: kpt on* **14/1**

9 shd **Distant Piper (IRE)**[9] 6350 4-9-1 77.............................. IJBrennan[(10)] 3 72
(Adrian McGuinness, Ire) *hld up: rdn and kpt on wout threatening fr 2f out* **16/1**

10 ½ **Nans Best (IRE)**[5] 6444 3-9-3 72.............................. PShanahan 11 66
(Liam McAteer, Ire) *trckd ldrs: rdn and no imp fr 2f out* **7/1**[3]

11 ¾ **Dianella (IRE)**[17] 6163 3-9-1 73..............................(b) PBBeggy[(3)] 18 65
(David P Myerscough, Ire) *trckd ldrs: 4th 2f out: sn rdn and no imp* **10/1**

12 1 ¾ **Waitingforanalibi**[31] 5788 4-9-9 75.............................. WMLordan 12 63
(T J O'Mara, Ire) *a towards rr* **14/1**

13 1 ¼ **Littleton Telchar (USA)**[203] 986 7-9-7 73.............................. CDHayes 6 58
(S W Hall) *hld up: prog into 10th 3f out: sn no imp* **12/1**

14 shd **Mac Don (IRE)**[5] 6444 3-9-6 75..............................(b[1]) KJManning 4 60
(Eamon Tyrrell, Ire) *a towards rr* **25/1**

15 1 ¼ **Tar (IRE)**[8] 6369 3-9-0 69..............................(b) DPMcDonogh 17 51
(Kevin Prendergast, Ire) *mid-div: rdn and wknd fr 2f out* **14/1**

16 2 ½ **Famous Seamus (IRE)**[7] 6396 4-8-10 69.............................. PTownend[(7)] 19 46
(T J O'Mara, Ire) *a towards rr* **16/1**

17 ½ **Out Of Nothing**[7] 6396 4-9-0 73.............................. AmyKathleenParsons[(7)] 14 49
(F J Bowles, Ire) *mid-div: wknd fr 3f out* **14/1**

18 1 ½ **Dane Blue (IRE)**[7] 6396 5-9-0 73.............................. MHarley[(7)] 13 46
(S J Treacy, Ire) *trckd ldrs: rdn and wknd fr 2 1/2f out* **14/1**

19 1 ¼ **Hanicor (IRE)**[24] 6000 6-8-13 75.............................. JMHarney[(10)] 20 45
(Ms F M Crowley, Ire) *trckd ldrs: wknd fr 2 1/2f out* **25/1**

20 3 ½ **Rose Hip (IRE)**[17] 6163 3-9-1 73.............................. CPGeoghegan[(3)] 16 35
(Joseph G Murphy, Ire) *in tch early: wknd fr 2 1/2f out* **14/1**

1m 41.2s (-3.20) **Going Correction** -0.25s/f (Firm)
WFA 3 from 4yo+ 3lb **20** Ran SP% **158.0**
Speed ratings: **106,105,105,103,103 102,102,102,102,101 101,99,98,97,96 94,93,92,90,87**
CSF £84.75 CT £452.15 TOTE £18.00: £3.40, £1.80, £1.60, £4.10; DF 100.60.
Owner Mrs Eimear Rogers **Bred** Gestut Park Wiedingen **Trained** Ardee, Co. Louth

NOTEBOOK
Littleton Telchar(USA), stepping back up in trip and with the ground to suit, never got involved after being held up.

6555a ELMWOOD H'CAP 1m 6f

4:25 (4:29) (60-90,85) 3-Y-0+ **£7,003** (£1,631; £719; £415)

RPR

1 **Rockys Choice (IRE)**[8] 6368 4-9-3 75..............................(b) KarenKenny[(10)] 3 86+
(Peter Casey, Ire) *trckd ldrs: 2nd 3f out: rdn to ld 1f out: kpt on wl* **8/1**

2 ¾ **Queen Althea (IRE)**[42] 5125 3-7-12 65..............................(p) EJMcNamara[(10)] 1 72
(Noel Meade, Ire) *sn led: jnd briefly 1/2-way: rdn and jnd again 2f out: hdd 1f out: kpt on same pce fnl f* **5/2**[1]

3 1 ½ **Hearthstead Dream**[29] 5847 6-9-10 72..............................(b) PJSmullen 5 77
(D K Weld, Ire) *trckd ldrs: rdn to dispute ld 2f out: hdd 1f out: no ex* **11/2**[2]

4 2 **Caltra Princess (IRE)**[43] 5461 3-8-11 68.............................. PShanahan 8 70
(Tracey Collins, Ire) *in rr of mid-div: 10th 5f out: kpt on wout threatening to go 4th ins fnl f* **14/1**

5 1 **Tangible**[38] 5586 5-8-13 61.............................. MCHussey 4 62
(Liam McAteer, Ire) *mid-div: 10th 1/2-way: rdn and kpt on fr 3f out* **14/1**

6 3 **Luminous One (IRE)**[15] 6217 3-10-0 85..............................(p) KJManning 6 82
(J S Bolger, Ire) *mid-div: 6th 3f out: rdn and kpt on one pce st* **14/1**

7 ½ **Passarelle (USA)**[8] 6368 3-9-2 73.............................. JAHeffernan 10 69
(M J Grassick, Ire) *trckd ldrs: 8th 3f out: sn rdn and no imp* **8/1**

8 1 ¼ **Not To Know**[17] 6164 3-8-13 70.............................. FMBerry 15 64
(John A Quinn, Ire) *bhd: kpt on fr 3f out* **11/1**

9 ½ **Flamingo Rainbow (GER)**[44] 5439 5-9-7 69.............................. WJSupple 7 62
(H Rogers, Ire) *mid-div: rdn and no imp fr 3f out* **16/1**

10 ½ **El Cerro**[12] 3892 3-8-11 68.............................. MJKinane 19 61
(Joseph Crowley, Ire) *towards rr: prog fr 1/2-way: no imp fr 3f out* **12/1**

11 1 **King Of Prussia (IRE)**[39] 5577 3-9-2 73.............................. WJLee 20 64
(Ms F M Crowley, Ire) *towards rr: rdn and no imp fr 3f out* **25/1**

12 2 ½ **King Of Redfield (IRE)**[24] 5999 3-8-4 61.............................. WMLordan 2 49
(J P Broderick, Ire) *trckd ldrs: rdn and wknd fr 3f out* **14/1**

13 3 **Golden Hare (IRE)**[8] 6368 6-9-2 64.............................. RPCleary 11 48
(Aidan Anthony Howard, Ire) *trckd ldrs: rdn and wknd fr 4f out* **14/1**

14 nk **Hyde Park Flight (IRE)**[19] 6118 3-7-11 61.............................. KTO'Neill[(7)] 14 44
(C P Donoghue, Ire) *nvr a factor* **50/1**

15 2 **Pretty Demanding (IRE)**[8] 6368 3-9-3 74.............................. DPMcDonogh 16 54
(M G Quinlan) *in rr of mid-div: rdn and no imp fr 3f out* **7/1**[3]

16 27 **Kalinina (IRE)**[19] 6117 4-9-9 74.............................. PBBeggy[(3)] 12 17
(Miss A M Winters, Ire) *mid-div: rdn and wknd fr 3f out: t.o* **33/1**

17 shd **Keel Castle Maine (IRE)**[40] 5547 6-8-13 61.............................. CDHayes 13 3
(Patrick Joseph Hayes, Ire) *dwlt and in rr: rdn and sme prog 1/2-way: sn wknd: t.o* **16/1**

18 3 ½ **Newlands North (IRE)**[52] 5105 6-9-0 72.............................. NiamhMurphy[(10)] 17 10
(M J P O'Brien, Ire) *prom: disp ld briefly 1/2-way: rdn and wknd fr 4f out: t.o* **14/1**

3m 1.06s (-4.84) **Going Correction** -0.25s/f (Firm)
WFA 3 from 4yo+ 9lb **20** Ran SP% **155.2**
Speed ratings: **103,102,101,100,100 98,98,97,97,96 96,94,93,92,91 76,76,74**
CSF £34.97 CT £141.39 TOTE £14.20: £4.70, £1.60, £1.70, £2.90; DF 58.50.
Owner J Bowe **Bred** James Nally **Trained** Stamullen, Co Meath

■ Stewards' Enquiry : Karen Kenny caution: careless riding

NOTEBOOK
Pretty Demanding(IRE), having her fifth race of the season in Ireland, put up a rare disappointing effort and may have had enough for the year. (op 6/1)

T/Jkpt: @1,226.30. Pool of @4,905.50 - 3 winning units. T/Plt: @79.00. Pool of @8,616.00. II

6554 - (Foreign Racing) - See Raceform Interactive

5239 **LEOPARDSTOWN** (L-H)

Monday, October 29

OFFICIAL GOING: Good to firm

6555a ELMWOOD H'CAP 1m 6f

4:25 (4:29) (60-90,85) 3-Y-O+ **£7,003** (£1,631; £719; £415)

RPR

1 **Rockys Choice (IRE)**[8] 6368 4-9-3 75.....................(b) KarenKenny(10) 3 86+
(Peter Casey, Ire) *trckd ldrs: 2nd 3f out: rdn to ld 1f out: kpt on wl* **8/1**

2 ¾ **Queen Althea (IRE)**[42] 5125 3-7-12 65..................(p) EJMcNamara(10) 1 72
(Noel Meade, Ire) *sn led: jnd briefly 1/2-way: rdn and jnd again 2f out: hdd 1f out: kpt on same pce fnl f* **5/2**[1]

3 1 ½ **Hearthstead Dream**[29] 5847 6-9-10 72..........................(b) PJSmullen 5 77
(D K Weld, Ire) *trckd ldrs: rdn to dispute ld 2f out: hdd 1f out: no ex* **11/2**[2]

4 2 **Caltra Princess (IRE)**[43] 5461 3-8-11 68......................... PShanahan 8 70
(Tracey Collins, Ire) *in rr of mid-div: 10th 5f out: kpt on wout threatening to go 4th ins fnl f* **14/1**

5 1 **Tangible**[38] 5586 5-8-13 61.. MCHussey 4 62
(Liam McAteer, Ire) *mid-div: 10th 1/2-way: rdn and kpt on fr 3f out* **14/1**

6 3 **Luminous One (IRE)**[15] 6217 3-10-0 85.........................(p) KJManning 6 82
(J S Bolger, Ire) *mid-div: 6th 3f out: rdn and kpt on one pce st* **14/1**

7 ½ **Passarelle (USA)**[8] 6368 3-9-2 73.................................. JAHeffernan 10 69
(M J Grassick, Ire) *trckd ldrs: 8th 3f out: sn rdn and no imp* **8/1**

8 1 ¼ **Not To Know**[17] 6164 3-8-13 70... FMBerry 15 64
(John A Quinn, Ire) *bhd: kpt on fr 3f out* **11/1**

9 ½ **Flamingo Rainbow (GER)**[44] 5439 5-9-7 69...................... WJSupple 7 62
(H Rogers, Ire) *mid-div: rdn and no imp fr 3f out* **16/1**

10 ½ **El Cerro**[12] 3892 3-8-11 68.. MJKinane 19 61
(Joseph Crowley, Ire) *towards rr: prog fr 1/2-way: no imp fr 3f out* **12/1**

11 1 **King Of Prussia (IRE)**[39] 5577 3-9-2 73................................ WJLee 20 64
(Ms F M Crowley, Ire) *towards rr: rdn and no imp fr 3f out* **25/1**

12 2 ½ **King Of Redfield (IRE)**[24] 5999 3-8-4 61........................ WMLordan 2 49
(J P Broderick, Ire) *trckd ldrs: rdn and wknd fr 3f out* **14/1**

13 3 **Golden Hare (IRE)**[8] 6368 6-9-2 64..................................... RPCleary 11 48
(Aidan Anthony Howard, Ire) *trckd ldrs: rdn and wknd fr 4f out* **14/1**

14 nk **Hyde Park Flight (IRE)**[19] 6118 3-7-11 61...................... KTO'Neill(7) 14 44
(C P Donoghue, Ire) *nvr a factor* **50/1**

15 2 **Pretty Demanding (IRE)**[8] 6368 3-9-3 74.................. DPMcDonogh 16 54
(M G Quinlan) *in rr of mid-div: rdn and no imp fr 3f out* **7/1**[3]

16 27 **Kalinina (IRE)**[19] 6117 4-9-9 74.................................... PBBeggy(3) 12 17
(Miss A M Winters, Ire) *mid-div: rdn and wknd fr 3f out: t.o* **33/1**

17 shd **Keel Castle Maine (IRE)**[40] 5547 6-8-13 61....................... CDHayes 13 3
(Patrick Joseph Hayes, Ire) *dwlt and in rr: rdn and sme prog 1/2-way: sn wknd: t.o* **16/1**

18 3 ½ **Newlands North (IRE)**[52] 5105 6-9-0 72............... NiamhMurphy(10) 17 10
(M J P O'Brien, Ire) *prom: disp ld briefly 1/2-way: rdn and wknd fr 4f out: t.o* **14/1**

3m 1.06s (-4.84) **Going Correction** -0.25s/f (Firm)
WFA 3 from 4yo+ 9lb **20** Ran SP% **155.2**
Speed ratings: **103,102,101,100,100 98,98,97,97,96 96,94,93,92,91 76,76,74**
CSF £34.97 CT £141.39 TOTE £14.20: £4.70, £1.60, £1.70, £2.90; DF 58.50.
Owner J Bowe **Bred** James Nally **Trained** Stamullen, Co Meath
■ Stewards' Enquiry : Karen Kenny caution: careless riding

NOTEBOOK

Pretty Demanding(IRE), having her fifth race of the season in Ireland, put up a rare disappointing effort and may have had enough for the year. (op 6/1)

T/Jkpt: @1,226.30. Pool of @4,905.50 - 3 winning units. T/Plt: @79.00. Pool of @8,616.00. II

6556 - (Foreign Racing) - See Raceform Interactive

6325 **CATTERICK** (L-H)

Tuesday, October 30

OFFICIAL GOING: Good (good to firm in places; 9.4)

Wind: Light, across Weather: Fine and dry

6557 COWTHORPE MEDIAN AUCTION MAIDEN STKS 5f 212y

1:30 (1:32) (Class 6) 2-Y-O **£2,730** (£806; £403) **Stalls** Low

Form RPR

65 1 **Seta Pura**[11] 6306 2-8-12 0.. RoystonFfrench 1 61
(Mrs A Duffield) *trckd ldrs: swtchd lft and hdwy wl over 1f out: rdn to ld ins fnl f: kpt on wl* **6/1**[3]

2 hd **Premier Danseur (IRE)** 2-9-3 0....................................... GregFairley 9 65
(M Johnston) *s.i.s: in tch 1/2-way: hdwy to chse ldrs 2f out: rdn and styng on whn nt clr run ins fnl f: kpt on wl towards fin* **4/1**[2]

03 3 ½ **Bishopbriggs (USA)**[11] 6303 2-9-3 0................................... TPQueally 5 64
(D J Murphy) *t.k.h: cl up: effrt and ev ch wl over 1f out: sn rdn: drvn ins fnl f and one pce towards fin* **11/8**[1]

2020 4 1 ½ **Tanley**[17] 6326 2-9-3 56... DavidAllan 4 59
(J F Coupland) *led: rdn along wl 2f out: drvn over 1f out: hdd & wknd ins fnl f* **16/1**

0 5 ¾ **Royal Acclamation (IRE)**[10] 6326 2-9-3 0............. SilvestreDeSousa 7 57
(G A Harker) *stdd s: hld up towards rr: hdwy 2f out: styd on ins fnl f: nrst fin* **8/1**

0 6 1 ½ **Stagecoach Topaz (USA)**[68] 4733 2-9-3 0.............. DeanMcKeown 10 52
(M Johnston) *chsd ldrs: rdn along wl over 2f out and grad wknd* **12/1**

50 7 4 **Laureldean Breeze (USA)**[22] 6065 2-8-12 0................ PaulHanagan 6 37+
(R A Fahey) *chsd ldrs: rdn along 1/2-way: sn btn* **14/1**

5 8 7 **Riki Wiki Wheels**[123] 3065 2-9-3 0.................................. MickyFenton 3 19
(P T Midgley) *in tch: rdn along 1/2-way: sn wknd* **25/1**

9 13 **Make A Bid** 2-8-9 0.. AndrewMullen(3) 8 —
(J R Norton) *s.i.s: a bhd* **50/1**

05 P **Aerialist**[8] 6384 2-8-12 0... TomEaves 2 —
(A Berry) *s.i.s and bhd: swvd bdly lft 2f out and sn p.u* **40/1**

1m 15.0s (1.00) **Going Correction** +0.05s/f (Good) **10** Ran SP% **116.0**
Speed ratings (Par 93): **95,94,94,92,91 89,83,74,57,—**
CSF £29.65 TOTE £7.20: £2.00, £1.80, £1.10; EX 32.30.
Owner Miss K Rausing **Bred** Miss K Rausing **Trained** Constable Burton, N Yorks

FOCUS

A modest maiden but solid enough, although limited as the proximity of the 56-rated fourth suggests.

NOTEBOOK

Seta Pura had to be niggled along through the early stages and this sharp track was not ideal, but she ran on gamely in the straight. She would probably have been beaten had the runner-up enjoyed a better trip, and the bare form looks modest, but at least she has the right attitude. (op 11-2 tchd 5-1)

Premier Danseur(IRE) ◆, son of Noverre, half-brother to among others top-class US filly Balletto, a multiple winner over 1m-1m1f on dirt, out of a dual 1m4f winner, looked unlucky not to make a winning debut. He had just a small gap to try and get through for much of the way up the straight and looked intimidated by the other jockeys' whips, and it was too late by the time he finally got in the clear. The bare form is modest, but he should improve plenty. (op 11-4)

Bishopbriggs(USA), dropped back from 1m, showed plenty of speed, albeit he was a little keen, but just found a couple too strong in the straight. He is now qualified for a handicap mark. (op 13-8 tchd 2-1)

Tanley ran a big race in defeat but, rated just 56, his proximity does little for the form. He will be better off in low-grade handicaps. (op 20-1 tchd 14-1)

Royal Acclamation(IRE) is still learning and he should find his level once handicapped. (op 10-1)

Riki Wiki Wheels Official explanation: jockey said colt slipped turning into home straight

6558 RACINGUK.TV H'CAP 1m 3f 214y

2:00 (2:00) (Class 6) (0-60,60) 3-Y-O+ **£2,730** (£806; £403) **Stalls** High

Form RPR

4024 1 **Star Of Angels**[14] 6257 3-9-2 60.. GregFairley 11 74
(M Johnston) *hld up in rr: gd hdwy on inner 4f out: swtchd rt and chsd ldrs 2f out: rdn to ld appr fnl f: sn clr* **7/1**[3]

0060 2 6 **Intavac Boy**[10] 6330 6-8-10 50................................. MichaelJStainton(3) 9 55
(S P Griffiths) *in tch: hdwy to chse ldr 3f out: rdn to ld wl over 1f out: drvn and hdd appr fnl f: kpt on same pce* **14/1**

0055 3 ½ **Rigat**[14] 6258 4-9-3 54... PhillipMakin 8 58
(T D Barron) *hld up: hdwy over 4f out: rdn to chse ldng pair over 2f out: drvn and kpt on same pce appr fnl f* **9/2**[2]

2060 4 2 ½ **Ashwell Rose**[31] 5803 5-9-3 54.......................................(v) PatCosgrave 2 54
(J R Jenkins) *midfield: hdwy and in tch 4f out: rdn along 3f out: kpt on u.p fnl 2f* **33/1**

0035 5 3 **Eijaaz (IRE)**[35] 5704 6-9-3 54...............................(v[1]) SilvestreDeSousa 5 49
(G A Harker) *in tch: effrt over 3f out: sn rdn along and plugged on same pce* **8/1**

2300 6 nk **Starcross Maid**[10] 6325 5-8-11 48..................................... TPQueally 3 43
(J F Coupland) *midfield: hdwy 4f out: rdn along to chse ldrs 2f out: sn drvn and no imp* **50/1**

-050 7 5 **Annibale Caro**[10] 6330 5-8-11 51................................ MarkLawson(3) 15 38
(Grant Tuer) *led: clr 1/2-way: rdn along 3f out: hdd wl over 1f out and sn wknd* **22/1**

0220 8 1 **Boppys Pride**[14] 6258 4-9-5 56.. PaulHanagan 13 41
(R A Fahey) *in rr: pushed along and sme hdwy 3f out: sn rdn and kpt on appr fnl f: nvr nr ldrs* **11/4**[1]

0360 9 ¾ **Barbirolli**[16] 6196 5-9-6 60... LukeMorris(3) 12 44
(W M Brisbourne) *hld up towards rr: sme hdwy 3f out: sn rdn along and nvr a factor* **12/1**

1000 10 1 ¼ **Parchment (IRE)**[10] 6330 5-9-4 55....................................... TomEaves 4 37
(A J Lockwood) *chsd ldrs: rdn along over 3f out: wknd over 2f out* **16/1**

0350 11 2 **Matinee Idol**[8] 6383 4-8-12 49.................................. PaulMulrennan 10 28
(Mrs S Lamyman) *a in rr* **100/1**

6610 12 13 **Dispol Peto**[14] 6259 7-8-12 49.............................(vt) AdrianTNicholls 1 7
(R Johnson) *chsd ldrs: rdn along 3f out: sn drvn and wknd* **20/1**

4630 13 4 **Miss Sure Bond (IRE)**[28] 5890 4-8-9 51...................(p) SladeO'Hara(5) 7 3
(G R Oldroyd) *a in rr* **50/1**

2000 14 2 **English Archer**[5] 6453 4-8-4 48.................................. DeanHeslop(7) 6 —
(W M Brisbourne) *a in rr* **22/1**

4061 15 5 **Mcqueen (IRE)**[10] 6330 7-9-9 60.................................... MickyFenton 14 —
(J T Stimpson) *chsd clr ldr: rdn along 4f out: wknd 3f out* **11/1**

2m 39.63s (0.63) **Going Correction** +0.05s/f (Good)
WFA 3 from 4yo+ 7lb **15** Ran SP% **118.3**
Speed ratings (Par 101): **99,95,94,93,91 90,87,86,86,85 84,75,72,71,68**
CSF £91.17 CT £493.70 TOTE £7.10: £2.10, £3.60, £2.20; EX 125.30.
Owner R S Brookhouse **Bred** R S Brookhouse **Trained** Middleham Moor, N Yorks

FOCUS

A weak middle-distance handicap run at a strong early pace. The form is rated at face value through the third.

Dispol Peto Official explanation: jockey said gelding had no more to give

6559 GO RACING AT WETHERBY THIS FRIDAY H'CAP 5f 212y

2:30 (2:31) (Class 5) (0-75,74) 3-Y-O **£2,914** (£867; £433; £216) **Stalls** Low

Form RPR

1250 1 **Expensive Art (IRE)**[42] 5495 3-8-7 63............................... MickyFenton 1 70
(N A Callaghan) *dwlt: sn in tch: hdwy on inner 2f out: sn rdn: styd on appr fnl f: led last 100yds* **9/2**[3]

4015 2 1 **Feelin Foxy**[21] 6089 3-8-13 69... TPQueally 2 73
(J G Given) *chsd ldr tl led after 2f: rdn along wl over 1f out: drvn ent fnl f: hdd and no ex last 100yds* **13/2**

4134 3 nk **Distant Sun (USA)**[10] 6331 3-9-4 74................................(p) TomEaves 4 77
(I Semple) *trckd ldrs: effrt 2f out and ev ch tl rdn and nt qckn wl ins fnl f* **4/1**[2]

0540 4 1 ¼ **Argentine (IRE)**[18] 6157 3-8-12 73............................... GaryBartley(5) 6 72+
(L Lungo) *stdd s: hld up and bhd: hdwy 2f out: swtchd rt over 1f out: rdn and kpt on ins fnl f: nrst fin* **11/2**

6500 5 nk **Ingleby Princess**[24] 6020 3-8-11 67.................................. PaulFessey 8 65
(T D Barron) *in rr: hdwy on inner over 2f out: sn rdn and kpt on same pce* **14/1**

0310 6 nk **Umpa Loompa (IRE)**[6] 6424 3-8-5 61....................(v) SilvestreDeSousa 9 58
(D Nicholls) *led 2f: cl up: rdn along 2f out and ev ch tl drvn appr last and grad wknd* **7/1**

1453 7 shd **Rainbow Fox**[14] 6256 3-8-13 69....................................... PaulHanagan 5 66
(R A Fahey) *stmbld s and bhd: hdwy over 2f out: sn rdn and kpt on same pce* **7/2**[1]

0500 8 10 **Alloro**[38] 5622 3-8-4 60 oh15.. AdrianTNicholls 7 25
(D W Thompson) *a towards rr* **200/1**

000 9 12 **Bella Grande**[38] 5625 3-8-4 60 oh15........................... RoystonFfrench 3 —
(Garry Moss) *a towards rr* **200/1**

1m 13.74s (-0.26) **Going Correction** +0.05s/f (Good) **9** Ran SP% **109.3**
Speed ratings (Par 101): **103,101,101,99,99 98,98,85,69**
CSF £30.71 CT £113.63 TOTE £5.70: £1.80, £1.80, £1.90; EX 34.80.
Owner Matthew Green **Bred** Stone Ridge Farm **Trained** Newmarket, Suffolk
■ Stewards' Enquiry : T P Queally two-day ban: used whip with excessive force (Nov 10-11)

FOCUS
A modest sprint handicap but straightforward form with the first three to their marks.

6560 TURFTV.CO.UK H'CAP 7f
3:00 (3:01) (Class 4) (0-85,81) 3-Y-O+ £4,857 (£1,445; £722; £360) Stalls Low

Form RPR

6350 1 **Bel Cantor**[8] 6381 4-8-11 77 AndrewMullen(3) 1 86
(W J H Ratcliffe) *cl up: rdn along 2f out: swtchd rt and hdwy to ld over 1f out: sn drvn and edgd lft: kpt on wl* 16/1

4212 2 3/4 **Crocodile Bay (IRE)**[16] 6203 4-9-1 78 AdrianTNicholls 3 85
(D Nicholls) *in tch hdwy over 2f out: swtchd rt and rdn over 1f out: drvn and styd on ins fnl f* 5/1[1]

5011 3 nk **Nuit Sombre (IRE)**[10] 6331 7-9-0 77 (p) SilvestreDeSousa 9 83
(G A Harker) *sn led: rdn along and edgd lft over 2f out: hdd over 1f out: drvn and hung rt ins fnl f: kpt on same pce* 9/1

5500 4 2 **Inaminute (IRE)**[27] 5907 4-8-7 73 AndrewElliott(3) 4 79+
(K R Burke) *chsd ldrs: hdwy 2f out: rdn and styng on whn hmpd ent fnl f: kpt on* 20/1

0005 5 nk **Coleorton Dancer**[9] 6355 5-9-2 79 TPQueally 13 79
(K A Ryan) *chsd ldrs: hdwy over 2f out: rdn wl over 1f out: drvn and one pce ent fnl f* 12/1

0640 6 nk **Imperial Echo (USA)**[11] 6301 6-9-3 80 PaulFessey 10 79
(T D Barron) *hld up and bhd: gd hdwy on inner wl over 1f out: styng on whn n.m.r ins fnl f: nrst fin* 9/1

3040 7 nk **Prince Namid**[8] 6381 5-9-2 79 RoystonFfrench 11 77
(Mrs A Duffield) *towards rr tl styd on fnl 2f: nrst fin* 16/1

2000 8 1 1/2 **Il Castagno (IRE)**[24] 6016 4-9-2 79 TomEaves 8 73
(B Smart) *midfield: effrt and sme hdwy 1/2-way: rdn along 2f out and sn no imp* 15/2[3]

0-00 9 1/2 **Winged Flight (USA)**[18] 6155 3-9-1 80 GregFairley 15 73
(M Johnston) *bhd tl sme late hdwy* 25/1

1564 10 1/2 **Viva Volta**[8] 6391 4-9-0 77 (b) DavidAllan 6 69
(T D Easterby) *chsd ldrs: rdn along 2f out: hld whn n.m.r ent fnl f: wknd* 8/1

0632 11 2 1/2 **King Harson**[10] 6331 8-8-8 71 ow1 (v) PatCosgrave 2 56
(J D Bethell) *chsd ldrs: rdn along over 2f out: drvn wl over 1f out and sn wknd* 8/1

0155 12 5 **Hazelhurst (IRE)**[40] 5560 4-8-4 67 PaulHanagan 14 38
(J Howard Johnson) *in tch on outer: rdn along 1/2-way: sn wknd* 16/1

1064 13 2 1/2 **Balakiref**[38] 5617 8-9-4 81 PaulMulrennan 12 46
(M Dods) *s.i.s: a in rr* 28/1

3400 14 3/4 **Hiccups**[38] 5617 7-9-1 78 PhillipMakin 5 41
(M Dods) *in tch: rdn along over 2f out and sn wknd* 7/1[2]

1m 27.02s (-0.34) **Going Correction** +0.05s/f (Good)
WFA 3 from 4yo+ 2lb 14 Ran SP% 120.5
Speed ratings (Par 105): **103,102,101,99,99 98,98,96,96,95 92,87,84,83**
CSF £92.04 CT £807.43 TOTE £23.50: £6.90, £1.70, £3.40; EX 196.90.
Owner W J H Ratcliffe **Bred** Henry And Mrs Rosemary Moszkowicz **Trained** Wensley, N Yorks

FOCUS
A fair handicap run at a good pace, although the first two held those positions throughout, and rated through the third to his latest mark.
Hiccups Official explanation: jockey said gelding had no more to give

6561 BOOK RACEDAY HOSPITALITY ON 01748 810165 H'CAP 1m 7f 177y
3:30 (3:31) (Class 5) (0-70,68) 3-Y-O+ £2,914 (£867; £433; £216) Stalls Low

Form RPR

3602 1 **Ha'Penny Beacon**[10] 6330 4-9-7 61 (v) MickyFenton 2 70+
(D Carroll) *midfield: hdwy 4f out: rdn to chse ldng pair 2f out: drvn and styd on wl fnl f to ld nr fin* 8/1[3]

3-65 2 1/2 **Calatagan (IRE)**[25] 5968 8-9-9 63 PaulHanagan 15 71
(J M Jefferson) *led: rdn clr 2f out: drvn ins fnl f: hdd and no ex nr fin* 4/1[2]

0400 3 1 **Forrest Flyer (IRE)**[27] 5906 3-7-10 49 oh3 DuranFentiman(3) 13 56
(Miss L A Perratt) *in tch: hdwy to chse ldr over 4f out: drvn 2f out: styd on u.p fnl f* 33/1

6020 4 8 **Merrymaker**[10] 6341 7-9-9 63 GregFairley 4 60
(W M Brisbourne) *hld up in rr: hdwy over 3f out: rdn 2f out: plugged on: nvr nr ldrs* 14/1

5063 5 3 **Cripsey Brook**[10] 6325 9-9-9 68 (t) JamesReveley(5) 5 62
(K G Reveley) *hld up in rr: hdwy 3f out: sn rdn and kpt on appr fnl f: nvr nr ldrs* 12/1

2204 6 1 3/4 **Dance Sauvage**[11] 6308 4-8-12 52 DavidAllan 3 44
(C W Thornton) *hld up in rr: hdwy 6f out: rdn along and in tch over 2f out: sn no imp* 8/1[3]

306 7 3 **Devilfishpoker Com**[10] 6330 3-8-2 52 (b) PaulFessey 12 40
(R C Guest) *chsd ldr: rdn along 4f out: drvn 3f out and sn wknd* 28/1

0030 8 nk **Emotive**[18] 5626 4-8-12 52 PaulMulrenan 7 40
(F P Murtagh) *in tch: rdn along over 3f out: sn drvn and no imp fnl 2f* 80/1

4063 9 1/2 **The Diamond Bond**[22] 6070 3-7-13 49 oh3 SilvestreDeSousa 14 36
(G R Oldroyd) *chsd ldrs: rdn along 4f out: drvn 3f out: sn wknd* 12/1

5353 10 4 **Group Force (IRE)**[10] 6330 3-8-6 56 RoystonFfrench 8 38
(M H Tompkins) *chsd ldrs: rdn along 4f out: drvn 3f out and sn wknd* 4/1[2]

0113 11 1 1/4 **Go Amwell**[16] 6200 4-9-1 55 PatCosgrave 6 36
(J R Jenkins) *hld up in rr: hdwy 6f out: rdn along over 3f out and sn btn* 7/2[1]

2560 12 1 **True (IRE)**[10] 6330 6-8-9 49 oh4 TomEaves 11 29
(Mrs S Lamyman) *hld up in rr: hdwy 6f out: rdn along over 3f out and sn wknd* 25/1

600 13 1/2 **Winter Lane**[20] 6109 3-7-13 52 AndrewMullen(3) 10 31
(J R Norton) *nvr btr than midfield* 50/1

6/00 14 dist **Penmon Point (IRE)**[34] 5739 4-8-9 49 oh4 AdrianTNicholls 1 —
(R Johnson) *prom: rdn along 1/2-way: sn lost pl and t.o fnl 4f* 200/1

0-00 15 2 **Niza D'Alm (FR)**[164] 1849 6-8-6 49 oh4 AndrewElliott(3) 9 —
(A Crook) *a in rr: t.o fnl 4f* 200/1

3m 32.73s (1.33) **Going Correction** +0.05s/f (Good)
WFA 3 from 4yo+ 10lb 15 Ran SP% 120.9
Speed ratings (Par 103): **98,97,97,93,91 90,89,89,88,86 86,85,85,—,—**
CSF £38.62 CT £1025.47 TOTE £10.80: £2.60, £2.80, £9.50; EX 59.30.
Owner Imperial Racing **Bred** Bishop Wilton Stud **Trained** Sledmere, E Yorks
■ Stewards' Enquiry : Greg Fairley two-day ban: careless riding (Nov 10-11)

FOCUS
A moderate staying handicap run at a reasonable pace and rated around the placed horses, and could be a little higher.

6562 COME RACING AGAIN NEXT TUESDAY H'CAP 5f
4:00 (4:01) (Class 6) (0-65,64) 3-Y-O+ £2,730 (£806; £403) Stalls Low

Form RPR

0021 1 **Spirit Of Coniston**[1] 6528 4-8-10 56 6ex AdrianTNicholls 9 73+
(D Nicholls) *cl up: led 2f out: sn rdn and edgd lft over 1f out: sn clr* 13/8[1]

4000 2 3 **Kings College Boy**[40] 5552 7-9-4 64 (b) PaulHanagan 7 70
(R A Fahey) *in rr: hdwy 2f out: rdn over 1f out: styd on ins fnl f* 12/1

012 3 1 1/4 **Royal Composer (IRE)**[41] 5522 4-8-13 59 (b) DavidAllan 4 61
(T D Easterby) *dwlt and bhd: hdwy 1/2-way: swtchd rt and nt clr run over 1f out and ins fnl f: kpt on* 13/2[2]

2160 4 nk **No Time (IRE)**[9] 6360 7-9-0 60 PatCosgrave 11 61
(A J McCabe) *chsd ldrs: hdwy over 2f out: rdn wl over 1f out and kpt on same pce ins fnl f* 16/1

3310 5 1 1/4 **She's Our Beauty (IRE)**[26] 5930 4-8-1 50 oh5 (p) DuranFentiman(3) 5 46
(S T Mason) *led: rdn along and hdd 2f out: grad wknd* 20/1

4301 6 1/2 **Baybshambles (IRE)**[21] 6078 3-8-11 57 TomEaves 1 51
(R E Barr) *in tch: hdwy on inner 2f out: sn rdn and n.m.r over 1f out: sn one pce* 13/2[2]

3000 7 3/4 **Tenancy (IRE)**[18] 6149 3-8-4 50 oh1 (p) GregFairley 6 42
(A J McCabe) *cl up: rdn along 2f out: sn drvn and grad wknd* 25/1

5435 8 1/2 **Throw The Dice**[25] 5969 5-8-6 52 (v) RoystonFfrench 2 42
(A Berry) *in tch: rdn along over 2f out and sn btn* 8/1

5231 9 nk **Jadan (IRE)**[26] 5930 6-8-7 53 (b) MickyFenton 10 42
(E J Alston) *dwlt: a in rr* 15/2[3]

652 10 1 1/4 **Rue Soleil**[4] 6466 3-8-9 58 JamieMoriarty(3) 3 42
(J R Weymes) *chsd ldrs: rdn along over 2f out and sn wknd* 20/1

0600 11 nk **High Reach**[12] 6283 7-8-9 62 (b) DeanHeslop(7) 13 45
(T D Barron) *chsd ldrs on outer: rdn over 2f out and sn wknd* 20/1

400 12 3 1/2 **Champagne Mindy**[32] 5781 3-8-4 50 oh5 SilvestreDeSousa 8 21
(Garry Moss) *stmbld s: a in rr* 100/1

61.41 secs (0.81) **Going Correction** +0.20s/f (Good) 12 Ran SP% 120.3
Speed ratings (Par 101): **101,96,94,93,91 90,89,88,88,86 85,80**
CSF £21.50 CT £109.36 TOTE £2.60: £1.40, £3.70, £2.40; EX 29.00 Place 6 £69.42, Place 5 £58.24.
Owner Richardson Kelly O'Gara Partnership **Bred** Green Square Racing **Trained** Sessay, N Yorks

FOCUS
A moderate sprint handicap with the winner in fine form for new yard. The form is somewhat fluid with the previously out-of-form runner-up finishing so close.
Baybshambles(IRE) Official explanation: jockey said gelding was denied a clear run
Jadan(IRE) Official explanation: jockey said gelding was never travelling
T/Jkpt: Not won. T/Plt: £89.70 to a £1 stake. Pool: £63,222.00. 514.45 winning tickets. T/Qpdt: £48.10 to a £1 stake. Pool: £3,304.90. 50.80 winning tickets. JR

6501 WOLVERHAMPTON (A.W) (L-H)
Tuesday, October 30

OFFICIAL GOING: Standard
Wind: Light, across Weather: Fine

6563 PLAY AUSTRALIAN @ CENTREBET.COM APPRENTICE H'CAP 5f 216y(P)
1:20 (1:20) (Class 6) (0-50,50) 3-Y-O+ £2,115 (£624; £312) Stalls Low

Form RPR

0404 1 **Briery Blaze**[9] 6361 4-8-11 47 (b1) JackMitchell 9 54
(J W Unett) *mde all: rdn wl over 1f out: drvn out* 10/1

0P00 2 1 1/4 **Grand Palace (IRE)**[34] 5730 4-8-13 49 (v) KellyHarrison 3 52
(D Shaw) *a.p: chsd wnr wl over 1f out: rdn and nt qckn ins fnl f* 7/1[3]

004 3 hd **Canina**[22] 6064 4-8-9 50 ChrisHough(5) 7 52
(Paul Green) *a.p: rdn over 2f out: kpt on ins fnl f* 8/1

0056 4 hd **Sovereignty (JPN)**[13] 6264 5-9-0 50 WilliamCarson 11 52
(D K Ivory) *sn chsng wnr: rdn over 2f out: lost 2nd wl over 1f out: kpt on ins fnl f* 11/2[1]

0040 5 shd **Dazzler Mac**[27] 5908 6-8-11 47 ThomasO'Brien 8 48+
(N Bycroft) *in rr: rdn over 2f out: swtchd rt jst over 1f out: gd late hdwy: fin wl* 8/1

0000 6 1/2 **Desert Lover (IRE)**[4] 6479 5-8-9 48 (p) RobbieEgan(3) 12 48
(R J Price) *chsd ldrs: rdn over 2f out: edgd lft jst over 1f out: one pce fnl f* 6/1[2]

0500 7 2 1/2 **Aggbag**[22] 6064 3-8-12 49 HarryPoulton 6 41
(B P J Baugh) *mid-div: no hdwy fnl 2f* 18/1

0644 8 3/4 **Piccolo Diamante (USA)**[25] 5982 3-8-10 50 (t) MatthewDavies(3) 4 39
(D J Murphy) *s.i.s: in rr: c wd st: nvr nr ldrs* 7/1[3]

6000 9 1 **Blakeshall Quest**[168] 1753 7-8-12 48 (b) JackDean 13 34
(R Brotherton) *mid-div: rdn 3f out: sn wknd* 16/1

54/0 10 1 1/4 **Cost Analysis (IRE)**[32] 5778 5-8-9 48 JemmaMarshall(3) 1 30
(Mrs P Ford) *a towards rr* 20/1

/0-0 11 shd **Knickyknackienoo**[76] 4515 6-8-13 49 MCGeran 5 31
(T T Clement) *s.i.s: a in rr* 33/1

6260 12 1/2 **Petite Mac**[27] 5908 7-8-8 47 FrankiePickard(3) 10 27
(N Bycroft) *outpcd* 8/1

1m 15.58s (-0.23) **Going Correction** -0.125s/f (Stan)
WFA 3 from 4yo+ 1lb 12 Ran SP% 115.9
Speed ratings (Par 101): **96,94,94,93,93 93,89,88,87,85 85,84**
CSF £76.61 CT £600.53 TOTE £11.20: £3.50, £3.70, £3.00; EX 91.20.
Owner Philip Bourchier **Bred** Simon And Helen Plumbly **Trained** Preston, Shropshire
■ Stewards' Enquiry : M C Geran one-day ban: used whip when out of contention (Nov 10)
Jemma Marshall caution: used whip when out of contention

FOCUS
A very moderate affair won by a filly landing her first race. The form is ordinary, even for this grade, although sound enough rated around the winner and third.

6564 WE'VE GOT THE ASHES @ CENTREBET.COM H'CAP 1m 5f 194y(P)
1:50 (1:50) (Class 6) (0-65,65) 3-Y-O+ £2,115 (£624; £312) Stalls Low

Form RPR

2344 1 **Mr Mischief**[10] 6076 7-9-7 63 RussellKennemore(5) 5 73
(M C Chapman) *s.i.s: hld up towards rr: hdwy over 2f out: sn rdn: led ins fnl f: edgd lft towards fin: drvn out* 11/2[3]

1300 2 1 3/4 **Rare Coincidence**[21] 6077 6-9-12 63 (p) ChrisCatlin 8 71
(R F Fisher) *led early: a.p: led over 2f out: sn rdn: hdd ins fnl f: nt qckn* 16/1

0046 3 1 1/4 **Little Richard (IRE)**[7] 6407 8-9-1 55 (p) NeilChalmers(3) 2 61
(M Wellings) *hld up in tch: rdn over 2f out: styd on one pce fnl f* 7/2[1]

0210 **4** 2 ½ **Birthday Star (IRE)**[92] 4025 5-9-6 **57** .... AdamKirby 4 60
(A G Juckes) *s.i.s: hld up towards rr: rdn over 2f out: hdwy and squeezed through wl over 1f out: one pce fnl f* **25/1**
0034 **5** *shd* **York Cliff**[10] 6325 9-9-2 **53** .... LiamJones 1 56
(W M Brisbourne) *hld up in mid-div: rdn and hdwy whn edgd rt wl over 1f out: one pce fnl f* **10/1**
2015 **6** 2 **Stagecoach Emerald**[10] 6341 5-10-0 **65** ....(p) RobertHavlin 3 65
(R W Price) *sn chsng ldr: led over 3f out: sn rdn: hdd over 2f out: wknd over 1f out* **10/1**
0540 **7** *nk* **Royal Premier (IRE)**[20] 6102 4-9-6 **60** ....(v) JerryO'Dwyer(3) 13 59
(H J Collingridge) *hld up: sn in rr: reminders over 4f out: rdn over 2f out: no imp whn hung lft over 1f out* **20/1**
2020 **8** 5 **Synonymy**[19] 6131 4-9-12 **63** ....(b) LPKeniry 7 55
(M Blanshard) *hld up in tch: wknd over 2f out* **6/1**
0000 **9** 1 **Tromp**[26] 5948 6-9-12 **63** .... DaneO'Neill 6 54
(D J Coakley) *hld up in mid-div: hdwy on outside over 2f out: bmpd wl over 1f out: sn wknd* **7/1**
-430 **10** 12 **Escoffier**[3] 6501 5-9-6 **57** ....(t) GeorgeBaker 12 31
(M Appleby) *a in rr* **25/1**
5000 **11** 5 **West End Lad**[11] 6304 4-9-1 **52** ....(p) PaulEddery 10 19
(S R Bowring) *sn led: hdd over 3f out: sn rdn: wknd qckly over 2f out* **66/1**
1515 **12** 3 ½ **Heights Of Golan**[15] 6241 3-9-1 **61** ....(v) LeeEnstone 9 23
(I A Wood) *sn prom: rdn and wknd over 2f out* **9/2[2]**

3m 4.83s (-2.54) **Going Correction** -0.125s/f (Stan)
WFA 3 from 4yo+ 9lb **12** Ran SP% **120.6**
Speed ratings (Par 101): **102,101,100,98,98 97,97,94,94,87 84,82**
CSF £86.90 CT £356.81 TOTE £3.80: £1.70, £4.60, £2.00; EX 114.70.
Owner R A Gadd **Bred** Mrs Maureen Barbara Walsh **Trained** Market Rasen, Lincs

FOCUS
A fairly modest staying event with the runner-up the best guide and the form should work out.
York Cliff Official explanation: jockey said gelding had steering problems on the final bend
Heights Of Golan Official explanation: jockey said gelding stopped very quickly

6565 BET NOW AT CENTREBET.COM CLASSIFIED STKS 5f 20y(P)
2:20 (2:20) (Class 7) 3-Y-0+ **£1,706** (£503; £252) **Stalls Low**

Form RPR
-000 **1** **Commander Wish**[9] 6361 4-8-11 45 ....(tp) NeilChalmers(3) 2 63
(Lucinda Featherstone) *w ldr: led over 2f out: rdn over 1f out: r.o wl* **66/1**
0002 **2** 4 **Muktasb (USA)**[8] 6390 6-9-0 45 ....(v) AdamKirby 9 49+
(D Shaw) *s.i.s: hld up in rr: hdwy on ins over 2f out: rdn over 1f out: wnt 2nd towards fin: nt trble wnr* **3/1[1]**
0030 **3** 1 **Smart Cassie**[8] 6390 4-9-0 45 .... FergusSweeney 6 45
(H J Evans) *led: hdd over 2f out: edgd lft jst over 1f out: one pce* **11/1**
0604 **4** 1 **Detonate**[1] 6531 5-8-9 45 .... KirstyMilczarek(5) 11 41+
(I A Wood) *hld up in rr: nt clr run wl over 1f out: swtchd rt and hdwy ent fnl f: nrst fin* **9/1**
0000 **5** 1 **Bahamian Bay**[8] 6390 5-9-0 45 .... DaleGibson 4 38
(M Brittain) *chsd ldrs: rdn over 2f out: wknd ins fnl f* **20/1**
0500 **6** 2 ½ **Millsini**[15] 6240 3-9-0 45 ....(b[1]) J-PGuillambert 3 29
(Rae Guest) *hld up in mid-div: rdn over 2f out: wknd over 1f out* **14/1**
0000 **7** 1 **Dodaa (USA)**[8] 6390 4-9-0 45 .... MatthewHenry 12 25
(N Wilson) *hld up in mid-div: rdn over 2f out: c wd st: no hdwy* **8/1**
00-3 **8** *shd* **Rapid Flow**[8] 6390 5-9-0 45 .... SteveDrowne 7 25
(J W Unett) *hld up in mid-div: nt clr run wl over 1f out: no imp* **10/3[2]**
0000 **9** ¾ **Minimum Fuss (IRE)**[35] 5700 3-8-9 45 ....(b) RussellKennemore(5) 5 22
(M C Chapman) *s.i.s: a bhd* **25/1**
0504 **10** ¾ **Mind That Fox**[33] 5752 5-9-0 45 .... ChrisCatlin 8 19
(T Wall) *chsd ldrs: rdn over 2f out: wknd over 1f out* **16/1**
6503 **11** 1 ¼ **Violet's Pride**[25] 5970 3-9-0 45 .... HayleyTurner 1 15
(N Tinkler) *prom tl rdn and wknd over 1f out* **5/1[3]**
0000 **12** 4 **Borzoi Maestro**[61] 4974 6-8-9 45 ....(p) KevinGhunowa(5) 13 1
(G F Bridgwater) *sn in rr* **25/1**
000 **13** 2 ½ **Newgate Parisien**[40] 5567 4-9-0 45 .... LPKeniry 10 —
(Mark Campion) *a in rr* **66/1**

62.20 secs (-0.62) **Going Correction** -0.125s/f (Stan) **13** Ran SP% **122.2**
Speed ratings (Par 97): **99,92,91,89,87 83,82,82,80,79 77,71,67**
CSF £255.46 TOTE £189.20: £32.30, £1.30, £3.50; EX 1309.70.
Owner J Roundtree **Bred** P R Featherstone **Trained** Ashbourne, Derbyshire
■ Lucinda Featherstone's first winner since resuming training after a year out.

FOCUS
Low-grade stuff won by a horse that was impossible to find on all known form. The form looks dubious with the runner-up and fourth not having the clearest of runs on the bend.
Muktasb(USA) Official explanation: jockey said gelding fly-leapt at the start
Newgate Parisien Official explanation: trainer said gelding was found to be lame on returning home

6566 CENTREBET.COM POKER CLAIMING STKS 1m 141y(P)
2:50 (2:51) (Class 6) 2-Y-0 **£2,115** (£624; £312) **Stalls Low**

Form RPR
6050 **1** **Khana Ras (IRE)**[6] 6433 2-8-10 63 .... ChrisCatlin 4 64
(E J O'Neill) *a.p: rdn over 2f out: edgd lft over 1f out: led wl ins fnl f: r.o* **9/1[3]**
0220 **2** 1 **Hurstpierpoint (IRE)**[18] 6150 2-8-5 64 .... DaleGibson 12 57
(R A Fahey) *chsd ldr: led over 6f out: rdn and hdd wl ins fnl f: nt qckn* **13/2[2]**
0006 **3** ½ **Carry On Cleo**[38] 5644 2-8-2 53 .... MatthewHenry 2 53+
(P D Evans) *stdd s: in rr: hdwy on outside 3f out: sn rdn and edgd lft: r.o wl towards fin* **25/1**
4412 **4** *nk* **What's For Tea**[5] 6454 2-8-3 61 .... HayleyTurner 10 53
(Tom Dascombe) *led: hdd over 6f out: chsd ldr: rdn wl over 1f out: nt qckn ins fnl f* **8/15[1]**
0550 **5** 8 **Kabuku**[7] 6410 2-8-12 68 .... SaleemGolam 11 45
(M H Tompkins) *s.i.s: sn swtchd lft: stdy hdwy over 5f out: rdn and wknd over 2f out* **12/1**
050U **6** 4 **Little Finch (IRE)**[41] 5520 2-8-2 42 ow7 ....(v[1]) KirstyMilczarek(5) 5 32
(R C Guest) *prom: rdn over 3f out: wknd over 2f out* **66/1**
000 **7** 6 **Mio Fiore**[34] 5720 2-8-2 48 .... FrancisNorton 7 14
(M Blanshard) *hld up in mid-div: rdn 3f out: bhd fnl 2f* **33/1**
2500 **8** 1 **Ten On Line (IRE)**[38] 5644 2-8-6 51 .... LiamJones 1 16
(J G M O'Shea) *a towards rr* **25/1**
6403 **9** ¾ **Prunes**[11] 6305 2-8-2 55 .... PatrickMathers(3) 6 14
(A Berry) *prom: hrd rdn 3f out: sn wknd* **11/1**
0 **10** 1 ½ **Raines Boy**[118] 3205 2-8-10 0 .... JamesDoyle 3 16
(N P Littmoden) *bhd fnl 3f* **40/1**
4006 **11** 2 ½ **Lavemill (IRE)**[27] 5902 2-8-3 43 ow4 .... KevinGhunowa(5) 9 8
(R F Fisher) *a towards rr* **66/1**

1m 51.4s (-0.36) **Going Correction** -0.125s/f (Stan) **11** Ran SP% **120.6**
Speed ratings (Par 93): **96,95,94,94,87 83,78,77,76,75 73**
CSF £63.53 TOTE £8.40: £3.30, £1.90, £7.40; EX 93.20.
Owner ROA Racing Partnership VII **Bred** Dr M V O'Brien **Trained** Averham Park, Notts
■ Stewards' Enquiry : Hayley Turner one-day ban: careless riding (Nov 10)

FOCUS
A very modest claimer. The first four pulled well clear of the remainder.

NOTEBOOK
Khana Ras(IRE), who was nicely supported in the market, took a really long time to get going and only got on top well inside the final furlong. He should get further judged on this effort. (op 12-1)
Hurstpierpoint(IRE) made her bid for victory off the final bend but was worn down in the final furlong. She deserves a victory. (op 11-2)
Carry On Cleo stayed on well up the home straight but was never quite getting to the principals. Another step up in trip looks likely.
What's For Tea battled on well for pressure but was comfortably held by the first three. Despite finishing well clear of the fifth horse, there is a chance that she could need a break now. (op 4-6)
Kabuku has become very disappointing since a promising run in a Newmarket maiden in September. He looks harshly treated on what he has actually done. (op 10-1)
Little Finch(IRE) Official explanation: jockey said filly suffered interference in running
Ten On Line(IRE) Official explanation: jockey said colt changed its legs
Lavemill(IRE) Official explanation: jockey said filly hung both ways

6567 AUSSIE AUSSIE AUSSIE BET @ CENTREBET.COM H'CAP 1m 141y(P)
3:20 (3:20) (Class 6) (0-65,65) 3-Y-0 **£2,115** (£624; £312) **Stalls Low**

Form RPR
0052 **1** **Goose Green (IRE)**[8] 6387 3-8-13 **60** .... SteveDrowne 1 67
(R J Hodges) *led early: a.p: rdn to ld ent fnl f: edgd rt towards fin: r.o* **10/3[1]**
0002 **2** 1 ¾ **Putra Laju (IRE)**[15] 6226 3-9-1 **62** ....(p) GeorgeBaker 2 65
(J W Hills) *hld up: hdwy over 2f out: rdn wl over 1f out: tk 2nd cl home: nt trble wnr* **7/2[2]**
3323 **3** ½ **Cap St Jean (IRE)**[8] 6387 3-8-5 **57** .... RussellKennemore(5) 5 59
(R Hollinshead) *plld hrd: a.p: rdn and ev ch wl over 1f out: nt qckn ins fnl f* **4/1[3]**
0003 **4** *nk* **Run Free**[15] 6245 3-9-1 **62** .... DanielTudhope 9 63
(N Wilson) *sn led: hdd over 5f out: chsd ldr: rdn to ld 2f out: edgd rt wl over 1f out: hdd ent fnl f: one pce* **11/2**
6404 **5** 2 ½ **Joyful Tears (IRE)**[22] 6057 3-8-10 **60** .... NeilChalmers(3) 8 55
(M G Quinlan) *hld up in rr: c wd st: rdn and sme hdwy whn hung lft fr over 1f out: n.d* **20/1**
3465 **6** 8 **Cow Girl (IRE)**[12] 6278 3-8-9 **59** .... WilliamBuick(3) 4 36
(Miss Gay Kelleway) *t.k.h: prom: led over 5f out: rdn and hdd 2f out: sn wknd* **7/1**
5046 **7** ¾ **Just Oscar (GER)**[9] 6361 3-8-10 **57** ....(p) DaneO'Neill 7 32
(W M Brisbourne) *dwlt: t.k.h towards rr: rdn over 2f out: sn struggling* **14/1**
6060 **8** 13 **A Little More (IRE)**[113] 3367 3-9-4 **65** .... FrankieMcDonald 3 10
(P A Blockley) *prom tl rdn and wknd over 3f out* **25/1**

1m 51.03s (-0.73) **Going Correction** -0.125s/f (Stan) **8** Ran SP% **108.5**
Speed ratings (Par 99): **98,96,96,95,93 86,85,74**
CSF £13.55 CT £40.97 TOTE £2.80: £1.50, £1.70, £1.40; EX 10.80.
Owner Mrs S G Clapp **Bred** Liam Queally **Trained** Charlton Mackrell, Somerset

FOCUS
A modest handicap that contained a few maidens. The form appears sound rated but modest although the winner looks capable of following up.
Cow Girl(IRE) Official explanation: jockey said filly ran too freely

6568 CENTREBET.COM CASINO H'CAP 7f 32y(P)
3:50 (3:50) (Class 5) (0-75,75) 3-Y-0+ **£2,914** (£867; £433; £216) **Stalls High**

Form RPR
0050 **1** **Will He Wish**[24] 6016 11-9-6 **73** ....(b) IanMongan 2 85
(S Gollings) *a.p: rdn to ld and edgd rt 1f out: readily* **12/1**
0031 **2** 2 ½ **Teasing**[15] 6232 3-9-3 **72** .... RobertHavlin 9 77+
(J Pearce) *s.i.s: hld up and bhd: nt clr run on ins over 2f out: hdwy wl over 1f out: swtchd rt over 1f out: r.o ins fnl f: nt trble wnr* **11/4[1]**
1050 **3** 2 ½ **Diminuto**[17] 6173 3-8-12 **74** .... FrankiePickard(7) 7 73
(M D I Usher) *sn chsng ldr: led over 3f out: rdn and hdd 1f out: one pce* **33/1**
1426 **4** *nk* **Napoleon Dynamite (IRE)**[19] 6122 3-9-4 **73** .... GeorgeBaker 6 71
(J W Hills) *hld up in rr: hdwy on ins over 1f out: kpt on ins fnl f* **10/3[2]**
5234 **5** 1 ½ **Dvinsky (USA)**[13] 6273 6-9-3 **70** .... ChrisCatlin 3 64
(P Howling) *led: hdd over 3f out: rdn over 1f out: wknd ins fnl f* **8/1[3]**
0000 **6** 1 **Stanley George (IRE)**[88] 4135 3-9-3 **72** .... MatthewHenry 4 63
(M A Jarvis) *s.i.s: sn mid-div: rdn whn hung lft wl over 1f out: hung lft and wknd ins fnl f* **14/1**
2002 **7** 1 **Parkview Love (USA)**[150] 2256 6-9-3 **70** .... DaneO'Neill 11 58
(D Shaw) *hld up and bhd: rdn over 2f out: c wd st: sn hung lft: nvr nr ldrs* **14/1**
055 **8** ¾ **Jacquart (NZ)**[19] 6122 5-9-6 **73** ....(p) AdamKirby 12 59
(C G Cox) *prom: edgd lft wl over 1f out: wknd fnl f* **11/1**
0-10 **9** 3 ½ **White Bear (FR)**[171] 1655 5-9-0 **67** ....(b) LiamJones 10 44
(C R Dore) *prom: rdn over 2f out: wknd over 1f out* **9/1**
0046 **10** ¾ **Kelamon**[9] 6355 3-9-1 **73** .... WilliamBuick(3) 5 48
(M D I Usher) *rdn over 3f out: a bhd* **12/1**
12-0 **11** *hd* **Kapellmeister (IRE)**[235] 652 4-9-2 **69** .... FergusSweeney 1 43
(M S Saunders) *hld up in mid-div: rdn and wknd wl over 1f out* **10/1**

1m 29.17s (-1.23) **Going Correction** -0.125s/f (Stan)
WFA 3 from 4yo+ 2lb **11** Ran SP% **119.9**
Speed ratings (Par 103): **102,99,96,95,94 93,91,91,87,86 86**
CSF £45.95 CT £1120.63 TOTE £10.60: £3.80, £1.20, £8.80; EX 49.90.
Owner Mrs D Dukes **Bred** Mrs C Buckland **Trained** Scamblesby, Lincs

FOCUS
A competitive race for the grade and the form looks sound with the winner back to form.

6569 SP PLUS PLUS @ CENTREBET.COM CLASSIFIED STKS 1m 4f 50y(P)
4:20 (4:21) (Class 7) 3-Y-0+ **£1,706** (£503; £252) **Stalls Low**

Form RPR
0335 **1** **Summer Bounty**[7] 6407 11-9-5 42 .... LPKeniry 8 51+
(F Jordan) *hld up in rr: hdwy whn nt clr run and swtchd lft wl over 1f out: hung lft ins fnl f: r.o wl to ld towards fin* **5/1**
2 1 ¼ **Wishes Or Watches (IRE)**[10] 1699 7-9-5 45 .... GeorgeBaker 12 48
(John A Quinn, Ire) *set slow pce: qcknd 4f out: rdn clr 1f out: ct towards fin* **9/2[3]**

0000 **3** 1 1/2 **The Mighty Ogmore**[10] 6325 3-8-7 45..................(p) KirstyMilczarek(5) 6 45
(R C Guest) *a.p: outpcd over 3f out: rdn over 1f out: kpt on one pce ins fnl f* **20/1**

2403 **4** shd **Dream Master (IRE)**[12] 6292 4-9-5 45.............................. AdamKirby 2 45
(J Ryan) *hld up in mid-div: hdwy on ins wl over 1f out: kpt on ins fnl f* **5/2**[1]

-000 **5** 3/4 **Finnegans Rainbow**[23] 2118 5-9-0 45............ RussellKennemore(5) 11 44
(M C Chapman) *chsd ldr: rdn and ev ch over 2f out: no ex ins fnl f* **33/1**

0500 **6** 3/4 **Sea Frolic (IRE)**[27] 5916 6-9-5 42.............................. HayleyTurner 9 43
(Jennie Candlish) *hld up towards rr: hdwy on outside 3f out: rdn over 1f out: one pce* **25/1**

-004 **7** nk **Guadiana (GER)**[5] 6452 5-9-5 44...................................(v) JamesDoyle 3 42
(A W Carroll) *hld up towards rr: hdwy wl over 1f out: no further prog fnl f* **10/3**[2]

6450 **8** nk **Jenny Soba**[10] 6341 4-9-2 43.. NeilChalmers(3) 4 42
(Lucinda Featherstone) *hld up towards rr: rdn and swtchd rt over 1f out: sme late hdwy* **14/1**

00 **9** 6 **Bythehokey (IRE)**[28] 5886 6-9-5 44.................................. DaneO'Neill 7 32
(W M Brisbourne) *hld up in tch: rdn and outpcd over 3f out: wknd wl over 1f out* **12/1**

0026 **10** 3/4 **Master Ben (IRE)**[187] 1261 4-9-5 45.............................(b) PaulEddery 10 31
(S R Bowring) *hld up in rr: reminder over 4f out: rdn and struggling 3f out* **50/1**

460 **11** 3 **Van Ruymbeke (IRE)**[11] 6311 3-8-12 43.........................(t) LiamJones 5 26
(D J Murphy) *hld up in mid-div: rdn 3f out: sn wknd* **15/2**

000- **12** 25 **Garrya**[191] 3-8-12 45.. DanielTudhope 1 —
(B P J Baugh) *prom: rdn and outpcd over 3f out: wknd over 2f out: t.o* **25/1**

2m 45.14s (2.72) **Going Correction** -0.125s/f (Stan)
WFA 3 from 4yo+ 7lb 12 Ran SP% **130.0**
Speed ratings (Par 97): **85,84,83,83,82 82,81,81,77,77 75,58**
CSF £29.03 TOTE £10.50: £2.90, £1.80, £6.90; EX 42.80 Place 6 £267.00, Place 5 £51.43.
Owner Tim Powell **Bred** Berkshire Equestrian Services Ltd **Trained** Adstone, Northants

FOCUS
A very moderate event, run in a very slow time, won by an 11-year-old who was basically to form. and given the slow pace the race has been rated fairly negatively. The third has shown all of its best form at sprint trips.
Van Ruymbeke(IRE) Official explanation: jockey said gelding ran too freely
T/Plt: £239.90 to a £1 stake. Pool: £48,169.00. 146.55 winning tickets. T/Qpdt: £31.90 to a £1 stake. Pool: £3,272.90. 75.70 winning tickets. KH

6408 YARMOUTH (L-H)
Tuesday, October 30

OFFICIAL GOING: Good to soft (soft in places; straight 7.0, back straight 6.4)
Wind: Fresh, behind Weather: Partly cloudy

6570 CRYSTAL CLEANING (S) STKS 1m 2f 21y
1:10 (1:10) (Class 6) 3-4-Y-O **£1,943** (£578; £288; £144) **Stalls** Low

Form RPR

0002 **1** **Ful Of Grace (IRE)**[7] 6408 3-8-7 50..................................(b) TPO'Shea 6 53
(M G Quinlan) *hld up bhd: hdwy 4f out: chsd ldng trio 2f out: swtchd lft over 1f out: styd on u.p to ld last 100yds* **13/2**[3]

0650 **2** 2 **Mark Of The Fen**[5] 6458 3-8-12 50.............................(e) DarryllHolland 3 54
(Rae Guest) *chsd ldr tl led wl over 3f out: rdn and hdd over 2f out: led again ins fnl f: hdd last 100yds: no ex* **4/1**[2]

6 **3** 1/2 **Satindra (IRE)**[15] 6245 3-8-12 59..............................(p) JamieSpencer 10 53
(John A Harris) *t.k.h: hld up bhd: hdwy 3f out: sltly hmpd 2f out: edgd out rt 1f out: styd on wl wnt 3rd last strides* **7/2**[1]

6000 **4** nk **Danum Diva (IRE)**[180] 1423 3-8-7 37.................................. JohnEgan 12 47
(D J Murphy) *stdd s: racd wd: hld up bhd: hdwy over 4f out: led narrowly over 2f out: sn rdn: hdd ins fnl f: no ex last 100yds* **50/1**

00-0 **5** 3/4 **Swayze (IRE)**[230] 675 4-9-3 63...................................... JimmyFortune 8 51
(M Quinn) *hld up in midfield: hdwy on inner 4f out: ev ch and rdn 2f out: wknd last 100yds* **7/2**[1]

000- **6** 7 **Lucy Babe**[312] 6907 4-8-7 35... NicolPolli(5) 13 32
(G Prodromou) *hld up bhd: rdn and sme hdwy 3f out: no imp over 1f out* **40/1**

0-3 **7** 3/4 **Lap Of The Gods**[7] 6408 3-8-12 0...........................(p) AdrianMcCarthy 5 35
(Miss Z C Davison) *chsd ldrs: rdn 3f out: wkng whn edgd rt 2f out: wl btn after* **25/1**

0-00 **8** 3 **Scene Three**[18] 6152 3-8-7 42.................................... GrahamGibbons 9 24
(J J Quinn) *w.w in tch: rdn 4f out: wknd wl over 2f out* **25/1**

0050 **9** 1 **Lady Ambitious**[12] 6292 4-8-7 41.................................(b[1]) JamesO'Reilly(5) 7 22
(D K Ivory) *s.i.s: sn in midfield: hdwy to chse ldrs over 4f out: rdn and wknd wl over 2f out* **10/1**

0510 **10** 2 **Wickedish**[41] 5546 3-8-13 54..(t) RichardMullen 4 24
(M J Gingell) *hld up in midfield: rdn over 3f out: sn wknd* **8/1**

56-0 **11** 16 **Rainbow Prince**[16] 6212 4-9-3 44.............................. StephenDonohoe 11 —
(M J Gingell) *dwlt: hld up in rr: rdn wl over 3f out: sn t.o* **28/1**

0000 **12** 2 1/2 **Mr Chocolate Drop (IRE)**[36] 5688 3-9-4 45............(vt[1]) SamHitchcott 1 —
(Miss M E Rowland) *sn led: rdn and hdd wl over 3f out: wknd 3f out: t.o* **50/1**

0606 **13** 6 **First Frost**[7] 6408 3-8-4 39.. DominicFox(3) 2 —
(M J Gingell) *chsd ldrs: reminder 7f out: rdn and wknd qckly 4f out: t.o* **200/1**

2m 13.4s (5.30) **Going Correction** +0.525s/f (Yiel)
WFA 3 from 4yo 5lb 13 Ran SP% **116.0**
Speed ratings (Par 101): **99,97,97,96,96 90,89,87,86,85 72,70,65**
CSF £29.94 TOTE £8.50: £2.60, £1.80, £1.40; EX 39.30 Trifecta £149.20 Part won. Pool: £210.20 - 0.30 winning units..The winner was sold to Martin Pipe for 6,000gns.
Owner Mrs Jeanette Johnson **Bred** Mrs Mary Coonan **Trained** Newmarket, Suffolk

FOCUS
A decidedly weak event, even by selling standards. The third helps to set the lowly level.
First Frost Official explanation: jockey said filly hung right

6571 EBF/HAPPY BIRTHDAY PENNY MAY MAIDEN STKS 7f 3y
1:40 (1:41) (Class 5) 2-Y-O **£3,238** (£963; £481; £240) **Stalls** High

Form RPR

00 **1** **Tasheba**[26] 5951 2-9-3 0.. AdrianMcCarthy 7 75+
(P W Chapple-Hyam) *hld up in tch: pushed along and outpcd over 2f out: hdwy over 1f out: styd on steadily to ld towards fin* **14/1**

5000 **2** nk **Double On Red**[15] 6233 2-8-12 75..............................(b[1]) RichardMullen 3 68
(J M P Eustace) *led: rdn over 1f out: battled on wl tl hdd and no ex towards fin* **7/1**

0 **3** hd **Mardood**[14] 6248 2-9-3 0.. RHills 8 73+
(W J Haggas) *trckd ldrs: wnt 2nd over 3f out: rdn 2f out: ev ch ins fnl f: unable qckn* **5/1**[3]

4 3/4 **Viscountess (IRE)** 2-8-12 0.. DarryllHolland 1 66+
(M Johnston) *chsd ldr tl over 3f out: rdn over 2f out: sltly outpcd 2f out: rallied fnl f: kpt on* **6/1**

0 **5** 3/4 **No Rules**[11] 6296 2-9-3 0.. JimmyQuinn 5 69+
(M H Tompkins) *chsd ldrs: rdn and outpcd over 2f out: styd on steadily fnl f: nt rch ldrs* **10/1**

6 3/4 **Robert Burns (IRE)** 2-9-3 0... JimmyFortune 6 67
(J H M Gosden) *s.i.s: sn in tch: hdwy to chse ldng pair wl over 1f out: rdn 1f out: fdd last 100yds* **7/2**[2]

7 shd **Ebn Malk (IRE)** 2-9-3 0.. PhilipRobinson 4 67+
(M A Jarvis) *stdd s: hld up in tch: rdn and outpcd over 2f out: kpt on ins fnl f* **10/3**[1]

8 3 **Treasure Islands (IRE)** 2-8-5 0..................................... JCorrigan(7) 10 54
(S W Hall) *stdd s: hld up in tch in rr: hdwy 3f out: chsd ldrs and rdn 2f out: wknd 1f out* **100/1**

00 **9** 18 **Romford Car Two**[21] 6079 2-9-3 0.. JohnEgan 9 14
(Miss J Feilden) *hld up in tch: rdn 3f out: sn struggling: t.o over 1f out* **25/1**

6 **10** 1/2 **Palmer's Green**[40] 5570 2-9-3 0................................. TGMcLaughlin 11 13
(Mrs C A Dunnett) *v awkward leaving stalls: sn detached in last and rdn: no ch fr 1/2-way: t.o* **100/1**

11 1 1/4 **Astrodome** 2-9-3 0.. JamieMackay 2 10
(Sir Mark Prescott) *t.k.h: chsd ldrs tl 1/2-way: sn wknd: wl bhd last 2f: t.o* **25/1**

1m 28.61s (2.01) **Going Correction** +0.20s/f (Good) 11 Ran SP% **114.2**
Speed ratings (Par 95): **96,95,95,94,93 92,92,89,68,68 66**
CSF £102.91 TOTE £25.20: £5.10, £2.30, £1.80; EX 143.50 TRIFECTA Not won..
Owner Terry Benson **Bred** C R Mason **Trained** Newmarket, Suffolk

FOCUS
A fair juvenile maiden, run at an average pace. The first seven were closely bunched at the finish and the runner-up helps to set the level.

NOTEBOOK
Tasheba stepped up markedly on his two previous efforts and just did enough to edge it near the finish, winning with a little left up his sleeve. The drop back in trip was obviously no problem, but he did more than enough to suggest he is going to want a stiffer test next year and he can expect an official mark in the mid-70s after this. (op 12-1)
Double On Red, equipped with first-time blinkers, showed much-improved form on this return to a straight track and was only picked off by the winner near the line. She is proving somewhat frustrating to follow, but her official mark still looks to have her about right at present. (tchd 11-2)
Mardood, distinctly green on debut at Newmarket a fortnight previously, showed the clear benefit of that experience and was not beaten at all far. He is going the right way and will not mind returning to 1m now, but is no more than a Handicapper in the making on this evidence. (op 8-1)
Viscountess(IRE) ◆, whose dam won over 1m at three, hit a flat spot before coming back at the leaders at the business end and ran a debut race full of promise. Considering her breeding she will likely prove happier on faster ground and she looks the one to take from the race with the immediate future in mind. (op 11-2 tchd 13-2)
No Rules was another who got done for speed when the tempo became really serious, but finished his race well and this was definite step in the right direction. He will appreciate the return to 1m before too long and needs one more run for a nursery mark. (tchd 9-1)
Robert Burns(IRE), a 120,000gns purchase whose dam scored over 10f at three, was representing a leading yard with a decent past record in this maiden. He ultimately proved too green to shine, however, and could have done with seeing more cover during the race. No doubt he will be sharper next time out. (op 11-4)
Ebn Malk(IRE), a brother to his stable's Ommraan, who was successful on his only start last year, was another who proved notably green and lacked the speed to get serious when it really mattered. The manner in which he finished his race would suggest the experience will certainly not be lost on him. (op 7-2 tchd 4-1)

6572 WEATHERBYS BLOODSTOCK INSURANCE NURSERY 7f 3y
2:10 (2:14) (Class 5) (0-70,70) 2-Y-O **£2,914** (£867; £433; £216) **Stalls** High

Form RPR

4352 **1** **Carnival Queen**[11] 6307 2-9-7 **70**...............................(v[1]) JamieSpencer 15 73
(J R Fanshawe) *hld up bhd: hdwy 2f out: swtchd rt and rdn over 1f out: hung lft but styd on to ld last 50yds* **7/1**

0044 **2** 1 1/4 **Grand Cuvee**[16] 6201 2-9-6 **69**...................................... TGMcLaughlin 5 69
(D M Simcock) *bhd: rdn wl over 3f out: hdwy over 2f out: led jst ins fnl f: hdd and no ex last 50yds* **7/1**

3003 **3** 1 **Home**[8] 6379 2-9-5 **68**.. JimmyFortune 13 66+
(E A L Dunlop) *chsd ldrs: rdn and sltly outpcd over 2f out: rallied u.p over 1f out: 3rd and btn whn short of room and swtchd rt nr fin* **9/2**[1]

554 **4** 1 **Blitzen (IRE)**[22] 6065 2-9-4 **67**..................................... RichardMullen 9 62
(E S McMahon) *plld hrd: led over 5f out: rdn wl over 1f out: hdd jst ins fnl f: no ex last 100yds* **13/2**[3]

1040 **5** 1 3/4 **Shepherds Warning (IRE)**[33] 5746 2-9-4 **67**................ SamHitchcott 6 58
(N J Vaughan) *in tch in midfield: rdn over 3f out: outpcd over 2f out: rallied u.p fnl f: styd on: nt rch ldrs* **20/1**

000 **6** shd **Rock Me (IRE)**[20] 6106 2-7-11 **49**................................. DominicFox(3) 14 39
(N A Callaghan) *chsd ldrs: rdn over 2f out: wknd u.p fnl f* **66/1**

5060 **7** shd **Infinite Patience**[8] 6379 2-9-4 **67**..................................... JohnEgan 8 57
(J S Moore) *chsd ldrs: rdn 3f out: hdwy 2f out: ev ch over 1f out: wknd ins fnl f: eased nr fin* **16/1**

050 **8** nk **Hawa Khana (IRE)**[15] 6225 2-9-1 **64**..................... StephenDonohoe 12 53
(N P Littmoden) *stdd s: t.k.h: hld up bhd: hdwy over 3f out: rdn wl over 1f out: no imp after* **25/1**

0520 **9** 3/4 **Kashmina**[10] 6328 2-9-5 **68**.. TPO'Shea 10 55
(M R Channon) *stdd after s: hld up in rr: rdn over 2f out: no hdwy* **16/1**

044 **10** shd **Langham House**[20] 6107 2-9-7 **70**............................. GrahamGibbons 2 57
(J R Jenkins) *t.k.h: chsd ldrs: rdn over 2f out: wknd over 1f out* **25/1**

0240 **11** 1 **Binfield (IRE)**[24] 6012 2-9-4 **67**................................. PhilipRobinson 11 52
(B G Powell) *t.k.h: hld up in tch in midfield: rdn over 2f out: sn struggling* **12/1**

4522 **12** 9 **Glittering Prize (UAE)**[12] 6282 2-9-6 **69**.................... DarryllHolland 1 31
(M Johnston) *rearing in stalls: led tl over 5f out: chsd ldr tl over 2f out: wknd qckly wl over 1f out: eased ins fnl f* **5/1**[2]

0500 **13** 5 **Marie Camargo**[83] 4278 2-8-3 **52**.................................. JimmyQuinn 3 2
(R A Fahey) *hld up in midfield: lost pl and rdn over 3f out: no ch after: eased ins fnl f* **10/1**

000 **14** 1 **Sweet Dane (IRE)**[49] 5309 2-7-12 **54** ow2.............(p) AshleyMorgan(7) 7 —
(V Smith) *bhd: rdn and struggling 4f out: no ch last 3f: t.o* **18/1**

1m 29.04s (2.44) **Going Correction** +0.20s/f (Good) 14 Ran SP% **120.9**
Speed ratings (Par 95): **94,92,91,90,88 88,88,87,86,86 85,75,69,68**
CSF £53.33 CT £256.23 TOTE £5.80: £2.50, £3.00, £2.00; EX 50.90 Trifecta £224.20 Pool: £331.70 - 1.05 winning units..
Owner Cheveley Park Stud **Bred** Cheveley Park Stud Ltd **Trained** Newmarket, Suffolk

The Form Book, Raceform Ltd, Compton, RG20 6NL

FOCUS

A modest nursery, run at a sound pace. The form looks straightforward and sound enough.

NOTEBOOK

Carnival Queen, making her nusery bow in a first-time visor, took an age to hit her full stride yet eventually came to mow down her rivals and win this going away. She is not straightforward, but is clearly a fair filly in the making and should be high on confidence now. (op 5-1)

Grand Cuvee ◆, nibbled at in the betting ring, posted a solid effort and this was his best yet to date in defeat. Nicely clear in second, he now deserves to break his duck. (op 9-1)

Home kept to his task under pressure from 2f out and ran very close to his recent level in defeat. He rates a sound benchmark for the form, but probably wants all of 1m now. (op 10-3 tchd 5-1)

Blitzen(IRE), again the subject of some market support, ran too freely for his own good on this switch to a nursery and not surprisingly paid the price inside the final furlong. He is proving a little frustrating to follow now, but no doubt has a race or two in him when getting his act together. (op 9-1)

Shepherds Warning(IRE) was noted doing her best work towards the finish and did not prove suited by the drop abck in trip. This ground suited her better though and she is another who helps to set the standard of the form. (op 22-1 tchd 25-1)

Glittering Prize(UAE), a runner-up on her last two outings, dropped out tamely when pressed for the lead and ran well below her recent level. A drop back to 6f now looks in order. (op 6-1)

Sweet Dane(IRE) Official explanation: jockey said filly hung right

6573 WEATHERBYS PRINTING CLAIMING STKS 1m 3y

2:40 (2:46) (Class 6) 3-4-Y-O **£1,943** (£578; £288; £144) **Stalls High**

Form				RPR
0023	1		**Kassuta**[4] 6464 3-7-12 52 (p) AdrianMcCarthy 8 (John A Harris) *hld up in midfield: hdwy and rdn over 2f out: chsd ldr 2f out: led wl over 1f out: clr ins fnl f: comf* **8/1**	53
4033	2	3	**Casablanca Minx (IRE)**[3] 6504 4-9-1 62 (v) TGMcLaughlin 5 (P D Evans) *s.i.s: hld up towards rr: rdn over 3f out: hdwy over 2f out: chsd wnr over 1f out: one pce* **3/1**[1]	60
0032	3	½	**Al Rayanah**[7] 6412 4-8-2 49 NicolPolli(5) 12 (G Prodromou) *awkward leaving stalls and slowly away: bhd: stdy hdwy 3f out: chsd ldng pair 1f out: kpt on but nvr able to chal* **4/1**[2]	51
050	4	1 ½	**Grand Symphony**[19] 6121 3-9-4 60 (p) DarryllHolland 6 (W Jarvis) *hld up in last: hdwy wl over 1f out: chsd ldng trio ins fnl f: nvr nr ldrs* **25/1**	62
03	5	5	**Sibo Baggins (IRE)**[7] 6412 3-9-3 0 JohnEgan 1 (J S Moore) *hld up in midfield: hdwy 3f out: chsd ldrs and rdn 2f out: wknd 1f out* **8/1**	49
2205	6	shd	**Gifted Heir (IRE)**[57] 5083 3-8-13 59 JimmyFortune 10 (A Bailey) *hld up in rr: hdwy 2f out: sn rdn: no imp* **13/2**[3]	45
0004	7	½	**Smart Cat (IRE)**[6] 6429 4-8-7 48 (v) RichardMullen 11 (A P Jarvis) *t.k.h: chsd ldrs: rdn 3f out: wknd wl over 1f out* **16/1**	35
0200	8	shd	**Dance Spirit (IRE)**[28] 5893 4-9-6 62 JamieSpencer 7 (W R Muir) *led tl over 6f out: chsd ldr after tl 2f out: sn wknd* **7/1**	47
4254	9	hd	**Split Briefs (IRE)**[7] 6412 3-8-4 63 TPO'Shea 4 (C A Dwyer) *towards rr: rdn 3f out: swtchd lft over 2f out: np imp* **9/1**	34
0440	10	¾	**Zilli**[20] 6108 3-8-1 42 ow1 RichardThomas 3 (N P Littmoden) *tok t.k.h: chsd ldrs: rdn over 2f out: wknd 2f out* **40/1**	29
0000	11	1 ½	**Wizby**[14] 6250 4-7-10 38 NataliaGemelova(5) 9 (P D Evans) *racd keenly: led over 6f out: sn clr: hdd wl over 1f out: wknd* **33/1**	23

1m 41.96s (2.06) **Going Correction** +0.20s/f (Good)
WFA 3 from 4yo 3lb 11 Ran SP% **118.2**
Speed ratings (Par 101): **97,94,93,92,87 86,86,86,86,85 83**
CSF £31.86 TOTE £9.90: £2.40, £1.80, £1.90; EX 40.60 Trifecta £88.60 Pool: £362.19 - 2.90 winning units..Kassuta was claimed by M. J. Gingell for £5,000.
Owner Shaun Taylor **Bred** Sally, Nikki & Pippa Clifton & Dr Peter Rossdale **Trained** Eastwell, Leics

FOCUS

A typically moderate claimer, run at a solid pace. The form should be treated with caution and has been rated negatively.

6574 AYLSHAM BATHROOM & KITCHENS MAIDEN STKS 1m 3y

3:10 (3:15) (Class 5) 2-Y-O **£3,141** (£934; £467; £233) **Stalls High**

Form				RPR
6	1		**First Avenue**[26] 5951 2-9-3 0 PhilipRobinson 3 (M A Jarvis) *in tch: hdwy over 2f out: chsd ldr over 1f out: rdn to ld jst ins fnl f: readily* **9/4**[2]	82+
02	2	2	**Majeen**[14] 6246 2-9-3 0 RHills 14 (W J Haggas) *chsd ldr tl led over 4f out: rdn 2f out: hdd jst ins fnl f: one pce* **6/4**[1]	78
0	3	1 ½	**Art Value**[14] 6248 2-9-3 0 AdrianMcCarthy 13 (P W Chapple-Hyam) *in tch: hdwy to press ldrs jst over 2f out: rdn 2f out: kpt on same pce* **8/1**[3]	74
00	4	2 ½	**Crimson Mitre**[12] 6274 2-8-10 0 EddieSemaan(7) 4 (J Jay) *chsd ldrs: rdn over 2f out: outpcd 2f out: kpt on u.p fnl f* **100/1**	69
0	5	nk	**Great Charm (IRE)**[39] 5599 2-9-3 0 RichardMullen 2 (M L W Bell) *racd in midfield: rdn 3f out: hdwy wl over 1f out: kpt on fnl f: nvr nr ldrs* **33/1**	68
45	6	1 ¼	**Bookish**[31] 5811 2-8-12 0 DarryllHolland 5 (M Johnston) *led tl 4f out: rdn over 2f out: wknd wl over 1f out* **14/1**	60
0	7	1 ½	**Moscow Oznick**[27] 5904 2-9-3 0 SamHitchcott 15 (N J Vaughan) *s.i.s: sn prom: rdn over 3f out: wknd over 2f out* **100/1**	62
6	8	1 ¼	**Dark Prospect**[12] 6285 2-9-3 0 JamieMackay 9 (M A Jarvis) *a towards rr: rdn 1/2-way: lost tch 2f out* **33/1**	59
0	9	1 ¾	**Kiribati King (IRE)**[19] 6130 2-9-3 0 TPO'Shea 6 (M R Channon) *s.i.s: drvn 3f out: nvr on terms* **66/1**	55
0	10	1 ¾	**Blimey O'Riley (IRE)**[17] 6184 2-9-3 0 JimmyQuinn 7 (M H Tompkins) *a towards rr: rdn 3f out: sn lost tch* **20/1**	52
	11	3	**Trenchant** 2-9-3 0 JamieSpencer 12 (J R Fanshawe) *hld up bhd: hdwy over 3f out: rdn over 2f out: sn no imp* **8/1**[3]	45
	12	9	**Siena** 2-8-12 0 TGMcLaughlin 1 (Mrs C A Dunnett) *s.i.s: a bhd* **100/1**	20
00	13	hd	**Ray Diamond**[47] 5343 2-8-12 0 PatrickHills(5) 10 (N P Littmoden) *s.i.s: a bhd* **100/1**	25

1m 41.9s (2.00) **Going Correction** +0.20s/f (Good) 13 Ran SP% **115.8**
Speed ratings (Par 95): **98,96,94,92,91 90,88,87,85,84 81,72,72**
CSF £5.43 TOTE £2.80: £1.40, £1.20, £2.00; EX 5.60 Trifecta £26.60 Pool: £324.67 - 8.65 winning units..
Owner Michael Tabor **Bred** The National Stud Never Say Die Club Ltd **Trained** Newmarket, Suffolk

FOCUS

A fair maiden best rated through the runner-up.

NOTEBOOK

First Avenue, who ran with plenty of promise in a Newmarket maiden on his debut, did not need to improve a great deal to be a major player here. Although weak in the market beforehand, he did nothing wrong in the race itself, travelling up well before seeing the trip out strongly. He looks a useful middle-distance prospect for next year on this evidence. (op 6-4)

Majeen had shown enough at Leicester to suggest that he could win a race like this and, with his main rival First Avenue weak in the market, he assumed favouritism. Given every chance in the race itself, he found the Jarvis colt too strong at the finish, but this was another solid effort, and handicaps are now an option for him. (op 9-4)

Art Value, who ran with promise on his debut, stepped up on that effort and ran on well for third. He might be able to find a race on the Polytrack in the coming weeks, but will be eligible for a mark after one more run. (op 10-1)

Crimson Mitre is a half-brother to George The Second, a multiple winning sprinter, but he shapes as though he wants a trip. He has improved with each start and now looks an interesting prospect for modest handicaps. (op 66-1)

Great Charm(IRE), a half-brother to Fregate Island, a triple winner between 7f and 1m3f, is bred to appreciate a bit of cut in the ground and will be suited by stepping up to middle distances next season. He needs one more run for a mark. (op 25-1)

Bookish, for the third time in three starts, tried to make all, but she again fell short. She will have better options in handicap company.

6575 EAST COAST WASTE H'CAP 6f 3y

3:40 (3:44) (Class 5) (0-75,75) 3-Y-0+ **£2,914** (£867; £433; £216) **Stalls High**

Form				RPR
3506	1		**Tudor Prince (IRE)**[16] 6203 3-9-4 75 PhilipRobinson 16 (A W Carroll) *chsd ldrs: wnt 2nd over 2f out: rdn to ld narrowly over 1f out: asserted nr fin* **14/1**	85
1-01	2	¾	**Efisio Princess**[15] 6239 4-8-5 61 RichardThomas 13 (J E Long) *led: rdn 2f out: narrowly hdd over 1f out: kpt on wl tl no ex nr fin* **4/1**[1]	69
1411	3	1 ¾	**Memphis Man**[4] 6467 4-8-13 69 12ex TGMcLaughlin 11 (P D Evans) *v.s.a: wl bhd: hdwy 2f out: str run on stands' rail fnl f: wnt 3rd on line: nt rch ldrs* **5/1**[3]	71+
0004	4	shd	**Equuleus Pictor**[20] 6103 3-8-9 66 SamHitchcott 9 (J L Spearing) *chsd ldrs: rdn and ev ch 2f out: one pce fnl f: lost 3rd on line* **28/1**	68
0000	5	2	**Russian Rocket (IRE)**[9] 6360 5-8-6 62 TPO'Shea 10 (Mrs C A Dunnett) *racd in midfield: rdn over 2f out: styd on fnl f: nt rch ldrs* **40/1**	58
313	6	½	**Blackmalkin (USA)**[55] 5134 3-8-7 64 DarryllHolland 12 (C E Brittain) *racd in midfield: rdn and outpcd over 2f out: styd on u.p fnl f: nt rch ldrs* **14/1**	58
2115	7	1 ½	**Bobby Rose**[11] 6313 4-8-11 72 JamesO'Reilly(5) 3 (D K Ivory) *prom: ev ch 2f out: sn rdn: wknd fnl f* **25/1**	61
0605	8	¾	**Linda Green**[15] 6239 6-8-11 67 JohnEgan 15 (M R Channon) *bhd: rdn 1/2-way: sme late hdwy: n.d* **14/1**	54
4064	9	¾	**Tilly's Dream**[17] 6173 4-9-2 72 JimmyFortune 7 (G C Bravery) *racd in midfield: hdwy over 2f out: rdn 2f out: no imp over 1f out* **20/1**	56
6602	10	1 ¼	**Brunelleschi**[17] 6173 4-9-0 75 (b) TolleyDean(5) 14 (M G Quinlan) *s.i.s: bhd drvn 1/2-way: n.d* **9/2**[2]	55
0022	11	1 ½	**Mugeba**[7] 6415 6-8-0 61 oh7 (t) NicolPolli(5) 6 (Miss Gay Kelleway) *s.i.s: bhd: rdn over 2f out: n.d* **11/1**	37
2106	12	¾	**Polar Force**[12] 6287 7-8-5 61 JimmyQuinn 8 (Mrs C A Dunnett) *w ldr tl over 2f out: wknd wl over 1f out* **12/1**	34
3150	13	½	**Gleaming Spirit (IRE)**[40] 5552 3-8-11 68 RichardMullen 1 (A P Jarvis) *chsd ldrs: rdn 1/2-way: wknd over 2f out* **33/1**	40
4602	14	4	**Mr Cellophane**[12] 6283 4-8-12 68 JamieSpencer 4 (J R Jenkins) *t.k.h: hld up bhd: hdwy 2f out: no imp and eased 1f out* **7/1**	27
0031	15	1 ½	**John O'Groats (IRE)**[95] 3905 9-7-12 61 oh4 (p) AmyBaker(7) 17 (T T Clement) *a bhd* **33/1**	15

1m 14.7s (1.00) **Going Correction** +0.20s/f (Good)
WFA 3 from 4yo+ 1lb 15 Ran SP% **123.8**
Speed ratings (Par 103): **101,100,97,97,94 94,92,91,90,88 86,85,84,79,77**
CSF £65.54 CT £333.57 TOTE £17.50: £5.10, £3.10, £2.00; EX 106.30 TRIFECTA Not won..
Owner Wyck Hall Stud **Bred** Edmond And Richard Kent **Trained** Cropthorne, Worcs

FOCUS

An ordinary handicap but the form looks solid enough with the winner well handicapped, the runner-up a lightly-raced improver and the third chasing a hat-trick.

Mr Cellophane Official explanation: jockey said gelding lost its action

John O'Groats(IRE) Official explanation: vet said gelding had gone into atrial fibrilation after race

6576 AYLSHAM SLURRY SERVICES H'CAP 1m 2f 21y

4:10 (4:12) (Class 4) (0-85,84) 3-Y-0+ **£4,857** (£1,445; £722; £360) **Stalls Low**

Form				RPR
4623	1		**Kavachi (IRE)**[29] 5862 4-8-2 70 oh3 RossAtkinson(7) 6 (G L Moore) *hld up: hdwy over 2f out: trckd ldr wl over 1f out: n.m.r jst ins fnl f: swtchd rt: pushed along to ld last 50yds: readily* **16/1**	80+
1	2	1	**Rose Street (IRE)**[132] 2766 3-9-3 83 PhilipRobinson 1 (M A Jarvis) *chsd ldrs: wnt 2nd over 3f out: rdn and ev ch 2f out: led ins fnl f: hdd and no ex last 50yds* **2/1**[1]	88
0053	3	2	**Fusili (IRE)**[41] 5543 4-9-4 84 PatrickHills(5) 8 (N P Littmoden) *led: rdn over 2f out: edgd lft fr over 1f out: hdd ins fnl f: fdd last 50yds* **16/1**	85
5620	4	3 ½	**Folio (IRE)**[20] 6110 7-9-5 80 TPO'Shea 4 (W J Musson) *hld up bhd: hdwy on rail 3f out: rdn and chsd ldng trio 2f out: kpt on same pce* **10/1**	74
1304	5	½	**Yossi (IRE)**[17] 6185 3-8-13 79 (b) JimmyQuinn 3 (M H Tompkins) *s.i.s: hld up bhd: plld out and rdn 3f out: hdwy to chse ldrs 2f out: no imp after* **9/2**[3]	72
4164	6	2 ½	**Just Two Numbers**[15] 6236 3-8-12 78 JamieSpencer 5 (W Jarvis) *t.k.h: hld up in last pair: hdwy 3f out: sn no imp* **5/2**[2]	66
-102	7	8	**Awatuki (IRE)**[223] 726 4-9-5 80 RichardMullen 2 (A P Jarvis) *chsd ldrs: rdn over 3f out: wknd over 2f out* **14/1**	52
	8	7	**Sea Saga (IRE)**[100] 4-9-1 76 JimmyFortune 7 (L M Cumani) *hld up towards rr: rdn and effrt over 3f out: sn struggling: no ch last 2f: t.o* **12/1**	34
240-	9	14	**Novista (IRE)**[428] 4895 3-7-12 71 oh1 ow1 AshleyMorgan(7) 9 (M H Tompkins) *stdd s: plld v hrd: pressed ldr after 2f tl over 3f out: sn dropped out: t.o fnl f* **66/1**	1

2m 11.79s (3.69) **Going Correction** +0.525s/f (Yiel)
WFA 3 from 4yo+ 5lb 9 Ran SP% **116.8**
Speed ratings (Par 105): **106,105,103,100,100 98,92,86,75**
CSF £48.92 CT £545.81 TOTE £17.50: £3.40, £1.60, £3.60; EX 63.40 Trifecta £407.90 Part won. Pool: £574.56 - 0.70 winning units. Place 6 £27.26, Place 5 £17.63.

Owner Bryan Pennick & Roy Martin **Bred** Gainsborough Stud Management Ltd **Trained** Woodingdean, E Sussex
■ Ross Atkinson's first winner.

FOCUS
Not a strongly-run handicap and the form may not be entirely reliable with little solid behind the first two and the third the best guide.
Rose Street(IRE) Official explanation: jockey said filly ran greenly
Yossi(IRE) Official explanation: jockey said colt missed the break
Just Two Numbers Official explanation: jockey said colt was denied a clear run
T/Plt: £88.10 to a £1 stake. Pool: £56,589.95. 468.50 winning tickets. T/Qpdt: £4.30 to a £1 stake. Pool: £4,161.20. 711.70 winning tickets. SP

6528 KEMPTON (A.W) (R-H)
Wednesday, October 31

OFFICIAL GOING: Standard
Wind: Nil Weather: Mild

6577 KINGDOM OF SAUDI ARABIA H'CAP — 1m 2f (P)
6:20 (6:22) (Class 6) (0-60,58) 3-Y-0+ — **£2,047** (£604; £302) **Stalls** High

Form — RPR
4500 **1** **Bowl Of Cherries**[2] 6529 4-8-10 **47** ow1 (b) NCallan 4 — 57
(I A Wood) *dwlt: hld up towards rr: hdwy on inner 3f out: swtchd lft over 1f out: led 1f out: hung lft u.p: drvn out* **7/1**[3]
0606 **2** *1* **Hatch A Plan (IRE)**[21] 6102 6-9-1 **55** NeilChalmers(3) 12 — 63
(Mouse Hamilton-Fairley) *hld up in midfield: hdwy over 3f out: chsd ldrs 2f out: ev ch 1f out: carried lft and unable qckn fnl f* **16/1**
4343 **3** *shd* **Sopran Gath (ITY)**[8] 6407 4-9-7 **58** JamesDoyle 14 — 66
(J W Hills) *hld up in midfield: swtchd lft 2f out: ev ch 1f out: carried lft and unable qckn fnl f* **10/1**
6132 **4** *¾* **Alfie Tupper (IRE)**[6] 6458 4-9-7 **58** SimonWhitworth 3 — 64
(S Kirk) *hld up in rr: hdwy over 3f out: c wd 2f out: sn rdn: styd on steadily: nt rch ldrs* **11/4**[1]
5445 **5** *1 ½* **Wee Charlie Castle (IRE)**[14] 6260 4-9-4 **55** (b) OscarUrbina 1 — 58
(G C H Chung) *sn w ldr: rdn to ld narrowly over 1f out: hdd 1f out: wknd last 100yds* **14/1**
1053 **6** *1* **Blu Manruna**[17] 6196 4-9-6 **57** (b) PaulDoe 10 — 58
(J Akehurst) *hld up in last: hdwy 2f out: r.o but nvr nr ldrs* **17/2**
0050 **7** *hd* **Play Up Pompey**[14] 6260 5-9-4 **55** JimCrowley 2 — 56
(J J Bridger) *t.k.h: hld up: rdn and effrt over 2f out: kpt on u.p: nt pce to rch ldrs* **20/1**
3043 **8** *1 ½* **Recalcitrant**[14] 6265 4-9-4 **55** SebSanders 7 — 53
(S Dow) *led: rdn 2f out: headed over 1f out: wknd ins fnl f* **9/2**[2]
4630 **9** *13* **Isphahan**[16] 6226 4-9-4 **55** (p) FrancisNorton 5 — 27
(A M Balding) *missed break and rdn early: chsd ldrs and t.k.h after 2f: rdn and wknd wl over 2f out: eased fnl f* **8/1**
10 *5* **Goochie (IRE)**[56] 5149 3-9-0 **56** JamieSpencer 13 — 18
(John Joseph Murphy, Ire) *chsd ldrs: rdn over 3f out: wkng whn hmpd over 2f out: sn eased* **8/1**
00/0 **11** *hd* **Leighton (IRE)**[14] 6260 7-9-7 **58** FergusSweeney 11 — 20
(M S Saunders) *chsd ldrs: rdn and wkng whn hmpd 2f out: sn wl btn: eased fnl f* **33/1**
50-3 **12** *14* **Persona (IRE)**[231] 12 5-9-7 **58** AdrianMcCarthy 9 — —
(B J McMath) *racd in midfield: rdn 6f out: struggling whn rdr dropped whip over 3f out: sn wl bhd: virtually p.u fnl f* **14/1**

2m 4.80s (-4.20) **Going Correction** -0.225s/f (Stan)
WFA 3 from 4yo+ 5lb — **12** Ran SP% **126.1**
Speed ratings (Par 101): **107,106,106,105,104 103,103,102,91,87 87,76**
CSF £120.97 CT £1144.76 TOTE £8.70: £2.60, £5.20, £3.30; EX 287.80.
Owner Graham Bradbury **Bred** Eurostrait Ltd **Trained** Upper Lambourn, Berks

FOCUS
A moderate handicap, but the pace was good and the winning time was decent for the level. The third sets the level to her recent best with those immediately behind close to their marks.
Hatch A Plan(IRE) Official explanation: jockey said gelding was carried left-handed inside final furlong
Goochie(IRE) Official explanation: jockey said filly was unsettled by the floodlights

6578 KEMPTON.CO.UK MAIDEN AUCTION STKS — 1m (P)
6:50 (6:52) (Class 6) 2-Y-0 — **£2,047** (£604; £302) **Stalls** High

Form — RPR
0 **1** **Sassy Gal (IRE)**[10] 6365 2-8-8 0 JamieSpencer 8 — 70+
(John Joseph Murphy, Ire) *leggy: lw: hld up in tch: swtchd lft over 2f out: rdn to ld over 1f out: edgd rt but r.o strly fnl f* **6/4**[1]
04 **2** *2* **Magical Fantasy (USA)**[50] 5308 2-8-10 0 NCallan 5 — 68
(J Nicol) *trckd ldrs: gng wl: rdn and ev ch over 1f out: outpcd by wnr fnl f* **8/1**[3]
4340 **3** *shd* **Moment's Notice**[28] 5901 2-9-0 70 LPKeniry 6 — 74+
(S Kirk) *t.k.h: hld up in midfield: hdwy over 3f out: rdn and outpcd 2f out: styd on ins fnl f: nrly snatched 2nd* **16/1**
42 **4** *2* **Spiritofthestorm (USA)**[27] 5944 2-8-5 0 ChrisCatlin 13 — 58
(R A Teal) *led for 1f: chsd ldr tl rdn to ld again over 2f out: hdd over 1f out: outpcd fnl f* **15/8**[2]
0 **5** *2 ½* **Animator**[15] 6246 2-8-13 0 SebSanders 3 — 61
(P F I Cole) *w'like: str: hld up towards rr: rdn and effrt on outer wl over 2f out: kpt on steadily: nvr able to chal* **33/1**
6 *2* **Timbalier (USA)** 2-9-0 0 RichardMullen 12 — 57
(D M Simcock) *leggy: angular: s.i.s: wl bhd: swtchd lft and rdn over 2f out: styd on past btn horses fnl f: nvr nr ldrs* **33/1**
0 **7** *hd* **Ogmore Junction (IRE)**[109] 3550 2-9-0 0 MartinDwyer 14 — 57
(P D Cundell) *dwlt: led after 1f: hdd over 2f out: sn rdn: wknd wl over 1f out* **66/1**
00 **8** *hd* **Serious Choice (IRE)**[12] 6294 2-8-13 0 IanMongan 9 — 56
(J R Boyle) *bhd: rdn 3f out: kpt on fnl f: nvr nr ldrs* **66/1**
9 *2* **Lady Asheena** 2-8-6 0 LukeMorris(3) 2 — 47
(J Jay) *unf: t.k.h: chsd ldrs: rdn over 3f out: wknd over 2f out* **50/1**
0 **10** *2 ½* **Diamond Seeker**[12] 6295 2-8-1 0 WilliamBuick(3) 10 — 37
(V Smith) *trckd ldrs on inner: rdn over 2f out: wknd qckly 2f out* **50/1**
5 **11** *¾* **Rondeau (GR)**[14] 6262 2-8-9 0 PaulDoe 7 — 40
(P R Chamings) *w'like: leggy: s.i.s: sn in tch on outer: rdn and wknd qckly 2f out: virtually p.u ins fnl f* **12/1**
4 **12** *½* **Montefiore (IRE)**[28] 5901 2-8-12 0 (t) OscarUrbina 4 — 42
(M Botti) *unf: a bhd* **16/1**
562 **13** *33* **Melt (IRE)**[7] 6425 2-8-5 0 TPO'Shea 11 — —
(R Hannon) *racd in midfield: reminder over 5f out: wknd 3f out: virtually p.u last 2f: t.o* **8/1**[3]

1m 39.04s (-1.76) **Going Correction** -0.225s/f (Stan) — **13** Ran SP% **129.3**
Speed ratings (Par 93): **99,97,96,94,92 90,90,90,88,85 84,84,51**
CSF £15.87 TOTE £3.10: £1.10, £3.30, £5.90; EX 14.00.
Owner D W J Veitch **Bred** Derek Veitch And Saleh Ali Hammadi **Trained** Upton, Co. Cork

FOCUS
Just a modest maiden with the third the best guide to the level and the sixth and seventh limiting things.

NOTEBOOK
Sassy Gal(IRE) had shown plenty of ability in her native Ireland, most notably when seventh of 12 in a Group 3 and when second in a big-field maiden on her most recent start, and she found this a suitable opportunity to get off the mark at the sixth attempt. The surface was an unknown, but she handled it just fine and was a convincing winner. (tchd 13-8)
Magical Fantasy(USA), upped to 1m for the first time, confirmed the encouragement she showed when fourth at Lingfield on her previous start, but she proved no match for the winner. She will have more options now she is qualified for a handicap mark. (op 9-1)
Moment's Notice was reported to have a breathing problem when down the field at Newcastle on his previous start, but this was a respectable effort. (op 14-1)
Spiritofthestorm(USA) was a long way below the form she showed when a short-head second over course and distance on her previous start and this was very disappointing. (op 9-2)
Animator stepped up on the form he showed when down the field on his debut at Newcastle and could make his mark once handicapped.
Timbalier(USA), a 18,000gns Dixieland Band half-brother to Leyte Gulfe, who was placed over 1m2f-1m4f in France, out of a 1m winner at two, was noted doing some good late work after starting slowly and he should improve on this. (op 25-1)
Montefiore(IRE) Official explanation: jockey said colt had a breathing problem
Melt(IRE) Official explanation: jockey said filly moved poorly throughout

6579 DIGIBET.COM H'CAP — 1m (P)
7:20 (7:20) (Class 6) (0-60,60) 3-Y-0+ — **£2,047** (£604; £302) **Stalls** High

Form — RPR
4-30 **1** **Royal Embrace**[7] 6431 4-9-1 **54** (v) DeanMcKeown 3 — 60
(D Shaw) *hld up in last pair: hdwy 2f out: burst through to ld ins fnl f: pushed out* **10/1**
6515 **2** *nk* **Viable**[37] 5687 5-9-5 **58** MickyFenton 14 — 63
(Mrs P Sly) *sn led: rdn over 2f out: hung lft u.p but kpt on wl tl hdd ins fnl f: no ex last 100yds* **7/1**[3]
6-2 **3** *nk* **Forbidden (IRE)**[20] 6121 4-9-4 **60** (t) JerryO'Dwyer(3) 9 — 65
(Daniel Mark Loughnane, Ire) *hld up in midfield: hanging rt and rdn over 2f out: r.o u.p fnl f: nt quite rch ldrs* **5/1**[2]
0-36 **4** *nk* **Capania (IRE)**[50] 5315 3-9-1 **57** RichardMullen 10 — 61
(Pat Eddery) *s.i.s: hld up in rr: hdwy into midfield over 3f out: r.o u.p over 1f out: no ex last 100yds* **25/1**
3005 **5** *¾* **Simpsons Gamble (IRE)**[32] 5817 4-8-9 **48** ChrisCatlin 6 — 50
(R A Teal) *hld up in tch: rdn over 2f out: ev ch over 1f out: unable qckn fnl f* **10/1**
0560 **6** *¾* **High Class Problem (IRE)**[77] 4505 4-9-5 **58** JimCrowley 4 — 59
(P Winkworth) *t.k.h: hld up: towards rr: rdn wl over 2f out: plugged on fnl f: nvr able to chal* **25/1**
3005 **7** *hd* **Greenwood**[16] 6226 9-9-2 **55** RobertHavlin 11 — 55
(P G Murphy) *lw: hld up in midfield: hdwy on inner over 2f out: rdn and ev ch jst over 1f out: fdd ins fnl f* **12/1**
6000 **8** *1 ½* **Royal Orissa**[29] 5890 5-8-12 **51** (p) HayleyTurner 7 — 48
(D Haydn Jones) *plld hrd: chsd ldrs: rdn and ev ch over 1f out: wknd ins fnl f* **25/1**
5106 **9** *1 ¼* **Inquisitress**[16] 6226 3-9-2 **58** SebSanders 8 — 52
(J J Bridger) *hld up in tch: hdwy over 2f out: rdn and ev ch over 1f out: wknd qckly ins fnl f* **7/1**[3]
0055 **10** *nk* **Swiper Hill (IRE)**[20] 6123 4-9-5 **58** (t) TomEaves 5 — 51
(B Ellison) *lw: racd in midfield: rdn 3f out: nt pce to chal* **9/2**[1]
3-00 **11** *1 ½* **Jomus**[290] 130 6-9-1 **54** (b) GeorgeBaker 12 — 44
(L Montague Hall) *s.i.s: hld up in rr: n.d* **12/1**
500 **12** *nk* **The Slider**[21] 6100 3-8-7 **49** ow1 (p) LPKeniry 2 — 38
(Mrs L C Jewell) *chsd ldr: rdn wl over 2f out: wknd over 2f out* **50/1**
2102 **13** *hd* **Blue Empire (IRE)**[30] 5864 6-9-4 **57** (p) LiamJones 1 — 45
(C R Dore) *chsd ldrs tl wnt 2nd over 2f out: wkng whn short of room and snatched up over 1f out* **15/2**

1m 39.31s (-1.49) **Going Correction** -0.225s/f (Stan)
WFA 3 from 4yo+ 3lb — **13** Ran SP% **118.7**
Speed ratings (Par 101): **98,97,97,97,96 95,95,93,92,92 90,90,90**
CSF £74.80 CT £410.71 TOTE £14.50: £3.80, £3.30, £1.50; EX 273.30.
Owner Mrs B E Wilkinson **Bred** Wickfield Farm Partnership **Trained** Danethorpe, Notts
■ Stewards' Enquiry : Richard Mullen caution: careless riding

FOCUS
The pace was steady, resulting in a bunch finish and a winning time slower than the previous juvenile maiden. The form is very modest rated through the third and wants treating with caution.
Jomus Official explanation: jockey said gelding ran free and clipped heels

6580 DIGIBET MEDIAN AUCTION MAIDEN STKS — 6f (P)
7:50 (7:53) (Class 6) 3-4-Y-0 — **£2,047** (£604; £302) **Stalls** High

Form — RPR
1 **Realt Na Mara (IRE)**[55] 5181 4-9-4 64 SteveDrowne 1 — 65
(H Morrison) *lengthy: lw: chsd ldr: rdn over 2f out: ev ch 2f out: led jst ins fnl f: hld on gamely all out* **5/1**
6 **2** *shd* **Tubby Isaacs**[177] 1541 3-9-3 0 SebSanders 2 — 65
(P J Makin) *w'like: str: lw: t.k.h: chsd ldrs: hdwy to ld over 2f out: sn rdn: hdd jst ins fnl f: rallied last 50yds: jst hld* **3/1**[3]
560 **3** *nk* **Compulsion**[23] 6062 4-8-13 56 PaulEddery 6 — 59
(Pat Eddery) *led tl over 2f out: ev ch and rdn 2f out: unable qckn fnl f* **15/8**[1]
- **4** *2 ½* **Diriculous** 3-9-3 0 JamieSpencer 4 — 56
(T G Mills) *w'like: scope: bit bkwd: hld up in tch: swtchd lft and rdn over 2f out: sn outpcd: styd on fnl f: nvr trbld ldrs* **11/4**[2]
4060 **5** *shd* **Ruthles Philly**[68] 4787 3-8-12 52 RichardMullen 5 — 51
(G L Moore) *t.k.h early: stdd and bhd after 2f: rdn 3f out: outpcd over 2f out: styd on ins fnl f: nt trble ldrs* **12/1**

1m 12.82s (-0.88) **Going Correction** -0.225s/f (Stan)
WFA 3 from 4yo 1lb — **5** Ran SP% **110.8**
Speed ratings (Par 101): **96,95,95,92,92**
CSF £20.04 TOTE £5.20: £2.60, £2.30; EX 21.40.
Owner Mrs G C Maxwell & J D N Tillyard **Bred** J C Condon **Trained** East Ilsley, Berks
■ Stewards' Enquiry : Steve Drowne three-day ban: used whip with excessive frequency (Nov 12,14-15)

The Form Book, Raceform Ltd, Compton, RG20 6NL

FOCUS
An ordinary older-horse maiden, with the winner officially rated just 64, that developed into a three-horse war all the way up the home straight. The form looks very modest with the third the best guide and not a race to be with.

6581 DIGIBET SPORTS BETTING H'CAP 6f (P)
8:20 (8:20) (Class 6) (0-60,60) 3-Y-O+ **£2,047** (£604; £302) **Stalls** High

Form RPR
0006 **1** **Willhewiz**[7] 6424 7-9-3 **58**......(v) FergusSweeney 1 68
(M S Saunders) *mde all: sn crossed to rail: rdn 2f out: hld on wl fnl f* **14/1**
0002 **2** *nk* **Macademy Royal (USA)**[11] 6340 4-9-1 **59**......(t) TravisBlock(3) 6 68
(H Morrison) *chsd ldrs: wnt 2nd 2f out: tried to chal ins fnl f: unable qckn last 100yds* **6/1**[2]
-031 **3** *1 1/2* **Ruman (IRE)**[14] 6264 5-9-5 **60**...... IanMongan 9 64
(M J Attwater) *lw: t.k.h: rdn to chse ldng pair over 1f out: edgd rt fnl f: kpt on same pce* **7/4**[1]
3632 **4** *1 1/4* **Perlachy**[11] 6339 3-8-13 **58**......(v) StephaneBreux(3) 8 58
(Mrs N Macauley) *towards rr: rdn wl over 2f out: styd on u.p: chsd ldng trio ins fnl f: nvr able to chal* **20/1**
4103 **5** *1 1/4* **Ishibee (IRE)**[13] 6279 3-9-2 **58**......(p) SebSanders 4 54
(J J Bridger) *racd in midfield: rdn and effrt over 2f out: kpt on but nvr pce to threaten ldrs* **7/1**
2224 **6** *hd* **Musical Script (USA)**[7] 6428 4-9-4 **59**......(b) ChrisCatlin 2 55
(Mouse Hamilton-Fairley) *lw: t.k.h: chsd ldr tl 2f out: sn wknd* **10/1**
0-00 **7** *nk* **Theoretical**[28] 5907 3-8-11 **60**...... RobbieEgan(7) 10 55
(A J McCabe) *racd in midfield: swtchd rt and rdn over 2f out: sn struggling* **20/1**
2216 **8** *1/2* **Kindallachan**[21] 6101 4-9-4 **59**...... NCallan 3 52
(G C Bravery) *stdd after s: hld up bhd: n.d* **16/1**
005 **9** *3/4* **Barbar**[23] 6062 4-9-3 **58**...... DaneO'Neill 12 49+
(Eve Johnson Houghton) *t.k.h: racd in midfield: rdn and struggling whn hmpd over 2f out: no ch after* **9/1**
4000 **10** *nk* **Pivotal Era**[14] 6268 4-9-2 **57**...... RichardThomas 7 47
(Jim Best) *a towards rr: rdn over 3f out: n.d after* **14/1**
5000 **11** *8* **Guildenstern (IRE)**[16] 6239 5-9-4 **59**...... JamieSpencer 5 23
(P Howling) *hld up in rr: lost tch over 2f out: eased fnl f* **13/2**[3]

1m 11.99s (-1.71) **Going Correction** -0.225s/f (Stan)
WFA 3 from 4yo+ 1lb **11** Ran SP% **124.3**
Speed ratings (Par 101): **102,101,99,97,96 96,95,94,93,93 82**
CSF £101.23 CT £228.35 TOTE £18.10: £5.30, £2.80, £1.40; EX 126.50.
Owner Tim Bostwick **Bred** L T And M Foster **Trained** Green Ore, Somerset
■ Stewards' Enquiry : Robbie Egan one-day ban: careless riding (Nov 11)

FOCUS
A fair sprint handicap, but very few ever managed to get involved. However, the form looks sound enough rated around the runner-up and fourth.
Guildenstern(IRE) Official explanation: jockey said gelding hung left-handed

6582 DAY TIME, NIGHT TIME, GREAT TIME CLASSIFIED STKS 7f (P)
8:50 (8:50) (Class 6) 3-Y-O+ **£2,047** (£604; £302) **Stalls** High

Form RPR
0022 **1** **Royal Envoy (IRE)**[14] 6266 4-9-2 50...... DeanMcKeown 7 63
(D Shaw) *lw: stdd s: hld up bhd: hdwy over 2f out: chsd wnr over 1f out: led ins fnl f: r.o wl* **5/1**[3]
1360 **2** *1* **Contented (IRE)**[17] 6210 5-9-2 53......(p) LPKeniry 14 60
(Mrs L C Jewell) *lw: hld up in midfield: hdwy on inner over 2f out: led wl over 1f: sn rdn and hrd pressed: hdd ins fnl f: no ex* **16/1**
0000 **3** *3/4* **Foreign Edition (IRE)**[26] 5964 5-9-2 54......(p) TomEaves 12 58
(Miss J A Camacho) *t.k.h: hld up in midfield: rdn and hanging rt over 2f out: r.o fnl wl fnl f: nt rch ldng pair* **16/1**
-500 **4** *1 1/2* **Is It Time (IRE)**[16] 6239 3-8-7 55...... NBazeley(7) 8 54
(Mrs P N Dutfield) *hld up towards rr: hdwy on inner over 2f out: rdn and no imp over 1f out* **50/1**
0004 **5** *1 1/4* **Bold Argument (IRE)**[35] 5731 4-9-2 55...... RobertHavlin 5 51
(Mrs P N Dutfield) *sn chsng ldr: rdn over 2f out: wknd over 1f out* **12/1**
0642 **6** *1* **Ganache (IRE)**[21] 6100 5-9-2 52...... JimCrowley 13 48
(P R Chamings) *lw: trckd ldrs: rdn over 2f out: wknd wl over 1f out* **7/2**[2]
5200 **7** *1/2* **Bollywood (IRE)**[17] 6212 4-9-2 44...... FrankieMcDonald 11 47
(J J Bridger) *t.k.h: hld up in rr: detached last 1/2-way: sme late hdwy: nvr nr ldrs* **33/1**
0300 **8** *1 1/2* **Apollo Five**[30] 5860 3-9-0 55...... NCallan 10 42
(D J Coakley) *lw: hld up in tch: rdn over 2f out: wknd over 1f out* **6/1**
6-03 **9** *1 1/4* **Spice Gardens (IRE)**[12] 6309 3-9-0 52...... SebSanders 6 39
(W Jarvis) *lw: plld hrd: chsd ldrs on outer: rdn over 2f out: sn btn* **6/4**[1]
0000 **10** *5* **Centreboard (USA)**[31] 5834 3-9-0 55...... PaulMulrennan 1 26
(M W Easterby) *t.k.h: sn led and crossed to rail: rdn and hdd wl over 1f out: sn wknd* **33/1**

1m 25.75s (-1.05) **Going Correction** -0.225s/f (Stan)
WFA 3 from 4yo+ 2lb **10** Ran SP% **120.5**
Speed ratings (Par 101): **97,95,95,93,91 90,90,88,87,81**
CSF £81.97 TOTE £5.90: £2.30, £3.10, £4.40; EX 59.00.
Owner The Circle Bloodstock I Limited **Bred** Northern Lights Bloodstock **Trained** Danethorpe, Notts
■ Stewards' Enquiry : N Bazeley four-day ban: used whip with excessive frequency and without giving filly time to respond (Nov 11-12, 14-15)

FOCUS
A moderate classified event and, even though a few pulled hard early, the pace did look decent which proved to the advantage of those held up. The form makes sense rated around the principals.

6583 PANORAMIC BAR & RESTAURANT LOYALTY SCHEME H'CAP 1m 4f (P)
9:20 (9:20) (Class 6) (0-60,59) 3-Y-O+ **£2,047** (£604; £302) **Stalls** Centre

Form RPR
0050 **1** **Key Partners (IRE)**[14] 6265 6-9-4 **52**...... GeorgeBaker 12 58+
(P A Blockley) *stdd after s: hld up in last pair: smooth hdwy over 2f out: led 1f out: rdn and r.o wl: comf* **25/1**
0353 **2** *1 1/4* **Fenners (USA)**[23] 6056 4-9-9 **57**...... DaleGibson 8 61
(M W Easterby) *chsd ldrs: rdn to ld over 2f out: sn hdd: ev over 1f out: kpt on same pce* **5/1**[3]
54/3 **3** *1/2* **Master At Arms**[21] 6102 4-9-11 **59**...... NCallan 11 63+
(Daniel Mark Loughnane, Ire) *lw: hld up in midfield on inner: rdn over 2f out: styd on u.p over 1f out: nt rch ldrs* **11/4**[2]
0006 **4** *shd* **Gracechurch (IRE)**[17] 6196 4-9-7 **55**...... SteveDrowne 4 58
(R J Hodges) *w.w in midfield: rdn 3f out: chsd ldrs over 1f out: kpt on same pce fnl f* **12/1**
4355 **5** *nk* **Fantasy Ride**[23] 6056 5-9-7 **58**...... WilliamBuick(3) 5 61
(J Pearce) *stdd s: t.k.h: hld up in rr: rdn and effrt on outer over 2f out: styd on fnl f: nt rch ldrs* **7/1**

04-1 **6** *1 1/4* **Ndola**[13] 6292 8-9-2 **50**......(v) JamieSpencer 6 51
(B J Curley) *t.k.h: hld up in midfield: gd hdwy 3f out: rdn to ld jst over 2f out: hdd 1f out: sn wknd* **15/8**[1]
0005 **7** *2 1/2* **Silver Dreamer (IRE)**[56] 5138 5-8-11 **45**...... AdrianMcCarthy 3 42
(H S Howe) *t.k.h: chsd ldrs tl lost pl over 3f out: kpt on same pce last 2f* **20/1**
00-2 **8** *shd* **Gamesters Lady**[23] 6068 4-9-11 **59**...... SebSanders 10 56
(W M Brisbourne) *hld up in tch on inner: rdn wl over 2f out: no imp* **11/2**
0000 **9** *6* **Iceni Princess**[19] 6147 3-8-4 **45**...... LiamJones 1 32
(P Howling) *t.k.h: hld up in rr: n.d* **50/1**
0-00 **10** *2* **Safin (GER)**[11] 6342 7-9-9 **57**...... LPKeniry 13 41
(F Jordan) *chsd ldr tl 9f out: chsd ldrs after: wknd 3f out* **50/1**
0-44 **11** *3 1/2* **Fasuby (IRE)**[8] 6408 3-8-9 **50**...... TGMcLaughlin 2 28
(P D Evans) *s.i.s: hdwy to chse ldr 9f out tl rdn and wknd 3f out* **25/1**
0030 **12** *13* **Royal Axminster**[64] 4914 12-8-11 **45**...... RobertHavlin 9 3
(Mrs P N Dutfield) *led tl wl over 2f out: sn wknd: virtually p.u ins fnl f: t.o* **33/1**

2m 35.03s (-1.87) **Going Correction** -0.225s/f (Stan)
WFA 3 from 4yo+ 7lb **12** Ran SP% **133.0**
Speed ratings (Par 101): **97,96,95,95,95 94,93,93,89,87 85,76**
CSF £154.23 CT £477.99 TOTE £32.20: £5.90, £2.20, £1.50; EX 171.30 Place 6 £448.96, Place 5 £104.33.
Owner John Wardle **Bred** Michael Munnelly **Trained** Lambourn, Berks

FOCUS
Something of a stop-start gallop for this handicap and things became a bit messy over the last couple of furlongs. Those that were ridden patiently seemed to be at an advantage and the fourth ran to this year's form.
Key Partners(IRE) Official explanation: trainer's representative said, regarding improved form shown, gelding ran too free last time out and was able to settle better today
T/Plt: £644.60 to a £1 stake. Pool: £74,622.70. 84.50 winning tickets. T/Qpdt: £40.20 to a £1 stake. Pool: £5,614.00. 103.10 winning tickets. SP

6542 LINGFIELD (L-H)
Wednesday, October 31

OFFICIAL GOING: Standard
Wind: Modest, across Weather: cloudy mild

6584 LINGFIELD PARK FOR EXHIBITIONS NURSERY 7f (P)
1:00 (1:01) (Class 5) (0-70,70) 2-Y-O **£4,095** (£1,209; £604) **Stalls** Low

Form RPR
000 **1** **Points Of View**[19] 6138 2-9-7 **70**...... SebSanders 4 78+
(Sir Mark Prescott) *chsd ldrs: rdn to chse ldr over 1f out: led ins fnl f: r.o strly* **13/2**
5401 **2** *1 3/4* **Polar Annie**[35] 5729 2-9-6 **69**...... FrancisNorton 6 72
(M S Saunders) *t.k.h: chsd ldr tl led 6f out: rdn over 2f out: hdd ins fnl f: one pce* **5/1**[1]
065 **3** *1 1/4* **Addikt (IRE)**[27] 5937 2-9-6 **69**...... GeorgeBaker 13 69
(S Kirk) *dropped in after s: hld up in rr: hdwy jst over 1f out: swtchd rt ins fnl f: r.o strly: snatched 3rd on line* **8/1**
0350 **4** *shd* **Llab Nala**[6] 6449 2-8-6 **55**...... JohnEgan 5 55
(M R Channon) *in tch in midfield: reminder wl over 3f out: rdn and hdwy over 2f out: chsd ldng pair ins fnl f: no imp: lost 3rd on line* **20/1**
0050 **5** *1/2* **Jelly Mo**[29] 5883 2-9-2 **70**...... PatrickHills(5) 12 69
(J W Hills) *in tch on outer: rdn and hdwy over 2f out: chsd ldrs over 1f out: kpt on same pce fnl f* **33/1**
0041 **6** *1/2* **Maybe I Wont**[7] 6438 2-9-4 **67** 6ex...... DaneO'Neill 10 65
(S Dow) *hmpd s: bhd: c wd and rdn wl over 1f out: styd on fnl f: nt threaten ldrs* **6/1**[3]
603 **7** *nk* **Private Code**[50] 5309 2-9-4 **67**...... RobertHavlin 11 64
(B J Meehan) *chsd ldrs: wnt 2nd over 3f out tl wl over 1f out: wknd fnl f* **14/1**
0051 **8** *shd* **It's My Day (IRE)**[32] 5818 2-9-3 **66**...... JimCrowley 9 63
(Jane Chapple-Hyam) *hmpd s: bhd: rdn over 3f out: styd on wl ins fnl f: n.d* **5/1**[1]
1405 **9** *hd* **Maddy**[23] 6052 2-9-0 **63**...... JamesDoyle 7 59
(R M Beckett) *towards rr: hdwy 3f out: rdn and chsd ldrs over 2f out: no hdwy 1f out* **11/2**[2]
430 **10** *1* **Especially (IRE)**[19] 6140 2-9-4 **67**...... GregFairley 2 61
(M Johnston) *chsd ldrs: rdn 3f out: wknd jst over 1f out* **11/1**
6005 **11** *1/2* **Bazguy**[55] 5167 2-9-5 **68**...... TGMcLaughlin 8 60
(P D Evans) *wnt rt s: in tch in midfield: rdn over 2f out: wknd over 1f out* **16/1**
2100 **12** *10* **Never Sold Out (IRE)**[19] 6150 2-8-7 **56**...... PaulEddery 3 23
(J G M O'Shea) *led for 1f: chsd ldr tl over 3f out: wknd over 2f out: eased ins fnl f* **40/1**
000 **13** *1 1/2* **Victory Shout (USA)**[139] 2590 2-8-11 **60**...... MartinDwyer 1 24
(J R Best) *midfield tl rdn and lost pl over 4f out: wl bhd last 2f: eased fnl f* **33/1**

1m 24.56s (-1.33) **Going Correction** -0.225s/f (Stan) **13** Ran SP% **121.4**
Speed ratings (Par 95): **98,96,94,94,93 93,92,92,92,91 90,79,77**
CSF £38.19 CT £280.43 TOTE £6.30: £1.70, £2.60, £2.70; EX 56.50 TRIFECTA Not won..
Owner G Moore - Osborne House **Bred** Limestone And Tara Studs **Trained** Newmarket, Suffolk

FOCUS
A modest nursery - the proximity of fourth-placed Llab Nala suggests the form is limited - but competitive nonetheless and the form looks solid.

NOTEBOOK
Points Of View showed pretty limited form in three runs in maiden company and he hardly looked well treated off a mark of 70 on his handicap debut, but he produced a much-improved performance, as so many from this stable do once assessed. He sweated up badly beforehand, which cannot have been ideal, but he did everything right in the race itself. The bare form looks just modest, but he should continue to progress. (tchd 6-1)
Polar Annie, racing off a mark 6lb higher than when winning a weaker race over this trip at Kempton on her previous start, was a little keen through the early stages, but she had plenty left for the straight and ran well in second. (tchd 11-2)
Addikt(IRE) ◆ was hopelessly placed when the pace increased rounding the final bend and it is to his credit he managed to stay on for third. He gives the impression he is still learning and he looks capable of picking up a similar event at some point. (op 11-1)
Llab Nala only has a selling win to his name, but he is a tough sort and he ran about as well as could have been expected. He was due to be dropped 2lb.
Jelly Mo was brought rather wide into the straight, but she still ran well. She has shown bits and pieces of encouraging form.
Maybe I Wont, carrying a penalty for his recent success in a 6f claimer round here, was never that well placed after getting bumped at the start and was forced to come very wide into the straight. (op 9-1)

It's My Day(IRE), racing off a 6lb higher mark than when winning a lesser nursery over this trip at Kempton, was bumped as the stalls opened and was always struggling. He finally found his stride in the straight, but it was all too late and he looks in need of 1m plus now. (op 9-2 tchd 11-2)
Maddy has struggled since winning her maiden round here earlier in the season and she was never really going. (op 5-1 tchd 9-2)

6585 ARENALEISUREPLC.COM MEDIAN AUCTION MAIDEN STKS 1m 2f (P)

1:30 (1:32) (Class 5) 2-Y-O **£3,238** (£963; £481; £240) **Stalls** Low

Form				RPR
32	**1**		**All The Aces (IRE)**[32] 5813 2-9-3 0 PhilipRobinson 5 (M A Jarvis) *chsd ldr: rdn to ld 2f out: battled on wl fnl f: hld on wl* **13/8**[1]	80+
3320	**2**	*nk*	**Howdigo**[31] 5828 2-9-3 79 DaneO'Neill 2 (J R Best) *trckd ldrs: plld out and rdn wl over 1f out: r.o wl but a jst hld* **3/1**[2]	79+
6333	**3**	*6*	**Judgethemoment (USA)**[22] 6092 2-9-3 78 JohnEgan 3 (Jane Chapple-Hyam) *in tch: pushed along 8f out: rdn 3f out: outpcd 2f out: plugged on to go 3rd ins fnl f: no ch w ldng pair* **5/1**[3]	66
00	**4**	*1*	**Sendefaa (IRE)**[14] 6262 2-8-12 0 NCallan 8 (M Botti) *hld up in tch in midfield: rdn and effrt over 3f out: outpcd over 2f out: kpt on* **20/1**	59
4002	**5**	*hd*	**Higgy's Boy (IRE)**[9] 6379 2-9-3 71 PatDobbs 4 (R Hannon) *led tl rdn and hdd 2f out: wknd fnl f* **8/1**	64
0	**6**	*shd*	**Bosamcliff (IRE)**[7] 6434 2-8-7 0 KevinGhunowa(5) 10 (A B Haynes) *s.i.s: bhd: hdwy 5f out: rdn and struggling 3f out: kpt on fnl f: nvr nr ldrs* **50/1**	59
043	**7**	*1/2*	**Havanavich**[35] 5721 2-9-3 75 GeorgeBaker 9 (S Kirk) *hdwy to chse ldrs 8f out: rdn over 2f out: wknd over 1f out* **8/1**	63+
005	**8**	*1 1/4*	**Crimsonwing (IRE)**[13] 6274 2-8-7 64 PatrickHills(5) 7 (A M Hales) *chsd ldrs: rdn 3f out: wknd over 2f out* **33/1**	56
	9	*1*	**Bruki (IRE)** 2-8-12 0 (t) GregFairley 11 (M Botti) *s.i.s: hld up in rr: lost tch 3f out: kpt on fnl f* **33/1**	54
000	**10**	*1 1/2*	**Lord's Bidding**[28] 5895 2-9-3 44 RobertHavlin 6 (R Ingram) *racd in midfield: rdn 5f out: wknd over 3f out* **66/1**	56
0000	**11**	*1 1/4*	**Jermajesty (IRE)**[22] 6079 2-8-10 50 (v) HarryPoulton(7) 13 (J R Boyle) *hld up in rr: rdn 3f out: sn lost tch* **66/1**	54?
00	**12**	*shd*	**Millennium Storm (GER)**[76] 4527 2-9-3 0 FrancisNorton 12 (M F Harris) *t.k.h: hld up in rr: lost tch 3f out* **66/1**	54?
	13	*5*	**Rutba** 2-8-12 0 MartinDwyer 1 (M P Tregoning) *s.i.s: a bhd: lost tch 3f out* **16/1**	40

2m 6.09s (-1.70) **Going Correction** -0.225s/f (Stan) **13** Ran SP% **124.9**
Speed ratings (Par 95): **97,96,91,91,91 90,90,89,88,87 86,86,82**
CSF £6.32 TOTE £2.30: £1.10, £1.20, £1.60; EX 8.50 Trifecta £30.90 Pool: £368.03 - 8.44 winning tickets..
Owner A D Spence **Bred** Jack Ronan And Des Ver Hunt Farm Ltd **Trained** Newmarket, Suffolk

FOCUS
Just an ordinary maiden with the first two coming clear but the previous form of those behind tends to limit.

NOTEBOOK
All The Aces(IRE) confirmed the promise of his two runs on turf over shorter at Haydock, but he was made to work very hard by Howdigo. He will apparently be put away for the year now and should make a useful middle-distance/stayer next year. (op 6-4 tchd 7-4 in places)
Howdigo was beginning to look exposed, but he produced an improved performance stepped up fully three furlongs in trip. He was well clear of the remainder and should find a race over this sort of distance. (op 4-1)
Judgethemoment(USA) was badly outpaced on the turn for home and he proved no match whatsoever for the front pair. To be struggling to lay up when it matters over this trip at this stage of his career hardly bodes well, and he gives the impression he will need a strongly-run race to be seen at his best. (op 4-1)
Sendefaa(IRE) was beaten a fair way into fourth, but she will have more options now she is qualified for a handicap mark. (op 25-1 tchd 33-1)
Higgy's Boy(IRE) had every chance from the front, but this trip seemed to stretch him. (op 10-1)

6586 LINGFIELD PARK FOR CONFERENCES CLAIMING STKS 6f (P)

2:00 (2:01) (Class 5) 2-Y-O **£3,238** (£963; £481; £240) **Stalls** Low

Form				RPR
4301	**1**		**Countrywide Comet (IRE)**[12] 6305 2-9-1 57 (b) NCallan 1 (K A Ryan) *mde all: rdn 2f out: styd on wl fnl f* **6/1**	64
0030	**2**	*2*	**Mairead's Boy (IRE)**[9] 6388 2-8-10 53 (b) JohnEgan 5 (J S Moore) *chsd ldrs: rdn over 2f out: wnt 2nd ins fnl f: no imp on wnr* **14/1**	53
0503	**3**	*nk*	**Ramblin Bob**[21] 6099 2-8-12 65 ow1 SebSanders 2 (R M Beckett) *pressed wnr: rdn over 2f out: unable qck u.p over 1f out: one pce* **5/2**[1]	54
2054	**4**	*1/2*	**Redsensor**[11] 6329 2-9-1 75 (b[1]) PatDobbs 8 (R Hannon) *racd in midfield: rdn and effrt over 2f out: kpt on ins fnl f: nvr able to chal* **11/4**[2]	56
0025	**5**	*3/4*	**I Dont Do Walkin (USA)**[7] 6438 2-8-4 67 (p) NickyMackay 11 (B J Meehan) *chsd ldrs: rdn over 2f out: unable qck 2f out: plugged on* **9/2**[3]	42
02P3	**6**	*1 1/4*	**Ely Une (IRE)**[7] 6425 2-7-13 50 NataliaGemelova(5) 3 (J S Moore) *bmpd s: bhd and rdn along: hdwy on inner over 2f out: no imp fnl f* **16/1**	39
4220	**7**	*1 1/4*	**Mama Leo**[61] 5017 2-8-7 59 PaulEddery 9 (J G M O'Shea) *a bhd: rdn 1/2-way: nvr nr ldrs* **25/1**	38
0004	**8**	*1 1/2*	**Enchanted Lady**[36] 5706 2-8-2 52 FrancisNorton 10 (H J L Dunlop) *a outpcd in last trio: n.d* **16/1**	28
0406	**9**	*1 1/4*	**Kintyre Lass (IRE)**[50] 5302 2-8-3 50 (b) ChrisCatlin 7 (B R Millman) *racd in midfield: rdn 3f out: wknd 2f out* **25/1**	26
2000	**10**	*4*	**Vixens Daughter**[58] 5096 2-8-6 49 (t) HayleyTurner 4 (R T Phillips) *wnt lft s: a struggling in rr* **33/1**	17

1m 12.09s (-0.72) **Going Correction** -0.225s/f (Stan) **10** Ran SP% **116.8**
Speed ratings (Par 95): **95,92,91,91,90 88,86,84,83,77**
CSF £83.48 TOTE £8.60: £2.20, £5.00, £1.10; EX 84.60 Trifecta £184.90 Part won. Pool: £260.54 - 0.96 winning tickets..The winner was claimed by Paul Howling for £12,000.
Owner Countrywide Racing **Bred** Mrs R Leonard **Trained** Hambleton, N Yorks
■ Stewards' Enquiry : Nicky Mackay one-day ban: careless riding (Nov 11)

FOCUS
A moderate claimer in which the form is solid enough but limited by the time and the proximity of the runner-up.

NOTEBOOK
Countrywide Comet(IRE) followed up his recent success in a similar event over 7f at Redcar in convincing fashion, but his main rivals ran below form and this was not much of a race. He was claimed for £12,000 by Paul Howling. (op 11-2 tchd 5-1)
Mairead's Boy(IRE), lowered in grade, ran a respectable race in second, but he has already been beaten in sellers three times in the past. (op 25-1)
Ramblin Bob, dropped in trip with the blinkers left off this time, ran some way below his best and seems to be regressing. (op 3-1)
Redsensor, fitted with blinkers for the first time and switched to Polytrack, ran nowhere near his official mark of 75 and is another who is going the wrong way. (op 7-2)
I Dont Do Walkin(USA), with cheekpieces replacing blinkers, ran a moderate race and looks one to avoid for the time being. (op 3-1)

6587 CHRISTMAS PARTIES AT LINGFIELD PARK H'CAP 7f (P)

2:30 (2:33) (Class 6) (0-52,52) 3-Y-O+ **£2,590** (£770; £385; £192) **Stalls** Low

Form				RPR
3000	**1**		**Quantum Leap**[28] 5900 10-9-2 **52** (v) SebSanders 3 (S Dow) *racd in midfield: rdn over 2f out: hdwy on inner over 1f out: drvn to ld ins fnl f: hld on cl home* **15/2**	60
40	**2**	*nk*	**Majestical (IRE)**[8] 6415 5-9-1 **51** (e[1]) NCallan 10 (V Smith) *s.i.s: t.k.h: hld up in rr: hdwy over 2f out: rdn and nt qckn wl over 1f out: r.o ins fnl f: wnt 2nd last 100yds: hld nr fin* **8/1**	58
433	**3**	*1 1/2*	**Shunkawakhan (IRE)**[14] 6266 4-8-13 **49** (p) OscarUrbina 14 (G C H Chung) *w.w: in tch: hdwy wl over 2f out: ev ch 2f out: led jst over 1f out: sn hung lft: hdd ins fnl f: fnd nil* **5/1**[2]	52
622	**4**	*hd*	**Having A Ball**[70] 4711 3-8-12 **50** ChrisCatlin 4 (P D Cundell) *t.k.h: chsd ldrs: rdn wl over 2f out: ev ch 1f out: unable qck fnl f* **13/2**[3]	52
6000	**5**	*hd*	**Rafferty (IRE)**[14] 6268 8-8-5 **48** ThomasBubb(7) 8 (S Dow) *s.i.s: hdwy on outer over 3f out: ev ch on wd outside 2f out: unable qck ins fnl f* **25/1**	50
4000	**6**	*nk*	**Joy And Pain**[8] 6412 6-9-0 **50** (p) IanMongan 2 (M J Attwater) *t.k.h: stdd after s and hld up in rr: grad moved to outer 3f out: gd hdwy 2f out: chsd ldrs 1f out: no hdwy last 100yds* **16/1**	51
2155	**7**	*1 1/4*	**Knead The Dough**[27] 5947 6-8-7 **48** NataliaGemelova(5) 6 (A E Price) *chsd ldrs: rdn and ev ch 2f out: wknd last 100yds* **12/1**	46
5050	**8**	*1/2*	**Shava**[27] 5946 7-8-11 **47** FrancisNorton 5 (H J Evans) *hld up towards rr: shkn up and hdwy 2f out: no imp fnl f* **8/1**	43
0404	**9**	*shd*	**Tipsy Lad**[5] 6479 5-8-11 **47** (bt) FergusSweeney 11 (D J S Ffrench Davis) *s.i.s: bhd and rdn along: sme late hdwy: nvr on terms* **12/1**	43
6060	**10**	*2*	**Feelin Irie (IRE)**[27] 5946 4-8-7 **50** (p) HarryPoulton(7) 7 (J R Boyle) *chsd ldr tl rdn to ld jst over 2f out: hdd jst over 1f out: wknd qckly* **14/1**	41
0025	**11**	*1 1/2*	**Palais Polaire**[7] 6431 5-8-13 **52** TravisBlock(3) 9 (J A Geake) *taken down early: v.s.i.s: a bhd: n.d* **9/2**[1]	39
2000	**12**	*1/2*	**Neboisha**[42] 5528 3-8-11 **49** JimCrowley 12 (P Howling) *racd in midfield: rdn wl over 3f out: wknd over 2f out* **33/1**	34
0000	**13**	*nk*	**Under Fire (IRE)**[35] 5730 4-8-11 **47** HayleyTurner 1 (A W Carroll) *sn rdn along: chsd ldrs tl wknd 3f out: sn bhd* **25/1**	31
0030	**14**	*1 1/2*	**Suhayl Star (IRE)**[37] 5688 3-9-0 **52** NickyMackay 13 (M Wigham) *led tl jst over 2f out: wknd qckly wl over 1f out: heavily eased ins fnl f* **16/1**	32

1m 24.42s (-1.47) **Going Correction** -0.225s/f (Stan)
WFA 3 from 4yo+ 2lb **14** Ran SP% **126.6**
Speed ratings (Par 101): **99,98,96,96,96 96,94,94,94,91 90,89,89,87**
CSF £68.64 CT £348.95 TOTE £8.40: £1.90, £2.70, £2.10; EX 50.20 TRIFECTA Not won..
Owner Mrs M E O'Shea **Bred** L C And Mrs A E Sigsworth **Trained** Epsom, Surrey

FOCUS
A moderate but competitive handicap and straightforward form that is sound for the grade rated around the second and fourth.
Quantum Leap Official explanation: trainer's representative said, regarding improved form shown, gelding was badly drawn on its previous run
Palais Polaire Official explanation: jockey said mare missed the break

6588 LINGFIELD PARK FOR WEDDINGS NURSERY 6f (P)

3:00 (3:01) (Class 4) (0-85,83) 2-Y-O **£5,181** (£1,541; £770; £384) **Stalls** Low

Form				RPR
3322	**1**		**Fabuleux Cherie**[16] 6227 2-8-6 **68** FrancisNorton 5 (W R Muir) *t.k.h: chsd ldrs: rdn 2f out: r.o gamely to ld nr fin* **7/2**[3]	70
504	**2**	*hd*	**Castles In The Air**[34] 5745 2-8-10 **72** PaulEddery 2 (Pat Eddery) *chsd ldr: rdn wl over 2f out: ev ch ins fnl f: no ex last strides* **10/3**[2]	73
1	**3**	*1/2*	**Blue Jack**[21] 6104 2-8-13 **75** RichardMullen 4 (W R Muir) *hld up in rr: rdn and effrt over 1f out: ev ch ins fnl f: no ex nr fin* **11/4**[1]	75
0020	**4**	*1*	**Cocabana**[17] 6195 2-8-6 **68** JamesDoyle 1 (J G Portman) *led: rdn over 1f out: hdd wl ins fnl f: fdd nr fin* **20/1**	65
1000	**5**	*nk*	**Monaazalah (IRE)**[88] 4152 2-9-7 **83** MartinDwyer 6 (B W Hills) *v.s.a: hld up in rr: rdn and effrt wl over 1f out: no imp tl styd on last 100yds* **15/2**	79+
150	**6**	*hd*	**The Game**[17] 6195 2-9-1 **77** NCallan 7 (J R Boyle) *t.k.h: stdd after s and hld up in rr: hdwy and nt clr run 2f out: rdn and running on whn short of room and snatched up wl ins fnl f: nt rcvr* **7/1**	76+
5530	**7**	*3/4*	**Choisky (IRE)**[6] 6449 2-8-6 **68** ChrisCatlin 3 (J Akehurst) *chsd ldrs: rdn wl over 2f out: kpt on same pce fnl f* **13/2**	61

1m 12.71s (-0.10) **Going Correction** -0.225s/f (Stan) **7** Ran SP% **114.3**
Speed ratings (Par 97): **91,90,90,88,88 88,87**
CSF £15.58 TOTE £4.80: £2.00, £1.90; EX 15.50.
Owner David & Gwyn Joseph **Bred** J K Beckitt And Son **Trained** Lambourn, Berks

FOCUS
A modest winning time for a race like this, 0.62 seconds slower than the earlier claimer. The form is messy and best rated around the winner and sixth.

NOTEBOOK
Fabuleux Cherie has been in really good form since winning a seller at Windsor back in August, following up in a handicap and running several good races in defeat subsequently. Racing here off a career-high mark, she comes from a yard who are in decent form at present and she got on top close home under a strong ride from Norton. This consistent mare should continue to give a good account off a higher mark. (op 3-1)
Castles In The Air, who shaped well on a couple of occasions in maidens, looked on a reasonable mark for this handicap debut and he showed improved form, but just ran into a mare in hot form. He should have little trouble winning races, whether it be a maiden or handicap. (op 11-2)
Blue Jack made a good first impression when winning over 5f on debut at Nottingham and the step up to 6f on this nursery debut looked unlikely to pose him any problems. In rear early, he came to have his chance, but was outbattled and simply found the front pair too experienced. There should be more to come from the son of Cadeaux Genereux. (tchd 5-2 and 3-1)
Cocabana ran well to a point, but she is likely to remain vulnerable off this mark. (op 16-1)
Monaazalah(IRE) did not go on from her maiden success back in the summer, but she certainly showed more on this return from a break, running on well late on having been very sluggish out of the stalls. She is still on a stiff enough mark, but is clearly capable of better. (op 5-1)

The Game got no luck at all, getting blocked on more than one occasion when attempting to come with a run and passing the line with plenty still left in the tank. He can safely have the run ignored. Official explanation: jockey said colt was denied a clear run (op 9-1)

6589 LINGFIELDPARK.CO.UK H'CAP 5f (P)
3:30 (3:30) (Class 4) (0-85,82) 3-Y-0+
£6,232 (£1,866; £933; £467; £233; £117) **Stalls** High

Form RPR

3041 **1** **New York Oscar (IRE)**[8] 6406 3-8-12 **76** 6ex................(p) SebSanders 9 88+
(A J McCabe) *chsd ldrs: wnt 2nd jst over 2f out: led jst over 1f out: rdn and r.o strly fnl f: readily* **15/2**

3030 **2** *1 3/4* **Texas Gold**[16] 6231 9-9-1 **79**................ MartinDwyer 7 84
(W R Muir) *t.k.h: hld up in last pair: hdwy and rdn on inner 2f out: r.o to go 2nd ins fnl f: no ch w wnr* **7/2**[2]

132 **3** *nk* **Osiris Way**[19] 6141 5-9-4 **82**................ JimCrowley 3 86
(P R Chamings) *chsd ldr tl jst over 2f out: sn rdn and unable qckn: styd on ins fnl f* **15/8**[1]

2063 **4** *nk* **Bluebok**[8] 6405 6-8-11 **75**................(t) DaneO'Neill 2 78
(J M Bradley) *s.i.s: sn in tch in midfield: rdn over 2f out: kpt on same pce fnl f* **12/1**

0000 **5** *nk* **Sand Cat**[19] 6142 4-9-2 **80**................ GeorgeBaker 1 82
(G L Moore) *led: rdn 2f out: hdd jst over 1f out: no ch w wnr after: fdd last 100yds* **20/1**

4506 **6** *1/2* **Fromsong (IRE)**[14] 6273 9-9-0 **78**................ JohnEgan 8 78
(D K Ivory) *t.k.h: hld up in tch: lost pl bnd over 2f out: rdn wl over 1f out: kpt on same pce* **10/1**

0024 **7** *hd* **George The Second**[8] 6405 4-8-10 **74**................ RichardKingscote 6 73
(Mrs H Sweeting) *chsd ldrs: rdn wl over 2f out: one pce last 2f* **7/1**[3]

0101 **8** *nk* **Hereford Boy**[8] 6405 3-9-0 **78** 6ex................ RobertHavlin 5 76
(D K Ivory) *stdd after s: bhd: rdn and effrt wl over 1f out: nvr able to chal* **14/1**

0000 **9** *3/4* **Mambazo**[62] 4965 5-8-4 **75**................(e) WilliamCarson(7) 4 71
(S C Williams) *taken down early: hld up towards rr: rdn and effrt 2f out: sn no imp* **25/1**

0540 **10** *3 1/2* **Peter Island (FR)**[6] 6450 4-8-12 **76**................(b) NCallan 10 59
(J Gallagher) *s.i.s: sn racing in midfield: rdn over 2f out: wknd over 1f out* **14/1**

57.97 secs (-1.81) **Going Correction** -0.225s/f (Stan) **10 Ran SP% 120.0**
Speed ratings (Par 105): **105,102,101,101,100 99,99,99,97,92**
CSF £35.00 CT £72.50 TOTE £8.10: £2.30, £1.50, £1.20; EX 41.20 Trifecta £80.90 Pool: £512.12 - 4.49 winning tickets..
Owner Paul J Dixon and James Kennerley **Bred** Corduff Stud And J Judd **Trained** Babworth, Notts
■ Stewards' Enquiry : Dane O'Neill two-day ban: used whip with excessive frequency (Nov 11-12)

FOCUS
A fair sprint handicap run in a reasonable time; the form is taken at face value but somewhat limited by the proximity of the fourth and fifth.
Fromsong(IRE) Official explanation: jockey said gelding hung badly right

6590 PLAY GOLF @ LINGFIELD PARK H'CAP 1m 2f (P)
4:00 (4:00) (Class 6) (0-58,57) 3-Y-O **£2,590** (£770; £385; £192) **Stalls** Low

Form RPR

000 **1** **Formidable Guest**[35] 5728 3-8-2 46................ WilliamBuick(3) 2 49
(J Pearce) *hld up in tch: stdd to rr 6f out: hdwy 3f out: rdn over 2f out: styd on u.p to ld last strides* **6/1**[3]

5004 **2** *hd* **Always Best**[6] 6453 3-8-5 46................ GregFairley 10 48
(M Johnston) *chsd ldr tl 8f out: styd handy: rdn to chse ldr again 2f out: led wl ins fnl f: hdd last strides* **6/4**[1]

0000 **3** *shd* **Woodins Way**[23] 6062 3-8-9 50................ AmirQuinn 7 52
(P J Makin) *t.k.h: hld up in rr: hdwy on outer 3f out: rdn wl over 1f out: styd on u.p fnl f: clsng nr fin* **12/1**

0020 **4** *1* **My Monna**[2] 6529 3-8-2 50................ JosephWalsh(7) 8 50
(Miss Sheena West) *in tch: hdwy on outer to chse wnr 8f out: led over 6f out: hrd pressed and rdn over 2f out: hdd wl ins fnl f: fdd nr fin* **11/1**

3144 **5** *3/4* **Everyman**[13] 6292 3-8-12 53................(v) JimCrowley 1 52
(A W Carroll) *t.k.h: chsd ldrs: rdn wl over 1f out: kpt on one pce u.p* **11/2**[2]

0006 **6** *1* **Lordswood (IRE)**[17] 6206 3-8-4 45................ ChrisCatlin 4 42
(J J Bridger) *hld up in midfield: rdn and effrt on inner 2f out: no imp over 1f out* **14/1**

0450 **7** *nk* **Bold Saxon (IRE)**[11] 6344 3-9-1 56................ HayleyTurner 3 52
(M D I Usher) *led tl over 6f out: chsd ldr after: rdn over 2f out: wknd jst over 1f out* **14/1**

0000 **8** *1 1/2* **Christalini**[26] 5899 3-9-2 57................ PatDobbs 9 50
(J C Fox) *stdd s: hld up in rr: rdn and effrt 2f out: no imp over 1f out* **14/1**

005 **9** *1 3/4* **Emily's Rainbow (IRE)**[16] 6238 3-8-11 52................ LiamJones 6 41
(W J Haggas) *in tch: rdn 3f out: wknd over 2f out* **15/2**

2m 7.53s (-0.26) **Going Correction** -0.225s/f (Stan) **9 Ran SP% 117.5**
Speed ratings (Par 99): **92,91,91,90,90 89,89,88,86**
CSF £15.67 CT £107.45 TOTE £7.10: £1.80, £1.10, £2.80; EX 16.40 Trifecta £129.70 Pool: £263.09 - 1.44 winning tickets. Place 6 £43.11, Place 5 £16.77.
Owner Macniler Racing Partnership **Bred** Kingwood Bloodstock **Trained** Newmarket, Suffolk
■ Stewards' Enquiry : William Buick three-day ban: used whip with excessive frequency and without giving filly time to respond (Nov 11-13)

FOCUS
A poor quality handicap with the fourth to course form and a race to be against.
T/Plt: £43.60 to a £1 stake. Pool: £49,365.30. 825.95 winning tickets. T/Qpdt: £14.20 to a £1 stake. Pool: £3,511.50. 181.80 winning tickets. SP

6281 NOTTINGHAM (L-H)
Wednesday, October 31

OFFICIAL GOING: Good to firm (good in back straight; str 9.0, bck str 8.5, overall 8.8)
After another dry week the ground was described as 'near perfect'. The inside track was in use.
Wind: Light, half-against Weather: Fine and sunny

6591 TURFTV A MATTER OF COURSE (S) STKS 1m 54y
12:50 (12:51) (Class 6) 2-Y-O **£2,286** (£675; £337) **Stalls** Centre

Form RPR

4000 **1** **Heavenly Saint**[19] 6150 2-8-6 55................ TPO'Shea 9 58
(M R Channon) *trckd ldrs: smooth hdwy 3f out: rdn to ld over 1f out and sn edgd lft: styd on strly u.p ins fnl f* **11/2**[2]

1040 **2** *3* **Lord Deevert**[19] 6151 2-8-9 67................(p) JackDean(7) 12 61
(W G M Turner) *hld up: stdy hdwy on outer over 3f out: rdn to chal wl over 1f out and ev ch tl one pce ins fnl f* **7/1**

0050 **3** *1 1/4* **Alfredtheordinary**[51] 5268 2-8-11 53................ SamHitchcott 6 54
(M R Channon) *led 2f: cl up tl led again over 4f out: rdn along and hdd wl over 2f out: led again briefly 2f out and sn drvn: hdd and one pce over 1f out* **5/1**[1]

430 **4** *2* **Giggling Monkey**[65] 4875 2-8-6 50................ PaulHanagan 4 44
(P D Evans) *chsd ldrs: rdn along 3f out: drvn wl over 1f out and kpt on same pce* **11/2**[2]

006 **5** *2 1/2* **Korcula**[56] 5133 2-8-11 47................ TedDurcan 8 44
(M J Wallace) *midfield: effrt and sme hdwy over 2f out: sn rdn and no imp* **33/1**

6200 **6** *shd* **Magnol**[7] 6433 2-8-3 57................ LukeMorris(3) 11 39
(J G M O'Shea) *hld up in rr: hdwy 3f out: sn rdn along and nvr nr ldrs* **14/1**

0606 **7** *1 1/4* **Ochenvay**[7] 6427 2-8-1 50................ KirstyMilczarek(5) 5 36
(M Quinn) *prom: rdn along 3f out: drvn wl over 1f out and plugged on same pce* **11/2**[2]

4600 **8** *1 3/4* **Pay Pay Pay**[8] 6410 2-8-7 56 ow1................(v[1]) DavidAllan 13 33
(P D Evans) *t.k.h: chsd ldrs tl led after 2f: wd home turn and sn hdd: rdn to ld again wl over 2f out: drvn and hdd 2f out: sn wknd* **9/1**

005 **9** *3 1/2* **Racey Rachel (IRE)**[30] 5869 2-8-6 52................ RoystonFfrench 2 24+
(E F Vaughan) *dwlt: a in rr: sddle slipped* **6/1**[3]

0 **10** *nk* **Pembo**[113] 3404 2-8-11 0................ SteveDrowne 3 29
(B Palling) *chsd ldrs: rdn along on inner over 3f out and sn wknd* **20/1**

5000 **11** *1 1/2* **Miss Willoughby**[41] 5571 2-8-11 45................(e) AdamKirby 7 25
(J Ryan) *a bhd* **100/1**

0 **12** *11* **Dome Blonde**[16] 6234 2-8-7 0 ow1................(p) NeilPollard 10 —
(W J Musson) *a in rr* **66/1**

1m 46.68s (0.28) **Going Correction** -0.20s/f (Firm) **12 Ran SP% 116.5**
Speed ratings (Par 93): **90,87,85,83,81 81,79,78,74,74 72,61**
CSF £41.81 TOTE £9.10: £2.40, £2.90, £2.00; EX 60.60.The winner was sold to Mount Pleasant Farm Racing for 6,000gns.
Owner John Sheehan **Bred** Mrs E C Dowling **Trained** West Ilsley, Berks

FOCUS
A poor affair which saw the field finish strung out behind the ready winner who is rated to form.

NOTEBOOK
Heavenly Saint, who had shown little on her last three outings on Polytrack, bounced right back to form on this return to the turf and won her first race at the seventh time of asking. She did the job in good style too, making up her ground easily when asked to win the race, and the drop into this grade clearly worked the oracle. Now connections know she gets this trip without fuss it opens up more options and she can go in again. (tchd 6-1)
Lord Deevert came through to have his chance on the outside of the pack, but failed to match the winner's speed at the business end. The application of cheekpieces held a positive effect and, considering this was only his fourth outing on turf, he appeals as the sort to win again in this company. However, a drop back to 7f will probably help on that front. (tchd 15-2)
Alfredtheordinary, back down in grade, was ridden much more prominently this time and basically helped to set up the race for his winning stable companion. The application of some headgear may well help his cause. (op 9-2 tchd 6-1)
Giggling Monkey, another dropping back down in grade, was having her first outing for 65 days and was unable to land a serious blow. It is hard to say whether she truly stayed the trip. (op 6-1 tchd 5-1)
Korcula failed to get home on this step up in trip and looks one to avoid.
Ochenvay Official explanation: jockey said filly was unsuited by the fast ground
Racey Rachel(IRE) Official explanation: jockey said saddle slipped

6592 OATH MAIDEN STKS (C&G) (DIV I) 1m 54y
1:20 (1:21) (Class 4) 2-Y-O **£3,562** (£1,059; £529; £264) **Stalls** Centre

Form RPR

22 **1** **Doctor Fremantle**[28] 5918 2-9-0 0................ RyanMoore 10 76+
(Sir Michael Stoute) *hld up in rr: smooth hdwy over 5f out: qcknd to ld 3f out: clr over 1f out: easily* **8/13**[1]

40 **2** *5* **St Jean Cap Ferrat**[40] 5598 2-9-0 67................ DarryllHolland 7 65+
(G Wragg) *trckd ldrs: wnt 2nd over 2f out: kpt on: no ch w wnr* **22/1**

0 **3** *2* **Tajweed (IRE)**[40] 5598 2-9-0 0................ RHills 2 59+
(M Johnston) *dwlt: in rr: hdwy on wd outside whn hmpd 3f out: kpt on fnl f* **16/1**

6 **4** *1 1/4* **Stow**[12] 6296 2-9-0 0................ SteveDrowne 9 54
(H Morrison) *mid-div: sn pushed along: hdwy over 3f out: outpcd and swtchd outside over 1f out: styd on* **12/1**

5 *shd* **Wells Lyrical (IRE)** 2-9-0 0................ TomEaves 6 54
(B Smart) *s.i.s: last and reminders after 2f: hdwy over 2f out: kpt on fnl f* **50/1**

5 **6** *3/4* **Manalito**[12] 6294 2-9-0 0................ TPO'Shea 1 52
(M R Channon) *s.i.s: hld up in rr: kpt on fnl 3f: nvr nr ldrs* **7/1**[3]

2 **7** *2* **Etruscan (IRE)**[21] 6107 2-9-0 0................ TedDurcan 5 48
(Saeed Bin Suroor) *sn trcking ldrs: t.k.h: drvn 3f out: sn btn* **4/1**[2]

60 **8** *2* **Leitmotif (USA)**[20] 6127 2-9-0 0................ TPQueally 3 43
(J L Dunlop) *chsd ldrs: wkng whn sltly hmpd over 2f out* **50/1**

00 **9** *3 1/2* **Promised Gold**[7] 6417 2-9-0 0................ DavidKinsella 11 35
(J A Geake) *in rr: hdwy over 3f out: lost pl over 1f out* **100/1**

000 **10** *4* **Casual Garcia**[13] 6285 2-9-0 36................ JamieMackay 4 27
(Sir Mark Prescott) *led tl 3f out: sn wknd* **125/1**

0 **11** *1 1/2* **Rockjumper**[15] 6248 2-9-0 0................ RichardHughes 8 23
(H Morrison) *w ldr: wknd qckly over 2f out* **50/1**

1m 44.28s (-2.12) **Going Correction** -0.20s/f (Firm) **11 Ran SP% 120.0**
Speed ratings (Par 97): **102,97,95,93,93 92,90,88,85,81 79**
CSF £24.54 TOTE £1.50: £1.02, £6.00, £5.20; EX 24.10.
Owner K Abdulla **Bred** Juddmonte Farms Ltd **Trained** Newmarket, Suffolk
■ Stewards' Enquiry : Steve Drowne one-day ban: careless riding (Nov 11)

FOCUS
Much the quicker and stronger division, a massive 2.32 seconds faster than division two. An effortless winner but the runner-up is rated just 67 and limits the form to some extent.

NOTEBOOK
Doctor Fremantle, noisy in the pre-parade ring, looked a picture of wellbeing and is a fluent mover. He swept to the front and was clear with the race won in a matter of strides and should make a useful handicapper at three. (op 4-6 tchd 8-11)
St Jean Cap Ferrat, having his fourth start, is rated just 67. He would surely have been better off in a nursery. (op 20-1)
Tajweed(IRE), an immature type, had finished last on his previous outing five weeks earlier. He stayed on down the wide outside after a tardy start and taking a bump, but will not be at his best until next year.
Stow still looks very immature and should do better in handicap company at three. (op 14-1 tchd 16-1)
Wells Lyrical(IRE), by Sadler's Wells out of a half-sister to an Oaks winner, looks very weak at present. Clueless, he stayed on when it was all over and should improve over middle distances next year.

Manalito, a decent type, was by no means knocked about and should prove his true worth in handicap company at three. (op 10-1)
Etruscan(IRE), who looked very fit indeed, would not settle and dropped away in a matter of strides. (op 10-3)

6593 OATH MAIDEN STKS (C&G) (DIV II) 1m 54y
1:50 (1:52) (Class 4) 2-Y-O £3,562 (£1,059; £529; £264) **Stalls** Centre

Form RPR

3 **1** **Turn Left (IRE)**[19] 6138 2-9-0 0 AdamKirby 4 70+
(R M Beckett) *in tch: hdwy and nt clr run 2f out: sn swtchd rt and rdn over 1f out: styd on strly to ld nr fin* **4/1**[2]

3 **2** ½ **Just Rob**[21] 6107 2-8-9 0 RussellKennemore(5) 2 69
(R Hollinshead) *trckd ldrs: hdwy on inner 4f out: n.m.r and swtchd rt 2f out: rdn to ld wl over 1f out: drvn ins fnl f: hdd and no ex nr fin* **6/1**[3]

0 **3** hd **Elliwan**[7] 6417 2-9-0 0 RHills 5 69
(M Johnston) *towards rr: gd hdwy on outer 3f out: rdn to chal wl over 1f out and ev ch tl drvn and nt qckn ins fnl f* **12/1**

4 ¾ **Moyenne Corniche** 2-9-0 0 DarryllHolland 10 67+
(G Wragg) *s.i.s and bhd: gd hdwy on outer 3f out: rdn to chse ldrs over 1f out: kpt on ins fnl f* **11/1**

5040 **5** ½ **Eton Fable (IRE)**[9] 6379 2-8-11 68 AndrewMullen(3) 3 66
(W J H Ratcliffe) *led: rdn along and hdd 3f out: drvn wl over 1f out and kpt on u.p ins fnl f* **9/1**

44 **6** ¾ **Fearless Warrior**[40] 5599 2-9-0 0 TPQueally 1 64
(J L Dunlop) *trckd ldrs: smooth hdwy 3f out and sn ev ch: rdn 2f out: drvn and one pce appr fnl f* **7/2**[1]

7 nk **Hawk Flight (IRE)** 2-9-0 0 RichardHughes 6 64
(W R Muir) *dwlt: sn prom: led 3f out and sn rdn: drvn and hdd wl over 1f out: grad wknd* **20/1**

8 3½ **Smetana** 2-9-0 0 RyanMoore 8 56
(H Morrison) *in rr: sme hdwy 3f out: sn rdn and nvr a factor* **15/2**

9 1½ **Asian Classic (IRE)** 2-9-0 0 SteveDrowne 9 53
(R Charlton) *s.i.s and bhd: hdwy on inner over 3f out: rdn along over 2f out and no imp* **9/1**

6 **10** 5 **No Nukes**[6] 6456 2-9-0 0 DavidAllan 7 42
(P D Evans) *in tch: rdn along over 3f out and sn wknd* **80/1**

0 **11** ½ **Traitor's Gate**[18] 6177 2-9-0 0 RoystonFfrench 11 40
(M Johnston) *prom: rdn along and wknd 3f out: edgd lft 2f out and sn bhd* **20/1**

1m 46.6s (0.20) **Going Correction** -0.20s/f (Firm) 11 Ran SP% **115.1**
Speed ratings (Par 97): **91,90,90,89,89 88,88,84,83,78 77**
CSF £26.93 TOTE £4.50: £1.90, £2.20, £3.90; EX 29.90.
Owner R S G Jones & Norman Brunskill **Bred** Khorshed And Ian Deane **Trained** Whitsbury, Hants

FOCUS
A fair second division of the juvenile maiden, run at just an ordinary pace and 2.32 seconds slower than the other half. The first seven were closely covered at the finish which suggests the form is not worth much, and the fifth is the best guide to the form.

NOTEBOOK
Turn Left(IRE), third on his debut at Lingfield 19 days previously, ran out a gutsy winner on this turf bow and relished the extra furlong. He can be rated value for a little further than the bare margin as he had to overcome a troubled passage around the 2f marker and showed a likeable attitude when asked for maximum effort. Sure to enjoy around 10f as a three-year-old, he rates a nice handicapper in the making. (tchd 7-2)
Just Rob, third on debut over course and distance 21 days previously, was another who met a little trouble 2f out. He still came through to have every chance in the driving finish, however, and clearly has a fair amount of ability. (op 11-2 tchd 13-2)
Elliwan ◆ took time to get going, but arrived on the outside of the pace full of running passing 2f out and looked the likely winner. He probably got there a bit too soon, however, and he ran green when put under maximum pressure late on, just losing out. It rates a big improvement on his Bath debut and this scopey colt can soon be placed to get off the mark. (op 11-1)
Moyenne Corniche ◆, the first foal of a smart 7-10f winner for this stable, lost his race coming out of the stalls and ran a big race in defeat in the circumstances. He eventually made his challenge at the same time as the winner, but had spent too much energy by that point and was not surprisingly one paced at the business end. A bundle of improvement likely for this debut experience and he evidently has a future. (tchd 12-1)
Eton Fable(IRE), held from a mark of 68 in a nursery last time, got very much the run of the race out in front and probably performed very close to his official rating in defeat. He is pretty much exposed now and puts this form into some perspective. (op 11-1)
Fearless Warrior looked likely to have a big say in the finish when making up his ground at the top of the home straight, but he eventually found just the same pace when it really mattered. Surely he will be seen to better effect off a stronger pace and now has the options of nurseries. (op 10-3 tchd 3-1)
Smetana Official explanation: jockey said colt was denied a clear run

6594 STUART JACKSON "LIFETIME IN RACING" H'CAP 5f 13y
2:20 (2:23) (Class 5) (0-70,69) 3-Y-O+ £3,238 (£963; £481; £240) **Stalls** Low

Form RPR

4524 **1** **Make My Dream**[13] 6279 4-8-11 62 TPO'Shea 4 69
(J Gallagher) *racd far side: in rr: hdwy 2f out: led that gp ins fnl f: jst hld on: 1st of 6 that gp* **12/1**

0320 **2** shd **Brandywell Boy (IRE)**[13] 6287 4-8-12 63 RichardThomas 15 70+
(D J S Ffrench Davis) *racd towards stands' side: mid-div: hdwy over 2f out: led that gp 1f out: jst failed* **6/1**[1]

0400 **3** nk **Registrar**[8] 6415 5-8-5 56 oh2 ow1 SaleemGolam 1 62
(Mrs C A Dunnett) *dwlt: racd far side: in rr: hdwy 2f out: no ex ins fnl f: 2nd of 6 that gp* **25/1**

2630 **4** nk **Lake Chini (IRE)**[13] 6283 5-9-4 69 (b) DaleGibson 5 74
(M W Easterby) *racd far side: trckd ldrs: led that side over 1f out: hdd nr fin: 3rd of 6 that gp* **14/1**

6643 **5** hd **Niteowl Lad (IRE)**[13] 6287 5-8-9 60 DavidAllan 3 64
(J Balding) *racd far side: chsd ldrs: kpt on same pce fnl f: 4th of 6 that gp* **7/1**[2]

1204 **6** 1 **Joyeaux**[12] 6313 5-9-1 69 DuranFentiman(3) 16 70
(J Hetherton) *dwlt: racd stands' side: styd on fnl 2f: nvr nr ldrs* **10/1**

1320 **7** ¾ **Dancing Mystery**[8] 6405 13-8-12 63 (b) AdamKirby 12 61
(E A Wheeler) *racd stands' side: chsd ldrs: fdd appr fnl f* **14/1**

546 **8** 1¾ **Rainbow Bay**[34] 5753 4-8-7 65 (v) MCGeran(7) 17 57
(P D Evans) *racd stands' side: mid-div: nvr nr ldrs* **7/1**[2]

2310 **9** hd **Jadan (IRE)**[1] 6562 6-8-4 55 oh2 (b) AdrianTNicholls 7 46
(E J Alston) *swtchd rt s and racd stands' side: sn chsng ldr: wknd 1f out* **12/1**

2102 **10** nk **Silver Prelude**[10] 6360 6-9-2 67 TedDurcan 2 57
(D K Ivory) *racd far side: w ldrs: wknd over 1f out: 5th of 6 that gp* **9/1**

0003 **11** nk **Blessed Place**[2] 6542 7-8-7 65 (t) BillyCray(7) 10 54
(D J S Ffrench Davis) *overall ldr towards centre: hdd 1f out: sn wknd* **8/1**[3]

0056 **12** ½ **Azygous**[10] 6360 4-9-0 65 TPQueally 6 52
(J Akehurst) *led far side gp of 6: hdd & wknd over 1f out: last of 6 that gp* **14/1**

1400 **13** 1 **Never Without Me**[34] 5747 7-9-1 66 MickyFenton 14 49
(J F Coupland) *racd stands' side: chsd ldrs: wknd fnl 2f* **28/1**

0064 **14** ½ **Isobel Rose (IRE)**[123] 3110 3-8-5 56 PaulHanagan 13 37
(J L Spearing) *racd stands' side: mid-div: hdwy over 2f out: sn wknd* **22/1**

60.38 secs (-1.42) **Going Correction** -0.20s/f (Firm) 14 Ran SP% **116.5**
Speed ratings (Par 103): **103,102,102,101,101 99,98,95,95,95 94,93,92,91**
CSF £77.72 CT £1824.31 TOTE £11.90: £4.30, £2.70, £8.80; EX 113.70.
Owner Mrs Irene Clifford **Bred** The Valentines **Trained** Moreton-in-Marsh, Gloucs

FOCUS
A modest sprint handicap and a large blanket would have covered the first five at the line. They raced in two separate groups but there was nothing between them as they converged near the line. The form makes sense with the third, fourth and fifth to their marks, although those racing stands' side could be rated higher.

6595 ROBIN KNOTT MEMORIAL MAIDEN STKS 5f 13y
2:50 (2:50) (Class 5) 2-Y-O £2,914 (£867; £433; £216) **Stalls** Low

Form RPR

0 **1** **Chartist**[12] 6295 2-9-3 0 RichardHughes 12 80+
(R Hannon) *racd towards far side: mde most: rdn over 1f out: drvn and edgd lft ins fnl f: kpt on wl* **10/3**[2]

45 **2** 1½ **Incomparable**[13] 6281 2-9-3 0 AdamKirby 2 75
(A J McCabe) *chsd ldrs: hdwy 2f out: rdn to chse wnr ent fnl f: sn drvn and nt qckn* **5/2**[1]

3 2 **Quaroma** 2-8-12 0 TPQueally 14 62
(Jane Chapple-Hyam) *racd wd: prom: rdn along and ev ch whn hung bdly lft appr fnl f: sn drvn and kpt on same pce* **33/1**

4 hd **Lindelaan (USA)** 2-8-12 0 RyanMoore 8 62+
(Sir Michael Stoute) *s.i.s and bhd: hdwy wl over 1f out: styd on wl fnl f: nrst fin* **7/2**[3]

3 **5** 4 **Filligree (IRE)**[21] 6105 2-8-12 0 JamieMackay 3 47
(Rae Guest) *in tch: hdwy on inner 2f out: sn rdn and kpt on ins fnl f: nrst fin* **10/1**

05 **6** nk **Caprio (IRE)**[16] 6237 2-9-3 0 SteveDrowne 11 51
(R Charlton) *towards rr: hdwy 2f out: sn rdn and hung lft: styd on ins fnl f: nrst fin* **17/2**

500 **7** 2 **Curio**[22] 6073 2-8-12 56 DeanMcKeown 13 39
(R M Whitaker) *racd wd: gd spd tl rdn and hung bdly lft wl over 1f out: wknd* **40/1**

53 **8** ¾ **Heron (IRE)**[18] 6177 2-9-0 0 LukeMorris(3) 5 41
(N P Littmoden) *chsd wnr: rdn along over 2f out: sn wknd* **12/1**

9 ¾ **Carmine Rock** 2-8-12 0 GrahamGibbons 7 34
(R Hollinshead) *rrd s: a bhd* **50/1**

0 **10** 1¼ **Rocketry**[20] 6125 2-9-0 0 EmmettStack(3) 6 34
(T Keddy) *in tch: rdn along 1/2-way: sn wknd* **125/1**

11 1¼ **Noche De Reyes** 2-9-3 0 DavidAllan 1 30
(E J Alston) *a towards rr* **20/1**

0600 **12** 1¼ **Eastbourne**[14] 6263 2-9-3 51 (b) MickyFenton 4 25
(Eve Johnson Houghton) *chsd ldrs: rdn along 1/2-way and sn wknd* **100/1**

50 **13** 2½ **Midnight Oasis**[68] 4756 2-8-12 0 J-PGuillambert 10 11
(Rae Guest) *chsd ldrs: rdn along 1/2-way: sn wknd* **50/1**

60.51 secs (-1.29) **Going Correction** -0.20s/f (Firm) 13 Ran SP% **117.0**
Speed ratings (Par 95): **102,99,96,96,89 89,86,84,83,81 79,77,73**
CSF £11.23 TOTE £4.20: £1.70, £1.60, £9.40; EX 14.40.
Owner J A Leek & Michael Pescod **Bred** Poulton Farm Stud **Trained** East Everleigh, Wilts

FOCUS
A modest juvenile maiden, run at a solid pace. It was a decent winning time for a race of its type, just 0.13 seconds slower than the preceding older-horse handicap.

NOTEBOOK
Chartist showed the clear benefit of his Newmarket debut 12 days previously and opened his account in good style. The drop back to this distance was to his liking, as was the quicker ground, and he looks a useful sprinting prospect for next term. (op 9-2 tchd 3-1)
Incomparable ran his best race to date in defeat and finished a clear second-best. He ought to be found a winning opportunity if kept going during the winter and he now qualifies for a nursery mark, but he may just prefer returning to another furlong. (op 10-3)
Quaroma, whose dam was a dual winner over this trip as two, was one of two runners to race more towards the stands' side early on yet eventually hung her way over to join the pack nearing the final furlong. She showed a deal of speed and, considering she covered more ground than the first pair, this rates a fair debut effort in defeat. Official explanation: jockey said filly hung left-handed (op 25-1)
Lindelaan(USA) ◆, a $500,000 purchase whose dam was a useful turf winner in the US, proved easy to back on this belated racecourse bow considering her connections. She fluffed the start and was always getting there too late in the day, which is not too surprising considering she is really bred to need a stiffer test. One to look out for next time. (op 2-1)
Caprio(IRE) was racing on ground this quick for the first time and again showed some quirks, but still hinted at ability in defeat. He now becomes eligible for a nursery mark. (op 10-1)
Curio Official explanation: jockey said filly hung left-handed

6596 ROBIN HOOD H'CAP 1m 54y
3:20 (3:20) (Class 4) (0-85,84) 3-Y-O+ £6,477 (£1,927; £963; £481) **Stalls** Centre

Form RPR

0122 **1** **Red Somerset (USA)**[7] 6423 4-8-12 74 RichardHughes 8 86+
(R J Hodges) *trckd ldrs: smooth hdwy 3f out: shkn up to ld 1f out: drew clr: readily* **9/4**[1]

5053 **2** 5 **Apex**[10] 6359 6-8-13 80 (p) HaddenFrost(5) 2 80
(M Hill) *led: rdn and edgd rt over 2f out: hdd 1f out: wknd towards fin* **11/2**

4151 **3** hd **Boundless Prospect (USA)**[8] 6412 8-9-3 84 6ex NicolPolli(5) 4 84
(Miss Gay Kelleway) *chsd ldrs: pushed along over 5f out: styd on wl fnl f* **10/1**

4065 **4** 1¾ **Knapton Hill**[65] 4907 3-8-9 79 RussellKennemore(5) 3 75
(R Hollinshead) *trckd ldrs: rdn over 2f out: one pce* **50/1**

4400 **5** 1¼ **Street Warrior (IRE)**[7] 6423 4-8-5 74 MarkCoumbe(7) 1 67
(G H Yardley) *s.s: in rr: kpt on fnl 3f: nvr rchd ldrs* **33/1**

0100 **6** 3 **Namid Reprobate (IRE)**[17] 6203 4-8-13 80 TolleyDean(5) 7 66
(P F I Cole) *in rr and sn pushed along: kpt on fnl 2f: nvr on terms* **14/1**

2214 **7** shd **Central Force**[62] 4960 3-8-11 76 RyanMoore 5 62
(E A L Dunlop) *hld up in rr: sme hdwy over 3f out: sn rdn: nvr on terms* **3/1**[2]

0020 **8** ¾ **Bustan (IRE)**[25] 6016 8-9-7 83 J-PGuillambert 6 67
(G C Bravery) *w ldr: rdn and wknd over 2f out* **4/1**[3]

1m 43.03s (-3.37) **Going Correction** -0.20s/f (Firm)
WFA 3 from 4yo+ 3lb 8 Ran SP% **111.8**
Speed ratings (Par 105): **108,103,102,101,99 96,96,95**
CSF £14.40 CT £99.28 TOTE £3.50: £1.20, £1.50, £2.70; EX 14.70.

Owner Fieldspring Racing **Bred** Haras D'Etreham **Trained** Charlton Mackrell, Somerset

FOCUS

A sound pace and a very ready winner of what was basically a weak handicap. The third is rated to this year's form but the fourth limits confidence.

Street Warrior(IRE) Official explanation: jockey said gelding missed the break

Central Force Official explanation: jockey said filly was never travelling

6597 TURFTV.CO.UK MAIDEN STKS — 1m 54y

3:50 (3:53) (Class 5) 3-Y-O — **£3,238** (£963; £481; £240) **Stalls** Centre

Form — RPR

-533 **1** **Hint Of Spring**[37] 5678 3-8-12 65 .... TedDurcan 3 — 64
(Saeed Bin Suroor) *cl up: led 1/2-way: rdn along 2f out: drvn ins fnl f and styd on gamely towards fin* **5/1**[2]

2 **2** *nk* **Tazeez (USA)**[28] 5915 3-9-3 0 .... RHills 15 — 68
(J H M Gosden) *in tch: effrt to chse ldrs 3f out and sn rdn along: styd on u.p and ev ch ins fnl f: no ex nr fin* **4/6**[1]

4232 **3** *shd* **Red Blossom**[16] 6238 3-8-12 65 ....(b) RyanMoore 4 — 63
(Sir Mark Prescott) *in tch: hdwy 3f out: rdn to chse wnr over 1f out: drvn and ev ch ins fnl f: no ex towards fin* **6/1**[3]

00-0 **4** *2 1/2* **Arthur's Edge**[22] 6094 3-8-12 48 .... TolleyDean(5) 11 — 62
(B Palling) *prom: effrt to chse wnr over 2f out and sn rdn: drvn over 1f out and grad wknd* **100/1**

5-5 **5** *3/4* **Samahir (USA)**[22] 6094 3-8-12 0 .... DavidAllan 14 — 55
(T T Clement) *hld up towards rr: gd hdwy over 2f out: rdn over 1f out: kpt on ins fnl f: nrst fin* **33/1**

02 **6** *3* **African Pursuits (USA)**[159] 1995 3-9-3 0 .... SteveDrowne 12 — 53
(H Morrison) *in tch on inner: rdn along 3f out: sn one pce* **18/1**

4 **7** *1/2* **Naledi**[22] 6094 3-9-3 0 ....(b) PaulMulrennan 17 — 52
(J R Norton) *hld up towards rr: hdwy on outer 3f out: rdn and edgd lft 2f out: sn no imp* **28/1**

0-0 **8** *2 1/2* **Dawn Mystery**[177] 1523 3-8-12 0 .... JamieMackay 6 — 41
(Rae Guest) *dwlt and in rr tl sme late hdwy* **100/1**

9 *shd* **Ruwain** 3-9-3 0 .... NeilPollard 16 — 46
(W J Musson) *hld up in rr: effrt over 3f out: sn rdn along and nvr a factor* **20/1**

0360 **10** *1/2* **New Light**[17] 6204 3-8-12 48 .... J-PGuillambert 7 — 40
(Eve Johnson Houghton) *towards rr: effrt and sme hdwy on outer 3f out: sn rdn and n.d* **100/1**

0- **11** *3 1/2* **Montrose Man**[386] 5890 3-9-3 0 .... RichardHughes 5 — 37
(B J Meehan) *led: pushed along and hdd 1/2-way: rdn 3f out and sn wknd* **16/1**

0 **12** *1 1/4* **Boppys Diamond**[12] 6309 3-8-12 0 .... MickyFenton 9 — 29
(P T Midgley) *chsd ldrs: rdn along over 3f out and sn wknd* **125/1**

13 *12* **Kielty's Folly** 3-9-3 0 .... DanielTudhope 10 — —
(B P J Baugh) *s.i.s: a bhd* **150/1**

000 **14** *1 1/4* **Rosemary And Thyme**[41] 5562 3-8-12 35 .... RoystonFfrench 8 — —
(Mrs S Lamyman) *a towards rr* **200/1**

15 *26* **Karaoke Queen** 3-8-12 0 .... SaleemGolam 1 — —
(G C Bravery) *s.i.s: a bhd* **100/1**

1m 45.24s (-1.16) **Going Correction** -0.20s/f (Firm) — **15** Ran SP% **119.2**

Speed ratings (Par 101): **97,96,96,94,93 90,89,87,87,86 83,82,70,68,42**

CSF £8.18 TOTE £8.30: £1.90, £1.10, £1.50; EX 13.00.

Owner Godolphin **Bred** Darley **Trained** Newmarket, Suffolk

FOCUS

A weak three-year-old maiden that produced a tight three-way finish. The 48-rated fourth puts the form into perspective.

6598 SAWFISH SOFTWARE H'CAP (FOR LADY AMATEUR RIDERS) — 1m 1f 213y

4:20 (4:21) (Class 6) (0-65,65) 3-Y-O+ — **£2,307** (£709; £354) **Stalls** Low

Form — RPR

2502 **1** **Zelos (IRE)**[11] 6344 3-10-5 65 ....(bt) MissFayeBramley 14 — 77
(D J S Ffrench Davis) *chsd ldrs: led over 2f out: styd on wl* **16/1**

3661 **2** *1 1/4* **Gala Sunday (USA)**[12] 6304 7-10-3 58 ....(bt) MissSBrotherton 5 — 67
(M W Easterby) *in tch: swtchd rt 2f out: r.o: nt rch wnr* **9/4**[1]

4424 **3** *2* **Kylkenny**[113] 3403 12-9-7 53 ....(t) MissVCartmel(5) 15 — 58
(H Morrison) *hld up in rr: hdwy 3f out: styd on wl fnl f* **11/1**

0305 **4** *1* **Wulimaster (USA)**[12] 6304 4-10-2 57 .... MissADeniel 6 — 60
(D W Barker) *sn mid-div: hdwy on ins 3f out: kpt on same pce fnl 2f* **8/1**[3]

0000 **5** *nk* **Spume (IRE)**[12] 6310 3-10-5 65 ....(bt[1]) MsKWalsh 10 — 67
(D J Murphy) *hld up towards rr: stdy hdwy over 3f out: chal over 1f out: rdn and hung lft: fnd little* **16/1**

0021 **6** *nk* **Ours (IRE)**[14] 6266 4-9-7 53 .... MissLAllan(5) 16 — 55
(John A Harris) *t.k.h in midfield: hdwy over 3f out: hung lft over 1f out: kpt on same pce* **10/1**

2010 **7** *1 1/4* **Gallego**[4] 6500 5-10-5 65 .... MissABevan(5) 11 — 64
(R J Price) *s.i.s: hdwy over 2f out: kpt on fnl f* **7/1**[2]

1665 **8** *3* **Global Traffic**[15] 6259 3-10-0 60 ....(b) MissEFolkes 13 — 53
(P D Evans) *mid-div: hdwy over 3f out: hung lft and wknd over 1f out* **14/1**

-006 **9** *3/4* **Alekhine (IRE)**[19] 6146 6-10-0 60 .... MissJCWilliams(5) 7 — 52
(J W Unett) *mid-div: hdwy over 3f out: nvr trbld ldrs* **25/1**

6015 **10** *1* **Singleb (IRE)**[12] 6310 3-10-1 61 .... MrsCBartley 12 — 51
(T D Barron) *mid-div: sme hdwy whn sltly hmpd over 2f out: nvr nr ldrs* **12/1**

1560 **11** *1 3/4* **Thornaby Green**[15] 6258 6-10-3 61 .... MissARyan(3) 8 — 47
(T D Barron) *w ldr: wknd over 2f out* **12/1**

3200 **12** *3/4* **Measured Response**[48] 5366 5-9-12 53 .... MissRDavidson 3 — 38
(J G M O'Shea) *mid-div: effrt over 3f out: nvr on terms* **22/1**

0600 **13** *3/4* **Emperor's Well**[28] 5905 8-10-2 60 .... MissJCoward(3) 2 — 43
(M W Easterby) *prom: lost pl over 2f out* **25/1**

0650 **14** *3/4* **First Friend (IRE)**[12] 6316 6-9-11 57 .... MissMichelleSaunders(5) 1 — 39
(M Hill) *w ldrs: led 3f out: sn hdd: wknd over 1f out* **50/1**

130/ **15** *6* **Atacama Star**[755] 4431 5-10-3 65 .... MissCLWills(7) 9 — 35
(B G Powell) *s.i.s: in rr: bhd fnl 2f* **50/1**

300 **16** *3* **Credential**[12] 6315 5-10-0 55 ....(p) MrsMMorris 4 — 19
(John A Harris) *mde most: hdd 3f out: sn wknd* **25/1**

2m 9.69s (-0.01) **Going Correction** -0.20s/f (Firm)

WFA 3 from 4yo+ 5lb — **16** Ran SP% **125.4**

Speed ratings (Par 101): **92,91,89,88,88 88,87,84,84,83 81,81,80,80,75 72**

CSF £49.65 CT £443.20 TOTE £19.90: £4.10, £2.60, £3.30, £2.30; EX 85.80 Place 6 £55.20, Place 5 £27.57.

Owner Gary Lee Jones **Bred** Dermot Brennan And Associates Ltd **Trained** Lambourn, Berks

■ Stewards' Enquiry : Miss S Brotherton one-day ban: careless riding (Nov 12)

FOCUS

A low-grade lady amateur riders' handicap run at a steady pace. The winner had first run on the placed horses and the runner-up sets the standard, with the third and fourth close to recent runs, but not that solid a race.

T/Plt: £65.70 to a £1 stake. Pool: £47,737.25. 530.05 winning tickets. T/Qpdt: £27.60 to a £1 stake. Pool: £2,533.50. 67.90 winning tickets. JR

6584 LINGFIELD (L-H)

Thursday, November 1

OFFICIAL GOING: Standard

Wind: Light, half behind, races 1-3, light, half against, races 4-7 Weather: Fine, mild

6601 EBF SCOTS GROUP QUAICH MAIDEN FILLIES' STKS — 7f (P)

1:10 (1:15) (Class 4) 2-Y-O — **£4,210** (£1,252; £625; £312) **Stalls** Low

Form — RPR

65 **1** **Debonnaire**[26] 6015 2-9-0 0 .... GregFairley 4 — 75+
(M Johnston) *w'like: pressed ldr: led jst over 2f out: wd bnd sn after: jnd and drvn ent fnl f: fnd ex and hld on wl* **4/1**[2]

4 **2** *shd* **Anne Of Kiev (IRE)**[13] 6306 2-9-0 0 .... JimmyFortune 8 — 75+
(J H M Gosden) *trckd ldrs: effrt and wd bnd 2f out: swtchd ins and chal 1f out: w wnr after: jst hld* **9/4**[1]

0 **3** *2 1/2* **Welsh Opera**[9] 6409 2-9-0 0 .... JimCrowley 5 — 69
(Mrs A J Perrett) *leggy: trckd ldng pair: rdn to chal over 1f out: outpcd fnl f* **8/1**[3]

00 **4** *shd* **Silky Steps (IRE)**[17] 6228 2-9-0 0 .... EddieAhern 6 — 68
(P J Makin) *trckd ldrs gng wl: prog over 2f out: to chal over 1f out: sn rdn and fnd nil* **25/1**

00 **5** *3 1/2* **Badoura**[34] 5766 2-9-0 0 .... NickyMackay 14 — 60
(G A Butler) *reluctant to go to post: plld hrd early: hld up in last trio: outpcd 2f out: pushed along and kpt on fnl f* **12/1**

05 **6** *3/4* **Sarah's First**[13] 6296 2-9-0 0 .... RyanMoore 12 — 58+
(E A L Dunlop) *racd wd in midfield: rdn 3f out: outpcd wl over 1f out: n.d after* **4/1**[2]

00 **7** *hd* **Miss Okaloosa**[33] 5811 2-9-0 0 .... RichardMullen 7 — 57
(D M Simcock) *led to jst over 2f out: btn whn intimidated over 1f out and gave up* **100/1**

0 **8** *nk* **Oriental Girl**[15] 6262 2-9-0 0 .... RichardThomas 11 — 56
(J A Geake) *t.k.h: hld up towards rr: rdn 3f out: outpcd fr wl over 1f out* **66/1**

9 *3* **Moluccella** 2-9-0 0 .... RobertHavlin 2 — 49
(H Morrison) *w'like: bit bkwd: dwlt: settled towards rr: rdn over 2f out: outpcd wl over 1f out* **25/1**

0 **10** *2* **Super Starlet (IRE)**[26] 6015 2-9-0 0 .... NCallan 3 — 44
(M Botti) *w'like: trckd ldrs on inner: rdn 3f out: wknd rapidly fr 2f out* **100/1**

65 **11** *3* **Rowan Dancer**[23] 6082 2-9-0 0 .... TedDurcan 9 — 36
(J R Boyle) *a in rr: struggling and btn over 2f out* **33/1**

00 **12** *3 1/2* **Flower Song**[8] 6418 2-9-0 0 .... FergusSweeney 10 — 28
(A King) *unf: a in last pair: bhd fnl 3f* **33/1**

1m 24.59s (-1.30) **Going Correction** -0.175s/f (Stan) — **12** Ran SP% **106.6**

Speed ratings (Par 95): **100,99,97,96,92 92,91,91,88,85 82,78**

CSF £10.32 TOTE £3.60: £1.70, £1.40, £2.00; EX 11.00 Trifecta £49.20 Pool £193.59 - 2.79 winning units..

Owner Ali Saeed **Bred** Gainsborough Stud Management Ltd **Trained** Middleham Moor, N Yorks

■ Siren Sound was withdrawn (7/1, unruly in stalls). R4 applies, deduct 10p in the £.

FOCUS

This was run at a decent pace and the winning time was 0.46 seconds quicker than the colts' equivalent which followed. The form looks solid and the principals are probably worth following.

NOTEBOOK

Debonnaire ◆, who had shown some ability in two turf maidens, eventually ground out a dour victory but had nothing like a straightforward passage. Always up with the pace, she firstly met trouble when Miss Okaloosa pushed her against the rail on the home bend and then she was inclined to hang out to the centre of the track once in line for home. That is usually not a bad thing here though, as she ended up on the faster strip, and she then showed the sort of gameness that typifies runners from the yard to hold off the favourite by the skin of her teeth. There should be more to come from her. (tchd 9-2)

Anne Of Kiev(IRE) ◆, up a furlong from her Redcar debut, was forced very wide on the home bend, but the winner hanging right meant that she made her effort up her inside. She appeared to have every chance, but she ran into a Johnston inmate at her most determined. It should not be long before she goes one better. (op 2-1 tchd 5-2)

Welsh Opera was always in a good position just behind the leaders and battled on to win the separate race for third. She appreciated the extra furlong and should have little difficulty getting a mile in time. She will qualify for a mark after one more run and that is likely to be where her future lies. (op 10-1)

Silky Steps(IRE), who had only managed to beat one home in each of her two previous outings, travelled really well behind the leaders and looked sure to play a part when delivered with her effort, but after her rider administered a few desperate taps with the whip down the shoulder to try and stop her hanging she did not find very much, though to be fair she was carried over to the slower inside rail. This was still a big improvement and she now qualifies for a mark. (op 28-1 tchd 33-1)

Badoura, out of her depth in the Watership Down Sales Race last time, does seem to have a bit of an attitude but, as on her debut, she did show a bit of ability as the race progressed. She is another for whom handicaps now become an option. (op 10-1)

Sarah's First ◆ was probably not helped by the drop in trip on this switch to sand and was off the bridle on the wide outside from a long way out. At least she now qualifies for a mark after this and, as she seems to have inherited some stamina from the dam's side of her pedigree, middle-distance handicaps are likely to see better from her in due course. (op 9-2)

Miss Okaloosa, beaten out of sight in her first two starts, ran much better than her odds suggested she should, but after coming off worse after trying to bully the winner against the rail on the home bend, did not seem to fancy it all soon after and threw in the towel.

Flower Song Official explanation: jockey said filly hung left

6602 EBF TAGWORLDWIDE.COM MAIDEN STKS — 7f (P)

1:40 (1:42) (Class 5) 2-Y-O — **£4,210** (£1,252; £625; £312) **Stalls** Low

Form — RPR

00 **1** **Traphalgar (IRE)**[97] 3896 2-9-3 0 .... TQuinn 3 — 75
(P F I Cole) *chsd ldr: rdn fr 1/2-way: chal 2f out: gained upper hand ins fnl f* **10/1**

60 **2** *1/2* **Silent Master (USA)**[41] 5580 2-9-3 0 .... GregFairley 4 — 74
(M Johnston) *unf: led: gng strly 3f out: rdn and pressed 2f out: worn down ins fnl f* **11/1**

0 **3** *2 1/2* **Segal (IRE)**[21] 6126 2-9-3 0 .... EddieAhern 7 — 68
(J Noseda) *t.k.h: hld up in 7th: rdn and outpcd 3f out: styd on to take 3rd ins fnl f: no ch w ldng pair* **9/1**

4 *nk* **Hawk Island (IRE)** 2-9-3 0 .... SteveDrowne 5 — 67+
(G Wragg) *w'like: scope: scratchy to post: chsd ldng pair: hung bdly rt bnd 2f out and lost grnd: kpt on again ins fnl f* **16/1**

5 ¾ **Stormbeam (USA)** 2-9-3 0 ... NickyMackay 9 65
(G A Butler) *w'like: bit bwkd: t.k.h early: hld up in 8th: outpcd and rdn 3f out: styd on fnl f* **16/1**

6 nk **Gainsborough's Art (IRE)** 2-9-3 0 ... SebSanders 6 64+
(D R C Elsworth) *leggy: bit bkwd: hld up in 6th: gng wl enough 3f out but sn outpcd: pushed along and sme prog 2f out: no imp after* **5/1[3]**

7 ½ **Distinctive Image (USA)** 2-9-3 0 ... JimmyFortune 8 63+
(J H M Gosden) *unf: scope: s.i.s: rn green in last: bhd fr 3f out: modest late prog* **11/4[2]**

44 8 ½ **Autumn Blades (IRE)**[30] 5880 2-9-3 0 ... RyanMoore 1 62
(J W Hills) *leggy: chsd ldng pair: outpcd over 2f out: drvn and fnd nil over 1f out: stl 3rd ent fnl f: wknd* **5/2[1]**

0 9 1 ¾ **Hla Tun (USA)**[15] 6267 2-9-3 0 ... AdamKirby 2 57
(W R Swinburn) *chsd ldng quartet: rdn 3f out: wknd wl over 1f out* **14/1**

1m 25.05s (-0.84) **Going Correction** -0.175s/f (Stan) **9** Ran SP% **117.8**
Speed ratings (Par 96): **97,96,93,93,92 92,91,90,88**
CSF £115.39 TOTE £14.30: £3.00, £3.30, £2.50; EX 127.90 Trifecta £244.10 Part won. Pool £343.92 - 0.35 winning units..

Owner The Fairy Story Partnership **Bred** Deepwood Farm Stud **Trained** Whatcombe, Oxon

FOCUS
The front pair dominated this from the start and nothing else ever really got into it. This did not looks as competitive as the preceding fillies' maiden over the same trip and the time was 0.46 seconds slower, but there should still be races to be won with a few of these.

NOTEBOOK
Traphalgar(IRE) ◆ had not got home in either of his two outings on turf in July, but the form of both contests has worked out well. Given a nice break since, he was a different proposition this time and he battled on well to get the better of a protracted duel with the runner-up. He is bred to get much further and looks a nice middle-distance handicapper in the making. (op 8-1)

Silent Master(USA), ridden much more positively on this switch to Polytrack, made a bold bid to make every yard and went down with all guns blazing. Like his rival, there is plenty of stamina on the dam's side of his pedigree and he is another that will appreciate stepping up in trip now that he qualifies for a mark. (op 7-1 tchd 12-1)

Segal(IRE), all the better for his Newbury debut, came off the bridle a fair way out but stayed on to win the separate race for third. He is no star, but should be able to win an ordinary maiden on this surface. (op 12-1)

Hawk Island(IRE), a 75,000gns colt out of a winner at up to 1m3f, looked very much in need of this debut and hung badly out to his right on the home bend, so he did well to finish where he did under the circumstances. As is the case with most from the yard, plenty of improvement can be expected from two to three. (op 14-1)

Stormbeam(USA) ◆, a $130,000 half-brother to a multiple winning sprinter in the US, showed definite signs of ability towards the end of the contest and looks sure to do better. (op 20-1)

Gainsborough's Art(IRE), a 32,000euros half-brother to three winners including Nights Cross, travelled well for a long way but was caught for foot rounding the home bend and there was no way back. He should have learnt from this. (op 7-1)

Distinctive Image(USA), out of a half-sister to a couple of top-class performers in the US, was bred to go on the surface but lack of experience proved his main obstacle, though he did suggest at the very end that he is not without some ability. There is a chance that he will take a big step forward after this, but he will need to. (op 3-1 tchd 10-3)

Autumn Blades(IRE) was disappointing as he was in a good position throughout, but found nothing once off the bridle and did not get home. Official explanation: jockey said colt hung both ways (op 3-1)

6603 RUDRIDGE H'CAP — 1m 2f (P)
2:10 (2:11) (Class 5) (0-75,75) 3-Y-O+ **£2,817** (£838; £418; £209) **Stalls** Low

Form — RPR

2223 1 **Optimus (USA)**[30] 5885 5-9-8 **75** ... TQuinn 4 84
(B G Powell) *lw: trckd ldrs: effrt delayed tl shkn up to chse clr ldr over 1f out and clsd rapidly: led last 100yds: sn clr* **13/2[3]**

0 2 1 ½ **Jago (SWI)**[22] 6102 4-8-8 **61** ... LPKeniry 14 67
(A M Hales) *stdd s: hld up in last trio: prog towards inner fr 2f out: r.o to take 2nd nr fin: no ch w wnr* **33/1**

0562 3 shd **Royal Fantasy (IRE)**[27] 5979 4-9-6 **73** ... JamieSpencer 12 79+
(J R Fanshawe) *hld up and sn last: gng wl but stl last 2f out: nt clr run and taken to wd outside over 1f out: r.o strly to take 3rd nr fin: far too much to do* **9/2[2]**

5602 4 ½ **Cinematic (IRE)**[40] 5645 4-9-2 **69** ... AmirQuinn 6 74
(J R Boyle) *hld up off the pce: effrt on wd outside 2f out: rdn over 1f out: r.o fnl f: no ch of rching ldrs* **15/2**

4-64 5 nk **Art Man**[8] 6439 4-9-3 **70** ... RyanMoore 1 74+
(G L Moore) *lw: mostly in midfield: rdn over 2f out: no prog tl r.o fnl f: nrst fin* **7/4[1]**

5300 6 ¾ **Sky Quest (IRE)**[18] 6199 9-8-8 **68** ... HarryPoulton(7) 8 71
(J R Boyle) *hld up in tch: prog to ld 1/2-way: drew clr fr 3f out: 5 l ahd over 1f out: wknd rapidly and hdd last 100yds* **33/1**

0602 7 shd **Resplendent Ace (IRE)**[15] 6272 3-9-0 **71** ... JimmyFortune 10 74
(P Howling) *chsd ldrs: rdn and no prog over 2f out: kpt on fnl f* **10/1**

6003 8 1 ½ **St Petersburg**[18] 6203 7-9-8 **75** ... NCallan 5 75
(J R Boyle) *hld up towards rr: rdn over 2f out: no real prog over 1f out: one pce* **17/2**

0446 9 4 **Pop Music (IRE)**[164] 1905 4-8-13 **66** ... (p) JamesDoyle 13 58
(Miss J Feilden) *prom: rdn over 2f out: no imp on clr ldr: wknd fnl f* **33/1**

1200 10 hd **Uig**[21] 6129 6-8-8 **61** oh2 ... TedDurcan 7 52
(H S Howe) *pushed up to ld: hdd 1/2-way: chsd clr ldr to over 1f out: wknd* **22/1**

0000 11 1 ½ **Pagan Crest**[16] 6253 4-8-9 **62** ... (p) JimCrowley 3 50
(Mrs A J Perrett) *chsd ldrs: rdn over 2f out: no imp: wknd over 1f out* **33/1**

5000 12 shd **Where's Broughton**[36] 5733 4-8-8 **61** ... EddieAhern 2 49
(W J Musson) *snatched up after 1f: mostly in last trio: nt clr run briefly over 1f out: nudged along and no prog* **20/1**

2m 5.52s (-2.27) **Going Correction** -0.175s/f (Stan)
WFA 3 from 4yo+ 4lb **12** Ran SP% **120.1**
Speed ratings (Par 103): **102,100,100,100,100 99,99,98,95,94 93,93**
CSF £212.95 CT £1051.70 TOTE £7.50: £2.30, £7.90, £1.80; EX 242.80 Trifecta £232.10 Part won. Pool £327.00 - 0.35 winning units..

Owner Andrew P Wyer **Bred** Strategy Bloodstock **Trained** Lambourn, Berks

FOCUS
An ordinary if competitive handicap, but something of a messy race and the whole complexion of the contest changed in the last furlong. Therefore the form may not be totally reliable.

Royal Fantasy(IRE) Official explanation: jockey said, regarding running and riding, from a wide draw his orders were to settle the filly as she was an awkward ride, and he was unable to make his run due to trouble in running from turning off final bend, having needed to produce her late in order to get home

Where's Broughton Official explanation: jockey said filly did not face kickback

6604 EBF GREENHAM ONE STOP FILLIES' STKS (REGISTERED AS THE FLEUR DE LYS STAKES) (LISTED RACE) — 1m (P)
2:40 (2:41) (Class 1) 3-Y-O+
£14,762 (£5,595; £2,800; £1,396; £699; £351) **Stalls** High

Form — RPR

0020 1 **Sesmen**[49] 5354 3-8-12 98 ... (t) OscarUrbina 12 94
(M Botti) *fast away fr wd draw and pressed ldr: led 5f out: kicked on over 2f out: hld on u.p nr fin* **7/1**

3214 2 hd **Fidelia (IRE)**[33] 5799 3-8-12 87 ... SteveDrowne 2 93
(G Wragg) *trckd ldrs: effrt to go 3rd 2f out: drvn to chse wnr jst over 1f out: clsd fnl f: jst failed* **4/1[2]**

-430 3 1 ¼ **Wagtail**[13] 6299 4-9-0 89 ... (t) SebSanders 6 90
(E A L Dunlop) *lw: hld up in rr: prog and reminders over 2f out: nt qckn over 1f out: styd on fnl f to take 3rd last stride* **7/2[1]**

0064 4 hd **Tiana**[33] 5794 4-9-0 88 ... (b) JimCrowley 10 90
(Mrs A J Perrett) *prom: chsd wnr over 3f out: drvn and nt qckn over 1f out: one pce after* **16/1**

66 5 ¾ **Enforce (USA)**[126] 3028 4-9-0 91 ... JamieSpencer 4 88
(E A L Dunlop) *hld up in last pair: keen 3f out: last 2f out: effrt on wd outside over 1f out: hanging but styd on fnl f: no ch of rching ldrs* **14/1**

0030 6 nk **Daniella**[13] 6300 5-9-0 85 ... (b) NCallan 9 88
(Rae Guest) *lw: dwlt: hld up in last: effrt over 2f out: drvn and styd on fr over 1f out: nt pce to trble ldrs* **16/1**

100 7 nk **Persian Express (USA)**[8] 6437 4-9-0 89 ... MichaelHills 1 87
(B W Hills) *hld up towards rr on inner: prog wl over 1f out: no imp fnl f* **11/1**

0050 8 1 ¼ **Precocious Star (IRE)**[113] 3430 3-9-1 86 ... FergusSweeney 5 87
(K R Burke) *racd wd: towards rr: prog to chse ldrs 3f out: outpcd 2f out: n.d after* **33/1**

06 9 nk **Lady Livius (IRE)**[49] 5354 4-9-0 94 ... RyanMoore 11 83
(R Hannon) *led for 3f: chsd ldr to over 3f out: wknd u.p over 1f out* **10/1**

1006 10 ½ **Ivory Lace**[8] 6437 6-9-0 87 ... TPQueally 8 82
(S Woodman) *hld up towards rr: rdn 2f out: wknd over 1f out* **16/1**

-500 11 hd **Chatila (USA)**[43] 5544 4-9-0 90 ... JimmyFortune 7 82
(J H M Gosden) *lw: awkward s: rcvrd to chse ldrs after 1f: effrt 3f out: fdd over 1f out* **11/2[3]**

0000 12 nk **Tanzanite (IRE)**[13] 6299 5-9-0 87 ... TedDurcan 3 81
(D W P Arbuthnot) *dwlt: hld up in rr: rdn and no prog 2f out* **16/1**

1m 36.57s (-2.86) **Going Correction** -0.175s/f (Stan)
WFA 3 from 4yo+ 2lb **12** Ran SP% **120.7**
Speed ratings (Par 108): **107,106,105,105,104 104,104,102,102,101 101,101**
CSF £35.74 TOTE £10.10: £2.60, £2.00, £1.90; EX 31.70 Trifecta £186.80 Part won. Pool £263.13 - 0.75 winning units..

Owner Scuderia Rencati Srl **Bred** Peter Ebdon Racing **Trained** Newmarket, Suffolk

FOCUS
A competitive fillies' Listed event run at a sound pace. Not strong form for the grade, with Sesmen not needing to improve on her summer form.

NOTEBOOK
Sesmen, a winner on Polytrack on her racecourse debut and a Group 3 winner on turf, had upwards of 8lb in hand of her rivals on adjusted official ratings. Fast away from her wide draw, she was travelling comfortably in front once taking it up at halfway and then showed plenty of grit to see her race out and win with nothing to spare. She is likely to head for the sales next month. (op 8-1)

Fidelia(IRE), like the winner having her first race on Polytrack since her racecourse debut, was in a great position for most of the way, but she took a while to hit full stride once in line for home and only just failed to get up. She would have been 11lb better off with the winner in a handicap, so emerges with plenty of credit. (op 7-2)

Wagtail, a winner over course and distance on her racecourse debut last year, was back over a more suitable trip and stayed on well to grab a place in the frame. This was a decent effort and she finished closer to Sesmen than at Bath in August, as she was entitled to on the revised terms.. (op 9-2)

Tiana, making her sand debut, was never far from the pace and kept plugging away, but lacked a decisive turn of foot. On a line through the two fillies immediately in front of her, she ran right up to her mark. (tchd 20-1)

Enforce(USA), trying sand for the first time, was returning from four months off and was always likely to find this too sharp. Given plenty to do, she was not surprisingly doing her best work late down the wide outside and looks worth stepping back up in trip. Official explanation: jockey said filly hung left (op 10-1)

Daniella, one of those worst in at the weights, was trying this trip for the first time since her second start at three. Ridden to get it, she stayed on but was never a threat.

6605 EUROPEAN BREEDERS' FUND RIVER EDEN FILLIES' STKS (LISTED RACE) — 1m 5f (P)
3:10 (3:10) (Class 1) 3-Y-O+
£14,762 (£5,595; £2,800; £1,396; £699; £351) **Stalls** Low

Form — RPR

4210 1 **Loulwa (IRE)**[19] 6168 3-8-9 90 ... (t) SebSanders 3 99
(J Noseda) *hld up in midfield: rdn and effrt over 2f out: prog and hung rt to centre of crse over 1f out: drvn and r.o to ld nr fin* **10/1**

2112 2 ¾ **Market Forces**[14] 6284 3-8-9 97 ... TedDurcan 4 98
(H R A Cecil) *lw: trckd ldrs: effrt to ld narrowly 2f out: jnd fnl f: kpt on wl but hdd nr fin* **2/1[1]**

-006 3 shd **Guilia**[13] 6299 4-9-2 96 ... NCallan 9 98
(Rae Guest) *hld up towards rr: prog 3f out to chse ldng pair 2f out: drvn and upsides fnl f: outpcd nr fin* **10/1**

2122 4 hd **Pivotal Answer (IRE)**[28] 5940 3-8-9 92 ... TPQueally 7 98
(J Noseda) *trckd ldrs: effrt on inner 2f out: upsides fnl f: outpcd nr fin* **7/2[2]**

0214 5 1 ½ **Elegant Hawk**[36] 5725 3-8-9 81 ... PaulDoe 1 95
(W J Knight) *lw: stdd s: hld up in last: effrt over 2f out: styd on fr over 1f out: nvr rchd ldrs* **25/1**

22-3 6 ¾ **Gower Song**[179] 1506 4-9-2 101 ... TQuinn 5 94
(D R C Elsworth) *hld up in last pair: outpcd over 2f out: rdn and kpt on: n.d* **8/1[3]**

0043 7 hd **Kerriemuir Lass (IRE)**[38] 5686 4-9-2 86 ... (p) PhilipRobinson 11 94
(M A Jarvis) *led at stdy pce: tried to kick on 3f out: narrowly hdd 2f out: wknd ins fnl f* **16/1**

0305 8 hd **Mussoorie (FR)**[13] 6299 4-9-2 99 ... JimmyFortune 2 95+
(J H M Gosden) *hld up in rr: effrt on inner 2f out: chsng ldrs 1f out: fdd* **8/1[3]**

-461 9 6 **Peppertree**[41] 5593 4-9-2 87 ... FergusSweeney 10 85
(E F Vaughan) *awkward s: sn chsd ldrs: rdn wl over 2f out: wknd wl over 1f out* **20/1**

0305 **10** *8* **Dance Of Light (USA)**[34] 5767 3-8-9 94........................ RyanMoore 12 73
(Sir Michael Stoute) *chsd ldr to 3f out: wknd rapidly* **8/1**[3]

2m 44.04s (-4.26) **Going Correction** -0.175s/f (Stan)
WFA 3 from 4yo 7lb **10** Ran SP% **121.6**
Speed ratings (Par 108): **106,105,105,105,104 103,103,103,100,95**
CSF £31.66 TOTE £13.80: £3.30, £1.70, £3.40; EX 48.80 Trifecta £264.50 Part won. Pool £372.55 - 0.10 winning units..
Owner Saleh Al Homeizi & Imad Al Sagar **Bred** W Maxwell Ervine **Trained** Newmarket, Suffolk

FOCUS
The front four finished in a line across the track and this is not strong form for the grade. The form is rated through the third. Although the early pace did not look that strong they certainly quickened things up later on and the final time was quite reasonable.

NOTEBOOK
Loulwa(IRE), who had run well enough in her one previous try on this surface, has been shaping as though she would relish this longer trip and so it proved. Despite hanging under pressure once in line for home, at least she was hanging over to the faster strip and she finished strongly to mug the trio on her inside. She had a bit to find with a few of these on official ratings so this was a decent effort.
Market Forces had no doubts over her stamina and the only question was whether she would have the necessary speed on this quick surface. She was given every chance and battled on in very game style to edge out her two nearest rivals, but the winner's late swoop down the outside of the track proved too much for all of them. (op 9-4)
Guilia, fifth in this race last year in her only previous try on sand, only returned to the track in August and is gradually returning to form. She was brought through to hold every chance on this occasion and only went down narrowly, but she is without a win since her racecourse debut. (op 9-1)
Pivotal Answer(IRE), a stable companion of the winner and never out of the first two in four previous tries on Polytrack, travelled well throughout and looked a big danger to all when produced between horses a furlong out, but just lacked a decisive turn of foot. (op 9-2)
Elegant Hawk was proven on this surface, but had plenty to find on these terms and though she stayed on she was never a threat.
Gower Song was best in at the weights, but she had only managed one outing in the past year. She was never a threat, but can be rated a little closer as she was forced very wide on the home bend. (op 15-2)
Kerriemuir Lass(IRE), a long way behind Pivotal Answer at Kempton last time, had the run of the race out in front but still emptied once in line for home.
Mussoorie(FR), still without a win since arriving from France, had a good chance at the weights but did not improve for the switch to sand and would only have been marginally closer had she not run out of room close home. Official explanation: jockey said filly was checked in the closing stages (tchd 15-2)

6606 GEMINI PRESS H'CAP — 7f (P)
3:40 (3:43) (Class 3) (0-95,96) 3-Y-0+
£6,855 (£2,052; £1,026; £513; £256; £128) **Stalls** Low

Form RPR
1021 **1** **Capricorn Run (USA)**[8] 6437 4-9-7 **96** 6ex..................(v) SebSanders 7 105+
(A J McCabe) *lw: hld up towards rr: prog on outer over 2f out: wnt 2nd over 1f out: drvn and r.o to ld last strides* **2/1**[1]
2100 **2** *nk* **Salient**[13] 6301 3-8-9 **85**.. PaulDoe 8 93
(J Akehurst) *led: kicked on over 2f out: styd on inner in st: hdd nr fin* **16/1**
1022 **3** *1 1/2* **Tender The Great (IRE)**[10] 6391 4-8-10 **85**.......................... TQuinn 6 89
(B G Powell) *t.k.h: hld up at bk of main gp: effrt over 2f out: styd on fr over 1f out: tk 3rd nr fin* **6/1**[2]
4 *3/4* **Orpenindeed (IRE)**[46] 4-9-3 **92**.. NCallan 11 94
(M Botti) *prom: chsd ldr 3f out: drvn and no imp 2f out: lost 2nd over 1f out: one pce* **50/1**
0540 **5** *1/2* **Roman Maze**[8] 6437 7-8-12 **87**.. EddieAhern 9 88
(W M Brisbourne) *hld up at bk of main gp: effrt on wd outside 2f out: styd on fnl f: nt rch ldrs* **12/1**
-000 **6** *nk* **Cupid's Glory**[33] 5797 5-9-0 **89**..................................(p) LPKeniry 3 89
(Mrs L C Jewell) *trckd ldrs: rdn over 2f out: nt qckn and no imp fr over 1f out* **40/1**
-146 **7** *1* **Mofarij**[153] 2212 3-9-5 **95**..(t) TedDurcan 14 92
(Saeed Bin Suroor) *t.k.h: trckd ldrs: rdn wl over 1f out: wknd fnl f* **10/1**
6560 **8** *nk* **Bomber Command (USA)**[20] 6143 4-8-12 **92**...........(p) PatrickHills[(5)] 4 88
(J W Hills) *hld up in rr: outpcd over 2f out: plugging on one pce whn nt clr run briefly ins fnl f* **16/1**
3051 **9** *2* **The Kiddykid (IRE)**[18] 6209 7-8-13 **88**......................... TGMcLaughlin 5 81
(P D Evans) *mistimed s: rcvrd to chse ldr to 3f out: wknd over 1f out: eased ins fnl f* **12/1**
1000 **10** *2* **Guilded Warrior**[26] 6013 4-8-12 **87**............................ FergusSweeney 1 72
(W S Kittow) *trckd ldrs on inner: lost pl over 2f out: rdn and no prog over 1f out* **25/1**
5032 **11** *shd* **Forest Dane**[8] 6437 7-8-7 **82**...................................... JamieSpencer 10 67
(Mrs N Smith) *racd wd in midfield: wknd tamely 2f out* **13/2**[3]
2204 **12** *3* **Yandina (IRE)**[37] 5712 4-8-7 **82**.................................... MichaelHills 2 59
(B W Hills) *hld up at bk of main gp: rdn and no response wl over 1f out* **25/1**
0002 **13** *4* **Sir Xaar (IRE)**[26] 6013 4-9-3 **92**...............................(bt) TomEaves 12 58
(B Smart) *lw: drvn in last and sn detached: nvr wnt a yard* **10/1**

1m 23.22s (-2.67) **Going Correction** -0.175s/f (Stan)
WFA 3 from 4yo+ 1lb **13** Ran SP% **118.4**
Speed ratings (Par 107): **108,107,105,105,104 104,103,102,100,98 98,94,90**
CSF £36.34 CT £171.41 TOTE £3.10: £1.70, £4.60, £2.30; EX 38.00 Trifecta £239.20 Pool £835.67 - 2.48 winning units..
Owner Paul J Dixon And Placida Racing **Bred** Santa Rosa Partners **Trained** Babworth, Notts

FOCUS
A decent handicap run at a true pace and a race that demonstrated the advantages of coming up the centre in the home straight. The form looks pretty solid.

NOTEBOOK
Capricorn Run(USA), carrying a 6lb penalty for his recent course-and-distance victory, adopted the same tactic as then of being brought wide with his effort in the home straight, which had also worked so well for Sanders in the preceding contest. He always looked like picking up the runner-up and may not have stopped winning yet. (op 7-4 tchd 13-8)
Salient, a dual winner over course and distance at around this time last year, tried to do it the hard way and considering he stuck tight against the rail once into the straight, he did well to keep all bar the favourite at bay. He is still 6lb higher than for his last win on sand, but looks capable of winning off this sort of mark. (op 14-1)
Tender The Great(IRE), up another 3lb, was given a fair amount to do, but finished well from off the pace if not to the same effect as the winner. She is running consistently well on Polytrack at the moment, but may just be better over a mile these days. (op 9-1)
Orpenindeed(IRE) ◆, a three-time winner in Italy at up to 1m, showed up for a long way on this British debut and looks well worth persevering with on this surface on this evidence.
Roman Maze, over four lengths behind Capricorn Run over course and distance last time and 6lb better off, came even wider into the straight than the favourite and although he stayed on, he could not stop his old rival from running away from him once again. (op 14-1)
Cupid's Glory, formerly a Group 3 winner for Sir Mark Prescott, is very much on the decline these days but he is in freefall down the handicap as a result and this was by far his best effort for his new connections on his third outing for them.
Forest Dane, 6lb better off for a two-length beating by Capricorn Run here the previous week, was still in touch running towards the home bend but he folded very tamely and this was too bad to be true. (op 6-1 tchd 11-2)

6607 PREMIER SHOWFREIGHT H'CAP — 7f (P)
4:10 (4:12) (Class 6) (0-60,60) 3-Y-0+ **£2,047** (£604; £302) **Stalls** Low

Form RPR
0003 **1** **Ever Cheerful**[18] 6210 6-9-1 **56**....................................(p) SteveDrowne 7 65
(A B Haynes) *t.k.h: pressed ldr: led 4f out: kicked on 2f out: kpt on wl fnl f* **13/2**[2]
3010 **2** *1 1/4* **Solicitude**[19] 6179 4-8-11 **52**...(p) RobertHavlin 2 58
(D Haydn Jones) *stdd s: t.k.h and sn in midfield: prog over 2f out: chsd wnr jst over 1f out: no real imp* **12/1**
5104 **3** *1/2* **Dasheena**[23] 6089 4-8-7 **55**......................................(be) SophieDoyle[(7)] 10 59
(A J McCabe) *wnt rt s: hld up towards rr: effrt and nt clr run briefly wl over 1f out: styd on after: nrst fin* **11/1**
0030 **4** *nk* **Special Place**[99] 3851 4-9-5 **60**.. OscarUrbina 4 63
(J A R Toller) *t.k.h: hld up in midfield: effrt over 2f out: styd on fnl f: nt rch ldrs* **15/2**[3]
0105 **5** *shd* **Vivi Belle**[16] 6256 3-9-0 **56**... JamieSpencer 3 59
(M L W Bell) *b: trckd ldrs: effrt over 2f out: drvn to dispute 2nd over 1f out: one pce fnl f* **8/1**
2331 **6** *1 3/4* **Prince Valentine**[37] 5708 6-8-5 **46**.........................(p) RichardMullen 11 47+
(G L Moore) *lw: squeezed out s: wl in rr: effrt 2f out: no ch whn squeezed out again jst over 1f out: kpt on* **6/1**[1]
1600 **7** *nk* **Border Artist**[9] 6413 8-9-0 **55**... TPQueally 9 53
(J Pearce) *t.k.h: hld up in last: effrt over 2f out: kpt on fr over 1f out: n.d* **12/1**
040 **8** *1/2* **Inwaan (IRE)**[8] 6424 4-9-1 **56**..(t) ChrisCatlin 1 52
(P R Webber) *chsd ldrs on inner: rdn and no imp 2f out: fdd* **10/1**
6100 **9** *1* **Mulberry Lad (IRE)**[199] 1064 5-8-12 **56**........................ TravisBlock[(3)] 8 50
(P W Hiatt) *chsd ldng pair to wl over 1f out: wknd* **16/1**
4340 **10** *1/2* **Marmooq**[9] 6415 4-8-11 **52**..(v) TQuinn 5 44
(M J Attwater) *led to 4f out: chsd wnr to over 1f out: wknd* **6/1**[1]
0043 **11** *1 1/4* **Rubilini**[14] 6277 3-8-4 **46**... FrancisNorton 13 35
(M R Channon) *t.k.h: racd wd in midfield: prog over 2f out: wknd over 1f out* **14/1**
4210 **12** *3/4* **King After**[17] 6226 5-9-1 **56**..(v) DaneO'Neill 12 43
(J R Best) *t.k.h: hld up towards rr: effrt on wd outside 2f out: wknd over 1f out* **8/1**
0406 **13** *3* **Noddledoddle (IRE)**[73] 4661 3-8-4 **46** oh1.......................(bt) PaulDoe 6 25
(J Ryan) *dwlt: hld up in rr: no prog over 2f out* **50/1**
0000 **14** *6* **Simplify**[68] 4807 5-8-5 **46** oh1...............................(p) FrankieMcDonald 14 9
(T M Jones) *nvr bttr than midfield: wkng whn n.m.r over 2f out: sn bhd* **66/1**

1m 24.64s (-1.25) **Going Correction** -0.175s/f (Stan)
WFA 3 from 4yo+ 1lb **14** Ran SP% **124.7**
Speed ratings (Par 101): **100,98,98,97,97 95,95,94,93,92 91,90,87,80**
CSF £85.56 CT £885.21 TOTE £8.40: £2.60, £2.60, £4.20; EX 120.80 TRIFECTA Not won..
Owner Abacus Employment Services Ltd **Bred** Southill Stud **Trained** Limpley Stoke, Bath
■ Stewards' Enquiry : Sophie Doyle one-day ban: careless riding (Nov 12)

FOCUS
A modest handicap in which the pace was only ordinary and the winning time was 1.42 seconds slower than the preceding handicap over the same trip, though given the difference in class it was about right. Solid form.
T/Jkpt: Not won. T/Plt: £131.90 to a £1 stake. Pool: £64,971.80. 359.45 winning tickets. T/Qpdt: £7.80 to a £1 stake. Pool: £4,452.00. 418.80 winning tickets. JN

6563 WOLVERHAMPTON (A.W) (L-H)
Thursday, November 1

OFFICIAL GOING: Standard
Wind: Light behind Weather: Overcast

6608 WOLVERHAMPTON-RACECOURSE.CO.UK H'CAP — 5f 216y(P)
6:50 (6:51) (Class 6) (0-55,55) 3-Y-0+ **£2,047** (£604; £302) **Stalls** Low

Form RPR
4305 **1** **Punching**[12] 6339 3-8-12 **54**.. WilliamBuick[(3)] 13 65
(Eve Johnson Houghton) *mde all: pushed clr over 1f out: eased nr fin* **16/1**
024 **2** *1 1/2* **Littledodayno (IRE)**[3] 6542 4-9-0 **53**........................... NickyMackay 7 59
(M Wigham) *mid-div: hdwy over 2f out: rdn over 1f out: r.o: nt rch wnr* **4/1**[1]
4000 **3** *hd* **Maison Dieu**[14] 6288 4-9-2 **55**.................................(b[1]) GrahamGibbons 1 61
(E J Alston) *hld up in tch: rdn over 1f out: nt clr run ins fnl f: r.o* **9/1**
004 **4** *3/4* **Siraj**[22] 6101 8-9-2 **55**...(p) BrettDoyle 8 58
(J Ryan) *sn pushed along and prom: rdn over 2f out: styd on same pce fnl f* **7/1**
4040 **5** *nk* **Mulligan's Gold (IRE)**[29] 5908 4-9-2 **55**....................(p) JamieSpencer 6 57+
(T D Easterby) *hld up: swtchd rt and hdwy over 1f out: rdn and hung lft ins fnl f: nt rch ldrs* **5/1**[2]
4404 **6** *1/2* **Kennington**[9] 6415 7-9-1 **54**.. LiamJones 5 55
(Mrs C A Dunnett) *chsd ldrs: rdn over 2f out: no ex fnl f* **8/1**
5006 **7** *2 1/2* **Phinerine**[14] 6288 4-8-11 **55**...(b) TolleyDean[(5)] 10 48
(Miss J E Foster) *chsd wnr: rdn over 2f out: wknd fnl f* **40/1**
6662 **8** *1/2* **Endless Summer**[8] 6424 10-8-10 **54**........................... KellyHarrison[(5)] 4 45
(A W Carroll) *s.i.s: hld up: nvr nr to chal* **6/1**[3]
3103 **9** *1* **Drum Dance (IRE)**[107] 3618 5-8-8 **52**.......................(b) HaddenFrost[(5)] 3 40
(M Hill) *s.i.s: hld up: hmpd 1/2-way: n.d* **9/1**
0650 **10** *3 1/2* **Ocean Gift**[14] 6290 5-9-2 **55**... PaulHanagan 9 32
(N Tinkler) *hld up: hmpd 1/2-way: n.d* **14/1**
0560 **11** *nk* **Lady Lafitte (USA)**[8] 6424 3-9-1 **54**............................(p) AdamKirby 2 30
(M Wellings) *s.i.s: hdwy 1/2-way: rdn and wknd wl over 1f out* **28/1**
20 **12** *4* **Diamond Hurricane (IRE)**[24] 6064 3-8-12 **54**......... NeilChalmers[(3)] 11 17
(M Wellings) *s.i.s: n.d* **33/1**
-100 **13** *10* **Inkjet (IRE)**[9] 6402 3-9-2 **55**... DavidAllan 12 —
(P D Evans) *chsd ldrs: rdn 4f out: wknd 1/2-way* **66/1**

1m 14.98s (-0.83) **Going Correction** -0.125s/f (Stan) **13** Ran SP% **117.4**
Speed ratings (Par 101): **100,98,97,96,96 95,92,91,90,85 85,79,66**
CSF £75.94 CT £652.16 TOTE £12.30: £3.70, £1.50, £3.00; EX 125.80.
Owner Anthony Pye-Jeary And Mel Smith **Bred** Cheveley Park Stud Ltd **Trained** Blewbury, Oxon

FOCUS
Ordinary form for the grade. The winner had the run of things and was able to set his own modest pace.
Mulligan's Gold(IRE) Official explanation: jockey said gelding ran too freely.
Drum Dance(IRE) Official explanation: jockey said gelding ran too keenly

6609 WOLVERHAMPTON HOLIDAY INN CLASSIFIED STKS 7f 32y(P)
7:20 (7:20) (Class 7) 3-Y-0+ **£1,911** (£564; £282) **Stalls** High

Form RPR
4006 1 **Silver Hotspur**[23] 6083 3-8-13 45 NickyMackay 4 57
(M Wigham) *chsd ldrs: rdn to ld over 1f out: r.o* **16/1**
2140 2 1 3/4 **Sion Hill (IRE)**[3] 6532 6-9-0 45 (p) SebSanders 5 53
(John A Harris) *mde most tl rdn and hdd over 1f out: styd on same pce* **8/1**
0000 3 1 1/2 **Blythe Spirit**[14] 6288 8-9-0 45 (b) LiamJones 8 49
(Mrs L Williamson) *hld up: hdwy over 1f out: sn rdn: r.o* **33/1**
6051 4 hd **Snow Bunting**[10] 6390 9-9-6 45 PaulHanagan 7 55
(Jedd O'Keeffe) *hld up: hdwy over 1f out: r.o u.p: nt rch ldrs* **11/4**[1]
0005 5 1/2 **Hornpipe**[13] 6311 5-8-9 45 HaddenFrost(5) 9 47
(M Hill) *chsd ldrs: rdn over 1f out: sn edgd lft: no ex ins fnl f* **9/1**
0022 6 nk **Muktasb (USA)**[2] 6565 6-9-0 45 (v) AdamKirby 11 47
(D Shaw) *s.s: hld up: hdwy over 1f out: nt trble ldrs* **3/1**[2]
0000 7 3 **Bold Nevison (IRE)**[27] 5967 3-8-10 45 NeilChalmers(3) 3 38
(B Smart) *chsd ldrs: rdn over 2f out: wknd fnl f* **33/1**
2204 8 1 **High Five Society**[5] 6505 3-8-13 45 (b) PaulEddery 12 35
(S R Bowring) *mid-div: hdwy over 2f out: rdn: hung lft and wknd over 1f out* **11/2**[3]
0240 9 8 **Miss Mujahid Times**[10] 6390 4-9-0 45 (b) GrahamGibbons 6 15
(A D Brown) *chsd ldrs: drvn along over 5f out: wknd 3f out* **28/1**
00/0 10 nk **Lady Fas (IRE)**[86] 4258 4-8-9 45 KellyHarrison(5) 2 15
(A W Carroll) *s.i.s: a in rr* **66/1**
0000 11 10 **Cadogen Square**[6] 6467 5-9-0 45 (b) PaulMulrennan 1 —
(D W Chapman) *w ldr tl rdn over 3f out: wknd 2f out* **33/1**
0033 12 3 **Mis Chicaf (IRE)**[13] 6311 6-9-0 45 DavidAllan 10 —
(D Carroll) *mid-div: sn drvn along: lost pl over 4f out: sn wknd* **10/1**

1m 29.73s (-0.67) **Going Correction** -0.125s/f (Stan)
WFA 3 from 4yo+ 1lb 12 Ran SP% **116.9**
Speed ratings (Par 97): **98,96,94,94,93 93,89,88,79,79 67,64**
CSF £130.31 TOTE £13.60: £4.10, £2.30, £9.90; EX 169.40.
Owner D Hassan **Bred** Theobalds Stud **Trained** Newmarket, Suffolk

FOCUS
Good form for the grade, but it proved difficult to come from too far back. The winner is rated to his best form of this year.

6610 SPONSOR A RACE BY CALLING 0870 220 2442 H'CAP 7f 32y(P)
7:50 (7:50) (Class 5) (0-70,70) 3-Y-0+ **£3,238** (£963; £481; £240) **Stalls** High

Form RPR
1416 1 **Hessian (IRE)**[18] 6208 3-9-4 70 NCallan 3 78+
(P Howling) *hld up: hdwy over 1f out: nt clr run sn after: rdn to ld wl ins fnl f: edgd lft: r.o* **5/1**
0404 2 3/4 **Elusive Warrior (USA)**[14] 6290 4-8-5 56 oh1 (p) PaulHanagan 7 62
(R A Fahey) *chsd ldr: rdn to ld over 1f out: sn hung lft: hdd ins fnl f: styd on* **12/1**
0201 3 nk **Sedge (USA)**[20] 6148 7-9-5 70 (b) MickyFenton 2 75
(P T Midgley) *chsd ldrs: rdn to ld ins fnl f: sn hdd and unable qck* **7/2**[2]
0232 4 1/2 **Obe Royal**[6] 6463 3-8-11 63 (p) TGMcLaughlin 1 67
(P D Evans) *s.i.s: hld up: hdwy over 1f out: nt rch ldrs* **10/3**[1]
6000 5 1 1/2 **My Learned Friend (IRE)**[31] 5874 3-9-2 68 FrancisNorton 5 68
(A M Balding) *hld up in tch: racd keenly: rdn over 1f out: styd on* **10/1**
0511 6 1 1/4 **Wadnagin (IRE)**[7] 6455 3-8-12 64 6ex JamieSpencer 8 60
(I A Wood) *hld up: rdn over 1f out: nt clr run ins fnl f: nvr trbld ldrs* **4/1**[3]
1000 7 1 1/2 **No Grouse**[14] 6290 7-8-6 57 ow1 GrahamGibbons 4 49
(E J Alston) *sn led: rdn and hdd over 1f out: wknd ins fnl f* **20/1**
1021 8 1 **Jilly Why (IRE)**[20] 6149 6-8-13 64 (b) SebSanders 6 54
(Paul Green) *hld up: rdn and wknd over 1f out* **8/1**
0535 9 3 **Bold Indian (IRE)**[12] 6344 3-8-12 64 (p) TomEaves 10 46
(I Semple) *s.s: hdwy over 5f out: rdn over 2f out: sn hung lft and wknd* **12/1**

1m 30.33s (-0.07) **Going Correction** -0.125s/f (Stan)
WFA 3 from 4yo+ 1lb 9 Ran SP% **122.3**
Speed ratings (Par 103): **95,94,93,93,91 90,88,87,83**
CSF £66.66 CT £243.38 TOTE £7.90: £2.00, £2.90, £1.90; EX 86.90.
Owner Miss T J Fitzgerald **Bred** Rathbarry Stud **Trained** Newmarket, Suffolk

FOCUS
This looked a reasonable race for the class beforehand, but a few of these were inconvenienced by the steady pace. The form makes plenty of sense though and Hessian can rate higher.
Wadnagin(IRE) Official explanation: jockey said filly ran flat and hung right
No Grouse Official explanation: jockey said gelding lost its action in closing stages

6611 HORIZONS RESTAURANT MAIDEN FILLIES' STKS 1m 141y(P)
8:20 (8:20) (Class 5) 2-Y-0 **£3,238** (£963; £481; £240) **Stalls** Low

Form RPR
0022 1 **Fandangerina**[7] 6449 2-9-0 71 SebSanders 5 78+
(Sir Mark Prescott) *mde all: edgd rt ins fnl f: rdn out* **5/2**[2]
042 2 1 3/4 **Counterclaim**[11] 6358 2-9-0 0 TedDurcan 6 74+
(Saeed Bin Suroor) *a.p: rdn to chse wnr and hung lft over 1f out: styd on* **7/2**[3]
36 3 5 **Snowy Indian**[33] 5811 2-9-0 0 JamieSpencer 2 64
(Sir Michael Stoute) *chsd ldrs: rdn over 3f out: styd on same pce fnl 2f* **2/1**[1]
0533 4 1 **Sweet Hope (USA)**[15] 6267 2-9-0 75 NCallan 7 62+
(K A Ryan) *chsd wnr tl rdn wl over 1f out: hmpd sn after: no ex* **4/1**
5 1/2 **Queen's Speech (IRE)** 2-9-0 0 RobertHavlin 4 61
(J H M Gosden) *s.i.s: hld up: rdn over 2f out: hung lft over 1f out: nvr trbld ldrs* **16/1**
50 6 11 **Bewdley**[14] 6289 2-9-0 0 TGMcLaughlin 3 38
(P D Evans) *s.i.s: hld up: wknd 3f out* **66/1**
06 7 shd **Daisy Nook**[29] 5919 2-9-0 0 JDSmith 8 37
(S Kirk) *sn pushed along in rr: wknd over 3f out* **66/1**

1m 50.03s (-1.73) **Going Correction** -0.125s/f (Stan) 7 Ran SP% **113.0**
Speed ratings (Par 93): **102,100,96,95,94 84,84**
CSF £11.42 TOTE £3.20: £2.00, £1.70; EX 10.20.
Owner Miss K Rausing **Bred** Miss K Rausing **Trained** Newmarket, Suffolk
■ Stewards' Enquiry : Ted Durcan caution: careless riding

FOCUS
Some powerful stables were represented, but this was a pretty ordinary fillies' maiden. However the first two finished clear and produced decent enough form.

NOTEBOOK
Fandangerina shaped as though she would benefit from a step up in trip when just held in a 7f nursery off a mark of 71 at Brighton on her previous start and this was an improved performance. She was allowed her own way out in front, but still set a reasonable pace and had her rivals on the stretch when kicking for home off the final bend. She may have had more to do had the runner-up not hung under pressure, but this was still a fair effort and she should stay even further. (op 3-1)
Counterclaim, stepped up to her furthest trip to date, blew any chance she may have had of getting to the winner by hanging badly left in the straight. Her attitude is questionable. (op 11-4)
Snowy Indian has not progressed as many expected from a highly encouraging debut at Salisbury and this was a modest effort. (op 9-4 tchd 5-2)
Sweet Hope(USA) travelled quite well, but she found little when it mattered and was some way below her official mark of 75. This trip seemed to stretch her. (tchd 9-2)
Queen's Speech(IRE), a 38,000gns daughter of Medicean, out of a 1m winner at three, was unfancied and was well held. (op 14-1)

6612 HOTEL & CONFERENCING AT WOLVERHAMPTON H'CAP 1m 1f 103y(P)
8:50 (8:50) (Class 6) (0-68,67) 3-Y-0+ **£2,218** (£654; £327) **Stalls** Low

Form RPR
1031 1 **Lobengula (IRE)**[7] 6458 5-9-5 67 6ex DanielTudhope 1 81+
(I W McInnes) *mde all: rdn clr over 2f out: sn hung rt: styd on* **2/1**[1]
2206 2 3 **My Michelle**[12] 6343 6-8-9 60 WilliamBuick(3) 5 66
(B Palling) *prom: outpcd 1/2-way: hdwy over 1f out: no ch w wnr* **11/1**
6263 3 1 1/2 **Airman (IRE)**[12] 6344 4-9-1 63 JamieSpencer 3 66
(W M Brisbourne) *hld up in tch: outpcd over 2f out: rallied over 1f out: styd on* **9/2**[3]
6026 4 shd **Siena Star (IRE)**[12] 6342 9-9-2 64 MickyFenton 9 67
(Stef Liddiard) *hld up: hdwy over 1f out: nvr nrr* **14/1**
5540 5 hd **Breaking Shadow (IRE)**[15] 4494 5-8-7 62 DeanHeslop(7) 6 64
(M A Peill) *chsd wnr: rdn over 2f out: no ex fnl f* **33/1**
3600 6 nk **Multicultural**[26] 6007 4-9-5 67 RichardMullen 7 69
(D M Simcock) *s.i.s: hld up: rdn over 3f out: styd on fr over 1f out: nt trble ldrs* **4/1**[2]
0222 7 2 1/2 **Emily's Place (IRE)**[12] 6342 4-9-3 65 SebSanders 2 62
(J Pearce) *chsd ldrs: hmpd over 2f out: sn rdn: wknd fnl f* **4/1**[2]
550 8 7 **Legend Erry (IRE)**[17] 6238 3-8-9 60 RobertHavlin 8 43
(Jane Chapple-Hyam) *hld up: rdn over 3f out: n.d* **25/1**
5406 9 3 1/2 **Mowadeh (IRE)**[61] 5034 3-8-11 62 (p) PaulEddery 4 38
(J R Gask) *s.i.s: hld up: a in rr* **33/1**
0 10 12 **Winter Cruise (IRE)**[14] 6293 3-8-7 58 RichardThomas 10 10
(Ian Williams) *chsd ldrs: rdn 1/2-way: wknd over 3f out* **50/1**

2m 0.83s (-1.79) **Going Correction** -0.125s/f (Stan)
WFA 3 from 4yo+ 3lb 10 Ran SP% **118.2**
Speed ratings (Par 101): **102,99,98,97,97 97,95,89,85,75**
CSF £25.93 CT £92.03 TOTE £2.50: £1.30, £3.70, £2.00; EX 21.70.
Owner Colin G R Booth **Bred** A S O'Brien And Lars Pearson **Trained** Catwick, E Yorks
■ Stewards' Enquiry : Dean Heslop four-day ban: used whip with excessive frequency (Nov 12, 14-16)

FOCUS
Just a modest handicap. The improving Lobengula set a reasonable pace, but caught his rivals out when kicking clear leaving the back straight. There is more to come from him.

6613 ENJOY EVENING RACING AT WOLVERHAMPTON H'CAP 1m 4f 50y(P)
9:20 (9:20) (Class 6) (0-50,50) 3-Y-0+ **£2,047** (£604; £302) **Stalls** Low

Form RPR
0056 1 **Lord Laing (USA)**[15] 6265 4-8-10 46 RichardMullen 1 55
(H J Collingridge) *chsd ldrs: styd on u.p to ld wl ins fnl f* **13/2**[3]
0602 2 1 1/4 **Intavac Boy**[2] 6558 6-8-11 50 (p) MichaelJStainton(3) 4 57
(S P Griffiths) *chsd ldr: led 2f out: rdn over 1f out: edgd rt and hdd wl ins fnl f* **7/2**[2]
4006 3 3 **Diktatorship (IRE)**[53] 4994 4-9-0 50 GregFairley 2 52
(Jennie Candlish) *led: rdn and hdd 2f out: no ex fnl f* **10/1**
0603 4 1 1/4 **Squirtle (IRE)**[23] 6076 4-9-0 50 SebSanders 3 50
(W M Brisbourne) *chsd ldrs: rdn over 3f out: styd on same pce appr fnl f* **7/1**
0252 5 3 **Cragganmore Creek**[14] 6292 4-8-11 47 (v) JamieSpencer 6 42+
(D Morris) *hld up: hdwy u.p over 1f out: n.d* **11/4**[1]
0024 6 3/4 **Bobering**[35] 5756 7-9-0 50 TGMcLaughlin 5 44
(B P J Baugh) *hld up: plld hrd: hdwy over 2f out: swtchd lft over 1f out: wknd fnl f* **14/1**
0600 7 nk **Tabulate**[15] 6265 4-8-10 49 WilliamBuick(3) 7 43
(P Howling) *chsd ldrs: rdn over 2f out: hung lft and wknd over 1f out* **8/1**
0550 8 15 **Musicmaestroplease (IRE)**[13] 6316 4-8-12 48 DanielTudhope 8 18
(S Parr) *hld up: a in rr* **33/1**
66-0 9 hd **Champion Lion (IRE)**[16] 6259 8-8-12 48 FrancisNorton 9 17
(R Allan) *s.s: hld up: effrt over 3f out: sn wknd* **9/1**
0-00 10 1 1/4 **Meantime (USA)**[7] 6453 4-8-7 50 (p) CharlotteKerton(7) 11 17
(G Prodromou) *hld up: hdwy 7f out: wknd over 3f out* **100/1**
040 11 29 **Camerooney**[12] 6325 4-9-0 50 GrahamGibbons 12 —
(A D Brown) *hld up: wknd over 3f out* **25/1**

2m 41.49s (-0.93) **Going Correction** -0.125s/f (Stan) 11 Ran SP% **119.4**
Speed ratings (Par 101): **98,97,95,94,92 91,91,81,81,80 61**
CSF £29.62 CT £231.35 TOTE £9.80: £3.20, £1.80, £3.50; EX 28.20 Place 6 £484.20, Place 5 £160.56..
Owner Maynard Durrant Partnership II **Bred** Echo Valley Horse Farm Inc **Trained** Exning, Suffolk

FOCUS
A moderate handicap and, with the pace steady, it was an advantage to race on the pace. The form is rated around the second and the race could work out despite the slow time.
Champion Lion(IRE) Official explanation: jockey said gelding hung right
T/Plt: £999.10 to a £1 stake. Pool: £107,440.70. 78.50 winning tickets. T/Qpdt: £24.50 to a £1 stake. Pool: £7,891.60. 237.90 winning tickets. CR

6460 SAINT-CLOUD (L-H)
Thursday, November 1

OFFICIAL GOING: Very soft

6614a PRIX PERTH (GROUP 3) 1m
1:20 (1:21) 3-Y-0+ **£27,027** (£10,811; £8,108; £5,405; £2,703)

RPR
1 **Chopastair (FR)**[38] 6-9-0 J-BEyquem 11 107
(T Lemer, France) *racd in 2nd tl led narrowly 2f out: hld on wl u.p fr over 1f out* **179/10**

The Form Book, Raceform Ltd, Compton, RG20 6NL

2 ½ **Cicerole (FR)**[34] 5792 3-8-8 .... C-PLemaire 2 102
(J-C Rouget, France) *trckd ldrs: 4th st: rdn over 1 1/2f out: n.m.r briefly over 1f out: tk 2nd 100yds out: kpt on* **27/10**[1]

3 ¾ **Athanor (FR)**[19] 6188 5-9-0 .... DBonilla 10 105
(F Head, France) *in tch on outside: 3rd st: kpt on same pce fr over 2f out* **59/10**[3]

4 ½ **Stop Making Sense**[23] 5-9-0 .... SPasquier 5 104
(A Fabre, France) *hld up: 9th on ins st: styd on steadily fnl 1 1/2f* **16/1**

5 hd **Gwenseb (FR)**[19] 6188 4-8-11 ....(b) MBlancpain 8 100
(C Laffon-Parias, France) *hld up on outside: 8th st: effrt on outside over 1 1/2f out: kpt on at one pce* **29/1**

6 ½ **Hujum (IRE)**[21] 3-8-12 .... TGillet 4 102
(J E Hammond, France) *led to 2f out: one pce* **41/10**[2]

7 ¾ **Satri (IRE)**[53] 5259 5-9-0 .... JMurtagh 9 101
(J-M Beguigne, France) *s.i.s: towards rr tl hdwy arnd outside to go 5th st: rdn under 2f out: unable qck* **61/10**

8 2 ½ **Plaisir Bere (FR)**[19] 6188 4-9-0 ....(b) TJarnet 3 96
(A Junk, France) *hld up in rr: last st: nvr a factor* **27/1**

9 nse **Hotel Du Cap**[41] 5588 4-9-0 .... DarryllHolland 1 96
(G Wragg) *midfield on ins: 7th st: effrt over 2f out: sn outpcd* **15/1**

10 1 ½ **Hello My Lord (FR)**[75] 4627 3-8-12 .... RichardHughes 6 93
(Mme C Head-Maarek, France) *missed break: racd keenly in last: 10th st: nvr a factor* **15/2**

11 **Rageman**[19] 6188 7-9-0 .... CSoumillon 7 93
(M Cheno, France) *cl up: 6th st: rdn and btn 2f out: eased fnl f* **16/1**

1m 46.5s (-1.00)
WFA 3 from 4yo+ 2lb 11 Ran SP% **117.2**
PARI-MUTUEL: WIN 18.90; PL 4.20, 1.60, 1.90; DF 32.60.
Owner Mlle G Ivoula & P Blazy **Bred** Alain Chopard & Mme Maryse Delteil **Trained** France

NOTEBOOK
Chopastair(FR) is a very genuine gelding who seems to be getting better with age. He looked magnificent in the paddock, was always in the leading group in the race itself and went to the head of affairs a furlong and a half out. He stayed on strongly at the end and will no doubt continue in similar events next season.
Cicerole(FR), who was given every possible chance, was tucked in on the rail behind the leading group early on and made a forward move from halfway up the straight. She never looked like pegging back the winner, though.
Athanor(FR), never far from the leaders, was given every chance and ran on well but one-paced from the two-furlong marker.
Stop Making Sense, who wore cheekpieces, did not have the luckiest of races but was putting in his best work at the finish.
Hotel Du Cap stumbled rounding the final turn on the rail and never really got in a blow.

6615a CRITERIUM INTERNATIONAL (GROUP 1) (C&F) 1m
1:50 (1:51) 2-Y-O **£96,520** (£38,615; £19,307; £9,645; £4,831)

RPR

1 **Thewayyouare (USA)**[19] 6187 2-9-0 .... SPasquier 2 117
(A Fabre, France) *hld up in 5th: 4th st: swtchd towards rails to chal over 2f out: rdn over 1f out: drvn to ld 100yds out: r.o* **14/10**[1]

2 ½ **Hello Morning (FR)**[13] 2-9-0 .... C-PLemaire 3 116
(Mme C Head-Maarek, France) *hld up: 5th st: chal on outside over 2f out: led 2f out: drvn over 1f out: hdd 100yds out: r.o* **58/10**

3 6 **Redolent (IRE)**[19] 6170 2-9-0 .... JMurtagh 5 103
(R Hannon) *led tl ent st: hrd rdn over 2f out: ev ch wl over 1f out: last 1f out: kpt on u.p to take 3rd fnl 100yds* **82/10**

4 ½ **Yankadi (USA)**[27] 5972 2-9-0 .... RichardHughes 4 102
(B W Hills) *reluctant to load: pressed ldr: cl 3rd st: ev ch 2f out: sn rdn and one pce* **12/1**

5 ½ **Blue Chagall (FR)**[40] 5660 2-9-0 .... JVictoire 1 101
(H-A Pantall, France) *trckd ldr: led ent st to 2f out: one pce* **4/1**[3]

6 ½ **Sceptre Rouge (IRE)**[11] 6378 2-9-0 .... CSoumillon 6 100
(A De Royer-Dupre, France) *hld up: last st: slipped through on rails to have ev ch over 1f out: sn rdn and one pce* **34/10**[2]

1m 45.3s (-2.20) 6 Ran SP% **117.7**
PARI-MUTUEL: WIN 2.40; PL 1.40, 2.20; SF 8.60.
Owner S Mulryan **Bred** Barnett Enterprises **Trained** Chantilly, France
■ Stewards' Enquiry : Richard Hughes €100 fine - whip abuse

NOTEBOOK
Thewayyouare(USA) was winning his fourth consecutive race and on this occasion he was workmanlike but still efficient. Fifth for much of the mile, he was moved left towards the rail a furlong and a half out and took up the running for a short time before being passed at the furlong marker. He then rallied in the last 100 yards and was going away from the runner-up at the end. The ground was a little on the sticky side and he showed great courage for such a young horse. There is no definite plan for next year except that he will be raced over longer distances and be entered for all the Derbys.
Hello Morning(FR) looked to have this Group 1 event wrapped up at the furlong marker but he could not quite keep up the good work to the post. Fourth for much of the race, he was brought up the centre of the track to make his run. He quickened well to lead a furlong out before failing to repel the renewed challenge of the winner. He certainly appreciated the cut in the ground.
Redolent(IRE) was asked to make all the running and stuck to his task until the bitter end. He came under pressure early in the straight and then just stayed on gamely to hold third place. His connections were delighted with the effort and he will be raced over longer distances next year.
Yankadi(USA), always well up and on the outside, ran well enough and had no excuses. He just stayed on one-paced throughout the final furlong and a half.

6332
NEWMARKET (ROWLEY) (R-H)
Friday, November 2

OFFICIAL GOING: Good (8.3)
Wind: Light across Weather: Cloudy with sunny spells

6616 PRESTIGE VEHICLES EBF MAIDEN STKS (C&G) (DIV I) 7f
12:15 (12:17) (Class 4) 2-Y-O **£4,857** (£1,445; £722; £360) **Stalls** High

Form RPR

03 1 **Black Rain**[14] 6296 2-9-0 0 ....(t) JamieSpencer 12 80
(P J McBride) *chsd ldr: led over 2f out: rdn and edgd rt ins fnl f: sn hdd: styd on: hmpd nr fin: fin 2nd, shd: awrdd r* **3/1**[2]

43 2 shd **Classic Descent**[10] 6403 2-9-0 0 .... SebSanders 9 79
(P J Makin) *hld up: hdwy over 1f out: rdn to ld wl ins fnl f: edgd lft nr fin: fin 1st, shd: disq: plcd 2nd* **9/1**

00 3 2 ½ **Tharawaat (IRE)**[28] 5971 2-9-0 0 .... RHills 5 73
(B W Hills) *led over 4f: rdn and edgd rt over 1f out: styd on same pce* **11/4**[1]

40 4 hd **Driven (IRE)**[8] 6451 2-9-0 0 .... JimCrowley 8 73
(Mrs A J Perrett) *chsd ldrs: rdn over 2f out: outpcd over 1f out: styd on ins fnl f* **33/1**

5 ½ **Kingdom Of Fife** 2-9-0 0 .... RyanMoore 4 71+
(Sir Michael Stoute) *dwlt: hld up: rdn over 2f out: hdwy over 1f out: nt trble ldrs* **8/1**

6 ½ **Beggars End (USA)** 2-9-0 0 .... TedDurcan 10 70
(E F Vaughan) *chsd ldrs: rdn over 2f out: sn outpcd: styd on ins fnl f* **10/1**

0 7 1 ¾ **Tyfos**[31] 5880 2-9-0 0 .... JohnEgan 2 66
(W M Brisbourne) *chsd ldrs: rdn over 2f out: styd on same pce appr fnl f* **100/1**

8 ½ **Navajo Joe (IRE)** 2-9-0 0 .... StephenDonohoe 1 64
(B J Meehan) *s.i.s: hld up: rdn over 2f out: n.d* **11/2**[3]

0 9 ½ **Chinese Profit**[28] 5971 2-9-0 0 .... OscarUrbina 7 63
(G C Bravery) *hld up in tch: plld hrd: rdn and wknd over 1f out* **150/1**

10 nk **Star Pattern (USA)** 2-9-0 0 .... JimmyFortune 11 62+
(J H M Gosden) *s.s: hdwy 1/2-way: rdn over 1f out: wknd ins fnl f* **8/1**

11 shd **Dubai's Wonder (IRE)** 2-9-0 0 .... MichaelHills 3 62
(B W Hills) *dwlt: rn green: a in rr* **25/1**

12 ¾ **Burnbrake** 2-9-0 0 .... RobertHavlin 6 60
(J A R Toller) *mid-div: lost pl 4f out: wknd over 2f out* **100/1**

1m 28.14s (1.64) **Going Correction** +0.15s/f (Good) 12 Ran SP% **117.8**
Speed ratings (Par 98): **95,96,93,92,92 91,89,89,88,88 88,87**
CSF £29.33 TOTE £4.20: £1.40, £2.40, £1.30; EX 26.30.
Owner PMRacing **Bred** Kirtlington Stud And Gilridge Bloodstock **Trained** Newmarket, Suffolk
■ A race that could have a big bearing on the outcome of the jockeys' title.

FOCUS
The slower of the two divisions by 0.58sec and probably only ordinary maiden form for the track. The first two finished clear but the time was modest and this did not appeal as a great race.

NOTEBOOK
Black Rain came out second best in the battle to the line but won the race in the Stewards' room with Spencer arguing that his title challenger's mount had drifted into him in the closing stages, hampering his ability to use the stick in his right hand. Given the narrowness of his defeat he had a fair case, and the result stood following an appeal. (op 11-4 tchd 10-3)
Classic Descent had shown enough in two previous starts to suggest that he could win an average maiden, and in drawing clear of the rest he did so again. Unfortunately for him he edged left into Black Rain as the pair of them knuckled down for a final-furlong duel, in the process hampering his rival jockey's ability to use his whip in his right hand. The margin of victory was so slender that the Stewards decided to reverse the placings, and the decision was upheld after an appeal by his connections. (op 15-2)
Tharawaat(IRE) finished seventh in a stronger heat than this over the course and distance last time and that form had been given a boost by the subsequent maiden success of the sixth. Backed into favouritism, he proved a little disappointing, but he has now had the requisite three runs for a mark, and should not be overburdened when he comes back for handicaps next year. (op 7-2 tchd 4-1 in places)
Driven(IRE) ran a better race down in trip as one might expect of a half-brother to Ayr Gold Cup winner Advanced. He too is now eligible for a mark after this third outing in a relatively short space of time, and better will be seen of him at three.
Kingdom Of Fife's dam won a Listed race over 1m2f so it is a little disappointing that her previous three foals have failed to get off the mark. This was a solid enough debut effort and a longer trip should suit him next year. (op 7-1)
Beggars End(USA), a first foal of a half-sister to First Word, a triple winner at around 6f to 1m1f in the US, did not cost too much at the sales but ran with plenty of encouragement on his debut. (op 14-1 tchd 9-1)
Navajo Joe(IRE) cost 180,000gns as a yearling, but that is understandable because he is a brother to Cheveley Park and Coronation Stakes winner Indian Ink. He did not show a great deal on this debut, but should improve for the experience and obviously one would imagine that softer ground will suit him too. (op 5-1 tchd 6-1)

6617 EUROPEAN BREEDERS' FUND MAIDEN STKS 6f
12:45 (12:52) (Class 4) 2-Y-O **£5,181** (£1,541; £770; £384) **Stalls** High

Form RPR

45 1 **Almoutaz (USA)**[56] 5194 2-9-3 0 .... RHills 1 79+
(B W Hills) *racd centre: led that pair tl overall ldr over 1f out: edgd rt fnl f: rdn out* **3/1**[1]

0 2 1 **The Gatekeeper**[160] 2041 2-9-3 0 .... TedDurcan 6 76
(M H Tompkins) *hld up: racd far side: hdwy over 1f out: rdn and hung rt ins fnl f: styd on* **20/1**

46 3 ¾ **Cotton Reel**[32] 5868 2-9-3 0 .... TQuinn 4 74
(P F I Cole) *racd centre: chsd wnr: rdn and ev ch over 1f out: styd on same pce: sddle slipped* **7/1**[2]

4 2 ½ **Kenton Street** 2-9-3 0 .... RobertHavlin 5 66
(J A R Toller) *racd far side: chsd ldrs: rdn and hung rt fr over 1f out: no ex fnl f* **12/1**[3]

0 5 1 **Benedetto**[9] 6436 2-9-3 0 .... JimCrowley 9 63
(Mrs A J Perrett) *racd far side: hld up: hdwy over 1f out: no ex fnl f* **50/1**

6 1 **Brother Barry (USA)** 2-9-3 0 .... NeilPollard 8 60+
(W J Musson) *racd far side: trckd ldrs: racd keenly: stmbld wl over 1f out: styd on same pce* **66/1**

0 7 2 **Opera Prince**[56] 5206 2-9-3 0 .... RyanMoore 13 54
(S Kirk) *racd far side: chsd ldr: led overall 3f out: sn rdn and hdd: wknd ins fnl f* **12/1**[3]

8 ½ **Moon Sister (IRE)** 2-8-12 0 .... TPQueally 11 48+
(W Jarvis) *racd far side: s.s: a in rr* **20/1**

9 shd **Amicable Terms** 2-8-12 0 .... ChrisCatlin 7 47
(Rae Guest) *racd far side: prom: rdn over 2f out: sn wknd* **50/1**

10 2 ½ **First In Show** 2-8-9 0 .... WilliamBuick(3) 2 40
(A M Balding) *s.s: swtchd to r far side sn after s: outpcd* **33/1**

11 2 ½ **Unlicensed** 2-9-3 0 .... RichardHughes 10 37
(R Hannon) *racd far side: overall ldr 4f: wknd fnl f* **16/1**

1m 14.11s (1.01) **Going Correction** +0.15s/f (Good) 11 Ran SP% **76.6**
Speed ratings (Par 98): **99,97,96,93,92 90,88,87,87,83 80**
CSF £27.48 TOTE £2.20: £1.10, £5.20, £1.70; EX 28.00.
Owner Hamdan Al Maktoum **Bred** Shadwell Farm **Trained** Lambourn, Berks
■ Frivolous 11/8 was withdrawn: broke loose at stalls (deduct 40p in the £ under Rule 4).

FOCUS
Another ordinary-looking maiden for the track, rendered even less competitive when the favourite Frivolous got loose before the start and was withdrawn. The winner ran to form and sets the level.

NOTEBOOK
Almoutaz(USA) stuck towards the centre of the track and that certainly seemed to be an advantage as both he and Cotton Reel, who finished third, appeared to benefit from racing on slightly quicker ground. His rider did not need to get too serious with him to score and he looks the type to make up into a useful handicapper next term, when he should also stay further. (op 7-2 tchd 11-4)
The Gatekeeper had not been seen out since finishing down the field in a maiden here back in May, but he ran well, coming out of the main group that raced towards the far-side rail and staying on takingly once he hit the rising ground. He could well win a maiden on the Polytrack before the year is out. (op 33-1)

Cotton Reel raced with the winner towards the centre of the track and that might have been a bit of an advantage. He could not match that rival's pace at the finish but still looked to have put up his best performance to date in third. He is now eligible for a mark. Official explanation: jockey said saddle slipped (op 6-1 tchd 11-2)
Kenton Street, a half-brother to Encores, a winner over 7f and 1m at three, hung right inside the last furlong, which did not help his cause, but there was promise in the run. (op 33-1)
Benedetto showed a lot more than on his debut when too keen, especially as racing next to the far-side rail may not have been to his advantage. (op 40-1)
Brother Barry(USA), whose stable has not won a two-year-old maiden in the last five seasons, looked a big baby and was not given a hard time. He showed he has ability, though, and should be a different proposition next year once handicapped.

6618 PRESTIGE VEHICLES EBF MAIDEN STKS (C&G) (DIV II) 7f
1:20 (1:23) (Class 4) 2-Y-O £4,857 (£1,445; £722; £360) **Stalls** High

Form RPR
5 **1** **Foolin Myself**[28] 5977 2-9-0 0 JamieSpencer 11 83+
(B W Hills) *hld up in tch: led over 1f out: rdn out* **11/8**[1]
2 *1 1/4* **Tartan Bearer (IRE)** 2-9-0 0 RyanMoore 2 83+
(Sir Michael Stoute) *s.s: sn chsng ldrs: ev ch whn hmpd and outpcd over 1f out: r.o ins fnl f* **9/4**[2]
3 *3/4* **Sundowner (IRE)** 2-9-0 0 NickyMackay 9 78+
(G A Butler) *hld up: rdn over 2f out: hdwy and hung lft fr over 1f out: styd on* **25/1**
0 **4** *3/4* **Emerald Crystal (IRE)**[6] 6493 2-9-0 0 RichardHughes 1 76
(B J Meehan) *led: rdn and edgd lft fr over 2f out: hdd over 1f out: no ex ins fnl f* **33/1**
5 *2* **Day Of Destiny (IRE)** 2-9-0 0 MichaelHills 6 71+
(B W Hills) *chsd ldrs: nt clr run and swtchd rt 2f out: sn rdn: hmpd over 1f out: nt clr run and wknd ins fnl f* **16/1**
6 *nk* **Nayef Star** 2-9-0 0 TPQueally 5 70+
(J Noseda) *s.i.s: sn chsng ldrs: rdn over 2f out: hmpd over 1f out: styd on same pce* **11/1**
0 **7** *3 1/2* **Pacifism (UAE)**[17] 6248 2-9-0 0 PhilipRobinson 10 62+
(M A Jarvis) *chsd ldr: rdn over 2f out: hmpd and wknd over 1f out* **7/1**[3]
8 *3* **Perez Prado (USA)** 2-9-0 0 TedDurcan 7 54
(W Jarvis) *hld up: nt clr run over 2f out: wknd over 1f out* **33/1**
60 **9** *1 1/2* **Redarsene**[24] 6079 2-8-9 0 JamieJones(5) 8 50+
(M G Quinlan) *hld up: plld hrd: hung rt fr over 2f out: n.d* **40/1**
10 *1 1/4* **Zhebe** 2-9-0 0 JimmyFortune 4 47+
(P J McBride) *s.s: hld up: nt clr run over 2f out: effrt and hung rt over 1f out: sn wknd and eased* **22/1**

1m 27.56s (1.06) **Going Correction** +0.15s/f (Good) **10** Ran SP% **116.1**
Speed ratings (Par 98): **99,97,96,95,93 93,89,85,84,82**
CSF £4.10 TOTE £2.20: £1.10, £1.40, £6.80; EX 5.40.
Owner W J Gredley **Bred** Middle Park Stud Ltd **Trained** Lambourn, Berks

FOCUS
The quicker of the two divisions by 0.58sec. The whole field came up the centre of the track and drifted towards the stands'-side rail from halfway this time. The form looks fair and the first two should go on from this.

NOTEBOOK
Foolin Myself, who ran a promising race on his debut, built on that experience and put up a professional display to get off the mark at the second time of asking. However, he was perhaps a little lucky to beat the newcomer Tartan Bearer, who he contributed to hampering on the rail approaching the final furlong. Given his pedigree he is likely to have no trouble staying 1m4f next year. (tchd 6-4, 13-8 in places)
Tartan Bearer(IRE) ◆, who is a brother to 2000 Guineas and King George winner Golan, looked a little unlucky not to make a winning debut. He was being pushed along but staying on when the gap he was going for next to the rail approaching the furlong pole shut on him as a consequence of the eventual winner edging left and carrying the eventual fourth with him. Snatched up, he was then switched off the rail and finished strongly to take second. There was plenty to like about this performance and he looks sure to make up into a very useful three-year-old. (op 5-2 tchd 2-1)
Sundowner(IRE), a half-brother to 1m2f winner Regal Sunset, was another who stayed on well. With this experience under his belt he should be able to win a maiden on the Polytrack in the coming weeks. (op 22-1)
Emerald Crystal(IRE) is the ninth foal of a mare who has already produced four Group winners, including Crystal Music, who won the Group 1 Fillies' Mile. Unsuited by soft ground on his debut six days earlier, this son of Green Desert showed dramatic improvement on this better surface, and is another capable of winning his maiden before the year is out. (op 28-1)
Day Of Destiny(IRE), a half-brother to Putra Laju, a 7f winner at two, and three times winning hurdler Ever Special, did not get the clearest of runs or the greatest of rides but, like the fifth, it would be stretching things to suggest he could have been placed. Official explanation: jockey said colt hung left-handed (op 14-1)
Nayef Star, a half-brother to Strawberry Leaf, a winner at 1m and 1m1f at three, and Zabaglione, a triple winner between 6f and 1m1f, got bumped about a bit approaching the furlong pole, but he would not have troubled the first four anyway. (op 8-1)
Zhebe Official explanation: jockey said colt lost its action

6619 EBF BOSRA SHAM FILLIES' STKS (LISTED RACE) 6f
1:55 (1:56) (Class 1) 2-Y-O
£15,046 (£5,702; £2,854; £1,423; £712; £357) **Stalls** High

Form RPR
2031 **1** **Spinning Lucy (IRE)**[14] 6306 2-8-12 82 MichaelHills 8 100
(B W Hills) *mde all: rdn clr fnl f: eased last strides* **10/1**
4106 **2** *1* **Dubai Princess (IRE)**[20] 6167 2-8-12 98 JamieSpencer 1 97+
(J A Osborne) *swvd lft s: hld up: nt clr run over 2f out: swtchd rt and hdwy over 1f out: rdn and hung lft ins fnl f: nt rch wnr* **7/2**[2]
3 **3** *1/2* **Bett's Spirit (IRE)**[35] 5784 2-8-12 0 RichardHughes 7 96
(M J Grassick, Ire) *a.p: rdn and edgd lft over 1f out: styd on same pce* **9/1**
1163 **4** *3/4* **Sophie's Girl**[35] 5766 2-8-12 89 KDarley 6 93
(P W Chapple-Hyam) *a.p: rdn to chse wnr over 1f out: no ex ins fnl f* **10/1**
61 **5** *1 1/4* **Festivale (IRE)**[146] 2457 2-8-12 88 EddieAhern 3 90+
(J L Dunlop) *hld up: rdn and hung rt over 1f out: nt trble ldrs* **9/1**
510 **6** *nk* **Irish Pearl (IRE)**[41] 5614 2-8-12 87 PhillipMakin 10 89
(K R Burke) *chsd ldrs: rdn over 2f out: styd on same pce appr fnl f* **33/1**
1 **7** *nk* **Masada (IRE)**[9] 6419 2-8-12 0 RyanMoore 2 88
(B J Meehan) *hld up: hdwy over 2f out: rdn and hung rt fr over 1f out: no ex fnl f* **8/1**[3]
6160 **8** *3* **Sudden Impact (IRE)**[20] 6182 2-8-12 93 TPQueally 5 79
(Paul Green) *chsd ldrs: rdn over 2f out: wknd over 1f out* **16/1**
41 **9** *nk* **Insaaf**[14] 6295 2-8-12 90 RHills 12 78
(W J Haggas) *chsd ldrs: rdn over 1f out: wknd fnl f* **2/1**[1]
1406 **10** *1 1/2* **Mey Blossom**[20] 6182 2-8-12 85 DeanMcKeown 11 73
(R M Whitaker) *chsd wnr tl rdn over 2f out: wknd over 1f out* **33/1**
015 **11** *3 1/2* **Jennifer's Dream (IRE)**[39] 5692 2-8-12 81 TedDurcan 9 63
(K A Ryan) *hld up: wknd 2f out* **66/1**
31 **12** *1/2* **Danseuse Volante (IRE)**[24] 6082 2-8-12 70 TQuinn 4 61
(J W Hills) *hld up: hdwy over 3f out: rdn and wknd over 1f out* **66/1**

1m 12.56s (-0.54) **Going Correction** +0.15s/f (Good) **12** Ran SP% **119.6**
Speed ratings (Par 101): **109,107,107,106,104 103,103,99,99,97 92,91**
CSF £44.66 TOTE £11.90: £2.80, £2.00, £2.70; EX 62.40 Trifecta £401.00 Part won. Pool: £564.80 - 0.50 winning units..
Owner Steve Jenkins **Bred** Patrick Cummins **Trained** Lambourn, Berks

FOCUS
A competitive Listed contest on paper but not the classiest although the time was very good for the grade. A big step up from the winner with the form rated around the fourth, fifth and sixth.

NOTEBOOK
Spinning Lucy(IRE), whose stable is in terrific form, took a while to get off the mark but she did so in decisive fashion at Redcar last time, and she underlined her well-being by running out a cosy winner of this Listed contest. She showed good pace throughout, was never really challenged, and looks the type who could do well in a Guineas trial early next season. (op 11-1 tchd 12-1 in places)
Dubai Princess(IRE), not disgraced in the Cornwallis Stakes last time out, was held up to challenge late but never got much of a clear run. Once a gap was eventually found the winner had gone beyond recall, but she ran on strongly inside the last, and the assumption must be that she would have given Spinning Lucy more to do had she got going sooner. (op 5-1)
Bett's Spirit(IRE), who beat some useful performers on the sand at Dundalk on her previous start, had previously finished third in this grade at the Curragh. She brought solid form to the table and ran a fair race, just lacking the pace of the winner, and her performance helps set the level of the form. (op 8-1)
Sophie's Girl was third in a sales race last time out and finished in front of Insaaf that day, so she was entitled to respect in this company. Well placed throughout, she had every chance and ran a sound race.
Festivale(IRE), clear-cut winner of a Lingfield maiden last time out in June, has clearly had her problems in the interim, and this was a good return. She travelled well for much of the race and it was probably just lack of a recent run that found her out towards the finish. (op 8-1)
Irish Pearl(IRE) has failed to build on the promise of her Windsor maiden win. (op 25-1)
Masada(IRE), reappearing just nine days after winning her maiden at Bath, threatened to get involved two furlongs out, but in the end lack of experience in this grade found her out. She looks the type to improve, though, and it would not be a surprise to see her succeed at this level next season. (op 6-1)
Insaaf, who won her maiden over this course and distance a fortnight earlier, raced furthest away from the centre of the track where the ground appeared to be fastest, but she should still have done better than this. Perhaps she has just had enough for the year as this was not her form. (tchd 9-4, 5-2 in places)

6620 EBF SPACEWORKS FURNITURE HIRE FILLIES' H'CAP 1m 4f
2:30 (2:31) (Class 3) (0-90,86) 3-Y-0+
£8,724 (£2,612; £1,306; £653; £326; £163) **Stalls** Centre

Form RPR
6644 **1** **Oh Glory Be (USA)**[14] 6302 4-9-10 **86** (v[1]) RichardHughes 3 94
(R Hannon) *hld up: hdwy over 2f out: rdn to ld wl ins fnl f* **11/1**
5420 **2** *1/2* **Vale De Lobo**[14] 6299 5-8-12 **74** TedDurcan 5 81
(B R Millman) *a.p: chsd ldr 5f out: led over 3f out: rdn over 1f out: hdd wl ins fnl f* **20/1**
053 **3** *1 1/4* **Postage Stampe**[61] 5067 4-8-13 **78** WilliamBuick(3) 1 83
(D M Simcock) *hld up: hdwy over 4f out: rdn over 1f out: edgd lft ins fnl f: styd on same pce* **14/1**
12 **4** *hd* **Watchful (IRE)**[25] 6061 3-9-0 **82** JimmyFortune 6 87
(L M Cumani) *hld up in tch: rdn and hung lft fr over 2f out: styd on* **10/11**[1]
5321 **5** *8* **Sister Maria (USA)**[28] 5979 3-8-10 **78** DaneO'Neill 8 70
(E A L Dunlop) *led: rdn and hdd over 3f out: edgd rt and wknd over 1f out* **5/1**[2]
5203 **6** *1 3/4* **Apply Dapply**[22] 6129 4-9-4 **80** RyanMoore 2 69
(H Morrison) *prom: rdn 4f out: wknd over 2f out* **6/1**[3]
0502 **7** *hd* **Shimoni**[9] 6422 3-8-9 **77** (v) PaulDoe 7 66
(W J Knight) *hld up: hdwy 5f out: rdn and wknd over 1f out* **16/1**
5050 **8** *20* **Tcherina (IRE)**[21] 6158 5-8-11 **73** JohnEgan 4 30
(T D Easterby) *chsd ldr tl rdn 5f out: wknd over 3f out* **14/1**

2m 33.96s (0.46) **Going Correction** +0.15s/f (Good)
WFA 3 from 4yo+ 6lb **8** Ran SP% **115.6**
Speed ratings (Par 104): **104,103,102,102,97 96,96,82**
CSF £198.20 CT £3064.72 TOTE £10.70: £2.70, £3.50, £2.90; EX 212.70.
Owner I A N Wight **Bred** W S Farish **Trained** East Everleigh, Wilts

FOCUS
An ordinary fillies' handicap that did not take much winning and rated around the placed horses.

NOTEBOOK
Oh Glory Be(USA), wearing a visor for the first time and back on a sounder surface, ran on well from off the pace to get up inside the last. She had dropped back to a fair mark so was entitled to go close if the headgear worked. (op 9-1)
Vale De Lobo was out of her depth in a Listed race last time but had built up a strong of consistent efforts prior to that. Back in the right grade, she bounced back to form. (op 16-1)
Postage Stampe did not look to be crying out for the extra two furlongs. She has not had a busy season and races on the Polytrack should be to her liking in the coming weeks as she is on a good mark on her best sand form. (op 12-1)
Watchful(IRE) looked to have been found a good opportunity as most of the field had an exposed look about them, and she was a well-backed favourite. She proved a little disappointing in the race itself, though, wandering about as they hit the rising ground, eventually ending up on the stands'-side rail. It was probably just inexperience and she should be capable of winning off her current mark. Official explanation: jockey said filly hung left-handed closing stages (op Evens tchd 11-10 in places)
Sister Maria(USA), who was only 2lb higher than when successful over 1m2f here last month, made much of the running but looked a blatant non-stayer. (op 7-1)
Apply Dapply was another who had her stamina to prove over this longer trip and failed the test. (tchd 13-2)
Tcherina(IRE) Official explanation: jockey said mare lost its action

6621 NGK SPARK PLUGS CONDITIONS STKS 6f
3:05 (3:05) (Class 4) 2-3-Y-O
£5,608 (£1,679; £839; £420; £209; £105) **Stalls** High

Form RPR
31 **1** **Paco Boy (IRE)**[42] 5591 2-8-8 87 ow2 RyanMoore 4 94+
(R Hannon) *hld up: hdwy over 2f out: sn rdn: led ins fnl f: r.o* **9/4**[2]
-002 **2** *3/4* **Wid (USA)**[14] 6300 3-9-6 95 RHills 3 90
(J L Dunlop) *chsd ldr tl led over 3f out: rdn over 1f out: hdd ins fnl f: styd on* **7/4**[1]
3 *1/2* **Baharah (USA)** 3-9-3 0 JamieSpencer 5 85+
(G A Butler) *s.i.s: hld up: hdwy over 1f out: shkn up ins fnl f: r.o* **10/1**
0530 **4** *1 1/4* **Tadalavil**[6] 6486 2-8-7 85 ow1 ChrisCatlin 2 85
(M R Channon) *chsd ldrs: rdn over 2f out: edgd rt and styd on same pce ins fnl f* **14/1**

01 **5** *1 ¾* **Red Rumour (IRE)**42 5595 2-8-6 87 .... SebSanders 6 79
(R M Beckett) *chsd ldrs: rdn over 2f out: wknd fnl f* **3/1**3

2200 **6** *4* **Miss Ippolita**77 4574 3-9-6 75 .... EddieAhern 7 66
(J R Jenkins) *led: hdd over 3f out: sn rdn: wknd over 1f out* **100/1**

1000 **7** *2* **Shamrock Lady (IRE)**29 5939 2-7-12 78 .... LukeMorris(3) 1 55
(Pat Eddery) *s.i.s: hld up: rdn over 2f out: sn wknd* **40/1**

1m 12.64s (-0.46) **Going Correction** +0.15s/f (Good) **7** Ran SP% **111.3**
Speed ratings: **109,108,107,105,103 98,95**
CSF £6.20 TOTE £2.70: £1.90, £1.40; EX 8.30.
Owner The Calvera Partnership **Bred** Mrs Joan Browne **Trained** East Everleigh, Wilts

FOCUS
A clash of three-year-olds and juveniles which has now been won by a youngster in five of the last six years. The form is not rock-solid with the runner-up slightly below her level and the fourth to his nursery form.

NOTEBOOK
Paco Boy(IRE) won his maiden nicely at Newbury last time and took a successful step up in class. He was receiving 14lb from the runner-up, albeit reduced by 2lb due to his rider's overweight, and that proved enough for him to continue the juveniles' recent dominance in this race. (op 15-8 tchd 5-2)
Tadalavil, who appears held off his current mark in handicaps, looks a difficult horse to place at present and things might not get any easier for him at three. (op 16-1 tchd 12-1)
Red Rumour(IRE), a maiden winner here in September, was a bit disappointing. Perhaps the ground was not as quick as he would have liked, or he may just have had enough for the year. (op 4-1)

6622 ALFIE WESTWOOD LIFETIME IN RACING H'CAP 2m
3:40 (3:43) (Class 3) (0-90,80) 3-Y-O+ **£7,772** (£2,312; £1,155; £577) **Stalls** Centre

Form RPR

1131 **1** **Double Banded (IRE)**14 6308 3-9-0 75 .... SebSanders 1 92+
(J L Dunlop) *hld up: hdwy to ld over 1f out: hung lft: rdn clr* **2/1**1

0330 **2** *5* **Dr Sharp (IRE)**13 6335 7-9-13 79 .... MickyFenton 9 85
(T P Tate) *bmpd s: led over 14f out: rdn over 2f out: hdd over 1f out: styd on same pce* **5/2**2

0122 **3** *1 ¾* **Lord Oroko**9 6421 3-8-9 70 .... VinceSlattery 5 74
(J G M O'Shea) *hld up: hdwy over 3f out: rdn over 1f out: no ex* **11/1**

3-00 **4** *3* **Altenburg (FR)**29 5938 5-9-4 70 .... HayleyTurner 3 70
(Mrs N Smith) *hld up: hdwy over 3f out: sn rdn: styd on same pce fnl 2f* **25/1**

/003 **5** *1* **Inchpast**11 6383 6-9-0 73 ....(b) AshleyMorgan(7) 7 72
(M H Tompkins) *hld up: hdwy 10f out: rdn over 2f out: edgd lft and wknd over 1f out* **33/1**

0311 **6** *2* **Featherlight**34 5820 3-8-11 72 ....(b) RobertHavlin 8 69
(Jamie Poulton) *edgd rt s: hld up: hdwy 10f out: rdn and wknd over 1f out* **10/1**

0230 **7** *nk* **Mister Completely (IRE)**7 6473 6-8-12 64 ....(v) JamesDoyle 6 60
(Ms J S Doyle) *hld up: rdn over 2f out: sn wknd* **20/1**

5042 **8** *2 ½* **Kayf Aramis**20 6181 5-9-5 71 ....(p) ChrisCatlin 4 64
(J L Spearing) *chsd ldrs: rdn over 4f out: wknd over 2f out* **6/1**3

4121 **9** *20* **Annambo**81 4460 7-10-0 80 .... EddieAhern 10 49
(P J McBride) *led: hdd over 14f out: chsd ldr: rdn and wknd over 2f out* **14/1**

2150 **10** *13* **Dar Es Salaam**21 6144 3-9-2 77 .... RyanMoore 2 31
(E A L Dunlop) *hld up: rdn over 4f out: wknd 3f out* **8/1**

3m 28.25s (1.33) **Going Correction** +0.15s/f (Good)
WFA 3 from 5yo+ 9lb **10** Ran SP% **122.9**
Speed ratings (Par 107): **102,99,98,97,96 95,95,94,84,77**
CSF £7.32 CT £45.59 TOTE £3.30: £1.40, £1.80, £3.30; EX 8.90.
Owner Sir Thomas Pilkington **Bred** Sir Thomas Pilkington **Trained** Arundel, W Sussex

FOCUS
Just a fair stayers' contest, but another impressive performance from Double Banded, who has a most progressive profile. The placed horses are the best guides to the level although the fourth and fifth raise doubts.

NOTEBOOK
Double Banded(IRE), a progressive stayer this backend, shrugged off a 9lb rise in the weights for his previous win at Redcar and drew clear for another easy win. Given his profile one would imagine that races like the Ascot Stakes and Cesarewitch will be in his programme next season. (op 9-4 tchd 11-4, 3-1 in places)
Dr Sharp(IRE), who made all to win this race last year off a 4lb higher mark, had to work to get to the front as neither Annambo nor Kayf Aramis was willing to hand that role to him on a plate again. He ran a sound race, fighting off the rest to take an honourable second, and was just unlucky to be beaten by a highly-progressive three-year-old. (tchd 11-4)
Lord Oroko kept on well enough but had no chance with the easy winner. He looks vulnerable off his current mark but could improve with a winter on his back. (op 14-1)
Altenburg(FR), who came into the race on the back of a lighter campaign than most, is well handicapped on his best form but he is still a maiden and his attitude has been questioned in the past.
Inchpast came back to the track in September having been absent for almost two years and he has yet to prove he retains his ability. (op 22-1)
Kayf Aramis, runner-up in this race last year off the same mark, failed to run up to that form. (op 10-1)
Annambo, having his first outing since August, stopped as if shot once he came under pressure.

6623 TURFTV APPRENTICE STKS (H'CAP) (IN MEMORY OF GEORGE COLLING) 1m
4:10 (4:14) (Class 5) (0-75,72) 3-Y-O **£3,238** (£963; £481; £240) **Stalls** High

Form RPR

4-44 **1** **Drawn Gold**15 6286 3-8-12 65 .... RussellKennemore 6 71
(R Hollinshead) *wnt lft s: trckd ldrs: racd keenly: led over 1f out: edgd lft: rdn out* **8/1**

5033 **2** *nk* **Aussie Blue (IRE)**14 6310 3-8-6 62 .... WilliamCarson(3) 9 67
(R M Whitaker) *prom: outpcd over 2f out: rallied over 1f out: r.o* **7/1**3

5065 **3** *nk* **Convivial Spirit**38 5708 3-8-5 58 ....(t) NicolPolli 2 62
(E F Vaughan) *hld up in tch: rdn over 1f out: r.o* **20/1**

104 **4** *½* **Mick Is Back**10 6413 3-8-8 61 ....(p) NeilBrown 4 64
(G G Margarson) *hmpd s: hld up: r.o ins fnl f: nrst fin* **8/1**

020 **5** *hd* **Flying Valentino**13 6331 3-9-1 71 .... GaryBartley(3) 8 74
(G A Swinbank) *hld up: swtchd rt over 2f out: hdwy over 1f out: r.o* **8/1**

410 **6** *nk* **Sun Of The Sea**90 4184 3-9-5 72 .... PatrickHills 7 74
(N P Littmoden) *s.i.s: hld up: hdwy over 2f out: rdn and ev ch over 1f out: edgd rt and unable qckn wl ins fnl f* **5/2**1

1110 **7** *hd* **Mountain Cat (IRE)**27 6002 3-9-0 72 .... DebraEngland(5) 1 73
(W J Musson) *trckd ldrs: racd keenly: rdn over 1f out: styd on* **9/2**2

0430 **8** *nk* **Astroangel**32 5860 3-8-2 60 .... AshleyMorgan(5) 5 61
(M H Tompkins) *hmpd s: hld up: hdwy over 1f out: sn rdn: styd on same pce ins fnl f* **12/1**

0203 **9** *2* **Mini Mosa**4 6546 3-9-3 70 .... AshleyHamblett 10 66
(J H M Gosden) *chsd ldrs: rdn over 2f out: sn rdn and hdd: wknd ins fnl f* **9/1**

0066 **10** *1* **Lordship (IRE)**6 6492 3-8-7 65 .... MarkCoumbe(5) 3 59
(A W Carroll) *led: racd keenly: hdd 2f out: wknd fnl f* **20/1**

-310 **11** *28* **Brave Quest (IRE)**202 1039 3-8-12 65 .... TolleyDean 11 —
(Mrs L J Mongan) *mid-div: rdn over 4f out: wknd 3f out* **40/1**

1m 40.7s (1.33) **Going Correction** +0.15s/f (Good) **11** Ran SP% **122.2**
Speed ratings (Par 102): **99,98,98,97,97 97,97,96,94,93 65**
CSF £64.00 CT £1125.11 TOTE £11.50: £3.00, £2.40, £6.20; EX 89.80 Place 6 £ 84.47, Place 5 £ 53.44.
Owner Tim Leadbeater **Bred** Longdon Stud Ltd **Trained** Upper Longdon, Staffs

FOCUS
A modest handicap for the track in which there was no pace on early, and the race developed into a bit of a sprint with a bunched finish. The form is somewhat messy but makes sense with the second and fifth close to their marks.
T/Jkpt: £7,100.00 to a £1 stake. Pool: £10,000.00. 1.00 winning ticket. T/Plt: £63.40 to a £1 stake. Pool: £50,964.80. 586.45 winning tickets. T/Qpdt: £28.30 to a £1 stake. Pool: £3,756.50. 98.00 winning tickets. CR

6608 WOLVERHAMPTON (A.W) (L-H)
Friday, November 2

OFFICIAL GOING: Standard
Wind: Almost nil Weather: Fine

6624 MACE RACING AT WOLVERHAMPTON NURSERY 5f 20y(P)
7:00 (7:02) (Class 6) (0-65,65) 2-Y-O **£2,047** (£604; £302) **Stalls** Low

Form RPR

5224 **1** **Loose Caboose (IRE)**11 6388 2-9-4 62 .... SebSanders 1 66
(A J McCabe) *led after 1f: rdn over 1f out: drvn out* **7/2**1

3003 **2** *nk* **A Wish For You**11 6386 2-9-2 65 .... JamesO'Reilly(5) 2 68
(D K Ivory) *a.p: rdn and ev ch fr over 1f out: r.o* **8/1**

000 **3** *2* **Lambrini Lace (IRE)**15 6281 2-9-5 63 .... LiamJones 8 59
(Mrs L Williamson) *led 1f: chsd wnr tl rdn wl over 1f out: kpt on same pce* **33/1**

500 **4** *2* **Yankee Storm**90 4181 2-8-11 55 .... ChrisCatlin 11 44
(M J Wallace) *a.p: rdn over 2f out: one pce* **15/2**

5003 **5** *nk* **Diademas (USA)**27 6023 2-9-4 65 ....(e1) JerryO'Dwyer(3) 9 52
(V Smith) *in rr: c wd st: sn rdn: hdwy fnl f: nvr nrr* **12/1**

0004 **6** *hd* **Ile Royale**9 6426 2-8-10 54 ....(be) StephenDonohoe 12 41
(C N Allen) *wnt rt s: sn mid-div: rdn and no real prog fnl 2f* **22/1**

0651 **7** *¾* **Too Grand**9 6426 2-8-12 59 6ex ....(v) NeilChalmers(3) 5 43
(A M Balding) *hld up and bhd: nt clr run over 2f out: hdwy on ins wl over 1f out: n.d* **4/1**2

0056 **8** *¾* **Emef Princess**8 6454 2-8-9 53 ....(b) PaulMulrennan 7 34
(K A Ryan) *mid-div: rdn over 2f out: edgd lft jst over 1f out: no hdwy* **22/1**

6500 **9** *3 ½* **Charlotti Carlotti (IRE)**15 6282 2-9-7 65 ....(p) TomEaves 6 34
(D W Chapman) *a in rr* **11/1**

000 **10** *½* **Captain Crooner (IRE)**23 6104 2-8-3 47 .... PaulHanagan 4 14
(D Shaw) *a towards rr* **7/1**3

2020 **11** *2 ½* **Culzean Bay**38 5715 2-8-8 52 .... GregFairley 13 10
(Miss Diana Weeden) *s.i.s: sn in mid-div: rdn and hdwy over 2f out: wknd over 1f out* **33/1**

1403 **12** *2* **Rightcar Ellie (IRE)**18 6227 2-9-2 60 ....(b) LPKeniry 10 11
(Peter Grayson) *a towards rr* **8/1**

000 **13** *2* **Brough (IRE)**57 5154 2-7-13 50 ....(t) ThomasLeaper(7) 3 —
(J O'Reilly) *mid-div: rdn over 2f out: sn struggling* **66/1**

62.43 secs (-0.39) **Going Correction** -0.125s/f (Stan) **13** Ran SP% **120.8**
Speed ratings (Par 94): **98,97,94,91,90 90,89,87,82,81 77,74,71**
CSF £30.25 CT £833.45 TOTE £4.40: £1.30, £2.30, £27.70; EX 35.50.
Owner Paul J Dixon & Greg McCabe **Bred** Paradime Ltd **Trained** Babworth, Notts
■ Stewards' Enquiry : Seb Sanders caution: used whip with excessive frequency

FOCUS
Not many got into this low-grade sprint nursery but with the time reasonable the form should prove sound.

NOTEBOOK
Loose Caboose(IRE) had the cheekpieces left off for this first run over the minimum trip. She held on gamely after reverting to more aggressive tactics. (tchd 10-3)
A Wish For You nearly took advantage of being 3lb lower than when last in a handicap and lost nothing in defeat. (op 9-1 tchd 10-1)
Lambrini Lace(IRE), reverting back to 5f on her sand debut, was 2lb better off than when finishing two lengths ahead of the runner-up over this trip at Warwick in June.
Yankee Storm was tackling the minimum distance for the first time on his handicap debut. (op 22-1)
Diademas(USA) ◆, dropped 6lb, should do better back on Fibresand when Southwell reopens next month. (tchd 14-1)
Ile Royale was down 2lb despite a better effort when fitted with the headgear for the first time at Kempton last week.
Too Grand Official explanation: jockey said filly missed the break
Rightcar Ellie(IRE) Official explanation: jockey said filly had no more to give

6625 STAY AT THE WOLVERHAMPTON HOLIDAY INN H'CAP 5f 216y(P)
7:30 (7:30) (Class 5) (0-70,70) 3-Y-O+ **£3,076** (£915; £457; £228) **Stalls** Low

Form RPR

1000 **1** **Sweet Pickle**41 5648 6-9-2 68 ....(e) GeorgeBaker 12 75
(J R Boyle) *w ldr: rdn to ld nr fin* **7/1**

5500 **2** *nk* **Came Back (IRE)**15 6288 4-8-10 65 .... MichaelJStainton(3) 10 71
(J Mackie) *led: rdn over 1f out: hdd nr fin* **11/4**1

021 **3** *1 ½* **Gimme Some Lovin (IRE)**49 5386 3-8-6 61 .... WilliamBuick(3) 1 62+
(D W P Arbuthnot) *in rr: pushed along over 3f out: c v wd st: sn rdn: gd hdwy fnl f: nrst fin* **10/3**2

043 **4** *1* **Canina**3 6563 4-8-4 56 oh6 .... GregFairley 5 54
(Paul Green) *s.i.s: in rr: rdn and hdwy wl over 1f out: one pce fnl f* **11/1**

0055 **5** *½* **Cerebus**185 1377 5-8-13 65 ....(bt) StephenDonohoe 7 61
(A J McCabe) *hld up: swtchd rt after 1f: lost pl over 2f out: c wd st: rdn and kpt on ins fnl f: nvr trbld ldrs* **14/1**

1040 **6** *½* **Woqoodd**14 6313 3-9-0 66 .... PaulHanagan 9 61
(R A Fahey) *prom: rdn over 2f out: wknd ins fnl f* **14/1**

4100 **7** *¾* **Nusoor (IRE)**16 6273 4-9-0 66 ....(b) LPKeniry 6 58
(Peter Grayson) *hld up: sme hdwy 2f out: no further prog* **12/1**

0250 **8** *2* **Steel City Boy (IRE)**7 6467 4-9-4 70 .... DavidAllan 8 56
(D Carroll) *prom: rdn over 2f out: edgd rt jst over 1f out: wknd fnl f* **5/1**3

0000 **9** *5* **Diamond Josh**19 6210 5-8-4 56 oh11 .... RichardMullen 4 26
(M Mullineaux) *w ldrs early: lost pl over 3f out: sn bhd* **50/1**

3023 **10** 5 **Zarzu**[172] 1718 8-9-2 **68** .... LiamJones 11 22
(C R Dore) *prom: rdn over 2f out: sn wknd* **7/1**

1m 14.39s (-1.42) **Going Correction** -0.125s/f (Stan) **10** Ran SP% **122.7**
Speed ratings (Par 103): **104,103,101,100,99 98,97,95,88,81**
CSF £28.07 CT £81.10 TOTE £9.60: £3.70, £1.20, £2.00; EX 39.30.
Owner M Khan X2 **Bred** C T Van Hoorn **Trained** Epsom, Surrey

FOCUS
A slowly-run minor sprint handicap where it paid to be close to the pace. The winner is rated close to her best.

6626 HOTEL & CONFERENCING MEDIAN AUCTION MAIDEN FILLIES' STKS 1m 141y(P)
7:55 (7:56) (Class 6) 2-Y-O **£2,047** (£604; £302) **Stalls** Low

Form RPR
6 **1** **Astrodonna**[31] 5882 2-9-0 0 .... PaulMulrennan 7 67+
(M H Tompkins) *hld up: hdwy 3f out: rdn 2f out: led ins fnl f: r.o wl* **10/3**[3]
0005 **2** 3 ½ **Miss Bouggy Wouggy**[15] 6289 2-9-0 52 .... PaulHanagan 4 60
(M Blanshard) *chsd ldr: rdn and ev ch over 2f out: hung lft over 1f out and ins fnl f: one pce* **25/1**
03 **3** 1 **Express Princess (IRE)**[28] 5984 2-8-9 0 .... AshleyHamblett(5) 3 58
(M Botti) *led: rdn over 1f out: hdd and no ex ins fnl f* **9/4**[2]
0056 **4** ¾ **Lella Beya**[29] 5944 2-9-0 68 .... LPKeniry 2 56
(S Kirk) *hld up: rdn and sme hdwy over 1f out: nvr trbld ldrs* **17/2**
5 **5** 4 **Sweet Sara**[52] 5301 2-9-0 0 .... SebSanders 6 48
(C E Brittain) *prom: rdn over 3f out: wknd wl over 1f out: eased whn btn fnl f* **15/8**[1]
6 5 **Green Wonder (GER)** 2-9-0 0 .... RichardMullen 1 37
(D M Simcock) *prom: rdn 3f out: sn wknd* **10/1**
000 **7** ½ **Chica Guapa (IRE)**[45] 5501 2-9-0 51 .... GregFairley 5 36
(Paul Green) *hld up and bhd: rdn 3f out: sn struggling* **66/1**

1m 52.57s (0.81) **Going Correction** -0.125s/f (Stan) **7** Ran SP% **113.6**
Speed ratings (Par 91): **91,87,87,86,82 78,77**
CSF £71.69 TOTE £4.40: £1.80, £5.70; EX 65.40.
Owner Mystic Meg Limited **Bred** Mystic Meg Limited **Trained** Newmarket, Suffolk

FOCUS
A poor maiden with the 52-rated runner-up casting doubts over the form.

NOTEBOOK
Astrodonna duly appreciated the longer trip on this switch to sand. The further she went the better she looked and middle distances may well be on the agenda next year. (tchd 3-1)
Miss Bouggy Wouggy, back up in distance, has improved since switching to Polytrack, albeit at a low level. All she wanted to do was hang left in the home straight.
Express Princess(IRE) could not keep the hanging second at bay never mind the winner. (op 3-1)
Lella Beya was unable to make her presence felt. (op 13-2)
Sweet Sara was disappointing on this switch to sand and came home in her own time. (tchd 9-4)

6627 CALL WOLVERHAMPTON RACECOURSE ON 0870 220 2442 H'CAP 1m 1f 103y(P)
8:25 (8:25) (Class 6) (0-55,55) 3-Y-O+ **£2,047** (£604; £302) **Stalls** Low

Form RPR
0042 **1** **Mighty Mover (IRE)**[14] 6315 5-8-12 **51** .... ChrisCatlin 11 60
(B Palling) *led after 1f: rdn over 1f out: edgd rt ins fnl f: all out* **14/1**
0-01 **2** nk **Kirstys Lad**[7] 6480 5-8-12 **51** 6ex .... RichardMullen 10 59
(M Mullineaux) *led 1f: chsd wnr: rdn and edgd rt over 1f out: ev ch ins fnl f: r.o* **9/1**
5511 **3** 1 ¼ **Prince Noel**[14] 6315 3-8-12 **54** .... SebSanders 13 59
(N Wilson) *hld up and bhd: hdwy on outside over 2f out: rdn over 1f out: nt qckn ins fnl f* **7/4**[1]
1054 **4** 1 **Dancing Storm**[30] 5917 4-9-0 **53** .... LPKeniry 1 56
(W S Kittow) *t.k.h: a.p: hrd rdn over 1f out: no ex ins fnl f* **10/1**
2000 **5** ½ **Cadwell**[43] 5565 3-8-12 **54** .... GregFairley 2 56
(T J Pitt) *hld up in mid-div: rdn and hdwy 2f out: one pce fnl f* **8/1**[3]
0000 **6** 1 **Tanforan**[9] 6431 5-9-1 **54** .... DavidAllan 9 54
(B P J Baugh) *hld up towards rr: rdn and hdwy on ins wl over 1f out: hrd rdn and one pce fnl f* **20/1**
040 **7** hd **George's Flyer (IRE)**[20] 6179 4-8-13 **52** ....(b) PaulHanagan 6 52
(R A Fahey) *hld up in mid-div: hdwy on ins over 2f out: hrd rdn wl over 1f out: no ex ins fnl f* **8/1**[3]
0030 **8** nk **Greenmeadow**[16] 6260 5-9-2 **55** .... GeorgeBaker 3 54
(S Kirk) *hld up in mid-div: lost pl 6f out: rdn and hdwy wl over 1f out: no further prog fnl f* **9/1**
0001 **9** 1 **Zantero**[81] 2619 5-8-10 **54** ....(tp) RussellKennemore(5) 5 51
(K M Prendergast) *stdd s: plld hrd in rr: rdn wl over 1f out: n.d* **66/1**
0064 **10** 2 **Don Pasquale**[4] 6529 5-8-8 **52** ow3 ....(v) JamesO'Reilly(5) 7 45
(J T Stimpson) *hld up and bhd: hrd rdn over 1f out: no rspnse* **13/2**[2]
5000 **11** 1 **Red Barnet**[52] 5299 3-8-5 **47** .... DaleGibson 8 38
(M W Easterby) *prom: rdn over 2f out: sn wknd* **66/1**
1226 **12** 3 **Charlottebutterfly**[20] 6179 7-8-10 **52** .... NeilChalmers(3) 12 36
(P J McBride) *hld up in mid-div: rdn over 2f out: sn bhd* **11/1**

2m 1.63s (-0.99) **Going Correction** -0.125s/f (Stan)
WFA 3 from 4yo+ 3lb **12** Ran SP% **123.8**
Speed ratings (Par 101): **99,98,97,96,96 95,95,94,94,92 91,88**
CSF £138.53 CT £336.45 TOTE £13.00: £3.70, £3.70, £1.10; EX 117.60.
Owner Bryn Palling **Bred** Humphrey Okeke **Trained** Tredodridge, Vale Of Glamorgan

FOCUS
A tightly-knit moderate affair run at a modest pace but the form is sound with the winner and third setting the level.
Zantero Official explanation: jockey said gelding ran too freely

6628 JOIN WBX.COM FOR FREE FOOTBALL SHIRT H'CAP 1m 141y(P)
8:55 (8:55) (Class 5) (0-70,70) 3-Y-O+ **£3,076** (£915; £457; £228) **Stalls** Low

Form RPR
164 **1** **Abbondanza (IRE)**[21] 6146 4-9-7 **70** ....(p) TomEaves 3 79
(I Semple) *chsd ldr tl over 3f out: rdn and wnt 2nd again wl over 1f out: hrd rdn to ld cl home* **3/1**[1]
3405 **2** ½ **Pab Special (IRE)**[6] 6504 4-9-3 **69** ....(p) AndrewElliott(3) 4 77
(K R Burke) *led: rdn jst over 1f out: hdd cl home* **10/3**[2]
4351 **3** 1 **Pelham Crescent (IRE)**[14] 6316 4-9-1 **64** .... RichardKingscote 8 73+
(B Palling) *hld up towards rr: c v wd st: hdwy over 1f out: edgd lft and r.o fnl f: nrst fin* **4/1**[3]
0303 **4** shd **Waterline Twenty (IRE)**[9] 6423 4-9-4 **67** .... TGMcLaughlin 5 72
(P D Evans) *hld up and bhd: hdwy whn nt clr run and swtchd lft wl over 1f out: rdn and kpt on ins fnl f* **7/1**
330 **5** 1 ½ **Tom Paris**[16] 6269 3-9-4 **70** .... RichardMullen 7 72
(W R Muir) *hld up towards rr: nt clr run on ins and swtchd rt over 1f out: rdn and kpt on fnl f* **7/1**
0000 **6** ¾ **Thumpers Dream**[11] 6380 4-9-4 **67** ....(b) DanielTudhope 6 68
(I W McInnes) *prom: chsd ldr over 3f out: rdn over 2f out: lost 2nd and edgd lft wl over 1f out: wknd fnl f* **40/1**
6266 **7** 3 **Shifty**[190] 1264 8-9-2 **65** .... DavidAllan 9 59
(D Carroll) *hld up in mid-div: rdn over 2f out: wknd over 1f out* **33/1**
650- **8** 1 ½ **Follow The Colours (IRE)**[202] 6070 4-8-13 **67** ....(t) PatrickHills(5) 1 58
(J W Hills) *hld up towards rr: hdwy over 3f out: rdn and wknd wl over 1f out* **9/1**
5600 **9** 25 **Magic Warrior**[37] 5733 7-8-12 **61** .... PatDobbs 2 —
(J C Fox) *hld up in tch: lost pl over 3f out: sn rdn and bhd: t.o* **16/1**

1m 50.44s (-1.32) **Going Correction** -0.125s/f (Stan)
WFA 3 from 4yo+ 3lb **9** Ran SP% **114.3**
Speed ratings (Par 103): **100,99,98,98,97 96,93,92,70**
CSF £12.96 CT £39.47 TOTE £5.20: £2.10, £1.50, £2.60; EX 18.10.
Owner Joseph Leckie & Sons Ltd **Bred** M Nolan **Trained** Carluke, S Lanarks

FOCUS
It paid to be near the pace in this moderate contest with a couple trying to come from behind meeting trouble in running. The form is not solid with the winner the best guide.

6629 BOOK ONLINE AT WOLVERHAMPTON-RACECOURSE.CO.UK H'CAP 1m 141y(P)
9:20 (9:20) (Class 6) (0-52,54) 3-Y-O+ **£2,047** (£604; £302) **Stalls** Low

Form RPR
0541 **1** **Time To Regret**[7] 6479 7-9-2 **54** 6ex ....(p) DanielTudhope 4 63
(I W McInnes) *a.p: rdn to ld 1f out: r.o* **13/8**[1]
2003 **2** 1 **General Feeling (IRE)**[14] 6316 6-8-13 **51** ....(t) TomEaves 2 58+
(S T Mason) *hld up in rr: c wd st: rdn and gd hdwy fnl f: fin wl* **14/1**
6541 **3** 1 **Reveur**[6] 6505 4-8-13 **51** 6ex .... RichardMullen 6 55
(M Mullineaux) *hld up in mid-div: stdy hdwy over 3f out: rdn 2f out: swtchd rt 1f out: kpt on ins fnl f* **11/1**
0300 **4** ¾ **Wodhill Gold**[14] 6316 6-9-0 **52** ....(v) HayleyTurner 9 55
(D Morris) *a.p: led over 4f out tl over 3f out: rdn and ev ch wl over 1f out: no ex ins fnl f* **20/1**
5300 **5** ¾ **Uhuru Peak**[7] 6479 6-8-12 **50** ....(t) PaulMulrennan 7 51
(M W Easterby) *led: hdd over 5f out: led over 3f out: rdn and hdd 1f out: one pce* **20/1**
0262 **6** nk **Machinate (USA)**[7] 6479 5-9-0 **52** .... LiamJones 3 52
(W M Brisbourne) *hld up in mid-div: lost pl over 5f out: hdwy over 2f out: rdn and hung rt 1f out: one pce* **13/2**[2]
-006 **7** 2 **Davidia (IRE)**[81] 605 4-8-10 **48** .... RichardKingscote 11 44
(Tom Dascombe) *hld up and bhd: rdn and sme hdwy whn edgd lft 1f out: n.d* **7/1**[3]
0324 **8** ½ **Domesday (UAE)**[36] 5756 6-8-6 **47** .... DuranFentiman(3) 10 42
(W G Harrison) *hld up in mid-div: rdn and hdwy on outside over 2f out: wknd wl over 1f out* **10/1**
5000 **9** ¾ **Band**[8] 6458 7-8-10 **48** .... GrahamGibbons 13 41
(E S McMahon) *hld up towards rr: rdn 3f out: no rspnse* **14/1**
P002 **10** ¾ **Grand Palace (IRE)**[3] 6563 4-8-6 **49** ....(v) KellyHarrison(5) 8 41
(D Shaw) *a bhd* **12/1**
0-00 **11** nk **Ocean Valentine**[14] 6315 4-8-10 **48** .... ChrisCatlin 5 39
(J T Stimpson) *a bhd* **33/1**
660 **12** 1 ½ **Spring Creek**[115] 3402 3-8-9 **50** .... DaleGibson 1 38
(M W Easterby) *plld hrd: prom: rdn over 3f out: wknd over 2f out* **50/1**
3300 **13** 61 **Beamsley Beacon**[7] 6479 6-8-10 **48** .... StephenDonohoe 12 —
(S T Mason) *sn rdn along: hdwy over 6f out: led over 5f out tl over 4f out: wknd over 3f out: eased whn no ch 2f out* **33/1**

1m 50.58s (-1.18) **Going Correction** -0.125s/f (Stan)
WFA 3 from 4yo+ 3lb **13** Ran SP% **119.7**
Speed ratings (Par 101): **100,99,98,97,96 96,94,94,93,93 92,91,37**
CSF £24.88 CT £201.61 TOTE £2.20: £1.10, £4.50, £2.90; EX 64.00 Place 6 £ 82.17, Place 5 £ 32.03.
Owner Horses 4 Courses **Bred** Speedlith Group **Trained** Catwick, E Yorks

FOCUS
A competitive basement-level contest best rated through the third to her latest mark.
T/Plt: £59.10 to a £1 stake. Pool: £107,639.75. 1,329.45 winning tickets. T/Qpdt: £22.60 to a £1 stake. Pool: £6,585.20. 214.70 winning tickets. KH

5719 MAISONS-LAFFITTE (R-H)
Friday, November 2

OFFICIAL GOING: Soft

6630a PRIX MIESQUE (GROUP 3) (FILLIES) 7f (S)
12:50 (12:50) 2-Y-O **£27,027** (£10,811; £8,108; £5,405; £2,703)

RPR
1 **Modern Look**[29] 2-8-11 .... SPasquier 7 107+
(D Smaga, France) *a.p: led over 1 1/2f out: drew clr ins fnl f: rdn out* **37/10**[3]
2 2 ½ **Lady Deauville (FR)**[6] 6498 2-8-11 .... JMurtagh 5 101
(P A Blockley) *racd in 6th or 7th tl hdwy to ld narrowly over 2f out: hdd over 1 1/2f out: no ex ins fnl f* **9/1**
3 1 ½ **Verba (FR)**[22] 2-8-11 .... TThulliez 6 97
(R Gibson, France) *hld up: plld hrd early: styd on steadily fr over 1f out* **8/1**
4 1 ½ **Ensis (SPA)**[35] 5791 2-8-11 .... IMendizabal 3 94
(O Rodriguez, Spain) *cl up on ins: kpt on at one pce fnl 2f* **28/1**
5 hd **Alsace**[38] 2-8-11 .... YLerner 10 93
(C Lerner, France) *plld hrd: cl up in 4th or 5th on outside: effrt over 2f out: unable qck* **27/10**[2]
6 ¾ **Lips Arrow (GER)**[33] 5848 2-8-11 .... THellier 4 91
(Andreas Lowe, Germany) *hld up towards rr: nvr a factor* **25/1**
7 ½ **Ossun (FR)**[35] 5791 2-8-11 .... C-PLemaire 2 90
(J-C Rouget, France) *midfield pulling hrd: effrt over 2f out: sn btn* **21/10**[1]
8 ¾ **Fleurina (FR)**[5] 2-8-11 .... RonanThomas 8 88
(Robert Collet, France) *a in rr* **20/1**
9 15 **Boccatenera (GER)**[33] 2-8-11 .... CSoumillon 1 51
(Rod Collet, France) *led to over 2f out: wknd qckly* **25/1**

1m 27.1s (-3.20) **9** Ran SP% **117.6**
PARI-MUTUEL: WIN 4.70; PL 2.00, 2.90, 3.00; DF 18.60.
Owner K Abdulla **Bred** Juddmonte Farms Ltd **Trained** Lamorlaye, France

FOCUS
The runner-up is the best guide, with a big step up from Modern Look.

The Form Book, Raceform Ltd, Compton, RG20 6NL

NOTEBOOK
Modern Look could develop into Classic material next season the way she is going. She was landing a hat-trick in her first Group race and did it in style. Smartly away, she was always one of the leaders, and when she quickened impressively at the furlong marker she looked in a different class to the other eight runners. She is now likely to be aimed at either the English or French 1000 Guineas.
Lady Deauville(FR) ran a very promising race. She made a forward move a furlong and a half out and looked dangerous for a moment, but she could not go through with her challenge and just stayed on one-paced as the race drew to an end. Her rider felt that he made his move a little too early, but it did not affect the end result.
Verba(FR) ran with credit considering that this was just her second race. Very green in the early stages, she was switched towards the outside to challenge at the furlong marker and ran on well from that point.
Ensis(SPA), always well up near the stands' rail, battled well but could not quicken when the race warmed up from a furlong and a half out.

6631a CRITERIUM DE MAISONS-LAFFITTE (GROUP 2) 6f (S)
1:20 (1:22) 2-Y-0 **£73,176** (£28,243; £13,480; £8,986; £4,493)

RPR
1 **Pomellato (GER)**[19] 6222 2-9-0 .... AStarke 1 117
(P Schiergen, Germany) *prom tl led 2f out: sn rdn and hung rt: drvn clr* **9/2**[2]
2 *3* **Norman Invader (USA)**[61] 5070 2-9-0 .... JMurtagh 3 108
(K J Condon, Ire) *hld up: hdwy to go 2nd over 1 1/2f out: kpt on u.str.p but no imp on wnr* **2/1**[1]
3 *1* **Equiano (FR)**[26] 2-9-0 .... JVictoire 7 105
(M Delcher, Spain) *hld up: hdwy on outside to go 3rd over 1f out: kpt on at one pce tl tired cl home: jst hld on for 3rd* **25/1**
4 *hd* **Salut L'Africain (FR)**[22] 6136 2-9-0 .... CSoumillon 8 104
(Robert Collet, France) *hld up: sltly outpcd in rr over 2f out: styd on wl down stands' side fnl f* **5/1**[3]
5 *hd* **Sehrezad (IRE)**[30] 2-9-0 .... THellier 6 104
(Andreas Lowe, Germany) *hld up: last and outpcd over 2f out: styd on wl down outside fnl f* **40/1**
6 *2* **Domingues**[22] 6136 2-9-0 .... DPMcDonogh 2 98
(Edward Lynam, Ire) *prom: rdn over 2f out: sn btn* **61/10**
7 *nk* **Quam Celerrime**[24] 6080 2-9-0 .... C-PLemaire 4 97
(P A Blockley) *hld up chsng ldrs: kpt on at one pce fnl 2f* **14/1**
8 *3* **Perfect Polly**[28] 5973 2-8-11 .... PJSmullen 9 85
(Andrew Oliver, Ire) *cl up tl wknd 2f out* **56/10**
9 *20* **Hammadi (IRE)**[20] 6167 2-9-0 .... NCallan 5 28
(K A Ryan) *led to 2f out: wknd qckly: eased* **13/1**

1m 13.6s (-0.40) **9** Ran SP% **117.5**
PARI-MUTUEL: WIN 5.50; PL 2.20, 1.40, 4.30; DF 11.40.
Owner Gestut Ittlingen **Bred** Gestut Hof Ittlingen **Trained** Germany

NOTEBOOK
Pomellato(GER), judging by this effort, should be Classic material back in his homeland as he made his rivals look pretty ordinary in this Group 2 event. Smartly away and always well up, he began to draw away from a furlong and a half out. He appeared to enjoy the soft ground which he did not have in his previous outing in Italy and passed the post on his own. He will probably be aimed at the German 2000 Guineas next year.
Norman Invader(USA), who was behind in the early part of the race, began to make a forward move as the winner took control. He made his run near the stands' rail but never looked like taking first place. He would have preferred better ground and has been entered in the 2000 Guineas at Newmarket, but he might be campaigned in the US next year.
Equiano(FR), a Spanish colt, ran a decent race. Held up in the early stages, he made a forward move before the furlong marker and battled on gamely to hold third place.
Salut L'Africain(FR), who has been on the go since the early part of the season, is one of the most consistent horses in training. Dropped out early on, he was putting in his best work up the stands' rail inside the final furlong.
Quam Celerrime, settled behind the leaders, was being pushed along by the halfway stage and was never dangerous from a furlong and a half out.
Hammadi(IRE) was smartly out of the stalls but a totally spent force with 300 yards left to run. He dropped back to finish a remote last and this could not have been his true running.

6633a PRIX DE SEINE-ET-OISE (GROUP 3) 6f (S)
2:20 (2:20) 3-Y-0+ **£27,027** (£10,811; £8,108; £5,405; £2,703)

RPR
1 **Tiza (SAF)**[26] 6039 5-8-13 .... CSoumillon 16 114
(A De Royer-Dupre, France) *hld up in rr on outside: hdwy 2f out: led appr fnl f: r.o strly* **26/10**[1]
2 *3* **Advanced**[13] 6338 4-8-11 .... NCallan 5 103
(K A Ryan) *a in tch: disp ld in centre over 3f out: hrd rdn and ev ch appr fnl f: one pce* **52/10**[2]
3 *shd* **Mariol (FR)**[25] 6071 4-8-11 .... DBoeuf 13 103
(Robert Collet, France) *mid-div on outside: hdwy 2f out: r.o one pce fnl f* **69/10**
4 *1/2* **Slade (GER)**[14] 5-8-8 .... FilipMinarik 15 99
(M Trybuhl, Germany) *a.p on outside: 3rd and rdn 2f out: kpt on one pce* **32/1**
5 *1/2* **Derison (USA)**[26] 6039 5-8-11 ....(b) TJarnet 4 100
(P Van De Poele, France) *trckd ldrs nr rails early: jnd main gp in middle over 2f out: kpt on but nvr nr to chal* **13/2**[3]
6 *snk* **Loda (FR)**[25] 6071 4-8-8 .... SPasquier 7 97
(C Baillet, France) *trckd ldrs: rdn and no ex fr wl over 1f out* **88/10**
7 *shd* **Biniou (IRE)**[25] 6071 4-8-11 .... JMurtagh 14 99
(R M H Cowell) *prom: led 1/2-way to appr fnl f: wknd grad* **34/1**
8 *3/4* **Sabasha (FR)**[54] 5259 4-8-8 .... RMarchelli 10 94
(Mlle S-V Tarrou, France) *racd stands' side and last overall over 2f out: rdn and btn wl over 1f out* **90/1**
8 *dht* **Rakiza (IRE)**[25] 6071 3-8-8 .... DBonilla 2 94
(F Head, France) *racd in mid-div nr stands' rails: rdn 2f out: nvr a factor* **24/1**
10 *2* **Arc De Triomphe (GER)**[14] 5-8-11 .... JVictoire 3 91
(D Fechner, Germany) *w ldr stands' side gp: prom tl rdn and btn 2f out* **35/1**
0 **Patavellian (IRE)**[13] 6338 9-8-11 ....(b) SteveDrowne 6 —
(R Charlton) *nvr a factor* **18/1**
0 **Tycoon's Hill (IRE)**[15] 8-8-11 .... SMaillot 12 —
(Robert Collet, France) *a outpcd* **69/10**
0 **Matrix (GER)**[40] 6-8-11 .... C-PLemaire 9 —
(Frau Y Vollmer, Germany) *led in middle to 1/2-way: sn wknd* **52/1**
0 **Bahama Mama (IRE)**[14] 3-8-8 .... AStarke 8 —
(W Hickst, Germany) *pressed ldrs in middle tl wknd wl over 1f out* **9/1**
0 **Val Jaro (FR)**[68] 4871 4-8-11 .... THuet 1 —
(S Morineau, France) *led stands' side gp tl wknd fr 1/2-way* **26/1**
0 **Zut Alors (IRE)**[15] 3-8-8 .... GBenoist 11 —
(Robert Collet, France) *a towards rr* **50/1**

1m 13.05s (-0.95) **16** Ran SP% **129.3**
PARI-MUTUEL: WIN 3.60; PL 1.60, 1.90, 2.60; DF 9.00.
Owner J C Seroul & R Plersch **Bred** Wilgerbosdrift **Trained** Chantilly, France

NOTEBOOK
Tiza(SAF), an ex-South African horse, ran out an impressive winner. Last for a long way in the group running up the middle of the track, he was brought wide with a challenge from a furlong and a half out and took the lead at the furlong marker. He then drew away and was in a class of his own. This winning performance will no doubt earn him an invitation to the Hong Kong Sprint as this was his second Group 3 success in France this season.
Advanced, always in the middle group, was given every possible chance. He was one of the leaders just over a furlong out but could not quicken to trouble the winner in any way at all inside the final furlong. He won the Ayr Gold Cup and it should not be long before he adds a Group race to his record.
Mariol(FR) was another to be held up for a late run and he was also in the main group up the centre of the track. He came with the winner and battled well, losing second place by just inches.
Slade(GER), well up throughout on the outside, ran a respectable race. She was there with the leaders just over a furlong and a half out but was then a little one-paced inside the final furlong.
Biniou(IRE) put up a sound performance and could not have been given a better ride. He was smartly into his stride but gradually dropped out of contention inside the final furlong.
Patavellian(IRE) raced with the small group on the stands' rail early on but was then taken across to join the main group. He never really got in a blow, though, and eventually finished in 11th place.

6461 AYR (L-H)
Saturday, November 3

OFFICIAL GOING: Heavy
Wind: Light, half behind Weather: Cloudy

6634 JOHN SMITH'S MAIDEN STKS 7f 50y
12:55 (12:55) (Class 5) 2-Y-O **£3,562** (£1,059; £529; £264) **Stalls** Low

Form RPR
3320 1 **Doon Haymer (IRE)**[50] 5397 2-9-3 78 ....(v[1]) TomEaves 7 79+
(I Semple) *mde all: rdn over 2f out: styd on strly to go clr fnl f* **5/2**[1]
0 2 *3 1/2* **Ninefineirishmen (IRE)**[22] 6156 2-9-0 0 .... AndrewElliott(3) 11 70
(K R Burke) *hld up in tch: effrt over 2f out: hdwy and wandered over 1f out: chsd wnr ins fnl f: no imp* **10/1**
32 3 *1 1/2* **Roman Legion (IRE)**[10] 6417 2-9-3 0 .... JamieSpencer 10 67
(P A Blockley) *pressed wnr: effrt and ev ch over 2f out: no ex and lost 2nd ins fnl f* **5/2**[1]
5 4 *3 1/2* **Pavershooz**[22] 6156 2-9-3 0 .... DanielTudhope 9 58
(N Wilson) *prom: effrt and hung lft over 2f out: no ex over 1f out* **5/1**[2]
5 *1* **Staten (USA)** 2-9-3 0 .... PhillipMakin 2 56
(T D Barron) *hld up in tch: hdwy 3f out: sn pushed along and no imp* **25/1**
5 6 *1/2* **Orpen Bid (IRE)**[8] 6461 2-8-12 0 .... AdrianTNicholls 3 50
(A M Crow) *cl up tl rdn and wknd over 1f out* **33/1**
7 *3/4* **Mufasa** 2-9-3 0 .... TonyHamilton 6 53
(Miss L A Perratt) *towards rr: rdn over 3f out: sn no ex* **50/1**
45 8 *1 3/4* **Red Tarn**[18] 6255 2-9-0 0 .... MarkLawson(3) 1 48
(B Smart) *in tch: drvn 3f out: sn wknd* **14/1**
033 9 *1 1/4* **Bishopbriggs (USA)**[4] 6557 2-8-12 0 .... JamesO'Reilly(5) 8 45
(D J Murphy) *t.k.h: hld up: rdn over 2f out: sn btn* **6/1**[3]
000 10 *2 1/2* **Spooky**[14] 6329 2-9-0 51 .... DominicFox(3) 5 39
(W Storey) *bhd: rdn 1/2-way: sn btn* **100/1**

1m 40.77s (8.05) **Going Correction** +1.125s/f (Soft) **10** Ran SP% **113.6**
Speed ratings (Par 96): **99,95,93,89,88 87,86,84,83,80**
CSF £28.32 TOTE £3.50: £1.40, £3.30, £1.30; EX 24.10.
Owner Gordon McDowall **Bred** Roland Lerner **Trained** Carluke, S Lanarks

FOCUS
Not the strongest of maidens but a fair test of stamina in these testing conditions. The form should prove sound enough, rated around the front three.

NOTEBOOK
Doon Haymer(IRE), tried in a visor, had the run of the race and proved himself fully effective in heavy ground. He showed a good attitude to land this uncompetitive event and may be capable of further progress granted a sufficient stamina test. (tchd 11-4)
Ninefineirishmen(IRE), who hinted at ability on his debut at York, bettered that form, despite wandering off a true line when pressure was applied. He should have no problems with 1m and is likely to be placed to best advantage. (tchd 11-1)
Roman Legion(IRE), who had shown ability on his first two starts, failed to see out this trip in the conditions anywhere near as well as the first two. Nevertheless he is qualified for a handicap mark and may do better in run-of-the-mill company. (op 7-4)
Pavershooz had shaped well on his debut when in front of Ninefineirishmen at York but failed to confirm those placings in this much more testing ground. He will be worth another chance in modest handicaps back on better ground. (op 13-2 tchd 7-1)
Staten(USA), a $45,000 half-brother to a 1m2f winner in Italy, was easy to back and only hinted at ability on this racecourse debut. He will be of much more interest over further in ordinary handicap company in due course. (op 22-1)
Orpen Bid(IRE), dropped in distance, again hinted at ability but is likely to continue to look vulnerable in this type of event. (tchd 40-1)
Red Tarn Official explanation: jockey said colt was unsuited by the heavy ground
Spooky Official explanation: jockey said gelding was unsuited by the heavy ground

6635 JOHN SMITH'S NURSERY 6f
1:25 (1:25) (Class 5) (0-75,75) 2-Y-O **£3,562** (£1,059; £529; £264) **Stalls** Low

Form RPR
0062 1 **Paint Stripper**[8] 6462 2-7-13 56 .... DominicFox(3) 7 61
(W Storey) *prom: rdn to dispute ld appr fnl f: kpt on wl: led cl home* **4/1**[2]
0000 2 *shd* **Red Skipper (IRE)**[12] 6379 2-8-2 56 .... PaulHanagan 8 61
(N Wilson) *led: jnd appr fnl f: kpt on wl: hdd cl home* **8/1**
2444 3 *2 1/2* **Style Award**[35] 5802 2-9-1 72 .... AndrewMullen(3) 6 69
(W J H Ratcliffe) *cl up: ev ch over 1f out: sn one pce* **10/3**[1]
4030 4 *nk* **Prunes**[4] 6566 2-7-9 52 oh1 ....(p) DuranFentiman(3) 3 48
(A Berry) *prom: drvn 2f out: sn one pce* **7/1**[3]
3100 5 *1 3/4* **Andrasta**[14] 6328 2-8-13 70 .... PatrickMathers(3) 4 61
(A Berry) *in tch: effrt 2f out: outpcd fnl f* **12/1**
321 6 *1 3/4* **Tobar Suil Lady (IRE)**[32] 5888 2-9-7 75 .... JamieSpencer 5 61
(K A Ryan) *stdd in last but in tch: effrt and ev ch over 1f out: sn rdn and btn* **10/3**[1]

346 **7** *14* **On Instinct (IRE)**[25] 6075 2-8-11 **65** .... TomEaves 1 9
(B Smart) *t.k.h: cl up tl wknd qckly wl over 1f out* **7/1**[3]

1m 18.95s (5.28) **Going Correction** +0.75s/f (Yiel) 7 Ran SP% **110.0**
Speed ratings (Par 96): **94,93,90,90,87 85,66**
CSF £32.22 CT £108.22 TOTE £4.50: £2.20, £5.30; EX 19.30.
Owner Gremlin Racing **Bred** Mrs J A Prescott **Trained** Muggleswick, Co Durham

FOCUS
A weakish event in which the field raced far side (stalls on that side). The pace was fair.

NOTEBOOK
Paint Stripper, who ran his best race when chasing home a progressive sort on his handicap debut over course and distance on his previous start, showed a good attitude to go one better in this ordinary event. He will have no problems with 7f and, as he should not be going up too much in the weights, may do a bit better away from progressive sorts. (tchd 9-2)
Red Skipper(IRE), dropped to sprinting and back in testing ground, ran his best race and showed a good attitude in the closing stages. He pulled clear of the remainder, will not mind the return to 7f and is more than capable of winning a similar event. (op 12-1)
Style Award, an exposed but consistent sort, did not fail through lack of stamina back over 6f for only the second time. She should continue to give a good account but she has little margin for error from her current mark. (op 3-1 tchd 7-2 in a place)
Prunes was not disgraced returned to sprinting in the first-time cheekpieces but, although the step back up to 7f is going to be in her favour, she is not really one to be lumping on until getting her head in front where it matters. (op 8-1)
Andrasta fared better back in trip than she had done at Catterick over 7f on her previous start but she may be ideally suited by a sounder surface. (tchd 11-1)
Tobar Suil Lady(IRE), who had improved steadily with every outing, proved a bit of a disappointment on this nursery debut but these testing conditions were almost certainly to blame and she will be worth another chance back on either Polytrack or a sound surface. Official explanation: jockey said filly was unsuited by the heavy ground (op 3-1 tchd 7-2)

6636 JOHN SMITH'S EXTRA COLD H'CAP 1m 1f 20y
1:55 (1:55) (Class 4) (0-85,82) 3-Y-0+
£6,232 (£1,866; £933; £467; £233; £117) **Stalls** Low

Form RPR
0351 **1** **Suits Me**[8] 6475 4-9-4 **79** .... MickyFenton 6 89
(T P Tate) *mde all: hrd pressed over 1f out: edgd lft ins fnl f: hld on gamely* **5/2**[2]
1660 **2** *3/4* **Hawkit (USA)**[8] 6465 6-8-9 **70** .... PaulMulrennan 1 78
(P Monteith) *trckd ldrs gng wl: ev ch over 1f out: shkn up fnl f: hld last 75yds* **10/1**
5622 **3** *6* **Rudry Dragon (IRE)**[8] 6465 3-9-1 **79** .... JamieSpencer 5 75
(P A Blockley) *dwlt: hld up in tch: effrt over 2f out: no ex over 1f out* **7/4**[1]
1513 **4** *4* **Boundless Prospect (USA)**[3] 6596 8-9-3 **78** .... TomEaves 7 66
(Miss Gay Kelleway) *prom: effrt over 2f out: wknd over 1f out* **13/2**[3]
0000 **5** *1/2* **Blue Spinnaker (IRE)**[8] 6465 8-8-8 **69** ....(p) DaleGibson 3 56
(M W Easterby) *chsd ldrs: outpcd over 2f out: n.d after* **11/1**
320 **6** *shd* **Getrah**[7] 6492 3-8-8 **72** .... PaulHanagan 4 59
(N Wilson) *chsd ldrs tl rdn and wknd fr 2f out* **15/2**
1420 **7** *2* **Ahlawy (IRE)**[7] 6499 4-9-0 **82** .... NSLawes(7) 2 65
(M W Easterby) *missed break: bhd: rdn and hung lft over 2f out: sn btn* **25/1**

2m 8.41s (8.41) **Going Correction** +1.125s/f (Soft)
WFA 3 from 4yo+ 3lb 7 Ran SP% **111.3**
Speed ratings (Par 105): **107,106,101,97,97 96,95**
CSF £25.45 TOTE £3.20: £1.90, £2.70; EX 20.80.
Owner D E Cook **Bred** R S A Urquhart **Trained** Tadcaster, N Yorks
■ Stewards' Enquiry : Paul Hanagan one-day ban: dropped hands and failed to ride out to line (Nov 14)

FOCUS
A fair handicap in which the pace was only fair at best. Nothing got into it from the rear. The form, rated through the runner-up, is sound.

6637 JOHN SMITH'S EXTRA SMOOTH H'CAP 1m
2:30 (2:30) (Class 3) (0-90,87) 3-Y-0+ **£7,772** (£2,312; £1,155; £577) **Stalls** Low

Form RPR
6345 **1** **Smokey Oakey (IRE)**[35] 5805 3-9-3 **86** .... PaulMulrennan 3 98
(M H Tompkins) *in tch: smooth hdwy to ld 2f out: pushed clr fnl f* **11/4**[2]
0046 **2** *6* **Emerald Bay (IRE)**[43] 5585 5-8-10 **77** .... TomEaves 9 76
(I Semple) *t.k.h: prom: effrt and ev ch 2f out: kpt on fnl f: nt rch wnr* **12/1**
0031 **3** *1* **Vicious Warrior**[8] 6465 8-9-6 **87** .... DeanMcKeown 4 84
(R M Whitaker) *led to 2f out: sn rdn and nt qckn* **5/1**[3]
2340 **4** *4* **Osteopathic Remedy (IRE)**[7] 6492 3-8-10 **79** .... PhillipMakin 2 68
(M Dods) *t.k.h: in tch: hdwy and ev ch over 2f out: hung lft and wknd over 1f out* **15/2**
5000 **5** *9* **Scotty's Future (IRE)**[12] 6380 9-8-1 **73** oh23 .... KellyHarrison(5) 5 43
(A Berry) *s.i.s: sn wl bhd: nvr on terms* **66/1**
1245 **6** *3/4* **Montrachet**[7] 6497 3-8-7 **76** ow1 .... JamieSpencer 1 44
(M L W Bell) *prom: effrt over 2f out: wkng whn hmpd over 1f out* **2/1**[1]
15-0 **7** *3 1/2* **Celtic Step**[10] 6439 3-8-11 **80** .... GregFairley 6 41
(M Johnston) *pressed ldr: rdn and ev ch over 2f out: wkng whn hung lft over 1f out* **5/1**[3]
1000 **8** *10* **Fern House (IRE)**[30] 5930 5-8-6 **73** oh21 .... PaulHanagan 8 13
(Garry Moss) *in tch: outpcd over 3f out: sn btn* **100/1**
0006 **9** *1 1/4* **Stanley Wolfe (IRE)**[40] 5672 4-8-7 **74** oh28 ow1 .... MickyFenton 7 11
(Garry Moss) *bhd: struggling 1/2-way: nvr on terms* **100/1**

1m 50.99s (7.50) **Going Correction** +1.125s/f (Soft)
WFA 3 from 4yo+ 2lb 9 Ran SP% **116.3**
Speed ratings (Par 107): **107,101,100,96,87 86,82,72,71**
CSF £35.49 CT £158.81 TOTE £4.40: £1.50, £2.60, £1.80; EX 50.50.
Owner Judi Dench and Bryan Agar **Bred** Hyde Park Stud **Trained** Newmarket, Suffolk

FOCUS
A fair handicap and one in which the pace was decent considering the conditions. There is some doubt as to whether the winner improved as much as the bare form suggests.

NOTEBOOK
Smokey Oakey(IRE), a consistent sort, appreciated the drop in trip and the return to testing ground when posting a career-best effort. These conditions suit him ideally but he is going to find life much tougher after reassessment. (op 3-1)
Emerald Bay(IRE), from a stable going well, ran creditably in these testing conditions. He has slipped to a fair mark and goes on any ground but it is worth bearing in mind that all his wins have been on a sound surface. (op 11-1)
Vicious Warrior, who has a decent record at this course, had the run of the race and seemed to give it his best shot. He looks a good guide to the worth of this form but he has little margin for error from his current mark. (op 4-1)
Osteopathic Remedy(IRE), back in testing ground, did not get home in the conditions. He has not won since his debut, is the type that needs things to drop right and, as such, would not be one to be taking too short a price about. (op 9-1 tchd 7-1)
Scotty's Future(IRE) was not totally disgraced in terms of the bare form from 23lb out of the handicap but he is a very tricky ride who is of little immediate interest. (tchd 80-1)
Montrachet, a consistent sort who knows how to win, looked to have conditions to suit but she ran poorly for no apparent reason. She will be worth another chance in similar company, though. Official explanation: jockey said filly hung left-handed throughout and suffered interference (op 9-4)
Celtic Step, turned out quickly on this second start after a lengthy break, failed by a long chalk to reproduce his fair reappearance run. This may well have come too quickly and he is not one to write off just yet. (op 11-2 tchd 6-1)

6638 JOHN SMITH'S FILLIES' H'CAP 7f 50y
3:05 (3:06) (Class 5) (0-70,67) 3-Y-0+ **£3,238** (£963; £481; £240) **Stalls** Low

Form RPR
0220 **1** **Mugeba**[4] 6575 6-8-7 **55** ....(t) MickyFenton 2 65
(Miss Gay Kelleway) *hld up: smooth hdwy to ld over 1f out: sn rdn: kpt on wl fnl f* **9/2**[2]
0240 **2** *1/2* **Eternal Legacy (IRE)**[8] 6467 5-8-6 **54** .... DavidAllan 5 63
(E J Alston) *prom: effrt and ev ch fr 2f out: no ex wl ins fnl f* **9/2**[2]
106 **3** *5* **Neil's Legacy (IRE)**[8] 6465 5-9-0 **67** .... NeilBrown(5) 6 63
(Miss L A Perratt) *cl up: led over 3f out to over 1f out: sn no ex* **6/1**[3]
0000 **4** *1 1/4* **Karmest**[8] 6467 3-8-4 **53** ....(v[1]) SilvestreDeSousa 8 45
(A D Brown) *prom: effrt over 2f out: hung lft and no ex over 1f out* **20/1**
2150 **5** *3 1/2* **Catherines Cafe (IRE)**[15] 6304 4-8-2 **53** oh3 .... AndrewMullen(3) 1 36
(A C Whillans) *in tch: rdn over 2f out: btn over 1f out* **12/1**
3220 **6** *3/4* **Mystical Ayr (IRE)**[8] 6465 5-9-0 **67** .... GaryBartley(5) 7 48
(Miss L A Perratt) *in tch: drvn over 2f out: sn btn* **4/1**[1]
3001 **7** *1 1/4* **Grethel (IRE)**[8] 6464 3-8-4 **56** .... PatrickMathers(3) 3 34
(A Berry) *hld up: effrt u.p over 2f out: sn no imp* **17/2**
2300 **8** *5* **Queen's Echo**[149] 2388 6-8-5 **53** oh2 .... PaulHanagan 4 18
(P Monteith) *led to over 3f out: wknd over 2f out* **7/1**
6300 **9** *10* **Ducal Pip Squeak**[13] 6361 3-9-1 **64** .... PhillipMakin 9 3
(M Dods) *cl up tl wknd over 2f out: t.o* **11/1**

1m 40.53s (7.81) **Going Correction** +1.125s/f (Soft)
WFA 3 from 4yo+ 1lb 9 Ran SP% **114.5**
Speed ratings (Par 100): **100,99,93,92,88 87,86,80,68**
CSF £24.83 CT £122.31 TOTE £5.60: £2.00, £1.50, £2.00; EX 24.10.
Owner M M Foulger **Bred** Broughton Bloodstock And M Billings **Trained** Exning, Suffolk

FOCUS
A modest event but a fair test of stamina in the conditions. As in the previous race, the winner raced closest to the stands rail in the straight. The first two finished clear but this is not form to take too literally given the bad ground.

6639 JOHN SMITH'S NO NONSENSE H'CAP 6f
3:40 (3:43) (Class 4) (0-80,82) 3-Y-0+
£5,608 (£1,679; £839; £420; £209; £105) **Stalls** Low

Form RPR
6006 **1** **Paris Bell**[22] 6157 5-8-12 **72** .... DavidAllan 7 85
(T D Easterby) *dwlt: bhd far side: hdwy 2f out: led ins fnl f: styd on strly* **7/1**
0003 **2** *1 1/2* **Pieter Brueghel (USA)**[45] 5535 8-9-1 **75** .... JamieSpencer 4 83
(D Nicholls) *midfield far side: hdwy and ev ch ins fnl f: kpt on same pce nr fin* **9/1**
4413 **3** *3/4* **Charles Parnell (IRE)**[22] 6157 4-9-2 **76** .... PhillipMakin 14 82
(M Dods) *prom far side: led over 1f out to ins fnl f: no ex* **8/1**
1100 **4** *1/2* **Prospect Court**[13] 6363 5-9-1 **78** .... AndrewMullen(3) 12 82
(A C Whillans) *in tch far side: drvn and effrt 2f out: no imp fnl f* **6/1**[3]
6410 **5** *3 1/2* **Yorkshire Blue**[19] 6243 8-8-13 **73** .... DanielTudhope 9 67
(J S Goldie) *bhd far side tl hdwy fnl 2f: nrst fin* **12/1**
3501 **6** *1* **Bel Cantor**[4] 6560 4-9-1 **82** 6ex .... LanceBetts(7) 5 73
(W J H Ratcliffe) *led far side to over 1f out: sn no ex* **5/1**[2]
4500 **7** *hd* **Sea Salt**[22] 6157 4-8-12 **72** .... PaulHanagan 6 62
(R A Fahey) *cl up far side: rdn over 2f out: no ex over 1f out* **14/1**
4340 **8** *1 1/2* **Goodbye Cash (IRE)**[28] 6006 3-9-0 **77** .... JamieMoriarty(3) 1 63
(P D Evans) *midfield: drvn and outpcd after 2f: no imp after* **25/1**
4113 **9** *shd* **Memphis Man**[4] 6575 4-8-9 **69** .... TGMcLaughlin 13 54+
(P D Evans) *missed break: racd w one other stands' side: kpt on fnl 2f: no ch w far side* **4/1**[1]
0000 **10** *1/2* **Varadouro (BRZ)**[35] 5806 5-8-13 **73** .... AdrianTNicholls 11 57
(D Nicholls) *chsd far side ldrs tl wknd over 1f out* **16/1**
5000 **11** *nk* **Stellite**[8] 6463 7-8-1 **64** oh2 .... DuranFentiman(3) 15 47
(J S Goldie) *hld up far side: effrt over 2f out: btn over 1f out* **25/1**
3364 **12** *3 1/2* **Howards Tipple**[18] 6256 3-8-7 **67** ....(p) TomEaves 8 39
(I Semple) *midfield far side: effrt over 2f out: wknd over 1f out* **22/1**
0023 **13** *2* **Steel Blue**[16] 6283 7-8-10 **70** .... DeanMcKeown 3 36
(R M Whitaker) *prom far side tl wknd over 2f out* **14/1**
-000 **14** *1 1/2* **Johnston's Diamond (IRE)**[24] 6103 9-8-1 **64** oh1(b) PatrickMathers(3) 16 26
(E J Alston) *racd w one other stands' side: hung lft u.p and struggling over 2f out* **33/1**
6400 **15** *1* **Baltimore Jack (IRE)**[13] 6355 3-9-3 **77** .... DaleGibson 10 36
(M W Easterby) *prom far side tl rdn and wknd over 2f out* **66/1**
0200 **16** *1* **Rothesay Dancer**[8] 6467 4-7-13 **64** .... KellyHarrison(5) 2 20
(J S Goldie) *hld up far side: rdn over 2f out: sn btn* **40/1**

1m 17.13s (3.46) **Going Correction** +0.75s/f (Yiel) 16 Ran SP% **130.4**
Speed ratings (Par 105): **106,104,103,102,97 96,96,94,93,93 92,88,85,83,82 80**
CSF £68.79 CT £556.30 TOTE £8.10: £2.50, £2.50, £2.60, £2.40; EX 82.40.
Owner Ryedale Partners No 8 **Bred** M H Easterby **Trained** Great Habton, N Yorks
■ Stewards' Enquiry : Patrick Mathers one-day ban: failed to ride to draw (Nov 14)

FOCUS
An open handicap and one in which the bulk of the field raced far side. Pretty solid form given the ground, the third the best guide.
Varadouro(BRZ) Official explanation: jockey said gelding lost its action

6640 JOHN SMITH'S AT AYR RACECOURSE H'CAP 1m 1f 20y
4:15 (4:15) (Class 6) (0-60,60) 3-Y-0+ **£3,238** (£963; £481; £240) **Stalls** Low

Form RPR
6-60 **1** **Little Bob**[18] 6258 6-9-3 **56** ....(b) GrahamGibbons 10 66
(J D Bethell) *mde all: hrd pressed fr over 2f out: edgd lft ins fnl f: hld on gamely* **12/1**
4056 **2** *hd* **Thunderwing (IRE)**[40] 5676 5-8-13 **55** .... PJMcDonald(3) 2 65
(James Moffatt) *in tch: hdwy to chal over 1f out: kpt on fnl f: hld cl home* **10/1**
1502 **3** *2 1/2* **Zain (IRE)**[30] 5936 3-9-0 **56** ....(t) PaulMulrennan 11 61
(J G Given) *chsd wnr: effrt and ev ch over 2f out to over 1f out: nt qckn fnl f* **5/1**[2]
5400 **4** *1* **Tidy (IRE)**[106] 3721 7-9-5 **58** ....(v) GregFairley 9 61
(Micky Hammond) *midfield: effrt over 2f out: one pce over 1f out* **12/1**
0500 **5** *3/4* **Bijou Dan**[18] 6259 6-9-7 **60** ....(p) TonyHamilton 3 62
(D W Thompson) *bhd tl kpt on fr 2f out: nrst fin* **16/1**

0133 6 9 **Oeuf A La Neige**[8] 6463 7-9-1 **57**............................ JamieMoriarty(3) 4 41
(Miss L A Perratt) *hld up: pushed along over 2f out: n.d* **9/1**

4105 7 2 1/2 **Lauro**[38] 5738 7-9-0 **60**............................ DawnRankin(7) 1 39
(Miss J A Camacho) *hld up on ins: drvn over 2f out: sn n.d* **14/1**

53 8 1 1/4 **Camolin (IRE)**[40] 5694 4-9-1 **54**............................(b) JamieSpencer 8 30
(Michael McElhone, Ire) *hld up: effrt and wd over 2f out: edgd lft and sn wknd* **2/1**[1]

0650 8 dht **Tracer**[15] 6310 3-9-4 **60**............................ DaleGibson 13 36
(M W Easterby) *hld up in tch: rdn over 2f out: sn btn* **28/1**

0002 10 3/4 **Moonstreaker**[18] 6247 4-9-0 **53**............................ DeanMcKeown 14 28
(R M Whitaker) *bhd: drvn over 3f out: nvr on terms* **10/1**

0600 11 3/4 **Dictatrix**[59] 5132 4-9-0 **53**............................ TomEaves 6 26
(P D Niven) *s.i.s: a bhd* **50/1**

3020 12 2 1/2 **Apache Nation (IRE)**[18] 6258 4-9-7 **60**............................ PhillipMakin 5 28
(M Dods) *prom tl rdn and wknd over 2f out* **6/1**[3]

2305 13 44 **Beaumont Boy**[30] 5936 3-8-13 **55**............................ PaulHanagan 12 —
(A G Foster) *prom to 1/2-way: sn lost pl* **33/1**

2m 10.8s (10.80) **Going Correction** +1.125s/f (Soft)
WFA 3 from 4yo+ 3lb **13** Ran SP% **128.8**
Speed ratings (Par 101): **97,96,94,93,93 85,82,81,81,81 80,78,39**
CSF £134.88 CT £699.24 TOTE £10.80: £3.10, £3.10, £2.20; EX 106.10 Place 6 £62.29, Place 5 £48.22.
Owner Robert Gibbons **Bred** R F Gibbons **Trained** Middleham Moor, N Yorks
■ Stewards' Enquiry : Graham Gibbons caution: careless riding

FOCUS
A modest handicap in which those held up failed to land a blow. The time was slow and this is not form to take literally, with not many coping with the ground.
T/Plt: £122.60 to a £1 stake. Pool: £62,373.55. 371.30 winning tickets. T/Qpdt: £16.20 to a £1 stake. Pool: £2,910.20. 132.60 winning tickets. RY

6577 KEMPTON (A.W) (R-H)

Saturday, November 3

OFFICIAL GOING: Standard
Wind: Nil Weather: Dark

6641 EUROPEAN BREEDERS' FUND MEDIAN AUCTION MAIDEN STKS 6f (P)
6:20 (6:20) (Class 5) 2-Y-O £3,141 (£934; £467; £233) Stalls High

Form RPR

4 1 **Torch Of Freedom (IRE)**[44] 5575 2-9-3 0............................ SebSanders 2 76+
(Sir Mark Prescott) *trckd ldr: rdn to ld jst over 1f out: drew clr last 100yds* **13/8**[2]

00 2 1 1/2 **Emperors Jade**[19] 6234 2-9-3 0............................ NCallan 6 72
(A P Jarvis) *led: rdn and hdd jst over 1f out: one pce* **20/1**

2 3 1 1/4 **Barnaby Rudge (IRE)**[19] 6234 2-9-3 0............................ JohnEgan 3 68
(Jane Chapple-Hyam) *t.k.h early: trckd ldng pair: racd awkwardly over 2f out: sn nt qckn: kpt on same pce* **4/6**[1]

0 4 3 **Coole Dodger (IRE)**[11] 6403 2-8-10 0............................ KylieManser(7) 5 59
(B G Powell) *wnt lft s: hld up in 5th: outpcd 2f out: nudged along and kpt on steadily* **66/1**

0000 5 3 **Berties Goodenough**[10] 6419 2-9-0 52............................ EmmettStack(3) 7 50
(Andrew Turnell) *t.k.h early: trckd ldng pair tl wknd wl over 1f out* **50/1**

0 6 4 **Love And Glory (FR)**[10] 6419 2-8-10 0............................ RossAtkinson(7) 1 38
(G L Moore) *s.i.s: rn green in 6th: lost tch sn after 1/2-way* **50/1**

7 9 **The Lady Lapwing** 2-8-12 0............................ SteveDrowne 4 6
(G Wragg) *s.s: a t.o* **16/1**[3]

1m 13.2s (-0.50) **Going Correction** -0.20s/f (Stan) **7** Ran SP% **114.1**
Speed ratings (Par 96): **95,93,91,87,83 78,66**
CSF £30.02 TOTE £3.40: £1.20, £3.50; EX 38.30.
Owner J Fishpool - Osborne House **Bred** Kilcarn Stud **Trained** Newmarket, Suffolk

FOCUS
An ordinary maiden run at a steady early pace. With the favourite failing to repeat his debut form, the winner had little to beat.

NOTEBOOK
Torch Of Freedom(IRE) was unfancied on his debut at Yarmouth but he ran with promise that day and this was a weaker event. He did the job in a professional style and looks likely to appreciate another furlong. (op 15-8 tchd 2-1, 9-4 in a place)
Emperors Jade ran his best race to date on his third career start. This sounder surface suited him and handicaps are now an option for connections. (op 16-1)
Barnaby Rudge(IRE) ran with promise on soft ground on his debut at Windsor and, while this was a different test, he looked to hold strong claims in what looked a weak race. He was a bit too keen for his own good off the steady early gallop, though, and when brought to have every chance up the centre of the track he could only plug on one-paced. (op 8-13)
Coole Dodger(IRE), a half-brother to four winners, mostly at around a mile, showed a lot more than on his debut and looks one for handicaps over further after one more run.
Berties Goodenough will be of more interest in moderate handicap company or selling grade.

6642 SURREY HERALD CLAIMING STKS 1m (P)
6:50 (6:50) (Class 6) 3-4-Y-O £2,047 (£604; £302) Stalls High

Form RPR

060 1 **General Knowledge (USA)**[7] 6504 4-9-6 72............................(t) SebSanders 11 58
(B G Powell) *chsd ldrs: eased out and effrt over 2f out: prog to ld 1f out: rdn clr* **11/4**[2]

5334 2 1 3/4 **Not Now Lewis (IRE)**[223] 776 3-9-2 66............................ SteveDrowne 4 52
(J A Osborne) *settled in midfield: rdn and nt qckn over 2f out: prog over 1f out: r.o to take 2nd last 100yds* **8/1**

0056 3 1 **Polish Prospect (IRE)**[40] 5690 3-8-3 40............................ AdrianMcCarthy 10 36
(H S Howe) *towards rr: effrt over 2f out: styd on wl fnl f to take 3rd last strides* **33/1**

-000 4 shd **Mycenean Prince (USA)**[34] 4526 4-9-0 42............................(b) PaulEddery 7 45
(R C Guest) *chsd ldr to over 4f out: sn u.p and struggling: lost pl over 1f out: styd on again ins fnl f* **20/1**

0000 5 1/2 **Wizby**[4] 6573 4-8-7 38 ow2............................ JohnEgan 5 37
(P D Evans) *s.i.s: wl in rr: rdn over 2f out: styd on fnl f: nrst fin* **25/1**

0000 6 shd **Rebellious Spirit**[83] 4418 4-9-4 75............................ JimCrowley 2 48
(P W Hiatt) *prom: chsd ldr over 4f out: rdn to chal over 1f out: upsides sn after: wknd ins fnl f* **7/4**[1]

0000 7 1/2 **Pont Wood**[35] 5817 3-8-10 47............................ StephenDonohoe 6 40
(Mrs N S Evans) *sttd awkwardly and slowly: mostly in last: rdn 3f out: styd on wl fnl f: nrst fin* **33/1**

600P 8 1/2 **I'm Agenius**[10] 6420 4-8-5 42 ow1............................ NeilChalmers(3) 8 35
(C Roberts) *hld up in rr: sme prog on inner over 2f out: shuffled along and no hdwy over 1f out: keeping on whn no room nr fin* **66/1**

1515 9 1/2 **The Jailer**[20] 6199 4-8-6 54............................(p) MCGeran(7) 3 39
(J G M O'Shea) *led: drvn and hdd 1f out: wknd* **9/2**[3]

0300 10 shd **Hayley's Flower (IRE)**[10] 6429 3-8-7 53............................(p) RichardSmith 9 35
(J C Fox) *chsd ldrs: rdn and no imp over 2f out: wknd ins fnl f* **33/1**

5500 11 3 1/2 **Franky'N'Jonny**[13] 6361 4-8-7 42............................(v) ChrisCatlin 1 25
(M J Attwater) *t.k.h: racd wd: prog after 3f: lost pl over 3f out: sn btn* **12/1**

1m 39.01s (-1.79) **Going Correction** -0.20s/f (Stan)
WFA 3 from 4yo 2lb **11** Ran SP% **118.9**
Speed ratings (Par 101): **100,98,97,97,96 96,96,95,95,94 91**
CSF £22.98 TOTE £3.60: £1.40, £1.80, £10.90; EX 26.60.
Owner I S Smith **Bred** Juddmonte Farms Inc **Trained** Lambourn, Berks

FOCUS
A very poor claimer in which the form horses were not at their best.
I'm Agenius Official explanation: jockey said filly hung badly right-handed

6643 ANDREA CHAPMAN 30TH BIRTHDAY H'CAP 2m (P)
7:20 (7:21) (Class 6) (0-65,61) 3-Y-O+ £2,047 (£604; £302) Stalls High

Form RPR

3000 1 **Dark Parade (ARG)**[45] 5533 6-9-9 61............................(b) JamieJones(5) 3 72
(G L Moore) *dwlt and drvn to stay in tch 1st 2f: prog to trck ldrs gng strly over 4f out: effrt over 1f out: rdn to ld ins fnl f: sn clr* **25/1**

0-21 2 2 1/2 **Spanish Conquest**[11] 6407 3-9-1 57............................ SebSanders 6 65
(Sir Mark Prescott) *hld up bhd ldrs: wnt 2nd 5f out: drvn to ld 2f out: one pce in front: hdd and outpcd ins fnl f* **4/9**[1]

0004 3 1 1/2 **Ronsard (IRE)**[14] 6341 5-9-3 50............................ JohnEgan 7 56
(P D Evans) *stdd s: t.k.h early and hld up in last pair: stdy prog over 4f out: rdn to chse clr ldng trio 3f out: kpt on to take 3rd wl ins fnl f* **20/1**

6-60 4 1/2 **Haatmey**[20] 6200 5-9-5 52............................(v) JimCrowley 8 58
(P R Chamings) *sn hld up towards rr: sltly hmpd over 4f out: drvn over 3f out: styd on fr over 1f out: nrst fin* **12/1**[3]

4042 5 1/2 **Arabian Sun**[14] 6341 3-9-5 61............................(v) ChrisCatlin 4 66
(M J Attwater) *chsd ldrs: reminders 6f out: outpcd over 4f out: kpt on u.p fnl 2f* **5/1**[2]

5240 6 nk **Sovietta (IRE)**[92] 4124 6-9-0 50............................(t) TravisBlock(3) 10 55
(A G Newcombe) *hld up in last pair: outpcd over 4f out: rdn over 2f out: styd on fnl f: nrst fin* **33/1**

0044 7 1 **Moonshine Beach**[12] 6383 9-9-3 50............................ StephenDonohoe 2 53
(P W Hiatt) *pressed ldr: led over 5f out: drvn 3f out: hdd 2f out: wknd ins fnl f* **14/1**

00-5 8 1 1/2 **Hereditary**[231] 242 5-8-12 45............................(p) SteveDrowne 1 47
(Mrs L C Jewell) *hld up in tch: outpcd over 4f out: effrt 3f out: no imp on ldrs 2f out: wknd ins fnl f* **16/1**

5000 9 1 3/4 **Lysander's Quest (IRE)**[45] 5533 9-8-12 45............................(b) EddieAhern 5 45
(R Ingram) *sn trckd ldng pair: trapped bhd wkng rival 5f out: dropped to rr and lost all ch* **33/1**

2535 10 23 **Sadler's Leap (IRE)**[37] 5754 4-10-0 61............................ PaulEddery 9 33
(Pat Eddery) *led to over 5f out: wknd rapidly: t.o* **25/1**

3m 27.8s (-3.60) **Going Correction** -0.20s/f (Stan)
WFA 3 from 4yo+ 9lb **10** Ran SP% **124.5**
Speed ratings (Par 101): **101,99,99,98,98 98,97,97,96,84**
CSF £37.75 CT £304.30 TOTE £35.20: £6.80, £1.10, £5.40; EX 49.90.
Owner N J Jones **Bred** Firmamento **Trained** Woodingdean, E Sussex

FOCUS
An ordinary handicap. Dark Parade is rated back to his best but Spanish Conquest was a big disappointment.
Dark Parade(ARG) Official explanation: trainer's rep said, regarding apparent improvement in form, that the gelding had benefited from a 45-day break, and this race was slightly weaker.
Arabian Sun Official explanation: jockey said gelding never travelled
Lysander's Quest(IRE) Official explanation: jockey said gelding hung right-handed and suffered interference on bend

6644 DIGIBET SPORTS BETTING CONDITIONS STKS 7f (P)
7:50 (7:51) (Class 3) 2-Y-O
£6,232 (£1,866; £933; £467; £233; £117) Stalls High

Form RPR

1 1 **Storm Force (IRE)**[22] 6138 2-9-3 0............................ TedDurcan 6 91
(Saeed Bin Suroor) *trckd ldng pair: effrt to ld over 1f out: rdn and r.o wl fnl f* **13/8**[1]

1 2 2 1/2 **Seasider**[33] 5872 2-9-3 0............................ RyanMoore 4 85
(Sir Michael Stoute) *hld up in 5th: prog to chal 2f out: chsd wnr jst over 1f out: readily outpcd* **13/8**[1]

2104 3 1 **Quick Release (IRE)**[40] 5691 2-9-3 79............................ RichardHughes 1 82
(D M Simcock) *t.k.h: trckd ldr: rdn to chal and upsides wl over 1f out: sn outpcd* **40/1**

3 4 1 1/4 **Transfer**[23] 6119 2-8-11 0............................ NeilChalmers(3) 7 76
(A M Balding) *led and sn t.k.h: drvn and hdd over 1f out: wknd ins fnl f* **33/1**

16 5 1 1/2 **Legislation**[74] 4694 2-9-3 88............................ JimmyFortune 3 75+
(J H M Gosden) *hld up in last: effrt but wl outpcd over 2f out: pushed along and wnt 5th over 1f out: no ch of rching ldrs* **3/1**[2]

4020 6 1 **Thunder Gorge (USA)**[23] 6128 2-9-0 75............................ SteveDrowne 5 70
(Mouse Hamilton-Fairley) *mostly in 6th: rdn and no prog over 2f out: no ch after* **66/1**

0010 7 2 **Tamara Moon (IRE)**[7] 6498 2-8-9 76............................ ChrisCatlin 2 60
(M R Channon) *t.k.h early: trckd ldng trio: hanging and nt qckn over 2f out: sn btn* **20/1**[3]

1m 24.73s (-2.07) **Going Correction** -0.20s/f (Stan) **7** Ran SP% **112.8**
Speed ratings (Par 100): **103,100,99,97,95 94,92**
CSF £4.31 TOTE £2.60: £1.40, £1.80; EX 6.00.
Owner Godolphin **Bred** Gerrardstown House Stud **Trained** Newmarket, Suffolk

FOCUS
They went a good pace and broke the juvenile track record by over a second. The form looks solid for the grade, rated around the third. Storm Force looks potentially smart if building on this.

NOTEBOOK
Storm Force(IRE), who made an impressive winning debut at Lingfield, was strong in the market beforehand and found a nice turn of foot to mark himself out as a useful juvenile. He has only run on Polytrack so far but his pedigree suggests turf will be no problem, and he looks an interesting prospect for next year. (op 9-4)
Seasider, who made a winning debut at Windsor last month, had relinquished outright favouritism by the off having earlier traded at odds-on. Brought to have every chance down the centre of the track, he kept on well enough but did not have the change of pace of the winner. (op Evens tchd 10-11)
Quick Release(IRE), whose performance anchors the form somewhat, was never far off the pace and while he lacked the class of the winner, he kept on well enough and posted a solid effort on his Polytrack debut. (tchd 33-1)
Transfer was pretty free out in front and kept on quite well in the circumstances. He will be eligible for handicaps after one more run.

Legislation, was third-favourite for the Group 3 Acomb Stakes on his last start back in August, but he ran poorly that day and this performance was no better. He has plenty to prove now. (op 4-1 tchd 9-2)

6645 FLOODLIT STKS (LISTED RACE) 1m 4f (P)
8:20 (8:22) (Class 1) 3-Y-0+

£14,762 (£5,595; £2,800; £1,396; £699; £351) **Stalls** Centre

Form				RPR
2515	1		**Dansant**[30] 5952 3-8-11 101 EddieAhern 2 (G A Butler) *stdd s: hld up: last wl over 2f out: rdn and prog on outer wl over 1f out: sustained run fnl f to ld last strides* **7/2**[2]	108+
-540	2	nk	**Into The Dark**[42] 5618 6-9-3 107 TedDurcan 3 (Saeed Bin Suroor) *trckd ldng trio: effrt over 3f out: drvn over 2f out: wnt 2nd over 1f out: styd on to ld jst ins fnl f: collared last strides* **9/2**[3]	108
2140	3	3/4	**Illustrious Blue**[15] 6298 4-9-8 108 PaulDoe 5 (W J Knight) *dwlt: hld up in rr: pushed along and prog on outer over 3f out: drvn over 2f out: clsd on ldrs 1f out: jst outpcd last 100yds* **10/1**	112
	4	2	**Miramare (GER)**[182] 3-8-6 0 JohnEgan 1 (B J Curley) *reluctant to enter stalls: racd freely and set mostly str pce: kicked on over 3f out: hdd jst ins fnl f: fdd* **11/1**	99
-002	5	3	**Young Mick**[5] 6538 5-9-3 103 (v) NCallan 4 (G G Margarson) *hld up in rr: effrt 3f out: drvn and no imp on ldrs 2f out: wknd fnl f* **9/4**[1]	99
02-0	6	2	**Cold Turkey**[19] 6230 7-9-3 87 SimonWhitworth 6 (G L Moore) *dwlt: hld up in last: effrt on inner 3f out: no imp on ldrs 2f out: fdd* **33/1**	96
0511	7	3/4	**Pinch Of Salt (IRE)**[23] 6124 4-9-3 87 MartinDwyer 8 (A M Balding) *prom: chsd ldr 1/2-way to over 1f out: wknd* **6/1**	94
0220	8	6	**Dunaskin (IRE)**[22] 6153 7-9-3 107 SebSanders 7 (Karen McLintock) *chsd ldr to 1/2-way: wknd over 3f out* **10/1**	85

2m 30.48s (-6.42) **Going Correction** -0.20s/f (Stan)
WFA 3 from 4yo+ 6lb **8** Ran SP% **114.9**
Speed ratings (Par 111): **113,112,112,110,108 107,107,103**
CSF £19.78 TOTE £4.70: £1.40, £2.40, £3.80; EX 23.50.
Owner Mrs Barbara M Keller **Bred** Mrs Cino Del Duca **Trained** Blewbury, Oxon
■ The first running of this Listed event.

FOCUS
They broke the track record by over a second in this Listed race that was run at a good pace. It is ordinary form for the grade, though, with the placed horses the best guide. An improved effort from Dansant.

NOTEBOOK
Dansant, who stays further than this, appreciated the good gallop and came home strongly having been last early in the straight. He looks the type who might improve again as a stayer next year. (op 5-1)
Into The Dark, who has been lightly raced this season, was missing the usual tongue tie. Always well placed, he looked to have been delivered with a well-timed challenge until the winner came and collared him close home. He had not run on the All-Weather before but the surface seemed to suit him. (op 6-1)
Illustrious Blue had his stamina to prove on this step up in distance and it ended up being a real test at the trip given the pace set by the leader. He proved he gets 1m4f well, though, and he comes out of the race the best horse at the weights. This should open up new opportunities for him. (op 12-1 tchd 14-1)
Miramare(GER), who had not run since winning her maiden in good style on her debut in Germany back in May, was making her debut for the Curley stable. None too co-operative before the start, she was very keen in the race itself, soon in front and pulling for her head. In the circumstances it was a great effort to be still in front at the furlong pole, and it was only inside the last that she tired. She has plenty of ability on this evidence and should be capable of winning at this level if taught to settle better. (op 10-1 tchd 14-1)
Young Mick, another who has enjoyed a light campaign, never looked like getting involved. This was disappointing as he had looked to be returning to form at Leicester last time. (op 15-8)
Cold Turkey failed to build on last month's reappearance from a significant spell on the sidelines.
Pinch Of Salt(IRE) was impressive in winning a handicap off 75 last time, but he was out of his depth in this grade.
Dunaskin(IRE) is at his best when allowed to lead, and he was denied that role this time by Miramare. (op 7-1 tchd 13-2)

6646 DIGIBET H'CAP 1m (P)
8:50 (8:50) (Class 4) (0-80,79) 3-Y-0+ **£4,728** (£1,406; £702; £351) **Stalls** High

Form				RPR
3034	1		**Waterline Twenty (IRE)**[1] 6628 4-8-8 67 JohnEgan 10 (P D Evans) *hld up in midfield: prog on inner over 2f out: rdn to ld narrowly 1f out: hld on wl fnl f* **8/1**	78
2661	2	nk	**Pendulum Star**[17] 6269 3-9-1 76 AdamKirby 12 (W R Swinburn) *t.k.h: prom: eased out and effrt 2f out: w wnr 1f out: jst hld last 100yds* **15/8**[1]	86
0650	3	1 1/4	**The Snatcher (IRE)**[10] 6435 4-9-3 76 RichardHughes 4 (R Hannon) *led to over 4f out: pressed ldr: led over 2f out to 1f out: one pce* **7/1**[3]	83
0021	4	shd	**Gaelic Princess**[16] 6293 7-9-1 77 TravisBlock[(3)] 5 (A G Newcombe) *t.k.h: hld up bhd ldrs: nt qckn 2f out: styd on fnl f: nrly snatched 3rd* **14/1**	84
1220	5	1 1/4	**Landucci**[20] 6209 6-9-1 79 PatrickHills[(5)] 7 (J W Hills) *t.k.h: hld up in midfield: effrt over 2f out: nt pce to rch ldrs over 1f out: kpt on* **10/1**	83
0201	6	1 1/4	**Touch Of Style (IRE)**[35] 5819 3-9-1 76 SebSanders 2 (J R Boyle) *t.k.h: hld up in last trio: drvn on wd outside over 2f out: no real imp* **15/2**	77
6000	7	3/4	**Binnion Bay (IRE)**[31] 5917 6-8-10 69 ow1 (b) AmirQuinn 1 (J J Bridger) *stdd s: hld up in last pair: urged along and no prog over 2f out: r.o fnl f: nrst fin* **40/1**	68
1022	8	1/2	**Reeling N' Rocking (IRE)**[17] 6269 4-8-12 71 ChrisCatlin 8 (B W Hills) *t.k.h: chsd ldr for 3f: lost pl and struggling 2f out* **6/1**[2]	69
0061	9	nk	**Strawberry Lolly**[29] 5985 4-9-4 77 NCallan 9 (M Botti) *hld up towards rr: rdn and effrt over 2f out: keeping on one pce whn squeezed out over 1f out: no ch after* **10/1**	77+
1400	10	1	**Tyzack (IRE)**[10] 6423 6-8-9 73 TolleyDean[(5)] 3 (Stef Liddiard) *hld up: plld way through to ld over 4f out: hdd over 2f out: wknd over 1f out* **16/1**	68
0000	11	1 1/4	**Silent Storm**[7] 6504 7-8-9 68 AdrianMcCarthy 6 (Peter Grayson) *t.k.h: hld up in last pair: rdn and no prog over 2f out* **40/1**	60

1m 39.32s (-1.48) **Going Correction** -0.20s/f (Stan)
WFA 3 from 4yo+ 2lb **11** Ran SP% **120.1**
Speed ratings (Par 105): **99,98,97,97,96 94,94,93,93,92 91**
CSF £23.78 CT £115.81 TOTE £12.90: £3.30, £1.30, £2.20; EX 40.80.
Owner Waterline Racing Club **Bred** Mountarmstrong Stud **Trained** Pandy, Monmouths

FOCUS
A steadily-run handicap run in a time slower than the earlier claimer. The form seems to make sense.
Tyzack(IRE) Official explanation: jockey said gelding ran too free

6647 DIGIBET CASINO APPRENTICE H'CAP 7f (P)
9:20 (9:20) (Class 6) (0-65,65) 3-Y-0+ **£2,047** (£604; £302) **Stalls** High

Form				RPR
1330	1		**Jools**[10] 6431 9-8-8 53 PatrickHills 1 (D K Ivory) *hld up in last pair: urged along and prog 2f out: led jst ins fnl f: kpt on wl* **9/2**[2]	60
0-	2	nk	**Silver Snipe**[14] 6348 3-8-2 53 MatthewDavies[(5)] 7 (John Joseph Murphy, Ire) *t.k.h: trckd ldr after 3f: led over 2f out: hdd jst ins fnl f: kpt on but a hld* **16/1**	59
0060	3	2	**Coseadrom (IRE)**[22] 6157 5-8-12 62 JosephWalsh[(5)] 4 (M F Harris) *hld up in last pair: prog on inner 2f out: chsd ldrs 1f out: one pce after* **12/1**	63
0001	4	1 1/2	**Vanadium**[16] 6290 5-9-1 65 JemmaMarshall[(5)] 2 (G L Moore) *t.k.h: hld up bhd ldrs: effrt over 2f out: one pce and no imp over 1f out* **10/11**[1]	62
4401	5	1 3/4	**Zazous**[181] 1507 6-8-13 58 TolleyDean 3 (J J Bridger) *sn trckd ldrs: effrt to chal and w ldr over 2f out to over 1f out: wknd* **10/1**	50
0602	6	1 1/4	**Looks Could Kill (USA)**[25] 6083 5-8-12 62 PNolan[(5)] 8 (A B Haynes) *pushed up to ld: hdd over 2f out: wknd over 1f out* **15/2**[3]	51
0066	7	13	**Buzzin'Boyzee (IRE)**[5] 6533 4-8-1 51 oh6 (b[1]) RichardEvans[(5)] 6 (P D Evans) *plld hrd and racd wd: chsd ldr tl wd bnd 4f out and lost pl: bhd fnl 2f* **9/1**	5

1m 26.24s (-0.56) **Going Correction** -0.20s/f (Stan)
WFA 3 from 4yo+ 1lb **7** Ran SP% **115.0**
Speed ratings (Par 101): **95,94,92,90,88 87,72**
CSF £68.68 CT £806.45 TOTE £5.80: £2.10, £6.10; EX 48.80 Place 6 £36.36, Place 5 £13.23 .
Owner Dean Ivory **Bred** Tsarina Stud **Trained** Radlett, Herts

FOCUS
They went a good gallop here and the winner came from off the pace. The form has been rated through the winner and he may not even had had to run to his recent marks to win this pretty soft race.
Buzzin'Boyzee(IRE) Official explanation: jockey said filly ran too free
T/Plt: £76.30 to a £1 stake. Pool: £74,622.85. 713.35 winning tickets. T/Qpdt: £13.20 to a £1 stake. Pool: £5,726.30. 320.70 winning tickets. JN

6616 NEWMARKET (ROWLEY) (R-H)
Saturday, November 3

OFFICIAL GOING: Good
Wind: Light, half-behind Weather: Overcast

6648 BET365 E B F MAIDEN FILLIES' STKS (DIV I) 7f
12:00 (12:01) (Class 4) 2-Y-0 **£4,857** (£1,445; £722; £360) **Stalls** Low

Form				RPR
0	1		**La Coveta (IRE)**[32] 5881 2-9-0 0 SteveDrowne 10 (B J Meehan) *chsd ldrs: rdn to ld 1f out: r.o* **20/1**	76+
	2	nk	**Dar Re Mi** 2-9-0 0 JimmyFortune 11 (J H M Gosden) *hld up in tch: rdn over 1f out: r.o ins fnl f* **10/1**	75+
66	3	3/4	**Wannabe Free**[17] 6267 2-9-0 0 TPQueally 2 (J Noseda) *a.p: rdn over 1f out: r.o* **20/1**	73
	4	1 1/2	**Quirina** 2-9-0 0 DavidKinsella 16 (J H M Gosden) *hld up: hdwy over 2f out: rdn over 1f out: edgd lft ins fnl f: r.o* **22/1**	70+
	5	shd	**Danae** 2-9-0 0 TQuinn 1 (H Candy) *s.i.s: hld up: hdwy over 1f out: hung rt ins fnl f: r.o: nt rch ldrs* **40/1**	69+
36	6	shd	**Sayedati Elhasna (IRE)**[25] 6093 2-9-0 0 MartinDwyer 14 (J L Dunlop) *led: rdn and hdd 1f out: styd on same pce* **14/1**	69
66	7	hd	**Secret Gem (IRE)**[31] 5913 2-9-0 0 PhilipRobinson 18 (C G Cox) *chsd ldr: rdn over 1f out: styd on same pce* **25/1**	69
	8	hd	**Almoutezah (USA)** 2-9-0 0 RHills 15 (M A Jarvis) *trckd ldrs: rdn over 1f out: styd on same pce* **11/4**[1]	68+
	9	1 1/2	**Selsey** 2-9-0 0 KDarley 8 (Sir Michael Stoute) *hld up in tch: outpcd over 2f out: styd on fnl f* **16/1**	64+
	10	hd	**Certain Promise (USA)** 2-9-0 0 RyanMoore 17 (Sir Michael Stoute) *hld up: rdn over 2f out: hdwy over 1f out: nvr nrr* **11/2**[2]	64+
	11	3/4	**Sabancaya** 2-9-0 0 SebSanders 20 (W J Haggas) *hld up: rdn and hung rt over 1f out: nvr nrr* **10/1**	62
	12	nk	**Music In Exile (USA)** 2-8-11 0 WilliamBuick[(3)] 9 (B W Hills) *hld up: shkn up 1/2-way: nvr trbld ldrs* **33/1**	61
	13	nk	**Ice Bellini** 2-9-0 0 HayleyTurner 12 (J M P Eustace) *prom: rdn 1/2-way: wknd fnl f* **66/1**	61
	14	nk	**Finmore Queen (USA)** 2-9-0 0 OscarUrbina 4 (J R Fanshawe) *s.i.s: a bhd* **33/1**	60
	15	hd	**Arabian Art (USA)** 2-9-0 0 TedDurcan 3 (H R A Cecil) *hld up: hdwy over 2f out: sn rdn and hung rt: wknd over 1f out* **9/1**[3]	59
	16	2	**Marie Tempest** 2-9-0 0 MichaelHills 7 (B W Hills) *s.i.s: hld up: nvr nr to chal* **12/1**	54
0	17	3/4	**Lady Florence**[29] 5977 2-9-0 0 EddieAhern 13 (A B Coogan) *chsd ldrs over 5f* **150/1**	52
	18	5	**Binyamina** 2-9-0 0 RichardKingscote 5 (E F Vaughan) *s.i.s: a in rr* **66/1**	40
	19	1	**Syriana** 2-9-0 0 NCallan 19 (A Bailey) *s.i.s: a in rr* **100/1**	37

1m 27.1s (0.60) **Going Correction** +0.125s/f (Good) **19** Ran SP% **121.2**
Speed ratings (Par 95): **101,100,99,98,97 97,97,97,95,95 94,94,93,93,93 91,90,84,83**
CSF £188.04 TOTE £23.40: £6.00, £3.50, £7.00; EX 265.60.
Owner Mrs Wendy English **Bred** Mrs Noelle Walsh **Trained** Manton, Wilts

FOCUS
The quicker of the two divisions by 1.13sec, but the field was fairly compressed and it is hard to believe the standard is very much better than it has been rated.

NOTEBOOK
La Coveta(IRE), who caught the eye when finishing in mid-division in a Warwick maiden on her debut, was probably not given enough credit in the market, especially considering that she had that invaluable edge on experience over most of her rivals. She should get 1m next year, but perhaps not too much further. (op 28-1)

The Form Book, Raceform Ltd, Compton, RG20 6NL

Dar Re Mi ◆, whose dam won the Prix Vermeille, is a half-sister to River Dancer (formerly Diaghilev), a smart 1m4f colt at home and later top class over 1m2f in Hong Kong, high-class 1m4f winner Darazari, high-class stayer Dariyoun, and smart pair Rhagaas and Kilimajaro, so she has plenty to live up to. This was a very pleasing debut as she really got going once she hit the rising ground and finished well. Middle distances will bring out the best in her next term. (op 12-1 tchd 14-1)

Wannabe Free appreciated this stiffer track and again shaped as though she is going to appreciate a longer trip. She has now had the requisite three runs for a mark, but ought to be able to win a maiden over 1m on Polytrack. (op 22-1 tchd 25-1)

Quirina, a half-sister to seven winners, including Quito, a high-class and prolific winner between 6f and 1m, and Quarter Note, a high-class miler, was the lesser fancied of the Gosden pair but she showed potential, too. She looks sure to come on for the experience. (op 25-1)

Danae, a half-sister to Gorse, a high-class multiple 6f winner, and Puya, a dual 7f winner, was putting in some good work late on under hand riding. She hails from a stable whose juveniles tend to come on quite a bit for their debuts. (op 50-1)

Sayedati Elhasna(IRE), her owner's second string on jockey bookings, tried to put her experience to good use and dominate this field, but she was brushed aside as they exited the Dip. She appears to have her limitations. (op 16-1)

Secret Gem(IRE) was another with a couple of runs under her belt who was given a positive ride against rivals largely lacking in racing experience. While her form to date is only modest, she should do better in handicap company.

Almoutezah(USA), who cost a cool $2,300,000, is a half-sister to Summer Colony, a top-class prolific winner at 1m plus in the US, and Sainted Colony, a multiple winner at 1m plus in the US. She threatened to get involved around two furlongs out when brought to challenge towards the far side, but her challenge petered out. Quicker ground will probably suit her and she can do better with this run under her belt. (op 5-2 tchd 3-1)

Selsey, who is a sister to Leadership, a top-class multiple winner at between 7f and 1m4f, shapes as though she will come into her own over further next year.

Certain Promise(USA), who is a sister to Spanish Sun and Spanish Moon, who both won on their only start at two, could not continue that family tradition. (op 9-2)

6649 BET365 E B F MAIDEN FILLIES' STKS (DIV II) 7f

12:30 (12:37) (Class 4) 2-Y-O **£4,857** (£1,445; £722; £360) **Stalls** Low

Form				RPR
	1		**Infallible** 2-9-0 0 ... JimmyFortune 8 (J H M Gosden) *hld up in tch: swtchd lft over 1f out: rdn to ld 1f out: r.o wl* **11/2**[2]	75+
	2	*1 ¾*	**Elmaleeha** 2-9-0 0 ... RHills 18 (J L Dunlop) *hld up: hdwy over 2f out: rdn over 1f out: edgd lft: r.o* **12/1**	70+
	3	*nk*	**Isabella Glyn (IRE)** 2-9-0 0 ... EddieAhern 14 (J Noseda) *hld up in tch: rdn over 1f out: r.o* **11/1**	69+
	4	*1*	**La Troupe (IRE)** 2-9-0 0 ... RobertHavlin 16 (J H M Gosden) *chsd ldrs: rdn over 1f out: hung lft ins fnl f: styd on* **7/1**[3]	67+
00	**5**	*¾*	**River N' Blues (IRE)**[10] 6417 2-8-9 0 ... KevinGhunowa(5) 2 (Dr J R J Naylor) *led: hung rt over 2f out: rdn and hdd 1f out: no ex* **50/1**	65
	6	*nk*	**Ada River** 2-8-11 0 ... NeilChalmers(3) 20 (A M Balding) *s.i.s: rdn over 2f out: r.o ins fnl f: nt rch ldrs* **40/1**	64+
	7	*½*	**Basanti (USA)** 2-9-0 0 ... MichaelHills 7 (B W Hills) *s.i.s: hld up: hdwy over 2f out: rdn and hung rt over 1f out: styd on* **14/1**	63+
	8	*½*	**Shindy (FR)** 2-9-0 0 ... OscarUrbina 5 (J A R Toller) *hld up: hdwy over 1f out: nvr trbld ldrs* **66/1**	62+
0	**9**	*1 ¼*	**Pentandra (IRE)**[52] 5329 2-9-0 0 ... TPQueally 3 (J G Given) *prom: rdn over 1f out: hung lft and wknd ins fnl f* **66/1**	59
	10	*¾*	**Filigree Lace (USA)** 2-9-0 0 ... KDarley 11 (Sir Michael Stoute) *chsd ldrs: rdn over 2f out: wknd fnl f* **11/1**	57
	11	*¾*	**Piano Sonata** 2-9-0 0 ... RichardHughes 1 (B W Hills) *hld up in tch: rdn and wknd over 1f out* **8/1**	55
	12	*hd*	**La Gazzetta (IRE)** 2-9-0 0 ... TQuinn 19 (D R C Elsworth) *hld up: n.d* **16/1**	54
	13	*hd*	**Perfect Silence** 2-9-0 0 ... PhilipRobinson 15 (C G Cox) *mid-div: rdn over 2f out: wknd over 1f out* **9/1**	54
0	**14**	*½*	**Lady Petrus**[10] 6432 2-9-0 0 ... TedDurcan 4 (H J L Dunlop) *chsd ldrs: lost pl over 4f out: wknd over 2f out* **20/1**	53
	15	*½*	**Charming Tale (USA)** 2-9-0 0 ... SteveDrowne 10 (B J Meehan) *s.s: a in rr* **16/1**	51
00	**16**	*hd*	**Coloratura (IRE)**[11] 6414 2-9-0 0 ... StephenDonohoe 17 (E A L Dunlop) *s.s: a in rr* **33/1**	51
	17	*nk*	**Victoria Reel** 2-8-11 0 ... WilliamBuick(3) 12 (R Hannon) *s.i.s: a in rr* **20/1**	50
	18	*½*	**Aura** 2-9-0 0 ... RyanMoore 9 (Sir Michael Stoute) *chsd ldrs over 5f* **5/1**[1]	49
00	**19**	*12*	**Marfeng**[16] 6289 2-9-0 0 ... LiamJones 6 (W M Brisbourne) *chsd ldrs over 4f* **66/1**	19
0	**20**	*3*	**Mellifluous (IRE)**[10] 6434 2-9-0 0 ... (t) MartinDwyer 13 (J W Hills) *mid-div: rdn 1/2-way: sn wknd* **100/1**	—

1m 28.23s (1.73) **Going Correction** +0.125s/f (Good) **20 Ran SP% 130.8**
Speed ratings (Par 95): **95,93,92,91,90 90,89,89,87,86 86,85,85,85,84 84,83,83,69,66**
CSF £68.30 TOTE £6.00: £2.70, £5.10, £4.50; EX 88.40.
Owner Cheveley Park Stud **Bred** Cheveley Park Stud Ltd **Trained** Newmarket, Suffolk

FOCUS

The slower of the two divisions by 1.13sec, but a taking performance from the winner in a finish dominated by newcomers. They were fairly compressed behind her, however, and again the standard is unlikely to be much better than it has been rated.

NOTEBOOK

Infallible, whose dam was a smart sprinter and won at Listed level at three, had more speed in her pedigree than most of her rivals and that counted for plenty in what was a steadily-run maiden. She quickened up well in the closing stages to win in good style, but it must be stressed that she beat rivals who will be mainly plying their trade over middle distances next season, whereas she will probably struggle to get beyond 1m. Nevertheless, she looks a smart filly in the making. (tchd 5-1 and 6-1)

Elmaleeha, a half-sister to quite useful dual 7f juvenile winner Mutahayya, 1m4f winner Majhud, and Qusoor, a three-time winning sprinter at two, challenged towards the far side, which was probably not the ideal place to be as the majority of winners the previous day and in the first race on the card came up the centre of the track. Running on well without being knocked about, she put up a very promising debut effort, and she can only improve as she steps up to middle distances next year.

Isabella Glyn(IRE) is closely related to Trumbaka, a high-class winner in France between 1m and 1m2f, and is a half-sister Arctic Hunt, a useful multiple winner in France at around the same distance. Another bred to come into her own as she steps up to 1m2f plus next season, she ran with a deal of promise, and softer ground ought not to concern her. (op 12-1)

La Troupe(IRE), a half-sister to Magic Instinct, a dual winner over middle distances, Cabinet, a winner over 7f at two and 1m2f at three, and Ryedale Ovation, a 5f winner at two, came in for good support despite appearing to be the stable's second string. Prominent throughout, she ran a sound first race. (op 9-1)

River N' Blues(IRE) had not shown a great deal in two previous starts but she did at least have an edge in experience over most of the field, and she put it to good use by making the running at just an ordinary pace. Well positioned in a race that developed into a bit of a sprint, she probably achieved her maximum.

Ada River, who is a sister to Don't Dili Dali, a smart, triple winner between 7f and 1m at two and three, was running on at the finish and looks sure to derive plenty from this debut experience, as most of her stable's juveniles do. (op 33-1)

Basanti(USA), who cost 260,000gns, is closely related to Amusing Time, useful 1m2f winner at three, and Musalsal, a useful performer between 1m and 1m2f. Another bred to want a trip next season, she would not have been suited by the way this race was run and can improve when granted a stiffer test of stamina. (op 10-1 tchd 16-1)

Shindy(FR), a half-sister to Shersha, a smart, triple winner between 6f and 1m, and Sherzabad, a dual 1m3f winner, showed ability and will do better at three. (op 50-1)

Pentandra(IRE) Official explanation: jockey said filly lost its action

Aura, who cost 115,000gns, is a sister to Far Hope, a smart, multiple winner over 6f to 1m in Italy, and to a winner in Greece. Unlike many in the field she looked to be running over her optimum distance, but she was ultimately disappointing. (op 13-2)

6650 BET365 ZETLAND CONDITIONS STKS 1m 2f

1:05 (1:09) (Class 2) 2-Y-O

£9,348 (£2,799; £1,399; £700; £349; £175) **Stalls** Low

Form				RPR
1	**1**		**Twice Over**[30] 5951 2-9-0 0 ... RichardHughes 9 (H R A Cecil) *hld up: racd keenly: nt clr run over 2f out: sn swtchd rt: hdwy over 1f out: shkn up to ld ins fnl f: r.o: edgd rt nr fin* **4/5**[1]	95+
21	**2**	*1 ½*	**Planetarium**[26] 6051 2-9-0 88 ... RHills 5 (M Johnston) *led: rdn: hung rt and hdd over 1f out: styd on* **11/4**[2]	90
5321	**3**	*nk*	**Stubbs Art (IRE)**[43] 5600 2-9-0 82 ... SebSanders 4 (D R C Elsworth) *trckd ldrs: racd keenly: rdn to ld over 1f out: edgd lft and hdd ins fnl f: styd on same pce* **11/2**[3]	90
0026	**4**	*2 ½*	**Double Attack (FR)**[37] 5746 2-8-9 77 ... EddieAhern 1 (M Johnston) *trckd ldrs: nt clr run wl over 1f out: sn rdn: styd on same pce* **33/1**	80
51	**5**	*¾*	**King Columbo (IRE)**[17] 6262 2-9-0 77 ... JerryO'Dwyer 6 (Miss J Feilden) *chsd ldrs: rdn and ev ch over 1f out: wknd ins fnl f* **33/1**	84
1354	**6**	*5*	**Donegal (USA)**[28] 6001 2-9-0 98 ... MartinDwyer 2 (A M Balding) *chsd ldrs: rdn over 3f out: wknd over 1f out* **12/1**	75
0	**7**	*1 ¼*	**Duntulm**[87] 4273 2-9-0 0 ... TQuinn 10 (H Candy) *hld up: effrt over 2f out: wknd over 1f out* **50/1**	73
56	**8**	*5*	**Challow Hills (USA)**[71] 4764 2-8-9 0 ... MichaelHills 7 (B W Hills) *s.i.s: sn chsng ldrs: rdn over 3f out: wknd over 2f out* **40/1**	59

2m 5.39s (-0.32) **Going Correction** +0.125s/f (Good) **8 Ran SP% 115.6**
Speed ratings (Par 102): **106,104,104,102,101 97,96,92**
CSF £3.10 TOTE £1.60: £1.10, £1.30, £1.60; EX 3.90.
Owner K Abdulla **Bred** Juddmonte Farms Ltd **Trained** Newmarket, Suffolk
■ Stewards' Enquiry : Richard Hughes caution: careless riding

FOCUS

Traditionally just about the most significant test there is over here over for juveniles over this extended trip, but the bare form this time is nothing special, although the time was faster than the older horse Listed race over the same trip. The winner outclassed his rivals and looks a very nice prospect, but strictly on form he still has plenty to prove.

NOTEBOOK

Twice Over made an impressive winning debut here over 1m last month and proved untroubled by the extra two furlongs on this step up in class. Held up in rear, taking a keen enough hold, he quickened up well when switched and he beat some slower types convincingly. While the bare form is nothing to get excited about, he looks a smart prospect, and he was given quotes of around 25-1 for the Derby. He is likely to take in one of the trials in the spring. (tchd 10-11 tchd evens in places)

Planetarium, who won a maiden over this trip at Pontefract last time, enjoyed the run of the race out in front. Hugging the stands'-side rail, he was able to dictate a pace to suit himself. He could not match the acceleration of the winner but kept on well enough and should develop into a very useful handicapper over middle distances and beyond next season. (op 7-2)

Stubbs Art(IRE), who won a nursery off 72 last time out, was not suited by the fairly steady early gallop and refused to settle. In the circumstances he did well to stay on in the latter stages. (op 7-1 tchd 15-2)

Double Attack(FR), whose last two starts over 1m suggested that she would appreciate this longer trip, tracked her stablemate on the rail and did not get the gaps when she needed them. As a galloper lacking the turn of foot of the winner, she takes a while to get into top gear and that ended her chance of finishing in the places. She will stay further next year.

King Columbo(IRE), running on turf for the first time having won a Polytrack maiden last time out, got warm beforehand. He found the opposition a bit too tough for him at this stage of his career, but looks the type to do better at three. (tchd 40-1)

Donegal(USA) finished third to Rio De La Plata in the Vintage Stakes earlier in the year, but he has not progressed from there. As he is likely to begin his three-year-old career on a stiff mark he is going to be difficult to place. (op 8-1)

6651 BET365 H'CAP 7f

1:35 (1:39) (Class 4) (0-85,85) 3-Y-O+ **£5,181** (£1,541; £770; £384) **Stalls** Low

Form				RPR
0355	**1**		**Purus (IRE)**[15] 6301 5-9-4 **83** ... ChrisCatlin 9 (R A Teal) *chsd ldrs: rdn to ld ins fnl f: r.o* **11/2**[2]	93
0000	**2**	*½*	**Bahiano (IRE)**[28] 6013 6-9-1 **80** ... RyanMoore 2 (C E Brittain) *hld up: hdwy over 1f out: r.o wl ins fnl f: nt rch wnr* **14/1**	89
334	**3**	*½*	**Summer Dancer (IRE)**[42] 5635 3-8-10 **76** ... TQuinn 12 (D R C Elsworth) *hld up: hdwy 2f out: nt clr run over 1f out: sn hrd rdn: edgd lft ins fnl f: styd on* **7/1**[3]	84
1424	**4**	*1 ¾*	**Nadawat (USA)**[44] 5560 3-9-5 **85** ... RHills 7 (J L Dunlop) *chsd ldrs: rdn over 1f out: styd on same pce* **16/1**	88
3010	**5**	*1 ¼*	**Blue Java**[20] 6203 6-8-6 **74** ow1 ... TravisBlock(3) 3 (H Morrison) *prom: rdn over 2f out: sn outpcd: rallied over 1f out: styd on* **12/1**	74
0603	**6**	*hd*	**Masterofthecourt (USA)**[16] 6278 4-8-5 **70** ... EddieAhern 13 (H Morrison) *prom: lost pl over 4f out: hdwy u.p over 1f out: styd on* **14/1**	69
3464	**7**	*¾*	**Super Frank (IRE)**[13] 6355 4-8-5 **70** ... MartinDwyer 11 (J Akehurst) *led: rdn over 1f out: hdd and no ex ins fnl f* **12/1**	67
1201	**8**	*¾*	**The Fifth Member (IRE)**[25] 6081 3-8-13 **79** ... IanMongan 4 (J R Boyle) *prom: rdn over 2f out: styd on same pce appr fnl f* **11/2**[2]	74
0-50	**9**	*½*	**Sotik Star (IRE)**[156] 2180 4-8-8 **73** ... RichardMullen 8 (P J Makin) *s.i.s: hld up: nt clr run 2f out: rdn over 1f out: nt trble ldrs* **40/1**	67
1300	**10**	*shd*	**Barons Spy (IRE)**[5] 6539 6-8-9 **79** ... RussellKennemore(5) 14 (R J Price) *chsd ldrs: rdn over 1f out: wknd ins fnl f* **20/1**	72
1021	**11**	*3 ½*	**Trivia (IRE)**[28] 6025 3-8-6 **75** ... WilliamBuick(3) 6 (N A Callaghan) *s.i.s: sn chsng ldrs: rdn and wknd over 1f out* **8/1**	59
3113	**12**	*nk*	**Goodbye**[8] 6465 3-9-0 **80** ... TedDurcan 5 (G A Swinbank) *prom: rdn over 2f out: hung lft over 1f out: wknd fnl f* **5/1**[1]	63

0500 **13** *4* **Grizedale (IRE)**[20] 6203 8-8-5 **70** oh3................................(t) PaulDoe 15 42
(J Akehurst) *chsd ldrs: rdn over 2f out: sn wknd* **25/1**

5416 **14** *22* **Neon Blue**[44] 5556 6-8-7 **72**..(v) HayleyTurner 10 —
(R M Whitaker) *sn pushed along in rr: wknd 1/2-way* **16/1**

1m 25.58s (-0.92) **Going Correction** +0.125s/f (Good)
WFA 3 from 4yo+ 1lb **14** Ran SP% **122.6**
Speed ratings (Par 105): **110,109,108,106,105 105,104,103,102,102 98,98,93,68**
CSF £80.16 CT £571.32 TOTE £9.50: £3.50, £3.90, £2.20; EX 107.40.

Owner J Morton **Bred** K Nercessian **Trained** Headley, Surrey

FOCUS
A competitive handicap and straightforward form to rate, with the winner rated 4lb higher than the best of his summer efforts and the second back to form off a reduced mark..
Goodbye Official explanation: jockey said filly had no more to give
Grizedale(IRE) Official explanation: jockey said gelding ran too flat

6652 BET365.COM E B F MONTROSE FILLIES' STKS (LISTED RACE) 1m
2:05 (2:10) (Class 1) 2-Y-O

£12,491 (£4,734; £2,369; £1,181; £591; £297) **Stalls** Low

Form RPR
1 **1** **Classic Legend**[31] 5913 2-8-12 0.. IanMongan 3 93
(B J Meehan) *chsd ldrs: led 3f out: rdn over 1f out: r.o* **11/2**[2]

3031 **2** *shd* **Jazz Jam**[37] 5746 2-8-12 78.. TQuinn 5 92
(P F I Cole) *chsd ldr: rdn and ev ch fr over 1f out: r.o* **12/1**

20 **3** *1/2* **Queen Of Naples**[27] 6040 2-8-12 0.. JimmyFortune 2 91
(J H M Gosden) *led 5f: outpcd over 1f out: r.o u.p ins fnl f* **5/4**[1]

0220 **4** *shd* **Dalkey Girl (IRE)**[14] 6336 2-8-12 89................................ WilliamBuick 1 91
(V Smith) *hld up: rdn over 1f out: r.o ins fnl f* **11/1**

1 **5** *shd* **Comeback Queen**[22] 6140 2-8-12 0............................ RichardHughes 8 91
(S Kirk) *chsd ldrs: rdn and ev ch fr over 1f out tl unable qckn nr fin* **8/1**

23 **6** *1 1/4* **Sayyedati Symphony (USA)**[23] 6130 2-8-12 0.................... JohnEgan 9 88
(C E Brittain) *s.i.s: hld up: hdwy 1/2-way: rdn over 1f out: styd on same pce fnl f* **25/1**

1002 **7** *nk* **Shaker (IRE)**[18] 6251 2-8-12 84.. RobertHavlin 7 87
(M L W Bell) *chsd ldrs: nt clr run over 2f out: rdn and edgd lft over 1f out: styd on same pce fnl f* **16/1**

32 **8** *3 1/2* **Saleima (IRE)**[23] 6127 2-8-12 0.. SebSanders 6 80
(J Noseda) *hld up: rdn over 1f out: wknd fnl f* **6/1**[3]

3441 **9** *1/2* **Relinquished**[9] 6449 2-8-12 72.. RyanMoore 10 79
(J Noseda) *hld up: rdn and wknd over 1f out* **20/1**

043 **10** *1/2* **Jollyhockeysticks**[10] 6418 2-8-12 0................................ ChrisCatlin 4 77
(M R Channon) *hld up: bmpd sn after s: rdn over 2f out: sn wknd* **50/1**

1m 41.71s (2.34) **Going Correction** +0.125s/f (Good) **10** Ran SP% **117.7**
Speed ratings (Par 101): **93,92,92,92,92 90,90,87,86,86**
CSF £67.98 TOTE £7.30: £1.80, £3.40, £1.30; EX 83.80 Trifecta £293.40 Part won. Pool: £413.30 - 0.70 winning tickets..

Owner Mrs Moira McNamara **Bred** B Walters **Trained** Manton, Wilts

FOCUS
A steady pace contributed to a bunched finish and the time was very ordinary for the grade. Modest form for the class of contest and well below the usual standard for this race, although the winner remains unbeaten and gives the impression there is more to come.

NOTEBOOK
Classic Legend won at a big price on her racecourse debut and successfully negotiated this rise in grade, albeit narrowly. The majority of her juvenile stablemates that have won first time up this season have gone on to prove themselves Pattern class and she was following that trend. Brian Meehan certainly seems to have a wealth of talent in the two-year-old division, and he pointed the way to an Oaks trial with this daughter of Galileo. (op 5-1 tchd 9-2 tchd 6-1 in places)
Jazz Jam won a nursery off 72 last time out, which puts the form in context, but she has improved for the step up to 1m and gained valuable black type here. She looks the type to progress at three. (op 11-1 tchd 14-1)
Queen Of Naples came into the race a maiden, but she was a well-backed favourite on the strength of her seventh place in the Marcel Boussac last time out and so was a shade disappointing. A stronger pace would probably have suited her better, as she was running on again at the finish. (op 11-8 tchd 6-5 tchd 6-4 in places)
Dalkey Girl(IRE), whose rider was unable to claim, has been highly tried since her maiden win. She ran on towards the stands' side and got into the mix late on, only narrowly failing to pick up a place. (op 12-1)
Comeback Queen, who won her Polytrack maiden in good fashion, appeared to have every chance on this step up in class, but she was another who would have been suited by a stronger pace. (op 15-2 tchd 9-1)
Sayyedati Symphony(USA), another who has yet to win a race, was not up to it on this step up in class, but she should be able to win an ordinary maiden. (tchd 33-1)

6653 BET365 CALL 08000 322365 JAMES SEYMOUR STKS (LISTED RACE) 1m 2f
2:40 (2:42) (Class 1) 3-Y-O+

£14,762 (£5,595; £2,800; £1,396; £699; £351) **Stalls** Low

Form RPR
3002 **1** **Mashaahed**[15] 6298 4-9-2 112.. RHills 2 105
(B W Hills) *mde all: rdn over 1f out: r.o* **9/4**[2]

3321 **2** *nk* **Fairmile**[22] 6153 5-9-2 113.. TedDurcan 5 104+
(Saeed Bin Suroor) *hld up: hdwy over 1f out: rdn to chse wnr and hung lft ins fnl f: r.o* **8/11**[1]

2400 **3** *1* **Pinpoint (IRE)**[28] 6011 5-9-2 109.. AdamKirby 1 102
(W R Swinburn) *chsd wnr: rdn over 1f out: styd on same pce ins fnl f* **7/1**[3]

1614 **4** *2 1/2* **Viva La Flag (USA)**[42] 5639 3-8-7 82................................(t) EddieAhern 4 92
(J L Dunlop) *chsd ldrs: rdn and edgd rt over 1f out: styd on same pce* **33/1**

4310 **5** *7* **Silca Key**[15] 6299 3-8-7 90.. JohnEgan 3 78
(M R Channon) *hld up in tch: rdn over 2f out: edgd rt and wknd over 1f out* **33/1**

2 **6** *13* **Rock Of Veio (IRE)**[50] 5378 3-8-12 90................................ JimmyFortune 6 57
(P W Chapple-Hyam) *racd alone tl jnd main gp over 8f out: hld up: rdn: hung rt and wknd over 1f out* **33/1**

2m 7.16s (1.45) **Going Correction** +0.125s/f (Good)
WFA 3 from 4yo+ 4lb **6** Ran SP% **110.0**
Speed ratings (Par 111): **99,98,97,95,90 79**
CSF £4.05 TOTE £2.80: £1.70, £1.10; EX 4.70.

Owner Hamdan Al Maktoum **Bred** Lightbody Celebration Cakes **Trained** Lambourn, Berks

FOCUS
A tactical race and dubious form as a result with the first three below form and the fourth to his best.

NOTEBOOK
Mashaahed usually competes in better races than this, and he had shown his well-being with a good second in a Group 3 race here last month. Richard Hills has his critics but he is dangerous when allowed an easy lead, and that is what he got here. He set steady fractions early on before winding things up, and always had things under control. The colt will now continue his career in Dubai. (tchd 2-1 and 5-2)
Fairmile could not match his recent York form in what was a tactical affair. Held up out the back, the steady early pace was all against him and he did not settle. Nevertheless, he picked up well to challenge the leader inside the last but just could not get by. He was the best horse in the race but things did not fall his way. (op 4-5 tchd 5-6)
Pinpoint(IRE) tracked the winner throughout and could not get by him. He had every chance and has the look of a twilight horse now. (op 11-2 tchd 8-1)
Viva La Flag(USA), beaten in a handicap off 83 last time out, had little chance against some smart opponents, but he beat his fellow rags well enough. (op 28-1)
Rock Of Veio(IRE) Official explanation: jockey said colt moved poorly

6654 BET365 BEST ODDS GUARANTEED ON EVERY RACE H'CAP 1m
3:15 (3:18) (Class 2) (0-100,95) 3-Y-O+

£12,464 (£3,732; £1,866; £934; £466; £234) **Stalls** Low

Form RPR
6030 **1** **Very Wise**[28] 6011 5-9-5 **94**.. JimmyFortune 7 107
(W J Haggas) *hld up in tch: led 2f out: sn rdn and hung lft: r.o* **7/1**[3]

2051 **2** *1 1/4* **Kinsya**[5] 6539 4-9-4 **93** 6ex.. SebSanders 2 103
(M H Tompkins) *hld up in tch: rdn and nt clr run 2f out: swtchd lft over 1f out: chsd wnr ins fnl f: r.o* **5/1**[1]

0003 **3** *3 1/2* **Capable Guest (IRE)**[15] 6301 5-8-13 **88**........................(v) ChrisCatlin 5 90
(M R Channon) *hld up: rdn over 3f out: nt clr run over 2f out: r.o ins fnl f: nt trble ldrs* **8/1**

4020 **4** *2* **Prince Of Thebes (IRE)**[15] 6301 6-8-11 **86**........................ PaulDoe 11 83
(J Akehurst) *prom: chsd ldr 3f out: sn rdn: wknd fnl f* **15/2**

2100 **5** *hd* **Bid For Glory**[22] 6155 3-9-1 **92**.. RichardHughes 1 89
(H J Collingridge) *trckd ldrs: rdn over 2f out: wknd ins fnl f* **10/1**

0300 **6** *1* **Blue Rocket (IRE)**[8] 6472 3-8-13 **90**.. JohnEgan 4 85
(D J Murphy) *hld up: hdwy and hung lft over 1f out: wknd ins fnl f* **40/1**

2550 **7** *shd* **Chicken Soup**[21] 6183 5-9-6 **95**.. NCallan 8 89
(D J Murphy) *s.i.s: hld up: hdwy over 1f out: wknd ins fnl f* **33/1**

3213 **8** *nk* **Voliere**[20] 6208 4-8-6 **81** oh1.. EddieAhern 13 75
(S C Williams) *hld up: hdwy over 2f out: rdn to chse wnr over 1f out: sn hung lft: wknd ins fnl f* **20/1**

0650 **9** *1 1/2* **Rain Stops Play (IRE)**[5] 6539 5-8-3 **81** oh3............... WilliamBuick(3) 6 71
(M Quinn) *led: rdn and hung rt over 2f out: sn hdd: wkng whn nt clr run fnl f* **16/1**

0061 **10** *shd* **Damika (IRE)**[15] 6301 4-9-6 **95**.. TedDurcan 3 85+
(R M Whitaker) *hld up: rdn over 2f out: nt clr run over 1f out: n.d* **9/1**

1040 **11** *1* **Danehillsundance (IRE)**[15] 6301 3-9-2 **93**.................... RyanMoore 10 81
(R Hannon) *s.i.s: hld up: effrt over 1f out: n.d* **6/1**[2]

2100 **12** *1 1/2* **South Cape**[15] 6301 4-8-10 **92**.. MatthewDavies(7) 14 76
(M R Channon) *chsd ldrs: wkng whn n.m.r over 1f out* **25/1**

2303 **13** *1 3/4* **Hazzard County (USA)**[22] 6143 3-8-10 **87**................ RichardMullen 12 67
(D M Simcock) *hld up in tch: rdn over 2f out: wknd over 1f out* **16/1**

0P6 **14** *4* **Zero Tolerance (IRE)**[21] 6172 7-8-10 **85**........................ MartinDwyer 9 56
(T D Barron) *chsd ldr tl rdn over 3f out: wknd 2f out* **10/1**

1m 38.48s (-0.89) **Going Correction** +0.125s/f (Good)
WFA 3 from 4yo+ 2lb **14** Ran SP% **120.3**
Speed ratings (Par 109): **109,107,104,102,102 101,100,100,99,99 98,96,94,90**
CSF £40.05 CT £292.87 TOTE £8.40: £3.00, £2.10, £2.70; EX 54.20 Trifecta £634.00 Pool: £982.34 - 1.10 winning tickets..

Owner J M Greetham **Bred** J M Greetham **Trained** Newmarket, Suffolk

FOCUS
A competitive handicap on paper but a number of these looked to have had enough for the year. The time was reasonable, however, and the form appears solid enough rated around the principals.

NOTEBOOK
Very Wise bounced back to his Lincoln-winning form and relished the climb to the line from the Dip, staying on really well for an authoritative win. He will no doubt be aimed at the Lincoln again next spring, and will deserve respect in his bid to repeat. (tchd 8-1)
Kinsya came out of the pack to chase the winner home. This was a good effort under his 6lb penalty, and for the second year running he is ending the turf campaign in great form. (op 11-2 tchd 6-1)
Capable Guest(IRE) stayed on from off the pace but was never a threat to the first two. He comprehensively reversed recent course form with Damika, but has never been the easiest to predict and has a poor strike-rate for a horse of his ability.
Prince Of Thebes(IRE) had work to do off his new mark but performed creditably. At his best in a small field on fast ground, his record on good to firm over 7f and 1m in a field of nine runners or fewer is four wins from five starts. (op 8-1)
Bid For Glory, running off a mark just 2lb higher than when successful at Nottingham in June, came into the race fresher than most, having enjoyed a three-month break in the summer. He ran no more than a fair race, though. (tchd 9-1)
Blue Rocket(IRE), who is not a miler, has run all her best races fresh. She won her maiden first time out, ran third in the Nell Gwyn on her seasonal reappearance and, on her return from a summer's break, finished third in a Listed race at Hamilton. Her other efforts do not compare with those performances. (op 33-1)
Chicken Soup did not get the clearest of runs but made little headway once the gap finally did arrive. (op 40-1)
Hazzard County(USA) Official explanation: jockey said colt was unsuited by the good ground
Zero Tolerance(IRE) Official explanation: jockey said gelding lost its action and was unsuited by the good ground

6655 BET365 BEN MARSHALL STKS (LISTED RACE) 1m
3:50 (3:50) (Class 1) 3-Y-O+

£14,762 (£5,595; £2,800; £1,396; £699; £351) **Stalls** Low

Form RPR
5004 **1** **Jalmira (IRE)**[14] 6349 6-8-11 0.. WJLee 1 107
(C F Swan, Ire) *hld up: hdwy over 2f out: rdn to ld wl ins fnl f: r.o* **8/1**

0124 **2** *nk* **Tell**[15] 6298 4-8-13 111..(b) EddieAhern 10 108
(J L Dunlop) *chsd ldrs: rdn and edgd lft over 1f out: ev ch ins fnl f: styd on* **3/1**[1]

4300 **3** *nk* **Caldra (IRE)**[14] 6332 3-8-11 104.. RichardHughes 5 107
(S Kirk) *led: rdn over 1f out: hdd wl ins fnl f* **14/1**

3150 **4** *nk* **Kapil (SAF)**[14] 6338 5-9-2 0..(b[1]) RyanMoore 3 110
(M F De Kock, South Africa) *hld up: swtchd rt and hdwy over 1f out: sn rdn: r.o* **5/1**[3]

-043 **5** *4* **Caradak (IRE)**[28] 6018 6-8-13 108.. TedDurcan 8 97
(Saeed Bin Suroor) *chsd ldrs: rdn over 1f out: edgd lft and no ex fnl f* **7/2**[2]

0201 **6** *10* **Smart Enough**[20] 6198 4-8-13 105.. SteveDrowne 6 74
(M A Magnusson) *chsd ldr: rdn over 2f out: wknd over 1f out* **7/2**[2]

5200 **7** *2* **Striving Storm (USA)**[77] 4627 3-8-11 105 JimmyFortune 7 70
(P W Chapple-Hyam) *prom 5f* **20/1**

101 **8** *6* **European Dream (IRE)**[21] 3513 4-8-13 103 JohnEgan 9 56
(R C Guest) *sn pushed along in rr: rdn 1/2-way: sn wknd* **16/1**

1m 37.52s (-1.85) **Going Correction** +0.125s/f (Good)
WFA 3 from 4yo+ 2lb **8** Ran SP% **114.5**
Speed ratings (Par 111): **114,113,113,113,109 99,97,91**
CSF £32.34 TOTE £9.30: £2.30, £1.60, £3.90; EX 33.20 TRIFECTA Not won. Place 6 £92.30, Place 5 £16.61.
Owner Green Dragon Syndicate **Bred** Ivan & Mrs Eileen Heanen **Trained** Cloughjordan, Co Tipperary

FOCUS
An ordinary race by Listed standards, despite the sound gallop, but improved form again from the winner.

NOTEBOOK
Jalmira(IRE) has been in great form this autumn, winning a Listed race at Cork on her last start, but that meant she had a penalty to carry. That left her with a bit to do, but she travelled well off the pace before seeing out the trip in good fashion on her first start in this country. She is progressing and could be capable of winning a Group race abroad on this evidence. (op 12-1)
Tell had run well in Group 3 races on his last two starts so was understandably favoured on this drop in class. He raced on the outside of the field, which may not have been an advantage, but he had every chance and came up just short. (op 11-4)
Caldra(IRE) made the running up the stands' rail, which looked to be the place to be, and took a bit of passing. This was a good effort considering his best performances have been on easier ground. (op 12-1)
Kapil(SAF), who had his first race for six months over 6f here on Champions Day, was back over a more suitable trip this time and ran on late once switched out wide. The first-time blinkers seemed to have their effect but a stronger pace would have suited him. (tchd 11-2)
Caradak(IRE) was a Group 1 winner last autumn but he has been in nowhere near that form this term. This was another disappointing effort. (tchd 10-3 and 4-1)
Smart Enough, who won a conditions event at Bath last time, could not match that performance here and was another who badly disappointed. (op 4-1 tchd 9-2)
Striving Storm(USA) Official explanation: jockey said colt hung left
European Dream(IRE) Official explanation: jockey said gelding had no more to give
T/Plt: £197.50 to a £1 stake. Pool: £71,543.25. 264.35 winning tickets. T/Qpdt: £7.20 to a £1 stake. Pool: £5,448.30. 556.00 winning tickets. CR

6663 - (Foreign Racing) - See Raceform Interactive

6601 LINGFIELD (L-H)
Sunday, November 4

OFFICIAL GOING: Standard
Wind: Almost nil Weather: Fine

6664 LINGFIELD PARK FOR WEDDINGS MEDIAN AUCTION MAIDEN FILLIES' STKS 7f (P)
1:00 (1:00) (Class 6) 2-Y-O **£2,832** (£836; £418) **Stalls** Low

Form RPR

5 **1** **Al Aqabah (IRE)**[12] 6403 2-9-0 0 GregFairley 6 73
(B Gubby) *hld up in tch: n.m.r over 5f out: pushed along and prog over 2f out: rdn on outer and r.o to ld last 100yds: sn clr* **4/1**[3]

3353 **2** *1 1/4* **Monashee Rock (IRE)**[6] 6535 2-9-0 77 DaneO'Neill 4 70
(M Salaman) *cl up on inner: effrt to ld 1f out: hdd and outpcd last 100yds* **11/8**[1]

3 *1* **Spanish Springs (IRE)** 2-9-0 0 JimmyFortune 3 67
(J H M Gosden) *in tch: effrt 2f out: shkn up over 1f out: styd on fnl f: nt pce to trble wnr* **10/3**[2]

4 *3/4* **Shesha Bear** 2-9-0 0 MartinDwyer 2 65
(W R Muir) *dwlt: settled in last: promising prog on inner wl over 1f out: pushed along and outpcd last 150yds* **14/1**

5 *1 1/4* **Istria (USA)** 2-9-0 0 JamesDoyle 9 62
(R M Beckett) *off the pce in last pair: pushed along over 2f out: picked up and r.o ins fnl f: nrst fin* **16/1**

635 **6** *1 1/4* **Oceana Blue**[31] 5944 2-9-0 71 SteveDrowne 5 59
(A M Balding) *mostly chsd ldr to wl over 1f out: sn btn* **15/2**

000 **7** *nk* **Lady Docker (IRE)**[12] 6403 2-9-0 42 RobertHavlin 8 58
(H J L Dunlop) *led: gng wl enough 2f out: hdd & wknd 1f out* **66/1**

00 **8** *6* **Les Allues (IRE)**[58] 5186 2-9-0 0 AdrianMcCarthy 7 43
(H S Howe) *prom on outer: pushed along 3f out: wknd 2f out* **100/1**

1m 25.74s (-0.15) **Going Correction** -0.20s/f (Stan) **8** Ran SP% **112.0**
Speed ratings (Par 91): **92,90,89,88,87 85,85,78**
CSF £9.44 TOTE £4.00: £1.20, £1.50, £1.60; EX 13.20 Trifecta £39.50 Part won. Pool £55.56 - 0.10 winning units..
Owner Brian Gubby **Bred** Ocal Bloodstock **Trained** Bagshot, Surrey

FOCUS
A fair maiden likely to produce its share of winners but rated slightly negatively around the runner-up and sixth.

NOTEBOOK
Al Aqabah(IRE), a keeping-on fifth over 6f at the course on debut, caught the eye of many that day and this step up to 7f was expected to prove much more suitable. Again towards the rear early, she got a little outpaced turning in, but ran on strongly down the outside and finished well on top close home. This run suggests she will get 1m in time and there should be more to come from the daughter of Redback. (op 9-2)
Monashee Rock(IRE) has been running well in fair maidens at some of the bigger tracks, so it was easy to see whyt she was a short-priced favourite. However, the inside is not the place to be here at the moment and, having gone to the front over a furlong out, the winner swept past her. She has shown enough to suggest a small race will come her way, although 77 is a stiff enough mark for when she goes handicapping. (op 15-8 tchd 2-1 in a place)
Spanish Springs(IRE), a half-sister to high-class UAE sprinter Conroy, comes from a yard that is more than capable of readying one to win first time up and she appeared to know her job, but just lacked the pace to make a race of it with the front pair. This was a pleasing start and finding a similar race should prove a formality. (op 11-4 tchd 7-2)
Shesha Bear, a 16,000gns daughter of Tobougg, comes from a yard that is going well at the moment and she shaped with plenty of potential on this racecourse debut, running on well down the straight despite racing towards the inner. The experience will not be lost on her and she looks another ready-made winner. (op 11-1)
Istria(USA) showed distinct signs of inexperience on this racecourse debut, but she was at least finishing off to good effect and can be expected to come on for the run. Her yard does well with their juveniles and she looks capable of winning a small maiden. (op 12-1)

6665 LINGFIELDPARK.CO.UK NURSERY 7f (P)
1:30 (1:30) (Class 5) (0-75,75) 2-Y-O **£3,886** (£1,156; £577; £288) **Stalls** Low

Form RPR

0033 **1** **Flying Applause**[54] 5314 2-8-12 66 DaneO'Neill 2 70
(A King) *chsd ldr over 4f out: rdn to ld wl over 1f out: styd on wl fnl f* **4/1**[3]

0063 **2** *1 1/4* **Splash The Cash**[11] 6438 2-8-7 61 MartinDwyer 4 62
(K A Ryan) *hld up in last pair: gd prog on inner fr 3f out: chsd wnr ins fnl f: kpt on but no imp* **6/1**

0433 **3** *1 1/4* **Hit The Roof**[27] 6058 2-9-7 75 RyanMoore 9 73
(R Hannon) *chsd ldr to over 4f out: sn rdn: struggling over 2f out: styd on again fr over 1f out to take 3rd ins fnl f* **7/2**[2]

0200 **4** *3/4* **Vigano (IRE)**[95] 4065 2-9-2 70 JDSmith 5 66
(S Kirk) *hld up in last trio: effrt on wd outside 2f out: stl in last trio over 1f out: rdn and r.o wl fnl f: nrst fin* **50/1**

662 **5** *shd* **Wavertree Princess (IRE)**[51] 5380 2-9-7 75 JamesDoyle 1 70
(N P Littmoden) *trckd ldrs: wnt 3rd over 2f out: no imp over 1f out: one pce* **16/1**

046 **6** *3/4* **Tense (IRE)**[50] 5428 2-9-3 71 JimCrowley 11 64
(J A Osborne) *hld up towards rr on outer: outpcd over 2f out: shkn up ent fnl f: styd on: nvr nr ldrs* **16/1**

0050 **7** *hd* **Bazguy**[4] 6584 2-9-0 68 (b[1]) TGMcLaughlin 8 61
(P D Evans) *led to wl over 1f out: wknd fnl f* **33/1**

3460 **8** *2 1/2* **Black Dahlia**[9] 6471 2-9-0 68 SteveDrowne 10 54
(A J McCabe) *chsd ldrs: rdn over 2f out: no prog over 1f out: wknd fnl f* **10/3**[1]

3040 **9** *hd* **Park Royal (UAE)**[10] 6449 2-9-4 72 GregFairley 6 58
(M Johnston) *nvr gng wl and sn pushed along in last pair: modest late prog* **13/2**

200 **10** *2 1/2* **Toasted Special (USA)**[18] 6267 2-8-10 64 RobertHavlin 5 43
(B J Meehan) *lost midfield pl 4f out: struggling in rr 3f out* **33/1**

0310 **11** *5* **Geordie Girl**[15] 6328 2-8-11 68 DuranFentiman[(3)] 7 34
(R C Guest) *nvr beyond midfield: pushed along over 3f out: wknd 2f out* **33/1**

1m 25.06s (-0.83) **Going Correction** -0.20s/f (Stan) **11** Ran SP% **115.5**
Speed ratings (Par 96): **96,94,93,92,92 91,91,88,88,85 79**
CSF £26.83 CT £92.86 TOTE £4.30: £1.70, £2.60, £1.40; EX 34.20 Trifecta £43.50 Pool £98.22 - 1.60 winning units..
Owner Four Mile Racing **Bred** G H Beeby And Viscount Marchwood **Trained** Barbury Castle, Wilts

FOCUS
A modest nursery run in a quicker time than the opening maiden and solid enough form rated through the third.

NOTEBOOK
Flying Applause has been running well in defeat off similar marks and a reproduction of his latest effort, when third at the course on turf, was good enough for him to get off the mark. This was not a good race, but he was always well positioned to strike and fully deserved the victory. He will need to progress further to defy a rise though. (op 7-1)
Splash The Cash, dropped 6lb having been beaten in a claimer at the course last month, was making his debut for the Ryan yard and showed a marked improvement in form for the step up in trip. His best chance of winning may still be in claimers. (tchd 5-1)
Hit The Roof showed a consistent level of fair form in maidens, including on Polytrack, but he was found wanting for pace on this drop back to 7f. He was unsurprisingly going on well close home and should find a similar race back at 1m. (op 9-2 tchd 3-1)
Vigano(IRE) had disappointed on two previous tries in handicaps, but he had slipped to a mark of 70 and made rapid progress out wide inside the final furlong to claim a never-nearer fourth. This seems the way to ride him and he will always require a slice of luck in running, but this effort suggested a race will come his way before long. (op 66-1)
Wavertree Princess(IRE) ran her best race to date on this step up in trip, but was always likely to prove vulnerable under top weight and could not race on in the straight. (op 14-1)
Tense(IRE) was another to make some good late headway having been well in rear early on, seeming to improve for the extra furlong. She is another who will be interesting in a similar contest off this sort of mark. (op 12-1)
Black Dahlia reportedly had no more to give in the straight and was the main disappointment of the race. Official explanation: jockey said filly had no more to give (tchd 7-2)

6666 ARENALEISUREPLC.COM H'CAP 1m 5f (P)
2:05 (2:05) (Class 5) (0-75,73) 3-Y-O+ **£3,238** (£963; £481; £240) **Stalls** Low

Form RPR

-066 **1** **Grande Caiman (IRE)**[24] 6132 3-9-3 72 RyanMoore 3 87+
(R Hannon) *trckd ldng trio: wnt 2nd wl over 2f out: rdn to ld over 1f out: styd on wl* **7/2**[2]

-440 **2** *1 1/2* **Wraith**[17] 6286 3-9-1 70 MartinDwyer 7 83
(H R A Cecil) *trckd ldr after 3f: led wl over 3f out: drvn and hdd over 1f out: clr of rest and kpt on but readily hld* **9/2**[3]

316 **3** *7* **Wait For The Will (USA)**[78] 4597 11-9-1 70 (b) RossAtkinson[(7)] 1 72
(G L Moore) *blind stl on whn stalls opened: hld up in last pair: outpcd over 2f out: pushed along to take modest 3rd jst ins fnl f: styd on: no ch* **8/1**

3314 **4** *3* **Constant Cheers (IRE)**[25] 6102 4-9-2 64 (p) AdamKirby 2 62
(W R Swinburn) *trckd ldr 3f: styd cl up tl easily outpcd fr over 2f out: wknd fnl f* **3/1**[1]

5310 **5** *1/2* **Top Tiger**[23] 6158 3-9-2 71 PaulMulrennan 5 68
(M H Tompkins) *plld hrd: hld up in 5th: lost grnd on inner wl over 2f out: no ch after and no prog* **9/2**[3]

/0-0 **6** *shd* **Kingkohler (IRE)**[19] 3567 8-9-0 62 JamesDoyle 6 59
(K A Morgan) *stdd s: hld up in last pair: effrt 3f out: sn wl outpcd and btn* **33/1**

6160 **7** *15* **Global Strategy**[17] 6276 4-9-11 73 ChrisCatlin 4 47
(Rae Guest) *led to over 3f out: wknd rapidly over 2f out: t.o* **6/1**

2m 45.04s (-3.26) **Going Correction** -0.20s/f (Stan)
WFA 3 from 4yo+ 7lb **7** Ran SP% **111.9**
Speed ratings (Par 103): **102,101,96,94,94 94,85**
CSF £18.65 TOTE £3.60: £2.00, £2.50; EX 18.80.
Owner I A N Wight **Bred** Sweet Retreat Syndicate **Trained** East Everleigh, Wilts

FOCUS
Two drew clear of the steady gallop in what was a modest handicap. The form may not be the most solid but the first two were clear and they can win more races.
Top Tiger Official explanation: jockey said colt ran too free

6667 LINGFIELD PARK GOLF COURSE H'CAP 6f (P)
2:35 (2:35) (Class 4) (0-80,78) 3-Y-O+ **£5,181** (£1,541; £770; £384) **Stalls** Low

Form RPR

3360 **1** **Sunoverregun**[29] 6002 3-9-2 76 PatCosgrave 8 83
(J R Boyle) *pressed ldr: disp ld fr over 3f out: minimal advantage over 1f out: jst hld on* **33/1**

3321 **2** *shd* **Hotham**[38] 5747 4-8-12 72 ChrisCatlin 3 78
(N Wilson) *t.k.h: hld up bhd ldrs: rdn and effrt 2f out: styd on to chal fnl f: jst failed* **10/1**

530 **3** *nk* **Idle Power (IRE)**[21] 6205 9-8-13 73 AmirQuinn 4 78
(J R Boyle) *led to over 3f out: styd w ldrs: upsides fnl f: no ex last strides* **5/1**[3]

1501 **4** *shd* **Cativo Cavallino**[24] 6122 4-8-13 **78**........................ NataliaGemelova(5) 9 83
(J E Long) *jnd ldrs on outer over 3f out: disp after tl over 1f out: kpt on fnl f but jst hld* **2/1**[1]

311 **5** *nk* **Carcinetto (IRE)**[16] 6313 5-9-2 **76**.................................. TGMcLaughlin 5 80
(P D Evans) *chsd ldrs: rdn wl over 2f out: styd on fr over 1f out on wd outside: nrst fin* **9/1**

3440 **6** *shd* **Carmenero (GER)**[20] 6232 4-8-13 **73**............................... MartinDwyer 2 77
(W R Muir) *hld up in last trio: prog on inner 2f out: effrt to chal ins fnl f: one pce last 75yds* **13/2**

-502 **7** *1 3/4* **Bertie Southstreet**[18] 6273 4-9-0 **74**.................................. DaneO'Neill 7 72
(J R Best) *dwlt: t.k.h and hld up in last trio: outpcd whn dash for home started wl over 1f out: no imp after* **9/2**[2]

6430 **8** *1 1/4* **Buxton**[8] 6492 3-9-4 **78**...(b[1]) RobertHavlin 1 72
(R Ingram) *dwlt: sn in tch on outer: outpcd fr 2f out* **12/1**

5325 **9** *6* **Twosheetstothewind**[17] 6279 3-8-7 **67**............................. GregFairley 6 42
(C R Dore) *a in rr: bhd over 1f out* **20/1**

1m 11.5s (-1.31) **Going Correction** -0.20s/f (Stan) **9** Ran SP% **116.0**
Speed ratings (Par 105): **100,99,99,99,98 98,96,94,86**
CSF £328.75 CT £1952.94 TOTE £28.70: £3.70, £4.70, £2.30; EX 183.50 TRIFECTA Not won..
Owner Inside Track Racing Club **Bred** Howard Barton Stud **Trained** Epsom, Surrey

FOCUS
A shambles of a race with the slow early pace resulting in the first six home being separated by three short heads and two necks. The form has to be treated with caution but the principals were close to their marks.

6668 LINGFIELD PARK FOR CONFERENCES H'CAP 6f (P)
3:10 (3:11) (Class 3) (0-95,96) 3-Y-0+

£7,790 (£2,332; £1,166; £583; £291; £146) **Stalls** Low

Form RPR

2221 **1** **Tamagin (USA)**[9] 6472 4-9-5 **96**... RyanMoore 9 107
(K A Ryan) *taken down early: mde all and set str pce: rdn and wd bnd wl over 1f out: hrd pressed fnl f: kpt on gamely* **2/1**[1]

0006 **2** *3/4* **King's Caprice**[9] 6472 6-8-9 **89**....................................(t) TravisBlock(3) 7 98
(J A Geake) *taken down early: awkward s: sn pushed up and mostly chsd wnr: effrt on inner 2f out: nrly upsides ins fnl f: nt qckn nr fin* **12/1**

1020 **3** *1 1/4* **Little Edward**[15] 6327 9-8-12 **89**....................................... SteveDrowne 5 94+
(R J Hodges) *taken down early: hld up towards rr: effrt on wd outside 2f out: hanging and nt qckn over 1f out: styd on fnl f to take 3rd last stride* **8/1**

5100 **4** *hd* **Diane's Choice**[31] 5954 4-8-10 **87**.................................... DaneO'Neill 10 91
(J Akehurst) *gd spd fr wd draw to press ldrs: effrt to chal over 1f out: nt qckn last 150yds: lost 3rd fnl stride* **25/1**

0-00 **5** *1* **Andronikos**[161] 2058 5-9-2 **93**....................................(t) NelsonDeSouza 3 94
(P F I Cole) *trckd ldng quartet: drvn and nt qckn 1f out: one pce* **25/1**

0004 **6** *shd* **Resplendent Alpha**[47] 5512 3-8-10 **87**............................. ChrisCatlin 4 87
(P Howling) *pushed along in last trio 4f out: nvr on terms: kpt on u.p fnl f* **25/1**

4511 **7** *1/2* **Ajigolo**[14] 6355 4-9-3 **94**.. SamHitchcott 8 93
(M R Channon) *taken down early: racd wd in midfield: effrt over 1f out: no imp: fdd ins fnl f* **9/2**[3]

0433 **8** *1/2* **Wyatt Earp (IRE)**[9] 6472 6-8-8 **88**................................ JamieMoriarty(3) 6 92+
(R A Fahey) *pushed along in last pair and nvr gng the pce: starting to stay on but no ch whn nt clr run ins fnl f* **11/4**[2]

0100 **9** *1/2* **One More Round (USA)**[29] 6003 9-8-8 **90**................(b) PatrickHills(5) 2 86
(N P Littmoden) *dwlt: hld up in last pair: rdn and one pce on inner over 1f out* **12/1**

4600 **10** *9* **Cav Okay (IRE)**[21] 6197 3-8-7 **84**.................................... DavidKinsella 1 51
(R Hannon) *taken down early: prom: drvn and lost pl wl over 2f out: t.o* **50/1**

1m 10.56s (-2.25) **Going Correction** -0.20s/f (Stan) course record **10** Ran SP% **118.2**
Speed ratings (Par 107): **107,106,104,104,102 102,101,101,100,88**
CSF £26.92 CT £164.42 TOTE £2.90: £1.50, £4.10, £2.20; EX 35.20 TRIFECTA Not won..
Owner Tariq Al Nisf **Bred** Stonehaven Farm LLC **Trained** Hambleton, N Yorks

FOCUS
A good handicap run at a strong pace thanks to the winner and the form looks solid.

NOTEBOOK
Tamagin(USA) has shown greatly-improved form since joining current connections, finishing either first or second on all six starts coming into this, and he defied a further 7lb rise under an excellent ride from Moore. Asked to use up some gas in order to get the lead from his high draw, he went on to set a fast gallop and kept finding under pressure, having come wide into the straight. His rider was unable to pull him up after the line and he went on to complete almost another circuit, suggesting he still had plenty left. There is more to come and he looks capable of adding a valuable prize to his collection on Polytrack this winter. (op 5-2)
King's Caprice, 15lb lower than when last seen on Polytrack back in March, had to be ridden to gain a decent position, but came with his challenge towards the inside in the straight and was never quite getting to the winner. He has slipped to a very favourable mark and it will be surprising if he cannot take advantage before long. (op 11-1)
Little Edward, 7lb higher than when last winning, has never been the most consistent, but he was kept wide throughout here and ran one of his better races, finishing strongly having originally hung fire with his challenge. He is likely to continue to find a few too good off this mark.
Diane's Choice bounced back from a couple of modest efforts on turf and seemed to appreciate the return to Polytrack. She too burned up plenty of early pace in trying to overcome a wide draw.
Andronikos had his chance and could not quicken in the straight, but he has slipped to a career-low mark now and this was easily his best effort for some time.
Resplendent Alpha could make only limited late headway having been outpaced.
Ajigolo, on a hat-trick following wins over course and distance and more recently Wolverhampton, was up a further 4lb and he disappointed, failing to last home having been kept wide. (tchd 11-2)
Wyatt Earp(IRE) has been running well, but he was struggling from an early stage here and then got blocked when trying to come with a run late on. (op 7-2 tchd 5-2)

6669 HOTEL COMING TO LINGFIELD PARK H'CAP 1m 2f (P)
3:40 (3:40) (Class 4) (0-85,85) 3-Y-0+ **£5,181** (£1,541; £770; £384) **Stalls** Low

Form RPR

1423 **1** **Evident Pride (USA)**[41] 5685 4-9-8 **85**............................... DaneO'Neill 7 94
(B R Johnson) *trckd ldrs: prog over 3f out to go 3rd over 2f out: rdn to ld jst over 1f out: hld on nr fin* **2/1**[1]

4323 **2** *nk* **Mafeking (UAE)**[23] 6145 3-8-12 **79**.................................... RyanMoore 9 87
(M R Hoad) *hld up towards rr: stdy prog over 2f out: produced to chal ins fnl f: kpt on but nt qckn and hld nr fin* **11/4**[2]

0555 **3** *3/4* **Baylini**[8] 6492 3-8-11 **78** ow1... AdamKirby 11 85
(Ms J S Doyle) *hld up towards rr: stdy prog over 2f out: drvn over 1f out: styd on fnl f: nrst fin* **16/1**

0010 **4** *1 1/2* **Stargazer Jim (FR)**[14] 6359 5-9-2 **79**............................ PaulMulrennan 6 83
(W J Haggas) *t.k.h: hld up in rr of main gp: effrt over 2f out: rdn and r.o fr over 1f out to take 4th nr fin* **8/1**

6610 **5** *nk* **Wise Little Girl**[23] 6144 3-8-13 **80**................................ PhilipRobinson 2 83
(M A Jarvis) *prom: stl cl up over 1f out: nt qckn after* **13/2**[3]

4504 **6** *nk* **Wavertree Warrior (IRE)**[23] 6143 5-9-8 **85**....................(b) JamesDoyle 8 87
(N P Littmoden) *prom: jnd ldr over 2f out gng wl: upsides over 1f out: drvn and fnd nil: lost pls fnl f* **14/1**

4300 **7** *3* **Oakley Heffert (IRE)**[11] 6422 3-8-2 **74**..............(b) NataliaGemelova(5) 4 70
(R Hannon) *prom: led over 3f out: hdd on inner jst over 1f out: wknd* **20/1**

0-06 **8** *1* **Basra (IRE)**[23] 6143 4-8-12 **80**..................................... KevinGhunowa(5) 1 74
(Miss Jo Crowley) *led 2f: stdd: lost pl bdly over 3f out: bmpd along and one pce after* **14/1**

0600 **9** *2 1/2* **Seal Point (USA)**[11] 6435 3-8-12 **82**........................(b[1]) TravisBlock(3) 13 71
(Christian Wroe) *racd wd in midfield: cl enough over 3f out: sn rdn and lost pl* **66/1**

2515 **10** *1* **Morning Farewell**[179] 1584 3-8-10 **77**................................. MartinDwyer 10 64
(P W Chapple-Hyam) *led after 2f to over 3f out: sn btn* **14/1**

250- **11** *1/2* **Obrigado (USA)**[385] 5990 7-9-7 **84**...................................... ChrisCatlin 5 70
(Karen George) *t.k.h: hld up in rr of main gp: sme prog on wd outside 1/2-way: lost pl over 2f out: wknd* **40/1**

1-60 **12** *hd* **Circus Polka (USA)**[11] 6439 3-8-8 **75**........................ NelsonDeSouza 12 61
(P F I Cole) *a in last pair: detached and btn over 2f out* **16/1**

50 **13** *7* **Marsam (IRE)**[22] 6186 4-8-13 **76**................................... TGMcLaughlin 3 48
(M G Quinlan) *s.s: a detached in last: rdn and no prog 3f out* **33/1**

2m 4.42s (-3.37) **Going Correction** -0.20s/f (Stan)
WFA 3 from 4yo+ 4lb **13** Ran SP% **127.8**
Speed ratings (Par 105): **105,104,104,102,102 102,100,99,97,96 96,95,90**
CSF £7.59 CT £75.01 TOTE £3.30: £1.20, £1.90, £4.30; EX 12.80 Trifecta £60.80 Pool £180.90 - 2.11 winning units..
Owner C Lefevre **Bred** Juddmonte Farms Inc **Trained** Ashtead, Surrey

FOCUS
A most competitive handicap run at a good gallop and the form looks sound rated around the third and fourth.
Basra(IRE) Official explanation: jockey said gelding ran too flat
Seal Point(USA) Official explanation: jockey said colt hung right
Marsam(IRE) Official explanation: jockey said gelding never travelled

6670 BOOK YOUR CHRISTMAS PARTY NOW MEDIAN AUCTION MAIDEN STKS 7f (P)
4:10 (4:10) (Class 6) 3-5-Y-0 **£2,832** (£836; £418) **Stalls** Low

Form RPR

04-2 **1** **Multakka (IRE)**[25] 6097 4-9-4 80... RHills 6 74+
(M P Tregoning) *mde all: drew rt away fnl 2f: easily* **2/11**[1]

000 **2** *6* **Takaamul**[71] 4801 4-9-4 50... JamesDoyle 5 58
(K A Morgan) *in tch: chsd wnr over 2f out: kpt on but lft bhd fnl 2f* **12/1**[3]

000 **3** *4* **Batchworth Fleur**[27] 6062 4-8-13 45..................................... AdamKirby 1 42
(E A Wheeler) *hld up in last pair: prog to chse ldng pair 2f out: sn lft bhd* **25/1**

4 *1/2* **Cyril The Squirrel** 3-9-3 0.. ChrisCatlin 2 46
(Karen George) *s.s: hld up in last pair: outpcd over 2f out: plugged on fnl 2f* **33/1**

00 **5** *hd* **Rollin 'n Tumblin**[47] 5494 3-8-12 0............................ KirstyMilczarek(5) 7 45
(W Jarvis) *t.k.h: racd wd and in tch: outpcd over 2f out: no ch after* **12/1**[3]

46 **6** *1 3/4* **Imperial Amber**[202] 1068 5-8-10 0..................................... JerryO'Dwyer(3) 4 36
(Karen George) *dwlt: t.k.h and sn chsd wnr: rdn and wknd over 2f out* **10/1**[2]

000 **7** *2* **Ring Of Charm**[38] 5752 5-8-10 38..................................... TravisBlock(3) 3 30
(C J Down) *cl up on inner tl pushed along and lost pl 3f out: wknd over 1f out* **40/1**

1m 24.07s (-1.82) **Going Correction** -0.20s/f (Stan)
WFA 3 from 4yo+ 1lb **7** Ran SP% **118.3**
Speed ratings (Par 101): **102,95,90,90,89 87,85**
CSF £4.06 TOTE £1.20: £1.10, £3.20; EX 4.00 Place 6 £61.27, Place 5 £46.78..
Owner Hamdan Al Maktoum **Bred** Shadwell Estate Company Limited **Trained** Lambourn, Berks

FOCUS
As weak a maiden as you will find and Multakka could not help but win. The form is rated using the time with the placed horses not that solid.
T/Plt: £130.50 to a £1 stake. Pool: £51,478.75. 287.95 winning tickets. T/Qpdt: £70.60 to a £1 stake. Pool: £3,286.00. 34.40 winning tickets. JN

6624 WOLVERHAMPTON (A.W) (L-H)
Sunday, November 4

OFFICIAL GOING: Standard
Wind: Almost nil Weather: Overcast

6671 HORIZONS RESTAURANT H'CAP 5f 216y(P)
12:40 (12:40) (Class 6) (0-65,65) 3-Y-0+ **£2,184** (£644; £322) **Stalls** Low

Form RPR

0054 **1** **Figaro Flyer (IRE)**[6] 6533 4-9-0 **61**............................. SimonWhitworth 9 71
(P Howling) *hld up and bhd: hdwy over 2f out: rdn over 1f out: edgd lft and led wl ins fnl f: drvn out* **9/4**[1]

3150 **2** *1/2* **Tag Team (IRE)**[45] 5565 6-8-12 **59**............................ StephenDonohoe 8 67
(John A Harris) *led over 1f: led wl over 2f out: rdn wl over 1f out: hdd wl ins fnl f* **12/1**

5000 **3** *1/2* **Strathmore (IRE)**[17] 6283 3-9-3 **64**.................................. PaulHanagan 10 70
(R A Fahey) *hld up in rr: rdn and hung lft over 1f out: r.o ins fnl f: nrst fin* **25/1**

-500 **4** *3/4* **Wicked Uncle**[38] 5753 8-9-3 **64**.................................(v) J-PGuillambert 4 68
(S Gollings) *hld up in mid-div: hdwy on ins over 2f out: rdn to chse ldr wl over 1f out: nt qckn whn n.m.r wl ins fnl f* **40/1**

1630 **5** *1/2* **Plateau**[26] 6083 8-9-4 **65**... GeorgeBaker 6 67
(C R Dore) *chsd ldrs: rdn over 2f out: one pce fnl f* **15/2**

5000 **6** *shd* **Gilded Cove**[25] 6103 7-9-3 **64**.. JamieSpencer 5 66
(R Hollinshead) *s.i.s: in rr: c v wd st: rdn over 1f out: r.o ins fnl f: nvr nrr* **7/1**

0420 **7** *3/4* **Overwing (IRE)**[17] 6287 4-9-2 **63**...................................... OscarUrbina 2 63
(R M H Cowell) *sn prom: led over 4f out: hdd wl over 2f out: sn briefly nt clr run: rdn wl over 1f out: fdd ins fnl f* **6/1**[3]

2503 **8** *nk* **Monte Major (IRE)**[14] 6360 6-9-3 **64**............................... DeanMcKeown 11 63
(D Shaw) *hld up and sn in rr: hdwy wl over 1f out: rdn and no ex ins fnl f* **7/1**

300 **9** *2* **The Fisio**[20] 6239 7-9-1 **62**...(v) TomEaves 12 54
(S Gollings) *chsd ldrs: c wd st: rdn and wknd 1f out* **33/1**

3031 **10** *3 1/2* **Mistral Sky**[25] 6101 8-9-2 **63**...(v) MickyFenton 3 44
(Stef Liddiard) *s.i.s: sn mid-div: nt clr run on ins and lost pl wl over 3f out: sn bhd* **5/1**[2]

The Form Book, Raceform Ltd, Compton, RG20 6NL

-000 11 1 1/4 **Mulligans Pursuit (IRE)**[15] 6344 3-8-10 **57**..................(v) HayleyTurner 7 34
(M D I Usher) *bhd fnl 3f* **40/1**

1m 15.31s (-0.50) **Going Correction** -0.05s/f (Stan) **11** Ran SP% **117.8**

Speed ratings (Par 101): **101,100,99,98,98 97,96,96,93,89 87**

CSF £30.92 CT £536.07 TOTE £3.50: £1.50, £2.30, £8.80; EX 49.30.

Owner S J Hammond **Bred** Mohammad Al Qatami **Trained** Newmarket, Suffolk

■ Stewards' Enquiry : Stephen Donohoe caution: careless riding

FOCUS

A moderate sprint handicap run at a strong pace and not easy to rate with the runner-up the best guide.

Plateau Official explanation: jockey said gelding hung right

6672 RINGSIDE CONFERENCE SUITE H'CAP 1m 4f 50y(P)

1:10 (1:10) (Class 6) (0-65,66) 3-Y-0+ **£2,184** (£644; £322) **Stalls** Low

Form RPR

0-20 **1** **Gamesters Lady**[4] 6583 4-9-8 **59**.............................. GrahamGibbons 6 69
(W M Brisbourne) *mde all: rdn clr over 2f out: drvn out* **12/1**

0241 **2** 1 **Star Of Angels**[5] 6558 3-9-9 **66** 6ex.............................. J-PGuillambert 2 74
(M Johnston) *hld up towards rr: hdwy on ins 3f out: sn swtchd rt and rdn: r.o one pce fnl f* **7/4**[2]

4060 **3** 1/2 **Opera Writer (IRE)**[257] 507 4-9-3 **54**.............................. GeorgeBaker 8 61
(R Hollinshead) *stdd s: hld up in rr: hdwy whn nt clr run and swtchd lft 2f out: sn rdn: kpt on same pce fnl f* **7/1**[3]

5330 **4** 7 **Bret Maverick (IRE)**[13] 6380 3-8-9 **52**.............................. FrancisNorton 5 48
(B P J Baugh) *t.k.h: chsd ldr: disp ld 6f out tl over 3f out: wknd wl over 1f out* **33/1**

1450 **5** 2 1/2 **Desert Hawk**[15] 6342 6-9-4 **55**.............................. LiamJones 3 47
(W M Brisbourne) *hld up towards rr: hdwy on outside whn forced wd over 2f out: sn rdn: wknd wl over 1f out* **12/1**

6050 **6** 19 **Newcorp Lad**[38] 5750 7-8-5 **45**..............................(p) AndrewElliott(3) 7 7
(Mrs G S Rees) *prom: rdn over 3f out: sn wknd* **25/1**

5003 **7** 4 **My Sara**[195] 1194 3-9-2 **59**.............................. PaulHanagan 4 14
(R A Fahey) *hld up in mid-div: rdn over 3f out: sn bhd* **20/1**

4244 **8** 20 **Golden Wave (IRE)**[30] 5980 3-9-7 **64**.............................. JamieSpencer 1 —
(D M Simcock) *hld up in tch: rdn over 3f out: hld whn hmpd on ins 2f out: sn eased* **13/8**[1]

2m 41.12s (-1.30) **Going Correction** -0.05s/f (Stan)

WFA 3 from 4yo+ 6lb **8** Ran SP% **113.9**

Speed ratings (Par 101): **102,101,101,96,94 82,79,66**

CSF £32.76 CT £163.45 TOTE £13.00: £1.70, £1.50, £2.70; EX 41.80.

Owner Gamesters Partnership **Bred** D Timmis **Trained** Great Ness, Shropshire

FOCUS

A moderate handicap and the form looks good for the grade. The pace was just ordinary, but the winning time was still 0.41 seconds quicker than the following 56-70.

Golden Wave(IRE) Official explanation: jockey said filly never travelled

6673 BUY TICKETS ONLINE H'CAP 1m 4f 50y(P)

1:40 (1:40) (Class 5) (0-70,70) 3-Y-0 **£3,071** (£906; £453) **Stalls** Low

Form RPR

2350 **1** **Vallemeldee (IRE)**[16] 6308 3-9-4 **70**.............................. FrancisNorton 2 77+
(P W D'Arcy) *led 1f: a.p: led 2f out: hung lft wl over 1f out: eased cl home* **6/1**[3]

0035 **2** 1 1/4 **Zefooha (FR)**[16] 6308 3-8-12 **64**.............................. GrahamGibbons 3 68
(T D Walford) *hld up in tch: rdn over 3f out: outpcd 2f out: hung lft jst over 1f out: styd on to take 2nd post* **8/1**

4221 **3** hd **Pearl (IRE)**[11] 6420 3-9-4 **70**.............................. LiamJones 7 74
(W J Haggas) *led after 1f: rdn and hdd 2f out: kpt on same pce fnl f* **9/2**[2]

2213 **4** 3 1/2 **Bond Casino**[16] 6314 3-8-8 **60**.............................. TomEaves 1 58
(G R Oldroyd) *prom early: hld up: pushed along over 6f out: rdn 4f out: hdwy on ins wl over 1f out: no further prog* **8/1**

6650 **5** 3 **Global Traffic**[4] 6598 3-8-7 **66**.............................. RichardEvans(7) 6 59
(P D Evans) *stdd s: in rr: wl bhd 7f out: nvr nr ldrs* **20/1**

0654 **6** 2 1/2 **Iceman George**[20] 6235 3-8-11 **63**..............................(v) StephenDonohoe 5 52
(D Morris) *sn prom: disp ld over 4f out: wknd 2f out* **11/1**

4311 **7** 25 **Polyquest (IRE)**[18] 6265 3-8-13 **65**.............................. JamieSpencer 8 14
(G A Butler) *hld up: rdn over 3f out: sn struggling: eased whn no ch wl over 1f out* **5/4**[1]

2m 41.53s (-0.89) **Going Correction** -0.05s/f (Stan) **7** Ran SP% **112.2**

Speed ratings (Par 102): **100,99,99,96,94 93,76**

CSF £49.57 CT £233.78 TOTE £11.10: £3.10, £2.10; EX 61.80.

Owner Mrs Dot Burlton **Bred** Celbridge Estates Ltd **Trained** Newmarket, Suffolk

FOCUS

A modest handicap and, with the pace steady for much of the way, the winning time was 0.41 seconds slower than the previous 51-65. The form is weakened with the favourite running poorly but the first three were pretty close to some of their best form.

Pearl(IRE) Official explanation: jockey said eventual winner wobbled off the rails in front of his filly, meaning he had to stop riding temporarily to avoid clipping heels

Iceman George Official explanation: jockey said gelding lost its action

6674 SPONSOR A RACE BY CALLING 0870 220 2442 H'CAP 1m 141y(P)

2:15 (2:15) (Class 4) (0-85,86) 3-Y-0+ **£4,857** (£1,445; £722; £360) **Stalls** Low

Form RPR

0036 **1** **Master Pegasus**[25] 6110 4-9-2 **80**.............................. GeorgeBaker 8 91+
(C F Wall) *hld up in rr: rdn and hdwy to ld wl ins fnl f: r.o* **11/2**

0260 **2** 1 1/4 **Dichoh**[23] 6143 4-9-4 **82**.............................. MatthewHenry 3 90
(M A Jarvis) *sn chsng ldr: led 2f out: rdn over 1f out: hdd wl ins fnl f* **10/1**

5052 **3** shd **Fiefdom (IRE)**[11] 6435 5-9-4 **82**.............................. DanielTudhope 1 93+
(I W McInnes) *hld up towards rr: nt clr run 2f out and over 1f out: hung lft ins fnl f: r.o* **5/1**

0231 **4** nk **Councellor (FR)**[13] 6385 5-9-2 **80**..............................(t) MickyFenton 7 87
(Stef Liddiard) *a.p: ev ch 2f out: rdn and nt qckn ins fnl f* **14/1**

3105 **5** hd **Magical Music**[21] 6208 4-9-7 **85**.............................. JamieSpencer 6 91
(J Pearce) *hld up towards rr: rdn wl over 1f out: kpt on ins fnl f* **4/1**[2]

0501 **6** 1 1/2 **Gallantry**[13] 6391 5-9-8 **86**.............................. DeanMcKeown 5 89
(D Shaw) *s.i.s: hld up in mid-div: hdwy over 2f out: rdn wl over 1f out: no ex ins fnl f* **7/2**[1]

5204 **7** nk **Full Victory (IRE)**[6] 6539 5-9-2 **80**..............................(p) FrancisNorton 2 82
(R A Farrant) *led early: hld up in tch: rdn and sltly outpcd over 1f out: n.d after* **9/2**[3]

6000 **8** hd **Kamanda Laugh**[8] 5776 6-8-8 **75**..............................(b[1]) AndrewMullen(3) 4 77
(K A Ryan) *sn led: rdn and hdd 2f out: wknd wl ins fnl f* **16/1**

1m 50.23s (-1.53) **Going Correction** -0.05s/f (Stan) **8** Ran SP% **114.1**

Speed ratings (Par 105): **104,102,102,102,102 101,100,100**

CSF £57.78 CT £293.35 TOTE £5.00: £1.70, £4.20, £3.00; EX 47.30.

Owner Mrs J Roberts **Bred** Mrs Sally Roberts **Trained** Newmarket, Suffolk

FOCUS

A fair, competitive handicap run at a strong pace and the pace was sound. They finished in a bunch, but that is basically because there was not much between them. The third and fifth are the best guides to the level.

Magical Music Official explanation: jockey said filly hung right in straight

6675 STAY AT THE WOLVERHAMPTON HOLIDAY INN MEDIAN AUCTION MAIDEN STKS 1m 141y(P)

2:45 (2:45) (Class 6) 2-Y-0 **£2,184** (£644; £322) **Stalls** Low

Form RPR

6332 **1** **Formation (USA)**[11] 6436 2-9-3 77.............................. JamieSpencer 1 79+
(E A L Dunlop) *mde all: pushed clr whn flashed tail and edgd lft 1f out: easily* **4/11**[1]

24 **2** 4 **Tamasou (IRE)**[16] 6307 2-9-0 0.............................. DominicFox(3) 2 69
(S Parr) *a.p: wnt 2nd over 2f out: rdn over 1f out: no ch w wnr* **6/1**[2]

40 **3** 8 **Gaitskell**[83] 4459 2-9-3 0.............................. GrahamGibbons 4 52
(R Hollinshead) *hld up: hdwy over 2f out: rdn and wknd over 1f out* **20/1**[3]

06 **4** 4 **Bainisteoir**[24] 6125 2-9-3 0.............................. GeorgeBaker 5 44
(S Kirk) *chsd wnr tl hung rt over 2f out: rn wd ent st: sn wknd* **6/1**[2]

0 **5** 16 **Make Acquaintance**[37] 5770 2-8-12 0.............................. LiamJones 3 —
(M Mullineaux) *hld up: rdn over 3f out: sn toiling* **66/1**

1m 53.01s (1.25) **Going Correction** -0.05s/f (Stan) **15** Ran SP% **108.1**

Speed ratings (Par 94): **92,88,81,77,63**

CSF £2.88 TOTE £1.20: £1.02, £2.30; EX 1.50.

Owner Highclere Thoroughbred Racing (Tamarisk) **Bred** Loch Lea Farm **Trained** Newmarket, Suffolk

FOCUS

An uncompetitive maiden and not form to dwell on with the pace steady.

NOTEBOOK

Formation(USA) was far too good for this lot, but he was still unconvincing when asked to go and settle the race, hanging to his left and continually flashing his tail quite violently. Despite winning, he looks like one to avoid.

Tamasou(IRE), switched to Polytrack for the first time, showed ability in second, confirming the promise of his two previous runs, and should not be underestimated now he is qualified for a handicap mark. (tchd 13-2)

Gaitskell shaped nicely when fourth on his debut over 5f in April, but he showed nothing off the back of a four-month break over 6f round here last time. Returning from another absence, this time almost three months, he was beaten a long way and probably did not achieve a great deal in third. He will have more options now he is qualified for a handicap mark, but he has plenty to prove.

Bainisteoir, stepped up to his furthest trip to date and switched to Polytrack for the first time, did not appear to stay. He is now qualified for a handicap mark and could do better back over shorter. Official explanation: jockey said gelding hung right-handed under pressure (op 11-2)

6676 WOLVERHAMPTON-RACECOURSE.CO.UK H'CAP 5f 20y(P)

3:20 (3:20) (Class 3) (0-95,94) 3-Y-0+ **£8,970** (£2,668; £1,333; £666) **Stalls** Low

Form RPR

12-4 **1** **Chief Editor**[36] 5810 3-8-11 **87**.............................. JamieSpencer 6 99+
(M J Wallace) *hld up and bhd: nt clr run and swtchd rt wl over 1f out: edgd lft ent fnl f: r.o wl u.p to ld last stride* **9/4**[1]

0240 **2** shd **Turn On The Style**[94] 4090 5-9-2 **92**..............................(b) PaulHanagan 5 99
(J Balding) *w ldr: led over 3f out: clr over 2f out: rdn and edgd lft 1f out: hdd last stride* **4/1**[2]

1500 **3** nk **Invincible Force (IRE)**[15] 6327 3-9-4 **94**.............................. FrancisNorton 4 100
(Paul Green) *a.p: rdn over 1f out: r.o towards fin* **17/2**

0000 **4** nk **Golden Dixie (USA)**[9] 6472 8-9-0 **93**.............................. LukeMorris(3) 1 98
(R A Harris) *outpcd: r.o ins fnl f* **16/1**

2022 **5** 1/2 **Come Out Fighting**[41] 5673 4-9-1 **91**.............................. GrahamGibbons 7 94
(P A Blockley) *chsd ldrs: rdn wl over 1f out: kpt on ins fnl f* **5/1**[3]

1510 **6** 1/2 **Topflightcoolracer**[22] 6173 3-8-3 **82**.............................. AndrewElliott(3) 2 83
(Mrs G S Rees) *chsd ldrs: rdn whn nt clr run and swtchd rt 1f out: nt qckn whn n.m.r cl home* **14/1**

011U **7** shd **Kay Two (IRE)**[8] 6487 5-8-10 **86**..............................(p) HayleyTurner 3 87
(R J Price) *led over 1f: chsd ldr: rdn and edgd lft 1f out: no ex* **15/2**

1402 **8** 3 1/2 **River Thames**[36] 5806 4-8-7 **83**.............................. TomEaves 8 71
(K A Ryan) *outpcd* **9/1**

61.51 secs (-1.31) **Going Correction** -0.05s/f (Stan) **8** Ran SP% **112.3**

Speed ratings (Par 107): **108,107,107,106,106 105,105,99**

CSF £10.69 CT £61.38 TOTE £2.90: £1.40, £2.20, £2.50; EX 14.20.

Owner Mrs P Good **Bred** J R And Mrs P Good **Trained** Newmarket, Suffolk

■ Stewards' Enquiry : Luke Morris one-day ban: used whip with excessive frequency (Nov 15)

FOCUS

A very good sprint handicap with the runner-up a solid guide to the form.

NOTEBOOK

Chief Editor would have been unlucky loser had he not got up, as he was denied a clear run and had to switch round horses at the top of the straight. He had it all to do by the time he finally got in the clear, but he responded most willingly to strong pressure to reel in the tiring Turn On The Style. Racing for only the second time this year, he was able to confirm the promise he showed on his belated reappearance at Haydock and is a handicapper on the up. He is likely to be put away for the year now. (op 11-4 tchd 3-1)

Turn On The Style, although running some good races in defeat, failed to win on turf, but he had landed his last three starts on sand earlier in the year. Having shown bags of early speed, he held a clear lead early in the straight, but began to tire late on and was just reeled in by Chief Editor who, to be fair, would have been unlucky had he not won. His form figures over 5f on Polytrack now read 821112. (tchd 7-2)

Invincible Force(IRE), trying Polytrack for the first time on his 23rd-career outing, had every chance and ran to a very useful level in defeat. (op 10-1 tchd 11-1 and 8-1)

Golden Dixie(USA) has improved on turf lately and was racing off a mark 8lb higher than when last seen on sand. He lacked to speed to hold his position from his inside draw, but he kept on nicely in the straight and remains in good order. (op 14-1)

Come Out Fighting, having just his second outing on Polytrack and his first at Wolverhampton, had every chance. (op 11-2 tchd 9-2)

Topflightcoolracer had to switch off the far rail in the straight, and her apprentice had to stop riding near the line, but she was not unlucky. (op 12-1)

Kay Two(IRE), trying Polytrack for the first time (he once ran on dirt in Dubai), had his chance. (op 13-2)

River Thames was never going the pace. (op 11-1)

6677 CHRISTMAS PARTY TIME H'CAP 7f 32y(P)

3:50 (3:50) (Class 5) (0-70,76) 3-Y-0+ **£3,071** (£906; £453) **Stalls** High

Form RPR

0020 **1** **Parkview Love (USA)**[5] 6568 6-9-5 **70**..............................(v) DeanMcKeown 2 77
(D Shaw) *hld up in mid-div: hdwy over 4f out: rdn to ld ins fnl f: r.o* **16/1**

4042 **2** 1/2 **Elusive Warrior (USA)**[3] 6610 4-8-5 **56** oh1..............................(p) PaulHanagan 1 62
(R A Fahey) *led early: a.p: rdn and kpt on ins fnl f* **11/4**[1]

0210 **3** *hd* **Jilly Why (IRE)**^{3} [6610] 6-8-13 **64**..................................(b) FrancisNorton 8 69
(Paul Green) *sn chsng ldr: led over 2f out: rdn over 1f out: hdd ins fnl f: nt qckn* **25/1**

2324 **4** *2* **Obe Royal**^{3} [6610] 3-8-3 **62**..(p) RichardEvans$^{(7)}$ 3 62
(P D Evans) *hld up towards rr: n.m.r on ins wl over 4f out: hdwy over 1f out: rdn and one pce ins fnl f* **8/1**

0503 **5** *½* **Methaaly (IRE)**^{16} [6313] 4-9-3 **68**...................................... GeorgeBaker 7 66+
(M Mullineaux) *s.i.s: hdwy on outside whn hung rt over 2f out: rn wd ent st: kpt on same pce fnl f* **7/1**

-542 **6** *hd* **Robinzal**^{8} [6504] 5-8-9 **63**... LukeMorris$^{(3)}$ 4 61
(A W Carroll) *hld up towards rr: rdn and hdwy 2f out: no imp fnl f* **7/1**

4161 **7** *2½* **Hessian (IRE)**^{3} [6610] 3-9-10 **76** 6ex.............................. J-PGuillambert 5 67+
(P Howling) *broke wl: sn stdd towards rr: nt clr run and swtchd rt over 1f out: n.d* **10/3**^{2}

2400 **8** *1* **Moves Goodenough**^{11} [6423] 4-8-13 **64**......................(b) HayleyTurner 6 52
(Andrew Turnell) *hld up in mid-div: lost pl over 3f out: sn rdn and bhd* **25/1**

3601 **9** *2* **Another Genepi (USA)**^{33} [5893] 4-9-2 **67**..................(b) JamieSpencer 9 55
(K A Ryan) *dwlt: sn prom: rdn over 2f out: wknd over 1f out: eased whn btn ins fnl f* **4/1**^{3}

0100 **10** *½* **Kims Rose (IRE)**^{80} [4545] 4-8-5 **56** oh1............................. LiamJones 10 38
(R A Harris) *sn led: rdn and hdd over 2f out: wknd over 1f out* **66/1**

1m 29.86s (-0.54) **Going Correction** -0.05s/f (Stan)
WFA 3 from 4yo+ 1lb **10** Ran SP% **120.9**
Speed ratings (Par 103): **101,100,100,97,97 97,94,93,90,90**
CSF £61.42 CT £1172.38 TOTE £22.80: £4.50, £1.50, £5.90; EX 71.50 Place 6 £180.12, Place 5 £70.53..
Owner Danethorpe Racing Partnership **Bred** Mark Johnston Racing Ltd **Trained** Danethorpe, Notts

FOCUS
There was no pace on early and this was a rather messy race. The form should not be taken too literally despite the winner and third running to their marks.
Methaaly(IRE) Official explanation: jockey said filly hung right on bend
Another Genepi(USA) Official explanation: jockey said filly missed the break
T/Plt: £157.00 to a £1 stake. Pool: £38,035.85. 176.85 winning tickets. T/Qpdt: £32.40 to a £1 stake. Pool: £2,858.30. 65.10 winning tickets. KH

6523 CAPANNELLE (R-H)
Sunday, November 4

OFFICIAL GOING: Soft

6686a PREMIO C. & F. ALOISI (EX PREMIO UMBRIA) (GROUP 3) 6f
1:30 (1:35) 2-Y-0+ **£24,628** (£10,836; £5,911; £2,955)

RPR

1 **Dream Impact (USA)**^{112} 6-9-9 .... GMarcelli 2 108
(L Riccardi, Italy) *a cl up on rails: led 1f out: r.o wl (11.16/1)* **112/10**

2 *1¾* **Le Cadre Noir (IRE)**^{21} [6224] 3-9-12 .... MDemuro 5 106
(A Renzoni, Italy) *pressed ldr: led over 2f out: hrd rdn over 1f out: hdd 1f out: one pce* **3/20**^{1}

3 *nk* **Titus Shadow (IRE)**^{49} 3-9-9 .... DVargiu 6 102
(B Grizzetti, Italy) *led to over 2f out: kpt on steadily* **13/1**

4 *shd* **Velvet Revolver (IRE)**^{21} [6224] 4-9-5 .... EddieAhern 1 98
(L Riccardi, Italy) *towards rr on rails to 1/2-way: styd on fr over 1f out to jst miss 3rd* **94/10**^{2}

5 *nk* **Vago (IRE)**^{504} 4-9-9 .... MSanna 7 101
(M Gasparini, Italy) *outpcd early: hdwy on outside over 2f out: styd on one pce u.p* **154/10**

6 *6* **Lady Marmelade (ITY)**^{141} 4-9-5 .... MEsposito 4 79
(D Ducci, Italy) *nvr nr to chal* **22/1**

7 *3* **Reykon (IRE)**^{112} 3-9-9 .... GBietolini 8 74
(A Renzoni, Italy) *chsd ldrs tl wknd wl over 1f out* **98/10**^{3}

8 *2* **Hand And Seal (ARG)** 5-9-9 .... PAragoni 3 68
(M Grassi, Italy) *s.i.s: a outpcd* **44/1**

69.20 secs (-1.10) **8** Ran SP% **133.8**
(including one euro stakes): WIN 12.16; PL 1.33, 1.03, 1.37; DF 4.40.
Owner Scuderia Quattro Mori **Bred** Sez Who Thoroughbreds **Trained** Italy

6687a PREMIO RIBOT (GROUP 2) 1m
2:30 (2:42) 3-Y-0+ **£38,767** (£17,057; £9,304; £4,652)

RPR

1 **Santiago (GER)**^{28} [6045] 5-9-2 .... EBotti 6 112
(H Blume, Germany) *hld up: 8th st: gd hdwy over 1f out: led 150yds out: rdn clr: sn on top: r.o wl* **27/20**^{1}

2 *3* **Miles Gloriosus (USA)**^{14} [6372] 4-9-2 .... CFiocchi 10 106
(Maria Rita Salvioni, Italy) *hld up: 7th st: hdwy fr wl over f out: led 1f out to 150yds out: one pce* **31/10**^{2}

3 *3* **Il Cadetto**^{36} [5821] 3-9-1 .... EddieAhern 2 101
(L Di Dio, Italy) *a.p: 3rd st: ev ch wl over 1f out: one pce* **72/10**

4 *nse* **Sopran Promo (IRE)**^{21} [6223] 3-9-1 .... DVargiu 7 101
(B Grizzetti, Italy) *hld up: last to 2f out: gd hdwy on outside fnl f to jst miss 3rd* **71/10**

5 *nk* **Freemusic (IRE)**^{63} 3-9-1 .... MDemuro 5 100
(L Riccardi, Italy) *a.p: 2nd st: led 2f out to 1f out: one pce* **109/10**

6 *4½* **Ceprin (IRE)**^{203} 6-9-2 .... SLandi 3 90
(A & G Botti, Italy) *led to 2f out* **13/2**^{3}

7 *2* **Allied Winner (ARG)**^{140} 5-9-2 .... GMarcelli 4 86
(M Grassi, Italy) *trckd ldrs on outside: 5th st: btn over 2f out* **29/1**

8 *4½* **Amante Latino**^{49} 3-9-1 .... CColombi 9 78
(V Caruso, Italy) *prom: 6th st: btn 2f out* **67/10**

9 *4* **Adorabile Fong**^{532} [1872] 4-9-2 .... MEsposito 8 69
(M Guarnieri, Italy) *pressed ldrs: 4th st: wknd 2f out* **27/1**

1m 38.0s (-1.80)
WFA 3 from 4yo+ 2lb **9** Ran SP% **133.1**
WIN 2.35; PL 1.37, 1.46, 2.05; DF 4.66.
Owner Gestut Hof Vesterberg **Bred** Gestut Hof Vesterberg **Trained** Germany

6688a PREMIO GIUSEPPE VALIANI (EX PREMIO BUONTALENTA) (LISTED RACE) (F&M) 1m 2f
3:00 (3:17) 3-Y-0+ **£18,919** (£8,324; £4,541; £2,270)

RPR

1 **Les Fazzani (IRE)**^{7} [6524] 3-8-9 .... EddieAhern 4 104
(M J Wallace) *mid-div: 7th st: hdwy 3f out: drvn to ld wl over 1f out: rdn out* **31/10**^{1}

2 *1½* **Mimetico (IRE)**^{7} [6524] 3-8-9 ....(b) DVargiu 13 101
(B Grizzetti, Italy)

3 *3* **Penthouse Serenade (IRE)**^{141} 3-8-12 .... PConvertino 8 98
(M Massimi Jr, Italy)

4 *2½* **Mia Kross (IRE)**^{21} [6221] 4-8-11 .... NCallan 6 89
(B Grizzetti, Italy)

5 *nk* **Lasciatelapassare (IRE)**^{35} 3-8-12 .... GBietolini 18 93
(R Brogi, Italy)

6 *½* **Bertha Von Suttner**^{35} 3-8-12 .... TThulliez 17 92
(F Folco, Italy)

7 *hd* **Digital Photo (ITY)**^{35} 4-9-1 .... GErcegovic 2 91
(V di Napoli, Italy)

8 *hd* **Cockayne (IRE)**^{8} [6519] 4-8-11 .... CColombi 1 86
(V Valiani, Italy)

9 *1* **Camafin (IRE)** 3-8-9 .... MVargiu 15 86
(L Camici, Italy)

10 *6* **Paint In Green (IRE)**^{81} 3-8-12 .... EBotti 7 78
(A & G Botti, Italy)

11 *3* **Carta Canta (IRE)** 4-8-11 .... MSanna 3 67
(M Gasparini, Italy)

12 *hd* **Lamentation**^{35} 3-8-9 .... GMarcelli 16 69
(M Gasparini, Italy)

13 *½* **Madame Esperance**^{379} 3-8-9 .... SLandi 5 68
(A & G Botti, Italy)

14 *1* **Jasmine Joli (IRE)**^{35} 3-8-9 .... SBasile 11 66
(Mafalda Osthaus, Italy)

15 *nse* **Shibuni's Thea (IRE)**^{35} 3-8-9 .... NPinna 10 66
(V Valiani, Italy)

16 *1* **Miss Lorella (IRE)**^{511} [2493] 4-8-11 .... OFancera 14 62
(L Camici, Italy)

17 *hd* **Randomity (IRE)**^{424} 3-8-12 .... MEsposito 9 67
(M Guarnieri, Italy)

18 *1* **Vinea Federspiel (IRE)**^{28} [6046] 3-9-3 ....(b) MDemuro 12 70
(Werner Glanz, Germany)

2m 3.20s (-0.10)
WFA 3 from 4yo 4lb **18** Ran SP% **24.4**
WIN 4.10; PL 2.22, 3.08, 3.49; DF 23.91.
Owner Mike & Denise Dawes **Bred** J Erhardt & Mrs J Schonwalder **Trained** Newmarket, Suffolk

NOTEBOOK
Les Fazzani(IRE), sixth in a Group 1 race over this course and distance a week earlier, appreciated the underfoot conditions and drop in class and gained herself some valuable black type.

6689a PREMIO ROMA AT THE RACES (GROUP 1) 1m 2f
3:30 (3:59) 3-Y-0+ **£72,973** (£32,108; £17,514; £8,757)

RPR

1 **Pressing (IRE)**^{36} [5821] 4-9-2 .... NCallan 10 118
(M A Jarvis) *racd in 3rd: led over 2f out: drvn clr: r.o wl (exact odds 2.42/1)* **24/10**^{2}

2 *1½* **Monachesi (IRE)**^{19} 4-9-2 .... OFancera 5 115
(F & L Camici, Italy) *7th st: stl 7th 3f out: rdn and hdwy over 2f out: disp 2nd 100yds out: drvn to take 2nd cl home* **73/1**

3 *nse* **Boris De Deauville (IRE)**^{29} [6032] 4-9-2 .... TThulliez 2 115
(S Wattel, France) *a in tch: 4th st: wnt 2nd 2f out: one pce fnl f: lost 2nd cl home* **19/10**^{1}

4 *1½* **Cherry Mix (FR)**^{136} [2787] 6-9-2 .... EddieAhern 9 112
(Saeed Bin Suroor) *pressed ldr on outside: 2nd st: pushed along over 3f out: kpt on at one pce* **5/2**^{3}

5 *½* **Vol De Nuit**^{35} 6-9-2 .... MPasquale 1 111
(L Brogi, Italy) *led to over 2f out: stl 3rd 1f out: one pce* **15/2**

6 *½* **First Stream (GER)**^{42} [5671] 3-9-0 .... THellier 4 112
(Mario Hofer, Germany) *hld up: 8th st: styd on at one pce fnl 2f: nvr nr to chal* **56/10**

7 *3* **Distant Way (USA)**^{21} [6223] 6-9-2 .... MDemuro 3 105
(L Brogi, Italy) *last to 2f out: nvr a factor* **15/2**

8 *1½* **Speciano**^{36} [5821] 4-9-2 .... SLandi 6 102
(E Borromeo, Italy) *9th st: a bhd* **68/1**

9 *3* **Laverock (IRE)**^{21} [6223] 5-9-2 .... TedDurcan 7 96
(Saeed Bin Suroor) *midfield: cl 6th on outside st: 5th 3f out: rdn and btn over 2f out* **5/2**^{3}

10 *1½* **Hattan (IRE)**^{35} [5831] 5-9-2 .... JohnEgan 8 93
(C E Brittain) *5th st: 6th and rdn wl over 2f out: eased whn btn over 1f out* **76/10**

2m 2.10s (-1.20)
WFA 3 from 4yo+ 4lb **10** Ran SP% **174.1**
(including 1 Euro stake): WIN 3.42; PL 1.54, 6.25, 1.50; DF 113.08.
Owner Gary A Tanaka **Bred** Azienda Agricola Del Parco **Trained** Newmarket, Suffolk

NOTEBOOK
Pressing(IRE), winner of a Group 3 race at San Siro last time out, was sent for home with two furlongs to run in order to try and burn off the stouter stayers in the field, and the tactic worked. He could now go to Hong Kong.
Cherry Mix(FR) made all in this race last year but was denied an uncontested lead this time. Held early in the straight, he plugged on for fourth.
Laverock(IRE), who is ideally suited by 1m4f, lacked the pace to get involved.
Hattan(IRE), runner-up in this race last year, failed to run to anywhere near that form, but in fairness the ground was much softer than he would have liked.

6218 COLOGNE (R-H)

Sunday, November 4

OFFICIAL GOING: Soft

6690a KOLNER HERBST-STUTEN-MEILE (GROUP 3) (F&M) 1m

2:40 (3:11) 3-Y-O+ **£21,622** (£6,757; £3,378; £2,027)

RPR

1 **Vincennes**[17] 3-8-13 .... JVictoire 4 104
(H-A Pantall, France) *mde all: hrd rdn whn strly pressed under 2f out: hld on gamely u.p* **1/2**[1]

2 ¾ **Contentious (USA)**[16] 6299 3-8-13 .... DBoeuf 5 102
(J L Dunlop) *racd in 3rd: wnt 2nd on ins over 2f out: sn rdn to press wnr: ev ch tl no ex cl home* **118/10**

3 3½ **Laeya Star (GER)**[21] 6218 3-8-13 .... ABoschert 6 95
(U Ostmann, Germany) *racd in 2nd: 3rd over 2f out: kpt on but nt pce of first two* **37/10**[2]

4 2½ **Scoubidou (GER)**[126] 3148 3-8-13 .... J-PCarvalho 7 90
(H Blume, Germany) *racd in 4th or 5th: 4th st: one pce fr over 2f out* **51/10**[3]

5 1¼ **Tanja Belle (GER)**[21] 6218 4-9-2 .... JiriPalik 9 89
(W Hickst, Germany) *in tch on outside: pushed along bef 1/2-way: 5th st: sn rdn and nt qckn* **20/1**

6 2½ **Ledicea**[21] 6218 3-8-13 .... TMundry 8 83
(P Rau, Germany) *hld up in 7th: effrt on outside over 2f out: sn no imp* **143/10**

7 10 **Sasphee (GER)**[21] 6218 3-8-13 .... PVanDeKeere 2 63
(E Kurdu, Germany) *racd in 6th: nvr a factor* **47/1**

8 28 **Highness (GER)**[28] 6046 3-8-13 .... AStarke 1 7
(W Baltromei, Germany) *last virtually thrght: t.o fr over 1f out* **174/10**

1m 43.13s (4.74)
WFA 3 from 4yo 2lb 8 Ran SP% **131.0**
(including ten euro stakes): WIN 15; PL 11, 17, 12: SF 62.
Owner Sheikh Mohammed **Bred** Darley **Trained** France

NOTEBOOK
Contentious(USA) ran a blinder on her final start before crossing the Atlantic but, having virtually drawn level with Vincennes two furlongs out, she could never get past and had to give best in the last 50 yards.

5850 HANOVER (L-H)

Sunday, November 4

OFFICIAL GOING: Soft

6691a GROSSER PREIS DES AUTORING HANNOVER (GROUP 3) 1m

1:20 (1:42) 3-Y-O+ **£21,622** (£6,757; £3,378; £2,027)

RPR

1 **Mharadono (GER)**[28] 6045 4-9-4 .... WPanov 4 108
(P Hirschberger, Germany) *led 2f: pressed ldr tl led again ent st: drvn out* **6/1**

2 nk **Waky Love (GER)**[36] 3-8-6 .... JLermyte 6 98
(Frau J Meyer, Germany) *a cl up: 3rd st: chal wl over 1f out: hrd rdn and ev ch ins fnl f: no ex fnl 100yds* **53/10**

3 ¾ **Idealist (GER)**[28] 6045 5-9-0 .... WMongil 8 102
(J Hirschberger, Germany) *hld up: last 1/2-way: 5th st: hdwy over 2f out: hrd rdn and ev ch appr fnl f: one pce* **56/10**

4 3½ **Wonderful Day (GER)**[21] 6220 5-8-9 .... MKolb 7 90
(Frau C Brandstatter, Germany) *hld up: 7th st: styd on at one pce: nvr able to chal* **15/1**

5 4½ **Molly Max (GER)**[14] 6370 3-8-13 .... FilipMinarik 2 87
(Frau K Haustein, Germany) *led after 2f tl hdd ent st: btn over 1f out* **22/10**[1]

6 ½ **Lord Areion (GER)**[28] 6045 5-9-2 .... EPedroza 5 87
(C Sprengel, Germany) *6th st: nvr a factor* **4/1**[3]

7 nk **Global Champion**[30] 3-8-13 .... AHelfenbein 1 85
(Mario Hofer, Germany) *disp 3rd: 4th st: sn btn* **27/10**[2]

8 9 **Genios (GER)**[91] 4217 6-9-0 .... IMendizabal 3 66
(Dr A Bolte, Germany) *last st: a in rr* **23/1**

1m 46.59s (106.59)
WFA 3 from 4yo+ 2lb 8 Ran SP% **134.0**
(including 10 Euro stake): WIN 70; PL 18, 20, 21; SF 666.
Owner Stall Sonnenschein **Bred** Ralf Paulick **Trained** Germany

6671 WOLVERHAMPTON (A.W) (L-H)

Monday, November 5

OFFICIAL GOING: Standard

Wind: Moderate behind becoming fresh across Weather: Brief heavy shower after Race 3

6692 CENTREBET.COM CASINO MEDIAN AUCTION MAIDEN STKS 5f 20y(P)

1:50 (1:50) (Class 5) 2-Y-O **£2,968** (£876; £438) **Stalls Low**

Form RPR

62 1 **Another Socket**[14] 6386 2-8-12 0 .... GrahamGibbons 7 69+
(E S McMahon) *s.i.s: hld up in tch: wnt 2nd 2f out: rdn to ld ins fnl f: r.o* **11/8**[1]

455 2 ½ **Wild Bill Tracey**[30] 6004 2-9-3 72 .... JamieSpencer 1 72
(M J Wallace) *led: rdn over 1f out: hdd ins fnl f: nt qckn* **9/2**

0 3 ½ **My Mate Pete (IRE)**[26] 6105 2-9-3 0 .... SebSanders 3 70
(R M Beckett) *w ldr 3f: hrd rdn 1f out: kpt on towards fin* **7/2**[3]

0264 4 3 **Mandelieu (IRE)**[27] 6073 2-9-3 75 .... LiamJones 5 59
(W J Haggas) *w ldrs: rdn 2f out: wknd over 1f out* **10/3**[2]

000 5 2 **Feeling Fresh (IRE)**[11] 6456 2-9-3 60 ....(v[1]) FrancisNorton 2 52
(Paul Green) *s.i.s: rdn over 2f out: a bhd* **33/1**

00 6 5 **Stoneacre Baby (USA)**[21] 6225 2-8-12 0 .... LPKeniry 6 29
(Peter Grayson) *hld up: rdn over 2f out: sn struggling* **100/1**

62.35 secs (-0.47) **Going Correction** -0.10s/f (Stan) 6 Ran SP% **109.5**
Speed ratings (Par 96): **99,98,97,92,89 81**
CSF £7.62 TOTE £2.10: £1.30, £1.60; EX 6.40.
Owner Mrs J McMahon **Bred** Mrs J McMahon **Trained** Lichfield, Staffs
■ Stewards' Enquiry : Seb Sanders three-day ban: used whip with excessive force (Nov 16-17,19)

FOCUS
A weak and uncompetitive maiden on paper, but at least they went a good clip and the final time was not bad. The front three came well clear of the others.

NOTEBOOK
Another Socket, whose second over course and distance last month has already started to work out well, was well backed to go one better. She was not best away once again thanks to Stoneacre Baby carrying her out to her right after the stalls opened, but it did not stop her from taking a decent position just behind the leading trio. Taken inside as the leader hung off the final bend, she made full use of the opportunity and battled on well to score. She should be able to hold her own in nurseries on this surface if given the chance. (op 13-8 tchd 7-4 and 15-8 in places)
Wild Bill Tracey, given a positive ride from the inside draw, did not look an easy ride and was inclined to carry his head at a funny angle as he hung off the rail turning for home. He did try to respond when the favourite was delivered on his inside in the home straight, but was outbattled. (op 4-1)
My Mate Pete(IRE), just behind Another Socket on his Nottingham debut last month, was always up with the pace and stayed on pretty well under a very strong ride. Although by a sprinter, his three winning half-brothers included one who scored over 2m, so he will probably appreciate further himself. (tchd 10-3)
Mandelieu(IRE), making his sand debut in his fifth outing, had his chance but again did not get home. As he is officially rated 3lb higher than the runner-up, it seems probable that he did not run close to his mark and is starting to look exposed. (op 3-1 tchd 7-2)
Feeling Fresh(IRE), taking a dramatic drop in trip and blinkered for the first time, had plenty to find on official ratings. As soon as he fluffed the start his race was virtually over.
Stoneacre Baby(USA), wayward leaving the stalls, was never in the race and has now only beaten one horse in three outings, though even that rival was virtually pulled up with a slipping saddle. She now qualifies for handicaps, but will still need to improve a ton when switched to that sphere.

6693 CENTREBET.COM POKER (S) STKS 7f 32y(P)

2:20 (2:21) (Class 6) 2-Y-O **£2,047** (£604; £302) **Stalls High**

Form RPR

600 1 **Marino Prince (FR)**[9] 6503 2-8-6 66 .... TolleyDean[(5)] 5 62+
(W G M Turner) *hld up in mid-div: nt clr run over 2f out: hdwy wl over 1f out: sn briefly n.m.r: rdn to ld wl ins fnl f: r.o* **4/1**[2]

2505 2 ¾ **Mister Beano (IRE)**[12] 6426 2-8-8 51 ....(v) JerryO'Dwyer[(3)] 6 59
(V Smith) *t.k.h in tch: rdn to ld jst ins fnl f: sn hdd: nt qckn* **6/1**

0001 3 ½ **Heavenly Saint**[5] 6591 2-8-11 55 .... JamieSpencer 4 58
(S Parr) *hld up towards rr: hdwy on outside over 2f out: c v wd st: rdn over 1f out: edgd lft and kpt on ins fnl f* **9/2**[3]

00 4 2 **Libertytyne**[23] 6177 2-8-6 0 .... SimonWhitworth 7 48
(S Kirk) *w ldr: led over 2f out: rdn wl over 1f out: hdd jst ins fnl f: no ex towards fin* **25/1**

0606 5 ½ **Pretty Bonnie**[12] 6438 2-8-6 53 .... JamesDoyle 1 47
(J G Portman) *chsd ldrs: rdn and ev ch wl over 1f out: wknd wl ins fnl f* **11/1**

2345 6 1¾ **Liani (IRE)**[21] 6242 2-8-6 53 .... MartinDwyer 11 43
(P D Evans) *sn prom: lost pl over 5f out: rdn over 3f out: hdwy on outside over 2f out: c wd st: edgd lft 1f out: sn wknd* **8/1**

0402 7 1½ **Lord Deevert**[5] 6591 2-8-9 67 ....(p) JackDean[(7)] 9 49
(W G M Turner) *hld up in mid-div: rdn over 1f out: wknd fnl f* **7/2**[1]

8 2½ **Lujano** 2-8-11 0 .... TomEaves 8 38
(Ollie Pears) *w ldrs: ev ch over 2f out: rdn and wknd wl over 1f out* **16/1**

3320 9 2 **Shipboard Romance (IRE)**[55] 5302 2-8-6 50 .... ChrisCatlin 12 28
(P D Evans) *hld up in mid-div: rdn over 3f out: sn bhd* **22/1**

40 10 nk **Ridgeway Jazz**[17] 6312 2-8-6 0 .... HayleyTurner 10 27
(M D I Usher) *s.i.s: rdn over 3f out: a in rr* **66/1**

0000 11 ½ **Brough (IRE)**[3] 6624 2-8-4 50 .... RachelCowley[(7)] 3 31
(J O'Reilly) *s.i.s: a in rr* **100/1**

0030 12 10 **Seventh Cloud (IRE)**[61] 5133 2-8-3 50 ....(v[1]) AndrewElliott[(3)] 2 1
(A P Jarvis) *led: hdd over 2f out: sn wknd* **16/1**

1m 31.03s (0.63) **Going Correction** -0.10s/f (Stan) 12 Ran SP% **116.6**
Speed ratings (Par 94): **92,91,90,88,87 85,84,81,78,78 77,66**
CSF £26.93 TOTE £5.00: £1.40, £2.20, £2.00; EX 27.80 Trifecta £151.80 Part won. Pool £213.90 - 0.85 winning units..There were no bids for the winner. Heavenly Saint was claimed by R Price for £6,000.
Owner John McGrath **Bred** Newsells Park Stud Ltd **Trained** Sigwells, Somerset

FOCUS
An ordinary seller though quite a competitive one and several still had a chance starting up the home straight. Even though the winning time was 2.73 seconds faster than the following maiden, it was still only about what you would expect for a race like this.

NOTEBOOK
Marino Prince(FR), down in class after showing a little ability in three Polytrack maidens, was caught up in traffic on the home bend and then looked as though he would not get through when brought with his effort starting up the home straight, but his rider persisted in going for the gap and was eventually rewarded. He would have been 15lb worse off with the runner-up in a handicap and 11lb worse off with the third, so in theory he should be lowered for this and is likely to struggle in nurseries otherwise. (tchd 7-2)
Mister Beano(IRE), trying this trip for the first time, hit the front halfway up the home straight and did not do a lot wrong, but could not withstand the winner's late surge on his inside. There should be a seller in him over this sort of trip on sand. (op 9-1)
Heavenly Saint, dropped a furlong in trip after landing a turf seller, ran a creditable race under her penalty and can be considered to have performed even better as she was forced extremely wide on the home bend, yet was not beaten far. (op 10-3 tchd 5-1)
Libertytyne, dropped in grade and upped in trip after showing little in two Polytrack maidens, was ridden aggressively and ran a much-improved race as a result. She is not without hope at this level. (op 16-1)
Pretty Bonnie tried to sneak up the inside on the crown over the home bend, but her effort eventually came to little. She looks totally exposed now. (tchd 10-1)
Liani(IRE), poorly drawn, was still in touch when she briefly lost her footing as she came wide around the home bend and there was no way back.
Lord Deevert, 5lb better off with Heavenly Saint for a three-length beating at Nottingham last time, never offered a threat and has nothing in the way of scope. (op 9-2)

6694 SP PLUS PLUS @CENTREBET.COM MAIDEN STKS 7f 32y(P)

2:50 (2:51) (Class 5) 2-Y-O **£2,968** (£876; £438) **Stalls High**

Form RPR

6 1 **Romantic Verse**[13] 6409 2-8-12 0 .... LiamJones 6 63
(W J Haggas) *chsd ldr: led 2f out: rdn out* **3/1**[2]

04 2 1 **Artistic Light**[18] 6289 2-8-12 0 .... MartinDwyer 5 61
(W R Muir) *hld up in tch: ev ch over 2f out: rdn and hung lft over 1f out: nt qckn ins fnl f* **8/1**

3 hd **E Major** 2-9-3 0 .... KDarley 2 69+
(Sir Michael Stoute) *dwlt: hld up: hdwy over 3f out: rdn over 2f out: hung lft whn swtchd rt and clipped heels jst over 1f out: hung lft ins fnl f: r.o* **2/1**[1]

0 4 1 3/4 **Silver Sprite**[45] 5605 2-9-3 0 .... DeanMcKeown 4 61
(D Shaw) *led: hdd 2f out: btn whn sltly hmpd towards fin* **66/1**

5 2 1/2 **Uno Dos Tres** 2-9-3 0 .... JamieSpencer 7 55
(Jane Chapple-Hyam) *hld up in mid-div: rdn 3f out: c wd st: no ch whn hung lft over 1f out* **6/1**

6 1 3/4 **Our Dolly** 2-8-9 0 .... DominicFox(3) 1 46
(S Parr) *prom tl wknd over 2f out* **66/1**

0 7 hd **Police Officer**[13] 6409 2-9-3 0 .... NeilPollard 8 50
(W J Musson) *bhd fnl 3f* **100/1**

8 shd **Hollow Point (IRE)** 2-9-3 0 .... GregFairley 3 50
(M Johnston) *t.k.h: a in rr* **7/2**[3]

1m 33.76s (3.36) **Going Correction** -0.10s/f (Stan) 8 Ran SP% **109.9**
Speed ratings (Par 96): **76,74,74,72,69 67,67,67**
CSF £24.46 TOTE £5.00: £2.10, £1.90, £1.10; EX 24.80 Trifecta £59.50 Pool £278.56 - 3.32 winning units..

Owner Romantic Verse Partnership **Bred** Cheveley Park Stud Ltd **Trained** Newmarket, Suffolk

FOCUS
A very poor maiden, run at a dawdle in a time 2.73 seconds slower than the preceding seller. The form looks very moderate.

NOTEBOOK
Romantic Verse, all the better for her Yarmouth debut, was always in a good position in a slowly-run race and showed a good attitude after taking it up turning in. The form is probably moderate due to the way the race was run, but she is still unexposed. (tchd 10-3)

Artistic Light had every chance, but was not helped by the slow pace as she probably needs further and could never quite find the pace to get to the winner. She now qualifies for a mark. Official explanation: jockey said filly was struck into (op 7-1)

E Major, a half-brother to four winners, missed the break and already looked an awkward ride even before clipping Artistic Light's heels and was lucky not to come down. He is bred to stay further, but has a question mark against him after this. Official explanation: jockey said colt ran green (op 9-4 tchd 15-8)

Silver Sprite, beaten 33 lengths when last of 12 on his debut here in September, made much of the running and had run his race when hampered against the rail by the errant E Major close to the line. His proximity does not do a lot for the form.

Uno Dos Tres, a half-brother to four winners including Montosari, did not show a great deal on this debut especially after racing too wide around the home bend, but to be fair a slowly-run race over this trip was never going to suit him on breeding. He may well improve once handicapped over further. (tchd 13-2)

Hollow Point(IRE), a 30,000euros daughter of the top-class Squeak, showed nothing on this debut and will need to improve a huge amount in order to win a race. (tchd 10-3)

6695 BET NOW AT CENTREBET.COM H'CAP 1m 141y(P)
3:20 (3:20) (Class 6) (0-67,67) 3-Y-O £2,047 (£604; £302) Stalls Low

Form RPR

5113 1 **Prince Noel**[3] 6627 3-7-13 57 oh2 ow1 .... LanceBetts(7) 7 64
(N Wilson) *hld up in mid-div: hdwy 3f out: edgd lft and led wl ins fnl f: rdr lost whip cl home: r.o* **9/2**[3]

1421 2 1/2 **Magroom**[22] 6199 3-8-10 61 .... MartinDwyer 6 67
(R J Hodges) *hld up in mid-div: hdwy 3f out: led 1f out: sn rdn: edgd rt and hdd wl ins fnl f: kpt on* **4/1**[2]

2502 3 3 **Tri Chara (IRE)**[21] 6245 3-8-11 62 .... (p) JamieSpencer 5 61
(R Hollinshead) *s.i.s: hld up towards rr: hdwy wl over 1f out: sn rdn: no ex ins fnl f* **11/4**[1]

2002 4 1/2 **Alexander Guru**[11] 6457 3-9-2 67 .... FrancisNorton 2 67+
(M Blanshard) *a.p: rdn over 1f out: hmpd ins fnl f: one pce* **12/1**

6630 5 nk **Fine Ruler (IRE)**[25] 1039 3-9-2 67 .... GeorgeBaker 4 66+
(M R Bosley) *led: rdn and hdd 1f out: hmpd ins fnl f: one pce* **16/1**

460 6 5 **Fowey (USA)**[22] 6206 3-8-7 58 oh1 ow2 .... SebSanders 8 44
(Sir Mark Prescott) *hld up and bhd: rdn and sme hdwy over 2f out: wknd over 1f out* **5/1**

1606 7 1/2 **Tommy Tobougg**[65] 5035 3-8-7 58 .... TomEaves 9 43
(I Semple) *hld up and bhd: short-lived effrt on outside over 2f out* **11/1**

1530 8 1 1/2 **Krakatau (FR)**[34] 5879 3-8-11 62 .... SamHitchcott 1 43
(D J Wintle) *prom: rdn 2f out: sn wknd* **16/1**

3350 9 2 **Fish Called Johnny**[15] 6360 3-9-1 66 .... LPKeniry 3 43
(Peter Grayson) *s.i.s: a in rr* **22/1**

4045 10 23 **Joyful Tears (IRE)**[6] 6567 3-8-9 60 .... TGMcLaughlin 10 —
(M G Quinlan) *prom tl wknd wl over 2f out: eased whn no ch over 1f out* **33/1**

1m 49.78s (-1.98) **Going Correction** -0.10s/f (Stan) 10 Ran SP% **116.6**
Speed ratings (Par 98): **104,103,100,100,100 95,95,93,92,71**
CSF £22.88 CT £58.53 TOTE £5.90: £1.90, £1.50, £1.60; EX 24.10 Trifecta £22.50 Pool £238.89 - 7.52 winning units..

Owner The Giggle Factor Partnership **Bred** P And Mrs A G Venner **Trained** Flaxton, N Yorks

■ Stewards' Enquiry : Martin Dwyer two-day ban (reduced from three days on appeal): careles riding (Nov 16-17)

FOCUS
A fair handicap run at a true pace and the form looks solid enough for the grade with the front pair progressing.

Alexander Guru Official explanation: jockey said gelding suffered inteference in running

6696 PLAY AUSTRALIAN @ CENTREBET.COM H'CAP 1m 141y(P)
3:50 (3:50) (Class 5) (0-75,76) 3-Y-O+ £2,968 (£876; £438) Stalls Low

Form RPR

1641 1 **Abbondanza (IRE)**[3] 6628 4-9-10 76 6ex .... (p) TomEaves 5 83
(I Semple) *a.p: wnt 2nd over 3f out: rdn to ld and edgd rt ins fnl f: edgd lft: r.o* **11/4**[2]

0001 2 1/2 **One Night In Paris (IRE)**[9] 6504 4-9-7 73 .... JamieSpencer 3 78
(M J Wallace) *led: edgd rt over 1f out: rdn and hdd ins fnl f: kpt on* **5/2**[1]

2300 3 3/4 **Bolton Hall (IRE)**[16] 6344 5-8-11 63 .... PaulHanagan 4 67
(R A Fahey) *s.v.s: hld up: hdwy over 2f out: rdn wl over 1f out: kpt on ins fnl f* **20/1**

0332 4 1 1/4 **Casablanca Minx (IRE)**[6] 6573 4-8-10 62 .... (v) TGMcLaughlin 6 63
(P D Evans) *hld up: hdwy on ins over 1f out: rdn and and nt qckn ins fnl f* **6/1**

4001 5 nk **Very Well Red**[12] 6423 4-9-3 69 .... JimCrowley 1 69
(P W Hiatt) *chsd ldr 2f: prom: rdn over 1f out: one pce* **11/2**

0062 6 shd **Daring Affair**[16] 6343 6-9-3 69 .... (p) SebSanders 2 69
(K R Burke) *hld up: rdn over 3f out: hdwy on outside over 2f out: btn over 1f out* **9/2**[3]

1m 50.62s (-1.14) **Going Correction** -0.10s/f (Stan) 6 Ran SP% **107.9**
Speed ratings (Par 103): **101,100,99,98,98 98**
CSF £9.19 TOTE £4.50: £2.30, £1.50; EX 12.70.

Owner Joseph Leckie & Sons Ltd **Bred** M Nolan **Trained** Carluke, S Lanarks

FOCUS
A tight little handicap, but they only went a modest early pace and it developed into something of a sprint. The runner-up is the best guide but not form to take too literally.

6697 WE'VE GOT THE ASHES @CENTREBET.COM H'CAP 1m 5f 194y(P)
4:20 (4:22) (Class 6) (0-65,62) 3-Y-O+ £2,047 (£604; £302) Stalls Low

Form RPR

6630 1 **Princely Ted (IRE)**[22] 6196 6-9-6 54 .... GrahamGibbons 11 62
(D Burchell) *led 1f: chsd ldr: led over 4f out: rdn clr over 1f out: drvn out* **33/1**

4006 2 1 1/4 **Party Palace**[7] 6534 3-8-3 45 .... AdrianMcCarthy 3 52
(H S Howe) *hld up towards rr: hdwy on ins whn swtchd rt over 2f out: rdn and edgd rt over 1f out: styd on ins fnl f: nt rch wnr* **50/1**

1065 3 1 1/2 **Royal Melbourne (IRE)**[16] 6330 7-9-8 56 .... DavidAllan 5 60
(A D Brown) *hld up in tch: rdn 2f out: edgd lft ins fnl f: styd on one pce* **25/1**

2 4 1 **Wishes Or Watches (IRE)**[6] 6569 7-8-11 45 .... JamieSpencer 1 48
(John A Quinn, Ire) *hld up and bhd: hdwy over 2f out: rdn over 1f out: one pce* **8/1**[3]

036- 5 shd **Easibet Dot Net**[78] 6256 7-9-7 55 .... (p) TomEaves 7 58
(I Semple) *hld up in mid-div: reminders 4f out: lost pl on outside over 2f out: c wd st: styd on ins fnl f* **25/1**

-212 6 1 1/4 **Spanish Conquest**[2] 6643 3-9-1 57 .... SebSanders 8 58
(Sir Mark Prescott) *hld up in tch: chsd wnr over 3f out: hrd rdn over 2f out: no ex ins fnl f* **10/11**[1]

4044 7 nk **Carlton Scroop (FR)**[11] 5453 4-9-7 55 .... (b) PaulEddery 6 56
(J Jay) *hld up and bhd: rdn over 4f out: nvr trbld ldrs* **10/1**

0345 8 3 1/2 **York Cliff**[6] 6564 9-9-5 53 .... LiamJones 9 49
(W M Brisbourne) *a bhd* **16/1**

5154 9 1 **Theflyingscottie**[11] 6459 5-9-2 50 .... DeanMcKeown 2 44
(D Shaw) *a bhd* **6/1**[2]

0605 10 nk **Figaro's Quest (IRE)**[29] 5235 5-8-11 45 .... (b) ChrisCatlin 10 39
(C N Kellett) *led after 1f tl over 4f out: wknd over 2f out* **66/1**

0500 11 2 1/2 **Mighty Kitchener (USA)**[11] 6459 4-10-0 62 .... SimonWhitworth 12 52
(P Howling) *prom: rdn over 3f out: sn wknd* **16/1**

4034 P **Dream Master (IRE)**[6] 6569 4-8-11 45 .... AdamKirby 4 —
(J Ryan) *a in rr: rdn 5f out: t.o whn p.u over 2f out* **14/1**

3m 5.31s (-2.06) **Going Correction** -0.10s/f (Stan)
WFA 3 from 4yo+ 8lb 12 Ran SP% **119.4**
Speed ratings (Par 101): **101,100,99,98,98 98,97,95,95,95 93,—**
CSF £1125.73 CT £34191.88 TOTE £47.30: £8.60, £10.80, £7.00; EX 871.20 TRIFECTA Not won. Place 6 £215.55, Place 5 £133.33..

Owner M S Heath **Bred** Thomas C Kerr **Trained** Briery Hill, Blaenau Gwent

FOCUS
An ordinary staying handicap, especially with the odds-on favourite disappointing, and the time was about what you would expect for a race of its grade. The form is rated around the winner and fourth.

Dream Master(IRE) Official explanation: jockey said gelding lost its action; trainer said gelding was found to have pulled a muscle in its hindquarters

T/Jkpt: Not won. T/Plt: £1,618.80 to a £1 stake. Pool: £72,517.10. 32.70 winning tickets. T/Qpdt: £193.10 to a £1 stake. Pool: £4,802.30. 18.40 winning tickets. KH

6557 CATTERICK (L-H)
Tuesday, November 6

OFFICIAL GOING: Good to firm (10.3)
Wind: Light across Weather: Sunny

6698 GODOLPHIN STABLE STAFF AWARDS - NOMINATE NOW MAIDEN AUCTION STKS 7f
1:40 (1:41) (Class 6) 2-Y-O £2,730 (£806; £403) Stalls Low

Form RPR

1 **San Silvestro (IRE)** 2-8-13 0 .... PaulMulrennan 2 68
(Mrs A Duffield) *sn chsng ldrs on inner: pushed along 2f out: swtchd rt and rdn to chal over 1f out: styd on u.p to ld last 50yds* **6/1**[2]

06 2 hd **Stagecoach Topaz (USA)**[7] 6557 2-9-2 0 .... J-PGuillambert 12 70
(M Johnston) *a.p: rdn to chal over 1f out: sn ev ch: drvn and edgd rt ins fnl f: kpt on* **7/1**[3]

3 1/2 **The Mighty One** 2-9-2 0 .... LeeEnstone 1 69
(P C Haslam) *led after 1f: rdn over 1f out: drvn ins fnl f: hdd and no ex last 50yds* **8/1**

6332 4 3/4 **Elusive Lady (IRE)**[10] 6503 2-8-1 60 .... AndrewElliott(3) 8 55
(J R Weymes) *in tch: hdwy to chse ldrs on outer 1/2-way: rdn wl over 1f out: drvn and one pce ins fnl f* **9/4**[1]

0 5 3/4 **Roger's Revenge**[101] 3951 2-8-9 0 .... TomEaves 5 58+
(B Smart) *plld hrd: chsd ldrs: effrt whn carried hd high and hung lft wl over 1f out: kpt on towards fin* **11/1**

0 6 1 3/4 **Sweet Andromeda**[18] 6312 2-8-4 0 .... LiamJones 10 49
(T J Fitzgerald) *midfield: hdwy over 2f out: kpt on ins fnl f: nrst fin* **40/1**

00 7 4 **Generous Boy**[29] 6051 2-8-11 0 .... DavidAllan 6 45
(T D Easterby) *chsd ldrs: rdn along 2f out and sn btn* **8/1**

0 8 2 **Graze On And On**[15] 6384 2-8-4 0 .... SilvestreDeSousa 3 33
(J J Quinn) *nvr nr ldrs* **20/1**

6000 9 3/4 **Carlton Mac**[18] 6307 2-8-6 48 .... (v[1]) AndrewMullen(3) 9 36
(N Bycroft) *nvr nr ldrs* **66/1**

0056 10 3 1/2 **Northwest**[17] 6329 2-8-11 52 .... TonyHamilton 4 29
(A Berry) *led 1f: prom tl rdn along over 2f out and sn wknd* **22/1**

0060 11 2 **Howe's Jack (IRE)**[34] 5901 2-8-6 40 .... DominicFox(3) 11 22
(M C Chapman) *s.i.s: a bhd* **150/1**

0R 12 17 **Fellrunner (IRE)**[74] 4784 2-8-7 0 ow1 .... PJMcDonald(3) 13 —
(A Berry) *a in rr* **200/1**

00 U **Traitor's Gate**[6] 6593 2-9-1 0 .... GregFairley 7 —
(M Johnston) *stmbld and uns rdr s* **15/2**

1m 27.84s (0.48) **Going Correction** 0.0s/f (Good) 13 Ran SP% **114.1**
Speed ratings (Par 94): **97,96,96,95,94 92,87,85,84,80 78,59,—**
CSF £42.99 TOTE £7.90: £2.50, £1.60, £3.60; EX 56.90.

Owner Middleham Park Racing Xiv **Bred** Canice M Farrell Jnr **Trained** Constable Burton, N Yorks

■ Stewards' Enquiry : Paul Mulrennan five-day ban: used whip with excessive frequency without giving colt time to respond (Nov 17, 19-22)

FOCUS
A modest maiden and it was no surprise to see it fall the way of a newcomer.

The Form Book, Raceform Ltd, Compton, RG20 6NL

NOTEBOOK

San Silvestro(IRE), whose dam is a half-sister to formerly high-class sprinter Fayr Jag, was well supported in the market beforehand and a big run was clearly expected on this racecourse debut. Always in a good position, he picked up well to hold every chance racing inside the final furlong and got on top close home. This was not a good race, but he could do no more than win and should be capable of better in handicaps. (op 10-1)

Stagecoach Topaz(USA), bred to be suited by this step up in trip, improved on his debut effort when sixth at the course last month and he took another step forward, keeping on but just finding the winner too strong. There is clearly a small race in him, possibly once going handicapping. (op 6-1)

The Mighty One, who cost 30,000gns as a two-year-old, showed up well for a long way on this racecourse debut, taking advantage of a good draw, but he could not repel the front pair inside the final half a furlong and was just run out of it. The experience should not be lost on him and a similarly modest maiden should come his way. (op 5-1)

Elusive Lady(IRE) set the standard, albeit a modest one, and it was no surprise to see her find a few too good. She has done enough to win a race, but is likely to remain vulnerable to improvers. (tchd 7-4)

Roger's Revenge, off since running poorly on his debut at Newcastle back in July, failed to settle on this return to the track, but was still keeping on towards the finish and certainly showed he has ability. It was slightly disconcerting to see him carry his head awkwardly under pressure, but that may have still been down to greenness. Official explanation: jockey said gelding hung badly left-handed throughout (op 15-2 tchd 7-1)

6699 CHRISTINE ROBINSON 60TH BIRTHDAY NURSERY 5f 212y

2:10 (2:10) (Class 4) (0-85,84) 2-Y-0 **£4,210** (£1,252; £625; £312) **Stalls** Low

Form RPR

1022 **1** **Ramatni**[8] 6544 2-9-5 **82** .... GregFairley 2 85
(M Johnston) *mde all: rdn and qcknd clr wl over 1f out: kpt on* **3/1**[1]

400 **2** 1 1/4 **The Real Guru**[23] 6195 2-8-7 **70** ....(v[1]) PaulMulrennan 1 69
(Mrs A Duffield) *trckd ldrs: hdwy to chse wnr 2f out: sn rdn: kpt on same pce ins fnl f* **16/1**

3563 **3** 1/2 **Chivola (IRE)**[11] 6462 2-8-12 **75** .... TomEaves 3 73
(B Smart) *t.k.h: chsd ldrs: hdwy 2f out: rdn over 1f out: kpt on same pce ins fnl f* **9/2**[2]

2022 **4** 3/4 **Lady Benjamin**[33] 5932 2-8-8 **78** ....(b[1]) PatrickDonaghy(7) 4 74
(P C Haslam) *hld up in tch: effrt over 2f out and sn rdn: drvn to chse ldrs and hanging lft over 1f out: kpt on same pce* **11/2**[3]

5201 **5** 1 1/2 **Elijah Pepper (USA)**[18] 6312 2-8-10 **73** .... PhillipMakin 5 64
(T D Barron) *cl up: rdn along and hung rt over 2f out: drvn wl over 1f out and sn wknd* **7/1**

26 **6** 3 1/2 **Atephobia**[28] 6072 2-8-0 **66** .... AndrewElliott(3) 9 47
(K R Burke) *wnt rt s: cl up: rdn along and hung rt over 2f out: sn btn* **14/1**

2100 **7** 1 3/4 **Nawaaff**[31] 6004 2-9-7 **84** .... PaulHanagan 8 59
(M R Channon) *rrd s: in tch: rdn along over 2f out and sn btn* **15/2**

1506 **8** 6 **The Game**[6] 6588 2-9-0 **77** .... NCallan 7 40+
(J R Boyle) *dwlt: a towards rr* **9/2**[2]

1m 14.04s (0.04) **Going Correction** 0.0s/f (Good) **8** Ran SP% **113.6**

Speed ratings (Par 98): **99,97,96,95,93 89,86,78**

CSF £51.70 CT £192.25 TOTE £3.30: £1.10, £4.50, £1.90; EX 49.80.

Owner Sheikh Ahmed Al Maktoum **Bred** Darley **Trained** Middleham Moor, N Yorks

FOCUS

A fair nursery.

NOTEBOOK

Ramatni, a tough and consistent filly who twice ran well to finish second last month, was bounced out in front from her low draw and never saw another rival, shooting clear from over a furlong out and sticking on gamely. This was her tenth run of the campaign, but she seems to be getting better and would be entitled to respect next time, even after a rise. (op 7-2)

The Real Guru, a maiden winner at Pontefract back in the summer, has since struggled in a few handicaps, but he has slipped 11lb in the ratings as a result and ran a much-improved race here in the first-time visor. Whether the headgear has the same affect in future is open to debate, but he is clearly capable of winning more races. (op 20-1)

Chivola(IRE), who failed to last home in soft ground at Ayr last time, ran a lot better on this faster surface and kept plugging away without being able to reach the winner. He looks worth a try over 7f now. (op 6-1)

Lady Benjamin, like the winner, has had a busy season, but she has run well more often than not and this was another respectable effort considering she was up 5lb following a couple of solid placed efforts. (op 6-1)

Elijah Pepper(USA), off the mark in a moderate maiden at Wolverhampton last time, ran reasonably well on this return to handicaps, but started to hang inside the final quarter mile and could find no more.

The Game was never involved following a sluggish start. Official explanation: trainer's rep said, regarding running, that the race may have come too soon for colt (op 100-30)

6700 ENTRIES OPEN - GODOLPHIN STABLE STAFF AWARDS MAIDEN STKS 1m 3f 214y

2:40 (2:40) (Class 5) 3-Y-0+ **£2,914** (£867; £433; £216) **Stalls** High

Form RPR

0604 **1** **Ashwell Rose**[7] 6558 5-9-4 54 ....(v) NCallan 6 51+
(J R Jenkins) *trckd ldrs: hdwy 3f out: rdn to ld wl over 1f out: sn clr* **11/8**[1]

0 **2** 4 **Lyon's Hill**[21] 6257 3-9-3 0 .... TomEaves 7 49
(M Mullineaux) *led 1f: cl up: rdn along over 2f out: drvn wl over 1f out: kpt on same pce* **5/1**[2]

3 3/4 **Spares And Repairs**[144] 4-9-9 0 .... PaulHanagan 3 48
(Mrs S Lamyman) *dwlt: t.k.h and hld up in rr: hdwy 3f out: rdn along wl over 1f out: kpt on ins fnl f* **16/1**

3500 **4** 3/4 **Matinee Idol**[7] 6558 4-9-4 46 .... PaulMulrennan 5 42
(Mrs S Lamyman) *hld up in rr: hdwy over 3f out: rdn to chse ldrs 2f out: sn drvn and one pce* **14/1**

0-00 **5** 1 **Telling**[181] 1579 3-9-0 43 .... AndrewMullen(3) 8 45
(Mrs A Duffield) *t.k.h and hdwy to ld after 1f: rdn along over 2f out: drvn and hdd wl over 1f out: sn wknd* **20/1**

0630 **6** shd **The Diamond Bond**[7] 6561 3-8-12 46 .... SladeO'Hara(5) 9 45
(G R Oldroyd) *trckd ldrs: rdn along 3f out: drvn wl over 1f out: sn edgd lft and wknd* **5/1**[2]

0 **7** 1 3/4 **Troys Steps**[19] 6286 3-8-12 0 .... DavidAllan 1 37
(E J Alston) *trckd ldrs: rdn along 3f out: sn wknd* **50/1**

600- **8** 2 **The Rebound Kid**[71] 1265 5-9-9 58 .... PhillipMakin 4 39
(J R Weymes) *hld up in tch: effrt and sme hdwy 3f out: sn rdn and btn* **12/1**

9 1 3/4 **Topwell**[415] 6-9-9 0 .... GrahamGibbons 2 36
(R C Guest) *s.i.s and bhd: hdwy and in tch 1/2-way: rdn along over 4f out and sn wknd* **13/2**[3]

2m 42.86s (3.86) **Going Correction** 0.0s/f (Good)

WFA 3 from 4yo+ 6lb **9** Ran SP% **115.7**

Speed ratings (Par 103): **87,84,83,83,82 82,81,80,78**

CSF £8.35 TOTE £1.90: £1.30, £1.60, £4.20; EX 10.10.

Owner Mr & Mrs C Schwick **Bred** Cromlech Bloodstock **Trained** Royston, Herts

FOCUS

As bad a maiden as you will find and unsurprisingly the winning time was moderate. The form is best rated through the runner-up.

6701 BOOK ON-LINE AT CATTERICKBRIDGE.CO.UK H'CAP 7f

3:10 (3:16) (Class 4) (0-80,78) 3-Y-0+ **£4,857** (£1,445; £722; £360) **Stalls** Low

Form RPR

0113 **1** **Nuit Sombre (IRE)**[7] 6560 7-9-3 **77** ....(v) SilvestreDeSousa 7 83
(G A Harker) *qckly away and sn clr: rdn wl over 1f out: hld on gamely* **9/2**[1]

0260 **2** 1/2 **Okikoki**[13] 6435 3-8-8 **74** ....(b) TolleyDean(5) 1 79
(W R Muir) *chsd ldrs: effrt and hdwy 2f out: swtchd lft and rdn 1f out: n.m.r and swtchd rt ins fnl f: styd on* **8/1**[3]

6402 **3** 1/2 **Champain Sands (IRE)**[37] 5840 8-8-7 **67** .... GrahamGibbons 14 71+
(E J Alston) *s.i.s and bhd: hdwy 1/2-way: rdn to chse ldrs whn nt clr run and swtchd rt ins fnl f: sn drvn and styd on* **14/1**

4054 **4** 1 **Esoterica (IRE)**[11] 6463 4-8-7 **67** ....(b) LiamJones 6 68+
(J S Goldie) *bhd: rdn along and hdwy 2f out: drvn and styng on whn nt clr run and swtchd lft ins fnl f: swtchd rt and styd on wl towards fin* **8/1**[3]

0400 **5** nk **Prince Namid**[7] 6560 5-9-1 **78** .... AndrewMullen(3) 9 78
(Mrs A Duffield) *prom: rdn along over 2f out: drvn to chse wnr over 1f out: wknd wl ins fnl f* **10/1**

4032 **6** 1 **Red Romeo**[22] 6243 6-9-4 **78** ....(p) DaleGibson 4 75
(N Wilson) *in tch: hdwy on inner over 2f out: sn rdn and styng on whn n.m.r 1f out: kpt on* **13/2**[2]

33 **7** nk **Angaric (IRE)**[17] 6331 4-8-13 **73** .... TomEaves 5 70
(B Smart) *prom: rdn along over 2f out: drvn and wknd appr fnl f* **9/2**[1]

0410 **8** hd **Dispol Isle (IRE)**[17] 6331 5-8-9 **69** .... PaulFessey 2 65
(T D Barron) *chsd wnr: rdn along 2f out: drvn over 1f out: hld whn n.m.r and wknd ins fnl f* **20/1**

/000 **9** nk **High Window (IRE)**[11] 6475 7-8-3 **70** oh19 ow6........ NSLawes(7) 3 65?
(G P Kelly) *bhd: rdn along 2f out: hdwy over 1f out: styng on whn n.m.r ins fnl f: kpt on* **250/1**

5004 **10** 3/4 **Triple Shadow**[37] 5834 3-8-1 **69** oh7 ow5........ DeanHeslop(7) 12 62
(M A Peill) *in rr: hdwy on outer 2f out: sn rdn: kpt on same pce ins fnl f* **66/1**

6320 **11** 3/4 **King Harson**[7] 6560 8-8-10 **70** .... NCallan 11 61
(J D Bethell) *chsd ldrs: rdn along over 2f out: drvn and wknd over 1f out* **12/1**

205 **12** hd **Flying Valentino**[4] 6623 3-8-7 **71** .... PJMcDonald(3) 13 62
(G A Swinbank) *a towards rr* **10/1**

0503 **13** 1 1/4 **Social Rhythm**[12] 6450 3-8-9 **73** .... JerryO'Dwyer(3) 8 60
(H J Collingridge) *towards rr: hdwy on outer 2f out: sn rdn and wknd over 1f out* **10/1**

5000 **14** 6 **Stoic Leader (IRE)**[17] 6331 7-8-13 **73** .... PaulHanagan 10 44
(R F Fisher) *a towards rr* **20/1**

1m 26.28s (-1.08) **Going Correction** 0.0s/f (Good)

WFA 3 from 4yo+ 1lb **14** Ran SP% **125.0**

Speed ratings (Par 105): **106,105,104,103,103 102,101,101,101,100 99,99,97,91**

CSF £40.67 CT £497.92 TOTE £5.60: £2.20, £3.70, £3.80; EX 64.30.

Owner P I Harker **Bred** M P B Bloodstock Ltd **Trained** Thirkleby, N Yorks

FOCUS

A fair handicap although the winner may not have need to improve on recent course and distance form to score.

Social Rhythm Official explanation: jockey said filly never travelled

6702 GO RACING IN YORKSHIRE CLAIMING STKS 5f

3:40 (3:44) (Class 6) 3-Y-0+ **£2,730** (£806; £403) **Stalls** Low

Form RPR

0410 **1** **Brut**[34] 5908 5-9-0 72 ....(p) TonyHamilton 6 70
(D W Barker) *qckly away: mde all: rdn wl over 1f out and kpt on strly* **9/4**[1]

0264 **2** 1 1/2 **Guto**[31] 6020 4-9-7 73 .... AndrewMullen(3) 2 74
(W J H Ratcliffe) *trckd ldrs: hdwy to chse wnr wl over 1f out: drvn ent fnl f and no imp* **9/4**[1]

2600 **3** 1 1/2 **Whozart (IRE)**[34] 5908 4-9-4 48 .... DanielTudhope 1 63
(A Dickman) *in tch on inner: hdwy 2f out: sn rdn and styd on ins fnl f* **9/1**

4350 **4** 1 1/2 **Throw The Dice**[7] 6562 5-8-8 52 ....(v) PhillipMakin 3 48
(A Berry) *chsd ldrs: rdn along 2f out: sn one pce* **6/1**[2]

-040 **5** 5 **Swallow Senora (IRE)**[14] 6412 5-7-10 40 .... DominicFox(3) 4 21
(M C Chapman) *s.i.s and bhd: rdn and hdwy 2f out: kpt on: nt rch ldrs* **100/1**

5260 **6** nk **Whats Your Game (IRE)**[17] 6339 3-8-7 48 ow1.....(b) PaulMulrennan 10 28
(A Berry) *cl up: rdn over 2f out and sn wknd* **50/1**

5220 **7** shd **Jember Red**[180] 1594 4-8-13 42 ....(v) TomEaves 13 33
(B Smart) *racd wd: towards rr: hdwy 2f out: sn rdn and kpt on: nvr nr ldrs* **28/1**

0060 **8** shd **Laith (IRE)**[42] 5711 4-8-10 44 ....(p) LiamJones 5 30
(Miss V Haigh) *towards rr: hdwy on inner 2f out: sn rdn and kpt on: nvr nr ldrs* **20/1**

0303 **9** 1 1/2 **Pegasus Dancer (FR)**[49] 5506 3-9-10 71 ....(b) NCallan 14 38
(K A Ryan) *chsd ldrs: rdn over 2f out and sn wknd* **17/2**[3]

000 **10** 3 **Sharp Hat**[28] 6078 13-8-4 45 .... DaleGibson 9 8
(D W Chapman) *nvr nr ldrs* **25/1**

0000 **11** 1 3/4 **Diamond Josh**[4] 6625 5-8-10 40 .... GregFairley 12 7
(M Mullineaux) *midfield: rdn along 1/2-way: sn wknd* **33/1**

40 **12** 1 **Suspender (IRE)**[168] 1913 3-8-9 0 .... PaulHanagan 8 3
(S T Mason) *s.i.s: a bhd* **80/1**

0000 **13** 1/2 **Musical Parkes**[21] 6247 3-7-10 43 .... DuranFentiman(3) 7 —
(W J H Ratcliffe) *a towards rr* **50/1**

0606 **14** nk **The Brat**[32] 5969 3-8-1 43 ow2 ....(p) PaulFessey 15 —
(Miss Tracy Waggott) *chsd ldrs towards outer: rdn along 1/2-way: sn wknd* **80/1**

60.47 secs (-0.13) **Going Correction** 0.0s/f (Good) **14** Ran SP% **118.7**

Speed ratings (Par 101): **101,98,96,93,85 85,85,85,82,77 75,73,72,72**

CSF £5.87 TOTE £3.30: £1.60, £1.60, £2.80; EX 9.90.

Owner D W Barker **Bred** Mrs Deborah O'Brien **Trained** Scorton, N Yorks

FOCUS

The two standout candidates dominated in what was a fair but uncompetitive race for the grade. The runner-up ran basically to form.

6703 NATIONAL HUNT SEASON STARTS ON 5TH DECEMBER H'CAP 1m 5f 175y

4:10 (4:10) (Class 5) (0-75,73) 3-Y-0+ **£2,914** (£867; £433; £216) **Stalls** Low

Form RPR

23-0 **1** **Hernando's Boy**[24] 6186 6-9-7 **64** .... TomEaves 2 74
(K G Reveley) *trckd ldrs: smooth hdwy 4f out: swtchd rt and effrt 2f out: sn led: rdn clr appr fnl f and styd on strly* **17/2**

4040 **2** 3½ **Mighty Moon**[11] 6473 4-9-9 71................................(tp) JamesO'Reilly(5) 7 76
(J O'Reilly) *s.i.s and sn rdn along in rr: hdwy 1/2-way: rdn to chse ldrs wl over 2f out: drvn over 1f out: styd on fnl f* **6/1**[3]
5120 **3** 2 **Sporting Gesture**[10] 6500 10-10-0 71.......................... PaulMulrennan 1 73
(M W Easterby) *led: hdd 1/2-way: led again over 3f out: rdn over 2f out: hdd wl over 1f out: kpt on same pce* **8/1**
5206 **4** 2 **Young Scotton**[45] 5626 7-8-6 52 oh3.......................... AndrewElliott(3) 8 52
(J D Bethell) *hld up in rr: hdwy over 4f out: rdn along over 3f out: kpt on u.p fnl 2f: nrst fin* **14/1**
-301 **5** ¾ **Hall Of Fame**[39] 5774 3-9-4 69.................................... GrahamGibbons 5 67
(R C Guest) *prom: hdwy to ld 1/2-way: rdn along 4f out: sn hdd: drvn over 2f out and sn wknd* **16/1**
-002 **6** 3½ **Dollar Chick (IRE)**[32] 5968 3-9-8 73................................. GregFairley 3 67
(M Johnston) *trckd ldr: rdn along 4f out: drvn over 3f out and sn wknd* **6/4**[1]
205 **7** shd **Boxhall (IRE)**[15] 6383 5-9-3 60...................................... DanielTudhope 4 53
(N Wilson) *in tch: pushed along over 4f out: rdn over 3f out and n.d* **7/2**[2]
5010 **8** 29 **Mystified (IRE)**[28] 6076 4-9-0 57...............................(b) PaulHanagan 6 10
(R F Fisher) *a in rr: rdn along 6f out and sn wl bhd* **33/1**

3m 4.70s (0.20) **Going Correction** 0.0s/f (Good)
WFA 3 from 4yo+ 8lb **8** Ran SP% **113.6**
Speed ratings (Par 103): **99,97,95,94,94 92,92,75**
CSF £57.49 CT £423.78 TOTE £12.50: £3.50, £1.50, £2.00; EX 53.00 Place 6 £76.02, Place 5 £23.00..
Owner Crack of Dawn Partnership **Bred** T E Pocock **Trained** Lingdale, Redcar & Cleveland
■ Stewards' Enquiry : James O'Reilly three-day ban: used whip above shoulder height (Nov 17, 19-20)

FOCUS
A modest staying handicap with the winner rated back to his best.
T/Jkpt: £15,525.90 to a £1 stake. Pool: £21,867.50. 0.50 winning tickets. T/Plt: £103.00 to a £1 stake. Pool: £70,825.70. 501.70 winning tickets. T/Qpdt: £17.80 to a £1 stake. Pool: £3,880.40. 160.50 winning tickets. JR

6664 LINGFIELD (L-H)
Tuesday, November 6

OFFICIAL GOING: Standard
The middle of the track looked to be riding significantly quicker than the far rail in the straight, as seems to be the case so often on the Lingfield Polytrack.
Wind: Moderate, against Weather: Sunny

6704 GODOLPHIN STABLE STAFF AWARDS - NOMINATE NOW MEDIAN AUCTION MAIDEN STKS 1m (P)
1:00 (1:00) (Class 6) 3-5-Y-O £2,388 (£705; £352) **Stalls High**

Form RPR
1 **Hope Island (IRE)**[32] 5986 3-8-12 0...................................... LPKeniry 8 62
(E F Vaughan) *dwlt: hld up in last pair but wl in tch: effrt over 2f out: rdn and r.o fr over 1f out to ld last 100yds* **6/1**
20 **2** ¾ **Distant Drama (USA)**[22] 6240 3-8-12 0.......................... SebSanders 3 61
(J Noseda) *trckd ldrs: effrt over 2f out: rdn and r.o to chal ins fnl f: outpcd by wnr last 100yds* **5/2**[1]
4300 **3** ¾ **Astroangel**[4] 6623 3-8-12 60.. MartinDwyer 2 59
(M H Tompkins) *dwlt: trckd ldrs: effrt on inner 2f out: led 1f out: hdd and one pce last 100yds* **3/1**[2]
44 **4** 1¼ **Fair Sailing (IRE)**[22] 6229 3-8-12 0................................... EddieAhern 4 56
(J W Hills) *cl up: effrt to ld over 2f out: hdd and fdd 1f out* **10/3**[3]
464 **5** 1½ **Massams Lane**[12] 6457 3-9-3 58... AdamKirby 9 58
(G C Bravery) *t.k.h: prom: led over 3f out: rdn and hdd over 2f out: fdd fnl f* **8/1**
030 **6** 1¼ **Princess Danehill (IRE)**[34] 5898 3-8-5 55...................... DTDaSilva(7) 6 50
(P F I Cole) *plld hrd: racd wd: in tch: v wd bnd 2f out and lost all ch* **16/1**
0000 **7** 2½ **Rangali Belle**[70] 4918 3-8-12 48.................................. SimonWhitworth 5 44
(C A Horgan) *t.k.h: led to over 3f out: awkward over 2f out: sn wknd* **66/1**
8 30 **Mystic Spin (IRE)** 3-9-0 0.. EmmettStack(3) 1 —
(K J Burke) *s.s: a last: t.o whn eased over 2f out* **28/1**

1m 38.74s (-0.69) **Going Correction** -0.15s/f (Stan)
WFA 3 from 5yo 2lb **8** Ran SP% **112.9**
Speed ratings (Par 101): **97,96,95,94,92 91,89,59**
CSF £20.83 TOTE £6.40: £2.10, £3.00, £1.10; EX 22.60 Trifecta £92.30 Pool £245.84 - 1.89 winning units..
Owner Ryder Cup Racing Syndicate **Bred** Canice Farrell Jnr **Trained** Newmarket, Suffolk

FOCUS
A moderate maiden. The winning time was 1.83 seconds slower than the closing 56-70 apprentice handicap.

6705 BOOK YOUR CHRISTMAS PARTY HERE MAIDEN AUCTION STKS 6f (P)
1:30 (1:30) (Class 6) 2-Y-O £2,388 (£705; £352) **Stalls Low**

Form RPR
40 **1** **Storey Hill (USA)**[15] 6386 2-8-10 0............................. DeanMcKeown 5 72
(D Shaw) *mde all: rdn over 2f out: kpt on and clr fnl f* **7/2**[2]
2000 **2** 2½ **Dhhamaan (IRE)**[20] 6267 2-8-10 75.................................. SebSanders 3 65
(C E Brittain) *pressed wnr: reminder after 2f: rdn over 2f out: nt qckn and hld wl over 1f out* **2/5**[1]
3 2 **Silver Waters** 2-8-9 0.. MarcHalford(3) 6 61
(D R C Elsworth) *s.s: m green in last: urged along 1/2-way: wd bnd 2f out: styd on fnl f to take 3rd last stride* **9/1**[3]
0 **4** hd **Forever Changes**[13] 6425 2-8-7 0 ow1................................ LPKeniry 4 55+
(L Montague Hall) *racd on outer: mostly chsd ldng pair: hanging and outpcd wl over 1f out: lost 3rd last stride* **66/1**
0 **5** 3 **Tobouggornotobougg**[32] 5984 2-8-11 0.......................... DaneO'Neill 2 50
(D Shaw) *t.k.h: hld up in tch: effrt over 2f out: wknd rapidly over 1f out* **33/1**
0060 **6** 8 **Liz Long**[45] 5644 2-8-5 53.. ChrisCatlin 1 20
(P Howling) *in tch tl wknd rapidly over 2f out* **33/1**

1m 12.89s (0.08) **Going Correction** -0.15s/f (Stan) **6** Ran SP% **111.0**
Speed ratings (Par 94): **93,89,87,86,82 72**
CSF £5.21 TOTE £5.10: £1.60, £1.10; EX 7.00.
Owner Jim Goose **Bred** And Mrs Richard S Kaster **Trained** Danethorpe, Notts

FOCUS
A modest, uncompetitive sprint maiden in which the runner-up was well below his official mark of 75.

NOTEBOOK
Storey Hill(USA) ◆ had shown ability on both his previous starts, including when not given the best of rides over 5f at Wolverhampton on his previous start, and he found this a good opportunity to get off the mark. Allowed an easy lead, he was kept wide of the far rail rounding the final bend, although he did drift left late on, and was always holding the favourite. He is flattered by the bare form, as there is no way the runner-up ran to his official mark of 75, but he still looks a fair sort in the making. It just has to be hoped the Handicapper does not overreact.
Dhhamaan(IRE) already looked held by the eventual winner when switching to unfavoured far rail in the straight. He showed fair form on his first two starts, but has not progressed and was some way below his official mark of 75. He may do better stepped back up in trip. (op 4-9 tchd 1-2 in a place)
Silver Waters ◆, a 10,000gns yearling but not sold at 9,500gns this year, is by Fantastic Light and the first foal of a mare who was unplaced over 7f-1m3f in a light career. He ran to just a modest level on his racecourse debut, but was green through the early stages and would have found this trip plenty short enough. He very much gave the impression he can leave this form behind in time, especially when stepped up in trip. (op 8-1)
Forever Changes failed to beat a rival on her debut over 5f at Kempton, but this was better. (op 50-1)
Tobouggornotobougg will find things easier in low-grade handicaps and he needs one more run for a mark.

6706 LINGFIELD PARK FOR WEDDINGS H'CAP 7f (P)
2:00 (2:04) (Class 6) (0-50,50) 3-Y-0+ £2,525 (£745; £372) **Stalls Low**

Form RPR
0006 **1** **Joy And Pain**[6] 6587 6-8-12 48.................................(p) IanMongan 7 57
(M J Attwater) *hld up in midfield: prog over 2f out: rdn to ld 1f out: r.o wl* **7/2**[1]
020- **2** 2 **Grand Assault**[311] 6983 4-9-0 50.................................... AdamKirby 6 54
(G C Bravery) *hld up in midfield: prog over 2f out: swtchd to inner and effrt to chal 1f out: styd on same pce* **14/1**
0000 **3** shd **Hannahbecc**[20] 6272 3-8-13 50...............................(e[1]) SaleemGolam 12 57+
(S C Williams) *hld up towards rr: prog 2f out: effrt whn nt clr run jst over 1f out: got through and r.o to take 3rd nr fin* **25/1**
0005 **4** ½ **Almondillo (IRE)**[14] 6402 3-8-12 49............................(b[1]) SebSanders 3 51
(C F Wall) *cl up: wnt 2nd over 2f out: drvn to ld over 1f out: hdd 1f out: outpcd* **7/1**[2]
6662 **5** nk **Double Valentine**[13] 6429 4-8-7 48.......................... JackMitchell(5) 13 49
(R Ingram) *dwlt: mostly last tl prog towards inner 2f out: eased to outer and styd on fnl f: nt pce to threaten ldrs* **8/1**[3]
0000 **6** ¾ **James Street (IRE)**[13] 6431 4-8-5 48.............................(b) RyanHill(7) 5 47
(Peter Grayson) *chsd ldr to over 2f out: bmpd along and grad outpcd* **16/1**
060 **7** 1 **Park Valley Prince**[49] 5499 3-8-13 50.......................... MartinDwyer 10 46
(W R Muir) *racd wd: trckd ldrs: gng wl 3f out: wd bnd 2f out and lost grnd: kpt on fnl f* **10/1**
3400 **8** 1 **Marmooq**[5] 6607 4-9-0 50...(v) ChrisCatlin 4 44
(M J Attwater) *led to over 1f out: wknd fnl f* **7/2**[1]
404 **9** ½ **Stagnite**[80] 4595 7-8-3 46 oh1............................... TimothyMeadows(7) 9 38
(Karen George) *hld up in rr: no real prog wl over 1f out: plugged on* **33/1**
0360 **10** shd **Tokyo Jo (IRE)**[19] 6277 3-8-10 47..............................(p) TGMcLaughlin 11 39
(T T Clement) *racd wdst of all: wl in rr: v wd bnd 2f out: no ch after* **33/1**
0000 **11** ½ **Shantina's Dream (USA)**[8] 6542 3-8-13 50.................... EddieAhern 14 41
(J R Boyle) *restless in stalls: hld up wl in rr: shkn up and no prog wl over 1f out* **50/1**
005 **12** ½ **Lily La Belle**[47] 5567 3-8-13 50.. JimCrowley 8 39
(A W Carroll) *prom towards outer: pushed along 3f out: grad lost pl* **22/1**
2405 **13** 1 **Batchworth Blaise**[22] 6229 4-8-8 49.................. RussellKennemore(5) 2 36
(E A Wheeler) *dwlt: sn in midfield on inner: wknd wl over 1f out* **11/1**
300 **14** 3 **Epidaurian King (IRE)**[17] 6339 4-9-0 50...................... DeanMcKeown 1 29
(D Shaw) *dwlt: rousted along on inner and sn chsd ldng pair: wknd over 2f out* **12/1**

1m 24.32s (-1.57) **Going Correction** -0.15s/f (Stan)
WFA 3 from 4yo+ 1lb **14** Ran SP% **121.8**
Speed ratings (Par 101): **102,99,99,99,98 97,96,95,94,94 94,93,92,89**
CSF £54.79 CT £1116.74 TOTE £4.90: £2.00, £4.60, £7.80; EX 65.40 TRIFECTA Not won..
Owner Phones Direct Partnership **Bred** Jonathan Shack **Trained** Epsom, Surrey

FOCUS
A moderate handicap.

6707 ARENA LEISURE PLC H'CAP 6f (P)
2:30 (2:32) (Class 4) (0-85,84) 3-Y-0+ £4,857 (£1,445; £722; £360) **Stalls Low**

Form RPR
3201 **1** **Ebraam (USA)**[16] 6360 4-8-9 75................................. DeanMcKeown 7 87+
(D Shaw) *t.k.h: pressed ldr: urged along to ld over 1f out: clr ins fnl f* **4/1**[2]
0302 **2** 1¾ **Texas Gold**[6] 6589 9-8-13 79... MartinDwyer 3 85
(W R Muir) *trckd ldrs: effrt on inner 2f out: styd on to take 2nd last 100yds: no ch w wnr* **9/1**
2200 **3** hd **Buy On The Red**[13] 6437 6-9-3 83..............................(p) SaleemGolam 4 88
(W R Muir) *led at modest pce: kicked on over 2f out: hdd over 1f out and nt qckn: lost 2nd fnl 100yds* **14/1**
4606 **4** ¾ **Mandarin Spirit (IRE)**[15] 6391 7-8-9 75........................(b) OscarUrbina 5 78
(G C H Chung) *hld up in 5th: outpcd 2f out: styd on same pce fr over 1f out* **14/1**
0411 **5** 1 **New York Oscar (IRE)**[6] 6589 3-8-12 78 6ex................(p) SebSanders 8 78
(A J McCabe) *t.k.h: hld up in 4th: outpcd 2f out: nt qckn and wl btn over 1f out* **5/4**[1]
3023 **6** 1¾ **Rainbow Mirage (IRE)**[16] 6355 3-9-4 84........................(b[1]) DaneO'Neill 6 78
(E S McMahon) *dwlt: hld up in last pair: outpcd 2f out: n.d after* **5/1**[3]
0310 **7** 1½ **Compton Classic**[24] 6173 5-8-9 75................................(p) JimCrowley 2 64
(J R Boyle) *stdd s: t.k.h: hld up in last pair: outpcd 2f out: no ch after* **25/1**

1m 12.58s (-0.23) **Going Correction** -0.15s/f (Stan) **7** Ran SP% **108.3**
Speed ratings (Par 105): **95,92,92,91,90 87,85**
CSF £34.33 CT £399.03 TOTE £5.70: £2.70, £2.30; EX 31.00 Trifecta £327.50 Pool £507.53 - 1.10 winning units..
Owner The Circle Bloodstock I Limited **Bred** Shadwell Farm LLC **Trained** Danethorpe, Notts

FOCUS
A good sprint handicap, but they went no pace through the early stages, resulting in a few of these taking a grip, and the winning time was unsurprisingly very modest, just 0.31 seconds faster than the earlier two-year-old maiden.

Rainbow Mirage(IRE) Official explanation: jockey said colt missed the break

6708 BUY TICKETS ONLINE H'CAP 5f (P)
3:00 (3:00) (Class 5) (0-75,75) 3-Y-0+ **£3,238** (£963; £481; £240) **Stalls** High

Form RPR
1552 **1** **Desperate Dan**[14] 6405 6-9-4 **75** SebSanders 5 83
(A B Haynes) *racd on outer in midfield: rdn and effrt over 1f out: r.o to ld last 150yds: sn clr* **3/1**[2]

3365 **2** *1 1/4* **Tony The Tap**[22] 6231 6-9-3 **74** (b[1]) SaleemGolam 6 78
(W R Muir) *pushed along in last trio: no prog tl r.o wl fnl f: tk 2nd nr fin* **6/1**

2342 **3** *1/2* **Financial Times (USA)**[190] 1363 5-9-4 **75** (t) MickyFenton 7 77
(Stef Liddiard) *led: drvn and hdd last 150yds: outpcd* **5/1**[3]

3212 **4** *shd* **Hotham**[2] 6667 4-9-1 **72** ChrisCatlin 3 73
(N Wilson) *stdd s: t.k.h and sn trckd ldrs: effrt on inner over 1f out: nt qckn ent fnl f: one pce* **9/4**[1]

015- **5** *shd* **Mogok Ruby**[405] 5606 3-8-13 **70** IanMongan 2 71
(L Montague Hall) *trckd ldrs: rdn and cl enough jst over 1f out: nt qckn and sn btn* **33/1**

5000 **6** *1 1/2* **Egyptian Lord**[14] 6405 4-8-12 **69** LPKeniry 4 65
(Peter Grayson) *dwlt: settled in last trio: effrt 2f out: styd on same pce fr over 1f out: nt rch ldrs* **28/1**

5146 **7** *1 1/4* **Fizzlephut (IRE)**[203] 1080 5-9-0 **71** PaulFitzsimons 8 62
(Miss J R Tooth) *mostly chsd ldr to 1f out: fdd* **25/1**

0634 **8** *1/2* **Bluebok**[6] 6589 6-9-3 **74** (t) DaneO'Neill 1 80+
(J M Bradley) *trckd ldrs: n.m.r wl over 1f out: hmpd 1f out: nt rcvr and eased* **8/1**

5400 **9** *3/4* **Peter Island (FR)**[6] 6589 4-9-4 **75** (v) JimCrowley 10 62
(J Gallagher) *racd on outer in last trio: lost grnd bnd 2f out: no ch after* **20/1**

000 **10** *1 3/4* **Peopleton Brook**[16] 6360 5-8-5 **67** (b) KevinGhunowa[(5)] 9 47
(J M Bradley) *pressed ldrs on outer: hanging and nt qckn wl over 1f out: sn btn* **33/1**

58.30 secs (-1.48) **Going Correction** -0.15s/f (Stan) 10 Ran SP% **115.8**
Speed ratings (Par 103): **105,103,102,102,101 99,97,96,95,92**
CSF £19.44 CT £85.22 TOTE £3.30: £1.20, £2.40, £1.80; EX 22.30 Trifecta £126.00 Pool £813.06 - 4.58 winning units..
Owner Joe McCarthy **Bred** Sheikh Amin Dahlawi **Trained** Limpley Stoke, Bath

FOCUS
A decent sprint handicap run at a true pace and yet again those that were brought with their efforts down the middle of the track held sway.
Bluebok Official explanation: jockey said gelding was denied a clear run

6709 PLAY GOLF COME RACING H'CAP 1m 4f (P)
3:30 (3:30) (Class 5) (0-75,81) 3-Y-0+ **£3,238** (£963; £481; £240) **Stalls** Low

Form RPR
622 **1** **Generous Lad (IRE)**[89] 4318 4-9-8 **71** (p) DaneO'Neill 6 77
(A B Haynes) *hld up in last pair: effrt wl over 1f out: urged along and styd on to ld ins fnl f: in command after* **4/1**[2]

5505 **2** *3/4* **Venir Rouge**[13] 6422 3-9-6 **75** TGMcLaughlin 2 80
(M Salaman) *settled in last pair: rdn over 3f out: effrt on outer over 2f out: styd on fnl f to take 2nd nr fin* **6/1**[3]

3201 **3** *1/2* **River Deuce**[23] 6211 3-9-6 **75** SebSanders 1 79
(M H Tompkins) *trckd ldr: rdn to ld jst over 2f out: hdd u.p ins fnl f: one pce* **9/4**[1]

2361 **4** *shd* **Know The Law**[8] 6545 3-9-9 **81** 6ex MarcHalford[(3)] 4 85
(D R C Elsworth) *sn trckd ldng pair: effrt 2f out: drvn and upsides 1f out: nt qckn* **9/4**[1]

6604 **5** *4* **Ocean Avenue (IRE)**[26] 6124 8-9-7 **70** JimCrowley 3 68
(C A Horgan) *sn settled in 4th: rdn and outpcd fr 2f out: no ch after* **15/2**

66-0 **6** *3/4* **River City (IRE)**[26] 6131 10-8-12 **61** SamHitchcott 5 57
(Noel T Chance) *led: rdn 3f out: hdd jst over 2f out: sn btn* **20/1**

2m 32.23s (-2.16) **Going Correction** -0.15s/f (Stan)
WFA 3 from 4yo+ 6lb 6 Ran SP% **112.4**
Speed ratings (Par 103): **101,100,100,100,97 96**
CSF £27.22 TOTE £4.30: £1.60, £3.40; EX 27.40.
Owner Mike Bowden **Bred** Frank Towey **Trained** Limpley Stoke, Bath
■ Stewards' Enquiry : Dane O'NeillM one-day ban: used whip down shoulder in forehand position (Nov 17)

FOCUS
A rather messy contest as the early pace was by no means strong and it developed into a sprint over the last three furlongs.

6710 LINGFIELDPARK.CO.UK APPRENTICE H'CAP 1m (P)
4:00 (4:00) (Class 5) (0-70,73) 3-Y-0+ **£3,276** (£967; £483) **Stalls** High

Form RPR
4400 **1** **Satin Braid**[8] 6547 3-8-13 **64** AmyBaker 2 71
(D R C Elsworth) *hld up in midfield: effrt 2f out: urged along and styd on fr over 1f out: led last 50yds* **10/1**

3000 **2** *3/4* **Meditation**[8] 6547 5-9-3 **66** JamieJones 4 71
(I A Wood) *chsd ldr: outpcd 3f out but clr of rest: clsd u.p fnl f: led last 75yds: sn hdd and one pce* **20/1**

0341 **3** *nk* **Waterline Twenty (IRE)**[3] 6646 4-9-5 **73** 6ex RichardEvans[(5)] 3 78
(P D Evans) *stdd s: hld up in last pair: effrt over 2f out: styd on fnl f: nt quite rch ldng pair* **7/2**[3]

1311 **4** *nk* **Samuel Charles**[20] 6268 9-9-7 **70** (p) JackMitchell 6 74
(C R Dore) *chsd ldng pair: rdn over 3f out: sn outpcd: kpt on again fnl f and clsng at fin* **11/4**[1]

0004 **5** *hd* **Royal Amnesty**[22] 6226 4-8-8 **57** MCGeran 7 60
(G C H Chung) *hld up in last pair: effrt on outer 2f out: styd on fnl f: nt rch ldrs* **3/1**[2]

0044 **6** *nk* **Border Edge**[12] 6447 9-8-8 **57** (v) JackDean 8 60
(J J Bridger) *racd on outer in midfield: outpcd 3f out: sn struggling in last pair: styd on again fnl f* **14/1**

5116 **7** *hd* **Seneschal**[12] 6447 6-8-13 **67** PNolan[(5)] 5 69
(A B Haynes) *led: drew clr over 3f out: 3l up over 1f out but styd on inner: swamped last 75yds* **9/2**

1206 **8** *9* **Rowan Lodge (IRE)**[14] 6412 5-8-10 **62** MatthewDavies[(3)] 1 44
(J R Boyle) *t.k.h: hld up in midfield: wknd over 2f out: sn bhd* **12/1**

1m 36.91s (-2.52) **Going Correction** -0.15s/f (Stan)
WFA 3 from 4yo+ 2lb 8 Ran SP% **120.3**
Speed ratings (Par 103): **106,105,104,104,104 104,103,94**
CSF £187.63 CT £847.23 TOTE £9.80: £2.80, £5.70, £2.00; EX 197.40 Trifecta £344.80 Part won. Pool £485.73 - 0.10 winning units. Place 6 £103.22, Place 5 £67.92..
Owner Wyck Hall Stud **Bred** Wyck Hall Stud Ltd **Trained** Newmarket, Suffolk

FOCUS
Seneschal set a decent pace from the off, too quick as things turned out, and the winning time was 1.83 seconds quicker than the opening maiden.
T/Plt: £103.20 to a £1 stake. Pool: £47,022.00. 332.35 winning tickets. T/Qpdt: £50.20 to a £1 stake. Pool: £3,133.00. 46.10 winning tickets. JN

6663 FLEMINGTON (L-H)
Tuesday, November 6

OFFICIAL GOING: Good

6711a THE LAVAZZA LONG BLACK (H'CAP) 1m 6f
12:45 (12:00) 3-Y-0+ **£26,815** (£5,847; £5,847; £1,613; £806)

RPR
1 **Red Lord (AUS)**[10] 6516 4-8-13 NashRawiller 13 102
(A Cummings, Australia) **17/1**

2 *2* **Dirt Music (AUS)** 6-8-5 (b) SebastianMurphy 14 91
(G Baker, Australia) **50/1**

2 *dht* **Completion (NZ)** 5-8-6 DNikolic 8 92
(G Rogerson, Australia) **17/10**[1]

4 *1 3/4* **Vicello (NZ)**[184] 3-8-5 DwayneDunn 15 88
(P Stokes, Australia) **6/1**[2]

5 *1* **Daneheart (AUS)** 5-8-5 (b) DMoor 10 87
(G Moloney, Australia)

6 *1/2* **Chiefcomingfirst (NZ)** 5-8-5 CBrown 4 86
(B Laming, Australia)

7 *nk* **Southern Courage (NZ)**[13] 5-9-2 CNewitt 12 97
(Mick Price, Australia)

8 *1 1/4* **Special Scene (AUS)**[10] 6516 9-8-6 MPegus 2 85
(Dan O'Sullivan, New Zealand)

9 *shd* **Aces High (NZ)**[17] 6-8-8 (b) WHernan 11 87
(Tom Cowan, Australia)

10 *1 1/4* **Epona Miss (AUS)** 6-8-5 RCartwright 18 82
(D Saxon)

11 *2 1/2* **Satinspin (NZ)**[13] 6-8-6 (b) BShinn 3 80
(R Smerdon, Australia)

12 *shd* **Dicktator (NZ)**[10] 6516 7-8-6 (b) SSeamer 1 79
(R Laing, Australia)

F **Bay Story (USA)**[31] 6033 5-9-2 MZahra 19 —
(B Ellison) *sn racing in 2nd 1 l off ldr: led gng wl appr st and stl in ld whn broke down and fell 150yds out: destroyed* **16/1**[3]

B **Bling Bling (NZ)**[10] 6516 6-8-7 (b) GChilds 7 —
(M Moroney, Australia)

2m 58.12s (178.12)
WFA 3 from 4yo+ 8lb 14 Ran SP% **64.7**

Owner Diamond Thoroughbreds et al **Bred** Strawberry Hill Stud **Trained** Australia

NOTEBOOK
Bay Story(USA), who missed the cut for the Melbourne Cup, broke his near hind leg while still in front in the closing stages and he had to be destroyed.

6712a EMIRATES MELBOURNE CUP (GROUP 1) (H'CAP) 2m
4:00 (12:00) 3-Y-0+
£1,250,000 (£302,419; £151,210; £80,645; £50,403; £44,355)

RPR
1 **Efficient (NZ)**[10] 6517 4-8-9 MRodd 10 123
(G Rogerson, Australia) *racd in 12th: n.m.r and taken bk 4f out: swtchd out over 3f out: 15th and wdst of all st: str run on outside to ld last 50yds* **16/1**

2 *1/2* **Purple Moon (IRE)**[17] 6354 4-8-7 DMOliver 15 120
(L M Cumani) *racd in 8th: hdwy to go 3rd st: disputing ld whn rdn 1 1/2f out: led appr fnl f: hung lft: hdd and no ex last 50yds* **9/2**[2]

3 *2 1/2* **Mahler**[52] 5408 3-8-0 SBaster 6 119
(A P O'Brien, Ire) *sn wnt 2nd: led wl over 3f out: hdd appr fnl f: kpt on gamely whn strly pressed fr 100yds out to hold 3rd* **9/1**

4 *nk* **Zipping (AUS)**[3] 6663 6-8-8 DNikolic 22 118
(G Rogerson, Australia) *hld up in 15th: hdwy and 10th towards outside st: r.o to press for 3rd 100yds out: one pce clsng stages* **13/2**[3]

5 *1* **Dolphin Jo (AUS)**[10] 6516 5-8-2 ClareLindop 1 111
(Terry & Karina O'Sullivan, Australia) *racd in 5th: 6th st: kpt on steadily down inner* **60/1**

6 *snk* **On A Jeune (AUS)**[17] 7-8-4 KerrinMcEvoy 4 113
(A Payne, Australia) *hld up in 13th: 14th st: styd on towards outside fnl 2f* **30/1**

7 *1 3/4* **Blue Monday**[17] 6354 6-8-12 NashRawiller 14 119
(D Hayes, Australia) *racd in 6th: 7th st: kpt on at one pce fnl 2f* **30/1**

8 *2* **Master O'Reilly (NZ)**[17] 6354 5-8-7 VDuric 17 112
(Danny O'Brien, Australia) *racd in 16th: 13th st towards outside: kpt on at one pce* **28/10**[1]

9 *1 1/4* **Sculptor (NZ)**[3] 5-8-3 LisaCropp 8 106
(P McKenzie, Australia) *2nd early: sn relegated to 3rd: 2nd st: sn rdn and one pce* **30/1**

10 *3/4* **Lazer Sharp (AUS)**[10] 6516 4-8-4 BShinn 16 107
(D Hayes, Australia) *racd in 10th: 8th st: sn rdn and one pce* **50/1**

11 *shd* **Douro Valley (AUS)**[3] 6663 6-8-2 (b) JWinks 13 104
(Danny O'Brien, Australia) *racd in 7th: 5th st: outpcd fnl 1 1/2f* **40/1**

12 *shd* **Sirmione (AUS)**[3] 6663 4-8-2 (b) PMertens 20 104
(J B Cummings, Australia) *racd in 18th: 16th st: nvr a factor* **12/1**

13 *1 1/2* **Princess Coup (AUS)**[3] 6663 4-8-1 NoelHarris 9 102
(M Walker, New Zealand) *racd in 17th: a in rr* **12/1**

14 *3 1/2* **Tawqeet (USA)**[3] 6663 5-9-0 (b) DwayneDunn 3 111
(D Hayes, Australia) *racd in 9th: 12th st: sn btn* **60/1**

15 *2 3/4* **Eskimo Queen (NZ)**[10] 6517 4-8-1 (b) CNewitt 5 95
(M Moroney, Australia) *racd in 11th: n.d* **25/1**

16 *hd* **Scenic Shot (AUS)**[3] 6663 5-8-4 CraigAWilliams 19 98
(D Morton, Australia) *hld up in last: a bhd* **100/1**

17 *2 1/2* **Black Tom (AUS)**[3] 7-8-7 (b) PHall 21 98
(D Hayes, Australia) *racd in 14th: 9th st: sn wknd* **200/1**

18 *1 1/2* **Sarrera (AUS)**[10] 6516 7-8-3 SebastianMurphy 23 92
(M Moroney, Australia) *racd in 20th: a bhd* **100/1**

19 *snk* **Blutigeroo (AUS)**[17] 6354 6-8-11 LNolen 12 100
(C Little, Australia) *racd in 4th: wknd over 2f out* **60/1**

20 6 **Railings (AUS)**[3] 6663 6-8-11 ....(b) SArnold 18 93
(Roger James, New Zealand) *racd in 19th: a bhd* **200/1**

21 25 **Tungsten Strike (USA)**[73] 4803 6-8-8 .... DarryllHolland 2 63
(Mrs A J Perrett) *set stdy early pce: led to wl over 3f out: wknd qckly* **30/1**

3m 23.34s (3.70)
WFA 3 from 4yo+ 9lb **21** Ran SP% **118.1**
(including $1 stake): WIN 22.40; PL 7.00, 1.80, 4.00; DF 76.10; SF 176.90.
Owner Mr & Mrs L J Williams et al **Bred** Bloodstock Resources Ltd & Cambridge Hunt Ltd
Trained Australia

FOCUS
A tremendously competitive race as usual, although the gallop was not that strong and plenty of them held a chance turning in. The principal British and Irish challengers acquitted themselves with huge credit. Mahler's stablemate Scorpion was due to run but incurred a career-ending injury a few days before the race.

NOTEBOOK
Efficient(NZ) came back to form after a long spell in the wilderness since his success in the Victoria Derby last year. Connections removed the blinkers he wore last time in the Caulfield Cup and even schooled him over hurdles during the week before this race which, combined, seemed to spark him back into life. He was due to take part in this race last year, but was scratched just before the event as they felt he was not quite ready. His task looked a big one rounding the final bend, as he had virtually nothing behind him, but his jockey galvanised a big effort out of him and he ended up quite a cosy winner. One suspects that his very wealthy owner will target this race for the horse from now, and he looks sure to come back next year, all being well, with a big chance.
Purple Moon(IRE) looked all set to end his Australian adventure with a win in the country's biggest race. Given every chance by his jockey and in front approaching the final furlong, he looked the winner until Efficient loomed large on his outside. He kept battling away for pressure but did not help himself by edging left. That said, the winner is very good on his day. He will return to England with his reputation enhanced and remains a versatile sort with regards to trip.
Mahler was given an enterprising ride off his low weight. Never far from the lead and in front inside the last half mile, he kept on strongly and ran a blinder, especially when one considers he was by far the youngest in the field. As long as the whole experience does not have a detrimental effect on him, he will make a fine stayer. Indeed he could prove a key member of Coolmore's 2008 team.
Zipping(AUS), who is in the same ownership as the winner, kept on well for his jockey but was not going to get to the leaders. Fourth in this race last year carrying 4lb less, he is the right sort for this race and looks sure to be a regular feature in the Cup.
Master O'Reilly(NZ) looked the one to beat after his victory in the Caulfield Cup. However, he never got involved and was most disappointing. The jury is out as to whether he stays the 2m trip.
Tungsten Strike(USA) was given a very prominent ride but, despite not setting a quick pace, dropped out very tamely under pressure. This was clearly not his running and the trip down to Australia must have got to him.

6641 KEMPTON (A.W) (R-H)
Wednesday, November 7

OFFICIAL GOING: Standard
Wind: Moderate, across

6713 DAY TIME, NIGHT TIME, GREAT TIME H'CAP 1m 2f (P)
6:20 (6:20) (Class 6) (0-52,56) 3-Y-0+ **£2,047** (£604; £302) **Stalls** High

Form RPR

3456 1 **Dinner Date**[9] 6529 5-9-2 **52** .... J-PGuillambert 7 62
(T Keddy) *mid-div: hdwy 5f out: drvn and styd on wl to ld fnl 100yds* **8/1**[3]

0-04 2 nk **Arthur's Edge**[7] 6597 3-8-3 **48** .... TolleyDean(5) 6 58
(B Palling) *lw: sn chsng ldr: rdn to ld over 1f out: hdd sn after: rallied to retake 2nd cl home but a jst hld by wnr* **14/1**

6413 3 nk **Lilac Moon (GER)**[19] 6315 3-8-12 **52** .... RichardKingscote 13 61
(N J Vaughan) *chsd ldrs: rdn 2f out: led 1f out: hdd fnl 100yds: outpcd for 2nd cl home* **11/2**[2]

5001 4 1 3/4 **Bowl Of Cherries**[7] 6577 4-9-2 **52** 6ex....................(b) SebSanders 10 58
(I A Wood) *lw: chsd ldrs: rdn 2f out: styd on same pce u.p fnl f* **4/1**[1]

3351 5 1 1/4 **Summer Bounty**[8] 6569 11-9-1 **51** 6ex.................... LPKeniry 11 54
(F Jordan) *s.i.s: in rr: rdn 3f out: kpt on fr over 1f out: nt rch ldrs* **20/1**

0243 6 nk **Granary Girl**[13] 6452 5-8-13 **52** .... WilliamBuick(3) 4 54
(J Pearce) *in rr: rdn over 2f out: styd on wl fnl f: gng on cl home* **10/1**

0040 7 3/4 **Garibaldi (GER)**[19] 6304 5-8-11 **52**....................(b) JamesO'Reilly(5) 5 53
(J O'Reilly) *s.i.s: hdwy into mid-div 5f out: rdn 3f out: one pce fnl 2f* **16/1**

0020 8 2 1/2 **Centenary (IRE)**[54] 5388 3-8-10 **50** .... EddieAhern 1 46
(D E Cantillon) *s.i.s: in rr: rdn 4f out: sme prog fnl f* **14/1**

0000 9 hd **Windy Prospect**[14] 6431 5-9-0 **50** ....(p) IanMongan 14 46
(Mrs L J Mongan) *chsd ldrs: rdn 3f out: wknd fr 2f out* **25/1**

0306 10 3/4 **Ernmoor**[23] 6238 5-8-8 **47** .... JerryO'Dwyer(3) 2 41
(J R Jenkins) *racd towards outside: nvr in contention* **66/1**

00-2 11 3/4 **Montana Sky (IRE)**[9] 6529 4-8-6 **47** .... KevinGhunowa(5) 3 40
(R A Harris) *chsd ldrs: rdn 4f out: wknd over 2f out* **8/1**[3]

0041 12 1 **Sekula Pata (NZ)**[9] 6529 8-9-1 **56** 6ex....................(v) SCreighton(5) 12 47
(E J Creighton) *chsd ldrs: rdn 4f out: wknd fr 3f out* **8/1**[3]

0200 13 3 **Storm Path (IRE)**[9] 6529 3-8-12 **52** .... DaneO'Neill 8 37
(D R C Elsworth) *in rr: hdwy 1/2-way: wknd 3f out* **11/1**

005 14 2 1/2 **Surdoue**[9] 6529 7-9-0 **50** .... AdrianMcCarthy 9 30
(D Morris) *led tl hdd over 1f out: sn wknd: eased whn no ch* **14/1**

2m 6.22s (-2.78) **Going Correction** -0.225s/f (Stan)
WFA 3 from 4yo+ 4lb **14** Ran SP% **122.1**
Speed ratings (Par 101): **102,101,101,100,99 98,98,96,96,95 94,94,91,89**
CSF £114.63 CT £679.49 TOTE £9.50: £2.60, £5.00, £2.00; EX 175.50.
Owner Mrs H Keddy **Bred** J M Greetham **Trained** Newmarket, Suffolk

FOCUS
A moderate handicap around the inner loop and there seemed a fair pace on thanks to Surdoue. There appeared no particular bias towards or against front-runners, as the second and third were always handy whilst the winner came from off the pace. Solid form.
Sekula Pata(NZ) Official explanation: jockey said gelding returned lame
Surdoue Official explanation: jockey said gelding lost its action

6714 PANORAMIC RESTAURANT LOYALTY SCHEME MAIDEN AUCTION STKS 7f (P)
6:50 (6:50) (Class 6) 2-Y-0 **£2,047** (£604; £302) **Stalls** High

Form RPR

43 1 **Southpaw Lad**[15] 6404 2-8-10 0 .... DaneO'Neill 1 72+
(J R Best) *hld up in rr: stl plenty to do over 2f out whn swtchd rt to ins and rapid hdwy over 1f out: str chal ins fnl f to ld cl home: hld on all out* **15/8**[1]

05 2 shd **Border Owl (IRE)**[11] 6494 2-9-0 0 .... RichardHughes 2 76+
(R Hannon) *lw: mid-div: shkn up over 2f out: rapid hdwy ins fnl f: fin strly: jst failed* **9/2**[3]

0 3 1/2 **Candida's Beau**[35] 5895 2-9-0 0 .... SebSanders 3 75
(R M Beckett) *chsd ldrs: rdn and styd on fr over 1f out to take narrow ld ins fnl f: hdd and no ex cl home* **7/1**

0 4 3 **Bertbrand**[15] 6401 2-8-12 0 .... EddieAhern 8 66
(M Botti) *lw: chsd ldr: led 2f out: rdn over 1f out: hdd ins fnl f: btn whn hmpd cl home* **7/1**

002 5 1 1/2 **Randama Bay (IRE)**[15] 6404 2-8-11 76.................... RichardThomas 12 61
(I A Wood) *lw: chsd ldrs: rdn over 2f out: styd chsng ldrs tl hmpd and wknd ins fnl f* **7/2**[2]

00 6 2 1/2 **Star Grazer**[16] 6384 2-8-8 0.................... MartinDwyer 4 52+
(C F Wall) *s.i.s: in rr: pushed along over 3f out: mod prog fnl f* **16/1**

0000 7 nk **La Varrosa**[15] 6404 2-8-5 52 ow1.................... GregFairley 11 48
(Mrs P N Dutfield) *led tl hdd 2f out: wknd fnl f* **50/1**

00 8 3/4 **Wogan's Sister**[15] 6401 2-8-8 0.................... JamesDoyle 6 49
(I A Wood) *chsd ldrs: rdn over 2f out: wknd over 1f out* **50/1**

0 9 2 **Black Or Red (IRE)**[11] 6503 2-8-13 0.................... DavidKinsella 10 49
(I A Wood) *w'like: outpcd most of way* **33/1**

00P 10 1 3/4 **Valentine Blue**[24] 6202 2-8-11 0.................... SamHitchcott 9 43
(A B Haynes) *chsd ldrs: rdn 3f out: wknd fr 2f out* **25/1**

000 11 6 **Westwood Dawn**[12] 6477 2-9-0 25....................(v) DanielTudhope 7 31
(Mrs N Macauley) *w'like: slowly away: a in rr* **100/1**

060 12 51 **Help (IRE)**[83] 4539 2-8-4 45....................(b) ChrisCatlin 5 —
(Mrs P N Dutfield) *a in rr: t.o* **66/1**

1m 26.5s (-0.30) **Going Correction** -0.225s/f (Stan) **12** Ran SP% **119.3**
Speed ratings (Par 94): **92,91,91,87,86 83,82,82,79,77 70,12**
CSF £10.04 TOTE £2.60: £1.40, £1.80, £3.10; EX 8.70.
Owner SN Racing II **Bred** S Nunn **Trained** Hucking, Kent
■ Stewards' Enquiry : Seb Sanders four-day ban: used whip with excessive frequency (Nov 20-23)

FOCUS
This looked just an ordinary maiden auction event and little separated the front three at the line, whilst a couple met trouble inside the last furlong and the front five cn be considered to have pulled even further further clear from the others than the margins might suggest.

NOTEBOOK
Southpaw Lad, fractionally behind Randama Bay at Lingfield last time, was again given plenty to do but was produced with his effort in plenty of time on this occasion and the longer home straight was probably a big help. Diving to the inside after the intersection, he was inclined to hang left once in front, causing problems for a couple, and in the end was all out to hold on. He may be the type that needs to be delivered as late as possible, but should have a future in fair handicaps next year. He was on his toes and got warm beforehand, but that's probably just him. (op 2-1 tchd 13-8 and 9-4 in places)
Border Owl(IRE) ◆, who has been struggling to get home over longer trips in his first two starts in soft ground on turf, if anything found this too sharp. His strong late finish only just failed and he would be of obvious interest over 1m on this surface, especially as he can now be handicapped. (op 3-1)
Candida's Beau, who showed a little ability on his debut over course and distance last month, was ridden handily again but, despite coming off the bridle a long way out, he never stopped trying and went down with all guns blazing. He is entitled to improve again from this. (tchd 13-2)
Bertbrand, an eye-catcher on his debut, was always up there and had every chance but seemed to have run his race when squeezed out well inside the last furlong. He has not had much luck in both of his outings now and has the ability to win a race on this surface, especially once handicapped after one more run. (op 8-1)
Randama Bay(IRE), who finished just in front of the winner at Lingfield last time, had every chance until his old rival hung across him inside the last furlong. He would not have won, but would have been closer and his mark of 76 provides something of a benchmark to the form. (op 4-1 tchd 5-1)

6715 DIGIBET NURSERY 1m (P)
7:20 (7:20) (Class 6) (0-70,76) 2-Y-0 **£2,047** (£604; £302) **Stalls** High

Form RPR

0001 1 **Points Of View**[7] 6584 2-9-13 **76** 6ex.................... SebSanders 7 83+
(Sir Mark Prescott) *swtg: trckd ldrs: rdn and bmpd 2f out: drvn to ld wl over 1f out: styd on wl: readily* **1/1**[1]

5505 2 2 1/2 **Greek Theatre (USA)**[13] 6449 2-9-4 **67**....................(e) JamesDoyle 11 66+
(Mrs A J Perrett) *lw: chsd ldrs: hmpd and lost pl 5f out: hdwy fr 2f out: fin wl but no ch w wnr* **8/1**[2]

0305 3 nk **Bid Art (IRE)**[51] 5471 2-8-13 **65**.................... WilliamBuick(3) 4 64
(A M Balding) *lw: slowly away: in rr: pushed along 3f out and edgd rt: str run over 1f out: fin wl to press for 2nd cl home but nvr any ch w wnr* **16/1**

0060 4 nk **Shadows Fall (USA)**[14] 6433 2-8-13 **62**.................... NelsonDeSouza 5 60
(P F I Cole) *chsd ldrs: rdn to press ldrs over 1f out: one pce ins fnl f* **50/1**

000 5 2 **Clear Daylight**[15] 6404 2-9-1 **64**.................... DaneO'Neill 2 57
(J R Best) *mid-div: hdwy and swtchd rt 2f out: pressed ldrs 1f out: sn n.m.r and one pce* **12/1**

0100 6 hd **Love Valentine (IRE)**[16] 6379 2-9-7 **70**.................... GregFairley 1 63
(M Johnston) *in rr: rdn 3f out: styd on fr over 1f out: nvr gng pce to be competitive* **9/1**[3]

0304 7 nk **Little Toto**[24] 6202 2-9-2 **65**.................... AdamKirby 12 57
(C G Cox) *led 2f: styd chsng ldr: upsides fr 2f out tl wknd ins fnl f* **12/1**

000 8 shd **Fareeha**[57] 5301 2-9-3 **66**.................... MartinDwyer 13 58+
(J H M Gosden) *chsng ldrs whn hmpd and lost pl 5f out: hdwy whn hmpd 2f out: nt rcvr* **16/1**

0502 9 hd **Towy Boy (IRE)**[15] 6401 2-9-4 **67**.................... RichardThomas 8 58
(I A Wood) *plld hrd: led after 2f: hung lft 2f out: hdd sn after and wknd ins fnl f* **14/1**

6540 10 1 1/4 **Bozeman Trail**[35] 5914 2-9-0 **68**.................... TolleyDean(5) 6 57
(P F I Cole) *in rr: rdn and hdwy fr 3f out: nvr gng pce to rch ldrs and wknd fnl f* **25/1**

0030 11 1 1/2 **Ledgerwood**[13] 6449 2-9-2 **65**.................... TQuinn 10 50
(J W Hills) *chsd ldrs: hmpd 5f out: styd front rnk tl hmpd 2f out: sn wknd* **25/1**

1000 12 15 **Ocean Glory (IRE)**[11] 6502 2-9-3 **66**.................... LPKeniry 3 17
(Peter Grayson) *outpcd most of way* **66/1**

0010 13 9 **King Supreme (IRE)**[53] 5423 2-9-5 **68**.................... RichardHughes 14 —
(R Hannon) *lw: chsd ldrs: rdn 3f out: wknd ins fnl 2f* **9/1**[3]

1m 39.57s (-1.23) **Going Correction** -0.225s/f (Stan) **13** Ran SP% **126.1**
Speed ratings (Par 94): **97,94,94,93,91 91,91,91,91,89 88,73,64**
CSF £9.72 CT £98.87 TOTE £2.10: £1.30, £1.80, £4.40; EX 12.70.
Owner G Moore - Osborne House **Bred** Limestone And Tara Studs **Trained** Newmarket, Suffolk

FOCUS
A modest nursery in which there was a bit of trouble and both the second and third compromised their chances at different stages, but even so the winner proved different class especially as things did not go perfectly for him either.

NOTEBOOK
Points Of View, carrying a 6lb penalty for his Lingfield success, was trying this trip for the first time. He can be given extra credit for this win as he was sweating badly beforehand, just as he did last time, and saw a lot of daylight as he raced keenly around the outside. Despite all of that he found plenty when asked and had little difficulty forging clear. There should be more to come from him. (tchd 11-10 and 6-5 in a place)

The Form Book, Raceform Ltd, Compton, RG20 6NL

Greek Theatre(USA) ◆, up in trip for this sand debut after finishing unplaced in four starts on turf, ran a tremendous race to finish so close as he was lucky to stay on his feet after appearing to clip heels racing towards the end of the back straight. He looks the type that will continue to progress with racing and it should not be long before he goes one better. (op 9-1)
Bid Art(IRE) ◆, another trying this trip for the first time on his sand debut, completely fluffed the start and gave his rivals a few lengths start, so he did well to make the frame and the way he powered home down the outside suggests he should be up to winning a race like this when he breaks on terms.
Shadows Fall(USA), well beaten in all five of his outings so far and reverting to 1m after a couple of tries over further, had every chance on this handicap debut and this was a major improvement. There seemed no fluke about it. (op 40-1)
Clear Daylight ◆, making his handicap debut after finishing well beaten in three maidens, was the eye-catcher of the race. Switched right over to the inside rail after the intersection in order to get a run, his rider then eased him off possibly in the anticipation of Little Toto hanging further across him that he did, and he was not given a hard time from then on. He is one to watch out for next time. (op 16-1)
Love Valentine(IRE), who landed her maiden over course and distance, was dropped in from the outside stall, but did not get going until it was far too late and probably needs further now. (op 8-1)
Fareeha, making her sand and nursery debuts, got caught in the backwash after Greek Theatre got hampered down the back straight and was again at the end of a chain reaction passing the intersection, so can be rated a bit closer. (op 14-1)

6716 DIGIBET.COM H'CAP 1m (P)
7:50 (7:50) (Class 6) (0-65,65) 3-Y-0+ **£2,047** (£604; £302) **Stalls** High

Form RPR
025 **1** **Smokin Joe**[9] 6547 6-9-3 **62**....(b) GeorgeBaker 7 71
(J R Best) *hld up in rr: hdwy and swtchd rt 2f out: led 1f out: drvn out* **4/1**[2]
0000 **2** *1 1/2* **Turn Me On (IRE)**[39] 5476 4-9-0 **59**.... GrahamGibbons 4 65
(T D Walford) *mid-div: rdn and hdwy over 2f out: styd on u.p fnl f to take 2nd cl home but a hld by wnr* **5/1**
1060 **3** *nk* **Inquisitress**[7] 6579 3-8-11 **58**.... EddieAhern 8 63
(J J Bridger) *chsd ldrs: rdn to ld over 2f out: hdd 1f out: styd on same pce and ct for 2nd cl home* **16/1**
5411 **4** *2* **Time To Regret**[5] 6629 7-9-2 **61** 6ex....(p) DanielTudhope 6 61
(I W McInnes) *lw: chsd ldrs: rdn 3f out: wknd fnl f* **3/1**[1]
6000 **5** *1 3/4* **Magic Warrior**[5] 6628 7-9-2 **61**.... PatDobbs 9 57+
(J C Fox) *in tch: effrt whn hmpd 2f out: styd on same pce after* **16/1**
1044 **6** *1/2* **Mick Is Back**[5] 6623 3-8-13 **60**....(p) SebSanders 12 55+
(G G Margarson) *chsd ldrs: rdn and n.m.r 2f out: sn outpcd* **9/2**[3]
3114 **7** *1* **Justcallmehandsome**[19] 6316 5-8-6 **58**....(v) SophieDoyle(7) 3 51
(D J S Ffrench Davis) *racd wd thrght: nvr gng pce to trble ldrs* **9/2**[3]
0040 **8** *1 1/2* **Smash Hit (IRE)**[24] 6196 4-8-13 **61**.... NeilChalmers(3) 1 50+
(David Pinder) *t.k.h: hdwy to chse ldrs 3f out: rdn and one pce whn hmpd 2f out and sn btn* **33/1**
0600 **9** *1 1/2* **Fancy You (IRE)**[9] 6537 4-8-3 **51** oh6.... LukeMorris(3) 5 37
(A W Carroll) *w ldr: led 3f out: hdd over 2f out: sn wknd* **50/1**
260/ **10** *2 1/2* **Aldbury Grey (IRE)**[778] 5394 4-9-1 **60**.... DaneO'Neill 11 40
(A B Haynes) *slowly away: a in rr* **50/1**
0000 **11** *1/2* **Top Gear**[25] 6175 5-9-6 **65**....(b) IanMongan 10 44
(Mrs L J Mongan) *sn led: hdd 3f out: wkng whn hmpd ins fnl 2f* **25/1**
000 **12** *1 1/2* **Elegans**[20] 6286 3-8-4 **51** oh6.... ChrisCatlin 2 27
(Mrs C A Dunnett) *chsd ldrs: rdn 3f out: sn wknd* **66/1**

1m 39.18s (-1.62) **Going Correction** -0.225s/f (Stan)
WFA 3 from 4yo+ 2lb **12** Ran SP% **122.0**
Speed ratings (Par 101): **99,97,97,95,93 92,91,90,88,86 85,84**
CSF £24.30 CT £297.88 TOTE £4.80: £1.60, £2.10, £3.60; EX 27.00.
Owner G G Racing **Bred** Alan Spargo Ltd **Trained** Hucking, Kent
■ Stewards' Enquiry : George Baker caution: careless riding; three-day ban: careless riding (Nov 19-21)
Ian Mongan two-day ban: struck gelding in annoyance with whip (Nov 19-20)

FOCUS
An ordinary handicap and the early tempo was only modest, but even so those that set it faded out of it and the front two came from off the pace. The bulk of the field tended to lug over to the inside rail after the intersection and a few met trouble. The form is rated through the winner and third.

6717 DIGIBET SPORTS BETTING H'CAP 7f (P)
8:20 (8:21) (Class 6) (0-65,65) 3-Y-0+ **£2,047** (£604; £302) **Stalls** High

Form RPR
3136 **1** **Blackmalkin (USA)**[8] 6575 3-9-3 **64**.... SebSanders 8 72
(C E Brittain) *in tch: rdn 3f out: str run fr over 1f out to ld last 110yds: drvn out* **4/1**[2]
0250 **2** *1/2* **Palais Polaire**[7] 6587 5-8-6 **52**.... DavidKinsella 2 59
(J A Geake) *wnt lft s and s.i.s: rapid hdwy to ld after 1f: rdn: hung rt and rdr lost whip appr fnl f: hdd and one pce last 110yds* **14/1**
4202 **3** *1/2* **Beneking**[14] 6431 7-8-9 **55**....(p) ChrisCatlin 6 61
(D Burchell) *led 1f: styd chsng ldr: rdn over 2f out: kpt on ins fnl f but nvr quite gng pce of ldng duo* **9/2**[3]
3200 **4** *1* **Tilsworth Charlie**[15] 6413 4-8-11 **57**....(b) EddieAhern 11 62+
(J R Jenkins) *chsd ldrs: effrt u.p over 1f out: one pce ins fnl f and wknd cl home* **14/1**
5116 **5** *2* **Wadnagin (IRE)**[6] 6610 3-9-2 **63**.... RichardThomas 3 61
(I A Wood) *in rr: rdn along over 3f out: mod prog fnl f* **12/1**
0014 **6** *3 1/2* **Vanadium**[4] 6647 5-9-5 **65**.... GeorgeBaker 5 53
(G L Moore) *chsd ldrs: rdn 3f out: wknd ins fnl 2f* **3/1**[1]
0404 **7** *shd* **Mythical Charm**[14] 6431 8-8-8 **54**....(t) J-PGuillambert 9 42
(J J Bridger) *a in rr* **12/1**
0415 **8** *4* **Monashee Prince (IRE)**[15] 6415 5-8-13 **59**....(v) DaneO'Neill 4 36
(J R Best) *t.k.h: in tch: rdn 3f out: wknd 2f out* **9/2**[3]
001/ **9** *20* **Growler**[144] 6-8-9 **55**.... GrahamGibbons 7 —
(T D Walford) *sn bhd: eased whn no ch fnl f* **14/1**

1m 25.51s (-1.29) **Going Correction** -0.225s/f (Stan)
WFA 3 from 4yo+ 1lb **9** Ran SP% **116.7**
Speed ratings (Par 101): **98,97,96,95,93 89,89,84,61**
CSF £58.59 CT £265.40 TOTE £5.50: £2.00, £4.00, £1.80; EX 54.70.
Owner Sheikh Marwan Al Maktoum **Bred** Darley **Trained** Newmarket, Suffolk

FOCUS
A modest handicap and not many ever got into it. There was little separating the front four at the line and the form, rated around the placed horses, looks ordinary but sound.
Growler Official explanation: jockey said gelding stopped quickly

6718 TFM NETWORKS H'CAP 6f (P)
8:50 (8:50) (Class 6) (0-52,52) 3-Y-0+ **£2,047** (£604; £302) **Stalls** High

Form RPR
6440 **1** **Piccolo Diamante (USA)**[8] 6563 3-8-12 **50**....(t) GrahamGibbons 1 59
(D J Murphy) *s.i.s: in rr: stl plenty to do whn rapid hdwy on ins over 1f out: styd on u.p to ld last strides* **14/1**
1030 **2** *hd* **Drum Dance (IRE)**[6] 6608 5-8-9 **52**.... HaddenFrost(5) 6 60
(M Hill) *in tch: rdn 2f out: rapid hdwy ins fnl f to take narrow ld cl home: ct last strides* **10/1**
6500 **3** *shd* **Duke Of Milan (IRE)**[9] 6542 4-8-11 **49**.... SebSanders 4 57
(G C Bravery) *lw: hld up: smooth hdwy fr 2f out: pushed along to chal ins fnl f and upsides nr fin: no ex last strides* **15/2**
5302 **4** *nk* **Davids Mark**[21] 6264 7-8-12 **50**.... EddieAhern 12 57+
(J R Jenkins) *in tch: drvn to ld wl over 1f out: hdd and outpcd cl home* **7/2**[1]
0000 **5** *1* **Gone'N'Dunnett (IRE)**[9] 6542 8-8-7 **50**....(v) KirstyMilczarek(5) 11 54
(Mrs C A Dunnett) *chsd ldrs: rdn 2f out: styd wl there tl wknd ins fnl f* **16/1**
5023 **6** *hd* **Mister Elegant**[21] 6264 5-8-6 **51**.... SophieDoyle(7) 8 54
(J L Spearing) *in tch: rdn over 2f out: styd on ins fnl f but nvr quite gng pce to rch ldrs* **4/1**[2]
0030 **7** *6* **Blessed Place**[7] 6594 7-9-0 **52**....(t) FergusSweeney 3 36
(D J S Ffrench Davis) *led: hdd wl over 1f out: sn wknd* **6/1**[3]
0663 **8** *1 1/4* **Hephaestus**[48] 5564 3-8-10 **48**.... LPKeniry 2 28
(Peter Grayson) *a towards rr* **8/1**
0-00 **9** *3* **Knickyknackienoo**[8] 6563 6-8-8 **49**.... NeilChalmers(3) 9 19
(T T Clement) *in rr most of way* **50/1**
0515 **10** *5* **Christian Bendix**[176] 1753 5-9-0 **52**....(p) ChrisCatlin 10 6
(P Howling) *rrd stalls: drvn to chse ldrs: wknd 3f out* **10/1**
0-0 **11** *3 1/2* **Surely Truly (IRE)**[46] 5643 4-8-12 **50**.... RobertHavlin 5 —
(A E Jones) *chsd ldrs tl wknd qckly ins fnl 3f* **14/1**

1m 12.5s (-1.20) **Going Correction** -0.225s/f (Stan) **11** Ran SP% **118.7**
Speed ratings (Par 101): **99,98,98,98,96 96,88,86,82,76 71**
CSF £148.00 CT £1162.51 TOTE £16.50: £4.50, £5.30, £3.40; EX 118.00.
Owner W Mckay, D Cornan, M Morris, P Reid **Bred** Pamela Linahan **Trained** Bawtry, S Yorks

FOCUS
Another modest handicap run at what appeared a solid early pace, and the first three came from the rear. The front quartet finished in a heap but this is fair form for the grade.
Gone'N'Dunnett(IRE) Official explanation: jockey said gelding stumbled soon after start

6719 BARRETTSTOWN STUD H'CAP 1m 3f (P)
9:20 (9:20) (Class 6) (0-60,60) 3-Y-0+ **£2,047** (£604; £302) **Stalls** High

Form RPR
0060 **1** **Ryedale Ovation (IRE)**[99] 4038 4-9-3 **59**.... HaddenFrost(5) 2 68+
(M Hill) *in rr: rapid hdwy fr 3f out to ld ins fnl 2f: styd on strly* **33/1**
0430 **2** *2* **Recalcitrant**[7] 6577 4-9-1 **55**.... WilliamBuick(3) 6 61
(S Dow) *chsd ldrs: rdn to ld over 2f out: sn hdd and btn* **15/2**[3]
5005 **3** *nk* **Barry Island**[24] 6196 8-9-9 **60**.... SebSanders 14 65
(D R C Elsworth) *lw: in rr: hdwy towards outside fr 2f out: fin wl fnl f but nvr any ch of rching wnr* **11/2**[1]
0001 **4** *shd* **Mixing**[13] 6453 5-8-10 **52**.... PatrickHills(5) 5 57+
(J Akehurst) *lw: in rr: swtchd rt to far rail and hdwy over 1f out: fin wl* **15/2**[3]
0501 **5** *hd* **Key Partners (IRE)**[7] 6583 6-9-7 **58** 6ex.... GeorgeBaker 12 63+
(P A Blockley) *s.i.s: in rr: hdwy fr over 2f out: styd on wl fnl f but nvr quite gng pce to rch ldrs* **15/2**[3]
3555 **6** *nk* **Fantasy Ride**[7] 6583 5-9-7 **58**.... OscarUrbina 7 62
(J Pearce) *in rr: hdwy and hung rt over 2f out: kpt on ins fnl f: nt rch ldrs* **6/1**[2]
4003 **7** *1/2* **Soldier Field**[26] 6147 3-8-9 **54**....(p) NeilChalmers(3) 10 58
(A M Balding) *chsd ldrs: rdn fr 3f out: styd on ins fnl f: nt pce to be competitive* **12/1**
1505 **8** *nk* **Spunger**[11] 6500 4-9-9 **60**....(v) EddieAhern 4 63
(H J L Dunlop) *chsd ldrs: rdn 3f out: one pce fnl 2f* **14/1**
0500 **9** *3 1/2* **Play Up Pompey**[7] 6577 5-9-4 **55**.... J-PGuillambert 8 52
(J J Bridger) *in rr: rdn 3f out: kpt on ins fnl f but nvr in contention* **20/1**
3062 **10** *3/4* **Prince Of Medina**[68] 5007 4-9-0 **51**.... DaneO'Neill 11 47
(J R Best) *chsd ldrs: rdn 3f out: wknd ins fnl 2f* **8/1**
5354 **11** *1 1/4* **Laugh 'n Cry**[21] 6261 6-8-12 **54**....(p) JamesO'Reilly(5) 1 48
(Eoin Doyle, Ire) *in tch: rdn and hdwy 4f out: wknd 2f out* **25/1**
0/60 **12** *3/4* **Mejhar (IRE)**[15] 6407 7-9-1 **55**.... AlanCreighton(3) 3 47
(E J Creighton) *in tch: rdn 3f out and sn btn* **25/1**
1 **13** *2* **Raydan (IRE)**[172] 1592 5-9-6 **57**.... MickyFenton 9 46
(D R Gandolfo) *chsd ldr: chal fr over 3f out tl over 2f out: wknd qckly* **11/2**[1]
5520 **14** *4* **Chiff Chaff**[107] 3803 3-9-4 **60**.... LiamJones 13 42
(C R Dore) *led tl hdd 2f out: wknd qckly* **14/1**

2m 20.09s (-2.59) **Going Correction** -0.225s/f (Stan)
WFA 3 from 4yo+ 5lb **14** Ran SP% **127.9**
Speed ratings (Par 101): **100,98,98,98,98 97,97,97,94,94 93,92,91,88**
CSF £270.94 CT £1611.45 TOTE £26.80: £9.30, £3.00, £2.40; EX 381.30 Place 6 £264.02, Place 5 £94.91.
Owner Martin Hill **Bred** Hascombe And Valiant Studs **Trained** Broadhempston, Devon
■ Stewards' Enquiry : Patrick Hills two-day ban: careless riding (Nov 19-20)

FOCUS
A modest handicap and a few did not see much daylight at various points in the home straight. The runner-up is the best guide to the level.
Key Partners(IRE) Official explanation: jockey said gelding was denied a clear run
Play Up Pompey Official explanation: jockey said gelding ran too free early
T/Plt: £378.40 to a £1 stake. Pool: £76,461.40. 147.50 winning tickets. T/Qpdt: £75.90 to a £1 stake. Pool: £6,273.10. 61.10 winning tickets. ST

6591 NOTTINGHAM (L-H)
Wednesday, November 7

OFFICIAL GOING: Good to firm (8.9)
Wind: Fresh, half-against Weather: Overcast and breezy and cool

6720 EVENTMASTERS FOR HORSERACING HOSPITALITY H'CAP 5f 13y
12:10 (12:12) (Class 6) (0-55,55) 3-Y-0+ **£2,047** (£604; £302) **Stalls** High

Form RPR
4003 **1** **Registrar**[7] 6594 5-8-12 **51**.... SaleemGolam 16 58+
(Mrs C A Dunnett) *dwlt and bhd: hdwy 2f out: swtchd lft and rdn over 1f out: styng on whn hit in face by opponent's whip ins fnl f: led last 100yds: hld on wl* **7/2**[1]
0405 **2** *nk* **George The Best (IRE)**[44] 5672 6-8-13 **52**.... PaulHanagan 1 58+
(Micky Hammond) *bhd: swtchd lft and gd hdwy over 1f out: str run ins fnl f: fin wl* **11/1**
2304 **3** *1/2* **The Cube**[23] 6240 3-8-11 **50**.... DavidAllan 9 54
(J Balding) *chsd ldrs: effrt and n.m.r wl over 1f out: squeezed through to ld appr fnl f: sn rdn: hdd and nt qckn last 100yds* **14/1**

0621 **4** ½ **Mickleberry (IRE)**[41] 5752 3-8-11 **50**................................ SebSanders 8 52
(J D Bethell) *trckd ldrs: hdwy 2f out: rdn and ev ch ins fnl f: sn drvn and one pce* **8/1**[3]
3245 **5** *nk* **Cleveland**[101] 4008 5-8-8 **52**............................... RussellKennemore(5) 14 53+
(R Hollinshead) *trckd ldrs towards stands' rail: effrt and n.m.r wl over 1f out: swtchd rt and rdn ent fnl f: kpt on* **6/1**[2]
1550 **6** ¾ **Knead The Dough**[7] 6587 6-8-4 **48**..................... NataliaGemelova(5) 15 46+
(A E Price) *in rr: hdwy and n.m.r 2f out: swtchd lft and nt clr run over 1f out and again ent fnl f: styd on: nrst fin* **8/1**[3]
0000 **7** *shd* **Limonia (GER)**[21] 6264 5-8-5 **49** ow1..................... KevinGhunowa(5) 11 47
(Mike Murphy) *s.i.s: sn in tch: rdn to chse ldrs 2f out: kpt on same pce* **16/1**
8 ½ **Tullyorior Glory (IRE)**[18] 6347 3-8-12 **54**................(t) JerryO'Dwyer(3) 3 50
(Emmanuel Hughes, Ire) *in tch on outer: rdn along and hdwy 2f out: drvn appr fnl f and one pce* **14/1**
066 **9** ½ **The Carpet Man**[38] 5834 3-8-9 **48**.................................... LiamJones 10 42+
(A W Carroll) *in rr: hdwy wl over 1f out: swtchd lft and rdn ent fnl f: styd on: nrst fin* **28/1**
4051 **10** ¾ **Splendidio**[43] 5716 3-9-1 **54**.. NCallan 4 46
(A Crook) *prom: rdn along 2f out and grad wknd* **14/1**
6000 **11** *hd* **Mr Loire**[14] 6424 3-9-2 **55**..(b) DeanMcKeown 2 46
(A J Chamberlain) *a towards rr* **50/1**
050 **12** *1* **Maromito (IRE)**[29] 6078 10-8-11 **50**........................... DanielTudhope 13 37
(R Bastiman) *prom: rdn along 2f out: sn edgd lft and wknd over 1f out* **14/1**
0500 **13** *nk* **Whistler**[55] 5349 10-8-8 **47**...(p) PaulFitzsimons 17 33
(Miss J R Tooth) *chsd ldrs on stands' rail: rdn along 2f out: bmpd and wknd ent fnl f* **22/1**
1003 **14** ½ **Beechside (IRE)**[12] 6466 3-8-8 **52**............................... JackMitchell(5) 7 37
(W A Murphy, Ire) *s.i.s and bhd: swtchd wd and sme hdwy 1/2-way: sn rdn and nvr a factor* **14/1**
0000 **15** *shd* **Tenancy (IRE)**[8] 6562 3-8-11 **50** ow1............................(p) AdamKirby 12 34
(A J McCabe) *hld up in tch: effrt and n.m.r 2f out: sn rdn and btn* **20/1**
0000 **16** 1¼ **Maktavish**[55] 5349 8-8-11 **50**...(b) TomEaves 6 30
(R Brotherton) *led: rdn along 2f out: hdd and bmpd over 1f out: wknd qckly* **33/1**

61.43 secs (-0.37) **Going Correction** -0.15s/f (Firm) **16** Ran SP% **123.7**
Speed ratings (Par 101): **96,95,94,93,93 92,92,91,90,89 88,87,86,86,85 83**
CSF £39.85 CT £518.08 TOTE £4.40: £1.20, £3.30, £3.60, £1.50; EX 68.00.
Owner The Smart Syndicate **Bred** Cheveley Park Stud Ltd **Trained** Hingham, Norfolk

FOCUS
The race was full of exposed older horses taking on moderate three-year-olds and, a somewhat messy contest best rated around the third and fourth . Most of the field came down the middle and avoided the far side. The inside track was used, the wind was fairly biting and the ground may have been riding a bit faster than the official going description.
George The Best(IRE) Official explanation: jockey said, regarding running and riding, he has won three times on the gelding and was led to believe he should employ the usual tactics, adding that it needs to be delivered late and, with the field going to the stands side, he felt it prudent to drop in behind, things went well and it just failed to get up on the line

6721 LOVELL PARTNERSHIPS MAIDEN STKS 5f 13y
12:40 (12:49) (Class 5) 2-Y-O **£3,238** (£963; £481; £240) **Stalls** High

Form RPR
3 **1** **Quaroma**[7] 6595 2-8-12 0.. JohnEgan 13 69
(Jane Chapple-Hyam) *w ldr: led over 1f out: jst hld on* **11/2**[3]
63 **2** *shd* **Doric Lady**[23] 6228 2-8-12 0.. EddieAhern 1 69
(J A R Toller) *trckd ldrs: chal 1f out: jst failed* **8/1**
3 ½ **Bussell Up** 2-8-12 0... SaleemGolam 15 67
(S C Williams) *s.v.s: hdwy and swtchd lft over 2f out: styd on strly ins fnl f* **40/1**
0004 **4** ½ **Fast Feet**[18] 6326 2-9-3 72.. NCallan 17 70
(K A Ryan) *led tl over 1f out: kpt on same pce ins fnl f* **11/2**[3]
5 *2* **Requisite** 2-8-12 0.. PatCosgrave 2 58
(Jane Chapple-Hyam) *sn chsng ldrs on outside: wknd ins fnl f* **20/1**
32 **6** 1½ **Recent Times**[28] 6105 2-8-12 0.. DavidAllan 4 53+
(T D Easterby) *chsd ldrs: kpt on same pce fnl 2f* **4/1**[1]
04 **7** ½ **Saranome (IRE)**[14] 6419 2-9-3 0............................... RichardKingscote 7 56
(R Charlton) *mid-div: kpt on fnl 2f: nvr nr ldrs* **9/2**[2]
8 *nk* **Nimbelle (IRE)** 2-8-12 0... SteveDrowne 8 50
(T F Lacy, Ire) *mid-div: kpt on fnl 2f: nvr a threat* **25/1**
500 **9** *1* **Sir Joey**[40] 5771 2-8-12 52................................ RussellKennemore(5) 16 51
(J T Stimpson) *in rr: kpt on fnl 2f: nvr a factor* **100/1**
0 **10** ½ **Monte Cassino (IRE)**[12] 6468 2-8-12 0.................. JamesO'Reilly(5) 10 50
(J O'Reilly) *chsd ldrs: outpcd fnl 2f* **66/1**
0 **11** 1¼ **Blakeshall Diamond**[16] 6386 2-8-12 0......................... DeanMcKeown 9 40
(A J Chamberlain) *chsd ldrs: lost pl over 1f out* **50/1**
3 **12** 3½ **Warners Bay (IRE)**[16] 6384 2-9-3 0................................ SebSanders 12 32
(R Bastiman) *mid-div: rdn 2f out: sn lost pl* **12/1**
44 **13** *1* **My Kaiser Chief**[86] 4447 2-9-3 0................................. PaulMulrennan 14 29
(W J H Ratcliffe) *chsd ldrs: lost pl over 1f out* **17/2**
00 **14** *32* **Rose De Rita**[28] 6104 2-8-12 0.. ChrisCatlin 5 —
(L P Grassick) *sn outpcd and in rr: bhd fnl 2f: t.o* **100/1**

61.13 secs (-0.67) **Going Correction** -0.15s/f (Firm) 14 Ran SP% **114.8**
Speed ratings (Par 96): **99,98,98,97,94 91,90,90,88,87 85,80,78,27**
CSF £44.23 TOTE £7.10: £2.40, £3.50, £10.60; EX 49.50.
Owner Franconson Partners **Bred** Lady Fairhaven **Trained** Newmarket, Suffolk

FOCUS
A modest-looking sprint maiden. Fast Feet is the one to rate the race around, but one suspects he is about 5lb too high in the weights at the moment.

NOTEBOOK
Quaroma and Doric Lady passed the post almost in union and it was the former who just got her nose in front. She had shown plenty of promise on her debut over the course last time and improved enough to take this, despite edging left under pressure. This, however, might be the last time we see her, as the trainer did mention after the race that this well-bred filly had done her job now and may go to the paddocks. (op 5-1 tchd 9-2)
Doric Lady moved well for much of the race and was only just denied in a driving finish. Another ordinary maiden is well within her grasp, especially against her own sex. (op 13-2)
Bussell Up ◆ fell out of the stalls and missed the break badly. Her jockey gave her time to recover and nothing was finishing quicker than her inside the final furlong. One would suspect that she will be winning races fairly soon. (op 33-1)
Fast Feet, officially rated 72, looked so promising at the start of the year but his form has levelled out this autumn after a summer break. He did nothing wrong up the stands'-side rail but was well held by the first three. (tchd 5-1 and 6-1)
Requisite showed plenty of promise for the future despite hanging. The experience will not have been lost on her. (op 18-1)
Recent Times was never really in the hunt and failed to get involved. One would suspect that handicaps will be in her future now.
Saranome(IRE) ◆ was outpaced early before staying on well from the rear of the pack. The drop in trip has not been a positive for him since his debut effort over six and a half furlongs, and one would expect to see a better effort again when raised in trip. (op 5-1)

6722 BLUES CONSULTANTS LTD NURSERY 5f 13y
1:10 (1:14) (Class 6) (0-65,68) 2-Y-O **£2,914** (£867; £433; £216) **Stalls** High

Form RPR
6160 **1** **Leading Edge (IRE)**[12] 6462 2-9-4 **62**............................. ChrisCatlin 14 69
(M R Channon) *hld up: swtchd lft and hdwy over 2f out: rdn over 1f out: led ins fnl f and kpt on* **14/1**
0600 **2** *1* **Lieutenant Pigeon**[26] 6154 2-9-4 **62**................................... DavidAllan 9 65
(T D Easterby) *chsd ldrs: rdn along wl over 1f out: kpt on wl u.p ins fnl f* **11/1**
66 **3** *nk* **Gain Share**[40] 5772 2-9-7 **65**.. TomEaves 12 67
(T D Barron) *sn led: rdn along wl over 1f out: drvn and hdd ins fnl f: kpt on* **9/1**[3]
0260 **4** ¾ **New Balls Please (IRE)**[14] 6426 2-8-4 **53**...............(p) JackMitchell(5) 4 53
(P M Phelan) *in tch on outer: hdwy 2f out: sn rdn and styd on ins fnl f* **18/1**
2241 **5** *hd* **Loose Caboose (IRE)**[5] 6624 2-9-10 **68** 6ex.................. SebSanders 5 67
(A J McCabe) *prom: rdn along after 110yds: drvn 2f out: kpt on same pce* **11/4**[1]
5000 **6** 1¼ **Curio**[7] 6595 2-8-9 **56**.. MichaelJStainton(3) 2 50
(R M Whitaker) *towards rr: hdwy 2f out: sn rdn: kpt on ins fnl f: nrst fin* **25/1**
5055 **7** *shd* **Copperbottomed (IRE)**[16] 6388 2-9-3 **61**........................ JimCrowley 7 55
(R Hollinshead) *dwlt: midfield and pushed along 1/2-way: rdn wl over 1f out: kpt on ins fnl f: nrst fin* **12/1**
0603 **8** ½ **Joss Stick**[14] 6426 2-8-12 **56**.. EddieAhern 10 48+
(P J Makin) *prom: rdn along wl over 1f out: drvn and one pce appr fnl f* **8/1**[2]
3040 **9** ½ **Linnet Park**[36] 5887 2-9-0 **58**... KDarley 8 48
(J G Given) *chsd ldr: rdn along over 2f out: grad wknd* **14/1**
0000 **10** *1* **Zahwah**[14] 6438 2-8-9 **53**...(b[1]) HayleyTurner 3 40
(J G Portman) *outpcd and bhd tl styd on fnl 2f: nvr nr ldrs* **33/1**
0035 **11** 1¼ **Fraamington**[37] 5863 2-8-4 **48** ow1................................. GregFairley 13 30
(M R Channon) *midfield: rdn along over 2f out and sn wknd* **22/1**
600 **12** ¾ **Bahia Palace**[13] 6454 2-8-1 **45**... JamieMackay 1 25
(M D I Usher) *racd wd: a towards rr* **40/1**
3144 **13** *nk* **Echostar**[163] 2087 2-9-2 **60**... MickyFenton 6 39
(Stef Liddiard) *nvr bttr than midfield* **25/1**
066 **14** *1* **Lunar Lass**[34] 5931 2-8-2 **46**.. LiamJones 15 21
(G Woodward) *in tch: rdn along over 2f out and sn wknd* **50/1**
2016 **15** *nk* **Princess Rhianna (IRE)**[16] 6388 2-9-6 **64**..................... PaulHanagan 17 38
(Mrs G S Rees) *a towards rr* **8/1**[2]
0000 **16** *6* **Vixens Daughter**[7] 6586 2-8-0 **49**.......................(t) NataliaGemelova(5) 11 —
(R T Phillips) *in tch: rdn along over 2f out: sn wknd* **40/1**
0000 **17** 3½ **Captain Crooner (IRE)**[5] 6624 2-8-3 **47**................(v[1]) FrancisNorton 16 —
(D Shaw) *s.i.s: a bhd* **25/1**

60.99 secs (-0.81) **Going Correction** -0.15s/f (Firm) **17** Ran SP% **119.2**
Speed ratings (Par 94): **100,98,97,96,96 94,94,93,92,91 89,87,87,85,85 75,70**
CSF £140.91 CT £1475.11 TOTE £21.20: £4.00, £2.70, £2.10, £7.70; EX 173.10.
Owner M Channon **Bred** Rathasker Stud **Trained** West Ilsley, Berks

FOCUS
This looked a modest nursery beforehand but was the fastest of the three races over the trip.

NOTEBOOK
Leading Edge(IRE) did well to come from behind and, making her challenge at the quarter-mile pole, wore down those that had raced prominently and had enough in hand to hold off the late finishers. Her previous success had been over 6f on soft ground and her stamina at this shorter trip came in useful.
Lieutenant Pigeon, who has been dropped 13lb in his last two outings, appreciated the return to the minimum trip, over which he scored on his debut. He tried his best but just could not get to the winner. (op 16-1)
Gain Share showed plenty of speed on this handicap debut and looks capable of winning a similar contest, although at this stage of the season it is likely to be on Polytrack. (op 8-1 tchd 15-2)
New Balls Please(IRE), who had conditions to suit, ran on late to edge favourite Loose Caboose out of the frame and the return of cheekpieces seemed to have a positive effect. (op 20-1)
Loose Caboose(IRE) ran his race under a 6lb penalty, but his two wins have been on Polytrack and he is likely to prove more effective back on that surface. (tchd 3-1 and 10-3 in places)
Joss Stick showed a fair amount of early pace but his jockey reported that she hung left under pressure. Official explanation: jockey said gelding hung left (op 10-1)
Princess Rhianna(IRE) Official explanation: jockey said filly was unsuited by the good to firm ground

6723 EVENTMASTERS FOR FOOTBALL HOSPITALITY MAIDEN STKS (DIV I) 1m 54y
1:45 (1:50) (Class 5) 2-Y-O **£2,590** (£770; £385; £192) **Stalls** Centre

Form RPR
0F33 **1** **Laterly (IRE)**[19] 6307 2-9-3 73.. MickyFenton 2 76
(T P Tate) *mde all: drvn 2f out: styd on wl* **4/1**[3]
2 1½ **Fiulin** 2-9-3 0... NCallan 3 76+
(M Botti) *chsd ldrs: wnt 2nd over 3f out: kpt on same pce: no imp* **5/1**
65 **3** 1¾ **Wannarock (IRE)**[43] 5707 2-9-3 0............................. StephenDonohoe 6 69
(E A L Dunlop) *trckd ldrs: effrt over 3f out: styd on same pce fnl 2f* **25/1**
04 **4** 3½ **Ibrox (IRE)**[19] 6303 2-9-3 0.. DeanMcKeown 1 61+
(R M Whitaker) *s.i.s: hdwy over 3f out: fdd fnl f* **33/1**
54 **5** *1* **Simone Martini (IRE)**[11] 6494 2-9-3 0............................ SteveDrowne 8 59
(R Charlton) *chsd ldrs: effrt 3f out: wknd over 1f out* **3/1**[2]
6 ¾ **Emerald Rock (CAN)** 2-9-3 0.. ChrisCatlin 4 57
(N J Vaughan) *chsd ldrs: drvn over 3f out: wknd over 1f out* **12/1**
7 *nk* **Millie's Rock (IRE)** 2-8-12 0.. EddieAhern 10 52+
(M R Channon) *in rr: hdwy over 2f out: nvr nr ldrs* **14/1**
54 **8** ½ **Piermarini**[56] 5321 2-9-3 0... GregFairley 11 56
(M Johnston) *trckd ldrs: effrt 3f out: wknd over 1f out* **9/4**[1]
00 **9** *15* **Bid To The Beat**[64] 5116 2-9-3 0... JohnEgan 12 23
(H J Collingridge) *sn bhd: sme hdwy over 3f out: wknd and eased 2f out* **150/1**
10 3½ **Soundbyte** 2-9-3 0.. JimCrowley 5 15
(J Gallagher) *s.i.s: sn wl bhd* **150/1**
11 *10* **Lake Nayasa** 2-8-12 0.. RobertHavlin 9 —
(H Morrison) *s.s: sn wl bhd* **66/1**
00 **12** *1* **Fongster**[42] 5721 2-9-0 0... JerryO'Dwyer(3) 7 —
(A M Hales) *sn bhd* **200/1**

1m 45.83s (-0.57) **Going Correction** -0.15s/f (Firm) **12** Ran SP% **116.9**
Speed ratings (Par 96): **96,94,92,89,88 87,87,86,71,68 58,57**
CSF £23.46 TOTE £6.20: £2.00, £2.00, £4.30; EX 30.00.
Owner S M Racing **Bred** Gestut Fahrhof Stiftung **Trained** Tadcaster, N Yorks

FOCUS
The winner was one of the most experienced horses in the race, so was entitled to go close after the favourite ran below par.

NOTEBOOK
Laterly(IRE), who made all the running, came from a yard in form and had been progressing with racing. Showing a good attitude, he looks a fair prospect for middle-distance handicaps next season. (op 9-2 tchd 7-2)
Fiulin put up the most encouraging performance of the newcomers, chasing the winner most of the way up the straight. This son of Galileo from the family of Falbrav showed plenty of ability despite running green and he should have learnt a good deal for the experience. (op 6-1 tchd 13-2)
Wannarock(IRE), whose first two runs were seperated by three months, produced a fair effort and now qualifies for a handicap mark. (op 22-1)
Ibrox(IRE) did best of those coming from off the pace and, progressing with racing, this half-brother to five winners should be emulating his relatives before long. (op 40-1)
Simone Martini(IRE) did not build on his Newbury effort, but this ground was much faster and he did not look totally at home on it. (op 5-2 tchd 10-3)
Emerald Rock(CAN), a nicely-bred son of Johannesburg, was somewhat buzzy beforehand but was supported in the market despite that. He showed plenty of promise prior to weakening out of contention in the final quarter-mile, and should come on a fair amount for this. (op 16-1)
Millie's Rock(IRE) is a daughter of Miletrian, who won the Ribblesdale and Park Hill for the same connections. She made good headway from the rear early in the straight before being unable to sustain the effort, and a good deal more is likely from her over longer trips next season. (op 12-1)
Piermarini appeared to have a sound chance on his performance behind the useful Kandahar Run last time but ran no sort of race. He may have had excuses as the stable is not really firing at present and he was left standing in the stalls for a long time on a cold day while the others were being loaded. (tchd 2-1 and 5-2)
Lake Nayasa Official explanation: jockey said filly never travelled
Fongster Official explanation: jockey said gelding never travelled

6724 EVENTMASTERS FOR FOOTBALL HOSPITALITY MAIDEN STKS (DIV II) 1m 54y
2:20 (2:21) (Class 5) 2-Y-O **£2,590** (£770; £385; £192) **Stalls** Centre

Form RPR
1 **Wintercast** 2-9-3 0 AdamKirby 5 86+
(W R Swinburn) *hld up in tch: smooth hdwy to trck ldrs 3f out: swtchd rt and effrt 2f out: led over 1f out: rdn and kpt on ins fnl f* **6/1**
0 2 1 **West With The Wind**[12] 6468 2-9-3 0 MickyFenton 10 82+
(T P Tate) *hld up: hdwy on outer 3f out: pushed along to chse ldrs 2f out: styd on wl fnl f* **3/1**[1]
6 3 1 1/4 **Amanjena**[19] 6294 2-8-12 0 FrancisNorton 7 74
(A M Balding) *t.k.h: chsd ldrs: pushed along and outpcd over 4f out: rdn and hdwy over 2f out: styd on wl fnl f* **11/2**[3]
56 4 shd **Clovis**[22] 6248 2-9-3 0 GregFairley 11 79
(M Johnston) *prom: rdn to ld over 2f out: drvn and hdd over 1f out: wknd ins fnl f* **15/2**
0 5 4 **Wing Play (IRE)**[14] 6418 2-9-3 0 SteveDrowne 9 73+
(H Morrison) *towards rr: hdwy wl over 2f out: rdn and kpt on appr fnl f: nrst fin* **100/1**
40 6 1 **African Flight**[12] 6470 2-8-12 0 HayleyTurner 8 63
(M L W Bell) *in rr: pushed along and hdwy 3f out: rdn 2f out: kpt on ins fnl f: nrst fin* **20/1**
7 1/2 **Amerigo (IRE)** 2-9-3 0 PhilipRobinson 3 69+
(M A Jarvis) *bhd tl styd on fnl 2f: nrst fin* **9/1**
8 1 1/4 **Ejeed (USA)** 2-9-3 0 RHills 6 65+
(J H M Gosden) *hld up towards rr: effrt and hdwy over 3f out: rdn along over 2f out: sn btn* **7/2**[2]
0 9 1 **Starlight Prince**[14] 6418 2-8-12 0 RussellKennemore(5) 4 62
(R Hollinshead) *chsd ldrs: rdn along 3f out: wknd 2f out* **100/1**
0 10 1 1/2 **Molly Ann (IRE)**[12] 6470 2-8-12 0 DavidAllan 1 53
(T D Easterby) *chsd ldrs on inner: rdn along 3f out and sn wknd* **100/1**
11 4 **Shady Gloom (IRE)** 2-9-3 0 NCallan 2 50
(K A Ryan) *cl up: led 3f out: rdn and hdd over 2f out: sn wknd* **14/1**
0 12 shd **Good Return**[28] 6106 2-9-3 0 PatCosgrave 12 49
(Jane Chapple-Hyam) *sn led: rdn along and hdd 3f out: wknd over 2f out* **40/1**

1m 45.14s (-1.26) **Going Correction** -0.15s/f (Firm) 12 Ran SP% **115.5**
Speed ratings (Par 96): **100,99,97,97,93 92,92,90,89,88 84,84**
CSF £23.09 TOTE £7.90: £3.40, £1.70, £2.10; EX 31.90.
Owner Mrs P W Harris **Bred** Pendley Farm **Trained** Aldbury, Herts

FOCUS
The leaders seemed to go a fair pace early and it was noticeable that there were some finishers from off the pace inside the final furlong. It was the quickest of the three divisions of the race.

NOTEBOOK
Wintercast ◆ took the eye in the paddock, being a fine-looking chestnut. He was settled in behind the early gallop and could be called the winner about 2f from home. Once asked to quicken, he quickly put daylight between himself and the rest of the field to win nicely. He looks something to look forward to next season for connections. (op 7-1)
West With The Wind ◆ really caught the eye on his debut at Doncaster but, once again, got outpaced at the halfway point. However, once he found his stride, he kept on really gamely but never looked like troubling the winner. He looks sure to stay well next year (op 7-2 tchd 4-1)
Amanjena, a half-sister to Presto Vento, was somewhere near the rear during the race and was another to be pushed along rounding the bend, probably more to do with greenness than any lack of pace. She kept going for her jockey but never looked like getting on terms. (op 13-2)
Clovis looked far more the finished article than most in the field and gave his running. He is another that will do better over further. (op 6-1 tchd 8-1)
Wing Play(IRE) who was given a kind ride once it was obvious he was not going to win. He probably wants more experience. (op 80-1)
African Flight still looked clueless under pressure and should be better with another year behind her. (op 16-1)
Amerigo(IRE), an already gelded son of Daylami, looked as though the race may bring him on in the paddock and he then messed about down at the start. He was stone last and not doing too much with a furlong to go, but all of a sudden the penny dropped and he decided to pick up, shaping promisingly. However, he does not seem a straightforward character and is one to treat with slight caution. (op 7-1)
Ejeed(USA) was keen early and never really got involved at all. Being out of 1000 Guineas winner Lahan, one would have hoped for better. (op 10-3)
Shady Gloom(IRE) has plenty of size about him and will be better in time. His effort was not without promise. (op 12-1)

6725 EVENTMASTERS FOR FOOTBALL HOSPITALITY MAIDEN STKS (DIV III) 1m 54y
2:55 (2:57) (Class 5) 2-Y-O **£2,590** (£770; £385; £192) **Stalls** Centre

Form RPR
2 1 **Cuban Missile**[22] 6248 2-9-3 0 SteveDrowne 11 81+
(R Charlton) *trckd ldrs: shkn up to ld appr fnl f: r.o wl: readily* **10/11**[1]
2 3/4 **French Riviera** 2-9-3 0 KDarley 6 80+
(Sir Michael Stoute) *in rr: effrt on ins 3f out: hmpd and swtchd rt: styd on wl appr fnl f* **9/2**[3]
05 3 1 **Fly With The Stars (USA)**[20] 6285 2-9-3 0 GregFairley 2 77
(M Johnston) *mde most: hdd appr fnl f: kpt on one pce* **12/1**
2 4 2 1/2 **Celtic Dragon**[14] 6418 2-9-3 0 JimCrowley 10 72
(Mrs A J Perrett) *w ldrs: wnt 2nd over 2f out: kpt on same pce appr fnl f* **4/1**[2]
5 5 1 3/4 **Prairie Storm**[14] 6418 2-9-3 0 LPKeniry 7 68
(A M Balding) *mid-div: outpcd over 2f out: styd on fnl f* **14/1**
00 6 4 **Stealth Project**[11] 6494 2-9-3 0 HayleyTurner 4 59
(A M Hales) *w ldrs: wknd over 1f out* **100/1**
00 7 2 1/2 **Supporting Role (IRE)**[12] 6469 2-9-3 0 NCallan 1 54
(E S McMahon) *mid-div: wknd 2f out* **28/1**
8 shd **Taikoo** 2-9-3 0 RobertHavlin 8 53
(H Morrison) *in rr: drvn 6f out: nvr a factor* **33/1**
0 9 20 **Doubloon**[36] 5880 2-9-3 0 RichardThomas 3 9+
(J Gallagher) *stdd s: t.k.h: sn trcking ldrs: wknd 3f out: t.o* **200/1**
10 36 **Sawpit Solitaire** 2-8-12 0 FrancisNorton 9 —
(J L Spearing) *s.s: detached in rr: t.o 3f out* **50/1**

1m 45.43s (-0.97) **Going Correction** -0.15s/f (Firm) 10 Ran SP% **114.8**
Speed ratings (Par 96): **98,97,96,93,92 88,85,85,65,29**
CSF £4.96 TOTE £2.10: £1.10, £1.50, £3.10; EX 6.70.
Owner Mountgrange Stud **Bred** Dermot Brennan & Associates Ltd **Trained** Beckhampton, Wilts

FOCUS
A competitive-looking maiden won by a well-backed favourite. The race should produce winners.

NOTEBOOK
Cuban Missile looked to be the one to be with after his very promising debut effort, and those who invested in him did not have too many worries, as he swept to the front over a furlong out and never looked like being caught. Gelded already, it will be interesting to see what sort of route connections take with him in the future. (tchd Evens, 11-10 in places)
French Riviera cost 150,000gns at the sales and is from a family that the trainer Patrick Chamings has had success with. He was green in the early stages but looked to have plenty to give when meeting a bit of trouble as the race took shape. Once Darley got a clear run, he kept on really well to suggest better to come. He will stay 1m4f next season.
Fly With The Stars(USA) had more experience than the front two and did most of the running. He was far from disgraced on this quick ground and handicaps can be won with him. (op 14-1)
Celtic Dragon made an encouraging start to his career at Bath a couple of weeks ago and looked to hold an obvious chance before the off. He was never far away and had every chance, but could not quicken in the same way the winner did. Much like the runner-up, middle distances should suit this half-brother to Spice Route next season and, possibly, more ease in the ground. (op 7-2)
Prairie Storm pretty much repeated his debut run behind the fourth. He stayed on from the rear and is probably the sort for handicaps in time. (op 16-1)
Stealth Project was keen in the early stages and was never going to have much left for the finish.
Taikoo, whose dam was placed in the Musidora and has produced some nice sorts in the past, travelled well for a long time before inexperience got the better of him. Once he has learned what the game is about, he will be winning races. (tchd 40-1)

6726 NESTLE CONDITIONS STKS 1m 54y
3:30 (3:30) (Class 2) 3-Y-O+
£9,971 (£2,985; £1,492; £747; £372; £187) **Stalls** Centre

Form RPR
-606 1 **Medicine Path**[135] 2952 3-8-8 103 NCallan 7 98
(E J O'Neill) *plld hrd: hld up towards rr: hdwy on outer 2f out: rdn and qcknd to ld ins fnl f: kpt on* **13/8**[2]
2304 2 1 1/4 **Fajr (IRE)**[9] 6541 5-8-10 107 SebSanders 4 95
(Miss Gay Kelleway) *trckd ldng pair: hdwy and cl up over 2f out: rdn wl over 1f out and ev ch tl nt qckn ins fnl f* **11/10**[1]
3006 3 nk **Blue Rocket (IRE)**[4] 6654 3-8-3 90 FrancisNorton 5 89
(D J Murphy) *led 1f: chsd ldr tl led again wl over 2f out: sn rdn: drvn over 1f out: hdd and one pce ins fnl f* **8/1**[3]
12-0 4 11 **Petrovich (USA)**[25] 6175 4-8-10 100 (b[1]) JohnEgan 6 69
(Jane Chapple-Hyam) *wnt rt and reminders s: led after 1f and sn clr: rdn along over 3f out: hdd wl over 2f out and sn wknd* **14/1**
1256 5 2 **Gleneagles (IRE)**[42] 5737 3-8-11 77 LiamJones 3 67
(T Wall) *trckd ldrs: hdwy 4f out: rdn along wl over 2f out and sn wknd* **33/1**
4400 6 22 **Little Darlin**[9] 6538 3-8-3 0 HayleyTurner 1 9
(G J Smith) *sn outpcd and a bhd* **500/1**

1m 44.47s (-1.93) **Going Correction** -0.15s/f (Firm)
WFA 3 from 4yo+ 2lb 6 Ran SP% **106.6**
Speed ratings (Par 109): **103,101,101,90,88 66**
CSF £3.29 TOTE £2.30: £1.30, £1.40; EX 4.00.
Owner J C Fretwell **Bred** Jenny Hall Bloodstock Ltd **Trained** Averham Park, Notts

FOCUS
Two of these looked a class above the rest on current form, and fought out the finish. The third casts a little doubt on how strong the form is, as she was not beaten that far, and sets the level.

NOTEBOOK
Medicine Path took a little while to get going but ended up winning with a bit in hand. The trainer is keen to finish him for the season now, after giving him plenty of time and care this season, and is looking forward to seeing him in some good races next season. (op 9-4)
Fajr(IRE) got the strong pace he likes and looked a big danger approaching the final furlong. He was always getting the better of his battle with Blue Rocket but possibly did not stride out fully on the ground. (op 10-11)
Blue Rocket(IRE) casts a little bit of doubt on the form, as she has shown most of her best form after an absence and over shorter. She did not quite see out the trip but was not disgraced. (op 9-1 tchd 11-1)
Petrovich(USA), making his debut for the Jane Chapple-Hyam stable, missed the break slightly but was pushed up to lead, and set a good gallop. The first-time blinkers may have set him alight, but he had no more to give up the home straight and dropped out after he was given a reminder at the 4f pole. The jury is very much out as to whether he retains much, if any, of his old ability. (op 8-1)

6727 EVENTMASTERS FOR CRICKET HOSPITALITY H'CAP 1m 1f 213y
4:00 (4:00) (Class 5) (0-75,76) 3-Y-O+ **£3,238** (£722; £722; £240) **Stalls** Low

Form RPR
6403 1 **Sforzando**[22] 6258 6-8-11 66 TomEaves 3 74+
(Mrs L Stubbs) *s.i.s: hld up: hdwy and nt clr run over 2f out: styd on wl to ld towards fin* **12/1**
3344 2 nk **Trouble Mountain (USA)**[22] 6258 10-8-10 65 (t) DaleGibson 7 72
(M W Easterby) *in rr: sn pushed along: hdwy on ins 3f out: styd on wl appr fnl f: no ex nr fin* **9/1**[3]
4204 2 dht **Titinius (IRE)**[16] 6380 7-8-8 63 KDarley 2 70
(Micky Hammond) *chsd ldrs: styd on to ld jst ins fnl f: hdd nr fin* **10/1**
3133 4 nk **Rawdon (IRE)**[22] 6253 6-9-1 70 (v) HayleyTurner 5 76
(M L W Bell) *trckd ldrs: hrd rdn 2f out: no ex towards fin* **8/1**[2]

6005 **5** *shd* **Davenport (IRE)**[22] 6253 5-9-2 **76** ow2..................(p) JamesMillman(5) 12 82
(B R Millman) *mid-div: hdwy on outside over 2f out: hung rt: kpt on wl fnl f* **12/1**

00 **6** *nk* **Shabahar (IRE)**[24] 6203 3-9-2 **75**.. JohnEgan 14 81
(M J McGrath) *stdd and swtchd rt sn after s: hdwy on outside over 2f out: hung lft and kpt on wl fnl f* **28/1**

4321 **7** *1 3/4* **Prime Number (IRE)**[35] 5916 5-9-4 **73**...................... PhilipRobinson 13 75
(J Akehurst) *sn chsng ldrs: drvn over 3f out: one pce fnl 2f* **5/2**[1]

0100 **8** *1 1/4* **Gallego**[7] 6598 5-8-5 **65**... KirstyMilczarek(5) 4 65
(R J Price) *s.i.s: t.k.h in rr: hdwy over 3f out: nvr trbld ldrs* **12/1**

4015 **9** *hd* **King Of The Moors (USA)**[12] 6465 4-9-1 **75**................. NeilBrown(5) 1 74
(T D Barron) *led: qcknd clr 3f out: hdd jst ins fnl f: wknd: eased towards fin* **9/1**[3]

0264 **10** *1 1/4* **Siena Star (IRE)**[6] 6612 9-8-9 **64**.................................... MickyFenton 11 61+
(Stef Liddiard) *chsd ldrs: outpcd whn hmpd over 1f out* **16/1**

5100 **11** *hd* **She's Our Lass (IRE)**[14] 6422 6-9-4 **73**........................... DavidAllan 15 69
(D Carroll) *chsd ldrs on outer: wknd over 1f out* **25/1**

6403 **12** *1 1/4* **Haasem (USA)**[13] 6447 4-8-9 **64**....................................... JimCrowley 8 58
(J R Jenkins) *mid-div: effrt over 3f out: wkng whn edgd lft over 1f out* **20/1**

0000 **13** *1 3/4* **Riley Boys (IRE)**[33] 5985 6-9-3 **72**................................ PaulHanagan 10 62
(J G Given) *hld up in rr: nvr on terms* **20/1**

2500 **14** *3* **Old Romney**[22] 6253 3-9-0 **73**.. PaulMulrennan 9 57
(M W Easterby) *s.i.s: a in rr* **33/1**

0600 **15** *3/4* **Flores Sea (USA)**[11] 6492 3-8-13 **72**................................ PhillipMakin 6 55
(T D Barron) *a in rr: nvr a factor* **66/1**

2m 9.26s (-0.44) **Going Correction** -0.15s/f (Firm)
WFA 3 from 4yo+ 4lb **15** Ran SP% **119.0**
Speed ratings (Par 103): **95,94,94,94,94 94,92,91,91,90 90,89,88,85,85**
WIN: Sforzando £13.80. PL: £3.50, Trouble Mountain £2.30, Titinius £2.40. EX: S/TM £45.30, S/T £54.30. CSF: S/TM £51.97, S/T £56.87. TRIC: S/TM/T £566.36, S/T/TM £571.42. Place 6 £161.98, Place 5 £67.63.
Owner Mrs L Stubbs **Bred** M E Wates **Trained** Norton, N. Yorks

FOCUS
A modest-looking handicap that resulted in a very tight finish and the form is sound but ordinary. The early tempo seemed strong thanks to King Of The Moors, but the time was modest for the grade.
Shabahar(IRE) Official explanation: jockey said colt hung left-handed
T/Jkpt: Not won. T/Plt: £541.90 to a £1 stake. Pool: £48,629.10. 65.50 winning tickets. T/Qpdt: £89.60 to a £1 stake. Pool: £3,418.00. 28.20 winning tickets. JR

5964 MUSSELBURGH (R-H)
Thursday, November 8

OFFICIAL GOING: Good (8.1)
Wind: Strong half against Weather: Sunny

6728 SCOTTISH RACING GENTLEMAN AMATEUR RIDERS' H'CAP 1m 4f
1:00 (1:00) (Class 5) (0-70,60) 4-Y-0+ **£3,123** (£968; £484; £242) **Stalls** High

Form RPR

0-25 **1** **Living On A Prayer**[54] 5426 4-10-10 **46**........................... MrSDobson 5 51
(T McLaughlin, Ire) *hld up in tch: smooth hdwy 3f out: led 1 1/2f out: sn rdn and styd on strly ins fnl f* **9/4**[2]

0553 **2** *3 1/2* **Rigat**[9] 6558 4-11-4 **54**.. MrSWalker 8 53
(T D Barron) *plld hrd: hld up in rr: hdwy 1/2-way: effrt 3f out: rdn to chal 2f out and ev ch tl drvn and one pce ent fnl f* **6/4**[1]

4505 **3** *nk* **Desert Hawk**[4] 6672 6-11-0 **55**..............................(b) MrBMcHugh(5) 7 54
(W M Brisbourne) *trckd ldrs: hdwy over 4f out: led wl over 2f out and sn rdn: hdd 1 1/2f out and kpt on same pce* **3/1**[3]

-050 **4** *1 3/4* **Grafty Green (IRE)**[14] 6458 4-11-5 **60**................. MrBenBrisbourne(5) 1 56
(W M Brisbourne) *hld up towards rr: hdwy on outer 3f out: rdn 2f out: sn drvn and no imp* **18/1**

0/00 **5** *3* **Stravonian**[69] 5000 7-10-2 **45**... MrOJMurphy(7) 3 36
(D A Nolan) *chsd ldrs: rdn along over 3f out: drvn and wknd 2f out* **100/1**

100/ **6** *4* **Wroot Danielle (IRE)**[877] 2566 7-10-9 **52**........................ MrCWhillans(7) 4 37
(D W Whillans) *plld hrd: cl up: rdn along over 3f out: wknd 2f out* **16/1**

0000 **7** *hd* **Royal Sailor (IRE)**[22] 5087 5-10-2 **45**.................... MrDavidMcMinn(7) 2 29
(J Ryan) *hld up: a towards rr* **66/1**

000- **8** *3 1/2* **Lazzoom (IRE)**[410] 5553 4-10-2 **45**................................ MrGRSmith(7) 6 24
(Miss Tracy Waggott) *led: rdn along over 3f out: hdd wl over 2f out and sn wknd* **100/1**

2m 44.94s (8.04) **Going Correction** +0.125s/f (Good) **8** Ran SP% **110.4**
Speed ratings (Par 103): **78,75,75,74,72 69,69,67**
CSF £5.52 CT £8.05 TOTE £3.60: £1.10, £1.60, £1.10; EX 7.30.
Owner Mrs C D Taylor **Bred** Beaumont Hall Bloodstock **Trained** Rathmullan, Co Donegal
■ The first winner for Irish-based trainer Tom McLaughlin.

FOCUS
A weak race and several of these had no chance. They virtually walked the first couple of furlongs and a few pulled hard as a result. The field fanned right out as they ran into the headwind up the home straight and those that came up the middle of the track, who included the first two, seemed to be at an advantage.

6729 EUROPEAN BREEDERS' FUND MAIDEN STKS 5f
1:30 (1:31) (Class 5) 2-Y-0 **£3,238** (£963; £481; £240) **Stalls** Low

Form RPR

3422 **1** **Hamish McGonagall**[27] 6156 2-9-3 81.............................. DavidAllan 1 73+
(T D Easterby) *led 1f: swtchd rt and cl up 1/2-way: led over 1f out and sn clr* **8/15**[1]

033 **2** *5* **Capefly**[15] 6419 2-8-12 74.. JamieSpencer 2 50
(P F I Cole) *cl up: led after 1f: rdn along wl over 1f out: sn hdd and one pce* **9/4**[2]

0000 **3** *shd* **Mchepple**[23] 6254 2-8-9 43... DominicFox(3) 3 50
(W Storey) *trckd ldrs: effrt 2f out: sn rdn and kpt on same pce* **250/1**

632 **4** *4* **Firewalker**[136] 2934 2-8-12 70... TomEaves 4 36
(B Smart) *prom: rdn along 2f out: sn drvn and wknd* **10/1**[3]

3000 **5** *5* **Jazz Stick (IRE)**[13] 6462 2-9-3 50.........................(bt) SilvestreDeSousa 5 23
(D A Nolan) *a in rr* **100/1**

62.94 secs (2.44) **Going Correction** +0.40s/f (Good) **5** Ran SP% **106.5**
Speed ratings (Par 96): **96,88,87,81,73**
CSF £1.77 TOTE £1.40: £1.02, £2.00; EX 2.20.
Owner Reality Racing Syndicate No 1 **Bred** J P Coggan And Whitsbury Manor Stud **Trained** Great Habton, N Yorks

FOCUS
A very uncompetitive maiden and one-way traffic through the final furlong, the winner impressing despite not having to run up to his best.

NOTEBOOK
Hamish McGonagall was back over the minimum trip after two decent runs over 6f and had no problem with it. His rider was looking around for non-existent dangers as he loomed alongside his market rival and fairly scooted clear. With the second-favourite probably running below form he only did as much as he was entitled to, but should still develop into a nice sprint handicapper next season. (op 4-6 tched 8-11 in places)
Capefly soon crossed over to bag the stands' rail in front, but once the favourite was unleashed her goose was cooked. The fact that she only just edged out a rival rated 31lb lower than her, whilst she was only 2lb badly in with the winner, strongly suggests that she did not run anywhere near her mark. (op 2-1 thced 5-2 in a place)
Mchepple had been beaten out of sight in all four of her previous starts to date, all of them over 7f. She appeared to show much improved form over this shorter trip and only just failed to catch a rival rated 31lb higher than her, whilst she had another rival rated 27lb higher a long way behind. Taking peformances like this at face value is a very dangerous game and it would be unwise to do so here, but one probable conclusion is that she is a sprinter. (op 150-1)
Firewalker had already run well at this track before and should have finished much closer on official ratings, but she dropped out very disappointingly. (op 6-1)
Jazz Stick(IRE) seems to have completely lost his way.

6730 RECTANGLE GROUP (S) STKS 5f
2:00 (2:03) (Class 6) 3-Y-0+ **£2,590** (£770; £385; £192) **Stalls** Low

Form RPR

0062 **1** **Monashee Brave (IRE)**[21] 6287 4-9-5 58...................... PaulHanagan 9 68
(J J Quinn) *prom: effrt 2f out: rdn to ld over 1f out: kpt on u.p ins fnl f* **4/1**[2]

0032 **2** *2* **Pieter Brueghel (USA)**[5] 6639 8-9-5 75....................... JamieSpencer 7 61
(D Nicholls) *trckd ldrs: hdwy 2f out: rdn over 1f out: drvn to chse wnr ins fnl f: one pce* **8/11**[1]

0653 **3** *nk* **Rebel Duke (IRE)**[19] 6340 3-9-10 73............................ TonyHamilton 10 65
(D W Barker) *trckd ldrs: effrt wl over 1f out: sn rdn and one pce ins fnl f* **5/1**[3]

000/ **4** *3* **African Storm (IRE)**[847] 3465 5-9-2 0......................... JerryO'Dwyer(3) 8 49
(T McLaughlin, Ire) *towards rr: hdwy 2f out sn rdn and kpt on appr fnl f: n.d* **66/1**

0265 **5** *1 1/4* **Valiant Romeo**[30] 6078 7-9-2 45................................(v) PJMcDonald(3) 3 44
(R Bastiman) *outpcd and towards rr: hdwy 2f out: styd on ins fnl f: n.d* **16/1**

6060 **6** *1/2* **The Brat**[2] 6702 3-9-0 43..(p) PaulFessey 11 38
(Miss Tracy Waggott) *in tch on outer: rdn along 2f out: sn drvn and wknd over 1f out* **100/1**

0600 **7** *1 1/4* **Alexia Rose (IRE)**[35] 5930 5-9-0 43..................................(t) TomEaves 6 33
(A Berry) *s.i.s: a in rr* **33/1**

4060 **8** *3/4* **Noddledoddle (IRE)**[7] 6607 3-9-0 40...........................(bt) ChrisCatlin 1 30
(J Ryan) *chsd ldrs: rdn along 2f out and sn wknd* **66/1**

0640 **9** *3/4* **Ashes (IRE)**[19] 6340 5-9-2 56... AndrewElliott(3) 4 33
(K R Burke) *led: rdn along over 2f out: hdd & wknd over 1f out* **20/1**

00-0 **10** *22* **Scottish Spirit (IRE)**[181] 1625 3-9-5 25............................. PhillipMakin 2 —
(J S Haldane) *prom: rdn along 1/2-way and sn wknd* **200/1**

62.40 secs (1.90) **Going Correction** +0.40s/f (Good) **10** Ran SP% **112.6**
Speed ratings (Par 101): **100,96,96,91,89 88,86,85,84,49**
CSF £6.84 TOTE £4.50: £1.60, £1.10, £1.50; EX 8.90.The winner was sold to Mark Brisbourne for 7,000gns.
Owner The Mushroom Men **Bred** Golden Vale Stud **Trained** Settrington, N Yorks

FOCUS
There were a couple of fair sorts in this seller, as well as some very ordinary ones, but they are both disappointng types and neither were at their best. The winner was by no means one of those best in at the weights, but the fourth and sixth both limit the form.
Pieter Brueghel(USA) Official explanation: jockey said gelding bled from the nose
Alexia Rose(IRE) Official explanation: jockey said mare missed the break

6731 DAILY RECORD FIRST FOR RACING H'CAP 7f 30y
2:30 (2:30) (Class 4) (0-85,80) 3-Y-0 **£5,505** (£1,637; £818; £408) **Stalls** Low

Form RPR

3206 **1** **Cha Cha Cha**[19] 6331 3-8-12 **71**....................................... JamieSpencer 7 77
(K A Ryan) *chsd ldr: hdwy over 2f out: led over 1f out and sn rdn: drvn ins fnl f and hld on wl* **9/2**[2]

2545 **2** *hd* **Charlie Tipple**[44] 5703 3-8-13 **72**.. DavidAllan 1 77
(T D Easterby) *hld up in rr: swtchd lft and hdwy 2f out: rdn and styd on strly ins fnl f: jst failed* **9/2**[2]

000 **3** *1 1/4* **Kompete**[20] 6301 3-9-4 **80**...(v[1]) JerryO'Dwyer(3) 3 82
(V Smith) *led: clr 1/2-way: rdn 2f out: hdd over 1f out: drvn and kpt on same pce* **14/1**

0364 **4** *1/2* **Sparkling Eyes**[16] 6406 3-9-0 **73**................................ PhilipRobinson 5 74
(C E Brittain) *prom: rdn along over 2f out: drvn over 1f out: kpt on same pce* **7/1**

44-4 **5** *nk* **Until When (USA)**[20] 6309 3-8-11 **70**................................. TomEaves 6 70
(B Smart) *hld up towards rr: hdwy over 2f out: nt clr run and swtchd lft over 1f out: sn rdn and kpt on* **16/1**

5404 **6** *hd* **Argentine (IRE)**[9] 6559 3-9-0 **73**...................................... PaulHanagan 9 72
(L Lungo) *chsd ldrs: hdwy 2f out: swtchd lft and rdn over 1f out: drvn and one pce ins fnl f* **4/1**[1]

533- **7** *1/2* **Inspirina (IRE)**[439] 4815 3-8-10 **72**................................ PJMcDonald(3) 2 70
(R Ford) *stdd s: hld up and bhd: hdwy on outer over 2f out: rdn to chse ldrs over 1f out: no imp ins fnl f* **40/1**

1343 **8** *1/2* **Distant Sun (USA)**[9] 6559 3-9-1 **74**................................ TonyHamilton 8 73+
(I Semple) *hld up in rr: hdwy over 2f out: nt clr run over 1f out: no ch after* **6/1**

6451 **9** *16* **Chin Wag (IRE)**[15] 6429 3-8-3 **62**....................................... ChrisCatlin 4 15
(J S Goldie) *in tch on outer: rdn along over 2f out and sn wknd* **11/2**[3]

1m 30.13s (0.19) **Going Correction** +0.125s/f (Good) **9** Ran SP% **113.5**
Speed ratings (Par 104): **103,102,101,100,100 100,99,99,80**
CSF £24.60 CT £260.18 TOTE £6.00: £2.20, £1.70, £3.50; EX 27.80.
Owner Guy Reed **Bred** G Reed **Trained** Hambleton, N Yorks

FOCUS
A tight little handicap according to the market and the pace was fair thanks to Kompete, but despite the size of the field there were a couple that met plenty of trouble in running inside the last couple of furlongs. The winner improved a touch, and the second ran to form.

6732 TURFTV CLAIMING STKS 1m
3:00 (3:01) (Class 6) 4-Y-0+ **£2,590** (£770; £385; £192) **Stalls** Low

Form RPR

2000 **1** **Defi (IRE)**[78] 4713 5-8-11 64..(b) TomEaves 8 70
(I Semple) *led over 3f: cl up tl led again 2f out: rdn clr ent fnl f: styd on wl* **11/1**

1336 **2** *4* **Oeuf A La Neige**[5] 6640 7-8-12 57...................................... PhillipMakin 9 61
(Miss L A Perratt) *in tch: hdwy over 2f out: rdn to chse wnr ins fnl f: no imp* **5/1**[2]

The Form Book, Raceform Ltd, Compton, RG20 6NL

0000 **3** *1* **Campo Bueno (FR)**[13] 6467 5-8-13 47........ PaulHanagan 3 60
(A Berry) *prom: effrt over 2f out and sn rdn: drvn over 1f out and kpt on same pce* **50/1**

4000 **4** *½* **Sarraaf (IRE)**[13] 6479 11-8-8 53........ PaulFessey 12 54
(I Semple) *chsd ldrs: rdn along over 2f out: drvn and styd on ins fnl f* **12/1**

0000 **5** *¾* **Wahoo Sam (USA)**[13] 6463 7-8-11 62........(p) TonyHamilton 2 55
(D W Barker) *cl up: led over 4f out: rdn along and hdd 2f out: drvn and wknd ent fnl f* **8/1**

2350 **6** *nk* **El Coto**[23] 6253 7-8-12 69........(p) JamieSpencer 6 56
(K A Ryan) *chsd ldrs: effrt over 2f out and sn rdn: drvn and one pce appr fnl f* **9/4**[1]

06-0 **7** *nk* **Star Of The Desert (IRE)**[37] 1198 4-8-13 64........(p) PaulMulrennan 7 56
(Mrs K Walton) *towards rr: hdwy over 2f out: sn rdn and styd on ins fnl f: nt rch ldrs* **33/1**

-404 **8** *nk* **Mister Pete (IRE)**[20] 6304 4-8-7 50........ DominicFox(3) 5 52
(W Storey) *midfield: hdwy on outer 3f out: rdn along to chse ldrs 2f out: sn drvn and one pce* **14/1**

0065 **9** *nk* **Lago D'Orta (IRE)**[52] 5479 7-8-13 64........ SilvestreDeSousa 4 55
(D Nicholls) *hld up in rr: hdwy on wd outside over 2f out: sn rdn and kpt on same pce appr fnl f* **8/1**

3000 **10** *4* **Pianoforte (USA)**[20] 6304 5-9-0 58........ DavidAllan 10 46
(E J Alston) *midfield: effrt 3f out: sn rdn along and nvr a factor* **11/2**[3]

000- **11** *3½* **Familiar Affair**[19] 343 6-8-6 55........ AndrewMullen(3) 11 33
(A Berry) *a towards rr* **66/1**

0406 **12** *3½* **Second Reef**[139] 2828 5-8-8 47........ PJMcDonald(3) 14 27
(T A K Cuthbert) *a towards rr* **80/1**

-000 **13** *7* **Insubordinate**[43] 5479 6-8-7 44........(p) ChrisCatlin 13 7
(J S Goldie) *a in rr* **50/1**

000- **14** *30* **Longy The Lash**[455] 4297 4-8-8 40........ KellyHarrison(5) 1 —
(Paul Murphy) *a bhd* **200/1**

1m 41.98s (-0.52) **Going Correction** +0.125s/f (Good) **14** Ran SP% **117.8**
Speed ratings (Par 101): **107,103,102,101,100 100,100,99,99,95 92,88,81,51**
CSF £62.81 TOTE £14.50: £3.40, £1.70, £16.70; EX 86.20.
Owner Gordon McDowall **Bred** Skymarc Farm Inc And Dr A J O'Reilly **Trained** Carluke, S Lanarks

FOCUS
A moderate claimer, but a cracking gallop with Defi and Wahoo Sam taking each other on from the start. Despite the strong pace, very few ever got into it and the principals were always towards the fore. The runner-up looks the best guide to the form, suggesting the winner was a shade off this year's best despite his wide-margin success.
Second Reef Official explanation: jockey said gelding moved poorly throughout

6733 TURFTV H'CAP 2m
3:30 (3:31) (Class 4) (0-80,74) 3-Y-0+ £6,477 (£1,927; £963; £481) Stalls Low

Form RPR

0110 **1** **Estate**[13] 6473 5-9-13 **73**........ ChrisCatlin 3 80+
(E J O'Neill) *hld up rr: stdy hdwy over 2f out: rdn to chse ldrs on inner whn n.m.r: swtchd lft and drvn to ld ins fnl f: edgd rt: styd on* **8/1**

5460 **2** *1¼* **Danzatrice**[20] 6308 5-8-13 **59**........ TomEaves 4 64
(C W Thornton) *hld up and bhd: stdy hdwy over 3f out: rdn wl over 1f out: styd on strly ins fnl f: tk 2nd nr fin* **16/1**

06 **3** *shd* **Los Nadis (GER)**[12] 5933 3-9-4 **73**........ PaulHanagan 2 78
(P Monteith) *trckd ldrs: hdwy to ld over 7f out: rdn clr wl over 2f out: drvn over 1f out: hdd ins fnl f: hld whn n.m.r nr fin* **20/1**

4623 **4** *hd* **Bukit Tinggi (IRE)**[20] 6308 3-9-2 **71**........ PhilipRobinson 9 76
(M A Jarvis) *trckd ldrs: hdwy to chse ldr 2f out: rdn over 1f out: drvn and wandered ent fnl f: one pce* **13/8**[1]

62-2 **5** *12* **Sharp Reply (USA)**[40] 5478 5-9-10 **73**........ PJMcDonald(3) 5 63
(Mrs S C Bradburne) *hld up and bhd: rdn along 3f out: nvr a factor* **7/2**[2]

4000 **6** *8* **Trance (IRE)**[13] 6473 7-10-0 **74**........(p) PhillipMakin 8 55
(T D Barron) *hld up and bhd: effrt wl over 2f out: sn rdn and nvr a factor* **22/1**

3P **7** *11* **Jafaru**[119] 3450 3-8-10 **65**........(b) JamieSpencer 1 32
(G A Butler) *midfield: effrt to chse ldrs over 3f out: sn rdn and wknd* **6/1**[3]

61-0 **8** *12* **Trew Style**[47] 5623 5-9-12 **72**........ PaulMulrennan 7 25
(M H Tompkins) *chsd ldr: rdn along over 3f out: drvn over 2f out and sn wknd* **22/1**

0445 **9** *5* **Nero West (FR)**[35] 5933 6-9-8 **68**........(b) PaulFessey 6 15
(I Semple) *led: hdd 7f out: rdn along over 3f out and sn wknd* **12/1**

3m 33.56s (-0.34) **Going Correction** +0.125s/f (Good)
WFA 3 from 5yo+ 9lb **9** Ran SP% **112.7**
Speed ratings (Par 105): **105,104,104,104,98 94,88,82,80**
CSF £116.01 CT £2428.21 TOTE £7.90: £2.00, £4.40, £6.70; EX 94.90 Place 6 £ 79.36, Place 5 £ 74.27.
Owner R S Brookhouse **Bred** Stratford Place Stud & Watership Down Stud **Trained** Averham Park, Notts

FOCUS
Quite a decent staying handicap and they went a good pace, which made it a proper test of stamina. Thefirst four finished a very long way clear. The winner, a half-brother to Champion Hurdle winner Sublimity, continues showing improvement on the Flat in line with last season's hurdles form.
T/Plt: £52.50 to a £1 stake. Pool: £41,667.55. 578.65 winning tickets. T/Qpdt: £48.30 to a £1 stake. Pool: £2,543.30. 38.90 winning tickets. JR

6692 WOLVERHAMPTON (A.W) (L-H)
Thursday, November 8

OFFICIAL GOING: Standard
Wind: Strong across Weather: Shower after Race 1

6734 BOOK TICKETS ONLINE AT WOLVERHAMPTON-RACECOURSE.CO.UK MAIDEN AUCTION STKS 5f 216y(P)
6:50 (6:52) (Class 6) 2-Y-0 £1,892 (£566; £283; £141; £70) Stalls Low

Form RPR

4430 **1** **Easy Wonder (GER)**[20] 6324 2-8-7 0........ SebSanders 6 71
(I A Wood) *w ldr: rdn over 2f out: led ins fnl f: r.o* **2/1**[1]

03 **2** *1* **Young Ivanhoe**[27] 6151 2-9-0 0........(t) NCallan 1 75
(P J McBride) *a.p: rdn over 2f out: led wl over 1f out: edgd rt and hdd ins fnl f: nt qckn* **3/1**[2]

46 **3** *½* **Nice Wee Girl (IRE)**[16] 6404 2-8-7 0........ LPKeniry 7 67
(S Kirk) *hld up in tch: rdn 2f out: kpt on ins fnl f* **5/1**

650 **4** *2½* **Street Diva (USA)**[15] 6432 2-8-7 70........ JamieSpencer 5 59
(P A Blockley) *led: rdn and hdd wl over 1f out: wknd ins fnl f* **4/1**[3]

0 **5** *3* **Where's Killoran**[24] 6228 2-8-8 0........ AdrianMcCarthy 4 51
(Peter Grayson) *s.i.s: hdwy 4f out: rdn and wknd over 2f out* **66/1**

2P36 **6** *2½* **Ely Une (IRE)**[8] 6586 2-7-13 59........ NataliaGemelova(5) 8 40
(J S Moore) *sn bhd* **18/1**

0 **7** *½* **Hula Hula**[16] 6409 2-8-7 0........ TGMcLaughlin 2 41
(E A L Dunlop) *s.i.s: outpcd* **16/1**

5 **8** *11* **Eastern Pride**[59] 5267 2-8-4 0........ FrankieMcDonald 3 5
(P A Blockley) *towards rr: rdn over 3f out: sn struggling* **20/1**

1m 16.72s (0.91) **Going Correction** -0.025s/f (Stan) **8** Ran SP% **112.4**
Speed ratings (Par 94): **92,90,90,86,82 79,78,64**
CSF £7.78 TOTE £3.00: £1.20, £1.40, £1.60; EX 13.60.
Owner Paddy Barrett **Bred** H K Gutschow **Trained** Upper Lambourn, Berks

FOCUS
A modest juvenile maiden rated, without much confidence, through the winner.

NOTEBOOK
Easy Wonder(GER) looked to be in a bit of trouble when coming off the bridle rounding the final bend, and she was carried right by Street Diva, but she showed a good attitude to get on top in the closing stages. She is likely to find things tougher from now on, but is clearly very game. (op 11-4 tchd 3-1)
Young Ivanhoe, who showed ability on his debut at Yarmouth before running third in a claimer over this course and distance, had no easy task conceding upwards of 6lb all round. He ran a solid race in defeat and looks capable of picking up a similar event, although he will also now have the option of going handicapping. (op 4-1 tchd 5-2)
Nice Wee Girl(IRE) ran well on this drop in trip and will have more options now that she is eligible for a handicap mark. (op 9-2)
Street Diva(USA), dropped back in trip, looked one of the more likely winners rounding the final bend, but she was inclined to drift to her right and did not see out her race. She now has something to prove. (op 11-4)

6735 DINE IN THE HORIZONS RESTAURANT CLAIMING STKS 5f 216y(P)
7:20 (7:21) (Class 6) 3-Y-0+ £1,943 (£578; £288; £144) Stalls Low

Form RPR

0321 **1** **Magic Glade**[10] 6531 8-9-5 87........ RichardKingscote 5 80
(Tom Dascombe) *hld up in mid-div: hdwy over 3f out: rdn over 1f out: led wl ins fnl f: r.o wl* **5/6**[1]

130R **2** *3* **Quiet Times (IRE)**[201] 1163 8-8-13 78........(b) NCallan 13 64
(K A Ryan) *sn prom: led wl over 3f out: rdn over 1f out: hdd and no ex wl ins fnl f* **22/1**

2340 **3** *½* **Mango Music**[25] 6205 4-8-6 80........ MatthewDavies(7) 4 62
(M R Channon) *w ldrs: rdn over 1f out: one pce* **10/3**[2]

5000 **4** *½* **Spy Gun (USA)**[12] 6505 7-8-2 44........(p) LukeMorris(3) 3 53
(T Wall) *led over 2f: rdn and outpcd 3f out: kpt on ins fnl f* **100/1**

2043 **5** *1¼* **Ochre Bay**[17] 6385 4-8-9 70........(p) GrahamGibbons 6 53
(R Hollinshead) *s.i.s: in rr: rdn 4f out: swtchd rt jst ins fnl f: r.o* **6/1**[3]

0000 **6** *hd* **Almora Guru**[35] 5947 3-8-1 45........ LiamJones 8 44
(W M Brisbourne) *s.i.s: in rr: hdwy on outside fnl f: nvr nrr* **50/1**

6003 **7** *3½* **Whozart (IRE)**[2] 6702 4-8-11 48........ DanielTudhope 12 43
(A Dickman) *hld up: hdwy on outside over 2f out: sn rdn: wknd over 1f out* **16/1**

6044 **8** *1½* **Detonate**[9] 6565 5-8-5 45........ RichardThomas 9 32
(I A Wood) *s.i.s: sme hdwy whn nt clr run briefly over 2f out: no further prog* **33/1**

5365 **9** *1½* **Dunn Deal (IRE)**[35] 5930 7-8-4 44........ PatrickMathers(3) 2 29
(J Balding) *hld up in mid-div: rdn over 2f out: sn bhd* **40/1**

0600 **10** *1* **Laith (IRE)**[2] 6702 4-8-9 44........(p) MickyFenton 7 28
(Miss V Haigh) *s.i.s: sn chsng ldrs: rdn over 3f out: wknd 2f out* **66/1**

0000 **11** *3½* **Creme Brulee**[49] 5566 4-8-6 44........ FrancisNorton 11 —
(P T Dalton) *w ldrs: rdn over 2f out: wknd wl over 1f out* **100/1**

0603 **12** *4* **Formidable Will (FR)**[36] 5897 5-8-2 50........(vt) WilliamBuick(3) 1 —
(D Shaw) *prom: lost pl on ins over 3f out: rdn and sme hdwy over 1f out: no imp whn wnt lame ins fnl f* **20/1**

0000 **13** *4* **Tia Jade**[25] 6206 3-8-1 45........ AdrianMcCarthy 10 —
(G Prodromou) *a in rr* **100/1**

1m 15.32s (-0.49) **Going Correction** -0.025s/f (Stan) **13** Ran SP% **118.7**
Speed ratings (Par 101): **102,98,97,96,95 94,90,88,86,84 80,74,69**
CSF £29.34 TOTE £1.80: £1.10, £4.00, £1.50; EX 21.50.Magic Glade was claimed by P. Grayson for £18,000.
Owner Alan Solomon **Bred** Juddmonte Farms **Trained** Lambourn, Berks

FOCUS
A reasonable claimer but the form is limited by the performance of the fourth.
Laith(IRE) Official explanation: jockey said gelding became unbalanced in home straight
Formidable Will(FR) Official explanation: jockey said gelding pulled up lame

6736 RINGSIDE NURSERY 7f 32y(P)
7:50 (7:52) (Class 6) (0-65,65) 2-Y-0 £1,943 (£578; £288; £144) Stalls High

Form RPR

0002 **1** **Chrystal Venture (IRE)**[10] 6536 2-9-5 **63**........(p) SebSanders 4 67
(A J McCabe) *mde all: clr 2f out: edgd rt over 1f out: hrd rdn fnl f: jst hld on* **11/4**[1]

000 **2** *shd* **Last Of The Line**[15] 6436 2-9-7 **65**........ FrancisNorton 6 69
(H J L Dunlop) *hld up in mid-div: hdwy over 2f out: rdn and r.o fnl f: jst failed* **15/2**

2206 **3** *1* **Natural Rhythm (IRE)**[17] 6379 2-9-5 **63**........ DanielTudhope 1 64
(D W Chapman) *hld up towards rr: c v wd st: hdwy fnl f: nrst fin* **7/1**

000 **4** *1¾* **Ogre (USA)**[37] 5881 2-9-7 **65**........ JamieSpencer 10 62
(J A Osborne) *s.i.s: hld up towards rr: hdwy on outside over 2f out: rdn over 1f out: one pce* **5/1**[3]

006 **5** *¾* **Run From Nun**[18] 6358 2-8-8 **52**........ RichardSmith 3 47
(J A Osborne) *chsd ldrs: rdn wl over 1f out: no ex fnl f* **25/1**

0003 **6** *4* **Melwood Dreams**[24] 6242 2-8-10 **59**........ RussellKennemore(5) 5 44
(Paul Green) *hld up in mid-div: rdn over 3f out: bhd fnl 2f* **12/1**

3011 **7** *5* **Countrywide Comet (IRE)**[8] 6586 2-9-5 **63** 6ex........(b) NCallan 9 36
(P Howling) *t.k.h: chsd wnr tl rdn wl over 1f out: sn wknd* **3/1**[2]

300 **8** *2* **Boot Strap Bill**[22] 6281 2-9-7 **65**........(p) PaulFitzsimons 7 33
(Miss J R Tooth) *hld up in mid-div: rdn 2f out: sn wknd* **33/1**

0600 **9** *hd* **She's Our Dream**[30] 6074 2-8-13 **57**........(t) GrahamGibbons 11 25
(R C Guest) *s.i.s: a bhd* **33/1**

0050 **10** *nk* **Night Robe**[10] 6536 2-8-8 **52**........ TGMcLaughlin 8 19
(P D Evans) *chsd ldrs: rdn 3f out: wknd 2f out* **33/1**

000 **11** *½* **Chica Guapa (IRE)**[6] 6626 2-8-7 **51**........ DeanMcKeown 2 17
(Paul Green) *a in rr* **66/1**

1m 31.86s (1.46) **Going Correction** -0.025s/f (Stan) **11** Ran SP% **114.5**
Speed ratings (Par 94): **90,89,88,86,85 81,75,73,73,72 72**
CSF £21.86 CT £131.90 TOTE £4.70: £1.80, £2.20, £1.60; EX 26.20.
Owner Paul J Dixon And The Chrystal Maze Ptn **Bred** Gestut Gorlsdorf **Trained** Babworth, Notts

FOCUS
A modest, but competitive nursery for the grade, and simple enough to assess rated through the winner and third.

NOTEBOOK
Chrystal Venture(IRE) went off very quickly, but she had most of her rivals on the stretch as a result and was just able to hold on, despite getting tired near the finish. She had shaped well when second in a big-field nursery at Leicester on her previous start and showed herself to be on the up with a game victory. (tchd 9-4 and 3-1)
Last Of The Line ◆ was one of the more interesting runners on his handicap debut, having enjoyed no luck in a Lingfield maiden on his previous start, and he only just failed. He looks sure to pick up a similar event. (op 11-2 tchd 8-1)
Natural Rhythm(IRE) was a real springer in the market and justified the support with a sound effort in defeat. Held up well out the back through the early stages, the strong pace played into his hands, but he had to switch wide with his challenge into the straight. (op 14-1)
Ogre(USA), who flauffed the start, looked in trouble a fair way from the finish and probably did well to finish so close. She gives the impression she will benefit from a step up in trip and ought to find a handicap. (op 9-2 tchd 7-2)
Run From Nun, making her nursery debut, ran creditably and should build on this.
Countrywide Comet(IRE) came into this on the back of a couple of wins in claiming company for Kevin Ryan, the most recent success coming over 6f at Lingfield, but he was too keen for his own good on his debut for new connections. (op 10-3 tchd 7-2)
She's Our Dream Official explanation: jockey said filly lost its action

6737 SPONSOR A RACE BY CALLING 0870 220 2442 MEDIAN AUCTION MAIDEN STKS — 1m 141y(P)
8:20 (8:20) (Class 6) 2-Y-O — **£2,047** (£604; £302) **Stalls** Low

Form				RPR
2	1		**Detonator (IRE)**[37] 5880 2-9-3 0 ... GregFairley 7 (M Johnston) *sn led: clr over 2f out: rdn 1f out: unchal* **1/2**[1]	79+
000	2	9	**Sunshine Lady (IRE)**[24] 6237 2-8-12 43 ... HayleyTurner 8 (D Haydn Jones) *a.p: chsd wnr over 6f out: rdn and btn over 2f out* **66/1**	55
33	3	4	**Almamia**[13] 6461 2-8-12 0 ... SebSanders 3 (Sir Mark Prescott) *led early: prom: reminders 4f out: rdn and wknd over 2f out* **2/1**[2]	47
0	4	1	**Lady Asheena**[8] 6578 2-8-9 0 ... LukeMorris[(3)] 5 (J Jay) *hld up in tch: rdn over 3f out: sn wknd* **66/1**	45
00	5	3 ½	**Festival Dreams**[10] 6530 2-9-3 0 ... AdrianMcCarthy 1 (Miss J S Davis) *hld up: pushed along over 5f out: rdn 4f out: sn struggling* **100/1**	42
0	6	2 ½	**Toll Gate (IRE)**[15] 6417 2-8-12 0 ... RichardKingscote 2 (R Charlton) *rdn 4f out: a bhd* **16/1**[3]	32
60	7	13	**No Nukes**[8] 6593 2-9-3 0 ... TGMcLaughlin 6 (P D Evans) *a in rr: lost tch fnl 3f* **66/1**	—

1m 51.26s (-0.50) **Going Correction** -0.025s/f (Stan) — 7 Ran SP% **111.4**
Speed ratings (Par 94): **101,93,89,88,85 83,71**
CSF £44.33 TOTE £1.30: £1.10, £42.90; EX 33.70.
Owner Sheikh Mohammed **Bred** Darley **Trained** Middleham Moor, N Yorks

FOCUS
A weak juvenile maiden which saw the winner score as he was entitled to with his main rival failing to run her race.

NOTEBOOK
Detonator(IRE) set a good gallop and looked to have this won leaving the back straight. He had shaped very nicely when overcoming his inexperience to run second in a 7f maiden at Warwick and has clearly gone the right way since then but, with his only serious rival running well below form, he could only win this as he was entitled to. No doubt he will stay further next term and he could be very useful. (op 8-11)
Sunshine Lady(IRE) came into this rated just 43 and, although she is evidently better than that rating indicates, her proximity very much puts this form into perspective. (op 50-1)
Almamia, an Irish Oaks entry, ran nowhere near the form she had shown when third on her first two starts. It is too early to be giving up on her yet and, now qualified for a handicap mark, she ought to do better over middle distances next year. (op 13-8)
Lady Asheena settled better and improved a touch on her debut form. She ought to be of a bit more interest when eligible for a handicap mark after her next outing. (op 50-1)

6738 STAY AT THE WOLVERHAMPTON HOLIDAY INN H'CAP — 1m 1f 103y(P)
8:50 (8:50) (Class 5) (0-75,73) 3-Y-O+
£2,710 (£811; £405; £203; £101; £50) **Stalls** Low

Form				RPR
6024	1		**Cinematic (IRE)**[7] 6603 4-9-3 69 ... AmirQuinn 1 (J R Boyle) *hld up in mid-div: hdwy wl over 1f out: led ent fnl f: hrd rdn: r.o* **5/1**[2]	77
2463	2	hd	**Chia (IRE)**[21] 6293 4-8-10 62 ...(p) HayleyTurner 2 (D Haydn Jones) *led early: a.p: rdn and ev ch ins fnl f: r.o* **6/1**[3]	70
4056	3	¾	**Baan (USA)**[12] 6504 4-9-0 66 ...(b) GregFairley 6 (M Johnston) *sn chsng ldr: led over 2f out: rdn and hdd ent fnl f: nt qckn* **15/2**	72
0104	4	1 ½	**Grand Diamond (IRE)**[24] 6245 3-8-7 62 ... LPKeniry 4 (J S Goldie) *hld up in tch: rdn 3f out: hung lft 1f out: one pce* **8/1**	65
5623	5	1	**Royal Fantasy (IRE)**[7] 6603 4-9-7 73 ... JamieSpencer 7 (J R Fanshawe) *hld up towards rr: hdwy over 2f out: rdn and hung lft wl over 1f out: one pce fnl f* **5/4**[1]	74
0006	6	4	**Street Life (IRE)**[23] 6253 9-8-13 65 ... NeilPollard 3 (W J Musson) *a in rr* **9/1**	58
0110	7	5	**Moheebb (IRE)**[13] 6465 3-9-3 72 ... LiamJones 5 (D W Chapman) *rdn over 4f out: a bhd* **10/1**	54
0340	8	5	**Red Contact (USA)**[37] 5893 6-9-2 68 ...(p) DanielTudhope 9 (A Dickman) *t.k.h: sn led: hdd over 2f out: rdn and wknd over 1f out* **25/1**	40
6400	9	9	**Jabraan (USA)**[42] 5752 5-8-0 59 oh14 ...(p) FrankiePickard[(7)] 8 (D W Chapman) *a in rr* **100/1**	12

2m 1.83s (-0.79) **Going Correction** -0.025s/f (Stan)
WFA 3 from 4yo+ 3lb — 9 Ran SP% **122.2**
Speed ratings (Par 103): **102,101,101,99,98 95,90,86,78**
CSF £37.28 CT £230.01 TOTE £7.60: £1.90, £1.90, £2.50; EX 32.80.
Owner Inside Track Racing Club **Bred** A Brosnan **Trained** Epsom, Surrey
■ Stewards' Enquiry : Hayley Turner caution: used whip with excessive frequency

FOCUS
A modest handicap, run at a sound pace. The first three came clear and the form looks solid enough rated around the runner-up and third.

6739 WOLVERHAMPTON-RACECOURSE.CO.UK H'CAP — 1m 5f 194y(P)
9:20 (9:21) (Class 4) (0-85,82) 3-Y-O+
£4,549 (£1,362; £681; £340; £170; £85) **Stalls** Low

Form				RPR
1111	1		**Boz**[13] 6481 3-9-1 77 ... JamieSpencer 7 (L M Cumani) *hld up: stdy hdwy over 6f out: hrd rdn 3f out: led wl over 1f out: drvn out* **10/3**[3]	87+
0534	2	½	**Heathyards Pride**[18] 6357 7-9-9 82 ... RussellKennemore[(5)] 8 (R Hollinshead) *broke wl: sn stdd: hld up and bhd: rdn over 2f out: hdwy fnl f: nt rch wnr* **20/1**	89
6224	3	½	**Maslak (IRE)**[13] 6475 3-8-13 75 ... LPKeniry 2 (P W Hiatt) *led 2f: a.p: rdn over 1f out: styd on ins fnl f* **16/1**	81
3102	4	shd	**Salute (IRE)**[18] 6356 8-9-9 77 ... RobertHavlin 4 (P G Murphy) *a.p: led 3f out: rdn and hdd wl over 1f out: nt qckn ins fnl f* **9/1**	83
5221	5	1 ¼	**Right Option (IRE)**[12] 6506 3-8-1 68 ... KevinGhunowa[(5)] 6 (J L Flint) *led after 2f: hdd 3f out: rdn and ev ch over 1f out: no ex ins fnl f* **11/1**	72
1-21	6	1	**Bank On Benny**[20] 6314 5-9-7 75 ... FrancisNorton 1 (P W D'Arcy) *hld up in mid-div: hdwy on ins wl over 1f out: sn rdn: one pce ins fnl f* **11/4**[2]	78
3111	7	2 ½	**Bold Adventure**[14] 6459 3-8-5 67 ... AdrianMcCarthy 3 (W J Musson) *hld up towards rr: rdn and hdwy on outside over 2f out: wknd wl over 1f out* **9/4**[1]	67
3060	8	7	**Three Boars**[14] 6459 5-8-9 66 ...(b) WilliamBuick[(3)] 5 (S Gollings) *hld up in rr: rdn over 2f out: no rspnse: eased whn no ch ins fnl f* **20/1**	56

3m 5.43s (-1.94) **Going Correction** -0.025s/f (Stan)
WFA 3 from 5yo+ 8lb — 8 Ran SP% **114.3**
Speed ratings (Par 105): **104,103,103,103,102 102,100,96**
CSF £64.26 CT £919.63 TOTE £5.60: £1.70, £2.10, £4.70; EX 47.60 Place 6 £ 42.62, Place 5 £ 31.18.
Owner Aston House Stud **Bred** Aston House Stud **Trained** Newmarket, Suffolk
■ Stewards' Enquiry : Jamie Spencer three-day ban: used whip with excessive force and frequency (Nov 19-21)

FOCUS
A good handicap for the grade, run at an average early pace, and as a result the form may not be too reliable. The winner remains most progressive, however.
T/Plt: £55.80 to a £1 stake. Pool: £90,812.20. 1,187.20 winning tickets. T/Qpdt: £42.30 to a £1 stake. Pool: £5,229.50. 91.40 winning tickets. KH

6728 MUSSELBURGH (R-H)
Friday, November 9

OFFICIAL GOING: Good (good to firm in places on round course; 8.6)
Wind: Fresh, half-against Weather: Sunny and blustery

6740 EUROPEAN BREEDERS' FUND MAIDEN STKS — 1m
1:00 (1:03) (Class 5) 2-Y-O — **£3,886** (£1,156; £577; £288) **Stalls** Low

Form				RPR
2	1		**Endless Luck (USA)**[24] 6252 2-9-3 0 ... GregFairley 4 (M Johnston) *cl up: led wl over 2f out: rdn clr over 1f out: edgd rt and kpt on wl fnl f* **6/5**[1]	88+
6	2	5	**Tighnabruaich (IRE)**[27] 6184 2-9-3 0 ... PhilipRobinson 5 (M A Jarvis) *slt ld: rdn along over 3f out: hdd wl over 2f out: drvn over 1f out and sn one pce* **15/8**[2]	77
26	3	4	**Azure Mist**[49] 5580 2-8-12 0 ... SebSanders 8 (M H Tompkins) *chsd ldng pair: rdn along over 2f out: sn drvn and no imp* **10/1**[3]	63
3520	4	2 ½	**Royal Applord**[24] 6255 2-9-3 74 ... JamieSpencer 2 (K A Ryan) *midfield: effgort and hdwy 2f out: sn rdn and no imp* **11/1**	63
	5	nk	**Beauchamp Warrior** 2-9-0 0 ... WilliamBuick[(3)] 10 (G A Butler) *dwlt and bhd: hdwy over 2f out: kpt on ins fnl f: nrst fin* **80/1**	62
5	6	hd	**Wells Lyrical (IRE)**[9] 6592 2-9-3 0 ... TomEaves 3 (B Smart) *s.i.s and in rr: hdwy on outer over 2f out: kpt on ins fnl f: nrst fin* **20/1**	62+
53	7	8	**World Tour**[47] 5663 2-9-3 0 ... PhillipMakin 9 (I Semple) *midfield: rdn along over 3f out and sn wknd* **50/1**	44
0	8	2 ½	**Mufasa**[6] 6634 2-9-3 0 ... PaulHanagan 7 (Miss L A Perratt) *in tch: rdn along 3f out: sn wknd* **100/1**	39
	9	2 ½	**Jim's Boy (USA)** 2-9-3 0 ... J-PGuillambert 6 (M Johnston) *chsd ldrs: rdn along over 3f out: sn wknd* **33/1**	33
	10	2	**Colleoni (IRE)** 2-9-3 0 ... EddieAhern 1 (G A Butler) *a towards rr* **14/1**	29

1m 40.37s (-2.13) **Going Correction** -0.10s/f (Good) 2y crse rec — 10 Ran SP% **116.2**
Speed ratings (Par 96): **106,101,97,94,94 94,86,83,81,79**
CSF £3.36 TOTE £2.30: £1.10, £1.30, £2.20; EX 4.90.
Owner Leung Kai Fai & Vincent Leung **Bred** Roger W Clark **Trained** Middleham Moor, N Yorks

FOCUS
A fair juvenile maiden which saw the field come home fairly strung out behind the impressive winner who stepped up on his debut form.

NOTEBOOK
Endless Luck(USA) ◆, second to a decent prospect on his debut at Leicester last time, confirmed the promise of that effort and ran out a taking winner under a positive ride. There was a great deal to like about the manner in which he put daylight between himself and the fancied runner-up here, with the quicker surface looking in his favour. He looks a typically relentless galloper from his stable and rates a smart middle-distance prospect for next season. (op 5-4 tchd 11-8, 6-4 in places)
Tighnabruaich(IRE) was fancied to leave his York debut running behind, and duly did so, but he was firmly put in his place by the winner nearing the final furlong. He still finished a clear second-best, however, and this scopey colt also rates a nice middle-distance prospect for next term. (tchd 13-8)
Azure Mist had a perfect sit in behind the first pair for most of the way, but simply lacked a change of foot to get really serious at any stage. She too will stay further as a three-year-old and, while she has a small maiden within her compass, she now also has the option of handicapping. (op 12-1)
Royal Applord, up again in trip, ran an improved race on this return to quicker ground without ever threatening. He kept on well enough towards the finish and helps to set the level of this form, but may just be a little flattered by his current official rating. Official explanation: jockey said colt hung left-handed throughout (op 17-2 tchd 8-1)
Beauchamp Warrior, bred to come into his own over further in time, proved friendless in the betting ring and duly ran green early on. He was noted doing some decent work towards the finish, however, and this experience will certainly not be lost on him. (op 66-1)

6741 CRAIGLEITH MASONRY NURSERY — 5f
1:30 (1:30) (Class 4) (0-85,85) 2-Y-O — **£5,181** (£1,541; £770; £384) **Stalls** Low

Form				RPR
4443	1		**Style Award**[6] 6635 2-8-5 72 ... AndrewMullen[(3)] 5 (W J H Ratcliffe) *chsd ldrs: rdn along 2f out: hdwy over 1f out: led ins fnl f and kpt on* **5/1**[3]	75
210	2	1	**Blue Eyed Miss (IRE)**[48] 5614 2-9-7 85 ... JamieSpencer 3 (P A Blockley) *cl up: rdn over 1f out: edgd rt and led briefly ent fnl f: sn drvn: hdd and one pce* **7/2**[2]	84

0531 **3** *nk* **Angle Of Attack (IRE)**[25] 6227 2-8-8 **72**........................ PaulHanagan 2 70
(R A Fahey) *led: rdn along wl over 1f out: drvn and hdd ent fnl f: one pce* **2/1**[1]

1421 **4** *1* **Choisette**[57] 5365 2-8-7 **71**........................ TomEaves 1 65
(B Smart) *trckd ldrs on inner: effrt and n.m.r appr fnl f: sn rdn and one pce* **7/2**[2]

1015 **5** *½* **Speedy Senorita (IRE)**[20] 6326 2-8-1 **68**........................ AndrewElliott[(3)] 6 61
(K R Burke) *cl up: rdn along wl over 1f out: drvn and wknd appr fnl f* **12/1**

6626 **6** *¾* **Eager Diva (USA)**[18] 6384 2-8-9 **73**........................ DarryllHolland 4 63
(K A Ryan) *sn outpcd and pushed along: a in rr* **9/1**

60.88 secs (0.38) **Going Correction** +0.15s/f (Good) **6** Ran SP% **112.1**
Speed ratings (Par 98): **102,100,99,98,97 96**
CSF £22.52 TOTE £7.80: £2.90, £2.10; EX 25.60.
Owner Bolton Hall Partnership 1 **Bred** Mrs S F Dibben **Trained** Wensley, N Yorks

FOCUS
A fair little nursery, run at a solid pace. The form makes sense.

NOTEBOOK
Style Award quickened up through horses in the final 100 yards to get her head in front again and gain reward for some consistent efforts. This is clearly her optimum trip at present and she has developed into a very likeable filly. (op 13-2 tchd 7-1)
Blue Eyed Miss(IRE), outclassed in Group 3 company last time, travelled nicely through the first three furlongs on the pace yet eventually lacked the required change of gears on this return to the minimum. She was still not beaten far, however, and this rates a fair effort under top weight. (op 9-4)
Angle Of Attack(IRE), 7lb higher, had every chance under a positive ride. He looks held by the Handicapper now, but remains in good heart and rates a solid benchmark for the form. (op 5-2)
Choisette, 8lb higher than when winning at Wolverhampton two months ago, did nothing wrong in defeat yet is another who now looks to be in the Handicapper's grip. She is entitled to come on a bit for the run, however, and her consistency may still be rewarded when she returns to the Polytrack. (op 9-2)

6742 EUROPEAN BREEDERS' FUND MAIDEN FILLIES' STKS 7f 30y
2:00 (2:00) (Class 5) 2-Y-O **£3,886** (£1,156; £577; £288) **Stalls** Low

Form RPR
6423 **1** **Hieroglyph**[19] 6358 2-9-0 78........................ GregFairley 2 75
(M Johnston) *trckd ldr: hdwy over 3f out: led wl over 2f out: rdn wl over 1f out and styd on wl* **5/4**[1]

2 *2* **Somerset Falls (UAE)** 2-9-0 0........................ J-PGuillambert 7 70
(M Johnston) *led: rdn along and hdd over 2f out: kpt on same pce appr fnl f* **12/1**

053 **3** *¾* **Island Music (IRE)**[21] 6306 2-9-0 66........................ GrahamGibbons 4 68
(J J Quinn) *t.k.h: chsd ldrs: hdwy 3f out: rdn along 2f out: drvn and one pce appr fnl f* **5/1**[3]

4 *3 ½* **Salerosa (IRE)** 2-9-0 0........................ SebSanders 5 59
(Mrs A Duffield) *s.i.s: hdwy 3f out: rdn along over 2f out: kpt on appr fnl f: nt rch ldrs* **10/1**

5 *hd* **Al Cobra (IRE)** 2-9-0 0........................ PhilipRobinson 1 59
(M A Jarvis) *hld up: effrt and rn green 3f out: kpt on appr fnl f* **11/4**[2]

0 **6** *5* **Berry Baby (IRE)**[38] 5881 2-8-11 0........................ WilliamBuick[(3)] 3 46
(G A Butler) *sn outpcd and a in rr* **12/1**

00 **7** *½* **Reel Cool**[24] 6254 2-9-0 0........................ TomEaves 8 45
(B Smart) *t.k.h: chsd ldrs: rdn along 3f out and sn wknd* **100/1**

1m 30.74s (0.80) **Going Correction** -0.10s/f (Good) **7** Ran SP% **113.2**
Speed ratings (Par 93): **91,88,87,83,83 77,77**
CSF £17.82 TOTE £2.10: £1.20, £4.80; EX 11.20.
Owner Gainsborough **Bred** Gainsborough Stud Management Ltd **Trained** Middleham Moor, N Yorks

FOCUS
A modest juvenile fillies' maiden. The third helps to set the level.

NOTEBOOK
Hieroglyph came good at the fifth attempt on this return to turf and did the job in workmanlike fashion. Her previous experience told here, but her confidence will have been done a world of good now and the step up to 1m should now bring about some further improvement. (op 7-4)
Somerset Falls(UAE) ◆, a half-sister to her stable's high-class middle-distance performer Boscobel among others, knew her job and was soon racing at the head of affairs. She kept to her task gamely when headed by her winning stable companion and, with improvement looking assured from this experience, she looks the one to really take from the race with the future in mind. (op 10-1 tchd 9-1)
Island Music(IRE) had his chance, but took time to settle early on and could only find the one pace when it mattered. He may just be better off reverting to 6f for the short term and ought to find life easier when switching to handicapping. (op 7-2 tchd 10-3)
Salerosa(IRE), half-sister to a winning hurdler, came through after a tardy start to run a pleasing enough debut and ought to improve a bundle for the experience. (op 9-1 tchd 8-1)
Al Cobra(IRE), half-sister to Arc winner Marienbard, was the subject of late market support for this belated racecourse bow. She ultimately proved far too green to do herself justice and the penny only really dropped inside the final furlong. (op 9-2)

6743 TURFTV H'CAP 5f
2:30 (2:32) (Class 4) (0-85,84) 3-Y-O+ **£5,181** (£1,541; £770; £384) **Stalls** Low

Form RPR
0500 **1** **Blazing Heights**[41] 5810 4-8-13 **79**........................ DanielTudhope 7 88+
(J S Goldie) *hld up: swtchd rt and gd hdwy wl over 1f out: str run to ld jst ins fnl f: rdn and r.o* **7/1**[3]

0200 **2** *½* **Avertuoso**[18] 6381 3-9-2 **82**........................ TomEaves 5 89
(B Smart) *chsd ldrs: hdwy over 1f out: rdn and ev ch ent fnl f: kpt on* **16/1**

0002 **3** *1 ¼* **First Order**[21] 6313 6-8-12 **78**........................(v) SebSanders 1 81
(I Semple) *hld up: hdwy wl over 1f out: effrt and nt clr run ent fnl f: rdn and styd on towards fin* **5/1**[2]

0605 **4** *nk* **The Nifty Fox**[18] 6381 3-8-13 **79**........................(b) DavidAllan 10 80
(T D Easterby) *cl up: rdn and led briefly ent fnl f: sn drvn and hdd: nt qckn* **10/1**

011 **5** *nk* **Sandwith**[25] 6244 4-8-1 **70** oh5........................(p) AndrewElliott[(3)] 4 70
(J S Wainwright) *hld up towards rr: hdwy over 1f out: sn rdn and styd on wl fnl f: nrst fin* **10/1**

1004 **6** *shd* **Malapropism**[18] 6381 7-9-3 **83**........................(v) DarryllHolland 13 83
(M R Channon) *a.p: effrt and ev ch over 1f out: sn rdn and one pce ins fnl f* **8/1**

4120 **7** *nk* **Inspainagain (USA)**[88] 4452 3-8-6 **72**........................ PaulFessey 14 71
(T D Barron) *prom on outer: effrt and ev ch over 1f out: sn rdn and one pce ent fnl f* **50/1**

3242 **8** *nk* **Harry Up**[35] 5969 6-9-2 **82**........................(p) JamieSpencer 9 80
(K A Ryan) *sn led: rdn along wl over 1f out: drvn and hdd ent fnl f: wknd* **7/2**[1]

202 **9** *shd* **Valley Of The Moon (IRE)**[28] 6157 3-8-6 **72**........................ PaulHanagan 11 69
(R A Fahey) *in tch: effrt and nt clr run over 1f out: swtchd rt and rdn: styd on ins fnl f* **8/1**

P000 **10** *hd* **Mr Lambros**[18] 6391 6-8-1 **70** oh1........................(vt) WilliamBuick[(3)] 8 67
(Miss Gay Kelleway) *chsd ldrs: rdn along wl over 1f out: sn one pce* **20/1**

5250 **11** *1* **Strensall**[34] 6020 10-8-1 **70** oh3........................ DuranFentiman[(3)] 6 63
(R E Barr) *a towards rr* **50/1**

35 **12** *¾* **Zahour Al Yasmeen**[26] 6197 3-8-11 **84**........................ MatthewDavies[(7)] 3 74
(M R Channon) *chsd ldrs: rdn along 2f out: grad wknd* **12/1**

0345 **13** *¾* **Baileys Outshine**[88] 4452 3-8-9 **75**........................ J-PGuillambert 12 63
(J G Given) *cl up: rdn and ev ch wl over 1f out tl drvn and wknd ent fnl f* **50/1**

2642 **14** *1 ¾* **Guto**[3] 6702 4-8-4 **73**........................(p) AndrewMullen[(3)] 2 54
(W J H Ratcliffe) *n.d* **12/1**

60.54 secs (0.04) **Going Correction** +0.15s/f (Good) **14** Ran SP% **123.7**
Speed ratings (Par 105): **105,104,102,101,101 101,100,100,99,99 98,96,95,92**
CSF £113.90 CT £633.25 TOTE £9.00: £3.20, £4.60, £2.30; EX 164.00.
Owner Jim Goldie Racing Club **Bred** Jim Goldie **Trained** Uplawmoor, E Renfrews
■ Stewards' Enquiry : Matthew Davies caution: careless riding

FOCUS
A fair and competitive sprint for the class, run at a strong early pace. The third to the tenth finished very closely covered and the form looks sound enough.
Guto Official explanation: jockey said gelding hung right-handed throughout

6744 BANK OF SCOTLAND CORPORATE WILLIE PARK TROPHY H'CAP 1m 6f
3:00 (3:01) (Class 2) (0-100,95) 3-Y-O+
£15,580 (£4,665; £2,332; £1,167; £582; £292) **Stalls** High

Form RPR
5130 **1** **Gee Dee Nen**[20] 6335 4-9-1 **83**........................ PaulMulrennan 2 92
(M H Tompkins) *trckd ldng pair: hdwy 3f out: rdn to ld over 1f out: drvn and hdd ins fnl f: rallied wl to ld nr fin* **6/1**[3]

1311 **2** *nk* **Double Banded (IRE)**[7] 6622 3-8-6 **82** 6ex ow1........................ SebSanders 3 91
(J L Dunlop) *hld up in tch: smooth hdwy 3f out: chal on outer wl over 1f out: rdn: edgd lft and led ins fnl f: sn drvn and edgd rt: hdd and no ex towards fin* **4/6**[1]

0040 **3** *4* **Greenwich Meantime**[20] 6335 7-9-13 **95**........................ PaulHanagan 4 98
(R A Fahey) *trckd ldr: hdwy 3f out: led over 2f out: rdn and hdd over 1f out: sn drvn and wknd* **10/1**

2511 **4** *1* **Rehearsed (IRE)**[13] 6500 4-8-8 **76** oh3........................ SteveDrowne 6 78
(H Morrison) *trckd ldrs: pushed along 6f out: rdn over 3f out: drvn along 2f out and sn one pce* **9/2**[2]

0006 **5** *½* **Trance (IRE)**[1] 6733 7-8-8 **76** oh2........................(p) PaulFessey 5 77
(T D Barron) *in rr: pushed along 1/2-way: hdwy on outer over 3f out: sn rdn: drvn along over 2f out and sn btn* **33/1**

0150 **6** *14* **King Of The Moors (USA)**[2] 6727 4-8-8 **76** oh1........................ PhillipMakin 7 57
(T D Barron) *led: rdn along over 3f out: hdd wl over 2f out and sn wknd* **33/1**

3m 4.16s (-1.54) **Going Correction** -0.10s/f (Good)
WFA 3 from 4yo+ 8lb **6** Ran SP% **107.4**
Speed ratings (Par 109): **100,99,97,96,96 88**
CSF £9.60 TOTE £6.30: £2.20, £1.10; EX 11.50.
Owner David P Noblett **Bred** Kingwood Bloodstock **Trained** Newmarket, Suffolk

FOCUS
A good staying handicap, run at an uneven pace. The first two came clear but the form is not the strongest, with the winner up 3lb but the favourite and the fourth below their best.

NOTEBOOK
Gee Dee Nen, midfield in the Cesarewitch last time, gamely resumed winning ways on this drop back down in class from a mark just 1lb higher than his last success. He stuck his head out to repel the runner-up where it mattered and continues his stable's decent end to the current turf campaign. (op 7-1 tchd 15-2 in a place)
Double Banded(IRE), bidding for his fifth success from his last six outings, had to wait for his challenge in the home straight yet still came there with every chance. He simply failed to go through with his effort when it really mattered, however, and, despite the fact he would have enjoyed a stronger early pace over this sharper test, he did not overly convince with his head carriage at the business end. It is still hard to crab one with his recent progressive profile, but he is already due to race from a 3lb higher mark in the future and did have a pretty hard race. (op 8-13 tchd 8-11 in places)
Greenwich Meantime, well behind the winner in the Cesarewitch last time, showed his true colours on this return to suitably faster ground and ran with credit under top weight. He helps to set the level of this form. (op 8-1)
Rehearsed(IRE), bidding for a hat-trick, was racing from 3lb out of the weights and therefore 4lb higher than her Newbury win. She ran below par, however, and probably found the uneven gallop against her. She is now likely to head off to the paddocks. (tchd 4-1, 5-1 in a place)

6745 LOTHIAN INDEPENDENT DENTAL PRACTITIONERS MAIDEN STKS 1m 4f
3:30 (3:31) (Class 5) 3-5-Y-O **£3,886** (£1,156; £577; £288) **Stalls** High

Form RPR
33 **1** **Alma Mater**[126] 3284 4-9-4 0........................ SebSanders 5 66
(Sir Mark Prescott) *t.k.h: led: rdn along and jnd 3f out: drvn and hdd over 1f out: rallied gamely u.p ins fnl f to ld last 75yds: edgd lft and styd on* **15/8**[1]

35U3 **2** *1 ¼* **Propaganda (IRE)**[22] 6275 3-8-12 68........................ EddieAhern 2 64
(L M Cumani) *trckd ldrs: hdwy 3f out: rdn to chal wl over 1f out: drvn to ld appr fnl f: edgd lft: hdd and no ex last 75yds* **9/2**[3]

4023 **3** *½* **Lochiel**[24] 6257 3-9-3 63........................ PaulMulrennan 7 68
(Mrs S C Bradburne) *trckd ldng pair: hdwy 3f out: rdn and ch whn n.m.r on inner and swtchd lft wl over 1f out: sn chal and ev ch tl drvn: edgd rt and no ex last 75yds* **12/1**

63 **4** *3* **Mythical Story (IRE)**[22] 6286 3-8-12 0........................ JamieSpencer 4 58
(J R Fanshawe) *t.k.h: cl up: effrt 3f out: rdn over 2f out and ev ch tl drvn and wkng whn rdr dropped whip appr fnl f* **2/1**[2]

0004 **5** *13* **Danum Diva (IRE)**[10] 6570 3-8-12 37........................ GrahamGibbons 6 37
(D J Murphy) *a in rr: bhd fnl 3f* **100/1**

3036 **6** *12* **Compton Falcon**[22] 6275 3-9-0 73........................ WilliamBuick[(3)] 1 23
(G A Butler) *t.k.h: rn wd bnd after 1f and in rr: effrt 4f out: sn rdn and nvr a factor* **6/1**

2m 36.63s (-0.27) **Going Correction** -0.10s/f (Good)
WFA 3 from 4yo 6lb **6** Ran SP% **109.3**
Speed ratings (Par 103): **96,95,94,92,84 76**
CSF £10.09 TOTE £2.40: £1.10, £2.00; EX 9.40.
Owner Miss K Rausing **Bred** Miss K Rausing & Abbey Bloodstock **Trained** Newmarket, Suffolk
■ Stewards' Enquiry : Seb Sanders caution: used whip with excessive frequency

FOCUS
A modest maiden, run at a sound pace. The second and third rather limit the form.

6746 REDMAN FISHER H'CAP 1m
4:00 (4:01) (Class 4) (0-80,78) 3-Y-0+ **£5,181** (£1,541; £770; £384) **Stalls** Low

Form RPR
2210 **1** **Ansells Pride (IRE)**[14] 6465 4-8-10 **68** TomEaves 2 78
(B Smart) *sn led on outer: rdn along over 2f out: drvn over 1f out: kpt on gamely u.p ins fnl f* **40/1**
0544 **2** *1* **Esoterica (IRE)**[3] 6701 4-8-9 **67** (b) DanielTudhope 10 75
(J S Goldie) *dwlt: hdwy into midfield 1/2-way: effrt to chse ldrs 2f out: swtchd rt and rdn over 1f out: ev ch ins fnl f: no ex towards fin* **9/2**[3]
2122 **3** *½* **Crocodile Bay (IRE)**[10] 6560 4-9-6 **78** JamieSpencer 3 85
(D Nicholls) *hld up in tch: hdwy 3f out: rdn and ch wl over 1f out: drvn and one pce wl ins fnl f* **2/1**[1]
0011 **4** *¾* **Spinning**[14] 6463 4-8-10 **68** (b) SebSanders 7 73
(T D Barron) *hld up in rr: hdwy 3f out: swtchd outside and rdn wl over 1f out: kpt on ins fnl f: nrst fin* **15/2**
0462 **5** *¾* **Emerald Bay (IRE)**[6] 6637 5-9-5 **77** PhillipMakin 4 80
(I Semple) *chsd ldrs: hdwy 3f out: rdn and ev ch wl over 1f out: sn drvn and one pce appr fnl f* **7/2**[2]
1063 **6** *nk* **Neil's Legacy (IRE)**[6] 6638 5-8-9 **67** PaulHanagan 8 69
(Miss L A Perratt) *prom: rdn along over 2f out: grad wknd* **12/1**
5134 **7** *1* **Boundless Prospect (USA)**[6] 6636 8-9-6 **78** MickyFenton 1 78
(Miss Gay Kelleway) *towards rr: hdwy over 2f out: sn rdn and no imp* **14/1**
3600 **8** *¾* **Milliegait**[14] 6474 3-8-11 **71** GrahamGibbons 9 69
(T D Easterby) *chsd ldrs: hdwy 3f out: cl up and rdn over 2f out: sn drvn and wknd appr fnl f* **16/1**
6650 **9** *1* **Neardown Beauty (IRE)**[93] 4268 4-9-1 **78** NeilBrown(5) 6 74
(R E Barr) *towards rr: hdwy on outer over 2f out: rdn and btn wl over 1f out* **25/1**
010 **10** *1 ½* **Monsoon Wedding**[24] 6258 3-8-10 **70** GregFairley 5 63
(M Johnston) *prom: rdn along wl over 2f out and sn wknd* **16/1**

1m 40.68s (-1.82) **Going Correction** -0.10s/f (Good)
WFA 3 from 4yo+ 2lb **10 Ran SP% 117.9**
Speed ratings (Par 105): **105,104,103,102,102 101,100,99,98,97**
CSF £215.01 CT £555.37 TOTE £23.30: £3.30, £1.80, £1.60; EX 223.40 Place 6 £34.24, Place 5 £30.66..
Owner Ansells Of Watford **Bred** E Lonergan **Trained** Hambleton, N Yorks
FOCUS
A modest handicap, run at a fair pace. The second and third set the level.
T/Plt: £36.20 to a £1 stake. Pool: £54,256.05. 1,092.50 winning tickets. T/Qpdt: £14.50 to a £1 stake. Pool: £3,106.80. 157.50 winning tickets. JR

6734 WOLVERHAMPTON (A.W) (L-H)
Friday, November 9

OFFICIAL GOING: Standard
Wind: Fresh behind Weather: Overcast

6747 MACE RACING AT WOLVERHAMPTON APPRENTICE H'CAP 5f 216y(P)
7:00 (7:01) (Class 5) (0-70,68) 3-Y-0+ **£2,968** (£876; £438) **Stalls** Low

Form RPR
3200 **1** **Norcroft**[17] 6415 5-8-13 **65** (p) KirstyMilczarek(3) 8 73
(Mrs C A Dunnett) *led early: prom: chsd ldr over 1f out: edgd lft: r.o to ld wl ins fnl f* **9/1**
6464 **2** *nk* **Chatshow (USA)**[38] 5879 6-8-12 **61** LukeMorris 13 68
(A W Carroll) *hld up: hdwy over 1f out: sn rdn: r.o* **7/1**[3]
0310 **3** *hd* **Mistral Sky**[5] 6671 8-8-11 **63** (p) TolleyDean(3) 5 69
(Stef Liddiard) *mid-div: sn pushed along: hdwy over 1f out: nt clr run ins fnl f: swtchd rt: r.o* **16/1**
0030 **4** *nk* **Metal Guru**[22] 6283 3-8-13 **65** RussellKennemore(3) 9 70+
(R Hollinshead) *hld up: nt clr run and edgd lft over 2f out: hdwy over 1f out: r.o* **16/1**
3051 **5** *nk* **Punching**[8] 6608 3-8-4 **60** 6ex RichardEvans(7) 2 64
(Eve Johnson Houghton) *s.i.s: rcvrd to ld 5f out: rdn and edgd lft fr over 1f out: hdd wl ins fnl f* **5/1**[2]
005 **6** *5* **Inka Dancer (IRE)**[14] 6476 5-8-9 **58** RichardKingscote 4 46
(B Palling) *sn led: hdd 5f out: chsd ldrs: rdn over 2f out: sn outpcd: no ch whn hung lft ins fnl f* **14/1**
2000 **7** *1 ¾* **Ken's Girl**[23] 6273 3-9-0 **66** ow1 JamesMillman(3) 1 48
(W S Kittow) *chsd ldrs: rdn over 1f out: wknd fnl f* **20/1**
0405 **8** *½* **Jord (IRE)**[52] 5495 3-9-0 **68** (p) RobbieEgan(5) 11 49
(A J McCabe) *hld up: hdwy u.p over 2f out: sn wknd* **16/1**
5002 **9** *shd* **Came Back (IRE)**[7] 6625 4-9-2 **65** MichaelJStainton 6 46
(J Mackie) *chsd ldrs: rdn and wknd over 1f out* **7/4**[1]
6364 **10** *1* **Charlotte Grey**[19] 6360 3-8-9 **63** MCGeran(5) 12 40
(C N Allen) *hld up: plld hrd: a in rr* **33/1**
2160 **11** *¾* **Kindallachan**[9] 6581 4-8-10 **59** LiamJones 7 34
(G C Bravery) *hld up: hmpd over 3f out: a in rr* **25/1**
0 **12** *2* **Bungie**[22] 6287 3-9-0 **63** TravisBlock 3 32
(Paul Green) *chsd ldrs over 4f* **50/1**
0415 **13** *1 ¼* **Megalo Maniac**[14] 6463 4-9-2 **65** JamieMoriarty 10 30
(R A Fahey) *dwlt: hld up: hmpd over 3f out: a in rr* **8/1**

1m 15.16s (-0.65) **Going Correction** -0.10s/f (Stan) **13 Ran SP% 124.5**
Speed ratings (Par 103): **100,99,99,98,98 91,89,88,88,87 86,83,82**
CSF £71.08 CT £1057.29 TOTE £17.70: £2.00, £2.20, £7.80; EX 67.80.
Owner G R Price **Bred** Norcroft Park Stud **Trained** Hingham, Norfolk
FOCUS
A modest sprint handicap, but very competitive. Ordinary form.
Came Back(IRE) Official explanation: jockey said colt ran flat

6748 HOTEL & CONFERENCING AT WOLVERHAMPTON RACECOURSE MAIDEN STKS 7f 32y(P)
7:30 (7:30) (Class 5) 2-Y-0 **£2,968** (£876; £438) **Stalls** High

Form RPR
032 **1** **Mafioso**[11] 6530 2-9-3 0 JamieSpencer 5 77+
(M Johnston) *sn led: rdn over 1f out: styd on wl* **4/11**[1]
50 **2** *3* **Jerry Hamilton (USA)**[16] 6436 2-9-3 0 DeanMcKeown 3 70
(M Johnston) *a.p: rdn to chse wnr over 1f out: no imp* **20/1**
2604 **3** *6* **Harbour Blues**[18] 6379 2-9-3 68 HayleyTurner 8 55
(C E Brittain) *chsd wnr tl rdn over 1f out: wknd fnl f* **13/2**[2]
00 **4** *5* **Special Feature (IRE)**[16] 6417 2-9-3 0 RobertHavlin 1 43
(C R Egerton) *in rr: effrt 1/2-way: wknd over 2f out* **25/1**
5 *1* **Loveofmylife** 2-8-12 0 SebSanders 6 35
(R M Beckett) *chsd ldrs: rdn over 2f out: sn wknd* **8/1**[3]
0 **6** *7* **Astrodome**[10] 6571 2-9-3 0 StephenDonohoe 7 23
(Sir Mark Prescott) *s.i.s: outpcd* **150/1**
00 **7** *1 ¼* **Aleatricis**[11] 6530 2-9-3 0 JamieMackay 4 20
(Sir Mark Prescott) *s.i.s: outpcd: bhd whn hung lft fnl f* **150/1**
0006 **8** *7* **Jimmy Dean**[22] 6289 2-9-3 49 (b) DaneO'Neill 9 3
(M Wellings) *chsd ldrs tl rdn and wknd over 2f out* **100/1**

1m 29.88s (-0.52) **Going Correction** -0.10s/f (Stan) **8 Ran SP% 108.7**
Speed ratings (Par 96): **98,94,87,82,80 72,71,63**
CSF £12.01 TOTE £1.30: £1.02, £3.50, £1.50; EX 10.10.
Owner Sheikh Mohammed **Bred** Darley **Trained** Middleham Moor, N Yorks
FOCUS
An uncompetitive maiden in which the third did not to run up to his official mark of 68. The time was fair.
NOTEBOOK
Mafioso had shaped nicely on his last two starts, including when runner-up in a stronger maiden at Kempton on his previous start, and he found this a straightforward opportunity to get off the mark at the fourth time of asking. He did not have a great deal to beat, and things are going to be tougher from now on, but he looks a nice handicapper in the making. (op 8-13)
Jerry Hamilton(USA) ◆, a half-brother to Shamardal, had not shown much on his two previous starts, but this was an encouraging effort behind his stablemate. He was not given an unnecessarily hard time once his chance had gone and he should come into his own when stepped up in trip and sent handicapping. (op 14-1)
Harbour Blues, dropped in trip and returned to maiden company, was well placed if good enough, but he weakened out of contention rather tamely. He was well below his official mark of 68. (op 9-2 tchd 7-1)
Special Feature(IRE) had not shown much in a couple of runs over 1m, but a drop in trip was not the answer for this Derby entry. He is now qualified for a handicap mark and it would be no surprise to see him leave this form behind in time.
Loveofmylife, a 31,000gns daughter of Dr Fong, half-sister to 7f-1m performer Hucking Hot, showed little on her racecourse debut and seemed to need the experience. (op 11-2)
Astrodome can be expected to do much better in middle-distance/staying handicaps next year. (op 100-1)
Aleatricis, like his stablemate in sixth, should leave this form well behind when stepped up in trip and sent handicapping. (op 100-1)

6749 HORIZONS RESTAURANT OVERLOOKS THE TRACK H'CAP 7f 32y(P)
7:55 (7:57) (Class 6) (0-62,66) 3-Y-0+ **£2,047** (£604; £302) **Stalls** High

Form RPR
0022 **1** **Northern Boy (USA)**[14] 6476 4-9-0 **60** SebSanders 12 71
(M W Easterby) *hld up: hdwy over 2f out: rdn over 1f out: hung lft ins fnl f: r.o to ld nr fin* **13/2**[3]
0010 **2** *¾* **Four Tel**[37] 5905 3-9-1 **62** SamHitchcott 10 71
(N J Vaughan) *sn led: rdn over 1f out: hdd nr fin* **8/1**
0421 **3** *½* **Encores**[11] 6533 3-9-5 **66** 6ex JamieSpencer 1 74
(M G Quinlan) *hld up in tch: chsd ldr over 1f out: hrd rdn ins fnl f: styd on same pce* **13/8**[1]
5204 **4** *3* **Carlitos Spirit (IRE)**[29] 6123 3-8-13 **60** FergusSweeney 5 60
(B R Millman) *ld early: chsd ldrs: rdn and edgd rt over 1f out: wknd ins fnl f* **10/1**
020- **5** *2 ½* **Kensington (IRE)**[346] 6642 6-8-12 **58** TGMcLaughlin 8 51
(P D Evans) *prom: rdn over 2f out: wknd over 1f out* **25/1**
630 **6** *nk* **Tyrannosaurus Rex (IRE)**[76] 4808 3-8-13 **60** LeeEnstone 6 52
(K R Burke) *prom: chsd ldr 1/2-way sn rdn: wknd over 1f out* **5/1**[2]
0406 **7** *½* **Winged Farasi**[39] 5860 3-8-7 **59** KevinGhunowa(5) 4 50
(R A Harris) *sn pushed along in rr: styd on u.p fr over 1f out: nvr nrr* **20/1**
/062 **8** *1* **Nok Twice (IRE)**[21] 6316 6-9-0 **60** DeanMcKeown 3 48
(D Carroll) *hld up: rdn over 2f out: wknd over 1f out* **10/1**
3003 **9** *1* **Spanish Needle**[14] 6476 3-8-13 **60** DaneO'Neill 2 45
(P R Webber) *s.i.s: rdn over 2f out: a in rr* **14/1**
2540 **10** *¾* **Split Briefs (IRE)**[10] 6573 3-8-12 **59** AdrianMcCarthy 7 42
(C A Dwyer) *chsd ldrs: lost pl 4f out: sn bhd* **80/1**
2601 **11** *3 ½* **Ten To The Dozen**[11] 6537 4-8-13 **59** 6ex ChrisCatlin 11 33
(P W Hiatt) *chsd ldrs over 4f* **20/1**
5400 **12** *2 ½* **Regal Royale**[107] 3852 4-9-2 **62** LPKeniry 9 29
(Peter Grayson) *hld up: a in rr: rdn and wknd over 2f out* **40/1**

1m 29.57s (-0.83) **Going Correction** -0.10s/f (Stan)
WFA 3 from 4yo+ 1lb **12 Ran SP% 121.1**
Speed ratings (Par 101): **100,99,98,95,92 91,91,90,89,88 84,81**
CSF £55.17 CT £127.28 TOTE £7.20: £1.60, £2.60, £1.50; EX 49.90.
Owner East Riding Horse Racing Syndicate Ltd **Bred** Phil Booker **Trained** Sheriff Hutton, N Yorks
FOCUS
A modest but competitive handicap. Ordinary form, the winner back to his spring level.

6750 STAY AT THE WOLVERHAMPTON HOLIDAY INN NURSERY 1m 141y(P)
8:25 (8:26) (Class 5) (0-75,82) 2-Y-0 **£2,968** (£876; £438) **Stalls** Low

Form RPR
3403 **1** **Moment's Notice**[9] 6578 2-9-4 **70** LPKeniry 5 76+
(S Kirk) *hld up in tch: led over 1f out: edgd rt ins fnl f: rdn out* **12/1**
0011 **2** *1* **Points Of View**[2] 6715 2-10-2 **82** 12ex SebSanders 12 86
(Sir Mark Prescott) *hld up: hdwy over 2f out: rdn and edgd lft over 1f out: hung lft ins fnl f: styd on* **4/5**[1]
005 **3** *1 ½* **Title Role**[74] 4882 2-9-0 **71** TolleyDean(5) 10 72
(P F I Cole) *s.i.s: hld up: racd keenly: rdn over 1f out: r.o ins fnl f: nrst fin* **9/1**[3]
3506 **4** *hd* **Duke Of Touraine (IRE)**[67] 5081 2-9-2 **68** DeanMcKeown 7 68
(P C Haslam) *hld up: nt clr run wl over 1f out: r.o ins fnl f: nt rch ldrs* **20/1**
0225 **5** *½* **Ten Pole Tudor**[15] 6451 2-9-2 **73** KevinGhunowa(5) 3 72
(R A Harris) *chsd ldr: led over 2f out: rdn and hdd over 1f out: styd on same pce* **25/1**
3605 **6** *1* **Eternal Optimist (IRE)**[14] 6478 2-8-5 **57** ChrisCatlin 1 54
(C W Thornton) *led: hdd 7f out: chsd ldrs: rdn over 2f out: styd on same pce fnl f* **40/1**
0431 **7** *shd* **Suzi Spends (IRE)**[25] 6233 2-9-7 **73** JamieSpencer 4 70
(M Johnston) *hld up: hdwy over 2f out: rdn and hung lft over 1f out: no ex* **9/2**[2]
0003 **8** *2* **Titfer (IRE)**[16] 6427 2-8-5 **57** FrancisNorton 9 50
(A W Carroll) *sn pushed along and prom: led 7f out: rdn and hdd over 2f out: wknd over 1f out* **14/1**
5624 **9** *1* **Elusive Deal (USA)**[14] 6478 2-8-9 **61** (p) TonyHamilton 2 52
(R A Fahey) *hld up: pushed along 1/2-way: rdn over 2f out: n.d* **14/1**
0053 **10** *5* **Kiwi Princess**[59] 5298 2-8-6 **58** DaleGibson 6 38
(M Brittain) *chsd ldrs: rdn over 3f out: wknd over 1f out* **50/1**
3400 **11** *1 ½* **Karky Schultz (GER)**[13] 6486 2-9-1 **67** HayleyTurner 11 44
(J M P Eustace) *prom: rdn over 2f out: wknd wl over 1f out* **25/1**

The Form Book, Raceform Ltd, Compton, RG20 6NL

0036 **12** ½ **Melwood Dreams**[1] 6736 2-8-5 **60** ow1 NeilChalmers(3) 8 36
(Paul Green) *rdn 1/2-way: a in rr* **40/1**

1m 51.18s (-0.58) **Going Correction** -0.10s/f (Stan) **12** Ran SP% **124.1**
Speed ratings (Par 96): **98,97,95,95,95 94,94,92,91,87 85,85**
CSF £21.75 CT £108.68 TOTE £19.20: £3.30, £1.30, £1.70; EX 41.30.
Owner C Wright & The Hon Mrs J M Corbett **Bred** Stratford Place Stud **Trained** Upper Lambourn, Berks

FOCUS
A decent nursery and the form looks solid.

NOTEBOOK
Moment's Notice was due to be raised to a mark of 81 following his recent third in a Kempton maiden, so he was 11lb well-in this time and he took full advantage. He got a dream run round the inside and stayed on strongly in the straight to deny the odds-on favourite, who was forced to come wide. He is going to find things much tougher from now on, but is clearly going the right way. (op 7-1)
Points Of View, bidding for the hat-trick just two days after picking up a similar event at Kempton, was 6lb higher under his double penalty and he found one too strong. He was forced to make up his ground a little wider than ideal and was always just being held after the eventual winner got first run towards the inside. This was still a useful effort under his big weight. (op 5-4)
Title Role ♦, stepped up in trip on his handicap debut, was in a hopeless position turning for home, but he stayed on strongly when switched out wide in the straight. He looks well up to winning off this sort of mark. (op 13-2 tchd 10-1)
Duke Of Touraine(IRE), a beaten favourite in a 6f claimer at Hamilton on his previous start, ran much better stepped up in trip and switched to Polytrack for the first time. He was a little short of room at the top of the straight, but was not unlucky. (op 16-1)
Ten Pole Tudor was trying his furthest trip to date on his Polytrack debut, but his stamina gave out late on. He could find a similar race back over a little shorter. (op 16-1)
Suzi Spends(IRE) never really looked like defying a 4lb rise in the weights for her Windsor success. (op 11-2)

6751 BOOK ONLINE AT WOLVERHAMPTON-RACECOURSE.CO.UK MEDIAN AUCTION MAIDEN STKS — 1m 4f 50y(P)
8:55 (8:55) (Class 6) 3-5-Y-O **£2,047** (£604; £302) **Stalls** Low

Form RPR
220 **1** **Vivacita**[26] 6211 3-8-12 59 ChrisCatlin 4 67
(E J O'Neill) *trckd ldrs: plld hrd: rdn to ld ins fnl f: styd on* **3/1**[3]
3023 **2** *nk* **Dart**[11] 6534 3-8-12 60 JamieSpencer 11 67
(J R Fanshawe) *chsd ldr 10f out: rdn to ld and wandered over 1f out: hdd ins fnl f: nt qckn* **2/1**[1]
6000 **3** *5* **Covert Mission**[26] 6196 4-9-4 55 TGMcLaughlin 7 59
(P D Evans) *s.i.s: hld up: hdwy 3f out: sn rdn: styd on same pce fnl 2f* **25/1**
0304 **4** *5* **Verbatim**[41] 5803 3-8-9 61 WilliamBuick(3) 3 51
(A M Balding) *chsd ldrs: rdn over 4f out: wknd over 2f out* **11/2**
4232 **5** *2* **Sweet Request**[32] 6070 3-8-12 64 (p) SebSanders 1 48
(R M Beckett) *led: rdn and bmpd wl over 1f out: sn hdd: wknd fnl f* **5/2**[2]
00 **6** *8* **Cumae (USA)**[41] 5816 3-8-12 0 DavidKinsella 9 35
(J Pearce) *hld up: hdwy 4f out: wknd 3f out* **100/1**
0 **7** *9* **Lord Of The Lake**[121] 3436 3-9-3 0 (t) FrancisNorton 2 26
(P J McBride) *hld up in tch: rdn over 3f out: sn wknd* **10/1**
0 **8** *8* **Karrumba (IRE)**[210] 1024 3-8-12 0 AdrianMcCarthy 10 8
(B J McMath) *hld up: bhd fnl 7f* **100/1**
00-0 **9** *100* **Garrya**[10] 6569 3-9-3 35 LeeEnstone 8 —
(B P J Baugh) *chsd ldr early: lost pl 7f out: bhd fnl 6f* **100/1**

2m 41.18s (-1.24) **Going Correction** -0.10s/f (Stan)
WFA 3 from 4yo 6lb **9** Ran SP% **118.2**
Speed ratings (Par 101): **100,99,96,93,91 86,80,75,—**
CSF £9.65 TOTE £4.00: £1.50, £1.60, £7.50; EX 12.20.
Owner Mrs A G Kavanagh **Bred** The National Stud Owner Breeders Club Ltd **Trained** Averham Park, Notts

FOCUS
A modest maiden, but the pace was strong. The runner-up is probably the best guide.
Vivacita Official explanation: trainer said, regarding apparent improvement in form, that he had no explanation

6752 EVENING RACING - MISS THE TRAFFIC H'CAP — 5f 20y(P)
9:20 (9:20) (Class 6) (0-60,62) 3-Y-O+ **£2,047** (£604; £302) **Stalls** Low

Form RPR
0001 **1** **Commander Wish**[10] 6565 4-8-6 **51** 6ex (tp) NeilChalmers(3) 5 68
(Lucinda Featherstone) *chsd ldrs: rdn to ld 1f out: r.o* **5/1**[2]
0211 **2** *1 ½* **Spirit Of Coniston**[10] 6562 4-9-6 **62** 12ex JamieSpencer 9 74
(D Nicholls) *hld up: hdwy over 1f out: rdn to chse wnr ins fnl f: no imp* **6/4**[1]
100 **3** *2 ½* **Hello Roberto**[16] 6424 6-8-8 **55** (p) KevinGhunowa(5) 4 58
(R A Harris) *hld up: hdwy over 1f out: nt rch ldrs* **14/1**
0006 **4** *½* **Matterofact (IRE)**[25] 6244 4-9-1 **57** FergusSweeney 7 58
(M S Saunders) *prom: rdn 1/2-way: styd on same pce appr fnl f* **25/1**
2110 **5** *hd* **Sofinella (IRE)**[25] 6244 4-9-1 **60** LukeMorris(3) 13 60
(A W Carroll) *chsd ldrs: led over 1f out: sn rdn and hdd: no ex ins fnl f* **20/1**
000 **6** *1 ½* **Theoretical**[9] 6581 3-9-4 **60** (p) SebSanders 6 55
(A J McCabe) *sn outpcd: styd on ins fnl f: nvr nrr* **14/1**
0043 **7** *½* **Briery Lane (IRE)**[16] 6424 6-9-2 **58** StephenDonohoe 2 51
(J M Bradley) *sn outpcd: nvr nrr* **7/1**
2120 **8** *¾* **Thoughtsofstardom**[25] 6244 4-9-2 **58** TGMcLaughlin 1 48
(G C Bravery) *s.i.s: outpcd* **16/1**
0006 **9** *1 ½* **Avoca Dancer (IRE)**[50] 5564 4-8-6 **48** JamieMackay 8 33
(M Wigham) *dwlt: outpcd* **33/1**
3340 **10** *½* **Gifted Lass**[25] 6244 5-9-1 **60** MarcHalford(3) 3 43
(J Balding) *led over 3f: wknd fnl f* **10/1**
0253 **11** *1 ½* **Triskaidekaphobia**[16] 6428 4-8-13 **55** (t) PaulFitzsimons 11 33
(Miss J R Tooth) *w ldr: rdn 1/2-way: wknd over 1f out* **11/2**[3]

62.49 secs (-0.33) **Going Correction** -0.10s/f (Stan) **11** Ran SP% **124.4**
Speed ratings (Par 101): **98,95,91,90,90 88,87,86,83,82 80**
CSF £13.35 CT £107.61 TOTE £14.80: £3.20, £1.20, £2.20; EX 23.90 Place 6 £14.98, Place 5 £2.73..
Owner J Roundtree **Bred** P R Featherstone **Trained** Ashbourne, Derbyshire
■ Stewards' Enquiry : Paul Fitzsimons one-day ban: failed to ride to draw (Nov 20)

FOCUS
A good sprint handicap for the grade dominated by a couple of horses who came into this ahead of the Handicapper. The early pace was very strong.
T/Plt: £37.80 to a £1 stake. Pool: £114,054.90. 2,198.20 winning tickets. T/Qpdt: £3.90 to a £1 stake. Pool: £6,575.80. 1,220.10 winning tickets. CR

6486 DONCASTER (L-H)
Saturday, November 10

OFFICIAL GOING: Good to firm
3mm water overall and 6mm over the final four furlongs over the previous day resulted in 'good to firm, lovely ground for the last turf meeting of the year'.
Wind: Moderate half-against Weather: overcast

6753 TONY HALLATT MEMORIAL APPRENTICE H'CAP — 7f
12:00 (12:03) (Class 4) (0-85,85) 3-Y-O+ **£5,181** (£1,541; £770; £384) **Stalls** High

Form RPR
2541 **1** **Gunfighter (IRE)**[26] 6243 4-8-13 **78** PJMcDonald 19 92+
(J S Wainwright) *hld up in rr: swtchd rt and smooth hdwy 2f out: shkn upand qcknd to ld last 100yds* **7/1**[1]
0002 **2** *¾* **Bahiano (IRE)**[7] 6651 6-9-4 **83** LiamJones 5 93
(C E Brittain) *in tch on outer: hdwy over 2f out: rdn over 1f out: kpt on ins fnl f* **8/1**[3]
6206 **3** *1 ¼* **Grimes Faith**[26] 6243 4-8-7 **72** (b) LukeMorris 8 79
(K A Ryan) *trckd ldrs: hdwy over 2f out: led wl over 1f out: rdn and edgd lft ent fnl f: hdd and nt qckn last 100yds* **18/1**
6000 **4** *½* **Geojimali**[26] 6243 5-8-8 **78** GaryBartley(5) 12 84
(J S Goldie) *in rr: swtchd outside and gd hdwy wl over 1f out: rdn and styd on strly ins fnl f: nrst fin* **11/1**
1004 **5** *hd* **Jacaranda Ridge**[14] 6497 3-8-10 **76** WilliamBuick 11 81
(M A Jarvis) *trckd ldrs: hdwy to ld briefly jst over 2f out: sn rdn and hdd wl over 1f out: drvn and one pce ins fnl f* **12/1**
060 **6** *¾* **Makshoof (IRE)**[50] 5584 3-9-2 **82** AndrewMullen 3 85
(K A Ryan) *chsd ldrs on outer: effrt over 2f out and ch tl rdn over 1f out and grad wknd ins fnl f* **33/1**
4105 **7** *shd* **Yorkshire Blue**[7] 6639 8-8-2 **72** KellyHarrison(5) 9 75
(J S Goldie) *in tch: effrt over 2f out: sn rdn and kpt on same pce appr fnl f* **16/1**
0002 **8** *¾* **Curzon Prince (IRE)**[14] 6492 3-8-10 **81** RobbieEgan(5) 16 82+
(C F Wall) *trckd ldrs: nt clr run and lost pl 2f out: sn swtchd rt and rdn: styd on ins fnl f: nrst fin* **7/1**[1]
6430 **9** *1 ¾* **Bonnie Prince Blue**[17] 6435 4-8-9 **77** PatrickHills(3) 21 73
(B W Hills) *in tch: effrt 2f out: sn rdn: edgd lft and kpt on same pce* **12/1**
2350 **10** *¾* **Barkass (UAE)**[14] 6492 3-8-7 **73** ow1 JamieMoriarty 13 67
(B Ellison) *in rr: hdwy 2f out: sn rdn and kpt on ins fnl f: nt rch ldrs* **33/1**
2500 **11** *½* **Bailieborough (IRE)**[28] 6185 8-8-13 **85** LanceBetts(7) 18 78
(N Wilson) *hld up in rr: effrt and sme hdwy 2f out: sn rdn and nt rch ldrs* **50/1**
0046 **12** *¾* **Macedon**[85] 4566 4-8-12 **80** TolleyDean(3) 7 71
(J S Moore) *nvr bttr then midfield* **15/2**[2]
1430 **13** *1 ¼* **Bid For Gold**[39] 5885 3-8-8 **74** MichaelJStainton 15 61
(Jedd O'Keeffe) *chsd ldrs: rdn along and edgd rt over 2f out: sn wknd* **50/1**
6660 **14** *½* **Katie Boo (IRE)**[22] 6300 5-8-13 **83** WilliamCarson(5) 10 69
(A Berry) *chsd ldrs: rdn along 2f out: sn wknd* **50/1**
0000 **15** *3* **Medici Pearl**[15] 6474 3-8-6 **72** DuranFentiman 22 50
(T D Easterby) *chsd ldrs: rdn along wl over 2f out and grad wknd* **50/1**
2106 **16** *¾* **Starlight Gazer**[22] 6301 4-9-2 **81** TravisBlock 14 57
(J A Geake) *towards rr fr 1/2-way* **11/1**
5400 **17** *¾* **Yerevan**[22] 6313 3-8-2 **73** SophieDoyle(5) 20 47
(R T Phillips) *chsd ldrs: rdn along wl over 2f out and sn wknd* **80/1**
2601 **18** *½* **Rydal Mount (IRE)**[32] 6088 4-8-1 **73** ow1 TimothyMeadows(7) 6 45
(W S Kittow) *chsd ldrs on outer: rdn along 2f out and sn wknd* **25/1**
0640 **19** *1* **Balakiref**[11] 6560 8-8-7 **79** JohnCavanagh(7) 17 49
(M Dods) *led: rdn along and hdd over 2f out: sn wknd* **40/1**
6406 **20** *nk* **Imperial Echo (USA)**[11] 6560 6-8-11 **79** NeilBrown(3) 2 48
(T D Barron) *racd far side: prom tl rdn along 3f out and sn wknd* **12/1**
5004 **21** *4* **Inaminute (IRE)**[11] 6560 4-8-8 **73** AndrewElliott 1 31
(K R Burke) *racd far side: prom tl rdn along 3f out and sn wknd* **20/1**

1m 26.17s (-1.60) **Going Correction** -0.075s/f (Good)
WFA 3 from 4yo+ 1lb **21** Ran SP% **124.8**
Speed ratings (Par 105): **106,105,103,103,102 102,101,101,99,98 97,96,95,94,91 90,89,89,87,87 83**
CSF £55.09 CT £1009.76 TOTE £6.60: £2.10, £2.60, £4.90, £2.50; EX 38.10 TRIFECTA Not won..
Owner M Sawers **Bred** Round Hill Stud **Trained** Kennythorpe, N Yorks

FOCUS
A big field but a convincing winner who can make further progress. Overall the form looks very solid, with the placed horses looking pretty exposed.

6754 FIRST TRANSFORMING TRAVEL IN DONCASTER E B F MAIDEN STKS (DIV I) — 6f
12:30 (12:36) (Class 4) 2-Y-O **£4,857** (£1,445; £722; £360) **Stalls** High

Form RPR
452 **1** **Incomparable**[10] 6595 2-9-3 75 SebSanders 4 77+
(A J McCabe) *chsd ldrs: drvn to ld 2f out: hdd 1f out: lft in ld last 75yds: bdly hmpd by loose horse nr fin* **11/4**[2]
2 *1* **Orange Pip** 2-8-12 0 RyanMoore 6 66
(R Hannon) *mid-div: hdwy over 2f out: rdn whn hmpd 1f out: kpt on ins fnl f* **8/1**
50 **3** *1* **Climaxtackledotcom**[32] 6073 2-9-3 0 PaulMulrennan 3 68
(M W Easterby) *hld up: hdwy 2f out: kpt on to snatch 3rd nr line* **100/1**
622 **4** *hd* **Alwaabel**[12] 6540 2-9-3 82 RHills 2 67
(J L Dunlop) *w ldrs: rdn and bdly hmpd 1f out: nt rcvr* **2/1**[1]
5 *5* **Signora (IRE)** 2-8-12 0 DarryllHolland 5 47
(M Johnston) *in rr: kpt on fnl 2f: nvr a factor* **14/1**
04 **6** *hd* **Horatio Carter**[29] 6156 2-9-3 0 JamieSpencer 8 52
(K A Ryan) *mid-div: effrt over 2f out: sn wl outpcd* **11/2**
0 **7** *5* **Jumpin Johnnie**[15] 6469 2-9-3 0 SteveDrowne 9 37
(R T Phillips) *hld up in rr: effrt over 2f out: sn lost pl* **33/1**
6 **8** *hd* **Persistent (IRE)**[29] 6139 2-9-3 0 MickyFenton 11 36
(P T Midgley) *s.i.s: a in rr* **50/1**
0 **9** *nk* **Super Tuscan (IRE)**[15] 6469 2-9-3 0 TomEaves 1 35
(J G Given) *led tl 2f out: wkng whn hmpd 1f out: eased* **100/1**
U **Omnicat (USA)** 2-9-3 0 (t) EddieAhern 12 77+
(Saeed Bin Suroor) *w ldrs: stdd after 1f: effrt & hung lft over 2f out: hung bdly lft & led 1f out: hrd rdn & veered bdly rt wl ins fnl f & uns rdr* **9/2**[3]

1m 13.95s (-0.35) **Going Correction** -0.075s/f (Good) **10** Ran SP% **118.2**
Speed ratings (Par 98): **99,97,96,96,89 89,82,82,81,—**
CSF £25.18 TOTE £3.90: £1.70, £2.10, £8.50; EX 27.20 TRIFECTA Not won..

Owner Paul J Dixon and Michael F Maguire **Bred** Mrs Yvette Dixon **Trained** Babworth, Notts

FOCUS

The quicker division and a dramatic outcome, putting Seb Sanders two ahead in the jockeys' table. The winner was very definitely only second best and the race has been rated around him. The third might well have been flattered.

NOTEBOOK

Incomparable, who has plenty of size and scope, was handed it on a plate. He was definitely only second best but is the type to progress further at three. (op 5-2)

Orange Pip, a late April foal, is on the leg and narrow. She showed ability on her racecourse debut and will be stronger next year. (op 11-1)

Climaxtackledotcom, unplaced in both his previous starts, stayed on and took third place on the line but was probably only fifth-best on the day.

Alwaabel, up in the air, was starting to get the worst of the argument when Omnicat shot across his bows. He looked third-best and should make a better three-year-old. (op 9-4 tchd 5-2 in places)

Signora(IRE), out of a mare that finished runner-up in the Italian Oaks, is lightly-made and very weak at present. She should be capable of better over further next year. (op 12-1)

Horatio Carter was not up to the task but should improve and make his mark in handicap company at three. (op 13-2)

Omnicat(USA), a rangy, rather delicate newcomer, was dropped in after the first furlong. He hung badly left before hitting the front but once there went right across to the far rail. With his rider throwing everything at him to stop him hitting the rail, he then swerved badly right giving his jockey no chance. He would have won by about three lengths and, though wilful, clearly has plenty of ability. Gelding looks the right option, he is clearly in need of careful handling. (op 5-1)

6755 FIRST TRANSFORMING TRAVEL IN DONCASTER E B F MAIDEN STKS (DIV II) 6f

1:00 (1:04) (Class 4) 2-Y-O **£4,857** (£1,445; £722; £360) **Stalls** High

Form | | | | RPR
2 **1** **Premier Danseur (IRE)**[11] 6557 2-9-3 0 DarryllHolland 7 74+
(M Johnston) *in tch: hdwy 2f out: swtchd rt and rdn to chse ldr ent fnl f: kpt on wl u.p to ld nr fin* **1/1**[1]
0 **2** *nk* **Minus Fifteen (IRE)**[22] 6295 2-9-3 0 JamieSpencer 1 73
(K A Ryan) *cl up on outer: hdwy to ld over 2f out: rdn over 1f out: drvn and edgd lft ins fnl f: hdd and no ex towards fin* **9/2**[2]
3 *1* **Beauchamp Wizard** 2-9-3 0 NickyMackay 4 70
(G A Butler) *in tch: hdwy to chse ldrs over 2f out: rdn over 1f out and ch: kpt on same pce ins fnl f* **28/1**
05 **4** *1 1/4* **Royal Acclamation (IRE)**[11] 6557 2-9-3 0 SilvestreDeSousa 2 66
(G A Harker) *towards rr: hdwy 2f out: sn rdn and kpt on ins fnl f: nrst fin* **16/1**
5 *hd* **Wise Hawk** 2-9-3 0 MichaelHills 8 66
(W J Haggas) *cl up: rdn and ev ch 2f out: sn drvn and wknd appr fnl f* **8/1**[3]
6 *1 1/4* **Novellen Lad (IRE)** 2-9-3 0 KDarley 9 62
(E J Alston) *sn led: rdn along and hdd over 2f out: grad wknd appr fnl f* **10/1**
05 **7** *1/2* **Benedetto**[8] 6617 2-9-3 0 JimCrowley 11 60
(Mrs A J Perrett) *in rr: hdwy 2f out: sn rdn and kpt on ins fnl f: nt rch ldrs* **12/1**
8 *3/4* **Asian Lady** 2-8-12 0 SteveDrowne 10 53
(R Charlton) *in tch: hdwy to chse ldrs 3f out: rdn over 2f out and sn wknd* **8/1**[3]
9 *22* **Be Superior** 2-8-12 0 PaulMulrennan 6 —
(J Balding) *prom: pushed along and lost pl over 3f out: sn bhd* **100/1**

1m 14.89s (0.59) **Going Correction** -0.075s/f (Good) **9** Ran SP% **117.5**
Speed ratings (Par 98): **93,92,91,89,89 87,87,86,56**
CSF £5.75 TOTE £2.00: £1.30, £1.60, £6.30; EX 6.90 Trifecta £78.20 Pool £439.87 - 3.99 winning units..

Owner Sheikh Mohammed **Bred** Darley **Trained** Middleham Moor, N Yorks

FOCUS

The weaker, slower division and the winner probably did not have to improve on his debut effort.

NOTEBOOK

Premier Danseur(IRE) made hard work of it but got there in the end. He should be capable of better over 7f plus at three. (op 11-8)

Minus Fifteen(IRE), having just his second start, is still up in the air and rather immature. He travelled strongly but was edged out near the line, and is sure to go on to better at three. (op 4-1 tchd 5-1 in places)

Beauchamp Wizard, long in the back, looked very inexperienced beforehand. He made a pleasing start to his career and there ought to be better to come.

Royal Acclamation(IRE), about three lengths behind the winner at Catterick last week, seemed to run to about the same level of form. This opens up the handicap route for him at three. Official explanation: jockey said colt moved poorly throughout

Wise Hawk, a tall, January foal, showed ability and will be more the finished article at three.

Novellen Lad(IRE), a late May foal, is out of a speedy dam line that has served this yard well. He showed bags of toe and should be able to make his mark in sprint company at three. (tchd 9-1)

6756 BET IN-PLAY AT TOTESPORT.COM NURSERY 6f

1:30 (1:33) (Class 4) (0-85,85) 2-Y-O **£6,477** (£1,927; £963; £481) **Stalls** High

Form | | | | RPR
531 **1** **Generous Thought**[44] 5745 2-9-2 **80** JamieSpencer 5 91+
(P Howling) *hld up in rr: stdy hdwy over 2f out: hrd rdn and edgd lft over 1f out: led ins fnl f: r.o* **4/1**[1]
3210 **2** *1 1/4* **Rash Judgement**[36] 5974 2-9-2 **80** FergusSweeney 7 87+
(W S Kittow) *hld up towards rr: stdy hdwy over 2f out: led over 1f out: hdd and no ex ins fnl f* **9/1**[3]
4100 **3** *1 3/4* **Mudhish (IRE)**[49] 5629 2-8-11 **75** (b[1]) SebSanders 13 77
(C E Brittain) *chsd ldrs: rdn and edgd lft appr fnl f: kpt on same pce* **16/1**
040 **4** *nk* **Dubai Petal (IRE)**[17] 6432 2-8-7 **71** JohnEgan 16 72
(J S Moore) *in rr: sn pushed along: hdwy over 2f out: kpt on wl fnl f* **16/1**
5304 **5** *3/4* **Tadalavil**[8] 6621 2-9-7 **85** JimmyFortune 15 84
(M R Channon) *mid-div: hdwy over 2f out: kpt on fnl f* **10/1**
6625 **6** *shd* **Wavertree Princess (IRE)**[6] 6665 2-8-11 **75** JamesDoyle 3 74
(N P Littmoden) *chsd ldrs: kpt on same pce fnl 2f* **33/1**
3000 **7** *1 1/2* **Fathsta (IRE)**[35] 6017 2-8-6 **70** FrancisNorton 1 64
(S Kirk) *chsd ldrs on outer: led over 2f out tl over 1f out: sn wknd* **7/1**[2]
3505 **8** *3/4* **Soopacal (IRE)**[25] 6251 2-9-2 **80** TomEaves 18 72
(B Smart) *chsd ldrs: one pce fnl 2f* **28/1**
5162 **9** *nk* **Prigsnov Dancer (IRE)**[21] 6326 2-8-7 **71** AndrewMullen(3) 10 65
(J O'Reilly) *mid-div: kpt on same pce fnl 2f: nvr rchd ldrs* **50/1**
1440 **10** *nk* **River Bounty**[41] 5828 2-8-2 **69** AndrewElliott(3) 4 59
(A P Jarvis) *led tl over 2f out: wknd over 1f out* **28/1**
1425 **11** *1* **Ridge Wood Dani (IRE)**[42] 5802 2-8-4 **68** MatthewHenry 22 55
(E J Alston) *fractious in stalls: chsd ldrs: wknd over 1f out* **10/1**
0120 **12** *nk* **Piscean (USA)**[28] 6182 2-9-2 **80** MickyFenton 14 66
(T Keddy) *in rr: sme hdwy 2f out: nvr on terms* **16/1**
41 **13** *1/2* **Indian Diva (IRE)**[18] 6403 2-9-5 **83** (b) EddieAhern 9 68
(P A Blockley) *chsd ldrs: wknd 2f out* **10/1**
51 **14** *nk* **Peter's Storm (USA)**[19] 6386 2-9-5 **83** NCallan 21 67
(K A Ryan) *chsd ldrs stands' side: outpcd fnl 2f* **9/1**[3]
0330 **15** *1 1/4* **Bishopbriggs (USA)**[7] 6634 2-8-7 **71** GrahamGibbons 19 51
(D J Murphy) *mid-div: outpcd over 2f out: sn lost pl* **20/1**
3221 **16** *3 1/2* **Fabuleux Cherie**[10] 6588 2-8-7 **71** MartinDwyer 12 40
(W R Muir) *in tch: effrt over 2f out: sn wknd* **14/1**
0224 **17** *1 1/4* **Lady Benjamin**[4] 6699 2-8-7 **78** PatrickDonaghy(7) 17 44
(P C Haslam) *a in rr* **20/1**
4041 **18** *nk* **Blue Zenith (IRE)**[17] 6425 2-8-4 **73** NataliaGemelova(5) 8 38
(J S Moore) *w ldrs on outer: wknd over 1f out* **28/1**

1m 12.72s (-1.58) **Going Correction** -0.075s/f (Good) **18** Ran SP% **128.9**
Speed ratings (Par 98): **107,105,103,102,101 101,99,98,98,97 96,95,95,94,93 88,86,86**
CSF £36.64 CT £549.48 TOTE £4.30: £1.70, £3.70, £3.20, £4.70; EX 86.50 Trifecta £388.00 Part won. Pool £546.60 - 0.20 winning units..

Owner Liam Sheridan **Bred** Aston Mullins Stud **Trained** Newmarket, Suffolk

FOCUS

A competitive nursery won in convincing fashion by the unexposed winner. The form looks strong at this level rated through the third, fourth and fifth.

NOTEBOOK

Generous Thought, who really took the eye beforehand, came from way off the pace to run out a convincing winner in the end. Highly regarded, he should go on to better things at three over 7f plus. (op 7-2 tchd 9-2)

Rash Judgement travelled equally as well as the winner. After taking charge, in the end he was very much second best. (op 10-1)

Mudhish(IRE), in first-time blinkers, has slipped down the ratings and this marked a return to form.

Dubai Petal(IRE), who still looks very immature, struggled to keep up but was putting in all her best work at the finish. She can improve over much further at three. (op 14-1)

Tadalavil ran a tremendous race under top-weight but his lack of size and scope will count against him in the longer term. (op 11-1)

Wavertree Princess(IRE), from a stable that has endured a lean spell, did not improve for the drop back in trip.

6757 TOTESPORT 0800 221 221 E B F GILLIES FILLIES' STKS (LISTED RACE) 1m 2f 60y

2:05 (2:05) (Class 1) 3-Y-O+ **£17,781** (£6,723; £3,360; £1,680) **Stalls** Low

Form | | | | RPR
2-36 **1** **Gower Song**[9] 6605 4-9-0 101 TQuinn 10 98
(D R C Elsworth) *hld up: stdy hdwy on outer over 4f out: chsd ldrs over 2f out: rdn to ld 1f out: drvn ins fnl f and hld on wl* **4/1**[1]
1-60 **2** *hd* **Lake Toya (USA)**[43] 5767 5-9-0 100 EddieAhern 3 98
(Saeed Bin Suroor) *led: rdn along over 2f out: hdd 1f out: drvn: edgd rt and rallied to have ev ch ins fnl f: no ex towards fin* **9/2**[2]
5401 **3** *2* **Sudoor**[25] 6249 3-8-10 98 RHills 6 94
(J L Dunlop) *trckd ldr: effrt over 2f out: sn rdn and ev ch: drvn whn n.m.r ent fnl f: one pce* **4/1**[1]
665 **4** *1* **Enforce (USA)**[9] 6604 4-9-0 91 RyanMoore 12 92
(E A L Dunlop) *hld up towards rr: hdwy on outer 3f out: rdn to chse ldrs wl over 1f out: drvn and one pce ent fnl f* **9/1**[3]
2314 **5** *hd* **Gull Wing (IRE)**[79] 4748 3-8-10 98 JamieSpencer 1 94+
(M L W Bell) *trckd ldrs on inner: n.m.r and lost postion 3f out: sn swtchd rt and rdn: styd on u.p ins fnl f* **4/1**[1]
4406 **6** *1 3/4* **Restless Soul**[17] 6420 3-8-10 75 J-PGuillambert 5 89?
(C A Cyzer) *towards rr: hdwy 3f out: swtchd outside and rdn over 1f out: kpt on ins fnl f: nrst fin* **125/1**
1003 **7** *nk* **Intiquilla (IRE)**[37] 5940 3-8-10 76 JimCrowley 13 88
(Mrs A J Perrett) *chsd ldrs: rdn along 3f out: wknd fnl 2f* **33/1**
3050 **8** *1* **Mussoorie (FR)**[9] 6605 4-9-0 99 JimmyFortune 9 86
(J H M Gosden) *in tch: hdwy to chse ldrs 4f out: rdn over 2f out: sn drvn and wknd appr fnl f* **9/1**[3]
320- **9** *1 1/4* **Kahlua Kiss**[380] 6190 4-9-0 96 MartinDwyer 11 84
(W R Muir) *dwlt: a in rr* **16/1**
0063 **10** *3/4* **Blue Rocket (IRE)**[3] 6726 3-8-10 90 JohnEgan 8 82
(D J Murphy) *nvr bttr than midfield* **16/1**
3105 **11** *2* **Silca Key**[7] 6653 3-8-10 90 DarryllHolland 2 79
(M R Channon) *a towards rr* **33/1**
6020 **12** *3 1/2* **Wassfa**[58] 5352 4-9-0 85 (t) NCallan 4 72
(C E Brittain) *chsd ldng pair: rdn along 3f out: sn wknd* **25/1**
0654 **13** *4* **Knapton Hill**[10] 6596 3-8-10 79 KDarley 7 64
(R Hollinshead) *in tch: rdn along 4f out: sn wknd* **66/1**

2m 7.71s (-4.12) **Going Correction** -0.20s/f (Firm)
WFA 3 from 4yo+ 4lb **13** Ran SP% **122.0**
Speed ratings (Par 108): **108,107,106,105,105 103,103,102,101,101 99,96,93**
CSF £21.62 TOTE £4.80: £2.10, £2.50, £2.20; EX 25.00 Trifecta £108.00 Pool £593.51 - 3.90 winning units..

Owner Usk Valley Stud **Bred** R E Crutchley **Trained** Newmarket, Suffolk

FOCUS

A rather weak Listed fillies' race run at a strong pace. The proximity of the lowly-rated sixth and seventh hold down the overall value of the form.

NOTEBOOK

Gower Song, sidelined all summer, finds this trip her bare minimum and in the end she scrambled home.

Lake Toya(USA), who took the corresponding event on soft ground run at Windsor a year ago, was having just her third start since. Absent six weeks after a poor effort, she set a strong pace and to her credit fought back hard all the way to the line. (op 13-2)

Sudoor, her confidence boosted, probably ran to her very best. (tchd 9-2)

Enforce(USA), already a winner over hurdles, proved better suited by going left-handed and gained some valuable black type. (op 8-1)

Gull Wing(IRE) lost a good pitch early in the straight, not helped by her basic lack of pace. Pulled wide, she was putting in some solid work at the finish and this trip was very much on the sharp side for her. (op 7-2)

Restless Soul, a modest maiden, not for the first time flattered when asked to swim out of her depth. (op 100-1)

Intiquilla(IRE) had a lot to find and seemed to run way above her official rating of just 76.

Blue Rocket(IRE) Official explanation: jockey said filly failed to stay

6758 TOTETENTOFOLLOW.CO.UK WENTWORTH STKS (LISTED RACE) 6f

2:35 (2:36) (Class 1) 3-Y-O+ **£23,708** (£8,964; £4,480; £2,240) **Stalls** High

Form | | | | RPR
1203 **1** **Galeota (IRE)**[21] 6338 5-9-6 107 RyanMoore 11 112
(R Hannon) *w ldrs: chal 1f out: styd on to ld last strides* **8/1**
2204 **2** *shd* **Borderlescott**[21] 6338 5-9-3 110 SebSanders 1 109
(R Bastiman) *led: rdn over 1f out: hdd towards fin* **4/1**[2]

3006 **3** ¾ **Knot In Wood (IRE)**[21] 6338 5-9-3 103....................(p) PaulHanagan 10 106
(R A Fahey) *trckd ldrs: effrt 2f out: kpt on wl fnl f* **11/1**

1341 **4** *shd* **Sunrise Safari (IRE)**[14] 6487 4-9-3 94....................(v) TomEaves 6 106
(I Semple) *hld up: effrt and swtchd lft over 1f out: kpt on wl* **14/1**

3011 **5** ½ **Greek Renaissance (IRE)**[21] 6338 4-9-9 114.................. EddieAhern 7 110+
(Saeed Bin Suroor) *trckd ldrs: effrt over 1f out: n.m.r: kpt on same pce* **9/4**[1]

6000 **6** ½ **Rising Shadow (IRE)**[28] 6183 6-9-6 100.................... FrancisNorton 12 106
(N Wilson) *dwlt: hld up: hdwy over 2f out: kpt on: nvr rchd ldrs* **40/1**

0242 **7** *hd* **Aegean Dancer**[14] 6487 5-9-3 90.............................. JimmyFortune 2 102
(B Smart) *trckd ldrs: t.k.h: effrt 2f out: wknd towards fin* **28/1**

0140 **8** ¾ **Zidane**[21] 6338 5-9-3 106.. JamieSpencer 8 106+
(J R Fanshawe) *hld up: effrt and nt clr run over 1f out: nt rcvr* **11/2**[3]

1452 **9** *nk* **Advanced**[8] 6633 4-9-3 113... NCallan 4 99
(K A Ryan) *chsd ldrs: kpt on same pce fnl 2f* **8/1**

0050 **10** ½ **Dhaular Dhar (IRE)**[28] 6183 5-9-3 95........................ DanielTudhope 5 97
(J S Goldie) *mid-div: kpt on fnl 2f: nvr a threat* **33/1**

2302 **11** 2½ **Commando Scott (IRE)**[15] 6472 6-9-3 94................ PaulMulrennan 13 89
(I W McInnes) *in rr: rdn over 2f out: nvr on terms* **25/1**

5210 **12** ½ **Senor Benny (USA)**[20] 6363 8-9-6 0........................... MartinDwyer 14 91
(M McDonagh, Ire) *hld up in rr: effrt over 2f out: nvr on terms* **33/1**

0022 **13** *15* **Wid (USA)**[8] 6621 3-8-12 95... RHills 3 35
(J L Dunlop) *w ldr: wknd over 1f out: heavily eased and sn bhd* **20/1**

1m 12.39s (-1.91) **Going Correction** -0.075s/f (Good) **13 Ran SP% 123.8**
Speed ratings (Par 111): **109,108,107,107,107 106,106,105,104,104 100,100,80**
CSF £38.40 TOTE £11.60: £3.10, £1.90, £4.30; EX 57.20 Trifecta £342.20 Pool £1,422.17 - 2.95 winning units..

Owner Robin Blunt **Bred** W Maxwell Ervine **Trained** East Everleigh, Wilts

■ Stewards' Enquiry : Seb Sanders two-day ban: used whip with excessive frequency (Nov 26-27)

FOCUS

A sound renewal of this Listed race and not a lot to choose between the first ten at the line. Overall the form does not look totally reliable, but take nothing away from the first two.

NOTEBOOK

Galeota(IRE), meeting Greek Renaissance on better terms, proved very willing and put his head in front right on the line. Hong Kong is now on the agenda.

Borderlescott, happy to sit in front, went for home and looked nailed on but he was caught in the very last stride, robbing Seb Sanders of outright victory in the jockeys' championship. (op 9-2 tchd 5-1)

Knot In Wood(IRE), tried in cheekpieces, seemed to show improved form and at last made a real impression in Listed company. (tchd 12-1)

Sunrise Safari(IRE) has ended the year in fine form and connections are hoping this best ever effort will book his ticket for Dubai this winter.

Greek Renaissance(IRE), who had the first two behind him at Newmarket, had a penalty to shoulder on much quicker ground. He was only keeping on in his own time when tightended up. (op 3-1)

Rising Shadow(IRE), who took this a year ago on soft ground at Windsor, has changed stables and the move has hopefully revitalised him.

Aegean Dancer looked a picture of wellbeing and travelled strongly, but he barely stays 6f. This was a good effort considering he had plenty to find. (tchd 25-1)

Zidane as usual travelled strongly, but he was denied racing room at a crucial stage. He deserves to make his mark at this level in 2008. (tchd 6-1)

Advanced, runner-up in a weak Group 3 in France a week earlier, does not appreciate the ground as quick as this. (op 7-1)

Wid(USA) Official explanation: jockey said filly lost her action

6759 TOTESPORT.COM NOVEMBER H'CAP (HERITAGE HANDICAP) 1m 4f

3:10 (3:11) (Class 2) 3-Y-0+

£46,740 (£13,995; £6,997; £3,502; £1,747; £877) **Stalls Low**

Form RPR

1401 **1** **Malt Or Mash (USA)**[35] 6014 3-8-10 **97**........................... RyanMoore 13 107+
(R Hannon) *hld up towards rr: swtchd outside and rapid hdwy to ld 2f out: sn rdn clr and styd on* **5/1**[2]

4122 **2** 1½ **Sanbuch**[35] 6014 3-8-12 **99**... JimmyFortune 17 107+
(L M Cumani) *hld up in rr: hdwy on outer over 2f out: sn rdn and hung lft: styd on ins fnl f: nrst fin* **13/2**[3]

0016 **3** *hd* **Night Crescendo (USA)**[14] 6499 4-8-13 **94**.................. MartinDwyer 19 102
(Mrs A J Perrett) *hld up towards rr: gd hdwy over 2f out: rdn to chse wnr over 1f out: sn drvn and no imp* **50/1**

211 **4** 2½ **Tropical Strait (IRE)**[39] 5892 4-8-5 **86**........................ FergusSweeney 2 90
(D W P Arbuthnot) *midfield: n.m.r over 2f out: sn rdn and styd on ins fnl f: nrst fin* **12/1**

-241 **5** *hd* **New Guinea**[12] 6538 4-9-10 **105**................................... DarryllHolland 4 110+
(Saeed Bin Suroor) *hld up in midfield: hdwy over 3f out: nt clr run and swtchd rt 2f out: sn rdn and kpt on ins fnl f: nrst fin* **16/1**

0641 **6** *nk* **Heaven Knows**[14] 6499 4-8-13 **94**.. RHills 10 97
(W J Haggas) *hld up towards rr: hdwy on outer 3f out: rdn along 2f out: kpt on same pce appr fnl f* **13/2**[3]

0401 **7** *1* **La Estrella (USA)**[20] 6357 4-8-3 **84**.................................... ChrisCatlin 9 85
(D E Cantillon) *chsd ldrs: rdn along over 3f out: drvn 2f out and kpt on same pce* **50/1**

111 **8** *nk* **Pippa Greene**[32] 6091 3-8-10 **97**.................................... JamieSpencer 7 98
(P F I Cole) *hld up and bhd: swtchd outside and hdwy 3f out: rdn wl over 1f out: styd on ins fnl f: nt rch ldrs* **9/2**[1]

4230 **9** ¾ **Lundy's Lane (IRE)**[41] 5830 7-9-2 **97**............................ FrancisNorton 15 97
(A M Balding) *hld up towards rr: hdwy wl over 2f out: sn rdn and kpt on appr fnl f: nvr nr ldrs* **33/1**

4032 **10** *3* **Bandama (IRE)**[14] 6490 4-8-9 **90**.................................... JimCrowley 16 85
(Mrs A J Perrett) *trckd ldrs: hdwy 3f out and sn ev ch: rdn 2f out and grad wknd* **16/1**

0000 **11** ½ **Bazart**[14] 6490 5-8-3 **87**...................................... AndrewElliott(3) 1 81
(K R Burke) *midfield: effrt and sme hdwy 3f out: sn rdn and no imp fnl 2f* **100/1**

205 **12** *shd* **John Terry (IRE)**[14] 6490 4-8-10 **91**................................ SebSanders 6 85
(Mrs A J Perrett) *trckd ldrs: effrt over 3f out: rdn along over 2f out: sn wknd* **22/1**

-554 **13** *shd* **Inchloch**[14] 6490 5-8-1 **82**.. DaleGibson 3 76
(B G Powell) *hld up towards rr: hdwy 3f out: rdn along 2f out: nvr nr ldrs* **25/1**

3100 **14** *1* **Heron Bay**[81] 4692 3-9-4 **105**.. SteveDrowne 18 97
(G Wragg) *midfield: hdwy on outer to chse ldrs 3f out: rdn along over 2f out and sn wknd* **14/1**

0120 **15** *3* **Realism (FR)**[35] 6014 7-8-8 **89**.................................. PaulMulrennan 5 76
(M W Easterby) *a bhd* **100/1**

0003 **16** *shd* **Akarem**[14] 6490 6-8-9 **90**.. KDarley 11 77
(K R Burke) *trckd ldng pair: effrt to chal 3f out: sn rdn and ev ch tl drvn 2f out: sn wknd* **20/1**

5500 **17** 1¼ **Chicken Soup**[7] 6654 5-8-11 **92**.. NCallan 14 77
(D J Murphy) *hld up: nvr bttr than midfield* **50/1**

2-55 **18** *16* **Rampallion**[41] 5830 4-9-1 **96**.. EddieAhern 12 56
(Saeed Bin Suroor) *prom: hdwy to ld 3 1/2f out: rdn along whn hdd over 2f out: hung lft and sn wknd* **25/1**

51 **19** *10* **Dzesmin (POL)**[49] 5623 5-7-13 **83**.....................(p) DuranFentiman(3) 23 27
(R C Guest) *in tch: hdwy on outer to chse ldrs 1/2-way: rdn along over 3f out and sn wknd* **16/1**

1310 **20** *5* **Turn Of Phrase (IRE)**[29] 6158 8-7-9 **79** oh4..........(b) WilliamBuick(3) 21 15
(N Wilson) *nvr bttr than midfield* **100/1**

0134 **21** 1¾ **Philanthropy**[42] 5805 3-8-3 **90**...................................... PaulHanagan 22 23
(K A Ryan) *sn led: rdn along 4f out: sn hdd & wknd* **16/1**

2m 29.23s (-6.30) **Going Correction** -0.20s/f (Firm)
WFA 3 from 4yo+ 6lb **21 Ran SP% 128.0**
Speed ratings (Par 109): **113,112,111,110,110 109,109,109,108,106 106,106,106,105,103 103,102,91,85,81 80**
CSF £34.37 CT £1506.63 TOTE £6.10: £2.30, £2.30, £17.20, £3.30; EX 25.90 Trifecta £3240.10 Pool £10,952.55 - 2.40 winning units..

Owner A P Patey **Bred** Delahanty Stock Farm **Trained** East Everleigh, Wilts

■ The winner's handler Richard Hannon ended the turf season top trainer numerically with a total of 134 winners.

FOCUS

A strong and competitive renewal, for once run on fast ground, and three-year-olds filled the first two places. The form should work out well and throw up winners at a higher level next year.

NOTEBOOK

Malt Or Mash(USA) ◆, 6lb higher, confirmed placings with the runner-up. He swept to the front and, likely to stay further, should take much higher grade at four. (op 6-1 tchd 9-2)

Sanbuch has his quirks but basically does little wrong. Hard at work once in line for home, he stayed on down the outer but in truth he was never going to seriously trouble the winner. Official explanation: jockey said colt hung left

Night Crescendo(USA), back after a two-week break, bounced back and neither the trip nor the fast ground proved a problem.

Tropical Strait(IRE) ◆, who looked very wintry, was putting in all his best work at the finish after encountering traffic problems. He is suited by 1m6f and is still relatively unexposed.

New Guinea, lumbered with top-weight, had no luck in running and deserves plenty of credit. It was just his fourth start this year and if he goes to Dubai he will be a relatively fresh horse. Official explanation: jockey said gelding was denied a clear run

Heaven Knows, 6lb higher, finds this trip stretching him to almost breaking point. (op 7-1)

La Estrella(USA), who changed hands at last month's sales for 32,000gns, ran with credit and should make a useful novice hurdler.

Pippa Greene ◆, defending his unbeaten record from a 7lb higher mark, fell out of the stalls. He made very hard work of it but was staying on steadily in his own time towards the finish. This was only his fourth start and he looks a bright prospect for next year. (op 11-2)

Akarem was 47-year-old Kevin Darley's final mount before retirement. Champion apprentice in 1978, he was champion jockey in 2000 and rode 2451 winners in Britain.

Rampallion Official explanation: jockey said gelding hung left

6760 TOTESPORTGAMES.COM H'CAP 2m 110y

3:40 (3:40) (Class 2) (0-100,97) 3-Y-0+ **£16,192** (£4,817; £2,407; £1,202) **Stalls Low**

Form RPR

1305 **1** **Inchnadamph**[21] 6335 7-9-0 83....................................(t) JamieSpencer 4 93
(T J Fitzgerald) *hld up: t.k.h: smooth hdwy over 2f out: shkn up to ld over 1f out: rdn clr: readily* **9/4**[1]

2246 **2** *8* **Kasthari (IRE)**[21] 6335 8-9-12 95................................... DarryllHolland 3 95
(J D Bethell) *chsd ldrs: styd on to go 2nd 1f out: no ch w wnr* **11/4**[2]

0020 **3** *1* **Dium Mac**[15] 6473 6-8-9 78 oh1...................................... FrancisNorton 2 77
(N Bycroft) *trckd ldrs: tk fierce hold: jnd ldr 9f out: led over 3f out: hdd over 1f out: kpt on same pce* **14/1**

3244 **4** *5* **Chocolate Caramel (USA)**[12] 6545 5-9-1 84.................. JimCrowley 9 77
(Mrs A J Perrett) *hld up: hdwy 4f out: chal over 2f out: wknd fnl f* **14/1**

0050 **5** 1¾ **Bulwark (IRE)**[57] 5375 5-10-0 97............................. StephenDonohoe 5 88
(Ian Williams) *hld up in last: t.o 6f out: styd on wl fnl 2f* **16/1**

3302 **6** ½ **Dr Sharp (IRE)**[8] 6622 7-8-13 82...................................... MickyFenton 8 73
(T P Tate) *led and sn clr: jnd 9f out: hdd over 3f out: wknd over 1f out* **7/2**[3]

2440 **7** *3* **Ned Ludd (IRE)**[21] 6335 4-8-12 81.................................... EddieAhern 6 68
(J G Portman) *chsd ldrs: rdn 4f out: lost pl 2f out* **6/1**

3m 34.52s (-7.44) **Going Correction** -0.20s/f (Firm) **7 Ran SP% 113.2**
Speed ratings (Par 109): **109,105,104,102,101 101,99**
CSF £8.46 CT £65.53 TOTE £2.50: £1.70, £2.20; EX 6.90 Trifecta £102.40 Pool £799.37 - 5.54 winning units. Place 6 £121.23, Place 5 £48.75..

Owner R N Cardwell **Bred** Bloomsbury Stud & R & A Craddock **Trained** Malton, N Yorks

■ Jamie Spencer's 190th winner of the turf season, earning him a last-gasp share of the jockeys' championship with Seb Sanders.

FOCUS

Not a strong handicap and everything went the winner's way. Although impressive, improvement at his stage of life is unlikely and he has just been rated to the best of his old form.

NOTEBOOK

Inchnadamph, with the race set up for him by Dr Sharp, travelled strongly. It was no surprise when Jamie Spencer left nothing at all to chance. (op 15-8)

Kasthari(IRE), who dead-heated in the 2004 Doncaster Cup, likes it round here and did enough to secure a modest second spot. (tchd 3-1 in a place)

Dium Mac took a fierce grip and made Dr Sharp go even quicker in front. In the end the winner and the second saw out the trip too well for him.

Chocolate Caramel(USA) travelled almost as well as the winner but in the end a truly-run 2m seemed to stretch him to breaking point. (op 16-1 tchd 12-1)

Bulwark(IRE), who left Amanda Perrett's yard a week earlier for 36,000gns, is a moody individual. He sulked in the rear until staying on when it was all over. No doubt his new connections will be hoping he turns over a new leaf over hurdles. (op 14-1)

Dr Sharp(IRE), who needs much more give underfoot, made sure there was no hanging about but he simply set the race up for the winner, an out-and-out stayer. (op 4-1 tchd 9-2)

Ned Ludd(IRE) made no appeal in the paddock and ended up well beaten, a 14th start without success on the level for this useful hurdler. (op 8-1)

T/Jkpt: £15,764.70 to a £1 stake. Pool: £55,509.74. 2.50 winning tickets. T/Plt: £74.50 to a £1 stake. Pool: £108,289.50. 1,061.00 winning tickets. T/Qpdt: £13.10 to a £1 stake. Pool: £6,746.80. 379.40 winning tickets. JR

6747 **WOLVERHAMPTON (A.W)** (L-H)

Saturday, November 10

OFFICIAL GOING: Standard

This fixture did not count towards the 'turf' season championships.

Wind: Moderate, half behind

6761 CENTREBET.COM CASINO MEDIAN AUCTION MAIDEN STKS 5f 216y(P)

7:00 (7:02) (Class 5) 2-Y-O £2,968 (£876; £438) Stalls Low

Form RPR

00 1 **Tyfos**[8] 6616 2-9-3 0 ... JohnEgan 3 80
(W M Brisbourne) *led after 1f: clr over 1f out: pushed out: comf* **12/1**

5304 2 3 ½ **Red Amaryllis**[12] 6535 2-8-12 72 ... RichardKingscote 1 65
(H J L Dunlop) *led for 1f: chsd wnr: wknd fnl f* **4/1**[2]

64 3 ½ **Capone (IRE)**[23] 6281 2-9-0 0 ... DominicFox(3) 5 68
(S Parr) *slowly away: t.k.h: rdn 1/2-way: sme late prog* **11/2**[3]

0 4 1 **Rosie Says No**[12] 6535 2-8-12 0 ... ChrisCatlin 4 60
(R M H Cowell) *outpcd: rdn 1/2-way: sme hdwy fnl f* **20/1**

000 5 ¾ **John Potts**[20] 6358 2-9-3 47 ... DeanMcKeown 2 63?
(B P J Baugh) *sn rdn: in tch but hanging lft and btn fnl 2f* **80/1**

52 6 nk **Showtime Ice**[50] 5603 2-8-12 0 ... EddieAhern 6 57
(M J Wallace) *chsd ldrs: rdn over 2f out: wknd over 1f out* **4/6**[1]

1m 15.73s (-0.08) **Going Correction** -0.125s/f (Stan) **6** Ran SP% **109.1**

Speed ratings (Par 96): **95,90,89,88,87 86**

CSF £54.98 TOTE £13.40: £3.20, £1.50; EX 67.10.

Owner J Tomlinson/G Williams **Bred** J Tomlinson And G Williams **Trained** Great Ness, Shropshire

FOCUS

A modest juvenile maiden rated around the second and third.

NOTEBOOK

Tyfos showed ability when seventh of 12 in a 7f maiden at Newmarket on his previous start and he progressed again dropped in trip. He is out of a winner of a bumper and hurdles, but he clearly gets his speed from his sire Bertolini, and was too quick for this lot. There should be more to come. (op 15-2)

Red Amaryllis, back on Polytrack for the first time since her debut, proved no match for the winner and was some way below her official mark of 72. (op 7-2)

Capone(IRE) got going too late and failed to build on the promise of his recent Nottingham effort, but he is now eligible for a handicap mark and could do better over further. (op 13-2 tchd 7-1)

Rosie Says No ran better than when beating just one home on her debut at Leicester and can find her level once stepped up in trip and sent handicapping. (tchd 25-1)

John Potts has an official rating of just 47 and his proximity suggests the form is limited. Official explanation: jockey said gelding hung left-handed (op 100-1)

Showtime Ice had not been seen since blowing a winning chance by hanging under pressure over this course and distance nearly two months previously and this was a most disappointing return to action. She is, though, now eligible for a handicap mark. Official explanation: trainer had no explanation for the poor form shown (op 5-6)

6762 CENTREBET.COM POKER H'CAP 5f 216y(P)

7:30 (7:31) (Class 5) (0-75,73) 3-Y-O+ £2,968 (£876; £438) Stalls Low

Form RPR

0555 1 **Cerebus**[8] 6625 5-8-9 64 ...(bt) StephenDonohoe 5 72
(A J McCabe) *mde all: rdn over 2f out: clr appr fnl f: hld on nr fin* **16/1**

2124 2 nk **Hotham**[4] 6708 4-9-3 72 ... ChrisCatlin 1 79
(N Wilson) *t.k.h: sn chsd ldrs: rdn 2f out: r.o to go cl 2nd nr fin* **2/1**[1]

5035 3 nk **Methaaly (IRE)**[6] 6677 4-8-13 68 ... LiamJones 10 74+
(M Mullineaux) *in rr tl hdwy over 1f out: r.o wl fnl f: nvr nrr* **9/2**[3]

2103 4 3 ½ **Jilly Why (IRE)**[6] 6677 6-8-4 64 ...(b) RussellKennemore(5) 3 59
(Paul Green) *sn chsd wnr: rdn over 1f out: wknd fnl f* **15/2**

2405 5 1 **Louphole**[69] 5064 5-9-4 73 ... EddieAhern 11 65
(P J Makin) *towards rr: rdn over 2f out: swtchd rt over 1f out: nvr nr to chal* **14/1**

0640 6 shd **Tilly's Dream**[11] 6575 4-8-13 71 ... AndrewMullen(3) 6 62
(G C Bravery) *in rr: rdn and sme hdwy over 1f out: nvr nr to chal* **25/1**

0503 7 1 ½ **Diminuto**[11] 6568 3-8-10 72 ... FrankiePickard(7) 9 59
(M D I Usher) *outpcd: a in rr* **25/1**

0534 8 1 ¾ **After The Show**[23] 6283 6-8-11 66 ... NCallan 4 47
(Rae Guest) *s.i.s: rdn 1/2-way: edgd lft over 1f out and nvr nr to chal* **4/1**[2]

016 9 5 **Memphis Marie**[16] 6455 3-8-1 59 oh1 ... LukeMorris(3) 8 24
(C N Allen) *mid-div on outside: rdn 1/2-way: c wd into st: nvr on terms* **33/1**

5330 10 1 ½ **Game Lady**[26] 6239 3-8-12 67 ... JohnEgan 2 27
(I A Wood) *prom tl rdn and wknd qckly 1/2-way* **10/1**

1m 14.3s (-1.51) **Going Correction** -0.125s/f (Stan) **10** Ran SP% **115.6**

Speed ratings (Par 103): **105,104,104,99,98 98,96,93,87,85**

CSF £47.01 CT £179.15 TOTE £22.70: £5.00, £1.20, £1.80; EX 74.10.

Owner Paul J Dixon **Bred** Rookley Holdings **Trained** Babworth, Notts

■ Stewards' Enquiry : Stephen Donohoe three-day ban: used whip with excessive frequency (Nov 21-23)

FOCUS

A modest but competitive sprint handicap, and straightforward to rate through the runner-up and third.

Game Lady Official explanation: jockey said filly lost its action

6763 SP PLUS PLUS @CENTREBET.COM MAIDEN AUCTION STKS 1m 141y(P)

7:55 (7:55) (Class 5) 2-Y-O £2,968 (£876; £438) Stalls Low

Form RPR

23 1 **Mystery Star (IRE)**[28] 6184 2-9-1 0 ... PaulMulrennan 10 83
(M H Tompkins) *in tch: rdn over 3f out: hdwy to ld over 1f out: rn green: r.o wl ins fnl f* **11/8**[1]

042 2 1 **Magical Fantasy (USA)**[10] 6578 2-8-10 77 ... JohnEgan 4 76
(J Nicol) *chsd ldrs: led 2f out: rdn and hdd over 1f out: kpt on one pce fnl f* **2/1**[2]

242 3 6 **Tamasou (IRE)**[6] 6675 2-8-9 0 ... DominicFox(3) 7 65
(S Parr) *trckd ldr: led briefly over 2f out: sn rdn: wknd fnl f* **12/1**

05 4 2 **Animator**[10] 6578 2-8-12 0 ... LPKeniry 3 61
(P F I Cole) *t.k.h: prom: tl outpcd over 2f out* **16/1**

6 5 2 ½ **Timbalier (USA)**[10] 6578 2-9-1 0 ... StephenDonohoe 8 59
(D M Simcock) *nvr bttr than mid-div* **14/1**

6 nk **Black Heart** 2-8-10 0 ... NicolPolli(5) 1 58
(M Botti) *in rr: t.k.h: mde sme late hdwy* **28/1**

7 4 **Willkandoo (USA)** 2-9-1 0 ... NCallan 9 50
(K A Ryan) *led tl hdd over 2f out: sn wknd* **7/1**[3]

0 8 4 **Princess Gee**[18] 6414 2-8-1 0 ... AndrewMullen(3) 5 30
(B J McMath) *hmpd on bnd after 2f: a bhd* **100/1**

9 ½ **Pie O My (IRE)** 2-8-9 0 ... LukeMorris(3) 6 37
(J Jay) *slowly away: a bhd* **50/1**

1m 50.86s (-0.90) **Going Correction** -0.125s/f (Stan) **9** Ran SP% **114.6**

Speed ratings (Par 96): **99,98,92,91,88 88,84,81,80**

CSF £4.11 TOTE £2.40: £1.10, £1.10, £2.40; EX 5.10.

Owner John Brenchley **Bred** R Coffey **Trained** Newmarket, Suffolk

FOCUS

An ordinary maiden, but they went a good pace and the form looks sound.

NOTEBOOK

Mystery Star(IRE) confirmed the promise he showed when placed in a couple of turf maidens on his first two starts. He ultimately proved hard enough work for Paul Mulrennan in the straight, but he was always going to win and gave the impression that this experience can bring him on again. (op 6-4 tchd 13-8)

Magical Fantasy(USA), officially rated 77, set a fair standard and she ensured the favourite had to be kept up to his work. She finished well clear of the remainder and can win a similar event. (op 3-1)

Tamasou(IRE) had every chance, but he was no match for the front two and will probably be better off in handicap company. (op 10-1)

Animator did not help his chance by taking a bit of a grip early on and he finished up well held. He might be capable of better in handicaps over further, although he will have to learn to settle. (op 14-1)

Timbalier(USA) was poorly positioned throughout and he could not build on the promise he showed on his debut at Kempton. He might be more of a handicap prospect.

6764 BET NOW AT CENTREBET.COM H'CAP 7f 32y(P)

8:25 (8:26) (Class 5) (0-68,67) 3-Y-O+ £2,968 (£876; £438) Stalls High

Form RPR

0006 1 **Tanforan**[8] 6627 5-8-4 55 oh3 ... ChrisCatlin 1 67
(B P J Baugh) *mid-div: hdwy on ins 2f out: rdn and r.o to ld wl ins fnl f* **8/1**

0000 2 shd **Rabbit Fighter (IRE)**[16] 6455 3-8-0 55 ... AndrewElliott(3) 12 66
(D Shaw) *outpcd: hdwy on outside over 2f out: hung lft u.p bef led over 1f out: hdd wl ins fnl f* **7/1**[3]

0006 3 3 ½ **Gilded Cove**[6] 6671 7-8-8 64 ... RussellKennemore(5) 5 66
(R Hollinshead) *towards rr: hdwy over 2f out: wl there whn bmpd over 1f out: one pce fnl f* **6/1**[2]

315 4 shd **Our Kes (IRE)**[29] 6146 5-9-2 67 ... SimonWhitworth 3 69
(P Howling) *in rr: hdwy over 1f out: kpt on one pce* **4/1**[1]

0603 5 1 **Coseadrom (IRE)**[7] 6647 5-8-9 60 ... JohnEgan 2 59
(M F Harris) *prom: rdn to ld 2f out: hdd over 1f out: wknd ins fnl f: broke stirrup irons* **4/1**[1]

0000 6 ½ **Silent Storm**[7] 6646 7-9-0 65 ... LPKeniry 8 63
(Peter Grayson) *outpcd: hdwy on ins 2f out: wknd fnl f* **11/1**

3030 7 ¾ **Strut The Stage (IRE)**[25] 6247 3-8-5 57 ...(tp) WandersonD'Avila 4 53+
(B W Duke) *trckd ldr to 2f out: hung lft appr fnl f: wknd* **14/1**

00- 8 4 **Tahafut**[36] 5993 3-8-1 56 ... AndrewMullen(3) 7 41
(R A Fahey) *slowly away: a bhd* **33/1**

5405 9 4 **Breaking Shadow (IRE)**[9] 6612 5-8-3 61 ... DeanHeslop(7) 11 35
(M A Peill) *chsd ldrs tl rdn and wknd 2f out* **12/1**

2205 10 2 ½ **Prince Rossi (IRE)**[45] 5741 3-8-0 55 ...(p) WilliamBuick(3) 10 22
(J D Bethell) *chsd ldrs tl wknd over 2f out* **8/1**

600 11 ¾ **Calypso King**[20] 6360 4-9-0 65 ... AdamKirby 6 30
(Peter Grayson) *led tl hdd 2f out: wknd qckly* **28/1**

1m 29.79s (-0.61) **Going Correction** -0.125s/f (Stan)

WFA 3 from 4yo+ 1lb **11** Ran SP% **118.1**

Speed ratings (Par 103): **98,97,93,93,92 92,91,86,82,79 78**

CSF £63.33 CT £370.05 TOTE £12.80: £4.20, £2.10, £1.60; EX 92.10.

Owner F Gillespie **Bred** Bearstone Stud **Trained** Audley, Staffs

FOCUS

A moderate handicap run at a strong pace. It has been rated through the third to his latest form for now.

Coseadrom(IRE) Official explanation: jockey said stirrup iron broke

Calypso King Official explanation: jockey said gelding ran too freely

6765 PLAY AUSTRALIAN @ CENTREBET.COM H'CAP 1m 1f 103y(P)

8:55 (8:55) (Class 3) (0-95,90) 3-Y-O+ £7,124 (£2,119; £1,059; £529) Stalls Low

Form RPR

3034 1 **Vainglory (USA)**[27] 6203 3-8-5 82 ... KirstyMilczarek(5) 9 93+
(D M Simcock) *mid-div: hdwy on ins over 1f out: edgd rt: drvn to ld cl home* **4/1**[1]

0342 2 hd **Del Mar Sunset**[12] 6545 8-8-7 76 ... LiamJones 8 83
(W J Haggas) *stdd s: hdwy 2f out: led jst ins fnl f: kpt on: hdd nr fin* **7/1**

0104 3 1 ¼ **Stargazer Jim (FR)**[6] 6669 5-8-10 79 ... PaulMulrennan 5 83
(W J Haggas) *trckd ldrs: rdn 3f out: styd prom: one pce fnl f* **9/2**[2]

0030 4 ½ **William's Way**[75] 4888 5-8-13 82 ... SebSanders 3 85
(I A Wood) *hld up in rr: styd on fnl f: nvr nr to chal* **9/2**[2]

5161 5 ½ **Secret Liaison**[38] 5921 4-8-13 85 ... DominicFox(3) 7 87
(S Parr) *mid-div: hdwy 4f out: swtchd lft over 1f out: bmpd ins fnl f: nt rcvr* **25/1**

3500 6 nk **Invasian (IRE)**[21] 6337 6-9-6 89 ... JohnEgan 4 90
(P W D'Arcy) *led tl rdn: edgd lft and hdd jst ins fnl f: wknd* **11/2**[3]

0523 7 3 ½ **Fiefdom (IRE)**[6] 6674 5-8-13 82 ... DanielTudhope 1 76
(I W McInnes) *hld up: effrt whn swtchd rt over 1f out: nvr on terms* **6/1**

-000 8 1 ½ **Winged Flight (USA)**[11] 6560 3-8-5 77 ... DeanMcKeown 6 68
(M Johnston) *trckd ldr to 2f out: wkng whn hmpd over 1f out* **16/1**

0533 9 2 **Fusili (IRE)**[11] 6576 4-9-2 90 ... PatrickHills(5) 2 77
(N P Littmoden) *in tch tl outpcd over 4f out: bhd fnl 3f* **11/1**

2m 0.52s (-2.10) **Going Correction** -0.125s/f (Stan)

WFA 3 from 4yo+ 3lb **9** Ran SP% **116.6**

Speed ratings (Par 107): **104,103,102,102,101 101,98,97,95**

CSF £32.59 CT £131.40 TOTE £5.70: £1.70, £2.60, £2.00; EX 47.60.

Owner DXB Bloodstock Ltd **Bred** Darley **Trained** Newmarket, Suffolk

■ Stewards' Enquiry : Kirsty Milczarek three-day ban: careless riding (Nov 21-23)

FOCUS

A good handicap best rated through the front-running sixth. The pace was reasonable and the winning time was 0.36 quicker than the following maiden.

NOTEBOOK

Vainglory(USA) ◆ won his maiden over 6f, but he had been finding 1m an inadequate test in recent starts and he produced an improved performance stepped up to his furthest trip to date. He did not help his chance by hanging right inside the final furlong, but he looks capable of stepping forward again. (op 13-2 tchd 8-1)

Del Mar Sunset stepped up on his recent second over 1m4f at Lingfield and was just denied by an improving type. (op 11-2)

Stargazer Jim(FR), a stablemate of the runner-up, seemed to have every chance and this was another solid run in defeat. (op 5-1)

William's Way ran an encouraging race off the back of a 75-day break and should be able to build on this. (tchd 5-1)

Secret Liaison, claimed out of Sir Mark Prescott's yard for £24,000 after winning at Salisbury on his previous start, ran creditably faced with quite a stiff task on his debut for new connections. He was short of room as the eventual winner came by inside the final furlong, but he was not unlucky. (op 20-1)
Invasian(IRE) was well held with the eye-shield left off on his return to sand. (op 8-1)
Fiefdom(IRE) looked very unlucky over this course and distance on his previous start, but this was disappointing. (op 9-2 tchd 4-1)

6766 WE'VE GOT THE ASHES @ CENTREBET.COM MAIDEN STKS 1m 1f 103y(P)
9:20 (9:20) (Class 5) 3-Y-O+ **£2,968** (£876; £438) **Stalls** Low

Form RPR
65 **1** **Kissing**[23] 6286 3-8-12 0 .... SebSanders 9 78+
(Sir Mark Prescott) *sn led: mde rest: drvn out fnl f* **5/2**[1]
23 **2** 2 ½ **Demisemiquaver**[17] 6420 3-8-12 70 .... (v[1]) JohnEgan 12 73
(J Noseda) *in tch: hdwy 4f out: chsd wnr over 2f out: hung lft and no imp fnl f* **5/2**[1]
0344 **3** 6 **Emperor Court (IRE)**[35] 6005 3-9-3 70 .... AdamKirby 1 65
(P J Makin) *mid-div: hdwy to chse ldrs 3f out: wknd over 1f out* **10/3**[2]
4 11 **Signs Of Love (FR)**[253] 4-9-6 67 .... SamHitchcott 10 42
(Noel T Chance) *mid-div: rdn 4f out: no hdwy fnl 2f* **9/1**[3]
530 **5** 1 ½ **Passing True (IRE)**[17] 6423 3-8-12 61 .... DeanMcKeown 3 34
(M Johnston) *broke wl: in tch tl wknd 2f out* **20/1**
0000 **6** 1 ½ **Cat Six (USA)**[14] 6506 3-8-12 55 .... (b[1]) ChrisCatlin 2 31
(T Wall) *rdn over 3f out: nvr bttr than mid-div* **40/1**
00-6 **7** nk **Silvabella (IRE)**[16] 6457 4-9-1 38 .... (p) RobertHavlin 6 30
(D Haydn Jones) *mid-div tl rdn and wknd over 2f out* **125/1**
5/ **8** ½ **Menkaura**[149] 5397 4-9-6 67 .... VinceSlattery 7 34
(John R Upson) *trckd ldrs tl rdn and wknd 3f out* **50/1**
0060 **9** 7 **Hill Of Clare (IRE)**[17] 6420 5-8-12 38 .... DominicFox(3) 5 14
(G H Jones) *a in rr* **150/1**
10 1 ¾ **Flight Dream (FR)**[30] 4-9-6 0 .... TGMcLaughlin 11 16
(M G Quinlan) *v.s.a: a bhd* **12/1**
000 **11** ¾ **Mays Louise**[19] 6385 3-8-12 40 .... DanielTudhope 4 9
(B P J Baugh) *slowly away: a bhd* **100/1**
12 20 **Tarte Tatin (IRE)** 3-8-12 0 .... J-PGuillambert 8 —
(J L Dunlop) *slowly away: a bhd: t.o fnl 2f* **9/1**[3]

2m 0.88s (-1.74) **Going Correction** -0.125s/f (Stan)
WFA 3 from 4yo+ 3lb 12 Ran SP% **119.5**
Speed ratings (Par 103): **102,99,94,84,83 82,81,81,75,73 72,55**
CSF £8.50 TOTE £4.10: £1.70, £1.50, £1.50; EX 13.50 Place 6 £45.11, Place 5 £7.82.
Owner Lordship Stud **Bred** Lordship Stud **Trained** Newmarket, Suffolk
■ A winner for Seb Sanders, a few hours after being crowned joint-champion jockey for the turf season.

FOCUS
An uncompetitive and modest maiden rated through the runner-up to the best view of her previous form. The winning time was 0.36 slower than the earlier 81-95 handicap.
T/Plt: £62.50 to a £1 stake. Pool: £104,533.15. 1,219.35 winning tickets. T/Qpdt: £10.20 to a £1 stake. Pool: £6,880.60. 497.50 winning tickets. JS

6527 SAN SIRO (R-H)
Saturday, November 10

OFFICIAL GOING: Good

6767a PREMIO CHIUSURA (GROUP 3) 7f
2:40 (2:50) 2-Y-O+ **£24,628** (£10,836; £5,911; £2,955)

RPR
1 **Icelandic**[146] 5-9-6 .... MDemuro 8 107
(Frank Sheridan, Italy) *s.i.s: last 2f out: moved outside and hdwy: led 1f out: drvn clr: pushed out fnl 100yds* **52/10**[3]
2 ¾ **Alamanni (USA)**[13] 6524 3-9-3 .... CColombi 6 103
(E Borromeo, Italy) *a cl up: fnd gap over 1f out: tk 2nd ins fnl f: r.o* **37/10**[2]
3 ¾ **My Sea Of Love**[517] 2493 4-9-3 .... EBotti 3 100
(A & G Botti, Italy) *a.p: disp 2nd appr fnl f: kpt on one pce* **71/10**
4 nk **Ricine (IRE)**[20] 6370 5-9-6 .... F-XBertras 2 102
(F Rohaut, France) *trckd ldr on rails: fnd gap ins fnl 2f: ev ch 1f out: one pce* **11/10**[1]
5 hd **Salisburgo (ITY)**[182] 4-9-6 .... WMongil 9 102
(V di Napoli, Italy) *pressed ldr: ev ch 1f out: one pce* **12/1**
6 shd **Zenone (IRE)** 3-9-6 .... PConvertino 7 102
(Laura Grizzetti, Italy) *mid-div: styd on u.p fr over 1f out: nrest at fin* **121/10**
7 1 ¾ **Key To Pleasure (GER)**[20] 6370 7-9-10 .... AHelfenbein 12 100
(Mario Hofer, Germany) *s.i.s: hdwy on outside 1/2-way: btn over 1f out* **103/10**
8 1 ½ **Magic Box (ITY)**[174] 4-9-6 .... MPasquale 5 92
(F & L Brogi, Italy) *led to 1f out: one pce* **137/10**
9 11 **Recoaro (IRE)**[511] 2670 3-9-6 .... GArena 1 62
(B Grizzetti, Italy) *nvr nrr than mid-div: bhd fnl 2f* **87/1**
10 1 ¾ **Docksil**[27] 6224 3-9-6 .... DVargiu 11 57
(B Grizzetti, Italy) *disp 3rd on outside to 2f out: sn wknd* **18/1**
11 3 **Fancy Groom**[13] 6523 2-8-1 .... GSanna 10 50
(B Grizzetti, Italy) *prom on outside to 3f out: wknd qckly 2f out* **35/1**

1m 24.1s (-4.10)
WFA 2 from 3yo 21lb 3 from 4yo+ 1lb 11 Ran SP% **137.5**
(including one euro stakes): WIN 6.20; PL 2.11, 2.19, 2.36; DF 15.53.
Owner Scuderia A 4/5 **Bred** Cheveley Park Stud Limited **Trained** Italy

TOULOUSE
Saturday, November 10

OFFICIAL GOING: Soft

6770a PRIX FILLE DE L'AIR (GROUP 3) (F&M) 1m 2f 110y
2:15 (2:20) 3-Y-O+ **£27,027** (£10,811; £8,108; £5,405; £2,703)

RPR
1 **Tashelka (FR)**[16] 6460 3-9-1 .... (b) JVictoire 1 111
(A Fabre, France) *trckd ldr: racing keenly: led ent st (wl over 1f out): drvn out and r.o wl* **17/1**
2 1 **Doe Ray Me**[35] 6030 3-8-8 .... DBoeuf 9 102
(H-A Pantall, France) *a cl up: 5th st: chsd wnr fnl f: r.o same pce u.p* **14/1**
3 1 ½ **Synopsis (IRE)**[35] 6030 3-9-1 .... SPasquier 3 106
(A Fabre, France) *reluctant to load: a cl up: 4th st: rdn over 1f out: rchd 3rd ins fnl f: kpt on one pce* **36/10**[2]
4 1 **Anabaa's Creation (IRE)**[20] 6376 3-8-8 .... TThulliez 2 97
(A De Royer-Dupre, France) *trckd ldr on ins: 3rd st: disp 2nd over 1f out: one pce fr 1f out* **7/5**[1]
5 1 **Kibaar (USA)**[22] 4-8-11 .... TGillet 10 93
(J E Hammond, France) *hld up in rr: 9th and brought wd st: styd on fnl f: nrest at fin* **13/1**
6 ½ **Singapore Creek (FR)**[16] 6460 3-8-8 .... IMendizabal 4 94
(Robert Collet, France) *racd in 6th to st: rdn and btn over 1f out* **52/1**
7 1 **Artistica (IRE)**[86] 4557 3-8-8 .... CSoumillon 8 93
(A Fabre, France) *hld up in rr: 7th st: nvr a factor* **8/1**
8 1 **Mayano Sophia (IRE)**[20] 3-8-8 .... JAuge 7 91
(J E Hammond, France) *hld up towards rr: pushed along 3f out: 8th st: no hdwy* **38/1**
9 ¾ **Never Green (IRE)**[69] 5079 3-8-8 .... OPeslier 5 89
(C Laffon-Parias, France) *led to ent st (wl over 1f out): sn wknd* **6/1**[3]
10 nse **Voxna (FR)**[20] 3-8-8 .... AlxiBadel 6 89
(J F Bernard, France) *last st: a in rr* **18/1**

2m 10.74s (130.74)
WFA 3 from 4yo 4lb 10 Ran SP% **117.9**
PARI-MUTUEL (including one euro stakes): WIN 2.90 (coupled with DoeRay Me & Synopsis); PL 3.10, 3.10, 2.40; DF 34.70.
Owner Sheikh Mohammed **Bred** H H The Aga Khan's Studs S C **Trained** Chantilly, France

NOTEBOOK
Tashelka(FR) was always well up before taking control of the race early in the straight and the first-time blinkers clearly made a huge difference. She lengthened her stride and stayed on really strongly during the final stages. This was her second Group 3 success of the season and she may well be seen around again in 2008.
Doe Ray Me raced on the outside and was fifth on the final turn. She tried to get on terms with the winner throughout the final furlong and a half but was held comfortably throughout the straight. She is another who might be left in training next year.
Synopsis(IRE), well up from the start and given every possible chance, she made her run up the far rail and stayed on one paced throughout the final furlong and a half. This filly could be retired at the end of the season.
Anabaa's Creation(IRE) was a rather disappointing favourite. Always well placed, she came on the outside to challenge early in the straight. Soon under pressure, she was very one-paced in the run to the line. Her trainer reported that she had travelled badly and that the ground was not soft enough for her to show her best

AQUEDUCT (L-H)
Saturday, November 10

OFFICIAL GOING: Firm

6771a RED SMITH H'CAP (GRADE 2) 1m 3f
8:44 (8:46) 3-Y-O+
£45,918 (£15,306; £7,653; £3,827; £2,296; £219)

RPR
1 **Dave (USA)**[21] 6-8-2 .... JBravo 10 103
(B Tagg, U.S.A) **148/10**
2 1 **True Cause (USA)**[462] 4126 4-8-3 .... (b) JRVelazquez 9 102
(Saeed Bin Suroor) **69/20**[1]
3 1 **Musketier (GER)**[32] 6095 5-8-4 .... J-LSamyn 4 101
(P Bary, France) **176/10**
4 hd **Crown Point (USA)**[36] 5-8-3 .... (b) JLEspinoza 11 100
(D Donk, U.S.A) **32/1**
5 2 ½ **Presious Passion (USA)**[50] 4-8-5 .... (b) StewartElliott 7 97
(Mary Hartmann, U.S.A) **325/10**
6 1 ½ **Sunshine Kid (USA)**[29] 6153 3-8-3 ow2 .... WHMcCauley 12 98
(J H M Gosden) **123/10**
7 1 ¾ **Dreadnaught (USA)**[36] 7-8-5 ow2 .... JCaraballo 2 91
(T Voss, U.S.A) **98/10**
8 1 **Tricky Causeway (USA)** 4-8-4 .... NArroyoJr 8 89
(J Jerkens, U.S.A) **193/10**
9 ¾ **Operation Red Dawn (USA)**[13] 5-8-2 .... CHill 6 85
(Christophe Clement, U.S.A) **68/10**
10 2 ¼ **Encinas (GER)**[274] 412 6-8-3 .... AGarcia 1 82
(K McLaughlin, U.S.A) *ruled the official pari-mutuel favourite* **69/20**[2]
11 ¾ **Golden Strategy (USA)**[49] 4-8-3 .... ECastro 5 81
(M D Wolfson, U.S.A) **62/10**[3]
12 1 ½ **Bee Charmer (IRE)**[36] 5-8-4 .... JLezcano 3 79
(M Matz, U.S.A) **135/10**

2m 21.45s (141.45)
WFA 3 from 4yo+ 5lb 12 Ran SP% **118.0**
PARI-MUTUEL (including $2 stake): WIN 31.60; PL (1-2) 11.80, 5.00;SHOW (1-2-3) 8.30, 3.40, 10.60; SF 191.00.
Owner The Three Colleens Stable and Partingglass Stable **Bred** Joe W Gerrity **Trained** USA

NOTEBOOK
True Cause(USA), last seen in Britain finishing fifth of eight in a Listed race at Glorious Goodwood, is an improved performer in the US.
Sunshine Kid(USA), second in a conditions race at York last time, continues to look difficult to place.

6373 WOODBINE (R-H)
Saturday, November 10

OFFICIAL GOING: Fast

6772a MAPLE LEAF STKS (F&M) (ALL-WEATHER) 1m 2f (D)
9:28 (9:32) 3-Y-O+
£59,210 (£15,351; £8,443; £4,605; £2,303; £175)

RPR
1 **Like A Gem (CAN)**[55] 4-8-7 .... (b) EmmaJayneWilson 6 —
(D Vella, Canada) **15/2**
2 ½ **I'm In Love (USA)**[28] 4-8-7 .... PHusbands 10 —
(K McLaughlin, U.S.A) **73/20**[2]

3 ½ **Tell It As It Is (USA)**[70] 5060 3-8-4 ow4 JMcAleney 3 —
(James J Smith, U.S.A) **137/10**

4 1¾ **Wow Me Free (USA)**[48] 3-8-0 (b) ChantalSutherland 1 —
(D Vella, Canada) **178/10**

5 1¾ **Russian Rosie (IRE)**[52] 5544 3-8-0 ERamsammy 8 —
(J G Portman) *towards rear, last & ridden over 2f out, stayed on from over 1f out, nearest at finish (actual SP 20.55/1)* **41/2**

6 nk **Yousaidido (USA)**[49] 3-8-4 ow4 (b) RLandry 7 —
(Stanley Baresich, U.S.A) **355/10**

7 1 **Serenading (USA)**[49] 3-8-3 ow3 DavidClark 5 —
(Josie Carroll, Canada) **167/20**

8 1¾ **Monashee (USA)**[28] 5-8-9 (b) JStein 2 —
(L Tracy McCarthy, U.S.A) **8/5**[1]

9 1 **Cryptoquip (USA)**[35] 4-8-7 TKabel 4 —
(H G Motion, U.S.A) **49/10**[3]

10 2¼ **Dancing Band (USA)**[315] 4-8-6 ow1 JonoJones 9 —
(Niall M O'Callaghan, U.S.A) **375/10**

2m 3.51s (123.51)
WFA 3 from 4yo+ 4lb **10** Ran SP% **121.5**
PARI-MUTUEL (including $CAN2 stakes): WIN 17.00; PL (1-2) 6.60, 5.00;SHOW (1-2-3) 5.30, 3.60, 6.80; SF 71.30.
Owner Hillsbrook Farm **Bred** Garland E Williamson **Trained** In Canada

NOTEBOOK
Russian Rosie(IRE), held in Listed company this season on turf back in Britain, was running on dirt for the first time. Towards the back of the field in the early stages, she made late progress inside the final two furlongs, but never got close enough to threaten for the win. Reverting to more positive tactics is likely to suit her in future.

6713 KEMPTON (A.W) (R-H)

Sunday, November 11

OFFICIAL GOING: Standard
Wind: medium, half-against Weather: overcast

6773 DAY TIME, NIGHT TIME, GREAT TIME H'CAP — 5f (P)

1:30 (1:32) (Class 6) (0-52,53) 3-Y-O+ **£2,047** (£604; £302) **Stalls** High

Form RPR

5406 1 **Sweetsformysweet (USA)**[22] 6339 3-8-13 **49** EddieAhern 9 58
(J Noseda) *s.i.s: sn in midfield: hdwy over 1f out: styd on wl to ld last strides* **12/1**

6003 2 hd **Sir Loin**[13] 6528 6-9-0 **50** (v) MickyFenton 11 58
(P Burgoyne) *led for 1f: chsd clr ldr after: rdn wl over 1f out: led wl ins fnl f: hdd last strides* **14/1**

0530 3 ½ **One Way Ticket**[30] 6149 7-8-12 **48** (b) HayleyTurner 10 54
(J M Bradley) *chsd ldr tl led after 1f: sn clr: rdn wl over 1f out: hdd wl ins fnl f: no ex* **11/2**

3024 4 nk **Davids Mark**[4] 6718 7-9-0 **50** LiamJones 6 55
(J R Jenkins) *racd in midfield: rdn wl over 1f out: r.o fnl f: nt rch ldrs* **9/2**[2]

5003 5 shd **Duke Of Milan (IRE)**[4] 6718 4-8-11 **47** J-PGuillambert 5 52+
(G C Bravery) *stdd s: hld up wl bhd: swtchd rt and hdwy over 1f out: r.o strly fnl f: n.m.r nr fin: nt rch ldrs* **5/1**[3]

6002 6 nk **Fastrac Boy**[13] 6528 4-9-3 **53** JimCrowley 12 57
(J R Best) *chsd ldrs: rdn 2f out: kpt on but nt pce to rch ldrs* **4/1**[1]

0024 7 ½ **Dysonic (USA)**[22] 6340 5-8-10 **51** (v) TolleyDean(5) 3 53
(J Balding) *chsd ldrs: rdn 1/2-way: kpt on but nt pce to chal ldrs* **11/1**

0440 8 1¾ **Detonate**[3] 6735 5-9-0 **50** DarryllHolland 2 46
(I A Wood) *bhd: kpt on u.p fnl f: nvr able to chal* **14/1**

/0-0 9 1 **Maraagel (USA)**[54] 5499 4-8-7 **50** (t) WilliamCarson(7) 4 42
(C Drew) *a bhd: n.d* **8/1**

3004 10 nk **Kilvickeon (IRE)**[37] 5970 3-8-11 **47** LPKeniry 7 38
(Peter Grayson) *dwlt: a bhd: nvr trbld ldrs* **33/1**

0300 11 hd **Blessed Place**[4] 6718 7-9-2 **52** (t) FergusSweeney 1 42
(D J S Ffrench Davis) *racd wd: a towards rr* **12/1**

0040 12 5 **Legal Set (IRE)**[33] 6078 11-8-9 **50** (b) AnnStokell(5) 8 22
(Miss A Stokell) *rrd leaving stalls: a struggling in rr* **33/1**

59.32 secs (-1.08) **Going Correction** -0.225s/f (Stan) **12** Ran SP% **124.3**
Speed ratings (Par 101): **99,98,97,97,97 96,95,93,91,91 90,82**
CSF £177.04 CT £745.40 TOTE £16.30: £3.40, £5.30, £2.20; EX 185.00.
Owner Mrs Susan Roy **Bred** New Farm **Trained** Newmarket, Suffolk

FOCUS
A weak sprint handicap, run at a strong early pace. The fourth and sixth set the level.

6774 TOM TOWNSEND LIFETIME IN RACING CLAIMING STKS — 1m 2f (P)

2:00 (2:01) (Class 6) 3-Y-O+ **£2,047** (£604; £302) **Stalls** High

Form RPR

1111 1 **Birkside**[25] 6261 4-9-11 70 DavidAllan 9 74
(D Carroll) *stdd s: hld up in midfield: hdwy over 2f out: ev ch jst over 1f out: led ins fnl f: r.o wl* **7/2**[3]

1221 2 ½ **Bridgewater Boys**[17] 6452 6-9-3 60 (b) FergusSweeney 5 65
(G L Moore) *trckd ldrs: rdn wl over 1f out: ev ch over 1f out: chsd wnr ins fnl f: unable qck* **10/3**[2]

0250 3 1 **Don Pietro**[30] 6145 4-9-11 73 EddieAhern 1 71
(D J Coakley) *trckd ldng pair: wnt 2nd over 2f out: led wl over 1f out: sn rdn: hdd ins fnl f: no ex* **3/1**[1]

3324 4 2 **Casablanca Minx (IRE)**[6] 6696 4-9-2 62 (b) StephenDonohoe 8 58
(P D Evans) *s.i.s: towards rr: rdn and hdwy 2f out: swtchd rt over 1f out: r.o fnl f: nt rch ldrs* **7/1**

0040 5 1 **Climate (IRE)**[16] 6476 8-8-5 58 ow1 (v) RussellKennemore(5) 7 50
(R Hollinshead) *t.k.h: hld up in tch: rdn and effrt on outer over 2f out: kpt on same pce fnl f* **20/1**

4520 6 shd **Speagle (IRE)**[63] 5255 5-8-10 75 JamieKyne(7) 10 57
(D Carroll) *t.k.h: hld up in tch: plld out and effrt wl over 1f out: sn edgd lft: kpt on same pce fnl f* **9/1**

02/0 7 ½ **Strength 'n Honour**[25] 6261 7-9-3 68 DarryllHolland 11 56
(Karen George) *stdd s: t.k.h: hld up in last: shkn up 1f out: sme late hdwy: n.d* **16/1**

5000 8 ¾ **Franky'N'Jonny**[8] 6642 4-8-2 40 DaleGibson 4 39
(M J Attwater) *s.i.s: hld up in rr: rdn and effrt wl over 1f out: kpt on but nvr threatened ldrs* **50/1**

06 9 ¾ **Itsy Bitsy**[15] 6501 5-8-6 0 NeilPollard 2 42
(W J Musson) *s.i.s: hld up in rr: rdn 2f out: kpt on but nvr pce to trble ldrs* **66/1**

0012 10 1¼ **Dawson Creek (IRE)**[15] 6505 3-9-7 51 J-PGuillambert 3 58
(B Gubby) *chsd ldr tl wl over 2f out: sn rdn: wknd wl over 1f out* **25/1**

-600 11 ½ **Circus Polka (USA)**[7] 6669 3-9-7 75 (bt[1]) ChrisCatlin 12 57
(P F I Cole) *t.k.h: led tl rdn and hdd wl over 1f out: wknd qckly over 1f out* **8/1**

2m 6.20s (-2.80) **Going Correction** -0.225s/f (Stan)
WFA 3 from 4yo+ 4lb **11** Ran SP% **121.9**
Speed ratings (Par 101): **102,101,100,99,98 98,97,97,96,95 95**
CSF £15.73 TOTE £4.60: £2.00, £1.90, £2.00; EX 13.10.The winner was the subject of a friendly claim.
Owner Document Express Ltd **Bred** Pendley Farm **Trained** Sledmere, E Yorks

FOCUS
A reasonable claimer with the first three home making sense.
Climate(IRE) Official explanation: jockey said gelding ran too free
Circus Polka(USA) Official explanation: jockey said colt ran too free

6775 WBX.COM NURSERY (DIV I) — 1m (P)

2:30 (2:31) (Class 6) (0-60,60) 2-Y-O **£1,706** (£503; £252) **Stalls** High

Form RPR

0000 1 **Fernlawn Hope (IRE)**[39] 5896 2-9-3 **56** EddieAhern 6 59
(J A Osborne) *in tch: rdn wl over 2f out: sltly outpcd over 1f out: rallied u.p fnl f: led nr fin* **10/1**

6004 2 nk **Silca Destination**[13] 6536 2-8-13 **52** DarryllHolland 2 54
(M R Channon) *chsd ldrs: rdn to ld wl over 1f out: r.o but ct nr fin* **8/1**[3]

0063 3 1½ **Tapas Lad (IRE)**[13] 6536 2-9-2 **55** (v) PatCosgrave 4 54+
(V Smith) *s.i.s: sn rdn into midfield: rdn and outpcd wl over 2f out: styd on u.p fnl f: wnt 3rd last 100yds: nt rch ldng pair* **4/1**[1]

0000 4 1¼ **Oli James (USA)**[17] 6454 2-8-13 **57** (b[1]) TolleyDean(5) 13 53
(P F I Cole) *chsd ldr for 2f: styd chsng ldrs: rdn over 2f out: one pce fnl f* **14/1**

060 5 1 **Evette**[23] 6303 2-8-11 **50** J-PGuillambert 8 43
(M Johnston) *hld up towards rr: rdn and hdwy over 2f out: styd on fnl f: nt pce to rch ldrs* **16/1**

0402 6 ½ **Imaginemysurprise**[16] 6478 2-9-1 **59** HaddenFrost(5) 5 51
(J A Geake) *chsd ldrs: wnt 2nd after 2f: rdn to ld narrowly over 2f out: hdd wl over 1f out: wknd ins fnl f* **9/1**

0006 7 1½ **Rock Me (IRE)**[12] 6572 2-8-6 **45** MickyFenton 11 34
(N A Callaghan) *led: rdn and hdd over 2f out: wknd jst over 1f out* **9/2**[2]

0456 8 1½ **Janet's Delight**[15] 6503 2-9-7 **60** PaulDoe 1 45
(S Curran) *hld up in midfield: hdwy on outer over 3f out: chsd ldrs over 2f out: wknd jst over 1f out* **11/1**

000U 9 shd **Mister Cafnex (IRE)**[34] 6051 2-8-6 **45** WandersonD'Avila 10 30
(B W Duke) *s.i.s: a bhd: sme modest late hdwy: n.d* **66/1**

000 10 1¾ **Zarees**[65] 5186 2-9-2 **55** LiamJones 3 36
(Miss Gay Kelleway) *t.k.h: hld up in midfield: rdn wl over 2f out: wknd over 1f out* **12/1**

060 11 1 **Fort Hull (IRE)**[28] 6202 2-9-3 **56** (b[1]) JimCrowley 9 35
(Mrs A J Perrett) *s.i.s: a bhd* **8/1**[3]

000 12 ¾ **Millennium Storm (GER)**[11] 6585 2-8-11 **50** FergusSweeney 7 27
(M F Harris) *racd in midfield: rdn and lost pl 3f out: no ch after* **14/1**

304 13 1¼ **Giggling Monkey**[11] 6591 2-8-10 **49** TGMcLaughlin 12 23
(P D Evans) *racd in midfield tl dropped to rr 1/2-way: no ch last 3f* **16/1**

1m 40.05s (-0.75) **Going Correction** -0.225s/f (Stan) **13** Ran SP% **122.1**
Speed ratings (Par 94): **94,93,92,90,89 89,87,86,86,84 83,82,81**
CSF £89.77 CT £381.75 TOTE £13.40: £3.90, £3.70, £2.50; EX 177.10.
Owner Martyn and Elaine Booth **Bred** James Mulligan **Trained** Upper Lambourn, Berks
■ Stewards' Enquiry : Pat Cosgrave two-day ban: used whip above shoulder height (Nov 22-23)

FOCUS
A moderate nursery, run at a fair pace.

NOTEBOOK
Fernlawn Hope(IRE), 4lb lower, dug deep when under maxmum pressure from the 2f marker and came good at the fifth time of asking. She was clearly much more suited to being ridden more prominently this time and she still ought to have a little more to offer from a likely future higher mark. (op 11-1 tchd 12-1)
Silca Destination showed the benefit of a 4lb drop in the weights and her best race to date in defeat. She only got reeled in near the finish and finished nicely clear in second, reversing her Newbury form with the third. (op 9-1)
Tapas Lad(IRE), in front of the runner-up over 7f at Newbury 13 days previously, did not help his cause with a sluggish start and had to be ridden early to recover. He then hit a flat spot before staying on again, but the first pair had gone beyond recall. This proves he gets the trip, and he is capable of better, but it also shows just why he sports a visor. (op 9-2)
Oli James(USA) showed his best form to date in the first-time visor on this step back up in grade, but was still well held and looks in need of further respite in the weights. (op 12-1)
Evette, making her nursery debut, took too long to find her full stride from off the pace and a more prominent ride over this trip should bring about some further improvement. Her pedigree also suggests a stiffer test will suit in due course. (op 12-1)

6776 WBX.COM NURSERY (DIV II) — 1m (P)

3:00 (3:05) (Class 6) (0-60,60) 2-Y-O **£1,706** (£503; £252) **Stalls** High

Form RPR

0503 1 **Alfredtheordinary**[11] 6591 2-9-5 **58** SamHitchcott 10 65
(M R Channon) *sn pushed into ld: mde rest: hung lft fr 2f out: styd on wl* **6/1**[3]

0000 2 1½ **Lord's Bidding**[11] 6585 2-8-11 **50** (b[1]) RobertHavlin 2 54
(R Ingram) *chsd ldrs: chsd wnr wl over 2f out: no imp fnl f* **20/1**

0063 3 4 **Carry On Cleo**[12] 6566 2-9-3 **56** StephenDonohoe 5 51
(P D Evans) *sn bhd and rdn along: swtchd rt over 2f out: r.o to go 3rd towards fin: nvr nr ldrs* **13/2**

3504 4 nk **Llab Nala**[11] 6584 2-9-2 **55** ChrisCatlin 9 49
(M R Channon) *hld up towards rr: rdn and lost pl over 3f out: swtchd lft wl over 2f out: hdwy 2f out: chsd ldng pair over 1f out: no imp: lost 3rd towards fin* **5/1**[2]

6100 5 hd **Ten Spot (IRE)**[28] 6207 2-9-7 **60** MickyFenton 12 54
(Stef Liddiard) *hld up in rr: c wd and rdn over 2f out: styd on past btn horses fnl f: nvr nr ldrs* **7/1**

004 6 ½ **Shot Through (USA)**[64] 5226 2-8-1 **47** (v[1]) PatrickDonaghy(7) 6 40
(P C Haslam) *sn bhd: rdn and hdwy on outer over 3f out: no imp fnl 2f* **14/1**

0000 7 ½ **Casual Garcia**[11] 6592 2-8-6 **45** JamieMackay 1 37
(Sir Mark Prescott) *chsd ldr tl rdn over 3f out: wknd over 2f out* **12/1**

0000 8 ¾ **Agon Eyes (USA)**[62] 5268 2-8-11 **50** DarryllHolland 4 40
(D J Coakley) *hld up in midfield on inner: rdn and effrt over 2f out: outpcd over 1f out* **10/1**

0000 9 hd **Talamahana**[44] 5766 2-9-3 **56** SimonWhitworth 8 46+
(S Kirk) *hld up towards rr: rdn over 2f out: bmpd and swtchd rt over 1f out: no hdwy* **9/2**[1]

The Form Book, Raceform Ltd, Compton, RG20 6NL

0000 **10** *hd* **Anabaa's Secret (IRE)**[18] 6427 2-9-1 **54**......................(b[1]) EddieAhern 7 43
(J A Osborne) *t.k.h: hld up in tch on outer: rdn and hung lft wl 2f out: no imp after* **10/1**

0061 **11** *3* **Rosy Dawn**[18] 6433 2-9-3 **56**......................(v) JamesDoyle 11 39
(Ms J S Doyle) *chsd ldrs: wnt 2nd over 3f out tl wl over 2f out: wknd qckly over 1f out* **9/1**

1m 40.07s (-0.73) **Going Correction** -0.225s/f (Stan) **11** Ran SP% **122.3**
Speed ratings (Par 94): **94,92,88,88,88 87,87,86,86,85 82**
CSF £123.25 CT £832.59 TOTE £6.80: £2.10, £6.50, £2.20; EX 180.10.
Owner The Lord Ilsley Racing Club **Bred** Norman Court Stud **Trained** West Ilsley, Berks

FOCUS
This second division of the nursery was another weak affair. The first two came clear.

NOTEBOOK
Alfredtheordinary, raised 5lb for finishing third in a seller last time, finally opened his account at the tenth attempt on this All-Weather debut. He did not looks straightforward when in front, but still won this readily enough and could well be an improver on this surface. (op 13-2)
Lord's Bidding had shown very little in four previous outings, but the application of a first-time visor had a positive effect and he put in a much-improved effort. Whether the headgear has the same effect next time remains to be seen, however. (op 12-1)
Carry On Cleo had to be ridden from an early stage and by the time she eventually found her stride the race was effectively over. The evidence of her recent runs would suggest she really needs a stiffer test now. (op 6-1 tchd 11-2)
Llab Nala looked far from straightforward here, hitting a flat spot before halfway and then hanging when switched out for his effort in the home straight. (op 9-2 tchd 4-1)
Ten Spot(IRE), making her debut for new connections, was not helped by being carried wide on the final bend and by the time she fully recovered it was too late. She is a little better than the bare form. (tchd 15-2)
Talamahana was never going that well from off the pace and failed to really prove she stayed the trip. (op 10-1)

6777 EUROPEAN BREEDERS' FUND MEDIAN AUCTION MAIDEN FILLIES' STKS 1m (P)
3:30 (3:35) (Class 6) 2-Y-O **£2,388** (£705; £352) **Stalls High**

Form RPR

1 **Burriscarra**[7] 6678 2-8-11 0.. JerryO'Dwyer(3) 6 77
(Eamon Tyrrell, Ire) *chsd ldr tl led over 3f out: rdn over 2f out: hdd over 1f out: looked btn tl rallied u.p last 100yds to ld again nr fin* **12/1**

2 *hd* **Girl Of Pangaea (GER)** 2-9-0 0.............................. StephenDonohoe 7 77+
(E A L Dunlop) *s.i.s: t.k.h: hld up towards rr: gd hdwy on inner over 2f out: rdn to ld over 1f out: looked wnr tl worn down nr fin* **9/1**

56 **3** *1 3/4* **Pampas (USA)**[122] 3446 2-9-0 0.............................. DarryllHolland 10 73
(R Charlton) *hld up in tch: rdn jst over 2f out: outpcd 2f out: styd on ins fnl f: nt rch ldng pair* **7/4**[1]

4 *3* **Sensible** 2-9-0 0.. EddieAhern 5 66
(M J Wallace) *chsd ldrs: rdn and ev ch over 2f out: outpcd wl over 1f out* **16/1**

5002 **5** *1* **Spectrana**[24] 6274 2-9-0 68.. JimCrowley 4 64
(Mrs A J Perrett) *wl in tch towards rr: pushed along over 3f out: rdn wl over 2f out: kpt on but nvr pce to threaten ldrs* **7/1**[3]

0 **6** *nk* **Treasure Islands (IRE)**[12] 6571 2-9-0 0...................... TGMcLaughlin 9 63
(S W Hall) *s.i.s: sn wl in tch in midfield: rdn wl over 2f out: sn outpcd: kpt on* **25/1**

7 *nk* **Ucetek (IRE)** 2-9-0 0.. JDSmith 3 63
(Sir Michael Stoute) *in tch on outer: rdn wl over 2f out: kpt on same pce after* **8/1**

00 **8** *1/2* **Amicus**[13] 6530 2-8-9 0.. PatrickHills(5) 1 61
(D K Ivory) *stdd and dropped in bhd after s: rdn and hdwy over 2f out: sn no imp* **66/1**

424 **9** *3/4* **Spiritofthestorm (USA)**[11] 6578 2-9-0 75.......................... ChrisCatlin 2 60+
(R A Teal) *t.k.h: hld up in tch on outer: rdn over 2f out: wknd wl over 1f out: eased towards fin* **2/1**[2]

0 **10** *10* **Tenraninthemist (IRE)**[30] 6139 2-9-0 0.......................... RobertHavlin 8 38
(T D McCarthy) *led tl hdd 3f out: wknd over 2f out: sn wl bhd* **66/1**

1m 40.84s (0.04) **Going Correction** -0.225s/f (Stan) **10** Ran SP% **123.7**
Speed ratings (Par 91): **90,89,88,85,84 83,83,82,82,72**
CSF £120.28 TOTE £14.60: £3.80, £3.10, £1.20; EX 163.90.
Owner M McLoughlin **Bred** Broughton Bloodstock **Trained** The Curragh, Co Kildare

FOCUS
A modest juvenile maiden. The first pair came clear in a driving finish and the level has been set by the third and fifth.

NOTEBOOK
Burriscarra, eighth on debut at Leopardstown a week previously, showed the benefit of that experience and ran out a very gutsy winner on this British bow. She also proved suited by this change in surfaces and the step up to this extra furlong was also much to her liking. (op 14-1 tchd 10-1)
Girl Of Pangaea(GER) ◆, a 105,000gns purchase whose dam was a useful juvenile miler in Germany; ran a pleasing race on this belated racecourse bow and looked the most likely winner entering the final furlong. However, her reluctance to settle through the early parts eventually cost her and she was just reeled in. It is fair to expect her to soon make amends, however, now she has this experience under her belt. (op 8-1 tchd 10-1)
Pampas(USA), well backed on this return from a 122-day break, simply too too long to find top gear over this extra furlong and lacked the pace of the first pair. She now has the option of handicapping and ought to come on for the run again, but has become expensive to follow all the same. (op 5-2)
Sensible, a 35,000euros half-sister to a Polytrack winner over this trip and beyond, put up a pleasing debut display and looks sure to come on a good deal for the run. She will also get a little further on this evidence. (op 10-1)
Spectrana again took time to get going on this switch to the All-Weather and is clearly not straightforward. She still goes some way to helping set the level of this form. (op 8-1 tchd 6-1)
Ucetek(IRE), whose dam won over 1m and is a sister to Spectrum, was clearly expected to need this debut run and performed accordingly. She could leave this form behind next time. (op 6-1)
Spiritofthestorm(USA) was again the subject of market support, but she pulled too hard early on and eventually emptied out when it mattered in the home straight. (op 9-4 tchd 11-4)

6778 TFM NETWORKS MEDIAN AUCTION MAIDEN STKS 1m (P)
4:00 (4:01) (Class 6) 3-5-Y-0 **£2,047** (£604; £302) **Stalls High**

Form RPR

0503 **1** **Jessica Wigmo**[21] 6361 4-8-11 44.............................. LukeMorris(3) 11 52
(A W Carroll) *hld up wl bhd: gd hdwy on inner over 1f out: chsd ldng pair 1f out: hung lft but r.o wl to ld towards fin* **20/1**

0055 **2** *nk* **Simpsons Gamble (IRE)**[11] 6579 4-9-5 46.......................... EddieAhern 5 57
(R A Teal) *trckd ldrs: chalng and carried lft over 1f out: drvn and ev ch ins fnl f: kpt on nr fin* **4/1**[2]

3630 **3** *nk* **Alecia (IRE)**[18] 6423 3-8-9 62.. NeilChalmers(3) 8 51
(A M Balding) *chsd ldrs: wnt 2nd 3f out: rdn to ld and edgd lft over 1f out: hdd and no ex towards fin* **7/2**[1]

-654 **4** *2* **Murrisk**[51] 5602 3-9-0 0..(b[1]) JerryO'Dwyer(3) 6 51
(Eamon Tyrrell, Ire) *led: rdn over 2f out: hdd over 1f out: btn whn sltly hmpd ins fnl f* **7/1**[3]

0520 **5** *3 1/2* **Anthea**[18] 6420 3-8-12 58.. FergusSweeney 9 38
(B R Millman) *chsd ldr tl 3f out: rdn over 2f out: outpcd jst over 1f out* **4/1**[2]

06- **6** *nk* **Wind Flow**[455] 4388 3-9-3 0.. AdrianMcCarthy 10 43
(C A Dwyer) *racd in midfield: reminder after 1f: rdn wl over 2f out: no imp last 2f* **20/1**

0 **7** *hd* **Tagula Sands (IRE)**[29] 6176 3-9-3 0.............................. RichardSmith 12 42
(J C Fox) *t.k.h: hld up wl in tch: drvn over 2f out: no imp over 1f out* **66/1**

0 **8** *1 1/2* **Ruwain**[11] 6597 3-9-3 0.. NeilPollard 7 39
(W J Musson) *s.i.s: bhd: hmpd over 4f out: sme late hdwy: nvr nr ldrs* **9/1**

5503 **9** *1 1/4* **Smart Pick**[16] 6480 4-9-0 49.. LiamJones 13 31
(Mrs L Williamson) *a in rr: rdn and effrt 3f out: nvr able to chal* **10/1**

0040 **10** *1 1/2* **Pajada**[15] 6497 3-8-12 42..(v) HayleyTurner 3 27
(M D I Usher) *chsd ldrs: rdn wl over 2f out: wknd 2f out* **25/1**

11 *5* **Rasmani** 3-8-12 0..(t) MickyFenton 1 16
(Miss Gay Kelleway) *s.i.s: a bhd: n.d* **16/1**

12 *1 1/2* **Bakers Boy** 3-9-3 0.. RichardThomas 4 17
(J E Long) *a in rr: wandered over 4f out: rdn wl over 3f out: nvr on terms* **16/1**

6602 **13** *3* **Nawayea**[21] 6361 3-8-9 45..(t) PatrickHills(5) 2 6
(C N Allen) *hld up in tch on outer: hdwy 3f out: rdn and btn over 2f out* **14/1**

0 **14** *3/4* **Night Rider**[27] 6240 3-8-10 0.. AmyBaker(7) 14 9
(Miss J Feilden) *racd in midfield: rdn and lost pl 3f out: sn wl bhd* **50/1**

1m 39.07s (-1.73) **Going Correction** -0.225s/f (Stan)
WFA 3 from 4yo 2lb **14** Ran SP% **129.1**
Speed ratings (Par 101): **99,98,98,96,92 92,92,90,89,88 83,81,78,77**
CSF £100.99 TOTE £24.10: £5.60, £1.80, £1.60; EX 152.30.
Owner J Wigmore Racing Partnership **Bred** J Wigmore **Trained** Cropthorne, Worcs

FOCUS
A poor maiden, run at a sound pace. The winner is value for a little further than the winning margin.
Nawayea Official explanation: jockey said filly hung left

6779 TFM NETWORKS H'CAP 6f (P)
4:30 (4:31) (Class 6) (0-55,59) 3-Y-0+ **£2,047** (£604; £302) **Stalls High**

Form RPR

0242 **1** **Littledodayno (IRE)**[10] 6608 4-9-1 **53**.............................. JamieMackay 11 65+
(M Wigham) *sn bhd: pushed along 1/2-way: swtchd rt over 2f out: str run on rail to ld last 100yds: sn in command* **6/1**[3]

402 **2** *1 3/4* **Majestical (IRE)**[11] 6587 5-9-2 **54**..............................(e) DarryllHolland 10 60
(V Smith) *bhd: c wd wl over 2f out: rdn over 1f out: r.o ins fnl f: snatched 2nd on post: nt rch wnr* **6/1**[3]

4046 **3** *shd* **Kennington**[10] 6608 7-9-1 **53**.. NeilPollard 7 59
(Mrs C A Dunnett) *led: rdn 2f out: battled on wl tl hdd last 100yds: nt pce of wnr after: lost 2nd on post* **20/1**

056 **4** *hd* **Faithful Ruler (USA)**[198] 1282 3-9-2 **54**.............................. EddieAhern 1 59+
(M A Magnusson) *wnt lft s: bhd: rdn and effrt on outer over 2f out: rn wl on fnl f: nt rch wnr* **16/1**

3516 **5** *shd* **Stormburst (IRE)**[19] 6415 3-8-10 **55**.......................... WilliamCarson(7) 3 60
(S C Williams) *wnt rt s: sn in tch: hdwy over 3f out: drvn over 2f out: kpt on ins fnl f* **5/1**[2]

0515 **6** *1* **Punching**[2] 6747 3-9-2 **59**.. PatrickHills(5) 12 61
(Eve Johnson Houghton) *trckd ldrs on inner: effrt jst over 2f out: ev ch over 1f out: no ex ins fnl f* **11/4**[1]

031 **7** *hd* **Crimson Fern (IRE)**[21] 6361 3-9-3 **55**.............................. FergusSweeney 5 56
(M S Saunders) *s.i.s: t.k.h: sn in tch in midfield: hdwy wl over 2f out: chsd ldrs and rdn wl over 1f out: no ex ins fnl f* **6/1**[3]

5660 **8** *3/4* **Mr Forthright**[18] 6424 3-9-1 **53**.. LPKeniry 9 51
(J M Bradley) *hld up towards rr: rdn and effrt over 2f out: kpt on but nvr threatened ldrs* **33/1**

9 *nk* **Trammon Ventre (IRE)**[163] 2228 3-8-12 **53**...........(b[1]) JerryO'Dwyer(3) 6 51
(Eamon Tyrrell, Ire) *bmpd s: chsd ldr for 2f: prom tl rdn wl over 2f out: outpcd over 1f out* **50/1**

0060 **10** *1/2* **Amber Isle**[23] 6310 3-8-12 **50**.. DavidAllan 8 46
(D Carroll) *sn pushed along in rr: nvr trbld ldrs* **25/1**

0236 **11** *hd* **Mister Elegant**[4] 6718 5-8-6 **51**.............................. SophieDoyle(7) 4 46
(J L Spearing) *t.k.h: chsd ldr 4f out: ev over 2f out: rdn over 1f out: wknd fnl f* **6/1**[3]

1m 12.35s (-1.35) **Going Correction** -0.225s/f (Stan) **11** Ran SP% **119.9**
Speed ratings (Par 101): **100,97,97,97,97 95,95,94,94,93 93**
CSF £41.00 CT £688.27 TOTE £8.20: £2.10, £2.40, £4.40; EX 23.70.
Owner W L Bamforth & John Williams P'ship **Bred** Lodge Park Stud **Trained** Newmarket, Suffolk

FOCUS
A moderate sprint handicap, run at a strong early pace.

6780 JUMP RACING HERE ON TUESDAY H'CAP 1m 3f (P)
5:00 (5:00) (Class 6) (0-65,65) 3-Y-0+ **£2,047** (£604; £302) **Stalls High**

Form RPR

1 **Fresh Mint (IRE)**[156] 2437 3-8-6 **53**.............................. EddieAhern 3 64
(M J Wallace) *t.k.h: led for 1f: chsd ldrs after: rdn to chse ldr over 2f out: led ins fnl f: drvn out* **16/1**

0506 **2** *1 1/4* **Watchmaker**[38] 5948 4-9-4 **60**.. ChrisCatlin 2 69
(Miss Tor Sturgis) *t.k.h: hdwy to ld after 1f: rdn and hung lft 2f out: hdd and no ex ins fnl f* **9/2**[3]

1141 **3** *4* **Majehar**[25] 6260 5-9-2 **61**.. TravisBlock(3) 8 63+
(A G Newcombe) *t.k.h: hld up in midfield: lost pl and bhd 4f out: hdwy on outer 2f out: chsd ldng pair 1f out: kpt on but nvr nr to chal* **7/2**[2]

2640 **4** *1 1/4* **Siena Star (IRE)**[4] 6727 9-9-7 **63**.............................. MickyFenton 13 63
(Stef Liddiard) *hld up in midfield: hdwy and rdn over 2f out: chsd ldng pair over 1f out: no imp and lost 3rd 1f out* **12/1**

0003 **5** *2 1/2* **The Mighty Ogmore**[12] 6569 3-8-1 **51** oh6...............(p) LukeMorris(3) 12 47
(R C Guest) *s.i.s: hld up in rr: rdn and effrt on inner over 2f out: kpt on but nvr nr ldrs* **40/1**

13-6 **6** *nk* **Zed Candy (FR)**[283] 319 4-9-7 **63**.. DaleGibson 4 58
(J T Stimpson) *t.k.h: hld up in midfield: short of room and swtchd lft wl over 2f out: sn rdn and no imp* **16/1**

0050 **7** *nk* **Silver Surprise**[13] 6534 3-7-13 **51** oh6.............................. NicolPolli(5) 10 46
(J J Bridger) *chsd ldrs: rdn wl over 3f out: wknd jst over 2f out* **50/1**

060 **8** *hd* **Colinca's Lad (IRE)**[91] 4418 5-8-13 **55**.............................. DarryllHolland 1 49
(T T Clement) *t.k.h: chsd ldr 9f out: upsides 7f out tl wl over 2f out: rdn 2f out: sn btn* **16/1**

0001 **9** *1* **Pothos Way (GR)**[22] 6342 4-9-9 **65**.................................... JimCrowley 11 58
(P R Chamings) *chsd ldrs on inner: rdn and effrt over 2f out: wknd over 1f out* **10/3**[1]

6000 **10** *1* **Darghan (IRE)**[20] 6380 7-9-5 **61**.. NeilPollard 6 52
(W J Musson) *stdd after s: hld up wl in rr: drvn over 3f out: nvr nr ldrs* **14/1**

0061 **11** *nk* **Sagunt (GER)**[17] 6447 4-9-5 **61**.. PaulDoe 9 51
(S Curran) *hld up towards rr: c wd and rdn wl over 2f out: no hdwy* **9/2**[3]

0606 **12** *nk* **Medieval Maiden**[31] 6124 4-8-13 **62**.......................... DebraEngland(7) 5 52
(W J Musson) *hld up in rr: hdwy on outer wl over 4f out: lost pl wl over 2f out: no ch after* **25/1**

0001 **13** *1 3/4* **Theatre Royal**[32] 6096 4-8-8 **53**.................................(b) NeilChalmers(3) 7 40
(Mouse Hamilton-Fairley) *hld up in midfield: n.m.r wl over 2f out: rdn 2f out: no imp* **16/1**

2m 20.28s (-2.40) **Going Correction** -0.225s/f (Stan)
WFA 3 from 4yo+ 5lb **13** Ran SP% **127.8**
Speed ratings (Par 101): **99,98,95,94,92 92,92,91,91,90 90,89,88**
CSF £91.64 CT £325.37 TOTE £14.00: £3.80, £1.70, £2.20; EX 117.10 Place 6 £196.08, Place 5 £26.64.
Owner Rick Barnes **Bred** Grange Con Holdings **Trained** Newmarket, Suffolk

FOCUS
A poor handicap, run at an uneven pace. The winner could rate a little higher.
T/Jkpt: Not won. T/Plt: £289.60 to a £1 stake. Pool: £63,651.20. 160.40 winning tickets. T/Qpdt: £50.80 to a £1 stake. Pool: £3,904.10. 56.80 winning tickets. SP

6046 FRANKFURT (L-H)
Sunday, November 11

OFFICIAL GOING: Soft

6781a GROSSER PREIS DER HELABA - HESSEN POKAL 2007 (GROUP 3) 1m 2f
2:30 (2:40) 3-Y-0+ **£21,622** (£6,757; £3,378; £2,027)

RPR

1 **Fair Breeze (GER)**[14] 6524 4-8-12 .... AHelfenbein 2 101
(Mario Hofer, Germany) *a cl up: jnd ldr on fnl turn: led over 2f out and c to middle: swvd sharply rt 1f out: drvn out* **2/1**[1]

2 *2* **Scatina (IRE)**[42] 5849 3-8-12 .... AStarke 10 101
(Mario Hofer, Germany) *a.p: 4th st: chsd wnr fr wl over 1f out: kpt on same pce* **67/10**

3 *1 1/2* **Soudaine (GER)**[35] 4-8-11 ow1.. FSpanu 3 93
(J Hirschberger, Germany) *hld up: towards rr tl r.o wl fnl f to take 3rd last strides* **44/10**[3]

4 *shd* **Lord Hill (GER)**[56] 5464 3-8-12 .... HGrewe 9 98
(C Zeitz) *a cl up: 3rd st: one pce fr over 1f out: lost 3rd last strides* **18/1**

5 *1 1/2* **White Lightning (GER)**[22] 6353 5-9-0 .... JBojko 6 93
(U Stech, Norway) *hld up in rr and pulling early: styd towards far side and 6th st: one pce fr over 1f out* **22/1**

6 *hd* **La Dancia (IRE)**[17] 6460 4-9-0 .... TMundry 8 93
(P Rau, Germany) *cl up: 7th st: sn btn* **42/10**[2]

7 *1/2* **Ioannina**[36] 6030 4-8-12 .... WMongil 4 90
(J Hirschberger, Germany) *led to over 2f out: 2nd st: sn btn* **49/10**

8 *shd* **Fighting Johan (GER)**[39] 5929 3-8-12 .... J-PCarvalho 7 94
(H Blume, Germany) *a in rr* **30/1**

9 *8* **Negus (GER)**[35] 3-8-10 .... EPedroza 1 76
(A Wohler, Germany) *mid-div: hdwy on ins over 3f out: 5th st: sn btn* **79/10**

10 *3* **Beiramar (IRE)**[28] 6220 4-8-13 ow1.. PHeugl 5 70
(W Hickst, Germany) *plld hrd and rushed up to press ldr after 2f: wknd 4f out* **12/1**

2m 17.41s (8.84)
WFA 3 from 4yo+ 4lb **10** Ran SP% **132.8**
(including 10 Euro stake): WIN 30; PL 14, 19, 15; SF 134.
Owner Stall Margarethe **Bred** Frau Margrit Wetzel **Trained** Germany

6614 SAINT-CLOUD (L-H)
Sunday, November 11

OFFICIAL GOING: Very soft

6782a CRITERIUM DE SAINT-CLOUD (GROUP 1) (C&F) 1m 2f
2:45 (2:46) 2-Y-0 **£96,520** (£38,615; £19,307; £9,645; £4,831)

RPR

1 **Full Of Gold (FR)**[17] 2-9-0 .... TGillet 2 107+
(Mme C Head-Maarek, France) *led 2f: a cl up: 3rd st: led 1 1/2f out: rdn out* **21/10**[2]

2 *2* **Hannouma (IRE)**[21] 6377 2-9-0 .... CSoumillon 5 103
(D Smaga, France) *hld up in rr: 4th st: r.o fnl f to take 2nd last strides* **7/5**[1]

3 *snk* **Putney Bridge (USA)**[20] 2-9-0 .... SPasquier 6 103
(Mme C Head-Maarek, France) *trckd ldrs: tk narrow ld ent st (over 2 1/2f out): sn drvn: hdd 1 1/2f out: one pce and lost 2nd last strides* **38/10**[3]

4 *snk* **New Zealand (IRE)**[37] 5990 2-9-0 .... CO'Donoghue 1 102
(A P O'Brien, Ire) *led after 2f tl ent st (over 2 1/2f out): sn drvn: kpt on steadily* **18/1**

5 *3/4* **Siberian Tiger (IRE)**[20] 6382 2-9-0 .... TPO'Shea 4 101
(M R Channon) *hld up in rr: last st: hdwy 2f out: rdn and outpcd over 1f out: rallied cl home* **89/10**

6 *3* **Tale Of Two Cities (IRE)**[22] 6352 2-9-0 .... JAHeffernan 3 96
(A P O'Brien, Ire) *disp 3rd to 3f out: 5th st: bhd fnl 2f* **13/1**

2m 18.1s (2.10) **Going Correction** +0.45s/f (Yiel) **6** Ran SP% **117.3**
Speed ratings: **109,107,107,107,106 104**
PARI-MUTUEL: WIN 3.10; PL 1.40, 1.40; SF 6.80.
Owner A Head **Bred** Alec & Mme Ghislaine Head **Trained** Chantilly, France
■ Stewards' Enquiry : C O'Donoghue €200 fine: whip abuse

FOCUS
A race with a modest recent history, and this renewal did seem to fall short of its Group 1 billing, but Full Of Gold was an impressive winner.

NOTEBOOK
Full Of Gold(FR), an imposing individual, quickens well and also has plenty of stamina. Racing in second place early on, he was third on the rail rounding the final turn before coming with a progressive run in the straight. He quickened from a furlong and a half out and then dominated the opposition. This was his fourth race and he is going from strength to strength. He will be entered in all the European Classics and the now shortened Jockey Club looks sure to be one of his main targets next season. He still has plenty of scope for further improvement.
Hannouma(IRE) had no excuses. He was held up in the early stages and came with his run up the stands' rail. Put under strong pressure halfway up the straight, he then fought well to take second place well inside the final furlong. He was brave to the bitter end and his trainer thinks he will get a little further next year, when he will be campaigned in top-class company.
Putney Bridge(USA), never far from the leading group, moved up to share the lead rounding the final turn and took over at the head of affairs early in the straight. He was passed by the winner with just over a furlong left to run and then lost second place close home. His trainer felt that he should have been held up a little longer before making his challenge for the lead, and that he may not have been totally at home on the very testing ground.
New Zealand(IRE) gave a brave performance in trying to make all the running. He gave up his lead early in the straight but then continued to battle and was running on again in the final stages. In a few more strides he may well have ended up in the third position.
Siberian Tiger(IRE), last early on, began to make progress up the centre of the track from a furlong and a half out and finished well. His rider felt that he was not at home on the very soft ground but was pleased with his effort.
Tale Of Two Cities(IRE) failed to build on his initial effort and steadily dropped away.

6783 - 6789a (Foreign Racing) - See Raceform Interactive

6771 AQUEDUCT (L-H)
Sunday, November 11

OFFICIAL GOING: All-weather - fast; turf course - good

6790a LONG ISLAND H'CAP (GRADE 3) (F&M) 1m 4f (T)
7:48 (7:50) 3-Y-0+

£45,918 (£15,306; £7,653; £3,826; £2,295; £510)

RPR

1 **Dalvina**[58] 5396 3-8-4 ow1.. CVelasquez 3 111
(E A L Dunlop) *missed break & raced in last, good hdwy on outside over 2f out, 2nd str, led over 1f out, ran on well, driven out SP 11-2* **11/2**[3]

2 *3 1/2* **Barancella (FR)**[21] 6373 6-8-7 .... JRVelazquez 4 102
(R J Frankel, U.S.A) **57/20**[2]

3 *3/4* **My Rachel (USA)** 5-8-4 ow1.......................................(b) EPrado 5 98
(T Pletcher, U.S.A) **188/10**

4 *hd* **Green Girl (FR)**[42] 5853 5-8-3 .... AGarcia 1 96
(Christophe Clement, U.S.A) **13/2**

5 *4 1/4* **Rising Cross**[29] 6168 4-8-3 .... ECastro 2 89
(J R Best) *struggled to go pace early in 5th place, last 2f out, never a factor SP 57-20* **57/20**[2]

6 *3 1/2* **Royal Highness (GER)**[43] 5822 5-8-10 .... JCastellano 6 90
(Christophe Clement, U.S.A) **11/10**[1]

7 *1 1/2* **Mary Louhana**[69] 4-8-5 ow2... RMaragh 8 83
(Leigh Delacour, U.S.A) **396/10**

8 *27* **Miracle Moment (USA)**[64] 4-8-3 .... ECoa 7 35
(B Tagg, U.S.A) **97/10**

2m 34.35s (3.32)
WFA 3 from 4yo+ 6lb **8** Ran SP% **145.1**
PARI-MUTUEL (Including $2 stake): WIN 13.00; PL (1-2) 6.50, 3.70;SHOW (1-2-3) 5.10, 2.60, 6.40; SF 57.00.
Owner A Stone **Bred** Normandie Stud Ltd **Trained** Newmarket, Suffolk

NOTEBOOK
Dalvina, the only three-year-old in the field, was dropping in grade on this US debut. Held up out the back in the early stages, she came four wide in the straight, picked up well and ran out a convincing winner in the end. The plan had been for her to go to the paddocks at the end of this season but she may now be kept in training as a four-year-old.
Rising Cross, who has struggled for most of this year, never got competitive.

6704 LINGFIELD (L-H)
Monday, November 12

OFFICIAL GOING: Standard
Wind: Very modest, against Weather: Bright, partly cloudy

6791 LINGFIELDPARK.CO.UK MAIDEN AUCTION STKS 7f (P)
1:10 (1:10) (Class 6) 2-Y-0 **£2,590** (£770; £385; £192) **Stalls** Low

Form RPR

4 **1** **Roaring Forte (IRE)**[38] 5977 2-9-1 0................................... LiamJones 6 82+
(W J Haggas) *in tch: chsd ldr 5f out: led over 2f out: sn pushed clr: eased towards fin* **1/10**[1]

2 *8* **Celtic Charlie (FR)** 2-9-0 0.. JimCrowley 2 57+
(P M Phelan) *s.i.s: bhd tl hdwy on outer over 3f out: chsd wnr and rdn 2f out: sn no ch w wnr: kpt on* **8/1**[2]

00 **3** *2* **Banjo Bandit (IRE)**[88] 4540 2-9-1 0....................................... JohnEgan 1 53
(J S Moore) *sn pushed into ld: rdn and hdd over 2f out: sn wl outpcd* **16/1**

00 **4** *nk* **Duneen Dream (USA)**[18] 6454 2-9-0 0................................ NeilPollard 5 51
(W J Musson) *t.k.h: hld up: hdwy over 2f out: rdn and no imp wl over 1f out* **16/1**

00 **5** *12* **Police Officer**[7] 6694 2-9-1 0.. EddieAhern 3 21
(W J Musson) *in tch: rdn 3f out: sn wl bhd: t.o* **14/1**[3]

000 **6** *1* **Avril Valley**[29] 6207 2-8-4 40.......................................(p) RichardThomas 4 —
(D J S Ffrench Davis) *chsd ldr tl 5f out: rdn 3f out: sn wl bhd: t.o* **33/1**

1m 23.96s (-1.93) **Going Correction** -0.30s/f (Stan) 2y crse rec **6** Ran SP% **123.4**
Speed ratings (Par 94): **99,89,87,87,73 72**
CSF £2.67 TOTE £1.10: £1.02, £3.10; EX 3.10.
Owner Flying Tiger Partnership **Bred** Grangecon Stud **Trained** Newmarket, Suffolk

FOCUS
An uncompetitive maiden, but still a useful effort from the long odds-on favourite, who broke the juvenile course record. The winning time was 0.98 seconds quicker than the later two-year-old claimer, but 0.76 seconds slower than the later 61-75 handicap for older horses.

NOTEBOOK
Roaring Forte(IRE), a promising fourth on his debut at Newmarket, had next to nothing to beat this time, as his odds suggested, but he still managed to lower the juvenile course record. Considered a big baby by his connections, he is likely to be put away for the year now. (op 1-12 tchd 1-8 in places)

Celtic Charlie(FR), a 24,000gns son of Until Sundown, who was placed in a Grade 1 on dirt over 1m1f in the US, is a half-brother to 1m4f winner Piper Bere and was not without support. He was no match for the above-average winner, but finished a clear second and this was a satisfactory debut. (op 10-1)
Banjo Bandit(IRE) had finished last in a couple of 7f maidens at Salisbury on his first two starts, but this was a little better and he is now qualified for a handicap mark.
Duneen Dream(USA), who beat just three home in a claimer at Wolverhampton on his previous start, did not help his chance by racing keenly and was well beaten. He is now qualified for a handicap mark, but needs to improve significantly to win a race.
Police Officer, like his stablemate in fourth, is now qualified for a handicap mark, but there was no promise whatsoever in this effort. His breeding suggests he may do better over further.

6792 PLAY GOLF @ LINGFIELD PARK CLASSIFIED STKS — 1m 2f (P)
1:45 (1:45) (Class 7) 3-Y-O+ — **£2,047** (£604; £302) **Stalls** Low

Form — RPR

30 **1** — **Bernabeu (IRE)**[22] 6361 5-9-2 43 .... PaulDoe 9 — 50
(S Curran) *pressed ldr tl led 6f out: hrd pressed and drvn over 2f out: hld on gamely u.p fnl f: all out* **11/2**[2]

000- **2** *hd* **Barton Sands (IRE)**[433] 5097 10-9-2 43 .... (t) JimCrowley 10 — 50
(Andrew Reid) *w.w in midfield: hdwy 3f out: str chal ins fnl f: hld cl home* **12/1**

6040 **3** *½* **Abbeygate**[18] 6458 6-9-2 42 .... J-PGuillambert 12 — 49
(T Keddy) *in tch: rdn and ev ch 2f out: hung rt and nt qckn fnl f* **9/2**[1]

0004 **4** *2½* **Mycenean Prince (USA)**[9] 6642 4-9-2 45 .... (b) RichardHughes 7 — 44
(R C Guest) *t.k.h: led for 1f: chsd ldr after: rdn and chsd wnr briefly over 2f out: no ex fnl f* **11/2**[2]

0066 **5** *½* **Lordswood (IRE)**[12] 6590 3-8-9 45 .... NeilChalmers(3) 2 — 43
(J J Bridger) *s.i.s: hld up in rr: hdwy 3f out: chsd ldrs over 1f out: kpt on same pce fnl f* **8/1**[3]

0000 **6** *1¼* **Oasis Sun (IRE)**[29] 6212 4-9-2 43 .... (b[1]) EddieAhern 11 — 40
(J R Best) *s.i.s: rdn and effrt on inner over 2f out: no imp fnl f* **16/1**

5000 **7** *½* **The Slider**[12] 6579 3-8-12 45 .... (p) LPKeniry 14 — 39
(Mrs L C Jewell) *hld up in rr: hdwy wl over 2f out: kpt on u.p but nvr pce to chal* **33/1**

0005 **8** *nk* **Wizby**[9] 6642 4-8-9 42 .... RichardEvans(7) 5 — 39
(P D Evans) *racd wd: hld up in midfield: hdwy wl over 2f out: kpt on u.p but nvr nr ldrs* **20/1**

2305 **9** *1* **Height Of Spirits**[14] 6532 5-9-2 45 .... (p) JohnEgan 13 — 37
(T D McCarthy) *stdd s: t.k.h: hld up in rr: rdn and hdwy on inner over 2f out: styng on whn swtchd rt ins fnl f: nvr nr ldrs* **9/2**[1]

-340 **10** *1½* **Piquet**[302] 129 9-9-2 44 .... MickyFenton 1 — 34
(J J Bridger) *t.k.h: hld up wl in tch: rdn and chsd ldrs wl over 1f out: fdd fnl f* **22/1**

0100 **11** *1¾* **Alqaayid**[76] 4915 6-9-2 43 .... JamesDoyle 6 — 30
(P W Hiatt) *t.k.h: chsd ldrs: wnt 2nd 5f out tl over 2f out: sn drvn and wknd* **8/1**[3]

6000 **12** *3½* **Time For Change (IRE)**[7] 6531 3-8-12 44 .... RobertHavlin 3 — 23
(P G Murphy) *stdd after s: hld up wl in rr: n.d* **50/1**

00-0 **13** *1¾* **Little Hotpotch**[147] 2718 3-8-12 45 .... StephenDonohoe 8 — 20
(M J Gingell) *led after 1f tl 6f out: rdn and lost pl wl over 4f out: n.d last 2f* **66/1**

6500 **14** *½* **Red Raptor**[88] 4533 6-9-2 44 .... (t) RichardThomas 4 — 19
(J A Geake) *t.k.h: hld up in midfield: rdn wl over 2f out: sn bhd* **16/1**

2m 5.62s (-2.17) **Going Correction** -0.30s/f (Stan)
WFA 3 from 4yo+ 4lb — **14** Ran SP% **124.3**
Speed ratings (Par 97): **96,95,95,93,93 92,91,91,90,89 88,85,83,83**
CSF £68.54 TOTE £8.00: £2.30, £3.80, £2.30; EX 83.40.
Owner G D Peck **Bred** Mrs Joan M Langmead **Trained** Faringdon, Oxon

FOCUS
A moderate but competitive classified contest, and sound form for the grade. The principals avoided the far rail in the straight.
Height Of Spirits Official explanation: jockey said gelding hung both ways
Red Raptor Official explanation: jockey said gelding ran too free

6793 LINGFIELD PARK FOR WEDDINGS CLAIMING STKS — 7f (P)
2:15 (2:15) (Class 6) 2-Y-O — **£2,047** (£604; £302) **Stalls** Low

Form — RPR

0544 **1** — **Redsensor**[12] 6586 2-8-13 69 .... RichardHughes 6 — 74+
(R Hannon) *in tch: rdn over 3f out: drvn to chse ldr over 2f out: led jst over 1f out: sn clr: eased towards fin* **2/1**[1]

0302 **2** *4* **Mairead's Boy (IRE)**[12] 6586 2-8-8 55 .... (b) JohnEgan 1 — 58
(J S Moore) *w ldrs: led over 3f out: rdn over 2f out: hung rt u.p: hdd jst over 1f out: sn outpcd by wnr* **5/1**[3]

4124 **3** *1¾* **What's For Tea**[13] 6566 2-8-4 61 .... HayleyTurner 3 — 49
(Tom Dascombe) *sn pushed along: led narrowly tl over 3f out: chsd ldrs u.p after: outpcd wl over 1f out: plugged on* **5/2**[2]

0000 **4** *1¼* **La Varrosa**[5] 6714 2-7-9 52 .... KMay(7) 7 — 44
(Mrs P N Dutfield) *racd in midfield: hdwy to chse ldrs over 2f out: rdn and no imp over 1f out* **20/1**

40 **5** *2* **Miss Solo**[115] 3718 2-8-2 0 .... PatrickDonaghy(7) 4 — 46
(P C Haslam) *s.i.s: sn in tch in midfield: rdn and struggling over 3f out: n.d after* **15/2**

6040 **6** *½* **Chemise (IRE)**[48] 5715 2-8-2 46 ow2 .... RichardThomas 8 — 37
(R J Hodges) *prom on outer: rdn wl over 2f out: outpcd over 2f: n.d after* **20/1**

2243 **7** *3* **Bollywood Style**[19] 6433 2-8-6 55 .... EddieAhern 2 — 34
(J R Best) *racd in midfield: rdn and effrt over 2f out: sn no hdwy: eased ins fnl f* **8/1**

00 **8** *3* **Alannah (IRE)**[42] 5869 2-8-8 0 .... RobertHavlin 5 — 28
(Mrs P N Dutfield) *a bhd: rdn and struggling over 3f out: nvr on terms* **50/1**

0 **9** *1½* **Valtat**[19] 6436 2-9-2 0 .... FrankieMcDonald 9 — 32
(B R Johnson) *wnt rt s and s.i.s: a bhd: rdn over 4f out: nvr on terms* **16/1**

1m 24.94s (-0.95) **Going Correction** -0.30s/f (Stan) — **9** Ran SP% **117.9**
Speed ratings (Par 94): **93,88,86,85,82 82,78,75,73**
CSF £12.52 TOTE £2.80: £1.20, £2.10, £1.40; EX 13.60.
Owner The Waney Racing Group Inc **Bred** Waney Racing Group Inc **Trained** East Everleigh, Wilts

FOCUS
A moderate claimer, but solid enough form. The pace was good, but the winning time was 0.98 seconds slower than the earlier maiden. The principals avoided the far rail in the straight.

NOTEBOOK
Redsensor was disappointing when only fourth in this grade when fitted with first-time blinkers over 6f round here on his previous start, but he had the headgear left off this time and benefited from the step up in trip. He came off the bridle early in the straight, but responded well to pressure and was well on top at the line. (op 9-4, tchd 5-2 in a place)
Mairead's Boy(IRE) was given a positive ride, but he was unable to confirm recent 6f form with Redsensor. He is still a maiden, but looks up to winning a seller. (op 13-2)
What's For Tea, dropped in trip, was never going at any stage and proved disappointing. On this evidence she needs a step back up in trip. (tchd 11-4)
La Varrosa, carrying a feather weight, did not run badly but she probably needs returning to selling company. (tchd 33-1)
Miss Solo looked one of the more interesting runners beforehand having shown ability in maiden company on soft turf, but she had not been seen for almost four months and was well beaten. (op 5-1)
Valtat Official explanation: jockey said gelding hung badly right

6794 LINGFIELDPARK.CO.UK H'CAP — 5f (P)
2:50 (2:50) (Class 5) (0-75,75) 3-Y-O+ — **£2,914** (£867; £433; £216) **Stalls** High

Form — RPR

1406 **1** — **Halsion Chancer**[20] 6406 3-8-10 **67** .... JohnEgan 4 — 78
(J R Best) *trckd ldrs: rdn to chse ldr over 1f out: led ins fnl f: r.o wl* **7/2**[2]

3423 **2** *¾* **Financial Times (USA)**[6] 6708 5-9-4 **75** .... (t) MickyFenton 6 — 84
(Stef Liddiard) *sn pushed into ld: rdn 2f out: hdd ins fnl f: no ex* **10/3**[1]

501 **3** *1* **Expensive Art (IRE)**[13] 6559 3-8-11 **68** ow1 .... RichardHughes 7 — 73
(N A Callaghan) *stdd after s: hld up in rr: hdwy 2f out: drvn wl over 1f out: r.o fnl f: wnt 3rd last 100yds: nt rch ldrs* **7/1**

6340 **4** *nk* **Bluebok**[6] 6708 6-9-3 **74** .... (t) StephenDonohoe 3 — 78+
(J M Bradley) *chsd ldrs tl short of room and lost pl over 4f out: rdn and effrt over 2f out: r.o fnl f: nt rch ldrs* **8/1**

1020 **5** *shd* **Silver Prelude**[12] 6594 6-8-8 **65** .... OscarUrbina 10 — 69
(D K Ivory) *chsd ldr: rdn wl over 1f out: fdd last 100yds* **8/1**

5241 **6** *½* **Make My Dream**[12] 6594 4-8-7 **64** .... GregFairley 8 — 66+
(J Gallagher) *hld up towards rr on outer: rdn 2f out: kpt on but nvr pce to rch ldrs* **4/1**[3]

4000 **7** *nk* **Peter Island (FR)**[6] 6708 4-9-2 **73** .... (v) JimCrowley 5 — 74
(J Gallagher) *in tch: rdn over 2f out: kpt on same pce* **20/1**

0000 **8** *3½* **Peopleton Brook**[6] 6708 5-8-10 **67** .... (b) HayleyTurner 1 — 55
(J M Bradley) *s.i.s: sn chsng ldrs: rdn over 2f out: wknd jst over 1f out* **33/1**

3200 **9** *1¾* **Rocker**[51] 5642 3-8-11 **68** .... FrankieMcDonald 2 — 50
(B R Johnson) *racd in midfield tl dropped to rr wl over 3f out: lost tch 3f out: no ch after* **12/1**

58.05 secs (-1.73) **Going Correction** -0.30s/f (Stan) — **9** Ran SP% **115.4**
Speed ratings (Par 103): **101,99,98,97,97 96,96,90,87**
CSF £15.61 CT £76.51 TOTE £4.50: £1.40, £1.50, £2.00; EX 20.70.
Owner Halsion Ltd **Bred** Mrs S Hansford **Trained** Hucking, Kent

FOCUS
Just a fair sprint handicap, but the form looks sound and should work out. Once again most of these were keen to race off the far rail in the straight.

6795 LINGFIELD PARK FOR PARTIES H'CAP — 7f (P)
3:20 (3:21) (Class 5) (0-75,75) 3-Y-O+ — **£2,914** (£867; £433; £216) **Stalls** Low

Form — RPR

0130 **1** — **Titan Triumph**[29] 6203 3-9-4 **75** .... (t) PaulDoe 1 — 89+
(W J Knight) *hld up towards rr: hdwy 3f out: rdn wl over 1f out: str run to ld last 50yds* **4/1**[1]

0312 **2** *¾* **Teasing**[13] 6568 3-9-1 **72** .... RobertHavlin 9 — 80
(J Pearce) *hld up wl bhd: hdwy jst over 2f out: swtchd lft over 1f out: r.o wl fnl f: wnt 2nd nr fin* **13/2**[2]

4406 **3** *nk* **Carmenero (GER)**[8] 6667 4-9-3 **73** .... LiamJones 10 — 80
(W R Muir) *r din midfield: hdwy over 2f out: rdn to chse ldr over1f out: led ins fnl f: hdd and no ex last 50yds* **10/1**

065 **4** *nk* **Satyricon**[44] 5819 3-9-2 **73** .... (v) GregFairley 5 — 79
(M Botti) *chsd ldr: led over 2f out: rdn wl over 1f out: hdd ins fnl f: no ex last 100yds* **9/1**

0350 **5** *hd* **Perfect Treasure (IRE)**[18] 6450 4-9-3 **73** .... EddieAhern 6 — 79
(J A R Toller) *chsd ldrs: rdn to chse ldng pair over 1f out: kpt on same pce fnl f* **22/1**

0510 **6** *hd* **High 'n Dry (IRE)**[24] 6300 3-8-12 **69** .... (p) HayleyTurner 14 — 74+
(M A Allen) *dropped in bhd after s: wl bhd: stl last over 2f out: hdwy wl over 1f out: swtchd rt over 1f out: r.o strly fnl f: nt rch ldrs* **33/1**

0000 **7** *¾* **Binnion Bay (IRE)**[9] 6646 6-8-10 **66** .... (b) MickyFenton 2 — 69
(J J Bridger) *s.i.s: t.k.h: hld up wl in rr: rdn wl over 1f out: styd on fnl f: nt rch ldrs* **20/1**

1/40 **8** *1* **Tango Step (IRE)**[21] 6393 7-8-5 **61** .... (p) MCHussey 8 — 62
(Bernard Lawlor, Ire) *t.k.h: in tch: rdn 3f out: kpt on same pce u.p fnl f* **25/1**

6064 **9** *¾* **Mandarin Spirit (IRE)**[6] 6707 7-9-5 **75** .... (b) OscarUrbina 3 — 74
(G C H Chung) *racd in midfield: hdwy and rdn 2f out: no imp over 1f out* **9/1**

0002 **10** *nk* **Meditation**[6] 6710 5-8-5 **66** ow3 .... JamieJones(5) 11 — 64
(I A Wood) *chsd ldrs: rdn over 2f out: wknd over 1f out* **8/1**[3]

0200 **11** *1½* **Laish Ya Hajar (IRE)**[59] 5383 3-9-0 **71** .... RichardHughes 12 — 65
(P R Webber) *racd in midfield: rdn wl over 2f out: no hdwy* **10/1**

-100 **12** *1¼* **White Bear (FR)**[13] 6568 5-8-10 **66** .... (b) JohnEgan 4 — 56
(C R Dore) *a bhd: rdn 4f out: neve ron terms* **20/1**

1551 **13** *½* **Im Ova Ere Dad (IRE)**[14] 6547 4-9-4 **74** .... JimCrowley 13 — 63
(D E Cantillon) *dropped in bhd after s: a bhd* **4/1**[1]

32-0 **14** *6* **Mumaathel (IRE)**[35] 6062 4-9-4 **74** .... J-PGuillambert 7 — 47
(M A Buckley) *led at str pce: rdn and hdd over 2f out: wknd qckly over 1f out* **20/1**

1m 23.2s (-2.69) **Going Correction** -0.30s/f (Stan)
WFA 3 from 4yo+ 1lb — **14** Ran SP% **128.0**
Speed ratings (Par 103): **103,102,101,101,101 101,100,99,98,97 96,94,94,87**
CSF £28.02 CT £262.80 TOTE £5.80: £2.20, £2.20, £3.30; EX 38.80.
Owner Canisbay Bloodstock **Bred** Hesmonds Stud Ltd **Trained** Patching, W Sussex

FOCUS
A fair handicap run at a very strong pace, which favoured those held up. Good form for the grade, with the winner less exposed than most.
Binnion Bay(IRE) Official explanation: jockey said gelding missed the break
White Bear(FR) Official explanation: jockey said gelding hung right
Im Ova Ere Dad(IRE) Official explanation: jockey said gelding never travelled

6796 LINGFIELD PARK FOR CONFERENCES APPRENTICE H'CAP — 1m (P)
3:50 (3:52) (Class 6) (0-55,55) 3-Y-O+ — **£2,047** (£604; £302) **Stalls** High

Form — RPR

1 — **Confidentiality (IRE)**[47] 5743 3-8-7 **48** .... RobbieEgan(3) 10 — 57+
(M Wigham) *hld up in rr: stl last jst over 2f out: rdn and gd hdwy over 1f out: r.o strly to ld last 50yds: readily* **4/1**[2]

0021 **2** *¾* **Almahaza (IRE)**[35] 6060 3-9-3 **55** .... (b) HarryPoulton 4 — 59
(A J Chamberlain) *hld up in midfield: hdwy gng wl over 2f out: plld out jst over 1f out: rdn and r.o fnl f: wnt 2nd nr fin: nt pce of wnr* **10/1**

4040 **3** *nk* **Mythical Charm**[5] 6717 8-9-4 **54**......(t) JackDean 7 57
(J J Bridger) *s.i.s: t.k.h: hld up in midfield: hdwy over 3f out: rdn to ld over 1f out: clr jst ins fnl f: hdd and no ex last 50yds* **13/2**[3]

4600 **4** *¾* **Trevian**[20] 6407 6-9-3 **53**...... GaryBartley 8 55
(J M Bradley) *hld up bhd: hdwy jst over 2f out: r.o u.p fnl f: unable to chal* **10/1**

0323 **5** *¾* **Al Rayanah**[13] 6573 4-9-4 **54**...... JackMitchell 3 54
(G Prodromou) *s.i.s: hld up in midfield: rdn and hdwy on inner 2f out: kpt on fnl f: nt trble ldrs* **8/1**

6 *¾* **Railway Express (IRE)**[21] 6399 3-8-6 **47**...... JemmaMarshall(3) 11 45
(Bernard Lawlor, Ire) *hld up towards rr: hdwy over 3f out: chsd ldrs and rdn 2f out: keeping on same pce whn n.m.r and swtchd rt ins fnl f* **25/1**

333 **7** *nk* **Shunkawakhan (IRE)**[12] 6587 4-8-13 **49**......(p) WilliamCarson 5 47
(G C H Chung) *chsd ldr: rdn and ev ch 2f out: sn fnd little: btn 1f out* **3/1**[1]

4322 **8** *2 ½* **Shaheer (IRE)**[139] 2963 5-8-10 **53**......(v) SineadLogush(7) 1 45
(J Gallagher) *chsd ldr tl led over 5f out: hdd over 1f out: btn whn bmpd ins fnl f* **12/1**

62-0 **9** *1 ¾* **Coastal Breeze**[20] 6407 4-8-12 **53**...... MarkCoumbe(5) 6 41
(A J Chamberlain) *chsd ldrs: rdn wl over 2f out: wknd wl over 1f out* **50/1**

604 **10** *nk* **Witchingham**[31] 6480 3-8-9 **54**...... CharlesEddery(7) 9 41
(R Hannon) *led tl over 5f out: sn in midfield and pushed along: rdn wl over 2f out: no ch after* **14/1**

4040 **11** *2* **Tipsy Lad**[12] 6587 5-8-6 **45**......(bt) MatthewDavies(3) 2 28
(D J S Ffrench Davis) *a bhd: rdn and no rspnse 3f out* **8/1**

1000 **12** *13* **Inkjet (IRE)**[11] 6608 3-8-7 **50**...... RichardEvans(5) 12 3
(P D Evans) *racd wd: a bhd: rdn and btn over 2f out: hung lft wl over 1f out: t.o* **66/1**

1m 38.3s (-1.13) **Going Correction** -0.30s/f (Stan)
WFA 3 from 4yo+ 2lb **12** Ran SP% **120.4**
Speed ratings (Par 101): **93,92,91,91,90 89,89,86,85,84 82,69**
CSF £44.15 CT £264.49 TOTE £6.90: £2.20, £3.10, £2.80; EX 49.70 Place 6 £17.20, Place 5 £15.99.
Owner J M Cullinan **Bred** Kevin Foley **Trained** Newmarket, Suffolk
■ Stewards' Enquiry : Jemma Marshall two-day ban: careless riding (Nov 23-24)

FOCUS
A weak handicap restricted to apprentices who had not ridden more than 25 winners. The fiorm has been rated through the third and the fifth and the winner could go in again. The pace was steady and the winning time was modest, even for a race like this.
Inkjet(IRE) Official explanation: jockey said filly did not get the trip
T/Plt: £41.80 to a £1 stake. Pool: £47,159.85. 822.35 winning tickets. T/Qpdt: £12.00 to a £1 stake. Pool: £3,878.50. 237.50 winning tickets. SP

6761 WOLVERHAMPTON (A.W) (L-H)
Monday, November 12

OFFICIAL GOING: Standard
Wind: Nil Weather: Fine and dry

6797 BOOK TICKETS ONLINE AMATEUR RIDERS' H'CAP (DIV I) 1m 5f 194y(P)
1:00 (1:00) (Class 6) (0-65,65) 3-Y-0+ **£1,648** (£507; £253) **Stalls** Low

Form RPR

3406 **1** **Rickety Bridge (IRE)**[25] 6276 4-11-0 **65**...... MrSGoswell(7) 6 71
(P R Chamings) *hld up and bhd: gd hdwy on inner over 3f out: swtchd outside and effrt wl over 1f out: rdn to ld ent fnl f and sn clr* **3/1**[1]

1540 **2** *2 ½* **Theflyingscottie**[7] 6697 5-10-6 **50**......(v) MrsMMorris 5 53
(D Shaw) *hld up in rr: stdy hdwy 1/2-way: trckd ldng pair 3f out: swtchd rt and rdn to ld briefly over 1f out: drvn and hdd ent fnl f: one pce* **11/2**

3400 **3** *½* **Blue Hills**[84] 4670 6-10-10 **57**......(b) MrsMarieKing(3) 2 59
(P W Hiatt) *t.k.h: set stdy pce tl hdd after 5f: cl up on inner: effrt over 2f out: sn rdn and ev ch tl one pce appr fnl f* **4/1**[2]

4100 **4** *1* **I'll Do It Today**[30] 5364 6-10-6 **55**...... MissNJefferson(5) 7 55
(J M Jefferson) *hld up in rr: hdwy over 2f out: swtchd rt wl over 1f out: kpt on ins fnl f: nrst fin* **5/1**[3]

-000 **5** *nk* **Katie Kingfisher**[88] 4526 3-9-1 **46** oh1......(p) MrJPearce(7) 13 46
(M Wigham) *s.i.s and bhd: hdwy and in tch 1/2-way: rdn along wl over 2f out: swtchd lft over 1f out: kpt on ins fnl f: nrst fin* **80/1**

0500 **6** *1 ¾* **Lady's Law**[144] 2810 4-9-9 **46** oh1...... MissEmma-JaneJenkins(7) 3 44
(Rae Guest) *t.k.h: trckd ldrs: hdwy to ld 1/2-way: rdn along over 2f out: drvn and hdd over 1f out: wknd* **20/1**

0400 **7** *3* **Integration**[99] 2946 7-10-2 **51** oh1 ow5...... MrAMerriam(5) 12 44
(Miss M E Rowland) *in tch: chsd ldrs 1/2-way: sn rdn and wknd over 3f out* **28/1**

000- **8** *4* **Zalzaar (IRE)**[400] 5831 5-10-1 **52**...... MrAWedge(7) 1 40
(R T Phillips) *mdifield: rdn along 1/2-way: sn wknd* **33/1**

0052 **9** *5* **On Every Street**[43] 5835 6-10-1 **50**......(vt) MissRBastiman(5) 11 31
(R Bastiman) *prom: rdn along over 3f out: wknd over 2f out* **12/1**

4500 **10** *8* **Jenny Soba**[13] 6569 4-9-11 **46** oh1...... MrJPFeatherstone(5) 8 16
(Lucinda Featherstone) *prom: rdn along over 4f out and sn wknd* **28/1**

021- **11** *¾* **Kick And Prance**[233] 6068 4-10-7 **58**......(t) MissAGarner(7) 4 27
(J A Geake) *t.k.h: cl up: led after 5f: hdd and rdn along 1/2-way: sn wknd: bhd fnl 3f* **7/1**

3m 11.63s (4.26) **Going Correction** +0.025s/f (Slow)
WFA 3 from 4yo+ 8lb **11** Ran SP% **113.1**
Speed ratings (Par 101): **88,86,86,85,85 84,82,80,77,73 72**
CSF £17.48 CT £65.08 TOTE £4.80: £3.00, £2.00, £1.90; EX 22.30 Trifecta £40.00 Pool: £76.11 - 1.35 winning units..
Owner Mrs Ann Jenkins **Bred** Jockey Hall Kriva Syndicate **Trained** Baughurst, Hants
■ A first winner on his 12th ride for amateur jockey Simon Goswell, who was unseated while pulling up.

FOCUS
They went no pace at all early in this modest amateur event which caused a few to pull, but although things quickened up appreciably over the last half-mile the winning time was still 2.6 seconds slower than the second division. Pretty weak form.

6798 BOOK TICKETS ONLINE AMATEUR RIDERS' H'CAP (DIV II) 1m 5f 194y(P)
1:35 (1:35) (Class 6) (0-65,59) 3-Y-0+ **£1,648** (£507; £253) **Stalls** Low

Form RPR

06-6 **1** **Snowberry Hill (USA)**[23] 6341 4-10-10 **53**...... MrJPFeatherstone(5) 4 58
(Lucinda Featherstone) *hld up in tch: hdwy to trck ldrs 4f out: cl up on outer 2f out: rdn over 1f out: drvn ins fnl f and styd on to ld nr fin* **9/1**[3]

6402 **2** *nk* **Zalkani (IRE)**[20] 6407 7-11-4 **59**...... MrSPearce(3) 11 63
(J Pearce) *hld up in rr: stdy hdwy over 4f out: chsd ldrs over 2f out: rdn to ld over 1f out: edgd lft ins fnl f: hdd and no ex towards fin* **11/4**[1]

-140 **3** *nk* **Cumbrian Knight (IRE)**[30] 4096 9-11-0 **57**...... MissNJefferson(5) 7 61
(J M Jefferson) *dwlt: sn in midfield: hdwy over 4f out: squeezed through over 2f out and sn ev ch: rdn wl over 1f out: kpt on ins fnl f* **11/4**[1]

2000 **4** *½* **Mango Masher (IRE)**[60] 5347 3-10-5 **58**......(p) MrRPFlint(7) 5 61
(J L Flint) *t.k.h: trckd ldrs: hdwy to ld over 4f out: rdn 2f out: drvn and hdd over 1f out: kpt on u.p* **3/1**[2]

0000 **5** *1* **Royal Sailor (IRE)**[4] 6728 5-10-0 **45**...... MrDavidMcMinn(7) 6 47
(J Ryan) *hld up towards rr: hdwy over 4f out: rdn to chse ldrs wl over 1f out: kpt on u.p ins fnl f: nrst fin* **33/1**

00-4 **6** *3* **Larad (IRE)**[99] 4200 6-10-7 **45**......(b) MrsSMoore 8 42
(J S Moore) *in tch: hdwy 4f out: rdn to chse ldrs wl over 1f out: sn drvn and no imp* **9/1**[3]

0650 **7** *5* **Kitebrook**[23] 6341 6-10-0 **45**...... MissCSchaefer(7) 10 35
(Mrs Mary Hambro) *midfield: rdn along 4f out and sn outpcd* **80/1**

00U0 **8** *11* **Gatecrasher**[84] 4670 4-10-10 **55**......(b[1]) MrSeanKerr(7) 12 30
(G H Yardley) *prom: rdn along over 4f out and sn wknd* **33/1**

460 **9** *½* **Rusty Roof**[17] 6480 4-10-0 **45**...... MissEmma-JaneJenkins(7) 3 19
(Rae Guest) *led: rdn along and hdd over 4f out: drvn along 3f out and sn wknd* **40/1**

0400 **10** *5* **Always Baileys (IRE)**[101] 4124 4-10-7 **52**...... MrAWEdwards(5) 2 19
(T Wall) *dwlt: a in rr* **14/1**

603/ **11** *13* **Onefourseven**[1548] 4216 14-10-7 **45**...... MissFayeBramley 9 —
(Lucinda Featherstone) *prom: rdn along over 4f out and sn wknd* **25/1**

3m 9.03s (1.66) **Going Correction** +0.025s/f (Slow)
WFA 3 from 4yo+ 8lb **11** Ran SP% **118.4**
Speed ratings (Par 101): **96,95,95,95,94 93,90,83,83,80 73**
CSF £33.05 CT £88.86 TOTE £13.80: £3.10, £1.30, £1.20; EX 59.50 Trifecta £190.10 Part won. Pool: £267.75 - 0.85 winning units..
Owner J M Roundtree **Bred** Russell S Fisher And Joe Sagginario **Trained** Ashbourne, Derbyshire
■ Stewards' Enquiry : Mr J P Featherstone five-day ban: used whip with excessive force (Nov 27, Dec 3, 10, Jan 4, 14)

FOCUS
A more solid gallop than the first division and the time was 2.6 seconds faster, but a couple were still inclined to take a hold. Similarly weak form to division one, rated through the third with proximity of the fifth a worry.

6799 HOTEL & CONFERENCING AT WOLVERHAMPTON RACECOURSE MAIDEN STKS 5f 216y(P)
2:05 (2:07) (Class 5) 2-Y-0 **£2,968** (£876; £438) **Stalls** Low

Form RPR

2 **1** **Haybrook**[20] 6403 2-9-3 0...... ChrisCatlin 2 81
(E J O'Neill) *sn led: rdn clr wl over 1f out: drvn out* **13/8**[2]

4 **2** *1* **Lindelaan (USA)**[12] 6595 2-8-12 0...... RyanMoore 11 73+
(Sir Michael Stoute) *midfield: rdn along 1/2-way: hdwy on outer 2f out: str run on ent fnl f: kpt on: nt rch wnr* **6/4**[1]

5200 **3** *1 ¾* **Hawk Eyed Lady (IRE)**[48] 5707 2-8-12 73...... AdamKirby 3 68
(J A Osborne) *sn chsng ldrs: hdwy to chse wnr 2f out: sn rdn and kpt on same pce appr fnl f* **14/1**

002 **4** *1 ½* **Town And Gown**[28] 6228 2-8-12 73...... JimmyFortune 4 63
(J H M Gosden) *in tch on inner: hdwy to chse ldrs over 2f out: sn rdn and kpt on same pce appr fnl f* **4/1**[3]

5 **5** *1 ¾* **Annes Rocket (IRE)**[32] 6125 2-9-3 0...... PatDobbs 8 63
(J C Fox) *s.i.s: sn in midfield: hdwy to chse ldrs 1/2-way: rdn 2f out and kpt on same pce* **33/1**

6 *3* **Inontime (IRE)** 2-8-9 0...... AndrewElliott(3) 7 49
(K R Burke) *in rr tl styd on fnl 2f* **80/1**

5 **7** *½* **Ricci De Mare**[14] 6540 2-8-12 0...... JamieMackay 12 48
(Sir Mark Prescott) *s.i.s: a in rr* **66/1**

0400 **8** *shd* **Plaka (FR)**[47] 5729 2-8-12 63...... DavidKinsella 10 47
(J A Osborne) *chsd ldrs: rdn along 1/2-way: sn wknd* **66/1**

0204 **9** *1* **Tanley**[13] 6557 2-9-3 61...... DavidAllan 5 49
(J F Coupland) *cl up: rdn along 1/2-way: drvn 2f out and sn wknd* **50/1**

10 *1 ½* **Hollow Dream (IRE)** 2-8-7 0...... KevinGhunowa(5) 9 40
(R A Harris) *chsd ldrs to 1/2-way: sn wknd* **100/1**

04 **11** *2* **Silver Sprite**[7] 6694 2-9-3 0...... DeanMcKeown 13 39
(D Shaw) *in rr fr 1/2-way* **66/1**

00 **12** *nk* **Didntcomeback**[22] 6358 2-9-3 0...... FergusSweeney 1 38
(M S Saunders) *dwlt: a towards rr* **150/1**

1m 15.52s (-0.29) **Going Correction** +0.025s/f (Slow) **12** Ran SP% **117.0**
Speed ratings (Par 96): **102,100,98,96,94 90,89,89,87,85 83,82**
CSF £4.24 TOTE £2.70: £1.20, £1.40, £2.40; EX 5.80 Trifecta £22.10 Pool: £480.34 - 15.37 winning units..
Owner Mrs S J Brookhouse **Bred** Canary Thoroughbreds **Trained** Averham Park, Notts
■ Stewards' Enquiry : Tolley Dean two-day ban: struck filly before start with whip (Nov 23-24)

FOCUS
A very uncompetitive maiden despite the size of the field as several had little chance. The race eventually only concerned the market leaders, but the time was good so the principals are probably worth following, with the winner building on his nice debut.

NOTEBOOK
Haybrook ◆ confirmed the promise of his Lingfield second, form which has already been boosted, and bossed the race from the start. He should develop into a nice sprint handicapper. (op 2-1)
Lindelaan(USA) did not have the best of draws, but although she eventually flew home down the outside her market rival was already home and hosed. She improved for the extra furlong from Nottingham, but on this evidence she needs to go up in trip again. (op 7-4 tchd 15-8 and 11-8)
Hawk Eyed Lady(IRE), making her sand debut in her sixth outing, had every chance starting up the home straight but lacked the pace to get to the winner. This trip looked better than the 7f she attempted at Brighton last time and though she looks exposed now, she has the ability to win a routine Polytrack maiden. (op 10-1)
Town And Gown tried to get into the race on the home turn, but although she plodded on she could never land a blow. A line through the third suggests she did not quite run up to her official mark. (op 7-2 tchd 9-2)
Annes Rocket(IRE) was not totally disgraced on this sand debut and may be capable of a little improvement now that he can be handicapped. (op 25-1)

6800 COMBINE BUSINESS WITH PLEASURE WOLVERHAMPTON RACECOURSE NOVICE STKS 7f 32y(P)
2:40 (2:41) (Class 5) 2-Y-0 **£2,968** (£876; £438) **Stalls** High

Form RPR

2255 **1** **Ten Pole Tudor**[3] 6750 2-8-7 73...... KevinGhunowa(5) 4 74
(R A Harris) *prom: rdn to ld wl over 1f out: edgd lft ins fnl f: kpt on* **3/1**[2]

41 **2** *2* **Torch Of Freedom (IRE)**[9] 6641 2-9-2 83...... JamieMackay 5 73+
(Sir Mark Prescott) *unruly stalls and s.i.s: rapid hdwy to ld 1/2-way: rdn and hdd wl over 1f out: one pce* **8/11**[1]

0000 **3** *3* **Galley Slave (IRE)**[14] 6536 2-8-7 52...... RussellKennemore(5) 2 62
(M C Chapman) *prom: rdn along: n.m.r and lost pl 1/2-way: sn rdn and kpt on fr over 1f out* **100/1**

3025 **4** 1 1/2 **Little Bones**23 6329 2-8-7 56 DavidAllan 7 53
(J F Coupland) *in rr: hdwy over 2f out: sn rdn and kpt on same pce* **33/1**
05 **5** 3 **Waterloo Dock**99 4192 2-8-12 0 FrancisNorton 1 50
(M Quinn) *led: hdd and rdn 1/2-way: wknd over 2f out* **50/1**
1410 **6** 3 **Ambrose Princess (IRE)**17 6478 2-8-7 61 (p) ChrisCatlin 6 38
(R A Harris) *a in rr* **20/1**
4120 **U** **Thompsons Walls (IRE)**73 4995 2-9-0 83 (t) LeeEnstone 3 —
(P C Haslam) *t.k.h: trckd ldng pair whn clipped heels and uns rdr after 1f* **5/1**3

1m 31.25s (0.85) **Going Correction** +0.025s/f (Slow) 7 Ran SP% **110.2**
Speed ratings (Par 96): **96,93,90,88,85 81,—**
CSF £5.15 TOTE £3.10: £1.80, £1.10; EX 6.20.
Owner Mrs Jan Adams **Bred** Rockdown Investments **Trained** Earlswood, Monmouths

FOCUS
An eventful race with the odds-on favourite blowing the start and the third-favourite losing his rider after a furlong. The winner did it nicely, but is only ran to his pre-race mark, but the form may not be totally reliable.

NOTEBOOK
Ten Pole Tudor, back in a maiden and over a more suitable trip, responded well to pressure to get on top but his two market rivals made it much easier for him and he had little else to beat. (op 4-1)
Torch Of Freedom(IRE), up a furlong in trip, gave problems in the stalls and then gave away a significant amount of ground on breaking, probably as much as he was beaten by. He did get back into the race and was given every chance, but did not have enough in reserve to repel his main market rival. (op 4-5)
Galley Slave(IRE), making his sand debut after failing to make the first three in 12 outings on turf, on the face of it ran a cracker given how badly in he was at the weights, but this was a very unsatisfactory race so it may be best not to get too carried away.
Little Bones was not totally disgraced, but may be better off in modest handicaps over further. (op 28-1)
Thompsons Walls(IRE), best in at the weights and making his sand debut, raced very keenly just behind the leaders before losing his rider when clipping heels on the first bend. (op 7-2 tchd 11-2)

6801 WOLVERHAMPTON-RACECOURSE.CO.UK H'CAP (DIV I) 1m 1f 103y(P)
3:10 (3:10) (Class 6) (0-58,58) 3-Y-0+ **£1,706** (£503; £252) **Stalls** Low

Form RPR
3602 **1** **Waterloo Corner**24 6304 5-8-13 54 PaulMulrennan 9 61
(R Craggs) *trckd ldr: hdwy 3f out: rdn to ld wl over 1f out: kpt on* **4/1**3
0421 **2** 1 1/2 **Mighty Mover (IRE)**10 6627 5-9-2 57 ChrisCatlin 8 61
(B Palling) *led: rdn along over 2f out: drvn and hdd wl over 1f out: kpt on* **10/3**2
0246 **3** nk **Bobering**11 6613 7-8-7 48 DeanMcKeown 10 51+
(B P J Baugh) *hld up towards rr: hdwy over 4f out: rdn to chse ldrs 2f out: drvn and kpt on ins fnl f: nrst fin* **3/1**1
3022 **4** nk **Dot's Delight**47 5739 3-8-5 54 KevinGhunowa(5) 5 58
(R A Harris) *in tch: effrt to chse ldrs 3f out: rdn 2f out and kpt on same pce appr fnl f* **17/2**
3040 **5** 2 1/2 **Ella Y Rossa**21 6387 3-9-0 58 TGMcLaughlin 2 56
(P D Evans) *chsd ldrs: rdn along over 3f out: drvn over 2f out: grad wknd* **10/1**
00 **6** hd **Winter Cruise (IRE)**11 6612 3-8-9 53 FergusSweeney 7 51
(Ian Williams) *towards rr: hdwy 3f out: sn rdn and kpt on appr fnl f: nrst fin* **66/1**
6000 **7** 1 1/2 **Dictatrix**9 6640 4-8-9 50 (p) TomEaves 4 44
(P D Niven) *bhd tl sme late hdwy* **40/1**
5100 **8** 3 **Moyoko (IRE)**14 6529 4-8-11 52 PaulHanagan 3 39
(M Blanshard) *chsd ldrs: rdn along 3f out: sn drvn and wknd fnl 2f* **15/2**
5000 **9** 9 **Floodlight Fantasy**38 5983 4-8-12 53 (b) DaleGibson 1 22
(Jedd O'Keeffe) *chsd ldrs on inner: rdn along 4f out: wknd 3f out* **14/1**
0-00 **10** 2 **Oakley Absolute**15 1521 5-9-3 58 PatDobbs 6 22
(J C Fox) *a in rr* **25/1**
11 shd **Paddy's Isle (IRE)**110 3860 4-8-2 46 oh1 AndrewElliott(3) 11 —
(A J McCabe) *a in rr* **25/1**
6000 **12** 8 **No Inkling (IRE)**136 2795 4-8-5 46 oh1 FrancisNorton 12 —
(Miss M E Rowland) *a in rr* **125/1**

2m 1.84s (-0.78) **Going Correction** +0.025s/f (Slow)
WFA 3 from 4yo+ 3lb 12 Ran SP% **118.5**
Speed ratings (Par 101): **104,102,102,102,99 99,98,95,87,85 85,78**
CSF £17.07 CT £45.86 TOTE £4.90: £1.50, £2.00, £1.50; EX 20.80 Trifecta £56.40 Pool: £270.38 - 3.40 winning units..
Owner Ray Craggs **Bred** R Craggs **Trained** Sedgefield, Co Durham

FOCUS
A very moderate handicap, and hard to rate the form positively. The pace was ordinary and the front pair were always prominent.
Oakley Absolute Official explanation: jockey said gelding hung left

6802 WEATHERBYS PRINTING H'CAP 2m 119y(P)
3:40 (3:40) (Class 5) (0-75,79) 3-Y-0+ **£2,968** (£876; £438) **Stalls** Low

Form RPR
0035 **1** **Inchpast**10 6622 6-9-6 67 (b) PaulMulrennan 4 76
(M H Tompkins) *in tch: hdwy to chse ldrs 1/2-way: rdn along on inner 4f out: swtchd outside and drvn wl over 1f out: styd on wl u.p ins fnl f to ld last 75yds* **14/1**
2000 **2** 1 **Noble Minstrel**64 5256 4-9-8 69 (t) SaleemGolam 2 77
(S C Williams) *trckd ldrs: hdwy to chse clr ldr over 4f out: led 3f out: rdn clr wl over 1f out: drvn ins fnl f: hdd and no ex last 75yds* **15/2**3
3441 **3** 2 **Mr Mischief**13 6564 7-9-0 66 RussellKennemore(5) 13 72
(M C Chapman) *hld up in rr: stdy hdwy over 5f out: trckd ldrs 3f out: rdn to chse ldr 2f out: sn rdn: edgd lft and one pce ent fnl f* **8/1**
1101 **4** 2 1/2 **Estate**4 6733 5-9-11 79 6ex MCGeran(7) 7 82
(E J O'Neill) *hld up in rr: hdwy 4f out: rdn along 2f out: dxriven and kpt on ins fnl f* **15/8**1
2215 **5** hd **Right Option (IRE)**4 6739 3-8-7 68 KevinGhunowa(5) 6 70
(J L Flint) *hld up: hdwy to chse ldrs over 4f out: rdn to chse ldr over 2f out: sn drvn and wknd* **8/1**
-433 **6** 6 **Golano**18 6459 7-9-9 70 PatDobbs 9 65
(P R Webber) *hld up towards rr: hdwy 5f out: rdn along over 3f out and sn no imp* **10/1**
0425 **7** 5 **Arabian Sun**9 6643 3-8-4 60 (v) ChrisCatlin 3 49
(M J Attwater) *bhd: rdn along 1/2-way: nvr a factor* **7/1**2
-652 **8** 5 **Calatagan (IRE)**13 6561 8-9-7 68 PaulHanagan 12 51
(J M Jefferson) *led and sn clr: rdn along 4f out: hdd 3f out and sn wknd* **14/1**
3005 **9** 5 **Victory Quest (IRE)**35 6054 7-8-12 59 (v) TomEaves 5 36
(Mrs S Lamyman) *prom: rdn along over 4f out and sn wknd* **25/1**
/665 **10** 28 **Rightful Ruler**79 3927 5-8-2 56 oh1 LanceBetts(7) 11 —
(N Wilson) *prom: rdn along 6f out: sn wknd* **33/1**
0-00 **11** 7 **Honduras (SWI)**16 6490 6-10-0 75 GeorgeBaker 8 10
(G L Moore) *chsd ldrs: rdn along over 5f out and sn wknd* **12/1**
0006 **P** **Jamaican Flight (USA)**154 2505 14-8-6 56 oh11 AndrewMullen(3) 1 —
(Mrs S Lamyman) *chsd ldrs tl lost pl qckly and p.u after 7f* **100/1**

3m 38.57s (-4.56) **Going Correction** +0.025s/f (Slow)
WFA 3 from 4yo+ 9lb 12 Ran SP% **119.2**
Speed ratings (Par 103): **111,110,109,108,108 105,103,100,98,85 81,—**
CSF £114.48 CT £912.00 TOTE £20.70: £4.40, £2.20, £3.80; EX 194.50 TRIFECTA Not won..
Owner Marcoe Racing Welwyn **Bred** Stanley Estate And Stud Co **Trained** Newmarket, Suffolk
■ Stewards' Enquiry : Kevin Ghunowa four-day ban: failed to ride out for 4th place (Nov 23-26)

FOCUS
A very decent winning time for a race of its class, although it was just about the only truly-run race on the card. Good form for the grade, and it should work out.
Honduras(SWI) Official explanation: jockey said gelding had no more to give
Jamaican Flight(USA) Official explanation: trainer later said colt was found to have pulled muscles in hindquarters

6803 HOLIDAY INN WOLVERHAMPTON H'CAP 1m 4f 50y(P)
4:10 (4:10) (Class 6) (0-65,67) 3-Y-0+ **£2,047** (£604; £302) **Stalls** Low

Form RPR
00-1 **1** **Alonso De Guzman (IRE)**37 6026 3-8-11 57 PatCosgrave 4 61+
(J R Boyle) *hld up in tch: hdwy 3f out: rdn to chse ldrs over 1f out: drvn and styd on ins fnl f to ld last 75yds* **7/4**1
5130 **2** nk **Raquel White**98 4231 3-8-9 60 KevinGhunowa(5) 10 64
(J L Flint) *t.k.h: trckd ldr: hdwy to chal 3f out: rdn to ld over 1f out: drvn ins fnl f: hdd and no ex last 75yds* **8/1**
0130 **3** hd **Giddywell**46 5755 3-8-7 53 ow1 DeanMcKeown 8 57
(R Hollinshead) *hld up towards rr: hdwy whn n.m.r 3f out and again 2f out: swtchd lft and rdn over 1f out: styd on wl fnl f* **25/1**
0/00 **4** 1 1/2 **Leighton (IRE)**12 6577 7-9-0 54 (v1) FergusSweeney 9 55
(M S Saunders) *hld up in rr: hdwy on outer over 3f out: rdn to chse ldrs wl over 1f out: drvn and one pce ins fnl f* **28/1**
5 1/2 **Nora Chrissie (IRE)**57 5461 5-8-13 56 (v1) JerryO'Dwyer(3) 7 56
(Niall Moran, Ire) *hld up towards rr: hdwy and in tch 1/2-way: rdn along to chse ldrs over 2f out: sn drvn and one pce* **16/1**
00-0 **6** 1/2 **Always Sparkle (CAN)**126 3366 3-8-13 59 ChrisCatlin 2 59
(B Palling) *led: rdn along over 3f out: drvn over 2f out: hdd over 1f out and grad wknd* **14/1**
4031 **7** 1 1/2 **Sforzando**5 6727 6-9-13 67 6ex TomEaves 5 64
(Mrs L Stubbs) *trckd ldrs: effrt over 2f out and sn rdn along: hld whn n.m.r over 1f out* **4/1**3
2410 **8** 1 1/2 **Compton Dragon (USA)**16 6500 8-9-8 62 GeorgeBaker 3 57
(W M Brisbourne) *hld up: a in rr* **11/4**2
-000 **9** 9 **Safin (GER)**12 6583 7-9-0 54 TGMcLaughlin 1 34
(F Jordan) *chsd ldrs on inner: rdn along over 3f out: drvn over 2f out and sn wknd* **40/1**
0/00 **10** 32 **Dashing Dane**62 5299 7-8-8 48 oh3 DaleGibson 6 —
(Mrs Marjorie Fife) *chsd ldrs: rdn along 4f out: sn wknd* **150/1**

2m 42.49s (0.07) **Going Correction** +0.025s/f (Slow)
WFA 3 from 5yo+ 6lb 10 Ran SP% **117.1**
Speed ratings (Par 101): **100,99,99,98,98 98,97,96,90,68**
CSF £16.54 CT £263.53 TOTE £2.70: £1.20, £2.80, £2.40; EX 19.70 Trifecta £133.50 Pool: £560.40 - 2.98 winning units..
Owner M Khan X2 **Bred** G And Mrs Middlebrook **Trained** Epsom, Surrey
■ Stewards' Enquiry : Pat Cosgrave one-day ban: used whip in incorrect place without giving gelding time to respond (Nov 24)

FOCUS
A weakish handicap which was slowly run. The winner did not need to improve but is very likely to rate higher.

6804 WOLVERHAMPTON-RACECOURSE.CO.UK H'CAP (DIV II) 1m 1f 103y(P)
4:40 (4:40) (Class 6) (0-58,57) 3-Y-0+ **£1,706** (£503; £252) **Stalls** Low

Form RPR
1600 **1** **Moonlight Fantasy (IRE)**10 6179 4-8-10 50 TGMcLaughlin 2 56
(Lucinda Featherstone) *rrd and lost svrl ls: midfield and t.k.h after 3f: hdwy to chse ldrs 2f out: rdn ent fnl f: squeezed through on inner to ld last 100yds* **18/1**
001 **2** 1/2 **Formidable Guest**12 6590 3-8-6 49 DavidKinsella 1 54
(J Pearce) *a.p: cl up over 3f out: rdn wl over 1f out and ev ch tl drvn ins fnl f and no ex last 100yds* **13/2**
-012 **3** 1 1/2 **Kirstys Lad**10 6627 5-9-2 56 GeorgeBaker 4 58
(M Mullineaux) *led: rdn along over 2f out: drvn over 1f out: hdd and no ex last 100yds* **11/4**1
2043 **4** 1/2 **Weet Yer Tern (IRE)**18 6458 5-8-13 53 FergusSweeney 6 54
(W M Brisbourne) *hld up: stdy hdwy to trck ldrs over over 3f out: effrt 2f out: sn rdn and kpt on ins fnl f* **3/1**2
4046 **5** 1 1/2 **Komreyev Star**101 4129 5-8-5 45 PaulHanagan 3 43
(R E Peacock) *prom: effrt 3f out: rdn along 2f out and ev ch tl drvn and wknd ent fnl f* **11/2**3
0000 **6** 9 **Oh Danny Boy**12 5704 6-8-5 48 DominicFox(3) 8 27
(M C Chapman) *chsd ldrs: rdn along over 3f out: drvn and wknd over 2f out* **50/1**
6/60 **7** 6 **Grey Gurkha**33 6100 6-9-1 55 TomEaves 5 21
(B Ellison) *in tch: rdn along 1/2-way: wknd 4f out* **10/1**
060- **8** 1 **Dark Society**436 4585 9-8-11 51 VinceSlattery 11 15
(A W Carroll) *a in rr* **33/1**
0-05 **9** 1 **Swayze (IRE)**13 6570 4-9-3 57 FrancisNorton 10 19
(M Quinn) *chsd ldrs: rdn along over 3f out: drvn over 2f out and sn wknd: bled fr nose* **8/1**
0- **10** 17 **Summerville Star (IRE)**72 5056 3-8-8 54 ow1 JerryO'Dwyer(3) 7 —
(Michael McElhone, Ire) *a in rr* **25/1**
50P **P** **Istibian (IRE)**29 6206 3-8-5 55 GHannon(7) 9 —
(Mrs H Sweeting) *chsd ldrs tl rn wd bnd after 3f: sn virtually ref to r and t.o: p.u over 3f out* **66/1**

2m 3.46s (0.84) **Going Correction** +0.025s/f (Slow)
WFA 3 from 4yo+ 3lb 11 Ran SP% **116.1**
Speed ratings (Par 101): **97,96,95,94,93 85,80,79,78,63 —**
CSF £125.72 CT £427.78 TOTE £23.40: £3.20, £2.30, £1.40; EX 132.20 Trifecta £441.30 Pool: £621.69 - 1.00 winning units. Place 6 £9.91, Place 5 £6.54.
Owner J Roundtree **Bred** Rockhart Trading Ltd **Trained** Ashbourne, Derbyshire

FOCUS
The pace was nowhere near as strong in this second division. Weak form, and dubious too.
Swayze(IRE) Official explanation: jockey said gelding had bled from the nose
T/Plt: £10.80 to a £1 stake. Pool: £45,951.50. 3,082.25 winning tickets. T/Qpdt: £6.50 to a £1 stake. Pool: £2,495.40. 282.50 winning tickets. JR

6773 KEMPTON (A.W) (R-H)
Wednesday, November 14

OFFICIAL GOING: Standard
Wind: Nil Weather: Chilly

6805 EUROPEAN BREEDERS' FUND MEDIAN AUCTION MAIDEN STKS 1m (P)
6:20 (6:20) (Class 6) 2-Y-O **£2,388** (£705; £352) **Stalls** High

Form				RPR
3202	1		**Howdigo**[14] 6585 2-9-3 81 GeorgeBaker 14 (J R Best) *lw: hld up in tch in midfield: swtchd lft 2f out: shkn up and hdwy over 1f out: qcknd to ld last 100yds: comf* **10/11**[1]	79+
	2	1	**Two Left Feet** 2-9-3 0 AdamKirby 8 (W R Swinburn) *w'like: chsd ldng pair: hdwy to ld over 1f out: hdd and outpcd by wnr last 100yds* **16/1**	73
	3	1 1/4	**Cozy Tiger (USA)** 2-9-3 0 NeilPollard 9 (W J Musson) *str: w'like: bit bkwd: hld up towards rr: hdwy on inner wl over 1f out: r.o wl to go 3rd ins fnl f: nt rch ldrs* **50/1**	70
04	4	2	**Coole Dodger (IRE)**[11] 6641 2-9-3 0 TQuinn 3 (B G Powell) *t.k.h: chsd ldr tl led 6f out: rdn and hdd over 1f out: wknd ins fnl furlong* **25/1**	66
	5	1/2	**Danse The Blues** 2-8-12 0 TPQueally 13 (E A L Dunlop) *leggy: scope: lw: hld up in midfield: hdwy over 2f out: chsd ldrs and rdn over 1f out: wknd 1f out* **9/2**[2]	60
00	6	1/2	**Kiribati King (IRE)**[15] 6574 2-9-3 0 DarryllHolland 6 (M R Channon) *chsd ldrs: rdn over 2f out: outpcd over 1f out: kpt on* **33/1**	63
2004	7	1 1/4	**Vigano (IRE)**[10] 6665 2-9-3 70 JDSmith 7 (S Kirk) *in tch in midfield: rdn 3f out: kpt on same pce last 2f* **9/1**[3]	61
0	8	nk	**Whitcombe Spirit**[42] 5919 2-9-3 0 PaulDoe 10 (Jamie Poulton) *s.i.s: bhd: rdn wl over 2f out: styd on past btn horses fnl f: n.d* **14/1**	60+
0	9	1/2	**Smetana**[14] 6593 2-9-3 0 RobertHavlin 1 (H Morrison) *leggy: chsd ldrs: rdn over 2f out: wknd over 1f out* **20/1**	59
04	10	2	**Jasoora**[20] 6456 2-8-12 0 PatDobbs 2 (M P Tregoning) *a towards rr: rdn wl over 2f out: no hdwy* **25/1**	50
06	11	shd	**Astrodome**[5] 6748 2-9-3 0 JamieMackay 11 (Sir Mark Prescott) *s.i.s: a bhd* **66/1**	54+
	12	2 1/2	**Neyraan** 2-8-12 0 GregFairley 12 (M Johnston) *unf: led tl 6f out: chsd ldr tl over 2f out: sn wknd* **14/1**	44
0	13	2	**Rutba**[14] 6585 2-8-12 0 RHills 5 (M P Tregoning) *a bhd: plld out and rdn over 2f out: no hdwy* **25/1**	39
60	14	32	**Palmer's Green**[15] 6571 2-9-3 0 TGMcLaughlin 4 (Mrs C A Dunnett) *s.i.s: sn rdn along: a bhd: virtually p.u fnl f: t.o* **100/1**	—

1m 39.87s (-0.93) **Going Correction** -0.15s/f (Stan) **14** Ran SP% **123.5**
Speed ratings (Par 94): **98,97,95,93,93 92,91,91,90,88 88,86,84,52**
CSF £17.11 TOTE £1.70: £1.10, £4.90, £6.70; EX 25.30.
Owner G G Racing **Bred** J R Wills **Trained** Hucking, Kent

FOCUS
A real range of abilities on show – a couple were fairly exposed, a couple had shown a modicum of promise in limited tries and a couple of interesting newcomers – so quite what the form will amount to is anyone's guess. Howdigo did not need to quite match his good Lingfield run to score.

NOTEBOOK
Howdigo looked to have been given enough chances to win already and his form figures did not look that promising. Things seemed fairly bleak for him two furlongs from home, but all of a sudden he picked up and won with a bit in hand. He will have a break now and come back next year. (op 11-10 tchd 5-4 in places)
Two Left Feet, who had already been gelded before this debut, travelled nicely throughout and looked to have made a winning move just over a furlong from home. There was no denying the promise of this effort and he can win his maiden. (op 12-1)
Cozy Tiger(USA), a 20,000gns newcomer by Hold That Tiger, was towards the rear early but came with a nice-looking effort up the home straight. The ability is definitely there and he too looks sure to pick up a race. (op 33-1)
Coole Dodger(IRE) was quite keen early on and held the lead until caught about a furlong from home. A drop back down in trip will be in his favour. (op 20-1)
Danse The Blues was solid in the market for her debut and ran a reasonable race. Lack of experience may have cost her.
Kiribati King(IRE) found this quicker surface much more to his liking and will be interesting when moved into handicap company. (op 25-1)
Vigano(IRE) had every chance and was not good enough. (op 8-1)
Astrodome is built like his half-sister, Alambic, and will no doubt do better at three.

6806 REUTERS FIRST FOR NEWS CLAIMING STKS 1m (P)
6:50 (6:50) (Class 6) 3-Y-O+ **£2,047** (£604; £302) **Stalls** High

Form				RPR
0006	1		**Rebellious Spirit**[11] 6642 4-9-1 72 EddieAhern 14 (P W Hiatt) *mde al: hrd pressed and rdn 2f out: r.o gamely: all out* **12/1**	73
0000	2	nk	**Pianoforte (USA)**[6] 6732 5-9-3 58 (b) MickyFenton 12 (E J Alston) *t.k.h: hld up in midfield: hdwy on inner over 2f out: n.m.r 1f out: swtchd lft ins fnl f: r.o: nt quite rch wnr* **20/1**	74
-420	3	3/4	**Given A Choice (IRE)**[29] 6253 5-9-3 82 TPQueally 8 (J G Given) *hld up bhd: hdwy and nt clr run over 2f out: swtchd rt 2f out: r.o wl fnl f: wnt 3rd last strides: nt rch ldrs* **11/2**[2]	72
06	4	hd	**Benllech**[91] 4509 3-8-13 82 LPKeniry 10 (S Kirk) *t.k.h: hld up wl in tch: hdwy to trck wnr gng wl over 2f out: shkn up 2f out: ev ch and drvn 1f out: fnd little: fdd last 100yds* **13/2**	70
3114	5	1	**Samuel Charles**[8] 6710 9-9-1 70 (p) AdamKirby 11 (C R Dore) *lw: chsd wnr tl over 2f out: sn drvn: kpt on same pce* **7/2**[1]	68
6030	6	1/2	**Zennerman (IRE)**[66] 5253 4-9-3 74 (p) DaneO'Neill 1 (K A Ryan) *hld up in midfield: rdn over 2f out: c wd wl over 1f out: styd on fnl f: nt trble ldrs* **6/1**[3]	68
2202	7	1	**Chief Exec**[51] 5687 5-9-3 69 HaddenFrost(5) 2 (B J Llewellyn) *s.i.s: hld up in midfield on outer: rdn and hdwy over 3f out: no imp last 2f* **16/1**	71
4650	8	nk	**Mountain Pass (USA)**[162] 2331 5-8-2 56 (p) DavidProbert(7) 7 (B J Llewellyn) *s.i.s: hld up bhd: rdn over 2f out: styd on past btn horses fnl f: n.d* **40/1**	57
0601	9	shd	**General Knowledge (USA)**[11] 6642 4-9-7 72 (t) TQuinn 5 (B G Powell) *lw: t.k.h: in tch: rdn over 2f out: sn outpcd* **10/1**	69
0200	10	shd	**Bustan (IRE)**[14] 6596 8-9-11 81 J-PGuillambert 4 (G C Bravery) *trckd ldng pair: ev ch and rdn wl over 2f out: wknd 2f out* **11/2**[2]	73
0000	11	2 1/2	**Pont Wood**[11] 6642 3-8-7 46 SimonWhitworth 13 (Mrs N S Evans) *s.i.s: t.k.h: hld up in rr: nvr on terms* **66/1**	51
0440	12	1/2	**Meeting Of Minds**[57] 5497 3-8-4 50 HayleyTurner 3 (W Jarvis) *s.i.s: a bhd* **66/1**	47
600	13	3/4	**Art Gallery**[9] 5894 3-8-7 47 (b) FergusSweeney 9 (G L Moore) *t.k.h: hld up in midfield: rdn wl over 2f out: sn btn* **50/1**	48
-640	14	nk	**Schoenberg (USA)**[44] 5873 3-8-9 70 (p) RobertHavlin 6 (C R Egerton) *t.k.h: chsd ldr: rdn 3f out: wknd over 2f out* **14/1**	50

1m 39.56s (-1.24) **Going Correction** -0.15s/f (Stan)
WFA 3 from 4yo+ 2lb **14** Ran SP% **122.1**
Speed ratings (Par 101): **100,99,98,98,97 97,96,95,95,95 93,92,92,91**
CSF £240.12 TOTE £20.50: £5.70, £5.50, £2.80; EX 556.00.
Owner Mrs Lucia Stockley & Ken Read **Bred** Car Colston Hall Stud **Trained** Hook Norton, Oxon
■ Stewards' Enquiry : T P Queally two-day ban: used whip above shoulder height with excessive force (Nov 26-27)

FOCUS
Plenty of old favourites lined up for this competitive race. General Knowledge had beaten the winner last time, but that form was reversed. There are doubts over how solid this form will prove.

6807 DIGIBET MEDIAN AUCTION MAIDEN STKS 1m 3f (P)
7:20 (7:21) (Class 6) 3-5-Y-O **£2,047** (£604; £302) **Stalls** High

Form				RPR
5004	1		**Highest Esteem**[16] 6534 3-9-3 56 (p) GeorgeBaker 5 (G L Moore) *a gng wl: trckd ldng pair: plld out and shkn up to chal over 2f out: pushed into ld over 1f out: rdn clr: eased nr fin* **5/4**[1]	72+
6425	2	4	**Auntie Mame**[47] 5783 3-8-12 58 TPQueally 6 (D J Coakley) *mounted on crse: chsd ldr: rdn and ev ch over 2f out: nt pce of wnr fnl f: wnt 2nd ins fnl f* **5/1**[3]	55
	3	hd	**Scary** 3-9-3 0 TQuinn 9 (P F I Cole) *unf: scope: b.hind: sn rdn to ld: rdn over 2f out: hdd over 1f out: sn outpcd by wnr: lost 2nd ins fnl f* **5/2**[2]	60
5355	4	5	**Scaramouscha**[231] 808 4-9-8 52 NeilPollard 1 (G C Bravery) *hld up towards rr: hdwy to chse ldrs over 4f out: rdn and btn 3f out* **10/1**	51
	5	3	**Imminent Victory**[242] 4-9-8 0 EddieAhern 4 (R M H Cowell) *s.i.s: sn pushed up to chse ldrs: rdn and btn over 2f out* **11/1**	46
0000	6	1 1/2	**Keagles (ITY)**[28] 6266 4-9-3 35 RichardThomas 8 (J E Long) *in tch in midfield: reminders over 6f out: rdn over 3f out: wknd 3f out* **66/1**	39
	7	20	**Highlands Skye** 3-8-12 0 LPKeniry 2 (L Montague Hall) *w'like: s.i.s: a wl bhd: t.o last 3f* **50/1**	5
000-	8	2	**Fun Thai**[331] 6859 3-8-12 38 HayleyTurner 10 (A J Chamberlain) *a bhd: rdn and lost tch 5f out: t.o* **66/1**	1
60/0	9	13	**Aldbury Grey (IRE)**[7] 6716 4-9-3 60 DaneO'Neill 7 (A B Haynes) *a wl bhd: t.o last 3f* **25/1**	—
0	10	1/2	**The Flying Phenom**[160] 573 4-9-3 0 HaddenFrost(5) 3 (J D Frost) *racd wd: t.k.h: in tch in midfield tl rdn and lost pl 6f out: t.o over 2f out* **33/1**	—

2m 21.79s (-0.89) **Going Correction** -0.15s/f (Stan)
WFA 3 from 4yo 5lb **10** Ran SP% **118.8**
Speed ratings (Par 101): **97,94,93,90,88 87,72,71,61,61**
CSF £7.97 TOTE £2.30: £1.10, £1.30, £1.50; EX 9.90.
Owner Paul Green **Bred** Paul Green **Trained** Woodingdean, E Sussex

FOCUS
A weak maiden in which the first two set a pretty modest standard, and it is unlikely to prove very informative in the future.
Aldbury Grey(IRE) Official explanation: jockey said filly lost its action

6808 DIGIBET.COM H'CAP 1m 3f (P)
7:50 (7:50) (Class 6) (0-65,65) 3-Y-O **£2,047** (£604; £302) **Stalls** High

Form				RPR
6004	1		**Altos Reales**[54] 5606 3-8-5 52 oh6 ow1 DeanMcKeown 6 (D Shaw) *hld up in last: rdn and gd hdwy to ld 2f out: hung lft over 1f out: r.o strly fnl f* **12/1**	58
3110	2	2 1/2	**Polyquest (IRE)**[10] 6673 3-9-4 65 NickyMackay 2 (G A Butler) *lw: hld up in tch: rdn and effrt 3f out: kpt on u.p but nt pce of wnr: wnt 2nd towards fin* **5/2**[3]	67
012	3	nk	**Formidable Guest**[2] 6804 3-8-4 51 oh2 DavidKinsella 3 (J Pearce) *hld up trcking ldng pair: led gng wl over 2f out: sn rdn: kpt on same pce u.p fnl f* **9/4**[2]	52
0-30	4	11	**Lap Of The Gods**[15] 6570 3-8-4 51 oh4 (p) ChrisCatlin 5 (Miss Z C Davison) *chsd ldr tl 4f out: sn rdn: wknd 3f out* **20/1**	34
0-10	5	8	**Me Fein**[37] 6056 3-8-9 56 TPQueally 4 (B J Curley) *lw: led: rdn and hdd over 2f out: sn btn: eased fnl f* **6/4**[1]	25

2m 22.33s (-0.35) **Going Correction** -0.15s/f (Stan) **5** Ran SP% **111.8**
Speed ratings (Par 98): **95,93,92,84,79**
CSF £42.08 TOTE £20.70: £4.70, £1.40; EX 32.50.
Owner Danethorpe Racing Partnership **Bred** Goldford Stud And P E Clinton **Trained** Danethorpe, Notts

FOCUS
This was a weakish event after a couple of withdrawals. The third is the best guide to the form. The winner is still unexposed and can win again, while Ma Fein has lost the plot after a good start to the year.
Me Fein Official explanation: trainer had no explanation for the poor form shown

6809 DIGIBET SPORTS BETTING H'CAP 7f (P)
8:20 (8:20) (Class 6) (0-52,52) 3-Y-O+ **£2,047** (£604; £302) **Stalls** High

Form				RPR
6016	1		**Ceris Star (IRE)**[18] 6505 3-8-11 50 ChrisCatlin 11 (B R Millman) *t.k.h: chsd ldrs: rdn to ld over 1f out: drvn and doing enough fnl f* **7/1**[3]	58
6600	2	nk	**Perfect Practice**[173] 2008 3-8-13 52 AdamKirby 14 (C G Cox) *chsd ldrs: rdn and effrt on inner over 2f out: ev ch over 1f out: kpt on u.p: wnt 2nd nr fin* **10/1**	59
6426	3	hd	**Ganache (IRE)**[14] 6582 5-9-0 52 JimCrowley 1 (P R Chamings) *chsd ldr: rdn over 2f out: ev ch over 1f out: kpt on u.p: lost 2nd nr fin* **9/1**	58
0640	4	1 1/2	**Isobel Rose (IRE)**[14] 6594 3-8-13 52 FrancisNorton 10 (J L Spearing) *hld up in midfield: rdn and hdwy over 2f out: styd on u.p fnl f: nt pce to rch ldrs* **16/1**	54
5031	5	1/2	**Jessica Wigmo**[3] 6778 4-8-8 51 6ex RussellKennemore(5) 4 (A W Carroll) *stdd and dropped in after s: hld up in rr: hdwy wl over 2f out: kpt on same pce u.p fnl f* **8/1**	52
2502	6	shd	**Palais Polaire**[7] 6717 5-8-13 51 DavidKinsella 13 (J A Geake) *taken down early: s.i.s: sn pushed up into midfield: effort and hung rt over 2f out: chsd ldrs and rdn over 1f out: no imp* **4/1**[1]	52

5004 **7** *nk* **Is It Time (IRE)**[14] 6582 3-8-13 **52**.................... RobertHavlin 8 52
(Mrs P N Dutfield) *sn led: rdn over 2f out: hdd over 1f out: fdd ins fnl f* **25/1**

3000 **8** *1* **Epidaurian King (IRE)**[8] 6706 4-8-12 **50**.................. DeanMcKeown 12 47
(D Shaw) *hld up in rr: hdwy on inner over 2f out: no imp jst over 1f out* **14/1**

0000 **9** *2* **Royal Orissa**[14] 6579 5-8-11 **49**.......................... HayleyTurner 7 41
(D Haydn Jones) *taken down early: t.k.h: chsd ldr: rdn 3f out: sn struggling* **6/1[2]**

0605 **10** *½* **Ruthles Philly**[14] 6580 3-8-13 **52**.......................... FergusSweeney 9 43
(G L Moore) *t.k.h: hld up in midfield: rdn wl over 2f out: sn outpcd* **20/1**

3300 **11** *2* **Mind Alert**[151] 2664 6-9-0 **52**..........................(v) DaneO'Neill 2 37
(D Shaw) *awkward leaving stalls: hld up bhd: swtchd lft and rdn over 2f out: nvr nr ldrs* **12/1**

-003 **12** *2* **Dado Mush**[16] 6537 4-8-12 **50**..........................(p) TGMcLaughlin 5 30
(T T Clement) *t.k.h: in tch in midfield: rdn 3f out: sn outpcd* **20/1**

06-0 **13** *½* **Opus Magnus (IRE)**[305] 124 4-8-13 **51**.................... EddieAhern 3 29
(P J Makin) *lw: racd wd: in tch in midfield: rdn and lost pl 3f out: sn wl btn* **11/1**

-000 **14** *½* **Mocha Java**[65] 5275 4-8-12 **50**..........................(p) RichardKingscote 6 27
(B G Powell) *a bhd* **28/1**

1m 25.62s (-1.18) **Going Correction** -0.15s/f (Stan)
WFA 3 from 4yo+ 1lb **14** Ran SP% **122.4**
Speed ratings (Par 101): **100,99,99,97,97 97,96,95,93,92 90,88,87,86**
CSF £72.44 CT £663.83 TOTE £9.00: £2.30, £4.90, £3.30; EX 136.30.
Owner Mrs S A J Kinsella-Hurley **Bred** Peter Harms **Trained** Kentisbeare, Devon

FOCUS
There was not a great deal between all of these on official figures and plenty held a chance with a couple of furlongs to go. Very modest, banded-class form.

6810 REUTERS FIRST FOR NEWS H'CAP — 6f (P)
8:50 (8:53) (Class 6) (0-65,65) 3-Y-0+ **£2,047** (£604; £302) **Stalls** High

Form RPR

3202 **1** **Brandywell Boy (IRE)**[14] 6594 4-9-3 **64**.................. RichardThomas 11 75
(D J S Ffrench Davis) *racd in midfield: rdn and hdwy 2f out: led ins fnl f: r.o strly* **9/2[1]**

5113 **2** *1* **Lord Of The Reins (IRE)**[57] 5495 3-9-4 **65**.................. DaneO'Neill 7 73+
(D Shaw) *lw: hld up in midfield: plld out and rdn over 2f out: r.o to chse wnr ins fnl f: no imp last 100yds* **5/1[2]**

3000 **3** *½* **The Fisio**[10] 6671 7-9-1 **62**..........................(v) ChrisCatlin 4 68
(S Gollings) *chsd ldr: rdn and ev ch over 2f out: no ex ins fnl f* **33/1**

3050 **4** *1* **Hucking Hope (IRE)**[57] 5495 3-9-1 **62**.................... GeorgeBaker 9 65
(J R Best) *hld up towards rr: rdn and effrt 2f out: kpt on u.p fnl f: nt rch ldrs* **11/1**

0061 **5** *shd* **Willhewiz**[14] 6581 7-9-2 **63**..........................(v) FergusSweeney 5 65
(M S Saunders) *sn led: rdn over 1f out: hdd ins fnl f: fdd last 100yds* **13/2[3]**

5004 **6** *shd* **Wicked Uncle**[10] 6671 8-8-12 **64**..................(v) RussellKennemore(5) 10 66
(S Gollings) *hld up bhd: rdn and hdwy over 1f out: r.o fnl f: nt rch ldrs* **12/1**

3106 **7** *nk* **Rosie Cross (IRE)**[32] 6174 3-8-11 **63**.................... PatrickHills(5) 8 64
(Eve Johnson Houghton) *chsd ldrs: rdn to chse ldng pair over 1f out: no ex ins fnl f* **14/1**

6305 **8** *hd* **Plateau**[10] 6671 8-9-4 **65**.......................... AdamKirby 6 66
(C R Dore) *stdd after s: hld up bhd: rdn and effrt over 2f out: kpt on u.p: nvr trbld ldrs* **10/1**

-405 **9** *hd* **Toucantini**[20] 6455 3-9-1 **62**.................... RichardKingscote 12 62
(R Charlton) *s.i.s: bhd: racd awkwardly bnd 4f out: rdn and effrt on inner over 2f out: nvr trbld ldrs* **14/1**

1000 **10** *1 ½* **Hollow Jo**[22] 6406 7-9-4 **65**.......................... EddieAhern 3 60
(J R Jenkins) *hld up towards rr: rdn and struggling over 2f out* **8/1**

2001 **11** *4* **Norcroft**[5] 6747 5-8-11 **65**..........................(p) RobbieEgan(7) 1 47
(Mrs C A Dunnett) *lw: chsd ldrs: rdn 3f out: wknd wl over 2f out* **9/2[1]**

4203 **12** *1 ¾* **Rann Na Cille (IRE)**[30] 6244 3-9-1 **62**..................(b) MickyFenton 2 39
(P T Midgley) *chsd ldrs: rdn 3f out: wknd over 2f out* **16/1**

1m 11.83s (-1.87) **Going Correction** -0.15s/f (Stan) **12** Ran SP% **124.7**
Speed ratings (Par 101): **106,104,104,102,102 102,102,101,101,99 94,91**
CSF £28.10 CT £698.02 TOTE £6.60: £2.00, £1.90, £13.20; EX 24.50.
Owner P B Gallagher **Bred** Mountarmstrong Stud **Trained** Lambourn, Berks
■ Stewards' Enquiry : Robbie Egan one-day ban: used whip when out of contention and gelding showing no response (Nov 26)

FOCUS
The winning time was very quick and the form should work out. Brandywell Boy and Lord Of The Reins look capable of going in again.

6811 REUTERS H'CAP — 2m (P)
9:20 (9:20) (Class 6) (0-65,64) 3-Y-0+ **£2,047** (£604; £302) **Stalls** High

Form RPR

0152 **1** **Up In Arms (IRE)**[34] 6132 3-9-1 **60**.................... JimCrowley 6 70+
(P Winkworth) *w.w in midfield: hdwy to chse ldrs 3f out: wnt 2nd over 2f out: led over 1f out: sn rdn clr: easily* **7/2[1]**

-604 **2** *2* **Haatmey**[11] 6643 5-9-1 **51**..........................(v) LPKeniry 8 56
(P R Chamings) *chsd ldrs tl wnt 2nd 9f out: led over 3f out: rdn over 2f out: hdd over 1f out: no ch w wnr* **7/1**

6033 **3** *¾* **Serhaaphim**[104] 4104 3-8-8 **56**.................... JerryO'Dwyer(3) 4 60
(N B King) *hld up wl in tch: rdn and effrt on inner over 2f out: kpt on same pce fnl f* **4/1[2]**

3500 **4** *1* **Moon Emperor**[140] 2996 10-9-6 **56**..........................(b) EddieAhern 2 59
(J R Jenkins) *hld up in last pair: hdwy over 2f out: plugged on u.p fnl f: nvr threatened wnr* **10/1**

0202 **5** *hd* **Pocket Too**[18] 6500 4-9-9 **62**.................... NeilChalmers(3) 1 65
(M Salaman) *in tch in midfield: rdn along briefly 6f out: drvn to chse ldrs over 2f out: wknd 1f out* **4/1[2]**

0043 **6** *1 ½* **Ronsard (IRE)**[11] 6643 5-9-0 **50**.................... StephenDonohoe 5 51
(P D Evans) *v s.i.s: hld up in last: hdwy on outer over 3f out: rdn wl over 2f out: no imp last 2f* **11/2[3]**

0300 **7** *5* **Isa'Af (IRE)**[253] 628 8-8-9 **45**.......................... ChrisCatlin 10 40
(P W Hiatt) *plld hrd: hld up in tch: rdn and btn over 2f out* **25/1**

3130 **8** *12* **Critical Stage (IRE)**[30] 6241 8-9-9 **64**.................... HaddenFrost(5) 9 44
(J D Frost) *led for 2f: chsd ldr tl 9f out and again over 3f out: sn rdn: wknd qckly over 2f out* **8/1**

0000 **9** *2* **Lysander's Quest (IRE)**[11] 6643 9-8-9 **45**..............(b) FergusSweeney 7 23
(R Ingram) *chsd ldr tl led after 2f out: hdd and rdn over 3f out: sn wknd* **20/1**

3m 28.16s (-3.24) **Going Correction** -0.15s/f (Stan)
WFA 3 from 4yo+ 9lb **9** Ran SP% **118.9**
Speed ratings (Par 101): **102,101,100,100,100 99,96,90,89**
CSF £29.42 CT £103.59 TOTE £4.60: £3.00, £2.80, £1.20; EX 37.40 Place 6 £206.86, Place 5 £121.29.
Owner P Winkworth **Bred** John O'Dwyer And J Ryan **Trained** Chiddingfold, Surrey
■ Stewards' Enquiry : L P Keniry one-day ban: careless riding (Nov 26)

FOCUS
A modest handicap. Most of these either couldn't win or had forgotten how to, so it would be surprising if anything of note emerges from the race in the coming weeks.
Critical Stage(IRE) Official explanation: jockey said gelding had no more to give
Lysander's Quest(IRE) Official explanation: jockey said gelding hung right throughout
T/Plt: £224.60 to a £1 stake. Pool: £76,772.35. 249.50 winning tickets. T/Qpdt: £18.40 to a £1 stake. Pool: £5,937.80. 238.00 winning tickets. SP

6797 WOLVERHAMPTON (A.W) (L-H)
Wednesday, November 14

OFFICIAL GOING: Standard
Wind: Almost nil Weather: Cloudy with sunny spells

6812 CENTREBET.COM CASINO NURSERY — 5f 216y(P)
1:10 (1:11) (Class 6) (0-65,68) 2-Y-0 **£2,047** (£604; £302) **Stalls** Low

Form RPR

663 **1** **Gain Share**[7] 6722 2-9-7 **65**.......................... PhillipMakin 3 72
(T D Barron) *mde all: rdn over 1f out: styd on* **4/1[1]**

4521 **2** *1 ¼* **Wiseman's Diamond (USA)**[16] 6536 2-9-4 **62**.................... NCallan 7 65
(K A Ryan) *hld up: hdwy over 2f out: rdn to chse wnr over 1f out: styd on same pce ins fnl f* **9/2[2]**

1601 **3** *nk* **Leading Edge (IRE)**[7] 6722 2-9-10 **68** 6ex.................... ChrisCatlin 2 70+
(M R Channon) *prom: n.m.r and lost pl 5f out: hdwy and nt clr run over 2f out: rdn and swtchd rt over 1f out: edgd lft ins fnl f: r.o* **13/2[3]**

024 **4** *½* **Gunner Fly (IRE)**[19] 6477 2-9-3 **64**.................... JamieMoriarty(3) 5 65
(R A Fahey) *s.i.s: outpcd: hdwy and hmpd over 2f out: rdn over 1f out: styd on same pce ins fnl f* **13/2[3]**

0550 **5** *2 ½* **Copperbottomed (IRE)**[7] 6722 2-9-3 **61**..................(e[1]) JimCrowley 10 54+
(R Hollinshead) *hld up: rdn and nt clr run over 1f out: hung lft and r.o ins fnl f: nvr nrr* **8/1**

0460 **6** *1 ¼* **Rich James (IRE)**[58] 5477 2-8-10 **54**.................... GrahamGibbons 1 43
(J D Bethell) *prom: rdn over 1f out: wknd fnl f* **8/1**

0560 **7** *1* **Sistos Fascination**[18] 6502 2-9-6 **64**..................(b[1]) GregFairley 4 50
(M Botti) *sn pushed along and prom: rdn 2f out: wknd ins fnl f* **11/1**

0000 **8** *3* **Lord Of The Wing**[25] 6326 2-8-4 **48**.................... FrankieMcDonald 6 25
(P T Midgley) *chsd ldrs: lost pl 5f out: n.d after* **66/1**

0046 **9** *½* **Ile Royale**[12] 6624 2-8-9 **53** ow2..................(be) StephenDonohoe 9 29
(C N Allen) *hld up: hdwy over 2f out: rdn and wknd over 1f out* **20/1**

030 **10** *3* **East Coast Girl (IRE)**[42] 5901 2-9-7 **65**.................... TGMcLaughlin 8 32
(S W Hall) *chsd ldrs: rdn over 2f out: sn wknd* **20/1**

5000 **11** *½* **Charlotti Carlotti (IRE)**[12] 6624 2-9-4 **62**..................(p) TomEaves 13 27
(D W Chapman) *prom over 3f* **20/1**

0564 **12** *5* **Lella Beya**[12] 6626 2-9-6 **64**.......................... JohnEgan 11 14
(S Kirk) *son pushed along in rr: wknd wl over 2f out* **14/1**

0000 **13** *2* **In Decorum**[50] 5715 2-8-1 **45**..........................(v[1]) DavidKinsella 12 —
(J A Geake) *prom to 1/2-way* **66/1**

1m 16.26s (0.45) **Going Correction** -0.025s/f (Stan) **13** Ran SP% **119.3**
Speed ratings (Par 94): **96,94,93,93,89 88,86,82,82,78 77,70,68**
CSF £20.07 CT £115.72 TOTE £5.70: £1.60, £2.50, £1.50; EX 23.60 Trifecta £41.20 Pool: £125.39 - 2.16 winning tickets..
Owner Dastardly And Muttley **Bred** Baroness Bloodstock & Redmyre Bloodstock **Trained** Maunby, N Yorks

FOCUS
A modest nursery but the first three came here in good heart and the form looks solid for the grade.

NOTEBOOK
Gain Share, who ran well on his handicap debut on turf behind Leading Edge, was 6lb better off with that rival for just over a length's beating, so had a strong chance on the book. He showed plenty of pace from the off, dominated throughout and justified favouritism in good style. (tchd 7-2)
Wiseman's Diamond(USA), whose Leicester win had been advertised by the subsequent success of the runner-up, was missing the cheekpieces she wore to that win. Racing off a 7lb higher mark and down a furlong in distance, she was a little tight for room rounding the turn into the straight, but stayed on well, suggesting a return to 7f will suit. (op 4-1 tchd 5-1)
Leading Edge(IRE) beat Gain Share by a length and a quarter at Nottingham last time but a 6lb penalty was always going to make things difficult for her in her attempt to confirm the form. She ran well in the circumstances, staying on after enjoying less than a clear run. (op 7-1 tchd 6-1)
Gunner Fly(IRE), running in a handicap for the first time, was again slowly away, but he came home well, finishing clear of the rest. Not for the first time he shaped as though he will be suited by a longer trip. (tchd 15-2)
Copperbottomed(IRE), who finished seventh in the Nottingham race in which Leading Edge and Gain Share finished first and third respectively, wore an eye-shield for the first time, but he was drawn out wide and, although he stayed on while hanging left in the straight, he could never get in a blow from off the pace. (op 9-1)
Rich James(IRE), who finished in mid-division in a Musselburgh seller last time out, has been dropped 12lb since his handicap debut in August but does not appear to be progressing at all. (op 16-1)

6813 CENTREBET.COM POKER MAIDEN AUCTION STKS — 5f 20y(P)
1:40 (1:41) (Class 6) 2-Y-0 **£2,047** (£604; £302) **Stalls** Low

Form RPR

4036 **1** **Valhillen**[35] 6098 2-8-9 61.......................... PatCosgrave 1 63
(M J Wallace) *chsd ldr: rdn over 1f out: styd on to ld wl ins fnl f* **3/1[1]**

3500 **2** *nk* **Mission Impossible**[25] 6328 2-8-8 66.................... PatrickDonaghy(7) 4 68
(P C Haslam) *in tch: rdn 1/2-way: hung lft and r.o ins fnl f* **7/2[2]**

0003 **3** *½* **Lambrini Lace (IRE)**[12] 6624 2-8-10 62.................... LiamJones 3 61
(Mrs L Williamson) *led: rdn and hung rt over 1f out: hdd and unable qck wl ins fnl f* **5/1[3]**

006 **4** *½* **Queens Mantle**[21] 6425 2-8-6 57.......................... ChrisCatlin 6 55
(P J Makin) *chsd ldrs: rdn 1/2-way: edgd rt ins fnl f: kpt on* **33/1**

5 *shd* **Hucking Harkness** 2-9-1 0.......................... DaneO'Neill 10 64
(J R Best) *prom: hung rt and outpcd 1/2-way: rdn and edgd lft ins fnl f: styd on* **10/1**

4500 **6** ½ **Tommytush (IRE)**[23] 6384 2-8-13 60 DavidAllan 2 60
(E J Alston) *sn pushed along in rr: hdwy u.p over 1f out: unable qck wl ins fnl f* **11/1**

6000 **7** 1 **Holly Golightley**[16] 6535 2-8-6 60 JohnEgan 8 51+
(K A Ryan) *prom: rdn over 2f out: styng on same pce whn n.m.r wl ins fnl f* **8/1**

30 **8** 5 **Warners Bay (IRE)**[7] 6721 2-8-13 0 DanielTudhope 9 39
(R Bastiman) *sn outpcd* **20/1**

530 **9** 1 ¼ **Heron (IRE)**[14] 6595 2-9-1 71 NCallan 7 36
(N P Littmoden) *chsd ldrs: rdn and hung lft 1/2-way: wknd fnl f* **11/2**

63.34 secs (0.52) **Going Correction** -0.025s/f (Stan) 9 Ran SP% **115.5**
Speed ratings (Par 94): **94,93,92,91,91 90,89,81,79**
CSF £13.53 TOTE £3.20: £1.20, £1.50, £2.50; EX 18.00 Trifecta £61.90 Pool: £92.56 - 1.06 winning tickets..
Owner Andy Viner **Bred** Lady Hardy **Trained** Newmarket, Suffolk

FOCUS
Very moderate maiden form rated around the winner and third.

NOTEBOOK
Valhillen, back in maiden company and returning to the minimum trip, tracked the leader on the rail for most of the way before swinging off it to challenge down the centre of the track. He just edged a tight finish and this looks to be his trip. (op 7-2)
Mission Impossible, another dropping back in distance, was running on Polytrack for the first time. He ran on well at the end and, while he shapes as though he should appreciate 6f more, his best two runs have now arguably come over the minimum trip. (tchd 4-1)
Lambrini Lace(IRE), third in a nursery off 63 over this course and distance last time out, attempted to make every yard. She probably ran to her recent form in defeat. (op 11-2 tchd 6-1)
Queens Mantle appears to be progressing steadily but her chances will be stronger in handicap company off her current mark. (op 20-1)
Hucking Harkness, who cost 20,000gns, is out of a sister to Prix Morny winner Hoh Magic. In what was a moderate maiden, he ran a sound first race from his wide draw, and he should be suited by further in time. (op 6-1)
Holly Golightley Official explanation: jockey said filly was short of room closing stages

6814 SP PLUS @CENTREBET.COM CLAIMING STKS 1m 141y(P)
2:10 (2:10) (Class 6) 2-Y-O **£2,047** (£604; £302) **Stalls** Low

Form RPR

6001 **1** **Marino Prince (FR)**[9] 6693 2-8-4 66 JackDean(7) 12 64
(W G M Turner) *hld up: hdwy 5f out: chsd ldr over 2f out: led over 1f out: rdn and edgd rt fnl f: r.o* **7/4**[1]

2202 **2** 2 ½ **Hurstpierpoint (IRE)**[15] 6566 2-8-12 61 TonyHamilton 1 60
(R A Fahey) *chsd ldrs: rdn and hung lft over 1f out: styd on* **9/4**[2]

00 **3** ¾ **Mujahope**[71] 5116 2-9-2 0 (p) AshleyHamblett(5) 7 67
(M Botti) *chsd ldr tl led over 2f out: rdn and hdd over 1f out: styd on same pce* **10/1**

0 **4** ½ **Sheer Fantastic**[133] 3199 2-8-11 0 (v[1]) PatrickDonaghy(7) 4 63
(P C Haslam) *prom: n.m.r over 3f out: sn rdn: styd on* **9/1**[3]

0040 **5** ½ **Flashy Max**[26] 6307 2-8-3 45 ChrisCatlin 2 47
(Jedd O'Keeffe) *hld up: rdn over 2f out: styd on appr fnl f: nt rch ldrs* **14/1**

3040 **6** 1 **Giggling Monkey**[3] 6775 2-7-12 49 (v[1]) NickyMackay 8 40
(P D Evans) *hld up: rdn over 1f out: edgd rt: nt rch ldrs* **10/1**

0000 **7** nk **Balais Folly (FR)**[21] 6427 2-8-13 55 RichardKingscote 10 54
(B Palling) *s.i.s: hld up: hdwy over 2f out: sn rdn: styd on same pce* **16/1**

065 **8** hd **Korcula**[14] 6591 2-8-10 46 PatCosgrave 9 51
(M J Wallace) *unruly in stalls: hld up in tch: rdn over 2f out: hung rt over 1f out: no ex* **12/1**

00 **9** 20 **Madame Montom (USA)**[21] 6438 2-8-4 0 LiamJones 3 3
(S W Hall) *hld up: bhd fr 1/2-way* **50/1**

0000 **10** 9 **Brough (IRE)**[9] 6693 2-8-10 40 ow8 JamesO'Reilly(5) 5 —
(J O'Reilly) *led: rdn and hdd over 2f out: sn wknd* **33/1**

2000 **11** 3 **Distant Noble**[96] 4363 2-8-11 50 TomEaves 11 —
(R Brotherton) *chsd ldrs over 5f* **50/1**

1m 53.27s (1.51) **Going Correction** -0.025s/f (Stan) 11 Ran SP% **122.4**
Speed ratings (Par 94): **92,89,89,88,88 87,87,86,69,61 58**
CSF £5.90 TOTE £3.80: £2.00, £1.40, £2.30; EX 5.90 Trifecta £48.20 Pool: £168.02 - 2.47 winning tickets..Marino Prince was claimed by Joe McCarthy for £9,000.
Owner John McGrath **Bred** Newsells Park Stud Ltd **Trained** Sigwells, Somerset
■ Stewards' Enquiry : Patrick Donaghy one-day ban: careless riding (Nov 26)

FOCUS
Modest but solid form rated around the winner and fifth.

NOTEBOOK
Marino Prince(FR), winner of a seller over 7f here last time, was best in at the weights and never looked in any danger after his rider sent him for home turning into the straight. He got the longer trip well. (tchd 13-8 and 2-1)
Hurstpierpoint(IRE), runner-up in a similar course-and-distance claimer last time, would have been 6lb better off with the winner had this been a handicap. She again ran a solid race in defeat. (op 11-4)
Mujahope, dropping into a claimer having failed to show much in a couple of maidens, had cheekpieces on for the first time. He ran his best race to date and looks to have found his level. (op 9-1)
Sheer Fantastic is a half-brother to a turf and dirt sprint winner in the US but his sire is more of an influence for stamina and this should be his trip at the moment. He made no show on his debut in a maiden at Catterick back in July but wore a visor on this drop in class and shaped a lot better. (op 8-1 tchd 10-1)
Flashy Max has not shown much ability in five starts on turf and this Polytrack debut confirmed him as banded class.
Giggling Monkey ran a bit better in the first-time visor but is another who is no better than banded class. (tchd 9-1)

6815 BET NOW AT CENTREBET.COM (S) STKS 1m 4f 50y(P)
2:40 (2:40) (Class 6) 3-5-Y-O **£2,047** (£604; £302) **Stalls** Low

Form RPR

1 **Veloso (FR)**[815] 5-9-2 0 JohnEgan 12 65+
(Ronald O'Leary, Ire) *s.i.s: hld up: racd keenly: hdwy over 3f out: chsd ldr over 1f out: rdn to ld wl ins fnl f* **3/1**[2]

5206 **2** 1 **Speagle (IRE)**[3] 6774 5-9-2 75 DavidAllan 3 63
(D Carroll) *chsd ldrs: led over 2f out: rdn clr over 1f out: hdd wl ins fnl f* **6/5**[1]

-400 **3** 10 **History Prize (IRE)**[257] 607 4-9-2 45 LPKeniry 1 47
(A G Newcombe) *hld up: hdwy 1/2-way: rdn and wknd over 1f out: hung lft ins fnl f* **50/1**

0060 **4** ½ **Davidia (IRE)**[12] 6629 4-9-2 47 RichardKingscote 6 46
(Tom Dascombe) *prom: rdn over 2f out: wknd over 1f out* **8/1**

2104 **5** 1 ¼ **Birthday Star (IRE)**[15] 6564 5-9-8 56 AdamKirby 8 50
(A G Juckes) *hld up: rdn over 2f out: n.d* **7/1**[3]

0600 **6** ½ **Slip Silver**[16] 6534 3-8-5 40 (p) ChrisCatlin 9 38
(P J Makin) *led: rdn and hdd over 2f out: wknd over 1f out* **33/1**

5060 **7** 2 ½ **Hook Money (IRE)**[25] 6325 3-8-10 48 (b) StephenDonohoe 2 39
(A J McCabe) *s.i.s: pushed along 1/2-way: a in rr* **12/1**

505 **8** ¾ **Island King (IRE)**[69] 5157 4-9-2 42 DanielTudhope 4 38
(R Bastiman) *hld up: rdn over 2f out: a in rr* **50/1**

0035 **9** 1 ¾ **The Mighty Ogmore**[3] 6780 3-8-2 45 (p) DuranFentiman(3) 11 30
(R C Guest) *prom: rdn over 4f out: wknd over 2f out* **18/1**

-505 **10** nk **Taran Tregarth**[18] 6501 3-8-5 40 LiamJones 5 30
(W M Brisbourne) *hld up: rdn and wknd over 2f out* **50/1**

0360 **11** nk **Homecroft Boy**[9] 4673 3-8-5 43 ow2 (p) RichardEvans(7) 7 36
(P D Evans) *s.i.s: sn pushed along in rr: wknd over 2f out* **50/1**

4300 **12** 26 **Escoffier**[15] 6564 5-9-2 54 (v[1]) DaneO'Neill 10 —
(M Appleby) *chsd ldr tl rdn over 3f out: sn wknd* **22/1**

2m 42.42s **Going Correction** -0.025s/f (Stan)
WFA 3 from 4yo+ 6lb 12 Ran SP% **122.2**
Speed ratings (Par 101): **99,98,91,91,90 90,88,88,86,86 86,69**
CSF £6.82 TOTE £3.30: £1.70, £1.10, £13.50; EX 7.30 Trifecta £196.60 Pool: £373.90 - 1.35 winning tickets..The winner was bought in for 5,500gns. Speagle was claimed by J. S. Wainwright for £6,000.
Owner Mrs Ronald O'Leary **Bred** Jean Louis Pariente **Trained** Killaloe, Co. Clare

FOCUS
A typically weak seller, run at a sound pace. The first pair came well clear and the form looks fair enough.

6816 PLAY AUSTRALIAN @ CENTREBET.COM H'CAP 1m 141y(P)
3:10 (3:11) (Class 5) (0-70,70) 3-Y-O+ **£2,968** (£876; £438) **Stalls** Low

Form RPR

5445 **1** **Hoh Wotanite**[24] 6359 4-9-5 68 (v[1]) NCallan 5 82
(R Hollinshead) *hld up: hdwy over 2f out: led over 1f out: hung lft and rdn clr* **3/1**[2]

2062 **2** 4 **My Michelle**[13] 6612 6-8-13 62 ChrisCatlin 3 66
(B Palling) *chsd ldrs: nt clr run over 2f out: rdn and ev ch over 1f out: styd on same pce* **17/2**

0521 **3** 1 ½ **Goose Green (IRE)**[15] 6567 3-9-0 66 JimCrowley 9 67
(R J Hodges) *chsd ldrs: led over 2f out: rdn and hdd over 1f out: no ex* **11/2**[3]

6500 **4** 6 **Rain Stops Play (IRE)**[11] 6654 5-9-7 70 FrancisNorton 7 57
(M Quinn) *sn led: rdn and hdd over 2f out: wknd over 1f out* **13/2**

3513 **5** 1 **Pelham Crescent (IRE)**[12] 6628 4-9-2 65 RichardKingscote 8 50
(B Palling) *hld up: rdn over 3f out: wkng whn hung lft over 1f out* **7/4**[1]

1006 **6** 1 **Life's A Whirl**[22] 6413 5-8-7 56 (p) JohnEgan 4 39
(Mrs C A Dunnett) *chsd ldr: rdn over 3f out: ev ch over 2f out: sn wknd* **14/1**

650- **7** 9 **Shopfitter**[515] 2644 4-8-7 56 oh11 FrankieMcDonald 6 18
(P T Midgley) *s.i.s: hld up: racd keenly: rdn over 3f out: sn wknd* **66/1**

6040 **8** 5 **King's Ransom**[16] 6547 4-8-13 62 (p) TomEaves 2 12
(S Gollings) *prom 6f* **8/1**

0000 **9** 5 **Fan Club**[19] 6463 3-8-8 60 DaleGibson 1 —
(D W Chapman) *hld up: rdn 1/2-way: wknd 3f out* **28/1**

1m 50.35s (-1.41) **Going Correction** -0.025s/f (Stan)
WFA 3 from 4yo+ 3lb 9 Ran SP% **123.3**
Speed ratings (Par 103): **105,101,100,94,93 93,85,80,76**
CSF £31.12 CT £140.79 TOTE £4.10: £1.50, £1.70, £2.10; EX 27.30 Trifecta £288.60 Pool: £902.65 - 2.22 winning tickets..
Owner The Three R'S **Bred** Dunchurch Lodge Stud Co **Trained** Upper Longdon, Staffs
■ Stewards' Enquiry : Frankie McDonald one-day ban: used whip when out of contention (Nov 26)

FOCUS
A moderate handicap, run at a strong early pace. The winner came from behind and posted a career-best.
Fan Club Official explanation: jockey said gelding suffered interference

6817 WE'VE GOT THE ASHES @CENTREBET.COM H'CAP 1m 5f 194y(P)
3:40 (3:45) (Class 6) (0-65,65) 3-Y-O+ **£2,047** (£604; £302) **Stalls** Low

Form RPR

0204 **1** **Merrymaker**[15] 6561 7-10-0 61 NCallan 9 71
(W M Brisbourne) *hld up: hdwy over 3f out: led 1f out: rdn clr* **6/1**

0062 **2** 2 ½ **Party Palace**[9] 6697 3-8-5 46 AdrianMcCarthy 8 52
(H S Howe) *hld up: hdwy u.p over 3f out: swtchd rt over 1f out: styd on* **8/1**

4162 **3** ¾ **Papradon**[20] 6459 3-9-4 59 (v) DaneO'Neill 2 64
(J R Best) *prom: jnd ldr 3f out: rdn and ev ch whn edgd lft 1f out: styd on same pce* **11/4**[1]

4206 **4** 1 ¼ **Composing (IRE)**[21] 6421 3-8-11 55 (vt[1]) TravisBlock(3) 4 58
(H Morrison) *chsd ldr tl led over 11f out: rdn over 2f out: hdd 1f out: wknd towards fin* **4/1**[3]

5006 **5** 1 ¾ **Sea Frolic (IRE)**[15] 6569 6-8-12 45 HayleyTurner 6 46
(Jennie Candlish) *hld up: hdwy over 1f out: nt rch ldrs* **25/1**

2500 **6** 3 **Zaffeu**[18] 6501 6-9-0 52 RussellKennemore(5) 3 49
(A G Juckes) *hld up: hdwy over 3f out: rdn over 2f out: wknd over 1f out* **33/1**

2201 **7** 1 ¼ **Vivacita**[5] 6751 3-9-10 65 6ex ChrisCatlin 5 60
(E J O'Neill) *trckd ldrs: racd keenly: rdn over 2f out: wknd over 1f out* **3/1**[2]

0000 **8** 6 **Iceni Princess**[14] 6583 3-8-4 45 LiamJones 1 31
(P Howling) *hld up: rdn over 3f out: sn wknd* **80/1**

9 18 **Sesaro Express (IRE)**[10] 3718 6-8-12 45 LPKeniry 10 6
(John A Quinn, Ire) *led: hdd over 11f out: chsd ldr: rdn over 5f out: wknd wl over 3f out* **20/1**

3530 **10** 6 **Group Force (IRE)**[15] 6561 3-9-0 55 PaulMulrennan 12 8
(M H Tompkins) *chsd ldrs: rdn over 3f out: sn wknd* **10/1**

000 **11** 62 **Shady Bay**[19] 6464 3-8-1 45 DuranFentiman(3) 11 —
(D W Chapman) *s.s: a in rr: lost tch fnl 4f* **100/1**

3m 8.52s (1.15) **Going Correction** -0.025s/f (Stan)
WFA 3 from 6yo+ 8lb 11 Ran SP% **119.9**
Speed ratings (Par 101): **95,93,93,92,91 89,89,85,75,71 36**
CSF £51.53 CT £163.95 TOTE £8.30: £2.30, £2.60, £1.40; EX 44.10 Trifecta £340.60 Pool: £676.52 - 1.41 winning tickets..
Owner The Blacktoffee Partnership **Bred** Hascombe And Valiant Studs **Trained** Great Ness, Shropshire

FOCUS
There was no great pace on early here and the race developed into a bit of a sprint over the last half-mile. As a result the winning time was modest. Modest form, the winner having dropped steadily in the weights.

Group Force(IRE) Official explanation: jockey said filly stopped very quickly

6818 AUSSIE AUSSIE AUSSIE BET @ CENTREBET.COM H'CAP 5f 216y(P)

4:10 (4:11) (Class 5) (0-70,69) 3-Y-0+ **£2,968** (£876; £438) **Stalls** Low

Form RPR

4150 **1** **Monashee Prince (IRE)**[7] 6717 5-8-8 **59**....................(v) JimCrowley 12 71
(J R Best) *hld up: hdwy over 1f out: hung lft and led ins fnl f: drvn out* **10/1**

4642 **2** *1 1/4* **Chatshow (USA)**[5] 6747 6-8-3 **61**................................ MarkCoumbe(7) 2 69
(A W Carroll) *chsd ldrs: rdn over 2f out: styd on* **2/1**[1]

1502 **3** *3/4* **Tag Team (IRE)**[10] 6671 6-8-8 **59**........................... StephenDonohoe 11 65
(John A Harris) *chsd ldr tl led over 2f out: rdn over 1f out: hdd and unable qck ins fnl f* **15/2**[3]

0040 **4** *shd* **Triple Shadow**[8] 6701 3-8-6 **57**.................................... FrancisNorton 4 62
(M A Peill) *s.i.s: hld up: hdwy over 1f out: sn ev ch: styd on same pce ins fnl f* **12/1**

4530 **5** *1/2* **Rainbow Fox**[15] 6559 3-9-3 **68**.................................... TonyHamilton 3 72+
(R A Fahey) *hld up: rdn over 1f out: r.o ins fnl f: nt rch ldrs* **12/1**

453 **6** *shd* **Royal Challenge**[16] 6531 6-9-2 **67**................................ DanielTudhope 8 70
(I W McInnes) *prom: rdn over 2f out: styd on same pce fnl f* **8/1**

5500 **7** *hd* **Winthorpe (IRE)**[19] 6467 7-8-2 **56**............................. AndrewMullen(3) 6 59
(J J Quinn) *hld up: rdn over 3f out: styd on ins fnl f: nt trble ldrs* **9/1**

0320 **8** *shd* **Boreana**[27] 6290 4-8-6 **57**.. DaleGibson 13 59
(Jedd O'Keeffe) *hld up: hdwy over 1f out: nt rch ldrs* **20/1**

2345 **9** *1/2* **Dvinsky (USA)**[15] 6568 6-9-4 **69**.................................. ChrisCatlin 1 70
(P Howling) *chsd ldrs: rdn over 2f out: no ex fnl f* **9/2**[2]

2455 **10** *1/2* **Cleveland**[7] 6720 5-8-6 **62**................................ RussellKennemore(5) 10 61
(R Hollinshead) *chsd ldrs: hung rt: rdn and ev ch over 2f out: no ex fnl f* **12/1**

434 **11** *4* **Canina**[12] 6625 4-8-4 **55** oh5.. LiamJones 9 41
(Paul Green) *chsd ldrs: rdn over 2f out: wknd fnl f* **28/1**

0000 **12** *2* **Creme Brulee**[6] 6735 4-8-1 **55** oh10.............................. DominicFox(3) 5 35
(P T Dalton) *sn led: rdn and hdd over 2f out: wknd fnl f* **66/1**

00 **13** *3* **Exit Strategy (IRE)**[20] 6455 3-8-9 **60**...............................(b) JohnEgan 7 30
(R A Harris) *s.i.s: outpcd* **18/1**

1m 15.3s (-0.51) **Going Correction** -0.025s/f (Stan) 13 Ran SP% **131.5**
Speed ratings (Par 103): **102,100,99,99,98 98,98,98,97,96 91,88,84**
CSF £32.82 CT £181.69 TOTE £13.80: £3.60, £2.00, £1.80; EX 67.80 Trifecta £111.60 Pool: £361.81 - 2.30 winning tickets. Place 6 £11.60, Place 5 £6.69.
Owner Michael Hurd, Ray Rooks, Paul Rooks **Bred** Mrs Dolores Gleeson **Trained** Hucking, Kent

FOCUS

An ordinary sprint handicap in which the early pace was fair - they took longer to cover the first couple of furlongs than in the earlier nursery over the same trip - but the final time was close to par for the grade. Sound form.

Rainbow Fox ◆ Official explanation: jockey said gelding was denied a clear run
Cleveland Official explanation: jockey said gelding hung right throughout
T/Plt: £8.80 to a £1 stake. Pool: £46,516.60. 3,818.95 winning tickets. T/Qpdt: £4.70 to a £1 stake. Pool: £2,767.10. 430.50 winning tickets. CR

6791 LINGFIELD (L-H)

Thursday, November 15

OFFICIAL GOING: Standard

Wind: Virtually nil Weather: Sunny

6819 DINE IN THE TRACKSIDE CARVERY APPRENTICE H'CAP 1m 5f (P)

1:20 (1:20) (Class 5) (0-75,78) 3-Y-0+ **£2,817** (£838; £418; £209) **Stalls** Low

Form RPR

0661 **1** **Grande Caiman (IRE)**[11] 6666 3-9-1 **78** 6ex............ CharlesEddery(7) 5 86+
(R Hannon) *hld up: plenty to do 2f out: rapid prog on inner to ld 1f out: sn clr* **5/6**[1]

0606 **2** *2* **Flame Creek (IRE)**[132] 3279 11-9-8 **74**........................ BarrySavage(3) 7 79
(E J Creighton) *trckd ldng pair: wnt 2nd over 3f out: rdn to ld over 1f out: hdd and outpcd 1f out* **25/1**

0-06 **3** *3 1/2* **Kingkohler (IRE)**[11] 6666 8-8-8 **62**.......................... DeclanCannon(5) 2 62
(K A Morgan) *mostly in 4th: outpcd over 2f out: plugged on to take 3rd ins fnl f* **25/1**

221 **4** *1 3/4* **Generous Lad (IRE)**[9] 6709 4-9-9 **77** 6ex...........................(p) PNolan(5) 3 74
(A B Haynes) *s.s: hld up in last: easily outpcd fr 3f out: nvr any ch after* **10/3**[2]

3010 **5** *nk* **Musango**[61] 5422 4-9-4 **67**...(t) MatthewDavies 4 64
(B R Johnson) *led for 3f: led over 4f out tl hdd & wknd over 1f out* **5/1**[3]

-000 **6** *15* **Honduras (SWI)**[3] 6802 6-9-12 **75**.........................(b[1]) JemmaMarshall 6 49
(G L Moore) *led after 3f and maintained gd pce: hdd over 4f out: wknd over 3f out: t.o* **10/1**

2m 43.72s (-4.58) **Going Correction** -0.05s/f (Stan)
WFA 3 from 4yo+ 7lb 6 Ran SP% **111.1**
Speed ratings (Par 103): **112,110,108,107,107 98**
CSF £23.69 TOTE £1.80: £1.10, £10.20; EX 27.90.
Owner I A N Wight **Bred** Sweet Retreat Syndicate **Trained** East Everleigh, Wilts

FOCUS

An ordinary handicap but they went a good gallop and that resulted in a very smart winning time for a race of its type. The form is on the weak side for the grade but should prove sound.

6820 EUROPEAN BREEDERS' FUND MEDIAN AUCTION MAIDEN STKS 5f (P)

1:50 (1:50) (Class 5) 2-Y-0 **£3,465** (£1,030; £515; £257) **Stalls** High

Form RPR

00 **1** **Blakeshall Diamond**[8] 6721 2-8-5 0........................... MarkCoumbe(7) 9 64
(A J Chamberlain) *mde all: rdn 2 l clr ins fnl f: unchal after* **33/1**

00 **2** *1 1/4* **Yamanmickmccann**[23] 6403 2-9-3 0.............................. DaneO'Neill 7 64
(R Hannon) *pushed along to chse ldrs: effrt on outer 2f out: drvn and styd on to take 2nd nr fin: no imp wnr* **6/1**

0 **3** *hd* **Little Lovely (IRE)**[22] 6419 2-8-12 0................................. LPKeniry 10 58
(A G Newcombe) *chsd wnr to over 2f out: drvn to go 2nd again 1f out: no imp: lost 2nd nr fin* **5/1**[3]

4 *nk* **Archilini** 2-9-3 0.. JamesDoyle 2 62
(K A Morgan) *towards rr: effrt 2f out: rn green over 1f out: n.m.r ent fnl f: kpt on: n.d* **16/1**

5 *1/2* **My Pin Up** 2-8-12 0.. SaleemGolam 8 56+
(Christian Wroe) *s.s: t.k.h: hld up in last: effrt 2f out: nowhere to go 1f out: kpt on: nt rcvr* **20/1**

04 **6** *1 1/2* **Forever Changes**[9] 6705 2-8-12 0................................... RobertHavlin 6 50
(L Montague Hall) *prom: nt qckn over 1f out: stl cl up ent fnl f: wknd last 100yds* **14/1**

06 **7** *hd* **Love And Glory (FR)**[12] 6641 2-9-3 0............................. GeorgeBaker 4 54
(G L Moore) *settled in last trio: stl in last pair 1f out: pushed along and styd on: nvr nr ldrs* **12/1**

8 *nk* **Art Exhibition (IRE)** 2-9-3 0.. JimmyFortune 1 53
(J Noseda) *towards rr: effrt on inner 2f out: no prog jst over 1f out: fdd* **7/2**[2]

9 *1 1/2* **Hero Heart** 2-9-3 0.. PatCosgrave 3 48
(Jane Chapple-Hyam) *prom: chsd wnr over 2f out to 1f out: wknd* **5/2**[1]

00 **10** *3* **Epsom Salts**[23] 6403 2-9-3 0.. ChrisCatlin 5 37
(P M Phelan) *s.i.s: racd wd and hld up in last trio: lost tch after c v wd bnd 2f out* **8/1**

60.49 secs (0.71) **Going Correction** -0.05s/f (Stan) 10 Ran SP% **120.8**
Speed ratings (Par 96): **92,90,89,89,88 86,85,85,82,78**
CSF £227.86 TOTE £51.80: £8.20, £2.60, £2.20; EX 378.10 Trifecta £221.10 Part won. Pool £311.45 - 0.10 winning units..
Owner M Bishop **Bred** M P Bishop **Trained** Ashton Keynes, Wilts

FOCUS

A poor maiden, no better than plating class.

NOTEBOOK

Blakeshall Diamond, a half-sister to Wrenlane, a dual 1m winner at three, Offtoworhwego, a 5f winner at two and Zinging, a multiple 5f-7f winner, had not shown much in two previous starts, but she was ridden far more positively this time and the change in tactics paid off handsomely. It is difficult to believe that the form is much better than plating class, but she should have improvement in her. She was Adrian Chamberlain's first winner for a staggering 11 years. (op 50-1)

Yamanmickmccann stayed on late after struggling to go the early pace. This was his best effort to date, but the opposition was poor and he is likely to want to return to 6f plus in future. Official explanation: jockey said colt hung left (op 8-1)

Little Lovely(IRE), who finished in mid-division in an ordinary maiden on her debut, is a half-sister to three winners. She probably did not have to improve much on her Bath effort to place here. (tchd 11-2)

Archilini, whose dam was a 6f winner at three, was first home of the newcomers, who as a bunch proved disappointing up against plating-class opposition. He is at least open to improvement, however, as he showed distinct signs of greenness here. (tchd 14-1)

My Pin Up, a half-sister to Makabul, a multiple winning sprinter, Brave Chief, a triple winner between 6f and 7f, and 7f winner Bint Makbul, did not get the best of runs when trying to make up ground from the back, and she is entitled to come on for her debut. Official explanation: jockey said filly was denied a clear run in home straight (op 14-1)

Love And Glory(FR) Official explanation: jockey said colt hung left

Hero Heart, who is closely related to Cyclonic (by Pivotal), a triple sprint winner as a four-year-old abroad, was being introduced in a weak maiden and came in for good support. He disappointed badly, though. (op 7-2 tchd 4-1)

6821 LINGFIELDPARK.CO.UK MAIDEN STKS 1m 4f (P)

2:20 (2:21) (Class 5) 3-Y-0+ **£2,817** (£838; £418; £209) **Stalls** Low

Form RPR

6 **1** **Praxiteles (IRE)**[181] 1812 3-9-3 0.. NCallan 4 91+
(Sir Michael Stoute) *trckd ldrs: effrt between rivals whn squeezed out over 1f out: swtchd ins and led last 150yds: sprinted clr* **4/6**[1]

4402 **2** *3 1/2* **Wraith**[11] 6666 3-9-3 70... TPQueally 2 78
(H R A Cecil) *led: rdn and pressed over 1f out: hdd and easily outpcd last 150yds* **2/1**[2]

0 **3** *3* **Sweet Mischief (IRE)**[22] 6420 3-8-12 0............................ JimmyFortune 6 68
(J H M Gosden) *trckd ldrs: wnt 2nd over 2f out: upsides whn bmpd over 1f out: sn outpcd* **14/1**

0 **4** *5* **Clear Reef**[31] 6238 3-9-3 0.. PatCosgrave 7 65
(Jane Chapple-Hyam) *mostly chsd ldr to over 2f out: sn btn u.p* **25/1**

42 **5** *1* **Accusation (IRE)**[32] 6204 3-8-12 0.................................... EddieAhern 1 59
(L M Cumani) *trckd ldrs: cl up gng wl 2f out: sn outpcd aned btn* **8/1**[3]

463 **6** *3* **Kokkokila**[32] 6204 3-8-12 64... MickyFenton 5 54
(Lady Herries) *in tch: rdn 5f out: lft bhd fr 3f out* **25/1**

00-0 **7** *8* **You're My Son**[309] 94 5-9-9 45..................................... GeorgeBaker 8 46
(K O Cunningham-Brown) *stdd s: hld up in last: brief effrt over 4f out: sn lost tch and bhd* **66/1**

05 **8** *2 1/2* **Stroppi Poppi**[43] 5898 3-8-12 0................................ FrankieMcDonald 3 37
(Jean-Rene Auvray) *a in rr: struggling 5f out: sn bhd* **66/1**

2m 31.03s (-3.36) **Going Correction** -0.05s/f (Stan)
WFA 3 from 5yo 6lb 8 Ran SP% **121.8**
Speed ratings (Par 103): **109,106,104,101,100 98,93,91**
CSF £2.36 TOTE £1.60: £1.10, £1.10, £2.70; EX 3.10 Trifecta £16.50 Pool £473.00 - 20.35 winning units..
Owner Ballymacoll Stud **Bred** Ballymacoll Stud Farm Ltd **Trained** Newmarket, Suffolk

FOCUS

A modest maiden but it was won in a decent time for the class of contest and the winner looks a very useful type in the making. The form could have been rated 5lb higher.

You're My Son Official explanation: jockey said gelding hung left

6822 EUROPEAN BREEDERS' FUND FILLIES' H'CAP 1m 2f (P)

2:50 (2:56) (Class 3) (0-90,80) 3-Y-0

£8,724 (£2,612; £1,306; £653; £326; £163) **Stalls** Low

Form RPR

5553 **1** **Baylini**[11] 6669 3-9-1 **77**... JamesDoyle 3 85
(Ms J S Doyle) *hld up: prog to chse clr ldr over 1f out: hung rt but r.o to ld last 100yds: sn clr* **3/1**[2]

3162 **2** *1 1/2* **Music Review**[24] 6389 3-9-2 **78**.................................... PaulHanagan 1 83
(R A Fahey) *led: kicked on 3f out: over 2 l clr 2f out: styd on inner in st: hdd and outpcd last 100yds* **7/2**[3]

0125 **3** *1/2* **Candy Mountain**[20] 6474 3-9-0 **76**.............................. JimmyFortune 6 80
(L M Cumani) *hld up in last pair: rdn on outer over 3f out: no prog tl styd on wl fnl f: nrst fin* **11/4**[1]

1612 **4** *3/4* **Lawyers Choice**[47] 5819 3-9-2 **78**.................................. DaneO'Neill 5 81
(Pat Eddery) *chsd ldrs: rdn and no imp over 2f out: kpt on same pce after: n.d* **6/1**

1050 **5** *2 1/2* **Silca Key**[5] 6757 3-8-13 **75**...................................... DarryllHolland 4 73
(M R Channon) *mostly chsd ldr to over 1f out: wknd* **7/1**

6330 **6** *shd* **World's Heroine (IRE)**[32] 6208 3-9-4 **80**......................... EddieAhern 2 77
(G A Butler) *hld up in last pair: lft wl bhd 3f out: shuffled along over 1f out: r.o fnl f: nvr in the r* **15/2**

2m 6.37s (-1.42) **Going Correction** -0.05s/f (Stan) 6 Ran SP% **112.4**
Speed ratings (Par 103): **103,101,101,100,98 98**
CSF £13.88 TOTE £3.30: £2.00, £2.30; EX 14.50.
Owner Ms J S Doyle **Bred** Templeton Stud **Trained** Upper Lambourn, Berks

FOCUS

A decent and tight little fillies' handicap in which Music Review set an even tempo. Once again the bias towards those that came down the middle of the track was evident. The winner ran to her recent C/D mark but the form is a bit shaky.

NOTEBOOK

Baylini, who ran a cracker against the boys from 1lb wrong over course and distance earlier in the month, was given a very intelligent ride and reaped the dividends. Settled travelling well in the pack, she was switched inside to cut the corner on the home bend, but had to be brought out wider to challenge the leader once into the straight - also because she was hanging slightly - and maintained her effort to swoop past. She does seem to love it here so there is no reason why she cannot find another opportunity. (op 10-3)

Music Review ◆, who has been running over further in recent months, had little choice but to try and make use of her stamina and although front-runners do not have as bad a record over this trip as over further here, it was still a big ask. She did make a brave fist of it though and was helped by not being taken on which enabled her to dictate at her own pace, but she stuck right against the inside rail once into the straight which made it almost inevitable that she would be cut down. This was still a good effort though and, as she remains unexposed on sand, she should be able to find a race or two on this surface. (op 5-1)

Candy Mountain, given a patient ride, tried to get closer around the outside racing down the side of the track, but she had to be hard ridden to do so. The way she came home strongly down the middle of the track in the slipstream of the winner suggests she is worth another try over further on this surface. (tchd 5-2)

Lawyers Choice, raised another 5lb after her narrow defeat at Kempton last time, was trying this trip for the first time and although close enough running to the final bend, did not find a great deal off the bridle. She did not really prove her stamina one way or the other. Official explanation: trainer said filly lost an off-fore shoe (tchd 13-2)

Silca Key, 15lb lower than on grass but still 9lb higher than when last on sand, raced closest to the leader for most of the way but she was also a little keen and had little more to offer once into the straight. She is totally exposed, having raced 25 times already in her life, and has nothing in the way of scope. (op 5-1)

World's Heroine(IRE) ◆, trying further than 1m for the first time, was given a strange ride. Settled at the back possibly to help her see out the trip, there did not appear to be much urgency as she lost touch with the rest of the field racing towards the home bend and she was not given much of a hard time in the straight either. It will be fascinating to see how she runs next time, especially if sticking to this trip. (op 7-1 tchd 8-1)

6823 WEDDINGS AT LINGFIELD PARK NURSERY 7f (P)

3:20 (3:21) (Class 4) (0-85,78) 2-Y-O **£4,533** (£1,348; £674; £336) **Stalls** Low

Form			Horse	Jockey	RPR
4520	1		**Geezers Colours**[19] 6503 2-8-10 **67**	FergusSweeney 7	71
			(K R Burke) *t.k.h: pressed ldr in slowly run r: chal over 1f out: narrow ld ins fnl f: jst prevailed* **12/1**		
1	2	*hd*	**King Hafhafah**[23] 6404 2-9-6 **77**	NCallan 2	80
			(I A Wood) *trckd ldng pair in slowly run r: effrt on inner 2f out: chal and w wnr ins fnl f: jst pipped* **8/1**		
0011	3	*¾*	**Cross Fell (USA)**[26] 6328 2-9-7 **78**	PatCosgrave 3	79
			(J R Boyle) *led: set v slow pce tl kicked on over 2f out: hdd and nt qckn ins fnl f* **2/1**[1]		
41	4	*hd*	**Afram Blue**[127] 3424 2-9-7 **78**	PaulDoe 1	79+
			(W J Knight) *hld up in 4th in slowly run r: effrt 2f out: styd on fr over 1f out but a hld* **11/2**		
0035	5	*shd*	**Diademas (USA)**[13] 6624 2-8-8 **65**	(e) DarryllHolland 6	65+
			(V Smith) *hld up in 6th in slowly run r: prog on outer over 2f out: drvn and nt qckn over 1f out: styd on last 100yds* **14/1**		
031	6	*1*	**Hucking Hero (IRE)**[23] 6401 2-9-0 **71**	DaneO'Neill 5	69+
			(J R Best) *s.s: hld up in 5th in slowly run r: effrt 2f out: chsng ldrs but hld whn nt clr run ins fnl f* **7/2**[2]		
1005	7	*5*	**Liberty Belle (IRE)**[59] 5480 2-9-5 **76**	GeorgeBaker 4	61
			(J R Best) *s.s: hld up in last in slowly run r: outpcd over 2f out: detached after* **9/2**[3]		

1m 29.06s (3.17) **Going Correction** -0.05s/f (Stan) **7** Ran SP% **114.6**

Speed ratings (Par 98): **79,78,77,77,77 76,70**

CSF £100.72 TOTE £17.10: £5.80, £2.70; EX 74.20.

Owner C Waters **Bred** Bloodhorse International Limited **Trained** Middleham Moor, N Yorks

FOCUS

A nonsense of a contest. Firstly the two John Best-trained horses fell out of the stalls, though they did not have much trouble catching up as the rest of the field went off at a crawl, and then a couple met plenty of trouble in the home straight. The form looks highly dubious because of that and, hardly surprisingly, the winning time was very moderate for a race like this.

NOTEBOOK

Geezers Colours returned to form after a dire effort at Wolverhampton last time and probably won this because he was best positioned throughout given the nature of the track and the way the race was run. He had nothing to spare at the line though and whether he was the best horse on the day is highly debatable. (op 11-1 tchd 14-1)

King Hafhafah, shock winner of a course-and-distance maiden on his debut, was given every chance but he was forced to make his challenge closer to the inside rail than ideal and just missed out. He has every right to be considered the moral winner, but this was a contest in which it is hard to draw any concrete conclusions about the form. (op 7-1)

Cross Fell(USA), bidding for a hat-trick off a 9lb higher mark on his debut for the yard, dictated at a very slow pace which enabled his pilot to commit when he wanted. His supporters can have no complaints over the route he took, as he was brought off the rail after turning in and it was lack of a bit of finishing toe in a race that developed into a sprint that proved his downfall. (op 11-4 tchd 3-1 in a place)

Afram Blue, up in trip for this nursery debut, was given a patient ride before being delivered in the home straight, but he became short of room on a couple of occasions inside the last furlong and would have gone even closer otherwise. (op 4-1 tchd 7-2)

Diademas(USA), racing beyond an extended 5f for the first time in his tenth outing, would have been suited by the way the race was run and kept on well down the outside to the line, but he enjoyed a trouble-free run whilst others did not and he is much more exposed than those that beat him. This contest also did not truly prove his stamina for the trip. (op 20-1)

Hucking Hero(IRE), who recorded a slightly faster time than King Hafhafah when winning the other division of the same maiden over course and distance last month, fell out of the stalls, and although the pedestrian pace meant he had little problem catching up, he then endured a nightmare passage when trying to get through against the inside in the home straight. This effort can probably be ignored. Official explanation: jockey said colt was denied a clear run (tchd 4-1)

Liberty Belle(IRE), up in trip for this sand debut, like her stable-companion walked out of the stalls but she never looked like getting involved. (op 5-1)

6824 LINGFIELD PARK FOR CHRISTMAS PARTIES H'CAP 1m (P)

3:50 (3:51) (Class 5) (0-75,73) 3-Y-O+ **£2,817** (£838; £418; £209) **Stalls** High

Form			Horse	Jockey	RPR
0020	1		**Meditation**[3] 6795 5-8-10 **63**	JamesDoyle 1	67
			(I A Wood) *mde all: set mod pce tl kicked on over 2f out: over a l clr 1f out: jst hld on* **9/1**		
5620	2	*shd*	**Run For Ede'S**[64] 5342 3-8-9 **64**	(p) EddieAhern 5	68
			(P M Phelan) *plld hrd: cl up: effrt on inner 2f out: r.o to chse wnr ins fnl f: jst failed* **12/1**		
3436	3	*nk*	**Aggravation**[17] 6547 5-9-1 **68**	JimmyFortune 6	71+
			(D R C Elsworth) *hld up in last trio: plenty to do whn plld out and effrt over 1f out: r.o wl fnl f: gaining at fin* **5/2**[1]		
0006	4	*¾*	**Stanley George (IRE)**[16] 6568 3-9-1 **70**	NCallan 4	71
			(M A Jarvis) *trckd ldr: rdn and no imp wl over 1f out: one pce and lost 2 pls ins fnl f* **12/1**		
0042	5	*1 ¼*	**Ninth House (USA)**[24] 6385 5-9-3 **73**	TravisBlock(3) 8	71
			(N P Littmoden) *hld up in last trio: effrt over 2f out: drvn and styd on fr over 1f out but only at same pce as ldrs* **4/1**[2]		
0251	6	*1*	**Smokin Joe**[8] 6716 6-9-0 **67** 6ex	(b) GeorgeBaker 9	63
			(J R Best) *t.k.h: hld up tl trckd ldrs on outer over 4f out: nt qckn over 1f out: sn outpcd* **4/1**[2]		
305	7	*1 ¼*	**Tom Paris**[13] 6628 3-9-0 **69**	SaleemGolam 7	62
			(W R Muir) *stdd s: hld up in last: outpcd whn pce lifted over 2f out: no ch after* **8/1**[3]		
3000	8	*4*	**Leptis Magna**[31] 6236 3-9-2 **71**	DaneO'Neill 2	55
			(D R C Elsworth) *plld hrd: trckd ldrs: rdn over 2f out: sn wknd* **8/1**[3]		

1m 38.71s (-0.72) **Going Correction** -0.05s/f (Stan)

WFA 3 from 5yo+ 2lb **8** Ran SP% **116.2**

Speed ratings (Par 103): **101,100,100,99,98 97,96,92**

CSF £109.73 CT £355.11 TOTE £8.40: £1.70, £3.20, £1.10; EX 90.70 Trifecta £340.90 Part won. Pool £480.25 - 0.96 winning units. Place 6 £425.73, Place 5 £259.73..

Owner Paddy Barrett **Bred** P E Barrett **Trained** Upper Lambourn, Berks

FOCUS

An ordinary handicap and one which developed into a tactical affair. The early pace was not strong and a couple pulled hard as a result, but they quickened appreciably over the last couple of furlongs. Not form to trust.

Smokin Joe Official explanation: jockey said gelding ran too free

T/Plt: £521.70 to a £1 stake. Pool: £49,991.50. 69.95 winning tickets. T/Qpdt: £53.40 to a £1 stake. Pool: £4,603.50. 63.70 winning tickets. JN

6819 LINGFIELD (L-H)

Friday, November 16

OFFICIAL GOING: Standard

Wind: Virtually nil

6825 LINGFIELDPARK.CO.UK H'CAP (DIV I) 7f (P)

12:00 (12:00) (Class 6) (0-60,60) 3-Y-O+ **£1,706** (£503; £252) **Stalls** Low

Form			Horse	Jockey	RPR
0001	1		**Quantum Leap**[16] 6587 10-9-1 **56**	(v) TQuinn 5	63
			(S Dow) *mid-div: hdwy over 1f out: str run to ld nr fin* **9/1**		
0031	2	*shd*	**Ever Cheerful**[15] 6607 6-9-5 **60**	(p) SteveDrowne 7	67
			(A B Haynes) *led: rdn ent fnl f: r.o: ct cl home* **5/1**[1]		
4022	3	*nk*	**Majestical (IRE)**[5] 6779 5-8-13 **54**	(e) DarryllHolland 4	60+
			(V Smith) *stdd s: hdwy whn short of room appr fnl f: r.o strly towards fin* **11/2**[2]		
0501	4	*nk*	**Rhapsilian**[18] 6542 3-8-7 **56**	KMay(7) 3	61
			(J A Geake) *trckd ldrs: rdn and ev ch ent fnl f: nt qckn nr fin* **8/1**		
2000	5	*shd*	**Convallaria (FR)**[24] 6413 4-9-0 **55**	(t) ChrisCatlin 13	60
			(G Wragg) *in rr tl hdwy on outside and str run ins fnl f: nvr nrr* **20/1**		
2100	6	*½*	**King After**[15] 6607 5-9-0 **55**	(v) DaneO'Neill 11	58
			(J R Best) *mid-div: rdn and hdwy 2f out: ev ch ins fnl f tl fdd nr fin* **10/1**		
0420	7	*nk*	**Sophia Gardens**[22] 6455 3-9-4 **60**	FergusSweeney 10	63
			(D W P Arbuthnot) *prom: hdwy on outside over 2f out: nt qckn ins fnl f* **16/1**		
0003	8	*½*	**Hannahbecc**[10] 6706 3-8-8 **50**	(e) SaleemGolam 8	51
			(S C Williams) *t.k.h: rdn 2f out: r.o fnl f* **12/1**		
6000	9	*1 ½*	**Border Artist**[15] 6607 8-8-12 **53**	RobertHavlin 9	50
			(J Pearce) *stdd s: racd keenly: nvr bttr than mid-div* **12/1**		
6	10	*½*	**Railway Express (IRE)**[4] 6796 3-8-5 **47**	PaulEddery 1	43
			(Bernard Lawlor, Ire) *in tch tl wknd fnl f* **16/1**		
0046	11	*hd*	**Lady Duxyana**[11] 4596 4-8-5 **46** oh1	(v) HayleyTurner 14	41
			(M D I Usher) *outpcd: in rr tl sme late hdwy* **33/1**		
00	12	*nk*	**Diamond Hurricane (IRE)**[15] 6608 3-8-5 **50**	NeilChalmers(3) 6	44
			(M Wellings) *t.k.h: prom tl rdn 2f out: sn btn* **50/1**		
2004	13	*1 ¾*	**Tilsworth Charlie**[9] 6717 4-9-2 **57**	(v) EddieAhern 2	47
			(J R Jenkins) *prom tl wknd appr fnl f* **12/1**		
0350	14	*1 ¾*	**Nikki Bea (IRE)**[33] 6210 4-9-3 **58**	PaulDoe 12	43
			(Jamie Poulton) *racd wd: rdn 2f out: sn wknd* **7/1**[3]		

1m 24.27s (-1.62) **Going Correction** -0.20s/f (Stan)

WFA 3 from 4yo+ 1lb **14** Ran SP% **119.3**

Speed ratings (Par 101): **101,100,100,100,100 99,99,98,96,96 96,95,93,91**

CSF £52.00 CT £277.11 TOTE £12.00: £3.90, £1.90, £1.60; EX 34.60 Trifecta £43.00 Part won. Pool: £60.60, 0.50 winning units..

Owner Mrs M E O'Shea **Bred** L C And Mrs A E Sigsworth **Trained** Epsom, Surrey

FOCUS

A competitive enough handicap for the grade in which each of the runners had some previous course experience. It was run at a sound early pace and the first six were closely covered at the finish, with the form making sense through the runner-up and fourth.

6826 PLAY GOLF @ LINGFIELD PARK CLAIMING STKS 6f (P)

12:25 (12:28) (Class 6) 3-Y-O+ **£2,047** (£604; £302) **Stalls** Low

Form			Horse	Jockey	RPR
1000	1		**One More Round (USA)**[12] 6668 9-9-7 90	(b) GeorgeBaker 10	77+
			(N P Littmoden) *stdd s: hld up in rr: c wd into st: hdwy bef hung lft fnl f: kpt on to ld nr fin* **9/4**[1]		
0005	2	*½*	**Mannello**[23] 6429 4-8-3 44 ow1	RichardThomas 7	57
			(Jim Best) *mid-div: hdwy over 1f out: r.o wl to snatch 2nd post* **33/1**		
3030	3	*shd*	**Pegasus Dancer (FR)**[10] 6702 3-9-5 71	(p) JohnEgan 5	73
			(K A Ryan) *led: rdn ent fnl f: hdd and lost 2nd nr fin* **16/1**		
5035	4	*hd*	**Regal Raider (IRE)**[18] 6531 4-8-9 63	(p) EddieAhern 4	62
			(A M Hales) *in tch: hdwy over 1f out: ev ch ins fnl f: no ex nr fin* **8/1**[3]		
0000	5	*nk*	**Pivotal Era**[16] 6581 4-8-7 55	(b[1]) FrancisNorton 8	59
			(Jim Best) *racd on outside: rdn over 1f out: r.o wl fnl f: nvr nrr* **25/1**		
0002	6	*¾*	**Mine Behind**[24] 6406 7-8-11 69	DaneO'Neill 9	61
			(J R Best) *towards rr: hdwy over 1f out: r.o: nt rch ldrs* **9/4**[1]		
3403	7	*shd*	**Mango Music**[8] 6735 4-8-13 80	MatthewDavies(7) 3	70
			(M R Channon) *prom: rdn over 2f out: one pce fnl f* **4/1**[2]		
4400	8	*1 ½*	**Detonate**[5] 6773 5-7-12 50	SophieDoyle(7) 11	50
			(I A Wood) *t.k.h: prom tl one pce fnl f* **50/1**		
1000	9	*hd*	**Mulberry Lad (IRE)**[15] 6607 5-8-10 55	ChrisCatlin 6	55
			(P W Hiatt) *prom tl rdn and wknd 1f out* **16/1**		
0300	10	*2*	**Bahamian Duke**[69] 5232 4-8-8 59	DeclanCannon(7) 1	54
			(K R Burke) *hmpd sn after s: mid-div: wknd ins fnl 2f* **50/1**		
0400	11	*3*	**Legal Set (IRE)**[5] 6773 11-8-9 50 ow1	(b) AnnStokell(5) 2	44
			(Miss A Stokell) *plld hrd in mid-div: wknd over 1f out* **50/1**		

500 **12** *9* **Ka'u Mauna Kea**[37] 6097 3-7-9 44 ow2 KMay[(7)] 12 —
(J A Geake) *racd wd in mid-div: wknd over 2f out* **80/1**

1m 12.06s (-0.75) **Going Correction** -0.20s/f (Stan) **12** Ran SP% **118.3**
Speed ratings (Par 101): **97,96,96,95,95 94,94,92,92,89 85,73**
CSF £94.36 TOTE £3.00: £1.60, £6.80, £4.30; EX 96.10 TRIFECTA Not won..The winner was claimed by Diamond Racing Ltd for £13,000

Owner Nigel Shields **Bred** Kenneth L Ramsey And Sarah K Ramsey **Trained** Newmarket, Suffolk

FOCUS
A typical claimer run at a modest pace and dubious form. Not a race to be with.
Regal Raider(IRE) Official explanation: jockey said gelding hung right
Ka'u Mauna Kea Official explanation: jockey said filly hung left

6827 LINGFIELDPARK.CO.UK MAIDEN AUCTION STKS 7f (P)
1:00 (1:01) (Class 6) 2-Y-O **£2,047** (£604; £302) **Stalls** Low

Form RPR

0002 **1** **Dhhamaan (IRE)**[10] 6705 2-8-11 75 (v[1]) HayleyTurner 1 71
(C E Brittain) *mde all: kicked clr ent fnl f: tiring towards fin: hld on* **7/1**[2]

2 *½* **Pravda Street** 2-9-3 0 TQuinn 9 75+
(P F I Cole) *a.p: chsd wnr fr 1/2-way: sltly outpcd ent fnl f: styd on towards fin* **3/1**[1]

463 **3** *1¼* **Nice Wee Girl (IRE)**[8] 6734 2-8-12 0 FrancisNorton 7 67
(S Kirk) *t.k.h in mid-div: hdwy over 1f out: r.o fnl f* **7/1**[2]

0 **4** *nk* **Burnbrake**[14] 6616 2-8-13 0 RobertHavlin 10 67
(J A R Toller) *slowly away: in rr: reminders 2f out: styd on wl fnl f: nvr nrr* **25/1**

04 **5** *nk* **Nordic Commander (IRE)**[20] 6503 2-8-13 0 TPQueally 3 66
(E A L Dunlop) *hld up: rdn and hdwy over 1f out: styd on one pce after* **3/1**[1]

6 *1½* **Gallic Charm (IRE)** 2-8-8 0 LPKeniry 11 58+
(D R C Elsworth) *sn bhd: styd on fnl f: nvr nr to chal* **20/1**

50 **7** *hd* **Rondeau (GR)**[16] 6578 2-8-9 0 PaulDoe 5 58
(P R Chamings) *v.s.a: hdwy on outside 2f out: nvr rchd ldrs* **9/1**[3]

4 **8** *shd* **Shesha Bear**[12] 6664 2-8-10 0 DarryllHolland 2 59
(W R Muir) *in tch: rdn over 2f out: wknd fnl f* **7/1**[2]

9 *hd* **Orange Square (IRE)** 2-9-1 0 RichardSmith 8 63+
(R Hannon) *mid-div: hdwy on ins whn hmpd over 1f out: no ch after* **14/1**

0065 **10** *4* **Coral Shores**[18] 6536 2-8-8 54 ChrisCatlin 12 46
(P W Hiatt) *mid-div: rdn over 2f out: sn wknd* **16/1**

00 **11** *½* **Dickie Valentine**[32] 6237 2-8-13 0 AdamKirby 6 50
(M R Bosley) *trckd wnr to 1/2-way: wknd over 1f out* **66/1**

1m 24.85s (-1.04) **Going Correction** -0.20s/f (Stan) **11** Ran SP% **120.1**
Speed ratings (Par 94): **97,96,95,94,94 92,92,92,92,87 86**
CSF £28.39 TOTE £7.70: £2.40, £1.60, £2.10; EX 32.60 Trifecta £89.50 Part won. Pool: 126.08, 0.72 winning units..

Owner C E Brittain **Bred** D Veitch And Musagd Abo Salim **Trained** Newmarket, Suffolk

FOCUS
A moderate juvenile maiden, which lost most of its interest when the likely warm order Whitcombe Minister was declared a non-runner. It was run at a solid early pace.

NOTEBOOK
Dhhamaan(IRE), 75-rated, made amends for a costly defeat over 6f at this venue ten days previously and just had enough in the tank to make every yard of the running. The application of a first-time visor had the desired effect and he got the extra furlong without any fuss this time. He is probably rated about right at present and his confidence should be higher now, but one will have to be wary of the headgear having the same effect next time when he steps outside of maiden company. (op 15-2 tchd 8-1)
Pravda Street, a newcomer, was prominent in the betting and clearly knew his job as he was quick to adopt a handy position. He had every chance, but just ran green passing the final furlong marker and, by the time he hit full-stride again, the winner was home and dry. He looked suited by this trip, but ought to get further in time and should really be placed to win one of these during the winter. (op 9-4)
Nice Wee Girl(IRE) moved kindly enough until turning for home, where she started to make heavy weather of it. She was keeping on towards the finish, albeit at the same pace, and had little trouble with the return to this extra furlong. Her life should be easier when she switches to nursery company and she rates a fair benchmark for this form. (tchd 15-2)
Burnbrake, not beaten all that far despite finishing last on his debut over this distance at Newmarket a fortnight previously, got himself outpaced through the first half of the race and looked well held turning for home. However, he stayed on stoutly inside the final furlong and evidently has some ability. A step up to 1m is well worth a try on this evidence and he will be eligible for a nursery mark after his next assignment.
Nordic Commander(IRE), fourth over this trip at Wolverhampton last time, proved a bit free just in behind the leaders and lacked the pace to land a significant blow when it mattered. He now qualifies for a nursery mark, however, and it would not be a surprise to see him fare better in that sphere when faced with another furlong. (op 9-2)
Gallic Charm(IRE), who cost 11,000gns, proved too green to do herself full justice on this racecourse bow. She was noted keeping on in the home straight and can be expected to prove sharper next time out.

6828 HOSPITALITY PACKAGES AVAILABLE (S) STKS 6f (P)
1:35 (1:36) (Class 6) 2-Y-O **£2,047** (£604; £302) **Stalls** Low

Form RPR

266 **1** **Atephobia**[10] 6699 2-8-11 66 FergusSweeney 11 72+
(K R Burke) *mde all: clr over 1f out: rdn out* **11/1**

6510 **2** *3½* **Too Grand**[14] 6624 2-8-8 59 (v) NeilChalmers[(3)] 6 61
(A M Balding) *stdd s: towards rr tl hdwy over 1f out: r.o to go 2nd nr fin: no ch w wnr* **12/1**

3100 **3** *¾* **Tan Bonita (USA)**[106] 4098 2-8-11 77 EddieAhern 5 59
(M J Wallace) *prom: wnt briefly 2nd 1f out: one pce ins fnl f* **11/4**[1]

3022 **4** *hd* **Mairead's Boy (IRE)**[4] 6793 2-8-11 55 (b) JohnEgan 9 58
(J S Moore) *chsd ldrs: rdn 2f out: one pce fnl f* **5/1**[2]

0416 **5** *2* **Maybe I Wont**[16] 6584 2-9-2 67 DarryllHolland 12 57
(S Dow) *in rr: hdwy fnl f: nvr nr to chal* **11/4**[1]

5260 **6** *2* **Redbrick Girl**[39] 6066 2-8-6 60 ChrisCatlin 8 41
(K A Ryan) *sn trckd wnr: wknd fnl f* **25/1**

4300 **7** *¾* **Freudian Slip**[23] 6432 2-8-6 66 (b[1]) PaulDoe 4 39
(S Curran) *s.i.s: in rr tl sme late hdwy* **8/1**[3]

P366 **8** *½* **Ely Une (IRE)**[8] 6734 2-8-6 59 (p) LPKeniry 7 37
(J S Moore) *mid-div: rdn 1/2-way: no hdwy fnl 2f* **50/1**

6160 **9** *hd* **Sharps Gold**[18] 6536 2-8-11 61 (t) SteveDrowne 10 42
(P J McBride) *chsd ldrs tl wknd over 1f out* **20/1**

040 **10** *nk* **Dusk Ballet**[37] 6099 2-8-6 54 SaleemGolam 1 36
(S C Williams) *prom tl outpcd over 2f out* **33/1**

00 **11** *3* **Doubloon**[9] 6725 2-8-11 0 RichardThomas 2 32
(J Gallagher) *t.k.h: mid-div tl wknd 2f out* **66/1**

0420 **12** *2½* **Orpen's Art (IRE)**[58] 5534 2-8-11 59 SimonWhitworth 3 24
(N A Callaghan) *trckd ldrs tl wknd 2f out* **11/1**

1m 11.31s (-1.50) **Going Correction** -0.20s/f (Stan) 2y crse rec **12** Ran SP% **120.5**
Speed ratings (Par 94): **102,97,96,96,93 90,89,89,88,88 84,81**
CSF £129.83 TOTE £14.30: £4.00, £3.10, £1.20; EX 155.60 TRIFECTA Not won..There was no bid for the winner. Maybe I Won't was claimed by Robert Stronge for £6,000

Owner P Timmins & A Rhodes Haulage **Bred** Ms Z N Watkins **Trained** Middleham Moor, N Yorks

FOCUS
A competitive enough seller on paper and the form looks strong for the grade and solid.

NOTEBOOK
Atephobiaovercame his wide draw by blasting out of the gates and, managing to lead after a furlong, kicked again early in the straight and came away for an easy success. This was a fair effort considering he raced on the supposedly disadvantageous rail for most of the way, and he looks capable of making a positive impact when returned to handicap-company. (op 14-1)
Too Grand, winner of a weak 5f handicap at Kempton two starts back, got too far back following a slow start at Wolverhampton last time and once again found herself with too much ground to make up, running on to finish a never-nearer second. This looks her right trip for the time being, but a more prominent ride would not go amiss in future. (tchd 14-1)
Tan Bonita(USA) had not been seen since finishing down the field in the Hilary Needler at Beverley back in May, and she set a decent standard being officially rated some 10lb higher than anything else in the field. However, having travelled well in midfield and briefly taken second in the straight, she was unable to get anywhere near the winner and in the end just held on for third. She would have been done no favours by racing towards the rail in the straight and it would be no surprise to see her do better in a similar race next time. Official explanation: jockey said filly did not stay (op 3-1)
Mairead's Boy(IRE), down slightly in grade having finished second in a couple of claimers at the course, was making a quick reappearance and looked a leading player, but in the end he was found wanting for a change of pace. He may be better at 7f. (op 9-2)
Maybe I Wont, a course and distance winner in a claimer last month, struggled to make an impact back in a handicap last time and he would have been expected to fare a lot better here, but just got too far behind. (tchd 3-1 in places)
Redbrick Girl, back down in grade having finished well-beaten in a handicap at Wolverhampton last month, gradually dropped away having been up there early and winning races is likely to remain a stern challenge.
Ely Une(IRE) Official explanation: jockey said filly suffered interference just after start
Sharps Gold Official explanation: jockey said filly had no more to give
Doubloon Official explanation: jockey said gelding ran too free

6829 BOOK ONLINE AT LINGFIELDPARK.CO.UK H'CAP 5f (P)
2:10 (2:11) (Class 5) (0-75,81) 3-Y-O+ **£2,817** (£838; £418; £209) **Stalls** High

Form RPR

4232 **1** **Financial Times (USA)**[4] 6794 5-9-4 **75** (t) MickyFenton 5 84
(Stef Liddiard) *slowly away: in rr tl hdwy over 1f out: rdn and r.o to ld nr fin* **11/4**[2]

4061 **2** *½* **Halsion Chancer**[4] 6794 3-9-2 **73** 6ex JohnEgan 2 80
(J R Best) *in tch: hdwy on ins to ld jst ins fnl f: r.o: hdd nr fin* **9/4**[1]

5521 **3** *nk* **Desperate Dan**[10] 6708 6-9-10 **81** 6ex DaneO'Neill 7 87
(A B Haynes) *mid-div: hdwy over 1f out: r.o fnl f to go 3rd nr fin* **3/1**[3]

15-5 **4** *½* **Mogok Ruby**[10] 6708 3-8-13 **70** RobertHavlin 6 74
(L Montague Hall) *trckd ldrs: rdn and ev ch 1f out: no ex nr fin* **16/1**

1001 **5** *shd* **Desert Opal**[27] 6340 7-9-3 **74** (b) TPQueally 1 78
(C R Dore) *towards rr: r.o fnl f: nvr nrr* **14/1**

1460 **6** *nk* **Fizzlephut (IRE)**[10] 6708 5-9-0 **71** PaulFitzsimons 4 74
(Miss J R Tooth) *led tl rdn and hdd jst ins fnl f: fdd cl home* **16/1**

2416 **7** *nk* **Make My Dream**[4] 6794 4-8-7 **64** GregFairley 9 66
(J Gallagher) *trckd ldr: rdn 2f out: wknd fnl f* **11/1**

4400 **8** *3* **Back In The Red (IRE)**[36] 6122 3-8-13 **70** ChrisCatlin 8 61
(R A Harris) *racd on outside: in rr fnl 2f* **20/1**

0000 **9** *1½* **Mambazo**[16] 6589 5-8-8 **72** (e) WilliamCarson[(7)] 10 57
(S C Williams) *stdd s: rdn over 2f out: nvr on terms* **22/1**

58.43 secs (-1.35) **Going Correction** -0.20s/f (Stan) **9** Ran SP% **118.3**
Speed ratings (Par 103): **102,101,100,99,99 99,98,94,91**
CSF £9.65 CT £19.58 TOTE £3.80: £1.60, £1.10, £1.80; EX 12.20 Trifecta £16.10 Pool: £357.62, 15.68 winning units.

Owner Mrs Stef Liddiard **Bred** Patricia Elia And Christopher Elia **Trained** Great Shefford, Berks

■ Stewards' Enquiry : Paul Fitzsimons one-day ban: used whip down shoulder in forehand position (Nov 27)

FOCUS
A fair handicap in which many of these had recent form that tied in with each other. The form looks reasonable although the proximity of the fourth raises doubts.

6830 LINGFIELD PARK FOR WEDDINGS MAIDEN STKS 7f (P)
2:45 (2:45) (Class 5) 3-Y-O **£2,968** (£876; £438) **Stalls** Low

Form RPR

304- **1** **Den's Gift (IRE)**[396] 6014 3-9-3 73 AdamKirby 7 79+
(C G Cox) *led for 2f: led again 2f out: hdd ent fnl f: rallied to ld again ins: all out* **7/1**[2]

3 **2** *shd* **Baharah (USA)**[14] 6621 3-8-12 0 EddieAhern 6 74+
(G A Butler) *t.k.h: prom: led seemingly gng wl ent fnl f: shkn up and sn hdd: no ex cl home* **2/9**[1]

0 **3** *10* **Accolation**[32] 6238 3-9-3 0 PatDobbs 3 52
(Pat Eddery) *led after 2f: rdn and hdd 2f out: sn no ch w first 2* **9/1**[3]

-060 **4** *1* **Falcon Flyer**[80] 4914 3-8-12 41 JohnEgan 1 44
(J R Best) *in rr: mde sme late hdwy* **33/1**

0 **5** *½* **Virgilia (IRE)**[306] 127 3-8-12 0 DaneO'Neill 8 43
(R Hannon) *a towards rr* **20/1**

0000 **6** *½* **Acece**[148] 2801 3-9-3 40 RobertHavlin 5 46
(D K Ivory) *prom tl wknd wl over 1f out* **33/1**

00 **7** *5* **Qatar Way (GR)**[157] 2541 3-8-12 0 JimCrowley 2 28
(P R Chamings) *prom tl rdn and wknd over 2f out* **50/1**

1m 24.57s (-1.32) **Going Correction** -0.20s/f (Stan) **7** Ran SP% **116.9**
Speed ratings (Par 102): **99,98,87,86,85 85,79**
CSF £9.33 TOTE £5.80: £2.50, £1.02; EX 13.80 Trifecta £43.70 Pool: £454.81, 7.38 winning units.

Owner Mrs Olive Shaw **Bred** Mrs J A Dene **Trained** Lambourn, Berks

FOCUS
A weak maiden that was run at just a steady early pace and, although the first pair came well clear, there was little solid in behind.
Accolation Official explanation: jockey said gelding ran too free

6831 LINGFIELDPARK.CO.UK H'CAP (DIV II) 7f (P)
3:20 (3:20) (Class 6) (0-60,60) 3-Y-O+ **£1,706** (£503; £252) **Stalls** Low

Form RPR

0003 **1** **Millfield (IRE)**[23] 6429 4-9-1 **55** GeorgeBaker 10 64+
(P R Chamings) *bhd tl hdwy over 1f out: r.o to ld wl ins fnl f* **7/2**[1]

4015 **2** 1 1/4 **Zazous**[13] 6647 6-9-4 **58** MickyFenton 6 64
(J J Bridger) *in tch: rdn to ld 1f out: kpt on u.p: hdd wl ins fnl f* **12/1**
0600 **3** 1 1/4 **Park Valley Prince**[10] 6706 3-8-9 **50** SaleemGolam 2 57+
(W R Muir) *t.k.h: nt clr run over 1f out: styd on to go 3rd cl home* **8/1[3]**
0005 **4** *hd* **Rafferty (IRE)**[16] 6587 8-8-4 **51** ow3 ThomasBubb(7) 14 53
(S Dow) *racd wd: hdwy over 1f out: styd on: nvr nrr* **20/1**
5606 **5** *shd* **High Class Problem (IRE)**[16] 6579 4-9-1 **55** JimCrowley 8 57
(P Winkworth) *prom: led wl over 1f out: hdd 1f out: no ex ins fnl f* **8/1[3]**
0400 **6** *1* **Pajada**[5] 6778 3-7-11 **45** (v) FrankiePickard(7) 1 44
(M D I Usher) *prom on outside: effrt over 1f out: kpt on ins fnl f* **25/1**
0120 **7** *nk* **Forced Upon Us**[24] 6415 3-9-5 **60** (b) EddieAhern 3 58
(P J McBride) *trckd ldrs: rdn on ins over 1f out: wknd ins fnl f* **7/2[1]**
540 **8** *shd* **Thea Di Bisanzio (IRE)**[27] 6339 3-9-2 **57** NickyMackay 9 55
(G A Butler) *nvr bttr than mid-div* **16/1**
0000 **9** 3/4 **Edin Burgher (FR)**[73] 5121 6-8-5 **45** (v[1]) HayleyTurner 7 41
(T T Clement) *trckd ldr to 2f out: wknd appr fnl f* **25/1**
-000 **10** *1* **Baba Ghanoush**[205] 1251 5-9-3 **57** PaulDoe 12 50
(J Akehurst) *a in rr* **14/1**
1043 **11** *shd* **Dasheena**[15] 6607 4-8-8 **55** (be) SophieDoyle(7) 4 48
(A J McCabe) *led tl hdd wl over 1f out: wknd qckly ins fnl f* **8/1[3]**
0403 **12** *3* **With Confidence**[46] 5866 3-9-2 **57** TQuinn 13 42
(D R C Elsworth) *towards rr on outside: hung rt over 1f out and no ch after* **15/2[2]**
5500 **13** *5* **Legend Erry (IRE)**[15] 6612 3-9-0 **55** JohnEgan 5 26
(Jane Chapple-Hyam) *sn in rr and styd there* **16/1**
0002 **14** 2 1/2 **Takaamul**[12] 6670 4-8-10 **50** ChrisCatlin 11 15
(K A Morgan) *in tch: rdn and wknd over 2f out* **12/1**

1m 24.09s (-1.80) **Going Correction** -0.20s/f (Stan)
WFA 3 from 4yo+ 1lb **14** Ran SP% **135.8**
Speed ratings (Par 101): **102,100,99,98,98 97,97,97,96,95 95,91,85,83**
CSF £54.83 CT £345.05 TOTE £5.20: £2.20, £3.80, £4.00; EX 66.80 TRIFECTA Not won..
Owner Patrick Chamings Sprint Club **Bred** Limestone Stud **Trained** Baughurst, Hants

FOCUS
This second division of the 7f handicap was run at a fair pace and was the quickest of the pair. The race looks sound with the first two and the fourth to form.
Park Valley Prince Official explanation: jockey said colt was denied a clear run
With Confidence Official explanation: jockey said filly hung right throughout
Legend Erry(IRE) Official explanation: jockey said gelding suffered interference in running

6832 DINE IN THE TRACKSIDE CARVERY H'CAP 1m 4f (P)
3:55 (3:56) (Class 6) (0-52,53) 3-Y-0+ **£2,047** (£604; £302) **Stalls** Low

Form RPR
6200 **1** **War Of The Roses (IRE)**[24] 6407 4-9-3 **52** J-PGuillambert 9 57
(R Brotherton) *in tch: rdn to ld jst ins fnl f: rdn out* **9/2[3]**
0014 **2** *2* **Mixing**[9] 6719 5-8-12 **52** KirstyMilczarek(5) 2 54
(J Akehurst) *trckd ldr: led 2f out: hdd jst ins fnl f: kpt on wl* **4/1[2]**
0006 **3** *shd* **Oasis Sun (IRE)**[4] 6792 4-8-11 **46** oh1 (b) JohnEgan 7 48
(J R Best) *hld up: hdwy over 1f out: r.o fnl f: nvr nrr* **14/1**
0-00 **4** *shd* **Henry Holmes**[37] 6096 4-8-13 **48** RichardThomas 6 50
(Mrs L Richards) *mid-div: rdn over 2f out: styd on fnl f* **40/1**
0204 **4** *dht* **My Monna**[16] 6590 3-8-6 **50** NeilChalmers(3) 14 52
(Miss Sheena West) *trckd ldrs: rdn over 2f out: kpt on one pce fnl f* **25/1**
6023 **6** 1/2 **Maria Antonia (IRE)**[22] 6453 4-8-10 **52** GHannon(7) 4 53+
(P A Blockley) *t.k.h in mid-div: rdn over 1f out: one pce fnl f* **16/1**
0400 **7** 1/2 **Garibaldi (GER)**[9] 6713 5-8-13 **53** ow1 (b) JamesO'Reilly(5) 1 53
(J O'Reilly) *s.i.s: sn in tch: rdn over 1f out: fdd ins fnl f* **16/1**
-013 **8** *nk* **Faraday (IRE)**[18] 6529 4-8-13 **48** TPQueally 3 48+
(B J Curley) *mid-div: effrt over 1f out: nt qckn ins fnl f* **7/2[1]**
0500 **9** 1 1/2 **Silver Surprise**[5] 6780 3-8-0 **46** oh1 NicolPolli(5) 12 43
(J J Bridger) *led tl hdd 2f out: wknd ins fnl f* **25/1**
5500 **10** *nk* **Big Ralph**[210] 1119 4-8-11 **46** oh1 JimCrowley 16 43
(D K Ivory) *stdd s: a towards rr* **22/1**
0620 **11** 1 1/2 **Prince Of Medina**[9] 6719 4-9-2 **51** DaneO'Neill 13 45
(J R Best) *stdd s: rdn over 2f out: nvr on terms* **10/1**
0-21 **12** 1/2 **Krasivi's Boy (USA)**[164] 496 5-9-2 **51** (b) GeorgeBaker 15 45
(G L Moore) *in tch: rdn 2f out: wknd fnl f* **11/2**
0004 **13** *1* **Mid Valley**[24] 6407 4-8-11 **46** oh1 EddieAhern 10 38
(J R Jenkins) *a bhd* **9/1**
566 **14** 1 1/4 **Beresford Lady**[28] 6315 3-8-5 **46** ChrisCatlin 8 36
(A D Brown) *in tch tl lost pl 3f out: sn btn* **25/1**
/0-0 **15** 1 1/2 **True Ruby**[23] 6430 4-8-4 **46** oh1 (b[1]) MatthewCosham(7) 5 34
(Dr J R J Naylor) *a struggling in rr* **66/1**
-000 **16** 3 1/2 **Jaufrette**[48] 5820 4-8-11 **46** FergusSweeney 11 28
(Dr J R J Naylor) *chsd ldrs: rdn over 3f out: sn wknd* **66/1**

2m 33.1s (-1.29) **Going Correction** -0.20s/f (Stan)
WFA 3 from 4yo+ 6lb **16** Ran SP% **134.6**
Speed ratings (Par 101): **96,94,94,94,94 94,93,93,92,92 91,91,90,89,88 86**
4th Place Tote: HH 3.30, MM 2.10. CSF £23.87 CT £253.73 TOTE £6.70: £1.80, £1.70, £3.40; EX 37.20 Trifecta £130.50 Pool £312.58, 1.70 winning units. Place 6 £ 15.12, Place 5 £ 7.48.
Owner P S J Croft **Bred** Mrs J Bailey **Trained** Elmley Castle, Worcs

FOCUS
A moderate handicap, run at a steady early gallop. The form should be treated with some caution with very little worthwhile form amongst those close up, and the race is rated negatively.
T/Plt: £18.60 to a £1 stake. Pool: £42,517.65. 1,661.55 winning tickets. T/Qpdt: £6.60 to a £1 stake. Pool: £3,276.30. 363.00 winning tickets. JS

6812 WOLVERHAMPTON (A.W) (L-H)
Friday, November 16

OFFICIAL GOING: Standard
Wind: Almost nil Weather: Overcast

6833 MACE RACING AT WOLVERHAMPTON CLAIMING STKS 1m 1f 103y(P)
7:00 (7:00) (Class 6) 3-Y-0 **£2,730** (£806; £403) **Stalls** Low

Form RPR
060 **1** **Without Excuse (USA)**[165] 2305 3-9-5 76 (b[1]) GregFairley 2 67
(M Botti) *hld up: rdn over 3f out: hdwy over 1f out: hung rt ins fnl f: r.o u.p to ld post* **9/1**
1130 **2** *hd* **Red Current**[32] 6245 3-9-0 65 LPKeniry 5 61
(R A Harris) *hld up: hdwy over 2f out: rdn to ld 1f out: hdd post* **7/2[2]**
63 **3** *hd* **Satindra (IRE)**[17] 6570 3-8-10 55 (tp) PhillipMakin 3 57
(John A Harris) *a.p: chsd ldr over 3f out: rdn and ev ch fr over 1f out: styd on* **5/1[3]**
0062 **4** *3* **Stay Active (USA)**[21] 6464 3-8-9 50 (v) TonyHamilton 6 50
(I Semple) *led: rdn and hdd 1f out: no ex* **7/2[2]**

3342 **5** *7* **Not Now Lewis (IRE)**[13] 6642 3-8-11 65 SteveDrowne 7 37
(J A Osborne) *chsd ldrs: rdn over 2f out: hung lft and wknd over 1f out* **15/8[1]**
0-00 **6** *7* **Bronco's Filly (IRE)**[39] 6060 3-7-13 38 ow1 MCGeran(7) 4 17
(J G M O'Shea) *s.i.s: hld up: rdn and wknd over 2f out* **100/1**
0563 **7** *10* **Polish Prospect (IRE)**[13] 6642 3-8-4 42 AdrianMcCarthy 1 —
(H S Howe) *trckd ldr 6f: sn rdn: wknd 2f out* **11/1**

2m 2.95s (0.33) **Going Correction** 0.0s/f (Stan) **7** Ran SP% **115.2**
Speed ratings (Par 98): **98,97,97,94,88 82,73**
CSF £40.97 TOTE £7.00: £4.20, £1.90; EX 37.10.
Owner A Nencini **Bred** Cashmark Farms Inc **Trained** Newmarket, Suffolk

FOCUS
A routine claimer run at just an ordinary early pace. With the front three finishing in a line across the track, the form is reasonably sound but probably means little outside of this grade.
Bronco's Filly(IRE) Official explanation: jockey said filly missed the break
Polish Prospect(IRE) Official explanation: jockey said filly finished lame

6834 KNOW PAINT GET GLIDDEN NURSERY 5f 20y(P)
7:30 (7:30) (Class 5) (0-75,72) 2-Y-0 **£2,968** (£876; £438) **Stalls** Low

Form RPR
3510 **1** **Weet A Surprise**[27] 6326 2-9-2 **67** HayleyTurner 9 71
(R Hollinshead) *hld up: nt clr run over 1f out: r.o u.p ins fnl f to ld last strides* **11/2**
4205 **2** *nk* **Wreningham**[20] 6502 2-8-12 **66** JerryO'Dwyer(3) 4 69
(T Keddy) *chsd ldrs: rdn to ld ins fnl f: hdd last strides* **9/2[3]**
1040 **3** 1 3/4 **Sinead Of Aglish (IRE)**[41] 6017 2-9-7 **72** (b[1]) LPKeniry 6 69
(Peter Grayson) *sn pushed along in rr: rdn 1/2-way: r.o ins fnl f: nt rch ldrs* **20/1**
2210 **4** *shd* **Fabuleux Cherie**[6] 6756 2-9-6 **71** FrancisNorton 5 67
(W R Muir) *prom: rdn over 1f out: styd on same pce ins fnl f* **4/1[2]**
0032 **5** *hd* **A Wish For You**[14] 6624 2-9-5 **70** SteveDrowne 1 66
(D K Ivory) *sn led: rdn over 1f out: hdd ins fnl f: edgd rt and styd on same pce* **9/1**
5313 **6** 1 1/4 **Angle Of Attack (IRE)**[7] 6741 2-9-7 **72** PaulHanagan 3 63
(R A Fahey) *chsd ldrs: rdn and hung rt 1/2-way: edgd lft over 1f out: wknd ins fnl f* **7/2[1]**
0204 **7** *nk* **Cocabana**[16] 6588 2-9-1 **66** JamesDoyle 8 56
(J G Portman) *chsd ldrs: rdn and hung rt over 1f out: no ex fnl f* **14/1**
002 **8** *1* **The Real Guru**[10] 6699 2-9-5 **70** (p) PaulMulrennan 2 56
(Mrs A Duffield) *chsd ldr: rdn 1/2-way: wknd fnl f* **5/1**

63.36 secs (0.54) **Going Correction** 0.0s/f (Stan) **8** Ran SP% **113.9**
Speed ratings (Par 96): **95,94,91,91,91 89,88,87**
CSF £30.12 CT £461.51 TOTE £7.60: £2.80, £1.20, £6.60; EX 27.20.
Owner Ed Weetman (haulage & Storage) Ltd **Bred** Longdon Stud Ltd **Trained** Upper Longdon, Staffs

FOCUS
An ordinary nursery in which they went hard up front early and rather set it up for the closers. The form looks fair rated around the principals.

NOTEBOOK
Weet A Surprise ◆, 4lb higher than when winning a similar event over course and distance last month, again found the strong early pace to her liking and she scythed her way through the field up the home straight to get up near the line. As she only does as much as is necessary, she may not be easy for the Handicapper to keep tabs with and she may also be worth another try over an extra furlong if ridden this way. (op 8-1)
Wreningham ◆, whose previous outings had all been over 6f, had every chance and was unfortunate to have the race snatched from him near the line. This trip probably suits him better and he should be able to find a similar event in which to break his duck. (op 6-1)
Sinead Of Aglish(IRE) ◆, making her debut on sand and for the yard in her 11th outing, seemed to find everything happening too quickly early, but she was putting in some sterling late work against the inside rail. She may be exposed on turf, but she is not on sand and there should be races to be won with her on this surface, possibly back over 6f. (op 11-1)
Fabuleux Cherie, narrowly beaten by Weet A Surprise over course and distance last month, was 4lb worse off with her here having been successful in the meantime. She could never land a blow on this occasion. (tchd 9-2)
A Wish For You, raised 5lb for a narrow defeat here earlier in the month, blitzed away from the rails draw and set a strong pace, but only succeeded in running herself into the ground. (op 13-2)
Angle Of Attack(IRE), 7lb higher than when winning at Lingfield last month, never looked happy and was always struggling to go the pace. (op 3-1)
Cocabana, closely matched with Fabulous Cherie on Lingfield running, did not help herself by hanging out into the centre of the track in the home straight. (tchd 16-1)

6835 STAY AT THE WOLVERHAMPTON HOLIDAY INN H'CAP 1m 5f 194y(P)
7:55 (7:56) (Class 6) (0-52,53) 3-Y-0+ **£2,047** (£604; £302) **Stalls** Low

Form RPR
2064 **1** **Young Scotton**[10] 6703 7-8-12 **49** AndrewElliott(3) 1 59
(J D Bethell) *a.p: chsd ldr over 2f out: rdn to ld 1f out: styd on* **7/1[3]**
6040 **2** *1* **Bugsy's Boy**[34] 6178 3-8-10 **52** LiamJones 4 60
(P W D'Arcy) *led 1f: chsd ldr tl led over 3f out: rdn and hdd 1f out: styd on same pce* **3/1[1]**
5000 **3** *5* **Jenny Soba**[4] 6797 4-8-8 **45** (p) NeilChalmers(3) 8 46
(Lucinda Featherstone) *hld up: styd on appr fnl f: nrst fin* **16/1**
6034 **4** 1 1/2 **Squirtle (IRE)**[15] 6613 4-8-13 **47** StephenDonohoe 5 46+
(W M Brisbourne) *s.i.s: hld up: hdwy over 1f out: nvr nrr* **7/1[3]**
0200 **5** *2* **Centenary (IRE)**[9] 6713 3-8-8 **50** (p) FrancisNorton 9 46
(D E Cantillon) *hld up in tch: rdn and lost pl over 5f out: n.d after* **10/1**
-000 **6** 3 1/2 **Ice And Fire**[27] 6330 8-8-7 **46** (b) AshleyHamblett(5) 10 37
(J T Stimpson) *hld up: hdwy over 2f out: rdn and wknd over 1f out* **20/1**
2525 **7** *1* **Cragganmore Creek**[15] 6613 4-8-12 **46** (v) TGMcLaughlin 11 36
(D Morris) *hld up: hdwy 6f out: rdn and wknd over 2f out* **12/1**
0063 **8** 2 1/2 **Diktatorship (IRE)**[15] 6613 4-9-2 **50** (p) GregFairley 6 36
(Jennie Candlish) *led after 1f: rdn and hdd over 3f out: wknd 2f out* **9/2[2]**
0065 **9** *19* **Sea Frolic (IRE)**[2] 6817 6-8-11 **45** HayleyTurner 7 5
(Jennie Candlish) *hld up: a in rr: wknd over 3f out: eased* **16/1**
0-63 **10** *nk* **Shamrock Bay**[178] 1590 5-8-12 **46** AdamKirby 13 5
(C R Dore) *hld up in tch: rdn 5f out: wknd over 3f out* **15/2**
5050 **11** *nk* **Taran Tregarth**[2] 6815 3-7-10 **45** Julie-AnneCumine(7) 3 4
(W M Brisbourne) *hld up in tch: rdn and wknd 4f out* **66/1**
3304 **12** *14* **Bret Maverick (IRE)**[12] 6672 3-8-11 **53** ow1 DanielTudhope 12 —
(B P J Baugh) *chsd ldrs: rdn 7f out: wknd 4f out* **16/1**
01-0 **13** *11* **Princess Of Aeneas (IRE)**[23] 6431 4-9-1 **49** LPKeniry 2 —
(Peter Grayson) *s.i.s: hld up: rdn and wknd 4f out* **33/1**

3m 5.42s (-1.95) **Going Correction** 0.0s/f (Stan)
WFA 3 from 4yo+ 8lb **13** Ran SP% **123.6**
Speed ratings (Par 101): **105,104,101,100,99 97,97,95,84,84 84,76,70**
CSF £28.73 CT £340.12 TOTE £9.00: £2.80, £2.50, £5.50; EX 55.70.
Owner Elliott Brothers **Bred** Lady Bland & Miss Anthea Gibson-Fleming **Trained** Middleham Moor, N Yorks

FOCUS
A moderate staying handicap, but they went a decent pace, the field finished well spread out and the form looks sound. Despite the solid gallop, the front pair were always up there and not many ever got into it.

6836 WOLVERHAMPTON-RACECOURSE.CO.UK H'CAP — 5f 216y(P)
8:25 (8:26) (Class 4) (0-85,85) 3-Y-0+ **£4,857** (£1,445; £722; £360) **Stalls** Low

Form RPR

2400 **1** **Curtail (IRE)**[26] 6355 4-9-3 **84** .... PhillipMakin 7 93
(I Semple) *led: rdn: edgd lft and hdd ins fnl f: rallied to ld nr fin* **18/1**

0332 **2** *shd* **Abunai**[41] 6006 3-9-1 **82** .... SteveDrowne 10 91
(R Charlton) *chsd ldrs: rdn to ld and edgd lft ins fnl f: hdd nr fin* **9/2**[2]

6012 **3** *1 ½* **Westport**[25] 6381 4-8-12 **79** .... FrancisNorton 3 83
(K A Ryan) *chsd ldrs: rdn over 1f out: sn ev ch: styd on same pce ins fnl f* **4/1**[1]

4110 **4** *1* **Cornus**[22] 6450 5-8-13 **80** ....(be) JamesDoyle 4 81
(A J McCabe) *chsd ldrs: rdn over 2f out: sn outpcd: styd on ins fnl f* **16/1**

0020 **5** *½* **Russian Symphony (USA)**[41] 6006 6-8-12 **79** .... RobertHavlin 6 78
(C R Egerton) *chsd ldrs: rdn 1/2-way: outpcd and hung lft wl over 1f out: styd on ins fnl f* **15/2**

2003 **6** *½* **Buy On The Red**[10] 6707 6-9-2 **83** ....(p) SaleemGolam 5 80
(W R Muir) *hld up: hdwy over 2f out: rdn over 1f out: styd on same pce ins fnl f* **16/1**

2002 **7** *¾* **Avertuoso**[7] 6743 3-9-1 **82** .... PaulHanagan 8 77
(B Smart) *chsd wnr tl rdn 2f out: wknd ins fnl f* **12/1**

5405 **8** *shd* **Roman Maze**[15] 6606 7-9-4 **85** .... GeorgeBaker 9 80
(W M Brisbourne) *hld up: pushed along 1/2-way: styd on ins fnl f: nt pce to chal* **11/2**

0 **9** *1* **Dress To Impress (IRE)**[96] 4429 3-8-11 **78** .... PatCosgrave 2 70
(G A Butler) *s.i.s: hld up: n.d* **22/1**

-000 **10** *¾* **Stolt (IRE)**[25] 6381 3-8-12 **79** .... DanielTudhope 13 68
(N Wilson) *s.i.s: in rr: bhd 1/2-way: n.d* **66/1**

302 **11** *1 ½* **Pawan (IRE)**[134] 3240 7-8-8 **80** ow1........(b) AnnStokell(5) 12 64
(Miss A Stokell) *mid-div: hdwy 1/2-way: rdn over 2f out: wknd over 1f out* **40/1**

0004 **12** *1* **Ingleby Arch (USA)**[64] 5356 4-8-12 **84** .... NeilBrown(5) 1 65
(T D Barron) *s.i.s: a in rr* **5/1**[3]

2042 **13** *1 ½* **Sir Nod**[26] 6355 5-9-0 **81** .... PaulMulrennan 11 57
(Miss J A Camacho) *hld up: plld hrd: hung rt and hdwy over 2f out: wknd wl over 1f out* **9/1**

1m 14.56s (-1.25) **Going Correction** 0.0s/f (Stan) **13** Ran SP% **125.0**
Speed ratings (Par 105): **108,107,105,104,103 103,102,102,100,99 97,96,94**
CSF £100.59 CT £417.85 TOTE £24.60: £13.70, £1.80, £2.00; EX 145.50.
Owner Gordon McDowall **Bred** Highfort Stud **Trained** Carluke, S Lanarks

FOCUS
This was a hot little sprint handicap run at a decent pace and te form looks reasonable assessed through the runner-up. As in the previous race, those that raced handily dominated throughout and nothing else ever really got involved.
Sir Nod Official explanation: jockey said gelding hung right

6837 BOOK YOUR 2008 CONFERENCE NOW H'CAP — 1m 1f 103y(P)
8:55 (8:55) (Class 6) (0-65,64) 3-Y-0+ **£2,047** (£604; £302) **Stalls** Low

Form RPR

1131 **1** **Prince Noel**[11] 6695 3-8-9 **62** 6ex........ LanceBetts(7) 3 70+
(N Wilson) *a.p: rdn to ld over 1f out: hung lft ins fnl f: r.o* **4/1**[3]

2126 **2** *nk* **Keisha Kayleigh (IRE)**[25] 6380 4-9-4 **61**........(v) J-PGuillambert 6 65
(B Ellison) *hld up: hdwy u.p over 1f out: hung lft: r.o* **6/1**

6001 **3** *¾* **Moonlight Fantasy (IRE)**[4] 6804 4-8-13 **56** 6ex........ TGMcLaughlin 5 59
(Lucinda Featherstone) *stdd s: hld up: hdwy over 2f out: rdn and ev ch over 1f out: styd on* **8/1**

5600 **4** *½* **Thornaby Green**[16] 6598 6-9-3 **60** .... PhillipMakin 4 62
(T D Barron) *chsd ldr tl led over 2f out: rdn and hdd over 1f out: styng on same pce whn nt clr run ins fnl f* **12/1**

4413 **5** *3* **Lord Of Dreams (IRE)**[36] 6124 5-9-7 **64** .... GeorgeBaker 8 59
(G L Moore) *hld up: hdwy over 3f out: rdn and hung lft fr over 1f out: no ex* **11/4**[1]

000- **6** *4* **Shaydreambeliever**[328] 6929 4-9-7 **64** .... PaulHanagan 1 51
(R A Fahey) *chsd ldrs: rdn over 5f out: wknd 3f out* **33/1**

0006 **7** *1* **Thumpers Dream**[14] 6628 4-9-5 **62**........(b) DanielTudhope 2 47
(I W McInnes) *led: rdn and hdd over 2f out: wknd over 1f out* **15/2**

1500 **8** *1* **Mandalay Prince**[20] 6506 3-8-10 **56** .... NeilPollard 9 39
(W J Musson) *hld up: hdwy over 4f out: wknd 3f out* **20/1**

3600 **9** *2 ½* **Barbirolli**[17] 6558 5-8-12 **55** .... LiamJones 7 33
(W M Brisbourne) *chsd ldrs: rdn over 4f out: wknd over 2f out* **7/2**[2]

2m 2.68s (0.06) **Going Correction** 0.0s/f (Stan)
WFA 3 from 4yo+ 3lb **9** Ran SP% **121.4**
Speed ratings (Par 101): **99,98,98,97,94 91,90,89,87**
CSF £29.94 CT £188.71 TOTE £3.10: £1.30, £2.20, £4.10; EX 38.20.
Owner The Giggle Factor Partnership **Bred** P And Mrs A G Venner **Trained** Flaxton, N Yorks
■ Stewards' Enquiry : Lance Betts three-day ban: careless riding (Nov 27,28,30)

FOCUS
An ordinary handicap in which they did not did not go a great pace early and there was not much separating the front four at the line.

6838 HOTEL AND CONFERENCING AT WOLVERHAMPTON H'CAP — 1m 141y(P)
9:20 (9:20) (Class 5) (0-70,68) 3-Y-0+ **£2,968** (£876; £438) **Stalls** Low

Form RPR

0114 **1** **Spinning**[7] 6746 4-9-7 **68** ....(b) PhillipMakin 1 77
(T D Barron) *hld up: hdwy over 4f out: rdn over 2f out: edgd lft and led ins fnl f: styd on u.p* **11/2**[3]

0563 **2** *½* **Baan (USA)**[8] 6738 4-9-5 **66** ....(b) GregFairley 7 74
(M Johnston) *chsd clr ldr: led wl over 1f out: sn rdn: edgd lft and hdd ins fnl f: styd on* **6/4**[1]

5665 **3** *3 ½* **Swift Cut (IRE)**[93] 4515 3-8-12 **65** .... AndrewElliott(3) 3 65
(A P Jarvis) *chsd ldrs: rdn over 4f out: hung rt over 2f out: styd on same pce appr fnl f* **8/1**

6305 **4** *2* **Fine Ruler (IRE)**[11] 6695 3-9-3 **67** .... GeorgeBaker 6 62
(M R Bosley) *led: clr 7f out: rdn and hdd wl over 1f out: wknd fnl f* **11/2**[3]

3244 **5** *¾* **Obe Royal**[12] 6677 3-8-12 **62** ....(p) TGMcLaughlin 4 56
(P D Evans) *hld up: racd keenly: effrt over 2f out: sn wknd* **10/3**[2]

6 *¾* **Rock Of Tarik (IRE)**[27] 6351 3-8-11 **64**........(t) JerryO'Dwyer(3) 2 56
(M J Grassick, Ire) *hld up: rdn over 3f out: wknd 2f out* **10/1**

1m 51.23s (-0.53) **Going Correction** 0.0s/f (Stan)
WFA 3 from 4yo 3lb **6** Ran SP% **114.0**
Speed ratings (Par 103): **102,101,98,96,96 95**
CSF £14.62 TOTE £6.40: £4.20, £2.40; EX 7.90.
Owner Mrs J Hazell **Bred** Cheveley Park Stud **Trained** Maunby, N Yorks

FOCUS
A modest handicap and not very competitive either due to the small field and the form looks weak. The early pace was strong with Fine Ruler going off at a rated of knots, but the others ignored him and once he folded the contest only ever really concerned the front pair.
Fine Ruler(IRE) Official explanation: jockey said gelding ran too freely
T/Plt: £409.70 to a £1 stake. Pool: £101,145.85. 180.20 winning tickets. T/Qpdt: £12.40 to a £1 stake. Pool: £6,617.80. 394.20 winning tickets. CR

6839 - 6846a (Foreign Racing) - See Raceform Interactive

6825 LINGFIELD (L-H)
Saturday, November 17

OFFICIAL GOING: Standard
Wind: Modest, behind Weather: Overcast

6847 EUROPEAN BREEDERS' FUND MAIDEN FILLIES' STKS (DIV I) — 7f (P)
12:00 (12:00) (Class 5) 2-Y-0 **£3,141** (£934; £467; £233) **Stalls** Low

Form RPR

1 **Fantasy Princess (USA)** 2-9-0 0........ NickyMackay 1 73
(G A Butler) *s.i.s: sn in midfield: hdwy on inner jst over 2f out: qcknd to ld last 100yds: sn hung rt: hld on* **12/1**

2 *hd* **Crystal Capella** 2-9-0 0........ NCallan 6 73+
(Sir Michael Stoute) *s.i.s: bhd: hdwy 3f out: rdn over 2f out: str run on outer fnl f: jst hld* **4/1**[2]

0 **3** *½* **Shindy (FR)**[14] 6649 2-9-0 0........ OscarUrbina 5 71
(J A R Toller) *in tch: rdn wl over 1f out: r.o ins fnl f: wnt 3rd nr fin* **12/1**

6053 **4** *1* **Acquifer**[33] 6225 2-9-0 74........ EddieAhern 4 69
(J L Dunlop) *trckd ldrs: rdn to chse ldr 2f out: ev ch over 1f out: outpcd last 100yds* **7/2**[1]

0 **5** *nk* **Arabian Art (USA)**[14] 6648 2-9-0 0........ TPQueally 8 68+
(H R A Cecil) *led at stdy pce: rdn jst over 2f out: hdd and hmpd ins fnl f: outpcd last 100yds* **15/2**[3]

0 **6** *1 ¾* **Sinaaf**[24] 6434 2-9-0 0........ RHills 10 64
(M P Tregoning) *chsd ldr tl 2f out: rdn and kpt on same pce over 1f out* **9/1**

7 *hd* **Rhadegunda** 2-9-0 0........ JimmyFortune 9 63+
(J H M Gosden) *s.i.s: bhd: rdn and plld out over 1f out: kpt on but nvr nr ldrs* **4/1**[2]

00 **8** *4* **Oriental Girl**[16] 6601 2-9-0 0........ RichardThomas 11 53
(J A Geake) *hld up in midfield tl lost pl over 3f out: no ch last 2f* **33/1**

0 **9** *½* **La Gazzetta (IRE)**[14] 6649 2-9-0 0........ TQuinn 7 52
(D R C Elsworth) *in tch: rdn 3f out: wknd jst over 2f out* **14/1**

10 *5* **Tessie Bear** 2-9-0 0........ JimCrowley 3 39
(Andrew Reid) *hld up in midfield: short of room and lost pl 5f out: sn pushed along and struggling: no ch fr 1/2-way* **33/1**

11 *8* **Peggle** 2-9-0 0........ TomEaves 2 19
(M H Tompkins) *nvr gng pce and sn pushed along in last: wl bhd fr 1/2-way: t.o* **33/1**

1m 25.51s (-0.38) **Going Correction** -0.175s/f (Stan) **11** Ran SP% **114.9**
Speed ratings (Par 93): **95,94,94,93,92 90,90,85,85,79 70**
CSF £57.31 TOTE £23.40: £4.20, £3.70, £2.90; EX 66.00 TRIFECTA Not won..
Owner A D Spence **Bred** Budget Stables **Trained** Blewbury, Oxon

FOCUS
An ordinary maiden, though despite a modest early pace the winning time was still 0.38 seconds faster than the second division and this is probably the stronger leg. There was little covering the principals at the line so the form does not look anything special.

NOTEBOOK
Fantasy Princess(USA), a 250,000euros half-sister to a couple of winners at up to 7f, was not best away but the modest pace meant that she was not inconvenienced and she travelled particularly well. She initially made her effort closest to the inside rail in the straight, but hung out towards the centre once in front and, given the narrow margin and the way the track has been riding, that may have made the difference between victory and defeat. The form is nothing special, but she is entitled to improve and her breeding suggests this will be as far as she wants. (op 11-1)
Crystal Capella, out of a dual 7f winner at two, was given a patient ride on this debut and was right alongside the eventual winner running to the last bend. She was briefly stopped on the turn, but flew down the wide outside late and she would have got there with a little further to go. She cannot really be considered unlucky though, as she ended up making her effort down the favoured centre of the track and, though she may be nothing special, clearly has the ability to win races. (op 10-3)
Shindy(FR) improved from her Newmarket debut and was staying on well at the end. She looks the type that will really come into her own in handicaps over a bit further.
Acquifer, the most exposed in the field, was trying this trip for the first time yet was still exposed for toe where it mattered. She is surely worth a try in a nursery now.
Arabian Art(USA), ridden in contrasting style to her Newmarket debut, proved a sitting duck for the finishers and, although she was done no favours by the winner late on, she was already beaten at the time. (tchd 8-1)
Sinaaf, ridden much closer to the pace than on her debut here last month, had every chance but found little when let down. Related to a whole host of winners on the dam's side, her two efforts to date suggest she will need to improve plenty to uphold the family tradition and her best hope is that she will be improve for a longer trip next term.

6848 SCOTT COMBUSTION H'CAP — 1m 2f (P)
12:25 (12:27) (Class 5) (0-75,75) 3-Y-0+ **£2,817** (£838; £418; £209) **Stalls** Low

Form RPR

2634 **1** **Kindlelight Blue (IRE)**[21] 6506 3-8-10 **67** .... JamesDoyle 9 72
(N P Littmoden) *hld up in midfield: hdwy on outer to ld 5f out: mde rest: hrd pressed and rdn over 2f out: edgd lft ins fnl f: styd on wl to assert last 75yds* **6/1**[2]

02 **2** *1* **Jago (SWI)**[16] 6603 4-8-9 **62** .... LPKeniry 1 65
(A M Hales) *t.k.h: trckd ldrs: effrt on inner over 2f out: ev ch over 1f out: edgd rt and unable qckn wl ins fnl f* **8/1**[3]

0536 **3** *nk* **Blu Manruna**[17] 6577 4-8-3 **61** oh5........(b) KirstyMilczarek(5) 6 63
(J Akehurst) *mostly 2nd: rdn over 2f out: kpt on u.p: wnt 3rd nr fin* **12/1**

3000 **4** *nk* **Oakley Heffert (IRE)**[13] 6669 3-9-1 **72**........(b) RichardHughes 2 74+
(R Hannon) *led at stdy pce tl 5f out: rdn and ev ch over 2f out: btn whn short of room last 50yds* **7/2**[1]

0401 **5** *½* **Topiary Ted**[233] 819 5-9-7 **74** .... RichardKingscote 3 75
(Tom Dascombe) *t.k.h: hld up wl in tch towards rr: rdn 3f out: hdwy over 2f out: kpt on but nt quite rch ldrs* **8/1**[3]

6036 **6** *nk* **Masterofthecourt (USA)**[14] 6651 4-9-8 **75** .... SteveDrowne 5 75
(H Morrison) *t.k.h: hld up in tch: rdn 3f out: outpcd wl over 1f out: kpt on fnl f* **7/2**[1]

3413 **7** *nk* **Waterline Twenty (IRE)**[11] 6710 4-9-6 **73** .... JohnEgan 10 73+
(P D Evans) *hld up in rr: hdwy over 3f out: chsd ldrs and rdn 2f out: keeping on same pce whn nt clr run last 50yds* **11/1**

150- **8** 2 **Bay Hawk**[343] 6766 5-8-10 **70**.. KylieManser(7) 4 66
(B G Powell) *s.i.s: t.k.h: hld up in midfield: rdn and effrt on inner wl over 1f out: nvr threatened ldrs* **33/1**

3164 **9** 1 **Burgundy**[30] 6276 10-9-2 **69**..(b) TPQueally 7 63
(R A Teal) *hld up in last: n.d* **10/1**

6020 **10** shd **Resplendent Ace (IRE)**[16] 6603 3-8-13 **70**.................. ChrisCatlin 8 63
(P Howling) *t.k.h: hld up in rr: nvr trbld ldrs* **11/1**

0050 **11** 7 **Title Deed (USA)**[94] 4511 3-8-5 **65**........................ AndrewElliott(3) 11 44
(A P Jarvis) *s.i.s: t.k.h: chsd ldrs tl rdn and lost pl over 2f out: sn bhd* **20/1**

2m 9.04s (1.25) **Going Correction** -0.175s/f (Stan)
WFA 3 from 4yo+ 4lb **11** Ran SP% **122.1**
Speed ratings (Par 103): **88,87,86,86,86 86,85,84,83,83 77**
CSF £55.64 CT £571.31 TOTE £9.20: £2.50, £2.40, £7.00; EX 54.60 TRIFECTA Not won..
Owner Kindlelight Ltd **Bred** Benedikt Fassbender **Trained** Newmarket, Suffolk

FOCUS
An ordinary contest run at a modest pace resulting in a moderate time, and those that raced handily seemed to be at an advantage. The principals finished in a heap though, so the form looks messy and probably does not amount to much.
Jago(SWI) ◆ Official explanation: jockey said gelding hung right in straight
Waterline Twenty(IRE) Official explanation: jockey said filly was denied a clear run

6849 EUROPEAN BREEDERS' FUND MAIDEN FILLIES' STKS (DIV II) 7f (P)
12:50 (12:51) (Class 5) 2-Y-O **£3,141** (£934; £467; £233) **Stalls** Low

Form RPR

1 **Mafasina (USA)** 2-9-0 0.. EddieAhern 7 64+
(Christian Wroe) *s.i.s: hld up bhd: gd hdwy jst over 1f out: swtchd rt ins fnl f: str run to ld towards fin: readily* **16/1**

06 **2** 1 **Marraasi (USA)**[24] 6432 2-9-0 0.. RHills 9 62
(M P Tregoning) *trckd ldrs tl chsd ldr over 2f out: rdn to ld over 1f out: hdd and outpcd towards fin* **10/3**[2]

0200 **3** ¾ **Smokey Rye**[23] 6449 2-9-0 58..(b[1]) FergusSweeney 3 60
(G L Moore) *in tch in midfield: swished tail over 2f out: styd on wl u.p fnl f* **25/1**

4 shd **Belotto (IRE)** 2-9-0 0.. SteveDrowne 8 60+
(R Charlton) *hld up in midfield on outer: hdwy and rdn 2f out: kpt on ins fnl f* **12/1**

456 **5** ¾ **Bookish**[18] 6574 2-9-0 63.. GregFairley 6 58
(M Johnston) *chsd ldr tl over 2f out: sn rdn: wknd over 1f out* **13/2**

53 **6** shd **Edie Superstar (USA)**[36] 6140 2-9-0 0.................. DarryllHolland 10 58
(M A Magnusson) *t.k.h: led: rdn over 2f out: hdd over 1f out: wknd ins fnl f* **9/4**[1]

66 **7** 2 **Rakeekah**[25] 6411 2-9-0 0.. JimmyFortune 4 53+
(J H M Gosden) *t.k.h: in tch: rdn over 2f out: keeping on same pce whn squeezed out jst ins fnl f* **7/2**[3]

8 ½ **Spitfire Jane (IRE)** 2-8-11 0.. AndrewElliott(3) 5 51
(K R Burke) *s.i.s: sn bhd and pushed along: sme late hdwy: n.d* **16/1**

9 hd **Bon Ton Roulet** 2-9-0 0.. RichardHughes 2 51
(R Hannon) *s.i.s: hld up bhd: nt clr run briefly over 2f out: c wd 2f out: n.d* **10/1**

1m 25.89s **Going Correction** -0.175s/f (Stan) **9** Ran SP% **121.8**
Speed ratings (Par 93): **93,91,91,90,90 89,87,87,86**
CSF £72.72 TOTE £18.00: £4.80, £1.40, £4.50; EX 86.20 TRIFECTA Not won..
Owner Prime Equestrian **Bred** Gainesway Thoroughbreds Ltd **Trained** Kimpton, Hants

FOCUS
Like the first division this looked an ordinary maiden especially with the third horse, who sets the level, rated just 58. Although the early pace was stronger than in division one, the final time was 0.38 seconds slower.

NOTEBOOK
Mafasina(USA), a 45,000gns two-year-old who is a half-sister to two winners in the US and one in Japan, was ridden with the utmost confidence and the only worry was whether she would get a gap when she needed it. Happily she did and she produced an impressive turn of foot, on admittedly the fastest trip, to cut down the runner-up near the line. The form may be nothing special, but she is entitled to improve from this. (tchd 20-1)
Marraasi(USA) was always in a good position and had every chance, but once she hit the front she hung over to the inside rail and the winner's turn of foot swamped her completely. She looks ordinary even though this was her best effort to date, but she can now be handicapped which widens her options. (op 9-2 tchd 5-1)
Smokey Rye, the most exposed in the field though this was her sand debut, seemed to be improved by the first-time blinkers and finished strongly to snatch third, but she showed her disgust when hit with the whip so may not be straightforward and her proximity does not do much for the form.
Belotto(IRE) ◆, out of a winner over 1m 4f, stayed on nicely down the wide outside in the closing stages and, as the stable's youngsters normally improve with racing, this was a more than satisfactory debut. She should really come into her own over middle-distances in due course. (op 11-1)
Bookish had every chance, but found little once in line for home. She will continue to be vulnerable to improvers in races like this, but the fact that she finished behind a rival rated 5lb lower than her does not suggest she is on a lenient handicap mark either. (tchd 7-1)
Edie Superstar(USA), down a furlong, was able to set her own tempo but once into the straight she was cut down rather easily. At least she now qualifies for a mark. (op 5-2 tchd 2-1)
Rakeekah, who showed some ability in two soft-ground maidens on turf, had every chance but was held when running out of room late on. (tchd 4-1)

6850 EUROPEAN BREEDERS' FUND MAIDEN STKS (C&G) 7f (P)
1:20 (1:22) (Class 5) 2-Y-O **£3,465** (£1,030; £515; £257) **Stalls** Low

Form RPR

1 **Wasan** 2-9-0 0.. RHills 6 71+
(E A L Dunlop) *s.i.s: sn pushed up in to midfield: hdwy to join ldrs over 2f out: rdn to ld jst ins fnl f: hld on* **7/2**[1]

03 **2** nk **Segal (IRE)**[16] 6602 2-9-0 0.. EddieAhern 14 70
(J Noseda) *hld up in midfield: hdwy over 3f out: chsd ldrs and rdn jst over 2f out: racd awkwardly and briefly outpcd over 1f out: rallied fnl f: wnt 2nd nr fin: nt quite rch wnr* **4/1**[2]

3 nk **Moothir (USA)** 2-9-0 0.. GregFairley 11 70+
(M Johnston) *chsd ldrs: hdwy to join ldr over 2f out: sn rdn: ev ch tl no ex wl ins fnl f* **5/1**[3]

0 **4** hd **Unlicensed**[15] 6617 2-9-0 0.. RichardHughes 1 69
(R Hannon) *trckd ldrs on inner: drvn wl over 1f out: kpt on but unable qckn last 100yds* **20/1**

5 **5** 2½ **Stormbeam (USA)**[16] 6602 2-9-0 0.. NickyMackay 13 63
(G A Butler) *stdd after s: hld up bhd: hdwy over 3f out: rdn and effrt over 1f out: kpt on but nt pce to rch ldrs* **11/2**

6 ½ **Master Spy** 2-9-0 0.. JimmyFortune 7 62+
(J H M Gosden) *s.i.s: bhd: nudged along wl over 2f out: swtchd rt over 1f out: kpt on fnl f: nt trble ldrs* **13/2**

7 ½ **Mick's Dancer** 2-9-0 0.. SaleemGolam 10 60+
(W R Muir) *hld up in midfield: rdn wl over 2f out: outpcd over 2f out: kpt on same pce after* **25/1**

4 **8** ½ **Bad Moon Rising**[19] 6540 2-9-0 0.. ChrisCatlin 2 59
(J Akehurst) *led: hrd pressed and rdn over 2f out: hdd jst ins fnl f: wknd* **20/1**

9 3 **King Of Cadeaux (IRE)** 2-9-0 0.. DarryllHolland 4 52
(M A Magnusson) *t.k.h: in tch on inner: lost pl jst over 2f out: rdn and no imp wl over 1f out* **16/1**

0 **10** 4 **Hennessy Island (USA)**[31] 6267 2-9-0 0.. SteveDrowne 5 42
(T G Mills) *in tch in midfield: rdn over 2f out: wknd on outer 2f out* **8/1**

11 1¼ **Impure Thoughts** 2-9-0 0.. HayleyTurner 3 38
(J R Best) *t.k.h: chsd ldr tl over 2f out: hung rt bnd jst over 2f out: sn wknd* **25/1**

12 3 **Mr Plod** 2-9-0 0.. JimCrowley 8 31
(Andrew Reid) *s.i.s: sn detached in last pair* **50/1**

13 shd **Tortola (IRE)** 2-9-0 0.. TomEaves 12 31
(M H Tompkins) *s.i.s: sn rdn: a bhd in last pair* **33/1**

1m 25.12s (-0.77) **Going Correction** -0.175s/f (Stan) **13** Ran SP% **126.7**
Speed ratings (Par 96): **97,96,96,96,93 92,92,91,88,83 82,78,78**
CSF £16.85 TOTE £5.20: £2.00, £1.90, £3.10; EX 19.70 Trifecta £130.60 Pool £265.02 - 1.44 winning units..
Owner Hamdan Al Maktoum **Bred** Belgrave Bloodstock **Trained** Newmarket, Suffolk

FOCUS
A much stronger early pace than in the two divisions of the fillies' maiden though in relative terms the final time was not that much quicker and with the first four finishing in a bunch difficult to rate higher. This still looked a race that will provide its share of winners though, as there were some eye-catching performances by a few.

NOTEBOOK
Wasan ◆, a 525,000gns half-brother to a couple of winners at up to 1m 4f, travelled well behind the leaders and showed a decent attitude when asked for his effort to just prevail in a bunch finish. He still has a long way to go to recoup his purchase price, but this was the perfect start and he will probably appreciate further in time. (op 4-1)
Segal(IRE), drawn widest of all, as here last time was doing all his best work late and he would have got there with a little further to go. He now qualifies for a mark and appears to be crying out for another furlong. (op 11-4)
Moothir(USA) ◆, out of a sister to the 1000 Guineas-winner Shadayid, was always up with the pace and never gave up. He should come on for this and a maiden should not be hard to find. (op 6-1)
Unlicensed ◆, last on his Newmarket debut earlier this month, improved from that and did well to finish so close as he was trying to put in his finishing effort tight against the inside rail. He is bred to get further and should win a race if brought back here.
Stormbeam(USA) stayed on well over the last couple of furlongs without offering a threat, but it is debatable whether this was an improvement as he finished further behind Segal than on his debut here earlier in the month. He may be one for handicaps after one more run. (op 6-1)
Master Spy ◆, a half-brother to three winners at up to 1m, stayed on steadily in the home straight without being by any means knocked about and he can be expected to come on a lot from this. (op 11-2)

6851 ARENALEISUREPLC.COM H'CAP 6f (P)
1:55 (1:55) (Class 2) (0-100,105) 3-Y-O+
£9,971 (£2,985; £1,492; £747; £372; £187) **Stalls** Low

Form RPR

0233 **1** **Ceremonial Jade (UAE)**[24] 6437 4-8-13 **95**..................(tp) OscarUrbina 2 105+
(M Botti) *hld up in midfield: hdwy jst over 2f out: rdn over 1f out: swtchd rt ins fnl f: r.o wl to ld nr fin* **5/2**[1]

0062 **2** nk **King's Caprice**[13] 6668 6-8-6 **91**..(t) TravisBlock(3) 11 98
(J A Geake) *t.k.h: chsd ldr: rdn over 2f out: kpt on u.p ins fnl f: wnt 2nd nr fin* **13/2**

2402 **3** hd **Turn On The Style**[13] 6676 5-8-12 **94**..(b) EddieAhern 6 100
(J Balding) *hld up in midfield: hdwy and rdn over 1f out: styd on u.p ins fnl f: snatched 3rd nr fin* **6/1**[3]

1000 **4** hd **Maltese Falcon**[34] 6205 7-9-9 **105**..(t) NelsonDeSouza 9 111
(P F I Cole) *led: rdn jst over 2f out: kpt on wl u.p tl hdd and lost pls nr fin* **16/1**

5600 **5** ¾ **Tony James (IRE)**[42] 6003 5-8-8 **90**.. PatDobbs 7 93
(K O Cunningham-Brown) *chsd ldrs: rdn over 2f out: keeping on same pce whn squeezed for room ins fnl f* **20/1**

0203 **6** hd **Little Edward**[13] 6668 9-8-8 **90** ow1.. SteveDrowne 1 93+
(R J Hodges) *t.k.h: hld up in last trio: hdwy over 1f out: styd on steadily fnl f: nt rch ldrs* **12/1**

6000 **7** ¾ **Lucayos**[23] 6450 4-8-4 **86**.. HayleyTurner 3 86
(Mrs H Sweeting) *chsd ldrs: rdn over 2f out: kpt on same pce over 1f out* **33/1**

-005 **8** 2 **Andronikos**[13] 6668 5-8-9 **91**..(t) TQuinn 5 85
(P F I Cole) *t.k.h: hld up in last trio: rdn and no imp over 1f out* **12/1**

0046 **9** hd **Resplendent Alpha**[13] 6668 3-8-4 **86** oh1.. ChrisCatlin 4 79
(P Howling) *t.k.h: hld up in last trio: short of room after 1f out: nvr threatened ldrs* **16/1**

4000 **10** 2 **Binanti**[24] 6437 7-8-7 **89**.. JimCrowley 10 76
(P R Chamings) *hld up in midfield on outer: rdn over 2f out: sn struggling* **8/1**

-505 **11** ¾ **Fyodor (IRE)**[21] 6487 6-9-6 **102**.. JimmyFortune 8 86
(W J Haggas) *s.i.s: t.k.h: hld up in midfield: rdn over 2f out: wknd wl over 1f out: eased ins fnl f* **4/1**[2]

69.95 secs (-2.86) **Going Correction** -0.175s/f (Stan) course record **11** Ran SP% **122.2**
Speed ratings (Par 109): **112,111,111,111,110 109,108,106,105,103 102**
CSF £19.82 CT £93.84 TOTE £3.80: £1.50, £2.50, £2.70; EX 27.70 Trifecta £74.30 Pool: £340.25 - 3.25 winning units..
Owner Giuliano Manfredini **Bred** Darley **Trained** Newmarket, Suffolk
■ Stewards' Enquiry : Oscar Urbina two-day ban; careless riding (Nov 28, 30)

FOCUS
A fiercely competitive sprint handicap and, although the expected battle for the early lead did not materilise, the pace set by Maltese Falcon was a decent one and the final time was very solid. The form looks solid rated around the fourth and fifth to last year's form and the runner-up to his latest mark.

NOTEBOOK
Ceremonial Jade(UAE), having his first try over a trip this short on sand and only his second go over it in all, was ridden with a lot of confidence but he had to rather make his own gap once into the straight. That proved a race-winning if illegal move and he got up to win with little to spare. The cheekpieces seemed to have helped him and he should continue to do well in similarly decent handicaps here. (op 3-1)
King's Caprice, 2lb higher than when runner-up over course and distance last time, took a handy position in the slipstream of Maltese Falcon and battled on really well all the way up the home straight, only just losing out. This was a decent effort from the outside stall and he really does deserve to go one better. (op 7-1)

Turn On The Style, raised 2lb after being just touched off at Wolverhampton, was ridden more patiently than he usually is and connections may have been mindful of there being so many potential front-runners in the field. Although he stayed on well down the outside in the straight, he was never quite doing it quickly enough and he will need to find a bit more improvement if he is to defy a mark 6lb higher than for his last win. (tchd 11-2)

Maltese Falcon, a three-time winner over this course and distance, was given his usual attacking ride and, despite there being so many other potential pacesetters in the field, he ended up with an uncontested lead. It looked for a long way as though he might succeed, but he was swamped by the front three in the very closing stages. Despite his inflated mark, he can never be written off here. (tchd 20-1)

Tony James(IRE) had become disappointing, but a 4lb drop in the weights brought about a much-improved effort here and he would have gone even closer still had the winner not hampered him inside the last furlong. If he can build on this there are races to be won with him here this winter.

Little Edward was carrying 1lb overweight so he was just 1lb better off with King's Caprice after finishing a couple of lengths behind him here last time. He soon sacrificed his rails draw and was content to race out the back, but once switched out for his effort in the home straight he stayed on very nicely without being beaten up. Despite now being 10lb higher than for his last win on sand, it would be dangerous to suggest he cannot win off this sort of mark. (op 17-2)

Fyodor(IRE) is probably better over 5f, but he has won over this trip on Polytrack so this was just too bad to be true. (tchd 9-2)

6852 LINGFIELD PARK FOR CONFERENCES H'CAP — 1m (P)

2:30 (2:30) (Class 2) (0-100,103) 3-Y-0+ **£9,971** (£2,985; £1,492; £747; £372; £187) **Stalls** High

Form / RPR

33-0 **1** **Military Cross**[150] 2755 4-8-13 **93** .... EddieAhern 4 104+
(L M Cumani) *hld up towards rr on inner: hdwy on inner jst over 2f out: led ins fnl f: hung rt: rdn out* **14/1**

0001 **2** ½ **Troubadour (IRE)**[36] 6143 6-8-13 **93** .... SteveDrowne 7 102+
(W Jarvis) *hld up in rr: hdwy wl over 1f out: swtchd lft and burst through to chse wnr ins fnl f: hld last 50yds* **8/1**

3060 **3** 1 ½ **Evens And Odds (IRE)**[29] 6301 3-8-12 **94** .... NCallan 3 100
(K A Ryan) *chsd ldrs: rdn over 2f out: kpt on u.p fnl f* **6/1**

0515 **4** shd **Orchard Supreme**[34] 6203 4-9-6 **100** .... RichardHughes 5 106
(R Hannon) *t.k.h: hld up in midfield: hdwy jst over 2f out: drvn over 1f out: kpt on same pce fnl f* **9/2**[2]

0033 **5** hd **Capable Guest (IRE)**[14] 6654 5-8-8 **88** ....(v) ChrisCatlin 1 93
(M R Channon) *rn in snatches: hdwy on inner 3f out: drvn and chsd ldrs over 1f out: one pce ins fnl f* **9/1**

0002 **6** nk **Babodana**[19] 6541 7-9-1 **95** .... TomEaves 12 100
(M H Tompkins) *led for 2f: rdn and ev ch over 2f out: led again over 1f out: hdd ins fnl f: fdd last 100yds* **14/1**

1400 **7** 1 **Party Boss**[197] 1448 5-9-8 **102** .... DarryllHolland 8 104
(C E Brittain) *chsd ldr tl led 6f out: rdn and hdd over 1f out: wknd ins fnl f* **16/1**

2353 **8** ½ **Waterside (IRE)**[83] 4851 8-9-9 **103** .... GeorgeBaker 2 104
(G L Moore) *taken down early: chsd ldrs: rdn jst over 2f out: wknd 1f out* **16/1**

0500 **9** 3 ½ **Precocious Star (IRE)**[16] 6604 3-8-1 **86** .... AndrewElliott(3) 11 79
(K R Burke) *chsd ldrs: lost pl jst over 2f out: rdn and btn 2f out* **20/1**

0211 **10** 1 ½ **Capricorn Run (USA)**[16] 6606 4-9-6 **100** ....(v) StephenDonohoe 9 90
(A J McCabe) *s.i.s: a bhd* **11/2**[3]

3005 **11** 1 **Elusive Flash (USA)**[77] 5047 3-9-0 **96** .... NelsonDeSouza 10 83
(P F I Cole) *t.k.h: early: racd in midfield: rdn over 4f out: bhd last 2f* **50/1**

0301 **12** 7 **Very Wise**[14] 6654 5-9-6 **100** .... JimmyFortune 6 71
(W J Haggas) *v.s.a: a last: rdn and no hdwy wl over 1f out: eased ins fnl f* **10/3**[1]

1m 35.83s (-3.60) **Going Correction** -0.175s/f (Stan) course record
WFA 3 from 4yo+ 2lb — 12 Ran SP% **123.9**
Speed ratings (Par 109): **111,110,109,108,108 108,107,106,103,101 100,93**
CSF £127.11 CT £763.12 TOTE £19.10: £4.80, £3.00, £2.60; EX 142.60 Trifecta £315.40 Part won. Pool: £444.36 - 0.10 winning units..
Owner R Thompson & A Bengough **Bred** Cheveley Park Stud Ltd **Trained** Newmarket, Suffolk

FOCUS
Another hot handicap, though a little devalued by the favourite Very Wise fluffing it at the start. The time was good though and the form still looks strong rated around those immediately behind the principals.

NOTEBOOK
Military Cross, making his sand debut in his 13th outing, was also returning from five months off but that did not bother him at all and he took to the surface like a duck to water. Patiently ridden, he was a little fortunate to get a lovely gap on the inside around the home bend and once in front he was inclined to hang away to his right into the centre of the track, but that is no bad thing here and he was always doing enough. If another opportunity can be found, he should be able to win again on this surface. (tchd 12-1)

Troubadour(IRE), raised 5lb for his successful sand debut over course and distance last month, was also given a patient ride and had to pick his way through the pack once into the straight. Eventually forced to challenge up the inside of the hanging winner though never inconvenienced, he finished strongly but could never quite get there. There are still more races to be won with him on this surface. (op 7-1)

Evens And Odds(IRE), third behind a couple of much higher-rated rivals in a Listed race here in March in his only previous try on sand, ran another fine race in defeat here having been close to the pace from the off. He remains unexposed on this surface and there should be another day. (op 8-1)

Orchard Supreme, rated 13lb higher on sand than on turf, travelled well behind the leaders as he often does and battled on well under pressure once in line for home. He loves this surface and should continue to do his best, but he does look to be handicapped to the hilt these days. (op 5-1)

Capable Guest(IRE), still relatively unexposed on sand, had every chance and was presented with a huge gap on the inside as the winner hung away to his right inside the last furlong, but he was still probably not on the ideal part of the track and was run out of the placings in the very dying strides. (op 8-1)

Babodana, whose four previous tries on sand had all been in Pattern company here, is gradually dropping down the handicap and was ridden up with the pace from the outside stall, but he was eventually done for foot in the last furlong. (op 16-1 tchd 12-1)

Capricorn Run(USA), bidding for a hat-trick off a 4lb higher mark, had shown nothing in two previous tries over this sort of trip but he was immediately up against it after a sloppy start and never got into it. Official explanation: jockey said gelding missed the break (op 13-2)

Very Wise, raised 6lb for his Newmarket win, still had the hood on when the stalls opened and as a result he gave away too much ground. He never got into the race at all and it was later reported that he had an irregular heartbeat. Official explanation: jockey said he was unable to remove the blind and consequently missed the break; vet said gelding was found to have an irregular heart beat (op 7-2)

6853 LINGFIELD PARK FOR PARTIES H'CAP — 1m 4f (P)

3:00 (3:00) (Class 4) (0-85,85) 3-Y-0+ **£4,605** (£1,378; £689; £344; £171) **Stalls** Low

Form / RPR

124 **1** **Watchful (IRE)**[15] 6620 3-8-13 **82** .... JimmyFortune 5 91+
(L M Cumani) *chsd clr ldr and clr of remainder: rdn and clsd over 2f out: led wl over 1f out: pressed ins fnl f: fnd ex last 50yds* **3/1**[1]

0013 **2** 1 **Polish Power (GER)**[21] 6500 7-9-8 **85** .... JohnEgan 1 93
(J S Moore) *hld up off the pce in midfield: hdwy to chse ldng pair over 2f out: rdn to chse wnr over 1f out: ch ins fnl f: no ex last 50yds* **11/2**

26/1 **3** 1 ¼ **Crete (IRE)**[37] 6132 5-8-13 **76** .... LiamJones 3 82
(W J Haggas) *hld up off the pce in main gp: rdn and hdwy over 2f out: edgd rt fr wl over 1f out: kpt on but nvr threatened wnr* **10/3**[2]

4313 **4** 1 **Risque Heights**[27] 6357 3-9-1 **84** .... SteveDrowne 4 88
(G A Butler) *hld up wl off the pce in main gp: rdn and hdwy over 2f out: nvr able to chal* **4/1**[3]

2231 **5** shd **Optimus (USA)**[16] 6603 5-9-3 **80** .... TQuinn 9 84
(B G Powell) *hld up wl off the pce in rr: rdn and kpt on fr wl over 1f out: nvr able to chal* **6/1**

1210 **6** 9 **Annambo**[15] 6622 7-9-0 **77** .... RobertHavlin 7 66
(P J McBride) *hld up wl off the pce in last pair: n.d: no ch last 3f* **33/1**

3614 **7** ½ **Know The Law**[11] 6709 3-8-12 **81** ....(b) RichardHughes 6 70
(D R C Elsworth) *racd freely: led: clr 8f out: reminders over 3f out: rdn over 2f out: hdd wl over 1f out: immediately btn* **8/1**

630/ **8** nk **Warningcamp (GER)**[217] 4852 6-9-0 **77** .... PatDobbs 8 65
(Lady Herries) *wl off the pce in main gp: rdn over 2f out: sn no hdwy: eased ins fnl f* **33/1**

2m 28.95s (-5.44) **Going Correction** -0.175s/f (Stan) course record
WFA 3 from 5yo+ 6lb — 8 Ran SP% **114.7**
Speed ratings (Par 105): **111,110,109,108,108 102,102,102**
CSF £20.01 CT £55.95 TOTE £3.80: £2.30, £1.90, £1.90; EX 34.50 Trifecta £34.60 Pool: £273.90 - 5.61 winning units..
Owner De La Warr Racing **Bred** Neville O'Byrne **Trained** Newmarket, Suffolk

FOCUS
Unlike most races over this trip here, this was run at a scorching pace and very few ever got into it. The winning time was smart for the grade and the form looks rock-solid rated around the placed horses and the fifth.

Optimus(USA) Official explanation: trainer's rep said gelding knocked its head on leaving stalls

6854 LINGFIELD PARK FOR EXHIBITIONS H'CAP — 7f (P)

3:35 (3:35) (Class 5) (0-70,70) 3-Y-0+ **£2,817** (£838; £418; £209) **Stalls** Low

Form / RPR

4030 **1** **Haasem (USA)**[10] 6727 4-8-13 **63** .... JimCrowley 5 68
(J R Jenkins) *dwlt: sn prom: chsd ldr over 5f out: rdn 2f out: led ins fnl f: r.o wl last 50yds* **10/1**

0343 **2** ½ **Maysarah (IRE)**[25] 6406 3-8-12 **66** .... WilliamBuick(3) 4 69
(G A Butler) *plld hrd: hld up wl in tch in rr: rdn and hdwy over 1f out: ev ch last 100yds: unable qckn towards fin* **7/4**[1]

-004 **3** hd **Onenightinlisbon (IRE)**[26] 6385 3-9-4 **69** .... FergusSweeney 3 72
(K R Burke) *t.k.h: in tch: rdn and effrt 2f out: ev ch ins fnl f: kpt on* **8/1**[3]

010 **4** nk **Night Wolf (IRE)**[162] 2414 7-8-9 **59** ....(t) PaulDoe 8 61
(Jamie Poulton) *sn led: rdn over 2f out: hdd ins fnl f: no ex last 50yds* **8/1**[3]

546P **5** hd **Dowlleh**[110] 4029 3-9-5 **70** .... TGMcLaughlin 2 71
(T T Clement) *hld up wl in tch in last pair: rdn and hdwy over 1f out: ev ch ins fnl f: no ex last 75yds* **33/1**

/400 **6** ½ **Tango Step (IRE)**[5] 6795 7-8-8 **61** .... JerryO'Dwyer(3) 1 61
(Bernard Lawlor, Ire) *t.k.h: chsd ldr for 2f out: rdn over 2f out: ev ch jst ins fnl f: fdd last 50yds* **10/1**

0304 **7** 1 **Special Place**[16] 6607 4-8-10 **60** .... OscarUrbina 7 57
(J A R Toller) *t.k.h: hld up wl in tch on outer: rdn and effrt 2f out: sn edgd lft: no imp fnl f* **2/1**[2]

1m 25.07s (-0.82) **Going Correction** -0.175s/f (Stan)
WFA 3 from 4yo+ 1lb — 7 Ran SP% **113.0**
Speed ratings (Par 103): **97,96,96,95,95 95,93**
CSF £27.38 CT £149.62 TOTE £16.50: £4.10, £1.60; EX 41.90 Trifecta £160.80 Pool: £464.31 - 2.05 winning units. Place 6 £360.15, Place 5 £122.21.
Owner Robin Stevens & Stephen Bullock **Bred** Shadwell Farm LLC **Trained** Royston, Herts

FOCUS
A nonsense of a race in which they dawdled early and it developed into a sprint. With only around three lengths covering the seven runners at the line, the form has a distinctly dodgy look to it.
T/Plt: £851.30 to a £1 stake. Pool: £46,357.60. 39.75 winning tickets. T/Qpdt: £78.00 to a £1 stake. Pool: £2,995.90. 28.40 winning tickets. SP

6833 WOLVERHAMPTON (A.W) (L-H)

Saturday, November 17

OFFICIAL GOING: Standard

Wind: fresh, half-behind Weather: overcast

6855 EUROPEAN BREEDERS' FUND MAIDEN STKS — 1m 141y(P)

7:00 (7:00) (Class 5) 2-Y-0 **£3,465** (£1,030; £515; £257) **Stalls** Low

Form / RPR

05 **1** **Wing Play (IRE)**[10] 6724 2-9-0 0 .... TravisBlock(3) 8 74+
(H Morrison) *s.i.s: hld up: hdwy over 2f out: led and hung lft 1f out: r.o* **5/1**[3]

00 **2** 1 ¾ **Martyr**[22] 6468 2-9-3 0 .... PatDobbs 11 70
(R Hannon) *led: hdd 4f out: led again over 1f out: sn rdn and hdd: styd on same pce* **18/1**

3 ¾ **Spring Style (IRE)** 2-8-12 0 .... ChrisCatlin 12 64+
(E J O'Neill) *chsd ldrs: rdn over 2f out: edgd lft and outpcd over 1f out: styd on ins fnl f* **16/1**

24 **4** ½ **Freedom Song**[36] 6140 2-8-12 0 .... SteveDrowne 5 63
(R Charlton) *s.i.s: sn chsng ldr: led 4f out: rdn and hdd over 1f out: no ex ins fnl f* **11/8**[1]

60 **5** hd **Red Twist**[21] 6494 2-9-3 0 .... RobertHavlin 6 67
(H Morrison) *prom: racd keenly: rdn over 1f out: no ex ins fnl f* **14/1**

0 **6** 1 **Hawk Flight (IRE)**[17] 6593 2-9-3 0 .... SaleemGolam 2 65
(W R Muir) *mid-div: lost pl 1/2-way: styd on u.p appr fnl f: nvr trbld ldrs* **14/1**

7 ¾ **Pharaohs Justice (USA)** 2-9-3 0 PatCosgrave 13 64+
(Jane Chapple-Hyam) *mid-div: hdwy over 5f out: hung lft over 1f out: styd on same pce* **33/1**

8 ¾ **Ephorus (USA)** 2-9-3 0 NCallan 10 62
(Sir Michael Stoute) *hld up: rdn over 3f out: hdwy over 2f out: wknd fnl f* **5/2[2]**

0 9 6 **Lechero (IRE)**[56] 5621 2-9-3 0 J-PGuillambert 7 49
(P A Blockley) *hld up: rdn over 2f out: n.d* **66/1**

05 10 1 **Tobouggornotobougg**[11] 6705 2-9-3 0 DeanMcKeown 4 47
(D Shaw) *sn outpcd* **50/1**

00 11 12 **Bagenalstown (IRE)**[105] 4162 2-9-3 0 AdamKirby 1 22
(M Wellings) *hld up in tch: rdn 1/2-way: wknd 3f out* **200/1**

1m 53.21s (1.45) **Going Correction** 0.0s/f (Stan) 11 Ran SP% **118.7**
Speed ratings (Par 96): **93,91,90,90,90 89,88,87,82,81 71**
CSF £88.70 TOTE £6.10: £1.80, £5.00, £4.70; EX 85.50.
Owner Watching Brief **Bred** Churchtown House Stud **Trained** East Ilsley, Berks

FOCUS
A fair maiden and the winner is likely to go on to better things.

NOTEBOOK
Wing Play(IRE) has improved with each of his three runs and this win saw him step up on a recent fifth at Nottingham. He will progress again when stepped up in trip next season. (op 11-2 tchd 9-2)
Martyr, who had finished down the field in maidens at Newbury and Doncaster, found the competition more to his liking here and ran well under a positive ride. He is now eligible for nurseries and his immediate future will obviously be determined by the mark he gets. (op 16-1)
Spring Style(IRE), out of a half-sister to a couple of winners in France, drifted in the market. She was never far away and, after getting a bit outpaced on the home turn, kept on encouragingly in the straight for a respectable third. She can only improve for the experience. (op 12-1)
Freedom Song, a shade disappointing when fourth of eleven at Lingfield last time, again failed to deliver on the promise she had shown when runner-up on her debut at Kempton in September and is looking very one-paced at present. (op 6-4 tchd 13-8 and 5-4, 7-4 in places)
Red Twist ◆ did not help himself by taking a grip, but more significantly now qualifies for a mark.
Ephorus(USA), a half-brother to Singalong and Potentiale, showed little on this debut and now has it all to prove. (op 4-1)

6856 STANLEY SMITH 80TH BIRTHDAY FILLIES' H'CAP 1m 1f 103y(P)
7:30 (7:30) (Class 5) (0-70,71) 3-Y-0+ **£2,968** (£876; £438) **Stalls** Low

Form RPR

1 **Coral Creek (IRE)**[14] 6661 3-9-3 **67** EddieAhern 1 73
(M J Grassick, Ire) *hld up in tch: rdn over 1f out: hung lft and styd on u.p to ld post* **16/1**

4632 2 shd **Chia (IRE)**[9] 6738 4-9-2 **63** (p) HayleyTurner 8 69
(D Haydn Jones) *trckd ldr: racd keenly: led over 5f out: rdn over 1f out: hdd post* **7/2[1]**

3350 3 1 ¼ **Ochre (IRE)**[26] 6387 3-8-10 **60** PaulHanagan 9 63
(R A Fahey) *hld up: hdwy over 4f out: chsd ldr over 2f out: sn rdn: styd on same pce fnl f* **20/1**

2213 4 shd **Pearl (IRE)**[13] 6673 3-9-7 **71** LiamJones 5 74
(W J Haggas) *led: hdd over 5f out: rdn over 2f out: styd on same pce fnl f* **7/2[1]**

5026 5 7 **Jeu D'Esprit (IRE)**[91] 4615 4-9-5 **66** TPQueally 3 55
(J G Given) *prom: rdn over 3f out: wknd over 1f out* **7/1[3]**

0015 6 2 ½ **Very Well Red**[12] 6696 4-9-6 **67** JimCrowley 7 51
(P W Hiatt) *prom: chsd ldr over 3f out tl rdn over 2f out: wknd over 1f out* **15/2**

-430 7 ½ **Niqaab**[96] 4458 3-9-3 **67** NeilPollard 2 50
(W J Musson) *prom: rdn over 3f out: sn wknd* **22/1**

5003 8 ½ **Naughty Thoughts (IRE)**[19] 6547 3-8-12 **65** EmmettStack(3) 4 47
(Andrew Turnell) *dwlt: hld up: hdwy over 2f out: sn rdn and wknd* **8/1**

-201 9 8 **Gamesters Lady**[13] 6672 4-9-4 **65** NCallan 6 31
(W M Brisbourne) *dwlt: hld up: rdn and hmpd over 3f out: wknd over 2f out* **4/1[2]**

2m 1.38s (-1.24) **Going Correction** 0.0s/f (Stan)
WFA 3 from 4yo 3lb 9 Ran SP% **114.8**
Speed ratings (Par 100): **105,104,103,103,97 95,94,94,87**
CSF £71.07 CT £1145.69 TOTE £15.10: £2.90, £1.50, £4.20; EX 126.40.
Owner M C Grassick **Bred** John Malone **Trained** Pollardstown, Co Kildare

FOCUS
A modest affair though the winning time was not at all bad for a race of its type. The form is rated through the runner-up and fourth.

6857 EUROPEAN BREEDERS' FUND AT WOLVERHAMPTON MAIDEN STKS 1m 1f 103y(P)
7:55 (7:56) (Class 5) 2-Y-0 **£3,465** (£1,030; £515; £257) **Stalls** Low

Form RPR

43 1 **Dandy Erin (IRE)**[23] 6451 2-9-3 0 TPQueally 7 82
(J A Osborne) *chsd ldr 3f: rdn to go 2nd again 2f out: styd on u.p to ld wl ins fnl f* **8/1**

42 2 1 ¾ **Heritage Coast (USA)**[36] 6140 2-8-12 0 NCallan 8 74
(Sir Michael Stoute) *sn led: rdn and hung lft over 1f out: hdd wl ins fnl f* **1/1[1]**

64 3 6 **Stow**[17] 6592 2-9-3 0 SteveDrowne 13 67
(H Morrison) *mid-div: sn pushed along: hdwy over 6f out: chsd ldr over 3f out tl rdn 2f out: wknd over 1f out* **12/1**

0 4 1 **Orkney (IRE)**[29] 6303 2-9-3 0 TomEaves 12 65
(Miss J A Camacho) *dwlt: hld up: hdwy over 4f out: rdn over 2f out: sn wknd* **33/1**

045 5 1 ½ **Tyrrells Wood (IRE)**[65] 5361 2-9-3 76 PaulHanagan 10 63
(T G Mills) *prom: chsd ldr over 6f out tl rdn over 3f out: wknd over 2f out* **5/2[2]**

564 6 nk **Clovis**[10] 6724 2-9-3 78 GregFairley 9 62
(M Johnston) *s.s: hdwy over 7f out: rdn and wknd 3f out* **7/1[3]**

0 7 7 **Moluccella**[16] 6601 2-8-12 0 EddieAhern 5 44
(H Morrison) *chsd ldrs 7f* **40/1**

0002 8 9 **Lord's Bidding**[6] 6776 2-9-3 50 (b) RobertHavlin 2 32
(R Ingram) *s.i.s: sn pushed along in rr: rdn and wknd over 3f out* **33/1**

9 1 **Valvigneres (IRE)** 2-9-3 0 StephenDonohoe 3 30
(E A L Dunlop) *s.s: outpcd* **25/1**

10 5 **Menorca (IRE)** 2-8-12 0 PatCosgrave 4 15
(Jane Chapple-Hyam) *mid-div: rdn and wknd over 4f out* **66/1**

000 11 18 **Honest Yankee (USA)**[134] 3270 2-9-3 40 (p) LPKeniry 6 —
(Mrs L C Jewell) *prom: lost pl over 5f out: wknd 4f out* **200/1**

0 12 13 **Jim's Boy (USA)**[8] 6740 2-9-3 0 J-PGuillambert 1 —
(M Johnston) *bhd fr 1/2-way* **33/1**

2m 1.86s (-0.76) **Going Correction** 0.0s/f (Stan) 12 Ran SP% **127.0**
Speed ratings (Par 96): **103,101,96,95,93 93,87,79,78,74 58,46**
CSF £17.06 TOTE £7.50: £2.10, £1.30, £4.40; EX 20.90.
Owner St James Partnership **Bred** Michael Collins **Trained** Upper Lambourn, Berks

FOCUS
Some nicely-bred maidens on show here, and the front two pulled clear of their rivals in the straight, giving the form a solid look.

NOTEBOOK
Dandy Erin(IRE), who had appeared to find 1m on the sharp side on her two previous starts, showed his appreciation of this step up in distance as he outstayed the favourite in the final furlong to win in the manner of a horse who will get further next year. (op 9-1)
Heritage Coast(USA), who was also stepping up from 1m, ensured there was no hanging about and had managed to shake off all but the winner by the two-furlong mark. She should find a similar event before long. (op 11-10 tchd 5-4)
Stow was never far away on this All-Weather debut, but was already feeling the pinch by the home turn. (op 11-1)
Orkney(IRE) stepped up on her debut ninth at Redcar and could be of interest once handicapped. (op 40-1)
Tyrrells Wood(IRE), who had shown some promise on turf at Sandown, was disappointing on this switch to the All-Weather especially as the market suggested better was expected. (op 9-2)
Lord's Bidding Official explanation: jockey said colt missed the break

6858 PD EDENHALL LTD MAIDEN STKS 1m 141y(P)
8:25 (8:26) (Class 5) 3-Y-0+ **£2,968** (£876; £438) **Stalls** Low

Form RPR

1 **Silver Tide (USA)**[27] 6369 3-8-12 0 EddieAhern 4 61
(M J Grassick, Ire) *s.i.s: sn chsng ldrs: led over 1f out: rdn out* **10/11[1]**

2323 2 ½ **Red Blossom**[17] 6597 3-8-12 67 (b) JamieMackay 3 60
(Sir Mark Prescott) *a.p: nt clr run and swtchd rt over 1f out: swtchd lft ins fnl f: sn hrd rdn: styd on* **7/2[3]**

-3R0 3 5 **Moral Code (IRE)**[38] 6109 3-9-3 69 ChrisCatlin 6 54
(E J O'Neill) *led over 7f out: rdn and hdd over 1f out: wknd ins fnl f* **3/1[2]**

004 4 ¾ **Interactive (IRE)**[19] 6546 4-9-3 73 EmmettStack(3) 10 52
(Andrew Turnell) *hld up: hdwy over 3f out: rdn and hmpd over 1f out: hung lft and wknd ins fnl f* **9/1**

00 5 5 **Ruwain**[6] 6778 3-9-3 0 NeilPollard 11 40
(W J Musson) *s.i.s: hld up: rdn over 2f out: n.d* **16/1**

0 6 ½ **Kielty's Folly**[17] 6597 3-9-3 0 DanielTudhope 8 39
(B P J Baugh) *hld up: rdn over 3f out: nvr nrr* **66/1**

0050 7 3 **Broad Town Girl**[19] 6546 4-8-8 30 KylieManser(7) 1 27
(Mrs H Sweeting) *s.i.s: hdwy over 3f out: rdn and wknd over 1f out* **100/1**

0000 8 5 **Pont Wood**[3] 6806 3-9-3 46 StephenDonohoe 5 21
(Mrs N S Evans) *s.i.s: a in rr: rdn 1/2-way: sn wknd* **25/1**

0000 9 17 **Elegans**[10] 6716 3-8-12 26 TGMcLaughlin 7 —
(Mrs C A Dunnett) *sn led: hdd over 7f out: chsd ldr tl rdn over 3f out: sn wknd* **80/1**

0560 10 19 **Village Storm (IRE)**[84] 4795 4-9-6 32 TomEaves 9 —
(C J Teague) *prom: rdn 1/2-way: sn wknd* **100/1**

000/ 11 4 **Miss St Albans**[1127] 6228 6-8-8 35 WilliamCarson(7) 2 —
(G C H Chung) *mid-div: rdn and wknd 1/2-way* **66/1**

1m 50.89s (-0.87) **Going Correction** 0.0s/f (Stan)
WFA 3 from 4yo+ 3lb 11 Ran SP% **125.5**
Speed ratings (Par 103): **103,102,98,97,93 92,89,85,70,53 49**
CSF £4.80 TOTE £2.20: £1.10, £1.20, £1.60; EX 4.00.
Owner Oliver Murphy **Bred** Christopher Grosso **Trained** Pollardstown, Co Kildare
■ Stewards' Enquiry : Jamie Mackay caution: careless riding

FOCUS
Some well-exposed and moderate maidens on display here. Poor form, rated negatively through the runner-up.

6859 BOOK ONLINE AT WOLVERHAMPTON-RACECOURSE.CO.UK H'CAP 1m 141y(P)
8:55 (8:55) (Class 6) (0-60,60) 3-Y-0+ **£2,047** (£604; £302) **Stalls** Low

Form RPR

2626 1 **Machinate (USA)**[15] 6629 5-8-11 **52** LiamJones 2 61
(W M Brisbourne) *chsd ldrs: led 2f out: sn rdn: hung rt ins fnl f: styd on* **9/1**

0216 2 ¾ **Ours (IRE)**[17] 6598 4-8-11 **52** StephenDonohoe 4 59
(John A Harris) *mid-div: hdwy over 3f out: edgd lft over 2f out: rdn and hung lft over 1f out: carried rt ins fnl f: kpt on* **9/2[2]**

-301 3 1 ¾ **Royal Embrace**[17] 6579 4-9-3 **58** (v) DeanMcKeown 3 61
(D Shaw) *hld up: hdwy and n.m.r over 2f out: rdn over 1f out: styd on* **13/2**

0002 4 shd **Turn Me On (IRE)**[10] 6716 4-9-5 **60** DanielTudhope 5 63
(T D Walford) *hld up in tch: outpcd over 2f out: rallied over 1f out: styd on* **3/1[1]**

0020 5 3 ½ **Postmaster**[12] 6431 5-9-0 **55** SteveDrowne 12 50
(R Ingram) *hld up: rdn over 2f out: styd on ins fnl f: nt trble ldrs* **11/2[3]**

5000 6 shd **Norwegian**[28] 6342 6-9-5 **60** (p) FergusSweeney 13 54
(Ian Williams) *led 7f out: rdn and hdd 2f out: wknd ins fnl f* **20/1**

6560 7 2 ½ **Vesuvio**[36] 6146 3-8-8 **55** PJMcDonald(3) 7 44
(C W Thornton) *s.i.s: hdwy over 6f out: rdn over 2f out: sn wknd* **20/1**

030 8 hd **Lincolneurocruiser**[45] 5916 5-8-13 **59** (v) RussellKennemore(5) 9 47
(Mrs N Macauley) *s.i.s: hdwy over 6f out: rdn and ev ch over 2f out: wknd over 1f out* **20/1**

3004 9 1 ½ **Wodhill Gold**[15] 6629 6-8-11 **52** (v) HayleyTurner 8 37
(D Morris) *led: hdd over 7f out: chsd ldrs: rdn and wknd over 2f out* **13/2**

050 10 nk **Katie Lawson (IRE)**[114] 3868 4-9-0 **55** (p) RobertHavlin 1 39
(D Haydn Jones) *mid-div: hdwy whn hmpd 2f out: sn wknd* **33/1**

400 11 1 ¼ **George's Flyer (IRE)**[15] 6627 4-8-9 **50** (b) PaulHanagan 11 31
(R A Fahey) *hld up: a in rr* **10/1**

0000 12 3 **Iced Diamond (IRE)**[88] 4685 8-8-3 **47** EmmettStack(3) 6 21
(S Wynne) *hld up: a in rr* **66/1**

1m 51.55s (-0.21) **Going Correction** 0.0s/f (Stan)
WFA 3 from 4yo+ 3lb 12 Ran SP% **123.0**
Speed ratings (Par 101): **100,99,97,97,94 94,92,92,90,90 89,86**
CSF £47.90 CT £241.12 TOTE £9.40: £4.40, £1.60, £2.60; EX 59.50.
Owner D Slingsby **Bred** Gaines-Gentry Thoroughbreds And William Condren **Trained** Great Ness, Shropshire
■ Stewards' Enquiry : Stephen Donohoe two-day ban: careless riding (Nov 28,30)
Liam Jones four-day ban: careless riding (Nov 28, 30, Dec 1,3)

FOCUS
A weak affair and something of a rough race with the winner carrying the runner-up halfway across the track. Modest form.

6860 BLACKHEATH PRODUCTS SPRINT H'CAP 5f 20y(P)
9:20 (9:21) (Class 5) (0-70,70) 3-Y-0+ **£2,968** (£876; £438) **Stalls** Low

Form RPR

5000 1 **Tartatartufata**[27] 6355 5-9-3 **69** (v) DeanMcKeown 4 81
(D Shaw) *mde all: rdn out* **4/1[2]**

The Form Book, Raceform Ltd, Compton, RG20 6NL

5030 2 nk **Monte Major (IRE)**[13] 6671 6-8-6 63 PatrickHills(5) 8 74
(D Shaw) *s.i.s: hdwy u.p over 1f out: edgd lft: r.o* 15/2
1050 3 ½ **Our Fugitive (IRE)**[44] 5942 5-8-10 62 JimCrowley 3 71
(A W Carroll) *chsd wnr: rdn over 1f out: sn hung lft: styd on* 9/1
0115 4 1¼ **Sandwith**[8] 6743 4-8-6 61 (p) PJMcDonald(3) 5 70+
(J S Wainwright) *hld up: hdwy over 1f out: nt clr run ins fnl f: nvr able to chal* 3/1[1]
1061 5 2 **El Potro**[30] 6287 5-8-9 61 SteveDrowne 2 58
(J R Holt) *chsd ldrs: rdn 1/2-way: sn outpcd* 5/1[3]
061 6 ½ **Stoneacre Boy (IRE)**[35] 6174 4-8-11 63 LPKeniry 6 59
(Peter Grayson) *chsd ldrs fr over 1f out: styd on same pce* 17/2
0002 7 1¼ **Kings College Boy**[18] 6562 7-8-13 65 (b) PaulHanagan 12 56
(R A Fahey) *sn pushed along in rr: nvr trbld ldrs* 12/1
0005 8 nk **Almaty Express**[27] 6360 5-9-3 69 (b) TomEaves 7 59
(J R Weymes) *prom: rdn 1/2-way: wknd fnl f* 8/1
0006 9 1½ **Egyptian Lord**[11] 6708 4-9-0 66 AdamKirby 9 51
(Peter Grayson) *s.i.s: a in rr* 16/1

62.79 secs (-0.03) **Going Correction** 0.0s/f (Stan) 9 Ran SP% 118.6
Speed ratings (Par 103): **100,99,98,96,93 92,90,90,87**
CSF £35.08 CT £260.17 TOTE £6.50: £1.90, £2.30, £3.20; EX 18.60 Place 6 £212.15, Place 5 £43.04..
Owner Danethorpe Racing Partnership **Bred** Dr A Ramkaran **Trained** Danethorpe, Notts

FOCUS
A modest, but competitive sprint handicap. The winner took advantage of a good mark and the form should work out.
Sandwith Official explanation: jockey said gelding was denied a clear run
Almaty Express Official explanation: jockey said gelding was unsuited by being unable to dominate
T/Plt: £176.00 to a £1 stake. Pool: £85,662.35. 355.25 winning tickets. T/Qpdt: £11.30 to a £1 stake. Pool: £5,960.30. 387.40 winning tickets. CR

6686 CAPANNELLE (R-H)
Sunday, November 18

OFFICIAL GOING: Heavy

6863a PREMIO ROMA VECCHIA (LISTED RACE) 1m 6f
3:00 (3:21) 3-Y-O+ £18,919 (£8,324; £4,541; £2,270)

RPR
1 **Place In Line**[33] 5-9-1 GBietolini 2 106
(Gianluca Bietolini, Italy)
2 1½ **Cocodrail (IRE)**[49] 6-9-1 FBranca 5 105
(F & L Brogi, Italy)
3 5 **Montalegre (IRE)**[22] 6518 5-9-1 DVargiu 12 98
(A & G Botti, Italy)
4 ½ **Next King (ITY)**[392] 6123 3-8-11 MMonteriso 7 101
(A & G Botti, Italy)
5 nk **Lear Cavern**[154] 3-8-9 PConvertino 9 99
(Laura Grizzetti, Italy)
6 15 **Chicchirichi (IRE)**[154] 3-8-9 GMarcelli 4 80
(M Gasparini, Italy)
7 1½ **Vicveris (ITY)**[196] 1518 5-9-1 LSorrentino 1 76
(S Billeri, France)
8 1 **Spanish Hidalgo (IRE)**[22] 6518 3-9-3 MDemuro 10 84
(J L Dunlop) *prom: 3rd on ins st: pushed along to chal 3 1/2f out: wknd 2f out SP 92-100F*
9 ½ **Cape Martin (IRE)** 5-9-3 CColombi 3 76
(V Valiani, Italy)
10 4 **Sidereus (IRE)**[182] 1875 3-8-11 OFancera 8 72
(F & L Camici, Italy)

3m 7.30s (6.90)
WFA 3 from 5yo+ 8lb 10 Ran
(Including 1 Euro stake): WIN 9.01; PL 2.30, 2.49, 1.55; DF 70.88.
Owner Mario Brancato **Bred** Loughtown Stud **Trained** Italy

NOTEBOOK
Spanish Hidalgo(IRE) looked to have this race at his mercy on form, but faded tamely two furlongs out after having moved smoothly up to challenge entering the straight. Undoubtedly this was a disappointing run on ground that should have suited, but probably not one to hold against the colt indefinitely.

6805 KEMPTON (A.W) (R-H)
Monday, November 19

OFFICIAL GOING: Standard
Wind: blustery, half behind Weather: frequent heavy downpours

6864 BET NOW AT WBX.COM CLASSIFIED STKS 5f (P)
12:50 (12:51) (Class 7) 3-Y-O+ £1,365 (£403; £201) Stalls High

Form RPR
0226 1 **Muktasb (USA)**[18] 6609 6-9-0 45 (v) AdamKirby 4 57
(D Shaw) *reminders in stalls: awkward s: rcvrd to chse ldrs after 2f: got through 1f out to ld jst ins fnl f: sn clr* 4/1[3]
4606 2 2 **Time Share (IRE)**[30] 6340 3-9-0 45 (be) HayleyTurner 5 50
(G C Bravery) *stdd s: wl in rr: gd prog on inner jst over 2f out to chse ldrs over 1f out: styd on to take 2nd last 50yds: no ch w wnr* 16/1
0500 3 1 **Maromito (IRE)**[12] 6720 10-9-0 45 PatCosgrave 8 46
(R Bastiman) *led 1f: pressed ldr: led wl over 1f out: hdd and easily outpcd jst ins fnl f* 7/1
0465 4 shd **Tibinta**[36] 6210 3-9-0 45 TGMcLaughlin 10 46
(P D Evans) *reminder after 1f: cl up: effrt on inner to join ldr wl over 1f out: stl upsides 1f out: sn outpcd* 15/2
5000 5 hd **Lady Hopeful (IRE)**[55] 5716 5-9-0 44 (b) AdrianMcCarthy 3 45
(Peter Grayson) *towards rr: rdn and effrt wl over 1f out: trying to cl whn nt clr run jst over 1f out: styd on ins fnl f* 33/1
406 6 nk **Tumbleweed Di**[52] 5781 3-8-8 45 ow1 WilliamCarson(7) 7 45
(G R Oldroyd) *wl in rr: struggling by 1/2-way: styd on fnl f: nrst fin* 14/1
0055 7 hd **Hornpipe**[18] 6609 5-8-9 45 HaddenFrost(5) 2 43
(M Hill) *chsd ldrs: rdn 2f out: stl 4th ent fnl f: wknd* 3/1[1]
0303 8 ½ **Smart Cassie**[20] 6565 4-9-0 44 FergusSweeney 1 42
(H J Evans) *chsd ldrs and racd on outer: v wd bnd 2f out and lost plenty of grnd: styd on again fnl f* 14/1
0000 9 1½ **Kitchen Sink (IRE)**[102] 4312 5-9-0 45 (e) FrankieMcDonald 9 36
(Jean-Rene Auvray) *outpcd and rdn over 3f out: nvr on terms after* 25/1
5040 10 1¼ **Mind That Fox**[20] 6565 5-8-11 44 NeilChalmers(3) 11 32
(T Wall) *lost pl and struggling over 3f out: n.d after* 33/1
6630 11 2 **Hephaestus**[12] 6718 3-9-0 45 DaneO'Neill 12 24
(Peter Grayson) *led on inner after 1f to wl over 1f out: sn wknd* 7/2[2]
0/ 12 28 **Nathan Jones**[59] 5607 8-9-0 44 MickyFenton 6 —
(M G Quinlan) *t.k.h: hmpd in rr after 1f: sn bhd: virtually p.u over 1f out* 16/1

59.63 secs (-0.77) **Going Correction** -0.25s/f (Stan) 12 Ran SP% 126.3
Speed ratings (Par 97): **96,92,91,91,90 90,89,89,86,84 81,36**
CSF £69.98 TOTE £4.40: £1.60, £9.00, £2.90; EX 66.60.
Owner Derek Shaw **Bred** Shadwell Farm LLC **Trained** Danethorpe, Notts
■ Stewards' Enquiry : Adrian McCarthy two-day ban: careless riding (Nov 30, Dec 1)

FOCUS
Only a 0-45, but quite competitive and probably not bad form for the grade. It has been rated through the second and third.
Hornpipe Official explanation: jockey said gelding hung right
Smart Cassie Official explanation: jockey said filly hung left
Hephaestus Official explanation: jockey said gelding hung left
Nathan Jones Official explanation: jockey said gelding suffered interference in running

6865 WBX.COM WORLD BET EXCHANGE CLAIMING STKS 1m 2f (P)
1:20 (1:20) (Class 6) 2-Y-O £2,047 (£604; £302) Stalls High

Form RPR
04 1 **Sheer Fantastic**[5] 6814 2-9-3 0 (b[1]) J-PGuillambert 6 64
(P C Haslam) *pressed ldrs on outer: rdn 3f out: lost grnd bnd 2f out: looked less than keen over 1f out: r.o wl fnl f to ld nr fin* 5/1[3]
0610 2 ½ **Rosy Dawn**[8] 6776 2-8-6 56 (b[1]) SaleemGolam 11 52
(Ms J S Doyle) *led: kpt on wl whn hrd pressed jst over 1f out: hdd and no ex nr fin* 12/1
0633 3 1¼ **Tapas Lad (IRE)**[8] 6775 2-9-1 55 (vt) PatCosgrave 7 59
(V Smith) *t.k.h: chsd ldrs: prog to go 2nd over 1f out: sn chalng: fnd nil and hld last 100yds: wknd nr fin* 9/4[1]
2430 4 1¼ **Bollywood Style**[7] 6793 2-8-12 55 DaneO'Neill 8 54
(J R Best) *prom: rdn to chse ldr over 2f out to over 1f out: wknd ins fnl f* 13/2
00 5 ½ **Has To Be Abacus (IRE)**[67] 5344 2-8-13 0 DavidKinsella 12 54
(A B Haynes) *hld up in last pair and off the pce: prog over 1f out and swtchd to inner: shuffled along and styd on: nvr nr ldrs* 50/1
0633 6 hd **Carry On Cleo**[8] 6776 2-8-6 56 FergusSweeney 9 46
(P D Evans) *chsd ldrs: pushed along 4f out: stl chsng over 1f out: wknd ins fnl f* 4/1[2]
400 7 ¾ **Ridgeway Jazz**[14] 6693 2-8-2 35 HayleyTurner 3 41
(M D I Usher) *mostly chsd ldr to over 2f out: wknd over 1f out* 100/1
405 8 3½ **Miss Solo**[7] 6793 2-7-13 0 PatrickDonaghy(7) 2 39
(P C Haslam) *a towards rr: rdn 3f out: no prog* 8/1
0050 9 4 **Racey Rachel (IRE)**[19] 6591 2-8-12 52 TPQueally 5 37
(E F Vaughan) *t.k.h: hld up in rr: rdn 3f out: no prog and struggling 2f out* 8/1
00 10 14 **Valtat**[7] 6793 2-8-13 0 (v[1]) FrankieMcDonald 1 13
(B R Johnson) *stdd s: plld hrd: hld up: a last: t.o fnl 2f* 33/1

2m 8.55s (-0.45) **Going Correction** -0.25s/f (Stan) 10 Ran SP% 116.6
Speed ratings (Par 94): **91,90,89,88,88 88,87,84,81,70**
CSF £62.33 TOTE £4.60: £1.50, £1.80, £1.70; EX 35.00.
Owner Middleham Park Racing Xviii **Bred** Newsells Park Stud Limited **Trained** Middleham Moor, N Yorks

FOCUS
A very moderate juvenile claimer. The winner ran basically to form and might be capable of a bit better.

NOTEBOOK
Sheer Fantastic, with blinkers replacing a visor, managed to build on the form he showed when a running-on fourth in a stronger race than this over an extended 1m on his return from a break at Wolverhampton, but he was far from convincing. Having pulled hard through the early stages, he looked reluctant when put under pressure at the top of the straight, before eventually deciding to run on and peg back the tiring leader. This might have helped his confidence, and he should stay even further next year, but he looks to have an attitude. (op 7-2)
Rosy Dawn, the winner of a similar race over this trip at Lingfield two starts back, ran better than when last in a 1m nursery here on her previous outing with blinkers replacing the visor. She was allowed her own way out in front and looked likely to take advantage of the easy lead for much of the way in the straight, but she was just reeled in. (op 10-1)
Tapas Lad(IRE), tried in a tongue tie, could not take advantage of the drop in grade on this step up in trip. (op 3-1)
Bollywood Style, trying this trip for the first time, seemed to have every chance if good enough. (op 11-2)
Has To Be Abacus(IRE) ◆ had shown very limited form on his first two starts, but he caught the eye stepped up in trip and dropped in grade off the back of a two-month break. Poorly positioned for much of the way, he could never threaten the principals, but he ran on nicely in the straight without being given too hard a time. He is now qualified for handicaps and is definitely one to look out for off a lowly mark.

6866 WBX.COM H'CAP (DIV I) 1m 2f (P)
1:50 (1:52) (Class 6) (0-60,60) 3-Y-O+ £1,706 (£503; £252) Stalls High

Form RPR
0440 1 **Fateful Attraction**[25] 6458 4-9-8 60 (b) DaneO'Neill 9 73
(I A Wood) *trckd ldrs: prog to go 2nd over 2f out: rdn to ld over 1f out: steadily drew away* 8/1[3]
5062 2 3 **Watchmaker**[8] 6780 4-9-8 60 FergusSweeney 3 67
(Miss Tor Sturgis) *pushed up fr tardy s to trck ldrs: effrt to ld 3f out: drvn and hdd over 1f out: no ch w wnr after* 11/10[1]
2-00 3 ½ **Mutamaasek (USA)**[34] 6259 5-8-12 55 KirstyMilczarek(5) 4 61
(Lady Herries) *hld up in last pair: rapid prog fr 4f out to go 3rd wl over 2f out: effrt flattened out and one pce fnl 2f* 15/2[2]
2436 4 1 **Granary Girl**[12] 6713 5-9-0 52 DavidKinsella 5 56
(J Pearce) *hld up in last trio: shuffled along over 2f out: sn outpcd: rdn and kpt on fr over 1f out* 11/1
0000 5 1½ **Dark Planet**[25] 6452 4-9-0 52 (v) RobertHavlin 10 53
(D Burchell) *cl up: trapped bhd rival fr 3f out to 2f out: drvn and no rspnse over 1f out* 16/1
0300 6 2½ **Greenmeadow**[17] 6627 5-9-1 53 SteveDrowne 1 49
(S Kirk) *nvr beyond midfield: rdn and no prog wl over 2f out* 11/1
0446 7 hd **Border Edge**[13] 6710 9-9-3 55 (v) StephenDonohoe 11 51
(J J Bridger) *rdn and won battle for ld: led to 3f out: sn u.p and btn* 10/1
4400 8 ½ **Ashmolian (IRE)**[61] 5531 4-8-10 48 oh1 ow2 SamHitchcott 8 43
(Miss Z C Davison) *nvr beyond midfield: rdn over 3f out: sn btn* 25/1

0000 **9** ½ **Roxie Princess (IRE)**[33] 6272 3-9-2 **58** .... TPQueally 7 52
(J A R Toller) *tried to ld but unable to: chsd ldr to over 3f out: sn u.p and btn* **25/1**

0054 **10** 12 **Mon Petite Amour**[180] 1951 4-9-1 **58** .... AshleyHamblett[(5)] 6 28
(D W P Arbuthnot) *a in last trio: rdn and struggling 3f out: t.o* **10/1**

0600 **11** ¾ **Myrtle Bay (IRE)**[36] 6212 4-8-8 **51** oh1 ow5.............(v) HaddenFrost[(5)] 2 19
(J C Tuck) *chsd ldrs: reminder 6f out: wknd over 3f out: t.o* **66/1**

2m 5.31s (-3.69) **Going Correction** -0.25s/f (Stan)
WFA 3 from 4yo+ 4lb **11** Ran SP% **120.4**
Speed ratings (Par 101): **104,101,101,100,99 97,97,96,96,86 86**
CSF £17.28 CT £74.69 TOTE £9.60: £2.10, £1.20, £2.40; EX 23.40.
Owner M I Forbes **Bred** Vidin Gate Stud **Trained** Upper Lambourn, Berks

FOCUS
A moderate handicap, but probably fair form for the level, and the time was reasonable. The sectionals suggested the pace was similar to the second division through the early stages, but the final time was 0.76 seconds quicker.
Mon Petite Amour Official explanation: jockey said filly banged its head on stalls

6867 WBX.COM H'CAP (DIV II) 1m 2f (P)
2:20 (2:23) (Class 6) (0-60,60) 3-Y-0+ **£1,706** (£503; £252) **Stalls** High

Form RPR

6062 **1** **Hatch A Plan (IRE)**[19] 6577 6-9-2 **57** .... NeilChalmers[(3)] 11 66
(Mouse Hamilton-Fairley) *hld up in midfield: lost grnd bhd wkng rival 4f out: effrt over 2f out: chsd ldr fnl f: coaxed along and styd on to ld last stride* **7/2**[1]

4561 **2** shd **Dinner Date**[12] 6713 5-9-6 **58** .... J-PGuillambert 2 67
(T Keddy) *trckd ldrs: gng wl fr 3f out: effrt to ld over 1f out: styd on fnl f: hdd last stride* **4/1**[2]

3300 **3** 1¼ **And Again (USA)**[25] 6447 4-9-3 **55** ....(p) OscarUrbina 3 61
(R A Teal) *hld up in rr: pushed along over 3f out: prog and rdn 2f out: styd on fnl f: nvr able to chal* **7/1**

0504 **4** 1½ **Grafty Green (IRE)**[11] 6728 4-8-13 **51** .... MartinDwyer 10 54
(W M Brisbourne) *hld up in last pair: prog on inner over 2f out: rdn and nt qckn over 1f out: one pce after* **8/1**

2200 **5** ¾ **Boppys Pride**[20] 6558 4-9-3 **55** ....(p) DaleGibson 8 57
(R A Fahey) *trckd ldrs: nt qckn wl over 1f out: squeezed out sn after: kpt on fnl f* **5/1**[3]

3220 **6** ¾ **Shaheer (IRE)**[7] 6796 5-9-1 **53** ....(v) JimCrowley 1 53
(J Gallagher) *mostly trckd ldr: led over 4f out to over 1f out: wknd fnl f* **8/1**

5000 **7** 3½ **Play Up Pompey**[12] 6719 5-9-0 **52** .... MickyFenton 7 45
(J J Bridger) *dwlt: t.k.h: hld up tl prog to join ldr over 4f out: wknd over 1f out* **9/1**

-000 **8** 10 **Knickyknackienoo**[12] 6718 6-8-3 **46** oh1 .... KirstyMilczarek[(5)] 5 19
(T T Clement) *awkward s: t.k.h: hld up in midfield: wknd 3f out: sn bhd* **66/1**

5205 **9** 13 **Anthea**[8] 6778 3-9-2 **58** ....(b[1]) DaneO'Neill 9 5
(B R Millman) *racd freely: led to over 4f out: wknd rapidly: t.o* **22/1**

-030 **10** 29 **Kings Topic (USA)**[72] 5237 7-9-8 **60** .... SamHitchcott 6 —
(A B Haynes) *reluctant to enter stalls: nvr gng wl: t.o fnl 3f: b.b.v* **16/1**

2m 6.07s (-2.93) **Going Correction** -0.25s/f (Stan)
WFA 3 from 4yo+ 4lb **10** Ran SP% **115.3**
Speed ratings (Par 101): **101,100,99,98,98 97,94,86,76,53**
CSF £17.17 CT £92.09 TOTE £4.80: £2.20, £1.60, £1.90; EX 20.30.
Owner Hamilton-Fairley Racing **Bred** Camogue Stud Ltd **Trained** Bramshill, Hants

FOCUS
A moderate handicap. The form has been rated through the third and fourth with the winner 4lb off this year's best. According to the sectionals, the pace was very similar to the first division through the early stages, but the winning time was 0.76 seconds slower.
Kings Topic(USA) Official explanation: vet said gelding had bled from the nose

6868 EBF WBX.COM MEDIAN AUCTION MAIDEN STKS 1m (P)
2:50 (2:51) (Class 5) 2-Y-0 **£3,238** (£963; £481; £240) **Stalls** High

Form RPR

0002 **1** **Last Of The Line**[11] 6736 2-9-3 69.................................. SteveDrowne 7 70+
(H J L Dunlop) *trckd ldrs: gng wl but nt clr run over 2f out to over 1f out: prog to ld 1f out: r.o wl: readily* **10/1**

3 **2** ¾ **Pharaohs Queen (IRE)**[27] 6401 2-8-12 0......................... TPQueally 11 63+
(E A L Dunlop) *dwlt and rousted along early: sn trckd ldrs: effrt on inner 2f out: chal and upsides 1f out: chsd wnr after: r.o but a hld* **7/1**

3 2½ **Parson's Punch** 2-9-3 0... MartinDwyer 6 63+
(P D Cundell) *racd wd in tch: outpcd over 2f out and rdn: styd on again to take 3rd ins fnl f* **11/2**[3]

0033 **4** 1½ **Home**[20] 6572 2-9-3 69... PatCosgrave 8 60
(J R Boyle) *cl up: rdn to ld narrowly 2f out to 1f out: sn wknd* **4/1**[2]

064 **5** nk **High Plains (FR)**[24] 6469 2-9-3 75..................................... DaneO'Neill 9 59
(R Hannon) *pressed ldr: chal and w new ldr 2f out: upsides 1f out: sn wknd* **4/1**[2]

00 **6** 4 **Diamond Seeker**[19] 6578 2-8-5 0............................. AshleyMorgan[(7)] 4 45
(V Smith) *t.k.h and hld up in rr: prog on inner 2f out: chsng ldrs over 1f out: sn wknd* **100/1**

7 ½ **Dear Will** 2-9-3 0... OscarUrbina 2 49
(J R Fanshawe) *dwlt: hld up in last: prog over 4f out and in tch: swtchd ins over 1f out: sn wknd* **25/1**

5 **8** 1¾ **Uno Dos Tres**[14] 6694 2-9-3 0... DaleGibson 5 45
(Jane Chapple-Hyam) *plld hrd on outer: restrained in bhd after 2f: rdn over 4f out: brief effrt on inner 2f out: wknd* **33/1**

03 **9** 1 **Grapes Of Wrath (UAE)**[25] 6456 2-8-12 0................ J-PGuillambert 12 38
(M Johnston) *mde most to 2f out: wknd* **25/1**

5052 **U** **Greek Theatre (USA)**[12] 6715 2-9-3 69.......................(e) JimCrowley 10 —
(Mrs A J Perrett) *lunged s and uns rdr* **11/4**[1]

1m 40.76s (-0.04) **Going Correction** -0.25s/f (Stan) **10** Ran SP% **115.3**
Speed ratings (Par 96): **90,89,86,85,84 80,80,78,77,—**
CSF £74.26 TOTE £8.80: £2.60, £1.60, £2.00; EX 57.70.
Owner Woodcote Stud Ltd **Bred** Ridgecourt Stud **Trained** Lambourn, Berks

FOCUS
A modest maiden and, with no pace on through the early stages, the form wants treating with some caution. The winner probably did not need to step up to score. The sectionals show they covered the first two furlongs in a slower time than the earlier 1m2f two-year-old claimer, and the field were still covered by around four or five lengths inside the final quarter mile.

NOTEBOOK
Last Of The Line, a real eye-catcher on two of his previous three starts in maiden company before being beaten just a short-head on his nursery debut off a mark of 65 over 7f at Wolverhampton, improved for the step up in trip and was able to get off the mark at the fifth attempt. Having travelled well just in behind the pace, he stayed on strongly once switched into the clear and did this quite well. He should progress into a fair handicapper. (op 8-1)
Pharaohs Queen(IRE), like the eventual winner, travelled strongly just in behind the leaders and she stayed on well once in the clear. This was an improvement on the form she showed when third over 7f on her debut at Lingfield. (op 6-1)
Parson's Punch ◆, a 20,000gns gelded son of Beat Hollow, half brother to Fransiscan, who was placed over 1m-1m4f, out of a multiple middle-distance winner, made a pleasing debut. He lacked the pace of the front two, but kept on nicely for third and should do well over further next year. (op 6-1 tchd 13-2)
Home was well held in fourth on his first start since leaving Ed Dunlop's yard. (op 5-1 tchd 7-2)
High Plains(FR) found disappointingly little stepped up to 1m for the first time on his Polytrack debut. (op 11-4)
Greek Theatre(USA) got rid of his rider as the stalls opened. (op 3-1)

6869 BET NOW AT WBX.COM H'CAP 7f (P)
3:20 (3:27) (Class 6) (0-65,64) 3-Y-0+ **£2,047** (£604; £302) **Stalls** High

Form RPR

3301 **1** **Jools**[16] 6647 9-8-11 **56**.. HayleyTurner 5 64
(D K Ivory) *t.k.h: hld up in rr: stdy prog fr 2f out: wl-timed effrt to ld last 100yds: styd on wl* **8/1**

0061 **2** ½ **Tanforan**[9] 6764 5-9-2 **61**.. TGMcLaughlin 14 68
(B P J Baugh) *trckd ldrs: rdn to cl fr 2f out: upsides ins fnl f: jst outpcd by wnr* **12/1**

0002 **3** ½ **Rabbit Fighter (IRE)**[9] 6764 3-9-0 **60**.......................... FergusSweeney 3 66
(D Shaw) *dropped in fr wd draw and hld up in rr: prog on outer fr 2f out: styd on fnl f: nvr quite able to chal* **3/1**[1]

0221 **4** nk **Northern Boy (USA)**[10] 6749 4-9-5 **64**............................ DaleGibson 10 69
(M W Easterby) *dwlt: rousted along early then plld hrd in midfield: effrt over 2f out: hrd rdn to chse ldrs over 1f out: styd on same pce* **9/2**[2]

3103 **5** shd **Mistral Sky**[10] 6747 8-9-5 **64**..(v) MickyFenton 4 69
(Stef Liddiard) *pressed ldr: rdn to ld narrowly over 1f out: hdd and one pce last 100yds* **16/1**

4401 **5** dht **Piccolo Diamante (USA)**[12] 6718 3-8-5 **51**..............(t[1]) MartinDwyer 12 59+
(D J Murphy) *s.s: plld hrd and hld up wl in rr: prog on inner 2f out: clsng on ldrs whn nt clr run ins fnl f: styd on last 100yds* **10/1**

5030 **7** 1¼ **Takitwo**[86] 4807 4-8-11 **63**.. JamieHamblett[(7)] 9 64
(P D Cundell) *trckd ldrs: rdn and nt qckn wl over 1f out: styd on same pce fnl f* **6/1**[3]

0660 **8** ½ **Buzzin'Boyzee (IRE)**[16] 6647 4-8-5 **50** oh5................... SaleemGolam 8 50+
(P D Evans) *hld up wl in last: effrt and sme prog whn nt clr run over 1f out: kpt on same pce after* **40/1**

0541 **9** 1 **Figaro Flyer (IRE)**[15] 6671 4-9-5 **64**........................ SimonWhitworth 11 61
(P Howling) *led: pushed along 2f out: narrowly hdd over 1f out: steadily lost pls ins fnl f* **9/2**[2]

0005 **10** 5 **Penny Glitters**[21] 6541 4-8-2 **50**................................(b) DominicFox[(3)] 2 34
(S Parr) *hld up in midfield: effrt over 2f out: wknd wl over 1f out* **50/1**

5300 **11** nk **Krakatau (FR)**[14] 6695 3-9-0 **60**...................................... SamHitchcott 13 43
(D J Wintle) *pressed ldng pair: wknd on inner over 1f out* **25/1**

6026 **12** 6 **Looks Could Kill (USA)**[16] 6647 5-9-1 **60**................(b) SteveDrowne 7 27
(A B Haynes) *walked to post: chsd ldrs tl wknd tamely 3f out* **25/1**

0146 **13** 2 **Vanadium**[12] 6717 5-9-5 **64**... TPQueally 1 25
(G L Moore) *tk fierce hold on outer: pressed ldrs 3f: lost grnd bnd 3f out: sn bhd* **14/1**

1m 25.12s (-1.68) **Going Correction** -0.25s/f (Stan)
WFA 3 from 4yo+ 1lb **13** Ran SP% **128.2**
Speed ratings (Par 101): **99,98,97,97,97 97,95,95,94,88 88,81,79**
CSF £104.34 CT £374.06 TOTE £11.80: £3.30, £4.30, £2.50; EX 191.40.
Owner Dean Ivory **Bred** Tsarina Stud **Trained** Radlett, Herts

FOCUS
Ordinary form for the grade, rated through the second and third. The leaders went off too fast.
Piccolo Diamante(USA) Official explanation: jockey said gelding was denied a clear run

6870 WBX.COM WORLD BET EXCHANGE H'CAP 6f (P)
3:50 (3:56) (Class 6) (0-63,64) 3-Y-0+ **£2,047** (£604; £302) **Stalls** High

Form RPR

0313 **1** **Ruman (IRE)**[19] 6581 5-9-0 **60**.. AdamKirby 12 77+
(M J Attwater) *plld hrd early: sn trckd ldrs: effrt on inner to ld over 1f out: styd on wl* **7/2**[2]

0312 **2** 1¼ **Ever Cheerful**[3] 6825 6-9-0 **60**......................................(p) SteveDrowne 8 69
(A B Haynes) *mde most: drvn and hdd over 1f out: nt qckn and readily hld after* **5/2**[1]

1000 **3** 1¼ **Anfield Dream**[27] 6415 5-8-12 **58**..................................(t) MickyFenton 9 63
(J R Jenkins) *pressed ldr: upsides 2f out: nt qckn over 1f out: fdd ins fnl f* **20/1**

0213 **4** 2 **Gimme Some Lovin (IRE)**[17] 6625 3-9-0 **60**............. FergusSweeney 5 59
(D W P Arbuthnot) *hld up in last trio: prog on inner over 2f out: chsd clr ldng trio fnl f: no imp* **6/1**[3]

0105 **5** 1 **Desert Light (IRE)**[26] 6428 6-8-13 **59**........................ J-PGuillambert 2 61+
(D Shaw) *t.k.h and hld up in last: prog and swtchd to inner over 2f out: kpt on: n.d* **8/1**

1501 **6** nk **Monashee Prince (IRE)**[5] 6818 5-9-4 **64** 6ex................(v) JimCrowley 4 59
(J R Best) *dwlt: settled in rr: prog 3f out: chsd ldrs but no imp 2f out: fdd* **6/1**[3]

00U0 **7** 1½ **Puskas (IRE)**[32] 6287 4-9-1 **61**.................................(v) StephenDonohoe 6 52
(J M Bradley) *pressed ldng pair to over 2f out: steadily wknd* **33/1**

6035 **8** ½ **Coseadrom (IRE)**[9] 6764 5-8-13 **59**............................(t) SamHitchcott 7 48
(M F Harris) *nvr beyond midfield: rdn and btn over 2f out* **14/1**

0-20 **9** 2 **Herb Paris (FR)**[21] 6533 3-9-0 **60**...................................... TPQueally 11 43
(P M Phelan) *trckd ldrs tl lost pl u.p over 2f out* **20/1**

0001 **10** 2 **Green Lagonda (AUS)**[26] 6428 5-9-1 **61**.......................... HayleyTurner 3 38
(J G Given) *rrd s: t.k.h: hld up in rr: effrt but no real prog 2f out: sn wknd* **15/2**

000 **11** 3 **Pauvic (IRE)**[202] 1377 4-9-0 **60**...................................... SaleemGolam 1 28
(Mrs A Duffield) *rdn in midfield bef 1/2-way: sn struggling* **50/1**

1m 11.34s (-2.36) **Going Correction** -0.25s/f (Stan) **11** Ran SP% **123.3**
Speed ratings (Par 101): **105,103,101,99,97 97,95,94,91,89 85**
CSF £12.80 CT £152.88 TOTE £4.20: £1.80, £1.90, £5.20; EX 15.80.
Owner The Attwater Partnership **Bred** Noel And Michael Buckley **Trained** Epsom, Surrey

FOCUS
A moderate sprint handicap and very few got involved. Solid form, and the winner could prove a bit better than the grade.

6871 WORLD BET EXCHANGE H'CAP 1m 4f (P)
4:20 (4:23) (Class 6) (0-60,62) 3-Y-0+ **£2,047** (£604; £302) **Stalls** Centre

Form RPR

0041 **1** **Highest Esteem**[5] 6807 3-9-6 **62** 6ex........................(p) FergusSweeney 2 74+
(G L Moore) *trckd ldrs: n.m.r briefly over 2f out: got through to ld over 1f out: in command after* **11/8**[1]

5556 **2** 1 1/4 **Fantasy Ride**[12] 6719 5-9-8 **58** .... OscarUrbina 11 65
(J Pearce) *trckd ldr: led over 2f out to over 1f out: kpt on but no imp on wnr ins fnl f* **7/1**

3532 **3** 1 **Fenners (USA)**[19] 6583 4-9-8 **58** ....(b) DaleGibson 3 63
(M W Easterby) *dwlt: hld up in rr: rdn 4f out: prog over 2f out: styd on to take 3rd ins fnl f* **6/1**[3]

/200 **4** 1 **Beliar (GER)**[33] 6271 4-9-9 **59** ....(p) PatCosgrave 6 63
(Eoin Doyle, Ire) *chsd ldng pair: chalng 2f out: sn nt qckn and outpcd: styd on again ins fnl f* **40/1**

1623 **5** hd **Papradon**[5] 6817 3-9-2 **58** ....(v) J-PGuillambert 10 61
(J R Best) *t.k.h: restrained bhd ldrs: effrt over 2f out: n.m.r briefly sn after: drvn and kpt on same pce* **11/2**[2]

4302 **6** 1 1/4 **Recalcitrant**[12] 6719 4-8-11 **54** .... JamieHamblett(7) 5 55
(S Dow) *t.k.h: hld up in midfield: nt qckn over 2f out: kpt on same pce fr over 1f out* **8/1**

6130 **7** 2 **Squiffy**[110] 4067 4-9-2 **52** .... SimonWhitworth 14 50
(P D Cundell) *hld up in rr: shuffled along and kpt on fr over 2f out: nvr nr ldrs* **25/1**

4600 **8** 7 **Sir Sandicliffe (IRE)**[21] 6534 3-8-10 **52** .... TGMcLaughlin 12 39+
(W M Brisbourne) *hld up wl in rr: prog on inner gng wl enough over 2f out: hmpd wl over 1f out: nt rcvr* **25/1**

0040 **9** 2 1/2 **Full Of Promise (USA)**[27] 6407 3-8-13 **55** .... JimCrowley 7 38
(Mrs A J Perrett) *chsd ldrs: u.p over 4f out: lost pl over 2f out* **50/1**

0030 **10** 3 **Divine River**[12] 6265 4-9-3 **53** .... TPQueally 13 31
(J G Portman) *dwlt: hld up in last: nvr on terms* **66/1**

10 **11** 1 **Raydan (IRE)**[12] 6719 5-9-7 **57** ....(b) MickyFenton 4 34
(D R Gandolfo) *hld up: prog on outer to trck ldrs over 3f out: wknd 2f out* **20/1**

-000 **12** 3/4 **Itsawindup**[164] 2425 3-8-13 **55** .... SteveDrowne 1 30
(W J Knight) *hld up wl in rr: nvr on terms: wknd over 2f out* **50/1**

2204 **13** 1 3/4 **Bolckow**[211] 1181 4-9-5 **60** .... AshleyHamblett(5) 9 33
(J T Stimpson) *led to over 2f out: heavily eased whn btn over 1f out* **20/1**

2m 34.06s (-2.84) **Going Correction** -0.25s/f (Stan)
WFA 3 from 4yo+ 6lb **13** Ran SP% **120.5**
Speed ratings (Par 101): **99,98,97,96,96 95,94,89,88,86 85,85,83**
CSF £10.10 CT £47.29 TOTE £3.00: £1.40, £2.30, £1.80; EX 14.40 Place 6 £64.90, Place 5 £16.90..
Owner Paul Green **Bred** Paul Green **Trained** Woodingdean, E Sussex

FOCUS
A weak middle-distance handicap run at an ordinary pace. Sound form, with the progressive winner value for 3l.
Itsawindup Official explanation: jockey said gelding had no more to give
T/Plt: £64.90 to a £1 stake. Pool: £44,660.25. 502.15 winning tickets. T/Qpdt: £16.90 to a £1 stake. Pool: £3,473.20. 151.20 winning tickets. JN

6855 WOLVERHAMPTON (A.W) (L-H)
Monday, November 19

OFFICIAL GOING: Standard
Wind: light, half against Weather: Dry

6872 PONTIN'S BOOK EARLY CLAIMING STKS 5f 216y(P)
1:00 (1:02) (Class 6) 2-Y-0 **£2,047** (£604; £302) **Stalls** Low

Form RPR

6043 **1** **Harbour Blues**[10] 6748 2-8-13 67 ....(t) LiamJones 6 80
(C E Brittain) *cl up: led over 2f out: rdn clr over 1f out: easily* **3/1**[1]

1005 **2** 6 **Andrasta**[16] 6635 2-8-3 68 .... PatrickMathers(3) 4 55
(A Berry) *trckd ldrs: hdwy over 2f out: rdn to chse wnr ent fnl f: sn drvn and no imp* **4/1**[3]

552 **3** 2 **Wild Bill Tracey**[14] 6692 2-9-2 72 ....(p) DarryllHolland 1 59
(M J Wallace) *led: rdn along and hdd over 2f out: sn drvn and kpt on same pce appr fnl f* **4/1**[3]

0 **4** nk **Dancing Maite**[31] 6303 2-8-13 0 .... PaulEddery 10 55
(S R Bowring) *towards rr: hdwy 2f out: sn rdn and styd on ins fnl f: nrst fin* **66/1**

1060 **5** nk **Little Firecracker**[28] 6379 2-8-1 64 ow1 .... AndrewElliott(3) 3 45
(Miss M E Rowland) *dwlt and bhd tl styd on appr fnl f: nrst fin* **12/1**

2100 **6** hd **Rievaulx Valentino**[68] 5331 2-8-13 74 ....(p) NCallan 7 54
(K A Ryan) *in midfield: rdn along 1/2-way: nvr a factor* **7/2**[2]

0140 **7** hd **Bahamarama (IRE)**[42] 6066 2-7-11 64 .... DavidProbert(7) 8 44
(R A Harris) *nvr bttr than midfield* **18/1**

0410 **8** nk **Mister Christie**[106] 4193 2-8-13 70 .... DeanMcKeown 9 52
(J G Given) *cl up on outer: rdn along wl over 2f out and sn wknd* **9/1**

0640 **9** 4 **Whistful Miss**[86] 4824 2-8-4 48 .... ChrisCatlin 2 31
(P Howling) *chsd ldrs: rdn along and wknd 1/2-way: sn bhd* **40/1**

0000 **10** 19 **Somarini**[69] 5302 2-8-7 48 .... LPKeniry 5 —
(T T Clement) *s.i.s: a bhd* **80/1**

1m 16.01s (0.20) **Going Correction** 0.0s/f (Stan) **10** Ran SP% **115.3**
Speed ratings (Par 94): **98,90,87,86,86 86,86,85,80,54**
CSF £14.91 TOTE £3.20: £1.60, £1.40, £1.40; EX 16.50 Trifecta £62.30 Pool £245.93 - 2.80 winning units..Harbour Blues was claimed by Mr A. W. Carroll for £12,000.
Owner A J Richards **Bred** Ewar Stud Farms **Trained** Newmarket, Suffolk

FOCUS
This was a very moderate claimer except for the winner who absolutely bolted up in a fair time for the grade, showing improved form. The pace was decent and very few ever got into this.

NOTEBOOK
Harbour Blues was by no means well treated at these weights, but he was well supported in the market and the drop to this trip for the first time since his debut, and possibly the first-time tongue-tie, made all the difference. He was running all over the early leader from a long way out and once sent for home he quickened right away. He was subsequently snapped up by Tony Carroll for £12,000 and it will be interesting to see what the Handicapper does with him after this. (op 7-2 tchd 4-1)
Andrasta, marginally best in on adjusted official ratings, emerged from the pack to finish a clear second-best but the winner was in a different parish. She is totally exposed now and this effort does not suggest that she is particularly well handicapped at the moment either. (op 9-2 tchd 5-1)
Wild Bill Tracey, having his first try beyond the minimum trip in the first-time cheekpieces, seemed to travel well enough in front, but he could do nothing once the favourite went past him and patently failed to stay. (op 10-3)
Dancing Maite, who hung badly when last of 11 on his Redcar debut, stayed on to finish amongst the bunch battling for third place, but was never a threat to the front pair. He is entitled to improve a bit more from this though. (op 50-1)
Little Firecracker, having her first start for her third different trainer in only her fifth outing, ran as though she found this too sharp but she should still have done better at the weights, even with the 1lb overweight, and has it to prove now. (op 10-1)
Rievaulx Valentino was another to run below form on the evidence of adjusted official ratings and seems to have gone the wrong way. (tchd 4-1)

6873 WOLVERHAMPTON-RACECOURSE.CO.UK (S) STKS 7f 32y(P)
1:30 (1:30) (Class 6) 3-Y-0+ **£2,047** (£604; £302) **Stalls** High

Form RPR

1 **Golden Surprice (IRE)**[15] 5-9-7 0 .... PConvertino 3 79+
(Aldo Locatelli, Italy) *hld up: hdwy 1/2-way: cl up whn pushed wd home turn: rdn to ld over 1f out: sn clr: kpt on* **1/1**[1]

0004 **2** 5 **Sarraaf (IRE)**[11] 6732 11-9-1 52 .... PhillipMakin 1 60+
(I Semple) *hld up in rr: hdwy 1/2-way: effrt whn n.m.r 2f out: swtchd outside over 1f out: rdn to chse wnr ins fnl f: no imp* **12/1**

3500 **3** 1 1/2 **Tobago Reef**[44] 6024 3-9-0 68 ....(p) DarryllHolland 7 56
(Mrs L Stubbs) *chsd ldrs: effrt and n.m.r 2f out: sn rdn and kpt on same pce appr fnl f* **13/2**[3]

1000 **4** 1 1/2 **Island Green (USA)**[196] 1527 4-9-7 60 .... DanielTudhope 5 58
(D Carroll) *in tch: effrt 3f out: n.m.r 2f out: sn rdn and kpt on same pce* **9/1**

2403 **5** nk **Calloff The Search**[27] 6402 3-8-7 53 ....(v) JackDean(7) 11 51
(W G M Turner) *chsd ldrs: rdn along on outer 2f out: sn drvn and kpt on same pce* **20/1**

0054 **6** shd **Rafferty (IRE)**[3] 6831 8-9-1 48 .... PaulDoe 6 51
(S Dow) *chsd ldng pair: hdwy 3f out: rdn and hung rt home turn: sn drvn and one pce* **6/1**[2]

660 **7** 4 **Trinculo (IRE)**[26] 6424 10-9-7 53 ....(b) LPKeniry 2 46
(R A Harris) *led: rdn along over 2f out: drvn and hdd over 1f out: wknd* **25/1**

0106 **8** 2 **Bert's Memory**[21] 6537 3-9-1 53 ....(p) NCallan 9 36
(K A Ryan) *a in rr* **20/1**

4000 **9** 4 **Marmooq**[13] 6706 4-9-7 48 ....(v) ChrisCatlin 4 30
(M J Attwater) *sn outpcd and a in rr* **12/1**

0505 **10** 1/2 **Swing On A Star (IRE)**[40] 6101 3-8-2 55 .... AmyBaker(7) 10 17
(Miss J Feilden) *cl up: rdn along 3f out: wknd 2f out* **33/1**

300 **11** 19 **Foxy Diplomat**[25] 6457 3-9-0 50 ....(b[1]) FrancisNorton 12 —
(Miss J R Tooth) *plld hrd: prom on outer over 2f: sn lost pl and bhd* **66/1**

1m 30.25s (-0.15) **Going Correction** 0.0s/f (Stan)
WFA 3 from 4yo+ 1lb **11** Ran SP% **120.8**
Speed ratings (Par 101): **100,94,92,90,90 90,85,83,78,78 56**
CSF £13.99 TOTE £1.30: £1.10, £4.30, £2.70; EX 16.80 Trifecta £131.30 Part won. Pool £180.97 - 0.71 winning units..The winner was bought in for 11,500gns. Call Off The Search was claimed by Mrs Stef Liddiard for £6,000.
Owner Chevaux de Prestige Italia Sas **Bred** Scuderia Golden Horse S R L **Trained** Italy

FOCUS
What had looked a bog-standard Wolverhampton seller was made much more interesting by the presence of the Italian-trained favourite, who duly bolted up and is clearly a cut above this grade.

6874 PONTIN'S BOOK EARLY PRICE PROMISE H'CAP 1m 141y(P)
2:00 (2:00) (Class 6) (0-66,66) 3-Y-0+ **£2,047** (£604; £302) **Stalls** Low

Form RPR

0622 **1** **My Michelle**[5] 6816 6-8-11 **62** .... NCallan 1 70
(B Palling) *cl up on inner: led 3f out: rdn clr wl over 1f out: drvn and edgd rt ins fnl f: kpt on* **9/2**[3]

0001 **2** 3/4 **Defi (IRE)**[11] 6732 5-8-7 **58** ....(b) FrancisNorton 4 64
(I Semple) *trckd ldrs: hdwy 3f out: rdn to chse wnr over 1f out: styd on wl fnl f* **11/1**

0022 **3** 1/2 **Putra Laju (IRE)**[20] 6567 3-8-10 **64** ....(p) JamesDoyle 10 69+
(J W Hills) *hld up towards rr: hdwy 3f out: nt clr run 2f out: sn swtchd outside: rdn and styd on wl fnl f* **14/1**

154 **4** 1/2 **Our Kes (IRE)**[3] 6764 5-9-0 **65** .... ChrisCatlin 6 69
(P Howling) *in tch: hdwy over 3f out: rdn to chse ldrs 2f out: sn drvn and kpt on same pce appr fnl f* **10/3**[1]

0653 **5** 1 1/4 **Convivial Spirit**[17] 6623 3-8-12 **66** ....(t) LPKeniry 12 67+
(E F Vaughan) *hld up towards rr: hdwy over 3f out: rdn along 2f out: kpt on same pce* **11/1**

3504 **6** 1 1/2 **Xpres Maite**[110] 4075 4-9-1 **66** .... PaulEddery 8 64
(S R Bowring) *in tch: rdn along and outpcd 3f out: kpt on appr fnl f: nrst fin* **50/1**

0061 **7** 1 3/4 **Surprise Act**[32] 6277 3-8-11 **65** .... PaulDoe 2 61
(P R Chamings) *led: rdn along and hdd 3f out: drvn 2f out and sn wknd* **4/1**[2]

1044 **8** nk **Grand Diamond (IRE)**[11] 6738 3-8-7 **61** .... LiamJones 13 54
(J S Goldie) *hld up: a towards rr* **9/1**

6-23 **9** 1 **Forbidden (IRE)**[19] 6579 4-8-7 **61** ....(t) JerryO'Dwyer(3) 9 52
(Daniel Mark Loughnane, Ire) *s.i.s: a in rr* **10/1**

4114 **10** 5 **Time To Regret**[12] 6716 7-8-7 **61** ....(p) AndrewElliott(3) 5 40
(I W McInnes) *chsd ldrs: rdn along over 3f out: grad wknd* **14/1**

4460 **11** 3/4 **Pop Music (IRE)**[18] 6603 4-8-7 **65** ....(p) AmyBaker(7) 7 42
(Miss J Feilden) *chsd ldrs: rdn along over 3f out: wknd 2f out* **25/1**

3-34 **12** 4 **Boogie Dancer**[155] 2691 3-8-12 **66** .... DarryllHolland 3 34
(H S Howe) *chsd ldrs: rdn along over 3f out: sn wknd* **18/1**

1m 51.69s (-0.07) **Going Correction** 0.0s/f (Stan)
WFA 3 from 4yo+ 3lb **12** Ran SP% **121.4**
Speed ratings (Par 101): **100,99,98,98,97 96,94,94,93,88 88,84**
CSF £54.98 CT £664.19 TOTE £4.90: £1.50, £3.70, £4.00; EX 66.40 Trifecta £128.30 Part won. Pool £180.71 - 0.10 winning units..
Owner Flying Eight Partnership **Bred** Snowdrop Stud Co Ltd **Trained** Tredodridge, Vale Of Glamorgan

FOCUS
An ordinary handicap in which the pace was only fair and the front pair were always handy. The winner was back to her best.
Surprise Act Official explanation: jockey said gelding had no more to give
Grand Diamond(IRE) Official explanation: jockey said gelding suffered interference on the bend
Boogie Dancer Official explanation: jockey said filly hung left-handed final three furlongs

6875 PONTIN'S GREAT FAMILY HOLIDAYS H'CAP 2m 119y(P)
2:30 (2:30) (Class 5) (0-75,75) 3-Y-0+ **£2,968** (£876; £438) **Stalls** Low

Form RPR

36-5 **1** **Easibet Dot Net**[14] 6697 7-8-9 **56** oh1 ....(p) PhillipMakin 5 63
(I Semple) *rdn along in rr sn after s: hld up: hdwy 3f out: swtchd outside and rdn over 1f out: styd on strly to ld wl ins fnl f* **10/1**

1014 **2** 1 1/2 **Estate**[7] 6802 5-10-0 **75** .... ChrisCatlin 4 80
(E J O'Neill) *hld up towards rr: gd hdwy to join ldrs over 4f out: cl up over 2f out and sn rdn: drvn over 1f out: kpt on ins fnl f* **2/1**[1]

6062 **3** shd **Flame Creek (IRE)**[4] 6819 11-9-10 **74** .... AlanCreighton(3) 3 79
(E J Creighton) *hld up towards rr: hdwy 4f out: rdn to chse ldrs 2f out: drvn and kpt on ins fnl f: nrst fin* **14/1**

4526 **4** *shd* **Champagne Shadow (IRE)**[29] 6356 6-10-0 **75**...............(p) PatDobbs 8 80
(Miss Tor Sturgis) *chsd ldrs: pushed along and outpcd 5f out: swtchd outside and rdn wl over 2f out: styd on strly ins fnl f* **12/1**

0440 **5** *shd* **Moonshine Beach**[16] 6643 9-8-8 **58** oh8 ow2............. TravisBlock(3) 10 63
(P W Hiatt) *cl up: led 1/2-way: rdn along 3f out: hdd wl ins fnl f: no ex* **16/1**

0001 **6** *4* **Dark Parade (ARG)**[16] 6643 6-9-2 **68**.........................(b) JamieJones(5) 7 68
(G L Moore) *t.k.h: hld up in tch: hdwy on inner 4f out: chsd ldrs 2f out: sn rdn and one pce* **7/1**

4336 **7** *1 1/2* **Golano**[7] 6802 7-9-8 **69**...(p) NCallan 1 67+
(P R Webber) *t.k.h: trckd ldrs on inner: pushed along and outpcd 5f out: rdn and hdwy over 2f out: sn drvn and kpt on fnl f* **11/2**[2]

2243 **8** *4* **Maslak (IRE)**[11] 6739 3-9-5 **75**... LPKeniry 11 68
(P W Hiatt) *hld up in rr: stdy hdwy 1/2-way: cl up 4f out: rdn and ev ch over 2f out: sn drvn and wknd over 1f out* **6/1**[3]

11-3 **9** *1/2* **Market Watcher (USA)**[31] 6323 6-9-1 **65**.................(t) JerryO'Dwyer(3) 2 58
(Seamus Fahey, Ire) *chsd ldrs: rdn along 3f out: drvn wl over 1f out and grad wknd* **9/1**

0644 **10** *12* **Naughty Nod (IRE)**[166] 2367 4-8-2 **56** oh4............... DeclanCannon(7) 9 34
(K R Burke) *in midfield: rdn along over 3f out: sn btn* **28/1**

50-6 **11** *78* **Salawat**[42] 6070 4-8-9 **56** oh11... DeanMcKeown 6 —
(T T Clement) *led to 1/2-way: lost pl over 6f out and sn bhd* **100/1**

3m 42.68s (-0.45) **Going Correction** 0.0s/f (Stan)
WFA 3 from 4yo+ 9lb **11** Ran SP% **119.3**
Speed ratings (Par 103): **101,100,100,100,100 98,97,95,95,89 53**
CSF £30.67 CT £294.32 TOTE £12.10: £2.90, £1.10, £3.50; EX 30.80 Trifecta £153.10 Part won. Pool £215.65 - 0.36 winning units..
Owner Raeburn Brick Limited **Bred** L A C Ashby Newhall Estate Farm **Trained** Carluke, S Lanarks
■ Stewards' Enquiry : Alan Creighton two-day ban: careless riding (Nov 30, Dec 1)

FOCUS
An ordinary staying handicap in which the early pace seemed solid enough and the complexion of the race changed dramatically over the last half-mile, with the front three all coming from the back of the field. Modest form, rated around the first three.
Market Watcher(USA) Official explanation: jockey said gelding was denied a clear run

6876 PONTINS.COM H'CAP 5f 20y(P)
3:00 (3:01) (Class 3) (0-95,95) 3-Y-0+ **£7,124** (£2,119; £1,059; £529) **Stalls** Low

Form RPR

2420 **1** **Aegean Dancer**[9] 6758 5-9-1 **92**....................................... PhillipMakin 5 105+
(B Smart) *in tch: wd st: gd hdwy over 1f out: rdn to ld and edgd lft jst ins fnl f: sn hung bdly rt and jst hld on* **7/2**[2]

2011 **2** *nk* **Ebraam (USA)**[13] 6707 4-8-4 **81**.................................... DeanMcKeown 1 93+
(D Shaw) *in tch: hdwy 2f out: rdn ent fnl f and sn ev ch: drvn: edgd lft and nt qckn nr fin* **13/8**[1]

3211 **3** *1* **Magic Glade**[11] 6735 8-8-9 **86**.. LPKeniry 3 94
(Peter Grayson) *in tch on inner: gd hdwy 2f out: rdn over 1f out: drvn and ev ch ins fnl f: nt qckn last 100yds* **14/1**

5110 **4** *1 1/2* **Ajigolo**[15] 6668 4-9-3 **94**... DarryllHolland 8 97
(M R Channon) *in midfield: hdwy on outer 2f out: rdn over 1f out: styd on ins fnl f: nrst fin* **7/1**[3]

4000 **5** *shd* **Northern Empire (IRE)**[51] 5810 4-8-3 **83**.................. AndrewMullen(3) 6 85
(K A Ryan) *s.i.s and bhd: hdwy wl over 1f out: sn rdn and styd on strly ins fnl f: nrst fin* **11/1**

4115 **6** *1/2* **New York Oscar (IRE)**[13] 6707 3-8-3 **83**.............(p) PatrickMathers(3) 12 83
(A J McCabe) *chsd ldrs: rdn along wl over 1f out: sn drvn and one pce appr fnl f* **20/1**

5106 **7** *3/4* **Topflightcoolracer**[15] 6676 3-8-1 **81**........................... AndrewElliott(3) 4 79
(Mrs G S Rees) *chsd ldrs: rdn along 2f out: grad wknd appr fnl f* **18/1**

6/00 **8** *nk* **Playful**[36] 6197 4-8-9 **86**.. JamesDoyle 2 83
(R M Beckett) *prom: rdn wl over 1f out: wknd ent fnl f* **25/1**

5003 **9** *3* **Invincible Force (IRE)**[15] 6676 3-9-4 **95**...................... FrancisNorton 13 81
(Paul Green) *s.i.s: a towards rr* **18/1**

2000 **10** *shd* **Yungaburra (IRE)**[30] 6327 3-8-13 **90**............................... PatDobbs 7 76
(D J Murphy) *racd wd: effrt and hdwy 2f out: sn rdn and no imp appr fnl f* **33/1**

0010 **11** *shd* **Godfrey Street**[28] 6381 4-8-9 **86** ow1..................................(b) NCallan 11 71
(K A Ryan) *led: rdn over 1f out: drvn and hdd jst ins fnl f: sn wknd* **12/1**

11U0 **12** *shd* **Kay Two (IRE)**[15] 6676 5-8-7 **84**.................................(p) LiamJones 10 69
(R J Price) *chsd ldrs: rdn wl over 1f out: sn drvn and wknd* **16/1**

5001 **13** *1 3/4* **Blazing Heights**[10] 6743 4-8-6 **83**.................................. ChrisCatlin 9 61
(J S Goldie) *s.i.s: hld up: a bhd* **14/1**

61.57 secs (-1.25) **Going Correction** 0.0s/f (Stan) **13** Ran SP% **130.1**
Speed ratings (Par 107): **110,109,107,105,105 104,103,102,98,97 97,97,94**
CSF £10.24 CT £78.81 TOTE £3.50: £1.50, £1.60, £5.80; EX 16.30 Trifecta £27.30 Pool £237.62 - 6.17 winning units..
Owner Pinnacle Piccolo Partnership **Bred** Theobalds Stud **Trained** Hambleton, N Yorks

FOCUS
A cracking sprint handicap run at a strong pace in a good time. They finished spread out right across the track and the form looks rock-solid. The first two can rate higher still.

NOTEBOOK
Aegean Dancer, on a career-high mark after his decent effort in a Doncaster Listed event last time, was very well supported on this first try on Polytrack. He was forced to make his effort very wide, but that did not bother him and he found enough for pressure despite hanging right over to the stands' rail near the line. He could be of interest at Kempton if an opportunity could be found. (op 9-2 tchd 11-2)
Ebraam(USA), bidding for a hat-trick off a 6lb higher mark, travelled well behind the leaders on the inside after breaking from the rails draw. A nice gap opened up for him just when he needed it and he did little wrong, but he could never quite get to the winner. (op 9-4)
Magic Glade, making his debut for the yard after winning a couple of Polytrack claimers, was 1lb lower than when last in a handicap on sand. He stayed on well over on the inside of the track and, as he goes equally well on Fibresand, should provide his new connections with plenty of fun throughout the winter. (op 11-1 tchd 16-1)
Ajigolo, 4lb higher than he has ever won off, found the drop back to the minimum trip against him and was doing his best work late. Official explanation: jockey said colt hung right-handed throughout (op 10-1)
Northern Empire(IRE) ◆, having his first try on sand in his 13th outing, did well to finish where he did as he completely missed the break and had to come from a fair way back. He is on a career-low mark now and is one to very much keep an eye on. (op 12-1)
New York Oscar(IRE), only 1lb better off with Ebraam for a near four-length beating at Lingfield, had every chance and deserves some credit for running as well as he did from a bad draw. (op 16-1)
Invincible Force(IRE) jumped in the air as the stalls opened and from his draw that was the end of that. Official explanation: jockey said gelding was awkward leaving the stalls (op 16-1 tchd 22-1)
Yungaburra(IRE) was forced very wide around the home bend, but so was the winner. (op 28-1)
Godfrey Street did far too much too soon. (tchd 10-1)

6877 HOTEL & CONFERENCING AT WOLVERHAMPTON MAIDEN STKS 5f 216y(P)
3:30 (3:32) (Class 5) 3-Y-0+ **£2,968** (£876; £438) **Stalls** Low

Form RPR

62 **1** **Tubby Isaacs**[19] 6580 3-9-3 0.. NCallan 10 61+
(P J Makin) *t.k.h: trckd ldrs: hdwy over 2f out: rdn: green and edgd lft over 1f out: swtchd lft ins fnl f: styd on under hand riding to ld on line* **10/3**[3]

6324 **2** *shd* **Perlachy**[19] 6581 3-9-3 58..................................(v) DanielTudhope 5 61
(Mrs N Macauley) *in tch: pushed along over 2f out: swtchd rt and rdn over 1f out: styd on to ld jst ins fnl f: sn drvn: ct on line* **3/1**[2]

0 **3** *1/2* **Music Box Express**[31] 6309 3-9-3 0............................. FrancisNorton 8 59+
(D J Murphy) *in rr: stdy hdwy over 2f out: swtchd outside and rdn over 1f out: styd on strly ins fnl f* **40/1**

2 **4** *shd* **Sintenis Mac (GER)**[42] 6062 4-9-3 0............................ DarryllHolland 13 59+
(P J O'Gorman) *dwlt: rapid hdwy to join ldrs after 2f: rdn to ld wl over 1f out: hdd jst ins fnl f: sn drvn and kpt on* **2/1**[1]

0600 **5** *5* **Cape Of Storms**[47] 5915 4-8-10 46.................................. JackDean(7) 11 43
(R Brotherton) *cl up: rdn and ev ch 2f out: sn drvn and wknd appr fnl f* **33/1**

6 *1/2* **Eleanor Eloise (USA)** 3-8-12 0.. LiamJones 2 36
(J R Gask) *s.i.s and bhd tl sme late hdwy* **20/1**

7 *3/4* **Bers Treasure (IRE)**[18] 4982 4-8-9 0.........................(t) JerryO'Dwyer(3) 9 34
(Seamus Fahey, Ire) *a in midfield* **25/1**

2200 **8** *nk* **Jember Red**[13] 6702 4-8-12 42..................................(v) PhillipMakin 3 33
(B Smart) *chsd ldrs on inner: rdn along over 2f out: grad wknd* **14/1**

060 **9** *hd* **Belinda Rose (IRE)**[163] 2455 3-8-12 55............................ ChrisCatlin 1 32
(E J Alston) *led: rdn along over 2f out: hdd wl over 1f out and sn wknd* **8/1**

-060 **10** *3/4* **The Power Of Phil**[238] 786 3-8-12 48............... RussellKennemore(5) 4 35
(Miss Joanne Priest) *a towards rr* **16/1**

0 **11** *9* **Raihanah**[25] 6457 3-8-12 0.. DeanMcKeown 12 1
(D Shaw) *a in rr* **40/1**

0 **12** *5* **Flashin Amber**[30] 6339 3-9-3 0.. LPKeniry 7 —
(Peter Grayson) *a in rr* **100/1**

13 *1 1/2* **Pennygee** 3-8-12 0.. PaulEddery 6 —
(S R Bowring) *s.i.s: sn chsng ldrs: rdn along wl over 2f out and sn wknd* **33/1**

1m 16.07s (0.26) **Going Correction** 0.0s/f (Stan) **13** Ran SP% **125.4**
Speed ratings (Par 103): **98,97,97,97,90 89,88,88,88,87 75,68,66**
CSF £13.64 TOTE £4.90: £1.60, £1.50, £12.00; EX 17.70 TRIFECTA Not won..
Owner John Khan & Arnold Bros **Bred** J W Ford **Trained** Ogbourne Maisey, Wilts

FOCUS
This was basically a weak maiden, as races like this for older horses tend to be at this time of year, and the winning time was fractionally slower than the earlier two-year-old claimer. The front four pulled well clear, but that does not say much for the others.

6878 GO PONTIN'S H'CAP 1m 4f 50y(P)
4:00 (4:00) (Class 5) (0-75,73) 3-Y-0+ **£2,968** (£876; £438) **Stalls** Low

Form RPR

5011 **1** **Robert The Brave**[28] 6387 3-9-3 **73**..................................... ChrisCatlin 7 82+
(P R Webber) *trckd ldrs: hdwy 4f out: rdn to chal wl over 1f out: sn drvn and styd on to ld wl ins fnl f* **11/2**[3]

2603 **2** *1/2* **Esclarmonde (IRE)**[32] 6276 3-8-12 **68**.....................(b[1]) DarryllHolland 8 74
(L M Cumani) *trckd ldr: led 4f out: jnd and rdn over 2f out: drvn wl over 1f out: hdd and no ex wl ins fnl f* **13/2**

0611 **3** *1 1/4* **Spirit Of Adjisa (IRE)**[40] 6102 3-9-3 **73**...........................(b) PatDobbs 6 77
(Pat Eddery) *trckd ldrs: hdwy over 3f out: effrt 2f out: sn rdn and ch tl drvn over 1f out and kpt on same pce* **7/4**[1]

430- **4** *3/4* **Deccan Express (IRE)**[45] 5999 3-8-11 **67**............................ LPKeniry 2 70
(Seamus Fahey, Ire) *trckd ldrs: effrt 3f out: sn rdn along and sltly outpcd: kpt on u.p ins fnl f* **7/1**

6345 **5** *3 1/2* **Golan Way**[33] 6272 3-8-12 **68**... NCallan 3 65
(I A Wood) *hld up: effrt and sme hdwy wl over 2f out: sn rdn and no imp* **9/2**[2]

1661 **6** *7* **Pitbull**[28] 6380 4-8-12 **62**...(p) LiamJones 9 48
(Mrs G S Rees) *hld up in rr: gd hdwy 4f out: rdn to chal 2f out: sn drvn and wknd wl over 1f out* **12/1**

3000 **7** *3/4* **Top Spec (IRE)**[75] 5145 6-9-8 **72**.................................. DeanMcKeown 5 57
(J Pearce) *hld up: a towards rr* **16/1**

/600 **8** *26* **Mejhar (IRE)**[12] 6719 7-8-3 **58** oh5.............................(b) SCreighton(5) 1 —
(E J Creighton) *led: rdn along and hdd 4f out: lost pl qckly and sn bhd* **33/1**

2m 41.88s (-0.54) **Going Correction** 0.0s/f (Stan)
WFA 3 from 4yo+ 6lb **8** Ran SP% **112.3**
Speed ratings (Par 103): **101,100,99,99,97 92,91,74**
CSF £39.22 CT £86.08 TOTE £5.50: £1.70, £2.90, £1.10; EX 26.10 Trifecta £31.00 Pool £214.26 - 4.90 winning units. Place 6 £42.98, Place 5 £28.56..
Owner T R Pearson **Bred** Alan Gibson **Trained** Mollington, Oxon

FOCUS
A fair handicap for the grade, won by a progressive type in Robert The Brave. The pace was only ordinary.
Top Spec(IRE) Official explanation: jockey said gelding moved poorly throughout
T/Jkpt: Not won. T/Plt: £17.50 to a £1 stake. Pool: £58,723.30. 2,435.85 winning tickets. T/Qpdt: £10.90 to a £1 stake. Pool: £3,495.40. 236.10 winning tickets. JR

6416 DEAUVILLE (R-H)
Monday, November 19

OFFICIAL GOING: Standard

6879a PRIX DE LA BOSSONNIERE (C&G) (ALL-WEATHER) 6f 110y
12:15 (12:14) 2-Y-0 **£9,459** (£3,784; £2,838; £1,892; £946)

RPR

1 **Barnaby Rudge (IRE)**[16] 6641 2-8-9 .... JohnEgan 8 67
(Jane Chapple-Hyam) *mde all: 3l clr over 1f out: drvn out* **23/10**[1]

2 *1 1/2* **El Puerto (FR)**[22] 2-9-2 ....(b) JLermyte 4 70
(M Boutin, France)

3 *2 1/2* **Polochon (FR)**[8] 2-8-13 .... RonanThomas 9 61
(J-M Beguigne, France)

4 *shd* **Carlior (FR)** 2-8-13 .... IMendizabal 6 61
(J-C Rouget, France)

The Form Book, Raceform Ltd, Compton, RG20 6NL

5 1 1/2 **Green Ascot (IRE)**[109] 2-8-9 .... TThulliez 1 53
(R Gibson, France)
6 1/2 **French Gallery (FR)**[87] 2-8-9 .... SRuis 3 52
(J-P Gallorini, France)
7 4 **Elle Of A Star (FR)**[55] 2-8-9 .... JCrocquevieille 2 43
(P Laloum, France)
8 6 **Source Du Nil (FR)** 2-8-9 .... ACrastus 7 29
(Y De Nicolay, France)

1m 18.3s (78.30) **8** Ran SP% **30.3**
PARI-MUTUEL (including 1 Euro stake): WIN 3.30; PL 1.60, 3.10, 1.60;DF 17.70.
Owner Mrs S Harniman **Bred** Eclipse Thoroughbreds Inc **Trained** Newmarket, Suffolk

NOTEBOOK
Barnaby Rudge(IRE), who had decent form in two runs in maidens and also had previous experience of Polytrack, had been too keen under restraint last time and was allowed to bowl along this time. He ran out a clear-cut winner and the tactics clearly suited.

6872 WOLVERHAMPTON (A.W) (L-H)
Tuesday, November 20

OFFICIAL GOING: Standard
Wind: Light, against Weather: Light rain after 3.20

6880 WOLVERHAMPTON-RACECOURSE.CO.UK CLAIMING STKS 7f 32y(P)
1:20 (1:20) (Class 6) 2-Y-0 £2,047 (£604; £302) Stalls High

Form RPR
600 1 **Berrynarbor**[27] 6417 2-8-10 62 .... FergusSweeney 2 59
(A G Newcombe) *sn towards rr: rdn over 3f out: hdwy over 2f out: led wl ins fnl f: r.o* 7/1[3]
0061 2 1 **Rich Kid (IRE)**[64] 5471 2-9-1 70 .... PaulDoe 5 62+
(R A Harris) *prom: lost pl bnd after 1f: sn rcvrd: wnt 2nd over 3f out: rdn and ev ch over 2f out: struck on hd by rival jockey's whip wl ins fnl f: edgd lft: kpt on* 5/6[1]
40 3 1 1/4 **Kamal**[135] 3341 2-9-1 0 .... FrancisNorton 6 58
(K A Ryan) *sn led: rdn over 2f out: hdd wl ins fnl f: edgd lft and n.m.r nr fin* 15/2
0505 4 nk **Scientific**[32] 6305 2-8-9 48 ....(b[1]) DaleGibson 4 52
(R A Fahey) *in rr: rdn over 4f out: hdwy over 1f out: r.o ins fnl f* 12/1
0400 5 5 **Dusk Ballet**[4] 6828 2-7-7 54 ow2 .... AmyBaker(7) 8 31
(S C Williams) *chsd ldrs: rdn over 2f out: wknd over 1f out* 4/1[2]
50 6 11 **Riki Wiki Wheels**[21] 6557 2-8-13 0 .... MickyFenton 7 17
(P T Midgley) *s.i.s: sn rcvrd: chsd ldr after 1f tl rdn over 3f out: wknd over 2f out* 33/1
0 7 12 **Make A Bid**[21] 6557 2-8-6 0 ....(v[1]) DeanMcKeown 1 —
(J R Norton) *led early: rdn and wknd over 4f out* 80/1

1m 31.67s (1.27) **Going Correction** 0.0s/f (Stan) 7 Ran SP% **110.7**
Speed ratings (Par 94): **92,90,89,89,83 70,57**
CSF £12.44 TOTE £7.40: £2.50, £1.70; EX 18.10 Trifecta £61.20 Pool: £284.88 - 3.30 winning units..Kamal was claimed by W. R. Muir for £8,000. Rich Kid was the subject of a friendly claim.
Owner Mrs Jayne Bramhill **Bred** Overbury Partnership **Trained** Yarnscombe, Devon

FOCUS
A reasonable claimer run at a good pace, resulting in a winning time 0.04 seconds quicker than the later two-year-old maiden. The winner is rated back to his selling-race form.

NOTEBOOK
Berrynarbor, dropped in grade and trip on her first start on Polytrack, looked held for much of the way up the straight, but the leaders fell away and she stayed on strongest of all. She should be suited by a return to 1m. (tchd 13-2)
Rich Kid(IRE) looked to be going the right way when winning a weak Leicester nursery off a mark of 65 for Richard Hannon, so it was a surprise to see him turn up in this grade for a different trainer after a two-month break. He was produced with every chance, but did not look to be striding out that well when placed under maximum pressure in the straight and was held when hit over the head by another rider's whip inside the final furlong. He looks like one to avoid. Official explanation: jockey said, regarding running and riding, that his orders were to get a good break and a prominent position, adding that whilst he got a level break, the colt jumped awkwardly leaving the stalls and initially had to be bustled along to hold its position, eventually coming wide to avoid kickback and make up ground thereafter, being all out to the line despite attempting to bite the third inside final furlong; trainer confirmed, adding it is very coltish and was considering having it cut. (op 4-5 tchd Evens)
Kamal, dropped in grade on his return from over four months off the track, set a good pace but failed to sustain his effort in the straight. He was entitled to need the run and has now joined William Muir. (tchd 13-2 and 8-1)
Scientific, fitted with blinkers for the first time, got going too late and should be suited by a step up in trip. (op 14-1)
Dusk Ballet will probably be better off back in selling company. (tchd 7-2 and 9-2)
Riki Wiki Wheels Official explanation: jockey said colt had a breathing problem

6881 PONTIN'S BOOK EARLY PRICE PROMISE NURSERY 5f 216y(P)
1:50 (1:50) (Class 6) (0-60,60) 2-Y-0 £2,047 (£604; £302) Stalls Low

Form RPR
056 1 **Caprio (IRE)**[20] 6595 2-9-5 58 .... RichardKingscote 13 66+
(R Charlton) *mde all: rdn 2f out: r.o wl ins fnl f* 13/2[3]
5004 2 2 **Yankee Storm**[18] 6624 2-9-0 53 .... PatCosgrave 3 55
(M J Wallace) *a.p: rdn wl over 1f out: r.o ins fnl f* 7/2[1]
0006 3 1 **Curio**[13] 6722 2-8-9 51 .... MichaelJStainton(3) 4 50
(R M Whitaker) *w wnr: rdn and ev ch 1f out: no ex ins fnl f* 6/1[2]
0005 4 hd **Feeling Fresh (IRE)**[15] 6692 2-9-3 56 .... FrancisNorton 9 54
(Paul Green) *hld up: hdwy over 2f out: rdn over 1f out: kpt on ins fnl f* 33/1
0005 5 2 1/2 **John Potts**[10] 6761 2-9-7 60 .... J-PGuillambert 8 51
(B P J Baugh) *hld up in mid-div: hdwy on ins over 2f out: sn rdn: one pce fnl f* 33/1
0500 6 hd **Hawa Khana (IRE)**[21] 6572 2-9-7 60 .... StephenDonohoe 6 50
(N P Littmoden) *bhd: hrd rdn wl over 1f out: kpt on fnl f: nvr nrr* 8/1
0000 7 shd **Talamahana**[9] 6776 2-9-3 56 .... LPKeniry 2 46
(S Kirk) *prom: rdn over 3f out: outpcd over 2f out: sme late hdwy* 10/1
0556 8 3/4 **Alabama Spirit (USA)**[34] 6263 2-9-6 59 .... DeanMcKeown 10 47
(D Shaw) *prom tl rdn and wknd wl over 1f out* 7/2[1]
0304 9 1/2 **Prunes**[17] 6635 2-8-8 50 ....(b[1]) PatrickMathers(3) 11 36
(A Berry) *a bhd* 16/1
5000 10 1 **Sir Joey**[13] 6721 2-8-10 54 ....(b[1]) RussellKennemore(5) 12 37
(J T Stimpson) *sn chsng ldrs: rdn over 3f out: wknd 2f out* 40/1
1440 11 2 **Echostar**[13] 6722 2-9-2 55 .... MickyFenton 7 32
(Stef Liddiard) *a bhd* 33/1
4420 12 3 **No Point (IRE)**[62] 5520 2-8-7 53 .... SophieDoyle(7) 1 21+
(P A Blockley) *s.i.s: sn mid-div: hmpd on ins over 3f out: sn bhd* 11/1
0000 13 4 **Ocean Glory (IRE)**[13] 6715 2-9-0 60 .... RyanHill(7) 5 16
(Peter Grayson) *t.k.h in mid-div: lost pl 3f out: sn eased: sddle slipped* 50/1

1m 16.17s (0.36) **Going Correction** 0.0s/f (Stan) 13 Ran SP% **119.7**
Speed ratings (Par 94): **97,94,93,92,89 89,89,88,87,86 83,79,74**
CSF £28.36 CT £151.72 TOTE £8.30: £3.00, £1.20, £3.10; EX 26.20 Trifecta £88.00 Pool: £163.71 - 1.32 winning units..
Owner Beckhampton Stables Ltd 1 **Bred** P Rabbitte **Trained** Beckhampton, Wilts

FOCUS
A moderate nursery and nothing got involved from off the pace. The placed horses give the form a solid feel.

NOTEBOOK
Caprio(IRE) bolted to post on his first two outings, but he had still displayed ability on all three of his starts in maiden company and showed himself on a very fair mark on his nursery debut, running out a convincing winner after showing good speed to overcome his wide draw. This was not much of a race, but he should be competitive off higher marks and would be very dangerous if turned out under a penalty. (op 5-1)
Yankee Storm was never too far away and this was a respectable effort. He looks capable of winning a similar race. (op 10-3)
Curio, trying Polytrack for the first time, kept the eventual winner honest up front and had every chance. (op 15-2 tchd 11-2)
Feeling Fresh(IRE) ran better with the visor left off this time and fared best of those held up.
John Potts had been raised 13lb following his recent fifth in a course-and-distance maiden.
Alabama Spirit(USA) Official explanation: jockey said filly became unbalanced on leaving stalls and again around bend
Sir Joey Official explanation: jockey said gelding didn't face the first-time blinkers
No Point(IRE) Official explanation: jockey said filly hung badly right causing her to become unbalanced
Ocean Glory(IRE) Official explanation: jockey said saddle slipped coming round bend

6882 PONTIN'S BOOK EARLY AND SAVE (S) STKS 1m 141y(P)
2:20 (2:20) (Class 6) 3-Y-0+ £2,047 (£604; £302) Stalls Low

Form RPR
6000 1 **Circus Polka (USA)**[9] 6774 3-8-12 71 ....(bt) ChrisCatlin 3 67
(P F I Cole) *led over 1f: chsd ldr: led wl over 2f out: clr whn hrd rdn over 1f out: r.o* 9/2[1]
0020 2 3 **Moonstreaker**[17] 6640 4-9-1 59 .... DeanMcKeown 10 60
(R M Whitaker) *chsd ldrs: wnt 2nd over 1f out: one pce* 15/2[3]
0550 3 2 1/2 **Swiper Hill (IRE)**[20] 6579 4-9-1 56 ....(vt[1]) J-PGuillambert 11 54
(B Ellison) *hld up in rr: hdwy on outside over 2f out: one pce fnl f* 8/1
3506 4 nk **El Coto**[12] 6732 7-9-7 67 ....(p) FrancisNorton 6 60
(K A Ryan) *hld up towards rr: rdn over 3f out: hdwy over 2f out: one pce fnl f* 11/2[2]
0066 5 1 3/4 **Local Poet**[29] 6385 6-9-1 60 ....(b) PhillipMakin 13 50+
(I Semple) *hld up in rr: c wd st: hdwy over 1f out: n.d* 9/1
0405 6 1 1/2 **Climate (IRE)**[9] 6774 8-9-2 58 ....(v) RussellKennemore(5) 7 52
(R Hollinshead) *hld up towards rr: rdn and hdwy on ins wl over 1f out: no imp fnl f* 12/1
0003 7 1 1/2 **Blythe Spirit**[19] 6609 8-9-7 45 ....(b) LiamJones 4 49
(Mrs L Williamson) *nvr nr ldrs* 50/1
2660 8 3 **Shifty**[18] 6628 8-9-1 63 .... DanielTudhope 8 36
(D Carroll) *hld up in mid-div: hdwy over 2f out: wknd over 1f out* 14/1
3-36 9 1 1/4 **Namibian Pink (IRE)**[43] 6057 3-8-7 59 ....(b[1]) JamesDoyle 2 28
(R M Beckett) *hld up in mid-div: rdn over 3f out: wknd 2f out* 14/1
0005 10 1 1/4 **Wahoo Sam (USA)**[12] 6732 7-9-7 63 ....(p) PatCosgrave 12 36
(D W Barker) *led 7f out tl wl over 2f out: sn rdn: wknd over 1f out* 8/1
6060 11 7 **Middleton Grey**[45] 6024 9-9-1 62 ....(b) FergusSweeney 5 14
(A G Newcombe) *a in rr* 15/2[3]
2000 12 15 **Dance Spirit (IRE)**[21] 6573 4-9-1 59 .... MartinDwyer 1 —
(W R Muir) *hld up in mid-div: rdn 3f out: wkng whn hmpd over 2f out* 16/1
2606 13 3 1/2 **Shannon Arms (USA)**[150] 2874 6-8-12 45 ....(p) AndrewMullen(3) 9 —
(R Brotherton) *chsd ldrs 1st: rdn over 3f out: wknd over 2f out* 66/1

1m 51.1s (-0.66) **Going Correction** 0.0s/f (Stan)
WFA 3 from 4yo+ 3lb 13 Ran SP% **119.7**
Speed ratings (Par 101): **102,99,97,96,95 93,92,89,88,87 81,68,65**
CSF £37.69 TOTE £3.70: £1.80, £2.90, £3.60; EX 61.50 TRIFECTA Not won..The winner was sold to Ray Salter for 8,500gns.
Owner Allport, Jefferson, Meyrick, Thomas **Bred** Hedgewood Farm **Trained** Whatcombe, Oxon

FOCUS
A good race for the grade and the winning time was 3.42 seconds quicker than the later 56-70 handicap. The form is limited by the runner-up and seventh.
Swiper Hill(IRE) Official explanation: jockey said gelding hung left down the home straight
Climate(IRE) Official explanation: jockey said gelding was denied a clear run
Middleton Grey Official explanation: jockey said gelding had no more to give
Dance Spirit(IRE) Official explanation: jockey said gelding was hampered on final bend

6883 GO PONTIN'S HOLIDAYS H'CAP 1m 4f 50y(P)
2:50 (2:50) (Class 6) (0-65,65) 3-Y-0+ £2,047 (£604; £302) Stalls Low

Form RPR
4/33 1 **Master At Arms**[20] 6583 4-9-2 60 .... JerryO'Dwyer(3) 7 68+
(Daniel Mark Loughnane, Ire) *a.p: wnt 2nd over 6f out: led 4f out: rdn over 1f out: drvn out* 9/4[1]
4500 2 1 1/4 **Punta Galera (IRE)**[102] 4353 4-9-10 65 .... FrancisNorton 5 71
(Paul Green) *chsd ldr over 5f: rdn wl over 1f out: kpt on to take 2nd nr fin* 33/1
0603 3 1/2 **Opera Writer (IRE)**[16] 6672 4-9-2 57 .... DeanMcKeown 3 62
(R Hollinshead) *hld up and bhd: hdwy over 2f out: rdn and nt qckn ins fnl f* 9/2[2]
3054 4 3/4 **Wulimaster (USA)**[20] 6598 4-9-0 55 .... HayleyTurner 2 59
(D W Barker) *hld up in rr: hdwy wl over 1f out: rdn and nt qckn ins fnl f* 11/2[3]
463 5 1 1/2 **Little Richard (IRE)**[21] 6564 8-8-13 54 ....(p) AdamKirby 10 55
(M Wellings) *hld up in tch: rdn wl over 1f out: one pce fnl f* 6/1
0004 6 1/2 **Mango Masher (IRE)**[8] 6798 3-8-11 58 ....(p) FergusSweeney 8 59
(J L Flint) *hld up in mid-div: rdn and lost pl 3f out: sme late hdwy* 10/1
4100 7 shd **Compton Dragon (USA)**[8] 6803 8-9-2 62 .... KirstyMilczarek(5) 11 62
(W M Brisbourne) *hld up in rr: short-lived effrt on outside over 2f out* 12/1
-306 8 1/2 **Scutch Mill (IRE)**[10] 6459 5-9-1 63 ....(t) PatrickDonaghy(7) 4 63
(P C Haslam) *bmpd s: hld up in mid-div: hdwy 5f out: rdn and wknd over 1f out* 12/1
055U 9 5 **Mysterious World (IRE)**[35] 6259 3-8-13 60 .... PhillipMakin 6 52
(Mrs K Walton) *hld up towards rr: rdn over 3f out: no rspnse* 66/1

1-30 **10** *12* **Market Watcher (USA)**[1] 6875 6-9-7 **65**....................(t) TravisBlock(3) 1 37
(Seamus Fahey, Ire) *led: sn clr: hdd 4f out: rdn and wknd over 2f out* **17/2**

2m 42.08s (-0.34) **Going Correction** 0.0s/f (Stan)
WFA 3 from 4yo+ 6lb **10** Ran SP% **118.1**
Speed ratings (Par 101): **101,100,99,99,98 98,97,97,94,86**
CSF £90.35 CT £320.70 TOTE £1.90: £1.10, £9.60, £1.60; EX 69.50 Trifecta £114.70 Part won. Pool: £161.64 - 0.36 winning units..
Owner T J Doran **Bred** Fittocks Stud **Trained** Trim, Co Meath
■ The first winner in Britain for Irish trainer Mark Loughnane.

FOCUS
A moderate handicap run at an ordinary pace and best rated around the placed horses.

6884 EUROPEAN BREEDERS' FUND MEDIAN AUCTION MAIDEN STKS 7f 32y(P)
3:20 (3:20) (Class 5) 2-Y-O **£3,465** (£1,030; £515; £257) **Stalls** High

Form RPR
02 **1** **The Gatekeeper**[18] 6617 2-9-3 0...................................... MartinDwyer 6 73+
(M H Tompkins) *hld up: hdwy over 3f out: rdn and edgd lft fr over 1f out: led wl ins fnl f: r.o* **15/8**[1]

055 **2** *1* **Penchesco (IRE)**[39] 6138 2-9-3 76...................................... PatDobbs 3 71+
(Pat Eddery) *a.p: led wl over 1f out: rdn and hdd wl ins fnl f* **11/4**[2]

322 **3** *nk* **Safebreaker**[33] 6289 2-9-3 75...................................... JimCrowley 2 70
(N Tinkler) *led: hdd wl over 1f out: nt clr run and swtchd rt ins fnl f: r.o towards fin* **11/4**[2]

05 **4** *3* **Great Charm (IRE)**[21] 6574 2-9-3 0...................................... HayleyTurner 8 63
(M L W Bell) *s.i.s: hld up: swtchd lft jst over 1f out: styd on ins fnl f* **8/1**[3]

5 *1/2* **Chesterton (IRE)** 2-9-0 0...................................... JerryO'Dwyer(3) 1 62
(John Joseph Murphy, Ire) *hld up: rdn over 2f out: sme hdwy on ins over 1f out: one pce ins fnl f* **14/1**

403 **6** *2 1/2* **Gaitskell**[16] 6675 2-9-3 60...................................... DeanMcKeown 7 56
(R Hollinshead) *s.i.s: hld up: rdn and short-lived effrt over 1f out* **33/1**

0005 **7** *1/2* **Transcendent (IRE)**[26] 6456 2-9-0 48...................... AndrewElliott(3) 4 54
(J D Bethell) *w ldr: ev ch over 2f out: hung lft and wknd over 1f out* **66/1**

1m 31.71s (1.31) **Going Correction** 0.0s/f (Stan) **7** Ran SP% **110.3**
Speed ratings (Par 96): **92,90,90,87,86 83,83**
CSF £6.69 TOTE £2.90: £1.40, £2.50; EX 7.50 Trifecta £10.50 Pool: £288.68 - 19.42 winning units..
Owner Mrs S Ashby **Bred** Dullingham Park **Trained** Newmarket, Suffolk

FOCUS
An ordinary maiden. The winning time was 0.04 seconds slower than the earlier two-year-old claimer and not a race to be with on balance.

NOTEBOOK
The Gatekeeper confirmed the promise he showed when second over 6f at Newmarket on his previous start to get off the mark at the third time of asking. He looked set to win quite well when swooping down the outside on the turn for home, but he continually drifted to his left, doing the eventual third few favours in the process. He could progress into a fair handicapper if whatever was making him go left can be ironed out. (tchd 7-4 and 2-1 in places)
Penchesco(IRE) travelled well for much of the way, but he just found one too strong. He should pick up a similar race. (op 10-3)
Safebreaker ◆, having his first start since leaving Mark Johnston, may have been a touch unlucky as he was just beginning to hit top stride when short of room around a furlong from the finish and he was staying on again at the line. He will be one to be with when stepped up to 1m. (op 9-4 tchd 3-1)
Great Charm(IRE) will have more options now he is qualified for a handicap mark. (tchd 9-1)
Chesterton(IRE), a Namid colt, half-brother to among others quite useful Master Papa, a dual 5f-7f winner at two who was also a multiple winner over jumps, has been given an entry in the Irish 2000 Guineas. This was just a satisfactory introduction and he should learn from the experience. (op 12-1 tchd 11-1)

6885 GO PONTIN'S SHORT BREAKS H'CAP 1m 141y(P)
3:50 (3:50) (Class 5) (0-70,74) 3-Y-O+ **£2,968** (£876; £438) **Stalls** Low

Form RPR
4451 **1** **Hoh Wotanite**[6] 6816 4-9-8 **74** 6ex....................(v) RussellKennemore(5) 6 74+
(R Hollinshead) *hld up: hdwy over 2f out: led wl over 1f out: drvn out* **10/11**[1]

1311 **2** *1* **Prince Noel**[4] 6837 3-8-12 **69** 6ex...................................... LanceBetts(7) 3 66+
(N Wilson) *a.p: rdn and ev ch ins fnl f: nt qckn* **2/1**[2]

6-00 **3** *1 1/2* **Star Of The Desert (IRE)**[12] 6732 4-9-1 **62**.................(p) PhillipMakin 1 56
(Mrs K Walton) *led: rdn and hdd wl over 1f out: no ex fnl f* **12/1**

1034 **4** *5* **Jilly Why (IRE)**[10] 6762 6-9-3 **64**...............................(b) FrancisNorton 5 47
(Paul Green) *prom: rdn and wknd over 1f out* **5/1**[3]

1m 54.52s (2.76) **Going Correction** 0.0s/f (Stan)
WFA 3 from 4yo+ 3lb **4** Ran SP% **110.1**
Speed ratings (Par 103): **87,86,84,80**
CSF £3.07 TOTE £1.70; EX 2.80.
Owner The Three R'S **Bred** Dunchurch Lodge Stud Co **Trained** Upper Longdon, Staffs

FOCUS
Just the four runners, but an interesting contest. Unsurprisingly considering the small field, they went a steady pace through the early stages and the winning time was 3.42 seconds slower than the earlier seller. The form looks dubious as a result.

6886 BOOK A CHRISTMAS BREAK AT PONTIN'S H'CAP (DIV I) 5f 216y(P)
4:20 (4:20) (Class 6) (0-52,52) 3-Y-O+ **£1,706** (£503; £252) **Stalls** Low

Form RPR
0006 **1** **Fast Freddie**[48] 5897 3-8-9 **47**...................................(e[1]) FrancisNorton 7 61
(D J Murphy) *chsd ldr: led over 3f out: r.o wl* **12/1**

0020 **2** *1 3/4* **Grand Palace (IRE)**[18] 6629 4-8-11 **49**...............(v) DeanMcKeown 5 57
(D Shaw) *a.p: ev ch over 1f out: rdn and nt qckn ins fnl f* **11/2**[2]

3004 **3** *3/4* **Mister Always**[61] 5564 3-8-10 **48**...................................... DanielTudhope 1 57+
(I W McInnes) *hld up in tch: nt clr run on ins over 2f out: swtchd rt and n.m.r ent st: rdn and r.o one pce fnl f* **7/1**[3]

0352 **4** *1* **Two Acres (IRE)**[22] 6542 4-8-7 **52**...................................... JackDean(7) 9 55
(A G Newcombe) *a.p: rdn wl over 1f out: edgd lft ent fnl f: one pce* **9/2**[1]

0000 **5** *nk* **Fern House (IRE)**[17] 6637 5-8-11 **52**...................................... MarkLawson(3) 2 54
(Garry Moss) *hld up and bhd: hdwy over 2f out: rdn over 1f out: kpt on ins fnl f* **40/1**

6500 **6** *3 1/2* **Ocean Gift**[19] 6608 5-9-0 **52**...(p) JimCrowley 4 43
(N Tinkler) *towards rr: rdn 4f out: hdwy 1f out: n.d* **20/1**

6304 **7** *hd* **The Salwick Flyer (IRE)**[25] 6467 4-8-10 **51**........... AndrewMullen(3) 12 41
(I Semple) *in rr: rdn over 3f out: hdwy 1f out: n.d* **15/2**

3043 **8** *3/4* **The Cube**[13] 6720 3-8-12 **50**...................................... MickyFenton 11 38
(J Balding) *hld up: hdwy over 3f out: rdn and wknd fnl f* **12/1**

0004 **9** *1/2* **Spy Gun (USA)**[12] 6735 7-8-8 **49**...............................(p) NeilChalmers(3) 10 35
(T Wall) *mid-div: rdn and wknd over 2f out* **14/1**

4000 **10** *1 3/4* **Detonate**[4] 6826 5-8-3 **48**...................................... RobbieEgan(7) 3 28
(I A Wood) *mid-div: rdn over 2f out: wknd wl over 1f out* **12/1**

2260 **11** *3/4* **Monda**[25] 6467 5-8-10 **48**...................................... PhillipMakin 6 26
(Miss J A Camacho) *bhd fnl 3f* **7/1**[3]

0335 **12** *1* **Jojesse**[51] 5834 3-9-0 **52**...................................... PatCosgrave 8 27
(Jennie Candlish) *s.i.s: a bhd* **7/1**[3]

000 **13** *1 3/4* **Diamond Hurricane (IRE)**[4] 6825 3-8-12 **50**.............(b[1]) AdamKirby 13 19
(M Wellings) *led: hdd over 3f out: wknd 2f out* **50/1**

1m 14.88s (-0.93) **Going Correction** 0.0s/f (Stan) **13** Ran SP% **121.7**
Speed ratings (Par 101): **106,103,102,101,100 96,96,95,94,92 91,89,87**
CSF £76.99 CT £528.80 TOTE £14.80: £5.60, £2.10, £3.00; EX 144.20 TRIFECTA Not won..
Owner Gordon Crawford **Bred** New Hall Stud **Trained** Bawtry, S Yorks
■ Stewards' Enquiry : Jack Dean one-day ban: careless riding (Dec 1)

FOCUS
A very moderate sprint handicap rated around the placed horses. The winning time was 0.55 seconds quicker than the second division.
Mister Always Official explanation: jockey said gelding was denied a clear run
Diamond Hurricane(IRE) Official explanation: jockey said gelding hung right

6887 BOOK A CHRISTMAS BREAK AT PONTIN'S H'CAP (DIV II) 5f 216y(P)
4:50 (4:51) (Class 6) (0-52,52) 3-Y-O+ **£1,706** (£503; £252) **Stalls** Low

Form RPR
5400 **1** **Bond Becks (IRE)**[70] 5295 7-8-10 **48**...................................... ChrisCatlin 8 58
(G R Oldroyd) *mde all: rdn over 1f out: r.o wl* **25/1**

4340 **2** *2* **Canina**[6] 6818 4-8-12 **50**...................................... FrancisNorton 12 54+
(Paul Green) *hld up towards rr: hdwy whn swtchd rt ins fnl f: edgd lft cl home: r.o* **9/1**

2233 **3** *hd* **Midmaar (IRE)**[201] 1436 6-9-0 **52**...............................(b) JamieMackay 4 55
(M Wigham) *a.p: rdn over 1f out: one pce fnl f* **9/2**[2]

0005 **4** *hd* **Gone'N'Dunnett (IRE)**[13] 6718 8-8-4 **47**...............(v) KirstyMilczarek(5) 6 49
(Mrs C A Dunnett) *s.i.s: in rr: rdn wl over 1f out: hdwy on outside fnl f: r.o* **10/1**

0240 **5** *3/4* **Dysonic (USA)**[9] 6773 5-8-10 **51**...............................(v) AndrewElliott(3) 3 51
(J Balding) *a.p: chsd wnr wl over 1f out: sn rdn: no ex ins fnl f* **5/1**[3]

4041 **6** *3/4* **Briery Blaze**[21] 6563 4-8-8 **51**...............................(b) JackMitchell(5) 5 49
(J W Unett) *a.p: rdn over 1f out: no ex fnl f* **7/2**[1]

0020 **7** *1 1/4* **Wodhill Be**[48] 5900 7-8-10 **48**...................................... HayleyTurner 13 42
(D Morris) *hld up and bhd: hdwy over 1f out: one pce fnl f* **20/1**

660 **8** *3/4* **The Carpet Man**[13] 6720 3-8-9 **47**...................................... LiamJones 7 38
(A W Carroll) *towards rr: n.m.r over 3f out: n.d after* **12/1**

6450 **9** *hd* **Bonnet O'Bonnie**[33] 6288 3-8-8 **49**...................................... DominicFox(3) 9 40
(J Mackie) *mid-div: rdn over 3f out: bhd fnl 2f* **14/1**

0510 **10** *3 1/2* **Splendidio**[13] 6720 3-8-9 **52**...................................... KellyHarrison(5) 10 31
(A Crook) *t.k.h: prom tl wknd wl over 1f out* **33/1**

3000 **11** *2* **Mind Alert**[6] 6809 6-9-0 **52**...............................(v) DeanMcKeown 11 25
(D Shaw) *s.i.s: a bhd* **16/1**

0514 **12** *1 3/4* **Snow Bunting**[19] 6609 9-8-10 **48**...................................... MickyFenton 1 15
(Jedd O'Keeffe) *s.i.s: a bhd* **9/2**[2]

1m 15.43s (-0.38) **Going Correction** 0.0s/f (Stan) **12** Ran SP% **126.1**
Speed ratings (Par 101): **102,99,99,98,97 96,95,94,93,89 86,84**
CSF £244.81 CT £1239.68 TOTE £22.70: £6.00, £3.30, £2.20; EX 253.20 Trifecta £202.20 Pool: £387.42 - 1.36 winning units. Place 6 £13.15, Place 5 £9.26.
Owner R C Bond **Bred** Dr Paschal Carmody **Trained** Brawby, N Yorks

FOCUS
Another very moderate sprint handicap rated around the first two and the fifth. The winning time was 0.55 seconds slower than the first division.
Gone'N'Dunnett(IRE) Official explanation: jockey said gelding attempted to dive under the stalls
Snow Bunting Official explanation: jockey said gelding did not stride out
T/Jkpt: £15,672.40 to a £1 stake. Pool: £44,147.75. 2.00 winning tickets. T/Plt: £47.90 to a £1 stake. Pool: £60,553.35. 921.35 winning tickets. T/Qpdt: £12.40 to a £1 stake. Pool: £3,557.90. 211.20 winning tickets. KH

2384 FONTAINEBLEAU
Tuesday, November 20

OFFICIAL GOING: Very soft

6888a PRIX ZEDDAAN (LISTED RACE) 6f
12:30 (12:31) 2-Y-O **£17,568** (£7,027; £5,270; £3,514; £1,757)

RPR
1 **Lady Deauville (FR)**[18] 6630 2-8-12 .... DBoeuf 10 101
(P A Blockley) *trckd ldr on outside: rdn to ld over 1f out: rdn out* **16/10**[1]

2 *1 1/2* **Badaria (FR)**[8] 2-8-8 .... J-BHamel 11 93
(Robert Collet, France)

3 *snk* **Shishangaan (IRE)**[23] 6527 2-8-8 .... SPasquier 9 92
(M Rulec, Germany)

4 *snk* **Salut L'Africain (FR)**[18] 6631 2-9-2 .... SMaillot 7 100
(Robert Collet, France)

5 *1* **Galaktea (IRE)**[40] 6136 2-8-12 .... MBlancpain 8 93
(C Laffon-Parias, France)

6 *3/4* **Sahara Boy (GER)**[37] 6219 2-8-11 .... EPedroza 2 89
(A Wohler, Germany)

7 *1 1/2* **Zoriana (FR)**[203] 2-8-8 .... F-XBertras 1 82
(F Rohaut, France)

8 *3* **Bid Again**[23] 6525 2-8-8 .... TJarnet 6 73
(R Pritchard-Gordon, France)

9 *1* **Valse Des Coeurs (FR)**[101] 2-8-8 .... SRuis 4 70
(G Pannier, France)

10 *8* **Pull The Plug (USA)**[23] 6525 2-8-8 .... TGillet 5 46
(Rod Collet, France)

0 **English Way (FR)** 2-8-11 .... FBlondel 3 —
(S-A Ghoumrassi, France)

1m 10.5s (70.50) **11** Ran SP% **38.5**
PARI-MUTUEL (including 1 Euro stake): WIN 2.60; PL 1.40, 3.60, 2.40;DF 19.90.
Owner P J Hughes Developments Ltd **Bred** Aerial Bloodstock Et Al **Trained** Lambourn, Berks

NOTEBOOK
Lady Deauville(FR), who had been placed in Group 3 company on two previous visits to France, found the return to a slightly lower grade in her favour and recorded her second Listed success. She handles any going but is clearly well suited by soft ground.

6889a PRIX SOLITUDE (LISTED RACE) (FILLIES) 1m 1f
1:30 (1:33) 3-Y-O **£17,568** (£7,027; £5,270; £3,514; £1,757)

RPR
1 **Lady Gloria**[35] 6249 3-8-12 .... TPQueally 9 101
(J G Given) *hld up: pushed along and hdwy 2f out: rdn to chal 1f out: styd on to ld nr fin* **283/10**[2]
2 ½ **In The Light**[33] 3-8-12 .... SPasquier 3 100
(A Fabre, France)
3 ¾ **Soft Morning**[37] 6220 3-8-12 .... J-BEyquem 12 99
(Sir Mark Prescott) *racd in 2nd: pushed along to ld 3f out to 2f out: styd on: lost 2nd cl home* **83/10**[1]
4 *hd* **Beatrix Kiddo (FR)**[80] 5058 3-9-2 .... TThulliez 11 102
(Robert Collet, France)
5 3 **Castellina**[104] 3-8-12 .... IMendizabal 7 92
(J-C Rouget, France)
6 *nk* **Une Pivoine (FR)**[15] 3-8-12 .... THuet 4 92
(J E Pease, France)
7 6 **Noble Ginger (FR)**[26] 6460 3-9-2 .... TGillet 1 85
(J E Pease, France)
8 4 **Rocky Mistress**[35] 3-8-12 .... ACrastus 5 73
(Y De Nicolay, France)
9 4 **Victoria College (FR)**[30] 3-8-12 .... DBoeuf 6 65
(D Smaga, France)
10 ¾ **Fontcia (FR)**[26] 6460 3-9-2 .... JVictoire 10 68
(D Sepulchre, France)
0 **Viola Carlita (FR)**[18] 6632 3-8-12 .... SRuis 13 —
(J-P Gallorini, France)
0 **Minar Salam (IRE)**[166] 3-8-12 ....(b) RMarchelli 2 —
(F Poulsen, France)
0 **Now Again (GER)** 3-8-12 .... AStarke 8 —
(W Hickst, Germany)

1m 55.5s (115.50) **13** Ran SP% **14.2**
PARI-MUTUEL: WIN 29.30; PL 7.30, 2.10, 3.30; DF 41.40.
Owner M H Tourle **Bred** M H And Mrs G Tourle **Trained** Willoughton, Lincs

NOTEBOOK
Lady Gloria has shown in the past that she handles soft ground and got up late in a close finish to record her first Listed success. She has progressed well since making her debut in a Southwell maiden back in January and she may be capable of winning over a little further if kept in training next year.

6864 KEMPTON (A.W) (R-H)
Wednesday, November 21

OFFICIAL GOING: Standard
There was a definite bias towards those racing prominently on what was a tough evening for the horses in the driving rain. The far rail was also favoured.
Wind: Almost nil Weather: Steady rain throughout

6890 BOOK NOW FOR BOXING DAY H'CAP 5f (P)
6:20 (6:20) (Class 6) (0-65,65) 3-Y-O+ **£2,047** (£604; £302) **Stalls** High

Form RPR
0040 1 **Smokin Beau**[29] 6413 10-8-13 **60** .... JimCrowley 12 72
(N P Littmoden) *mde all fr ins draw: drvn 2 l clr over 1f out: styd on* **15/2**[3]
0000 2 ¾ **Hollow Jo**[7] 6810 7-9-4 **65** .... MickyFenton 6 74
(J R Jenkins) *wl in rr: gd prog on inner over 1f out: chsd wnr last 100yds: clsng at fin but nvr able to chal* **16/1**
000 3 1 ½ **Calypso King**[11] 6764 4-9-1 **62** .... LPKeniry 11 66
(Peter Grayson) *prom: chsd wnr wl over 1f out: no imp fnl f: lost 2nd last 100yds* **9/1**
0010 4 ¾ **Green Lagonda (AUS)**[2] 6870 5-9-0 **61** .... HayleyTurner 8 62
(J G Given) *trckd ldrs gng wl: rdn and nt qckn over 1f out: one pce after* **3/1**[1]
1060 5 ¾ **Rosie Cross (IRE)**[7] 6810 3-8-11 **63** .... PatrickHills(5) 3 62+
(Eve Johnson Houghton) *wl in rr: brought wdst of all in st: r.o wl fnl f: no ch to rch ldrs* **12/1**
1200 6 *hd* **Thoughtsofstardom**[12] 6752 4-8-8 **55** ....(be) TGMcLaughlin 10 53
(G C Bravery) *awkward s: rcvring whn n.m.r on inner after 1f: chsd ldrs 2f out: disp 2nd over 1f out: fdd* **20/1**
0026 7 1 ½ **Fastrac Boy**[10] 6773 4-8-6 **53** .... JohnEgan 9 45
(J R Best) *towards rr: effrt over 1f out and swtchd rt: no hdwy after* **11/2**[2]
0560 8 *shd* **Azygous**[21] 6594 4-9-1 **62** .... DaneO'Neill 1 54
(J Akehurst) *chsd ldrs on outer: rdn bef 1/2-way: outpcd over 1f out: plugged on* **8/1**
1604 9 1 **No Time (IRE)**[22] 6562 7-8-12 **59** ....(p) SteveDrowne 4 48
(A J McCabe) *a towards rr on outer: struggling fr 1/2-way* **12/1**
2530 10 2 ½ **Triskaidekaphobia**[12] 6752 4-8-7 **54** ....(t) PaulFitzsimons 7 34
(Miss J R Tooth) *chsd wnr to wl over 1f out: wknd rapidly* **16/1**
3640 11 ¾ **Charlotte Grey**[12] 6747 3-8-13 **60** .... NCallan 5 37
(C N Allen) *outpcd and a bhd* **20/1**
5303 12 ½ **One Way Ticket**[10] 6773 7-8-4 **51** oh3 ....(b) FrancisNorton 2 26
(J M Bradley) *prom on outer tl wknd over 1f out: no ch whn hmpd wl ins fnl f* **15/2**[3]

59.63 secs (-0.77) **Going Correction** -0.125s/f (Stan) **12** Ran SP% **121.7**
Speed ratings (Par 101): **101,99,97,96,95 94,92,92,90,86 85,84**
CSF £124.54 CT £1112.80 TOTE £8.80: £2.90, £4.40, £3.90; EX 127.20.
Owner Miss Vanessa Church **Bred** Alan Spargo **Trained** Newmarket, Suffolk

FOCUS
This was a strongly run handicap and the form has been rated fairly positively. The winner produced his best run since the spring.

6891 DREAMS COME TRUE CLAIMING STKS 6f (P)
6:50 (6:51) (Class 6) 3-Y-O+ **£2,047** (£604; £302) **Stalls** High

Form RPR
3100 1 **Compton Classic**[15] 6707 5-9-2 73 ....(v) HarryPoulton(7) 12 77
(J R Boyle) *hld up bhd ldrs on inner: prog over 2f out: led over 1f out: shkn up and readily in command* **12/1**
30R2 2 1 ½ **Quiet Times (IRE)**[13] 6735 8-9-5 76 ....(b) NCallan 11 69
(K A Ryan) *mde most to over 1f out: kpt on but no match for wnr* **9/4**[2]
0000 3 *hd* **Dickie Le Davoir**[61] 5584 3-9-5 85 .... FergusSweeney 8 77+
(K R Burke) *hld up in last: covered up tl swtchd lft and effrt over 1f out: r.o wl fnl f but wnr already gone beyond recall* **2/1**[1]
0000 4 ¾ **Mulberry Lad (IRE)**[5] 6826 5-8-10 55 .... ChrisCatlin 9 57
(P W Hiatt) *blindfold stl on as stalls opened: hld up in last pair: prog on inner over 2f out: chsd ldng pair 1f out: no imp: lost 3rd nr fin* **12/1**
2360 5 ½ **Mister Elegant**[10] 6779 5-8-13 50 .... FrancisNorton 10 58
(J L Spearing) *t.k.h: trckd ldng pair: poised to chal gng strly over 2f out: rdn and no rspnse over 1f out* **14/1**
4120 6 1 ¼ **Hart Of Gold**[60] 5635 3-9-9 75 .... LPKeniry 6 64
(R A Harris) *chsd ldrs: nt qckn over 1f out: n.d after* **6/1**[3]
000 7 ¾ **Cayman Breeze**[51] 5864 7-8-9 44 .... SteveDrowne 7 48
(J M Bradley) *hld up towards rr: rdn and nt qckn over 1f out: no imp after* **33/1**
0300 8 1 **Shavoulin (USA)**[71] 5315 3-9-1 72 .... SamHitchcott 2 50
(Christian Wroe) *pressed ldr: upsides over 2f out to over 1f out: wknd* **33/1**
460 9 2 **Rainbow Bay**[21] 6594 4-8-13 64 ....(v) TGMcLaughlin 1 42
(P D Evans) *chsd ldrs and racd on outer: wknd wl over 1f out* **11/1**
6600 10 7 **Parkside Pursuit**[87] 4853 9-8-7 45 .... JohnEgan 5 14
(J M Bradley) *in tch on outer over 3f: sn wknd* **40/1**

1m 13.13s (-0.57) **Going Correction** -0.125s/f (Stan) **10** Ran SP% **117.1**
Speed ratings (Par 101): **98,96,95,94,94 92,91,90,87,78**
CSF £39.01 TOTE £11.00: £2.40, £1.20, £1.30; EX 32.30.
Owner M Khan X2 **Bred** James Thom And Sons And Peter Orr **Trained** Epsom, Surrey

FOCUS
A competitive enough claimer, run at a steady pace. The fifth limits the form and the principals are not running to their marks at present.
Dickie Le Davoir Official explanation: jockey said gelding was denied a clear run
Shavoulin(USA) Official explanation: jockey said gelding hung right-handed

6892 DIGIBET.COM NURSERY 6f (P)
7:20 (7:21) (Class 5) (0-75,79) 2-Y-O **£3,238** (£963; £481; £240) **Stalls** High

Form RPR
0500 1 **Bazguy**[17] 6665 2-8-13 **65** ....(b) TGMcLaughlin 4 68
(P D Evans) *mde all: drew at least 2 l clr 2f out: looked vulnerable ent fnl f: kpt on wl* **16/1**
000 2 1 ¼ **Desiderio**[25] 6493 2-8-1 **53** ow1 .... FrancisNorton 7 52
(R Hannon) *sn last: rdn and prog on inner over 2f out: chsd wnr 1f out and looked dangerous briefly: readily hld last 75yds* **12/1**
6125 3 ½ **Maryolini**[93] 4669 2-9-4 **70** .... SamHitchcott 8 68
(N J Vaughan) *racd in 3rd tl rdn to chse wnr over 2f out: no imp: one pce and lost 2nd 1f out* **4/1**[2]
6013 4 1 ½ **Leading Edge (IRE)**[7] 6812 2-9-0 **66** .... ChrisCatlin 6 59
(M R Channon) *chsd ldng trio: rdn over 2f out: no imp: wl btn over 1f out* **5/4**[1]
4400 5 2 **River Bounty**[11] 6756 2-8-12 **67** .... AndrewElliott(3) 2 54
(A P Jarvis) *chsd wnr to over 2f out: sn lost pl u.p* **13/2**[3]
430 6 7 **Klarity**[29] 6409 2-9-1 **67** ....(e[1]) RobertHavlin 5 33
(J Pearce) *stdd s: hld up in last pair: rdn over 2f out: no rspnse: wknd over 1f out* **12/1**
605 7 1 ½ **Hold That Call (USA)**[29] 6409 2-9-0 **66** .... DaneO'Neill 3 28
(R Hannon) *rrd s: t.k.h: in tch on outer to over 2f out: wknd* **7/1**

1m 13.18s (-0.52) **Going Correction** -0.125s/f (Stan) **7** Ran SP% **111.5**
Speed ratings (Par 96): **98,96,95,93,91 81,79**
CSF £172.48 CT £904.97 TOTE £19.20: £5.30, £5.00; EX 176.80.
Owner B McCabe & K J Mercer **Bred** Usk Valley Stud **Trained** Pandy, Monmouths

FOCUS
Three of the original ten defected from this nursery and Bazguy caused a minor surprise in winning, having the run of the race in front and stepping up on recent efforts.

NOTEBOOK
Bazguy, too keen over 7f at Lingfield in the first-time blinkers last time, put his speed to good use on this drop in trip and found himself in a clear lead racing inside the final quarter mile. He began to wander inside the final half-furlong, but responded well to pressure and was always just doing enough. He should not be put up too much for this and remains capable of better. (op 14-1)
Desiderio improved on the moderate form he showed in three maidens, keeping on well in second without being able to get to the winner. He had done all his previous racing at 1m and looks capable of winning a small race off his lowly mark. (op 10-1)
Maryolini has only been lightly raced since winning back in the summer and she had to leave a terrible effort at Wolverhampton last time well behind if she were to stand any realistic chance. She ran well, sticking on gamely back in third, but lacked the pace to challenge the winner.
Leading Edge(IRE), twice a winner earlier in the season off marks of 60 and 62, ran well off a 2lb higher mark to finish third at Wolverhampton last week and she looked the one to beat. However, she was being driven as they straightened for home and never really looked like picking up. She is better than this and probably deserves another chance. (tchd 11-10)
River Bounty ran well in a couple of decent handicaps earlier in the season, but she has been struggling for form of late and, having showed good early speed, gradually dropped away. (op 7-1 tchd 15-2)
Klarity Official explanation: jockey said filly ran too free
Hold That Call(USA) Official explanation: jockey said gelding ran too free

6893 DIGIBET MEDIAN AUCTION MAIDEN STKS 1m 4f (P)
7:50 (7:50) (Class 6) 3-5-Y-O **£2,047** (£604; £302) **Stalls** Low

Form RPR
5 1 **Imminent Victory**[7] 6807 4-9-9 0 ....(p) ChrisCatlin 3 52
(R M H Cowell) *led after 1f: mde rest: pushed along 5f out: kpt on whn pressed 2f out and whn jnd ins fnl f* **6/1**[3]
0000 2 ¾ **Franky'N'Jonny**[10] 6774 4-9-4 40 .... DaneO'Neill 1 46
(M J Attwater) *settled in 4th: rdn and effrt over 2f out: wnt 2nd over 1f out: jnd wnr ins fnl f: gave up nr fin* **16/1**
545 3 3 **Summerofsixtynine**[28] 6430 4-9-9 60 .... RobertHavlin 5 46
(J G M O'Shea) *led 1f: chsd wnr to 1/2-way: nt qckn over 2f out: plugged on* **7/2**[2]
0- 4 1 ¼ **Tralanza (IRE)**[28] 6444 3-8-12 0 .... TPQueally 2 39
(P J Prendergast, Ire) *trckd ldng pair: wnt 2nd 1/2-way: gng best over 2f out: shkn up 2f out and no rspnse: folded tamely* **4/9**[1]
00GP 5 21 **Zameliana**[104] 4309 3-8-5 41 .... MatthewCosham(7) 4 6
(Dr J R J Naylor) *a last: wknd over 2f out: t.o* **40/1**

2m 35.66s (-1.24) **Going Correction** -0.125s/f (Stan)
WFA 3 from 4yo 6lb **5** Ran SP% **114.1**
Speed ratings (Par 101): **99,98,96,95,81**
CSF £73.55 TOTE £9.20: £2.10, £4.00; EX 45.20.
Owner Khalifa Dasmal **Bred** Khalifa Abdulla Dasmal **Trained** Six Mile Bottom, Cambs
■ Stewards' Enquiry : Dane O'Neill two-day ban: careless riding (Dec 3-4)

FOCUS
A very weak event, with the runner-up having been beaten in banded races. The winner was up 9lb on his previous form here.

6894 DIGIBET SPORTS BETTING H'CAP 1m (P)
8:20 (8:21) (Class 6) (0-65,65) 3-Y-O+ **£2,047** (£604; £302) **Stalls** High

Form RPR
1 **1** **Confidentiality (IRE)**[9] 6796 3-8-4 **51** oh3 NickyMackay 9 65+
(M Wigham) *cl up on inner: got through to ld 2f out: drvn and in command whn edgd lft fr over 1f out* **6/4**[1]
0050 **2** *2* **Shouldntbethere (IRE)**[30] 6387 3-8-13 **60** RobertHavlin 4 68+
(Mrs P N Dutfield) *s.i.s: hld up wl in rr: gng wl whn nt clr run over 2f out and whn same story and hmpd over 1f out: r.o strly fnl f: tk 2nd last strides* **25/1**
0005 **3** *nk* **Magic Warrior**[14] 6716 7-9-0 **59** PatDobbs 13 65+
(J C Fox) *hld up bhd ldrs on inner: n.m.r over 2f out: prog to chse wnr fnl f: no imp: lost 2nd last strides* **16/1**
600 **4** *shd* **Colinca's Lad (IRE)**[10] 6780 5-8-10 **55** HayleyTurner 1 59+
(T T Clement) *dropped in fr wd draw and hld up in last pair: taken to outer and drvn 2f out: styd on wl but nt rch ldrs* **20/1**
5152 **5** *nk* **Viable**[21] 6579 5-9-1 **60** MickyFenton 8 63
(Mrs P Sly) *pressed ldr: led over 3f out: hdd u.p 2f out: plugged on* **10/1**
0003 **6** *hd* **Hucking Heat (IRE)**[53] 5819 3-9-3 **64** (v) DaneO'Neill 10 67
(J R Best) *hld up in midfield: rdn and effrt 2f out: styd on but nt pce to chal* **12/1**
2135 **7** *nk* **Wrighty Almighty (IRE)**[51] 5862 5-9-2 **61** JimCrowley 11 63
(P R Chamings) *s.i.s: hld up in midfield: rdn and effrt over 2f out: kpt on: nvr able to chal* **7/1**
0603 **8** *2 1/2* **Inquisitress**[14] 6716 3-8-11 **58** TPQueally 12 54
(J J Bridger) *s.i.s: hld up in rr: effrt on inner whn nt clr run over 2f out: no imp on ldrs fnl f* **16/1**
0006 **9** *1/2* **Silent Storm**[11] 6764 7-9-4 **63** LPKeniry 2 58
(Peter Grayson) *dropped in fr wd draw and hld up in last trio: rdn 2f out: kpt on but nvr a factor* **25/1**
0400 **10** *1 1/2* **Smash Hit (IRE)**[14] 6716 4-8-13 **61** NeilChalmers(3) 3 53
(David Pinder) *wl in rr: u.p 1/2-way: hanging bdly 2f out: n.d* **25/1**
6404 **11** *hd* **Isobel Rose (IRE)**[7] 6809 3-8-5 **52** FrancisNorton 7 43
(J L Spearing) *trckd ldrs: no prog 2f out: fdd* **16/1**
042 **12** *nk* **Katiypour (IRE)**[35] 6268 10-9-6 **65** RichardThomas 6 55
(B R Johnson) *prom: cl 3rd 3f out: wknd wl over 1f out* **5/1**[2]
0000 **13** *6* **Merlins Quest**[173] 2196 3-8-4 **51** oh4 (b[1]) LiamJones 14 28
(J M Bradley) *led to over 3f out: wknd over 2f out* **50/1**
-230 **14** *4* **Forbidden (IRE)**[2] 6874 4-8-13 **61** (t) JerryO'Dwyer(3) 5 28
(Daniel Mark Loughnane, Ire) *racd wd: chsd ldrs: u.p sn after 1/2-way: wknd over 2f out* **13/2**[3]

1m 39.0s (-1.80) **Going Correction** -0.125s/f (Stan)
WFA 3 from 4yo+ 2lb **14** Ran SP% **135.2**
Speed ratings (Par 101): **104,102,101,101,101 101,100,98,97,96 96,95,89,85**
CSF £59.99 CT £540.47 TOTE £2.30: £1.40, £10.90, £5.20; EX 97.80.
Owner J M Cullinan **Bred** Kevin Foley **Trained** Newmarket, Suffolk

FOCUS
A moderate handicap, but the form looks sound. The winner could still be ahead of the handicapper.
Shouldntbethere(IRE) Official explanation: jockey said gelding was denied a clear run
Smash Hit(IRE) Official explanation: jockey said gelding was denied a clear run
Isobel Rose(IRE) Official explanation: jockey said filly lost its action

6895 TFM NETWORKS H'CAP 7f (P)
8:50 (8:54) (Class 6) (0-55,55) 3-Y-O+ **£2,047** (£604; £302) **Stalls** High

Form RPR
0564 **1** **Faithful Ruler (USA)**[10] 6779 3-9-1 **54** FergusSweeney 13 67+
(M A Magnusson) *sn trckd ldrs on inner: smooth prog to go 2nd over 2f out: rdn to cl fr over 1f out: led last 100yds: sn clr* **5/1**[1]
5150 **2** *2 1/2* **The Jailer**[18] 6642 4-8-8 **53** MCGeran(7) 8 60
(J G M O'Shea) *led: drew 3 l clr and had all bar wnr in trble over 2f out: plugged on but hdd last 100yds* **16/1**
0223 **3** *3* **Majestical (IRE)**[5] 6825 5-9-2 **54** (e) PatDobbs 12 53
(V Smith) *towards rr: rdn 3f out: prog to take 3rd over 1f out: no ch w ldng pair* **5/1**[1]
0552 **4** *1* **Cabourg (IRE)**[47] 5966 4-9-2 **54** SteveDrowne 1 50
(R Bastiman) *wl in rr and sn pushed along: prog on outer fr 2f out: styd on: n.d* **10/1**
3602 **5** *3/4* **Contented (IRE)**[21] 6582 5-9-2 **54** (p) LPKeniry 3 48
(Mrs L C Jewell) *wl in rr: sme prog on inner over 2f out: kpt on but n.d* **20/1**
5-55 **6** *nk* **Samahir (USA)**[21] 6597 3-9-2 **55** HayleyTurner 11 48
(T T Clement) *last and nt gng wl 1st 2f: sme prog fr 1/2-way: chsd ldrs but nt on terms over 2f out: disp 3rd over 1f out: one pce* **10/1**
0061 **7** *5* **Joy And Pain**[15] 6706 6-9-1 **53** (p) OscarUrbina 4 33
(M J Attwater) *towards rr on outer: struggling and no prog 3f out: no ch after* **13/2**[3]
2023 **8** *1 1/4* **Beneking**[14] 6717 7-9-3 **55** (p) ChrisCatlin 7 31
(D Burchell) *chsd ldrs: u.p sn after 1/2-way: lost pl and wl btn over 2f out* **13/2**[3]
4010 **9** *3 1/2* **Smash N'Grab (IRE)**[34] 6277 3-9-1 **54** LiamJones 14 21
(J R Jenkins) *chsd ldr to over 2f out: wknd* **25/1**
0203 **10** *1* **Bens Georgie (IRE)**[29] 6415 5-9-2 **54** JimCrowley 10 18
(D K Ivory) *chsd ldrs: u.p 1/2-way: wknd over 2f out* **8/1**
4340 **11** *5* **Task Complete**[34] 6290 4-9-3 **55** DaneO'Neill 6 5
(Jean-Rene Auvray) *chsd ldrs on outer: hanging and wd bnd over 3f out: sn wl bhd* **25/1**
0001 **12** *2* **Sarah's Art (IRE)**[53] 5817 4-9-3 **55** MickyFenton 5 —
(Stef Liddiard) *dwlt: wl in rr on outer: carried v wd bnd 3f out: no ch after* **6/1**[2]
035 **13** *5* **Sibo Baggins (IRE)**[22] 6573 3-9-2 **55** JohnEgan 9 —
(J S Moore) *chsd ldrs 3f: sn wknd rapidly* **10/1**

1m 24.86s (-1.94) **Going Correction** -0.125s/f (Stan)
WFA 3 from 4yo+ 1lb **13** Ran SP% **131.0**
Speed ratings (Par 101): **106,103,99,98,97 97,91,90,86,85 79,77,71**
CSF £94.18 CT £436.65 TOTE £6.10: £2.30, £5.80, £2.40; EX 112.90.
Owner Eastwind Racing Ltd and Martha Trussell **Bred** WinStar Farm LLC **Trained** Upper Lambourn, Berks

FOCUS
Not much got into this and the front two did well to come clear. The winner is progressive.
Beneking Official explanation: trainer had no explanation for the poor form shown
Sarah's Art(IRE) Official explanation: vet said gelding was lame on right-fore

6896 BARRETTSTOWN STUD H'CAP 1m 3f (P)
9:20 (9:22) (Class 6) (0-50,51) 3-Y-O+ **£2,047** (£604; £302) **Stalls** High

Form RPR
3515 **1** **Summer Bounty**[14] 6713 11-9-4 **50** LPKeniry 9 55+
(F Jordan) *dwlt: hld up in last: prog on inner over 2f out: hmpd wl over 1f out: rdn and r.o to ld narrowly ins fnl f: hld on* **12/1**
0004 **2** *hd* **Karmest**[18] 6638 3-8-13 **50** DaneO'Neill 14 53
(A D Brown) *hld up in midfield: effrt towards inner over 2f out: rdn to ld over 1f out: narrowly hdd ins fnl f: jst hld* **12/1**
-550 **3** *hd* **Mariaverdi**[49] 5894 3-8-11 **48** SteveDrowne 13 51
(P G Murphy) *settled midfield: pushed along 5f out: prog on inner over 2f out: chal over 1f out: jst hld fnl f* **20/1**
0041 **4** *3/4* **Altos Reales**[7] 6808 3-9-0 **51** 6ex DeanMcKeown 4 53+
(D Shaw) *hld up wl in rr: prog on outer over 2f out: hanging over 1f out: shuffled along and no imp on ldng trio fnl f* **11/8**[1]
-004 **5** *nk* **Henry Holmes**[5] 6832 4-9-2 **48** RichardThomas 8 49
(Mrs L Richards) *hld up towards rr: effrt and sme prog 2f out: rdn and styd on same pce fnl f* **8/1**
0640 **6** *1 1/4* **Kilmeena Magic**[90] 4739 5-9-0 **46** oh1 PatDobbs 5 45
(J C Fox) *led at stdy pce to 1/2-way: trckd ldr: led again over 2f out gng wl: hdd and nt qckn over 1f out* **33/1**
005 **7** *1* **Rollin 'n Tumblin**[17] 6670 3-8-10 **47** PaulDoe 11 44
(W Jarvis) *trckd ldrs: n.m.r briefly 2f out: pushed along and no imp after* **20/1**
123 **8** *nk* **Formidable Guest**[7] 6808 3-8-12 **49** DavidKinsella 10 46+
(J Pearce) *dwlt: hld up wl in rr: nt clr run over 2f out to over 1f out: one pce after* **6/1**[3]
5544 **9** *1* **Magic Amigo**[13] 6096 6-9-1 **47** (v) JimCrowley 1 42
(J R Jenkins) *stdd s: hld up wl in rr: prog on outer 6f out into midfield: effrt on outer 2f out: sme hdwy over 1f out: wknd ins fnl f* **11/2**[2]
0-46 **10** *2* **Larad (IRE)**[9] 6798 6-9-0 **46** oh1 (b) JohnEgan 6 38
(J S Moore) *hld up in midfield: no real prog fnl 2f* **10/1**
0665 **11** *2* **Lordswood (IRE)**[9] 6792 3-8-9 **46** oh1 ChrisCatlin 12 34
(J J Bridger) *t.k.h: prom tl wknd 2f out* **16/1**
-000 **12** *3* **Ocean Valentine**[19] 6629 4-8-9 **46** oh1 RussellKennemore(5) 2 29
(J T Stimpson) *t.k.h: trckd ldr to 1/2-way: styd prom tl wknd 2f out* **25/1**
3400 **13** *1 3/4* **Piquet**[9] 6792 9-9-0 **46** oh1 MickyFenton 7 26
(J J Bridger) *t.k.h: cl up tl wknd 2f out* **25/1**
/00- **14** *4* **The Stafford (IRE)**[603] 778 6-9-0 **46** oh1 SamHitchcott 3 20
(L Wells) *hld up in last trio: plld hrd and rapid prog to ld 1/2-way: hdd over 2f out: wknd rapidly* **50/1**

2m 25.33s (2.65) **Going Correction** -0.125s/f (Stan)
WFA 3 from 4yo+ 5lb **14** Ran SP% **135.4**
Speed ratings (Par 101): **85,84,84,84,83 83,82,82,81,79 78,76,75,72**
CSF £152.81 CT £2917.02 TOTE £18.10: £3.20, £5.80, £5.40; EX 445.80 Place 6 £9,793.26, Place 5 £1,836.26.
Owner Tim Powell **Bred** Berkshire Equestrian Services Ltd **Trained** Adstone, Northants
■ Stewards' Enquiry : Dane O'Neill two-day ban: used whip with excessive frequency (Dec 5-6)

FOCUS
A very moderate winning time.
Formidable Guest Official explanation: jockey said filly was denied a clear run
T/Plt: £2,724.40 to a £1 stake. Pool: £80,615.25. 21.60 winning tickets. T/Qpdt: £1,555.10 to a £1 stake. Pool: £6,935.10. 3.30 winning tickets. JN

6847 LINGFIELD (L-H)
Wednesday, November 21

OFFICIAL GOING: Standard
Wind: Fresh, half behind Weather: bright partly cloudy

6897 PONTIN'S BOOK EARLY E B F MAIDEN STKS 6f (P)
1:00 (1:05) (Class 5) 2-Y-O **£3,141** (£934; £467; £233) **Stalls** Low

Form RPR
1 **Classic Fortune (IRE)** 2-9-3 0 TQuinn 9 73+
(D R C Elsworth) *w'like: scope: lw: v.s.a: t.k.h: hld up in midfield: gd hdwy to chse ldrs over 2f out: rdn over 1f out: chsd ldr ins fnl f: r.o wl to ld last stride* **5/6**[1]
0044 **2** *shd* **Fast Feet**[14] 6721 2-9-3 75 FrancisNorton 12 70
(K A Ryan) *w'like: chsd ldr tl led over 3f out: rdn wl over 1f out: clr ins fnl f: r.o but ct last stride* **15/2**[3]
3 *1 3/4* **Salt Of The Earth (IRE)** 2-9-3 0 JohnEgan 11 65+
(T G Mills) *w'like: bit bkwd: in tch: hdwy 3f out: chsd ldr over 2f out: sn rdn: kpt on same pce fnl f* **10/1**
4 *1 3/4* **Steele Tango (USA)** 2-9-3 0 ChrisCatlin 8 60+
(R A Teal) *t.k.h: hld up in midfield: rdn wl over 2f out: outpcd 2f out: styd on ins fnl f* **14/1**
005 **5** *3/4* **River N' Blues (IRE)**[18] 6649 2-8-12 70 FergusSweeney 4 52
(Dr J R J Naylor) *t.k.h: chsd ldrs: rdn over 2f out: wknd 1f out* **14/1**
35 **6** *2 1/2* **Filligree (IRE)**[21] 6595 2-8-12 0 JamieMackay 1 45
(Rae Guest) *sn pushed along to go prom: rdn over 2f out: sn struggling: kpt on same pce* **25/1**
2003 **7** *3/4* **Hawk Eyed Lady (IRE)**[9] 6799 2-8-12 73 MartinDwyer 10 43
(J A Osborne) *in tch tl short of room and lost pl after 1f: bhd: rdn over 2f out: nvr trbld ldrs* **7/2**[2]
0 **8** *nk* **Yattendon**[115] 3991 2-9-3 0 SimonWhitworth 7 47
(S Kirk) *v.s.a: a bhd* **20/1**
50 **9** *3/4* **Ricci De Mare**[9] 6799 2-8-12 0 J-PGuillambert 5 39
(Sir Mark Prescott) *w'like: s.i.s: sn in tch in midfield: lost pl bnd over 2f out: no ch after* **33/1**
10 *1/2* **Scots W'Hae** 2-9-3 0 JimCrowley 6 43+
(S C Williams) *unf: bit bkwd: s.i.s: t.k.h: hld up in rr: c wd bnd over 2f out: n.d* **66/1**
10 *dht* **Mister New York (USA)** 2-9-3 0 JosedeSouza 2 43
(Noel T Chance) *w'like: leggy: bit bkwd: t.k.h: led tl over 3f out: rdn and wknd over 2f out* **40/1**

1m 12.75s (-0.06) **Going Correction** -0.125s/f (Stan) **11** Ran SP% **126.4**
Speed ratings (Par 96): **95,94,92,90,89 85,84,84,83,82 82**
CSF £8.39 TOTE £2.10: £1.20, £1.90, £3.00; EX 12.00 Trifecta £63.80 Pool: £160.88 - 1.79 winning tickets..
Owner Fung Lok Li **Bred** Mrs C R Philipson & Mrs H G Lascelles **Trained** Newmarket, Suffolk

FOCUS
A reasonable sprint maiden for the time of year and although the form is limited the race should produce some winners. Classic Fortune can go on to better things.

NOTEBOOK

Classic Fortune(IRE) ◆, a 70,000gns son of Royal Applause, first foal of a quite useful triple 6f-7f winner at two to four, justified significant market confidence on his racecourse debut, but only just. Having been slowly into his stride after being kept in the stalls for an unsatisfactory length of time, he was forced to race a little wider than ideal for much of the way and still had plenty to do at the top of the straight. He gradually got the idea, though, and picked up in good style to grab Fast Feet, who was not exactly stopping in front, literally on the line. He can be rated better than the bare form and is open to loads of improvement. (op Evens tchd 5-4)

Fast Feet ◆ would have taken advantage of the eventual winner's inexperience had he not had to use up so much energy to get to the front from the widest stall of all. He has not progressed as one might have hoped, but this was just his second start over 6f and he looks he looks well up to winning a similar event. (tchd 6-1)

Salt Of The Earth(IRE), a £50,000 son of Invincible Spirit, first foal of a mare who was unplaced over 6f-1m2f, made a pleasing debut in third. He is open to some improvement and it will be disappointing if he cannot win a similar race during the winter. (op 15-2)

Steele Tango(USA) ◆, a 30,000gns son of Okawango, half-brother to a three-year-old winner in Japan, and to Greatrakes, a winner over hurdles, made a pleasing debut for a trainer who has made a bright start to his career. He should improve plenty with the benefit of this experience and appeals as one to keep on side. (op 12-1 tchd 9-1)

River N' Blues(IRE) had shown ability in three turf maidens, most notably when fifth over 7f at Newmarket on her latest start, but this was a little disappointing. Dropping to this trip for the first time, she showed plenty of speed to race in a handy position, but she did not offer much under pressure when it mattered. (tchd 20-1 in a place)

Hawk Eyed Lady(IRE) was poorly placed after finding a bit of trouble soon after the start and she never posed a threat. (op 7-1)

Ricci De Mare is now qualified for a handicap mark and she is likely to leave this form behind when stepped up in trip next year. (tchd 40-1)

6898 PONTIN'S SHORT BREAKS CLAIMING STKS — 7f (P)

1:30 (1:31) (Class 6) 2-Y-O — £2,047 (£604; £302) Stalls Low

Form				RPR
5201	1		**Geezers Colours**[6] 6823 2-8-11 67 ... FergusSweeney 4 (K R Burke) *led for 2f: chsd ldr tl led again over 2f out: rdn wl over 1f out: r.o strly to go clr last 100yds* **9/4**[2]	76+
032	2	2 ½	**Ike Quebec (FR)**[83] 4963 2-9-0 74 ... RichardHughes 5 (R Hannon) *lw: hld up wl in tch: hdwy and rdn over 2f out: chsd wnr over 1f out: outpcd last 100yds: eased towards fin* **3/1**[3]	74+
5410	3	3	**Wee Buns**[25] 6502 2-8-6 68 ... LPKeniry 6 (S Kirk) *in tch in last pair: rdn over 2f out: outpcd over 1f out: kpt on to go 3rd ins fnl f* **6/1**	57
120U	4	1 ¾	**Thompsons Walls (IRE)**[9] 6800 2-8-11 83 ... (t) NickyMackay 2 (P C Haslam) *sn chsng ldr: led after 2f: rdn and hdd over 2f out: wknd 1f out* **13/8**[1]	57

1m 25.31s (-0.58) **Going Correction** -0.125s/f (Stan) — 4 Ran SP% **108.2**

Speed ratings (Par 94): **98,95,91,89**

CSF £8.93 TOTE £3.10; EX 6.90.

Owner C Waters **Bred** Bloodhorse International Limited **Trained** Middleham Moor, N Yorks

FOCUS

This looked like a good claimer beforehand, even allowing for the small field, but they went no pace through the early stages and the form needs treating with caution. A slight step up from Geezers Colours.

NOTEBOOK

Geezers Colours was always well placed considering the steady pace and he followed up his win in a course-and-distance nursery in straightforward fashion. He is progressing into a fair type. (op 11-4)

Ike Quebec(FR) had shown plenty of ability in three runs in maiden company, but he had been a beaten favourite on two of those starts. Trying 7f for the first time on this drop in grade, he did not help his chance by racing against the often unfavoured far rail in the straight, but he was basically no match for the winner and probably would have preferred a stronger-run race. (op 7-4)

Wee Buns ran a little better than when well beaten at Wolverhampton on his previous start, but he was never seen with a winning chance. (tchd 11-2 and 13-2)

Thompsons Walls(IRE) had upwards of 10lb in hand at the weights, but he dropped out very tamely in the straight. (op 9-4)

6899 GO PONTIN'S NOW NURSERY — 1m (P)

2:00 (2:01) (Class 4) (0-85,77) 2-Y-O — £4,533 (£1,348; £674; £336) Stalls High

Form				RPR
001	1		**Traphalgar (IRE)**[20] 6602 2-9-5 75 ... TQuinn 7 (P F I Cole) *lw: chsd ldr: rdn and ev ch 2f out: led over 1f out: hld on wl u.p* **10/3**[2]	78
602	2	nk	**Silent Master (USA)**[20] 6602 2-9-3 73 ... J-PGuillambert 6 (M Johnston) *lw: sn led: pressed and rdn 2f out: hdd over 1f out: unable qck last 100yds* **11/4**[1]	75
0316	3	hd	**Hucking Hero (IRE)**[6] 6823 2-9-0 70 ... DaneO'Neill 2 (J R Best) *t.k.h: hld up towards rr: hdwy and rdn jst over 2f out: chsd ldng pair jst ins fnl f: r.o* **11/1**	72+
0630	4	1 ½	**Tiger's Rocket (IRE)**[29] 6410 2-8-5 61 ... FrancisNorton 10 (R Hannon) *t.k.h: chsd ldrs: rdn over 2f out: kpt on same pce u.p fnl f* **13/2**	59
5441	5	1 ¾	**Redsensor**[9] 6793 2-9-5 75 6ex ... RichardHughes 5 (R Hannon) *lw: in tch: rdn over 2f out: chsd ldng pair 2f out: wknd jst over 1f out* **5/1**[3]	69
0000	6	shd	**Fathsta (IRE)**[11] 6756 2-8-13 69 ... SimonWhitworth 8 (S Kirk) *t.k.h: hld up towards rr on outer: rdn 2f out: kpt on but nvr pce to trble ldrs* **15/2**	63
3243	7	1 ¼	**Straight And Level (CAN)**[23] 6543 2-9-7 77 ... ChrisCatlin 9 (Miss Jo Crowley) *hld up and rdn and effrt over 2f out: no hdwy* **16/1**	68
600	8	¾	**Magical Song**[50] 5888 2-7-12 54 ... NickyMackay 4 (P A Blockley) *chsd ldrs: pushed along over 4f out: rdn over 2f out: wknd jst over 1f out* **33/1**	44
0340	9	1 ½	**Landikhaya (IRE)**[27] 6449 2-9-2 72 ... MartinDwyer 1 (D K Ivory) *s.i.s: sn in tch in midfield: pushed along 4f out: wknd wl over 1f out: eased ins fnl f* **14/1**	58

1m 38.49s (-0.94) **Going Correction** -0.125s/f (Stan) — 9 Ran SP% **115.3**

Speed ratings (Par 98): **99,98,98,97,95 95,93,93,91**

CSF £12.92 CT £89.54 TOTE £4.30: £1.90, £1.70, £2.70; EX 9.50 Trifecta £58.10 Pool: £220.14 - 2.69 winning tickets..

Owner The Fairy Story Partnership **Bred** Deepwood Farm Stud **Trained** Whatcombe, Oxon

FOCUS

A fair nursery, but they went just a steady pace and those who raced handy were at an advantage. Traphalgar confirmed recent superiority over Silent Master and this form should work out.

NOTEBOOK

Traphalgar(IRE), who had today's runner-up behind in second when winning his maiden over 7f round here on his previous start, was always in a good position considering the way the race was run and stayed on strongly in the straight to follow up. He looks up to completing the hat-trick. (op 9-4)

Silent Master(USA), upped in trip on his nursery debut, ran his race after being allowed an easy lead, but he was unable to reverse recent form with Traphalgar. He should find a similar race. (op 3-1)

Hucking Hero(IRE) took an age to hit top stride once in the clear in the straight and didn't exactly look to be helping his rider, carrying his head at a slight angle, but he still fared best of those held up. (tchd 12-1)

Tiger's Rocket(IRE) held a good position just in behind the leaders for much of the way, but he lacked a change of pace. Official explanation: jockey said colt jumped awkwardly leaving stalls (op 11-1)

Redsensor was 3lb wrong under the penalty he picked up for his recent success in a 7f claimer round here and he was found out by both the better company and the step up in trip. (op 6-1)

Landikhaya(IRE) needs further and a more galloping track.

6900 CDL LIGHTING MAINTENANCE H'CAP — 7f (P)

2:30 (2:32) (Class 4) (0-85,85) 3-Y-O+ — £4,728 (£1,406; £702; £351) Stalls Low

Form				RPR
1034	1		**Golden Desert (IRE)**[38] 6209 3-9-3 84 ... JohnEgan 9 (T G Mills) *t.k.h: led for 1f: stdd and hld up in tch after: hdwy and n.m.r 1f out: sn swtchd lft: r.o wl ins fnl f to ld towards fin* **7/1**[3]	93+
1430	2	nk	**Danetime Lord (IRE)**[215] 1133 4-8-9 75 ... FrancisNorton 4 (K A Ryan) *chsd ldrs: rdn and ev ch wl over 1f out: led jst over 1f out: hdd and no ex towards fin* **11/1**	81
5046	3	¾	**Wavertree Warrior (IRE)**[17] 6669 5-9-4 84 ... (b) SteveDrowne 11 (N P Littmoden) *lw: chsd ldr: rdn jst over 2f out: ev ch over 1f out: unable qck wl ins fnl f* **6/1**[2]	88
343	4	nk	**Summer Dancer (IRE)**[18] 6651 3-8-11 78 ... TQuinn 2 (D R C Elsworth) *plld hrd: hld up in rr: edgd to outer bnd jst over 2f out: r.o u.p fnl f: nt rch ldrs* **9/2**[1]	81+
0060	5	hd	**Desert Dreamer (IRE)**[31] 6355 6-8-10 76 ... NickyMackay 5 (G A Butler) *hld up wl in tch in midfield: rdn and effrt 2f out: chsd ldrs 1f out: kpt on same pce ins fnl f* **10/1**	79
0223	6	shd	**Tender The Great (IRE)**[20] 6606 4-9-5 85 ... RichardKingscote 12 (B G Powell) *dropped in bhd after s: rdn and hdwy on inner over 1f out: r.o but nt rch ldrs* **6/1**[2]	87+
0005	7	¾	**Sand Cat**[21] 6589 4-8-13 79 ... FergusSweeney 10 (G L Moore) *t.k.h: hld up wl in tch in midfield: hdwy over 2f out: rdn 2f out: kpt on same pce fnl f* **25/1**	79
5000	8	shd	**China Cherub**[40] 6142 4-9-2 82 ... (b) RichardHughes 6 (R Hannon) *in tch in midfield: rdn jst over 2f out: hdwy u.p over 1f out: no imp last 100yds* **14/1**	82
0132	9	shd	**Minaash (USA)**[37] 6232 3-8-9 76 ... MartinDwyer 13 (D M Simcock) *lw: t.k.h: chsd ldrs: rdn jst over 2f out: btn whn short of room jst ins fnl f* **8/1**	76
0320	10	½	**Forest Dane**[20] 6606 7-8-10 83 ... MCGeran(7) 7 (Mrs N Smith) *s.i.s: hld up in rr: rdn and effrt wl over 1f out: nvr trbld ldrs* **16/1**	81
4000	11	½	**Princess Valerina**[25] 6497 3-8-11 78 ... DaneO'Neill 3 (B W Hills) *s.i.s: sn rcvrd and led after 1f: rdn 2f out: hdd jst over 1f out: wknd ins fnl f* **16/1**	75
2330	12	1	**Fabuleux Millie (IRE)**[96] 4574 3-8-11 78 ... AdamKirby 8 (R M Beckett) *w.w towards rr: hdwy over 2f out: rdn 2f out: sn struggling* **18/1**	72
010-	13	½	**Steely Dan**[604] 763 8-9-0 80 ... LPKeniry 14 (Mrs L C Jewell) *bit bkwd: t.k.h: dropped in bhd after s: nvr trbld ldrs* **33/1**	73
0004	14	¾	**Happy As Larry (USA)**[31] 6359 5-8-13 79 ... (t) MickyFenton 1 (D J Murphy) *lw: s.i.s: a bhd* **14/1**	70

1m 24.04s (-1.85) **Going Correction** -0.125s/f (Stan)

WFA 3 from 4yo+ 1lb — 14 Ran SP% **124.9**

Speed ratings (Par 105): **105,104,103,103,103 103,102,102,102,101 100,99,99,98**

CSF £85.23 CT £514.58 TOTE £6.20: £1.80, £4.80, £2.70; EX 84.60 TRIFECTA Not won..

Owner S Parker **Bred** Mervyn Stewkesbury **Trained** Headley, Surrey

■ Stewards' Enquiry : Francis Norton caution: careless riding

FOCUS

A good, competitive handicap, but they went no great pace. The winner is generally progressive on sand and the fifth looks the best guide to this form.

Summer Dancer(IRE) Official explanation: jockey said gelding ran too free

6901 PONTINS.COM MAIDEN STKS — 1m 2f (P)

3:00 (3:01) (Class 5) 3-Y-O+ — £2,817 (£838; £418; £209) Stalls Low

Form				RPR
3442	1		**Alpes Maritimes**[23] 6546 3-9-3 75 ... FergusSweeney 6 (G L Moore) *lw: hld up in last: hdwy over 2f out: rdn wl over 1f out: edgd rt ins fnl f: styd on to ld last 50yds* **1/1**[1]	75
232	2	2	**Demisemiquaver**[11] 6766 3-8-12 70 ... (v) JohnEgan 7 (J Noseda) *led: sn clr: rdn jst over 2f out: jinked rt wl ins fnl f: sn hdd and btn* **13/8**[2]	66
0-0	3	hd	**Montrose Man**[21] 6597 3-9-3 0 ... RobertHavlin 4 (B J Meehan) *chsd ldrs: wnt 2nd and rdn over 2f out: kpt on u.p* **25/1**	71
2030	4	6	**Mini Mosa**[19] 6623 3-8-12 68 ... JimmyFortune 3 (J H M Gosden) *chsd ldr tl over 2f out: sn rdn: wknd wl over 1f out* **13/2**[3]	54
	5	6	**Stratn Jack**[14] 3-9-3 0 ... TQuinn 2 (B G Powell) *w'like: leggy: plld hrd: hld up towards rr: rdn and wknd over 2f out* **25/1**	47
0	6	6	**Tarte Tatin (IRE)**[11] 6766 3-8-12 0 ... DaneO'Neill 8 (J L Dunlop) *leggy: s.i.s: sn in tch in midfield: rdn and wknd wl over 2f out* **33/1**	30
050-	7	1 ¼	**Dories Dream**[443] 5052 3-8-12 43 ... LPKeniry 1 (Jane Southcombe) *bit bkwd: chsd ldrs: rdn and lost pl over 3f out: wl bhd last 2f* **66/1**	27

2m 6.40s (-1.39) **Going Correction** -0.125s/f (Stan)

WFA 3 from 6yo 4lb — 7 Ran SP% **113.6**

Speed ratings (Par 103): **100,98,98,93,88 83,82**

CSF £2.74 TOTE £1.90: £2.20, £1.10; EX 3.50 Trifecta £27.20 Pool: £544.23 - 14.16 winning tickets..

Owner R A Green **Bred** J L C Pearce **Trained** Woodingdean, E Sussex

FOCUS

A weak, uncompetitive maiden run in a slow time. The winner was the clear form pick.

6902 PONTINSBINGO.COM AMATEUR RIDERS' H'CAP — 1m 4f (P)

3:30 (3:30) (Class 5) (0-70,70) 3-Y-O+ — £2,717 (£842; £421; £210) Stalls Low

Form				RPR
0450	1		**Blue Hedges**[44] 6068 5-10-7 56 oh5 ... MrSWalker 6 (H J Collingridge) *hld up wl in tch in midfield: gd hdwy on outer 3f out: led over 2f out: sn rdn clr: styd on wl* **14/1**	64

1326 **2** *3* **Apache Fort**[39] 6186 4-11-0 **66** MrSPearce(3) 1 69
(T Keddy) *in tch: rdn and hdwy jst over 2f out: chsd wnr ins fnl f: kpt on but nvr threatened wnr* **7/4**[1]

1302 **3** *1* **Raquel White**[9] 6803 3-9-12 **60** MrRPFlint(7) 10 62
(J L Flint) *lw: t.k.h: chsd ldr: rdn and chsd wnr over 2f out: no imp: lost 2nd ins fnl f* **15/2**[3]

5363 **4** *1 1/4* **Blu Manruna**[4] 6848 4-10-0 **56** (b) MrAdamWest(7) 8 56
(J Akehurst) *led tl 8f out: led again over 3f out: hdd over 2f out: sn rdn: kpt on same pce* **6/1**[2]

0250 **5** *nk* **Calculating (IRE)**[31] 5870 3-10-11 **66** MrLeeNewnes 4 67+
(M D I Usher) *in tch: short of room and lost pl over 2f out: swtchd rt over 1f out: kpt on u.p fnl f* **10/1**

4365 **6** *nk* **Cavendish**[30] 6387 3-9-11 **59** (b) MrDJEustace(7) 3 58
(J M P Eustace) *in tch on inner: rdn over 1f out: kpt on same pce* **11/1**

0005 **7** *3/4* **Royal Sailor (IRE)**[9] 6798 5-10-0 **56** oh11 MrDavidMcMinn(7) 5 53
(J Ryan) *s.i.s: hld up in rr: rdn and effrt wl over 1f out: kpt on but nvr trbld ldrs* **66/1**

163 **8** *nk* **Wait For The Will (USA)**[17] 6666 11-11-1 **69** (b) MissHayleyMoore(5) 9 66
(G L Moore) *in tch on outer: rdn over 1f out: sn outpcd* **8/1**

5015 **9** *2* **Atlantic Gamble (IRE)**[35] 6261 7-10-8 **62** (p) MissKellyBurke(5) 2 56
(K R Burke) *trckd ldrs on inner: rdn and btn over 1f out* **11/1**

5006 **10** *16* **Lady's Law**[9] 6797 4-10-0 **56** oh11 MissEmma-JaneJenkins(7) 11 24
(Rae Guest) *chsd ldrs tl led 8f out: hdd over 3f out: wkng whn short of room and lost pl over 2f out: no ch after* **66/1**

1260 **11** *1 1/4* **Salut Saint Cloud**[188] 1793 6-11-2 **68** DanielHutchison(3) 12 34
(G L Moore) *hld up in rr: lost tch over 3f out* **8/1**

5/0 **P** **Very Green (FR)**[109] 4188 5-10-8 **64** MrOJMurphy(7) 7 —
(Mrs A L M King) *stdd after s: t.k.h: hld up in rr: rdn and lost tch qckly over 4f out: t.o and p.u 2f out* **33/1**

2m 33.25s (-1.14) **Going Correction** -0.125s/f (Stan)
WFA 3 from 4yo+ 6lb 12 Ran SP% **123.0**
Speed ratings (Par 103): **98,96,95,94,94 94,93,93,92,81 80,—**
CSF £40.00 CT £213.86 TOTE £13.80: £6.20, £1.50, £2.60; EX 51.80 TRIFECTA Not won. Place 6 £41.81, Place 5 £29.58.
Owner N H Gardner **Bred** S C E A Des Bissons **Trained** Exning, Suffolk
■ Stewards' Enquiry : Mr O J Murphy two-day ban: used whip when out of contention (Dec 4-5)

FOCUS
A moderate amateur riders' handicap run at an ordinary pace. The presence of the seventh casts doubts over the form, and the winner himself was 5lb wrong although well treated on his form last year.
Very Green(FR) Official explanation: jockey said gelding had bled from the nose
T/Plt: £61.80 to a £1 stake. Pool: £55,506.20. 655.55 winning tickets. T/Qpdt: £13.50 to a £1 stake. Pool: £3,527.50. 192.30 winning tickets. SP

6880 WOLVERHAMPTON (A.W) (L-H)
Thursday, November 22

OFFICIAL GOING: Standard
Wind: Fresh across Weather: Cloudy

6903 PONTIN'S HOLIDAYS MEDIAN AUCTION MAIDEN STKS 7f 32y(P)
6:50 (6:50) (Class 6) 2-Y-O **£2,047** (£604; £302) **Stalls High**

Form RPR

1 **Desert Clover (USA)** 2-9-3 0 TQuinn 5 72+
(P F I Cole) *mde all: edgd rt fnl f: drvn out* **5/4**[1]

00 **2** *1 1/2* **Molly Ann (IRE)**[15] 6724 2-8-12 0 JohnEgan 1 63
(T D Easterby) *a.p: chsd wnr over 2f out: rdn over 1f out: no ex towards fin* **20/1**

3 *3 1/2* **Prince Hamlet (IRE)** 2-9-3 0 SteveDrowne 3 59
(B Smart) *chsd ldrs: pushed along 1/2-way: hung lft and styd on same pce fnl 2f* **7/1**

00 **4** *5* **Karmei**[69] 5380 2-9-3 0 J-PGuillambert 2 47
(J W Hills) *prom: lost pl 6f out: rdn over 2f out: sn wknd* **6/1**

5 *1 3/4* **Eloquent Isle (IRE)** 2-8-9 0 AndrewMullen(3) 7 38
(Mrs A Duffield) *hld up: hdwy 1/2-way: rdn and wknd 2f out* **16/1**

5 **6** *2* **Istria (USA)**[18] 6664 2-8-12 0 AdamKirby 8 33
(R M Beckett) *dwlt: in rr: effrt over 2f out: sn wknd* **3/1**[2]

560 **7** *1* **Keep Your Head (USA)**[51] 5882 2-8-12 65 TPQueally 9 31
(J A Osborne) *chsd wnr 6f out tl rdn over 2f out: sn wknd* **11/2**[3]

1m 31.0s (0.60) **Going Correction** -0.10s/f (Stan) 7 Ran SP% **122.3**
Speed ratings (Par 94): **92,90,86,80,78 76,75**
CSF £32.86 TOTE £2.30: £1.10, £7.20; EX 43.70.
Owner Frank Stella **Bred** Delehanty Stock Farm Inc **Trained** Whatcombe, Oxon

FOCUS
A modest juvenile maiden and the form is somewhat guessy.

NOTEBOOK
Desert Clover(USA), a son of Mutakddim, half-brother to multiple US turf winner Waltzing Camel, and 1m US winner Outback, out of a very useful juvenile scorer on the turf in the US, justified strong market support on his racecourse debut. His trainer said beforehand he would have been disappointed had he been beaten and his confidence proved spot on, as the colt was always going well in front having broken best of all. He had a persistent challenger in the form of Molly Ann for much of the way up the straight, but he was always keeping that rival at bay. The bare form is pretty modest, but he should not get too harsh a handicap mark as a result and he could win again this winter. (op 13-8 tchd 7-4)
Molly Ann(IRE) found this easier than the two 1m turf maidens she had contested and this was a good effort in second. Well clear of the remainder, she might be able to find a similarly weak race and will also now have the option of going handicapping.
Prince Hamlet(IRE), by Fantastic Light, first foal of a mare who was placed in US sprints at two, showed just moderate form on his racecourse debut but is open to improvement. (op 11-2)
Karmei, returning from over two months off, failed to build on the form he showed in a couple of sprint maidens and was disappointing. (op 5-1)
Eloquent Isle(IRE), a 16,000gns daughter of Mull Of Kintyre, half-sister to multiple 1m-1m4f Mersyka and triple 1m2f scorer Moonlight Fantasy, was well held on her racecourse bow.
Istria(USA) showed ability on her debut at Lingfield, but she was always struggling after starting very slowly this time. Official explanation: jockey said filly was never travelling; vet said filly was stiff in the back (tchd 7-2)

6904 PONTIN'S GREAT FAMILY HOLIDAYS MEDIAN AUCTION MAIDEN STKS 1m 141y(P)
7:20 (7:20) (Class 6) 3-5-Y-O **£2,047** (£604; £302) **Stalls Low**

Form RPR

202 **1** **Distant Drama (USA)**[16] 6704 3-8-12 62 (p) TPQueally 10 57
(J Noseda) *hld up: rdn over 3f out: hdwy over 2f out: led ins fnl f: drvn out* **11/4**[2]

0050 **2** *1* **Johnston's Glory (IRE)**[27] 6464 3-8-12 45 MickyFenton 8 55
(E J Alston) *hld up: nt clr run over 2f out: hdwy over 1f out: sn rdn: r.o* **16/1**

0024 **3** *2* **Alexander Guru**[17] 6695 3-9-3 67 FrancisNorton 6 55
(M Blanshard) *chsd ldrs: led over 3f out: rdn and edgd rt over 1f out: rdr dropped whip sn after: hdd and no ex ins fnl f* **15/8**[1]

550 **4** *2* **Botham (USA)**[34] 6315 3-9-3 48 (b) SteveDrowne 3 51
(D J Murphy) *chsd ldrs: rdn over 2f out: styd on same pce appr fnl f* **13/2**

55 **5** *1* **Idun**[39] 6211 3-8-12 0 AdrianMcCarthy 7 44
(P W Chapple-Hyam) *chsd ldrs: rdn and ev ch over 1f out: wknd ins fnl f* **8/1**

0-40 **6** *1 1/2* **Santera (IRE)**[153] 2840 3-8-9 34 AndrewMullen(3) 9 40
(Mrs A Duffield) *prom: rdn over 3f out: wknd over 1f out* **66/1**

4 **7** *5* **Cyril The Squirrel**[18] 6670 3-9-3 0 ChrisCatlin 5 34
(Karen George) *s.i.s: rdn over 3f out: n.d* **16/1**

466 **8** *1 1/2* **Imperial Amber**[18] 6670 5-8-12 58 JerryO'Dwyer(3) 11 25
(Karen George) *s.s: a in rr* **16/1**

00 **9** *3/4* **Josama**[34] 6309 3-8-12 0 PhillipMakin 1 23
(R Bastiman) *prom: rdn 1/2-way: wknd over 2f out* **66/1**

40-0 **10** *shd* **Genoa Star**[15] 5750 4-9-1 41 (be) FergusSweeney 2 23
(D J Murphy) *hld up in tch: rdn 1/2-way: wknd over 2f out* **66/1**

0455 **11** *5* **Semi Detached (IRE)**[28] 6457 4-9-6 59 AdamKirby 4 30
(J W Unett) *led: hdd over 3f out: rdn and wknd 2f out* **11/2**[3]

1m 51.3s (-0.46) **Going Correction** -0.10s/f (Stan)
WFA 3 from 4yo+ 3lb 11 Ran SP% **123.4**
Speed ratings (Par 101): **98,97,95,93,92 91,86,85,84,84 80**
CSF £49.00 TOTE £4.70: £1.10, £5.90, £1.10; EX 85.80.
Owner Ballylinch Stud **Bred** Jim Ryan And Geraldine Ryan **Trained** Newmarket, Suffolk

FOCUS
A moderate maiden and not form to dwell on.
Alexander Guru Official explanation: trainer said jockey dropped his whip 1 1/2f out
Semi Detached(IRE) Official explanation: trainer said gelding was found to have mucus in its throat

6905 GO PONTIN'S H'CAP 5f 20y(P)
7:50 (7:50) (Class 5) (0-75,71) 3-Y-O **£2,817** (£838; £418; £209) **Stalls Low**

Form RPR

4000 **1** **Back In The Red (IRE)**[6] 6829 3-9-3 **70** JohnEgan 9 77
(R A Harris) *chsd ldrs: rdn over 3f out: edgd lft and r.o to ld nr fin* **12/1**

5030 **2** *3/4* **Diminuto**[12] 6762 3-8-10 **70** FrankiePickard(7) 5 74
(M D I Usher) *chsd ldrs: rdn over 1f out: led wl ins fnl f: hdd nr fin* **7/1**

1132 **3** *nk* **Lord Of The Reins (IRE)**[8] 6810 3-8-12 **65** DaneO'Neill 10 68+
(D Shaw) *sn pushed along in rr: hdwy over 1f out: swtchd rt ins fnl f: r.o* **3/1**[2]

020 **4** *hd* **Valley Of The Moon (IRE)**[13] 6743 3-9-4 **71** DaleGibson 6 73
(R A Fahey) *chsd ldrs: rdn 1/2-way: r.o* **5/1**[3]

6533 **5** *3/4* **Rebel Duke (IRE)**[14] 6730 3-9-3 **70** PhillipMakin 7 70
(D W Barker) *chsd ldr: rdn over 1f out: styd on same pce ins fnl f* **11/4**[1]

3450 **6** *nk* **Baileys Outshine**[13] 6743 3-9-3 **70** TPQueally 1 68
(J G Given) *led: rdn over 1f out: hdd and no ex ins fnl f* **13/2**

222- **7** *2 1/2* **Wibbadune (IRE)**[328] 6975 3-8-6 **59** LPKeniry 3 48
(Peter Grayson) *chsd ldrs: rdn 1/2-way: wknd ins fnl f* **16/1**

0006 **8** *2 1/2* **Black Moma (IRE)**[30] 6405 3-9-3 **70** SteveDrowne 8 50
(A B Haynes) *hld up: rdn 1/2-way: n.d* **8/1**

0600 **9** *9* **Saint Remus (IRE)**[38] 6240 3-8-4 **57** oh12 (b) AdrianMcCarthy 4 5
(Peter Grayson) *sn outpcd* **66/1**

06-0 **10** *11* **Ava's World (IRE)**[148] 2988 3-8-9 **69** RyanHill(7) 2 —
(Peter Grayson) *s.i.s: outpcd* **28/1**

62.32 secs (-0.50) **Going Correction** -0.10s/f (Stan) 10 Ran SP% **123.8**
Speed ratings (Par 102): **100,98,98,98,96 96,92,88,73,56**
CSF £99.12 CT £333.39 TOTE £18.90: £4.70, £2.30, £1.10; EX 155.90.
Owner Mrs Ruth M Serrell **Bred** Mrs Rachanee Butler **Trained** Earlswood, Monmouths

FOCUS
A modest sprint handicap but the form looks sound enough rated through the runner-up.
Lord Of The Reins(IRE) ◆ Official explanation: jockey said gelding hung right
Saint Remus(IRE) Official explanation: jockey said gelding hung right

6906 GO PONTIN'S HOLIDAYS H'CAP 1m 1f 103y(P)
8:20 (8:20) (Class 6) (0-55,60) 3-Y-O+ **£2,047** (£604; £302) **Stalls Low**

Form RPR

11 **1** **Confidentiality (IRE)**[1] 6894 3-8-13 **54** 6ex NickyMackay 10 74+
(M Wigham) *hld up: hdwy over 3f out: led over 1f out: edgd lft: rdn out* **5/4**[1]

5532 **2** *2* **Rigat**[14] 6728 4-9-1 **53** PhillipMakin 5 62
(T D Barron) *dwlt: hld up: hdwy over 1f out: sn rdn: edgd lft and r.o: nt rch wnr* **11/2**[3]

-042 **3** *1 3/4* **Arthur's Edge**[15] 6713 3-8-12 **53** FergusSweeney 13 59
(B Palling) *sn led: rdn and hdd over 1f out: styd on same pce* **13/2**

6021 **4** *3/4* **Waterloo Corner**[10] 6801 5-9-1 **60** 6ex LanceBetts(7) 11 64
(R Craggs) *chsd ldrs: rdn over 1f out: styd on same pce* **16/1**

5000 **5** *1* **Morbick**[122] 3783 3-8-13 **54** TGMcLaughlin 3 56
(W M Brisbourne) *mid-div: hdwy over 3f out: sn rdn: nt clr run over 1f out: no ex* **25/1**

5413 **6** *1* **Reveur**[20] 6629 4-9-0 **52** GeorgeBaker 2 52
(M Mullineaux) *hld up: hdwy over 2f out: rdn over 1f out: no ex* **16/1**

2030 **7** *2 1/2* **Saucy**[19] 6662 6-8-11 **49** JohnEgan 7 44
(Daniel Mark Loughnane, Ire) *chsd ldrs: rdn and ev ch fr over 2f out: edgd rt over 1f out: sn wknd* **9/2**[2]

2463 **8** *5* **Bobering**[10] 6801 7-8-10 **48** DeanMcKeown 1 32
(B P J Baugh) *hld up: effrt over 2f out: wknd over 1f out* **14/1**

5260 **9** *2* **Keon (IRE)**[220] 1066 5-8-10 **53** RussellKennemore(5) 8 33
(R Hollinshead) *hld up: plld hrd: rdn over 3f out: n.d* **33/1**

2620 **10** *5* **Buscador (USA)**[185] 1907 8-8-11 **54** AshleyHamblett(5) 12 23
(W M Brisbourne) *chsd ldr: rdn over 3f out: wknd over 2f out* **20/1**

4533 **11** *1 1/2* **Zabeel Tower**[27] 6479 4-8-9 **50** AndrewElliott(3) 6 16
(R Allan) *hld up: rdn over 3f out: sn wknd* **14/1**

6300 **12** *4* **Miss Sure Bond (IRE)**[23] 6558 4-8-10 **48** (v[1]) ChrisCatlin 9 6
(G R Oldroyd) *s.i.s: hdwy over 6f out: rdn over 3f out: sn wknd* **25/1**

2m 0.34s (-2.28) **Going Correction** -0.10s/f (Stan)
WFA 3 from 4yo+ 3lb 12 Ran SP% **131.8**
Speed ratings (Par 101): **106,104,102,102,101 100,98,93,91,87 86,82**
CSF £9.07 CT £39.71 TOTE £2.00: £1.40, £2.60, £2.00; EX 14.80.
Owner J M Cullinan **Bred** Kevin Foley **Trained** Newmarket, Suffolk

FOCUS
This was a modest handicap on paper, but they went a very decent pace and the time was good so this is very solid form for the grade.
Saucy Official explanation: trainer said mare lost her action

The Form Book, Raceform Ltd, Compton, RG20 6NL

Keon(IRE) Official explanation: jockey said gelding had no more to give

6907 BOOK A CHRISTMAS BREAK AT PONTIN'S H'CAP 5f 216y(P)
8:50 (8:52) (Class 4) (0-80,82) 3-Y-O+ £4,728 (£1,054; £1,054; £351) Stalls Low

Form RPR

115 **1** **Carcinetto (IRE)**[18] 6667 5-9-0 76 TGMcLaughlin 10 85
(P D Evans) *a.p: chsd ldr over 4f out: rdn to ld over 1f out: hung rt ins fnl f: r.o* 5/1[3]

0055 **2** 1 3/4 **Coleorton Dancer**[23] 6560 5-9-1 77 JohnEgan 2 81
(K A Ryan) *a.p: rdn over 1f out: nt clr run and swtchd lft ins fnl f: styd on* 2/1[1]

1104 **2** dht **Cornus**[6] 6836 5-9-4 80 (be) AdamKirby 4 84+
(A J McCabe) *chsd ldrs: rdn over 1f out: styd on* 13/2

000 **4** 3 **Eloquent Rose (IRE)**[188] 1820 3-8-5 70 AndrewMullen(3) 3 64
(Mrs A Duffield) *s.i.s: hld up: rdn over 2f out: hdwy over 1f out: nt rch ldrs* 25/1

5001 **5** nk **Whitbarrow (IRE)**[35] 6288 8-9-1 82 ow2 (b) JamesMillman(5) 8 75
(B R Millman) *led: rdn and hdd over 1f out: wknd ins fnl f* 4/1[2]

5000 **6** 1 3/4 **Sea Salt**[19] 6639 4-8-8 70 DaleGibson 7 57
(R A Fahey) *hld up in tch: rdn over 2f out: wknd over 1f out* 8/1

0600 **7** 3/4 **Cool Sands (IRE)**[136] 3388 5-8-8 70 (v) DeanMcKeown 1 55
(D Shaw) *sn outpcd: nvr nrr* 16/1

1300 **8** 2 1/2 **Sir Douglas**[211] 1252 4-8-10 72 (p) LPKeniry 9 49
(R A Harris) *prom: rdn over 2f out: sn wknd* 8/1

/00- **9** 1 1/2 **Oversighted (GER)**[412] 5796 6-8-10 72 MickyFenton 5 44
(Mrs Y Dunleavy, Ire) *chsd ldrs: rdn over 2f out: wknd over 1f out* 25/1

4065 **10** 6 **Josh**[131] 3549 5-8-11 73 ChrisCatlin 6 26
(K A Ryan) *s.i.s: outpcd* 7/1

1m 13.85s (-1.96) **Going Correction** -0.10s/f (Stan) 10 Ran SP% 131.6
Speed ratings (Par 105): **109,106,106,102,102 99,98,95,93,85**
TOTE £5.10: £2.70 TRIFECTA 2nd pl C 2.50, CD 2.00; Ex C-C 18.00, C-CD 11.60; CSF C-C 21.45, C-CD 8.80; T/C C-C-CD 45.58, C-CD-C 36.26.
Owner Mrs Sally Edwards **Bred** M A Doyle **Trained** Pandy, Monmouths

FOCUS
A very decent sprint handicap in which Whitbarrow made sure there was no hanging about and the winning time was good. The form looks very solid for the grade.

6908 WOLVERHAMPTON-RACECOURSE.CO.UK CLASSIFIED STKS 7f 32y(P)
9:20 (9:21) (Class 7) 3-Y-O+ £1,619 (£481; £240; £120) Stalls High

Form RPR

0500 **1** **Dancing Deano (IRE)**[174] 2220 5-8-9 45 (v) RussellKennemore(5) 3 52
(R Hollinshead) *prom: chsd ldr over 5f out: rdn to ld and hung rt fr over 1f out: all out* 8/1

1402 **2** nk **Sion Hill (IRE)**[11] 6609 6-9-0 45 (p) TPQueally 8 51
(John A Harris) *sn led: rdn and hdd over 1f out: hung rt: styd on u.p* 4/1[2]

0602 **3** 1/2 **Only A Grand**[24] 6537 3-8-13 45 (b) PhillipMakin 4 50
(R Bastiman) *chsd ldrs: rdn over 2f out: styd on* 7/1[3]

4040 **4** 1 **Stagnite**[16] 6706 7-8-11 45 JerryO'Dwyer(3) 1 47+
(Karen George) *hld up: hdwy u.p and edgd rt over 1f out: nt rch ldrs* 11/1

0006 **5** hd **Almora Guru**[14] 6735 3-8-13 45 LiamJones 9 47
(W M Brisbourne) *sn pushed along in rr: swtchd lft and hdwy over 1f out: nt rch ldrs* 8/1

0400 **6** 1/2 **Tipsy Lad**[10] 6796 5-9-0 45 (bt) FergusSweeney 11 45
(D J S Ffrench Davis) *hld up: hdwy u.p over 2f out: edgd rt: styd on* 15/2

3005 **7** 1 **Fistral**[24] 6537 3-8-13 45 DaleGibson 12 43
(Ollie Pears) *hld up: rdn over 1f out: r.o ins fnl f: nt rch ldrs* 14/1

3600 **8** 1 **Tokyo Jo (IRE)**[16] 6706 3-8-13 45 (v) TGMcLaughlin 2 43
(T T Clement) *chsd ldrs: rdn 1/2-way: eased whn btn ins fnl f* 8/1

4063 **9** 1 3/4 **Kathleen Kennet**[24] 6532 7-9-0 45 ChrisCatlin 5 35
(C Tinkler) *sn pushed along in rr: rdn over 2f out: n.d* 7/2[1]

2050 **10** 3 **Beat The Bully**[110] 4165 3-8-13 45 VinceSlattery 6 27
(D J Wintle) *chsd ldrs: rdn 1/2-way: wknd over 1f out* 7/1[3]

0454 **11** nk **Following Flow (USA)**[51] 5083 5-8-9 45 KellyHarrison(5) 7 26
(R Allan) *s.i.s: outpcd* 16/1

1m 30.42s (0.02) **Going Correction** -0.10s/f (Stan)
WFA 3 from 4yo+ 1lb 11 Ran SP% 133.2
Speed ratings (Par 97): **95,94,94,92,92 92,91,89,87,84 84**
CSF £45.65 TOTE £13.10: £4.30, £1.70, £2.50; EX 79.70.
Owner Ron Wood **Bred** Mrs Olivia Farrell **Trained** Upper Longdon, Staffs
■ Stewards' Enquiry : Russell Kennemore three-day ban: used whip with arm above shoulder height (Dec 3-5)

FOCUS
A race that before this year would have been known as a banded contest, but whatever you call it this was dire and the fact that the field finished in a heap says a lot about the ability of these horses. The principals were always up with the pace and when they hung right over towards the stands' rail in the straight, the herd instinct of those behind saw them follow suit. The placed horses set the level.

T/Plt: £21.00 to a £1 stake. Pool: £90,875.25. 3,147.50 winning tickets. T/Qpdt: £9.10 to a £1 stake. Pool: £6,240.30. 502.50 winning tickets. CR

6903 WOLVERHAMPTON (A.W) (L-H)
Friday, November 23

OFFICIAL GOING: Standard (meeting abandoned after race 3 (7.55) due to the course being unsafe)
Wind: Almost nil

6910 MACE RACING AT WOLVERHAMPTON APPRENTICE H'CAP 5f 216y(P)
7:00 (7:00) (Class 6) (0-58,67) 3-Y-O+ £2,047 (£604; £302) Stalls Low

Form RPR

1130 **1** **Memphis Man**[20] 6639 4-8-7 62 RichardEvans(5) 2 73
(P D Evans) *slowly away: hdwy on outside over 2f out: rdn and edgd rt bef led ins fnl f: kpt up to work* 5/1[3]

536 **2** 2 **Royal Challenge**[9] 6818 6-9-3 67 LanceBetts 5 72
(I W McInnes) *trckd ldr: led 2f out: rdn and hdd ins fnl f: one pce* 6/1

0003 **3** 1 1/4 **Strathmore (IRE)**[19] 6671 3-8-11 64 JamesRogers(3) 10 65
(R A Fahey) *towards rr: effrt on outside over 2f out: rdn and edgd lft bef r.o ins fnl f* 17/2

6422 **4** shd **Chatshow (USA)**[9] 6818 6-8-12 62 (v[1]) MarkCoumbe 7 63
(A W Carroll) *mid-div: hdwy on outside over 3f out: kpt on fnl f* 11/4[1]

1055 **5** 3/4 **Desert Light (IRE)**[4] 6870 6-8-9 59 PatrickDonaghy 3 57
(D Shaw) *mid-div: rdn over 2f out: hung lft and one pce fnl f* 4/1[2]

0000 **6** 3 **Diamond Josh**[17] 6702 5-8-0 55 oh10 RossAtkinson(5) 4 44
(M Mullineaux) *in tch: rdn over 2f out: wknd over 1f out* 100/1

6000 **7** 1 1/4 **High Reach**[24] 6562 7-8-7 57 DeanHeslop 9 42
(T D Barron) *led tl hdd 2f out: wknd over 1f out* 9/1

3500 **8** nk **Fish Called Johnny**[18] 6695 3-8-6 63 RyanHill(7) 1 47
(Peter Grayson) *a bhd and nvr on terms* 25/1

0031 **9** 1 **Registrar**[16] 6720 5-8-1 56 AshleyMorgan(5) 6 37
(Mrs C A Dunnett) *t.k.h: a in rr* 8/1

0600 **10** 5 **Noddledoddle (IRE)**[15] 6730 3-8-5 55 oh10 (tp) FrankiePickard 8 20
(J Ryan) *prom: rdn 1/2-way: sn wknd* 100/1

1m 15.42s (-0.39) **Going Correction** -0.025s/f (Stan) 10 Ran SP% 115.1
Speed ratings (Par 101): **101,98,96,96,95 91,89,89,88,81**
CSF £34.31 CT £253.94 TOTE £4.20: £2.70, £2.20, £2.50; EX 27.10.
Owner M D Jones **Bred** R T And Mrs Watson **Trained** Pandy, Monmouths
■ The first winner since turning professional for Richard Evans, son of the winning trainer.
■ Stewards' Enquiry : Mark Coumbe seven-day ban: used whip with excessive frequency and without giving gelding time to respond (Dec 4-10)

FOCUS
A modest handicap for inexperienced apprentices with the form rated through the runner-up to his latest mark but limited by the proximity of the sixth.

6911 PONTIN'S BOOK EARLY H'CAP 1m 5f 194y(P)
7:30 (7:31) (Class 6) (0-60,60) 3-Y-O+ £2,047 (£604; £302) Stalls Low

Form RPR

4003 **1** **Blue Hills**[11] 6797 6-9-8 57 (b) PhillipMakin 10 64
(P W Hiatt) *led after 1f: mde rest: rdn 2f out: styd on fnl f* 9/1

0641 **2** 1 1/2 **Young Scotton**[7] 6835 7-9-1 53 6ex AndrewElliott(3) 3 59+
(J D Bethell) *a in tch: rdn to chse wnr fnl f* 6/4[1]

2134 **3** 3/4 **Bond Casino**[19] 6673 3-9-2 59 ChrisCatlin 5 63
(G R Oldroyd) *led for 1f: trckd wnr tl rdn and one pce fnl f* 15/2[2]

6200 **4** 2 1/2 **Prince Of Medina**[7] 6832 4-9-1 50 DaneO'Neill 13 50
(J R Best) *mid-div: rdn over 3f out: styd on ins fnl 2f: nvr nr to chal* 11/1

4022 **5** 1/2 **Zalkani (IRE)**[11] 6798 7-9-10 59 DeanMcKeown 9 59
(J Pearce) *hld up: hdwy over 3f out: rdn over 2f out: one pce fr over 1f out* 8/1[3]

6 nk **Simple Jim (FR)**[32] 3-9-3 60 PaulMulrennan 6 59
(A D Brown) *mid-div: rdn over 3f out: hmpd over 2f out: one pce after* 16/1

0064 **7** 2 1/2 **Gracechurch (IRE)**[23] 6583 4-9-6 55 SteveDrowne 2 51
(R J Hodges) *in tch: rdn over 2f out: wknd over 1f out* 10/1

0003 **8** 1 1/4 **Covert Mission**[14] 6751 4-9-8 57 TGMcLaughlin 12 51
(P D Evans) *slowly away: a towards rr* 33/1

050 **9** shd **Hill Cloud**[86] 4948 5-9-3 52 LiamJones 8 46
(W M Brisbourne) *trckd ldrs: rdn 3f out: wknd 2f out* 66/1

5400 **10** 10 **Royal Premier (IRE)**[24] 6564 4-9-5 57 (v) JerryO'Dwyer(3) 4 37
(H J Collingridge) *mid-div: rdn over 4f out: sn btn* 14/1

5015 **11** 14 **Key Partners (IRE)**[16] 6719 6-9-9 58 GeorgeBaker 11 18
(P A Blockley) *hld up: rdn over 3f out: a bhd* 8/1[3]

/004 **P** **Leighton (IRE)**[11] 6803 7-9-5 54 (v) FergusSweeney 1 —
(M S Saunders) *hld up: bhd whn p.u over 2f out: dead* 25/1

3m 11.62s (4.25) **Going Correction** -0.025s/f (Stan)
WFA 3 from 4yo+ 8lb 12 Ran SP% 122.2
Speed ratings (Par 101): **86,85,84,83,83 82,81,80,80,74 66,—**
CSF £23.20 CT £115.27 TOTE £8.50: £2.00, £1.20, £3.40; EX 23.40.
Owner Tom Pratt **Bred** Darley **Trained** Hook Norton, Oxon

FOCUS
A moderate staying handicap run at a crawl for over a circuit and unsurprisingly those that raced prominently dominated the finish. The form is not the most solid despite the runner-up running to his latest mark.

Royal Premier(IRE) Official explanation: trainer said gelding coughed post-race
Key Partners(IRE) Official explanation: jockey said gelding ran too freely off a slow pace

6912 PONTIN'S BOOK EARLY AND SAVE MAIDEN AUCTION STKS 7f 32y(P)
7:55 (8:04) (Class 6) 2-Y-O £2,047 (£604; £302) Stalls High

Form RPR

3324 **1** **Elusive Lady (IRE)**[17] 6698 2-8-4 65 (p) ChrisCatlin 7 65
(J R Weymes) *trckd ldrs: wnt 2nd 3f out: rdn to ld over 1f out: sn clr* 10/3[3]

63 **2** 4 **Hellfire Bay**[25] 6540 2-8-13 0 JohnEgan 3 64
(K A Ryan) *towards rr: rdn and hdwy 3f out: styd on to go 2nd wl ins fnl f* 5/2[1]

033 **3** 1/2 **Express Princess (IRE)**[21] 6626 2-8-3 64 ow2 AshleyHamblett(5) 6 58
(M Botti) *trckd ldr: led 4f out: hdd over 1f out: sn btn and lost 2nd wl ins fnl f* 9/2

0 **4** 1 3/4 **Didana (IRE)**[25] 6535 2-8-7 0 ow1 J-PGuillambert 2 53
(M G Quinlan) *trckd ldrs: rdn 3f out: no hdwy ins fnl 2f* 11/4[2]

5 5 **Ros Cuire (IRE)**[33] 6362 2-8-9 0 SteveDrowne 8 42
(W A Murphy, Ire) *towards rr: edgd lft and one pce fr over 1f out* 50/1

6 8 **Fortunes Maid (IRE)** 2-8-0 0 ow1 AshleyMorgan(7) 4 21
(M H Tompkins) *sn outpcd: nvr on terms* 25/1

06 **7** nk **Sweet Andromeda**[17] 6698 2-8-4 0 LiamJones 5 17
(T J Fitzgerald) *mid-div: rdn 1/2-way: sn btn* 33/1

8 2 **Embra (IRE)** 2-8-13 0 NickyMackay 10 21
(T J Etherington) *mid-div: rdn 1/2-way: wknd over 2f out* 16/1

9 4 **Cool Fashion (IRE)** 2-8-4 0 DaleGibson 1 2
(Ollie Pears) *led for 3f: wknd 2f out* 33/1

10 1 3/4 **Crossing Bridges** 2-8-7 0 ow1 DeanMcKeown 9 1
(T D Barron) *v.s.a: outpcd thrght* 20/1

1m 30.8s (0.40) **Going Correction** -0.025s/f (Stan) 10 Ran SP% 118.8
Speed ratings (Par 94): **96,91,90,88,83 74,73,71,66,64**
CSF £11.65 TOTE £3.90: £1.40, £1.40, £1.70; EX 14.60 Place 6 £5.48, Place 5 £2.08.
Owner T A Scothern **Bred** Liam Queally **Trained** Middleham Moor, N Yorks

FOCUS
An ordinary auction maiden dominated by those with previous experience with the winner to her mark backed up by the third and solid form. The track had to be harrowed prior to this race due to falling temperatures, but despite that the kickback looked particularly heavy.

NOTEBOOK
Elusive Lady(IRE), who ran well when runner-up in a similar event on her All-Weather debut over course and distance last month, had cheekpieces on for the first time and that and the return to this surface enabled her to get off the mark at the tenth attempt. She came right away in the end and should be able to win a handicap if the assessor does not put her up too much . (op 5-2 tchd 9-4)
Hellfire Bay, who was heavily backed down to favourite on this All-Weather debut, struggled to go the early pace but ran on at the finish without making any impression on the winner from the home turn. He now qualifies for a handicap mark and should do better with experience of the surface under his belt. (op 6-1 tchd 7-1)
Express Princess(IRE), a diminutive filly who has done all her racing on Polytrack, was made plenty of use of on this drop in trip. She was unable to respond when tackled by the winner in the straight and may need to be dropped a few pounds to be competitive in handicaps. (tchd 4-1 and 5-1)

Didana(IRE), a half-sister to Babodana, showed up for much of the trip on this All-Weather debut and can do better in time and once handicapped. (op 3-1)
Ros Cuire(IRE), who finished last on his debut at the Curragh, missed the break before running on steadily, and although this was an improvement he was beaten a fair way. (op 33-1)
Embra(IRE), a brother to the stable's useful sprinter Fullandby, made headway to join the leaders at the end of the back straight before weakening and, like his sibling, is likely to be seen to better effect as he gets older. (op 12-1 tchd 20-1)
Cool Fashion(IRE), a half-sister to a 5f juvenile winner, showed good early pace before dropping right out but should come on for the outing. (op 40-1)

6913 GO PONTIN'S NOW MEDIAN AUCTION MAIDEN STKS 7f 32y(P)
() (Class 6) 3-5-Y-O £

6914 GO PONTIN'S SHORT BREAKS H'CAP 1m 141y(P)
() (Class 5) (0-75,) 3-Y-0+ £

6915 PONTINS.COM H'CAP 1m 1f 103y(P)
() (Class 4) (0-80,) 3-Y-0+ £

T/Plt: £4.20 to a £1 stake. Pool: £109,772.45. 18,858.55 winning tickets. T/Qpdt: £1.10 to a £1 stake. Pool: £6,572.40. 4,942.60 winning tickets. JS

6839 DUNDALK (A.W) (L-H)
Friday, November 23

OFFICIAL GOING: Standard

6916a LADBROKESPOKER.COM RACE 6f
6:45 (6:45) 3-Y-0+ £5,836 (£1,359; £599; £346)

RPR

1 **Blue Rocket (IRE)**13 6757 3-9-0 ....(b1) PJSmullen 3 69+
(D J Murphy) *chsd ldrs: 6th ent st: nt clr run under 2f out: sn swtchd to inner: r.o wl to ld fnl 100yds* **7/2**2

2 ¾ **Herotozero (IRE)**35 6317 3-8-8 77....(b) SFoley(7) 1 68+
(Gerard O'Leary, Ire) *chsd ldrs: chal 2f out: led 1 1/2f out: rdn and hdd fnl 100yds: no ex* **12/1**

3 ½ **Romeo's On Fire (IRE)**7 6840 3-9-12 81.... KJManning 2 78+
(G M Lyons, Ire) *chsd ldrs: rdn in 4th 2f out: styd on into cl 3rd under 1f out: kpt on* **7/1**3

4 shd **Seven Gold Rings (IRE)**30 6441 4-9-0 77....(b) JAHeffernan 5 65+
(J F O'Shea, Ire) *chsd ldrs: rdn in 5th 2f out: 4th and kpt on fr 1f out* **14/1**

5 1 ¼ **Diamonds For Luck (IRE)**32 6393 5-9-5 63.... DPMcDonogh 6 66
(Desmond McDonogh, Ire) *chsd ldrs: impr to ld ent st: chal 2f out: hdd 1 1/2f out: no ex fnl f* **14/1**

6 shd **Gandolfini (IRE)**14 6784 4-9-1 61....(b) WJSupple 4 62
(H Rogers, Ire) *mid-div: 7th and rdn 2f out: no imp: kpt on one pce* **16/1**

7 1 ¾ **Distant Times**32 6393 6-8-12 63.... MHarley(7) 8 61
(Liam McAteer, Ire) *towards rr: sme late hdwy: nvr a danger* **33/1**

8 shd **Nastrelli (IRE)**7 6840 4-9-5 90....(b) JMurtagh 14 61
(M Halford, Ire) *mid-div: rdn in 8th under 2f out: no imp* **7/4**1

9 1 **Zaharath Al Bustan**44 6117 4-9-0 72....(t) JPFahy(7) 7 60
(E D Delany, Ire) *towards rr for most: nvr a factor* **16/1**

10 3 **Upper Village**35 6317 3-8-8 73.... SHunter(7) 13 45
(Joseph G Murphy, Ire) *led: rdn and hdd ent st: no ex fr 1 1/2f out* **14/1**

11 nk **Champion's Way (IRE)**35 6317 5-9-1 65.... WJLee 10 44
(Daniel William O'Sullivan, Ire) *a towards rr* **20/1**

12 nk **Talk Of Excitment**513 2994 3-8-10 75.... WMLordan 12 38
(Charles O'Brien, Ire) *towards rr: sme hdwy into 9th 2f out: sn no ex* **20/1**

13 8 **Maid Ofiron (IRE)**32 6393 3-9-0 64.... PShanahan 11 18
(M O Quigley, Ire) *in rr of mid-div: nvr a factor: trailing fnl f* **66/1**

14 2 ½ **Prince Livius (IRE)**32 6396 4-9-12 71....(t) FMBerry 9 22
(B P Galvin, Ire) *mid-div: rdn and no imp ent st: eased fnl f* **33/1**

1m 12.2s (72.20) **14 Ran SP% 127.4**
CSF £45.50 TOTE £4.30: £1.40, £3.40, £3.80; DF 58.10.
Owner W McKay, J Barton, T Sinclair **Bred** Mrs John McEnery **Trained** Bawtry, S Yorks

NOTEBOOK
Blue Rocket(IRE), making her All-Weather debut and fitted with blinkers for the first time, was also taking a big drop in trip. The combination had the right effect and she finished well to become the first British-trained winner of an Irish All-Weather contest. (op 3/1)
Nastrelli(IRE) Official explanation: jockey said gelding ran wide on the home bend and lost ground as a result
Champion's Way(IRE) Official explanation: jockey said gelding was slowly away and lost ground shortly after the start

6920a LADBROKESBINGO.COM RACE 1m
8:45 (8:46) 3-Y-0+ £9,237 (£2,710; £1,291; £439)

RPR

1 **Latino Magic (IRE)**32 6398 7-9-2 100.... PJSmullen 1 90+
(D K Weld, Ire) *chsd ldrs: 4th 1/2-way: 6th 2f out: impr to cl 3rd over 1f out: led under 1f out: kpt on wl* **4/1**2

2 nk **Dynamo Dancer (IRE)**25 6554 4-9-9 104.... JMurtagh 11 96+
(G M Lyons, Ire) *chsd ldrs: 6th 1/2-way: rdn in 7th 2f out: 4th 1f out: kpt on wl fnl f to press wnr* **4/1**2

3 2 **Warriors Key (IRE)**73 5319 3-9-4 99.... DPMcDonogh 9 89
(Kevin Prendergast, Ire) *in rr of mid-div: hdwy into 5th 2f out: rdn to chal in cl 2nd 1 1/2f out: kpt on* **7/2**1

4 ½ **Chicken Soup**13 6759 5-9-2 ....(b1) KJManning 12 84
(D J Murphy) *in rr of mid-div: hdwy into 4th 2f out: led 1 1/2f out: hdd under 1f out: no ex: kpt on* **5/1**3

5 5 ¼ **Palmistry**406 5951 4-9-2 .... WJSupple 3 76
(John G Carr, Ire) *mid-div: nt clr run 2f out: 7th 1f out: kpt on: fin 6th, plcd 5th* **33/1**

6 1 ¼ **Cotocachi (IRE)**32 6399 3-8-9 .... WMLordan 4 68
(Edward P Harty, Ire) *towards rr: sme late hdwy: n.d: fin 7th, plcd 6th* **66/1**

7 shd **Tin Town Boy (IRE)**19 6685 6-8-9 72....(t) MHarley(7) 14 73
(H Rogers, Ire) *chsd ldrs: impr to chal 2f out: sn no ex: wknd fr 1 1/2f out fin 8th, plcd 7th* **25/1**

8 4 ½ **Zakfree (IRE)**44 6117 6-8-6 63....(b) EJMcNamara(10) 10 63
(Liam McAteer, Ire) *chsd ldrs: led and disp after 2f: 2nd and rdn 2f out: wknd fr 1 1/2f out: fin 9th, plcd 8th* **50/1**

9 ½ **There's A Light (IRE)**34 6351 3-8-9 66....(b) PShanahan 2 57
(Tracey Collins, Ire) *sn led: disp after 2f: led 2f out: rdn and hdd 1 1/2f out: sn wknd: fin 10th, plcd 9th* **25/1**

10 1 **Foreigner (IRE)**40 5461 4-8-13 70.... DJMoran(3) 7 60
(C W J Farrell, Ire) *a towards rr: fin 11th, plcd 10th* **50/1**

11 2 **Le Louvre (IRE)**20 6656 3-8-9 .... FMBerry 5 51
(John M Oxx, Ire) *chsd ldrs: rdn and wknd ent st: fin 12th, plcd 11th* **25/1**

12 8 **Derby Desire (IRE)**42 6163 3-8-6 .... PBBeggy(3) 6 33
(Michael McElhone, Ire) *a towards rr: trailing st: fin 13th, plcd 12th* **66/1**

13 9 **Avelian (IRE)**272 5868 4-9-2 64....(bt1) WJLee 13 18
(S J Mahon, Ire) *s.i.s and a trailing: fin 14th, plcd 13th* **66/1**

D 3 ½ **Belle Artiste (IRE)**7 6843 5-8-11 97.... JAHeffernan 8 9
(Joseph Crowley, Ire) *mid-div: styd on into mod 5th under 1f out: nvr nrr fin 5th, nk, 2l, ½l, & 3½l: disq* **7/2**1

1m 38.3s (98.30)
WFA 3 from 4yo+ 2lb **14 Ran SP% 124.0**
CSF £19.46 TOTE £4.50: £2.10, £1.60, £2.10; DF 14.80.
Owner Hassen Adams **Bred** Ces Racing Ltd **Trained** The Curragh, Co Kildare
■ Stewards' Enquiry : J A Heffernan caution: failed to weigh in

NOTEBOOK
Chicken Soup, like his winning stable companion earlier in the card, was dropping in trip and had the blinkers on for the first time. On a surface that suits him better than turf, he ran quite well although a little below last season's form. (op 5/1 tchd 9/2)
Belle Artiste(IRE) Official explanation: vet said mare was struck into behind in running and finished slightly lame

6921 - 6922a (Foreign Racing) - See Raceform Interactive

LE CROISE-LAROCHE
Friday, November 23

OFFICIAL GOING: Heavy

6923a PRIX RENT A CAR (H'CAP) 1m 2f 110y
4:25 (4:29) 4-Y-0+ £5,405 (£2,162; £1,622; £1,081; £541)

RPR

1 **Cuban (FR)**30 4-8-6 ....(b) BRaballand(5) —
(J-P Delaporte, France)

2 4 **Yaya Gold (FR)**9 5-9-4 .... RMarchelli —
(P Lenogue, France)

3 ½ **Red Tune (FR)**9 6-8-9 ....(b) TPiccone(2) —
(C Boutin, France)

4 ½ **Mister Des Aigles (FR)**30 4-9-5 ....(b) —
(Mme C Barande-Barbe, France)

5 4 **Paging The King (FR)**38 7-9-2 ....(b) —
(B Dutruel, France)

6 ¾ **Lizzy's Girl (FR)**79 4-9-4 .... —
(R Crepon, France)

7 1 ½ **Kiwi Des Mottes (FR)**29 9-9-6 .... —
(E Lellouche, France)

8 3 ½ **Alqaayid**11 6792 6-8-11 .... DBreux —
(P W Hiatt) *nvr nrr than mid-div* **31/1**1

9 1 **Chope Royale (FR)**325 5-9-6 .... —
(J-Y Artu, France)

10 3 **Sakkaline (IRE)**30 7-9-6 ....(b) —
(F Chappet, France)

0 **Song Of War (IRE)**9 8-8-11 .... —
(F-M Cottin, France)

0 **Anselme Royal (FR)**600 7-9-2 .... —
(J-Y Artu, France)

0 **Indanehill (IRE)**403 5-9-4 .... —
(P Monfort, France)

0 **Mazel Baby (FR)**84 4-8-10 .... —
(Mlle C Azzoulai, France)

2m 17.09s (137.09) **14 Ran SP% 3.1**
PARI-MUTUEL (including one euro stakes): WIN 7.10; PL 2.50, 3.20,3.20; DF 33.50.
Owner J-P Delaporte **Bred** J-P Delaporte **Trained** France

NOTEBOOK
Alqaayid, a regular visitor to France, was disqualified after being beaten a neck on his last appearance on this track. This time, however, he never got into contention.

3340 HOLLYWOOD PARK (L-H)
Friday, November 23

OFFICIAL GOING: Firm

6924a CITATION H'CAP (GRADE 1) (TURF) 1m 110y(T)
12:30 (12:46) 3-Y-0+ £122,449 (£40,816; £24,490; £12,245; £4,082)

RPR

1 **Lang Field (USA)**96 4-8-2 ....(b) JKCourt 3 110
(Art Sherman, U.S.A) **188/10**

2 nk **Zann (USA)**47 4-8-3 ....(b) GKGomez 7 110
(M Machowsky, U.S.A) **21/10**1

3 ½ **Proudinsky (GER)**383 4-8-2 .... RBejarano 8 108
(R J Frankel, U.S.A) **27/10**2

4 hd **Silent Name (JPN)**27 6511 5-8-5 .... BBlanc 6 111
(R J Frankel, U.S.A) **57/10**

5 2 **Crested**55 4-8-2 ....(b) MCBaze 9 103
(W Dollase, U.S.A) **202/10**

6 1 ¼ **Palace Episode (USA)**26 4-8-3 .... JValdivia 1 102
(Saeed Bin Suroor) **53/10**3

7 1 ½ **Visa Parade (ARG)**81 4-8-2 .... JRosario 4 98
(J W Sadler, U.S.A) **468/10**

8 ¾ **Independent George (USA)**48 4-8-7 .... CNakatani 2 101
(H G Motion, U.S.A) **96/10**

9 4 **Willow O Wisp (USA)**146 5-8-4 .... MGarcia 5 90
(V Cerin, U.S.A) **123/10**

1m 39.72s (-1.40) **9 Ran SP% 118.9**
PARI-MUTUEL (Including $2 stake): WIN 39.60; PL (1-2) 12.80, 4.00;SHOW (1-2-3) 6.00, 2.40, 3.20; DF 65.80.
Owner Nigel R Shields **Bred** Freddy Lewis Jr **Trained** USA

NOTEBOOK
Palace Episode(USA) has had very little racing since being purchased by Godolphin, and his recent campaign in the USA has been only marginally successful.

6897 LINGFIELD (L-H)

Saturday, November 24

OFFICIAL GOING: Standard

Wind: Modest, half-behind Weather: overcast cold

6925 LADBROKES 24/7 FREE PHONE BETTING 0800 777 888 H'CAP (DIV I) 6f (P)

12:05 (12:06) (Class 6) (0-60,62) 3-Y-0+ **£1,706** (£503; £252) **Stalls** Low

Form RPR

3056 **1** **Lost All Alone**[51] 5946 3-8-0 47 .... KirstyMilczarek(5) 1 55
(D M Simcock) *led tl wl over 3f out: styd pressing ldr tl led again jst over 1f out: hld on gamely last 100yds* **15/2**

2006 **2** *hd* **Thoughtsofstardom**[3] 6890 4-8-13 55 .... TGMcLaughlin 4 62
(G C Bravery) *stdd s: hld up in tch in midfield: hdwy and rdn 2f out: swtchd lft ins fnl f: r.o and ev ch wl ins fnl f: hld nr fin* **25/1**

3122 **3** *nk* **Ever Cheerful**[5] 6870 6-9-6 62 ....(p) SteveDrowne 2 69
(A B Haynes) *chsd ldr: led wl over 3f out: rdn over 2f out: hdd jst over 1f out: unable qck last 100yds* **5/2**[1]

5165 **4** *½* **Stormburst (IRE)**[13] 6779 3-8-6 55 .... WilliamCarson(7) 6 60
(S C Williams) *chsd ldrs: rdn and effrt 2f out: kpt on same pce u.p fnl f* **4/1**[2]

0152 **5** *hd* **Zazous**[8] 6831 6-9-3 59 .... MickyFenton 11 63
(J J Bridger) *dropped in bhd after s: rdn 2f out: r.o wl fnl f: nt rch ldrs* **12/1**

5014 **6** *nk* **Rhapsilian**[8] 6825 3-9-0 56 .... JimmyFortune 3 60
(J A Geake) *chsd ldrs: chsd ldng pair and rdn over 2f out: kpt on same pce u.p fnl f* **9/2**[3]

0000 **7** *nk* **Mind Alert**[4] 6887 6-8-8 50 ....(v) DeanMcKeown 7 53
(D Shaw) *stdd s and hld up in bhd: hdwy on inner 2f out: kpt on but nt pce to rch ldrs* **25/1**

0004 **8** *2* **Mulberry Lad (IRE)**[3] 6891 5-8-11 53 .... ChrisCatlin 10 50
(P W Hiatt) *a towards rr: rdn 2f out: plugged on ins fnl f: nvr threatened ldrs* **13/2**

4000 **9** *¾* **Regal Royale**[15] 6749 4-9-2 58 .... LPKeniry 9 52
(Peter Grayson) *a towards rr: sltly hmpd over 4f out: nvr trbld ldrs* **33/1**

6000 **10** *½* **Parkside Pursuit**[3] 6891 9-7-12 47 oh1 ow1 .... PietroRomeo(7) 5 40
(J M Bradley) *chsd ldrs: rdn and wknd wl over 1f out* **100/1**

5150 **11** *14* **Christian Bendix**[17] 6718 5-8-6 48 ....(p) SimonWhitworth 8 —
(P Howling) *racd in midfield on outer: rdn over 3f out: wl bhd wl over 1f out: t.o* **25/1**

1m 10.74s (-2.07) **Going Correction** -0.20s/f (Stan) **11** Ran SP% **115.0**

Speed ratings (Par 101): **105,104,104,103,103 103,102,99,98,98 79**

CSF £180.60 CT £511.71 TOTE £8.40: £2.30, £8.00, £1.60; EX 196.10 TRIFECTA Not won..

Owner Tick Tock Partnership **Bred** B Whitehouse **Trained** Newmarket, Suffolk

FOCUS

A moderate but competitive sprint handicap. Sound form. The winning time was 0.13 seconds quicker than the second division.

6926 E B F LADBROKES.COM LEADS THE WAY MAIDEN STKS 5f (P)

12:40 (12:41) (Class 5) 2-Y-0 **£2,914** (£867; £433; £216) **Stalls** High

Form RPR

6256 **1** **Wavertree Princess (IRE)**[14] 6756 2-8-12 73 .... NCallan 2 72
(N P Littmoden) *t.k.h: trckd ldrs: rdn to chal over 1f out: led ins fnl f: hld on wl* **9/4**[1]

4 **2** *nk* **Fastella (IRE)**[40] 6225 2-8-12 0 .... NickyMackay 4 71
(G A Butler) *in tch: rdn and effrt jst over 2f out: kpt on wl ins fnl f: chsd wnr last 75yds: hld cl home* **7/2**[3]

0024 **3** *nk* **Town And Gown**[12] 6799 2-8-12 72 .... JimmyFortune 6 70
(J H M Gosden) *led: rdn jst over 2f out: hdd ins fnl f: no ex last 75yds* **5/2**[2]

0325 **4** *½* **A Wish For You**[8] 6834 2-8-12 70 .... SteveDrowne 7 68
(D K Ivory) *chsd ldr: rdn and ev ch wl over 1f out: one pce ins fnl f* **8/1**

5 **5** *3 ½* **Hucking Harkness**[10] 6813 2-9-3 0 .... GeorgeBaker 10 60
(J R Best) *racd on outer: in midfield tl rdn 3f out: outpcd over 2f out: n.d after* **17/2**

60 **6** *1 ¾* **Whitcombe Flyer (USA)**[69] 5448 2-9-3 0 ....(p) RobertHavlin 5 54
(Jamie Poulton) *sn bhd: styd on past btn horses fnl f: n.d* **40/1**

7 *1 ¼* **Martingrange Boy (IRE)** 2-9-3 0 .... FrancisNorton 1 50
(D J Murphy) *stdd s: hld up towards rr on inner: hdwy over 2f out: outpcd and edging rt wl over 1f out: n.d after* **16/1**

05 **8** *1* **Where's Killoran**[16] 6734 2-8-12 0 .... LPKeniry 8 41+
(Peter Grayson) *plld hrd: in tch in midfield: hdwy wl over 2f out: outpcd and hung rt wl over 1f out: no ch after* **100/1**

0 **9** *2* **Hero Heart**[9] 6820 2-9-3 0 .... JohnEgan 9 39
(Jane Chapple-Hyam) *chsd ldrs: rdn over 2f out: wknd wl over 1f out* **22/1**

0 **10** *3* **Impure Thoughts**[7] 6850 2-9-3 0 .... JimCrowley 3 28
(J R Best) *hld up in tch in midfield: outpcd jst over 2f out: no ch after* **33/1**

58.61 secs (-1.17) **Going Correction** -0.20s/f (Stan) 2y crse rec **10** Ran SP% **119.8**

Speed ratings (Par 96): **101,100,100,99,93 90,88,87,84,79**

CSF £10.51 TOTE £2.80: £1.10, £2.10, £1.20; EX 13.70 Trifecta £36.60 Pool: £495.33 - 9.60 winning tickets..

Owner Wavertree Racing Partnership D **Bred** Hans Vermeulen **Trained** Newmarket, Suffolk

FOCUS

Just a modest sprint maiden on paper, but surprisingly the juvenile course record was lowered.

NOTEBOOK

Wavertree Princess(IRE) proved suited by the drop back in trip and was able to gain her first success at the sixth attempt. She was a little keen through the early stages, but still had plenty left in the straight and was always holding challengers on both sides. She is going to find things tougher from now on, but has the right attitude. (op 5-2 tchd 11-4)

Fastella(IRE), fourth in an ordinary 6f maiden on her debut round here, had every chance but was always being held by the eventual winner. She looks capable of winning a similarly modest event and will also have the option of handicaps after one more run. (op 4-1)

Town And Gown, dropped back to 5f for the first time, had every chance and basically just found a couple of these too good. (op 11-4 tchd 9-4)

A Wish For You did not run up to her official mark of 70 and was disappointing. (op 11-1)

Hucking Harkness is not without ability and should find his level once handicapped. (op 8-1 tchd 9-1)

Martingrange Boy(IRE) Official explanation: jockey said gelding hung right in straight

Hero Heart Official explanation: jockey said colt hung left throughout

6927 LADBROKES 24/7 FREE PHONE BETTING 0800 777 888 H'CAP (DIV II) 6f (P)

1:10 (1:10) (Class 6) (0-60,60) 3-Y-0+ **£1,706** (£503; £252) **Stalls** Low

Form RPR

0202 **1** **Grand Palace (IRE)**[4] 6886 4-8-7 49 ....(v) DeanMcKeown 5 60
(D Shaw) *t.k.h: chsd ldrs: hdwy to chal wl over 1f out: led over 1f out: r.o wl* **2/1**[1]

056 **2** *¾* **Inka Dancer (IRE)**[15] 6747 5-8-13 55 .... NCallan 11 64
(B Palling) *t.k.h: chsd ldrs: chsd ldr over 2f out tl wl over 1f out: kpt on same pce u.p ins fnl f* **8/1**

6040 **3** *1* **No Time (IRE)**[3] 6890 7-9-3 59 .... SteveDrowne 9 65
(A J McCabe) *t.k.h: hld up towards rr: hdwy wl over 2f out: chsd ldrs over 1f out: kpt on u.p* **6/1**[3]

0003 **4** *hd* **Anfield Dream**[5] 6870 5-9-2 58 ....(t) MickyFenton 1 63
(J R Jenkins) *led: hdd over 1f out: rdn jst ins fnl f: fdd and lost 2 pls wl ins fnl f* **4/1**[2]

6062 **5** *nk* **Time Share (IRE)**[5] 6864 3-8-4 45 ....(be) HayleyTurner 10 50
(G C Bravery) *stdd s: plld hrd and hld up in rr: rdn and hdwy over 1f out: r.o but nt rch ldrs* **9/1**

4520 **6** *½* **Minnow**[26] 6528 3-8-6 55 ....(e) WilliamCarson(7) 6 58
(S C Williams) *missed break: sn in tch in midfield and t.k.h: rdn and outpcd 2f out: rallied fnl f: styd on* **10/1**

0000 **7** *1* **Mr Loire**[17] 6720 3-8-10 52 ....(b) J-PGuillambert 2 52
(A J Chamberlain) *t.k.h: in tch on inner: rdn over 2f out: wknd over 1f out* **14/1**

000 **8** *2 ½* **Cayman Breeze**[3] 6891 7-8-4 45 .... LiamJones 3 38
(J M Bradley) *t.k.h: hld up in rr: rdn and hmpd bnd over 2f out: no ch after* **16/1**

0402 **9** *shd* **Lawdy Miss Clawdy**[40] 6240 3-8-5 47 .... ChrisCatlin 8 39
(D W P Arbuthnot) *stdd after s: hld up in rr: nvr trbld ldrs* **16/1**

400- **10** *7* **Edward (IRE)**[600] 858 5-8-13 55 .... JohnEgan 4 26
(M Madgwick) *t.k.h: chsd ldr tl over 2f out: wkng whn edgd lft bnd jst over 2f out: sn bhd* **33/1**

1m 10.87s (-1.94) **Going Correction** -0.20s/f (Stan) **10** Ran SP% **119.2**

Speed ratings (Par 101): **104,103,101,101,101 100,99,95,95,86**

CSF £19.33 CT £87.76 TOTE £2.90: £1.20, £2.20, £2.40; EX 26.50 Trifecta £154.60 Part won. Pool: £217.82 - 0.72 winning tickets..

Owner ownaracehorse.co.uk (Shakespeare) **Bred** D McDonnell And Tower Bloodstock **Trained** Danethorpe, Notts

FOCUS

Another moderate sprint handicap, but probably slightly stronger than the first division. The form should prove reliable for the grade. The winning time was 0.13 seconds slower than the first division.

6928 "EDDIE STARR" MEMORIAL (S) STKS 1m (P)

1:40 (1:40) (Class 6) 2-Y-0 **£2,047** (£604; £302) **Stalls** High

Form RPR

601 **1** **Caltire (GER)**[41] 6207 2-8-11 51 ....(b) JamieJones(5) 1 59
(M G Quinlan) *s.i.s: hld up in tch: hdwy over 3f out: trckd ldrs 2f out: rdn and effrt jst over 1f out: led last 100yds: r.o wl* **8/1**

4165 **2** *¾* **Maybe I Wont**[8] 6828 2-9-2 65 .... GeorgeBaker 10 57
(R M Stronge) *in tch: rdn and effrt 2f out: ev ch ins fnl f: nt pce of wnr last 50yds* **13/8**[1]

5044 **3** *2* **Llab Nala**[13] 6776 2-9-2 55 .... JohnEgan 5 53
(M R Channon) *led at stdy gallop: rdn and hung rt over 1f out: hdd ins fnl f: sn btn* **6/1**[3]

1000 **4** *shd* **Adam Eterno (IRE)**[31] 6433 2-9-2 52 .... SteveDrowne 9 52
(A B Haynes) *chsd ldrs: rdn and ev ch 2f out: sltly hmpd 1f out: kpt on same pce after* **33/1**

0004 **5** *shd* **Oli James (USA)**[13] 6775 2-8-11 56 .... TQuinn 8 47
(P F I Cole) *prom: ev ch and rdn 2f out: carried rt and sltly hmpd jst over 1f out: one pce after* **3/1**[2]

000 **6** *1 ¾* **Alannah (IRE)**[12] 6793 2-8-8 31 ow2 .... RobertHavlin 6 40
(Mrs P N Dutfield) *t.k.h: in tch: chsd ldrs and drvn 2f out: no imp jst over 1f out* **66/1**

6336 **7** *nk* **Carry On Cleo**[5] 6865 2-8-7 56 ow1 .... TGMcLaughlin 12 39
(P D Evans) *in tch on outer: rdn to chse ldrs jst over 2f out: no imp fnl f* **8/1**

5205 **8** *hd* **La Belle Joannie**[74] 5302 2-8-6 53 .... AdrianMcCarthy 11 37
(S Curran) *stdd s: t.k.h: hld up in rr: nvr trbld ldrs* **33/1**

0600 **9** *1 ½* **Help (IRE)**[17] 6714 2-8-8 40 ow2 ....(b) FergusSweeney 3 36
(Mrs P N Dutfield) *in tch in midfield: rdn and effrt on inner 2f out: swished tail u.p: wknd over 1f out* **66/1**

3000 **10** *6* **Freudian Slip**[8] 6828 2-8-6 65 ....(p) PaulDoe 7 21
(S Curran) *s.i.s: a bhd: rdn and struggling wl over 2f out: no ch after* **7/1**

5000 **11** *15* **Smokeyourpipe (IRE)**[40] 6242 2-9-2 49 ....(p) JimCrowley 4 —
(R M Stronge) *racd in midfield: pushed along over 4f out: lost tch over 3f out: t.o* **40/1**

00 **12** *hd* **Tenraninthemist (IRE)**[13] 6777 2-8-6 0 .... ChrisCatlin 2 —
(T D McCarthy) *s.i.s: t.k.h in midfield: rdn over 4f out: wl bhd last 3f: t.o* **66/1**

1m 40.16s (0.73) **Going Correction** -0.20s/f (Stan) **12** Ran SP% **124.9**

Speed ratings (Par 94): **88,87,85,85,85 83,83,82,81,75 60,60**

CSF £22.09 TOTE £10.90: £2.70, £1.40, £2.30; EX 37.80 Trifecta £135.30 Part won. Pool: £190.70 - 0.86 winning tickets..The winner was bought in for 8,800gns.

Owner N J Jones **Bred** L & K Zimmermann **Trained** Newmarket, Suffolk

FOCUS

Not a bad race for the grade.

NOTEBOOK

Caltire(GER), picked up out of Jamie Osborne's yard after winning a very weak course-and-distance claimer on his previous start, showed improved form - 9lb according to RPRs - to follow up on his debut for new connections. He had to wait for a gap at the top of the straight, but his rider remained confident throughout and he picked up well once in the clear. He looks slightly better than this level. (op 10-1 tchd 7-1)

Maybe I Wont, having his first run since leaving Simon Dow, ran well stepped up to 1m for the first time and finished clear of the remainder in second. (op 5-2 tchd 11-4 in places)

Llab Nala only has a 5f win in this grade to his name, but there wasn't much wrong with this effort. (op 13-2 tchd 7-1)

Adam Eterno(IRE), dropped in trip and grade, ran well at a big price and only just missed out on third.

Oli James(USA) could not take advantage of the drop in grade with the blinkers left off this time.
Official explanation: jockey said colt suffered interference in running (tchd 10-3)

6929 E B F PLAY POKER AT LADBROKES.COM FILLIES' H'CAP 1m (P)
2:10 (2:10) (Class 4) (0-85,85) 3-Y-0+ £5,505 (£1,637; £818; £408) Stalls High

Form RPR
3360 1 **Bussel (USA)**[52] 5907 3-8-0 **72**.................................. KirstyMilczarek(5) 4 76
(D M Simcock) *in tch: chsd ldrs and rdn wl over 1f out: drvn ins fnl f: r.o wl to ld towards fin* **16/1**
6124 2 *nk* **Lawyers Choice**[9] 6822 3-8-10 **77**.................................. MartinDwyer 6 81
(Pat Eddery) *led at stdy gallop: hrd pressed and rdn 2f out: battled on gamely tl hdd and no ex towards fin* **5/1[2]**
3221 3 *¾* **Princess Taylor**[68] 5475 3-8-8 **75**..................................(t) JohnEgan 10 77
(M Botti) *w ldr: ev ch and rdn jst over 2f out: no ex wl ins fnl f* **5/1[2]**
6116 4 *shd* **Nice To Know (FR)**[66] 5537 3-8-9 **76**.................................. AdamKirby 2 78+
(G L Moore) *t.k.h: hld up wl in tch on inner: rdn wl over 1f out: str run ins fnl f: nt rch ldrs* **9/1**
5106 5 *¾* **High 'n Dry (IRE)**[12] 6795 3-8-4 **71** oh2..................................(p) PaulDoe 5 71
(M A Allen) *t.k.h: hld up wl in tch in rr: edgd to outer wl over 2f out: rdn and no imp tl r.o last 100yds: nt rch ldrs* **8/1[3]**
0302 6 *hd* **Regal Quest (IRE)**[52] 5907 3-8-11 **78**.................................. J-PGuillambert 1 78
(S C Williams) *s.i.s: t.k.h: sn wl in tch: rdn and tried to chal on inner jst over 1f out: no ex last 100yds* **7/2[1]**
0000 7 *hd* **Tanzanite (IRE)**[23] 6604 5-9-6 **85**.................................. FergusSweeney 3 84+
(D W P Arbuthnot) *s.i.s: hld up in last pair: hdwy over 1f out: nt clr run and swtchd rt ins fnl f: r.o but nvr able to chal* **9/1**
0406 8 *¾* **Labor Day (IRE)**[26] 6546 3-8-4 **71** oh3.................................. DavidKinsella 8 68
(J H M Gosden) *racd on outer: hdwy to join ldrs after 2f: ev ch and rdn jst over 2f out: fdd last 100yds* **14/1**
0060 9 *½* **Ivory Lace**[23] 6604 6-9-6 **85**.................................. JimCrowley 11 81
(S Woodman) *dropped in bhd after s: nvr trbld ldrs* **14/1**
0610 10 *hd* **Strawberry Lolly**[21] 6646 4-8-11 **76**.................................. OscarUrbina 9 72
(M Botti) *in tch: rdn and effrt 2f out: no imp whn edgd lft ins fnl f* **12/1**
003 11 *2* **Kompete**[16] 6731 3-8-7 **77** ow2..................................(v) JerryO'Dwyer(3) 7 68
(V Smith) *chsd ldrs tl rdn and lost pl over 2f out: no ch over 1f out* **8/1[3]**

1m 37.86s (-1.57) **Going Correction** -0.20s/f (Stan)
WFA 3 from 4yo+ 2lb 11 Ran SP% **124.7**
Speed ratings (Par 102): **99,98,97,97,97 96,96,95,95,95 93**
CSF £99.86 CT £484.90 TOTE £21.20: £4.80, £1.90, £1.70; EX 134.40 TRIFECTA Not won..
Owner DXB Bloodstock Ltd **Bred** John Weld **Trained** Newmarket, Suffolk

FOCUS
A steadily-run handicap that turned into something of a sprint and the form is not entirely reliable. The race has been rated fairly negatively.
Nice To Know(FR) Official explanation: jockey said filly ran too free
Tanzanite(IRE) Official explanation: jockey said mare was denied a clear run

6930 PLAY CASINO AT LADBROKES.COM STKS (REGISTERED AS THE GOLDEN ROSE STAKES) (LISTED RACE) 6f (P)
2:45 (2:49) (Class 1) 3-Y-0+
£14,762 (£5,595; £2,800; £1,396; £699; £351) Stalls Low

Form RPR
0004 1 **Maltese Falcon**[7] 6851 7-9-2 105..................................(t) NelsonDeSouza 8 103
(P F I Cole) *mde all: rdn over 1f out: hld on wl* **13/2**
2042 2 *½* **Borderlescott**[14] 6758 5-9-2 109.................................. MartinDwyer 7 102
(R Bastiman) *s.i.s: sn chsng ldrs: rdn wl over 1f out: edgd rt 1f out: styd on wl but nvr quite getting to wnr* **9/4[1]**
0253 3 *nk* **Desert Lord**[48] 6039 7-9-2 111..................................(b) NCallan 9 101
(K A Ryan) *awkward leaving stalls: t.k.h: chsd wnr: rdn 2f out: edgd sltly rt 1f out: unable qck ins fnl f: lost 2nd nr fin* **10/3[2]**
061 4 *nk* **Bonus (IRE)**[49] 6003 7-9-2 104.................................. NickyMackay 10 100
(G A Butler) *s.i.s: t.k.h: hld up in tch towards rr: hdwy on outer jst over 2f out: nt clr run and swtchd lft 1f out: r.o but nt rch ldrs* **4/1[3]**
0063 5 *nk* **Knot In Wood (IRE)**[14] 6758 5-9-2 103..................................(p) DaleGibson 2 99
(R A Fahey) *in tch in midfield: rdn and outpcd jst over 2f out: rallied u.p fnl f: r.o: nt rch ldrs* **6/1**
4000 6 *hd* **Murfreesboro**[41] 6198 4-9-2 90..................................(e[1]) DeanMcKeown 4 98
(K J Burke) *hld up in last: plld out and hdwy over 1f out: r.o but nvr able to chal* **33/1**
2036 7 *¾* **Little Edward**[7] 6851 9-9-2 89.................................. SteveDrowne 5 96
(R J Hodges) *t.k.h: hld up wl in tch in midfield: rdn over 1f out: keeping on same pce whn n.m.r towards fin* **20/1**
6400 8 *¾* **Woodnook**[126] 3746 4-8-11 95.................................. JohnEgan 6 89
(J A R Toller) *chsd ldrs: rdn wl over 1f out: wknd jst ins fnl f* **16/1**
5013 9 *1* **Expensive Art (IRE)**[12] 6794 3-8-11 67.................................. ChrisCatlin 1 86
(N A Callaghan) *hld up in last trio: nvr trbld ldrs* **33/1**

69.80 secs (-3.01) **Going Correction** -0.20s/f (Stan) course record 9 Ran SP% **118.0**
Speed ratings (Par 111): **112,111,110,110,110 109,108,107,106**
CSF £21.62 TOTE £8.40: £2.30, £1.40, £1.40; EX 27.00 Trifecta £57.30 Pool: £710.72 - 8.80 winning tickets..
Owner Christopher Wright **Bred** Stratford Place Stud **Trained** Whatcombe, Oxon
■ Stewards' Enquiry : Nicky Mackay caution: careless riding
N Callan four-day ban (includes three deferred days): careless riding (Dec 5-8)

FOCUS
A classy sprint for the track. Maltese Falcon enjoyed the run of things out in front and lowered the track record in the process of winning. The sixth, seventh and ninth all finished closer than they ought to have and so the first five home were all a bit below form.

NOTEBOOK
Maltese Falcon, who likes it round here, was soon out in front and dominated throughout. A smart performer on Polytrack, he is dangerous when allowed an uncontested lead, and he was always comfortably holding his rivals in the closing stages, setting a new track record in the process. His form figures over this course and distance now read an impressive 1152141. (op 6-1 tchd 15-2)
Borderlescott, running on the All-Weather for the first time, put in a determined late effort but was never quite going to get there. A consistent performer at this level, he has not won this year but has held his form very well. (op 3-1)
Desert Lord, who won over this course and distance earlier in his career, was last seen finishing third in the Abbaye. Never far off the pace, he had every chance, but 5f probaby suits him best. (op 3-1)
Bonus(IRE), who came from off the pace, did not get the clearest of runs in the straight but he could not be considered an unlucky loser. (tchd 7-2 and 9-2)
Knot In Wood(IRE) was never far off the inside rail in the straight, which is not the place to be, and did not run badly in the circumstances. A more galloping track suits him best. (op 15-2)

Murfreesboro, wearing an eye-shield for the first time, had plenty on in this company and was not disgraced, especially as the race was not really run to suit him. (tchd 50-1)

6931 PLAY BINGO AT LADBROKES.COM STKS (REGISTERED AS THE CHURCHILL STAKES) (LISTED RACE) 1m 2f (P)
3:15 (3:15) (Class 1) 3-Y-0+
£15,614 (£5,918; £2,961; £1,476; £739; £371) Stalls Low

Form RPR
5350 1 **Grand Passion (IRE)**[36] 6298 7-9-2 105.................................. SteveDrowne 9 99
(G Wragg) *hld up towards rr: hdwy jst over 2f out: drvn wl over 1f out: styd on wl to ld last stride* **7/2[2]**
1100 2 *shd* **Gentleman's Deal (IRE)**[43] 6155 6-9-6 108.................................. PaulMulrennan 2 103
(M W Easterby) *chsd ldr: rdn over 2f out: upsides wl over 1f out: kpt on u.p cl home: wnt 2nd on post* **9/4[1]**
5005 3 *shd* **Millville**[26] 6538 7-9-2 110.................................. NCallan 3 99
(M A Jarvis) *t.k.h: chsd ldng pair: rdn and upsides wl over 1f out: led narrowly 1f out: hdd and lost 2 pls nr fin* **8/1[3]**
2130 4 *nk* **Voliere**[21] 6654 4-8-11 80.................................. J-PGuillambert 7 93
(S C Williams) *stdd s and slowly away: hld up in last: stl gng wl over 1f out: shkn up and hdwy on inner jst over 1f out: rdn ins fnl f: kpt on* **66/1**
0512 5 *hd* **Kinsya**[21] 6654 4-9-2 96.................................. GeorgeBaker 4 98
(M H Tompkins) *t.k.h early: w.w in tch: rdn wl over 1f out: styd on u.p ins fnl f* **9/1**
4321 6 *shd* **World Spirit**[41] 6208 3-8-7 82.................................. ChrisCatlin 5 92
(Rae Guest) *w.w in tch: rdn wl over 2f out: no hdwy tl over 1f out: styd on wl ins fnl f: nt quite rch ldrs* **8/1[3]**
1265 7 *1 ¼* **Banknote**[76] 5265 5-9-6 108.................................. FrancisNorton 6 99
(A M Balding) *t.k.h: led: rdn 2f out: hdd 1f out: fdd last 100yds* **7/2[2]**
0341 8 *1* **Vainglory (USA)**[14] 6765 3-8-12 85.................................. MartinDwyer 8 93
(D M Simcock) *hld up wl in tch: rdn over 2f out: wknd 1f out* **20/1**
20-0 9 *6* **Kahlua Kiss**[14] 6757 4-8-11 92.................................. PaulDoe 1 76
(W R Muir) *stdd s: hld up in last pair: rdn and effrt 3f out: outpcd over 2f out: no ch after* **33/1**

2m 4.53s (-3.26) **Going Correction** -0.20s/f (Stan)
WFA 3 from 4yo+ 4lb 9 Ran SP% **116.6**
Speed ratings (Par 111): **105,104,104,104,104 104,103,102,97**
CSF £11.74 TOTE £4.70: £1.80, £1.40, £3.60; EX 12.70 Trifecta £41.70 Pool: £522.56 - 8.88 winning tickets..
Owner H H Morriss **Bred** Mr & Mrs H H Morriss **Trained** Newmarket, Suffolk
■ Stewards' Enquiry : Paul Mulrennan two-day ban: used whip with excessive frequency without giving horse time to respond (Dec 5-6)

FOCUS
This was another steadily-run affair and it turned into something of a sprint. The proximity of a couple of horses rated in the low 80s casts doubt on the form and the first three are all rated 10lb+ off their marks.

NOTEBOOK
Grand Passion(IRE), who won this race in 2004, did not have the race run entirely to suit and was forced to challenge just one off the inside rail, but he still proved good enough to edge a bunch finish by the shortest of margins. He is a credit to his trainer and clearly remains a smart performer on this surface. (tchd 4-1)
Gentleman's Deal(IRE), previously unbeaten in seven starts on the All-Weather including when edging out Grand Passion in the Winter Derby over this course and distance in March, went for home at the top of the straight but could never get clear. He was only narrowly beaten by his old rival at the line and another campaign geared towards a defence of his Winter Derby crown looks likely now. (op 2-1)
Millville was ridden more prominently than he was in this race last year and ran a better race as a result. He remains at his best over further, though, and will appreciate a return to 1m4f plus. (op 15-2)
Voliere ◆, back on the Polytrack, appears to have put up a career-best effort on the face of it, bustling up rivals rated about a stone and a half superior to her. Indeed, she may have done even better as she was travelling well entering the straight but her rider took her to race right next to the inside rail where the surface is slowest. She will make plenty of appeal if turned out quickly off her current mark of 80 in handicap company.
Kinsya, who likes a bit of give on turf and continued his steady career progress this season, ran a sound enough race on his All-Weather debut. He was in the best position to challenge in the straight, though, widest of the group. (op 11-1)
World Spirit was another staying on well at the finish, although the fact that she won a handicap off just 72 last time out does mean that there are some big question marks over the value of the form. Having said that, she is fairly unexposed on the surface and is clearly going the right way.
Official explanation: vet said filly returned lame on left-fore (tchd 9-1)
Banknote had every chance on the ratings but he had his stamina to prove and, having set a steady pace out in front, he dropped out tamely from the entrance to the straight. (op 4-1 tchd 9-2)
Kahlua Kiss Official explanation: jockey said filly missed the break

6932 PLAY DEAL OR NO DEAL AT LADBROKES.COM H'CAP 7f (P)
3:50 (3:51) (Class 2) (0-100,100) 3-Y-0+
£9,971 (£2,985; £1,492; £747; £372; £93) Stalls Low

Form RPR
2110 1 **Capricorn Run (USA)**[7] 6852 4-9-5 100..................................(v) SteveDrowne 6 110
(A J McCabe) *prom: chsd ldr 4f out: led 2f out: drvn clr ins fnl f: in command after* **11/2[3]**
3042 2 *½* **Fajr (IRE)**[17] 6726 5-9-5 100.................................. JohnEgan 12 109
(Miss Gay Kelleway) *hld up and bhd: hdwy jst over 2f out: rdn wl over 1f out: r.o to chse wnr ins fnl f: clsng nr fin* **9/2[2]**
0050 3 *1* **Andronikos**[7] 6851 5-8-7 88..................................(t) TQuinn 4 94+
(P F I Cole) *t.k.h: hld up towards rr: short of room briefly bnd over 2f out: swtchd lft over 1f out: r.o strly: nt rch wnr* **16/1**
3530 4 *½* **Waterside (IRE)**[7] 6852 8-9-5 100.................................. GeorgeBaker 11 105
(G L Moore) *hld up towards rr: gd hdwy on inner bnd over 2f out: kpt on u.p fnl f: nt pce to chal wnr* **12/1**
1002 5 *1 ½* **Salient**[23] 6606 3-8-6 88.................................. PaulDoe 10 89
(J Akehurst) *led for 1f: styd prom: ev ch and rdn jst over 2f out: outpcd by wnr 1f out: fdd and lost 2nd ins fnl f* **9/1**
0510 6 *shd* **The Kiddykid (IRE)**[23] 6606 7-8-7 88.................................. TGMcLaughlin 8 88
(P D Evans) *t.k.h: hld up towards rr: short of room 5f out: swtchd to outer and hdwy 3f out: drvn 2f out: kpt on but nvr threatened ldrs* **20/1**
4 6 *dht* **Orpenindeed (IRE)**[23] 6606 4-8-11 92..................................(t) OscarUrbina 7 92
(M Botti) *t.k.h: hld up in midfield: lost pl and dropped to rr over 3f out: swtchd to inner 3f out: hdwy and rdn 2f out: no imp ins fnl f* **22/1**
4010 8 *1 ¾* **Philharmonic**[42] 6183 6-9-3 98.................................. DaleGibson 3 94
(R A Fahey) *racd in midfield: rdn whn short of room and lost pl bnd jst over 2f out: sme late hdwy: nt trble ldrs* **33/1**
6005 9 *¾* **Tony James (IRE)**[7] 6851 5-8-8 89.................................. DeanMcKeown 5 83
(K O Cunningham-Brown) *prom tl led after 1f: rdn and hdd 2f out: wknd over 1f out* **22/1**

0603 **10** 1 1/4 **Evens And Odds (IRE)**[7] 6852 3-8-12 94..............................(p) NCallan 1 84
(K A Ryan) *chsd ldrs: rdn over 3f out: wknd over 2f out* **3/1**[1]
6000 **11** 1 **Partners In Jazz (USA)**[43] 6155 6-8-10 91........................ PhillipMakin 2 79
(T D Barron) *racd in midfield: rdn wl over 2f out: struggling whn edgd rt bnd over 2f out: n.d after* **12/1**
0622 **12** 3/4 **King's Caprice**[7] 6851 6-8-8 92....................................(t) TravisBlock(3) 14 77
(J A Geake) *s.i.s: racd on outer: rdn 3f out: sn struggling* **10/1**
0006 **13** 2 **Cupid's Glory**[23] 6606 5-8-6 87..(p) LPKeniry 13 67
(Mrs L C Jewell) *racd in midfield: rdn and struggling over 2f out: no ch after* **33/1**
4000 **14** 4 **Party Boss**[7] 6852 5-9-5 100.. JimmyFortune 9 69
(C E Brittain) *prom tl 4f out: sn dropped out: bhd last 3f* **8/1**

1m 22.44s (-3.45) **Going Correction** -0.20s/f (Stan) course record
WFA 3 from 4yo+ 1lb **14** Ran SP% **129.4**
Speed ratings (Par 109): **111,110,109,108,107 106,106,104,104,102 101,100,98,93**
CSF £30.68 CT £400.68 TOTE £9.30: £2.60, £2.00, £5.30; EX 41.00 Trifecta £409.70 Part won. Pool: £577.12 - 0.10 winning tickets. Place 6 £16.37, Place 5 £6.98.
Owner Paul J Dixon And Placida Racing **Bred** Santa Rosa Partners **Trained** Babworth, Notts

FOCUS
A decent handicap run at a good pace. Good form, which looks pretty solid and should work out.

NOTEBOOK
Capricorn Run(USA) can ruin his chance with a slow start, as he did here a week earlier, but on this occasion he jumped smartly and was in the box position throughout. He kept on well in the straight to run out a commanding winner and notch his third win from his last four starts, and he now looks to have developed into a Listed-class performer on this surface. He may go to Dubai in the new year for the carnival. (op 8-1)
Fajr(IRE), successful in five of his previous six races at this track, ran on from the back of the field for second, but he found the highly progressive winner had gone beyond recall. There is an argument for saying that he remains fairly handicapped despite a three-figure mark. (tchd 5-1)
Andronikos, who is on a long losing run, was back up in trip and kept on well, especially considering that he made his move towards the inside in the straight. He clearly retains plenty of ability and it would not be a surprise to see him pop up in the near future.
Waterside(IRE), who is back on his last winning mark, ran a better race for his reappearance outing here a week earlier. He helps set the level of the form and will not be without hope in similar company. (tchd 14-1)
Salient, 3lb higher for his good effort here last time, was not given an easy time of it in front and he eventually paid for helping to set a pretty strong pace. He will be interesting when he looks likely to get the run of the race out in front. (op 11-1)
Orpenindeed(IRE), who shaped quite well on his All-Weather debut 23 days earlier, had a tongue tie on this time. He was far from disgraced given that his rider took the rail route rounding the turn into the straight and all the way home. (op 25-1)
The Kiddykid(IRE) ran a bit better than his finishing position suggests as he came widest round the bend into the straight. (op 25-1)
Evens And Odds(IRE) was struggling from some way out and proved disappointing in the first-time cheekpieces. (op 4-1)
T/Plt: £23.00 to a £1 stake. Pool: £54,601.15. 1,731.25 winning tickets. T/Qpdt: £11.40 to a £1 stake. Pool: £3,275.90. 211.00 winning tickets. SP

6910 WOLVERHAMPTON (A.W) (L-H)
Saturday, November 24

OFFICIAL GOING: Standard
Much milder temperatures meant the problems of the previous evening were never going to resurface.
Wind: Light behind Weather: Light showers

6933 TRY C BEECH FOR STEEL 01384 456 654 CLAIMING STKS 1m 141y(P)
7:00 (7:01) (Class 6) 2-Y-O **£2,047** (£604; £302) **Stalls** Low

Form RPR
0011 **1** **Marino Prince (FR)**[10] 6814 2-8-12 64.............................. SteveDrowne 2 71+
(A B Haynes) *played up in stalls: s.i.s: hld up: swtchd rt and hdwy wl over 1f out: led ins fnl f: readily* **5/2**[1]
003 **2** 1 1/2 **Mujahope**[10] 6814 2-8-8 67......................................(p) AshleyHamblett(5) 1 65
(M Botti) *a.p: rdn to ld 1f out: hdd ins fnl f: nt qckn* **8/1**
0334 **3** 1 1/2 **Home**[5] 6868 2-9-0 69...(p) HayleyTurner 5 63
(J R Boyle) *hld up: c wd st: hdwy 1f out: sn edgd lft: kpt on* **7/2**[2]
0604 **4** shd **Shadows Fall (USA)**[17] 6715 2-9-0 62........................ NelsonDeSouza 8 63
(P F I Cole) *a.p: hung rt bnd 3f out: sn rdn: edgd lft ins fnl f: kpt on* **9/2**[3]
0045 **5** 2 **Desert Life (IRE)**[72] 5363 2-8-7 65.. LPKeniry 4 51
(R A Harris) *hld up in tch: swtchd lft over 1f out: sn hrd rdn: one pce* **10/1**
2022 **6** 2 **Hurstpierpoint (IRE)**[10] 6814 2-8-6 60................................ DaleGibson 6 46
(R A Fahey) *led: rdn and hdd 1f out: wknd ins fnl f* **15/2**
4026 **7** 1 1/4 **Imaginemysurprise**[13] 6775 2-8-0 59.................................. DavidKinsella 7 38
(J A Geake) *chsd ldr: rdn and ev ch over 2f out: wknd 1f out* **11/1**
0034 **8** 7 **Novestar (IRE)**[65] 5572 2-8-7 60.. ChrisCatlin 9 30
(G J Smith) *rdn over 5f out: a in rr* **14/1**
00 **9** 7 **Dome Blonde**[24] 6591 2-8-4 0...(b[1]) NickyMackay 3 12
(W J Musson) *swished tail: hld up: rdn 4f out: sn bhd* **100/1**

1m 52.43s (0.67) **Going Correction** -0.05s/f (Stan) **9** Ran SP% **116.9**
Speed ratings (Par 94): **95,93,92,92,90 88,87,81,75**
CSF £23.79 TOTE £2.90: £1.30, £3.20, £1.50; EX 29.60.The winner was claimed by T Wall for £13,000.
Owner Joe McCarthy **Bred** Newsells Park Stud Ltd **Trained** Limpley Stoke, Bath
■ Stewards' Enquiry : Ashley Hamblett two-day ban: used whip with excessive frequency (Dec 5-6)

FOCUS
This ordinary claimer was tightly-knit based on official ratings.

NOTEBOOK
Marino Prince(FR) lost ground at the start after a stalls handler had to be in with him when the gates opened. Continuing on a roll, he had little difficulty completing a hat-trick and changed hands again, this time being claimed by Trevor Wall for £13,000. (tchd 3-1)
Mujahope was readily brushed aside despite being 9lb better off than when beaten just over three lengths by the much improved winner here last time. (op 6-1)
Home had cheekpieces fitted for this drop in grade and was inclined to drift left in the closing stages. (op 5-1)
Shadows Fall(USA) hung right and did not handle the bend at all well before being inclined to go the other way late on. (op 15-2)
Desert Life(IRE) was back up to a mile having tried cheekpieces on his previous outing a couple of months ago. (op 8-1 tchd 11-1)
Hurstpierpoint(IRE) had more use made of her than when a two and a half-length second to the progressive winner in a similar contest on 7lb worse terms here last time. (op 7-1 tchd 6-1)

6934 BRAMBLES 70TH MAIDEN STKS 1m 141y(P)
7:30 (7:30) (Class 5) 2-Y-O **£2,968** (£876; £438) **Stalls** Low

Form RPR
04 **1** **Cossack Prince**[31] 6417 2-9-3 0.. RobertHavlin 6 78
(B J Meehan) *mde all: rdn over 1f out: drvn out* **11/4**[2]
3 **2** 1 **Cozy Tiger (USA)**[10] 6805 2-9-3 0.. NeilPollard 8 76
(W J Musson) *sn chsng wnr: rdn and kpt on same pce fnl f* **11/4**[2]
05 **3** 6 **Tevez**[64] 5598 2-9-3 0.. PaulMulrennan 1 63
(M H Tompkins) *a.p: rdn 2f out: sn btn* **13/8**[1]
4 2 **Caribana** 2-8-12 0.. J-PGuillambert 2 54
(M A Jarvis) *hld up: rdn over 2f out: no hdwy* **14/1**
0052 **5** 2 **Miss Bouggy Wouggy**[22] 6626 2-8-12 66..................... FrancisNorton 7 50
(M Blanshard) *prom: rdn over 2f out: wknd wl over 1f out* **14/1**
6 3 1/2 **Opening Act** 2-9-3 0.. NelsonDeSouza 9 48+
(P F I Cole) *s.i.s: nvr gng wl in rr: rdn whn hung lft over 2f out* **12/1**[3]
7 3 **Arabesque Dancer** 2-8-7 0.. AshleyHamblett(5) 3 36
(M Botti) *hld up in rr: pushed along 3f out: no rspnse* **20/1**

1m 51.37s (-0.39) **Going Correction** -0.05s/f (Stan) **7** Ran SP% **117.2**
Speed ratings (Par 96): **99,98,92,91,89 86,83**
CSF £11.27 TOTE £3.60: £2.30, £1.40; EX 16.60.
Owner Wyck Hall Stud **Bred** Wyck Hall Stud Ltd **Trained** Manton, Wilts

FOCUS
This minor maiden was run at a modest pace.

NOTEBOOK
Cossack Prince had less to do on this sand debut and kept the runner-up at bay after again benefiting from a soft lead. (op 9-2)
Cozy Tiger(USA) stuck to his task but could not peg back the winner. (op 13-8 tchd 10-3)
Tevez, trying a longer trip on this switch to sand, could not go with the leading pair from the quarter-mile marker. (op 7-2 tchd 11-8)
Caribana is bred to do better over longer distances next year. (op 11-1 tchd 9-1)
Miss Bouggy Wouggy had more on her plate than when runner-up over course and distance last time. (op 12-1)

6935 PONTIN'S BOOK EARLY PRICE PROMISE (S) STKS 1m 141y(P)
7:55 (7:58) (Class 6) 3-5-Y-O **£2,047** (£604; £302) **Stalls** Low

Form RPR
0060 **1** **Zaafira (SPA)**[152] 2948 3-8-9 49..............................(t) StephenDonohoe 3 55
(E J Creighton) *hld up in mid-div: hdwy over 2f out: styd on to ld cl home* **20/1**
0604 **2** 1/2 **Davidia (IRE)**[10] 6815 4-8-10 47.................................. RichardKingscote 2 52
(Tom Dascombe) *led: clr whn rdn over 1f out: hdd cl home* **11/4**[2]
0050 **3** 2 **My Mirasol**[167] 2490 3-8-9 60..(p) TPQueally 7 49
(D E Cantillon) *chsd ldr: rdn over 2f out: no ex wl ins fnl f* **1/1**[1]
0000 **4** 4 **Dance Spirit (IRE)**[4] 6882 4-8-10 59........................(b[1]) FrancisNorton 11 38
(W R Muir) *faultered sn after s: sn mid-div: hdwy on ins over 2f out: no further prog* **5/1**[3]
-000 **5** 4 **Tamworth (IRE)**[2] 3730 5-8-10 35..............................(vt) PaulMulrennan 5 29
(E J Creighton) *prom: n.m.r and lost pl after 1f: sn bhd: n.d after* **25/1**
56 **6** 1 **Ugenius**[256] 670 3-8-7 45.. LPKeniry 1 26
(R A Harris) *prom tl rdn and wknd over 2f out* **16/1**
0-60 **7** 3 1/2 **Silvabella (IRE)**[14] 6766 4-8-5 38....................................(b[1]) LiamJones 4 13
(D Haydn Jones) *hld up in tch: rdn and wknd over 2f out* **33/1**
00-0 **8** 8 **Tahafut**[14] 6764 3-8-2 54... DaleGibson 8 —
(R A Fahey) *s.i.s: t.k.h: sn in mid-div: pushed along 4f out: bhd fnl 3f* **14/1**
4006 **9** 18 **Little Darlin**[17] 6726 3-8-3 28 ow1.. ChrisCatlin 10 —
(G J Smith) *sn chsng ldrs: wknd over 5f out: t.o* **33/1**

1m 52.94s (1.18) **Going Correction** -0.05s/f (Stan)
WFA 3 from 4yo+ 3lb **9** Ran SP% **120.4**
Speed ratings (Par 101): **92,91,89,86,82 81,78,71,55**
CSF £75.41 TOTE £21.00: £4.50, £1.40, £1.10; EX 109.80.There was no bid for the winner. My Mirasol was subject to a friendly claim for £6,000.
Owner The Vixens **Bred** Cuadra The Vixens **Trained** East Garston, Berks
■ Stewards' Enquiry : Stephen Donohoe two-day ban: used whip with excessive frequency (Dec 5-6)

FOCUS
Not many got into this weak seller in which the early pace seemed over-strong.

6936 PONTIN'S GREAT FAMILY HOLIDAYS NURSERY 7f 32y(P)
8:25 (8:26) (Class 4) (0-85,83) 2-Y-O **£4,210** (£1,252; £625; £312) **Stalls** High

Form RPR
2551 **1** **Ten Pole Tudor**[12] 6800 2-9-0 **76**.. ChrisCatlin 4 78
(R A Harris) *s.i.s: hdwy on ins over 5f out: hrd rdn to ld wl ins fnl f: r.o* **5/1**[2]
5660 **2** 1/2 **The Last Bottle (IRE)**[79] 5153 2-8-2 **64**............................. LiamJones 1 65
(W M Brisbourne) *sn led: rdn over 1f out: hdd wl ins fnl f* **17/2**[3]
0064 **3** 1 1/2 **Weet By Far**[30] 6454 2-8-0 **62** oh5 ow2.............................. HayleyTurner 7 59
(R Hollinshead) *hld up in rr: hdwy on ins wl over 1f out: rdn and nt qckn ins fnl f* **20/1**
502 **4** nk **Jerry Hamilton (USA)**[15] 6748 2-8-12 **74**.................... DeanMcKeown 3 70
(M Johnston) *hld up: rdn and hung lft fr over 1f out: kpt on towards fin* **2/1**[1]
0113 **5** nk **Cross Fell (USA)**[9] 6823 2-9-2 **78**.. GeorgeBaker 5 74
(J R Boyle) *led early: w ldr: ev ch 2f out: rdn over 1f out: one pce* **2/1**[1]
1330 **6** 4 **Semah Harold**[44] 6120 2-9-1 **77**................................... StephenDonohoe 2 63
(E S McMahon) *prom: rdn over 2f out: wknd wl over 1f out* **14/1**
001 **7** 3 1/2 **Tyfos**[14] 6761 2-9-7 **83**.. TGMcLaughlin 6 60
(W M Brisbourne) *t.k.h: prom: rdn and wknd over 2f out* **9/1**

1m 30.34s (-0.06) **Going Correction** -0.05s/f (Stan) **7** Ran SP% **115.3**
Speed ratings (Par 98): **98,97,95,95,95 90,86**
CSF £46.15 TOTE £5.00: £3.10, £4.80; EX 120.30.
Owner Mrs Jan Adams **Bred** Rockdown Investments **Trained** Earlswood, Monmouths

FOCUS
A low-key nursery.

NOTEBOOK
Ten Pole Tudor, 3lb higher than when fifth in a stretch mile nursery here two starts ago, showed the right sort of attitude to follow up his course-and-distance win in a novice stakes. (tchd 9-2 and 11-2)
The Last Bottle(IRE), previously trained by Thomas Tate, was making his sand debut. This was his best effort since being gelded. (op 11-1 tchd 8-1)
Weet By Far, carrying a couple of pounds overweight, was effectively 7lb higher than her correct mark. (op 25-1)
Jerry Hamilton(USA) was not helping his jockey in the home straight and may do better over further. (op 15-8 tchd 6-4)

Cross Fell(USA) was probably not helped by having competition for the lead. (op 10-3 tchd 7-2)

6937 GO PONTIN'S H'CAP 1m 4f 50y(P)
8:55 (8:55) (Class 6) (0-55,56) 3-Y-O+ £2,047 (£604; £302) Stalls Low

Form RPR

0455 1 **Moment Of Clarity**[33] 6380 5-8-8 **53**....................(p) KrishGundowry(7) 8 63+
(R C Guest) *mde all: clr 2f out: rdn jst over 1f out: r.o* **20/1**

5053 2 3 1/2 **Desert Hawk**[16] 6728 6-9-2 **54**...(b) LiamJones 6 58
(W M Brisbourne) *hld up in mid-div: hdwy over 2f out: sn rdn: styd on ins fnl f: nt trble wnr* **12/1**

1634 3 1 1/2 **Regency Red (IRE)**[63] 5647 9-8-10 **55**............. Julie-AnneCumine(7) 10 60+
(W M Brisbourne) *hld up: sn in tch: lost pl 4f out: nt clr run over 2f out: sn swtchd rt: styd on fnl f* **20/1**

0434 4 1/2 **Weet Yer Tern (IRE)**[12] 6804 5-9-1 **53**........................... GeorgeBaker 3 54
(W M Brisbourne) *hld up towards rr: hdwy over 2f out: sn rdn: n.m.r jst over 1f out and ins fnl f: kpt on* **13/2**[3]

3055 5 3/4 **Autograph Hunter**[26] 6534 3-8-10 **54**................................. LPKeniry 12 54
(Peter Grayson) *hld up in rr: rdn over 3f out: styd on fnl f: nvr nrr* **8/1**

1303 6 3/4 **Giddywell**[12] 6803 3-8-7 **56**.................................. RussellKennemore(5) 7 54
(R Hollinshead) *hld up towards rr: hdwy over 4f out: edgd rt jst over 1f out: fdd ins fnl f* **7/1**

0005 7 shd **Cadwell**[22] 6627 3-8-10 **54**.. RobertHavlin 9 52
(T J Pitt) *hld up towards rr: hdwy over 6f out: chsd wnr over 3f out: rdn over 2f out: wknd ins fnl f* **9/2**[2]

6022 8 1 1/4 **Intavac Boy**[23] 6613 6-8-11 **52**............................(p) MichaelJStainton(3) 1 48+
(S P Griffiths) *prom: hmpd and lost pl over 3f out: nt clr run on ins over 2f out: n.d after* **4/1**[1]

2064 9 1 1/4 **Composing (IRE)**[10] 6817 3-8-7 **54**........................(bt[1]) TravisBlock(3) 4 48
(H Morrison) *hld up in tch: stdd after 2f: sn bhd: n.d after* **9/2**[2]

2000 10 3 1/2 **Bulberry Hill**[47] 6069 6-8-7 **52**................................(t) SoniaEaton(7) 11 41
(R W Price) *plld hrd: hdwy over 8f out: wknd 2f out* **33/1**

00-0 11 20 **Peephole**[115] 215 4-9-0 **52**... HayleyTurner 2 9
(M A Allen) *prom over 6f: t.o* **28/1**

5/0 12 5 **Menkaura**[14] 6766 4-9-3 **55**.................................(v[1]) VinceSlattery 5 4
(John R Upson) *t.k.h: prom: chsd wnr 5f out tl rdn over 3f out: sn wknd: t.o* **50/1**

2m 42.0s (-0.42) **Going Correction** -0.05s/f (Stan)
WFA 3 from 4yo+ 6lb **12** Ran SP% **118.9**
Speed ratings (Par 101): **99,96,95,95,94 94,94,93,92,90 76,73**
CSF £228.76 CT £4806.40 TOTE £22.60: £2.90, £3.80, £1.80; EX 260.70.
Owner Andrew Sheddon **Bred** Lordship Stud **Trained** Carburton, Notts
■ A first winner for Mauritius-born apprentice Krishlovy Gundowry.

FOCUS
They went no pace in this closely-knit, low-grade handicap with the winner taking advantage of a soft lead, although it is doubtful if he was flattered. The form seems sound enough.
Regency Red(IRE) Official explanation: jockey said gelding was denied a clear run
Giddywell Official explanation: jockey said filly hung right-handed throughout
Intavac Boy Official explanation: jockey said gelding was denied a clear run

6938 BOOK A CHRISTMAS BREAK AT PONTIN'S H'CAP 5f 216y(P)
9:20 (9:23) (Class 5) (0-75,75) 3-Y-O+ £2,968 (£876; £438) Stalls Low

Form RPR

652 1 **Tony The Tap**[18] 6708 6-9-4 **75**..................................(b) HayleyTurner 9 87
(W R Muir) *stdd s: sn in rr and swtchd lft: hdwy on ins over 2f out: led jst ins fnl f: r.o wl* **9/2**[2]

0033 2 2 1/2 **Strathmore (IRE)**[1] 6910 3-8-7 **64**...................................... DaleGibson 5 68
(R A Fahey) *hld up and bhd: hdwy over 2f out: rdn and wandered 1f out: r.o to take 2nd nr fin* **11/2**[3]

0353 3 1/2 **Methaaly (IRE)**[14] 6762 4-8-12 **69**...................................... LiamJones 4 71
(M Mullineaux) *stmbld s: prom: led over 1f out: rdn and hdd jst ins fnl f: nt qckn* **3/1**[1]

3005 4 1 1/4 **Tous Les Deux**[32] 6405 4-8-12 **69**... LPKeniry 1 67
(Peter Grayson) *s.i.s: hld up and bhd: hdwy over 2f out: rdn over 1f out: one pce fnl f* **12/1**

0015 5 2 **Desert Opal**[8] 6829 7-9-2 **73**....................................(b) TPQueally 2 65
(C R Dore) *prom: ev ch wl over 1f out: sn rdn and edgd lft: wknd wl ins fnl f* **9/1**

0006 6 1 1/2 **River Kirov (IRE)**[36] 6313 4-9-1 **72**.............................. NickyMackay 8 59
(M Wigham) *hld up in rr: hdwy 1f out: nvr trbld ldrs* **9/2**[2]

5541 7 3/4 **Mafaheem**[50] 5981 5-9-1 **72**.. SteveDrowne 7 57
(A B Haynes) *mid-div: lost pl 3f out: n.d after* **7/1**

0060 8 2 1/2 **Egyptian Lord**[7] 6860 4-8-6 **63**............................... AdrianMcCarthy 11 40
(Peter Grayson) *s.i.s: sn in mid-div: wknd over 2f out* **33/1**

1260 9 nk **Count Cougar (USA)**[130] 3608 7-9-0 **74**............. MichaelJStainton(3) 10 50
(S P Griffiths) *plld hrd: led early: led over 3f out: rdn and hdd over 1f out: wknd ins fnl f* **18/1**

-234 10 2 **Le Masque**[287] 423 3-8-10 **67**.. PaulMulrennan 3 36
(B Smart) *t.k.h: sn led: hdd over 3f out: wknd over 1f out* **28/1**

1000 11 shd **Nusoor (IRE)**[22] 6625 4-8-5 **65**............................(b) PatrickMathers(3) 6 34
(Peter Grayson) *prom: rdn 3f out: sn wknd* **33/1**

1m 14.88s (-0.93) **Going Correction** -0.05s/f (Stan) **11** Ran SP% **121.5**
Speed ratings (Par 103): **104,100,100,98,95 93,92,89,88,86 86**
CSF £30.11 CT £88.18 TOTE £4.60: £1.30, £2.10, £1.70; EX 45.60 Place 6 £853.78, Place 5 £545.10.
Owner K J Mercer & Mrs S Mercer **Bred** K J Mercer **Trained** Lambourn, Berks

FOCUS
Several came into this moderate affair in reasonable form. Solid form, the winner running pretty close to this year's turf level.
T/Plt: £162.90 to a £1 stake. Pool: £99,750.80. 446.80 winning tickets. T/Qpdt: £51.40 to a £1 stake. Pool: £5,843.50. 84.10 winning tickets. KH

6782 SAINT-CLOUD (L-H)
Saturday, November 24

OFFICIAL GOING: Heavy

6939a PRIX ISONOMY (LISTED RACE) 1m
1:10 (1:10) 2-Y-O £17,568 (£7,027; £5,270; £3,514; £1,757)

RPR

1 **Vadsalina (IRE)**[13] 2-8-8 .... SPasquier 6 —
(A De Royer-Dupre, France)

2 nse **Fleurina (FR)**[7] 6861 2-8-8 .... RonanThomas 3 —
(Robert Collet, France)

3 1/2 **Destare**[85] 2-8-8 .... THuet 1 —
(J E Pease, France)

4 1 **Indigo Blue (FR)**[23] 2-8-11 .... SRuis 7 —
(J-P Gallorini, France)

5 1 **Silk Affair (IRE)**[29] 6461 2-8-8 .... J-BEyquem 4 —
(M G Quinlan) *led 3f: 2nd 1/2-way: drvn st: u.p 1 1/2f out: one pce fnl f* **12/1**[1]

6 shd **Major D'Helene (FR)**[121] 2-8-11 .... JVictoire 5 —
(F-X de Chevigny, France)

7 2 **Fortunate Isles (USA)**[69] 2-8-8 .... TThulliez 2 —
(P Bary, France)

8 4 **Sambatiger (GER)** 2-8-11 .... WMongil 8 —
(T Horwart, Germany)

1m 50.4s (2.90) **8** Ran SP% **7.7**
PARI-MUTUEL: WIN 2.40; PL 1.20, 2.00, 1.60; DF 11.20.
Owner H H Aga Khan **Bred** Haras De Son Altesse L'Aga Khan **Trained** Chantilly, France

NOTEBOOK
Silk Affair(IRE) was smartly away and with the leaders early on. She held her position until the straight and then battled on well until the furlong marker where she began to fade out of contention. This was a fair effort on this step up in class.

6940a PRIX CERES (LISTED RACE) (FILLIES) 7f
2:15 (2:17) 3-Y-O £17,568 (£7,027; £5,270; £3,514; £1,757)

RPR

1 **Air Bag (FR)**[22] 6632 3-8-11 .... MBlancpain 10 100
(Mme C Barande-Barbe, France)

2 shd **Mary D'Or (FR)**[42] 3-8-11 .... TThulliez 2 100
(N Clement, France)

3 2 **Danse Du Soir (FR)**[49] 3-8-11 .... DBoeuf 14 95
(H-A Pantall, France)

4 1 **Brofalya (FR)**[37] 3-8-11 .... J-BEyquem 1 92
(J-C Rouget, France)

5 2 **Titree**[10] 3-8-11 .... GBenoist 9 87
(C Laffon-Parias, France)

6 1/2 **Banderella (IRE)** 3-8-11 .... AStarke 12 85
(W Hickst, Germany)

7 1 **Antonym (USA)** 3-8-11 .... AlxiBadel 6 82
(Mario Hofer, Germany)

8 shd **Anoush (USA)**[82] 5107 3-8-11 .... TJarnet 4 82
(P Bary, France)

9 1 1/2 **Katoomba**[23] 3-8-11 .... JVictoire 3 78
(H-A Pantall, France)

10 8 **Mimisel**[55] 5850 3-8-11 .... DBonilla 5 57
(Rae Guest) *racd in 3rd on ins: 4th and drvn st: one pce 1 1/2f out: eased fnl 150yds* **54/1**[1]

0 **Fairy Dress (USA)**[22] 3-8-11 .... SMaillot 7 —
(Robert Collet, France)

0 **Macheera (IRE)**[22] 6632 3-8-11 .... J-BHamel 11 —
(Robert Collet, France)

1m 33.1s (0.90) **12** Ran SP% **1.8**
PARI-MUTUEL: WIN 7.70; PL 2.40, 3.60, 4.60; DF 44.50.
Owner Mme C Barande-Barbe **Bred** Patrick & Mme Corinne Barbe **Trained** France

NOTEBOOK
Mimisel was well placed until early in the straight. Slightly hampered two out, she was soon beaten and her trainer felt she may need a longer trip in the future.

6941a PRIX DENISY (LISTED RACE) 1m 7f 110y
2:45 (2:47) 3-Y-O+ £17,568 (£7,027; £5,270; £3,514; £1,757)

RPR

1 **El Tango (GER)**[28] 6518 5-9-7 .... AStarke 8 106
(P Schiergen, Germany)

2 snk **Loup De Mer (GER)**[27] 6526 5-9-1 .... DBoeuf 12 100
(W Baltromei, Germany)

3 1 1/2 **Incanto Dream**[57] 5793 3-8-7 .... YLerner 5 99
(C Lerner, France)

4 shd **Latin Mood (FR)**[27] 6526 4-9-4 .... TThulliez 2 101
(P Demercastel, France)

5 3/4 **Brisant (GER)**[27] 6526 5-9-4 .... WMongil 9 101
(M Trybuhl, Germany)

6 nk **Darsha (FR)**[8] 6846 3-8-10 .... MPoirier 3 101
(A De Royer-Dupre, France)

7 6 **Shaking**[85] 3-8-4 .... SPasquier 7 89
(A Fabre, France)

8 snk **Dance The Classics (IRE)**[44] 6137 3-8-4 ....(b) DBonilla 4 89
(J L Dunlop) *led 5f: 4th and pushed along st: rdn 2f out: no ex fr over 1f out* **31/1**[1]

9 4 **Art Martial (FR)**[57] 5793 3-8-7 .... SDevesse 11 88
(A De Royer-Dupre, France)

10 1 1/2 **Ponte Tresa (FR)**[27] 6526 4-9-4 .... ACrastus 6 89
(Y De Nicolay, France)

0 **Sac A Puces (FR)**[13] 10-9-1 .... RonanThomas 1 —
(J-P Gallorini, France)

0 **Savoisien (FR)**[18] 7-9-1 .... ABonnefoy 13 —
(J-V Toux, France)

0 **Gallo's Wells (IRE)**[23] 4-9-1 .... SRuis 10 —
(J-P Gallorini, France)

0 **Caprice (GER)**[24] 6600 4-8-11 .... JVictoire 14 —
(A De Royer-Dupre, France)

3m 42.5s (3.80)
WFA 3 from 4yo+ 8lb **14** Ran SP% **3.1**
PARI-MUTUEL: WIN 5.60; PL 3.00, 5.90, 6.90; DF 72.20.
Owner Stall Mydlinghoven **Bred** Gestut Wittekindshof **Trained** Germany

NOTEBOOK
Dance The Classics(IRE) was smartly into her stride and soon at the head of affairs. She led until halfway up the straight and then dropped out of contention as if finding this trip beyond her. She has apparently now been retired to stud.

The Form Book, Raceform Ltd, Compton, RG20 6NL

TOKYO (L-H)

Saturday, November 24

OFFICIAL GOING: Standard

6942a JAPAN CUP DIRT (GRADE 1) (DIRT) 1m 2f 110y

6:20 (6:20) 3-Y-0+

£572,950 (£227,410; £143,722; £85,763; £55,746; £39,022)

RPR

1 **Vermilion (JPN)**[24] 5-9-0 .... YTake 7 118
(S Ishizaka, Japan)

2 1 ¼ **Field Rouge (JPN)**[28] 5-9-0 .... NYokoyama 11 116
(M Nishizono, Japan)

3 3 ½ **Sunrise Bacchus (JPN)**[24] 5-9-0 .... KAndo 1 109
(H Otonashi, Japan)

4 1 ¼ **Meisho Tokon (JPN)**[68] 5-9-0 .... KTake 8 107
(I Yasuda, Japan)

5 nk **Wild Wonder (JPN)**[28] 5-9-0 .... YIwata 6 106
(T Kubota, Japan)

6 1 ¼ **Dragon Fire (JPN)**[56] 3-8-10 .... KatsuharuTanaka 12 105
(T Kubota, Japan)

7 1 ¾ **Blue Concorde (JPN)**[24] 7-9-0 .... HMiyuki 13 100
(T Hattori, Japan)

8 2 ½ **Student Council (USA)**[56] 5-9-0 .... RMigliore 2 96
(V Cerin, U.S.A)

9 nk **Wonder Speed (JPN)**[27] 5-9-0 .... FKomaki 10 95
(T Hatsuki, Japan)

10 2 ½ **Furioso (JPN)**[24] 3-8-10 .... HUchida 4 91
(M Kawashima, Japan)

11 dist **Fusaichi Ho O (JPN)**[34] 3-8-10 .... OPeslier 14 —
(K Matsuda, Japan)

12 1 ¾ **Jack Sullivan (USA)**[41] 6198 6-9-0 .... EddieAhern 15 —
(G A Butler) *mid-div: n.d* **122/1**[2]

13 nk **Eishin Lombard (USA)**[28] 5-9-0 .... YFukunaga 9 —
(K Kozaki, Japan)

14 nk **Bonneville Record (JPN)**[27] 5-9-0 .... YShibata 16 —
(M Horii, Japan)

15 2 ½ **Kandidate**[80] 5142 5-9-0 .... RyanMoore 3 —
(C E Brittain) *racd in 3rd on ins: disp ld 3 1/2f out: rdn and led ent st: hdd 2f out: wknd* **82/1**[1]

16 10 **Cafe Olympus (USA)**[28] 6-9-0 .... HGoto 5 —
(Y Matsuyama, Japan)

2m 6.70s (126.70)
WFA 3 from 5yo+ 4lb **16** Ran SP% **2.0**
(Including Y100 stake): WIN 230; PL 130, 250, 420; DF 1,350.
Owner Sunday Racing Co Ltd **Bred** Northern Farm **Trained** Japan

NOTEBOOK

Jack Sullivan(USA) was taking a step up in both trip and class, having been campaigned at around 7f in Britain this season. He not surprisingly failed to figure in this competitive contest.

Kandidate, who has been globetrotting this season, was given a positive ride but weakened pretty quickly once in line for home.

6942 TOKYO (L-H)

Sunday, November 25

OFFICIAL GOING: Firm

6943a JAPAN CUP (GRADE 1) 1m 4f

6:20 (6:22) 3-Y-0+

£1,088,250 (£433,448; £272,470; £162,950; £107,204; £75,043)

RPR

1 **Admire Moon (JPN)**[28] 4-9-0 .... YIwata 4 124
(H Matsuda, Japan) *a cl up: 4th st on ins: wnt 2nd 2f out: led dist: rdn out and r.o wl to hold on* **99/10**

2 hd **Pop Rock (JPN)**[28] 6-9-0 .... OPeslier 2 123
(Katsuhiko Sumii, Japan) *a cl up: 5th st: rdn and hdwy in middle over 1f out: wnt 2nd 100yds out: r.o wl: jst failed* **19/2**

3 nk **Meisho Samson (JPN)**[28] 4-9-0 .... YTake 10 123
(S Takahashi, Japan) *mid-div: c wd on turn: hdwy over 2f out: rdn over 1f out: 4th 1f out: r.o* **4/5**[1]

4 1 **Vodka (JPN)**[42] 3-8-5 .... HShii 11 118
(Katsuhiko Sumii, Japan) *hld up in rr: last 4f out: hdwy and moved to outside fr 2 1/2f out: styd on wl tl no ex fnl 100yds* **51/10**[2]

5 1 ¼ **Delta Blues (JPN)**[28] 6-9-0 .... YKawada 18 119
(Katsuhiko Sumii, Japan) *a cl up: 6th st: kpt on one pce fnl 2f* **146/1**

6 nk **Chosan (JPN)**[28] 5-9-0 .... NYokoyama 5 119
(T Shimizu, Japan) *led after 1f tl hdd at dist: one pce* **62/1**

7 2 **Papal Bull**[65] 5589 4-9-0 .... RyanMoore 7 116
(Sir Michael Stoute) *s.i.s: towards rr to st: styd on fr over 1f out: nvr a factor* **51/1**

8 ¾ **Artiste Royal (IRE)**[50] 6-9-0 .... (b) JTalamo 8 115
(N Drysdale, U.S.A) *in tch: 7th st: rdn 2f out: one pce* **36/1**

9 nk **Fusaichi Pandora (JPN)**[14] 4-8-10 .... SFujita 12 110
(T Shirai, Japan) *first to show: trckd ldrs: 3rd st: wnt 2nd 2 1/2f out: stl 3rd 1f out: wknd qckly* **74/1**

10 1 ½ **Inti Raimi (JPN)**[49] 5-9-0 .... TSato 9 112
(S Sasaki, Japan) *mid-div to st: effrt on outside 2f out: sn btn* **64/10**[3]

11 hd **Saddex**[49] 6043 4-9-0 .... TMundry 16 111
(P Rau, Germany) *hld up towards rr: 17th st: hung lft and bmpd rival over 2f out: nvr a factor* **72/1**

12 ½ **Erimo Harrier (JPN)**[49] 7-9-0 .... KTake 1 111
(H Tadokoro, Japan) *a towards rr* **204/1**

13 ¾ **Cosmo Bulk (JPN)**[28] 6-9-0 .... MMatsuoka 3 109
(K Tabe, Japan) *trckd ldr: 2nd st: wknd 2f out* **109/1**

14 ½ **Dream Passport (JPN)**[252] 4-9-0 .... KAndo 14 109
(H Matsuda, Japan) *a towards rr* **15/1**

15 1 **Rosenkreuz (JPN)**[28] 5-9-0 .... YFujioka 15 107
(K Hashiguchi, Japan) *last st: bmpd over 2f out: a bhd* **224/1**

16 5 **Hiraboku Royal (JPN)**[35] 3-8-10 .... (b) HGoto 13 101
(R Okubo, Japan) *prom to appr st: sn btn* **258/1**

17 3 **Halicarnassus (IRE)**[65] 5589 3-8-10 .... DarryllHolland 17 96
(M R Channon) *mid-div: pushed along on outside over 3f out: btn over 2f out* **165/1**

18 7 **Victory (JPN)**[35] 3-8-10 .... C-PLemaire 6 85
(H Otonashi, Japan) *mid-div: btn over 2f out* **47/1**

2m 24.7s (-0.80)
WFA 3 from 4yo+ 6lb **18** Ran SP% **124.9**
(including 100 yen stakes): WIN 1,090; PL 240, 180, 110; DF 3,660; SF 8,100.
Owner Darley Japan Farm Co Ltd **Bred** Northern Farm **Trained** Japan

FOCUS

This looked a strong renewal of this big international even and the form appears solid.

NOTEBOOK

Admire Moon(JPN), a consistent performer whose wins this season include the Dubai Duty Free in the spring, handled the step up in trip well and battled on bravely to score. He will now retire to Darley's Japanese Stud for next season.

Pop Rock(JPN), who was narrowly beaten in last season's Melbourne Cup, has had several near misses since and very nearly caught his old rival, who had beaten him at Hanshin earlier in the year. He deserves to win a big race.

Meisho Samson(JPN), who had been beaten half-a length by the winner at Hanshin in June, ran to that form again, having beaten both of the first two in the meantime and for that reason he was sent off favourite.

Papal Bull had the ground to suit but missed the break and never looked that happy. However, he did stay on without ever looking likely to reach a challenging position.

Halicarnassus(IRE), who beat Papal Bull at Newbury in September, had a stiff task all all known form and was in trouble soon after turning in.

6925 LINGFIELD (L-H)

Monday, November 26

OFFICIAL GOING: Standard

Wind: nil Weather: partly overcast

6944 LINGFIELD PARK FOR WEDDINGS MAIDEN STKS (DIV I) 1m (P)

12:00 (12:02) (Class 5) 2-Y-O **£2,493** (£741; £277; £277) **Stalls** High

Form RPR

00 1 **Jaser**[53] 5951 2-9-3 0 .... AdrianMcCarthy 9 70
(P W Chapple-Hyam) *trckd ldrs: upsides ldr 3f out: rdn 2f out: led 1f out: forged ahd last 75yds* **12/1**

2 ¾ **Mrs Summersby (IRE)** 2-8-12 0 .... SteveDrowne 8 63+
(H Morrison) *hld up towards rr: hdwy into midfield wl over 2f out: rdn wl over 1f out: styd on wl fnl f: wnt 2nd nr fin* **16/1**

3 ½ **Hasty Retreat** 2-9-3 0 .... StephenDonohoe 12 67
(E A L Dunlop) *w.w wl in tch in midfield: hdwy to chse ldng pair and rdn over 2f out: kpt on u.p fnl f* **12/1**

0 3 dht **Orange Square (IRE)**[10] 6827 2-9-3 0 .... RichardHughes 6 67+
(R Hannon) *led for 1f: chsd ldr tl led again 3f out: rdn jst over 2f out: hdd 1f out: ev ch tl no ex last 75yds* **3/1**[1]

06 5 ½ **Berry Baby (IRE)**[17] 6742 2-8-12 0 .... NickyMackay 10 61
(G A Butler) *hld up in rr: c wd and hdwy over 1f out: styd on wl fnl f: nt rch ldrs* **33/1**

6 1 **Warringah** 2-9-3 0 .... DeanMcKeown 7 64
(Sir Michael Stoute) *in tch: rdn over 2f out: kpt on same pce fnl f* **5/1**[3]

7 1 ¼ **Desert Sands (IRE)** 2-9-0 0 .... JerryO'Dwyer(3) 3 61+
(John Joseph Murphy, Ire) *stdd s: hld up towards rr: rdn wl over 1f out: kpt on but nvr trbld ldrs* **20/1**

8 1 ¼ **E'Cusson** 2-8-12 0 .... NCallan 5 53
(M A Jarvis) *in tch: rdn and struggling whn short of room bnd jst over 2f out: n.d after* **5/1**[3]

9 1 **Mischief Making (USA)** 2-8-12 0 .... TGMcLaughlin 11 51
(E A L Dunlop) *sn pushed along in rr: rdn 4f out: nvr nr ldrs* **12/1**

00 10 hd **Black Tor Figarro (IRE)**[30] 6493 2-8-10 0 .... GHannon(7) 4 56
(B W Duke) *led after 1f: hdd 3f out: wknd wl over 1f out* **50/1**

02 11 ¾ **Colorado Springs**[28] 6543 2-8-12 0 .... ChrisCatlin 2 49
(W Jarvis) *t.k.h: chsd ldrs on inner: rdn and wknd 2f out: hanging lft over 1f out* **4/1**[2]

1m 38.76s (-0.67) **Going Correction** -0.15s/f (Stan) **11** Ran SP% **117.0**
Speed ratings (Par 96): **97,96,95,95,95 94,93,91,90,90 89**
3rd place Tote: Hasty Retreat 2.60, Orange Square £0.60 CSF £182.76 TOTE £21.80: £3.60, £5.10; EX 305.30 TRIFECTA Not won..
Owner Ziad A Galadari **Bred** Galadari Sons Stud Company Limited **Trained** Newmarket, Suffolk
■ Stewards' Enquiry : Stephen Donohoe caution: careless riding

FOCUS

Some powerful connections were represented and this looked a reasonable maiden for the time of the year, although there was not much previous form to go on. They went steady through the early stages, but the gallop increased significantly inside the final half mile. The winning time was 0.48 seconds quicker than the second division.

NOTEBOOK

Jaser had hinted at ability on a couple of starts in good maiden company at Newmarket and he stepped up on those efforts with a convincing success off the back of a near two-month break. He looks a nice prospect for next year. (op 11-1)

Mrs Summersby(IRE) ◆, 45,000euros daughter of King's Best, first foal of a top-class multiple winner in South Africa, made a very pleasing debut. Ridden with patience through the early stages, she could easily have been caught out when the pace increased inside the final half mile, but she made good headway to move into a challenging position and maintained her effort all the way to the line. This run should bring her on and she can win a maiden before stepping up in class. She should make a lovely three-year-old.

Hasty Retreat, by King's Best, out of a multiple 5f-6f winner at two to three, shaped nicely on his racecourse debut. He is open to improvement. (op 7-2)

Orange Square(IRE) stepped up on the form he showed on his debut over 7f round here and is going the right way. (op 7-2)

Berry Baby(IRE) ◆ had shown just moderate form in a couple of turf maidens over 7f, but this was much better. She can be rated even better than the bare form suggests as she was given plenty to do and was caught out when the pace increased. She should be one to look out for in handicap company.

Warringah ◆, a Galileo colt, half-brother to high-class Hi Calypso, a multiple 7f-1m7f winner, out of a quite useful 1m winner, showed ability on his debut and should come into his when stepped up to middle-distances in time. (op 11-2 tchd 6-1)

Desert Sands(IRE) ◆, a 38,000gns son of Dubai Destination, half-brother to quite useful Silk Dress, Group-3 placed over 7f at two, was short of room when trying to make a move rounding the final bend and he is better than he was able to show.

E'Cusson, a daughter of Singspiel, half-sister to Love On The Rocks, who was placed over 1m at two, was well held on her racecourse debut and probably needs a bit more time. (op 4-1)

Colorado Springs was hanging in the straight and was well below the form she showed when runner-up over course and distance on her previous start. (tchd 9-2)

6945 LINGFIELD PARK FOR CONFERENCES H'CAP (DIV I) 7f (P)

12:30 (12:33) (Class 6) (0-58,60) 3-Y-0+ **£1,706** (£503; £252) **Stalls** Low

Form RPR

6003 **1** **Park Valley Prince**[10] 6831 3-8-8 **49**.. PaulDoe 6 57+
(W R Muir) *led for 1f: chsd ldr after: rdn over 1f out: led ins fnl f: r.o wl* **10/3**[1]

5000 **2** ¾ **Aggbag**[27] 6563 3-8-1 **45**.. AndrewElliott[(3)] 4 51
(B P J Baugh) *t.k.h: hld up in tch: rdn over 1f out: swtchd rt ins fnl f: r.o u.p: wnt 2nd wl ins fnl f: nt rch ldr* **25/1**

4015 **3** ½ **Piccolo Diamante (USA)**[7] 6869 3-8-10 **51**...............(t) FrancisNorton 5 59+
(D J Murphy) *t.k.h in midfield: swtchd to outer and rdn 3f out: styd on u.p fnl f: wnt 3rd wl ins fnl f* **7/2**[2]

0040 **4** ¾ **Tilsworth Charlie**[10] 6825 4-9-1 **55**......................................(b) NCallan 11 58
(J R Jenkins) *hld up in tch in rr: rdn and hdwy over 1 fout: no imp last 100yds* **14/1**

0040 **5** shd **Mulberry Lad (IRE)**[2] 6925 5-8-13 **53**................................. ChrisCatlin 1 55
(P W Hiatt) *chsd ldrs on inner: rdn jst over 2f out: kpt on same pce fnl f* **8/1**

2333 **6** 1 **Midmaar (IRE)**[6] 6887 6-8-12 **52**...............................(b) JamieMackay 12 52
(M Wigham) *t.k.h: hld up in tch: hdwy to chse ldrs and rdn 2f out: sn nt qckn and no hdwy* **11/2**

1006 **7** shd **King After**[10] 6825 5-9-1 **55**..(v) GeorgeBaker 7 54
(J R Best) *t.k.h: hld up in tch on outer: rdn to chse ldrs 2f out: sn no hdwy and btn* **9/2**[3]

0460 **8** shd **Lady Duxyana**[10] 6825 4-8-5 **45**..................................(v) HayleyTurner 13 44
(M D I Usher) *hld up in detached last: rdn and hdwy over 1f out: nvr trbld ldrs* **25/1**

6030 **9** 1 **Inquisitress**[5] 6894 3-9-3 **58**.. MickyFenton 3 54
(J J Bridger) *led after 1f: rdn 2f out: hdd ins fnl f: wknd qckly* **12/1**

2-00 **10** 3 **Coastal Breeze**[14] 6796 4-8-9 **48** ow1........................(b[1]) SteveDrowne 10 37
(A J Chamberlain) *racd in midfield on inner: rdn wl over 2f out: wknd 2f out* **25/1**

1m 25.6s (-0.29) **Going Correction** -0.15s/f (Stan)
WFA 3 from 4yo+ 1lb **10** Ran SP% **115.9**
Speed ratings (Par 101): **95,94,93,92,92 91,91,91,90,86**
CSF £88.83 CT £305.48 TOTE £4.80: £2.00, £6.10, £2.00; EX 117.70 TRIFECTA Not won..
Owner Middleham Park Racing Xxi **Bred** Usk Valley Stud **Trained** Lambourn, Berks
■ Stewards' Enquiry : Jamie Mackay one-day ban: careless riding (Dec 7)

FOCUS
A weak handicap which was slowly run. The form has been rated fairly negatively around the winner and third. The winning time was 0.76 seconds slower than the second division, and 1.53 seconds slower than the claimer.

6946 LINGFIELDPARK.CO.UK H'CAP 6f (P)

1:00 (1:02) (Class 5) (0-70,70) 3-Y-0+ **£2,817** (£838; £418; £209) **Stalls** Low

Form RPR

0354 **1** **Regal Raider (IRE)**[10] 6826 4-8-7 **62**..........................(p) AndrewElliott[(3)] 8 74+
(A M Hales) *t.k.h: hld up in midfield on outer: stl gng wl 2f out: shkn up and hdwy jst over 1f out: rdn and str run fnl f to ld last strides* **12/1**

2021 **2** nk **Brandywell Boy (IRE)**[12] 6810 4-9-2 **68**..................... RichardThomas 9 75
(D J S Ffrench Davis) *hld up in rr: rdn and gd hdwy jst over 1f out: led wl ins fnl f: hdd last strides* **7/2**[1]

1 **3** nk **Realt Na Mara (IRE)**[26] 6580 4-8-12 **64**.......................... SteveDrowne 4 71
(H Morrison) *led: hrd pressed and rdn 2f out: battled on wl tl hdd and no ex wl ins fnl f* **7/1**

2134 **4** hd **Gimme Some Lovin (IRE)**[7] 6870 3-8-8 **60**................. FrancisNorton 2 66
(D W P Arbuthnot) *chsd ldrs: rdn and hdwy over 2f out: ev ch fnl f: no ex last 50yds* **13/2**[3]

4006 **5** 1¼ **Tango Step (IRE)**[9] 6854 7-8-8 **63** ow3.....................(p) JerryO'Dwyer[(3)] 7 65
(Bernard Lawlor, Ire) *hld up bhd: gd hdwy on inner bnd over 2f out: ev ch ins fnl f: fdd last 50yds* **16/1**

0026 **6** shd **Mine Behind**[10] 6826 7-9-3 **69**.. GeorgeBaker 11 71
(J R Best) *dropped in after s: hld up in rr: swtchd rt and hdwy over 1f out: r.o fnl f: nt rch ldrs* **8/1**

3450 **7** nk **Dvinsky (USA)**[12] 6818 6-9-0 **66**.. ChrisCatlin 5 67
(P Howling) *chsd ldr tl 2f out: wknd u.p 1f out* **6/1**[2]

4160 **8** ½ **Make My Dream**[10] 6829 4-8-12 **64**............................. J-PGuillambert 12 63
(J Gallagher) *chsd ldrs: rdn over 2f out: wknd over 1f out* **16/1**

3050 **9** 2 **Plateau**[12] 6810 8-8-10 **62**.. AdamKirby 10 55
(C R Dore) *in tch in midfield: rdn over 2f out: sn outpcd* **14/1**

2-00 **10** ¾ **Mumaathel (IRE)**[14] 6795 4-9-2 **68**................................... MickyFenton 3 58
(M A Buckley) *stdd s and hld up towards rr: plld hrd: hdwy to chse ldrs over 2f out: wknd over 1f out* **20/1**

6005 **11** ¾ **Who's Winning (IRE)**[32] 6450 6-8-11 **70**....................... KylieManser[(7)] 1 58
(B G Powell) *a bhd: pushed along 4f out: bhd last 2f* **14/1**

1010 **12** 5 **Calabaza**[32] 6450 5-8-13 **65**.. PaulDoe 6 37
(J Akehurst) *prom on outer tl rdn and wknd qckly 2f out* **11/1**

1m 10.96s (-1.85) **Going Correction** -0.15s/f (Stan) **12** Ran SP% **119.3**
Speed ratings (Par 103): **106,105,105,104,103 103,102,102,99,98 97,90**
CSF £54.06 CT £331.89 TOTE £16.20: £3.80, £1.50, £2.20; EX 66.00 TRIFECTA Not won..
Owner Brick Farm Racing **Bred** Gerard Callanan **Trained** Preston Capes, Northants

FOCUS
A modest sprint handicap run at a strong pace and producing a decent time. The form has been rated at face value through the second and third.
Realt Na Mara(IRE) ◆ Official explanation: jockey said gelding hung right
Mine Behind Official explanation: jockey said gelding was denied a clear run
Who's Winning(IRE) Official explanation: jockey said gelding did not face kickback

6947 LINGFIELD PARK FOR CHRISTMAS PARTIES CLAIMING STKS 7f (P)

1:30 (1:30) (Class 6) 3-Y-0+ **£2,047** (£604; £302) **Stalls** Low

Form RPR

0043 **1** **Onenightinlisbon (IRE)**[9] 6854 3-8-8 69..................... PaulMulrennan 3 63
(K R Burke) *in tch: rdn and hdwy jst over 2f out: chsd ldr over 1f out: kpt on u.p to ld wl ins fnl f* **6/1**[3]

0001 **2** nk **One More Round (USA)**[10] 6826 9-9-6 87................(b) GeorgeBaker 10 73
(Ollie Pears) *dropped in bhd after s: hdwy on outer over 2f out: chal 1f out: sn rdn: nt qckn nr fin* **13/8**[1]

2020 **3** nk **Chief Exec**[12] 6806 5-8-9 69.. DavidProbert[(7)] 8 68
(B J Llewellyn) *chsd ldrs: wnt 2nd over 3f out: led and rdn jst over 2f out: hrd pressed 1f out: hdd and no ex wl ins fnl f* **16/1**

1000 **4** 1¾ **Ceredig**[75] 5062 4-8-11 48.. TGMcLaughlin 2 61
(Mrs L J Mongan) *t.k.h: chsd ldr tl over 3f out: rdn over 2f out: short of room and hmpd wl over 1f out: kpt on u.p fnl f* **50/1**

0000 **5** nk **China Cherub**[5] 6900 4-9-1 82.............................(b) RichardHughes 6 62
(R Hannon) *racd in midfield: rdn 2f out: outpcd over 1f out: kpt on again ins fnl f* **2/1**[2]

0006 **6** 2½ **Only If I Laugh**[74] 5368 6-8-11 43...................................... AdamKirby 4 51
(M J Attwater) *in tch towards rr: rdn 4f out: wknd 2f out* **66/1**

0566 **7** ½ **Mozakhraf (USA)**[40] 6268 5-8-12 62..................(p) NataliaGemelova[(5)] 9 56
(K A Ryan) *taken down early: racd freely: led tl jst over 2f out: wknd over 1f out* **14/1**

1000 **8** 3 **White Bear (FR)**[14] 6795 5-9-0 64...............................(b) HayleyTurner 7 45
(C R Dore) *hld up in last: nvr on terms* **12/1**

0005 **S** **Pivotal Era**[10] 6826 4-8-10 55.....................................(b) RichardThomas 1 —
(Jim Best) *racd in midfield: rdn whn slipped up bnd over 2f out: dead* **16/1**

1m 24.07s (-1.82) **Going Correction** -0.15s/f (Stan)
WFA 3 from 4yo+ 1lb **9** Ran SP% **115.3**
Speed ratings (Par 101): **104,103,103,101,100 98,97,94,—**
CSF £16.10 TOTE £7.60: £2.10, £1.40, £3.90; EX 17.80 Trifecta £159.10 Part won. Pool: £224.20, 0.66 winning units..The winner was claimed by J. R. Boyle for £9,000
Owner Nigel Shields **Bred** Stephen Moloney **Trained** Middleham Moor, N Yorks

FOCUS
A good claimer on paper, but the proximity of the fourth and sixth does little for the form. The winning time was 1.53 seconds quicker than the first division of the 7f handicap, and 0.77 seconds quicker than the second division.

6948 LINGFIELD PARK FOR WEDDINGS MAIDEN STKS (DIV II) 1m (P)

2:00 (2:15) (Class 5) 2-Y-0 **£2,493** (£741; £370; £185) **Stalls** High

Form RPR

0422 **1** **Magical Fantasy (USA)**[16] 6763 2-8-12 76........................... NCallan 10 70
(J Nicol) *t.k.h: chsd ldrs: wnt 2nd over 2f out: rdn to ld over 1f out: jst hld on* **2/1**[1]

2 hd **Agente Romano (USA)** 2-9-3 0................................. NickyMackay 11 75+
(G A Butler) *bhd: pushed along early: hdwy 2f out: r.o wl fnl f: jst hld* **13/2**[2]

0 **3** 2 **Valvigneres (IRE)**[9] 6857 2-9-3 0.............................. TGMcLaughlin 12 70
(E A L Dunlop) *t.k.h: hdwy to ld after 2f: rdn 3f out: hdd over 1f out: one pce fnl f* **50/1**

6 **4** 1 **Flash Of Colour**[162] 2687 2-9-3 0.. PatDobbs 8 68
(Mrs A J Perrett) *led for 2f: chsd ldr after: rdn 3f out: lost 2nd over 2f out: kpt on same pce* **40/1**

04 **5** ¾ **Unlicensed**[9] 6850 2-9-3 0.. RichardHughes 3 66
(R Hannon) *in tch: hdwy to chse ldrs over 2f out: hung bdly rt bnd jst over 2f out: nt rcvr* **7/1**[3]

6 1¼ **Dynamo Dave (USA)** 2-9-3 0.. IanMongan 2 63
(B J Meehan) *t.k.h: chsd ldrs: rdn 2f out: wknd over 1f out* **2/1**[1]

00 **7** 1½ **Shaftesbury (IRE)**[33] 6418 2-9-3 0................................ J-PGuillambert 4 60
(M Johnston) *racd in midfield: rdn and effrt over 2f out: nvr pce to rch ldrs* **9/1**

45 **8** nk **Autumn Charm**[34] 6401 2-8-12 0... SteveDrowne 6 54
(W Jarvis) *t.k.h: in tch in midfield: rdn wl over 2f out: wknd 2f out* **20/1**

9 nk **Nino Cochise (IRE)** 2-9-3 0.................................... StephenDonohoe 9 58
(C R Egerton) *s.i.s: a bhd* **20/1**

10 ¾ **Kannon** 2-8-12 0.. PaulDoe 5 51
(W J Knight) *v.s.a: a bhd* **16/1**

0 **11** ¾ **Tessie Bear**[9] 6847 2-8-12 0.. HayleyTurner 7 50
(Andrew Reid) *bhd: rdn 5f out: sn wl bhd* **66/1**

12 ¾ **Killcara Boy** 2-9-3 0.. AdamKirby 1 53
(H Candy) *s.i.s: sn rdn along in rr: nvr on terms* **25/1**

1m 39.24s (-0.19) **Going Correction** -0.15s/f (Stan) **12** Ran SP% **127.6**
Speed ratings (Par 96): **94,93,91,90,90 88,87,87,86,85 85,84**
CSF £16.58 TOTE £2.80: £1.20, £1.90, £15.80; EX 17.30 Trifecta £341.80 Part won. Pool: £481.41, 0.36 winning units..
Owner Miss Anita Farrell **Bred** Rodes S Parrish & Charles Beach Iv **Trained** Newmarket, Suffolk

FOCUS
Probably the weaker of the two divisions and the winning time was 0.48 seconds slower. The winner was a bit below her best and it remains to be seen how reliable this form proves.

NOTEBOOK
Magical Fantasy(USA) had shown plenty of ability on all four of her previous starts and she found this a suitable opportunity to get off the mark. Having travelled well on the pace throughout, she picked up when asked to go on at the top of the straight and had just enough in hand to hold off the fast-finishing runner-up. She should hold her own in handicaps. (op 9-4 tchd 15-8 and 5-2 in places)
Agente Romano(USA), a $70,000 son of Street Cry, half-brother to a dual sprint winner at three in the US, out of a dual winner at 1m plus at three, including on turf in the US, was given quite a bit to do but finished strongly once getting the hang of things. He should be well up to winning a similar event provided he goes the right way. (op 10-1)
Valvigneres(IRE) showed nothing on his debut over an extended 1m1f at Wolverhampton, but this was much better. He should come into his own over further next year. (op 40-1)
Flash Of Colour was tailed off on his debut over 6f at Folkestone back in June, but this was much better and he has clearly benefited from a bit of time off the track. He should find his level once handicapped. (op 50-1 tchd 33-1)
Unlicensed could not really build on the form he showed when fourth over 7f round here on his previous start, hanging badly right close home, but he will have more options now he is qualified for a handicap mark. Official explanation: jockey said gelding hung right (op 7-2)
Dynamo Dave(USA), a son of Distorted Dave, half-brother to dual US sprint winner Mama Theresa, and Mercy Matters, a prolific winner on turf in US, out of a smart prolific winner at around 6f-1m1f in the US, was all the rage in the market, but was seemingly in need of the run. (op 4-1 tchd 9-2 in places)
Kannon Official explanation: jockey said filly jumped awkwardly

6949 PLAY GOLF @ LINGFIELD PARK H'CAP 1m (P)

2:30 (2:42) (Class 4) (0-85,82) 3-Y-0+ **£4,728** (£1,406; £702; £351) **Stalls** High

Form RPR

2314 **1** **Councellor (FR)**[22] 6674 5-9-4 **80**...................................(t) MickyFenton 4 85
(Stef Liddiard) *t.k.h: trckd ldrs on inner: effrt to chse ldr 2f out: rdn to ld jst over 1f out: hld on wl* **12/1**

2120 **2** ½ **New World Order (IRE)**[49] 6067 3-8-9 **76**...............(t) AndrewElliott[(3)] 9 80
(K R Burke) *sn pushed up to ld: rdn jst over 2f out: hdd jst over 1f out: kpt on same pce fnl f* **22/1**

1301 **3** ½ **Titan Triumph**[14] 6795 3-9-1 **79**...(t) PaulDoe 1 82+
(W J Knight) *hld up in rr: edgd to outer after 3f: hdwy on outer bnd over 2f out: chsd ldrs 1f out: kpt on same pce ins fnl f* **9/4**[1]

0014 **4** shd **Alfresco**[51] 6006 3-9-3 **81**..(b) PatDobbs 5 84+
(I A Wood) *stdd and dropped in bhd after s: hdwy and nt clr run and bmpd 1f out: sn swtchd lft: r.o wl: nt rch ldrs* **7/1**[3]

306 **5** nk **Monkey Glas (IRE)**[49] 6053 3-8-12 **76**......................... PaulMulrennan 8 78
(K R Burke) *t.k.h: chsd ldrs: rdn jst over 2f out: kpt on same pce fnl f* **14/1**

2300 **6** *1* **Mataram (USA)**[79] 5221 4-9-4 **80** SteveDrowne 2 80
(W Jarvis) *t.k.h: hld up in rr: hdwy over 1f out: r.o fnl f: nvr rchd ldrs* **8/1**

5230 **7** *nk* **Fiefdom (IRE)**[16] 6765 5-9-6 **82** AdamKirby 7 81
(I W McInnes) *hld up wl in tch in midfield: hdwy and edgd lft 1f out: styd on but nvr trbld ldrs* **11/1**

4300 **8** *2* **Buxton**[22] 6667 3-8-13 **77** PaulFitzsimons 12 71
(R Ingram) *w.w in tch in midfield: rdn wl over 1f out: fdd fnl f* **25/1**

-004 **9** *1* **Danski**[33] 6435 4-9-6 **82** NCallan 6 74
(P J Makin) *hld up wl in tch in midfield: hdwy to chse ldrs wl over 1f out: wknd 1f out* **4/1**[2]

2016 **10** *hd* **Touch Of Style (IRE)**[23] 6646 3-8-13 **77** ow1 RichardHughes 3 69
(J R Boyle) *t.k.h: hld up in tch on inner: rdn jst over 2f out: wknd fnl f* **12/1**

5-00 **11** *1 1/4* **Celtic Step**[23] 6637 3-8-13 **77** (b) J-PGuillambert 11 66
(M Johnston) *chsd ldr: rdn over 2f out: lost 2nd 2f out: wknd over 1f out* **11/1**

0640 **12** *1/2* **Mandarin Spirit (IRE)**[14] 6795 7-8-11 **73** OscarUrbina 10 61
(G C H Chung) *in tch in midfield: rdn wl over 2f out: wknd 2f out* **16/1**

1m 36.51s (-2.92) **Going Correction** -0.15s/f (Stan)
WFA 3 from 4yo+ 2lb **12** Ran SP% **127.2**
Speed ratings (Par 105): **108,107,107,106,106 105,105,103,102,102 100,100**
CSF £265.61 CT £834.77 TOTE £12.80: £4.50, £6.00, £1.30; EX 353.80 Trifecta £185.50 Part won. Pool: £261.28, 0.72 winning units..
Owner ownaracehorse.co.uk **Bred** Janus Bloodstock & Pontchartrain Stud **Trained** Great Shefford, Berks

FOCUS
A good handicap which did not look strongly run despite the seemingly fair time. A negative view has been taken of the form due to the proximity of the runner-up and the fifth.

6950 LINGFIELD PARK FOR CONFERENCES H'CAP (DIV II) 7f (P)
3:00 (3:09) (Class 6) (0-58,58) 3-Y-0+ **£1,706** (£503; £252) **Stalls** Low

Form RPR

0610 **1** **Joy And Pain**[5] 6895 6-8-12 **53** (p) AdamKirby 1 61
(M J Attwater) *t.k.h: hld up towards rr: hdwy to chse ldrs 2f out: rdn jst over 1f out: r.o wl to ld nr fin* **9/2**[2]

6400 **2** *nk* **Imperium**[31] 6476 6-9-3 **58** (b) PatDobbs 5 65
(Jean-Rene Auvray) *t.k.h: hld up in tch: hdwy to chse ldng pair and rdn wl over 1f out: swtchd lft 1f out: led last 100yds: hdd and no ex nr fin* **14/1**

0005 **3** *1/2* **Convallaria (FR)**[10] 6825 4-9-0 **55** (t) SteveDrowne 10 61
(G Wragg) *bhd: pushed along 3f out: rdn and hdwy over 1f out: r.o ins fnl f: wnt 3rd nr fin: nt rch ldrs* **7/2**[1]

5026 **4** *nk* **Palais Polaire**[12] 6809 5-8-8 **52** (p) TravisBlock(3) 9 57
(J A Geake) *t.k.h: prom tl led 5f out: rdn and carried hd awkwardly 2f out: hdd last 100yds: sn btn* **6/1**

6500 **5** *1/2* **Mountain Pass (USA)**[12] 6806 5-8-8 **56** (p) DavidProbert(7) 11 59
(B J Llewellyn) *t.k.h: hld up in rr: hdwy 2f out: rdn wl over 1f out: styd on but nt pce to rch ldrs* **11/1**

0546 **6** *1 1/2* **Rafferty (IRE)**[7] 6873 8-8-4 **51** ow4 ThomasBubb(7) 6 51
(S Dow) *v.s.a: sn in tch on inner: rdn wl over 1f out: kpt on but nvr threatened ldrs* **9/1**

0006 **7** *3/4* **King Of Charm (IRE)**[28] 6542 4-7-12 **46** oh1 (b) RossAtkinson(7) 3 43
(G L Moore) *restless in stalls: t.k.h: chsd ldr: ev ch and rdn 2f out: wknd qckly jst ins fnl f* **20/1**

0043 **8** *1* **Mister Always**[6] 6886 3-8-3 **48** AndrewElliott(3) 4 43
(I W McInnes) *t.k.h: led for 1f: chsd ldrs after tl rdn and wknd jst over 2f out* **5/1**[3]

-000 **9** *1 3/4* **Patavium Prince (IRE)**[33] 6428 4-8-9 **50** ChrisCatlin 7 40
(Miss Jo Crowley) *t.k.h: hld up in midfield: lost pl and bhd over 3f out: no ch after* **20/1**

4006 **10** *1* **Pajada**[10] 6831 3-8-4 **46** oh1 (v) HayleyTurner 2 33
(M D I Usher) *pushed up to ld after 1f tl 5f out: rdn and wknd wl over 2f out* **33/1**

0030 **11** *shd* **Hannahbecc**[10] 6825 3-8-8 **50** (e) J-PGuillambert 12 37
(S C Williams) *racd on outer: a towards rr: rdn and bhd 2f out: no ch after* **8/1**

1m 24.84s (-1.05) **Going Correction** -0.15s/f (Stan)
WFA 3 from 4yo+ 1lb **11** Ran SP% **119.9**
Speed ratings (Par 101): **100,99,99,98,98 96,95,94,92,91 91**
CSF £65.11 CT £253.04 TOTE £5.10: £1.70, £2.70, £2.10; EX 55.50 Trifecta £118.80 Pool: £222.70, 1.33 winning units.
Owner Phones Direct Partnership **Bred** Jonathan Shack **Trained** Epsom, Surrey

FOCUS
A moderate handicap. Ordinary form which could have been rated a bit higher. The winning time was 0.76 seconds faster than the first division, but 0.77 seconds slower than the claimer.

6951 BOOK ONLINE FOR DISCOUNTED PRICES H'CAP 1m 2f (P)
3:30 (3:37) (Class 6) (0-62,66) 3-Y-0+ **£2,047** (£604; £302) **Stalls** Low

Form RPR

0340 **1** **Stark Contrast (USA)**[42] 6235 3-9-2 **62** RichardHughes 10 70
(J Akehurst) *chsd ldr tl over 6f out: rdn to chse ldr again over 1f out: sn ev ch: led last 100yds: r.o wl* **16/1**

4133 **2** *1/2* **Lilac Moon (GER)**[19] 6713 3-8-10 **56** RichardKingscote 13 63
(N J Vaughan) *led: rdn over 2f out: hrd pressed over 1f out: hdd and no ex last 100yds* **8/1**

1324 **3** *3/4* **Alfie Tupper (IRE)**[26] 6577 4-9-3 **59** SimonWhitworth 2 65+
(S Kirk) *t.k.h: hld up towards rr: hdwy over 2f out: r.o wl fnl f: wnt 3rd nr fin: nt rch ldrs* **9/2**[2]

6404 **4** *nk* **Siena Star (IRE)**[15] 6780 9-9-5 **61** MickyFenton 12 66
(Stef Liddiard) *chsd ldrs: wnt 2nd over 6f out: rdn 3f out: lost 2nd over 1f out: kpt on same pce* **14/1**

0045 **5** *hd* **Royal Amnesty**[20] 6710 4-8-13 **55** OscarUrbina 8 60
(G C H Chung) *t.k.h: hld up in tch: hdwy to chse ldrs over 2f out: sn rdn: kpt on same pce fnl f* **13/2**[3]

-000 **6** *nk* **Just Intersky (USA)**[52] 5964 4-9-1 **57** (e[1]) DeanMcKeown 4 61
(V Smith) *t.k.h: hld up towards rr: hdwy on inner over 2f out: kpt on fnl f: nt rch ldrs* **33/1**

4401 **7** *1/2* **Fateful Attraction**[7] 6866 4-9-10 **66** 6ex (b) NCallan 1 69
(I A Wood) *in tch: rdn and effrt jst over 2f out: kpt on u.p but nt pce to rch ldrs* **7/1**

0053 **8** *nk* **Barry Island**[19] 6719 8-9-4 **60** HayleyTurner 7 62+
(D R C Elsworth) *v.s.a: dropeed in bhd in last: stl wl bhd over 2f out: sme hdwy on inner over 1f out: n.d* **11/4**[1]

0540 **9** *shd* **Mon Petite Amour**[7] 6866 4-9-2 **58** FrancisNorton 14 60
(D W P Arbuthnot) *hld up towards rr: rdn and effrt over 1f out: nvr threatened ldrs* **33/1**

0300 **10** *1/2* **Mr Napoleon (IRE)**[32] 6452 5-8-13 **55** SteveDrowne 11 56
(G L Moore) *w.w in midfield: rdn over 2f out: no hdwy* **7/1**

2206 **11** *hd* **Shaheer (IRE)**[7] 6867 5-8-11 **53** J-PGuillambert 6 54
(J Gallagher) *chsd ldr over 2f out: wknd wl over 1f out* **25/1**

0010 **12** *1/2* **Theatre Royal**[15] 6780 4-8-7 **52** (b) NeilChalmers(3) 3 52
(Mouse Hamilton-Fairley) *w.w in midfield: rdn and effrt on outer over 2f out: nvr threatened ldrs* **40/1**

3244 **13** *3/4* **Casablanca Minx (IRE)**[15] 6774 4-9-3 **59** (v) TGMcLaughlin 5 57
(P D Evans) *hld up in rr: n.d* **16/1**

3003 **14** *1 3/4* **And Again (USA)**[7] 6867 4-8-13 **55** (p) ChrisCatlin 9 50
(R A Teal) *hld up in rr: hmpd 6f out: n.d* **14/1**

2m 6.89s (-0.90) **Going Correction** -0.15s/f (Stan)
WFA 3 from 4yo+ 4lb **14** Ran SP% **131.6**
Speed ratings (Par 101): **97,96,96,95,95 95,94,94,94,94 94,93,93,91**
CSF £147.28 CT £697.68 TOTE £20.50: £7.00, £2.50, £2.10; EX 311.90 TRIFECTA Not won. Place 6 £ 45.83, Place 5 £ 17.73.
Owner A D Spence **Bred** Grousemont Farm **Trained** Epsom, Surrey

FOCUS
This looked a reasonable handicap for the level, but it was steadily run and it proved an advantage to race on the pace. There was not much between the whole field at the line.
T/Plt: £45.00 to a £1 stake. Pool: £34,119.80. 553.30 winning tickets. T/Qpdt: £8.10 to a £1 stake. Pool: £4,327.00. 391.80 winning tickets. SP

6888 FONTAINEBLEAU
Monday, November 26

OFFICIAL GOING: Very soft

6952a PRIX RADIO EVASION FM (PRIX DU LOING) (C&G) 1m
11:50 (11:51) 2-Y-0 **£9,459** (£3,784; £2,838; £1,892; £946)

RPR

1 **Townsville (FR)**[62] 2-8-9 MSautjeau 2 74
(B Secly, France)

2 *shd* **Celebrissime (IRE)**[70] 2-8-9 DBonilla 8 74
(F Head, France)

3 *2* **Penny (FR)** 2-8-9 DBoeuf 5 70
(Mme C Head-Maarek, France)

4 *3/4* **Su Doku (FR)** 2-9-2 THuet 9 75
(J E Pease, France)

5 *1* **Kocham Cie (GER)** 2-8-9 IMendizabal 10 66
(M Trybuhl, Germany)

6 *3* **Camfair (FR)**[85] 2-9-2 ACardine 3 67
(G Chirurgien, France)

7 *1/2* **Sudamy (FR)** 2-8-9 J-BHamel 1 59
(Robert Collet, France)

8 *hd* **Crimson Mitre**[27] 6574 2-8-9 JimCrowley 4 58
(J Jay) *prom on ins: 2nd 1/2-way: rdn 2f out: wknd 1 1/2f out* **28/1**[1]

9 *8* **River Cry (FR)** 2-8-9 RMarchelli 7 42
(P Lenogue, France)

10 *2* **Not Only One (FR)**[4] 2-8-9 RBriard 6 37
(Robert Collet, France)

1m 43.6s (103.60) **10** Ran SP% **3.4**
PARI-MUTUEL (Including 1 Euro stake): WIN 15.20; PL 3.30, 1.30, 3.20; DF 28.60.
Owner P Elliott **Bred** P-D Allaire **Trained** France

NOTEBOOK
Crimson Mitre had shown only modest form in maidens but was below par on this softer surface.

6953a PRIX BELLE DE NUIT (LISTED RACE) (FILLES & MARES) 1m 4f 110y
1:20 (1:26) 3-Y-0+ **£17,568** (£7,027; £5,270; £3,514; £1,757)

RPR

1 **Alma Mater**[17] 6745 4-9-0 J-BEyquem 8 100
(Sir Mark Prescott) *mde all: pushed along st: qcknd up and 1 1/2l clr 1 1/2f out: r.o wl to line: drvn out* **29/10**[1]

2 *4* **Sworn Mum (GER)**[22] 3-8-8 DBoeuf 11 95
(W Baltromei, Germany)

3 *snk* **Silver Mitzva (IRE)**[30] 6519 3-8-8 (b) MMonteriso 3 95
(M Botti) *hld up on ins: pushed along st: rdn and hdwy 2f out: disputing 2nd fnl f: styd on* **16/1**[2]

4 *hd* **Scotch Bonnet (IRE)**[21] 3-8-8 (b) DBonilla 13 95
(R Gibson, France)

5 *1 1/2* **Sureyya (GER)**[46] 6137 4-9-0 GFaucon 12 91
(E Lellouche, France)

6 *2* **Fleche Brisee (USA)**[41] 3-8-8 SPasquier 6 89
(A Fabre, France)

7 *1 1/2* **Lady Needles (IRE)**[144] 5-9-0 RMarchelli 15 86
(M Rolland, France)

8 *nk* **Rhapsody In Blue (GER)**[22] 4-9-0 PHeugl 7 86
(D K Richardson, Germany)

9 *2* **Penkinella (FR)**[32] 6460 4-9-0 AClement 10 83
(A Couetil, France)

10 *2* **Carolines Secret**[29] 3-8-8 AHelfenbein 5 81
(Mario Hofer, Germany)

0 **Double Mix (FR)**[26] 6600 4-9-0 TThulliez 17 —
(Rod Collet, France)

0 **Ragazza Mio (IRE)**[178] 2330 4-9-0 AlxiBadel 9 —
(A De Royer-Dupre, France)

0 **Queen Of Stars (FR)**[46] 6137 4-9-0 SMaillot 1 —
(M Delzangles, France)

0 **Aramina (GER)**[22] 4-9-0 TJarnet 16 —
(P Schiergen, Germany)

0 **Cherryxma (FR)**[158] 3-8-8 JVictoire 2 —
(A Fabre, France)

0 **Intiquilla (IRE)**[16] 6757 3-8-8 JimCrowley 14 —
(Mrs A J Perrett) *trckd ldr: 2nd 1/2-way: drvn st: sn u.p: wknd: fin 12th* **70/1**[3]

0 **Lounamix (FR)**[107] 3-8-8 IMendizabal 4 —
(J-C Rouget, France)

2m 43.4s (163.40)
WFA 3 from 4yo+ 6lb **17** Ran SP% **32.9**
PARI-MUTUEL: WIN 3.90; PL 2.10, 13.00, 6.50; DF 162.90.
Owner Miss K Rausing **Bred** Miss K Rausing & Abbey Bloodstock **Trained** Newmarket, Suffolk

NOTEBOOK
Alma Mater, a lightly-raced half-sister to Alborada and Albanova, had got off the mark in a Musselburgh maiden early in the month but secured her paddock value but running out a decisive winner of this Listed contest. If she is kept in training she could well win at Group level.

Silver Mitzva(IRE), whose trainer done really well with her, ran off 72 on her last outing in Britain but has now been placed in two Listed races which increases her paddock value.
Intiquilla(IRE), who has shown her form in ordinary handicaps, was out of her depth at this level.

6954a PRIX CONTESSINA (LISTED RACE) 6f
1:50 (1:58) 3-Y-0+ **£17,568** (£7,027; £5,270; £3,514; £1,757)

RPR
1 **Biniou (IRE)**[24] 6633 4-8-11 RobertHavlin 6 103
(R M H Cowell) *in tch: cl 7th 1/2-way: pushed along over 2f out: chal appr fnl f: rdn to ld 150yds out: comf* **372/10**[2]
2 1 1/2 **Kourka (FR)**[49] 6071 5-8-12 RonanThomas 3 99
(J-M Beguigne, France)
3 shd **Mariol (FR)**[24] 6633 4-9-2 DBoeuf 8 103
(Robert Collet, France)
4 hd **Derison (USA)**[24] 6633 5-9-2 (b) TJarnet 7 102
(P Van De Poele, France)
5 snk **Loda (FR)**[24] 6633 4-8-12 TThulliez 9 98
(C Baillet, France)
6 1/2 **Jodhpur**[24] 3-8-11 SPasquier 11 95
(A Fabre, France)
7 snk **Asque**[57] 4-8-8 IMendizabal 13 92
(G Henrot, France)
8 nk **Very Very Risky (FR)**[25] 7-8-8 LHuart 12 91
(L Cendra, France)
9 2 1/2 **Mood Music**[43] 6224 3-9-2 (b) AHelfenbein 10 91
(Mario Hofer, Germany)
10 4 **Slade (GER)**[24] 6633 5-8-12 WMongil 4 75
(M Trybuhl, Germany)
11 5 **Miss Donovan**[99] 4643 4-8-8 J-BEyquem 2 56
(Patrick J Moloney, Ire) *in tch: 5th 1/2-way: sn pushed along: rdn and one pce fr 1 1/2f out* **30/1**[1]
12 1 **Farnesina (FR)**[46] 5-8-8 (b) JCabre 1 53
(E Danel, France)

68.50 secs (68.50) **12** Ran SP% **5.8**
PARI-MUTUEL: WIN 38.20; PL 5.90, 2.10, 1.60; DF 93.00.
Owner Dasmal,Stennett,Rix,Barr,Mrs Penney **Bred** Kilfrush And Knocktoran Studs **Trained** Six Mile Bottom, Cambs

NOTEBOOK
Biniou(IRE), who finished fourth in the Prix de L'Abbaye last season, has returned to France regularly since joining his current trainer but this was his first success. He scored with a little in hand and will continue to look for opportunities on the continent so could well be up to winning Group races next season.

6933 WOLVERHAMPTON (A.W) (L-H)
Tuesday, November 27

OFFICIAL GOING: Standard
Wind: Light, behind Weather: Overcast

6955 PONTINS.COM AMATEUR RIDERS' H'CAP (DIV I) 1m 141y(P)
12:50 (12:50) (Class 6) (0-60,60) 3-Y-0+ **£1,648** (£507; £253) **Stalls** Low

Form RPR
2260 1 **Charlottebutterfly**[25] 6627 7-10-11 **50** MrSWalker 13 58
(P J McBride) *hld up: hdwy over 2f out: rdn to ld nr fin* **8/1**
6261 2 hd **Machinate (USA)**[10] 6859 5-10-13 **57** MrPCollington(5) 4 64
(W M Brisbourne) *chsd ldrs: led over 1f out: sn rdn: hdd nr fin* **9/2**[2]
0031 3 1 1/4 **Millfield (IRE)**[11] 6831 4-11-2 **60** MrSGoswell(5) 7 65+
(P R Chamings) *s.s: hld up: hdwy over 2f out: rdn over 1f out: r.o* **3/1**[1]
0060 4 1/2 **Empire Dancer (IRE)**[35] 6413 4-11-7 **60** MrSDobson 9 64
(I W McInnes) *sn led: rdn and hdd over 1f out: sn hung lft: styd on same pce* **11/2**
0006 5 3 **Desert Lover (IRE)**[28] 6563 5-10-1 **47** MrMPrice(7) 8 44
(R J Price) *trckd ldrs: rdn over 1f out: edgd lft and no ex* **12/1**
1540 6 2 1/2 **Gee Ceffyl Bach**[122] 3965 3-10-13 **55** MissFayeBramley 5 47
(R C Guest) *chsd ldr over 2f: wnt 2nd again over 3f out: rdn over 1f out: sn wknd* **25/1**
050 7 1 3/4 **Riolo (IRE)**[85] 5090 5-10-6 **52** oh1 ow6 (b) MrSBest(7) 6 40
(K F Clutterbuck) *prom: rdn over 2f out: hung lft and wknd over 1f out* **80/1**
0123 8 3/4 **Kirstys Lad**[15] 6804 5-10-13 **57** MissMMullineaux(5) 2 43
(M Mullineaux) *hld up in tch: rdn over 2f out: sn wknd* **5/1**[3]
000 9 2 **High Window (IRE)**[21] 6701 7-10-4 **46** oh1 MissJCoward(3) 10 28
(G P Kelly) *chsd ldr 6f out to over 3f out: wknd 2f out* **22/1**
0010 10 3 1/2 **Zantero**[25] 6627 5-11-0 **53** (tp) MrWBiddick 1 27
(K M Prendergast) *stdd s: a in rr* **18/1**
3220 11 1 3/4 **Danelor (IRE)**[197] 1732 9-10-12 **51** (p) MrsMMorris 11 21
(D Shaw) *hld up in tch: racd keenly: wknd over 2f out* **16/1**
0400 12 nk **Mind That Fox**[8] 6864 5-10-0 **46** oh1 MrAWEdwards(7) 3 —
(T Wall) *hld up: a in rr: wknd 3f out* **80/1**
0045 13 3 **Danum Diva (IRE)**[18] 6745 3-10-4 **46** oh1 MsKWalsh 12 —
(D J Murphy) *rrd s and wl bhd: effrt 1/2-way: wknd 3f out* **20/1**

1m 53.03s (1.27) **Going Correction** +0.01s/f (Slow)
WFA 3 from 4yo+ 3lb **13** Ran SP% **120.6**
Speed ratings (Par 101): **94,93,92,92,89 87,85,85,83,80 78,78,75**
CSF £42.10 CT £139.96 TOTE £14.10: £4.30, £2.10, £1.70; EX 59.80 TRIFECTA Not won..
Owner Future Electrical Services Ltd **Bred** J T O'Neill **Trained** Newmarket, Suffolk
■ Stewards' Enquiry : Ms K Walsh one-day ban: used whip when out of contention (Dec 10)

FOCUS
A competitive race for the grade, but the winning time was much slower than the second division. The lack of pace means that the form is not solid.

6956 PONTINS.COM AMATEUR RIDERS' H'CAP (DIV II) 1m 141y(P)
1:25 (1:25) (Class 6) (0-60,60) 3-Y-0+ **£1,648** (£507; £253) **Stalls** Low

Form RPR
3503 1 **Ochre (IRE)**[10] 6856 3-11-1 **60** MissARyan(3) 3 74
(R A Fahey) *hld up: hdwy over 3f out: rdn to ld ins fnl f: r.o* **15/2**
0004 2 3/4 **Ceredig**[7] 6947 4-10-2 **48** MissHWarbrick(7) 5 61
(Mrs L J Mongan) *trckd ldr: racd keenly: led over 3f out: clr over 2f out: shkn up: hung rt: hdd and unbalanced ins fnl f: edgd lft and styd on towards fin* **16/1**
1140 3 5 **Justcallmehandsome**[20] 6716 5-11-5 **58** (v) MissFayeBramley 1 59
(D J S Ffrench Davis) *chsd ldrs: rdn over 2f out: styd on same pce appr fnl f* **5/1**[2]
0205 4 nk **Postmaster**[10] 6859 5-10-8 **54** MissSSawyer(7) 11 54
(R Ingram) *hld up: hdwy over 1f out: hung lft ins fnl f: nt rch ldrs* **10/1**
0040 5 2 1/2 **Wodhill Gold**[10] 6859 6-10-5 **51** MrBMMorris(7) 13 46
(D Morris) *prom: lost pl over 3f out: n.d after* **20/1**
0024 6 1 1/4 **Turn Me On (IRE)**[10] 6859 4-11-4 **60** MrMWalford(3) 7 52
(T D Walford) *hld up: hdwy u.p over 1f out: wknd fnl f* **9/4**[1]
0605 7 3 **Gifted Flame**[46] 6152 8-10-2 **46** oh1 MissLAllan(5) 10 31
(Miss A Stokell) *s.s: hld up: sme hdwy 2f out: n.d* **40/1**
5245 8 3/4 **Angel Voices (IRE)**[54] 5934 4-10-6 **52** MissLEBurke(7) 4 35
(K R Burke) *chsd ldrs: rdn over 2f out: sn wknd* **12/1**
0000 9 1 3/4 **Border Artist**[11] 6825 8-10-9 **51** MrSPearce(3) 2 30
(J Pearce) *hld up: rdn over 2f out: n.d* **7/1**[3]
4002 10 1 1/4 **Primeshade Promise**[29] 6532 6-10-0 **46** (p) MrRPFlint(7) 12 22
(J L Flint) *hld up: rdn over 2f out: n.d* **16/1**
6460 11 1/2 **Beck**[60] 5782 3-9-13 **46** oh1 (p) MrPCollington(5) 9 21
(W M Brisbourne) *chsd ldrs: rdn over 3f out: hung lft and wknd over 1f out* **20/1**
0044 12 7 **Mycenean Prince (USA)**[15] 6792 4-10-0 **46** oh1 (b) MrCAHarris(7) 8 5
(R C Guest) *led: rdn and hdd over 3f out: sn wknd* **16/1**
0000 13 2 1/2 **Knickyknackienoo**[8] 6867 6-10-0 **46** oh1 (v[1]) MrDavidMcMinn(7) 6 —
(T T Clement) *s.i.s: hld up: wknd over 3f out* **66/1**

1m 51.66s (-0.10) **Going Correction** +0.01s/f (Slow)
WFA 3 from 4yo+ 3lb **48** Ran SP% **119.6**
Speed ratings (Par 101): **100,99,94,94,92 91,88,87,86,85 84,78,76**
CSF £116.11 CT £500.61 TOTE £10.10: £3.10, £4.90, £2.30; EX 140.50 TRIFECTA Not won..
Owner D Brennan **Bred** Darley **Trained** Musley Bank, N Yorks

FOCUS
Arguably, this looked weaker on paper than the first division, but it produced a quicker winning time and the form looks pretty solid, with the first pair clear.
Border Artist Official explanation: jockey said gelding never travelled

6957 PONTIN'S HOLIDAYS H'CAP 5f 20y(P)
2:00 (2:00) (Class 6) (0-53,53) 3-Y-0+ **£2,047** (£604; £302) **Stalls** Low

Form RPR
0061 1 **Fast Freddie**[7] 6886 3-9-0 **53** 6ex (e) NCallan 11 66+
(D J Murphy) *chsd ldr: led 2f out: rdn and edgd rt ins fnl f: r.o* **7/2**[1]
600 2 hd **Trinculo (IRE)**[8] 6873 10-9-0 **53** (b) ChrisCatlin 1 61
(R A Harris) *chsd ldrs: rdn 1/2-way: hung lft and r.o ins fnl f* **13/2**[3]
2261 3 1/2 **Muktasb (USA)**[8] 6864 6-8-12 **51** 6ex (v) AdamKirby 12 58
(D Shaw) *s.s: reminders sn after s: hdwy u.p over 1f out: hung lft ins fnl f: r.o* **9/1**
0052 4 1/2 **Mannello**[11] 6826 4-8-13 **52** EddieAhern 3 57+
(Jim Best) *hld up: rdn over 1f out: edgd lft and r.o ins fnl f: nt rch ldrs* **8/1**
0060 5 1/2 **Phinerine**[26] 6608 4-8-11 **53** (b) MichaelJStainton(3) 8 56
(Miss J E Foster) *mid-div: n.m.r 4f out: hdwy u.p over 1f out: edgd lft: r.o* **22/1**
1000 6 1/2 **Kims Rose (IRE)**[23] 6677 4-8-7 **53** MCGeran(7) 13 54
(R A Harris) *s.i.s: in rr tl r.o ins fnl f: nvr nrr* **40/1**
0032 7 1 1/2 **Sir Loin**[16] 6773 6-8-13 **52** (v) LPKeniry 5 48
(P Burgoyne) *led 3f: sn rdn: wknd ins fnl f* **13/2**[3]
4232 8 nk **Blackheath (IRE)**[90] 4939 11-8-8 **52** KellyHarrison(5) 10 47
(S T Mason) *chsd ldrs: rdn over 1f out: wknd ins fnl f* **20/1**
0302 9 hd **Drum Dance (IRE)**[20] 6718 5-8-8 **52** HaddenFrost(5) 6 46
(M Hill) *s.i.s: sn pushed along: styd on ins fnl f: nvr nrr* **11/2**[2]
140- 10 3/4 **Sir Don (IRE)**[340] 6922 8-9-0 **53** (p) StephenDonohoe 4 44
(E S McMahon) *mid-div: sn drvn along: outpcd fr 1/2-way* **14/1**
0463 11 nk **Kennington**[16] 6779 7-9-0 **53** NeilPollard 7 43
(Mrs C A Dunnett) *chsd ldrs: rdn over 3f out: edgd rt over 2f out: styd on same pce appr fnl f* **12/1**
6000 12 4 **Futuristic Dragon (IRE)**[82] 5174 3-9-0 **53** TGMcLaughlin 2 29
(D Shaw) *hld up: sme hdwy u.p over 1f out: wknd fnl f* **25/1**
1004 13 3 **Tajjree**[29] 6528 4-8-13 **52** (tp) AdrianMcCarthy 9 17
(H J Collingridge) *chsd ldrs: rdn whn hmpd 1/2-way: wknd over 1f out* **16/1**

62.81 secs (-0.01) **Going Correction** +0.01s/f (Slow) **13** Ran SP% **121.0**
Speed ratings (Par 101): **100,99,98,98,97 96,94,93,93,92 91,85,80**
CSF £24.55 CT £200.52 TOTE £3.80: £1.30, £3.40, £4.00; EX 37.20 TRIFECTA Not won..
Owner Gordon Crawford **Bred** New Hall Stud **Trained** Bawtry, S Yorks

FOCUS
A good race for the grade, run at a decent pace, although they finished in something of a heap. The form is pretty sound.
Muktasb(USA) Official explanation: jockey said gelding missed the break

6958 WOLVERHAMPTON-RACECOURSE.CO.UK (S) STKS 7f 32y(P)
2:35 (2:36) (Class 6) 2-Y-0 **£2,047** (£604; £302) **Stalls** High

Form RPR
5505 1 **Copperbottomed (IRE)**[13] 6812 2-8-12 58 (e) JimCrowley 8 66
(R Hollinshead) *chsd ldr tl led 1/2-way: clr whn hung lft over 1f out: styd on wl* **10/3**[2]
5052 2 3 **Mister Beano (IRE)**[22] 6693 2-8-9 62 (v) JerryO'Dwyer(3) 6 59
(V Smith) *a.p: rdn over 2f out: styd on same pce fnl f* **11/4**[1]
3016 3 1/2 **Lady Bower**[83] 5127 2-8-12 62 J-PGuillambert 12 57
(M Johnston) *led to 1/2-way: rdn over 2f out: no ex fnl f* **4/1**[3]
0000 4 3 **Sir Joey**[7] 6881 2-8-7 54 RussellKennemore(5) 4 50
(J T Stimpson) *hld up: rdn over 2f out: styd on ins fnl f: nvr nrr* **33/1**
4660 5 shd **Rio Rocket (IRE)**[34] 6426 2-8-7 54 HayleyTurner 9 45
(Tom Dascombe) *hld up: rdn 1/2-way: styd on ins fnl f: nrst fin* **13/2**
0455 6 1 1/2 **Desert Life (IRE)**[3] 6933 2-8-12 65 (b[1]) ChrisCatlin 1 46
(R A Harris) *s.s: hdwy over 5f out: rdn over 2f out: wknd over 1f out* **11/2**
0500 7 1 **Racey Rachel (IRE)**[8] 6865 2-8-7 52 (b[1]) LPKeniry 10 39
(E F Vaughan) *dwlt: plld hrd and sn prom: rdn 1/2-way: wknd over 1f out* **20/1**
0 8 2 1/2 **Yippyiayippyio**[37] 6358 2-8-8 0 ow1 MickyFenton 7 34
(Mrs C A Dunnett) *hld up: bhd fr 1/2-way* **66/1**
0400 9 3 1/2 **Polish Priory (IRE)**[32] 6462 2-8-7 53 (b[1]) TGMcLaughlin 11 24
(P D Evans) *hld up in tch: rdn and wknd over 2f out* **16/1**

1m 32.08s (1.68) **Going Correction** +0.01s/f (Slow) **9** Ran SP% **113.5**
Speed ratings (Par 94): **90,86,86,82,82 80,79,76,72**
CSF £12.45 TOTE £3.90: £1.70, £1.10, £1.60; EX 13.90 Trifecta £29.10 Pool: £406.37 - 9.91 winning units..The winner was bought in for 4,750gns. Lady Bower was claimed by J. Ryan for £6,000. Mister Beano was claimed by R. J. Price for £6,000.
Owner John L Marriott **Bred** Paul McEnery **Trained** Upper Longdon, Staffs

FOCUS
This was pretty much a one-horse race from the home bend. The winner apart, the form looks moderate.

NOTEBOOK
Copperbottomed(IRE), who shaped with promise last time, found the ease in grade exactly what was needed and came right away. The only negative was his ungainly head carriage under pressure. (op 7-2 tchd 3-1)
Mister Beano(IRE) finished well but was never a threat to the winner at any stage. He can probably win a race but is one to take on most times. (tchd 10-3)
Lady Bower tried to make every yard of the running but was collared rounding the final bend and was unable to respond. It was a fair effort after her break and her new connections - she was claimed after the race - should find her something similar soon. (op 5-1)
Sir Joey, who had the headgear removed, stayed on nicely down the home straight but was never a threat. Official explanation: jockey said gelding hung left leaving back straight (op 28-1)
Rio Rocket(IRE) never really got out of the rear group on her first start since leaving Alan Swinbank. (op 6-1 tchd 7-1)
Desert Life(IRE) showed very little in first-time blinkers. (op 9-2)
Polish Priory(IRE) Official explanation: jockey said filly had no more to give

6959 PONTIN'S GREAT FAMILY HOLIDAYS MAIDEN STKS 1m 4f 50y(P)
3:10 (3:10) (Class 5) 3-Y-0+ **£2,968** (£876; £438) **Stalls** Low

Form RPR
4066 **1** **Restless Soul**[17] 6757 3-8-12 80 .... NCallan 7 65
(C A Cyzer) *chsd ldrs: led 3f out: rdn over 1f out: all out* **2/1**[2]
5U32 **2** *shd* **Propaganda (IRE)**[18] 6745 3-8-12 66 .... EddieAhern 6 64
(L M Cumani) *hld up: hdwy 5f out: chsd ldr 4f out: rdn and ev ch fr over 1f out: edgd lft: styd on* **7/4**[1]
3 **3** *4* **Spares And Repairs**[21] 6700 4-9-9 0 .... PaulMulrennan 2 63
(Mrs S Lamyman) *sn pushed along in rr: hdwy over 3f out: rdn over 1f out: styd on: nt trble ldrs* **25/1**
03 **4** *2* **Sweet Mischief (IRE)**[12] 6821 3-8-12 0 .... RobertHavlin 4 55
(J H M Gosden) *s.i.s: hld up: rdn and hung lft over 4f out: hdwy over 3f out: hung lft and wknd over 1f out* **3/1**[3]
3R03 **5** *27* **Moral Code (IRE)**[10] 6858 3-9-3 65 .... ChrisCatlin 1 17
(E J O'Neill) *led over 10f out: rdn and hdd 3f out: wknd over 2f out* **8/1**
00 **6** *24* **Troys Steps**[21] 6700 3-8-12 0 .... MickyFenton 5 —
(E J Alston) *led: hdd over 10f out: chsd ldr tl rdn over 4f out: wknd over 3f out* **100/1**
4/00 **7** *41* **Cost Analysis (IRE)**[28] 6563 5-9-9 43 ....(t) HayleyTurner 3 —
(Mrs P Ford) *chsd ldrs 7f* **100/1**

2m 40.45s (-1.97) **Going Correction** +0.01s/f (Slow)
WFA 3 from 4yo+ 6lb **7 Ran SP% 111.6**
Speed ratings (Par 103): **106,105,103,101,83 67,40**
CSF £5.58 TOTE £2.90: £2.40, £1.10; EX 6.00.
Owner Mrs Charles Cyzer **Bred** C A Cyzer **Trained** Maplehurst, W Sussex
■ Stewards' Enquiry : Eddie Ahern two-day ban: used whip with excessive frequency in incorrect place (Dec 8-9)

FOCUS
A very modest maiden, despite the official handicap mark of the winner. The third probably holds the form down and the winner was some way below her best.
Troys Steps Official explanation: jockey said filly had a breathing problem

6960 EUROPEAN BREEDERS' FUND NOVICE STKS 1m 141y(P)
3:40 (3:41) (Class 5) 2-Y-0 **£4,533** (£1,348; £674; £336) **Stalls** Low

Form RPR
1 **1** **Hilbre Court (USA)**[29] 6543 2-9-2 0 .... IanMongan 1 83
(B J Meehan) *chsd ldrs: rdn to ld and edgd rt over 1f out: edgd lft ins fnl f: r.o* **6/1**[3]
4 **2** *1 ½* **King Kenny**[32] 6468 2-8-12 0 ....(e[1]) NCallan 4 76
(D J Murphy) *hld up: hdwy over 3f out: hung rt over 2f out: rdn and edgd lft over 1f out: ev ch whn hung rt ins fnl f: nt run on* **4/5**[1]
0 **3** *1 ¼* **Zhebe**[25] 6618 2-8-12 0 ....(t) RobertHavlin 7 73
(P J McBride) *s.i.s: hld up: hung rt over 2f out: rdn and hung lft over 1f out: styd on ins fnl f: nt trble ldrs* **40/1**
1 **4** *¾* **Orpen Fire (IRE)**[31] 6503 2-8-9 0 .... StephenDonohoe 2 69
(E S McMahon) *s.i.s: sn prom: chsd ldr 6f out: led over 2f out: rdn and hdd over 1f out: edgd lft and no ex ins fnl f* **6/1**[3]
4621 **5** *5* **Celtic Strand (IRE)**[39] 6303 2-9-0 76 .... MickyFenton 3 63
(T P Tate) *sn pushed along to ld: rdn and hdd over 2f out: wknd fnl f* **7/2**[2]
0510 **6** *hd* **It's My Day (IRE)**[27] 6584 2-9-0 66 .... PatCosgrave 6 63
(Jane Chapple-Hyam) *chsd ldrs: pushed along 6f out: rdn over 3f out: sn wknd* **16/1**

1m 51.9s (0.14) **Going Correction** +0.01s/f (Slow) **6 Ran SP% 114.7**
Speed ratings (Par 96): **99,97,96,95,91 91**
CSF £11.69 TOTE £5.70: £4.00, £1.10; EX 16.30.
Owner E H Jones (paints) Ltd **Bred** Richard Nip & Omar Trevino **Trained** Manton, Wilts

FOCUS
A fair-looking contest run at a sound pace. The winner looks progressive, while the favourite is one to avoid on this evidence. The winning time was quicker than the amateur-rider events that started the card.

NOTEBOOK
Hilbre Court(USA), a fair winner on his debut, managed to hang on despite looking fairly green when hitting the front. One would suspect he has plenty more to come and he rates an interesting prospect. (op 7-1 tchd 8-1)
King Kenny, who showed plenty of promise on his turf debut, looked in trouble rounding the final bend and rolled around under pressure. His jockey managed to straighten him out to have another pop at the eventual winner, but he hung out to his right when he got to Hilbre Court's quarters, looking far from straightforward once again. It will take a very cool ride to get him to put his head in front. (op 5-6 tchd 10-11 in places and evens in a place)
Zhebe kept plugging away up the home straight and ran a very respectable race, considering his debut effort. A bigger sort than most of his rivals, he seems sure to stay further. (tchd 50-1)
Orpen Fire(IRE), who went off at 33/1 on her debut, showed quite a lot of pace but did not truly get home against these rivals. A drop in trip will probably be to her advantage. (op 9-2 tchd 4-1)
Celtic Strand(IRE), trying Polytrack for the first time, was firmly put in his place off the final bend. It was disappointing that he did not show a bit more. (op 9-2)
It's My Day(IRE), who went off joint favourite for a nursery last time, was readily dropped by the rest of the field rounding the final bend, and never looked like taking a hand in the finish after that. (op 22-1)

6961 GO PONTIN'S H'CAP 1m 5f 194y(P)
4:10 (4:11) (Class 5) (0-75,75) 3-Y-0+ **£2,968** (£876; £438) **Stalls** Low

Form RPR
2041 **1** **Merrymaker**[13] 6817 7-9-6 67 .... NCallan 7 79+
(W M Brisbourne) *dwlt: hld up: hdwy over 4f out: led 2f out: sn rdn: clr whn edgd lft fnl f: eased towards fin* **11/4**[2]
4061 **2** *5* **Rickety Bridge (IRE)**[15] 6797 4-9-9 70 .... JimCrowley 4 73
(P R Chamings) *s.i.s: hld up: hdwy over 4f out: rdn and ev ch 2f out: edgd lft and wknd ins fnl f* **7/4**[1]
0050 **3** *2 ½* **Victory Quest (IRE)**[15] 6802 7-8-10 57 ....(v) ChrisCatlin 2 57
(Mrs S Lamyman) *chsd ldrs: rdn over 3f out: wknd over 1f out* **18/1**
1-00 **4** *hd* **Trew Style**[19] 6733 5-9-4 65 .... PaulMulrennan 5 64
(M H Tompkins) *led after 1f: rdn and hdd 2f out: wknd over 1f out* **15/2**
6301 **5** *20* **Princely Ted (IRE)**[22] 6697 6-8-12 59 .... MickyFenton 3 30
(D Burchell) *led 1f: chsd ldr: disp ld fr over 8f out tl rdn 3f out: wknd 2f out* **10/3**[3]
/13- **6** *34* **Mr Excel (IRE)**[318] 6655 4-9-9 75 .... HaddenFrost[(5)] 8 —
(G A Ham) *chsd ldrs over 9f* **12/1**

3m 5.86s (-1.51) **Going Correction** +0.01s/f (Slow) **6 Ran SP% 110.8**
Speed ratings (Par 103): **104,101,99,99,88 68**
CSF £7.77 CT £62.17 TOTE £4.90: £2.10, £1.20; EX 8.90 Trifecta £41.80 Pool: £564.53 - 9.57 winning units..
Owner The Blacktoffee Partnership **Bred** Hascombe And Valiant Studs **Trained** Great Ness, Shropshire

FOCUS
A weak handicap and the form is far fom solid. The finish concerned two last-time-out winners, and it was Merrymaker who had too much pace for his market rival.
Princely Ted(IRE) Official explanation: trainer had no explanation for the poor form shown
Mr Excel(IRE) Official explanation: jockey said gelding lost its action

6962 GO PONTIN'S HOLIDAYS FILLIES' H'CAP 5f 216y(P)
4:40 (4:40) (Class 5) (0-70,70) 3-Y-0+ **£2,968** (£876; £438) **Stalls** Low

Form RPR
6406 **1** **Tilly's Dream**[17] 6762 4-9-2 68 .... AdamKirby 6 80
(G C Bravery) *chsd ldrs: rdn to ld 1f out: edgd lft: r.o* **8/1**[3]
1654 **2** *¾* **Stormburst (IRE)**[3] 6925 3-8-0 57 oh1 ow1 .... KirstyMilczarek[(5)] 13 66+
(S C Williams) *broke wl: stdd and lost pl 5f out: hdwy over 1f out: hung lft and r.o ins fnl f: nt rch wnr* **8/1**[3]
0430 **3** *1* **Dasheena**[11] 6831 4-7-13 56 oh2 ....(be) NataliaGemelova[(5)] 2 62
(A J McCabe) *mid-div: hdwy over 2f out: sn rdn: r.o* **14/1**
001 **4** *½* **Sweet Pickle**[25] 6625 6-9-4 70 ....(e) GeorgeBaker 1 74
(J R Boyle) *s.i.s: hld up: hdwy over 2f out: rdn over 1f out: edgd lft: styd on* **7/2**[1]
4050 **5** *1 ¼* **Jord (IRE)**[18] 6747 3-8-7 66 .... RobbieEgan[(7)] 11 66+
(A J McCabe) *hld up: hdwy over 1f out: nt rch ldrs* **25/1**
0304 **6** *nk* **Metal Guru**[18] 6747 3-8-8 65 .... RussellKennemore[(5)] 9 64
(R Hollinshead) *led 1f: chsd ldr tl led over 2f out: rdn and hdd 1f out: wknd towards fin* **13/2**[2]
6010 **7** *½* **Another Genepi (USA)**[23] 6677 4-9-1 67 ....(b) NCallan 3 65
(K A Ryan) *s.i.s: hdwy over 4f out: rdn and hung lft over 1f out: wknd ins fnl f* **7/2**[1]
4200 **8** *½* **Overwing (IRE)**[23] 6671 4-8-10 62 .... EddieAhern 8 58
(R M H Cowell) *led 5f out: rdn and hdd over 2f out: wknd ins fnl f* **11/1**
3200 **9** *nk* **Boreana**[13] 6818 4-8-4 56 oh1 .... DaleGibson 7 51
(Jedd O'Keeffe) *prom: rdn 1/2-way: edgd lft over 1f out: wknd fnl f* **16/1**
6050 **10** *hd* **Linda Green**[28] 6575 6-9-0 66 .... ChrisCatlin 10 61
(M R Channon) *sn outpcd* **9/1**
0605 **11** *½* **Rosie Cross (IRE)**[6] 6890 3-8-9 61 .... HayleyTurner 4 54
(Eve Johnson Houghton) *hld up: rdn 1/2-way: n.d* **14/1**
6000 **12** *2 ½* **Alexia Rose (IRE)**[19] 6730 5-7-13 56 oh11 ....(t) KellyHarrison[(5)] 12 41
(A Berry) *s.s: outpcd* **100/1**
600 **13** *3* **Safranine (IRE)**[49] 6078 10-8-10 67 oh11 ow11 .... AnnStokell[(5)] 5 42
(Miss A Stokell) *chsd ldrs: rdn and hung rt over 2f out: sn wknd* **100/1**

1m 15.15s (-0.66) **Going Correction** +0.01s/f (Slow) **13 Ran SP% 123.4**
Speed ratings (Par 100): **104,103,101,101,99 98,98,97,97,96 96,92,88**
CSF £72.64 CT £927.28 TOTE £9.50: £3.00, £3.50, £4.80; EX 110.20 TRIFECTA Not won. Place 6 £17.48, Place 5 £10.00.
Owner Richard Withers And Meddler Bloodstock **Bred** Southill Stud **Trained** Newmarket, Suffolk

FOCUS
A modest but competitive sprint for fillies and mares, run at a reasonable pace. The form is ordinary for the grade, but pretty sound, rated through the winner and third.
T/Plt: £34.70 to a £1 stake. Pool: £54,500.15. 1,145.80 winning tickets. T/Qpdt: £4.50 to a £1 stake. Pool: £4,657.80. 750.00 winning tickets. CR

6890 KEMPTON (A.W) (R-H)
Wednesday, November 28

OFFICIAL GOING: Standard
Wind: Moderate, half behind Weather: Dark

6963 BOOK NOW FOR BOXING DAY MEDIAN AUCTION MAIDEN STKS 6f (P)
6:20 (6:21) (Class 6) 3-5-Y-0 **£2,047** (£604; £302) **Stalls** High

Form RPR
-4 **1** **Diriculous**[28] 6580 3-9-3 0 .... JohnEgan 10 66
(T G Mills) *prom: trckd ldr over 3f out: led over 2f out: hrd rdn fnl f: jst hld on* **4/1**[2]
306 **2** *hd* **Tyrannosaurus Rex (IRE)**[19] 6749 3-9-3 58 ....(v[1]) PaulMulrennan 9 65
(K R Burke) *prom: rdn over 2f out: chsd wnr wl over 1f out: drvn and clsd grad fnl f: nt quite get up* **9/4**[1]
6600 **3** *4* **The Carpet Man**[8] 6887 3-9-3 47 .... RichardKingscote 4 53
(A W Carroll) *fractious preliminaries: dwlt: hld up in last: prog on inner over 2f out: shkn up over 1f out: styd on to take 3rd fnl f: no ch w ldng pair* **33/1**
4020 **4** *½* **Lawdy Miss Clawdy**[4] 6927 3-8-12 47 .... JimCrowley 7 46
(D W P Arbuthnot) *hld up in last trio: prog wl over 2f out: chsd clr ldrs over 1f out: kpt on* **11/1**
4035 **5** *3 ½* **Calloff The Search**[9] 6873 3-9-3 53 .... MickyFenton 5 40
(Stef Liddiard) *chsd ldrs: rdn over 2f out: sn outpcd and btn* **9/2**[3]
0 **6** *½* **Elizabeth Spirit (IRE)**[39] 6339 3-8-12 0 .... J-PGuillambert 12 33
(E S McMahon) *racd freely: led to over 2f out: wknd over 1f out* **25/1**
5603 **7** *3* **Compulsion**[28] 6580 4-8-12 56 .... EddieAhern 1 24
(Pat Eddery) *stdd and wnt lft s: hld up in last trio: taken to wd outside in st: no ch after: plugged on* **9/2**[3]
0000 **8** *1* **Rangali Belle**[22] 6704 3-8-12 45 .... SimonWhitworth 8 20
(C A Horgan) *t.k.h: hld up towards rr: outpcd over 2f out: no ch after* **66/1**
4066 **9** *2 ½* **Tumbleweed Di**[9] 6864 3-8-8 45 ow1 .... SladeO'Hara[(5)] 2 13
(G R Oldroyd) *chsd ldrs but r.o wd outside: lost grnd over 2f out: sn struggling* **20/1**
0000 **10** *1 ½* **Merlins Quest**[7] 6894 3-9-3 47 ....(b) ChrisCatlin 11 13
(J M Bradley) *chsd ldr to over 3f out: wknd over 2f out* **40/1**
0306 **11** *1 ¾* **Princess Danehill (IRE)**[22] 6704 3-8-12 52 ....(t) NelsonDeSouza 3 2
(P F I Cole) *prom on outer: lost pl rapidly over 2f out: sn no ch* **16/1**

003 **12** *1* **Batchworth Fleur**[24] 6670 4-8-12 45 StephenCarson 6 —
(E A Wheeler) *hld up towards rr: wknd over 2f out: b.b.v* **33/1**

1m 12.54s (-1.16) **Going Correction** -0.075s/f (Stan) 12 Ran SP% **119.8**
Speed ratings (Par 101): **104,103,98,97,93 92,88,87,83,81 79,78**
CSF £12.58 TOTE £4.90: £1.40, £2.20, £6.90; EX 12.40.
Owner Sherwoods Transport Ltd **Bred** Sherwoods Transport Ltd **Trained** Headley, Surrey

FOCUS
A weak sprint maiden, but probably a reasonable winner in Diriculous who turned around course form with the seventh. The form is relatively weak despite the first three appearing to have improved.
Batchworth Fleur Official explanation: jockey said filly bled from the nose

6964 EUROPEAN BREEDERS' FUND MEDIAN AUCTION MAIDEN FILLIES' STKS 6f (P)
6:50 (6:53) (Class 6) 2-Y-O **£2,388** (£705; £352) **Stalls** High

Form RPR

2003 **1** **Smokey Rye**[11] 6849 2-9-0 66 (b) GeorgeBaker 4 70+
(G L Moore) *trckd ldrs: rdn and prog over 2f out: flashed tail u.p: styd on to ld last 150yds: pushed out* **11/4**[1]

5 **2** *nk* **My Pin Up**[13] 6820 2-9-0 0 PatDobbs 11 69
(Christian Wroe) *trckd ldrs gng wl: wnt 2nd over 2f out: drvn to chal 1f out and upsides: jst outpcd last 100yds* **7/1**

3 *¾* **Miss Mujanna** 2-9-0 0 J-PGuillambert 2 67+
(J Akehurst) *trckd ldrs on outer: lost grnd bnd 3f out: shkn up 2f out: styd on wl fnl f to take 3rd last strides* **12/1**

4 *nk* **Wise Melody** 2-9-0 0 TPQueally 9 66
(W J Haggas) *led on inner after 1f: gng wl 2f out: rdn and pressed 1f out: hdd and one pce last 150yds* **4/1**[2]

0 **5** *1* **Tallulah Sunrise**[135] 3589 2-8-7 0 GHannon(7) 7 63
(M D I Usher) *prom: chsd ldr wl over 2f out and hanging: nt qckn over 1f out: bmpd along and kpt on* **40/1**

6 *½* **Maggie Kate** 2-9-0 0 PaulFitzsimons 8 61
(R Ingram) *dwlt: sn wl in tch: chsd ldrs 2f out: one pce and no imp fnl f* **50/1**

7 *4* **Sunley Smiles** 2-9-0 0 LPKeniry 12 49
(D R C Elsworth) *dwlt: hld up towards rr: effrt on inner over 2f out: no prog over 1f out* **11/2**[3]

04 **8** *3* **Rosie Says No**[18] 6761 2-9-0 0 ChrisCatlin 3 40
(R M H Cowell) *hld up in rr and racd wd: lost tch over 2f out* **12/1**

0 **9** *½* **The Lady Lapwing**[25] 6641 2-9-0 0 SteveDrowne 10 39
(G Wragg) *dwlt: a wl in rr* **20/1**

10 *5* **Sparkling Silver** 2-9-0 0 RobertHavlin 1 24
(D K Ivory) *s.s: sn detached in last: a bhd* **33/1**

3042 **11** *¾* **Red Amaryllis**[18] 6761 2-8-7 70 VictorSantos(7) 6 22
(H J L Dunlop) *racd v wd: led 1f: lost much grnd fr 1/2-way: unbalanced and struggling in rr fnl 2f* **11/2**[3]

1m 14.11s (0.41) **Going Correction** -0.075s/f (Stan) 11 Ran SP% **117.4**
Speed ratings (Par 91): **94,93,92,92,90 90,84,80,80,73 72**
CSF £21.61 TOTE £3.80: £1.70, £2.60, £4.40; EX 21.10.
Owner Darrell Hinds Susan Bell Pat Butcher **Bred** Jeremy Hinds **Trained** Woodingdean, E Sussex
■ Stewards' Enquiry : Victor SantosA caution: used whip when out of contention

FOCUS
A modest fillies' maiden and, with the pace ordinary through the early stages, the first six were covered by around two and a half lengths at the line. The winning time was 0.38 seconds slower than the later nursery.

NOTEBOOK
Smokey Rye had not progressed as one might have hoped after running second at Brighton earlier in the season, but she shaped with some promise when third in first-time blinkers over 7f at Lingfield on her previous start and confirmed she is on the right track now with a narrow success. She flashed her tail when hit with the whip, but she has done that in the past and it clearly didn't slow her down. She only had a neck to spare at the line, but always looked likely to get up. She is already rated 66 and is likely to find things tougher from now on. (op 11-2 tchd 6-1 in a place)
My Pin Up made her debut in just an ordinary 5f maiden at Lingfield, but she was unlucky not to finish quite a bit closer than fifth having been denied a clear run, and she confirmed the promise of that effort with a close second. She travelled every bit as well as the winner into the straight, but was just run out of it close home. She might be able to find a similarly weak race and will also have the option of handicaps after one more run. (op 5-1)
Miss Mujanna ◆, a daughter of Mujahid, half-sister to triple 6f-7f winner Aastral Magic, out of a mare who was placed over 1m5f-1m6f, made a very encouraging debut in third. She lost ground when coming wide round the final bend and took a while to pick up in the straight, but she gradually got the hang of things and came home nicely. The bare form does not amount to a great deal, but she is open to a fair bit of improvement.
Wise Melody, a daughter of Zamindar, half-sister to among others quite useful 5f two-year-old winner Racina, out of a 5f juvenile scorer, made a satisfactory introduction. Allowed an easy enough time of things towards the front against the rail, she stayed on for pressure in the straight before eventually giving way inside the final furlong. She is entitled to improve and gives the impression she will do even better over 5f.
Tallulah Sunrise improved on the form she showed when down the field over 5f at Windsor on her debut over four months ago. (tchd 50-1)
Red Amaryllis was well beaten, but she raced very wide throughout under an inexperienced apprentice and this run is best ignored. (op 4-1)

6965 DIGIBET.COM HYDE STKS (LISTED RACE) 1m (P)
7:20 (7:21) (Class 1) 3-Y-0+
£14,762 (£5,595; £2,800; £1,396; £699; £351) **Stalls** High

Form RPR

2162 **1** **Ventura (USA)**[32] 6497 3-8-9 91 JimCrowley 7 109+
(Mrs A J Perrett) *trckd ldrs gng easily: led 2f out and sn kicked at least 3l clr: drvn out: unchal* **16/1**

4060 **2** *2½* **Wise Dennis**[40] 6298 5-9-2 104 JohnEgan 1 107
(A P Jarvis) *hld up in last pair: rdn over 2f out: prog on outer over 1f out: styd on to take 2nd fnl f: no ch w wnr* **6/1**

-403 **3** *nk* **Raptor (GER)**[30] 6541 4-9-2 100 EddieAhern 8 106
(K R Burke) *w.w in midfield: rdn over 2f out: prog to dispute 2nd over 1f out: no ch w wnr: kpt on* **11/2**[3]

5154 **4** *2½* **Orchard Supreme**[11] 6852 4-9-2 100 RichardHughes 4 100
(R Hannon) *w.w in midfield: rdn over 2f out: prog to dispute 2nd over 1f out: wknd ins fnl f* **7/2**[2]

5011 **5** *hd* **Appalachian Trail (IRE)**[32] 6491 6-9-4 111 (b) J-PGuillambert 12 102+
(I Semple) *hld up in last: rdn and nt clr run briefly 2f out: styd on fnl f: no ch* **9/4**[1]

5304 **6** *2* **Waterside (IRE)**[4] 6932 8-9-2 100 GeorgeBaker 6 95
(G L Moore) *mostly chsd ldr: upsides 2f out: wknd over 1f out* **13/2**

0-45 **7** *3½* **Highway To Glory (IRE)**[200] 1661 4-8-11 90 (t) GregFairley 9 82
(M Botti) *dwlt: rcvrd to go prom: drvn over 2f out: sn lost pl and btn* **25/1**

0026 **8** *¾* **Babodana**[11] 6852 7-9-2 94 PaulMulrennan 2 85
(M H Tompkins) *pressed ldrs tl wknd fr 2f out* **25/1**

3010 **9** *shd* **Very Wise**[11] 6852 5-9-2 100 TPQueally 3 85
(W J Haggas) *pushed up to ld: hdd 2f out: wknd rapidly over 1f out* **10/1**

1m 37.32s (-3.48) **Going Correction** -0.075s/f (Stan)
WFA 3 from 4yo+ 2lb 9 Ran SP% **118.7**
Speed ratings (Par 111): **114,111,111,108,108 106,103,102,102**
CSF £111.48 TOTE £15.60: £3.00, £2.80, £1.60; EX 268.60.
Owner K Abdulla **Bred** Juddmonte Farms Inc **Trained** Pulborough, W Sussex

FOCUS
A good field for the first running of this Listed event and a decent race for the grade. Ventura was value for extra and is rated up a stone. They went a strong pace from the outset and the form looks solid. The winning time was 3.39 seconds quicker than the later Class 6 handicap.

NOTEBOOK
Ventura(USA) had plenty to find strictly on the book having come into this rated just 91, but she has been most progressive this year and took another significant step forward with an impressive victory. Always travelling nicely off the decent gallop, she quickened up smartly in the straight and settled the contest in a matter of strides. She had only managed second off a mark of 89 in a handicap at Newbury on her most recent start, but her connections felt the ground was too soft that day and this much more consistent surface clearly suited. It remains to be seen whether she stays in training, as she is clearly a very valuable broodmare prospect now, but she has the potential to make a very smart filly if persevered with next year. (tchd 20-1)
Wise Dennis was unproven on this surface, had only ever won over 7f and had a poor draw to overcome, but he was the second best in on official figures. The strong pace suited and he ran a solid race in defeat, but the winner was simply in a different league. Official explanation: jockey said gelding hung right-handed (op 8-1)
Raptor(GER), a Listed winner when trained in Germany last year, acquitted himself with real credit in both the Lincoln and in the Cambridgeshire this season, and he confirmed himself pretty smart when third in a good conditions contest over 7f at Leicester on his most recent start. This was another decent effort in defeat and he looks capable of landing a nice prize. It will be interesting to see if his connections are tempted by the Dubai Carnival. (op 8-1)
Orchard Supreme developed into a smart sand performer last winter and the evidence of his recent fourth in a hot handicap at Lingfield off a mark of 100 suggested he would continue to progress this winter. This was a solid effort and he appeals as one to keep on side in the coming weeks. (op 3-1 tchd 4-1)
Appalachian Trail(IRE) has enjoyed a terrific season, but he endured a nightmare trip this time, being blocked in his run when trying to make a move in the straight, and he is better than he was able to show. He would probably have been second with a clear run, but it is hard to know whether he would have troubled the impressive winner. (op 15-8)
Waterside(IRE) proved he is as good as ever when fourth over 7f at Lingfield off a mark of 100 on his previous start, but he chased quite a strong pace this time and could not sustain his challenge in the straight. (op 8-1)
Babodana was well held and probably finds this company a bit hot these days. (op 20-1)
Very Wise showed pretty smart form on sand last winter, but he was tailed off on his return to Polytrack at Lingfield last time after starting very slowly and was reported by the vet to have an irregular heart beat. Away from the stalls okay this time, he may have gone off a touch too fast, but even allowing for that it was disappointing to see him drop away so tamely in the straight. (op 8-1)

6966 DIGIBET.COM NURSERY 6f (P)
7:50 (7:51) (Class 6) (0-65,71) 2-Y-O **£2,047** (£604; £302) **Stalls** High

Form RPR

0561 **1** **Caprio (IRE)**[8] 6881 2-9-6 64 6ex RichardKingscote 4 67
(R Charlton) *mostly chsd ldr: rdn over 2f out: clsd to chal fnl f: led last strides* **11/8**[1]

2060 **2** *hd* **Kaystar Ridge**[40] 6312 2-8-13 62 JamesO'Reilly(5) 5 65
(D K Ivory) *rrd s: hld up in last gp tl prog over 2f out: styd on u.str.p to ld narrowly last 75yds: hdd last strides* **50/1**

5001 **3** *hd* **Bazguy**[7] 6892 2-9-6 71 6ex (b) RichardEvans(7) 6 73
(P D Evans) *led: 2l clr bef 1/2-way to jst over 1f out: urged along fnl f: hdd last 75yds* **5/1**[2]

1243 **4** *1* **What's For Tea**[16] 6793 2-9-2 60 HayleyTurner 11 59
(Tom Dascombe) *dwlt: hld up wl in rr: prog on inner fr over 2f out: chsd ldrs fnl f: nt qckn* **13/2**[3]

4106 **5** *shd* **Ambrose Princess (IRE)**[16] 6800 2-9-0 58 LPKeniry 10 57
(R A Harris) *a chsng ldrs: rdn over 2f out: kpt on fr over 1f out: nvr able to chal* **20/1**

000 **6** *1½* **Dickie Valentine**[12] 6827 2-8-9 53 (v[1]) PatDobbs 12 47
(M R Bosley) *dwlt: in rr on inner: rdn over 2f out: kpt on fr over 1f out: n.d* **33/1**

0355 **7** *hd* **Diademas (USA)**[13] 6823 2-9-4 65 (e) JerryO'Dwyer(3) 1 59
(V Smith) *hld up in last pair fr wd draw: effrt on outer 2f out: prog over 1f out: kpt on same pce fnl f* **11/1**

000 **8** *3* **My Flame**[30] 6540 2-8-11 55 (v[1]) JimCrowley 2 40
(J R Jenkins) *hld up towards rr: prog on outer 2f out: no imp over 1f out: wknd ins fnl f* **33/1**

5102 **9** *1¼* **Too Grand**[12] 6828 2-8-13 60 (v) NeilChalmers(3) 8 41
(J J Bridger) *nvr bttr than midfield: struggling whn n.m.r wl over 1f out: fdd* **9/1**

4000 **10** *1¼* **Plaka (FR)**[16] 6799 2-9-2 60 TPQueally 3 37
(J A Osborne) *chsd ldrs on outer: awkward bnd 3f out: sn lost pl u.p* **16/1**

0110 **11** *½* **Countrywide Comet (IRE)**[20] 6736 2-9-7 65 ChrisCatlin 7 41
(P Howling) *dwlt: t.k.h: hld up towards rr: rdn 3f out: no prog and btn 2f out* **10/1**

4000 **12** *1* **Nothing Likea Dame**[87] 5063 2-9-6 64 AdamKirby 9 37
(D J Coakley) *sn rdn to chse ldrs: u.p whn nt clr run 2f out: no ch after* **20/1**

1m 13.73s (0.03) **Going Correction** -0.075s/f (Stan) 12 Ran SP% **122.8**
Speed ratings (Par 94): **96,95,95,94,94 92,91,87,86,84 83,82**
CSF £116.50 CT £305.85 TOTE £2.40: £1.40, £10.50, £1.90; EX 108.40.
Owner Beckhampton Stables Ltd 1 **Bred** P Rabbitte **Trained** Beckhampton, Wilts
■ Stewards' Enquiry : James O'Reilly two-day ban: used whip with excessive frequency and with whip arm above shoulder height (Dec 9-10)

FOCUS
A modest but competitive nursery and they went a strong pace from the off. The winning time was 0.38 seconds quicker than the earlier juvenile maiden.

NOTEBOOK
Caprio(IRE) was 2lb well-in under the penalty he picked up for his recent success in a similar contest at Wolverhampton, but he made hard work of this. He looked held for much of the way up the straight and was not helped by Bazguy, who continually drifted to his left, but he gradually wore that one down and came out on top in a three-way finish. He is not the most straightforward, as he showed when again being awkward on his way to the start, but he has ability and may progress again once gelded. (op 7-4)
Kaystar Ridge showed he was on a reasonable mark on his first start in a handicap with a close second. He was left with plenty to do after fluffing the start, but he came home well under a forceful ride and was just held. (op 40-1)

Bazguy was 2lb wrong under the penalty he picked up for winning a similar race over course and distance the previous week, but he made a bold bid to follow up and was just held. Soon in the clear having gone off at a strong pace, he looked like he might take a bit of catching for much of the way up the straight, but he did not help his chance by continually drifting left and was just reeled in. (op 6-1 tchd 13-2)
What's For Tea had hardly been shaping as though she would be suited by this drop in trip, but she acquitted herself most creditably. She is holding her form well and may do even better when stepped back up in trip. (op 7-1 tchd 6-1)
Ambrose Princess(IRE) had not shown a great deal since being picked up out of Stan Moore's yard, but she is in good hands and this was a little better. (op 16-1)

6967 DIGIBET CASINO H'CAP 1m 4f (P)
8:20 (8:21) (Class 6) (0-65,65) 3-Y-O **£2,047** (£604; £302) **Stalls** Centre

Form RPR
1 **1** **Fresh Mint (IRE)**17 6780 3-8-13 **60** EddieAhern 1 70+
(M J Wallace) *trckd ldr 3f: styd handy: prog to ld 2f out: r.o wl and sn clr: 4l up fnl f: eased last 100yds* **9/4**1
6000 **2** *1 3/4* **Sir Sandicliffe (IRE)**9 6871 3-8-6 **53** ow1 JohnEgan 10 57
(W M Brisbourne) *hld up towards rr: prog 2f out: styd on to take 2nd last 100yds: no ch w wnr* **9/2**3
0414 **3** *3/4* **Altos Reales**7 6896 3-8-8 **55** DeanMcKeown 8 58+
(D Shaw) *hld up in last: swtchd bhd rivals over 2f out and tried to weave way through: shuffled along and styd on to take 3rd nr fin: no ch* **3/1**2
0 **4** *1 1/2* **Goochie (IRE)**28 6577 3-8-6 **56** JerryO'Dwyer(3) 5 56
(John Joseph Murphy, Ire) *led: kicked on over 3f out: hdd 2f out: one pce after* **12/1**
4300 **5** *1 1/2* **Niqaab**11 6856 3-9-4 **65** TPQueally 9 63
(W J Musson) *hld up in last pair: effrt and sme prog over 2f out: outpcd and no imp fr over 1f out* **11/1**
5000 **6** *2* **Silver Surprise**12 6832 3-7-13 **51** oh6 NicolPolli(5) 4 46
(J J Bridger) *hld up towards rr on outer: rdn wl over 2f out: outpcd sn after* **33/1**
0-06 **7** *3/4* **Always Sparkle (CAN)**16 6803 3-8-11 **58** ChrisCatlin 6 52
(B Palling) *plld hrd: hld up bhd ldrs: outpcd fr 2f out* **9/1**
8 *shd* **Welcome Cat (USA)**37 3-9-3 **64** PaulMulrennan 3 57
(A D Brown) *dwlt: hld up towards rr: rdn and struggling whn bmpd over 2f out: no ch after* **7/1**
0000 **9** *3* **Bali Belony**112 4292 3-8-4 **51** oh6 (v) HayleyTurner 7 40
(J R Jenkins) *trckd ldrs on inner: n.m.r briefly over 3f out: sn rdn and btn* **66/1**
66 **10** *8* **Bothar Brugha (IRE)**45 6211 3-8-8 **55** RobertHavlin 2 31
(J G M O'Shea) *s.s: t.k.h and rcvrd to trck ldr after 3f to 3f out: wknd rapidly* **40/1**

2m 37.09s (0.19) **Going Correction** -0.075s/f (Stan) **10** Ran SP% **119.3**
Speed ratings (Par 98): **96,94,94,93,92 91,90,90,88,83**
CSF £12.87 CT £31.30 TOTE £3.50: £1.70, £2.10, £1.40; EX 16.70.
Owner Rick Barnes **Bred** Grange Con Holdings **Trained** Newmarket, Suffolk
■ Stewards' Enquiry : T P Queally two-day ban: careless riding (Dec 9-10)

FOCUS
Just a modest middle-distance handicap and they went a noticeably steady pace for much of the way. The overall form is a little dubious but the well-in Fresh Mint was value for double the actual margin.

6968 KEMPTON.CO.UK H'CAP 1m (P)
8:50 (8:52) (Class 6) (0-52,52) 3-Y-O+ **£2,047** (£604; £302) **Stalls** High

Form RPR
0000 **1** **Under Fire (IRE)**28 6587 4-8-10 **46** oh1 HayleyTurner 4 55
(A W Carroll) *prom: chsd ldr over 3f out: rdn to cl fr over 2f out: led jst over 1f out: hld on: all out* **11/1**
2405 **2** *hd* **Royal Guest**33 6466 3-8-10 **48** EddieAhern 14 57
(J R Jenkins) *dwlt: hld up wl in rr: stdy prog and hanging 2f out: hrd rdn to press wnr wl ins fnl f: a jst hld* **8/1**
00/2 **3** *nk* **Smokey The Bear**13 6212 5-8-8 **47** NeilChalmers(3) 11 55
(Miss Sheena West) *hld up in midfield: prog on inner over 2f out: pressed wnr fnl f: nt qckn and lost 2nd nr fin* **9/2**1
6625 **4** *1* **Double Valentine**22 6706 4-8-7 **48** JackMitchell(5) 7 54+
(R Ingram) *dwlt: hld up in last: nt clr run over 2f out: swtchd to outer and gd prog over 1f out: chsd ldrs fnl f: no imp last 100yds* **6/1**3
0000 **5** *2 1/2* **Josr's Magic (IRE)**97 4742 3-8-9 **52** HaddenFrost(5) 5 52
(H J Collingridge) *t.k.h: sn trckd ldrs: cl enough but nt qckn over 1f out: kpt on same pce after* **11/2**2
0050 **6** *nk* **Emily's Rainbow (IRE)**28 6590 3-8-12 **50** (b1) TPQueally 2 49
(W J Haggas) *hld up in midfield: lost pl over 2f out: kpt on again fr over 1f out* **11/1**
0000 **7** *1* **Shantina's Dream (USA)**22 6706 3-8-8 **46** oh1 PatCosgrave 12 43
(J R Boyle) *t.k.h: cl up on inner: rdn over 2f out: grad fdd fr over 1f out* **33/1**
3101 **8** *3/4* **Kinsman (IRE)**30 6532 10-8-13 **49** (p) JohnEgan 3 44
(T D McCarthy) *t.k.h: hld up in rr: shkn up and nt qckn over 2f out: one pce after* **13/2**
-000 **9** *2 1/2* **Jomus**28 6579 6-9-2 **52** (bt) RobertHavlin 8 41
(L Montague Hall) *dwlt and stdd s: rapid prog on outer to ld over 4f out and sn 3 l clr: wknd and hdd jst over 1f out* **10/1**
0/6- **10** *3 1/2* **Blakeshall Hope**373 6544 5-9-0 **50** DeanMcKeown 1 31
(A J Chamberlain) *mde most to over 4f out: chsd ldr to over 3f out: wknd u.p over 1f out* **14/1**
00-0 **11** *1 3/4* **Ticking**121 4031 4-8-13 **49** J-PGuillambert 13 26
(T Keddy) *dwlt: sn in midfield on inner: drvn over 2f out: no prog: wknd over 1f out* **11/1**
04-P **12** *3/4* **Frank's Quest (IRE)**304 273 7-8-3 **46** oh1 GemmaElford(7) 9 22
(A B Haynes) *hld up and sn racd on outer: bhd fr over 2f out* **25/1**
0000 **13** *10* **Diamond Hurricane (IRE)**8 6886 3-8-8 **46** oh1 (e) ChrisCatlin 6 —
(M Wellings) *hld up but t.k.h and wnt prom after 3f: wknd 3f out: eased fnl 2f: t.o* **16/1**

1m 40.71s (-0.09) **Going Correction** -0.075s/f (Stan)
WFA 3 from 4yo+ 2lb **13** Ran SP% **125.7**
Speed ratings (Par 101): **97,96,96,95,93 92,91,90,88,84 83,82,72**
CSF £101.42 CT £482.12 TOTE £18.60: £3.50, £3.70, £2.00; EX 167.70.
Owner Marita Bayley and Trevor Turner **Bred** Mrs Marita Bayley **Trained** Cropthorne, Worcs

FOCUS
A banded-class handicap and four of these, including the winner, were racing from out of the weights. Reasonable form for the lowly grade. The pace was steady through the early stages, but increased significantly when the free-running Jomus went to the front just before the first bend about 4f from the finish. The winning time was 3.39 seconds slower than the earlier Listed contest.
Under Fire(IRE) Official explanation: trainer said, regarding the improved form shown, his string have been out of form lately and this gelding had been rested since its last outing
Jomus Official explanation: jockey said gelding ran too free
Blakeshall Hope Official explanation: jockey said gelding cut its head in stalls
Diamond Hurricane(IRE) Official explanation: jockey said colt hung badly right throughout

6969 PANORAMIC RESTAURANT LOYALTY SCHEME H'CAP 1m 3f (P)
9:20 (9:26) (Class 6) (0-52,56) 3-Y-O+ **£2,047** (£604; £302) **Stalls** High

Form RPR
0063 **1** **Oasis Sun (IRE)**12 6832 4-8-12 **46** (b) JohnEgan 13 56
(J R Best) *hld up in midfield: prog over 3f out: rdn to ld jst over 1f out: r.o wl and sn clr* **9/1**
0142 **2** *3* **Mixing**12 6832 5-8-13 **52** KirstyMilczarek(5) 1 57
(J Akehurst) *t.k.h: trckd ldrs: prog to ld over 2f out: pushed along and hdd jst over 1f out: no ch w wnr* **4/1**2
0042 **3** *1* **Karmest**7 6896 3-8-11 **50** PaulMulrennan 5 54+
(A D Brown) *led for 2f: remained prom: rdn to chal wl over 1f out: hld fnl f: snatched up last strides* **10/1**
5151 **4** *shd* **Summer Bounty**7 6896 11-9-8 **56** 6ex LPKeniry 8 59+
(F Jordan) *hld up wl in rr: prog and nt clr run on inner over 2f out: styd on fr over 1f out: nt pce to chal* **12/1**
2000 **5** *1 3/4* **Storm Path (IRE)**21 6713 3-8-9 **48** EddieAhern 3 48
(D R C Elsworth) *trckd ldrs: nt qckn over 2f out: one pce after* **16/1**
0345 **6** *1 3/4* **Black Mogul**34 6459 3-8-10 **49** JimCrowley 4 46
(R Hollinshead) *prom: cl enough 2f out: nt qckn over 1f out: wknd* **9/1**
0561 **7** *1/2* **Lord Laing (USA)**27 6613 4-9-3 **51** PatDobbs 7 47
(H J Collingridge) *trckd ldrs on inner: nt qckn over 2f out: wknd fnl f* **7/2**1
4000 **8** *1* **Garibaldi (GER)**12 6832 5-8-12 **51** (b) JamesO'Reilly(5) 12 46
(J O'Reilly) *hld up wl in rr: prog to trck ldrs over 3f out: hrd rdn and wknd 2f out* **12/1**
0050 **9** *nk* **Certifiable**241 866 6-8-13 **52** RobynBrisland(5) 10 46
(Miss Z C Davison) *dwlt: hld up in last: nvr a factor: modest late prog* **33/1**
-210 **10** *5* **Krasivi's Boy (USA)**12 6832 5-9-3 **51** (b) GeorgeBaker 14 37
(G L Moore) *hld up wl in rr: shkn up and no prog over 2f out* **8/1**3
0-20 **11** *6* **Montana Sky (IRE)**21 6713 4-8-13 **47** ChrisCatlin 6 22
(R A Harris) *nvr beyond midfield: u.p and struggling over 3f out* **9/1**
0000 **12** *4* **Dictatrix**16 6801 4-8-13 **47** (p) SteveDrowne 2 16
(P D Niven) *reluctant to go to post: s.s: rapid prog to ld after 2f: hdd over 2f out: wknd rapidly* **33/1**
5044 **13** *8* **Grafty Green (IRE)**9 6867 4-9-3 **51** TGMcLaughlin 9 6
(W M Brisbourne) *hld up in midfield: hit rail bdly 6f out: dropped to last sn after: nt rcvr* **12/1**

2m 22.12s (-0.56) **Going Correction** -0.075s/f (Stan)
WFA 3 from 4yo+ 5lb **13** Ran SP% **127.3**
Speed ratings (Par 101): **99,96,96,96,94 93,93,92,92,88 84,81,75**
CSF £47.85 CT £383.09 TOTE £10.40: £3.60, £1.60, £3.10; EX 41.70 Place 6 £48.33, Place 5 £26.15.
Owner Mrs J Schabacker **Bred** Peter Jones And G G Jones **Trained** Hucking, Kent
■ Stewards' Enquiry : Kirsty Milczarek one-day ban: careless riding (Dec 9)
Eddie Ahern 11-day ban: improper riding - used whip with excessive frequency, excessive force and without giving time to respond (Dec 14-27)

FOCUS
A moderate middle-distance handicap in which the early pace was just steady. The form seems sound enough, with the winner up 5lb in a race rated through the second and third.
Lord Laing(USA) Official explanation: trainer said gelding coughed post race
T/Plt: £188.80 to a £1 stake. Pool: £87,810.15. 339.35 winning tickets. T/Qpdt: £87.50 to a £1 stake. Pool: £6,303.70. 53.30 winning tickets. JN

6944 LINGFIELD (L-H)
Friday, November 30

OFFICIAL GOING: Standard
Wind: Strong, behind Weather: Overcast

6970 CRAWLEY NEWS H'CAP (DIV I) 6f (P)
12:10 (12:10) (Class 4) (0-85,85) 3-Y-O+ **£4,404** (£1,310; £654; £327) **Stalls** Low

Form RPR
0050 **1** **Distinctly Game**39 6381 5-8-9 **76** ChrisCatlin 8 84
(K A Ryan) *dwlt: rousted along and sn pressed ldr: drvn to chal 2f out: led jst ins fnl f: hld on wl* **10/1**
4300 **2** *1/2* **Bonnie Prince Blue**20 6753 4-8-9 **76** (b) SteveDrowne 4 83
(B W Hills) *dwlt: hld up in rr: prog towards inner wl over 1f out: styd on wl to take 2nd nr fin* **15/2**
0050 **3** *nk* **Sand Cat**9 6900 4-8-12 **79** PatDobbs 6 85
(G L Moore) *trckd ldrs: effrt 2f out: drvn to chal fnl f: nt qckn and hld last 100yds* **11/1**
2236 **4** *3/4* **Tender The Great (IRE)**9 6900 4-9-4 **85** TQuinn 10 89+
(B G Powell) *chsd ldrs on outer: rdn 2f out: kpt on wl fnl f: nvr able to chal* **6/1**2
000 **5** *nk* **Secret Night**161 2835 4-9-3 **84** EddieAhern 7 87
(J A R Toller) *hld up towards rr: prog 2f out: drvn to press ldrs fnl f: 4th and hld whn eased nr fin* **14/1**
1156 **6** *1/2* **New York Oscar (IRE)**11 6876 3-8-9 **83** (p) RobbieEgan(7) 5 85
(A J McCabe) *led: drvn over 2f out: hdd jst ins fnl f: hld whn n.m.r nr fin* **7/1**3
323 **7** *5* **Osiris Way**30 6589 5-9-1 **82** JimCrowley 3 68
(P R Chamings) *hld up bhd ldrs: effrt 2f out: cl up 1f out: wknd and eased last 100yds* **15/8**1
240 **8** *1* **George The Second**30 6589 4-8-6 **73** HayleyTurner 9 56
(Mrs H Sweeting) *w ldrs to 1/2-way: grad wknd* **16/1**
-505 **9** *1 1/2* **Spoof Master (IRE)**193 1900 3-9-1 **82** SimonWhitworth 1 61
(N A Callaghan) *a in last trio: struggling over 2f out* **25/1**
2200 **10** *1 1/4* **Hucking Hill (IRE)**46 6232 3-8-5 **72** (b) NickyMackay 2 47
(J R Best) *outpcd in last and drvn after 2f: a bhd* **11/1**

1m 10.43s (-2.38) **Going Correction** -0.225s/f (Stan) course record **10** Ran SP% **115.5**
Speed ratings (Par 105): **106,105,104,103,103 102,96,94,92,91**
CSF £82.00 CT £843.92 TOTE £11.90: £3.00, £2.30, £3.30; EX 115.40 TRIFECTA Not won..
Owner Mr & Mrs Julian And Rosie Richer **Bred** J A Forsyth **Trained** Hambleton, N Yorks
■ Stewards' Enquiry : Pat Dobbs two-day ban: careless riding (Dec 11-12)

FOCUS
A fair handicap for the track, and a fast time, suggesting the form is sound with the four immedaitely behind the winner close to their recent marks.

Osiris Way Official explanation: jockey said gelding hung right; vet said gelding returned lame

6971 CROYDON ADVERTISER (S) STKS 1m 4f (P)
12:40 (12:41) (Class 6) 3-Y-O+ £2,047 (£604; £302) Stalls Low

Form RPR

0105 **1** **Musango**[15] 6819 4-9-11 65 ....(t) FrankieMcDonald 2 71+
(B R Johnson) *hld up towards rr: prog gng wl 3f out: nt clr run briefly over 2f out: sustained hdwy to ld 1f out: sn rdn clr* **3/1**[2]

2106 **2** 2 ½ **Annambo**[13] 6853 7-9-11 75 .... RobertHavlin 11 67
(P J McBride) *trckd ldrs: led gng easily wl over 2f out: drvn and hdd 1f out: one pce* **8/11**[1]

330- **3** shd **Bucks**[467] 4626 10-9-6 67 .... ChrisCatlin 1 62
(Mike Murphy) *cl up on inner: rdn and effrt over 2f out: chal and upsides 1f out: one pce* **12/1**

0224 **4** 3 ½ **Dot's Delight**[18] 6801 3-8-9 54 .... TGMcLaughlin 6 51
(R A Harris) *uns rdr and bolted bef s: racd wd: prog and prom 5f out: chsd ldr over 2f out to wl over 1f out: fdd* **10/1**[3]

0500 **5** 5 **Missie Baileys**[36] 6452 5-9-1 45 ....(p) TolleyDean(5) 8 48
(Mrs L J Mongan) *chsd ldrs: u.p fr 1/2-way: struggling over 3f out: plugged on* **25/1**

3000 **6** 5 **Isa'Af (IRE)**[16] 6811 8-8-13 41 .... WilliamCarson(7) 5 40
(P W Hiatt) *hld up in rr: prog to ld 1/2-way: hdd wl over 2f out: wknd* **33/1**

0300 **7** 5 **Divine River**[11] 6871 4-9-1 53 .... GeorgeBaker 3 27
(J G Portman) *stdd s: hld up in last: outpcd fr 3f out: no ch after* **33/1**

0-00 **8** 2 ½ **You're My Son**[15] 6821 5-9-6 46 .... JamesDoyle 9 28
(K O Cunningham-Brown) *dwlt: hld up in last pair: hanging bdly and lft bhd fr 3f out* **66/1**

60 **9** 9 **Royalties**[132] 3730 5-9-1 34 ....(t) PaulDoe 10 9
(M A Allen) *racd freely: led to 1/2-way: wknd 4f out: t.o* **100/1**

0200 **10** 10 **Gunner's View**[36] 3420 3-9-0 70 ....(p) EddieAhern 7 —
(A Ennis) *t.k.h: chsd ldr to over 6f out: wknd 4f out: t.o* **12/1**

2m 32.58s (-1.81) **Going Correction** -0.225s/f (Stan)
WFA 3 from 4yo+ 6lb **10** Ran SP% **119.6**
Speed ratings (Par 101): **97,95,95,92,89 86,82,81,75,68**
CSF £5.49 TOTE £4.80: £1.20, £1.10, £3.20; EX 8.60 Trifecta £33.60 Pool: £309.54 - 6.53 winning tickets..The winner was sold to Ron Harris for 9,800gns. Annambo was claimed by A. S. Reid for £6,000.
Owner Tann Racing **Bred** Juddmonte Farms Ltd **Trained** Ashtead, Surrey

FOCUS
An above-average seller, with the first three home all rated 65 or above but little solid form behind.
You're My Son Official explanation: jockey said gelding hung left
Gunner's View Official explanation: jockey said colt had a breathing problem

6972 CRAWLEY NEWS H'CAP (DIV II) 6f (P)
1:10 (1:13) (Class 4) (0-85,85) 3-Y-O+ £4,404 (£1,310; £654; £327) Stalls Low

Form RPR

0000 **1** **Lucayos**[13] 6851 4-8-11 85 .... KylieManser(7) 6 92
(Mrs H Sweeting) *chsd ldr: rdn and hanging bdly over 1f out: kpt on fnl f to ld last strides* **10/1**

021- **2** shd **Hello Man (IRE)**[85] 5180 4-8-5 72 .... JamieMackay 3 79
(Eamon Tyrrell, Ire) *chsd ldng pair: effrt over 1f out: upsides fnl f: jst pipped* **14/1**

2420 **3** shd **Harry Up**[21] 6743 6-8-13 80 .... ChrisCatlin 5 87
(K A Ryan) *led: urged along and kicked on over 2f out: hrd pressed fnl f: hdd last strides* **8/1**

0005 **4** 1 **China Cherub**[4] 6947 4-8-10 82 ....(b) HaddenFrost(5) 1 86
(R Hannon) *trckd ldrs: rdn 2f out: kpt on and cl up ins fnl f: no imp nr fin* **12/1**

0605 **5** hd **Desert Dreamer (IRE)**[9] 6900 6-8-9 76 .... NickyMackay 8 79+
(G A Butler) *stdd s: hld up in last pair: plenty to do 2f out: gd prog fnl f: gaining at fin* **9/2**[2]

5020 **6** shd **Bertie Southstreet**[26] 6667 4-8-6 73 .... EddieAhern 9 76
(J R Best) *t.k.h: trckd ldrs: nt qckn over 1f out: kpt on fnl f: nvr able to chal* **7/2**[1]

0040 **7** 1 ¾ **Happy As Larry (USA)**[9] 6900 5-8-12 79 ....(t) MickyFenton 2 77
(D J Murphy) *mostly in last pair: struggling over 2f out: modest late prog on inner* **25/1**

521 **8** ½ **Tony The Tap**[6] 6938 6-9-0 81 6ex ....(b) HayleyTurner 4 77
(W R Muir) *towards rr: rdn over 2f out: no prog and btn after* **5/1**[3]

0460 **9** 1 ¼ **Resplendent Alpha**[13] 6851 3-9-2 83 .... TPQueally 10 75
(P Howling) *chsd ldrs and racd on outer: struggling 2f out: no ch after* **9/1**

5213 **10** 3 ½ **Desperate Dan**[14] 6829 6-9-1 82 .... SteveDrowne 7 64
(A B Haynes) *most reluctant to go to post: dwlt: in tch: rdn over 2f out: sn btn* **13/2**

1m 10.6s (-2.21) **Going Correction** -0.225s/f (Stan) **10** Ran SP% **118.8**
Speed ratings (Par 105): **105,104,104,103,103 103,100,100,98,93**
CSF £142.83 CT £1183.02 TOTE £16.50: £4.60, £4.10, £2.40; EX 248.50 TRIFECTA Not won. ..
Owner Alex Sweeting **Bred** P Sweeting **Trained** Lockeridge, Wilts

FOCUS
Like the first division, a race of reasonable quality for the track, and a fast time. The runner-up sets the standard but the form may not prove that solid.

6973 EAST GRINSTEAD OBSERVER NURSERY 7f (P)
1:40 (1:45) (Class 5) (0-75,75) 2-Y-O £3,238 (£963; £481; £240) Stalls Low

Form RPR

322 **1** **Ike Quebec (FR)**[9] 6898 2-9-1 74 .... HaddenFrost(5) 10 76+
(R Hannon) *trckd ldr: led 2f out: hrd pressed fnl f: styd on wl and holding on nr fin* **12/1**

1120 **2** nk **Only A Game (IRE)**[85] 5167 2-8-13 67 ow1 .... AdamKirby 4 68
(Miss M E Rowland) *trckd ldng pair: rdn to chse wnr over 1f out: str chal fnl f: hld nr fin* **25/1**

0466 **3** 1 ½ **Tense (IRE)**[26] 6665 2-9-1 69 .... TPQueally 1 67
(J A Osborne) *trckd ldrs: rdn over 2f out: prog to chse ldng pair fnl f: no imp after* **16/1**

0653 **4** ½ **Addikt (IRE)**[30] 6584 2-9-1 69 .... GeorgeBaker 12 65+
(S Kirk) *hld up towards rr: shkn up over 3f out: prog u.p over 1f out: styd on wl: nrst fin* **3/1**[1]

052U **5** hd **Greek Theatre (USA)**[11] 6868 2-9-1 69 ....(e) JamesDoyle 5 65
(Mrs A J Perrett) *hld up in midfield: effrt on inner 2f out: rdn and kpt on: nrst fin* **14/1**

0021 **6** nk **Last Of The Line**[11] 6868 2-9-7 75 6ex .... SteveDrowne 7 70
(H J L Dunlop) *chsd ldrs: rdn over 2f out: wl in tch but hanging bdly lft over 1f out: nt qckn* **13/2**

3163 **7** 1 ¼ **Hucking Hero (IRE)**[9] 6899 2-9-1 69 .... HayleyTurner 13 61
(J R Best) *plld hrd early: hld up in last pair: stl last of main gp 2f out: shkn up and styd on fr over 1f out: nvr nr ldrs* **9/2**[3]

5020 **8** 1 ¼ **Towy Boy (IRE)**[23] 6715 2-8-11 65 .... ChrisCatlin 2 54
(I A Wood) *chsd ldrs: rdn over 2f out: wknd over 1f out* **20/1**

044 **9** nk **Coole Dodger (IRE)**[16] 6805 2-9-0 68 .... MickyFenton 9 56
(B G Powell) *plld hrd early: hld up in last pair: wnt v wd fr 4f out: last and lost all ch whn wd bnd 2f out: kpt on* **33/1**

0140 **10** ½ **Affirmatively**[161] 2812 2-9-7 75 .... LPKeniry 14 62
(D R C Elsworth) *hld up in midfield: rdn and effrt over 2f out: no prog over 1f out: wknd* **20/1**

0431 **11** 1 ¾ **Harbour Blues**[11] 6872 2-9-5 73 6ex ....(t) JimCrowley 8 55
(A W Carroll) *led to 2f out: wknd rapidly on inner over 1f out* **7/2**[2]

0005 **12** nk **Clear Daylight**[23] 6715 2-8-8 62 .... EddieAhern 11 44
(J R Best) *chsd ldrs: u.p and losing pl fr 3f out* **12/1**

1m 24.97s (-0.92) **Going Correction** -0.225s/f (Stan) **12** Ran SP% **123.0**
Speed ratings (Par 96): **96,95,93,93,93 92,91,89,89,89 87,86**
CSF £290.60 CT £4825.08 TOTE £9.60: £2.90, £8.00, £5.90; EX 288.50 TRIFECTA Not won..
Owner R Hannon **Bred** Elevage De Bois Carrouges **Trained** East Everleigh, Wilts

FOCUS
An ordinary but competitive nursery and solid enough for rated through the runner-up.

NOTEBOOK
Ike Quebec(FR), backed from 20-1, had previously done well on this surface and showed that he was worth another chance at 7f last time. Though this looked a stronger race, he improved again and scored gamely. (op 20-1)
Only A Game(IRE) has done well at 5f and 6f, but showed here that 7f is right up his street these days. Only going down narrowly with his rider putting up 1lb overweight, he looks capable of winning a similar race. (op 28-1)
Tense(IRE), probably still a couple of pounds too high in the weights, is well at home on this surface and in this company.
Addikt(IRE) gets this trip really well, and ought to stay a mile on this evidence. He is inching closer to a first win. (op 10-3 tchd 4-1)
Greek Theatre(USA) was dropping from a mile, but he is not short of stamina and a return to an extra furlong should be in his favour. (tchd 16-1)
Last Of The Line may have found the 6lb penalty more of a problem than the drop in distance. However, he can do a bit better if becoming less unbalanced than he did here in the home straight. Official explanation: jockey said colt hung left in straight (op 6-1)
Hucking Hero(IRE) is on a fair mark at present, and looks capable of finding a race either at 7f or 1m if he times his run better. (op 5-1 tchd 4-1)
Coole Dodger(IRE) Official explanation: jockey said colt hung right throughout

6974 SURREY MIRROR CONDITIONS STKS 7f (P)
2:15 (2:16) (Class 3) 2-Y-O £6,855 (£2,052; £1,026; £513; £256; £128) Stalls Low

Form RPR

1 **Amazing Star (IRE)**[69] 5652 2-9-0 0 .... MickyFenton 1 84+
(M Halford, Ire) *trckd ldng pair: effrt on inner whn nt clr run and swtchd rt over 1f out: drvn to ld last 150yds: styd on* **10/1**

2 **2** nk **Regal Bird (USA)**[190] 1960 2-8-9 0 .... EddieAhern 5 79
(M A Magnusson) *hld up in 4th: rdn over 2f out: effrt on outer over 1f out: chsd wnr last 100yds: kpt on: jst hld* **9/4**[2]

1 **3** 1 **Burriscarra**[19] 6777 2-8-9 0 .... PatCosgrave 4 76
(Eamon Tyrrell, Ire) *trckd ldr: effrt to chal over 1f out: upsides ent fnl f: nt qckn* **9/1**

1204 **4** ¾ **Eastern Gift**[48] 6171 2-8-12 95 .... HaddenFrost(5) 3 82
(R Hannon) *t.k.h: led: set stdy pce to 1/2-way: rdn and styd against rail in st: hdd and fdd last 150yds* **6/4**[1]

0 **5** 2 ½ **Dinarius**[169] 2596 2-9-0 0 .... J-PGuillambert 2 73
(K J Burke) *hld up in last pair: rdn whn pce lifted 1/2-way: struggling after: plugged on* **33/1**

01 **6** nk **Port Quin**[45] 6246 2-9-3 79 .... SteveDrowne 6 75
(G Wragg) *restrained s: hld up in last: outpcd and pushed along over 2f out: nvr on terms after* **4/1**[3]

1m 24.9s (-0.99) **Going Correction** -0.225s/f (Stan) **6** Ran SP% **112.8**
Speed ratings (Par 100): **96,95,94,93,90 90**
CSF £33.14 TOTE £12.20: £4.60, £1.50; EX 42.70.
Owner Peter Yip **Bred** Glending Bloodstock **Trained** the Curragh, Co Kildare

FOCUS
Eastern Gift set a good standard for the track, but the early pace was steady. The form is best rated around the placed horses.

NOTEBOOK
Amazing Star(IRE), an Irish maiden, was reported by Fenton to have still been green but overcame that problem to gain a workmanlike victory against more obvious rivals. With only one previous run to his name, he is entitled to improve again. (op 8-1 tchd 12-1)
Regal Bird(USA) had finished second on her only previous outing, on turf in May. This was a fine run following the long absence, and she looks capable of winning on sand before picking up the thread on grass next year. (op 11-4)
Burriscarra handled the drop in trip alright, but it was still a solid effort. She should continue to make her mark at either 7f or 1m. (op 11-1 tchd 8-1)
Eastern Gift had the run of the race, as well as the best form on offer, but was rather disappointing when it came to the crunch. This was his first run on Polytrack, and he has yet to prove he is as good on it as he is on turf. (op 13-8 tchd 15-8)
Dinarius had been well beaten on turf in his only previous race, so this was not a bad debut on sand considering his price, though he was essentially outclassed. An extra furlong should suit. (op 25-1)
Port Quin made a modest All-Weather debut, and needs to prove himself on the surface now. (op 7-2 tchd 3-1 and 9-2)

6975 EAST SUSSEX AND SURREY NEWS & MEDIA MAIDEN STKS 1m 2f (P)
2:45 (2:46) (Class 5) 3-Y-O £2,817 (£838; £418; £209) Stalls Low

Form RPR

2322 **1** **Demisemiquaver**[9] 6901 3-8-12 70 ....(b[1]) SteveDrowne 5 62
(J Noseda) *trckd ldng pair: effrt on inner 2f out: led 1f out: jst hld on* **9/4**[1]

3230 **2** shd **Paradise Dancer (IRE)**[46] 6232 3-8-12 68 .... EddieAhern 3 62
(J A R Toller) *trckd ldrs: brought to outer and effrt wl over 1f out: styd on fnl f: jst failed* **7/2**[2]

5242 **3** ½ **Power Player**[35] 6480 3-9-3 65 .... AdamKirby 11 66
(D J Coakley) *pushed up to trck ldr: drvn over 3f out: tried to chal over 1f out: kpt on same pce* **11/1**

6250 **4** shd **Saviour Sand (IRE)**[142] 3420 3-9-3 75 .... LPKeniry 7 66
(D R C Elsworth) *led: drvn 2f out: hdd and nt qckn 1f out* **5/1**[3]

0 **5** nk **Muscovado (USA)**[37] 6420 3-8-12 0 .... NickyMackay 4 60
(L M Cumani) *trckd ldrs: brought wd in st and effrt: nt qckn and hld fnl f* **7/1**

-556 **6** *10* **Samahir (USA)**[9] 6895 3-8-12 55 ChrisCatlin 8 40
(T T Clement) *hld up in last pair: outpcd sn after 1/2-way: effrt to chse clr ldng quintet over 3f out: no imp over 1f out: wknd* **14/1**

0030 **7** *1* **Bonne D'Argent (IRE)**[38] 6413 3-8-12 64 PatCosgrave 10 38
(J R Boyle) *hld up: lft bhd sn after 1/2-way: no ch after* **12/1**

2044 **8** *1 1/2* **My Monna**[14] 6832 3-8-9 50 NeilChalmers(3) 1 35
(Miss Sheena West) *hld up in rr: lft bhd sn after 1/2-way: no ch after* **12/1**

05 **9** *3/4* **Virgilia (IRE)**[14] 6830 3-8-12 0 PatDobbs 2 34
(R Hannon) *awkward s: in tch tl wknd u.p over 4f out* **33/1**

10 *25* **Ela Mario (CYP)** 3-9-3 0 GeorgeBaker 6 —
(Mrs H Sweeting) *in tch tl wknd rapidly sn after 1/2-way: wl t.o* **14/1**

2m 5.71s (-2.08) **Going Correction** -0.225s/f (Stan) **10** Ran SP% **122.2**
Speed ratings (Par 102): **99,98,98,98,98 90,89,88,87,67**
CSF £10.50 TOTE £2.70: £1.70, £1.80, £2.40; EX 13.00 Trifecta £20.70 Pool: £397.85 - 13.63 winning tickets..
Owner Lady Carolyn Warren, Duke Of Roxburghe **Bred** Highclere Stud And Floors Farming **Trained** Newmarket, Suffolk

FOCUS
A routine maiden for the track, and a blanket finish seems to reflect that fact. The form rated through the third is modest.
Power Player Official explanation: jockey said gelding hung left
Ela Mario(CYP) Official explanation: jockey said gelding had a breathing problem

6976 CARAVAN CLUB CENTENARY H'CAP 5f (P)
3:20 (3:20) (Class 5) (0-70,73) 3-Y-O+ **£2,817** (£838; £418; £209) **Stalls** High

Form RPR

0205 **1** **Silver Prelude**[18] 6794 6-8-9 65 JamesO'Reilly(5) 10 75
(D K Ivory) *mde most: clr w runner-up after 2f: rdn and kpt on wl fr over 1f out* **7/1**

5600 **2** *3/4* **Azygous**[9] 6890 4-8-11 62 ChrisCatlin 7 70
(J Akehurst) *pressed wnr thrght and clr of rest after 2f: kpt on but hld fnl f* **8/1**

5-54 **3** *1* **Mogok Ruby**[14] 6829 3-9-4 69 IanMongan 3 73
(L Montague Hall) *hld up in last pair: rdn over 2f out: styd on to take 3rd fnl f: clsng at fin but no ch* **9/2**[3]

0615 **4** *3/4* **Willhewiz**[16] 6810 7-8-11 62 EddieAhern 1 64
(M S Saunders) *settled to chse ldng pair: rdn and no imp 2f out: one pce after* **4/1**[2]

003 **5** *nk* **Calypso King**[9] 6890 4-8-11 62 LPKeniry 2 63
(Peter Grayson) *hld up in midfield and off the pce: effrt on inner wl over 1f out: disp 3rd fnl f* **7/2**[1]

4606 **6** *1 3/4* **Fizzlephut (IRE)**[14] 6829 5-9-4 69 (p) PaulFitzsimons 6 63
(Miss J R Tooth) *chsd ldng trio: drvn and no prog 2f out: wknd fnl f* **11/1**

4250 **7** *1/2* **Hythe Bay**[43] 6279 3-8-13 64 J-PGuillambert 4 57
(J R Best) *stdd s: hld up in last pair: c wdst of all bnd 2f out: n.d after* **12/1**

0001 **8** *1/2* **Back In The Red (IRE)**[8] 6905 3-9-8 73 6ex SteveDrowne 8 64
(R A Harris) *sn rdn to stay in tch: struggling 2f out: fdd* **11/2**

57.87 secs (-1.91) **Going Correction** -0.225s/f (Stan) **8** Ran SP% **115.4**
Speed ratings (Par 103): **106,104,103,102,101 98,97,97**
CSF £61.52 CT £281.86 TOTE £8.40: £2.10, £2.60, £1.70; EX 65.20 Trifecta £252.80 Part won. Pool: £356.07 - 0.36 winning tickets. Place 6 £1,858.20, Place 5 £344.68.
Owner Mrs A Shone **Bred** Bearstone Stud **Trained** Radlett, Herts

FOCUS
A moderate race in terms of ratings, but containing proven speedsters at this level, and the time was good. The placed horses ran to their recent marks.
T/Plt: £2,557.60 to a £1 stake. Pool: £44,495.55. 12.70 winning tickets. T/Qpdt: £300.50 to a £1 stake. Pool: £4,873.40. 12.00 winning tickets. JN

6955 WOLVERHAMPTON (A.W) (L-H)
Friday, November 30

OFFICIAL GOING: Standard
Wind: Fresh, behind Weather: Raining

6977 MACE RACING AT WOLVERHAMPTON CLAIMING STKS 5f 20y(P)
7:00 (7:00) (Class 6) 2-Y-O **£2,388** (£705; £352) **Stalls** Low

Form RPR

0006 **1** **Ten Down**[55] 6004 2-8-11 76 TPQueally 1 73
(J A Osborne) *mde all: rdn and edgd rt over 1f out: all out* **8/1**

4005 **2** *shd* **River Bounty**[9] 6892 2-8-8 67 (v[1]) NeilPollard 2 70
(A P Jarvis) *a.p: rdn to chse wnr over 1f out: sn ev ch: r.o* **8/1**

6030 **3** *1* **Joss Stick**[23] 6722 2-8-6 56 (p) JamieMackay 6 64+
(P J Makin) *s.i.s and hmpd s: in rr: nt clr run over 2f out: hdwy over 1f out: r.o* **20/1**

621 **4** *hd* **Golden Dane (IRE)**[55] 6023 2-8-9 68 JimCrowley 8 66
(I A Wood) *prom: outpcd 1/2-way: rdn over 1f out: r.o ins fnl f* **4/1**[1]

6002 **5** *1 1/4* **Lieutenant Pigeon**[23] 6722 2-9-2 65 (b[1]) PaulMulrennan 7 69
(T D Easterby) *edgd lft s: chsd ldrs: rdn over 1f out: edgd lft: styd on same pce ins fnl f* **8/1**

460 **6** *1 1/2* **Longoria (IRE)**[67] 5692 2-8-6 68 GregFairley 11 53
(M G Quinlan) *s.i.s: in rr: swtchd lft over 1f out: r.o ins fnl f: nrst fin* **7/1**

661 **7** *nk* **Atephobia**[14] 6828 2-8-13 68 AndrewElliott(3) 4 62
(K R Burke) *w wnr tl rdn over 2f out: wknd ins fnl f* **11/2**[3]

523 **8** *1 3/4* **Wild Bill Tracey**[11] 6872 2-8-9 72 (v[1]) TGMcLaughlin 5 49
(M J Wallace) *s.i.s: hld up: hdwy 1/2-way: rdn over 1f out: wknd ins fnl f* **5/1**[2]

010 **9** *3 1/2* **Ingleby Star (IRE)**[198] 1772 2-9-2 81 PaulFessey 12 43
(T D Barron) *hld up: rdn over 1f out: a in rr* **16/1**

1600 **10** *nk* **Sharps Gold**[14] 6828 2-7-13 57 (t) DuranFentiman(3) 3 28
(P J McBride) *mid-div: lost pl 4f out: rdn and hung rt over 2f out: n.d after* **33/1**

2606 **11** *3* **Redbrick Girl**[14] 6828 2-8-1 53 (b[1]) NataliaGemelova(5) 9 22
(K A Ryan) *sn pushed along: a in rr* **33/1**

0005 **12** *6* **Berties Goodenough**[27] 6641 2-8-7 52 HayleyTurner 13 —
(Andrew Turnell) *chsd ldrs: rdn and hung rt 1/2-way: sn wknd* **33/1**

63.32 secs (0.50) **Going Correction** 0.0s/f (Stan) **12** Ran SP% **117.4**
Speed ratings (Par 94): **96,95,94,93,91 89,89,86,80,80 75,65**
CSF £66.88 TOTE £12.20: £4.10, £4.60, £7.30; EX 52.40.Golden Dane was claimed by C. R. Dore for £8,000.
Owner Piers Pottinger And Ten **Bred** Baydon House Stud **Trained** Upper Lambourn, Berks
■ Stewards' Enquiry : Hayley Turner jockey said gelding hung right-handed throughout

FOCUS
The usual mixed bag but, although the pace was strong, those attempting to come from off the pace were at a disadvantage. The principals came down the centre and although the form looks fairly solid the 56-rated third holds it down.

NOTEBOOK
Ten Down has been disappointing since his maiden win at Windsor in May but he had a decent chance at the weights and showed a fine attitude dropped in grade and with the headgear left off. Life is going to be tougher back in handicap company from his current mark of 76, though. (op 5-1)
River Bounty has been a bit disappointing in handicaps since her maiden success on turf in August but she ran creditably dropped in grade in the first-time visor. Consistency has not been her strongest suit though, and it remains to be seen whether the headgear will have the same effect next time. (op 12-1)
Joss Stick ran creditably in the face of a stiff task in the first-time cheekpieces, especially in a race where the leaders did not come back. He is worth another try over 6f and may be capable of picking up a small event but he may not be entirely straightforward and life will be tougher after reassessment.
Golden Dane(IRE), a selling winner over this course and distance on his previous start, was unable to dominate in this stronger event but ran creditably and left the impression that he would be worth another try over 6f. (op 17-2)
Lieutenant Pigeon, who returned to form after some disappointing efforts on his second run for the yard last time, was not disgraced on this All-Weather debut and shaped as though the return to 6f would be in his favour. (op 10-1)
Longoria(IRE), a consistent sort, was not disgraced in a race where the leaders did not come back to the field on this All-Wweather debut. The return to 6f will be in her favour. (op 15-2 tchd 8-1)
Berties Goodenough Official explanation: jockey said gelding hung right-handed throughout

6978 PONTIN'S BOOK EARLY NURSERY 1m 141y(P)
7:30 (7:30) (Class 5) (0-75,70) 2-Y-O **£2,914** (£867; £433; £216) **Stalls** Low

Form RPR

054 **1** **Animator**[20] 6763 2-9-0 68 TolleyDean(5) 8 70
(P F I Cole) *chsd ldr tl led over 2f out: rdn and edgd lft over 1f out: styd on* **15/2**[3]

000 **2** *1 1/4* **It's Josr**[44] 6262 2-9-3 66 JimCrowley 1 65
(I A Wood) *a.p: rdn over 2f out: chsd wnr ins fnl f: styd on* **18/1**

6333 **3** *1* **Tapas Lad (IRE)**[11] 6865 2-8-6 55 (v) ChrisCatlin 6 52
(V Smith) *s.i.s: sn drvn along: hdwy over 5f out: rdn over 2f out: styd on u.p* **7/2**[1]

534 **4** *hd* **Tiger Spice**[40] 6358 2-9-5 68 TPQueally 9 65
(M J Haggas) *chsd ldrs: rdn over 2f out: edgd lft fnl f: styd on* **11/2**[2]

0040 **5** *1 1/2* **Vigano (IRE)**[16] 6805 2-9-4 67 LPKeniry 3 61
(S Kirk) *s.i.s: hld up: rdn over 2f out: styd on ins fnl f: nt trble ldrs* **9/1**

5235 **6** *hd* **Funseeker (UAE)**[32] 6543 2-9-5 68 GregFairley 5 61
(M Johnston) *led: rdn and hdd over 2f out: no ex fnl f* **7/2**[1]

0350 **7** *4* **Boomtown**[58] 5914 2-9-0 70 MarieLussiana(7) 7 55+
(M Johnston) *hld up: effrt and hung lft over 1f out: n.d* **10/1**

0000 **8** *6* **Aberavon**[97] 4810 2-8-12 61 (p) EddieAhern 2 33
(P D Evans) *hld up in tch: rdn over 3f out: wknd over 2f out* **15/2**[3]

5033 **9** *2 1/2* **Ramblin Bob**[30] 6586 2-8-13 62 NeilPollard 4 29
(W J Musson) *stdd s: plld hrd: a in rr: rdn and wknd over 2f out* **8/1**

1m 53.21s (1.45) **Going Correction** 0.0s/f (Stan) **9** Ran SP% **118.8**
Speed ratings (Par 96): **93,91,91,90,89 89,85,80,78**
CSF £133.33 CT £564.01 TOTE £12.00: £3.80, £4.50, £1.50; EX 195.10.
Owner Strategic Thoroughbred Racing **Bred** Stowell Park Stud **Trained** Whatcombe, Oxon

FOCUS
An ordinary nursery run at an modest pace but the form looks reasonable. Those up with the pace were again favoured and the winner came up the inside rail in the straight.

NOTEBOOK
Animator, who showed ability in maidens on Polytrack, is from a yard among the winners and he turned in an improved effort on this handicap debut. He should have no problems with 1m2f and appeals as the type to win more races. (op 8-1 tchd 9-1)
It's Josr, who has improved a fair bit with every start, turned in his best effort yet on this handicap debut. He will be suited by the step up to 1m2f and appeals as the type to win an ordinary event. (op 14-1)
Tapas Lad(IRE) once again ran creditably in terms of form over this shorter trip with the tongue-tie omitted but, while the return to further should suit, he looked anything but straightforward and the colt, who carries his head high, looks one to tread carefully with. (op 9-2 tchd 10-3)
Tiger Spice, up in trip for this nursery debut, was not disgraced and left the impression that an even stiffer test of stamina would suit. She has little margin for error from her current mark but is in good hands and is likely to be placed to best advantage. (op 7-2 tchd 13-2)
Vigano(IRE), an exposed maiden, again had his limitations exposed on Polytrack back in nursery company. While worth the a try over a bit further, he has something to prove at present from his current mark. (op 8-1 tchd 10-1)
Funseeker(UAE), who showed ability in maiden company on turf and Polytrack in autumn, had the run of the race but proved a bit of a disappointment on this nursery debut. She will have to show more before she is a strong betting proposition. (op 4-1 tchd 3-1)

6979 PONTIN'S BOOK EARLY PRICE PROMISE H'CAP 1m 141y(P)
7:55 (7:55) (Class 6) (0-55,55) 3-Y-O+ **£2,047** (£604; £302) **Stalls** Low

Form RPR

0423 **1** **Arthur's Edge**[8] 6906 3-8-5 53 TolleyDean(5) 13 68
(B Palling) *chsd ldr tl led over 6f out: rdn clr over 1f out: jst hld on* **5/2**[1]

6450 **2** *nk* **Glenridding**[57] 5945 3-8-7 50 JimCrowley 7 64
(J G Given) *led: hdd over 6f out: remained handy: chsd wnr over 2f out: sn rdn: r.o* **25/1**

2162 **3** *3* **Ours (IRE)**[13] 6859 4-8-8 55 MarkCoumbe(7) 5 62+
(John A Harris) *hld up: hdwy over 1f out: sn rdn: r.o: nt rch ldrs* **8/1**

0065 **4** *2 1/2* **Desert Lover (IRE)**[3] 6955 5-8-7 47 (v) EddieAhern 9 49
(R J Price) *hld up in tch: rdn over 1f out: wkng whn edgd lft fnl f* **7/1**

0130 **5** *2 1/2* **Faraday (IRE)**[14] 6832 4-8-7 47 TPQueally 11 43
(A P Stringer) *hld up: hdwy 1/2-way: rdn over 2f out: hung lft and wknd over 1f out* **4/1**[2]

36-0 **6** *1* **Art Elegant**[41] 6348 5-8-1 48 (p) AmyKathleenParsons(7) 8 42
(T G McCourt, Ire) *mid-div: hdwy over 2f out: rdn: edgd lft and wknd over 1f out* **14/1**

004 **7** *1 3/4* **Colinca's Lad (IRE)**[9] 6894 5-9-0 54 HayleyTurner 2 44
(T T Clement) *hld up: rdn over 2f out: n.d* **6/1**[3]

5600 **8** *1 1/4* **Vesuvio**[13] 6859 3-8-10 53 GregFairley 10 40
(C W Thornton) *prom: chsd wnr over 5f out tl rdn over 2f out: wknd over 1f out* **33/1**

660 **9** *3 1/2* **I Will If You Will**[192] 1913 3-8-10 53 PaulMulrennan 4 32
(K A Ryan) *s.i.s: sn pushed along: a in rr* **33/1**

006 **10** *1* **Winter Cruise (IRE)**[18] 6801 3-8-7 50 ChrisCatlin 1 26
(Ian Williams) *s.i.s: outpcd* **20/1**

2600 **11** *1* **Keon (IRE)**[8] 6906 5-8-8 53 RussellKennemore(5) 12 27
(R Hollinshead) *chsd ldrs: rdn over 3f out: wknd wl over 1f out* **28/1**

4136 **12** *1 1/4* **Reveur**[8] 6906 4-8-12 52 TGMcLaughlin 6 23
(M Mullineaux) *mid-div: rdn over 3f out: wknd over 2f out* **14/1**

000 **13** *4* **George's Flyer (IRE)**[13] 6859 4-8-8 **48**..........................(v) DaleGibson 3 10
(R A Fahey) *sn pushed along: a in rr: wknd over 3f out* **20/1**

1m 51.56s (-0.20) **Going Correction** 0.0s/f (Stan)
WFA 3 from 4yo+ 3lb **13** Ran SP% **122.5**
Speed ratings (Par 101): **100,99,97,94,92 91,90,89,85,85 84,83,79**
CSF £80.59 CT £466.15 TOTE £4.00: £2.20, £7.80, £2.00; EX 109.70.
Owner Mrs Annabelle Mason **Bred** Christopher J Mason **Trained** Tredodridge, Vale Of Glamorgan

FOCUS
A low-grade handicap in which the pace was just fair. Those up with the pace were again favoured and the winner, who sets the standard, raced against the inside rail in the straight.

6980 PONTIN'S GREAT FAMILY HOLIDAYS MAIDEN AUCTION STKS 7f 32y(P)
8:25 (8:25) (Class 6) 2-Y-O **£2,047** (£604; £302) **Stalls** High

Form RPR
34 **1** **Swift Gift**[98] 4784 2-9-1 0.................................... RobertHavlin 4 82+
(B J Meehan) *hld up: hdwy over 2f out: led over 1f out: rdn clr* **6/5**[1]

2443 **2** *4* **Spiritofthetiger (USA)**[67] 5682 2-8-6 68.......................... EddieAhern 5 63
(R A Teal) *chsd ldrs: nt clr run 2f out: sn rdn: styd on same pce fnl f* **4/1**[3]

00 **3** *hd* **Black Or Red (IRE)**[23] 6714 2-8-12 0............................ JimCrowley 1 69
(I A Wood) *led early: chsd ldr: led over 2f out: rdn and hdd over 1f out: styd on same pce* **20/1**

4633 **4** *shd* **Nice Wee Girl (IRE)**[14] 6827 2-8-8 67.............................. LPKeniry 7 64
(S Kirk) *hld up: swtchd rt and hdwy over 1f out: sn rdn: styd on same pce fnl f* **9/4**[2]

5 **5** *2 ½* **Wise Hawk**[20] 6755 2-8-11 0...................................... TPQueally 3 61
(W J Haggas) *hld up: outpcd over 3f out: hdwy and edgd lft over 1f out: nt rch ldrs* **11/2**

00 **6** *5* **Lechero (IRE)**[13] 6855 2-8-9 0........................... J-PGuillambert 8 47
(P A Blockley) *sn led: rdn and hdd over 2f out: wknd over 1f out* **33/1**

7 *8* **Amyann (IRE)** 2-8-5 0.. ChrisCatlin 6 23
(J R Holt) *s.i.s: sn pushed along in rr: wknd 3f out* **25/1**

0000 **8** *½* **Westwood Dawn**[23] 6714 2-8-12 25................................ HayleyTurner 9 29
(Mrs N Macauley) *s.i.s: sn chsng ldrs: rdn and wknd 2f out* **66/1**

1m 31.25s (0.85) **Going Correction** 0.0s/f (Stan) **8** Ran SP% **124.7**
Speed ratings (Par 94): **95,90,90,90,87 81,72,71**
CSF £7.12 TOTE £2.30: £1.40, £1.80, £2.40; EX 10.00.
Owner Social and Affordable Racing Partnership **Bred** Glebe Stud And J F Dean **Trained** Manton, Wilts

FOCUS
An uncompetitive maiden run at just a fair gallop and one in which the winner, who came down the centre in the straight, proved a cut above his rivals. He sets the standard and the form looks believable.

NOTEBOOK
Swift Gift ◆, who shaped well in a race that threw up winners on his debut, failed to build on that next time but he confirmed debut promise on this All-Weather debut. This was not much of a race but, although life will be tougher from a mark around 80 in handicaps, he may well be capable of better. (op 2-1 tchd 11-10)
Spiritofthetiger(USA) is starting to look exposed but she is a consistent sort who is the best guide to the worth of this form. While vulnerable to the more progressive types in this grade, she ought to pick up a small event at some point. (op 7-2 tchd 9-2)
Black Or Red(IRE), well beaten on his previous two starts, had the run of the race at a course that has been favouring those up with the pace and he turned in his best effort. He is likely to remain vulnerable in this grade but may do better in handicaps. (tchd 25-1)
Nice Wee Girl(IRE) is another consistent sort who ran creditably. She looks well worth a try over 1m and may be able to pick up a small handicap when the emphasis is more on stamina. (op 10-3 tchd 7-2)
Wise Hawk, easy to back, was not knocked about on this All-Weather debut and only second start. He is in very good hands and may be the sort to fare best once handicapped. (op 3-1 tchd 6-1)
Lechero(IRE), having this third run, was again soundly beaten and his short-term future at least lies in low-grade handicap company.

6981 GO PONTIN'S H'CAP 7f 32y(P)
8:55 (8:55) (Class 4) (0-85,86) 3-Y-O+ **£4,857** (£1,445; £722; £360) **Stalls** High

Form RPR
3141 **1** **Councellor (FR)**[4] 6949 5-9-6 **86** 6ex..........................(t) MickyFenton 7 94
(Stef Liddiard) *mde all: rdn and edgd rt over 1f out: styd on* **9/2**[2]

0236 **2** *1 ¼* **Rainbow Mirage (IRE)**[24] 6707 3-9-3 **84**..................... J-PGuillambert 8 89
(E S McMahon) *hld up: hdwy over 4f out: rdn and edgd lft fr over 1f out: styd on* **12/1**

1151 **3** *1* **Carcinetto (IRE)**[8] 6907 5-8-9 **82** 6ex....................... RichardEvans[(7)] 5 84
(P D Evans) *hld up in tch: lost pl 4f out: hdwy over 1f out: sn rdn: styd on* **5/1**[3]

0036 **4** *nk* **Buy On The Red**[14] 6836 6-9-2 **82**..............................(p) HayleyTurner 1 83
(W R Muir) *chsd ldrs: rdn and edgd rt over 1f out: styd on u.p* **13/2**

0040 **5** *5* **Ingleby Arch (USA)**[14] 6836 4-9-0 **80**.............................. PaulFessey 10 68
(T D Barron) *chsd ldrs: rdn over 2f out: wknd over 1f out* **14/1**

0003 **6** *¾* **Dickie Le Davoir**[9] 6891 3-9-4 **85**.................................. EddieAhern 3 71
(K R Burke) *hld up: styd on fnl f: nvr nrr* **8/1**

6500 **7** *shd* **Neardown Beauty (IRE)**[21] 6746 4-8-6 **75**............ DuranFentiman[(3)] 6 61
(R E Barr) *s.i.s: hld up: styd on ins fnl f: nvr nrr* **20/1**

0326 **8** *½* **Red Romeo**[24] 6701 6-8-12 **78**.. ChrisCatlin 12 62
(N Wilson) *prom: racd keenly: trckd ldr 5f out: rdn over 2f out: nt clr run over 1f out: sn wknd* **11/1**

4050 **9** *1 ¼* **Roman Maze**[14] 6836 7-9-4 **84**...................................... GeorgeBaker 4 65
(W M Brisbourne) *hld up: rdn over 1f out: sn wknd* **4/1**[1]

1042 **10** *1* **Cornus**[8] 6907 5-8-13 **79**..(be) NeilPollard 11 57
(A J McCabe) *chsd ldrs: rdn over 3f out: wknd 2f out* **10/1**

1260 **11** *7* **Yakimov (USA)**[120] 4105 8-9-5 **85**................................... VinceSlattery 2 44
(D J Wintle) *prom: lost pl over 5f out: sn bhd* **25/1**

1m 29.86s (-0.54) **Going Correction** 0.0s/f (Stan)
WFA 3 from 4yo+ 1lb **11** Ran SP% **119.7**
Speed ratings (Par 105): **103,101,100,100,94 93,93,92,91,90 82**
CSF £58.75 CT £284.86 TOTE £4.80: £2.50, £3.90, £2.30; EX 90.70.
Owner ownaracehorse.co.uk **Bred** Janus Bloodstock & Pontchartrain Stud **Trained** Great Shefford, Berks

FOCUS
A fair event but an ordinary gallop meant those held up were again at a big disadvantage. The winner made the running and raced in the centre while the placed horses set the level for the form.

6982 BOOK A CHRISTMAS BREAK AT PONTIN'S H'CAP 1m 1f 103y(P)
9:20 (9:20) (Class 5) (0-75,75) 3-Y-O+ **£2,914** (£867; £433; £216) **Stalls** Low

Form RPR
0311 **1** **Lobengula (IRE)**[29] 6612 5-9-4 **74**............................. AndrewElliott[(3)] 7 88+
(I W McInnes) *mde all: clr over 2f out: edgd lft towards fin: rdn out* **7/2**[2]

1111 **2** *2* **Birkside**[19] 6774 4-8-10 **70**... JamieKyne[(7)] 11 80
(D Carroll) *s.i.s: hld up: hdwy over 3f out: rdn to chse wnr 2f out: hung lft fr over 1f out: styd on* **7/1**

5632 **3** *2 ½* **Baan (USA)**[14] 6838 4-9-1 **68**.......................................(v[1]) GregFairley 8 73
(M Johnston) *hld up: styd on appr fnl f: nt rch ldrs* **4/1**[3]

2220 **4** *½* **Emily's Place (IRE)**[29] 6612 4-8-12 **65**.......................... PatCosgrave 4 69
(J Pearce) *hld up: styd on appr fnl f: nvr nrr* **11/1**

1310 **5** *shd* **Kansas Gold**[41] 6342 4-8-13 **66**.............................. PaulMulrennan 10 70
(J Mackie) *chsd ldrs: rdn over 3f out: wkng whn hung lft fnl f* **10/1**

0066 **6** *1 ½* **Street Life (IRE)**[22] 6738 9-8-10 **63**................................ NeilPollard 6 64
(W J Musson) *s.i.s: hld up: styd on appr fnl f: nvr nrr* **16/1**

4106 **7** *3 ½* **Sun Of The Sea**[28] 6623 3-9-1 **71**................................... GeorgeBaker 1 64
(N P Littmoden) *chsd ldrs: rdn over 2f out: sn wknd* **10/3**[1]

514 **8** *2 ½* **Windbeneathmywings (IRE)**[80] 5316 3-9-2 **72**.............. EddieAhern 12 60
(M J Grassick, Ire) *hld up: bhd fnl 3f* **9/1**

0- **9** *3 ½* **Annunzio**[27] 6662 4-8-3 **63**..........................(p) AmyKathleenParsons[(7)] 5 44
(T G McCourt, Ire) *chsd wnr tl rdn 2f out: sn wknd* **66/1**

1-5F **10** *4* **Stravita**[202] 1672 3-9-0 **75**............................. RussellKennemore[(5)] 13 47
(R Hollinshead) *mid-div: rdn and wknd over 3f out* **40/1**

0650 **11** *6* **Josh**[8] 6907 5-9-6 **73**... ChrisCatlin 3 33
(K A Ryan) *mid-div: rdn 1/2-way: wknd over 3f out* **20/1**

2m 1.79s (-0.83) **Going Correction** 0.0s/f (Stan)
WFA 3 from 4yo+ 3lb **11** Ran SP% **119.8**
Speed ratings (Par 103): **103,101,99,98,98 97,94,91,88,85 79**
CSF £28.52 CT £104.08 TOTE £5.70: £2.20, £2.80, £1.20; EX 33.80 Place 6 £177.24, Place 5 £34.38.
Owner Colin G R Booth **Bred** A S O'Brien And Lars Pearson **Trained** Catwick, E Yorks

FOCUS
An ordinary handicap but, although the pace was sound throughout, the leader once again failed to come back to the pack at this meeting. The winner and second ended up on or towards the inside rail in the straight.
T/Plt: £274.20 to a £1 stake. Pool: £116,699.30. 310.60 winning tickets. T/Qpdt: £6.40 to a £1 stake. Pool: £8,327.50. 951.80 winning tickets. CR

6983 - 6989a (Foreign Racing) - See Raceform Interactive

6963 KEMPTON (A.W) (R-H)
Saturday, December 1

OFFICIAL GOING: Standard
Wind: strong, across Weather: fine until rain after race 5

6990 AZURE MAIDEN AUCTION STKS 6f (P)
1:10 (1:12) (Class 6) 2-Y-O **£2,047** (£604; £302) **Stalls** High

Form RPR
002 **1** **Yamanmickmccann**[16] 6820 2-8-12 67 ow1............... RichardHughes 8 77
(R Hannon) *mde all: rdn and pressed 2f out: kpt on wl to assert fnl f* **6/4**[1]

2 *1 ½* **Sempre Libera (IRE)** 2-8-7 0...................................... HayleyTurner 9 67
(P W Chapple-Hyam) *dwlt: sn trckd ldrs: effrt on inner to chal 2f out: no ex and hld fnl f* **13/2**[3]

00 **3** *2 ½* **Super Tuscan (IRE)**[21] 6754 2-8-12 0.............................. TPQueally 4 64
(J G Given) *trckd ldng pair: tried to chal 2f out: hung bdly lft jst over 1f out: one pce* **16/1**

04 **4** *1 ¼* **Bertbrand**[24] 6714 2-8-11 0....................................... EddieAhern 5 59
(M Botti) *mostly trckd wnr to 2f out: fdd u.p* **15/8**[2]

5 *1 ½* **Fantadot** 2-8-10 0.. LPKeniry 1 54
(D J S Ffrench Davis) *wnt bdly lft s: mostly last: rdn and outpcd over 2f out: kpt on fr over 1f out* **33/1**

606 **6** *½* **Whitcombe Flyer (USA)**[7] 6926 2-8-12 59.................(p) RobertHavlin 6 54
(Jamie Poulton) *hld up in tch: outpcd over 2f out: hanging and nt keen after: plugged on fnl f* **12/1**

7 *6* **Golden Horus (USA)** 2-8-9 0................................ JerryO'Dwyer[(3)] 3 35
(P J O'Gorman) *dwlt: rousted along early in last pair: in tch tl wknd over 2f out* **25/1**

0000 **8** *3 ½* **Somarini**[12] 6872 2-8-6 45...(b[1]) ChrisCatlin 7 18
(T T Clement) *t.k.h: in tch tl wknd over 2f out* **50/1**

004 **9** *9* **Libertytyne**[26] 6693 2-8-7 51................................... SimonWhitworth 2 —
(S Kirk) *in tch on outer to 1/2-way: sn wknd: t.o* **14/1**

1m 13.79s (0.09) **Going Correction** -0.10s/f (Stan) **9** Ran SP% **117.1**
Speed ratings (Par 94): **95,93,89,88,86 85,77,72,60**
CSF £12.11 TOTE £2.60: £1.10, £1.80, £3.50; EX 11.00.
Owner J R May **Bred** Helshaw Grange Stud & T & S Dhaliwel **Trained** East Everleigh, Wilts
■ Stewards' Enquiry : Richard Hughes one-day ban: used whip in incorrect place (Dec 12)

FOCUS
A modest race, with the winner looking a cut above the rest.

NOTEBOOK
Yamanmickmccann missed an engagement at Lingfield the previous day to run here, and landed a gamble in the process. Making all despite the wide draw, he found more than enough to hold on despite the 1lb overweight, and looks capable of scoring again at this trip. (op 11-4)
Sempre Libera(IRE) ◆, a 15,000gns daughter of the miler Statue Of Liberty, made a promising debut to beat all but the well-backed winner and should find a similar event. Her dam won at 7f as a juvenile, so she should stay farther than this, but 6f seemed to suit well enough. (op 3-1)
Super Tuscan(IRE), making his All-Weather debut, finished closer than he had in two races on turf. A 16,000gns son of the smart 6f-7f performer Fath, he has a number of winners in the family and looks a likely sort for handicaps now he is qualified. (op 20-1)
Bertbrand has not been quite up to it in maiden company, and the drop in trip was not the answer. However, he is likely to switch to handicaps soon, and that will be more his scene. (op 2-1)
Fantadot, a gelding by Fantastic Light out of an unraced half-sister to the prolific winner Attorney, cost just 7,000gns as a yearling. However, he made a satisfactory debut and looks the sort to improve over longer trips. (op 25-1)
Whitcombe Flyer(USA) has shown a glimmer of ability without being convincing. The time has come for him to take his chance in handicaps, but he lacks the pace for sprints, so would be worth trying at 7f. (op 11-1 tchd 9-1)

6991 AZURE MEDIAN AUCTION MAIDEN STKS 1m 4f (P)
1:45 (1:47) (Class 6) 3-5-Y-O **£2,047** (£604; £302) **Stalls** Centre

Form RPR
342- **1** **Crazy Bear (IRE)**[581] 1307 4-9-3 68.......................... DeanMcKeown 6 57+
(K J Burke) *hld up in midfield: prog gng easily over 2f out: led jst over 1f out: shkn up and sn clr* **14/1**

5 **2** *2 ½* **Kadouchski (FR)**[201] 1725 3-9-3 0.............................. MickyFenton 8 58
(Miss E C Lavelle) *t.k.h early: trckd ldrs: pushed along over 3f out: kpt on to ld 2f out: hdd and easily outpcd jst over 1f out* **11/4**[1]

4-45 **3** *1* **Bramcote Lorne**[307] 278 4-9-8 51............................... HayleyTurner 10 56
(R C Guest) *t.k.h: trckd ldrs: effrt on inner to chal over 2f out: one pce fr over 1f out* **9/1**

-550 **4** ¾ **Whaxaar (IRE)**[115] 4270 3-9-3 55 RobertHavlin 2 55+
(R Ingram) *stdd s: hld up in last pair: sme prog over 2f out: pushed along and styd on steadily fnl f: nvr nr ldrs* **7/1**

3044 **5** 1 **Verbatim**[22] 6751 3-8-12 57 LPKeniry 7 48
(A M Balding) *trckd ldr for 3f: styd prom: rdn over 2f out: nt qckn: fdd over 1f out* **11/2**[3]

04 **6** nk **Clear Reef**[16] 6821 3-9-3 0 PatCosgrave 3 53
(Jane Chapple-Hyam) *dwlt: t.k.h and rcvrd to press ldr after 3f: upsides over 2f out: sn btn* **4/1**[2]

0366 **7** 1 **Compton Falcon**[22] 6745 3-9-3 70 EddieAhern 11 51
(G A Butler) *led: set stdy pce for 5f: hdd 2f out: wknd over 1f out* **6/1**

0 **8** 4 **Ocean Waves (IRE)**[38] 6429 4-9-3 42 FergusSweeney 5 40
(Miss Tor Sturgis) *hld up in last pair: shkn up and wknd over 2f out* **33/1**

0002 **9** 3 **Franky'N'Jonny**[10] 6893 4-9-3 47 ChrisCatlin 4 35
(M J Attwater) *hld up in rr: rdn and no prog over 2f out: sn bhd* **14/1**

0 **10** nk **Rasmani**[20] 6778 3-8-12 0 (t) TPQueally 9 34
(Miss Gay Kelleway) *stdd s: hld up in rr: shkn up and wknd over 2f out* **28/1**

2m 36.34s (-0.56) **Going Correction** -0.10s/f (Stan)
WFA 3 from 4yo 5lb **10** Ran SP% **118.6**
Speed ratings (Par 101): **97,95,94,94,93 93,92,89,87,87**
CSF £53.44 TOTE £6.70: £2.30, £1.60, £3.60; EX 37.40.
Owner J Bourke **Bred** John Murphy **Trained** Bourton-on-the-Water, Gloucs

FOCUS
A modest race on the whole and steadily run, but the winner looked capable of much better.
Ocean Waves(IRE) Official explanation: jockey said filly hung right in straight
Rasmani Official explanation: jockey said filly made a noise

6992 AZURE CONDITIONS STKS 7f (P)
2:15 (2:15) (Class 4) 3-Y-O+ **£5,829** (£1,734; £866; £432) **Stalls** High

Form RPR

32 **1** **Baharah (USA)**[15] 6830 3-8-9 0 EddieAhern 4 104+
(G A Butler) *hld up in 4th: effrt 2f out: rdn to cl over 1f out: styd on wl to ld jst ins fnl f: sn clr* **11/2**[2]

1544 **2** 2 **Orchard Supreme**[3] 6965 4-9-0 100 (b[1]) RichardHughes 1 104
(R Hannon) *racd freely: led: gng strly over 2f out: rdn over 1f out: hdd and nt qckn jst ins fnl f* **7/4**[1]

0422 **3** hd **Fajr (IRE)**[7] 6932 5-9-0 100 MickyFenton 3 104
(Miss Gay Kelleway) *chsd ldr: rdn to cl fr 2f out: ch 1f out: no ex u.p* **7/4**[1]

0006 **4** 5 **Murfreesboro**[7] 6930 4-9-0 90 (be[1]) DeanMcKeown 5 90
(K J Burke) *stdd and bmpd s: hld up in last: urged along and no prog over 2f out* **12/1**

6301 **5** 6 **Blue Rocket (IRE)**[8] 6916 3-8-9 87 (e[1]) ChrisCatlin 2 69
(D J Murphy) *disp 2nd pl tl wknd over 2f out* **6/1**[3]

1m 25.23s (-1.57) **Going Correction** -0.10s/f (Stan) **5** Ran SP% **110.1**
Speed ratings (Par 105): **104,101,101,95,88**
CSF £15.60 TOTE £6.10: £3.10, £1.60; EX 22.40.
Owner Erik Penser **Bred** Darley **Trained** Blewbury, Oxon

FOCUS
A small field, but the pace was reasonable, the joint favourites set a decent standard and ran close to their relative official marks.

6993 TFM NETWORKS H'CAP 7f (P)
2:50 (2:52) (Class 6) (0-65,65) 3-Y-O+ **£2,047** (£604; £302) **Stalls** High

Form RPR

0313 **1** **Millfield (IRE)**[4] 6955 4-9-0 **61** ow1 GeorgeBaker 8 73
(P R Chamings) *hld up in midfield: shkn up and prog 2f out: led jst ins fnl f: styd on wl and sn clr* **9/2**[1]

0023 **2** 3 **Rabbit Fighter (IRE)**[12] 6869 3-8-13 **60** (v[1]) FergusSweeney 12 64+
(D Shaw) *t.k.h early: hld up in midfield on inner: nt clr run 2f out and again briefly 1f out: r.o wl to snatch 2nd last stride* **11/2**[2]

104 **3** shd **Night Wolf (IRE)**[14] 6854 7-8-12 **59** (t) PaulDoe 6 63
(Jamie Poulton) *led after 1f: 2l clr 2f out: hdd and one pce jst ins fnl f* **12/1**

20-5 **4** nk **Kensington (IRE)**[22] 6749 6-8-10 **57** (p) TGMcLaughlin 11 60
(P D Evans) *led for 1f: chsd ldr: tried to cl over 1f out: kpt on same pce* **15/2**

4002 **5** ½ **Imperium**[5] 6950 6-8-11 **58** (b) PatDobbs 5 60
(Jean-Rene Auvray) *trckd ldrs: rdn to dispute 2nd over 1f out: one pce after* **7/1**[3]

3011 **6** ½ **Jools**[12] 6869 9-8-12 **59** HayleyTurner 10 66+
(D K Ivory) *trckd ldrs on inner: nowhere to go fr 2f out despite travelling strly: lost pl ins fnl f* **7/1**[3]

4-50 **7** nk **Gwyllion (USA)**[154] 3110 3-9-4 **65** EddieAhern 13 65
(Charles O'Brien, Ire) *settled in rr: rdn and no prog over 2f out: styd on fnl f: nrst fin* **16/1**

5000 **8** 1 **Fish Called Johnny**[8] 6910 3-8-11 **58** LPKeniry 14 55
(Peter Grayson) *hld up in rr: rdn over 2f out: kpt on fr over 1f out: n.d* **33/1**

5213 **9** hd **Goose Green (IRE)**[17] 6816 3-9-4 **65** SteveDrowne 9 61
(R J Hodges) *cl up tl wknd u.p over 2f out* **11/2**[2]

30 **10** 2 **Granakey (IRE)**[51] 6123 4-8-10 **57** JamieMackay 2 48
(M Wigham) *dropped in fr wd draw: hld up: nvr on terms struggling over 2f out* **20/1**

1035 **11** 3 **Ishibee (IRE)**[31] 6581 3-8-9 **56** (p) MickyFenton 7 39
(J J Bridger) *hld up towards rr on outer: rdn and no prog over 2f out* **25/1**

0060 **12** ½ **Silent Storm**[10] 6894 7-8-6 **60** RyanHill[(7)] 1 42
(Peter Grayson) *eventually dropped in fr wd draw and hld up in last: detached fr 1/2-way: shuffled along and no ch fnl 2f* **33/1**

0022 **13** dist **Macademy Royal (USA)**[31] 6581 4-8-12 **62** (t) TravisBlock[(3)] 3 —
(H Morrison) *hit hd in stalls: pressed ldrs tl wknd rapidly 1/2-way: t.o and eased last 2f* **15/2**

1m 26.98s (0.18) **Going Correction** -0.10s/f (Stan) **13** Ran SP% **125.5**
Speed ratings (Par 101): **94,90,90,90,89 88,88,87,87,84 81,80,—**
CSF £28.89 CT £296.56 TOTE £4.70: £1.50, £2.90, £6.90; EX 32.60.
Owner Patrick Chamings Sprint Club **Bred** Limestone Stud **Trained** Baughurst, Hants

FOCUS
Most of these were just moderate handicappers, but the winner put up a performance that rates a bit better than that. The early pace was good but the overall time was ordinary.
Rabbit Fighter(IRE) ◆ Official explanation: jockey said colt was denied a clear run
Jools Official explanation: jockey said gelding was denied a clear run
Macademy Royal(USA) Official explanation: jockey said gelding banged its head in stalls and bled from the nose

6994 WILD FLOWER STKS (LISTED RACE) 1m 4f (P)
3:25 (3:25) (Class 1) 3-Y-O+
£14,762 (£5,595; £2,800; £1,396; £699; £351) **Stalls** Centre

Form RPR

5151 **1** **Dansant**[28] 6645 3-9-2 105 EddieAhern 6 119+
(G A Butler) *hld up: smooth prog over 3f out: led over 2f out: shkn up and drew clr wl over 1f out* **5/4**[1]

1224 **2** 5 **Pivotal Answer (IRE)**[30] 6605 3-8-9 97 TPQueally 4 102
(J Noseda) *hld up in tch: stdy prog over 3f out: shkn up to chal over 2f out: sn no match for wnr u.p* **5/2**[2]

5006 **3** 8 **Invasian (IRE)**[21] 6765 6-9-5 87 MickyFenton 8 94
(P W D'Arcy) *led at decent pce: kicked on 4f out: hdd over 2f out: brushed aside by ldng pair* **16/1**

0030 **4** 7 **Akarem**[8] 6759 6-9-5 88 FergusSweeney 1 83
(K R Burke) *mostly chsd ldr to jst over 3f out: sn lft wl bhd* **12/1**

1304 **5** ¾ **Voliere**[7] 6931 4-9-0 80 GeorgeBaker 2 77
(S C Williams) *stdd s: hld up in last: effrt over 3f out: rdn and struggling over 2f out: wknd* **14/1**

6612 **6** 3 **St Savarin (FR)**[49] 6169 6-9-5 95 SteveDrowne 5 77
(R A Fahey) *chsd ldrs tl wknd 3f out* **15/2**[3]

100 **7** 8 **Strategic Mount**[91] 5049 4-9-5 98 (b) RichardHughes 3 64
(P F I Cole) *hld up in rr: shkn up on outer over 3f out: sn btn: eased fnl 2f* **10/1**

0661 **8** 6 **Restless Soul**[4] 6959 3-8-9 80 DeanMcKeown 9 49
(C A Cyzer) *prom to 4f out: wknd rapidly: t.o* **33/1**

2m 31.03s (-5.87) **Going Correction** -0.10s/f (Stan)
WFA 3 from 4yo+ 5lb **8** Ran SP% **117.1**
Speed ratings (Par 111): **115,111,106,101,101 99,93,89**
CSF £4.56 TOTE £2.30: £1.10, £1.40, £4.10; EX 5.00.
Owner Mrs Barbara M Keller **Bred** Mrs Cino Del Duca **Trained** Blewbury, Oxon

FOCUS
Not a great field for the first running of this Listed event with the exception of the winner, who looks Group 3 material. The pace was good and the time above average for the grade,while the form looks pretty solid with the placed horses close to handicap form.

NOTEBOOK
Dansant ◆, top-rated on official figures, appreciated the strong gallop again and won in the style of a high-class horse in the making. An impressive sort, he will be very much at home in Group 3 company, and connections will now take him to Dubai in search of big money. (op 13-8 tchd 7-4 in places)
Pivotal Answer(IRE) is very consistent, but with hindsight second was the best her connections could realistically hope for here. Though rated only a pound behind the winner going into the race, that rival is very progressive, and time may show she had an impossible task. (op 11-4)
Invasian(IRE) had a tough job at the weights. However, he just about ran his race, especially as he went off at a cracking good pace and in effect merely set the race up for the two market leaders. (op 20-1)
Akarem has lost his Flat form on turf, and last week's win over hurdles suggests his future may lie over jumps. This was a fair Polytrack debut, but no more than that. Official explanation: jockey said horse hung right (tchd 11-1)
Voliere did not finish as close as official ratings suggested, and would be suited by a return to 1m2f. (op 10-1)
St Savarin(FR) is probably more at home in handicaps, but should still have done a bit better than this. (op 6-1)
Strategic Mount Official explanation: jockey said colt had no more to give

6995 AZURE CATERING H'CAP 1m 3f (P)
3:55 (3:55) (Class 3) (0-95,92) 3-Y-O+
£6,855 (£2,052; £1,026; £513; £256; £128) **Stalls** High

Form RPR

1005 **1** **Bid For Glory**[28] 6654 3-9-2 **90** RichardHughes 6 95
(H J Collingridge) *trckd ldr 2f: styd prom: rdn 3f out: narrow ld 2f out: battled on wl whn hrd pressed after* **5/1**[3]

5110 **2** nk **Pinch Of Salt (IRE)**[28] 6645 4-9-4 **91** NeilChalmers[(3)] 8 98+
(A M Balding) *hld up bhd ldrs: effrt over 2f out: nt clr run in tightly bunched field over 1f out: styd on fnl f to take 2nd last strides* **11/2**

1043 **3** hd **Stargazer Jim (FR)**[21] 6765 5-8-8 **78** PaulMulrennan 5 83
(W J Haggas) *hld up towards rr: effrt over 2f out: drvn to press ldrs 1f out: kpt on: a jst hld* **8/1**

4 hd **Eumene (IRE)**[13] 4-9-3 **87** ChrisCatlin 3 91
(C C Bealby) *trckd ldr after 2f to 2f out: kpt on u.p fnl f: a jst hld* **33/1**

1020 **5** shd **Awatuki (IRE)**[32] 6576 4-8-12 **82** TPQueally 4 86
(A P Jarvis) *sn led: drvn and narrowly hdd 2f out: kpt on u.p but a jst hld* **6/1**

4020 **6** 1 **Speedy Sam**[49] 6172 4-9-5 **92** AndrewElliott[(3)] 7 94
(K R Burke) *hld up in midfield: effrt over 2f out: clsd on ldrs 1f out: one pce u.p fnl f* **3/1**[1]

0304 **7** 2½ **William's Way**[21] 6765 5-8-12 **82** ow1 AdamKirby 1 80
(I A Wood) *dwlt: t.k.h and hld up: prog to press ldrs over 2f out: sn nt qckn: fdd over 1f out* **12/1**

3134 **8** 2 **Risque Heights**[14] 6853 3-8-9 **83** SteveDrowne 9 78
(G A Butler) *stdd s: hld up in last: effrt against far rail 2f out: hanging rt and wknd* **7/2**[2]

2m 21.0s (-1.68) **Going Correction** -0.10s/f (Stan)
WFA 3 from 4yo+ 4lb **8** Ran SP% **115.3**
Speed ratings (Par 107): **102,101,101,101,101 100,98,97**
CSF £32.79 CT £216.63 TOTE £6.20: £2.10, £2.10, £2.20; EX 44.90.
Owner Harraton Court One **Bred** Llety Stud **Trained** Exning, Suffolk
■ Stewards' Enquiry : Richard Hughes two-day ban: careless riding (Dec 13-14)

FOCUS
A middling handicap, but the steady early pace helped create a bunched finish. The form, best rated around the winner and third, looks ordinary for the grade.

NOTEBOOK
Bid For Glory only scraped home on this Polytrack debut but, in doing so, proved he handles the surface. His trainer more or less ruled out taking him to either Lingfield or Wolverhampton, but he will be interesting if returning, as seems likely, to Kempton in the spring. (op 13-2)
Pinch Of Salt(IRE), a massive 16lb higher than in his last handicap two races ago, showed the Handicapper had got it right with a splendid effort. In fine form at present, he is improving so fast that there is likely to be a bit more to come on a surface that suits him perfectly.
Stargazer Jim(FR) ran really well over a longer trip than usual and looks well worth another try beyond 1m2f. (op 13-2 tchd 6-1)
Eumene(IRE) had been disappointing over hurdles, but connections need not worry about that now because this was a fine Polytack debut from this useful former French middle-distance horse. He could well win a race around this trip or slightly farther.

Awatuki(IRE) has done well at this track in the past, and appreciated the return to Polytrack after having a pipe-opener on turf last time. This is his surface, and he should be there or thereabouts in similar company for the time being. (tchd 5-1)
Speedy Sam is still useful at his best, on turf and Polytrack. Though not quite good enough here, he was not beaten far. (tchd 7-2)
Risque Heights Official explanation: jockey said gelding hung right

6996 THE PANORAMIC RESTAURANT H'CAP (DIV I) 1m (P)
4:25 (4:30) (Class 5) (0-75,75) 3-Y-O+ **£2,590** (£770; £385; £192) **Stalls** High

Form RPR
04-1 **1** **Den's Gift (IRE)**[15] 6830 3-9-2 **73** AdamKirby 9 89+
(C G Cox) *led for 2f: pressed ldr tl led again 3f out: drew clr 2f out: styd on strly* **15/8**[1]
2456 **2** *2* **Nicada (IRE)**[45] 6272 3-8-7 **69** TolleyDean(5) 8 78
(Stef Liddiard) *trckd ldrs: rdn to chse wnr over 2f out: styd on but no imp fnl 2f* **13/2**[3]
4130 **3** *2 1/2* **Waterline Twenty (IRE)**[14] 6848 4-9-2 **72** TGMcLaughlin 10 76
(P D Evans) *hld up in rr: stdy prog through rivals fr 3f out: styd on to take 3rd 1f out: no ch w ldng pair* **11/1**
1340 **4** *3/4* **Boundless Prospect (USA)**[22] 6746 8-8-6 **67** NicolPolli(5) 4 69+
(Miss Gay Kelleway) *hld up in last trio: hrd rdn and kpt on fr over 2f out: nrst fin but n.d* **12/1**
516 **5** *1 3/4* **Smokin Joe**[16] 6824 6-9-0 **70** ow2 (b) GeorgeBaker 5 68
(J R Best) *hld up towards rr and racd wd: rdn and nt keen over 2f out: kpt on fr over 1f out* **8/1**
6322 **6** *1 3/4* **Chia (IRE)**[14] 6856 4-8-9 **65** (p) HayleyTurner 7 59
(D Haydn Jones) *mostly in midfield: outpcd over 2f out: plugged on one pce after* **5/1**[2]
0 **7** *3/4* **Dushstorm (IRE)**[44] 6293 6-8-5 **66** (p) AshleyHamblett(5) 2 58
(M Botti) *prom on outer: rdn and cl enough over 2f out: sn nt qckn and btn* **16/1**
005 **8** *hd* **Cape Of Luck (IRE)**[45] 6273 4-9-0 **75** JackMitchell(5) 3 67
(P M Phelan) *dropped in last fr wd draw: plld hrd early: effrt and hrd rdn on outer over 2f out: plugged on but no ch* **12/1**
1002 **9** *1* **Torquemada (IRE)**[33] 6547 6-8-9 **70** KirstyMilczarek(5) 1 59
(J Akehurst) *hld up towards rr: sme prog u.p over 2f out: no hdwy and wl btn over 1f out* **8/1**
0002 **10** *1* **Pianoforte (USA)**[17] 6806 5-8-13 **69** (b) MickyFenton 13 56
(E J Alston) *hld up in midfield: prog on inner to dispute 2nd over 2f out: wknd over 1f out* **11/1**
0-40 **11** *11* **Racing Stripes (IRE)**[39] 6406 3-8-9 **66** ow1 SteveDrowne 12 28
(K O Cunningham-Brown) *dwlt: hld up wl in rr: rdn and struggling over 2f out: lost action over 1f out and eased* **50/1**
2050 **12** *3/4* **Blacktoft (USA)**[127] 3926 4-9-3 **73** (e) J-PGuillambert 11 33
(S C Williams) *mostly midfield tl wknd rapidly over 2f out: t.o* **8/1**
6653 **13** *shd* **Swift Cut (IRE)**[15] 6838 3-8-3 **63** AndrewElliott(3) 6 23
(A P Jarvis) *t.k.h: led after 2f to 3f out: wknd rapidly: t.o* **20/1**

1m 38.58s (-2.22) **Going Correction** -0.10s/f (Stan)
WFA 3 from 4yo+ 1lb **13** Ran SP% **142.8**
Speed ratings (Par 103): **107,105,102,101,100 98,97,97,96,95 84,83,83**
CSF £17.63 CT £129.68 TOTE £3.40: £1.60, £3.00, £3.10; EX 32.90.
Owner Mrs Olive Shaw **Bred** Mrs J A Dene **Trained** Lambourn, Berks
■ Stewards' Enquiry : Adam Kirby one-day ban: used whip in incorrect place (Dec 12)

FOCUS
A fair handicap, run at a good gallop, and won by a progressive sort. The form looks good for the grade with the three immediately behind the principals sound form guides.
Torquemada(IRE) Official explanation: jockey said gelding ran flat
Racing Stripes(IRE) Official explanation: jockey said gelding hung right

6997 THE PANORAMIC RESTAURANT H'CAP (DIV II) 1m (P)
4:55 (4:55) (Class 5) (0-75,74) 3-Y-O+ **£2,590** (£770; £385; £192) **Stalls** High

Form RPR
5500 **1** **Spring Goddess (IRE)**[51] 6124 6-9-0 **69** RichardHughes 13 83+
(A P Jarvis) *hld up in midfield: prog over 2f out: nt clr run over 1f out and swtchd lft: r.o to ld last 150yds: sn clr* **10/1**
0036 **2** *2* **Hucking Heat (IRE)**[10] 6894 3-8-7 **63** (v) HayleyTurner 12 70
(J R Best) *dwlt: hld up in last: rdn and detached over 3f out: prog over 2f out: styd on wl fnl f to take 2nd nr fin* **12/1**
1350 **3** *nk* **Hypocrisy**[22] 6789 4-9-2 **71** EddieAhern 11 78
(Garvan Donnelly, Ire) *trckd ldrs: effrt on inner over 2f out: led over 1f out tl hdd last 150yds: one pce and lost 2nd nr fin* **15/2**
1-00 **4** *3/4* **Hanbrin Bhoy (IRE)**[26] 6235 3-8-12 **68** MickyFenton 9 73
(R Dickin) *hld up in rr: effrt on wd outside over 2f out: rdn and styd on fr over 1f out: nrst fin* **16/1**
0000 **5** *1/2* **Binnion Bay (IRE)**[19] 6795 6-8-10 **65** (b) AmirQuinn 3 69
(J J Bridger) *dwlt: wl in rr: rdn on inner over 2f out: styd on fr over 1f out: nrst fin* **8/1**
5510 **6** *nk* **Im Ova Ere Dad (IRE)**[19] 6795 4-9-5 **74** StephenDonohoe 10 77
(D E Cantillon) *dwlt: wl in rr: prog fr 1/2-way: effrt to chal 2f out: nt qckn over 1f out: fdd* **11/2**[2]
4052 **7** *1/2* **Pab Special (IRE)**[29] 6628 4-9-0 **72** (p) AndrewElliott(3) 8 74
(K R Burke) *led: hrd rdn over 2f out: hdd over 1f out: fdd* **9/2**[1]
1065 **8** *1 1/2* **High 'n Dry (IRE)**[7] 6929 3-8-13 **69** (p) PaulDoe 7 68
(M A Allen) *mostly pressed ldr: upsides over 2f out to over 1f out: wknd* **10/1**
4212 **9** *nk* **Magroom**[26] 6695 3-8-7 **66** TravisBlock(3) 4 64
(R J Hodges) *mostly midfield: no imp u.p 2f out: steadily wknd* **7/1**[3]
3003 **10** *9* **Bolton Hall (IRE)**[26] 6696 5-8-8 **63** (p) DaleGibson 2 40
(R A Fahey) *s.s and rousted along: wl in rr: drvn on outer 3f out: nvr a factor* **16/1**
064 **11** *3/4* **Benllech**[17] 6806 3-9-0 **70** LPKeniry 6 45
(S Kirk) *t.k.h: pressed ldrs tl wknd rapidly over 2f out* **10/1**
2000 **12** *6* **Laish Ya Hajar (IRE)**[19] 6795 3-8-12 **68** ChrisCatlin 5 30
(P R Webber) *t.k.h: prom tl lost pl rapidly over 3f out: sn bhd: t.o* **16/1**
0061 **13** *hd* **Rebellious Spirit**[17] 6806 4-9-3 **72** GeorgeBaker 1 33
(P W Hiatt) *trckd ldrs tl wknd rapidly jst over 3f out: t.o* **12/1**

1m 38.58s (-2.22) **Going Correction** -0.10s/f (Stan)
WFA 3 from 4yo+ 1lb **13** Ran SP% **129.2**
Speed ratings (Par 103): **107,105,104,103,103 103,102,101,100,91 91,85,84**
CSF £134.80 CT £683.00 TOTE £14.20: £4.50, £6.10, £2.80; EX 222.40 Place 6 £46.12, Place 5 £25.91..
Owner Grant & Bowman Limited **Bred** Ballyhane Stud **Trained** Twyford, Bucks

FOCUS
A fair handicap, with the back-to-form winner looking a bit better than that. The form is not as strong as the first division though.
Rebellious Spirit Official explanation: jockey said gelding hung right

T/Plt: £66.80 to a £1 stake. Pool: £51,912.35. 567.00 winning tickets. T/Qpdt: £18.90 to a £1 stake. Pool: £2,992.60. 116.70 winning tickets. JN

6977 WOLVERHAMPTON (A.W) (L-H)
Saturday, December 1

OFFICIAL GOING: Standard
Wind: moderate to strong, behind Weather: showers

6998 PONTIN'S BOOK EARLY PRICE PROMISE MAIDEN STKS 5f 216y(P)
7:00 (7:03) (Class 5) 2-Y-O **£2,968** (£876; £438) **Stalls** Low

Form RPR
6266 **1** **Eager Diva (USA)**[22] 6741 2-8-12 73 (b1) PaulMulrennan 7 71
(K A Ryan) *in tch: rdn over 3f out: r.o to ld wl ins fnl f* **11/1**
5 **2** *1* **Requisite**[24] 6721 2-8-12 0 PatCosgrave 10 68
(Jane Chapple-Hyam) *a.p: rdn to ld jst over 1f out: hdd wl ins fnl f: nt qckn* **12/1**
0004 **3** *1 1/4* **Bahamian Lad**[35] 6502 2-9-3 67 DeanMcKeown 8 69
(R Hollinshead) *led: rdn and hdd jst over 1f out: styd on same pce ins fnl f* **8/1**[3]
3 **4** *nk* **Brazilian Brush (IRE)**[51] 6125 2-9-3 0 SteveDrowne 9 68
(H Morrison) *a.p: rdn and ev ch over 1f out: kpt on same pce ins fnl f* **5/4**[1]
54 **5** *1 3/4* **Farpedon**[64] 5771 2-9-3 0 FergusSweeney 5 63
(H Candy) *racd keenly: in tch: rdn over 2f out: one pce fr over 1f out* **3/1**[2]
6 *5* **Polychrome** 2-8-12 0 NeilPollard 3 43
(John Berry) *missed break: detached and outpcd: styd on fnl f: nt pce to trble ldrs* **80/1**
50 **7** *1* **Ella Junior (USA)**[50] 6138 2-8-12 0 (b1) NickyMackay 6 40
(B J Meehan) *w ldr: rdn and wknd over 2f out* **20/1**
00 **8** *3* **Jumpin Johnnie**[21] 6754 2-9-3 0 RobertHavlin 4 36
(R T Phillips) *hld up: rdn 3f out: no imp* **33/1**
0 **9** *1 1/2* **King Of Cadeaux (IRE)**[14] 6850 2-9-3 0 PatDobbs 1 31
(M A Magnusson) *hld up: rdn 3f out: nvr on terms* **20/1**
0 **10** *1 3/4* **Human Touch**[43] 6295 2-8-12 0 TPQueally 12 21
(E A L Dunlop) *racd keenly: hld up: pushed along over 2f out: no imp: wknd over 1f out* **14/1**
000 **11** *2* **Cealtra Star (IRE)**[33] 6535 2-8-7 49 NataliaGemelova(5) 2 15
(K A Ryan) *in tch: rdn 4f out: wknd over 3f out* **66/1**

1m 16.68s (0.87) **Going Correction** -0.025s/f (Stan) **11** Ran SP% **118.4**
Speed ratings (Par 96): **93,91,90,89,87 80,79,75,73,70 68**
CSF £126.43 TOTE £10.50: £2.10, £3.20, £2.20; EX 121.30.
Owner Hillen, McIntosh, Walsh And Partners **Bred** D Brown & Lendy Brown **Trained** Hambleton, N Yorks

FOCUS
A moderate maiden and the winner's official rating of 73 probably provides an accurate benchmark to the form.

NOTEBOOK
Eager Diva(USA), the most exposed member of the field, found the hoped-for improvement in first-time blinkers to get off the mark at the ninth attempt. She did need some strong driving to get there, and it remains to be seen whether the headgear proves as effective once she gets accustomed to it. (op 12-1 tchd 14-1)
Requisite finished a modest fifth at Nottingham on her debut last month, but stepped up on that effort with a solid second and she is learning fast. (tchd 14-1)
Bahamian Lad, rated 6lb inferior to Eager Diva in current handicap lists, ran right up to form in third. (op 15-2)
Brazilian Brush(IRE) was a warm order on the strength of his debut third at Newbury, but he was unable to build on that promise and it may be that he is not going to be as effective on the All-Weather. (tchd Evens and 11-8)
Farpedon attracted market support, but he could not find the change of gear needed to get in an effective blow in the straight. (op 9-2)

6999 WOLVERHAMPTON-RACECOURSE.CO.UK CLAIMING STKS 1m 5f 194y(P)
7:30 (7:31) (Class 6) 3-Y-O+ **£2,047** (£604; £302) **Stalls** Low

Form RPR
1024 **1** **Salute (IRE)**[23] 6739 8-9-9 77 RobertHavlin 3 81
(P G Murphy) *in tch: chsd ldr 4f out: led 3f out: dashed abt 3l clr 2f out: edgd rt sltly over 1f out: drvn out and hld on wl towards fin* **5/4**[1]
1003 **2** *nk* **Drizzi (IRE)**[35] 6501 6-8-13 62 AdamKirby 6 71
(A W Carroll) *in midfield: rdn and hdwy 3f out: chsd wnr 2f out: clsd and ev ch ins fnl f: r.o* **4/1**[2]
6306 **3** *15* **The Diamond Bond**[25] 6700 3-8-4 45 ChrisCatlin 10 48
(G R Oldroyd) *led for 1f: regained ld after 4f: hdd 3f out: lost tch w front pair wl over 1f out* **28/1**
6- **4** *8* **Flash Harry**[75] 4620 3-8-9 53 J-PGuillambert 2 42
(M G Quinlan) *hld up: rdn and sme hdwy over 2f out: no imp on ldrs* **16/1**
5006 **5** *1 1/2* **Zaffeu**[17] 6817 6-8-6 50 RussellKennemore(5) 11 35
(A G Juckes) *s.i.s: towards rr: niggled along several times: sme hdwy on outside 2f out: nvr able to trble ldrs* **33/1**
0/00 **6** *1/2* **Just Superb**[188] 285 8-9-5 40 PatDobbs 13 42
(P A Pritchard) *hld up: rdn 3f out: nvr able to trble ldrs* **100/1**
00-0 **7** *10* **Airedale Lad (IRE)**[19] 1086 6-9-4 40 MichaelJStainton(3) 1 30
(R M Whitaker) *prom: rdn 4f out: wkng whn hmpd wl over 2f out* **50/1**
040- **8** *1 1/2* **Polygonal (FR)**[511] 3294 7-9-13 91 MickyFenton 4 34
(Miss Gay Kelleway) *racd keenly: hld up: hdwy 4f out: nt rch ldrs: rdn and wknd over 2f out* **9/2**[3]
9 *8* **Monsheramie (IRE)**[499] 3691 5-8-8 0 AmyKathleenParsons(7) 5 11
(T G McCourt, Ire) *led after 1f: hdd after 4f: remained prom: rdn over 3f out: sn wknd* **40/1**
-040 **10** *8* **Sualda (IRE)**[49] 4318 8-9-7 69 SteveDrowne 8 6
(Ollie Pears) *in midfield: hdwy 4f out: rdn and wknd over 2f out: eased over 1f out* **9/1**
6006 **11** *8* **Slip Silver**[17] 6815 3-7-13 39 (p) JamieMackay 12 —
(P J Makin) *prom: rdn 5f out: wkng whn hmpd over 3f out* **33/1**
6606 **12** *5* **Prince Golan (IRE)**[127] 3919 3-9-0 76 PaulMulrennan 7 —
(K A Ryan) *dropped to midfield after 4f: rdn and wknd over 5f out* **14/1**
55U0 **13** *8* **Mysterious World (IRE)**[11] 6883 3-9-0 57 TPQueally 9 —
(Mrs K Walton) *in midfield: rdn 7f out: wknd over 4f out* **66/1**

3m 5.97s (-1.40) **Going Correction** -0.025s/f (Stan)
WFA 3 from 5yo+ 7lb **13** Ran SP% **121.4**
Speed ratings (Par 101): **103,102,94,89,88 88,82,81,77,72 68,65,60**
CSF £5.84 TOTE £2.20: £1.50, £1.50, £3.30; EX 7.10.Drizzi was claimed by Mr P. T. Midgley for £6,000. Prince Golan was claimed by Mr M. E. Hughes for £10,000.
Owner The Golden Anorak Partnership **Bred** Ahmed M Foustok **Trained** East Garston, Berks

FOCUS
An average claimer in which the front pair in the market predictably dominated. The form makes sense rated around the placed horses and sixth.

Polygonal(FR) Official explanation: vet said gelding moved very poorly
Sualda(IRE) Official explanation: jockey said gelding had no more to give

7000 PONTIN'S GREAT FAMILY HOLIDAYS MAIDEN STKS 5f 20y(P)
7:55 (7:57) (Class 5) 2-Y-O £2,968 (£876; £438) Stalls Low

Form RPR
0442 1 **Fast Feet**[10] 6897 2-9-3 79 PaulMulrennan 1 75
(K A Ryan) *mde all: rdn over 1f out: r.o* 6/4[1]
5633 2 1 1/4 **Chivola (IRE)**[25] 6699 2-9-3 75 EddieAhern 3 71
(B Smart) *chsd ldrs: rdn over 1f out: styd on to take 2nd towards fin: no imp on wnr* 5/2[2]
3 nk **Taine (IRE)** 2-9-3 0 SteveDrowne 2 70
(W J Haggas) *in tch: rdn to chse wnr over 1f out: lost 2nd and nt qckn towards fin* 8/1
55 4 1 1/2 **Annes Rocket (IRE)**[19] 6799 2-9-3 0 PatDobbs 10 64
(J C Fox) *racd keenly: in midfield: hdwy and hung lft over 1f out: one pce towards fin* 20/1
2644 5 1 1/2 **Mandelieu (IRE)**[26] 6692 2-9-3 69 TPQueally 6 59
(W J Haggas) *plld hrd: hld up: hdwy wl over 1f out: sn rdn: one pce ins fnl f* 7/1[3]
0063 6 nk **Curio**[11] 6881 2-8-9 51 MichaelJStainton(3) 8 53
(R M Whitaker) *prom: rdn wl over 1f out: wknd ins fnl f* 25/1
0 7 1 3/4 **Carmine Rock**[31] 6595 2-8-7 0 RussellKennemore(5) 5 47
(R Hollinshead) *s.i.s: towards rr: sme hdwy into midfield wl over 1f out: no imp fnl f* 40/1
4306 8 nk **Klarity**[10] 6892 2-8-12 63 RobertHavlin 7 46
(J Pearce) *prom: lugged rt over 2f out: sn wknd* 25/1
4 9 1 1/2 **Archilini**[16] 6820 2-9-3 0 JamesDoyle 4 45
(K A Morgan) *chsd ldrs tl outpcd over 3f out* 11/1
10 6 **Primos Dream** 2-9-3 0 MickyFenton 9 24
(Ollie Pears) *s.s: a wl outpcd* 66/1

63.45 secs (0.63) **Going Correction** -0.025s/f (Stan) 10 Ran SP% 116.9
Speed ratings (Par 96): **93,91,90,88,85 85,82,81,79,69**
CSF £4.87 TOTE £2.20: £1.10, £1.20, £2.60; EX 5.70.
Owner J Duddy,B McDonald,A Heeney,M McMenamin **Bred** P A Mason **Trained** Hambleton, N Yorks

FOCUS
Another ordinary maiden in which the favourite made full use of the rails draw and was never in much danger. The form looks solid and should work out.

NOTEBOOK
Fast Feet had the best form in this weak maiden and, having been touched off over 6f at Lingfield last time, he was always doing enough to hold his pursuers over this shorter trip, which is more suitable for him at present. (op 13-8 tchd 11-8)
Chivola(IRE), rated 4lb inferior to Fast Feet in current handicap lists, ran right up to form on this All-Weather debut but is finding it hard to win. (op 10-3)
Taine(IRE), a 50,000gns newcomer and half-brother to Celtic Sultan, shaped with promise and normal improvement should bring a win for him in a similar race before long (op 6-1)
Annes Rocket(IRE) was not disgraced over a trip that looks on the sharp side and there is probably a little race to be found for him. (op 18-1)
Mandelieu(IRE) is starting to look a short runner so the last thing he needed to do was take a grip. (op 15-2 tchd 9-1)

7001 SPONSOR A RACE BY CALLING 0870 220 2442 (S) STKS 1m 141y(P)
8:25 (8:26) (Class 6) 3-Y-0+ £2,047 (£604; £302) Stalls Low

Form RPR
520 1 **Arctic Desert**[82] 5275 7-9-0 63 (t) HayleyTurner 4 62
(Miss Gay Kelleway) *racd keenly: in tch: clsd over 2f out: r.o to ld ins fnl f: pushed out* 3/1[1]
2056 2 1 1/4 **Gifted Heir (IRE)**[7] 6573 3-8-12 57 MickyFenton 1 59
(A Bailey) *led: rdn over 1f out: hdd ins fnl f: nt qckn* 5/1[3]
0065 3 3 **Almora Guru**[9] 6908 3-8-12 45 TGMcLaughlin 5 52
(W M Brisbourne) *chsd ldrs: rdn over 2f out: one pce ins fnl f* 14/1
0601 4 1/2 **Zaafira (SPA)**[7] 6935 3-8-12 53 (t) StephenDonohoe 12 51
(E J Creighton) *in midfield: hdwy over 3f out: sn rdn: chsd ldr over 2f out tl over 1f out: no ex ins fnl f* 15/2
4056 5 4 **Climate (IRE)**[11] 6882 8-9-5 55 (v) FergusSweeney 7 47
(R Hollinshead) *in midfield: rdn over 2f out: no imp* 9/2[2]
1060 6 hd **Bert's Memory**[12] 6873 3-8-12 50 (p) PaulMulrennan 8 41
(K A Ryan) *chsd ldrs: losing pl whn n.m.r over 3f out: tried to cl wl over 1f out: sn no imp on ldrs* 20/1
1663 7 1 1/2 **Mountain Climb (IRE)**[50] 6152 5-9-0 44 HaddenFrost(5) 13 43
(J D Frost) *hld up: hdwy 3f out: rdn over 2f out: edgd lft and wknd over 1f out: lame* 17/2
0000 8 1 1/2 **Ocean Valentine**[10] 6896 4-8-9 42 RussellKennemore(5) 11 34
(J T Stimpson) *in tch: wnt 2nd over 3f out tl rdn over 2f out: wknd over 1f out* 20/1
0030 9 hd **Blythe Spirit**[11] 6882 8-9-0 50 (b) TolleyDean(5) 10 39
(Mrs L Williamson) *a bhd* 20/1
0000 10 3/4 **Diamond Hurricane (IRE)**[3] 6968 3-8-9 42 NeilChalmers(3) 9 32
(M Wellings) *s.i.s: a bhd* 33/1
6050 11 nk **Gifted Flame**[4] 6956 8-8-9 43 (b[1]) AnnStokell(5) 2 32
(Miss A Stokell) *s.i.s: racd keenly: in midfield: nt clr run wl over 1f out: sn wknd* 16/1
0004 12 24 **Dance Spirit (IRE)**[7] 6935 4-9-0 48 (b) SteveDrowne 6 —
(W R Muir) *prom: rdn over 3f out: sn wknd* 11/1
13 16 **Momaha** 3-8-12 0 LPKeniry 3 —
(J M Bradley) *s.i.s: pushed along 4f out: a bhd* 66/1

1m 51.13s (-0.63) **Going Correction** -0.025s/f (Stan)
WFA 3 from 4yo+ 2lb 13 Ran SP% 121.7
Speed ratings (Par 101): **101,99,97,96,93 93,91,90,90,89 89,67,53**
CSF £16.42 TOTE £4.50: £1.90, £2.60, £2.80; EX 21.40.There was no bid for the winner.
Owner bettingjobs.com **Bred** Whatton Manor Stud **Trained** Exning, Suffolk

FOCUS
An average seller dominated by the two highest-rated horses. The level of the form is doubtful and this is not a race to be with.
Mountain Climb(IRE) Official explanation: vet said gelding returned lame right-fore
Dance Spirit(IRE) Official explanation: jockey said gelding had no more to give

7002 GO PONTIN'S H'CAP 1m 1f 103y(P)
8:55 (8:55) (Class 4) (0-85,85) 3-Y-0+ £4,857 (£1,445; £722; £360) Stalls Low

Form RPR
4511 1 **Hoh Wotanite**[11] 6885 4-8-8 78 (v) RussellKennemore(5) 4 86+
(R Hollinshead) *racd keenly: hld up: pushed along over 2f out: hdwy over 1f out: r.o strly to ld fnl stride* 7/2[1]
315 2 hd **Princess Cocoa (IRE)**[36] 6475 4-8-8 73 DaleGibson 11 79
(R A Fahey) *in tch: chsd ldr 2f out: rdn over 1f out: edgd lft and led wl ins fnl f: hdd fnl stride* 5/1[2]
4202 3 3/4 **Vale De Lobo**[29] 6620 5-8-11 76 ChrisCatlin 7 81
(B R Millman) *a.p: led 3f out: rdn over 1f out: hdd wl ins fnl f: nt qckn* 8/1
0601 4 3/4 **Without Excuse (USA)**[15] 6833 3-8-9 76 (b) GregFairley 8 79
(M Botti) *s.i.s: in rr: hdwy over 2f out: rdn over 1f out: styd on ins fnl f: nt pce to rch ldrs* 18/1
5000 5 3 **Bailieborough (IRE)**[21] 6753 8-8-4 76 LanceBetts(7) 2 73
(N Wilson) *s.i.s: in midfield: rdn whn nt clr run over 1f out: nt pce to trble ldrs* 16/1
0560 6 1/2 **Kingsholm**[48] 6203 5-8-4 72 AndrewElliott(3) 10 68
(I W McInnes) *chsd ldrs: rdn over 2f out: one pce fnl f* 7/1
1055 7 1/2 **Magical Music**[27] 6674 4-9-6 85 RobertHavlin 1 80
(J Pearce) *in midfield: hdwy over 2f out: rdn and edgd rt over 1f out: wknd ins fnl f* 7/1
2040 8 hd **Full Victory (IRE)**[27] 6674 5-9-0 79 (p) SteveDrowne 6 74
(R A Farrant) *chsd ldrs: rdn over 2f out: wknd over 1f out* 8/1
0313 9 1/2 **Vicious Warrior**[28] 6637 8-9-0 79 DeanMcKeown 3 73
(R M Whitaker) *led: hdd 3f out: rdn and wknd over 1f out* 11/2[3]
1402 10 shd **Sudden Impulse**[106] 4582 6-8-8 73 ow1 PaulMulrennan 5 66
(A D Brown) *a bhd* 25/1
0-00 11 1 **Rookwith (IRE)**[28] 6659 7-7-13 71 oh12 AmyKathleenParsons(7) 9 62
(T G McCourt, Ire) *hld up: racd wd ent st wl over 1f out: no imp* 33/1

2m 1.55s (-1.07) **Going Correction** -0.025s/f (Stan)
WFA 3 from 4yo+ 2lb 11 Ran SP% 119.4
Speed ratings (Par 105): **103,102,102,101,98 98,97,97,97,97 96**
CSF £20.82 CT £133.32 TOTE £4.30: £2.30, £2.30, £1.10; EX 16.50.
Owner The Three R'S **Bred** Dunchurch Lodge Stud Co **Trained** Upper Longdon, Staffs
■ Stewards' Enquiry : Dale Gibson one-day ban: used whip with excessive frequency (Dec 12)

FOCUS
A fair handicap run at a sound gallop but the form is ordinary for the grade.
Without Excuse(USA) Official explanation: jockey said gelding hung right
Magical Music Official explanation: jockey said filly hung right

7003 PONTINS.COM H'CAP 7f 32y(P)
9:20 (9:21) (Class 6) (0-55,55) 3-Y-0+ £2,047 (£604; £302) Stalls High

Form RPR
2203 1 **Alto Vertigo**[57] 5982 4-8-2 50 PatrickDonaghy(7) 1 71+
(P C Haslam) *mde all: kicked clr 2f out: r.o wl: eased towards fin* 8/1
5000 2 6 **Winthorpe (IRE)**[17] 6818 7-8-13 54 PaulMulrennan 10 59
(J J Quinn) *chsd ldrs: rdn and outpcd over 2f out: kpt on to take 2nd ins fnl f: no ch w wnr* 14/1
3 1 3/4 **Lucky Clio (IRE)**[71] 5611 3-9-0 55 EddieAhern 9 55
(M J Grassick, Ire) *prom: rdn to chse wnr over 2f out: no imp: lost 2nd and no ex ins fnl f* 7/1[3]
0416 4 2 **Briery Blaze**[11] 6887 4-8-6 52 ow1 (b) JackMitchell(5) 8 47
(J W Unett) *in midfield: hdwy over 4f out: rdn over 2f out: wknd over 1f out* 25/1
6006 5 nk **Haroldini (IRE)**[36] 6476 5-8-11 55 (p) PatrickMathers(3) 2 49
(J Balding) *racd keenly in midfield: lost pl over 5f out: hdwy wl over 1f out: one pce fnl f* 15/2
0102 6 1 1/4 **Solicitude**[30] 6607 4-8-12 53 (p) HayleyTurner 12 43
(D Haydn Jones) *sn in midfield: rdn over 2f out: outpcd over 1f out* 8/1
5-50 7 nk **Hits Only Jude (IRE)**[33] 6533 4-9-0 55 DeanMcKeown 5 45+
(J Pearce) *towards rr: n.m.r and hmpd over 3f out: rdn over 1f out: no imp* 7/2[2]
5206 8 nk **Minnow**[7] 6927 3-8-5 53 (e) WilliamCarson(7) 7 42
(S C Williams) *hld up: rdn on wd outside over 2f out: no imp* 16/1
3402 9 hd **Canina**[11] 6887 4-8-3 51 AndrewHeffernan(7) 3 39
(Paul Green) *in tch: lost pl 5f out: outpcd fnl 2f* 16/1
0161 10 3/4 **Ceris Star (IRE)**[17] 6809 3-8-12 53 ChrisCatlin 6 39
(B R Millman) *racd keenly in midfield: pushed along 2f out: wknd wl over 1f out* 3/1[1]
6600 11 15 **Mr Forthright**[20] 6779 3-8-10 51 SteveDrowne 4 —
(J M Bradley) *a bhd: eased whn n.d ins fnl f* 33/1
0000 12 3 **Trickle (USA)**[77] 5424 3-9-0 55 MickyFenton 11 —
(Miss D Mountain) *chsd wnr over 5f out tl over 3f out: wkng whn hmpd over 2f out: eased whn btn ins fnl f* 33/1

1m 29.4s (-1.00) **Going Correction** -0.025s/f (Stan) 12 Ran SP% 121.9
Speed ratings (Par 101): **104,97,95,92,92 91,90,90,90,89 72,68**
CSF £115.47 CT £842.92 TOTE £11.60: £4.00, £3.20, £2.30; EX 167.40 Place 6 £88.93, Place 5 £15.07..
Owner Middleham Park Racing XXXI **Bred** Ercan Dogan **Trained** Middleham Moor, N Yorks
■ Stewards' Enquiry : William Carson one-day ban: used whip when out of contention (Dec 12)

FOCUS
A modest handicap that looked competitive enough beforehand, but the unexposed winner turned it into a procession. The form appears sound enough rated around the placed horses.
Trickle(USA) ◆ Official explanation: jockey said filly had a breathing problem
T/Plt: £175.10 to a £1 stake. Pool: £101,856.70. 424.55 winning tickets. T/Qpdt: £44.10 to a £1 stake. Pool: £7,212.00. 120.80 winning tickets. DO

6998 WOLVERHAMPTON (A.W) (L-H)
Monday, December 3

OFFICIAL GOING: Standard
Wind: Fresh, half-behind Weather: Fine

7004 PONTIN'S BOOK EARLY PRICE PROMISE H'CAP FOR AMATEUR RIDERS 1m 5f 194y(P)
1:10 (1:10) (Class 6) (0-65,65) 3-Y-0+ £1,977 (£608; £304) Stalls Low

Form RPR
0436 1 **Ronsard (IRE)**[19] 6811 5-10-5 49 MissEFolkes 3 56+
(P D Evans) *hld up in tch: nt clr run and swtchd lft over 2f out: sn rdn to chse ldr: led wl ins fnl f: drvn out* 9/1
1403 2 3/4 **Cumbrian Knight (IRE)**[21] 6798 9-10-9 58 MissNJefferson(5) 4 64
(J M Jefferson) *s.i.s: hld up in rr: hdwy on ins over 2f out: swtchd rt wl ins fnl f: styd on* 13/2[2]
3424 3 1/2 **Born West (USA)**[65] 5820 3-11-0 65 MrJOwen 1 70
(P W Chapple-Hyam) *sn prom: led over 4f out: rdn over 2f out: edgd lft and hdd wl ins fnl f: no ex* 8/1
0006 4 3/4 **Pocketwood**[37] 6500 5-11-0 65 MissJMHindle(7) 2 72+
(Jean-Rene Auvray) *s.i.s: hld up in rr: hdwy over 1f out: styd on towards fin* 11/1

0225 **5** 1 ½ **Zalkani (IRE)**[10] 6911 7-10-12 **59**........ MrSPearce(3) 7 61
(J Pearce) *hld up in rr: hdwy on ins over 3f out: rdn over 1f out: one pce ins fnl f* **15/2**

3023 **6** ¾ **Raquel White**[12] 6902 3-10-4 **62**........ MrRPFlint(7) 6 63
(J L Flint) *prom: rdn over 3f out: wknd wl over 1f out* **7/1**[3]

0050 **7** 5 **Royal Sailor (IRE)**[12] 6902 5-9-13 **50**........ MrDavidMcMinn(7) 12 44
(J Ryan) *broke wl: hld up and sn towards rr: rdn and hdwy on ins over 2f out: wknd fnl f* **33/1**

-251 **8** 1 ¾ **Living On A Prayer**[25] 6728 4-10-0 **51**........ MrTPMcGettigan(7) 9 43
(T McLaughlin, Ire) *hld up in mid-div: stdy hdwy over 5f out: rdn over 3f out: wknd 2f out* **7/1**[3]

0031 **9** 1 ¾ **Blue Hills**[10] 6911 6-11-4 **62**........(b) MissEJJones 11 51
(P W Hiatt) *sn w ldr: led over 8f out tl over 4f out: rdn and wknd 2f out* **13/2**[2]

-002 **10** 24 **Dubai Ace (USA)**[47] 6271 6-11-2 **65**........(p) MrAMerriam(5) 8 21
(Miss Sheena West) *hld up in tch: pushed along 7f out: wknd over 5f out: t.o fnl 3f* **5/1**[1]

0U00 **11** 11 **Gatecrasher**[21] 6798 4-10-3 **54** ow2........(b) MrSeanKerr(7) 10 —
(G H Yardley) *led: hdd over 8f out: wknd over 5f out: t.o fnl 4f* **80/1**

0-44 **12** 23 **Proper Article (IRE)**[293] 453 5-10-6 **55**........(bt) MissJFoster(5) 5 —
(Miss J E Foster) *a towards rr: t.o fnl 5f* **33/1**

3m 10.09s (2.72) **Going Correction** +0.025s/f (Slow)
WFA 3 from 4yo+ 7lb **12 Ran SP% 116.7**
Speed ratings (Par 101): **93,92,92,91,91 90,87,86,85,72 65,52**
CSF £64.67 CT £492.70 TOTE £8.30: £3.30, £2.70, £4.50; EX 75.40 Trifecta £159.40 Part won. Pool: £224.57 - 0.36 winning tickets..
Owner Mrs I M Folkes **Bred** Liscannor Stud Ltd **Trained** Pandy, Monmouths
■ Stewards' Enquiry : Mr R P Flint caution: used whip with excessive frequency
Mr J Owen two-day ban: used whip with excessive force (Jan 4,14)

FOCUS
A wide-open, low-grade handicap, run at a steady pace. Fairly sound form, and the winner could have been rated a little higher.
Raquel White Official explanation: trainer's rep said filly had lost a front shoe

7005 PONTIN'S BOOK EARLY AND SAVE H'CAP (DIV I) 5f 20y(P)
1:40 (1:40) (Class 6) (0-65,71) 3-Y-0+ **£1,706** (£503; £252) **Stalls Low**

Form RPR

0503 **1** **Our Fugitive (IRE)**[16] 6860 5-9-1 **62**........ NCallan 8 73
(A W Carroll) *sn led: rdn and edgd lft over 1f out: r.o* **4/1**[2]

0005 **2** ¾ **Russian Rocket (IRE)**[34] 6575 5-8-12 **59**........ MickyFenton 4 67
(Mrs C A Dunnett) *sn chsng wnr: rdn and ev ch ins fnl f: nt qckn* **10/1**

003 **3** 1 **Hello Roberto**[24] 6752 6-8-7 **54**........(p) ChrisCatlin 9 58
(R A Harris) *a.p: rdn and kpt on same pce fnl f* **14/1**

6214 **4** nk **Mickleberry (IRE)**[26] 6720 3-8-1 **51** oh2........ AndrewElliott(3) 10 54+
(J D Bethell) *hld up and bhd: swtchd lft 3f out: rdn and hdwy on ins wl over 1f out: kpt on ins fnl f* **15/2**

1154 **5** 1 ½ **Sandwith**[16] 6860 4-9-0 **61**........(p) EddieAhern 1 59+
(J S Wainwright) *led early: chsd ldrs: rdn over 1f out: one pce* **5/4**[1]

0600 **6** 2 **Egyptian Lord**[9] 6938 4-8-13 **60**........ LPKeniry 5 51
(Peter Grayson) *s.i.s: hld up and bhd: rdn and sme hdwy whn edgd lft 1f out: n.d* **14/1**

0005 **7** nk **Lady Hopeful (IRE)**[14] 6864 5-8-4 **51** oh6........(b) AdrianMcCarthy 2 41
(Peter Grayson) *chsd ldrs: rdn over 1f out: wknd ins fnl f* **33/1**

0060 **8** 1 ½ **Blushing Russian (IRE)**[218] 1317 5-8-1 **53** oh6 ow2(p) KirstyMilczarek(5) 3 37
(J M Bradley) *hld up and bhd: shortlived effrt 2f out* **40/1**

0404 **9** hd **Triple Shadow**[19] 6818 3-8-10 **57**........ SteveDrowne 6 41
(M A Peill) *s.i.s: a bhd* **6/1**[3]

0064 **10** 5 **Matterofact (IRE)**[24] 6752 4-8-8 **55**........ FergusSweeney 7 21
(M S Saunders) *prom tl rdn and wknd 2f out* **14/1**

62.68 secs (-0.14) **Going Correction** +0.025s/f (Slow) **10 Ran SP% 125.0**
Speed ratings (Par 101): **102,100,99,98,96 93,92,90,89,81**
CSF £47.29 CT £540.41 TOTE £7.30: £1.80, £2.60, £2.90; EX 70.30 Trifecta £72.70 Pool: £171.07 - 1.67 winning tickets..
Owner Serafino Agodino **Bred** Dr Paschal Carmody **Trained** Cropthorne, Worcs

FOCUS
The first three were always up with the pace in this moderate contest, run in a time 0.2 seconds slower than the other division. The form has been rated at face value.
Matterofact(IRE) Official explanation: jockey said filly had hung right-handed

7006 WOLVERHAMPTON-RACECOURSE.CO.UK (S) STKS 7f 32y(P)
2:10 (2:12) (Class 6) 3-Y-0+ **£2,047** (£604; £302) **Stalls High**

Form RPR

5005 **1** **Mountain Pass (USA)**[7] 6950 5-8-13 56........(p) DavidProbert(7) 3 63
(B J Llewellyn) *hld up in mid-div: hdwy 5f out: led on bit 2f out: rdn clr 1f out: r.o* **8/1**[3]

0306 **2** ¾ **Zennerman (IRE)**[19] 6806 4-9-6 73........ NCallan 9 61
(K A Ryan) *hld up towards rr: hdwy on ins 3f out: chsd wnr fnl f: hung lft: kpt on* **4/5**[1]

5040 **3** 1 ¼ **Ruffie (IRE)**[35] 6537 4-9-1 60........(e) MickyFenton 12 53
(Miss Gay Kelleway) *hld up towards rr: hdwy on outside over 3f out: c wd st: rdn over 1f out: kpt on ins fnl f* **20/1**

1-50 **4** ½ **Amorist (IRE)**[68] 5737 5-9-0 70........ PaulMulrennan 11 50
(D W Chapman) *sn prom: rdn over 2f out: one pce fnl f* **20/1**

5140 **5** shd **Snow Bunting**[13] 6887 9-9-6 48........ TPQueally 10 56
(Jedd O'Keeffe) *hld up towards rr: hdwy wl over 1f out: sn rdn: one pce fnl f* **25/1**

0500 **6** ½ **Katie Lawson (IRE)**[16] 6859 4-8-9 53........(p) RobertHavlin 5 47
(D Haydn Jones) *s.i.s: in rr: hdwy over 1f out: nt clr run and swtchd rt ins fnl f: nvr trbld ldrs* **33/1**

2120 **7** 1 ¾ **Halfwaytoparadise**[35] 6537 4-8-10 49........(p) TolleyDean(5) 7 45
(W G M Turner) *hld up in mid-div: rdn over 2f out: wknd wl over 1f out* **14/1**

0010 **8** 3 **Tequila Sheila (IRE)**[60] 5935 5-9-1 51........ PaulDoe 1 37
(M A Allen) *led: hdd 2f out: sn rdn: wknd 1f out* **40/1**

5003 **9** shd **Tobago Reef**[14] 6873 3-8-7 62........(p) KristinStubbs(7) 8 36
(Mrs L Stubbs) *hld up in mid-div: bhd fnl 2f* **11/2**[2]

2000 **10** 7 **Put It On The Card**[48] 6256 3-9-6 62........(v) SteveDrowne 6 23
(J S Wainwright) *chsd ldr to 3f out: wknd wl over 1f out* **14/1**

2-05 **11** 2 **Cape Thea**[206] 1633 3-8-9 65........ EddieAhern 2 6
(Mark Gillard) *prom tl lost pl over 4f out: sn rdn and bhd* **16/1**

1m 32.32s (1.92) **Going Correction** +0.025s/f (Slow) **11 Ran SP% 120.0**
Speed ratings (Par 101): **90,89,87,87,87 86,84,81,80,72 70**
CSF £14.15 TOTE £9.90: £2.60, £1.10, £4.20; EX 20.60 Trifecta £184.30 Part won. Pool: £259.61 - 0.56 winning tickets..The winner was bought in for 7,000gns. Zennerman was claimed by Miss J. E. Foster for £6,000.
Owner B J Llewellyn **Bred** Marablue Farm **Trained** Fochriw, Caerphilly
■ The first winner for 19-year-old apprentice David Probert.

FOCUS
An ordinary seller run ina slow time. The winner was close to his best but the runner-up was way off form, as were the next two home.
Put It On The Card Official explanation: jockey said gelding lost its action in final 2f

7007 GO PONTIN'S HOLIDAYS NURSERY (DIV I) 1m 141y(P)
2:40 (2:41) (Class 6) (0-65,65) 2-Y-0 **£1,706** (£503; £252) **Stalls Low**

Form RPR

5212 **1** **Wiseman's Diamond (USA)**[19] 6812 2-9-6 **64**........ NCallan 2 68+
(K A Ryan) *hld up towards rr: hmpd over 3f out: hdwy and swtchd lft over 2f out: swtchd rt wl over 1f out: edgd lft ins fnl f: r.o to ld last strides* **11/8**[1]

0405 **2** hd **Flashy Max**[19] 6814 2-8-0 **47**........ AndrewElliott(3) 6 50
(Jedd O'Keeffe) *led: rdn over 1f out: hdd last strides* **22/1**

6056 **3** 1 ¼ **Eternal Optimist (IRE)**[24] 6750 2-8-12 **56**........ EddieAhern 5 56
(C W Thornton) *a.p: wnt 2nd 2f out: rdn over 1f out: nt qckn ins fnl f* **11/2**[3]

0002 **4** 6 **Sunshine Lady (IRE)**[25] 6737 2-9-4 **62**........ HayleyTurner 4 50
(D Haydn Jones) *hld up in tch: edgd lft over 3f out: wknd 2f out* **20/1**

2063 **5** shd **Natural Rhythm (IRE)**[25] 6736 2-9-7 **65**........ PaulMulrennan 3 53
(D W Chapman) *hld up in mid-div: bmpd over 3f out: hdwy over 2f out: sn rdn: wknd over 1f out* **7/2**[2]

0650 **6** 3 **Coral Shores**[17] 6827 2-8-10 **54**........ ChrisCatlin 1 35
(P W Hiatt) *hld up in mid-div: wknd over 2f out* **16/1**

6200 **7** ¾ **Twilight Belle (IRE)**[38] 6478 2-9-0 **58**........(p) FergusSweeney 8 38
(K R Burke) *chsd ldr: ev ch over 2f out: sn rdn and lost 2nd: wknd wl over 1f out* **16/1**

6240 **8** 2 ½ **Elusive Deal (USA)**[24] 6750 2-9-1 **59**........(p) DaleGibson 9 33
(R A Fahey) *a bhd* **10/1**

6000 **9** 4 **Frammenti**[44] 6329 2-8-8 **52**........(p) SteveDrowne 7 18
(A J McCabe) *prom: rdn over 2f out: sn wknd* **50/1**

006 **10** 2 ½ **Diamond Seeker**[14] 6868 2-7-13 **50**........ AshleyMorgan(7) 10 11
(V Smith) *a in rr* **33/1**

1m 52.91s (1.15) **Going Correction** +0.025s/f (Slow) **10 Ran SP% 114.6**
Speed ratings (Par 94): **95,94,93,88,88 85,84,82,79,76**
CSF £41.02 CT £133.49 TOTE £2.10: £1.10, £5.00, £1.20; EX 37.40 Trifecta £112.30 Part won. Pool: £158.28 - 0.10 winning tickets..
Owner Wright, Hillen and Hatta **Bred** Hatta Bloodstock International **Trained** Hambleton, N Yorks

FOCUS
This moderate nursery was 0.2 seconds faster than the other division, with the stretch mile finding a lot of these out. The first three finished clear but the form is nothing to get excited about.

NOTEBOOK
Wiseman's Diamond(USA) ◆ overcame more than her fair share of trouble in running and would have been an unlucky loser had she failed to get up. This step up in distance suited her well and she is better than this bare form suggests. (op 6-4 tchd 6-5, 13-8 in a place)
Flashy Max, switching to front-running tactics on his handicap debut, left his previous form behind and could be on the upgrade. (op 20-1)
Eternal Optimist(IRE) was a springer in the market after a couple of fair efforts over course and distance. She could not overhaul the winner despite having dropped a total of 7lb. (op 11-1)
Sunshine Lady(IRE) looked harshly treated after being well beaten by a hot favourite when second in a maiden over course and distance last month. (op 14-1)
Natural Rhythm(IRE), raised 2lb, should have appreciated the return to a longer trip. (op 9-2 tchd 5-1)

7008 GO PONTIN'S SHORT BREAKS H'CAP 2m 119y(P)
3:10 (3:10) (Class 5) (0-75,72) 3-Y-0+ **£2,968** (£876; £438) **Stalls Low**

Form RPR

0351 **1** **Inchpast**[21] 6802 6-9-13 **72**........(b) PaulMulrennan 5 84+
(M H Tompkins) *hld up: hdwy over 4f out: led over 3f out: rdn wl over 1f out: styd on wl* **11/4**[1]

1521 **2** 4 **Up In Arms (IRE)**[19] 6811 3-8-13 **66**........ StephenCarson 3 73
(P Winkworth) *hld up in rr: hdwy over 4f out: ev ch over 2f out: sn rdn: btn whn edgd lft jst ins fnl f* **4/1**[3]

3002 **3** 5 **Rare Coincidence**[34] 6564 6-9-5 **64**........(p) EddieAhern 2 65
(R F Fisher) *led: hdd over 3f out: wknd 2f out* **17/2**

2155 **4** 4 **Right Option (IRE)**[21] 6802 3-8-11 **67**........ TravisBlock(3) 1 63
(J L Flint) *chsd ldr 4f: rdn and wknd 4f out* **11/2**

3360 **5** 11 **Golano**[14] 6875 7-9-8 **67**........(p) ChrisCatlin 6 56
(P R Webber) *prom: chsd ldr after 4f tl over 3f out: sn wknd* **8/1**

5-22 **6** 30 **To Arms**[37] 6200 5-9-1 **60**........ NCallan 4 7
(K J Burke) *hld up: rdn over 3f out: sn struggling: t.o fnl 2f* **3/1**[2]

3m 41.26s (-1.87) **Going Correction** +0.025s/f (Slow)
WFA 3 from 5yo+ 8lb **6 Ran SP% 108.7**
Speed ratings (Par 103): **105,103,100,98,93 79**
CSF £13.01 TOTE £3.60: £1.70, £2.10; EX 16.00.
Owner Marcoe Racing Welwyn **Bred** Stanley Estate And Stud Co **Trained** Newmarket, Suffolk

FOCUS
Despite a bit of a stop-start gallop in this little staying handicap the pace seemed reasonable overall and they finished well strung out. Inchpast improved on his latest win but will still be well treated on his old form.
To Arms Official explanation: trainer had no expalantion for the poor form shown

7009 PONTINS.COM H'CAP 1m 1f 103y(P)
3:40 (3:42) (Class 6) (0-55,55) 3-Y-0+ **£2,047** (£604; £302) **Stalls Low**

Form RPR

5322 **1** **Rigat**[11] 6906 4-9-0 **55**........ PaulMulrennan 13 68+
(T D Barron) *swtchd lft sn after s: t.k.h early in rr: hdwy on wd outside 3f out: rdn wl over 1f out: led ent fnl f: rdn out* **7/2**[1]

0050 **2** 2 ½ **Cadwell**[9] 6937 3-8-11 **54**........ RobertHavlin 6 59
(T J Pitt) *a.p: led over 2f out: rdn wl over 1f out: hdd ent fnl f: nt qckn* **10/1**

0212 **3** 1 ½ **Almahaza (IRE)**[21] 6796 3-8-5 **55**........(b) HarryPoulton(7) 7 57
(A J Chamberlain) *hld up and bhd: gd hdwy 6f out: rdn over 1f out: one pce fnl f* **7/1**

6010 **4** ¾ **Montemayorprincess (IRE)**[48] 6247 3-8-5 **48**........(p) HayleyTurner 12 48
(D Haydn Jones) *a.p: rdn wl over 1f out: one pce* **28/1**

0003 **5** ¾ **Woodins Way**[33] 6590 3-8-10 **53**........ EddieAhern 1 52
(P J Makin) *hld up in mid-div: hdwy on ins over 2f out: rdn over 1f out: one pce fnl f* **5/1**[3]

0066 **6** 1 **Life's A Whirl**[19] 6816 5-8-13 **54**........(p) MickyFenton 4 51
(Mrs C A Dunnett) *led: hdd over 4f out: wknd 2f out* **20/1**

4344 **7** hd **Weet Yer Tern (IRE)**[9] 6937 5-8-11 **52**........ FergusSweeney 3 48
(W M Brisbourne) *hld up towards rr: sme hdwy wl over 1f out: no real prog fnl f* **9/1**

504 **8** 2 ½ **Botham (USA)**[11] 6904 3-8-9 **52**........(bt) SteveDrowne 5 43
(D J Murphy) *hld up and bhd: rdn over 2f out: no rspnse* **25/1**

0014 **9** 2 ½ **Bowl Of Cherries**[26] 6713 4-8-12 **53**..............................(b) NCallan 10 39
(I A Wood) *hld up in tch: rdn and wknd over 2f out* **9/2**[2]
3006 **10** shd **Greenmeadow**[14] 6866 5-8-4 **52** ow1...................... MatthewBirch(7) 11 37
(S Kirk) *prom: lost pl over 3f out: bhd fnl 2f* **25/1**
2244 **11** 1 **Dot's Delight**[3] 6971 3-8-11 **54**..............................(b) TGMcLaughlin 8 37
(R A Harris) *hld up in mid-div: hdwy over 5f out: led over 4f out: rdn and hdd over 2f out: wknd over 1f out* **12/1**
4364 **12** nk **Granary Girl**[14] 6866 5-8-10 **51**.............................. J-PGuillambert 9 34
(J Pearce) *a towards rr* **14/1**
6-00 **13** 7 **Opus Magnus (IRE)**[19] 6809 4-8-7 **48**.............................. ChrisCatlin 2 16
(P J Makin) *prom tl wknd 4f out* **40/1**
2m 2.95s (0.33) **Going Correction** +0.025s/f (Slow)
WFA 3 from 4yo+ 2lb **13** Ran SP% **121.4**
Speed ratings (Par 101): **99,96,95,94,94 93,93,90,88,88 87,87,81**
CSF £37.16 CT £239.80 TOTE £4.90: £1.80, £2.60, £3.60; EX 57.00 Trifecta £110.20 Part won. Pool: £155.33 - 0.20 winning tickets..
Owner Mrs Janis Macpherson **Bred** Mrs M Chaworth-Musters **Trained** Maunby, N Yorks
■ Stewards' Enquiry : N Callan three-day ban: careless riding (Dec 14-16)
FOCUS
A closely-knit, low-grade affair. Rigat is rated better than the bare form and has obviously taken well to Wolverhampton.
Montemayorprincess(IRE) Official explanation: jockey said filly hung left

7010 GO PONTIN'S HOLIDAYS NURSERY (DIV II) 1m 141y(P)
4:10 (4:10) (Class 6) (0-65,65) 2-Y-0 **£1,706** (£503; £252) **Stalls** Low

Form RPR
0500 **1** **Ostinata (IRE)**[84] 5268 2-8-4 **48**.............................. WandersonD'Avila 10 51
(B W Duke) *hld up in tch: hung lft wl over 1f out: sn rdn: r.o to ld wl ins fnl f* **25/1**
0004 **2** nk **Ogre (USA)**[25] 6736 2-9-6 **64**.............................. TPQueally 5 67
(J A Osborne) *s.i.s: hld up in rr: nt clr run over 2f out: hdwy wl over 1f out: sn rdn: r.o ins fnl f* **7/2**[1]
3333 **3** ¾ **Tapas Lad (IRE)**[3] 6978 2-9-0 **58**.............................. PatCosgrave 8 59
(V Smith) *hld up in tch: wnt 2nd over 2f out: sn rdn: nt qckn ins fnl f* **7/1**
5006 **4** ½ **Hawa Khana (IRE)**[13] 6881 2-9-1 **59**.............................. StephenDonohoe 9 59
(N P Littmoden) *t.k.h: w ldrs: led over 6f out: rdn over 2f out: hdd wl ins fnl f: no ex* **10/1**
6011 **5** 1 **Caltire (GER)**[9] 6928 2-8-13 **62**..............................(b) JamieJones(5) 3 60
(M G Quinlan) *hld up and bhd: c wd st: sn rdn and hung lft: kpt on ins fnl f: nvr able to chal* **9/2**[3]
0000 **6** ½ **Balais Folly (FR)**[19] 6814 2-8-11 **55**..............................(p) ChrisCatlin 1 52
(B Palling) *hld up in tch: n.m.r briefly over 2f out: sn rdn and no hdwy* **22/1**
6044 **7** 3 **Shadows Fall (USA)**[9] 6933 2-9-2 **65**.............................. TolleyDean(5) 4 56
(P F I Cole) *w ldrs: rdn over 2f out: wknd ins fnl f* **4/1**[2]
0000 **8** 6 **Kay One (IRE)**[131] 3841 2-8-3 **52**.............................. KirstyMilczarek(5) 2 30
(R J Price) *led: hdd over 6f out: n.m.r on ins briefly over 2f out: sn wknd* **50/1**
6523 **9** ½ **Space Pirate**[41] 6410 2-8-13 **57**.............................. DavidKinsella 6 34
(J Pearce) *hld up and bhd: rdn over 3f out: sn struggling* **7/2**[1]
1m 53.11s (1.35) **Going Correction** +0.025s/f (Slow) **9** Ran SP% **114.4**
Speed ratings (Par 94): **95,94,94,93,92 92,89,84,83**
CSF £108.22 CT £703.12 TOTE £36.70: £6.10, £2.20, £2.40; EX 190.00 TRIFECTA Not won..
Owner Tom & Evelyn Yates **Bred** Miss Patricia Beston **Trained** Lambourn, Berks
■ The first winner in Britain for Wanderson D'Avila who has ridden around 250 winners in his native Brazil.
FOCUS
This looked weaker than the first division and was 0.2 seconds slower. Modest form, but solid enough.
NOTEBOOK
Ostinata(IRE), dropped 4lb, came through to spring a surprise after hanging left on the home turn.
Ogre(USA) ♦, trying a longer trip, did not get the run of the race and deserves another chance. (tchd 10-3)
Tapas Lad(IRE), raised 3lb, had the visor left off for this quick reappearance and continued his run of third places. (op 11-2)
Hawa Khana(IRE) was just run out of it and could have settled better on this step up to a mile. (op 9-1 tchd 12-1)
Caltire(GER) was up in class on this hat-trick bid and could never quite make his presence felt after hanging left.
Balais Folly(FR), tried in cheekpieces, was 6lb lower than when previously in a nursery. (op 20-1)

7011 PONTIN'S BOOK EARLY AND SAVE H'CAP (DIV II) 5f 20y(P)
4:40 (4:41) (Class 6) (0-65,64) 3-Y-0+ **£1,706** (£503; £252) **Stalls** Low

Form RPR
5300 **1** **Triskaidekaphobia**[12] 6890 4-8-6 **52**..............................(t) PaulFitzsimons 2 63
(Miss J R Tooth) *mde all: rdn fnl f: jst hld on* **6/1**[3]
0046 **2** hd **Wicked Uncle**[19] 6810 8-9-2 **62**..............................(v) ChrisCatlin 1 72
(S Gollings) *mid-div: hdwy on ins over 2f out: chsd wnr jst over 1f out: hrd rdn and r.o ins fnl f: jst failed* **4/1**[2]
3214 **3** 2 **By The Edge (IRE)**[38] 6466 3-8-9 **55**.............................. PaulFessey 4 58
(T D Barron) *a.p: chsd wnr over 3f out tl rdn jst over 1f out: one pce* **17/2**
0035 **4** 1 ¼ **Calypso King**[3] 6976 4-9-1 **61**.............................. LPKeniry 11 60
(Peter Grayson) *hld up in rr: sn swtchd lft: hdwy on ins wl over 1f out: rdn and no further prog fnl f* **8/1**
1060 **5** hd **Polar Force**[34] 6575 7-9-0 **60**.............................. SaleemGolam 6 58
(Mrs C A Dunnett) *stdd s: hld up and bhd: hdwy on ins over 2f out: rdn jst over 1f out: one pce* **12/1**
0621 **6** ¾ **Monashee Brave (IRE)**[25] 6730 4-9-2 **62**.............................. PaulDoe 7 57
(R A Harris) *prom: rdn 2f out: edgd lft and wknd over 1f out* **7/2**[1]
0U00 **7** 1 ¾ **Puskas (IRE)**[17] 6870 4-8-9 **55**..............................(v) StephenDonohoe 10 44
(J M Bradley) *sn swtchd lft: outpcd in rr: n.d* **18/1**
0403 **8** ½ **No Time (IRE)**[9] 6927 7-8-12 **58**.............................. SteveDrowne 5 45
(A J McCabe) *chsd wnr over 1f: wknd over 2f out* **4/1**[2]
2500 **9** 1 ¼ **Strensall**[24] 6743 10-8-1 **50** oh2.............................. DuranFentiman(3) 9 32
(R E Barr) *s.i.s: a bhd* **20/1**
4654 **10** 1 ¼ **Tibinta**[14] 6864 3-8-1 **50** oh5..............................(b[1]) AndrewElliott(3) 8 28
(P D Evans) *t.k.h early in mid-div: bhd fnl 2f* **16/1**
6-00 **11** 18 **Ava's World (IRE)**[11] 6905 3-8-11 **64**.............................. RyanHill(7) 3 —
(Peter Grayson) *s.i.s: outpcd* **66/1**
62.48 secs (-0.34) **Going Correction** +0.025s/f (Slow) **11** Ran SP% **123.2**
Speed ratings (Par 101): **103,102,99,97,97 95,93,92,90,88 59**
CSF £31.81 CT £182.38 TOTE £8.40: £2.70, £1.60, £2.00; EX 35.20 TRIFECTA Not won. Place 6 £97.05, Place 5 £20.59.
Owner Raymond Tooth And Steve Gilbey **Bred** K Bowen **Trained** Lambourn, Berks
FOCUS
This was 0.2 seconds quicker than the first division, in which the winner also made all. The form seems fairly sound.

Puskas(IRE) Official explanation: jockey said gelding did not face the kick-back early on
T/Jkpt: Not won. T/Plt: £123.10 to a £1 stake. Pool: £72,287.55. 428.60 winning tickets. T/Qpdt: £9.80 to a £1 stake. Pool: £5,545.40. 416.50 winning tickets. KH

6970 LINGFIELD (L-H)
Tuesday, December 4

OFFICIAL GOING: Standard
Wind: Strong, behind Weather: Overcast, drizzly

7012 JUMPING HERE ON DECEMBER 15TH AMATEUR RIDERS' H'CAP 2m (P)
12:20 (12:21) (Class 6) (0-60,58) 3-Y-0+ **£1,873** (£581; £290; £145) **Stalls** Low

Form RPR
0006 **1** **Ice And Fire**[18] 6835 8-10-8 **45**..............................(b) MrSDobson 13 53
(J T Stimpson) *stdd s: hld up in last pair: gd prog fr 4f out to trck ldrs 3f out: wnt 2nd over 1f out: r.o to ld nr fin* **33/1**
6042 **2** ½ **Haatmey**[20] 6811 5-11-0 **51**..............................(v) MrSWalker 3 58
(P R Chamings) *lw: trckd ldrs: effrt 3f out: rdn to ld wl over 1f out: collared nr fin* **11/4**[1]
-140 **3** ½ **Enthusius**[182] 1026 4-10-10 **52**.............................. MissHayleyMoore(5) 6 58
(G L Moore) *hld up towwards rr: rdn and prog fr 3f out: styd on fr over 1f out: clsng at fin* **4/1**[2]
0046 **4** 2 ½ **Mango Masher (IRE)**[14] 6883 3-10-5 **57**..............................(p) MrRPFlint(7) 10 61+
(J L Flint) *hld up towards rr: rdn and prog over 4f out: hmpd on inner over 2f out: kpt on fr over 1f out: nvr able to chal* **17/2**
4405 **5** 1 ¼ **Moonshine Beach**[15] 6875 9-11-4 **58**.............................. MrsMarieKing(3) 9 60
(P W Hiatt) *led after 1f: mde most to 3f out: steadily outpcd fnl 2f* **9/1**
1/4- **6** 2 **Cayman Calypso (IRE)**[530] 40 6-10-3 **45**................ MissLAllan(5) 12 45
(Mrs P Sly) *hld up in midfield: prog over 4f out: led 3f out to wl over 1f out: wknd* **8/1**[3]
7 ½ **Deimne (IRE)**[35] 6114 4-10-3 **45**.............................. MrIPopham(5) 11 44
(John Joseph Murphy, Ire) *prom: rdn over 3f out: outpcd and btn over 2f out* **25/1**
5004 **8** 5 **Moon Emperor**[20] 6811 10-11-5 **56**..............................(b) MrLeeNewnes 2 49
(J R Jenkins) *hld up in last trio: outpcd over 3f out: plugged on fnl 2f: n.d* **12/1**
006- **9** 2 **Stolen Song**[511] 3382 7-10-3 **47**.............................. MrDavidMcMinn(7) 1 38
(J Ryan) *bit bkwd: led 1f: prom tl bmpd along and lost pl fr 4f out* **66/1**
5402 **10** 7 **Theflyingscottie**[22] 6797 5-11-0 **51**..............................(v) MrsMMorris 14 33
(D Shaw) *t.k.h: racd wd: hld up: prog over 4f out: outpcd over 3f out: fdd* **17/2**
006/ **11** 6 **Charleston**[940] 450 6-10-13 **55**.............................. MissAWallace(5) 5 30
(R Rowe) *bit bkwd: t.k.h: prom: w ldrs 7f out to over 4f out: wknd over 3f out* **66/1**
0440 **12** 4 **My Monna**[4] 6975 3-10-0 **50**.............................. MrAMerriam(5) 7 20
(Miss Sheena West) *pressed ldr after 3f tl over 4f out: wknd* **14/1**
30-0 **13** 6 **Escobar (POL)**[176] 2055 6-10-5 **47**.............................. MrsCThompson(5) 4 10
(Mrs P Townsley) *nvr on terms w ldrs: wknd 5f out: sn bhd* **33/1**
0005 **14** 4 **Katie Kingfisher**[22] 6797 3-9-7 **45**..............................(p) MrJPearce(7) 8 3
(M Wigham) *a in rr: bhd fnl 3f* **16/1**
3m 24.66s (-4.13) **Going Correction** -0.20s/f (Stan)
WFA 3 from 4yo+ 8lb **14** Ran SP% **121.8**
Speed ratings (Par 101): **102,101,101,100,99 98,98,95,94,91 88,86,83,81**
CSF £121.19 CT £468.07 TOTE £27.40: £7.20, £1.50, £1.90; EX 152.60 TRIFECTA Not won..
Owner J T Stimpson & B W Trubshaw **Bred** Abdullah Saeed Belhab **Trained** Newcastle-Under-Lyme, Staffs
FOCUS
A moderate staying handicap, although at least the pace was better than is often the case round here. The form is rated around the runner-up and fourth.
Escobar(POL) Official explanation: jockey said gelding had breathing problems

7013 PONTIN'S BOOK EARLY PRICE PROMISE H'CAP (DIV I) 6f (P)
12:50 (12:52) (Class 6) (0-57,59) 3-Y-0+ **£1,619** (£481; £240; £120) **Stalls** Low

Form RPR
0611 **1** **Fast Freddie**[7] 6957 3-9-4 **59** 6ex..............................(e) RichardHughes 1 69+
(D J Murphy) *trckd ldrs on inner: effrt 2f out: led jst over 1f out: hung rt fnl f: drvn out* **7/2**[2]
6542 **2** ½ **Stormburst (IRE)**[7] 6962 3-9-0 **55**.............................. EddieAhern 6 64+
(S C Williams) *lw: hld up in midfield: rdn 2f out: prog towards over 1f out: drvn to chse wnr wl ins fnl f: a hld* **10/3**[1]
0062 **3** ½ **Thoughtsofstardom**[10] 6925 4-8-11 **57**.................. KirstyMilczarek(5) 2 63+
(G C Bravery) *dwlt: hld up on inner: prog on inner wl over 1f out: trying to cl whn nt clr run briefly ins fnl f: styd on* **5/1**[3]
0040 **4** shd **Is It Time (IRE)**[20] 6809 3-8-9 **50**.............................. RobertHavlin 11 54
(Mrs P N Dutfield) *t.k.h: sn prom on outer: tried to chal over 1f out: nt qckn fnl f* **33/1**
0350 **5** nk **Ishibee (IRE)**[3] 6993 3-9-1 **56**..............................(p) GeorgeBaker 3 59
(J J Bridger) *hld up in last trio: prog over 1f out: styd on fnl f: nvr able to chal* **12/1**
0060 **6** nk **King Of Charm (IRE)**[8] 6950 4-8-5 **46** oh1..............................(b) PaulDoe 5 48
(G L Moore) *hld up in midfield: rdn and nt qckn 2f out: kpt on* **20/1**
2613 **7** nk **Muktasb (USA)**[7] 6957 6-8-10 **51**..............................(v) FergusSweeney 12 52
(D Shaw) *lw: rrd and s.s: mostly in last trio: stl there over 1f out: r.o fnl f: nrst fin* **8/1**
-200 **8** ¾ **Herb Paris (FR)**[15] 6870 3-9-2 **57**..............................(p) IanMongan 4 56
(P M Phelan) *led to jst over 1f out: fdd* **16/1**
0000 **9** hd **Royal Orissa**[20] 6809 5-8-6 **47**..............................(p) ChrisCatlin 9 45
(D Haydn Jones) *prog to press ldr over 3f out to over 1f out: wknd* **11/1**
4640 **10** nk **Arfinnit (IRE)**[75] 5565 6-8-13 **54**..............................(v) GregFairley 8 52
(Mrs A L M King) *awkward s: sn in midfield on outer: no imp on ldrs over 1f out: fdd* **20/1**
0034 **11** 2 ½ **Anfield Dream**[10] 6927 5-9-2 **57**..............................(t) MickyFenton 10 47
(J R Jenkins) *racd wd in rr: no prog whn v wd bnd 2f out: no ch after* **11/1**
0006 **12** shd **Polish Prize**[80] 5420 3-8-9 **50**.............................. AdamKirby 7 40
(W R Swinburn) *chsd ldr to over 3f out: wknd 2f out* **16/1**
1m 11.91s (-0.90) **Going Correction** -0.20s/f (Stan) **12** Ran SP% **121.7**
Speed ratings (Par 101): **98,97,96,96,96 95,95,94,94,93 90,90**
CSF £15.60 CT £60.79 TOTE £3.50: £1.40, £2.00, £1.60; EX 13.10 Trifecta £40.00 Pool £271.25 - 4.81 winning units..
Owner Gordon Crawford **Bred** New Hall Stud **Trained** Bawtry, S Yorks
■ Stewards' Enquiry : Richard Hughes caution: careless riding
FOCUS
They were spread out all over the track in the straight and finished in a heap. Add to that the winning time was 0.89 seconds slower than the second division and this looks like form to treat with caution. That said, the first three are all fair types for the grade.
Muktasb(USA) Official explanation: jockey said gelding missed the break

Polish Prize Official explanation: jockey said colt suffered interference on home bend

7014 PONTIN'S BOOK EARLY PRICE PROMISE H'CAP (DIV II) 6f (P)
1:20 (1:23) (Class 6) (0-57,57) 3-Y-O+ **£1,619** (£481; £240; £120) **Stalls** Low

Form RPR

4001 **1** **Bond Becks (IRE)**[14] 6887 7-8-13 **54** ChrisCatlin 11 64
(G R Oldroyd) *fast away fr wd draw: mde all: drvn over 1f out: tired nr fin: hld on* **14/1**

2246 **2** ½ **Musical Script (USA)**[34] 6581 4-8-13 **57** (p) TravisBlock(3) 1 65
(Mouse Hamilton-Fairley) *prom: rdn over 2f out: chsd wnr wl over 1f out: no imp tl styd on nr fin: jst hld* **8/1**

2021 **3** *hd* **Grand Palace (IRE)**[10] 6927 4-8-9 **55** (v) PatrickHills(5) 5 62
(D Shaw) *b: chsd ldrs: pushed along over 2f out: rdn and clsd fnl f: a hld* **9/4**[1]

0000 **4** *hd* **Mind Alert**[10] 6925 6-8-7 **48** (v) JamesDoyle 7 55
(D Shaw) *settled in midfield: effrt 2f out: nt qckn over 1f out: r.o fnl f: nrst fin* **11/1**

0524 **5** *shd* **Mannello**[7] 6957 4-8-11 **52** EddieAhern 12 62+
(Jim Best) *dwlt: hld up in last pair: pushed along 2f out: limited prog tl rdn and r.o wl fnl f: too much to do* **4/1**[2]

4030 **6** *hd* **With Confidence**[18] 6831 3-9-2 **57** TQuinn 3 63
(D R C Elsworth) *dwlt: hld up towards rr: effrt on inner 2f out: styd on fnl f: nvr quite rchd ldrs* **16/1**

0405 **7** *1* **Mulberry Lad (IRE)**[8] 6945 5-8-10 **51** JimCrowley 6 54
(P W Hiatt) *settled wl in rr: prog wl over 1f out: chsd ldrs fnl f: one pce last 100yds* **13/2**[3]

0625 **8** *nk* **Time Share (IRE)**[10] 6927 3-8-0 **46** oh1 KirstyMilczarek(5) 10 48
(G C Bravery) *swtg: awkward s: hld up in last pair: stl keen over 2f out: rdn and r.o fnl f: no ch of rching ldrs* **11/1**

3000 **9** *3* **Bahamian Duke**[18] 6826 4-9-2 **57** FergusSweeney 9 50
(K R Burke) *hld up in midfield: shkn up wl over 1f out: btn whn n.m.r jst ins fnl f: fdd* **9/1**

2000 **10** *6* **Elmasong**[41] 6429 3-8-5 **46** oh1 NelsonDeSouza 8 21
(J J Bridger) *nvr on terms w ldrs on outer: struggling over 2f out* **66/1**

-050 **11** *1¾* **Iron Pearl**[265] 679 3-9-2 **57** AdamKirby 2 27
(J Ryan) *chsd wnr to wl over 1f out: wknd rapidly* **66/1**

00-0 **12** *1* **Edward (IRE)**[10] 6927 5-8-9 **50** StephenCarson 4 17
(M Madgwick) *prom over 2f: sn lost pl and struggling* **50/1**

1m 11.02s (-1.79) **Going Correction** -0.20s/f (Stan) **12** Ran SP% **119.4**
Speed ratings (Par 101): **103,102,102,101,101 101,100,99,95,87 85,84**
CSF £122.04 CT £356.66 TOTE £12.20: £2.10, £2.60, £1.70; EX 136.50 TRIFECTA Not won..

Owner R C Bond **Bred** Dr Paschal Carmody **Trained** Brawby, N Yorks

■ Stewards' Enquiry : Jim Crowley caution: careless riding

FOCUS
Like the first division, moderate sprint form, if pretty solid, but they went a good pace from the outset and the winning time was 0.89 seconds quicker. It proved difficult to make up significant amounts of ground from off the pace.

With Confidence Official explanation: jockey said filly missed the break

Time Share(IRE) Official explanation: jockey said filly suffered interference on home bend

Bahamian Duke Official explanation: jockey said gelding was hampered and suffered interference in home straight

Iron Pearl Official explanation: jockey said filly had no more to give

7015 PONTIN'S BOOK EARLY NOVICE STKS 6f (P)
1:50 (1:52) (Class 4) 2-Y-O **£3,886** (£1,156; £577; £288) **Stalls** Low

Form RPR

21 **1** **Haybrook**[22] 6799 2-9-5 86 ChrisCatlin 1 87
(E J O'Neill) *trckd ldng pair: rdn to go 2nd wl over 1f out: chal fnl f: drvn ahd last 75yds* **4/1**[2]

1 **2** *nk* **Classic Fortune (IRE)**[13] 6897 2-9-5 0 TQuinn 5 86
(D R C Elsworth) *lw: t.k.h: led after 2f: rdn over 1f out: worn down last 75yds* **8/11**[1]

0021 **3** *2½* **Dhhamaan (IRE)**[18] 6827 2-9-0 71 (v) RichardHughes 2 74
(C E Brittain) *trckd ldrs: rdn and nt qckn over 1f out: one pce after* **12/1**

0 **4** *4* **Mister New York (USA)**[13] 6897 2-8-12 0 JosedeSouza 3 60
(Noel T Chance) *settled in last pair: pushed along and outpcd fnl 2f* **66/1**

5 *3* **Kingsgate Castle** 2-8-8 0 JimCrowley 6 47
(J R Best) *w'like: str: dwlt: a in last pair: shkn up and outpcd over 2f out: sn no ch* **6/1**[3]

45 **6** *2* **Pretty Ballerina (USA)**[101] 4833 2-8-7 0 EddieAhern 4 40
(John Joseph Murphy, Ire) *leggy: led 2f: chsd wnr to wl over 1f out: wknd tamely* **10/1**

1m 11.21s (-1.60) **Going Correction** -0.20s/f (Stan) 2y crse rec **6** Ran SP% **110.5**
Speed ratings (Par 98): **102,101,98,92,88 86**
CSF £7.08 TOTE £6.00: £2.20, £1.10; EX 8.30.

Owner Mrs S J Brookhouse **Bred** Canary Thoroughbreds **Trained** Averham Park, Notts

FOCUS
This looked like a very good novice event beforehand, but the bare form is probably not as strong as it might have been. The third is probably the best guide.

NOTEBOOK
Haybrook followed up in his recent Wolverhampton maiden success in determined style. It remains to be seen how strong a race this was, but the runner-up looked a very useful prospect when winning over this course and distance on his debut, and this must rate as a decent effort. He is progressing nicely and could now head to Dubai for the Carnival. (op 7-2)

Classic Fortune(IRE) looked a nice prospect when narrowly landing a maiden over course and distance on his debut, but this was much tougher. He ran a respectable race, finishing clear of all bar the improving winner, and he should progress again. (op 10-11 tchd Evens)

Dhhamaan(IRE), the winner of a 7f maiden round here on his previous start, came into this rated just 71 and he proved no match for the front pair. (op 10-1)

Mister New York(USA) beat just one rival when behind Classic Fortune on his debut over course and distance, recording an RPR of just 43 in the process, so his proximity does little for the form.

Kingsgate Castle, a 70,000gns son of Kyllachy, half-brother to multiple 6f-7f winner Mugeba, out of a 5f winner at three, had been due to make his debut in a Listed contest back in May, but was withdrawn due to passport irregularities. His trainer has a good record in this race, but he proved easy to back on course and was too green to do himself justice. He will know a lot more next time. (op 4-1)

Pretty Ballerina(USA) was highly tried and showed some useful form in Ireland earlier in the year, but she had not been seen since finishing a tailed-off last of five behind New Approach in a Group 2 in August. Trying Polytrack for the first time, she showed plenty of early speed but offered very little when it mattered. (tchd 11-1)

7016 GO PONTIN'S NURSERY 1m (P)
2:20 (2:21) (Class 4) (0-95,78) 2-Y-O **£4,731** (£1,416; £708; £354; £176) **Stalls** High

Form RPR

1630 **1** **Hucking Hero (IRE)**[4] 6973 2-9-1 **72** ow1 GeorgeBaker 3 74
(J R Best) *hld up in 4th: shkn up and effrt to press ldrs over 2f out: rdn to ld 1f out: hld on u.p* **7/2**[3]

2011 **2** *nk* **Geezers Colours**[13] 6898 2-9-6 **77** FergusSweeney 4 78
(K R Burke) *swtg: t.k.h: trckd ldr: led over 2f out: drvn and hdd 1f out: styd on: a jst hld* **6/1**

414 **3** *shd* **Afram Blue**[19] 6823 2-9-7 **78** PaulDoe 1 79
(W J Knight) *lw: hld up in last in modly run r: rdn 2f out: picked up fnl f: clsd on ldng pair last 100yds: nt qckn nr fin* **9/4**[1]

1 **4** *3* **Mafasina (USA)**[17] 6849 2-9-1 **72** EddieAhern 2 66
(Christian Wroe) *lw: trckd ldng pair: nt qckn over 2f out: outpcd over 1f out: no ch after* **3/1**[2]

4231 **5** *2* **Hieroglyph**[25] 6742 2-9-3 **74** GregFairley 5 64
(M Johnston) *led at mod pce: rdn and hdd over 2f out: wknd over 1f out* **4/1**

1m 39.34s (-0.09) **Going Correction** -0.20s/f (Stan) **5** Ran SP% **112.3**
Speed ratings (Par 98): **92,91,91,88,86**
CSF £23.32 TOTE £4.40: £2.60, £3.40; EX 18.10.

Owner Hucking Horses **Bred** Mrs A Hughes **Trained** Hucking, Kent

FOCUS
A fair nursery on paper, but they went no pace. The principals were close to form but this is not a race to place great faith in.

NOTEBOOK
Hucking Hero(IRE) had not had things go his way in three starts since landing his maiden over 7f round here in October, but everything fell kindly this time, despite the lack of early pace, and he ran out a narrow winner. He was made to work quite hard, but can probably step forward again off a stronger gallop. (op 4-1)

Geezers Colours was chasing a hat-trick following wins in a nursery and a claimer over 7f round here, but he was 10lb higher this time and was just held. (tchd 11-2)

Afram Blue was caught out when the pace increased and, although staying on, he narrowly failed to reverse recent course form with Geezers Colours. (op 11-4)

Mafasina(USA), off the mark on her debut in a 7f maiden round here, was one of the last off the bridle, but she found little. On this evidence she will probably be better off back over shorter. (op 10-3 tchd 7-2)

Hieroglyph, the winner of a 7f Musselburgh maiden on her previous start, enjoyed the run of the race out in front, but she was another who found very little when it mattered. (op 10-3)

7017 PONTINS.COM H'CAP 1m (P)
2:50 (2:50) (Class 4) (0-80,92) 3-Y-O+ **£4,605** (£1,378; £689; £344; £171) **Stalls** High

Form RPR

1604 **1** **Atlantic Story (USA)**[71] 5685 5-9-5 **80** (t) EddieAhern 10 89+
(M W Easterby) *t.k.h early: hld up in midfield: prog 2f out: rdn to ld 1f out: idled nr fin: jst hld on* **7/2**[1]

-060 **2** *shd* **Basra (IRE)**[30] 6669 4-9-3 **78** AdamKirby 8 86
(Miss Jo Crowley) *lw: prom: effrt to ld over 2f out: drvn and hdd 1f out: kpt on wl: jst failed* **8/1**

165 **3** *nk* **Smokin Joe**[3] 6996 6-8-7 **68** (b) JimCrowley 1 75
(J R Best) *stdd s: hld up in rr: effrt on outer 2f out: r.o wl fnl f: gaining at fin* **12/1**

0214 **4** *nk* **Gaelic Princess**[31] 6646 7-8-13 **77** TravisBlock(3) 9 84
(A G Newcombe) *hld up in last trio: prog on outer 2f out: drvn and r.o fnl f: nrst fin* **12/1**

0201 **5** *1¼* **Meditation**[19] 6824 5-8-6 **67** ow1 JamesDoyle 7 71
(I A Wood) *led 1f: styd prom: chal over 2f out: nt qckn over 1f out: one pce after* **11/1**

065 **6** *nk* **Monkey Glas (IRE)**[8] 6949 3-9-0 **76** IanMongan 3 79
(K R Burke) *racd freely: led after 1f to over 2f out: wknd fnl f* **6/1**[2]

2213 **7** *nk* **Princess Taylor**[10] 6929 3-8-13 **75** (t) GregFairley 4 77
(M Botti) *trckd ldrs: pushed along over 2f out: lost pl over 1f out: reminders ent fnl f: kpt on same pce* **8/1**

5361 **8** *shd* **Gazboolou**[54] 6121 3-8-12 **74** FergusSweeney 12 76
(David Pinder) *hld up in last trio: rdn and effrt 2f out: sme prog 1f out: one pce ins fnl f* **14/1**

0260 **9** *4* **Trans Sonic**[49] 6253 4-9-1 **76** RichardHughes 2 69
(A P Jarvis) *t.k.h early: hld up in midfield: effrt on inner 2f out: no prog u.p over 1f out: wknd and eased* **13/2**[3]

5-0P **10** *2* **Sri Pekan Two**[218] 1365 3-9-1 **77** TQuinn 5 65
(P F I Cole) *t.k.h early: hld up in midfield: lost pl 2f out: wknd* **8/1**

10-0 **11** *2* **Steely Dan**[13] 6900 8-9-3 **78** ChrisCatlin 11 62
(Mrs L C Jewell) *a last: lost tch over 2f out* **33/1**

1m 37.12s (-2.31) **Going Correction** -0.20s/f (Stan)
WFA 3 from 4yo+ 1lb **11** Ran SP% **116.5**
Speed ratings (Par 105): **103,102,102,102,101 100,100,100,96,94 92**
CSF £31.07 CT £309.03 TOTE £4.00: £1.80, £2.70, £3.70; EX 27.90 TRIFECTA Not won..

Owner Matthew Green **Bred** A I Appleton **Trained** Sheriff Hutton, N Yorks

FOCUS
A fair handicap run at a reasonable pace. The winner was back to his best and the form has a sound look to it.

Trans Sonic Official explanation: jockey said gelding ran too free

7018 PONTIN'S GREAT FAMILY HOLIDAYS H'CAP 1m 2f (P)
3:20 (3:20) (Class 4) (0-80,80) 3-Y-O+ **£4,605** (£1,378; £689; £344; £171) **Stalls** Low

Form RPR

4421 **1** **Alpes Maritimes**[13] 6901 3-9-3 **76** GeorgeBaker 5 86+
(G L Moore) *lw: hld up in rr: stdy prog fr 3f out: effrt to ld jst ins fnl f: in command after* **3/1**[1]

6341 **2** *1* **Kindlelight Blue (IRE)**[17] 6848 3-8-11 **70** JamesDoyle 7 77+
(N P Littmoden) *lw: hld up in last pair: effrt over 2f out: nt clr run over 1f out: r.o to chse wnr ins fnl f: a hld* **7/1**[3]

3232 **3** *½* **Mafeking (UAE)**[30] 6669 3-9-7 **80** PaulDoe 11 85+
(M R Hoad) *hld up in rr: prog on wd outside over 2f out: lost grnd bnd sn after: r.o fnl f to take 3rd last strides* **3/1**[1]

0400 **4** *shd* **Dragon Slayer (IRE)**[39] 6475 5-9-7 **77** GregFairley 4 82
(P A Blockley) *t.k.h: prom: drvn to dispute 2nd over 1f out: kpt on same pce* **20/1**

3344 **5** *½* **Resonate (IRE)**[38] 6499 9-9-3 **73** FergusSweeney 10 77
(A G Newcombe) *led after 2f: kicked on wl over 2f out: hdd and btn jst ins fnl f* **13/2**[2]

4335 **6** *1* **Inside Story (IRE)**[54] 6121 5-9-4 **74**....................(b) EddieAhern 6 76
(M W Easterby) *hld up towards rr: prog to chse ldrs 2f out: nt qckn over 1f out: kpt on* **9/1**

0200 **7** *1 1/2* **Resplendent Ace (IRE)**[17] 6848 3-8-9 **68**.................... MickyFenton 2 67
(P Howling) *trckd ldrs: lost pl over 3f out and rdn: effrt on inner over 1f out: no real imp* **20/1**

0160 **8** *3/4* **Touch Of Style (IRE)**[8] 6949 3-8-10 **76**.................... HarryPoulton(7) 8 74
(J R Boyle) *cl up: nt qckn over 2f out: hmpd wl over 1f out: btn after* **25/1**

3401 **9** *3/4* **Stark Contrast (USA)**[8] 6951 3-8-9 **68** 6ex.................... ChrisCatlin 9 64
(J Akehurst) *moslty chsd ldr fr 7f out to over 1f out: wknd* **9/1**

300 **10** *6* **Spirit Of The Mist (IRE)**[59] 6002 3-9-7 **80**....................(b[1]) RichardHughes 1 64
(D J Murphy) *plld hrd early: led 2f: cl up tl btn 2f out: eased whn no ch* **7/1[3]**

2600 **11** *19* **Salut Saint Cloud**[13] 6902 6-8-3 **66**....................(p) JemmaMarshall(7) 3 12
(G L Moore) *struggling in last over 4f out: t.o* **25/1**

2m 4.57s (-3.22) **Going Correction** -0.20s/f (Stan)
WFA 3 from 5yo+ 3lb **11** Ran SP% **125.5**
Speed ratings (Par 105): **104,103,102,102,102 101,100,99,99,94 79**
CSF £25.22 CT £70.35 TOTE £3.60: £1.90, £2.40, £1.90; EX 25.30 TRIFECTA Pool £225.39 - 3.42 winning units. Place 6 £56.28, Place 5 £30.92..
Owner R A Green **Bred** J L C Pearce **Trained** Woodingdean, E Sussex

FOCUS
A fair handicap run at a moderate pace. The form is fairly sound and there coulbe be more to come from Alpes Maritimes.
T/Plt: £45.30 to a £1 stake. Pool: £52,085.10. 838.85 winning tickets. T/Qpdt: £15.80 to a £1 stake. Pool: £2,819.10. 132.00 winning tickets. JN

7004 WOLVERHAMPTON (A.W) (L-H)
Tuesday, December 4

OFFICIAL GOING: Standard
Wind: Light behind, becoming fresher Weather: Overcast

7019 PONTIN'S HOLIDAYS MAIDEN STKS 5f 20y(P)
1:00 (1:00) (Class 5) 3-Y-0+ £2,968 (£876; £438) Stalls Low

Form RPR

03 **1** **Music Box Express**[15] 6877 3-9-3 0....................(e[1]) SteveDrowne 9 61
(D J Murphy) *trckd ldrs: racd keenly: hung lft fr over 1f out: sn rdn: r.o to ld wl ins fnl f* **9/4[1]**

22-0 **2** *1* **Wibbadune (IRE)**[12] 6905 3-8-12 56.................... LPKeniry 11 52
(Peter Grayson) *led 4f out: rdn over 1f out: sn edgd lft: hdd and unable qck wl ins fnl f* **12/1**

3242 **3** *1 1/4* **Perlachy**[15] 6877 3-9-0 58....................(v) DuranFentiman(3) 4 53
(Mrs N Macauley) *chsd ldrs: rdn 1/2-way: styd on* **5/2[2]**

4 *nk* **Irish Conection (IRE)** 4-9-0 0.................... JerryO'Dwyer(3) 3 51+
(T McLaughlin, Ire) *s.s: swtchd lft and hdwy over 1f out: nt rch ldrs* **10/1**

0660 **5** *nk* **Tumbleweed Di**[6] 6963 3-8-9 45 ow2....................(p) SladeO'Hara(5) 2 47
(G R Oldroyd) *prom: nt clr run and lost pl 4f out: hdwy over 1f out: styd on* **11/1**

2606 **6** *3/4* **Whats Your Game (IRE)**[28] 6702 3-9-3 47....................(b) PaulMulrennan 7 48
(A Berry) *led 1f: chsd ldrs: rdn over 1f out: no ex ins fnl f* **16/1**

0000 **7** *1 3/4* **Our Archie**[64] 5867 3-9-3 40....................(p) PatDobbs 6 41
(M J Attwater) *prom: rdn over 1f out: wknd fnl f* **50/1**

0040 **8** *1 1/4* **Kilvickeon (IRE)**[23] 6773 3-9-3 44.................... AdrianMcCarthy 12 37
(Peter Grayson) *mid-div: hdwy over 3f out: rdn and wknd over 1f out* **25/1**

0350 **9** *shd* **Boppys Dream**[46] 6309 5-8-12 40....................(p) FrankieMcDonald 10 31
(P T Midgley) *sn pushed along in rr: nvr nrr* **33/1**

0000 **10** *4* **Stoneacre Donny (IRE)**[130] 3924 3-8-10 45.................... RyanHill(7) 13 22
(Peter Grayson) *dwlt: a in rr* **80/1**

0006 **11** *1 1/2* **Acece**[18] 6830 3-9-3 40.................... HayleyTurner 8 17
(D K Ivory) *chsd ldrs to 1/2-way* **12/1**

12 *shd* **Chocolate Sands** 3-9-3 0.................... TPQueally 5 16
(J G Given) *hld up: effrt and nt clr run 1/2-way: a in rr* **7/1[3]**

0000 **13** *16* **Flying Princess (IRE)**[97] 4938 3-8-12 30....................(b[1]) StephenDonohoe 1 —
(A Berry) *sn outpcd* **150/1**

63.25 secs (0.43) **Going Correction** +0.025s/f (Slow) **13** Ran SP% **121.2**
Speed ratings (Par 103): **97,95,93,92,92 91,88,86,86,79 77,77,51**
CSF £30.38 TOTE £3.40: £1.60, £2.80, £1.40; EX 32.50 Trifecta £26.40 Pool £157.88 - 4.25 winning units..
Owner Willie McKay **Bred** Dachel Stud **Trained** Bawtry, S Yorks

FOCUS
Mainly exposed sorts in what was in essence a weak sprint maiden.

7020 STAY AT THE WOLVERHAMPTON HOLIDAY INN CLAIMING STKS 5f 216y(P)
1:30 (1:31) (Class 6) 3-Y-0+ £2,047 (£604; £302) Stalls Low

Form RPR

0020 **1** **Strabinios King**[17] 6476 3-8-7 55.................... PaulMulrennan 9 66
(P C Haslam) *s.i.s: hld up: hdwy over 2f out: rdn and hung lft fr over 1f out: styd on to ld whn rdr dropped reins wl ins fnl f* **11/1**

600 **2** *1* **Rainbow Bay**[13] 6891 4-8-13 59....................(v) StephenDonohoe 12 69
(P D Evans) *s.i.s: hld up: hdwy 2f out: rdn to ld 1f out: hdd wl ins fnl f* **14/1**

0063 **3** *1 1/4* **Gilded Cove**[24] 6764 7-9-3 63.................... RichardKingscote 13 69
(R Hollinshead) *hld up: hdwy over 1f out: sn rdn: edgd lft: nt rch ldrs* **7/1[2]**

3605 **4** *2* **Mister Elegant**[13] 6891 5-8-11 52.................... SteveDrowne 2 56
(J L Spearing) *mid-div: hdwy over 2f out: rdn and ev ch 1f out: no ex* **20/1**

6420 **5** *1* **Guto**[25] 6743 4-9-0 72.................... MCGeran(7) 4 63
(W J H Ratcliffe) *w ldr tl led 4f out: rdn and hdd 1f out: wknd wl ins fnl f* **10/1**

5660 **6** *3/4* **Mozakhraf (USA)**[8] 6947 5-9-3 62....................(p) PatCosgrave 5 59+
(K A Ryan) *prom: nt clr run over 2f out: sn outpcd* **9/1[3]**

0104 **7** *1/2* **Green Lagonda (AUS)**[13] 6890 5-9-7 60.................... HayleyTurner 3 59
(J G Given) *s.i.s: styd on fnl f: nvr nrr* **14/1**

1206 **8** *3/4* **Hart Of Gold**[13] 6891 3-9-5 73....................(p) LPKeniry 1 55
(R A Harris) *chsd ldrs: rdn and edgd rt over 2f out: wknd fnl f* **11/1**

00/4 **9** *1 3/4* **African Storm (IRE)**[26] 6730 5-9-4 0.................... JerryO'Dwyer(3) 10 51
(T McLaughlin, Ire) *chsd ldrs over 4f* **66/1**

0605 **10** *hd* **Phinerine**[7] 6957 4-8-4 53....................(b) TolleyDean(5) 7 39
(Miss J E Foster) *chsd ldrs: rdn over 1f out: wknd fnl f* **33/1**

1 **11** *hd* **Golden Surprice (IRE)**[15] 6873 5-9-7 0.................... OscarUrbina 6 50
(Aldo Locatelli, Italy) *sn pushed along: a in rr* **6/5[1]**

2340 **12** *10* **Le Masque**[10] 6938 3-9-0 62.................... MarkLawson(3) 8 14
(B Smart) *led 2f: sn rdn: hmpd over 2f out: sn wknd* **33/1**

1m 15.46s (-0.35) **Going Correction** +0.025s/f (Slow) **12** Ran SP% **119.2**
Speed ratings (Par 101): **103,101,100,97,96 95,94,93,91,90 90,77**
CSF £149.89 TOTE £15.20: £4.30, £5.00, £2.40; EX 193.30 TRIFECTA Not won..The winner was claimed by Miss Gay Kelleway for £5,000.
Owner Middleham Park Racing XLIV **Bred** Newsells Park Stud Limited **Trained** Middleham Moor, N Yorks

FOCUS
Mainly exposed sorts in this claimer but the fastest of the three races over the trip on the day. The form should work out well in this grade.
Golden Surprice(IRE) Official explanation: trainer had no explanation for the poor form shown
Le Masque Official explanation: jockey said gelding ran flat

7021 WOLVERHAMPTON-RACECOURSE.CO.UK (S) STKS 5f 216y(P)
2:00 (2:00) (Class 6) 2-Y-0 £2,047 (£604; £302) Stalls Low

Form RPR

0 **1** **Lujano**[29] 6693 2-9-0 0.................... PaulMulrennan 9 60
(Ollie Pears) *chsd ldrs: rdn and hung lft fr over 1f out: led ins fnl f: styd on* **16/1**

1652 **2** *1* **Maybe I Wont**[10] 6928 2-9-3 63.................... DuranFentiman(3) 7 63
(R M Stronge) *hld up: rdn over 2f out: hdwy u.p fr over 1f out: nt rch wnr* **5/2[1]**

5006 **3** *2* **Tommytush (IRE)**[20] 6813 2-9-0 60....................(t) DeanMcKeown 4 51
(E J Alston) *chsd ldr: rdn over 1f out: hung lft and no ex fnl f* **8/1**

0361 **4** *3/4* **Valhillen**[20] 6813 2-9-6 62.................... PatCosgrave 8 55
(M J Wallace) *chsd ldrs: rdn over 3f out: sn outpcd: styd on u.p ins fnl f* **10/3[2]**

6605 **5** *1/2* **Rio Rocket (IRE)**[7] 6958 2-8-9 54....................(b[1]) RichardKingscote 5 42+
(Tom Dascombe) *led: rdn over 1f out: wknd and hdd ins fnl f* **9/2[3]**

0000 **6** *2* **Zarees**[23] 6775 2-9-0 52....................(v[1]) SteveDrowne 2 41
(Miss Gay Kelleway) *chsd ldrs: rdn over 2f out: wknd fnl f* **16/1**

1400 **7** *3* **Bahamarama (IRE)**[15] 6872 2-9-1 61.................... LPKeniry 11 33
(R A Harris) *s.i.s: nvr nrr* **20/1**

00 **8** *1 1/2* **Primer Lugar**[69] 5734 2-8-2 0.................... MCGeran(7) 6 23
(W J H Ratcliffe) *s.i.s: outpcd* **66/1**

3040 **9** *2 1/2* **Prunes**[14] 6881 2-8-10 50 ow1....................(b) StephenDonohoe 3 16
(A Berry) *s.s: outpcd* **16/1**

3000 **10** *4* **Boot Strap Bill**[26] 6736 2-9-0 59....................(b[1]) HayleyTurner 12 8
(Miss J R Tooth) *chsd ldrs over 3f* **33/1**

4000 **11** *22* **Polish Priory (IRE)**[7] 6958 2-8-2 53....................(v) RichardEvans(7) 13 —
(P D Evans) *sn pushed along in rr: effrt over 3f out: wkng whn hung rt sn after* **16/1**

R **Clip Clop (IRE)** 2-8-2 0....................[1] AmyBaker(7) 1 —
(Miss J Feilden) *ref to r: tk no part* **12/1**

1m 16.65s (0.84) **Going Correction** +0.025s/f (Slow) **12** Ran SP% **121.4**
Speed ratings (Par 94): **95,93,91,90,89 86,82,80,77,72 42,—**
CSF £56.46 TOTE £22.00: £6.00, £1.90, £3.00; EX 102.70 Trifecta £176.80 Part won. Pool £249.02 - 0.30 winning units..There was no bid for the winner. Maybe I Wont was subject to a friendly claim.
Owner David Scott and Co (Pattern Makers) Ltd **Bred** D Scott **Trained** Norton, N Yorks
■ A first Flat winner for trainer Ollie Pears, who gained his first jumps winner the previous week.

FOCUS
A fair gallop to this juvenile seller but a slower time than the two older-horse races over the trip. Average form for the grade.

NOTEBOOK
Lujano, dropping in trip on only his second start, improved on his debut effort to run out a ready winner. A box-walker who lives outside, he may improve a little more and could make his mark in claimers or small nurseries. (op 14-1)
Maybe I Wont, dropping back in trip after finishing second over a mile on his previous start, kept on to finish a creditable second. (op 3-1 tchd 9-4)
Tommytush(IRE), who showed up from the outset, ran better back over this trip with the tongue tie back on. (tchd 10-1)
Valhillen could not confirm previous course running with the third on 10lb worse terms. (op 5-2 tchd 7-2)
Rio Rocket(IRE), tried in blinkers, broke well, showed plenty of speed and led until into the straight, but faded. (op 8-1)

7022 PONTIN'S GREAT FAMILY HOLIDAYS NURSERY 1m 141y(P)
2:30 (2:31) (Class 6) (0-65,65) 2-Y-0 £2,047 (£604; £302) Stalls Low

Form RPR

006 **1** **Kryptonite (IRE)**[132] 3849 2-9-3 **61**.................... SteveDrowne 12 65
(J W Hills) *hld up: hdwy over 2f out: led and hung lft fr over 1f out: sn rdn: r.o* **16/1**

042 **2** *1/2* **Artistic Light**[29] 6694 2-9-2 **60**.................... HayleyTurner 7 63
(W R Muir) *trckd ldrs: racd keenly: rdn over 1f out: r.o* **4/1[2]**

4000 **3** *3/4* **Ridgeway Jazz**[15] 6865 2-8-1 **45**.................... NickyMackay 2 46
(M D I Usher) *hld up: hdwy and nt clr run over 1f out: swtchd lft ins fnl f: r.o* **25/1**

0000 **4** *4* **Saturday Boy**[60] 5984 2-8-12 **63**.................... AndrewHeffernan(7) 9 56
(Paul Green) *hld up: plld hrd: hdwy over 1f out: no imp ins fnl f* **25/1**

6304 **5** *3/4* **Tiger's Rocket (IRE)**[13] 6899 2-9-3 **61**.................... PatDobbs 6 52
(R Hannon) *trckd ldrs: rdn over 2f out: wknd ins fnl f* **3/1[1]**

0525 **6** *nk* **Miss Bouggy Wouggy**[10] 6934 2-9-7 **65**.................... TPQueally 13 56
(M Blanshard) *chsd ldrs: rdn and ev ch over 1f out: wknd ins fnl f* **20/1**

1065 **7** *1 1/4* **Ambrose Princess (IRE)**[6] 6966 2-9-0 **58**.................... LPKeniry 10 46
(R A Harris) *led: hdd 7f out: chsd ldr: rdn over 1f out: sn hung lft and wknd* **10/1**

500 **8** *2* **Laureldean Breeze (USA)**[35] 6557 2-8-3 **47**.................... DaleGibson 8 31
(R A Fahey) *mid-div: rdn 1/2-way: wknd over 2f out* **9/2[3]**

0000 **9** *1 1/4* **Lord Of The Wing**[20] 6812 2-8-1 **45**.................... FrankieMcDonald 5 26
(P T Midgley) *sn outpcd* **50/1**

030 **10** *3 1/2* **Grapes Of Wrath (UAE)**[15] 6868 2-8-9 **53**.................... J-PGuillambert 11 27
(M Johnston) *chsd ldrs 6f* **8/1**

036 **11** *1/2* **Gaitskell**[14] 6884 2-9-2 **60**.................... PaulMulrennan 4 33+
(R Hollinshead) *led 7f out: rdn and hdd over 1f out: wknd and eased ins fnl f* **12/1**

0460 **U** **Ile Royale**[20] 6812 2-8-0 **49**....................(be) NicolPolli(5) 1 —
(C N Allen) *swvd rt and uns rdr s* **16/1**

1m 54.34s (2.58) **Going Correction** +0.025s/f (Slow) **12** Ran SP% **117.3**
Speed ratings (Par 94): **89,88,87,84,83 83,82,80,79,76 75,—**
CSF £75.06 CT £1654.08 TOTE £9.30: £4.20, £1.90, £7.30; EX 122.00 TRIFECTA Not won..
Owner R J Tufft **Bred** Pat Jones **Trained** Upper Lambourn, Berks
■ Stewards' Enquiry : Nicky Mackay one-day ban: careless riding (Dec 15)

FOCUS
A nursery run at a modest gallop and 4.45sec slower than the following older-horse handicap. Solid form for the grade, the first three clear.

NOTEBOOK

Kryptonite(IRE), who was making his nursery debut after a break of over four months, came from off the pace and travelled up well on the outside on the turn. He hung left when first asked for his effort, but though he then edged right in the final furlong, he ran on to score a shade comfortably. This was his first try at this trip and, though it was not a true test, it clearly suited him and he can win again. (op 12-1)

Artistic Light, another lightly-raced sort making her handicap debut, ran well enough in second to suggest she can pick up a race and the fact that she took a keen hold in the early stages may have cost her in the run to the line. (op 5-1)

Ridgeway Jazz, dropping in trip, had run in a seller and a claimer on her previous two outings but this was more encouraging and she was clear of the rest.

Saturday Boy put up an improved effort compared with his previous runs over course and distance despite having pulled hard.

Tiger's Rocket(IRE), dropping in grade after a fair effort on his previous outing, travelled well just off the pace, but could not quicken when asked. (op 11-4 tchd 5-2)

Gaitskell, though he had the run of the race, dictated the moderate gallop but dropped out very quickly in the straight. Official explanation: jockey said after making the running, colt had no more to give (tchd 14-1)

7023 GO PONTIN'S H'CAP — 1m 141y(P)

3:00 (3:00) (Class 6) (0-64,63) 3-Y-0+ — **£2,047** (£604; £302) **Stalls** Low

Form — RPR

111 **1** **Confidentiality (IRE)**[12] 6906 3-9-3 **63** .... NickyMackay 7 — 88+
(M Wigham) *hld up: hdwy over 2f out: led ins fnl f: shkn up and edgd lft: r.o wl* **6/4**[1]

0400 **2** *4* **King's Ransom**[20] 6816 4-9-2 **60** .... PaulMulrennan 8 — 69
(S Gollings) *mid-div: hdwy over 3f out: led over 1f out: sn rdn: hung lft and hdd ins fnl f: no ex* **14/1**

1262 **3** *1 3/4* **Keisha Kayleigh (IRE)**[18] 6837 4-9-5 **63** ....(v) J-PGuillambert 5 — 68
(B Ellison) *dwlt: hld up: hdwy u.p over 1f out: nt rch ldrs* **11/2**[3]

0060 **4** *1/2* **Western Roots**[96] 4959 6-9-1 **62** ....(p) NeilChalmers(3) 10 — 66
(M Appleby) *hld up: hdwy 2f out: sn rdn: wknd ins fnl f* **28/1**

4600 **5** *1/2* **Pop Music (IRE)**[15] 6874 4-9-2 **63** ....(p) JerryO'Dwyer(3) 3 — 66
(Miss J Feilden) *chsd ldr tl led 3f out: rdn and hdd over 1f out: wknd ins fnl f* **16/1**

0221 **6** *1/2* **Royal Envoy (IRE)**[34] 6582 4-8-12 **56** .... DeanMcKeown 6 — 58
(D Shaw) *hld up: hdwy over 2f out: wknd fnl f* **7/2**[2]

1140 **7** *6* **Time To Regret**[15] 6874 7-8-10 **59** ....(p) NataliaGemelova(5) 4 — 47
(I W McInnes) *chsd ldrs: rdn over 2f out: wknd wl over 1f out* **16/1**

0633 **8** *9* **Muncaster Castle (IRE)**[92] 5084 3-8-11 **57** .... SteveDrowne 9 — 24
(R F Fisher) *chsd ldrs: rdn over 2f out: wknd wl over 1f out* **10/1**

6016 **9** *1 1/2* **Cavallo Di Ferro (IRE)**[145] 3456 3-9-3 **63** .... StephenDonohoe 2 — 27
(M J Gingell) *hld up: rdn 1/2-way: wknd over 2f out* **40/1**

053- **10** *nk* **Todwick Owl**[431] 5647 3-9-1 **61** .... TPQueally 1 — 24
(J G Given) *led: racd keenly: hdd 3f out: wknd wl over 1f out* **25/1**

1m 49.89s (-1.87) **Going Correction** +0.025s/f (Slow)
WFA 3 from 4yo+ 2lb — 10 Ran SP% **114.9**
Speed ratings (Par 101): **109,105,103,103,103 102,97,89,87,87**
CSF £24.47 CT £94.30 TOTE £2.70: £1.30, £3.50, £1.90; EX 17.90 Trifecta £112.20 Pool £512.24 - 3.24 winning units..
Owner J M Cullinan **Bred** Kevin Foley **Trained** Newmarket, Suffolk

FOCUS
A fair gallop to this handicap and the time was 4.45sec faster than the preceding nursery and very decent for the grade. The form is rated through the third, and impressive winner Confidentiality was value for extra.
Muncaster Castle(IRE) Official explanation: jockey said gelding hung badly left

7024 GO PONTIN'S HOLIDAYS H'CAP (DIV I) — 7f 32y(P)

3:30 (3:31) (Class 6) (0-62,62) 3-Y-0+ — **£1,706** (£503; £252) **Stalls** High

Form — RPR

4303 **1** **Dasheena**[7] 6962 4-8-5 **54** ....(be) PatrickMathers(3) 6 — 65
(A J McCabe) *s.i.s: hld up: hdwy u.p over 1f out: led ins fnl f: r.o* **6/1**[3]

612 **2** *1 1/2* **Tanforan**[15] 6869 5-9-2 **62** .... PaulMulrennan 3 — 69
(B P J Baugh) *trckd ldrs: led over 1f out: hdd and unable qck ins fnl f* **9/2**[1]

0300 **3** *1/2* **Takitwo**[15] 6869 4-9-2 **62** .... LPKeniry 4 — 68
(P D Cundell) *chsd ldrs: rdn over 1f out: edgd lft and styd on same pce fnl f* **5/1**[2]

0604 **4** *2* **Empire Dancer (IRE)**[7] 6955 4-8-11 **60** .... AndrewElliott(3) 9 — 60
(I W McInnes) *s.i.s: hld up: hdwy u.p over 1f out: nvr nrr* **6/1**[3]

0200 **5** *1 3/4* **Radiator Rooney (IRE)**[37] 6344 4-8-5 **51** ....(p) HayleyTurner 10 — 46
(Patrick Morris, Ire) *chsd ldrs: led over 2f out: rdn and hdd over 1f out: wknd ins fnl f* **13/2**

3300 **6** *1/2* **Wiltshire (IRE)**[114] 4423 5-8-8 **54** .... FrankieMcDonald 8 — 50
(P T Midgley) *hld up: nt clr run over 2f out: siwtched lft over 1f out: nt trble ldrs* **20/1**

00 **7** *1 1/4* **Bungie**[25] 6747 3-8-5 **58** .... AndrewHeffernan(7) 11 — 49
(Paul Green) *hld up: rdn over 2f out: n.d* **28/1**

0000 **8** *2* **Stoic Leader (IRE)**[28] 6701 7-9-0 **60** .... SteveDrowne 1 — 49
(R F Fisher) *led over 4f: wknd fnl f* **7/1**

300 **9** *nk* **Lincolneurocruiser**[17] 6859 5-8-12 **58** ....(v) TPQueally 12 — 43
(Mrs N Macauley) *s.i.s: hld up: hdwy over 2f out: rdn and wknd fnl f* **9/1**

0 **10** *3 1/2* **Hazelwood Ridge (IRE)**[60] 5994 4-8-11 **57** .... DaleGibson 7 — 32
(Joseph Fox, Ire) *s.i.s: sn chsng ldrs: rdn 1/2-way: wknd over 2f out* **25/1**

0006 **11** *2 1/2* **Kims Rose (IRE)**[7] 6957 4-8-7 **53** .... LiamJones 5 — 21
(R A Harris) *w ldr tl rdn over 2f out: wknd over 1f out* **12/1**

1m 30.43s (0.03) **Going Correction** +0.025s/f (Slow) — 11 Ran SP% **119.0**
Speed ratings (Par 101): **100,98,97,95,93 92,91,89,88,84 81**
CSF £32.73 CT £147.73 TOTE £8.10: £2.40, £1.10, £2.20; EX 31.90 Trifecta £181.60 Pool £299.35 - 1.17 winning units..
Owner Paul J Dixon **Bred** Mrs Yvette Dixon **Trained** Babworth, Notts

FOCUS
An open handicap run at a strong early gallop but fractionally slower than the second division. The winner is rated back to her best and the form seems sound.
Lincolneurocruiser Official explanation: jockey said gelding hung right-handed in home straight

7025 GO PONTIN'S HOLIDAYS H'CAP (DIV II) — 7f 32y(P)

4:00 (4:02) (Class 6) (0-62,62) 3-Y-0+ — **£1,706** (£503; £252) **Stalls** High

Form — RPR

5524 **1** **Cabourg (IRE)**[13] 6895 4-8-9 **55** ow1 .... SteveDrowne 4 — 64
(R Bastiman) *a.p: rdn to ld ins fnl f: edgd lft: r.o* **11/2**[3]

3121 **2** *1 1/2* **The City Kid (IRE)**[39] 6476 4-9-1 **61** .... SaleemGolam 11 — 66
(S C Williams) *hld up: nt clr run over 2f out: hdwy over 1f out: rdn and swtchd lft ins fnl f: r.o: nt rch wnr* **7/2**[2]

2050 **3** *hd* **Prince Rossi (IRE)**[24] 6764 3-8-4 **53** ....(p) AndrewElliott(3) 6 — 57
(J D Bethell) *led 6f out: rdn over 1f out: hdd and unable qck ins fnl f* **33/1**

3003 **4** *3/4* **Astroangel**[28] 6704 3-8-12 **58** .... PaulMulrennan 3 — 60
(M H Tompkins) *hld up in tch: rdn 1/2-way: outpcd over 2f out: rallied over 1f out: no ex wl ins fnl f* **12/1**

060- **5** *hd* **Smirfys Systems**[427] 5752 8-8-5 **51** oh3 .... NickyMackay 8 — 53+
(E S McMahon) *hld up: hdwy over 2f out: rdn over 1f out: styd on same pce* **40/1**

0232 **6** *3/4* **Rabbit Fighter (IRE)**[3] 6993 3-9-0 **60** ....(v) TPQueally 10 — 60+
(D Shaw) *hld up: hdwy u.p over 1f out: nt trble ldrs* **5/2**[1]

2445 **7** *3/4* **Obe Royal**[18] 6838 3-8-7 **60** ....(p) RichardEvans(7) 9 — 60+
(P D Evans) *s.i.s: hld up: nt clr run over 2f out: rdn and hmpd over 1f out: n.d* **10/1**

0003 **8** *3/4* **Campo Bueno (FR)**[26] 6732 5-8-10 **56** .... StephenDonohoe 2 — 52
(A Berry) *prom: chsd ldr over 4f out: rdn and ev ch 2f out: wknd fnl f* **22/1**

0 **9** *1 3/4* **Trammon Ventre (IRE)**[23] 6779 3-8-5 **51** oh1 ....(b) JamieMackay 1 — 42
(Eamon Tyrrell, Ire) *led 1f: chsd ldr to over 4f out: remained handy: rdn over 2f out: edgd lft and wknd over 1f out* **66/1**

-543 **10** *2* **Far Seeking**[67] 5781 3-9-2 **62** .... LiamJones 12 — 48
(R A Harris) *s.i.s: hld up: nt clr run over 2f out: rdn and hung lft over 1f out: n.d* **12/1**

4164 **11** *3/4* **Briery Blaze**[3] 7003 4-8-5 **51** ....(b) HayleyTurner 5 — 35
(J W Unett) *hld up: a in rr* **11/1**

0422 **12** *nk* **Elusive Warrior (USA)**[30] 6677 4-8-11 **57** ....(p) DaleGibson 7 — 40
(R A Fahey) *chsd ldrs over 4f* **6/1**

1m 30.11s (-0.29) **Going Correction** +0.025s/f (Slow) — 12 Ran SP% **124.5**
Speed ratings (Par 101): **102,100,100,99,98 98,97,96,94,92 91,90**
CSF £25.73 CT £613.23 TOTE £6.40: £2.30, £1.70, £11.60; EX 31.30 Trifecta £266.50 Part won. Pool £375.49 - 0.20 winning units..
Owner Ms M Austerfield **Bred** Swettenham Stud **Trained** Cowthorpe, N Yorks

FOCUS
The second division of the 7f handicap, run 0.32sec faster than the first leg. The form looks pretty solid.
Trammon Ventre(IRE) Official explanation: jockey said filly became unbalanced in straight

7026 PONTINS.COM H'CAP — 5f 216y(P)

4:30 (4:32) (Class 5) (0-75,75) 3-Y-0+ — **£2,968** (£876; £438) **Stalls** Low

Form — RPR

21-2 **1** **Hello Man (IRE)**[4] 6972 4-8-12 **72** .... JerryO'Dwyer(3) 3 — 89+
(Eamon Tyrrell, Ire) *trckd ldrs: n.m.r and lost pl 4f out: hdwy over 2f out: swtchd rt over 1f out: sn hung lft: led ins fnl f: rdn out* **13/8**[1]

5023 **2** *1 1/2* **Tag Team (IRE)**[20] 6818 6-8-1 **61** oh1 .... AndrewElliott(3) 7 — 69
(John A Harris) *chsd ldr: led over 4f out: rdn over 1f out: hdd and unable qckn ins fnl f* **8/1**

0344 **3** *1* **Jilly Why (IRE)**[14] 6885 6-7-12 **62** ....(b) AndrewHeffernan(7) 2 — 67
(Paul Green) *mid-div: n.m.r and lost pl 4f out: hdwy u.p over 1f out: no ex towards fin* **16/1**

0505 **4** *3/4* **Jord (IRE)**[7] 6962 3-8-9 **66** .... SteveDrowne 1 — 68
(A J McCabe) *led: hdd over 4f out: rdn over 2f out: styd on same pce* **12/1**

0054 **5** *1* **Tous Les Deux**[10] 6938 4-8-10 **67** .... LPKeniry 5 — 66
(Peter Grayson) *s.i.s: hld up: hdwy u.p over 1f out: edgd lft: nt rch ldrs* **10/1**

0332 **6** *1 1/4* **Strathmore (IRE)**[10] 6938 3-8-7 **64** ....(p) DaleGibson 12 — 62+
(R A Fahey) *hld up: nt clr run wl over 1f out: styd on ins fnl f: nt trble ldrs* **8/1**

0330 **7** *2* **Highland Song (IRE)**[62] 5908 4-8-4 **61** oh12 .... DavidKinsella 11 — 50
(R F Fisher) *chsd ldrs: rdn over 2f out: wknd fnl f* **66/1**

1301 **8** *1/2* **Memphis Man**[11] 6910 4-8-5 **69** .... RichardEvans(7) 8 — 56
(P D Evans) *hld up: hdwy over 3f out: rdn over 2f out: wknd over 1f out* **4/1**[2]

00 **9** *nk* **Hill Of Lujain**[163] 2912 3-8-11 **68** .... StephenDonohoe 9 — 54
(Ian Williams) *s.s: outpcd* **50/1**

6000 **10** *1/2* **Cool Sands (IRE)**[12] 6907 5-8-11 **68** ....(v) DeanMcKeown 6 — 53
(D Shaw) *prom over 3f* **12/1**

3665 **11** *5* **Swinbrook (USA)**[43] 6385 6-9-2 **73** .... PatCosgrave 10 — 42
(R A Fahey) *chsd ldrs: rn wd 1/2-way: sn rdn and wknd: b.b.v* **5/1**[3]

6-1 **12** *6* **Fustaan (IRE)**[307] 311 3-9-4 **75** .... PatDobbs 4 — 24
(A G Newcombe) *prom: n.m.r over 2f out: sn rdn and wknd* **16/1**

1m 15.5s (-0.31) **Going Correction** +0.025s/f (Slow) — 12 Ran SP% **136.7**
Speed ratings (Par 103): **103,101,99,98,97 95,93,92,91,91 84,76**
CSF £19.02 CT £187.47 TOTE £3.10: £1.30, £3.40, £5.20; EX 19.70 Trifecta £320.70 Part won. Pool £451.75 0 - 0.46 winning units. Place 6 £116.56, Place 5 £78.53..
Owner Tailor Made Syndicate **Bred** William Moloney **Trained** The Curragh, Co Kildare

FOCUS
Just an ordinary gallop to this 6f handicap and slightly slower than the earlier claimer. Few featured and front runners were possibly favoured. The form seems sound.
Strathmore(IRE) Official explanation: jockey said gelding was denied a clear run
Hill Of Lujain Official explanation: jockey said gelding missed the break
Swinbrook(USA) Official explanation: trainer said gelding bled from the nose
T/Jkpt: Not won. T/Plt: £38.90 to a £1 stake. Pool: £42,638.20. 798.35 winning tickets. T/Qpdt: £4.70 to a £1 stake. Pool: £4,356.00. 679.10 winning tickets. CR

6909 DEAUVILLE (R-H)

Tuesday, December 4

OFFICIAL GOING: Standard

7027a PRIX CHINGACGOOK (C&G) (ALL-WEATHER) — 7f 110y

10:20 (10:20) 2-Y-O — **£11,149** (£4,459; £3,345; £2,230; £1,115)

RPR

1 **Traphalgar (IRE)**[13] 6899 2-9-0 .... SPasquier 7 — 80
(P F I Cole) *prom: 2nd and chalng st: led 1 1/2f out: styd on wl to line* **6/5**[1]

2 *1 1/2* **Surething (FR)**[22] 2-8-13 .... MMartinez(5) 1 — 80
(M Rolland, France)

3 *1* **Unidentified Thief (FR)** 2-8-7 .... DelphineSantiago 8 — 67
(J E Hammond, France)

4 *1 1/2* **Barnaby Rudge (IRE)**[15] 6879 2-9-0 .... TGMcLaughlin 6 — 71
(Jane Chapple-Hyam) *led: drvn st: hdd 1 1/2f out: no ex* **49/10**[2]

5 *hd* **Lone Star (GER)** 2-8-10 .... FSpanu 4 — 66
(M Trybuhl, Germany)

6 *nse* **Adagio (BEL)** 2-9-0 .... OPlacais 2 — 70
(Andre Hermans, Belgium)

7 *3* **Enrisy (FR)** 2-9-0 .... WMongil 3 — 63
(Mme L Audon, France)

The Form Book, Raceform Ltd, Compton, RG20 6NL

8 5 **Pimlico Dralliv (FR)** 2-9-0 .... GPardon 5 51
(J-P Gauvin, France)

1m 29.8s (89.80) **8** Ran SP% **62.4**
PARI-MUTUEL (Including 1 Euro stake): WIN 2.20; PL 1.30, 2.10, 4.10; DF 8.50.
Owner The Fairy Story Partnership **Bred** Deepwood Farm Stud **Trained** Whatcombe, Oxon

NOTEBOOK
Traphalgar(IRE), twice a winner - over 7f and 1m at Lingfield last month - was well suited by this intermediate distance and, starting a well-backed favourite, scored in good style. There could be more to come.
Barnaby Rudge(IRE), who made all when scoring over a furlong shorter here last month, adopted the same tactics but could not get a break on his rivals and did not last home.

6990 KEMPTON (A.W) (R-H)

Wednesday, December 5

OFFICIAL GOING: Standard
Wind: Strong, half behind Weather: Overcast

7028 KEMPTON FOR CONFERENCES APPRENTICE H'CAP 1m (P)

6:20 (6:20) (Class 6) (0-58,58) 3-Y-0+ **£2,047** (£604; £302) **Stalls** High

Form RPR
2044 **1** **Carlitos Spirit (IRE)**[26] 6749 3-9-3 **58** .... JamesMillman 14 69
(B R Millman) *mde all: kicked clr 3f out: at least 5 l ahd over 1f out: tired and drvn out: unchal* **4/1**[2]

3013 **2** *3 1/2* **Royal Embrace**[18] 6859 4-9-4 **58** ....(v) PatrickHills 6 61+
(D Shaw) *hld up towards rr: prog 1/2-way: rdn and nt keen over 2f out: styd on to go 2nd 1f out and sn clr of rest: no ch w wnr* **7/2**[1]

060 **3** *2 1/2* **Winged Farasi**[26] 6749 3-8-13 **57** .... WilliamCarson(3) 7 54
(R A Harris) *prom: chsd wnr over 5f out to over 2f out: under pressed after: plugged on* **11/1**

1330 **4** *shd* **Earl Kraul (IRE)**[275] 616 4-8-7 **52** .... RossAtkinson(5) 10 49
(G L Moore) *hld up in rr: gd prog against rail 3f out to chse ldrs over 2f out: wnt 2nd over 1f out to 1f out: no ex* **17/2**

3000 **5** *3/4* **Krakatau (FR)**[16] 6869 3-8-12 **58** .... MatthewDavies(5) 12 53
(D J Wintle) *chsd ldrs: outpcd by wnr whn effrt over 2f out: kpt on same pce* **25/1**

0000 **6** *3/4* **Baba Ghanoush**[19] 6831 5-9-1 **55** .... KirstyMilczarek 13 49
(J Akehurst) *chsd wnr to over 5f out and again over 2f out to over 1f out: wknd fnl f* **14/1**

0446 **7** *1/2* **Mick Is Back**[28] 6716 3-9-0 **58** ....(p) JackMitchell(3) 9 50
(G G Margarson) *hld up wl in rr: effrt 3f out: plugged on u.p: no ch* **8/1**

0315 **8** *nk* **Jessica Wigmo**[21] 6809 4-8-6 **49** .... KellyHarrison(3) 5 41
(A W Carroll) *dwlt: wl in rr: prog on inner over 2f out: no imp over 1f out: fdd fnl f* **9/1**

0403 **9** *1/2* **Mythical Charm**[23] 6796 8-8-11 **54** ....(t) JackDean(3) 8 45
(J J Bridger) *pushed along early: sn chsd ldrs gng wl enough 3f out: sn rdn and fnd nil* **6/1**[3]

0355 **10** *8* **Calloff The Search**[7] 6963 3-8-11 **52** .... TolleyDean 11 24
(Stef Liddiard) *t.k.h: hld up in rr: effrt and drvn over 2f out: sn no prog: eased fnl f: t.o* **12/1**

6025 **11** *3 1/2* **Contented (IRE)**[14] 6895 5-8-10 **53** ....(p) SCreighton(3) 1 17
(Mrs L C Jewell) *nvr bttr than midfield: wknd over 2f out: t.o* **12/1**

3-65 **12** *1/2* **Claws**[282] 571 4-8-12 **52** .... HaddenFrost 3 15
(A J Lidderdale) *chsd ldrs tl wknd rapidly over 2f out: t.o* **12/1**

5406 **13** *1/2* **Gee Ceffyl Bach**[8] 6955 3-8-9 **55** .... KrishGundowry(5) 4 17
(R C Guest) *racd v wd: in tch tl lost plenty of grnd bnd over 3f out: sn bhd* **11/1**

1m 39.71s (-1.09) **Going Correction** 0.0s/f (Stan)
WFA 3 from 4yo+ 1lb **13** Ran SP% **138.4**
Speed ratings (Par 101): **105,101,99,98,98 97,96,96,96,88 84,84,83**
CSF £21.74 CT £164.90 TOTE £5.80: £2.10, £1.90, £4.00; EX 25.30.
Owner Karmaa Racing Limited **Bred** Tally-Ho Stud **Trained** Kentisbeare, Devon

FOCUS
A low-grade handicap. It was comfortable for Carlitos Spirit, but he was given an easy lead and there are doubts over the form.
Royal Embrace Official explanation: jockey said gelding lost its action
Claws Official explanation: jockey said filly ran too freely

7029 ANDREW TARBET MEDIAN AUCTION MAIDEN STKS 7f (P)

6:50 (6:52) (Class 6) 3-5-Y-0 **£2,047** (£604; £302) **Stalls** High

Form RPR
335 **1** **Affrettando (IRE)**[100] 4905 3-9-3 60 .... EddieAhern 10 63
(J A R Toller) *lw: t.k.h early: trckd ldng pair: rdn to ld wl over 1f out: kpt on wl whn pressed fnl f* **9/4**[1]

3325 **2** *3/4* **Towy Girl (IRE)**[51] 6240 3-8-12 65 .... JimCrowley 13 56
(A W Carroll) *hld up bhd ldrs: prog over 2f out: swtchd lft wl over 1f out: rdn to press wnr jst over 1f out: fnd little and a hld* **5/2**[2]

U0 **3** *1/2* **North South Divide (IRE)**[37] 6546 3-9-3 0 .... GeorgeBaker 4 64+
(R A Teal) *stdd s: hld up in last pair: effrt whn hmpd twice over 2f out: gd prog over 1f out: styd on wl fnl f: nrst fin* **10/1**

0000 **4** *1 1/4* **Ginger Pop**[212] 1541 3-9-3 55 .... J-PGuillambert 7 57
(G G Margarson) *t.k.h: led at stdy pce: kicked on over 2f out: hdd over 1f out: wknd ins fnl f* **25/1**

6 **5** *1 1/4* **Eleanor Eloise (USA)**[16] 6877 3-8-12 0 .... LiamJones 2 48
(J R Gask) *w'like: t.k.h: cl up: rdn over 2f out: one pce and btn over 1f out* **33/1**

4 **6** *nk* **Coloso**[172] 2674 3-9-3 0 .... ChrisCatlin 14 52
(P D Cundell) *lw: dwlt: hld up in last trio: rdn and prog on inner fr 2f out: kpt on: n.d* **10/1**

0604 **7** *1 1/4* **Falcon Flyer**[19] 6830 3-8-12 41 .... TPQueally 11 44
(J R Best) *t.k.h: hld up and sn in rr: rdn over 2f out: kpt on u.p but n.d* **20/1**

0243 **8** *3 1/2* **Alexander Guru**[13] 6904 3-9-3 65 .... SteveDrowne 3 40
(M Blanshard) *trckd ldrs: rdn over 2f out: wknd over 1f out* **7/2**[3]

9 *1 1/4* **Kilmeena Dream** 3-8-12 0 .... PatDobbs 12 31
(J C Fox) *dwlt: hld up wl in rr: effrt whn nt clr run 2f out: immediately wknd* **50/1**

00 **10** *2 1/2* **Tagula Sands (IRE)**[24] 6778 3-8-12 0 .... HaddenFrost(5) 6 29
(J C Fox) *t.k.h: w ldr to 3f out: wknd over 1f out* **33/1**

5 **11** *1 1/4* **Stratn Jack**[14] 6901 3-9-3 0 .... RichardKingscote 8 26
(B G Powell) *dwlt: racd wd in rr: effrt but lost grnd bnd 3f out: sn struggling* **16/1**

-060 **12** *shd* **Pink Salmon**[86] 5280 3-8-12 56 .... IanMongan 9 21
(Mrs L J Mongan) *sn drvn in midfield: wknd over 2f out* **40/1**

0 **13** *4* **Bakers Boy**[24] 6778 3-8-12 0 .... NataliaGemelova(5) 1 15
(J E Long) *drvn in midfield after 3f: struggling after: sn bhd* **40/1**

1m 27.83s (1.03) **Going Correction** 0.0s/f (Stan) **13** Ran SP% **127.0**
Speed ratings (Par 101): **94,93,92,91,89 89,87,83,82,79 78,78,73**
CSF £7.96 TOTE £3.40: £1.70, £1.40, £2.20; EX 11.10.
Owner Lady Sophia Topley **Bred** R Fagan **Trained** Newmarket, Suffolk

FOCUS
This was run at a steady pace and the time was slow compared with the nursery. Affretando might not have had to improve to land this moderate event and the form has been rated around the fourth and seventh.
Ginger Pop Official explanation: jockey said gelding hung left

7030 DIGIBET.COM CLAIMING STKS 6f (P)

7:20 (7:24) (Class 6) 2-Y-0 **£2,047** (£604; £302) **Stalls** High

Form RPR
0052 **1** **River Bounty**[5] 6977 2-8-8 64 ....(v) NeilPollard 5 61+
(A P Jarvis) *racd freely early: mde all: jnd over 1f out: styd on wl and in command ins fnl f* **15/8**[1]

0U6 **2** *1 1/2* **Little Finch (IRE)**[36] 6566 2-7-11 38 ....(b) DuranFentiman(3) 7 49
(R C Guest) *chsd wnr to 2f out: hld after: kpt on fnl f to take 2nd again last stride* **66/1**

0440 **3** *shd* **Coole Dodger (IRE)**[5] 6973 2-9-2 68 .... GeorgeBaker 6 64
(B G Powell) *wl in tch: prog on inner to press wnr 2f out: upsides over 1f out: outbattled fnl f: lost 2nd last stride* **11/4**[2]

0224 **4** *2* **Mairead's Boy (IRE)**[19] 6828 2-8-2 58 ....(b) TolleyDean(5) 3 49
(J S Moore) *chsd ldng pair: rdn over 2f out: sn nt qckn and hld: kpt on* **7/2**

0000 **5** *1/2* **Zahwah**[28] 6722 2-8-2 50 ....(b) ChrisCatlin 2 43
(J G Portman) *tended to r wd in last: rdn and effrt wl over 2f out: one pce over 1f out* **20/1**

0504 **6** *hd* **Her Name Is Rio (IRE)**[48] 6282 2-7-13 69 .... NataliaGemelova(5) 1 44
(J S Moore) *hanging lft and lost grnd bnd over 4f out to 3f out: struggling after* **3/1**[3]

1m 14.63s (0.93) **Going Correction** 0.0s/f (Stan) **6** Ran SP% **114.9**
Speed ratings (Par 94): **93,91,90,88,87 87**
CSF £82.30 TOTE £2.80: £1.60, £5.30; EX 39.80.Mairead's Boy was claimed by P. Butler for £6,000.
Owner Christopher Shankland **Bred** Limestone & Tara Studs **Trained** Twyford, Bucks

FOCUS
Not a race to be with but the form seems sound enough.

NOTEBOOK
River Bounty, back up in trip for this quick return to action, raced somewhat freely in the visor but was able to dicatate the pace and run out a workmanlike winner. She might stay 7f. (op 6-4 tchd 11-8)
Little Finch(IRE), down in trip and with blinkers back on in place of the visor, ran well above her official mark of just 38 and would be of interest if turned out before she is reassessed. (op 40-1)
Coole Dodger(IRE), back down in trip, challenged the winner on the inside in the straight but with the winning jockey's stick flailing there was never that much of a gap and he could not or would not go through it. Baker had to stop riding for a couple of strides inside the last and that cost him second. Official explanation: jockey said colt hung right throughout (op 4-1 tchd 9-2)
Mairead's Boy(IRE), who is edging up the weights, ran below his recent level. (op 11-2)
Her Name Is Rio(IRE) had a leading chance on her easy-ground turf form but ran most disappointingly on this sand debut. (op 5-2 tchd 7-2)

7031 DIGIBET NURSERY 7f (P)

7:50 (7:53) (Class 6) (0-65,65) 2-Y-0 **£2,047** (£604; £302) **Stalls** High

Form RPR
4565 **1** **Bookish**[18] 6849 2-9-6 **64** .... GregFairley 3 66
(M Johnston) *trckd ldng pair: rdn to chal 2f out: styd on wl to ld last 75yds* **17/2**

2434 **2** *1/2* **What's For Tea**[7] 6966 2-9-2 **60** .... RichardKingscote 7 61
(Tom Dascombe) *lw: led 1f: w ldr tl led again 3f out: drvn 2f out: worn down last 75yds* **11/4**[1]

050 **3** *nk* **Miss Phoebe (IRE)**[39] 6503 2-9-7 **65** .... GeorgeBaker 6 65
(S Kirk) *lw: towards rr on outer: rdn wl over 2f out: prog over 1f out: styd on to take 3rd ins fnl f: gaining at fin* **10/1**

1020 **4** *1 1/2* **Too Grand**[7] 6966 2-8-13 **60** ....(v) NeilChalmers(3) 2 57
(J J Bridger) *hld up in rr: prog on inner 2f out: kpt on same pce fnl f: nvr able to chal* **20/1**

6500 **5** *shd* **Athboy Auction**[39] 6502 2-9-0 **63** .... HaddenFrost(5) 10 59
(H J Collingridge) *prom: rdn over 2f out: cl enough but nt qckn over 1f out: one pce after* **7/1**[3]

0244 **6** *shd* **Gunner Fly (IRE)**[21] 6812 2-9-6 **64** .... DaleGibson 4 60
(R A Fahey) *lw: dwlt: rn in snatches in last pair: prog 2f out: styd on wl fnl f: nrst fin* **7/2**[2]

050 **7** *1* **Aim**[57] 6080 2-9-1 **59** .... JimCrowley 1 53
(J R Jenkins) *sn in last pair: rdn 2f out: prog over 1f out: styd on same pce fnl f* **50/1**

040 **8** *1 1/4* **Silver Sprite**[23] 6799 2-8-13 **57** .... DeanMcKeown 8 47
(D Shaw) *nvr bttr than midfield: drvn and struggling over 2f out: plugged on again fnl f* **33/1**

0602 **9** *1/2* **Kaystar Ridge**[7] 6966 2-9-4 **62** .... PatDobbs 9 51
(D K Ivory) *w.w in midfield: rdn to chse ldrs 2f out: no imp 1f out: wknd* **15/2**

5640 **10** *3/4* **Lella Beya**[21] 6812 2-9-5 **63** .... LPKeniry 12 50
(S Kirk) *prom tl lost pl u.p over 2f out: no ch after* **50/1**

1005 **11** *1/2* **Ten Spot (IRE)**[24] 6776 2-9-0 **58** .... MickyFenton 11 44
(Stef Liddiard) *wl in rr: rdn 3f out: no prog: kpt on* **14/1**

0333 **12** *nk* **Express Princess (IRE)**[12] 6912 2-9-6 **64** .... EddieAhern 13 49
(M Botti) *nvr beyond midfield: no prog over 2f out: wknd over 1f out* **15/2**

0260 **13** *5* **Imaginemysurprise**[11] 6933 2-8-12 **56** .... SteveDrowne 14 29
(J A Geake) *dwlt: rcvrd on inner to ld after 1f: hdd 3f out: wknd rapidly* **20/1**

1m 28.04s (1.24) **Going Correction** 0.0s/f (Stan) **13** Ran SP% **127.6**
Speed ratings (Par 94): **92,91,91,89,89 89,88,86,86,85 84,84,78**
CSF £32.67 CT £252.49 TOTE £10.10: £3.30, £1.60, £3.10; EX 57.90.
Owner Sheikh Mohammed **Bred** Darley **Trained** Middleham Moor, N Yorks

FOCUS
A very modest nursery with few progressive types on show. The form seems solid enough.

NOTEBOOK
Bookish, making her handicap debut, again raced prominently. She showed a decent attitude to get on top in the last half-furlong but, although she is a consistent filly, she might struggle to add to this. (op 10-1 tchd 8-1)
What's For Tea, returning to 7f, was back in front entering the staright and battled on, but just succumbed to the favourite's challenge late on. (op 4-1 tchd 5-2)
Miss Phoebe(IRE), on her nursery bow, finished well down the outside and looks ready for a try over a mile.

Too Grand, having her second start since leaving Andrew Balding, made good progress along the inside rail in the straight but the effort flattened out in the final furlong. Official explanation: jockey said filly missed the break (op 12-1)

Athboy Auction was still in third place entering the final furlong but the longer trip then seemed to find her out. (op 8-1 tchd 9-1)

Gunner Fly(IRE), tackling 7f for the first time, missed the break once again. He made good late progress when the race was over and things should click for him one day. (op 4-1)

7032 DIGIBET CASINO CLAIMING STKS 1m 3f (P)
8:20 (8:21) (Class 6) 3-Y-O £2,047 (£604; £302) Stalls High

Form RPR

2134 1 **Pearl (IRE)**[18] 6856 3-9-4 71 LiamJones 2 64
(W J Haggas) *lw: dwlt: sn prom: wnt 2nd 1/2-way: pushed into ld over 3f out: drvn and hrd pressed 2f out: styd on* 4/6[1]

0030 2 1 1/4 **Soldier Field**[28] 6719 3-8-0 53 (p) DavidProbert(7) 3 51
(A M Balding) *hld up: smooth prog 4f out: jnd wnr over 2f out to over 1f out: nt qckn fnl f* 4/1[2]

633 3 3/4 **Satindra (IRE)**[19] 6833 3-8-9 56 (tp) TPQueally 9 52
(John A Harris) *led to over 3f out: styd pressing wnr to over 2f out: kpt on same pce* 15/2

1302 4 1 1/4 **Red Current**[19] 6833 3-9-4 63 LPKeniry 7 59
(R A Harris) *lw: trckd ldrs: gng wl 3f out: rdn and no rspnse jst over 2f out* 6/1[3]

0000 5 nk **The Slider**[23] 6792 3-8-2 42 ChrisCatlin 1 42
(Mrs L C Jewell) *in tch: rdn 4f out: no imp on ldrs over 2f out: plugged on* 33/1

0006 6 1/2 **Sadler's Hill (IRE)**[69] 4473 3-8-7 40 HayleyTurner 4 46
(M J McGrath) *trckd ldr to 1/2-way: rdn over 4f out: wknd 2f out* 33/1

0005 7 2 1/2 **Snake Hips**[57] 6090 3-8-7 42 (p) RichardKingscote 5 42
(B Palling) *lw: a in rr: struggling over 3f out: brief effrt on inner over 2f out: sn btn* 14/1

00 8 48 **Flashin Amber**[16] 6877 3-9-1 0 AdamKirby 8 —
(Peter Grayson) *stdd s: a last: struggling bef 1/2-way: t.o over 3f out* 40/1

2m 22.88s (0.20) **Going Correction** 0.0s/f (Stan) 8 Ran SP% **121.0**
Speed ratings (Par 98): **99,98,97,96,96 96,94,59**
CSF £3.97 TOTE £1.70: £1.02, £1.30, £2.60; EX 4.60.The winner was claimed by I. A. Wood for £14,000. Soldier Field was claimed by J. S. Wainwright for £6,000.
Owner Mr & Mrs G Middlebrook **Bred** G And Mrs Middlebrook **Trained** Newmarket, Suffolk
■ Stewards' Enquiry : Liam Jones one-day ban: excessive use of the whip (Dec 16)

FOCUS
A weak and steadily-run claimer, and not form to take too seriously.
Flashin Amber Official explanation: jockey said gelding was never travelling

7033 TFM NETWORKS H'CAP 6f (P)
8:50 (8:53) (Class 5) (0-70,70) 3-Y-O+ £2,817 (£838; £418; £209) Stalls High

Form RPR

4500 1 **Dvinsky (USA)**[9] 6946 6-9-0 66 (v) TGMcLaughlin 8 75
(P Howling) *mde all: upped the pce fr 1/2-way: rdn and kpt on wl fnl 2f: nvr seriously chal* 6/1

0212 2 3/4 **Brandywell Boy (IRE)**[9] 6946 4-9-2 68 SteveDrowne 6 75+
(D J S Ffrench Davis) *lw: settled in midfield: rdn and effrt 2f out: styd on to take 2nd wl ins fnl f: nvr able to chal* 9/4[1]

3432 3 1/2 **Maysarah (IRE)**[18] 6854 3-9-0 66 TPQueally 1 71
(G A Butler) *hld up in last trio on outer: effrt 2f out: styd on wl fnl f to take 3rd nr fin* 7/1

6020 4 hd **Mr Cellophane**[36] 6575 4-9-0 66 EddieAhern 5 70
(J R Jenkins) *lw: t.k.h early: chsd wnr: rdn and no real imp fnl 2f: lost 2 pls wl ins fnl f* 5/1[3]

3000 5 shd **Sir Douglas**[13] 6907 4-9-4 70 (p) LPKeniry 10 74
(R A Harris) *plld v hrd: hld up bhd ldrs: 3rd and rdn 2f out: nt qckn fnl f* 10/1

0562 6 1/2 **Inka Dancer (IRE)**[11] 6927 5-8-5 57 ChrisCatlin 9 59
(B Palling) *swtg: t.k.h early: hld up in last trio on inner: grad taken to outer fnl 2f and pushed along: kpt on steadily: nvr nr ldrs* 9/1

1323 7 3/4 **Lord Of The Reins (IRE)**[13] 6905 3-9-0 66 DeanMcKeown 4 66
(D Shaw) *plld hrd early: hld up bhd ldrs: bmpd along and nt qckn over 2f out: fdd fnl f* 9/2[2]

0500 8 6 **Romany Nights (IRE)**[56] 6103 7-9-1 67 (bt) HayleyTurner 3 48
(Miss Gay Kelleway) *b: b.hind: dwlt: swtchd to inner: in tch tl wknd rapidly wl over 1f out* 20/1

3000 9 2 **Shavoulin (USA)**[14] 6891 3-8-8 60 SaleemGolam 2 34
(Christian Wroe) *prom tl wknd over 2f out: sn bhd* 66/1

1m 13.16s (-0.54) **Going Correction** 0.0s/f (Stan) 9 Ran SP% **117.7**
Speed ratings (Par 103): **103,102,101,101,100 100,99,91,88**
CSF £20.32 CT £99.61 TOTE £7.90: £2.40, £1.30, £2.30; EX 23.90.
Owner Richard Berenson **Bred** Eclipse Bloodstock & Tipperary Bloodstock **Trained** Newmarket, Suffolk

FOCUS
A moderate sprint handicap in which winner Dvinsky took advantage of an easy lead.
Sir Douglas Official explanation: jockey said colt ran too free
Shavoulin(USA) Official explanation: jockey said gelding hung right

7034 BARRETTSTOWN STUD CLASSIFIED STKS 1m (P)
9:20 (9:23) (Class 7) 3-Y-O+ £1,365 (£403; £201) Stalls High

Form RPR

5-00 1 **Ai Hawa (IRE)**[75] 5606 4-8-12 45 (b) JerryO'Dwyer(3) 3 54
(Eamon Tyrrell, Ire) *hld up wl in rr: prog fr 2f out on outer: sustained effrt fr over 1f out to ld last 75yds* 16/1

4022 2 3/4 **Sion Hill (IRE)**[13] 6908 6-9-1 45 (p) TPQueally 7 52
(John A Harris) *lw: led at decent pce: jnd over 1f out: kpt on wl: hdd last 75yds* 7/2[2]

000 3 nk **Kindkintyre (IRE)**[292] 484 3-9-0 45 DaleGibson 2 51
(R A Fahey) *cl up: effrt to chse ldr on inner 2f out: upsides over 1f out: hld last 100yds and lost 2nd sn after* 20/1

0000 4 2 **Epidaurian King (IRE)**[21] 6809 4-9-1 45 (v[1]) DeanMcKeown 4 47
(D Shaw) *t.k.h: hld up in midfield: gd prog over 2f out to dispute 2nd over 1f out: hanging and fnd nil* 6/1[3]

000 5 1 1/2 **Just Crystal**[44] 6385 3-9-0 45 TGMcLaughlin 5 43
(B P J Baugh) *dwlt: hld up wl in rr: rdn and prog fr 2f out: no ch of rching ldrs: one pce fnl f* 25/1

0664 6 1/2 **Future Deal**[37] 6532 6-9-1 45 JimCrowley 6 42
(C A Horgan) *rdn in midfield over 4f out: prog to chse ldrs 2f out: one pce and no imp after* 3/1[1]

0404 7 hd **Stagnite**[13] 6908 7-8-8 45 TimothyMeadows(7) 14 42
(Karen George) *mostly chsd ldr to 2f out: wknd* 10/1

4500 8 2 1/2 **Bonnet O'Bonnie**[15] 6887 3-8-11 45 DominicFox(3) 1 36
(J Mackie) *nvr beyond midfield: rdn 1/2-way: struggling fnl 2f* 12/1

6300 9 1 1/4 **Astorygoeswithit**[59] 4029 4-9-1 45 AdamKirby 8 33
(G C Bravery) *nvr bttr than midfield: wl btn fnl 2f* 7/1

0450 10 2 **Danum Diva (IRE)**[8] 6955 3-9-0 45 (bt) SteveDrowne 10 28
(D J Murphy) *dwlt: a towards rr: struggling over 2f out* 16/1

0520 11 hd **Firebird Annie (IRE)**[28] 3040 3-9-0 45 (b) MickyFenton 9 28
(A Bailey) *nvr on terms: last and struggling over 2f out* 20/1

566 12 3/4 **Ugenius**[11] 6935 3-9-0 45 ChrisCatlin 12 26
(R A Harris) *b: ldng trio tl wknd over 2f out* 20/1

0200 13 2 **Wodhill Be**[15] 6887 7-9-1 45 HayleyTurner 11 22
(D Morris) *trckd ldrs: rdn and nt qckn over 2f out: wknd rapidly over 1f out* 17/2

1m 40.37s (-0.43) **Going Correction** 0.0s/f (Stan)
WFA 3 from 4yo+ 1lb 13 Ran SP% **131.2**
Speed ratings (Par 97): **102,101,100,98,97 96,96,94,93,91 90,90,88**
CSF £74.55 TOTE £17.80: £5.60, £1.30, £10.90; EX 103.20 Place 6 £17.95, Place 5 £8.99.
Owner M McLoughlin **Bred** Derek Dunne **Trained** The Curragh, Co Kildare

FOCUS
Straightforward form to rate, with the runner-up the best guide.
T/Plt: £19.40 to a £1 stake. Pool: £85,554.50. 3,205.85 winning tickets. T/Qpdt: £7.20 to a £1 stake. Pool: £5,717.60. 587.00 winning tickets. JN

7035 - 7036a (Foreign Racing) - See Raceform Interactive

6983 DUNDALK (A.W) (L-H)
Wednesday, December 5

OFFICIAL GOING: Standard

7037a GREENORE RACE 7f
7:40 (7:41) 3-Y-O+ £8,797 (£2,581; £1,229; £418)

RPR

1 **Xinji (IRE)**[206] 1694 3-9-0 90 FMBerry 3 79
(John M Oxx, Ire) *led early: chsd ldrs after 1f: hdwy into 2nd ent st: impr to ld under 2f out: pressed cl home: kpt on wl* 5/2[2]

2 nk **Summit Surge (IRE)**[12] 6918 3-9-9 107 (t) KJManning 8 87+
(G M Lyons, Ire) *sn mid-div: 5th 1/2-way: cl 6th over 2f out: impr into 3rd 1 1/2f out: 2nd 1f out: styd on to press wnr cl home* 4/6[1]

3 3/4 **Chicken Soup**[12] 6920 5-9-9 (b) DPMcDonogh 1 85
(D J Murphy) *chsd ldrs: 4th 1/2-way: cl 5th over 2f out: impr into 2nd 1 1/2f out: cl 3rd fnl f: no ex cl home* 9/2[3]

4 2 1/2 **Regaleya (IRE)**[5] 6988 4-8-7 74 (bt) MHarley(7) 7 69
(H Rogers, Ire) *towards rr: hdwy into 5th 1 1/2f out: kpt on into 4th under 1f out* 20/1

5 1 1/2 **Funatfuntasia**[61] 5991 3-8-12 70 SJGray(7) 6 70
(Ms Joanna Morgan, Ire) *sn chsd ldr: 3rd and rdn 2f out: kpt on same pce in 4th fr 1 1/2f out* 25/1

6 3 **Give Me A Reason (IRE)**[220] 1323 3-8-11 47 WMLordan 4 53
(Daniel Mark Loughnane, Ire) *a towards rr* 100/1

7 2 **Nanita Bonita (IRE)**[5] 6989 3-8-8 DJMoran(3) 5 48
(Francis Ennis, Ire) *t.k.h to ld after 1f: rdn and hdd under 2f out: sn wknd* 100/1

8 3 **Mineral Star (IRE)**[43] 6412 5-9-9 WJLee 2 51
(R Donohoe, Ire) *dwlt: sn chsd ldrs: rdn in 4th over 2f out: sn wknd* 25/1

1m 26.8s (86.80) 8 Ran SP% **121.2**
CSF £4.71 TOTE £3.50: £2.20, £1.10, £2.50; DF 5.90.
Owner Horse Breeding Company **Bred** Horse Breeding Company **Trained** Currabeg, Co Kildare

NOTEBOOK
Chicken Soup, prominent enough throughout, went in pursuit of the winner a furlong and a half out, eventually switching to the inside inside the last half furlong, but she just was not quite good enough. (op 7/2)

7038 - 7041a (Foreign Racing) - See Raceform Interactive

7019 WOLVERHAMPTON (A.W) (L-H)
Thursday, December 6

OFFICIAL GOING: Standard
Wind: Fresh behind

7042 PONTIN'S BOOK EARLY NURSERY 5f 216y(P)
6:50 (6:52) (Class 6) (0-65,65) 2-Y-O £2,730 (£806; £403) Stalls Low

Form RPR

0054 1 **Feeling Fresh (IRE)**[16] 6881 2-8-8 55 PatrickMathers(3) 7 66+
(Paul Green) *s.i.s: in rr tl hdwy on outside 2f out: rdn to ld 1f out: r.o wl and sn clr* 6/1[2]

0042 2 3 1/2 **Yankee Storm**[16] 6881 2-8-11 55 EddieAhern 6 56
(M J Wallace) *broke wl: trckd ldrs: rdn over 1f out: styd on to go 2nd nr fin* 6/4[1]

5560 3 shd **Alabama Spirit (USA)**[16] 6881 2-8-10 59 TolleyDean(5) 5 59
(D Shaw) *hld up in rr: hdwy on ins wl over 1f out: styd on fnl f: nvr nrr* 7/1[3]

0000 4 nk **Holly Golightley**[22] 6813 2-8-12 56 JohnEgan 2 55
(K A Ryan) *led after 1f: rdn and hdd 1f out: one pce fnl f* 12/1

0440 5 2 **Shakespeare's Son**[57] 6098 2-9-1 62 DuranFentiman(3) 9 55
(H J Evans) *trckd ldrs: racd on outside: wnt briefly 2nd 2f out: wknd ent fnl f* 12/1

0605 6 1 1/2 **Little Firecracker**[17] 6872 2-9-2 65 ow4 JamesO'Reilly(5) 4 54
(Miss M E Rowland) *s.i.s: rdn 1/2-way: nvr on terms* 7/1[3]

403 7 3 1/2 **Kamal**[16] 6880 2-9-4 62 HayleyTurner 3 40
(W R Muir) *t.k.h: prom tl rdn and wknd ent fnl f* 15/2

0052 8 shd **Andrasta**[17] 6872 2-9-7 65 PhillipMakin 8 43
(A Berry) *led for 1f: trckd ldr to 2f out: sn wknd* 17/2

0000 9 21 **My Flame**[8] 6966 2-8-11 55 (v) JimCrowley 1 —
(J R Jenkins) *s.i.s: racd in tch on ins tl wknd over 2f out: t.o* 22/1

1m 16.72s (0.91) **Going Correction** +0.05s/f (Slow) 9 Ran SP% **121.3**
Speed ratings (Par 94): **95,90,90,89,87 85,80,80,52**
CSF £16.24 CT £68.23 TOTE £7.10: £2.70, £1.10, £4.00; EX 22.10.
Owner Max Kay **Bred** J Mahon **Trained** Lydiate, Merseyside

FOCUS
A moderate handicap run at a good pace with a decisive winner and sound form with the runner-up to his latest effort.

NOTEBOOK

Feeling Fresh(IRE), who caught the eye doing best of the closers in a race dominated by pace horses over this course and distance last time out, was under pressure from a fair way out, but he responded and, challenging wide into the straight, ran on strongly to finish up a decisive winner. He came in for good support here, is clearly going the right way, and shapes very much as though he will be suited by 7f. (op 10-1)

Yankee Storm, second in the course and distance handicap in which Feeling Fresh finished fourth last time out, was probably helped by racing towards the fore that day in a race which was dominated by pace horses. On this occasion they went a better gallop and the progressive Feeling Foxy, who was 3lb better off with him, comprehensively turned the form around. (tchd 11-8 and 13-8)

Alabama Spirit(USA) was another to benefit from the decent gallop. She stayed on from well off the pace but remains a maiden. (op 11-2 tchd 5-1 and 8-1)

Holly Golightley set a good gallop in front and paid for that later in the race, losing the runner-up place and having to settle for fourth in the closing stages.

Shakespeare's Son, relatively unexposed, settled better in this stronger-run race, but he was another who was seen off by the closers in the latter stages. (op 14-1 tchd 11-1)

Little Firecracker was beaten in a claimer last time and was racing from 4lb out of the handicap, but she was a market mover. She never gave her her supporters much hope in the race itself, though. (op 20-1)

7043 PONTIN'S BOOK EARLY PRICE PROMISE MEDIAN AUCTION MAIDEN STKS 5f 216y(P)

7:20 (7:20) (Class 6) 2-Y-O £2,047 (£604; £302) Stalls Low

Form				RPR
3	1		**The Mighty One**[30] 6698 2-8-10 0 ..... PatrickDonaghy(7) 6 (P C Haslam) *mde all: rdn over 1f out: in command fnl f* **13/8**[1]	69+
	2	1 ½	**Desert Pride** 2-9-3 0 ..... FergusSweeney 7 (W S Kittow) *sn trckd wnr: edgd lft over 1f out: kpt on one pce ins fnl f* **12/1**	65
00	3	1 ¼	**Yattendon**[15] 6897 2-9-3 0 ..... GeorgeBaker 1 (S Kirk) *hld up after broke wl: styd on fr over 1f out: nvr nr to chal* **13/2**	61
	4	1 ¼	**Moon Bound (IRE)** 2-9-3 0 ..... EddieAhern 5 (W R Muir) *in tch: rdn wl over 1f out: one pce after* **9/2**[3]	57
400	5	1	**Shabnaam**[143] 3596 2-8-12 65 ..... JohnEgan 2 (K A Ryan) *in tch: rdn 2f out: hung lft over 1f out: sn btn* **5/2**[2]	49
	6	15	**Saunders Encore** 2-8-12 0 ..... AdamKirby 3 (M S Saunders) *s.i.s: a outpcd in rr* **25/1**	4
	7	11	**Stoneacre Pat (IRE)** 2-9-3 0 ..... LPKeniry 4 (Peter Grayson) *slowly away: a struggling in rr* **40/1**	—

1m 17.54s (1.73) **Going Correction** +0.05s/f (Slow) 7 Ran SP% **112.2**
Speed ratings (Par 94): **90,88,86,84,83 63,48**
CSF £21.59 TOTE £2.90: £1.80, £6.40; EX 41.50.

Owner Middleham Park Racing Vi **Bred** Helescane Stud **Trained** Middleham Moor, N Yorks

FOCUS

Modest maiden form although the winner can do better in time.

NOTEBOOK

The Mighty One, who ran with promise on his debut at Catterick last month, put that experience to good use and made every yard. He probably did not need to improve to win this modest heat. (op 10-11 tchd 7-4)

Desert Pride, a half-brother to Alfred Sisley, a 7f winner at three, and Hambleden, a triple winner between 1m4f and 1m6f, shaped with promise on his debut, only finding the more experienced winner too strong. (op 14-1 tchd 16-1)

Yattendon ran his best race on his third start in maiden grade. A half-brother to Listed-class sprinter Prime Defender, he will be of interest in handicap company. (op 15-2)

Moon Bound(IRE), a half-brother to Group 3-winning sprinter Dixie Belle, never really threatened on his debut but kept on well enough and should improve for this experience. (op 7-2 tchd 5-1)

Shabnaam was very well backed but proved disappointing. She tracked the leader on the rail but, not for the first time, hung under pressure and weakened tamely. (op 7-1)

7044 WOLVERHAMPTON-RACECOURSE.CO.UK CLAIMING STKS 7f 32y(P)

7:50 (7:50) (Class 6) 2-Y-O £2,388 (£705; £352) Stalls High

Form				RPR
1135	1		**Cross Fell (USA)**[12] 6936 2-9-5 78 ..... PatCosgrave 4 (J R Boyle) *t.k.h: trckd ldr: led over 2f out: rdn over 1f out: hld on wl fnl f* **5/2**[2]	78
5051	2	½	**Copperbottomed (IRE)**[9] 6958 2-8-9 58 ..... (e) JimCrowley 3 (R Hollinshead) *s.i.s: hdwy on ins to go 2nd 2f out: ev ch 1f out but flashed tail and no imp cl home* **5/2**[2]	67
4342	3	5	**What's For Tea**[1] 7031 2-8-4 60 ..... HayleyTurner 6 (Tom Dascombe) *a.p: ev ch over 2f out: outpcd by first 2 fr over 1f out* **15/8**[1]	50
4103	4	¾	**Wee Buns**[15] 6898 2-8-9 68 ..... EddieAhern 2 (S Kirk) *prom whn hmpd on ins after 1f: hmpd again over 2f out: one pce after* **11/2**[3]	53+
0400	5	8	**Prunes**[2] 7021 2-8-1 50 ..... (b) DuranFentiman(3) 5 (A Berry) *bhd: rdn and hdwy on outside over 2f out: wknd over 1f out* **33/1**	28
3100	6	13	**Rio Taffeta**[97] 5015 2-8-9 66 ..... LPKeniry 1 (Peter Grayson) *led tl hdd over 2f out: sn btn* **20/1**	1

1m 32.48s (2.08) **Going Correction** +0.05s/f (Slow) 6 Ran SP% **115.0**
Speed ratings (Par 94): **90,89,83,82,73 58**
CSF £9.54 TOTE £5.10: £1.90, £1.60; EX 8.80.Copperbottomed (IRE) was claimed by Mustafa Khan for £8,000

Owner M Khan X2 **Bred** Darley **Trained** Epsom, Surrey

FOCUS

An average claimer with little strength in depth rated around the first two.

NOTEBOOK

Cross Fell(USA) looked to hold strong claims on this drop into claiming company and, although once again keen in the early stages, he got a dream run through on the inside as the field turned into the straight, and he got first run on the eventual runner-up. He was all out to score. (op 15-8 tchd 11-4)

Copperbottomed(IRE), who won a seller last time out, had more to do in this company as he would have been 10lb better off with the winner in a handicap, but he is in form and, having tracked Cross Fell through entering the straight, threw down a determined challenge inside the last, despite flashing his tail. (op 4-1)

What's For Tea, runner-up in a handicap at Kempton the previous day, was a bit disappointing as the first two pulled well clear of her in the closing stages. (op 5-2)

Wee Buns did not enjoy the best of luck in running and deserves rating a bit better than his finishing position suggests. (op 5-1 tchd 9-2 and 6-1)

Rio Taffeta Official explanation: jockey said gelding hung right throughout

7045 PONTIN'S GREAT FAMILY HOLIDAYS H'CAP 7f 32y(P)

8:20 (8:20) (Class 5) (0-75,73) 3-Y-O+ £3,238 (£963; £481; £240) Stalls High

Form				RPR
0	1		**Painted Sky**[40] 6500 4-9-0 72 ..... JamieMoriarty(3) 9 (R A Fahey) *in rr whn bmpd on ins sn after s: hdwy on outside over 2f out: led wl ins fnl f: hld on* **50/1**	80
3122	2	hd	**Teasing**[24] 6795 3-9-4 73 ..... RobertHavlin 10 (J Pearce) *hld up: hdwy whn swtchd lft over 1f out: n.m.r and swtchd lft ins fnl f: r.o wl to grab 2nd nr fin* **7/1**	83+
330	3	½	**Angaric (IRE)**[30] 6701 4-9-1 73 ..... MarkLawson(3) 2 (B Smart) *trckd ldrs: rdn and ev ch ins fnl f: no ex cl home* **6/1**[3]	79
4562	4	¾	**Nicada (IRE)**[5] 6996 3-8-9 69 ..... TolleyDean(5) 8 (Stef Liddiard) *chsd ldrs: led 2f out: rdn and hdd wl ins fnl f: no ex cl home* **4/1**[2]	73+
4063	5	2	**Carmenero (GER)**[24] 6795 4-9-4 73 ..... LiamJones 4 (W R Muir) *hld up: hmpd wl over 2f out: hdwy whn swtchd lft over 1f out: no ex ins fnl f* **10/1**	74+
2602	6	½	**Okikoki**[30] 6701 3-9-1 70 ..... (b) EddieAhern 3 (W R Muir) *chsd ldrs: rdn 2f out: wknd ins fnl f* **10/1**	68
0201	7	2 ½	**Parkview Love (USA)**[32] 6677 6-9-3 72 ..... (v) DeanMcKeown 5 (D Shaw) *in rr: hdwy over 2f out: wknd over 1f out* **11/1**	63
4640	8	1	**Pietersen (IRE)**[48] 6310 3-8-11 66 ..... (b) PaulFessey 1 (T D Barron) *s.i.s: outpcd and nvr on terms* **12/1**	54
1131	9	5	**Nuit Sombre (IRE)**[30] 6701 7-9-1 70 ..... (p) JimCrowley 11 (G A Harker) *led tl over 5f out: led again over 3f out: hdd 2f out: wknd qckly* **7/2**[1]	45
5426	10	3	**Robinzal**[32] 6677 5-8-7 62 ..... HayleyTurner 7 (A W Carroll) *chsd ldrs for 3f: sn wknd* **22/1**	29
2063	11	28	**Grimes Faith**[26] 6753 4-9-4 73 ..... (b) JohnEgan 6 (K A Ryan) *led over 5f out to over 3f out: wknd over 2f out* **6/1**[3]	—

1m 30.18s (-0.22) **Going Correction** +0.05s/f (Slow) 11 Ran SP% **123.8**
Speed ratings (Par 103): **103,102,102,101,99 98,95,94,88,85 53**
CSF £389.37 CT £2489.46 TOTE £30.80: £4.80, £2.40, £4.30; EX 123.50.

Owner J P M Syndicate **Bred** Juddmonte Farms Ltd **Trained** Musley Bank, N Yorks

FOCUS

A fair handicap run at a strong early pace, and the first two came from well back. The third is the best guide to the level.

Grimes Faith Official explanation: jockey said gelding moved badly

7046 GO PONTIN'S H'CAP 1m 4f 50y(P)

8:50 (8:50) (Class 5) (0-70,70) 3-Y-O+ £3,238 (£963; £481; £240) Stalls Low

Form				RPR
1112	1		**Birkside**[6] 6982 4-9-2 70 ..... JamieKyne(7) 4 (D Carroll) *hmpd on bnd sn after s: hld up: hdwy on outside 2f out: rdn and r.o to ld ins fnl f* **10/3**[2]	80+
11	2	1 ¼	**Fresh Mint (IRE)**[8] 6967 3-9-0 66 6ex ..... EddieAhern 8 (M J Wallace) *mid-div: hdwy over 4f out: wnt 2nd wl over 2f out: led wl over 1f out: rdn and hdd ins fnl f: kpt on one pce* **7/4**[1]	74
5002	3	2	**Punta Galera (IRE)**[16] 6883 4-9-2 66 ..... PatrickMathers(3) 6 (Paul Green) *hld up in tch: rdn wl over 1f out: kpt on one pce fnl f* **9/1**	71
5420	4	1 ½	**Evita**[40] 6506 3-9-1 67 ..... NickyMackay 5 (L M Cumani) *edgd lft s: mid-div: ev ch 2f out: edgd lft appr fnl f: sn no ex* **8/1**[3]	70
2010	5	5	**Gamesters Lady**[19] 6856 4-9-4 65 ..... LiamJones 2 (W M Brisbourne) *wnt rt s: chsd ldrs: rdn over 2f out: one pce after* **17/2**	60
6033	6	4	**Opera Writer (IRE)**[16] 6883 4-8-10 57 ..... (p) JimCrowley 3 (R Hollinshead) *hmpd s and bdly again sn after: effrt on outside over 2f out: wknd over 1f out* **11/1**	45
2062	7	3 ½	**Speagle (IRE)**[22] 6815 5-9-6 67 ..... DeanMcKeown 7 (A J Chamberlain) *in tch: wnt 2nd over 5f out tl wl over 2f out: sn hmpd and wknd* **22/1**	50
4212	8	½	**Mighty Mover (IRE)**[24] 6801 5-8-11 58 ..... ChrisCatlin 10 (B Palling) *trckd ldr: led over 5f out tl hdd & wknd wl over 1f out* **9/1**	40
5036	9	61	**Three Thieves (UAE)**[177] 2544 4-9-9 70 ..... AdamKirby 1 (M S Saunders) *wnt rt s and hmpd sn after: lost tch 4f out: t.o* **18/1**	—
2-00	10	5	**Kapellmeister (IRE)**[37] 6568 4-9-5 66 ..... FergusSweeney 9 (M S Saunders) *led tl hdd over 5f out: wknd 4f out: t.o* **33/1**	—

2m 41.86s (-0.56) **Going Correction** +0.05s/f (Slow)
WFA 3 from 4yo+ 5lb 10 Ran SP% **122.0**
Speed ratings (Par 103): **103,102,100,99,96 93,91,91,50,47**
CSF £10.06 CT £49.52 TOTE £4.40: £1.20, £1.40, £3.50; EX 12.80.

Owner Document Express Ltd **Bred** Pendley Farm **Trained** Sledmere, E Yorks

■ A winner for Jamie Kyne on only his third ride under Rules.

■ Stewards' Enquiry : Nicky Mackay seven-day ban: careless riding (Dec 17-Dec 26)
Eddie Ahern seven-day ban: careless riding (Dec 28-Jan 3)

FOCUS

Pretty straightforward form to rate with the third seemingly running up to his recent second here.

7047 PONTINS.COM H'CAP 1m 141y(P)

9:20 (9:20) (Class 5) (0-70,70) 3-Y-O+ £3,238 (£963; £481; £240) Stalls Low

Form				RPR
0223	1		**Putra Laju (IRE)**[17] 6874 3-8-13 65 ..... (p) EddieAhern 2 (J W Hills) *mid-div: hdwy over 2f out: hrd rdn fr over 1f out: led post* **9/2**[3]	74
4001	2	shd	**Satin Braid**[30] 6710 3-8-7 66 ..... AmyBaker(7) 4 (D R C Elsworth) *chsd ldrs: led wl over 1f out: kpt on: hdd post* **7/1**	75
050	3	1 ¼	**Tom Paris**[21] 6824 3-9-1 67 ..... (b) HayleyTurner 3 (W R Muir) *hld up in rr: hdwy 2f out: rdn and ev ch ins fnl f: no ex nr fin* **8/1**	73
0012	4	2	**Defi (IRE)**[17] 6874 5-8-10 60 ..... (b) PhillipMakin 8 (I Semple) *trckd ldr to 2f out: rdn and edgd lft 1f out: one pce after* **6/1**	62
2214	5	¾	**Northern Boy (USA)**[17] 6869 4-9-0 64 ..... DaleGibson 6 (M W Easterby) *s.i.s: t.k.h in mid-div: effrt on outside 2f out: one pce fnl f* **4/1**[2]	64
6221	6	½	**My Michelle**[17] 6874 6-9-2 66 ..... ChrisCatlin 5 (B Palling) *in tch tl rdn and one pce ins fnl 2f* **7/2**[1]	65
0064	7	2 ½	**Stanley George (IRE)**[21] 6824 3-9-3 69 ..... MatthewHenry 1 (M A Jarvis) *led tl hdd wl over 1f out: sn rdn and fdd ins fnl f* **12/1**	62
0156	8	1 ¾	**Very Well Red**[19] 6856 4-9-1 65 ..... JimCrowley 7 (P W Hiatt) *in tch tl outpcd over 3f out: sn rdn and nvr on terms after* **16/1**	54

0146 9 7 **United Nations**[90] 5197 6-8-13 **70** SamuelDrury(7) 9 43
(N Wilson) *racd wd: hdwy over 4f out: wknd 2f out* **11/1**

1m 51.3s (-0.46) **Going Correction** +0.05s/f (Slow)
WFA 3 from 4yo+ 2lb 9 Ran SP% **120.2**
Speed ratings (Par 103): **104,103,102,101,100 99,97,96,89**
CSF £37.60 CT £250.07 TOTE £6.10: £1.40, £2.90, £2.70; EX 57.60 Place 6 £ 76.89, Place 5 £ 53.80.
Owner F Lee **Bred** Rathasker Stud **Trained** Upper Lambourn, Berks

FOCUS
An ordinary handicap run at a fair pace and the form looks sound rated through the third.
T/Plt: £73.00 to a £1 stake. Pool: £100,683.30. 1,005.90 winning tickets. T/Qpdt: £44.30 to a £1 stake. Pool: £5,668.50. 94.60 winning tickets. JS

7027 DEAUVILLE (R-H)
Thursday, December 6

OFFICIAL GOING: Standard

7048a PRIX DU VEXIN NORMAND (FILLIES) (ALL-WEATHER) 6f 110y(S)
10:50 (10:51) 2-Y-0 £8,784 (£3,514; £2,635; £1,318)

RPR

1 **Lettre Spirituelle**[7] 2-9-2 RonanThomas 9 81
(J-C Rouget, France)

2 nse **Race Driver (IRE)**[17] 2-9-2 TJarnet 5 81
(E Leenders, France)

3 1 1/2 **Vytinna (FR)**[69] 5791 2-9-2 GFaucon 4 77
(D Sepulchre, France)

4 3/4 **Lady Cat (FR)**[62] 2-9-2 RPerruchot 12 76
(P Bary, France)

5 nk **El Shenandoah (FR)**[17] 2-9-2 TPiccone 11 75
(C Boutin, France)

6 nse **High Days (IRE)**[36] 6599 2-9-2 MGuyon 8 75
(H-A Pantall, France)

7 1 **Piece Of My Heart**[169] 2756 2-8-9 IMendizabal 3 66
(P F I Cole) *trckd ldr in 2nd: 3rd st: rdn 1 1/2f out: sn btn* **53/10**[1]

8 1 **La Madonetta (IRE)**[39] 6525 2-9-2 J-BHamel 10 70
(Robert Collet, France)

9 1 1/2 **Under The Sun**[112] 2-8-9 RMarchelli 7 60
(M Rolland, France)

10 shd **Frynia (USA)**[25] 2-8-13 MBlancpain 1 63
(C Laffon-Parias, France)

0 **Valse Des Coeurs (FR)**[16] 6888 2-8-13 SRuis 2 —
(G Pannier, France)

0 **Domalinoise (FR)**[22] 2-9-2 MMartinez 6 —
(Robert Collet, France)

1m 19.5s (0.30) 12 Ran SP% **15.9**
PARI-MUTUEL (Including 1 Euro stake): WIN 4.80; PL 2.00, 1.60, 3.70;DF 6.10.
Owner Baron E De Rothschild **Bred** Haras De Meautry **Trained** Pau, France

NOTEBOOK
Piece Of My Heart, a five-furlong winner on fast ground in the spring, was having her first outing since June and did not fare badly. The run should bring her on.

7049a PRIX PETITE ETOILE (LISTED RACE) (FILLIES) (ALL-WEATHER) 1m 1f 110y
2:35 (2:37) 3-Y-0 £17,568 (£7,027; £5,270; £3,514; £1,757)

RPR

1 **Soft Morning**[16] 6889 3-8-11 J-BEyquem 7 101
(Sir Mark Prescott) *mde all: pushed along and qcknd ent st: drvn clr appr fnl f: r.o wl* **11/2**[1]

2 2 **Daralara (FR)**[46] 3-8-11 IMendizabal 3 97
(J-C Rouget, France)

3 3 **In The Light**[16] 6889 3-8-11 SPasquier 2 91
(A Fabre, France)

4 1 **Muthabaie (FR)**[24] 3-8-11 THuet 9 89
(R Pritchard-Gordon, France)

5 nk **Shendaya (FR)**[14] 6909 3-8-11 FDiFede 11 88
(A De Royer-Dupre, France)

6 1 1/2 **Adonita**[12] 3-8-11 DMichaux 12 85
(H-A Pantall, France)

7 shd **Cable Beach (USA)**[23] 3-8-11 MBlancpain 10 85
(C Laffon-Parias, France)

8 snk **Anoush (USA)**[12] 6940 3-8-11 TJarnet 6 85
(P Bary, France)

9 1/2 **Clodovina (IRE)**[34] 6632 3-8-11 AlxiBadel 1 84
(A Fabre, France)

10 2 **Playing Star (FR)**[17] 3-8-11 TPiccone 5 80
(C Boutin, France)

11 **Elusive Flash (USA)**[19] 6852 3-9-1 FSpanu 8 —
(P F I Cole) *disp 3rd to over 3f out: 5th and rdn st: sn wknd* **23/1**[2]

12 **Altesse Imperiale (IRE)**[24] 3-8-11 ACrastus 4 —
(E Lellouche, France)

1m 58.1s (118.10) 12 Ran SP% **19.6**
PARI-MUTUEL: WIN 6.50; PL 2.10, 3.40, 1.50; DF 31.40.
Owner Miss K Rausing **Bred** Miss K Rausing **Trained** Newmarket, Suffolk

NOTEBOOK
Soft Morning, who won her maiden on Polytrack in January, has since progressed through handicaps on turf to be placed at this level. The return to this surface presented no problem and she gained her first Listed win in good style, so there may be more to come if she is kept in training.
Elusive Flash(USA), was placed on Polytrack early in her career, but has failed to build on that since and looks happiest on fast turf.

7012 LINGFIELD (L-H)
Friday, December 7

OFFICIAL GOING: Standard
Wind: Fresh, across

7050 LADBROKES.COM LEADS WAY CLAIMING STKS 1m 4f (P)
12:40 (12:41) (Class 6) 3-Y-0+ £2,047 (£604; £302) Stalls Low

Form RPR

501 1 **Nawamees (IRE)**[19] 6501 9-9-10 79 (p) GeorgeBaker 2 72+
(G L Moore) *set stdy gallop tl hdd 4f out: rdn and qcknd to ld again wl over 1f out: a holding rivals after* **8/11**[1]

3243 2 1/2 **Alfie Tupper (IRE)**[11] 6951 4-9-10 59 LPKeniry 5 71
(S Kirk) *hld up in tch: hdwy to chal jst over 2f out: unable qckn fnl f* **9/2**[2]

1051 3 nk **Musango**[7] 6971 4-9-8 65 RobertHavlin 3 69+
(Miss Gay Kelleway) *hld up in tch: dropped to last over 4f out: rdn and effrt jst over 2f out: hung lft 1f out: r.o nt pce to rch wnr* **9/2**[2]

-000 4 4 **Thyolo (IRE)**[102] 4910 6-8-9 70 KylieManser(7) 4 56
(B G Powell) *hld up in last tl hdwy to chse wnr 6f out: led 4f out tl rdn and hdd wl over 1f out: outpcd fnl f* **8/1**[3]

0236 5 1 1/4 **Maria Antonia (IRE)**[21] 6832 4-9-1 51 J-PGuillambert 6 53
(P A Blockley) *plld hrd: chsd ldr tl 6f out: rdn jst over 2f out: outpcd over 1f out* **16/1**

2m 39.55s (5.16) **Going Correction** -0.10s/f (Stan) 5 Ran SP% **111.3**
Speed ratings (Par 101): **78,77,77,74,73**
CSF £4.47 TOTE £1.80: £1.20, £1.80; EX 4.10.Alfie Tupper was claimed by Mustafa Khan for £12,000.
Owner Paul Stamp **Bred** Kilfrush Stud Ltd **Trained** Woodingdean, E Sussex

FOCUS
The winner is above the usual claiming race quality, but the small field and steady pace devalue the form to some extent with the fifth the best guide.
Musango Official explanation: jockey said gelding hung left and made a noise

7051 LADBROKES 24/7 FREE PHONE BETTING 0800 777 888 MAIDEN STKS 1m (P)
1:10 (1:12) (Class 5) 2-Y-0 £2,817 (£838; £418; £209) Stalls High

Form RPR

1 **Crosstar**[83] 2-9-3 0 OscarUrbina 7 71+
(M Botti) *hld up in midfield: rdn and hdwy over 1f out: led wl ins fnl f: in command after: eased nr fin* **20/1**

2 1 **Seattle Storm (IRE)** 2-9-3 0 LPKeniry 8 66+
(D R C Elsworth) *s.i.s: stdd and hld up in rr: hdwy on outer over 1f out: r.o wl: wnt 2nd wl ins fnl f: nt threaten wnr* **16/1**

3 1 **Strategic Knight (USA)** 2-9-3 0 ChrisCatlin 11 64
(P F I Cole) *led: hrd pressed and drvn jst over 2f out: hdd wl ins fnl f: no ex* **5/1**[3]

0 4 shd **Mick's Dancer**[20] 6850 2-9-3 0 MartinDwyer 3 64
(W R Muir) *hld up in midfield: rdn and gd hdwy 2f out: ev ch jst ins fnl f: no ex wl ins fnl f* **12/1**

0 5 hd **Pharaohs Justice (USA)**[20] 6855 2-9-3 0 JohnEgan 2 64
(Jane Chapple-Hyam) *chsd ldrs: rdn jst over 2f out: ev ch 1f out: one pce wl ins fnl f* **33/1**

2 6 shd **Agente Romano (USA)**[11] 6948 2-9-3 0 NickyMackay 1 63+
(G A Butler) *hld up towards rr: effrt and nt clr run wl over 1f out: styd on fr over 1f out: nvr rchd ldrs* **2/1**[1]

7 3/4 **Ace Of Spies (IRE)** 2-9-3 0 GregFairley 5 62
(M Johnston) *chsd ldr: ev ch and rdn jst over 2f out: wknd ins fnl f* **13/2**

03 8 3/4 **Art Value**[38] 6574 2-9-3 0 AdrianMcCarthy 12 60
(P W Chapple-Hyam) *t.k.h: chsd ldrs: rdn jst over 2f out: edgd rt jst over 1f out: wknd fnl f* **10/3**[2]

9 3/4 **Plumage** 2-8-12 0 SteveDrowne 4 53+
(M Blanshard) *s.i.s: sn in midfield: rdn 2f out: nt clr run jst over 1f out: kpt on but n.d* **50/1**

0 10 2 1/2 **The Twelve Steps**[41] 6493 2-9-3 0 EddieAhern 6 53
(P F I Cole) *t.k.h: chsd ldrs: rdn 2f out: wknd jst over 1f out* **33/1**

11 nk **Shoot Pontoon (IRE)** 2-9-3 0 PatDobbs 9 52+
(N A Callaghan) *s.i.s: a bhd* **66/1**

12 1 **Love Empire (USA)** 2-9-3 0 DeanMcKeown 10 50
(M Johnston) *s.i.s: a bhd: nvr trbld ldrs* **33/1**

1m 39.42s (-0.01) **Going Correction** -0.10s/f (Stan) 12 Ran SP% **117.0**
Speed ratings (Par 96): **96,95,94,93,93 93,92,92,91,88 88,87**
CSF £283.28 TOTE £22.90: £5.70, £5.60, £2.20; EX 434.40 TRIFECTA Not won..
Owner Giuliano Manfredini **Bred** R J Cornelius **Trained** Newmarket, Suffolk
■ Stewards' Enquiry : Adrian McCarthy one-day ban; careless riding (Dec 18)

FOCUS
The first three in this maiden in particular look potentially above-average for the track. The pace was modest and, although the bare form is limited, several should do better in time.

NOTEBOOK
Crosstar, a 28,000gns son of Cape Cross out of a successful 7f mare, is from a good family. A promising third on his debut in Italy in September, he adapted well to the Polytrack surface and won in the style of a likely improver, with his trainer reporting that he thought he would need the run. He is highly thought of at home, and will now be kept back for the turf season. (op 25-1)
Seattle Storm(IRE) ◆, a Robellino colt, is a half-brother to several winners from 6f to 1m2f, including the useful 1m2f performer Snoqualmie Boy. Patiently ridden after a slow start, he put in some excellent late work which suggests it will not take long for him to make his mark. (tchd 25-1)
Strategic Knight(USA) ◆, a $275,000 foal and 270,000gns yearling, is a Johannesburg half-brother to the multiple 6f-7f winner Resplendent Cee, and there are other winners in the family over a wide range of distances. He put in a bold bid to make all, and ought to find a similar event. (op 6-1)
Mick's Dancer, a 65,000gns son of top sprinter Pivotal, is a half-brother to five winners and his dam won over 7f as a juvenile. He improved a little on his recent debut here, and should find some suitable races, particularly when handicapped. (op 14-1)
Pharaohs Justice(USA), a $150,000 foal but recently unsold at 18,000gns, has shown some ability in his two races, and will be more effective when handicapped. (tchd 40-1)
Agente Romano(USA) was unable to capitalise on his promising debut here 11 days earlier. However, he was not ideally suited by the modest early tempo, and should not be discounted yet. (op 6-4)
Ace Of Spies(IRE), a Machiavellian colt out of the top-class 1m2f mare Nadia, is bred to win good races. Though he is unlikely to live up to those expectations, he showed enough on this debut to suggest there is something to work on for the future. (op 7-1 tchd 8-1)
Art Value has fallen short in maidens, but this was a fair Polytrack debut and he will be at home in handicaps. (op 3-1)

Plumage Official explanation: jockey said filly was denied a clear run

7052 PLAY POKER AT LADBROKES.COM NURSERY 6f (P)
1:45 (1:45) (Class 5) (0-85,77) 2-Y-O £4,210 (£1,252; £625; £312) Stalls Low

Form RPR
5060 1 **The Game**[31] 6699 2-9-7 77 PatCosgrave 1 81
(J R Boyle) *stdd s: t.k.h: hld up in last: hdwy on outer 2f out: edgd rt fnl f: led wl ins fnl f: r.o wl* 8/1[3]

0611 2 ½ **What Katie Did (IRE)**[43] 6454 2-8-12 73 TolleyDean(5) 3 76
(P F I Cole) *t.k.h: led: rdn wl over 1f out: hdd wl ins fnl f: no ex* 15/8[1]

1003 3 nk **Mudhish (IRE)**[27] 6756 2-9-5 75 (b) HayleyTurner 4 77+
(C E Brittain) *chsd ldng pair: short of room briefly wl over 1f out: rdn and edgd rt jst over 1f out: kpt on: wnt 3rd nr fin* 10/3[2]

13 4 nk **Blue Jack**[37] 6588 2-9-5 75 MartinDwyer 2 76
(W R Muir) *stdd s: t.k.h: hld up in tch: edgd out rt and hdwy wl over 1f out: ev ch 1f out: no ex last 50yds* 15/8[1]

0403 5 9 **Sinead Of Aglish (IRE)**[21] 6834 2-9-2 72 (b) LPKeniry 5 46
(Peter Grayson) *s.i.s: sn chsng ldr: ev ch and rdn 2f out: wknd over 1f out* 20/1

1m 11.77s (-1.04) **Going Correction** -0.10s/f (Stan) 5 Ran SP% 108.5
Speed ratings (Par 96): **102,101,100,100,88**
CSF £22.74 TOTE £10.20: £3.50, £1.40; EX 33.80.
Owner M Khan X2 **Bred** Aston House Stud **Trained** Epsom, Surrey

FOCUS
A fair nursery run in a good time, though the small field was disappointing

NOTEBOOK
The Game was unlucky in running here two outings ago, but made up for that with a battling victory. He has now dropped to a fairer mark, and should not go up much for this, so can remain more competitive now on a surface that clearly suits. (tchd 10-1)

What Katie Did(IRE), bought for £16,000 after winning a claimer last time, showed he can make his mark back in handicaps with a solid first effort at this track. He has handled Polytrack well elsewhere, and should have a good winter. (tchd 2-1 tchd 9-4 in a place)

Mudhish(IRE) ran another good race with the blinkers on, and should find a race eventually if they continue to do the trick. (op 3-1 tchd 11-4)

Blue Jack, though unable to justify joint-favouritism, only went under late in the day, and this lightly-raced colt should remain a live contender in handicap company. (op 2-1 tchd 9-4 in a place)

Sinead Of Aglish(IRE), by far the outsider of the party, ran well for a while, and looks worth dropping back to 5f. (op 14-1)

7053 PLAY CASINO AT LADBROKES.COM H'CAP 6f (P)
2:20 (2:21) (Class 3) (0-95,95) 3-Y-0+
£6,855 (£2,052; £1,026; £513; £256; £128) Stalls Low

Form RPR
4023 1 **Turn On The Style**[20] 6851 5-9-4 95 (b) EddieAhern 5 107+
(J Balding) *missed break and squeezed sn after s: hdwy into midfield 4f out: n.m.r 3f out: hdwy 2f out: swtchd lft 1f out: r.o strly to ld nr fin* 5/2[1]

0001 2 hd **Lucayos**[7] 6972 4-8-7 91 6ex KylieManser(7) 8 98
(Mrs H Sweeting) *chsd ldrs: wnt 2nd and rdn wl over 1f out: led and edgd rt jst over 1f out: hdd nr fin* 16/1

46 3 nk **Orpenindeed (IRE)**[13] 6932 4-8-13 90 (t) OscarUrbina 4 96
(M Botti) *t.k.h: in tch: hdwy to chse ldrs 2f out: kpt on u.p fnl f* 7/1[3]

0503 4 ½ **Andronikos**[13] 6932 5-8-12 89 (t) NelsonDeSouza 6 96+
(P F I Cole) *t.k.h: hld up in rr: hdwy and swtchd rt over 1f out: r.o strly fnl f: nt rch ldrs* 13/2[2]

1004 5 ½ **Diane's Choice**[33] 6668 4-8-9 86 MartinDwyer 11 89
(J Akehurst) *slowly away: sn chsng ldr: rdn over 2f out: lost 2nd over 1f out: fdd last 50yds* 20/1

6220 6 shd **King's Caprice**[13] 6932 6-8-12 92 (t) TravisBlock(3) 10 94
(J A Geake) *mounted on crse and taken down early: sn led: rdn jst over 2f out: hdd jst over 1f out: fdd last 50yds* 12/1

0360 7 shd **Little Edward**[13] 6930 9-8-12 89 SteveDrowne 7 91
(R J Hodges) *t.k.h: hld up in tch in midfield: rdn wl over 1f out: kpt on ins fnl f: nvr threatened ldrs* 8/1

0022 8 nk **Bahiano (IRE)**[27] 6753 6-8-10 87 LiamJones 12 88
(C E Brittain) *in midfield tl dropped to rr and rdn 3f out: kpt on fnl f: nt trble ldrs* 8/1

4000 9 1 **Woodnook**[13] 6930 4-9-1 92 JohnEgan 1 90
(J A R Toller) *hld up in rr: rdn and effrt wl over 1f out: nvr trbld ldrs* 7/1[3]

1104 10 1¾ **Ajigolo**[18] 6876 4-9-2 93 ChrisCatlin 2 85
(M R Channon) *in tch in midfield: rdn jst over 2f out: outpcd wl over 1f out* 7/1[3]

1m 10.44s (-2.37) **Going Correction** -0.10s/f (Stan) course record 10 Ran SP% 120.0
Speed ratings (Par 107): **111,110,110,109,109 108,108,108,107,104**
CSF £49.19 CT £258.24 TOTE £3.40: £1.30, £4.90, £3.00; EX 60.90 TRIFECTA Not won..
Owner The Haydock Badgeholders **Bred** J And Mrs Bowtell **Trained** Scrooby, Notts

FOCUS
A decent-quality, competitive sprint producing an exciting blanket finish, with the winner doing well to overcome considerable trouble in running. The form is rated fairly positively around the first two.

NOTEBOOK
Turn On The Style used to have problems with the stalls, but his current connections have corrected that and - though described by his trainer as "a bit of a character - a real monkey", Balding also paid tribute to his bravery following this remarkable success. 7lb above his highest winning mark, he had a nightmare run almost from start to finish, but he goes well round here and got there in the nick of time. He is developing into a smart sprinter. (op 11-4 tchd 3-1 in a place)

Lucayos nearly overcame his 6lb penalty, only being run down by the winner near the finish. He is back in form now, and can never be ruled out round here, despite being higher in the handicap these days. (op 11-1)

Orpenindeed(IRE) ◆ is acclimatising well, and his handicap mark looks a fair one now. He is capable of winning from 6f to 1m, and a first success in Britain should not be far away. (op 12-1)

Andronikos has never won a handicap, but recent efforts suggest he is on an attractive mark now, so he may put the record straight in the coming weeks. He is capable of winning at either 6f or 7f. (op 11-2)

Diane's Choice is running better now, despite being drawn wide in his last two races. With better luck, and a cleaner break, he could get himself back into the winner's enclosure.

King's Caprice ran much better than last time and was not beaten far despite finisihing out of the places. He has not won for over a year, but is now 7lb below his highest winning mark and that will keep him competitive on days when everything falls into place. (op 9-1)

Little Edward is still running well off a tough mark, and in doing so is not encouraging the Handicapper to show much leniency. (tchd 15-2)

Bahiano(IRE) found the trip too sharp, but his stamina was coming into to play late on. He has not won for nearly two years, but he is fairly handicapped at present and, though relatively unexposed on the All-Weather, acts well enough on Polytrack to be given a chance at 7f. (op 9-1 tchd 10-1)

7054 FRED GIBSON MEMORIAL H'CAP 6f (P)
2:55 (2:55) (Class 5) (0-75,73) 3-Y-0+ £2,817 (£838; £418; £209) Stalls Low

Form RPR
4030 1 **No Time (IRE)**[4] 7011 7-8-1 59 oh1 PatrickMathers(3) 7 66
(A J McCabe) *in tch: rdn and hdwy over 1f out: styd on wl u.p to ld towards fin* 11/2

2500 2 nk **Hythe Bay**[7] 6976 3-8-9 64 JimCrowley 6 70
(J R Best) *chsd ldr: drvn to ld 1f out: hdd and no ex towards finsh* 12/1

0302 3 1½ **Monte Major (IRE)**[20] 6860 6-8-10 65 DeanMcKeown 3 67
(D Shaw) *chsd ldrs: rdn and effrt on inner over 1f out: one pce last 100yds* 4/1[3]

0000 4 shd **Cool Sands (IRE)**[3] 7026 5-8-13 68 (v) AdamKirby 8 69
(D Shaw) *dropped in bhd after s: drvn and detached over 4f out: hung lft over 1f out: sme late hdwy but n.d* 7/1

0002 5 nk **Hollow Jo**[16] 6890 7-8-12 67 MickyFenton 5 67
(J R Jenkins) *stdd s: racd in last pair: detached 4f out: plugged on fnl f: n.d* 5/2[1]

400 6 nk **George The Second**[7] 6970 4-9-4 73 RichardKingscote 1 73
(Mrs H Sweeting) *led tl 1f out: wknd ins fnl f* 11/4[2]

1m 11.0s (-1.81) **Going Correction** -0.10s/f (Stan) 6 Ran SP% 110.8
Speed ratings (Par 103): **108,107,105,105,105 104**
CSF £60.36 CT £278.76 TOTE £7.10: £2.60, £2.80; EX 40.50 Trifecta £82.50 Pool £340.50 - 2.93 winning units..
Owner Paul J Dixon **Bred** Tally-Ho Stud **Trained** Babworth, Notts

FOCUS
A modest sprint contested by horses who just win in their turn. The time was decent and the form appears pretty straightforward.

George The Second Official explanation: jockey said colt hung right

7055 BET IN PLAY AT LADBROKES.COM H'CAP 1m 4f (P)
3:30 (3:30) (Class 4) (0-85,85) 3-Y-0+ £4,605 (£1,378; £689; £344; £171) Stalls Low

Form RPR
0630 1 **Sgt Schultz (IRE)**[111] 4597 4-9-1 79 LPKeniry 3 87+
(J S Moore) *t.k.h: hld up in midfield: hdwy to chse ldr 2f out: led ins fnl f: r.o wl* 7/2[2]

5124 2 1 **Pass The Port**[218] 1438 6-9-0 78 HayleyTurner 7 83
(D Haydn Jones) *slowly away: t.k.h: hld up in last: swtchd rt and hdwy over 1f out: r.o wl fnl f: wnt 2nd wl ins fnl f nt rch wnr* 9/1

-0R0 3 1½ **Willhego**[44] 6439 6-8-12 76 AdamKirby 8 78
(J R Best) *t.k.h: sn chsng ldr: led and rdn 2f out: hdd ins fnl f: no ex* 16/1

214 4 hd **Generous Lad (IRE)**[22] 6819 4-8-11 75 (p) SteveDrowne 2 77
(A B Haynes) *t.k.h: in tch: short of room jst over 2f out: kpt on u.p fnl f* 3/1[1]

2444 5 hd **Chocolate Caramel (USA)**[27] 6760 5-9-4 82 (b[1]) JimCrowley 6 83
(Mrs A J Perrett) *t.k.h: hld up in last trio: rdn and hdwy jst over 2f out: chsd ldng pair over 1f out: one pce fnl f* 3/1[1]

5020 6 nk **Shimoni**[35] 6620 3-8-10 79 (v) PaulDoe 1 80
(W J Knight) *in tch in midfield: rdn and nt qckn 2f out: kpt on fnl f: nt trble ldrs* 9/1

6140 7 3½ **Know The Law**[20] 6853 3-8-11 80 (b) PatDobbs 4 75
(D R C Elsworth) *t.k.h: hld up in rr: last and rdn 2f out: sn btn* 13/2[3]

2-04 8 8 **Petrovich (USA)**[30] 6726 4-9-7 85 JohnEgan 5 68
(Jane Chapple-Hyam) *led at stdy gallop: pushed along wl over 3f out: drvn 3f out: hdd and bmpd 2f out: sn wknd: eased fnl f* 16/1

2m 34.91s (0.52) **Going Correction** -0.10s/f (Stan)
WFA 3 from 4yo+ 5lb 8 Ran SP% 117.3
Speed ratings (Par 105): **94,93,92,92,92 91,89,84**
CSF £35.63 CT £448.99 TOTE £5.30: £1.60, £1.90, £4.10; EX 44.50 TRIFECTA Not won. Place 6 £674.77, Place 5 £517.69..
Owner Jim Barnes **Bred** Frank Dunne **Trained** Upper Lambourn, Berks

FOCUS
A fair handicap, but the pace was steady and the form may not prove that relaible.
T/Plt: £3,121.60 to a £1 stake. Pool: £39,127.65. 9.15 winning tickets. T/Qpdt: £192.80 to a £1 stake. Pool: £4,012.75. 15.40 winning tickets. SP

7042 WOLVERHAMPTON (A.W) (L-H)
Friday, December 7

OFFICIAL GOING: Standard
Wind: Fresh, behind Weather: Cloudy

7056 MACE RACING AT WOLVERHAMPTON APPRENTICE H'CAP 1m 1f 103y(P)
7:00 (7:00) (Class 6) (0-65,65) 3-Y-0+ £2,047 (£604; £302) Stalls Low

Form RPR
4551 1 **Moment Of Clarity**[13] 6937 5-8-10 59 (p) KrishGundowry(5) 6 69+
(R C Guest) *chsd ldrs: led 4f out: pushed clr 2f out: styd on* 11/4[1]

50- 2 1 **Dictation**[34] 6662 5-8-7 51 oh6 (b) SCreighton 5 54
(Mrs Valerie Keatley, Ire) *chsd ldrs: hmpd and lost pl over 3f out: rallied over 1f out: edgd lft: r.o* 40/1

6004 3 ½ **Thornaby Green**[21] 6837 6-8-13 60 DeanHeslop(3) 8 62
(T D Barron) *chsd ldr tl led over 5f out: hdd 4f out: rdn over 2f out: styd on* 7/1

2101 4 ½ **Mister Fizzbomb (IRE)**[23] 6325 4-9-3 61 (v) SladeO'Hara 7 62
(J S Wainwright) *outpcd: r.o ins fnl f: nrst fin* 7/1

4044 5 1¼ **Siena Star (IRE)**[11] 6951 9-9-3 61 JackDean 3 59
(Stef Liddiard) *hld up: hdwy over 5f out: outpcd over 3f out: hdwy u.p over 1f out: edgd lft: styd on same pce fnl f* 9/2[2]

0034 6 3½ **Run Free**[38] 6567 3-8-13 62 LanceBetts(3) 4 53
(N Wilson) *led 4f: rdn over 2f out: sn outpcd* 9/1

3640 7 1 **Granary Girl**[4] 7009 5-8-0 51 JosephineBruning(7) 2 40
(J Pearce) *chsd ldrs: no much room and lost pl over 6f out: n.d after* 22/1

50-0 8 8 **Follow The Colours (IRE)**[35] 6628 4-9-7 65 (t) JamieJones 10 37
(J W Hills) *hld up: plld hrd: hdwy over 5f out: rdn and wknd wl over 1f out* 10/1

3024 9 14 **Red Current**[2] 7032 3-9-3 63 WilliamCarson 9 6
(R A Harris) *chsd ldrs 7f* 5/1[3]

2m 2.90s (0.28) **Going Correction** -0.05s/f (Stan)
WFA 3 from 4yo+ 2lb 9 Ran SP% 112.4
Speed ratings (Par 101): **96,95,94,94,93 90,89,82,69**
CSF £113.21 CT £693.51 TOTE £4.00: £1.10, £9.70, £2.10; EX 123.20.
Owner Andrew Shedden **Bred** Lordship Stud **Trained** Carburton, Notts

FOCUS
A moderate affair with the winner value for a little further than the official margin, but not strong form rated around the third and fourth.
Red Current Official explanation: trainer said race came too soon for filly

7057 PONTIN'S HOLIDAYS CLAIMING STKS — 1m 141y(P)
7:30 (7:30) (Class 6) 3-Y-0+ — £2,388 (£705; £352) Stalls Low

Form — RPR

0425 **1** — **Ninth House (USA)**[22] 6824 5-9-4 71.......................(bt) GeorgeBaker 11 — 71
(N P Littmoden) *hld up: hdwy over 3f out: rdn to ld over 1f out: edgd lft: r.o* — 13/8[1]

111 **2** *nk* **Sawwaah (IRE)**[177] 2559 10-9-2 78.......................(v) RichardKingscote 6 — 68
(Tom Dascombe) *s.s: hld up: hdwy over 1f out: rdn ins fnl f: r.o* — 9/4[2]

-364 **3** *1/2* **Capania (IRE)**[37] 6579 3-8-5 57.......................... GregFairley 4 — 58
(Pat Eddery) *prom: racd keenly: chsd ldr 3f out: rdn and ev ch over 1f out: styd on same pce ins fnl f* — 8/1

0626 **4** *1 1/2* **Daring Affair**[32] 6696 6-9-1 68.......................(p) PhillipMakin 1 — 63
(K R Burke) *chsd ldrs: rdn and hmpd over 2f out: swtchd rt over 1f out: styd on* — 9/2[3]

006 **5** *4* **Maiden Investor**[162] 3031 4-8-3 40 ow1.................. TolleyDean(5) 10 — 46
(Stef Liddiard) *s.s: hld up: rdn over 1f out: nt trble ldrs* — 80/1

1420 **6** *hd* **Intersky Sports (USA)**[41] 694 3-9-0 63.................. DeanMcKeown 9 — 54
(K J Burke) *chsd ldr tl rdn and nt clr run over 1f out: wknd fnl f* — 28/1

3425 **7** *nk* **Not Now Lewis (IRE)**[21] 6833 3-8-6 62.................. TPQueally 2 — 45
(J A Osborne) *hld up: hdwy over 2f out: rdn and hmpd over 1f out: edgd lft and wknd fnl f* — 14/1

0406 **8** *nk* **Shadow Jumper (IRE)**[56] 6152 6-8-11 43......(v) RussellKennemore(5) 5 — 53
(J T Stimpson) *led: rdn and hdd over 1f out: wknd ins fnl f* — 40/1

0040 **9** *6* **Welsh Whisper**[221] 1362 8-8-2 41 ow1.................. ChrisCatlin 7 — 25
(S A Brookshaw) *chsd ldrs: rdn and hmpd over 2f out: wknd over 1f out* — 66/1

0000 **10** *14* **Diamond Hurricane (IRE)**[6] 7001 3-8-7 42...........(p) NeilChalmers(3) 8 — —
(M Wellings) *hld up: pushed along 5f out: wknd over 2f out* — 100/1

1m 50.72s (-1.04) **Going Correction** -0.05s/f (Stan)
WFA 3 from 4yo+ 2lb — 10 Ran SP% 114.4
Speed ratings (Par 101): **102,101,101,99,96 96,95,95,90,77**
CSF £5.13 TOTE £3.40: £1.30, £1.60, £1.80; EX 8.20.Capania was claimed by J Babb for £8,000.
Owner Nigel Shields **Bred** Juddmonte Farms Inc **Trained** Newmarket, Suffolk

FOCUS
An average claimer and limited form with some moderate sorts not beaten far.

7058 PONTIN'S BOOK EARLY AND SAVE MAIDEN FILLIES' STKS — 7f 32y(P)
7:55 (7:57) (Class 5) 2-Y-0 — £2,914 (£867; £433; £216) Stalls High

Form — RPR

320 **1** — **Applauded (IRE)**[48] 6336 2-9-0 89.......................(b[1]) RobertHavlin 11 — 78+
(B J Meehan) *trckd ldr 6f out: led over 3f out: sn clr: eased wl ins fnl f* — 8/11[1]

520 **2** *4* **Ceka Dancer (IRE)**[81] 5483 2-9-0 79.......................... ChrisCatlin 2 — 60
(E J O'Neill) *led 1f: racd keenly: rdn 1/2-way: chsd wnr over 1f out: no imp* — 2/1[2]

6 **3** *1* **Inontime (IRE)**[25] 6799 2-8-11 0.......................... AndrewElliott(3) 5 — 58
(K R Burke) *chsd ldrs: rdn over 2f out: styd on same pce* — 25/1

0 **4** *shd* **Spitfire Jane (IRE)**[20] 6849 2-8-7 0.................. DeclanCannon(7) 10 — 57
(K R Burke) *dwlt: hld up: hdwy u.p over 1f out: edgd lft: nt trble ldrs* — 50/1

00 **5** *hd* **Broughtons Flight (IRE)**[45] 6411 2-9-0 0.................. NeilPollard 8 — 57
(W J Musson) *hld up: effrt and hung lft over 2f out: n.d* — 50/1

043 **6** *5* **Naming Problems**[119] 4359 2-9-0 50.................. DeanMcKeown 9 — 45
(K J Burke) *hld up: shkn up over 2f out: hung lft over 1f out: nt trble ldrs* — 50/1

7 *nk* **Gayanula (USA)** 2-9-0 0.......................... PaulMulrennan 6 — 44
(Miss J A Camacho) *s.s: outpcd: nvr nrr* — 40/1

8 *2 1/2* **Jazenio** 2-9-0 0.......................... TPQueally 1 — 38
(K A Ryan) *s.i.s: hdwy to ld 6f out: hdd 1/2-way: sn rdn: wknd over 1f out* — 12/1[3]

0 **9** *3 1/2* **Hollow Dream (IRE)**[25] 6799 2-9-0 0.......................... LPKeniry 3 — 29
(R A Harris) *prom: rdn 1/2-way: wknd over 2f out* — 80/1

10 *1 3/4* **Nodservatory** 2-9-0 0.......................... PhillipMakin 4 — 25
(Miss J A Camacho) *s.s: outpcd* — 66/1

1m 31.33s (0.93) **Going Correction** -0.05s/f (Stan) — 10 Ran SP% 113.8
Speed ratings (Par 93): **92,87,86,86,85 80,79,77,73,71**
CSF £2.07 TOTE £1.70: £1.02, £1.80, £3.60; EX 2.00.
Owner Hugo Lascelles **Bred** Norelands Bloodstock **Trained** Manton, Wilts

FOCUS
An uncompetitive maiden and an easy winner, with the fifth and sixth setting a modest level.

NOTEBOOK
Applauded(IRE) was the form horse judged on his placed efforts in maidens at Newbury and Yarmouth before finding a step up in class to Group company too much to cope with last time. Fitted with blinkers for this All-Weather debut, he was always going like a winner and was value for twice the winning margin. (op 4-5 tchd 4-6)
Ceka Dancer(IRE), whose best run to date was a second over 6f at Kempton, raced keenly again and was left behind by the winner off the turn. It remains to be seen what he achieved here. (op 9-4 tchd 15-8)
Inontime(IRE) raced much more prominently than on her debut here last month, and ran better as a result. (op 28-1 tchd 33-1)
Spitfire Jane(IRE), who raced freely to halfway following a slowish start, was doing her best work late on and should appreciate further in time. (op 40-1)
Broughtons Flight(IRE), having her third start and first on the All-Weather, ran up to her turf form and now qualifies for a handicap mark. (op 40-1)

7059 PONTIN'S SHORT BREAKS H'CAP — 5f 20y(P)
8:25 (8:25) (Class 5) (0-75,74) 3-Y-0+ — £2,914 (£867; £433; £216) Stalls Low

Form — RPR

051 **1** — **Silver Prelude**[7] 6976 6-8-10 71 6ex.................. JamesO'Reilly(5) 3 — 87+
(D K Ivory) *mde all: rdn clr over 1f out: r.o* — 9/4[1]

6066 **2** *3* **Fizzlephut (IRE)**[7] 6976 5-8-13 69.................. PaulFitzsimons 4 — 74
(Miss J R Tooth) *prom: rdn to chse wnr fnl f: no imp* — 11/1

1001 **3** *1* **Compton Classic**[16] 6891 5-8-11 74.................(v) HarryPoulton(7) 5 — 75
(J R Boyle) *hld up: rdn over 1f out: hung lft and r.o ins fnl f: nrst fin* — 4/1[2]

0000 **4** *shd* **Stolt (IRE)**[21] 6836 3-9-3 73.................. DanielTudhope 8 — 74
(N Wilson) *s.i.s: hld up: r.o ins fnl f: nrst fin* — 22/1

0155 **5** *1/2* **Desert Opal**[13] 6938 7-9-2 72.......................(b) TPQueally 7 — 71
(C R Dore) *chsd ldrs: rdn over 3f out: styd on same pce fnl 2f* — 5/1[3]

0050 **6** *1* **Almaty Express**[20] 6860 5-8-6 67.................(b) AshleyHamblett(5) 6 — 63
(J R Weymes) *chsd wnr tl rdn over 1f out: wknd ins fnl f* — 13/2

0010 **7** *1* **Back In The Red (IRE)**[7] 6976 3-8-11 74.................. WilliamCarson(7) 1 — 66
(R A Harris) *sn outpcd* — 8/1

6000 **8** *11* **Bold Minstrel (IRE)**[45] 6405 5-9-0 70.................(v[1]) ChrisCatlin 2 — 22
(M Quinn) *s.i.s: outpcd* — 16/1

61.70 secs (-1.12) **Going Correction** -0.05s/f (Stan) — 8 Ran SP% 110.4
Speed ratings (Par 103): **106,101,99,99,98 97,95,77**
CSF £26.32 CT £87.11 TOTE £2.70: £1.40, £2.90, £1.60; EX 21.20.
Owner Mrs A Shone **Bred** Bearstone Stud **Trained** Radlett, Herts

FOCUS
A fair handicap with an impressive winner, and the form should prove reasonable despite the proximity of the fourth.

7060 GO PONTIN'S NOW H'CAP — 1m 4f 50y(P)
8:55 (8:55) (Class 6) (0-55,55) 3-Y-0+ — £2,047 (£604; £302) Stalls Low

Form — RPR

301 **1** — **Bernabeu (IRE)**[25] 6792 5-8-8 47.......................... PaulDoe 7 — 56+
(S Curran) *chsd ldr: led 3f out: rdn out* — 6/1

2 **2** *1* **Ilviz (FR)**[68] 5-9-0 53.......................... PaulMulrennan 12 — 57
(Ollie Pears) *mid-div: hdwy over 3f out: rdn over 1f out: r.o* — 16/1

4143 **3** *1/2* **Altos Reales**[9] 6967 3-8-11 55.................. DeanMcKeown 5 — 58
(D Shaw) *hld up: hdwy over 3f out: nt clr run over 2f out: rdn and swtchd lft over 1f out: r.o* — 8/1

5000 **4** *3/4* **Mandalay Prince**[21] 6837 3-8-10 54.................. TPQueally 11 — 56
(W J Musson) *s.i.s: hld up: hdwy 2f out: sn rdn and hung lft: styd on* — 15/2

0220 **5** *1* **Intavac Boy**[13] 6937 6-8-13 52.......................(p) ChrisCatlin 6 — 52
(S P Griffiths) *prom: rdn to chse ldr and hung lft over 2f out: no ex fnl f* — 5/1[2]

3036 **6** *1* **Giddywell**[13] 6937 3-8-6 55.................. RussellKennemore(5) 8 — 54
(R Hollinshead) *hmpd s: hld up: rdn over 2f out: nvr nrr* — 25/1

6200 **7** *3* **Buscador (USA)**[15] 6906 8-8-8 52.................. AshleyHamblett(5) 1 — 46
(W M Brisbourne) *led: rdn and hdd 3f out: wknd over 1f out* — 14/1

0002 **8** *shd* **Sir Sandicliffe (IRE)**[9] 6967 3-8-8 52.................. NeilPollard 4 — 46
(W M Brisbourne) *hld up: hdwy over 5f out: rdn over 3f out: wkng whn hung lft over 1f out* — 4/1[1]

6343 **9** *1/2* **Regency Red (IRE)**[13] 6937 9-8-9 55.................. Julie-AnneCumine(7) 9 — 48
(W M Brisbourne) *hld up: racd keenly: hdwy 9f out: rdn over 3f out: wknd 2f out: sn hung lft* — 12/1

0030 **10** *1 1/4* **Covert Mission**[14] 6911 4-8-9 55.................. RichardEvans(7) 3 — 46
(P D Evans) *mid-div: lost pl over 4f out: sn bhd* — 25/1

2005 **11** *1 1/2* **Boppys Pride**[18] 6867 4-8-12 54.................(p) JamieMoriarty(3) 2 — 43
(R A Fahey) *chsd ldrs: rdn over 3f out: wknd over 2f out* — 11/2[3]

2m 40.96s (-1.46) **Going Correction** -0.05s/f (Stan)
WFA 3 from 4yo+ 5lb — 11 Ran SP% 117.1
Speed ratings (Par 101): **102,101,101,100,99 99,97,97,96,95 94**
CSF £97.11 CT £766.93 TOTE £5.80: £2.00, £8.20, £2.80; EX 445.40.
Owner G D Peck **Bred** Mrs Joan M Langmead **Trained** Faringdon, Oxon

FOCUS
A moderate handicap runat a fair gallop and rated around the third and fourth, backed up by the sixth.
Sir Sandicliffe(IRE) Official explanation: jockey said gelding ran flat

7061 PONTINS.COM H'CAP — 1m 141y(P)
9:20 (9:22) (Class 4) (0-85,85) 3-Y-0+ — £4,857 (£1,445; £722; £360) Stalls Low

Form — RPR

6411 **1** — **Abbondanza (IRE)**[32] 6696 4-9-0 79.......................(p) PhillipMakin 2 — 92
(I Semple) *mde all: clr 2f out: rdn and hung rt over 1f out: styd on* — 5/2[2]

0144 **2** *5* **Alfresco**[11] 6949 3-9-0 81.......................(b) PatDobbs 7 — 82
(I A Wood) *hld up: hdwy over 2f out: rdn to chse wnr over 1f out: no imp* — 6/1[3]

0361 **3** *1 1/2* **Master Pegasus**[33] 6674 4-9-4 83.................. GeorgeBaker 6 — 81
(C F Wall) *hld up: hdwy over 3f out: rdn to chse wnr over 2f out: styd on same pce* — 5/2[2]

5411 **4** *2 1/2* **Gunfighter (IRE)**[27] 6753 4-9-6 85.................. PaulMulrennan 1 — 77
(J S Wainwright) *chsd clr ldrs: nt clr run wl over 2f out: effrt over 1f out: wknd ins fnl f* — 9/4[1]

3040 **5** *3/4* **Bee Stinger**[123] 4234 5-8-13 78.................. ChrisCatlin 4 — 68
(I A Wood) *chsd wnr tl rdn over 2f out: sn wknd* — 18/1

1m 49.99s (-1.77) **Going Correction** -0.05s/f (Stan)
WFA 3 from 4yo+ 2lb — 5 Ran SP% 107.5
Speed ratings (Par 105): **105,100,99,97,96**
CSF £15.90 TOTE £4.00: £2.10, £1.50; EX 11.50 Place 6 £59.65, Place 5 £27.69..
Owner Joseph Leckie & Sons Ltd **Bred** M Nolan **Trained** Carluke, S Lanarks

FOCUS
This fair handicap looked quite competitive, with three of the five runners coming into the race in winning form but Abbondanza turned it intoa procession.
Gunfighter(IRE) Official explanation: jockey said colt never travelled
T/Plt: £28.30 to a £1 stake. Pool: £103,700.85. 2,672.30 winning tickets. T/Qpdt: £8.60 to a £1 stake. Pool: £6,385.10. 547.50 winning tickets. CR

7062 - 7093a (Foreign Racing) - See Raceform Interactive

[7050] LINGFIELD (L-H)
Saturday, December 8

OFFICIAL GOING: Standard
Wind: Strong, behind Weather: Rain

7069 PLAY GOLF @ LINGFIELD PARK CLASSIFIED STKS — 1m 4f (P)
12:20 (12:20) (Class 7) 3-Y-0+ — £1,706 (£503; £252) Stalls Low

Form — RPR

00-2 **1** — **Barton Sands (IRE)**[26] 6792 10-9-3 45.......................(t) JimCrowley 4 — 59
(Andrew Reid) *hld up in midfield: hdwy over 2f out: led over 1f out: drvn out* — 8/1

056- **2** *hd* **Dishdasha (IRE)**[28] 1536 5-9-3 41.................. JamieSpencer 16 — 59
(Mrs A M Thorpe) *stdd s and swtchd to rail: dropped out last: swtchd outside and gd hdwy 2f out: chal 1f out: kpt on wl: jst hld* — 2/1[1]

5005 **3** *6* **Missie Baileys**[8] 6971 5-9-3 45.................(v[1]) TGMcLaughlin 5 — 49
(Mrs L J Mongan) *towards rr: rdn and r.o fnl 2f: wnt 3rd fnl 100yds: no ch w ldng pair* — 11/1

0005 **4** *1 1/2* **The Slider**[3] 7032 3-8-12 42.................. FergusSweeney 8 — 47
(Mrs L C Jewell) *hld up in midfield: hdwy over 2f out: jnd ldrs ent st: no ex fnl f* — 25/1

5000 **5** *1* **Big Ralph**[22] 6832 4-8-12 42.................. JamesO'Reilly(5) 10 — 45
(D K Ivory) *chsd ldrs: rdn whn squeezed and snatched up wl over 1f out: sn btn* — 10/1

0350 **6** *1 1/4* **The Mighty Ogmore**[24] 6815 3-8-7 43.................(p) KirstyMilczarek(5) 9 — 43
(R C Guest) *bhd: pushed along over 2f out: nrst fin* — 12/1

305 **7** 1 1/4 **War Feather**[45] 4914 5-9-3 45....(p) RobertHavlin 13 41
(T D McCarthy) *mid-div: rdn over 4f out: no hdwy fnl 2f* **16/1**

3063 **8** 1 **The Diamond Bond**[7] 6999 3-8-12 45.... ChrisCatlin 15 39
(G R Oldroyd) *in tch: effrt over 2f out: wknd over 1f out* **6/1**[3]

065/ **9** 1/2 **Ede's**[262] 3136 7-9-3 45.... IanMongan 12 39
(P M Phelan) *prom: led 3f out tl wknd over 1f out* **25/1**

-060 **10** 7 **Global Achiever**[18] 1719 6-8-12 42.... RussellKennemore(5) 7 27
(M J Gingell) *chsd ldrs: drvn along 4f out: sn wknd* **50/1**

0000 **11** shd **Simplify**[37] 6607 5-9-3 39.... FrankieMcDonald 3 27
(T M Jones) *in rr of mid-div: rdn and n.d fnl 3f* **66/1**

050 **12** 1 1/4 **The Iron Giant (IRE)**[24] 3397 5-9-3 45.... GeorgeBaker 1 25
(B G Powell) *pressed ldr: slt ld 6f out tl 3f out: sn wknd* **11/2**[2]

13 3 **Sumdancer (NZ)**[33] 5-9-3 45.... J-PGuillambert 14 21
(M Madgwick) *stdd s: t.k.h early: rdn 3f out: a bhd* **20/1**

3060 **14** 1 1/4 **Ernmoor**[31] 6713 5-9-0 45.... JerryO'Dwyer(3) 11 19
(J R Jenkins) *led tl 6f out: drvn along over 3f out: wknd 2f out* **25/1**

2m 32.3s (-2.09) **Going Correction** -0.125s/f (Stan)
WFA 3 from 4yo+ 5lb **14** Ran SP% **124.9**
Speed ratings (Par 97): **101,100,96,95,95 94,93,92,92,87 87,86,84,84**
CSF £23.42 TOTE £7.00: £2.40, £1.40, £2.90; EX 28.10 Trifecta £77.20 Part won. Pool: £108.78 - 0.50 winning units..
Owner A S Reid **Bred** Patrick Cassidy **Trained** Mill Hill, London NW7
■ Andrew Reid's first winner since resuming training after 19 months without a licence.

FOCUS
A very weak classified stakes, run at a sound gallop and the first three all came from off the pace. The form looks fair enough with the first pair coming clear.
The Iron Giant(IRE) Official explanation: jockey said gelding had no more to give

7070 LINGFIELD PARK FOR WEDDINGS MEDIAN AUCTION MAIDEN STKS 1m (P)
12:50 (12:54) (Class 6) 2-Y-O **£1,943** (£578; £288; £144) **Stalls** High

Form RPR

1 **Call Of Duty (IRE)** 2-9-3 0.... GregFairley 8 74+
(M Johnston) *towards rr: hdwy over 1f out: r.o strly to ld fnl 30yds* **8/1**

00 **2** 3/4 **Alcimedes**[113] 4584 2-9-3 0.... AdrianMcCarthy 2 71
(P W Chapple-Hyam) *sn prom: drvn to ld ins fnl f: hdd and nt qckn fnl 30yds* **11/2**[2]

02 **3** hd **Fair Gale**[44] 6456 2-9-3 0.... RichardHughes 11 71
(S Kirk) *hld up in rr: pushed along over 3f out: gd hdwy over 1f out: styd on wl u.p fnl f* **6/1**[3]

24 **4** 1/2 **Celtic Dragon**[31] 6725 2-9-3 0.... JimCrowley 12 70
(Mrs A J Perrett) *led: rdn over 2f out: hdd and one pce ins fnl f* **11/4**[1]

04 **5** 1 3/4 **Burnbrake**[22] 6827 2-9-3 0.... RobertHavlin 10 66+
(J A R Toller) *wd: hld up in rr of midfield: swtchd to ins rail and hdwy over 1f out: nt rch ldrs* **15/2**

2 **6** nk **Celtic Charlie (FR)**[26] 6791 2-9-3 0.... JamieSpencer 5 65+
(P M Phelan) *hld up last: effrt and v wd st: hdwy over 1f out: styd on: too much to do* **11/2**[2]

40 **7** 3/4 **My Shadow**[51] 6289 2-9-3 0.... JohnEgan 4 64
(S Dow) *t.k.h: chsd ldrs: drvn along 3f out: outpcd fnl 2f* **33/1**

0 **8** 3 1/2 **Golden Horus (USA)**[7] 6990 2-9-0 0.... JerryO'Dwyer(3) 1 56
(P J O'Gorman) *s.s: sn in tch on rail: effrt over 2f out: wknd over 1f out* **66/1**

5 **9** hd **Beauchamp Warrior**[29] 6740 2-9-3 0.... NickyMackay 7 56
(G A Butler) *t.k.h in midfield: rdn and no hdwy fnl 2f* **7/1**

0 **10** 7 **Princess Augusta (USA)**[40] 6535 2-8-12 0.... LPKeniry 6 35
(A M Balding) *prom tl wknd qckly wl over 1f out* **66/1**

0 **11** 4 **Dear Will**[19] 6868 2-9-3 0.... OscarUrbina 3 31
(J R Fanshawe) *t.k.h: chsd ldrs over 5f* **25/1**

00 **12** 1 **Super Starlet (IRE)**[37] 6601 2-8-12 0.... TPQueally 9 24
(M Botti) *broke wl: chsd ldrs tl stdd bk into midfield after 2f: wknd 3f out* **66/1**

1m 40.81s (1.38) **Going Correction** -0.125s/f (Stan) **12** Ran SP% **118.4**
Speed ratings (Par 94): **88,87,87,86,84 84,83,80,80,73 69,68**
CSF £50.02 TOTE £11.40: £3.10, £2.30, £2.30; EX 68.30 TRIFECTA Not won..
Owner Gainsborough **Bred** Gainsborough Stud Management Ltd **Trained** Middleham Moor, N Yorks

FOCUS
A modest juvenile maiden, run at a good pace. The winner could rate higher but the level of the form is a bit guessy.

NOTEBOOK
Call Of Duty(IRE) ◆, a half-brother to smart 10f performer and high-class hurdler Blythe Knight, ran out a ready winner at the first time of asking. He proved very easy to back, ran green through the first half of the race, but he showed a bit of class when the penny dropped and won going away in the end. His trainer is not afraid to put a classy prospect onto the Polytrack for its early education and he could prove to be a useful three-year-old.
Alcimedes, who showed modest ability in two Newmarket maidens during the summer, has been given time since having a gelding operation and his connections patience looks to have paid off as this was a much more encouraging effort on this Polytrack bow. He is entitled to come on for the run, now qualifies for a handicap mark, and looks well worth another try over this extra furlong. (op 13-2)
Fair Gale needed to be ridden nearing the home turn, but he responded for pressure and looked to run close to his recent level in defeat. He sets the standard for this form, is now qualified for a handicap mark, and could be ready to tackle a stiffer test now. (op 9-2)
Celtic Dragon had his chance from the front on this switch to the All-Weather and can have no excuses. He is another who probably needs a stiffer test and has more options now he is eligible for a handicap rating. (tchd 5-2 and 3-1 tchd 10-3 in a place)
Burnbrake was not helped by having to come wide for most of the way and got the longer trip well enough. He is another who can do better now he is qualified for a handicap mark. (op 8-1 tchd 9-1)
Celtic Charlie(FR), runner-up over 7f on debut 26 days previously, was given an ill-judged ride from off the pace over this longer trip and got going all too late in the day. He is capable of better. (op 15-2)
Dear Will Official explanation: jockey said gelding lost its action approaching final bend

7071 JUMPING HERE SATURDAY 15TH DECEMBER MAIDEN AUCTION STKS 5f (P)
1:25 (1:25) (Class 6) 2-Y-O **£1,943** (£578; £288; £144) **Stalls** High

Form RPR

0303 **1** **Joss Stick**[8] 6977 2-8-9 59....(p) TPQueally 2 66
(P J Makin) *chsd ldng pair: led 1f out: drvn out* **5/2**[2]

03 **2** 1 1/4 **Orange Square (IRE)**[12] 6944 2-8-11 0.... RichardHughes 4 64
(R Hannon) *sn pressing ldr: hrd rdn 1f out: kpt on* **5/4**[1]

0064 **3** 1 1/4 **Queens Mantle**[24] 6813 2-8-6 55.... ChrisCatlin 1 54
(P J Makin) *led: hrd rdn and hdd 1f out: one pce* **10/1**

4 5 **Plenty Of Action (USA)** 2-8-10 0.... JamieSpencer 3 40+
(M J Wallace) *s.i.s: last tl wnt mod 4th 1f out: n.d* **10/3**[3]

050 **5** 1 3/4 **Where's Killoran**[14] 6926 2-8-10 52.... LPKeniry 5 34
(Peter Grayson) *hld up in 4th: rdn 2f out: sn outpcd* **40/1**

58.84 secs (-0.94) **Going Correction** -0.125s/f (Stan) **5** Ran SP% **107.6**
Speed ratings (Par 94): **102,100,98,90,87**
CSF £5.75 TOTE £3.40: £1.80, £1.10; EX 5.20.
Owner Lady Davis J P Carrington D M Ahier **Bred** K W Green **Trained** Ogbourne Maisey, Wilts

FOCUS
A moderate juvenile maiden. The second and third set the level.

NOTEBOOK
Joss Stick, third in a claimer last time, did enough to get off the mark at the eighth attempt and rates full value for his winning margin. He is exposed on a mark of 59, and the fact he won here confirms the form is only moderate, but he has been improved by the application of cheekpieces the last twice. It may also be that he finds a little more improvement when tried over 6f again now he has got his head in front. (op 7-2)
Orange Square(IRE), dropping back from 1m, basically lacked the tactical speed of the winner when it mattered. He should not be too harsly judged on this effort, he now qualifies for a handicap mark, and has a race in him when reverting to a stiffer test. (op 11-8 tchd 6-5)
Queens Mantle ran a sound enough race in defeat from the front and helps to set the moderate level of this form. (op 11-1 tchd 9-1)
Plenty Of Action(USA), a $50,000 half-sister to winning sprinters, would not have had to be anything special to make a winning debut in this company yet she proved very easy to back. She ultimately proved too green to do herself justice and ought to know a deal more next time out. (op 2-1)

7072 LINGFIELDPARK.CO.UK NURSERY 5f (P)
2:00 (2:00) (Class 4) (0-85,79) 2-Y-O **£4,210** (£1,252; £625; £312) **Stalls** High

Form RPR

0061 **1** **Ten Down**[8] 6977 2-9-2 **74**.... TPQueally 4 77
(J A Osborne) *sn led: mde virtually all: hrd rdn over 1f out: hld on wl fnl f* **11/2**[3]

0013 **2** nk **Bazguy**[10] 6966 2-9-1 **73**....(b) TGMcLaughlin 2 75
(P D Evans) *sn rdn along in 5th: hdwy over 1f out: styd on to press wnr fnl 100yds: jst hld* **7/1**

2104 **3** 1 1/4 **Fabuleux Cherie**[22] 6834 2-8-12 **70**.... MartinDwyer 6 67
(W R Muir) *chsd wnr tl ins fnl f: one pce* **6/1**

4421 **4** 1 1/2 **Fast Feet**[7] 7000 2-9-7 **79**.... JohnEgan 5 71
(K A Ryan) *hdwy over 3f out: shkn up over 1f out: one pce* **3/1**[2]

2561 **5** nk **Wavertree Princess (IRE)**[14] 6926 2-9-2 **74**.... JamesDoyle 1 65
(N P Littmoden) *hld up in 6th: effrt over 1f out: nt pce to chal* **5/2**[1]

2052 **6** 2 **Wreningham**[22] 6834 2-8-9 **70**.... JerryO'Dwyer(3) 8 54
(T Keddy) *sn outpcd in rr* **10/1**

2040 **7** 2 1/2 **Cocabana**[22] 6834 2-8-7 **65**.... ChrisCatlin 3 40
(J G Portman) *chsd ldrs over 3f* **12/1**

58.76 secs (-1.02) **Going Correction** -0.125s/f (Stan) **7** Ran SP% **112.5**
Speed ratings (Par 98): **103,102,100,98,97 94,90**
CSF £41.22 CT £236.17 TOTE £7.90: £3.60, £2.20; EX 45.50 Trifecta £210.60 Pool: £456.94 - 1.54 winning units..
Owner Piers Pottinger And Ten **Bred** Baydon House Stud **Trained** Upper Lambourn, Berks

FOCUS
A fair nursery, run at a solid pace. Sound form, rated through the runner-up. Ten Down and previous race winner Joss Stick both came out of the same Wolverhampton claimer.

NOTEBOOK
Ten Down, off the mark in claiming company eight days previously, again did it from the front on this step back up in grade and just had enough in the locker to hold off the runner-up at the line. He has clearly enjoyed being able to race from the front the last twice and has improved since the headgear was discarded ahead of his previous outing. This course and distance looks perfect for him. (op 6-1 tchd 9-2)
Bazguy could not go the early pace on this drop back to the minimum trip, but he still came through to make the winner work all the way to the line. He remains in good heart and deserves to find another race again, but the return to another furlong looks in order. (op 13-2 tchd 8-1)
Fabuleux Cherie did nothing wrong in defeat and ran a fair race in defeat, helping to set the standard of this form. (op 13-2 tchd 7-1 and 11-2)
Fast Feet, finally off the mark at Wolverhampton a week previously, ran his race under top weight without ever seriously threatening. He looks in need of some respite from the assessor. (op 11-4 tchd 10-3)
Wavertree Princess(IRE) lacked the speed when it really mattered and is another who may now prefer a sixth furlong in this sort of company. (op 3-1)

7073 LINGFIELD PARK FOR CONFERENCES H'CAP 7f (P)
2:30 (2:32) (Class 5) (0-70,70) 3-Y-O+ **£2,817** (£838; £418; £209) **Stalls** Low

Form RPR

3541 **1** **Regal Raider (IRE)**[12] 6946 4-8-10 **65**....(p) AndrewElliott(3) 3 73+
(A M Hales) *mde all: rdn over 1f out: r.o wl: readily* **4/1**[1]

0431 **2** 2 **Onenightinlisbon (IRE)**[12] 6947 3-8-10 **69**.... HarryPoulton(7) 4 72
(J R Boyle) *mid-div: hdwy to chse wnr jst over 1f out: kpt on to hold 2nd nr fin* **10/1**

6535 **3** shd **Convivial Spirit**[19] 6874 3-9-0 **66**....(t) LPKeniry 6 69
(E F Vaughan) *towards rr: rdn and hdwy over 1f out: kpt on: jst hld for 2nd* **9/1**[3]

0266 **4** 1 3/4 **Mine Behind**[12] 6946 7-9-3 **69**.... GeorgeBaker 9 67
(J R Best) *bhd: hdwy and fair 4th over 1f out: no imp fnl f* **5/1**[2]

0-54 **5** 1 3/4 **Kensington (IRE)**[7] 6993 6-8-4 **56**....(p) SaleemGolam 2 49
(P D Evans) *mid-div: drvn along 3f out: no imp fnl 2f* **5/1**[2]

0005 **6** 1 1/2 **Sir Douglas**[3] 7033 4-9-4 **70**.... JohnEgan 1 62+
(R A Harris) *plld hrd: prom tl wknd over 1f out: eased whn btn ins fnl f* **5/1**[2]

0030 **7** 4 **Naughty Thoughts (IRE)**[21] 6856 3-8-12 **64**.... ChrisCatlin 7 42
(Andrew Turnell) *sn pushed along towards rr: n.d* **14/1**

46P5 **8** 2 1/2 **Dowlleh**[21] 6854 3-8-12 **69**....(p) KirstyMilczarek(5) 5 41
(T T Clement) *prom tl wknd qckly over 1f out: b.b.v* **20/1**

0301 **9** 1 3/4 **Haasem (USA)**[21] 6854 4-8-13 **65**.... JimCrowley 8 32
(J R Jenkins) *chsd ldrs tl hrd rdn and wknd wl over 1f out* **5/1**[2]

1m 24.53s (-1.36) **Going Correction** -0.125s/f (Stan) **9** Ran SP% **117.2**
Speed ratings (Par 103): **102,99,99,97,95 93,89,86,84**
CSF £45.44 CT £342.44 TOTE £3.50: £1.60, £2.10, £3.10; EX 29.30 Trifecta £292.50 Part won. Pool: £412.03 - 0.36 winning units..
Owner Brick Farm Racing **Bred** Gerard Callanan **Trained** Preston Capes, Northants

FOCUS
A modest handicap, run at an uneven pace. The winner rates value for a bit further with the runner-up setting the standard.
Sir Douglas Official explanation: jockey said colt did not stride out closing stages

Dowlleh Official explanation: trainer said gelding bled from the nose

7074 ARENALEISUREPLC.COM H'CAP — 1m (P)

3:05 (3:06) (Class 2) (0-100,103) 3-Y-O+

£9,971 (£2,985; £1,492; £747; £372; £187) **Stalls** High

Form				RPR
4223	1		**Fajr (IRE)**[7] 6992 5-9-8 **103** (b[1]) JamieSpencer 3 (Miss Gay Kelleway) *stdd s: hld up 2nd last: smooth hdwy over 2f out: hung lft and led 100yds out: drvn out* **15/8**[1]	111
0025	2	3/4	**Salient**[14] 6932 3-8-5 **87** PaulDoe 6 (J Akehurst) *led 3f: led over 3f out: hrd rdn and hdd 100yds out: n.m.r on rail: kpt on* **13/2**	94
0463	3	1 1/4	**Wavertree Warrior (IRE)**[17] 6900 5-8-6 **87** oh1 ow1...(b) JamesDoyle 2 (N P Littmoden) *hld up in 6th: hdwy and drvn along over 1f out: r.o fnl f* **10/1**	91
1411	4	*shd*	**Councellor (FR)**[8] 6981 5-8-9 **90** (t) MickyFenton 1 (Stef Liddiard) *chsd ldrs: rdn over 2f out: kpt on same pce appr fnl f* **11/2**[3]	93
5442	5	2	**Orchard Supreme**[7] 6992 4-9-5 **100** (b) RichardHughes 8 (R Hannon) *hdwy to ld 5f out: hdd over 3f out: hrd rdn and wknd 1f out* **7/2**[2]	99
0310	6	*hd*	**Just Bond (IRE)**[48] 6359 5-8-6 **87** ChrisCatlin 4 (G R Oldroyd) *s.s: bhd: rdn 3f out: styd on fnl f* **16/1**	85
6030	7	1/2	**Evens And Odds (IRE)**[14] 6932 3-8-12 **94** (p) JohnEgan 7 (K A Ryan) *prom: hrd rdn 3f out: wknd over 1f out: eased whn btn ins fnl f* **11/2**[3]	91
3046	8	*shd*	**Waterside (IRE)**[10] 6965 8-9-5 **100** GeorgeBaker 5 (G L Moore) *chsd ldrs: outpcd and lost pl over 2f out: n.d after* **14/1**	97

1m 37.33s (-2.10) **Going Correction** -0.125s/f (Stan)
WFA 3 from 4yo+ 1lb — **8** Ran SP% **122.7**
Speed ratings (Par 109): **105,104,103,102,100 100,100,100**
CSF £16.25 CT £103.53 TOTE £2.90: £1.40, £2.00, £2.40; EX 20.90 Trifecta £159.70 Pool: £672.92 - 2.99 winning units..

Owner The New Dawn Partnership **Bred** Shadwell Estate Company Limited **Trained** Exning, Suffolk

■ Jamie Spencer, on his first day's riding since the turf season ended, picked up what is likely to be a lengthy ban after this race.

■ Stewards' Enquiry : Jamie Spencer 17-day ban (takes into account previous offences): careless riding (Dec 21-Jan 5)

FOCUS

A decent handicap, run at a strong early pace. The form is rated around those in the frame behind the winner.

NOTEBOOK

Fajr(IRE), back up in trip, finally got his head back in front in the first-time blinkers. This was the first time he has been ridden by Spencer and it was not a surprise that the partnership came good, as the jockey's patient style clearly suited the horse. He still looked less than straightforward however, hanging markedly left when asked to win his race and his overall record dictates he is probably one to take on again next time out. That said, no doubt this success was deserved. (op 3-1)

Salient, not far off the winner over 7f last time, was done no favours as Fajr hung across him inside the final furlong. He was held by that rival at the time however, and it was not surprising the result stood in the subsequent Stewards' enquiry. This still rates a solid effort in defeat and he certainly does deserve to gain compensation now. (op 9-1)

Wavertree Warrior(IRE) ran his race, doing nothing wrong, and rates a fair benchmark for this form despite racing from 1lb out of the handicap. (op 9-1 tchd 12-1)

Councellor(FR), bidding for his fourth success from his last five outings, was far from disgraced off this 4lb higher mark in much better company than he has been keeping of late. He remains in good heart and is another benchmark for this form. (op 7-2)

Orchard Supreme, well backed, had finished in front of Fajr last time out and was 3lb better off with that rival so held obvious claims. However, he failed to really see out the extra furlong and performed below his recent level. (op 9-2)

Just Bond(IRE) struggled to go the early pace and was doing his best work towards the finish. He is on a career-high mark at present, but is capable of better than he showed here. (op 14-1)

Evens And Odds(IRE) Official explanation: jockey said colt had a breathing problem

7075 BOOK ONLINE FOR DISCOUNTED PRICES H'CAP — 1m 2f (P)

3:35 (3:35) (Class 4) (0-85,84) 3-Y-O+ **£4,605** (£1,378; £689; £344; £171) **Stalls** Low

Form				RPR
2323	1		**Mafeking (UAE)**[4] 7018 3-8-11 **80** AndrewElliott(3) 2 (M R Hoad) *towards rr: hdwy to trck ldr 6f out: led ins fnl f: pushed clr: readily* **8/11**[1]	88+
4004	2	1 1/2	**Dragon Slayer (IRE)**[4] 7018 5-9-0 **77** GregFairley 6 (P A Blockley) *chsd ldr: led 7f out tl ins fnl f: nt qckn* **7/2**[2]	82
50-0	3	3	**Obrigado (USA)**[34] 6669 7-9-3 **80** GeorgeBaker 7 (Karen George) *lost 6l s: hld up in rr: hdwy 2f out: wnt 3rd over 1f out: one pce fnl f* **12/1**	79
0060	4	*hd*	**Cupid's Glory**[14] 6932 5-9-7 **84** LPKeniry 3 (Mrs L C Jewell) *chsd ldrs: hrd rdn over 1f out: one pce* **14/1**	83
3213	5	7	**Lorikeet**[16] 1003 8-8-10 **73** JamesDoyle 4 (Noel T Chance) *led 3f: rdn 3f out: sn outpcd* **14/1**	58
242-	6	3 1/2	**Victor Trumper**[371] 6676 3-9-3 **83** FergusSweeney 1 (P W Chapple-Hyam) *bhd fnl 3f* **8/1**[3]	61
1006	7	1 1/4	**Cactus King**[25] 2512 4-9-4 **81** (p) IanMongan 5 (P M Phelan) *chsd ldrs tl wknd over 2f out* **14/1**	56

2m 7.52s (-0.27) **Going Correction** -0.125s/f (Stan)
WFA 3 from 4yo+ 3lb — **7** Ran SP% **118.9**
Speed ratings (Par 105): **96,94,92,92,86 83,82**
CSF £3.81 CT £16.92 TOTE £1.80: £1.40, £1.90; EX 5.10 Trifecta £38.10 Pool: £320.76 - 5.97 winning units. Place 6 £222.17, Place 5 £123.47..

Owner Mrs J E Taylor **Bred** Darley **Trained** Lewes, E Sussex

FOCUS

A fair handicap and the form is rated around the first two, although those behind are not that solid.

Obrigado(USA) Official explanation: jockey said gelding missed the break

T/Plt: £127.50 to a £1 stake. Pool: £52,294.50. 299.40 winning tickets. T/Qpdt: £23.10 to a £1 stake. Pool: £3,292.10. 105.40 winning tickets. LM

7056 WOLVERHAMPTON (A.W) (L-H)

Saturday, December 8

OFFICIAL GOING: Standard

Wind: Fresh, behind Weather: Overcast

7076 PONTIN'S BOOK EARLY PRICE PROMISE MAIDEN STKS — 1m 4f 50y(P)

7:00 (7:00) (Class 5) 3-Y-O+ **£2,968** (£876; £438) **Stalls** Low

Form				RPR
02	1		**Noble Plum (IRE)**[157] 3214 3-8-12 0 JamieMackay 6 (Sir Mark Prescott) *a.p: led over 1f out: shkn up and r.o: eased nr fin* **13/8**[2]	71+
2505	2	1 1/2	**Calculating (IRE)**[17] 6902 3-9-3 67 HayleyTurner 3 (M D I Usher) *hld up: hdwy over 5f out: rdn over 2f out: styd on* **17/2**	70
6032	3	1	**Esclarmonde (IRE)**[19] 6878 3-8-12 71 (b) NickyMackay 2 (L M Cumani) *led: rdn and hdd over 1f out: no ex ins fnl f* **6/4**[1]	63
2264	4	6	**Unreachable Star**[45] 6420 3-8-12 73 JimCrowley 8 (Mrs A J Perrett) *prom: chsd ldr 7f out: rdn and ev ch over 1f out: wknd ins fnl f: fin lame* **7/2**[3]	54
0-00	5	23	**Dickie Deano**[285] 569 3-9-3 45 PaulFitzsimons 1 (J M Bradley) *chsd ldrs over 7f: t.o* **150/1**	22
50-4	6	1 3/4	**Gouranga**[271] 270 4-8-12 55 KirstyMilczarek(5) 7 (A W Carroll) *s.i.s: hld up: rdn and wknd over 3f out: t.o* **40/1**	14
50-0	7	34	**Dories Dream**[17] 6901 3-8-12 43 ChrisCatlin 5 (Jane Southcombe) *chsd ldr 5f: wknd over 5f out: t.o* **100/1**	—

2m 41.17s (-1.25) **Going Correction** -0.025s/f (Stan)
WFA 3 from 4yo 5lb — 7 Ran SP% **114.9**
Speed ratings (Par 103): **103,102,101,97,82 80,58**
CSF £15.71 TOTE £2.70: £1.30, £3.70; EX 24.20.

Owner Sir Edmund Loder **Bred** Sir E J Loder **Trained** Newmarket, Suffolk

FOCUS

A modest, uncompetitive maiden in which the winner did not need to improve. The form is rated through the runner-up.

Unreachable Star Official explanation: vet said filly returned lame

Gouranga Official explanation: jockey said the filly had no more to give

7077 BOOK TICKETS ONLINE AT WOLVERHAMPTON-RACECOURSE.CO.UK CLAIMING STKS — 5f 216y(P)

7:30 (7:30) (Class 6) 3-Y-O+ **£2,047** (£604; £302) **Stalls** Low

Form				RPR
1040	1		**Green Lagonda (AUS)**[4] 7020 5-9-3 60 JimCrowley 5 (J G Given) *mde virually all: rdn clr over 1f out: edgd rt: styd on* **6/1**	73
0303	2	1 3/4	**Pegasus Dancer (FR)**[22] 6826 3-8-13 68 (p) JohnEgan 6 (K A Ryan) *chsd wnr: rdn over 2f out: styd on* **4/1**[3]	63
2320	3	*hd*	**Blackheath (IRE)**[11] 6957 11-8-4 50 KellyHarrison(5) 7 (S T Mason) *chsd ldrs: rdn over 2f out: edgd lft fnl f: styd on* **16/1**	58
410	4	1/2	**Mafaheem**[14] 6938 5-8-9 68 TGMcLaughlin 9 (A B Haynes) *s.s: in rr: hdwy u.p over 1f out: nrst fin* **13/8**[1]	57
5245	5	*hd*	**Mannello**[4] 7014 4-7-12 52 AdrianMcCarthy 1 (Jim Best) *chsd ldrs: outpcd 1/2-way: r.o ins fnl f* **7/2**[2]	45
6604	6	1 1/4	**Cyfrwys (IRE)**[68] 5861 6-7-12 44 (p) LiamJones 12 (B Palling) *prom: rdn 1/2-way: hung lft over 1f out: styd on same pce* **20/1**	41
0002	7	3	**Aggbag**[12] 6945 3-8-4 47 AndrewElliott(3) 10 (B P J Baugh) *s.i.s: n.d* **20/1**	40
0000	8	1	**Kitchen Sink (IRE)**[19] 6864 5-8-3 44 (e) FrankieMcDonald 8 (Jean-Rene Auvray) *sn outpcd* **66/1**	33
045-	9	*shd*	**Coranglais**[475] 4636 7-8-13 44 (p) PaulFitzsimons 3 (J M Bradley) *prom: rdn over 2f out: wknd over 1f out* **66/1**	43

1m 14.95s (-0.86) **Going Correction** -0.025s/f (Stan) — **9** Ran SP% **113.0**
Speed ratings (Par 101): **104,101,101,100,100 98,94,93,93**
CSF £28.35 TOTE £7.40: £2.00, £1.60, £4.40; EX 23.70.

Owner P J & Mrs Y Brain & R S G Jones **Bred** P J Brain **Trained** Willoughton, Lincs

FOCUS

An ordinary claimer, and an improved effort from winner Green Lagonda.

Kitchen Sink(IRE) Official explanation: jockey said gelding never travelled

7078 PONTIN'S GREAT FAMILY HOLIDAYS H'CAP — 5f 20y(P)

7:55 (7:57) (Class 4) (0-80,82) 3-Y-O+ **£4,857** (£1,445; £722; £360) **Stalls** Low

Form				RPR
0023	1		**First Order**[29] 6743 6-9-2 **78** (v) PhillipMakin 2 (I Semple) *chsd ldrs: swtchd rt over 2f out: sn rdn: r.o to ld wl ins fnl f* **4/1**[3]	90
4203	2	2	**Harry Up**[8] 6972 6-9-6 **82** (p) ChrisCatlin 6 (K A Ryan) *led 4f out: rdn over 1f out: edgd rt and hdd wl ins fnl f* **5/2**[1]	87
0001	3	1/2	**Tartatartufata**[21] 6860 5-8-11 **73** (v) DeanMcKeown 3 (D Shaw) *led 1f: chsd ldr: rdn over 1f out: no ex ins fnl f* **8/1**	76
3443	4	1/2	**Jilly Why (IRE)**[4] 7026 6-7-11 **66** oh4 (b) AndrewHeffernan(7) 1 (Paul Green) *sn outpcd: styd on appr fnl f: nvr trbld ldrs* **16/1**	67
0000	5	1/2	**Mr Lambros**[29] 6743 6-9-0 **76** (vt) HayleyTurner 7 (Miss Gay Kelleway) *sn outpcd: nt clr run over 1f out: r.o ins fnl f: nvr nrr* **22/1**	75
2321	6	4	**Financial Times (USA)**[22] 6829 5-9-4 **80** (t) MickyFenton 5 (Stef Liddiard) *s.i.s: sn pushed along in rr: rdn over 1f out: n.d* **11/4**[2]	65
0000	7	2	**Overstayed (IRE)**[85] 5379 4-8-10 **72** JimCrowley 8 (M Mullineaux) *prom to 1/2-way* **33/1**	50
0020	8	1/2	**Avertuoso**[22] 6836 3-9-4 **80** PaulMulrennan 4 (B Smart) *chsd ldrs: rdn whn hmpd over 2f out: edgd lft and wknd wl over 1f out* **6/1**	56

61.38 secs (-1.44) **Going Correction** -0.025s/f (Stan) — **8** Ran SP% **113.8**
Speed ratings (Par 105): **110,106,106,105,104 98,94,94**
CSF £14.29 CT £75.15 TOTE £5.60: £1.50, £1.50, £2.10; EX 12.00.

Owner Gordon McDowall **Bred** Mrs Hazel Conroy **Trained** Carluke, S Lanarks

FOCUS

A fair sprint handicap run at a strong pace, which suited the winner. He is rated to this year's best.

7079 CTD NEWS 1ST FOR NEWSPAPERS H'CAP — 1m 141y(P)

8:25 (8:25) (Class 6) (0-57,59) 3-Y-O+ **£2,047** (£604; £302) **Stalls** Low

Form				RPR
1230	1		**Kirstys Lad**[11] 6955 5-9-1 **57** GeorgeBaker 13 (M Mullineaux) *hld up: hdwy over 4f out: rdn to ld ins fnl f: r.o* **13/2**[3]	63
2612	2	*nk*	**Machinate (USA)**[11] 6955 5-9-3 **59** LiamJones 11 (W M Brisbourne) *s.i.s: hld up: hdwy over 3f out: rdn and ev ch ins fnl f: r.o* **3/1**[1]	64

The Form Book, Raceform Ltd, Compton, RG20 6NL

0042 **3** 3/4 **Sarraaf (IRE)**[19] 6873 11-8-11 **53** ow1 .... PhillipMakin 5 56
(I Semple) *broke wl: stdd and lost pl 7f out: hdwy u.p over 2f out: edgd lft over 1f out: r.o: nt rch ldrs* **15/2**

0502 **4** 1 1/4 **Johnston's Glory (IRE)**[16] 6904 3-8-10 **54** .... MickyFenton 1 58+
(E J Alston) *trckd ldrs: nt clr run and lost pl over 2f out: sn rdn: styd on* **10/1**

4600 **5** *shd* **Beck**[11] 6956 3-7-13 **46** oh1 .... DuranFentiman(3) 10 47
(W M Brisbourne) *prom: led over 2f out: rdn over 1f out: hdd and no ex ins fnl f* **33/1**

5030 **6** 1 3/4 **Smart Pick**[27] 6778 4-8-3 **50** ow2 .... TolleyDean(5) 9 47
(Mrs L Williamson) *hld up: hdwy u.p and edgd lft over 1f out: no ex ins fnl f* **25/1**

0500 **7** *nk* **Cove Mountain (IRE)**[40] 6529 5-8-0 **47** ow1 .... KirstyMilczarek(5) 6 43
(M G Rimell) *hld up: rdn over 1f out: edgd lft and styd on ins fnl f: nvr nrr* **25/1**

0000 **8** 3/4 **Sir Bond (IRE)**[50] 6316 6-8-8 **55** ow1 ....(t) SladeO'Hara(5) 2 49+
(G R Oldroyd) *trckd ldrs: nt clr run and lost pl over 2f out: n.d after* **15/2**

5503 **9** 1 1/2 **Swiper Hill (IRE)**[18] 6882 4-8-13 **55** ....(vt) J-PGuillambert 3 46
(B Ellison) *s.i.s and hmpd s: hld up: rdn over 1f out: n.d* **7/2**[2]

10 4 **Namiguest (IRE)**[59] 6111 3-7-9 **46** oh1 .... AndrewHeffernan(7) 4 28
(Paul Green) *wnt lft s: hld up: rdn over 3f out: a in rr* **50/1**

0000 **11** *nk* **Sofia Royale**[122] 4272 3-8-9 **53** .... ChrisCatlin 12 35
(B Palling) *chsd ldr over 6f out: rdn over 2f out: wknd over 1f out* **66/1**

0001 **12** 1 3/4 **Under Fire (IRE)**[10] 6968 4-8-7 **49** .... HayleyTurner 7 27
(A W Carroll) *chsd ldrs: rdn 1/2-way: wknd 3f out* **11/1**

/6-0 **13** 1 **Blakeshall Hope**[10] 6968 5-8-6 **48** oh1 ow2 .... DeanMcKeown 8 24
(A J Chamberlain) *led 7f out: rdn and hdd over 2f out: sn wknd* **16/1**

1m 51.19s (-0.57) **Going Correction** -0.025s/f (Stan)
WFA 3 from 4yo+ 2lb **13** Ran SP% **121.5**
Speed ratings (Par 101): **101,100,100,98,98 97,97,96,95,91 91,89,88**
CSF £25.58 CT £159.70 TOTE £8.60: £3.10, £1.90, £2.20; EX 32.00.
Owner S A Pritchard **Bred** T S And Mrs Wallace **Trained** Alpraham, Cheshire

FOCUS
A moderate handicap and a rather messy race, so there are doubts over the form. The form has been tentatively rated through the sixth.
Johnston's Glory(IRE) Official explanation: jockey said filly was denied a clear run
Swiper Hill(IRE) Official explanation: jockey said gelding was hampered leaving stalls

7080 PONTIN'S SHORT BREAKS H'CAP 1m 1f 103y(P)
8:55 (8:55) (Class 5) (0-70,70) 3-Y-O+ **£2,968** (£876; £438) **Stalls** Low

Form RPR
1111 **1** **Confidentiality (IRE)**[4] 7023 3-9-5 **70** 6ex .... NickyMackay 1 83+
(M Wigham) *hld up: hdwy over 1f out: led on bit ins fnl f: shkn up and r.o wl* **4/9**[1]

544 **2** 1 1/4 **Our Kes (IRE)**[19] 6874 5-9-2 **65** .... TGMcLaughlin 8 73
(P Howling) *hld up: rdn to chse wnr ins fnl f: r.o* **15/2**[2]

5201 **3** 3 1/2 **Arctic Desert**[7] 7001 7-9-0 **63** ....(t) HayleyTurner 3 64
(Miss Gay Kelleway) *hld up: plld hrd: hdwy over 2f out: led over 1f out: rdn and hdd ins fnl f: no ex* **10/1**[3]

0006 **4** 2 1/2 **Norwegian**[21] 6859 6-8-9 **58** ....(p) StephenDonohoe 2 54
(Ian Williams) *hld up: hdwy u.p and n.m.r over 2f out: wknd ins fnl f* **28/1**

-003 **5** *nk* **Star Of The Desert (IRE)**[18] 6885 4-8-11 **60** ....(p) PaulMulrennan 4 55
(Mrs K Walton) *led: hdd over 5f out: chsd ldr: rdn and hung lft over 1f out: wkng whn hung rt ins fnl f* **33/1**

6 4 **Rising Force (IRE)**[47] 6396 4-9-6 **69** .... AdamKirby 7 56
(J L Spearing) *chsd ldrs: led over 2f out: rdn: hung lft and hdd over 1f out: sn hung rt and wknd* **20/1**

0445 **7** 2 **Siena Star (IRE)**[1] 7056 9-8-12 **61** ....(e[1]) MickyFenton 6 44
(Stef Liddiard) *chsd ldr: led over 5f out: rdn and hdd over 2f out: hmpd and wknd sn after* **16/1**

425 **8** 1/2 **Accusation (IRE)**[23] 6821 3-9-1 **66** .... ChrisCatlin 5 48
(L M Cumani) *chsd ldrs: rdn and wknd 2f out* **12/1**

2m 2.36s (-0.26) **Going Correction** -0.025s/f (Stan)
WFA 3 from 4yo+ 2lb **8** Ran SP% **114.8**
Speed ratings (Par 103): **100,98,95,93,93 89,87,87**
CSF £4.20 CT £15.79 TOTE £1.40: £1.10, £1.50, £2.40; EX 5.20.
Owner J M Cullinan **Bred** Kevin Foley **Trained** Newmarket, Suffolk

FOCUS
A modest, uncompetitive handicap run at a steady pace. Confidentiality completed a five-timer with something in hand, and the form is rated through the runner-up.

7081 PONTINS.COM H'CAP 2m 119y(P)
9:20 (9:23) (Class 6) (0-65,76) 3-Y-O+ **£2,047** (£604; £302) **Stalls** Low

Form RPR
0402 **1** **Bugsy's Boy**[22] 6835 3-8-11 **56** .... LiamJones 11 69+
(P W D'Arcy) *chsd ldrs: led 5f out: rdn clr over 1f out* **3/1**[1]

0344 **2** 5 **Squirtle (IRE)**[22] 6835 4-8-9 **46** oh1 .... JohnEgan 12 53
(W M Brisbourne) *s.i.s: hld up: pushed along 1/2-way: hdwy over 5f out: chsd wnr 4f out: rdn over 2f out: edgd lft and styd on same pce appr fnl f* **7/1**

3 1 3/4 **All Native (IRE)**[475] 2963 8-8-9 **46** oh1 ....(t) PaulMulrennan 3 52+
(C P Donoghue, Ire) *hld up: nt clr run over 3f out: hdwy over 1f out: nvr nrr* **25/1**

3456 **4** 1 1/2 **Black Mogul**[10] 6969 3-8-2 **47** ....(p) HayleyTurner 13 50
(R Hollinshead) *chsd ldrs: rdn over 3f out: styd on same pce fnl 2f* **16/1**

6-51 **5** 1 1/2 **Easibet Dot Net**[19] 6875 7-9-9 **60** ....(p) PhillipMakin 9 61
(I Semple) *hld up: styd on ins fnl f: nvr nrr* **11/2**[2]

6443 **6** *shd* **Park's Prodigy**[11] 2552 3-7-12 **50** ....(t) PatrickDonaghy(7) 7 53+
(P C Haslam) *chsd ldrs: lost pl over 12f out: hdwy 6f out: hmpd and lost pl 4f out: n.d after* **11/2**[2]

0061 **7** 1 1/4 **Ice And Fire**[4] 7012 8-9-0 **51** 6ex ....(b) MickyFenton 2 51
(J T Stimpson) *sn pushed along in rr: rdn 1/2-way: hdwy over 2f out: hung rt and wknd over 1f out* **16/1**

0411 **8** 2 1/2 **Merrymaker**[11] 6961 7-10-11 **76** .... GeorgeBaker 1 73
(W M Brisbourne) *hld up: hdwy 5f out: rdn and wknd over 2f out* **6/1**[3]

1343 **9** 15 **Bond Casino**[15] 6911 3-9-1 **60** ....(p) ChrisCatlin 6 39
(G R Oldroyd) *chsd ldrs: rdn over 3f out: sn wknd* **8/1**

4361 **10** 1 1/2 **Ronsard (IRE)**[5] 7004 5-8-11 **55** 6ex .... RichardEvans(7) 5 32
(P D Evans) *s.i.s: hld up: hdwy 7f out: hmpd 4f out: sn wknd* **9/1**

11 58 **Curristown Pet (IRE)**[188] 2285 3-8-2 **47** ....(b[1]) JamieMackay 4 —
(C P Donoghue, Ire) *hld up: plld hrd: hdwy 12f out: hmpd and wknd 4f out: t.o* **50/1**

6000 **12** 1 1/2 **Pre Eminence (IRE)**[50] 6308 6-8-9 **46** oh1 ....(tp) StephenDonohoe 10 —
(L R James) *led: clr 10f out: hdd 5f out: wknd 4f out: t.o* **66/1**

3m 43.17s (0.04) **Going Correction** -0.025s/f (Stan)
WFA 3 from 4yo+ 8lb **12** Ran SP% **122.7**
Speed ratings (Par 101): **98,95,94,94,93 93,92,91,84,83 56,55**
CSF £24.82 CT £459.23 TOTE £4.60: £2.00, £1.90, £7.90; EX 28.00 Place 6 £51.48, Place 5 £15.84.
Owner Seaton Stud Limited **Bred** Mrs R S Evans **Trained** Newmarket, Suffolk

FOCUS
A decent staying handicap for the grade and they went a fair pace through the early stages. The unexposed winner is rated up 9lb.
T/Plt: £83.30 to a £1 stake. Pool: £102,727.40. 900.00 winning tickets. T/Qpdt: £5.50 to a £1 stake. Pool: £7,006.60. 930.50 winning tickets. CR

7069 LINGFIELD (L-H)
Sunday, December 9

OFFICIAL GOING: Standard
Wind: Moderate, across Weather: Sunny

7082 GO PONTIN'S HOLIDAYS APPRENTICE H'CAP 5f (P)
12:30 (12:30) (Class 6) (0-60,59) 3-Y-O+ **£2,137** (£635; £317; £158) **Stalls** High

Form RPR
1600 **1** **Sands Crooner (IRE)**[112] 4635 4-8-13 **56** ....(v) PatrickHills(3) 1 66+
(D Shaw) *s.i.s: sn in tch: smooth hdwy to ld over 1f out: rdn out* **15/2**

0260 **2** 1 3/4 **Fastrac Boy**[18] 6890 4-8-4 **51** .... KierenFox(7) 2 55
(J R Best) *a.p: ev ch 2f out: nt pce of wnr fnl f: jst hld on for 2nd* **8/1**

2060 **3** *shd* **Minnow**[8] 7003 3-8-6 **51** ow1 ....(v) WilliamCarson(5) 5 55
(S C Williams) *slowly away: sn chsd ldrs: effrt 1/2-way: kpt on one pce fnl f* **8/1**

0033 **4** 3/4 **Hello Roberto**[6] 7005 6-8-7 **54** ....(p) DavidProbert(7) 10 55
(R A Harris) *led after 1f: rdn and hdd over 1f out: one pce fnl f* **12/1**

5156 **5** *nk* **Punching**[28] 6779 3-9-2 **59** .... TolleyDean(3) 4 59
(Eve Johnson Houghton) *mid-div: rdn and one pce fr over 1f out* **9/2**[2]

006 **6** *nk* **Theoretical**[30] 6752 3-8-12 **57** ....(p) RobbieEgan(5) 6 56
(A J McCabe) *in rr: hung rt after 2f: r.o fnl f: nvr nrr* **22/1**

0623 **7** *nk* **Thoughtsofstardom**[5] 7013 4-9-0 **57** ....(be) HaddenFrost(3) 7 55
(G C Bravery) *chsd ldrs: rdn 2f out: one pce fnl f* **3/1**[1]

0066 **8** 1 1/2 **Piccostar**[66] 5947 4-8-6 **51** ow2 .... JackDean(5) 3 43
(A B Haynes) *a in rr* **12/1**

6400 **9** 3 1/2 **Charlotte Grey**[18] 6890 3-9-3 **57** .... GregFairley 8 37
(C N Allen) *led for 1f: wknd over 1f out* **33/1**

0320 **10** 3 **Sir Loin**[12] 6957 6-8-11 **51** ....(v) TravisBlock 9 20
(P Burgoyne) *rrd up leaving stalls: a bhd* **6/1**[3]

58.33 secs (-1.45) **Going Correction** -0.125s/f (Stan) **10** Ran SP% **114.1**
Speed ratings (Par 101): **106,103,103,101,101 100,100,98,92,87**
CSF £64.66 CT £492.77 TOTE £8.80: £2.10, £4.10, £3.60; EX 89.70 TRIFECTA Not won..
Owner Danethorpe Racing Partnership **Bred** Peter Molony **Trained** Danethorpe, Notts

FOCUS
An average sprint run at a good pace but the form is sound enough rated around the placed horses.
Sir Loin Official explanation: jockey said gelding hung right

7083 GO PONTIN'S NOW H'CAP (DIV I) 1m 2f (P)
1:00 (1:00) (Class 6) (0-60,60) 3-Y-O+ **£2,137** (£635; £317; £158) **Stalls** Low

Form RPR
0006 **1** **Just Intersky (USA)**[13] 6951 4-9-3 **56** ....(e) DeanMcKeown 3 64+
(V Smith) *stdd s: hld up in rr: hdwy on outside wl over 1f out: rdn and r.o to ld post* **11/2**[2]

-050 **2** *hd* **Forfeiter (USA)**[14] 5820 5-8-3 **49** .... JemmaMarshall(7) 11 57
(C Gordon) *sn led: hdd 6f out: styd prom and rdn to ld 1f out: kpt on: hdd post* **25/1**

06-6 **3** 1/2 **Wind Flow**[28] 6778 3-8-11 **53** .... AdrianMcCarthy 7 60
(C A Dwyer) *trckd ldrs: rdn over 2f out: ev ch 1f out: kpt on u.str.p* **14/1**

0000 **4** *shd* **Play Up Pompey**[20] 6867 5-8-10 **49** .... AmirQuinn 10 56
(J J Bridger) *plld hrd: led 6f out: hdd 1f out: kpt on fnl f* **16/1**

2036 **5** 1/2 **Sir Haydn**[20] 6260 7-9-5 **58** ....(v) RichardKingscote 6 64
(J R Jenkins) *hld up: hdwy on outside over 2f out: nt qckn ins fnl f* **11/2**[2]

0053 **6** *shd* **Magic Warrior**[18] 6894 7-9-6 **59** .... PatDobbs 9 65+
(J C Fox) *in rr: hdwy over 1f out: r.o fnl f: nvr nrr* **12/1**

5612 **7** 3/4 **Dinner Date**[20] 6867 5-9-7 **60** .... J-PGuillambert 1 64
(T Keddy) *mid-div: effrt over 2f out: nt qckn fnl f* **5/1**[1]

0405 **8** 3/4 **Ella Y Rossa**[27] 6801 3-9-0 **56** .... StephenDonohoe 5 59
(P D Evans) *hld up: rdn over 2f out: no hdwy appr fnl f* **10/1**

4426 **9** 1/2 **Slavonic Lake**[18] 6026 3-8-5 **47** ....(t) ChrisCatlin 8 49
(I A Wood) *chsd ldrs: rdn over 3f out: wknd ins fnl f* **17/2**

3026 **10** 3/4 **Recalcitrant**[20] 6871 4-8-7 **53** .... JamieHamblett(7) 2 53
(S Dow) *plld hrd: trckd ldrs: wknd ins fnl f* **6/1**[3]

0503 **11** 3 1/2 **My Mirasol**[15] 6935 3-8-3 **52** ....(p) MatthewDavies(7) 4 45
(D E Cantillon) *plld hrd: a in rr* **16/1**

12 3 **Cami Collins (FR)**[76] 5694 3-8-13 **55** .... JimCrowley 12 42
(J R Best) *hld up in rr: lost tch wl over 1f out* **10/1**

2m 8.46s (0.67) **Going Correction** -0.125s/f (Stan)
WFA 3 from 4yo+ 3lb **12** Ran SP% **120.4**
Speed ratings (Par 101): **92,91,91,91,90 90,90,89,89,88 85,83**
CSF £135.97 CT £1841.75 TOTE £7.00: £1.80, £7.80, £5.30; EX 250.70 TRIFECTA Not won..
Owner Tapas Partnership **Bred** Dreamfields Inc And Don Brady **Trained** Exning, Suffolk

FOCUS
A moderate handicap in which there was no great early pace on and that resulted in something of a sprint to the line and a bunch finish. It was the slower of the two divisions by 1.43sec and therefore not a race to be that positive about.

7084 GO PONTIN'S MAIDEN STKS 7f (P)
1:30 (1:32) (Class 5) 2-Y-O **£2,914** (£867; £433; £216) **Stalls** Low

Form RPR
222 **1** **Hold The Gold (IRE)**[58] 6138 2-9-3 **82** .... ChrisCatlin 6 81+
(E J O'Neill) *t.k.h: mid-div on outside: gd hdwy over 2f out: led over 1f out: r.o wl* **9/4**[1]

22 **2** 1 3/4 **Regal Bird (USA)**[9] 6974 2-8-12 **0** .... FergusSweeney 2 71
(M A Magnusson) *a in tch: rdn and r.o to go 2nd ins fnl f: no ch w wnr* **11/4**[2]

023 **3** 1/2 **Green Diamond**[81] 5541 2-9-3 **82** .... GregFairley 4 75
(M Johnston) *led tl rdn and hdd over 1f out: one pce and lost 2nd ins fnl f* **4/1**[3]

05 4 ½ **Tallulah Sunrise**[11] 6964 2-8-5 0 ... GHannon(7) 3 69
(M D I Usher) *trckd ldrs: rdn over 1f out: kpt on one pce* **33/1**
5 ½ **Rankayo Hitam (USA)** 2-9-3 0 ... JohnEgan 9 72
(J S Moore) *mid-div: rdn and hdwy over 2f out: styd on one pce fnl f* **6/1**
4 6 1 **Steele Tango (USA)**[18] 6897 2-9-3 0 ... GeorgeBaker 7 70+
(R A Teal) *mid-div: rdn over 2f out: no imp on ldrs fr over 1f out* **11/1**
7 nk **Street Power (USA)** 2-9-3 0 ... DeanMcKeown 5 69+
(J R Gask) *bmpd leaving stalls: plld v hrd in rr: mde sme late hdwy* **33/1**
3504 8 3½ **Threestoneburn (USA)**[73] 5746 2-8-12 66 ... RobertHavlin 11 55
(J R Boyle) *trckd ldr to over 2f out: wknd over 1f out* **33/1**
0 9 nk **Nino Cochise (IRE)**[13] 6948 2-9-3 0 ... SteveDrowne 1 59
(C R Egerton) *s.i.s: a bhd* **50/1**
00 10 3 **Hennessy Island (USA)**[22] 6850 2-9-3 0 ... JimCrowley 10 51
(T G Mills) *mid-div: rdn 2f out: nvr nr to chal* **33/1**
050 11 5 **Ryan's Rock**[61] 6079 2-9-3 49 ... LiamJones 12 38
(T D McCarthy) *in rr: rdn 1/2-way: sn lost tch* **100/1**
12 5 **Malt Empress (IRE)** 2-8-13 0 ow1 ... AdamKirby 13 21
(B W Duke) *prom: rdn 1/2-way: wknd over 2f out* **66/1**

1m 25.08s (-0.81) **Going Correction** -0.125s/f (Stan) 12 Ran SP% **116.3**
Speed ratings (Par 96): **99,97,96,95,95 94,93,89,89,86 80,74**
CSF £7.84 TOTE £3.50: £1.40, £1.70, £1.20; EX 9.20 Trifecta £11.50 Pool: £85.56 - 5.27 winning units..
Owner Roadmate Racing **Bred** B Firestone **Trained** Averham Park, Notts

FOCUS
Not a bad maiden, and the form looks solid enough with the principals all coming into the race with decent figures behind them.

NOTEBOOK
Hold The Gold(IRE), who was unlucky to run into a Godolphin good thing over this course and distance last time, travelled strongly into contention running down the hill and ran out a clear winner in the end. He deserved to win a race following a string of consistent efforts, and he could well do better again in handicap company, especially off a stronger pace, as he still tends to race a bit keenly. (tchd 2-1 tchd 5-2 in a place)
Regal Bird(USA), runner-up in a conditions event here last time, never threatened to win the race but ran on late to take second place away from Green Diamond. She should have little trouble winning a similar event this winter. (op 5-2)
Green Diamond, off the track since September and running on Polytrack for the first time, enjoyed the run of the race but was a sitting duck for the winner in the straight. A reproduction of this effort would be good enough to win most maidens on the sand this winter. (tchd 7-2)
Tallulah Sunrise, stepping up another furlong in distance, ran her best race to date. She is progressing the right way and handicaps ought to provide her with a stronger chance of recording a first win. (op 40-1)
Rankayo Hitam(USA), a half-brother to Northern Boy, a modest performer at around 7f to 1m, was not without his supporters on his debut despite appearing to have stiff opposition in the shape of the more experienced first three in the betting. He ran with undoubted promise and will no doubt face easier tasks than this in the future. (op 11-2)
Steele Tango(USA) ran a solid race up in trip and is another who can be expected to do better once qualified for handicaps. Official explanation: jockey said colt hung having got its tongue over the bit (op 14-1)

7085 PONTIN'S BOOK EARLY AND SAVE H'CAP 1m (P)
2:00 (2:01) (Class 6) (0-60,60) 3-Y-0+ **£2,137** (£635; £317; £158) **Stalls** High

Form RPR
1350 1 **Wrighty Almighty (IRE)**[18] 6894 5-9-5 60 ... JimCrowley 10 70
(P R Chamings) *trckd ldrs: r.o to ld ins fnl f: jst hld on* **5/1**[3]
0011 2 shd **Quantum Leap**[23] 6825 10-8-11 59 ... (v) ThomasBubb(7) 8 69
(S Dow) *mid-div: hdwy over 2f out: r.o to press wnr ins fnl f: jst failed* **11/1**
0031 3 1¾ **Park Valley Prince**[13] 6945 3-8-11 53 ... MartinDwyer 11 59+
(W R Muir) *trckd ldr: led wl over 1f out: rdn and hdd ins fnl f: no ex* **10/3**[1]
0060 4 nk **King After**[13] 6945 5-8-13 54 ... (v) JohnEgan 9 59
(J R Best) *t.k.h: a in tch: nt qckn ins fnl f* **9/2**[2]
4200 5 nk **Sophia Gardens**[23] 6825 3-9-3 59 ... SteveDrowne 12 64
(D W P Arbuthnot) *trckd ldrs: chal wl over 1f out: fdd ins fnl f* **16/1**
0404 6 1¼ **Tilsworth Charlie**[13] 6945 4-8-13 54 ... (b) ChrisCatlin 5 56
(J R Jenkins) *mid-div: rdn over 2f out: kpt on but nvr nr to chal* **20/1**
2054 7 nk **Postmaster**[12] 6956 5-8-13 54 ... RobertHavlin 4 55
(R Ingram) *hld up: rdn over 1f out: mde sme late hdwy* **5/1**[3]
03 8 nk **Dancing Duo**[67] 5900 3-9-1 57 ... (v) DeanMcKeown 1 57
(D Shaw) *in rr: hung lft over 1f out: nvr nr to chal* **14/1**
1525 9 2 **Zazous**[15] 6925 6-9-4 59 ... AmirQuinn 2 55
(J J Bridger) *hld up: a towards rr* **12/1**
3550 10 1¾ **Calloff The Search**[4] 7028 3-8-8 50 ... (v) MickyFenton 7 42
(Stef Liddiard) *led tl hdd wl over 1f out: wknd qckly* **16/1**
4000 11 1½ **Smash Hit (IRE)**[18] 6894 4-9-4 59 ... FergusSweeney 3 47
(David Pinder) *t.k.h: hld up in mid-div: rdn over 2f out: wknd over 1f out* **25/1**
2000 12 8 **Lucius Verrus (USA)**[152] 3409 7-9-3 58 ... (v) AdamKirby 6 28
(D Shaw) *s.i.s: rdn 3f out: sn btn: eased ins fnl f* **25/1**

1m 37.35s (-2.08) **Going Correction** -0.125s/f (Stan)
WFA 3 from 4yo+ 1lb 12 Ran SP% **121.5**
Speed ratings (Par 101): **105,104,103,102,102 101,101,100,98,96 95,87**
CSF £59.00 CT £210.75 TOTE £6.30: £2.10, £2.60, £1.70; EX 47.90 Trifecta £80.00 Part won. Pool: £112.77 - 0.10 winning units..
Owner The Boccy Hall Evans Tyrrell Partnership **Bred** P Heffernan **Trained** Baughurst, Hants

FOCUS
An ordinary handicap run at a sound pace and solid form with the first three close to their marks.
Tilsworth Charlie Official explanation: jockey said filly suffered interference at start
Dancing Duo Official explanation: jockey said filly hung badly left in straight

7086 PONTINS.COM H'CAP 1m 4f (P)
2:30 (2:30) (Class 3) (0-95,90) 3-Y-0 **£6,855** (£2,052; £1,026; £513; £256) **Stalls** Low

Form RPR
6611 1 **Grande Caiman (IRE)**[24] 6819 3-8-11 85 ... RichardHughes 6 97+
(R Hannon) *hld up in tch: hdwy to go 2nd 2f out: led ins fnl f: styd on wl* **4/5**[1]
0132 2 1 **Polish Power (GER)**[22] 6853 7-9-4 87 ... JohnEgan 5 93
(J S Moore) *hld up in rr: rdn over 2f out: hdwy over 1f out: styd on to go 2nd wl ins fnl f* **11/4**[2]
5330 3 1¾ **Fusili (IRE)**[29] 6765 4-9-4 87 ... IanMongan 3 90
(N P Littmoden) *trckd ldr: led over 2f out: rdn and hdd ins fnl f: no ex* **14/1**
2-06 4 8 **Cold Turkey**[36] 6645 7-9-6 89 ... GeorgeBaker 4 79
(G L Moore) *trckd ldrs: effrt over 2f out: sn btn* **13/2**[3]
6/0- 5 1½ **Jagger**[197] 7-9-7 90 ... MartinDwyer 1 78
(G A Butler) *led tl hdd over 2f out: sn fdd* **11/1**

2m 33.55s (-0.84) **Going Correction** -0.125s/f (Stan)
WFA 3 from 4yo+ 5lb 5 Ran SP% **110.6**
Speed ratings (Par 107): **97,96,95,89,88**
CSF £3.24 TOTE £1.80: £1.30, £1.60; EX 3.20.
Owner I A N Wight **Bred** Sweet Retreat Syndicate **Trained** East Everleigh, Wilts

FOCUS
A soundly-run handicap won by an improving type but not all that strong and best rated through the third.

NOTEBOOK
Grande Caiman(IRE) ran out a comfortable winner to record a hat-trick of successes at this track this winter. He benefited from a fair gallop but is clearly an improving three-year-old who could yet defy the Handicapper again in the coming weeks. (op 10-11 tchd evens in places)
Polish Power(GER), who came from the back of the field to win here in October, again challenged last and late, but the well-handicapped and improving three-year-old was always holding him. He has never won off a mark this high before but he is in the form of his life at present. (op 10-3)
Fusili(IRE) tried to nick the race when taking over running down the hill, but Grande Caiman always had her covered and in hindsight she may have gone for home too soon. That may be harsh, however, as the winner was undoubtedly well handicapped here. (op 11-1)
Cold Turkey is not in the best of form at present. (op 9-2)
Jagger, back with Gerard Butler now having been out in Australia since the spring of 2006, raced freely in front and stopped quickly when tackled by Fusili running down the hill. He is entitled to come on quite a bit for this first outing in 197 days and is undoubtedly well handicapped on his best British form. (op 9-1 tchd 12-1)

7087 VALERIE GILROY BIRTHDAY H'CAP 6f (P)
3:00 (3:00) (Class 4) (0-80,81) 3-Y-0+ **£4,857** (£1,445; £722; £180; £180) **Stalls** Low

Form RPR
0612 1 **Halsion Chancer**[23] 6829 3-8-13 75 ... JohnEgan 6 85+
(J R Best) *mde all: rdn over 1f out: r.o strly* **9/1**
3456 2 1¼ **Bazroy (IRE)**[83] 5473 3-9-2 78 ... (b) StephenDonohoe 4 84
(P D Evans) *stdd s: short of room and swtchd lft over 1f out: r.o wl to go 2nd nr fin* **14/1**
3013 3 ½ **Titan Triumph**[13] 6949 3-9-3 79 ... (t) PaulDoe 8 88+
(W J Knight) *hld up: hdwy on outside 1f out: r.o: nvr nrr* **9/4**[1]
3022 4 hd **Texas Gold**[33] 6707 9-9-4 80 ... MartinDwyer 7 84
(W R Muir) *mid-div: hdwy over 1f out: r.o fnl f* **7/1**[3]
0205 4 dht **Russian Symphony (USA)**[23] 6836 6-9-2 78 ... RobertHavlin 5 82
(C R Egerton) *a.p on ins: ev ch over 1f out: kpt on one pce* **10/1**
3433 6 ½ **Best One**[61] 6081 3-8-9 71 ... (t) HayleyTurner 12 73
(C E Brittain) *sn chsd wnr: wknd ins fnl f* **16/1**
0552 7 shd **Coleorton Dancer**[17] 6907 5-8-11 76 ... (p) AndrewMullen(3) 10 78
(K A Ryan) *plld hrd: effrt over 1f out: wknd ins fnl f* **7/1**[3]
0054 8 2½ **China Cherub**[9] 6972 4-9-0 81 ... (b) PatrickHills(5) 2 76
(S Dow) *a in rr* **14/1**
0503 9 ½ **Sand Cat**[9] 6970 4-9-3 79 ... GeorgeBaker 9 72
(G L Moore) *in tch: rdn 2f out: wknd ent fnl f* **7/2**[2]
0400 10 ½ **Happy As Larry (USA)**[9] 6972 5-8-13 75 ... (t) GregFairley 11 67
(D J Murphy) *towards rr on outside: effrt 2f out: wknd appr fnl f* **22/1**

1m 10.55s (-2.26) **Going Correction** -0.125s/f (Stan) course record 10 Ran SP% **120.6**
Speed ratings (Par 105): **110,108,107,107,107 106,106,103,102,101**
CSF £131.15 CT £384.79 TOTE £10.20: £2.50, £3.10, £1.40; EX 90.00 TRIFECTA Not won..
Owner Halsion Ltd **Bred** Mrs S Hansford **Trained** Hucking, Kent

FOCUS
There was a sound pace to this sprint handicap and the form looks solid.

7088 GO PONTIN'S NOW H'CAP (DIV II) 1m 2f (P)
3:30 (3:30) (Class 6) (0-60,60) 3-Y-0+ **£2,137** (£635; £317; £158) **Stalls** Low

Form RPR
-003 1 **Mutamaasek (USA)**[20] 6866 5-9-3 56 ... RichardHughes 6 68+
(Lady Herries) *trckd ldrs gng wl: shkn up to ld jst ins fnl f: rdn out* **9/4**[1]
3634 2 ½ **Blu Manruna**[18] 6902 4-9-7 60 ... (b) PaulDoe 11 71
(J Akehurst) *trckd ldr: led over 2f out: rdn and hdd jst ins fnl f: kpt on wl* **7/2**[2]
5400 3 5 **Mon Petite Amour**[13] 6951 4-9-3 56 ... SteveDrowne 8 57
(D W P Arbuthnot) *in rr: hdwy to chse ldrs over 2f out: kpt on fnl f* **13/2**
1230 4 1 **Formidable Guest**[18] 6896 3-8-10 52 ... DavidKinsella 9 51
(J Pearce) *mid-div: hdwy on ins wl over 1f out: kpt on one pce fnl f* **10/1**
4460 5 ¾ **Border Edge**[20] 6866 9-8-7 53 ... (v) JackDean(7) 5 51
(J J Bridger) *led tl hdd over 2f out: wknd over 1f out* **14/1**
0140 6 1¾ **Bowl Of Cherries**[6] 7009 4-9-1 54 ... (v) JimCrowley 12 48
(I A Wood) *in tch tl rdn and wknd over 1f out* **6/1**[3]
0000 7 ¾ **Christalini**[39] 6590 3-8-12 54 ... PatDobbs 4 47
(J C Fox) *mid-div: hdwy to chse ldrs over 1f out: wknd ins fnl f* **20/1**
5000 8 1¼ **Hey Presto**[47] 6407 7-8-7 46 oh1 ... ChrisCatlin 1 36
(R Rowe) *hld up: a in rr* **33/1**
5050 9 nk **Spunger**[32] 6719 4-9-6 59 ... (v) RobertHavlin 10 48
(H J L Dunlop) *mid-div tl lost pl over 2f out* **7/1**
0060 10 1½ **Pajada**[13] 6950 3-8-4 46 oh1 ... (v) JamieMackay 3 32
(M D I Usher) *a bhd* **40/1**
2200 11 5 **Danelor (IRE)**[12] 6955 9-8-11 50 ... (p) DeanMcKeown 2 26
(D Shaw) *slowly away and stirrup leather broke sn after s: out of control after and eventually fin last* **16/1**

2m 7.03s (-0.76) **Going Correction** -0.125s/f (Stan)
WFA 3 from 4yo+ 3lb 11 Ran SP% **124.9**
Speed ratings (Par 101): **98,97,93,92,92 90,90,89,88,87 83**
CSF £10.40 CT £47.58 TOTE £4.90: £2.00, £1.70, £2.50; EX 15.50 Trifecta £38.40 Pool: £314.11 - 5.80 winning units. Place 6 £88.58, Place 5 £17.38.
Owner Lady Herries **Bred** Shadwell Farm LLC **Trained** Patching, W Sussex

FOCUS
A steadily-run affair but still the quicker of the two divisions by 1.43sec. The first two home were always well placed and the form has been rated through the third and fourth.
Danelor(IRE) Official explanation: jockey said he lost an iron
T/Plt: £186.90 to a £1 stake. Pool: £51,059.95. 199.35 winning tickets. T/Qpdt: £3.20 to a £1 stake. Pool: £4,913.00. 1,101.80 winning tickets. LM

SHA TIN (R-H)
Sunday, December 9

OFFICIAL GOING: Good

7089a CATHAY PACIFIC HONG KONG SPRINT (GROUP 1) 6f
6:00 (6:02) 3-Y-0+
£449,409 (£173,456; £78,844; £44,678; £26,281; £15,769)

RPR
1 **Sacred Kingdom (AUS)**[22] 4-9-0 ... (t) GMosse 6 129+
(P F Yiu, Hong Kong) *mid-div: 8th st: hdwy and moved outside wl over 1f out: led 120yds out: r.o wl* **9/20**[1]

2 2 1/2 **Absolute Champion (AUS)**[22] 6-9-0 ....(p) BPrebble 3 121
(D Hall, Hong Kong) *a cl up: 5th st: hdwy 2f out: pressed ldr 1 1/2f out: styd on same pce* **9/1**[3]

3 nk **Royal Delight (AUS)**[49] 5-9-0 ....(b) SDye 4 120
(C Fownes, Hong Kong) *led to 120yds out: one pce* **18/1**

4 1 3/4 **Scintillation (AUS)**[22] 7-9-0 .... ESaint-Martin 7 115
(C S Shum, Hong Kong) *racd in mid-div outside wnr: 9th st: styd on fnl 2f: nrest at fin* **37/1**

5 nse **Sunny Power (AUS)**[14] 5-9-0 .... YTCheng 10 115
(K W Lui,) *11th st: hdwy and nt clr run over 1f out: styd on: nrest at fin* **25/1**

6 hd **Marchand D'Or (FR)**[64] 6029 4-9-0 .... DBonilla 5 114
(F Head, France) *hld up: 12th st on ins: hdwy fr over 1f out: nrst at fin* **100/1**

7 1 3/4 **Green Birdie (NZ)**[14] 4-9-0 ....(b[1]) LDettori 8 109
(C Fownes, Hong Kong) *last to st: effrt on outside: nvr nr to chal* **30/1**

8 1 3/4 **Tiza (SAF)**[37] 6633 5-9-0 .... CSoumillon 11 104
(A De Royer-Dupre, France) *towards rr to st: n.d* **100/1**

9 3 1/2 **Desert Lord**[15] 6930 7-9-0 ....(b) NCallan 9 93
(K A Ryan) *prom: 2nd st: wknd appr fnl f* **100/1**

10 3/4 **Miss Andretti (AUS)**[29] 6-8-10 ....(t) CNewitt 12 87
(Lee Freedman, Australia) *trckd ldrs: 6th st: sn rdn and btn* **37/10**[2]

11 2 1/4 **Why Be (AUS)**[23] 5-9-0 ....(t) NCallow 13 84
(L Laxon, Singapore) *cl up: 7th st on outside st: sn btn* **100/1**

12 hd **Sunny Sing (IRE)**[22] 5-9-0 ....(tp) DBeadman 1 84
(J Moore, Hong Kong) *4th on ins st: disp 2nd tl wkng 1 1/2f out* **71/1**

13 1 1/2 **Benbaun (IRE)**[63] 6039 6-9-0 ....(v) PJSmullen 2 79
(M J Wallace) *prom: 3rd st: rdn wl over 1f out: btn whn squeezed up over 1f out* **40/1**

68.40 secs (68.40) **13 Ran SP% 123.0**
(including $HK10 stakes): WIN 14.50; PL 10.50, 14.50, 17.50; DF 43.50.
Owner Sin Kang Yuk **Bred** Mrs N F Calvert & Estate Of The Late A M Calvert **Trained** Hong Kong

NOTEBOOK
Sacred Kingdom(AUS) beat the runner-up and fourth in the trial for this race last month but was 5lb worse off. He did not have much room turning for home, but once he found the gap he swept through to score going away from last year's impressive winner. He has claims to being regarded the best sprinter in the world after this.
Marchand D'Or(FR), who has been running consistently well in the top European races between 6f and 7f this season, ran on from well back to do best of the European raiders, but he never got close enough to trouble the principals.
Desert Lord, who finished last behind today's runner-up in this race last year, has not recaptured his 2006 form this season.
Miss Andretti(AUS) has had a fantastic season, but it has been an arduous one too, on top of which she had a wide draw and an unfamiliar right-handed turn to overcome. This can easily be forgiven.
Benbaun(IRE) has been in good form this season and came into this on a four-timer, but after showing up turning for home he was on the retreat when hampered approaching the final furlong. His rider reported he had to make a little too much use of him early, but that he ran as if over the top.

7090a CATHAY PACIFIC HONG KONG VASE (GROUP 1) 1m 4f
6:40 (6:40) 3-Y-0+
£524,310 (£202,365; £91,984; £52,562; £30,223; £18,397)

RPR

1 **Doctor Dino (FR)**[50] 6334 5-9-0 .... OPeslier 4 122
(R Gibson, France) *mid-div: 10th st: hdwy and moved out 2f out: hrd rdn appr fnl f: led abt 75yds out: drvn out* **31/4**[3]

2 1 1/2 **Quijano (GER)**[49] 6374 5-9-0 .... AStarke 1 119
(P Schiergen, Germany) *hld up: 11th st: moved outside and hdwy fr 2f out: r.o to take 2nd last strides* **87/10**

3 nk **Bussoni (GER)**[56] 6223 6-9-0 ....(t) CSoumillon 6 118
(H Blume, Germany) *wnt 2nd after 4f: led ent st: 2l clr 1f out: rdn and hdd abt 75yds out: one pce* **29/1**

4 1 **Arch Rebel (USA)**[49] 6376 6-9-0 ....(p) FMBerry 10 117
(Noel Meade, Ire) *hld up: 12th st on outside: stdy hdwy fnl 2f: nrest at fin* **88/1**

5 1/2 **Kocab**[49] 6376 5-9-0 .... SPasquier 2 116
(A Fabre, France) *a.p: 5th st: 2nd 1 1/2f out: one pce fnl f* **96/1**

6 1/2 **Egerton (GER)**[50] 6353 6-9-0 .... TMundry 3 115
(P Rau, Germany) *mid-div: hrd rdn and hdwy fr wl over 1f out: 4th 1f out: one pce* **100/1**

7 1 **Dylan Thomas (IRE)**[43] 6513 4-9-0 .... JMurtagh 7 113
(A P O'Brien, Ire) *hld up: last st on ins: btn 1 1/2f out* **7/10**[1]

8 shd **Ever Bright (NZ)**[28] 4-9-0 .... ODoleuze 5 113
(P O'Sullivan, New Zealand) *a mid-div* **40/1**

9 shd **Red Rocks (IRE)**[43] 6513 4-9-0 .... LDettori 8 113
(B J Meehan) *a cl up: 3rd st: disp 2nd tl wkng over 1f out* **58/10**[2]

10 3/4 **Hawkes Bay**[14] 5-9-0 .... GMosse 11 112
(D Hall, Hong Kong) *led over 1f: 6th st: sn btn* **48/1**

11 3 1/2 **Macleya (GER)**[42] 6526 5-8-10 .... RyanMoore 12 102
(A Fabre, France) *hld up tl wnt up qckly on outside to ld 7f out: hdd ent st: wknd over 1f out* **23/1**

12 1 **Viva Macau (FR)**[28] 4-9-0 ....(t) DBeadman 13 104
(J Moore, Hong Kong) *led after 1 1/2f to 7f out: 4th st: sn wknd* **22/1**

13 14 1/2 **Vital King (NZ)**[28] 5-9-0 ....(b) BPrebble 9 79
(P O'Sullivan, New Zealand) *mid-div to st: sn btn* **11/1**

2m 28.2s **13 Ran SP% 123.1**
WIN 87.50; PL 28.00, 32.00, 65.00; DF 272.50.
Owner J Martinez Salmean **Bred** Ecurie Pelder **Trained** Lamorlaye, France

FOCUS
This was the sixth successive time that a European horse has taken this race and the domination was highlighted by the fact that European raiders filled the first seven places.

NOTEBOOK
Doctor Dino(FR), whose six races this season have comprised two Group 1s in Europe, two in the USA and now two in Asia, has either won or been placed every time and took this on his first attempt at 1m4f. He is likely to remain in training next season and has more options open to him now.
Quijano(GER), who had a successful time in Dubai last winter, is another international traveller, having finished third in Canada last time. He ran well despite not getting the clearest of runs and is likely to return to Nad Al Sheba in the New Year.
Bussoni(GER), another German globetrotter, made a bold bid and was clear early in the straight, but was run down in the closing stages.
Dylan Thomas(IRE), for whom this was an alternative target after he was not allowed to take part in the Japan Cup, had put on a fair amount of condition whilst in quarantine but still went off the odds-on favourite. However, he ran no sort of race under a waiting ride and his career ends on an anti-climactic note. That said he has already proved himself at this level on numerous occasions and is likely to prove a valuable addition to the Coolmore stallion ranks.
Red Rocks(IRE), who has been held at this level since his win in the 2006 Breeders' Cup Turf, was given every chance in a race run at a less-than-frantic gallop but faded in the straight.

7091a CATHAY PACIFIC HONG KONG MILE (GROUP 1) 1m
7:50 (7:51) 3-Y-0+
£599,212 (£231,274; £105,125; £59,790; £34,823; £21,025)

RPR

1 **Good Ba Ba (USA)**[22] 5-9-0 ....(t) ODoleuze 6 124
(A Schutz, Hong Kong) *hld up: 9th st: hdwy on outside fr over 1f out: led 120yds out: r.o wl* **57/20**[1]

2 shd **Creachadoir (IRE)**[50] 6334 3-8-13 .... LDettori 12 124
(Saeed Bin Suroor) *a in tch: 7th st: hdwy 1 1/2f out: sn drvn: ev ch fnl 100yds: unable qckn cl home* **18/1**

3 1 1/4 **Darjina (FR)**[71] 5798 3-8-9 .... CSoumillon 9 117
(A De Royer-Dupre, France) *mid-div: 8th st: hdwy 1 1/2f out: drvn to take 3rd cl home* **39/10**[3]

4 1/2 **Floral Pegasus (AUS)**[22] 4-9-0 ....(t) GMosse 11 120
(A S Cruz, Hong Kong) *a.p: 4th st: led over 1f out to 120yds out: one pce* **79/10**

5 3/4 **Joyful Winner (AUS)**[22] 7-9-0 ....(t) DBeadman 7 118
(J Moore, Hong Kong) *12th st: hdwy on outside fr 1 1/2f out: kpt on steadily fnl f* **28/1**

6 nk **Spirito Del Vento (FR)**[64] 6031 4-9-0 .... OPeslier 13 117
(J-M Beguigne, France) *hld up: last st: hdwy on outside fr 1 1/2f out: kpt on same pce fnl f* **30/1**

7 3/4 **The Duke (AUS)**[22] 8-9-0 .... GBoss 3 116
(C Fownes, Hong Kong) *6th st: n.m.r over 1f out: one pce fnl f* **60/1**

8 1/2 **Excellent Art**[43] 6511 3-8-13 .... JMurtagh 5 115
(A P O'Brien, Ire) *hld up: 10th st: outpcd wl over 1f out: sme prog u.p fnl f: nvr a factor* **33/10**[2]

9 2 1/2 **Kongo Rikishio (IRE)**[63] 5-9-0 .... SFujita 1 109
(K Yamauchi, Japan) *led to over 1f out* **66/10**

10 1 3/4 **Able One (NZ)**[22] 5-9-0 .... MJKinane 2 105
(J Moore, Hong Kong) *3rd st: stl cl up whn n.m.r over 1f out: sn btn* **21/1**

11 3/4 **Visionario (IRE)**[157] 3255 3-8-13 .... NCallan 8 103
(S P C Woods, Hong Kong) *5th st on ins: btn 1 1/2f out* **100/1**

12 1 1/4 **Al Qasi (IRE)**[50] 6332 4-9-0 .... RyanMoore 10 100
(P W Chapple-Hyam) *11th st: a in rr* **100/1**

13 nse **Down Town (AUS)**[49] 5-9-0 ....(t) DWhyte 4 100
(C H Yip, Hong Kong) *trckd ldr: 2nd st: wknd over 1f out* **10/1**

1m 34.5s (-0.20)
WFA 3 from 4yo+ 1lb **13 Ran SP% 123.2**
WIN 38.50; PL 16.50, 44.50, 20.50; DF 520.50.
Owner John Yuen Se Kit **Bred** Haras Santa Maria De Araras **Trained** Hong Kong

NOTEBOOK
Good Ba Ba(USA), who scored at the trials meeting here last month, confirmed form from that race with today's fourth and fifth and held off the European raiders to give his former German-based trainer his biggest success since moving to Hong Kong.
Creachadoir(IRE), whose campaign started with Jim Bolger back in March, has yet to win anything better than a Group 3, but he has now been second three times at Group 1 level, including two Classics. Dropping back to 1m again, he was only just touched off, and this looks his best effort yet. He can make amends in 2008, when his first big target will be the Dubai Duty Free.
Darjina(FR), who has proved herself a top-class miler this season, stayed on late to snatch the minor placing. She has not had that much racing and will be kept in training next year, when she will be tried over longer distances.
Excellent Art, who had been narrowly beaten in three major mile races since winning the St James's Palace Stakes, failed to run up to that form. He now retires to stud.
Al Qasi(IRE), attempting this longer trip for the first time since his debut in June last year, has yet to prove he is up to this class and made no show.

7092a CATHAY PACIFIC HONG KONG CUP (GROUP 1) 1m 2f
8:30 (8:30) 3-Y-0+
£749,014 (£289,093; £131,406; £74,901; £43,364; £26,281)

RPR

1 **Ramonti (FR)**[71] 5798 5-9-0 ....(t) LDettori 4 124
(Saeed Bin Suroor) *racd keenly in 3rd to st: led appr fnl f: drvn out* **38/10**[2]

2 1/2 **Viva Pataca**[28] 5-9-0 .... MJKinane 3 124+
(J Moore, Hong Kong) *racd in 4th to st: sltly hmpd 1 1/2f out: r.o wl fnl f tl no ex last 50yds* **30/100**[1]

3 2 1/2 **Musical Way (FR)**[42] 6524 5-8-10 ....(p) RonanThomas 5 114
(P Van De Poele, France) *disp 4th: 5th st: styd on fnl f to take 3rd cl home* **100/1**

4 1/2 **Art Trader (USA)**[28] 6-9-0 ....(t) DBeadman 1 117
(J Moore, Hong Kong) *6th st: kpt on but nvr able to chal* **51/1**

5 1/2 **Shadow Gate (JPN)**[42] 5-9-0 ....(t) KatsuharuTanaka 2 116
(Y Kato, Japan) *led 1f: led again over 3f out to appr fnl f: one pce* **23/1**

6 hd **Vengeance Of Rain (NZ)**[22] 7-9-0 ....(t) ADelpech 7 116
(D Ferraris, Hong Kong) *hld up: last st on outside: no hdwy* **84/10**[3]

7 2 3/4 **Royal Prince**[22] 4-9-0 ....(t) BPrebble 6 110
(A S Cruz, Hong Kong) *rrd s: led after 1f to over 3f out: 2nd st: wknd over 1f out* **18/1**

2m 2.80s (1.40) **7 Ran SP% 120.7**
WIN 48.00; PL 11.00, 10.10, 16.50; DF 22.50.
Owner Godolphin **Bred** S P A Siba **Trained** Newmarket, Suffolk

NOTEBOOK
Ramonti(FR), a really consistent sort who proved himself the best miler in Europe this year, was stepping up to this longer trip for the first time since being touched off in the Derby Italiano back in 2005. He raced just off the pace and was quite keen but found plenty for pressure and recorded his fourth Group 1 success of the season at the expense of a rival who has an outstanding record at Sha Tin. Connections indicated he is likely to remain at this distance, which brings the Dubai World Cup into the picture.
Viva Pataca, who won the trial race for this last month, was reportedly unsuited by the steady pace and got going too late after meeting some trouble in the straight. His rider unsuccessfully objected to the winner.
Musical Way(FR), a three-time winner in France earlier in the autumn, ran really well but would have ideally preferred a softer surface.
Vengeance Of Rain(NZ), Hong Kong's horse of the year and winner of the Dubai Sheema Classic, failed to run to his form and was beaten before the turn in.

7082 LINGFIELD (L-H)

Monday, December 10

OFFICIAL GOING: Standard

Wind: Mostly strong, against Weather: Overcast becoming fine

7094 PONTIN'S HOLIDAYS CLAIMING STKS — 7f (P)

1:00 (1:00) (Class 6) 3-Y-0+ — **£1,943** (£578; £288; £144) Stalls Low

Form — RPR

6055 **1** **Desert Dreamer (IRE)**[10] 6972 6-9-5 76 ... EddieAhern 8 — 76+
(G A Butler) *taken down early: hld up: prog on outer fr 4f out: cl up 2f out: rdn to ld over 1f out: sn in command* — **5/2**[1]

3131 **2** 1 ½ **Millfield (IRE)**[9] 6993 4-9-5 68 ... GeorgeBaker 1 — 72+
(P R Chamings) *taken down early: hld up wl in rr: plenty to do whn effrt 2f out: prog and swtchd lft over 1f out: wnt 2nd ins fnl f: clsd but no ch w wnr* — **11/4**[2]

0203 **3** nk **Chief Exec**[14] 6947 5-8-8 69 ... DavidProbert(7) 3 — 67+
(B J Llewellyn) *dwlt: hld up in last pair: stl there over 1f out: r.o strly fnl f: nrly snatched 2nd: no ch* — **8/1**

0650 **4** 1 ½ **High 'n Dry (IRE)**[9] 6997 3-8-7 68 ... (p) HarryPoulton(7) 13 — 62
(M A Allen) *dropped in fr wd draw: hld up wl in rr: brought to wd outside 1/2-way: outpcd over 2f out: kpt on fr over 1f out: n.d* — **14/1**

6216 **5** shd **Monashee Brave (IRE)**[7] 7011 4-9-0 62 ... PaulDoe 9 — 62
(R A Harris) *prom: chsd ldr 3f out to wl over 1f out: fdd* — **20/1**

4050 **6** 1 ½ **Mulberry Lad (IRE)**[6] 7014 5-8-11 52 ... ChrisCatlin 11 — 55
(P W Hiatt) *led: kicked on over 2f out: hdd over 1f out: wknd ins fnl f* **33/1**

640 **7** nk **Benllech**[9] 6997 3-9-0 65 ... RichardHughes 10 — 57
(S Kirk) *dwlt: hld up in midfield: pushed along and prog to chse ldrs 2f out: no imp over 1f out: fdd* — **16/1**

0050 **8** 2 **Who's Winning (IRE)**[14] 6946 6-9-0 66 ... (v1) JohnEgan 7 — 52
(B G Powell) *t.k.h: hld up bhd ldrs: rdn and nt qckn over 2f out: fdd* **16/1**

4000 **9** 1 ¾ **Piquet**[19] 6896 9-8-4 42 ... NelsonDeSouza 4 — 37
(J J Bridger) *hld up in last pair: no real prog fnl 2f* — **80/1**

0654 **10** ¾ **Satyricon**[28] 6795 3-9-5 73 ... (v) GregFairley 5 — 50
(M Botti) *n.m.r on inner over 5f out: nvr beyond midfield: rdn and no prog on inner 2f out* — **7/2**[3]

0000 **11** 6 **Campbeltown (IRE)**[42] 6542 4-8-9 43 ... SteveDrowne 12 — 24
(A B Haynes) *mostly chsd ldr to 3f out: wknd 2f out* — **66/1**

0000 **12** ½ **Elmasong**[6] 7014 3-8-5 44 ... AdrianMcCarthy 6 — 18
(J J Bridger) *prom tl wknd 2f out: no ch whn hmpd 1f out* — **80/1**

1m 24.39s (-1.50) **Going Correction** -0.175s/f (Stan) — **12** Ran SP% **118.7**

Speed ratings (Par 101): **101,99,98,97,97 95,95,92,90,89 83,82**

CSF £9.13 TOTE £3.60: £1.30, £1.40, £3.30; EX 11.00 Trifecta £38.00 Pool: £162.72 - 3.04 winning tickets..Chief Exec was claimed by Horses First Racing Limited for £11,000.

Owner The Desert Dreamer Partnership **Bred** Gainsborough Stud Management Ltd **Trained** Blewbury, Oxon

■ Stewards' Enquiry : Chris Catlin one-day ban: careless riding (Dec 21)
George Baker two-day ban: careless riding (Dec 21-22)

FOCUS

An ordinary claimer in which the winner was the form pick.

7095 GO PONTIN'S SHORT BREAKS NURSERY — 7f (P)

1:30 (1:30) (Class 5) (0-85,80) 2-Y-0 — **£4,100** (£1,227; £613; £306; £152) Stalls Low

Form — RPR

0006 **1** **Fathsta (IRE)**[19] 6899 2-8-8 **67** ... LPKeniry 6 — 74
(S Kirk) *t.k.h early: hld up in last: prog over 2f out: clsd on ldng pair over 1f out: shkn up to ld ent fnl f: readily* — **5/1**[3]

031 **2** 1 ½ **Smokey Rye**[12] 6964 2-8-11 **70** ... (b) FergusSweeney 1 — 73
(G L Moore) *chsd ldr 1f: wnt 2nd again over 2f out: drvn to chal 1f out: nt pce of wnr fnl f* — **16/1**

6022 **3** 1 ¼ **Silent Master (USA)**[19] 6899 2-9-2 **75** ... GregFairley 2 — 75
(M Johnston) *sn led: tried to kick on over 2f out: hdd and nt qckn ent fnl f* — **4/7**[1]

5511 **4** 6 **Ten Pole Tudor**[16] 6936 2-9-7 **80** ... ChrisCatlin 5 — 64
(R A Harris) *chsd ldr after 1f to over 2f out: wknd* — **7/2**[2]

526 **5** 2 ½ **Showtime Ice**[30] 6761 2-9-6 **79** ... EddieAhern 3 — 57
(M J Wallace) *in tch: rdn 1/2-way: sn struggling: wknd over 2f out* **25/1**

1m 24.8s (-1.09) **Going Correction** -0.175s/f (Stan) — **5** Ran SP% **112.3**

Speed ratings (Par 96): **99,97,95,89,86**

CSF £61.64 TOTE £8.90: £2.00, £4.50; EX 61.50.

Owner Speedlith Group **Bred** Brian Miller **Trained** Upper Lambourn, Berks

FOCUS

A fair nursery run at a decent pace despite the small field. The winner is rated back to his best.

NOTEBOOK

Fathsta(IRE) was behind Silent Master on his one recent sand debut but returned to his best form with what was ultimately a cosy win. He settled better this time and it would not surprise to see him build on this here over the winter. (op 6-1 tchd 9-2)

Smokey Rye, off the mark in a 6f maiden at Kempton last time, improved on that form back in nursery company. Her tail-swishing traits were again in evidence, but not to the same extent as in recent races. (op 14-1)

Silent Master(USA) enjoyed the run of the race in front and attempted to kick away in the straight, but he could not offer much resistance once tackled. He ran close to the form of his brace of seconds to Traphalgar here last month, but this was still rather disappointing. (op 4-6 tchd 8-11, 10-11 in a place and 4-5 in a place)

Ten Pole Tudor, 4lb higher than when recording back-to-back wins at Wolverhampton, was below par on this first run at Lingfield. (tchd 3-1)

Showtime Ice was the first beaten on this nursery debut, before the extra furlong became a factor. (op 16-1 tchd 28-1)

7096 LADY LUCK'S (S) STKS — 6f (P)

2:00 (2:05) (Class 6) 2-Y-0 — **£1,943** (£578; £288; £144) Stalls Low

Form — RPR

6522 **1** **Maybe I Wont**[6] 7021 2-9-2 63 ... GeorgeBaker 3 — 64
(R M Stronge) *trckd ldng trio: prog jst over 2f out: led over 1f out: sn rdn clr* — **4/7**[1]

500 **2** 1 ½ **Just Mossie**[70] 5869 2-8-4 39 ... JackDean(7) 9 — 54
(W G M Turner) *sn drvn in last: stl struggling 2f out: r.o fr over 1f out to take 2nd last 50yds* — **66/1**

4556 **3** 1 **Desert Life (IRE)**[13] 6958 2-8-11 60 ... JohnEgan 5 — 51
(R A Harris) *settled in rr: rdn over 2f out: prog over 1f out: chsd wnr ins fnl f: one pce and lost 2nd last 50yds* — **9/2**[2]

0406 **4** ¾ **Chemise (IRE)**[28] 6793 2-8-6 46 ... NelsonDeSouza 4 — 44
(R J Hodges) *trckd ldng pair: sltly short of room and lost pl over 2f out: effrt again to dispute 2nd ent fnl f: one pce* — **14/1**

0004 **5** 1 ½ **La Varrosa**[28] 6793 2-8-6 52 ... GregFairley 7 — 40
(Mrs P N Dutfield) *trckd ldrs: wd bnd 2f out and sn outpcd: plugged on* — **20/1**

0 **6** 1 **Joshua**[47] 6419 2-8-11 0 ... EddieAhern 1 — 45+
(J R Gask) *dwlt: in tch: rdn over 2f out: prog on inner to press for a pl 1f out: nowhere to go and snatched up last 100yds* — **33/1**

0350 **7** 1 **Fraamington**[33] 6722 2-8-11 47 ... ChrisCatlin 8 — 39
(M R Channon) *a in last trio: rdn over 4f out: struggling after* — **16/1**

U62 **8** shd **Little Finch (IRE)**[5] 7030 2-8-4 38 ... (b) KrishGundowry(7) 6 — 38
(R C Guest) *w ldr to 2f out: sn wknd* — **14/1**

0005 **9** ½ **Zahwah**[5] 7030 2-8-6 50 ... (b) RichardKingscote 2 — 32
(J G Portman) *led to over 1f out: wknd rapidly* — **12/1**[3]

1m 12.86s (0.05) **Going Correction** -0.175s/f (Stan) — **9** Ran SP% **117.9**

Speed ratings (Par 94): **92,90,88,87,85 84,83,82,82**

CSF £71.57 TOTE £1.60: £1.10, £13.30, £1.60; EX 60.60 Trifecta £336.90 Part won. Pool: £474.51 - 0.46 winning tickets..There was no bid for the winner. Joshua was claimed by Don Cantillon for £6,000.

Owner Tim Whiting **Bred** Wheelersland Stud **Trained** Beedon Common, Berks

FOCUS

An ordinary seller. The winner is slightly better than this grade and the runner-up improved on the poor level of his previous form.

NOTEBOOK

Maybe I Wont, whose only win in a busy first season had been over course and distance in October, was a beaten favourite on his previous three starts but made no mistake this time with a decisive win. He is just as happy over 7f. (op 8-11 tchd 4-5, 10-11 in a place)

Just Mossie, having his first run on Polytrack, had shown little in three starts on turf, twice in this grade. He looked set to finish at the back after struggling to go the pace, but stayed on well inside the last to snatch second. Likely to appreciate a return to further, his official mark of just 39 will suffer for this. (op 50-1)

Desert Life(IRE), dropped in trip, was without the blinkers that had been tried last time. He is probably up to winning a race of this nature but does look a little tricky. (tchd 4-1)

Chemise(IRE), who is exposed as a poor performer, would have finished a shade closer had she enjoyed an uninterrupted run. (op 12-1)

Joshua, quickly down in grade after finishing tailed off in a Bath maiden on his debut, was endeavouring to stay on against the rail when he ran out of racing room inside the last and was eased. (op 25-1)

Zahwah, still in front going to the furlong pole, was weakening when hampered inside the last. (tchd 11-1)

7097 PONTIN'S GREAT FAMILY HOLIDAYS MEDIAN AUCTION MAIDEN FILLIES' STKS — 1m (P)

2:30 (2:35) (Class 6) 2-Y-0 — **£2,266** (£674; £337; £168) Stalls High

Form — RPR

6 **1** **Bauhaus Bourbon (USA)**[160] 3187 2-9-0 0 ... ChrisCatlin 4 — 71
(P F I Cole) *in tch in midfield: pushed along fr 1/2-way: prog 3f out: effrt on inner over 1f out: sustained run to ld last 150yds: styd on wl* — **14/1**

6334 **2** 1 ¾ **Nice Wee Girl (IRE)**[10] 6980 2-9-0 67 ... RichardHughes 9 — 67
(S Kirk) *led: drvn 2f out: hdd and outpcd last 150yds* — **5/1**[3]

3 1 **Ivory Silk** 2-9-0 0 ... DaneO'Neill 1 — 65+
(D K Ivory) *s.s: hld up wl in rr: stdy prog fr over 3f out: wd bnd 2f out: rdn over 1f out: styd on to take 3rd ins fnl f* — **25/1**

03 **4** 1 **Welsh Opera**[39] 6601 2-9-0 0 ... JimCrowley 2 — 63
(Mrs A J Perrett) *dwlt: sn trckd ldrs: rdn over 2f out: chsd ldr and ch over 1f out: nt qckn* — **6/4**[1]

6356 **5** ½ **Oceana Blue**[36] 6664 2-9-0 68 ... FergusSweeney 10 — 62
(A M Balding) *trckd ldrs: effrt over 2f out: rdn and nt qckn over 1f out* **8/1**

0 **6** 3 **Neyraan**[26] 6805 2-9-0 0 ... GregFairley 8 — 55
(M Johnston) *t.k.h: trckd ldr after 3f to over 1f out: wknd rapidly* — **14/1**

6 **7** 12 **Gallic Charm (IRE)**[24] 6827 2-9-0 0 ... LPKeniry 5 — 29+
(D R C Elsworth) *plld hrd early: hld up in midfield: eased fr 3f out: sddle slipped* — **11/4**[2]

8 2 ½ **Station Place** 2-9-0 0 ... SteveDrowne 3 — 23
(A B Haynes) *dwlt: a in rr: bhd over 3f out: t.o* — **33/1**

0 **9** ¾ **Sparkling Silver**[12] 6964 2-9-0 0 ... RobertHavlin 7 — 21
(D K Ivory) *a in rr: bhd over 3f out: t.o* — **66/1**

10 5 **Double R** 2-9-0 0 ... SamHitchcott 6 — 10
(A B Haynes) *v s.i.s: a in rr: bhd fnl 3f: t.o* — **50/1**

1m 39.21s (-0.22) **Going Correction** -0.175s/f (Stan) — **10** Ran SP% **118.0**

Speed ratings (Par 91): **94,92,91,90,89 86,74,72,71,66**

CSF £81.50 TOTE £15.20: £3.80, £1.50, £4.70; EX 67.70 Trifecta £338.90 Part won. Pool: £477.45 - 0.72 winning tickets..

Owner Frank Stella **Bred** Delehanty Stock Farm **Trained** Whatcombe, Oxon

FOCUS

An ordinary fillies' maiden with little strength in depth, although the winning time was marginally faster than the later old-horse handicap. The race should provide a winner or two and the race again showed that the usually dreaded inside rail was no handicap following the recent wet spell.

NOTEBOOK

Bauhaus Bourbon(USA), not seen since showing only a little ability on her debut here in July, proved well suited by the extra quarter-mile. Despite coming off the bridle before reaching the home bend, she responded well and scythed her way up the inside rail to win going away. A half-sister to three winners including the latest November Handicap winner Malt Or Mash, she should continue to progress. (tchd 16-1)

Nice Wee Girl(IRE), trying 1m for the first time, tried to make all the running and kept battling away but found the winner's turn of foot too much for her. She continues to find one or two too good for her and is now starting to look exposed, but her official rating of 67 does provide a fair benchmark to the form. (op 4-1)

Ivory Silk ◆, a 28,000gns half-sister to Pride Of Joy, did extremely well to give herself a chance of winning after completely fluffing the start and racing widest around the home bend. Her breeding suggests this trip would be as far as she wants, but with improvement likely she ought to be able to pick up a race or two in due course. (tchd 28-1)

Welsh Opera once again had every chance, but lacked the finishing pace to take advantage over this longer trip. This was a little disappointing in view of her third in a stronger-looking maiden here last time, but she does now qualify for a mark and could still be of interest in that sphere. (op 7-4 tchd 2-1 in a place)

Oceana Blue had every chance, but should have done better based on official ratings through the runner-up and she has not built on early promise. (op 7-1)

Neyraan ran a little better than on her Kempton debut last month, but was still comfortably seen off and is not amongst the stable's stars. (op 12-1)

Gallic Charm(IRE) pulled like a train early and then took a buffeting from those around her. It was probably then that her saddle slipped and she was eased right off approaching the home bend. This can be ignored. Official explanation: jockey said saddle slipped (op 7-2 tchd 4-1)

Sparkling Silver Official explanation: jockey said filly hung right

7098 PONTINS.COM H'CAP — 1m 2f (P)
3:00 (3:05) (Class 6) (0-52,52) 3-Y-0+ £1,943 (£578; £288; £144) Stalls Low

Form — RPR

0004 **1** **Play Up Pompey**[1] 7083 5-8-13 **49** AmirQuinn 14 57
(J J Bridger) *plld hrd early: hld up: rdn 4f out: prog on outer 3f out: struggling 2f out: styd on fr over 1f out: led last stride* **11/2**[2]

2060 **2** *shd* **Shaheer (IRE)**[14] 6951 5-9-0 **50** (v) JimCrowley 7 58
(J Gallagher) *trckd ldrs: effrt over 2f out: drvn to ld jst ins fnl f: collared last stride* **7/1**

0005 **3** *1 ½* **Josr's Magic (IRE)**[12] 6968 3-8-11 **50** EddieAhern 4 55
(H J Collingridge) *hld up wl in rr: stl there and rdn over 2f out: wd bnd sn after: styd on strly fnl f to take 3rd nr fin* **12/1**

0120 **4** *½* **Dawson Creek (IRE)**[29] 6774 3-8-12 **51** GregFairley 12 55
(B Gubby) *pressed ldng pair: led wl over 2f out: drvn over 1f out: hdd jst ins fnl f: no ex* **9/2**[1]

0/23 **5** *shd* **Smokey The Bear**[12] 6968 5-8-12 **48** ChrisCatlin 3 52
(Miss Sheena West) *plld hrd and heavily restrained to rr early: stl at bk of main gp and nowhere to go over 2f out: prog and hrd rdn over 1f out: one pce ins fnl f* **9/2**[1]

6000 **6** *1* **Mucho Loco (IRE)**[45] 3047 4-8-3 **46** (p) ThomasO'Brien(7) 9 48
(R Curtis) *mostly in midfield: effrt on inner over 2f out: chsng ldrs over 1f out: one pce* **25/1**

7 *1 ¾* **Jalandy (IRE)**[52] 5742 4-8-13 **49** AdrianMcCarthy 10 47
(S Curran) *mostly midfield: drvn over 2f out: no prog after* **12/1**

004 **8** *½* **Raise Again (IRE)**[11] 6100 4-8-9 **52** NBazeley(7) 1 49
(Mrs P N Dutfield) *settled wl in rr: effrt on inner 2f out: plugged on but no imp on ldrs* **33/1**

6254 **9** *nk* **Double Valentine**[12] 6968 4-8-7 **48** JackMitchell(5) 13 45
(R Ingram) *dwlt: hld up: prog fr 6f out: jnd ldrs on wd outside 3f out: wd and btn wl over 1f out* **12/1**

000- **10** *4* **Tuning Fork**[454] 5267 7-8-7 **48** KirstyMilczarek(5) 5 37
(M J Attwater) *racd keenly: led to wl over 2f out: wknd over 1f out* **25/1**

0000 **11** *¾* **Itsawindup**[21] 6871 3-8-13 **52** (v) PaulDoe 8 39
(W J Knight) *t.k.h: trckd ldrs: lost pl and struggling over 2f out* **50/1**

0423 **12** *¾* **Karmest**[12] 6969 3-8-12 **51** DaneO'Neill 11 37
(A D Brown) *mostly trckd ldr to 3f out: stl wl there 2f out: wknd tamely* **13/2**[3]

602- **13** *19* **Busy Man (IRE)**[407] 6232 8-8-3 **46** KrishGundowry(7) 6 —
(R C Guest) *s.v.s: plld hrd and hld up in last pair: wknd 4f out: t.o* **10/1**

2m 5.83s (-1.96) **Going Correction** -0.175s/f (Stan)
WFA 3 from 4yo+ 3lb **13** Ran SP% **122.3**
Speed ratings (Par 101): **100,99,98,98,98 97,96,95,95,92 91,91,75**
CSF £43.39 CT £455.39 TOTE £7.10: £2.90, £2.40, £4.10; EX 54.30 Trifecta £136.60 Part won. Pool: £192.47 - 0.46 winning tickets..
Owner double-r-racing.com **Bred** M Pollitt **Trained** Liphook, Hants

FOCUS
A routine and modest handicap of its type for the track and several still had a chance turning in. The principals all came down the centre of the track, but the evidence of recent days suggests those that stayed against the inside were not as inconvenienced as they usually are. The form makes sense.

Karmest Official explanation: jockey said filly hung left
Busy Man(IRE) Official explanation: jockey said gelding ran too free

7099 GO PONTIN'S NOW H'CAP — 1m (P)
3:30 (3:38) (Class 5) (0-75,75) 3-Y-0+ £3,238 (£963; £481; £240) Stalls High

Form — RPR

3221 **1** **Demisemiquaver**[10] 6975 3-8-13 **69** (b) SteveDrowne 5 76
(J Noseda) *dwlt: hld up towards rr: prog over 1f out: pushed along and r.o fnl f to ld nr fin: cleverly* **9/2**[3]

2015 **2** *nk* **Meditation**[6] 7017 5-8-11 **66** JamesDoyle 3 72
(I A Wood) *led: steadily increased pce fr 3f out: kpt on wl u.p over 1f out: hdd nr fin* **16/1**

1653 **3** *½* **Smokin Joe**[6] 7017 6-8-12 **67** (b) JimCrowley 2 74+
(J R Best) *t.k.h: hld up towards rr: effrt 2f out: nt clr run briefly 1f out: r.o to take 3rd nr fin: jst outpcd* **3/1**[1]

3000 **4** *shd* **Buxton**[14] 6949 3-9-5 **75** RobertHavlin 8 80
(R Ingram) *dropped in fr wd draw: hld up: prog on inner over 1f out and got through to look dangerous ins fnl f: one pce last 75yds* **9/1**

0362 **5** *1* **Hucking Heat (IRE)**[9] 6997 3-8-8 **64** (v) JohnEgan 10 66
(J R Best) *t.k.h: sn pressed ldr: upsides 2f out: nt qckn over 1f out: fdd nr fin* **7/2**[2]

3251 **6** *½* **Arena's Dream (USA)**[101] 4997 3-8-9 **65** PatCosgrave 6 66
(J R Boyle) *t.k.h: hld up in midfield: outpcd 2f out: styd on fnl f: n.d* **16/1**

0160 **7** *1 ¼* **Prince Of Charm (USA)**[145] 3646 3-8-12 **68** ow1 (p) DaneO'Neill 9 66
(R A Teal) *s.s: hld up in rr: rdn and outpcd over 2f out: plugged on fnl f* **25/1**

410/ **8** *2* **Maidanni (USA)**[1144] 6334 5-9-1 **70** EddieAhern 4 64
(J R Gask) *free to post: t.k.h: prom tl wknd over 1f out* **12/1**

0020 **9** *nk* **Torquemada (IRE)**[9] 6996 6-9-0 **69** PaulDoe 7 62
(J Akehurst) *t.k.h: pressed ldr: upsides 2f out: wknd rapidly jst over 1f out* **10/1**

0005 **10** *¾* **Binnion Bay (IRE)**[9] 6997 6-8-9 **64** (b) AmirQuinn 1 55
(J J Bridger) *s.s: plld hrd and hld up in last pair: rdn and struggling fr 3f out* **7/1**

1m 39.23s (-0.20) **Going Correction** -0.175s/f (Stan)
WFA 3 from 5yo+ 1lb **10** Ran SP% **120.3**
Speed ratings (Par 103): **94,93,93,93,92 91,90,88,88,87**
CSF £76.10 CT £253.74 TOTE £5.40: £1.60, £5.00, £1.60; EX 80.40 Trifecta £185.00 Pool: £534.32 - 2.05 winning tickets. Place 6 £368.92, Place 5 £248.79.
Owner Lady Carolyn Warren, Duke Of Roxburghe **Bred** Highclere Stud And Floors Farming **Trained** Newmarket, Suffolk

FOCUS
The early pace was modest and resulted in a moderate winning time for a race of its class, slightly slower than the earlier two-year-old fillies' maiden. The winner was up 3lb on her previous best and the runner-up is the best guide to the form.

Torquemada(IRE) Official explanation: trainer said gelding had a breathing problem
Binnion Bay(IRE) Official explanation: jockey said gelding ran flat

T/Jkpt: Not won. T/Plt: £352.00 to a £1 stake. Pool: £61,364.20. 127.25 winning tickets. T/Qpdt: £25.50 to a £1 stake. Pool: £4,773.80. 138.20 winning tickets. JN

7076 WOLVERHAMPTON (A.W) (L-H)
Monday, December 10

OFFICIAL GOING: Standard
Racing was put back for 15 minutes after the voided first race so that the ambulance which took Thyolo's rider to hospital could return to the track.
Wind: Moderate, across Weather: Fine

7100 PONTIN'S BOOK EARLY PRICE PROMISE AMATEUR RIDERS' H'CAP — 1m 1f 103y(P)
1:10 (1:10) (Class 5) (0-75,72) 3-Y-0+ £2,717 (£842; £421; £210) Stalls Low

Form — RPR

000- **V** **Candy Anchor (FR)**[584] 1467 8-10-7 **58** oh13 MissFayeBramley 12 —
(R E Peacock)

0000 **V** **Kamanda Laugh**[36] 6674 6-11-4 **72** MissARyan(3) 4 —
(K A Ryan)

0604 **V** **Western Roots**[6] 7023 6-10-4 **62** (p) MrJGoss(7) 5 —
(M Appleby)

0004 **V** **Thyolo (IRE)**[3] 7050 6-10-12 **70** MissLauraGray(7) 7 —
(B G Powell)

5606 **V** **Kingsholm**[9] 7002 5-11-4 **69** MrSDobson 6 —
(I W McInnes)

0500 **V** **Royal Sailor (IRE)**[7] 7004 5-10-0 **58** oh8 (b) MrDavidMcMinn(7) 10 —
(J Ryan)

4000 **V** **Mind That Fox**[13] 6955 5-10-0 **58** oh13 MrAWEdwards(7) 2 —
(T Wall)

42-1 **V** **Crazy Bear (IRE)**[9] 6991 4-10-10 **68** MrECookson(7) 8 —
(K J Burke)

0060 **V** **Lady's Law**[19] 6902 4-10-0 **58** oh13 MissEmma-JaneJenkins(7) 9 —
(Rae Guest)

0500 **V** **Riolo (IRE)**[13] 6955 5-10-0 **58** oh13 (b) MrSBest(7) 13 —
(K F Clutterbuck)

2106 **V** **Strike Force**[120] 4416 3-10-2 **60** MissALHutchinson(5) 1 —
(K F Clutterbuck)

0000 **V** **L'Oiseau De Feu (USA)**[6] 5886 3-9-12 **58** oh1 MissSPeacock(7) 3 —
(Mrs K Waldron)

11 **V** **Alonso De Guzman (IRE)**[28] 6803 3-10-2 **62** MrBAdams(7) 11 —
(J R Boyle)

■ Stewards' Enquiry : Miss Emma-Jane Jenkins seven-day ban: careless riding (Jan 4,14,18,23,27,29, Feb 1)

FOCUS
The race was voided for safety reasons. Thyolo was fatally injured in a fall after a furlong and was stricken on the track as the runners came round for the second circuit. The flagman alerted the other jockeys who pulled up on the entrance to the home straight. Lady's Law's rider was given a seven-day suspension for careless riding for her part in Thyolo's fall.

7101 GO PONTIN'S CLAIMING STKS — 1m 141y(P)
1:40 (1:58) (Class 6) 2-Y-O £2,730 (£806; £403) Stalls Low

Form — RPR

3360 **1** **Carry On Cleo**[16] 6928 2-8-3 52 ow1 (b[1]) MatthewHenry 1 53
(P D Evans) *hld up and bhd: hdwy on outside over 3f out: rdn 2f out: led jst over 1f out: drvn out* **14/1**

5054 **2** *nk* **Scientific**[20] 6880 2-8-7 55 (b) DaleGibson 8 56
(R A Fahey) *s.i.s: hld up towards rr: rdn 4f out: hdwy 3f out: ev ch ins fnl f: r.o* **11/1**[3]

5344 **3** *hd* **Tiger Spice**[10] 6978 2-9-0 68 LiamJones 7 63
(W J Haggas) *hld up in mid-div: hdwy over 5f out: rdn and ev ch 1f out: kpt on* **8/15**[1]

0406 **4** *2 ½* **Giggling Monkey**[26] 6814 2-8-1 47 ow1 (v) HayleyTurner 5 45
(P D Evans) *hld up in rr: rdn and hdwy over 1f out: styd on fnl f* **16/1**

0 **5** *½* **Arabesque Dancer**[16] 6934 2-9-0 0 OscarUrbina 4 57
(M Botti) *hld up in mid-div: rdn and flashed tail over 1f out: styd on fnl f* **28/1**

0004 **6** *1 ½* **Adam Eterno (IRE)**[16] 6928 2-8-7 55 (b) TGMcLaughlin 3 47
(A B Haynes) *led: hdd over 5f out: led 3f out: rdn and hdd jst over 1f out: edgd rt and wknd ins fnl f* **22/1**

3500 **7** *1* **Boomtown**[10] 6978 2-8-8 67 MarieLussiana(7) 10 52
(M Johnston) *w ldr: led over 5f out tl over 4f out: hung lft fr over 3f out: wknd wl over 1f out* **15/2**[2]

00U0 **8** *13* **Mister Cafnex (IRE)**[29] 6775 2-8-4 39 (p) NeilChalmers(3) 6 17
(B W Duke) *s.i.s: in rr: rdn over 3f out: sn struggling* **16/1**

0000 **9** *3 ½* **Lord Of The Wing**[6] 7022 2-8-9 41 ow2 (p) MickyFenton 9 12
(P T Midgley) *chsd ldrs: rdn over 5f out: led over 4f out to 3f out: sn wknd* **40/1**

0000 **10** *1 ¼* **Distant Noble**[26] 6814 2-8-13 46 (b[1]) J-PGuillambert 2 13
(R Brotherton) *prom: rdn over 3f out: wknd wl over 2f out* **100/1**

1m 53.27s (1.51) **Going Correction** +0.025s/f (Slow) **10** Ran SP% **115.0**
Speed ratings (Par 94): **94,93,93,91,90 89,88,77,74,72**
CSF £148.36 TOTE £11.30: £2.70, £2.60, £1.10; EX 77.60.
Owner J E Abbey **Bred** J E Abbey **Trained** Pandy, Monmouths

FOCUS
Pretty solid if decidedly modest form.

NOTEBOOK
Carry On Cleo found the fitting of blinkers doing the trick having worn a visor once in the past. Her trainer described it as a bad race for bad horses but was obviously relieved she had actually won something. (op 10-1)

Scientific does seem to have benefited from having blinkers fitted and lost nothing in defeat over a longer trip. (op 12-1 tchd 14-1)

Tiger Spice had shaped as though she would be suited by further than this here last time. It was still a bit disappointing that she could not win at this level but she did not run far off her form. (op 8-11)

Giggling Monkey, again in a visor, took a while to get going and might need a bit further still. (op 14-1 tchd 20-1)

Arabesque Dancer was quickly downgraded after showing nothing over course and distance on her debut last month. She stayed on late in the day despite showing some signs of temperament. (op 22-1 tchd 33-1)

Adam Eterno(IRE), who had previously tried blinkers back in June, failed to get home after making the running over this longer trip. (op 20-1)

7102 PONTINS.COM (S) STKS — 1m 4f 50y(P)
2:10 (2:25) (Class 6) 3-Y-O+ — £2,047 (£604; £302) Stalls Low

Form RPR
6540 1 **Mayadeen (IRE)**[14] 5676 5-9-8 50....(b) PhillipMakin 1 53
(I Semple) *hld up: rdn over 2f out: hdwy and n.m.r wl over 1f out: led ent fnl f: rdn out* 9/2[2]
4305 2 1 1/2 **Cool Isle**[53] 6292 4-8-13 42....(b) TGMcLaughlin 3 42
(P Howling) *chsd ldr: led 2f out: sn rdn: hdd ent fnl f: nt qckn* 17/2
4115 3 1 1/4 **Treetops Hotel (IRE)**[82] 5531 8-9-8 64.... FrankieMcDonald 6 51+
(B R Johnson) *stdd s: hld up sn in tch: nt clr run over 2f out and briefly jst over 1f out: rdn and kpt on ins fnl f* 5/6[1]
0000 4 1 1/4 **Ocean Valentine**[9] 7001 4-8-13 40.... RussellKennemore(5) 4 43
(J T Stimpson) *hld up: hdwy on outside over 2f out: rdn and ev ch over 1f out: wknd ins fnl f* 25/1
00-4 5 hd **Trackattack**[8] 5427 5-9-1 35....(p) NeilChalmers(3) 5 43
(M Appleby) *set stdy pce: rdn 3f out: hdd 2f out: wknd wl ins fnl f* 12/1
13-6 6 2 **Mr Excel (IRE)**[13] 6961 4-8-13 73.... HaddenFrost(5) 2 39
(G A Ham) *prom: rdn over 1f out: sn btn* 5/1[3]

2m 46.51s (4.09) **Going Correction** +0.025s/f (Slow) 6 Ran SP% 111.5
Speed ratings (Par 101): **87,86,85,84,84 82**
CSF £39.02 TOTE £6.50: £1.70, £4.70; EX 35.40.There was no bid for the winner. Treetops Hotel was claimed by R. Hollinshead for £6,000.
Owner Cheesie & The Quiet Men **Bred** Shadwell Estate Company Limited **Trained** Carluke, S Lanarks
■ Stewards' Enquiry : Russell Kennemore caution: careless riding.

FOCUS
A modest pace resulted in a very slow winning time, even for a seller. Very weak form.
Ocean Valentine Official explanation: jockey said gelding hung left

7103 GO PONTIN'S HOLIDAYS MAIDEN STKS — 1m 141y(P)
2:40 (2:55) (Class 5) 3-Y-O+ — £2,968 (£876; £438) Stalls Low

Form RPR
3232 1 **Red Blossom**[23] 6858 3-8-12 67....(b) JamieMackay 7 66
(Sir Mark Prescott) *a gng wl: led wl over 1f out: shkn up and qcknd clr ent fnl f: drvn out* 1/1[1]
2 5 **Ready To Crown (USA)**[33] 3-8-12 0.... DaleGibson 11 55
(Andrew Turnell) *s.s: hld up and bhd: hdwy 2f out: rdn and swtchd rt over 1f out: wnt 2nd ins fnl f: no ch w wnr* 15/2[3]
00 3 2 1/2 **Ocean Waves (IRE)**[9] 6991 4-8-11 42.... TravisBlock(3) 1 49
(Miss Tor Sturgis) *led early: a.p: ev ch wl over 1f out: sn rdn: one pce fnl f* 28/1
0-30 4 2 1/2 **Rapid Flow**[41] 6565 5-9-5 44.... AdamKirby 8 48
(J W Unett) *sn led: hdd over 6f out: led 3f out: rdn and hdd wl over 1f out: wknd ins fnl f* 20/1
40 5 1/2 **Naledi**[40] 6597 3-9-3 0....(b) PaulMulrennan 5 47
(J R Norton) *hmpd s: hld up and bhd: styd on fnl f: n.d* 14/1
06 6 1 **Kielty's Folly**[23] 6858 3-9-3 0.... DanielTudhope 3 45
(B P J Baugh) *hld up and bhd: hdwy whn n.m.r 2f out: wknd over 1f out* 66/1
6060 7 1 3/4 **Cantique (IRE)**[130] 4109 3-8-12 41.... LiamJones 9 36
(R J Price) *t.k.h in mid-div: rdn over 2f out: sn bhd: hung lft over 1f out* 40/1
3660 8 3/4 **Little Miss Tara (IRE)**[15] 6196 3-8-12 63.... TGMcLaughlin 6 34
(A B Haynes) *a bhd* 12/1
6202 9 3 **Run For Ede'S**[25] 6824 3-8-12 65....(p) MickyFenton 10 27
(P M Phelan) *sn prom: rdn and wknd wl over 1f out: hung rt ent fnl f* 15/8[2]
00-0 10 9 **Inchmarlow (IRE)**[79] 5625 4-8-12 40.... JamesRogers(7) 2 11
(T H Caldwell) *prom: led over 6f out to 3f out: wknd 2f out* 80/1

1m 50.83s (-0.93) **Going Correction** +0.025s/f (Slow)
WFA 3 from 4yo+ 2lb 10 Ran SP% 124.3
Speed ratings (Par 103): **105,100,98,96,95 94,93,92,89,81**
CSF £10.27 TOTE £2.40: £1.02, £3.10, £6.60; EX 17.70.
Owner Cheveley Park Stud **Bred** Cheveley Park Stud Ltd **Trained** Newmarket, Suffolk
■ Stewards' Enquiry : Adam Kirby one-day ban: used whip above shoulder height (Dec 21)

FOCUS
A poor maiden in which Red Blossom did not need to improve to score despite the big winning margin, with her only form rival well below par.

7104 WEATHERBYS PRINTING H'CAP — 1m 141y(P)
3:10 (3:25) (Class 5) (0-75,75) 3-Y-O+ — £2,968 (£876; £438) Stalls Low

Form RPR
0000 1 **Soviet Palace (IRE)**[44] 6492 3-9-4 73....(e[1]) PaulMulrennan 5 81
(K A Ryan) *mde all: rdn and edgd rt 1f out: drvn out* 8/1
6323 2 hd **Baan (USA)**[10] 6982 4-9-0 67....(v) DeanMcKeown 1 74
(M Johnston) *chsd ldrs: wnt 2nd over 3f out: rdn over 2f out: ev ch ins fnl f: r.o* 3/1[2]
5031 3 1 **Ochre (IRE)**[13] 6956 3-8-11 66.... TonyHamilton 8 71
(R A Fahey) *hld up: hdwy over 2f out: rdn whn hung lft and carried rt 1f out: nt qckn* 11/4[1]
0605 4 7 **Chookie Hamilton**[49] 6389 3-9-6 75....(p) PhillipMakin 3 64
(I Semple) *hld up: rdn over 3f out: sme hdwy on outside over 2f out: n.d* 5/1
-500 5 6 **Gwyllion (USA)**[9] 6993 3-8-8 63.... StephenDonohoe 4 38
(B J Meehan) *hld up: rdn over 3f out: bhd fnl 2f* 14/1
6044 6 5 **Empire Dancer (IRE)**[6] 7024 4-8-4 60.... AndrewElliott(3) 6 24
(I W McInnes) *sn chsng ldr: lost 2nd over 3f out: wknd over 2f out* 4/1[3]
4206 7 1 3/4 **Intersky Sports (USA)**[3] 7057 3-8-5 63.... PatrickMathers(3) 2 23
(K J Burke) *hld up and bhd: rdn over 4f out: sn struggling* 20/1

1m 51.02s (-0.74) **Going Correction** +0.025s/f (Slow)
WFA 3 from 4yo 2lb 7 Ran SP% 110.9
Speed ratings (Par 103): **104,103,102,96,91 86,85**
CSF £30.21 CT £79.45 TOTE £10.30: £5.40, £1.70; EX 47.30.
Owner David Reilly **Bred** Joe Rogers **Trained** Hambleton, N Yorks
■ Stewards' Enquiry : Dean McKeown three-day ban: used whip with excessive frequency (Dec 21,22,26)

FOCUS
They went a decent pace in this modest affair which did not turn out to be quite as competitive as expected. Soviet Palace was on a good mark on his spring form and was back to something like his best.

7105 PONTIN'S BOOK EARLY AND SAVE H'CAP — 5f 216y(P)
3:40 (3:55) (Class 5) (0-70,70) 3-Y-O+ — £2,968 (£876; £438) Stalls Low

Form RPR
362 1 **Royal Challenge**[17] 6910 6-9-1 67.... DanielTudhope 5 74
(I W McInnes) *t.k.h: a.p: led wl over 1f out: rdn ins fnl f: r.o wl* 5/1
2423 2 2 **Perlachy**[6] 7019 3-8-3 58....(v) DuranFentiman(3) 8 59
(Mrs N Macauley) *broke wl: led 1f: led 3f out: rdn and hdd wl over 1f out: nt qckn ins fnl f* 11/1
0462 3 1 **Wicked Uncle**[7] 7011 8-8-10 62....(v) PaulMulrennan 2 60
(S Gollings) *hld up: rdn and hdwy on outside wl over 1f out: kpt on same pce fnl f* 3/1[3]
0100 4 3/4 **Paddywack (IRE)**[45] 6476 10-8-0 57....(b) DanielleMcCreery(5) 4 52
(D W Chapman) *s.i.s: outpcd: kpt on ins fnl f: nvr nrr* 20/1
0040 5 3/4 **Spy Gun (USA)**[20] 6886 7-7-13 58 oh11 ow2....(p) PatrickDonaghy(7) 6 51?
(T Wall) *hld up: rdn over 2f out: kpt on ins fnl f* 40/1
0011 6 1/2 **Commander Wish**[31] 6752 4-8-4 59....(tp) NeilChalmers(3) 1 50
(Lucinda Featherstone) *w ldrs tl over 3f out: sn rdn and lost pl: n.d after* 5/2[1]
4061 7 1 3/4 **Tilly's Dream**[13] 6962 4-9-4 70.... AdamKirby 7 56
(G C Bravery) *hld up in tch: rdn wl over 1f out: wknd ins fnl f* 11/4[2]
406 8 1 3/4 **Just Spike**[203] 1904 4-8-13 65.... TGMcLaughlin 9 45
(B P J Baugh) *hld up: hdwy over 3f out: ev ch over 2f out: hung lft and wknd 1f out* 66/1
0006 9 5 **Diamond Josh**[17] 6910 5-7-11 56 oh11.... RossAtkinson(7) 3 20
(M Mullineaux) *rdr lost iron leaving stalls: led after 1f to 3f out: rdr sn lost weight cloth: wknd wl over 1f out* 66/1

1m 15.73s (-0.08) **Going Correction** +0.025s/f (Slow) 9 Ran SP% 115.4
Speed ratings (Par 103): **101,98,97,96,95 94,92,89,83**
CSF £54.70 CT £192.54 TOTE £5.90: £1.60, £2.60, £1.40; EX 31.20 Place 6 £52.90, Place 5 £46.64.
Owner Truck Export **Bred** Capt A L Smith-Maxwell **Trained** Catwick, E Yorks
■ Stewards' Enquiry : Duran Fentiman one-day ban: used whip with excessive frequency (Dec 21)

FOCUS
A low-key sprint handicap which did not take too much winning with the market leaders both disappointing. The fifth holds down the form.
Tilly's Dream Official explanation: jockey said filly ran flat
Diamond Josh Official explanation: jockey said gelding lost an iron leaving the stalls
T/Plt: £35.80 to a £1 stake. Pool: £58,557.40. 1,192.95 winning tickets. T/Qpdt: £40.90 to a £1 stake. Pool: £2,659.50. 48.10 winning tickets. KH

2343 SOUTHWELL (L-H)
Tuesday, December 11

OFFICIAL GOING: Standard
The first meeting to take place here since June 5th, the course having been closed since due to substantial flooding followed by extensive remedial work.
Wind: Light across Weather: Overcast

7106 PONTIN'S BOOK EARLY NURSERY — 5f (F)
12:00 (12:00) (Class 6) (0-75,75) 2-Y-O — £2,047 (£604; £302) Stalls High

Form RPR
5101 1 **Weet A Surprise**[25] 6834 2-9-4 72.... HayleyTurner 2 73
(R Hollinshead) *hld up in tch: swtchd lft 2f out: r.o u.p to ld wl ins fnl f* 5/2[1]
3254 2 nk **A Wish For You**[17] 6926 2-8-11 70.... JamesO'Reilly(5) 7 70
(D K Ivory) *chsd ldrs: rdn to ld over 1f out: edgd lft and hdd wl ins fnl f* 9/2[3]
0160 3 3/4 **Mac Dalia**[68] 5932 2-8-13 70.... JerryO'Dwyer(3) 6 67
(M G Quinlan) *s.i.s and hmpd s: hdwy 1/2-way: rdn and hung lft over 1f out: styd on same pce towards fin* 8/1
0100 4 1 1/2 **Ingleby Star (IRE)**[11] 6977 2-9-7 75.... PaulFessey 8 67
(T D Barron) *led 4f out: rdn and hdd over 1f out: edgd lft and no ex ins fnl f* 10/1
440 5 1/2 **My Kaiser Chief**[34] 6721 2-9-0 68.... PaulMulrennan 5 58
(W J H Ratcliffe) *led 1f: chsd ldr: rdn and ev ch over 1f out: no ex ins fnl f* 13/2
0003 6 5 **Galley Slave (IRE)**[29] 6800 2-8-3 60.... DominicFox(3) 3 32
(M C Chapman) *chsd ldrs: rdn 1/2-way: wknd fnl f* 12/1
4200 7 hd **Orpen's Art (IRE)**[25] 6828 2-8-1 55 ow1.... ChrisCatlin 1 26
(N A Callaghan) *hld up: racd keenly: rdn 1/2-way: sn outpcd* 7/2[2]

61.32 secs (1.02) **Going Correction** +0.125s/f (Slow) 7 Ran SP% 110.2
Speed ratings (Par 94): **96,95,94,91,91 83,82**
CSF £12.84 CT £70.38 TOTE £2.10: £1.50, £1.80; EX 8.30 Trifecta £31.60 Pool £116.87 - 2.62 winning units..
Owner Ed Weetman (haulage & Storage) Ltd **Bred** Longdon Stud Ltd **Trained** Upper Longdon, Staffs

FOCUS
The first race at Southwell in six months and too early to draw many conclusions over how the track was riding. The stalls were against the stands' rail as usual for this race, but the field all grouped down the centre of the track and gradually edged towards the far rail in the latter stages. There was not much strength in depth, but the principals should remain very competitive in forthcoming nurseries here.

NOTEBOOK
Weet A Surprise, raised 5lb for her Wolverhampton victory, had a bit to do at halway but knuckled down well under pressure and, racing closest to the far rail, got up to snatch the race near the line. The Fibresand was clearly no problem to her and she still looks worth another go over 6f. (op 9-4)
A Wish For You, just over two lengths behind Weet A Surprise at Wolverhampton and 5lb better off, raced up with the pace as she usually does and did not do much wrong, but was unable to hold off her old rival. She remains a maiden after eleven attempts which is a worry even though her attitude does not seem to be a problem. (op 7-2)
Mac Dalia, who showed little in one try on Polytrack though that was over 6f which looks beyond her, got messed about at the start but nonetheless travelled well before being produced to hold every chance. She kept on to the line and looks capable of winning a small race on sand. (op 7-1)
Ingleby Star(IRE), making his handicap debut, made much of the running but did not get home. He may be worth another try on the quicker Polytrack. (tchd 11-1)
My Kaiser Chief, making his sand and handicap debuts after showing some ability in three turf maidens, showed up for a long way and may not be totally without hope as he is not yet the finished article. (tchd 6-1)
Galley Slave(IRE), racing over the minimum trip for the first time since his racecourse debut, ended up well beaten and is already exposed as moderate. (op 14-1 tchd 11-1)

Orpen's Art(IRE), 1lb wrong, attracted significant market support despite being a maiden after ten attempts coming into this, but he was heavily restrained from the outside stall and was getting the worst of the kickback throughout. Obviously better was expected from him by someone. (op 13-2)

7107 PONTINS.COM H'CAP (DIV I) 6f (F)
12:30 (12:31) (Class 6) (0-57,62) 3-Y-O+ **£2,047** (£604; £302) **Stalls** Low

Form RPR
002 **1** **Trinculo (IRE)**[14] 6957 10-8-13 **54**........................(b) ChrisCatlin 10 66
(R A Harris) *chsd ldrs: led over 2f out: edgd fnl f: drvn out* **12/1**
0213 **2** 1 1/4 **Grand Palace (IRE)**[7] 7014 4-9-0 **55**........................(v) DeanMcKeown 7 63
(D Shaw) *chsd ldrs: rdn over 2f out: hung lft over 1f out: styd on* **9/2**[2]
4630 **3** 1 1/2 **Kennington**[14] 6957 7-8-11 **52**........................(b) NeilPollard 5 56
(Mrs C A Dunnett) *led: hdd over 4f out: rdn 1/2-way: styd on* **20/1**
0430 **4** 3/4 **Mister Always**[15] 6950 3-8-4 **48**........................(p) AndrewElliott(3) 3 49
(I W McInnes) *s.i.s: hld up: hdwy u.p over 1f out: nt rch ldrs* **15/2**[3]
4220 **5** 2 1/2 **Elusive Warrior (USA)**[7] 7025 4-8-13 **57**........................(p) JamieMoriarty(3) 1 51+
(R A Fahey) *s.i.s: outpcd: styd on fnl f: nvr nrr* **9/2**[2]
040 **6** hd **Savile's Delight (IRE)**[179] 2619 8-8-5 **46** oh1.......... RichardKingscote 9 39
(Tom Dascombe) *trckd ldr: led over 4f out: rdn and hdd over 2f out: wknd ins fnl f* **3/1**[1]
3010 **7** shd **Double Carpet (IRE)**[57] 6239 4-8-9 **50**........................ TGMcLaughlin 2 43
(G Woodward) *s.i.s: outpcd* **16/1**
3340 **8** 1 **Obe One**[46] 6467 7-8-2 **46** oh1........................ PatrickMathers(3) 6 36
(A Berry) *mid-div: sn drvn along: bhd fr 1/2-way* **33/1**
6111 **9** 1 **Fast Freddie**[7] 7013 3-9-7 **62** 6ex........................(e) NCallan 8 49
(D J Murphy) *trckd ldrs: rdn over 2f out: wknd over 1f out* **9/2**[2]
1500 **10** 27 **Christian Bendix**[17] 6925 5-8-5 **46** oh1........................(p) AdrianMcCarthy 4 —
(P Howling) *mid-div: sn drvn along: wknd over 3f out* **40/1**

1m 16.82s (-0.08) **Going Correction** -0.05s/f (Stan) **10** Ran SP% **115.0**
Speed ratings (Par 101): **98,96,94,93,90 89,89,88,86,50**
CSF £63.21 CT £1100.36 TOTE £8.10: £2.40, £1.70, £4.00; EX 46.50 Trifecta £224.80 Part won. Pool £316.72 - 0.36 winning units..
Owner Peter A Price **Bred** Humphrey Okeke **Trained** Earlswood, Monmouths
■ Stewards' Enquiry : Dean McKeownM caution: used whip with excessuive frequency

FOCUS
The winning time was 0.38 seconds slower than the second division, but 0.72 seconds faster than the seller. Again the action all took place centre to far side once the field had turned for home. Straightforward for, the winner rated to this year's best.

7108 PONTIN'S BOOK EARLY AND SAVE (S) STKS 6f (F)
1:00 (1:00) (Class 6) 3-Y-O+ **£2,047** (£604; £302) **Stalls** Low

Form RPR
6054 **1** **Mister Elegant**[7] 7020 5-9-0 52........................ AdamKirby 4 61
(J L Spearing) *hld up: hdwy over 3f out: led 2f out: drvn clr fnl f* **5/2**[2]
6050 **2** 3 1/2 **Phinerine**[7] 7020 4-9-2 52........................(e[1]) TolleyDean(5) 5 57
(Miss J E Foster) *hld up: hdwy 2f out: sn rdn: styd on* **16/1**
0R22 **3** nk **Quiet Times (IRE)**[20] 6891 8-9-7 70........................(b) NCallan 9 56
(K A Ryan) *blindfold removed late: s.s: hdwy over 4f out: rdn over 1f out: no ex ins fnl f* **8/13**[1]
3000 **4** 2 **Temtation (IRE)**[140] 3811 3-8-9 44........................ DeanMcKeown 7 38
(J A Pickering) *chsd ldrs: ev ch 2f out: sn rdn: styd on same pce* **33/1**
0060 **5** 3 1/2 **Stanley Wolfe (IRE)**[38] 6637 4-9-0 44........................ DaneO'Neill 8 33
(Garry Moss) *chsd ldrs: rdn 1/2-way: wknd over 1f out* **50/1**
3650 **6** 1/2 **Dunn Deal (IRE)**[33] 6735 7-9-0 44........................ PaulMulrennan 1 31
(J Balding) *led 4f: sn rdn and wknd* **12/1**[3]
0000 **7** 3 1/2 **Alexia Rose (IRE)**[14] 6962 5-8-6 43........................(b) AndrewMullen(3) 2 16
(A Berry) *s.s: outpcd* **20/1**
0050 **8** 2 1/2 **Heidi Hi**[13] 5627 3-8-9 41........................(t) PaulFessey 3 8
(J R Turner) *chsd ldrs: rdn over 4f out: sn lost pl* **33/1**

1m 17.54s (0.64) **Going Correction** -0.05s/f (Stan) **8** Ran SP% **116.7**
Speed ratings (Par 101): **93,88,87,85,80 79,75,71**
CSF £36.83 TOTE £3.80: £1.10, £6.50, £1.02; EX 24.10 Trifecta £75.80 Pool £350.42 - 3.28 winning units..There was no bid for the winner.
Owner M Lawrence & W Cooper **Bred** J Spearing And Kate Ive **Trained** Kinnersley, Worcs

FOCUS
The winning time was 0.72 seconds slower than the first division of the 6f handicap, and 1.1 seconds slower than the second division. This was a dreadful seller that will not live long in the memory, especially given the problems that befell the favourite. The first two were close to their marks.
Quiet Times(IRE) Official explanation: jockey said he had problems removing the blindfold
Dunn Deal(IRE) Official explanation: jockey said gelding hung right

7109 SOUTHWELL GOLF CLUB H'CAP 1m 3f (F)
1:30 (1:30) (Class 6) (0-65,60) 3-Y-O+ **£2,047** (£604; £302) **Stalls** Low

Form RPR
516- **1** **Friends Hope**[476] 4673 6-9-3 **57**........................ StephenDonohoe 4 76+
(P A Blockley) *hld up: hdwy over 3f out: led over 1f out: rdn clr: eased towards fin* **9/1**
4002 **2** 5 **King's Ransom**[7] 7023 4-9-6 **60**........................ PaulMulrennan 7 69
(S Gollings) *led: rdn and hdd over 1f out: styd on same pce* **11/4**[1]
2040 **3** 6 **Bolckow**[22] 6871 4-9-3 **57**........................ DaleGibson 9 56
(J T Stimpson) *chsd ldr tl rdn over 2f out: wknd over 1f out* **4/1**[2]
3630 **4** 5 **Anything Once (USA)**[9] 6265 4-8-3 **50**........................(v) JamieKyne(7) 10 41
(D Carroll) *s.i.s: hld up: styd on appr fnl f: nvr nrr* **12/1**
0030 **5** 2 **My Sara**[37] 6672 3-8-10 **54**........................(v) TonyHamilton 8 42
(R A Fahey) *chsd ldrs: lost pl 8f out: rdn 5f out: sn wknd* **20/1**
3006 **6** 1 1/4 **Starcross Maid**[42] 6558 5-9-1 **55**........................ ChrisCatlin 1 41
(J F Coupland) *chsd ldrs: rdn over 3f out: wknd 2f out* **8/1**
-453 **7** 2 1/2 **Bramcote Lorne**[10] 6991 4-9-1 **55**........................ PhillipMakin 3 37
(R C Guest) *chsd ldrs: rdn over 4f out: wknd over 2f out* **6/1**[3]
1445 **8** 6 **Everyman**[41] 6590 3-8-8 **52**........................(v) RichardKingscote 6 25
(A W Carroll) *prom over 7f* **7/1**
0000 **9** 1/2 **Boppys Dancer**[54] 6292 4-8-9 **49** oh1 ow3........................(p) MickyFenton 2 21
(P T Midgley) *hld up: rdn 1/2-way: hung lft and wknd over 4f out* **20/1**

2m 25.96s (-2.94) **Going Correction** -0.05s/f (Stan)
WFA 3 from 4yo+ 4lb **9** Ran SP% **111.8**
Speed ratings (Par 101): **108,104,100,96,94 94,92,87,87**
CSF £32.52 CT £114.01 TOTE £9.60: £2.40, £1.50, £1.90; EX 39.40 Trifecta £51.70 Pool £212.66 - 2.92 winning units..
Owner Mrs Joanna Hughes **Bred** Huish Bloodstock **Trained** Lambourn, Berks

FOCUS
The pace was decent in this handicap resulting in a smart winning time for a race of its type. They finished very well spread out and the form looks solid, with a career best from Friends Hope.

7110 GO PONTIN'S NOW H'CAP 1m 6f (F)
2:00 (2:01) (Class 5) (0-75,75) 3-Y-O+ **£2,968** (£876; £438) **Stalls** Low

Form RPR
0600 **1** **Three Boars**[33] 6739 5-8-13 **60**........................(b) NCallan 7 79+
(S Gollings) *hld up: hdwy over 4f out: led over 1f out: sn clr: eased ins fnl f* **3/1**[1]
0503 **2** 5 **Victory Quest (IRE)**[14] 6961 7-8-9 **56** oh1........................(v) ChrisCatlin 2 58
(Mrs S Lamyman) *prom: chsd ldr 6f out: rdn and ev ch 2f out: styd on same pce* **6/1**
0623 **3** 1 **Flame Creek (IRE)**[22] 6875 11-9-11 **75**........................ AlanCreighton(3) 3 76
(E J Creighton) *s.i.s: sn chsng ldrs: rdn over 3f out: styd on same pce fnl 2f* **7/2**[3]
3302 **4** 3 1/2 **Jackie Kiely**[50] 6380 6-9-11 **72**........................(t) J-PGuillambert 1 68
(R Brotherton) *trckd ldrs: racd keenly: rdn over 4f out: wknd over 2f out* **9/2**
6412 **5** 1/2 **Young Scotton**[18] 6911 7-8-6 **56** oh1........................ AndrewElliott(3) 4 51
(J D Bethell) *led: rdn over 2f out: hdd & wknd over 1f out* **10/3**[2]
6000 **6** 35 **Winter Lane**[42] 6561 3-8-2 **56** oh2........................(v[1]) LiamJones 5 2
(J R Norton) *chsd ldr 8f: sn rdn: wknd over 4f out: t.o* **66/1**
0 **7** 23 **Welcome Cat (USA)**[13] 6967 3-8-8 **62**........................ PaulMulrennan 6 —
(A D Brown) *s.i.s: hld up: rdn and wknd over 4f out: t.o* **20/1**

3m 8.80s (-0.80) **Going Correction** -0.05s/f (Stan)
WFA 3 from 5yo+ 7lb **7** Ran SP% **109.0**
Speed ratings (Par 103): **100,97,96,94,94 74,61**
CSF £19.22 TOTE £4.00: £1.10, £3.40; EX 15.80.
Owner P Whinham **Bred** J M Greetham **Trained** Scamblesby, Lincs

FOCUS
A modest staying handicap, run at a fairly steady pace. Impressive winner Three Boars is rated value for 12l in a race rated around the second and third's recent Polytrack form.
Three Boars Official explanation: trainer said, regarding apparent improvement in form, that the gelding had been dropped in class and the weights and also appeared suited by the track

7111 PONTINS.COM H'CAP (DIV II) 6f (F)
2:30 (2:30) (Class 6) (0-57,57) 3-Y-O+ **£2,047** (£604; £302) **Stalls** Low

Form RPR
0002 **1** **Winthorpe (IRE)**[10] 7003 7-8-13 **54** ow1........................(p) DanielTudhope 5 69
(J J Quinn) *mid-div: hdwy 1/2-way: chsd ldr over 1f out: rdn to ld and edgd lft ins fnl f: r.o* **7/4**[1]
0000 **2** 4 **Blakeshall Quest**[42] 6563 7-8-5 **46** oh1........................(b) PaulFessey 6 49
(R Brotherton) *led: rdn over 1f out: hdd and no ex ins fnl f* **16/1**
5000 **3** 1 3/4 **Bentley**[106] 4885 3-9-0 **55**........................(v) DaneO'Neill 9 53
(D Shaw) *s.i.s: rdn over 2f out: edgd lft and styd on fnl f: n.d* **7/1**[2]
0005 **4** 1 1/2 **Fern House (IRE)**[21] 6886 5-8-9 **50**........................ PaulMulrennan 7 43
(Garry Moss) *edgd rt s: chsd ldrs: rdn over 3f out: wknd fnl f* **7/1**[2]
0054 **5** shd **Gone'N'Dunnett (IRE)**[21] 6887 8-8-6 **47**........................(v) ChrisCatlin 10 40
(Mrs C A Dunnett) *sn pushed along and prom: rdn 1/2-way: edgd lft and wknd over 1f out* **7/1**[2]
0300 **6** nk **Toberogan (IRE)**[51] 6363 6-9-0 **55**........................ DaleGibson 3 47
(W A Murphy, Ire) *sn pushed along in rr: n.d* **9/1**[3]
0405 **7** 3/4 **Spy Gun (USA)**[1] 7105 7-7-12 **46** oh1........................(p) PatrickDonaghy(7) 1 36
(T Wall) *s.s: outpcd* **11/1**
0600 **8** 3/4 **Silent Storm**[10] 6993 7-8-9 **57**........................ RyanHill(7) 2 45
(Peter Grayson) *s.s: outpcd* **16/1**
00 **9** 8 **Pauvic (IRE)**[22] 6870 4-8-10 **54**........................ AndrewMullen(3) 4 18
(Mrs A Duffield) *chsd ldrs to 1/2-way* **33/1**
0000 **10** 1 3/4 **Dodaa (USA)**[42] 6565 4-8-5 **46** oh1........................ MatthewHenry 8 4
(N Wilson) *chsd ldr: rdn over 2f out: wknd over 1f out* **16/1**

1m 16.44s (-0.46) **Going Correction** -0.05s/f (Stan) **10** Ran SP% **112.8**
Speed ratings (Par 101): **101,95,93,91,91 90,89,88,78,75**
CSF £31.95 CT £158.42 TOTE £2.20: £1.10, £5.40, £3.20; EX 37.30 Trifecta £139.10 Part won. Pool £195.94 - 0.72 winning units..
Owner Green Roberts Savage Whittall Williams **Bred** M Conaghan **Trained** Settrington, N Yorks

FOCUS
A moderate sprint handicap. The winning time was 0.38 seconds quicker than the first division, and 1.10 seconds faster than the earlier seller. This was the best of the three C/D races, with Winthorpe rated to last winter's best form.
Silent Storm Official explanation: vet said gelding returned lame
Dodaa(USA) Official explanation: jockey said gelding had no more to give

7112 SOUTHWELL-RACECOURSE.CO.UK H'CAP 5f (F)
3:00 (3:00) (Class 3) (0-95,87) 3-Y-O+ **£7,772** (£2,312; £1,155; £577) **Stalls** High

Form RPR
0005 **1** **Northern Empire (IRE)**[22] 6876 4-9-1 **81**........................ NCallan 6 91
(K A Ryan) *s.i.s: hdwy 1/2-way: rdn to ld ins fnl f: r.o: hung rt towards fin* **10/3**[1]
020 **2** hd **Pawan (IRE)**[25] 6836 7-8-7 **78**........................(b) AnnStokell(5) 8 87
(Miss A Stokell) *chsd ldrs: hmpd ins fnl f: r.o* **25/1**
0000 **3** 3/4 **Yungaburra (IRE)**[22] 6876 3-9-6 **86**........................(b) MickyFenton 1 93
(D J Murphy) *chsd ldrs: rdn over 1f out: styd on* **25/1**
0100 **4** hd **Godfrey Street**[22] 6876 4-8-13 **82**........................(b) AndrewMullen(3) 4 88
(K A Ryan) *led: rdn over 1f out: edgd rt and hdd ins fnl f: styd on same pce* **14/1**
1566 **5** 2 **New York Oscar (IRE)**[11] 6970 3-9-2 **82**........................(v[1]) StephenDonohoe 5 81
(A J McCabe) *chsd ldrs over 3f out: outpcd 1/2-way: r.o ins fnl f* **11/1**
0112 **6** 1/2 **Ebraam (USA)**[22] 6876 4-9-3 **83**........................ DeanMcKeown 9 80
(D Shaw) *chsd ldrs: rdn over 1f out: no ex fnl f* **7/2**[2]
-330 **7** 3/4 **Grand Show**[60] 6142 5-9-4 **84**........................ AdamKirby 2 78
(W R Swinburn) *hld up: rdn 1/2-way: hdwy over 1f out: wknd ins fnl f* **9/2**[3]
2113 **8** 1 **Magic Glade**[22] 6876 8-9-5 **85**........................ LPKeniry 3 76
(Peter Grayson) *chsd ldrs: rdn over 1f out: wknd fnl f* **11/2**
5050 **9** 1 3/4 **Spoof Master (IRE)**[11] 6970 3-8-7 **78**........................ KirstyMilczarek(5) 7 62
(N A Callaghan) *sn outpcd* **33/1**
3000 **10** hd **Lethal**[152] 3464 4-9-4 **87**........................(e[1]) JamieMoriarty(3) 10 71
(R A Fahey) *s.i.s: outpcd* **11/1**

60.37 secs (0.07) **Going Correction** +0.125s/f (Slow) **10** Ran SP% **112.8**
Speed ratings (Par 107): **104,103,102,102,98 98,96,95,92,92**
CSF £86.43 CT £1808.09 TOTE £4.40: £1.70, £3.60, £7.10; EX 69.40 TRIFECTA Not won..
Owner Roger Peel **Bred** Denis McDonnell **Trained** Hambleton, N Yorks

FOCUS
A good sprint handicap, and sound form.

NOTEBOOK
Northern Empire(IRE) shaped well when fifth at Wolverhampton on his first try on sand and he stepped up on that effort switched to Fibresand. He was Listed placed as a two-year-old when trained by Brian Meehan and should still look reasonably treated once reassessed. (op 9-2 tchd 11-4)
Pawan(IRE) often runs well in these types of races and he would surely have won this under stronger handling. He is useful on his day and should have won more races over the years, with a record of six wins from 103 career starts not doing him justice. (tchd 33-1)
Yungaburra(IRE) ◆ returned to form with blinkers re-fitted. He was rated 100 in May, so is on a very attractive mark now and appeals as one to keep on side. (tchd 28-1)
Godfrey Street took them along at a good clip and this was a respectable effort. (op 12-1)
New York Oscar(IRE) did not run badly with a visor replacing cheekpices, but he has been finding things tougher of late. (op 17-2 tchd 8-1)
Ebraam(USA) beat just one home on his only previous try on this surface and he will probably be happier back on Polytrack. (op 3-1)
Grand Show was well beaten on his Fibresand debut and he looks a much better horse at Lingfield. (op 6-1)
Magic Glade ran well on his debut for these connections when third at Wolverhampton, but this was disappointing. (op 5-1)

7113 PONTINSBINGO.COM H'CAP 7f (F)
3:30 (3:30) (Class 6) (0-60,60) 3-Y-O+ £2,047 (£604; £302) Stalls Low

Form				RPR
3031	1		**Dasheena**[7] 7024 4-9-1 60 6ex (be) PatrickMathers(3) 8	77
			(A J McCabe) *s.i.s: outpcd: hdwy u.p over 1f out: r.o to ld ins fnl f: sn clr* 17/2	
2031	2	3 ½	**Alto Vertigo**[10] 7003 4-8-11 60 PatrickDonaghy(7) 2	68
			(P C Haslam) *s.i.s: sn chsng ldrs: led 5f out: rdn and hung lft 2f out: hdd and no ex ins fnl f* 3/1[2]	
0654	3	1 ½	**Desert Lover (IRE)**[11] 6979 5-8-5 47 (v) HayleyTurner 5	51
			(R J Price) *prom: rdn 1/2-way: swtchd lft and chsd ldr over 2f out: no ex fnl f* 15/2[3]	
0000	4	1 ¼	**Lucius Verrus (USA)**[2] 7085 7-9-2 58 (v) DeanMcKeown 4	58
			(D Shaw) *chsd ldrs: rdn 1/2-way: styd on same pce fnl 2f* 16/1	
0441	5	1 ¾	**Carlitos Spirit (IRE)**[6] 7028 3-8-13 60 ow2 JamesMillman(5) 9	55
			(B R Millman) *s.i.s: rdn over 2f out: n.d* 15/8[1]	
0153	6	1 ½	**Piccolo Diamante (USA)**[15] 6945 3-8-10 52 (t) MickyFenton 3	43
			(D J Murphy) *s.i.s: hdwy 1/2-way: rdn and wknd over 1f out* 15/2[3]	
6600	7	hd	**Shifty**[21] 6882 8-8-11 60 JamieKyne(7) 7	51
			(D Carroll) *outpcd* 16/1	
0400	8	3	**Government (IRE)**[49] 6412 6-8-0 47 NicolPolli(5) 1	30
			(M C Chapman) *chsd ldr: rdn 1/2-way: wknd 2f out* 25/1	
0100	9	1 ½	**Smash N'Grab (IRE)**[20] 6895 3-8-11 53 LiamJones 10	32
			(J R Jenkins) *mid-div: rdn 1/2-way: wknd over 2f out* 50/1	
4040	10	nk	**Isobel Rose (IRE)**[20] 6894 3-8-8 50 ChrisCatlin 6	28
			(J L Spearing) *sn outpcd* 25/1	

1m 29.21s (-1.59) **Going Correction** -0.05s/f (Stan) 10 Ran SP% **115.3**
Speed ratings (Par 101): **107,103,101,99,97 96,95,92,90,90**
CSF £33.23 CT £207.03 TOTE £8.20: £2.60, £1.40, £2.30; EX 60.40 Trifecta £141.40 Pool £346.76 - 1.74 winning units. Place 6 £36.61, Place 5 £20.23..
Owner Paul J Dixon **Bred** Mrs Yvette Dixon **Trained** Babworth, Notts

FOCUS
A moderate handicap, but it was strongly run and produced a decent winning time for the class. Fair form for the grade, with a much-improved effort from Dasheena.
Carlitos Spirit(IRE) Official explanation: jockey said gelding hung right
T/Plt: £55.10 to a £1 stake. Pool: £48,806.70. 646.00 winning tickets. T/Qpdt: £5.80 to a £1 stake. Pool: £2,788.40. 349.80 winning tickets. CR

7028 KEMPTON (A.W) (R-H)
Wednesday, December 12

OFFICIAL GOING: Standard
Wind: Nil Weather: Cold

7114 HALO SOLUTIONS MEDIAN AUCTION MAIDEN STKS 1m 2f (P)
6:20 (6:20) (Class 6) 2-Y-O £2,047 (£604; £302) Stalls High

Form				RPR
	1		**Relative Strength (IRE)** 2-9-3 0 LPKeniry 10	70
			(A M Balding) *bit bkwd: leggy: mde all: set stdy pce to 2f out: shkn up and styd on wl fnl f: readily* 12/1	
64	2	1 ½	**Flash Of Colour**[16] 6948 2-9-3 0 JimCrowley 7	67
			(Mrs A J Perrett) *lw: trckd ldng pair: rdn and effrt wl over 1f out: wnt 2nd 1f out: no imp on wnr* 7/1[3]	
0	3	¾	**Bruki (IRE)**[42] 6585 2-8-12 0 (t) JohnEgan 8	61
			(M Botti) *hld up in 8th: prog on outer over 2f out but lost grnd bnd sn after: drvn and r.o fnl f: nrst fin* 16/1	
00	4	nk	**Whitcombe Spirit**[28] 6805 2-9-3 0 PaulDoe 9	65
			(Jamie Poulton) *trckd ldng pair: rdn to dispute 2nd over 1f out: one pce after* 20/1	
2024	5	½	**Doctor Robert**[55] 6274 2-9-3 77 RichardKingscote 5	64
			(Tom Dascombe) *lw: hld up in midfield: prog on inner to dispute 2nd over 1f out: sn rdn and nt qckn* 6/5[1]	
0503	6	½	**Miss Phoebe (IRE)**[7] 7031 2-8-12 65 JDSmith 4	58
			(S Kirk) *hld up in 7th in slowly run r: effrt 2f out: styd on but no imp on ldrs* 9/2[2]	
50	7	¾	**Beauchamp Warrior**[4] 7070 2-9-3 0 NickyMackay 6	62
			(G A Butler) *hld up in last in modestly run r: effrt 2f out: kpt on but no inroads into ldrs* 7/1[3]	
6	8	1	**Black Heart**[32] 6763 2-9-3 0 OscarUrbina 1	60
			(M Botti) *w'like: hld up in midfield: lost pl fr 2f out: n.d after* 10/1	
005	9	2 ½	**Has To Be Abacus (IRE)**[23] 6865 2-9-3 53 SteveDrowne 2	55
			(A B Haynes) *w wnr to 2f out: shkn up and wknd over 1f out* 50/1	

2m 10.8s (1.80) **Going Correction** -0.15s/f (Stan) 9 Ran SP% **118.0**
Speed ratings (Par 94): **86,84,84,83,83 83,82,81,79**
CSF £94.95 TOTE £11.30: £2.80, £2.00, £4.60; EX 168.50.
Owner D H Caslon **Bred** Holborn Trust Co **Trained** Kingsclere, Hants

FOCUS
A modest juvenile maiden, run at an average early pace. The runner-up helps to set the level.

NOTEBOOK
Relative Strength(IRE), an 11,500gns purchase whose dam was a triple winner at up to 1m, clearly knew his job ahead of this racecourse bow as he was smart from the gates and never saw another rival en route to success. As a Derby entrant he was certainly one of the most interesting runners in this field and he clearly stays well. The sound surface was to his liking and he is open to a bundle of improvement, with his connections now likely to put him away until the spring. (op 16-1)
Flash Of Colour ran very close to his recent level over this extra 2f and did little wrong, but was never going to catch the winner. He now becomes eligible for a handicap mark, but is probably better off back over a sharper test for the short term. (op 6-1)
Bruki(IRE) took a step in the right direction with an improved effort and was doing all of her best work inside the final furlong. She looks likely to come on again for this outing and deserves to be ridden more positively in the future, but is probably one to be more interested in when qualifying for a handicap mark after her next run. (op 12-1)
Whitcombe Spirit improved as could have been expected for the step up to this longer trip. He is now eligible for a handicap mark and, on this evidence, will have little trouble getting another 2f next year. (op 25-1)
Doctor Robert, bought for 45,000gns by his new connections, ran well below his current official mark in defeat and has become very expensive to follow. He did not really convince he wanted this longer trip, however. (op 11-8 tchd 6-4)
Miss Phoebe(IRE), up in trip, was not seen to best effort by being held up off the modest early gallop. (op 7-2)

7115 AFM SERVICES DATA CENTRE CONSTRUCTION H'CAP 1m 2f (P)
6:50 (6:52) (Class 6) (0-55,55) 3-Y-O+ £2,047 (£604; £302) Stalls High

Form				RPR
3000	1		**Mr Napoleon (IRE)**[16] 6951 5-9-2 55 GeorgeBaker 8	63
			(G L Moore) *stdd s: hld up in last: pushed along and sme prog over 2f out: threaded through over 1f out: rdn to ld last 100yds: styd on strly* 11/2[3]	
6-63	2	½	**Wind Flow**[3] 7083 3-8-11 53 (b[1]) JohnEgan 4	60
			(C A Dwyer) *lw: hld up on outer: dropped to last and rdn over 2f out: swtchd to outer and str run over 1f out to chal last 100yds: a hld* 7/2[1]	
2601	3	shd	**Charlottebutterfly**[15] 6955 7-9-1 54 RobertHavlin 2	61
			(P J McBride) *hld up in last trio: nt clr run briefly 2f out: prog on outer over 1f out: str run to chal last 100yds: a hld nr fin* 14/1	
-060	4	1 ½	**Always Sparkle (CAN)**[14] 6967 3-8-13 55 ChrisCatlin 14	59
			(B Palling) *lw: led: tried to kick on over 2f out: kpt on u.p: hdd and outpcd by ldng trio last 100yds* 25/1	
330	5	1	**Shunkawakhan (IRE)**[30] 6796 4-8-5 49 (p) TolleyDean(5) 10	51
			(G C H Chung) *prom: chsd ldr 2f out: hld ent fnl f: sn outpcd* 12/1	
4030	6	½	**Mythical Charm**[7] 7028 8-8-8 54 (t) JackDean(7) 11	55
			(J J Bridger) *plld hrd: hld up bhd ldrs: effrt and cl enough over 1f out: sn outpcd* 16/1	
1406	7	nk	**Bowl Of Cherries**[3] 7088 4-9-1 54 (b) DaneO'Neill 7	54
			(I A Wood) *hld up towards rr: prog over 1f out: outpcd whn n.m.r ent fnl f: plugged on* 8/1	
2000	8	1	**Danelor (IRE)**[3] 7088 9-8-11 50 (p) OscarUrbina 12	48
			(D Shaw) *hld up towards rr: prog to trck ldrs gng strly over 2f out: cl enough over 1f out: outpcd whn n.m.r jst ins fnl f* 25/1	
0100	9	nk	**Theatre Royal**[16] 6951 4-8-8 50 (p) NeilChalmers(3) 3	49
			(Mouse Hamilton-Fairley) *hld up in last trio: prog to trck ldrs over 2f out: nt clr run over 1f out and lost pl: plugged on one pce* 20/1	
4502	10	5	**Glenridding**[12] 6979 3-8-13 55 TPQueally 13	43
			(J G Given) *chsd ldr to 2f out: sn lost pl and btn* 9/1	
0602	11	hd	**Shaheer (IRE)**[2] 7098 5-8-11 50 (v) GregFairley 5	37
			(J Gallagher) *chsd ldrs: rdn 3f out: losing pl and struggling 2f out* 4/1[2]	
6065	12	5	**High Class Problem (IRE)**[26] 6831 4-9-1 54 JimCrowley 1	31
			(P Winkworth) *t.k.h: trckd ldrs tl wknd over 2f out* 12/1	
2306	13	3	**Jarvo**[192] 2275 6-8-11 53 AndrewElliott(3) 9	24
			(I W McInnes) *raced wd thrght: nvr beyond midfield: u.p and wkng over 2f out* 14/1	

2m 6.57s (-2.43) **Going Correction** -0.15s/f (Stan)
WFA 3 from 4yo+ 3lb 13 Ran SP% **125.8**
Speed ratings (Par 101): **103,102,102,101,100 100,99,99,98,94 94,90,88**
CSF £25.76 CT £264.86 TOTE £8.20: £2.90, £2.00, £2.30; EX 48.20.
Owner Jason Gibbons **Bred** Forenaghts Stud **Trained** Woodingdean, E Sussex
■ Stewards' Enquiry : George Baker one-day ban: careless riding (26 Dec)

FOCUS
A moderate handicap, run at an uneven pace, and the first three came from the rear. The form looks sound enough for the class.

7116 DIGIBET H'CAP 5f (P)
7:20 (7:21) (Class 5) (0-75,75) 3-Y-O+ £2,817 (£838; £418; £209) Stalls High

Form				RPR
0401	1		**Smokin Beau**[21] 6890 10-8-8 65 JimCrowley 7	74
			(N P Littmoden) *lw: mde all: drvn over 1f out: hld on wl fnl f* 9/4[1]	
0662	2	¾	**Fizzlephut (IRE)**[5] 7059 5-8-10 67 PaulFitzsimons 6	73
			(Miss J R Tooth) *sltly awkward s: sn chsd ldng pair: shkn up to chse wnr over 1f out: kpt on but a hld* 3/1[3]	
4506	3	¾	**Baileys Outshine**[20] 6905 3-8-11 68 TPQueally 1	71
			(J G Given) *mostly in 4th: rdn and effrt on outer over 1f out: kpt on fnl f: nvr able to chal* 12/1	
3200	4	¾	**Dancing Mystery**[42] 6594 13-9-2 73 (b) StephenCarson 5	74
			(E A Wheeler) *awkward s and slowly away: nt on terms w ldrs in 5th: kpt on fnl f: no ch* 20/1	
6002	5	nk	**Azygous**[12] 6976 4-8-5 62 ChrisCatlin 3	62
			(J Akehurst) *pressed wnr to over 1f out: fdd* 5/2[2]	
616	6	13	**Stoneacre Boy (IRE)**[25] 6860 4-8-5 62 LiamJones 4	15+
			(Peter Grayson) *lw: jockey tk three attempts to remove blindfold as stalls opened: no ch and allowed to complete in own time* 11/2	

59.89 secs (-0.51) **Going Correction** -0.15s/f (Stan) 6 Ran SP% **112.2**
Speed ratings (Par 103): **98,96,95,94,93 73**
CSF £9.34 TOTE £3.30: £1.60, £1.20; EX 11.70.
Owner Miss Vanessa Church **Bred** Alan Spargo **Trained** Newmarket, Suffolk

FOCUS
A modest sprint, run at a solid pace and the form is straightforward.
Stoneacre Boy(IRE) Official explanation: jockey said blind was caught up when he tried to remove it and gelding was slowly away

7117 DIGIBET.COM NURSERY 1m (P)
7:50 (7:52) (Class 6) (0-65,65) 2-Y-O £2,047 (£604; £302) Stalls High

Form				RPR
0042	1		**Ogre (USA)**[9] 7010 2-9-6 64 TPQueally 2	67
			(J A Osborne) *awkward s: last and nt gng wl early: gd prog on inner fr 3f out: drvn to ld over 1f out: styd on wl* 7/2[1]	
2244	2	¾	**Mairead's Boy (IRE)**[7] 7030 2-9-0 58 (v[1]) JimCrowley 3	59
			(P Butler) *mde most: drvn and hdd over 1f out: kpt on u.p* 20/1	
460U	3	hd	**Ile Royale**[8] 7022 2-8-0 49 (be) NicolPolli(5) 10	50
			(C N Allen) *b: v.s.i.s: rcvrd into midfield: effrt on outer over 2f out: styd on fr over 1f out* 33/1	

0405 **4** *nk* **Vigano (IRE)**[12] 6978 2-9-7 **65** GeorgeBaker 9 65
(S Kirk) *lw: dwlt and rousted along to go prom: rdn and effrt over 2f out: nt qckn over 1f out: one pce fnl f* **15/2**[3]

3045 **5** *shd* **Tiger's Rocket (IRE)**[8] 7022 2-8-12 **61** HaddenFrost(5) 13 61
(R Hannon) *lw: prom: chsd ldr 1/2-way to wl over 1f out: one pce* **9/2**[2]

0240 **6** *3/4* **Lady Sandicliffe (IRE)**[49] 6427 2-8-13 **57** DaneO'Neill 14 55
(Miss Jo Crowley) *lw: chsd ldr to 1/2-way: styd cl up: u.p over 2f out: kpt on* **12/1**

004 **7** *1 1/4* **Duneen Dream (USA)**[30] 6791 2-8-11 **55** NeilPollard 12 51
(W J Musson) *lw: t.k.h: hld up bhd ldrs: hanging over 2f out: reminder over 1f out: no imp: eased nr fin* **16/1**

422 **8** *shd* **Artistic Light**[8] 7022 2-9-2 **60** HayleyTurner 1 55
(W R Muir) *lw: hld up in last trio and racd on outer: pushed along over 2f out: kpt on steadily: nvr nr ldrs* **15/2**[3]

0266 **9** *1 3/4* **I Certainly May**[70] 5896 2-9-4 **62** JohnEgan 4 54
(S Dow) *wl in rr: rdn and sme prog fr 2f out: no imp on ldrs fnl f* **9/1**

0050 **10** *3/4* **Ten Spot (IRE)**[7] 7031 2-9-0 **58** (v[1]) MickyFenton 7 48
(Stef Liddiard) *a towards rr: rdn and struggling over 3f out* **33/1**

5005 **11** *1 3/4* **Athboy Auction**[7] 7031 2-9-0 **63** TolleyDean(5) 6 49
(H J Collingridge) *nvr bttr than midfield on outer: limited prog 2f out: wknd fnl f* **14/1**

0042 **12** *1/2* **Silca Destination**[31] 6775 2-8-11 **55** ChrisCatlin 5 40
(M R Channon) *racd on outer and nvr on terms w ldrs: struggling over 2f out* **15/2**[3]

060 **13** *1 1/2* **Sweet Andromeda**[19] 6912 2-8-1 **50** DanielleMcCreery(5) 11 32
(T J Fitzgerald) *nvr beyond midfield: wknd 2f out* **66/1**

0300 **14** *8* **Ledgerwood**[35] 6715 2-9-4 **62** EddieAhern 8 26
(J W Hills) *prom tl wknd rapidly wl over 2f out: eased: t.o* **12/1**

1m 40.95s (0.15) **Going Correction** -0.15s/f (Stan) **14** Ran SP% **125.8**
Speed ratings (Par 94): **93,92,92,91,91 90,89,89,87,87 85,84,83,75**
CSF £83.15 CT £2104.58 TOTE £4.20: £2.10, £6.30, £14.20; EX 110.10.
Owner Michael Kerr-Dineen **Bred** Gulf Coast Farms LLC **Trained** Upper Lambourn, Berks

FOCUS
A moderate nursery, run at an average pace and the form is rated round the fourth and fifth. The winner is improving though and may be able to do a bit better.

NOTEBOOK
Ogre(USA), as was the case when second at Wolverhampton last time, again made an awkward start and did not convince through the early parts. She found plenty for pressure entering the home straight, however, and finally rewarded her rider's persistence by getting up late on. This was a moderate affair, but the Handicapper should not put her up too much for this. (tchd 4-1)
Mairead's Boy(IRE), with a first-time visor replacing blinkers, was suited by racing out in front and posted a solid effort in defeat on this debut for new connections. The step up in trip proved well within his compass. (op 25-1)
Ile Royale, who unseated in the stalls last time, again proved tricky at the start and fell out of the gates. She kept on nicely as she eventually hit full stride, however, and this was a much better effort in defeat.
Vigano(IRE), another who needed to be ridden from an early stage, was not beaten too far and ran right up to his official mark in defeat. A further step up in trip could help now. Official explanation: jockey said gelding missed the break (op 9-1)
Tiger's Rocket(IRE) was another to run right up to his official mark in defeat, reversing Wolverhampton form with Artistic Light, and rates a fair benchmark for this race. (op 6-1 tchd 13-2)
Duneen Dream(USA) Official explanation: jockey said gelding was hanging
Ten Spot(IRE) Official explanation: jockey said filly was denied a clear run
Ledgerwood Official explanation: jockey said gelding stumbled at start

7118 DIGIBET CASINO CLASSIFIED STKS 6f (P)
8:20 (8:21) (Class 6) 3-Y-0+ **£2,047** (£604; £302) **Stalls** High

Form RPR

2450 **1** **Angel Voices (IRE)**[15] 6956 4-8-7 50 (p) DeclanCannon(7) 8 61
(K R Burke) *mde all: rdn over 1f out: hld on u.p fnl f* **5/1**[3]

4046 **2** *3/4* **Tilsworth Charlie**[3] 7085 4-9-0 54 (b) EddieAhern 4 59
(J R Jenkins) *hld up in tch gng wl: prog over 2f out: chsd wnr jst over 1f out: nt qckn and a jst hld* **3/1**[1]

0000 **3** *3/4* **Regal Royale**[18] 6925 4-9-0 54 (b) LPKeniry 5 56
(Peter Grayson) *cl up: chsd wnr 1/2-way to jst over 1f out: kpt on same pce* **7/2**[2]

300 **4** *2* **Strut The Stage (IRE)**[32] 6764 3-9-0 55 (tp) DaneO'Neill 2 50
(B W Duke) *t.k.h: hld up in rr: effrt over 2f out: kpt on but no imp on ldrs fnl f* **7/2**[2]

040- **5** *4* **Micky Mac (IRE)**[491] 4228 3-8-11 53 DuranFentiman(3) 6 37
(T D Walford) *bit bkwd: chsd wnr to 1/2-way: sn drvn and btn* **16/1**

0-00 **6** *5* **Earl Compton (IRE)**[76] 5752 3-9-0 50 (t[1]) MickyFenton 7 21
(Stef Liddiard) *dwlt: hld up in last pair: effrt over 2f out: sn no prog: wknd tamely over 1f out* **25/1**

0004 **7** *10* **Ginger Pop**[7] 7029 3-9-0 55 JohnEgan 1 —
(G G Margarson) *chsd ldrs: u.p bef 1/2-way: wknd over 2f out: eased: t.o* **7/2**[2]

0000 **8** *3* **Auction Oasis**[125] 4312 3-9-0 43 ChrisCatlin 3 —
(B Palling) *bit bkwd: dwlt: a in last pair: bhd fnl 2f: t.o* **40/1**

1m 12.61s (-1.09) **Going Correction** -0.15s/f (Stan) **8** Ran SP% **120.5**
Speed ratings (Par 101): **101,100,99,96,91 84,71,67**
CSF £21.64 TOTE £6.80: £2.10, £1.50, £1.50; EX 22.10.
Owner Mrs Elaine M Burke **Bred** W Haggas And W Jarvis **Trained** Middleham Moor, N Yorks

FOCUS
A weak classified sprint. The first three came clear and the regressive winner, who was allowed an easy lead, was the third horse on the card to make all.
Ginger Pop Official explanation: jockey said gelding hung badly left-handed

7119 PETER HAUGHTON HALF CENTURY H'CAP 6f (P)
8:50 (8:50) (Class 6) (0-65,64) 3-Y-0+ **£2,047** (£604; £302) **Stalls** High

Form RPR

2326 **1** **Rabbit Fighter (IRE)**[8] 7025 3-9-0 **60** (v) PaulMulrennan 7 80+
(D Shaw) *in tch: prog on inner to chse ldr over 2f out: led over 1f out: drvn wl clr* **9/2**[2]

6154 **2** *4* **Willhewiz**[12] 6976 7-9-1 **61** (v) FergusSweeney 9 68
(M S Saunders) *led to over 1f out: no ch w wnr but hld on for 2nd* **8/1**

1223 **3** *nk* **Ever Cheerful**[18] 6925 6-9-3 **63** (p) SteveDrowne 10 69
(A B Haynes) *lw: dwlt: sn prom: chsd ldr over 3f out to over 2f out: nt qckn u.p* **5/1**[3]

1600 **4** *1/2* **Make My Dream**[16] 6946 4-9-3 **63** JimCrowley 1 67
(J Gallagher) *towards rr of main gp: effrt on outer over 2f out: drvn and kpt on: n.d* **16/1**

2462 **5** *1 1/2* **Musical Script (USA)**[8] 7014 4-8-8 **57** (p) TravisBlock(3) 8 57
(Mouse Hamilton-Fairley) *chsd ldrs: rdn over 2f out: no prog fr over 1f out* **6/1**

0504 **6** *2* **Hucking Hope (IRE)**[28] 6810 3-9-1 **61** DaneO'Neill 4 54+
(J R Best) *dwlt: off the pce in 8th: pushed along and sme prog over 2f out: nvr nr ldrs: eased last 100yds* **16/1**

5002 **7** *1 1/2* **Hythe Bay**[5] 7054 3-9-0 **60** HayleyTurner 6 48
(J R Best) *chsd ldr to over 3f out: steadily lost pl* **5/1**[3]

5410 **8** *3/4* **Figaro Flyer (IRE)**[23] 6869 4-9-4 **64** TGMcLaughlin 2 50
(P Howling) *chsd ldrs on outer: pushed along 1/2-way: btn over 2f out: steadily wknd* **3/1**[1]

01/0 **9** *13* **Growler**[35] 6717 6-8-3 **52** DuranFentiman(3) 3 —
(T D Walford) *s.s: a detached in last: t.o* **33/1**

1m 11.13s (-2.57) **Going Correction** -0.15s/f (Stan) **9** Ran SP% **116.6**
Speed ratings (Par 101): **111,105,105,104,102 99,97,96,79**
CSF £40.64 CT £187.60 TOTE £6.30: £2.40, £2.80, £1.40; EX 54.20.
Owner Market Avenue Racing Club Ltd **Bred** Hawthorn Villa Stud **Trained** Danethorpe, Notts

FOCUS
A modest sprint handicap run at a strong gallop, and the course record was lowered by the winner. The form looks solid rated through the runner-up, third and fourth.

7120 CITY & SUBURBAN PARKING H'CAP 1m 4f (P)
9:20 (9:21) (Class 6) (0-52,53) 3-Y-0+ **£2,047** (£604; £302) **Stalls** Centre

Form RPR

5000 **1** **Legend Erry (IRE)**[26] 6831 3-8-11 **52** JohnEgan 8 60
(Jane Chapple-Hyam) *cl up: trckd ldr over 3f out: rdn over 2f out: styd on to ld jst ins fnl f: clr nr fin* **5/2**[2]

3011 **2** *1 1/4* **Bernabeu (IRE)**[5] 7060 5-9-3 **53** 6ex PaulDoe 1 59
(S Curran) *dwlt: sn wl in tch: prog to trck ldr 5f out: led over 3f out: drvn over 2f out: hdd jst ins fnl f: wknd nr fin* **6/4**[1]

5440 **3** *shd* **Magic Amigo**[21] 6896 6-8-10 **46** EddieAhern 10 52
(J R Jenkins) *trckd ldrs: rdn and effrt over 2f out: no imp tl styd on ins fnl f: nrly snatched 2nd* **12/1**

4020 **4** *1* **Theflyingscottie**[8] 7012 5-9-1 **51** (v) DeanMcKeown 11 55
(D Shaw) *hld up: gng strly over 3f out: effrt over 2f out: rdn and kpt on same pce fnl 2f* **8/1**[3]

6050 **5** *4* **Phoenix Hill (IRE)**[17] 3598 5-9-1 **51** SteveDrowne 9 49
(D R Gandolfo) *hld up in rr: rdn and effrt 3f out: plugged on one pce fnl 2f* **9/1**

2004 **6** *hd* **Prince Of Medina**[19] 6911 4-8-13 **49** JimCrowley 6 47
(J R Best) *hld up in rr: pushed along 4f out: effrt u.p over 2f out: no imp on ldrs* **17/2**

0050 **7** *4* **Night Groove (IRE)**[175] 1342 4-8-4 **47** (p) JackDean(7) 4 38
(P Butler) *hld up in last: struggling over 3f out: nvr on terms after* **50/1**

006 **8** *22* **Cumae (USA)**[33] 6751 3-8-5 **46** oh1 ChrisCatlin 5 2
(J Pearce) *a in rr: t.o over 3f out* **66/1**

3554 **9** *nk* **Scaramoushca**[28] 6807 4-9-2 **52** (b) NeilPollard 12 7
(G C Bravery) *led to over 3f out: sn wknd rapidly: t.o* **20/1**

002R **10** *nk* **Prince Des Neiges (FR)**[71] 5886 4-8-11 **50** AndrewElliott(3) 7 5
(M R Hoad) *reluctant to go to post: mostly trckd ldr to 5f out: reluctant after and t.o over 2f out* **14/1**

0000 **11** *6* **Iceni Princess**[28] 6817 3-8-5 **46** oh1 HayleyTurner 2 —
(P Howling) *prom to 1/2-way: wknd over 4f out: t.o 3f out* **66/1**

2m 34.13s (-2.77) **Going Correction** -0.15s/f (Stan)
WFA 3 from 4yo+ 5lb **11** Ran SP% **124.3**
Speed ratings (Par 101): **103,102,102,101,98 98,95,81,81,80 76**
CSF £6.92 CT £38.53 TOTE £3.60: £1.40, £1.20, £2.60; EX 9.50 Place 6 £274.41, Place 5 £36.73.
Owner Mrs A Cantillon **Bred** Dermot Cantillon And Forenaghts Stud **Trained** Newmarket, Suffolk

FOCUS
A poor handicap, but the well-backed winner has scope to improve further and the second ran to form.
T/Jkpt: Not won. T/Plt: £577.60 to a £1 stake. Pool: £98,085.60. 123.95 winning tickets. T/Qpdt: £22.00 to a £1 stake. Pool: £8,318.50. 279.60 winning tickets. JN

7106 SOUTHWELL (L-H)
Wednesday, December 12

OFFICIAL GOING: Standard
Wind: Nil Weather: Dry and sunny

7121 PONTINSBINGO.COM MAIDEN AUCTION STKS 1m (F)
12:30 (12:31) (Class 6) 2-Y-0 **£2,047** (£604; £302) **Stalls** Low

Form RPR

1 **Commit To Memory**[12] 6985 2-8-10 0 EddieAhern 6 78
(Andrew Oliver, Ire) *trckd ldrs: effrt over 2f out and sn rdn: styd on to ld appr fnl f: hung rt and drvn clr ins fnl f* **3/1**[1]

2 *6* **Blue Law (IRE)**[12] 6986 2-8-12 0 ow2 DaneO'Neill 8 67
(Andrew Oliver, Ire) *cl up: rdn over 2f out: led wl over 1f out: drvn and hdd over 1f out: kpt on same pce ins fnl f* **15/2**

0002 **3** *1 3/4* **It's Josr**[12] 6978 2-8-10 68 TPQueally 5 61
(I A Wood) *cl up: effrt to ld wl over 2f out: sn rdn and hdd wl over 1f out: drvn and one pce fr over 1f out* **9/2**[3]

0032 **4** *4* **Mujahope**[18] 6933 2-8-11 68 (p) NCallan 9 53
(M Botti) *cl up on outer: effrt 3f out: sn rdn and ev ch tl wknd wl over 1f out* **7/2**[2]

0 **5** *7* **Crossing Bridges**[19] 6912 2-8-5 0 PaulFessey 2 32
(T D Barron) *led: rdn along 3f out: sn hdd and grad wknd* **66/1**

000 **6** *1 1/2* **Lancaster Lad (IRE)**[90] 5344 2-8-10 44 ow1 TGMcLaughlin 4 33
(A B Haynes) *in rr: sme hdwy 3f out: sn rdn and no imp* **100/1**

00 **7** *nk* **Smetana**[28] 6805 2-8-10 0 TravisBlock(3) 7 36
(H Morrison) *chsd ldrs: rdn along wl over 2f out: sn wknd* **7/2**[2]

6506 **8** *7* **Coral Shores**[9] 7007 2-8-5 54 ChrisCatlin 10 12
(P W Hiatt) *a towards rr* **33/1**

0 **9** *3* **Hollow Point (IRE)**[37] 6694 2-8-13 0 GregFairley 3 14
(M Johnston) *dwlt: a in rr* **14/1**

10 *4* **Acela (IRE)** 2-8-5 0 SaleemGolam 1 —
(R A Fahey) *chsd ldrs on inner: rdn along 3f out and sn wknd* **40/1**

1m 45.53s (0.93) **Going Correction** +0.10s/f (Slow) **10** Ran SP% **113.9**
Speed ratings (Par 94): **99,93,91,87,80 78,78,71,68,64**
CSF £25.12 TOTE £3.30: £1.90, £2.80, £1.10; EX 28.10 Trifecta £50.00 Pool: £146.58 - 2.08 winning tickets..
Owner Mrs M P Oliver **Bred** Ian H Stephenson **Trained** Caledon, Co. Tyrone
■ Stewards' Enquiry : Eddie Ahern caution: careless riding; caution: used whip with excessive frequency

FOCUS
Just a modest maiden, but the winner seems to be improving and could still be a bit better.

NOTEBOOK

Commit To Memory ran well behind the potentially smart Plan at Leopardstown two starts back before running a fair fifth off a mark of 78 on his nursery debut at Dundalk and he found this a suitable opportunity to get off the mark at the fifth time of asking. He proved well suited by the step up to 1m and, okay on the surface, he totally outclassed his nine rivals. This was not much of a race, but he looks a useful handicapper in the making. (op 5-2 tchd 10-3)

Blue Law(IRE), carrying 2lb overweight, confirmed the promise he showed when fifth on his debut at Dundalk, but he was no match for his stablemate. (op 13-2)

It's Josr, second off a mark of 66 in an extended 1m nursery at Wolverhampton on his previous start, travelled well into the straight, but he did not help his chance by hanging right and proved no match for the Irish raiders. (tchd 5-1 tchd 11-2 in a place)

Mujahope had been beaten in claimers on his last two starts and this was tougher.

Smetana failed to justify market support, but he will have more options now he is qualified for a handicap mark. (op 5-1)

7122 PONTIN'S BOOK EARLY PRICE PROMISE CLAIMING STKS 6f (F)

1:00 (1:00) (Class 6) 2-Y-O £2,047 (£604; £302) Stalls Low

Form RPR

606 **1** **Longoria (IRE)**[12] 6977 2-8-7 65 ... JerryO'Dwyer[(3)] 1 68
(M G Quinlan) *led 1f: chsd ldng pair: pushed along and sltly outpcd 3f out: styd on to ld appr fnl f: kpt on* **13/8**[1]

1006 **2** *2* **Rievaulx Valentino**[23] 6872 2-9-2 68 ... (p) NCallan 5 68
(K A Ryan) *cl up: led after 1f: rdn along over 2f out: drvn and hdd over 1f out: kpt on same pce* **2/1**[2]

0520 **3** *6* **Andrasta**[6] 7042 2-8-7 65 ... PatrickMathers[(3)] 4 44
(A Berry) *chsd ldrs: rdn along over 2f out: sn drvn and kpt on same pce* **10/3**[3]

0600 **4** *5* **Howe's Jack (IRE)**[36] 6698 2-8-11 40 ... RussellKennemore[(5)] 3 35
(M C Chapman) *sn rdn along and outpcd in rr: hdwy on wd outside over 2f out: sn drvn: edgd lft and wknd* **100/1**

R **5** *1 3/4* **Clip Clop (IRE)**[8] 7021 2-7-11 0 ... AmyBaker[(7)] 8 18
(Miss J Feilden) *s.v.s: a bhd* **25/1**

0 **6** *10* **Primos Dream**[11] 7000 2-8-11 0 ... MickyFenton 7 —
(Ollie Pears) *sn cl up: rdn along wl over 2f out: sn drvn and wknd qckly 2f out* **12/1**

1m 19.32s (2.42) **Going Correction** +0.10s/f (Slow) **6** Ran SP% **107.0**

Speed ratings (Par 94): **87,84,76,69,67 54**

CSF £4.59 TOTE £2.70: £2.00, £1.20; EX 4.90 Trifecta £8.00 Pool: £234.16 - 20.64 winning tickets..

Owner John Hanly **Bred** Cathal Ryan **Trained** Newmarket, Suffolk

FOCUS

A modest claimer in which the winner probably just ran to form and very little strength in depth with only three runners with any sort of chance.

NOTEBOOK

Longoria(IRE), the best off at the weights, benefited from the return to 6f and found this a straightforward opportunity to double her career tally. This was a weak race, but she was a clear-cut winner and should continue to go well in this sort of company. (op 7-4 tchd 2-1)

Rievaulx Valentino was not at his best in a similar event at Wolverhampton on his previous start, but this was better and he finished well clear of the remainder. (tchd 15-8)

Andrasta had a real squeak at the weights, but she was well below form at Wolverhampton on her previous start and this was another moderate effort. (op 5-2)

7123 BUY TICKETS ON-LINE H'CAP 1m 4f (F)

1:30 (1:30) (Class 5) (0-70,69) 3-Y-O+ £2,968 (£876; £438) Stalls Low

Form RPR

4243 **1** **Kylkenny**[42] 6598 12-9-2 **67** ... (t) TravisBlock[(3)] 3 77
(H Morrison) *trckd ldng pair: hdwy to chse ldr over 2f out: rdn wl over 1f out: drvn ins fnl f: styd on wl to ld nr fin* **5/1**[3]

500 **2** *nk* **Marsam (IRE)**[17] 6669 4-9-7 **69** ... EddieAhern 1 78
(M G Quinlan) *led 1f: cl up tl led again 3f out: rdn along wl over 1f out: drvn ins fnl f: hdd and no ex nr fin* **2/1**[1]

0032 **3** *2* **Drizzi (IRE)**[11] 6999 6-9-3 **65** ... MickyFenton 5 71
(P T Midgley) *hld up in tch: hdwy over 4f out: chsd ldng pair over 2f out: sn rdn and ev ch tl drvn and one pce ins fnl f* **10/3**[2]

0000 **4** *11* **Bulberry Hill**[18] 6937 6-8-10 **58** oh5 ow3 ... SamHitchcott 6 46
(R W Price) *cl up: led after 1f: rdn along and hdd 3f out: sn wknd* **20/1**

2025 **5** *1 1/2* **Pocket Too**[6] 6811 4-8-13 **61** ... (p) TGMcLaughlin 4 47
(M Salaman) *chsd ldrs: rdn along over 4f out: wknd over 3f out* **10/3**[2]

51 **6** *50* **Imminent Victory**[21] 6893 4-8-7 **55** oh2 ... (p) ChrisCatlin 2 —
(R M H Cowell) *in tch: pushed along 1/2-way: rdn over 4f out and sn wknd* **12/1**

2m 43.08s (0.99) **Going Correction** +0.10s/f (Slow) **6** Ran SP% **108.6**

Speed ratings (Par 103): **100,99,98,91,90 56**

CSF £14.42 TOTE £6.60: £2.40, £2.00; EX 12.80.

Owner Mrs M D W Morrison **Bred** R M , P J And S R Payne **Trained** East Ilsley, Berks

■ Stewards' Enquiry : Eddie Ahern three-month ban: breach of rule 220 (iii): misuse of whip in order to trigger beginning of a "totting up" penalty (Jan 4-Apr 3)

FOCUS

A fair race for the grade and the form looks solid. Course specialist Kylkenny was racing off his lowest sand mark for five years and he was 8lb off last winter's best form round here.

7124 PONTIN'S SHORT BREAKS (S) STKS 7f (F)

2:00 (2:00) (Class 6) 3-Y-O+ £2,047 (£604; £302) Stalls Low

Form RPR

5001 **1** **Dancing Deano (IRE)**[20] 6908 5-8-13 47 ... (v) RussellKennemore[(5)] 3 62
(R Hollinshead) *cl up: led wl over 2f out: rdn clr wl over 1f out: edgd rt ins fnl f: kpt on* **9/2**[2]

0403 **2** *3 1/2* **Ruffie (IRE)**[9] 7006 4-8-13 60 ... (e) RobertHavlin 1 48
(Miss Gay Kelleway) *hld up in tch: hdwy wl over 2f out: rdn to chse wnr over 1f out: sn drvn and no imp ins fnl f* **11/4**[1]

6020 **3** *1 3/4* **Nawayea**[31] 6778 4-8-2 45 ... (t) KirstyMilczarek[(5)] 8 37
(C N Allen) *in tch: hdwy 3f out: rdn to chse ldrs 2f out: drvn and edgd lft ins fnl f: kpt on same pce* **7/1**

0066 **4** *8* **Only If I Laugh**[16] 6947 6-8-12 45 ... DaneO'Neill 5 22
(M J Attwater) *towards rr: hdwy 1/2-way: rdn over 2f out: styd on appr fnl f* **11/2**[3]

0000 **5** *1 3/4* **Mr Chocolate Drop (IRE)**[43] 6570 3-8-13 49 ... (v) JamesO'Reilly[(5)] 2 23
(Miss M E Rowland) *led: rdn along over 3f out: hdd wl over 2f out and grad wknd* **33/1**

5000 **6** *2* **Capital Lass**[218] 1569 4-8-13 47 ... HayleyTurner 10 13
(A J McCabe) *prom: rdn along to chse wnr over 2f out: drvn and wknd wl over 1f out* **9/1**

0300 **7** *2* **Kingsmaite**[225] 1379 6-8-12 48 ... PaulEddery 11 7
(S R Bowring) *in tch: hdwy to chse ldrs 1/2-way: rdn along wl over 2f out and sn btn* **11/2**[3]

0330 **8** *shd* **A Teen**[83] 5566 9-9-4 44 ... TGMcLaughlin 7 12
(P Howling) *towards rr: sme hdwy on outer 3f out: rdn over 2f out and sn wknd* **33/1**

6-00 **9** *19* **Sir Mikeale**[44] 6542 4-8-12 43 ... SaleemGolam 6 —
(G Prodromou) *a bhd* **25/1**

0600 **10** *1 1/2* **Abadia**[142] 3789 3-8-8 43 ow1 ... (p) PaulMulrennan 4 —
(J G Given) *t.k.h: prom: pushed along 4f out: sn rdn and wknd* **25/1**

1m 31.8s (1.00) **Going Correction** +0.10s/f (Slow) **10** Ran SP% **111.7**

Speed ratings (Par 101): **98,94,92,82,80 78,76,76,54,52**

CSF £15.72 TOTE £5.70: £1.90, £1.40, £1.70; EX 17.30 Trifecta £40.70 Pool: £180.19 - 3.14 winning tickets..There was no bid for the winner.

Owner Ron Wood **Bred** Mrs Olivia Farrell **Trained** Upper Longdon, Staffs

FOCUS

A standard seller. Not easy to rate though, the winner and third not having run here before. The winner is rated back to his latter 3yo form.

Only If I Laugh Official explanation: jockey said gelding suffered interference in running

7125 GO PONTIN'S MEDIAN AUCTION MAIDEN STKS 1m 3f (F)

2:30 (2:30) (Class 6) 3-5-Y-O £2,047 (£604; £302) Stalls Low

Form RPR

0232 **1** **Dart**[33] 6751 3-8-12 63 ... JamieSpencer 9 73+
(J R Fanshawe) *trckd ldrs: smooth hdwy to ld wl over 2f out: sn clr: eased ins fnl f: easily* **1/2**[1]

0000 **2** *7* **West End Lad**[43] 6564 4-9-7 48 ... (p) DeanMcKeown 8 51
(S R Bowring) *in tch: hdwy to chse ldrs 4f out: rdn along wl over 2f out: drvn and styd on same pce appr fnl f* **33/1**

4605 **3** *hd* **Grizebeck (IRE)**[86] 5478 5-9-7 66 ... ChrisCatlin 11 51
(R F Fisher) *cl up: led after 3f: rdn along 3f out: sn hdd: drvn wl over 1f out and kpt on same pce* **3/1**[2]

636 **4** *7* **Piano Key**[106] 4914 3-8-5 42 ... GHannon[(7)] 4 34
(M D I Usher) *in tch: hdwy on inner wl over 2f out: sn rdn and plugged on same pce* **25/1**

50 **5** *1 1/4* **King Of Connacht**[100] 5102 4-9-7 0 ... (p) TPQueally 2 37
(M Wellings) *in rr tl sme late hdwy* **20/1**

0020 **6** *hd* **Franky'N'Jonny**[11] 6991 4-9-2 45 ... DaneO'Neill 5 31
(M J Attwater) *midfield: hdwy 3f out: rdn to chse ldrs 2f out: sn drvn and no imp* **22/1**

7 *nk* **Lady Nimue (FR)** 3-8-12 0 ... EddieAhern 3 31
(J Jay) *hld up: hdwy and in tch 4f out: rdn along wl over 2f out and no further prog* **12/1**[3]

00 **8** *6* **Rasmani**[11] 6991 3-8-12 0 ... (vt[1]) HayleyTurner 7 21
(Miss Gay Kelleway) *cl up: rdn along over 3f out: drvn over 2f out: sn edgd lft and wknd* **33/1**

4/ **9** *3* **Hill Farm Shanty**[899] 2956 5-9-7 0 ... MickyFenton 1 20
(J T Stimpson) *t.k.h: led 3f: cl up tl rdn along 1/2-way and sn wknd* **40/1**

0560 **10** *36* **Betterlatethanever (IRE)**[65] 6057 3-9-3 41 ... (p) TGMcLaughlin 10 —
(C J Teague) *a in rr: bhd fr 1/2-way* **66/1**

11 *35* **Rosandwil (IRE)**[18] 3-8-12 0 ... PaulMulrennan 6 —
(A D Brown) *s.i.s: a in rr: bhd fr 1/2-way* **66/1**

2m 30.57s (1.67) **Going Correction** +0.10s/f (Slow)

WFA 3 from 4yo+ 4lb **11** Ran SP% **123.6**

Speed ratings (Par 101): **97,91,91,86,85 85,85,81,78,52 27**

CSF £34.82 TOTE £1.80: £1.02, £7.80, £1.30; EX 31.00 Trifecta £190.40 Pool: £413.12 - 1.54 winning tickets..

Owner Dr Catherine Wills **Bred** St Clare Hall Stud **Trained** Newmarket, Suffolk

FOCUS

A terrible maiden in which the third, the only danger to Dart, was well below his best. The winner was worth a lot better than the bare form.

7126 SOUTHWELL-RACECOURSE.CO.UK H'CAP 6f (F)

3:00 (3:00) (Class 4) (0-85,83) 3-Y-O+ £4,728 (£1,406; £702; £351) Stalls Low

Form RPR

0405 **1** **Ingleby Arch (USA)**[12] 6981 4-8-13 **77** ... PaulFessey 7 92
(T D Barron) *mde all: rdn and qcknd clr 1 1/2f out: styd on strly* **9/2**[2]

4600 **2** *2 1/2* **Resplendent Alpha**[12] 6972 3-9-1 **79** ... TGMcLaughlin 4 86
(P Howling) *awkward s: towards rr: hdwy 2f out: swtchd lft and rdn over 1f out: styd on strly ins fnl f: nt rch wnr* **16/1**

5016 **3** *1 1/4* **Bel Cantor**[39] 6639 4-8-1 **68** ... (p) AndrewMullen[(3)] 3 71
(W J H Ratcliffe) *chsd ldrs: rdn 2f out: drvn over 1f out: kpt on ins fnl f* **5/1**[3]

0123 **4** *3/4* **Westport**[26] 6836 4-9-1 **79** ... NCallan 8 80+
(K A Ryan) *chsd ldrs: hdwy on outer over 2f out: rdn to chse wnr wl over 1f out: sn drvn and wknd ins fnl f* **6/4**[1]

4000 **5** *2 1/2* **Happy As Larry (USA)**[3] 7087 5-8-11 **75** ... (t) MickyFenton 6 68
(D J Murphy) *stmbld s and bhd: hdwy 2f out: swtchd rt over 1f out: rdn ent fnl f: styd on wl: nrst fin* **20/1**

4020 **6** *2 1/2* **River Thames**[38] 6676 4-9-2 **80** ... ChrisCatlin 5 65
(K A Ryan) *hld up: hdwy to chse ldrs 2f out: sn rdn and wknd over 1f out* **12/1**

0015 **7** *1/2* **Whitbarrow (IRE)**[20] 6907 8-9-0 **83** ow3 ... (b) JamesMillman[(5)] 9 66
(B R Millman) *cl up: rdn along over 2f out: sn drvn and wknd* **7/1**

2130 **8** *3* **Desperate Dan**[12] 6972 6-9-4 **82** ... (b) TPQueally 1 56
(A B Haynes) *chsd ldng pair: rdn along 1/2-way: sn drvn and wknd over 2f out* **20/1**

0302 **9** *1/2* **Diminuto**[20] 6905 3-8-2 **71** ... KirstyMilczarek[(5)] 2 43
(M D I Usher) *chsd ldrs: rdn over 2f out: grad wknd* **16/1**

1m 16.27s (-0.63) **Going Correction** +0.10s/f (Slow) **9** Ran SP% **116.3**

Speed ratings (Par 105): **108,104,103,102,98 95,94,90,90**

CSF £73.08 CT £370.11 TOTE £6.00: £1.40, £3.30, £1.90; EX 80.10 Trifecta £326.70 Part won. Pool: £460.15 - 0.36 winning tickets..

Owner Dave Scott **Bred** Alexander-Groves Thoroughbreds **Trained** Maunby, N Yorks

FOCUS

A fair sprint handicap. The form looks solid and should work out well. The winner is rated to his latter turf form.

Happy As Larry(USA) Official explanation: jockey said, regarding the running and riding, his orders were to jump out and ride the race as he found it and that the gelding was outpaced in the early stages before staying on past beaten horses in the final 2f, adding that he didn't feel the gelding moved well in the home straight and, further, he stated to the trainer post race that the gelding be fitted with blinkers in future; trainer's rep added that the gelding has a history of physical problems and may benefit from being raced over a longer trip in future

7127 PONTINS.COM H'CAP 1m (F)
3:30 (3:30) (Class 6) (0-62,62) 3-Y-0+ £2,047 (£604; £302) Stalls Low

Form RPR

0030 1 **Dado Mush**[28] 6809 4-8-0 **50** oh5 ....(p) KirstyMilczarek(5) 7 63
(T T Clement) *prom: hdwy 3f out: rdn to ld over 2f out: styd on wl u.p ins fnl f* **28/1**

1623 2 3 1/2 **Ours (IRE)**[12] 6979 4-8-10 **55** .... StephenDonohoe 6 60
(John A Harris) *hld up towards rr: hdwy wl over 2f out: rdn to chse wnr wl over 1f out: sn edgd lft and kpt on same pce* **9/4**[1]

0502 3 1 1/4 **Cadwell**[9] 7009 3-8-8 **54** .... RobertHavlin 5 56
(T J Pitt) *trckd ldrs: hdwy to chse ldr over 2f out and sn ev ch tl rdn wl over 1f out and kpt on same pce* **9/4**[1]

0202 4 1 1/4 **Moonstreaker**[22] 6882 4-9-0 **59** .... DeanMcKeown 2 58
(R M Whitaker) *hld up in rr: hdwy 3f out: rdn along 2f out: sn drvn and no imp appr fnl f* **10/3**[2]

0034 5 6 **Astroangel**[8] 7025 3-8-12 **58** .... PaulMulrennan 1 43
(M H Tompkins) *trckd ldrs on inner: effrt 3f out: sn rdn along and wknd fnl 2f* **9/1**[3]

1400 6 3 1/2 **Time To Regret**[8] 7023 7-9-0 **59** ....(p) DanielTudhope 3 36
(I W McInnes) *chsd ldrs: rdn along over 3f out: sn wknd* **10/1**

0500 7 3 1/2 **Gifted Flame**[11] 7001 8-8-4 **54** oh5 ow4........................ AnnStokell(5) 8 23
(Miss A Stokell) *in tch on outer: hdwy to chse ldrs 3f out: sn rdn and wknd* **40/1**

3000 8 1/2 **Rebel Pearl (IRE)**[47] 6463 3-8-13 **62** .... JerryO'Dwyer(3) 4 30
(M G Quinlan) *led: rdn along 3f out: hdd over 2f out and sn wknd* **16/1**

1m 43.5s (-1.10) **Going Correction** +0.10s/f (Slow)
WFA 3 from 4yo+ 1lb 8 Ran SP% **115.5**
Speed ratings (Par 101): **109,105,104,103,97 93,90,89**
CSF £91.98 CT £209.00 TOTE £27.30: £5.20, £1.90, £1.10; EX 162.60 Trifecta £437.20 Part won. Pool: £615.83 - 0.66 winning tickets. Place 6 £14.80, Place 5 £7.22.
Owner Dr M Edres **Bred** Bellow Hill Stud **Trained** Newmarket, Suffolk

FOCUS
Moderate form but probably sound for the grade. The time was decent and the winner is rated back to his 3yo best.
Rebel Pearl(IRE) Official explanation: jockey said filly had no more to give
T/Plt: £25.20 to a £1 stake. Pool: £59,534.35. 1,718.20 winning tickets. T/Qpdt: £11.90 to a £1 stake. Pool: £3,621.30. 224.60 winning tickets. JR

7048 DEAUVILLE (R-H)
Wednesday, December 12

OFFICIAL GOING: Standard

7128a PRIX LYPHARD (LISTED RACE) (ALL-WEATHER) 1m 1f 110y
2:05 (2:11) 3-Y-0+ £17,568 (£7,027; £5,270; £3,514; £1,757)

RPR

1 **Willywell (FR)**[25] 6862 5-9-2 .... FBlondel 3 107
(J-P Gauvin, France)

2 1 1/2 **Major Grace (FR)**[20] 6909 4-8-12 .... ACrastus 10 100
(Y De Nicolay, France)

3 nse **Stop Making Sense**[20] 6909 5-8-12 .... SPasquier 9 100
(A Fabre, France)

4 nk **Soft Morning**[6] 7049 3-8-11 .... F-XBertras 11 101
(Sir Mark Prescott) *sn led: pushed along st: rdn 1 1/2f out: hdd 150yds out: lost 2nd fnl strides* **66/10**[1]

5 nk **Miss Salvador (FR)**[26] 6846 4-8-9 .... TJarnet 1 96
(S Wattel, France)

6 1 1/2 **Touch Of Land (FR)**[25] 6862 7-9-2 .... JAuge 12 100
(H-A Pantall, France)

7 shd **Mondovino (FR)**[25] 6862 4-8-12 .... THuet 15 96
(Rod Collet, France)

8 1 1/2 **Royal Pennekamp (FR)**[13] 4-8-12 .... DMichaux 7 93
(H-A Pantall, France)

9 shd **Kingvati (FR)**[20] 6909 5-8-12 ....(b) GFaucon 5 92
(Y De Nicolay, France)

10 1 **Criticism**[25] 6862 3-8-11 .... RonanThomas 4 92
(H-A Pantall, France)

0 **Sirene Doloise (FR)**[20] 4-8-9 .... RMarchelli 6 —
(A Bonin, France)

0 **Risky Nizzy**[48] 4-8-9 .... MBlancpain 2 —
(C Lerner, France)

0 **Softlanding (IRE)**[13] 4-8-9 .... J-BHamel 13 —
(Robert Collet, France)

0 **Thunder Storm Cat (USA)**[152] 3514 3-8-11 ....(b) AHelfenbein 14 —
(M Rulec, Germany)

0 **Kankakee (USA)**[20] 4-8-9 .... DBonilla 8 —
(J E Pease, France)

1m 55.5s (115.50)
WFA 3 from 4yo+ 2lb 15 Ran SP% **13.2**
PARI-MUTUEL (Including 1 Euro stake): WIN 15.70; PL 4.60, 12.60, 2.10;DF 275.00.
Owner H Gauvin **Bred** Henri Gauvin **Trained** France

NOTEBOOK
Soft Morning, a winner in similar grade over this course and distance last time out, albeit against her own sex, tried to make all the running again. She probably ran to a similar level under her penalty against this tougher opposition as she did six days earlier.

7100 WOLVERHAMPTON (A.W) (L-H)
Thursday, December 13

OFFICIAL GOING: Standard
Wind: Nil Weather: Fine and cold

7129 PONTIN'S GREAT FAMILY HOLIDAYS MAIDEN AUCTION STKS 5f 216y(P)
6:50 (6:52) (Class 6) 2-Y-0 £2,730 (£806; £403) Stalls Low

Form RPR

5002 1 **Mission Impossible**[29] 6813 2-8-6 67........................ PatrickDonaghy(7) 2 70
(P C Haslam) *chsd ldr: led 2f out: sn rdn and hung lft: r.o* **15/8**[2]

6324 2 3/4 **Firewalker**[35] 6729 2-8-4 67........................ ChrisCatlin 1 59
(B Smart) *led 4f: sn rdn: ev ch ins fnl f: no ex towards fin* **4/1**[3]

2 3 3 **Sempre Libera (IRE)**[12] 6990 2-8-7 0........................ HayleyTurner 4 53
(P W Chapple-Hyam) *a.p: rdn and one pce fnl 2f* **5/4**[1]

5 4 nk **Fantadot**[12] 6990 2-8-10 0........................ RichardThomas 5 55
(D J S Ffrench Davis) *hung rt most of way: bhd: rdn 3f out: kpt on ins fnl f: n.d* **20/1**

0 5 1 1/2 **Mad Man Will (IRE)**[101] 5097 2-8-12 0........................ SaleemGolam 3 53
(S C Williams) *hld up in tch: rdn over 2f out: wknd over 1f out* **33/1**

1m 16.1s (0.29) **Going Correction** +0.125s/f (Slow) 5 Ran SP% **106.9**
Speed ratings (Par 94): **103,102,98,97,95**
CSF £8.98 TOTE £4.20: £1.10, £2.50; EX 8.90.
Owner Vyas Ltd & M T Buckley **Bred** Rodney Meredith **Trained** Middleham Moor, N Yorks

FOCUS
A small field and a modest race on paper, but very few ever got into it and the winning time was 0.31 seconds faster than the older-horse maiden later on the card. The race has been rated around the winner to his recent mark.

NOTEBOOK
Mission Impossible, always up with the pace on this return to 6f, looked like winning comfortably when edging ahead of the leader on the crown of the home bend, but the runner-up made sure he had to be ridden right out to make sure of it. He struggled when put into handicap company turf, but is on a lower mark now so he may find another opportunity on this surface. (op 13-8)
Firewalker, making her sand debut, was given a positive ride from the rails draw and to be fair she battled back very gamely after the winner edged past her. There should be a small race in her on this surface. (op 9-2 tchd 11-2)
Sempre Libera(IRE) did not look that happy from some way out and could do nothing to stop the front pair from running right away from her. She did not confirm the promise of her debut effort and this performance rather backs up the view that the Kempton contest was a moderate one. (tchd 11-8)
Fantadot, more than five lengths behind Sempre Libera on his Kempton debut when badly drawn, did not look happy going this way around and, even though he finished much closer to his old rival this time, he probably achieved very little. (op 16-1 tchd 14-1)
Mad Man Will(IRE), friendless in the market, never looked like winning but, although he is by a top-class sprinter, there is more stamina on the dam's side and he is likely to show more once handicapped after one more run. (op 16-1)

7130 PONTINS.COM MEDIAN AUCTION MAIDEN STKS 7f 32y(P)
7:20 (7:21) (Class 6) 2-Y-0 £2,730 (£806; £403) Stalls High

Form RPR

1 **My Mate Max** 2-8-12 0........................ RussellKennemore(5) 3 74
(R Hollinshead) *in rr: hdwy wl over 1f out: rdn to ld wl ins fnl f: r.o wl* **25/1**

2356 2 1 3/4 **Funseeker (UAE)**[13] 6978 2-8-12 66........................ GregFairley 6 65
(M Johnston) *sn led: rdn over 2f out: hdd and nt qckn ins fnl f* **7/2**[3]

3 3 1 **Hasty Retreat**[17] 6944 2-9-3 0........................ StephenDonohoe 5 67
(E A L Dunlop) *hld up: rdn 3f out: hung lft 1f out: r.o towards fin* **11/8**[1]

0643 4 1/2 **Weet By Far**[19] 6936 2-8-12 61........................ HayleyTurner 4 61
(R Hollinshead) *led early: sn stdd and hld up: hdwy 3f out: one pce fnl f* **14/1**

5 1 1/2 **Liberty Valance (IRE)** 2-9-3 0........................ GeorgeBaker 2 62
(S Kirk) *prom: wnt 2nd over 3f out: hung rt and rn green bnd over 2f out: wknd wl ins fnl f* **2/1**[2]

5 6 3 **Ros Cuire (IRE)**[20] 6912 2-9-3 0........................ DaleGibson 1 55
(W A Murphy, Ire) *hld up in tch: hung lft over 1f out: wknd fnl f* **50/1**

0360 7 10 **Melwood Dreams**[34] 6750 2-9-0 55........................(v1) PatrickMathers(3) 7 31
(Paul Green) *sn chsng ldr: rdn and lost 2nd over 3f out: sn hung rt and lost pl* **50/1**

1m 31.41s (1.01) **Going Correction** +0.125s/f (Slow) 7 Ran SP% **112.1**
Speed ratings (Par 94): **99,97,95,95,93 90,78**
CSF £105.72 TOTE £25.50: £16.10, £2.80; EX 125.40.
Owner Tim Leadbeater **Bred** Tim Leadbeater **Trained** Upper Longdon, Staffs

FOCUS
A weak and uncompetitive maiden, but the time was a fair one for the grade and the winner, who was making his racecourse debut, can only improve. The runner-up's recent efforts helps set the level, with the third and fourth also giving the form quite a solid look.

NOTEBOOK
My Mate Max ◆, out of a half-sister to three winners including the prolific sprinter Fearby Cross, was not obviously expected according to the market but he showed a decent attitude to run past some experienced rivals and it will be a surprise if he cannot gain further success. (op 20-1)
Funseeker(UAE), back in a maiden after disappointing in a nursery here last month, was given another positive ride on this drop back in trip, but again lack of finishing pace proved her downfall in the run to the line. She now looks exposed, but her official rating of 66 does provide a benchmark to the form.
Hasty Retreat, all the rage after his promising Lingfield debut, was probably not helped by the drop in trip but this did look a decent opportunity and it was disappointing that he could not take advantage. He is worth another chance back over further. Official explanation: jockey said colt hung left throughout (op 15-8)
Weet By Far, a stablemate of the winner, had every chance back in a maiden and probably ran to a similar level of form as of late. She looks well and truly exposed now. (op 8-1)
Liberty Valance(IRE), a 46,000gns half-brother to three winners including the smart Tolpuddle, was close enough on the home bend but then tended to show his inexperience and did not get home. The market support for him suggests he has ability and he should have learned something from this. (tchd 9-4)
Ros Cuire(IRE) Official explanation: jockey said colt hung left

7131 PONTINSBINGO.COM H'CAP 1m 141y(P)
7:50 (7:50) (Class 5) (0-70,76) 3-Y-0+ £2,817 (£838; £418; £209) Stalls Low

Form RPR

1111 1 **Confidentiality (IRE)**[5] 7080 3-9-12 **76** 12ex........................ NickyMackay 7 87+
(M Wigham) *hld up: smooth hdwy on ins wl over 1f out: led on bit ins fnl f* **4/9**[1]

5030 2 nk **Swiper Hill (IRE)**[5] 7079 4-8-7 **55** .... PaulMulrennan 4 58
(B Ellison) *chsd ldr: rdn to ld wl over 1f out: hung lft and hdd ins fnl f: kpt on* **10/1**[3]

2440 **3** *1 ¾* **Casablanca Minx (IRE)**[17] 6951 4-8-9 **57**..............(v) StephenDonohoe 5 56
(P D Evans) *hld up: swtchd lft and hdwy over 1f out: nt qckn ins fnl f* **14/1**

2013 **4** *½* **Arctic Desert**[5] 7080 7-9-1 **63**..(t) HayleyTurner 2 61
(Miss Gay Kelleway) *plld hrd in tch: nt clr run wl over 1f out: swtchd rt ins fnl f: one pce* **5/1**[2]

-5F0 **5** *1 ¼* **Stravita**[13] 6982 3-9-1 **70**.. RussellKennemore(5) 6 65
(R Hollinshead) *prom: rdn 2f out: btn over 1f out* **28/1**

6 *1 ¼* **Sharp Liquor (IRE)**[512] 3653 4-8-6 **54** oh9..................(b) JamieMackay 3 46?
(G T Lynch, Ire) *a bhd* **66/1**

1320 **7** *nk* **Corrib (IRE)**[62] 6146 4-9-1 **63**.. ChrisCatlin 1 54
(B Palling) *led: rdn and hdd wl over 1f out: wknd ins fnl f* **18/1**

1m 53.16s (1.40) **Going Correction** +0.125s/f (Slow)
WFA 3 from 4yo+ 2lb 7 Ran SP% **111.9**
Speed ratings (Par 103): **98,97,96,95,94 93,93**
CSF £5.69 TOTE £1.20: £1.10, £6.80; EX 7.80.
Owner J M Cullinan **Bred** Kevin Foley **Trained** Newmarket, Suffolk

FOCUS
An ordinary handicap lit up by Confidentiality who managed to record a remarkable sixth straight handicap victory. The pace was modest however, as was the winning time and the form is messy and not that solid.

7132 GO PONTIN'S HOLIDAYS APPRENTICE H'CAP 1m 4f 50y(P)
8:20 (8:20) (Class 5) (0-75,77) 3-Y-0+ **£2,817** (£838; £418; £209) **Stalls** Low

Form RPR

5624 **1** **The King And I (IRE)**[69] 5983 3-8-11 **68**..............(b[1]) KrishGundowry(5) 4 80
(Miss E C Lavelle) *stdd s: hld up and bhd: hdwy over 2f out: rdn and edgd rt 1f out: led ins fnl f: r.o* **9/2**[2]

1121 **2** *1 ¼* **Birkside**[7] 7046 4-9-11 **77** 6ex.. JamieKyne(5) 5 87
(D Carroll) *hld up in tch: rdn to ld wl over 1f out: edgd rt and hdd ins fnl f: nt qckn* **5/4**[1]

0023 **3** *3 ½* **Punta Galera (IRE)**[7] 7046 4-9-0 **66**...................... AndrewHeffernan(5) 6 70
(Paul Green) *plld hrd: chsd ldr: led over 7f out: rdn over 2f out: hdd wl over 1f out: no ex fnl f* **5/1**[3]

2-1V **4** *1 ¾* **Crazy Bear (IRE)**[3] 7100 4-9-7 **68**.................................... MatthewDavies 1 69
(K J Burke) *hld up: hdwy over 2f out: wknd over 2f out* **7/1**

604V **5** *½* **Western Roots**[3] 7100 6-9-1 **62**.................................... PatrickDonaghy 3 62
(M Appleby) *stdd s: nvr nr ldrs* **16/1**

5000 **6** *4* **Mighty Kitchener (USA)**[38] 6697 4-8-13 **60**...................... LanceBetts 2 54
(P Howling) *set stdy pce: hdd over 7f out: chsd ldr tl over 2f out: wknd wl over 1f out* **6/1**

2m 43.0s (0.58) **Going Correction** +0.125s/f (Slow)
WFA 3 from 4yo+ 5lb 6 Ran SP% **112.0**
Speed ratings (Par 103): **103,102,99,98,98 95**
CSF £10.55 TOTE £6.50: £4.90, £1.10; EX 21.30.
Owner The Villains **Bred** Lisieux Stud **Trained** Wildhern, Hants

FOCUS
A modest middle-distance handicap and, with no pace on early, the form, rated around the placed horses, wants treating with caution.

7133 WOLVERHAMPTON-RACECOURSE.CO.UK CLASSIFIED STKS 1m 1f 103y(P)
8:50 (8:50) (Class 7) 3-Y-0+ **£1,295** (£385; £192; £96) **Stalls** Low

Form RPR

0000 **1** **Shantina's Dream (USA)**[15] 6968 3-8-12 45.................. HayleyTurner 3 45
(J R Boyle) *a.p: rdn over 1f out: led wl ins fnl f: r.o* **20/1**

-660 **2** *hd* **Ponte Vecchio (IRE)**[45] 6532 3-8-12 45.......................... PatCosgrave 6 44
(J R Boyle) *led: rdn and edgd rt wl over 1f out: hdd wl ins fnl f: r.o* **5/1**[2]

202- **3** *nk* **Veneer (IRE)**[569] 1914 5-9-0 45.. StephenDonohoe 1 43
(Mrs N S Evans) *hld up in mid-div: rdn and hdwy on ins wl over 1f out: ev ch ins fnl f: r.o* **12/1**

0/00 **4** *1* **Princess Zaha**[149] 3619 5-9-0 45.. LPKeniry 5 41
(A G Newcombe) *a.p: rdn over 2f out: kpt on same pce ins fnl f: fin 5th, hd, nk, ½l & ½l: plcd 4th* **28/1**

-005 **5** *shd* **Telling**[37] 6700 3-8-9 45.. AndrewMullen(3) 11 41
(Mrs A Duffield) *s.i.s: t.k.h in rr: stmbld over 5f out: hdwy on outside over 2f out: edgd lft ins fnl f: one pce: fin 6th: plcd 5th* **14/1**

0005 **6** *½* **Just Crystal**[8] 7034 3-8-12 45.. TGMcLaughlin 12 40
(B P J Baugh) *swtchd lft sn after s: sn w ldr: ev ch 2f out: rdn and hung rt ins fnl f: one pce: fin 7th: plcd 6th* **11/1**[3]

-406 **7** *1 ¼* **Santera (IRE)**[8] 6904 3-8-12 45...................................... PaulMulrennan 8 37
(Mrs A Duffield) *hld up in tch: rdn 2f out: wknd over 1f out: fin 8th: plcd 7th* **22/1**

0403 **8** *shd* **Abbeygate**[31] 6792 6-9-0 44..(p) NickyMackay 10 41+
(T Keddy) *hld up towards rr: n.m.r over 2f out: hmpd wl over 1f out: n.d after: fin 9th: plcd 8th* **1/1**[1]

0060 **9** *½* **Ten Black**[18] 6060 3-8-12 45.. J-PGuillambert 4 36
(R Brotherton) *hld up in mid-div: pushed along over 3f out: bhd fnl 2f: fin 10th: plcd 9th* **33/1**

0600 **D** **The Power Of Phil**[24] 6877 3-8-7 45.................... RussellKennemore(5) 9 46+
(Miss Joanne Priest) *t.k.h in rr: nt clr run over 2f out: swtchd rt and rn wd ent st: rdn and hung lft fr over 1f out: gd late hdwy: fin 4th: disqualified for failing to weigh-in* **5/1**[2]

2m 5.46s (2.84) **Going Correction** +0.125s/f (Slow)
WFA 3 from 5yo+ 2lb 10 Ran SP% **121.5**
Speed ratings (Par 97): **92,91,91,90,90 90,89,88,88,91**
CSF £117.30 TOTE £33.40: £7.80, £1.50, £2.10; EX 135.50.
Owner David Grieve **Bred** S Peskoff **Trained** Epsom, Surrey

■ Stewards' Enquiry : Russell Kennemore three-day ban: failed to weigh-in (Dec 26-28)
Pat Cosgrave two-day ban: used whip with arm above shoulder height (Dec 26-27)
T G McLaughlin two-day ban: careless riding (Dec 26-27)

FOCUS
A moderate contest and, with the pace just ordinary the winning time was modest, even for a race like this, and they finished in a bit of a bunch. The form looks particularly weak.

7134 GO PONTIN'S SHORT BREAKS MEDIAN AUCTION MAIDEN STKS 5f 216y(P)
9:20 (9:22) (Class 6) 3-5-Y-0 **£2,047** (£604; £302) **Stalls** Low

Form RPR

20-2 **1** **Grand Assault**[37] 6706 4-9-3 50.......................................(be) AdamKirby 3 58
(G C Bravery) *hld up: hdwy whn hung lft 2f out: rdn to ld jst ins fnl f: sn edgd rt: drvn out* **5/4**[1]

0600 **2** *2* **Belinda Rose (IRE)**[24] 6877 3-8-12 52.......................... DavidAllan 9 47
(E J Alston) *led early: a.p: rdn 3f out: r.o one pce ins fnl f* **16/1**

5500 **3** *½* **Calloff The Search**[4] 7085 3-9-3 50..............................(v) MickyFenton 4 50
(Stef Liddiard) *s.i.s: sn chsng ldrs: wnt 2nd over 2f out: rdn and hung lft over 1f out: ev ch ent fnl f: nt qckn* **5/1**[3]

6003 **4** *¾* **The Carpet Man**[15] 6963 3-9-3 48.............................. RichardKingscote 8 48
(A W Carroll) *hld up: hdwy on ins wl over 1f out: sn hung lft: one pce fnl f* **11/4**[2]

06 **5** *3 ½* **Elizabeth Spirit (IRE)**[15] 6963 3-8-12 0.................... StephenDonohoe 2 31
(E S McMahon) *racd keenly: sn led: rdn over 2f out: hdd jst ins fnl f: wknd* **9/1**

6000 **6** *6* **Saint Remus (IRE)**[21] 6905 3-9-3 41.....................................(b) LPKeniry 6 17
(Peter Grayson) *bhd fnl 3f* **50/1**

0 **7** *2 ½* **Chocolate Sands**[9] 7019 3-9-3 0.................................... J-PGuillambert 5 9
(J G Given) *t.k.h: prom: hung rt over 2f out: wknd wl over 1f out* **12/1**

400 **8** *7* **Suspender (IRE)**[37] 6702 3-8-12 38............................ PaulMulrennan 7 —
(S T Mason) *s.i.s: sn outpcd* **40/1**

1m 16.41s (0.60) **Going Correction** +0.125s/f (Slow) 8 Ran SP% **115.8**
Speed ratings (Par 101): **101,98,97,96,92 84,80,71**
CSF £25.14 TOTE £2.10: £1.20, £2.70, £1.20; EX 18.70.
Owner Russell Reed **Bred** Mrs Elizabeth J Reed **Trained** Newmarket, Suffolk

FOCUS
A very moderate maiden but the form is pretty sound if limited.
T/Plt: £88.00 to a £1 stake. Pool: £94,009.25. 779.40 winning tickets. T/Qpdt: £16.90 to a £1 stake. Pool: £6,236.60. 271.90 winning tickets. KH

7121 SOUTHWELL (L-H)
Friday, December 14

OFFICIAL GOING: Standard to slow
Wind: Light across Weather: Overcast

7135 PONTIN'S BOOK EARLY PRICE PROMISE APPRENTICE H'CAP 1m 4f (F)
11:50 (11:55) (Class 6) (0-65,66) 3-Y-0+ **£2,047** (£604; £302) **Stalls** Low

Form RPR

60- **1** **Hugs 'n Kisses (IRE)**[55] 6350 3-9-1 **65**.......................... JamieJones(5) 5 73
(John Joseph Murphy, Ire) *hld up: hdwy over 3f out: rdn and hung lft over 1f out: sn hung rt: styd on to ld wl ins fnl f* **28/1**

6001 **2** *¾* **Three Boars**[3] 7110 5-9-12 **66** 6ex.....................................(b) GregFairley 4 73
(S Gollings) *hld up in tch: led and hung rt fr over 1f out: rdn and hdd wl ins fnl f* **2/5**[1]

3610 **3** *nk* **Ronsard (IRE)**[6] 7081 5-8-8 **55** 6ex.............................. RichardEvans(7) 2 61
(P D Evans) *s.i.s: hld up: hdwy over 2f out: rdn over 1f out: styd on* **20/1**

4045 **4** *8* **Sand Repeal (IRE)**[61] 6200 5-9-5 **64**...............................(v) AmyBaker(5) 7 58
(Miss J Feilden) *led: rdn and hdd over 1f out: wknd fnl f* **10/1**[3]

604- **5** *2 ½* **Sorbiesharry (IRE)**[367] 6795 8-8-10 **50** oh5.................. DuranFentiman 8 40
(Mrs N Macauley) *chsd ldr over 3f: remained handy: rdn and ev ch over 2f out: wknd over 1f out* **100/1**

0006 **6** *10* **Isa'Af (IRE)**[14] 6971 8-8-5 **50** oh5.................................. WilliamCarson(5) 6 24
(P W Hiatt) *prom: chsd ldr over 8f out: rdn over 3f out: wknd 2f out: eased fnl f* **50/1**

2365 **7** *11* **Maria Antonia (IRE)**[7] 7050 4-8-6 **51**.......................... KellyHarrison(5) 1 7
(P A Blockley) *hld up: rdn and nt clr run over 3f out: sn wknd* **12/1**

4501 **8** *nk* **Blue Hedges**[23] 6902 5-9-6 **63**.. NicolPolli(3) 3 18
(H J Collingridge) *chsd ldrs: rdn over 3f out: wknd over 2f out* **7/1**[2]

2m 44.22s (2.13) **Going Correction** +0.175s/f (Slow)
WFA 3 from 4yo+ 5lb 8 Ran SP% **111.9**
Speed ratings (Par 101): **99,98,98,92,91 84,77,77**
CSF £39.00 CT £272.21 TOTE £33.00: £5.90, £1.10, £4.40; EX 89.50 TRIFECTA Not won..
Owner O Finetto **Bred** Highfort Stud **Trained** Upton, Co. Cork
■ Stewards' Enquiry : William Carson three-day ban: weighed-in 3lb heavy (Dec 26-28)

FOCUS
A modest middle-distance handicap best rated through the third to his summer form.

7136 PONTIN'S GREAT FAMILY HOLIDAYS NURSERY 6f (F)
12:20 (12:26) (Class 6) (0-65,65) 2-Y-0 **£2,047** (£604; £302) **Stalls** Low

Form RPR

0500 **1** **Night Robe**[36] 6736 2-8-3 **47** ow2.................................... MatthewHenry 5 49
(P D Evans) *s.i.s and hmpd s: hld up: hdwy over 2f out: rdn to ld ins fnl f: r.o* **14/1**

06 **2** *1 ¼* **Rich James (IRE)**[30] 6812 2-8-4 **51**.............................. AndrewElliott(3) 10 49
(J D Bethell) *chsd ldrs: led over 2f out: sn rdn: hdd and unable qckn ins fnl f* **7/2**[2]

0650 **3** *shd* **Ambrose Princess (IRE)**[10] 7022 2-8-13 **57**...................... LPKeniry 6 55
(R A Harris) *chsd ldrs: rdn whn n.m.r over 1f out: styd on* **10/3**[1]

030 **4** *¾* **Santa Clara**[51] 6434 2-9-5 **63**.. PatCosgrave 3 59
(Jane Chapple-Hyam) *edgd rt s: sn chsng ldrs: rdn and edgd rt fr over 2f out: sn ev ch: no ex wl ins fnl f* **9/2**[3]

1100 **5** *shd* **Countrywide Comet (IRE)**[16] 6966 2-9-4 **62**............(b) TGMcLaughlin 4 57
(P Howling) *hmpd s: hld up: hdwy over 2f out: sn rdn: styd on* **6/1**

2200 **6** *11* **Mama Leo**[44] 6586 2-8-8 **52**.. PaulEddery 7 14
(J G M O'Shea) *led 1f: sn rdn and lost pl: wknd over 2f out* **12/1**

0000 **7** *½* **Frammenti**[11] 7007 2-8-9 **53** ow1.................................(be[1]) SteveDrowne 2 14
(A J McCabe) *led 5f out: rdn and hdd over 2f out: hmpd and wknd sn after* **10/1**

0005 **8** *1 ½* **Wynberg (IRE)**[60] 6227 2-8-8 **57**.............................. KirstyMilczarek(5) 8 13
(N A Callaghan) *s.i.s: hld up: rdn and wknd over 2f out* **7/1**

1m 19.75s (2.85) **Going Correction** +0.175s/f (Slow) 8 Ran SP% **113.7**
Speed ratings (Par 94): **88,86,86,85,85 70,69,67**
CSF £61.89 CT £206.86 TOTE £19.30: £4.80, £1.50, £1.20; EX 81.90 Trifecta £122.50 Pool £184.68 - 1.07 winning units..
Owner G E Amey **Bred** G E Amey **Trained** Pandy, Monmouths

FOCUS
A very moderate nursery - the winning time was 0.84 seconds slower than the later juvenile maiden - and not form to dwell on.

NOTEBOOK
Night Robe had shown very limited form on her previous seven starts, including when beating just one home over 7f at Wolverhampton last time, but she proved suited by both the drop in trip and switch to Fibresand and was able to get off the mark. She carried 2lb overweight, but that put her on a mark of just 47. This is her sort of level. Official explanation: trainer's rep said, regarding apparent improvement in form, that the filly was suited by the Fibresand and had shown sings of maturing over the past month (op 16-1)
Rich James(IRE) has tumbled in the weights since first contesting a nursery and this was a respectable effort in second. This was his first try on Fibresand and the surface seemed to suit. (op 5-1)
Ambrose Princess(IRE), whose two wins to date have been gained in selling company, might have been second with a clear run. (op 4-1 tchd 3-1)
Santa Clara had shown some ability in maiden company, but she was conceding weight all round on her nursery debut and was well held in fourth. (op 7-2)
Countrywide Comet(IRE) has not progressed since leaving Kevin Ryan's yard. (op 13-2 tchd 11-2)

Wynberg(IRE) Official explanation: jockey said gelding hung left up straight

7137 PROTEC GROUP (SHEPSHED) LTD H'CAP (DIV I) 5f (F)
12:55 (1:00) (Class 6) (0-52,52) 3-Y-0+ £2,047 (£604; £302) Stalls High

Form RPR

0545 **1** **Gone'N'Dunnett (IRE)**[3] 7111 8-8-2 **47**...(p) KirstyMilczarek(5) 1 58
(Mrs C A Dunnett) *s.i.s: sn pushed along: hdwy u.p over 1f out: r.o to ld nr fin* **8/1**

3524 **2** *nk* **Two Acres (IRE)**[24] 6886 4-8-11 **51**... DaneO'Neill 5 61
(A G Newcombe) *s.i.s: outpcd and hung lft: hdwy 1/2-way: rdn to ld over 1f out: hdd nr fin* **5/2**[1]

0000 **3** *3 1/2* **Tenancy (IRE)**[37] 6720 3-8-3 **46** oh1...(p) PatrickMathers(3) 3 43
(A J McCabe) *chsd ldrs: rdn over 1f out: styd on same pce* **7/1**[3]

0000 **4** *3/4* **Kissi Kissi**[46] 6537 4-8-6 **46** oh1... AdrianMcCarthy 2 41
(M J Attwater) *mid-div: sn drvn along: hdwy over 1f out: nt trble ldrs* **25/1**

0000 **5** *2* **Dodaa (USA)**[3] 7111 4-8-6 **46** oh1...(b) MatthewHenry 8 34
(N Wilson) *led: rdn and hdd over 1f out: wknd ins fnl f* **15/2**

0506 **6** *1* **Prime Recreation**[110] 4857 10-8-6 **46** oh1... RichardThomas 9 30
(P S Felgate) *chsd ldrs: rdn over 1f out: sn wknd* **33/1**

035 **7** *shd* **Celeb Style (IRE)**[153] 3537 3-8-12 **52**... JimCrowley 6 36
(Paul Green) *mid-div: sn drvn along: outpcd fr 1/2-way* **11/2**[2]

0030 **8** *3/4* **Luloah**[46] 6531 4-8-8 **48**... PaulEddery 4 29
(J G M O'Shea) *chsd ldrs over 3f* **12/1**

0000 **9** *hd* **Maktavish**[37] 6720 8-8-3 **46** oh1...(b) AndrewMullen(3) 12 26
(R Brotherton) *chsd ldrs over 3f* **12/1**

6000 **10** *nk* **Noddledoddle (IRE)**[21] 6910 3-8-6 **46** oh1...(tp) NeilPollard 11 25
(J Ryan) *sn outpcd* **20/1**

0030 **11** *2 1/2* **Beechside (IRE)**[37] 6720 3-8-9 **49**... DaleGibson 10 19
(W A Murphy, Ire) *s.s: outpcd* **12/1**

0060 **12** *hd* **Polish Prize**[10] 7013 3-8-11 **51** ow1... AdamKirby 13 20
(W R Swinburn) *sn outpcd* **16/1**

-000 **13** *7* **Skiddaw Fox**[196] 2195 3-8-6 **46** oh1...(p) LiamJones 7 —
(Mrs L Williamson) *sn outpcd* **66/1**

61.74 secs (1.44) **Going Correction** +0.30s/f (Slow) **13** Ran SP% **121.3**
Speed ratings (Par 101): **100,99,93,92,89 87,87,86,86,85 81,81,70**
CSF £27.62 CT £142.42 TOTE £6.40: £2.10, £1.60, £2.40; EX 17.50 Trifecta £61.50 Part won. Pool £86.74 - 0.50 winning units..
Owner Christine Dunnett Racing **Bred** Ocal Bloodstock **Trained** Hingham, Norfolk

FOCUS
They went a good pace in this sprint and the first two came from well off the pace. The winner has been rated as performing right up to this year's best form. The winning time was 0.20 seconds slower than the second division.
Luloah Official explanation: jockey said filly had no more to give
Beechside(IRE) Official explanation: jockey said filly missed the break
Skiddaw Fox Official explanation: jockey said colt hung right

7138 PROTEC GROUP (SHEPSHED) LTD H'CAP (DIV II) 5f (F)
1:30 (1:36) (Class 6) (0-52,52) 3-Y-0+ £2,047 (£604; £302) Stalls High

Form RPR

0404 **1** **Is It Time (IRE)**[10] 7013 3-8-10 **50**... RobertHavlin 5 61
(Mrs P N Dutfield) *sn pushed along in rr: hdwy u.p and n.m.r over 1f out: r.o to ld and hung lft wl ins fnl f* **6/1**[3]

5000 **2** *1 1/4* **The Geester**[66] 6078 3-8-9 **49**...(b) PaulEddery 13 55
(S R Bowring) *trckd ldrs: led over 1f out: hdd wl ins fnl f* **12/1**

0000 **3** *3/4* **Creme Brulee**[30] 6818 4-8-3 **46** oh1... DominicFox(3) 7 49
(P T Dalton) *led over 3f: styd on same pce ins fnl f* **16/1**

0502 **4** *1* **Phinerine**[3] 7108 4-8-7 **52**...(e) TolleyDean(5) 4 52
(Miss J E Foster) *hld up: hdwy u.p and n.m.r over 1f out: styd on* **4/1**[1]

6506 **5** *2 1/2* **Dunn Deal (IRE)**[3] 7108 7-8-8 **48** oh1 ow2... PaulMulrennan 12 39
(J Balding) *free to post: sn outpcd: hung rt 1/2-way: rdn over 1f out: nvr nrr* **8/1**

6-06 **6** *shd* **College Queen**[280] 653 9-8-6 **46** oh1... GregFairley 3 36
(S Gollings) *chsd ldrs: rdn over 1f out: wknd ins fnl f* **9/1**

350 **7** *1/2* **Jojesse**[24] 6886 3-8-8 **48**... PatCosgrave 9 37
(Jennie Candlish) *sn outpcd: rdn 1/2-way: nvr nrr* **5/1**[2]

3105 **8** *1 1/2* **She's Our Beauty (IRE)**[45] 6562 4-8-3 **46** oh1...(p) DuranFentiman(3) 2 29
(S T Mason) *chsd ldrs: rdn whn hmpd and wknd over 1f out* **5/1**[2]

0000 **9** *1/2* **Mujart**[94] 5303 3-8-7 **47**... DeanMcKeown 10 28
(J A Pickering) *s.i.s: sn prom: wknd 1/2-way* **16/1**

0060 **10** *nk* **Diamond Josh**[4] 7105 5-7-13 **46** oh1... RossAtkinson(7) 11 26
(M Mullineaux) *chsd ldrs to 1/2-way* **28/1**

0000 **11** *3 1/2* **Our Archie**[10] 7019 3-8-6 **46** oh1... AdrianMcCarthy 6 14
(M J Attwater) *chsd ldrs over 3f* **16/1**

0600 **12** *7* **Percy Douglas**[289] 581 7-8-5 **50** oh1 ow4...(b) AnnStokell(5) 1 —
(Miss A Stokell) *mid-div: sn pushed along: wknd 1/2-way* **50/1**

61.54 secs (1.24) **Going Correction** +0.30s/f (Slow) **12** Ran SP% **119.5**
Speed ratings (Par 101): **102,100,98,97,93 93,92,89,89,88 82,71**
CSF £76.73 CT £1121.30 TOTE £7.70: £2.50, £3.90, £5.20; EX 84.10 TRIFECTA Not won..
Owner G Payne **Bred** Century Bloodstock **Trained** Axmouth, Devon

FOCUS
Another sprint run at a good gallop, and the winning time was 0.20 seconds quicker than the first division. It has been rated through the runner-up.
Creme Brulee Official explanation: jockey said filly lost a front shoe
Dunn Deal(IRE) Official explanation: jockey said gelding hung right throughout

7139 GO PONTIN'S HOLIDAYS MEDIAN AUCTION MAIDEN STKS 6f (F)
2:05 (2:11) (Class 6) 2-Y-0 £2,047 (£604; £302) Stalls Low

Form RPR

00 **1** **The Twelve Steps**[7] 7051 2-9-3 0... SteveDrowne 5 67+
(P F I Cole) *hmpd s: hld up: hdwy over 2f out: rdn over 1f out: led ins fnl f: sn clr: comf* **3/1**[2]

0 **2** *3* **Martingrange Boy (IRE)**[20] 6926 2-9-3 0...(t) GregFairley 7 58
(D J Murphy) *trckd ldrs: racd keenly: led over 1f out: hdd and unable qckn ins fnl f* **8/1**

0 **3** *3/4* **Fools Gold**[63] 6156 2-9-3 0... DavidAllan 6 56
(T D Easterby) *chsd ldrs: rdn and ev ch over 2f out: styd on same pce fnl f* **10/1**

04 **4** *3/4* **Dancing Maite**[25] 6872 2-9-3 0... PaulEddery 2 54
(S R Bowring) *sn led: rdn over 2f out: hdd over 1f out: no ex ins fnl f* **15/2**

5 *1 3/4* **Jakam (IRE)** 2-9-3 0... DaneO'Neill 3 48
(E J O'Neill) *edgd rt s: chsd ldrs: rdn over 2f out: wknd over 1f out* **2/1**[1]

54 **6** *12* **Pinewood Lulu**[53] 6384 2-8-9 0... DuranFentiman(3) 4 7
(R C Guest) *hmpd s: prom: rdn and hung lft 2f out: sn wknd* **9/2**[3]

0 **7** *2 1/2* **Cool Fashion (IRE)**[21] 6912 2-8-12 0... PaulMulrennan 1 —
(Ollie Pears) *in tch: rdn over 3f out: sn wknd* **33/1**

8 *17* **Chalford** 2-9-0 0...(b[1]) PatrickMathers(3) 8 —
(J Balding) *mid-div: hung rt and droped rr over 4f out: bhd fr 1/2-way* **40/1**

1m 18.91s (2.01) **Going Correction** +0.175s/f (Slow) **8** Ran SP% **113.9**
Speed ratings (Par 94): **93,89,88,87,84 68,65,42**
CSF £26.84 TOTE £3.70: £1.70, £2.20, £3.40; EX 30.30 Trifecta £146.30 Pool £369.07 - 1.79 winning units..
Owner D N Green **Bred** Wickfield Farm Partnership **Trained** Whatcombe, Oxon

FOCUS
A very modest maiden and despite the clear winner not a race to get carried away with. The winning time was 0.84 seconds quicker than the earlier 0-65 nursery.

NOTEBOOK
The Twelve Steps had finished down the field in two runs in reasonable maiden company over 1m, but this was a very weak race and he was able to get off the mark at the third time of asking. Dropping a couple of furlongs in trip, he looked in a bit of trouble turning for home, but stayed on strongly in the straight to ultimately run out a decisive winner. He should not be too harshly treated by the Handicapper and could go on from this, possibly back over slightly further. (op 5-1)
Martingrange Boy(IRE), seventh of ten over 5f at Lingfield on his debut, ran a little better fitted with a tongue-tie. He will have more options once qualified for a handicap mark. (op 7-1 tchd 9-1)
Fools Gold showed very little on his debut at York back in October, but this was considerably easier and he ran a respectable race. (tchd 9-1 and 11-1)
Dancing Maite, fourth in a claimer at Wolverhampton on his previous start, was well held in fourth but will have more options now he is qualified for a handicap mark. (op 8-1 tchd 9-1 and 7-1)
Jakam(IRE), a gelded son of Diktat, half-brother to 1m2f winner Alexander Goldmine, was sent off a well-backed favourite and has presumably been showing plenty at home, but he could only manage fifth. He is worth another chance. (op 5-2 tchd 7-4 tchd 11-4 in places)
Pinewood Lulu was hampered at the start and could not confirm the promise of her two turf efforts, but she is now qualified for a handicap mark. Official explanation: jockey said filly was unsuited by the Fibresand (op 11-4 tchd 5-1 in places)

7140 PONTINS.COM MAIDEN STKS 7f (F)
2:40 (2:46) (Class 5) 2-Y-0 £2,968 (£876; £438) Stalls Low

Form RPR

3223 **1** **Safebreaker**[24] 6884 2-9-3 75... JimCrowley 6 74
(N Tinkler) *a.p: rdn to chse ldr over 1f out: r.o to ld wl ins fnl f* **7/4**[1]

002 **2** *1* **Molly Ann (IRE)**[22] 6903 2-8-12 70... DavidAllan 5 67
(T D Easterby) *chsd ldrs tl led 1/2-way: rdn clr over 2f out: hdd wl ins fnl f* **7/1**

00 **3** *1/2* **Nino Cochise (IRE)**[5] 7084 2-9-3 0... RobertHavlin 9 70
(C R Egerton) *sn pushed along in rr: hdwy u.p and hung lft fr over 2f out: nt rch ldrs* **20/1**

4 *1* **Barons Court** 2-9-3 0... GregFairley 4 68
(M Johnston) *s.s: outpcd: hdwy and hung lft fr over 1f out: nrst fin* **4/1**[3]

632 **5** *2* **Hellfire Bay**[21] 6912 2-9-3 67... PaulMulrennan 10 63
(K A Ryan) *prom: rdn 1/2-way: chsd clr ldr over 2f out to over 1f out: styd on same pce* **3/1**[2]

60 **6** *5* **Persistent (IRE)**[34] 6754 2-9-3 0... FrankieMcDonald 8 50
(P T Midgley) *sn outpcd* **50/1**

00 **7** *2 1/2* **King Of Cadeaux (IRE)**[13] 6998 2-9-3 0... FergusSweeney 7 44
(M A Magnusson) *prom over 4f* **40/1**

0 **8** *1* **Shoot Pontoon (IRE)**[7] 7051 2-8-10 0... BradleyRoper(7) 1 42
(N A Callaghan) *s.i.s: outpcd* **50/1**

0340 **9** *8* **Novestar (IRE)**[20] 6933 2-9-3 54...(p) AdamKirby 3 22
(G J Smith) *led: hdd over 4f out: sn rdn: wknd over 2f out* **33/1**

3052 **10** *15* **Spic 'n Span**[74] 5863 2-9-3 74... LPKeniry 2 —
(R A Harris) *chsd ldr tl led over 4f out: hdd 1/2-way: rdn and wknd over 2f out* **7/1**

1m 32.22s (1.42) **Going Correction** +0.175s/f (Slow) **10** Ran SP% **120.4**
Speed ratings (Par 96): **98,96,96,95,92 87,84,83,74,56**
CSF £14.87 TOTE £2.90: £1.20, £2.20, £4.50; EX 18.80 Trifecta £90.60 Pool £458.39 - 3.59 winning units..
Owner Elite Racing Club **Bred** Gainsborough Stud Management Ltd **Trained** Langton, N Yorks

FOCUS
A reasonable maiden for the track/time of year and sound form.

NOTEBOOK
Safebreaker ◆ shaped well when third at Wolverhampton on his first start since leaving Mark Johnston's yard and he was able to confirm that promise to get off the mark at the fifth attempt. Just as at Wolverhampton he very much gave the impression he will do even better when stepped up to 1m. (op 15-8 tchd 2-1)
Molly Ann(IRE) probably ran to about the same sort of level she showed when second in a similar event at Wolverhampton on her previous start, but the winner was too good. (op 8-1 tchd 9-1 in places)
Nino Cochise(IRE) ran his best race yet in third and offered plenty of encouragement. He is now qualified for a handicap mark and should come into his own over further next year. (op 25-1)
Barons Court, a son of Pivotal, an half-brother to useful triple 5f-1m winner Zosima, and 1m2f scorer Violin Time, out of a useful winner at around 1m-1m2f, has plenty of size and shaped very nicely on his debut. He was soon in trouble after starting slowly, but he finally began to understand what was required in the straight and came home nicely. He should improve plenty and ought to be up to winning next time. Official explanation: jockey said colt missed the break (tchd 9-2)
Hellfire Bay, gambled on when second in a weak Wolverhampton maiden on his previous start, found this tougher and was well held. (op 4-1)
Spic 'n Span Official explanation: jockey said gelding lost its action

7141 WILLIAM BRIMSTED 60TH BIRTHDAY H'CAP 1m (F)
3:15 (3:20) (Class 5) (0-75,73) 3-Y-0+ £2,968 (£876; £438) Stalls Low

Form RPR

0000 **1** **Kabeer**[254] 915 9-8-12 **71**...(t) NataliaGemelova(5) 2 86
(A J McCabe) *mde all: rdn and hung lft over 1f out: hung rt ins fnl f: all out* **16/1**

5106 **2** *1/2* **Im Ova Ere Dad (IRE)**[13] 6997 4-9-5 **73**... TPQueally 6 87
(D E Cantillon) *hld up in tch: rdn to chse wnr 2f out: sn hung lft: styd on u.p* **11/4**[1]

0610 **3** *10* **Rebellious Spirit**[13] 6997 4-9-2 **70**... JimCrowley 1 61
(P W Hiatt) *stmbld s: chsd wnr tl rdn 2f out: sn wknd* **6/1**

3404 **4** *5* **Boundless Prospect (USA)**[13] 6996 8-8-11 **65**... AdamKirby 5 45
(Miss Gay Kelleway) *chsd ldrs: rdn 1/2-way: wknd over 2f out* **7/2**[3]

2010 **5** *2* **Parkview Love (USA)**[8] 7045 6-9-4 **72**...(v) DeanMcKeown 4 47
(D Shaw) *prom over 5f* **8/1**

3062 **6** *6* **Zennerman (IRE)**[11] 7006 4-9-0 **73**...(p) TolleyDean(5) 7 34
(Miss J E Foster) *hld up: bhd fr 1/2-way* **16/1**

0366 **U** **Masterofthecourt (USA)**[27] 6848 4-9-5 **73**... SteveDrowne 3 —
(H Morrison) *stmbld and uns rdr s* **3/1**[2]

1m 44.47s (-0.13) **Going Correction** +0.175s/f (Slow) **7** Ran SP% **111.1**
Speed ratings (Par 103): **107,106,96,91,89 83,—**
CSF £56.43 TOTE £20.40: £6.20, £1.90; EX 68.50 Place 6 £107.59, Place 5 £79.00..
Owner Placida Racing **Bred** Shadwell Estate Company **Trained** Babworth, Notts
■ Stewards' Enquiry : Natalia Gemelova one-day ban: used whip with excessive frequency (Dec 26)

FOCUS
Not a strong race but two pulled clear in a race run in a fair time for the grade and the winner is rated in line with last winter's form.
T/Plt: £183.30 to a £1 stake. Pool: £47,181.35. 187.90 winning tickets. T/Qpdt: £45.30 to a £1 stake. Pool: £3,564.20. 58.10 winning tickets. CR

7129 WOLVERHAMPTON (A.W) (L-H)
Friday, December 14

OFFICIAL GOING: Standard
Wind: Almost nil Weather: Fine and cold

7142 MACE RACING AT WOLVERHAMPTON CLAIMING STKS — 7f 32y(P)
7:00 (7:01) (Class 6) 2-Y-O — £2,047 (£604; £302) Stalls High

Form — RPR
0405 **1** **Shepherds Warning (IRE)**[45] 6572 2-8-8 63 .... RichardKingscote 3 — 68
(N J Vaughan) *hld up: hdwy over 5f out: led over 2f out: rdn over 1f out: r.o wl* — **5/2**[2]
221 **2** 1 3/4 **Maybe I Wont**[4] 7096 2-8-4 63 .... DuranFentiman(3) 2 — 62
(R M Stronge) *led early: hld up in tch: rdn and chsd wnr jst over 2f out: no imp fnl f* — **11/4**[3]
6056 **3** 1 **Little Firecracker**[8] 7042 2-8-1 61 .... AndrewElliott(3) 7 — 57
(Miss M E Rowland) *sn led: hdd over 4f out: nt clr run and swtchd rt over 2f out: kpt on same pce fnl f* — **14/1**
1034 **4** 2 1/2 **Wee Buns**[8] 7044 2-8-9 68 .... LPKeniry 5 — 56
(S Kirk) *prom tl rdn and wknd over 1f out* — **7/1**
0512 **5** nk **Copperbottomed (IRE)**[8] 7044 2-8-8 66 ....(e) HarryPoulton(7) 1 — 61
(J R Boyle) *t.k.h: prom: lost pl over 3f out: rdn wl over 1f out: no rspnse* — **2/1**[1]
0000 **6** 2 **Nothing Likea Dame**[16] 6966 2-8-8 58 .... ChrisCatlin 4 — 49
(D J Coakley) *a bhd* — **20/1**
436 **7** 23 **Naming Problems**[7] 7058 2-7-12 50 ....(v) JamieMackay 6 — —
(K J Burke) *s.i.s: hdwy over 5f out: led over 4f out: hung rt and hdd over 2f out: sn eased* — **33/1**

1m 31.62s (1.22) **Going Correction** +0.025s/f (Slow) — **7** Ran SP% **115.4**
Speed ratings (Par 94): **94,92,90,88,87 85,59**
CSF £10.07 TOTE £3.30: £1.60, £2.10; EX 15.50.
Owner A Black **Bred** T M Jennings **Trained** Malpas, Cheshire

FOCUS
A modest contest full of exposed juveniles. The runner-up and third help set the standard.

NOTEBOOK
Shepherds Warning(IRE) took advantage of being back in a claimer and was always finding enough in the home straight. (op 4-1)
Maybe I Wont, who landed a Lingfield seller earlier in the week, continues to hold his form and did not mind being back up in distance. (op 7-4 tchd 3-1)
Little Firecracker, another reverting to a longer trip, stuck to her task after being forced to switch on the home turn.
Wee Buns had no excuses on this occasion but did manage to turn around recent course and distance form with the free-running Copperbottomed on 6lb better terms. (op 6-1 tchd 15-2)
Copperbottomed(IRE) could not confirm his near six-length superiority over Wee Buns here last week on 6lb worse terms after running freely for his young apprentice early on. (op 5-2)
Naming Problems Official explanation: jockey said bit slipped through filly's mouth

7143 PONTIN'S BOOK EARLY H'CAP — 7f 32y(P)
7:30 (7:30) (Class 6) (0-65,65) 3-Y-O+ — £2,047 (£604; £302) Stalls High

Form — RPR
0102 **1** **Four Tel**[35] 6749 3-9-3 **64** .... SamHitchcott 9 — 73+
(N J Vaughan) *s.i.s: sn prom: rdn to ld and hung lft over 1f out: r.o* — **11/4**[1]
3054 **2** 1 1/4 **Fine Ruler (IRE)**[28] 6838 3-9-4 **65** .... GeorgeBaker 6 — 71
(M R Bosley) *prom: lost pl over 5f out: rdn over 3f out: rallied 2f out: kpt on ins fnl f* — **10/1**
3 nk **Ginger Princess (IRE)**[21] 6921 5-8-5 **52** ....(t) SaleemGolam 2 — 57
(Oliver McKiernan, Ire) *s.i.s: hld up in rr: hdwy over 1f out: rdn and kpt on ins fnl f* — **16/1**
0050 **4** nk **Northern Desert (IRE)**[135] 4063 8-9-3 **64** .... PaulDoe 5 — 68
(S Curran) *hld up towards rr: hdwy 2f out: c wd st: rdn over 1f out: hung lft ins fnl f: kpt on* — **14/1**
6122 **5** 1 1/4 **Tanforan**[10] 7024 5-9-1 **62** .... ChrisCatlin 1 — 63
(B P J Baugh) *led early: sn towards rr: hdwy 2f out: rdn over 1f out: one pce ins fnl f* — **10/3**[2]
0020 **6** 1/2 **Pianoforte (USA)**[13] 6996 5-9-4 **65** ....(b) DavidAllan 8 — 65
(E J Alston) *hld up in mid-div: hdwy over 2f out: rdn and ev ch over 1f out: no ex whn carried lft ins fnl f* — **12/1**
0132 **7** nk **Royal Embrace**[9] 7028 4-8-11 **58** ....(v) DeanMcKeown 4 — 57
(D Shaw) *hld up in rr: rdn and sme hdwy over 1f out: no further prog fnl f* — **7/2**[3]
000 **8** 1 **Lincolneurocruiser**[10] 7024 5-8-11 **58** ....(v) HayleyTurner 10 — 54
(Mrs N Macauley) *sn w ldr: led over 2f out: hdd over 1f out: fdd ins fnl f* — **20/1**
6000 **9** 4 **Tancredi (SWE)**[175] 2831 5-9-0 **64** .... JerryO'Dwyer(3) 11 — 49
(N B King) *s.i.s: sn prom: rdn over 2f out: sn wknd* — **12/1**
6 **10** 1/2 **Sharp Liquor (IRE)**[1] 7131 4-8-4 **51** oh6 ....(b) JamieMackay 3 — 35
(G T Lynch, Ire) *prom tl wknd over 3f out: eased whn no ch wl ins fnl f* — **16/1**
0/ **11** 5 **Shafrons Canyon (IRE)**[415] 6183 4-9-1 **62** .... GregFairley 7 — 32
(P M Rogers, Ire) *sn led: hdd over 2f out: wknd wl over 1f out* — **28/1**

1m 30.2s (-0.20) **Going Correction** +0.025s/f (Slow) — **11** Ran SP% **123.1**
Speed ratings (Par 101): **102,100,100,99,98 97,97,96,91,91 85**
CSF £33.33 CT £394.18 TOTE £4.50: £1.40, £2.80, £4.60; EX 32.50.
Owner Owen Promotions Limited **Bred** Owen Promotions Ltd **Trained** Malpas, Cheshire
■ Stewards' Enquiry : Paul Doe caution: careless riding

FOCUS
This moderate handicap was run at a reasonable pace. The winner os progressing and the fifth is the best guide.
Pianoforte(USA) Official explanation: jockey said gelding hung left-handed

7144 PONTIN'S BOOK EARLY AND SAVE MEDIAN AUCTION MAIDEN STKS — 1m 141y(P)
7:55 (7:56) (Class 6) 3-5-Y-O — £2,047 (£604; £302) Stalls Low

Form — RPR
065 **1** **Maiden Investor**[7] 7057 4-9-0 40 .... MickyFenton 6 — 51
(Stef Liddiard) *dwlt: hld up in rr: hdwy on ins 2f out: led jst over 1f out: rdn ins fnl f: jst hld on* — **10/1**[3]
6303 **2** hd **Alecia (IRE)**[33] 6778 3-8-9 48 .... NeilChalmers(3) 1 — 51
(A M Balding) *led: hdd 7f out: prom: rdn jst over 1f out: r.o ins fnl f: jst failed* — **2/1**[2]
60/ **3** 2 **Blackbury**[18] 6623 5-9-0 0 .... TGMcLaughlin 3 — 46
(W M Brisbourne) *hld up: rdn and c wd st: edgd rt 1f out: kpt on ins fnl f* — **28/1**
53-0 **4** 3/4 **Todwick Owl**[10] 7023 3-9-0 61 .... JerryO'Dwyer(3) 4 — 50
(J G Given) *hld up: rdn and hdwy over 2f out: edgd lft over 1f out: one pce fnl f* — **10/1**[3]
5024 **5** 2 **Johnston's Glory (IRE)**[6] 7079 3-8-12 54 .... DavidAllan 5 — 40
(E J Alston) *led 7f out: rdn and hdd jst over 1f out: wknd ins fnl f* — **5/4**[1]
6600 **6** hd **Little Miss Tara (IRE)**[4] 7103 3-8-12 63 ....(b[1]) SamHitchcott 7 — 40
(A B Haynes) *s.i.s: hdwy 7f out: rdn 3f out: wknd 2f out* — **14/1**
0203 **7** 6 **Nawayea**[2] 7124 4-8-9 45 ....(t) KirstyMilczarek(5) 2 — 26
(C N Allen) *prom: chsd ldr over 6f out tl 2f out: sn wknd* — **12/1**

1m 53.28s (1.52) **Going Correction** +0.025s/f (Slow)
WFA 3 from 4yo+ 2lb — **7** Ran SP% **113.8**
Speed ratings (Par 101): **94,93,92,91,89 89,84**
CSF £30.15 TOTE £16.30: £5.00, £1.20; EX 32.40.
Owner R A Webb **Bred** D R Botterill **Trained** Great Shefford, Berks

FOCUS
A moderate winning time for this weak event, 0.25 seconds slower than the following two-year-old conditions event over the same trip. The runner-up is the best guide to the level.

7145 PONTIN'S SHORT BREAKS CONDITIONS STKS — 1m 141y(P)
8:25 (8:25) (Class 3) 2-Y-O
£6,045 (£1,810; £905; £452; £226; £113) Stalls Low

Form — RPR
11 **1** **Hilbre Court (USA)**[17] 6960 2-9-3 85 .... RobertHavlin 3 — 77
(B J Meehan) *hld up: hdwy on ins over 2f out: swtchd rt wl over 1f out: rdn to ld ins fnl f: drvn out* — **4/6**[1]
0213 **2** 1 1/4 **Dhhamaan (IRE)**[10] 7015 2-9-0 71 ....(v) HayleyTurner 1 — 71
(C E Brittain) *led early: chsd ldr: led over 3f out: rdn over 1f out: edgd rt and hdd ins fnl f: kpt on* — **11/2**[3]
0 **3** hd **Ace Of Spies (IRE)**[7] 7051 2-9-0 0 .... GregFairley 4 — 71
(M Johnston) *a.p: rdn over 1f out: ev ch jst ins fnl f: nt qckn* — **4/1**[2]
5202 **4** 1 1/4 **Ceka Dancer (IRE)**[7] 7058 2-8-9 79 .... ChrisCatlin 5 — 63
(E J O'Neill) *hld up: hdwy over 2f out: rdn whn bmpd wl over 1f out: one pce fnl f* — **10/1**
05 **5** 2 **Dinarius**[14] 6974 2-9-0 0 .... DeanMcKeown 6 — 64
(K J Burke) *sn led: hdd over 3f out: wknd 2f out* — **28/1**
00 **6** 3/4 **Ever Dreaming (USA)**[110] 4852 2-8-9 0 .... LPKeniry 2 — 58
(A M Balding) *hld up in rr: rdn over 1f out: no rspnse* — **14/1**

1m 53.03s (1.27) **Going Correction** +0.025s/f (Slow) — **6** Ran SP% **114.6**
Speed ratings (Par 100): **95,93,93,92,90 90**
CSF £5.13 TOTE £1.50: £1.20, £2.70; EX 5.50.
Owner E H Jones (paints) Ltd **Bred** Richard Nip & Omar Trevino **Trained** Manton, Wilts
■ Stewards' Enquiry : Robert Havlin three-day ban: careless riding (Dec 26-28)

FOCUS
Not a great race for the grade. The runner-up sets the level for the race, and the winner will have to improve to complete the hat-trick.

NOTEBOOK
Hilbre Court(USA) produced what was required after rather barging his way through once in line for home and Havlin earned himself a three-day Christmas holiday. (op 8-11 tchd 4-5 in places)
Dhhamaan(IRE) did not mind a return to a mile and got back up to secure the runner-up spot. (op 8-1)
Ace Of Spies(IRE), making a fairly quick reappearance after his Lingfield debut, had no excuses and it was a shade disappointing that he could not quite hold on to second. He is likely to need further next year. (tchd 9-2)
Ceka Dancer(IRE), done no favours by the winner off the home turn, appeared to get the longer trip reasonably well. (op 11-2 tchd 5-1)
Dinarius adopted totally different tactics on this step up to a mile. (op 25-1)

7146 PONTINSBINGO.COM H'CAP — 1m 1f 103y(P)
8:55 (8:55) (Class 6) (0-60,63) 3-Y-O+ — £2,047 (£604; £302) Stalls Low

Form — RPR
2432 **1** **Alfie Tupper (IRE)**[7] 7050 4-9-6 **60** .... PatCosgrave 8 — 77+
(J R Boyle) *hld up and bhd: hdwy on outside 3f out: chsd clr ldr wl over 1f out: led wl ins fnl f: r.o wl* — **5/2**[1]
5511 **2** 1 3/4 **Moment Of Clarity**[7] 7056 5-8-12 **59** ....(p) KrishGundowry(7) 4 — 72+
(R C Guest) *hld up in mid-div: hdwy to ld over 2f out: clr whn rdn wl over 1f out: hdd and no ex wl ins fnl f* — **11/4**[2]
4403 **3** 6 **Casablanca Minx (IRE)**[1] 7131 4-8-10 **57** ....(v) RichardEvans(7) 2 — 58+
(P D Evans) *hld up: sn towards rr: nt clr run over 2f out: hdwy on ins wl over 1f out: nt clr run over 1f out: r.o ins fnl f: nvr nr ldrs* — **14/1**
2301 **4** 1 1/2 **Kirstys Lad**[6] 7079 5-9-9 **63** 6ex .... GeorgeBaker 11 — 61
(M Mullineaux) *hld up in mid-div: hdwy 2f out: edgd lft over 1f out: one pce* — **14/1**
0013 **5** 1/2 **Moonlight Fantasy (IRE)**[28] 6837 4-9-2 **56** .... TGMcLaughlin 10 — 53+
(Lucinda Featherstone) *s.i.s: hld up and bhd: nt clr run on ins over 2f out: swtchd rt wl over 1f out: hung lft fr jst over 1f out: nvr nr ldrs* — **20/1**
6 1/2 **Scott Summerland (HOL)**[46] 6552 4-9-4 **58** .... LPKeniry 12 — 54
(Mervyn Torrens, Ire) *led 7f out tl over 2f out: sn rdn and btn* — **50/1**
0540 **7** nk **Chasing Memories (IRE)**[56] 6304 3-9-0 **56** .... HayleyTurner 3 — 51
(W K Goldsworthy) *sn led: hdd 7f out: rdn over 2f out: wknd wl over 1f out* — **12/1**
0302 **8** 1 1/2 **Swiper Hill (IRE)**[1] 7131 4-9-1 **55** .... PaulMulrennan 6 — 47
(B Ellison) *wnt lft s: prom tl wknd over 2f out* — **9/1**
5005 **9** 3/4 **Bijou Dan**[5] 6640 6-9-5 **59** ....(p) MickyFenton 9 — 50
(D W Thompson) *hld up and bhd: rdn 3f out: no rspnse* — **20/1**
0064 **10** nk **Norwegian**[6] 7080 6-9-4 **58** ....(p) StephenDonohoe 7 — 48
(Ian Williams) *a bhd* — **20/1**
530 **11** 1/2 **Camolin (IRE)**[41] 6640 4-9-0 **54** ....(b) GregFairley 1 — 43
(Michael McElhone, Ire) *led early: prom tl wknd over 3f out* — **28/1**
0-10 **12** 8 **Sonic Anthem (USA)**[15] 2145 5-9-5 **59** .... ChrisCatlin 5 — 32
(J T Stimpson) *hmpd s: hld up and bhd: hdwy over 6f out: wknd qckly over 2f out* — **40/1**
1332 **13** 9 **Lilac Moon (GER)**[18] 6951 3-9-2 **58** .... RichardKingscote 13 — 13
(N J Vaughan) *prom tl wknd 2f out* — **7/1**[3]

2m 1.74s (-0.88) **Going Correction** +0.025s/f (Slow)
WFA 3 from 4yo+ 2lb — **13** Ran SP% **120.9**
Speed ratings (Par 101): **104,102,97,95,95 94,94,93,92,92 91,84,76**
CSF £8.43 CT £81.63 TOTE £1.90: £2.00, £1.70, £3.10; EX 13.80.
Owner M Khan X2 **Bred** Stone Ridge Farm **Trained** Epsom, Surrey

FOCUS
They went 7/1 bar the first two home in this low-grade affair. The time was decent and the form looks good for the grade.

7147 PONTINS.COM H'CAP 1m 4f 50y(P)
9:20 (9:20) (Class 3) (0-95,93) 3-Y-0+ £7,124 (£2,119; £1,059; £529) Stalls Low

Form RPR
0063 1 **Invasian (IRE)**[13] 6994 6-9-6 90 MickyFenton 3 96
(P W D'Arcy) *mde all: drvn out ins fnl f* 5/4[1]
4 2 1 3/4 **Eumene (IRE)**[13] 6995 4-9-3 87 ChrisCatlin 2 90
(C C Bealby) *chsd wnr to 5f out: wnt 2nd again 3f out: rdn and nt qckn fnl f* 8/1[2]
2144 3 3 **Generous Lad (IRE)**[7] 7055 4-8-9 79 oh4 (p) TGMcLaughlin 1 77
(A B Haynes) *hld up: rdn 4f out: hdwy on ins wl over 1f out: one pce fnl f* 17/2[3]
1102 4 15 **Pinch Of Salt (IRE)**[13] 6995 4-9-6 93 NeilChalmers(3) 4 67
(A M Balding) *prom: chsd wnr 5f out tl rdn 3f out: sn wknd* 5/4[1]
2m 40.21s (-2.21) **Going Correction** +0.025s/f (Slow) 4 Ran SP% **110.5**
Speed ratings (Par 107): **108,106,104,94**
CSF £11.05 TOTE £2.70; EX 20.80 Place £47.09, Place 5 £17.14..
Owner Dr K Sanderson **Bred** Dr Karen Monica Sanderson **Trained** Newmarket, Suffolk

FOCUS
This took even less winning with Pinch Of Salt running well below par. The form makes sense with the placed horses to their recent marks.

NOTEBOOK
Invasian(IRE) adopted his usual front-running tactics and only had to be kept up to his work in the final 200 yards. (op 2-1)
Eumene(IRE) was clearly playing second fiddle from the furlong pole. (op 4-1)
Generous Lad(IRE) could not sustain his effort in the home straight after looking in trouble with fully half a mile to go. (op 15-2)
Pinch Of Salt(IRE) may have shown a liking for Kempton but was most disappointing on his first visit to Dunstall Park. Official explanation: jockey said gelding ran flat (op 11-8 tchd 11-10)
T/Plt: £87.90 to a £1 stake. Pool: £112,056.45. 930.60 winning tickets. T/Qpdt: £13.60 to a £1 stake. Pool: £5,445.90. 294.20 winning tickets. KH

7135 SOUTHWELL (L-H)
Saturday, December 15

OFFICIAL GOING: Standard to slow
Wind: almost nil Weather: misty

7148 GO PONTIN'S H'CAP (DIV I) 7f (F)
11:30 (11:32) (Class 6) (0-53,53) 3-Y-0+ £2,047 (£604; £302) Stalls Low

Form RPR
3040 1 **The Salwick Flyer (IRE)**[25] 6886 4-8-12 47 PhillipMakin 4 57
(I Semple) *chsd ldrs: rdn over 2f out: r.o to ld post* 9/2[2]
4060 2 hd **Shadow Jumper (IRE)**[8] 7057 6-8-10 45 (v) DaleGibson 7 54
(J T Stimpson) *chsd ldr: led 2f out: rdn ins fnl f: edgd lft: hdd post* 8/1
3000 3 5 **Astorygoeswithit**[10] 7034 4-8-11 46 ow1 (p) AdamKirby 5 42
(G C Bravery) *led 5f: sn rdn: wknd ins fnl f* 14/1
0000 4 1 1/4 **Royal Orissa**[11] 7013 5-8-10 45 (p) ChrisCatlin 8 37
(D Haydn Jones) *s.i.s: in rr whn hung rt 1/2-way: r.o appr fnl f: nvr nrr* 8/1
0-00 5 1 1/4 **Maraagel (USA)**[34] 6773 4-8-12 47 (t) J-PGuillambert 2 36
(S C Williams) *s.i.s: sn prom: rdn 1/2-way: wknd over 1f out* 5/1[3]
0011 6 1 3/4 **Dancing Deano (IRE)**[3] 7124 5-8-13 53 6ex (v) RussellKennemore(5) 1 37
(R Hollinshead) *s.i.s: sn pushed along in rr: hmpd over 4f out: hdwy u.p 2f out: wknd fnl f* 13/8[1]
4600 7 2 1/2 **Van Ruymbeke (IRE)**[46] 6569 3-8-10 45 (bt[1]) GregFairley 3 22
(D J Murphy) *s.i.s: rdn over 2f out: n.d* 14/1
0100 8 6 **Tequila Sheila (IRE)**[12] 7006 5-9-0 49 PaulDoe 11 10
(M A Allen) *chsd ldrs: rdn 1/2-way: wknd over 2f out* 33/1
0656 9 2 1/2 **Maeve (IRE)**[196] 2260 3-8-7 45 AlanCreighton(3) 6 —
(E J Creighton) *s.i.s: rdn 1/2-way: a in rr* 100/1
455 10 14 **Cryptic Clue (USA)**[246] 1031 3-8-12 47 (p) LiamJones 10 —
(D W Chapman) *chsd ldrs over 4f* 50/1
0060 11 10 **Scruffy (IRE)**[57] 6315 3-8-11 46 ow1 (v[1]) TGMcLaughlin 9 —
(C J Teague) *mid-div: rdn over 4f out: sn lost pl: wknd 1/2-way* 80/1
1m 31.91s (1.11) **Going Correction** +0.125s/f (Slow) 11 Ran SP% **115.6**
Speed ratings (Par 101): **98,97,92,90,89 87,84,77,74,58 47**
CSF £39.04 CT £466.35 TOTE £5.40: £1.80, £2.70, £4.40; EX 50.70 Trifecta £103.00 Part won. Pool £145.09 - 0.20 winning units..
Owner The Irish Mafia **Bred** Piercetown Stud **Trained** Carluke, S Lanarks
■ Stewards' Enquiry : Dale Gibson one-day ban: used whip with excessive frequency (Dec 26)

FOCUS
A very moderate handicap in which there were four vying for the early lead and the early pace was much stronger than in the second division, but they were going pretty slowly at the end and the winning time was 0.37 seconds slower. Nevertheless the form looks sound rated around the principals.
Dancing Deano(IRE) Official explanation: jockey said gelding was never travelling

7149 PLAY GOLF COME RACING NURSERY 1m (F)
12:00 (12:01) (Class 6) (0-65,65) 2-Y-0 £2,047 (£604; £302) Stalls Low

Form RPR
0003 1 **Ridgeway Jazz**[11] 7022 2-8-2 46 HayleyTurner 8 47
(M D I Usher) *sn pushed along and prom: rdn to ld over 1f out: jst hld on* 10/1
0300 2 shd **Grapes Of Wrath (UAE)**[11] 7022 2-8-6 50 GregFairley 1 51
(M Johnston) *a.p: rdn over 2f out: swtchd lft over 1f out: ev ch ins fnl f: r.o* 11/1
0400 3 1 **Silver Sprite**[10] 7031 2-8-10 54 DeanMcKeown 2 53
(D Shaw) *chsd ldr: rdn and ev ch over 1f out: styd on same pce ins fnl f* 7/1
6560 4 3 **Afton View (IRE)**[79] 5745 2-9-2 65 (e[1]) JamesO'Reilly(5) 3 57
(D J Murphy) *trckd ldrs: rdn over 1f out: styd on same pce* 6/1
2446 5 nk **Gunner Fly (IRE)**[10] 7031 2-9-3 64 JamieMoriarty(3) 4 56
(R A Fahey) *led 7f out: rdn and hdd over 1f out: wknd ins fnl f* 10/3[1]
0635 6 nk **Natural Rhythm (IRE)**[12] 7007 2-9-7 65 DanielTudhope 7 56
(D W Chapman) *dwlt: outpcd: hdwy over 3f out: rdn over 2f out: styd on same pce appr fnl f* 9/2[3]
3333 7 shd **Tapas Lad (IRE)**[12] 7010 2-9-0 58 (t) PatCosgrave 6 49
(V Smith) *s.i.s: hdwy over 5f out: rdn over 2f out: styd on same pce appr fnl f* 7/2[2]
0000 8 39 **Kay One (IRE)**[12] 7010 2-8-3 47 LiamJones 5 —
(R J Price) *sn pushed along in rr: hung rt 5f out: wknd 1/2-way* 33/1
1m 46.79s (2.19) **Going Correction** +0.125s/f (Slow) 8 Ran SP% **110.6**
Speed ratings (Par 94): **94,93,92,89,89 89,89,50**
CSF £104.40 CT £790.50 TOTE £9.70: £2.40, £2.60, £2.00; EX 80.60 TRIFECTA Not won..
Owner The Ridgeway Bloodstock Company Ltd **Bred** Templeton Stud And Bricklow Ltd **Trained** Upper Lambourn, Berks
■ Stewards' Enquiry : Hayley Turner three-day ban: used whip with excessive frequency (Dec 26-28)

FOCUS
Not a great nursery and weak form. They were spread right across the track racing up the home straight and all bar one of these still had a chance coming to the last furlong.

NOTEBOOK
Ridgeway Jazz, who showed signs of coming into form at Wolverhampton last time, confirmed that with a dour winning performance. Just about in front halfway up the home straight, she came up the centre of the track whilst her main rival stuck tight against the far rail. How much difference that made is hard to say, but she showed a good attitude and seems to be going the right way. (op 8-1)
Grapes Of Wrath(UAE), who had appeared to be going the wrong way, finished around 13 lengths behind Ridgeway Jazz at Wolverhampton last time and was only 4lb better off. However, she performed much better here and battled on all the way up the home straight tight against the far rail, only losing out to her old rival on the nod. She may be no star, but there should be a small race in her and she shapes as though she will appreciate further.
Silver Sprite, who has shown little in four starts on Polyrack, plugged on down the home straight to reach the frame and may be able to pick up a very small race here during the winter. (op 15-2 tchd 13-2)
Afton View(IRE), making his sand and nursery debuts after three months off and sporting a first-time eyeshield, showed up for a long way but looked one-paced in the latter stages. He looks high enough in the weights on what he has achieved. (op 11-2)
Gunner Fly(IRE) made much of the running, but did not see out the extra furlong on this testing surface. (op 3-1 tchd 7-2)
Natural Rhythm(IRE), who is totally exposed, gave away too much ground with a sloppy start and that is usually fatal on this surface. (op 11-2)
Tapas Lad(IRE) was another that basically blew it at the start and, although he managed to get back into contention, he was making very hard work of it from some way out.

7150 PONTIN'S BOOK EARLY CLAIMING STKS 1m 3f (F)
12:30 (12:30) (Class 6) 3-4-Y-0 £2,047 (£604; £302) Stalls Low

Form RPR
00-6 1 **Shaydreambeliever**[29] 6837 4-8-9 62 TonyHamilton 2 62
(R A Fahey) *chsd ldrs: rdn to ld 2f out: hung rt ins fnl f: styd on u.p* 7/1[3]
4-6 2 nk **Bedouin Blue (IRE)**[70] 6007 4-9-4 69 (b[1]) PaulMulrennan 4 71
(P C Haslam) *edgd rt s: sn trcking ldr: led 4f out: rdn and hdd 2f out: ev ch whn hung rt ins fnl f: nt run on* 5/4[1]
0513 3 6 **Musango**[8] 7050 4-9-7 67 (t) RobertHavlin 1 64
(Miss Gay Kelleway) *hld up in tch: chsd ldr over 3f out: rdn and ev ch over 1f out: wknd fnl f* 6/4[2]
4500 4 17 **Danum Diva (IRE)**[10] 7034 3-7-12 41 (e[1]) LiamJones 3 18
(D J Murphy) *led: racd keenly: hdd 4f out: rdn and wknd 3f out* 33/1
0-00 5 3/4 **Genoa Star**[23] 6904 4-7-13 37 (e[1]) DuranFentiman(3) 5 17
(D J Murphy) *hmpd s: outpcd: lost tch fnl 4f* 80/1
034P 6 56 **Dream Master (IRE)**[40] 6697 4-8-13 45 (b[1]) AdamKirby 6 —
(J Ryan) *chsd ldrs: rdn over 4f out: sn wknd: virtually p.u fnl f* 14/1
2m 30.46s (1.56) **Going Correction** +0.125s/f (Slow)
WFA 3 from 4yo 4lb 6 Ran SP% **107.8**
Speed ratings (Par 101): **99,98,94,82,81 40**
CSF £15.02 TOTE £7.90: £3.00, £1.10; EX 15.90.
Owner The Matthewman Partnership **Bred** T & Mrs Brudenell, P Deal, J Boughey, P Wiener **Trained** Musley Bank, N Yorks
■ Stewards' Enquiry : Paul Mulrennan one-day ban: used whip with excessive frequency (Dec 26)

FOCUS
A poor claimer in which four of the six runners were sporting some sort of headgear for the first time. At least the pace was sound with Danum Diva and Bedouin Blue taking each other on from the start and they finished in exactly the order that adjusted official ratings suggested they should.
Musango Official explanation: jockey said gelding was unsuited by the standard to slow fibresand

7151 PONTIN'S BOOK EARLY AND SAVE MAIDEN STKS 1m 4f (F)
1:05 (1:05) (Class 5) 3-4-Y-0 £2,968 (£876; £438) Stalls Low

Form RPR
2430 1 **Maslak (IRE)**[26] 6875 3-9-3 73 ChrisCatlin 2 75
(P W Hiatt) *trckd ldrs: led 7f out: hrd rdn and hung lft fr over 1f out: all out* 3/1[2]
5052 2 1/2 **Calculating (IRE)**[7] 7076 3-9-3 70 HayleyTurner 1 74
(M D I Usher) *a.p: rdn to chse wnr 2f out: edgd lft over 1f out: hung rt and unable qckn nr fin* 5/1[3]
25-2 3 4 **Counting House (IRE)**[27] 5594 4-9-8 80 SteveDrowne 5 68
(J A B Old) *led 11f out: hdd 7f out: chsd wnr tl rdn 4f out: styd on same pce fnl 2f* 8/11[1]
33 4 shd **Spares And Repairs**[18] 6959 4-9-8 0 PaulMulrennan 3 67
(Mrs S Lamyman) *s.i.s: sn prom: rdn to chse wnr 4f out: hung lft and styd on same pce appr fnl f* 33/1
0600 5 20 **Phone In**[49] 3617 4-9-8 45 J-PGuillambert 4 35
(R Brotherton) *plld hrd: led 1f: stdd and lost pl sn after: rdn over 4f out: wknd over 3f out* 20/1
2m 43.73s (1.64) **Going Correction** +0.125s/f (Slow)
WFA 3 from 4yo 5lb 5 Ran SP% **107.3**
Speed ratings (Par 103): **99,98,96,95,82**
CSF £16.47 TOTE £4.30: £1.90, £1.60; EX 14.80.
Owner Clive Roberts **Bred** Shadwell Estate Company Limited **Trained** Hook Norton, Oxon

FOCUS
A very moderate maiden run at a modest pace until the eventual winner seized the initiative just before halfway. The form, rated through the runner-up, probably does not add up to a great deal.
Phone In Official explanation: jockey said gelding lost its action

7152 EUROPEAN BREEDERS' FUND MAIDEN STKS 1m (F)
1:40 (1:41) (Class 5) 2-Y-0 £3,562 (£1,059; £529; £264) Stalls Low

Form RPR
3 1 **Prince Hamlet (IRE)**[23] 6903 2-9-3 0 J-PGuillambert 3 74
(B Smart) *mde virtually all: rdn out* 5/1[3]
5646 2 1 1/4 **Clovis**[28] 6857 2-9-3 73 GregFairley 6 71
(M Johnston) *a.p: chsd wnr over 3f out: sn rdn and ev ch: unable qckn ins fnl f* 7/4[1]
3 3 1 1/4 **Strategic Knight (USA)**[8] 7051 2-9-3 0 ChrisCatlin 4 69
(P F I Cole) *chsd ldrs: shkn up over 4f out: rdn over 2f out: styd on* 2/1[2]
4 1 1/2 **Si Belle (IRE)** 2-8-12 0 JamieMackay 7 60
(Rae Guest) *s.i.s: hld up: r.o ins fnl f: nt trble ldrs* 11/1

0522 **5** *3* **Mister Beano (IRE)**[18] 6958 2-8-12 62............................ TolleyDean(5) 8 59
(R J Price) *hld up: hdwy over 3f out: rdn over 2f out: wknd fnl f* **17/2**

6 *10* **Grail Knight** 2-8-12 0.. NicolPolli(5) 1 37
(Miss Gay Kelleway) *s.s: hdwy over 4f out: sn rdn and wknd* **40/1**

0 **7** *hd* **Love Empire (USA)**[8] 7051 2-9-3 0.............................. DeanMcKeown 5 36
(M Johnston) *s.s: sn prom: rdn and wknd over 2f out* **16/1**

0 **8** *32* **Al Mogeer (IRE)**[73] 5904 2-9-3 0.................................. PaulMulrennan 2 —
(K A Ryan) *chsd wnr: reminders 5f out: wknd over 3f out* **66/1**

1m 44.94s (0.34) **Going Correction** +0.125s/f (Slow) **8** Ran SP% **115.0**
Speed ratings (Par 96): **103,101,100,99,96 86,85,53**
CSF £14.28 TOTE £6.80: £1.80, £1.50, £1.30; EX 20.20 Trifecta £58.00 Pool £333.37 - 4.08 winning units..
Owner H E Sheikh Rashid Bin Mohammed **Bred** Darley **Trained** Hambleton, N Yorks

FOCUS
Probably not a bad maiden as a few of these had already shown some ability and the winning time was 1.85 seconds quicker than the earlier nursery. The form looks quite solid.

NOTEBOOK
Prince Hamlet(IRE) ◆, who hinted at ability on his Wolverhampton debut and attracted market support here, earned his cigar with a game all-the-way victory and he showed a good attitude to keep the favourite at bay. Whether he will be seen again before the turf season is uncertain, but he can win again if he is and he should get further. (op 7-1)
Clovis, who did not seem to stay the longer trip at Wolverhampton last time, arrived to hold every chance against the stands' rail up the home straight but was inclined to carry his head a little to one side and was never quite doing enough. (op 9-4 tchd 13-8)
Strategic Knight(USA), who ran with plenty of promise on his Lingfield debut, drifted significantly in the market and did not look happy from a very long way out. He did plug on to make the frame, but unless the different surface was the reason for this ordinary effort he has a few questions to answer now. (op 11-10)
Si Belle(IRE) ◆, whose dam was a smart performer at up to 7f in France, was noted doing some decent work from well off the pace over the last couple of furlongs. She obviously has ability and should improve, but the very best of her is likely to be seen once she is handicapped. (op 33-1)
Mister Beano(IRE), by far the most experienced in the field, has already been beaten in sellers and would have been 11lb better off with the runner-up in a handicap. He tried to lay down a challenge, but was eventually found out in this company. (op 11-1 tchd 8-1)

7153 GO PONTIN'S H'CAP (DIV II) 7f (F)
2:15 (2:15) (Class 6) (0-53,53) 3-Y-0+ **£2,047** (£604; £302) **Stalls** Low

Form RPR
0065 **1** **Haroldini (IRE)**[14] 7003 5-9-0 **53**..............................(p) PaulMulrennan 1 62+
(J Balding) *hld up: hdwy over 2f out: led 1f out: sn rdn and hung rt: r.o wl* **3/1**[2]

0003 **2** *2 1/2* **Kindkintyre (IRE)**[10] 7034 3-8-7 **46** oh1............................ DaleGibson 9 49
(R A Fahey) *chsd ldrs: led 2f out: rdn and hdd 1f out: styd on same pce ins fnl f* **10/1**

0500 **3** *1 1/4* **Shava**[16] 6587 7-8-1 **47** oh1 ow1.............................. DeclanCannon(7) 6 46
(H J Evans) *chsd ldrs: rdn and ev ch over 1f out: no ex ins fnl f* **8/1**

0000 **4** *nk* **Time For Change (IRE)**[33] 6792 3-8-7 **46** oh1..........(e[1]) DavidKinsella 5 45
(P G Murphy) *s.i.s: reminders sn after s: rdn 1/2-way: hung lft fr over 1f out: nt run on* **14/1**

6543 **5** *hd* **Desert Lover (IRE)**[4] 7113 5-8-8 **47**..........................(p) HayleyTurner 11 45
(R J Price) *mid-div: hdwy 1/2-way: rdn over 2f out: no ex fnl f* **5/2**[1]

0006 **6** *1* **James Street (IRE)**[39] 6706 4-8-8 **47**.................................(b) LPKeniry 4 42
(Peter Grayson) *chsd ldrs: rdn over 4f out: no ex fnl f* **15/2**[3]

5000 **7** *nk* **Gifted Flame**[3] 7127 8-8-5 **49** oh1 ow3............................ AnnStokell(5) 2 43
(Miss A Stokell) *hld up: hdwy over 1f out: sn rdn: no etxra fnl f* **40/1**

3000 **8** *1 1/2* **Kingsmaite**[3] 7124 6-8-9 **48**...(b) PaulEddery 8 38
(S R Bowring) *led: edgd lft sn after s: rdn and hdd 2f out: wknd ins fnl f* **10/1**

0300 **9** *2 1/2* **Blythe Spirit**[14] 7001 8-8-7 **46** oh1....................................(v) LiamJones 3 30
(Mrs L Williamson) *hld up: rdn over 2f out: wknd fnl f* **20/1**

0000 **10** *10* **One And Gone (IRE)**[110] 4426 3-8-4 **46** oh1............ AndrewElliott(3) 10 3
(Miss M E Rowland) *sn pushed along and prom: lost pl 5f out: wknd 1/2-way* **66/1**

-004 **11** *5* **Preskani**[193] 2343 5-8-4 **46** oh1..................................(v) DuranFentiman(3) 7 —
(Mrs N Macauley) *hmpd s: sn chsng ldrs: rdn over 2f out: wknd over 1f out* **22/1**

1m 31.54s (0.74) **Going Correction** +0.125s/f (Slow) **36** Ran SP% **114.3**
Speed ratings (Par 101): **100,97,95,95,95 94,93,91,89,77 71**
CSF £30.53 CT £220.41 TOTE £4.10: £1.90, £1.90, £3.30; EX 42.30 Trifecta £155.80 Part won. Pool £219.54 - 0.36 winning units..
Owner Tykes And Terriers Racing Club **Bred** Michael O'Mahony **Trained** Scrooby, Notts

FOCUS
Another moderate handicap in which seven of the 11 runners were a little out of the handicap and the form is sound but limited. The pace was not as strong in the first half of the contest as it was in the first division, but the pace held up better in the second half of the race and the winning time was 0.37 seconds faster.
Gifted Flame Official explanation: jockey said gelding hung right

7154 MARK MCKAY 21ST BIRTHDAY H'CAP 1m 6f (F)
2:50 (2:50) (Class 5) (0-75,74) 3-Y-0+ **£2,968** (£876; £438) **Stalls** Low

Form RPR
5032 **1** **Victory Quest (IRE)**[4] 7110 7-8-9 **55**..............................(v) ChrisCatlin 3 65
(Mrs S Lamyman) *a.p: chsd ldr over 5f out: led over 3f out: sn rdn: styd on wl* **9/4**[1]

5040 **2** *5* **Botham (USA)**[12] 7009 3-8-2 **55** oh7...................................(e[1]) LiamJones 7 58
(D J Murphy) *hld up: hdwy u.p over 4f out: edgd lft over 1f out: styd on same pce* **14/1**

0310 **3** *1/2* **Blue Hills**[12] 7004 6-9-0 **60**...(b) PhillipMakin 1 62
(P W Hiatt) *chsd ldr tl led 1/2-way: rdn and hdd over 3f out: no ex fnl f* **6/1**

6-61 **4** *hd* **Snowberry Hill (USA)**[33] 6798 4-8-6 **55**..................... NeilChalmers(3) 6 57
(Lucinda Featherstone) *hld up: hdwy 5f out: rdn over 3f out: styd on same pce appr fnl f* **10/3**[2]

-063 **5** *12* **Kingkohler (IRE)**[17] 6819 8-8-5 **58**..........................(p) DeclanCannon(7) 2 43
(K A Morgan) *chsd ldrs over 9f* **12/1**

0-50 **6** *17* **Almanshood (USA)**[27] 5025 5-9-0 **60**...............................(tp) GregFairley 4 21
(T Hogan, Ire) *led to 1/2-way: sn rdn: wknd 5f out* **8/1**

6233 **7** *nk* **Flame Creek (IRE)**[4] 7110 11-9-9 **74**..............................(t) SCreighton(5) 5 35
(E J Creighton) *s.s: hld up: rdn and wknd over 4f out* **5/1**[3]

3m 9.69s (0.09) **Going Correction** +0.125s/f (Slow)
WFA 3 from 4yo+ 7lb **7** Ran SP% **110.3**
Speed ratings (Par 103): **104,101,100,100,93 84,84**
CSF £31.73 CT £155.01 TOTE £3.00: £1.80, £5.20; EX 34.10 Trifecta £88.70 Pool £417.69 - 3.34 winning units..
Owner P Lamyman **Bred** Miss Veronica Henley **Trained** Ruckland, Lincs

FOCUS
An ordinary staying handicap, but there went a good pace and it developed into a proper decent test of stamina. The winner is a standing dish around here and the form, rated around the third and fourth, looks reliable and fairly sound.

7155 PONTINS.COM H'CAP 1m (F)
3:20 (3:20) (Class 6) (0-65,65) 3-Y-0+ **£2,047** (£604; £302) **Stalls** Low

Form RPR
5054 **1** **Jord (IRE)**[11] 7026 3-9-0 **64**... AndrewElliott(3) 5 75
(A J McCabe) *mde all: rdn over 1f out: r.o* **7/1**

320 **2** *3 1/2* **Crow's Nest Lad**[57] 6310 3-8-9 **61**.................................. JamesO'Reilly(5) 8 64
(J O'Reilly) *chsd wnr: rdn over 2f out: styd on same pce fnl f* **16/1**

3400 **3** *1 3/4* **Red Contact (USA)**[37] 6738 6-9-5 **65**......................(p) DanielTudhope 10 64
(A Dickman) *chsd ldrs: rdn over 2f out: no ex fnl f* **9/2**[2]

2600 **4** *hd* **Valley Observer (FR)**[62] 6199 3-9-3 **64**............................ AdamKirby 7 62
(W R Swinburn) *chsd ldrs: rdn over 3f out: styd on same pce fnl 2f* **7/2**[1]

1560 **5** *2* **Very Well Red**[9] 7047 4-9-3 **63**.. ChrisCatlin 3 57
(P W Hiatt) *hld up: hdwy 2f out: sn rdn and no imp* **13/2**

5046 **6** *2 1/2* **Xpres Maite**[26] 6874 4-9-4 **64**... PaulEddery 9 52
(S R Bowring) *hld up: hdwy over 3f out: sn rdn: nt trble ldrs* **5/1**[3]

4004 **7** *10* **Tidy (IRE)**[19] 6640 7-8-11 **57**......................................(v) PaulMulrennan 1 22
(Micky Hammond) *sn outpcd* **10/1**

0610 **8** *6* **Surprise Act**[26] 6874 3-9-4 **65**.. PaulDoe 4 16
(P R Chamings) *chsd ldrs over 4f* **9/2**[2]

5/0- **9** *33* **Breeder's Folly**[23] 771 5-8-5 **51** oh6............................(t) HayleyTurner 6 —
(E J Creighton) *prom: rdn over 5f out: sn lost pl: bhd fr 1/2-way* **50/1**

1m 44.68s (0.08) **Going Correction** +0.125s/f (Slow)
WFA 3 from 4yo+ 1lb **9** Ran SP% **118.0**
Speed ratings (Par 101): **104,100,98,98,96 94,84,78,45**
CSF £112.54 CT £566.26 TOTE £5.60: £1.90, £3.10, £2.20; EX 75.50 TRIFECTA Not won. Place 6 £213.97, Place 5 £70.66..
Owner Paul J Dixon **Bred** M Channon **Trained** Babworth, Notts

FOCUS
A moderate handicap, but another race in which they went a good pace. Not many ever got into it and the order hardly changed at all throughout the contest so there re slight doubts over the form.
T/Plt: £163.60 to a £1 stake. Pool: £42,536.55. 189.80 winning tickets. T/Qpdt: £8.30 to a £1 stake. Pool: £3,245.50. 287.50 winning tickets. CR

7142 WOLVERHAMPTON (A.W) (L-H)
Saturday, December 15

OFFICIAL GOING: Standard
The jockeys were unhappy about the kickback and the surface balling but most punters were not complaining with every favourite winning.
Wind: Nil Weather: Fine and cold

7156 PONTIN'S GREAT FAMILY HOLIDAYS CLAIMING STKS 1m 1f 103y(P)
7:00 (7:00) (Class 5) 2-Y-0 **£2,968** (£876; £438) **Stalls** Low

Form RPR
3443 **1** **Tiger Spice**[5] 7101 2-8-10 68...(b[1]) LiamJones 2 63
(W J Haggas) *chsd ldr tl over 6f out: rdn and wnt 2nd again over 2f out: led wl ins fnl f: r.o* **7/4**[1]

3343 **2** *1/2* **Home**[21] 6933 2-9-5 67...(p) PatCosgrave 1 71
(J R Boyle) *set slow pce: qcknd over 3f out: rdn and edgd lft jst over 1f out: hdd wl ins fnl f: kpt on* **2/1**[2]

3601 **3** *3/4* **Carry On Cleo**[5] 7101 2-8-2 52.................................(b) MatthewHenry 3 53
(P D Evans) *hld up: rdn and sltly outpcd over 3f out: hdwy over 2f out: kpt on ins fnl f* **11/2**[3]

0000 **4** *9* **Talamahana**[25] 6881 2-8-4 53.. ChrisCatlin 5 38
(S Kirk) *prom: chsd ldr over 6f out tl wknd over 2f out* **11/2**[3]

4064 **5** *1 1/4* **Giggling Monkey**[5] 7101 2-7-11 47...........................(v) DuranFentiman(3) 6 31
(P D Evans) *hld up in tch: rdn over 3f out: sn wknd* **10/1**

0004 **6** *1* **Sir Joey**[18] 6958 2-8-7 50 ow1.................................. RussellKennemore(5) 4 41
(J T Stimpson) *stdd s: hld up in rr: rdn over 3f out: sn struggling* **33/1**

2m 6.75s (4.13) **Going Correction** +0.05s/f (Slow) **6** Ran SP% **112.5**
Speed ratings (Par 96): **83,82,81,73,72 71**
CSF £5.57 TOTE £2.80: £1.40, £1.70; EX 5.90.
Owner M S Bloodstock Ltd **Bred** P D And Mrs Player **Trained** Newmarket, Suffolk

FOCUS
The fact they went no pace resulted in a very slow winning time, even for a race like this. The form looks reasonable rated around the first two.

NOTEBOOK
Tiger Spice found the first-time blinkers enabling her to turn around a near length defeat by Carry On Cleo in a similar event over the stretch mile here earlier in the week on 3lb better terms. (tchd 2-1)
Home could not hold the winner after waiting in front and was again inclined to go left-handed. (tchd 15-8 and 9-4)
Carry On Cleo was 3lb worse off than when beating the winner by just over a length over a slightly shorter trip here at the start of the week. She may well have been unsuited by the way the race was run. (op 4-1)

7157 PONTINSBINGO.COM H'CAP 1m 4f 50y(P)
7:30 (7:30) (Class 6) (0-60,60) 3-Y-0+ **£2,047** (£604; £302) **Stalls** Low

Form RPR
5323 **1** **Fenners (USA)**[26] 6871 4-9-7 **58**.. DaleGibson 2 65
(M W Easterby) *hld up in tch: rdn over 2f out: led ins fnl f: drvn out* **9/4**[1]

0-45 **2** *1 1/2* **Trackattack**[5] 7102 5-8-5 **45**.. NeilChalmers(3) 9 50
(M Appleby) *led after 1f: rdn over 3f out: hdd ins fnl f: nt qckn* **40/1**

-105 **3** *1* **Me Fein**[31] 6808 3-8-12 **54**... TPQueally 5 57
(A P Stringer) *t.k.h in mid-div: smooth hdwy on outside over 2f out: rdn and hung lft jst over 1f out: no ex ins fnl f* **8/1**

4 *5* **Arondo (GER)**[22] 6921 4-9-3 **54**.. ChrisCatlin 6 49
(Mervyn Torrens, Ire) *hld up in tch: rdn over 2f out: wknd wl over 1f out* **11/2**

5 *2* **All Tied Up (IRE)**[10] 7040 3-9-4 **60**.................................... JimCrowley 3 52
(T Hogan, Ire) *led 1f: prom: rdn and wknd over 1f out* **5/1**[3]

2255 **6** *2 1/2* **Zalkani (IRE)**[12] 7004 7-9-6 **57**...................................... GeorgeBaker 1 45
(J Pearce) *hld up in mid-div: stdy hdwy over 5f out: rdn and wknd wl over 1f out* **10/3**[2]

/40- **7** *1 1/2* **Tanning**[408] 3594 5-8-8 **45**..(p) LiamJones 7 31
(M Appleby) *hld up and bhd: rdn over 4f out: sn struggling* **25/1**

6600 **8** *3 1/2* **I Will If You Will**[15] 6979 3-8-8 **50**................................ PaulMulrennan 4 30
(K A Ryan) *prom tl wknd 2f out* **11/1**

0 **9** *3 ½* **Namiguest (IRE)**[7] 7079 3-7-10 **45** AndrewHeffernan(7) 8 20
(Paul Green) *bhd fnl 5f* **66/1**

000/ **10** *48* **Litigious**[1610] 3431 10-8-8 **45** PaulEddery 10 —
(B P J Baugh) *a bhd: t.o fnl 4f* **100/1**

2m 43.89s (1.47) **Going Correction** +0.05s/f (Slow)
WFA 3 from 4yo+ 5lb **10** Ran SP% **114.1**
Speed ratings (Par 101): **97,96,95,92,90 89,88,85,83,51**
CSF £104.26 CT £619.64 TOTE £3.60: £1.40, £9.40, £2.50; EX 31.00.
Owner K Wreglesworth **Bred** Darley **Trained** Sheriff Hutton, N Yorks

FOCUS
A poor handicap limited by the proximity of the runner-up.

7158 WOLVERHAMPTON-RACECOURSE.CO.UK H'CAP 7f 32y(P)
7:55 (8:00) (Class 5) (0-75,76) 3-Y-0+ **£2,968** (£876; £438) **Stalls** High

Form RPR

1222 **1** **Teasing**[9] 7045 3-9-5 **76** RobertHavlin 1 86+
(J Pearce) *hld up in mid-div: hdwy over 1f out: rdn to ld wl ins fnl f: r.o wl* **9/4**[1]

3610 **2** *1 ¼* **Gazboolou**[11] 7017 3-9-3 **74** FergusSweeney 5 78
(David Pinder) *hld up in mid-div: hdwy over 2f out: rdn to ld briefly wl ins fnl f: nt qckn* **11/1**

000 **3** *1 ¼* **Hill Of Lujain**[11] 7026 3-8-6 **63** ow1 StephenDonohoe 9 64
(Ian Williams) *chsd ldr: rdn to ld over 2f out: hdd and no ex wl ins fnl f* **14/1**

3503 **4** *½* **Hypocrisy**[14] 6997 4-9-0 **71** TPQueally 8 70
(Garvan Donnelly, Ire) *hld up and bhd: hdwy on outside 2f out: rdn over 1f out: one pce fnl f* **11/4**[2]

2061 **5** *1 ¼* **Cha Cha Cha**[37] 6731 3-9-4 **75** PaulMulrennan 10 71
(K A Ryan) *prom: rdn over 1f out: fdd ins fnl f* **6/1**[3]

6153 **6** *1* **Inca Soldier (FR)**[108] 4942 4-8-6 **63** PaulEddery 7 56
(R C Guest) *s.i.s: hld up in rr: rdn 2f out: nvr trbld ldrs* **12/1**

0006 **7** *nk* **Sea Salt**[23] 6907 4-8-10 **67** TonyHamilton 6 59
(R A Fahey) *led early: t.k.h: prom tl rdn and wknd wl over 1f out* **13/2**

131- **8** *6* **Outlook**[112] 4-9-2 **73** MickyFenton 4 49
(P T Midgley) *sn led: hdd over 2f out: wknd over 1f out* **25/1**

100- **9** *14* **Grenane (IRE)**[400] 6428 4-9-3 **74** TGMcLaughlin 2 12
(P D Evans) *a in rr: lost tch fnl 3f: b.b.v* **33/1**

1m 30.53s (0.13) **Going Correction** +0.05s/f (Slow) **9** Ran SP% **114.5**
Speed ratings (Par 103): **101,99,98,97,96 95,94,87,71**
CSF £28.01 CT £282.83 TOTE £3.10: £1.30, £2.40, £3.60; EX 30.20.
Owner D Leech **Bred** Chippenham Lodge Stud Ltd **Trained** Newmarket, Suffolk
■ Stewards' Enquiry : Tony Hamilton three-day ban: used whip down the shoulder in the forehand position (Dec 26-28)

FOCUS
A modest contest rated through the runner-up, although there may be more to come from the winner.
Grenane(IRE) Official explanation: trainer's rep said gelding bled from the nose

7159 SPONSOR A RACE BY CALLING 0870 220 2442 MAIDEN STKS 7f 32y(P)
8:25 (8:26) (Class 5) 3-Y-0+ **£2,968** (£876; £438) **Stalls** High

Form RPR

42-5 **1** **Kirk Michael**[210] 1839 3-9-3 **85** DaneO'Neill 4 94+
(H Candy) *mde all: clr wl over 1f out: easily* **4/6**[1]

2 *12* **Dancing Wizard** 3-9-3 **0** AdamKirby 8 58
(C G Cox) *s.i.s: pushed along over 5f out: hdwy wl over 1f out: tk 2nd nr fin: no ch w wnr* **9/1**

6005 **3** *½* **Beck**[7] 7079 3-9-0 **44** DuranFentiman(3) 10 57
(W M Brisbourne) *hld up in tch: chsd wnr over 2f out: sn rdn and btn* **12/1**

03 **4** *4* **Accolation**[29] 6830 3-9-3 **0** PatDobbs 7 46
(Pat Eddery) *w wnr tl rdn and wknd over 2f out* **13/2**[3]

5 *¾* **Elusive Hawk (IRE)** 3-9-3 **0** TPQueally 5 44
(A P Stringer) *s.i.s: short-lived effrt 3f out* **5/1**[2]

0- **6** *4* **Miss Hoolie**[425] 6015 3-8-5 **0** JackDean(7) 11 28
(W G M Turner) *chsd ldrs: rdn over 3f out: wknd over 2f out* **33/1**

00- **7** *3* **Nanosecond (USA)**[466] 5086 4-9-3 **0** ChrisCatlin 3 25
(N A Callaghan) *outpcd* **16/1**

0500 **8** *shd* **Broad Town Girl**[28] 6858 4-8-6 **38** ow1 KylieManser(7) 6 21
(Mrs H Sweeting) *s.s: a wl bhd* **50/1**

0000 **9** *20* **Bella Grande**[46] 6559 3-8-12 **33** FergusSweeney 2 —
(Garry Moss) *chsd ldrs tl wknd over 3f out: t.o* **66/1**

1m 29.7s (-0.70) **Going Correction** +0.05s/f (Slow) **9** Ran SP% **120.0**
Speed ratings (Par 103): **106,92,91,87,86 81,78,78,55**
CSF £8.33 TOTE £1.80: £1.30, £1.50, £2.50; EX 6.70.
Owner Girsonfield Ltd **Bred** Girsonfield Ltd **Trained** Kingston Warren, Oxon

FOCUS
This moderate maiden turned into a one-horse race but the form is limited by the proximity of the third.

7160 PONTIN'S BOOK EARLY PRICE PROMISE H'CAP 1m 1f 103y(P)
8:55 (8:55) (Class 4) (0-85,85) 3-Y-0+ **£4,857** (£1,445; £722; £360) **Stalls** Low

Form RPR

3111 **1** **Lobengula (IRE)**[15] 6982 5-9-6 **82** DanielTudhope 5 93+
(I W McInnes) *mde all: edgd rt 1f out: sn rdn: r.o* **15/8**[1]

1600 **2** *1 ¼* **Touch Of Style (IRE)**[11] 7018 3-8-9 **73** (p) PatCosgrave 4 79
(J R Boyle) *chsd wnr: rdn over 2f out: lost 2nd wl over 1f out: carried rt ins fnl f: kpt on to take 2nd towards fin* **16/1**

1312 **3** *hd* **Millfield (IRE)**[5] 7094 4-8-6 **68** JimCrowley 6 74
(P R Chamings) *hld up: hdwy over 2f out: chsd wnr wl over 1f out: edgd lft ins fnl f: rdn and lost 2nd towards fin* **7/2**[3]

3356 **4** *5* **Inside Story (IRE)**[11] 7018 5-8-12 **74** (b) DaneO'Neill 2 70
(M W Easterby) *s.i.s: hld up: rdn over 2f out: no rspnse* **9/2**

0433 **5** *4* **Stargazer Jim (FR)**[14] 6995 5-9-2 **78** PaulMulrennan 1 65
(W J Haggas) *prom: rdn over 3f out: wknd over 2f out* **2/1**[2]

2m 1.39s (-1.23) **Going Correction** +0.05s/f (Slow)
WFA 3 from 4yo+ 2lb **5** Ran SP% **114.4**
Speed ratings (Par 105): **107,105,105,101,97**
CSF £27.52 TOTE £3.10: £1.60, £3.20; EX 35.90.
Owner Colin G R Booth **Bred** A S O'Brien And Lars Pearson **Trained** Catwick, E Yorks

FOCUS
A fair handicap which lost some interest due to the withdrawal of Confidentiality but the winner improved again and the form makes sense rated around the placed horses.
Stargazer Jim(FR) Official explanation: jockey said gelding ran flat

7161 GO PONTIN'S HOLIDAYS H'CAP 5f 216y(P)
9:20 (9:23) (Class 5) (0-75,73) 3-Y-0+ **£2,968** (£876; £438) **Stalls** Low

Form RPR

13 **1** **Realt Na Mara (IRE)**[19] 6946 4-8-12 **64** RobertHavlin 3 73
(H Morrison) *sn chsng ldr: hrd rdn over 1f out: r.o to ld cl home* **2/1**[1]

3533 **2** *1* **Methaaly (IRE)**[21] 6938 4-9-2 **68** GeorgeBaker 6 74
(M Mullineaux) *led: rdn over 1f out: hdd cl home* **7/2**[3]

3326 **3** *shd* **Strathmore (IRE)**[11] 7026 3-8-11 **63** (p) TonyHamilton 5 69
(R A Fahey) *hld up: hdwy 2f out: r.o ins fnl f* **8/1**

0001 **4** *nk* **Scarlett Heart (IRE)**[33] 6402 3-8-1 **56** DuranFentiman(3) 1 61
(J G Burns, Ire) *hld up in rr: hdwy on outside wl over 1f out: sn rdn and hung lft: kpt on ins fnl f* **20/1**

3621 **5** *1 ¾* **Royal Challenge**[5] 7105 6-9-7 **73** 6ex DanielTudhope 4 72
(I W McInnes) *hld up: rdn over 1f out: no real prog fnl f* **11/4**[2]

2122 **6** *1 ½* **Brandywell Boy (IRE)**[10] 7033 4-9-3 **69** RichardThomas 2 63
(D J S Ffrench Davis) *hld up in tch: sltly outpcd over 3f out: hdwy on ins wl over 1f out: rdn and wknd ins fnl f* **7/1**

4434 **7** *1 ½* **Jilly Why (IRE)**[7] 7078 6-8-3 **62** (b) AndrewHeffernan(7) 7 52
(Paul Green) *t.k.h: prom: rdn and wknd wl over 1f out* **12/1**

1m 15.31s (-0.50) **Going Correction** +0.05s/f (Slow) **7** Ran SP% **118.3**
Speed ratings (Par 103): **105,103,103,103,100 98,96**
CSF £9.88 CT £46.27 TOTE £3.90: £2.10, £2.70; EX 15.70 Place 6 £ 19.74, Place 5 £ 14.57.
Owner Mrs G C Maxwell & J D N Tillyard **Bred** J C Condon **Trained** East Ilsley, Berks

FOCUS
A competitive little handicap rated around the placed horses and the fifth and the form should prove reliable.
T/Plt: £17.40 to a £1 stake. Pool: £100,295.15. 4,184.95 winning tickets. T/Qpdt: £7.20 to a £1 stake. Pool: £6,021.80. 611.40 winning tickets. KH

7114 KEMPTON (A.W) (R-H)
Sunday, December 16

OFFICIAL GOING: Standard
Wind: moderate, across Weather: sunny and cold

7162 BEAULIEU HOMES MEDIAN AUCTION MAIDEN STKS 5f (P)
1:00 (1:03) (Class 6) 3-5-Y-0 **£2,047** (£604; £302) **Stalls** High

Form RPR

2-02 **1** **Wibbadune (IRE)**[12] 7019 3-8-12 52 LPKeniry 3 50
(Peter Grayson) *mde all: drvn 5l clr over 1f out: being ct fnl 50yds but a holding on: rdn out* **15/8**[1]

-006 **2** *¾* **Earl Compton (IRE)**[4] 7118 3-9-3 50 (bt[1]) MickyFenton 4 52
(Stef Liddiard) *rrd s: bhd: effrt and nt clr run ins fnl 2f: r.o to take 2nd fnl 100yds: clsng at fin but a hld* **6/1**

0034 **3** *1 ¼* **The Carpet Man**[3] 7134 3-9-3 48 RichardKingscote 6 48
(A W Carroll) *in tch: outpcd jst over 2f out: kpt on fnl f* **9/4**[2]

60 **4** *1 ½* **Yurchenko**[208] 1923 3-8-9 0 NeilChalmers(3) 7 37
(M Wellings) *chsd ldrs: wnt 2nd 2f out: outpcd by wnr over 1f out: lost 2nd fnl 100yds* **16/1**

44- **5** *2 ½* **New Spirit (IRE)**[37] 6785 3-8-9 0 JerryO'Dwyer(3) 5 28
(John Joseph Murphy, Ire) *chsd wnr tl 2f out: wknd over 1f out* **5/1**[3]

0000 **6** *½* **Stoneacre Donny (IRE)**[12] 7019 3-9-3 42 AdamKirby 2 32
(Peter Grayson) *wd and sn rdn along: chsd ldrs: hrd rdn 2f out: sn wknd* **28/1**

60.70 secs (0.30) **Going Correction** -0.20s/f (Stan) **6** Ran SP% **105.8**
Speed ratings (Par 101): **89,87,85,83,79 78**
CSF £11.81 TOTE £2.50: £1.10, £2.90; EX 13.50.
Owner Simon Mapletoft Racing I **Bred** Ballyhane Stud **Trained** Formby, Lancs

FOCUS
A weak maiden and a very moderate winning time.

7163 HAVE YOU GOT THE WINNING EDGE H'CAP 1m 2f (P)
1:30 (1:30) (Class 3) (0-95,92) 3-Y-0+
£6,855 (£2,052; £1,026; £513; £256; £128) **Stalls** High

Form RPR

4231 **1** **Evident Pride (USA)**[42] 6669 4-9-6 **88** DaneO'Neill 7 104+
(B R Johnson) *hld up towards rr: hdwy on rails over 2f out: led 1f out: rdn and r.o wl: readily* **6/4**[1]

10 **2** *1 ¼* **Northern Spy (USA)**[51] 6465 3-8-11 **82** PatDobbs 5 90
(S Dow) *stdd s: hld up: hdwy wd and rdn st: r.o appr fnl f: wnt 2nd fnl 75yds* **10/1**

0205 **3** *2* **Awatuki (IRE)**[15] 6995 4-9-0 **82** JohnEgan 3 86
(A P Jarvis) *hld up: rdn and hdwy 4f out: disp 2nd 2f out: one pce* **8/1**

0051 **4** *¾* **Bid For Glory**[15] 6995 3-9-7 **92** (p) RichardHughes 1 95
(H J Collingridge) *sn led: reminder 7f out: hdd and no ex 1f out* **6/1**[3]

0604 **5** *2* **Cupid's Glory**[8] 7075 5-8-13 **81** LPKeniry 8 80
(Mrs L C Jewell) *chsd ldrs tl wknd over 1f out* **16/1**

0042 **6** *2* **Dragon Slayer (IRE)**[8] 7075 5-8-10 **78** GregFairley 4 73
(P A Blockley) *stdd s: t.k.h: hdwy and prom 6f out: wknd jst ins fnl 2f* **12/1**

3303 **7** *1 ½* **Fusili (IRE)**[7] 7086 4-9-5 **87** GeorgeBaker 2 79
(N P Littmoden) *prom tl wknd 3f out* **10/1**

4111 **8** *17* **Abbondanza (IRE)**[9] 7061 4-9-3 **85** (p) PhillipMakin 6 43+
(I Semple) *plld hrd: in tch: crowded and stdd 6f out: wknd qckly over 2f out: eased whn no ch fnl f* **4/1**[2]

2m 4.77s (-4.23) **Going Correction** -0.20s/f (Stan)
WFA 3 from 4yo+ 3lb **8** Ran SP% **117.2**
Speed ratings (Par 107): **108,107,105,104,103 101,100,86**
CSF £18.68 CT £94.67 TOTE £2.30: £1.10, £3.00, £2.50; EX 35.30.
Owner C Lefevre **Bred** Juddmonte Farms Inc **Trained** Ashtead, Surrey

FOCUS
A fair handicap run at a fair gallop and a good time. The winner is progressive at the trip and may be even better than the bare form.

NOTEBOOK
Evident Pride(USA) ◆ was well backed, and looks to be on the upgrade followng this stylish victory. He travelled well, and settled it with a good turn of foot, and appears to be ahead of the Handicapper. (op 2-1)
Northern Spy(USA), patiently ridden from the back, got going too late down the wide outside for his new stable. This was a promising All-Weather debut, with the extra furlong definitely in his favour, and even longer trips now looking an option. (op 12-1 tchd 14-1 in places)
Awatuki(IRE) ran another good race at a track where he has done well in the past, but this inconsistent sort can probably do even better even though he is a little higher in the weights these days.
Bid For Glory, wearing first-time cheekpieces, opted to make the pace over this slightly shorter trip but ended up running himself into the ground. (op 5-1)

Cupid's Glory continues to disappoint, despite his plummeting handicap mark. (tchd 14-1)
Dragon Slayer(IRE), keen - as he often is - folded tamely turning for home. Most of his best form has been on left-handed tracks. (tchd 11-1)
Abbondanza(IRE) paid the penalty for trying to pull his rider's arms off. Official explanation: jockey said gelding ran too free (op 7-2)

7164 BEAULIEU HOMES H'CAP 7f (P)
2:00 (2:00) (Class 5) (0-70,70) 3-Y-0+ **£2,817** (£838; £418; £209) **Stalls** High

Form RPR
6533 **1** **Smokin Joe**[6] 7099 6-9-3 **69**....(b) GeorgeBaker 14 83+
(J R Best) *hld up towards rr: hdwy and n.m.r ins fnl 2f: rdn to ld jst ins fnl f* **7/2**[1]
6400 **2** *2* **Pietersen (IRE)**[10] 7045 3-8-13 **65**....(b) PaulFessey 12 74+
(T D Barron) *sn rdn along towards rr: sme hdwy whn n.m.r over 2f out: styd on wl to take 2nd fnl 50yds* **14/1**
3505 **3** *¾* **Corlough Mountain**[62] 6232 3-9-1 **67**.... JohnEgan 1 74
(M J McGrath) *chsd ldr: led 3f out tl jst ins fnl f: one pce* **25/1**
0600 **4** *hd* **Messiah Garvey**[59] 6278 3-8-8 **60**.... ChrisCatlin 9 66
(M R Channon) *plld hrd early: prom: rdn over 3f out: one pce appr fnl f* **16/1**
0116 **5** *nk* **Jools**[15] 6993 9-8-7 **59**.... HayleyTurner 7 65+
(D K Ivory) *hld up in rr: n.m.r and hdwy 2f out: kpt on fnl f: nvr able to chal* **7/1**
5001 **6** *½* **Dvinsky (USA)**[11] 7033 6-9-4 **70**....(v) TGMcLaughlin 4 74
(P Howling) *chsd ldrs: drvn along over 2f out: one pce appr fnl f* **14/1**
3003 **7** *½* **Takitwo**[12] 7024 4-8-8 **60**.... LPKeniry 10 63
(P D Cundell) *in tch on rails: effrt over 2f out: no imp over 1f out* **9/2**[3]
1160 **8** *1 ¼* **Seneschal**[40] 6710 6-9-1 **67**.... RichardHughes 6 67
(A B Haynes) *wd: hld up in midfield: rdn over 2f out: no imp* **8/1**
5624 **9** *2* **Nicada (IRE)**[10] 7045 3-8-13 **70**.... TolleyDean(5) 2 64
(Stef Liddiard) *hld up in rr of midfield: outpcd over 2f out: n.d after* **4/1**[2]
0012 **10** *1* **Satin Braid**[10] 7047 3-8-10 **69**.... AmyBaker(7) 3 60
(D R C Elsworth) *bhd: rdn and wd st: nvr trbld ldrs* **10/1**
6530 **11** *4* **Swift Cut (IRE)**[15] 6996 3-8-8 **60**.... NeilPollard 5 41
(A P Jarvis) *s.i.s: bhd: rdn and n.d fnl 3f* **33/1**
-050 **12** *nk* **Cape Thea**[13] 7006 3-8-5 **64** ow4....(b1) JackDean(7) 8 44
(Mark Gillard) *mid-div tl wknd over 2f out* **66/1**
6P50 **13** *1 ¼* **Dowlleh**[8] 7073 3-8-12 **69**....(p) KirstyMilczarek(5) 13 45
(T T Clement) *prom tl n.m.r and wknd 2f out* **33/1**
-400 **14** *5* **Racing Stripes (IRE)**[15] 6996 3-8-5 **60**....(b1) NeilChalmers(3) 11 23
(K O Cunningham-Brown) *sn led: hdd 3f out: wknd qckly 2f out* **66/1**

1m 24.84s (-1.96) **Going Correction** -0.20s/f (Stan) **14 Ran SP% 125.0**
Speed ratings (Par 103): **103,100,99,99,99 98,98,96,94,93 88,88,86,81**
CSF £54.55 CT £1123.15 TOTE £5.10: £2.10, £5.30, £6.00; EX 50.70.
Owner G G Racing **Bred** Alan Spargo Ltd **Trained** Hucking, Kent
■ Stewards' Enquiry : Paul Fessey one-day ban: careless riding (Dec 27)

FOCUS
Moderate quality, but a competitive race run at a decent pace and the form looks sound. The winner is gradually getting back to last winter's form.

7165 100% SIGN-UP BONUS AT BETBROKERS POKER H'CAP 1m (P)
2:30 (2:30) (Class 4) (0-85,85) 3-Y-0+ **£4,728** (£1,406; £702; £351) **Stalls** High

Form RPR
6041 **1** **Atlantic Story (USA)**[12] 7017 5-9-3 **83**....(bt1) DaneO'Neill 14 93
(M W Easterby) *hld up in tch: effrt 2f out: led ins fnl f: rdn out: holding runner-up fnl 50yds* **5/2**[1]
1060 **2** *nk* **Apache Dawn**[137] 4080 3-8-13 **80**.... AdamKirby 2 89
(G L Moore) *towards rr: gd hdwy over 1f out: r.o to press wnr ins fnl f: jst hld fnl 50yds* **25/1**
0020 **3** *1 ¾* **Curzon Prince (IRE)**[36] 6753 3-9-0 **81**.... RichardHughes 6 86
(C F Wall) *hld up in midfield: effrt over 2f out: styd on to take 3rd fnl 100yds* **11/2**[2]
3006 **4** *½* **Mataram (USA)**[20] 6949 4-8-13 **79**.... SteveDrowne 13 83
(W Jarvis) *mid-div: rdn to chse ldrs ins fnl 2f: kpt on fnl f* **9/1**
1036 **5** *hd* **Carnivore**[53] 6435 5-9-0 **80**.... PaulFessey 5 83
(T D Barron) *led over 6f out: qcknd tempo and wnt 4l clr 1/2-way: hdd & wknd ins fnl f* **10/1**
2602 **6** *¾* **Dichoh**[42] 6674 4-9-2 **82**.... MatthewHenry 3 84
(M A Jarvis) *sn led at weak pce: hdd over 6f out: prom tl no ex over 1f out* **9/1**
0000 **7** *½* **Lopinot (IRE)**[113] 4827 4-8-6 **79**.... KylieManser(7) 12 79
(M R Bosley) *bhd tl pushed along and styd on fnl 2f: nvr nrr* **66/1**
1340 **8** *shd* **Risque Heights**[15] 6995 3-9-1 **82**.... HayleyTurner 8 82
(G A Butler) *hld up last: sme hdwy 2f out: rdn and styd on: nt rch ldrs* **16/1**
5000 **9** *1* **Precocious Star (IRE)**[29] 6852 3-9-2 **83**.... FergusSweeney 11 81
(K R Burke) *prom tl wknd 2f out* **9/1**
2364 **10** *nk* **Tender The Great (IRE)**[16] 6970 4-9-5 **85**.... GeorgeBaker 10 82
(B G Powell) *hld up in tch: effrt over 2f out: hrd rdn and wknd over 1f out* **13/2**[3]
2300 **11** *5* **Fiefdom (IRE)**[20] 6949 5-9-0 **80**.... DanielTudhope 7 66
(I W McInnes) *in midfield on outside: hrd rdn and wknd 3f out* **10/1**
0600 **12** *1* **Ivory Lace**[22] 6929 6-9-3 **83**.... JimCrowley 9 66
(S Woodman) *bhd: rdn along 1/2-way: nvr nr ldrs* **33/1**
4302 **13** *8* **Danetime Lord (IRE)**[25] 6900 4-8-12 **78**.... ChrisCatlin 4 43
(K A Ryan) *broke wl: chsd ldrs: rdn over 3f out: sn wknd* **14/1**

1m 38.08s (-2.72) **Going Correction** -0.20s/f (Stan)
WFA 3 from 4yo+ 1lb **13 Ran SP% 126.3**
Speed ratings (Par 105): **105,104,102,102,102 101,101,100,99,99 94,93,85**
CSF £82.01 CT £348.91 TOTE £3.60: £2.00, £10.10, £1.70; EX 105.70.
Owner Matthew Green **Bred** A I Appleton **Trained** Sheriff Hutton, N Yorks
■ Stewards' Enquiry : Matthew Henry three-day ban: careless riding (Dec 27-29)

FOCUS
A decent race with an improving winner who can score again. The pace was weak for the first 3f, but Carnivore soon increased the tempo into a good gallop.

7166 BEAULIEU HOMES CHRISTMAS H'CAP (DIV I) 1m (P)
3:00 (3:02) (Class 6) (0-55,55) 3-Y-0+ **£2,047** (£604; £302) **Stalls** High

Form RPR
/600 **1** **Grey Gurkha**[34] 6804 6-9-1 **52**.... DanielTudhope 4 61+
(I W McInnes) *hld up towards rr: n.m.r over 2f out: gd hdwy over 1f out: led ins fnl f: rdn out* **8/1**
0000 **2** *2 ½* **Korty**[129] 4336 3-8-12 **50**.... RichardHughes 12 50
(W J Musson) *hld up in tch on rails: rdn to chse ldr over 1f out: one pce fnl f* **14/1**
0000 **3** *1 ¼* **Trickle (USA)**[15] 7003 3-8-11 **49**....(t) PaulEddery 11 46
(Miss D Mountain) *t.k.h towards rr: hdwy to chse ldrs 3f out: styd on same pce appr fnl f* **33/1**
6040 **4** *½* **Falcon Flyer**[11] 7029 3-8-7 **45**.... JohnEgan 7 41
(J R Best) *bhd: rdn and hdwy fnl 2f: nrst fin* **14/1**
0000 **5** *¾* **Detonate**[26] 6886 5-8-3 **45**.... KirstyMilczarek(5) 3 39
(I A Wood) *sn led: shkn up over 1f out: hdd and no ex ins fnl f* **14/1**
6002 **6** *1* **Perfect Practice**[32] 6809 3-9-1 **53**.... AdamKirby 13 45
(C G Cox) *chsd ldrs: effrt 3f out: wknd over 1f out* **5/4**[1]
0664 **7** *1* **Only If I Laugh**[4] 7124 6-8-8 **45**....(v) LPKeniry 5 35
(M J Attwater) *mid-div: rdn whn n.m.r and lost pl over 2f out: n.d after* **11/1**
0000 **8** *shd* **Piquet**[6] 7094 9-8-5 **45**.... NeilChalmers(3) 9 34
(J J Bridger) *chsd ldrs tl hrd rdn and wknd over 2f out* **16/1**
0402 **9** *nk* **Megalala (IRE)**[33] 6452 6-8-8 **45**.... ChrisCatlin 8 34
(J J Bridger) *in tch on outside tl outpcd fnl 3f* **5/1**[2]
0000 **10** *3 ½* **Compton Express**[64] 6175 4-8-8 **45**.... RobertHavlin 1 26
(Jamie Poulton) *in rr of midfield: outpcd over 2f out: n.d after* **16/1**
0 **11** *¾* **Cami Collins (FR)**[7] 7083 3-9-3 **55**.... GeorgeBaker 6 34
(J R Best) *settled last: sme hdwy on rails over 2f out: sn rdn and btn* **14/1**
0000 **12** *5* **Christalini**[7] 7088 3-9-2 **54**.... PatDobbs 2 21
(J C Fox) *dwlt: sn prom: wknd over 2f out* **8/1**[3]

1m 38.78s (-2.02) **Going Correction** -0.20s/f (Stan)
WFA 3 from 4yo+ 1lb **12 Ran SP% 129.6**
Speed ratings (Par 101): **102,99,98,97,97 96,95,94,94,91 90,85**
CSF £184.37 CT £5440.21 TOTE £15.90: £3.80, £4.10, £8.70; EX 269.10.
Owner Robert E Cook **Bred** R E And Mrs G M Cook **Trained** Catwick, E Yorks

FOCUS
Selling quality at best and hard to be too positive about the form. The gallop was no better than a medium one, but the winning time was just over a second quicker than the second division.
Perfect Practice Official explanation: jockey said filly had no more to give

7167 BEAULIEU HOMES CHRISTMAS H'CAP (DIV II) 1m (P)
3:30 (3:32) (Class 6) (0-55,55) 3-Y-0+ **£2,047** (£604; £302) **Stalls** High

Form RPR
32-5 **1** **My Jeanie (IRE)**[340] 93 3-9-0 **52**.... PatDobbs 6 55
(J C Fox) *hld up in tch: effrt over 2f out: r.o to ld fnl 100yds* **16/1**
0552 **2** *¾* **Simpsons Gamble (IRE)**[35] 6778 4-9-2 **53**.... JimCrowley 3 54
(R A Teal) *led after 1f tl over 4f out: led over 2f out tl fnl 100yds: kpt on* **7/4**[1]
4050 **3** *nk* **Batchworth Blaise**[40] 6706 4-8-10 **47**.... StephenCarson 8 47+
(E A Wheeler) *hld up towards rr: rdn and hdwy 2f out: chsd ldng pair ins fnl f: kpt on* **13/2**[3]
0000 **4** *¾* **Jomus**[18] 6968 6-8-12 **49**.... RobertHavlin 4 48+
(L Montague Hall) *s.i.s and stdd sn after s: hld up in rr: gd hdwy over 1f out: nrst fin* **6/1**[2]
000/ **5** *shd* **Rhuby River (IRE)**[12] 6474 5-8-8 **45**.... MickyFenton 10 43
(R Dickin) *mid-div: rdn 4f out: hdwy fnl 2f: nvr nrr* **50/1**
-000 **6** *1 ½* **Coastal Breeze**[20] 6945 4-8-9 **46** ow1....(b) SteveDrowne 13 41
(A J Chamberlain) *chsd ldng pair tl no ex over 1f out* **20/1**
030 **7** *½* **Bear Bottom**[228] 1398 3-9-3 **55**.... NeilPollard 2 49
(W J Musson) *hld up in midfield: shkn up over 2f out: nvr rchd ldrs* **16/1**
0000 **8** *nk* **My Spring Rose**[39] 6453 3-8-7 **45**.... GregFairley 12 38
(J R Jenkins) *led 1f: led over 4f out tl over 2f out: wknd over 1f out* **16/1**
00-0 **9** *nk* **Lady Firecracker (IRE)**[137] 4078 3-9-1 **53**.... HayleyTurner 7 45
(J R Best) *towards rr: rdn over 2f out: n.d* **16/1**
4-P0 **10** *¾* **Frank's Quest (IRE)**[18] 6968 7-8-1 **45**.... GemmaElford(7) 9 36
(A B Haynes) *in tch on outside: lost pl 3f out: n.d after* **33/1**
2000 **11** *1* **Bollywood (IRE)**[46] 6582 4-8-8 **45**.... ChrisCatlin 5 33
(J J Bridger) *chsd ldrs: drvn along and wknd 3f out* **8/1**
0-00 **12** *nk* **Edward (IRE)**[12] 7014 5-8-8 **45**.... LPKeniry 1 33
(M Madgwick) *stdd s: bhd: sme hdwy on rails 2f out: sn rdn and wknd* **33/1**
-04U **13** *16* **Ma Ridge**[129] 4321 3-9-3 **55**.... JohnEgan 11 6
(T D McCarthy) *t.k.h: chsd ldrs: nt handle bnd and wknd 3f out: eased whn no ch over 1f out* **7/1**

1m 39.85s (-0.95) **Going Correction** -0.20s/f (Stan)
WFA 3 from 4yo+ 1lb **13 Ran SP% 123.7**
Speed ratings (Par 101): **96,95,94,94,94 92,92,91,91,90 89,89,73**
CSF £44.39 CT £219.76 TOTE £14.90: £3.40, £1.50, £2.10; EX 26.30.
Owner Rob Hurst & Rick Kavanagh **Bred** S Connolly **Trained** Collingbourne Ducis, Wilts

FOCUS
Like division one, no more than a selling-quality contest. The early pace looked a bit stronger than the first division, but the winning time was just over a second slower.
Ma Ridge Official explanation: jockey said colt hung left

7168 OPEN AN ACCOUNT AT BETBROKERS.COM H'CAP 1m 4f (P)
4:00 (4:02) (Class 6) (0-50,50) 3-Y-0+ **£2,047** (£604; £302) **Stalls** Centre

Form RPR
/235 **1** **Smokey The Bear**[6] 7098 5-8-9 **48**.... NeilChalmers(3) 6 54+
(Miss Sheena West) *hld up towards rr: gd hdwy on bit to ld over 1f out: rdn clr: readily* **7/2**[1]
0040 **2** *2 ½* **Mid Valley**[30] 6832 4-8-9 **45**.... J-PGuillambert 3 49+
(J R Jenkins) *stdd s: hld up in rr: gd hdwy to press ldrs whn nt clr run over 1f out: swtchd lft: r.o wl to take 2nd on line* **12/1**
0045 **3** *shd* **Henry Holmes**[25] 6896 4-8-12 **48**.... RichardThomas 5 50+
(Mrs L Richards) *chsd ldrs: rdn to chal over 1f out: one pce* **8/1**
-000 **4** *¾* **Only Hope**[54] 6412 3-8-9 **50**....(p) PaulEddery 9 53+
(Miss Diana Weeden) *stdd s: t.k.h in rr of midfield: hdwy to press ldrs whn hmpd over 1f out: rallied and r.o fnl f* **66/1**
5503 **5** *nk* **Mariaverdi**[25] 6896 3-8-9 **50**.... SteveDrowne 4 50
(P G Murphy) *mid-div: rdn to press ldrs 2f out: one pce fnl f* **14/1**
0050 **6** *½* **Ghaill Force**[37] 4259 5-8-9 **45**.... JimCrowley 10 45
(P Butler) *s.s: bhd: rdn over 2f out: nrst fin* **25/1**
0502 **7** *¾* **Forfeiter (USA)**[7] 7083 5-8-6 **49**.... JemmaMarshall(7) 11 47
(C Gordon) *led tl over 1f out: no ex fnl f: eased whn btn fnl 50yds* **5/1**[3]
0-00 **8** *3* **Dawn Mystery**[46] 6597 3-8-9 **50**.... MickyFenton 2 44
(Rae Guest) *in tch tl hrd rdn and btn 2f out* **5/1**[3]
0005 **9** *3* **Storm Path (IRE)**[18] 6969 3-8-5 **46**.... HayleyTurner 1 35
(D R C Elsworth) *chsd ldrs: rdn 4f out: wknd 3f out* **9/2**[2]
0 **10** *¾* **Deimne (IRE)**[12] 7012 4-8-9 **48** ow3.... JerryO'Dwyer(3) 7 36
(John Joseph Murphy, Ire) *chsd ldrs tl hrd rdn and wknd over 2f out* **16/1**
0100 **11** *9* **Smoothie (IRE)**[247] 1026 9-8-10 **46**.... PaulFitzsimons 12 19
(E G Bevan) *stdd s: hld up in rr of midfield: hrd rdn over 2f out: sn bhd* **25/1**

24 12 1 3/4 **Wishes Or Watches (IRE)**[24] 6697 7-8-11 **47**....................(b) LPKeniry 8 17
(John A Quinn, Ire) *pressed ldr tl wknd over 2f out* **12/1**

2m 33.26s (-3.64) **Going Correction** -0.20s/f (Stan)
WFA 3 from 4yo+ 5lb **12** Ran SP% **122.0**
Speed ratings (Par 101): **104,102,102,101,101 101,100,98,96,96 90,89**
CSF £48.04 CT £324.54 TOTE £4.40: £1.90, £4.10, £3.50; EX 57.10 Place 6 £239.23, Place 5 £127.06..
Owner Graham Flight **Bred** A P Jones **Trained** Falmer, E Sussex

FOCUS
The overall form is probably poor despite a solid winning time, but the winner is unexposed over the trip and may be capable of more.
Wishes Or Watches(IRE) Official explanation: jockey said gelding ran too free
T/Jkpt: Part won. £52,827.50 to a £1 stake. Pool: £74,405.00. 0.50 winning tickets. T/Plt: £693.00 to a £1 stake. Pool: £101,067.80. 106.45 winning tickets. T/Qpdt: £1,326.60 to a £1 stake. Pool: £5,916.30. 3.30 winning tickets. LM

7156 WOLVERHAMPTON (A.W) (L-H)

Monday, December 17

OFFICIAL GOING: Standard to slow
Wind: Moderate against Weather: Fine and cold

7169 PONTIN'S BOOK EARLY PRICE PROMISE H'CAP 1m 141y(P)
1:10 (1:10) (Class 6) (0-52,51) 3-Y-0+ **£2,047** (£604; £302) **Stalls** Low

Form RPR

0053 1 **Beck**[2] 7159 3-8-3 **45**.. DuranFentiman(3) 9 52+
(W M Brisbourne) *hld up in tch: led wl over 1f out: sn rdn: drvn out* **9/2**[1]

0465 2 1 1/4 **Komreyev Star**[35] 6804 5-8-8 **45**.................................. PaulMulrennan 6 49
(R E Peacock) *chsd ldrs: led over 3f out: rdn and hdd over 1f out: no ex wl ins fnl f* **9/2**[1]

6-00 3 3 **Blakeshall Hope**[9] 7079 5-8-8 **45**................................ DeanMcKeown 4 42
(A J Chamberlain) *hld up in mid-div: hdwy over 3f out: rdn and one pce fnl 2f* **20/1**

0050 4 1 **Wizby**[35] 6792 4-8-8 **45**.. StephenDonohoe 7 40
(P D Evans) *hld up in rr: rdn and hdwy over 2f out: one pce fnl f* **16/1**

0400 5 nk **Mister Benji**[143] 3922 8-8-13 **50**.................................... PhillipMakin 11 44
(B P J Baugh) *hld up towards rr: rdn and hdwy over 2f out: one pce fnl f* **11/1**

-001 6 3/4 **Ai Hawa (IRE)**[12] 7034 4-8-7 **47**...............................(b) JerryO'Dwyer(3) 1 42+
(Eamon Tyrrell, Ire) *hld up towards rr: rdn and hdwy whn hung lft over 1f out: one pce fnl f* **11/2**[2]

6000 7 5 **Keon (IRE)**[17] 6979 5-8-9 **51**...........................(p) RussellKennemore(5) 5 32
(R Hollinshead) *hld up towards rr: hdwy 3f out: rdn wl over 1f out: wknd ent fnl f* **8/1**[3]

3600 8 3/4 **Homecroft Boy**[33] 6815 3-8-2 **48** ow3...................(v) RichardEvans(7) 12 27
(P D Evans) *hld up and bhd: swtchd lft sn after s: nvr nr ldrs* **22/1**

0653 9 1/2 **Almora Guru**[16] 7001 3-8-12 **51**.. LiamJones 2 29
(W M Brisbourne) *hld up towards rr: rdn and hdwy over 2f out: wknd 1f out* **8/1**[3]

5000 10 4 **Susiedil (IRE)**[7] 4249 6-8-8 **45**................................(b[1]) PaulFessey 8 14
(S T Mason) *sn w ldr: rdn and wknd over 2f out* **33/1**

0400 11 1 3/4 **Welsh Whisper**[10] 7057 8-8-8 **45**................................... ChrisCatlin 3 10
(S A Brookshaw) *hld up in mid-div: pushed along over 5f out: bhd fnl 3f* **20/1**

0306 12 2 **Smart Pick**[9] 7079 4-8-4 **46**.................................(b[1]) TolleyDean(5) 13 6
(Mrs L Williamson) *s.i.s: sn prom: n.m.r on ins 3f out: sn wknd* **12/1**

0000 13 2 **Glenargo (USA)**[21] 5368 4-8-3 **45**...................... DanielleMcCreery(5) 10 —
(S T Lewis) *led: hdd over 3f out: rdn and wknd 2f out* **80/1**

1m 52.91s (1.15) **Going Correction** +0.225s/f (Slow)
WFA 3 from 4yo+ 2lb **13** Ran SP% **113.9**
Speed ratings (Par 101): **103,101,99,98,98 97,92,92,91,88 86,84,83**
CSF £20.77 CT £362.98 TOTE £5.90: £2.50, £1.40, £8.20; EX 31.00 Trifecta £145.00 Part won. Pool £204.31 - 0.10 winning units.
Owner Steve Roberts **Bred** The Duke Of Devonshire **Trained** Great Ness, Shropshire

FOCUS
An open-looking modest affair which his best summed up by the fact that eight of the runners were carrying more than their handicap marks because they were rated less than 45. The pace was sound and the form could be rated higher but has been treated with caution.

7170 PONTIN'S SHORT BREAKS MAIDEN AUCTION STKS 5f 20y(P)
1:45 (1:45) (Class 6) 2-Y-0 **£2,047** (£604; £302) **Stalls** Low

Form RPR

003 1 **Super Tuscan (IRE)**[16] 6990 2-8-13 65.............................. TPQueally 3 71
(J G Given) *trckd ldrs: rdn and edgd rt ins fnl f: led towards fin: r.o* **7/2**[2]

3242 2 1 **Firewalker**[4] 7129 2-8-4 67.. ChrisCatlin 5 58
(B Smart) *sn led: rdn over 1f out: hdd and nt qckn towards fin* **10/11**[1]

0033 3 4 **Lambrini Lace (IRE)**[33] 6813 2-8-11 62.............................. LiamJones 4 51
(Mrs L Williamson) *led early: prom: wkng whn edgd rt 1f out* **9/2**[3]

0000 4 1 **Westwood Dawn**[17] 6980 2-8-10 33............................ DuranFentiman(3) 1 49?
(Mrs N Macauley) *s.i.s: hdwy on outside over 2f out: c wd st: hung lft fr over 1f out: nt run on* **100/1**

005 5 3/4 **Seductive Witch**[54] 6425 2-8-6 58.................................. SaleemGolam 2 39
(M D I Usher) *bhd: effrt whn hung lft over 1f out: swtchd rt ins fnl f: n.d* **16/1**

0243 6 1 1/2 **Jastaanhi**[140] 4026 2-8-1 57.. AndrewElliott(3) 6 32
(J A Pickering) *prom: wkng whn edgd rt jst over 1f out* **8/1**

64.22 secs (1.40) **Going Correction** +0.225s/f (Slow) **6** Ran SP% **110.8**
Speed ratings (Par 94): **97,95,89,87,86 83**
CSF £6.89 TOTE £4.10: £1.90, £1.40; EX 6.60.
Owner Hintlesham Racing **Bred** J & J Waldron **Trained** Willoughton, Lincs

FOCUS
A weak contest.

NOTEBOOK
Super Tuscan(IRE), who had hung badly left at Kempton last time, eventually got the better of a good battle with the favourite. (tchd 4-1)
Firewalker had run a very similar race in defeat over 6f here last time. (tchd 5-6 and evens in places)
Lambrini Lace(IRE) failed to progress on turf and seems to have gone the same way on sand. (op 6-1)
Westwood Dawn, an habitual poor starter, was again without the visor and did not look very co-operative on his first try over the minimum distance.

7171 DOWDING & MILLS CHRISTMAS CELEBRATION (S) STKS 5f 216y(P)
2:15 (2:15) (Class 6) 2-Y-0 **£2,047** (£604; £302) **Stalls** Low

Form RPR

3614 1 **Valhillen**[13] 7021 2-9-3 60.. PatCosgrave 9 63
(M J Wallace) *led 1f: w ldr: led 2f out: hrd rdn fnl f: r.o* **3/1**[2]

0063 2 1 1/2 **Tommytush (IRE)**[13] 7021 2-8-12 57..........................(t) DeanMcKeown 2 54
(E J Alston) *led after 1f: rdn over 1f out: no ex wl ins fnl f* **9/4**[1]

5002 3 1 1/2 **Just Mossie**[7] 7096 2-8-5 39......................................(p) JackDean(7) 4 49
(W G M Turner) *s.i.s: outpcd: rdn and hdwy over 1f out: kpt on ins fnl f* **6/1**

5563 4 shd **Desert Life (IRE)**[7] 7096 2-8-12 60...............................(p) ChrisCatlin 7 49
(R A Harris) *bhd: rdn and hdwy over 2f out: kpt on ins fnl f* **5/1**[3]

4000 5 2 **Bahamarama (IRE)**[13] 7021 2-8-12 55..................... StephenDonohoe 1 43
(R A Harris) *s.i.s: outpcd: swtchd rt over 2f out: c wd st: hdwy and edgd lft over 1f out: one pce fnl f* **12/1**

4064 6 1 **Chemise (IRE)**[7] 7096 2-8-7 46.. LiamJones 3 35
(R J Hodges) *prom: lost pl over 3f out: n.d after* **12/1**

2600 7 1/2 **Imaginemysurprise**[12] 7031 2-8-7 54.................................. LPKeniry 6 33
(J A Geake) *chsd ldrs: rdn and wknd over 2f out* **10/1**

400 8 5 **Silver Deal**[102] 5176 2-8-4 43................................ DuranFentiman(3) 8 18
(J A Pickering) *prom: rdn over 2f out: sn wknd* **40/1**

1m 18.3s (2.49) **Going Correction** +0.225s/f (Slow) **8** Ran SP% **113.6**
Speed ratings (Par 94): **92,90,88,87,85 83,83,76**
CSF £10.04 TOTE £3.70: £1.50, £1.40, £1.60; EX 10.60 Trifecta £19.20 Pool £313.59 - 11.59 winning units..There was no bid for the winner
Owner Andy Viner **Bred** Lady Hardy **Trained** Newmarket, Suffolk

FOCUS
The form of this seller looks solid and could be rated a little higher.

NOTEBOOK
Valhillen showed the right sort of attitude under his penalty for winning a weak maiden over 5f here last month. (op 11-4)
Tommytush(IRE) was a pound better off than when two lengths behind the winner over the minimum distance here last month. (op 10-3 tchd 7-2)
Just Mossie, tried in cheekpieces, just snatched third place and again shaped as though he requires a longer trip. (tchd 11-2 and 13-2)
Desert Life(IRE) had finished a length behind Just Mossie in a similar event at Lingfield last week. (tchd 9-2 and 13-2)
Bahamarama(IRE) has not progressed since changing hands for 12,000 guineas after landing a 5f seller here at the end of August. Official explanation: jockey said filly moved poorly (tchd 10-1 and 14-1)
Chemise(IRE) Official explanation: jockey said filly hung left throughout

7172 GO PONTIN'S HOLIDAYS H'CAP 1m 5f 194y(P)
2:45 (2:46) (Class 6) (0-55,53) 3-Y-0+ **£2,047** (£604; £302) **Stalls** Low

Form RPR

635 1 **Little Richard (IRE)**[27] 6883 8-9-4 **53**............................(p) AdamKirby 3 61
(M Wellings) *a.p: led wl over 1f out: drvn out* **9/2**[3]

0060 2 3/4 **Winter Cruise (IRE)**[17] 6979 3-8-6 **48**.............................. ChrisCatlin 7 55
(Ian Williams) *hld up in mid-div: hdwy over 3f out: rdn wl over 1f out: styng on whn edgd lft cl home* **11/1**

3442 3 1 **Squirtle (IRE)**[9] 7081 4-8-11 **46**.. LiamJones 1 52+
(W M Brisbourne) *dwlt: hld up in rr: rdn and hdwy over 2f out: styd on wl towards fin* **9/2**[3]

0422 4 hd **Haatmey**[13] 7012 5-9-4 **53**...(v) LPKeniry 10 58
(P R Chamings) *sn chsng ldr: led 3f out: rdn and hdd wl over 1f out: edgd rt ins fnl f: nt qckn* **11/4**[1]

6103 5 3/4 **Ronsard (IRE)**[3] 7135 5-8-9 **51**................................... RichardEvans(7) 9 56+
(P D Evans) *s.i.s: hld up towards rr: nt clr run 3f out: hdwy over 1f out: no ex ins fnl f* **7/2**[2]

1045 6 5 **Birthday Star (IRE)**[33] 6815 5-8-13 **53**...........(p) RussellKennemore(5) 2 50
(A G Juckes) *hld up towards rr: rdn whn pce qcknd 4f out: nvr trbld ldrs* **10/1**

04-5 7 1 **Sorbiesharry (IRE)**[3] 7135 8-8-7 **45**........................ DuranFentiman(3) 8 41
(Mrs N Macauley) *hld up in mid-div: rdn over 2f out: sn struggling* **25/1**

0004 8 1 3/4 **Reminiscent (IRE)**[199] 2222 8-9-2 **51**........................(p) PaulMulrennan 11 44
(B P J Baugh) *hld up in tch: rdn and wknd wl over 1f out* **20/1**

000 9 6 **Mustakhlas (USA)**[169] 2434 6-8-10 **45**................................ PaulEddery 5 30
(B P J Baugh) *set slow pce: qcknd 4f out: hdd 3f out: sn rdn: wknd 2f out* **22/1**

3m 11.68s (4.31) **Going Correction** +0.225s/f (Slow)
WFA 3 from 4yo+ 7lb **9** Ran SP% **115.6**
Speed ratings (Par 101): **96,95,95,94,94 91,91,90,86**
CSF £50.51 CT £235.58 TOTE £5.40: £1.60, £3.30, £1.80; EX 60.20 Trifecta £236.70 Pool £333.44 - 1.00 winning unit..
Owner Mark Wellings Racing **Bred** Rathbarry Stud **Trained** Six Ashes, Shropshire
■ Stewards' Enquiry : Chris Catlin one-day ban: careless riding (Dec 28)

FOCUS
The tempo finally quickened at the half-mile pole in this slowly-run low-grade staying handicap and the form, rated through the fourth, is not that solid.

7173 PONTINS.COM H'CAP 1m 1f 103y(P)
3:15 (3:15) (Class 5) (0-75,72) 3-Y-0+ **£2,968** (£876; £438) **Stalls** Low

Form RPR

4555 1 **Scamperdale**[102] 5178 5-9-6 **72**.. TPQueally 3 81+
(B P J Baugh) *wnt rt and bmpd s: hld up: swtchd rt and hdwy over 1f out: hung lft and led wl ins fnl f: r.o wl* **8/1**

606V 2 2 **Kingsholm**[7] 7100 5-9-3 **69**....................................... DanielTudhope 4 74
(I W McInnes) *hmpd s: hld up: hdwy over 2f out: rdn over 1f out: kpt on ins fnl f* **7/2**[2]

4204 3 nk **Evita**[11] 7046 3-8-7 **66**..(b[1]) AshleyHamblett(5) 5 70
(L M Cumani) *wnt lft s: hld up in tch: led over 2f out: rdn over 1f out: hdd and no ex wl ins fnl f* **13/2**

0 4 3 **Manathon (FR)**[102] 5178 4-9-2 **68**................................... RobertHavlin 1 66
(A E Jones) *chsd ldr to 3f out: sn rdn: wknd fnl f* **14/1**

0620 5 1/2 **Speagle (IRE)**[11] 7046 5-8-13 **65**............................... DeanMcKeown 2 62
(A J Chamberlain) *prom: lost pl on ins over 3f out: n.d after* **20/1**

3105 6 shd **Kansas Gold**[17] 6982 4-8-12 **64**................................ PaulMulrennan 7 60
(J Mackie) *set stdy pce: qcknd 4f out: hdd over 2f out: wknd over 1f out* **5/1**[3]

3221 **7** 1 1/4 **Rigat**[14] 7009 4-8-11 **63** .... PhillipMakin 6 57
(T D Barron) *t.k.h: stdy hdwy over 5f out: outpcd over 3f out: rallied on outside and hung rt over 2f out: wknd wl over 1f out* **6/4**[1]

2m 7.67s (5.05) **Going Correction** +0.225s/f (Slow)
WFA 3 from 4yo+ 2lb 7 Ran SP% **114.8**
Speed ratings (Par 103): **86,84,83,81,80 80,79**
CSF £36.23 TOTE £6.70: £2.90, £2.60; EX 45.00.
Owner Saddle Up Racing **Bred** Mrs J A Prescott **Trained** Audley, Staffs

FOCUS
A very slow winning time for a race of its class which developed into something of a sprint in the last half-mile. The third sets the standard but the time was slow.

7174 PONTINSBINGO.COM MAIDEN STKS 1m 1f 103y(P)
3:45 (3:48) (Class 5) 3-Y-0+ **£2,968** (£876; £438) **Stalls** Low

Form RPR
40-0 **1** **Pelican Waters (IRE)**[31] 6843 3-8-12 0 .... TPQueally 6 81+
(E F Vaughan) *hld up in tch: led wl over 1f out: drew clr fnl f: easily* **6/5**[1]
044 **2** 9 **Granary**[96] 5335 3-8-12 60 .... DaneO'Neill 1 62
(H Candy) *led: rdn and hdd wl over 1f out: no ch w wnr* **15/2**
2504 **3** 1 1/2 **Saviour Sand (IRE)**[17] 6975 3-9-3 72 .... LPKeniry 10 64
(D R C Elsworth) *a.p: rdn and one pce fnl 2f* **11/2**[3]
0 **4** 1 3/4 **Flight Dream (FR)**[37] 6766 4-9-0 0 .... JamieJones(5) 8 60+
(M G Quinlan) *wnt lft and stdd s: hld up and bhd: styd on fnl 2f: n.d* **11/4**[2]
0-0 **5** 17 **Me No Puppet**[251] 991 3-8-12 0 .... DavidAllan 9 19
(E J Alston) *hld up towards rr: hdwy over 4f out: rdn and wknd over 4f out* **66/1**
5430 **6** 1/2 **Far Seeking**[13] 7025 3-9-3 60 .... ChrisCatlin 5 23
(R A Harris) *chsd ldr tl rdn and wknd over 2f out* **16/1**
7 10 **Hayley's Pearl**[207] 8-9-0 0 .... GregFairley 3 —
(Mrs P Ford) *s.s: a in rr* **150/1**
8 9 **Tewkesbury (IRE)** 3-9-3 0 .... VinceSlattery 2 —
(Mrs K Waldron) *s.i.s: sn mid-div: bhd fnl 5f* **66/1**
60/3 **9** 3/4 **Blackbury**[3] 7144 5-9-0 0 .... TGMcLaughlin 7 —
(W M Brisbourne) *prom early: hld up in mid-div: rdn 4f out: sn bhd* **20/1**
00/ **10** 17 **Capricorn Red**[18] 4200 7-8-9 0 .... RussellKennemore(5) 4 —
(R Hollinshead) *hld up in tch: rdn over 5f out: wknd over 4f out: t.o* **150/1**

2m 3.45s (0.83) **Going Correction** +0.225s/f (Slow)
WFA 3 from 4yo+ 2lb 10 Ran SP% **114.2**
Speed ratings (Par 103): **105,97,95,94,79 78,69,61,61,45**
CSF £10.10 TOTE £2.20: £1.10, £1.70, £1.40; EX 10.90 TRIFECTA Pool £333.81 - 14.87 winning units. Place 6 £36.24, Place 5 £17.54..
Owner Michael M Sammon **Bred** J M Ryan **Trained** Newmarket, Suffolk

FOCUS
This moderate maiden turned into a one-horse race and the form appears sound rated around the placed horses.
T/Plt: £27.90 to a £1 stake. Pool: £64,183.65. 1,677.35 winning tickets. T/Qpdt: £12.30 to a £1 stake. Pool: £5,160.00. 310.30 winning tickets. KH

7148 SOUTHWELL (L-H)
Tuesday, December 18

OFFICIAL GOING: Standard to slow
Wind: Nil Weather: Overcast

7175 GO PONTIN'S HOLIDAYS CLAIMING STKS 1m 3f (F)
12:40 (12:40) (Class 6) 3-Y-0+ **£2,047** (£604; £302) **Stalls** Low

Form RPR
6126 **1** **St Savarin (FR)**[17] 6994 6-9-4 94 .... JamieMoriarty(3) 4 83+
(R A Fahey) *trckd ldr: smooth hdwy over 2f out: led on bit wl over 1f out: pushed clr ent fnl f* **2/5**[1]
2600 **2** 3 **Yakimov (USA)**[18] 6981 8-9-6 84 .... VinceSlattery 1 72
(D J Wintle) *trckd ldrs: hdwy on outer over 2f out: rdn to chse wnr over 1f out: sn drvn and one pce* **14/1**
6505 **3** 3/4 **Global Traffic**[9] 6673 3-8-10 64 ....(v[1]) StephenDonohoe 5 64
(P D Evans) *hld up in rr: hdwy over 4f out: rdn along to chse ldrs 2f out: kpt on u.p ins fnl f* **18/1**
0316 **4** 2 1/2 **Sweet World**[64] 6235 3-8-11 64 .... AndrewElliott(3) 2 64
(A P Jarvis) *led: rdn along 3f out: drvn and hdd wl over 1f out: sn wknd* **9/1**[3]
0005 **5** 33 **Bailieborough (IRE)**[17] 7002 8-9-7 73 .... DanielTudhope 3 11
(N Wilson) *hld up in rr: effrt over 4f out: sn rdn along and wknd* **8/1**[2]
0410 **6** 38 **Lady Romanov (IRE)**[51] 3243 4-8-10 74 .... PatrickMathers(3) 6 —
(D G Bridgwater) *chsd ldrs: pushed along 1/2-way: sn rdn and wknd wl over 4f out* **20/1**

2m 29.65s (0.75) **Going Correction** +0.175s/f (Slow)
WFA 3 from 4yo+ 4lb 6 Ran SP% **109.2**
Speed ratings (Par 101): **104,101,101,99,75 47**
CSF £6.81 TOTE £1.40: £1.30, £3.30; EX 4.10.The winner was claimed by B. R. Johnson for £15,000. Bailieborough (IRE) was claimed by Brian Ellison for £15,000.
Owner J H Tattersall **Bred** F W Holtkotter **Trained** Musley Bank, N Yorks

FOCUS
A claimer in which the winner stood out on official ratings and the fourth may prove to be the best guide to the form.

7176 SOUTHWELL-RACECOURSE.CO.UK NURSERY 7f (F)
1:10 (1:10) (Class 6) (0-65,65) 2-Y-0 **£2,047** (£604; £302) **Stalls** Low

Form RPR
4300 **1** **Especially (IRE)**[48] 6584 2-9-6 **64** .... GregFairley 6 67
(M Johnston) *chsd ldrs: hdwy over 2f out: rdn to ld over 1f out: drvn ins fnl f and kpt on wl* **5/1**[2]
6356 **2** 1 1/4 **Natural Rhythm (IRE)**[3] 7149 2-9-7 **65** .... DanielTudhope 5 65
(D W Chapman) *sn rdn along and outpcd in rr: gd hdwy on outer over 2f out: rdn to chal over 1f out and ev ch tl drvn and nt qckn fnl 100yds* **5/1**[2]
1000 **3** 1/2 **Ballycroy Boy (IRE)**[135] 4193 2-9-2 **63** .... NeilChalmers(3) 1 62
(A Bailey) *wnt bdly rt s: in tch on inner: smooth hdwy over 2f out: chal over 1f out and ev ch tl rdn: edgd lft and one pce ins fnl f* **8/1**
000 **4** 5 **Twilight Belle (IRE)**[15] 7007 2-8-10 **54** ow1 ....(b) PhillipMakin 9 40
(K R Burke) *sn led: rdn over 2f out: drvn and hdd over 1f out: grad wknd* **15/2**[3]
0060 **5** 1 1/4 **Rock Me (IRE)**[37] 6775 2-8-1 **45** ....(b) JamieMackay 2 28
(N A Callaghan) *hmpd s: sn in tch: rdn along over 2f out and no imp* **8/1**
050 **6** 3/4 **Tobouggornotobougg**[31] 6855 2-8-8 **52** .... DeanMcKeown 3 33
(D Shaw) *bdly hmpd s and bhd: rdn along 1/2-way: hdwy on inner 2f out: sn no imp* **10/1**
5000 **7** 1 **Laureldean Breeze (USA)**[14] 7022 2-8-1 **45** ....(b[1]) DaleGibson 8 24
(R A Fahey) *sn rdn along and a towards rr* **20/1**
0036 **8** 2 1/2 **Galley Slave (IRE)**[7] 7106 2-8-11 **60** .... RussellKennemore(5) 7 32
(M C Chapman) *in tch: rdn along 3f out and sn wknd* **20/1**
0632 **9** 4 **Splash The Cash**[44] 6665 2-9-6 **64** .... ChrisCatlin 10 26
(K A Ryan) *cl up: effrt over 2f out: sn rdn and ev ch tl edgd lft wl over 1f out and sn wknd* **3/1**[1]
6004 **10** 3 1/2 **Howe's Jack (IRE)**[6] 7122 2-7-12 **45** .... DominicFox(3) 4 —
(M C Chapman) *chsd ldrs: rdn along 3f out and sn wknd* **66/1**

1m 33.13s (2.33) **Going Correction** +0.175s/f (Slow) **10** Ran SP% **112.4**
Speed ratings (Par 94): **93,91,91,85,83 83,81,79,74,70**
CSF £28.29 CT £199.32 TOTE £6.20: £2.10, £1.60, £2.50; EX 26.30 Trifecta £171.20 Pool: £330.48, 1.37 winning units.
Owner Sheikh Mohammed **Bred** Darley **Trained** Middleham Moor, N Yorks

FOCUS
A moderate nursery but a good finish. Especially went on near the quarter-mile pole and battled on well to hold off Natural Rhythm and Ballycroy Boy, who challenged on either side of her. The form looks solid enough without being exceptional.

NOTEBOOK
Especially(IRE), disappointing in two runs on Polytrack after showing promise on turf, went on near the quarter-mile pole and battled on well to hold off the placed horses who challenged on either side of her. She is not very big, but she showed the right attitude and is likely to be kept on the go, having shown a liking for this surface. (op 7-2)
Natural Rhythm(IRE) broke better than on his previous run here, but got outpaced and was last of all at halfway. However, he picked up well to challenge in the straight, only to find the winner too resolute. (op 13-2 tchd 9-2)
Ballycroy Boy(IRE), a winner over the minimum trip here in the spring, went sharply right from the stalls and gave Rock Me a bump. He travelled well into the race and had every chance, but did not look that keen under pressure. (op 10-1)
Twilight Belle(IRE), runner-up to a decent sort at a respectful distance here at the last meeting before the floods in early June when trained by Brian Meehan, showed plenty of pace but was soon left behind when the principals joined issue. (op 12-1)
Rock Me(IRE) did not run badly after getting involved in the early scrimmaging, travelling well turning in before fading. (op 9-1)
Tobouggornotobougg was another to run with credit after suffering in the early mayhem, staying on up the inside rail in the straight. (op 15-2 tchd 11-1)
Splash The Cash, who had shown ability in four runs on the Lingfield Polytrack, showed up well early but dropped out disappointingly in the last quarter-mile. (op 5-2 tchd 9-4)
Howe's Jack(IRE) Official explanation: jockey said gelding hung right throughout

7177 PONTINS.COM (S) STKS 7f (F)
1:40 (1:45) (Class 6) 2-Y-0 **£2,047** (£604; £302) **Stalls** Low

Form RPR
450 **1** **Autumn Charm**[22] 6948 2-8-6 60 .... GregFairley 6 59
(W Jarvis) *trckd ldrs: hdwy and ev ch wl over 1f out: sn rdn: drvn ins fnl f: styd on to ld nr line* **10/3**[2]
5046 **2** hd **Her Name Is Rio (IRE)**[13] 7030 2-8-4 64 ow3 .... TolleyDean(5) 4 62
(J S Moore) *cl up: rdn 2f out: led over 1f out: drvn and edgd lft ins fnl f: hdd and no ex nr line* **5/2**[1]
4020 **3** 3 1/2 **Lord Deevert**[43] 6693 2-8-9 65 ....(p) JackDean(7) 7 60
(W G M Turner) *cl up on outer: hdwy to ld narrowly wl over 1f out: sn hdd: rdn and hung lft: one pce ent fnl f* **10/3**[2]
006 **4** 2 **Nothing To Add**[108] 5033 2-8-11 45 ....(b[1]) ChrisCatlin 1 50
(K A Ryan) *sn rdn along on inner: drvn and lost pl 1/2-way: sn in rr* **7/2**[3]
0360 **5** 35 **Gaitskell**[14] 7022 2-8-11 57 ....(e[1]) DeanMcKeown 2 —
(R Hollinshead) *sn led: rdn along over 2f out: sn hdd & wknd* **8/1**

1m 33.07s (2.27) **Going Correction** +0.175s/f (Slow) 5 Ran SP% **108.1**
Speed ratings (Par 94): **94,93,89,87,47**
CSF £11.51 TOTE £4.70: £2.50, £1.60; EX 12.10.The winner was sold to D W Chapman for 4,100gns
Owner The All Seasons Partnership **Bred** Brick Kiln Farming **Trained** Newmarket, Suffolk

FOCUS
A modest juvenile seller run fractionally faster than the earlier nursery. Despite the lack of numbers this was an open betting heat and produced a good finish but the form looks shaky.

NOTEBOOK
Autumn Charm, rated 4lb inferior to Her Name Is Rio, was helped by the drop in grade and the surface seemed to suit as she wore down her rival near the line, the pair finishing clear. (op 11-4 tchd 7-2)
Her Name Is Rio(IRE) also seemed to appreciate the Fibresand but was just outstayed and the 3lb overweight put up by her rider made the difference. She looks capable of picking up a similar race back here. (tchd 3-1)
Lord Deevert had already won a claimer and a seller on Polytrack and had the same chance as the winner judged on official ratings and taking the fillies' allowance into account, but he was well beaten on his first try on this surface. (op 7-2 tchd 3-1)
Nothing To Add had a lot to find judged on official ratings, but was fitted with blinkers for the first time on this drop in grade and was well backed. However, supporters knew their fate early as he was being ridden along leaving the back straight and, although keeping on, never got competitive. (op 7-1 tchd 3-1)
Gaitskell made the running in the first time eyeshield, but dropped right away in the straight. Official explanation: jockey said colt had a breathing problem (op 5-1)

7178 PONTINSBINGO.COM H'CAP 2m (F)
2:10 (2:16) (Class 5) (0-75,69) 3-Y-0+ **£2,968** (£876; £438) **Stalls** Low

Form RPR
0321 **1** **Victory Quest (IRE)**[3] 7154 7-9-9 **61** 6ex ....(v) ChrisCatlin 6 73
(Mrs S Lamyman) *trckd ldr: hdwy to ld over 4f out: rdn over 2f out: styd on strly appr fnl f* **5/2**[3]
0012 **2** 3 **Three Boars**[4] 7135 5-10-0 **66** 6ex ....(b) PaulMulrennan 4 74
(S Gollings) *trckd ldrs: hdwy to trck wnr 4f out: shkn up wl over 2f out: sn rdn and one pce fr wl over 1f out* **9/4**[2]
-210 **3** 2 1/2 **Hora**[59] 6341 3-8-9 **55** .... JamieMackay 1 60
(Sir Mark Prescott) *led: rdn along and hdd over 4f out: drvn along wl over 2f out: kpt on same pce* **2/1**[1]
0040 **4** 10 **Moon Emperor**[14] 7012 10-9-1 **53** ....(b) LiamJones 2 46
(J R Jenkins) *chsd ldrs: rdn along 4f out and sn wknd* **22/1**
2300 **5** 16 **Mister Completely (IRE)**[46] 6622 6-10-0 **66** .... JamesDoyle 3 40
(Ms J S Doyle) *in rr: reminders 1/2-way and sn rdn along: sme hdwy 4f out: sn drvn and btn* **12/1**
3000 **6** 1 1/4 **Letham Island (IRE)**[26] 4542 3-9-9 **69** .... AdamKirby 5 42
(R M Stronge) *trckd ldrs on outer: reminders 1/2-way: rdn along 6f out: sn wknd and bhd fnl 4f* **16/1**

3m 46.96s (2.42) **Going Correction** +0.175s/f (Slow)
WFA 3 from 5yo+ 8lb 6 Ran SP% **110.6**
Speed ratings (Par 103): **100,98,97,92,84 83**
CSF £8.28 TOTE £3.60: £2.10, £1.10; EX 9.80.
Owner P Lamyman **Bred** Miss Veronica Henley **Trained** Ruckland, Lincs

The Form Book, Raceform Ltd, Compton, RG20 6NL

FOCUS
A staying handicap featuring several regulars in this type of contest with the winner rated back to his best.
Mister Completely(IRE) Official explanation: jockey said gelding never travelled

7179 PONTIN'S BOOK EARLY H'CAP 5f (F)
2:40 (2:46) (Class 4) (0-85,85) 3-Y-0+ **£4,728** (£1,406; £702; £351) **Stalls** High

Form RPR
2600 **1** **Count Cougar (USA)**[24] 6938 7-8-5 72 ChrisCatlin 2 82
(S P Griffiths) *chsd ldng pair: pushed along 1/2-way: rdn wl over 1f out: styd on ins fnl f to ld last 100yds* **7/2**[3]
0013 **2** ¾ **Tartatartufata**[10] 7078 5-8-6 73 (v) DeanMcKeown 5 80
(D Shaw) *cl up: led 1 1/2f out: rdn ent fnl f: hdd and no ex last 100yds* **11/4**[1]
202 **3** *shd* **Pawan (IRE)**[7] 7112 7-8-6 78 (b) AnnStokell(5) 4 85
(Miss A Stokell) *chsd ldrs: rdn along and outpcd 1/2-way: styd on u.p ins fnl f: nrst fin* **10/3**[2]
2010 **4** 2 **Proud Killer**[64] 6239 4-8-4 71 oh4 (v[1]) LiamJones 7 71
(J R Jenkins) *blind removed late and s.i.s: bhd tl styd on appr fnl f: nvr a factor* **10/1**
1004 **5** 2 **Godfrey Street**[7] 7112 4-8-10 82 (b) NataliaGemelova(5) 3 75
(K A Ryan) *led: rdn along 2f out: hdd 1 1/2f out and sn wknd* **11/4**[1]
61.12 secs (0.82) **Going Correction** +0.30s/f (Slow) **5** Ran SP% **107.7**
Speed ratings (Par 105): **105,103,103,100,97**
CSF £12.75 TOTE £4.90: £2.40, £1.80; EX 13.60.
Owner M Grant **Bred** Angus Glen Farm (1996) Ltd **Trained** Easingwold, N Yorks
FOCUS
A fair sprint despite the non-runners and the form looks solid rated around the placed horses.

7180 PONTIN'S BOOK EARLY PRICE PROMISE H'CAP 7f (F)
3:10 (3:15) (Class 6) (0-65,64) 3-Y-0+ **£2,968** (£876; £438) **Stalls** Low

Form RPR
-545 **1** **Kensington (IRE)**[10] 7073 6-8-13 55 (p) StephenDonohoe 6 64
(P D Evans) *hld up: hdwy wl over 2f out: rdn to ld 1 1/2f out: drvn ent fnl f: hld on gamely towards fin* **5/1**[2]
0311 **2** ½ **Dasheena**[7] 7113 4-9-5 64 6ex (be) PatrickMathers(3) 2 72
(A J McCabe) *in tch: pushed along 3f out: hdwy over 2f out: chal over 1f out: sn drvn and ev ch tl no ex last 50yds* **11/10**[1]
0346 **3** 2½ **Run Free**[11] 7056 3-9-4 60 DanielTudhope 1 61
(N Wilson) *chsd ldrs on inner: hdwy 2f out: sn rdn and ev ch tl drvn and one pce appr fnl f* **15/2**
040- **4** 1¼ **Pauline's Prince**[442] 5740 5-8-13 60 RussellKennemore(5) 7 58
(R Hollinshead) *t.k.h: cl up: led over 2f out: rdn and hdd 1 1/2f out: grad wknd* **15/2**
5300 **5** 1¼ **Swift Cut (IRE)**[2] 7164 3-9-1 60 (v[1]) AndrewElliott(3) 3 54
(A P Jarvis) *led: rdn along 3f out: hdd over 2f out: drvn and wknd wl over 1f out* **28/1**
0000 **6** 2 **Imperial Sword**[53] 6467 4-9-3 59 PhillipMakin 8 48
(T D Barron) *chsd ldrs on outer: rdn along 3f out: drvn 2f out and sn btn* **11/2**[3]
1004 **7** 9 **Paddywack (IRE)**[8] 7105 10-8-10 57 (b) DanielleMcCreery(5) 5 22
(D W Chapman) *s.i.s: a in rr* **25/1**
1m 31.75s (0.95) **Going Correction** +0.175s/f (Slow) **7** Ran SP% **110.5**
Speed ratings (Par 101): **101,100,97,96,94 92,82**
CSF £10.16 CT £36.52 TOTE £6.30: £3.30, £1.10; EX 11.00 Trifecta £141.80 Pool: £667.10 - 3.34 winning units. Place 6 £ 21.25, Place 5 £ 17.25.
Owner Derek Buckley **Bred** Mountarmstrong Stud **Trained** Pandy, Monmouths
■ Stewards' Enquiry : Stephen Donohoe two-day ban: used whip with excessive frequency (Dec 29-30)
Patrick Mathers two-day ban: used whip with excessive frequency (Dec 29-30)
FOCUS
A modest handicap that was run 1.32 seconds faster than the two earlier juvenile races over the trip. The form looks sound and could rate higher in time.
T/Plt: £19.50 to a £1 stake. Pool: £55,092.70. 2,053.85 winning tickets. T/Qpdt: £5.00 to a £1 stake. Pool: £5,185.80. 757.80 winning tickets. JR

7162 KEMPTON (A.W) (R-H)
Wednesday, December 19
OFFICIAL GOING: Standard
Wind: Light, half behind Weather: Clear, cold

7181 EUROPEAN BREEDERS' FUND MEDIAN AUCTION MAIDEN STKS 1m (P)
6:20 (6:22) (Class 6) 2-Y-0 **£2,388** (£705; £352) **Stalls** High

Form RPR
023 **1** **Fair Gale**[11] 7070 2-9-3 73 RichardHughes 5 71
(S Kirk) *chsd ldr after 2f: pushed along 1/2-way: rdn to ld narrowly wl over 1f out: in command whn edgd rt fnl f* **7/4**[2]
2 **2** 1½ **Seattle Storm (IRE)**[12] 7051 2-9-3 0 LPKeniry 2 68
(D R C Elsworth) *led after 1f: rdn jst over 2f out: hdd wl over 1f out: hld whn n.m.r and swtchd lft ins fnl f* **4/5**[1]
3 6 **Henry James (IRE)**[121] 4680 2-9-3 0 JohnEgan 6 55
(M Botti) *hld up in rr: rdn and prog over 3f out to chse ldng pair over 2f out: no imp after* **14/1**
4 3½ **Hiss And Boo** 2-9-3 0 (b[1]) J-PGuillambert 3 47
(P Howling) *led 1f: restrained: green and hanging over 2f out: wknd* **40/1**
5 5 **Walton House (USA)** 2-9-0 0 NeilChalmers(3) 4 36
(A M Balding) *s.s: in tch 5f: wknd* **12/1**[3]
6 5 **Toballa** 2-8-12 0 (t) TPQueally 1 20
(H J Collingridge) *s.s: t.k.h and hld up in tch: wknd 3f out* **20/1**
1m 40.66s (-0.14) **Going Correction** -0.125s/f (Stan) **6** Ran SP% **113.5**
Speed ratings (Par 94): **95,93,87,84,79 74**
CSF £3.53 TOTE £2.80: £1.30, £1.10; EX 3.90.
Owner Norman Ormiston **Bred** Hesmonds Stud Ltd **Trained** Upper Lambourn, Berks
■ Stewards' Enquiry : Richard Hughes caution: careless riding
FOCUS
The first two are streets ahead of the rest in the terms of potential, so it would not a be a surprise to see this have a lop-sided looks to it, form wise, in the future.
NOTEBOOK
Fair Gale overhauled the long-time leader over a furlong out after taking a while to get on top. Well regarded at home, he had not had the best of luck in his races before this victory, and it might be that he turns out to be a little better than his official rating. (op 2-1 tchd 13-8)
Seattle Storm(IRE), a promising second on his Lingfield debut, contributed to his own defeat here, as he raced freely in front, and so, not surprisingly, was limited in what he could produce under pressure. Described by his trainer as "wild", he clearly has some maturing to do, but once everything clicks he might well prove himself to be quite useful. (tchd 10-11 and evens in a place)
Henry James(IRE), making his British bow after three uninspiring starts in Ireland, improved greatly on his final two outings. That said, he was still beaten a long way by the runner-up, and is clearly nothing more than moderate. (op 16-1)
Hiss And Boo, wearing blinkers on his racecourse debut, was not completely disgraced and will find his level in time. (op 33-1)
Walton House(USA) Official explanation: jockey said gelding missed the break
Toballa wore a tongue tie on her racecourse debut and did not show a great deal. (tchd 25-1)

7182 DIGIBET SPORTS BETTING NURSERY 7f (P)
6:50 (6:53) (Class 6) (0-60,60) 2-Y-0 **£2,047** (£604; £302) **Stalls** High

Form RPR
4030 **1** **Kamal**[13] 7042 2-9-7 60 HayleyTurner 1 64
(W R Muir) *stdd s and dropped in fr wd draw: hld up in last pair and plld hrd early: rapid prog on inner over 2f out: led over 1f out: sn clr: hung lft but kpt on* **16/1**
5603 **2** 1¼ **Alabama Spirit (USA)**[13] 7042 2-9-6 59 DeanMcKeown 14 60
(D Shaw) *taken down early: t.k.h and hld up towards rr: prog on inner 1/2-way: upsides over 1f out: chsd wnr after: urged along and kpt on* **11/2**[2]
60U3 **3** *shd* **Ile Royale**[7] 7117 2-8-5 49 (be) NicolPolli(5) 7 50
(C N Allen) *s.s: t.k.h and hld up in rr: prog whn nt clr run and swtchd to outer over 2f out: hdwy over 1f out: styd on fnl f* **7/1**
0000 **4** 2 **In Decorum**[35] 6812 2-8-1 45 (v) KirstyMilczarek(5) 10 41
(J A Geake) *t.k.h early: hld up towards rr: prog 2f out: chsd ldrs 1f out: one pce fnl f* **66/1**
6400 **5** ¾ **Lella Beya**[14] 7031 2-9-6 59 RichardHughes 12 53
(S Kirk) *chsd ldrs: rdn and cl up over 1f out: fdd fnl f* **9/1**
000 **6** ¾ **Viola Rosa (IRE)**[136] 4192 2-8-11 50 DaneO'Neill 11 42
(D Shaw) *hld up towards rr: reminder over 2f out: shuffled along and kpt on steadily fnl 2f: nvr nr ldrs* **20/1**
620 **7** 1¾ **Little Finch (IRE)**[9] 7096 2-8-8 50 (b) DuranFentiman(3) 4 38
(R C Guest) *led at str pce to wl over 1f out: wknd fnl f* **33/1**
0500 **8** ½ **Ten Spot (IRE)**[7] 7117 2-9-3 56 (v) TPQueally 8 42
(Stef Liddiard) *chsd ldrs: rdn over 3f out: lost pl over 2f out: n.d after* **10/1**
0330 **9** ½ **Ramblin Bob**[19] 6978 2-9-0 60 DebraEngland(7) 2 45
(W J Musson) *t.k.h: sn chsd ldr: upsides wl over 1f out: pushed along and sn wknd* **14/1**
0204 **10** ¾ **Too Grand**[14] 7031 2-9-3 59 (v) NeilChalmers(3) 5 42
(J J Bridger) *t.k.h: cl up: rdn sn after 1/2-way: struggling over 2f out* **5/1**[1]
0163 **11** 1 **Lady Bower**[22] 6958 2-9-6 59 AdamKirby 13 40
(J Ryan) *trckd ldng pair: narrow ld briefly wl over 1f out: sn wknd* **8/1**
6503 **12** 3½ **Ambrose Princess (IRE)**[5] 7136 2-9-4 57 LPKeniry 6 29
(R A Harris) *rrd s: sn trckd ldrs: wd and losing pl bnd 3f out: sn btn* **6/1**[3]
0500 **13** ¾ **Aim**[14] 7031 2-9-3 56 JimCrowley 3 26
(J R Jenkins) *racd wd in midfield: struggling fr wl over 2f out* **10/1**
000 **14** 2½ **Up The Wycombe**[68] 6138 2-8-13 52 (b[1]) JohnEgan 9 16
(S Dow) *s.s: t.k.h and hld up in last pair: wknd over 2f out* **16/1**
1m 27.2s (0.40) **Going Correction** -0.125s/f (Stan) **14** Ran SP% **125.8**
Speed ratings (Par 94): **92,90,90,88,87 86,84,83,83,82 81,77,76,73**
CSF £104.69 CT £715.93 TOTE £25.90: £6.90, £1.50, £2.70; EX 69.00.
Owner C L A Edginton **Bred** Coln Valley Stud **Trained** Lambourn, Berks
FOCUS
A low-grade contest won in good style by the winner. The form is probably sound for the grade, although the winning time was only moderate.
NOTEBOOK
Kamal defied top weight and the outside draw to score. He was helped by a very strong pace and quickened well to hit the front. If anything, he got to the lead sooner than his rider would have wanted. Claimed out of a Wolverhampton race last month, he has had plenty of niggles, but his new trainer went through a similar scenario with half-brother Texas Gold, and Kamal could end up a good bit better than the 60 rating he ran off here.
Alabama Spirit(USA) came from off the pace, but she never looked likely to overhaul the winner. Nevertheless, this was a most solid effort. (op 5-1)
Ile Royale found herself with nowhere to go early in the straight. She lost all momentum when stopped, which means her staying-on third was very respectable. She has had plenty of chances but will surely win at some point (op 8-1)
In Decorum showed more than in any of her previous races to plug on into fourth.
Lella Beya came here as the least exposed runner in the field, and she emerges from the race as perhaps one to note, as she caught the eye mid-pack being given what looked a considerate ride. She is better than her bare form indicates and could pop up at a big price beforelong. (op 14-1)
Viola Rosa(IRE) Official explanation: jockey said filly hung left
Little Finch(IRE) was not beaten that far despite setting off at a strong pace. (op 25-1)
Up The Wycombe Official explanation: jockey said blinkers became loose in running

7183 DIGIBET H'CAP 6f (P)
7:20 (7:22) (Class 6) (0-65,65) 3-Y-0+ **£2,047** (£604; £302) **Stalls** High

Form RPR
3261 **1** **Rabbit Fighter (IRE)**[7] 7119 3-9-4 65 6ex (v) PaulMulrennan 9 76+
(D Shaw) *trckd ldrs: effrt on inner and nt clr run jst over 2f out: swtchd lft and prog to chse ldr ins fnl f: styd on wl to ld last strides* **8/11**[1]
0146 **2** *nk* **Rhapsilian**[25] 6925 3-8-9 56 SteveDrowne 8 66
(J A Geake) *trckd ldrs: prog 2f out to ld over 1f out: styd on: collared last strides* **20/1**
201 **3** 1 **Strabinios King**[15] 7020 3-8-13 60 ChrisCatlin 10 67
(R A Harris) *plld hrd and hld up in rr: prog fr 1/2-way: eased to outer fr 2f out: r.o fnl f: nrst fin* **13/2**[2]
555 **4** ½ **Desert Light (IRE)**[26] 6910 6-8-11 58 (v) J-PGuillambert 7 63
(D Shaw) *plld hrd early: hld up in last trio and wl off the pce: prog on wd outside fr over 2f out: styd on: nrst fin* **25/1**
5046 **5** *nk* **Hucking Hope (IRE)**[7] 7119 3-9-0 61 JohnEgan 1 65
(J R Best) *chsd ldrs: rdn and nt qckn over 2f out: kpt on fr over 1f out: nvr able to chal* **28/1**
0301 **6** *nk* **No Time (IRE)**[12] 7054 7-8-13 63 PatrickMathers(3) 12 66
(A J McCabe) *prom: disp 2nd 2f out: fdd over 1f out* **14/1**
1542 **7** *nk* **Willhewiz**[7] 7119 7-9-0 61 (v) FergusSweeney 11 63
(M S Saunders) *led to over 1f out: wknd and lost several pls last 100yds* **8/1**[3]
5016 **8** 2 **Monashee Prince (IRE)**[30] 6870 5-9-2 63 (v) GeorgeBaker 5 59
(J R Best) *awkward s: nvr bttr than midfield: no imp on ldrs 2f out: fdd* **12/1**
0025 **9** 2 **Imperium**[18] 6993 6-8-12 59 (b) DaneO'Neill 6 48
(Jean-Rene Auvray) *dwlt: hld up in last pair: a bhd* **14/1**
0401 **10** 2½ **Green Lagonda (AUS)**[11] 7077 5-9-2 63 JimCrowley 2 44
(J G Given) *mostly chsd ldr to 2f out: wknd* **16/1**

52 11 ¾ **Kadouchski (FR)**[18] 6991 3-9-4 65 .... DeanMcKeown 4 44
(Miss E C Lavelle) *dwlt: hld up in last trio and sn off wl off the pce: a bhd* **33/1**

1m 11.68s (-2.02) **Going Correction** -0.125s/f (Stan) 11 Ran SP% **124.3**
Speed ratings (Par 101): **108,107,106,105,105 104,104,101,99,95 94**
CSF £24.91 CT £72.00 TOTE £1.80: £1.30, £3.70, £2.80; EX 32.20.
Owner Market Avenue Racing Club Ltd **Bred** Hawthorn Villa Stud **Trained** Danethorpe, Notts
■ Stewards' Enquiry : Fergus Sweeney two-day ban: careless riding (Dec 30-31)

FOCUS
A competitive sprint run at a solid pace. The form looks reliable with the four immediately behind the principals close to recent form.
Hucking Hope(IRE) Official explanation: jockey said filly hung right

7184 DIGIBET.COM SUNBURY STKS (LISTED RACE) 7f (P)
7:50 (7:53) (Class 1) 3-Y-O+
£14,762 (£5,595; £2,800; £1,396; £699; £351) Stalls High

Form RPR
614 1 **Bonus (IRE)**[25] 6930 7-9-2 104 .... HayleyTurner 1 96+
(G A Butler) *wnt lft s: hld up and dropped in last fr wd draw: gd prog gng strly over 2f out: led over 1f out: hrd rdn fnl f: all out* **7/1**[3]
1513 2 nk **Carcinetto (IRE)**[19] 6981 5-8-11 81 .... TGMcLaughlin 10 90
(P D Evans) *prom: effrt to chal over 1f out: chsd wnr after: clsd last 100yds: jst hld* **33/1**
4114 3 1 ¾ **Councellor (FR)**[11] 7074 5-9-2 90 ....(t) TPQueally 7 90
(Stef Liddiard) *led after 3f: drvn and hdd over 1f out: hld on for 3rd nr fin* **8/1**
0220 4 nk **Bahiano (IRE)**[12] 7053 6-9-2 87 .... LiamJones 13 89
(C E Brittain) *hld up: hmpd against rail after 2f: rdn and prog on inner 2f out: kpt on fnl f: unable to chal* **8/1**
0043 5 shd **Chicken Soup**[14] 7037 5-9-2 98 ....(e[1]) RichardHughes 3 89
(D J Murphy) *dwlt: hld up in rr: rdn over 2f out: kpt on fnl 2f: nvr pce to threaten ldrs* **8/1**
3026 6 nk **Regal Quest (IRE)**[25] 6929 3-8-11 78 ....(t) J-PGuillambert 2 83
(S C Williams) *hld up in last pair: rdn over 2f out: styd on fr over 1f out: nt rch ldrs* **33/1**
1101 7 ¾ **Capricorn Run (USA)**[25] 6932 4-9-2 106 ....(v) SteveDrowne 11 86
(A J McCabe) *s.s: had to work hrd to rch midfield after 3f: u.p and struggling over 2f out* **7/4**[1]
005 8 1 ¼ **Secret Night**[19] 6970 4-8-11 84 .... JohnEgan 12 78
(J A R Toller) *hld up in midfield: prog to press ldrs 2f out: wknd over 1f out* **33/1**
2321 9 1 **Red Blossom**[9] 7103 3-8-11 67 ....(b) JamieMackay 9 75
(Sir Mark Prescott) *wl in tch: prog and cl up 2f out: fdd tamely over 1f out* **16/1**
0-05 10 shd **Big Timer (USA)**[86] 5673 3-9-2 100 .... PhillipMakin 6 80
(I Semple) *reluctant to enter stalls: chsd ldrs: wd bnd 3f out and lost grnd: steadily wknd fnl 2f* **13/2**[2]
5034 11 1 ¼ **Andronikos**[12] 7053 5-9-2 89 ....(t) LPKeniry 4 76
(P F I Cole) *in tch in midfield: rdn and wknd 2f out* **14/1**
3000 12 11 **Mimisel**[25] 6940 3-8-11 90 .... ChrisCatlin 8 42
(Rae Guest) *dwlt: nvr on terms: bhd fnl 2f* **50/1**
2-0 13 19 **Taita (GER)**[47] 3-8-11 92 .... AdamKirby 5 —
(C G Cox) *led 3f: sn wknd rapidly: t.o* **66/1**

1m 24.27s (-2.53) **Going Correction** -0.125s/f (Stan) 13 Ran SP% **120.4**
Speed ratings (Par 111): **109,108,106,106,106 105,105,103,102,102 100,88,66**
CSF £229.55 TOTE £7.50: £2.00, £12.70, £2.80; EX 310.50.
Owner The Bonus Partnership **Bred** A Stroud & J Hanly **Trained** Blewbury, Oxon

FOCUS
Not a strong contest for the first running of this Listed race, although three of them were rated over 100, and ordinary form for the grade.

NOTEBOOK
Bonus(IRE) was given a great ride by Hayley Turner, who had to steer him from a stall-one start. He actually got to the front too soon, but given how fast he scythed through the field there was nothing that could be done to avoid that. One of only three members of the field holding a three-figure mark, he was much too classy for his rivals, and he will remain a force in the better sand races. There is Listed race over 6f at Lingfield February that would be an ideal target for him next. (op 11-2)
Carcinetto(IRE), five times a Wolverhampton handicap winner this year, posted a personal best to take second. Never far off the lead, she battled on all the way to the line and, by finishing second, greatly enhanced her paddock value.
Councellor(FR) made most of the running and was another who exceeded his previous best. (op 12-1)
Bahiano(IRE) was badly hampered leaving the back straight and did particularly well to stay on into fourth. However, he finds it almost impossible to win, and is not one to follow blindly next time. (op 16-1)
Chicken Soup, in a first-time eyeshield, finished better than most but was never quite getting there. (op 10-1)
Regal Quest(IRE) was far from disgraced but will have to hope the Handicapper does not take this form too literally, or she could get a hefty rise in the weights.
Capricorn Run(USA), having his first taste of Kempton after a successful time around Lingfield, has a high official mark but had not been tried in anything like this sort of company since his days with Godolphin - all his previous form for current connections had come in handicaps. He did not seem up to this grade and will find things fairly difficult unless a return to Lingfield seriously improves his form again. Official explanation: jockey said gelding missed the break (tchd 15-8)
Big Timer(USA), a Group 3-winning juvenile last year, was reluctant to lead and then showed little in the race itself, not helping his own cause by taking a very wide route around the bend. (op 9-2)

7185 DIGIBET CASINO MEDIAN AUCTION MAIDEN STKS 1m 3f (P)
8:20 (8:25) (Class 6) 3-5-Y-O
£2,047 (£604; £302) Stalls High

Form RPR
4252 1 **Auntie Mame**[35] 6807 3-8-12 54 .... TPQueally 2 44
(D J Coakley) *hld up bhd ldrs: prog over 2f out: led over 1f out: idled and sn jnd: hrd rdn to assert last 150yds* **9/4**[1]
0445 2 ½ **Verbatim**[18] 6991 3-8-9 55 ....(v[1]) NeilChalmers(3) 7 43
(A M Balding) *prom: lost pl 6f out: plld out and effrt over 2f out: limited prog tl styd on wl fnl f to take 2nd nr fin* **7/2**[3]
0050 3 nk **Rollin 'n Tumblin**[28] 6896 3-8-12 46 .... KirstyMilczarek(5) 3 48
(W Jarvis) *t.k.h: hld up tl prog to trck ldr 6f out: rdn and nt qckn over 2f out: styd on again ins fnl f* **5/1**
0005 4 nk **Big Ralph**[11] 7069 4-9-7 42 .... JimCrowley 8 47
(D K Ivory) *cl up: pushed along 4f out: drvn and effrt to join wnr 1f out: sn hld: wknd nr fin* **7/1**
5 ½ **Amical Risks (FR)**[248] 3-9-3 65 .... NeilPollard 4 46
(W J Musson) *cl up: effrt to ld over 3f out: rdn and hdd over 1f out: nt qckn* **10/3**[2]
40 6 nk **Cyril The Squirrel**[27] 6904 3-9-3 0 .... ChrisCatlin 6 46
(Karen George) *t.k.h: hld up in last trio: rdn on wd outside over 2f out: plugged on fr over 1f out: nvr able to chal* **20/1**
0060 7 8 **Haydock Express (IRE)**[251] 1008 3-9-3 44 .... LPKeniry 5 32
(Peter Grayson) *a in last trio: struggling 3f out: bhd after* **40/1**
0000 8 18 **Elmasong**[9] 7094 3-8-12 43 .... DaneO'Neill 1 —
(J J Bridger) *mde most to over 3f out: wknd rapidly: t.o* **50/1**

2m 22.7s (0.02) **Going Correction** -0.125s/f (Stan)
WFA 3 from 4yo 4lb 8 Ran SP% **114.4**
Speed ratings (Par 101): **94,93,93,93,92 92,86,73**
CSF £10.15 TOTE £3.20: £1.30, £1.50, £2.10; EX 8.70.
Owner Finders Keepers Partnership **Bred** Eclipse-Rogers Partnership **Trained** West Ilsley, Berks

FOCUS
An ordinary maiden run in a moderate winning time and the form looks very moderate.

7186 TFM NETWORKS H'CAP 1m 3f (P)
8:50 (8:55) (Class 6) (0-60,60) 3-Y-O+
£1,326 (£1,326; £302) Stalls High

Form RPR
0365 1 **Sir Haydn**[10] 7083 7-9-6 58 ....(v) J-PGuillambert 4 66
(J R Jenkins) *hld up towards rr: prog on inner to chse ldr wl over 1f out: sustained chal fnl f: forced dead-heat last stride* **14/1**
6053 1 dht **Noah Jameel**[95] 5421 5-8-9 47 .... FergusSweeney 8 55
(A G Newcombe) *trckd ldrs: prog to ld over 2f out: hrd pressed fr over 1f out: jnd on line* **5/1**[2]
4455 3 1 ¼ **Wee Charlie Castle (IRE)**[49] 6577 4-9-2 54 .... JimCrowley 9 60
(G C H Chung) *dwlt: hld up wl in rr: smooth prog to chse ldng pair over 1f out: kpt on but no imp fnl f* **8/1**
4560 4 3 **Beech Games**[79] 5865 3-9-0 56 .... TGMcLaughlin 11 57
(F Jordan) *hld up in rr: effrt on inner over 2f out: limited prog and no imp on ldrs* **50/1**
0-00 5 ¾ **Mujobliged (IRE)**[63] 6268 4-8-8 46 oh1 .... JohnEgan 2 46
(J R Best) *t.k.h: hld up in last: pushed along and prog fr 3f out: no imp on ldrs over 1f out* **50/1**
0-00 6 3 **Otaki (IRE)**[337] 149 3-8-4 46 oh1 .... JamieMackay 10 40
(Sir Mark Prescott) *t.k.h: prom: chsd ldr over 3f out: upsides over 2f out: sn wknd* **7/1**
005 7 1 **Ruwain**[32] 6858 3-8-8 50 .... TPQueally 3 43
(W J Musson) *hld up in midfield: gng wl enough 3f out: asked for effrt over 2f out and no rspnse* **3/1**[1]
5562 8 1 ¼ **Fantasy Ride**[30] 6871 5-9-7 59 .... RobertHavlin 6 50
(J Pearce) *trckd ldrs tl wknd fr 2f out* **3/1**[1]
0621 9 5 **Hatch A Plan (IRE)**[30] 6867 6-9-5 60 .... NeilChalmers(3) 7 42
(Mouse Hamilton-Fairley) *hld up in rr and racd wd: effrt over 2f out: sn rdn and wknd* **13/2**[3]
0000 10 hd **Hey Presto**[10] 7088 7-8-8 46 oh1 .... ChrisCatlin 1 28
(R Rowe) *chsd ldr to over 3f out: steadily wknd* **50/1**
0610 11 1 ¼ **Sagunt (GER)**[20] 6780 4-9-8 60 .... PaulDoe 5 40
(S Curran) *led to over 2f out: wknd rapidly* **33/1**

2m 20.49s (-2.19) **Going Correction** -0.125s/f (Stan)
WFA 3 from 4yo+ 4lb 11 Ran SP% **119.1**
Speed ratings (Par 101): **102,102,101,98,98 96,95,94,90,90 89**
WIN: Sir Haydn £6.00, Noah Jameel £3.80; PL: SH £2.80, NJ £2.40, WCC £2.90; EX: SH £40.80, NJ £48.40; CSF: SH £41.17, NJ £35.64; TRICAST: SH £303.52, NJ £275.61.
Owner Alan Sowle **Bred** D Leggate, Miss N Kent & Helshaw Grange Stud **Trained** Royston, Herts
Owner S Langridge **Bred** Michael Ng **Trained** Yarnscombe, Devon

FOCUS
Modest but sound form rated around the third to his recent best.
Mujobliged(IRE) Official explanation: jockey said gelding ran too free

7187 BARRETTSTOWN STUD H'CAP 1m 4f (P)
9:20 (9:22) (Class 6) (0-55,55) 3-Y-O+
£2,047 (£604; £302) Stalls Centre

Form RPR
4000 1 **Royal Premier (IRE)**[26] 6911 4-9-1 55 ....(v) JerryO'Dwyer(3) 1 61
(H J Collingridge) *pressed ldr in slowly run r: led over 3f out: drvn clr over 2f out: edgd lft but unchal* **8/1**
5504 2 1 ¼ **Whaxaar (IRE)**[18] 6991 3-8-13 55 .... RobertHavlin 4 59+
(R Ingram) *stdd s: t.k.h and hld up towards rr: prog over 2f out: nt clr run briefly 1f out: got through to take 2nd nr fin* **8/1**
0631 3 nk **Oasis Sun (IRE)**[21] 6969 4-9-2 53 ....(b) JohnEgan 3 57
(J R Best) *trckd ldrs: rdn over 3f out: disp 2nd over 2f out to over 1f out: kpt on* **3/1**[2]
0402 4 ½ **Mid Valley**[3] 7168 4-8-9 46 oh1 .... J-PGuillambert 2 49
(J R Jenkins) *stdd s: hld up in last pair: outpcd fr 3f out: styd on fnl 2f on outer: n.d to wnr* **5/1**[3]
56-2 5 hd **Dishdasha (IRE)**[11] 7069 5-9-4 55 .... GeorgeBaker 8 58
(Mrs A M Thorpe) *stdd s: smmoth prog to chse wnr over 2f out: sn rdn and nt qckn: lost pls wl ins fnl f* **15/8**[1]
1514 6 1 ¼ **Summer Bounty**[21] 6969 11-9-4 55 .... LPKeniry 10 56
(F Jordan) *stdd s: hld up in midfield: smooth prog over 2f out: rdn and nt qckn sn after* **14/1**
0500 7 6 **Certifiable**[21] 6969 6-8-9 51 .... RobynBrisland(5) 6 42
(Miss Z C Davison) *plld hrd: hld up in midfield: outpcd fr over 2f out* **33/1**
4003 8 ¾ **History Prize (IRE)**[35] 6815 4-8-11 48 .... DaneO'Neill 5 38
(A G Newcombe) *hld up in rr: outpcd wl over 2f out: no hdwy after* **16/1**
0066 9 7 **Sadler's Hill (IRE)**[14] 7032 3-8-4 46 oh1 .... HayleyTurner 9 25
(M J McGrath) *led at stdy pce: hdd over 3f out: wknd over 2f out* **40/1**
3506 10 ¾ **The Mighty Ogmore**[11] 7069 3-8-1 46 oh1 ....(p) DuranFentiman(3) 7 24
(R C Guest) *a last: lost tch and struggling 3f out* **33/1**

2m 34.62s (-2.28) **Going Correction** -0.125s/f (Stan)
WFA 3 from 4yo+ 5lb 10 Ran SP% **119.5**
Speed ratings (Par 101): **102,101,100,100,100 99,95,95,90,90**
CSF £70.95 CT £239.05 TOTE £10.10: £2.60, £2.70, £1.50; EX 108.60 Place 6 £102.53, Place 5 £95.37.
Owner Maynard Durrant Partnership I **Bred** Mrs Anne Hughes **Trained** Exning, Suffolk

FOCUS
Not a bad race for the grade, but it was most unsatisfactory, in that the early pace was sedate. It has been rated around the winner to his All-Weather mark and the third to her latest win.
T/Plt: £130.50 to a £1 stake. Pool: £80,443.45. 449.70 winning tickets. T/Qpdt: £32.70 to a £1 stake. Pool: £6,366.20. 143.70 winning tickets. JN

[7094]LINGFIELD (L-H)

Wednesday, December 19

OFFICIAL GOING: Standard

Wind: Very modest, against Weather: bright after a frosty start

7188 PONTIN'S BOOK EARLY AND SAVE H'CAP (DIV I) 6f (P)

12:10 (12:13) (Class 6) (0-55,55) 3-Y-0+ £1,943 (£578; £288; £144) Stalls Low

Form RPR

2132 1 **Grand Palace (IRE)**[8] 7107 4-9-0 55.........................(v) DeanMcKeown 6 65+
(D Shaw) *a gng wl: hld up wl in tch: hdwy 2f out: led 1f out: r.o wl* 11/4[2]

6400 2 *nk* **Arfinnit (IRE)**[15] 7013 6-8-11 52.........................(v) GregFairley 4 61
(Mrs A L M King) *s.i.s: sn in midfield: hdwy on inner 2f out: swtchd lft over 1f out: pressed wnr fnl f: a hld* 20/1

0003 3 *1 1/2* **Regal Royale**[7] 7118 4-8-13 54......................... LPKeniry 1 58
(Peter Grayson) *trckd ldrs: rdn and effrt over 1f out: kpt on same pce ins fnl f* 13/2[3]

3200 4 *3/4* **Sir Loin**[10] 7082 6-8-5 51.........................(v) DanielleMcCreery(5) 2 53
(P Burgoyne) *led: rdn and edgd rt over 1f out: hdd 1f out: outpcd ins fnl f* 20/1

0600 5 *1/2* **Blushing Russian (IRE)**[16] 7005 5-7-13 47 oh1 ow1(p) PietroRomeo(7) 8 47
(J M Bradley) *stdd after s: hld up and bhd: rdn and hdwy on inner 2f out: kpt on fnl f: nt pce to rch ldrs* 50/1

5466 6 *shd* **Rafferty (IRE)**[23] 6950 8-8-8 49 ow1.........................(p) JohnEgan 3 49
(S Dow) *towards rr: hdwy 3f out: rdn 2f out: styd on fnl f: nt trble ldrs* 12/1

5003 7 *3/4* **Calloff The Search**[6] 7134 3-8-7 48.........................(v) HayleyTurner 5 46
(Stef Liddiard) *chsd ldr tl over 1f out: wknd 1f out* 11/1

0000 8 *hd* **Patavium Prince (IRE)**[23] 6950 4-8-7 48 ow1.......... SimonWhitworth 7 45
(Miss Jo Crowley) *towards rr: rdn and effrt on outer 2f out: nvr trbld ldrs* 25/1

6540 9 *nk* **Tibinta**[16] 7011 3-8-5 46 oh1......................... MatthewHenry 10 42
(P D Evans) *sn outpcd in last: hdwy u.p 2f out: nvr trbld ldrs* 25/1

2455 10 *1/2* **Mannello**[11] 7077 4-8-11 52......................... RichardThomas 12 46
(Jim Best) *sn bustled along in midfield on outer: drvn 2f out: no imp* 8/1

5242 11 *1 1/4* **Two Acres (IRE)**[5] 7137 4-8-10 51......................... TPQueally 11 41
(A G Newcombe) *chsd ldrs tl lost pl and dropped to rr wl over 3f out: n.d after* 9/4[1]

0000 12 *5* **Bahamian Duke**[15] 7014 4-8-11 55.........................(v[1]) AndrewElliott(3) 9 29
(K R Burke) *chsd ldrs: rdn over 2f out: wknd qckly 2f out* 14/1

1m 12.03s (-0.78) **Going Correction** -0.025s/f (Stan) 12 Ran SP% 123.7
Speed ratings (Par 101): **104,103,101,100,99 99,98,98,98,97 95,89**
CSF £65.63 CT £349.67 TOTE £4.10: £1.40, £6.40, £2.80; EX 67.70 Trifecta £69.20 Part won. Pool: £97.60 - 0.10 winning tickets..
Owner ownaracehorse.co.uk (Shakespeare) **Bred** D McDonnell And Tower Bloodstock **Trained** Danethorpe, Notts

FOCUS
A moderate sprint handicap run at a fair gallop and the form looks solid rated around the first three.
Sir Loin Official explanation: jockey said gelding hung right throughout
Blushing Russian(IRE) Official explanation: trainer said gelding lost a shoe
Two Acres(IRE) Official explanation: jockey said gelding hung left downhill

7189 PONTIN'S SHORT BREAKS CLAIMING STKS 1m 2f (P)

12:40 (12:43) (Class 6) 3-Y-0+ £1,943 (£578; £288; £144) Stalls Low

Form RPR

0662 1 **King's Majesty (IRE)**[36] 5916 5-9-0 70......................... VinceSlattery 5 72
(V R A Dartnall) *t.k.h: racd in midfield: hdwy to trck ldng pair 3f out: rdn to ld over 1f out: styd on wl* 11/4[2]

112 2 *nk* **Sawwaah (IRE)**[12] 7057 10-9-4 75.........................(v) RichardKingscote 2 76
(Tom Dascombe) *slowly away: hld up in rr: hdwy wl over 3f out: chsd ldng pair over 1f out: wnt 2nd ins fnl f: styd on but nvr quite getting to wnr* 9/2

1202 3 *1 1/4* **New World Order (IRE)**[19] 6949 3-8-12 77.........................(t) AndrewElliott(3) 7 73
(K R Burke) *t.k.h: led tl rdn and hdd over 1f out: kpt on same pce u.p fnl f* 5/2[1]

1-00 4 *3 1/2* **Ryan's Future (IRE)**[53] 6490 7-9-0 78......................... JohnEgan 11 62
(J S Moore) *trckd ldng pair: wnt 2nd over 4f out: ev ch and rdn over 2f out: wknd over 1f out* 7/2[3]

0530 5 *3 1/2* **Barry Island**[23] 6951 8-9-8 60......................... GeorgeBaker 10 63
(D R C Elsworth) *slowly away: hld up in rr: hdwy wl over 3f out: chsd ldrs and rdn 2f out: wl btn 1f out* 8/1

0000 6 *5* **Anduril**[130] 4383 6-9-0 58.........................(b) MatthewHenry 9 45
(Miss M E Rowland) *v.s.a: a wl bhd: lost tch over 2f out: kpt on past btn horses fnl f* 33/1

000 7 *1* **Tagula Song (IRE)**[135] 4235 3-8-0 23.........................(v[1]) JamieMackay 4 32
(J A Geake) *racd in midfield: rdn to chse ldrs 3f out: wknd over 2f out* 66/1

0600 8 *1/2* **Pink Salmon**[14] 7029 3-8-6 50......................... HayleyTurner 6 37
(Mrs L J Mongan) *t.k.h: hld up in midfield: rdn over 4f out: bhd last 2f* 66/1

0006 9 *shd* **Keagles (ITY)**[35] 6807 4-8-13 35......................... RichardThomas 8 41
(J E Long) *racd in midfield: rdn over 4f out: bhd last 2f* 100/1

-005 10 *11* **Dickie Deano**[11] 7076 3-8-9 43......................... PaulFitzsimons 1 18
(J M Bradley) *chsd ldr tl over 4f out: rdn and wknd over 3f out: t.o* 66/1

2m 6.30s (-1.49) **Going Correction** -0.025s/f (Stan)
WFA 3 from 4yo+ 3lb 10 Ran SP% 115.2
Speed ratings (Par 101): **104,103,102,99,97 93,92,91,91,83**
CSF £15.12 TOTE £3.80: £1.60, £1.40, £1.20; EX 17.30 Trifecta £14.60 Pool: £327.76 - 15.93 winning tickets..The winner was claimed by T. J. Pitt for £8,000. Anduril was claimed by I. W. McInnes for £8,000. New World Order was claimed by Vetlab Supplies Ltd for £10,000.
Owner Drink Up **Bred** Mrs T V Ryan **Trained** Brayford, Devon

FOCUS
This was a pretty good claimer, with the first four rated in the 70s, and a few of these are well up to winning in handicap company, although those outside the frame suggest the principals ran below their marks.
Sawwaah(IRE) Official explanation: jockey said gelding missed the break
Anduril Official explanation: jockey said gelding missed the break

7190 EBF PONTIN'S GREAT FAMILY HOLIDAYS MAIDEN FILLIES' STKS 7f (P)

1:10 (1:10) (Class 5) 2-Y-0 £2,914 (£867; £433; £216) Stalls Low

Form RPR

5334 1 **Sweet Hope (USA)**[48] 6611 2-9-0 72.........................(b[1]) PaulMulrennan 4 82+
(K A Ryan) *w ldr: rdn to ld jst over 1f out: sn clr: r.o strly* 6/1

3 2 *5* **Miss Mujanna**[21] 6964 2-9-0 0......................... J-PGuillambert 7 69
(J Akehurst) *chsd ldng pair: rdn jst over 2f out: sn outpcd by wnr: kpt on to go 2nd ins fnl f: no ch w wnr* 9/2[3]

4663 3 *2* **Tense (IRE)**[19] 6973 2-9-0 69.........................(b[1]) JimCrowley 2 64
(J A Osborne) *led: rdn and hdd jst over 1f out: sn outpcd by wnr: lost 2nd ins fnl f* 7/1

663 4 *hd* **Wannabe Free**[46] 6648 2-9-0 73......................... TPQueally 1 63
(J Noseda) *sn pushed along in last trio: short of room and dropped to last over 5f out: swtchd wd and drvn 3f out: styd on u.p over 1f out: wnt 4th nr fin: n.d* 11/4[1]

00 5 *nk* **Contessina (IRE)**[56] 6434 2-9-0 0......................... ChrisCatlin 6 63
(P F I Cole) *chsd ldrs: rdn wl over 2f out: wl outpcd 2f out: plugged on* 13/2

6 *1 3/4* **To Be Or Not To Be** 2-9-0 0......................... SteveDrowne 3 58
(W Jarvis) *s.i.s: towards rr: hdwy and in tch wl over 2f out: rdn and outpcd whn hung lft wl over 1f out: wl btn after* 40/1

2250 7 *3 1/2* **Forsyte Saga**[54] 6471 2-9-0 71......................... GregFairley 5 49
(M Johnston) *chsd ldrs tl 4f out: sn lost pl: wl bhd last 2f* 7/2[2]

8 *4* **Capriccioso** 2-9-0 0......................... FergusSweeney 8 38
(G L Moore) *s.i.s: hdwy and in tch over 4f out: rdn over 2f out: sn wknd: eased ins fnl f* 20/1

1m 24.77s (-1.12) **Going Correction** -0.025s/f (Stan) 8 Ran SP% 114.4
Speed ratings (Par 93): **105,99,97,96,96 94,90,85**
CSF £33.08 TOTE £6.30: £2.00, £1.40, £2.20; EX 39.90 Trifecta £97.30 Pool: £283.85 - 2.07 winning tickets..
Owner Highbank Syndicate **Bred** Castleton Lyons & Kilboy Estate, Inc **Trained** Hambleton, N Yorks

FOCUS
A fair maiden but a very smart winning time for a race of its type, 1.18 seconds faster than the colts and geldings equivalent which followed. The third is the best guide to the form.

NOTEBOOK
Sweet Hope(USA), blinkered for the first time, proved in a different league to her rivals on the day. She looks as though she would be at least as well suited by 1m, and that probably helped her with the way the race panned out. This was by far her best performance in six starts, it is likely the blinkers accounted for some, if not all, of the improvement. (op 5-1 tchd 13-2)
Miss Mujanna had shaped promisingly on her debut over 6f at Kempton three weeks earlier, staying on after losing ground on the bend, and she again kept on well enough to suggest a maiden is hers for the taking. (op 5-1 tchd 11-2)
Tense(IRE) has the ability to win a maiden or weak nursery, and was blinkered for the first time. She showed a lot of speed before weakening, and it may be that she is dropped back to 6f next time. (tchd 13-2)
Wannabe Free, whose third at Newmarket at the start of last month was easily the best form on offer, found herself adrift of the remainder halfway through the race and, although keeping on strongly in the straight, was always going to have too much to do. Official explanation: jockey said filly never travelled (op 5-2 tchd 3-1)
Forsyte Saga had regressed in four starts on turf and showed no sign of returning to form on this All-Weather debut. (tchd 3-1)

7191 EBF GO PONTIN'S MAIDEN STKS (C&G) 7f (P)

1:40 (1:46) (Class 5) 2-Y-0 £2,914 (£867; £433; £216) Stalls Low

Form RPR

0 1 **Parisian Gift (IRE)**[57] 6409 2-9-0 0......................... RichardKingscote 10 72
(Tom Dascombe) *t.k.h: in tch: hdwy and rdn jst over 2f out: chal over 1f out: led ins fnl f: r.o wl* 7/2[1]

64 2 *nk* **Taken (IRE)**[144] 3958 2-9-0 0......................... TPQueally 6 71
(J R Fanshawe) *hld up in midfield: hdwy over 2f out: edgd lft u.p jst ins fnl f: r.o to go 2nd nr fin* 7/2[1]

3 *shd* **General Blucher (IRE)** 2-9-0 0......................... AdrianMcCarthy 8 71
(P W Chapple-Hyam) *chsd ldr for 2f and again wl over 1f out: rdn to ld over 1f out: hdd jst ins fnl f: kpt on same pce: lost 2nd nr fin* 12/1

3 4 *3/4* **Beauchamp Wizard**[39] 6755 2-9-0 0......................... HayleyTurner 1 69
(G A Butler) *t.k.h: chsd ldrs: rdn and short of room jst ins fnl f: kpt on same pce after* 8/1[3]

5 *1/2* **Admiral Dundas (IRE)** 2-9-0 0......................... J-PGuillambert 4 68
(W Jarvis) *s.i.s: in rr on inner: edgd out off rail 3f out: nt clr run over 2f out: hdwy and rdn wl over 1f out: kpt on but nt rch ldrs* 33/1

6 *1* **Sacrilege** 2-9-0 0......................... LPKeniry 12 65
(D R C Elsworth) *s.i.s: bhd: rdn and hdwy jst over 2f out: swtchd rt jst ins fnl f: r.o: nt rch ldrs* 22/1

7 *2* **Pentathlon (IRE)** 2-9-0 0......................... GregFairley 11 60
(M Johnston) *hdwy to chse ldr 5f out: rdn over 2f out: lost 2nd wl over 1f out: wknd qckly 1f out* 5/1[2]

40 8 *shd* **Archilini**[18] 7000 2-9-0 0......................... JamesDoyle 7 60
(K A Morgan) *led tl rdn and hdd over 1f out: wknd qckly 1f out* 40/1

9 *3/4* **Petomic (IRE)** 2-9-0 0......................... PatDobbs 13 58
(Christian Wroe) *v s.i.s: bhd: hdwy on inner wl over 1f out: nvr trbld ldrs* 33/1

10 *1 1/2* **Kibitzer** 2-9-0 0......................... SteveDrowne 2 54
(J W Hills) *s.i.s: sn in tch on inner: rdn over 2f out: wknd 2f out* 8/1[3]

40 11 *1 1/4* **Bad Moon Rising**[32] 6850 2-9-0 0......................... DaneO'Neill 5 51
(J Akehurst) *a towards rr: rdn and btn 2f out* 14/1

12 *8* **Musical Feud (IRE)** 2-9-0 0.........................(b[1]) PatCosgrave 9 31
(Jane Chapple-Hyam) *v s.i.s: sn pushed along in last pair: wl bhd fr 1/2-way* 33/1

13 *shd* **Ubenkor (IRE)** 2-9-0 0......................... SaleemGolam 14 31
(Christian Wroe) *racd wd in midfield tl rdn and wknd over 2f out* 66/1

1m 25.95s (0.06) **Going Correction** -0.025s/f (Stan) 13 Ran SP% 114.8
Speed ratings (Par 96): **98,97,97,96,96 94,92,92,91,90 88,79,79**
CSF £12.73 TOTE £3.90: £1.60, £1.50, £4.20; EX 15.00 Trifecta £107.30 Part won. Pool: £151.14 - 0.70 winning tickets..
Owner The PG Tipsters **Bred** Bakewell Bloodstock And Freynestown Stud **Trained** Lambourn, Berks

FOCUS
This looked an above-average maiden for this course, and a trappy one for punters. The winning time, though, was more than a second slower than the preceding maiden for fillies.

NOTEBOOK
Parisian Gift(IRE) had shaped with plenty of promise on his debut on soft ground at Yarmouth in October, and even more so here in justifying market support a bit more comfortably than the winning margin suggests. His trainer said he would now be put away for the turf season next spring. (op 6-1 tchd 10-3)
Taken(IRE) had shown enough on his two turf outings to warrant some respect and again ran well. He will get a handicap mark now and can be placed to win, perhaps over a bit further. (tchd 11-4)
General Blucher(IRE), a 30,000gns two-year-old who is a half-brother to a dual winner abroad, was always in the firing line and was just a short head back in third on his debut. He should get a bit further. (op 8-1)
Beauchamp Wizard had made an encouraging beginning to his career when third at Doncaster last month and this was also a fair performance in what was probably a contest of similar standard. (tchd 15-2)

Admiral Dundas(IRE), a 36,000gns half-brother to Sans Reserve, put in a fair display on his debut.
Sacrilege, a 15,000gns half-brother to a winner on the Flat and over hurdles, was not disgraced on this debut. (tchd 20-1)
Pentathlon(IRE), a half-brother to No Excuse Needed, faded after being prominent early. He will improve for the experience. (op 11-2)

7192 PONTIN'S BOOK EARLY AND SAVE H'CAP (DIV II) 6f (P)
2:15 (2:16) (Class 6) (0-55,55) 3-Y-0+ **£1,943** (£578; £288; £144) **Stalls** Low

Form RPR
40-0 **1** **Sir Don (IRE)**[22] 6957 8-8-11 **52**....(p) StephenDonohoe 9 59
(E S McMahon) *chsd ldr tl led wl over 2f out: rdn and clr 2f out: hld on wl last 50yds* **16/1**
0506 **2** *hd* **Mulberry Lad (IRE)**[9] 7094 5-8-10 **51**....(p) ChrisCatlin 6 57
(P W Hiatt) *chsd ldrs: rdn to chse wnr 2f out: kpt on u.p fnl f: hld last 50yds* **3/1**[1]
6130 **3** *1 1/2* **Muktasb (USA)**[15] 7013 6-8-11 **52** ow1....(v) AdamKirby 5 54+
(D Shaw) *s.i.s: bhd: hdwy on outer bnd over 2f out: r.o wl fnl f: snatched 3rd on post: nt rch ldrs* **10/3**[2]
3336 **4** *shd* **Midmaar (IRE)**[23] 6945 6-8-10 **51**....(b) JamieMackay 8 52
(M Wigham) *t.k.h early: in tch: rdn and nt qckn jst over 2f out: rallied u.p over 1f out: kpt on same pce fnl f* **11/2**[3]
0000 **5** *shd* **Mr Loire**[25] 6927 3-8-7 **48**....(b) DeanMcKeown 7 49
(A J Chamberlain) *in tch in midfield: rdn 2f out: kpt on steadily u.p fnl f: nt pce to rch ldrs* **9/1**
6250 **6** *3/4* **Time Share (IRE)**[15] 7014 3-8-5 **45**.... HayleyTurner 1 45
(G C Bravery) *t.k.h: hld up in bhd on inner: hrd rdn and hdwy wl over 1f out: kpt on but nvr threatened ldrs* **15/2**
0000 **7** *1* **Fish Called Johnny**[18] 6993 3-9-0 **55**.... LPKeniry 11 50
(Peter Grayson) *hld up in rr: stl last 2f out: sn rdn: sme late hdwy but nvr trbld ldrs* **16/1**
000 **8** *hd* **Balerno**[130] 4397 8-8-12 **53**.... AmirQuinn 4 48
(Mrs L J Mongan) *a towards rr: pushed along wl over 3f out: plugged on u.p but n.d* **11/1**
0000 **9** *nk* **Cayman Breeze**[25] 6927 7-8-5 **45**....(b[1]) LiamJones 2 40
(J M Bradley) *t.k.h: hld up in midfield on inner: rdn and hdwy 2f out: chsd ldrs jst over 1f out: wknd last 100yds* **25/1**
2000 **10** *4* **Herb Paris (FR)**[15] 7013 3-9-0 **55**....(b[1]) TPQueally 10 36
(P M Phelan) *led tl over 2f out: sn rdn: wknd wl over 1f out* **10/1**
45-0 **11** *2* **Coranglais**[11] 7077 7-8-5 **45**....(p) PaulFitzsimons 12 21
(J M Bradley) *t.k.h: in tch in midfield on outer: rdn and wknd over 2f out* **28/1**

1m 12.5s (-0.31) **Going Correction** -0.025s/f (Stan) **11** Ran SP% **121.7**
Speed ratings (Par 101): **101,100,98,98,98 97,96,95,95,90 87**
CSF £65.98 CT £209.12 TOTE £11.80: £3.00, £1.60, £1.60; EX 76.50 Trifecta £129.40 Pool: £311.88 - 1.71 winning tickets..
Owner Mrs Dian Plant **Bred** C And R O'Brien **Trained** Lichfield, Staffs

FOCUS
The winning time was half a second slower than the first division of this handicap. This race could be rated higher but the winner is exposed.

7193 POWER 2000 H'CAP 1m 2f (P)
2:50 (2:50) (Class 4) (0-80,78) 3-Y-0+ **£4,857** (£1,445; £722; £360) **Stalls** Low

Form RPR
2144 **1** **Gaelic Princess**[15] 7017 7-9-5 **77**.... DaneO'Neill 8 84
(A G Newcombe) *hld up in tch in midfield: rdn wl over 1f out: styd on wl u.p fnl f to ld nr fin* **13/2**
0152 **2** *nk* **Meditation**[9] 7099 5-8-8 **66**.... JamesDoyle 2 72
(I A Wood) *led at stdy pce: rdn over 2f out: hdd narrowly over 1f out: battled on wl tl no ex nr fin* **12/1**
0004 **3** *shd* **Oakley Heffert (IRE)**[32] 6848 3-8-7 **73**....(b) NataliaGemelova[(5)] 5 79
(R Hannon) *in tch: pushed along to chal 2f out: sn rdn and led narrowly: hld hd high and fnd little after: hdd nr fin* **9/1**
1303 **4** *hd* **Waterline Twenty (IRE)**[18] 6996 4-8-13 **71**.... JohnEgan 4 76
(P D Evans) *chsd ldng pair: rdn and effrt over 1f out: ev ch ins fnl f: no ex last 50yds* **11/2**[3]
3434 **5** *1* **Summer Dancer (IRE)**[28] 6900 3-9-3 **78**.... LPKeniry 3 83+
(D R C Elsworth) *t.k.h: hld up in tch in midfield: hdwy wl over 1f out: keeping on whn nt clr run wl ins fnl f* **3/1**[1]
3232 **6** *1/2* **Baan (USA)**[9] 7104 4-8-9 **67**....(v) GregFairley 1 69
(M Johnston) *chsd ldr: rdn over 2f out: lost pl over 1f out: one pce u.p after* **10/3**[2]
0-03 **7** *1* **Obrigado (USA)**[11] 7075 7-9-5 **77**.... GeorgeBaker 6 77
(Karen George) *stdd and dropped in after s: hld up in last pair: rdn over 1f out: kpt on same pce* **8/1**
6014 **8** *3* **Without Excuse (USA)**[18] 7002 3-9-1 **76**....(b) TPQueally 7 70
(M Botti) *stdd s and dropped in bhd: hld up in last: rdn and effrt on outer over 2f out: no imp* **8/1**

2m 9.42s (1.63) **Going Correction** -0.025s/f (Stan)
WFA 3 from 4yo+ 3lb **8** Ran SP% **116.7**
Speed ratings (Par 105): **92,91,91,91,90 90,89,87**
CSF £80.82 CT £705.89 TOTE £8.10: £2.20, £2.50, £2.80; EX 70.80 TRIFECTA Not won..
Owner M K F Seymour **Bred** Mrs N Quinn **Trained** Yarnscombe, Devon

FOCUS
An interesting handicap, in that the majority of the field were attempting a distance that should have suited but that they had not tried before, or rarely. The winner's time was more than three seconds slower than the winner of the claimer, accounted for by the dawdling early gallop, with the third to his All-Weather mark.
Summer Dancer(IRE) Official explanation: jockey said gelding was denied a clear run
Without Excuse(USA) Official explanation: jockey said gelding hung right in straight

7194 PONTINS.COM H'CAP 1m 4f (P)
3:20 (3:20) (Class 5) (0-75,75) 3-Y-0+ **£2,817** (£838; £418; £209) **Stalls** Low

Form RPR
0031 **1** **Mutamaasek (USA)**[10] 7088 5-8-3 **62** 6ex.... KirstyMilczarek[(5)] 7 72+
(Lady Herries) *chsd ldrs: hdwy and upsides ldr 2f out: pushed into ld over 1f out: in command after: pushed out* **2/1**[1]
-000 **2** *nk* **Greek Easter (IRE)**[52] 4-9-0 **68**.... JamieMackay 4 77+
(David P Myerscough, Ire) *in tch: nt clr run and shuffled bk over 2f out: sn swtchd rt and rdn: hdwy and swtchd lft 1f out: r.o wl fnl f: wnt 2nd towards fin* **16/1**
002/ **3** *nk* **Masked (IRE)**[962] 1387 6-9-7 **75**.... GeorgeBaker 5 81
(R M Beckett) *hld up in last trio: hdwy wl over 3f out: trckd ldrs 2f out: rdn over 1f out: kpt on fnl f* **9/1**
03/0 **4** *1/2* **Dash Of Grey (IRE)**[59] 6368 8-8-10 **64**....(b) TPQueally 2 69
(Ruaidhri Joseph Tierney, Ire) *led: rdn and qcknd over 2f out: hdd over 1f out: kpt on same pce fnl f: lost 2 pls towards fin* **33/1**
1102 **5** *1 1/2* **Polyquest (IRE)**[35] 6808 3-8-6 **65**.... HayleyTurner 6 68
(G A Butler) *s.i.s: t.k.h: hld up in rr: rdn and hdwy over 2f out: kpt on u.p but nt pce to threaten ldrs* **15/2**
3210 **6** *2* **Prime Number (IRE)**[28] 6727 5-9-5 **73**.... ChrisCatlin 10 72
(J Akehurst) *in tch in midfield: rdn and effrt to chse ldrs 2f out: wknd 1f out* **11/2**[3]
6000 **7** *1 3/4* **Prime Contender**[13] 6422 5-8-10 **64**....(b) FergusSweeney 9 61
(G L Moore) *hld up in midfield: rdn 2f out: fnd nil and sn btn* **9/4**[2]
4020 **8** *1 3/4* **Sudden Impulse**[18] 7002 6-9-3 **71**.... PaulMulrennan 3 65
(A D Brown) *taken down early: chsd ldr tl over 2f out: sn rdn: wknd 2f out* **12/1**
6000 **9** *9* **Salut Saint Cloud**[15] 7018 6-8-4 **65**....(p) JemmaMarshall[(7)] 8 44
(G L Moore) *awkward leaving stalls and slowly away: bhd: rdn and struggling over 2f out: sn lost tch* **20/1**

2m 35.65s (1.26) **Going Correction** -0.025s/f (Stan)
WFA 3 from 4yo+ 5lb **9** Ran SP% **122.5**
Speed ratings (Par 103): **94,93,93,93,92 90,89,88,82**
CSF £38.48 CT £252.20 TOTE £3.20: £1.10, £5.80, £2.60; EX 43.80 Trifecta £284.60 Part won. Pool: £400.94 - 0.10 winning tickets. Place 6 £150.77, Place 5 £63.61.
Owner Lady Herries **Bred** Shadwell Farm LLC **Trained** Patching, W Sussex

FOCUS
A competitive enough handicap with only the two Irish raiders looking unlikely winners beforehand, although in the end they were among the first four. The winning time was moderate for the class though.
Salut Saint Cloud Official explanation: jockey said gelding missed the break
T/Plt: £69.30 to a £1 stake. Pool: £54,271.05. 570.95 winning tickets. T/Qpdt: £24.70 to a £1 stake. Pool: £3,541.70. 105.90 winning tickets. SP

7175 SOUTHWELL (L-H)
Thursday, December 20

OFFICIAL GOING: Standard to slow
Wind: Nil Weather: Damp and misty

7195 PONTIN'S GREAT FAMILY HOLIDAYS NURSERY 5f (F)
12:30 (12:30) (Class 6) (0-65,62) 2-Y-0 **£2,047** (£604; £302) **Stalls** High

Form RPR
0000 **1** **Captain Crooner (IRE)**[43] 6722 2-8-4 **45**.... LiamJones 2 48
(D Shaw) *s.i.s: sn bhd and rdn along: swtchd to far side and hdwy wl over 1f out: styd on strly ins fnl f to ld nr fin* **14/1**
3456 **2** *1/2* **Liani (IRE)**[45] 6693 2-8-6 **50**.... AndrewMullen[(3)] 1 51
(J R Norton) *chsd ldrs: rdn along 1/2-way: drvn over 1f out: styd on ins fnl f* **4/1**
0004 **3** *shd* **Holly Golightley**[14] 7042 2-9-0 **55**....(b[1]) PaulMulrennan 7 56
(K A Ryan) *sn led: rdn wl over 1f out: drvn ent fnl f: hdd and no ex nr fin* **10/3**[2]
4405 **4** *nk* **Shakespeare's Son**[14] 7042 2-9-4 **59**.... DeanMcKeown 3 59
(H J Evans) *cl up: rdn 2f out: drvn over 1f out: kpt on same pce ins fnl f* **11/4**[1]
436 **5** *5* **Maid In Bloom**[114] 4924 2-9-4 **62**.... MarkLawson[(3)] 5 44
(B Smart) *chsd ldrs: hdwy 2f out: sn rdn and wknd ent fnl f* **7/2**[3]
0000 **6** *3* **Ocean Glory (IRE)**[30] 6881 2-9-1 **56**.... LPKeniry 4 27
(Peter Grayson) *cl up: rdn along 1/2-way: wknd wl over 1f out* **11/2**

63.40 secs (3.10) **Going Correction** +0.475s/f (Slow) **6** Ran SP% **114.0**
Speed ratings (Par 94): **94,93,93,92,84 79**
CSF £69.09 TOTE £19.20: £7.50, £2.30; EX 106.60.
Owner Danethorpe Racing Partnership **Bred** Peter Molony **Trained** Danethorpe, Notts

FOCUS
The leaders went quick enough here and set it up for Captain Crooner, who had struggled to keep up in the early stages. Poor form but solid rated around the second and third.

NOTEBOOK
Captain Crooner(IRE) was slowly away and struggled to go the early pace, but in the end he benefited from the fact that the leaders went off quickly, and he stayed on best of all to notch an unlikely success. Matched at the ceiling price of 1000 on the machine, he paid for one lucky punter's Christmas. (op 16-1)
Liani(IRE), dropping back in distance from 7f and debuting for her new stable, also benefited from the strong pace and stayed on to edge out the speedy Holly Golightley for second. (tchd 7-2)
Holly Golightley had blinkers fitted for the first time and set a fast pace out in front, too fast in fact, as she fell in a hole inside the last and was passed by two rivals. She has the ability to win a similar race. (tchd 3-1 and 4-1)
Shakespeare's Son, dropping back in trip, took on Holly Golightley in the early stages but could not match her pace and eventually paid for trying to keep tabs on her. (op 4-1)
Maid In Bloom, off the track since August, was running in a handicap for the first time having shown modest ability in maiden company. She ran as though needing the outing. Official explanation: jockey said filly was never travelling (op 5-2)

7196 PONTIN'S BOOK EARLY MAIDEN AUCTION STKS 7f (F)
1:00 (1:01) (Class 6) 2-Y-0 **£2,047** (£604; £302) **Stalls** Low

Form RPR
04 **1** **Didana (IRE)**[27] 6912 2-8-9 0.... PatDobbs 6 69+
(M G Quinlan) *led 1f: cl up tl led again wl over 1f out: sn rdn and styd on fnl f* **1/1**[1]
6434 **2** *2* **Weet By Far**[7] 7130 2-8-4 61.... HayleyTurner 1 59
(R Hollinshead) *trckd ldrs: hdwy over 2f out: rdn wl over 1f out: drvn ent fnl f and kpt on same pce: tk 2nd nr line* **6/4**[2]
0 **3** *nk* **Amyann (IRE)**[20] 6980 2-8-7 0.... ChrisCatlin 4 61
(J R Holt) *hdwy to ld after 1f: rdn along over 2f out: drvn and hdd over 1f out: kpt on same pce: lost 2nd nr line* **25/1**
00 **4** *9* **Landed Gent (IRE)**[116] 4852 2-8-8 0.... AndrewElliott[(3)] 7 43
(Miss V Haigh) *trckd ldng pair: rdn along 3f out: drvn over 2f out and sn wknd* **40/1**
5 *5* **Jane's Payoff (IRE)** 2-8-7 0.... LPKeniry 3 26
(Mrs L C Jewell) *dwlt: hld up in rr: effrt and sme hdwy over 2f out: sn rdn and wknd* **10/1**[3]
0 **6** *26* **Chalford**[6] 7139 2-9-1 0....(b) PaulMulrennan 5 —
(J Balding) *plld hrd towards rr: rdn along over 3f out: sn wknd and bhd* **66/1**

1m 34.74s (3.94) **Going Correction** +0.35s/f (Slow) **6** Ran SP% **106.9**
Speed ratings (Par 94): **91,88,88,78,72 42**
CSF £2.37 TOTE £1.90: £1.40, £1.10; EX 2.60.
Owner The Spurs **Bred** Keatly Overseas Ltd **Trained** Newmarket, Suffolk
■ Stewards' Enquiry : Hayley Turner caution: used whip with excessive frequency

The Form Book, Raceform Ltd, Compton, RG20 6NL

FOCUS
Very modest maiden form rated through the runner-up.
NOTEBOOK
Didana(IRE) only had to be pushed out to get off the mark in this weak maiden. She should not be harshly rated for handicaps on the back of this and is open to improvement, especially back on turf, where soft ground is likely to suit her. (op 5-4)
Weet By Far looked to hold solid claims in what was a weak affair, but she bumped into a less-exposed rival with improvement in her. She was always playing second fiddle. (op 5-4 tchd 6-5)
Amyann(IRE), whose unraced dam is a half-sister to Group 3 winner Notable Guest, ran a much better race than on her debut and perhaps this slower surface suited her. (op 20-1 tchd 28-1)
Landed Gent(IRE) has shown little in three starts to date and is likely to struggle to get into handicaps off what will undoubtedly prove to be a lowly mark. (op 33-1 tchd 50-1)

7197 PONTINSBINGO.COM (S) STKS — 1m (F)
1:30 (1:31) (Class 6) 3-Y-0+ — £2,047 (£604; £302) Stalls Low

Form — RPR
4400 **1** **Meeting Of Minds**[36] 6806 3-8-9 45 .... HayleyTurner 10 — 53
(W Jarvis) *hld up in midfield: smooth hdwy on outer 3f out: led 1 1/2f out: sn rdn and styd on wl* **14/1**
6000 **2** 1 1/4 **Shifty**[9] 7113 8-8-8 60 .... JamieKyne[(7)] 6 — 55
(D Carroll) *trckd ldrs: hdwy 2f out: ev ch whn n.m.r wl over 1f out: kpt on same pce ins fnl f* **4/1[2]**
6042 **3** 1 1/2 **Davidia (IRE)**[26] 6935 4-8-12 47 .... AndrewElliott[(3)] 9 — 52
(D W Thompson) *towards rr: pushed along 3f out: hdwy on outer 2f out: rdn and edgd lft ent fnl f: kpt on same pce* **11/1**
4032 **4** 4 **Ruffie (IRE)**[8] 7124 4-9-2 58 ....(e) RobertHavlin 1 — 43
(Miss Gay Kelleway) *trckd ldrs on inner: hdwy over 2f out: rdn to chal and ev ch wl over 1f out: wknd appr fnl f* **3/1[1]**
000L **5** 1 1/2 **By Storm**[28] 3840 4-8-5 37 .... KirstyMilczarek[(5)] 11 — 34
(Miss J E Foster) *chsd ldrs: rdn along over 2f out: drvn wl over 1f out and grad wknd* **25/1**
0004 **6** nk **Time For Change (IRE)**[5] 7153 3-9-6 42 ....(e) DavidKinsella 4 — 44
(P G Murphy) *in rr: hdwy over 2f out: rdn wl over 1f out and sn no imp* **14/1**
0222 **7** shd **Sion Hill (IRE)**[15] 7034 6-9-7 45 ....(p) TPQueally 2 — 44
(John A Harris) *sn led: rdn along over 2f out: drvn and hdd 1 1/2f out: sn wknd* **5/1[3]**
0005 **8** 1 1/4 **Mr Chocolate Drop (IRE)**[8] 7124 3-9-1 49 ....(b[1]) JamesO'Reilly[(5)] 3 — 41
(Miss M E Rowland) *midfield: effrt and sme hdwy on inner over 2f out: sn rdn and n.d* **66/1**
5151 **9** 2 1/2 **Louisiade (IRE)**[259] 932 6-9-7 63 ....(p) StephenDonohoe 12 — 35
(John A Harris) *in rr and rdn along 1/2-way: a bhd* **8/1**
-504 **10** 4 **Amorist (IRE)**[17] 7006 5-9-1 65 .... LiamJones 5 — 20
(D W Chapman) *towards rr: rdn along 1/2-way: bhd after* **11/2**
0600 **11** 1/2 **Global Achiever**[12] 7069 6-9-1 40 ....(b) SamHitchcott 8 — 19
(M J Gingell) *midfield: rdn along 3f out: sn btn* **50/1**
50-0 **12** hd **Shopfitter**[36] 6816 4-9-1 40 ....(p) FrankieMcDonald 7 — 19
(P T Midgley) *cl up: rdn along over 3f out and sn wknd* **20/1**

1m 47.13s (2.53) **Going Correction** +0.35s/f (Slow)
WFA 3 from 4yo+ 1lb — 12 Ran SP% **121.9**
Speed ratings (Par 101): **101,99,98,94,92 92,92,91,88,84 84,83**
CSF £69.30 TOTE £12.40: £4.60, £1.30, £3.60; EX 115.70 TRIFECTA Not won..The winner was sold to Paul Blockley for 5,800gns
Owner William Jarvis **Bred** C Platts And Miss S E Hall **Trained** Newmarket, Suffolk
FOCUS
An ordinary seller and the form is pretty weak.
Sion Hill(IRE) Official explanation: jockey said gelding hung right

7198 ARCHER ELECTRICAL H'CAP — 1m 4f (F)
2:00 (2:00) (Class 5) (0-70,70) 3-Y-0+ — £2,968 (£876; £438) Stalls Low

Form — RPR
5045 **1** **Bentley Brook (IRE)**[213] 1907 5-8-9 56 oh3 ow2..... StephenDonohoe 6 — 64+
(P A Blockley) *trckd ldng pair: hdwy 3f out: led over 2f out: rdn over 1f out and styd on wl* **4/1**
0522 **2** 1 3/4 **Calculating (IRE)**[5] 7151 3-9-4 70 .... HayleyTurner 8 — 74
(M D I Usher) *hld up towards rr: hdwy over 2f out: rdn to chse wnr ent fnl f: sn drvn and kpt on* **11/4[1]**
2152 **3** 4 **They All Laughed**[139] 4124 4-9-7 68 .... ChrisCatlin 7 — 65
(P W Hiatt) *hld up in rr: hdwy over 3f out: rdn to chse wnr wl over 1f out: drvn and kpt on same pce ent fnl f* **7/2[3]**
2040 **4** 1 1/2 **Dreams Jewel**[11] 6056 7-8-4 54 oh3............ NeilChalmers[(3)] 2 — 49
(C Roberts) *chsd ldrs: rdn along and outpcd 4f out: kpt on under pressure fnl 2f* **25/1**
0066 **5** 7 **Starcross Maid**[9] 7109 5-8-5 55 .... PatrickMathers[(3)] 5 — 39
(J F Coupland) *hld up: hdwy on inner 4f out: rdn along over 2f out and sn btn* **9/1**
- **6** 1/2 **Jeu De Roseau (IRE)**[30] 2017 3-9-0 66 .... TPQueally 1 — 49
(A P Stringer) *chsd ldr: effrt 3f out: rdn aover 2f out and sn btn* **16/1**
0403 **7** 5 **Bolckow**[9] 7109 4-8-10 57 .... DaleGibson 3 — 32
(J T Stimpson) *led: rdn along 3f out: hdd over 2f out and sn wknd* **10/3[2]**

2m 46.86s (4.77) **Going Correction** +0.35s/f (Slow)
WFA 3 from 4yo+ 5lb — 7 Ran SP% **111.7**
Speed ratings (Par 103): **98,96,94,93,88 88,84**
CSF £14.67 CT £39.99 TOTE £5.40: £2.80, £1.70; EX 16.60 Trifecta £40.40 Pool: £501.68, 8.80 winning units.
Owner John Wardle **Bred** Christopher Maye **Trained** Lambourn, Berks
FOCUS
A pleasing effort from the winner and solid enough form rated through the second.
Starcross Maid Official explanation: jockey said mare hung right

7199 GO PONTIN'S HOLIDAYS MAIDEN STKS — 1m 3f (F)
2:30 (2:31) (Class 5) 3-Y-0+ — £2,968 (£876; £438) Stalls Low

Form — RPR
6333 **1** **Satindra (IRE)**[15] 7032 3-9-0 56............(tp) AndrewElliott[(3)] 5 — 65
(John A Harris) *trckd ldr: led over 4f out: rdn along and hdd 3f out: rallied to ld wl over 1f out: sn drvn and styd on* **9/1**
U322 **2** 2 **Propaganda (IRE)**[23] 6959 3-8-12 70............ ChrisCatlin 11 — 57
(L M Cumani) *trckd ldrs: smooth hdwy to ld 3f out: pushed along and hdd wl over 1f out: sn rdn and hung lft: one pce* **1/1[1]**
5050 **3** 14 **Island King (IRE)**[36] 6815 4-9-7 40............ DanielTudhope 2 — 38
(R Bastiman) *hld up: hdwy 4f out: rdn along over 2f out and sn no imp* **100/1**
0302 **4** 1/2 **Soldier Field**[15] 7032 3-9-3 55............(p) TonyHamilton 10 — 37
(J S Wainwright) *hld up towards rr: hdwy on outer 4f out: chsd ldrs 3f out: sn rdn and plugged on one pce fnl 2f* **8/1[3]**
3 **5** 2 **Scary**[36] 6807 3-9-3 0............ LPKeniry 3 — 34
(P F I Cole) *chsd ldrs on inner: rdn along over 3f out and sn btn* **11/4[2]**
0600 **6** 7 **Reflective Glory (IRE)**[22] 4449 3-8-12 36............(p) PaulMulrennan 1 — 17
(J S Wainwright) *led: rdn along and hdd over 4f out: sn wknd* **66/1**
400 **7** 6 **Long Gone**[65] 6250 4-8-9 31............(p) MarkCoumbe[(7)] 8 — 6
(John A Harris) *chsd ldrs: rdn along 4f out and sn wknd* **50/1**
8 5 **Wordy's Girl**[41] 4-9-2 0............(b[1]) StephenDonohoe 7 — —
(M J Gingell) *a bhd* **150/1**
9 15 **Swimandyouwin (IRE)** 4-9-0 0............ MHarley[(7)] 9 — —
(Shaun Harley, Ire) *hld up: hdwy on outer and in tch over 4f out: rdn along wl over 2f out and sn wknd* **10/1**

2m 32.87s (3.97) **Going Correction** +0.35s/f (Slow)
WFA 3 from 4yo 4lb — 9 Ran SP% **112.0**
Speed ratings (Par 103): **99,97,87,87,85 80,76,72,61**
CSF £17.82 TOTE £8.10: £2.00, £1.10, £12.30; EX 22.00 TRIFECTA Not won..
Owner Miss Laura Morgan **Bred** D H W Dobson **Trained** Eastwell, Leics
FOCUS
A poor maiden and difficult to rate but unlikely to be a source of future winners.
Soldier Field Official explanation: trainer said gelding lost a hind shoe

7200 COME RACING TOMORROW H'CAP — 1m (F)
3:00 (3:02) (Class 5) (0-75,77) 3-Y-0+ — £2,968 (£876; £438) Stalls Low

Form — RPR
0001 **1** **Kabeer**[6] 7141 9-9-2 77 6ex............(t) NataliaGemelova[(5)] 4 — 91
(A J McCabe) *t.k.h: cl up tl led 1/2-way: pushed wl clr ins fnl 2f: kpt on* **5/2[2]**
000 **2** 12 **Spirit Of The Mist (IRE)**[16] 7018 3-9-4 75............(e[1]) JohnEgan 3 — 61
(D J Murphy) *t.k.h and led to 1/2-way: chsng wnr and rdn along over 2f out: sn drvn and one pce* **15/8[1]**
2516 **3** nk **Arena's Dream (USA)**[10] 7099 3-8-8 65............ PatCosgrave 2 — 51
(J R Boyle) *cl up whn n.m.r over 4f out: rdn 3f out: drvn over 2f out and sn one pce* **9/2**
1100 **4** 6 **Moheebb (IRE)**[42] 6738 3-8-10 67............ LiamJones 5 — 39
(D W Chapman) *cl up on outer: rdn along 3f out: sn wknd* **7/2[3]**
1460 **5** 13 **United Nations**[14] 7047 6-8-8 71 ow3............ SamuelDrury[(7)] 1 — 13
(N Wilson) *cl up on inner tl rdn along 3f out and sn wknd* **16/1**

1m 45.21s (0.61) **Going Correction** +0.35s/f (Slow)
WFA 3 from 5yo+ 1lb — 5 Ran SP% **109.6**
Speed ratings (Par 103): **110,98,97,91,78**
CSF £7.54 TOTE £3.80: £1.50, £1.50; EX 8.80.
Owner Placida Racing **Bred** Shadwell Estate Company **Trained** Babworth, Notts
■ Stewards' Enquiry : Natalia Gemelova two-day ban: used whip with excessive frequency and when clearly winning (Dec 31, Jan 1)
FOCUS
The market suggested that this was quite a competitive little heat, but Kabeer turned it into a procession. The winner has been rated back to his very best.

7201 PONTINS.COM H'CAP — 1m (F)
3:30 (3:31) (Class 6) (0-58,56) 3-Y-0 — £2,047 (£604; £302) Stalls Low

Form — RPR
6023 **1** **Only A Grand**[28] 6908 3-8-2 45............(b) AndrewMullen[(3)] 4 — 59
(R Bastiman) *chsd ldrs: hdwy to chal 3f out: led over 2f out: rdn clr over 1f out: styd on wl* **15/2**
6004 **2** 6 **The Power Of Phil**[7] 7133 3-8-5 45............ HayleyTurner 7 — 45
(Miss Joanne Priest) *in tch: hdwy to chse ldrs 3f out: rdn over 2f out: drvn and styd on appr last: tk 2nd on line* **5/1[3]**
5023 **3** shd **Cadwell**[8] 7127 3-9-2 56............ RobertHavlin 2 — 56
(T J Pitt) *cl up: led over 4f out: rdn along and hdd over 2f out: sn drvn and kpt on same pce: lost 2nd nr line* **5/4[1]**
03 **4** 5 **Winged Farasi**[15] 7028 3-8-8 55............ WilliamCarson[(7)] 1 — 43
(R A Harris) *sn rdn along and sulked in rr: bhd 1/2-way: sme hdwy fnl 2f: nvr a factor* **3/1[2]**
0606 **5** 5 **Bert's Memory**[19] 7001 3-8-8 48............(p) PaulMulrennan 6 — 25
(K A Ryan) *chsd ldrs: rdn along 3f out: drvn over 2f out and sn one pce* **9/1**
0-04 **6** 13 **Pretty Game**[310] 454 3-8-5 45............ PaulFessey 5 — —
(K A Ryan) *chsd ldrs: rdn along over 3f out and sn wknd* **16/1**
0006 **7** shd **The Light Fandango**[276] 708 3-8-5 45............ LiamJones 3 — —
(R A Harris) *s.i.s: a in rr* **33/1**
004 **8** 1 **Coleorton Dagger**[303] 506 3-8-5 45............ ChrisCatlin 8 — —
(J R Holt) *led: pushed along and hdd over 4f out: rdn over 3f out and sn wknd* **25/1**

1m 46.26s (1.66) **Going Correction** +0.35s/f (Slow) — 8 Ran SP% **120.5**
Speed ratings (Par 98): **105,99,98,93,88 75,75,74**
CSF £47.15 CT £79.61 TOTE £9.20: £2.30, £1.40, £1.50; EX 64.90 Trifecta £112.10 Pool: £521.48, 3.30 winning units. Place 6 £ 96.99, Place 5 £ 10.08.
Owner S Lorimer **Bred** Shade Oak Stud **Trained** Cowthorpe, N Yorks
FOCUS
Very ordinary handicap form rated around the third.
T/Plt: £122.80 to a £1 stake. Pool: £41,232.50. 245.05 winning tickets. T/Qpdt: £27.60 to a £1 stake. Pool: £4,053.40. 108.50 winning tickets. JR

7169 WOLVERHAMPTON (A.W) (L-H)
Thursday, December 20

OFFICIAL GOING: Standard
Wind: Almost nil Weather: Fine and cold

7202 PONTIN'S BOOK EARLY PRICE PROMISE NOVICE STKS — 5f 216y(P)
6:50 (6:51) (Class 5) 2-Y-0 — £2,817 (£838; £418; £209) Stalls Low

Form — RPR
1355 **1** **Gross Prophet**[68] 6171 2-9-10 87............ RichardKingscote 2 — 88+
(Tom Dascombe) *chsd ldrs: rdn to ld ent fnl f: sn edgd rt: r.o* **7/4[1]**
21 **2** 2 **Ike Quebec (FR)**[20] 6973 2-8-13 78............ HaddenFrost[(5)] 4 — 76
(R Hannon) *chsd ldr over 1f: led jst over 2f out: rdn wl over 1f out: hdd ent fnl f: sn edgd rt: no ex* **5/2[3]**
0240 **3** 10 **Russian Reel**[75] 6017 2-9-7 89............ PaulMulrennan 3 — 49
(K A Ryan) *s.i.s: sn rcvrd: wnt 2nd over 4f out: sn hung rt: wknd wl over 1f out* **15/8[2]**
1300 **4** 4 **Piece Of My Heart**[14] 7048 2-9-2 81............ NelsonDeSouza 1 — 32
(P F I Cole) *led: hdd jst over 2f out: sn rdn: wknd over 1f out* **12/1**

1m 18.51s (2.70) **Going Correction** +0.55s/f (Slow) — 4 Ran SP% **107.4**
Speed ratings (Par 96): **104,101,88,82**
CSF £6.29 TOTE £3.40; EX 8.30.
Owner Alan Solomon **Bred** A D Solomon **Trained** Lambourn, Berks

FOCUS
An interesting little contest best rated through the runner-up.

NOTEBOOK
Gross Prophet looked very well on this return following a two-month break. Quite highly tried since winning a Newbury nursery in September, he found this much easier despite again displaying a tendency to go right-handed. (op 6-4 tchd 15-8 and 2-1 in a place)
Ike Quebec(FR), reverting to 6f, was unable to cope with a rival he would have been meeting on 3lb better terms in a handicap. (op 11-4 tchd 9-4)
Russian Reel began to hang right at the end of the back straight and proved a most difficult ride on his sand debut. Official explanation: jockey said colt hung right throughout (op 5-2)
Piece Of My Heart was not beaten far on her comeback run on the sand at Deauville a fortnight ago but got put in her place here. (op 7-1)

7203 WOLVERHAMPTON-RACECOURSE.CO.UK MEDIAN AUCTION MAIDEN STKS — 1m 5f 194y(P)
7:20 (7:21) (Class 6) 3-5-Y-O — **£2,047** (£604; £302) **Stalls** Low

Form — RPR
0046 **1** **Prince Of Medina**[8] 7120 4-9-10 49 .... GeorgeBaker 3 — 50
(J R Best) *hld up: stdy hdwy 7f out: rdn over 3f out: led wl over 1f out: edgd lft ins fnl f: styd on* **10/11**[1]
0440 **2** *2* **Wavertree One Off**[28] 5573 5-9-10 40 .... AdamKirby 6 — 48
(J Ryan) *chsd ldr: led over 3f out: sn rdn: hdd wl over 1f out: nt qckn ins fnl f* **16/1**
364 **3** *4* **Piano Key**[8] 7125 3-8-5 42 .... GHannon(7) 5 — 37
(M D I Usher) *hld up in tch: pushed along over 5f out: edgd lft over 4f out: rdn and hung lft over 2f out: one pce* **11/1**
020 **4** *6* **Red**[115] 4877 3-8-12 60 .... DaneO'Neill 1 — 29
(R M Stronge) *s.s: t.k.h in rr: rdn 4f out: short-lived effrt over 2f out* **9/4**[2]
0500 **5** *8* **Arabellas Homer**[69] 6152 3-8-12 42 .... StephenDonohoe 7 — 17
(Mrs N S Evans) *t.k.h: led tl over 3f out: rdn and wknd over 2f out* **25/1**
0004 **6** *3/4* **Ocean Valentine**[10] 7102 4-9-5 40 .... RussellKennemore(5) 4 — 21
(J T Stimpson) *s.s: plld hrd in rr: rdn over 3f out: sn struggling* **11/1**
0500 **7** *46* **Hill Cloud**[27] 6911 5-9-10 50 .... TGMcLaughlin 2 — —
(W M Brisbourne) *hld up in tch: rdn and wkng whn hmpd and stmbld bdly and nrly uns rdr over 4f out: sn t.o* **8/1**[3]

3m 18.29s (10.92) **Going Correction** +0.55s/f (Slow)
WFA 3 from 4yo+ 7lb — **7** Ran SP% **120.7**
Speed ratings (Par 101): **90,88,86,83,78 78,51**
CSF £20.27 TOTE £1.90: £1.20, £5.50; EX 21.20.
Owner G G Racing **Bred** Slatch Farm Stud **Trained** Hucking, Kent
■ Stewards' Enquiry : G Hannon four-day ban: careless riding (Dec 31, Jan 1-3)

FOCUS
They went no great pace in this poor maiden which is best rated through the winner.
Hill Cloud Official explanation: jockey said gelding suffered interference in running

7204 PONTINS.COM NURSERY — 1m 1f 103y(P)
7:50 (7:50) (Class 5) (0-75,73) 2-Y-0 — **£2,968** (£876; £438) **Stalls** Low

Form — RPR
002 **1** **Martyr**[33] 6855 2-9-7 73 .... PatDobbs 5 — 79+
(R Hannon) *mde all: rdn over 1f out: r.o wl* **6/1**
0115 **2** *2 1/2* **Caltire (GER)**[17] 7010 2-8-7 64 ow2 .... JamieJones(5) 7 — 65
(M G Quinlan) *hld up in rr: rdn and hdwy on ins wl over 1f out: kpt on ins fnl f: nt trble wnr* **12/1**
0111 **3** *1 1/2* **Marino Prince (FR)**[26] 6933 2-8-13 72 .... PatrickDonaghy(7) 3 — 70
(T Wall) *hld up and bhd: rdn and hdwy over 2f out: hung lft ins fnl f: no ex* **11/1**
5000 **4** *3 1/2* **Ten Spot (IRE)**[1] 7182 2-8-4 56 .... (v) HayleyTurner 2 — 48
(Stef Liddiard) *hld up and bhd: rdn over 3f out: styd on fnl f: n.d* **20/1**
6462 **5** *5* **Clovis**[5] 7152 2-9-7 73 .... (b[1]) GregFairley 6 — 55
(M Johnston) *w wnr tl rdn over 2f out: hung lft over 1f out: wknd fnl f* **11/4**[2]
053 **6** *3 1/2* **Tevez**[26] 6934 2-9-5 71 .... PaulMulrennan 1 — 47
(M H Tompkins) *prom: rdn over 2f out: wknd over 1f out* **7/2**[3]
0061 **7** *6* **Kryptonite (IRE)**[16] 7022 2-9-0 66 .... SteveDrowne 4 — 30
(J W Hills) *prom tl rdn and wknd over 2f out: eased whn no ch over 1f out* **5/2**[1]
0000 **8** *1/2* **Morforwyn**[146] 3923 2-7-5 50 oh4 .... DavidProbert(7) 8 — 13
(A Bailey) *t.k.h: prom tl rdn and wknd over 3f out* **100/1**

2m 9.06s (6.44) **Going Correction** +0.55s/f (Slow) — **8** Ran SP% **113.5**
Speed ratings (Par 96): **93,90,89,86,81 78,73,73**
CSF £72.28 CT £767.32 TOTE £6.60: £1.90, £4.60, £4.00; EX 82.00.
Owner Highclere Thoroughbred Racing (Delilah) **Bred** D Maroun **Trained** East Everleigh, Wilts

FOCUS
Half of the field had won a total of seven races between them but only one of these were outside selling or claiming company. the third is rated just below recent form.

NOTEBOOK
Martyr ◆ adopted the same tactics as when second in a stretch-mile maiden here last month. The longer trip held no terrors for him and there should be plenty of opportunities if he is kept on the go this winter. (op 11-2)
Caltire(GER) showed no tendency to hang this time with the blinkers left off but was never going to peg back a winner who appears on the upgrade. (op 14-1 tchd 11-1)
Marino Prince(FR) looked reasonably treated on his first venture into a handicap but had nothing more to offer after hanging left in the closing stages. (op 6-1)
Ten Spot(IRE), trying a longer trip, could never get competitive after his run at Kempton the previous evening. (op 22-1)
Clovis, tried in blinkers after his second at Southwell last weekend, has yet to prove he stays beyond a mile and may be better suited to Fibresand. (tchd 3-1)
Tevez did not find a step up in distance the answer and now has something to prove. (op 11-2)
Kryptonite(IRE), raised 5lb for his win here, was most disappointing over this slightly longer trip. Official explanation: jockey said colt was never travelling (tchd 3-1)

7205 GO PONTIN'S H'CAP — 1m 4f 50y(P)
8:20 (8:21) (Class 5) (0-75,74) 3-Y-0 — **£2,968** (£876; £438) **Stalls** Low

Form — RPR
3043 **1** **Abounding**[14] 6506 3-8-9 65 .... JamesDoyle 1 — 72
(M J Attwater) *chsd ldr: rdn to ld over 2f out: drvn out* **12/1**
6241 **2** *nk* **The King And I (IRE)**[7] 7132 3-8-12 68 .... (b) ChrisCatlin 2 — 75+
(Miss E C Lavelle) *hld up in rr: rdn over 3f out: styd on ins fnl f: nt rch wnr* **5/2**[2]
021 **3** *1 1/4* **Noble Plum (IRE)**[12] 7076 3-9-4 74 .... JamieMackay 3 — 79
(Sir Mark Prescott) *hld up: wnt 2nd wl over 1f out: sn hung lft: nt qckn ins fnl f* **5/6**[1]
3501 **4** *4* **Vallemeldee (IRE)**[46] 6673 3-9-4 74 .... LPKeniry 4 — 72
(P W D'Arcy) *led tl over 2f out: sn rdn: wknd ins fnl f* **10/3**[3]

2m 50.02s (7.60) **Going Correction** +0.55s/f (Slow) — **4** Ran SP% **113.9**
Speed ratings (Par 102): **96,95,94,92**
CSF £41.02 TOTE £10.50; EX 34.20.
Owner The Attwater Partnership **Bred** A D G Oldrey **Trained** Epsom, Surrey
■ Stewards' Enquiry : Chris Catlin three-day ban: used whip with excessive force (Dec 31, Jan 1-2)

FOCUS
This quite interesting little handicap was a slowly-run afffair and it is doubtful if the form is solid.

7206 PONTIN'S SHORT BREAKS H'CAP — 5f 20y(P)
8:50 (8:52) (Class 6) (0-65,65) 3-Y-0+ — **£2,047** (£604; £302) **Stalls** Low

Form — RPR
2143 **1** **By The Edge (IRE)**[17] 7011 3-8-7 54 .... PaulFessey 3 — 66
(T D Barron) *mde all: rdn 1f out: drvn out* **12/1**
3023 **2** *1/2* **Monte Major (IRE)**[13] 7054 6-8-13 65 .... PatrickHills(5) 2 — 75
(D Shaw) *s.i.s: hld up and bhd: hdwy over 1f out: r.o ins fnl f: hung rt towards fin* **11/4**[1]
031 **3** *1 3/4* **Music Box Express**[16] 7019 3-8-13 60 .... (e) SteveDrowne 13 — 64
(D J Murphy) *a.p: rdn over 1f out: kpt on same pce fnl f* **10/1**
2005 **4** *shd* **Radiator Rooney (IRE)**[16] 7024 4-8-4 58 .... (b) JamesPSullivan(7) 8 — 62+
(Patrick Morris, Ire) *mid-div: c wd st: hung rt over 1f out: r.o ins fnl f* **11/1**
6001 **5** *1/2* **Sands Crooner (IRE)**[11] 7082 4-8-9 56 .... (v) DeanMcKeown 6 — 58
(D Shaw) *hld up in mid-div: hdwy 2f out: rdn 1f out: no ex ins fnl f* **7/2**[2]
4623 **6** *shd* **Wicked Uncle**[10] 7105 8-9-3 64 .... (v) PaulMulrennan 10 — 65
(S Gollings) *hld up and bhd: rdn and hdwy over 1f out: swtchd lft ins fnl f: kpt on* **9/1**[3]
0000 **7** *1/2* **Overstayed (IRE)**[12] 7078 4-9-4 65 .... (be) GeorgeBaker 7 — 65
(M Mullineaux) *a.p: rdn over 1f out: wknd ins fnl f* **16/1**
3046 **8** *1 1/4* **Metal Guru**[23] 6962 3-8-12 64 .... RussellKennemore(5) 12 — 59
(R Hollinshead) *hld up and bhd: c wd st: rdn and edgd lft fnl f: n.d* **14/1**
0334 **9** *2 1/2* **Hello Roberto**[11] 7082 6-8-6 53 .... (p) ChrisCatlin 4 — 39
(R A Harris) *chsd ldrs tl wknd wl over 1f out* **11/1**
0350 **10** *hd* **Celeb Style (IRE)**[6] 7137 3-8-2 52 .... PatrickMathers(3) 9 — 37
(Paul Green) *s.i.s: hld up and bhd: rdn over 1f out: no rspnse* **33/1**
0354 **11** *2* **Calypso King**[17] 7011 4-8-12 59 .... (b) LPKeniry 5 — 37
(Peter Grayson) *t.k.h in mid-div: nt clr run on ins wl over 1f out: n.d after* **12/1**
6400 **12** *1 1/4* **Ashes (IRE)**[42] 6730 5-8-8 62 .... DeclanCannon(7) 1 — 36
(K R Burke) *prom tl wknd fnl f* **18/1**
000 **13** *9* **Bungie**[16] 7024 3-8-1 55 .... (v[1]) AndrewHeffernan(7) 11 — —
(Paul Green) *swvd rt and lft s: a wl in rr* **50/1**

64.65 secs (1.83) **Going Correction** +0.55s/f (Slow) — **13** Ran SP% **122.7**
Speed ratings (Par 101): **107,106,103,103,102 102,101,99,95,95 91,89,75**
CSF £46.11 CT £373.50 TOTE £15.90: £3.10, £1.80, £4.80; EX 68.60.
Owner J Starbuck **Bred** A M Burke **Trained** Maunby, N Yorks

FOCUS
A low-key sprint handicap but run at a good pace and the form looks solid.

7207 PONTIN'S BOOK EARLY AND SAVE H'CAP — 7f 32y(P)
9:20 (9:21) (Class 6) (0-58,60) 3-Y-0+ — **£2,047** (£604; £302) **Stalls** High

Form — RPR
2030 **1** **Bens Georgie (IRE)**[29] 6895 5-8-6 53 .... JamesO'Reilly(5) 10 — 62
(D K Ivory) *hld up in mid-div: hdwy over 3f out: sn briefly nt clr run: rdn over 2f out: led 1f out: drvn out* **16/1**
0244 **2** *hd* **Green Pirate**[55] 6476 5-9-2 58 .... (v) GeorgeBaker 5 — 66
(W M Brisbourne) *n.m.r sn after s: sn swtchd lft: hld up and bhd: swtchd rt ent st: hdwy over 1f out: rdn and ev ch wl ins fnl f: r.o* **4/1**[3]
1536 **3** *4* **Piccolo Diamante (USA)**[9] 7113 3-8-10 52 .... (t) SteveDrowne 12 — 49
(D J Murphy) *swtchd lft s: hld up and bhd: c wd st: hdwy over 1f out: kpt on ins fnl f* **14/1**
0313 **4** *2* **Park Valley Prince**[11] 7085 3-8-11 53 .... HayleyTurner 3 — 45
(W R Muir) *a.p: edgd lft wl over 1f out: wknd ins fnl f* **11/4**[1]
00 **5** *hd* **Granakey (IRE)**[19] 6993 4-8-13 55 .... JamieMackay 2 — 46
(M Wigham) *bhd: forced wd st: hung lft over 1f out: nvr trbld ldrs* **25/1**
-650 **6** *hd* **Claws**[15] 7028 4-8-8 50 .... JamesDoyle 1 — 41
(A J Lidderdale) *led over 1f: prom: n.m.r wl over 1f out: wknd ins fnl f* **40/1**
62 **7** *3/4* **Tyrannosaurus Rex (IRE)**[22] 6963 3-9-2 58 .... (v) PaulMulrennan 7 — 47
(K R Burke) *hld up in mid-div: lost pl over 4f out: n.d after* **3/1**[2]
60-5 **8** *2 1/2* **Smirfys Systems**[16] 7025 8-8-7 49 .... StephenDonohoe 9 — 31
(E S McMahon) *hld up in mid-div: hdwy over 3f out: led 2f out: sn rdn: hdd 1f out: wknd* **17/2**
0021 **9** *1* **Trinculo (IRE)**[9] 7107 10-9-4 60 6ex .... (b) ChrisCatlin 11 — 39
(R A Harris) *prom: led briefly over 2f out: bmpd wl over 1f out: wknd fnl f* **20/1**
0230 **10** *1 1/4* **Beneking**[29] 6895 7-8-12 54 .... DaneO'Neill 6 — 30
(D Burchell) *prom: led over 5f out: rdn and hdd over 2f out: wknd wl over 1f out* **12/1**
0-00 **11** *10* **The Bronx**[162] 3429 3-8-11 53 .... (v[1]) PatCosgrave 4 — 2
(M J Wallace) *chsd ldrs: n.m.r after 1f: rdn over 3f out: sn lost pl* **8/1**

1m 33.57s (3.17) **Going Correction** +0.55s/f (Slow) — **11** Ran SP% **124.6**
Speed ratings (Par 101): **103,102,98,95,95 95,94,91,90,89 77**
CSF £82.26 CT £977.78 TOTE £21.40: £5.40, £1.90, £4.00; EX 112.30 Place 6 £3,708.77, Place 5 £1,368.30.
Owner Marcoe Electrical **Bred** Mrs Maureen Barbara Walsh **Trained** Radlett, Herts

FOCUS
Another low-grade handicap with the first two finishing clear.
T/Plt: £1,771.60 to a £1 stake. Pool: £84,943.65. 35.00 winning tickets. T/Qpdt: £130.90 to a £1 stake. Pool: £6,582.10. 37.20 winning tickets. KH

7195 SOUTHWELL (L-H)
Friday, December 21

OFFICIAL GOING: Standard to slow
Wind: almost nil Weather: dull and cold

7208 PONTIN'S BOOK EARLY PRICE PROMISE MAIDEN STKS — 1m (F)
12:20 (12:20) (Class 5) 2-Y-0 — **£2,968** (£876; £438) **Stalls** Low

Form — RPR
05 **1** **Pharaohs Justice (USA)**[14] 7051 2-9-3 0 .... PatCosgrave 8 — 74
(Jane Chapple-Hyam) *trckd ldrs: chal over 2f out: led over 1f out: hld on towards fin* **4/1**[2]
30 **2** *3/4* **Leamington (USA)**[68] 6202 2-8-9 0 .... AndrewElliott(3) 3 — 67
(M Johnston) *led: rdn over 2f out: hung lft: wandered and hdd over 1f out: no ex ins fnl f* **7/2**[1]
4 **3** *nk* **Caribana**[27] 6934 2-8-12 0 .... J-PGuillambert 7 — 66
(M A Jarvis) *sn trcking ldrs on outside: outpcd over 2f out: styd on wl ins fnl f* **4/1**[2]

0 4 2½ **Taikoo**[44] 6725 2-9-3 0 .... SteveDrowne 1 66+
(H Morrison) *outpcd and lost pl after 1f: hdwy over 2f out: kpt on fnl f* **8/1**

5 2 **Yes Mr President (IRE)** 2-9-3 0 .... GregFairley 6 61+
(M Johnston) *s.i.s: sn bhd: styd on fnl 2f: nt rch ldrs* **7/2**[1]

60 6 5 **Black Heart**[9] 7114 2-9-3 0 .... OscarUrbina 5 50
(M Botti) *w ldrs: drvn over 4f out: sn outpcd* **15/2**[3]

00 7 23 **Hollow Dream (IRE)**[14] 7058 2-8-12 0 .... LiamJones 4 —
(R A Harris) *w ldrs: reminders 5f out: outpcd over 3f out: sn lost pl and bhd* **66/1**

8 8 **Tiegan An Josh** 2-8-12 0 .... PaulMulrennan 2 —
(A Crook) *s.i.s: sn bhd: t.o over 3f out* **50/1**

1m 45.74s (1.14) **Going Correction** +0.075s/f (Slow) **8 Ran SP% 110.8**
Speed ratings (Par 96): **97,96,95,93,91 86,63,55**
CSF £17.19 TOTE £4.60: £2.00, £1.90, £1.40; EX 17.70 Trifecta £66.50 Part won. Pool £93.78 - 0.72 winning units..
Owner Franconson Partners **Bred** The Answer LLC **Trained** Newmarket, Suffolk

FOCUS
A modest maiden rated for the time being through the runner-up.

NOTEBOOK
Pharaohs Justice(USA), having his third start, proved suited by this flatter track. He worked hard to master the leader but at the line there was precious little to spare. (op 9-2 tchd 7-2)
Leamington(USA) took them along but hung and wandered under pressure and in the end seemed to be worried out of it.
Caribana, tapped for toe once in line for home, put in some solid late work and will be suited by another step up in trip. (op 7-2)
Taikoo, whose only previous outing was on turf, stayed on after getting outpaced and will fare better in handicap company over further at three. (op 6-1)
Yes Mr President(IRE), a late foal, is on the leg and weak. Clueless, after a tardy start he was steadily pulling back the leaders in the home straight. He should improve a good deal for the experience. (tchd 4-1)

7209 GO PONTIN'S (S) STKS 6f (F)
12:55 (12:55) (Class 6) 3-Y-0+ **£2,047** (£604; £302) **Stalls Low**

Form RPR

2165 1 **Monashee Brave (IRE)**[11] 7094 4-9-5 60 .... PaulDoe 4 66
(R A Harris) *mde virtually all: carried hd high and kpt on: hld on towards fin* **5/1**[3]

6606 2 nk **Mozakhraf (USA)**[17] 7020 5-9-5 58 .... (p) PaulMulrennan 7 65
(K A Ryan) *chsd ldrs: drvn 3f out: chal 1f out: no ex towards fin* **9/4**[1]

0541 3 1½ **Mister Elegant**[10] 7108 5-9-5 52 .... SteveDrowne 2 60
(J L Spearing) *in tch: drvn and outpcd 3f out: styd on fnl f* **11/4**[2]

5000 4 nk **Pappas Image**[239] 1266 3-8-9 45 .... (p) PatrickMathers(3) 6 52
(A J McCabe) *hmpd s: hdwy over 2f out: hung lft and kpt on fnl f* **16/1**

4000 5 ½ **Charlotte Grey**[12] 7082 3-9-0 57 .... GregFairley 9 53
(C N Allen) *chsd ldrs: kpt on same pce fnl 2f* **7/1**

0000 6 1½ **Bold Nevison (IRE)**[50] 6609 3-8-9 42 .... MarkLawson(3) 8 46
(B Smart) *mid-div: edgd rt and kpt on same pce fnl f* **22/1**

0000 7 ¾ **Put It On The Card**[18] 7006 3-9-5 60 .... (v) TonyHamilton 12 50
(J S Wainwright) *chsd ldrs on outer: hung lft and one pce fnl 2f* **20/1**

2030 8 ½ **Nawayea**[7] 7144 4-8-2 45 .... (t) KirstyMilczarek(5) 3 37
(C N Allen) *w wnr: wknd fnl f* **14/1**

0000 9 shd **Stepaside (IRE)**[34] 5525 3-8-5 44 .... (b) SBushby(7) 13 42
(A D Brown) *bhd: hdwy on outer over 2f out: nvr nr ldrs* **33/1**

P000 10 1¾ **Cape Dancer (IRE)**[53] 6537 3-8-7 42 .... (p) PaulFessey 5 31
(J S Wainwright) *a towards rr* **33/1**

11 3½ **Brunton (IRE)**[62] 6347 5-8-12 41 .... StephenDonohoe 1 25
(A Berry) *mid-div: drvn over 4f out: sn outpcd and lost pl* **40/1**

5-00 12 11 **Ten For Tosca (IRE)**[92] 5564 3-8-12 48 .... LiamJones 11 —
(R A Harris) *mid-div: lost pl over 3f out: sn bhd* **50/1**

1m 18.81s (1.91) **Going Correction** +0.075s/f (Slow) **12 Ran SP% 118.5**
Speed ratings (Par 101): **90,89,87,87,86 84,83,82,82,80 75,61**
CSF £15.36 TOTE £5.20: £2.10, £1.30, £1.20; EX 25.20 Trifecta £39.50 Pool £148.84 - 2.67 winning units..There was no bid for the winner.
Owner Miss Sarah Anne Phillips **Bred** Golden Vale Stud **Trained** Earlswood, Monmouths

FOCUS
An ordinary seller but the form looks sound at this level rated around the first four.

7210 SOUTHWELL-RACECOURSE.CO.UK NURSERY 6f (F)
1:30 (1:30) (Class 6) (0-65,71) 2-Y-0 **£2,047** (£604; £302) **Stalls Low**

Form RPR

0422 1 **Yankee Storm**[15] 7042 2-8-11 55 .... PatCosgrave 6 60
(M J Wallace) *mde all: qckND over 2f out: clr over 1f out: readily* **11/4**[1]

3423 2 2½ **What's For Tea**[15] 7044 2-9-4 62 .... RichardKingscote 2 60
(Tom Dascombe) *swvd rt s: sn chsng ldrs: wnt 2nd over 1f out: kpt on: no ch w wnr* **7/2**[2]

01 3 2½ **Lujano**[17] 7021 2-9-2 60 .... PaulMulrennan 8 50
(Ollie Pears) *w ldrs on outside: effrt over 2f out: kpt on same pce* **7/2**[2]

0021 4 ¾ **Mission Impossible**[8] 7129 2-9-6 71 6ex .... PatrickDonaghy(7) 7 59
(P C Haslam) *w ldrs: wknd over 1f out* **4/1**[3]

1005 5 hd **Countrywide Comet (IRE)**[7] 7136 2-9-4 62 .... (b) TGMcLaughlin 5 49
(P Howling) *sltly hmpd s: sn chsng ldrs: edgd lft and one pce fnl 2f* **16/1**

5001 6 ¾ **Night Robe**[7] 7136 2-8-8 52 6ex ow1 .... StephenDonohoe 1 37
(P D Evans) *sn outpcd and in rr: hdwy on outer over 2f out: nvr on terms* **7/1**

1m 18.68s (1.78) **Going Correction** +0.075s/f (Slow) **6 Ran SP% 109.5**
Speed ratings (Par 94): **91,87,84,83,83 82**
CSF £11.91 CT £29.71 TOTE £3.20: £1.30, £2.60; EX 10.00 Trifecta £40.30 Pool £282.63 - 4.97 winning units..
Owner Greenstead Hall Racing **Bred** Mark Johnston Racing Ltd **Trained** Newmarket, Suffolk

FOCUS
An improved effort from the in-form winner. The race has been rated through the runner-up but has a dubious look about it.

NOTEBOOK
Yankee Stormis thriving and racing with real enthusiasm always looked in total charge. (op 10-3)
What's For Tea continues in good form but that second career success is proving elusive. In the end she was no match. (op 5-1)
Lujano, trapped on the outer, tended to do too much and in the end was firmly put in his place. Hopefully the experience will not be lost on him. (tchd 10-3 and 4-1)
Mission Impossible, back in handicap company, was anchored by the penalty for his maiden-race success. (op 11-4)
Countrywide Comet(IRE), left short of room at the start, ended up racing towards the far side and never threatened. (op 14-1)
Night Robe, under her penalty, was soon struggling to keep up. (op 6-1)

7211 PONTINS.COM H'CAP 1m 3f (F)
2:05 (2:05) (Class 5) (0-70,68) 3-Y-0 **£2,968** (£876; £438) **Stalls Low**

Form RPR

046 1 **Clear Reef**[20] 6991 3-9-0 64 .... TGMcLaughlin 6 75
(Jane Chapple-Hyam) *stdd s: hld up in last: pushed along over 5f out: styd on to ld over 1f out: kpt on wl* **8/1**[3]

0 2 2½ **Pertemps Networks**[15] 5704 3-8-5 55 .... DaleGibson 3 62
(M W Easterby) *trckd ldrs: shkn up to ld over 2f out: hdd over 1f out: kpt on same pce* **15/8**[2]

510 3 4 **Stringsofmyheart**[172] 3170 3-9-4 68 .... (e[1]) PaulMulrennan 4 68
(Miss Gay Kelleway) *sn led: hdd over 2f out: kpt on same pce* **8/1**[3]

11V 4 ¾ **Alonso De Guzman (IRE)**[11] 7100 3-8-12 62 .... PatCosgrave 7 61
(J R Boyle) *chsd ldrs: drvn over 2f out: one pce* **11/8**[1]

4564 5 13 **Black Mogul**[13] 7081 3-7-12 55 oh9 ow1 .... (b) PatrickDonaghy(7) 1 32
(R Hollinshead) *led early: chsd ldrs: wknd over 2f out* **12/1**

0305 6 3½ **My Sara**[10] 7109 3-8-4 54 .... (b[1]) SaleemGolam 2 25
(R A Fahey) *chsd ldrs: drvn over 2f out: sn lost pl* **16/1**

2m 27.37s (-1.53) **Going Correction** +0.075s/f (Slow) **6 Ran SP% 112.7**
Speed ratings (Par 102): **108,106,103,102,93 90**
CSF £23.69 TOTE £8.80: £3.20, £1.60; EX 32.30.
Owner Chapple-Hyam Serrell Tegel Ward **Bred** Hesmonds Stud Ltd **Trained** Newmarket, Suffolk

FOCUS
With the favourite flopping it did not take that much winning. The winner, on his handicap debut, showed improved form to account for a recent hurdle-race winner.

7212 PONTIN'S SHORT BREAKS H'CAP 6f (F)
2:40 (2:40) (Class 4) (0-85,85) 3-Y-0+ **£4,728** (£1,406; £702; £351) **Stalls Low**

Form RPR

11-0 1 **Crimson King (IRE)**[61] 6355 6-8-8 75 .... JamieMackay 6 92+
(R W Price) *hld up: smooth hdwy 2f out: rdn to ld jst ins fnl f: r.o strly* **12/1**

6002 2 2½ **Resplendent Alpha**[9] 7126 3-8-12 79 .... TGMcLaughlin 7 86
(P Howling) *sn in rr and pushed along: hdwy over 2f out: styd on to take 2nd ins fnl f: no ch w wnr* **11/4**[1]

5520 3 ¾ **Coleorton Dancer**[12] 7087 5-8-9 76 .... (p) PaulMulrennan 5 81
(K A Ryan) *w ldrs: led over 1f out: hdd jst ins fnl f: no ex* **11/4**[1]

0013 4 3 **Compton Classic**[14] 7059 5-8-6 73 .... (v) GregFairley 3 68
(J R Boyle) *w ldrs: led 3f out: hdd over 1f out: sn btn* **5/1**[2]

5665 5 3 **New York Oscar (IRE)**[10] 7112 3-8-12 82 .... (v) PatrickMathers(3) 4 67
(A J McCabe) *chsd ldrs: rdn over 3f out: wknd over 1f out* **15/2**

-210 6 3½ **Doubtful Sound (USA)**[246] 1108 3-8-9 76 .... PaulFessey 2 50
(T D Barron) *led tl 3f out: lost pl over 1f out* **11/2**[3]

3015 7 1¼ **Blue Rocket (IRE)**[20] 6992 3-8-11 85 .... (e) DeclanCannon(7) 1 55
(D J Murphy) *chsd ldrs: wknd 2f out* **11/1**

1m 17.36s (0.46) **Going Correction** +0.075s/f (Slow) **7 Ran SP% 113.2**
Speed ratings (Par 105): **99,95,94,90,86 82,80**
CSF £44.14 TOTE £10.40: £3.80, £1.80; EX 47.80.
Owner Rothmere Racing Limited **Bred** Hazel Kelly **Trained** Newmarket, Suffolk

FOCUS
A lightly-raced and progressive winner. The race has been rated around the placed horses.

7213 PONTIN'S BOOK EARLY AND SAVE POUNDS H'CAP 1m (F)
3:15 (3:15) (Class 6) (0-65,70) 3-Y-0+ **£2,047** (£604; £302) **Stalls Low**

Form RPR

0301 1 **Dado Mush**[9] 7127 4-8-0 51 6ex .... (p) KirstyMilczarek(5) 8 70+
(T T Clement) *chsd ldr: led 3f out: drvn clr appr fnl f: readily* **15/8**[1]

0541 2 5 **Jord (IRE)**[6] 7155 3-9-6 70 6ex .... AndrewElliott(3) 7 78
(A J McCabe) *led: hdd 3f out: kpt on: no ch w wnr* **8/1**

0214 3 1¼ **Waterloo Corner**[29] 6906 5-8-13 59 .... PaulMulrennan 6 64
(R Craggs) *chsd ldrs: outpcd and lost pl over 4f out: hdwy 2f out: kpt on to take modest 3rd jst ins fnl f* **11/2**[2]

5605 4 2½ **Very Well Red**[6] 7155 4-8-12 63 .... JamieJones(5) 9 62
(P W Hiatt) *trckd ldrs: one pce fnl 2f* **16/1**

4044 5 1 **Boundless Prospect (USA)**[7] 7141 8-9-0 65 .... (e[1]) NicolPolli(5) 4 62
(Miss Gay Kelleway) *s.i.s: bhd: sme hdwy over 3f out: nvr nr ldrs* **8/1**

4652 6 6 **Komreyev Star**[4] 7169 5-8-5 51 oh6 .... (p) LiamJones 3 34
(R E Peacock) *chsd ldrs: drvn 4f out: edgd lft and wknd over 1f out* **7/1**[3]

5-01 7 10 **Oakbridge (IRE)**[315] 402 5-9-0 60 .... VinceSlattery 5 20
(R Brotherton) *mid-div: drvn over 3f out: sn lost pl* **16/1**

4003 8 ½ **Red Contact (USA)**[6] 7155 6-9-5 65 .... (p) DanielTudhope 1 24
(A Dickman) *chsd ldrs: rdn over 2f out: lost pl over 1f out* **15/2**

0035 9 5 **Star Of The Desert (IRE)**[13] 7080 4-8-10 56 .... (p) PhillipMakin 2 4
(Mrs K Walton) *s.i.s: sn mid-div: lost pl over 3f out: sn bhd and eased* **16/1**

000- 10 10 **Boogie Magic**[532] 3263 7-8-5 51 oh6 .... JamieMackay 10 —
(R W Price) *sn in rr and pushed along: bhd fnl 3f: eased* **50/1**

1m 43.53s (-1.07) **Going Correction** +0.075s/f (Slow)
WFA 3 from 4yo+ 1lb **10 Ran SP% 116.3**
Speed ratings (Par 101): **108,103,101,99,98 92,82,81,76,66**
CSF £17.38 CT £71.33 TOTE £2.60: £1.10, £2.90, £2.10; EX 18.70 Trifecta £96.80 Pool £625.03 - 4.58 winning units. Place 6 £18.18, Place 5 £11.85..
Owner Dr M Edres **Bred** Bellow Hill Stud **Trained** Newmarket, Suffolk

FOCUS
An improved effort from the winner, the placed horses ran to their pre-race marks.
Red Contact(USA) Official explanation: jockey said gelding stopped very quickly in home straight
T/Plt: £52.60 to a £1 stake. Pool: £34,495.40. 478.30 winning tickets. T/Qpdt: £37.70 to a £1 stake. Pool: £3,360.80. 65.90 winning tickets. WG

7202 WOLVERHAMPTON (A.W) (L-H)
Friday, December 21

OFFICIAL GOING: Standard
Wind: Almost nil Weather: Fine and cold

7214 MACE RACING AT WOLVERHAMPTON APPRENTICE H'CAP 1m 1f 103y(P)
7:00 (7:00) (Class 6) (0-65,71) 3-Y-0+ **£2,218** (£654; £327) **Stalls Low**

Form RPR

0536 1 **Magic Warrior**[12] 7083 7-9-1 59 .... PatrickDonaghy 4 69
(J C Fox) *stdd s: hld up: hdwy over 2f out: r.o wl u.p to ld nr fin* **12/1**

4033 2 ½ **Casablanca Minx (IRE)**[7] 7146 4-8-8 57 .... (v) RichardEvans(5) 3 66
(P D Evans) *hld up: hdwy on ins over 2f out: rdn over 1f out: led briefly cl home: r.o* **11/2**[2]

0- **3** *1* **Breaker Morant (IRE)**[60] 6396 5-8-11 **60**............(b) JamesPSullivan(5) 5 67
(J G Burns, Ire) *hld up in tch: led wl over 2f out: clr wl over 1f out: sn rdn: hdd and no ex cl home* **11/2**[2]

4321 **4** *6* **Alfie Tupper (IRE)**[7] 7146 4-9-8 **71** 6ex.......................... JamieKyne(5) 1 65
(J R Boyle) *stdd s: t.k.h and sn wl in rr: hdwy on outside over 3f out: rdn over 2f out: wknd wl over 1f out* **6/5**[1]

0043 **5** *2 1/2* **Thornaby Green**[14] 7056 6-9-2 **60**.................................... DeanHeslop 6 49
(T D Barron) *led tl wl over 2f out: sn rdn: wknd wl over 1f out* **8/1**[3]

452 **6** *4* **Trackattack**[6] 7157 5-8-4 **51** oh6..................................(p) SoniaEaton(3) 8 32
(M Appleby) *sn chsng ldr: wknd over 4f out* **33/1**

6122 **7** *7* **Machinate (USA)**[13] 7079 5-8-10 **61**.................... Julie-AnneCumine(7) 9 27
(W M Brisbourne) *prom: wnt 2nd over 5f out: wknd over 2f out* **9/1**

0000 **8** *25* **Where's Broughton**[50] 6603 4-8-8 **57**........................ DebraEngland(5) 2 —
(W J Musson) *prom tl wknd over 3f out: eased whn no ch fnl 2f* **16/1**

2m 3.39s (0.77) **Going Correction** +0.15s/f (Slow)
WFA 3 from 4yo+ 2lb **8** Ran SP% **113.9**
Speed ratings (Par 101): **102,101,100,95,93 89,83,61**
CSF £75.37 CT £407.70 TOTE £7.00: £1.50, £1.80, £1.90; EX 73.50.

Owner Miss H J Flower **Bred** Patrick Eddery Ltd **Trained** Collingbourne Ducis, Wilts

FOCUS
A run-of-the-mill handicap in which the pace seemed fair and the form looks sound. The action unfolded against the inside rail in the straight.

Where's Broughton Official explanation: jockey said filly was never travelling

7215 POONTIN'S BOOK EARLY H'CAP 5f 20y(P)

7:30 (7:32) (Class 5) (0-75,78) 3-Y-O+ **£3,238** (£963; £481; £240) **Stalls** Low

Form RPR

0004 **1** **Stolt (IRE)**[14] 7059 3-9-0 **71**.. DanielTudhope 2 83
(N Wilson) *t.k.h: a.p: led over 1f out: rdn and edgd lft wl ins fnl f: r.o* **7/2**[2]

3010 **2** *shd* **Memphis Man**[17] 7026 4-8-5 **69**.................................. RichardEvans(7) 4 81
(P D Evans) *s.i.s and n.m.r: hld up in rr: hdwy whn nt clr run and swtchd lft 1f out: ev ch wl ins fnl f: r.o* **8/1**

0132 **3** *2 1/2* **Tartatartufata**[3] 7179 5-8-11 **73**....................................(v) TolleyDean(5) 7 76
(D Shaw) *hld up in tch: rdn over 1f out: no ex towards fin* **11/4**[1]

0506 **4** *1 3/4* **Almaty Express**[14] 7059 5-8-7 **64**..........................(b) StephenDonohoe 8 61
(J R Weymes) *prom: rdn over 2f out: sltly outpcd over 1f out: kpt on towards fin* **12/1**

6622 **5** *3/4* **Fizzlephut (IRE)**[9] 7116 5-8-11 **68**................................ PaulFitzsimons 3 62
(Miss J R Tooth) *hld up: hdwy on ins wl over 1f out: rdn and wknd ins fnl f* **4/1**[3]

5063 **6** *nk* **Baileys Outshine**[9] 7116 3-8-11 **68**...................................... TPQueally 6 61
(J G Given) *w ldr: led 2f out: rdn and hdd over 1f out: wknd ins fnl f* **8/1**

6001 **7** *3* **Count Cougar (USA)**[3] 7179 7-9-4 **78** 6ex........... MichaelJStainton(3) 1 60
(S P Griffiths) *led: hdd 2f out: rdn and wknd 1f out* **11/2**

63.55 secs (0.73) **Going Correction** +0.15s/f (Slow) **7** Ran SP% **114.2**
Speed ratings (Par 103): **100,99,95,93,91 91,86**
CSF £30.74 CT £86.59 TOTE £4.10: £2.90, £4.90; EX 47.60.

Owner Dixon, McIntyre, Tobin **Bred** Seamus Phelan **Trained** Flaxton, N Yorks

FOCUS
Exposed performers in this ordinary event but the early pace seemed just fair and the first two were clear of a solid favourite. The principals raced against the inside rail in the straight.

7216 PONTIN'S HOLIDAYS MEDIAN AUCTION MAIDEN FILLIES' STKS 5f 216y(P)

7:55 (7:59) (Class 6) 2-Y-O **£2,047** (£604; £302) **Stalls** Low

Form RPR

4 **1** **Wise Melody**[23] 6964 2-9-0 0.. LiamJones 6 70+
(W J Haggas) *led early: a.p: squeezed through on ins to ld 2f out: clr over 1f out: r.o wl* **15/8**[1]

2 *6* **Kool Katie** 2-8-7 0.. IanCraven(7) 3 52+
(Mrs G S Rees) *s.i.s: bhd tl hdwy and swtchd lft 1f out: kpt on ins fnl f: no ch w wnr* **16/1**

0 **3** *1 1/2* **Topflightrebellion**[109] 5097 2-9-0 0.................................. DaleGibson 1 48
(Mrs G S Rees) *prom: lost pl over 3f out: nt clr run on ins 2f out: rallied over 1f out: kpt on same pce ins fnl f* **50/1**

0 **4** *1* **Jazenio**[14] 7058 2-9-0 0.. PaulFessey 5 45
(K A Ryan) *sn led: hdd 2f out: rdn over 1f out: one pce* **20/1**

64 **5** *3/4* **Doric Dream**[94] 5501 2-9-0 0.. PhillipMakin 9 42
(B Smart) *sn prom: ev ch 2f out: sn rdn: one pce* **9/2**[3]

52 **6** *1* **My Pin Up**[23] 6964 2-9-0 0... PatDobbs 10 39
(Christian Wroe) *hld up in tch: rdn and no hdwy fnl 2f* **4/1**[2]

00 **7** *3 1/2* **Far Song (IRE)**[163] 3417 2-9-0 0... LPKeniry 8 29
(A M Balding) *hld up in tch: rdn and wknd over 1f out* **10/1**

8 *hd* **Tilly Ann (IRE)** 2-8-9 0.. ColinHaddon(5) 2 28
(Peter Grayson) *dwlt: outpcd* **40/1**

9 *3 1/2* **Marie Claude** 2-9-0 0.. TPQueally 4 18
(J Noseda) *s.i.s: outpcd* **5/1**

1m 17.35s (1.54) **Going Correction** +0.15s/f (Slow) **9** Ran SP% **113.8**
Speed ratings (Par 91): **95,87,85,83,82 81,76,76,71**
CSF £34.30 TOTE £3.00: £1.10, £3.70, £7.70; EX 62.00.

Owner Wise Move UK Limited **Bred** I A Southcott **Trained** Newmarket, Suffolk

FOCUS
An ordinary bunch with the exception of the winner, who turned in an improved display to win in the centre of the course, looks one to keep on the right side.

NOTEBOOK
Wise Melody ◆, who shaped with a bit of promise on her debut at Kempton, turned in an improved display. As is the case with many of her stable companions, she took a good hold but fairly sprinted away in the straight to win with a good deal in hand and she looks the sort to hold her own in a bit better company. (tchd 2-1)

Kool Katie, out of a multiple winner, showed ability on this racecourse debut but, while entitled to improve, is the sort to fare best in ordinary events over further once handicapped. She is one to keep an eye on. (op 25-1)

Topflightrebellion, soundly beaten on her debut over this course and distance on her sole previous run in September, fared much better this time but, as with her stable companion, her future lies in ordinary handicap company.

Jazenio, well beaten on his debut at this course earlier in the month, fared a bit better this time but is likely to continue to look vulnerable in this type of event. (op 12-1)

Doric Dream showed ability at a modest level on turf but failed to build on that for this All-Weather debut and first start for three months. She is in good hands but is another that is going to continue to look vulnerable in maiden company. (op 4-1 tchd 7-2)

My Pin Up, who had shown progressive form at a modest level in maidens, proved a disappointment on this first start at this course. She is better than she showed here though, and is worth another chance in ordinary company. (op 9-2 tchd 5-1)

7217 PONTIN'S GREAT FAMILY HOLIDAYS MAIDEN STKS 7f 32y(P)

8:25 (8:27) (Class 5) 2-Y-O **£2,968** (£876; £438) **Stalls** High

Form RPR

1 **Fadhb Ar Bith (IRE)** 2-9-3 0...(t) LPKeniry 3 73
(John A Quinn, Ire) *t.k.h: chsd ldr: led 2f out: rdn 1f out: edgd lft wl ins fnl f: drvn out* **40/1**

2 *1* **Moosley (IRE)** 2-9-3 0.. AdrianMcCarthy 4 71
(P W Chapple-Hyam) *hld up: hdwy on ins wl over 1f out: sn rdn: edgd rt towards fin: nt rch wnr* **1/1**[1]

0 **3** *2* **Benedict Spirit (IRE)**[86] 5734 2-9-3 0.............................. SaleemGolam 2 66
(M H Tompkins) *a.p: pushed along over 3f out: rdn wl over 1f out: one pce fnl f* **20/1**

4 **4** *1 1/4* **Barons Court**[7] 7140 2-9-3 0.. GregFairley 1 63
(M Johnston) *led: hdd 2f out: rdn over 1f out: wknd ins fnl f* **15/8**[2]

034 **5** *hd* **Spice Trade**[72] 6106 2-9-3 75...(v[1]) TPQueally 6 62
(J Noseda) *s.i.s: hld up: rdn and hdwy over 2f out: hung lft over 1f out: wknd ins fnl f* **6/1**[3]

6 *15* **Princess Zhukova (IRE)** 2-8-7 0................................. TolleyDean(5) 7 20
(R J Price) *s.i.s: hld up in rr: rdn over 2f out: sn struggling* **100/1**

1m 32.23s (1.83) **Going Correction** +0.15s/f (Slow) **6** Ran SP% **107.3**
Speed ratings (Par 96): **95,93,91,90,89 72**
CSF £75.02 TOTE £19.00: £4.60, £1.80; EX 132.30.

Owner Ju Ju Partnership **Bred** Glending Bloodstock **Trained** Blackmiller Hill, Co. Kildare

FOCUS
An ordinary maiden, especially with Barons Court disappointing and the form is somewhat guessy. The action unfolded against the inside rail.

NOTEBOOK
Fadhb Ar Bith(IRE), a 36,000gns half brother to winners over 7f and 1m, was very easy to back but showed a fair level of form in a tongue-tie on this racecourse debut. He travelled well for a long way and may be capable of better. (op 28-1)

Moosley(IRE) ◆, a 100,000gns half-brother to prolific middle distance stayer Isa'af, failed to justify the market support but ran creditably on this racecourse debut and left the impression that he would be winning races, especially granted a stiffer test of stamina. (tchd 8-11)

Benedict Spirit(IRE), well beaten on his debut at Redcar in September, fared better in this ordinary event on this racecourse debut and may be capable of a bit better granted a stiffer test of stamina in run-of-the-mill handicap company. (op 12-1 tchd 25-1)

Barons Court, who shaped with a degree of promise in an ordinary event at Southwell the previous week, had the run of the race but failed to build on that this time. This may have come too quickly but he is not one to write off just yet. (op 11-4)

Spice Trade, who showed ability at a modest level in maiden company, looked to have reasonable prospects in this ordinary event for this All-Wweather debut but he looked less than straightforward in the blinkers and was below his best. He is likely to remain vulnerable in this type of event. (op 5-1 tchd 9-2 and 13-2)

Princess Zhukova(IRE), a half-sister to Chester Vase winner Red Lancer, refused to enter the stalls on her intended debut and was soundly beaten when consenting to race this time. She has plenty to prove. (op 80-1)

7218 GO PONTIN'S HOLIDAYS H'CAP 1m 141y(P)

8:55 (8:56) (Class 6) (0-55,55) 3-Y-O+ **£2,047** (£604; £302) **Stalls** Low

Form RPR

0000 **1** **Sir Bond (IRE)**[13] 7079 6-8-9 **53**.................................... SladeO'Hara(5) 5 62
(G R Oldroyd) *hld up in tch: pushed along over 3f out: rdn over 1f out: r.o to ld cl home* **13/2**

0531 **2** *1/2* **Beck**[4] 7169 3-8-10 **51** 6ex.. TGMcLaughlin 8 59
(W M Brisbourne) *t.k.h: a.p: rdn to ld wl over 1f out: sn edgd lft: hdd cl home* **4/1**[2]

6232 **3** *shd* **Ours (IRE)**[9] 7127 4-9-2 **55**... StephenDonohoe 1 63
(John A Harris) *hld up in mid-div: rdn and hdwy over 2f out: swtchd lft 1f out: kpt on ins fnl f* **2/1**[1]

0565 **4** *4* **Climate (IRE)**[20] 7001 8-8-13 **52**... TPQueally 7 51
(R Hollinshead) *hld up and bhd: rdn and hdwy over 2f out: one pce fnl f* **13/2**

0550 **5** *2 1/2* **Hornpipe**[8] 6864 5-8-7 **46** oh1.......................................(be[1]) JamesDoyle 4 39
(M Hill) *led: rdn and hdd wl over 1f out: wknd 1f out* **16/1**

0504 **6** *2* **Wizby**[4] 7169 4-8-7 **46** oh1...(v) MatthewHenry 10 34
(P D Evans) *hld up and bhd: rdn over 2f out: nvr nr ldrs* **16/1**

3000 **7** *shd* **Hayley's Flower (IRE)**[48] 6642 3-8-9 **50**................................ PatDobbs 2 38
(J C Fox) *hld up and bhd: rdn and swtchd rt ent st: nvr nr ldrs* **33/1**

0600 **8** *3* **Cantique (IRE)**[11] 7103 3-8-5 **46** oh1................................. LiamJones 6 27
(R J Price) *hld up in rr: swtchd rt over 1f out: n.d* **40/1**

0 **9** *4* **Major Melody (IRE)**[88] 5696 5-8-7 **46** oh1............................ LPKeniry 3 18
(J J Lennon, Ire) *hld up in tch: pushed along over 3f out: wknd 2f out* **16/1**

0423 **10** *3* **Sarraaf (IRE)**[13] 7079 11-9-0 **53**.................................... PhillipMakin 11 18
(I Semple) *hld up in mid-div: rdn 3f out: sn bhd* **6/1**[3]

-003 **11** *1* **Blakeshall Hope**[4] 7169 5-8-4 **50** oh1 ow4.................. MarkCoumbe(7) 9 13
(A J Chamberlain) *t.k.h: prom tl rdn and wknd 3f out* **20/1**

1m 52.42s (0.66) **Going Correction** +0.15s/f (Slow)
WFA 3 from 4yo+ 2lb **11** Ran SP% **122.1**
Speed ratings (Par 101): **103,102,102,98,96 94,94,92,88,85 85**
CSF £33.40 CT £73.97 TOTE £9.40: £1.90, £1.80, £1.40; EX 51.50.

Owner R C Bond **Bred** Seamus Phelan **Trained** Brawby, N Yorks

FOCUS
A modest event run at a fair pace which again unfolded close to the inside rail and the form looks reasonable rated around the first and third.

7219 PONTINS.COM H'CAP 1m 4f 50y(P)

9:20 (9:20) (Class 6) (0-55,57) 3-Y-O+ **£2,218** (£654; £327) **Stalls** Low

Form RPR

0020 **1** **Sir Sandicliffe (IRE)**[14] 7060 3-8-10 **52**......................... TGMcLaughlin 2 63
(W M Brisbourne) *hld up: hdwy over 3f out: rdn to ld 2f out: r.o* **13/2**[3]

31-3 **2** *hd* **Twist Bookie (IRE)**[38] 215 7-9-0 **51**..................................... LPKeniry 3 62
(S Lycett) *hld up in tch: rdn wl over 1f out: chsd wnr fnl f: r.o* **6/5**[1]

3430 **3** *2* **Regency Red (IRE)**[14] 7060 9-8-9 **53**................. Julie-AnneCumine(7) 5 60
(W M Brisbourne) *hld up and bhd: hdwy over 3f out: rdn over 2f out: one pce fnl f* **12/1**

5000 **4** *8* **Cove Mountain (IRE)**[13] 7079 5-8-3 **45**................... KirstyMilczarek(5) 9 40
(M G Rimell) *hld up: rdn over 2f out: sme hdwy on ins wl over 1f out: nvr nr ldrs* **12/1**

0003 **5** *nk* **Jenny Soba**[35] 6835 4-8-8 **45**..(p) LiamJones 8 39
(Lucinda Featherstone) *hld up: hdwy over 8f out: led over 5f out tl over 3f out: rdn over 2f out: wknd wl over 1f out* **12/1**

2205 **6** 3 1/2 **Intavac Boy**[14] 7060 6-8-10 **50**.........................(v[1]) MichaelJStainton(3) 10 39
(S P Griffiths) *prom: led over 3f out: rdn and hdd over 2f out: wknd over 1f out* **4/1**[2]
6304 **7** 23 **Anything Once (USA)**[10] 7109 4-8-6 **50**......................(v) JamieKyne(7) 6 —
(D Carroll) *plld hrd early: set slow pce tl qcknd 7f out: hdd over 5f out: rdn and wknd wl over 3f out* **14/1**
0060 **8** 1 **Cumae (USA)**[9] 7120 3-8-3 **45**..................................(p) AdrianMcCarthy 4 —
(J Pearce) *plld hrd early: prom: rdn 5f out: sn wknd* **66/1**
000- **9** 24 **Lord Adonis (IRE)**[280] 5862 4-8-13 **50**........................ NelsonDeSouza 1 —
(S A Brookshaw) *a bhd: rdn over 7f out: t.o fnl 4f* **20/1**

2m 44.62s (2.20) **Going Correction** +0.15s/f (Slow)
WFA 3 from 4yo+ 5lb **9** Ran SP% **114.8**
Speed ratings (Par 101): **98,97,96,91,91 88,73,72,56**
CSF £14.57 CT £92.47 TOTE £8.00: £1.50, £1.30, £2.30; EX 16.10 Place 6 £67.19, Place 5 £18.60..
Owner The Blacktoffee Partnership **Bred** James Lombard **Trained** Great Ness, Shropshire

FOCUS
A run-of-the-mill handicap in which the early pace was slow and this bare form may not prove reliable. The principals raced towards the inside rail in the straight.
T/Plt: £315.40 to a £1 stake. Pool: £101,070.70. 233.90 winning tickets. T/Qpdt: £10.10 to a £1 stake. Pool: £9,236.80. 676.00 winning tickets. KH

7188 LINGFIELD (L-H)
Saturday, December 22

OFFICIAL GOING: Standard
Wind: Almost nil Weather: Overcast

7220 PLAY GOLF @ LINGFIELD PARK (S) STKS — 6f (P)
1:00 (1:02) (Class 6) 2-Y-O **£1,943** (£578; £288; £144) **Stalls** Low

Form RPR
02 **1** **Martingrange Boy (IRE)**[8] 7139 2-8-11 0....................(t) SteveDrowne 3 69
(D J Murphy) *taken down early: mde all: shkn up and drew clr over 1f out: styd on wl* **11/2**[3]
6610 **2** 3 1/2 **Atephobia**[22] 6977 2-8-11 67.. FergusSweeney 2 59
(K R Burke) *t.k.h: trckd wnr 2f and again over 2f out whn poised to chal: rdn and fnd nil wl over 1f out* **11/10**[1]
0344 **3** 1 **Wee Buns**[8] 7142 2-9-2 63.. LPKeniry 5 61
(S Kirk) *hld up: prog to chse ldng pair over 2f out: sn rdn and nt qckn* **15/2**
6066 **4** 10 **Whitcombe Flyer (USA)**[21] 6990 2-8-11 57......................(b[1]) PaulDoe 6 26
(Jamie Poulton) *dwlt: rcvrd to chse wnr 4f out to over 2f out: wknd* **10/1**
0 **5** 6 **Stoneacre Pat (IRE)**[16] 7043 2-8-11 0................................. AdamKirby 1 8
(Peter Grayson) *dwlt: in tch tl wknd over 2f out: sn wl bhd* **66/1**
0062 **6** 14 **Rievaulx Valentino**[10] 7122 2-9-2 68.....................................(p) NCallan 4 —
(K A Ryan) *chsd ldrs over 2f: sn wknd: t.o* **3/1**[2]

1m 11.82s (-0.99) **Going Correction** -0.225s/f (Stan) **6** Ran SP% **110.4**
Speed ratings (Par 94): **97,92,91,77,69 51**
CSF £11.65 TOTE £5.60: £2.30, £1.50; EX 12.70.The winner was bought in for 13,200gns.
Owner Willie McKay **Bred** James Drynan & Tom Wallace **Trained** Bawtry, S Yorks

FOCUS
A modest seller that was run in at a good tempo and fairly good form for the grade and time of year.

NOTEBOOK
Martingrange Boy(IRE), who looked a bit of a monkey before the off, flew out of the stalls and never got headed. Having his first start in selling company, he won with plenty in hand and connections were forced to go to 13,200gns to retain him. (op 9-2 tchd 4-1)
Atephobia, who won a course and distance seller last month, was much more exposed than the winner and was firmly put in his place as the race started in earnest down the home straight. (op 6-5 tchd 5-4 and 11-8 in a place)
Wee Buns, trying selling grade for the first time, got a bit behind early but made a move on the final bend that, for a brief moment, looked threatening. However, that effort soon petered out and he was not able to get past Atephobia let alone the winner. (tchd 8-1)
Whitcombe Flyer(USA) ran well up to a point but was readily left behind when the tempo increased. (op 12-1 tchd 14-1)
Stoneacre Pat(IRE) showed very little for the second time in a row.
Rievaulx Valentino did not find the drop into selling company any easier than the claimers he has been beaten in recently. That said, this effort was well below the majority of his form and one would suspect something was not quite right with him. Official explanation: jockey said colt lost its action (tchd 10-3)

7221 CWB CONTROLS H'CAP — 5f (P)
1:35 (1:35) (Class 5) (0-70,70) 3-Y-O+ **£2,817** (£838; £418; £209) **Stalls** High

Form RPR
3032 **1** **Pegasus Dancer (FR)**[14] 7077 3-9-1 **67**..............................(p) NCallan 5 76
(K A Ryan) *mde all: kicked clr 2f out: in no real danger fnl f: drvn out* **9/2**[3]
1555 **2** 1 1/4 **Desert Opal**[15] 7059 7-9-4 **70**...(b) TPQueally 4 74
(C R Dore) *prom: chsd wnr over 2f out: sn outpcd: no real imp after: hld on for 2nd* **11/2**
5340 **3** shd **After The Show**[42] 6762 6-8-13 **65**.................................. ChrisCatlin 6 69
(Rae Guest) *hld up in rr: prog on wd outside bnd 2f out: drvn and styd on fnl f to press for 2nd* **4/1**[2]
-543 **4** nk **Mogok Ruby**[22] 6976 3-9-3 **69**...................................... RobertHavlin 8 72
(L Montague Hall) *hld up in rr: prog 1/2-way: drvn to chse ldrs over 1f out: kpt on same pce* **10/3**[1]
0545 **5** 2 1/2 **Tous Les Deux**[18] 7026 4-8-13 **65**... LPKeniry 3 59
(Peter Grayson) *s.i.s: hld up: effrt and sme prog 2f out: sn no imp* **11/2**
0000 **6** 3 **Mambazo**[36] 6829 5-9-2 **68**..(e) HayleyTurner 7 51
(S C Williams) *taken down early: s.s: in tch in rr: outpcd 2f out: no ch whn hmpd 1f out* **12/1**
0060 **7** 1 3/4 **Black Moma (IRE)**[30] 6905 3-9-0 **66**............................. SteveDrowne 2 43
(A B Haynes) *chsd wnr to over 2f out: wknd rapidly fnl f* **16/1**
0000 **8** 3/4 **Nusoor (IRE)**[28] 6938 4-8-11 **63**.. AdamKirby 1 37
(Peter Grayson) *chsd ldrs: u.p fr 1/2-way: wknd over 1f out* **16/1**
6-10 **9** nk **Fustaan (IRE)**[18] 7026 3-9-1 **70**................................. TravisBlock(3) 10 43
(A G Newcombe) *drvn and struggling in rr after 2f: nvr a factor* **20/1**

58.69 secs (-1.09) **Going Correction** -0.225s/f (Stan) **9** Ran SP% **116.2**
Speed ratings (Par 103): **99,97,96,96,92 87,84,83,83**
CSF £29.69 CT £107.21 TOTE £3.60: £2.00, £2.40, £1.50; EX 23.30 Trifecta £32.20 Pool: £381.20 - 8.39 winning units..
Owner Rievaulx Racing Syndicate **Bred** Jean-Claude Campos Et Al **Trained** Hambleton, N Yorks

FOCUS
A modest-looking affair run at a sound pace. However, the winner had been beaten in claimers recently, which makes the form slightly suspect.

7222 BOOK ONLINE @ LINGFIELDPARK.CO.UK NOVICE STKS — 1m (P)
2:10 (2:10) (Class 5) 2-Y-O **£3,886** (£1,156; £577; £288) **Stalls** High

Form RPR
2430 **1** **Straight And Level (CAN)**[31] 6899 2-8-12 72.................. AdamKirby 1 70
(Miss Jo Crowley) *chsd ldng pair: rdn 3f out: looked hld tl styd on u.p fnl f to ld nr fin* **8/1**[3]
1 **2** nk **Call Of Duty (IRE)**[14] 7070 2-9-0 0............................... J-PGuillambert 4 71
(M Johnston) *trckd ldr: chal 2f out but green after: led 1f out: idled in front and collared nr fin* **4/5**[1]
4143 **3** 1 1/4 **Afram Blue**[18] 7016 2-9-0 79... PaulDoe 2 69
(W J Knight) *led: drvn 2f out: hdd 1f out: no ex* **13/8**[2]
00 **4** 11 **Tessie Bear**[26] 6948 2-8-7 0.. JimCrowley 3 37
(Andrew Reid) *s.i.s: a last: wknd over 3f out: t.o* **50/1**

1m 38.83s (-0.60) **Going Correction** -0.225s/f (Stan) **4** Ran SP% **106.7**
Speed ratings (Par 96): **94,93,92,81**
CSF £15.02 TOTE £6.60; EX 13.60.
Owner Mrs Liz Nelson **Bred** Dr Jerry Bilinski & David Cassidy **Trained** Whitcombe, Dorset
■ The first winner for trainer Jo Crowley, a former assistant to Gay Kelleway.

FOCUS
A very small field, in which only three had any obvious chance. The winning time was modest, as they went very slowly in the early stages and only really quickened up in the final quarter.

NOTEBOOK
Straight And Level(CAN) looked a very unlikely winner inside the final furlong, but he picked up in great style under a forceful ride and got his nose in front where it counted. However, it would be dangerous to take this form to literally, considering all of his previous form and the moderate winning time. (op 15-2 tchd 7-1 and 9-1)
Call Of Duty(IRE) is an enthusiastic sort but still looked green under pressure. He seemed sure to win as he passed Afram Blue inside the final furlong, but he did not do a great deal once in front and got mugged close to the line. This run should have done him the world of good for experience, and he can make up into a useful performer on the surface. He also has the build to make more physical improvement. (op 8-11 tchd 4-6)
Afram Blue did virtually all of the donkey work in front and only weakened inside the final 50yards. A consistent sort, his turn will come soon. (op 2-1)

7223 LINGFIELD PARK FOR WEDDINGS CONDITIONS STKS — 1m (P)
2:40 (2:41) (Class 4) 3-Y-O+ **£4,731** (£1,416; £708; £354; £176) **Stalls** High

Form RPR
550 **1** **Jack Sullivan (USA)**[28] 6942 6-9-3 102...........................(t) TPQueally 2 113
(G A Butler) *hld up in last pair: effrt 2f out: shkn up and prog to ld jst over 1f out: sn clr* **9/4**[2]
4033 **2** 3 1/2 **Raptor (GER)**[24] 6965 4-8-12 102.................................. FergusSweeney 1 100
(K R Burke) *cl up: nudged by rival after 2f: chsd ldr over 2f out to over 1f out: kpt on up to take 2nd again ins fnl f* **7/4**[1]
0300 **3** 1 1/2 **Evens And Odds (IRE)**[14] 7074 3-8-11 94.........................(b[1]) NCallan 5 97
(K A Ryan) *v keen: led after 3f: hdd and easily outpcd jst over 1f out* **9/2**
0435 **4** 3/4 **Chicken Soup**[3] 7184 5-8-12 98.................................(be) SteveDrowne 6 95
(D J Murphy) *led 3f: trckd ldr to over 2f out: shkn up over 1f out: nt qckn* **7/2**[3]
5 42 **Joe Rich** 3-8-11 0.. LPKeniry 4 —
(Mrs L C Jewell) *in tch 3f: sn wknd and t.o* **100/1**

1m 36.0s (-3.43) **Going Correction** -0.225s/f (Stan) course record
WFA 3 from 4yo+ 1lb **5** Ran SP% **108.5**
Speed ratings (Par 105): **108,104,103,102,60**
CSF £6.39 TOTE £3.30: £1.40, £1.40; EX 5.80.
Owner The International Carnival Partnership **Bred** Hermitage Farm L L C **Trained** Blewbury, Oxon

FOCUS
Despite the small field this was a decent little conditions event, and it was run at a good gallop.

7224 JUMPING HERE JANUARY 4TH H'CAP — 1m 2f (P)
3:10 (3:11) (Class 5) (0-70,75) 3-Y-O+ **£2,817** (£838; £418; £209) **Stalls** Low

Form RPR
0002 **1** **Greek Easter (IRE)**[3] 7194 4-9-6 **68**............................ JamieMackay 8 78+
(David P Myerscough, Ire) *trckd ldng trio: prog 3f out: led wl over 1f out and sn kicked clr: awkward last 50yds but in n.d* **9/2**[2]
5331 **2** 1 3/4 **Smokin Joe**[6] 7164 6-9-13 **75** 6ex.............................(b) HayleyTurner 7 82+
(J R Best) *stdd s: hld up in last: stl in last pair over 1f out: rapid prog fnl f to take 2nd nr fin: no ch of catching wnr* **7/1**[3]
2302 **3** nk **Paradise Dancer (IRE)**[22] 6975 3-9-3 **68**........................ RobertHavlin 5 74
(J A R Toller) *settled in 7th: rdn over 2f out: prog over 1f out: kpt on to take 3rd nr fin* **7/1**[3]
0-21 **4** nk **Barton Sands (IRE)**[14] 7069 10-8-7 **55**.........................(t) JimCrowley 6 60
(Andrew Reid) *hld up in last trio: rdn and prog on wd outside over 2f out: kpt on fnl f: nvr able to chal* **15/2**
4010 **5** 3/4 **Stark Contrast (USA)**[18] 7018 3-9-0 **65**.............................. TPQueally 3 69
(J Akehurst) *hld up in 6th: smooth prog over 2f out: drvn to chse wnr 1f out: no imp: wknd last 100yds* **9/1**
1522 **6** 2 1/2 **Meditation**[3] 7193 5-9-7 **69**.. JamesDoyle 4 68
(I A Wood) *trckd ldr: rdn and nt qckn over 2f out: sn lost pl and btn* **8/1**
6522 **7** nk **Best Selection**[70] 6175 3-9-4 **69**...................................... TGMcLaughlin 2 67
(Mrs L J Mongan) *settled in 5th: rdn over 2f out: no prog and btn over 1f out* **16/1**
622 **8** nk **Watchmaker**[33] 6866 4-9-1 **63**.. ChrisCatlin 1 61
(Miss Tor Sturgis) *sn led: drvn over 2f out: hdd wl over 1f out: wknd* **3/1**[1]
6500 **9** 6 **Josh**[22] 6982 5-9-5 **67**...(b[1]) NCallan 10 53
(K A Ryan) *stdd s: hld up in last: rdn over 2f out: no prog* **20/1**
026 **10** 1 3/4 **African Pursuits (USA)**[52] 6597 3-9-4 **69**........................ SteveDrowne 9 51
(H Morrison) *rousted along to press ldr: drvn 3f out: wknd over 2f out* **14/1**

2m 4.34s (-3.45) **Going Correction** -0.225s/f (Stan)
WFA 3 from 4yo+ 3lb **10** Ran SP% **118.4**
Speed ratings (Par 103): **104,102,102,102,101 99,99,99,94,92**
CSF £36.71 CT £220.52 TOTE £6.50: £2.30, £2.70, £2.00; EX 34.00 Trifecta £264.40 Part won. Pool: £372.43 - 0.20 winning units..
Owner Ms Charlotte Musgrave **Bred** J Hanly **Trained** Newbridge, Co Kildare
■ The first winner in Britain for Irish-based David Myerscough.

FOCUS
A competitive-looking handicap featuring a number of in-form horses.

7225 ROBERT LEECH QUEBEC STKS (LISTED RACE) 1m 2f (P)
3:40 (3:40) (Class 1) 3-Y-0+

£14,762 (£5,595; £2,800; £1,396; £699; £351) Stalls Low

Form RPR
1002 1 **Gentleman's Deal (IRE)**[28] 6931 6-9-7 108 PaulMulrennan 2 108+
(M W Easterby) *mde all: set stdy pce tl kicked on 3f out: drvn at least 2l clr over 1f out: jst hld on* **5/4**[1]
3501 2 shd **Grand Passion (IRE)**[28] 6931 7-9-5 105 SteveDrowne 3 106+
(G Wragg) *hld up in 5th: effrt on outer over 2f out but plenty to do: r.o to take 2nd 1f out: clsng fast fin: jst failed* **7/2**[2]
3045 3 1 1/4 **Voliere**[21] 6994 4-8-12 90 J-PGuillambert 6 96
(S C Williams) *hld up in last: effrt whn rn into bk of wkng rival 2f out: prog on wd outside 1f out: styd on to take 3rd nr fin* **10/1**
0053 4 1/2 **Millville**[28] 6931 7-9-3 105 NCallan 4 100
(M A Jarvis) *trckd ldng pair: rdn to chse wnr over 2f out: no imp over 1f out: fdd fnl f* **5/1**[3]
0012 5 nk **Troubadour (IRE)**[35] 6852 6-9-3 97 TPQueally 1 100
(W Jarvis) *cl up: rdn to dispute 2nd on inner wl over 1f out: no imp: fdd fnl f* **5/1**[3]
0-00 6 10 **Kahlua Kiss**[28] 6931 4-8-12 87 HayleyTurner 5 75
(W R Muir) *t.k.h: w wnr tl lost pl rapidly over 2f out: t.o* **28/1**

2m 6.82s (-0.97) **Going Correction** -0.225s/f (Stan) 6 Ran SP% **112.5**
Speed ratings (Par 111): **94,93,92,92,92 84**
CSF £5.89 TOTE £2.10: £1.10, £2.30; EX 6.30 Place 6 £89.25, Place 5 £57.47.
Owner Stephen J Curtis **Bred** C H Wacker Iii **Trained** Sheriff Hutton, N Yorks

FOCUS
A steadily-run Listed contest which turned into something of a sprint, as a resut of which the form is somewhat messy.

NOTEBOOK
Gentleman's Deal(IRE) dominated throughout in a steadily-run contest and, once he kicked on the turn into the straight, he soon put distance between himself and the rest. Sticking to the inside rail was not the best move though, and he almost got collared in a traditional Lingfield finish as Grand Passion flew down the outside and almost caught him at the line. He had been narrowly beaten by that rival over this course and distance last month but was 2lb better off at the weights this time, and there is clearly not a lot between the pair. They will probably bump into each other again this winter, and both have the Winter Derby as their aim in the spring. (op 13-8 tchd 15-8)
Grand Passion(IRE), who just got up to beat Gentleman's Deal in a similar race over this course and distance last month, came with his customary late finish but just failed this time. In theory the 2lb turnaround in the weights beat him but in reality the way the race panned out was far more significant. (op 3-1 tchd 11-4)
Voliere, a close fourth in a similar contest here last month in which Grand Passion and Gentleman's Deal finished first and second, was beaten further this time but again stayed on well from off the pace having been held up at the tail of the field. She gained some valuable black type and looked far more effective back over this shorter trip. Official explanation: jockey said filly suffered interference in running (op 11-1 tchd 12-1 and 9-1)
Millville did not get as close to the first two as he did last month. The way the race was run would not have suited him as he is essentially a 1m4f horse. (op 9-2)
Troubadour(IRE) has done most of his winning at around a mile in handicap company and he did not see this trip out as well as the others, despite the steady early pace. (tchd 11-2)
T/Plt: £202.40 to a £1 stake. Pool: £62,866.45. 226.70 winning tickets. T/Qpdt: £69.30 to a £1 stake. Pool: £3,645.60. 38.90 winning tickets. JN

7214 WOLVERHAMPTON (A.W) (L-H)
Saturday, December 22

OFFICIAL GOING: Standard (meeting abandoned after race 2 (7.30) due to fog)
Racing was put back 30 minutes because of bad visibilty and the meeting was abandoned when the fog closed in again after the second race.
Wind: Nil Weather: Intermittent fog

7226 PONTIN'S GREAT FAMILY HOLIDAYS CLAIMING STKS 1m 4f 50y(P)
7:00 (7:31) (Class 6) 3-Y-0+ £2,388 (£705; £352) Stalls Low

Form RPR
011 1 **Nawamees (IRE)**[15] 7050 9-9-10 78 (p) AdamKirby 7 77+
(G L Moore) *a.p: led over 4f out: clr over 2f out: eased wl ins fnl f* **13/8**[1]
-515 2 7 **Easibet Dot Net**[14] 7081 7-9-2 58 (p) PhillipMakin 3 58
(I Semple) *hld up and bhd: hdwy over 3f out: sn rdn: styd on ins fnl f: no ch w wnr* **6/1**
00 3 1 1/2 **Welcome Cat (USA)**[11] 7110 3-9-5 57 (b[1]) DanielTudhope 5 64
(A D Brown) *hld up in rr: rdn and hdwy on outside over 2f out: kpt on same pce* **40/1**
5133 4 1/2 **Musango**[7] 7150 4-9-6 66 (t) RobertHavlin 8 59
(Miss Gay Kelleway) *hld up and bhd: hdwy over 5f out: bmpd over 3f out: sn chsng wnr: no imp* **3/1**[2]
5400 5 7 **Chasing Memories (IRE)**[8] 7146 3-8-10 53 AdrianMcCarthy 1 43
(W K Goldsworthy) *hld up in mid-div: rdn and short-lived effrt on ins over 2f out* **20/1**
3052 6 2 1/2 **Cool Isle**[12] 7102 4-8-7 41 (b) ChrisCatlin 9 31
(P Howling) *chsd ldr: led over 6f out tl over 4f out: wkng whn hmpd on ins over 3f out* **16/1**
3-66 7 3 **Mr Excel (IRE)**[12] 7102 4-9-4 65 RichardKingscote 6 37
(G A Ham) *hld up towards rr: hdwy 4f out: rdn 3f out: wknd wl over 1f out* **33/1**
0150 8 26 **Atlantic Gamble (IRE)**[31] 6902 7-9-3 60 (p) AndrewElliott(3) 4 —
(K R Burke) *prom: pushed along over 5f out: rdn and wknd over 2f out: t.o* **4/1**[3]
0600 P **Diamond Josh**[8] 7138 5-8-9 42 RossAtkinson(7) 2 —
(M Mullineaux) *half-rrd s: plld hrd: led: sddle sn slipped: hdd over 6f out: wknd over 5f out: t.o whn p.u over 2f out* **100/1**

2m 43.9s (1.48) **Going Correction** +0.20s/f (Slow)
WFA 3 from 4yo+ 5lb 9 Ran SP% **114.4**
Speed ratings (Par 101): **103,98,97,97,92 90,88,71,—**
CSF £11.52 TOTE £2.40: £1.10, £2.10, £6.00; EX 13.60.
Owner Paul Stamp **Bred** Kilfrush Stud Ltd **Trained** Woodingdean, E Sussex

FOCUS
An uncompetitive claimer in which Nawamees stood out at the weights.
Musango Official explanation: jockey said gelding hung left and suffered a breathing problem

7227 PONTINSBINGO.COM H'CAP 5f 216y(P)
7:30 (8:00) (Class 6) (0-60,61) 3-Y-0+ £2,047 (£604; £302) Stalls Low

Form RPR
4232 1 **Perlachy**[12] 7105 3-8-12 57 (v) DuranFentiman(3) 4 65
(Mrs N Macauley) *a.p: rdn over 2f out: led 1f out: drvn out* **16/1**
0066 2 nk **Theoretical**[13] 7082 3-8-10 55 (p) PatrickMathers(3) 6 62
(A J McCabe) *sn bhd and rdn along: c wd ent st: gd hdwy and edgd lft ins fnl f: fin wl* **12/1**
0021 3 shd **Winthorpe (IRE)**[11] 7111 7-9-5 61 (p) DanielTudhope 1 68
(J J Quinn) *hld up in mid-div: hdwy wl over 1f out: rdn and ev ch ins fnl f: r.o* **6/1**[2]
2013 4 hd **Strabinios King**[3] 7183 3-9-4 60 PaulMulrennan 7 66
(R A Harris) *hld up in mid-div: nt clr run 2f out: hdwy over 1f out: rdn and nt clr run whn swtchd rt and faltered ins fnl f: r.o* **9/4**[1]
0000 5 shd **Guildenstern (IRE)**[52] 6581 5-8-13 55 TGMcLaughlin 9 61
(P Howling) *sn outpcd: swtchd rt jst over 1f out: hdwy and swtchd lft ins fnl f: fin wl* **20/1**
1533 6 2 **Toms Laughter**[147] 3950 3-9-3 59 LiamJones 3 58
(R A Harris) *s.i.s: outpcd: c wd st: late hdwy: nrst fin* **12/1**
0011 7 1 **Bond Becks (IRE)**[18] 7014 7-9-1 57 ChrisCatlin 12 53
(G R Oldroyd) *a.p: led 2f out: rdn and hdd 1f out: wknd wl ins fnl f* **8/1**
0116 8 hd **Commander Wish**[12] 7105 4-9-0 59 (tp) NeilChalmers(3) 13 55
(Lucinda Featherstone) *hld up in mid-div: hdwy on outside over 3f out: rdn over 1f out: wknd ins fnl f* **20/1**
0605 9 3/4 **Polar Force**[19] 7011 7-8-12 59 KirstyMilczarek(5) 5 52
(Mrs C A Dunnett) *chsd ldrs: hung lft and wknd 1f out* **6/1**[2]
0052 10 7 **Russian Rocket (IRE)**[19] 7005 5-9-4 60 JamesDoyle 11 31
(Mrs C A Dunnett) *chsd ldrs: rdn over 2f out: wknd wl over 1f out* **11/1**
0210 11 5 **Trinculo (IRE)**[2] 7207 10-8-9 58 (b) WilliamCarson(7) 2 13
(R A Harris) *led: rdn and hdd 2f out: sn wknd: eased whn no ch fnl f* **14/1**
1200 12 1 1/4 **Forced Upon Us**[36] 6831 3-8-13 60 (b) RussellKennemore(5) 8 11
(P J McBride) *s.i.s: outpcd* **15/2**[3]

1m 17.03s (1.22) **Going Correction** +0.20s/f (Slow) 12 Ran SP% **128.0**
Speed ratings (Par 101): **99,98,98,98,98 95,94,93,92,83 76,75**
CSF £209.96 CT £1323.86 TOTE £17.50: £3.30, £4.20, £2.30; EX 91.50 Place 6 £9.48, Place 5 £4.65.
Owner Mrs N Macauley **Bred** J James **Trained** Sproxton, Leics
■ Norma Macauley's first winner for over a year.

FOCUS
A blanket finish to this low-grade sprint handicap.
Forced Upon Us Official explanation: jockey said gelding missed the break and resented the kickback

7228 JOIN WBX.COM FREE FOOTBALL SHIRT H'CAP 1m 5f 194y(P)
() (Class 5) (0-70,) 3-Y-0+ £

7229 GO PONTIN'S H'CAP 7f 32y(P)
() (Class 5) (0-75,) 3-Y-0+ £

7230 PONTINS.COM MEDIAN AUCTION MAIDEN STKS 1m 1f 103y(P)
() (Class 6) 3-5-Y-0 £

7231 WBX.COM £25 BET FOR NEW ACCOUNTS H'CAP 1m 1f 103y(P)
() (Class 6) (0-52,) 3-Y-0+ £

T/Plt: £4.50 to a £1 stake. Pool: £118,012.50. 18,858.15 winning tickets. KH

7226 WOLVERHAMPTON (A.W) (L-H)
Wednesday, December 26

OFFICIAL GOING: Standard
Wind: Light, behind Weather: Fine

7232 PONTIN'S BOOK EARLY PRICE PROMISE NOVICE STKS 7f 32y(P)
1:30 (1:30) (Class 5) 2-Y-0 £2,968 (£876; £438) Stalls High

Form RPR
0112 1 **Geezers Colours**[22] 7016 2-9-5 78 FergusSweeney 2 82
(K R Burke) *trckd ldr: led jst over 2f out: drvn out and r.o wl fnl f* **13/8**[1]
3342 2 1 3/4 **Nice Wee Girl (IRE)**[16] 7097 2-8-7 69 SimonWhitworth 1 66
(S Kirk) *racd keenly: led: hdd jst over 2f out: nt qckn fnl f* **9/4**[2]
3 1 1/4 **Chinese Temple (IRE)**[118] 4983 2-9-5 0 PatDobbs 4 75
(M G Quinlan) *hld up: pushed along to trck ldng pair over 2f out: kpt on same pce fnl f* **11/4**[3]
0504 4 7 **Weetfromthechaff**[79] 6066 2-8-12 57 VinceSlattery 3 51
(R Hollinshead) *racd keenly: trckd ldrs: pushed along 3f out: outpcd fnl 2f* **7/1**

1m 31.72s (1.32) **Going Correction** +0.125s/f (Slow) 4 Ran SP% **108.0**
Speed ratings (Par 96): **97,95,93,85**
CSF £5.51 TOTE £2.30; EX 5.10.
Owner C Waters **Bred** Bloodhorse International Limited **Trained** Middleham Moor, N Yorks

FOCUS
A fair novice event but a comfortable winner who continued his recent good run of form.

NOTEBOOK
Geezers Colours, who has done really well at Lingfield of late, had a major chance if he could transfer the improvement back to this course. In the event he did so without too much fuss and looks capable of adding to his score this winter. (op 15-8 tchd 6-4)
Nice Wee Girl(IRE), who has done all her racing on Polytrack, set the pace and, although she kept on, found the winner too strong. She is pretty consistent and, although still a maiden, may be worth a try in handicaps. (op 3-1 tchd 10-3)
Chinese Temple(IRE), a winner over 5f when trained in Ireland, was making his British and All-Weather debut for new connections. He moved onto the heels of the leaders on the home turn but could find nothing extra from that point and may be better at a shorter. (op 7-4 tchd 13-8)
Weetfromthechaff had a good deal to find on official ratings and was left behind off the turn in. (op 11-1)

7233 PONTIN'S BOOK EARLY AND SAVE CLAIMING STKS 7f 32y(P)
2:00 (2:01) (Class 6) 3-Y-0+ £2,388 (£705; £352) Stalls High

Form RPR
0036 1 **Dickie Le Davoir**[26] 6981 3-9-1 80 FergusSweeney 5 72
(K R Burke) *midfield: hdwy over 2f out: r.o to ld ins fnl f: sn edgd rt: kpt on* **4/1**[2]

4450 **2** *hd* **Obe Royal**[22] 7025 3-8-4 58........................(b[1]) RichardEvans(7) 3 67
(P D Evans) *hld up: hdwy 2f out: ev ch whn carried sltly rt ins fnl f: kpt on* **9/1**

2442 **3** *2* **Green Pirate**[6] 7207 5-8-7 58........................(v) LiamJones 1 58
(W M Brisbourne) *sn in midfield: rdn and hdwy 2f out: edgd lft ins fnl f: styd on: no imp on front pair towards fin* **3/1**[1]

6400 **4** *2 1/2* **Benllech**[16] 7094 3-8-9 63........................ SimonWhitworth 9 53
(S Kirk) *trckd ldrs: wnt 2nd over 2f out: rdn to ld over 1f out: sn edgd lft: hdd ins fnl f: no ex towards fin* **10/1**

0000 **5** *1 1/4* **Gifted Flame**[11] 7153 8-8-8 42........................ AnnStokell(5) 2 53
(Miss A Stokell) *in tch: lost pl over 3f out: kpt on again fnl f: no imp on ldrs* **28/1**

0001 **6** *1 1/4* **Circus Polka (USA)**[36] 6882 3-9-1 67........................(t) ChrisCatlin 7 52
(W M Brisbourne) *prom: rdn over 3f out: wknd over 2f out* **4/1**[2]

0100 **7** *shd* **Another Genepi (USA)**[29] 6962 4-8-8 66........................(b) GregFairley 8 45
(K A Ryan) *s.s: hdwy to go prom after 1f: led over 4f out: hdd over 1f out: wknd ins fnl f* **5/1**[3]

0000 **8** *12* **Rebel Pearl (IRE)**[14] 7127 3-8-5 62 ow2........................(b[1]) JamieJones(5) 10 14
(M G Quinlan) *racd keenly: sn led: hdd over 4f out: rdn over 2f out: wknd over 1f out* **20/1**

0040 **9** *1/2* **Preskani**[11] 7153 5-8-6 40........................(v) DuranFentiman(3) 4 12
(Mrs N Macauley) *a bhd* **66/1**

0046 **10** *1* **Time For Change (IRE)**[6] 7197 3-8-5 42........................(e) DavidKinsella 6 5
(P G Murphy) *hld up: hdwy to chse ldrs 5f out: sn drvn: wknd over 2f out* **33/1**

0030 **11** *4* **Calloff The Search**[7] 7188 3-8-7 48........................(be[1]) SaleemGolam 11 —
(Stef Liddiard) *s.s: a bhd* **25/1**

1m 30.5s (0.10) **Going Correction** +0.125s/f (Slow) **11 Ran SP% 117.2**
Speed ratings (Par 101): **104,103,101,98,97 95,95,81,81,80 75**
CSF £36.77 TOTE £5.70: £1.90, £2.40, £1.60; EX 41.90 Trifecta £123.20 Pool: £262.10 - 1.51 winning tickets..
Owner Bigwigs Bloodstock II **Bred** P And Mrs A G Venner **Trained** Middleham Moor, N Yorks
■ Stewards' Enquiry : Fergus Sweeney one-day ban: careless riding (Jan 6)

FOCUS
A typically uncompetitive claimer but run at a sound gallop and a good finish nonetheless. The winner and third did not need to be at their best.
Another Genepi(USA) Official explanation: jockey said filly missed the break
Calloff The Search Official explanation: jockey said gelding missed the break

7234 GO PONTIN'S HOLIDAYS NURSERY 1m 141y(P)
2:40 (2:42) (Class 4) (0-85,76) 2-Y-0 **£4,210** (£1,252; £625; £312) **Stalls** Low

Form RPR

3241 **1** **Elusive Lady (IRE)**[33] 6912 2-8-12 67........................(p) ChrisCatlin 3 70
(J R Weymes) *hld up bhd ldrs: wnt 2nd over 3f out: led over 2f out: r.o ins fnl f* **5/2**[1]

0024 **2** *1 1/2* **Sunshine Lady (IRE)**[23] 7007 2-8-0 58........................ AndrewElliott(3) 5 58
(D Haydn Jones) *s.i.s: sn rcvrd and w ldr: led 5f out: rdn and hdd over 2f out: continued to press wnr: nt qckn towards fin* **8/1**

055 **3** *3 1/2* **Dinarius**[12] 7145 2-9-2 71........................ JimCrowley 2 64
(K J Burke) *led: hdd 5f out: outpcd over 3f out: no imp after* **9/2**[3]

3562 **4** *3/4* **Natural Rhythm (IRE)**[8] 7176 2-8-4 62........................(p) DuranFentiman(3) 4 53
(D W Chapman) *racd keenly: hld up: effrt to take 2nd over 4f out: lost 2nd over 3f out: one pce after* **3/1**[2]

1m 54.68s (2.92) **Going Correction** +0.125s/f (Slow) **4 Ran SP% 82.9**
Speed ratings (Par 98): **92,90,87,86**
CSF £10.76 TOTE £2.20; EX 6.60.
Owner T A Scothern **Bred** Liam Queally **Trained** Middleham Moor, N Yorks
■ The Last Bottle (11/4) was withdrawn (reared up and got leg caught over stall): Rule 4 applies, deduct 25p in £ from all bets.

FOCUS
A modest nursery weakened by three non-runners and dominated by the fillies. Not form to place much faith in.

NOTEBOOK
Elusive Lady(IRE) has taken well to this surface and, raised just 2lb for a clear-cut win here last month, followed up in similar fashion, although she had to work a little harder this time. The extra furlong or so did not inconvenience her and there looks to be more to come. (op 2-1)
Sunshine Lady(IRE), dropped 4lb after finishing well beaten here earlier in the month, put up a much better effort and did not go down without a fight. However, she may need to drop a few pounds more before she is on a winning mark. (op 11-1)
Dinarius, making his handicap debut, was supported in the betting ring and again made the running. However, he could not respond when taken on at the end of the back straight and only ran on when the race was over. He is another who looks harshly handicapped at present. (op 7-1)
Natural Rhythm(IRE), who ran well in a lower-grade handicap over 7f at Southwell recently; was rather lit up by the first-time cheekpieces and did too much early, as a result of which he got tired in the straight. (op 9-2)

7235 PONTINS.COM MAIDEN STKS 5f 216y(P)
3:10 (3:10) (Class 5) 2-Y-0 **£2,968** (£876; £438) **Stalls** Low

Form RPR

554 **1** **Annes Rocket (IRE)**[25] 7000 2-9-3 70........................ PatDobbs 4 67
(J C Fox) *hld up: hdwy 3f out: r.o to ld ins fnl f: pushed out towards fin* **6/4**[1]

2 *nk* **Roundthetwist (IRE)** 2-9-0 0........................ AndrewElliott(3) 1 66
(K R Burke) *led for 1f: pushed along and outpcd over 2f out: rallied and ev ch whn n.m.r 1f out: continued to press wnr: nt qckn towards fin* **8/1**[3]

5 **3** *1/2* **Liberty Valance (IRE)**[13] 7130 2-9-3 0........................ SimonWhitworth 2 65
(S Kirk) *upset in stalls: racd keenly: a.p: led 2f out: sn rdn: hdd ins fnl f: no ex towards fin* **2/1**[2]

4 **4** *2 1/2* **Plenty Of Action (USA)**[18] 7071 2-8-12 0........................ PhillipMakin 3 52
(M J Wallace) *led after 1f: hdd 2f out: one pce after* **17/2**

0006 **5** *7* **Dickie Valentine**[28] 6966 2-9-3 51........................(v) AdamKirby 6 36
(M R Bosley) *prom: lost pl 4f out: rdn 3f out: tried to rally over 2f out: wknd over 1f out* **12/1**

06 **6** *7* **Joshua**[16] 7096 2-9-3 0........................ JimCrowley 5 15
(D E Cantillon) *a outpcd* **12/1**

7 *3* **Arrabiata** 2-8-12 0........................ ChrisCatlin 7 1
(C N Kellett) *s.i.s: a outpcd* **20/1**

1m 17.46s (1.65) **Going Correction** +0.125s/f (Slow) **7 Ran SP% 115.1**
Speed ratings (Par 96): **94,93,92,89,80 70,66**
CSF £14.68 TOTE £2.20: £1.20, £3.40; EX 14.30.
Owner Mrs Anne Coughlan **Bred** S Coughlan **Trained** Collingbourne Ducis, Wilts

FOCUS
A modest maiden producing a decent finish. The winner ran to form, with the third stepping up slightly.

NOTEBOOK
Annes Rocket(IRE) has gradually been finding his feet on this surface and the step up from 5f enabled him to get off the mark. He was value for slightly more than the official margin and should be able to win again, although he does not look especially well handicapped. (op 9-4)
Roundthetwist(IRE) ◆, a 30,000euros half-brother to the decent dual-purpose performer Kentucky Blue amongst others, ran very well on this debut and did not have a lot of room against the rail in the straight. He looks capable of winning races on this evidence. (op 17-2 tchd 15-2)
Liberty Valance(IRE), who showed promise over 7f here earlier in the month, got upset in the stalls and ran far too keenly on this drop in trip. He was not beaten far in the end and can do better if learning to settle. (op 7-4)
Plenty Of Action(USA) showed improvement from her debut at Lingfield and set the pace, but she could not pick up when taken on. (op 5-1)

7236 PONTINSBINGO.COM H'CAP 1m 4f 50y(P)
3:40 (3:41) (Class 4) (0-85,83) 3-Y-0+ **£4,857** (£1,445; £722; £360) **Stalls** Low

Form RPR

1212 **1** **Birkside**[13] 7132 4-9-4 80........................ DanielTudhope 8 89+
(D Carroll) *hld up: hdwy over 2f out: led over 1f out: kpt on wl* **7/1**

1242 **2** *1 1/4* **Pass The Port**[19] 7055 6-9-4 80........................ AdamKirby 9 87
(D Haydn Jones) *hld up: nt clr run 2f out: swtchd rt and hdwy wl over 1f out: r.o to take 2nd ins fnl f: nt rch wnr* **15/2**

2412 **3** *2* **The King And I (IRE)**[6] 7205 3-7-13 73........................(b) KrishGundowry(7) 4 77
(Miss E C Lavelle) *s.i.s: hld up: hdwy over 2f out: led wl over 1f out: sn hung rt and hdd: styd on same pce ins fnl f* **13/2**[3]

4010 **4** *1 1/2* **La Estrella (USA)**[26] 6759 4-9-7 83........................ JimCrowley 7 84
(D E Cantillon) *midfield: hdwy 6f out: pushed along whn n.m.r 2f out: sn outpcd: kpt on ins fnl f: no imp on ldrs* **7/2**[1]

0002 **5** *1 1/4* **Noble Minstrel**[44] 6802 4-8-10 72........................(t) SaleemGolam 2 71
(S C Williams) *prom: rdn over 1f out: sn wknd* **7/1**

0111 **6** *1/2* **Robert The Brave**[17] 6878 3-8-10 77........................ ChrisCatlin 1 76
(P R Webber) *midfield: pushed along 4f out: effrt 2f out: one pce fnl f* **4/1**[2]

1025 **7** *5* **Fregate Island (IRE)**[182] 2994 4-9-7 83........................ J-PGuillambert 6 74
(J G Given) *led: rdn and hdd wl over 1f out: sn wknd: eased whn btn fnl f* **12/1**

-000 **8** *8* **Celtic Step**[30] 6949 3-8-6 73........................ GregFairley 3 51
(M Johnston) *prom: rdn and ev ch 2f out: wknd over 1f out* **14/1**

2023 **P** **Vale De Lobo**[25] 7002 5-8-9 76........................ TolleyDean(5) 5 —
(B R Millman) *in tch: wnt wrong and lost pl qckly over 6f out: sn p.u* **7/1**

2m 41.1s (-1.32) **Going Correction** +0.125s/f (Slow)
WFA 3 from 4yo+ 5lb **9 Ran SP% 119.2**
Speed ratings (Par 105): **109,108,106,105,105 104,101,96,—**
CSF £60.25 CT £363.03 TOTE £7.70: £2.50, £1.80, £2.70; EX 60.70 Trifecta £179.80 Part won. Pool: £253.24 - 0.20 winning tickets..
Owner Document Express Ltd **Bred** Pendley Farm **Trained** Sledmere, E Yorks
■ Stewards' Enquiry : Adam Kirby one-day ban: used whip with excessive force and with whip arm above shoulder height (Jan 6)

FOCUS
A decent handicap run at a good gallop and a clear-cut winner in the progressive Birkside. Sound form, rated through the runner-up.

7237 PONTIN'S WISHES YOU A HAPPY CHRISTMAS FILLIES' H'CAP 1m 1f 103y(P)
4:10 (4:11) (Class 5) (0-70,70) 3-Y-0+ **£2,968** (£876; £438) **Stalls** Low

Form RPR

16-1 **1** **Friends Hope**[15] 7109 6-8-11 70........................ GHannon(7) 4 80
(P A Blockley) *s.i.s: hld up: hdwy 2f out: led over 1f out: r.o* **5/1**

3226 **2** *2* **Chia (IRE)**[25] 6996 4-8-13 65........................(p) AdamKirby 3 71
(D Haydn Jones) *led after 1f: rdn and hdd over 1f out: nt qckn ins fnl f* **11/4**[2]

6264 **3** *1 1/4* **Daring Affair**[19] 7057 6-9-0 66........................ FergusSweeney 5 69
(K R Burke) *trckd ldrs: rdn and outpcd 2f out: kpt on ins fnl f* **9/2**[3]

2204 **4** *3/4* **Emily's Place (IRE)**[26] 6982 4-8-11 63........................ J-PGuillambert 1 65
(J Pearce) *midfield: hdwy 2f out: rdn and ev ch briefly over 2f out: no ex ins fnl f* **9/2**[3]

442 **5** *1/2* **Our Kes (IRE)**[18] 7080 5-9-1 67........................ SimonWhitworth 6 68
(P Howling) *hld up: effrt 2f out: no imp* **5/2**[1]

0240 **6** *3* **Red Current**[19] 7056 3-8-8 62........................ ChrisCatlin 2 56
(R A Harris) *led for 1f: remained prom: rdn over 2f out: ev ch wl over 1f out: wknd ins fnl f* **14/1**

5F05 **7** *1* **Stravita**[13] 7131 3-8-11 65........................ VinceSlattery 7 57
(R Hollinshead) *pushed along over 3f out: a bhd* **25/1**

100 **8** *shd* **Bahhmirage (IRE)**[145] 4129 4-8-1 56 oh7........................(p) AndrewElliott(3) 8 48
(C N Kellett) *racd keenly: prom: rdn 2f out: wknd over 1f out* **33/1**

2m 3.82s (1.20) **Going Correction** +0.125s/f (Slow)
WFA 3 from 4yo+ 2lb **8 Ran SP% 121.7**
Speed ratings (Par 100): **99,97,96,95,95 92,91,91**
CSF £20.57 CT £68.77 TOTE £6.90: £2.50, £1.40, £1.50; EX 42.30 Trifecta £92.80 Pool: £300.79 - 2.30 winning tickets. Place 6 £109.57, Place 5 £47.97 .
Owner Mrs Joanna Hughes **Bred** Huish Bloodstock **Trained** Lambourn, Berks

FOCUS
A modest fillies' handicap won by an improving mare in Friends Hope. The runner-up is the best guide. Gabriel Hannon's first winner since resuming riding after a three-year-break.
T/Plt: £38.00 to a £1 stake. Pool: £33,915.25. 650.80 winning tickets. T/Qpdt: £18.90 to a £1 stake. Pool: £2,326.80. 90.90 winning tickets. DO

7208 SOUTHWELL (L-H)
Thursday, December 27

OFFICIAL GOING: Standard
Wind: fresh, half-behind Weather: overcast and mild

7238 PONTIN'S GREAT FAMILY HOLIDAYS CLAIMING STKS 5f (F)
12:00 (12:01) (Class 6) 3-Y-0+ **£2,047** (£604; £302) **Stalls** High

Form RPR

0040 **1** **Axis Shield (IRE)**[50] 6078 4-7-11 45........................ NicolPolli(5) 10 58
(M C Chapman) *mde all: edgd lft over 1f out: hld on ins fnl f* **40/1**

0020 **2** *3/4* **Came Back (IRE)**[48] 6747 4-9-1 66........................ GregFairley 4 68
(J Mackie) *w wnr: carried lft and no ex ins fnl f* **15/8**[1]

0/40 **3** *5* **African Storm (IRE)**[23] 7020 5-8-3 0........................ DaleGibson 1 38
(T McLaughlin, Ire) *chsd ldrs: one pce fnl 2f* **17/2**

0005 **4** *2* **Detonate**[11] 7166 5-8-3 44........................ ChrisCatlin 7 31
(I A Wood) *s.i.s: hdwy 2f out: nvr nr ldrs* **8/1**[3]

0134 **5** *hd* **Compton Classic**[6] 7212 5-9-2 73........................(v) HarryPoulton(7) 8 50
(J R Boyle) *t.k.h in rr: effrt: n.m.r and swtchd rt over 2f out: nvr nr ldrs* **7/2**[2]

0004 **6** *3* **Kissi Kissi**[13] 7137 4-8-4 40 AdrianMcCarthy 6 21
(M J Attwater) *mid-div: hrd rdn and edgd lft and kpt on fnl f: nvr a factor* **22/1**

0000 **7** *1* **Minimum Fuss (IRE)**[58] 6565 3-7-13 43 DominicFox(3) 9 15
(M C Chapman) *s.i.s: in rr: hung lft over 1f out: nvr a factor* **50/1**

6000 **8** *1 1/4* **Percy Douglas**[13] 7138 7-8-8 41 (b) AnnStokell(5) 2 21
(Miss A Stokell) *w ldrs: lost pl over 2f out* **100/1**

00 **9** *3* **Chocolate Sands**[14] 7134 3-8-11 0 ow2 J-PGuillambert 11 9
(J G Given) *racd towards stands' side: in rr: sn drvn along: nvr on terms* **66/1**

3400 **10** *7* **Gifted Lass**[48] 6752 5-8-2 58 AndrewElliott(3) 5 —
(J Balding) *taken down early and v free to post: chsd ldrs 2f: sn lost pl* **7/2**[2]

59.84 secs (-0.46) **Going Correction** -0.05s/f (Stan) **10** Ran SP% **112.1**
Speed ratings (Par 101): **101,99,91,88,88 83,81,79,75,63**
CSF £109.69 TOTE £52.20: £8.20, £1.40, £2.20; EX 154.00 TRIFECTA Not won..
Owner Dr A Shubsachs **Bred** Mrs P Grubb **Trained** Market Rasen, Lincs
■ Stewards' Enquiry : Nicol Polli caution: used whip with excessive frequency
Adrian McCarthy three-day ban: used whip with excessive frequency (Jan 7-9)

FOCUS
A very modest claimer best rated through the runner-up.
Gifted Lass Official explanation: jockey said mare boiled over in the preliminaries

7239 PONTIN'S SHORT BREAKS MAIDEN STKS 6f (F)
12:30 (12:33) (Class 5) 3-Y-0+ **£2,968** (£876; £438) **Stalls** Low

Form RPR

6000 **1** **Van Ruymbeke (IRE)**[12] 7148 3-9-3 41 (e[1]) LiamJones 14 54
(D J Murphy) *in rr: edgd rt after 1f: hdwy on inner over 2f out: styd on to ld nr fin* **18/1**

6005 **2** *hd* **Cape Of Storms**[38] 6877 4-9-3 45 PaulMulrennan 5 53
(R Brotherton) *w ldr: led over 1f out: hdd and no ex towards fin* **20/1**

-005 **3** *1 1/4* **Maraagel (USA)**[12] 7148 4-9-3 45 (t) J-PGuillambert 2 49
(S C Williams) *led tl over 1f out: kpt on same pce* **6/1**[3]

24 **4** *1 1/4* **Sintenis Mac (GER)**[38] 6877 4-9-3 0 GregFairley 10 45
(P J O'Gorman) *awkward to load: trckd ldrs: kpt on same pce appr fnl f* **11/10**[1]

4 **5** *3* **Irish Conection (IRE)**[23] 7019 4-9-0 0 JerryO'Dwyer(3) 12 35
(T McLaughlin, Ire) *chsd ldrs: sn drvn along: wknd fnl f* **7/2**[2]

2000 **6** *1 1/4* **Jember Red**[38] 6877 4-8-9 42 (v) MarkLawson(3) 11 26
(B Smart) *sn chsng ldrs: one pce fnl 2f* **14/1**

0-6 **7** *nk* **Miss Hoolie**[12] 7159 3-8-6 0 ow1 JackDean(7) 9 26
(W G M Turner) *chsd ldrs: edgd rt and wknd over 1f out* **25/1**

000 **8** *3* **High Window (IRE)**[30] 6955 7-8-10 44 NSLawes(7) 8 21
(G P Kelly) *sltly hmpd s: in rr: sme hdwy 2f out: nvr a factor* **33/1**

56 **9** *1* **Good Cause (IRE)**[24] 1296 6-9-3 0 ChrisCatlin 3 18
(Mrs S Lamyman) *s.s: swtchd rt after s: hdwy on outer 4f out: lost pl 3f out* **11/1**

0 **10** *1/2* **Brunton (IRE)**[6] 7209 5-9-3 41 PhillipMakin 13 16
(A Berry) *mid-div: sn drvn along: hdwy over 3f out: lost pl over 2f out* **50/1**

0- **11** *9* **Sweet Seville (FR)**[503] 4323 3-8-12 0 DaleGibson 6 —
(Mrs G S Rees) *swvd rt s: chsd ldrs: lost pl 3f out* **33/1**

0 **12** *2 1/2* **Tewkesbury (IRE)**[10] 7174 3-9-3 0 VinceSlattery 1 —
(Mrs K Waldron) *in rr: bhd fnl 2f* **100/1**

0 **13** *2* **Pennygee**[38] 6877 3-8-12 0 PaulEddery 7 —
(S R Bowring) *sltly hmpd s: mid-div and sn drvn along: bhd fnl 2f* **66/1**

1m 17.37s (0.47) **Going Correction** -0.125s/f (Stan) **13** Ran SP% **123.3**
Speed ratings (Par 103): **91,90,89,87,83 81,81,77,76,75 63,60,57**
CSF £335.54 TOTE £25.70: £4.40, £2.70, £2.00; EX 328.60 TRIFECTA Not won..
Owner Gordon Crawford & Willie McKay **Bred** Victor Stud And Brendan Cummins **Trained** Bawtry, S Yorks

FOCUS
A very weak maiden with the winner rated just 41 and the placed horses only 45.

7240 GO PONTIN'S HOLIDAYS (S) STKS 5f (F)
1:05 (1:05) (Class 6) 2-Y-0 **£2,047** (£604; £302) **Stalls** High

Form RPR

1603 **1** **Mac Dalia**[16] 7106 2-8-9 70 JerryO'Dwyer(3) 4 68+
(M G Quinlan) *trckd ldrs gng wl: shkn up over 1f out: led last 100yds: readily* **11/4**[2]

021 **2** *1 1/4* **Martingrange Boy (IRE)**[5] 7220 2-9-3 0 (t) GregFairley 1 69
(D J Murphy) *led: rdn and edgd rt over 1f out: hdd and no ex ins fnl f* **6/4**[1]

5230 **3** *1 3/4* **Wild Bill Tracey**[27] 6977 2-8-12 69 PaulMulrennan 6 57
(M J Wallace) *w ldr: swtchd lft jst ins fnl f: kpt on same pce* **7/2**[3]

0632 **4** *2 1/2* **Tommytush (IRE)**[10] 7171 2-8-12 57 (t) DeanMcKeown 7 48
(E J Alston) *chsd ldrs: effrt over 2f out: sn outpcd* **5/1**

4000 **5** *4* **Silver Deal**[10] 7171 2-8-7 43 ChrisCatlin 3 29
(J A Pickering) *sn chsng ldrs: lost pl over 1f out* **66/1**

0045 **6** *5* **La Varrosa**[17] 7096 2-8-0 50 AmyBaker(7) 2 11
(Mrs P N Dutfield) *chsd ldrs: rdn and edgd lft over 2f out: sn wknd* **28/1**

7 *2 1/2* **Orphan Boy** 2-8-8 0 ow1 JamieJones(5) 5 8
(M G Quinlan) *dwlt: sn outpcd in rr: bhd fnl 2f* **18/1**

60.21 secs (-0.09) **Going Correction** -0.05s/f (Stan) **7** Ran SP% **115.8**
Speed ratings (Par 94): **98,96,93,89,82 74,70**
CSF £7.49 TOTE £4.40: £2.20, £1.60; EX 10.50.The winner was sold to A J McCabe Racing Ltd for 8,500gns. Martingrange Boy was the subject of a friendly claim for £6,000.
Owner Dr Angelo Macchi **Bred** Chippenham Lodge Stud **Trained** Newmarket, Suffolk

FOCUS
A much better than average selling race with the first two looking a cut above this level pre-race. Solid form, and strong for the grade.

NOTEBOOK
Mac Dalia, tackling selling company for the first time, travelled easily under a confident ride and made this look plain sailing. She changed hands at the auction. (op 4-1)
Martingrange Boy(IRE), who cost connections dear to retain him just five days earlier, is a very keen type. He set the pace but the winner always looked to have his hand well covered. Connections were able to retain him when their friendly claim came first out of the hat. (op 11-8 tchd 7-4)
Wild Bill Tracey matched strides with the leader but had to switch when he went across his bows. He met two above-average sorts here and can surely find a similar race. (tchd 11-4)
Tommytush(IRE) had a fair bit to find and simply found this opposition too tough. There will be much easier opportunities in the New Year. (op 13-2 tchd 9-2)

7241 J.A. HUTCHINSON LTD DENTAL LABORATORY H'CAP 1m (F)
1:40 (1:41) (Class 5) (0-75,80) 3-Y-0+ **£2,968** (£876; £438) **Stalls** Low

Form RPR

0313 **1** **Ochre (IRE)**[17] 7104 3-8-10 66 DaleGibson 9 82
(R A Fahey) *chsd ldrs: shkn up to ld appr fnl f: drvn clr* **8/1**

366U **2** *3* **Masterofthecourt (USA)**[13] 7141 4-9-1 73 TravisBlock(3) 5 82
(H Morrison) *w ldrs: led 2f out: hdd appr fnl f: no ch w wnr* **7/1**[3]

0005 **3** *5* **Happy As Larry (USA)**[15] 7126 5-9-4 73 (t[1]) MickyFenton 7 71
(D J Murphy) *sn in rr and pushed along: hdwy over 3f out: kpt on fnl f: tk modest 3rd nr fin* **11/2**[2]

0011 **4** *hd* **Kabeer**[7] 7200 9-9-6 80 6ex (t) NataliaGemelova(5) 1 77
(A J McCabe) *w ldrs: led after 1f: hdd 2f out: wknd ins fnl f* **6/4**[1]

0000 **5** *4* **Speed Dial Harry (IRE)**[63] 6447 5-8-10 65 (v) LiamJones 3 53
(C R Dore) *chsd ldrs: sn drvn along: lost pl over 5f out: bhd tl kpt on fnl f* **33/1**

0520 **6** *1* **Pab Special (IRE)**[26] 6997 4-8-12 70 AndrewElliott(3) 4 56
(K R Burke) *led 1f: chsd ldrs: rdn over 3f out: lost pl over 1f out* **11/2**[2]

000V **7** *nk* **Kamanda Laugh**[17] 7100 6-9-3 72 PaulMulrennan 2 57
(K A Ryan) *chsd ldrs: rdn and lost pl over 4f out: kpt on fnl f* **33/1**

0502 **8** *5* **Shouldntbethere (IRE)**[36] 6894 3-8-7 63 AdrianMcCarthy 8 36
(Mrs P N Dutfield) *s.s: bhd and drvn along over 3f out* **11/1**

6103 **9** *1 1/2* **Rebellious Spirit**[13] 7141 4-8-13 68 ChrisCatlin 6 38
(P W Hiatt) *chsd ldrs: lost pl over 1f out* **14/1**

1m 42.38s (-2.22) **Going Correction** -0.125s/f (Stan)
WFA 3 from 4yo+ 1lb **9** Ran SP% **115.3**
Speed ratings (Par 103): **106,103,98,97,93 92,92,87,86**
CSF £62.54 CT £334.42 TOTE £8.50: £2.10, £2.70, £2.20; EX 71.70 Trifecta £245.40 Part won. Pool: £345.69 - 0.36 winning units..
Owner D Brennan **Bred** Darley **Trained** Musley Bank, N Yorks

FOCUS
A fair handicap, but the pace was not strong and the favourite Kabeer was not at his best.
Happy As Larry(USA) Official explanation: jockey said gelding had a breathing problem

7242 PONTINS.COM H'CAP 1m 4f (F)
2:15 (2:15) (Class 5) (0-75,71) 3-Y-0+ **£2,968** (£876; £438) **Stalls** Low

Form RPR

0451 **1** **Bentley Brook (IRE)**[7] 7198 5-8-2 59 6ex ow2 GHannon(7) 1 70
(P A Blockley) *trckd ldrs: slt advantage over 3f out: kpt on wl ins fnl f* **2/1**[1]

2431 **2** *1/2* **Kylkenny**[15] 7123 12-9-4 71 (t) TravisBlock(3) 6 81
(H Morrison) *sn trcking ldrs: chal 3f out: no ex ins fnl f* **7/1**

4301 **3** *8* **Maslak (IRE)**[12] 7151 3-9-2 71 ChrisCatlin 4 68
(P W Hiatt) *trckd ldrs: t.k.h: drvn over 3f out: styd on same pce* **10/3**[2]

334 **4** *1/2* **Spares And Repairs**[12] 7151 4-9-3 67 PaulMulrennan 7 63
(Mrs S Lamyman) *swtched lft s and t.k.h early: trckd ldrs: drvn over 4f out: one pce fnl 3f* **12/1**

3331 **5** *1 1/2* **Satindra (IRE)**[7] 7199 3-8-4 62 6ex (tp) AndrewElliott(3) 3 56
(John A Harris) *set modest pce: qcknd over 4f out: hdd over 3f out: one pce* **13/2**

1554 **6** *3* **Right Option (IRE)**[24] 7008 3-8-7 67 ow1 JamieJones(5) 5 56
(J L Flint) *sn trcking ldrs: drvn over 3f out: hung rt and wknd over 1f out* **4/1**[3]

560- **7** *21* **Impostor (IRE)**[276] 5628 4-9-6 70 (b) LiamJones 2 25
(R A Harris) *in rr and sn pushed along: lost tch 6f out: t.o 3f out* **25/1**

2m 39.77s (-2.32) **Going Correction** -0.125s/f (Stan)
WFA 3 from 4yo+ 5lb **7** Ran SP% **113.8**
Speed ratings (Par 103): **102,101,96,96,95 93,79**
CSF £16.57 TOTE £3.60: £2.00, £2.10; EX 10.50.
Owner John Wardle **Bred** Christopher Maye **Trained** Lambourn, Berks

FOCUS
The in-form first two pulled well clear in the end in a race that developed into a 5f dash.

7243 SOUTHWELL-RACECOURSE.CO.UK NURSERY 5f (F)
2:50 (2:50) (Class 6) (0-75,74) 2-Y-0 **£2,047** (£604; £302) **Stalls** High

Form RPR

1011 **1** **Weet A Surprise**[16] 7106 2-9-7 74 LPKeniry 1 79
(R Hollinshead) *w ldrs: shkn up to ld over 1f out: edgd rt: hld on wl* **13/8**[1]

0360 **2** *1* **Galley Slave (IRE)**[9] 7176 2-8-0 58 NicolPolli(5) 3 59
(M C Chapman) *chsd ldrs: rdn and outpcd over 2f out: kpt on to take 2nd ins fnl f: no real imp* **14/1**

5203 **3** *1 1/4* **Andrasta**[15] 7122 2-8-2 58 AndrewMullen(3) 7 55
(A Berry) *s.i.s: racd stands' side: hdwy to join ldrs over 2f out: kpt on same pce fnl f* **10/1**

4562 **4** *1* **Liani (IRE)**[7] 7195 2-7-9 51 oh1 DuranFentiman(3) 4 44
(J R Norton) *chsd ldrs: rdn and outpcd over 2f out: kpt on fnl f* **7/1**

3550 **5** *3/4* **Carnival Dream**[90] 5766 2-8-10 63 ChrisCatlin 5 53
(R A Harris) *w ldrs: edgd lft over 1f out: kpt on same pce* **4/1**[3]

4405 **6** *nk* **My Kaiser Chief**[16] 7106 2-8-11 64 PaulMulrennan 2 53
(W J H Ratcliffe) *sn w ldr: hung rt and wknd fnl f* **10/3**[2]

200 **7** *1 1/4* **Little Finch (IRE)**[8] 7182 2-7-12 51 oh1 (b) AdrianMcCarthy 6 36
(R C Guest) *mde most tl hdd over 1f out: sn wknd* **25/1**

60.98 secs (0.68) **Going Correction** -0.05s/f (Stan) **7** Ran SP% **113.3**
Speed ratings (Par 94): **92,90,88,86,85 85,83**
CSF £25.84 TOTE £2.20: £1.10, £5.70; EX 24.30.
Owner Ed Weetman (haulage & Storage) Ltd **Bred** Longdon Stud Ltd **Trained** Upper Longdon, Staffs

FOCUS
The winner is progressing nicely and the runner-up can surely find a selling race.

NOTEBOOK
Weet A Surprise, 2lb higher, travelled best and was always doing just enough giving plenty of weight away all round. (op 11-8 tchd 7-4)
Galley Slave(IRE) stuck on to claim second spot, his second placing on his 16th start. He can surely be placed to success in selling company. (tchd 16-1)
Andrasta, well treated on her turf form, raced alone towards the stands' side and this trip is short of her best. (op 9-1 tchd 15-2)
Liani(IRE), having just her second outing for this yard, lacks size. (op 11-2 tchd 5-1)
Carnival Dream was making her sand debut for her new yard. (op 13-2 tchd 7-1 in a place)
My Kaiser Chief, meeting the winner on 6lb better terms, wanted to do nothing but hang right. Official explanation: jockey said colt hung right (op 11-2)

7244 PONTIN'S BOOK EARLY H'CAP 1m (F)
3:25 (3:25) (Class 6) (0-57,62) 3-Y-0+ **£2,047** (£604; £302) **Stalls** Low

Form RPR

3011 **1** **Dado Mush**[6] 7213 4-9-3 62 6ex (p) KirstyMilczarek(5) 6 74
(T T Clement) *trckd ldrs: n.m.r 3f out: swtchd rt and led over 2f out: rdn and styd on strly: readily* **11/10**[1]

0231 **2** *2* **Only A Grand**[7] 7201 3-8-7 51 6ex (b) AndrewMullen(3) 2 58
(R Bastiman) *chsd ldrs: sn drvn along: sltly hmpd over 2f out: styd on to go 2nd over 1f out: no real imp* **4/1**[2]

4-50 **3** *5* **Sorbiesharry (IRE)**[10] 7172 8-8-2 45 (p) DuranFentiman(3) 5 41
(Mrs N Macauley) *sn outpcd and in rr: hdwy on outside over 3f out: hmpd over 2f out: one pce fnl 2f* **20/1**

405 **4** 1 1/2 **Naledi**[17] 7103 3-9-0 **55**........ PaulMulrennan 8 47
(J R Norton) *s.i.s: reminders and hdwy to chse ldrs over 3f out: led and hung bdly lft over 2f out: sn hdd: wknd fnl f* **14/1**

0040 **5** 3/4 **Raise Again (IRE)**[17] 7098 4-8-2 **49**........ AmyBaker(7) 3 39
(Mrs P N Dutfield) *chsd ldrs: drvn 5f out: sn outpcd: kpt on fnl 2f* **16/1**

1020 **6** 2 **Blue Empire (IRE)**[57] 6579 6-9-1 **55**........(v[1]) AdamKirby 1 41
(C R Dore) *chsd ldrs: reminders over 4f out: wknd over 1f out* **8/1**

4000 **7** 3/4 **Government (IRE)**[16] 7113 6-8-0 **45**........ NicolPolli(5) 7 29
(M C Chapman) *led tl over 2f out: lost pl over 1f out* **10/1**

3305 **8** 11 **Shunkawakhan (IRE)**[15] 7115 4-8-9 **49**........(b) ChrisCatlin 4 8
(G C H Chung) *t.k.h: hdwy to join ldrs after 2f: lost pl 2f out* **7/1**[3]

1m 43.3s (-1.30) **Going Correction** -0.125s/f (Stan)
WFA 3 from 4yo+ 1lb — 8 Ran SP% **117.6**
Speed ratings (Par 101): **101,99,94,92,91 89,89,78**
CSF £5.82 CT £56.07 TOTE £2.00: £1.10, £1.70, £4.30; EX 5.30 Trifecta £26.70 Pool: £120.60 - 3.20 winning units. Place 6 £200.70, Place 5 £88.13.
Owner Dr M Edres **Bred** Bellow Hill Stud **Trained** Newmarket, Suffolk
■ Stewards' Enquiry : Kirsty Milczarek two-day ban: careless riding (Jan 7-8)

FOCUS
The winner continues on the upgrade but it was a very steady pace and the form is anything but solid.
T/Plt: £1,083.00 to a £1 stake. Pool £31,231.10. 21.05 winning units. T/Qpdt: £12.80 to a £1 stake. Pool £3,158.70. 182.50 winning units. WG

7232 WOLVERHAMPTON (A.W) (L-H)

Thursday, December 27

OFFICIAL GOING: Standard
Wind: Fresh, behind Weather: Overcast

7245 PONTIN'S HOLIDAYS NURSERY — 7f 32y(P)
6:50 (6:52) (Class 6) (0-65,65) 2-Y-O — £2,730 (£806; £403) Stalls High

Form — RPR

0455 **1** **Tiger's Rocket (IRE)**[15] 7117 2-8-13 **62**........ HaddenFrost(5) 2 64
(R Hannon) *chsd ldrs: rdn and hmpd over 1f out: led ins fnl f: r.o* **4/1**[1]

005 **2** 1 **Broughtons Flight (IRE)**[20] 7058 2-9-6 **64**........ GeorgeBaker 8 64
(W J Musson) *s.i.s: hld up: rdn 1/2-way: hdwy over 2f out: hung lft over 1f out: r.o* **4/1**[1]

5604 **3** hd **Afton View (IRE)**[12] 7149 2-9-4 **62**........(e) SteveDrowne 4 61
(D J Murphy) *chsd ldrs: rdn to ld 2f out: hdd and unable qck ins fnl f* **11/2**[3]

0055 **4** 1 **John Potts**[37] 6881 2-8-13 **57**........ PhillipMakin 9 54
(B P J Baugh) *s.i.s: hld up: hdwy over 1f out: nrst fin* **16/1**

3565 **5** 2 **Oceana Blue**[17] 7097 2-9-4 **65**........(v[1]) NeilChalmers(3) 1 57
(A M Balding) *hld up: hdwy over 2f out: rdn over 1f out: hung lft and no ex ins fnl f* **16/1**

5225 **6** 1/2 **Mister Beano (IRE)**[12] 7152 2-8-13 **62**........(v) TolleyDean(5) 11 52
(R J Price) *chsd ldr: led 3f out: hdd 2f out: rdn and hung rt over 1f out: wknd ins fnl f* **14/1**

0U33 **7** 1/2 **Ile Royale**[8] 7182 2-8-1 **50**........(be) NicolPolli(5) 10 39
(C N Allen) *s.s: hld up: nt clr run over 2f out: styd on ins fnl f: nvr nrr* **8/1**

0000 **8** 1/2 **Plaka (FR)**[29] 6966 2-8-12 **56**........ LiamJones 12 44
(W M Brisbourne) *mid-div: effrt over 2f out: sn outpcd* **40/1**

0506 **9** 9 **Tobouggornotobougg**[9] 7176 2-8-8 **52**........ DeanMcKeown 3 18
(D Shaw) *edgd rt s: hld up: rdn 1/2-way: wknd over 2f out* **12/1**

3002 **10** 4 **Grapes Of Wrath (UAE)**[12] 7149 2-8-8 **52**........ GregFairley 7 8
(M Johnston) *chsd ldrs over 4f* **7/1**

003 **11** 1 1/2 **Yattendon**[21] 7043 2-9-7 **65**........ SimonWhitworth 5 18
(S Kirk) *led 4f: wknd over 1f out* **5/1**[2]

1m 32.43s (2.03) **Going Correction** +0.15s/f (Slow) — 11 Ran SP% **124.2**
Speed ratings (Par 94): **94,92,92,91,89 88,88,87,77,72 70**
CSF £20.74 CT £94.23 TOTE £4.10: £1.80, £2.10, £2.30; EX 24.20.
Owner M Mulholland **Bred** Bryan Ryan **Trained** East Everleigh, Wilts

FOCUS
A modest nursery but the form seems sound enough.

NOTEBOOK
Tiger's Rocket(IRE) had managed just one placing in ten previous starts but has been performing pretty consistently. He has been running over 1m recently and this drop in trip probably suited him, especially as the race was run at a good clip, but he was inclined to flash his tail in the closing stages and may not be entirely straightforward. (op 3-1 tchd 9-2)
Broughtons Flight(IRE) was gambled on for this nursery debut, but she showed clear signs of greenness, being slow to get competitive and then hanging when asked for her effort in the straight. The penny was dropping with her late on, and she will no doubt be winning before long, but the price will be on the skinny side after this effort and the value has been lost for now. (op 8-1 tchd 7-2)
Afton View(IRE), who finished behind Grapes Of Wrath at Southwell last time, reversed placings with that rival back down in trip. (op 8-1)
John Potts, eased 3lb in the weights, was doing his best work at the finish on this return to a longer trip. (tchd 20-1)
Oceana Blue was visored for the first time on this nursery debut and ran only respectably. (op 12-1)
Mister Beano(IRE) Official explanation: jockey said colt ran too freely
Grapes Of Wrath(UAE), 2lb higher than when runner-up over a mile at Southwell, was in trouble turning for home, and perhaps the Fibresand is her surface. (op 7-2)
Yattendon Official explanation: jockey said gelding had no more to give

7246 PONTIN'S BOOK EARLY AND SAVE CLAIMING STKS — 5f 216y(P)
7:20 (7:20) (Class 5) 2-Y-O — £3,238 (£963; £481; £240) Stalls Low

Form — RPR

212 **1** **Ike Quebec (FR)**[7] 7202 2-8-13 **78**........ HaddenFrost(5) 4 74+
(R Hannon) *chsd ldr: led 2f out: sn rdn and hung lft: r.o* **4/6**[1]

5125 **2** 1 **Copperbottomed (IRE)**[13] 7142 2-8-10 **67**........(be[1]) JimCrowley 3 63+
(J R Boyle) *chsd ldrs: rdn and edgd lft over 1f out: r.o* **4/1**[3]

6102 **3** 1 **Atephobia**[5] 7220 2-8-9 **67**........ FergusSweeney 1 59+
(K R Burke) *led: rdn and hdd 2f out: styd on same pce ins fnl f* **11/4**[2]

4 5 **Modern Practice (IRE)** 2-9-2 **0**........ MickyFenton 2 51
(Miss V Haigh) *s.s: sn pushed along in rr: wknd over 2f out: hung lft over 1f out: hung rt ins fnl f* **40/1**

1m 17.36s (1.55) **Going Correction** +0.15s/f (Slow) — 4 Ran SP% **109.1**
Speed ratings (Par 96): **95,93,92,85**
CSF £3.78 TOTE £1.50; EX 2.80.Ike Quebec was claimed by J. R. Boyle for £17,000.
Owner R Hannon **Bred** Elevage De Bois Carrouges **Trained** East Everleigh, Wilts

FOCUS
The race could have been rated higher, but the time was slow and the fourth a little too close for comfort.

NOTEBOOK
Ike Quebec(FR) was best in on official figures and always looked like winning in the straight. He hung left when taking it up and then idled in front, needing to be kept up to his work to the line to hold the runner-up. (tchd 8-11 and 4-5 in a place)
Copperbottomed(IRE), who won a 7f seller here last month, had blinkers added to the eyeshield. He was running on well at the finish, despite flashing his tail under pressure, and is probably better over further. (op 5-1 tchd 11-2)
Atephobia, who found little off the bridle at Lingfield last time, was simply not good enough at the weights on this occasion. (op 5-2 tchd 9-4 and 3-1)
Modern Practice(IRE), a half-brother to five winners, is with a trainer not noted for her success with two-year-old debutants. He was very green and got left behind in the straight. (op 28-1)

7247 WOLVERHAMPTON-RACECOURSE.CO.UK MEDIAN AUCTION MAIDEN STKS — 1m 141y(P)
7:50 (7:50) (Class 6) 3-5-Y-O — £2,047 (£604; £302) Stalls Low

Form — RPR

5020 **1** **Glenridding**[15] 7115 3-9-3 53........ JimCrowley 2 69
(J G Given) *mde all: drvn out* **5/2**[2]

2 1 **Steig (IRE)**[236] 4745 4-9-5 0........ JamesDoyle 1 67
(Carl Llewellyn) *a.p: chsd wnr over 3f out: rdn and hung lft fr over 1f out: styd on* **2/1**[1]

3032 **3** 5 **Alecia (IRE)**[13] 7144 3-8-9 50........ NeilChalmers(3) 3 51
(A M Balding) *chsd ldrs: lost pl and edgd lft 7f out: hdwy over 2f out: sn rdn: styd on same pce* **5/2**[2]

000 **4** 11 **Sun Bian**[14] 5817 5-9-5 45........ VinceSlattery 4 33
(L P Grassick) *chsd ldr 5f: rdn and wknd over 2f out* **33/1**

0206 **5** 1 1/4 **Franky'N'Jonny**[15] 7125 4-9-0 41........ AdamKirby 7 25
(M J Attwater) *prom 6f* **20/1**

00 **6** 1/2 **Willie Ever**[201] 2477 3-9-3 0........ FergusSweeney 6 29
(W J Musson) *s.i.s: hld up: rdn and wknd over 2f out* **8/1**[3]

000 **7** 59 **Rasmani**[15] 7125 3-8-12 28........(vt) MickyFenton 5 —
(Miss Gay Kelleway) *s.i.s: hld up: hmpd 7f out: rdn 1/2-way: wknd over 2f out: eased over 1f out* **40/1**

1m 51.13s (-0.63) **Going Correction** +0.15s/f (Slow)
WFA 3 from 4yo+ 2lb — 7 Ran SP% **111.7**
Speed ratings (Par 101): **108,107,102,92,91 91,38**
CSF £7.49 TOTE £4.20: £2.40, £1.80; EX 9.70.
Owner Tremousser Partnership **Bred** Bolton Grange **Trained** Willoughton, Lincs

FOCUS
A weak maiden but an improved effort from Glenridding. The form is rated through the third.

7248 GO PONTIN'S NOW H'CAP — 1m 141y(P)
8:20 (8:20) (Class 6) (0-60,60) 3-Y-O+ — £2,218 (£654; £327) Stalls Low

Form — RPR

1220 **1** **Machinate (USA)**[6] 7214 5-9-6 **60**........ LiamJones 4 65
(W M Brisbourne) *trckd ldrs: led over 1f out: edgd lft: rdn out* **5/2**[1]

40-4 **2** nk **Pauline's Prince**[9] 7180 5-9-6 **60**........ JimCrowley 5 64
(R Hollinshead) *hld up: nt clr run over 2f out: hdwy and swtchd lft over 1f out: sn rdn: r.o* **9/2**[3]

106V **3** 1 1/2 **Strike Force**[17] 7100 3-8-13 **60**........ KirstyMilczarek(5) 10 61
(K F Clutterbuck) *chsd ldr tl led over 2f out: rdn and hdd over 1f out: styd on same pce* **10/1**

40-5 **4** nk **Micky Mac (IRE)**[15] 7118 3-8-5 **50**........ DuranFentiman(3) 2 50
(T D Walford) *hld up: nt clr run over 2f out: hmpd over 1f out: carried lft and r.o ins fnl f: nvr able to chal* **20/1**

500V **5** 1 1/4 **Riolo (IRE)**[17] 7100 5-8-7 **47** oh1 ow1........(b) JamesDoyle 6 45
(K F Clutterbuck) *prom: rdn 3f out: hung lft and styd on same pce fnl f* **20/1**

6013 **6** 1 **Charlottebutterfly**[15] 7115 7-8-12 **57**........ HaddenFrost(5) 1 53
(P J McBride) *hld up: hdwy over 2f out: rdn over 1f out: edgd lft and no ex fnl f* **3/1**[2]

00 **7** 8 **Namiguest (IRE)**[12] 7157 3-7-11 **46** oh1........ AndrewHeffernan(7) 7 25
(Paul Green) *plld hrd and prom: rdn whn hmpd over 2f out: sn wknd* **80/1**

5005 **8** 3 **Gwyllion (USA)**[17] 7104 3-9-4 **60**........(b[1]) NickyMackay 8 33
(B J Meehan) *led: rdn and hdd over 2f out: wknd over 1f out* **6/1**

0050 **9** 6 **Just Crystal**[14] 7133 3-8-2 **47** oh1 ow1........ AndrewElliott(3) 3 7
(B P J Baugh) *s.i.s: hld up: effrt over 2f out: sn wknd* **8/1**

1m 53.05s (1.29) **Going Correction** +0.15s/f (Slow)
WFA 3 from 5yo+ 2lb — 9 Ran SP% **117.0**
Speed ratings (Par 101): **100,99,98,98,97 96,89,86,81**
CSF £13.96 CT £96.77 TOTE £4.00: £1.10, £1.60, £5.20; EX 16.10.
Owner D Slingsby **Bred** Gaines-Gentry Thoroughbreds And William Condren **Trained** Great Ness, Shropshire
■ Stewards' Enquiry : Jim Crowley one-day ban: careless riding (Jan 7)

FOCUS
The time was moderate and this was a somewhat messy affair. The form is not too solid.
Charlottebutterfly Official explanation: jockey said mare had no more to give

7249 STAY AT THE WOLVERHAMPTON HOLIDAY INN H'CAP — 1m 4f 50y(P)
8:50 (8:50) (Class 6) (0-65,65) 3-Y-O+ — £2,218 (£654; £327) Stalls Low

Form — RPR

0105 **1** **Gamesters Lady**[21] 7046 4-9-5 **63**........ LiamJones 3 70
(W M Brisbourne) *led: hdd over 10f out: chsd ldr: pushed along 5f out: led 3f out: rdn over 1f out: edgd rt ins fnl f: styd on* **8/1**

1433 **2** 3/4 **Altos Reales**[20] 7060 3-8-7 **56**........ DeanMcKeown 4 62
(D Shaw) *hld up: hdwy over 3f out: rdn over 1f out: styd on* **6/1**[3]

0236 **3** shd **Raquel White**[24] 7004 3-8-7 **61**........ TolleyDean(5) 5 67
(J L Flint) *s.i.s and hmpd s: hdwy over 9f out: rdn over 2f out: styd on: eased whn nt clr run last strides* **11/1**

1V4 **4** 3/4 **Alonso De Guzman (IRE)**[6] 7211 3-8-6 **62**........ PatrickDonaghy(7) 2 66
(J R Boyle) *trckd ldrs: rdn over 1f out: edgd rt fnl f: styd on u.p* **3/1**[1]

6205 **5** 10 **Speagle (IRE)**[10] 7173 5-9-0 **65**........ MarkCoumbe(7) 7 53
(A J Chamberlain) *chsd ldrs tl rdn and wknd 2f out* **12/1**

0233 **6** 5 **Punta Galera (IRE)**[14] 7132 4-9-7 **65**........ MickyFenton 6 45
(Paul Green) *chsd ldr: led over 10f out: rdn and hdd 3f out: wknd wl over 1f out* **4/1**[2]

2623 **7** 4 **Keisha Kayleigh (IRE)**[23] 7023 4-9-5 **63**........(v) PaulMulrennan 9 37
(B Ellison) *stdd s: hld up and bhd: rdn over 3f out: nvr any ch* **7/1**

3020 **8** 1 **Swiper Hill (IRE)**[13] 7146 4-8-11 **55**........ J-PGuillambert 1 27
(B Ellison) *hld up and bhd: rdn over 3f out: nvr any ch* **11/1**

1153 **9** 3 1/2 **Treetops Hotel (IRE)**[17] 7102 8-9-4 **62**........ GeorgeBaker 8 29
(R Hollinshead) *stdd s: hld up and bhd: rdn over 3f out: nvr any ch* **8/1**

2m 43.05s (0.63) **Going Correction** +0.15s/f (Slow)
WFA 3 from 4yo+ 5lb — 9 Ran SP% **118.4**
Speed ratings (Par 101): **103,102,102,101,95 91,89,88,86**
CSF £56.67 CT £536.83 TOTE £10.90: £4.20, £1.70, £2.40; EX 52.90.
Owner Gamesters Partnership **Bred** D Timmis **Trained** Great Ness, Shropshire

■ Stewards' Enquiry : Tolley Dean seven-day ban: failed to ride out to finish and lost second place (Jan 7-13)

FOCUS

Just a moderate pace on here, and it paid to race handily. Modest form, but sound enough.

Speagle(IRE) Official explanation: jockey said gelding hung left

7250 PONTINSBINGO.COM H'CAP — 7f 32y(P)

9:20 (9:21) (Class 6) (0-50,51) 3-Y-0+ — **£2,218** (£654; £327) **Stalls** High

Form — RPR

4304 **1** **Mister Always**[16] 7107 3-8-9 **47** ....(e[1]) JimCrowley 7 — 57
(I W McInnes) *hld up: hdwy over 1f out: rdn to ld and hung lft wl ins fnl f: r.o* **7/1[3]**

6506 **2** ½ **Claws**[7] 7207 4-8-12 **50** .... JamesDoyle 1 — 59
(A J Lidderdale) *led 1f: chsd ldrs: rdn and ev ch ins fnl f: r.o* **16/1**

5312 **3** hd **Beck**[6] 7218 3-8-10 **51** 6ex .... DuranFentiman(3) 3 — 59
(W M Brisbourne) *s.i.s: hld up: hdwy and nt clr run fr over 2f out tl rdn and swtchd lft 1f out: r.o* **5/4[1]**

5435 **4** ¾ **Desert Lover (IRE)**[12] 7153 5-8-3 **46** oh1 ....(p) KirstyMilczarek(5) 8 — 52
(R J Price) *s.i.s: hld up: hdwy over 2f out: rdn over 1f out: edgd lft ins fnl f: styd on* **5/1[2]**

4005 **5** ½ **Mister Benji**[10] 7169 8-8-12 **50** ....(p) PhillipMakin 6 — 55
(B P J Baugh) *hld up in tch: n.m.r over 2f out: rdn over 1f out: edgd lft: styd on* **12/1**

0061 **6** ½ **Silver Hotspur**[56] 6609 3-8-12 **50** .... NickyMackay 10 — 54
(M Wigham) *trckd ldrs: led 2f out: rdn and hdd wl ins fnl f* **8/1**

3054 **7** 10 **Ask No More**[241] 1349 4-8-9 **47** ....(b) LiamJones 9 — 24
(J Ryan) *led 6f out: rdn and hdd 2f out: sn wknd* **14/1**

0602 **8** 1 **Shadow Jumper (IRE)**[12] 7148 6-8-10 **48** ....(v) DaleGibson 2 — 22
(J T Stimpson) *chsd ldrs: hmpd 1/2-way: sn rdn: wknd 2f out* **11/1**

4400 **9** 1 **Marist Madame**[174] 3286 3-8-9 **47** .... GregFairley 5 — 18
(T J Pitt) *sn pushed along in rr: wknd over 2f out* **33/1**

5330 **10** nk **Zabeel Tower**[35] 6906 4-8-11 **49** ....(p) PaulMulrennan 11 — 20
(R Allan) *prom: rdn over 2f out: wknd fnl f: eased* **8/1**

1m 31.69s (1.29) **Going Correction** +0.15s/f (Slow) — **10** Ran SP% **127.3**

Speed ratings (Par 101): **98,97,97,96,95 95,83,82,81,81**

CSF £122.17 CT £240.16 TOTE £9.60: £1.70, £5.20, £1.10; EX 155.10 Place 6 £28.25, Place 5 £17.24.

Owner Barrie Kirby **Bred** K McAuliffe **Trained** Catwick, E Yorks

FOCUS

A moderate but open-looking handicap. Sound form which should work out.

Desert Lover(IRE) Official explanation: jockey said gelding missed the break and hung left

Ask No More Official explanation: jockey said gelding ran too freely

T/Plt: £73.70 to a £1 stake. Pool: £100,778.25. 997.10 winning tickets. T/Qpdt: £18.80 to a £1 stake. Pool: £7,577.90. 297.80 winning tickets. CR

7220 LINGFIELD (L-H)

Friday, December 28

OFFICIAL GOING: Standard

Wind: strong behind Weather: overcast

7251 PONTINSBINGO.COM APPRENTICE CLAIMING STKS — 1m (P)

12:40 (12:44) (Class 6) 3-Y-0+ — **£1,943** (£578; £288; £144) **Stalls** High

Form — RPR

4251 **1** **Ninth House (USA)**[21] 7057 5-9-1 73 ....(bt) HarryPoulton(3) 2 — 79
(N P Littmoden) *s.i.s: t.k.h: hld up in midfield: hdwy over 2f out: jnd ldr gng wl over 1f out: led 1f out: shkn up ins fnl f: r.o wl* **5/2[1]**

0504 **2** 1 **Northern Desert (IRE)**[14] 7143 8-8-13 62 .... KirstyMilczarek 6 — 72
(S Curran) *hld up in tch in rr: hdwy over 2f out: n.m.r briefly wl over 1f out: chsd wnr jst ins fnl f: kpt on but nt threaten wnr* **5/1[3]**

3625 **3** 1¾ **Hucking Heat (IRE)**[18] 7099 3-8-6 64 ....(v) KierenFox(7) 10 — 69
(J R Best) *stdd s: hld up in last: hdwy over 2f out: swtchd rt over 1f out: chsd ldng pair ins fnl f: nvr able to chal* **7/1**

0361 **4** 2½ **Dickie Le Davoir**[2] 7233 3-8-8 80 .... DeclanCannon(7) 8 — 65
(K R Burke) *hld up in rr: hdwy on outer jst over 2f out: styd on fnl f: nvr rchd ldrs* **7/2[2]**

0051 **5** nk **Mountain Pass (USA)**[25] 7006 5-8-8 64 ....(p) DavidProbert(7) 5 — 63
(B J Llewellyn) *t.k.h: chsd ldrs: wnt 2nd over 2f out: rdn to ld wl over 1f out: hdd 1f out: fdd fnl f* **14/1**

420 **6** 1 **Katiypour (IRE)**[37] 6894 10-9-0 63 .... PatrickHills 7 — 60
(B R Johnson) *t.k.h: hld up in tch: rdn and slipped bnd jst over 2f out: no imp over 1f out* **5/1[3]**

0-00 **7** 1¼ **Steely Dan**[24] 7017 8-9-7 75 ....(p) JamieJones 4 — 64
(Mrs L C Jewell) *led: rdn over 2f out: edgd rt wl over 1f out: sn hdd: btn and eased ins fnl f* **16/1**

6014 **8** nk **Zaafira (SPA)**[27] 7001 3-8-7 51 ow2 ....(t) SCreighton(3) 1 — 53
(E J Creighton) *chsd ldrs: rdn 3f out: wknd over 2f out* **33/1**

50 **9** 9 **Stratn Jack**[23] 7029 3-8-8 0 .... KylieManser(5) 3 — 36
(B G Powell) *stdd s: sn chsng ldr: wkng whn short of room over 2f out: wl bhd over 1f out* **66/1**

-300 **10** 2 **Unlimited**[112] 5191 5-9-0 53 ....(p) RyanClark(7) 9 — 38
(R Simpson) *v free to post: racd in midfield on outer: wknd over 2f out: sn wl bhd* **33/1**

1m 39.21s (-0.22) **Going Correction** -0.125s/f (Stan)

WFA 3 from 5yo+ 1lb — **10** Ran SP% **116.6**

Speed ratings (Par 101): **96,95,93,90,90 89,88,87,78,76**

CSF £15.04 TOTE £3.50: £1.40, £1.80, £2.10; EX 15.20 Trifecta £63.90 Pool £305.37 - 3.39 winning units..Hucking Heat was claimed by M Khan for £8,000.

Owner Nigel Shields **Bred** Juddmonte Farms Inc **Trained** Newmarket, Suffolk

FOCUS

Not a bad claimer, but the sedate early pace caught a few out.

Stratn Jack Official explanation: jockey said gelding suffered interference in running

7252 PONTIN'S BOOK EARLY AND SAVE MEDIAN AUCTION MAIDEN STKS — 1m (P)

1:10 (1:11) (Class 6) 2-Y-O — **£1,943** (£578; £288; £144) **Stalls** High

Form — RPR

1 **Age Of Reason (UAE)** 2-9-3 0 .... GregFairley 3 — 80+
(M Johnston) *chsd ldr after 1f: rdn to ld 2f out: clr jst over 1f out: rdn out* **9/2[3]**

454 **2** 3½ **Mcconnell (USA)**[80] 6080 2-9-3 74 .... GeorgeBaker 2 — 72
(J R Best) *stdd s: hld up in rr: hdwy over 2f out: chsd wnr jst ins fnl f: kpt on but nvr able to chal* **6/1**

5 **3** 1¼ **Rankayo Hitam (USA)**[19] 7084 2-9-3 0 .... JohnEgan 7 — 69
(J S Moore) *t.k.h: hld up in tch in midfield: rdn and outpcd wl over 2f out: styd on fnl f: nt rch ldrs* **11/4[1]**

400 **4** nk **My Shadow**[20] 7070 2-9-3 66 .... DeanMcKeown 9 — 68
(S Dow) *stdd after s and sn detached in last: hdwy and in tch 4f out: outpcd wl over 2f out: styd on fnl f: nvr nr ldrs* **66/1**

2 **5** 2 **Mrs Summersby (IRE)**[32] 6944 2-8-12 0 .... SteveDrowne 6 — 59
(H Morrison) *in tch drvn and outpcd over 2f out: n.d after* **3/1[2]**

26 **6** 2½ **Celtic Charlie (FR)**[20] 7070 2-9-3 0 .... JimCrowley 1 — 59
(P M Phelan) *s.i.s: sn rcvrd and led after 1f: clr w wnr over 2f out: hdd 2f out: sn outpcd: lost 2nd jst ins fnl f: wknd qckly* **12/1**

002 **7** 1¾ **Alcimedes**[20] 7070 2-9-3 74 .... AdrianMcCarthy 5 — 55
(P W Chapple-Hyam) *led for 1f: styd prom tl rdn and outpcd over 2f out: wknd over 1f out* **9/2[3]**

0 **8** 3½ **Arrewig Lissome (USA)**[98] 5599 2-9-3 0 .... LPKeniry 4 — 47
(A M Balding) *in tch in midfield: rdn and struggling over 3f out: wl bhd last 2f* **33/1**

04 **9** 18 **Lacala (IRE)**[97] 5646 2-8-12 0 .... PatCosgrave 8 — 2
(Jane Chapple-Hyam) *racd in midfield: rdn and lost pl over 4f out: t.o last 2f* **16/1**

1m 38.82s (-0.61) **Going Correction** -0.125s/f (Stan) — **9** Ran SP% **120.3**

Speed ratings (Par 94): **98,94,93,92,90 88,86,83,65**

CSF £33.14 TOTE £5.90: £1.70, £2.20, £1.60; EX 39.90 Trifecta £226.80 Pool £351.46 - 1.10 winning units..

Owner Sheikh Mohammed **Bred** Darley **Trained** Middleham Moor, N Yorks

FOCUS

A fair juvenile maiden, run at just an average pace, and the impressive winner should rate a good bit higher.

NOTEBOOK

Age Of Reason(UAE) ◆, a 200,000gns purchase whose dam was a very useful miler in France, got his career off to a perfect start with a taking debut success. He knew his job and was soon racing handily, which proved to his advantage off the modest early pace, but there was a lot to like about the manner in which he quickened to settle the issue when asked to win his race. He should be rated value for a little further than the winning margin and this gelding looks yet another bright prospect for his leading stable, with the likelihood of a step up in trip suiting him as he matures. (op 15-2)

Mcconnell(USA) ◆, officially rated 74 after three previous runs on turf, stayed on late in the day without seriously threatening the winner over this extra furlong. The lack of real early pace would not have helped his cause and, with this outing likely to bring him on, it would not be surprising to see him placed to deservedly go one better in something similar soon. (op 11-2 tchd 5-1)

Rankayo Hitam(USA), runner-up over 7f at this track on his debut earlier in the month, was another not seen to best advantage in being held up off the modest early pace and took time to settle. He kept on nicely when hitting his full stride and is clearly going the right way. Official explanation: jockey said colt suffered interference on leaving the stalls (op 9-4)

My Shadow, who pulled hard on his previous outing, was not that surprisingly restrained after a tardy start and again ran freely. He still showed ability again, without ever seriously threatening, and ought to learn more from this experience. It may be that he would like a stiffer test, however. Official explanation: jockey said colt got upset in the stalls and missed the break

Mrs Summersby(IRE), runner-up over course and distance last month, proved tricky at the start yet still had her chance, only to prove one-paced when it mattered. (op 7-2 tchd 9-2)

7253 GO PONTIN'S H'CAP — 7f (P)

1:40 (1:44) (Class 5) (0-75,75) 3-Y-0+ — **£2,817** (£838; £418; £209) **Stalls** Low

Form — RPR

0220 **1** **Reeling N' Rocking (IRE)**[55] 6646 4-8-13 **70** .... SteveDrowne 10 — 78
(B W Hills) *racd in midfield: rdn along over 4f out: hdwy jst over 1f out: styd on u.p to ld nr fin* **8/1**

0635 **2** nk **Carmenero (GER)**[22] 7045 4-9-1 **72** .... SaleemGolam 4 — 79
(W R Muir) *in tch: short of room over 3f out: rdn and chsd ldrs 2f out: styd on to chal ins fnl f: styd on* **9/1**

3016 **3** ½ **No Time (IRE)**[9] 7183 7-8-6 **63** .... JamesDoyle 5 — 69
(A J McCabe) *chsd ldrs: rdn over 2f out: chsd ldr 1f out: led last 100yds: hdd and no ex towards fin* **20/1**

4640 **4** ¾ **Super Frank (IRE)**[55] 6651 4-9-4 **75** .... J-PGuillambert 9 — 79
(J Akehurst) *led: rdn jst over 2f out: hdd last 100yds: fdd towards fin* **11/4[1]**

2033 **5** ½ **Chief Exec**[18] 7094 5-8-4 **68** .... DavidProbert(7) 14 — 70
(J R Gask) *stdd after s and dropped in wl bhd: hdwy on outer bnd 2f out: styd on wl fnl f: nt rch ldrs* **12/1**

5206 **6** ¾ **Pab Special (IRE)**[1] 7241 4-8-13 **70** ....(v) FergusSweeney 12 — 70
(K R Burke) *t.k.h: hld up in midfield: rdn and hdwy wl over 1f out: kpt on u.p: nvr threatened ldrs* **11/1**

0206 **7** 1 **Bertie Southstreet**[28] 6972 4-9-1 **72** .... GeorgeBaker 7 — 70
(J R Best) *t.k.h: hld up towards rr: effrt whn nt clr run and snatched up wl over 1f out: styd on on fnl f: nvr trbld ldrs* **7/1[3]**

0025 **8** nk **Hollow Jo**[21] 7054 7-8-10 **67** .... MickyFenton 11 — 64
(J R Jenkins) *chsd ldr: rdn 2f out: lost 2nd 1f out: wknd fnl f* **20/1**

050 **9** shd **Cape Of Luck (IRE)**[27] 6996 4-9-1 **72** ....(t) JimCrowley 3 — 69
(P M Phelan) *s.i.s: rdn 4f out: kpt on fnl f: nvr threatened ldrs* **6/1[2]**

3351 **10** nk **Affrettando (IRE)**[23] 7029 3-8-10 **67** .... JohnEgan 13 — 63
(J A R Toller) *in tch in midfield on outer: rdn and struggling over 2f out: kpt on same pce* **12/1**

32 **11** nk **Tamino (IRE)**[64] 6450 4-9-0 **71** .... TGMcLaughlin 2 — 66
(P Howling) *hld up bhd: effrt on inner wl over 1f out: nvr nr ldrs* **9/1**

-340 **12** ½ **Boogie Dancer**[39] 6874 3-8-8 **65** .... AdrianMcCarthy 8 — 59
(H S Howe) *chsd ldrs: rdn wl over 3f out: wknd over 2f out* **50/1**

-526 **13** 1½ **Cavalry Guard (USA)**[215] 2059 3-9-2 **73** .... PatCosgrave 6 — 63
(J R Boyle) *hld up in midfield: rdn wl over 2f out: sn outpcd* **16/1**

0004 **14** shd **Cool Sands (IRE)**[21] 7054 5-8-10 **67** ....(v) DeanMcKeown 1 — 56
(D Shaw) *hld up in last pair: n.d* **16/1**

1m 24.19s (-1.70) **Going Correction** -0.125s/f (Stan) — **14** Ran SP% **131.5**

Speed ratings (Par 103): **104,103,103,102,101 100,99,99,99,98 98,97,96,96**

CSF £84.00 CT £1478.63 TOTE £10.00: £3.50, £3.60, £7.30; EX 89.90 TRIFECTA Not won..

Owner D M James **Bred** Richard F Barnes **Trained** Lambourn, Berks

FOCUS

A modest handicap, run at a strong pace, which saw the first six closely covered at the finish. Straightforward form, rated through the winner and third.

Bertie Southstreet Official explanation: jockey said gelding was denied a clear run

Hollow Jo Official explanation: jockey said gelding hung left

The Form Book, Raceform Ltd, Compton, RG20 6NL

Boogie Dancer Official explanation: jockey said filly hung left

7254 PONTIN'S BOOK EARLY PRICE PROMISE H'CAP 7f (P)
2:10 (2:11) (Class 2) (0-100,103) 3-Y-O+

£9,971 (£2,985; £1,492; £747; £372; £187) Stalls Low

Form RPR

0056 1 **Vortex**[98] 5588 8-9-7 **103**......(t) GeorgeBaker 7 109
(Miss Gay Kelleway) *stdd after s and dropped in bhd: hdwy to trck ldrs over 2f out: rdn to ld 1f out: in command after* **4/1**[2]

5000 2 1/2 **Ektimaal**[104] 5413 4-8-4 **86** oh1......(t) JamieMackay 8 91
(E A L Dunlop) *stdd and dropped in bhd after s: hdwy over 2f out: c wd st: r.o wl to chse wnr ins fnl f: clsng on wnr nr fin* **4/1**[2]

0252 3 1 1/4 **Salient**[20] 7074 3-8-6 **88**...... PaulDoe 5 89
(J Akehurst) *w ldr: led over 2f out: sn rdn: hdd 1f out: one pce fnl f* **9/4**[1]

0266 4 1/2 **Regal Quest (IRE)**[9] 7184 3-8-4 **86** oh8......(t) SaleemGolam 2 86
(S C Williams) *in tch: rdn to chse ldrs 2f out: kpt on same pce fnl f* **20/1**

0340 5 3/4 **Andronikos**[9] 7184 5-8-7 **89**......(t) NelsonDeSouza 3 87
(P F I Cole) *plld hrd: chsd ldrs: rdn wl over 1f out: kpt on same pce* **11/2**

143 6 hd **Councellor (FR)**[9] 7184 5-8-8 **90**......(t) MickyFenton 4 87
(Stef Liddiard) *t.k.h: led tl rdn and hdd over 2f out: wknd fnl f* **9/2**[3]

P 7 1 1/4 **Markab**[118] 5031 4-8-7 **89**...... JamesDoyle 6 83
(K A Morgan) *towards rr: rdn and struggling 2f out: n.d after* **33/1**

0000 8 3/4 **Zafonical Storm (USA)**[70] 5833 3-8-4 **86** oh1......(t) NickyMackay 1 78
(B W Duke) *in tch on inner: rdn and lost pl 3f out: wknd wl over 1f out* **50/1**

1m 24.0s (-1.89) **Going Correction** -0.125s/f (Stan) **8** Ran SP% **114.0**
Speed ratings (Par 109): **105,104,103,102,101 101,99,99**
CSF £19.87 CT £43.48 TOTE £5.40: £1.50, £2.10, £1.50; EX 22.90 Trifecta £50.90 Pool £635.68 - 8.86 winning units..

Owner Coriolis Partnership **Bred** Juddmonte Farms **Trained** Exning, Suffolk

FOCUS
A decent handicap which saw the winner outclass his rivals under his big weight. It is doubtful whether he had to improve, with the fourth too close for comfort.

NOTEBOOK
Vortex, having his first outing since September, shot clear passing the final furlong and ran out a decisive winner, registering his first success since winning in Dubai back in February. This rates a decent effort under his big weight and he simply outclassed his rivals, but it is now hoped he does not go up again too much for this as he is due back for another campaign at Nad Al Sheba next year. (op 7-2 tchd 9-2)

Ektimaal ◆, returning from a 104-day break, took time to find his full stride from off the pace and was doing all of his best work late in the day. He is still open to further improvement and is obviously entitled to come on a deal for the run. (op 7-2)

Salient, runner-up to the winner's stable companion Fayr over course and distance last time, again did little wrong in defeat from this 1lb higher mark and helps to set the level of the form. He deserves to win again. (op 3-1)

Regal Quest(IRE) ran with real credit considering she was 8lb out of the handicap. No doubt the Handicapper will react to this, however. (op 16-1)

Markab Official explanation: jockey said colt hung right from 4f out

7255 LINGFIELDPARK.CO.UK H'CAP 6f (P)
2:45 (2:46) (Class 2) (0-100,105) 3-Y-O+

£9,971 (£2,985; £1,492; £747; £372; £187) Stalls Low

Form RPR

1126 1 **Ebraam (USA)**[17] 7112 4-8-1 **86** oh3...... DuranFentiman(3) 3 98
(D Shaw) *hld up towards rr: hdwy jst over 2f out: chal 1f out: sn led: r.o wl* **5/1**[3]

0231 2 1/2 **Turn On The Style**[21] 7053 5-9-3 **99**......(b) PaulMulrennan 1 109
(J Balding) *t.k.h: chsd ldrs on inner: effrt and rdn wl over 1f out: led 1f out: sn hdd: kpt on but a hld by wnr* **3/1**[1]

045 3 1 1/4 **Orpsie Boy (IRE)**[83] 6003 4-8-11 **93**...... JimCrowley 6 99
(N P Littmoden) *hld up in last pair: hdwy on outer jst over 2f out: r.o u.p fnl f: wnt 3rd nr fin: nt rch ldrs* **15/2**

0041 4 hd **Maltese Falcon**[34] 6930 7-9-9 **105**......(t) NelsonDeSouza 8 110
(P F I Cole) *awkward leaving stalls: sn chsng ldrs: drvn over 1f out: kpt on same pce fnl f* **9/2**[2]

0033 5 3/4 **Qadar (IRE)**[75] 6197 5-9-1 **97**......(b) GeorgeBaker 7 100
(N P Littmoden) *stdd s and dropped in bhd: rdn and effrt jst over 2f out: kpt on u.p fnl f: nt trble ldrs* **5/1**[3]

463 6 shd **Orpenindeed (IRE)**[21] 7053 4-8-9 **91**......(t) JohnEgan 9 94
(M Botti) *w ldr: rdn and ev ch wl over 1f out: fdd ins fnl f* **7/1**

0045 7 3/4 **Diane's Choice**[21] 7053 4-8-4 **86** oh1...... NickyMackay 4 86
(J Akehurst) *led: rdn over 2f out: hdd 1f out: wknd ins fnl f* **16/1**

0012 8 3/4 **Lucayos**[21] 7053 4-8-7 **96** ow3...... KylieManser(7) 2 94
(Mrs H Sweeting) *chsd ldrs: rdn 2f out: wknd over 1f out* **16/1**

0150 9 2 1/2 **Blue Rocket (IRE)**[7] 7212 3-8-4 **86** oh1......(e) LiamJones 5 76
(D J Murphy) *chsd ldrs tl over 4f out: sn rdn and lost pl: bhd last 2f* **25/1**

1m 10.58s (-2.23) **Going Correction** -0.125s/f (Stan) course record **9** Ran SP% **116.4**
Speed ratings (Par 109): **109,108,106,106,105 105,104,103,99**
CSF £20.57 CT £112.56 TOTE £6.60: £2.00, £1.60, £2.50; EX 27.00 Trifecta £128.80 Pool £760.17 - 4.19 winning units..

Owner The Circle Bloodstock I Limited **Bred** Shadwell Farm LLC **Trained** Danethorpe, Notts

FOCUS
A good sprint handicap for the class. The form looks sound and should work out.

NOTEBOOK
Ebraam(USA) posted a career-best effort to score in determined fashion on this return to the Polytrack. He showed a decent attitude when asked to win his race and has now won his last two races at this venue, so it will be very interesting to see how he now copes with a likely future weight rise. (op 10-1)

Turn On The Style, 4lb higher than when scoring narrowly over course and distance last time, was able to race handily again and lost nothing in defeat. He is a very likeable sprinter and rates a solid benchmark for the form. (tchd 11-4 and 10-3 in a place)

Orpsie Boy(IRE) struggled to go the early pace, but kept to his task under pressure and did more than enough to suggest he would come on for this first outing since October. (op 13-2 tchd 6-1)

Maltese Falcon lost his chance of bagging the early lead with a sluggish start and was always up against it thereafter. He had a tough enough task under top weight and was not disgraced. (op 4-1)

Qadar(IRE), having his first run since October, was given his usual patient ride after being slow to break. He came through to run his race and, while not one for win-only purposes, is entitled to come on for the outing. Official explanation: jockey said gelding missed the break (op 9-2 tchd 11-2)

Orpenindeed(IRE) Official explanation: jockey said colt ran too freely

7256 ARENALEISUREPLC.COM H'CAP 1m 5f (P)
3:15 (3:21) (Class 6) (0-65,64) 3-Y-O+ £1,943 (£578; £288; £144) Stalls Low

Form RPR

2001 1 **War Of The Roses (IRE)**[42] 6832 4-9-7 **58**...... J-PGuillambert 10 71
(R Brotherton) *hld up in rr: gd hdwy over 2f out: led jst over 1f out: sn clr: readily* **7/2**[1]

3/04 2 3 **Dash Of Grey (IRE)**[9] 7194 8-9-13 **64**......(b) JimCrowley 6 71
(Ruaidhri Joseph Tierney, Ire) *led: hrd pressed and rdn 2f out: hdd jst over 1f out: no ch w wnr* **12/1**

2351 3 1 **Smokey The Bear**[12] 7168 5-9-0 **54** 6ex...... NeilChalmers(3) 8 60
(Miss Sheena West) *t.k.h: hld up in rr: hdwy over 2f out: rdn wl over 1f out: styd on to go 3rd ins fnl f: nvr able to chal* **7/2**[1]

0453 4 3/4 **Henry Holmes**[12] 7168 4-8-11 **48**...... RichardThomas 5 53
(Mrs L Richards) *chsd ldrs: wnt 2nd 8f out: rdn and ev ch jst over 2f out: outpcd fnl f* **8/1**

2100 5 1/2 **Krasivi's Boy (USA)**[30] 6969 5-8-12 **49**......(b) FergusSweeney 11 53
(G L Moore) *t.k.h: chsd ldrs: rdn 3f out: outpcd wl over 1f out* **16/1**

5010 6 1 1/2 **Blue Hedges**[14] 7135 5-9-5 **59**...... JerryO'Dwyer(3) 4 61
(H J Collingridge) *hld up in rr: rdn and effrt jst over 2f out: nvr trbld ldrs* **7/1**[3]

1422 7 2 1/2 **Mixing**[30] 6969 5-8-11 **53**...... KirstyMilczarek(5) 9 51
(J Akehurst) *t.k.h: hld up towards rr: effrt on outer over 3f out: no imp over 2f out* **4/1**[2]

0500 8 3 **Night Groove (IRE)**[16] 7120 4-8-8 **45**......(v[1]) JamesDoyle 7 39
(P Butler) *racd in midfield: plld out and rdn 3f out: sn struggling: no ch wl over 1f out* **50/1**

0050 9 1 **Silver Dreamer (IRE)**[58] 6583 5-8-8 **45**...... AdrianMcCarthy 1 37
(H S Howe) *s.i.s: sn chsng ldrs: rdn 4f out: bhd last 2f* **25/1**

0006 10 34 **Silver Surprise**[30] 6967 3-8-2 **45**...... NickyMackay 3 —
(J J Bridger) *chsd ldr tl 8f out: rdn and wknd wl over 3f out: eased last 2f: t.o* **33/1**

2m 46.35s (-1.95) **Going Correction** -0.125s/f (Stan)
WFA 3 from 4yo+ 6lb **10** Ran SP% **110.4**
Speed ratings (Par 101): **101,99,98,98,97 96,95,93,92,71**
CSF £38.98 CT £118.58 TOTE £4.30: £1.80, £2.50, £1.60; EX 48.80 Trifecta £162.00 Pool £522.55 - 2.29 winning units..

Owner P S J Croft **Bred** Mrs Jane Bailey **Trained** Elmley Castle, Worcs

FOCUS
A moderate handicap won by a progressive sort. The pace was good and this is solid form.

Mixing Official explanation: jockey said gelding pulled very hard

7257 PONTINS.COM H'CAP 1m 2f (P)
3:45 (3:49) (Class 6) (0-65,65) 3-Y-O+ £1,943 (£578; £288; £144) Stalls Low

Form RPR

0001 1 **Mr Napoleon (IRE)**[16] 7115 5-9-2 **60**...... GeorgeBaker 10 70
(G L Moore) *hld up towards rr: gd hdwy to chse ldrs jst over 2f out: led jst over 1f out: r.o wl: readily* **7/2**[2]

4003 2 2 **Mon Petite Amour**[19] 7088 4-8-10 **54**...... SteveDrowne 8 60
(D W P Arbuthnot) *chsd ldrs: rdn to chse ldr 2f out: sn ev ch tl nt pce of wnr 1f out: kpt on* **9/1**

5163 3 shd **Arena's Dream (USA)**[8] 7200 3-9-4 **65**...... PatCosgrave 3 71
(J R Boyle) *hld up in tch in midfield: hdwy jst over 2f out: rdn and ev ch jst over 1f out: kpt on same pce fnl f* **10/1**

5361 4 nk **Magic Warrior**[7] 7214 7-8-8 **59**...... PatrickDonaghy(7) 14 64
(J C Fox) *hld up wl in rr: rdn and hdwy on outer jst over 2f out: styd on wl fnl f* **6/1**[3]

2000 5 3/4 **Resplendent Ace (IRE)**[24] 7018 3-9-4 **65**...... TGMcLaughlin 11 69
(P Howling) *hld up in tch in midfield: rdn and hdwy jst over 2f out: kpt on u.p fnl f: nt pce to trble wnr* **15/2**

0041 6 hd **Play Up Pompey**[18] 7098 5-8-10 **54** ow2...... AmirQuinn 2 58
(J J Bridger) *t.k.h: hld up towards rr: sltly hmpd and lost pl over 3f out: rdn and hdwy on inner 2f out: kpt on: nt rch ldrs* **8/1**

5000 7 2 **Certifiable**[9] 7187 6-8-2 **51**...... RobynBrisland(5) 7 51
(Miss Z C Davison) *t.k.h: chsd ldr tl led wl over 2f out: rdn and hdd wl over 1f out: fdd fnl f* **66/1**

4450 8 hd **Siena Star (IRE)**[20] 7080 9-9-0 **58**...... MickyFenton 9 57
(Stef Liddiard) *chsd ldrs: rdn to chse ldr wl over 2f out tl 2f out: wknd fnl f* **14/1**

3010 9 1 1/2 **Haasem (USA)**[20] 7073 4-9-7 **65**...... JimCrowley 13 61
(J R Jenkins) *t.k.h: dropped in bhd: rdn and effrt over 2f out: nvr trbld ldrs* **16/1**

00-0 10 1 **Nanosecond (USA)**[13] 7159 4-8-11 **55**...... SimonWhitworth 6 49
(N A Callaghan) *t.k.h: racd in midfield: rdn wl over 1f out: sn wknd* **33/1**

6342 11 2 **Blu Manruna**[19] 7088 4-9-5 **63**......(b) PaulDoe 12 53
(J Akehurst) *chsd ldrs: rdn wl over 2f out: wknd wl over 1f out* **3/1**[1]

0300 12 5 **Naughty Thoughts (IRE)**[20] 7073 3-8-10 **62**...... AshleyHamblett(5) 1 42
(Andrew Turnell) *led tl wl over 2f out: rdn over 2f out: wknd 2f out* **16/1**

055- 13 2 **Mrs Solese (IRE)**[446] 5830 4-8-13 **57**...... FergusSweeney 4 33
(J R Boyle) *stdd s: t.k.h: hld up in rr: n.d* **40/1**

00 14 nk **Cami Collins (FR)**[12] 7166 3-7-12 **52**...... KierenFox(7) 5 28
(J R Best) *hld up in rr: rdn over 3f out: no ch last 2f* **50/1**

2m 6.22s (-1.57) **Going Correction** -0.125s/f (Stan)
WFA 3 from 4yo+ 3lb **14** Ran SP% **130.7**
Speed ratings (Par 101): **101,99,99,99,98 98,96,96,95,94 92,88,87,87**
CSF £38.22 CT £309.17 TOTE £5.00: £2.20, £3.00, £4.20; EX 44.00 Trifecta £132.50 Pool £405.26 - 2.17 winning units. Place 6 £51.29, Place 5 £28.41..

Owner Jason Gibbons **Bred** Forenaghts Stud **Trained** Woodingdean, E Sussex

FOCUS
A modest handicap, run at a strong early pace.

Blu Manruna Official explanation: jockey said gelding ran flat

T/Plt: £84.30 to a £1 stake. Pool: £67,034.35. 580.45 winning tickets. T/Qpdt: £23.60 to a £1 stake. Pool: £4,943.30. 154.70 winning tickets. SP

[7245]WOLVERHAMPTON (A.W) (L-H)

Friday, December 28

OFFICIAL GOING: Standard

Wind: Strong behind Weather: Heavy showers

7258 MACE RACING AT WOLVERHAMPTON MAIDEN AUCTION STKS 7f 32y(P)

7:00 (7:01) (Class 6) 2-Y-O **£2,047** (£604; £302) **Stalls** High

Form RPR

5036 **1** **Miss Phoebe (IRE)**[16] 7114 2-8-6 65 JamesDoyle 8 72
(S Kirk) *sn w ldr: led over 2f out: rdn wl over 1f out: r.o wl* **11/4**[1]

6 **2** *4* **Maggie Kate**[30] 6964 2-8-4 0 DavidKinsella 9 60
(R Ingram) *a.p: rdn over 3f out: chsd wnr fnl f: no imp* **11/1**[3]

3 *1 1/4* **Ginger Minx (IRE)** 2-8-0 0 ow1 KirstyMilczarek(5) 4 58
(N J Vaughan) *s.s: hld up: hdwy on outside over 2f out: hung lft 1f out: styd on towards fin* **9/2**[2]

2225 **4** *3/4* **Southwest Star (IRE)**[62] 6503 2-8-12 66 LPKeniry 3 63
(J S Moore) *a.p: chsd wnr 2f out to 1f out: wknd ins fnl f* **11/4**[1]

4342 **5** *3 1/2* **Weet By Far**[8] 7196 2-8-1 62 DuranFentiman(3) 6 47
(R Hollinshead) *hld up in mid-div: rdn over 2f out: wknd over 1f out* **9/2**[2]

6 *2* **Asmodea** 2-8-7 0 LiamJones 7 45
(D J Coakley) *s.i.s: rdn over 2f out: a bhd* **12/1**

2436 **7** *5* **Jastaanhi**[11] 7170 2-8-6 57 DeanMcKeown 2 32
(J A Pickering) *led: hdd over 2f out: wkng whn nt clr run on ins ent st* **33/1**

8 *14* **Firespin (USA)** 2-8-7 0 GregFairley 1 —
(M Botti) *s.s: t.k.h in rr: rdn over 2f out: sn struggling* **14/1**

1m 31.89s (1.49) **Going Correction** +0.125s/f (Slow) 8 Ran SP% **115.3**
Speed ratings (Par 94): **96,91,90,89,85 82,77,61**
CSF £35.28 TOTE £3.80: £1.10, £4.00, £2.50; EX 21.10.

Owner Hedsor Stud Associates **Bred** Knockainey Stud **Trained** Upper Lambourn, Berks

FOCUS
A modest maiden in which the pace was only fair. Improved form from the winner.

NOTEBOOK
Miss Phoebe(IRE) had the run of the race and did not have to improve too much to land this modest event. She stays further but her short-term future in handicaps depends on how the handicapper views the level of this form. (op 4-1)

Maggie Kate, who shaped with a degree of promise in a modest event on her debut at Kempton, bettered that form in this uncompetitive event. She will stay 1m and may do better in run-of-the-mill handicap company. (op 17-2 tchd 15-2)

Ginger Minx(IRE), the first foal of a half-sister to several winners up to middle distances, showed ability at a modest level, despite her greenness, on this racecourse debut and should improve, especially granted a stiffer test of stamina. Official explanation: jockey said filly missed the break (op 13-2)

Southwest Star(IRE), an exposed maiden, again failed to get home over this trip and, although the step back to 6f may be in his favour, he is going to continue to look vulnerable in this type of event. (op 3-1 tchd 10-3)

Weet By Far, exposed as a modest performer, again had her limitations exposed in this type of event and she is also going to have to improve to win from her current mark back in handicap company. (op 4-1)

Asmodea, out of a juvenile winner in France, did not show enough on this racecourse debut to suggest she is of much immediate interest in this type of event. (op 17-2)

Firespin(USA) Official explanation: jockey said filly missed the break; vet said filly finished stiff behind

7259 PONTIN'S BOOK EARLY CLAIMING STKS 1m 141y(P)

7:30 (7:30) (Class 6) 2-Y-O **£2,388** (£705; £352) **Stalls** Low

Form RPR

6013 **1** **Carry On Cleo**[13] 7156 2-8-4 54 (b) SaleemGolam 7 60
(P D Evans) *hld up in rr: hdwy over 3f out: rdn over 2f out: led ins fnl f: r.o* **4/1**[3]

3432 **2** *2* **Home**[13] 7156 2-9-5 72 (p) PatCosgrave 4 71
(J R Boyle) *t.k.h: hdwy over 5f out: led over 4f out: edgd lft jst over 2f out: rdn and hung lft over 1f out: hdd ins fnl f: edgd rt towards fin: no ex* **1/1**[1]

0563 **3** *shd* **Little Firecracker**[14] 7142 2-7-13 60 DuranFentiman(3) 6 54
(Miss M E Rowland) *led early: chsd ldr: ev ch whn bmpd jst over 2f out: nt clr run on ins and swtchd rt over 1f out: kpt on towards fin* **3/1**[2]

05 **4** *13* **Arabesque Dancer**[18] 7101 2-8-12 0 GregFairley 1 37
(M Botti) *prom: rdn 4f out: sn wknd* **17/2**

R5 **5** *21* **Clip Clop (IRE)**[16] 7122 2-7-7 0 ow2 AmyBaker(7) 3 —
(Miss J Feilden) *sn led: hdd over 4f out: rdn over 3f out: wknd over 2f out: t.o* **50/1**

1m 53.6s (1.84) **Going Correction** +0.125s/f (Slow) 5 Ran SP% **107.5**
Speed ratings (Par 94): **96,94,94,82,63**
CSF £8.09 TOTE £3.60: £2.30, £1.10; EX 6.80.

Owner J E Abbey **Bred** J E Abbey **Trained** Pandy, Monmouths

FOCUS
A modest event, even for the grade, and a race run at just an ordinary gallop. The best effort yet from Carry On Cleo and fairly reliable form for the grade.

NOTEBOOK
Carry On Cleo is an improved performer in blinkers and she did enough in the headgear to notch her second win from her last three starts and in the process reversed latest placings with Home. She should continue to give a good account. (op 3-1 tchd 11-4)

Home looked the one to beat on his previous efforts in ordinary claiming company but he proved a disappointment this time and in the process looked a less than easy ride. While capable of winning a modest event, he does not look one to be taking too short a price about. (op 5-4 tchd 11-8, 6-4 in places)

Little Firecracker, who was not disgraced over 7f at this course on her previous outing, did not get the best of runs but it is unlikely that the placings were affected and she is going to have to improve to win from her current mark back in handicaps. (op 11-4 tchd 7-2)

Arabesque Dancer finished much further behind the winner than she had done over course and distance on her previous start earlier this month. She has plenty to prove at present. (op 8-1 tchd 7-1)

Clip Clop(IRE) was again soundly beaten and is of no immediate interest. (op 66-1)

7260 PONTIN'S SHORT BREAKS NURSERY 5f 216y(P)

7:55 (7:57) (Class 6) (0-75,73) 2-Y-O **£2,047** (£604; £302) **Stalls** Low

Form RPR

1253 **1** **Maryolini**[37] 6892 2-8-13 70 KirstyMilczarek(5) 3 73
(N J Vaughan) *led 2f: led over 2f out: rdn over 1f out: edgd rt ins fnl f: drvn out* **11/4**[2]

1202 **2** *1 1/2* **Only A Game (IRE)**[28] 6973 2-9-4 70 AdamKirby 2 69
(Miss M E Rowland) *a.p: rdn over 2f out: rdn to chse wnr and hung rt wl over 1f out: hung rt wl ins fnl f: one pce* **5/1**

54 **3** *1 1/4* **Tallulah Sunrise**[19] 7084 2-8-9 68 GHannon(7) 5 63
(M D I Usher) *a.p: rdn wl over 1f out: one pce fnl f* **8/1**

541 **4** *hd* **Feeling Fresh (IRE)**[22] 7042 2-8-12 64 PhillipMakin 1 58
(Paul Green) *s.i.s: hld up: rdn over 2f out: c wd st: hdwy over 1f out: one pce fnl f* **5/2**[1]

31 **5** *5* **The Mighty One**[22] 7043 2-9-0 73 PatrickDonaghy(7) 4 52
(P C Haslam) *w ldr: led 4f out tl over 2f out: rdn and wkng whn edgd lft over 1f out* **3/1**[3]

044 **6** *2* **Bertbrand**[27] 6990 2-9-1 67 GregFairley 7 40
(M Botti) *s.i.s: rdn over 2f out: a bhd* **25/1**

0001 **7** *12* **Captain Crooner (IRE)**[8] 7195 2-7-13 51 6ex LiamJones 6 —
(D Shaw) *sn outpcd* **28/1**

1m 16.78s (0.97) **Going Correction** +0.125s/f (Slow) 7 Ran SP% **115.3**
Speed ratings (Par 94): **98,96,94,94,87 84,68**
CSF £17.19 TOTE £4.20: £1.90, £3.10; EX 18.70.

Owner A Charlton P Jones I Smith K Warth **Bred** Ms M A Rowlands **Trained** Malpas, Cheshire

FOCUS
An ordinary nursery run in driving rain. The pace seemed fair.

NOTEBOOK
Maryolini, from a stable that has been among the winners of late, had the run of the race and did enough to land her second win over this course and distance. She is worth a try over further and may be capable of a bit better. (op 7-2)

Only A Game(IRE), who ran creditably on his first run for the stable at Lingfield on his previous start, left the impression that the return to 7f would be in his favour and he is capable of picking up a similar event. (op 6-1)

Tallulah Sunrise, who had progressed with each of her three previous starts, was not disgraced on this handicap debut and left the impression that the return to 7f would be more to her liking. (tchd 11-1)

Feeling Fresh(IRE), who beat subsequent winner Yankee Storm over course and distance on his previous outing, ran a fair race from this 9lb higher mark and may be a bit better than the bare form as this race suited those racing prominently. However he is going to have to improve to win from his current mark. (op 11-4 tchd 9-4)

The Mighty One, who won a modest maiden over course and distance on his previous start, had the run of the race but proved disappointing on this handicap debut. However he is only lightly raced and is in good hands so would not be one to write off just yet. (op 5-2)

Bertbrand, who showed ability at a modest level in maidens on Polytrack, was soundly beaten on this handicap debut and he has plenty to prove at present. Official explanation: jockey said colt was slowly away (op 20-1)

Captain Crooner(IRE), who looked flattered in a race where the leaders went off too quickly at Southwell on his previous start, was soundly beaten under a penalty in this stronger event on this quicker surface.

7261 GO PONTIN'S HOLIDAYS H'CAP 5f 216y(P)

8:25 (8:25) (Class 5) (0-75,73) 3-Y-O+ **£2,914** (£867; £433; £216) **Stalls** Low

Form RPR

0005 **1** **Mr Lambros**[20] 7078 6-9-4 73 (vt) MickyFenton 1 84
(Miss Gay Kelleway) *hld up in tch: wnt 2nd 3f out: led wl over 1f out: drvn out* **6/1**[3]

0134 **2** *1 1/4* **Strabinios King**[6] 7227 3-8-5 60 SaleemGolam 8 67
(R A Harris) *hld up: hung bdly lft fr 2 out: hdwy over 1f out: wnt 2nd ins fnl f: nt run on* **9/4**[1]

0105 **3** *1 3/4* **Parkview Love (USA)**[14] 7141 6-9-2 71 (v) DeanMcKeown 5 72+
(D Shaw) *hld up: nt clr run 3f out: hdwy 2f out: rdn over 1f out: one pce fnl f* **12/1**

0102 **4** *1* **Memphis Man**[7] 7215 4-8-7 69 RichardEvans(7) 2 67
(P D Evans) *s.i.s: hld up: hdwy on ins over 2f out: no ex ins fnl f* **3/1**[2]

0100 **5** *1 1/2* **Back In The Red (IRE)**[21] 7059 3-9-3 72 LiamJones 4 65
(R A Harris) *sn outpcd: sme hdwy over 1f out: nvr trbld ldrs* **28/1**

0010 **6** *3/4* **Norcroft**[44] 6810 5-8-7 67 (p) KirstyMilczarek(5) 6 58
(Mrs C A Dunnett) *chsd ldr 3f: fading whn nt clr run wl over 1f out: sn edgd lft* **7/1**

6215 **7** *1 1/2* **Royal Challenge**[13] 7161 6-9-3 72 DanielTudhope 10 58
(I W McInnes) *t.k.h: sn prom: rdn over 1f out: wknd fnl f* **10/1**

0630 **8** *3* **Grimes Faith**[22] 7045 4-9-4 73 (b) PaulMulrennan 7 50
(K A Ryan) *led: rdn and hdd wl over 1f out: wknd fnl f* **16/1**

003 **9** *18* **Hill Of Lujain**[13] 7158 3-8-5 60 AdrianMcCarthy 9 —
(Ian Williams) *prom 2f: eased whn no ch fnl 2f* **12/1**

1m 15.75s (-0.06) **Going Correction** +0.125s/f (Slow) 9 Ran SP% **116.4**
Speed ratings (Par 103): **105,103,101,99,97 96,94,90,66**
CSF £20.05 CT £159.54 TOTE £6.90: £1.90, £1.40, £3.70; EX 25.50.

Owner Winterbeck Manor Stud **Bred** Witney And Warren Enterprises Ltd **Trained** Exning, Suffolk

■ Stewards' Enquiry : Dean McKeown one-day ban: careelss riding (Jan 8)

FOCUS
A run-of-the-mill handicap in which the pace was fair. Sound form. The winner raced in the centre of the course in the straight.

Strabinios King Official explanation: jockey said gelding had hung in behind the winner

7262 PONTINSBINGO.COM MEDIAN AUCTION MAIDEN STKS 1m 4f 50y(P)

8:55 (8:55) (Class 6) 3-5-Y-O **£2,047** (£604; £302) **Stalls** Low

Form RPR

5453 **1** **Summerofsixtynine**[37] 6893 4-9-8 58 (p) TGMcLaughlin 3 52
(J G M O'Shea) *a.p: rdn over 3f out: led 2f out: styd on* **3/1**[2]

5000 **2** *1 1/4* **Hill Cloud**[8] 7203 5-9-8 50 (t) JamesDoyle 1 50
(W M Brisbourne) *hld up: hdwy 4f out: rdn 2f out: wnt 2nd and nt qckn ins fnl f* **33/1**

0630 **3** *2* **The Diamond Bond**[20] 7069 3-8-12 44 SladeO'Hara(5) 5 47
(G R Oldroyd) *led early: chsd ldr: led over 5f out: rdn and hdd 2f out: no ex wl ins fnl f* **8/1**[3]

0-46 **4** *5* **Gouranga**[20] 7076 4-8-10 53 MarkCoumbe(7) 7 34
(A W Carroll) *hld up in rr: styd on fnl 3f: nvr trbld ldrs* **11/1**

0402 **5** *2* **Botham (USA)**[13] 7154 3-9-3 55 (e) LiamJones 4 36
(D J Murphy) *sn led: hdd over 5f out: sn rdn: wknd over 2f out* **8/11**[1]

6 *36* **Mr Joe Platinum (IRE)**[29] 5-9-8 0 (t) PaulMulrennan 2 —
(E J Creighton) *hld up in tch: rdn 7f out: wknd over 3f out: t.o* **28/1**

/0-0 **7** *81* **Breeder's Folly**[13] 7155 5-9-0 35 AlanCreighton(3) 6 —
(E J Creighton) *a bhd: lost tch 6f out: t.o* **66/1**

2m 49.06s (6.64) **Going Correction** +0.125s/f (Slow)
WFA 3 from 4yo+ 5lb 7 Ran SP% **110.2**
Speed ratings (Par 101): **82,81,79,76,75 51,—**
CSF £77.03 TOTE £3.90: £1.50, £5.60; EX 52.00.

Owner Quality Pipe Supports (Q P S) Ltd **Bred** Mrs J A Gawthorpe **Trained** Elton, Gloucs

FOCUS
A low-grade maiden in which the pace was soon sound. The form is rated through the third.

7263 PONTINS.COM H'CAP 1m 1f 103y(P)
9:20 (9:20) (Class 5) (0-75,75) 3-Y-0+ **£2,914** (£867; £433; £216) **Stalls** Low

Form RPR
6005 **1** **Pop Music (IRE)**[24] 7023 4-8-6 **61**....................(p) JamesDoyle 1 70
(Miss J Feilden) *led 1f: chsd ldr: led wl over 2f out: hrd rdn over 1f out: r.o* **5/2**[3]
-330 **2** *½* **He's Mine Too**[158] 3785 3-8-8 **65** ow1.................... MickyFenton 6 73
(D G Bridgwater) *hld up: hdwy over 2f out: chsd wnr wl over 1f out: rdn and nt qckn wl ins fnl f* **16/1**
06V2 **3** *1 ¼* **Kingsholm**[11] 7173 5-9-0 **69**.................... DanielTudhope 4 74
(I W McInnes) *hld up: c wd st: hdwy over 1f out: rdn and one pce fnl f* **6/4**[1]
3-11 **4** *10* **Italian Romance**[267] 933 4-9-6 **75**.................... AdamKirby 7 59
(J W Unett) *led after 1f: rdn and hdd wl over 2f out: wknd over 1f out* **2/1**[2]
100 **5** *¾* **Tina's Ridge (IRE)**[39] 5555 3-8-5 **62**....................(p) AdrianMcCarthy 2 45
(Miss J S Davis) *hld up in tch: rdn over 3f out: wknd 2f out* **20/1**

2m 4.23s (1.61) **Going Correction** +0.125s/f (Slow)
WFA 3 from 4yo+ 2lb 5 Ran SP% **112.5**
Speed ratings (Par 103): **97,96,95,86,85**
CSF £33.62 TOTE £3.40: £1.70, £3.30; EX 25.70.
Owner Michael Jenner **Bred** John Foley **Trained** Exning, Suffolk

FOCUS
An ordinary handicap but the steady early pace means this bare form may not be entirely reliable. The third looks the best guide.
T/Plt: £204.80 to a £1 stake. Pool: £118,701.90. 422.95 winning tickets. T/Qpdt: £70.50 to a £1 stake. Pool: £7,645.50. 80.20 winning tickets. KH

7251 LINGFIELD (L-H)
Saturday, December 29

OFFICIAL GOING: Standard
Wind: fresh, half-behind Weather: bright

7264 LINGFIELDPARK.CO.UK MEDIAN AUCTION MAIDEN STKS 6f (P)
12:55 (12:56) (Class 6) 2-Y-0 **£1,943** (£578; £288; £144) **Stalls** Low

Form RPR
03 **1** **My Mate Pete (IRE)**[54] 6692 2-9-3 0.................... GeorgeBaker 2 74
(R M Beckett) *hld up in midfield: hdwy and rdn 2f out: chsd ldng pair and hung lft over 1f out: styd on to ld last 100yds: sn in command* **5/2**[2]
4 **2** *1 ½* **Moon Bound (IRE)**[23] 7043 2-9-3 0.................... ChrisCatlin 7 70
(W R Muir) *prom tl led over 4f out: rdn 2 l clr 2f out: hdd and no ex last 100yds* **16/1**
23 **3** *¾* **Sempre Libera (IRE)**[16] 7129 2-8-7 0.................... KirstyMilczarek(5) 3 62
(P W Chapple-Hyam) *led for 1f: styd prom: chsd ldr and rdn 2f out: kpt on same pce* **11/2**[3]
34 **4** *1 ¼* **Brazilian Brush (IRE)**[28] 6998 2-9-3 0....................(t) SteveDrowne 11 64
(H Morrison) *chsd ldrs: rdn and unable qck over 2f out: kpt on u.p fnl f: nt pce to rch ldrs* **2/1**[1]
2 **5** *¾* **Desert Pride**[23] 7043 2-9-3 0.................... FergusSweeney 1 61
(W S Kittow) *s.i.s: hld up in midfield: rdn and effrt 2f out: kpt on but nvr pce to rch ldrs* **9/1**
6 *nk* **Irish Music (IRE)** 2-9-3 0.................... NeilPollard 12 60
(A P Jarvis) *hld up in rr: rdn and effrt on inner wl over 1f out: kpt on but nvr pce to rch ldrs* **25/1**
0 **7** *½* **Felicia**[61] 6535 2-8-12 0.................... SaleemGolam 5 54
(S C Williams) *s.i.s: a towards rr: rdn over 2f out: kpt on but nvr nr ldrs* **16/1**
8 *shd* **Brunton Blue** 2-8-12 0.................... GregFairley 6 54
(W Jarvis) *t.k.h: in tch: rdn over 2f out: outpcd 2f: n.d after* **14/1**
9 *1 ¾* **Extreme North (USA)** 2-9-3 0.................... MickyFenton 4 53
(Miss V Haigh) *s.i.s: t.k.h: hld up towards rr: c wd and rdn bnd 2f out: nvr nr ldrs* **20/1**
00 **10** *5* **Impure Thoughts**[35] 6926 2-9-3 0.................... JimCrowley 9 38
(J R Best) *plld hrd: prom tl led after 1f: sn hdd: w ldrs tl wknd qckly 2f out* **33/1**
11 *25* **Piccolo Pride** 2-9-3 0.................... AdamKirby 10 —
(B G Powell) *s.i.s: sn rdn in detached last: t.o last 2f* **25/1**

1m 12.03s (-0.78) **Going Correction** -0.15s/f (Stan) 11 Ran SP% **121.1**
Speed ratings (Par 94): **99,97,96,94,93 92,92,92,89,83 49**
CSF £41.10 TOTE £3.90: £1.80, £3.20, £1.90; EX 34.10 Trifecta £165.10 Pool: £241.91. - 1.04 winning units..
Owner R A Pegum **Bred** Ballyhane Stud **Trained** Whitsbury, Hants

FOCUS
A modest juvenile maiden, run at a fair pace.

NOTEBOOK
My Mate Pete(IRE) relished the step up to 6f and he swooped inside the distance to win readily. This looks to be his ideal trip and he can expect an official mark of around 70 for this. (tchd 11-4)
Moon Bound(IRE) shaped with promise on his debut and he stepped up on that, making a bold bid for glory when skipping clear turning for home. He eventually had no answer to the winner, but still stayed on well enough to suggest that he will pick one of these up before long. (op 14-1)
Sempre Libera(IRE) again ran well without shaping as though she is improving to any serious degree and she is probably quite modest. She does have more options now she is eligible for a handicap mark. (op 9-2)
Brazilian Brush(IRE), tried in a tongue tie, was again disappointing despite attracting support in the market. He was not helped by being trapped wide from his high stall, but even so, he has yet to build on his promising debut effort. (op 11-4)
Desert Pride was doing some good late work after his tardy start and there is more to come from him. (op 8-1)

7265 LINGFIELD PARK FOR WEDDINGS H'CAP 6f (P)
1:30 (1:31) (Class 6) (0-52,54) 3-Y-0+ **£1,943** (£578; £288; £144) **Stalls** Low

Form RPR
1303 **1** **Muktasb (USA)**[10] 7192 6-8-13 **51**....................(v) AdamKirby 3 63
(D Shaw) *hld up in rr: stl plenty to do and rdn 2f out: gd hdwy to chal 1f out: led ins fnl f: r.o wl* **3/1**[1]
6303 **2** *¾* **Kennington**[18] 7107 7-8-13 **51**....................(b) NeilPollard 6 60
(Mrs C A Dunnett) *chsd ldrs: wnt 2nd and sltly hmpd wl over 1f out: drvn to ld 1f out: hdd and unable qck ins fnl f* **10/1**
0204 **3** *2* **Lawdy Miss Clawdy**[31] 6963 3-8-8 **46** oh1.................... FergusSweeney 2 49
(D W P Arbuthnot) *hld up towards rr: travelling strly over 2f out: rdn and effrt wl over 1f out: kpt on to go 3rd towards fin* **12/1**
2004 **4** *nk* **Sir Loin**[10] 7188 6-8-11 **49**....................(v) MickyFenton 5 51
(P Burgoyne) *led: edgd rt wl over 1f out: hdd 1f out: no ex fnl f* **10/1**
5451 **5** *1 ½* **Gone'N'Dunnett (IRE)**[15] 7137 8-8-9 **52**....................(p) KirstyMilczarek(5) 1 49
(Mrs C A Dunnett) *in tch in midfield: rdn 3f out: effrt 2f out: kpt on same pce* **11/1**
034 **6** *2* **Accolation**[14] 7159 3-8-12 **50**.................... DaneO'Neill 4 41
(Pat Eddery) *t.k.h: hld up in midfield: rdn wl over 1f out: no imp* **7/1**
0603 **7** *1 ¾* **Minnow**[20] 7082 3-8-6 **51**....................(p) WilliamCarson(7) 9 36
(S C Williams) *chsd ldrs: wnt 2nd over 3f out: rdn wl over 2f out: losing pl whn sltly hmpd wl over 1f out: no ch after* **17/2**
4002 **8** *¾* **Arfinnit (IRE)**[10] 7188 6-9-2 **54**....................(v) GregFairley 8 37
(Mrs A L M King) *s.i.s: bhd: rdn and effrt on outer over 2f out: nvr on terms* **6/1**[3]
6000 **9** *½* **Safranine (IRE)**[32] 6962 10-8-4 **47** oh1 ow1.................... AnnStokell(5) 11 28
(Miss A Stokell) *in tch in midfield: struggling over 2f out: n.d after* **66/1**
0033 **10** *nk* **Regal Royale**[10] 7188 4-9-0 **52**.................... LPKeniry 7 32
(Peter Grayson) *sn rdn along in rr: n.d* **9/2**[2]
6305 **11** *2 ½* **Boisdale (IRE)**[68] 6390 9-8-8 **46** oh1.................... RichardThomas 10 18
(P S Felgate) *chsd ldrs: rdn and wknd over 2f out* **25/1**

1m 11.25s (-1.56) **Going Correction** -0.15s/f (Stan) 11 Ran SP% **120.0**
Speed ratings (Par 101): **104,103,100,99,97 95,92,91,91,90 87**
CSF £35.09 CT £323.85 TOTE £3.60: £1.40, £3.90, £4.00; EX 38.60 Trifecta £224.60 Pool: £351.22, 1.11 w/u.
Owner Miss Claire Comery **Bred** Shadwell Farm LLC **Trained** Danethorpe, Notts

FOCUS
A moderate sprint handicap run at a decent pace unlike several races on this card. The second and third set the level, with Muktasb posting his best form for over two years.
Lawdy Miss Clawdy Official explanation: jockey said filly ran too freely
Sir Loin Official explanation: jockey said gelding hung right

7266 PLAY GOLF @ LINGFIELD PARK MAIDEN STKS 7f (P)
2:00 (2:01) (Class 5) 2-Y-0 **£2,817** (£838; £418; £209) **Stalls** Low

Form RPR
4 **1** **Whitcombe Minister (USA)**[85] 5971 2-9-3 0.................... JohnEgan 14 77+
(Jamie Poulton) *mde all: drvn wl over 1f out: styd on* **7/4**[1]
32 **2** *1* **Miss Mujanna**[10] 7190 2-8-12 0.................... ChrisCatlin 7 69
(J Akehurst) *chsd wnr thrght: rdn over 2f out: kpt on but nvr quite able to chal wnr* **15/2**
3 **3** *1 ¼* **Ivory Silk**[19] 7097 2-8-12 0.................... DaneO'Neill 6 66
(D K Ivory) *in tch: chsd ldng pair 3f out: rdn over 2f out: kpt on same pce* **11/1**
04 **4** *4* **Mister New York (USA)**[25] 7015 2-9-3 0.................... JosedeSouza 3 61
(Noel T Chance) *hld up off the pce in midfield: hdwy on inner 2f out: kpt on fnl f: n.d* **20/1**
5 *shd* **Pippbrook Gold** 2-9-3 0.................... FergusSweeney 8 61
(J R Boyle) *s.i.s: wl off the pce in midfield: pushed along and hdwy 3f out: styd on steadily fnl f: nvr nr ldrs* **100/1**
5 **6** *3* **Kingsgate Castle**[25] 7015 2-9-3 0.................... GeorgeBaker 11 53
(J R Best) *hld up wl off the pce in midfield: rdn over 2f out: no hdwy* **13/2**[3]
7 *2 ½* **Nowzdetime (IRE)** 2-8-12 0.................... JamieJones(5) 12 47
(M G Quinlan) *s.i.s: a towards rr: sme modest hdwy over 1f out: nvr on terms* **25/1**
6 **8** *1 ¼* **Dynamo Dave (USA)**[33] 6948 2-9-3 0.................... SteveDrowne 4 44
(B J Meehan) *sn chsng ldrs: rdn over 3f out: wl outpcd over 2f out: no ch after* **5/2**[2]
9 *nk* **Usetheforce (IRE)** 2-9-3 0.................... PatCosgrave 10 43
(M J Wallace) *s.i.s: a in rr on outer: nvr on terms* **16/1**
10 *2* **Rich Harvest (USA)** 2-9-3 0.................... NeilPollard 2 38
(A P Jarvis) *s.i.s: plld hrd in rr: nvr on terms* **33/1**
00 **11** *9* **Yippyiayippyio**[32] 6958 2-8-12 0.................... MickyFenton 9 11
(Mrs C A Dunnett) *racd wd: sn outpcd: t.o last 3f* **100/1**
00 **12** *hd* **Princess Augusta (USA)**[21] 7070 2-8-12 0.................... LPKeniry 13 10
(A M Balding) *chsd ldrs: rdn 3f out: wknd qckly: t.o* **100/1**
13 *½* **Caffe Coretto** 2-8-6 0 ow1.................... KylieManser(7) 1 10
(B G Powell) *s.i.s: a wl bhd: t.o last 3f* **66/1**
0 **14** *1 ¼* **Peter's Joy (USA)**[205] 2398 2-9-3 0.................... FrankieMcDonald 5 11
(Jean-Rene Auvray) *s.i.s: a bhd: t.o last 2f* **100/1**

1m 24.82s (-1.07) **Going Correction** -0.15s/f (Stan) 14 Ran SP% **121.3**
Speed ratings (Par 96): **100,98,97,92,92 89,86,85,84,82 72,71,71,69**
CSF £15.20 TOTE £2.60: £1.20, £2.30, £2.50; EX 16.10 Trifecta £27.30 Pool: £318.63, 8.26 w/u.
Owner The Whitcombe Racing Partnership 1 **Bred** Dinwiddie Farm **Trained** Whitcombe, Dorset

FOCUS
A modest juvenile maiden. The winner did the job in taking fashion and looks a useful sort in the making. He is rated 6lb off his debut effort here but the initial level of the form is fluid.

NOTEBOOK
Whitcombe Minister(USA) ◆ pinged out from his outside stall to make all and open his account at the second attempt on this All-Weather bow. His connections think he is a decent horse in the making, with his trainer eyeing possible targets such as the Italian Guineas for him. He certainly ought to get a mile plus in time. (tchd 2-1)
Miss Mujanna ◆ again ran well in defeat, chasing the winner throughout and sticking to her task in game fashion. A similar contest would be at her mercy on this evidence and she now also qualifies for an official mark. (tchd 7-1)
Ivory Silk did well enough in third, pulling clear of the rest, to suggest she can be found a winning opportunity, especially back against her own sex. (op 10-1)
Mister New York(USA) was not given an overly hard time in fourth and looks an interesting one for nurseries now he is eligible for an official mark. (op 16-1)
Pippbrook Gold, first foal of a mare who was unplaced in four starts, shaped with a degree of promise on this debut.
Kingsgate Castle Official explanation: jockey said colt ran green
Dynamo Dave(USA), a $375,000 breeze-up purchase, failed to improve on the level of his debut effort and has to rate as disappointing. Official explanation: jockey said colt was never travelling (op 11-4 tchd 9-4)

7267 ARENALEISUREPLC.COM H'CAP 1m (P)
2:30 (2:30) (Class 2) (0-100,106) 3-Y-£9,971 (£2,985; £1,492; £747; £372) **Stalls** High

Form RPR
0411 **1** **Atlantic Story (USA)**[13] 7165 5-8-8 **89**....................(bt) ChrisCatlin 7 97
(M W Easterby) *heavily restrained after s and hld up in 3rd: rdn and effrt wl over 1f out: ev ch 1f out: led ins fnl f: r.o wl* **11/4**[2]
4425 **2** *¾* **Orchard Supreme**[21] 7074 4-9-5 **100**.................... SteveDrowne 2 106
(R Hannon) *hld up in last pair: rdn and effrt on inner over 1f out: ev ch 1f out: chsd wnr ins fnl f: one pce last 50yds* **7/2**[3]

2231 **3** ½ **Fajr (IRE)**[21] 7074 5-9-11 **106**..........(b) MickyFenton 6 111
(Miss Gay Kelleway) *hld up in tch: rdn and effrt on outer bnd 2f out: r.o to go 3rd ins fnl f: nt rch ldng pair* **9/4**[1]

4633 **4** 1 **Wavertree Warrior (IRE)**[21] 7074 5-8-6 **87** oh1 ow1...(b) JamesDoyle 3 90
(N P Littmoden) *led for 1f: w ldr after: drvn and upsides jst over 2f out tl 1f out: one pce fnl f* **9/2**

436 **5** nk **Councellor (FR)**[1] 7254 5-8-9 **90**..........(t) PatCosgrave 5 92
(Stef Liddiard) *t.k.h: led after 1f: rdn 2f out: hdd ins fnl f: no ex* **13/2**

1m 38.07s (-1.36) **Going Correction** -0.15s/f (Stan)
WFA 3 from 4yo+ 1lb **5** Ran SP% **111.2**
Speed ratings (Par 109): **100,99,98,97,97**
CSF £12.64 TOTE £3.10: £1.80, £1.30; EX 11.80.
Owner Matthew Green **Bred** A I Appleton **Trained** Sheriff Hutton, N Yorks

FOCUS
A very decent handicap, but it was run at a slow early pace and the time was relatively poor. The winner is on the up but the form may not prove reliable.

NOTEBOOK
Atlantic Story(USA) ◆, who loves this surface, was probably the one most unsuited by the slow early pace and his rider was at pains to get him settled. Despite that, he produced the best turn of foot when the sprint began at the top of the straight and he was always going to get up where it mattered. He could have the potential to bustle up his stablemate Gentleman's Deal in the Winter Derby, although his stamina for that 1m2f trip has yet to be proven. It is even possible he could head to Dubai. (op 9-4 tchd 3-1 in places)
Orchard Supreme really needs a stronger pace to be seen at his best and would not have been at his best here under a patient ride. A solid effort in the circumstances. (tchd 3-1)
Fajr(IRE) was undone by being held up in a slowly-run race. It would have taken a massive effort to come from last to first and, although he didn't manage it, this run suggests he remains at the top of his game. (tchd 5-2)
Wavertree Warrior(IRE) is hard to win with nowadays and had the run of the race for most of the way. He still helps to set the level of this form. (tchd 6-1)
Councellor(FR), unplaced at this track 24 hours previously, proved too keen in the lead and may need a break now after a busy winter. (op 10-1)

7268 LINGFIELD PARK FOR PARTIES H'CAP 1m (P)
3:05 (3:05) (Class 6) (0-60,60) 3-Y-O+ £1,943 (£578; £288; £144) Stalls High

Form RPR

0604 **1** **King After**[20] 7085 5-8-12 **53**..........(v) JimCrowley 3 63
(J R Best) *t.k.h: hld up in tch: hdwy to chse ldr 2f out: led 1f out: sn in command: rdn out* **3/1**[1]

000 **2** 1¼ **Napoletano (GER)**[32] 3615 6-8-13 **54**..........(p) JohnEgan 10 61
(S Dow) *hld up in last: swtchd lft and gd hdwy wl over 1f out: r.o wl to go 2nd towards fin: nvr able to chal wnr* **14/1**

0250 **3** ½ **Imperium**[10] 7183 6-9-2 **57**..........(b) DaneO'Neill 12 63
(Jean-Rene Auvray) *hld up towards rr: hdwy wl over 2f out: chsd wnr jst ins fnl f: kpt on same pce: lost 2nd towards fin* **10/1**

0005 **4** 2½ **Krakatau (FR)**[24] 7028 3-8-7 **56**.......... MatthewDavies(7) 7 56
(D J Wintle) *t.k.h: chsd ldrs for 2f: stdd and dropped bk to rr 4f out: rdn and effrt on outer 2f out: styd on ins fnl f: wnt 4th nr fin* **10/1**

4605 **5** hd **Border Edge**[20] 7088 9-8-9 **50**..........(b) ChrisCatlin 6 50
(J J Bridger) *prom: chsd ldr over 4f out: led over 2f out: sn rdn: hdd 1f out: fdd last 100yds* **15/2**

5241 **6** 1¼ **Cabourg (IRE)**[25] 7025 4-9-5 **60**.......... SteveDrowne 11 57
(R Bastiman) *chsd ldrs: rdn 2f out: wknd jst over 1f out* **4/1**[2]

030 **7** ½ **Dancing Duo**[20] 7085 3-8-9 **56**..........(v) TolleyDean(5) 8 52
(D Shaw) *racd in midfield: rdn 3f out: no hdwy u.p wl over 1f out* **12/1**

2005 **8** ½ **Sophia Gardens**[20] 7085 3-9-2 **58**.......... FergusSweeney 9 53
(D W P Arbuthnot) *racd in midfield on outer: rdn 3f out: no imp and btn wl over 1f out* **7/1**[3]

555 **9** 5 **Idun**[37] 6904 3-8-11 **53**.......... AdrianMcCarthy 5 36
(P W Chapple-Hyam) *led tl over 5f out: styd prom: rdn 3f out: struggling whn jostled jst over 2f out: sn btn* **16/1**

043 **10** 11 **Night Wolf (IRE)**[28] 6993 7-9-3 **58**..........(t) PaulDoe 1 16
(Jamie Poulton) *rrd in stalls and v.s.a: rapid hdwy on outer to ld over 5f out: hdd over 2f out: sn dropped out: eased wl over 1f out: t.o* **7/1**[3]

1m 38.19s (-1.24) **Going Correction** -0.15s/f (Stan)
WFA 3 from 4yo+ 1lb **10** Ran SP% **120.2**
Speed ratings (Par 101): **100,98,98,95,95 94,93,93,88,77**
CSF £48.73 CT £391.75 TOTE £4.10: £1.70, £5.00, £2.60; EX 72.10 TRIFECTA Not won..
Owner Miss Sara Furnival **Bred** Mrs J McCreery **Trained** Hucking, Kent
■ Stewards' Enquiry : Paul Doe three-day ban: careless riding (Jan 9-11)

FOCUS
A moderate handicap, run at an average pace. Sound enough form, the winner back to his best.
Night Wolf(IRE) Official explanation: jockey said gelding missed the break and suffered interference on the final bend

7269 LINGFIELD PARK FOR CONFERENCES H'CAP 7f (P)
3:35 (3:38) (Class 5) (0-70,76) 3-Y-O+ £2,817 (£838; £418; £209) Stalls Low

Form RPR

5053 **1** **Corlough Mountain**[13] 7164 3-9-1 **67**.......... JohnEgan 13 74
(M J McGrath) *pressed ldrs: rdn to chse ldr wl over 1f out: led wl ins fnl f: r.o wl* **10/1**

3312 **2** ½ **Smokin Joe**[7] 7224 6-9-10 **76**..........(b) GeorgeBaker 14 82+
(J R Best) *hld up in last trio: hdwy on outer over 2f out: rdn and nt qckn over 1f out: r.o u.p fnl f: wnt 2nd nr fin* **7/2**[2]

641 **3** hd **Faithful Ruler (USA)**[38] 6895 3-8-10 **62**.......... FergusSweeney 12 67
(M A Magnusson) *t.k.h: hld up in tch: rdn to chse ldrs over 1f out: kpt on fnl f: wnt 3rd nr fin: nt rch wnr* **7/4**[1]

0044 **4** shd **Interactive (IRE)**[42] 6858 4-9-4 **70**.......... ChrisCatlin 6 75
(Andrew Turnell) *v free to s: led: rdn 2f out: hrd pressed over 1f out: hdd wl ins fnl f: lost 2 pls nr fin* **16/1**

3500 **5** ½ **Nikki Bea (IRE)**[43] 6825 4-8-6 **58** ow1.......... PaulDoe 5 62
(Jamie Poulton) *t.k.h: hld up towards rr: rdn jst over 2f out: hdwy over 1f out: chsd ldrs ins fnl f: no imp last 50yds* **20/1**

4312 **6** nk **Onenightinlisbon (IRE)**[21] 7073 3-8-10 **69**.......... HarryPoulton(7) 7 72
(J R Boyle) *chsd ldrs: rdn over 2f out: kpt on same pce u.p fnl f* **14/1**

1344 **7** shd **Gimme Some Lovin (IRE)**[33] 6946 3-8-8 **60**.......... SimonWhitworth 10 63
(D W P Arbuthnot) *hld up towards rr: rdn and hdwy wl over 2f out: kpt on fnl f: nvr able to chal* **16/1**

1145 **8** shd **Samuel Charles**[45] 6806 9-9-2 **68**..........(b[1]) LiamJones 8 70
(C R Dore) *t.k.h: hld up in tch: lost pl over 2f out: rdn jst over 2f out: n.m.r over 1f out: keeping on whn nt clr run towards fin* **14/1**

4656 **9** nk **Cow Girl (IRE)**[60] 6567 3-8-5 **57**.......... NickyMackay 2 58
(Miss Gay Kelleway) *s.i.s: hld up in rr: rdn and effrt wl over 1f out: kpt on fnl f but nvr nr to chal* **20/1**

0112 **10** ½ **Quantum Leap**[20] 7085 10-8-4 **63**..........(v) ThomasBubb(7) 4 63
(S Dow) *hld up in rr: hdwy wl over 1f out: n.m.r fnl f: nvr able to chal* **8/1**[3]

5250 **11** ½ **Zazous**[20] 7085 6-8-6 **58**.......... AdrianMcCarthy 3 57
(J J Bridger) *s.i.s: sn in tch on inner: drvn jst over 2f out: outpcd over 1f out* **25/1**

006 **12** 1¼ **Follow The Flag (IRE)**[200] 2545 3-8-11 **63**.......... JimCrowley 1 58
(C F Wall) *t.k.h: hld up in tch in midfield on inner: lost pl over 2f out: rdn and effrt wl over 1f out: no imp* **14/1**

3163 **13** 1 **Metropolitan Chief**[65] 6455 3-8-7 **59**.......... LPKeniry 9 52
(P Burgoyne) *t.k.h: chsd ldr tl wl over 1f out: wknd jst over 1f out* **33/1**

1m 25.65s (-0.24) **Going Correction** -0.15s/f (Stan) **13** Ran SP% **126.9**
Speed ratings (Par 103): **95,94,94,94,93 93,93,92,92,92 91,90,88**
CSF £45.57 CT £95.15 TOTE £13.00: £3.10, £1.90, £1.30; EX 62.30 Trifecta £275.00 Pool: £464.79 - 1.20 winning units. Place 6 £70.58, Place 5 £26.01.
Owner Gallagher O'Rourke **Bred** Bottisham Heath Stud **Trained** Maidstone, Kent

FOCUS
A modest handicap, but it was slowly run and the form is not likely to prove too reliable. The first three home were all drawn high.
T/Plt: £57.00 to a £1 stake. Pool: £61,476.55. 787.20 winning tickets. T/Qpdt: £12.60 to a £1 stake. Pool: £3,534.40. 206.00 winning tickets. SP

7258 WOLVERHAMPTON (A.W) (L-H)
Saturday, December 29

OFFICIAL GOING: Standard
A pretty dire card with every race a class 6.
Wind: Moderate half behind Weather: Showers

7270 WOLVERHAMPTON-RACECOURSE.CO.UK MEDIAN AUCTION MAIDEN STKS 5f 20y(P)
7:00 (7:00) (Class 6) 2-Y-O £2,388 (£705; £352) Stalls Low

Form RPR

2542 **1** **A Wish For You**[18] 7106 2-8-7 71..........(p) JamesO'Reilly(5) 2 69
(D K Ivory) *w ldr: led wl over 1f out: rdn and r.o ins fnl f* **5/4**[1]

0043 **2** 1½ **Bahamian Lad**[28] 6998 2-9-3 72.......... DeanMcKeown 1 69
(R Hollinshead) *led: hdd wl over 1f out: rdn and nt qckn ins fnl f* **5/2**[2]

3 shd **Dunmore Dodger (IRE)** 2-9-3 0.......... TonyHamilton 5 69
(R A Fahey) *s.i.s and reminders: hld up: hdwy on ins over 3f out: rdn wl over 1f out: nt qckn ins fnl f* **16/1**

0526 **4** ½ **Wreningham**[21] 7072 2-9-0 69.......... JerryO'Dwyer(3) 4 67
(T Keddy) *hld up in tch: rdn wl over 1f out: kpt on towards fin* **5/1**[3]

5505 **5** 9 **Carnival Dream**[2] 7243 2-8-12 63.......... ChrisCatlin 3 29
(R A Harris) *prom: lost pl over 3f out: sn struggling* **15/2**

62.85 secs (0.03) **Going Correction** -0.025s/f (Stan) **5** Ran SP% **107.3**
Speed ratings (Par 94): **98,95,95,94,80**
CSF £4.30 TOTE £1.90: £1.10, £1.80; EX 3.70.
Owner Lesley Ivory And Cynthia Smith **Bred** Mrs Maureen Barbara Walsh **Trained** Radlett, Herts

FOCUS
A modest event with the first two and the fourth running close to their form.

NOTEBOOK
A Wish For You was hardly winning out of turn and gained a well deserved victory in first-time cheekpieces. (op 6-5)
Bahamian Lad could not hold the winner but hung on for second on what was a somewhat surprising return to the minimum trip. (op 7-2)
Dunmore Dodger(IRE), a half-brother to the multiple 2m winner Spitting Image, was certainly beginning his career at a low level. Apparently unfancied, he should come on for the experience and should do better when stepped up in distance. (op 14-1)
Wreningham ran as if he requires a return to 6f. (op 4-1)

7271 PONTIN'S BOOK EARLY PRICE PROMISE H'CAP 5f 216y(P)
7:30 (7:30) (Class 6) (0-65,65) 3-Y-O+ £2,730 (£806; £403) Stalls Low

Form RPR

4100 **1** **Figaro Flyer (IRE)**[17] 7119 4-9-2 **63**.......... SimonWhitworth 8 73
(P Howling) *hld up and bhd: hdwy jst over 1f out: hrd rdn fnl f: edgd rt and led last strides* **7/1**

1321 **2** hd **Grand Palace (IRE)**[10] 7188 4-8-12 **59**..........(v) DeanMcKeown 2 68
(D Shaw) *a.p: rdn to ld over 1f out: hdd last strides* **11/2**[2]

0232 **3** ¾ **Tag Team (IRE)**[25] 7026 6-8-12 **62**.......... AndrewElliott(3) 5 69
(John A Harris) *led: hdd over 1f out: sn rdn: kpt on ins fnl f* **9/2**[1]

1536 **4** ½ **Inca Soldier (FR)**[14] 7158 4-8-13 **60**.......... PaulEddery 7 65
(R C Guest) *hld up in mid-div: hdwy on ins 2f out: edgd rt jst over 1f out: rdn and nt qckn fnl f* **11/1**

5336 **5** hd **Toms Laughter**[7] 7227 3-8-11 **58**.......... ChrisCatlin 4 62
(R A Harris) *s.i.s: sn nt clr run and swtchd rt: hdwy on outside over 4f out: struck on hd by rival jockey's whip jst over 2f out: sn rdn: r.o one pce fnl f* **9/1**

3263 **6** ¾ **Strathmore (IRE)**[14] 7161 3-9-2 **63**..........(p) TonyHamilton 10 65
(R A Fahey) *t.k.h in tch: rdn over 1f out: one pce fnl f* **6/1**[3]

0633 **7** hd **Gilded Cove**[25] 7020 7-8-11 **63**.......... RussellKennemore(5) 3 64
(R Hollinshead) *hld up and bhd: nt clr run 2f out: swtchd rt wl over 1f out: r.o ins fnl f: nvr nrr* **7/1**

3230 **8** ¾ **Lord Of The Reins (IRE)**[24] 7033 3-8-13 **65**.......... TolleyDean(5) 1 64
(D Shaw) *hld up and bhd: rdn and hdwy on ins over 1f out: fdd ins fnl f* **8/1**

4060 **9** ½ **Just Spike**[19] 7105 4-8-13 **60**.......... JamesDoyle 6 57
(B P J Baugh) *hld up and bhd: c wd st: rdn over 1f out: n.d* **66/1**

4340 **10** 1½ **Jilly Why (IRE)**[14] 7161 6-8-13 **60**..........(b) PaulMulrennan 11 53
(Paul Green) *broke wl: sn stdd into mid-div: rdn over 1f out: no rspnse* **20/1**

0500 **11** 2 **Plateau**[33] 6946 8-9-0 **61**.......... AdamKirby 13 47
(C R Dore) *chsd ldr 4f: sn wknd* **25/1**

002 **12** nk **Rainbow Bay**[25] 7020 4-9-1 **62**..........(v) TGMcLaughlin 12 47
(P D Evans) *s.i.s: a in rr* **14/1**

1m 15.15s (-0.66) **Going Correction** -0.025s/f (Stan) **12** Ran SP% **119.1**
Speed ratings (Par 101): **103,102,101,101,100 99,99,98,97,95 93,92**
CSF £44.62 CT £198.56 TOTE £9.00: £2.40, £2.40, £1.60; EX 64.90.
Owner S J Hammond **Bred** Mohammad Al Qatami **Trained** Newmarket, Suffolk

FOCUS
Some old acquaintances reunited in this competitive low-grade handicap. Sound form.
Gilded Cove Official explanation: jockey said horse was denied a clear run

Plateau Official explanation: jockey said gelding had no more to give

7272 PONTIN'S GREAT FAMILY HOLIDAYS CLAIMING STKS 7f 32y(P)
7:55 (7:55) (Class 6) 2-Y-O £2,388 (£705; £352) Stalls High

Form RPR
4051 1 **Shepherds Warning (IRE)**[15] 7142 2-8-7 71.......... RichardKingscote 5 65
(N J Vaughan) *t.k.h: wnt 2nd over 5f out: rdn to ld wl over 1f out: r.o* **10/11**[1]
061 2 ¾ **Longoria (IRE)**[17] 7122 2-8-8 65 ow3.......... JerryO'Dwyer(3) 4 67
(M G Quinlan) *sn led: rdn and hdd wl over 1f out: nt qckn ins fnl f* **11/4**[2]
0203 3 1 ¾ **Lord Deevert**[11] 7177 2-8-2 64.......... (v[1]) JackDean(7) 2 61
(W G M Turner) *plld hrd: hdwy 3f out: sn rdn: one pce fnl f* **14/1**
0004 4 shd **Talamahana**[14] 7156 2-8-0 48.......... (b[1]) DuranFentiman(3) 3 55
(S Kirk) *hld up: rdn over 2f out: edgd lft wl over 1f out: styd on ins fnl f* **11/1**
0462 5 3 ½ **Her Name Is Rio (IRE)**[11] 7177 2-8-3 62.......... LiamJones 1 46
(J S Moore) *led early: prom: rdn over 2f out: wknd ins fnl f* **15/2**[3]
5634 6 2 **Desert Life (IRE)**[12] 7171 2-8-8 54.......... (p) ChrisCatlin 6 46
(R A Harris) *plld hrd: hdwy over 5f out: rdn over 2f out: sn wknd* **25/1**
3605 7 1 **Gaitskell**[11] 7177 2-8-8 57.......... (t) DeanMcKeown 8 44
(R Hollinshead) *s.i.s: sn swtchd lft: a in rr* **50/1**

1m 31.96s (1.56) **Going Correction** -0.025s/f (Stan) **7 Ran SP% 111.6**
Speed ratings (Par 94): **90,89,87,87,83 80,79**
CSF £3.30 TOTE £2.00: £1.30, £1.50; EX 3.70.
Owner A Black **Bred** T M Jennings **Trained** Malpas, Cheshire

FOCUS
Several of these proved difficult to settle in this slowly-run moderate affair. The principals did not need to find their best in a race anchored by the fourth

NOTEBOOK
Shepherds Warning(IRE) did not need to be at her best to follow up her win in a similar event over course and distance a fortnight earlier. (op 6-4)
Longoria(IRE), whose rider was unable to utilise his claim, did not mind the step up to 7f on this quicker surface. She may well have been better off setting a stronger pace but would have been meeting the winner on 7lb better terms in a handicap. (op 7-2)
Lord Deevert proved a real handful in the first-time visor and his jockey must have wished that they had gone a better gallop. (op 12-1 tchd 16-1)
Talamahana, tried in blinkers on her second start in claiming company, is struggling to find the right trip. (op 12-1 tchd 14-1)
Her Name Is Rio(IRE) does not appear to be as good on sand as she is in soft ground on turf despite her narrow defeat on the Fibresand surface last time which probably suits her better. (op 10-3)
Gaitskell Official explanation: jockey said colt had a breathing problem

7273 LENNIE LAWRENCE 60TH BIRTHDAY H'CAP 1m 4f 50y(P)
8:25 (8:25) (Class 6) (0-60,60) 3-Y-O+ £2,047 (£604; £302) Stalls Low

Form RPR
0602 1 **Winter Cruise (IRE)**[12] 7172 3-8-5 **49**.......... ChrisCatlin 10 59
(Ian Williams) *hld up in tch: rdn to ld ins fnl f: r.o* **5/1**[2]
0201 2 1 ¾ **Sir Sandicliffe (IRE)**[8] 7219 3-9-0 **58**.......... TGMcLaughlin 3 65
(W M Brisbourne) *hld up in rr: hdwy on outside over 2f out: styd on u.p despite hanging lft fnl f: nt trble wnr* **10/1**
4303 3 ¾ **Regency Red (IRE)**[8] 7219 9-9-2 **55**.......... LiamJones 12 61
(W M Brisbourne) *hld up in mid-div: hdwy over 5f out: led wl over 2f out: rdn and hdd ins fnl f: no ex* **10/1**
2000 4 1 ½ **Buscador (USA)**[22] 7060 8-8-11 **50**.......... RichardKingscote 6 53
(W M Brisbourne) *led: hdd wl over 2f out: sn rdn: ev ch 1f out: eased whn btn cl home* **14/1**
6060 5 2 **Medieval Maiden**[48] 6780 4-9-7 **60**.......... NeilPollard 1 60
(W J Musson) *hld up in rr: c wd st: styd on fnl f: n.d* **12/1**
2350 6 hd **Countback (FR)**[152] 2511 8-8-7 **46** oh1.......... (p) JamesDoyle 8 46
(A W Carroll) *hld up in rr: rdn over 1f out: sme late prog* **40/1**
0204 7 nk **Theflyingscottie**[17] 7120 5-8-11 **50**.......... (v) DeanMcKeown 9 49
(D Shaw) *s.i.s: sn swtchd lft: hld up in mid-div: hdwy over 3f out: rdn over 2f out: wknd wl over 1f out* **8/1**
2 8 1 ½ **Ilviz (FR)**[22] 7060 5-9-2 **55**.......... PaulMulrennan 7 52
(Ollie Pears) *hld up in tch: lost pl and rdn over 3f out: n.d after* **2/1**[1]
2556 9 nk **Zalkani (IRE)**[14] 7157 7-9-2 **55**.......... GeorgeBaker 5 52
(J Pearce) *hld up in rr: hdwy 2f out: rdn and hung lft over 1f out: wknd fnl f* **7/1**[3]
526 10 1 ½ **Trackattack**[8] 7214 5-8-5 **47**.......... NeilChalmers(3) 4 41
(M Appleby) *prom tl rdn and wknd over 3f out* **33/1**
0006 11 9 **Mighty Kitchener (USA)**[16] 7132 4-9-4 **57**.......... SimonWhitworth 11 37
(P Howling) *prom tl rdn and wknd 2f out* **16/1**

2m 41.11s (-1.31) **Going Correction** -0.025s/f (Stan)
WFA 3 from 4yo+ 5lb **11 Ran SP% 117.4**
Speed ratings (Par 101): **103,101,101,100,99 98,98,97,97,96 90**
CSF £54.24 CT £485.31 TOTE £6.30: £2.40, £2.40, £3.70; EX 79.40.
Owner Patrick Kelly **Bred** D H W Dobson **Trained** Portway, Worcs

FOCUS
Three runners from the Mark Brisbourne stable chased the winner home in this moderate affair. Sound enough form.
Ilviz(FR) Official explanation: jockey said gelding hung left

7274 GO PONTIN'S SHORT BREAKS H'CAP 1m 1f 103y(P)
8:55 (8:55) (Class 6) (0-60,60) 3-Y-O+ £2,047 (£604; £302) Stalls Low

Form RPR
0135 1 **Moonlight Fantasy (IRE)**[15] 7146 4-9-2 **56**.......... TGMcLaughlin 2 61
(Lucinda Featherstone) *stdd s: hld up in rr: hdwy and swtchd lft jst over 1f out: swtchd rt ins fnl f: r.o wl to ld cl home* **7/2**[1]
5654 2 1 **Climate (IRE)**[8] 7218 8-8-5 **50**.......... RussellKennemore(5) 10 53
(R Hollinshead) *t.k.h in tch: led over 2f out: rdn clr over 1f out: ct cl home* **11/2**[3]
0332 3 shd **Casablanca Minx (IRE)**[8] 7214 4-8-12 **59**.......... (v) RichardEvans(7) 11 62
(P D Evans) *hld up in rr: c wd st: hdwy on outside over 1f out: sn hung lft: r.o ins fnl f* **7/2**[1]
0640 4 1 **Norwegian**[15] 7146 6-9-0 **54**.......... (p) PaulEddery 5 55
(Ian Williams) *hld up in tch: rdn over 2f out: one pce fnl f* **7/1**
6526 5 hd **Komreyev Star**[8] 7213 5-8-9 **49** oh1 ow3.......... PaulMulrennan 7 50
(R E Peacock) *led early: a.p: chsd ldr over 2f out: sn rdn: no ex ins fnl f* **7/1**
00-V 6 1 ¼ **Candy Anchor (FR)**[19] 7100 8-8-3 **46** oh1.......... AndrewElliott(3) 6 44
(R E Peacock) *hld up: hdwy over 5f out: wknd wl over 1f out* **66/1**
04V5 7 1 ¾ **Western Roots**[16] 7132 6-9-3 **60**.......... (p) NeilChalmers(3) 1 54
(M Appleby) *hld up and bhd: nt clr run over 2f out: swtchd rt wl over 1f out: nvr nr ldrs* **5/1**[2]
2406 8 1 ½ **Come What July (IRE)**[198] 2595 6-8-3 **48** ow1.......... (v) TolleyDean(5) 8 39
(D Shaw) *a towards rr* **16/1**
0030 9 1 ¼ **Blakeshall Hope**[8] 7218 5-8-7 **47** oh1 ow1.......... DeanMcKeown 4 36
(A J Chamberlain) *t.k.h: prom: rdn over 2f out: wknd over 1f out* **33/1**
6000 10 6 **Cantique (IRE)**[8] 7218 3-8-4 **46** oh1.......... LiamJones 9 22
(R J Price) *plld hrd: sn led: hdd over 2f out: sn wknd* **40/1**

2m 3.02s (0.40) **Going Correction** -0.025s/f (Stan)
WFA 3 from 4yo+ 2lb **10 Ran SP% 114.3**
Speed ratings (Par 101): **97,96,96,95,94 93,92,90,89,84**
CSF £22.12 CT £71.11 TOTE £4.40: £1.30, £1.70, £1.90; EX 22.10.
Owner J Roundtree **Bred** Rockhart Trading Ltd **Trained** Ashbourne, Derbyshire

FOCUS
A competitive low-key handicap. The fifth and sixth cast doubt over the form and it is doubtful if the winner had to improve.
Cantique(IRE) Official explanation: jockey said filly ran too freely

7275 PONTINS.COM CLASSIFIED STKS 1m 141y(P)
9:20 (9:21) (Class 6) 3-Y-O+ £2,047 (£604; £302) Stalls Low

Form RPR
6500 1 **Zabeel House**[61] 6533 4-9-0 55.......... (p) DeanMcKeown 4 65
(John A Harris) *hld up: hdwy over 3f out: led 1f out: rdn and r.o wl* **9/1**
034 2 4 **Winged Farasi**[9] 7201 3-8-12 53.......... ChrisCatlin 7 56
(R A Harris) *s.i.s and reminders: hdwy 7f out: led jst over 2f out: rdn and hdd 1f out: one pce* **13/2**[3]
0005 3 shd **Morbick**[37] 6906 3-8-12 52.......... TGMcLaughlin 3 56
(W M Brisbourne) *a.p: rdn over 1f out: kpt on same pce fnl f* **13/2**[3]
3123 4 ¾ **Beck**[2] 7250 3-8-9 53.......... DuranFentiman(3) 5 54
(W M Brisbourne) *hld up and bhd: hdwy on outside over 2f out: c wd st: rdn and one pce fnl f* **11/8**[1]
651 5 1 ½ **Maiden Investor**[15] 7144 4-9-0 51.......... MickyFenton 9 51
(Stef Liddiard) *settled in rr: swtchd rt over 1f out: no real prog fnl f* **16/1**
1000 6 1 ½ **Theatre Royal**[17] 7115 4-8-11 50.......... (b) NeilChalmers(3) 8 47
(Mouse Hamilton-Fairley) *hld up: hdwy over 3f out: ev ch over 2f out: rdn and wknd wl over 1f out* **20/1**
6040 7 12 **Sky Chart (IRE)**[122] 4943 3-8-12 55.......... (p) SamHitchcott 2 20
(N J Vaughan) *led: hdd jst over 2f out: wknd qckly over 1f out* **3/1**[2]
0/30 8 6 **Blackbury**[12] 7174 5-9-0 47.......... (t) LiamJones 6 6
(W M Brisbourne) *chsd ldr tl over 3f out: wknd qckly* **33/1**

1m 51.1s (-0.66) **Going Correction** -0.025s/f (Stan)
WFA 3 from 4yo+ 2lb **8 Ran SP% 117.4**
Speed ratings (Par 101): **101,97,97,96,95 94,83,78**
CSF £67.40 TOTE £9.60: £3.00, £2.20, £2.70; EX 59.80 Place 6 £ 35.71, Place 5 £ 30.13.
Owner Cricklewood Timber **Bred** Plantation Stud **Trained** Eastwell, Leics

FOCUS
Only 8lb separated the field on adjusted official ratings in this weak contest. The winner did not need to improve on this year's best in a race rated through the third and the fifth.
T/Plt: £40.20 to a £1 stake. Pool: £116,758.75. 2,116.55 winning tickets. T/Qpdt: £18.50 to a £1 stake. Pool: £6,522.10. 259.80 winning tickets. KH

7264 LINGFIELD (L-H)
Sunday, December 30

OFFICIAL GOING: Standard
Wind: light, across Weather: Fine but cloudy

7276 PONTINS.COM H'CAP (DIV I) 7f (P)
12:40 (12:41) (Class 6) (0-52,53) 3-Y-O+ £1,943 (£578; £288; £144) Stalls Low

Form RPR
1204 1 **Dawson Creek (IRE)**[20] 7098 3-8-13 **51**.......... GregFairley 5 62
(B Gubby) *trckd ldr: effrt to ld over 2f out: rdn and styd on wl fr over 1f out* **2/1**[1]
004 2 1 ½ **Strut The Stage (IRE)**[18] 7118 3-8-7 **52**.......... (tp) GHannon(7) 1 59
(B W Duke) *trckd ldng pair: clr of rest over 2f out: rdn and styd on to take 2nd last 100yds: no real imp on wnr* **9/1**
00-0 3 1 ½ **Tuning Fork**[20] 7098 7-8-4 **47**.......... KirstyMilczarek(5) 2 50
(M J Attwater) *led: rdn and hdd over 2f out: fdd and lost 2nd ins fnl f* **20/1**
0000 4 1 **Bollywood (IRE)**[14] 7167 4-8-5 **46** oh1.......... (p) NeilChalmers(3) 3 46
(J J Bridger) *chsd ldng trio: rdn 1/2-way: sn outpcd: styd on fr over 1f out: unable to land a blow* **16/1**
0004 5 1 ¾ **Mind Alert**[26] 7014 6-8-10 **48**.......... (v) JamesDoyle 11 43
(D Shaw) *hld up in last trio: stl there but gng wl enough over 2f out: no ch whn nt clr run wl over 1f out: r.o after: nrst fin* **7/1**
3300 6 4 **A Teen**[18] 7124 9-8-8 **46** oh1.......... TGMcLaughlin 9 31
(P Howling) *racd wd: hld up in rr: outpcd 3f out: no ch whn wd bnd 2 out* **33/1**
0330 7 1 ¼ **Regal Royale**[1] 7265 4-9-0 **52**.......... LPKeniry 7 33
(Peter Grayson) *hld up in last trio: rdn over 3f out: sn outpcd and no ch* **5/1**[2]
-P00 8 ½ **Frank's Quest (IRE)**[14] 7167 7-8-9 **47** oh1 ow1.......... SamHitchcott 10 27
(A B Haynes) *nvr gng that wl: mostly in last trio tl sme prog on inner wl over 1f out: no ch: eased last 100yds* **50/1**
5062 9 1 ¾ **Mulberry Lad (IRE)**[11] 7192 5-9-1 **53**.......... ChrisCatlin 6 28
(P W Hiatt) *racd on outer in midfield: u.p fr 1/2-way: sn outpcd and no ch* **6/1**[3]
0000 10 ¾ **Itsawindup**[20] 7098 3-8-8 **46** oh1.......... (v) PaulDoe 4 19
(W J Knight) *chsd ldng trio: outpcd and rdn fr 3f out: wknd* **16/1**
4052 11 1 ½ **Royal Guest**[27] 6968 3-8-12 **50**.......... LiamJones 8 19
(J R Jenkins) *nvr bttr than midfield: drvn and struggling 1/2-way: sn btn* **13/2**

1m 24.59s (-1.30) **Going Correction** -0.15s/f (Stan) **11 Ran SP% 121.5**
Speed ratings (Par 101): **101,99,97,96,94 89,88,87,85,85 83**
CSF £21.74 CT £293.90 TOTE £2.90: £1.50, £2.50, £5.60; EX 23.60 TRIFECTA Not won..
Owner Brian Gubby **Bred** Eastersnow Stud **Trained** Bagshot, Surrey

FOCUS
A decidedly moderate handicap but the time was respectable for the grade.
Mind Alert Official explanation: jockey said gelding was denied a clear run
Frank's Quest(IRE) Official explanation: jockey said gelding lost its action

7277 PONTIN'S BOOK EARLY (S) STKS 1m 2f (P)
1:10 (1:10) (Class 6) 3-Y-O+ £1,943 (£578; £288; £144) Stalls Low

Form RPR
6006 1 **Little Miss Tara (IRE)**[16] 7144 3-8-6 51.......... (v) DavidKinsella 4 57
(A B Haynes) *trckd ldng pair: prog to ld wl over 2f out: kicked 4 l clr wl over 1f out: drvn rt out* **20/1**

5305 **2** 2½ **Barry Island**[11] 7189 8-9-0 60 .... LPKeniry 6 57
(D R C Elsworth) *hld up: prog over 2f out but wnr already flown: hanging but rdn to take 2nd last 100yds: clsd grad* **3/1**[2]

6400 **3** 2 **Granary Girl**[23] 7056 5-8-9 49 .... DeanMcKeown 8 48
(J Pearce) *chsd ldng pair: rdn to go 2nd jst over 2f out: no imp on wnr: lost 2nd last 100yds* **9/1**

-004 **4** 1½ **Ryan's Future (IRE)**[11] 7189 7-9-0 78 .... SteveDrowne 9 50
(J S Moore) *s.v.s: sn in tch: rdn on outer over 3f out: outpcd wl over 2f out: kpt on u.p* **11/10**[1]

/40- **5** nk **Grooms Affection**[36] 765 7-9-0 78 .... JamesDoyle 1 49
(K A Morgan) *dwlt: hld up in tch: outpcd fr 3f out: plugged on one pce after* **5/1**[3]

0000 **6** 2½ **Elms Schoolboy**[244] 1362 5-9-0 40 ....(b) TGMcLaughlin 5 44
(P Howling) *v.s.i.s: hld up in last pair: outpcd fr 3f out: no ch after* **33/1**

0000 **7** shd **Elmasong**[11] 7185 3-8-6 35 ....(p) ChrisCatlin 3 39
(J J Bridger) *led 1f: chsd ldr to 3f out: nudged along and sn lost pl* **80/1**

0160 **8** 1¾ **Cavallo Di Ferro (IRE)**[26] 7023 3-9-3 62 .... GregFairley 7 47
(M J Gingell) *led after 1f to wl over 2f out: wknd fnl 2f* **16/1**

2m 9.68s (1.89) **Going Correction** -0.15s/f (Stan)
WFA 3 from 4yo+ 3lb — 8 Ran SP% **114.1**
Speed ratings (Par 101): **86,84,82,81,80 78,78,77**
CSF £78.42 TOTE £23.30: £3.20, £1.20, £1.90; EX 72.20 TRIFECTA Not won..There was no bid for the winner.
Owner Mrs S Maine,K Wills,D Fuller,L Bloxsome **Bred** Keith Wills **Trained** Limpley Stoke, Bath

FOCUS
A poor seller run at a pedestrian pace.

7278 PONTINS.COM H'CAP (DIV II) — 7f (P)
1:45 (1:45) (Class 6) (0-52,52) 3-Y-O+ — **£1,943** (£578; £288; £144) **Stalls** Low

Form — RPR

0004 **1** **Epidaurian King (IRE)**[25] 7034 4-8-8 **46** oh1 ....(v) DeanMcKeown 9 59
(D Shaw) *hld up off the pce: prog fr 3f out to go 4th 2f out: rdn and r.o to ld last 150yds: sn in command* **15/2**

0020 **2** 1¼ **Takaamul**[44] 6831 4-8-10 **48** .... JamesDoyle 7 58
(K A Morgan) *hld up off the pce: stdy prog to go 3rd over 2f out: rdn to ld over 1f out: hdd and nt qckn last 150yds* **16/1**

0306 **3** 1¼ **Mythical Charm**[18] 7115 8-9-0 **52** ....(t) DaneO'Neill 3 59
(J J Bridger) *hld up in last trio: nt clr run briefly over 2f out: rdn and prog over 1f out: styd on to take 3rd ins fnl f: no ch to chal* **15/2**

-640 **4** ¾ **Riviera Red (IRE)**[336] 273 7-8-8 **46** oh1 .... TGMcLaughlin 10 51
(L Montague Hall) *hld up in last pair and wl off the pce: effrt on wd outside over 2f out and lost grnd bnd sn after: r.o fnl f: nrst fin* **16/1**

0264 **5** nk **Palais Polaire**[34] 6950 5-8-11 **52** ....(p) TravisBlock(3) 5 56
(J A Geake) *led 1f: chsd ldr: upsides and rdn 2f out: wd and nt qckn over 1f out: one pce after* **6/1**[3]

1000 **6** nk **Smash N'Grab (IRE)**[19] 7113 3-8-13 **51** .... LiamJones 11 54
(J R Jenkins) *mostly in last trio and wl off the pce: sme prog u.p wl over 1f out: kpt on: n.d* **16/1**

0564 **7** hd **Sovereignty (JPN)**[61] 6563 5-8-7 **50** .... PatrickHills(5) 12 52
(D K Ivory) *led after 1f and set decent pce: hdd over 1f out: wknd fnl f* **4/1**[1]

2540 **8** 2½ **Double Valentine**[20] 7098 4-8-9 **47** .... SteveDrowne 2 43
(R Ingram) *nvr beyond midfield: rdn 3f out: no imp on ldrs over 1f out* **5/1**[2]

6640 **9** ½ **Only If I Laugh**[14] 7166 6-8-8 **46** oh1 ....(v) DaleGibson 6 40
(M J Attwater) *chsd ldrs: u.p 3f out: struggling over 2f out: wknd* **12/1**

6-00 **10** 5 **Noble Mount**[90] 5866 6-8-8 **46** oh1 ....(p) DavidKinsella 4 27
(A B Haynes) *wl off the pce in last trio: rdn 3f out: sn btn* **25/1**

0300 **11** hd **Nawayea**[9] 7209 4-8-3 **46** oh1 ....(t) KirstyMilczarek(5) 8 26
(C N Allen) *pressed ldrs on outer tl wknd over 2f out* **22/1**

3364 **12** nk **Midmaar (IRE)**[11] 7192 6-8-12 **50** ....(b) JamieMackay 1 29
(M Wigham) *chsd ldrs but nvr gng wl: wknd on inner over 1f out: eased last 100yds* **6/1**[3]

1m 24.51s (-1.38) **Going Correction** -0.15s/f (Stan) — 12 Ran SP% **122.3**
Speed ratings (Par 101): **101,99,98,97,96 96,96,93,92,87 87,86**
CSF £125.17 CT £956.84 TOTE £7.50: £2.50, £4.50, £3.20; EX 133.50 TRIFECTA Not won..
Owner Derek Shaw **Bred** Shadwell Estate Company Limited **Trained** Danethorpe, Notts

FOCUS
Another mediocre handicap with very little winning form on display. It was run in an almost identical time to the first division.
Double Valentine Official explanation: jockey said filly was never travelling
Midmaar(IRE) Official explanation: jockey said gelding lost its action

7279 PONTIN'S BOOK EARLY AND SAVE CLAIMING STKS — 6f (P)
2:15 (2:15) (Class 6) 3-Y-O+ — **£1,943** (£578; £288; £144) **Stalls** Low

Form — RPR

4004 **1** **Benllech**[4] 7233 3-8-6 63 .... SimonWhitworth 4 75
(S Kirk) *hld up in midfield: prog 2f out to chse ldng trio: r.o to ld last 150yds: in command after* **14/1**

0012 **2** ¾ **One More Round (USA)**[34] 6947 9-9-0 83 ....(b) SteveDrowne 2 81
(Ollie Pears) *dwlt: hld up in last pair and wl off the pce: hrd rdn and gd prog fr 2f out: clsd on ldrs but nt qckn fnl 100yds: tk 2nd last strides* **11/4**[2]

100 **3** nk **Philharmonic**[36] 6932 6-9-5 96 .... TonyHamilton 10 85
(R A Fahey) *wl in tch: chsd clr ldng pair over 2f out: clsd on inner to chal and upsides 1f out: nt qckn: lost 2nd last strides* **9/4**[1]

3400 **4** 1¼ **Goodbye Cash (IRE)**[57] 6639 3-8-8 75 .... TGMcLaughlin 7 70
(P D Evans) *hld up in midfield: outpcd over 2f out: drvn and r.o fnl f: nrst fin* **16/1**

2032 **5** ½ **Harry Up**[22] 7078 6-9-3 82 .... ChrisCatlin 5 77
(K A Ryan) *led at str pce: clr w chalr 2f out: hdd & wknd last 150yds* **9/2**[3]

4000 **6** nk **Ashes (IRE)**[10] 7206 5-8-1 56 ....(p) AndrewElliott(3) 8 63
(K R Burke) *pressed ldr: clr of rest over 2f out: rdn to chal wl over 1f out: fnd nil and sn btn* **28/1**

3500 **7** 1¾ **Count Ceprano (IRE)**[155] 3944 3-8-4 82 .... GHannon(7) 9 65
(M D I Usher) *s.s: wl off the pce in last pair: pushed along and kpt on same pce fnl 2f* **9/1**

5066 **8** 1½ **Fromsong (IRE)**[60] 6589 9-8-10 76 .... PatrickHills(5) 1 64
(D K Ivory) *hld up and trbld passage towards rr on inner: limited prog over 1f out: no hdwy after* **8/1**

0005 **9** 4 **Charlotte Grey**[9] 7209 3-8-1 47 .... NickyMackay 12 37
(C N Allen) *hld up in rr fr wd draw: rdn and struggling on outer over 2f out* **50/1**

/06- **10** hd **Miss Brush**[568] 2433 4-8-9 73 .... JimCrowley 3 45
(J R Fanshawe) *prom tl wknd rapidly over 2f out* **20/1**

11 3½ **Kazakstan**[86] 5991 3-8-7 55 ow1 .... LPKeniry 11 31
(Mrs L C Jewell) *prom over 2f out: lost pl rapidly* **100/1**

0000 **12** ½ **Stargazy**[111] 5270 3-8-7 49 .... LiamJones 6 30
(W G M Turner) *racd wd and a wl in rr: no ch fnl 2f* **66/1**

1m 10.71s (-2.10) **Going Correction** -0.15s/f (Stan) — 12 Ran SP% **121.9**
Speed ratings (Par 101): **108,107,106,104,104 103,101,99,94,93 89,88**
CSF £52.50 TOTE £18.80: £3.60, £1.60, £1.50; EX 69.00 TRIFECTA Not won..Benllech was claimed by Jeff Pearce for £7,000.
Owner Speedlith Group **Bred** Speedlith Group **Trained** Upper Lambourn, Berks

FOCUS
A very mixed bag went to post for this claimer, with question marks hanging over a number of them.

7280 PONTIN'S SHORT BREAKS NURSERY — 6f (P)
2:45 (2:45) (Class 4) (0-85,80) 2-Y-O — **£3,886** (£1,156; £577; £288) **Stalls** Low

Form — RPR

0061 **1** **Fathsta (IRE)**[20] 7095 2-9-0 **73** .... LPKeniry 9 76
(S Kirk) *trckd ldng pair: effrt over 1f out: drvn to ld jst ins fnl f: sn jnd: hld on wl* **3/1**[1]

0312 **2** hd **Smokey Rye**[20] 7095 2-8-13 **72** ....(b) AdamKirby 2 74
(G L Moore) *hld up in 5th/6th: effrt and urged along over 1f out: hrd rdn and r.o last 150yds: jst failed* **10/1**

0601 **3** shd **The Game**[23] 7052 2-9-7 **80** .... PatCosgrave 4 82
(J R Boyle) *hld up in 5th/6th: effrt over 1f out: prog to chal ins fnl f and looked likely wnr: flattened out cl home* **3/1**[1]

2254 **4** 1¾ **Southwest Star (IRE)**[2] 7258 2-8-3 **67** ow1 .... TolleyDean(5) 1 64
(J S Moore) *dwlt: hld up in last pair of main gp: rdn over 2f out: styd on fr over 1f out to take 4th nr fin* **8/1**

0301 **5** ½ **Kamal**[11] 7182 2-8-6 **65** .... ChrisCatlin 6 60
(W R Muir) *stdd s: hld up in last pair of main gp: rdn 2f out: plugged on fnl f: no ch* **13/2**[2]

4214 **6** nk **Fast Feet**[22] 7072 2-9-6 **79** .... PaulMulrennan 8 73
(K A Ryan) *w ldr: upsides ent fnl f: fdd* **8/1**

0132 **7** nk **Bazguy**[22] 7072 2-8-9 **75** ....(b) RichardEvans(7) 5 68
(P D Evans) *led: increased pce fr 1/2-way: hdd jst ins fnl f: fdd* **7/1**[3]

0030 **8** 1 **Evenstorm (USA)**[108] 5357 2-8-5 **64** .... GregFairley 3 54
(B Gubby) *trckd ldng pair: cl up on inner jst over 1f out: wknd tamely* **25/1**

0050 **9** 14 **Liberty Belle (IRE)**[45] 6823 2-9-0 **73** .... DaneO'Neill 7 21
(J R Best) *lft at least 12 l s: trailed rnd and a t.o* **12/1**

1m 12.42s (-0.39) **Going Correction** -0.15s/f (Stan) — 9 Ran SP% **118.7**
Speed ratings (Par 98): **96,95,95,93,92 92,91,90,71**
CSF £36.37 CT £99.69 TOTE £3.10: £1.50, £3.80, £1.40; EX 51.70 Trifecta £244.30 Pool £378.53. - 1.10 winning units.
Owner Speedlith Group **Bred** Brian Miller **Trained** Upper Lambourn, Berks

FOCUS
A competitive-looking nursery featuring three last-time-out winners plus a couple who have been knocking on the door recently.

NOTEBOOK
Fathsta(IRE), successful on his last outing over 7f here, showed good character to follow up off a 6lb higher mark in what looked a tougher race. His jockey found himself in front sooner than he would have liked, but felt he had little choice but to race prominently from his wide draw, and he reported afterwards that he was taken with the way the colt stuck his neck out when they came at him late on. (op 5-1)
Smokey Rye, a tail-swisher, has been creeping up the weights for a series of good runs. She finished to good effect and it would be no surprise to see her in the mix again. (op 9-1 tchd 11-1)
The Game came there with what looked like a winning run in the closing stages, but was just unable to master the two who finished in front of him. Connections report that he ran a bit freer than they would have liked in the early parts. (op 5-2)
Southwest Star(IRE) has been bang there recently and as a consequence has been creeping up the weights. This was a tough assignment and he gave a good account of himself. (tchd 9-1)
Kamal, 5lb higher and down in trip, could never get into the action. (op 7-1 tchd 6-1)
Evenstorm(USA) Official explanation: jockey said filly was denied a clear run

7281 GO PONTIN'S HOLIDAYS H'CAP — 1m (P)
3:20 (3:21) (Class 4) (0-85,83) 3-Y-O+ — **£4,857** (£1,445; £722; £360) **Stalls** High

Form — RPR

1442 **1** **Alfresco**[23] 7061 3-9-2 **80** ....(b) DaneO'Neill 2 91
(I A Wood) *stdd s but sn in midfield: prog to go 4th 2f out: drvn and r.o to ld ins fnl f: a holding on after* **3/1**[1]

0602 **2** ¾ **Basra (IRE)**[26] 7017 4-9-5 **82** .... AdamKirby 11 91
(Miss Jo Crowley) *pressed ldrs: rdn over 2f out: nt qckn over 1f out: styd on again fnl f to take 2nd last stride* **11/2**[3]

6026 **3** hd **Dichoh**[14] 7165 4-9-4 **81** ....(b[1]) MatthewHenry 3 90
(M A Jarvis) *mde most to 3f out: styd pressing ldr: led again briefly 1f out: one pce and lost 2nd last stride* **11/1**

0405 **4** nk **Bee Stinger**[23] 7061 5-8-12 **75** .... JamesDoyle 1 83
(I A Wood) *chsd ldrs: u.p wl over 2f out and lost pl sltly: styd on wl again ins fnl f* **25/1**

3613 **5** ¾ **Master Pegasus**[23] 7061 4-9-0 **82** .... JackMitchell(5) 6 88
(C F Wall) *t.k.h: hld up in rr: effrt over 2f out: nt qckn over 1f out: styd on fnl f: nvr able to chal* **11/1**

3034 **6** hd **Waterline Twenty (IRE)**[11] 7193 4-8-8 **71** .... TGMcLaughlin 9 77
(P D Evans) *hld up towards rr: rdn and effrt on outer over 2f out: styd on fnl f: nrst fin* **16/1**

3400 **7** ½ **Risque Heights**[14] 7165 3-9-2 **80** .... PaulMulrennan 12 85
(G A Butler) *dropped in fr wd draw and hld up in last trio: effrt on inner 2f out: kpt on: nt pce to threaten* **16/1**

0000 **8** nk **Lopinot (IRE)**[14] 7165 4-8-7 **77** .... KylieManser(7) 4 81
(M R Bosley) *w ldrs: narrow ld 3f out to 1f out: wknd v tamely* **12/1**

3131 **9** 3½ **Ochre (IRE)**[3] 7241 3-8-8 **72** 6ex .... DaleGibson 10 68
(R A Fahey) *chsd ldrs: grad wknd fnl 2f* **13/2**

0004 **10** shd **Buxton**[20] 7099 3-8-13 **77** .... SteveDrowne 5 73
(R Ingram) *hld up towards rr: nt clr run over 2f out: no prog and no ch whn hmpd 1f out* **20/1**

00-0 **11** 5 **She's My Outsider**[204] 2450 5-8-13 **76** .... ChrisCatlin 8 60
(A W Carroll) *plld hrd early: hld up in last trio: brief effrt over 2f out on outer: sn wknd* **50/1**

213 **12** 11 **Zero Cool (USA)**[36] 6236 3-9-5 **83** .... GeorgeBaker 7 42
(G L Moore) *nvr gng wl: a last trio: t.o* **7/2**[2]

1m 37.56s (-1.87) **Going Correction** -0.15s/f (Stan)
WFA 3 from 4yo+ 1lb — 12 Ran SP% **122.6**
Speed ratings (Par 105): **103,102,102,101,101 100,100,100,96,96 91,80**
CSF £19.90 CT £168.58 TOTE £4.20: £1.90, £2.00, £3.70; EX 25.30 Trifecta £97.80 Pool £495.31 - 3.58 winning units.
Owner Mrs A M Riney **Bred** Usk Valley Stud **Trained** Upper Lambourn, Berks

FOCUS
A decent handicap run in a respectable time despite what appeared a moderate early gallop.

Risque Heights Official explanation: jockey said gelding hung right
She's My Outsider Official explanation: jockey said mare ran too freely
Zero Cool(USA) Official explanation: jockey said colt was never travelling

7282 LINGFIELDPARK.CO.UK MAIDEN STKS — 1m 2f (P)
3:50 (3:50) (Class 5) 3-Y-O — £2,817 (£838; £418; £209) Stalls Low

Form — RPR

66- **1** **The Carlton Cannes**[428] 6214 3-9-3 0 .... SteveDrowne 11 — 66
(G Wragg) *hld up in midfield: prog on outer 3f out: rdn to ld jst over 1f out: idled in front: hld on* **11/4**[1]

3443 **2** ½ **Emperor Court (IRE)**[50] 6766 3-9-3 67 .... ChrisCatlin 9 — 65
(P J Makin) *t.k.h: trckd ldrs: effrt over 2f out: chal and upsides jst over 1f out: nt qckn* **12/1**

0503 **3** nk **Rollin 'n Tumblin**[11] 7185 3-8-12 46 .... KirstyMilczarek(5) 2 — 64
(W Jarvis) *hld up in midfield: pushed along and prog over 2f out: cl enough but nt qckn over 1f out: styd on again ins fnl f* **28/1**

0323 **4** ½ **Esclarmonde (IRE)**[22] 7076 3-8-12 70 .... (b) NickyMackay 12 — 58
(L M Cumani) *tardy s: rushed up to trck ldr after 2f: drvn to ld wl over 1f out: hdd jst over 1f out: one pce* **5/1**[2]

L0 **5** 1 ¼ **Rose Row**[256] 1093 3-8-12 0 .... VinceSlattery 4 — 56
(Mrs Mary Hambro) *hld up in midfield: stdy prog to trck ldrs over 2f out: shkn up over 1f out: nt qckn fnl f* **100/1**

3023 **6** 5 **Paradise Dancer (IRE)**[8] 7224 3-8-7 68 .... PatrickHills(5) 5 — 46
(J A R Toller) *hld up towards rr: prog 3f out: chsng ldrs over 2f out: wknd over 1f out* **11/4**[1]

2 **7** ¾ **Ready To Crown (USA)**[20] 7103 3-8-12 0 .... DaleGibson 3 — 44
(Andrew Turnell) *nvr bttr than midfield: losing pl on inner wl over 2f out: n.d after* **8/1**

8 1 ¾ **National Day (IRE)** 3-8-12 0 .... LPKeniry 1 — 41
(D R C Elsworth) *s.s: hld up in rr: rdn on outer and no impact wl over 2f out* **16/1**

45 **9** 1 **Intersky Charm (USA)**[224] 1863 3-9-3 0 .... DeanMcKeown 6 — 44
(R M Whitaker) *t.k.h: prom tl wknd fr 3f out* **7/1**[3]

24 **10** 2 **Old Etonian (UAE)**[266] 956 3-8-10 0 .... RyanHill(7) 8 — 40
(Peter Grayson) *threw himself to the grnd bef ent stalls: led: racd awkwardly: hdd wl over 1f out: gave up* **8/1**

0-0 **11** 35 **Eau Sauvage**[350] 128 3-8-12 0 .... PaulDoe 10 — —
(J Akehurst) *a bhd: t.o 4f out* **80/1**

5 **12** 1 **Joe Rich**[8] 7223 3-9-3 0 .... DaneO'Neill 7 — —
(Mrs L C Jewell) *in tch to 5f out: sn bhd: t.o* **33/1**

2m 5.78s (-2.01) **Going Correction** -0.15s/f (Stan) — **12** Ran SP% **126.9**
Speed ratings (Par 102): **102,101,101,100,99 95,95,93,93,91 63,62**
CSF £42.31 TOTE £4.20: £1.70, £3.90, £6.40; EX 52.60 TRIFECTA Not won. Place 6 £143.90, Place 5 £62.19..
Owner J L C Pearce **Bred** J L C Pearce **Trained** Newmarket, Suffolk

FOCUS
Probably a decent maiden.
T/Plt: £226.00 to a £1 stake. Pool: £66,996.25. 216.35 winning tickets. T/Qpdt: £27.40 to a £1 stake. Pool: £5,428.40. 146.40 winning tickets. JN

7270 WOLVERHAMPTON (A.W) (L-H)
Monday, December 31

OFFICIAL GOING: Standard
Wind: Light, half-behind Weather: Overcast

7283 WILLIAM HILL 0800 44 40 40 H'CAP (DIV I) — 5f 20y(P)
12:50 (12:50) (Class 6) (0-55,55) 3-Y-O+ — £2,047 (£604; £302) Stalls Low

Form — RPR

1050 **1** **Ace Club**[293] 668 6-8-6 52 ow4 .... (b) MarkCoumbe(7) 10 — 57
(S Parr) *mde all: rdn over 1f out: edgd lft: jst hld on* **16/1**

0003 **2** shd **Bentley**[20] 7111 3-9-0 53 .... (v) DaneO'Neill 9 — 58
(D Shaw) *chsd ldrs: rdn over 1f out: hung lft ins fnl f: r.o* **2/1**[1]

0040 **3** 1 ½ **Taboor (IRE)**[160] 3829 9-8-9 48 .... PatCosgrave 4 — 48
(R M H Cowell) *hld up: hdwy 1/2-way: rdn over 1f out: edgd lft: r.o* **6/1**[3]

0006 **4** hd **Stoneacre Donny (IRE)**[15] 7162 3-8-7 46 oh1 .... LPKeniry 3 — 45
(Peter Grayson) *hld up: rdn over 1f out: r.o wl ins fnl f: nt rch ldrs* **28/1**

0005 **5** ½ **Dodaa (USA)**[17] 7137 4-8-7 46 oh1 .... MatthewHenry 7 — 43
(N Wilson) *chsd ldrs: rdn and ev ch over 1f out: no ex ins fnl f* **6/1**[3]

3340 **6** ½ **Hello Roberto**[11] 7206 6-8-13 52 .... (p) LiamJones 5 — 47
(R A Harris) *chsd ldrs: rdn 1/2-way: styd on same pce fnl f* **5/2**[2]

0000 **7** 1 ¾ **Percy Douglas**[4] 7238 7-8-3 47 oh1 ow1 .... (b) AnnStokell(5) 2 — 36
(Miss A Stokell) *chsd ldrs: rdn over 1f out: wknd ins fnl f* **33/1**

604 **8** nk **Yurchenko**[15] 7162 3-8-7 46 oh1 .... DaleGibson 1 — 34
(M Wellings) *mid-div: sn drvn along: nt trble ldrs* **25/1**

-000 **9** 3 **Ava's World (IRE)**[28] 7011 3-8-11 55 .... ColinHaddon(5) 6 — 32
(Peter Grayson) *s.i.s: outpcd* **33/1**

500 **10** ½ **Stoneacre Gareth (IRE)**[124] 4944 3-8-7 53 .... RyanHill(7) 8 — 28
(Peter Grayson) *rrd s: outpcd: sme hdwy 1/2-way: sn wknd* **20/1**

63.55 secs (0.73) **Going Correction** +0.05s/f (Slow) — **10** Ran SP% **114.3**
Speed ratings (Par 101): **96,95,93,93,92 91,88,88,83,82**
CSF £44.79 CT £225.40 TOTE £24.20: £5.40, £1.80, £1.70; EX 73.70 TRIFECTA Not won..
Owner Brooklands Racing **Bred** Helescane Stud **Trained** Carburton, Notts
■ Stewards' Enquiry : Mark Coumbe one-day ban: used whip with excessive frequency (Jan 11)

FOCUS
This was not a great race, evidenced by the performance of the fourth from out of the handicap, and very few ever got into it. The winning time was 0.42 seconds slower than the second division.

7284 WILLIAM HILL 0800 44 40 40 H'CAP (DIV II) — 5f 20y(P)
1:20 (1:20) (Class 6) (0-55,55) 3-Y-O+ — £2,047 (£604; £302) Stalls Low

Form — RPR

3001 **1** **Triskaidekaphobia**[28] 7011 4-9-2 55 .... (t) PaulFitzsimons 3 — 66
(Miss J R Tooth) *mde all: rdn over 1f out: edgd lft ins fnl f: r.o* **5/2**[2]

2144 **2** 1 ½ **Mickleberry (IRE)**[28] 7005 3-8-7 49 .... AndrewElliott(3) 6 — 55
(J D Bethell) *hld up: hdwy 1/2-way: rdn over 1f out: r.o* **9/4**[1]

0054 **3** ¾ **Fern House (IRE)**[20] 7111 5-8-9 48 .... (b[1]) PaulEddery 4 — 51
(Garry Moss) *sn trcking wnr: rdn over 1f out: no ex ins fnl f* **7/2**[3]

0050 **4** ¾ **Lady Hopeful (IRE)**[28] 7005 5-8-7 46 oh1 .... (b) AdrianMcCarthy 9 — 46
(Peter Grayson) *s.i.s: hdwy 1/2-way: rdn over 1f out: styd on same pce fnl f* **16/1**

-021 **5** 1 **Wibbadune (IRE)**[15] 7162 3-8-13 52 .... LPKeniry 1 — 49
(Peter Grayson) *chsd ldrs: rdn 1/2-way: wknd ins fnl f* **9/1**

0026 **6** 2 ½ **Orchestration (IRE)**[214] 2174 6-8-4 46 oh1 .... DominicFox(3) 2 — 34
(S Parr) *sn outpcd* **8/1**

0400 **7** 5 **Kilvickeon (IRE)**[27] 7019 3-8-5 49 oh1 ow3 .... ColinHaddon(5) 5 — 19
(Peter Grayson) *prom: lost pl whn n.m.r 3f out: sn wknd* **20/1**

63.13 secs (0.31) **Going Correction** +0.05s/f (Slow) — **7** Ran SP% **113.3**
Speed ratings (Par 101): **99,96,95,94,92 88,80**
CSF £8.40 CT £18.23 TOTE £4.30: £1.90, £1.70; EX 10.30 Trifecta £25.00 Pool: £133.84 - 3.80 winning tickets..
Owner Raymond Tooth And Steve Gilbey **Bred** K Bowen **Trained** Lambourn, Berks

FOCUS
Another modest sprint handicap and, as in the first division, the winner made all and very little else ever got into it. The winning time was 0.42 seconds faster, though, and the form looks sound enough.

7285 BET ONLINE @ WILLIAMHILL.CO.UK H'CAP — 1m 5f 194y(P)
1:50 (1:52) (Class 6) (0-60,60) 3-Y-O+ — £2,047 (£604; £302) Stalls Low

Form — RPR

4125 **1** **Young Scotton**[20] 7110 7-9-1 55 .... AndrewElliott(3) 4 — 64
(J D Bethell) *chsd ldr tl led over 2f out: rdn clr over 1f out: styd on* **17/2**

0336 **2** 3 **Opera Writer (IRE)**[25] 7046 4-9-5 56 .... GeorgeBaker 9 — 61
(R Hollinshead) *hld up: hdwy over 1f out: sn rdn: r.o: nt rch wnr* **9/1**

4332 **3** hd **Capitalise (IRE)**[44] 6383 4-9-2 56 .... JerryO'Dwyer(3) 6 — 61
(V Smith) *chsd ldrs: rdn over 2f out: edgd lft over 1f out: styd on same pce fnl f* **10/3**[1]

4423 **4** hd **Squirtle (IRE)**[14] 7172 4-8-4 46 .... KirstyMilczarek(5) 5 — 50
(W M Brisbourne) *s.i.s: hld up: hdwy whn rdr dropped whip over 1f out: r.o: nt rch ldrs* **4/1**[2]

351 **5** ½ **Little Richard (IRE)**[14] 7172 8-9-4 55 .... (p) AdamKirby 13 — 59
(M Wellings) *a.p: rdn to chse wnr over 1f out: no ex ins fnl f* **6/1**[3]

3 **6** 3 **All Native (IRE)**[23] 7081 8-8-9 46 .... (t) PatCosgrave 1 — 45
(C P Donoghue, Ire) *prom: rdn to chse wnr 2f out: edgd lft: wknd ins fnl f* **7/1**

1035 **7** ¾ **Ronsard (IRE)**[14] 7172 5-8-11 55 .... RichardEvans(7) 12 — 53
(P D Evans) *s.i.s: hld up: rdn over 2f out: n.d* **12/1**

0360 **8** 7 **Don Jose (USA)**[146] 4253 4-8-12 49 .... SamHitchcott 11 — 37
(N J Vaughan) *led: clr 10f out: rdn and hdd over 2f out: wknd over 1f out* **16/1**

0040 **9** 3 **Reminiscent (IRE)**[14] 7172 8-8-13 50 .... (p) PaulMulrennan 2 — 34
(B P J Baugh) *hld up: rdn and wknd over 2f out* **20/1**

1000 **10** 1 ¼ **Vanishing Dancer (SWI)**[65] 2860 10-9-2 60 .... PietroRomeo(7) 8 — 43
(Mrs D Thomas) *hld up: bhd fnl 4f* **50/1**

0505 **11** 2 ½ **Phoenix Hill (IRE)**[19] 7120 5-8-13 50 .... DaneO'Neill 7 — 29
(D R Gandolfo) *hld up: rdn and wknd over 2f out* **20/1**

003 **12** 24 **Welcome Cat (USA)**[9] 7226 3-9-2 60 .... (b) DanielTudhope 10 — 5
(A D Brown) *hld up: racd keenly: hdwy over 7f out: wknd 3f out* **22/1**

3m 7.83s (0.46) **Going Correction** +0.05s/f (Slow)
WFA 3 from 4yo+ 7lb — **12** Ran SP% **119.8**
Speed ratings (Par 101): **100,98,98,98,97 96,95,91,89,89 87,74**
CSF £79.34 CT £310.79 TOTE £10.60: £3.40, £3.10, £1.60; EX 57.20 TRIFECTA Not won..
Owner Elliott Brothers **Bred** Lady Bland & Miss Anthea Gibson-Fleming **Trained** Middleham Moor, N Yorks

FOCUS
A very modest staying handicap and, although the pace set by the clear leader Don Jose was not breakneck, it was solid enough to make this a reasonable test of stamina. Rated through the placed horses, the winner looks to be right back to his best.

7286 CHIPS @ WILLIAMHILLCASINO.COM (S) STKS — 1m 141y(P)
2:20 (2:20) (Class 6) 2-Y-O — £2,047 (£604; £302) Stalls Low

Form — RPR

0 **1** **Mission Control (IRE)**[94] 5780 2-8-12 0 .... PatCosgrave 5 — 58+
(J R Boyle) *s.s: hld up: hmpd wl over 3f out: hdwy over 1f out: sn rdn and hung lft: styd on to ld wl ins fnl f* **5/4**[1]

0542 **2** 1 **Scientific**[21] 7101 2-8-12 57 .... (b) DaleGibson 7 — 56
(R A Fahey) *hld up in tch: chsd ldr over 3f out: led over 1f out: sn rdn: hdd wl ins fnl f* **4/1**[3]

6000 **3** 1 ¾ **Sharps Gold**[31] 6977 2-8-10 50 .... (t) JerryO'Dwyer(3) 6 — 53
(P J McBride) *chsd ldrs: rdn and ev ch 2f out: styd on same pce fnl f* **22/1**

0023 **4** ½ **Just Mossie**[14] 7171 2-8-5 55 .... JackDean(7) 4 — 51
(W G M Turner) *hld up: rdn over 3f out: hdwy over 1f out: no imp fnl f* **11/1**

3330 **5** nk **Tapas Lad (IRE)**[16] 7149 2-8-12 58 .... (v) DavidKinsella 1 — 51
(V Smith) *hld up: nt clr run over 2f out: hdwy over 1f out: sn rdn: nt rch ldrs* **7/2**[2]

0006 **6** 1 ¾ **Nothing Likea Dame**[17] 7142 2-8-7 56 .... LiamJones 9 — 42
(D J Coakley) *led over 7f out: clr 5f out: rdn and hdd over 1f out: wknd ins fnl f* **12/1**

0046 **7** 2 **Sir Joey**[16] 7156 2-8-12 50 .... LPKeniry 2 — 43
(J T Stimpson) *led 1f: chsd ldr tl rdn over 3f out: wknd fnl f* **33/1**

3600 **8** 14 **Melwood Dreams**[18] 7130 2-8-12 50 .... PhillipMakin 3 — 13
(Paul Green) *chsd ldrs 6f* **20/1**

0645 **9** 1 ¾ **Giggling Monkey**[16] 7156 2-8-7 46 .... (b[1]) SaleemGolam 8 — 5
(P D Evans) *hld up: rdn over 3f out: sn rdn and wknd* **20/1**

1m 53.04s (1.28) **Going Correction** +0.05s/f (Slow) — **9** Ran SP% **119.5**
Speed ratings (Par 94): **96,95,93,93,92 91,89,77,75**
CSF £6.24 TOTE £2.20: £1.20, £1.70, £7.90; EX 9.00 Trifecta £69.80 Part won. Pool: £98.40 - 0.74 winning tickets..The winner was bought in for 10,500gns. Scientific was claimed by George Prodromou for £6,000.
Owner M Khan X2 **Bred** Darley **Trained** Epsom, Surrey

FOCUS
A modest seller and not very competitive either, but quite a dramatic event with the gambled-on winner overcoming all sorts of trouble to score. The performances of the runner-up and third limit the value of the form.

NOTEBOOK
Mission Control(IRE), who showed a glimmer of ability at this track on his only outing for Mark Johnston, was very well backed but could hardly have faced so many obstacles before eventually winning. Firstly, he fell out of the stalls and found himself stone last. Then he got into all sorts of trouble when trying to make headway exiting the back straight and was forced to circle the entire field to get a run, so the fact that he managed to maintain his effort to get up near the line means that he can be rated a good deal better than the official margin. He can probably hold his own in better company than this, an opinion shared by his connections who went to 10,500gns to get him back. (op 5-2 tchd 11-4)
Scientific had experience on his side and had run well over this course and distance in his last start. He came through to win his race and did not do much wrong, apart from run about a bit once in front, and can count himself unlucky to run into an unexposed rival in a race like this who will probably turn out to be rather better than a plater. There should be an ordinary seller in him. (op 10-3 tchd 3-1)
Sharps Gold had every chance and ran better than she has done of late, especially based on adjusted official ratings, but her penalty for winning a bad seller at Lingfield in September is proving too much of a handicap. (op 16-1)

Just Mossie, back up in trip after a couple of spins over 6f, had been shaping as though he would appreciate it but he never landed a blow and this effort did not really prove his stamina one way or the other. (op 8-1)

Tapas Lad(IRE), who has become totally exposed, was still going within himself when caught in traffic on the turn for home, but he did manage to reach the heels of the leaders after being switched inside and it would be wrong to make too many excuses for him. (op 4-1 tchd 10-3)

Giggling Monkey Official explanation: jockey said filly hung right

7287 HEADS-UP @ WILLIAMHILLPOKER.COM H'CAP 1m 1f 103y(P)

2:50 (2:50) (Class 2) (0-100,86) 3-Y-0+

£9,971 (£2,985; £1,492; £747; £372; £187) **Stalls** Low

Form				RPR
5111	1		**Hoh Wotanite**[30] 7002 4-8-11 82.....................(v) RussellKennemore(5) 1 (R Hollinshead) *hld up: hdwy and nt clr run over 2f out: rdn to ld over 1f out: sn hung rt: r.o* **7/2**[2]	90
3106	2	½	**Just Bond (IRE)**[23] 7074 5-9-1 86.................................. SladeO'Hara(5) 5 (G R Oldroyd) *hld up: hdwy over 2f out: rdn to chse wnr and hung rt fnl f: r.o* **4/1**[3]	93
0501	3	3	**Will He Wish**[62] 6568 11-9-2 82..................................... PaulMulrennan 4 (S Gollings) *chsd ldr: rdn and ev ch over 1f out: styd on same pce fnl f* **18/1**	83
6045	4	1 ¼	**Cupid's Glory**[15] 7163 5-8-11 77.. LPKeniry 2 (Mrs L C Jewell) *chsd ldr tl led over 2f out: rdn and hdd over 1f out: nt clr run sn after: no ex* **11/1**	75
1441	5	1 ¾	**Gaelic Princess**[12] 7193 7-8-13 79.................................. DaneO'Neill 6 (A G Newcombe) *trckd ldrs: rdn and hung lft over 1f out: wknd fnl f* **6/1**	73
1111	6	8	**Lobengula (IRE)**[16] 7160 5-9-5 85................................ DanielTudhope 3 (I W McInnes) *led: hung rt: rdn and hdd over 2f out: wknd over 1f out* **6/4**[1]	63

2m 1.32s (-1.30) **Going Correction** +0.05s/f (Slow) **6** Ran SP% **110.1**
Speed ratings (Par 109): **107,106,103,102,101 94**
CSF £16.94 TOTE £4.40: £2.30, £2.00; EX 16.00.

Owner The Three R'S **Bred** Dunchurch Lodge Stud Co **Trained** Upper Longdon, Staffs

FOCUS

A decent little handicap featuring several course specialists and a few of these came into the race at the top of their game. The early pace was by no means strong, but despite that the front pair both came from the back of the field and the final time was perfectly reasonable under the circumstances. The form looks sound enough rated through the runner-up.

NOTEBOOK

Hoh Wotanite, raised another 4lb in his bid for a four-timer, would have preferred an even stronger pace and was very keen in the first half of the contest, but despite that he made full use of the dream gap which appeared against the inside rail turning for home. He did tend to hang once in front, but nothing like as much as the runner-up and that may have made the difference. He absolutely adores this track. (op 10-3 tchd 3-1)

Just Bond(IRE), another course specialist, was switched off out the back alongside the eventual winner and was brought with his effort on the outside, whilst his main rival enjoyed the inside route. It looked for much of the home straight as though he would prevail, but despite his rider's best efforts he hung right over to the stands' rail and may have lost about as much ground as he was beaten by. (op 6-1)

Will He Wish, raised a whopping 9lb for his victory over 7f here in October, had run twice over hurdles and once in a bumper at the very start of his career, but this was the longest trip he had attemped in his 63rd outing on the level. He was not ridden as though stamina was thought to be an issue and had every chance, but could not go with the front pair down the home straight. (op 14-1)

Cupid's Glory ◆, down another 4lb and racing at this track for only the second time against a field of track specialists, led the field into the straight but was already beaten when the winner crossed him a furlong out. He may be a shadow of his former self, but it would not be a surprise if he were to drop to a mark he can win off sooner rather than later. (op 14-1)

Gaelic Princess, up 2lb for her recent Lingfield victory, had every chance but did not get home and probably found this company a bit too hot. (op 5-1)

Lobengula(IRE), winner of his last four starts, all over this course and distance, was up another 3lb in his bid for a five-timer. He certainly enjoyed the run of the race as he managed to gain the unconstested lead that is so important to him, but the distress signals were being sent out rounding the home bend as he started to hang and was quickly swamped. This was a tame end to his prolific spell, but perhaps this was his way of saying that he needs a rest. Official explanation: trainer said gelding hung right throughout and may have been feeling the effects of a busy campaign (op 11-8 tchd 7-4)

7288 PLAY BACKGAMMON @ WILLHILL.COM MAIDEN STKS 7f 32y(P)

3:20 (3:20) (Class 5) 2-Y-0 **£2,968** (£876; £438) **Stalls** High

Form				RPR
5220	1		**Glittering Prize (UAE)**[62] 6572 2-8-12 69.......................... GregFairley 4 (M Johnston) *a.p: chsd ldr 1/2-way: led over 2f out: rdn clr over 1f out* **6/4**[2]	68+
0022	2	6	**Molly Ann (IRE)**[17] 7140 2-8-12 69..................................... DavidAllan 3 (T D Easterby) *led: rdn and hdd over 2f out: wknd fnl f* **5/6**[1]	53
00	3	½	**Hollow Point (IRE)**[19] 7121 2-9-0 0............................. AndrewElliott(3) 5 (M Johnston) *s.s: outpcd: nvr nrr* **16/1**[3]	57
0	4	shd	**Gayanula (USA)**[24] 7058 2-8-13 0 ow1............................. PhillipMakin 1 (Miss J A Camacho) *chsd ldrs: rdn over 2f out: sn edgd lft and wknd* **20/1**	53
000	5	11	**Validity**[72] 6329 2-8-9 45.. PatrickMathers(3) 2 (A J McCabe) *chsd ldr over 5f out tl rdn 1/2-way: wknd over 2f out* **66/1**	25

1m 31.35s (0.95) **Going Correction** +0.05s/f (Slow) **5** Ran SP% **106.7**
Speed ratings (Par 96): **96,89,88,88,75**
CSF £2.83 TOTE £2.30: £2.00, £1.02; EX 3.10.

Owner Sheikh Mohammed **Bred** Darley **Trained** Middleham Moor, N Yorks

FOCUS

A very uncompetitive maiden which was basically a match, and with the odds-on favourite disappointing there could only be one winner so the form probably adds up to little.

NOTEBOOK

Glittering Prize(UAE), who showed a little ability in a couple of races on turf but was very disappointing last time, had little difficulty in picking off her only serious rival before bounding right away. She seemed to relish the surface, but the favourite probably failed to run her race leaving her with nothing to beat, so the form means little and she lacks scope. (op 11-8)

Molly Ann(IRE) finished runner-up for the third successive time on sand, but in truth this was a disappointing effort as she offered little resistance to the winner once headed, and the proximity of the third and fourth strongly suggests she did not run her race. (op Evens)

Hollow Point(IRE), a stablemate of the winner, was never going to win but can be given a little extra credit for this effort as he gave away a huge amount of ground at the start. He now qualifies for a mark and from his point of view hopefully this performance will be rated through the winner rather than the second. (op 12-1)

Gayanula(USA) looks very moderate, but at least she did show a bit of early pace this time. She may be capable of a bit more once handicapped. (tchd 16-1)

7289 CALL HOUSE @ WILLIAMHILLBINGO.COM H'CAP 7f 32y(P)

3:50 (3:50) (Class 4) (0-85,81) 3-Y-0+ **£4,857** (£1,445; £722; £360) **Stalls** High

Form				RPR
3260	1		**Red Romeo**[31] 6981 6-8-13 76...................................... DanielTudhope 2 (N Wilson) *led 1f: chsd ldr tl led over 2f out: rdn clr over 1f out: jst hld on* **14/1**	83
3020	2	nk	**Danetime Lord (IRE)**[15] 7165 4-9-1 78....................(p) PaulMulrennan 4 (K A Ryan) *chsd ldrs: lost pl 3f out: rallied 2f out: sn hung lft: r.o u.p* **14/1**	84
0656	3	1	**Monkey Glas (IRE)**[27] 7017 3-8-9 75........................... AndrewElliott(3) 1 (K R Burke) *led 6f out: hdd over 2f out: sn rdn: styd on* **7/2**[2]	78
3303	4	2 ½	**Angaric (IRE)**[25] 7045 4-8-9 75................................... MarkLawson(3) 3 (B Smart) *trckd ldrs: rdn over 1f out: styd on same pce* **13/2**[3]	71
1424	5	shd	**Divertimenti (IRE)**[109] 5367 3-8-12 75.................................. LPKeniry 6 (C R Dore) *hld up: nt clr run over 2f out: hdwy over 1f out: nt trble ldrs* **16/1**	71
0022	6	1 ½	**Resplendent Alpha**[10] 7212 3-9-2 79........................... TGMcLaughlin 7 (P Howling) *s.s: rdn over 2f out: n.d* **7/1**	71
2221	7	3 ½	**Teasing**[16] 7158 3-9-3 80.. PatCosgrave 5 (J Pearce) *hld up: rdn over 2f out: n.d* **13/8**[1]	63
0364	8	7	**Buy On The Red**[31] 6981 6-9-4 81..............................(p) SaleemGolam 8 (W R Muir) *chsd ldrs: rdn 1/2-way: wknd 2f out* **15/2**	45

1m 29.31s (-1.09) **Going Correction** +0.05s/f (Slow) **8** Ran SP% **117.1**
Speed ratings (Par 105): **108,107,106,103,103 101,97,89**
CSF £190.36 CT £843.27 TOTE £17.00: £4.00, £2.80, £1.70; EX 87.90 TRIFECTA Not won. Place 6 £13.13, Place 5 £7.05.

Owner Six Pound Note Club **Bred** J O'Mulloy **Trained** Flaxton, N Yorks

FOCUS

A fair handicap with which to end the 2007 Flat season. The pace was solid, those that raced handily were favoured, and the form looks reliable enough for the level.

Teasing Official explanation: jockey was unable to explain the poor run

T/Plt: £22.60 to a £1 stake. Pool: £66,098.25. 2,129.25 winning tickets. T/Qpdt: £12.90 to a £1 stake. Pool: £4,597.40. 262.10 winning tickets. CR

INDEX TO FLAT RACING

Horses are shown in alphabetical order; the trainer's name follows the name of the horse. The figures to the right are current master ratings for all-weather and turf; the all-weather rating is preceded by the letter 'a'.Underneath the horse's name is its age, colour and sex in abbreviated format e.g. 6 b g indicates the horse is six-years-old, bay in colour, and a gelding.The descriptive details are followed by the race numbers of the races in which it has taken part in chronological order; a superscript figure indicates its finishing position in that race (brackets indicate it was the winner of the race).

Aahayson *K R Burke* a86 109
3 b c Noverre(USA) —See You Later (Emarati (USA))
760[10] 1099[2] 1500[5] (1623) (1802) 2035[5] (3104) 4438a[4] 6071a[8]
Aah Haa *John Joseph Murphy* 60
2 b c King's Best(USA) —Snowtop (Thatching)
3438a[14]
Aaim For Applause *M R Channon* 81
2 b c Royal Applause—Picot (Piccolo)
2193[2] 2624[2] 2977[3] 3479[3] 3962[3] 4323[2] 4636[2] 4923[5] 5575[7] 5856[6]
Aaim To Storm (USA) *M R Channon* 83
2 ch g Storm Boot(USA) —Lenient (USA) (Mt. Livermore (USA))
1469[4] (1706) 2009[2] 2732[13] 3462[4] 3669[2] 3938[4] 4057[7] 5551[3]
Aaim To Succeed (IRE) *M R Channon* a58 71
2 b f Montjeu(IRE) —Dicharachera (Mark Of Esteem (IRE))
3270[6] 4947[7] 5596[6]
Aajel (USA) *M P Tregoning* a77 100
3 gr c Aljabr(USA) —Awtaan (USA) (Arazi (USA))
(386) 638[6] 1987[3] 4288[3] (5574)
Aaliyah (IRE) *E J Creighton*
4 b m Fasliyev(USA) —Rosie (FR) (Bering)
3732[9] 4312[13]
Aaron's Way *A W Carroll* 64
3 gb f Act One—Always On My Mind (Distant Relative)
1408[10] 2515[7] 2718[5] 3369[8] 3713[3]
Abadia *J G Given* a30 38
3 b f Bahamian Bounty—Shafaq (USA) (Dayjur (USA))
998[7] 1282[10] 1558[7] 1943[6] 2661[7] 3789[14] 7124[10]
Abandon (USA) *W J Haggas* a86 88
4 ch m Rahy(USA) —Caerless (IRE) (Caerleon (USA))
(1414)
Abbashiva (GER) *P Rau*
2 b c Tiger Hill(IRE) —Abba (GER) (Goofalik (USA))
6219a[3]
Abbey Express *M Dods* 52
2 b g Bahamian Bounty—Glimpse (Night Shift (USA))
3341[8] 3781[6] 4221[6] 5081[9] 6305[9]
Abbeygate *T Keddy* a54 47
6 b g Unfuwain(USA) —Ayunli (Chief Singer)
402[4] 4464[6] 5421[8] 6212[4] 6458[8] 6792[3] 7133[8]
Abbondanza (IRE) *I Semple* a92 79
4 b g Cape Cross(IRE) —Ninth Wonder (USA) (Forty Niner (USA))
1939[6] 3093[9] (4932) 5983[6] 6146[4] (6628) (6696) (7061) 7163[8]
Abbotts Account (USA) *Mrs A J Perrett* 54
3 b g Mr Greeley(USA) —Agenda (USA) (Private Account (USA))
1536[8] 2096[8] 3450[7]
Abby Road (IRE) *B J Meehan* 99
3 b f Danehill(USA) —Bells Are Ringing (USA) (Sadler's Wells (USA))
1808[4]
Aberavon *P D Evans* a33 58
2 b f Cadeaux Genereux—Dodo (IRE) (Alzao (USA))
2000[10] 2473[9] 3747[7] 4501[11] 4810[7] 6978[8]
Aberlady Bay (IRE) *T T Clement* a59 45
4 ch m Selkirk(USA) —Desert Serenade (USA) (Green Desert (USA))
2004[11] 2412[7]
Aberlady Lad *B Mactaggart*
2 br c Millkom—Lady El Ee (Komaite (USA))
5081[10] 5675[7]
Abeyance (IRE) *J Noseda* 54
2 ch c Dubai Destination(USA) —Peneia (USA) (Nureyev (USA))
5306[8] 5598[12]
Abfabfong (IRE) *P F I Cole* a50 45
2 b c Dr Fong(USA) —Flatter (IRE) (Barathea (IRE))
1201[9] 1519[5] 2478[10] 4022[5] 5002[7] 6207[10]
Abhisheka (IRE) *Saeed Bin Suroor* 108
4 b m Sadler's Wells(USA) —Snow Bride (USA) (Blushing Groom (FR))
546a[2] 1472[4] 2720[5]
Abientot (IRE) *D W Barker* a47 69
5 b g Danetime(IRE) —Clandolly (IRE) (Burslem)
97[3] 2989[6]
A Big Sky Brewing (USA) *T D Barron* 63
3 b g Arch(USA) —Runalpharun (USA) (Thunder Rumble (USA))
954[10] (1197) 1530[5] 1964[4] 2389[6] 4078[7]
Abitofafath (IRE) *J G Given* a9
2 b g Fath(USA) —Queen's Victory (Mujadil (USA))
5363[13]
Ablaan (USA) *M F De Kock* a86 66
2 ch c Sunday Break(JPN) —La Danzadora (ARG) (El Sembrador (ARG))
4584[11] 5321[8] 6262[2]
Able Mind *D W Thompson* a59 66
7 b g Mind Games—Chlo-Jo (Belmez (USA))
4219[7]
Able One (NZ) *J Moore* 121
5 b g Cape Cross(IRE) —Gardenia (NZ) (Danehill (USA))
7091a[10]
Abolition (USA) *M Johnston* a85 79
2 b c Harlan's Holiday(USA) —Open House (USA) (Deputy Minister (CAN))
1743[2] 2251[4] 3574a[5] (5236) 5590[5] 6001[7]
Aboriginie (USA) *J H M Gosden* a78 74
2 ch c Street Cry(IRE) —Native Roots (IRE) (Indian Ridge)
4393[3] 5200[2] 5538[5] 5919[13]
Abounding *M J Attwater* a72 72
3 b f Generous(IRE) —Ecstasy (Pursuit Of Love)
(2223) 3170[4] 4172[3] 4766[3] 5333[7] 6241[4] 6506[3] (7205)
Aboustar *M Brittain* a48 35
7 b g Abou Zouz(USA) —Three Star Rated (IRE) (Pips Pride)
221[7] 239[5]
Above And Below (IRE) *M Quinn* a58 34
3 b f Key Of Luck(USA) —Saramacca (IRE) (Kahyasi)
816[4] 1232[7] 2607[13] 3057[7]
Aboyne (IRE) *K F Clutterbuck* a54 33
4 b g Mull Of Kintyre(USA) —Never End (Alzao (USA))
5090[13] 5542[8]
Abraham Lincoln (IRE) *A P O'Brien* a95 102
3 b c Danehill(USA) —Moon Drop (Dominion)
(5392a) 5832[9]
Absolute Champion (AUS) *D Hall* 128
6 br g Marauding(NZ) —Beauty Belle (AUS) (Ideal Planet (AUS))
7089a[2]
Absolute Image (IRE) *D K Weld* a48 100
5 gr g Indian Ridge—Absolute Glee (USA) (Kenmare (FR))
3138a[13] 4051a[3]
Absolutelyfabulous (IRE) *David Wachman* 106
4 b m Mozart(IRE) —Lady Windermere (IRE) (Lake Coniston (IRE))
1171a[3] (1461a) 2050a[9] 2379a[3] 2586a[7] 5436a[4]
Absolutelythebest (IRE) *J G M O'Shea* a48 57
6 b g Anabaa(USA) —Recherchee (Rainbow Quest (USA))
5007[12]
Abstract Art (USA) *Miss Venetia Williams* a76 78
4 ch g Distorted Humor(USA) —Code From Heaven (USA) (Lost Code (USA))
1288[7] 1771[13]
Abstract Folly (IRE) *J D Bethell* a67 74
5 b g Rossini(USA) —Cochiti (Kris)
623[8] 3815[5] (4409) 4786[3] 5256[3] 5884[6]
Abtak (IRE) *P Burgoyne* 34
7 b m Royal Abjar(USA) —Takhiyra (Vayrann)
1501[7] 5121[11] 5315[10]
Abunai *R Charlton* a91 85
3 ch f Pivotal—Ingozi (Warning)
3944[8] 4607[7] 5092[3] 5635[3] 6006[2] 6836[2]
Abwaab *Eve Johnson Houghton* a59 86
4 br g Agnes World(USA) —Flitteriss Park (Beldale Flutter (USA))
1060[11] (1545) 2318[7] 2725[4] 4367[3] 4585[8] 4816[12] 5923[10] 6122[9]
Abydos *Saeed Bin Suroor* a73 83
3 b c King's Best(USA) —Polska (USA) (Danzig (USA))
4457[3] 4815[5] 5562[2] 6005[2] (6286)
Abyla *M P Tregoning* a68 69
3 b f Rock Of Gibraltar(IRE) —Animatrice (USA) (Alleged (USA))
2455[3] 3365[2] 4205[10] 5500[11]
Acapulco (IRE) *A P O'Brien* 113
3 b c Galileo(IRE) —Harasava (FR) (Darshaan)
1475[2] 2235[9] 4692[4] 5408[8] 5831[6]
Acapulco Bay *Miss J A Camacho* a51 47
3 b g Pursuit Of Love—Lapu-Lapu (Prince Sabo)
807[2] 1261[5] 1746[8] 3914[6] 6247[13] 6464[4]
Acceleration (IRE) *Karen McLintock* a51 61
7 b g Groom Dancer(USA) —Overdrive (Shirley Heights)
4[6]
Accent (IRE) *Miss Tor Sturgis* a13 14
4 b g Beckett(IRE) —Umlaut (Zafonic (USA))
1947[13]
Accentuate (IRE) *Charles O'Brien* a84 84
3 b c Danehill(USA) —Arcade (Rousillon (USA))
5460a[5] 5788a[9]
Accolation *Pat Eddery* a52 49
3 b g Royal Applause—Jasmine Breeze (Saddlers' Hall (IRE))
6238[7] 6830[3] 7159[4] 7265[6]
Accordello (IRE) *K G Reveley* 63
6 b m Accordion—Marello (Supreme Leader)
913[8]
According To Pete *J M Jefferson* 79
6 b g Accordion—Magic Bloom (Full Of Hope)
6158[3] 6473[13]
Accumulus *Noel T Chance* 50
7 b g Cloudings(IRE) —Norstock (Norwick (USA))
2981[5]
Accusation (IRE) *L M Cumani* a59 64
3 b f Barathea(IRE) —Uncertain Affair (IRE) (Darshaan)
5678[4] 6204[2] 6821[5] 7080[8]
Accused (IRE) *J Noseda* 71
2 b g Xaar—Danedrop (IRE) (Danehill (USA))
4818[3] 5397a[19] 5971[9]
Ace (IRE) *S Seemar* 118
6 b h Danehill(USA) —Tea House (Sassafras (FR))
330a[2] 600a[12]
Ace Baby *K J Burke* a17 52
4 b g First Trump—Mise En Scene (Lugana Beach)
525[8]
Acece *D K Ivory* a52
3 b c Muthahb(IRE) —Berry Brook (Magic Ring (IRE))
304[11] 537[10] 907[13] 2697[15] 2801[12] 6830[6] 7019[11]
Ace Club *S Parr* a57 23
6 ch g Indian Rocket—Presently (Cadeaux Genereux)
59[7] (430) 5621[11] 580[5] 668[10] (7283)
Acela (IRE) *R A Fahey*
2 ch f Hawk Wing(USA) —Altishaan (Darshaan)
7121[10]
Ace Of Hearts *C F Wall* a76 108
8 b g Magic Ring(IRE) —Lonely Heart (Midyan (USA))
1145[13] 1494[5] 2123[6] 2755[22] (4153) 4377[2] 4900[3] 5419[6] 6011[19]
Ace Of Spies (IRE) *M Johnston* a75
2 br c Machiavellian(USA) —Nadia (Nashwan (USA))
7051[7] 7145[3]
Aces High (NZ) *Tom Cowan* 87
6 b m Generous(IRE) —Sitting Pat (NZ) (Full On Aces (AUS))
6711a[9]
Acheekyone (IRE) *B J Meehan* a93 97
4 b g Indian Ridge—Tafrah (IRE) (Sadler's Wells (USA))
1145[6] 1524[6] 1842[12] 2476[5]
Achilles Of Troy (IRE) *A P O'Brien* 103
2 b c Danehill Dancer(IRE) —Twice The Ease (Green Desert (USA))
(1498) 2049a[4] 2737[14] 5324[2] 5975[5]
Achill Island (IRE) *A P O'Brien* 108
2 b c Sadler's Wells(USA) —Prawn Cocktail (USA) (Artichoke (USA))
5795[2] 6484a[2]
Acknowledgement *Carl Llewellyn* a65 77
5 b g Josr Algarhoud(IRE) —On Request (IRE) (Be My Guest (USA))
1526[10]
Acosta *Dr J R J Naylor* a40 50
3 b c Foxhound(USA) —Dancing Heights (IRE) (High Estate)
1633[7] 2081[6] 3450[6] 4595[6] 4961[6] 5311[6]
Acotango (GER) *Frau E Mader* 77
2 ch c Pentire—Anna Of Russia (GER) (Acatenango (GER))
5028a[7]
Acquifer *J L Dunlop* a73 72
2 b f Oasis Dream—Llyn Gwynant (Persian Bold)
3895[6] 4602[10] 5277[5] 6225[3] 6847[4]
Acropolis (IRE) *I Semple* 98
6 b g Sadler's Wells(USA) —Dedicated Lady (IRE) (Pennine Walk)
1109[5] 1805[3] 2462[4] 2859[11] 4117[7] 4376[3] 4690[8]
Actabou *M Dods* 74
2 b c Tobougg(IRE) —Carreamia (Weldnaas (USA))
4890[8] 5501[2] 6281[12]
Actilius (IRE) *M Botti* a67 50
3 gr c Medicean—Afto (USA) (Relaunch (USA))
3113[5] 3382[5] 4334[4]
Action Plan (AUS) *L Smith* 98
5 ch g Distorted Humor(USA) —Tondela (AUS) (Blazing Sword (AUS))
15a[9]
Active Asset (IRE) *M Quinn* a89 91
5 ch g Sinndar(IRE) —Sacristy (Godswalk (USA))
726[3] (829) 940[15] 1356[6] 1542[2] 2002[3] 2314[4] 3509[13] 3959[8] 4194[6] 4366[4] 4609[4] 4917[7] 5362[5] 5543[8] 5892[4] 6357[5]
Activist *D Carroll* a55 65
9 ch g Diesis—Shicklah (USA) (The Minstrel (CAN))
607[9] 677[9] 730[5] 767[11] 909[7] 1362[4] 1570[2] 1730[5]
Activity (IRE) *M J Gingell* a74 84
8 gr g Pennekamp(USA) —Actoris (USA) (Diesis)
(70) 151[2] 308[5] 367[9] 675[3] 770[3]
Activo (FR) *S Dow* a87 86
6 b g Trempolino(USA) —Acerbis (GER) (Rainbow Quest (USA))
164[7] 587[7]
Actodos (IRE) *B R Millman* a82 86
3 ro g Act One—Really Gifted (IRE) (Cadeaux Genereux)
(1030) 1584[3] 2185[3] 2816[13]
Act Sirius (IRE) *J Howard Johnson* 74
3 ch g Grand Lodge(USA) —Folgore (USA) (Irish River (FR))
1827[12] 3379[5]
Act Three *Mouse Hamilton-Fairley* 60
3 br f Beat Hollow—Rada's Daughter (Robellino (USA))
1217[5] 3847[6] 6420[10]
Actuality *Patrick Martin* a60 68
5 b g So Factual(USA) —Cottage Maid (Inchinor)
4865a[12]
Acuzio *W M Brisbourne* a59 67
6 b g Mon Tresor—Veni Vici (IRE) (Namaqualand (USA))
2531[2] 2935[2] 3533[4] 4124[4] 4194[4] 4558[3] 4732[3] 4994[5]
Adab (IRE) *J H M Gosden* 67
2 b c Invincible Spirit(IRE) —Acate (IRE) (Classic Music (USA))
1631[2]
Adabi *M P Tregoning* a63 47
3 b g Soviet Star(USA) —Clincher Club (Polish Patriot (USA))
208[11] 418[7] 1633[6]
Adage *David Pinder* a65 65
4 b m Vettori(IRE) —Aymara (Darshaan)
1026[11] 1254[5] (1730) 2142[2] 3047[6] (3598) 4067[9] (5364) 5779[6] 6271[6]
Adagio (BEL) *Andre Hermans* a70
2 b c Pyramus(USA) —Sweet Melody (BEL) (Sizzling Melody)
7027a[6]
Adamantinos *Frau E Mader* 96
3 b c Seattle Dancer(USA) —Aberdeen (GER) (Polish Precedent (USA))
4869a[5]
Adam Eterno (IRE) *A B Haynes* a52 48
2 ch g Spartacus(IRE) —Mermaid Melody (Machiavellian (USA))
1832[19] 2410[8] 2632[8] 3065[9] 4963[6] 5302[9] (5572) 5869[10] 6207[7] 6433[14] 6928[4] 7101[6]
Adantino *B R Millman* a81 87
8 b g Glory Of Dancer—Sweet Whisper (Petong)
419[4] 575[10] 697[4] 1063[3] 1200[3] 1545[2] 1971[4] (2318) 3104[12] 3481[15] 3802[5] 4456[8] 4965[8] 5223[10] 5648[7] 5874[4]
Adaptation *M Johnston* 86
3 b f Spectrum(IRE) —Key Academy (Royal Academy (USA))
1623[4] 2577[8] 3437[9] 4222[4]
Adare (GER) *T P Tate* 55
4 b g Saddlers' Hall(IRE) —Aughamore Beauty (IRE) (Dara Monarch)
2118[6]
Ada River *A M Balding* 64
2 b f Dansili—Miss Meltemi (IRE) (Miswaki Tern (USA))
6649[6]
Addictive *S C Williams* 68
3 b f Averti(IRE) —Shadow Bird (Martinmas)
2834[16] 3384[13] 4339[15]
Addikt (IRE) *S Kirk* a68 67
2 b c Diktat—Frond (Alzao (USA))
3991[7] 5344[6] 5937[5] 6584[3] 6973[4]
Addwaitya *C F Wall* a47 62
2 b c Xaar—Three White Sox (Most Welcome)
5771[14] 6119[13] 6469[6]
Adeje (IRE) *C G Cox* 20
2 b c Mull Of Kintyre(USA) —Comet Dust (Ezzoud (IRE))
6234[11]
Adenium (IRE) *W R Swinburn* a68
3 b g Desert Style(IRE) —Kelsey Rose (Most Welcome)
1166[7] 1440[3] 1904[4]
Adil (KSA) *J Gardel* a97
3 gr c Torrey Canyon(USA) —Bel Native (USA) (Mill Native (USA))
859a[3]
Adjami (IRE) *John A Harris* 47
6 b g Entrepreneur—Adjriyna (Top Ville)
3467[8] 3844[5] 4493[11]
Adlerflug (GER) *J Hirschberger* 120
3 ch c In The Wings—Aiyana (GER) (Last Tycoon (IRE))
(3146a) 5077a[2]
Admiral (IRE) *T J Pitt* 94
6 b g Alhaarth(IRE) —Coast Is Clear (IRE) (Rainbow Quest (USA))
1582[15]
Admiralcollingwood *J J Quinn* 55
2 b g Reel Buddy(USA) —Chocolate (IRE) (Brief Truce (USA))
3995[6] 5521[8] 5745[10] 6462[5]
Admiral Compton *B Storey* a64 66
6 ch g Compton Place—Sunfleet (Red Sunset)
2820[9]
Admiral Dundas (IRE) *W Jarvis* a68
2 b c Noverre(USA) —Brandish (Warning)
7191[5]
Admiralofthefleet (USA) *A P O'Brien* 115
3 b c Danehill(USA) —Rafina (USA) (Mr Prospector (USA))
948a[7] (1617) 2235[10] 3331[5] 4412a[4]
Admiral Savannah (IRE) *T D Easterby* 51
3 b g Dilshaan—Valmarana (USA) (Danzig Connection (USA))
2552[5] 3159[4] 3792[12] 4230[2] 4821[4]
Admiral's Cruise (USA) *B J Meehan* 116
5 b h A.P. Indy(USA) —Ladies Cruise (USA) (Fappiano (USA))
1144[5] 1495[2] 2856[4] 3461[9] 5589[5]
Admirals Way *C N Kellett* a13 45
2 ch g Observatory(USA) —Dockage (CAN) (Riverman (USA))
6065[10] 6409[13]
Admire Moon (JPN) *H Matsuda* 127
4 b h End Sweep(USA) —My Katies (JPN) (Sunday Silence (USA))
(862a) (6943a)
Adobe *W M Brisbourne* a54 63
12 b g Green Desert(USA) —Shamshir (Kris)
1539[5] 2214[11] 2490[11] 2716[12] 4966[7] 5708[10]
Adonita *H-A Pantall* a85 88
3 b f Singspiel(IRE) —Anna Palariva (IRE) (Caerleon (USA))
7049a[6]
Adopted Hero (IRE) *G L Moore* a49 76
7 b g Sadler's Wells(USA) —Lady Liberty (NZ) (Noble Bijou (USA))
2236[14] 2736[17]
Adorabella (IRE) *A King* a57 73
4 b m Revoque(IRE) —Febrile (USA) (Trempolino (USA))
2766[10] 3365[4] 4630[2] 5271[4] 6132[4]
Adorabile Fong *M Guarnieri* 96
4 b h Dr Fong(USA) —Divine Secret (Hernando (FR))
6687a[9]

Adore Moi *R W Price* 16
5 b m Keen—Dominuet (Dominion)
2153^{13} 4707^{7}

A Dream Come True *D K Ivory* a60
2 b f Where Or When(IRE) —Katy Ivory (IRE) (Night Shift (USA))
3213^{14} 3453^{4} 4273^{5} 5117^{9}

Advanced *K A Ryan* a105 119
4 b h Night Shift(USA) —Wonderful World (GER) (Dashing Blade)
1159^{5} 4150^{16} 4438a^{7} 4747^{2} 5214^{10} (5616) 6018^{4} 6338^{5} 6633a^{2} 6758^{9}

Advancement *R A Fahey* a73 75
4 b g Second Empire(IRE) —Lambast (Relkino)
1751^{7} 2550^{10} 2871^{6} 3301^{2} 3888^{4} 4732^{9} 5000^{14}

Adventuress *B J Meehan* a92 91
4 b m Singspiel(IRE) —Arriving (Most Welcome)
941^{9} 1287^{5} 1649^{3} 2123^{7} 2883^{10}

Adversane *J L Dunlop* a71 71
3 ch g Alhaarth(IRE) —Cragreen (Green Desert (USA))
1039^{2} 1810^{6} 2628^{3} 3473^{7} 3969^{8}

Adversity *Sir Michael Stoute* a78
2 b c Oasis Dream—Tuxford Hideaway (Cawston's Clown)
5498^{2} (6530)

Advertisement *C G Cox* 73
2 b g Averti(IRE) —Adhaaba (USA) (Dayjur (USA))
1469^{3} 2086^{2} 2510^{6} 3363^{11} 4903^{12} 5534^{7}

Advice *Saeed Bin Suroor* a58 109
6 b g Seeking The Gold(USA) —Anna Palariva (IRE) (Caerleon (USA))
413a^{7} 531a^{9}

Aegean Dancer *B Smart* a105 102
5 b g Piccolo—Aegean Flame (Anshan)
(1134) 1574^{3} 1854^{8} (2463) 4386^{10} 5044^{2} 5689^{4} 6487^{2} 6758^{7} *(6876)*

Aegean Prince *W R Muir* a84 84
3 b c Dr Fong(USA) —Dizzydaisy (Sharpo)
1275^{2} 1956^{8} 3235^{10} 4092^{16} 4551^{3} *5099^{6}* 5775^{5} 6110^{7}

Aegis (IRE) *B W Hills* a78 80
3 b g Beckett(IRE) —Silver Spoon (IRE) (College Chapel)
1440^{6} (1716) 2305^{6} 3689^{5} 4197^{7} 4510^{7} 4960^{7} 5307^{5} 5865^{5}

Aerialist *A Berry* 51
2 b f Mind Games—Polar Fair (Polar Falcon (USA))
6073^{8} 6384^{5} 6557^{P} (Dead)

Aeroplane *P W Chapple-Hyam* 110
4 b h Danehill Dancer(IRE) —Anita At Dawn (IRE) (Anita's Prince)
5416^{7}

Aesop (GER) *C Von Der Recke* 64
6 ch g Green Tune(USA) —Alisa (GER) (Daun (GER))
494a^{3}

Afaf (FR) *M Delzangles* 106
5 br m Spectrum(IRE) —Halawa (IRE) (Dancing Brave (USA))
397a^{8} 546a^{8}

Affiliation (IRE) *R Hannon* a60 56
3 b f Danehill Dancer(IRE) —Latin Beauty (IRE) (Sadler's Wells (USA))
1468^{6} 1726^{5} *2178^{2}*

Affirmatively *D R C Elsworth* a62 69
2 b f Diktat—Circlet (Lion Cavern (USA))
1101^{7} (1354) 1608^{4} 2812^{19} *6973^{10}*

Affrettando (IRE) *J A R Toller* a63 60
3 b g Danetime(IRE) —Trading Aces (Be My Chief (USA))
2593^{3} 3425^{3} 4905^{5} *(7029) 7253^{10}*

Afghan (USA) *S Seemar* a84 62
9 ch g Hennessy(USA) —Affirm The Gold (USA) (Golden Act (USA))
329a^{15}

A Foot In Front *N Tinkler* 23
3 b g Sugarfoot—Scoffera (Scottish Reel)
1912^{13}

Afrad (FR) *N J Henderson* 96
6 gr g Linamix(FR) —Afragha (IRE) (Darshaan)
1582^{16} 2736^{6} 4056^{2} 6335^{9}

Afram Blue *W J Knight* a79 61
2 b g Fraam—Tup Tim (Emperor Jones (USA))
2539^{4} *(3424) 6823^{4} 7016^{3} 7222^{3}*

African Concerto (IRE) *S Kirk* a65 54
4 b g Mozart(IRE) —Out Of Africa (IRE) (Common Grounds)
1729^{8} 1899^{10} *2331^{12}*

African Flight *M L W Bell* 64
2 b f Hawk Wing(USA) —Valiantly (Anabaa (USA))
6254^{4} 6470^{9} 6724^{6}

African Pursuits (USA) *H Morrison* a51 65
3 b g Johannesburg(USA) —Woodland Orchid (IRE) (Woodman (USA))
1523^{12} 1995^{2} 6597^{6} *7224^{10}*

African Rose *Mme C Head-Maarek* 99
2 ch f Observatory(USA) —New Orchid (USA) (Quest For Fame)
5493a^{3} 6416a^{3}

African Storm (IRE) *T McLaughlin* a51 49
5 b g Fasliyev(USA) —Out Of Africa (IRE) (Common Grounds)
6730^{4} *7020^{9} 7238^{3}*

Afric Star *John A Harris* a27 27
3 b f Woodborough(USA) —America Star (Norwick (USA))
1912^{10} 2718^{12} *3597^{10}* 4226^{18} 4488^{9}

After Market (USA) *J Shirreffs* 123
4 bb h Storm Cat(USA) —Tranquility Lake (USA) (Rahy (USA))
5823a^{2}

After Nine *F Watson*
3 b f Classic Cliche(IRE) —Eponine (Sharpo)
2420^{7} 3415^{7}

After The Show *Rae Guest* a82 83
6 b g Royal Applause—Tango Teaser (Shareef Dancer (USA))
432^{7} 3452^{6} 3791^{3} 4486^{4} 4816^{7} *5387^{5}* 6103^{3} 6283^{4} *6762^{8} 7221^{3}*

Afton View (IRE) *D J Murphy* a61 63
2 gr g Clodovil(IRE) —Moonlight Partner (IRE) (Red Sunset)
4733^{6} 5399^{5} 5521^{6} 5745^{8} *7149^{4} 7245^{3}*

Agent Eleven (IRE) *A J Lidderdale* a40 47
4 b g Desert Story(IRE) —Elizabethan Air (Elegant Air)
1950^{8} 2666^{6}

Agente Romano (USA) *G A Butler* a75
2 bb c Street Cry(IRE) —Dixie Bay (USA) (Dixieland Band (USA))
6948^{2} 7051^{6}

Age Of Chivalry (IRE) *John M Oxx* 89
2 b f Invincible Spirit(IRE) —Aravonian (Night Shift (USA))
(6392a)

Age Of Reason (UAE) *M Johnston* a80
2 b g Halling(USA) —Time Changes (USA) (Danzig (USA))
(7252)

Aggbag *B P J Baugh* a60 19
3 b g Fath(USA) —Emaura (Dominion)
40^{3} 202^{7} 335^{5} 5688^{14} *6064^{10} 6563^{7} 6945^{2} 7077^{7}*

Agglestone Rock *W G M Turner* a63 14
2 b g Josr Algarhoud(IRE) —Royalty (IRE) (Fairy King (USA))
3404^{8} 4540^{12} *5895^{3} 6401^{6}*

Aggravation *D R C Elsworth* a72 77
5 b g Sure Blade(USA) —Confection (Formidable (USA))
830^{6} 1036^{10} 1507^{12} (2004) (2514) 2722^{4} 4135^{10} 4455^{5} 5166^{6} 5559^{3} 5885^{4} 6063^{3} *6547^{6} 6824^{3}*

Agilete *J Pearce* a59 67
5 b g Piccolo—Ingerence (FR) (Akarad (FR))
464^{5} 617^{3} 741^{5} 2214^{4} 2716^{10} 3036^{3} 4231^{3} 4994^{4}

Agitator *Mrs G S Rees* a58
3 b g Lujain(USA) —Forum Girl (USA) (Sheikh Albadou)
4671^{4} 4977^{9}

Agnes Gift *Rae Guest* a46
4 b m Agnes World(USA) —Evocatrice (Persepolis (FR))
670^{7} 728^{6} 1119^{9}

Agnes Jedi (JPN) *Hideyuki Mori* a103
5 b h Agnes World(USA) —Lucky Pisces (CAN) (Crafty Prospector (USA))
597a^{5} 860a^{10}

Agon Eyes (USA) *D J Coakley* a48 47
2 b f Stravinsky(USA) —Dixie Eyes Blazing (USA) (Gone West (USA))
2468^{8} *3404^{7}* 4310^{10} 5268^{10} *6776^{8}*

Ahaz *J F Coupland* a40 21
5 b g Zaha(CAN) —Classic Faster (IRE) (Running Steps (USA))
579^{13} 625^{12} 730^{9}

Ahlawy (IRE) *M W Easterby* a63 86
4 gr g Green Desert(USA) —On Call (Alleged (USA))
1040^{12} *1180^{7}* 1288^{15} 1862^{4} 2095^{4} 2868^{6} 3093^{5} 4031^{2} (4228) (4817) 5296^{4} 6180^{2} 6499^{14} 6636^{7}

Aiakos (GER) *P Schiergen* 80
2 ch c Devil River Peek(USA) —Asuma (GER) (Surumu (GER))
6324a^{4}

Aide Memoir (IRE) *S Kirk* a74 92
2 b f Lend A Hand—Secret Justice (USA) (Lit De Justice (USA))
1533^{4} 1762^{6} (2488) 2812^{4} 3432^{9} 4046^{13} 5922^{4} *6270^{3}*

Ai Hawa (IRE) *Eamon Tyrrell* a54 57
4 b m Indian Danehill(IRE) —Arabian Princess (Taufan (USA))
4532^{9} *5606^{9} (7034) 7169^{6}*

Ailton (GER) *W Baltromei* 95
3 b g Fly To The Stars—Aznavour (GER) (Lagunas)
1054a^{5}

Aim *J R Jenkins* a53 56
2 b c Weetman's Weigh(IRE) —Ballet On Ice (FR) (Fijar Tango (FR))
4656^{10} 5570^{5} 6080^{9} *7031^{7} 7182^{13}*

Ainama (IRE) *M Wigham* a58 84
3 b g Desert Prince(IRE) —Gilah (IRE) (Saddlers' Hall (IRE))
567^{13} 700^{7} (3082) (3825) (3964) (5807) 5955^{5} 6473^{5}

Air Bag (FR) *Mme C Barande-Barbe* 103
3 b f Poliglote—Avrilana (FR) (Deep Roots)
436a^{3} 4873a^{5} (6940a)

Airbound (USA) *H J L Dunlop* a75 65
4 ch g Fusaichi Pegasus(USA) —Secrettame (USA) (Secretariat (USA))
316^{6}

Air Chief *H J L Dunlop* a49 59
2 ch g Dr Fong(USA) —Fly For Fame (Shaadi (USA))
2876^{13} 3551^{6} 4110^{11} *5127^{13}*

Airedale Lad (IRE) *R M Whitaker* a30 58
6 b g Charnwood Forest(IRE) —Tamarsiya (USA) (Shahrastani (USA))
1086^{9} *6999^{7}*

Air Guitar (IRE) *J Ryan* 69
7 b g Blues Traveller(IRE) —Money Talks (IRE) (Lord Chancellor (USA))
3468^{4} 3708^{14}

Airmail Special (IRE) *A Fabre* 108
3 b c Peintre Celebre(USA) —Shirley Blue (IRE) (Shirley Heights)
(2751a) 3566a^{4}

Airman (IRE) *W M Brisbourne* a68 68
4 b g Danehill(USA) —Jiving (Generous (IRE))
3079^{8} 4235^{6} 4908^{6} 5433^{2} *6148^{6} 6344^{3} 6612^{3}*

Aizen Myoo (IRE) *Seamus Fahey* a19 70
9 b g Balla Cove—Fly In Amber (IRE) (Doubletour (USA))
481^{11}

Ajaan *H R A Cecil* 94
3 br c Machiavellian(USA) —Alakananda (Hernando (FR))
2126^{8} 3335^{4} 3919^{3} (4288) (4779) 5574^{4}

Ajhar (USA) *M P Tregoning* 102
3 b g Diesis—Min Alhawa (USA) (Riverman (USA))
(1812) 5764^{2} 6499^{2}

Ajigolo *M R Channon* a104 102
4 ch h Piccolo—Ajig Dancer (Niniski (USA))
198^{5} 344^{4} 550^{11} (660) 867^{2} 1102^{6} 4090^{15} 4386^{9} 4614^{6} 4806^{13} 5050^{7} 5195^{4} 5449^{5} *(6231) (6355) 6668^{7} 6876^{4} 7053^{10}*

Ajzal (IRE) *M P Tregoning*
3 b g Alhaarth(IRE) —Alkaffeyeh (IRE) (Sadler's Wells (USA))
2909^{8}

Akarem *K R Burke* a83 111
6 b h Kingmambo(USA) —Spirit Of Tara (IRE) (Sadler's Wells (USA))
882a^{6} 1144^{7} 1650^{2} 1805^{4} 2216^{7} 2441^{3} 2856^{7} 3973^{5} 4690^{14} 5830^{9} 6169^{9} 6490^{3} 6759^{16} *6994^{4}*

Akash (IRE) *Miss J Feilden* a16 36
7 b g Dr Devious(IRE) —Akilara (IRE) (Kahyasi)
685^{9}

Akimbo (USA) *James Leavy* a77 105
6 b g Kingmambo(USA) —All At Sea (USA) (Riverman (USA))
247a^{8} 477a^{7} 3138a^{16}

Akiyama (IRE) *J Howard Johnson* 68
3 b g Traditionally(USA) —Dark Albatross (USA) (Sheikh Albadou)
2092^{8} 2740^{4} 3376^{9}

Akram (IRE) *Jonjo O'Neill* 95
5 b g Night Shift(USA) —Akdariya (IRE) (Shirley Heights)
993^{14} 1996^{8} 2452^{6} 3234^{8} 3715^{4} 4107^{9} 4731^{8}

Akshar (IRE) *P M Quinlan* a70 79
8 b g Danehill(USA) —Akilara (IRE) (Kahyasi)
6366a^{21}

Akua'Ba (IRE) *J S Bolger* a90 94
3 b f Sadler's Wells(USA) —Ghana (IRE) (Lahib (USA))
1777a^{6} *5761a^{3}* 6216a^{6}

Alabama Mama (IRE) *H J L Dunlop* a55 35
2 b f Fath(USA) —Radiance (IRE) (Thatching)
6087^{12} *6403^{6}*

Alabama Spirit (USA) *D Shaw* a60 67
2 bb f Dixie Union(USA) —Appealing Spirit (USA) (Valid Appeal (USA))
1992^{6} 3200^{2} 4026^{2} 4453^{4} *5199^{11} 5601^{11} 5887^{5} 6098^{5} 6263^{6} 6881^{8} 7042^{3} 7182^{2}*

Aladdins Cave *Sir Michael Stoute* 49
3 b g Rainbow Quest(USA) —Flight Of Fancy (Sadler's Wells (USA))
6286^{6}

Alaghiraar (IRE) *J L Dunlop* 84
3 b g Act One—Tarsheeh (USA) (Mr Prospector (USA))
(3685) 4617^{7} 5808^{5} 6186^{12}

Alagon (IRE) *Ian Williams* a60
7 b g Alzao(USA) —Forest Lair (Habitat)
39^{3} (100) 232^{6}

Alamanni (USA) *E Borromeo* 103
3 br f Elusive Quality(USA) —Altamura (USA) (El Gran Senor (USA))
6524a^{4} 6767a^{2}

Alambic *Sir Mark Prescott* a36 104
4 gr m Cozzene(USA) —Alexandrine (IRE) (Nashwan (USA))
2505^{2} 3333^{2} 3501^{5} 4089^{8} 4957a^{11}

Alan Devonshire *M H Tompkins* 94
2 b c Mtoto—Missed Again (High Top)
3733^{3} 4151^{6} (4578) 4991^{2} 5400^{2} 6382^{3}

Alannah (IRE) *Mrs P N Dutfield* a40 15
2 b f Alhaarth(IRE) —Aljeeza (Halling (USA))
2539^{17} 5869^{11} *6793^{8} 6928^{6}*

Alannahbeckaaoibhe (IRE) *Patrick J Flynn* 40
2 b f Tomba—Kanga (Primo Dominie)
6392a^{9}

Al Aqabah (IRE) *B Gubby* a73
2 ch f Redback—Snow Eagle (IRE) (Polar Falcon (USA))
6403^{5} (6664)

Alarazi (IRE) *John M Oxx* 99
3 b c Spectrum(IRE) —Alaya (IRE) (Ela-Mana-Mou)
948a^{6}

Alasil (USA) *R J Price* a67 72
7 bb g Swain(IRE) —Asl (USA) (Caro)
278^{10} 3907^{13} 4526^{5} 4856^{3} 5348^{11} *5756^{2} 6068^{10} 6479^{6}*

Alaska River (GER) *P Schiergen* 112
3 b c Anabaa(USA) —Ariosta (GER) (Scenic)
1005a^{7} 3581a^{4} 6370a^{2}

Alaska State (SWE) *J Malmborg*
3 ch g Bahamian Bounty—Baby Dancer (Rambo Dancer (CAN))
2548a^{3}

Alavana (IRE) *D W Barker* 57
3 b f Kyllachy—Grey Galava (Generous (IRE))
968^{8} (1236) 1410^{7} 1964^{6} 2422^{6} 2713^{6} 3029^{5} 4224^{8} 4705^{5} 5000^{12}

Al Azy (IRE) *J L Dunlop* 71
2 b c Nayef(USA) —Nasheed (USA) (Riverman (USA))
3856^{6} 4547^{5} 5417^{6} 5858^{4}

Albabilia (IRE) *C E Brittain* 103
2 b f King's Best(USA) —Sonachan (IRE) (Darshaan)
3507^{4} (3895) (4400) 5073a^{4} 5395a^{22}

Al Badeya (IRE) *Sir Michael Stoute* a60 69
3 ch f Pivotal—Out Of Africa (IRE) (Common Grounds)
2046^{4} 2429^{5} 2913^{2} 3447^{9} *5567^{3}* 6062^{4} *6339^{3}*

Albany Becky (IRE) *M G Quinlan* a40
2 br f Namid—Alchi (USA) (Alleged (USA))
4273^{12} 5097^{6} 5201^{10} 5363^{10}

Albany Hall (IRE) *F Poulsen* a36 98
5 b g Turtle Island(IRE) —Aughamore Beauty (IRE) (Dara Monarch)
1648a^{12}

Albaqaa *E A L Dunlop* 82
2 ch g Medicean—Basbousate Nadia (Wolfhound (USA))
1990^{9} 3095^{2} 3625^{7} 4501^{5} 6128^{6} 6449^{6}

Albaraari *Sir Michael Stoute* a68 63
2 b f Green Desert(USA) —Brigitta (IRE) (Sadler's Wells (USA))
4602^{9} *(5682)*

Alberts Story (USA) *R A Fahey* a62 62
3 b g Tale Of The Cat(USA) —Hazino (USA) (Hazaam (USA))
1894^{5} 2530^{13} (3997) 4354^{10} 4998^{2} 5704^{4} *5983^{5} 6178^{5}*

Alcharinga (IRE) *T J Etherington* a35 35
5 b g Ashkalani(IRE) —Bird In Blue (IRE) (Bluebird (USA))
138^{11}

Alcime (FR) *Robert Collet* a61 97
3 gr c Clerkenwell(USA) —Alshazam (IRE) (Petong)
436a^{6}

Alcimedes *P W Chapple-Hyam* a71 59
2 b g Domedriver(IRE) —Allegra (Niniski (USA))
3957^{9} 4584^{8} *7070^{2} 7252^{7}*

Al Cobra (IRE) *M A Jarvis* 58
2 b f Sadler's Wells(USA) —Marienbad (FR) (Darshaan)
6742^{5}

Alcomo (BRZ) *P Nickel Filho* a104
4 b h Rainbow Corner—Amazing Singer (BRZ) (Tokatee (USA))
175a^{14} 596a^{7}

Aldbury Grey (IRE) *A B Haynes* a40
4 gr m Alhaarth(IRE) —Alphilda (Ezzoud (IRE))
6716^{10} 6807^{9}

Alderney (USA) *M A Jarvis* 95
3 b f Elusive Quality(USA) —Adonesque (IRE) (Sadler's Wells (USA))
1502^{5} 2450^{4} 2757^{19}

Aleagueoftheirown (IRE) *David Wachman* 99
3 b f Danehill Dancer(IRE) —Golden Coral (USA) (Slew O'Gold (USA))
4237a^{6}

Aleatricis *Sir Mark Prescott* a32
2 bg g Kingmambo(USA) —Alba Stella (Nashwan (USA))
6358^{10} 6530^{12} 6748^{7}

Alecia (IRE) *A M Balding* a51 67
3 gr f Keltos(FR) —Ahliyat (USA) (Irish River (FR))
4659^{3} *5019^{6}* 5860^{3} 6423^{10} *6778^{3} 7144^{2} 7247^{3}*

Al Eile (IRE) *John Queally* 107
7 b g Alzao(USA) —Kilcsem Eile (IRE) (Commanche Run)
3090^{4} 6335^{4}

Alekhine (IRE) *J W Unett* a72 84
6 b g Soviet Star(USA) —Alriyaah (Shareef Dancer (USA))
1609^{12} 4231^{15} *6146^{6}* 6598^{9}

Aleph (IRE) *P Paciello*
2 b c Night Shift(USA) —Secrete Marina (IRE) (Mujadil (USA))
6527a^{6}

Aleron (IRE) *J J Quinn* a14 78
9 b g Sadler's Wells(USA) —High Hawk (Shirley Heights)
914^{3} 1532^{8}

Alessano *G L Moore* a94 99
5 ch g Hernando(FR) —Alessandra (Generous (IRE))
698^{5}

Aleutian *Doug Watson* a98 91
7 gr g Zafonic(USA) —Baked Alaska (Green Desert (USA))
104a^{3} 250a^{12} *410a^{3} 532a^{4} 601a^{3}*

Alexander Castle (USA) *K A Ryan* 108
2 b c Lemon Drop Kid(USA) —Palapa (USA) (Storm Cat (USA))
(4890) 5406^{2}

Alexander Guru *M Blanshard* a67 46
3 ch g Ishiguru(USA) —Superspring (Superlative)
1250^{2} 1725^{8} *3621^{8} 6457^{2} 6695^{4} 6904^{3} 7029^{8}*

Alexander Monarchy (IRE) *D W Barker* a59 58
2 b f Royal Applause—Alexander Confranc (IRE) (Magical Wonder (USA))
1533^{8} *(1728)* 2087^{5} 2549^{2} 4136^{4} 4484^{9} 4783^{4} *5015^{11}* 6075^{11}

Alexander Nepotism (IRE) *B J Meehan* 74
2 b f Fasliyev(USA) —Willowbridge (IRE) (Entrepreneur)
1101^{5} 1367^{2} 2316^{5}

Alexander Of Hales (USA) *A P O'Brien* 114
3 b c Danehill(USA) —Legend Maker (IRE) (Sadler's Wells (USA))
(2066a) 2293a^{16} 3142a^{2}

Alexander Tango (IRE) *T Stack* 109
3 ch f Danehill Dancer(IRE) —House In Wood (FR) (Woodman (USA))
1047a^{2} 1547a^{4} (1694a) 2065a^{4} (3578a) 4435a^{2} (5248a) 5822a^{7} (Dead)

Alexandra Rose (SAF) *M F De Kock* 105
5 b m Caesour(USA) —Alexander Bi (IRE) (Darshaan)
397a^{2} 546a^{5}

Alexandros *A Fabre* 111
2 ch c Kingmambo(USA) —Arlette (IRE) (King Of Kings (IRE))
(4009a) 4653a^{3}

Alexian *D W P Arbuthnot* a70 71
4 b g Almushtarak(IRE) —Rough Guess (IRE) (Believe It (USA))
623^{5} 1886^{14} 2055^{6} 2467^{14} *2946^{2}* (Dead)

Alexia Rose (IRE) *A Berry* a41 45
5 b m Mujadil(USA) —Meursault (IRE) (Salt Dome (USA))
1492^{9} 1707^{9} *2516^{10}* 2761^{5} 3017^{6} 3259^{7} 3347^{14} 3498^{7} 3787^{14} 4008^{8} 4525^{10} 4996^{6} 5836^{14} 5930^{7} 6730^{7} *6962^{12} 7108^{7}*

Alfathaa *W J Haggas* 107
2 b c Nayef(USA) —Arctic Char (Polar Falcon (USA))
4656^{3} (5206) 5795^{5}

Alfie Flits *G A Swinbank* a96 118
5 b g Machiavellian(USA) —Elhilmeya (IRE) (Unfuwain (USA))
761^{11} 2216^{5} 2462^{2} 2907^{6} 3119a^{3}

Alfie Lee (IRE) *D A Nolan* a3 37
10 ch g Case Law—Nordic Living (IRE) (Nordico (USA))
1707[8] 1891[8] 2249[8] 3374[10] 3498[9] 4379[5] 4478[8] 5481[11]

Alfie Tupper (IRE) *J R Boyle* a77 88
4 ch g Soviet Star(USA) —Walnut Lady (Forzando)
2318[9] 3234[9] *3851[12]* 4471[12] 4879[6] *(5366) 6260[3] 6458[2] 6577[4] 6951[3] 7050[2] (7146) 7214[4]*

Alfonso *P Monteith* a47 76
6 ch g Efisio—Winnebago (Kris)
1042[9] (1598) 2465[4] 2824[3]

Alfredian Park *S Kirk* a79 51
3 ch g Bertolini(USA) —Ulysses Daughter (IRE) (College Chapel)
184[8] 1956[10] 2943[6] 3235[12] 4505[12] *5233[8]*

Alfredtheordinary *M R Channon* a65 58
2 b g Hunting Lion(IRE) —Solmorin (Fraam)
999[9] 1367[4] 1858[6] 3348[4] 4202[7] 4524[9] 4783[5] 5268[7] 6591[3] *(6776)*

Alfresco *I A Wood* a91 76
3 b g Mtoto—Maureena (IRE) (Grand Lodge (USA))
498[6] 635[2] (694) (889) 1202[9] 1563[7] *2354[6] 2767[7] 3420[3]* 4313[7] *4889[7] (5223) 6006[4] 6949[4] 7061[2] (7281)*

Algarade *Sir Mark Prescott* a76 79
3 b f Green Desert(USA) —Alexandrine (IRE) (Nashwan (USA))
2475[2] 2999[5] 4735[5]

Alghaazy (IRE) *Micky Hammond* 31
6 b g Mark Of Esteem(IRE) —Kentmere (FR) (Galetto (FR))
913[14] 2252[15] 4280[8]

Ali Bruce *P A Blockley* a83 60
7 b g Cadeaux Genereux—Actualite (Polish Precedent (USA))
2[3] 341[2]

Alice Howe *W R Muir* a37 22
3 b f Vettori(IRE) —Peacock Alley (IRE) (Salse (USA))
3843[4] 4426[7]

Ali D *G Woodward* a51 69
9 b g Alhijaz—Doppio (Dublin Taxi)
3721[9] 4177[9] 4427[12]

Alimacdee *I Semple* 27
3 ch f Compton Place—Howards Heroine (IRE) (Danehill Dancer (IRE))
4000[8] 5036[7]

Alisar (IRE) *E J Creighton* a44 92
7 b g Entrepreneur—Aliya (IRE) (Darshaan)
48[14] 109[7] 159[7] 278[12] 372[8] 6152[8] 6292[10]

Alisdanza *N Wilson* a34 57
5 b m Namaqualand(USA) —Enchanting Eve (Risk Me (FR))
12[8] 1045[8] *1381[8]* 1893[11] 2118[9]

Alistair John *Mrs G S Rees* a58 39
4 b g Komaite(USA) —Young Rosein (Distant Relative)
137[8] 339[9] 523[2] 632[5] 746[7] 1360[11]

A Little More (IRE) *P A Blockley* a10 67
3 b c Princely Heir(IRE) —A Little While (Millfontaine)
1062[6] 1358[10] 1863[6] 3367[11] *6567[8]*

Aliysa (BRZ) *A Cintra Pereira* a82
4 ch m Music Prospector(USA) —Angra Dos Reis (BRZ) (Purple Mountain (USA))
249a[3] 474a[10]

Alizadora *Sir Mark Prescott* 77
2 b f Zilzal(USA) —Ballymac Girl (Niniski (USA))
(1636) 2271[2] 2812[14]

Al Khaleej (IRE) *E A L Dunlop* a86 103
3 b g Sakhee(USA) —Mood Swings (IRE) (Shirley Heights)
1956[2] (3745) 3940[3] *6143[9]*

All About Him (USA) *N I M Rossiter* 48
4 ch g Mt. Livermore(USA) —Inscrutable Dancer (USA) (Green Dancer (USA))
201[13]

Allahor *A Berry* 65
2 b g Rock City—Miss Puci (Puissance)
1963[7] 2451[7] (3024) 3373[3] 3635[4] 3909[8] 4524[15]

Allaire *M Johnston* a55 52
3 b f Keltos(FR) —Allegra (Niniski (USA))
884[4] 2763[9] 5045[4] 5481[3] *6026[12]*

Allanit (GER) *J Hirschberger* 91
3 b c Tiger Hill(IRE) —Astilbe (GER) (Monsun (GER))
1387a[3] 2102a[8]

All Began (IRE) *G Wragg* 63
3 b f Fasliyev(USA) —Sea Mistress (Habitat)
1105[13] 1408[7]

Allegretto (IRE) *Sir Michael Stoute* 115
4 ch m Galileo(IRE) —Alleluia (Caerleon (USA))
1823[5] (2125) 2787[9] (4091) 4723[2] 5376[3] (6526a)

Alleviate (IRE) *Sir Mark Prescott* a59 76
3 br f Indian Ridge—Alleluia (Caerleon (USA))
2362[8] 2793[2] *3624[8]* (4391) (4511) 4758[3]

Allez Mousson *A Bailey* 38
9 b g Hernando(FR) —Rynechra (Blakeney)
1942[8]

Allicansayis Wow (USA) *J S Bolger* a84 98
2 b f Street Cry(IRE) —Crown Of Jewels (USA) (Half A Year (USA))
5073a[5] 5395a[9]

Allied Powers (IRE) *M L W Bell* 46
2 b c Invincible Spirit(IRE) —Always Friendly (High Line)
6248[12]

Allied Winner (ARG) *M Grassi* 86
5 b h Allied Forces(USA) —Novara (ARG) (Saint Sever (FR))
6687a[7]

All In The Red (IRE) *Miss Gay Kelleway* 66
2 ch c Redback—Light-Flight (IRE) (Brief Truce (USA))
4733[5] 5065[3]

All Is Vanity (FR) *W J S Cargeeg* 108
3 ch f Gold Away(IRE) —Castilly (Inchinor)
(2290a) 4010a[11] 5661a[4]

All Ivory *I Mohammed* a19 106
5 ch g Halling(USA) —Ivorine (USA) (Blushing Groom (FR))
331a[7] 542a[10]

All Lit Up *A King* a56 37
2 b g Fantastic Light(USA) —Maiden Aunt (IRE) (Distant Relative)
4393[10] 5116[7] 6058[12]

All My Loving (IRE) *A P O'Brien* 114
3 b f Sadler's Wells(USA) —Jude (Darshaan)
1581[2] 2211[3] 2786[2] 3576a[3] 5352[2] 5767[2] 6030a[9] 6367a[3] 6509a[5]

All Native (IRE) *C P Donoghue* a52 43
8 b g Revoque(IRE) —Psyche (IRE) (Nashamaa)
7081[3] 7285[6]

All Of Me (IRE) *T G Mills* a85 57
3 b g Xaar—Silk Point (IRE) (Barathea (IRE))
(1228) 1439[6] 2943[8] 3857[7] 5508[8]

Alloro *D W Thompson* a50 63
3 ch g Auction House(USA) —Minette (Bishop Of Cashel)
1316[5] 2079[4] 2425[12] 2697[8] 3714[7] 3966[5] 4256[8] 5622[8] 6559[8]

Alls Fair *R Hannon* a67 71
2 br c Bertolini(USA) —Comme Ca (Cyrano De Bergerac)
3962[6] 4181[9] *4962[3]*

All Sorts Star (IRE) *Andrew Lee* 84
7 b g Accordion—Thank One's Stars (Alzao (USA))
3577a[16]

All Spirit (GER) *N Sauer* 111
5 b h Platini(GER) —All Saints (GER) (Goofalik (USA))
882a[8] 1689a[12] 2976a[8]

All Talk *M J Gingell* a41 40
3 b f Muhtarram(USA) —Bron Hilda (IRE) (Namaqualand (USA))
162[8] 1537[11] 2273[10] 2747[6] 3593[7] 3824[10] 4337[10] 4943[10]

All That Brass *E J O'Neill* 49
2 ch c Compton Place—Ebba (Elmaamul (USA))
2687[5]

All The Aces (IRE) *M A Jarvis* a76 79
2 b c Spartacus(IRE) —Lili Cup (FR) (Fabulous Dancer (USA))
5329[3] 5813[2] *(6585)*

All The Good (IRE) *G A Butler* a104 107
4 ch h Diesis—Zarara (USA) (Manila (USA))
940[6] 1822[10] (2245) 3119a[4] 4047[9] 4388[5] 4722[14] *4867a[2]* 5326[4] (5830)

All Tied Up (IRE) *T Hogan* a62 63
3 ch f Desert Prince(IRE) —Half-Hitch (USA) (Diesis)
7157[5]

All Woman *E J Creighton* a18 79
5 ch m Groom Dancer(USA) —Flight Soundly (IRE) (Caerleon (USA))
101[6]

Ally Makbul *Ian Emmerson* a65 54
7 b m Makbul—Clarice Orsini (Common Grounds)
1570[14]

All You Need (IRE) *R Hollinshead* a76 81
3 b g Iron Mask(USA) —Choice Pickings (IRE) (Among Men (USA))
1825[7] 2044[12] *(3924)* 4330[8] *4740[6] 5238[2] 5387[7] 5893[3]* 6283[7]

Al Maali (IRE) *Doug Watson* a52 92
8 b h Polar Falcon(USA) —Amwag (USA) (El Gran Senor (USA))
247a[6] 540a[8]

Almahaza (IRE) *A J Chamberlain* a60 56
3 b c Alzao(USA) —Morna's Moment (USA) (Timeless Moment (USA))
1725[9] 2127[12] 2320[10] 3876[7] *4277[7]* 4809[10] *5095[2] (6060) 6796[2] 7009[3]*

Almajd (IRE) *Sir Michael Stoute* 95
2 b c Marju(IRE) —Irish Valley (USA) (Irish River (FR))
(5977) 6495[5]

Alma Mater *Sir Mark Prescott* a74 100
4 b m Sadler's Wells(USA) —Alouette (Darshaan)
2766[3] 3284[3] (6745) (6953a)

Almamia *Sir Mark Prescott* a47 68
2 b f Hernando(FR) —Alborada (Alzao (USA))
5913[3] 6348[13] *6737[3]*

Almanshood (USA) *T Hogan* a66 66
5 b g Bahri(USA) —Lahan (Unfuwain (USA))
220[5] 369[11] 7154[6]

Almaram (USA) *D Selvaratnam* a100 94
7 b h A.P. Indy(USA) —Berasyim (Lion Cavern (USA))
105a[7] *(324a)* 409a[5] *543a[5]*

Al Martino (SWI) *M Weiss* 77
9 b g Llandaff(USA) —Annie Get Your Gun (Blakeney)
494a[4]

Almaty Express *J R Weymes* a84 62
5 b g Almaty(IRE) —Express Girl (Sylvan Express)
(154) (214) 251[2] (566) 835[2] 1363[9] 1854[15] 6020[14] *6360[5] 6860[8] 7059[6] 7215[4]*

Almavara (USA) *C P Morlock* a30 49
5 bb g Fusaichi Pegasus(USA) —Name Of Love (IRE) (Petardia)
2544[5] *2874[5]*

Almazaal (IRE) *D K Weld* 67
3 bb f Alhaarth(IRE) —Lovelyst (IRE) (Machiavellian (USA))
5460a[14]

Almizan (IRE) *G L Moore* a65 69
7 b g Darshaan—Bint Albaadiya (USA) (Woodman (USA))
16[7] 3448[10]

Al Mogeer (IRE) *K A Ryan* 9
2 b g Montjeu(IRE) —Jumbo Delight (IRE) (Don't Forget Me)
5904[15] *7152[8]*

Almolahek (IRE) *D K Weld* 74
2 b c Red Ransom(USA) —Daqtora (Dr Devious (IRE))
6443a[4]

Almondillo (IRE) *C F Wall* a51 45
3 b g Tagula(IRE) —Almond Flower (IRE) (Alzao (USA))
973[9] *1282[8] 6149[8] 6402[5] 6706[4]*

Almora Guru *W M Brisbourne* a52 60
3 b f Ishiguru(USA) —Princess Almora (Pivotal)
894[3] 1008[8] (1269) 1561[13] 2120[2] 2172[5] 3583[10] 4330[9] 5041[10] *5947[10] 6735[6] 6908[5] 7001[3] 7169[9]*

Almost Married (IRE) *J D Bethell* a54
3 b g Indian Ridge—Shining Hour (USA) (Red Ransom (USA))
1716[4] 3062[12]

Al Moulatham *R Ford* a68 77
8 b g Rainbow Quest(USA) —High Standard (Kris)
146[3] 220[10] 464[6] (628) 709[2] 994[13] *2148[3]* 3012[11] 3533[7] *5820[5] 6341[13]*

Almoutaz (USA) *B W Hills* 79
2 bb c Kingmambo(USA) —Dessert (USA) (Storm Cat (USA))
4571[4] 5194[5] (6617)

Almoutezah (USA) *M A Jarvis* 68
2 br f Storm Cat(USA) —Probable Colony (USA) (Pleasant Colony (USA))
6648[8]

Almowj *C E Brittain* a59 53
4 b g Fasliyev(USA) —Tiriana (Common Grounds)
350[2] 435[12] 557[5]

Al Muheer (IRE) *C E Brittain* a94 95
2 b c Diktat—Dominion Rose (USA) (Spinning World (USA))
1073[3] 2183[3] 2885[3] 3508[2] (4162) 5410[5] *6001[2]*

Almuraad (IRE) *Doug Watson* a88 98
6 b h Machiavellian(USA) —Wellspring (IRE) (Caerleon (USA))
178a[3] 325a[2] 473a[4] 542a[8]

Al Naahadth (USA) *Saeed Bin Suroor* 69
3 b g Storm Cat(USA) —Ajina (USA) (Strawberry Road (AUS))
4457[10] 5384[4]

Alnitak (USA) *B Olsen* 97
6 br h Nureyev(USA) —Very True (USA) (Proud Truth (USA))
2131a[9] 4218a[6] 5263a[4]

Alnwick *P D Cundell* a67 60
3 b g Kylian(USA) —Cebwob (Rock City)
790[4] 2801[2] 3082[6] 3189[2] 3945[6] 4113[5] 4809[3]

Alone He Stands (IRE) *J C Hayden* 92
7 b g Flying Spur(AUS) —Millennium Tale (FR) (Distant Relative)
3140a[5] 6363a[3]

Alone It Stands (IRE) *D Nicholls* a37 44
4 b g King Charlemagne(USA) —Golden Concorde (Super Concorde (USA))
1625[9] 2121[10] *2221[9]*

Along The Nile *K G Reveley* 91
5 b g Desert Prince(IRE) —Golden Fortune (Forzando)
850[12] 995[2] 1149[12] 2136[7] 5327[9] 5748[5]

Alonso De Guzman (IRE) *J R Boyle* a66 12
3 b g Dockslider(USA) —Addaya (IRE) (Persian Bold)
(6026) (6803) 7100 7211[4] 7249[4]

Alo Pura *M A Jarvis* a62 82
3 b f Anabaa(USA) —Rubies From Burma (USA) (Forty Niner (USA))
3710[2] (3992)

Alovera (IRE) *M R Channon* 96
3 ch f King's Best(USA) —Angelic Sounds (IRE) (The Noble Player (USA))
1391[5] 2914[8]

Alpacco (IRE) *Mario Hofer* a91 102
5 b g Desert King(IRE) —Albertville (GER) (Top Ville)
176a[8] (331a) *543a[8]* 642a[8] *4012a[7]*

Alpen Adventure (IRE) *Mrs L Stubbs* 68
2 b g Shinko Forest(IRE) —Alpina (USA) (El Prado (IRE))
845[7] 1622[4] 1938[4] 2166[5] 2819[2] 3296[P] (Dead)

Alpes Maritimes *G L Moore* a86 82
3 b g Danehill Dancer(IRE) —Miss Riviera (Kris)
1011[3] 1290[9] 2153[5] 2834[3] 3964[3] 4568[3] 5285[4] 6081[4] *6546[2] (6901) (7018)*

Alpha Jet *Patrick J Flynn* 66
7 b g Lando(GER) —Alpha City (Unfuwain (USA))
1330a[9]

Alphun (IRE) *N B King* a4 3
5 b g Orpen(USA) —Fakhira (IRE) (Jareer (USA))
1732[RR]

Alpine Eagle (IRE) *Mrs John Harrington* 102
3 b g Golan(IRE) —Alpine Symphony (Northern Dancer (CAN))
4035a[2] 4830a[5]

Alpino Chileno (ARG) *Rune Haugen* 101
8 gr h Alpino Fitz(ARG) —Fairyland (ARG) (Lode (USA))
4218a[9]

Alqaayid *P W Hiatt* a37 64
6 b g Machiavellian(USA) —One So Wonderful (Nashwan (USA))
1406[14] (2141) 4534[7] *4915[10] 6792[11]* 6923a[8]

Al Qasi (IRE) *P W Chapple-Hyam* a85 118
4 b h Elnadim(USA) —Delisha (Salse (USA))
1770[6] 2857[10] 3894[2] (4438a) 5832[5] 6332[2] 7091a[12]

Al Qudra (IRE) *J R Jenkins* a83 87
5 b h Cape Cross(IRE) —Alvilda (IRE) (Caerleon (USA))
3388[14]

Al Rayanah *G Prodromou* a54 68
4 b m Almushtarak(IRE) —Desert Bloom (FR) (Last Tycoon (IRE))
979[8] 2154[10] 2831[6] *3172[2]* 3247[11] 3826[6] *4063[9]* 4294[7] 4416[7] 6247[3] 6412[2] 6573[3] *6796[5]*

Alrida (IRE) *R A Fahey* a71 75
8 b g Ali-Royal(IRE) —Ride Bold (USA) (J O Tobin (USA))
515[5] 955[2] 1793[15] 2250[5] (Dead)

Alsace *C Lerner* 93
2 b f King's Best(USA) —Annex (Anabaa (USA))
6630a[5]

Alsadaa (USA) *Mrs L J Mongan* a69 79
4 b g Kingmambo(USA) —Aljawza (USA) (Riverman (USA))
930[8] 1040[16] *(1265) 1755[8] 2149[7]* 2256[15] 2431[3] 2810[9] 3042[5] 3155[7] 4355[3]

Alsadeek (IRE) *J L Dunlop* 78
2 b c Fasliyev(USA) —Khulan (USA) (Bahri (USA))
2424[2] 5587[3] 5910[10]

Alseraaj (USA) *Sir Michael Stoute* 58
2 ch f El Prado(IRE) —Barzah (IRE) (Darshaan)
6087[6]

Al Shemali *Sir Michael Stoute* 112
3 ch c Medicean—Bathilde (IRE) (Generous (IRE))
1097[4] 1473[13] 1790[3] 2789[2] 3142a[7]

Altar (IRE) *R Hannon* 77
3 b c Cape Cross(IRE) —Sophrana (IRE) (Polar Falcon (USA))
1974[10] (2598)

Altenburg (FR) *Mrs N Smith* a75 86
5 b g Sadler's Wells(USA) —Anna Of Saxony (Ela-Mana-Mou)
4630[7] 5938[7] 6622[4]

Altercation *W Jarvis* 49
2 ch f Polish Precedent(USA) —Show Off (Efisio)
1636[7] 2526[5] 3363[10] 4315[6] 5274[8]

Altesse Imperiale (IRE) *E Lellouche* a76 75
3 b f Rock Of Gibraltar(IRE) —Ange Bleu (USA) (Alleged (USA))
7049a[12]

Al Tharib (USA) *Sir Michael Stoute* a111 101
3 b c Silver Hawk(USA) —Ameriflora (USA) (Danzig (USA))
1306[5] (1605) 2813[9] *(4887) 5220[2]* 6298[9]

Altilhar (USA) *G L Moore* a86 83
4 b g Dynaformer(USA) —Al Desima (Emperor Jones (USA))
593[5] 6144[13] 6473[14]

Altitude *Sir Mark Prescott* a76 75
2 gr f Green Desert(USA) —Alouette (Darshaan)
2992[6] 3453[2] 3874[4] *5100[2] 5646[5]* 5914[2]

Alto Singer (IRE) *B R Millman*
2 b f Alhaarth(IRE) —Sonatina (Distant Relative)
972[11]

Altos Reales *D Shaw* a62 42
3 b f Mark Of Esteem(IRE) —Karsiyaka (IRE) (Kahyasi)
1904[8] 2520[8] 2948[8] 4078[9] 4632[6] 4846[7] *5368[7] 5606[4] (6808) 6896[4] 6967[3] 7060[3] 7249[2]*

Alto Taquari (BRZ) *P Nickel Filho* a88 95
4 ch h Yagli(USA) —Primeiranista (Never So Bold)
172a[6] *410a[9] 526a[3]* 641a[7]

Alto Vertigo *P C Haslam* a71 55
4 b g Averti(IRE) —Singer On The Roof (Chief Singer)
4795[2] 5082[2] 5231[7] *5982[3] (7003) 7113[2]*

Alucica *D Shaw* a51 50
4 b m Celtic Swing—Acicula (IRE) (Night Shift (USA))
106[9] 311[10] 440[10] 523[10] 632[7] 653[2] 690[10] 722[4] 1594[10] 2121[3] *(2592)* 2937[12]

Alugat (IRE) *Mrs A Duffield* a59 75
4 b g Tagula(IRE) —Notley Park (Wolfhound (USA))
2419[7] 2712[14] 4251[10]

Alujawill (IRE) *Evan Williams* a42 43
4 b g Erhaab(USA) —El-Libaab (Unfuwain (USA))
1673[14]

Alwaabel *J L Dunlop* 81
2 b c Green Desert(USA) —Etizaaz (USA) (Diesis)
2041[6] 2596[2] 6540[2] 6754[4]

Alwariah *Ms J S Doyle* a47 61
4 b m Xaar—Signs And Wonders (Danehill (USA))
431[6] 1347[10] 1539[14] 1740[12] *2331[7]* 2540[15] *2591[6]*

Always A Story *Miss D Mountain* a44 44
5 b g Lake Coniston(IRE) —Silk St James (Pas De Seul)
455[6] 559[5] 721[13] 1750[12] 2157[9] 2745[10] *6175[11]*

Always Attractive (IRE) *M Johnston* 38
2 ch f King's Best(USA) —Fife (IRE) (Lomond (USA))
5882[13]

Always Baileys (IRE) *T Wall* a69 75
4 ch g Mister Baileys—Dubiously (USA) (Jolie Jo (USA))
142[5] 215[5] 515[12] 3280[4] 3485[8] 4124[8] *6798[10]*

Always Best *M Johnston* a59 69
3 b g Best Of The Bests(IRE) —Come To The Point (Pursuit Of Love)
(917) 1194[5] 1536[7] 1916[5] *2259[10]* 2915[2] 3183[5] 3640[4] *4025[5]* 4391[13] 4894[5] *5364[9] 5980[8]* 6453[4] *6590[2]*

Always Brave *M Johnston* a32 69
2 ch g Danehill Dancer(IRE) —Digge Park (USA) (Capote (USA))
3625[15] 4028[4] 4852[4] 5470[6] *5984[9]*

Always Certain (USA) *M Johnston* 68
2 ch g Giant's Causeway(USA) —Mining Missharriet (USA) (Mining (USA))
5343[6] 6156[6]

Always Esteemed (IRE) *J O'Reilly* a99 69
7 b g Mark Of Esteem(IRE) —Always Far (USA) (Alydar (USA))
4082[12]

Always First *T Voss* 109
6 b g Barathea(IRE) —Pink Cristal (Dilum (USA))
4415a[5]

Always Fruitful *M Johnston* 90
3 b c Fruits Of Love(USA) —Jerre Jo Glanville (USA) (Skywalker (USA))
3503[16] 3940[11] 4399[5] 4617[3] 5141[7] 6091[4]

Always Ready *C E Brittain* a74 82
2 ch c Best Of The Bests(IRE) —Tahara (IRE) (Caerleon (USA))
1743[7] 2303[3] 3625[2] 4130[2] 4776[4] 5053[2] 5571[2] *6120[9]*

Always Sparkle (CAN) *B Palling* a59 57
3 ch c Grand Slam(USA) —Dancing All Night (USA) (Nijinsky (CAN))
3366[3] *6803[6] 6967[7] 7115[4]*

Always The Groom (IRE) *Patrick J Flynn* 77
5 br g Darshaan—Kyka (USA) (Blushing John (USA))
3577a[2]

Alzerra (UAE) *I Mohammed* a59 109
3 b f Pivotal—Belle Argentine (FR) (Fijar Tango (FR))
246a^{6}

Amadeus Wolf *K A Ryan* 120
4 b h Mozart(IRE) —Rachelle (IRE) (Mark Of Esteem (IRE))
(1770) 2857^{11} 3506^{12} 4746^{7} 5214^{12}

Amanda Carter *R A Fahey* 71
3 b f Tobougg(IRE) —Al Guswa (Shernazar)
954^{9} (2299) 2538^{2} 3183^{6} (3955) 4382^{7} 4993^{6}

Amandalini *B J Meehan* a49 50
2 b f Bertolini(USA) —Luxurious (USA) (Lyphard (USA))
6140^{10} 6470^{13}

Amanda's Lad (IRE) *M C Chapman* a48 61
7 b g Danetime(IRE) —Art Duo (Artaius (USA))
239^{6} 318^{10} 523^{7} 581^{6} 1112^{8} 1134^{7}

Amandus (USA) *Doug Watson* a84 90
7 b g Danehill(USA) —Affection Affirmed (USA) (Affirmed (USA))
331a^{6} 477a^{9}

Amanjena *A M Balding* 73
2 b f Beat Hollow—Placement (Kris)
6294^{6} 6724^{3}

Amante Latino *V Caruso* 99
3 b c Mujahid(USA) —Supercharger (Zamindar (USA))
1336a^{3} 2295a^{7} 6687a^{8}

Amarama (IRE) *David P Myerscough* 71
2 br f Fraam—Amarapura (FR) (Common Grounds)
4832a^{8}

Amaranda (IRE) *David Wachman* 61
2 b f Fasliyev(USA) —Top Table (Shirley Heights)
6443a^{5}

Amarna (USA) *Saeed Bin Suroor* a101 100
3 b c Danzig(USA) —Mysterial (USA) (Alleged (USA))
3881^{4} (4275) (4889) (5382) 6002^{2} (6155)

Amarula Ridge (IRE) *Niall Madden* a64 68
6 b g Indian Ridge—Mail Boat (Formidable (USA))
5761a^{11}

Amaryllis (GER) *T Hogan* 62
5 br m Law Society(USA) —Alyeska (GER) (Northjet)
6330^{4}

Amateis (GER) *P Rau* 98
4 b m Tiger Hill(IRE) —Adorea (GER) (Dashing Blade)
1517a^{6}

Amazing Day *John A Harris* a48 61
2 b g Averti(IRE) —Daynabee (Common Grounds)
971^{4} 1235^{4} 1728^{3} (1857) 2028^{U} 4027^{9}

Amazing King (IRE) *W G M Turner* a53 63
3 b g King Charlemagne(USA) —Kraemer (USA) (Lyphard (USA))
1399^{8} 2200^{3} 2893^{9} 3619^{4} 4591^{5}

Amazing Request *R Charlton* 84
3 b c Rainbow Quest(USA) —Maze Garden (USA) (Riverman (USA))
1106^{6} 1584^{P} 3590^{5} 3993^{11} 4572^{9}

Amazing Spirit *Miss V Haigh* 33
2 ch f Hawk Wing(USA) —Free Spirit (IRE) (Caerleon (USA))
1553^{8} 3507^{16} 3884^{7} 5322^{19}

Amazing Star (IRE) *M Halford* a84 63
2 b c Soviet Star(USA) —Sadika (IRE) (Bahhare (USA))
(6974)

Amber Bamber *D Burchell* 36
2 b f Piccolo—Martha P Perkins (IRE) (Fayruz)
5442^{8}

Amber Glory *K A Ryan* a66 60
4 b m Foxhound(USA) —Compton Amber (Puissance)
77^{11}

Amber Isle *D Carroll* a59 51
3 b g Weet-A-Minute(IRE) —Cloudy Reef (Cragador)
423^{5} 535^{8} 4224^{10} 5602^{6} 6310^{13} 6779^{10}

Amber Ridge *B P J Baugh* a40 54
2 b g Tumbleweed Ridge—Amber Brown (Thowra (FR))
2517^{7} 3283^{8} 3866^{6} 4527^{5} 5675^{4}

Ambrose Princess (IRE) *R A Harris* a57 57
2 b f Chevalier(IRE) —Mark One (Mark Of Esteem (IRE))
3592^{7} 4014^{6} 4363^{11} (4897) 5423^{4} (6242) 6478^{8} 6800^{6} 6966^{5} 7022^{7} 7136^{3} 7182^{12}

Ambrosiano *C G Cox* a66 77
3 b g Averti(IRE) —Secret Circle (Magic Ring (IRE))
(736) (931) 1076^{7} 2335^{4} 2633^{4} 3707^{6}

Ameeq (USA) *G L Moore* a90 87
5 bb g Silver Hawk(USA) —Haniya (IRE) (Caerleon (USA))
587^{2} 3509^{6}

Amended *D K Weld* 33
2 ch f Beat Hollow—Daki (USA) (Miswaki (USA))
6549a^{0}

Americain (USA) *A Fabre* 95
2 b c Dynaformer(USA) —America (IRE) (Arazi (USA))
4625a^{3}

American Art (IRE) *B W Hills* 77
2 b g Statue Of Liberty(USA) —Peshawar (Persian Bold)
1498^{6} 1832^{4} 2303^{9} (4285) 4991^{3}

America Nova (FR) *R Gibson* a69 97
3 gr f Verglas(IRE) —Las Americas (FR) (Linamix (FR))
1338a^{6} 1880a^{6}

American Welcome (IRE) *B J Meehan* 53
2 b c Statue Of Liberty(USA) —Double Opus (IRE) (Petorius)
4014^{7} 4454^{8} 4781^{9} 5571^{10} 5869^{9}

Amerigo (IRE) *M A Jarvis* 68
2 gr g Daylami(IRE) —Geminiani (IRE) (King Of Kings (IRE))
6724^{7}

Ames Souer (IRE) *P D Evans* a37 34
4 b m Fayruz—Taispeain (IRE) (Petorius)
135^{5} 225^{6}

Amhooj *M P Tregoning* a66 55
2 br f Green Desert(USA) —Harayir (USA) (Gulch (USA))
4094^{14} 6139^{3}

Amicable Terms *Rae Guest* 47
2 b f Royal Applause—Friendly Finance (Auction Ring (USA))
6617^{9}

Amical Risks (FR) *W J Musson* a46
3 bl g Take Risks(FR) —Miss High (FR) (Concorde Jr (USA))
7185^{5}

Amichi *G L Moore* a35 55
3 b f Averti(IRE) —Friend For Life (Lahib (USA))
3710^{11} 4457^{11} 5499^{10}

Amicus *D K Ivory* a60
2 br f Xaar—Kartuzy (JPN) (Polish Precedent (USA))
6262^{14} 6530^{10} 6777^{8}

Amie Magnificent (IRE) *P Winkworth* a55 55
2 b f Mujahid(USA) —Darbela (IRE) (Doyoun)
5061^{8} 5527^{5} 5944^{12}

Ammeyrr *A Crook* a69 57
3 b g Mark Of Esteem(IRE) —Walimu (IRE) (Top Ville)
537^{9} 711^{2} 1714^{P} 2554^{4} 3052^{4} 3502^{11} 4229^{8} 4563^{4} 4771^{6} 5525^{15}

Amnesty *G L Moore* a50 62
8 ch g Salse(USA) —Amaranthus (Shirley Heights)
2595^{8} 3280^{5} 4534^{9}

Amonita (GER) *Annette McMahon* 76
5 gr m Medaaly—Augreta (GER) (Simply Great (FR))
4240a^{8}

Amorist (IRE) *D W Chapman* a50
5 b g Anabaa(USA) —Moivouloirtoi (USA) (Bering)
2347^{5} 5737^{10} 7006^{4} 7197^{10}

Amoroso (GER) *P Rau* 96
6 br h Goofalik(USA) —Abazzia (GER) (Acatenango (GER))
4957a^{6}

A Mothers Love *P J McBride* a55 59
3 gr f Act One—Oiselina (FR) (Linamix (FR))
260^{8} 569^{8} 649^{9} 790^{2} (907) 1154^{6} 1579^{10} 2192^{2} 2793^{4} 3249^{10} 4069^{5}

Amouretta *T T Clement* a40 47
2 b f Daylami(IRE) —Allumette (Rainbow Quest (USA))
5202^{8} 6092^{U} 6297^{7}

Ampelio (IRE) *Doug Watson* a94 94
5 ch h Grand Lodge(USA) —Bordighera (USA) (Alysheba (USA))
248a^{3} 475a^{11} 529a^{10}

Amphibalus (IRE) *D K Ivory*
2 gr g Daylami(IRE) —Dramatically (USA) (Theatrical)
5679^{10}

Amusing (IRE) *John Joseph Murphy* 84
3 b f Danehill Dancer(IRE) —Belize Tropical (IRE) (Baillamont (USA))
1777a^{10}

Amwaal (USA) *J L Dunlop* 76
4 b h Seeking The Gold(USA) —Wasnah (USA) (Nijinsky (CAN))
1040^{13} 1395^{11} 1845^{15}

Amwell Brave *J R Jenkins* a71 89
6 b g Pyramus(USA) —Passage Creeping (IRE) (Persian Bold)
(88) 232^{4} 507^{4} 1152^{5} 1451^{4} 1822^{6} 2156^{4} 2833^{8} 3097^{7} 3217^{4} 3397^{4} 3912^{6} 5093^{2} 5500^{7} 5732^{5} 6102^{12}

Amwell House *J R Jenkins* 41
2 gr g Auction House(USA) —Amwell Star (USA) (Silver Buck (USA))
1021^{5} 1919^{10} 3479^{10} 4363^{8} 5306^{9} 6274^{11}

Amyann (IRE) *J R Holt* a59
2 b f Indian Lodge(IRE) —Moral Certainty (USA) (Seeking The Gold (USA))
6980^{7} 7196^{3}

Amylee (IRE) *C G Cox* 86
2 b f Danehill Dancer(IRE) —Igreja (ARG) (Southern Halo (USA))
2997^{3} 3895^{13} 4602^{2} 5395^{6}

Amy Lionheart *N Tinkler* 37
2 b f Makbul—So Generous (Young Generation)
1087^{13} 2549^{4} 2738^{5} 3835^{6} 4559^{4} 4770^{12}

Amy Louise (IRE) *T D Barron* 88
4 ch m Swain(IRE) —Mur Taasha (USA) (Riverman (USA))
1861^{6} (2742) 3201^{5} 3953^{3} 4581^{16}

Amy Storm (GER) *P Vovcenko* 93
4 b m Tannenkonig(IRE) —Amanwana (GER) (Platini (GER))
1517a^{8}

Anabaa's Creation (IRE) *A De Royer-Dupre* 112
3 b f Anabaa(USA) —Premiere Creation (FR) (Green Tune (USA))
1055a^{5} 1880a^{3} 2501a^{4} 5661a^{3} 6376a^{4} 6770a^{4}

Anabaa's Secret (IRE) *J A Osborne* a52 46
2 bb g Anabaa Blue—Rizo Amoro (USA) (Fit To Fight (USA))
3471^{7} 3596^{10} 3712^{8} 5423^{12} 6427^{8} 6776^{10}

Anamarka *H Candy* 57
2 b f Mark Of Esteem(IRE) —Anna Of Brunswick (Rainbow Quest (USA))
4875^{13} 5301^{10}

Anamato (AUS) *D Hayes* 104
4 br m Redoute's Choice(AUS) —Voltage (AUS) (Whiskey Road (USA))
6354a^{15}

Anatolian Prince *J M P Eustace* a53 63
3 b g Almutawakel—Flight Soundly (IRE) (Caerleon (USA))
931^{5} 1359^{11} 2153^{11} 3949^{7} 4516^{2} 4763^{8} 5497^{7}

Ancien Regime (IRE) *M A Jarvis* 93
2 b c King's Best(USA) —Sadalsud (IRE) (Shaadi (USA))
(4854) 5410^{4} 6059^{2}

Ancient Cross *M Johnston* 16
3 b g Machiavellian(USA) —Magna Graecia (IRE) (Warning)
3015^{8}

Ancient Culture *Sir Michael Stoute* 86
3 b c Sadler's Wells(USA) —Wemyss Bight (Dancing Brave (USA))
1358^{6} 1812^{4} 2308^{6} 3402^{3} 3908^{2} (4403) 4749^{11} 5955^{9}

Ancient Egypt *Annelie Larsson* a87 43
5 b g Singspiel(IRE) —Nekhbet (Artaius (USA))
1648a^{3}

Ancient Pride (IRE) *Miss L A Perratt* 51
3 br g Inchinor—Carrie Pooter (Tragic Role (USA))
5036^{6} 5082^{3} 5285^{5}

Ancient Site (USA) *B P J Baugh* a41 17
3 ch c Distant View(USA) —Victorian Style (Nashwan (USA))
253^{10} 3786^{12} 4416^{13}

Ancus Martius (FR) *R Biondi* 79
3 b c Almutawakel—White Evening (IRE) (Entitled)
1335a^{7}

And Again (USA) *R A Teal* a62 81
4 b m In The Wings—Garah (Ajdal (USA))
1434^{5} 1783^{6} 2321^{13} 2964^{4} 3397^{10} 3616^{2} 3946^{3} 4327^{3} 6260^{8} 6447^{10} 6867^{3} 6951^{14}

Andaman Sunset *G Wragg* 84
2 b c Red Ransom(USA) —Miss Amanpuri (Alzao (USA))
3747^{8} 4048^{13} 5281^{2} 5735^{4} 6493^{2}

And I *C A Horgan* a73 68
4 b m Inchinor—Fur Will Fly (Petong)
1609^{13} 2472^{14} 3191^{12}

Andmoreagain (USA) *J Noseda* a69 72
3 b f Distorted Humor(USA) —It's Personal (USA) (Personal Flag (USA))
2886^{3} 3827^{5} 4275^{3} (4575)

Andorn (GER) *J Hirschberger* 103
3 b c Monsun(GER) —Anthyllis (GER) (Lycius (USA))
5929a^{9}

Andorran (GER) *A Bailey* a54 54
4 gr g Lando(GER) —Adora (GER) (Danehill (USA))
1423^{4} 2091^{4} 2563^{7} 3814^{4} 4099^{6} 4449^{4} 4718^{2} 4860^{6} 5087^{6} 5389^{4} 5586^{10} 6265^{4}

Andrasta *A Berry* a58 71
2 b f Bertolini(USA) —Real Popcorn (IRE) (Jareer (USA))
1079^{4} 1445^{5} 1762^{8} 4903^{7} 5199^{9} 5931^{3} (6074) 6282^{7} 6328^{9} 6635^{5} 6872^{2} 7042^{8} 7122^{3} 7243^{3}

Andre Chenier (IRE) *P Monteith* 63
6 b g Perugino(USA) —Almada (GER) (Lombard (GER))
1042^{12} 3783^{7}

Andronikos *P F I Cole* a104 110
5 ch h Dr Fong(USA) —Arctic Air (Polar Falcon (USA))
1836^{15} 2058^{12} 6668^{5} 6851^{8} 6932^{3} 7053^{4} 7184^{11} 7254^{5}

Anduril *Miss M E Rowland* a71 76
6 ch g Kris—Attribute (Warning)
14^{3} 228^{5} 263^{13} 2169^{7} 2809^{10} 3926^{7} 4383^{7} 7189^{6}

And Your Point Is (USA) *C R Egerton* 58
3 b g Point Given(USA) —Ascend (USA) (Risen Star (USA))
3276^{8} 4138^{5} 4457^{8}

Aneebee (IRE) *R Hannon* a47 51
2 b f Fraam—Emilia Romagna (GER) (Acatenango (GER))
3213^{11} 4162^{11} 4875^{10} 5869^{2} 6207^{8} 6427^{12}

Anfield Dream *J R Jenkins* a81 65
5 b g Lujain(USA) —Fifth Emerald (Formidable (USA))
79^{9} 234^{12} 262^{7} 465^{10} 626^{8} 1252^{7} 1681^{11} (5340) 5731^{8} 6101^{8} 6415^{16} 6870^{3} 6927^{4} 7013^{11}

Angaric (IRE) *B Smart* a79 81
4 ch g Pivotal—Grannys Reluctance (IRE) (Anita's Prince)
953^{2} 1481^{2} 2466^{6} 3401^{8} 4140^{3} 6232^{3} 6331^{3} 6701^{7} 7045^{3} 7289^{4}

Angel De Madrid (CHI) *Rune Haugen* 100
6 ch g More Royal(USA) —Labrada (CHI) (Laguardia (USA))
2131a^{2} 4874a^{4} 5263a^{5}

Angel Kate (IRE) *H R A Cecil* 74
3 b f Invincible Spirit(IRE) —Lake Nyasa (IRE) (Lake Coniston (IRE))
1128^{5} 1409^{2} 2428^{4} 3387^{3} (5013)

Angelofthenorth *C J Teague* 64
5 b m Tomba—Dark Kristal (IRE) (Gorytus (USA))
4706^{12}

Angelonmyshoulder *John M Oxx* 102
3 b g King's Best(USA) —Angel Of The Gwaun (IRE) (Sadler's Wells (USA))
1547a^{9}

Angel Pie *R Charlton* a34 24
2 b f Diesis—Name Of Love (IRE) (Petardia)
3643^{10} 4402^{18}

Angel Rock (IRE) *P W Chapple-Hyam* 67
2 b c Rock Of Gibraltar(IRE) —Nomothetis (IRE) (Law Society (USA))
5321^{6}

Angel Sprints *C J Down* 88
5 b m Piccolo—Runs In The Family (Distant Relative)
1292^{6} 1984^{3} 2088^{4} 2472^{2} 3474^{3} 3682^{4} 3970^{4} (4396) 4816^{11} 5722^{6}

Angel Voices (IRE) *K R Burke* a64 63
4 b m Tagula(IRE) —Lithe Spirit (IRE) (Dancing Dissident (USA))
1177^{5} 2309^{3} 2988^{5} 3474^{5} 4157^{2} 4855^{4} 5934^{5} 6956^{8} (7118)

Angle Of Attack (IRE) *R A Fahey* a74 71
2 b g Acclamation—Travel Spot Girl (Primo Dominie)
1772^{5} 2021^{4} 2460^{4} 3841^{6} 4560^{2} 4923^{8} 4975^{5} 5932^{3} (6227) 6741^{3} 6834^{6}

Angus Newz *M Quinn* a79 100
4 ch m Compton Place—Hickleton Lady (IRE) (Kala Shikari)
551^{6} 847^{7} 1497^{9} 1670^{8} (1861) 2184^{6} 3104^{13} 3240^{4} 3511^{10} 3749^{8} 5195^{5} 5513^{2} (5954) 6300^{3}

Animated *A J McCabe* a38 50
3 b g Averti(IRE) —Anita Marie (IRE) (Anita's Prince)
237^{8}

Animator *P F I Cole* a70 44
2 b c Act One—Robsart (IRE) (Robellino (USA))
6246^{10} 6578^{5} 6763^{4} (6978)

Ankara *M Johnston* a39
3 ch f Elusive Quality(USA) —Maeander (FR) (Nashwan (USA))
449^{8}

Anko (POL) *J D Frost*
8 b g Saphir(GER) —Arietta (GER) (Kings Lake (USA))
3795^{11}

Anna Karenina (IRE) *David Wachman* 107
4 b m Green Desert(USA) —Simaat (USA) (Mr Prospector (USA))
2053a^{4} 4648a^{7} 5459a^{8}

Annaliesse (IRE) *R A Fahey* 71
2 ch f Rock Of Gibraltar(IRE) —Oh So Well (IRE) (Sadler's Wells (USA))
3192^{4} (3761) 5350^{13} 5613^{4}

Annambo *P J McBride* a82 82
7 ch g In The Wings—Anna Matrushka (Mill Reef (USA))
1272^{4} 2047^{4} (2471) 3112^{2} (4460) 6622^{9} 6853^{6} 6971^{2}

Anna Pavlova *R A Fahey* 113
4 b m Danehill Dancer(IRE) —Wheeler's Wonder (IRE) (Sure Blade (USA))
(875a) 1789^{2} 4691^{3} (5618) (6030a) 6526a^{6}

Anna's Rock (IRE) *J S Bolger* 104
3 b f Rock Of Gibraltar(IRE) —Anna Karenina (USA) (Atticus (USA))
3138a^{19} 6038a^{4}

Anna Towkaska *W R Swinburn* 56
3 b f Polish Precedent(USA) —Eliza Acton (Shirley Heights)
1928^{4} 2597^{12} 5005^{9} 5710^{7}

Anna Walhaan (IRE) *Ian Williams* a7 78
8 b g Green Desert(USA) —Queen's Music (USA) (Dixieland Band (USA))
5756^{13}

Anne Bonney *E J O'Neill* a55 53
3 b f Jade Robbery(USA) —Sanchez (Wolfhound (USA))
258^{3} 522^{7} 1964^{5} 3427^{10} 5386^{9}

Anne Bronte *M Johnston* a66 64
3 ro f Act One—Anka Britannia (USA) (Irish River (FR))
735^{4} 869^{2} 1044^{8} 2008^{3} 2223^{3} 2610^{13}

Annemasse *M Johnston* a93 103
3 b g Anabaa(USA) —Statua (IRE) (Statoblest)
(583) (725) 815^{3} (1603) 2037^{2} 2212^{5} 2788^{6} 3431^{9} 3745^{2} 3940^{5} (4385) 4745^{13} 5833^{4} 6011^{10}

Annenkov (IRE) *P Moody* 111
5 b h Danehill(USA) —Agathe (USA) (Manila (USA))
6354a^{8}

Anne Of Kiev (IRE) *J H M Gosden* a74 62
2 b f Oasis Dream—Top Flight Queen (Mark Of Esteem (IRE))
6306^{4} 6601^{2}

Annes Rocket (IRE) *J C Fox* a67 66
2 b c Fasliyev(USA) —Aguilas Perla (IRE) (Indian Ridge)
6125^{5} 6799^{5} 7000^{4} (7235)

Annia Faustina (IRE) *J L Spearing* a56 41
3 ch f Docksider(USA) —Benguela (USA) (Little Current (USA))
284^{5} 454^{11}

Annibale Caro *Grant Tuer* a22 50
5 b g Mtoto—Isabella Gonzaga (Rock Hopper)
3753^{10} 5835^{5} 6330^{9} 6558^{7}

Annie Skates (USA) *Jane Chapple-Hyam* a77 99
2 ch f Mr Greeley(USA) —Vivalita (USA) (Deputy Minister (CAN))
4774^{2} (5202) 6008^{3} 6482a^{2}

Annosh (TUR) *M Yigiter* 106
4 b m Nashwan(USA) —Anam (Persian Bold)
5264a^{5}

Annunzio *T G McCourt* a44 94
4 b g Big Shuffle(USA) —Abrakadabra (GER) (Aratikos (GER))
6982^{9}

A Nod And A Wink (IRE) *J C Fox* a52 53
3 b f Raise A Grand(IRE) —Earth Charter (Slip Anchor)
25^{4} 93^{2} 209^{7} 357^{9} 676^{6} 794^{3} 3652^{9} 4025^{10} 5708^{11}

Anosti *K A Ryan* 90
2 b f Act One—Apennina (USA) (Gulch (USA))
(3673) 4225^{2} 4899^{2} 5322^{11} 5766^{5} 5974^{2}

Another Choice (IRE) *N P Littmoden* a3 40
6 ch g Be My Guest(USA) —Gipsy Rose Lee (IRE) (Marju (IRE))
1438^{9} 1997^{10}

Another Decree *M Dods* 75
2 b c Diktat—Akhira (Emperor Jones (USA))
3781^{4} 4378^{4} 5974^{19}

Another Express (IRE) *T Stack* 93
2 b c Choisir(AUS) —Chantarella (IRE) (Royal Academy (USA))
2049a^{5} 3141a^{4} 5070a^{8}

Another Genepi (USA) *K A Ryan* a76 73
4 br m Stravinsky(USA) —Dawn Aurora (USA) (Night Shift (USA))
85^{11} 211^{9} 359^{4} 724^{8} 796^{2} 967^{3} (1280) 1309^{6} 1534^{2} 3414^{4} 4083^{3} 4462^{3} 4931^{6} 5155^{8} (5893) 6677^{9} 6962^{7} 7233^{7}

Another Gladiator (USA) *K A Ryan* a64 59
4 br h Danzig(USA) —Scarab Bracelet (USA) (Riverman (USA))
131^{8} 306^{6} (379)

Another Socket *E S McMahon* a74 55
2 b f Overbury(IRE) —Elsocko (Swing Easy (USA))
6105^{6} 6386^{2} (6692)

Another Toy *A D Brown* a43
4 b m Sugarfoot—Nampara Bay (Emarati (USA))
375^{7} 567^{8}

Another True Story *Z Koplik* 91
3 b c Piccolo—Lost In Lucca (Inchinor)
1005a[6]

Anoush (USA) *P Bary* a85 92
3 b f Giant's Causeway(USA) —Brianda (IRE) (Alzao (USA))
6940a[8] 7049a[8]

Ans Bach *D Selvaratnam* a107 97
4 b g Green Desert(USA) —Bezzaaf (Machiavellian (USA))
394a[2] 542a[6]

An Scaribh *P D Evans* 59
2 br c Where Or When(IRE) —Wadenhoe (IRE) (Persian Bold)
1919[9] 2303[4] 2539[12] 5771[11]

Ansells Pride (IRE) *B Smart* a75 78
4 b g King Charlemagne(USA) —Accounting (Sillery (USA))
204[2] 449[2] (559) 6465[13] (6746)

Anselme Royal (FR) *J-Y Artu* 60
7 b g Kaldounevees(FR) —Royal Bride (FR) (Garde Royale)
6923a[0]

Ansermo (GER) *Christina Bucher* 52
3 b c Hamond(GER) —Auenqueen (GER) (Big Shuffle (USA))
2503a[11]

An Tadh (IRE) *G M Lyons* a102 111
4 b h Halling(USA) —Tithcar (Cadeaux Genereux)
1049a[2] 2050a[11] 4864a[7] 5242a[18] 6038a[10]

Antek (GER) *H Blume* 106
3 br c Kallisto(GER) —Anna Of Cashel (GER) (Bishop Of Cashel)
2502a[5] 3146a[2]

Anthea *B R Millman* a62 65
3 b f Tobougg(IRE) —Blue Indigo (FR) (Pistolet Bleu (IRE))
1155[10] 1731[8] 2105[4] 2940[2] 3429[9] 4630[5] 5859[2] 6420[11] 6778[5] 6867[9]

Anthemion (IRE) *Mrs J C McGregor* a48 64
10 ch g Night Shift(USA) —New Sensitive (Wattlefield)
1488[5] 1627[10] 2388[3] 2827[4] 3376[11] 3816[3] 4159[9] 4704[10] 4966[4] 4998[10] 5035[5] 5476[10] 5890[4] 6479[5]

Anthill *I A Wood* a42 63
3 b f Slickly(FR) —Baddi Heights (FR) (Shirley Heights)
1409[6] 1838[8] 2425[7] 3087[2] 6455[7]

Antigoni (IRE) *A M Balding* a69 72
4 ch m Grand Lodge(USA) —Butter Knife (IRE) (Sure Blade (USA))
1507[16] 2257[2] 2592[9] 3409[9]

Anton Chekhov *U Ostmann* 108
3 b c Montjeu(IRE) —By Charter (Shirley Heights)
1185a[5] (1572a) 2235[12] 3146a[3] 4872a[6]

Antonym (USA) *Mario Hofer* 82
3 b f Bahri(USA) —Annaba (IRE) (In The Wings)
6940a[7]

Antrim Rose *E F Vaughan* a61 58
3 b f Giant's Causeway(USA) —Aunty Rose (IRE) (Caerleon (USA))
4327[8] 4742[3] 5783[6] 6290[6]

Anybody's Guess (IRE) *J S Wainwright* 42
3 b g Iron Mask(USA) —Credibility (Komaite (USA))
2300[10] 2829[12]

Any Given Day (IRE) *D M Simcock* a63 54
2 gr c Clodovil(IRE) —Five Of Wands (Caerleon (USA))
4110[13] 4539[7] 5541[8] (6427)

Any Given Saturday (USA) *T Pletcher* a127
3 bb c Distorted Humor(USA) —Weekend In Indy (USA) (A.P. Indy (USA))
1486a[8] 6514a[6]

Anything Once (USA) *D Carroll* a51 54
4 b g Elusive Quality(USA) —Bushy's Pride (USA) (Hagley's Reward (USA))
1167[12] 4427[10] 4920[8] 5525[4] 5557[8] 5739[3] 6019[6] 6250[3] 6265[7] 7109[4] 7219[7]

A One (IRE) *H J Manners* 41
8 b g Alzao(USA) —Anita's Contessa (IRE) (Anita's Prince)
2603[11] 3163[8] 3690[7] 4231[11] 4418 [10]

Apache Chant (USA) *A W Carroll* 62
3 b g War Chant(USA) —Sterling Pound (USA) (Seeking The Gold (USA))
2081[3] 2558[5] 3150[14] 4877[3] 5346[4]

Apache Dawn *G L Moore* a89 89
3 ch g Pursuit Of Love—Taza (Persian Bold)
1804[5] 2312[4] (3029) 3235[7] 3607[6] 4080[9] 7165[2]

Apache Fort *T Keddy* a70 75
4 b g Desert Prince(IRE) —Apogee (Shirley Heights)
126[DSQ] (203) (309) 1314[3] 1532[3] 1819[4] 2089[4] 2471[2] 2887[3] 3457[2] 3945[3] 4576[9] (5093) 5454[3] 5769[2] 6186[6] 6902[2]

Apache Nation (IRE) *M Dods* 69
4 b g Fruits Of Love(USA) —Rachel Green (IRE) (Case Law)
992[16] 1241[10] 1675[13] 1944[7] 2302[8] (2809) 3034[6] 3381[3] 3571[2] 3754[3] 3789[7] 5964[2] 6258[8] 6640[12]

Apache Point (IRE) *N Tinkler* a11 66
10 ch g Indian Ridge—Ausherra (USA) (Diesis)
1090[11] 1918[8] 2168[6] 2843[2] 3195[2] 3765[9] 4082[5] 4410[4] 4580[2] 5525[7] 5838[6] 6380[9]

A Peaceful Man *Mrs L C Jewell* a46 59
3 b g Tipsy Creek(USA) —My Hearts Desire (Deploy)
342[11] 1634[16] 2572[12] 4322[10]

Aperitif *D Nicholls* a72 77
6 ch g Pivotal—Art Deco Lady (Master Willie)
151[7] 468[8] 604[8] 681[8] 718[2] 895[4] 1066[12]

Apex *M Hill* a84 90
6 ch g Efisio—Royal Loft (Homing)
268[8] 366[6] 447[3] 524[5] 710[4] (976) (1251) 1378[2] (1765) (1886) 3001[4] 3527[5] 5593[8] 6067[5] 6359[3] 6596[2]

Aphorism *J R Fanshawe* a73 82
4 b m Halling(USA) —Applecross (Glint Of Gold)
4544[3] 5034[3] (5884) 6284[3]

Aphrodelta *P D Cundell* a52
5 b m Delta Dancer—Mouton (IRE) (Dolphin Street (FR))
189[6] 207[2] 1360[8]

Aphrodisia *S C Williams* a66 65
3 b f Sakhee(USA) —Aegean Dream (IRE) (Royal Academy (USA))
1901[8] 2913[10] 5279[2] 5531[2]

Apocalypto (IRE) *E J Creighton*
3 b c Auction House(USA) —Scared (Royal Academy (USA))
1587[13]

Apolina *Miss K B Boutflower* 38
3 b f Pursuit Of Love—Caerosa (Caerleon (USA))
2059[11] 2186[5] 2606[13] 3826[12] 4327[12]

Apollo Five *D J Coakley* a61 80
3 ch g Auction House(USA) —Dazzling Quintet (Superlative)
1500[10] 2400[12] 3235[11] 4015[14] 4760[3] 5475[8] 5860[11] 6582[8]

Apollo Shark (IRE) *J Howard Johnson* 78
2 ch g Spartacus(IRE) —Shot Of Redemption (Shirley Heights)
1859[4] (2739) (3373) 4743[18]

Apollo Star (GER) *Mario Hofer* 109
5 ch g Devil River Peek(USA) —Arwina (GER) (Windwurf (GER))
(881a) (2295a) 3581a[5] (4217a) 5670a[2] 6372a[7]

Appalachian Trail (IRE) *I Semple* a102 116
6 b g Indian Ridge—Karinski (USA) (Palace Music (USA))
247a[4] (400a) 528a[5] 847[4] 1656[8] 2857[18] 3088[2] 3894[8] 5213[5] 5616[9] (6018) (6491) 6965[5]

Appel Au Maitre (FR) *Wido Neuroth* 104
3 ch c Starborough—Rotina (FR) (Crystal Glitters (USA))
1387a[4] 2502a[2] 3146a[4] (5263a) 6376a[6]

Applauded (IRE) *B J Meehan* a81 88
2 b f Royal Applause—Frappe (IRE) (Inchinor)
4602[3] 5540[2] 6336[10] (7058)

Apple Blossom (IRE) *G Wragg* 80
3 b f Danehill Dancer(IRE) —Silk (IRE) (Machiavellian (USA))
977[2] 1620[8] 2429[2] (4178) 4848[14]

Appleby *J H M Gosden* a59 66
3 b f Anabaa(USA) —May Ball (Cadeaux Genereux)
1447[7] 1961[3] 2542[5] 3087[8] 5510[4] 6089[11]

Apple Pie Order (IRE) *R J Hodges*
2 b f Namid—Apple Sauce (Prince Sabo)
5162[18]

Apply Dapply *H Morrison* a60 89
4 b m Pursuit Of Love—Daring Destiny (Daring March)
(902) 1649[2] 2207[9] 3001[3] 3591[5] 4257[5] 4814[2] 5794[7] 6129[3] 6620[6]

Appointment *Mrs A J Perrett* a64 46
2 ch f Where Or When(IRE) —Shoshone (Be My Chief (USA))
5596[13] 5944[7] 6262[4]

April Fool *J A Geake* 60
3 ch g Pivotal—Palace Affair (Pursuit Of Love)
1297[5] 1726[13] 3429[3]

April Reigns *D Burchell* a14 18
2 ch f Ballet Master(USA) —Princess Oberon (IRE) (Fairy King (USA))
4756[12] 5302[15] 6151[10]

April's Quest (IRE) *David Pinder* a41 43
2 ch f Spectrum(IRE) —Coastal Jewel (IRE) (Kris)
3643[12] 4074[8] 4428[10] 5267[8] 5603[12]

April The Second *R J Price* a46 56
3 b g Tomba—Little Kenny (Warning)
1348[7] 1937[8] 2402[12]

Apsara *G M Moore* 74
6 br m Groom Dancer(USA) —Ayodhya (IRE) (Astronef)
1413[10] 2007[4] 2338[11] 3156[9] 3754[6] 4081[5] 5738[7]

A. P. Xcellent (USA) *J Shirreffs* a117 109
4 b h A.P. Indy(USA) —Exing (CHI) (Exceller (USA))
5824a[5]

Aqaleem *M P Tregoning* 117
3 b c Sinndar(IRE) —Dalayil (IRE) (Sadler's Wells (USA))
(1662) 2235[3] 4044[2]

Aqlaam *W J Haggas* 90
2 b c Oasis Dream—Bourbonella (Rainbow Quest (USA))
3991[3]

Aqmaar *J L Dunlop* a87 95
3 b c Green Desert(USA) —Hureya (USA) (Woodman (USA))
1124[4] (1471) 2037[13] 3503[13] 3940[10]

Aqraan *Kevin Prendergast* 98
3 ch f In The Wings—Elshamms (Zafonic (USA))
3576a[11]

Aqualung *D Broad* a44 49
6 b g Desert King(IRE) —Aquarelle (Kenmare (FR))
5788a[13]

Aquamarine Beauty (FR) *Sir Michael Stoute* 58
3 b f Daliapour(IRE) —Dix Huit Brumaire (FR) (General Assembly (USA))
3847[7] 5271[5]

Aquarian Dancer *Jedd O'Keeffe* 51
2 b f Mujahid(USA) —Admonish (Warning)
1193[9] 1963[8] 2504[13] 4278[8] 5702[5]

Aquaturbo (FR) *J-P Gauvin* 96
4 b g Northern Crystal—Basilissa (FR) (Gay Minstrel (FR))
3665a[12]

Aquilegia (IRE) *E S McMahon* 75
3 b f Desert Style(IRE) —Pyatshaw (Common Grounds)
1151[2] 1766[4] 2198[4] (Dead)

Arabellas Homer *Mrs N S Evans* a50 48
3 b f Mark Of Esteem(IRE) —Rush Hour (IRE) (Night Shift (USA))
65[5] 224[13] 335[7] 534[8] 1573[2] 2843[3] 4031[15] 4426[8] 4920[12] 5690[5] 5915[12] 6152[9] 7203[5]

Arabesque Dancer *M Botti* a57
2 b f Dubai Destination(USA) —Seven Of Nine (IRE) (Alzao (USA))
6934[7] 7101[5] 7259[4]

Arabian Art (USA) *H R A Cecil* a70 59
2 br f E Dubai(USA) —Slamya (USA) (Seattle Slew (USA))
6648[15] 6847[5]

Arabian Fern *M E Sowersby* 39
2 b f Tobougg(IRE) —Cryptogam (Zamindar (USA))
2738[4] 2838[5] 3296[5] 3751[7] 5524[8]

Arabian Gleam *J Noseda* a89 115
3 b c Kyllachy—Gleam Of Light (IRE) (Danehill (USA))
1452[2] (2175) 2752[3] 4045[5] (5409) 6332[6]

Arabian Gulf *Sir Michael Stoute* 107
3 b c Sadler's Wells(USA) —Wince (Selkirk (USA))
(1093) 1602[2]

Arabian Prince (USA) *Doug Watson* a100 109
4 b h Fusaichi Pegasus(USA) —Add (USA) (Spectacular Bid (USA))
413a[8] 643a[3]

Arabian Spirit *E A L Dunlop* a68 65
2 b c Oasis Dream—Royal Flame (IRE) (Royal Academy (USA))
5977[13] 6246[4] 6530[3]

Arabian Sun *M J Attwater* a68 64
3 b g Singspiel(IRE) —Bright Halo (IRE) (Bigstone (IRE))
2455[11] 2690[5] 3402[8] 3848[6] 4322[9] 5426[4] 5820[7] 5948[4] 6341[2] 6643[5] 6802[7]

Arabian Treasure (USA) *Sir Michael Stoute* 81
3 b f Danzig(USA) —Very Confidential (USA) (Fappiano (USA))
1105[6] (1408) 2369[4] 3591[6] 5210[5]

Arabiyah *L M Cumani* a38 60
3 b f Halling(USA) —Jumaireyah (Fairy King (USA))
1560[15] 2077[4] 2580[3] 3249[3] 4309[5] 4821[7] 5755[9] 6315[8]

Arab League (IRE) *M Johnston* 42
2 b g Dubai Destination(USA) —Johnny And Clyde (USA) (Sky Classic (CAN))
1498[7] 5707[9]

Arafan (IRE) *Dr R D P Newland* a72 69
5 b g Barathea(IRE) —Asmara (USA) (Lear Fan (USA))
1263[3] 1683[9] 1752[5]

Araglin *J T Stimpson* a47 30
8 b g Sadler's Wells(USA) —River Cara (USA) (Irish River (FR))
3927[7] 4638[8]

Aramina (GER) *P Schiergen* 103
4 ch m In The Wings—Akasma (GER) (Windwurf (GER))
6220a[6] 6953a[0]

Araschan (FR) *H Rogers* a64 78
4 ch g Lord Of Men—All The Glory (GER) (Lomitas)
6553a[7]

Arboraetas (GER) *W Figge* 48
2 b c Monsun(GER) —Alte Klasse (GER) (Royal Academy (USA))
6324a[11]

Arcadio (GER) *J Hirschberger* 118
5 b h Monsun(GER) —Assia (IRE) (Royal Academy (USA))
1872a[6] 2924a[5] 4013a[5]

Arcangela *Miss Tracy Waggott* a44 45
4 b m Galileo(IRE) —Crafty Buzz (USA) (Crafty Prospector (USA))
628[3] 913[13] 965[4] 2252[F] 2825[13] 3402[9]

Arc Bleu (GER) *A J Martin* 87
6 ch g Monsagem(USA) —Antala (FR) (Antheus (USA))
(3143a)

Arc De Triomphe (GER) *D Fechner* 106
5 b h Big Shuffle(USA) —Alepha (Celestial Storm (USA))
1800a[4] (2811a) 4190a[9] 4869a[8] 6633a[10]

Arcetri (IRE) *K A Ryan* 58
2 b f Galileo(IRE) —Shewillifshewants (IRE) (Alzao (USA))
3916[9] 5281[5] 5949[13]

Archduke Ferdinand (FR) *A King* a87 84
9 ch g Dernier Empereur(USA) —Lady Norcliffe (USA) (Norcliffe (CAN))
192[7]

Arch Folly *R J Price* a58 65
5 b g Silver Patriarch(IRE) —Folly Fox (Alhijaz)
4521[8] 5007[13]

Archiestown (USA) *J L Dunlop* 80
4 b g Arch(USA) —Second Chorus (IRE) (Scenic)
3060[10] (3711) 4166[8] 4814[7] 6203[14]

Archilini *K A Morgan* a62
2 b c Bertolini(USA) —Dizzy Knight (Distant Relative)
6820[4] 7000[9] 7191[8]

Archimage (USA) *T D Barron* 39
3 bb g Arch(USA) —Powerful Package (USA) (Star De Naskra (USA))
1923[12] 2740[10] 2894[8] 5282[9]

Archimboldo (USA) *T Wall* a74 62
4 ch g Woodman(USA) —Awesome Strike (USA) (Theatrical)
4352[10]

Archipenko (USA) *A P O'Brien* 114
3 b c Kingmambo(USA) —Bound (USA) (Nijinsky (CAN))
(1693a) 2235[17] 3331[7] 4058[5] 5261a[5]

Archived (IRE) *M G Quinlan* 87
2 b c Millkom—La Fija (USA) (Dixieland Band (USA))
2241[2] (2687) 3524[4] 4372[5] 4769[2] 5974[10] 6495[7]

Arch Of Titus (IRE) *M L W Bell* a84 76
3 ch c Titus Livius(FR) —Cap And Gown (IRE) (Royal Academy (USA))
73[2] 301[3] 522[3] (711) (935) 1257[6] 1994[6] 3078[6] 3943[21]

Arch Rebel (USA) *Noel Meade* 117
6 b g Arch(USA) —Sheba's Step (USA) (Alysheba (USA))
2064a[7] 2483a[3] 2851a[3] 3983a[5] 4647a[3] 5240a[2] 6376a[2] 7090a[4]

Arch Swing (USA) *John M Oxx* 115
3 b f Arch(USA) —Gold Pattern (USA) (Slew O'Gold (USA))
(946a) 1496[2] 2065a[11] 2814[4] 3433[3] 5241a[3]

Arctic Cape *M Johnston* 84
2 b c Cape Cross(IRE) —Arctic Air (Polar Falcon (USA))
3991[6] (4378) 5053[4]

Arctic Desert *Miss Gay Kelleway* a81 79
7 b g Desert Prince(IRE) —Thamud (IRE) (Lahib (USA))
6[7] 211[3] 261[7] 592[4] 739[4] 923[2] 1036[9] 3711[13] 4029[7] 4135[5] 4587[4] 4860[5] 5062[2] 5275[7] (7001) 7080[3] 7131[4]

Arctic Wings (IRE) *W R Muir* a69 75
3 b c In The Wings—Arctic Hunt (IRE) (Bering)
1289[4] (1724) 2112[6] 2602[15] 4069[4] 4910[4] 5432[3] 5732[10] 6145[12]

Arctiz (USA) *P F I Cole* a27 65
3 bb c Tiznow(USA) —Perfect Arc (USA) (Brown Arc (USA))
2690[4] 3113[9] 3476[11]

Ardbrae Lady *Joseph G Murphy* 104
4 b m Overbury(IRE) —Gagajulu (Al Hareb (USA))
(782a) 1548a[4] 2053a[10]

Ardennes (IRE) *M Botti* a56 42
3 b g Jade Robbery(USA) —Ribbon Glade (UAE) (Zafonic (USA))
2894[4] 4021[4] 5511[5]

Ardent Number *D A Nolan*
7 b g Alderbrook—Pretty Average (Skyliner)
1804[14]

Ardent Prince *Heather Dalton* a59 41
4 b g Polar Prince(IRE) —Anthem Flight (USA) (Fly So Free (USA))
3487[9] 4353[13] 4670[2] 5204[8] 5364[10] 6265[11]

Ardmaddy (IRE) *J A R Toller* a61 57
3 b g Generous(IRE) —Yazmin (IRE) (Green Desert (USA))
1343[12] 4815[11] 5366[2] 5894[2] 6147[2] 6534[11]

Arena's Dream (USA) *J R Boyle* a71 75
3 rg g Aljabr(USA) —Witching Well (IRE) (Night Shift (USA))
257[5] 744[4] 1076[4] 1247[3] 1676[2] 2092[4] 2464[2] 3015[3] 4138[2] 4424[5] (4997) 7099[6] 7200[3] 7257[3]

Arenti (NZ) *J Meagher* 107
6 b g O'Reilly(NZ) —Gio (NZ) (Centaine (AUS))
409a[2] 528a[3]

Areweplayingout (IRE) *Peter Grayson* a59 46
2 b f Namid—Bobbydazzle (Rock Hopper)
1033[5] 1285[12] 1889[7] 2247[3] (2517) 3392[2]

Areyaam (USA) *L M Cumani* a72 75
3 b f Elusive Quality(USA) —Yanaseeni (USA) (Trempolino (USA))
2429[3] 2873[3] 3454[3] 4112[9] 5367[5]

Areyoutalkingtome *C A Cyzer* a121 107
4 b h Singspiel(IRE) —Shot At Love (IRE) (Last Tycoon (IRE))
43[4] (118) (344) 551[5] 860a[12] 1305[9] 4747[10] 5112[6] 5416[4] 5797[20]

Arfinnit (IRE) *Mrs A L M King* a66 60
6 b g College Chapel—Tidal Reach (USA) (Kris S (USA))
189[3] 549[8] 557[7] 687[6] 750[3] 1899[7] 1969[7] (2174) 2555[10] 3618[5] 4180[8] (4668) 4973[4] 5340[6] 5430[4] 5565[9] 7013[10] 7188[2] 7265[8]

Arganil (USA) *K A Ryan* 51
2 ch c Langfuhr(CAN) —Sherona (USA) (Mr Greeley (USA))
5580[9]

Argentina (IRE) *R J Frankel* 113
5 b m Sadler's Wells(USA) —Airline (USA) (Woodman (USA))
5822a[5] 6509a[9]

Argentine (IRE) *L Lungo* a75 84
3 b g Fasliyev(USA) —Teller (ARG) (Southern Halo (USA))
5039[13] 5332[5] 5667[4] 6157[13] 6559[4] 6731[6]

Ariege (USA) *T Stack* 94
2 bb f Doneraile Court(USA) —Kostroma (Caerleon (USA))
4440a[4] 5353[11]

Aries Magic *S C Burrough* 9
2 b f High Tension(USA) —Mountain Magic (Magic Ring (IRE))
2103[13] 3552[14] 5161[5]

Ariodante *J M P Eustace* a70 72
5 b g Groom Dancer(USA) —Maestrale (Top Ville)
29[2] 195[12] 1295[8] 2531[9] 3617[10] 4318[9] 4915[13]

Aristi (IRE) *R M Stronge* a56 54
6 b m Dr Fong(USA) —Edessa (IRE) (Tirol)
1229[6]

Arithmatix (USA) *G A Butler* a61 58
3 b c Arch(USA) —Startarette (USA) (Dixieland Band (USA))
1403[12] 2477[6] 2913[7] 4433[8]

Arkadina (IRE) *David Wachman* 99
3 b f Danehill(USA) —Cumbres (FR) (Kahyasi)
4649a[3]

Arkando (IRE) *K R Burke* 45
2 b f Mull Of Kintyre(USA) —Arjan (IRE) (Paris House)
4076[9]

Armada *W J Haggas* a77
4 b g Anabaa(USA) —Trevillari (USA) (Riverman (USA))
351[10] 501[9] 604[10]

Armenian Heritage *Gianluca Bietolini* 83
4 b m Bluebird(USA) —Blueberry Walk (Green Desert (USA))
1337a[14]

Arminius (IRE) *I Mohammed* 99
4 b g Shinko Forest(IRE) —Tribal Rite (Be My Native (USA))
395a[3] 540a[4]

Armure *M A Jarvis* 77
2 gr f Dalakhani(IRE) —Bombazine (IRE) (Generous (IRE))
4094[7] 4796[4] 5812[3]

Army Of Angels (IRE) *Saeed Bin Suroor* 114
5 ch g King's Best(USA) —Angelic Sounds (IRE) (The Noble Player (USA))
646a[6] (1723) 2442[2]

Arniecoco *B J Meehan* a45
2 b c Dr Fong(USA) —Groovy (Shareef Dancer (USA))
3849[8]

Arnie's Joint (IRE) *N P Littmoden* a63 71
3 b g Golan(IRE) —Green Green Grass (Green Desert (USA))
385[6] 502[5] 659[5] 778[6] 974[3] 1219[8] 1346[2]

Arnuide (SPA) *R Martin-Vidania* 93
4 ch h Kahyasi—Value For Money (FR) (Highest Honor (FR))
3893a[8]

Aromatherapy *H R A Cecil* 74
2 b f Oasis Dream—Fragrant View (USA) (Distant View (USA))
5598[3] 6015[4]

Arondo (GER) *Mervyn Torrens* a59 36
4 ch g Areion(GER) —Arrancada (GER) (Riboprince (USA))
7157[4]

Arqaam *Saeed Bin Suroor* 108
3 b c Machiavellian(USA) —Khams-Alhawas (IRE) (Marju (IRE))
(5157) 6153[4]

Arrabiata *C N Kellett* a1
2 b f Piccolo—Paperweight (In The Wings)
7235[7]

Arravale (USA) *M Benson* 117
4 bb m Arch(USA) —Kalosca (FR) (Kaldoun (FR))
6509a[7]

Arrewig Lissome (USA) *A M Balding* a47 51
2 b c Black Tie Affair—Lissome (USA) (Lear Fan (USA))
5599[12] 7252[8]

Arrivee (FR) *Mrs P Sly* a54 92
4 bb m Anabaa(USA) —Quiet Dream (USA) (Seattle Slew (USA))
1472[8] 1661[8] 2573[11]

Arsad (IRE) *C E Brittain* a80 63
4 b m Cape Cross(IRE) —Astuti (IRE) (Waajib)
(62) 434[2] 1253[8] 1752[2] 2148[2] 4131[8] 5892[5]

Arson Squad (USA) *B Headley* a118 108
4 bb g Brahms(USA) —Majestic Fire (USA) (Green Dancer (USA))
5824a[7]

Art Advisor (IRE) *J Howard Johnson* 101
2 b c Noverre(USA) —Monarchy (IRE) (Common Grounds)
1772[2] (2071) 2785[2] 3779a[5] 4721[7] 6017[17]

Art Attack (GER) *Rune Haugen* 97
4 ch h Platini(GER) —A Real Work Of Art (IRE) (Keen)
2131a[7] 4874a[8] 6353a[9]

Art Collector (USA) *G L Moore*
2 ch c Mr Greeley(USA) —Fellwaati (USA) (Alydar (USA))
5011[15]

Art Currency (USA) *M J Wallace* a60 67
2 bb c Street Cry(IRE) —Lady In Silver (USA) (Silver Hawk (USA))
4393[6] 4683[2] 5399[6]

Artdeal *M J Wallace* a72 73
2 b g Fasliyev(USA) —Eternal Beauty (USA) (Zafonic (USA))
942[2] (1087) 1580[7] 2090[3] (2549) (3174)

Art Deco (IRE) *C R Egerton* 115
4 ch h Peintre Celebre(USA) —Sometime (IRE) (Royal Academy (USA))
1274[6]

Art Elegant *T G McCourt* a42 73
5 b g Desert Prince(IRE) —Elegant (IRE) (Marju (IRE))
5836[10] 6979[6]

Art Exhibition (IRE) *J Noseda* a53
2 ch c Captain Rio—Miss Dilletante (Primo Dominie)
6820[8]

Art Gallery *G L Moore* a42 56
3 ch g Indian Ridge—Party Doll (Be My Guest (USA))
1399[6] 2425[9] 5894[9] 6806[13]

Art Gamble (IRE) *N A Callaghan* 38
3 b g Shinko Forest(IRE) —Kiva (Indian Ridge)
2012[13] 2186[8] 2366[6]

Arthur Parker *J A B Old* a19 29
6 b g Cloudings(IRE) —Black H'Penny (Town And Country)
936[9] 1665[12] 2307[12]

Arthurs Dream (IRE) *A W Carroll* a41 51
5 b g Desert Prince(IRE) —Blueprint (USA) (Shadeed (USA))
907[7] 1362[7]

Arthur's Edge *B Palling* a71 62
3 b g Diktat—Bright Edge (Danehill Dancer (IRE))
6094[7] 6597[4] 6713[2] 6906[3] (6979)

Arthur's Girl *G Wragg* a67
2 b f Hernando(FR) —Maid Of Camelot (Caerleon (USA))
6225[5]

Artic Bliss *G F Bridgwater* a41
5 ch m Fraam—Eskimo Nel (IRE) (Shy Groom (USA))
349[8] 615[13]

Artic Cry (USA) *D K Weld* 84
2 b g Rahy(USA) —Sailing Minstrel (USA) (The Minstrel (CAN))
5397a[18]

Artie *T D Easterby* 62
8 b g Whittingham(IRE) —Calamanco (Clantime)
2989[11] 3298[9] 3515[10]

Artimino *J R Fanshawe* 106
3 b c Medicean—Palatial (Green Desert (USA))
1257[4] (2045) 2788[4] 3503[2] 4401[4] 6301[17]

Art Investor *D R C Elsworth* a73 74
4 b g Sinndar(IRE) —Maid For Romance (Pursuit Of Love)
120[3] 230[3] 458[7] 1152[13] 1578[4] 1811[14] 2157[2] 2833[7] 4610[8] 5640[7]

Artiste Royal (IRE) *N Drysdale* 115
6 b h Danehill(USA) —Agathe (USA) (Manila (USA))
6943a[8]

Artistica (IRE) *A Fabre* 97
3 ch f Spectrum(IRE) —Artistique (IRE) (Linamix (FR))
2270a[3] 4557a[10] 6770a[7]

Artistic Lad *Mrs John Harrington* 85
7 ch g Peintre Celebre(USA) —Maid For The Hills (Indian Ridge)
2018a[P] (Dead)

Artistic Liason *G C H Chung* a50 18
3 ch f Auction House(USA) —Homeoftheclassics (Tate Gallery (USA))
4470[4] 5781[8]

Artistic License (IRE) *M R Channon* 68
2 b f Chevalier(IRE) —Alexander Eliott (IRE) (Night Shift (USA))
(5065) 5766[7] 6154[12]

Artistic Light *W R Muir* a63 47
2 ch f Fantastic Light(USA) —Artisia (IRE) (Peintre Celebre (USA))
5633[10] 6289[4] 6694[2] 7022[2] 7117[8]

Artistic Style *B G Powell* a84 92
7 b g Anabaa(USA) —Fine Detail (IRE) (Shirley Heights)
3242[5] 3386[9]

Artist's Muse (USA) *M S Saunders* a2 66
4 b m Royal Academy(USA) —Atelier (Warning)
443[9]

Artless (USA) *Sir Mark Prescott* a75 89
4 b m Aptitude(USA) —Eternity (Suave Dancer (USA))
1714[3] 1937[2] 2274[4] (3371) (3584) 4371a[4]

Art Man *G L Moore* a76 73
4 b g Dansili—Persuasion (Batshoof)
5921[6] 6439[4] 6603[5]

Art Market (CAN) *G L Moore* a68 94
4 ch g Giant's Causeway(USA) —Fantasy Lake (USA) (Salt Lake (USA))
1836[11] 2399[11] 2835[13] 4234[10] 6293[6]

Art Martial (FR) *A De Royer-Dupre* 91
3 ch g Monsun(GER) —Veiled Wings (FR) (Priolo (USA))
6941a[9]

Art Master *S Kirk* a101 106
2 b c Peintre Celebre(USA) —Eurolinka (IRE) (Tirol)
3471[2] (3842) 5004[6] (6001) 6489[4]

Art Modern (IRE) *G L Moore* a88 84
5 ch g Giant's Causeway(USA) —Sinead (USA) (Irish River (FR))
96[9] 362[3] (652) (868) 1149[4] 1245[16] 2002[8] 3272[8] 4551[10] 5454[4] 6175[3]

Art Professor (IRE) *J W Hills* a73 76
3 b g In The Wings—Itab (USA) (Dayjur (USA))
456[6] 655[4] 3827[7] 4504[2] 5018[3] 5777[3]

Art Sale *G L Moore* 95
2 b c Compton Place—Bandanna (Bandmaster (USA))
2424[6] 3363[3] 3589[3] (4315) 4921[3] 5216[2] 5410[2]

Artsu *M L W Bell* 80
2 b g Bahamian Bounty—War Shanty (Warrshan (USA))
2510[4] (3037) 3524[7] 4775[2] 4995[4] 5773[6]

Art Trader (USA) *J Moore* 117
6 b g Arch(USA) —Math (USA) (Devil's Bag (USA))
7092a[4]

Art Value *P W Chapple-Hyam* a60 72
2 ch c Barathea(IRE) —Empty Purse (Pennine Walk)
6248[7] 6574[3] 7051[8]

Artzola (IRE) *C A Horgan* a58 54
7 b m Alzao(USA) —Polistatic (Free State)
495[9]

Asbury Park *M R Bosley* a56 66
4 b g Primo Valentino(IRE) —Ocean Grove (IRE) (Fairy King (USA))
1376[6]

Ascalon *Pat Eddery* 88
3 ch c Galileo(IRE) —Leaping Flame (USA) (Trempolino (USA))
1143[5] (1841) 2789[10] 4147[9] 6474[8]

Ascot Family (IRE) *A Lyon* 103
3 b f Desert Style(IRE) —Family At War (USA) (Explodent (USA))
1006a[0] 4190a[3] 4871a[9]

Ascot Lime *Sir Michael Stoute* 75
2 ch c Pivotal—Hector's Girl (Hector Protector (USA))
5323[6]

Asfurah's Dream (IRE) *M P Tregoning* a67
2 b f Nayef(USA) —Asfurah (USA) (Dayjur (USA))
6138[4]

Ashaawes (USA) *Kevin Prendergast* 109
4 b h Kingmambo(USA) —Crown Of Crimson (USA) (Seattle Slew (USA))
3144a[7]

Ashantee (GER) *M Rulec* 59
2 ch f Areion(GER) —Api Sa (IRE) (Zinaad)
2684a[9] 3147a[8]

Ashdown Express (IRE) *C F Wall* 119
8 ch g Ashkalani(IRE) —Indian Express (Indian Ridge)
400a[3] 528a[2] 644a[6] 1657[4] 2050a[5] 2695[5] 2858[13] 3894[11]

Ashes (IRE) *K R Burke* a72 76
5 b m General Monash(USA) —Wakayi (Persian Bold)
964[3] (1067) 1214[3] 1427[4] 1806[11] 2459[2] 2933[7] 3782[6] 4158[3] 4525[12] 5552[8] 5667[6] 5969[4] 6340[7] 6730[9] 7206[12] 7279[6]

Ashes Regained *B W Hills* a87 92
4 b h Galileo(IRE) —Hasty Words (IRE) (Polish Patriot (USA))
1166[3] (1905) 2469[5] 3437[2]

Ashkazar (FR) *A De Royer-Dupre* 107
3 b g Sadler's Wells(USA) —Asharna (IRE) (Darshaan)
2813[6] 3566a[5]

Ashleigh Anderson (FR) *Eamon Tyrrell* a33 68
3 b f Black Minnaloushe(USA) —Miswakette (USA) (Miswaki (USA))
3421[12] 4978[12]

Ashmal (USA) *J L Dunlop* 69
3 b f Machiavellian(USA) —Alabaq (USA) (Riverman (USA))
1127[9] 1785[3] 2620[3] 3176[6] 4282[2] 5157[2] 5859[4] 6420[2]

Ashmolian (IRE) *Miss Z C Davison* a43 53
4 b g Grand Lodge(USA) —Animatrice (USA) (Alleged (USA))
1998[10] 3232[4] 3485[4] 3901[12] 5531[11] 6866[8]

Ashwell Rose *J R Jenkins* a46 63
5 b m Anabaa(USA) —Finicia (USA) (Miswaki (USA))
3247[12] 3803[7] 4131[2] 4766[9] 5573[6] 5803[9] 6558[4] (6700)

Asian Alliance (IRE) *K A Ryan* a56 58
6 ch m Soviet Star(USA) —Indian Express (Indian Ridge)
71[6]

Asian Classic (IRE) *R Charlton* 53
2 b g Montjeu(IRE) —Yafoul (USA) (Torrential (USA))
6593[9]

Asian Lady *R Charlton* 53
2 br f Kyllachy—Prancing (Prince Sabo)
6755[8]

Asian Power (IRE) *P J O'Gorman* a70 71
2 ch g Bertolini(USA) —Cynara (Imp Society (USA))
2478[8] 2832[11] 3625[10] 4130[5] 4524[14] 4776[11] (5199) 5471[4] 6502[9]

Asiatic Boy (ARG) *M F De Kock* a121 121
4 b h Not For Sale(ARG) —S. S. Asiatic (USA) (Polish Navy (USA))
(173a) (414a) (596a) (859a) 4058[4] 4693[5]

Ask *Sir Michael Stoute* 123
4 b h Sadler's Wells(USA) —Request (Rainbow Quest (USA))
(1618) (5831) 6374a[2]

Askar Tau (FR) *M P Tregoning* 52
2 b c Montjeu(IRE) —Autriche (IRE) (Acatenango (GER))
5590[7] 6493[9]

Ask Jack (USA) *Joseph G Murphy* 72
3 ch c Mt. Livermore(USA) —Moll (USA) (Criminal Type (USA))
4114a[7]

Ask Jenny (IRE) *Patrick Morris* a52 46
5 b m Marju(IRE) —Waltzing Matilda (Mujtahid (USA))
46[9]

Ask No More *J Ryan* a73 30
4 b g Pyramus(USA) —Nordesta (IRE) (Nordico (USA))
130[11] 235[9] 341[4] 586[4] 680[3] 1120[7] 1262[5] 1349[4] 7250[7]

Ask The Butler *A W Carroll* 83
3 b g Dansili—Heronetta (Halling (USA))
1124[12] 1504[4] 1843[2] 2816[12]

Ask The Clerk (IRE) *Mrs J L Le Brocq* a62 71
6 b g Turtle Island(IRE) —Some Fun (Wolverlife)
5233[2]

Ask Yer Dad *Mrs P Sly* a65 67
3 b g Diktat—Heuston Station (IRE) (Fairy King (USA))
1155[4] 1726[6] 2083[3] 2749[5] 3646[3] 4394[12] 4778[5]

Aslan *T D Easterby* 36
3 b c Averti(IRE) —Opopmil (IRE) (Pips Pride)
1197[9] 1482[7] 2029[6] (Dead)

Asleep At The Back (IRE) *J G Given* a56 11
4 b g Halling(USA) —Molomo (Barathea (IRE))
87[3] 240[4]

Asmodea *D J Coakley* a42
2 b f Dr Fong(USA) —Latina (IRE) (King's Theatre (IRE))
7258[6]

Aspectus (IRE) *H Blume* 112
4 ch h Spectrum(IRE) —Anna Thea (IRE) (Turfkonig (GER))
880a[9] 1192a[3] 1699a[2] 2903a[2] (3581a) 4217a[3] 5265a[6] 6372a[5]

Aspen Shadow (USA) *David Wachman* 65
2 b f Fasliyev(USA) —Elegant As Always (USA) (Nashwan (USA))
2325a[8]

Asperity (USA) *J H M Gosden* 109
3 b c War Chant(USA) —Another Storm (USA) (Gone West (USA))
1306[3] (2499a) 3362a[6] 3987a[5]

Asque *G Henrot* a96 92
4 b m Dansili—Makara (Lion Cavern (USA))
31a[6] 6954a[7]

Asrar *Miss Lucinda V Russell* 43
5 b m King's Theatre(IRE) —Zandaka (FR) (Doyoun)
1491[7] 1804[12]

Assertive *R Hannon* 115
4 ch h Bold Edge—Tart And A Half (Distant Relative)
1102[2] 1770[5] (2319) 2857[16] 3894[4] 4045[10] 4438a[5] 5112[9] 5359[3] 5832[3] 6338[10]

Asset (IRE) *R Hannon* a106 121
4 b g Marju(IRE) —Snow Peak (Arazi (USA))
(1102) 2857[3] 3506[6] 4045[2] 5214[6] 5588[2] 6332[5]

Assir *C Hennessy*
5 gr m Daylami(IRE) —Etaaq (IRE) (Sadler's Wells (USA))
5696a[12]

Assistacat (IRE) *A P Jarvis* a44
3 br f Lend A Hand—Cattiva (ITY) (Lomond (USA))
6891[0]

Astania *P W D'Arcy* a54 72
2 b f Shahrastani(USA) —So Ambitious (Teenoso (USA))
2832[5] 3453[5] 5912[4]

Astarte *P R Chamings* a34
3 b f Slip Anchor—Nanouche (Dayjur (USA))
1816[8] 2542[11] 2766[13]

Aston Boy *M Blanshard* 41
2 ch c Dr Fong(USA) —Hectic Tina (Hector Protector (USA))
4508[13]

Aston Lad *Micky Hammond* 54
6 b g Bijou D'Inde—Fishki (Niniski (USA))
1745[6] 6259[3]

Astorygoeswithit *G C Bravery* a55 42
4 b g Foxhound(USA) —La Belle Mystere (Lycius (USA))
1891[1] 239[2] (320) 524[2] 586[9] 1349[12] 1569[6] 1933[3] 2937[11] 4029[10] 7034[9] 7148[3]

Astral Charmer *M H Tompkins* a63 4
3 b g Tobougg(IRE) —Blushing Sunrise (USA) (Cox's Ridge (USA))
1724[14] 2112[7] 4339[16]

Astroangel *M H Tompkins* a69 68
3 b f Groom Dancer(USA) —Nutmeg (IRE) (Lake Coniston (IRE))
899[4] 1091[2] 2133[8] 2607[5] 3826[2] 4064[9] 4579[4] 5563[3] 5860[7] 6623[8] 6704[3] 7025[4] 7127[5]

Astrobella *M H Tompkins* 80
4 ch m Medicean—Optimistic (Reprimand)
2011[9] 4365[8] 5884[9]

Astrodome *Sir Mark Prescott* a53 8
2 b g Domedriver(IRE) —Alexandrine (IRE) (Nashwan (USA))
6571[11] 6748[6] 6805[11]

Astrodonna *M H Tompkins* a67 60
2 ch f Carnival Dancer—Mega (IRE) (Petardia)
5882[6] (6626)

Astrol *T D Easterby* 41
2 b f Diktat—Magic Myth (IRE) (Revoque (IRE))
2371[9] 2739[8] 3560[6] 4578[12] 5252[7]

Astrolibra *M H Tompkins* a53 61
3 b f Sakhee(USA) —Optimistic (Reprimand)
901[4] 1024[4] 1917[8] 2609[9] 5710[3] 5894[3] 6178[4] 6529[9]

Astronomer Royal (USA) *A P O'Brien* 119
3 b c Danzig(USA) —Sheepscot (USA) (Easy Goer (USA))
1056a[6] (1703a) 2734[3] 3362a[4] 5261a[7]

Astronomic *J Howard Johnson* 80
7 b g Zafonic(USA) —Sky Love (USA) (Nijinsky (CAN))
2245[6] 2908[9]

Astronomical Odds (USA) *T D Barron* a71 61
4 b g Miswaki(USA) —Perfectly Polish (USA) (Polish Numbers (USA))
228[3] 346[7] 468[9] 651[13] 686[3]

Asturias *J W Hills* a63 63
3 b f Anabaa(USA) —Halcyon Daze (Halling (USA))
1901[3]

Atabaas Pride *M Johnston* 80
2 b c Pivotal—Atabaa (FR) (Anabaa (USA))
1411[4] 2166[2] 3582[2] 4152[2] (5281)

Atacama King (USA) *J H M Gosden* 60
3 b g Chester House(USA) —Santona (CHI) (Winning (USA))
1204[10]

Atacama Star *B G Powell* 35
5 ch g Desert King(IRE) —Aunty (FR) (Riverman (USA))
6598[15]

Ataensic *C N Allen* a13
2 b f Warningford—Enchanting Eve (Risk Me (FR))
3424[11] 3823[P]

Atamane (GER) *Mario Hofer* 98
4 b h Winged Love(IRE) —Adjani (Surumu (GER))
2976a[7]

Atayeb (USA) *M P Tregoning* a70 65
3 ch f Rahy(USA) —Sarayir (USA) (Mr Prospector (USA))
2219[9] 2625[4] 3827[4] 4277[2] (4738) 5333[10]

A Teen *P Howling* a57 49
9 ch g Presidium—Very Good (Noalto)
83[3] 189[10] (207) 350[9] 450[8] 556[6] 625[2] 682[6] 800[5] 978[4] 2343[14] 3163[3] 4741[3] 5566[10] 7124[8] 7276[6]

Atephobia *K R Burke* a68 65
2 bb c Auction House(USA) —Seren Teg (Timeless Times (USA))
1889[6] 2090[4] 2819[5] 3925[6] 4154[4] 4406[7] 5081[2] 6072[6] 6699[6] (6828) 6977[7] 7220[2] 7246[3]

Athanor (FR) *F Head* a103 105
5 ch g Ashkalani(IRE) —Leariva (USA) (Irish River (FR))
6614a[3]

Athboy Auction *H J Collingridge* a60 64
2 b f Auction House(USA) —Thabeh (Shareef Dancer (USA))
4232[7] 5065[6] 5357[5] 5883[8] 6502[8] 7031[5] 7117[11]

Athea Lad (IRE) *W K Goldsworthy* a37 46
3 b g Indian Danehill(IRE) —Persian Empress (IRE) (Persian Bold)
40[6]

Atheer Dubai (IRE) *C E Brittain* 88
2 b c Dubai Destination(USA) —Atheer (USA) (Lear Fan (USA))
2215[2] 2732[11] 3459[11] 4604[4] 4991[5] 5828[4] 6328[4]

Athenian Way (IRE) *J R Fanshawe* 105
3 b f Barathea(IRE) —Grecian Bride (IRE) (Groom Dancer (USA))
2702a[2] 2851a[2] 3576a[10] 5544[13] 6168[10]

Athlone (IRE) *A & G Botti* 106
3 b f Montjeu(IRE) —Almi Ad (USA) (Silver Hawk (USA))
4557a[8] 6519a[8]

Athlumney Lad (IRE) *Noel Meade* 84
8 b g Mujadil(USA) —Simouna (Ela-Mana-Mou)
6366a[13]

Atlantic Air (FR) *Y De Nicolay* 115
5 gr h Kaldounevees(FR) —Beg Meil (FR) (Tel Quel (FR))
531a[5] 624a[10] 2617a[3] (3665a) 4520a[2] 5719a[4]

Atlantic City *Mrs L Richards* a52 47
6 ch g First Trump—Pleasuring (Good Times (ITY))
89[9]

Atlantic Coast (IRE) *M Johnston* a49 87
3 b g In The Wings—Reasonably Devout (CAN) (St Jovite (USA))
3082[14] (3677) 3888[3] 4280[2] (4576) (4941) 5256[5] (5573) 5884[3] 6181[4]

Atlantic Dame (USA) *Mrs A J Perrett* a53 41
3 ch f Lemon Drop Kid(USA) —While Rome Burns (USA) (Overskate (CAN))
1785[9] 2793[12]

Atlantic Gamble (IRE) *K R Burke* a69 65
7 b g Darnay—Full Traceability (IRE) (Ron's Victory (USA))
(71) (182) (481) (514) 623[4] 740[6] 2810[4] 3063[5] (3684) 4096[5] 4249[9] (5422) 6261[5] 6902[9] 7226[8]

Atlantic Light *M Johnston* 86
3 gr f Linamix(FR) —Atlantic Destiny (IRE) (Royal Academy (USA))
1298[13] 2578[8] 4080[4] 4497[5]

Atlantic Quest (USA) *Miss Venetia Williams* a91 80
8 b g Woodman(USA) —Pleasant Pat (USA) (Pleasant Colony (USA))
96[3] 185[3] 255[4] 420[5] 488[5] 608[7] 2351[9] 3111[8] 3671[7]

Atlantic Rhapsody (FR) *B J Llewellyn* 75
10 b g Machiavellian(USA) —First Waltz (FR) (Green Dancer (USA))
3467[10]

Atlantic Sport (USA) *M R Channon* 99
2 b c Machiavellian(USA) —Shy Lady (FR) (Kaldoun (FR))
(3991) 5406[6]

Atlantic Story (USA) *M W Easterby* a97 79
5 bb g Stormy Atlantic(USA) —Story Book Girl (USA) (Siberian Express (USA))
(185) (351) 4176[6] 5221[13] 5685[4] (7017) (7165) (7267)

Atlantic Viking (IRE) *P D Evans* a55 71
12 b g Danehill(USA) —Hi Bettina (Henbit (USA))
138[6]

Atlantique Nord (FR) *D De Watrigant* 103
7 gr g Balleroy(USA) —La Narquoise (FR) (Al Nasr (FR))
2330a[5]

A To The Croft (USA) *K McPeek* a105 99
2 ch f Menifee(USA) —Heart Warmer (USA) (Devil's Bag (USA))
6507a[9]

Atraas (IRE) *M P Tregoning* 79
3 b g King's Best(USA) —Sundus (USA) (Sadler's Wells (USA))
(2077) 2598[11] 6269[12]

Attacca *J R Weymes* a59 61
6 b g Piccolo—Jubilee Place (IRE) (Prince Sabo)
801[3] 967[6] 1360[5] 1459[11] 1569[5] 2711[8] 2827[3] 3034[8] (3375) 3572[7] 3599[2] 4562[8] 4966[6] 5037[3] 5391[10] 5476[3] 5840[7] 5966[10] 6533[10]

Attercliffe (IRE) *Noel Meade* 102
4 b g Alhaarth(IRE) —Daraliya (IRE) (Kahyasi)
2851a[7] 4830a[4] 6367a[2]

At The Money *J M P Eustace* a68 80
4 b g Robellino(USA) —Coh Sho No (Old Vic)
1793[5]

Atticus Trophies (IRE) *Ms J S Doyle* a60 60
4 b g Mujadil(USA) —Nezool Almatar (IRE) (Last Tycoon (IRE))
610[14] 649[8] 723[10] 751[9] 888[9] 2176[7] 2332[10] 2511[10] 2656[7] 3232[6] 3428[8]

Attila's Peintre *P C Haslam* 63
3 b g Peintre Celebre(USA) —Atabaa (FR) (Anabaa (USA))
2116[6] 2565[2] 3792[16] 4246[4]

Attilius (BRZ) *E Charpy* a80 81
5 b h Dodge(USA) —Favorite Blass (BRZ) (Tokatee (USA))
245a[13] 400a[8] 597a[9]

Attribution *A B Haynes* a65 64
2 b c Royal Applause—Thrilling Day (Groom Dancer (USA))
2984[9] (3364) 4315[5] 4737[2] 4903[4] 5452[10] 6098[3] 6227[9]

Aube Claire (IRE) *L Brogi*
2 gr c Act One—Midefix (ITY) (Night Shift (USA))
6523a[9]

Auburndale *A Crook* 10
5 b g Mind Games—Primitive Gift (Primitive Rising (USA))
2298[13]

Auction Oasis *B Palling* a2 68
3 b f Auction House(USA) —Shining Oasis (IRE) (Mujtahid (USA))
1219[9] 1561[16] 2652[17] 3869[12] 4312[9] 7118[8]

Audience *J Akehurst* 98
7 b g Zilzal(USA) —Only Yours (Aragon)
848[6] 1145[7] 1842[4] 2446[2]

Audit (IRE) *Sir Michael Stoute* a84 77
3 b g Fusaichi Pegasus(USA) —Amethyst (IRE) (Sadler's Wells (USA))
1293[6] 1714[2] (1937) (2574)

Audley *M P Tregoning* 45
3 b f Averti(IRE) —Midnight Break (Night Shift (USA))
4666[RR] 4908[4]

Auenlove (GER) *M Weber*
2 ch f Dashing Blade—Auenburg (GER) (Big Shuffle (USA))
4837a[10]

Auenritter (GER) *Karin Suter* 98
3 b c Lando(GER) —Auenkronung (GER) (Shareef Dancer (USA))
2503a[8]

Auentraum (GER) *Ms J S Doyle* a64 57
7 br g Big Shuffle(USA) —Auenglocke (GER) (Surumu (GER))
82[9] 479[12] 687[9] 722[12] 750[10] 797[11] 2174[5] 2357[6] 2540[17]

Augmentation *P W D'Arcy* 44
2 br c Dansili—Moulin Rouge (Shareef Dancer (USA))
5951[15] 6285[7]

Augustine *P W Hiatt* a81 84
6 bb g Machiavellian(USA) —Crown Of Light (Mtoto)
205[7] 297[2] 362[6] 428[6] 652[9] 669[4] 740[4] 819[3] 997[4] 1090[5] 1199[3] 2027[2] 2113[2] 2621[2] 3232[3] 3301[4] 3854[4] 4040[3]

Augustus Caeser (IRE) *E J Creighton* a45 34
3 b g Beckett(IRE) —Miss Sabre (Sabrehill (USA))
884[7] 2454[9] 3274[6]

Augustus John (IRE) *T J Pitt* a82 79
4 gr g Danehill(USA) —Rizerie (FR) (Highest Honor (FR))
120[2] 564[2] 594[2] 1621[2]

Augustus Livius (IRE) *W Storey* a41 49
4 b g Titus Livius(FR) —Regal Fanfare (IRE) (Taufan (USA))
2[4] 305[9]

Auntie Mame *D J Coakley* a58 56
3 b f Diktat—Mother Molly (USA) (Irish River (FR))
3387[6] 3948[4] 5102[2] 5783[5] 6807[2] (7185)

Au Pair (IRE) *P W Chapple-Hyam* 72
2 ch f Domedriver(IRE) —Noble Dane (IRE) (Danehill (USA))
4602[5] 4832a[19] 6419[7]

Aura *Sir Michael Stoute* 49
2 b f Barathea(IRE) —Finger Of Light (Green Desert (USA))
6649[18]

Aureate *B Ellison* a79 93
3 ch g Jade Robbery(USA) —Anne D'Autriche (IRE) (Rainbow Quest (USA))
2246[3] 2426[6] (3081) 3273[5] 4059[11]

Ausone *Miss J R Gibney* a59
5 b m Singspiel(IRE) —Aristocratique (Cadeaux Genereux)
230[2] 389[9] 677[7]

Aussie Battler (IRE) *B W Duke* 69
2 b c Noverre(USA) —Dancerette (Groom Dancer (USA))
3957[5] 5795[11]

Aussie Blue (IRE) *R M Whitaker* 68
3 b g Bahamian Bounty—Luanshya (First Trump)
1197[6] 2206[6] 2892[2] 3583[6] 4078[3] 4354[5] 5159[7] 5253[3] 6310[3] 6623[2]

Aussie Cricket (FR) *D J Coakley* a68 66
3 gr f Verglas(IRE) —Coup De Colere (FR) (Pistolet Bleu (IRE))
1250[3] 1731[3] 2196[3] 2971[9] 3555[9]

Austintatious (USA) *B J Meehan* 87
2 ch c Distorted Humor(USA) —Fancy Ruler (USA) (Half A Year (USA))
4593[4] 5951[2]

Australia Day (IRE) *Charles O'Brien* 72
4 br g Key Of Luck(USA) —Atalina (FR) (Linamix (FR))
5460a[24]

Authorized (IRE) *P W Chapple-Hyam* 131
3 b c Montjeu(IRE) —Funsie (FR) (Saumarez)
(1790) (2235) 3331[2] (4693) 6043a[10]

Autocue *Sir Michael Stoute* 81
2 b c Dansili—Sing For Fame (USA) (Quest For Fame)
(3958) 6297[5]

Autograph Hunter *Peter Grayson* a83 30
3 b g Tobougg(IRE) —Kalindi (Efisio)
(886) 1076[14] 2045[17] 2771[10] 4021[9] 5233[3] 6026[10] 6265[5] 6534[5] 6937[5]

Autumn Blades (IRE) *J W Hills* a68 70
2 ch c Daggers Drawn(USA) —September Tide (IRE) (Thatching)
5337[4] 5880[4] 6602[8]

Autumn Charm *W Jarvis* a54 50
2 ch f Reel Buddy(USA) —Eurolink Cafe (Grand Lodge (USA))
5863[4] 6401[5] 6948[8] (7177)

Autumn Star (IRE) *M R Channon* 19
2 b f Mujadil(USA) —Second Omen (Rainbow Quest (USA))
4756[11]

Autumn Storm *R Ingram* a47 58
3 b f Auction House(USA) —Cozette (IRE) (Danehill Dancer (IRE))
1213[6] 2459[9]

Auvano (GER) *R Dzubasz* 92
3 b g Silvano(GER) —Auenfeuer (GER) (Big Shuffle (USA))
5929a[5]

Ava Gee *B De Haan* 63
2 br f Averti(IRE) —Spring Sunrise (Robellino (USA))
4254[6] 4506[7] 5110[7] 5357[9] 5939[8]

Avanti *Dr J R J Naylor* a49 74
11 gr g Reprimand—Dolly Bevan (Another Realm)
220[4] 416[10]

Avanti Polonia (GER) *P Schiergen* 108
3 br f Polish Precedent(USA) —Alisa (GER) (Daun (GER))
2294a[3] (3075a) 4651a[6] 5669a[5] 5849a[4]

Ava's World (IRE) *Peter Grayson* a63 82
3 b f Desert Prince(IRE) —Taibhseach (USA) (Secreto (USA))
2988[10] 6905[10] 7011[11] 7283[9]

Avelian (IRE) *S J Mahon* a18 75
4 b g Cape Cross(IRE) —Mashoura (Shareef Dancer (USA))
6920a[13]

Avening *Eve Johnson Houghton* 91
7 br g Averti(IRE) —Dependable (Formidable (USA))
4204[7] 4664[9] 5381[8] 5722[15]

Aventura (IRE) *S R Bowring* a59 49
7 b g Sri Pekan(USA) —La Belle Katherine (USA) (Lyphard (USA))
42[10] 252[9] 366[7] 533[10] (Dead)

Averoo *E A L Dunlop* a67 73
2 br g Averti(IRE) —Roo (Rudimentary (USA))
5200[8] 5679[5] 5951[8] 6329[2]

Averticus *B W Hills* a63 78
3 b g Averti(IRE) —Santa Vida (USA) (St Jovite (USA))
1099[6] 1450[8] 1667[3] 2395[5] 5092[7] 5635[6] 6081[8]

Avertis *M Botti* a71
2 b c Averti(IRE) —Double Stake (USA) (Kokand (USA))
(5895)

Averti Star *Mrs A Duffield* 46
3 b g Averti(IRE) —Zinzi (Song)
2535[7] 3029[10] 3639[11] 4943[12]

Avertitop *R Hannon* a68 77
2 b c Averti(IRE) —Lucayan Belle (Cadeaux Genereux)
1007[6] 1201[2] 1367[5] 2349[4] 3508[5]

Avertuoso *B Smart* a77 92
3 b g Averti(IRE) —First Musical (First Trump)
1160[5] 1825[3] 2022[5] 4567[11] 4898[2] 5505[7] 6381[10] 6743[2] 6836[7] 7078[8]

Avery *R J Hodges* a47 62
3 gr c Averti(IRE) —Bandanna (Bandmaster (USA))
404[6] 636[8] 900[5] 1004[14] 1164[10]

Avian Flew *J A Pickering* a26 48
2 b f Averti(IRE) —Ice Bird (Polar Falcon (USA))
3030[5] 3378[5] 3596[11] 4041[9] 5888[9]

Aviso (GER) *J Hirschberger* 108
3 b c Tertullian(USA) —Akasma (GER) (Windwurf (GER))
(1516a) 2903a[3] 4217a[4]

Avoca Dancer (IRE) *M Wigham* a43 74
4 ch m Compton Place—Kashra (IRE) (Dancing Dissident (USA))
1681[12] 1885[10] 3594[13] 5174[10] 5564[6] 6752[9]

Avoncreek *B P J Baugh* a51 51
3 b g Tipsy Creek(USA) —Avondale Girl (IRE) (Case Law)
253[6] 512[9] 1635[6] 2300[8] 3713[6] 3924[6] 4330[10]

Avontuur (FR) *D W Chapman* a54 55
5 ch g Kabool—Ipoh (FR) (Funambule (USA))
4138[4] 4381[12] 4479[7] 4768[6] (5566) 5890[7] 6064[9]

Avoriaz (IRE) *R A Fahey* 92
4 gr g Desert Prince(IRE) —Abbatiale (FR) (Kaldoun (FR))
(2822) 3558[RR]

Avril Valley *D J S Ffrench Davis* a21 33
2 b f Averti(IRE) —Shamrock Fair (IRE) (Shavian)
5343[15] 5727[11] 6207[11] 6791[6]

Awaken *Miss Tracy Waggott* 64
6 b m Zafonic(USA) —Dawna (Polish Precedent (USA))
3343[11] 4249[4] (4410) 4846[5] 5286[5]

Awash (USA) *D Broad* a54 58
5 ch g Coronado's Quest(USA) —All At Sea (USA) (Riverman (USA))
4114a[9]

Awatuki (IRE) *A P Jarvis* a89 85
4 b g Distant Music(USA) —Itkan (IRE) (Marju (IRE))
(353) 488[10] 726[2] 6576[7] 6995[5] 7163[3]

Awelmarduk (IRE) *A & G Botti* 105
3 b c Almutawakel—Claba Di San Jore (IRE) (Barathea (IRE))
(1875a)

Awesome Gem (USA) *Craig Dollase* a116 104
4 ch g Awesome Again(CAN) —Piano (USA) (Pentelicus (USA))
5824a[2] 6514a[3]

A Wish For You *D K Ivory* a70 68
2 ch f Tumbleweed Ridge—Peperonata (IRE) (Cyrano De Bergerac)
1445[7] 2333[7] 2663[3] 3030[3] 3426[8] 4903[10] 6386[3] 6624[2] 6834[5] 6926[4] 7106[2] (7270)

Awwal Malika (USA) *C E Brittain* a60 79
3 b f Kingmambo(USA) —First Night (IRE) (Sadler's Wells (USA))
2242[7] 2571[8] 3235[8] 3646[4] 3913[2] 4270[2] 4538[2] (4711) 5354[10] 5799[10]

Axiom *E A L Dunlop* a85 85
3 ch c Pivotal—Exhibitor (USA) (Royal Academy (USA))
1840[4] 3382[3] 4275[8] 5494[2] 5873[2] (6094)

Axis Mundi (IRE) *T J Etherington* a51 22
3 b f Titus Livius(FR) —Inventive (Sheikh Albadou)
3051[10] 4671[6] 5728[5] 6266[10]

Axis Shield (IRE) *M C Chapman* a58 64
4 b m Shinko Forest(IRE) —La Doyenne (IRE) (Masterclass (USA))
221[10] 317[8] 523[5] 715[11] 3708[12] 4485[4] 6078[9] (7238) (Dead)

Axxos (GER) *P Schiergen* 111
3 b c Monsun(GER) —Acerbis (GER) (Rainbow Quest (USA))
1387a[2] (2502a) 3566a[2] 5077a[5] 5929a[2]

Aye Aye Definitely (IRE) *R A Fahey* a48 74
3 b f Danetime(IRE) —Taispeain (IRE) (Petorius)
2821[2] 2867[4] 3158[6] 3784[7] 4158[11] 4379[3] 5648[12] 5934[P]

Aye Aye Digby (IRE) *H Candy* 84
2 b c Captain Rio—Jane Digby (IRE) (Magical Strike (USA))
3592[6] 4151[10] (4540) 5536[3] 6154[5]

Aypeeyes (IRE) *S Kirk* a74 73
3 b g King Charlemagne(USA) —Habaza (IRE) (Shernazar)
1722[14] 1974[12] 3456[3] 3799[2] 4309[2] 4504[9] 4687[5] (5604)

Azarole (IRE) *J S Moore* a103 108
6 b g Alzao(USA) —Cashew (Sharrood (USA))
172a[7] 331a[5] 411a[5] 540a[6] 4119[7] 4747[5] 5213[8]

Azeema (IRE) *B W Hills* 78
3 b f Averti(IRE) —Kazeem (Darshaan)
1128[6] (1620) 2243[9] 5768[14]

Azeer (USA) *P W Chapple-Hyam* 88
2 ch c Giant's Causeway(USA) —Touch Of Love (USA) (Alydar (USA))
2478[4] 2855[8]

Azreme *P Howling* a57 75
7 ch g Unfuwain(USA) —Mariette (Blushing Scribe (USA))
741[7] 1655[2] 1761[7] 2107[12] 2809[3] 2979[3] (3167) (3381) 3571[4] 3855[5] 5424[5] 6179[7] 6423[9]

Azure Mist *M H Tompkins* 68
2 ch f Bahamian Bounty—Inquirendo (USA) (Roberto (USA))
4028[2] 5580[6] 6740[3]

Azygous *J Akehurst* a70 86
4 ch g Foxhound(USA) —Flag (Selkirk (USA))
554[10] 692[10] 1023[9] 1214[2] 1630[4] 2399[10] 2694[7] 3179[7] 3594[8] 4944[3] 5160[10] 5642[7] 5726[5] 6360[6] 6594[12] 6890[8] 6976[2] 7116[5]

Baaher (USA) *M P Tregoning* a68
3 b c War Chant(USA) —Raajiya (USA) (Gulch (USA))
492[3]

Baan (USA) *M Johnston* a94 102
4 ch g Diesis—Madaen (USA) (Nureyev (USA))
2807[5] 3386[6] 3955[10] 4228[3] 4481[DSQ] 4843[7] 5334[4] 5732[8] 6131[5] 6504[6] 6738[3] 6838[2] 6982[3] 7104[2] 7193[6]

Baarrij *G A Huffer* a24 50
3 ch f Tobougg(IRE) —Bint Albaadiya (USA) (Woodman (USA))
1403[9] 3826[11] 4327[9] 4516[5] 5121[9]

Baba Ganouge (IRE) *B J Meehan* a55 81
3 ch f Desert Prince(IRE) —Le Montrachet (Nashwan (USA))
2320[3] (2620) 3081[4] 3458[9]

Baba Ghanoush *J Akehurst* a63 39
5 ch m Zaha(CAN) —Vrennan (Suave Dancer (USA))
556[9] 614[11] 1251[9] 6831[10] 7028[6]

Babilu *J G Given* 30
2 ch f Lomitas—Creeking (Persian Bold)
5193[8] 5770[11]

Babodana *M H Tompkins* a100 117
7 ch h Bahamian Bounty—Daanat Nawal (Machiavellian (USA))
1305[6] 1791[10] 2442[3] 3103[2] 4119[14] 4745[10] 6011[32] 6541[2] 6852[6] 6965[8]

Baby Barry *S Parr* a50 60
10 b g Komaite(USA) —Malcesine (IRE) (Auction Ring (USA))
715[10] 1086[3] 1368[9] 2258[7] 2370[7] 4449[5] 5503[11]

Baby Blue Eyes (IRE) *Patrick J Flynn* 109
4 ch m Cadeaux Genereux—Zalitzine (USA) (Zilzal (USA))
4051a[7] (4649a) 6216a[3]

Baby Dordan (IRE) *H J L Dunlop* a66 66
3 b f Desert Prince(IRE) —Three Owls (IRE) (Warning)
1155[5] 1534[4] 2061[4] 2607[4] 3178[8] 4361[2]

Baby Jack *D Nicholls* 57
2 b c Josr Algarhoud(IRE) —Mashmoon (USA) (Habitat)
2392[4] 2983[8] 3995[7] 4715[5] 5302[10] 5520[11]

Bachnagairn *R Charlton* a58 71
3 b g In The Wings—Purple Heather (USA) (Rahy (USA))
1211[2] 1370[2] 2132[3] 3170[7]

Back In The Red (IRE) *R A Harris* a77 79
3 ch g Redback—Fureur De Vivre (IRE) (Bluebird (USA))
918[6] 1248[4] 1437[5] (4661) (4759) 4919[4] 5358[4] 5747[9] 6122[10] 6829[8] (6905) 6976[8] 7059[7] 7261[5]

Backlash *A W Carroll* 27
6 b m Fraam—Mezza Luna (Distant Relative)
1002[11] 1380[12]

Backseat Rhythm (USA) *Patrick L Reynolds* a106 106
2 b f El Corredor(USA) —Kiss A Miss (USA) (Kissin Kris (USA))
6507a[3]

Badalona *M L W Bell* 79
2 b f Cape Cross(IRE) —Badawi (USA) (Diesis)
3706[2] 4094[2] 4796[2] (5811)

Badaria (FR) *Robert Collet* a89 93
2 b f Almutawakel—Green Maid (USA) (Green Dancer (USA))
6888a[2]

Baddam *M R Channon* 111
5 b g Mujahid(USA) —Aude La Belle (FR) (Ela-Mana-Mou)
1393[2] 2787[7] 2860[2] 4091[13] 5376[8] 5829[5] 6054[3] 6335[30]

Bad Girl Runs (SAF) *M F De Kock* 116
5 b m Western Winter(USA) —Badius (IRE) (Sadler's Wells (USA))
(547a) 862a[13]

Bad Moon Rising *J Akehurst* a59 51
2 ch c Piccolo—Janette Parkes (Pursuit Of Love)
6540[4] 6850[8] 7191[11]

Badoura *G A Butler* a59 59
2 ch f Dr Fong(USA) —Kalindi (Efisio)
5357[7] 5766[17] 6601[5]

Ba Dreamflight *H Morrison* a51
2 b g Noverre(USA) —Aunt Tate (Tate Gallery (USA))
5895[13] 6262[12] 6543[7]

Baffled (USA) *J Noseda* a78 96
2 bb f Distorted Humor(USA) —Surf Club (USA) (Ocean Crest (USA))
(1945) 2812[3] 3522[6] 4400[7]

Bagenalstown (IRE) *M Wellings* a23
2 b c Fath(USA) —Rhapsani (IRE) (Persian Bold)
3915[12] 4162[12] 6855[11]

Baggio (IRE) *Charles O'Brien* 101
6 b g Foxhound(USA) —Starring Role (IRE) (Glenstal (USA))
3140a[19] 5242a[13]

Bahalita (IRE) *L Riccardi* 89
4 b m Bluebird(USA) —Barriyah (Kris)
1337a[10]

Bahama Baileys *M Johnston* 75
2 ch g Bahamian Bounty—Baileys Silver (USA) (Marlin (USA))
1291[4] (1528) 1772[4] 2024[3] 3398[9] 4406[4] 4695[16] 5251[6] 5665[4]

Bahama Gold *D G Bridgwater* a49 27
3 b f Bahamian Bounty—Pictina (Petong)
417[3] 589[8] 676[12] 1008[9] 1210[16] 1782[14]

Bahama Mama (IRE) *W Hickst* 107
3 b f Invincible Spirit(IRE) —Nassma (IRE) (Sadler's Wells (USA))
1338a[3] 4213a[4] 4869a[3] 6633a[0]

Bahamarama (IRE) *R A Harris* a60 50
2 ch f Bahamian Bounty—Cole Slaw (Absalom)
2468[7] 2797[3] 3162[3] 3424[9] (5017) 5365[4] 6066[11] 6872[7] 7021[7] 7171[5]

Bahama Reef (IRE) *B Gubby* a32
6 b g Sri Pekan(USA) —Caribbean Dancer (Shareef Dancer (USA))
288[10]

Bahamian Ballad *J D Bethell* 68
2 ch f Bahamian Bounty—Record Time (Clantime)
3200[11] 4611[8] 5252[3] 5692[9]

Bahamian Ballet *E S McMahon* a83 91
5 ch g Bahamian Bounty—Plie (Superlative)
1574[12] 2025[3] (2479) (3836) 4664[4] 5029[6] 5379[13] 5891[7] 6381[3]
Bahamian Bay *M Brittain* a38 59
5 b m Bahamian Bounty—Moly (Inchinor)
771[3] 1349[11] 2791[14] 6390[9] 6565[5]
Bahamian Blue (IRE) *H J L Dunlop* a55 63
2 ch g Touch Of The Blues(FR) —Cattiva (ITY) (Lomond (USA))
3967[9] 4325[6] 5186[9] 5529[9] 5729[8]
Bahamian Duke *K R Burke* a54 67
4 ch g Bahamian Bounty—Madame Sisu (Emarati (USA))
1241[3] 3998[9] 4486[3] 4703[13] 5232[11] 6826[10] 7014[9] 7188[12]
Bahamian Gift *M Brittain* 61
2 ch f Bahamian Bounty—Desert Nomad (Green Desert (USA))
(2819)
Bahamian Lad *R Hollinshead* a69 75
2 b c Bahamian Bounty—Danehill Princess (IRE) (Danehill (USA))
4125[2] 5194[9] 5772[7] 6195[8] 6502[4] 6998[3] 7270[2]
Bahamian Love *B W Hills* a65 67
3 br f Bahamian Bounty—Asian Love (Petong)
520[9] 679[8] 925[5] 1437[3] 1932[7] 2260[7]
Bahamian Pirate (USA) *D Nicholls* a102 108
12 ch g Housebuster(USA) —Shining Through (USA) (Deputy Minister (CAN))
307[4] 391[5] (452) 660[5] 847[12] 1653[2] 1852[2] 2237[3] 2817[15] 3140a[4] 3500[5] 3975[9] 4614[14]
Bahamian Princess *E S McMahon* a24
2 ch f Bahamian Bounty—Cutlass Princess (USA) (Cutlass (USA))
5603[10]
Baharah (USA) *G A Butler* a104 85
3 b f Elusive Quality(USA) —Bahr (Generous (IRE))
6621[3] 6830[2] (6992)
Bahar Shumaal (IRE) *C E Brittain* a103 99
5 b h Dubai Millennium—High Spirited (Shirley Heights)
119[7] 264[5] 756[5] 1082[4] 5419[10]
Bahhmirage (IRE) *C N Kellett* a48 68
4 ch m Bahhare(USA) —Border Mirage (Selkirk (USA))
2343[13] (2716) 2979[11] 4129[12] 7237[8]
Bahia Breeze *Rae Guest* 109
5 b m Mister Baileys—Ring Of Love (Magic Ring (IRE))
1305[2] 2207[2] 3098[5] 3433[6] 4652a[2] 5396a[5] 6298[12]
Bahiano (IRE) *C E Brittain* a96 97
6 ch g Barathea(IRE) —Trystero (Shareef Dancer (USA))
41[3] 172a[8] 396a[10] 1474[5] 1653[15] 2670[7] 2817[18] 4133[8] 4401[9] 6013[15] 6651[2] 6753[2] 7053[8] 7184[4]
Bahia Palace *M D I Usher* a41 26
2 b f Zamindar(USA) —Inya Lake (Whittingham (IRE))
6023[6] 6151[9] 6454[10] 6722[12]
Bahrain Gold (IRE) *N P McCormack* a60 51
7 b g Great Commotion(USA) —Hassosi (IRE) (High Estate)
61[8] 221[9]
Bahrall *A P Jarvis* 31
4 b g Bahri(USA) —Navajo Love Song (IRE) (Dancing Brave (USA))
1044[14] 1350[11] 2540[8]
Bailador (IRE) *S Seemar* a45 77
7 b g Alzao(USA) —Alymatrice (USA) (Alysheba (USA))
328a[11]
Bailamos (GER) *C Von Der Recke* 106
7 b g Lomitas—Bandeira (GER) (Law Society (USA))
4957a[7]
Bailey (IRE) *B J Meehan* a79 80
2 ch g Captain Rio—Baileys Cream (Mister Baileys)
2424[4] 2949[2] 4273[2] 4776[5] 5109[3] 5937[2]
Baileys Best *J G M O'Shea* 62
5 b g Mister Baileys—Miss Rimex (IRE) (Ezzoud (IRE))
1002[10]
Baileys Outshine *J G Given* a71 76
3 ch f Inchinor—Red Ryding Hood (Wolfhound (USA))
958[2] 1067[6] 1484[3] 1932[2] (2172) 2513[10] 2867[3] 3061[4] 4452[5] 6743[13] 6905[6] 7116[3] 7215[6]
Bailieborough (IRE) *N Wilson* a83 97
8 b g Charnwood Forest(IRE) —Sherannda (USA) (Trempolino (USA))
846[12] 969[3] 1307[5] 1599[2] 1767[3] 2093[3] 2891[2] 3111[5] 3558[12] 6185[11] 6753[11] 7002[5] 7175[5]
Bainisteoir *S Kirk* a42 65
2 b g Tobougg(IRE) —Peruvian Jade (Petong)
5937[10] 6125[6] 6675[4]
Bairag (USA) *Mrs C A Dunnett* 63
2 b c Grand Slam(USA) —Brilliance (FR) (Priolo (USA))
5575[9] 6126[9]
Baizically (IRE) *J A Osborne* a95 94
4 ch g Galileo(IRE) —Baize (Efisio)
629[3] 777[6] 1208[2] 2245[7] 4091[15] 5640[2]
Bajan Parkes *E J Alston* 84
4 bb g Zafonic(USA) —My Melody Parkes (Teenoso (USA))
1852[10] 2374[5] 2986[6] 3346[3] 3530[4] 3755[3] 3955[4] 4382[2] 4909[3] (5197) 5215[7] 5677[5]
Bajan Pride *R Hannon* a78 85
3 b g Selkirk(USA) —Spry (Suave Dancer (USA))
1467[3] 1505[5] 1987[7] 2627[8] 3176[5] (3622) (3913) 4502[2] 4827[8] 5382[5] 5768[10] 6203[15]
Bajeel (IRE) *G A Butler* a69 50
3 b c Traditionally(USA) —Calypso Grant (IRE) (Danehill (USA))
1037[4] 1236[6] 3409[5] 3537[6]
Baker Of Oz *M A Doyle* a51 51
6 b g Pursuit Of Love—Moorish Idol (Aragon)
285[12] 333[11]

Bakers Boy *J E Long* a17
3 ch g Tipsy Creek(USA) —Unparalleled (Primo Dominie)
6778[12] 7029[13]
Bakhoor (IRE) *W Jarvis* 81
4 b m Royal Applause—First Waltz (FR) (Green Dancer (USA))
(2085) 2240[2] 2835[6]
Balais Folly (FR) *B Palling* a54 53
2 ch g Act One—Bhima (Polar Falcon (USA))
4656[8] 5186[7] 5858[8] 6427[14] 6814[7] 7010[6]
Balakar (IRE) *J J Lambe* 66
11 b g Doyoun—Balaniya (USA) (Diesis)
3677[2] 4380[3] 5283[2] (5586)
Balakiref *M Dods* a61 86
8 b g Royal Applause—Pluck (Never So Bold)
1574[11] (2088) 2744[5] 2762[5] 2912[6] (3569) (3953) 4581[14] 5584[6] 5617[4] 6560[13] 6753[19]
Balance (USA) *D Hofmans* a116
4 b m Thunder Gulch(USA) —Vertigineux (USA) (Kris S (USA))
5854a[4] 6512a[6]
Balance Of Power *D Broad* 89
5 b g Sadler's Wells(USA) —Cattermole (USA) (Roberto (USA))
2018a[5]
Balanchine Moon *M P Tregoning* a55 47
3 ch f Zilzal(USA) —Crescent Moon (Mr Prospector (USA))
4905[7] 5390[12]
Balata *B R Millman* 70
2 b g Averti(IRE) —Manila Selection (USA) (Manila (USA))
1201[5] 5470[2] 5868[3] 6419[5]
Bal De La Rose (IRE) *F Rohaut* a104 104
3 ch f Cadeaux Genereux—Lady Vettori (Vettori (IRE))
4010a[6] (6095a)
Baldemar *K R Burke* 80
2 b g Namid—Keen Melody (USA) (Sharpen Up)
3915[7] (4612) 4775[13] 5699[2] 5802[3]
Baldoria (IRE) *M Delcher-Sanchez* 98
4 b m In The Wings—Prickly Pearl (IRE) (Lahib (USA))
6030a[6]
Baldovina *Tom Dascombe* a68 88
3 b f Tale Of The Cat(USA) —Baldwina (FR) (Pistolet Bleu (IRE))
382[7] 491[3] 2691[5] 3367[12] 3731[9]
Balerno *Mrs L J Mongan* a63 60
8 b g Machiavellian(USA) —Balabina (USA) (Nijinsky (CAN))
292[8] 440[2] 637[7] (690) 797[2] 980[5] 2799[7] 3064[6] 3419[9] 3549[7] 4397[8] 7192[8]
Balfour House *C Roberts* a1 20
4 b g Wizard King—Tymeera (Timeless Times (USA))
5345[9] 5898[10]
Balian *Mrs P Sly* a58 67
4 b g Mujahid(USA) —Imperial Jade (Lochnager)
581[9] 723[9] 920[7] 1262[10]
Bali Belony *J R Jenkins* a40 23
3 b f Erhaab(USA) —Daarat Alayaam (IRE) (Reference Point)
418[10] 484[13] 2940[10] 3800[8] 4292[7] 6967[9]
Balius (IRE) *C Laffon-Parias* a104 113
4 b h Mujahid(USA) —Akhla (USA) (Nashwan (USA))
3665a[2]
Balkan Knight *D R C Elsworth* 114
7 b g Selkirk(USA) —Crown Of Light (Mtoto)
1650[3] 2125[2] (2462) (3333) 4091[4] 4691[2] 5376[6] 6044a[4] 6337[2]
Ballad Maker (IRE) *J H M Gosden* a70 60
3 b g Marju(IRE) —Cappella (IRE) (College Chapel)
5915[7] 6097[3] 6457[3]
Ballet Boy (IRE) *Sir Mark Prescott* a80 85
3 b g Sadler's Wells(USA) —Happy Landing (FR) (Homing)
(2727) 2801[3] 3379[6] (6077) 6241[2]
Balletic (IRE) *S Kirk* a49 40
2 b f Noverre(USA) —Feminine Touch (IRE) (Sadler's Wells (USA))
5162[13] 5681[8] 6530[7]
Balliasta (IRE) *B W Hills* 61
3 b f Grand Lodge(USA) —Obeah (Cure The Blues (USA))
1045[4] 2693[8] 4760[6] 5803[12]
Ballinskelligs Boy *R Hannon* 64
2 b c Compton Place—Autumn Affair (Lugana Beach)
1469[8] 1631[3] 2539[2] 2961[5]
Ballinteni *Miss Gay Kelleway* a86 100
5 b h Machiavellian(USA) —Silabteni (USA) (Nureyev (USA))
993[6] (1543) 1822[9] 2906[3] 3272[2] 4117[6] 4399[4] 5764[5] 6011[33] 6499[5]
Ballisodare *P W Chapple-Hyam* 67
2 b c Elusive Quality(USA) —River Jig (USA) (Irish River (FR))
6494[7]
Ballochroy (IRE) *B W Hills* 79
2 b c Mull Of Kintyre(USA) —Shonara's Way (Slip Anchor)
4350[8] 4761[4] 5328[2] (5813) 6471[12]
Ballora (FR) *S Kirk* a73 79
2 ro f Kendor(FR) —Vodka (FR) (Ali-Royal (IRE))
3895[11] 4875[2] (5727)
Ballroom Dancer (IRE) *J Noseda* a81 87
3 b f Danehill Dancer(IRE) —Dwell (USA) (Habitat)
1398[2] (2428) 4111[2] 4331[6]
Ballybunion (IRE) *R A Harris* a55 63
8 ch g Entrepreneur—Clarentia (Ballad Rock)
2555[14] 2652[12] 3169[7] 3368[14] 3618[2] 3829[8] 4252[13] 4312[11] 4668[12] 5349[14]
Ballycroy Boy (IRE) *A Bailey* a72 52
2 b g Captain Rio—Royal Baldini (USA) (Green Dancer (USA))
890[2] 952[8] (1713) 1897[7] 4022[10] 4193[7] 7176[3]
Ballyhealy Lady *D K Ivory* a40 45
2 b f Tobougg(IRE) —Amal (Top Ville)
1445[10] 2590[9] 3687[9] 4756[13]

Ballyhoctor (IRE) *James Vincent Slevin* 65
9 b g Commanche Run—Missus Dickler (IRE) (Horage)
4371a[5]
Ballyhurry (USA) *J S Goldie* a63 72
10 b g Rubiano(USA) —Balakhna (FR) (Tyrant (USA))
(2563) (2828) 2985[8] 3783[2] 3814[2]
Ballyshane Spirit (IRE) *N A Callaghan* a64 58
3 b c Distant Music(USA) —Nationalartgallery (IRE) (Tate Gallery (USA))
37[6] 157[4] (469) 624[2] 889[2] 1155[11]
Balnagore *J L Dunlop* 76
3 bb c Tobougg(IRE) —Bogus Mix (IRE) (Linamix (FR))
4608[5]
Balthazaar's Gift (IRE) *L M Cumani* 120
4 b h Xaar—Thats Your Opinion (Last Tycoon (IRE))
1294[4] 1656[7] 2319[5] 2858[3] 3506[17] (3894) 4150[6] 4813[2] 5214[3] 5832[14] 6332[4]
Baltic Belle (IRE) *R Hannon* a71 83
3 b f Redback—Skerries Bell (Taufan (USA))
720[5] 919[3] 1247[4] 1731[5] (2317) (3087) 3334[3] 4060[9] 4665[3] 6208[11]
Baltic King *H Morrison* 120
7 b h Danetime(IRE) —Lindfield Belle (IRE) (Fairy King (USA))
1102[4] 2319[8] 2857[7] 3894[5] 4196[2] 4798[10] 5832[10] 6338[16]
Baltic Princess (FR) *M Johnston* 78
4 ch m Peintre Celebre(USA) —Snow House (IRE) (Vacarme (USA))
914[8]
Baltimore Jack (IRE) *M W Easterby* a42 84
3 b g Night Shift(USA) —Itsibitsi (IRE) (Brief Truce (USA))
(1108) 1667[4] 2313[3] (2821) 3944[12] 4425[6] 4898[4] 5356[15] 6355[12] 6639[15]
Balwearie (IRE) *Miss L A Perratt* 65
6 b g Sesaro(USA) —Eight Mile Rock (Dominion)
1042[3]
Balyan (IRE) *J Howard Johnson* 85
6 b g Bahhare(USA) —Balaniya (USA) (Diesis)
914[5] 1490[2] 2031[4] 3027[4]
Bamboo Banks (IRE) *J L Dunlop* 71
4 b g Indian Lodge(IRE) —Emma's Star (ITY) (Darshaan)
5472[5] 6250[10]
Banana Belle *J Ryan* a24 46
3 b f Josr Algarhoud(IRE) —Scurrilous (Sharpo)
3163[7] 3353[3] 3627[11] 3708[11] 3873[8] 4226[17] 4689[13] 5861[6]
Band *E S McMahon* a66 61
7 b g Band On The Run—Little Tich (Great Nephew)
2716[8] 3067[11] 3922[5] 4532[7] 5421[7] 6458[11] 6629[9]
Bandama (IRE) *Mrs A J Perrett* a104 103
4 b h Green Desert(USA) —Orinoco (IRE) (Darshaan)
1477[4] 2351[2] 2859[14] 4043[10] 4376[9] 5049[4] 5631[9] 6014[3] 6490[2] 6759[10]
Banderella (IRE) *W Hickst* 85
3 b f Diktat—Baskama (GER) (Surumu (GER))
6940a[6]
Bandido Secreto (BRZ) *P Nickel Filho* a91 98
5 b h Romarin(BRZ) —Hail Secreto (USA) (Secreto (USA))
177a[5] 399a[10] 477a[11]
Bandos *M Smith* a49 61
7 ch g Cayman Kai(IRE) —Lekuti (Le Coq D'Or)
479[7] 625[4] 729[5] 2937[8] 3376[12] 4768[13] 5083[15]
Banjo Bandit (IRE) *J S Moore* a63 35
2 b c Mujadil(USA) —Common Cause (Polish Patriot (USA))
3551[13] 4540[13] 6791[3]
Bankable (IRE) *L M Cumani* 94
3 b c Medicean—Dance To The Top (Sadler's Wells (USA))
4815[8] (5285) (5768)
Banknote *A M Balding* a103 110
5 b h Zafonic(USA) —Brand (Shareef Dancer (USA))
(817) (1699a) 2705a[2] 3523[6] 5265a[5] 6931[7]
Bank On Benny *P W D'Arcy* a79 68
5 b g Benny The Dip(USA) —Green Danube (USA) (Irish River (FR))
48[2] (6314) 6739[6]
Bank On Bertie *M W Easterby* a6 39
2 b g Bertolini(USA) —Piggy Bank (Emarati (USA))
890[12] 1043[8] 1087[12] 1130[5] (Dead)
Banquet (IRE) *M R Channon* 45
2 ch c Dr Fong(USA) —Barbera (Barathea (IRE))
5918[14] 6494[15]
Bantham Bay *B J Meehan* a36 50
2 ch f Reel Buddy(USA) —Florentynna Bay (Aragon)
1354[13] 1727[9] 2488[11] 3446[7] 4783[11] 5302[7] 5572[9]
Bantry Bere (IRE) *J R Best* a68 60
3 b g Distant Music(USA) —Tirana (USA) (Fappiano (USA))
2445[8] 6506[6]
Banus Flyer (IRE) *N Tinkler* 35
2 b g Distant Music(USA) —Gracious Gretclo (Common Grounds)
1792[13] 2337[8]
Baraari (USA) *J L Dunlop* 74
2 bb f Nayef(USA) —Reem Al Barari (USA) (Storm Cat (USA))
3507[8] 4094[10] 5301[2] 5811[8]
Barancella (FR) *R J Frankel* a107 116
6 ch m Acatenango(GER) —Baranciaga (USA) (Bering)
6373a[3] 6790a[2]
Barashi *J Howard Johnson* 20
2 b g King's Best(USA) —Maid To Dance (Pyramus (USA))
3761[12]
Barataria *R Bastiman* 62
5 ch g Barathea(IRE) —Aethra (USA) (Trempolino (USA))
1944[12] (2203) 2714[9] 3375[3] 4029[11] 4562[12] 4966[10]

Barathea Blazer *K McAuliffe* a86 90
8 b g Barathea(IRE) —Empty Purse (Pennine Walk)
870[5]
Barathea Dreams (IRE) *J S Moore* a72 82
6 b g Barathea(IRE) —Deyaajeer (USA) (Dayjur (USA))
1446[5] 1819[8] 2218[11] 2467[11]
Barati (IRE) *B N Pollock* 62
6 b g Sadler's Wells(USA) —Oriane (Nashwan (USA))
2860[12]
Barawin (IRE) *K R Burke* 79
2 ch f Hawk Wing(USA) —Cosabawn (IRE) (Barathea (IRE))
4350[7] (5812) 6471[11]
Barbar *Eve Johnson Houghton* a49 58
4 b g Anabaa(USA) —Prends Ca (IRE) (Reprimand)
4908[9] 5315[8] 6062[5] 6581[9]
Barbarossa *R Hannon* a54 77
2 b c Beat All(USA) —Gagajulu (Al Hareb (USA))
2215[5] 2424[3] (2977) 3524[6] 4484[5] 5629[7] 6120[13]
Barbary Boy (FR) *M L W Bell* 79
2 b c Rock Of Gibraltar(IRE) —Don't Worry Me (IRE) (Dancing Dissident (USA))
5380[6] 5771[2] 6409[2]
Barbirolli *W M Brisbourne* a69 72
5 b g Machiavellian(USA) —Blushing Barada (USA) (Blushing Groom (FR))
110[4] 3530[2] 3907[6] 4159[6] 4582[14] 5674[3] 5916[6] 6196[10] 6558[9] 6837[9]
Barbossa *A J McCabe*
2 ch g Bahamian Bounty—Marjurita (IRE) (Marju (IRE))
3465[9] 4020[9]
Barbs Pink Diamond (USA) *Mrs A J Perrett* a60 60
3 b f Johannesburg(USA) —Unsaddled (USA) (Pancho Villa (USA))
2428[8] 2940[5] 3393[9] 4327[5] 4534[3] 5068[2] 5341[6] 5709[4]
Bar City (USA) *Linda Rice* 76
2 b f City Zip(USA) —Bar None (USA) (Major Impact (USA))
5293a[7]
Bariloche *J R Boyle* a77
4 b h Benny The Dip(USA) —Bella Lambada (Lammtarra (USA))
630[4] 909[12]
Barkass (UAE) *B Ellison* a77 77
3 b g Halling(USA) —Areydha (Cadeaux Genereux)
193[4] 418[4] 3952[2] 4281[3] 4797[5] 6492[9] 6753[10]
Barley Moon *T Keddy* a40 63
3 b f Vettori(IRE) —Trojan Desert (Troy)
1075[7] 1815[13] 3913[10] 4339[11]
Barliffey (IRE) *D J Coakley* 78
2 b c Bahri(USA) —Kildare Lady (IRE) (Indian Ridge)
3552[6] 4316[2] 4904[2] 5343[4]
Barnaby Rudge (IRE) *Jane Chapple-Hyam* a71 81
2 b c Danetime(IRE) —Gild (IRE) (Caerleon (USA))
6234[2] 6641[3] (6879a) 7027a[4]
Barndeh (IRE) *R McGlinchey* 77
4 b g Marju(IRE) —Sweetest Thing (IRE) (Prince Rupert (FR))
5696a[4]
Barney McGrew (IRE) *J A R Toller* a101 93
4 b g Mark Of Esteem(IRE) —Success Story (Sharrood (USA))
56[3] 261[2] 486[2] 1268[5] 1905[5] (2427) 2882[2] 3104[14] (4585) 5209[6] (6142) 6472[12]
Barney's Dancer *C L Popham* a45
2 b f Iron Mask(USA) —Alcalali (USA) (Septieme Ciel (USA))
304[10] 390[4] 534[10] 2454[3]
Barny's Barnato (IRE) *M Weiss* 34
6 b g Revoque(IRE) —Frisky Lady (Magic Ring (IRE))
438a[7]
Barodine *R J Hodges* a69 88
4 ch g Barathea(IRE) —Granted (FR) (Cadeaux Genereux)
444[7]
Baron De Feypo (IRE) *Patrick O Brady* 74
9 b g Simply Great(FR) —Fete Champetre (Welsh Pageant)
3577a[6]
Baron De'L (IRE) *Edward P Harty* a39 100
4 ch g In The Wings—Lightstorm (IRE) (Darshaan)
3577a[4] 6367a[6]
Baroness Richter (IRE) *J-C Rouget* 106
3 b f Montjeu(IRE) —Principium (USA) (Hansel (USA))
2786[4] 4557a[5]
Baroness Thatcher (USA) *F Parisel* a113 97
3 ch f Johannesburg(USA) —Natkeeta (USA) (Gulch (USA))
6483a[4]
Baronovici (IRE) *R Hannon* 73
2 b c Namid—Allegrina (IRE) (Barathea (IRE))
2510[2] 3902[2] (4014) 4775[7]
Barons Court *M Johnston* a68
2 ch c Pivotal—Grafin (USA) (Miswaki (USA))
7140[4] 7217[4]
Baron's Pit *E F Vaughan* a94 104
7 gr g Night Shift(USA) —Incendio (Siberian Express (USA))
1125[5] 1657[7] 2022[2] 2352[6] 2858[9] 3708[6] 4150[20] 4401[7] 5449[3]
Barons Spy (IRE) *R J Price* a84 84
6 b g Danzero(AUS) —Princess Accord (USA) (D'Accord (USA))
1765[2] 2038[2] 2469[10] 3239[5] 4418 [9] 4657[2] (5168) 5638[3] 6243[9] 6539[7] 6651[10]
Barraland *M R Channon* 74
2 b g Compton Place—Dance Land (IRE) (Nordance (USA))
1058[4] 1411[3] (1631) 2049a[7] 3398[8] 3734[2] 3867[2] 4152[7] 4560[9] 5452[4] 5534[4] 5802[8] 6059[4] 6195[5]
Barricado (FR) *R Charlton* 70
2 b c Anabaa(USA) —Aube D'Irlande (FR) (Selkirk (USA))
6246[3]

Barry Island *D R C Elsworth* a69 73
8 b g Turtle Island(IRE) —Pine Ridge (High Top)
30^{3} 117^{5} 594^{9} 5514^{8} 6196^{5} 6719^{3} 6951^{8} 7189^{5} 7277^{2}

Barry The Brave *Micky Hammond* a54 60
5 b g Mujadil(USA) —Rakli (Warning)
123^{6} 243^{12}

Barshiba (IRE) *D R C Elsworth* a84 111
3 ch f Barathea(IRE) —Dashiba (Dashing Blade)
(418) 1096^{5} 1496^{15} (2757) 3332^{2} $4010a^{4}$ 4503^{7} $5241a^{9}$ 6010^{6}

Bartola (ARG) *J C Maldotti* a103 103
4 b m Roy(USA) —Baronesita (ARG) (Political Ambition (USA))
$859a^{12}$

Barton Belle *C N Kellett* a52 61
5 b m Barathea(IRE) —Veronica (Persian Bold)
229^{8} 1566^{5} 2026^{7}

Barton Sands (IRE) *Andrew Reid* a60 58
10 b g Tenby—Hetty Green (Bay Express)
6792^{2} (7069) 7224^{4}

Barzak (IRE) *S R Bowring* a54 54
7 b g Barathea(IRE) —Zakuska (Zafonic (USA))
156^{7} 448^{11} 627^{5} 1379^{11} 1750^{5} 2145^{13} 3282^{8}

Basaata (USA) *M P Tregoning* a82 107
3 b f Dixieland Band(USA) —Asareer (USA) (Gone West (USA))
2599^{5} 4148^{4} 4633^{7} 5047^{3} 5451^{4}

Basanti (USA) *B W Hills* 63
2 ch f Galileo(IRE) —Ozone Friendly (USA) (Green Forest (USA))
6649^{7}

Baskerville *D Selvaratnam* a66 95
4 b g Foxhound(USA) —Miss Up N Go (Gorytus (USA))
$250a^{13}$ $473a^{11}$

Basko Hermoso (ARG) *Doug Watson* a51
4 ch h Engrillado(ARG) —Dark Beauty (ARG) (Mat-Boy (ARG))
$526a^{8}$

Ba Speedbird (IRE) *M R Channon* a19 38
2 b f Spartacus(IRE) —Missing Slate (IRE) (Dolphin Street (FR))
972^{7} 2443^{11} 5236^{4}

Basque Beauty *W J Haggas* 74
2 b f Nayef(USA) —River Cara (USA) (Irish River (FR))
4774^{3}

Basra (IRE) *Miss Jo Crowley* a91 88
4 b g Soviet Star(USA) —Azra (IRE) (Danehill (USA))
$3143a^{17}$ 6143^{6} 6669^{8} 7017^{2} 7281^{2}

Bastakiya (IRE) *J H M Gosden* a90 82
2 ch f Dubai Destination(USA) —Ting A Folie (ARG) (Careafolie)
1945^{2} (2344) 2756^{12}

Batchworth Blaise *E A Wheeler* a56 56
4 b g Little Jim—Batchworth Dancer (Ballacashtal (CAN))
1119^{8} 1541^{7} 1737^{8} 2664^{12} 4908^{2} 5001^{4} 5189^{7} 6229^{5} 6706^{13} 7167^{3}

Batchworth Fleur *E A Wheeler* a44 55
4 b m Little Jim—Batchworth Belle (Interrex (CAN))
2175^{9} 2878^{7} 3102^{2} 3388^{13} 4164^{4} 4853^{7} 5090^{15} 6062^{13} 6670^{3} 6963^{12}

Bateleur *M R Channon* a73 83
3 b g Fraam—Search Party (Rainbow Quest (USA))
2629^{6} 3418^{7} 3944^{6} 4269^{3} 4425^{3} 5051^{6} 5360^{4} 5768^{18}

Bathwick Breeze *A B Haynes* a63 63
3 ch g Sugarfoot—She's A Breeze (Crofthall)
694^{12} 834^{10} 1536^{4} 1917^{7} (2653) 3825^{11} 4758^{5} 5710^{6}

Bathwick Emma (IRE) *M A Doyle* a60 68
4 ch m Raise A Grand(IRE) —Lindas Delight (Batshoof)
(42) 109^{4} 252^{10} 298^{5} 425^{8} 518^{4} 620^{6} 666^{7} 768^{7} 2258^{9} 2431^{15}

Bathwick Fancy (IRE) *J G Portman* a56 63
3 b f Desert Sun—Fleetwood Fancy (Taufan (USA))
736^{2} 924^{9} 1432^{7} 2203^{9} 2511^{7} 3394^{8} 3651^{6} 4267^{7}

Bathwick Icon (IRE) *A B Haynes* 53
2 b f Xaar—Greek Icon (Thatching)
4310^{7} 4904^{8} 5267^{6} 6074^{10}

Bathwick Leti (IRE) *A M Balding* a22 39
3 b f Trans Island—Brandon Princess (Waajib)
5175^{11}

Bathwick Man *B R Millman* 60
2 b g Mark Of Esteem(IRE) —Local Abbey (IRE) (Primo Dominie)
4539^{9} 5088^{3} 5633^{9}

Bathwick Rox (IRE) *P D Evans* a61 35
4 b g Carrowkeel(IRE) —Byproxy (IRE) (Mujtahid (USA))
605^{10}

Battlecruiser (IRE) *M Johnston* a25 53
2 b c Red Ransom(USA) —First Fleet (USA) (Woodman (USA))
1390^{8} 3092^{8} 4604^{7} 5153^{9} 6263^{10}

Battle Paint (USA) *J-C Rouget* 116
3 b c Tale Of The Cat(USA) —Black Speck (USA) (Arch (USA))
$1056a^{2}$ $1703a^{9}$ $2499a^{4}$

Bauer (IRE) *L M Cumani* a47 104
4 gr h Halling(USA) —Dali's Grey (Linamix (FR))
1822^{7} 4288^{2} (5030) 5589^{6}

Bauhaus (IRE) *R T Phillips* 71
6 u g Second Empire(IRE) —Hi Bettina (Henbit (USA))
4056^{7} 4576^{15}

Bauhaus Bourbon (USA) *P F I Cole* a71
2 gr f Behrens(USA) —Southern Tradition (USA) (Family Doctor (USA))
3187^{6} (7097)

Baunagain (IRE) *M J Wallace* 54
2 b g No Excuse Needed—Manuka Honey (Mystiko (USA))
4854^{8}

Bavarian Nordic (USA) *E A L Dunlop* 78
2 b c Barathea(IRE) —Dubai Diamond (Octagonal (NZ))
3435^{13} 4037^{5} 4487^{5} 6233^{2} 6410^{2}

Bavarica *Miss J Feilden* a77 79
5 b m Dansili—Blue Gentian (USA) (Known Fact (USA))
112^{6} 299^{2} 358^{2} 1258^{10} 1567^{5} 2006^{2} 2361^{3} (2603) 2883^{4} 3100^{5} 4284^{2} 4994^{7} 5198^{7}

Bawaader (IRE) *D K Weld* 107
5 b g Indian Ridge—Alyakkh (IRE) (Sadler's Wells (USA))
$3138a^{6}$

Bayberry King (USA) *J S Goldie* a47 52
4 b g Lear Fan(USA) —Myrtle (Batshoof)
1488^{10} 2711^{17} 3052^{5} 3375^{12}

Bay Boy *Andrew Oliver* a83 84
5 b g Tomba—Gay Reign (Lord Gayle (USA))
211^{6} 340^{3} 501^{5} 568^{2} 587^{4} 669^{3} 747^{7} 1198^{9} 1939^{2} (2307) 6465^{7}

Baybshambles (IRE) *R E Barr* 63
3 b g Compton Admiral—Payvashooz (Ballacashtal (CAN))
1161^{6} 1425^{7} 2094^{3} (2895) 3342^{6} 3763^{6} 4425^{5} 4896^{4} 5139^{3} 5741^{7} (6078) 6562^{6}

Bay City Stroller (IRE) *A J McCabe* a37
3 ch f City On A Hill(USA) —Baywood (Emarati (USA))
1175^{6}

Bay Hawk *B G Powell* a74 76
5 b g Alhaarth(IRE) —Fleeting Vision (IRE) (Vision (USA))
6848^{8}

Baylani De S'Ena (IRE) *B Grizzetti* 98
3 b c Ashkalani(IRE) —Bayrika (IRE) (Kahyasi)
$1873a^{2}$

Baylaw Star *I W McInnes* a84 89
6 b g Case Law—Caisson (Shaadi (USA))
673^{9} 967^{10} 1459^{6} 1488^{3} (1711) 1892^{2} 3258^{7} 3814^{7} 3996^{6} 4479^{5} 4891^{6}

Baylini *Ms J S Doyle* a85 86
3 gr f Bertolini(USA) —Bay Of Plenty (FR) (Octagonal (NZ))
3900^{3} 4170^{7} 5092^{8} 5537^{5} 5768^{5} 6492^{5} 6669^{3} (6822)

Bay Of Light *P W Chapple-Hyam* 69
3 b f Fantastic Light(USA) —Lady Bankes (IRE) (Alzao (USA))
3913^{11} 4610^{6} 5046^{9} 5983^{13}

Bayonyx (IRE) *J Howard Johnson* 80
3 b g Montjeu(IRE) —Dafariyna (IRE) (Nashwan (USA))
1624^{2} 2808^{4}

Bay Story (USA) *B Ellison* 107
5 b g Kris S(USA) —Sweeping Story (USA) (End Sweep (USA))
$15a^{2}$ $6033a^{7}$ $6711a^{F}$

Baytown Blaze *Miss K B Boutflower* a67 74
2 ch f Zaha(CAN) —Lightning Blaze (Cosmonaut)
814^{7} (890) 1503^{3} 1580^{6} 1608^{2} 2183^{6} 2232^{12} 4605^{7} 5365^{5}

Baytown Paikea *P S McEntee* a56 59
3 b f Primo Valentino(IRE) —Mystical Song (Mystiko (USA))
54^{5} 194^{8} 219^{6}

Baytown Rosie (IRE) *P S McEntee* a43 28
3 ch f Intikhab(USA) —Masaniya (IRE) (Kris)
99^{4}

Baytown Valentina *R Brotherton* 43
4 b m Lugana Beach—Baytown Rhapsody (Emperor Jones (USA))
2304^{11} 4685^{5}

Bazart *K R Burke* a85 98
5 b g Highest Honor(FR) —Summer Exhibition (Royal Academy (USA))
1583^{7} 2209^{12} 6011^{30} 6490^{8} 6759^{11}

Bazergan (IRE) *C E Brittain* 103
2 b c Machiavellian(USA) —Lunda (IRE) (Soviet Star (USA))
4777^{7} 5323^{3} 5972^{4} 6382^{5}

Bazguy *P D Evans* a75 69
2 b g Josr Algarhoud(IRE) —Ewenny (Warrshan (USA))
942^{8} 2297^{5} 2510^{3} 3465^{6} 4669^{9} 4775^{15} 5167^{5} 6584^{11} 6665^{7} (6892) 6966^{3} 7072^{2} 7280^{7}

Bazroy (IRE) *P D Evans* a88 94
3 b g Soviet Star(USA) —Kunucu (IRE) (Bluebird (USA))
943^{7} 1099^{8} 2035^{7} 2395^{10} 3104^{10} 3553^{10} 4123^{13} 4389^{3} 5168^{4} 5358^{5} 5473^{6} 7087^{2}

Beach Bunny (IRE) *Kevin Prendergast* a70 56
2 b f High Chaparral(IRE) —Miss Hawai (FR) (Peintre Celebre (USA))
$6443a^{7}$

Beacon Lodge (IRE) *C G Cox* 102
2 b c Clodovil(IRE) —Royal House (FR) (Royal Academy (USA))
5193^{2} (6126) (6495)

Be Alert (SWE) *L Reuterskiold* a64
5 br g Diaghlyphard(USA) —Fairy Jane (IRE) (Fairy King (USA))
$1648a^{10}$

Beamish Prince *Mrs S A Watt*
8 ch g Bijou D'Inde—Unconditional Love (IRE) (Polish Patriot (USA))
6076^{13}

Beamsley Beacon *S T Mason* a55 52
6 ch g Wolfhound(USA) —Petindia (Petong)
287^{3} 320^{7} 1112^{4} 1163^{2} 1384^{4} 1493^{7} 2761^{7} 3169^{5} 4099^{5} 4410^{3} 4449^{3} 5179^{3} 5525^{10} 6479^{12} 6629^{13}

Bear Bottom *W J Musson* a59
3 b g Imperial Ballet(IRE) —Pigeon Hole (Green Desert (USA))
589^{7} 802^{3} 1398^{13} 7167^{7}

Bear Essential *Mrs P N Dutfield* a52
3 ch g Rambling Bear—Adar Jane (Ardar)
429^{9} 635^{6} 708^{10} 920^{10}

Bearna Bhui (IRE) *S Dow* a14 48
4 b m Daggers Drawn(USA) —Beechwood Quest (IRE) (River Falls)
1347^{12}

Bear Now (USA) *Reade Baker* a114
3 bb f Tiznow(USA) —Controlled (USA) (In Excess (IRE))
$6512a^{8}$

Beatrix Kiddo (FR) *Robert Collet* 111
3 b f Victory Note(USA) —Laquifan (USA) (Lear Fan (USA))
$989a^{5}$ $2501a^{5}$ $4654a^{3}$ $5058a^{4}$ $6889a^{4}$

Beatrix Potter (IRE) *Francis Ennis* 78
2 ch f Cadeaux Genereux—Great Joy (IRE) (Grand Lodge (USA))
$5395a^{13}$

Beat The Bully *D J Wintle* a33 58
3 b g Ishiguru(USA) —Edgeaway (Ajdal (USA))
2622^{3} 2665^{2} 3342^{14} 3875^{5} 4165^{12} 6908^{10}

Beat The Odds *V Caruso*
3 b c Beat Hollow—Biodotis (Warning)
$1191a^{7}$

Beat The Rain *J H M Gosden* a67 62
2 b f Beat Hollow—Love The Rain (Rainbow Quest (USA))
3706^{11} 4564^{11} 5100^{3}

Beau Bramble *C F Wall* a51
3 b g Gorse—Belle De Jour (Exit To Nowhere (USA))
4908^{12} 5494^{10} 6176^{7} 6542^{12}

Beauchamp Twist *M R Hoad* a29
5 b m Pharly(FR) —Beauchamp Cactus (Niniski (USA))
615^{12}

Beauchamp Viceroy *G A Butler* a98 95
3 ch g Compton Admiral—Compton Astoria (USA) (Lion Cavern (USA))
760^{5} 5031^{8} 5833^{9}

Beauchamp Viking *G A Butler* a45 55
3 b g Compton Admiral—Beauchamp Jade (Kalaglow)
1812^{11} 2666^{5}

Beauchamp Warrior *G A Butler* a61 62
2 b c Compton Admiral—Beauchamp Buzz (High Top)
6740^{5} 7070^{9} 7114^{7}

Beauchamp Wizard *G A Butler* a69 70
2 b c Compton Admiral—Compton Astoria (USA) (Lion Cavern (USA))
6755^{3} 7191^{4}

Beaufort *Mike Murphy* a52 43
5 b g Yaheeb(USA) —Royal Blaze (Scallywag)
1402^{U}

Beau Jazz *W De Best-Turner* a43 31
6 br g Merdon Melody—Ichor (Primo Dominie)
4204^{11}

Beau Michael *W R Swinburn* a43 71
3 b g Medicean—Tender Moment (IRE) (Caerleon (USA))
1522^{11} 2046^{6} 2726^{12} 3150^{6} (3450)

Beaumont Boy *A G Foster* 57
3 b g Foxhound(USA) —Play The Game (Mummy's Game)
1091^{7} 1489^{4} 1964^{8} 3202^{2} 3639^{3} 4224^{12} 5936^{5} 6640^{13}

Beau Sancy *R A Harris* a70 81
3 b g Tobougg(IRE) —Bride's Answer (Anshan)
58^{3} 122^{6} 196^{2} 294^{6} (370) 460^{4} 563^{4} 731^{3} 834^{2} 1059^{5} (1218) 1370^{4} 1722^{12} 2653^{4} (3351) (3570) 3848^{3} 4111^{12} 4847^{9} 5099^{8} 6475^{7}

Beautiful Dancer (IRE) *L M Cumani* a55 40
3 b f Danehill Dancer(IRE) —Beautiful France (IRE) (Sadler's Wells (USA))
5499^{5} 5915^{9}

Beautiful Madness (IRE) *M G Quinlan* a48 71
3 ch f Shinko Forest(IRE) —Dosha (Touching Wood (USA))
2749^{4} 3038^{5} 4324^{2} (4513) 4536^{4} 5489^{5}

Beautiful Mover (USA) *J E Long* a47 52
5 ch m Spinning World(USA) —Dancer's Glamour (USA) (Danzig Connection (USA))
20^{7} 115^{6} 1951^{9} 3186^{7}

Beautiful Reward (FR) *J R Fanshawe* 74
3 ch f Diesis—Toujours Elle (USA) (Lyphard (USA))
1127^{14} 2873^{6}

Beautiful Summer (IRE) *R A Fahey* a55 59
4 br m Zafonic(USA) —Sadler's Song (Saddlers' Hall (IRE))
1284^{8} 1626^{7}

Beau Torero (FR) *B N Pollock* a63
9 gr g True Brave(USA) —Brave Lola (FR) (Dom Pasquini (FR))
365^{3} 443^{3} 602^{7} 677^{5} 1732^{9} 1907^{11}

Beauty Is Truth (IRE) *Robert Collet* 117
3 b f Pivotal—Zelding (IRE) (Warning)
$1006a^{3}$ $1704a^{2}$ (2291a) 2733^{7} 4746^{10} $6039a^{16}$

Beauty Shine *M Johnston* 34
3 ch f Selkirk(USA) —Lines Of Beauty (USA) (Line In The Sand (USA))
3678^{5} 4229^{9}

Beaver (AUS) *J G M O'Shea* 65
8 b g Bite The Bullet(USA) —Mahenge (AUS) (Twig Moss (FR))
3721^{7} 4959^{5} 5676^{5} 6200^{9}

Beaver Patrol (IRE) *Eve Johnson Houghton* a108 108
5 ch g Tagula(IRE) —Erne Project (IRE) (Project Manager)
(1474) 1651^{5} 2237^{6} 2858^{11} 3104^{5} 4150^{5} 4456^{2} (5209) 5616^{4} 6003^{2}

Becharm *A G Newcombe* a67 62
3 b f Singspiel(IRE) —Zuleika Dobson (Cadeaux Genereux)
1416^{6} 1358^{9} 2472^{8} 2834^{7} 3875^{6}

Beck *W M Brisbourne* a59 49
3 ch g Cadeaux Genereux—River Cara (USA) (Irish River (FR))
2241^{4} 3736^{6} 3612^{2} 3997^{7} 4427^{5} 4971^{6} 5084^{4} 5625^{6} 5782^{10} 6956^{11} 7079^{5} 7159^{3} (7169) 7218^{2} 7250^{3} 7275^{4}

Beckenham's Secret *A W Carroll* a62 73
3 b g Foxhound(USA) —Berliese (IRE) (High Estate)
725^{7} 931^{6} 1726^{7} 2545^{4} 3150^{15} 3620^{12} 4326^{7} 4760^{10} 5095^{5} 5187^{2} 6147^{7} 6453^{6}

Beckermet (IRE) *R F Fisher* a61 114
5 b g Second Empire(IRE) —Razida (IRE) (Last Tycoon (IRE))
$400a^{7}$ $470a^{9}$ $597a^{12}$ 1159^{6} 1619^{2} 1826^{3} 2030^{3} 2396^{2} 2858^{19} 4150^{15} 4196^{9} 4600^{7} (4813) 5112^{5} (5416) 5588^{5} 5832^{6} 6338^{2}

Becky Quick (IRE) *Garry Moss*
2 b f Fantastic Light(USA) —Private Bluff (USA) (Pine Bluff (USA))
5675^{6}

Bedaly (FR) *A Bonin* a70 105
4 b g Medaaly—Pro Gold (FR) (Saumarez)
$3665a^{7}$

Bed Fellow (IRE) *A P Jarvis* a86 81
3 b g Trans Island—Moonlight Partner (IRE) (Red Sunset)
754^{4} 939^{3} 1773^{9} 2231^{9} 3553^{11} 4276^{11} 4608^{9} 5508^{3} 6475^{11}

Bedizen *Mrs P Sly* 79
4 b g Fantastic Light(USA) —Barboukh (Night Shift (USA))
1011^{2} 1259^{9} 3060^{4} 5870^{11}

Bedouin Beauty (IRE) *E A L Dunlop* a42
3 gr f King's Best(USA) —Manchaca (FR) (Highest Honor (FR))
2931^{1} 484^{8}

Bedouin Blue (IRE) *P C Haslam* a71 77
4 b g Desert Style(IRE) —Society Fair (FR) (Always Fair (USA))
6007^{6} 7150^{2}

Bee Charmer (IRE) *M Matz* 105
5 b h Anabaa(USA) —Bayourida (USA) (Slew O'Gold (USA))
$6771a^{12}$

Beech Games *F Jordan* a75 75
3 b g Mind Games—Dane Dancing (IRE) (Danehill (USA))
184^{6} 4659^{4} 4977^{5} 5390^{6} 5865^{11} 7186^{4}

Beechside (IRE) *W A Murphy* a19 53
3 b f Orpen(USA) —Tokurama (IRE) (Mtoto)
970^{3} 1240^{7} 1453^{6} 2939^{4} 4384^{4} 4935^{4} (5282) 5834^{7} 5930^{10} 6466^{3} 6720^{14} 7137^{11}

Bee Eater (IRE) *Sir Mark Prescott* 107
3 b f Green Desert(USA) —Littlefeather (IRE) (Indian Ridge)
(2393) 3099^{3} (3278) (3746) (4133) 4639^{3}

Bee Magic *C N Kellett* a54 23
4 ch g Magic Ring(IRE) —Miss Bananas (Risk Me (FR))
13^{2} 221^{8} 430^{6} 680^{11} 1136^{9} 2304^{13} (3597) 4252^{10} 4668^{8} 4973^{10}

Bee Sting *W R Swinburn* 84
3 b g Selkirk(USA) —Desert Lynx (IRE) (Green Desert (USA))
1841^{11} 2726^{5} (3079)

Bee Stinger *I A Wood* a86 89
5 b g Almaty(IRE) —Nest Egg (Prince Sabo)
1395^{8} 1962^{3} 2427^{11} 2995^{4} 4234^{11} 7061^{5} 7281^{4}

Beetuna (IRE) *B Smart* 76
2 b c Statue Of Liberty(USA) —High Atlas (Shirley Heights)
4784^{7} 5140^{2} 5502^{4}

Before You Go (IRE) *T G Mills* a96 106
4 b g Sadler's Wells(USA) —Here On Earth (USA) (Mr Prospector (USA))
3272^{6} 3989^{3} (4588) 5030^{7}

Befortyfour *M A Jarvis* 83
2 b g Kyllachy—Ivania (First Trump)
2337^{2} 2737^{13}

Beggars End (USA) *E F Vaughan* 70
2 rg g Mizzen Mast(USA) —Hasardeuse (USA) (Distant View (USA))
6616^{6}

Beiramar (IRE) *W Hickst* 99
4 br m Monsun(GER) —Be My Lady (GER) (Be My Guest (USA))
(6220a) $6781a^{10}$

Bel Cantor *W J H Ratcliffe* a71 86
4 b h Largesse—Palmstead Belle (IRE) (Wolfhound (USA))
1134^{10} 1481^{8} 1718^{5} 1847^{7} 2202^{3} 2744^{10} 2805^{6} 3686^{2} (4006) 4075^{2} 4381^{6} 5356^{3} 5923^{5} 6381^{8} (6560) 6639^{6} 7126^{3}

Beldon Hill (USA) *R A Fahey* a82 73
4 b m Rahy(USA) —Bevel (USA) (Mr Prospector (USA))
45^{2} (74) (112) 283^{3} (434) 507^{5} 2861^{7} 3243^{7}

Belgrave Square (USA) *A P O'Brien* 95
2 ch c Hennessy(USA) —Dream Profit (USA) (Deputy Minister (CAN))
4151^{2} 5048^{4}

Beliar (GER) *Eoin Doyle* a63 76
4 ch h Tertullian(USA) —Brighella (GER) (Lomitas)
$2018a^{2}$ $4114a^{12}$ 6271^{12} 6871^{4}

Believe Me (IRE) *J-M Beguigne* 112
3 ch f In The Wings—Golden Wings (USA) (Devil's Bag (USA))
$1880a^{2}$ $2501a^{6}$ $4055a^{2}$

Belinda Rose (IRE) *E J Alston* a47 53
3 b f Namid—Barathiki (Barathea (IRE))
1523^{11} 1725^{6} 2455^{12} 6877^{9} 7134^{2}

Bella Amica (GER) *Frau Marion Rotering* 67
2 b f Black Sam Bellamy(IRE) —Bennetta (FR) (Top Ville)
$5028a^{10}$

Bella Ciao (GER) *A Oertel*
2 b f Chato(USA) —Briscola (General Assembly (USA))
$5848a^{8}$

Bella Grande *Garry Moss* 12
3 ch f Primo Valentino(IRE) —Florie Nightingale (Tragic Role (USA))
3202^{11} 5082^{9} 5625^{11} 6559^{9} 7159^{9}

Bella Ida (FR) *J E Hammond* 92
3 b f Hernando(FR) —Bayourida (USA) (Slew O'Gold (USA))
$6400a^{5}$

Bellalatino (IRE) *Mrs Norma Pook* a54 54
2 b f Modigliani(USA) —Quaver (USA) (The Minstrel (CAN))
1445^{6} 2812^{17} 3348^{3} 3938^{10} 4162^{10} 4903^{11}

Bellalini *E J Alston* 6
4 b m Bertolini(USA) —Primum Tempus (Primo Dominie)
6309[12]

Bella Marie *L R James* 47
4 b m Kasakov—Onemoretime (Timeless Times (USA))
2315[10] 4177[14]

Bellamont Forest (USA) *O Larsen* a77 106
11 br g Hermitage(USA) —Teresa's Spirit (USA) (Master Derby (USA))
245a[14] 400a[12] 472a[10] 5262a[9]

Bellamy Cay *D K Weld* 117
5 b g Kris—Trellis Bay (Sadler's Wells (USA))
663a[6] 861a[8] 5437a[9]

Bella Natasha (IRE) *K A Ryan* a57 19
2 b f Intikhab(USA) —Baldemara (FR) (Sanglamore (USA))
942[4] 1302[10]

Bellapais Boy *T D Easterby* a50 41
3 b g Spectrum(IRE) —Denice (Night Shift (USA))
1224[11] 1579[15]

Bellas Chicas (IRE) *P T Midgley* 42
2 ch f Captain Rio—Persian Light (IRE) (Persian Heights)
1302[4] 4924[13] 5903[7]

Belle Aire (GER) *D K Richardson* a82
3 b f Areion(GER) —Birjama (GER) (Meinberg (GER))
1006a[0]

Belle Allure (IRE) *R Pritchard-Gordon* 99
2 ch f Numerous(USA) —Mare Aux Fees (Kenmare (FR))
5493a[4] 6040a[9]

Belle Artiste (IRE) *Joseph Crowley* a82 96
5 b m Namid—Beltisaal (FR) (Belmez (USA))
6920a[DSQ]

Belle Bellino (FR) *B R Millman* 65
2 b f Robellino(USA) —Hoh Chi Min (Efisio)
3152[7] 3796[9] 4540[10]

Belle Epine (FR) *J J Chavarrias* a36 84
5 ch m Lord Of Men—Belle Muse (FR) (Courtroom (FR))
6044a[6]

Belle Famille (IRE) *E Lellouche* 100
3 br f Linamix(FR) —Exocet (USA) (Deposit Ticket (USA))
6460a[10]

Belle Hernando (GER) *Dr A Bolte* 94
4 b m Hernando(FR) —Be Happy (GER) (Homing)
6519a[4]

Belle Isnarde (IRE) *V Caruso* 82
2 b f Desert Prince(IRE) —Attitre (FR) (Mtoto)
6047a[6]

Belle Of The Lodge (IRE) *John M Oxx* 90
3 b f Grand Lodge(USA) —Beldarian (IRE) (Last Tycoon (IRE))
6368a[3]

Bellini Star *G A Ham* a49 61
4 b g Fraam—Rewardia (IRE) (Petardia)
1368[11] 3405[12]

Bellomi (IRE) *M R Channon* 88
2 bg g Lemon Drop Kid(USA) —Reina Blanca (Darshaan)
4070[2] 4593[2] 5033[2] (5399) 5972[7]

Belmundo (GER) *P Schiergen* 105
3 b c Monsun(GER) —Bajonette (IRE) (Lomond (USA))
6353a[2]

Belotto (IRE) *R Charlton* a65
2 b f Peintre Celebre(USA) —Bel (Darshaan)
6849[4]

Belshazzar (USA) *D C O'Brien* a5 69
6 b g King Of Kings(IRE) —Bayou Bidder (USA) (Premiership (USA))
1251[12] 1592[14]

Beltanus (GER) *Frau Ira Ferentschak* 98
3 ch c Tertullian(USA) —Brighella (GER) (Lomitas)
2293a[17]

Belvedere Vixen *M J Wallace* a64 58
3 b f Foxhound(USA) —Aunt Susan (Distant Relative)
128[5] 290[7] 588[3] (659)

Ben *P G Murphy* a73 73
2 b c Bertolini(USA) —Bold Byzantium (Bold Arrangement)
814[4] 999[4] 1291[2] 1680[3] 2333[3] 2443[5] 3426[3] 3687[2] 4459[6] 5008[6] 5429[3] 5815[3] 6017[22]

Benandonner (USA) *R A Fahey* a80 96
4 ch g Giant's Causeway(USA) —Cape Verdi (IRE) (Caerleon (USA))
993[2] 1245[3] 2093[11] 3513[3] 3813[3] (4377) 4745[6] 5326[5] 5631[10] 6011[18]

Benbaun (IRE) *M J Wallace* 125
6 b g Stravinsky(USA) —Escape To Victory (Salse (USA))
(2050a) 2733[12] (5075a) (5436a) (6039a) 7089a[13]

Ben Chorley *P W Chapple-Hyam* a23 73
3 gr g Inchinor—Arantxa (Sharpo)
1978[8]

Bencoolen (IRE) *R Charlton* 79
2 b c Daylami(IRE) —Jakarta (IRE) (Machiavellian (USA))
3896[5] (4876) 5613[8]

Bencorr (USA) *M J Wallace* a68 35
2 ch c Proud Citizen(USA) —Exquisite Mistress (USA) (Nasty And Bold (USA))
2590[6] 2991[6] 3560[7] 4669[2] 4892[10] 5601[3] 6207[5]

Beneath The Trees (USA) *J A Osborne* 30
2 b c Forestry(USA) —Arabis (USA) (Deputy Minister (CAN))
5091[9]

Benedetti (AUS) *T Noonan* 116
6 bb g Second Empire(IRE) —Seattle Gem (NZ) (Khozaam (USA))
(395a) (531a) 646a[5]

Benedetto *Mrs A J Perrett* a49 63
2 b c Fasliyev(USA) —Inchyre (Shirley Heights)
6436[13] 6617[5] 6755[7]

Benedict Bay *J A Geake* a36 59
5 b g In The Wings—Persia (IRE) (Persian Bold)
1732[6]

Benedict Spirit (IRE) *M H Tompkins* a66 61
2 b c Invincible Spirit(IRE) —Kathy Caerleon (IRE) (Caerleon (USA))
5734[7] 7217[3]

Beneking *D Burchell* a66 61
7 bb g Wizard King—Gagajulu (Al Hareb (USA))
(50) 235[4] 346[4] 549[9] 560[6] 750[7] 888[6] 1436[4] 1947[4] 2336[2] 2656[8] 6431[2] 6717[3] 6895[8] 7207[10]

Benellino *R M Stronge* a29 47
4 b g Robellino(USA) —Benjarong (Sharpo)
2962[3] 3366[13] 4290[5] 5341[13]

Benhavis *J L Dunlop* 77
2 b c Lomitas—Northern Goddess (Night Shift (USA))
2215[11] 3471[3] 4316[3] 4852[5] 5721[2] (6307)

Benitez Bond *G R Oldroyd*
2 ch c Bahamian Bounty—Triple Tricks (IRE) (Royal Academy (USA))
5281[11]

Benllech *S Kirk* a84 76
3 b g Lujain(USA) —Four Legs Good (IRE) (Be My Guest (USA))
3797[9] 4509[6] 6806[4] 6997[11] 7094[7] 7233[4] (7279)

Bennie Blue (SAF) *M F De Kock* a95 95
5 ch h Rich Man's Gold(USA) —Biloxi Blue (SAF) (Al Mufti (USA))
250a[11] 398a[7] 475a[6] 529a[3] (643a)

Benny The Bat *K O Cunningham-Brown* a73 71
3 gr g Victory Note(USA) —Little Emily (Zafonic (USA))
275[4] 1247[7] 2177[10] 2558[7] 3969[7] 4544[8]

Benny The Bull (USA) *R Dutrow Jr* a118
4 bb h Lucky Lionel(USA) —Comet Cat (USA) (Birdonthewire (USA))
6510a[4]

Benny The Bus *Mrs G S Rees* a71 47
5 b g Komaite(USA) —Amy Leigh (IRE) (Imperial Frontier (USA))
621[10] 686[7] 806[2] 1064[8] 1280[7] 1673[12] 2225[4] (2947) 3285[3] 3409[4] 5330[12] 5643[7] 6148[7]

Benny The Rascal (IRE) *J Pearce* a59 46
5 b g Benny The Dip(USA) —Bolshoi Star (Soviet Star (USA))
630[3]

Bens Georgie (IRE) *D K Ivory* a62 73
5 ch m Opening Verse(USA) —Peperonata (IRE) (Cyrano De Bergerac)
1280[3] 1946[4] 2257[3] 2334[7] 2799[5] 3106[3] 3735[2] 3950[10] 5391[2] 5897[9] 6415[3] 6895[10] (7207)

Bentley *D Shaw* a70 62
3 b g Piccolo—April Lee (Superpower)
34[3] 103[2] (202) 290[4] (378) (404) 502[6] 2255[6] 2518[2] 2594[4] 2837[4] 3168[12] 3369[5] 3483[5] 3763[10] 4658[7] 4885[8] 7111[3] 7283[2]

Bentley Biscuit (AUS) *Mrs Gai Waterhouse* 123
6 ch g Peintre Celebre(USA) —Tycoon Joy (AUS) (Last Tycoon (IRE))
2733[20] 3506[10] 4214a[7]

Bentley Brook (IRE) *P A Blockley* a70 74
5 ch g Singspiel(IRE) —Gay Bentley (USA) (Riverman (USA))
10[5] 72[5] 1025[9] 1314[4] 1907[5] (7198) (7242)

Bentley's Ball (USA) *S Seemar* a80 75
6 br g Stravinsky(USA) —Slide By (Aragon)
105a[5]

Bentong (IRE) *P F I Cole* a72 108
4 b g Anabaa(USA) —Miss Party Line (USA) (Phone Trick (USA))
1474[10] 2440[2] 2858[15] 3505[14] 4150[14]

Benwilt Breeze (IRE) *G M Lyons* a103 107
5 b g Mujadil(USA) —Image Of Truce (IRE) (Brief Truce (USA))
1171a[5] 3140a[14] 4864a[2] 5394a[7] 5616[2] 5842a[3] 6036a[3] 6363a[17]

Berbatov *Paul Green* a58 51
3 b g Alhaarth(IRE) —Neptunalia (Slip Anchor)
3066[9] 3570[7] 3997[11] 4197[6] 4526[3]

Berbice (IRE) *R Hannon* 105
2 gr c Acclamation—Pearl Bright (FR) (Kaldoun (FR))
1989[3] 2232[4] (2624) 4743[4] 5630[3] 5922[2]

Bere Davis (FR) *P D Evans* 73
2 gr g Verglas(IRE) —Zerelda (Exhibitioner)
(2432) 2732[17] 3157[5]

Berenice Pancrisia (FR) *Mme M Bollack-Badel* a71 94
3 b f Kendor(FR) —Entretenue (FR) (Cadeaux Genereux)
6400a[9]

Beresford Lady *A D Brown* a47 47
3 b f Presidium—Coney Hills (Beverley Boy)
2137[9] 2792[4] 3917[10] 4641[5] 5945[6] 6315[6] 6832[14]

Beret Rouge (IRE) *A Fabre* 98
2 gr c Red Ransom(USA) —Bernimixa (FR) (Linamix (FR))
5660a[3]

Bergo (GER) *W Hefter* 111
4 b h Silvano(GER) —Bella Figura (USA) (Surumu (GER))
1689a[2]

Bergonzi (IRE) *J H M Gosden* a78 91
3 ch g Indian Ridge—Lady Windley (Baillamont (USA))
(1011) 1277[2] 1584[2] (1898) 2231[6] 2999[8] 5415[3] 5724[2]

Beringoer (FR) *A M Balding* a86 104
4 ch g Bering—Charmgoer (USA) (Nureyev (USA))
176a[11] 327a[11] 411a[11] 2755[26]

Berkhamsted (IRE) *Tom Dascombe* a85 81
5 b g Desert Sun—Accounting (Sillery (USA))
30[2] 117[8] 263[6] (Dead)

Berlin Bunker (IRE) *B Ellison* a52
6 b g Right Win(IRE) —Venture To Heaven (IRE) (The Parson)
1279[6] (Dead)

Berlioz (IND) *S Seemar* a70 81
6 b g Sri Pekan(USA) —Innocent Pleasures (IRE) (Night Shift (USA))
331a[9] 473a[7]

Bermacha *W R Muir* a74 66
2 ch f Bertolini(USA) —Machaera (Machiavellian (USA))
1960[5] 3648[8] 4181[6] 4975[4] 5527[3] 5896[2] 6150[2] (6456)

Bermuda Beauty (IRE) *J M Bradley* a48 42
4 b m Elnadim(USA) —Believing (Belmez (USA))
403[10] 442[12]

Bernabeu (IRE) *S Curran* a59 44
5 b g Mark Of Esteem(IRE) —Snow Ballet (IRE) (Sadler's Wells (USA))
4914[3] 6361[9] (6792) (7060) 7120[2]

Bernando (FR) *P Bary* a90 90
3 b c Hernando(FR) —Beggars Belief (IRE) (Common Grounds)
2499a[7]

Bernasconi (USA) *G A Swinbank* a77
3 b g Rahy(USA) —Argentina (USA) (Storm Cat (USA))
301[4] (375)

Bernix *T D Easterby* 71
5 gr g Linamix(FR) —Bernique (USA) (Affirmed (USA))
1044[6] 1259[3] 1479[2] 1849[5] 2201[7]

Berri Chis (ARG) *Vanja Sandrup* 98
5 b h Strawberry-Li(ARG) —Potrichis (ARG) (Potrillazo (ARG))
1647a[8] 5262a[3] 6370a[15]

Berry Baby (IRE) *G A Butler* a61 52
2 b f Rainbow Quest(USA) —Inchberry (Barathea (IRE))
5881[8] 6742[6] 6944[5]

Berry Hill Lass (IRE) *J G M O'Shea* 64
3 b f Alhaarth(IRE) —Gold Mist (Darshaan)
2359[5] 2620[4] 3794[3] 4960[10] 5346[7]

Berrymead *M W Easterby* a51 60
2 br f Killer Instinct—Mill End Quest (King's Signet (USA))
1087[4] 1713[4] 2251[5] 3398[6] 4975[6] 6536[14]

Berrynarbor *A G Newcombe* a62 59
2 b f Tobougg(IRE) —River Art (USA) (Irish River (FR))
2303[6] 4094[9] 6417[14] (6880)

Bers Treasure (IRE) *Seamus Fahey* a38 37
4 b m Tagula(IRE) —City Imp (IRE) (Mac's Imp (USA))
6877[7]

Bertbrand *M Botti* a75
2 b c Bertolini(USA) —Mi Amor (IRE) (Alzao (USA))
6401[7] 6714[4] 6990[4] 7260[6]

Bertha Von Suttner *F Folco* 93
3 ch f Noverre(USA) —Bandofpearls (USA) (Chimes Band (USA))
6688a[6]

Berti Bertolini *Rae Guest* a59 42
4 b g Bertolini(USA) —Cosmic Countess (IRE) (Lahib (USA))
1718[9] 2799[2] 3408[4] 5778[9]

Bertie Bear *G G Margarson* 41
4 b h Bertolini(USA) —Philarmonique (FR) (Trempolino (USA))
2187[9]

Berties Brother *D G Bridgwater* a38 29
4 ch g Forzando—Sweets (IRE) (Persian Heights)
51[10] 129[10]

Berties Goodenough *Andrew Turnell* a50 50
2 b g Bertolini(USA) —Goodenough Girl (Mac's Imp (USA))
2103[9] 2977[9] 4181[12] 6237[7] 6419[14] 6641[5] 6977[12]

Bertie Southstreet *J R Best* a78 81
4 bb g Bertolini(USA) —Salvezza (IRE) (Superpower)
4965[5] 5712[7] 6273[2] 6667[7] 6972[6] 7253[7]

Bertie Swift *J Gallagher* a68 67
3 b g Bertolini(USA) —Hollybell (Beveled (USA))
127[2] 290[2] 423[2] 1117[8] 1403[11] 2878[15]

Bertie Vista *T D Easterby* 62
2 b g Bertolini(USA) —Off Camera (Efisio)
3560[8] 5042[6]

Bertoliver *D K Ivory* a94 89
3 b g Bertolini(USA) —Calcavella (Pursuit Of Love)
1660[6] (1900) (2399) 2884[8] 4133[5] 5632[7] 5891[6] 6142[3] 6487[6]

Bertrada (IRE) *G P Enright* a53 27
3 b f King Charlemagne(USA) —Goldenfort Queen (IRE) (Distinctly North (USA))
136[4] 373[2] 469[2] 624[8] 708[7] 794[4] 4533[10] 4742[14] 6060[15]

Bertranicus (FR) *L Urbano-Grajales* a111 108
4 br g Take Risks(FR) —L'Etoile La Lune (IRE) (Groom Dancer (USA))
2100a[5] 2953a[2] (4012a) 5259a[3] 6031a[4]

Bert's Memory *K A Ryan* a59 66
3 b f Bertolini(USA) —Meg's Memory (IRE) (Superlative)
4023[9] 4480[9] 5936[10] (6247) 6464[12] 6537[6] 6873[8] 7001[6] 7201[5]

Beseech (IRE) *B J Meehan* 33
3 b f Danehill(USA) —Francfurter (Legend Of France (USA))
1659[10]

Beshairt *D Burchell* a46 40
3 b f Silver Wizard(USA) —Irja (Minshaanshu Amad (USA))
2654[7] 2978[10] 3595[7]

Besi *P Monteith*
5 b g Lavirco(GER) —Brangane (IRE) (Anita's Prince)
1627[14] 2254[15]

Bespoke Boy *P C Haslam* 97
2 b c Acclamation—Milly Fleur (Primo Dominie)
(1858) 2232[2] 2785[8] 4724[10] 5480[6]

Bessemer (JPN) *I W McInnes* a82 82
6 b g Carnegie(IRE) —Chalna (IRE) (Darshaan)
32[9] (252) 346[3] 2033[10] 2551[3] 2823[8] 2947[12]

Best Alibi (IRE) *Saeed Bin Suroor* 119
4 b h King's Best(USA) —Chauncy Lane (IRE) (Sadler's Wells (USA))
598a[6] 861a[10] 6153[3]

Best Lead *Ian Emmerson* a58 55
8 b g Distant Relative—Bestemor (Selkirk (USA))
318[4] (448) 580[3] 1262[12] 1753[12]

Best Name *Saeed Bin Suroor* 120
4 b h King's Best(USA) —Flawly (Old Vic)
600a[4] 862a[11]

Best Of Gold (IRE) *B J Meehan* 56
3 b c Montjeu(IRE) —Penny Fan (Nomination)
1081[7] 1812[14] 2081[4]

Best Of The Lot (USA) *R A Fahey* a61 79
5 b g Lear Fan(USA) —Aerosilver (USA) (Relaunch (USA))
1490[7] 1942[9] (2254) 3049[6] 4159[8] 4582[7] 4972[3] 5145[8] 5674[10]

Best Of Thurgau (GER) *Carmen Bocskai* 86
3 ch c Silvano(GER) —Bukett (GER) (Turfkonig (GER))
2503a[4]

Best One *C E Brittain* a73 77
3 ch g Best Of The Bests(IRE) —Nasaieb (IRE) (Fairy King (USA))
3244[11] 3349[11] 3827[3] 4291[3] 4641[4] 5064[3] 6081[3] 7087[6]

Best Option *W R Muir* a46 43
3 b f Best Of The Bests(IRE) —B'Elanna Torres (Entrepreneur)
55[3] 689[9] 832[7] 900[6]

Best Prospect (IRE) *M Dods* a74 101
5 b g Orpen(USA) —Bright Prospect (USA) (Miswaki (USA))
995[8] 1449[7] 1767[13] 3026[6] 3509[11] 4523[7] 5554[2] (5775) 6185[3] 6499[8]

Best Selection *Mrs L J Mongan* a71 71
3 ch f Inchinor—Manila Selection (USA) (Manila (USA))
764[4] 904[2] 1289[10] 2445[3] 3214[5] 3421[6] 5131[5] 5921[2] 6175[2] 7224[7]

Best Suited *J J Quinn* 62
2 b f Averti(IRE) —Scarlett Holly (Red Sunset)
2984[7] 3378[2] 4041[4] 4406[8] 4897[5] 5520[2]

Best Warning *J Ryan* a9 47
3 br f Best Of The Bests(IRE) —Just Warning (Warning)
1566[10] 2192[12] 2610[10] 4172[15]

Best Woman *P Howling* a50 51
3 b f Best Of The Bests(IRE) —Business Woman (Primo Dominie)
417[4] 534[6] 676[10] 794[2] 2454[4]

Be Superior *J Balding*
2 b f Superior Premium—Miss Tun (Komaite (USA))
6755[9]

Bethanys Boy (IRE) *M Wigham* a65 56
6 ch g Docksider(USA) —Daymoon (USA) (Dayjur (USA))
35[2] 215[7] 302[7] 623[11] (730) 808[7] 1279[3] 1368[4] 3282[4] 3595[2] (4533) (5237) 5569[11] 6199[12]

Beths Choice *J M Bradley* a17 39
6 b g Midnight Legend—Clare's Choice (Pragmatic)
3476[10] 4630[11] 4948[9]

Bet Noir (IRE) *W R Swinburn* 63
2 b f King's Best(USA) —Ivowen (USA) (Theatrical)
6470[10]

Betteras Bertie *M Brittain* a38 40
4 gr g Paris House—Suffolk Girl (Statoblest)
1177[9] 1259[8] 2894[5] 3765[7] 4673[7] 5739[9]

Better Built *Declan Gillespie* 79
2 b c Xaar—Quiz Show (Primo Dominie)
5397a[11]

Better Hand (IRE) *M R Channon* 88
2 b c Montjeu(IRE) —Silly Game (IRE) (Bigstone (IRE))
3270[2] (3856) 4598[8]

Better In Heaven *H J L Dunlop* a43 55
2 b c Zamindar(USA) —Peace (Sadler's Wells (USA))
5329[9] 6139[9]

Betterlatethanever (IRE) *C J Teague* 38
3 ch g Titus Livius(FR) —First Nadia (Auction Ring (USA))
3639[14] 4901[5] 5045[6] 6057[8] 7125[10]

Better Off Red (USA) *D M Simcock* a31 41
3 bb f Red Ransom(USA) —Unending Love (USA) (Dixieland Band (USA))
2192[13] 3151[5]

Better Talk Now (USA) *H G Motion* 121
8 bb g Talkin Man(CAN) —Bendita (USA) (Baldski (USA))
6513a[4]

Bett's Spirit (IRE) *M J Grassick* a85 96
2 b f Invincible Spirit(IRE) —Hi Bettina (Henbit (USA))
5435a[3] 6619[3]

Betty Burke *H J L Dunlop* a62 67
2 b f Choisir(AUS) —Island Lover (IRE) (Turtle Island (IRE))
1993[7] 3648[5] 4254[2] 4756[3] 4924[5] 5601[5] 6098[8]

Betty Oxo *B P J Baugh*
3 b f Mind Games—Kildine (IRE) (Common Grounds)
152[10] 237[11]

Bettys Touch *W J Musson* 55
2 b f Lujain(USA) —Fadaki Hawaki (USA) (Vice Regent (CAN))
2056[8] 2152[2] 2832[7] 4453[6]

Beverley Beau *Mrs L Stubbs* a52 57
5 b g Inchinor—Oriel Girl (Beveled (USA))
83[2] 201[8] 339[7] 557[10] 1594[7] 1707[4] 2357[7] 2761[9] 4351[4] 4741[4] 5276[13]

Beverly Hill Billy *A King* a81 82
3 b g Primo Valentino(IRE) —Miss Beverley (Beveled (USA))
1563[3] 3165[2] 3590[7]

Bewdley *P D Evans* a39 58
2 b f Best Of The Bests(IRE) —Garota De Ipanema (FR) (Al Nasr (FR))
5801[5] 6289[10] 6611[6]

Bewildering (IRE) *E J O'Neill* a64 64
3 b c Tagula(IRE) —Mystic Belle (IRE) (Thatching)
338[3] 492[8] 1289[15] 1722[4]

Be Wise Girl *A W Carroll* a38
6 ch m Fleetwood(IRE) —Zabelina (USA) (Diesis)
976[16] 1380[7] 1934[6] 2142[7] 2519[11]

Beyabi *J R Jenkins* 33
2 br f Tumbleweed Ridge—Sifat (Marju (IRE))
1896[12] 2365[8] 3245[11] 4359[7] 4824[8]

Beyond Belief (IRE) *M J Wallace*
4 b m Sadler's Wells(USA) —Adjriyna (Top Ville)
2661[3]

Beyond Compare (IRE) *J S Bolger* 60
2 ch f Galileo(IRE) —Gold Bust (Nashwan (USA))
6443a[6]

Bianca Capello *J R Fanshawe* 54
2 b f Medicean—Totom (Mtoto)
5541[6] 5882[7]

Bianconi (SAF) *S Seemar* a12 83
8 b g Rambo Dancer(CAN) —Coconut Ice (SAF) (Jungle Cove (USA))
244a[7] 401a[10]

Biarritz *Mrs J C McGregor*
6 b m Prince Daniel(USA) —Sweet Fun (Meadowbrook)
4496[10] 4891[13]

Biased Opinion (IRE) *H J L Dunlop* a61 55
2 b c Fasliyev(USA) —Atnab (USA) (Riverman (USA))
2041[19] 2575[10] 2949[6] 4065[5] 4669[6] 5096[8] 5715[5] 6426[6]

Bibi Leon (IRE) *R Feligioni*
2 b f Noverre(USA) —Crocus (IRE) (Mister Baileys)
6527a[10]

Bicoastal (USA) *B J Meehan* a88 103
3 ch f Gone West(USA) —Ocean Queen (USA) (Zilzal (USA))
1035[4] 1702a[7] 1958[5] 5047[4] 5794[9]

Bidable *B Palling* a65 66
3 b f Auction House(USA) —Dubitable (Formidable (USA))
1155[7] 1410[3] 2079[5] 3490[3] 3798[3] 4073[2] (4257) 4760[4] 5347[8] 5860[10]

Bid Again *R Pritchard-Gordon* 91
2 b f Auction House(USA) —Carn Maire (Northern Prospect (USA))
6525a[7] 6888a[8]

Bid Art (IRE) *A M Balding* a65 65
2 b g Hawk Wing(USA) —Crystal Theatre (IRE) (King's Theatre (IRE))
2103[12] 2473[10] 2961[3] 3508[9] 5471[5] 6715[3]

Bidders Itch *A Berry* 11
3 b f Auction House(USA) —Sharp Ego (USA) (Sharpen Up)
4001[7] 4714[9] 5041[14]

Bidding Time *M L W Bell* 48
3 b f Rock Of Gibraltar(IRE) —Bianca Nera (Salse (USA))
1128[11] 2606[11]

Bid For Fame (USA) *J Pearce* a68 55
10 bb g Quest For Fame—Shroud (USA) (Vaguely Noble)
618[11] 891[9]

Bid For Glory *H J Collingridge* a95 95
3 ch c Auction House(USA) —Woodland Steps (Bold Owl)
2045[2] (2578) 3460[16] 6155[10] 6654[5] (6995) 7163[4]

Bid For Gold *Jedd O'Keeffe* 76
3 b g Auction House(USA) —Gold And Blue (IRE) (Bluebird (USA))
1197[3] (2094) 2662[3] 3029[6] (3723) 4006[4] 4581[3] 5885[14] 6753[13]

Bid To The Beat *H J Collingridge* a54 38
2 b c Auction House(USA) —Sophies Symphony (Merdon Melody)
4130[10] 5116[8] 6723[9]

Bienheureux *Miss Gay Kelleway* a70 69
6 b g Bien Bien(USA) —Rochea (Rock City)
4[2] 62[3] 100[3] 213[5] 302[6] 1032[3] 1178[11] (1319) 1741[4] 2055[13] 2595[3] 3217[5] 3457[4] (3617) 4318[3] 4499[2] 4708[2] 5514[5] 5709[5] 6276[5]

Biff Tannen (ITY) *L D'Auria* 102
5 b h Shantou(USA) —Buenos Aires (ITY) (Mukaddamah (USA))
1518a[2]

Bigalos Bandit *D Nicholls* a80 89
5 ch g Compton Place—Move Darling (Rock City)
841[5] 1456[6] 1601[6] 1788[10] 2234[17]

Bigalo's Magic (UAE) *E J O'Neill* a61 66
2 ch c Halling(USA) —Roseate (USA) (Mt. Livermore (USA))
4362[9] 4916[4] 5749[4] 6486[7]

Big Booster (USA) *M Mitchell* a114 105
6 b g Accelerator(USA) —Waterside (USA) (Topsider (USA))
5824a[3]

Big Easy (NZ) *L Laxon* 104
6 b g Spinning World(USA) —Nicoles Niner (USA) (Forty Niner (USA))
1877a[8]

Bigfanofthat (IRE) *K R Burke* 78
2 b c Rock Of Gibraltar(IRE) —Miss Salsa (USA) (Unbridled (USA))
(2166)

Big Honor (IRE) *U Suter* a76 82
3 b c Big Shuffle(USA) —Pat's Honor (GER) (Great Lakes)
2503a[9]

Big Noise *Dr J D Scargill* a75 93
3 b c Lake Coniston(IRE) —Mitsubishi Video (IRE) (Doulab (USA))
(2186) 2570[2] (3099) (4170) 5635[2]

Big Ralph *D K Ivory* a47
4 ch g Mark Of Esteem(IRE) —Wish Me Luck (IRE) (Lycius (USA))
49[5] 272[5] 789[5] 907[11] 1119[10] 6832[10] 7069[5] 7185[4]

Big Robert *W R Muir* 105
3 b c Medicean—Top Flight Queen (Mark Of Esteem (IRE))
1103[6] 2066a[4] 2789[7] 3361a[3] (3683) 4044[6] 4803[9] 5351[6]

Big Slick (IRE) *M Brittain* 28
2 ch c Rossini(USA) —Why Worry Now (IRE) (College Chapel)
1792[11] 2804[9] 3024[9] 5550[16] 5901[10]

Big Spartan (BRZ) *P Nickel Filho* a92 54
4 b g Spend A Buck(USA) —Beautiful Maria (BRZ) (Ghadeer (FR))
326a[4] 597a[13]

Big Timer (USA) *I Semple* a92 102
3 ch g Street Cry(IRE) —Moonflute (USA) (The Minstrel (CAN))
760[9] 5673[5] 7184[10]

Bijou Dan *D W Thompson* a76 68
6 ch g Bijou D'Inde—Cal Norma's Lady (IRE) (Lyphard's Special (USA))
1069[5] 1751[6] (1944) (2168) 2823[3] 3343[10] 3955[5] 4333[9] 6259[7] 6640[5] 7146[9]

Bijouterie *T J Pitt* a26 69
3 ch f Tobougg(IRE) —Branston Gem (So Factual (USA))
583[7]

Bikini *H Candy* 65
2 b f Trans Island—Chimere (FR) (Soviet Lad (USA))
2968[7] 5882[3]

Bilboa *B R Millman* 45
2 b g Averti(IRE) —Anita Marie (IRE) (Anita's Prince)
2193[7] 2941[9]

Bilkie (IRE) *John Berry* a51 51
5 ch g Polish Precedent(USA) —Lesgor (USA) (Irish River (FR))
508[5]

Bill Bennett (FR) *J Jay* a53 70
6 b g Bishop Of Cashel—Concert (Polar Falcon (USA))
71[2] 1254[10]

Billberry *S C Williams* 47
2 gr g Diktat—Elderberry (Bin Ajwaad (IRE))
6540[6]

Billich *D E Cantillon* a91 84
4 ch h Observatory(USA) —Pomponette (USA) (Rahy (USA))
457[2] 662[9] 2449[9] 3112[8] (4786)

Billion Dollar Kid *R Hannon* 87
2 br c Averti(IRE) —Fredora (Inchinor)
2600[2] 3238[2] (5274) (5536)

Billy Dane (IRE) *R A Fahey* a87 91
3 b g Fayruz—Lomalou (IRE) (Lightning Dealer)
1768[5] 2037[3] 2231[10] 2788[22] 3559[7] 4640[9]

Billyford (IRE) *Liam Roche* a99 100
2 b c Lil's Boy(USA) —Alamanta (IRE) (Ali-Royal (IRE))
6161a[3] 6549a[3]

Billy Hot Rocks (IRE) *R M Beckett* 41
2 b c Intikhab(USA) —Rock Abbey (IRE) (College Chapel)
3550[13]

Billy One Punch *G G Margarson* a49 75
5 b g Mark Of Esteem(IRE) —Polytess (IRE) (Polish Patriot (USA))
928[U] 1078[8] 2338[10] 2665[6] 4031[4] 4340[2] 4517[2] 5280[2] 5514[3] 5983[11]

Billy Red *J R Jenkins* a65 69
3 ch g Dr Fong(USA) —Liberty Bound (Primo Dominie)
1022[6] 1269[5] 1932[4] 2594[6] 3353[4] (3879) 4546[7] 5051[4] 6287[5] 6413[15]

Billy Ruffian *T D Easterby* a67 62
3 ch g Kyllachy—Antonia's Folly (Music Boy)
280[3] 1484[5] 2363[8] 2939[6] 3837[11] 4330[12]

Binanti *P R Chamings* a85 99
7 b g Bin Ajwaad(IRE) —Princess Rosananti (IRE) (Shareef Dancer (USA))
1395[6] 2427[2] 2670[2] (2817) 3941[3] 4062[4] 4851[10] 5797[14] 6437[14] 6851[10]

Binario Uno *D Nicholls* 66
2 b g Bertolini(USA) —Madame Curie (Polish Precedent (USA))
2562[3] 2758[3]

Binary File (USA) *L Kelp* a110 104
9 b h Nureyev(USA) —Binary (Rainbow Quest (USA))
399a[7] 599a[5]

Binfield (IRE) *B G Powell* a59 67
2 b f Officer(USA) —Identify (IRE) (Persian Bold)
2724[7] 3233[2] 3643[4] 6012[8] 6572[11]

Binham Boy *M J Gingell* a40
3 ch g Pebble Powder—Northwold Star (USA) (Monteverdi)
53[8] 223[8] 386[10] 553[9]

Biniou (IRE) *R M H Cowell* a67 112
4 b h Mozart(IRE) —Cap Coz (IRE) (Indian Ridge)
1497[10] 1704a[9] 2352[9] 2811a[7] 4190a[7] 4485[2] 4813[3] 6071a[4] 6633a[7] (6954a)

Binnion Bay (IRE) *J J Bridger* a82 75
6 b g Fasliyev(USA) —Literary (Woodman (USA))
86[8] 310[8] (383) 461[4] 545[4] 556[2] 650[2] 739[3] (773) 865[4] (1036) 1401[8] (1446) (1666) 1969[12] 2358[5] 2626[6] 3215[13] 3525[10] 5917[10] 6646[7] 6795[7] 6997[5] 7099[10]

Binocular *B W Hills* 70
3 ch c Observatory(USA) —Well Beyond (IRE) (Don't Forget Me)
1001[3] 1412[3] 3365[5]

Binyamina *E F Vaughan* 40
2 b f Elmaamul(USA) —Latour (Sri Pekan (USA))
6648[18]

Birbalini *J R Best* a30 11
4 b m Bertolini(USA) —La Birba (IRE) (Prince Of Birds (USA))
2459[10]

Birdie Birdie *R A Fahey* a44 51
3 b f Superior Premium—Cautious Joe (First Trump)
335[6] 512[5] 667[6] 832[5] 1750[3] 2110[4] 2829[14]

Birdsville *Rae Guest* 38
2 b f Tobougg(IRE) —Fred's Dream (Cadeaux Genereux)
3043[10] 3801[4] 3923[10]

Birkintastic *B J Meehan* 75
2 ch g Dr Fong(USA) —Sharpe's Lady (Prince Des Coeurs (USA))
4350[4] 4775[10] 5194[3] 6052[10] 6471[15]

Birkside *D Carroll* a89 78
4 ch g Spinning World(USA) —Bright Hope (IRE) (Danehill (USA))
758[7] 870[6] 1216[5] 1368[3] 1559[3] 1765[5] (2140) (2667) 3048[7] 4015[11] 4763[5] (5310) (5690) (6019) (6261) (6774) 6982[2] (7046) 7132[2] (7236)

Birkspiel (GER) *S Dow* a81 107
6 b g Singspiel(IRE) —Beaute (GER) (Lord Udo (GER))
552[7] 882a[9]

Birthday Star (IRE) *A G Juckes* a67 58
5 b g Desert King(IRE) —White Paper (IRE) (Marignan (USA))
195[11] 363[10] 610[9] 767[4] 1314[11] 2222[2] (3595) 4025[7] 6564[4] 6815[5] 7172[6]

Bishop Auckland (IRE) *Mrs A Duffield* 38
3 b g Dockside(USA) —Chancel (USA) (Al Nasr (FR))
2554[12] 3415[5] 3804[12] 3825[13]

Bishopbriggs (USA) *D J Murphy* 69
2 ch g Victory Gallop(CAN) —Inny River (USA) (Seattle Slew (USA))
5910[8] 6303[3] 6557[3] 6634[9] 6756[15]

Bishop Court Hill (USA) *T Pletcher* a117
7 ch g Holy Bull(USA) —Just Cuz (USA) (Cormorant (USA))
860a[5]

Bite The Boss *E J O'Neill* 71
2 b c Mujahid(USA) —Clashfern (Smackover)
5038[5] 5485[3] 6051[4]

Bit Of A Monkey *L P Grassick*
3 b g Superior Premium—Rita's Rock Ape (Mon Tresor)
4530[15] 5688[16]

Bit Of Whimsy (USA) *B Tagg* 115
3 ch f Distorted Humor(USA) —Kristi B (USA) (El Prado (IRE))
5248a[2]

Bitooh *Saeed Bin Suroor* a50
2 b f Diktat—Sitara (Salse (USA))
5727[9]

Bivouac (UAE) *G A Swinbank* a47 55
3 b g Jade Robbery(USA) —Tentpole (USA) (Rainbow Quest (USA))
728[3] 1044[7] 1177[8] 2538[3] 3181[2] 3587[8]

Biz Bar *M Guarnieri* 98
3 b f Tobougg(IRE) —Ulanova (USA) (Barachois (CAN))
1701a[6] 2707a[5]

Blackat Blackitten (IRE) *G A Butler* a98 104
3 ch c Inchinor—Tara's Girl (IRE) (Fayruz)
3395[5] (3994) 4574[3] 4949[2] (5685) (5950)

Blackberry Boy (IRE) *D K Weld* 94
3 b c Desert Prince(IRE) —Summer Crush (USA) (Summer Squall (USA))
948a[8]

Blackberry Pie (USA) *R Charlton* a50 74
3 b f Gulch(USA) —Name Of Love (IRE) (Petardia)
1408[3] 2429[6] 5013[7] 5475[6] 5943[9]

Blackbury *W M Brisbourne* a46
5 b m Overbury(IRE) —Fenian Court (IRE) (John French)
7144[3] 7174[9] 7275[8]

Black Cat Crossing (USA) *A P O'Brien* 94
3 b c Storm Cat(USA) —Rings A Chime (USA) (Metfield (USA))
5459a[7]

Black Charmer (IRE) *M Johnston* a33 107
4 b g Black Minnaloushe(USA) —Abla (Robellino (USA))
1791[5] 2374[11] (2670) 2817[14] 3091[10] 3559[11]

Black Dahlia *A J McCabe* a53 72
2 br f Dansili—South Rock (Rock City)
4565[3] 5010[4] 5301[6] 6471[9] 6665[8]

Black Duke *M G Quinlan* a56 56
2 br c Diktat—Cool Question (Polar Falcon (USA))
1498[8] 3037[3] 3283[10] 5298[11] 5715[8] 6438[8]

Black Falcon (IRE) *M A Peill* a82 62
7 ch g In The Wings—Muwasim (USA) (Meadowlake (USA))
669[2] 811[2] 955[9] 2511[5]

Black Heart *M Botti* a59
2 b c Diktat—Blodwen (USA) (Mister Baileys)
6763[6] 7114[8] 7208[6]

Blackheath (IRE) *S T Mason* a69 82
11 ch g Common Grounds—Queen Caroline (USA) (Chief's Crown (USA))
536[2] 581[5] 688[3] 743[5] 1065[2] 1317[2] (1729) 1891[4] 2220[2] 2561[12] 2761[8] 3498[5] 3636[6] 4252[4] 4561[2] 4668[3] 4939[2] 6957[8] 7077[3]

Black Jacari (IRE) *A King* 78
2 b g Black Sam Bellamy(IRE) —Amalia (IRE) (Danehill (USA))
3552[8] 4876[5] (5344) 6194[5]

Blackmail (USA) *P Mitchell* a68 66
9 b g Twining(USA) —Black Penny (USA) (Private Account (USA))
115[4] 195[9] 309[2] 459[2] 612[12] 651[7] 805[10] 1451[14] (2332) 2595[11] 3617[6] 3730[3] 4318[6] 4739[4] 5120[9] 5341[9] 5709[7]

Blackmalkin (USA) *C E Brittain* a72 58
3 b f Forest Wildcat(USA) —Farrfesheena (USA) (Rahy (USA))
996[3] (1267) 5134[3] 6575[6] (6717)

Black Mamba (NZ) *J W Sadler* 111
4 b m Black Minnaloushe(USA) —Sneetch (NZ) (Grosvenor (NZ))
5825a[3]

Black Mambazo (IRE) *L Riccardi*
2 b c Statue Of Liberty(USA) —Rich Gift (Cadeaux Genereux)
2684a[3]

Black Meyeden (FR) *S W Hall* a43 4
3 b f Black Minnaloushe(USA) —Eye Witness (IRE) (Don't Forget Me)
2593[5] 3827[9]

Black Mogul *R Hollinshead* a53 54
3 b g Robellino(USA) —Brilliance (Cadeaux Genereux)
1522[7] 2192[6] 2456[9] 3082[12] 3652[11] 4292[2] 4687[3] 4943[7] 5427[3] 6147[4] 6459[5] 6969[6] 7081[4] 7211[5]

Black Moma (IRE) *A B Haynes* a75 79
3 b f Averti(IRE) —Sareb (FR) (Indian Ridge)
606[3] 639[3] 1099[12] 2513[4] 2631[3] (3086) 3688[3] 4204[9] 4664[8] 6173[17] 6405[6] 6905[8] 7221[7]

Black Or Red (IRE) *I A Wood* a69
2 b c Cape Cross(IRE) —Gentle Thoughts (Darshaan)
6503[10] 6714[9] 6980[3]

Black Oval *S Parr* a69 69
6 b m Royal Applause—Corniche Quest (IRE) (Salt Dome (USA))
217[3] 447[4] 562[2] 722[2] 841[6] 2993[11] 3535[10] 4021[5] 4141[13] 4180[17] 4449[8] 4595[12]

Black Rain *P J McBride* 83
2 b g Desert Prince(IRE) —Antigua (Selkirk (USA))
5951[11] 6296[3] (6616)

Black Rock (IRE) *M A Jarvis* a83 99
3 ch c Rock Of Gibraltar(IRE) —Biraya (Valiyar)
1143[3] 2127[3] (2674) 3460[8] (4617) (5619)

Black Sea Pearl *P W D'Arcy* a71 68
4 br m Diktat—Made Of Pearl (USA) (Nureyev (USA))
(150) 376[2] 686[10] 3455[5] 3591[7] 3950[5] 4063[10] 4135[4]

Blacktoft (USA) *S C Williams* a81 82
4 bb g Theatrical—Black Truffle (USA) (Mt. Livermore (USA))
(30) 319[2] 377[8] 1356[2] 1494[15] 2136[5] 2476[2] 2986[15] 3386[5] 3926[9] 6996[12]

Black Tom (AUS) *D Hayes* 108
7 ch h Langfuhr(CAN) —Narmada (USA) (Blushing Groom (FR))
15a[14] 6033a[8] 6354a[13] 6712a[17]

Black Tor Figarro (IRE) *B W Duke* a56 56
2 b c Rock Of Gibraltar(IRE) —Will Be Blue (IRE) (Darshaan)
6248[8] 6493[10] 6944[10]

Black Wadi *T Keddy* 32
5 br m Desert King(IRE) —Tamelia (USA) (Caerleon (USA))
1998[13] 3244[10] 6538[6]

Black Wish (IRE) *L Young* 39
8 b m Beveled(USA) —Ural Dancer (Corvaro (USA))
5696a[8]

Blades Girl *K A Ryan* 97
4 ch m Bertolini(USA) —Banningham Blade (Sure Blade (USA))
3746[9] 4119[8] 4990[12] 5804[14]

Blakeshall Boy *A J Chamberlain* a48 71
9 b g Piccolo—Giggleswick Girl (Full Extent (USA))
123[8]

Blakeshall Diamond *A J Chamberlain* a64 40
2 gr f Piccolo—Hi Hoh (IRE) (Fayruz)
6386[9] 6721[11] (6820)

Blakeshall Hope *A J Chamberlain* a49 47
5 ch g Piccolo—Elite Hope (USA) (Moment Of Hope (USA))
6968[10] 7079[13] 7169[3] 7218[11] 7274[9]

Blakeshall Quest *R Brotherton* a58 56
7 b m Piccolo—Corniche Quest (IRE) (Salt Dome (USA))
221[3] 296[4] 448[6] 586[8] 1436[12] 1753[7] 6563[9] 7111[2]

Blakeshall Rose *A J Chamberlain* a47 37
3 b f Tobougg(IRE) —Giggleswick Girl (Full Extent (USA))
970[10] 1163[RR]

Blandys Wood *M R Channon* a47 60
2 ch f Fleetwood(IRE) —Blandys (IRE) (Dolphin Street (FR))
1990[7] 2443[4] 2876[8] 4022[9] 5268[6] 5423[13] 5572[3] (5869) 6379[8]

Blatant *A Al Raihe* a115 117
8 ch g Machiavellian(USA) —Negligent (Ahonoora)
599a[3]

Blaze Trailer (IRE) *T G McCourt* a26 53
4 b g Indian Danehill(IRE) —Moonlight Melody (Merdon Melody)
2061[2]

Blazing Bullet (IRE) *N Wilson* a24 27
2 b g Tagula(IRE) —Shao (FR) (Alzao (USA))
845[12] 1087[17] 2021[9] 2247[6] 2517[9] 3410[6]

Blazing Heights *J S Goldie* a61 90
4 b g Compton Place—Harrken Heights (IRE) (Belmez (USA))
957[6] 1941[3] 2244[9] 2461[2] 2866[5] 3080[5] 3515[2] 3990[22] 5039[9] 5212[15] 5481[5] 5584[18] 5810[11] (6743) 6876[13]

Blazing Mask (IRE) *Mrs A Duffield* 47
2 b f Barathea(IRE) —Alphilda (Ezzoud (IRE))
4612[11] 4890[6] 5294[7] 5746[10]

Blendon Boy (IRE) *D W Thompson* a19 3
5 b g Brave Act—Negria (IRE) (Al Hareb (USA))
365[9]

Blessed Place *D J S Ffrench Davis* a67 77
7 ch g Compton Place—Cathedra (So Blessed)
161[10] 236[10] 2479[9] 2655[9] 2912[2] (2972) 3388[12] 3528[6] 3594[7] 3859[4] 4103[2] 4296[5] 4507[7] 4634[6] (4734) 5174[7] 6174[7] 6279[7] 6542[3] 6594[11] 6718[7] 6773[11]

Blessyourpinksox (IRE) *Peter Casey* 105
6 ch m Cadeaux Genereux—Kumta (IRE) (Priolo (USA))
1777a[4] 2053a[9]

Bleu Intense (FR) *J-M Beguigne* 109
3 gr c Kouroun(FR) —Bariola (FR) (Ksardar (FR))
2952a[2]

Blimey O'Riley (IRE) *M H Tompkins* 67
2 b c Kalanisi(IRE) —Kafayef (USA) (Secreto (USA))
6184[8] 6574[10]

Blindspin *M Dods* 66
2 b c Intikhab(USA) —Blinding (IRE) (High Top)
4125[12] 5328[4]

Bling Bling (NZ) *M Moroney* 75
6 b m Le Destin(FR) —Gemma Dilemma (AUS) (Bureaucracy (NZ))
6711a[B]

Blissfully *S Parr* a12 43
3 b f Kyllachy—Bliss (IRE) (Statoblest)
505[7] 670[10]

Blissphilly *M Mullineaux* a19 32
5 b m Primo Dominie—Majalis (Mujadil (USA))
13[8]

Blitzen (IRE) *E S McMahon* a55 64
2 bb c Indian Danehill(IRE) —Notable Dear (ITY) (Last Tycoon (IRE))
4702[5] 5470[5] 6065[4] 6572[4]

Blockley (USA) *Ian Williams* a51 59
3 b g Johannesburg(USA) —Saintly Manner (USA) (St Jovite (USA))
257[8] 2192[3] 2609[7] 3567[5] 3640[2] 3804[11] 4518[4]

Blue Admiral *M H Tompkins* 66
2 ch g Fleetwood(IRE) —Poly Blue (IRE) (Thatching)
5598[6] 5977[12]

Blue Aura (IRE) *R M Beckett* 81
4 b g Elnadim(USA) —Absent Beauty (IRE) (Dancing Dissident (USA))
1357[10] 2479[6] 2912[3] 3859[2] 4103[6] 4664[6] 5874[12]

Blue Bajan (IRE) *Andrew Turnell* a108 113
5 b g Montjeu(IRE) —Gentle Thoughts (Darshaan)
552[2] 761[5] (1245) 1600[2] 2856[5] 3271[3] 3974[8]

Blue Bamboo *Mrs A J Perrett* a67 66
3 b f Green Desert(USA) —Silver Bandana (USA) (Silver Buck (USA))
(1345) 1837[14] 2571[5] 5303[7] 6533[5]

Bluebelle Dancer (IRE) *W R Muir* a66 67
3 b f Danehill Dancer(IRE) —Spring To Light (USA) (Blushing Groom (FR))
1815[5] 2061[8] 4163[3] 4684[2] 4848[11] 5234[6] 5753[9] 6277[6]

Bluebell Ridge (IRE) *D W P Arbuthnot* a59
2 b f Distant Music(USA) —Miss Indigo (Indian Ridge)
5727[5] 6262[6]

Blue Bird's Dream *E J Alston* a59 58
4 b g Lake Coniston(IRE) —Bedtime Model (Double Bed (FR))
769[6] 1011[9] 1679[9] 3571[10] 3721[11] 4905[6] 5237[8] 5781[2] 6149[4] 6247[15]

Bluebok *J M Bradley* a80 91
6 ch g Indian Ridge—Blue Sirocco (Bluebird (USA))
1088[4] 1242[5] 1464[2] 1986[7] 2463[17] 4204[10] 5029[2] 5278[7] 5332[6] 6405[3] 6589[4] 6708[8] 6794[4]

Blue Chagall (FR) *H-A Pantall* 106
2 br c Testa Rossa(AUS) —Eloisey (IRE) (Pitskelly)
4625a[2] (5660a) 6615a[5]

Blue Charm *S Kirk* a79
3 b g Averti(IRE) —Exotic Forest (Dominion)
885[3]

Blue Ciel *P Bary* 93
2 b f Oasis Dream—Blue Fern (USA) (Woodman (USA))
6416a[5]

Blue Citadel (USA) *J H M Gosden* 77
2 ch c Dubai Destination(USA) —Cloud Castle (In The Wings)
5361[8] 5580[3] 5813[6] 6202[3] 6410[4]

Blue Concorde (JPN) *T Hattori* a113 105
7 b h Fusaichi Concorde(JPN) —Ebisu Family (JPN) (Brian's Time (USA))
6942a[7]

Bluecrop Boy *D J S Ffrench Davis* a47 44
3 b g Zaha(CAN) —Pearl Dawn (IRE) (Jareer (USA))
53[6] 386[13] 703[6] 1039[13] 1224[12] 2140[8] 4535[3]

Blue Cross Boy (USA) *J Howard Johnson* 71
2 rg c Sunday Break(JPN) —Introducer (USA) (Cozzene (USA))
2297[7] (4077) 4819[8]

Blue Damask (USA) *A Fabre* a83 107
4 br h Rahy(USA) —Blush Damask (USA) (Green Dancer (USA))
4190a[12]

Blue Denim *M A Jarvis* a35
3 b f Singspiel(IRE) —Velvet Lady (Nashwan (USA))
1566[7] 1816[6]

Blue Echo *M A Jarvis* 96
3 b f Kyllachy—Mazarine Blue (Bellypha)
1670[3] 2291a[11] 3511[4] 4726[5] (5403) 5666[11]

Blue Empire (IRE) *C R Dore* a64 68
6 b g Second Empire(IRE) —Paleria (USA) (Zilzal (USA))
80[6] 309[11] 579[14] 1260[5] 1539[7] 1918[5] 2336[4] 3615[9] 4294[2] (4449) 4978[11] 5864[2] 6579[13] 7244[6]

Blue Eyed Eloise *J M Bradley* a49
5 b m Overbury(IRE) —Galix (FR) (Sissoo)
1342[3] 3621[5]

Blue Eyed Miss (IRE) *P A Blockley* a73 84
2 b f Statue Of Liberty(USA) —Classic Jenny (IRE) (Green Desert (USA))
5126[2] (5357) 5614[11] 6741[2]

Blue Hedges *H J Collingridge* a67 61
5 b h Polish Precedent(USA) —Palagene (Generous (IRE))
39[11] 332[5] 1225[5] 1730[9] 2055[4] 4031[5] 6068[11] (6902) 7135[8] 7256[6]

Blue Hills *P W Hiatt* a75 63
6 br g Vettori(IRE) —Slow Jazz (USA) (Chief's Crown (USA))
62[5] 146[4] (302) 482[3] 585[2] (617) 683[2] 775[11] (808) 994[12] 1406[5] 1683[10] 1888[10] 2367[3] 3112[3] 3598[4] 4030[9] 4670[10] 6797[3] (6911) 7004[9] 7154[3]

Blue Jack *W R Muir* a76 71
2 b c Cadeaux Genereux—Fairy Flight (IRE) (Fairy King (USA))
(6104) 6588[3] 7052[4]

Bluejain *Miss Gay Kelleway* 60
2 b c Lujain(USA) —Belle Of The Blues (IRE) (Blues Traveller (IRE))
5143[8] 6281[7]

Blue Java *H Morrison* a62 82
6 ch g Bluegrass Prince(IRE) —Java Bay (Statoblest)
1984[2] 2626[2] 3234[2] 3943[6] 4268[5] 4657[3] 5115[9] (5712) 6203[10] 6651[5]

Blue Jet (USA) *R M Whitaker* 62
3 b g Black Minnaloushe(USA) —Clickety Click (USA) (Sovereign Dancer (USA))
1303[12] 1746[7] (3415) 3993[13] 5144[5] 5906[3] 6330[12]

Blue Knight (IRE) *P Howling* a60 64
8 ch g Bluebird(USA) —Fer De Lance (IRE) (Diesis)
86[7] 268[4] 447[6] 519[13] 721[9] 800[4] (920) 1360[3] 2187[8] 2664[6] 4396[11] 4471[3] 4685[9] 5090[9] 5336[11]

Blue Ksar (FR) *Saeed Bin Suroor* 116
4 b h Anabaa(USA) —Delicieuse Lady (Trempolino (USA))
(1664) 2233[2] (4005) 4805[3] 5451[6] 5798[6] 6298[3]

Blue Law (IRE) *Andrew Oliver* a68
2 ch g Fath(USA) —Mica Male (ITY) (Law Society (USA))
7121[2]

Blue Line *M Madgwick* a64 59
5 gr m Bluegrass Prince(IRE) —Out Line (Beveled (USA))
1038[4] (1629) 1951[3] 2654[4] 3644[13] 5001[8] 5118[7] 5708[4] 5917[5]

Blue Madeira *Mrs L Stubbs* a77 80
3 b g Auction House(USA) —Queen Of Scotland (IRE) (Mujadil (USA))
1851[12] 2872[5] 3335[10] 4155[6] 5967[11]

Blue Mistral (IRE) *W J Knight* a55 66
3 ch f Spinning World(USA) —Blue Sirocco (Bluebird (USA))
1430[5] 2178[11] (3352) 3615[11] 4270[10] 4760[5] 5347[10] (5710) 6206[7] 6534[13]

Blue Monday *D Hayes* 119
6 b g Darshaan—Lunda (IRE) (Soviet Star (USA))
6354a[4] 6712a[7]

Blue Monkey (IRE) *M L W Bell* a73 84
3 b c Orpen(USA) —Resurgence (Polar Falcon (USA))
114[3] 260[2] 565[3] 889[4] (1261) 1634[5] (2872) 3235[2] 3470[2] (3855) 4502[8] 5776[6]

Blue Mountie (IRE) *Edward P Harty* 67
3 b f Fath(USA) —Lady Of Bilston (IRE) (Bin Ajwaad (IRE))
5460a[11]

Blue On Blues (ARG) *S Seemar* a109 102
6 ch g Lode(USA) —Blue Baby Blue (ARG) (Forever Sparkle (USA))
177a[6] (410a) 599a[11]

Blue Opal *Miss S E Hall* a50 57
5 b m Bold Edge—Second Affair (IRE) (Pursuit Of Love)
1362[10]

Blue Patrick *P A Blockley* a8 68
7 gr g Wizard King—Great Intent (Aragon)
308[7]

Blue Quiver (IRE) *C A Horgan* a65 45
7 b g Bluebird(USA) —Paradise Forum (Prince Sabo)
416[8] 514[3] 2176[12] (2591) 3419[5] (5094) 6123[3] 6316[5]

Blue Rhapsody *L M Cumani* a77 74
2 b f Cape Cross(IRE) —Blue Symphony (Darshaan)
4169[9] 4662[10] (5308) 6012[5] 6410[9]

Blue Rocket (IRE) *D J Murphy* a76 93
3 ch f Rock Of Gibraltar(IRE) —Champagne Girl (Robellino (USA))
1096[3] 1496[20] 5666[3] 6300[12] 6472[17] 6654[6] 6726[3] 6757[10] (6916a) 6992[5] 7212[7] 7255[9]

Blues In The Night (IRE) *P J Makin* a81 87
4 ch g Bluebird(USA) —Always True (USA) (Geiger Counter (USA))
1845[14] 1971[8] 2573[6] 2995[9] 3525[13] 5330[5]

Blue Sky Basin *A M Balding* a76 76
2 b g Desert Prince(IRE) —Kimba (USA) (Kris S (USA))
4508[4] (4882) 5350[12] 6201[3]

Blue Sky God (USA) *Saeed Bin Suroor* a78
3 b c Stormy Atlantic(USA) —Godmother (USA) (Showem Slew (USA))
526a[5]

Blue Sky Thinking (IRE) *K R Burke* a92 89
8 b g Danehill Dancer(IRE) —Lauretta Blue (IRE) (Bluebird (USA))
420[6] 620[2] (674) (833) (1066) (1744) 2298[6]

Blues Minor (IRE) *R Hannon* 80
2 b c Acclamation—Narbayda (IRE) (Kahyasi)
2630[4] 4539[2] 4810[5] 5207[9] (5937)

Blue Space *P J Makin* a67 64
3 b f Mtoto—La Tour De Blay (USA) (Irish River (FR))
2428[7] 3651[3] 4392[4] (4742) 5068[10]

Blue Spinnaker (IRE) *M W Easterby* 97
8 b g Bluebird(USA) —Suedoise (Kris)
848[10] 1583[8] 1767[10] 2093[4] 2906[2] 3513[8] 4039[3] 4566[13] 4900[7] 5327[11] 5775[8] 6180[13] 6465[12] 6636[5]

Blue Tomato *J M Bradley* a74 97
6 b g Orpen(USA) —Ocean Grove (IRE) (Fairy King (USA))
1088[16] 1458[12] 1852[6] 1971[3] 2466[7]

Blue Trojan (IRE) *S Kirk* a87 94
7 b g Inzar(USA) —Roman Heights (IRE) (Head For Heights)
3330[17]

Blue Zenith (IRE) *J S Moore* a65 68
2 ch f Daggers Drawn(USA) —Secret Combe (IRE) (Mujadil (USA))
999[8] 2443[6] 4629[2] 5267[2] 5452[5] 5629[4] 6128[9] 6386[4] (6425) 6756[18]

Blu Manruna *J Akehurst* a71 65
4 ch g Zaha(CAN) —Vrennan (Suave Dancer (USA))
24[4] 229[3] 363[2] 4850[6] (5280) 5454[10] 5916[5] 6196[3] 6577[6] 6848[3] 6902[4] 7088[2] 7257[11]

Blumire (ITY) *A & G Botti*
2 ch f Blu Air Force(IRE) —Henutmire (ITY) (Trempolino (USA))
1485a[2]

Blushing Hilary (IRE) *Miss J A Camacho* a73 75
4 ch m City On A Hill(USA) —Trinida (Jaazeiro (USA))
3719[5] 4040[4] 4475[3] 4925[8] 5364[7]

Blushing King (FR) *J-L Guillochon* 108
5 b h Blush Rambler(USA) —Storm Warning (Tumble Wind)
663a[5] 880a[7] 1340a[7] 2617a[5] 3665a[9] 4655a[8]

Blushing Light (USA) *M A Magnusson* a62 63
4 bb g Mt. Livermore(USA) —Swan River (USA) (Hennessy (USA))
461[11] 3946[5] 4464[9]

Blushing Prince (IRE) *R C Guest* a51 51
9 b g Priolo(USA) —Eliade (IRE) (Flash Of Steel)
462[3] (579) 742[6] 1199[5] 3161[9] 3907[16] 4580[4] 5676[11]

Blushing Russian (IRE) *J M Bradley* a53 37
5 b g Fasliyev(USA) —Ange Rouge (Priolo (USA))
20[8] 137[5] (281) 562[10] 580[6] 690[6] 746[11] 1028[8] 1065[6] 1317[9] 7005[8] 7188[5]

Blush On Cue (USA) *J H M Gosden* a56 42
3 b f Theatrical—Goldminess (USA) (Mr Prospector (USA))
3214[9] 4403[6]

Blutigeroo (AUS) *C Little* 120
6 ch g Encounter(AUS) —Shanghai Sky (AUS) (Zamazaan (FR))
6354a[7] 6712a[19]

Bluto *P C Haslam*
3 b g Mtoto—Low Line (High Line)
2565[8]

Blythe Knight (IRE) *J J Quinn* a96 113
7 ch g Selkirk(USA) —Blushing Barada (USA) (Blushing Groom (FR))
255[2] 848[9] 1583[3] (1791) (2233) 4805[7] 5618[4] 6031a[3] 6298[7]

Blythe Spirit *Mrs L Williamson* a67 45
8 b g Bahamian Bounty—Lithe Spirit (IRE) (Dancing Dissident (USA))
137[3] 221[4] 241[4] 467[5] (586) (632) 654[9] 766[4] 1221[7] 1753[6] 2187[7] 3172[9] 3534[9] 3674[7] 6149[7] 6288[12] 6609[3] 6882[7] 7001[9] 7153[9]

Boanerges (IRE) *J M Bradley* a63 66
10 br g Caerleon(USA) —Sea Siren (Slip Anchor)
50[11] 135[10] (Dead)

Bobal Girl *E F Vaughan* a57 44
2 ch f Tobougg(IRE) —Al Guswa (Shernazar)
5294[9] 5881[11] 6177[2]

Bobansheil (IRE) *J S Wainwright* 70
3 b f Dushyantor(USA) —Bobanlyn (IRE) (Dance Of Life (USA))
1769[5] 2133[14] 2552[11]

Bob Baileys *P R Chamings* a55
5 b g Mister Baileys—Bob's Princess (Bob's Return (IRE))
625[3] 682[2] 812[6] 1592[12]

Bobbish *J E Mulhern* a63 77
3 b g Best Of The Bests(IRE) —Bella Bianca (IRE) (Barathea (IRE))
5460a[27]

Bobby Charles *Dr J D Scargill* a87 84
6 ch g Polish Precedent(USA) —Dina Line (USA) (Diesis)
1645 2351[10] 3060[5]

Bobby Darling (IRE) *M R Channon* 46
2 b f Montjeu(IRE) —Karinski (USA) (Palace Music (USA))
5162[16] 5721[8] 6202[6]

Bobby Rose *D K Ivory* a77 78
4 b g Sanglamore(USA) —Grown At Rowan (Gabitat)
1321[1] 222[7] (751) 992[14] 1200[6] 1589[7] 3106[5] 3388[3] 4103[3] 4486[6] 4689[8] 4853[2] (5731) (5909) 6313[5] 6575[7]

Bobering *B P J Baugh* a61 43
7 b g Bob's Return(IRE) —Ring The Rafters (Batshoof)
156[6] (266) 741[4] 976[9] 1227[8] 1435[7] 5179[2] 5756[4] 6613[6] 6801[3] 6906[8]

Bobski (IRE) *G A Huffer* a93 88
5 b g Victory Note(USA) —Vivid Impression (Cure The Blues (USA))
(259) 1448[6] 1818[12] 2835[7] 3437[8] 3650[7] 4195[4] 5196[6] 6209[2] 6435[3]

Bobsleigh *H S Howe* a63 63
8 b g Robellino(USA) —Do Run Run (Commanche Run)
213[7] 1526[6] 1925[4] 2430[6] 3397[9]

Bobs Surprise *B W Hills* 100
2 ch c Bertolini(USA) —Flourish (Selkirk (USA))
(2215) 2732[7] 3459[5] 4120[7]

Bob's Your Uncle *J G Portman* a70 71
4 br g Zilzal(USA) —Bob's Princess (Bob's Return (IRE))
976[10] 1609[3] 2332[2] (2595) 2996[2] 3397[3] 3945[5] 4576[5] 5007[6] 5426[13] 6453[2]

Bocabelle (FR) *J-C Rouget* 87
3 b f Celtic Swing—Bocanegra (FR) (Night Shift (USA))
2547a[8]

Boca Dancer (IRE) *Kevin Prendergast* a75 93
3 b f Indian Ridge—Rain Dancer (IRE) (Sadler's Wells (USA))
2851a[8]

Boccassini (GER) *M Rulec* 107
3 br f Artan(IRE) —Bella Monica (GER) (Big Shuffle (USA))
1006a[0] 1855a[6]

Boccatenera (GER) *Rod Collet* 76
2 b f Artan(IRE) —Bella Monica (GER) (Big Shuffle (USA))
6630a[9]

Bochinche (USA) *Saeed Bin Suroor* a60 13
3 b f Kingmambo(USA) —Hatoof (USA) (Irish River (FR))
5494[5] 5859[9]

Bodden Bay *I W McInnes* a66 66
5 b g Cayman Kai(IRE) —Badger Bay (IRE) (Salt Dome (USA))
292[7] 504[5] 743[2] 896[2] 1064[12] 1262[6] 5340[8] 5546[14]

Boekenhoutskloof (IRE) *E F Vaughan* a16 38
3 b f Selkirk(USA) —Labrusca (Grand Lodge (USA))
2620[10] 3214[13] 3908[7]

Bogaz (IRE) *Mrs H Sweeting* a41 46
5 b g Rossini(USA) —Fastnet (Forzando)
2273[6] 2559[5]

Bogside Katie *G M Moore* a50 49
3 b f Hunting Lion(IRE) —Enchanting Eve (Risk Me (FR))
40[5] 99[10]

Bogside Theatre (IRE) *G M Moore* 91
3 b f Fruits Of Love(USA) —Royal Jubilee (IRE) (King's Theatre (IRE))
(2253) 2506[6] (3501) 4288[4] 4749[12] 5808[2]

Bohobe (IRE) *J G Given* a50 70
2 b f Noverre(USA) —Green Life (Green Desert (USA))
2344[4] 2819[6] (3200) 4406[3] 5322[18] 6282[10]

Boisdale (IRE) *P S Felgate* a53 22
9 b g Common Grounds—Alstomeria (Petoski)
320[9] 523[11] 920[3] 1344[6] 2220[3] 2791[9] 6390[5] 7265[11]

Bolckow *J T Stimpson* a69 66
4 b g Marju(IRE) —Stamatina (Warning)
(242) 453[5] 503[2] 631[2] 733[8] 1181[4] 6871[13] 7109[3] 7198[7]

Bold Abbott (USA) *Mrs A J Perrett* 83
3 b c Mizzen Mast(USA) —Ms Isadora (USA) (Miswaki (USA))
(1468) 2243[4] 2671[3] 3480[5] 4111[6] 5712[6]

Bold Adventure *W J Musson* a73 48
3 ch g Arkadian Hero(USA) —Impatiente (USA) (Vaguely Noble)
2192[7] 3469[8] 3804[4] 4339[13] 5388[3] (5533) (5779) (6459) 6739[7]

Bold Argument (IRE) *Mrs P N Dutfield* a73 78
4 ch g Shinko Forest(IRE) —Ivory Bride (Domynsky)
1589[11] 1787[4] 2546[4] 3190[7] 3368[8] 3686[11] 5731[4] 6582[5]

Bold Bibi (IRE) *M Halford* 94
3 br f Hernando(FR) —Bibi Karam (IRE) (Persian Bold)
(4240a) 5998a[10]

Bold Bobby *J M P Eustace* a45 53
3 b f Pivotal—Mrs P (First Trump)
2606[5] 3031[3] 3395[8]

Bold Choice (IRE) *M A Jarvis* 94
2 b c Dubai Destination(USA) —Sheer Spirit (IRE) (Caerleon (USA))
3896[2] 5011[2] 5397a[15] 6382[4]

Bold Cross (IRE) *E G Bevan* a68 68
4 b g Cape Cross(IRE) —Machikane Akaiito (IRE) (Persian Bold)
1249[5] 1521[8] 1886[4] 2107[5] 2721[8] 3419[7] 3799[12] (5098) 5190[2] (5433) 5645[6] 6148[3] 6533[3]

Bold Diktator *Tom Dascombe* a83 85
5 b g Diktat—Madam Bold (Never So Bold)
(233) (427) 652[12] 765[6] (1308) 2180[7] 2469[6] 4672[7] 5383[8] 5985[6] 6025[4]

Bold Diva *A W Carroll* 42
2 ch f Bold Edge—Trina's Pet (Efisio)
1354[14] 1533[10] 2488[10] 2723[4] 3174[7] 4453[14] 4875[11] 5443[7] 6281[13]

Bold Finch (FR) *J M Bradley* 46
5 b g Valanour(IRE) —Eagle's Nest (FR) (King Of Macedon)
2089[8] 2214[7]

Bold Girl (IRE) *H-A Pantall* 92
3 b f Red Ransom(USA) —Bold Bold (IRE) (Sadler's Wells (USA))
989a[7] 1388a[P] (Dead)

Bold Glance *Saeed Bin Suroor* 80
3 gr c Kingmambo(USA) —Last Second (IRE) (Alzao (USA))
(5562) 6014[11]

Bold Haze *Miss S E Hall* 69
5 ch g Bold Edge—Melody Park (Music Boy)
2304[5] (2711) 3375[6] 3787[10] 4423[14] 5284[9] 5966[14]

Bold Heta (IRE) *Sabrina J Harty* 63
4 b m Namid—Bold Encounter (IRE) (Persian Bold)
5460a[8]

Bold Indian (IRE) *I Semple* a71 73
3 b g Indian Danehill(IRE) —Desert Gift (Green Desert (USA))
968[3] 1089[5] 1531[8] 1965[8] (2200) 3078[7] 3411[9] (4155) 4998[9] 5555[5] 6025[3] 6344[5] 6610[9]

Bold Josr *D J S Ffrench Davis*
3 b g Josr Algarhoud(IRE) —Skiddaw Bird (Bold Owl)
4948[14]

Bold Love *J Balding* a47 48
4 ch m Bold Edge—Noor El Houdah (IRE) (Fayruz)
61[5] 138[5] 1719[5]

Bold Marc (IRE) *K R Burke* a86 90
5 b g Bold Fact(USA) —Zara's Birthday (IRE) (Waajib)
1287[4] 1481[5] (2038) 2374[9] 2452[7] (2986) 3330[11] 3943[14] 4827[7] 5585[7]

Bold Minstrel (IRE) *M Quinn* a83 84
5 br g Bold Fact(USA) —Ponda Rosa (IRE) (Case Law)
554[8] 810[12] 1080[12] 1630[2] (2191) 2399[13] 4780[6] 5332[11] 6173[16] 6405[10] 7059[8]

Bold Nevison (IRE) *B Smart* a59 43
3 b g Danehill Dancer(IRE) —La Pieta (IRE) (Spectrum (IRE))
122[9] 1850[13] 5299[9] 5967[10] 6609[7] 7209[6]

Bold Phoenix (IRE) *B J Curley* a61 38
6 b g Dr Fong(USA) —Subya (Night Shift (USA))
64[8] 266[10] 1271[7] 1435[2]

Bold Saxon (IRE) *M D I Usher* a67 65
3 ch g Desert Sun—Sirdhana (Selkirk (USA))
111[5] 184[9] 1261[3] 2061[6] 2317[11] 2593[6] 5237[6] 5528[9] 5783[4] 6245[5] 6344[10] 6590[7]

Bold Tiger (IRE) *Miss Tracy Waggott* 48
4 b g Bold Fact(USA) —Heart Of The Ocean (IRE) (Soviet Lad (USA))
1221[8] 1423[12] 1527[7] 1744[14]

Bold Trump *Mrs N S Evans* a52 39
6 b g First Trump—Blue Nile (IRE) (Bluebird (USA))
62[4] 240[13]

Bolero De Aighenta (ITY) *P Cadeddu*
3 b c Astronef—Nunivak (ITY) (Big Reef)
1191a[8]

Boleyna (USA) *Rae Guest* a47 30
3 b f Officer(USA) —Cassation (USA) (Lear Fan (USA))
1175[5] 4182[8] 4513[7]

Bollin Derek *T D Easterby* a69 92
4 gr h Silver Patriarch(IRE) —Bollin Magdalene (Teenoso (USA))
811[6] 1300[5] (1794)
Bollin Dolly *T D Easterby* 73
4 ch m Bien Bien(USA) —Bollin Roberta (Bob's Return (IRE))
4128[7] 4615[5] 4846[4] 5300[9]
Bollin Felix *T D Easterby* 82
3 br c Generous(IRE) —Bollin Magdalene (Teenoso (USA))
893[4] (1637) 1917[3] (3159) (3379) 4570[3] 4749[15] 5619[3] 5911[6]
Bollin Fergus *T D Easterby* 62
3 br c Vettori(IRE) —Bollin Harriet (Lochnager)
931[11] 1965[3] 2829[6] 3029[7] 4902[5]
Bollin Franny *T D Easterby* 70
3 br c Bertolini(USA) —Bollin Ann (Anshan)
1286[7] 2255[2] 3054[6] 3413[7] 3763[5] 4939[10] 5139[6]
Bollin Freddie *A J Lockwood* 49
3 ch g Golden Snake(USA) —Bollin Roberta (Bob's Return (IRE))
2133[9] 2552[7] 3610[6] 4943[6]
Bollin Greta *T D Easterby* 24
2 b f Mtoto—Bollin Zola (Alzao (USA))
5524[7]
Bollin Guil *T D Easterby* 53
2 b c Helissio(FR) —Bollin Ann (Anshan)
1859[8] 2888[10] 4037[8]
Bollin Thomas *R Allan* 72
9 b g Alhijaz—Bollin Magdalene (Teenoso (USA))
3012[14] 3501[7]
Bollywood (IRE) *J J Bridger* a50 51
4 ch g Indian Rocket—La Fille De Cirque (Cadeaux Genereux)
789[12] 1317[4] *1344[8]* 1739[6] 2143[5] 2273[4] 3149[5] *3422[14]* 3799[8] 4469[5] 4595[2] 5001[9] *6212[9] 6582[7] 7167[11] 7276[4]*
Bollywood Style *J R Best* a55
2 b f Josr Algarhoud(IRE) —Dane Dancing (IRE) (Danehill (USA))
4359[2] 5133[2] 6207[4] 6433[3] 6793[7] 6865[4]
Bolodenka (IRE) *R A Fahey* a100 105
5 b g Soviet Star(USA) —My-Lorraine (IRE) (Mac's Imp (USA))
43[3] 325a[4] 473a[5] 848[8] 1145[14] 2891[5] 4051a[10] 4211a[8] (4900) 5242a[14] 5631[4]
Bolton Hall (IRE) *R A Fahey* a67 73
5 b g Imperial Ballet(IRE) —Muneera (USA) (Green Dancer (USA))
1455[6] 2007[11] 2302[13] 2660[8] 2865[3] 3816[2] *4063[3]* (4526) 4797[2] 4932[3] 5198[8] *6344[13] 6696[3] 6997[10]*
Bombardier Wells *Eve Johnson Houghton* 58
2 b c Red Ransom(USA) —Bow River Gold (Rainbow Quest (USA))
5591[5] 6125[10]
Bomber Command (USA) *J W Hills* a101 84
4 b g Stravinsky(USA) —Parish Manor (USA) (Waquoit (USA))
550[2] 658[2] 817[5] 1308[12] 1845[16] (3525) 3943[2] 4585[6] *4886[5] 5761a[6] 6143[8] 6606[8]*
Bo McGinty (IRE) *R A Fahey* a73 92
6 ch g Fayruz—Georges Park Lady (IRE) (Tirol)
957[8] 1223[12] 1574[2] *1754[4]* 2025[4] 2244[3] 2866[7] 2989[4] 3298[4] 3557[3] 3720[8] 3886[2] 4389[5] 4489[7] (5332) 5667[2] 5810[3] 6173[3] 6327[4] 6487[9]
Bona Fidelis (IRE) *A J McCabe* a38
2 b f Namid—Sacred Love (IRE) (Barathea (IRE))
5681[10]
Bonchester Bridge *N J Henderson* 43
6 b m Shambo—Cabriole Legs (Handsome Sailor)
2970[4]
Bond Angel Eyes *G R Oldroyd* a44 57
4 b m Dr Fong(USA) —Speedybird (IRE) (Danehill (USA))
800[11] 1162[6] 1423[9]
Bond Becks (IRE) *G R Oldroyd* a63 64
7 ch g Tagula(IRE) —At Amal (IRE) (Astronef)
2418[13] 4101[6] 4252[7] 4773[5] 4996[4] 5085[8] 5295[13] *(6887) (7014) 7227[7]*
Bond Boy *G R Oldroyd* a59 93
10 b g Piccolo—Arabellajill (Aragon)
1134[3] 1574[9] *1754[9]* 2841[9] 3197[2] 3298[2] 3515[4] 3791[7] 4095[9] 4780[5] 5552[16] 5740[10]
Bond Casino *G R Oldroyd* a65 54
3 b f Kyllachy—Songsheet (Dominion)
998[8] 1530[3] 2892[7] 3752[11] 4078[12] 4283[4] 4943[2] *5388[2] (5755) 6314[3] 6673[4] 6911[3] 7081[9]*
Bond City (IRE) *G R Oldroyd* a97 111
5 b g Trans Island—Where's Charlotte (Sure Blade (USA))
927[2] 1159[2] 1497[3] 1770[14] 2234[7] 2463[3] 3329[3] 3531[3] 4090[8] 4150[27] 5305[4] 5700[2] 5953[10] 6327[9]
Bond Cruz *D Burchell* a41 38
4 b g King's Best(USA) —Arabis (Arazi (USA))
2006[12]
Bond Diamond *P T Midgley* a67 70
10 gr g Prince Sabo—Alsiba (Northfields (USA))
833[6] (1086) 2007[10] *3405[5]* 4082[3] 4427[13]
Bond Free Spirit (IRE) *G R Oldroyd* a22 53
4 br m Shinko Forest(IRE) —Sawaki (Song)
806[11] 1136[8] *1750[11]*
Bond Playboy *G R Oldroyd* a73 62
7 b g Piccolo—Highest Ever (FR) (Highest Honor (FR))
67[3] 269[6] 368[5] 516[8] 3791[9] 3836[8] 4083[14] 4494[5] 4706[8] *5016[6] 5778[4] (6064) 6149[2]*
Bond Scissorsister (IRE) *G R Oldroyd* 46
2 b f Xaar—Musical Refrain (IRE) (Dancing Dissident (USA))
4125[9] 5281[6] 5766[20]
Bond Sea Breeze (IRE) *G R Oldroyd* a2 22
4 b m Namid—Gold Prospector (IRE) (Spectrum (IRE))
36[10] 186[6]
Bonecrusher *M Al Muhairi* a74 89
8 b g Revoque(IRE) —Eurolink Mischief (Be My Chief (USA))
244a[4] 328a[8]
Bongo Bello (DEN) *T Christensen* 96
6 b h Asaasy(USA) —Sypha (FR) (Saumarez)
4218a[8]
Bonjour Allure (IRE) *Mrs A Duffield* 80
2 b f Hawk Wing(USA) —Exact Replica (Darshaan)
3916[2] (4487) 5350[19]
Bonne D'Argent (IRE) *J R Boyle* a66 74
3 b f Almutawakel—Petite-D-Argent (Noalto)
2878[14] 3710[17] *5532[8] 6226[3]* 6413[11] *6975[7]*
Bonnet O'Bonnie *J Mackie* a54 45
3 br f Makbul—Parkside Prospect (Piccolo)
1175[4] 1386[4] 2080[6] *5386[4] 5982[5] 6288[7] 6887[9] 7034[8]*
Bonneville Record (JPN) *M Horii* 110
5 b h Assatis(USA) —Daiwa Stan (JPN) (Maruzensky (JPN))
6942a[14]
Bonnie Belle *J R Boyle* a15 61
4 b m Imperial Ballet(IRE) —Reel Foyle (USA) (Irish River (FR))
1931[14]
Bonnie Prince Blue *B W Hills* a88 90
4 ch g Tipsy Creek(USA) —Heart So Blue (Dilum (USA))
1060[6] *(1401)* 1818[8] 2239[13] *2573[3] 2771[9]* 3234[4] 3488[6] 4548[3] *4949[6] 5223[4] 6243[3] 6435[8]* 6753[9] *6970[2]*
Bon Nuit (IRE) *Mrs John Harrington* a77 103
5 b m Night Shift(USA) —Pray (IRE) (Priolo (USA))
875a[2] 1550a[5] 2053a[6] 4649a[5]
Bonny Rose *M Johnston* 70
2 ch f Zaha(CAN) —Marina Park (Local Suitor (USA))
4818[2] 5329[2] 5675[2] (5965) 6486[15]
Bonny's Babe *B Smart* a47 54
2 b f City On A Hill(USA) —Ashtree Belle (Up And At 'Em)
2147[7] (2533) 4154[7] 4484[7] *4975[7] 5644[7]* 6305[2]
Bonny Scotland (IRE) *I W McInnes* a21 46
3 b f Redback—Muckross Park (Nomination)
237[9] 378[7] 454[9] 506[5]
Bon Ton Roulet *R Hannon* a65
2 ch f Hawk Wing(USA) —Evangeline (Sadler's Wells (USA))
6849[9]
Bonus (IRE) *G A Butler* a109 102
7 b g Cadeaux Genereux—Khamseh (Thatching)
198[3] 470a[8] *762[2]* 1497[7] 2858[22] 4062[8] *4864a[6] (6003) 6930[4] (7184)*
Boo *K R Burke* a103 98
5 b g Namaqualand(USA) —Violet (IRE) (Mukaddamah (USA))
175a[11] 250a[9] 328a[9] *701[9] 761[6]* 846[14] 3513[9] 4105[5] *4867a[7]* 6475[8]
Boogie Board *S Parr* a51 40
3 b f Tobougg(IRE) —Royal Gift (Cadeaux Genereux)
1369[4] 1639[14] *2592[5] 3110[8] 3406[8]*
Boogie Dancer *H S Howe* a65 68
3 b f Tobougg(IRE) —Bolero (Rainbow Quest (USA))
2181[3] 2691[4] *6874[12] 7253[12]*
Boogie Magic *R W Price* a29 51
7 b m Wizard King—Dalby Dancer (Bustiki)
7213[10]
Bookiebasher Babe (IRE) *M Quinn* a57 20
2 b f Orpen(USA) —Jay Gee (IRE) (Second Set (IRE))
2344[7] 2746[6] *4428[8] 6433[2]*
Bookiebasher Dude *M Quinn* a73 72
2 b c Elnadim(USA) —Masaader (USA) (Wild Again (USA))
1033[3] 1585[5] 2333[10] *3423[2] 4065[3]* 4315[3] 4755[2] *5097[3]*
Bookiesindex Boy *J R Jenkins* a79 78
3 bb g Piccolo—United Passion (Emarati (USA))
1270[3] *1351[2]* 1820[2] 2513[12] 2837[7] *3212[2] 3452[7]* 4123[18] 4486[2] 5066[4] 5139[10] 5942[5]
Bookish *M Johnston* a67 61
2 b f Dubai Destination(USA) —Daybook (IRE) (Daylami (IRE))
5309[4] 5811[5] 6574[6] *6849[5] (7031)*
Book Of Days (IRE) *Evan Williams* a39 31
4 b m Barathea(IRE) —Beeper The Great (USA) (Whadjathink (USA))
2332[12] 3047[8]
Book Of Facts (FR) *J McAuley* a80 46
3 ch g Machiavellian(USA) —Historian (IRE) (Pennekamp (USA))
2045[16] 2662[6] *3111[9]* 3824[7]
Book Of Kings (USA) *S Seemar* a65 93
6 b g Kingmambo(USA) —Honfleur (IRE) (Sadler's Wells (USA))
325a[14] 401a[14] *529a[14]*
Book Of Music (IRE) *Saeed Bin Suroor* 113
4 b h Sadler's Wells(USA) —Novelette (Darshaan)
248a[6] 401a[2] (545a) 648a[9] 5402[5] 5976[6]
Boom Or Bust (IRE) *Karen George* a29 37
8 ch g Entrepreneur—Classic Affair (USA) (Trempolino (USA))
182[9]
Boomtown *M Johnston* a62 69
2 b c Fantastic Light(USA) —Ville D'Amore (USA) (Irish River (FR))
2532[2] 2803[6] 3435[10] 4524[3] 4892[5] 5914[8] *6978[7] 7101[7]*
Boot 'n Toot *C A Cyzer* a84 79
6 b m Mtoto—Raspberry Sauce (Niniski (USA))
702[4] 829[5] 1371[3] 3963[5] 4318[8] *(4917) 5205[2] 5422[2]*
Boot Strap Bill *Miss J R Tooth* a34 62
2 ch g Timeless Times(USA) —Nuthatch (IRE) (Thatching)
4904[3] 5628[10] 6281[11] *6736[8] 7021[10]*
Boppys Dancer *P T Midgley* a55 55
4 b g Clan Of Roses—Dancing Mary (Sri Pekan (USA))
12[6] 508[6] (716) 1717[5] 1966[5] 3260[6] 3815[10] 4333[10] 4843[10] *6292[9] 7109[9]*
Boppys Diamond *P T Midgley* 29
3 b f Clan Of Roses—Dancing Mary (Sri Pekan (USA))
6309[10] 6597[12]
Boppys Dream *P T Midgley* a40 47
5 ch m Clan Of Roses—Laurel Queen (IRE) (Viking (USA))
13[3] 524[10] 714[4] 1197[10] 1748[10] 2121[9] 2894[10] 4525[14] 4801[7] 5231[3] 5488[5] 6309[8] *7019[9]*
Boppys Pride *R A Fahey* a62 60
4 ch h Clan Of Roses—Joara (FR) (Radetzky)
89[8] 4772[7] 5557[2] 5750[2] 6258[9] 6558[8] *6867[5] 7060[11]*
Borasco (USA) *T D Barron* a67 69
2 ch f Stormy Atlantic(USA) —Seek (USA) (Devil's Bag (USA))
1963[3] 2532[6] (2889) 3524[8] 4126[3] *4669[3]*
Bora Shaamit (IRE) *M Scudamore* a28
5 b m Shaamit(IRE) —Bora Bora (Bairn (USA))
5816[10]
Bordello *K A Ryan* a60 74
4 b g Efisio—Blow Me A Kiss (Kris)
1287[14] *2521[8]* 4129[11] 4701[12]
Border Artist *J Pearce* a65 71
8 ch g Selkirk(USA) —Aunt Tate (Tate Gallery (USA))
379[4] 485[5] 549[2] 1847[14] 2458[6] *3067[6] 3419[13]* 3828[3] 4029[8] 4562[6] 4879[8] (5546) 5966[6] *6123[9]* 6413[7] *6607[7] 6825[9] 6956[9]*
Border Defence (IRE) *P A Blockley* a53 55
2 bb g Princely Heir(IRE) —Dakhira (Emperor Jones (USA))
890[10] 999[10] 4823[8] *5888[5]* 6154[9] *6388[11]*
Border Edge *J J Bridger* a71 70
9 b g Beveled(USA) —Seymour Ann (Krayyan)
1886[7] 2275[7] *2568[4]* 2877[4] 3234[7] 3350[12] 3799[9] *4063[11]* (4355) 4577[11] 4959[7] 5166[8] *6124[9]* 6278[4] 6447[4] *6710[6] 6866[7] 7088[5] 7268[5]*
Borderlescott *R Bastiman* a102 118
5 b g Compton Place—Jeewan (Touching Wood (USA))
1657[2] 2319[2] 2857[8] 3506[7] 4150[2] 4798[2] 5616[19] 6338[4] 6758[2] *6930[2]*
Border Music *A M Balding* a113 98
6 b g Selkirk(USA) —Mara River (Efisio)
(656) 762[10] 867[4] 1971[9] *2352[4]* (3526) 4122[7] 4456[4] 5689[6] *6003[6]*
Border Owl (IRE) *R Hannon* a79 70
2 b g Selkirk(USA) —Nightbird (IRE) (Night Shift (USA))
6202[12] 6494[5] *6714[2]*
Border Tale *James Moffatt* a69 63
7 b g Selkirk(USA) —Likely Story (IRE) (Night Shift (USA))
1225[3] 1532[10]
Bordonaro (USA) *B Spawr* a122
6 ch g Memo(CHI) —Miss Excitement (USA) (Rajab (USA))
6510a[6]
Boreana *Jedd O'Keeffe* a63 72
4 ch m Nashwan(USA) —Aliena (IRE) (Grand Lodge (USA))
1413[7] 2121[8] *2947[2] 3173[4] 3599[4] 4978[9] 5391[3] 5778[2] 6290[10] 6818[8] 6962[9]*
Boris De Deauville (IRE) *S Wattel* 118
4 b h Soviet Star(USA) —Logjam (IRE) (Royal Academy (USA))
663a[4] (880a) 1340a[4] 6032a[3] 6689a[3]
Borita (IRE) *M Scudamore* 51
4 ch m Lahib(USA) —Bora Bora (Bairn (USA))
3794[7] 4235[9] 4630[10] 5345[11]
Born For Diamonds (IRE) *R E Barr* a14 33
5 b m Night Shift(USA) —Kirri (IRE) (Lycius (USA))
2806[8]
Born West (USA) *P W Chapple-Hyam* a70 71
3 b g Gone West(USA) —Admirer (USA) (Private Terms (USA))
3804[3] 4339[4] 5626[2] *5820[4] 7004[3]*
Borodinsky *R E Barr* a42 69
6 b g Magic Ring(IRE) —Valldemosa (Music Boy)
80[8] 238[6] 1086[11] 1423[5] 2390[3] 2741[3] 3376[6] 3765[6] 3839[3] 4100[4] (4250) 4427[2] 4820[13] 6016[19]
Borora *R Lee* 59
8 gr g Shareef Dancer(USA) —Bustling Nelly (Bustino)
4352[9] 5007[8]
Borouj (IRE) *Philip Fenton* 72
5 ch g Unfuwain(USA) —Amanah (USA) (Mr Prospector (USA))
4371a[8]
Borsch (IRE) *Miss L A Perratt* 45
5 b g Soviet Star(USA) —Cheese Soup (USA) (Spectacular Bid (USA))
1895[5] 2252[12] 2567[9] 2825[9] 3584[9] 4246[6] 4475[5] 4972[8] 5283[10] 5835[7]
Borzoi Maestro *G F Bridgwater* a63 61
6 ch g Wolfhound(USA) —Ashkernazy (IRE) (Salt Dome (USA))
287[5] 1028[2] (1065) 1436[13] 1729[12] 2652[14] *3618[11] 4974[12] 6565[12]*
Bosamcliff (IRE) *A B Haynes* a55
2 b f Daylami(IRE) —L'Animee (Green Tune (USA))
6434[11] 6585[6]
Boscobel *M Johnston* a100 116
3 ch c Halling(USA) —Dunnes River (USA) (Danzig (USA))
(113) (483) 1476[2] (1803) (2813) 3142a[4] 4692[9]
Bosra's Valentine (USA) *R Bouresly* a49
7 b h Sadler's Wells(USA) —Bosra Sham (USA) (Woodman (USA))
399a[13]
Boston Lodge *Doug Watson* a111 84
7 ch g Grand Lodge(USA) —Ffestiniog (IRE) (Efisio)
325a[5] 477a[5] *(532a) (599a) 858a[14]*
Bosun Breese *P W D'Arcy* 85
2 b g Bahamian Bounty—Nellie Melba (Hurricane Sky (AUS))
1007[3] 2241[4] (2630) 4168[3] 4695[17] 5974[9] 6195[2]
Botanical (USA) *E Charpy* a102 83
6 b h Seeking The Gold(USA) —Satin Flower (USA) (Shadeed (USA))
249a[8] 324a[4] 597a[10]
Botham (USA) *D J Murphy* a58 46
3 bb g Cryptoclearance(USA) —Oval (USA) (Kris S (USA))
4330[7] 5037[8] *5894[5] 6026[5] 6315[9] 6904[4] 7009[8] 7154[2] 7262[5]*
Bothar Brugha (IRE) *J G M O'Shea* a53 57
3 b g Alexius(IRE) —Denise's Stride (IRE) (Fumo Di Londra (IRE))
5816[6] 6211[6] 6967[10]
Bottomless Wallet *F Watson* 48
6 ch m Titus Livius(FR) —Furry Dance (USA) (Nureyev (USA))
1744[8] 2253[8]
Boucheen *J W Unett* a47 50
4 b g Foxhound(USA) —Anytime Baby (Bairn (USA))
1380[10] 4671[5] 4920[9]
Bouggler *Miss J A Camacho* 50
2 b g Tobougg(IRE) —Rush Hour (IRE) (Night Shift (USA))
4037[12] 5904[6] 6307[6]
Bouguereau *P W Chapple-Hyam* 94
2 b c Alhaarth(IRE) —Blessed Honour (Ahonoora)
4151[7] 4625a[4] 5417[3]
Boulevin (IRE) *R J Price* a38 52
7 bb g Perugino(USA) —Samika (IRE) (Bikala)
182[7] 333[9]
Boundless Prospect (USA) *Miss Gay Kelleway* a79 89
8 b g Boundary(USA) —Cape (USA) (Mr Prospector (USA))
101[4] 308[4] 3039[6] 3855[7] 4496[3] *5203[9] 5338[3]* 5545[4] (5737) 6016[5] (6412) 6596[3] 6636[4] 6746[7] *6996[4] 7141[4] 7213[5]*
Bounty Quest *K A Ryan* a108 100
5 b h Fasliyev(USA) —Just Dreams (Salse (USA))
326a[2] 474a[2] 597a[2] 860a[13] 3708[5] 4183[3] 4798[6] 5407[21]
Bourbon Balistic *Mrs A Duffield* 61
2 ch c Piccolo—Last Ambition (IRE) (Cadeaux Genereux)
5558[4] 6072[5] 6384[13]
Bourbon Highball (IRE) *P C Haslam* 61
2 b g Catcher In The Rye(IRE) —Be Exciting (IRE) (Be My Guest (USA))
1938[8] 3718[5] 3977[3] 4524[10] 5736[9]
Bournonville *M Wigham* a47 43
4 b g Machiavellian(USA) —Amellnaa (IRE) (Sadler's Wells (USA))
180[9] 278[11] 372[2] 393[6] 496[15] 665[7] 716[7] 1271[9] *1570[6] 1934[7]* 2825[14] 3036[8]
Bourse (IRE) *J H M Gosden* 60
2 b g Dubai Destination(USA) —Quarter Note (USA) (Danehill (USA))
2041[11] 2424[11]
Bouzouki (USA) *Karen George* a60 43
4 bb g Distant Music(USA) —Pamina (IRE) (Perugino (USA))
1765[14] 2544[7] *2875[3] 3282[RR]*
Bovered (IRE) *A Berry* a15 19
3 b f Fayruz—Lucky Pick (Auction Ring (USA))
1623[6] 2135[5] 5082[8] 5625[13]
Bowder Stone (IRE) *M H Tompkins* 41
2 b c Rock Of Gibraltar(IRE) —Ghita (IRE) (Zilzal (USA))
4125[11]
Bowl Of Cherries *I A Wood* a63 44
4 b g Vettori(IRE) —Desert Nomad (Green Desert (USA))
2007[9] 2154[9] *2667[8] 2875[2] 2990[9] 3067[7] 3419[6] 4161[10]* 4340[6] *4945[4] 5132[5] 5389[8] 6529[7] (6577) 6713[4] 7009[9] 7088[6] 7115[7]*
Bowness *J G Given* a63 89
5 b m Efisio—Dominio (IRE) (Dominion)
1670[6] 2240[8] 3344[9] 3897[14]
Boxhall (IRE) *N Wilson* a63 78
5 b g Grand Lodge(USA) —March Hare (Groom Dancer (USA))
1263[4] 1677[2] 2026[3] 2250[3] 4179[8] 5257[2] 5839[7] 6383[5] 6703[7]
Boy Blue *D Nicholls* 85
2 b c Observatory(USA) —Rowan Flower (IRE) (Ashkalani (IRE))
4578[5] 5328[2] (5580)
Boy Dancer (IRE) *D W Barker* a60 67
4 ch g Danehill Dancer(IRE) —Mary Gabry (IRE) (Kris)
101[5] 228[11] 556[3] 831[6] 915[5] 1132[11] 1488[9] 2007[2] 2302[10]
Boz *L M Cumani* a84 53
3 gr c Grand Lodge(USA) —Dali's Grey (Linamix (FR))
973[12] *1166[12] 1522[10]* 3825[9] 4339[9] 4533[3] 4894[3] *(5421) (5647) (6027) (6481) (6739)*
Bozeman Trail *P F I Cole* a59 64
2 b c Averti(IRE) —Crystal Power (USA) (Pleasant Colony (USA))
3404[6] 4162[5] 5186[4] 5914[14] *6715[10]*
Brabazon (IRE) *Barry Potts* 77
4 b g In The Wings—Azure Lake (USA) (Lac Ouimet (USA))
1598[4] 2567[8] 4096[14]
Brace Of Doves *D W Whillans* a55 61
5 b g Bahamian Bounty—Overcome (Belmez (USA))
1198[16] 2256[14] 2714[13] 3999[8] 4477[8] 4966[11] 5503[14] 5838[11]
Brackenridge *Miss E C Lavelle* 29
3 b g Tumbleweed Ridge—I Have A Dream (SWE) (Mango Express)
1635[7] 2083[5] 2470[12]
Braddock (IRE) *T D Barron* a77 85
4 b h Pivotal—Sedna (FR) (Bering)
(1747) 3489[6] *6243[5] 6391[11]*
Brahminy Kite (USA) *R Bouresly* a95 96
5 b g Silver Hawk(USA) —Cope's Light (USA) (Copelan (USA))
175a[13] 248a[13] *329a[10]* 401a[13]
Bramcote Lorne *R C Guest* a57 67
4 b g Josr Algarhoud(IRE) —Dreamtime Quest (Blakeney)
148[4] 278[5] 6991[3] 7109[7]

Brandane (IRE) *Mrs A Duffield* 60
2 br g Danehill Dancer(IRE) —Oumaldaaya (USA) (Nureyev (USA))
4286[6] 4782[10]

Brandywell Boy (IRE) *D J S Ffrench Davis* a84 81
4 b g Danetime(IRE) —Alexander Eliott (IRE) (Night Shift (USA))
692[8] 1004[13] 1630[7] 1885[7] 1969[15] *3396[3] 3852[11]* 4236[10] 4767[2] 5009[7] *5387[8]* 5642[3] 5879[2] 6287[11] 6594[2] *(6810) 6946[2] 7033[2] 7161[6]*

Branston Tiger *Ian Emmerson* a71 76
8 b g Mark Of Esteem(IRE) —Tuxford Hideaway (Cawston's Clown)
3[4] (59) 323[8] 388[3] 1265[3] 1755[5]

Brasingaman Hifive *Mrs G S Rees* 73
2 b f High Estate—Our Miss Florence (Carlitin)
(5329) 6328[6]

Brass Hat (USA) *W Bradley* a117
6 b g Prized(USA) —Brassy (USA) (Dixie Brass (USA))
5059a[6]

Brassini *B R Millman* 82
2 bg g Bertolini(USA) —Silver Spell (Aragon)
926[4] 1201[3] 1919[3] (2526) (3486) 4255[6] 4605[3] 5008[7] 5629[15]

Brastar Jelois (FR) *R Hollinshead* a81 86
4 b m True Brave(USA) —Star Angels (FR) (Ski Chief (USA))
1083[7] *1279[2] 1567[2] 1951[8] 3063[4] 3282[3] 3595[3]* 4660[7] 4846[3] *(5235)* 5553[2] 5774[5]

Brave Dane (IRE) *K J Burke* a66 59
9 b g Danehill(USA) —Nuriva (USA) (Woodman (USA))
570[12]

Brave Falcon (IRE) *Leo J Temple* a57 70
3 b g Fasliyev(USA) —Don't Care (IRE) (Nordico (USA))
6339[4]

Brave Hiawatha (FR) *G J Smith* a10 46
5 b g Dansili—Alexandrie (USA) (Val De L'Orne (FR))
3598[12]

Brave Jack (IRE) *J R Best* a59 57
3 b g Royal Applause—Zaynah (IRE) (Kahyasi)
55[6] 231[7] 343[9] 636[4] 738[4] 924[4] 1154[9] 2489[3] 3351[7] 3652[12] *4591[7]* 5062[8] 5276[3] 5688[2] *5817[3] 5946[4] 6266[5]*

Bravely (IRE) *J S Bolger* 89
3 b g Rock Of Gibraltar(IRE) —Raghida (IRE) (Nordico (USA))
1047a[9] 5842a[7] 6036a[11]

Brave Mave *W Jarvis* 71
2 gr f Daylami(IRE) —Baalbek (Barathea (IRE))
3507[14] 4709[5] (6093)

Brave Prospector *P W Chapple-Hyam* 96
2 b c Oasis Dream—Simply Times (USA) (Dodge (USA))
5868[2] 6295[4] 6495[4]

Brave Quest (IRE) *Mrs L J Mongan* a62 67
3 b g Indian Danehill(IRE) —Mill Rainbow (FR) (Rainbow Quest (USA))
611[3] (904) *1039[12]* 6623[11]

Brave Tin Soldier (USA) *A P O'Brien* 104
3 b c Storm Cat(USA) —Bless (USA) (Mr Prospector (USA))
1703a[12] 5240a[6] 6038a[8]

Brave Vision *A C Whillans* a34 44
11 b g Clantime—Kinlet Vision (IRE) (Vision (USA))
1942[5] 2252[5]

Bravo Bolivar (IRE) *J L Dunlop* 46
2 b c Red Ransom(USA) —Fantasy Girl (IRE) (Marju (IRE))
4151[18] 4683[11] 5918[10]

Braydeen (IRE) *D K Weld* a83 80
3 b f Barathea(IRE) —Sparky's Song (Electric)
5761a[9]

Brazilian Bride (IRE) *Kevin Prendergast* 106
3 b f Pivotal—Braziliz (USA) (Kingmambo (USA))
946a[9]

Brazilian Brush (IRE) *H Morrison* a68 71
2 ch c Captain Rio—Ejder (IRE) (Indian Ridge)
6125[3] *6998[4] 7264[4]*

Brazilian Star (IRE) *Kevin Prendergast* a92 100
2 b g Galileo(IRE) —Braziliz (USA) (Kingmambo (USA))
1508a[8] 3980a[2] 5845a[4] *6161a[5]*

Breaker Morant (IRE) *J G Burns* a76 74
5 b g Montjeu(IRE) —Arcade (Rousillon (USA))
7214[3]

Breaking Shadow (IRE) *M A Peill* a64 87
5 br g Danehill Dancer(IRE) —Crimbourne (Mummy's Pet)
1040[15] 1198[12] *1718[12]* 2508[9] 2741[4] 3053[5] 3572[5] 3723[4] 4494[11] *6612[5] 6764[9]* (Dead)

Break 'N' Dish *B R Johnson*
3 b g Montjoy(USA) —Ship Of Gold (Glint Of Gold)
6060[16]

Break Out *J M Bradley* a40 48
3 b c Kayf Tara—Clifton Girl (Van Der Linden (FR))
2196[10] 2581[5] *3084[10]* 3804[14] 4533[12]

Brean Dot Com (IRE) *Mrs P N Dutfield* a60 61
3 b g Desert Sun—Anna Elise (IRE) (Nucleon (USA))
149[6] 520[6] 636[7] 790[6] 1266[3] 2456[6] 2916[9] *3622[12]* 4504[11] *4742[12]*

Breeder's Folly *E J Creighton* a45 41
5 b m Mujahid(USA) —Wynona (IRE) (Cyrano De Bergerac)
7155[9] 7262[7]

Breeze In (IRE) *R A Fahey* a36 40
4 b g Houmayoun(FR) —Breeze Up (Coquelin (USA))
144[9]

Breiz Dream's (FR) *Heather Dalton* 80
5 ch g East Of Heaven(IRE) —Impish (FR) (Epervier Bleu)
4717[10]

Bret Maverick (IRE) *B P J Baugh* a57 57
3 b g Josr Algarhoud(IRE) —Shady Street (USA) (Shadeed (USA))
1624[8] 2763[4] 3377[2] 3824[5] 4036[3] 4735[3] 6380[11] *6672[4] 6835[12]*

Bretton *J E Long* a40
6 b g Polar Prince(IRE) —Understudy (In The Wings)
1254[11] (Dead)

Bretwalda (IRE) *P T Midgley* 58
4 b g Imperial Ballet(IRE) —Prime Time Girl (Primo Dominie)
5488[3]

Brexca (IRE) *C G Cox* 78
2 b g Diktat—Hemaca (Distinctly North (USA))
5010[11] 5538[4] 6130[2]

Briannsta (IRE) *B Smart* a85 80
5 b g Bluebird(USA) —Nacote (IRE) (Mtoto)
190[4] 419[11] 1971[16] 2318[2] 2546[10] 2982[5] 3549[10] *6243[11] 6531[6]*

Briarwood Bear *M Blanshard* a60 21
3 ch g Woodborough(USA) —Bramble Bear (Beveled (USA))
93[9] 322[2] 392[4] 572[5]

Brick (IRE) *M Mullineaux* a43 29
2 b f Averti(IRE) —Wicked (Common Grounds)
5644[5] 5801[9]

Bricks And Porter (IRE) *John A Quinn* 94
7 b g College Chapel—Camassina (IRE) (Taufan (USA))
3138a[15]

Bridge It Jo *G G Margarson* a51 90
3 gr f Josr Algarhoud(IRE) —T G's Girl (Selkirk (USA))
1372[10] 2060[6] 3061[7] 4606[4] 4898[8] 5278[6] 5506[5] 5747[13] *6122[11]*

Bridge Of Fermoy (IRE) *Miss Gay Kelleway* a63 60
2 b c Danetime(IRE) —Banco Solo (Distant Relative)
3733[6] 3962[17] 4363[2] 4776[8] *5117[4] (5423)*

Bridget's Team *D G Bridgwater* a54 40
3 b f Elnadim(USA) —Overcome (Belmez (USA))
223[7] 619[6] 786[8] 1028[9]

Bridgewater Boys *G L Moore* a74 71
6 b g Atraf—Dunloe (IRE) (Shaadi (USA))
63[3] 205[3] 332[9] 445[10] 533[4] (630) 674[6] 733[4] 825[2] 3595[4] 3638[2] 4249[2] *4460[4]* (4663) *6102[2] 6265[2]* (6452) *6774[2]*

Brief Engagement (IRE) *T D McCarthy* 4
4 br m Namid—Brief Fairy (IRE) (Brief Truce (USA))
160[11] 1452[11] 3046[10] 4164[11]

Brief Goodbye *John Berry* 85
7 b g Slip Anchor—Queen Of Silk (IRE) (Brief Truce (USA))
1149[6] 1543[8] 2003[7] 2634[2] 3882[6] 4184[12] 5052[8] 5362[4] 5539[7] 5924[6]

Brierley Lil *J L Spearing* a50 50
3 ch f Intikhab(USA) —Pooka (Dominion)
37[7] 140[8] 534[8] 3244[4] 5542[4]

Briery Blaze *J W Unett* a54 58
4 b m Dansili—Sabonis (USA) (The Minstrel (CAN))
1197[14] 2298[10] 2938[6] 3204[12] 3996[7] 4736[2] *5094[5]* 5269[9] *5730[4]* 6247[16] *6361[4] (6563) 6887[6] 7003[4] 7025[11]*

Briery Lane (IRE) *J M Bradley* a64 69
6 ch g Tagula(IRE) —Branston Berry (IRE) (Mukaddamah (USA))
1212[4] 1640[4] 2576[9] 3829[2] 4397[15] (4635) 4996[2] 5160[11] 5867[8] 6287[4] 6424[3] *6752[7]*

Brigadore *J G Given* a62 79
8 b g Magic Ring(IRE) —Music Mistress (IRE) (Classic Music (USA))
(992) 1492[4] 1885[4] 1914[12] 2072[4] 2508[3] 2864[3] 3345[6] 3401[9] 3723[7] 3998[7] 4083[10] 4390[6] 5879[3] 6467[18]

Brigentia (GER) *Frau Ira Ferentschak*
4 ch m Hamond(GER) —Berlanga (GER) (Executive Pride)
2409a[8]

Bright *W K Goldsworthy* a11 28
4 ch g Mister Baileys—Razzle Dazzle (IRE) (Caerleon (USA))
240[12] 4530[9] 4663[6] *6097[9]*

Bright Falcon *D J Murphy* 83
2 ch c Hawk Wing(USA) —Cream Tease (Pursuit Of Love)
(6184)

Bright Mind *J H M Gosden* 86
3 b c Zamindar(USA) —Bright Spells (USA) (Alleged (USA))
4568[2] 5005[2]

Bright Sun (IRE) *N Tinkler* a68 76
6 b g Desert Sun—Kealbra Lady (Petong)
1158[7] 1621[10] 2117[3] 2338[4] 3346[11] 3705[13]

Brilliantsensation (IRE) *J G Given* 49
2 b g Danetime(IRE) —Looks Sensational (USA) (Majestic Light (USA))
2532[14] 3835[7] 4136[5] 4405[13] 4897[7]

Bring Back Matron (IRE) *J S Bolger* a19 91
3 b f Rock Of Gibraltar(IRE) —Elida (IRE) (Royal Academy (USA))
1777a[8] 5460a[30]

Bringbackmeboots *Liam Roche* a68 58
2 b c Piccolo—Piccante (Wolfhound (USA))
6392a[7]

Bring It On Home *G L Moore* a58 69
3 b g Beat Hollow—Dernier Cri (Slip Anchor)
2625[6] 3335[7] *4069[11]* 5068[8] 5273[6]

Brisant (GER) *M Trybuhl* 114
5 br g Goofalik(USA) —Beresina (Surumu (GER))
1190a[7] 1689a[8] 2409a[2] (4957a) 6526a[5] 6941a[5]

Briseida *P Schiergen* 95
2 ch f Pivotal—Party Doll (Be My Guest (USA))
6371a[3]

Brisk Breeze (GER) *H R A Cecil* 109
3 ch f Monsun(GER) —Bela-M (IRE) (Ela-Mana-Mou)
1127[2] 1663[2] (2081) 2816[10] 3434[4] 4089[4] 4748[2] 5352[3] (5767) 6168[4]

Britannic *T P Tate* 106
4 ch g Rainbow Quest(USA) —Anka Britannia (USA) (Irish River (FR))
5411[8] 6153[9]

British Isles *S Seemar* a89
5 b h Giant's Causeway(USA) —Wildwood Flower (Distant Relative)
410a[4] 532a[3]

Brixworth Scribe *B Smart* a61 73
2 b g Forzando—Segretezza (IRE) (Perugino (USA))
1540[10] 2086[3] 2758[2] (2984) 4484[8] 5331[12] *6151[4] 6502[10]*

Broad Town Girl *Mrs H Sweeting* a27
4 b m Woodborough(USA) —Fortunes Course (IRE) (Crash Course)
260[9] 565[8] 788[5] 6546[12] 6858[7] 7159[8]

Brofalya (FR) *J-C Rouget* 103
3 b f Fasliyev(USA) —Broad And High (USA) (Broad Brush (USA))
6940a[4]

Broghill *J H M Gosden* 97
3 ch c Selkirk(USA) —Mystify (Batshoof)
1103[7] 1475[4] 1957[3]

Brogue Lanterns (IRE) *E J Creighton* a30 81
5 ch m Dr Devious(IRE) —Landrail (USA) (Storm Bird (CAN))
129[12] 3616[11]

Broken Applause (IRE) *R A Fahey* 102
2 br f Acclamation—Pink Cashmere (IRE) (Polar Falcon (USA))
(2869) 3492[2] 4225[4] 5322[4] 5614[2] 6017[10]

Broken Moon *J R Fanshawe* 69
2 gr f Galileo(IRE) —Bedazzling (IRE) (Darshaan)
4774[9] 5881[3]

Bronco's Filly (IRE) *J G M O'Shea* a17 38
3 bb f Val Royal(FR) —Lady Esther (IRE) (Darnay)
2978[9] 6060[13] *6833[6]*

Bronte's Hope *M P Tregoning* a71
3 ch f Gorse—General Jane (Be My Chief (USA))
(55) 290[4]

Bronze Cannon (USA) *J H M Gosden* a87
2 bb c Lemon Drop Kid(USA) —Victoria Cross (IRE) (Mark Of Esteem (IRE))
5337[8] (5680) (6120)

Bronze Dancer (IRE) *G A Swinbank* 76
5 b g Entrepreneur—Scrimshaw (Selkirk (USA))
1239[2] 1677[3] 1794[8] (2391) 2567[5] 5777[8] 6325[2]

Bronze Star *J R Fanshawe* a70 71
4 b m Mark Of Esteem(IRE) —White House (Pursuit Of Love)
1258[8] 1764[4] 2156[2] 2833[3] (3629)

Bronzo Di Riace (IRE) *M G Quinlan* a35 23
3 b c Montjeu(IRE) —Afreeta (USA) (Afleet (CAN))
141[10]

Brookby (NZ) *Miss Sheena West* a74
7 b g Groom Dancer(USA) —Kappadios (NZ) (Great Charmer (USA))
211[5] 314[5]

Brook Lass (IRE) *T G McCourt* 39
3 b f Dilshaan—Polish Widow (Polish Precedent (USA))
5835[10]

Brooklyn Boy (USA) *J-C Rouget* 106
3 gr c Gone West(USA) —Moon Queen (IRE) (Sadler's Wells (USA))
2293a[9]

Broomielaw *E A L Dunlop* 97
3 ch c Rock Of Gibraltar(IRE) —Peony (Lion Cavern (USA))
1093[4] (4568)

Brother Barry (USA) *W J Musson* 60
2 bb g Forestry(USA) —Saratoga Sugar (USA) (Gone West (USA))
6617[6]

Brother Bobby (USA) *G Forster* a109
4 ch g Out Of Place(USA) —Doc's Destiny (USA) (Doc's Leader (USA))
5855a[5]

Brother's Valcour (FR) *K Schafflutzel* 52
9 b h River Mist(USA) —Lady De Valcour (FR) (Labus (FR))
356a[12] 494a[10]

Brough (IRE) *J O'Reilly* a31 38
2 b c Fasliyev(USA) —Metaphor (USA) (Woodman (USA))
4173[12] 4487[12] 5154[8] *6624[13] 6693[11] 6814[10]*

Broughtons Flight (IRE) *W J Musson* a64 56
2 ch f Hawk Wing(USA) —Aldburgh (Bluebird (USA))
6093[9] 6411[8] *7058[5] 7245[2]*

Broughtons Folly *W J Musson* a75 65
4 b m Groom Dancer(USA) —Cressida (Polish Precedent (USA))
117[7] 459[4] 1378[9] 2321[6] *(3407)*

Broughtons Revival *W J Musson* a74 88
5 b m Pivotal—Ella Lamees (Statoblest)
602[5] 769[3] 1521[3] (2156) *2765[3]* 3243[4] (3844) (5808)

Brouhaha *Miss Diana Weeden* a57 63
3 b g Bahhare(USA) —Top Of The Morning (Keen)
1399[7] 1634[18] 2915[8] 3913[5] 4856[10] *5945[2]*

Bruki (IRE) *M Botti* a60
2 b f Captain Rio—Coup De Coeur (IRE) (Kahyasi)
6585[9] 7114[3]

Brunelleschi *M G Quinlan* a59 84
4 ch g Bertolini(USA) —Petrovna (IRE) (Petardia)
1405[2] (1640) (1847) (2155) 2394[11] 2882[6] 4367[6] 4816[9] *6173[2] 6575[10]*

Brunton (IRE) *A Berry* a22 50
5 b g Charnwood Forest(IRE) —Lady Nathalie (IRE) (Bigstone (IRE))
7209[11] 7239[10]

Brunton Blue *W Jarvis* a58
2 b f Compton Place—Persian Blue (Persian Bold)
7264[8]

Brut *D W Barker* a58 75
5 b g Mind Games—Champenoise (Forzando)
448[2] 463[4] 668[12] 896[5] 1112[7] 1405[6] (1493) 1557[12] 2386[2] (2561) (2762) 3014[5] 3184[3] 3676[8] 5083[11] 5552[4] (5672) 5908[15] (6702)

Bruxcalina (FR) *A Fabre* 91
7 gr m Linamix(FR) —Brusca (USA) (Grindstone (USA))
5058a[3]

Brynris *Mrs G S Rees* a32 11
3 gr g Perryston View—Isle Of Mull (Elmaamul (USA))
122[5] 224[12] 1282[11] 2220[11] 2304[12]

Bsharpsonata (USA) *Timothy E Salzman* a75 102
2 b f Pulpit(USA) —Apasionata Sonata (USA) (Affirmed (USA))
6482a[4]

Buachaill Dona (IRE) *D Nicholls* 107
4 b g Namid—Serious Contender (IRE) (Tenby)
1826[4] 2034[6] 3990[16] 4696[3] (5039) 5407[12] 5616[24]

Bubbly Girl *P J McBride* a53 54
3 b f Tamayaz(CAN) —Alexander Star (IRE) (Inzar (USA))
1093[12] *1440[7]* 1841[8] 2727[14] *3394[4]* 3824[9] 4337[5]

Buccellati *A M Balding* 105
3 ch c Soviet Star(USA) —Susi Wong (IRE) (Selkirk (USA))
1275[4] 1835[5] 2231[4] 2788[21] 3460[5] 4092[6] (5327) (5805) (6169)

Bucharest *M Wigham* a77 69
4 b g Barathea(IRE) —Zorleni (Zafonic (USA))
(2556) *(3419) 3647[2]* 4250[6] *5118[10] 5234[3] 5387[4] 5731[2] 6406[9]*

Buckie Massa *S Kirk* a79 80
3 ch g Best Of The Bests(IRE) —Up On Points (Royal Academy (USA))
1658[10] 1900[6] 2335[6] 2415[2] 2601[3] 3483[4] 4123[12] (4269) 4574[10] 5092[4] *5684[8]* 5768[7] *6504[4]*

Buckle And Hyde *Mrs A L M King* a54 46
4 ch m Foxhound(USA) —Step On Degas (Superpower)
1400[10] 4416[4] *4673[12]* 5269[6] *5497[11]*

Bucks *Mike Murphy* a62 74
10 b g Slip Anchor—Alligram (USA) (Alysheba (USA))
6971[3]

Buckthorn *G Wragg* a57 70
3 ch c Lomitas—Emma Peel (Emarati (USA))
1093[11] 1358[8] 1722[5] *3456[7]*

Buddy Holly *Pat Eddery* 53
2 b c Reel Buddy(USA) —Night Symphonie (Cloudings (IRE))
5003[8] 6252[7]

Buds Dilemma *W M Brisbourne* a19 50
3 b f Anabaa(USA) —Lady Thynn (FR) (Crystal Glitters (USA))
2012[12] 2740[5] 3997[12] 4480[11] 4846[10] 5803[6] *6026[11]*

Buffy Boo *C R Egerton* 33
4 bb m Agnes World(USA) —Bunty Boo (Noalto)
2606[10]

Bugaku *Sir Michael Stoute* 56
2 ch c Montjeu(IRE) —Bryony Brind (IRE) (Kris)
6494[13]

Bugatti Royale (USA) *Peter Morgan* 91
7 b h Dynaformer(USA) —Cin Isa Luv (USA) (Private Account (USA))
6033a[13]

Bugsy's Boy *P W D'Arcy* a69
3 b g Double Trigger(IRE) —Bugsy's Sister (Aragon)
655[7] 1177[6] 1523[8] 5899[4] 6178[7] 6835[2] (7081)

Buju *N Tinkler* 50
2 b g Sugarfoot—Edge Of Darkness (Vaigly Great)
3024[14] 4448[7] 4770[3] 5298[12] 5572[5] 6305[8]

Bukit Tinggi (IRE) *M A Jarvis* a70 76
3 b g Peintre Celebre(USA) —Puteri Wentworth (Sadler's Wells (USA))
4568[6] *4948[4] 5683[6]* 5938[2] 6308[3] 6733[4]

Bulas Boy *E W Tuer* 37
2 ch g Exit To Nowhere(USA) —Bula Rose (IRE) (Alphabatim (USA))
6051[9]

Bulberry Hill *R W Price* a67 45
6 b g Makbul—Hurtleberry (IRE) (Tirol)
10[4] 146[2] 389[2] 2252[10] *2996[11] 6069[11] 6937[10] 7123[4]*

Bullet Man (USA) *L M Cumani* a76 70
2 bb c Mr Greeley(USA) —Silk Tapestry (USA) (Tank's Prospect (USA))
5088[2] *5780[3]*

Bullish Luck (USA) *A S Cruz* a114 122
8 b g Royal Academy(USA) —Wild Vintage (USA) (Alysheba (USA))
863a[3]

Bull Market (IRE) *J A Osborne* a80 84
4 b g Danehill(USA) —Paper Moon (IRE) (Lake Coniston (IRE))
2692[3] 3748[9] 4184[6] 4597[16] *4976[5]*

Bulwark (IRE) *Ian Williams* a107 111
5 b g Montjeu(IRE) —Bulaxie (Bustino)
1144[8] 1823[3] 2125[3] 2787[10] 4091[8] 5165[5] 5375[8] 6760[5]

Bunderos (IRE) *R A Fahey* 41
3 b f Areion(GER) —Bundheimerin (GER) (Ordos (GER))
1197[13] 2740[9] 4000[5] 4155[3] 4842[11]

Bundle Up *Mrs L J Mongan* a53 58
4 b m Diktat—Bundle (Cadeaux Genereux)
2219[7] *2666[4]* 3387[9]

Bungie *Paul Green* a64 58
3 gr g Forzando—Sweet Whisper (Petong)
54[4] 6287[14] *6747[12] 7024[7] 7206[13]*

Bunny Hug *T D Easterby* 47
2 b f Royal Applause—White Rabbit (Zilzal (USA))
4225[6] 4565[10]

Bunty Malenoir *I A Wood* a39 38
2 b f Silver Patriarch(IRE) —Captivating (IRE) (Wolfhound (USA))
2009[4] 2468[12] *3213[12]*

Burford Lass (IRE) *D K Ivory* a64 58
4 b m Quws—Dancing Willma (IRE) (Dancing Dissident (USA))
1207[8] *1947[2]* 2336[10] *2592[6] 3173[5] 3393[4]* (3873) 4978[6] 5386[2] *5731[12] 5981[6]*

Burgundy *R A Teal* a78 77
10 b g Lycius(USA) —Decant (Rousillon (USA))
195[5] 1451[7] 1591[10] 2765[4] 2964[2] *3416[2] 3641[3]* (3854) 4108[6] 6276[4] *6848[9]*

Burhaan (IRE) *J R Boyle* a67 54
5 b h Green Desert(USA) —Arjuzah (IRE) (Ahonoora)
86[3] (158) 276[6] (346) 379[3]

Burley Flame *J G Given* a62 82
6 b g Marju(IRE) —Tarsa (Ballad Rock)
1287[3] 2985[6]

Burnbrake *J A R Toller* a67 60
2 b c Mujahid(USA) —Duena (Grand Lodge (USA))
6616[12] *6827[4] 7070[5]*

Burningfold Babe *P Winkworth* a54 1
3 b f Muhtarram(USA) —Laser Light Lady (Tragic Role (USA))
194[2]

Burning Incense (IRE) *R Charlton* a67 105
4 b g Namid—Night Scent (IRE) (Scenic)
1474[17] 2858[6] 3104[7] 3941[5] 4601[9] 5254[10] 5809[5] 6205[4]

Burning Moon *S W Hall* a13 47
6 b g Bering—Triple Green (Green Desert (USA))
431[12] 514[11]

Burnley (IRE) *Mrs A L M King* a17 40
4 b g Distant Music(USA) —Dance Ahead (Shareef Dancer (USA))
1560[14] 2981[7] 3476[8]

Burnley Al (IRE) *Peter Grayson* a69 69
5 ch g Desert King(IRE) —Bold Meadows (Persian Bold)
124[7] 298[3] 485[3] 681[14] 1311[6]

Burn The Breeze (IRE) *H R A Cecil* 73
2 b f Beat Hollow—Madiyla (Darshaan)
4402[5] 5301[4] 5912[3]

Burntoakboy *Dr R D P Newland* 82
9 b g Sir Harry Lewis(USA) —Sainte Martine (Martinmas)
1300[8] 5938[13]

Burnwynd Boy *I Semple* 91
2 b g Tobougg(IRE) —Cadeau Speciale (Cadeaux Genereux)
(1743) (2009) 2732[10] 4372[7] 5665[3] 6182[15]

Burriscarra *Eamon Tyrrell* a76 61
2 b f Mujahid(USA) —Cressida (Polish Precedent (USA))
(6777) 6974[3]

Bury Treasure (IRE) *Miss Gay Kelleway* 56
2 ch c Choisir(AUS) —Future Treasure (Habitat)
2832[14] 3823[4] 4854[7]

Busaco *K J Condon* 41
5 b g Mister Baileys—War Shanty (Warrshan (USA))
4371a[9]

Buscador (USA) *W M Brisbourne* a66 50
8 ch g Crafty Prospector(USA) —Fairway Flag (USA) (Fairway Phantom (USA))
110[7] 286[3] 445[8] 539[4] 564[7] 741[3] 767[2] 1167[6] 1314[2] 1907[10] 6906[10] 7060[7] 7273[4]

Buscape (USA) *S Seemar* a76 70
5 bb m Repriced(USA) —Pyrite Pink (USA) (Formal Dinner (USA))
397a[12]

Bush Maiden (IRE) *Mrs Seamus Hayes* a97 100
7 b m Among Men(USA) —Moonbi Range (IRE) (Nordico (USA))
5242a[15] 6216a[15]

Bushy Dell (IRE) *Miss J Feilden* a69
2 br f King Charlemagne(USA) —Nisibis (In The Wings)
5202[5] (5984)

Bussel (USA) *D M Simcock* a76 69
3 ch f Royal Academy(USA) —Reigning Princess (USA) (Storm Boot (USA))
76[3] 4778[3] 5662[6] 5907[9] *(6929)*

Bussell Up *S C Williams* 67
2 b f Danehill Dancer(IRE) —Digamist Girl (IRE) (Digamist (USA))
6721[3]

Bussoni (GER) *H Blume* 118
6 br h Goofalik(USA) —Blumme (CHI) (Jadar (CHI))
882a[3] 1190a[2] (1689a) (3565a) 4442a[3] (5264a) 6223a[4] 7090a[3]

Bustan (IRE) *G C Bravery* a67 103
8 b g Darshaan—Dazzlingly Radiant (Try My Best (USA))
(1157) 1480[2] 1818[7] 2374[3] 2817[16] 4377[9] 5012[9] *5737[2]* 6016[11] 6596[8] *6806[10]*

Buster Hyvonen (IRE) *J R Fanshawe* a74 80
5 b g Dansili—Serotina (IRE) (Mtoto)
1272[3]

Bustin Justin (USA) *J Noseda* a74 94
4 b h Forestry(USA) —Designatoree (USA) (Alysheba (USA))
396a[11]

Busy Man (IRE) *R C Guest* a54 6
8 b g Darnay—Make Or Mar (Daring March)
7098[13]

Bute Street *R J Hodges* 33
2 b g Superior Premium—Hard To Follow (Dilum (USA))
5088[8] 5856[14]

Butlers Best *E J O'Neill* a60 42
3 b g Best Of The Bests(IRE) —Evening Charm (IRE) (Bering)
4718[9]

Butterfly Bud (IRE) *J O'Reilly* a35 70
4 b g Lend A Hand—Rathbawn Realm (Doulab (USA))
1640[3] 2121[4] 2206[4] 3839[10] 4180[13] 4822[13]

Buxton *R Ingram* a84 77
3 b g Auction House(USA) —Dam Certain (IRE) (Damister (USA))
1633[2] *(1904)* 2400[15] *2769[3] 4360[4] 4950[3]* 5168[6] *6231[4] 6273[3] 6492[12] 6667[8] 6949[8] 7099[4] 7281[10]*

Buy On The Red *W R Muir* a94 79
6 b g Komaite(USA) —Red Rosein (Red Sunset)
44[2] 198[4] 3613[7] (4236) 4320[5] 5064[2] 5711[2] *6142[11] 6437[7] 6707[3] 6836[6] 6981[4] 7289[8]*

Buzbury Rings *A M Balding* a58 54
3 b g Piccolo—Mory Kante (USA) (Icecapade (USA))
498[7] 752[11] 1373[7]

Buzzin'Boyzee (IRE) *P D Evans* a63 65
4 ch m Monashee Mountain(USA) —Las Bela (Welsh Pageant)
158[11] 183[3] 479[3] 699[4] 734[4] 793[10] 833[4] 932[4] 1027[6] 5190[7] *6064[11]* 6247[6] *6533[6] 6647[7] 6869[8]*

Bwana Bull (USA) *J Hollendorfer* a104
3 ch c Holy Bull(USA) —Shahalo (USA) (Halo (CAN))
1486a[15]

Byanita (IRE) *B Palling* a24
3 b f Anita's Prince—Byliny (IRE) (Archway (IRE))
68[8]

By Command *J L Dunlop* 69
2 b c Red Ransom(USA) —Rafha (Kris)
2632[4] 3552[5]

Bygone Days *Saeed Bin Suroor* 119
6 ch g Desert King(IRE) —May Light (Midyan (USA))
2319[4] 2857[6] 4214a[0] 5112[3] 5359[2]

Byron (GER) *W Hefter* 94
3 br c Monsun(GER) —Bandera (GER) (Sure Blade (USA))
3146a[10]

Byron Bay *I Semple* a91 89
5 b h My Best Valentine—Candarela (Damister (USA))
227[5] 451[2] 629[4] 846[9]

By Storm *Miss J E Foster* a39 53
4 b m Largesse—Polar Storm (IRE) (Law Society (USA))
1025[11] 2370[14] *3186[8]* 3428[10] 3840[LFT] *7197[5]*

By The Edge (IRE) *T D Barron* a66 56
3 b f Shinko Forest(IRE) —Magic Annemarie (IRE) (Dancing Dissident (USA))
2895[8] 3000[4] 3588[2] 3763[2] 3811[4] 4616[2] 4661[3] 4935[5] *5752[3]* 5970[2] *(6339)* 6466[4] *7011[3] (7206)*

Bythehokey (IRE) *W M Brisbourne* a32 44
6 b g Barathea(IRE) —Regal Portrait (IRE) (Royal Academy (USA))
5427[9] 5886[8] *6569[9]*

By The River *P Winkworth* 48
3 b g Zamindar(USA) —Baby Bunting (Wolfhound (USA))
2690[8] 3236[6] 3593[5] 3903[4]

Cabinet (IRE) *Sir Michael Stoute* a85 98
3 b c Grand Lodge(USA) —Passe Passe (USA) (Lear Fan (USA))
1956[4] 2448[6] (3882) 4799[4] 5805[2]

Cable Beach (USA) *C Laffon-Parias* a85 76
3 b f Langfuhr(CAN) —Curve (USA) (A.P. Indy (USA))
7049a[7]

Cabourg (IRE) *R Bastiman* a66 64
4 b g Danehill(USA) —Loire Valley (IRE) (Sadler's Wells (USA))
124[2] 334[7] 479[2] 549[4] 831[5] 1260[4] 1675[4] 2121[7] 3414[11] 4250[5] 4583[5] 5966[2] *6895[4] (7025) 7268[6]*

Cactus King *P M Phelan* a87 94
4 b g Green Desert(USA) —Apache Star (Arazi (USA))
(870) 1245[13] 2180[8] 2512[6] *7075[7]*

Cactus Rose *R Charlton* 96
3 b g Zamindar(USA) —Bolsena (USA) (Red Ransom (USA))
1839[7] 2477[2] (3349) 3960[2] (5012)

Cadeaux Cerise (IRE) *N I M Rossiter* 24
3 b f Cadeaux Genereux—Cerisette (IRE) (Polar Falcon (USA))
3968[8] 4575[8] 5013[14]

Cadeaux Rouge (IRE) *D W Thompson* 47
6 ch m Croco Rouge(IRE) —Gift Of Glory (FR) (Niniski (USA))
(2417) 3638[13] 4249[11]

Cadi May *W M Brisbourne* a24 50
3 b f Fasliyev(USA) —Sound Of Sleat (Primo Dominie)
1537[4] 2137[8] *3110[9]* 4220[9] 4416[12]

Cadogen Square *D W Chapman* a19 56
5 ch m Takhlid(USA) —Mount Park (IRE) (Colonel Collins (USA))
3257[8] (3534) 3816[12] 3920[3] 4141[4] 4250[11] 4822[15] 5627[9] 5964[12] 6467[9] *6609[11]*

Cadre (IRE) *J H M Gosden* 73
2 b c King's Best(USA) —Desert Frolic (IRE) (Persian Bold)
5971[8]

Cadwell *T J Pitt* a62 53
3 b g Pivotal—Sur Les Pointes (IRE) (Sadler's Wells (USA))
684[2] 849[10] 4701[14] *5565[12] 6627[5] 6937[7] 7009[2] 7127[3] 7201[3]*

Caesar Beware (IRE) *S Seemar* 91
5 b g Daggers Drawn(USA) —Red Shareef (Marju (IRE))
247a[9] 528a[9] 644a[10]

Cafe Olympus (USA) *Y Matsuyama* a107
6 ch h Grand Slam(USA) —Cognac Lady (USA) (Olympio (USA))
6942a[16]

Caffari (GER) *K R Burke* 47
2 ch f Seattle Dancer(USA) —Calarca (GER) (Goofalik (USA))
5811[7] 6254[6]

Caffe Coretto *B G Powell* a19
2 b f Mark Of Esteem(IRE) —Sempre Sorriso (Fleetwood (IRE))
7266[13]

Caffrey Kelly *J J Quinn* 4
2 b c Rock City—Mochras (Mtoto)
4002[9] 4897[10]

Cairnbrae *Miss J A Camacho* 59
2 ch g Where Or When(IRE) —Hill Welcome (Most Welcome)
2432[6] 2888[6] 3761[10] (Dead)

Caj (IRE) *Luke Comer* a56 56
3 b f Tagula(IRE) —Notley Park (Wolfhound (USA))
231[4] 382[8] 636[11] 3948[7]

Cake (IRE) *R Hannon* a66 102
2 b f Acclamation—Carpet Lady (IRE) (Night Shift (USA))
(1033) (1503) 1897[3] 2756[5] 3096[5] 4046[10] (4573) 4724[2] 5377[8] 6167[3]

Calabash Cove (USA) *Saeed Bin Suroor* a76 85
3 ch c Rahy(USA) —I Need A Holiday (USA) (Nureyev (USA))
527a[7] (1665) (2340) 3709[6] 5432[5]

Calabaza *J Akehurst* a37 73
5 ch g Zaha(CAN) —Mo Stopher (Sharpo)
1607[6] 1847[10] 2479[5] 2879[8] 3627[10] 4296[10] 5430[2] 5726[9] (5879) 6157[8] (6279) 6450[8] *6946[12]*

Calatagan (IRE) *J M Jefferson* a51 74
8 ch g Danzig Connection(USA) —Calachuchi (Martinmas)
5586[6] 5968[5] 6561[2] *6802[8]*

Calculating (IRE) *M D I Usher* a74 71
3 b g Machiavellian(USA) —Zaheemah (USA) (El Prado (IRE))
1098[5] 1468[5] 1815[11] 2727[7] 3176[2] 5198[5] 5870[7] *6902[5] 7076[2] 7151[2] 7198[2]*

Caldra (IRE) *S Kirk* 111
3 b g Elnadim(USA) —Lady Rachel (IRE) (Priolo (USA))
4543[4] 5213[3] 5618[10] 6332[12] 6655[3]

Caliban (IRE) *Ian Williams* a10
9 ch g Rainbows For Life(CAN) —Amour Toujours (IRE) (Law Society (USA))
126[11] 514[8]

California Laws *R M Beckett* a99 76
5 b g Pivotal—Noor El Houdah (IRE) (Fayruz)
(227) 2626[9]

Calistoga (DEN) *L Reuterskiold* 99
8 br g Richard Of York—Geneva (DEN) (Miami Springs (IRE))
2131a[3]

Calistos Quest *M Johnston* 72
2 b c Rainbow Quest(USA) —Carambola (IRE) (Danehill (USA))
3270[5] 4192[4] 4876[9]

Call For Liberty (IRE) *B Smart* a75 83
2 b c Statue Of Liberty(USA) —Give A Whistle (IRE) (Mujadil (USA))
3582[11] 4328[2] 4781[2] 5193[5]

Callisto Moon *Ian Williams* a69 69
3 b g Mujahid(USA) —Nursling (IRE) (Kahyasi)
565[5] 719[11] (1084) 1536[6]

Callitquits (IRE) *Jennie Candlish* a48 70
5 b g Desert Story(IRE) —Quits (IRE) (Brief Truce (USA))
1732[8] 2946[3] 3282[9] 3595[8] 3927[8]

Call Me Crazy (IRE) *Eamon Tyrrell* a51 73
4 b m Key Of Luck(USA) —Smile Awhile (USA) (Woodman (USA))
300[9]

Call Me Punch *E S McMahon* 66
6 ch g Bettergeton—Tradjazz (Alhijaz)
4530[3] 4905[10] 5917[2]

Call Me Rosy (IRE) *C F Wall* a65 40
3 ch f Shinko Forest(IRE) —Fanciful (IRE) (Mujtahid (USA))
2260[3] 3168[9] 5175[4] 6100[12]

Call My Bluff (FR) *Rae Guest* a81 69
4 b g Highest Honor(FR) —Baino Bluff (Be My Guest (USA))
(24) 110[3] 1264[5] 1862[10] 2623[2] 2831[5] 3352[5] 3711[6] 3854[6] *5099[4] 5985[4] 6293[5]*

Call Of Duty (IRE) *M Johnston* a74
2 br c Storming Home—Blushing Barada (USA) (Blushing Groom (FR))
(7070) 7222[2]

Calloff The Search *Stef Liddiard* a61 57
3 b g Piccolo—Unchain My Heart (Pursuit Of Love)
25[3] 348[4] 535[3] 636[6] 679[6] 974[5] 1782[9] *2331[9] 2798[2]* 3873[2] 4416[3] 5511[2] 5688[4] 6247[7] *6402[3] 6873[5] 6963[5] 7028[10] 7085[10] 7134[3] 7188[7] 7233[11]*

Call Of Ktulu (IRE) *J S Wainwright* 12
2 b g Noverre(USA) —Yankee Dancer (Groom Dancer (USA))
4784[13] 6305[12]

Callow Lake (IRE) *Mrs John Harrington* 85
7 b g Bahhare(USA) —Sharayif (IRE) (Green Desert (USA))
2067a[12]

Calmdownmate (IRE) *K R Burke* 89
2 b g Danehill Dancer(IRE) —Lady Digby (IRE) (Petorius)
2804[6] 3747[2] (4225) 4694[5] 5397a[10]

Calming Influence (IRE) *Saeed Bin Suroor* 92
2 b c King's Best(USA) —Idilic Calm (IRE) (Indian Ridge)
(6156)

Calming Waters *D W P Arbuthnot* a73 39
4 ch g Dr Fong(USA) —Faraway Waters (Pharly (FR))
2180[9] *2520[2]*

Caltire (GER) *M G Quinlan* a65 35
2 b g Pentire—Caluna (SWI) (Lagunas)
5646[6] 5869[8] *(6207) (6928) 7010[5] 7204[2]*

Caltra Princess (IRE) *Tracey Collins* 75
3 gr f Traditionally(USA) —Supercal (Environment Friend)
6555a[4]

Caluba *K R Burke* 56
3 ch f Daggers Drawn(USA) —Canlubang (Mujtahid (USA))
1620[7] 1995[5] 2464[6] 3202[5] 4354[8] 4705[6] 5476[8]

Calusa Lady (IRE) *J A Geake* a42 51
7 ch m Titus Livius(FR) —Solas Abu (IRE) (Red Sunset)
207[10]

Calypso Charms *M L W Bell* 76
2 b f Dansili—Chrysalis (Soviet Star (USA))
4402[12] 5541[4] 6470[5]

Calypso King *Peter Grayson* a78 88
4 gr g Agnes World(USA) —T G's Girl (Selkirk (USA))
1061[7] 1465[6] *1935[6] (2357) 3452[3]* 3676[6] 4606[15] *6360[9] 6764[11] 6890[3] 6976[5] 7011[4] 7206[11]*

Calza Di Seta *G M Moore* 39
2 b f Lujain(USA) —Isla Negra (IRE) (Last Tycoon (IRE))
2504[9]

Calzaghe (IRE) *A M Balding* a75 70
3 ch g Galileo(IRE) —Novelette (Darshaan)
1972[2] *2223[2]* 2602[6] 4113[3] 4570[5] *(5388)*

Camafin (IRE) *L Camici* 86
3 b f Davide Umbro(ITY) —Max Almabrouka (USA) (Hennessy (USA))
6688a[9]

Cambo (FR) *Miss Sheena West* a43 32
6 bb g Mansonnien(FR) —Royal Lie (FR) (Garde Royale)
2770[12] 2996[9] 4535[6]

Came Back (IRE) *J Mackie* a82 45
4 ch h Bertolini(USA) —Distant Decree (USA) (Distant View (USA))
33[2] 306[4] (467) 561[7] 621[8] 717[2] (803) (1165) 1226[5] 1935[5] 5981[12] 6288[8] *6625[2] 6747[9] 7238[2]*

Camellia's Girl *J J Bridger* 26
4 b m Golden Snake(USA) —Stormy Heights (Golden Heights)
3593[11] 3966[6]

Camerooney *A D Brown* a39 49
4 b g Sugarfoot—Enkindle (Relkino)
5562[7] *6070[4]* 6325[8] *6613[11]*

Camfair (FR) *G Chirurgien* 86
2 b c Charge D'Affaires—Camibas (FR) (Solicitor (FR))
6952a[6]

Cami Collins (FR) *J R Best* a42 60
3 ch g Colonel Collins(USA) —Camiriva (FR) (River River (FR))
7083[12] 7166[11] 7257[14]

Camille Pissarro (USA) *D J Wintle* a60 64
7 b g Red Ransom(USA) —Serenity (Selkirk (USA))
525[6] 681[3] 928[2] 1078[3] *1178[3]* 1559[5] (Dead)

Camissa *D K Ivory* a62 71
3 b f Averti(IRE) —Ambitious (Ardkinglass)
1270[5] *1948[7]* 2513[11] 3000[6] *3394[5]*

Camolin (IRE) *Michael McElhone* a43 58
4 b m Fantastic Light(USA) —Maritsa (IRE) (Danehill (USA))
2764[5] 4477[3] 6640[8] *7146[11]*

Campanologist (USA) *M Johnston* 91
2 b c Kingmambo(USA) —Ring Of Music (Sadler's Wells (USA))
(4110) 4694[4] (5217) 5795[10]

Camp Attack *S Dow* a57 57
4 b g Fleetwood(IRE) —Queen Of Tides (IRE) (Soviet Star (USA))
191[3] 315[8] 1025[10] 1319[7]

Campbells Lad *Mrs G S Rees* a60 62
6 b g Mind Games—T O O Mamma'S (IRE) (Classic Secret (USA))
936[5] 1907[9] (3638) 4003[4] 4249[3] *4670[5]*

Campbeltown (IRE) *A B Haynes* a55 83
4 b g Mull Of Kintyre(USA) —Jallaissine (IRE) (College Chapel)
366[3] 549[12] 613[9] 1431[8] 1899[11] 2273[9] *6542[11] 7094[11]*

Camp Counsellor *M J Gingell* a62 41
3 b g Royal Applause—Rash (Pursuit Of Love)
418[8] 484[9] 553[4] 2223[8] 2454[6] 3394[6] 4292[5] 4859[8]

Campeon (IRE) *J M Bradley* a68 57
5 b g Monashee Mountain(USA) —Arcticlead (USA) (Arctic Tern (USA))
287[8] 2104[11] 2555[9] 2652[11] 5276[5] 5349[10] 5866[11]

Campfire Glow (IRE) *D K Weld* 101
2 bb f Invincible Spirit(IRE) —Ski Lodge (IRE) (Persian Bold)
(4440a) 5395a[5]

Campli (IRE) *Micky Hammond* 68
5 b g Zafonic(USA) —Sept A Neuf (Be My Guest (USA))
1044[2] 1849[3] 2253[12] 4248[5] 4969[3] 5257[11] 5968[3]

Campo Bueno (FR) *A Berry* a54 88
5 b g Septieme Ciel(USA) —Herba Buena (FR) (Fabulous Dancer (USA))
953[11] 1619[10] 2528[13] 2871[4] 3201[3] 3401[11] 3572[10] 3754[9] 4006[8] 5556[13] 5934[8] 6467[19] 6732[3] *7025[8]*

Camps Bay (USA) *Mrs A J Perrett* 98
3 b c Cozzene(USA) —Seewillo (USA) (Pleasant Colony (USA))
(1974) 2627[3] (3590) 4059[2] 4749[9] 5574[5]

Camrose *J L Dunlop* 105
6 ch g Zafonic(USA) —Tularosa (In The Wings)
1304[3] 1805[2] 2907[7] 4117[8] 4588[2] 5411[3]

Canadian Danehill (IRE) *R M H Cowell* a93 98
5 b g Indian Danehill(IRE) —San Jovita (CAN) (St Jovite (USA))
97[2] (251) (318) (368) 513[3] (727) 810[4] 1292[8] *1754[2]* 1941[6] 2529[5] *3108[3]* 3179[5] 3749[3] 4095[21] 4780[3] (5009) 5379[3] (5513) 6036a[6]

Canary Girl *Mrs C A Dunnett* a40 41
4 br m Primo Valentino(IRE) —Cumbrian Concerto (Petong)
978[7] 1267[5] 3163[11] 4164[8] 4336[17]

Can Can Star *A W Carroll* a71 79
4 br h Lend A Hand—Carrie Can Can (Green Tune (USA))
84[2] (204) 445[2] 1002[2] (1295) 1922[4] 2106[9] 3386[2] 3844[4] 4419[8] 5432[2] 5774[2]

Candarli (IRE) *D R Gandolfo* a62 40
11 ch g Polish Precedent(USA) —Calounia (IRE) (Pharly (FR))
39[5] 4670[3]

Candela Bay (IRE) *W J Haggas* 72
2 b f Captain Rio—Incendio (Siberian Express (USA))
(5558) 6128[14]

Candida's Beau *R M Beckett* a78
2 b g Bertolini(USA) —Breezy Louise (Dilum (USA))
5895[8] 6714[3]

Candidato Roy (ARG) *W J Haggas* a71 116
6 ch g Roy(USA) —Candila (ARG) (Mariache (ARG))
4907[2] (5797) 6332[7]

Candle *H Candy* a81 91
4 br m Dansili—Celia Brady (Last Tycoon (IRE))
1783[3] 3844[3] 4572[3] (5940)

Candle Sahara (IRE) *M R Channon* 80
2 b f Noverre(USA) —Staylily (IRE) (Grand Lodge (USA))
3233[4] 4061[3] 4422[4] 5110[4]

Candy Anchor (FR) *R E Peacock* a44
8 b m Slip Anchor—Kandavu (Safawan)
7100 7274[6]

Candy Critic (ARG) *M F De Kock* 107
5 ch m Candy Stripes(USA) —Tough Dancer (ARG) (Tough Critic (USA))
401a[6] 475a[3] 648a[2] 4366[6]

Candyland (IRE) *M Quinn* a56 62
3 b f Bubble Gum Fellow(JPN) —Capoeira (USA) (Nureyev (USA))
54[6] 219[4] 404[3] 577[3] 974[2] 4513[4] 4918[8] (5511)

Candy Mountain *L M Cumani* a83 80
3 ch f Selkirk(USA) —Valthea (FR) (Antheus (USA))
1560[4] 2253[3] 2944[6] 4205[2] 4766[12] (5636) 5943[2] 6474[5] 6822[3]

Canina *Paul Green* a54 49
4 b m Foxhound(USA) —Fizzy Fiona (Efisio)
66[9] 2527[8] 3064[10] 6064[4] 6563[3] 6625[4] 6818[11] 6887[2] 7003[9]

Cankara (IRE) *D Carroll* a57
4 b m Daggers Drawn(USA) —Suddenly (Puissance)
383[7] (518) 741[12]

Cannonball (USA) *W Ward* a61 104
2 bb g Catienus(USA) —No Deadline (USA) (Skywalker (USA))
6484a[3]

Canongate *R Gibson* a84 89
3 gr c Highest Honor(FR) —Tremiere (FR) (Anabaa (USA))
2788[9]

Cantabilly (IRE) *R J Hodges* a88 79
4 b g Distant Music(USA) —Cantaloupe (Priolo (USA))
1003[2] 1253[4] 5924[9]

Cantique (IRE) *R J Price* a61 57
3 b f Danetime(IRE) —Bethania (Mark Of Esteem (IRE))
90[2] 1215[7] 1561[8] 1782[5] 2196[8] 2362[14] 2800[5] 2978[6] 3274[7] 3795[6] 4109[8] 7103[7] 7218[8] 7274[10]

Capable Guest (IRE) *M R Channon* a94 101
5 bb g Cape Cross(IRE) —Alexander Confranc (IRE) (Magical Wonder (USA))
576[5] 848[14] 993[10] (1307) 1651[12] 2755[16] 5031[6] 5419[8] 5833[13] 6011[13] 6301[3] 6654[3] 6852[5]

Capall An Ibre (IRE) *Edward Lynam* a78 74
2 b f Traditionally(USA) —Lidanna (Nicholas (USA))
5435a[7]

Capania (IRE) *Pat Eddery* a61 57
3 br f Cape Cross(IRE) —Gentle Papoose (Commanche Run)
4905[3] 5315[6] 6579[4] 7057[3]

Cape *P Howling* 92
4 b m Cape Cross(IRE) —Rubbiyati (Cadeaux Genereux)
2440[6] 2688[5] 3746[8] 5809[4] 6205[11] 6300[4]

Cape Amber (IRE) *P W Chapple-Hyam* 85
2 b f Cape Cross(IRE) —Maramba (Rainbow Quest (USA))
(4402)

Cape Cobra *J H M Gosden* a59 69
3 ch g Inchinor—Cape Merino (Clantime)
2059[4] 2541[2] 6176[3] (6309)

Cape Colony *R Hannon* 57
2 gr c Cape Town(IRE) —Lucky Princess (Bijou D'Inde)
5417[8]

Cape Dancer (IRE) *J S Wainwright* a28 63
3 b f Cape Cross(IRE) —Yankee Dancer (Groom Dancer (USA))
1482[6] 1916[8] 2796[6] 3540P 5299[13] 6309[7] 6537[12] 7209[10]

Cape Diamond (IRE) *W R Swinburn* a82 74
4 b g Cape Cross(IRE) —Jemalina (USA) (Trempolino (USA))
4266[2] 4667[3]

Capefly *P F I Cole* a57 70
2 b f Cape Cross(IRE) —Patacake Patacake (USA) (Bahri (USA))
5309[7] 5713[3] 6419[3] 6729[2]

Cape Greko *B G Powell* a92 89
5 ro g Loup Sauvage(USA) —Onefortheditch (USA) (With Approval (CAN))
56[5] 351[9] 1308[6] 1922[8] 2218[5] 5769[3]

Cape Hawk (IRE) *R Hannon* a91 83
3 b g Cape Cross(IRE) —Hawksbill Special (IRE) (Taufan (USA))
1522[2] 1839[2] (2354) 3553[4] (4276) 5221[4]

Cape Martin (IRE) *V Valiani* 76
5 b h Polish Precedent(USA) —Clara House (Shirley Heights)
6863a[9]

Cape Of Luck (IRE) *P M Phelan* a87 96
4 b g Cape Cross(IRE) —Fledgling (Efisio)
2239[2] 3527[6] 4377[7] 4601[6] 4949[7] 5413[6] 5712[8] 5923[7] 6273[5] 6996[8] 7253[9]

Cape Of Storms *R Brotherton* a60 60
4 b g Cape Cross(IRE) —Lloc (Absalom)
123[5] 217[7] 266[5] 742[2] 1206[15] 1435[6] 3241[9] 5915[14] 6877[5] 7239[2]

Cape Presto (IRE) *Mrs C A Dunnett* a79 78
4 b h Cape Cross(IRE) —Samhat Mtoto (Mtoto)
810[7] 1283[4] 1545[3] 1678[5] (Dead)

Cape Rock *C A Horgan* a64 51
2 b g Cape Cross(IRE) —Wildwood Flower (Distant Relative)
5628[9] 5919[11] 6436[5]

Cape Royal *J M Bradley* a94 102
7 b g Prince Sabo—Indigo (Primo Dominie)
927[6] 1088[2] (1242) 1601[12] 1788[13] 1853[5] 2234[16] 3268[4] 3526[5] 3990[8] 4386[2] 4696[7] 5212[10] 5305[5] 5689[2] 6197[11] 6487[7]

Cape Secret (IRE) *R M Beckett* a70 93
4 b g Cape Cross(IRE) —Baylands Sunshine (IRE) (Classic Secret (USA))
(1506) 2236[10] 3090[10] 4047[10] 4398[2] 5215[5] 6230[6]

Cape Sydney (IRE) *D W Barker* a31 47
4 b m Cape Cross(IRE) —Lady At War (Warning)
557[11] 812[8] 912[13] 1426[2]

Cape Thea *Mark Gillard* a64 53
3 b f Cape Cross(IRE) —Pasithea (IRE) (Celtic Swing)
1068[8] 1633[5] 7006[11] 7164[12]

Cape Vale (IRE) *D Nicholls* 83
2 b c Cape Cross(IRE) —Wolf Cleugh (IRE) (Last Tycoon (IRE))
(4782) (5582)

Cape Velvet (IRE) *J W Hills* a72 78
3 b f Cape Cross(IRE) —Material Lady (IRE) (Barathea (IRE))
996[4] 1961[2] 2541[7] 2998[5] 4060[8] 4828[3] 5367[2] 5645[8] 6199[6]

Capistrano *Mrs P Sly* a73 76
4 b g Efisio—Washita (Valiyar)
726[6] 921[7] 1083[6] 3828[13] 4107[10] 4272[10]

Capital Exposure (USA) *D K Weld* 103
3 b c Danzig(USA) —Suitably Discreet (USA) (Mr Prospector (USA))
2066a[7]

Capitalise (IRE) *V Smith* a64 64
4 b g City On A Hill(USA) —Prime Interest (IRE) (Kings Lake (USA))
578[8] 618[2] 677[3] 994[4] 5820[3] 5948[3] 6383[2] 7285[3]

Capital Lass *A J McCabe* a64 53
4 bb m Forzando—Fair Test (Fair Season)
(61) 150[3] 238[4] 374[7] 479[10] 579[9] 686[11] 932[5] 1265[9] 1379[12] 1569[10] 7124[6]

Capitana (GER) *N J Henderson* 81
6 ch m Lando(GER) —Capitolina (FR) (Empery (USA))
5210[8] 5594[6]

Capone (IRE) *S Parr* a64 69
2 b c Daggers Drawn(USA) —Order Of The Day (USA) (Dayjur (USA))
5903[6] 6281[4] 6761[3]

Cappanrush (IRE) *A Ennis* a41
7 gr g Medaaly—Introvert (USA) (Exbourne (USA))
458[11]

Capping (IRE) *W R Swinburn* a54 47
3 ch c Rahy(USA) —Hawksleys Jill (Mujtahid (USA))
1904[11] 2175[7] 2542[7] 3066[10] 4529[13]

Capriccioso *G L Moore* a38
2 b f Cape Cross(IRE) —Heart Of India (IRE) (Try My Best (USA))
7190[8]

Caprice (GER) *A De Royer-Dupre* 96
4 b m Monsun(GER) —Catella (GER) (Generous (IRE))
6941a[0]

Capricho (IRE) *J Akehurst* a71 74
10 gr g Lake Coniston(IRE) —Star Spectacle (Spectacular Bid (USA))
902[5] 1118[2] 1446[8] 1984[4] 2626[5] 3191[7] 3682[5] 4395[14] 4606[14] 4853[11] 6239[3]

Capricorn Red *R Hollinshead*
7 ch m Rashik—Bella Maggio (Rakaposhi King)
7174[10]

Capricorn Run (USA) *A J McCabe* a111 96
4 bb g Elusive Quality(USA) —Cercida (USA) (Copelan (USA))
1179[7] 1915[9] 2882[5] 3108[4] 3525[7] (5119) 5356[19] (5638) 6013[14] 6142[2] (6437) (6606) 6852[10] (6932) 7184[7]

Caprima (IRE) *M Brittain* a3 46
2 ch f Captain Rio—Titchwell Lass (Lead On Time (USA))
1285[13] 1772[9] 2934[5] 4173[10] 4349[6] 5484[9]

Caprio (IRE) *R Charlton* a68 56
2 ch c Captain Rio—Disarm (IRE) (Bahamian Bounty)
5872[7] 6237[5] 6595[6] (6881) (6966)

Cap St Jean (IRE) *R Hollinshead* a63 59
3 b g Cape Cross(IRE) —Karminiya (IRE) (Primo Dominie)
60[4] 375[4] 449[10] 894[13] 2248[2] 2796[9] 4073[5] 4354[3] 5299[3] 6026[2] 6387[3] 6567[3]

Captain Bolsh *J Pearce* a52 58
4 b g Tagula(IRE) —Bolshoi Star (Soviet Star (USA))
133[7] 179[4] 279[7] 372[10] 666[3] 721[11] 1271[4]

Captain Brilliance (USA) *J Noseda* 83
2 ch c Officer(USA) —Bloomin Genius (USA) (Beau Genius (CAN))
3462[2] (4132)

Captain Cole (IRE) *Peter Casey* 66
4 b g Soviet Star(USA) —Sylvella (Lear Fan (USA))
873a[12]

Captain Crooner (IRE) *D Shaw* a48 18
2 ch g Captain Rio—Kurfuffle (Bluebird (USA))
5176[8] 5363[8] 6104[8] 6624[10] 6722[17] (7195) 7260[7]

Captain Darling (IRE) *R W Price* a72 46
7 b g Pennekamp(USA) —Gale Warning (IRE) (Last Tycoon (IRE))
2990[13] 6268[12]

Captain Dunne (IRE) *T D Easterby* 72
2 b g Captain Rio—Queen Bodicea (IRE) (Revoque (IRE))
1792[7] (1993) 3157[4] 3562[3]

Captain Esteem *B W Hills* a71 72
2 b g Mark Of Esteem(IRE) —Daring Destiny (Daring March)
2215[4] 2596[6] 2949[4] 5314[13] 5705[6]

Captain General *J A R Toller* a79 72
5 br h In The Wings—Sea Quest (IRE) (Rainbow Quest (USA))
1591[5] 1949[7] 4917[4] 5500[12] 6144[11]

Captain Gerrard (IRE) *B Smart* 110
2 b c Oasis Dream—Delphinus (Soviet Star (USA))
1792[6] 2024[2] 2451[3] (3077) (3492) 4046[3] (4724) 5377[4] (5583) (6167)

Captain Hurricane *B J Meehan* a92 89
5 b g Desert Style(IRE) —Ravine (Indian Ridge)
1448[10] 1836[10] 2440[13] 3911[11] 4122[14] 4389[8] 5044[7] (Dead)

Captain Jack Black *M R Bosley* 17
2 br c Superior Premium—La Volta (Komaite (USA))
2510[13] 3669[6] 4755[13]

Captain Jacksparra (IRE) *K A Ryan* a84 91
3 b c Danehill(USA) —Push A Venture (Shirley Heights)
510[2] (670) (815) 1228[2] 1535[2] 1851[2] 2213[8] 3503[14] 3944[5] (5092)

Captain Kir (IRE) *B De Haan* a64 30
2 ch c Captain Rio—A Lot Of Kir (IRE) (Selkirk (USA))
4160[3] 4629[13]

Captain Macarry (IRE) *B Smart* 73
2 ch c Captain Rio—Grannys Reluctance (IRE) (Anita's Prince)
4636[6] (5143) 5410[9] 6017[20]

Captain Mainwaring *N P Littmoden* 59
2 b g Auction House(USA) —Shalyah (IRE) (Shalford (IRE))
5344[12] 5599[13] 6285[4]

Captain Marryat *J Akehurst* a47
6 ch g Inchinor—Finlaggan (Be My Chief (USA))
2332[11] 2875[8] 3397[11] 4535P

Captain Marvelous (IRE) *B W Hills* 116
3 b c Invincible Spirit(IRE) —Shesasmartlady (IRE) (Dolphin Street (FR))
1147[6] 5409[6] 5832[15] 6332[8]

Captain Nemo (USA) *T D Barron* 65
3 b g Officer(USA) —Macarena Macarena (CAN) (Gone West (USA))
3411[11] 4842[13] 5286[12] 5487[13] 5622[9]

Captain Oats (IRE) *Mrs P Ford* a54 54
4 b g Bahhare(USA) —Adarika (Kings Lake (USA))
110[10] 4660[3]

Captain Royale (IRE) *J Noseda* a61 88
2 ch c Captain Rio—Paix Royale (Royal Academy (USA))
2353[6] (2803) 4437a[6] 4762[12] 6486[10]

Captain Turbot (IRE) *D W Barker* 37
2 ch g Captain Rio—Kiriwas (ITY) (Alwasmi (USA))
4636[8] 5252[10] 5772[11] 6072[8]

Captain Webb *M Johnston* 73
2 br c Storming Home—Criquette (Shirley Heights)
(6274)

Capt Chaos (IRE) *Edward Lynam* 100
2 b c Captain Rio—Blusienka (IRE) (Blues Traveller (IRE))
5456a[8] 5845a[7] 6549a[7]

Captivate *A J McCabe* a53 49
4 ch m Hernando(FR) —Catch (USA) (Blushing Groom (FR))
16[9] 71[4] 215[8]

Caracciola (GER) *N J Henderson* 108
10 b g Lando(GER) —Capitolina (FR) (Empery (USA))
3153[3] 4375[2] (5446) 6335[2]

Caradak (IRE) *Saeed Bin Suroor* 118
6 b h Desert Style(IRE) —Caraiyma (IRE) (Shahrastani (USA))
4600[10] 5265a[4] 6018[3] 6655[5]

Caradoc Place *M P Tregoning* 67
2 b g Compton Place—Queen Linear (USA) (Polish Navy (USA))
3233[8] 3592[4] 4014[4] 5452[8] 5939[5] 6282[6]

Caraman (IRE) *J J Quinn* a73 69
9 ch g Grand Lodge(USA) —Caraiyma (IRE) (Shahrastani (USA))
297[6] 515[11] 4003[7]

Caravel (IRE) *Sir Mark Prescott* a54 98
3 ch g Medicean—Caraiyma (IRE) (Shahrastani (USA))
3062[9] 3276[11] 3447[6] 3997[2] (4270) (4354) (4847) (5156) (5696a)

Carcinetto (IRE) *P D Evans* a90 73
5 b m Danetime(IRE) —Dolphin Stamp (IRE) (Dolphin Street (FR))
50[8] 131[3] 367[4] (485) 516[9] 673[4] (1064) 1309[3] 1507[6] 1564[2] 2197[3] 2472[3] 2655[11] 5177[3] (5648) (6313) 6667[5] (6907) 6981[3] 7184[2]

Cardington Queen *M Mullineaux* a29 17
3 b f Cois Na Tine(IRE) —Bold Feliciter (Bold Arrangement)
2261[13] 2580[8] 2740[11] 4291[10] 4491[8] 4989[7]

Careenya (IRE) *R M Beckett* 29
2 b f Captain Rio—Carallia (IRE) (Common Grounds)
3364[5] 4311[7]

Carefree *G A Swinbank* a58
3 b f Medicean—Hertha (Hernando (FR))
(11) 469[13] (577) 6463[14]

Carefree Flapper *G A Swinbank* a42 52
3 ch f Generous(IRE) —Roaring Twenties (Halling (USA))
1348[6] 1746[5]

Careless Freedom *B J Meehan* 54
2 ch f Bertolini(USA) —Humble Pie (Known Fact (USA))
6419[11]

Caribana *M A Jarvis* a66
2 ch f Hernando(FR) —Carenage (IRE) (Alzao (USA))
6934[4] 7208[3]

Caribbean Coral *J J Quinn* 99
8 ch g Brief Truce(USA) —Caribbean Star (Soviet Star (USA))
1088[12] (1601) 2234[3] 3050[3] 3586[12] 4227[3] 4567[9] 5584[9] 5809[9] 6327[12] 6487[16]

Caribbean Cruiser *Garry Moss* 55
2 b g Diktat—Caribbean Star (Soviet Star (USA))
2819[7] 3341[5] 3951[15] 4328[12] 5902[9] 6329[10]

Carillon (IRE) *Doug Watson* a75 73
3 ch f Desert Prince(IRE) —Steeple (Selkirk (USA))
476a[6] 647a[4]

Carimo (IRE) *J-P Gallorini* 93
3 b c Fasliyev(USA) —Barnabas (ITY) (Slip Anchor)
1005a[4]

Carleton *M R Channon* 94
2 b g Hunting Lion(IRE) —Canadian Capers (Ballacashtal (CAN))
(1721) 2183[7] (2650) 2785[6] 3459[12] 4046[16] 4613[5] 4724[7] 5032[4] 5324[12] 5583[3] 5922[6] 6167[9]

Carlior (FR) *J-C Rouget* a61
2 b c Orpen(USA) —Carlitta (USA) (Olympio (USA))
6879a[4]

Carlitos Spirit (IRE) *B R Millman* a69 63
3 ch g Redback—Negria (IRE) (Al Hareb (USA))
3384[8] 3949[2] 4313[5] 4710[2] 5475[9] 6123[4] 6749[4] (7028) 7113[5]

Carlitos Tevez (IRE) *A & G Botti*
3 b c Lomitas—Enter (ITY) (Exit To Nowhere (USA))
1191a[3]

Carlowsantana (IRE) *Adrian Sexton* a83 85
4 b g Blue Ocean(USA) —Lees First Step (Reprimand)
4433[2] 5788a[3]

Carlton Mac *N Bycroft* 49
2 ch g Timeless Times(USA) —Julie's Gift (Presidium)
1859[10] 3760[11] 4077[12] 4405[6] 4770[13] 5520[9] 6307[7] 6698[9]

Carlton Scroop (FR) *J Jay* a69 64
4 ch g Priolo(USA) —Elms Schooldays (Emarati (USA))
(767) 1042[6] 1342[2] 1451[6] 1730[4] 2332[9] 5204[4] 5453[4] 6697[7]

Carmela Maria *C F Wall* 58
2 b f Medicean—Carmela Owen (Owington)
6125[7]

Carmenero (GER) *W R Muir* a81 83
4 b g Barathea(IRE) —Claire Fraser (USA) (Gone West (USA))
1209[3] 1765[7] 2004[12] (2358) 3111[6] 4068[7] 4135[7] 4949[3] 5312[4] 5532[4] 6232[8] 6667[6] 6795[3] 7045[5] 7253[2]

Carmine Rock *R Hollinshead* a47 35
2 ch f Arkadian Hero(USA) —Cloudy Reef (Cragador)
6595[9] 7000[7]

Carniolan *W R Swinburn* 73
2 b g Royal Applause—Dancing Feather (Suave Dancer (USA))
2600[3]

Carnival Dream *R A Harris* a53 65
2 b f Carnival Dancer—Reach The Wind (USA) (Relaunch (USA))
1938[5] 2504[4] 3205[4] 4077[2] 4422[3] 4560[5] 5501[5] 5766[13] 7243[5] 7270[5]

Carnival Queen *J R Fanshawe* 84
2 ch f Carnival Dancer—Irish Light (USA) (Irish River (FR))
3043[4] 4077[3] 5313[5] 6307[2] (6572)

Carnivore *T D Barron* a86 84
5 ch g Zafonic(USA) —Ermine (IRE) (Cadeaux Genereux)
1223[6] 1845[8] (2936) 3943[12] 6209[3] 6435[6] 7165[5]

Carole Os (IRE) *S W Hall* a48 64
2 b f Catcher In The Rye(IRE) —Kuda Chantik (IRE) (Lashkari)
5428[8] 5603[8]

Carolina Belle (USA) *M J Wallace* a74 74
2 bb f Dixie Union(USA) —Stormy Reply (USA) (Storm Cat (USA))
1445[2] 2457[3] (4160) 4724[9]

Carolina Blini *B J Meehan* a64 62
2 b f Bertolini(USA) —Key (Midyan (USA))
1079[5] 1354[10] 1519[3] 2488[4] 2797[2]

Carolines Secret *Mario Hofer* 98
3 ch f Inchinor—Blodwen (USA) (Mister Baileys)
2384a[7] 3075a[4] 6220a[2] 6953a[10]

Caro Mio (IRE) *R Charlton* 10
3 b f Danehill Dancer(IRE) —Our Hope (Dancing Brave (USA))
1128[16]

Carpet Ride *C W J Farrell* a61 52
5 ch g Unfuwain(USA) —Fragrant Oasis (USA) (Rahy (USA))
4142a[7]

Carr Hall (IRE) *Mrs J L Le Brocq* a63 58
4 b g Rossini(USA) —Pidgeon Bay (IRE) (Perugino (USA))
5647[3]

Carribean Sunset (IRE) *D K Weld* 92
2 b f Danehill Dancer(IRE) —Bonheur (IRE) (Royal Academy (USA))
5395a[3] 5843a[4]

Carrickmacross (IRE) *E S McMahon* a62 73
2 b c Mull Of Kintyre(USA) —Lady Corduff (IRE) (Titus Livius (FR))
1713[3] 1975[2] 2949[5] 3680[4] 4349[5] (5089) (5932)

Carrie McCurry (IRE) *Patrick Martin* a74 64
3 b f Fath(USA) —Simply Devious (IRE) (Dr Devious (IRE))
301[5]

Carry On Cleo *P D Evans* a60 53
2 ch f First Trump—Classy Cleo (IRE) (Mujadil (USA))
2392[3] 2797[8] 3596[7] 4453[11] 5015[7] 5644[6] 6566[3] 6776[3] 6865[6] 6928[7] (7101) 7156[3] (7259)

Carson's Spirit (USA) *W S Kittow* a73 81
3 ch g Carson City(USA) —Pascarina (FR) (Exit To Nowhere (USA))
1230[5] 1563[4] 1920[11]

Carta Canta (IRE) *M Gasparini* 67
4 ch m Dockside(USA) —Crudelia (IRE) (Great Commotion (USA))
6688a[11]

Cartimandua *E S McMahon* 111
3 b f Medicean—Agrippina (Timeless Times (USA))
1146[11] 1496[11] (1973) (2450)

Carus (GER) *D K Richardson* 102
8 br h Taishan(GER) —Contessina (FR) (Mistigri)
1689a[11] 2409a[5] 2976a[2] 4957a[8]

Casablanca Minx (IRE) *P D Evans* a76 60
4 br m Desert Story(IRE) —Conspire (IRE) (Turtle Island (IRE))
205[8] 314[7] 380[2] 568[8] 634[5] 825[5] 1038[7] 1311[4] 1562[11] 2603[7] 3156[3] 3286[2] 3826[4] (4023) 4259[10] 4433[6] (4978) 5020[2] 5237[3] 5569[4] 5985[7] 6343[3] 6504[3] 6573[2] 6696[4] 6774[4] 6951[13] 7131[3] 7146[3] 7214[2] 7274[3]

Casa Catalina (IRE) *M Johnston* a44 80
2 b f King's Best(USA) —Ruacana Falls (USA) (Storm Bird (CAN))
3850[9] (4448) 5395a[18]

Casa Mia (IRE) *R A Fahey* a9 51
2 b f Frenchmans Bay(FR) —Isla Bonita (Kings Lake (USA))
5501[6] 6242[11]

Cashel Mead *J L Spearing* a86 94
7 b m Bishop Of Cashel—Island Mead (Pharly (FR))
1363[7] 1630[8] 1854[3] 2694[8] 3080[7] (3268) 3586[8] 5666[9] *5891[10]* 6205[15]

Cashema (IRE) *James Moffatt* 33
6 b m Cape Cross(IRE) —Miss Shema (USA) (Gulch (USA))
1527[5] 1744[10]

Cashmere Jack *K G Reveley*
2 b g Daylami(IRE) —Cashmere (Barathea (IRE))
6255[12]

Cash On (IRE) *Karen George* a67 65
5 ch g Spectrum(IRE) —Lady Lucre (IRE) (Last Tycoon (IRE))
5500[9]

Casiluca (ITY) *M Marcialis*
2 b f Daro Sopran(GER) —Sopran Newar (Warning)
1485a[6]

Casino Night *J R Weymes* a66 63
2 ch f Night Shift(USA) —Come Fly With Me (Bluebird (USA))
2562[4] *3171[3]* 3471[5] 4278[6] (4770) 4991[7] 5471[6] 5624[5] 5837[7]

Casla Beag (IRE) *B Palling* 57
2 b f Acclamation—Carna (IRE) (Anita's Prince)
2103[4] 2651[10] 6104[4]

Caspian Rose *M J Attwater* a35 31
4 b m Paris House—Caspian Morn (Lugana Beach)
222[6] *321[6]* *435[10]*

Cassablanca *M L W Bell* 88
2 b f Royal Applause—Ravine (Indian Ridge)
5598[7] 6336[9]

Cassiara *J Pearce* a74 80
3 gr f Diktat—Heaven-Liegh-Grey (Grey Desire)
1105[2] *1386[2]* 1961[6] 2369[3] 3247[5] 3607[2] 3992[4] 4338[4] 4785[3] 5013[3] 5488[2] 5625[2] 5873[4]

Cassie's Choice (IRE) *B Smart* 68
3 b f Fath(USA) —Esteraad (IRE) (Cadeaux Genereux)
2534[4] 2988[11] 3413[3] 4658[3] 4934[7]

Castano *B R Millman* a51 74
3 br g Makbul—Royal Orchid (IRE) (Shalford (IRE))
798[5] 2366[2] 2631[5] (3046) 3688[9] 4186[10] 5473[7] 6083[4]

Castara Bay *R Hannon* a82 76
3 b c Sakhee(USA) —Mayaro Bay (Robellino (USA))
1358[4] 2625[2] 2944[2] 3689[11] 4541[7] 4960[8] (5472) 5921[3] *6121[8]*

Castellina *J-C Rouget* a105 92
3 ch f Medicean—Protectorate (Hector Protector (USA))
6889a[5]

Cast In Gold (USA) *B J Meehan* a84 91
3 b f Elusive Quality(USA) —Crystal Crossing (IRE) (Royal Academy (USA))
1146[4] 1809[5]

Castlebury (IRE) *G A Swinbank* 3
2 b g Spartacus(IRE) —La Vie En Rouge (IRE) (College Chapel)
3718[16]

Castle Durrow (IRE) *Seamus Fahey* a54 7
3 b f Strike Out(IRE) —Marylin Park (IRE) (Kendor (FR))
149[7] *478[5]* *678[9]*

Castle Heights (CAN) *M Mesic* 83
6 b g Cobra King(USA) —Texas Approved (USA) (With Approval (CAN))
6375a[8]

Castle Howard (IRE) *W J Musson* 99
5 b g Montjeu(IRE) —Termania (IRE) (Shirley Heights)
2002[2] (3105) 4047[11] 4722[7] 5375[6] 5800[8] 6169[11]

Castlereagh (UAE) *A Fabre* 110
3 b c Machiavellian(USA) —Spring Oak (Mark Of Esteem (IRE))
2293a[5]

Castles In The Air *Pat Eddery* a72 72
2 b c Oasis Dream—Dance Parade (USA) (Gone West (USA))
3233[5] 3747[11] 5745[4] *6588[2]*

Casual Affair *J D Bethell* a67 71
4 b g Golden Snake(USA) —Fontaine Lady (Millfontaine)
1673[2] 4105[3] 4493[4] (5257) 5486[5] 6186[2] 6473[11]

Casual Garcia *Sir Mark Prescott* a37 32
2 gr g Hernando(FR) —Frosty Welcome (USA) (With Approval (CAN))
5470[14] *5680[10]* 6285[9] 6592[10] *6776[7]*

Cat Belling (IRE) *R Bouresly* a79 86
7 br m Catrail(USA) —Lute And Lyre (IRE) (The Noble Player (USA))
174a[4] 247a[10] *327a[9]* 397a[10]

Catch Me (GER) *E J O'Grady* 84
5 br g Law Society(USA) —Calcida (GER) (Konigsstuhl (GER))
6367a[7]

Cat De Mille (USA) *P W Chapple-Hyam* 79
3 bb c Stormin Fever(USA) —De Mille (USA) (Nureyev (USA))
1851[6] 2633[8] 2881[10] 4287[3] 4735[2] 6132[9]

Categorical *K G Reveley* a69 78
4 b g Diktat—Zibet (Kris)
1890[4] 5486[4] 6308[6]

Caterina Ballerina (USA) *K A Ryan* a52
3 b f Catienus(USA) —La Serina (IRE) (Royal Academy (USA))
498[9] *906[3]*

Cate Washington *Mrs L Williamson* a14 47
4 b m Superior Premium—Willisa (Polar Falcon (USA))
33[12]

Cathedral Walk (USA) *K R Burke* 65
2 ch c Johannesburg(USA) —Hilarity (USA) (Kingmambo (USA))
3582[3] 5903[11]

Catherine Palace *E A L Dunlop* a56 56
3 b f Grand Lodge(USA) —Tereshkova (USA) (Mr Prospector (USA))
1988[6] 2359[9] *2766[8]*

Catherines Cafe (IRE) *A C Whillans* a58 67
4 b m Mull Of Kintyre(USA) —Wisecrack (IRE) (Lucky Guest)
1378[7] 2302[4] 2714[2] (2938) 3343[5] 6304[13] 6638[5]

Cativo Cavallino *J E Long* a84 76
4 ch g Bertolini(USA) —Sea Isle (Selkirk (USA))
(548) (687) (1118) 4165[4] (4594) *5312[5]* 5722[12] *(6122) 6667[4]*

Cat Junior (USA) *B J Meehan* 84
2 bb c Storm Cat(USA) —Luna Wells (IRE) (Sadler's Wells (USA))
(4201)

Catlivius (IRE) *K A Ryan* a59 61
3 ch f Titus Livius(FR) —Cat's Tale (IRE) (Catrail (USA))
40[7]

Cato Major (USA) *J Kimmel* 89
2 br f E Dubai(USA) —Love To Fight (CAN) (Fit To Fight (USA))
6482a[8]

Cat Shaker (USA) *C Callis* a84
5 br h Catienus(USA) —Diamonds N Pearls (USA) (Black Tie Affair)
5827a[4]

Cat Six (USA) *T Wall* a58 64
3 b f Tale Of The Cat(USA) —Hurricane Warning (USA) (Thunder Gulch (USA))
1639[8] 1988[5] 2413[5] *2801[10]* *3393[3]* 4129[5] 4257[9] 4632[8] 5188[12] 6109[9] *6506[9]* *6766[6]*

Catskill *Adrian McGuinness* a40 77
5 ch g Inchinor—Manhattan Sunset (USA) (El Gran Senor (USA))
4114a[10]

Catspraddle (USA) *R Hannon* a64 74
4 ch m High Yield(USA) —Beaux Dorothy (USA) (Dehere (USA))
555[3]

Cat Whistle *R A Fahey* 79
2 b f Dansili—Mighty Flyer (IRE) (Mujtahid (USA))
2039[4] 2710[3] 3747[5] (4406) 5974[11]

Caucasienne (FR) *J W Hills* a71 80
4 b m Galileo(IRE) —Carousel Girl (USA) (Gulch (USA))
(458) 578[6] 1216[3] (1741) 1884[3] 2082[4]

Caudillo (GER) *Dr A Bolte* 99
4 b h Acatenango(GER) —Corsita (Top Ville)
2409a[4] 4218a[2]

Caught In Paradise (IRE) *A B Haynes* 59
2 b c Catcher In The Rye(IRE) —Paradis (Bijou D'Inde)
1857[5] 2028[2] (2392) 3174[5] (3626) 4255[9] 4311[9] 4824[9]

Caught You Looking *W R Swinburn* a65 57
3 b f Observatory(USA) —Corndavon (USA) (Sheikh Albadou)
2878[5]

Caustic Wit (IRE) *M S Saunders* a68 81
9 b g Cadeaux Genereux—Baldemosa (FR) (Lead On Time (USA))
50[2] *132[6]* *467[4]* *654[6]* *724[12]* 1212[13] (2879) *3064[2]* 3368[2] (3449) 3594[4] *3852[3]* 3906[4] 4396[3] 4634[3] 4767[7] 5160[7] *5731[5]* 5942[2] 6239[13]

Cavalli (FR) *Dagmar Geissmann*
4 ch g Volochine(IRE) —Halle Aux Grains (IRE) (Shardari)
494a[11]

Cavallini (USA) *G L Moore* a77 84
5 bb g Bianconi(USA) —Taylor Park (USA) (Sir Gaylord)
844[8] *1591[2]* 2474[5] 3385[9] 3858[3] *5225[10]* 6200[7]

Cavallo Di Ferro (IRE) *M J Gingell* a63 57
3 b g Iron Mask(USA) —Lacinia (Groom Dancer (USA))
591[10] *694[10]* *937[6]* 1238[7] *(2178)* *3456[6]* *7023[9]* *7277[8]*

Cavalry Guard (USA) *J R Boyle* a63 78
3 ch g Officer(USA) —Leeward City (USA) (Carson City (USA))
1259[5] 1634[2] 2059[6] *7253[13]*

Cavalry Twill (IRE) *P F I Cole* a70 69
3 b g Alhaarth(IRE) —Blue Mantle (IRE) (Barathea (IRE))
1062[9] 1810[7] 2185[9] 2602[12] 4172[5] 5068[6] *5342[5]* 5955[6] *6481[3]*

Cavendish *J M P Eustace* a65 65
3 b g Pursuit Of Love—Bathwick Babe (IRE) (Sri Pekan (USA))
936[3] *1361[4]* 1917[10] *2520[5]* (3035) 3150[4] *3624[3]* 3876[6] *6387[5]* *6902[6]*

Caviar Heights (IRE) *Miss L A Perratt* 52
3 b g Golan(IRE) —Caviar Queen (USA) (Crafty Prospector (USA))
1303[13] 1491[6] 2453[4] 3183[11] 3587[6] 4424[8] 4936[2] 5040[5] 6464[5]

Cav Okay (IRE) *R Hannon* a82 96
3 gr g Fasliyev(USA) —Dane's Lane (IRE) (Danehill (USA))
841[4] 1502[6] *2352[10]* 6197[13] *6668[10]*

Cavort (IRE) *Pat Eddery* a73 76
3 ch f Vettori(IRE) —Face The Storm (IRE) (Barathea (IRE))
725[11] 1407[9] *(1731)* *2150[6]* 2691[2] *3731[8]* 4205[11] 4828[8] *5424[12]*

Cayman Breeze *J M Bradley* a60 59
7 b g Danzig(USA) —Lady Thynn (FR) (Crystal Glitters (USA))
50[7] *161[7]* *339[5]* 2576[7] 5190[13] 5864[10] *6891[7]* *6927[8]* *7192[9]*

Cayman Calypso (IRE) *Mrs P Sly* a45
6 ro g Danehill Dancer(IRE) —Warthill Whispers (Grey Desire)
7012[6]

Cayman Fox *James Moffatt* 74
2 ch f Cayman Kai(IRE) —Kalarram (Muhtarram (USA))
1043[4] 1285[2] 1848[6] 2451[6] 2717[3] 3492[5] 4098[9]

Cealtra Star (IRE) *K A Ryan* a15 48
2 b f Mujadil(USA) —Haraabah (USA) (Topsider (USA))
4733[7] 6306[9] 6535[13] *6998[11]*

Cearan (CZE) *F Jordan* 13
4 b g Rainbows For Life(CAN) —Ceara (CZE) (Corvaro (USA))
4421[6]

Cecina Marina *C W Thornton* 46
4 b m Sugarfoot—Chasetown Cailin (Suave Dancer (USA))
1045[11] 1995[11] 2792[5] 4449[10] 4521[3] 5158[6] 5698[4] 6308[13]

Cedar Mountain (IRE) *J H M Gosden* a96 96
4 b h Galileo(IRE) —Ventura (IRE) (Spectrum (IRE))
1296[2] *(1566)* *2351[3]* 2859[9] 4166[7]

Cee Bargara *J A Osborne* a91 99
2 b g Acclamation—Balsamita (FR) (Midyan (USA))
898[5] 1107[2] (1411) 2232[9] *(2353)* 2732[6] 3910[3] 4120[9] 4743[19] *5219[9]* 5583[8]

Cefalu (CHI) *Lee Freedman* 106
6 b g Dushyantor(USA) —Cristal (CHI) (Semenenko (USA))
6033a[6]

Ceka Dancer (IRE) *E J O'Neill* a75 71
2 ch f Danehill Dancer(IRE) —Tidal Reach (USA) (Kris S (USA))
4564[5] *5201[2]* 5483[8] *7058[2]* *7145[4]*

Celeberry (IRE) *J G Burns* 82
2 b c Val Royal(FR) —Caeribland (IRE) (Namaqualand (USA))
1706[4]

Celebration Song (IRE) *W R Swinburn* a86 85
4 b g Royal Applause—Googoosh (IRE) (Danehill (USA))
4234[6]

Celebrissime (IRE) *F Head* 74
2 ch c Peintre Celebre(USA) —Ring Beaune (USA) (Bering)
6952a[2]

Celeb Style (IRE) *Paul Green* a37 51
3 b f Tagula(IRE) —Lovely Me (IRE) (Vision (USA))
1620[11] 2894[3] 3537[5] *7137[7]* *7206[10]*

Celestial Halo (IRE) *B W Hills* 115
3 b g Galileo(IRE) —Pay The Bank (High Top)
(1044) 1306[6] 1602[3] 2790[11] 4059[12] 4749[2] 5408[7]

Celestial Sphere (USA) *J H M Gosden* 35
3 b c Dixieland Band(USA) —Skybox (USA) (Spend A Buck (USA))
6238[12]

Celt *L M Cumani* a56 58
2 b c Selkirk(USA) —Puce (Darshaan)
5343[7] *5680[6]*

Celtic Change (IRE) *M Dods* 82
3 br c Celtic Swing—Changi (IRE) (Lear Fan (USA))
1403[5] 1965[6] 2534[2] 2834[2] (3764) 4608[2] 6110[12]

Celtic Charlie (FR) *P M Phelan* a65
2 ch c Until Sundown(USA) —India Regalona (USA) (Dehere (USA))
6791[2] *7070[6]* *7252[6]*

Celtic Dane (IRE) *Kevin Prendergast* a78 103
3 b g Danetime(IRE) —Quelle Celtique (FR) (Tel Quel (FR))
4051a[5] *4867a[9]*

Celtic Dragon *Mrs A J Perrett* a70 73
2 b c Fantastic Light(USA) —Zanzibar (IRE) (In The Wings)
6418[2] 6725[4] *7070[4]*

Celticello (IRE) *Heather Dalton* a26 59
5 bb g Celtic Swing—Viola Royale (IRE) (Royal Academy (USA))
1559[4]

Celtic Empire (IRE) *Jedd O'Keeffe* a42 58
4 b g Second Empire(IRE) —Celtic Guest (IRE) (Be My Guest (USA))
585[7] 1942[10]

Celtic Memories (IRE) *M W Easterby* a16 57
3 ch f Selkirk(USA) —Memories (IRE) (Don't Forget Me)
655[10] 1045[12] *1353[6]* 1917[5] 2552[6] 2793[11] 3040[3] 3156[8]

Celtic Mill *D W Barker* a107 114
9 b g Celtic Swing—Madam Millie (Milford)
245a[4] 409a[3] *474a[6]* 547a[6] *762[8]* 1159[4] 1497[5] 2463[2] 3586[10] (3708) 4090[14] 4746[12]

Celtic Silence *R Bouresly* 85
9 b h Celtic Swing—Smart 'n Noble (USA) (Smarten (USA))
477a[10] 530a[9]

Celtic Slipper (IRE) *R M Beckett* 106
2 b f Anabaa(USA) —Celtic Silhouette (FR) (Celtic Swing)
2457[6] (4094) 4804[2] 5353[3] (6047a) 6222a[5]

Celtic Spa (IRE) *P D Evans* a58 76
5 gr m Celtic Swing—Allegorica (IRE) (Alzao (USA))
3904[6] 3999[10] 4257[2] 4317[4] 4455[6] 4632[2] 4880[5]

Celtic Spirit (IRE) *R M Beckett* a89 96
4 ch g Pivotal—Cavernista (Lion Cavern (USA))
940[4] (3002)

Celtic Step *M Johnston* a81 86
3 br g Selkirk(USA) —Inchiri (Sadler's Wells (USA))
6439[7] 6637[7] *6949[11]* *7236[8]*

Celtic Strand (IRE) *T P Tate* a63 72
2 b g Celtic Swing—Mur Taasha (USA) (Riverman (USA))
1963[4] 2739[4] 4819[6] 5526[2] (6303) *6960[5]*

Celtic Sultan (IRE) *T P Tate* 105
3 b c Celtic Swing—Farjah (IRE) (Charnwood Forest (IRE))
1298[4] 2044[3] 3431[4] 5254[4] 5804[3] (6013) 6491[4]

Celtic Thunder *T J Etherington* a67 64
6 b g Mind Games—Lake Mistassiu (Tina's Pet)
158[2] *(292)* *361[5]* (Dead)

Centenary (IRE) *D E Cantillon* a48 71
3 b g Traditionally(USA) —Catherinofaragon (USA) (Chief's Crown (USA))
931[13] 1530[15] 3161[7] 3997[13] *4064[12]* 4902[2] *5388[8]* *6713[8]* *6835[5]*

Centenerola (USA) *B W Hills* 63
2 b f Century City(IRE) —Lady Angharad (IRE) (Tenby)
6087[11] 6535[5]

Centennial (IRE) *J H M Gosden* 100
2 gr c Dalakhani(IRE) —Lurina (IRE) (Lure (USA))
3625[3] (4586) (5590) 6187a[2]

Central Force *E A L Dunlop* a50 80
3 ch f Pivotal—Lady Joyce (FR) (Galetto (FR))
1522[6] 1785[6] 2360[3] 2727[16] 3451[2] 4112[2] (4365) 4960[4] 6596[7]

Centreboard (USA) *M W Easterby* a26 68
3 rg f Mizzen Mast(USA) —Corsini (Machiavellian (USA))
4606[17] 5139[13] 5507[15] 5834[13] *6582[10]*

Ceol Eile (IRE) *D Haydn Jones* a34 51
4 b m Distant Music(USA) —Strina (IRE) (Indian Ridge)
121[10] 1206[7] 2140[6] 3593[4] 3795[5] *4460[7]*

Ceol Loch Aoidh (IRE) *J S Bolger* 77
2 b f Medecis—Margaree Mary (CAN) (Seeking The Gold (USA))
4832a[7]

Ceprin (IRE) *A & G Botti* 97
6 b h Desert Prince(IRE) —Black Wood (USA) (Woodman (USA))
6687a[6]

Cerbiatta (ITY) *M G Quinlan*
2 b f Kyllachy—Celestina (IRE) (Priolo (USA))
6527a[7]

Cerebus *A J McCabe* a73 65
5 b m Wolfhound(USA) —Bring On The Choir (Chief Singer)
102[7] *296[2]* *(376)* *467[6]* *513[12]* *626[3]* *(681)* *724[7]* 895[9] *1265[5]* *1377[5]* *6625[5]* *(6762)*

Ceredig *Mrs L J Mongan* a64 64
4 b g Lujain(USA) —Anneli Rose (Superlative)
282[2] *421[2]* *511[5]* *588[5]* *688[6]* 1112[5] 1207[6] *1379[9]* 1640[5] 1885[15] 1969[2] 2143[8] *2179[4]* 2561[9] 2622[7] *(2798)* *3067[8]* *3619[8]* 5062[7] *6947[4]* *6956[2]*

Ceremonial Jade (UAE) *M Botti* a105 98
5 b g Jade Robbery(USA) —Talah (Danehill (USA))
487[2] *840[7]* 1041[4] *1448[2]* 2817[7] 4062[11] 4401[2] 5209[3] *6437[3]* *(6851)*

Ceris Star (IRE) *B R Millman* a58 47
3 b g Cadeaux Genereux—Midsummernitedream (GER) (Thatching)
4707[6] 5347[12] *(6311)* *6505[6]* *(6809)* *7003[10]*

Certain Justice (USA) *Stef Liddiard* a82 78
9 gr g Lit De Justice(USA) —Pure Misk (Rainbow Quest (USA))
102[5] *191[2]* *307[5]* *486[4]* *509[9]* 4606[2] *4884[7]* 5638[8] 6088[7] 6278[2]

Certain Promise (USA) *Sir Michael Stoute* 64
2 b f El Prado(IRE) —Shining Bright (Rainbow Quest (USA))
6648[10]

Certifiable *Miss Z C Davison* a60 37
6 b g Deploy—Gentle Irony (Mazilier (USA))
29[9] *592[8]* *650[7]* *739[5]* *866[9]* *6969[9]* *7187[7]* *7257[7]*

Cerulean Rose *A W Carroll* a53 71
8 ch m Bluegrass Prince(IRE) —Elegant Rose (Noalto)
2982[6] 4075[7] 4396[8] 4545[10] 5009[6] 5190[14] (5349) 5726[7] 5861[5] 6424[11]

Cesare *J R Fanshawe* a95 123
6 b g Machiavellian(USA) —Tromond (Lomond (USA))
(1392) 2735[5] (3523) 4805[2] 5798[4] 6332[15]

Cesar Le Peintre (FR) *H-A Pantall* a71 92
3 b c Grape Tree Road—Saint Patricia (FR) (Assert)
2503a[2]

Cesc *P J Makin* a95 91
3 b c Compton Place—Mana Pools (IRE) (Brief Truce (USA))
760[12] *922[2]* 1124[9] 2213[10] 3960[7] 4093[6] 4811[11] 5382[8] *6002[4]* *6437[8]*

C'Est La Vie *Miss J E Foster* 28
5 ch m Bering—Action De Grace (USA) (Riverman (USA))
3805[12]

Cetshwayo *J M P Eustace* a61 62
5 ch g Pursuit Of Love—Induna (Grand Lodge (USA))
52[7]

Cha Cha Cha *K A Ryan* a71 77
3 b f Efisio—Shall We Dance (Rambo Dancer (CAN))
(998) 1286[3] 1786[2] 5662[7] 6331[6] (6731) *7158[5]*

Chaenomeles (USA) *M Johnston* a71 57
2 bb f Fusaichi Pegasus(USA) —Eliza (USA) (Mt. Livermore (USA))
5801[7] 6107[5] *6432[4]*

Chain Of Gold *E S McMahon* 70
2 ch c Bahamian Bounty—Beading (Polish Precedent (USA))
2297[4]

Chairman Bobby *D W Barker* a54 61
9 ch g Clantime—Formidable Liz (Formidable (USA))
1423[3] 1711[5] 2421[8] 2509[14] 2761[10] 4351[8] 4996[11] 5083[6]

Chakeera (IRE) *Matthieu Palussiere* 83
3 b f Orpen(USA) —Classic Heights (Shirley Heights)
4240a[2]

Chalentina *P Howling* a62 78
4 b m Primo Valentino(IRE) —Chantilly Myth (Sri Pekan (USA))
70[8] *366[4]* *497[10]* *796[3]* 1655[10] 2540[3] 4295[3] *5098[4]* 5190[9] *5391[5]* *5897[11]* *6268[3]*

Chalford *J Balding*
2 ch g Compton Place—Red Head And Dotty (Risk Me (FR))
7139[8] *7196[6]*

Chalice Welcome *C F Wall* a48 38
4 b g Most Welcome—Blue Peru (IRE) (Perugino (USA))
210[5] *350[4]* *789[4]* 1206[12]

Challis (IRE) *J Noseda* a79
3 b c Barathea(IRE) —Chalosse (Doyoun)
141[2] *(499)*

Challow Hills (USA) *B W Hills* a55 63
2 ch f Woodman(USA) —Cascassi (USA) (Nijinsky (CAN))
3643[5] 4764[6] 6650[8]

Chambord (IRE) *A Fabre* a102 101
4 ch h Green Desert(USA) —Kenmist (Kenmare (FR))
4012a[2]

Champagne Cracker *M Dods* 65
6 ch m Up And At 'Em—Kiveton Komet (Precocious)
964[5] 1404[8] 1493[8] (1748) 2315[5] 2553[15] 2933[10] 3782[8] 4583[10]

Champagne Dancer *D J S Ffrench Davis* 51
2 ch g Lomitas—Rosewood Belle (USA) (Woodman (USA))
2977[6] 3238[6] 4454[12] 5858[11]

Champagne Mindy *Garry Moss* 23
3 b f Superior Premium—Oakwell Ace (Clantime)
3846[4] 5082[10] *5781[9]* 6562[12]

Champagne Rossini (IRE) *M C Chapman* a26 38
5 b g Rossini(USA) —Alpencrocus (IRE) (Waajib)
504[9] 1221[10]

Champagne Shadow (IRE) *Miss Tor Sturgis* a83 71
6 b g Kahyasi—Moet (IRE) (Mac's Imp (USA))
4[3] 142[7] 2027[5] 2431[11] *(2800) (3063) (3282) (3945) 4067[4] 4915[5] 5779[2] 6356[6] 6875[4]*

Champagne Sue *D W Barker* 33
3 ch f Foxhound(USA) —Pigeon (Casteddu)
4616[11] 4938[5] 5282[13]

Champain Sands (IRE) *E J Alston* a61 74
8 b g Green Desert(USA) —Grecian Bride (IRE) (Groom Dancer (USA))
1132[6] 1413[4] *2225[3]* 2311[8] 2985[5] *3644[7]* 4100[3] (4177) 4353[4] 4820[6] 4932[4] 5559[9] 5840[2] 6701[3]

Champery (USA) *M Johnston* a97 106
3 b g Bahri(USA) —Ice Ballet (IRE) (Nureyev (USA))
1035[2] 1516a[3] (1873a) 2789[8] 3331[8] 4044[4] 4627a[7]

Champfleurie *G A Swinbank* 91
3 b f Efisio—Blossom (Warning)
(1840) 2872[2] (3094) 3430[8]

Champion Lion (IRE) *R Allan* a17 50
8 b g Sadler's Wells(USA) —Honey Bun (Unfuwain (USA))
6259[15] *6613[9]*

Championship Point (IRE) *M R Channon* 118
4 b h Lomitas—Flying Squaw (Be My Chief (USA))
244a[6] 401a[8] 1109[2] 1550a[3] 1985[7] (2815) (4043) 4435a[4] 4826[6] 5618[11] 6334[9]

Champion's Way (IRE) *Daniel William O'Sullivan* a55 27
5 b g Namid—Savage (IRE) (Polish Patriot (USA))
557[2] 627[4] 6916a[11]

Champlain *I Mohammed* a25 105
3 b c Seeking The Gold(USA) —Calando (USA) (Storm Cat (USA))
173a[10] 641a[5]

Champollion (SWE) *L Reuterskiold*
3 b g Dushyantor(USA) —Di's Pearl (IRE) (Diaghlyphard (USA))
(2548a)

Champs Elysees *A Fabre* 113
4 b h Danehill(USA) —Hasili (IRE) (Kahyasi)
(1571a) 2292a[5] 3565a[2] 4872a[3] 6223a[2]

Champus (GER) *C Von Der Recke* 87
3 ch c Banyumanik(IRE) —Cordona (GER) (Lagunas)
4366[5]

Chancellor (IRE) *D K Ivory* a87 102
9 ch h Halling(USA) —Isticanna (USA) (Far North (CAN))
2351[11] 3076[7] 3386[10]

Change Alley (USA) *M Johnston* a77 41
2 b c Elusive Quality(USA) —Fortune (IRE) (Night Shift (USA))
5771[13] *6138[9] 6477[2]*

Change Course *Sir Michael Stoute* 63
3 b f Sadler's Wells(USA) —Orford Ness (Selkirk (USA))
5013[5] 5803[3]

Change Tack (USA) *Mrs A J Perrett* a60 72
2 gr f Mizzen Mast(USA) —Jibe (USA) (Danzig (USA))
2457[2] *5603[3]*

Change The Grange (AUS) *S Seemar* a100
9 gr g Umatilla(NZ) —Je Reviens (AUS) (The Challenge (AUS))
175a[10] 329a[7]

Changing Skies (IRE) *B J Meehan* 73
2 b f Sadler's Wells(USA) —Magnificient Style (USA) (Silver Hawk (USA))
6127[3]

Chantaco (USA) *A M Balding* a79 101
5 b g Bahri(USA) —Dominant Dancer (Primo Dominie)
1109[4] 2093[12] 5326[8] 5764[8] (6110) 6499[10]

Chant De Guerre (USA) *P Mitchell* a59 70
3 bb f War Chant(USA) —Fatwa (IRE) (Lahib (USA))
1215[6] *1731[6] 2178[3] 2668[7] 3083[2]* (3428) 3876[U] (4472) 5068[3] 5865[2] 6235[3] 6276[9]

Chanteuse De Rue (IRE) *M Johnston* 46
2 b f Street Cry(IRE) —Mt Morna (USA) (Mt. Livermore (USA))
5550[13] 5965[5] 6461[6]

Chantilly Beauty (FR) *R Pritchard-Gordon* a74 100
5 b m Josr Algarhoud(IRE) —Lysabelle (FR) (Lesotho (USA))
1661[6]

Chantilly Tiffany *E A L Dunlop* 91
3 ch f Pivotal—Gaily Royal (IRE) (Royal Academy (USA))
(1100) 1466[4] (2001) 2757[16] 3332[6] 3961[6] 5047[8] 5354[15] 6249[4]

Chantra (GER) *P Rau* 98
3 b f Lando(GER) —Chalkidiki (GER) (Nebos (GER))
1338a[7] 2294a[10]

Chapel Court (IRE) *T M Walsh* 66
3 ch g Exit To Nowhere(USA) —Lucky Fourstars (IRE) (Fourstars Allstar (USA))
4114a[16]

Chapelizod (IRE) *T G McCourt* a41 67
4 b g Raphane(USA) —Fulminus Instar (IRE) (Classic Secret (USA))
4836a[6] 5840[4]

Chapter (IRE) *Mrs A L M King* a48 67
5 ch g Sinndar(IRE) —Web Of Intrigue (Machiavellian (USA))
1562[4] 2027[8] 2582[7] *4161[6]* 4355[13] *4945[8]* 5427[8] 5886[2] 6259[10]

Charanne *J M Bradley* a25 22
4 b m Diktat—Mystique (Mystiko (USA))
901[7]

Chariots Of Fire (IRE) *David Wachman* 105
3 b c Galileo(IRE) —Tadkiyra (IRE) (Darshaan)
1306[4] 1547a[6] 2752[12]

Charles Darwin (IRE) *M Blanshard* a93 95
4 ch g Tagula(IRE) —Seymour (IRE) (Eagle Eyed (USA))
927[5] 1474[26] 1653[12] 2058[4] 2339[7] 3240[8] 5356[16]

Charles Parnell (IRE) *M Dods* a76 82
4 b g Elnadim(USA) —Titania (Fairy King (USA))
1074[10] 1492[5] 1678[8] 2072[12] 2202[7] 2508[4] 2827[5] 3345[4] (3787) (3839) 4251[8] 4381[4] 4895[4] 4934[4] (5552) 6157[3] 6639[3]

Charleston *R Rowe* a30
6 ch g Pursuit Of Love—Discomatic (USA) (Roberto (USA))
7012[11]

Charlevoix (IRE) *C F Wall* a51 45
2 b f King Charlemagne(USA) —Cayman Sound (Turtle Island (IRE))
2724[10] *5126[6]* 6411[11]

Charley Fox *D C O'Brien* a22
3 ch g Lahib(USA) —Bumpse A Daisy (Lord Bud)
1587[12] 1928[14]

Charlie Be (IRE) *Mrs P N Dutfield* a47 57
2 ch g King Charlemagne(USA) —Miriana (IRE) (Bluebird (USA))
1586[6] 1781[8] 2539[11] 5268[14] *6401[8]*

Charlie Bear *Miss Z C Davison* a54 66
6 ch h Bahamian Bounty—Abi (Chief's Crown (USA))
773[4] 975[5] 1260[2] 1507[13] 2214[16] 2722[7] *5094[11]*

Charlie Cool *W J Haggas* a108 111
4 ch h Rainbow Quest(USA) —Tigwa (Cadeaux Genereux)
176a[3] (401a) 642a[4] *941[3]* 1494[16] 1985[4] (2368) 2815[3] 3523[8] 4805[6] 5464a[4]

Charlie Delta *J M Bradley* a82 86
4 b g Pennekamp(USA) —Papita (IRE) (Law Society (USA))
(9) 183[5] 513[8] 581[10] 724[10] 803[8] (978) 1379[2] 1946[2] (2187) (2540) 2877[14] 4236[8] 4767[10] *5177[6]* 5275[10] *5981[10]*

Charlie Farnsbarns (IRE) *B J Meehan* 114
3 b c Cape Cross(IRE) —Lafleur (IRE) (Grand Lodge (USA))
2124[2]

Charlie Green (IRE) *Paul Green* 35
2 b g Traditionally(USA) —Saninka (IRE) (Doyoun)
1993[8] 2526[9] 3995[11]

Charlie Oxo *B P J Baugh* 27
2 br g Puissance—Aegean Mist (Prince Sabo)
5192[11] 5772[13] 6105[9]

Charlies Girl (IRE) *K J Burke* a35
3 ch f Trans Island—Indian Charm (IRE) (Indian Ridge)
60[11] 534[7] 676[11]

Charlie Tipple *T D Easterby* 78
3 b g Diktat—Swing Of The Tide (Sri Pekan (USA))
1257[8] 1965[9] 2892[4] (3713) 3885[4] 4425[2] 4898[5] 5253[4] 5703[5] 6731[2]

Charlie Tokyo (IRE) *R A Fahey* a81 106
4 b g Trans Island—Ellistown Lady (IRE) (Red Sunset)
940[10] (995) 1245[2] 1583[4] (3558) 3974[6] 5618[7] 6153[5]

Charlotte Bronte *David Wachman* 95
2 b f Danehill Dancer(IRE) —Speak Softly To Me (USA) (Ogygian (USA))
3071a[3]

Charlottebutterfly *P J McBride* a61 52
7 b m Millkom—Tee Gee Jay (Northern Tempest (USA))
(22) 83[10] 383[8] 637[8] 800[7] 3826[13] 4029[6] 4596[5] *(5121) 5368[2] 6096[2] 6179[6] 6627[12] (6955) 7115[3] 7248[6]*

Charlotte Grey *C N Allen* a67 64
3 gr f Wizard King—Great Intent (Aragon)
122[4] 336[4] 404[2] 679[9] 1022[8] *(1313)* 1820[6] *2260[4]* 2950[8] *3281[2] 3649[6]* 3879[3] *4432[6] 6360[4] 6747[10] 6890[11] 7082[9] 7209[5] 7279[9]*

Charlotte Vale *Micky Hammond* 80
6 ch m Pivotal—Drying Grass Moon (Be My Chief (USA))
914[2] 2008[6] 2201[4] (2743) (3012) 3501[2] 3719[6]

Charlotti Carlotti (IRE) *D W Chapman* a35 78
2 b f Celtic Swing—Kunucu (IRE) (Bluebird (USA))
1848[2] 2134[6] (2818) 3499[4] 4168[6] 4476[5] 5153[11] 6282[12] *6624[9] 6812[11]*

Charmatic (IRE) *Andrew Turnell* a72 78
6 br m Charnwood Forest(IRE) —Instamatic (Night Shift (USA))
(1249) 1884[5] 2321[3] 2967[2]

Charmel's Lad *W R Swinburn* a54 64
2 ch g Compton Place—Fittonia (FR) (Ashkalani (IRE))
4540[5] *5337[12]* 6252[6]

Charming Ballet (IRE) *N P Littmoden* a53 68
4 b g Imperial Ballet(IRE) —Some Merit (Midyan (USA))
1080[8] *1589[9]* 1847[13] 2217[4] (2664) 2879[7] *4394[9]* 4853[6] *5174[8]* 5866[13] 6415[14]

Charming Tale (USA) *B J Meehan* 51
2 b f Kingmambo(USA) —Crystal Crossing (IRE) (Royal Academy (USA))
6649[15]

Charnwood Street (IRE) *D Shaw* a38 31
8 b g Charnwood Forest(IRE) —La Vigie (King Of Clubs)
87[6] 617[13] 1229[10]

Chart Express *J R Best* a45 34
3 b g Robellino(USA) —Emerald Angel (IRE) (In The Wings)
2175[10] 3616[9]

Chartist *R Hannon* 81
2 ch c Choisir(AUS) —Sareb (FR) (Indian Ridge)
6295[9] (6595)

Chart Oak *P Howling* a57
4 b g Robellino(USA) —Emerald Angel (IRE) (In The Wings)
204[4] 537[4] 683[8] 807[7] 1030[3] 2520[9]

Chasing Memories (IRE) *W K Goldsworthy* a62 62
3 b f Pursuit Of Love—Resemblance (State Diplomacy (USA))
1850[3] 2133[4] 2760[6] 3611[3] (3789) 4287[7] 4579[5] 5936[4] 6304[9] *7146[7] 7226[5]*

Chastity (IRE) *N Tinkler* 24
3 b f Dilshaan—Fanny Bay (IRE) (Key Of Luck (USA))
99[11]

Chateau (IRE) *M E Sowersby* a20 66
5 ch g Grand Lodge(USA) —Miniver (IRE) (Mujtahid (USA))
2091[5] 2298[5] 2843[4] *3405[11]* 4249[10] 4426[5]

Chateau Nicol *B G Powell* a74 70
8 b g Distant Relative—Glensara (Petoski)
4594[10] *4884[14]*

Chatham Islands (USA) *M Johnston* a67 76
2 b f Elusive Quality(USA) —Zelanda (IRE) (Night Shift (USA))
2071[5] *2992[4]* (4350) 4762[2] 5331[5]

Chatila (USA) *J H M Gosden* a82 93
4 b m Red Ransom(USA) —Silvester Lady (Pivotal)
1466[5] 4849[7] 5544[9] *6604[11]*

Chatshow (USA) *A W Carroll* a74 79
6 br g Distant View(USA) —Galanty Show (Danehill (USA))
1004[5] 1080[2] 1241[2] 1885[6] 2197[2] 2411[2] 2655[5] 2912[7] 3613[6] 4320[6] *5234[4] 5648[6]* 5879[4] *6747[2] 6818[2] 6910[4]*

Chattan Clan *R A Kvisla* a73 64
3 ch g Kyllachy—Shona (USA) (Lyphard (USA))
343[5] 489[4] (919) 1359[10] *3420[9] 4740[2] 5238[9] 5495[6]*

Cheap N Chic *K A Ryan* a79 78
4 ch m Primo Valentino(IRE) —Amber Mill (Doulab (USA))
697[12]

Cheap Street *J G Portman* 90
3 ch c Compton Place—Anneliina (Cadeaux Genereux)
1099[14] 1817[5] 2213[7] 2669[8] 3334[8] 4710[6] 5722[11]

Checkit (IRE) *R Bouresly* a62 91
7 br h Mukaddamah(USA) —Collected (IRE) (Taufan (USA))
245a[5] 331a[10] 394a[4] 470a[5]

Check Up (IRE) *B W Duke* 52
6 b g Frimaire—Melons Lady (IRE) (The Noble Player (USA))
4256[3]

Cheddar Island (IRE) *Kevin Prendergast* 101
5 b g Trans Island—Poker Dice (Primo Dominie)
3140a[9]

Cheeky Jack (USA) *B J Meehan* a52 64
3 b c A.P. Indy(USA) —Poetically (CAN) (Silver Deputy (CAN))
1100[8] *1375[6] 3113[7]*

Cheery Cat (USA) *D W Barker* a53 66
3 bb g Catienus(USA) —Olinka (USA) (Wolfhound (USA))
1266[6] 1712[10] 2203[2] (2910) 3029[3] 3342[4] 3583[4] (4078) 4250[3] 4940[7] 5701[6]

Chelsea Ballad (USA) *J H M Gosden* a51
3 b f Street Cry(IRE) —Chelsey Dancer (USA) (Affirmed (USA))
2455[8]

Chelsea Girl *C G Cox* 50
2 b f Kyllachy—Ghassanah (Pas De Seul)
2122[10]

Chemise (IRE) *R J Hodges* a44 44
2 b f Chevalier(IRE) —Louvolite (IRE) (Fayruz)
2488[9] 4311[6] 4629[10] *5133[4]* 5715[7] *6793[6] 7096[4] 7171[6]*

Cheonmado (USA) *Simon Earle* a46 65
3 ch g Miswaki(USA) —Academie Royale (IRE) (Royal Academy (USA))
1062[8] *1343[8]* 1433[4]

Cheque *J A Osborne* a73 61
2 b g Mujahid(USA) —Watheeqah (USA) (Topsider (USA))
4293[5] 4904[4] *(5116)* 5600[5]

Cherie's Dream *A M Balding* a65 73
3 b f Silver Wizard(USA) —Last Dream (IRE) (Alzao (USA))
(1587) 2425[3] *3645[6]*

Cherished Song *N A Callaghan* a56 53
2 b f Mark Of Esteem(IRE) —Waseyla (IRE) (Sri Pekan (USA))
5065[9] 5429[4] *5944[8]*

Cherokee Star *C C Bealby* a53
2 br g Primo Valentino(IRE) —Me Cherokee (Persian Bold)
5605[10]

Cherokee Triangle (USA) *Michael J Maker* 102
2 b c Cherokee Run(USA) —Brief Bliss (USA) (Navarone (USA))
6484a[11]

Cherri Fosfate *D Carroll* a79 74
3 b g Mujahid(USA) —Compradore (Mujtahid (USA))
(40) 147[3] 290[8] 510[4] 520[2] 589[2] 725[12] (744) 935[3] 1122[12] 1228[9] 1672[6] 2110[7] 4071[8] *4429[7]* 4842[5] 5037[11] *5233[9] 5367[6]* (5739) 6090[4]

Cherry Hinton *A P O'Brien* 103
3 b f Green Desert(USA) —Urban Sea (USA) (Miswaki (USA))
1777a[2] 2211[5] 2814[12] 3578a[3]

Cherry Mix (FR) *Saeed Bin Suroor* a97 121
6 gr h Linamix(FR) —Cherry Moon (USA) (Quiet American (USA))
1700a[4] 2787[8] 6689a[4]

Cherry Pickings (USA) *S Seemar* a95 18
10 b g Miner's Mark(USA) —Cherry D'Or (USA) (Cassaleria (USA))
471a[9]

Cherryxma (FR) *A Fabre* 93
3 gr f Linamix(FR) —Cherry Moon (USA) (Quiet American (USA))
6953a[0]

Cheshire Prince *W M Brisbourne* 73
3 br g Desert Prince(IRE) —Bundle Up (USA) (Miner's Mark (USA))
1238[5] 1536[9] 2133[3] 2530[2] 3587[5] 4197[3] (4283) (4735)

Cheshire Rose *T D Barron* 69
2 ch f Bertolini(USA) —Merch Rhyd-Y-Grug (Sabrehill (USA))
(3378) 4921[7] 5802[11] 6282[9] 6462[13]

Chesterton (IRE) *John Joseph Murphy* a61
2 bb c Namid—Beguine (USA) (Green Dancer (USA))
6884[5]

Chestoria (USA) *B Levine* 101
3 br f Chester House(USA) —R D Fille (USA) (Dixieland Band (USA))
5248a[5]

Cheveley Flyer *J Pearce* a57 55
4 ch g Forzando—Cavern Breeze (Lion Cavern (USA))
(3616) 4340[11]

Cheviot Red *B J Meehan* 59
2 b f Red Ransom(USA) —Cheviot Hills (USA) (Gulch (USA))
4602[13] 5162[7]

Cheyenne Star (IRE) *Ms F M Crowley* a108 112
4 b m Mujahid(USA) —Charita (IRE) (Lycius (USA))
782a[7] (2053a) (6216a)

Chia (IRE) *D Haydn Jones* a71 66
4 ch m Ashkalani(IRE) —Motley (Rainbow Quest (USA))
85[2] (299) 427[6] 933[2] 2491[3] *3407[4]* 4355[2] *5018[4] 5732[6] 6293[3] 6738[2] 6856[2] 6996[6] 7237[2]*

Chica Guapa (IRE) *Paul Green* a36 49
2 b f Carrowkeel(IRE) —Money Spinner (USA) (Teenoso (USA))
2039[7] 2504[11] 5501[10] *6626[7] 6736[11]*

Chicamia *M Mullineaux* 43
3 b f Kyllachy—Inflation (Primo Dominie)
2873[10] 3786[7] 4178[6] 4736[3] 5803[8]

Chicchirichi (IRE) *M Gasparini* 80
3 b c Celtic Swing—Velate (USA) (Spend A Buck (USA))
6863a[6]

Chicherova (IRE) *W M Brisbourne* a50 38
4 b m Soviet Star(USA) —Ruby Rose (Red Ransom (USA))
204[9] 768[11]

Chichi Creasy (FR) *Mme N Rossio* 117
3 b c Chichicastenango(FR) —Folle Garde (FR) (Garde Royale)
(1056a)

Chicken George (IRE) *D Nicholls* 78
3 ch g Observatory(USA) —Missing (Singspiel (IRE))
4616[7] (5036) 6331[5] 6492[4]

Chicken Soup *D J Murphy* a106 89
5 br g Dansili—Radiancy (IRE) (Mujtahid (USA))
(44) 656[5] 777[4] 817[2] 941[5] 2368[5] 6183[20] 6654[7] 6759[17] *6920a[4] 7037a[3] 7184[5] 7223[4]*

Chiefcomingfirst (NZ) *B Laming* 86
5 ch g Chief Bearhart(CAN) —Alchemy (NZ) (Noble Bijou (USA))
6711a[6]

Chief Commander (FR) *Jane Chapple-Hyam* a91 102
4 br g Commands(AUS) —Neeran (USA) (Fast Play (USA))
391[4] 656[9] 993[13] 1619[12] 2469[15]

Chief Dipper *D Morris* a50
5 b g Benny The Dip(USA) —Cuban Reef (Dowsing (USA))
425[12] 605[5]

Chief Editor *M J Wallace* a99 88
3 b g Tomba—Princess Zara (Reprimand)
5810[4] *(6676)*

Chief Eric *B I Case* 69
2 gr c Slickly(FR) —Last Romance (IRE) (Last Tycoon (IRE))
4764[5]

Chief Exec *J R Gask* a79 65
5 br g Zafonic(USA) —Shot At Love (IRE) (Last Tycoon (IRE))
44[4] 1629[9] 3056[4] *4063[2] 4394[2]* 4879[2] 5189[13] 5687[2] *6806[7] 6947[3] 7094[3] 7253[5]*

Chief Powderface (IRE) *Jedd O'Keeffe* a17 12
2 ch c Modigliani(USA) —Better Look (IRE) (College Chapel)
1087[14] *1713[9]* 2869[8] 3410[5]

Chiff Chaff *C R Dore* a68 64
3 b f Mtoto—Hen Harrier (Polar Falcon (USA))
1361[3] 1536[2] 1972[5] *2801[5] 3282[2]* 3803[9] *6719[14]*

Childish Thoughts *Mrs Norma Pook* a44 11
3 b f River Falls—Simmie's Special (Precocious)
17[8] 128[6] 194[7] 2077[12] *2331[14]*

Chill (FR) *J-C Rouget* 102
3 gr f Verglas(IRE) —Calithea (IRE) (Marju (IRE))
1388a[2] 2270a[4] 4055a[6] 4654a[5]

Chilsdown *J G Given* 42
4 b g Mozart(IRE) —Goodwood Blizzard (Inchinor)
2554[10] 3789[6] 5625[9]

Chimes At Midnight (USA) *Luke Comer* a50 65
10 b h Danzig(USA) —Surely Georgies (USA) (Alleged (USA))
349[3] 558[8] 615[11] 683[10] 2595[4]

China Cherub *S Dow* a93 94
4 ch m Inchinor—Ashlinn (IRE) (Ashkalani (IRE))
1063[6] 1200[7] *1525[5]* 2427[8] (2725) *2993[4] (3188)* 3472[2] 3746[2] 4373[5] 4806[7] 5923[9] *6142[7] 6900[8] 6947[5] 6972[4] 7087[8]*

Chinalea (IRE) *C G Cox* 81
5 b g Danetime(IRE) —Raise-A-Secret (IRE) (Classic Secret (USA))
1080[4] 1357[12] 1465[4] 1969[10] 2394[4] 2673[5] 2879[4] 3528[9] 3859[7]

Chinandega (FR) *P Demercastel* 106
3 ch f Chichicastenango(FR) —European Style (FR) (Ezzoud (IRE))
1055a[3] 1339a[4] 1880a[4] 4873a[8]

China Pink *Sir Mark Prescott* a36 47
2 b f Oasis Dream—Red Bouquet (Reference Point)
1945[10] 4037[9] 4422[9]

Chinese Profit *G C Bravery* 63
2 b g Acclamation—Tancholo (So Factual (USA))
5971[13] 6616[9]

Chinese Temple (IRE) *M G Quinlan* a75 80
2 b c Choisir(AUS) —Savage (IRE) (Polish Patriot (USA))
7232[3]

Chinese Whisper (IRE) *A P O'Brien* 107
3 b c Montjeu(IRE) —Majinskaya (FR) (Marignan (USA))
1057a[2] 1593a[3] 2293a[19] 2789[6] 3144a[6]

Chingford (IRE) *J G Portman* a62 46
3 ch f Redback—Beverley Macca (Piccolo)
290[9] 577[7] 894[7] 1430[6] 1883[6] 3425[7] 4536[5] 5716[13]

Chinkara *Doug Watson* a98 95
7 ch g Desert Prince(IRE) —You Make Me Real (USA) (Give Me Strength (USA))
175a[2] 329a[4] 398a[4] 529a[5] 601a[4]

Chin Wag (IRE) *J S Goldie* a76 86
3 b g Iron Mask(USA) —Sweet Chat (IRE) (Common Grounds)
1110[8] 1851[11] 3491[6] 5819[4] 6055[5] (6429) 6731[9]

Chip N Pin *T D Easterby* 57
3 b f Erhaab(USA) —Vallauris (Faustus (USA))
1111[7] 1236[4] 1579[2] 1850[10] 2132[4] 2793[8] 3570[8] 4283[3] 4424[2] 4718[3]

Chirango (FR) *P Demercastel* 86
2 gr c Chicastenango(FR) —European Style (FR) (Ezzoud (IRE))
6187a[4]

Chiron (GER) *Dr A Bolte* 106
6 b h Valanour(IRE) —Corsita (Top Ville)
4838a[8]

Chisel *M Wigham* 18
6 ch g Hector Protector(USA) —Not Before Time (IRE) (Polish Precedent (USA))
2006[13] 2825[11] 3036[7]

Chivola (IRE) *B Smart* a71 73
2 b c Invincible Spirit(IRE) —Boudica (IRE) (Alhaarth (IRE))
2983[4] 4378[3] 4782[5] 5192[6] 6462[3] 6699[3] 7000[2]

Chjimes (IRE) *K R Burke* a73 94
3 b g Fath(USA) —Radiance (IRE) (Thatching)
1176[4] 1603[6] 1978[4] 3029[2] 3334[2] 3762[2] 4778[2] 6205[2] 6492[3]

Chockdee (FR) *M J McGrath* a50
7 b g King's Theatre(IRE) —Chagrin D'Amour (IRE) (Last Tycoon (IRE))
4917[8]

Chocolate Caramel (USA) *Mrs A J Perrett* a92 89
5 b g Storm Creek(USA) —Sandhill (BRZ) (Baynoun)
3844[6] 4171[4] 4609[6] 4917[3] 5725[2] 6230[4] 6545[4] 6760[4] 7055[5]

Chocolate Sands *J G Given* a16
3 ch g Compton Place—Coffee Ice (Primo Dominie)
7019[12] 7134[7] 7238[9]

Choctaw Nation (USA) *S Seemar* a116 103
7 b g Louis Quatorze(USA) —Melisma (USA) (Well Decorated (USA))
601a[8]

Choiseau (IRE) *Pat Eddery* 74
2 b c Choisir(AUS) —Little Linnet (Be My Guest (USA))
4571[9] 5003[2]

Choisette *B Smart* a70 65
2 b f Choisir(AUS) —Final Pursuit (Pursuit Of Love)
1478[4] 2803[5] 3200[4] (4476) 4560[4] 5096[2] (5365) 6741[4]

Choisky (IRE) *J Akehurst* a67 61
2 b c Choisir(AUS) —Vinicky (USA) (Kingmambo (USA))
1762[10] 2349[5] 2630[9] 3426[5] 3680[5] 4274[3] 4683[5] 5199[5] 5705[3] 6449[12] 6588[7]

Chookie Hamilton *I Semple* a84 67
3 ch g Compton Place—Lady Of Windsor (IRE) (Woods Of Windsor (USA))
(111) (184) 1275[9] 1851[13] 2246[6] 3181[12] 4936[6] 5936[7] 6389[5] 7104[4]

Chookie Heiton (IRE) *I Semple* 105
9 br g Fumo Di Londra(IRE) —Royal Wolff (Prince Tenderfoot (USA))
2022[6] 3586[13] 4614[21] 5083[7]

Chookie Windsor *A G Juckes* a59 53
4 b g Lake Coniston(IRE) —Lady Of Windsor (IRE) (Woods Of Windsor (USA))
907[10]

Choose Your Moment *P C Haslam* 94
2 b c Choisir(AUS) —Time Will Show (FR) (Exit To Nowhere (USA))
(2983) 4613[3] (5251)

Chopastair (FR) *T Lerner* a110 107
6 b g Astair(FR) —Very Sol (FR) (Solicitor (FR))
437a[10] 3445a[9] (6614a)

Chope Royale (FR) *J-Y Artu* 75
5 ch g Sin Kiang(FR) —Gazette Royale (FR) (Garde Royale)
6923a[9]

Chord *Sir Michael Stoute* a87 74
3 ch g Pivotal—Choirgirl (Unfuwain (USA))
1665[3] (3284) 3993[7] (4976) 5205[7] 6144[8]

Choreography *D Nicholls* a77 79
4 ch g Medicean—Stark Ballet (USA) (Nureyev (USA))
672[7] 969[8] 1555[8] 2072[10] 2985[12] 3998[3] 4251[2] 4494[6] 4822[3] 5232[10] 5476[6] 5741[4] 5909[2] 6467[2]

Choristar *J Mackie* a62 69
6 ch g Inchinor—Star Tulip (Night Shift (USA))
377[9] 508[7] 623[7] 767[5] 976[2] (1090) 1295[F] (Dead)

Chosan (JPN) *T Shimizu* 119
5 b h Dance In The Dark(JPN) —Stay Young (JPN) (Soccer Boy (JPN))
6943a[6]

Choysia *D W Barker* 82
4 b m Pivotal—Bonica (Rousillon (USA))
1458[14] 1678[2] 1914[9] 2870[8] (3414) 4137[15] (4251) 4639[8] 5232[3] 5403[4]

Christalini *J C Fox* a57 78
3 b g Bertolini(USA) —Jay Tee (IRE) (Charnwood Forest (IRE))
1974[13] 2598[13] 4064[8] 5342[10] 5899[10] 6590[8] 7088[7] 7166[12]

Christian Bendix *P Howling* a58 41
5 ch g Presidium—Very Good (Noalto)
83[4] 189[5] 239[4] (524) 632[4] 723[4] 801[9] 980[10] 1120[8] 1349[5] (1400) 1753[5] 6718[10] 6925[11] 7107[10]

Christmas Truce (IRE) *M R Hoad* a62 69
8 b g Brief Truce(USA) —Superflash (Superlative)
115[8] 200[11] 288[3] 341[9] 363[13] 1206[10] 1318[3] 1612[7] 1740[6] 2275[5] 2559[4] 3083[9]

Christy Ryan (IRE) *M J Wallace*
3 b g Danetime(IRE) —Esterlina (IRE) (Highest Honor (FR))
139[9]

Chrystal Venture (IRE) *A J McCabe* a68 69
2 ch f Barathea(IRE) —Ukraine Venture (Slip Anchor)
3706[18] 4564[8] 5011[13] 5601[12] 6536[2] (6736)

Chunky's Choice (IRE) *J Noseda* a68 74
3 b g Key Of Luck(USA) —Indian Imp (Indian Ridge)
1840[8] 2177[9] 2627[11] 2945[6] 4821[6] 5158[2] (5709) 5899[8] (6276)

Chunsa *W Jarvis* a41
2 b c Makbul—Mynador (USA) (Forty Niner (USA))
5888[11] 6438[9]

Chun Tosaigh (USA) *J S Bolger* a70 93
2 ch c Street Cry(IRE) —In The Ghetto (USA) (Hennessy (USA))
3574a[3] 5397a[12]

Churchtown *K R Burke* a42 42
3 b g Kyllachy—Manhattan Diamond (Primo Dominie)
2167[4] 2938[11]

Ciccone *G L Moore* a63 82
4 ch m Singspiel(IRE) —Untold Riches (USA) (Red Ransom (USA))
181[2] 309[7] 363[5] 426[8] 2875[4] 3352[9] 3805[2] 4161[2] 4355[4] 4825[6]

Cicerole (FR) *J-C Rouget* 107
3 ch f Barathea(IRE) —Uryale (FR) (Kendor (FR))
1006a[8] 6614a[2]

Cigalas *B W Hills* 79
2 ch c Selkirk(USA) —Langoustine (AUS) (Danehill (USA))
4048[7] 5323[4]

Cima On Fly (IRE) *B Grizzetti* 60
2 b c Kris Kin(USA) —Peralta (IRE) (Green Desert (USA))
2684a[2] 6222a[9]

Cimyla (IRE) *C F Wall* a111 101
6 b g Lomitas—Coyaima (GER) (Night Shift (USA))
176a[6] 401a[5] 541a[7] 761[6] 941[7]

Cinaman (IRE) *R F Fisher* 31
3 b g Key Of Luck(USA) —Madame Nureyev (USA) (Nureyev (USA))
956[U]

Cincinnati Kid (TUR) *I Eser* 79
5 b h George Thomas(TUR) —Top Honor (TUR) (Highest Honor (FR))
5265a[11]

Cinematic (IRE) *J R Boyle* a79 82
4 b g Bahhare(USA) —Eastern Star (IRE) (Sri Pekan (USA))
28[10] 211[10] 381[3] 486[7] (594) 652[2] 1997[2] 2512[4] 3641[5] 4551[6] 4889[8] 5645[2] 6603[4] (6738)

Cinerama (IRE) *M P Tregoning* a61
2 b f Machiavellian(USA) —Disco Volante (Sadler's Wells (USA))
6434[7]

Cinnamon Bay *A Fabre* 103
3 ch f Zamindar(USA) —Trellis Bay (Sadler's Wells (USA))
2501a[10]

Cinnamon Girl *A M Hales* a5
4 ch m Erhaab(USA) —Distant Cheers (USA) (Distant View (USA))
1030[7]

Cinnamon Hill *Eve Johnson Houghton* a67 61
3 ch f Compton Place—Cajole (IRE) (Barathea (IRE))
5315[4] 6094[2] 6546[5]

Cinque Cento (AUS) *P Moody* 112
6 b m Nothin' Leica Dane(AUS) —Laydown Misere (AUS) (Varick (USA))
6354a[16]

Circle Of Love *J L Dunlop* 83
3 b f Sakhee(USA) —Claxon (Caerleon (USA))
2597[2] (3160) 3972[6]

Circle Of Truth *W G M Turner* a21 12
3 b g Makbul—Jade's Girl (Emarati (USA))
108[7] 254[12]

Circuit Dancer (IRE) *D Nicholls* a73 88
7 b g Mujadil(USA) —Trysinger (IRE) (Try My Best (USA))
692[9] 957[9] 1854[19] 2989[10] 3921[10] 5155[4] (5401) 5667[7] 5806[4] 6381[11]

Circular Quay (USA) *T Pletcher* a121 99
3 ch c Thunder Gulch(USA) —Circle Of Life (USA) (Belong To Me (USA))
1486a[6] 1882a[5]

Circus Polka (USA) *W M Brisbourne* a81
3 br c Stravinsky(USA) —Far Wiser (USA) (Private Terms (USA))
275[6] 6439[9] 6669[12] 6774[11] (6882) 7233[6]

Citronnade (USA) *R J Frankel* 117
4 b m Lemon Drop Kid(USA) —Primarily (USA) (Lord At War (ARG))
4413a[4] 5825a[2]

Citrus Chief (USA) *R A Harris* a59 59
3 b g Lemon Drop Kid(USA) —Tricky Indy (USA) (A.P. Indy (USA))
157[9] 267[10] 572[2] 790[3] 917[3] 1361[7] 2105[8] 3620[9]

City For Conquest (IRE) *John A Harris* a74 74
4 b m City On A Hill(USA) —Northern Life (IRE) (Distinctly North (USA))
97[6] 183[2] 254[2] 310[7] 561[9] 688[7] 1405[10] 1729[2] 2221[7] 2509[9] 3597[4] 3853[5]

City Hustler (USA) *J S Moore* a72 63
2 b c Century City(IRE) —French Buster (USA) (Housebuster (USA))
4293[9] 4539[4] 5116[2] 5294[5] 6139[2] 6404[4]

City Leader (IRE) *B J Meehan* 111
2 gr c Fasliyev(USA) —Kanmary (FR) (Kenmare (FR))
(3896) 5048[2] (5795) 6489[2]

City Miss *Miss L A Perratt* 51
4 br m Rock City—Miss Pigalle (Good Times (ITY))
1459[14] 1595[8] 1711[7] 2563[11] 2823[7] 3584[7] (4380) 4969[7] 5283[14] 5586[8]

City Of Dreams (IRE) *J S Moore* a31
2 b c Dubai Destination(USA) —America Calling (USA) (Quiet American (USA))
6433[13]

City Of The Kings (IRE) *R Hannon* a77 83
2 b c Cape Cross(IRE) —Prima Volta (Primo Dominie)
3462[8] 4586[4] (4947) (5400)

City Of Tribes (IRE) *G M Lyons* 102
3 b g Invincible Spirit(IRE) —Yellow Trumpet (Petong)
(1616) 2035[3] 2672[2] 3139a[5] 3431[19] 6036a[2]

City Roma (IRE) *A Peraino* 82
2 b c Mount Abu(IRE) —Tarrifa (IRE) (Mujtahid (USA))
3147a[7]

City Stable (IRE) *Sir Michael Stoute* 75
2 b c Machiavellian(USA) —Rainbow City (IRE) (Rainbow Quest (USA))
5541[2] 6058[2] 6451[3]

City Wizzard *M L W Bell* 38
2 ch g Bahamian Bounty—Aries (GER) (Big Shuffle (USA))
2398[11] 2941[15] (Dead)

Claire Et Bleu (FR) *Mme M Bollack-Badel* 96
3 b f Anabaa Blue—Clarte Du Soir (FR) (Kaldoun (FR))
989a[8] 2384a[3] 3564a[7]

Clara Allen (IRE) *John E Kiely* 106
9 b m Accordion—Deeco Valley (IRE) (Satco (FR))
1330a[4] 2161a[4]

Clare Park *H J Manners*
3 ch f Kier Park(IRE) —Shafayif (Ela-Mana-Mou)
3274[11] 3903[6]

Clarricien (IRE) *E J O'Neill* 76
3 br g Key Of Luck(USA) —Tango Two Thousand (IRE) (Sri Pekan (USA))
1237[4] 1827[16]

Classical Flair *M Kettle* 53
3 ch f Distant Music(USA) —Balleta (USA) (Lyphard (USA))
595a[6]

Classical Rhythm (IRE) *J R Boyle* a51 68
2 ch c Traditionally(USA) —Golden Angel (USA) (Slew O'Gold (USA))
2041[7] 2569[6] 4571[11] 5053[7] 5314[6] 5736[7]

Classical World (USA) *Sir Michael Stoute* 71
2 gr c El Prado(IRE) —Tethkar (Machiavellian (USA))
3747[15] (4247) 4776[13] 5109[7]

Classic Blue (IRE) *Ian Williams* a54 37
3 b f Tagula(IRE) —Palace Blue (IRE) (Dara Monarch)
5347[15] 5894[7] 6343[7] 6387[10]

Classic Caro (GER) *Frau Marion Rotering* 61
3 b c Seattle Dancer(USA) —Classic Cara (GER) (Nikos)
1387a[10]

Classic Croco (GER) *T Hogan* a84 78
6 gr g Croco Rouge(IRE) —Classic Light (IRE) (Classic Secret (USA))
5184a[10] 6366a[14]

Classic Descent *P J Makin* a76 79
2 b c Auction House(USA) —Polish Descent (IRE) (Danehill (USA))
5193[4] 6403[3] 6616[2]

Classic Encounter (IRE) *D M Simcock* a97 96
4 b g Lujain(USA) —Licence To Thrill (Wolfhound (USA))
344[6] 490[8] 818[7] 1242[6] (1464) 1986[6] 2352[5] 3708[10] 4090[16]

Classic Fortune (IRE) *D R C Elsworth* a86
2 b c Royal Applause—Injaaz (Sheikh Albadou)
(6897) 7015[2]

Classic Hall (IRE) *T Keddy* a31 25
4 b m Saddlers' Hall(IRE) —Classic Mix (IRE) (Classic Secret (USA))
1312[12] 1950[9] 3805[11] 4535[8] 5683[9]

Classic Legend *B J Meehan* 93
2 b f Galileo(IRE) —Lady Lahar (Fraam)
(5913) (6652)

Classic Punch (IRE) *D R C Elsworth* 114
4 b g Mozart(IRE) —Rum Cay (USA) (Our Native (USA))
(3097) (3912) 4599[5] 4825[2] 5411[7] 5831[7]

Classic Role *L Wells* 35
8 b g Tragic Role(USA) —Clare Island (Connaught)
3385[11]

Classira (IRE) *M A Jarvis* a66 81
3 b f Danehill(USA) —Alleged Devotion (USA) (Alleged (USA))
1408[2] 1841[2] (3454) 3745[3] 4170[5] 4710[4] 5312[11]

Claws *A J Lidderdale* a61 61
4 b m Marju(IRE) —Paws (IRE) (Brief Truce (USA))
179[6] 571[5] 7028[12] 7207[6] 7250[2]

Clean Sheet (USA) *W J Haggas* 50
2 b f Fasliyev(USA) —Starlight Night (USA) (Distant View (USA))
5540[12] 5745[P] (Dead)

Clear Daylight *J R Best* a58 64
2 b c Daylami(IRE) —Barbara Frietchie (IRE) (Try My Best (USA))
5595[10] 5937[7] 6404[9] 6715[5] 6973[12]

Clearing Sky (IRE) *J R Boyle* a40 62
6 gr m Exploit(USA) —Litchfield Hills (USA) (Relaunch (USA))
4165[13] 4606[11] 5425[10] 5730[10]

Clearly Foxy (USA) *M Casse* a92 100
2 b f Volponi(USA) —Sermon (USA) (Pulpit (USA))
(5293a) 6507a[6]

Clear Picture *A P Jarvis* a21 48
4 ch m Observatory(USA) —Defined Feature (IRE) (Nabeel Dancer (USA))
272[7] 1374[4]

Clear Reef *Jane Chapple-Hyam* a76 46
3 b c Hernando(FR) —Trinity Reef (Bustino)
6238[8] 6821[4] 6991[6] (7211)

Clear Sailing *Mrs A J Perrett* 83
4 b g Selkirk(USA) —Welsh Autumn (Tenby)
2634[5] 3882[9] 4184[11]

Cleaver *Lady Herries* a82 85
6 ch g Kris—Much Too Risky (Bustino)
850[4] 1591[4] 1949[3] 2634[3] 3093[2] 3242[2] 3753[9]

Cleide Da Silva (USA) *J Noseda* a81 69
3 gr f Monarchos(USA) —Sage Cat (USA) (Tabasco Cat (USA))
1153[4] 2317[5] (3110) 3418[9]

Cleveland *R Hollinshead* a73 53
5 b g Pennekamp(USA) —Clerio (Soviet Star (USA))
63[11] 306[2] 468[5] 686[2] 766[6] 1262[3] 1755[2] 2149[4] 4008[5] 6720[5] 6818[10]

Clew Bay (IRE) *Barry Potts* 19
8 b g Nicolotte—Lady Danjar (FR) (Nadjar (FR))
1596[14]

Clewer *P A Blockley* a56 57
3 b f Bahamian Bounty—Polisonne (Polish Precedent (USA))
791[9] 894[14]

Cliche (IRE) *Sir Michael Stoute* 104
3 b f Diktat—Sweet Kristeen (USA) (Candy Stripes (USA))
(1901) 2757[8] 3332[4] 4849[2]

Clifton Dancer *Tom Dascombe* 79
2 b f Fraam—Crofters Ceilidh (Scottish Reel)
2365[7] 4527[3] 4775[5] (5314) 5629[12] 6498[8]

Clifton Four (USA) *R Hannon* a59 72
2 b f Forest Wildcat(USA) —Black Truffle (USA) (Mt. Livermore (USA))
4602[6] 5277[3] 5682[6]

Climate (IRE) *R Hollinshead* a74 66
8 ch g Catrail(USA) —Burishki (Chilibang)
32[3] (109) (298) (364) 533[8] 620[3] 674[3] 768[9] 6146[10] 6344[4] 6476[9] 6774[5] 6882[6] 7001[5] 7218[4] 7274[2]

Climaxtackledotcom *M W Easterby* 68
2 b g Bahri(USA) —La Danseuse (Groom Dancer (USA))
3092[5] 6073[10] 6754[3]

Clip Clop (IRE) *Miss J Feilden* a16
2 b f Minardi(USA) —Vailmora (USA) (Mt. Livermore (USA))
7021[RR] 7122[5] 7259[5]

Clipper Hoy *Mrs H Sweeting* a74 56
5 ch g Bahamian Bounty—Indian Flag (IRE) (Indian Ridge)
566[12] 2350[9] 2879[11]

Clock Face (IRE) *M D I Usher* a44
3 b f Danetime(IRE) —Sugar River (FR) (Polish Precedent (USA))
678[10] 752[10] 906[4]

Clodovina (IRE) *A Fabre* a84 102
3 b f Rock Of Gibraltar(IRE) —Clodora (FR) (Linamix (FR))
7049a[9]

Closetocrazy (IRE) *Ms Joanna Morgan* a65 78
7 b m Blues Traveller(IRE) —Foulage (Picea)
5184a[5]

Close To Paradise (IRE) *E A L Dunlop* 74
2 gr f Clodovil(IRE) —Tropical Paradise (USA) (Manila (USA))
2832[9] 3706[4] (4074) 5322[8] 5692[11] 6201[11]

Clouded Leopard (USA) *J H M Gosden* a77 50
3 b f Danehill(USA) —Golden Cat (USA) (Storm Cat (USA))
3447[7]

Cloudy's Knight (USA) *Frank J Kirby* 121
7 ch g Lord Avie(USA) —Cloudy Spot (USA) (Solar City (USA))
(6374a)

Clovis *M Johnston* a71 78
2 b c Kingmambo(USA) —Darling Flame (USA) (Capote (USA))
6058[5] 6248[6] 6724[4] 6857[6] 7152[2] 7204[5]

Clowance *R Charlton* 73
2 b f Montjeu(IRE) —Freni (GER) (Sternkoenig (IRE))
6127[4]

Club Captain (USA) *T D McCarthy* a44 41
4 b g Red Ransom(USA) —Really Fancy (USA) (In Reality (USA))
6238[10]

Clueless *N G Richards* 90
5 b g Royal Applause—Pure (Slip Anchor)
2314[2] 2861[4] 3509[9] 5215[13] 5504[6] 5933[8] 6475[10]

Clytha *M L W Bell* 55
3 ch f Mark Of Esteem(IRE) —India Atlanta (Ahonoora)
1154[12] 1538[10]

C'Mon You Irons (IRE) *B Smart* 76
2 b c Orpen(USA) —Laissez Faire (IRE) (Tagula (IRE))
4702[4] (5675) 6017[12]

Cnoc Moy (IRE) *C F Wall* a74 86
3 b g Mull Of Kintyre(USA) —Ewar Sunrise (Shavian)
492[9] 569[6] 791[2] (924) 2834[8] (3384) (3689) 4234[2] 5889[7]

Cnoc Rua (IRE) *Timothy Doyle* 80
3 b g Redback—Tuft Hill (Grundy)
5696a[7]

Coach And Four (USA) *A P O'Brien* a50 71
2 b c Storm Cat(USA) —Tacha (USA) (Mr Prospector (USA))
6392a[4]

Coachhouse Lady (USA) *K A Ryan* a52 76
2 b f Rahy(USA) —Secret Advice (USA) (Secreto (USA))
2134[13] 2949[9] 4422[2] 4796[5] (6015)

Coalite (IRE) *A D Brown* a40 62
4 b g Second Empire(IRE) —Municipal Girl (IRE) (Mac's Imp (USA))
1349[13] (1596) 2561[10] 3195[6] 4668[10] 5037[6] 5503[16]

Coalseam (AUS) *Jim Taylor* 105
6 b g Desert Sun—Crow's Nest (Shirley Heights)
15a[U]

Coastal Breeze *A J Chamberlain* a41
4 b g Fasliyev(USA) —Classic Design (Busted)
6407[13] 6796[9] 6945[10] 7167[6]

Coastal Command *R Charlton* a67 74
3 b g Sakhee(USA) —Zenith (Shirley Heights)
1659[2] 2402[4] 5683[5]

Coastal Path *A Fabre* 114
3 b c Halling(USA) —Coraline (Sadler's Wells (USA))
(5258a) (6028a)

Coasting *Mrs A J Perrett* 96
2 b g Cape Cross(IRE) —Sweeping (Indian King (USA))
1540[3] (1832) 2732[15] (4121) 4372[10]

Cobbold Point *M W Easterby* 32
2 b g Tipsy Creek(USA) —Mofeyda (IRE) (Mtoto)
2739[9] 3037[10] 3761[11]

Cobo Bay *K A Ryan* a83 92
2 b c Primo Valentino(IRE) —Fisher Island (IRE) (Sri Pekan (USA))
2803[4] 3283[3] 4037[4] (4461) (4776) 5350[17] (5613)

Cocabana *J G Portman* a64 72
2 b f Captain Rio—Hiraeth (Petong)
1896[6] 2488[6] 2997[5] 3162[4] (4026) 4573[10] 4903[8] 5452[2] 6195[10] 6588[4] 6834[7] 7072[7]

Cockatoo (USA) *G L Moore* a62 66
4 b g Dynaformer(USA) —Enticed (USA) (Stage Door Johnny (USA))
618[7] 2430[3]

Cockayne (IRE) *V Valiani* 94
4 b m Barathea(IRE) —Clara House (Shirley Heights)
2296a[9] 6519a[3] 6688a[8]

Cockney Rebel (IRE) *G A Huffer* 124
3 b c Val Royal(FR) —Factice (USA) (Known Fact (USA))
(1473) (2051a) 2734[5]

Cocktail Shaker (USA) *B J Meehan* a4 59
2 b c Gulch(USA) —Carr Shaker (USA) (Carr De Naskra (USA))
4110[12] 4508[8] 5200[12] 5600[3]

Cocobean *M Appleby* a29 18
3 b g Josr Algarhoud(IRE) —Aker Wood (Bin Ajwaad (IRE))
2800[6] 3274[8] 3848[9] 4246[9]

Cocodrail (IRE) *F & L Brogi* a87 105
6 b h Croco Rouge(IRE) —Seattle Jey (ITY) (Seattle Dancer (USA))
4520a[0] 6863a[2]

Coconut Moon *E J Alston* a66 86
5 b m Bahamian Bounty—Lunar Ridge (Indian Ridge)
480[10] 566[8] 835[7] 1080[10] 1427[2] 2315[2] 2529[3] 3080[2] 3344[6] 3720[5] 4158[8] 4780[2] (5029) 5212[9] 5401[2] 5806[11]

Coconut Queen (IRE) *Mrs A Duffield* 74
3 b f Alhaarth(IRE) —Royal Bounty (IRE) (Generous (IRE))
1131[4] 1424[4] 1916[6] 2534[3] (2713) 2988[6] 3411[10] 3607[8] 4450[8] 5703[14]

Coda Agency *D W P Arbuthnot* a62 63
4 b g Agnes World(USA) —The Frog Lady (IRE) (Al Hareb (USA))
1888[11] 2430[5] 2770[4] 3033[6] 3945[7] 4531[11]

Code (IRE) *Miss Z C Davison* 45
6 b g Danehill(USA) —Hidden Meaning (USA) (Gulch (USA))
1998[11] 2274[6] 2996[12] 3280[6] 3473[6]

Coeur Courageux (FR) *G L Moore* a86 93
5 b g Xaar—Linoise (FR) (Caerwent)
660[6] 1195[7] 1651[22] 1996[6] 3401[4] 4100[7] (4462) 4672[6] 5312[9] 5685[10] 6145[4] 6504[7]

Coeur De Lionne (IRE) *R Charlton* a109 91
3 b g Invincible Spirit(IRE) —Lionne (Darshaan)
(1250) 2057[4] 3691[3] 4147[2] 4749[13] (5205) (5686)

Coffee Cup (IRE) *G A Swinbank* 61
2 b f Royal Academy(USA) —Christel Flame (Darshaan)
2984[6] 3916[4] (4783) 5153[10]

Coffin Dodger *C N Allen* a49 51
4 ch m Dracula(AUS) —Karakul (IRE) (Persian Bold)
1271[3] 1570[10] 2089[12] 2156[9] 2557[3] 3629[8] 4473[5]

Colchium (IRE) *H Morrison* a71 76
3 br f Elnadim(USA) —Dog Rose (SAF) (Fort Wood (USA))
1076[5] 1610[2] 2181[5] 2988[4] 3555[6] 5001[5] 5893[9]

Colditz (IRE) *D W Barker* a46 73
3 ch g Noverre(USA) —West Escape (Gone West (USA))
582[5] 917[2] 1194[7] 1708[4] 2340[7] 2565[3] 2759[8] 3181[8] 3377[4] 3587[2] 3765[4] 3785[4] 5286[10] 5487[3]

Cold Quest (USA) *J H M Gosden* a86 98
3 b g Seeking The Gold(USA) —Polaire (IRE) (Polish Patriot (USA))
3709[3] 4059[16]

Cold Turkey *G L Moore* a99 98
7 bb g Polar Falcon(USA) —South Rock (Rock City)
6230[8] 6645[6] 7086[4]

Coleorton Dagger *J R Holt* a25
3 ch f Daggers Drawn(USA) —Tayovullin (IRE) (Shalford (IRE))
237[10] 423[9] 506[4] 7201[8]

Coleorton Dancer *K A Ryan* a81 102
5 ch g Danehill Dancer(IRE) —Tayovullin (IRE) (Shalford (IRE))
1195[14] 1474[27] 1651[11] 2058[11] 5584[24] 6355[5] 6560[5] 6907[2] 7087[7] 7212[3]

Coleridge (AUS) *J C Fox* a80 79
8 ch g Yeats(USA) —Coco Cheval (AUS) (Zephyr Bay (AUS))
2995[6] 3420[8] 6199[14]

Colinca's Lad (IRE) *T T Clement* a63 71
5 b g Lahib(USA) —Real Flame (Cyrano De Bergerac)
2004[6] (2831) 3048[4] 3711[10] 4063[6] 4418 [12] 6780[8] 6894[4] 6979[7]

Colinette *R T Phillips* a66 67
4 b m Groom Dancer(USA) —Collide (High Line)
2431[5] 4458[2] 5807[12] 6314[4] 6481[5]

Collateral Damage (IRE) *T D Easterby* a84 94
4 b h Orpen(USA) —Jay Gee (IRE) (Second Set (IRE))
658[9] 848[11] 1583[5] 1767[11] 2093[5] 2807[3] 3558[3] 4043[12] 4388[6] 4720[12] 5327[7]

Collection (IRE) *W J Haggas* 85
2 b c Peintre Celebre(USA) —Lasting Chance (USA) (American Chance (USA))
5920[2] (6255)

College Land Boy *J J Quinn* 61
3 b g Cois Na Tine(IRE) —Welcome Lu (Most Welcome)
3302[10] 3917[13] 4642[8] 5041[12]

College Queen *S Gollings* a39 41
9 b m Lugana Beach—Eccentric Dancer (Rambo Dancer (CAN))
51[12] 653[6] 7138[6]

College Rebel *J F Coupland* a12 52
6 b m Defacto(USA) —Eccentric Dancer (Rambo Dancer (CAN))
302[8] 628[8] 683[11] 808[11] 4409[11] 4638[10] 4941[8]

College Scholar (GER) *E A L Dunlop* a65 93
3 ch c Dr Fong(USA) —Colina (GER) (Caerleon (USA))
1099[11] 1502[7] 2044[6] 3380[6] 4811[9] 5684[9]

Collematteo (IRE) *D J Wintle* 15
3 b g Alexius(IRE) —Saraho'Byrne (IRE) (Brief Truce (USA))
3846[6]

Colleoni (IRE) *G A Butler* a51 29
2 b c Sadler's Wells(USA) —Francfurter (Legend Of France (USA))
6740[10]

Collette's Choice *R A Fahey* a41 71
4 b m Royal Applause—Brilliance (Cadeaux Genereux)
1258[4] 1576[U] 1890[5] 3815[2] 4131[6] 4558[5] (4969) 5144[4] 5750[12]

Collingwood (IRE) *T M Walsh* a63 67
5 br g Machiavellian(USA) —Almaaseh (IRE) (Dancing Brave (USA))
5460a[7]

Collioure (USA) *P F I Cole* a59 28
3 b f Gulch(USA) —Saraa Ree (USA) (Caro)
1375[3] 1714[6] 1901[12]

Colloquial *H Candy* a90 98
6 b g Classic Cliche(IRE) —Celia Brady (Last Tycoon (IRE))
1844[12] (2449) 3090[15] 4375[3] 5446[2]

Collow (GER) *M Weiss* 104
7 b g Lando(GER) —Conga (Robellino (USA))
355a[3] 493a[3]

Colmar Magic (IRE) *R Hannon* a39 56
2 b f Dixie Union(USA) —On View (USA) (Distant View (USA))
4232[13] 4602[11] 5088[6] 5818[8] 6427[13]

Colonel Bilko (IRE) *Ms J S Doyle* a48 57
5 b g General Monash(USA) —Mari-Ela (IRE) (River Falls)
26[4] 273[4] 341[7] 789[14]

Colonel Cotton (IRE) *W J Knight* a55 76
8 b g Royal Applause—Cutpurse Moll (Green Desert (USA))
1681[7] 2143[14] 2412[2]

Colonel Flay *Mrs P N Dutfield* a68 69
3 ch g Danehill Dancer(IRE) —Bobbie Dee (Blakeney)
1504[3] 1974[6] 3367[10] 5014[10] 5899[5] 6271[5]

Colonel Gun (IRE) *C R Dore* 40
7 ch g Catrail(USA) —Return Again (IRE) (Top Ville)
499[12] 603[11]

Colonial Cross (IRE) *M Halford* a62 74
3 b g Cape Cross(IRE) —Maytpleasethecourt (IRE) (Persian Heights)
5788a[12]

Colony (IRE) *Sir Michael Stoute* 74
2 b c Statue Of Liberty(USA) —Funoon (IRE) (Kris)
5010[9] (6417)

Colophony (USA) *K A Morgan* a67
7 ch g Distant View(USA) —Private Line (USA) (Private Account (USA))
747[4]

Colorado Blue (IRE) *R Charlton* 78
2 ch g Nayef(USA) —Colouring (IRE) (Catrail (USA))
6468[5]

Colorado Rapid (IRE) *M Johnston* 103
3 b c Barathea(IRE) —Rafting (IRE) (Darshaan)
(1111) 1851[3] (2010) 2788[11] 3330[2]

Colorado Springs *W Jarvis* a64 52
2 b f Olden Times—Engulfed (USA) (Gulch (USA))
5882[10] 6543[2] 6944[11]

Coloratura (IRE) *E A L Dunlop* 57
2 b f Cape Cross(IRE) —Elauyun (IRE) (Muhtarram (USA))
5949[12] 6414[12] 6649[16]

Color Man *Mrs A J Perrett* a57 55
3 b g Rainbow Quest(USA) —Subya (Night Shift (USA))
157[6] 267[12] 553[5] 907[3] 1397[2] (2096) 2610[6]

Colorus (IRE) *M W Easterby* a54 85
4 b g Night Shift(USA) —Duck Over (Warning)
1112[12] (1299) 1565[7] (1854) 2244[7] 2866[10] 3197[6] 3720[12] 3954[10] 4289[7] 4703[3] 4800[5] 6157[11]

Coloso *P D Cundell* a52 11
3 ch g Compton Place—Nashville Blues (IRE) (Try My Best (USA))
2674[4] 7029[6]

Colourful Life (IRE) *K G Reveley* a64 75
11 ch g Rainbows For Life(CAN) —Rasmara (Kalaglow)
2537[8]

Colourful Score (USA) *Saeed Bin Suroor*
3 b c Storm Cat(USA) —Serena's Song (USA) (Rahy (USA))
3454[U] 4641[11]

Colour Trooper (IRE) *P Winkworth* 65
2 ch c Traditionally(USA) —Viola Royale (IRE) (Royal Academy (USA))
5010[12]

Colton *J M P Eustace* a79 76
4 b g Zilzal(USA) —Picot (Piccolo)
1416[8] 2403[14] 3249[8] 4610[7] 5018[7]

Columbus (IRE) *Jennie Candlish* 38
10 b g Sadler's Wells(USA) —Northern Script (USA) (Arts And Letters (USA))
1196[9] 1556[13]

Colwyn Bay (IRE) *Jane Chapple-Hyam* a65 70
5 b g Sadler's Wells(USA) —Stolen Tear (FR) (Cadeaux Genereux)
804[2] (1402) 1942[3] (2770) (3448) (4544) 5533[10]

Comandante Xara (BRZ) *P Nickel Filho* a88 21
4 gr h Bonapartiste(FR) —Massabielle (BRZ) (Executioner (USA))
173a[8] 396a[8] 471a[6] 526a[2] 641a[10]

Come April *Sir Mark Prescott* a79
3 b f Singspiel(IRE) —So Admirable (Suave Dancer (USA))
(2455)

Comeback Queen *S Kirk* a74 91
2 gb f Nayef(USA) —Miss Universe (IRE) (Warning)
(6140) 6652[5]

Come Bye (IRE) *Miss A M Newton-Smith*
11 b g Star Quest—Boreen Dubh (Boreen (FR))
5938[14]

Comeintothespace (IRE) *K J Burke* a57 53
5 b g Tagula(IRE) —Playa Del Sol (IRE) (Alzao (USA))
(273) 350[3] 435[2] 524[3] (616) 665[11] 742[8] 1025[6] (1254) (1342) 1907[4] 3927[12]

Come On Nellie (IRE) *J G M O'Shea* 44
3 b f Diktat—Bauci (IRE) (Desert King (IRE))
2541[8] 2873[7] 3365[U] 3794[9] 5347[16] 6147[11]

Come Out Fighting *P A Blockley* a94 101
4 b h Bertolini(USA) —Ulysses Daughter (IRE) (College Chapel)
1653[3] 1836[12] 3268[12] 4133[2] 4389[13] 5195[2] 5673[2] 6676[5]

Come What Augustus *R M Stronge* a52 11
5 b g Mujahid(USA) —Sky Red (Night Shift (USA))
16[3] 134[3] 482[6] 677[12]

Come What July (IRE) *D Shaw* a56 44
6 b g Indian Rocket—Persian Sally (IRE) (Persian Bold)
12[7] 78[8] 285[6] 333[2] 578[4] 618[6] 677[4] 792[6] 1254[8] 1347[2] 1592[4] 2055[8] 2595[6] 7274[8]

Come What May *Rae Guest* a45 63
3 b f Selkirk(USA) —Portelet (Night Shift (USA))
1429[3] 1943[16] 2661[8] (2837) 2939[5] 5420[10] 5908[14]

Comic Tales *M Mullineaux* a52 34
6 b g Mind Games—Glorious Aragon (Aragon)
125[9] 201[7] 271[8] 282[3]

Comma (USA) *Sir Michael Stoute* a78 66
3 b f Kingmambo(USA) —Flute (USA) (Seattle Slew (USA))
3645[2] 3913[4] 4338[5] 5816[2] 6420[8]

Commander Cave (USA) *R Hannon* a60
2 bb c Tale Of The Cat(USA) —Royal Shyness (Royal Academy (USA))
6139[5] 6436[9]

Commander Wish *Lucinda Featherstone* a68 35
4 ch g Arkadian Hero(USA) —Flighty Dancer (Pivotal)
4534[13] 4925[12] 6361[11] (6565) (6752) 7105[6] 7227[8]

Command Marshal (FR) *M Scudamore* 78
4 b g Commands(AUS) —Marsakara (IRE) (Turtle Island (IRE))
3496[3]

Commandment (IRE) *E A L Dunlop* a61 75
3 b g Titus Livius(FR) —Alpine Flair (IRE) (Tirol)
1725[2] 2520[3] 2962[2] (4470)

Commando Scott (IRE) *I W McInnes* a80 99
6 b g Danetime(IRE) —Faye (Monsanto (FR))
757[8] 1041[9] 1157[9] 1195[8] 1619[9] 1826[6] (2058) 2237[8] 4851[5] 5584[8] (5617) 5809[2] 6183[3] 6301[10] 6472[2] 6758[11]

Commemoration Day (IRE) *M F Harris* 70
6 b g Daylami(IRE) —Bequeath (USA) (Lyphard (USA))
(2430) 4056[15]

Commentator (USA) *N Zito* a123
6 ch g Distorted Humor(USA) —Outsource (USA) (Storm Bird (CAN))
6510a[7]

Commit To Memory *Andrew Oliver* a78 66
2 br c Best Of The Bests(IRE) —Simonida (IRE) (Royal Academy (USA))
(7121)

Common Purpose (USA) *J H M Gosden* a73 77
3 b g Elusive Quality(USA) —Kithira (Danehill (USA))
1062[4] 1523[3] 2425[2]

Competitor *J Akehurst* a67 39
6 b h Danzero(AUS) —Ceanothus (IRE) (Bluebird (USA))
195[7] (288) 363[7] (612) 753[10] 825[3] 1026[12] 1368[10] 2141[9] 2332[7]

Complete Frontline (GER) *K R Burke* 62
2 ch c Tertullian(USA) —Carola Rouge (Arazi (USA))
1107[8] 1422[5] 3560[2]

Completion (NZ) *G Rogerson* 92
5 b g Zabeel(NZ) —Royal Magic (NZ) (Lord Ballina (AUS))
6711a[2]

Completo (IRE) *F Castro*
4 b g Mull Of Kintyre(USA) —Bold Avril (IRE) (Persian Bold)
5262a[4]

Composing (IRE) *H Morrison* a66 68
3 b f Noverre(USA) —Aqaba (Lake Coniston (IRE))
1127[11] 1560[5] 2602[13] 3624[7] 4172[10] 4809[4] 5426[2] 5948[7] 6421[6] 6817[4] 6937[9]

Compromiznotension (IRE) *I Semple* 84
4 br g Key Of Luck(USA) —Music Khan (Music Boy)
850[7]

Compton Abbess *B R Millman* a44 55
2 ch f Compton Place—Celt Song (IRE) (Unfuwain (USA))
2122[11] 2969[6] 5110[12] 5534[13] 5882[9] 6098[10]

Compton Charlie *J G Portman* a49 64
3 b g Compton Place—Tell Tale Fox (Tel Quel (FR))
1399[14] 1726[11] 3082[13] 3593[2]

Compton Classic *J R Boyle* a77 82
5 b g Compton Place—Ayr Classic (Local Suitor (USA))
1112[9] 1707[2] 1891[7] 2461[5] (2712) (2830) 3014[2] 3184[7] 3347[9] 3374[3] (3782) 3886[4] 3954[6] (4381) 4703[12] 5581[3] (5969) 6173[15] 6707[7] (6891) 7059[3] 7212[4] 7238[5]

Compton Commander *E W Tuer* a62 66
9 ch g Barathea(IRE) —Triode (USA) (Sharpen Up)
1196[11] 1556[11] 2026[5] 2839[3] 3193[10] 4451[6]

Compton Court *John G Carr* a74 78
5 b g Compton Place—Loriner's Lass (Saddlers' Hall (IRE))
4114a[17]

Compton Dragon (USA) *W M Brisbourne* a62 67
8 ch g Woodman(USA) —Vilikaia (USA) (Nureyev (USA))
1895[8] 2531[3] (2764) 3012[2] 3496[4] (6056) 6500[10] 6803[8] 6883[7]

Compton Eclaire (IRE) *N Wilson* a57 63
7 ch m Lycius(USA) —Baylands Sunshine (IRE) (Classic Secret (USA))
4280[7] 4451[9] 5283[15]

Compton Eclipse *J J Lambe* a52 69
7 ch g Singspiel(IRE) —Fatah Flare (USA) (Alydar (USA))
3600[12] 6316[8] 6342[7]

Compton Express *Jamie Poulton* a53 46
4 gr m Compton Place—Jilly Woo (Environment Friend)
133[2] 416[3] 615[5] 775[13] 1396[5] 1926[7] 2361[7] 3186[10] 5001[11] 5422[10] 6175[8] 7166[10]

Compton Falcon *G A Butler* a51 73
3 ch g Peintre Celebre(USA) —Lesgor (USA) (Irish River (FR))
1369[3] 2436[7] 3366[3] 6275[6] 6745[6] 6991[7]

Compton Lad *D A Nolan* a11 50
4 b g Compton Place—Kintara (Cyrano De Bergerac)
1594[18] 3536[8] 3782[16] 4157[9] 4967[8] 5282[10] 5481[7] 5672[11] 5930[11]

Compton Micky *R F Marvin* a38 35
6 ch g Compton Place—Nunthorpe (Mystiko (USA))
137[6]

Compton Plume *M W Easterby* a55 65
7 ch g Compton Place—Brockton Flame (Emarati (USA))
892[11] 1241[4] 1675[3] 2033[15] 2421[5] 2947[6] 3636[3] 4083[5] 4423[6] 5284[15]

Compton Quay *Karen George* a42
5 ch g Compton Place—Roonah Quay (IRE) (Soviet Lad (USA))
1279[8]

Compton Ridge *Mrs A J Perrett* 67
2 b c Compton Place—Mana Pools (IRE) (Brief Truce (USA))
2473[5] 5872[4] 6079[4] (Dead)

Compton Rose *H Candy* 57
2 ch f Compton Place—Benjarong (Sharpo)
4016[5]

Compton's Eleven *M R Channon* a103 106
6 gr g Compton Place—Princess Tara (Prince Sabo)
409a[6] 470a[7] 1041[5] 1474[19] 1836[8] 2239[10] 2689[2] 2835[4] 3488[3] 3953[9] (4606) 5044[5] 5413[5] 5809[3] 5923[13] 6205[14]

Compton Special *J G Given* a50 41
3 ch f Compton Place—Spectina (Spectrum (IRE))
996[5] 1943[10] 3281[7] 3918[5] 4224[11] 4741[5] 5175[10]

Comptonspirit *B P J Baugh* a59 72
3 ch f Compton Place—Croeso Cynnes (Most Welcome)
301[10] 678[3] 998[4] 1437[6] 2262[4] 2718[3] 3168[4] 4330[6] 4661[2] (4935) 5139[4] 5401[6]

Compulsion *Pat Eddery* a60 46
4 br m Bertolini(USA) —Comme Ca (Cyrano De Bergerac)
2173[5] 5129[6] 6062[8] 6580[3] 6963[7]

Comrade Cotton *N A Callaghan* a66 66
3 b g Royal Applause—Cutpurse Moll (Green Desert (USA))
55[2] (290) 336[11] 1738[2] 1948[9] 2363[4] 2415[5] 3099[4] 3178[9] 6278[11] 6455[4]

Conbextra *J S Moore* a66 41
3 ch g Pivotal—Muffled (USA) (Mizaaya)
1398[9] 2173[4] 2470[11] (Dead)

Conceal *R Bouresly* a86 103
9 b g Cadeaux Genereux—Mystery Play (IRE) (Sadler's Wells (USA))
178a[4] 326a[8] (415a)

Concealment (IRE) *R M Beckett* a68
2 b f Iron Mask(USA) —Akatib (IRE) (Lahib (USA))
5603[6] (6022)

Concentric *A Fabre* 102
3 b f Sadler's Wells(USA) —Apogee (Shirley Heights)
6460a[2]

Concertmaster *R M Beckett* a80 72
2 b c Bertolini(USA) —Cumbrian Concerto (Petong)
814[2] 999[3] 1315[2] (2349) (3426) 4605[6] 5393a[6] 6059[6]

Condi (IRE) *A J Lidderdale* 52
3 b f Diktat—Bea's Ruby (IRE) (Fairy King (USA))
1725[7] 1901[10] 2219[12]

Conduit (IRE) *Sir Michael Stoute* a81 67
2 ch c Dalakhani(IRE) —Well Head (IRE) (Sadler's Wells (USA))
4362[7] *4947[3]* *(5646)*

Conference Call *P Bary* 111
2 b f Anabaa(USA) —Phone West (USA) (Gone West (USA))
6040a[2]

Confide In Me *G A Butler* a33
3 b g Medicean—Confidante (USA) (Dayjur (USA))
1398[12]

Confidence Trick (USA) *Sir Michael Stoute* 79
2 ch c Rahy(USA) —Hiaam (USA) (Alydar (USA))
4777[9] (5343)

Confidentiality (IRE) *M Wigham* a88 46
3 b f Desert Style(IRE) —Confidential (Generous (IRE))
(6796) (6894) (6906) (7023) (7080) (7131)

Confidential Lady *Sir Mark Prescott* 115
4 b m Singspiel(IRE) —Confidante (USA) (Dayjur (USA))
5618[13]

Confirm (IRE) *H Rogers* 63
3 b f In The Wings—Ashkirk (Selkirk (USA))
5279[7]

Confront *Sir Michael Stoute* 105
2 b c Nayef(USA) —Contiguous (USA) (Danzig (USA))
5628[2] (6171)

Confuchias (IRE) *Francis Ennis* 114
3 b c Cape Cross(IRE) —Schust Madame (IRE) (Second Set (IRE))
948a[2] 1547a[5] 2051a[7] (3088) 5842a[5] 6338[13]

Confucius Classic (IRE) *J R Boyle* a64 92
3 ch g Danehill Dancer(IRE) —Sublime Beauty (USA) (Caerleon (USA))
2470[9] 2878[9] *4066[3]* 4907[4] *5118[3]* 5588[4]

Congrio Dorado (USA) *C Von Der Recke* 42
5 b g Real Quiet(USA) —Cox Girl (USA) (Cox's Ridge (USA))
494a[5]

Conillon (GER) *A Wohler* 117
3 ch c Acatenango(GER) —Castilla (IRE) (Spectrum (IRE))
2502a[3] 3778a[2]

Conjecture *R Bastiman* a65 79
5 b g Danzig(USA) —Golden Opinion (USA) (Slew O'Gold (USA))
992[12] *1309[10]* 2418[5] 3347[2] 3627[3] 3829[4] 4180[2] 4706[3] 5284[2] 5741[11]

Connect *M H Tompkins* a87 100
10 b g Petong—Natchez Trace (Commanche Run)
218[6] *277[6]* 1195[10] 1474[20] 1788[12] 2440[12] 2882[7] 3802[3] 4351[6] 4585[14] 4895[7] 5064[11] (5535)

Connessa (IRE) *V Valiani* 74
3 b f Invincible Spirit(IRE) —Corbetta (IRE) (Polar Falcon (USA))
2707a[12]

Connor's Choice *Andrew Turnell* a31 78
2 b g Bertolini(USA) —Susan's Dowry (Efisio)
2349[10] 3589[8] 5343[2] 5937[3] 6448[2]

Connotation *A G Newcombe* a78 60
5 b m Mujahid(USA) —Seven Wonders (USA) (Rahy (USA))
121[5] *431[2]* *651[12]*

Conny Nobel (IRE) *C Roberts* a65 56
3 gr g Marju(IRE) —Beauharnaise (FR) (Linamix (FR))
140[7] *209[8]* *603[10]* *791[5]* *834[5]* 1059[6] *1164[9]* *2259[2]* 2490[5] *3624[11]* 3903[3] 4531[2] 4877[5]

Conorville (IRE) *B W Hills* a49
3 b g Compton Place—Courtenay (Vettori (IRE))
160[10] *573[9]* *678[7]*

Conquest (IRE) *W J Haggas* 113
3 b g Invincible Spirit(IRE) —Aguinaga (IRE) (Machiavellian (USA))
1770[17] 2291a[5] 2733[15] 4813[5] 5325[3] 5953[11] 6183[15]

Conquisto *C G Cox* 67
2 ch g Hernando(FR) —Seal Indigo (IRE) (Glenstal (USA))
1832[12] 4070[6] 5977[10]

Conrad *R A Fahey* a71 75
4 b g Royal Applause—Milly-M (Cadeaux Genereux)
102[3] *262[6]* *424[10]* *681[5]* *809[4]* *932[9]*

Conroy (USA) *A Manuel* a98 16
9 ch g Gone West(USA) —Crystal Gazing (USA) (El Gran Senor (USA))
249a[12]

Conservative *P G Murphy* a64 74
4 bb g Pivotal—Happy Omen (Warning)
651[10] *869[6]*

Consonant (IRE) *D G Bridgwater* a86 74
10 ch g Barathea(IRE) —Dina Lina (FR) (Top Ville)
205[12] *564[6]* *675[8]* 976[17] 1539[13]

Constant Cheers (IRE) *W R Swinburn* a70 67
4 b g Royal Applause—Juno Marlowe (IRE) (Danehill (USA))
3617[3] *4025[3]* (4458) *6102[4]* *6666[4]*

Consuelita *B J Meehan* a57 62
4 bb m Singspiel(IRE) —Green Rosy (USA) (Green Dancer (USA))
88[7]

Consular *I Mohammed* a99 103
5 br g Singspiel(IRE) —Language Of Love (Rock City)
475a[13]

Consulate (IRE) *David Wachman* 105
3 b c Rock Of Gibraltar(IRE) —Soha (USA) (Dancing Brave (USA))
2816[11]

Consul General *D K Weld* 101
3 b c Selkirk(USA) —West Dakota (USA) (Gone West (USA))
948a[4]

Contemplation *G A Swinbank* a67 64
4 b g Sunday Silence(USA) —Wood Vine (USA) (Woodman (USA))
1265[6] 1578[5] 1918[14] 3101[11] 3414[6] 4079[9] 4660[13] (5487) 6077[5] 6304[6]

Contented (IRE) *Mrs L C Jewell* a60 63
5 b g Orpen(USA) —Joyfullness (USA) (Dixieland Band (USA))
3950[12] 4397[6] (4853) 5090[3] 5942[6] *6210[12]* *6582[2]* *6895[5]* *7028[11]*

Contentious (USA) *J L Dunlop* 102
3 b f Giant's Causeway(USA) —Illicit (USA) (Mr Prospector (USA))
(2429) 3332[5] 4005[2] 5058a[12] 5794[3] 6299[8] 6690a[2]

Contessina (IRE) *P F I Cole* a66 50
2 ch f Medicean—Queen's Music (USA) (Dixieland Band (USA))
4061[10] *6434[8]* *7190[5]*

Contest (IRE) *David Wachman* 104
3 b c Danehill Dancer(IRE) —Mala Mala (IRE) (Brief Truce (USA))
2672[3] 5394a[10]

Continent *D Nicholls* a86 100
10 ch g Lake Coniston(IRE) —Krisia (Kris)
828[8] 1088[17] 1854[2] 2529[7] (2744) 2841[5] 3050[10] 3401[12] (4095) 4696[13] 5195[6] 5584[5] 5809[10]

Contingency Plan (IRE) *Patrick Tallis* a71 58
2 b f Choisir(AUS) —Dame Portia (IRE) (Approach The Bench (IRE))
6161a[11]

Contrada *R Charlton* 67
2 b c Medicean—Trounce (Barathea (IRE))
6127[7]

Contra Mundum (USA) *B S Rothwell* a59 78
4 ch g Giant's Causeway(USA) —Speak Softly To Me (USA) (Ogygian (USA))
98[8] *305[5]* *464[11]* *533[7]* *605[7]* 1086[12] 1239[7] 1671[8] 1744[9]

Controvento (IRE) *Eamon Tyrrell* a39 77
5 b m Midhish—La Maya (IRE) (Scenic)
(873a) 1806[9] 4103[4] 4158[7] 4498[8]

Convallaria (FR) *G Wragg* a64 64
4 b m Cape Cross(IRE) —Scarlet Davis (FR) (Ti King (FR))
1447[6] 2154[2] 2905[8] *5494[7]* 6413[17] *6825[5]* *6950[3]*

Converti *H J Manners* a57 54
3 b g Averti(IRE) —Conquestadora (Hernando (FR))
1039[11] *2454[2]* *2801[11]* *3082[5]* (3593) 4015[10]

Convince (USA) *J M Bradley* a48 70
6 ch g Mt. Livermore(USA) —Conical (Zafonic (USA))
751[6] 975[3] 1562[5] (1921) 2107[11] 2540[7] 5062[9] 5190[10] 5864[6] *5900[6]* *6179[12]*

Convivial Spirit *E F Vaughan* a72 64
3 b g Lake Coniston(IRE) —Ruby Princess (IRE) (Mac's Imp (USA))
219[2] *(336)* *502[3]* *(737)* *935[5]* 1658[9] 2335[10] *2518[4]* 4165[5] 4807[14] 5275[6] 5708[5] 6623[3] *6874[5]* *7073[3]*

Coolaw (IRE) *G G Margarson* a46
4 br m Priolo(USA) —Cool Gales (Lord Gayle (USA))
495[10] *615[14]*

Cool Box (USA) *Mrs A J Perrett* a88 82
3 b c Grand Slam(USA) —Frigidette (USA) (It's Freezing (USA))
1124[7] 1603[7] *1930[2]* 2476[8] *4068[6]* 5593[6] *6002[5]* *6435[5]*

Cool Ebony *M Dods* 83
4 br g Erhaab(USA) —Monawara (IRE) (Namaqualand (USA))
953[5] 1481[6] 2469[12] 2822[4] 3816[4] 4177[6] 4382[3] (5035) 5228[2] 5693[5] 6180[18]

Coole Dodger (IRE) *B G Powell* a65
2 ch c Where Or When(IRE) —Shining High (Shirley Heights)
6403[10] *6641[4]* *6805[4]* *6973[9]* *7030[3]*

Cool Fashion (IRE) *Ollie Pears* a2
2 b f Orpen(USA) —Fun Fashion (IRE) (Polish Patriot (USA))
6912[9] *7139[7]*

Cool Hunter *R C Guest* a62 89
6 ch g Polar Falcon(USA) —Seabound (Prince Sabo)
693[10]

Cool Isle *P Howling* a56 45
4 b m Polar Prince(IRE) —Fisher Island (IRE) (Sri Pekan (USA))
78[7] *1592[8]* 2055[11] 3593[9] *4460[5]* *5235[4]* 5542[3] *6212[10]* *6292[5]* *7102[2]* *7226[6]*

Cool Judgement (IRE) *M A Jarvis* 78
2 b c Peintre Celebre(USA) —Sadinga (IRE) (Sadler's Wells (USA))
3095[3] 4151[14] (6202)

Cool Panic (IRE) *M L W Bell* a74 93
5 b g Brave Act—Geht Schnell (Fairy King (USA))
1268[6] 1845[17] 5874[14]

Cool Sands (IRE) *D Shaw* a77 58
5 b g Trans Island—Shalerina (USA) (Shalford (IRE))
70[3] *131[11]* *292[3]* *(323)* *468[3]* *516[3]* *(561)* *672[5]* *717[5]* *(774)* *(1935)* *1977[8]* *3108[6]* *3188[8]* 3388[8] *6907[7]* *7026[10]* *7054[4]* *7253[14]*

Cool Sting (IRE) *M G Quinlan* a67 73
4 b g Bluebird(USA) —Honey Bee (Alnasr Alwasheek)
650[9] 1212[14]

Cool The Heels (IRE) *J S Moore* a58 59
2 b g Catcher In The Rye(IRE) —Alinea (USA) (Kingmambo (USA))
3552[10] *4393[7]* 5186[5]

Cool Tiger *P Howling* a56 65
4 ch g Vettori(IRE) —Juvenilia (IRE) (Masterclass (USA))
221[5] *383[6]* *548[8]* *627[6]* *722[7]* 980[16]

Cool Touch (IRE) *Peter Casey* a85 109
4 b g Marju(IRE) —Feather Star (Soviet Star (USA))
1330a[3] 2067a[4] 2483a[4] 2851a[4]

Coombe Centenary *L Montague Hall* a40
5 b m Robellino(USA) —Shining Dancer (Rainbow Quest (USA))
212[12] *500[9]*

Cooperstown *I Semple* a33 78
4 ch g Dr Fong(USA) —Heckle (In The Wings)
3015[2] 3994[3] 4716[10] *6480[6]*

Copernican *Sir Mark Prescott* a73 84
3 ch g Hernando(FR) —Wonderful World (GER) (Dashing Blade)
(2389) (2558) (2808) *3189[5]*

Copperbottomed (IRE) *J R Boyle* a67 61
2 ch g Redback—Stoneware (Bigstone (IRE))
5097[11] 5521[5] 5856[10] *6151[5]* *6388[5]* 6722[7] *6812[5]* *(6958)* *7044[2]* *7142[5]* *7246[2]*

Copper Dock (IRE) *T G McCourt* a51 62
3 b g Docksider(USA) —Sundown (Polish Precedent (USA))
5834[3]

Coppergirl (IRE) *G A Huffer* a48 65
3 b f Iron Mask(USA) —Scarlet Woman (Sri Pekan (USA))
3406[9] (3824) 5046[4] 5514[11] *6272[7]*

Copper King *J W Hills* a82 80
3 ch g Ishiguru(USA) —Dorissio (IRE) (Efisio)
113[3] *216[2]* *483[4]* *638[8]* 1076[2] 1563[6] 1603[3] 2040[8] 3690[4] (3996) *4462[6]* 4880[11] *5424[7]* *6024[10]*

Coppermalt (USA) *R Curtis* a51 66
9 b g Affirmed(USA) —Poppy Carew (IRE) (Danehill (USA))
315[9]

Copperwood *M Blanshard* 74
2 ch c Bahamian Bounty—Sophielu (Rudimentary (USA))
4761[2] 5329[4] 6126[5]

Coppington Melody (IRE) *B W Duke* a57 38
4 b m Ordway(USA) —Chorus (USA) (Darshaan)
71[8] *134[12]* *909[11]*

Copywriter *J H M Gosden* a81 93
2 b g Efisio—Copy-Cat (Lion Cavern (USA))
3625[4] *3850[5]* *(4883)* 5324[3] 5974[3]

Coquerelle (IRE) *J-C Rouget* 113
3 b f Zamindar(USA) —Cracovie (Caerleon (USA))
(1880a) 2501a[14]

Coral Creek (IRE) *M J Grassick* a73 72
3 b f Invincible Spirit(IRE) —Antapoura (IRE) (Bustino)
(6856)

Coral Shores *P W Hiatt* a48 61
2 b f Carnival Dancer—Leading Role (Cadeaux Genereux)
4265[3] 4904[11] 5110[14] *5984[6]* 6536[5] *6827[10]* *7007[6]* *7121[8]*

Coranglais *J M Bradley* a43 58
7 ch g Piccolo—Antonia's Folly (Music Boy)
7077[9] *7192[11]*

Corconte (FR) *R Avial Lopez* 84
2 b c Sagacity(FR) —Joie De Rose (FR) (Procida (USA))
6377a[4]

Cordell (IRE) *R Hannon* a78 76
2 b c Fasliyev(USA) —Urgele (FR) (Zafonic (USA))
1721[4] 3747[4] 4048[12] 4506[3] 5324[16] *(5679)* 6297[6]

Cordier *J Mackie* a83 49
5 b g Desert Style(IRE) —Slipper (Suave Dancer (USA))
1181[2] 1813[12] 4333[7]

Cordon Bleu (IRE) *M Johnston* a64 59
2 br c Key Of Luck(USA) —Blue Note (FR) (Habitat)
3560[10] 4174[3] *4963[3]* 5314[14] 5773[9] *6263[8]*

Corinthian (USA) *J Jerkens* a122
4 ch h Pulpit(USA) —Multiply (USA) (Easy Goer (USA))
5059a[4] *(6485a)*

Corking (IRE) *Eve Johnson Houghton* a37 52
2 b f Montjeu(IRE) —Scanno's Choice (IRE) (Pennine Walk)
5681[11] 6093[10]

Corkscrew Hill (IRE) *N A Callaghan* a47 50
3 b f Golan(IRE) —Perugia (IRE) (Perugino (USA))
2836[9] 3057[4] 3629[6] 4287[10]

Corlough Mountain *M J McGrath* a74 74
3 ch g Inchinor—Two Step (Mujtahid (USA))
2749[2] 3167[3] 3349[5] 3752[14] *6232[5]* *7164[3]* *(7269)*

Cormorant Wharf (IRE) *T E Powell* a74 75
7 b g Alzao(USA) —Mercy Bien (IRE) (Be My Guest (USA))
1609[7] 2055[9] 2467[3] 4356[2] 4597[9]

Cornell Precedent *J J Quinn* 48
3 ch g Polish Precedent(USA) —Shamwari (USA) (Shahrastani (USA))
2133[17] 2538[10] 3540[4] 4391[8] 4894[8]

Cornerstone *S C Williams* a41 58
3 ch g Pivotal—Splice (Sharpo)
127[10] *260[10]* *573[12]* 2661[4] 2750[3] 3713[8] (3949)

Cornus *A J McCabe* a84 87
5 ch g Inchinor—Demerger (USA) (Distant View (USA))
323[6] *(513)* *774[8]* *835[5]* 1061[8] 1200[5] 1847[3] 2088[2] 2394[6] 2744[3] 2882[11] 3053[3] *3599[8]* 3762[9] 4800[8] (5232) 5297[5] 5642[9] 5840[8] 5909[4] (6103) (6283) 6450[11] *6836[4]* *6907[2]* *6981[10]*

Coronado's Gold (USA) *B Ellison* a56 60
6 ch g Coronado's Quest(USA) —Debit My Account (USA) (Classic Account (USA))
(2431) *3067[13]* 4031[6] 4477[4] 4820[15]

Coronation Flight *F P Murtagh* a24 54
4 b m Missed Flight—Hand On Heart (IRE) (Taufan (USA))
1045[9] *1380[8]* 1744[6] 3538[6] 3996[9] (Dead)

Corre Solta (BRZ) *H J Brown* a58
4 gr m Ski Champ(USA) —Ion Drive (BRZ) (Clackson (BRZ))
246a[8] *647a[6]*

Correy *Miss J S Davis* a31 45
3 ch f Tobougg(IRE) —Numerate (Bishop Of Cashel)
3732[6] 4071[11] 4256[16] (4528) *6534[14]*

Corrib (IRE) *B Palling* a75 72
4 b m Lahib(USA) —Montana Miss (IRE) (Earl Of Barking (IRE))
895[8] 1564[7] 1787[7] 2654[3] 2980[5] 3487[15] (4577) 5189[3] 5348[2] *6146[7]* *7131[7]*

Corrib Eclipse *Ian Williams* a78 79
8 b g Double Eclipse(IRE) —Last Night's Fun (IRE) (Law Society (USA))
2860[9]

Corridor Creeper (FR) *J M Bradley* 112
10 ch g Polish Precedent(USA) —Sonia Rose (USA) (Superbity (USA))
1125[9] 1601[2] 1788[2] 2034[4] 2234[9] 2858[26] 3526[3] 3990[20] 4567[17] 4696[10] 5050[13] 5212[5] 5513[5] 6173[14]

Corriolanus (GER) *A M Balding* a102 101
7 b g Zamindar(USA) —Caesarea (GER) (Generous (IRE))
248a[5] 412a[11] 545a[9] 3461[11] 4376[6] 5255[9] 6172[7]

Corrybrough *H Candy* 92
2 ch c Kyllachy—Calamanco (Clantime)
5772[2] (6234)

Cortesia (IRE) *P W Chapple-Hyam* a72 84
4 ch m Courteous—Cecina (Welsh Saint)
1356[9] 1813[5] 2361[6] 3107[4] *3945[9]* 4576[13] 5514[6] *6068[5]*

Corum (IRE) *Mrs K Waldron* a89 92
4 b g Galileo(IRE) —Vallee Des Reves (USA) (Kingmambo (USA))
1582[9] 2047[3] *(3112)* 4288[8] 4786[6]

Corviglia *C E Longsdon* a17 48
4 b m Nashwan(USA) —Ski Run (Petoski)
2620[9] *3457[8]*

Coseadrom (IRE) *M F Harris* a63 82
5 b g Almutawakel—Madam Lightfoot (USA) (Vice Regent (CAN))
3836[3] 4389[11] 4585[11] 4800[10] 5430[6] 6157[17] *6647[3]* *6764[5]* *6870[8]*

Cosenza *H J L Dunlop* a45 69
2 b f Bahri(USA) —Dawnus (IRE) (Night Shift (USA))
1945[9] 2997[4] 4102[9]

Cosi *L Brogi* 94
3 b f Galileo(IRE) —Sopran Dandy (IRE) (Doyoun)
2707a[8]

Cosimo Primo *J A Geake* a47 44
3 b g Medicean—Cugina (Distant Relative)
1839[9] *5095[7]*

Cosmea *A King* a51 66
2 b f Compton Place—St James's Antigua (IRE) (Law Society (USA))
2968[6] *3423[7]* 4329[4] 4991[9] 6449[10]

Cosmic Apollo *Rae Guest* a42 44
5 ch g Pennekamp(USA) —Windmill Princess (Gorytus (USA))
1716[7] 2153[8]

Cosmic Art *E A L Dunlop* a90 95
2 b c Bertolini(USA) —Cosmic Song (Cosmonaut)
2333[6] *2569[2]* *(3283)* *(3925)* 4168[5] *(4431)* 4743[3]

Cosmic Destiny (IRE) *E F Vaughan* a67 76
5 b m Soviet Star(USA) —Cruelle (USA) (Irish River (FR))
613[7] *746[12]* *1067[3]* *1120[6]* 1321[4] 1669[13] 1991[4] *2221[5]* 2459[3] (2555) 2966[3] *3190[2]* *3853[2]* (4314) (4689) 5029[3] 5726[2] 6450[4]

Cosmo Bulk (JPN) *K Tabe* 121
6 b h Zagreb(USA) —Iseno Tosho (JPN) (Tosho Boy (JPN))
1877a[2] 6943a[13]

Cosmodrome (USA) *L M Cumani* a75 102
3 b f Bahri(USA) —Space Time (FR) (Bering)
(1312) (1958) 2786[7]

Cosmonaut (USA) *F Parisel* a107 118
5 rg h Lemon Drop Kid(USA) —Cosmic Fire (USA) (Capote (USA))
6511a[3]

Cossack Prince *B J Meehan* a78 66
2 b g Dubai Destination(USA) —Danemere (IRE) (Danehill (USA))
5977[11] 6417[4] *(6934)*

Cost Analysis (IRE) *Mrs P Ford* a37
5 ch g Grand Lodge(USA) —Flower Girl (Pharly (FR))
5778[11] *6563[10]* *6959[7]*

Costume *J H M Gosden* 114
3 b f Danehill(USA) —Dance Dress (USA) (Nureyev (USA))
1105[3] 1702a[4] (2341) 2757[3] 4118[2] 5248a[4]

Cotocachi (IRE) *Edward P Harty* a68 46
3 b f Imperial Ballet(IRE) —Mackem Beat (Aragon)
6920a[6]

Cottam Breeze *M W Easterby* a19 33
2 b f Diktat—Flower Breeze (USA) (Rahy (USA))
2904[10] 3760[9] 4487[11] 4796[13] *5100[8]*

Cottam Eclipse *I W McInnes* 52
6 b g Environment Friend—Che Gambe (USA) (Lyphard (USA))
968[7] 1259[6] 1676[6] 1918[13] 2203[10] 2937[4] 3376[7] 4294[13] 4488[6] 4802[10]

Cottam Grange *I W McInnes* a13 24
7 b g River Falls—Karminski (Pitskelly)
804[9] 965[6]

Cotton Eyed Joe (IRE) *G A Swinbank* a77 78
6 b g Indian Rocket—Cwm Deri (IRE) (Alzao (USA))
1752[4] *2148[4]* (2715) 2987[4] 3371[3] 3753[8] (4124) 4352[4] 4969[2] 5677[6]

Cotton Reel *P F I Cole* 74
2 b c Cape Cross(IRE) —Cotton House (IRE) (Mujadil (USA))
5587[4] 5868[6] 6617[3]

Cougar Bay (IRE) *David Wachman* 113
4 b g Daylami(IRE) —Delimara (IRE) (In The Wings)
3144a[3] 3579a[2] 4826[3] 5240a[5] 5459a[2]

Councellor (FR) *Stef Liddiard* a94 83
5 b g Gilded Time(USA) —Sudden Storm Bird (USA) (Storm Bird (CAN))
44[11] *190[12]* *351[3]* *427[3]* *(525)* *629[2]* *697[9]* *(842)* *1180[4]* 1996[4] 2401[12] 2719[7] 4268[4] *5221[11]* 5545[9] *6024[2]* *6121[3]* *(6385)* *6674[4]* *(6949)* *(6981)* *7074[4]* *7183[4]* *7254[6]* *7267[5]*

Counsel's Opinion (IRE) *C F Wall* a108 111
10 ch g Rudimentary(USA) —Fairy Fortune (Rainbow Quest (USA))
701[10] 995[7] 1245[8] *2351[6]* 3272[4] 3959[11] 4551[4] 4909[4] 5432[6]

Countback (FR) *A W Carroll* a52 16
8 b g Anabaa(USA) —Count Me Out (FR) (Kaldoun (FR))
39^{10} 134^{4} 285^{5} 496^{5} 615^{2} 792^{3} 1229^{5} 2511^{8} 7273^{6}

Count Ceprano (IRE) *M D I Usher* a87 86
3 b g Desert Prince(IRE) —Camerlata (Common Grounds)
1202^{4} 1439^{3} 2943^{5} 3553^{9} 3944^{10} 7279^{7}

Count Cougar (USA) *S P Griffiths* a82 19
7 b g Sir Cat(USA) —Gold Script (USA) (Seeking The Gold (USA))
(225) (306) 317^{2} (717) (905) 1565^{2} 1977^{6} 3608^{14} 6938^{9} (7179) 7215^{7}

Countdown *T D Easterby* a82 92
5 ch g Pivotal—Quiz Time (Efisio)
1481^{3} 1818^{5} 2339^{6} 2566^{5} 2841^{4} (3201) (3559) 3953^{6} 4195^{6} 4401^{10} 5031^{14} 5617^{8}

Counterclaim *Saeed Bin Suroor* a75 69
2 ch f Pivotal—Dusty Answer (Zafonic (USA))
5428^{7} 5881^{4} 6358^{2} 6611^{2}

Counterfactual (IRE) *B Smart* a48 56
4 br g Key Of Luck(USA) —Wakayi (Persian Bold)
7^{7} 72^{9} 732^{5} 1044^{5} 1918^{7} 2168^{8} 2582^{10} 5503^{7}

Countess Majella (IRE) *E J O'Neill* a54 50
3 b f Grand Lodge(USA) —Mrs Moonlight (Ajdal (USA))
386^{8}

Counting House (IRE) *J A B Old* a68 85
4 ch g King's Best(USA) —Inforapenny (Deploy)
5594^{2} 7151^{3}

Count Kristo *B G Powell* a56 78
5 br g Dr Fong(USA) —Aryadne (Rainbow Quest (USA))
259^{9} 422^{6}

Country Affair (USA) *P R Webber* a75 58
4 ch g Vettori(IRE) —Nany's Affair (USA) (Colonial Affair (USA))
422^{5} 568^{9}

Country Pursuit (USA) *C E Brittain* a91 88
5 ch g Theatrical—Jade Flush (USA) (Jade Hunter (USA))
95^{9} 1272^{6}

Country Rambler (USA) *Doug Watson* a62 74
5 b h Red Ransom(USA) —Country Garden (Selkirk (USA))
104a^{10}

Country Song (USA) *J Noseda* a92 98
3 bb c Fusaichi Pegasus(USA) —Eliza (USA) (Mt. Livermore (USA))
173a^{4} 414a^{4} 641a^{4}

Countrywide Comet (IRE) *P Howling* a62 60
2 b g Desert Style(IRE) —Darzao (IRE) (Alzao (USA))
1487^{5} 1889^{4} 2147^{5} 5298^{4} 5902^{3} 6150^{7} (6305) (6586) 6736^{7} 6966^{11} 7136^{5} 7210^{5}

Countrywide Style (IRE) *N P Littmoden* a19 52
3 b g Xaar—Nautical Light (Slip Anchor)
106^{11} 373^{13} 534^{9}

Count Trevisio (IRE) *Saeed Bin Suroor* 108
4 b g Danehill(USA) —Stylish (Anshan)
(104a) 398a^{2} 544a^{7} 2755^{21} 4167^{3}

County Crystal *T D Easterby* 36
2 b c Mujahid(USA) —Cumbrian Crystal (Mind Games)
3915^{10}

County Kerry (UAE) *Jean-Rene Auvray* a54 33
3 b f Jade Robbery(USA) —Limerick Belle (IRE) (Roi Danzig (USA))
114^{6} 720^{6} 864^{3} 4018^{8} 4392^{6} 4504^{10} 5894^{11}

Coup D'Etat *R A Harris* a52 91
5 b g Diktat—Megdale (IRE) (Waajib)
1434^{3} 1765^{9} 2311^{9} 2621^{6} 3572^{2} 3828^{4} 4418^{8} (4657) 4807^{13} 5693^{8} 5864^{3} 6024^{11}

Courant D'Air (IRE) *Lucinda Featherstone* 28
6 b g Indian Rocket—Red River Rose (IRE) (Red Sunset)
4535^{7} 4994^{9}

Court Masterpiece *Saeed Bin Suroor* a100 124
7 b h Polish Precedent(USA) —Easy Option (IRE) (Prince Sabo)
530a^{8} 858a^{5}

Court Of Appeal *B Ellison* a64 73
10 ch g Bering—Hiawatha's Song (USA) (Chief's Crown (USA))
(891) (966) (1554) 2342^{4} 2987^{3} 3496^{2} 4558^{6} 4941^{6}

Court One *R E Barr* 36
9 b g Shareef Dancer(USA) —Fairfields Cone (Celtic Cone)
2417^{4}

Cousteau *John Joseph Hanlon* a81 104
4 ch g Spinning World(USA) —Wavy Up (IRE) (Brustolon)
4211a^{12} 4867a^{10}

Coustou (IRE) *R M Stronge* a42 29
7 b g In Command(IRE) —Carranza (IRE) (Lead On Time (USA))
1003^{6}

Cove Mountain (IRE) *M G Rimell* a66 66
5 br m Indian Danehill(IRE) —Nordic Pride (Horage)
1251^{10} 2336^{13} 2656^{5} 3405^{9} 6529^{13} 7079^{7} 7219^{4}

Covert Mission *P D Evans* a59 59
4 b m Overbury(IRE) —Peg's Permission (Ra Nova)
5005^{5} 5271^{6} 5384^{8} 5777^{9} 6196^{11} 6751^{3} 6911^{8} 7060^{10}

Cow Girl (IRE) *Miss Gay Kelleway* a58 67
3 b f King's Best(USA) —Reveuse De Jour (IRE) (Sadler's Wells (USA))
3276^{4} 3561^{2} 3992^{9} 4321^{2} 4684^{5} 4989^{3} 5563^{4} 5865^{6} 6278^{5} 6567^{6} 7269^{9}

Cowtown Cat (USA) *T Pletcher* a111
3 ch c Distorted Humor(USA) —Tom's Cat (USA) (Storm Cat (USA))
1486a^{20}

Coy Coyote (USA) *M Dickinson* a103
3 b f Honour And Glory(USA) —Desert Prowler (USA) (Desert Wine (USA))
3810a^{6}

Coyote Creek *E F Vaughan* 82
3 b g Zilzal(USA) —High Barn (Shirley Heights)
1355^{3} 1887^{3} 2602^{2} 3883^{9} 4403^{3} 5113^{2}

Cozy Tiger (USA) *W J Musson* a76
2 gr g Hold That Tiger(USA) —Cozelia (USA) (Cozzene (USA))
6805^{3} 6934^{2}

C P West (USA) *N Zito* a114
3 b c Came Home(USA) —Queen's Legend (USA) (Dynaformer (USA))
1882a^{4} 2487a^{5}

Cracking (IRE) *R Hannon* 93
2 b c Acclamation—Adieu Cherie (IRE) (Bustino)
1058^{8} (1315) (1580) 2232^{5} 2785^{11} 4168^{3} 4812^{10} 5974^{23}

Cracking Nick (IRE) *W R Swinburn* a70 63
2 b g Cape Cross(IRE) —Enrich (USA) (Dynaformer (USA))
2590^{5} 3596^{3} 4328^{5}

Crafty Fox *John A Harris* a61 58
4 b g Foxhound(USA) —Surrealist (ITY) (Night Shift (USA))
138^{3} 497^{9} 560^{7} 690^{11} 866^{8} (1719) 2331^{4} 3191^{8} 3619^{3} 4219^{3} 4856^{11} 5338^{11} 6247^{18}

Crafty George (IRE) *J G Coogan* 35
2 ch g Rossini(USA) —Tidler (IRE) (Rainbows For Life (CAN))
4832a^{22}

Cragganmore Creek *D Morris* a63 31
4 b g Tipsy Creek(USA) —Polish Abbey (Polish Precedent (USA))
64^{3} 503^{4} 982^{8} 1402^{3} 1590^{12} 1934^{3} 2345^{7} 4535^{11} 4914^{2} 5389^{5} 6292^{2} 6613^{5} 6835^{7}

Craggy Cat (IRE) *L M Cumani* 90
2 b c Statue Of Liberty(USA) —Trexana (Kaldoun (FR))
3037^{3} 4130^{3} (4818) (5331) 6017^{6}

Craigstown *Saeed Bin Suroor* 75
2 b c Cape Cross(IRE) —Craigmill (Slip Anchor)
4151^{5} 4890^{4} 6418^{7}

Craig Y Nos *A Berry* 2
3 ch f Auction House(USA) —Thabeh (Shareef Dancer (USA))
3016^{4} 4178^{11} 5082^{11}

Cranworth Blaze *T J Etherington* a20 43
3 b f Diktat—Julietta Mia (USA) (Woodman (USA))
1709^{4} 2206^{10} 2951^{10} 4411^{4} 4997^{5}

Crathorne (IRE) *M Todhunter* a39 71
7 b g Alzao(USA) —Shirley Blue (IRE) (Shirley Heights)
2567^{3} 4280^{9}

Crazy About You (IRE) *B W Hills* 42
2 b f Montjeu(IRE) —Touch Of Magic (IRE) (Brief Truce (USA))
4774^{13}

Crazy Bear (IRE) *K J Burke* a69 53
4 ch m King Charlemagne(USA) —Specifiedrisk (IRE) (Turtle Island (IRE))
(6991) 7100 7132^{4}

Creachadoir (IRE) *Saeed Bin Suroor* 124
3 b c King's Best(USA) —Sadima (IRE) (Sadler's Wells (USA))
(948a) 1185a^{4} (1547a) 1703a^{2} 2051a^{2} 2734^{6} (6009) 6334^{4} 7091a^{2}

Creative (IRE) *M H Tompkins* 67
2 b g Acclamation—Pride Of Pendle (Grey Desire)
2056^{4} 2385^{2} 4335^{6} 4832a^{16} 5624^{3} 5901^{3}

Creative Mind (IRE) *E J O'Neill* a75 92
4 b m Danehill Dancer(IRE) —Inventive (Sheikh Albadou)
1157^{4} 1661^{3} 2450^{10}

Credential *John A Harris* a68 63
5 b h Dansili—Sabria (USA) (Miswaki (USA))
(1) 74^{2} 319^{5} 507^{8} 2531^{8} 3530^{8} 4488^{2} 4860^{3} 5341^{10} 6315^{11} 6598^{16}

Credit (IRE) *Jennie Candlish* a80 94
6 b g Intikhab(USA) —Tycooness (IRE) (Last Tycoon (IRE))
35^{3}

Credit Slip *J L Dunlop* a61 72
3 b c Slip Anchor—Credit-A-Plenty (Generous (IRE))
(1361) 2105^{2} (2610)

Credit Swap *L M Cumani* 67
2 b c Diktat—Locharia (Wolfhound (USA))
6409^{4}

Cree *W R Muir* a66 62
5 b g Indian Ridge—Nightitude (Night Shift (USA))
50^{4} 66^{6} 2143^{13} 2556^{12} (Dead)

Creme Brulee *P T Dalton* a61 53
4 b m College Chapel—Balinsky (IRE) (Skyliner)
296^{8} 580^{7} 690^{9} 4668^{13} 5566^{7} 6735^{11} 6818^{12} 7138^{3}

Crescentia *Jane Chapple-Hyam*
4 ch m Vitus—Another Nightmare (IRE) (Treasure Kay)
4430^{10} 5427^{12}

Cresta Gold *A Bailey* a105 104
4 b m Halling(USA) —Fleet Hill (IRE) (Warrshan (USA))
1844^{20} 2036^{6} 5402^{6} 6014^{14}

Crested *W Dollase* 111
4 ch g Fantastic Light(USA) —Dunnes River (USA) (Danzig (USA))
6924a^{5}

Crete (IRE) *W J Haggas* a82 80
5 b g Montjeu(IRE) —Paesanella (Seattle Song (USA))
(6132) 6853^{3}

Crime Scene (IRE) *Saeed Bin Suroor* 115
4 b g Royal Applause—Crime (USA) (Gulch (USA))
328a^{4} (475a) (648a) 5976^{4} (6496)

Crimson And Gold *L Reuterskiold* 100
5 b g Singspiel(IRE) —Rosia (IRE) (Mr Prospector (USA))
2131a^{6} 4874a^{6}

Crimson Fern (IRE) *M S Saunders* a56 15
3 ch f Titus Livius(FR) —Crimada (IRE) (Mukaddamah (USA))
6062^{12} 6240^{3} (6361) 6779^{7}

Crimson Flame (IRE) *A J Chamberlain* a48 73
4 b g Celtic Swing—Wish List (IRE) (Mujadil (USA))
45^{8} 180^{6}

Crimson King (IRE) *R W Price* a92
6 ch g Pivotal—Always Happy (Sharrood (USA))
6355^{13} (7212)

Crimson Mitre *J Jay* a48 67
2 b c Bishop Of Cashel—Pink Champagne (Cosmonaut)
5984^{7} 6274^{7} 6574^{4} 6952a^{8}

Crimson Monarch (USA) *Mrs A J Perrett* 76
3 b g Red Ransom(USA) —Tolltally Light (USA) (Majestic Light (USA))
1205^{3} 1355^{4} 1637^{8} 2628^{7} 3300^{5} 5938^{3} (6275)

Crimson Silk *B Smart* 79
7 ch g Forzando—Sylhall (Sharpo)
2318^{6}

Crimsonwing (IRE) *A M Hales* a54 59
2 b f Vettori(IRE) —Crimson Topaz (Hernando (FR))
5681^{9} 5944^{9} 6274^{5} 6585^{8}

Cripsey Brook *K G Reveley* 83
9 ch g Lycius(USA) —Duwon (IRE) (Polish Precedent (USA))
(997) (1078) 1288^{10} 1490^{4} 1668^{4} 2011^{6} 5623^{5} 6021^{14} 6158^{6} 6325^{3} 6561^{5}

Crispian (IRE) *W J Haggas* 72
3 b g Hernando(FR) —Continuous (IRE) (Darshaan)
849^{3} 2253^{6} 3041^{4}

Cristal Clear (IRE) *T D Easterby* 90
2 gr f Clodovil(IRE) —Spring To Light (USA) (Blushing Groom (FR))
(1107) 1821^{3} 2134^{4} 2756^{21} 3096^{7} 4406^{6} (4695) 4899^{3} 5322^{3} 5614^{5} 6017^{13}

Cristobal (USA) *J-C Rouget* 107
3 br c Aptitude(USA) —Balenciaga (USA) (Gulch (USA))
2751a^{4} (6400a)

Criterion *Sir Michael Stoute* 71
2 b g Dr Fong(USA) —Film Script (Unfuwain (USA))
3957^{10} 6418^{4}

Critical Stage (IRE) *J D Frost* a70 59
8 b g King's Theatre(IRE) —Zandaka (FR) (Doyoun)
213^{3} 354^{2} 578^{7} 640^{7} 3969^{3} (5204) 5426^{3} 6241^{8} 6811^{8}

Criticism *H-A Pantall* a92 106
3 b f Machiavellian(USA) —Innuendo (IRE) (Caerleon (USA))
6095a^{3} 7128a^{10}

Crocodile Bay (IRE) *D Nicholls* a80 85
4 b g Spectrum(IRE) —Shenkara (IRE) (Night Shift (USA))
1287^{9} 1765^{12} 2180^{2} 2358^{2} 2748^{8} 3215^{5} 3416^{7} 4581^{7} 5228^{5} 5330^{4} 5556^{2} (5905) 6203^{2} 6560^{2} 6746^{3}

Croeso Bach *J L Spearing* 54
3 b f Bertolini(USA) —Croeso-I-Cymru (Welsh Captain)
1635^{13} 2029^{5} 4314^{2} 4759^{2} 5139^{12}

Croeso Cusan *J L Spearing* 49
2 b f Diktat—Croeso Croeso (Most Welcome)
6237^{6}

Croft (IRE) *M S Saunders* a42 61
4 b g Mull Of Kintyre(USA) —Home Comforts (Most Welcome)
3487^{16} 3966^{7} (4256) 4532^{13} 4688^{4} 4880^{13} 5001^{13} 5269^{14} 5647^{7} 6292^{6}

Croix De Guerre (IRE) *P J Hobbs* 54
7 gr g Highest Honor(FR) —Esclava (USA) (Nureyev (USA))
2430^{4}

Croix Rouge (USA) *R J Smith* a39 70
5 b h Chester House(USA) —Rougeur (USA) (Blushing Groom (FR))
283^{5} 377^{10}

Crooked Throw (IRE) *C F Swan* 104
8 bb g Anshan—Mary's View (IRE) (Phardante (FR))
848^{7} 1184a^{6} 2755^{17} 3138a^{10} 4051a^{2} 6038a^{7}

Croon *T J Pitt* a82 85
5 b g Sinndar(IRE) —Shy Minstrel (USA) (The Minstrel (CAN))
362^{4} 434^{4} 662^{4}

Crooner (IRE) *Doug Watson* a97 82
4 b h Titus Livius(FR) —John's Ballad (IRE) (Ballad Rock)
324a^{3} 474a^{F}

Crosby Hall *N Tinkler* 56
4 b g Compton Place—Alzianah (Alzao (USA))
1260^{13} 1675^{12} 3375^{13}

Crosby Jemma *J R Weymes* 49
3 ch f Lomitas—Gino's Spirits (Perugino (USA))
1558^{2} 1894^{9} 3914^{5} 4178^{5} 4971^{2} 5084^{6} 5563^{7}

Crosby Millie *J R Weymes* 55
3 gr f Linamix(FR) —Calling Card (Bering)
1424^{6} 1916^{9} 3917^{14}

Crosby Vision *J R Weymes* 74
4 b g Agnes World(USA) —Aegean Blue (Warning)
1133^{4} 1747^{8} 1892^{7} 4177^{10} 4407^{5} 4704^{7} 4931^{12}

Crossbow Creek *M G Rimell* a90 89
9 b g Lugana Beach—Roxy River (Ardross)
2512^{5} (3416) 3671^{2} 4171^{10} 5225^{5} 6169^{13}

Cross Fell (USA) *J R Boyle* a79 79
2 b c Cherokee Run(USA) —Campsie Fells (UAE) (Indian Ridge)
2432^{10} 2991^{9} 5772^{8} (6066) (6328) 6823^{3} 6936^{5} (7044)

Crossing *William J Fitzpatrick* a87 106
6 b m Cape Cross(IRE) —Piney River (Pharly (FR))
4051a^{11} 4649a^{4} 5242a^{11} 6216a^{5}

Crossing Bridges *T D Barron* a32
2 ch f Dr Fong(USA) —Pontressina (USA) (St Jovite (USA))
6912^{10} 7121^{5}

Crossing The Line (IRE) *Sir Mark Prescott* a71 57
3 b g Cape Cross(IRE) —Tropical Zone (Machiavellian (USA))
3170^{2} 3450^{P} (Dead)

Cross Of Lorraine (IRE) *J Wade* a72 72
4 b g Pivotal—My-Lorraine (IRE) (Mac's Imp (USA))
67^{4} 727^{3} 1492^{3} 1597^{7} 2072^{2} 2864^{7} 3053^{4} 3585^{2} 3998^{5}

Crosstar *M Botti* a71
2 b c Cape Cross(IRE) —Pie High (Salse (USA))
(7051)

Cross The Line (IRE) *A P Jarvis* a95 87
5 b g Cape Cross(IRE) —Baalbek (Barathea (IRE))
759^{6} 840^{2} 1040^{5} 1395^{2} 2469^{4} 3525^{4} 4049^{12} 5585^{9} 5950^{6} 6437^{12}

Crowning Moment (IRE) *H Rogers* 45
3 b f Johannesburg(USA) —Moment Of Madness (USA) (Seattle Slew (USA))
5280^{13}

Crown Office (USA) *H Morrison* a65 61
3 ch f Horse Chestnut(SAF) —Great Verdict (AUS) (Christmas Tree (AUS))
720^{4} 1433^{3} 2219^{8} 6447^{9}

Crown Point (USA) *D Donk* a90 109
5 u h Honor Grades(USA) —Runaway Ashleigh (USA) (Runaway Groom (CAN))
4415a^{4} 6771a^{4}

Crow's Nest Lad *J O'Reilly* a64 74
3 b g Komaite(USA) —Miss Fit (IRE) (Hamas (IRE))
1351^{7} 1994^{7} 3568^{6} 5387^{13} 5701^{3} 6088^{2} 6310^{9} 7155^{2}

Crow Wood *J J Quinn* a100 93
8 b g Halling(USA) —Play With Me (IRE) (Alzao (USA))
57^{3} 345^{5}

Cruel Sea (USA) *B W Hills* 84
2 gr f Mizzen Mast(USA) —Storm Dove (USA) (Storm Bird (CAN))
(6470)

Cruise Director *Ian Williams* a85 89
7 b g Zilzal(USA) —Briggsmaid (Elegant Air)
1288^{4} 1621^{8} 1771^{5}

Crumpett (IRE) *J E Hammond* 93
4 b m Montjeu(IRE) —Pretty (IRE) (Darshaan)
5150a^{8}

Crush On You *R Hollinshead* a53 54
4 b m Golden Snake(USA) —Mourir D'Aimer (USA) (Trempolino (USA))
(271) 682^{10} 1086^{6} 1360^{7} 3156^{11} 3405^{3} 4449^{6} 5179^{12} 5782^{11}

Crusoe (IRE) *A Sadik* a56 31
10 b g Turtle Island(IRE) —Self Reliance (Never So Bold)
298^{8} 364^{2} 464^{8} 518^{7} 533^{12} 579^{8} 664^{8} 742^{10} 833^{7} 1311^{11} 1380^{9}

Crux *R E Barr* a40 57
5 b g Pivotal—Penny Dip (Cadeaux Genereux)
715^{12} 2121^{6} 2312^{7} 2554^{6} 3345^{18}

Cry And Catch Me (USA) *B Baffert* a110
2 b f Street Cry(IRE) —Please Sign In (USA) (Doc's Leader (USA))
(5826a)

Crying Aloud (USA) *P A Blockley* a58 78
2 bb f Street Cry(IRE) —Angelic Deed (USA) (Alydeed (CAN))
1101^{11} 1727^{5} 5063^{2} 5435a^{9} 6461^{4}

Cry Presto (USA) *R Hannon* a78 87
3 b g Street Cry(IRE) —Sabaah Elfull (Kris)
661^{7} (703) 1810^{8} 2185^{8} 2635^{5}

Cryptic Clue (USA) *D W Chapman* a51 50
3 b g Cryptoclearance(USA) —Nidd (USA) (Known Fact (USA))
336^{12} 429^{4} 807^{5} 1031^{5} 7148^{10}

Cryptonite Diamond (USA) *W R Swinburn* a34 54
2 ch f Hennessy(USA) —Cryptotoo (USA) (Cryptoclearance (USA))
2504^{8} 4232^{5} 5707^{6} 6150^{8}

Cryptoquip (USA) *H G Motion* a102
4 bb m Cryptoclearance(USA) —Rose Hips (USA) (Meadowlake (USA))
6772a^{9}

Crystal Annie *Heather Dalton* a24 52
4 b m Namaqualand(USA) —Crystal Canyon (Efisio)
4718^{7} 5364^{12}

Crystal Ball *Rae Guest* 45
3 b f Diktat—First Sapphire (Simply Great (FR))
3248^{5}

Crystal Capella *Sir Michael Stoute* a75
2 b f Cape Cross(IRE) —Crystal Star (Mark Of Esteem (IRE))
6847^{2}

Crystal Gazer (FR) *R Hannon* a86 77
3 b f Elnadim(USA) —Chrysalu (Distant Relative)
(885) (1588) 1837^{9} 3797^{2} 4017^{4} (5684) 6006^{13}

Crystal Plum (IRE) *B W Hills* a22 60
3 ch f Rock Of Gibraltar(IRE) —State Crystal (IRE) (High Estate)
2177^{13} 2668^{11}

Crystal Prince *T P Tate* 74
3 b g Marju(IRE) —Crystal Ring (IRE) (Kris)
1153^{2} 2436^{4} 4229^{3}

Crystal Reign (IRE) *P W Chapple-Hyam* a71 74
2 b g Noverre(USA) —Crystal Springs (IRE) (Kahyasi)
2473^{2} 3095^{9} 6544^{5}

Crystal Rock (IRE) *B W Hills* 82
2 br g Rock Of Gibraltar(IRE) —State Crystal (IRE) (High Estate)
3991^{13} 4454^{2} 5033^{3} 5350^{16}

Crystany (IRE) *H R A Cecil* 90
2 b f Green Desert(USA) —Crystal Music (USA) (Nureyev (USA))
3055^{4} 4061^{5} (5042) 5322^{2}

Cuban (FR) *J-P Delaporte* a64 75
4 b g Ski Chief(USA) —If Only (FR) (Highest Honor (FR))
(6923a)

Cuban Missile *R Charlton* 81
2 b g Danehill Dancer(IRE) —Lady Salsa (IRE) (Gone West (USA))
6248^{2} (6725)

Cuban Rhythm (USA) *R Charlton* 63
2 b f Kingmambo(USA) —Kournakova (IRE) (Sadler's Wells (USA))
6285[2]

Cubillas (BRZ) *M D Wolfson* 80
5 gr g Ski Champ(USA) —La Mora (BRZ) (Midnight Tiger (USA))
394a[6] 542a[9]

Culzean Bay *Miss Diana Weeden* a11 48
2 b f Mind Games—Florie Nightingale (Tragic Role (USA))
2605[6] 3037[8] 3246[9] *3392[7]* 3626[3] 4311[3] 4512[2] 5089[9] 5484[2] 5715[9] *6624[11]*

Cumae (USA) *J Pearce* a35 22
3 b f King Cugat(USA) —Jubilee Walk (Generous (IRE))
2693[13] *5816[13] 6751[6] 7120[8] 7219[8]*

Cumberland Road *C A Mulhall* a41 50
4 ch g Efisio—Thatcher's Era (IRE) (Never So Bold)
156[12] 518[9] 3914[12] 4494[2] 5231[11] 6309[9]

Cumbrian Knight (IRE) *J M Jefferson* a64 53
9 b g Presenting—Crashrun (Crash Course)
(39) 617[4] 4096[9] *6798[3] 7004[2]*

Cumin (USA) *B W Hills* 99
3 ch f Fusaichi Pegasus(USA) —User Cat (USA) (Storm Cat (USA))
3463[5] 3897[11] 4849[12]

Cupid's Glory *Mrs L C Jewell* a99 88
5 b g Pursuit Of Love—Doctor's Glory (USA) (Elmaamul (USA))
43[7] 5031[13] 5797[22] *6606[6] 6932[13] 7075[4] 7163[5] 7287[4]*

Cupids Ray (IRE) *Allan Smith* 80
6 b g Fayruz—Cupid Miss (Anita's Prince)
415a[12]

Cuppacocoa *C G Cox* a49 78
3 b f Bertolini(USA) —Coffee Time (IRE) (Efisio)
1151[3] (1373) 1577[8] 2513[7] 2631[8] 4314[5] 5051[2] 5272[6] 5358[9] 6173[13]

Cuprea (IRE) *E Polito* 87
3 ch f Best Of The Bests(IRE) —Verbena (IRE) (Don't Forget Me)
1701a[8]

Curio *R M Whitaker* a53 58
2 b f Captain Rio—Luanshya (First Trump)
2199[5] 2526[8] 6073[7] 6595[7] 6722[6] *6881[3] 7000[6]*

Curlin (USA) *S Asmussen* a131
3 ch c Smart Strike(CAN) —Sherriff's Deputy (USA) (Deputy Minister (CAN))
1486a[3] (1882a) 2487a[2] (5855a) (6514a)

Currahee *Miss J A Camacho* a16 45
3 b g Efisio—Dixie Favor (USA) (Dixieland Band (USA))
728[10] 1224[8] 3159[7] 3792[8] 5906[10]

Currency *J M Bradley* a72 74
10 b g Sri Pekan(USA) —On Tiptoes (Shareef Dancer (USA))
1681[8] 2187[2] 2390[2] (2546) 2664[2] 4634[4] 4853[10] *5130[11]* 5909[6]

Curristown Pet (IRE) *C P Donoghue* 47
3 b f Lil's Boy(USA) —Moorefield (USA) (Marquetry (USA))
7081[11]

Cursum Perficio *R Lee* a81 79
5 b g Tagula(IRE) —Simply Sooty (Absalom)
3926[13] 4390[10]

Curtail (IRE) *I Semple* a95 91
4 b g Namid—Nipitinthebud (USA) (Night Shift (USA))
255[5] 656[8] 1852[8] 2566[7] 2866[4] 3080[6] 3464[4] 3586[14] 4585[2] 4780[4] 5584[22] *6355[7] (6836)*

Curtain Call (FR) *Mrs John Harrington* 112
2 b c Sadler's Wells(USA) —Apsara (FR) (Darshaan)
4833a[2] (5845a) 6489[5]

Curule (USA) *Doug Watson* a98
10 bb h Go For Gin(USA) —Reservation (USA) (Cryptoclearance (USA))
410a[5] 471a[3]

Curzon Prince (IRE) *C F Wall* a88 88
3 b c Mujadil(USA) —Smooth Spirit (USA) (Alydar (USA))
1228[4] 1920[2] 2400[7] 3235[9] 5768[11] 6492[2] 6753[8] *7165[3]*

Cushat Law (IRE) *W Jarvis* 71
3 b f Montjeu(IRE) —Blush With Love (USA) (Mt. Livermore (USA))
2192[4] 2552[2] 2945[2] (3919) 4542[2] 4766[4]

Cusoon *G L Moore* a105 82
5 b g Dansili—Charming Life (Habitat)
264[2] 420[2] (552) 761[9]

Cute *C E Brittain* 89
2 b f Diktat—Gleam Of Light (IRE) (Danehill (USA))
2365[3] 2812[5] 3432[11] 3880[4]

Cute Ass (IRE) *K R Burke* 103
2 b f Fath(USA) —John's Ballad (IRE) (Ballad Rock)
2071[3] 2717[2] 3269[4] (4097) 4573[2] 5377[3] 6167[2]

Cut Ridge (IRE) *J S Wainwright* a36 55
8 b m Indian Ridge—Cutting Ground (IRE) (Common Grounds)
912[4] 967[5] 2553[8] 3185[11] 3259[9]

Cut The Cake (USA) *J Noseda* 73
3 b f Diesis—Wife For Life (USA) (Dynaformer (USA))
1408[4] (Dead)

Cutting Crew (USA) *W R Swinburn* 102
6 ch g Diesis—Poppy Carew (IRE) (Danehill (USA))
4572[4] 6014[4] 6302[2]

Cybersnow (USA) *Mrs A J Perrett* a77
3 b c Royal Anthem(USA) —Storm Dove (USA) (Storm Bird (CAN))
2455[2] 3084[5]

Cyfrwys (IRE) *B Palling* a52 49
6 b m Foxhound(USA) —Divine Elegance (IRE) (College Chapel)
1221[2] 1640[6] 1766[6] 1921[8] 5861[4] *7077[6]*

Cyril The Squirrel *Karen George* a46
3 b g Cyrano De Bergerac—All Done (Northern State (USA))
6670[4] 6904[7] 7185[6]

Daaly Babet (FR) *C Scandella* 102
4 gr m Medaaly—Osmyose (FR) (Sicyos (USA))
4652a[7]

Daaweitza *B Ellison* a82 88
4 ch g Daawe(USA) —Chichen Itza (Shareef Dancer (USA))
846[8] 1040[9] 1308[3] (1458) 1915[5] (1996) 2986[3] 3091[6] 5356[13] 5641[4] *6067[9]*

Dabawiyah (IRE) *L M Cumani* 60
3 b f Intikhab(USA) —The Perfect Life (IRE) (Try My Best (USA))
2597[8] 3176[3]

Dabbers Ridge (IRE) *B W Hills* 109
5 b h Indian Ridge—Much Commended (Most Welcome)
1651[18] 2817[3] 3505[13] 3941[21] 4747[13] (5809) 6183[6] 6491[9]

Da Bookie (IRE) *P A Blockley* a76 70
7 b g Woods Of Windsor(USA) —Hurgill Lady (Emarati (USA))
1629[10] 3690[10] 4256[4] *5237[10]*

Daddy Cool *W G M Turner* a75 82
3 b g Kyllachy—Addicted To Love (Touching Wood (USA))
(17) 188[2] 502[4] (778) (1160) 1616[6] 3061[8] 4123[20] 5278[9]

Daddy's Boy *Mrs A J Perrett* 65
2 ch g Selkirk(USA) —Narva (Nashwan (USA))
5206[5] 5918[11]

Dado Mush *T T Clement* a81 59
4 b g Almushtarak(IRE) —Princess Of Spain (King Of Spain)
2556[11] 3705[15] 6537[3] *6809[12] (7127) (7213) (7244)*

Dafarabad (IRE) *Jonjo O'Neill* 71
5 b g Cape Cross(IRE) —Daftara (IRE) (Caerleon (USA))
1149[9] 1356[13] 1811[11]

Dafaroun (IRE) *T Hogan* a67 82
6 b g Royal Applause—Dafayna (Habitat)
873a[14]

Daggerman *P A Blockley* a29 36
2 ch c Daggers Drawn(USA) —Another Mans Cause (FR) (Highest Honor (FR))
4882[10] 5428[14]

Dairy Maid *W J Knight* 43
3 b f Montjeu(IRE) —Eurolink Sundance (Night Shift (USA))
1632[8]

Daisy Nook *S Kirk* a38 45
2 b f Domedriver(IRE) —Kilbride (Selkirk (USA))
5162[12] 5919[6] *6611[7]*

Daiwa Major (JPN) *Hiroyuki Uehara* 123
6 ch h Sunday Silence(USA) —Scarlet Bouquet (JPN) (Northern Taste (CAN))
862a[3]

Dakota Rain (IRE) *Jennie Candlish* 88
5 br g Indian Ridge—Mill Rainbow (FR) (Rainbow Quest (USA))
1416[10] 1655[6] 2302[2] (2576) (3686) 4140[10] (4895) 5155[3] 5505[3]

Dalarossie *E J Alston* a55 65
2 br g Kyllachy—Damalis (IRE) (Mukaddamah (USA))
1107[6] 2071[4] 2526[3] 3562[5] *4020[5]* 4175[6]

Dal Cais (IRE) *Francis Ennis* 98
3 b c Noverre(USA) —Annieirwin (IRE) (Perugino (USA))
2066a[6] 2788[18]

Dalhaan (USA) *J L Dunlop* 68
2 b c Fusaichi Pegasus(USA) —Khazayin (USA) (Bahri (USA))
4151[9]

Dalkey Girl (IRE) *V Smith* 92
2 ch f Raise A Grand(IRE) —Tosca (Be My Guest (USA))
2333[4] (2746) 3096[6] 3508[4] 3880[8] 4372[9] 4769[3] 4812[4] 5350[10] 5597[2] 6012[2] 6336[8] 6652[4]

Dallma (IRE) *C E Brittain* a61 71
4 b m Daylami(IRE) —Play With Fire (FR) (Priolo (USA))
110[12] 426[10] 524[12]

Dalvina *E A L Dunlop* a80 111
3 ch f Grand Lodge(USA) —Foodbroker Fancy (IRE) (Halling (USA))
(1499) 2211[11] 2786[3] 4723[5] 5396a[3] (6790a)

Daly Daly (FR) *R Laplanche* 98
3 gr f Medaaly—Dame Phanie (FR) (Kaldoun (FR))
436a[5]

Damascus Gold *Miss Z C Davison* 7
3 b c Thowra(FR) —Damasquiner (Casteddu)
2726[14]

Damelza (IRE) *T D Easterby* a67 76
4 b m Orpen(USA) —Damezao (Alzao (USA))
1905[10] 2422[2] 2988[3] 3754[5] 3961[10] 4177[13] 4797[10]

Damhsoir (IRE) *H S Howe* a52 52
3 b f Invincible Spirit(IRE) —Ceide Dancer (IRE) (Alzao (USA))
1883[4] 2444[8] 4186[8] 4397[7] 5270[8] *5566[5] (6240) 6528[6]*

Damika (IRE) *R M Whitaker* 99
4 ch g Namid—Emly Express (IRE) (High Estate)
2841[11] 3089[3] 3401[2] 3559[3] 4006[9] (5044) 5254[7] 5584[20] 6013[6] (6301) 6654[10]

Danae *H Candy* 69
2 br f Dansili—Pervenche (Latest Model)
6648[5]

Danak (IRE) *John M Oxx* 118
4 br h Pivotal—Daniysha (IRE) (Doyoun)
(1184a) (1696a) 2064a[4] 4414a[6]

Danalova *R A Fahey* a40 58
3 b f Groom Dancer(USA) —Revival (Sadler's Wells (USA))
73[7] 222[10] 449[9] 907[4] 1271[6] *1353[4] 2223[6]* (3377) 3587[3] 3956[2]

Danamight (IRE) *G G Margarson* a65 64
2 gr f Danetime(IRE) —Nuit Chaud (USA) (Woodman (USA))
2000[8] 3796[8] 4162[9] *5127[5] 5423[3]* 5746[9]

Dana Music (USA) *M R Channon* a61 71
3 br g Silver Hawk(USA) —Inca Princess (USA) (Big Spruce (USA))
703[3] 936[4] 1415[5] 1916[2] 2610[3] 3351[9]

Danao (USA) *R Menichetti* 94
3 b c Richter Scale(USA) —Essie's Maid (USA) (Linkage (USA))
1336a[10] 1873a[5]

Danawi (IRE) *M R Hoad* a69 63
4 ch g Elnadim(USA) —Just Rainbow (FR) (Rainbow Quest (USA))
902[8] 1086[2] 1740[2] 2272[4] 2556[8] 3034[2] 3352[6] 3950[8] 4469[10] 6247[14]

Dan Buoy (FR) *A King* a54 78
4 b g Slip Anchor—Bramosia (Forzando)
1446[11] 2113[4] 2981[2] 3243[2] 3963[7]

Dance Easily *J L Dunlop* 36
2 b f Dansili—Crystal Flite (IRE) (Darshaan)
5162[15] 5720[15] 6451[9]

Danceinthevalley (IRE) *D K Ivory* a42 59
5 b g Imperial Ballet(IRE) —Dancing Willma (IRE) (Dancing Dissident (USA))
151[10] 605[8] 1152[12] *1362[12]* 2372[3] (2557) *2875[11]* 4319[13]

Dance Of Dreams *N P Littmoden* a62 63
3 ch g Johannesburg(USA) —Nunatak (USA) (Bering)
336[8] 535[7] (636) 738[6] 931[9] 3875[4] 4760[12] *5136[4] 5528[6]*

Dance Of Light (USA) *Sir Michael Stoute* a73 98
3 b f Sadler's Wells(USA) —Flamelight (IRE) (Seattle Slew (USA))
(1784) 2211[7] 3628[3] 4748[9] 5767[5] *6605[10]*

Dance Of Moonlight (FR) *Miss Susan A Finn* 32
4 b m Danehill Dancer(IRE) —Kengar (FR) (Adieu Au Roi (IRE))
1760a[11]

Dancer's Legacy *E A L Dunlop* 76
2 ch c Nayef(USA) —Blond Moment (USA) (Affirmed (USA))
2876[7] 3471[9] (4904) 5571[3] 5871[7]

Dance Sauvage *C W Thornton* 58
4 ch g Groom Dancer(USA) —Peace Dance (Bikala)
1671[9] 1966[2] 2434[8] 4475[6] 4972[2] 5087[2] 6056[9] 6308[4] 6561[6]

Dancesowell (IRE) *John Joseph Murphy* 68
3 b f Sadler's Wells(USA) —Aim For The Top (USA) (Irish River (FR))
6366a[18]

Dance Spirit (IRE) *W R Muir* a69 71
4 ch g Namid—Phantom Act (USA) (Theatrical)
3907[18] *5177[2] 5424[8] 5893[11]* 6573[8] *6882[12] 6935[4] 7001[12]*

Dance Steps *Miss K B Boutflower* a21 43
3 b f Golan(IRE) —Swift Baba (USA) (Deerhound (USA))
257[10] 3387[12] 3948[5]

Dance The Classics (IRE) *J L Dunlop* 100
3 b f Sadler's Wells(USA) —Head In The Clouds (IRE) (Rainbow Quest (USA))
4238a[5] 5150a[6] 6137a[5] 6941a[8]

Dancewiththestars (USA) *Miss J Feilden* a45 55
3 b f Cryptoclearance(USA) —Sir Harry's Waltz (IRE) (Sir Harry Lewis (USA))
1343[9] 1665[7] 1917[9] 2192[8] 2610[8] 3907[11] 4231[9] 4516[4]

Dance World *Miss J Feilden* a79 58
7 b g Spectrum(IRE) —Dansara (Dancing Brave (USA))
811[9] 2675[5] 3250[5] 3907[12]

Dan Chillingworth (IRE) *J R Fanshawe* a67 69
2 b c Indian Ridge—Shizao (IRE) (Alzao (USA))
5575[5] *6530[5]*

Dancing Abbie (USA) *M L W Bell* 77
2 ch f Theatrical—Sicy D'Alsace (FR) (Sicyos (USA))
6414[3]

Dancing Band (USA) *Niall M O'Callaghan* 102
4 b m Dixieland Band(USA) —Miss Ra He Ra (USA) (Rahy (USA))
6772a[10]

Dancing Bay *N J Henderson* a69 108
10 b g Suave Dancer(USA) —Kabayil (Dancing Brave (USA))
1582[13]

Dancing Beauty (IRE) *T T Clement* a44
5 b m Charnwood Forest(IRE) —Viennese Dancer (Prince Sabo)
60[3] 320[12] 632[14] 714[6]

Dancing Deano (IRE) *R Hollinshead* a62 70
5 b g Second Empire(IRE) —Ultimate Beat (USA) (Go And Go)
1260[11] 1739[5] 1921[9] *2220[9] (6908) (7124) 7148[6]*

Dancing Dik *Mrs A J Perrett* 67
2 b g Diktat—Maureena (IRE) (Grand Lodge (USA))
2885[8] 3552[7] 6493[6]

Dancing Duo *D Shaw* a62 58
3 b f Groom Dancer(USA) —Affaire Royale (IRE) (Royal Academy (USA))
1345[11] 1731[10] 1903[2] 2262[10] 2515[13] *5136[10] 5900[3] 7085[8] 7268[7]*

Dancing Ellie *P M Phelan*
2 b f Where Or When(IRE) —Eleonor Sympson (Cadeaux Genereux)
6202[11]

Dancing Guest (IRE) *G G Margarson* a88 93
4 ch m Danehill Dancer(IRE) —Saibhreas (IRE) (Last Tycoon (IRE))
979[5] *1588[5]*

Dancing Jest (IRE) *Rae Guest* a19 63
3 b f Averti(IRE) —Mezzannine (Sadler's Wells (USA))
1117[13] 3651[2] (4338) 4684[6] 5046[8] 5563[6]

Dancing Lady (FR) *J-M Beguigne* 108
3 b f Dansili—Aka Lady (FR) (Sanglamore (USA))
2270a[5] 4557a[3] 5258a[2] 6376a[8]

Dancing Lyra *R A Fahey* a78 83
6 b g Alzao(USA) —Badaayer (USA) (Silver Hawk (USA))
846[2] 5748[6] 6180[6] 6490[7]

Dancing Maite *S R Bowring* a54 11
2 ch c Ballet Master(USA) —Ace Maite (Komaite (USA))
6303[11] *6872[4] 7139[4]*

Dancing Marabout (IRE) *C R Egerton* a73 64
2 ch g Danehill Dancer(IRE) —Bluebell Wood (IRE) (Bluebird (USA))
3270[8] 3878[5] 4323[6] *(5601)* 5871[8] *6120[7]*

Dancing Melody *J A Geake* 56
4 b m Dr Fong(USA) —Spring Mood (FR) (Nashwan (USA))
2214[15]

Dancing Mystery *E A Wheeler* a88 75
13 b g Beveled(USA) —Batchworth Dancer (Ballacashtal (CAN))
79[6] 554[9] 810[10] 1969[16] 2479[8] 4233[11] 4689[6] 5160[3] (5430) 5867[3] 6279[2] *6405[7]* 6594[7] *7116[4]*

Dancing Sky (IRE) *D K Weld* 102
4 ch m Polish Precedent(USA) —Foreign Love (USA) (Gulch (USA))
2053a[8]

Dancing Storm *W S Kittow* a56 61
4 b m Trans Island—Stormswell (Persian Bold)
3110[6] (3615) 4257[7] 5189[5] 5917[4] *6627[4]*

Dancing Sword *H J L Dunlop* 33
2 b g Groom Dancer(USA) —Kristina (Kris)
5344[13]

Dancing Wizard *C G Cox* a58
3 ch g Dancing Spree(USA) —Magic Legs (Reprimand)
7159[2]

Dan Dare (USA) *Sir Michael Stoute* 91
4 b g Dynaformer(USA) —Etheldreda (USA) (Diesis)
(1529) 2093[7] 3105[2] 3989[7] 5049[3] 5554[7]

Dandy Erin (IRE) *J A Osborne* a82 75
2 b c Danehill Dancer(IRE) —Sanctuary Line (IRE) (Lake Coniston (IRE))
5680[4] 6451[3] *(6857)*

Dandy Man (IRE) *Tracey Collins* 122
4 b h Mozart(IRE) —Lady Alexander (IRE) (Night Shift (USA))
(1171a) 2324a[2] 2733[2] 3506[5] 4746[3] 5075a[2] 6039a[10]

Dandys Hurricane *M W Easterby* a23 48
4 br g Diktat—Bahamian Rhapsody (IRE) (Fairy King (USA))
1715[10] 3402[10] 3684[3]

Dane Blue (IRE) *S J Treacy* 77
5 ch m Danehill Dancer(IRE) —Palace Blue (IRE) (Dara Monarch)
6553a[18]

Danebury Hill *B J Meehan* a99 101
3 b c Danehill(USA) —Mackie (USA) (Summer Squall (USA))
839[3] 1095[5] 1471[7] 1835[7] 2788[19]

Daneheart (AUS) *G Moloney* 87
5 b g Danehill Dancer(IRE) —Princess Pushy (AUS) (Cossack Prince (NZ))
6711a[5]

Danehill Folly (IRE) *J M Bradley* a18
4 b g Danehill Dancer(IRE) —Theorique (IRE) (Theatrical)
3597[11] 4321[12] 5864[13]

Danehill Kikin (IRE) *B W Hills* a46 57
3 b f Danehill(USA) —Miletrian (IRE) (Marju (IRE))
1620[5] *2173[7]* 3875[10] 4529[8]

Danehill Music (IRE) *David Wachman* 106
4 b m Danehill Dancer(IRE) —Tuesday Morning (Sadler's Wells (USA))
782a[2] 1049a[4] (3144a) 3579a[3] 4648a[5]

Danehill Silver *R Hollinshead* a52 64
3 b g Silver Patriarch(IRE) —Danehill Princess (IRE) (Danehill (USA))
2530[6] 3159[13] *4742[6]* 5347[2] 5710[U]

Danehill Stroller (IRE) *A M Hales* a59 73
7 b g Danetime(IRE) —Tuft Hill (Grundy)
2652[2] 3045[4] *3618[9]* 4312[2]

Danehillsundance (IRE) *R Hannon* a73 100
3 b c Danehill Dancer(IRE) —Rosie's Guest (IRE) (Be My Guest (USA))
2243[2] (2577) (3334) 4640[8] (5355) 5797[11] 6053[4] 6301[12] 6654[11]

Danehill Warrior (IRE) *R C Guest* a34 29
3 b g Indian Danehill(IRE) —Karatisa (IRE) (Nishapour (FR))
684[7] 745[7] 807[9] 2453[11] 4155[8] 4424[7] 4920[U] 5687[12]

Danelor (IRE) *D Shaw* a57 42
9 b g Danehill(USA) —Formulate (Reform)
64[9] 187[5] 266[7] (372) 453[10] 616[3] 716[2] 1254[2] 1732[10] 6955[11] 7088[11] 7115[8]

Danethorpe (IRE) *D Shaw* a49 40
4 b g Monashee Mountain(USA) —Waroonga (IRE) (Brief Truce (USA))
838[3] 321[3] 430[5] 519[5] 632[8] 1594[5] 2844[9] 3752[13]

Danetime Lord (IRE) *K A Ryan* a87 70
4 b g Danetime(IRE) —Seven Sisters (USA) (Shadeed (USA))
102[6] (234) 424[3] (480) (614) 757[4] 827[3] 1133[9] *6900[2] 7165[13] 7289[2]*

Danetime Panther (IRE) *P F I Cole* a76 73
3 b c Danetime(IRE) —Annotate (Groom Dancer (USA))
1143[8] *(1348)* 1773[12]

Danetime Rose (IRE) *Miss V Haigh* a21
3 b f Danetime(IRE) —Amory (GER) (Goofalik (USA))
4066[10]

Danettie *W M Brisbourne* a55 42
6 b m Danzero(AUS) —Petite Heritiere (Last Tycoon (IRE))
479[8] 637[6] 801[4] 1227[13] 1435[5] 1534[8] 1951[7] 2258[12]

Daneway *P Howling* a56
4 ch m Danehill Dancer(IRE) —Scylla (Rock City)
365[6] 514[4] 630[10]

Dangerous Dancer (IRE) *R Charlton* 59
3 b f Danehill Dancer(IRE) —Elite Guest (IRE) (Be My Guest (USA))
1784[4] 2597[9] 4172[8]

Dangerously Good *J Howard Johnson* a65 72
9 b g Shareef Dancer(USA) —Ecologically Kind (Alleged (USA))
507[2]

Daniella *Rae Guest* a88 105
5 b m Dansili—Break Point (Reference Point)
2450[P] 3059[4] 3481[10] 3746[3] 4196[8] 5354[7] 5799[11] 6013[3] 6300[11] *6604[6]*

Danielle's Lad *B Palling* a60 69
11 b g Emarati(USA) —Cactus Road (FR) (Iron Duke (FR))
22[5] 2076[6] 447[11]

Daniel Thomas (IRE) *Mrs A L M King* a89 85
5 b g Dansili—Last Look (Rainbow Quest (USA))
340[6] 1984[5] 2427[9] 3039[5] *4068[10]* 4455[8] 5198[9] 6063[7]

Dani's Girl (IRE) *P A Fahy* a61 101
4 bb m Second Empire(IRE) —Quench The Lamp (IRE) (Glow (USA))
782a[5] 1548a[7] 2053a[5] 3578a[4] 4051a[15] 4211a[7]

Danish Art (IRE) *J A R Toller* 77
2 b c Danehill Dancer(IRE) —Lady Ounavarra (IRE) (Simply Great (FR))
5575[3] 6295[6]

Danish Blues (IRE) *D Nicholls* a67 67
4 b g Danetime(IRE) —Sing A Song (IRE) (Blues Traveller (IRE))
310[4] 504[2] 688[5] 751[3] 978[2] 1212[2] 1675[5] *1947[10] (3169)* 3597[3] 3837[2] 4083[2] (4478) *4974[RR]* 5232[5] 5535[RR]

Danish Rebel (IRE) *G A Charlton* a49 79
3 b g Danetime(IRE) —Wheatsheaf Lady (IRE) (Red Sunset)
(956) 1237[2] 1827[11] 3501[8]

Danjet (IRE) *J M Bradley* a70 80
4 bl m Danehill Dancer(IRE) —Jet Lock (USA) (Crafty Prospector (USA))
1854[18] 1999[10] 2191[7] 2972[8] 3086[7] 4103[11]

Danjoe *R Brotherton* a53 38
3 ch g Forzando—Baytown Rhapsody (Emperor Jones (USA))
2083[8] *3406[13]* 4530[6] 6062[16]

Danni Di Guerra (IRE) *J Barclay* 36
3 b g Soviet Star(USA) —Lina Bella (FR) (Linamix (FR))
1492[10] 1711[8] 2389[10] 2565[9]

Danny Boy Blue *Mrs L J Mongan* 29
2 b c Josr Algarhoud(IRE) —Rosina May (IRE) (Danehill Dancer (IRE))
1201[11] 1428[5] 2087[6]

Dansant *G A Butler* a119 106
3 b c Dansili—La Balagna (Kris)
(1358) 1803[2] 2448[3] 2790[12] 3883[2] 4749[5] (5375) 5952[5] *(6645) (6994)*

Danse Du Soir (FR) *H-A Pantall* a94 95
3 b f Nombre Premier—Dentelle (FR) (Apeldoorn (FR))
6940a[3]

Danse The Blues *E A L Dunlop* a59
2 br f Dansili—Dixie D'Oats (Alhijaz)
6805[5]

Danseuse *B J Meehan* a73 73
3 b f Dr Fong(USA) —Danemere (IRE) (Danehill (USA))
1105[14] 1535[9]

Danseuse Volante (IRE) *J W Hills* 69
2 ch f Danehill Dancer(IRE) —Termania (IRE) (Shirley Heights)
5591[3] (6082) 6619[12]

Dan's Heir *P C Haslam* a56 63
5 b g Dansili—Million Heiress (Auction Ring (USA))
10[3] 146[8]

Dansili Dancer *C G Cox* a102 107
5 b g Dansili—Magic Slipper (Habitat)
941[6] 1494[11] 2446[5] 4043[8] (4388) 5030[5] 5215[3]

Dansil In Distress *S Kirk* a69 56
3 b f Dansili—Just Speculation (IRE) (Ahonoora)
1310[3] 1731[4] 2181[10] 2697[4] *(3393)* 4111[10] 4684[12] *5122[12]*

Dansilver *D J Wintle* a57 54
3 b g Dansili—Silver Gyre (IRE) (Silver Hawk (USA))
3903[2] 4809[5]

Dansimar *M R Channon* a72 71
3 gr f Daylami(IRE) —Hylandra (USA) (Bering)
719[6] 1092[3] 1355[7] 1624[6] *3421[3] 3624[2]* 4139[3] 4409[2] 4531[3] *4951[8]* 5626[3] 5906[4] *6069[2] 6341[3]*

Danski *P J Makin* a87 89
4 b h Dansili—Manila Selection (USA) (Manila (USA))
5833[8] 6203[16] *6435[4] 6949[9]*

Dante's Diamond (IRE) *R Lee* a64 64
5 b g Orpen(USA) —Flower From Heaven (Baptism)
1559[7] 1921[4] *(2258) 3111[7]* 3549[4] *3599[3] 3922[8]*

Danticat (USA) *John J Coleman* 69
6 ch g Tale Of The Cat(USA) —Colonial Debut (USA) (Pleasant Colony (USA))
4475[RR]

Dan Tucker *B J Meehan* a75 74
3 b g Dansili—Shapely (USA) (Alleged (USA))
(791) (893) 1084[3] 1724[7] *2177[3] 2574[3] 3189[6]* 4113[8] 4511[5] *5131[6]* 6235[2]

Dan Tucket *M R Channon* a59 87
2 b c Dansili—Fanfare (Deploy)
1107[3] (1428) 1743[5] *2353[7]* (3508) 3909[3] 4372[6] (4812) 5217[3] 5597[3] 5828[8] 6486[12]

Danum *R Hollinshead* a51 57
7 b g Perpendicular—Maid Of Essex (Bustino)
126[7] 179[2] 402[12]

Danum Dancer *N Bycroft* 94
3 ch c Allied Forces(USA) —Branston Dancer (Rudimentary (USA))
847[8] 1099[5] 1473[22] 1825[6] 2841[10] 3380[5] 4080[8] 4898[13] 5522[8]

Danum Diva (IRE) *D J Murphy* a34 47
3 ch f Danehill Dancer(IRE) —Comprehension (USA) (Diesis)
583[8] 791[6] 907[14] 1301[10] 1423[15] 6570[4] 6745[5] *6955[13] 7034[10] 7150[4]*

Danvers *J L Dunlop* a62
2 b f Cape Cross(IRE) —Tyranny (Machiavellian (USA))
5201[5] 6228[7]

Danzare *J L Spearing* a63 58
5 b m Dansili—Shot Of Redemption (Shirley Heights)
(19) 72[8] 976[12] 1260[12] 1918[11] 2157[3] 2656[6] 3042[2] 3249[7] (3805) 4031[3]

Danzatrice *C W Thornton* 68
5 b m Tamure(IRE) —Miss Petronella (Petoski)
1042[7] 1457[2] 1598[2] 2031[5] 2824[5] 3371[4] (4096) 4380[6] 4969[6] 5257[5] 5839[4] 6259[6] 6308[8] 6733[2]

Danzig Fox *M Mullineaux* 70
2 b c Foxhound(USA) —Via Dolorosa (Chaddleworth (IRE))
(3341) 5551[6] 5773[7]

Danzig River (IRE) *D Nicholls* a66 82
6 b g Green Desert(USA) —Sahara Breeze (Ela-Mana-Mou)
44[9] 432[10] 609[8] 1134[8] (1292) 1483[6] 1852[7] 2025[9] 2394[7] (Dead)

Danzon (USA) *F Parisel* a109 109
4 b m Royal Academy(USA) —Zappeuse (USA) (Kingmambo (USA))
6509a[10]

Dapple Dawn (IRE) *Garvan Donnelly* a80 79
4 b m Celtic Swing—Lasting Chance (USA) (American Chance (USA))
101[3] 151[4] 300[2] (367) 592[2] 771[4] 5184a[9]

Dapple Grey (IRE) *T Stack* 82
4 gr m Aljabr(USA) —Asl (USA) (Caro)
3578a[11] 5459a[9]

Daraahem (IRE) *B W Hills* 70
2 ch c Act One—Shamah (Unfuwain (USA))
6468[9]

Daralara (FR) *J-C Rouget* a97 97
3 b f Barathea(IRE) —Darakiyla (IRE) (Last Tycoon (IRE))
2926a[7] *7049a[2]*

Daramas (IRE) *Rodger Sweeney* 74
5 b g Darshaan—Anima (Ajdal (USA))
6366a[7] (Dead)

Daramsar (FR) *A De Royer-Dupre* 114
4 b h Rainbow Quest(USA) —Daryaba (IRE) (Night Shift (USA))
990a[3] 1881a[5] 2292a[6]

Darcy's Pride (IRE) *D W Barker* 76
3 bb f Danetime(IRE) —Cox's Ridge (IRE) (Indian Ridge)
(918) 970[4] 1240[4] 1530[7] (2255) (2301) 2631[6] 3054[2] 3374[6] 3637[5] 4158[2] 4703[9] 5332[8] 5747[8]

Dareios (GER) *G A Swinbank* 48
2 ch g Numerous(USA) —Desert Chiara (USA) (Desert King (IRE))
3341[9] 4784[12]

Darenjan (IRE) *John Joseph Hanlon* 74
4 b g Alhaarth(IRE) —Darariyna (IRE) (Shirley Heights)
4114a[6]

Dar Es Salaam *E A L Dunlop* 84
3 ch g King's Best(USA) —Place De L'Opera (Sadler's Wells (USA))
2320[5] 2836[2] (3399) 4510[5] *6144[12]* 6622[10]

Darestan (IRE) *A De Royer-Dupre* 105
3 br c Sinndar(IRE) —Daralbayda (IRE) (Doyoun)
2816[9]

Darfour *J S Goldie* 77
3 b g Inchinor—Gai Bulga (Kris)
(1965) 2171[5] 3514[3] 3940[13] 4811[14] 6016[17]

Darghan (IRE) *W J Musson* a52 69
7 b g Air Express(IRE) —Darsannda (IRE) (Kahyasi)
2423[3] (4340) 5211[6] 5514[7] 6132[10] 6380[8] *6780[10]*

Daring Affair *K R Burke* a87 84
6 b m Bien Bien(USA) —Daring Destiny (Daring March)
96[5] (256) 451[P] 629[10] 1288[5] 1414[5] 1649[7] *1979[6]* 3972[8] *5225[9]* 5553[6] *6343[2] 6696[6] 7057[4] 7237[3]*

Daring Dream (GER) *T D Easterby* 74
2 ch c Big Shuffle(USA) —Daring Action (Arazi (USA))
2021[6] 2804[4] 3560[3] 4126[4] 5550[3] 5613[2] 6379[16]

Daring Racer (GER) *S Dow* a70 72
4 ch g Big Shuffle(USA) —Daring Action (Arazi (USA))
753[9] 1222[13] 2967[7] *3217[2]* 3692[2] 3858[4] *5204[11]*

Darjina (FR) *A De Royer-Dupre* 124
3 b f Zamindar(USA) —Darinska (IRE) (Zilzal (USA))
(1055a) (1702a) 2814[3] (4010a) (5261a) 5798[7] 7091a[3]

Dark Angel (IRE) *B W Hills* 114
2 gr c Acclamation—Midnight Angel (Machiavellian (USA))
1094[2] (1585) 2737[11] 3459[4] (4743) 5377[7] (5630) (5975) 6333[9]

Dark Camellia *H J L Dunlop* 53
2 b f Olden Times—Miss Mirror (Magic Mirror)
5628[11] 6093[8]

Dark Champion *R E Barr* a51 67
7 b g Abou Zouz(USA) —Hazy Kay (IRE) (Treasure Kay)
2033[7] 2421[3] (3203) 3608[5] 3921[2] 4289[9] 6020[7]

Dark Chapel *W J H Ratcliffe* a19
4 b g College Chapel—Possibility (Robellino (USA))
1749[9]

Dark Charm (FR) *R A Fahey* a71 79
8 b g Anabaa(USA) —Wardara (Sharpo)
969[7] 1287[10] 1655[12] 2117[2] 2551[5] 2868[2] 3182[6] 3403[10] 4496[2] (4716) 5086[4] 5553[7] 5674[8]

Dark Druid (IRE) *I A Wood* a55 42
3 b g Princely Heir(IRE) —Super Sonic Sonia (IRE) (Tirol)
720[7] 1523[6] 2196[12] 2916[11] 3652[13] 4339[14] *4591[10]*

Dark Energy *B Smart* 77
3 br g Observatory(USA) —Waterfowl Creek (IRE) (Be My Guest (USA))
1111[13] 1804[7] 2915[4] 3570[9] 5555[2] 6021[10] (6258)

Dark Islander (IRE) *J W Hills* a99 116
4 b h Singspiel(IRE) —Lamanka Lass (USA) (Woodman (USA))
3523[9] 4045[7] 4600[9]

Dark Mask (IRE) *J L Spearing* a14 22
3 b g Iron Mask(USA) —Darkness At Noon (USA) (Night Shift (USA))
2948[11] 3276[12]

Dark Missile *A M Balding* a93 113
4 b m Night Shift(USA) —Exorcet (FR) (Selkirk (USA))
1474[4] (2858) 3511[9] 4373[2] 5832[2] 6375a[7]

Dark Moon *D Shaw* a55 59
4 b m Observatory(USA) —Lady Donatella (Last Tycoon (IRE))
189[8] 296[3] (337) 447[10] 555[7] 743[10] 912[10] *2220[7]* 2304[6] *2591[8]*

Dark Parade (ARG) *G L Moore* a73 68
6 b g Parade Marshal(USA) —Charming Dart (ARG) (D'Accord (USA))
(1003) 1152[2] *1526[4]* 2055[3] 3273[7] *5204[7] 5533[13] (6643) 6875[6]*

Dark Planet *D Burchell* a66 65
4 ch g Singspiel(IRE) —Warning Shadows (IRE) (Cadeaux Genereux)
607[10] 740[8] 753[4] 1069[7] 1451[10] 6068[12] 6452[9] *6866[5]*

Dark Prospect *M A Jarvis* 57
2 b c Nayef(USA) —Miss Mirasol (Sheikh Albadou)
6285[6] 6574[8]

Dark Queen *D Carroll* a31 43
2 b f Bertolini(USA) —Abstone Queen (Presidium)
3410[4] 4074[10] 4447[8] *5017[5]*

Dark Society *A W Carroll* a32 50
9 b g Imp Society(USA) —No Candles Tonight (Star Appeal)
6804[8]

Dark Tara *R A Fahey* 75
2 br f Diktat—Karisal (IRE) (Persian Bold)
2904[4] (3560) 4152[6] 4695[14] 5582[9] 6052[7] 6462[6]

Darley Star *C E Brittain* a53 62
2 gr f King's Best(USA) —Amellnaa (IRE) (Sadler's Wells (USA))
4565[6] 5061[6] *5682[10]*

Darling Belinda *D K Ivory* a66 41
3 ch f Silver Wizard(USA) —Katyushka (IRE) (Soviet Star (USA))
34[5] 3924[5] 4536[8] *4919[8]* 5175[7]

Darraghs Day (IRE) *Miss Martina Anne Doran* 72
2 ch g Monashee Mountain(USA) —Persian Tapestry (Tap On Wood)
779a[9]

Dar Re Mi *J H M Gosden* 75
2 b f Singspiel(IRE) —Darara (Top Ville)
6648[2]

Darrfonah (IRE) *C E Brittain* a65 106
3 b f Singspiel(IRE) —Avila (Ajdal (USA))
246a[7] 1146[7] 1496[16] 2211[10] (2599) 4723[6] 5396a[6] 6010[8]

Darsalam (IRE) *A Shavuyev* 103
6 ch h Desert King(IRE) —Moonsilk (Solinus)
1689a[4]

Darsha (FR) *A De Royer-Dupre* 108
3 b f Sakhee(USA) —Darashandeh (IRE) (Darshaan)
4557a[2] 6030a[3] 6941a[6]

Dart *J R Fanshawe* a73 68
3 br f Diktat—Eilean Shona (Suave Dancer (USA))
5530[3] 5898[9] 6257[2] *6534[3] 6751[2] (7125)*

Daruma (IRE) *Peter Grayson* a51 48
3 b g Iron Mask(USA) —Mary's Way (GR) (Night Shift (USA))
103[6] 209[9]

Darusso *J S Moore* a55 66
4 ch g Daylami(IRE) —Rifada (Ela-Mana-Mou)
1078[7] 1470[9] 1683[6] 1888[8] 2471[4]

Daryal (IRE) *A King* 84
6 b g Night Shift(USA) —Darata (IRE) (Vayrann)
(4994) 5145[3] 5808[4]

Da Schadenfreude (USA) *W G M Turner* a54 59
3 bb g Tale Of The Cat(USA) —Conquistas Jessica (USA) (Boundary (USA))
93[7] 348[9] 460[8] 1561[10] *6268[13]*

Dasheena *A J McCabe* a77 62
4 b m Magic Ring(IRE) —Sweet And Lucky (Lucky Wednesday)
67[6] 161[8] 803[2] 1212[8] *1436[2] 1946[9] 2225[5] 2516[8] 3110[3] 4021[DSQ] 4361[5]* (5627) *5778[12]* 6089[4] *6607[3] 6831[11] 6962[3] (7024) (7113) 7180[2]*

Dashing Dane *Mrs Marjorie Fife* a36
7 b h Danehill(USA) —Baldemara (FR) (Sanglamore (USA))
4673[9] 5299[15] *6803[10]*

Dash Of Grey (IRE) *Ruaidhri Joseph Tierney* a71 82
8 gr g Simply Great(FR) —Donna Katrina (Kings Lake (USA))
6368a[20] *7194[4] 7256[2]*

Dash To The Front *J R Fanshawe* a73 103
4 b m Diktat—Millennium Dash (Nashwan (USA))
2136[6] (2720) 3434[6] 6168[6] 6496[6]

Dauberval (IRE) *S Kirk* 94
2 b g Noverre(USA) —Just In Love (FR) (Highest Honor (FR))
3233[7] 4540[2] (4852) 5414[3]

Davaye *K R Burke* a38 67
3 b f Bold Edge—Last Impression (Imp Society (USA))
1453[7] 2821[4] 3583[5] 4480[7] 4842[4] 5159[11] 5688[11] *6402[6]*

Dave (USA) *B Tagg* 110
6 b g Ends Well(USA) —Commadores Gold (USA) (Commodore C (USA))
(6771a)

Davenport (IRE) *B R Millman* a87 86
5 b g Bold Fact(USA) —Semence D'Or (FR) (Kaldoun (FR))
(101) 850[5] *1180[6]* 1288[14] 1819[9] 6253[5] 6727[5]

Davidia (IRE) *D W Thompson* a60 64
4 b g Barathea(IRE) —Green Life (Green Desert (USA))
2921[1] 497[8] 605[6] 6629[7] 6815[4] 6935[2] 7197[3]

Davidoff (GER) *P Schiergen* 106
3 b c Montjeu(IRE) —Dapprima (GER) (Shareef Dancer (USA))
(1054a) 1516a[4] 2102a[2] 3146a[5] 4958a[3] 5929a[3]

David's Cavalier *R Hollinshead* a58 60
3 b g Beat All(USA) —Foxtrot Pie (Shernazar)
257[6] 484[12] 769[9] 893[5] 1154[2]

Davids Mark *J R Jenkins* a58 56
7 b g Polar Prince(IRE) —Star Of Flanders (Puissance)
613[8] 797[7] 1405[5] *2221[3] 5947[7] 6264[2] 6718[4] 6773[4]*

Daweyrr (USA) *M P Tregoning* a16 71
3 b c Kingmambo(USA) —With Flair (USA) (Broad Brush (USA))
3881[5] 4334[3]

Dawla *Kevin Prendergast* 97
3 b f Alhaarth(IRE) —Za Aamah (USA) (Mr Prospector (USA))
3578a[7] 6363a[7]

Dawn At Sea *Mrs K Waldron* a45 68
5 b m Slip Anchor—Finger Of Light (Green Desert (USA))
618[10] 767[12]

Dawn Light (IRE) *Mrs A Duffield* 48
2 ch f Spartacus(IRE) —Erbaluce (Be My Guest (USA))
1073[4] 1193[10] 3750[5] 4027[2] 4405[9] 4770[4]

Dawn Mystery *Rae Guest* a48 41
3 gr f Daylami(IRE) —Frustration (Salse (USA))
1523[7] 6597[8] *7168[8]*

Dawn Sky *M A Jarvis* 83
3 b c Fantastic Light(USA) —Zacheta (Polish Precedent (USA))
2308[2] 2690[2] 3248[2] (3847) 4609[5]

Dawn Storm (IRE) *K R Burke*
2 ch g City On A Hill(USA) —Flames (Blushing Flame (USA))
3283[12]

Dawn Whisper *M E Sowersby* 28
2 ch f Rock City—Doodle Wood (Nomination)
2115[9] 5483[9] 5735[10]

Dawn Wind *I A Wood* a58
2 b f Vettori(IRE) —Topper (IRE) (Priolo (USA))
2768[8] 3453[7] 3643[7] 5127[3]

Dawson Creek (IRE) *B Gubby* a62 49
3 ch g Titus Livius(FR) —Particular Friend (Cadeaux Genereux)
342[10] 864[4] 1059[9] 2273[8] *(6212) 6505[2] 6774[10] 7098[4] (7276)*

Daybreak Dancer (IRE) *Doug Watson* a78 79
5 bb g Fasliyev(USA) —Darkling (IRE) (Grand Lodge (USA))
105a[4]

Day By Day *B J Meehan* a70 86
3 ch f Kyllachy—Dayville (USA) (Dayjur (USA))
1961[9] 2740[6] *3286[7] 3646[2] 4361[8]* (4514) *(4740)* (5051) 5358[2] 5666[5] 6300[17]

Day Flight *J H M Gosden* 119
6 b h Sadler's Wells(USA) —Bonash (Rainbow Quest (USA))
1833[2] 2216[6]

Daylami Dreams *J S Moore* a78 72
3 gr g Daylami(IRE) —Kite Mark (Mark Of Esteem (IRE))
(196) 294[3] 563[2] 1205[5] 1637[5] 4758[4]

Day Of Days (IRE) *M H Tompkins* 60
3 b g Spectrum(IRE) —Private Encore (IRE) (Niniski (USA))
1412[5] 1725[10] 2005[9]

Day Of Destiny (IRE) *B W Hills* 71
2 gr c Clodovil(IRE) —El Corazon (IRE) (Mujadil (USA))
6618[5]

Day Pass (USA) *Saeed Bin Suroor* a110
3 rg c Five Star Day(USA) —Authorized Staff (USA) (Relaunch (USA))
596a[4] 859a[9]

Day Shift (IRE) *Rae Guest* 28
2 gr f Night Shift(USA) —Persian Mistress (IRE) (Persian Bold)
2416[5] 3823[9] 4026[6]

Days Of Thunder (IRE) *G F Bridgwater* 21
2 b c Choisir(AUS) —Grazina (Mark Of Esteem (IRE))
1680[13] 3471[14] 3947[7]

Daytona (IRE) *M Johnston* a85 114
3 ch g Indian Ridge—Kyka (USA) (Blushing John (USA))
456[2] 567[2] (633)

Day To Remember *J J Quinn* a72 91
6 gr g Daylami(IRE) —Miss Universe (IRE) (Warning)
6490[11]

Dazed And Amazed *R Hannon* a102 98
3 b c Averti(IRE) —Amazed (Clantime)
943[3] 1394[5] 1502[4] *(2352)* 2733[19] 3329[7] 4090[12] 4374[5] 4726[15] 5050[12] *6003[8]* 6197[6]

Dazzler Mac *N Bycroft* a48 68
6 b g Komaite(USA) —Stilvella (Camden Town)
892[8] 2256[7] 2711[12] 3161[5] 3381[9] 3765[11] 4768[4] 5908[10] *6563[5]*

Dazzling Colours *J Noseda* 63
2 b c Oasis Dream—Dazzle (Gone West (USA))
5193[6]

Dea Caelestis (FR) *H R A Cecil* 71
2 b f Dream Well(FR) —Gwydion (USA) (Raise A Cup (USA))
2000[3] 2904[9]

Deadline (UAE) *P T Midgley* a74 76
3 ch c Machiavellian(USA) —Time Changes (USA) (Danzig (USA))
694[3] 816[3] 1131[3] 1529[2] 1851[9] 2092[6] 3964[8] (4282) 4640[4] 5043[3] 5156[5] 5703[6] 6021[15]

Dead Red (USA) *G-E Mikhalides* 103
4 ch g Out Of Place(USA) —Lonely Fact (USA) (Known Fact (USA))
6375a[5]

Deal Breaker *Edward Lynam* a85 97
2 ch g Night Shift(USA) —Photo Flash (IRE) (Bahamian Bounty)
5456a[3] *6161a[10]*

Deal Flipper *P Winkworth* a67 69
2 b f Xaar—Zibet (Kris)
1445[4] 2134[11] *2992[5]* 4152[5] 4453[3] *4964[8]*

Dear Maurice *E A L Dunlop* 67
3 b c Indian Ridge—Shamaiel (IRE) (Lycius (USA))
4666[4]

Dear One (IRE) *P A Blockley* a57
3 b f Montjeu(IRE) —Siamoise (Caerleon (USA))
73[10]

Dear Will *J R Fanshawe* a49
2 bb g Mark Of Esteem(IRE) —Sweet Wilhelmina (Indian Ridge)
6868[7] 7070[11]

Deauville (GER) *Frau E Mader* 94
4 b m Dashing Blade—Dea (GER) (Shareef Dancer (USA))
1189a[9] 4190a[11] 5468a[7]

Deauville Vision (IRE) *M Halford* 111
4 b m Danehill Dancer(IRE) —Alexia Reveuse (IRE) (Dr Devious (IRE))
1548a[3] 2053a[11] 3578a[6] 4051a[9] 4648a[6] 6216a[8]

Debdene Bank (IRE) *Mrs Mary Hambro* 41
4 b m Pivotal—Nedaarah (Reference Point)
3968[4]

Debonnaire *M Johnston* a74 68
2 b f Anabaa(USA) —Ultra Finesse (USA) (Rahy (USA))
5745[6] 6015[5] *(6601)*

Debord (FR) *Jamie Poulton* a59 67
4 ch g Sendawar(IRE) —Partie De Dames (USA) (Bering)
2157[7] 2367[2] 2675[8] 3467[11] 5924[8]

Decado (IRE) *Kevin Prendergast* 114
4 b h Danehill Dancer(IRE) —Pirie (USA) (Green Dancer (USA))
1184a[3] 1696a[3] (3579a) 4058[6] 4435a[3] 5459a[6] 6031a[8]

Deccan Express (IRE) *Seamus Fahey* a70 71
3 ch g Grand Lodge(USA) —Harda Arda (USA) (Nureyev (USA))
6878[4]

Decent Proposal *T D Easterby* 49
3 b f Montjeu(IRE) —Markova's Dance (Mark Of Esteem (IRE))
849[7] 1045[13] 2096[6] 2793[9]

Dechiper (IRE) *R Johnson* a35 68
5 bb g Almutawakel—Safiya (USA) (Riverman (USA))
732[10] 1044[4] 1488[14] *1715[7]* 2254[4] (3956) 4582[5] (4772) 5286[2] 5905[3] 6258[6]

Decider (USA) *J M Bradley* a63 59
4 ch g High Yield(USA) —Nikita Moon (USA) (Secret Hello (USA))
1669[7] 1885[8] *2516[7]* 2966[8] *3064[8] 3190[6]* 4635[6] 4734[7] 4881[7]

Decision Day *J A Geake* 58
3 b f Groom Dancer(USA) —Indubitable (Sharpo)
2998[6] 3447[12] 6421[P]

Deckguard *J S Moore* a61 59
2 ch c Bertolini(USA) —Aegean Blue (Warning)
2941[11] 3478[6] 4323[9] *4963[5] 5729[12] 6099[2] 6454[5]*

Declaration Of War (IRE) *P W Chapple-Hyam* 112
2 b c Okawango(USA) —Date Mate (USA) (Thorn Dance (USA))
(1846) (2232) 2732[8] 3504[2] 6041a[2] 6489[6]

Dedicate *R Charlton* 67
2 b f Beat Hollow—Total Devotion (Desert Prince (IRE))
6470[8]

Dedo (IRE) *Kevin Prendergast* 98
2 b c Modigliani(USA) —Scant (FR) (Septieme Ciel (USA))
4743[7] 5070a[6]

Dee Burgh *J Pearce* a53 39
3 b f Zaha(CAN) —Glensara (Petoski)
2747[4]

Dee Cee Elle *M Johnston* a76 73
3 b f Groom Dancer(USA) —Missouri (Charnwood Forest (IRE))
1092[2] (1224) *(1353)* 1637[4] (2132) *2574[4]* 2808[7] 3590[8] 4139[6] 4843[6]

Dee Jay Wells *B Ellison* 74
3 b g Ishiguru(USA) —Stravaig (IRE) (Sadler's Wells (USA))
968[11] 1256[4] 1708[3] 2305[5] 2916[13] (3611) 3816[10] 4287[5]

Deep Cover (IRE) *R M Flower* a52
3 ch c Boundary(USA) —Chibi (USA) (Dynaformer (USA))
93[10] 791[12]

Deeper In Debt *J Akehurst* a66 77
9 ch g Piccolo—Harold's Girl (FR) (Northfields (USA))
2514[11]

Deerpark (IRE) *John F Gleeson* 96
5 ch g Orpen(USA) —Early Fin (IRE) (Mukaddamah (USA))
3138a[23] (Dead)

Dee Valley Boy (IRE) *J D Bethell* 47
3 b g Val Royal(FR) —Canadian Girl (IRE) (Rainbows For Life (CAN))
834[11] 1224[6] 2096[12] 2565[10]

Defi (IRE) *I Semple* a75 76
5 b g Rainbow Quest(USA) —Danse Classique (IRE) (Night Shift (USA))
151[6] 427[5] 674[7] 2388[2] 2563[9] 3502[10] 4713[9] (6732) *6874[2] 7047[4]*

Defies Logic *J G Given* 48
2 ch g Domedriver(IRE) —Khandahar (Zamindar (USA))
5226[5] 5749[10]

Definate Spectacle (IRE) *Noel Meade* a86 88
7 b g Spectrum(IRE) —Silver Bubble (USA) (Silver Hawk (USA))
4867a[6]

Define (IRE) *J Motherway* a74 81
4 b g Definite Article—Lingering Melody (IRE) (Nordico (USA))
6368a[5]

Definite Guest (IRE) *R A Fahey* a60 14
9 gr g Definite Article—Nicea (IRE) (Dominion)
259[8] 538[12] 1132[14]

Defnikov *A B Haynes* a46
2 gr g Baryshnikov(AUS) —By Definition (IRE) (Definite Article)
942[9] 4527[12] 5856[13]

Deimne (IRE) *John Joseph Murphy* a44 30
4 bb m Mull Of Kintyre(USA) —Lake Poopo (IRE) (Persian Heights)
7012[7] 7168[10]

Deira Dubai *B W Hills* a72 69
2 b f Green Desert(USA) —Aspen Leaves (USA) (Woodman (USA))
4564[6] 5140[3] 5745[3] *6434[2]*

Delacroix (GER) *W Kujath* 53
2 b c Big Shuffle(USA) —Deborah (GER) (Law Society (USA))
6324a[10]

De La Grandera (USA) *David Wachman* a68 86
3 bb c Fusaichi Pegasus(USA) —Torros Straits (USA) (Boundary (USA))
2788[13]

De La Vista (GER) *W Hickst* 74
2 b f Big Shuffle(USA) —Dancing Flower (IRE) (Compton Place)
4837a[6] 5848a[2] 6324a[6]

Dellini (IRE) *M R Channon* 83
2 b f Green Desert(USA) —Belle Genius (USA) (Beau Genius (CAN))
4602[12] (4992) 5324[14] 5614[10]

Del Mar Sunset *W J Haggas* a86 86
8 b g Unfuwain(USA) —City Of Angels (Woodman (USA))
1356[4] (2003) 2403[9] 3671[6] 4184[9] 4909[8] 5362[3] 5593[4] *6545[2] 6765[2]*

Delorain (IRE) *N B King* 55
4 b g Kalanisi(IRE) —Lady Nasrana (FR) (Al Nasr (FR))
1925[6]

Delta Blues (JPN) *Katsuhiko Sumii* 123
6 b h Dance In The Dark(JPN) —Dixie Splash (USA) (Dixieland Band (USA))
6943a[5]

Delta Diva (USA) *P F I Cole* a69
2 b f Victory Gallop(CAN) —Tjinouska (USA) (Cozzene (USA))
(4273)

Delta Shuttle (IRE) *K R Burke* 66
3 b g Bluebird(USA) —Ibtihal (IRE) (Hamas (IRE))
1091[8] 1410[5] 1708[6] 2112[2] 2389[5] 3081[3] 5777[11] 6250[12]

Delude (IRE) *S Seemar* a87 76
9 ch g Be My Guest(USA) —Deceive (Machiavellian (USA))
327a[5] 410a[12]

Dematraf (IRE) *P D Evans* a30 69
5 gr m Atraf—Demolition Jo (Petong)
1891[2] (2249) 3017[2] (3277) 3368[15] 4881[4] (5191) 5272[10]

Demi Sec *Dr J D Scargill* a35 22
4 ch m Bahamian Bounty—Veuve (Tirol)
559[9] 714[7] 2304[9] 4596[11]

Demisemiquaver *J Noseda* a76 69
3 b f Singspiel(IRE) —Miss D'Ouilly (FR) (Bikala)
1659[11] 2359[2] 3908[4] 4989[2] 6420[3] *6766[2] 6901[2] (6975) (7099)*

Demolition *C A Cyzer* a24 80
3 ch g Starborough—Movie Star (IRE) (Barathea (IRE))
3084[11] 3948[2] 4510[2] (5005) 5385[6] 5724[5] 6055[6]

Demolition Molly *R F Marvin* 13
6 b m Rudimentary(USA) —Persian Fortune (Forzando)
1299[14]

Demure Princess *W G M Turner* a34 60
2 b f Tamure(IRE) —Princess Penny (King's Signet (USA))
1255[3] 1858[4] 2803[2] 3199[5] *3925[9]* 4193[4] 4762[14]

Denbera Dancer (USA) *M Johnston* 77
3 b c Danehill(USA) —Monevassia (USA) (Mr Prospector (USA))
3436[4] 3994[4]

Dendor *D W Barker* 63
3 b g Warningford—Dolphin Dancer (Dolphin Street (FR))
1236[8] 1425[5] 2312[11] 2892[3] 3786[2] (5935)

Deneuve *M G Quinlan* a55 48
4 ch m Tomba—Princess Sadie (Shavian)
129[5] (210) 517[8]

Den's Boy *J R Boyle* 2
2 b c Josr Algarhoud(IRE) —Den's-Joy (Archway (IRE))
4014[15]

Den's Gift (IRE) *C G Cox* a89 71
3 rg g City On A Hill(USA) —Romanylei (IRE) (Blues Traveller (IRE))
(6830) (6996)

Denton Hawk *M Dods* a58 56
3 b g Mujahid(USA) —Lamasat (USA) (Silver Hawk (USA))
223[2] 373[10] 1164[5] 1489[3] 2091[7] 3918[8] 4220[6]

Deo Valente (IRE) *B J Meehan* 84
2 b c Dubai Destination(USA) —Pack Ice (USA) (Wekiva Springs (USA))
5598[8] 5971[3]

De Port Heights (IRE) *M Madgwick*
3 bl g Redback—Raise-A-Secret (IRE) (Classic Secret (USA))
5873[14] *6546[13]*

Depp (ITY) *L D'Auria* 93
3 ch c City On A Hill(USA) —Drifa (ITY) (Hamas (IRE))
1875a[11]

Deputy Consort (USA) *M J P O'Brien* 67
4 b g Stravinsky(USA) —Possible Consort (USA) (Deputy Minister (CAN))
6368a[7]

Derby Desire (IRE) *Michael McElhone* a33
3 b f Swallow Flight(IRE) —Jaldi (IRE) (Nordico (USA))
6920a[12]

Derison (USA) *P Van De Poele* 109
5 b g Miesque's Son(USA) —Devolli (Saumarez)
5468a[2] 6039a[7] 6633a[5] 6954a[4]

Derpat (IRE) *J S Bolger* 73
3 b f Invincible Spirit(IRE) —No Tippling (IRE) (Unblest)
5841a[17]

Derricks Dotty *N J Vaughan* a64 50
3 br g Beat All(USA) —Pass The Rose (IRE) (Thatching)
2341[4] *2951[4] 3406[5]* 3999[14] *6361[7]*

Derringer (AUS) *J Salantri* 99
8 b g Creese—Derring Red (AUS) (Sovereign Red (NZ))
6033a[11]

Descargo *W G M Turner* a54 23
3 ch f Delta Dancer—Secret Miss (Beveled (USA))
36[2] 311[7] 1151[13]

Descartes *Saeed Bin Suroor* a102 67
5 b g Dubai Millennium—Gold's Dance (FR) (Goldneyev (USA))
329a[3] 5554[10]

Desert Anger *E Charpy* a83 85
6 b g Cadeaux Genereux—Chere Amie (USA) (Mr Prospector (USA))
250a[10] 398a[10]

Desert Chief *Saeed Bin Suroor* 90
5 b h Green Desert(USA) —Oriental Fashion (IRE) (Marju (IRE))
325a[3] 2374[8] 5413[13]

Desert Chill (USA) *Saeed Bin Suroor* 82
2 b f Red Ransom(USA) —Storm Song (USA) (Summer Squall (USA))
6087[3] 6470[2]

Desert Clover (USA) *P F I Cole* a76
2 bb c Mutakddim(USA) —Booly (USA) (Apalachee (USA))
(6903)

Desert Commander (IRE) *K A Ryan* a82 105
5 b g Green Desert(USA) —Meadow Pipit (CAN) (Meadowlake (USA))
1088[13] 1826[12] (2339) 3140a[12] 3586[16] 4227[8] 5254[11] *6243[8]*

Desert D'Argent (IRE) *H Morrison* a89 58
4 ch m Desert Story(IRE) —Petite-D-Argent (Noalto)
5225[2] 5940[7]

Desert Dew (IRE) *B W Hills* 111
3 ch c Indian Ridge—Blue Water (USA) (Bering)
(1275) 1617[2] 2789[3]

Desert Dreamer (IRE) *G A Butler* a87 88
6 b g Green Desert(USA) —Follow That Dream (Darshaan)
827[6] 1063[12] 1308[4] 1765[8] *1935[2]* 2180[5] 2318[11] 2965[4] (3350) *(3619) 4965[2] 5223[6]* 5617[7] *5891[8] 6209[6] 6355[9] 6900[5] 6972[5] (7094)*

Desert Dust *R M H Cowell* a58 48
4 b g Vettori(IRE) —Dust (Green Desert (USA))
317[4] 1384[3] 1902[11] 3347[16]

Deserted Dane (USA) *G A Swinbank* a81 91
3 b c Elusive Quality(USA) —Desertion (IRE) (Danehill (USA))
474a[9] 641a[8] 1160[7] 2135[4] 2461[9] (2989) 3380[4] 3749[6] 5039[6] 5506[6]

Deserter (IRE) *J A Osborne* a62
3 b f Desert Style(IRE) —Tianella (GER) (Acatenango (GER))
114[4] 258[8] 386[7] 491[4] (Dead)

Desert Fight (CHI) *S Seemar* a101
4 b m Hussonet(USA) —Mozinha (CHI) (Mocito Feliz (CHI))
476a[4]

Desert Hawk *W M Brisbourne* a62 61
6 b g Cape Cross(IRE) —Milling (IRE) (In The Wings)
71[3] (121) 180[8] 445[11] 612[14] 742[3] 1167[9] 1314[7] 2370[5] 2603[5] (2745) 2967[3] 3250[3] 3805[4] 3956[3] 4284[7] *4464[3]* (4860) 5676[4] 5886[5] *6342[8] 6672[5]* 6728[3] *6937[2]*

Desert Hunter (IRE) *Micky Hammond* a54 56
4 b g Desert Story(IRE) —She-Wolff (IRE) (Pips Pride)
2033[3] 2421[4] *3647[4]* 4137[7] 4223[12] 4562[13] 4701[15] 5295[4]

Desert Island Miss *W R Swinburn* a71 67
4 b m Medicean—Miss Castaway (Selkirk (USA))
2154[4] *2990[3]* 4860[7] *(5424)* 6063[6]

Desert Lark *G A Swinbank* 44
2 ch c Sakhee(USA) —Oyster Catcher (IRE) (Bluebird (USA))
4077[6] 5227[9]

Desert Leader (IRE) *R W Price* a79 55
6 b g Green Desert(USA) —Za Aamah (USA) (Mr Prospector (USA))
(142) 205[13] 428[4] 564[4] 4672[10] 4976[8] 5225[8] 6027[4] 6314[8]

Desert Life (IRE) *R A Harris* a63 63
2 b g Desert Style(IRE) —Vie Privee (Hernando (FR))
4683[7] 4876[8] *5015[4]* 5363[5] *6933[5] 6958[6] 7096[3] 7171[4] 7272[6]*

Desert Light (IRE) *D Shaw* a66 47
6 b g Desert Sun—Nacote (IRE) (Mtoto)
50[6] 132[4] 158[6] 236[8] 310[3] 442[3] 562[3] (622) 654[4] 743[4] 896[8] *(1309) 3408[10] 6428[5] 6870[5] 6910[5] 7183[4]*

Desert Lightning (IRE) *I W McInnes* a54 61
5 ch g Desert Prince(IRE) —Saibhreas (IRE) (Last Tycoon (IRE))
2168[5] 2372[6] 2820[3] 3629[3] 3868[5] 4426[13]

Desert Lord *K A Ryan* a101 119
7 b g Green Desert(USA) —Red Carnival (USA) (Mr Prospector (USA))
2324a[3] 2733[6] 4090[11] 4746[2] 5632[5] 6039a[3] *6930[3]* 7089a[9]

Desert Lover (IRE) *R J Price* a61 62
5 b g Desert Prince(IRE) —Crystal Flute (Lycius (USA))
131[13] 334[5] 447[8] 517[4] 571[2] (625) 682[3] 729[4] 806[10] 1027[10] 5817[12] *6479[7] 6563[6] 6955[5] 6979[4] 7113[3] 7153[5] 7250[4]*

Desert Master *C F Wall* a81 66
4 b g Green Desert(USA) —Khambani (IRE) (Royal Academy (USA))
186[5] 342[4] 489[3] (567) 835[3] 1061[9] 2191[4] 2608[4] *(5753)*

Desert Ocean (IRE) *G Collet* a97 93
3 b c Desert Sun—Skerray (Soviet Star (USA))
436a[7]

Desert Opal *C R Dore* a80 80
7 ch g Cadeaux Genereux—Nullarbor (Green Desert (USA))
155[7] 269[4] 835[6] (1074) *1363[4]* (1914) 3298[3] 3528[4] (3859) 4800[7] 6020[13] *(6340) 6829[5] 6938[5] 7059[5] 7221[2]*

Desert Pride *W S Kittow* a65
2 b c Desert Style(IRE) —Dalu (IRE) (Dancing Brave (USA))
7043[2] 7264[5]

Desert Quiet (IRE) *P Giannotti* 107
5 b m Desert Story(IRE) —Quiet Awakening (USA) (Secreto (USA))
2296a[11]

Desert Rat (IRE) *J T Gorman* 66
3 b g Desert Sun—Virtue Rewarded (IRE) (Darshaan)
4836a[8]

Desert Realm (IRE) *I Mohammed* a87 103
4 b g Desert Prince(IRE) —Fawaayid (USA) (Vaguely Noble)
250a[8] *329a[16]* 401a[12]

Desert Sands (IRE) *John Joseph Murphy* a61
2 b c Dubai Destination(USA) —Zvezda (USA) (Nureyev (USA))
6944[7]

Desert Sea (IRE) *D W P Arbuthnot* a90 89
4 b g Desert Sun—Sea Of Time (USA) (Gilded Time (USA))
1654[7] 2449[4] 3273[2] 3898[7] (4569) 6335[15]

Desert Showa (IRE) *P Paciello*
2 b f Intikhab(USA) —Feeling Free (IRE) (Alzao (USA))
1485a[3]

Desert Soul *R H York* a61 62
3 b g Fantastic Light(USA) —Jalousie (IRE) (Barathea (IRE))
738[7] 1091[15] 1894[2] 2248[7] 4687[8]

Desert Thistle (IRE) *H J L Dunlop* 75
2 b c Tamarisk(IRE) —Taajreh (IRE) (Mtoto)
5274[9] 5633[11] (6079)

Desiderio *R Hannon* a55 48
2 b c Oasis Dream—Pleasuring (Good Times (ITY))
5918[12] 6127[12] 6493[14] *6892[2]*

Desirable Dancer (IRE) *R A Harris* a40 47
3 b f Fath(USA) —Tender Time (Tender King)
136[10]

Desperate Dan *A B Haynes* a91 85
6 b g Danzero(AUS) —Alzianah (Alzao (USA))
452[3] 554[3] 810[9] 1063[16] 1431[6] 1999[2] 2479[7] 3449[4] 4233[7] *(4974)* 5272[5] *5648[5] 6405[2] (6708) 6829[3] 6972[10] 7126[8]*

Desperation (IRE) *M R Channon* a79 20
5 b g Desert Style(IRE) —Mauras Pride (IRE) (Cadeaux Genereux)
316[7]

Destare *J E Pease* 93
2 b f Desert Prince(IRE) —Contare (Shirley Heights)
6939a[3]

Destinys Dream (IRE) *Mrs A Duffield* 71
2 b f Mull Of Kintyre(USA) —Dream Of Jenny (Caerleon (USA))
1553[4] 1848[9] 3606[6] 4076[10] 4524[2] 4841[5] (5298) 5746[3] 5914[6]

Destour (IRE) *J Noseda* 73
3 b c Royal Applause—Wild Missy (USA) (Wild Again (USA))
1468[4] 2059[5] 2393[4] 4079[3]

Determind Stand (USA) *Sir Michael Stoute* a76 86
2 b c Elusive Quality(USA) —Sauterne (Rainbow Quest (USA))
2473[8] *2991[3]* 3625[5] 4501[6] *(4964)* 5350[6] 6471[2]

Detonate *I A Wood* a54 63
5 b g Mind Games—Bron Hilda (IRE) (Namaqualand (USA))
359[9] 485[10] 562[7] 653[9] 2357[3] 2540[6] 2652[3] *2798[13]* 4336[10] 5009[14] *6062[6] 6390[13] 6531[4] 6565[4] 6735[8] 6773[8] 6826[8] 6886[10] 7166[5] 7238[4]*

Detonator (IRE) *M Johnston* a79 74
2 b g Fantastic Light(USA) —Narwala (Darshaan)
5880[2] *(6737)*

Deuteronomio (IRE) *Maria Rita Salvioni* 87
2 ch c Intikhab(USA) —Discreet Option (IRE) (Night Shift (USA))
6523a[10]

Devilfishpoker Com *R C Guest* a48 51
3 ch g Dr Fong(USA) —Midnight Allure (Aragon)
136[8] 1303[4] 1573[3] 2096[9] 6330[6] 6561[7]

Devils Desire *J M Bradley*
3 b f Superior Premium—Ming Blue (Primo Dominie)
1203[13]

Devine Dancer *H Candy* a58 81
4 ch m Woodborough(USA) —Princess Londis (Interrex (CAN))
1061[12] 1465[5] 3859[10] 4204[12]

Devolution (IRE) *Miss C Dyson* a51
9 b g Distinctly North(USA) —Election Special (Chief Singer)
6124[8]

Devon Flame *R J Hodges* a67 86
8 b g Whittingham(IRE) —Uaeflame (IRE) (Polish Precedent (USA))
622[2] 688[2] 803[11] 1004[15] *1165[8]* 3869[8] 4236[13]

Devon House (USA) *J H M Gosden* 50
3 b f Chester House(USA) —Devon Heights (USA) (Mt. Livermore (USA))
1639[12]

Devonia Plains (IRE) *Mrs P N Dutfield* a64 62
5 ch g Danehill Dancer(IRE) —Marlfield Lake (Cadeaux Genereux)
1118[11] 1507[18] *4063[13]* 4505[9] *5730[14]*

Dexileos (IRE) *David Pinder* a56 71
8 b g Danehill(USA) —Theano (IRE) (Thatching)
94[7] 123[9] 341[10] 721[2] 1119[5] 1381[3] 2591[5] 2619[3] 3405[7] 3730[10] 4673[3] 5121[5] 5368[3] 5606[7] 5782[7]

Dezigna (NZ) *Wayne & Vanessa Hillis* 112
7 b g Volksraad—Label Basher (NZ) (Conquistarose (NZ))
1877a[11]

Dhaka Dazzle *M R Channon* 48
2 b g Josr Algarhoud(IRE) —Magical Flute (Piccolo)
1073[6] 1291[7] 1963[9] 3373[4] 4202[9] 4770[8] 5268[11] 5572[10]

Dharori (IRE) *M A Jarvis* 60
2 ch c Captain Rio—Sliding (Formidable (USA))
5771[6] 6065[P] (Dead)

Dhaular Dhar (IRE) *J S Goldie* a93 105
5 b h Indian Ridge—Pescara (IRE) (Common Grounds)
1041[2] 1242[10] 1601[7] (1619) 2030[4] 2237[14] 3088[7] 3329[6] 3505[4] 3941[20] 4196[4] 4614[11] 5031[11] 5616[25] 5797[5] 6183[16] 6758[10]

Dhehdaah *Mrs P Sly* a78 75
6 b g Alhaarth(IRE) —Carina Clare (Slip Anchor)
(1253) 1793[9] (2887) 5204[2] 5808[8] 6473[16]

Dhhamaan (IRE) *C E Brittain* a76 69
2 b c Dilshaan—Safe Care (IRE) (Caerleon (USA))
3957[3] 4393[2] 4784[9] 5974[26] 6267[7] 6705[2] (6827) 7015[3] 7145[2]

Dhurwah (IRE) *T Keddy* a43 42
4 b m Green Desert(USA) —Bintalbawadi (IRE) (Diesis)
2174[10] 4908[10] 5386[10]

Diable (GER) *H Hesse* 99
8 b h Big Shuffle(USA) —Diasprina (GER) (Aspros (GER))
1800a[6] 3581a[6]

Diacaro *H Blume* 94
2 b c Alhaarth(IRE) —Diacada (GER) (Cadeaux Genereux)
5028a[4] 6219a[9]

Diademas (USA) *V Smith* a70 70
2 bb c Grand Slam(USA) —Kona Kat (USA) (Mountain Cat (USA))
1680[2] (1975) 2090[5] 3562[4] 4358[5] 4903[14] 5365[7] 6023[3] 6624[5] 6823[5] 6966[7]

Diamantgottin (GER) *P Rau* 98
2 b f Fantastic Light(USA) —Dunnellon (Shareef Dancer (USA))
6371a[2]

Diamond Dan (IRE) *P D Evans* a62 60
5 b g Foxhound(USA) —Kawther (Tap On Wood)
371[9] 426[4]

Diamond Diva *J W Hills* a97 100
3 br f Dansili—Vivianna (Indian Ridge)
1610[3] 1837[5] (2518) 3059[6] (3670) 4062[2] 4639[2] 5403[2] 5799[2]

Diamond Flute *Mouse Hamilton-Fairley*
2 b f Piccolo—Diamond Park (IRE) (Alzao (USA))
3592[13]

Diamond Hurricane (IRE) *M Wellings* a65 73
3 b g Mujadil(USA) —Christoph's Girl (Efisio)
3480[10] 4351[5] 5041[2] 6064[8] 6608[12] 6825[12] 6886[13] 6968[13] 7001[10] 7057[10]

Diamond Josh *M Mullineaux* a58 62
5 ch g Primo Dominie—Exit (Exbourne (USA))
4706[16] 4973[12] 5430[8] 6210[10] 6625[9] 6702[11] 6910[6] 7105[9] 7138[10] 7226[P]

Diamond Katie (IRE) *N Tinkler* a52 64
5 b m Night Shift(USA) —Fayrooz (USA) (Gulch (USA))
123[3] 225[8]

Diamond Key (IRE) *M G Quinlan* a77 56
3 b f Key Of Luck(USA) —Aljeeza (Halling (USA))
423[10] 449[11] 3183[10] (3274) 3803[5] 3907[8] 5187[14] 5690[2] (5980) (6271) 6506[2]

Diamond Lass (IRE) *R A Fahey* 63
2 b f Rock Of Gibraltar(IRE) —Keralba (USA) (Sheikh Albadou)
3582[4] 4350[5] 5140[6]

Diamond Light (USA) *M Botti* a63 66
3 ch f Fantastic Light(USA) —Queen Of Women (USA) (Sharpen Up)
21[7] 267[2] 624[7] 904[9]

Diamond Necklace (USA) *A P O'Brien* 98
3 gr f Unbridled's Song(USA) —Helsinki (Machiavellian (USA))
1777a[9] 2065a[7] 2483a[5]

Diamond Orchid (IRE) *G A Harker* 48
7 gr m Victory Note(USA) —Olivia's Pride (IRE) (Digamist (USA))
1966[10]

Diamond Peak (IRE) *L D'Auria*
3 gr c Daylami(IRE) —De Puntillas (Distant Relative)
1191a[2]

Diamond Quest (SAF) *A M Balding* 111
6 b g Saumarez—Discover Diamonds (AUS) (Marscay (AUS))
172a[3] 328a[6] (473a) 531a[4] 645a[2] 2856[6]

Diamond Royal (IRE) *E A L Dunlop* 74
2 b f Red Ransom(USA) —Gaily Royal (IRE) (Royal Academy (USA))
6087[4]

Diamonds And Dust *F P Murtagh* a82 90
5 b g Mister Baileys—Dusty Shoes (Shareef Dancer (USA))
(115) (380) 2987[17]

Diamond Seeker *V Smith* a45 41
2 ch f Erhaab(USA) —Slavonic Dance (Muhtarram (USA))
6295[13] 6578[10] 6868[6] 7007[10]

Diamonds For Luck (IRE) *Desmond McDonogh* a68 68
5 bb g Key Of Luck(USA) —Aine's Pet (IRE) (Fayruz)
5460a[4] 6916a[5]

Diamond Soles (IRE) *B J Meehan* a22 46
2 b f Danetime(IRE) —Villa Nova (IRE) (Petardia)
1469[6] 2398[8] 4755[12] 5096[10]

Diamond Stripes (USA) *R Dutrow Jr* a113
4 rg g Notebook(USA) —Romantic Summer (USA) (On To Glory (USA))
5059a[3] 6514a[8]

Diamond Tycoon (USA) *B J Meehan* 110
3 b c Johannesburg(USA) —Palacoona (FR) (Last Tycoon (IRE))
(1143) 1473[9]

Diamond World *C A Horgan* a47 58
4 b m Agnes World(USA) —In A Twinkling (IRE) (Brief Truce (USA))
723[8] 5336[10] 6097[7]

Diamond Yas (IRE) *H R A Cecil* 72
2 b f Mull Of Kintyre(USA) —Balgren (IRE) (Ballad Rock)
5540[3]

Dianella (IRE) *David P Myerscough* a76 85
3 b f Gold Away(IRE) —Dictatrice (FR) (Anabaa (USA))
6553a[11]

Diane's Choice *J Akehurst* a92 92
4 ch m Komaite(USA) —Ramajana (USA) (Shadeed (USA))
1023[7] 1292[3] 1653[20] 2440[7] 3268[10] 4095[2] 4664[5] (4886) 5449[7] 5954[14] 6668[4] 7053[5] 7255[7]

Dichoh *M A Jarvis* a95 16
4 b g Diktat—Hoh Dancer (Indian Ridge)
28[6] 233[5] (451) (629) 846[17] 1180[2] 5685[6] 6143[11] 6674[2] 7165[6] 7281[3]

Dickens (GER) *H Blume* 114
4 b h Kallisto(GER) —Desidera (IRE) (Shaadi (USA))
2706a[4] 3778a[4] 4520a[7] 5671a[7] 6353a[3]

Dickensian (IRE) *E Charpy* 102
4 br h Xaar—Cappella (IRE) (College Chapel)
540a[5]

Dickie Deano *J M Bradley* a39
3 b g Sooty Tern—Chez Bonito (IRE) (Persian Bold)
338[7] 569[11] 7076[5] 7189[10]

Dickie Le Davoir *K R Burke* a78 93
3 b g Kyllachy—Downeaster Alexa (USA) (Red Ryder (USA))
1298[2] 1604[4] (1667) 2044[8] 2213[11] 3089[9] 3380[7] 5584[25] 6891[3] 6981[6] (7233) 7251[4]

Dickie Valentine *M R Bosley* a50 49
2 b g Diktat—Passionelle (Nashwan (USA))
5868[10] 6237[10] 6827[11] 6966[6] 7235[5]

Dick Morris (IRE) *J G Coogan* 88
2 b g Kalanisi(IRE) —Moet (IRE) (Mac's Imp (USA))
779a[6] 1508a[2]

Dicktator (NZ) *R Laing* 92
7 b g Yamanin Vital(NZ) —Gem Fire (NZ) (Noble Bijou (USA))
6033a[9] 6711a[12]

Dictation *Mrs Valerie Keatley* a54 47
5 b m Diktat—Monaiya (Shareef Dancer (USA))
7056[2]

Dictatrix *P D Niven* a72 72
4 gr m Diktat—Apennina (USA) (Gulch (USA))
979[6] 1252[6] 1589[10] 1766[11] 2309[6] 4856[12] 5132[12] 6640[11] 6801[7] 6969[12]

Didactic *A J McCabe* a49 48
3 b g Diktat—Scene (IRE) (Scenic)
1261[4] 1913[11] 2829[13] 3257[6] 5041[6] 5688[7]

Didana (IRE) *M G Quinlan* a67 60
2 br f Diktat—Daanat Nawal (Machiavellian (USA))
6535[7] 6912[4] (7196)

Didntcomeback *M S Saunders* a41 27
2 b g Oasis Dream—Latin Beauty (IRE) (Sadler's Wells (USA))
4014[14] 6358[8] 6799[12]

Didnt Tell My Wife *Miss K B Boutflower* a47 41
8 ch g Aragon—Bee Dee Dancer (Ballacashtal (CAN))
20[11] 51[9] 210[9] 243[10] 2370[15] 2795[7] 3616[5] 4294[14]

Diego Cao (IRE) *N J Gifford* a65 79
6 b g Cape Cross(IRE) —Lady Moranbon (USA) (Trempolino (USA))
1959[8] 6335[32] (Dead)

Dig Deep (IRE) *W J Haggas* a104 96
5 b g Entrepreneur—Diamond Quest (Rainbow Quest (USA))
79[2] 155[2] 1088[7] (1363) 1853[7] 2566[12] 3464[8] (3528) 3990[3] 4386[12] 4567[15] 5212[16] 5513[4] 5806[8] 6173[9] (6381)

Digger Boy *J Gallagher* a69 64
4 b g King's Best(USA) —Chameleon (Green Desert (USA))
48[13] 539[9] 603[9] 2084[9] 2493[10]

Dig Gold (USA) *M A Jarvis* 83
3 ch c Seeking The Gold(USA) —Sheroog (USA) (Shareef Dancer (USA))
1012[4] 1290[6] 3685[4] 3964[10] 4357[2] (4910)

Diggs Lane (IRE) *N A Callaghan* a54 49
3 b g Galileo(IRE) —Desert Bluebell (Kalaglow)
904[8]

Digital *M R Channon* a74 79
10 ch g Safawan—Heavenly Goddess (Soviet Star (USA))
793[7] 992[6] 1200[4] 1564[4] 1787[3] 1969[6] 2272[6] 2576[8] 3017[4] 3375[2] 3572[4] 3723[2] 3787[7] 4397[4] 4505[5] 4853[12] 4881[2] 5191[6] (5272) 5349[2] 5576[3] (5740) 5942[3] 6157[12]

Digital Photo (ITY) *V di Napoli* 91
4 b m Bahhare(USA) —Mamya (Shernazar)
6688a[7]

Dijeerr (USA) *Saeed Bin Suroor* 106
3 b c Danzig(USA) —Sharp Minister (CAN) (Deputy Minister (CAN))
1703a[11] 6198[2] 6491[2]

Dik Dik *J S Moore* a48 60
4 b g Diktat—Totom (Mtoto)
120[4] 270[5] 333[4] 380[6]

Diksie Dancer *K A Ryan* a69 67
3 br f Diktat—Careful Dancer (Gorytus (USA))
565[6] 1045[2] 1282[2] 1923[3] 2137[5] 3920[11] 4079[8] 4705[8] 5175[9] 5982[10]

Diktalex (IRE) *C J Teague* a34 26
4 b m Diktat—Kingdom Royale (IRE) (Royal Academy (USA))
3[13] 59[5] 318[11] 376[7] 504[6] 580[9]

Diktatorial *J Howard Johnson* a87 91
5 br g Diktat—Reason To Dance (Damister (USA))
2397[7] 4690[17]

Diktatorship (IRE) *Jennie Candlish* a65 59
4 b g Diktat—Polka Dancer (Dancing Brave (USA))
45[3] 71[5] (126) 203[6] 315[7] 578[10] 789[2] 1032[4] 1362[2] (1570) 1732[2] 1966[9] 3598[2] 3927[4] 4463[12] 4670[8] 4994[6] 6613[3] 6835[8]

Dilmoun (IRE) *A L T Moore* 11
5 b g Darshaan—Mannakea (USA) (Fairy King (USA))
4138[8]

Dilshaan's Prize (IRE) *R Pritchard-Gordon* 105
3 b c Dilshaan—Dancing Prize (IRE) (Sadler's Wells (USA))
5258a[6] 6137a[8]

Dilwin (IRE) *D Nicholls* 61
3 b g Dilshaan—Welsh Harp (Mtoto)
968[4] 2844[10] 3181[10] 3411[8]

Dimashq *J O'Reilly* 48
5 b m Mtoto—Agwaas (IRE) (Rainbow Quest (USA))
4246[5] 6325[6]

Dimenticata (IRE) *Kevin Prendergast* 111
3 b f Danetime(IRE) —Non Dimenticar Me (IRE) (Don't Forget Me)
782a[8] 1047a[5] 2065a[2] 3117a[9] 5392a[3] 6216a[4]

Diminuto *M D I Usher* a74 78
3 b f Iron Mask(USA) —Thicket (Wolfhound (USA))
147[2] 387[2] 520[8] 671[4] 707[2] 925[2] 1151[4] 1351[3] 1766[3] (1932) 2276[5] 2950[4] 3277[3] (3369) (3637) 4123[14] 5684[5] 6173[12] 6568[3] 6762[7] 6905[2] 7126[9]

Dinaha (FR) *X Thomas-Demeaulte* a93 91
6 b m Octagonal(NZ) —Dinah (FR) (Sillery (USA))
31a[15]

Dinarius *K J Burke* a73 53
2 b c Bertolini(USA) —Ambassadress (USA) (Alleged (USA))
2596[10] 6974[5] 7145[5] 7234[3]

Dingaan (IRE) *A M Balding* a94 93
4 b g Tagula(IRE) —Boughtbyphone (Warning)
1836[9] (2440) 2817[11] 3481[13] 3941[15] 4227[6] 4548[8] 4851[9] 4886[4] 5449[4] 6142[4] 6437[4]

Dinner Date *T Keddy* a67 65
5 ch g Groom Dancer(USA) —Misleading Lady (Warning)
2007[3] 2423[4] 4340[5] 6529[6] (6713) 6867[2] 7083[7]

Diplomatic Dan (IRE) *E J Alston*
4 b g Imperial Ballet(IRE) —Yaqatha (IRE) (Sadler's Wells (USA))
1259[11]

Directa (GER) *Andreas Lowe* 99
4 b m Acatenango(GER) —Directa Germania (IRE) (Priolo (USA))
3121a[5]

Directa's Digger (IRE) *M Scudamore* 64
3 b c Daggers Drawn(USA) —Chita Rivera (Chief Singer)
5807[5] 6259[4]

Direct Debit (IRE) *M L W Bell* a87 92
4 b g Dansili—Dimple (Fairy King (USA))
1145[10] 1524[11] 1962[9] 2835[3] 3039[2] (3482) 4134[3]

Diriculous *T G Mills* a66
3 b g Diktat—Sheila's Secret (IRE) (Bluebird (USA))
6580[4] (6963)

Dirt Music (AUS) *G Baker* 91
6 br m Jeune—Lochnarie (Kings Lake (USA))
6711a[2]

Dirty Dancing *B W Hills* a60 57
3 b g Green Desert(USA) —Shadow Dancing (Unfuwain (USA))
2175[6] 3062[7] 3968[2] 5166[12] 5475[7]

Discanti (IRE) *T D Easterby* a47 63
2 ch g Distant Music(USA) —Gertie Laurie (Lomond (USA))
1713[7] 2251[6] 2803[3] 3606[8] 4447[6]

Disco Dan *D K Ivory* a64 80
3 b g Danehill Dancer(IRE) —Ghay (USA) (Bahri (USA))
1099[17] 1930[7] 2570[9] 3038[3] 4269[P] (Dead)

Discotheque (USA) *P Howling* a70 65
4 ch m Not For Love(USA) —Disco Darlin' (USA) (Citidancer (USA))
72[2] 212[9] (286) 363[3] 426[2] 459[3]

Discover Roma (IRE) *F Magliari* 68
3 br f Rock Of Gibraltar(IRE) —Soltura (IRE) (Sadler's Wells (USA))
2070a[11]

Discreet Cat (USA) *Saeed Bin Suroor* a130
4 b h Forestry(USA) —Pretty Discreet (USA) (Private Account (USA))
863a[7] 5852a[3] 6485a[3]

Dishdasha (IRE) *Mrs A M Thorpe* a59
5 b g Desert Prince(IRE) —Counterplot (IRE) (Last Tycoon (IRE))
7069[2] 7187[5]

Disintegration (IRE) *A King* 62
3 b g Barathea(IRE) —Leave Me Alone (IRE) (Nashwan (USA))
1724[8] 1972[7] 2915[3] 3473[8]

Dispol Isle (IRE) *T D Barron* a65 78
5 gr m Trans Island—Pictina (Petong)
(967) 1488[11] 1710[3] (1892) 2742[2] 2988[7] 3512[4] 3790[3] 4281[8] 4705[7] 5253[12] 5701[4] (5840) 6331[11] 6701[8]

Dispol Katie *T D Barron* 79
6 ch m Komaite(USA) —Twilight Time (Aragon)
2033[14] 2256[11] 2576[12]

Dispol Peto *R Johnson* a62 57
7 gr g Petong—Plie (Superlative)
145[9] 242[4] 464[2] 579[6] 907[2] 3204[6] 3502[6] (3840) 6259[11] 6558[12]

Dispol Truly (IRE) *A G Newcombe* a27 50
3 b f Bold Fact(USA) —Beautyofthepeace (IRE) (Exactly Sharp (USA))
577[14] 1782[16]

Dispol Veleta *Miss T Spearing* a45 78
6 b m Makbul—Foxtrot Pie (Shernazar)
1627[4] 2214[14] 2660[2] 3182[7] 3789[5] 4667[8]

Distalino (FR) *F Doumen* 97
4 b g Poliglote—Distale (USA) (Trempolino (USA))
6137a[3]

Distant Charm (IRE) *R Hannon* 81
2 b c Distant Music(USA) —My Lucy Locket (IRE) (Mujadil (USA))
2539[5] (2876) (3275) 4121[8] 4501[8] 6201[6] 6471[7]

Distant Diamond (IRE) *W R Swinburn* a66 50
2 b c Distant Music(USA) —La Belle Katherine (USA) (Lyphard (USA))
3850[8] 4761[6] 5337[11] (5896)

Distant Drama (USA) *J Noseda* a61 71
3 ch f Distant View(USA) —To Act (USA) (Roberto (USA))
4808[2] 6240[7] 6704[2] (6904)

Distant Noble *R Brotherton* a34 54
2 b g Carnival Dancer—Fly In Style (Hernando (FR))
2510[9] 2605[2] 3283[7] 3642[12] 4363[12] 6814[11] 7101[10]

Distant Piper (IRE) *Adrian McGuinness* a73 82
4 b m Distant Music(USA) —Pipers Pool (IRE) (Mtoto)
6553a[9]

Distant Pleasure *M Dods* 62
3 b f Diktat—Our Pleasure (IRE) (Lake Coniston (IRE))
1558[6] 1913[10] (2535) 3570[4] 4287[9] 4971[7]

Distant Shores (IRE) *Miss T Spearing* a27 42
4 b m Averti(IRE) —Adeptation (USA) (Exceller (USA))
217[9]

Distant Sun (USA) *I Semple* a65 78
3 b g Distant View(USA) —The Great Flora (USA) (Unaccounted For (USA))
69[3] 208[2] 1197[8] 1625[4] 1903[7] (2167) 2821[5] 3413[5] 4078[2] 4479[4] (4714) 5662[3] 6331[4] 6559[3] 6731[8]

Distant Sunset (IRE) *B W Hills* a64 62
3 b g Distant Music(USA) —Blushing Libra (Perugino (USA))
1361[2] 1917[4] 2223[4]

Distant Times *Liam McAteer* a61 81
6 b g Orpen(USA) —Simply Times (USA) (Dodge (USA))
4836a[5] 6916a[7]

Distant Vision (IRE) *A Berry* a38 36
4 br m Distant Music(USA) —Najeyba (Indian Ridge)
321[12] 567[11] 743[9] 2298[8] 2709[5]

Distant Way (USA) *L Brogi* 118
6 b h Distant View(USA) —Grey Way (USA) (Cozzene (USA))
(1700a) 5467a[5] 6223a[8] 6689a[7]

Distiller (IRE) *W R Muir* a76 75
3 b g Invincible Spirit(IRE) —Bobbydazzle (Rock Hopper)
1117[9] 3384[2] 3691[9] 4111[7] (4424) 4960[9] 5405[4] 5777[7] 6146[3] (6245) 6504[9]

Distinction (IRE) *Sir Michael Stoute* 116
8 b g Danehill(USA) —Ivy Leaf (IRE) (Nureyev (USA))
4091[7] 4691[4] 5376[4] (5829) 6337[4]

Distinctive Image (USA) *J H M Gosden* a63
2 b c Mineshaft(USA) —Dock Leaf (USA) (Woodman (USA))
6602[7]

Distinctly Game *K A Ryan* a94 88
5 b g Mind Games—Distinctly Blu (IRE) (Distinctly North (USA))
79[4] (277) 490[3] 660[9] 828[3] 3464[12] 3586[7] 3911[13] 4567[7] 5044[8] 5379[10] 5581[5] 6381[16] (6970)

Dium Mac *N Bycroft* 85
6 b g Presidium—Efipetite (Efisio)
850[8] 1288[9] 1767[14] 2011[5] 2536[8] 2987[9] 6308[2] 6473[10] 6760[3]

Divalini *J Akehurst* a60 58
3 ch f Bertolini(USA) —Divine Grace (IRE) (Definite Article)
1786[6] (2276) 2459[7] 6244[4] 6428[8]

Diverse Forecast (IRE) *Mrs P Sly* 20
3 b g Fasliyev(USA) —Motley (Rainbow Quest (USA))
2308[12]

Divert (IRE) *Edward Lynam* a80 88
3 b f Averti(IRE) —Dawn Chorus (IRE) (Mukaddamah (USA))
2379a[8] 5394a[11]

Divertimenti (IRE) *C R Dore* a80 80
3 b g Green Desert(USA) —Ballet Shoes (IRE) (Ela-Mana-Mou)
231[5] (489) 694[5] 885[6] (1008) 1978[3] 3066[3] 3285[4] (4394) 4884[4] 5122[2] 5367[4] 7289[5]

Divine Love (IRE) *E J O'Neill* a69 58
3 b f Barathea(IRE) —Darling (Darshaan)
4424[6] 5036[4] 5347[11] 5819[13]

Divine Night (IRE) *David Wachman* 92
3 b f Danehill(USA) —Starlight Night (USA) (Distant View (USA))
1694a[3] 2757[11] 6216a[13]

Divine Power *R M Beckett* a73 72
2 b f Kyllachy—Tiriana (Common Grounds)
4102[2] 4662[3] 5357[4] 6432[2]

Divine Right *B J Meehan* 90
3 ch f Observatory(USA) —Grail (USA) (Quest For Fame)
2669[5] 3100[7] 3555[5] 4060[15]

Divine River *J G Portman* a75 79
4 b m Lujain(USA) —Berliese (IRE) (High Estate)
2467[15] 4128[8] 5111[8] 5690[3] 6265[12] 6871[10] 6971[7]

Divine Spirit *M Dods* a61 89
6 b g Foxhound(USA) —Vocation (IRE) (Royal Academy (USA))
992[9] 1074[6] 1405[3] 1597[6] 1681[2] 2386[8] 2509[3] 2712[2] 2830[2] 3608[3] 3782[2] (4038) (4103) 4489[9] 4703[4] (5481) (5581)

Divine Task (USA) *E Charpy* a61 65
9 ch g Irish River(FR) —Set In Motion (USA) (Mr Prospector (USA))
244a[9] 477a[14]

Divine White *P Bowen* a56 57
4 ch m College Chapel—Snowy Mantle (Siberian Express (USA))
1379[3] 2033[12] 3167[5] 3451[7] 4257[14] 5348[13] 6311[7]

Divinitus *M J Grassick* 85
2 b c Medicean—Divina Mia (Dowsing (USA))
6549a[13]

Dixey *M A Jarvis* a92 65
2 br f Diktat—Hoh Dancer (Indian Ridge)
(2768) 3522^5 4022^2
Dixieland Boy (IRE) *P J Makin* a71 78
4 b g Inchinor—Savannah Belle (Green Desert (USA))
(13) 323^4 4634^2 5722^2 5942^4
Dixie Meister (USA) *J Canani* a116
5 bb g Holzmeister(USA) —Dixity Do Dah (USA) (Dixieland Band (USA))
858a^4
Dixigold (FR) *Carmen Bocskai* 85
6 ch g Gold Away(IRE) —Dixiella (FR) (Fabulous Dancer (USA))
355a^4 493a^7
Diyakalanie (FR) *J Boisnard* 113
3 b f Ashkalani(IRE) —Diyawara (IRE) (Doyoun)
1339a^5 2501a^3 4055a^3 4654a^2 5465a^7 6042a^7
Diysem (USA) *B J Meehan* a81 85
3 b c Johannesburg(USA) —Technicolour (IRE) (Rainbow Quest (USA))
939^7 1099^9 1658^6
Dizzy Dreamer (IRE) *P W Chapple-Hyam* 101
4 b m Spinning World(USA) —Divine Prospect (IRE) (Namaqualand (USA))
1189a^{10} 1704a^8 3059^7
Djalalabad (FR) *Mrs C A Dunnett* 62
3 b f King's Best(USA) —Daraydala (IRE) (Royal Academy (USA))
1784^3 2360^4 2909^7 3964^{13} 4338^6 4856^6 5710^2 6109^8 6447^{11}
Django (SWE) *Caroline Stromberg* a88 96
4 b g Acatenango(GER) —Praeriens Drottning (SWE) (Elmaamul (USA))
4218a^4
Do As I Say *T D Easterby* 68
2 b g Diktat—Antonia's Choice (Music Boy)
2024^6 2460^3 2710^5
Docksil *B Grizzetti* 102
3 b f Docksider(USA) —Simil (USA) (Apalachee (USA))
(1337a) 1701a^{13} 3445a^{11} 6224a^4 6767a^{10}
Docofthebay (IRE) *J A Osborne* a72 110
3 ch c Docksider(USA) —Baize (Efisio)
1247^2 1359^2 (1851) 2045^3 2577^2 (3480) (4093) 4745^2 5797^3 6011^2 6298^6
Doctor Dino (FR) *R Gibson* 122
5 ch h Muhtathir—Logica (IRE) (Priolo (USA))
1340a^3 1877a^3 4414a^3 (5250a) 6334^3 (7090a)
Doctor Fremantle *Sir Michael Stoute* 81
2 b c Sadler's Wells(USA) —Summer Breeze (Rainbow Quest (USA))
4417^2 5918^2 (6592)
Doctor Hilary *S Seemar* a109 91
5 b g Mujahid(USA) —Agony Aunt (Formidable (USA))
326a^6
Doctor Ned *Miss Sheena West* a49 52
3 b g Bahamian Bounty—Sangra (USA) (El Gran Senor (USA))
635^7 700^6 (900) 1232^5 1561^7 2187^4 2916^5 3175^7 3949^8 5886^{16}
Doctor Of Laws *S Seemar* a93 93
4 b g Dr Fong(USA) —Mavourneen (USA) (Dynaformer (USA))
104a^2 328a^5
Doctor Robert *Tom Dascombe* a64 79
2 b c Sakhee(USA) —Please (Kris)
2991^{12} 4130^7 4764^2 5350^{14} 5871^2 6274^4 7114^5
Doctor's Cave *K O Cunningham-Brown* a80 61
5 b g Night Shift(USA) —Periquitum (Dilum (USA))
287^7 (440) (519) 681^{12} 1382^4 (1755) (2149) 2719^4 3149^6
Doctor Scott *M Johnston* a78 92
4 b g Medicean—Milly Of The Vally (Caerleon (USA))
1621^{11} (2031) 2245^4 2861^9 3412^5 4056^8 4398^4 4786^5 (5086) 5229^4 5677^7 6144^4 6356^4
Dodaa (USA) *N Wilson* a56 25
4 b g Dayjur(USA) —Ra'A (USA) (Diesis)
239^3 320^3 (523) 680^8 5672^8 5930^{14} 6390^7 6565^7 7111^{10} 7137^5 7283^5
Doe Ray Me *H-A Pantall* 102
3 b f Singspiel(IRE) —Ejlaal (IRE) (Caerleon (USA))
5150a^2 6030a^5 6770a^2
Dohasa (IRE) *G M Lyons* a93 98
2 b g Bold Fact(USA) —Zara's Birthday (IRE) (Waajib)
4832a^6
Dolce Dovo *W J Haggas* a76 80
4 b m Medicean—Dance To The Top (Sadler's Wells (USA))
936^2 1312^2 3015^4 3731^4 4131^{11}
Dollar Chick (IRE) *M Johnston* 78
3 b f Dansili—Dollar Bird (IRE) (Kris)
4716^{12} 5043^7 5968^2 6703^6
Dolly *Tom Dascombe* a43 26
5 b m Thowra(FR) —Sweet Symphony (IRE) (Orchestra)
18^8 210^{12} 699^7 920^4
Dolly Coughdrop (IRE) *K R Burke* a65 72
3 b f Titus Livius(FR) —Fairy Berry (IRE) (Fairy King (USA))
312^5 433^5 737^7 2171^6 2387^3 2713^{12}
Dolly No Hair *D W Barker* 70
2 ch g Reel Buddy(USA) —Champagne Grandy (Vaigly Great)
4076^{11} 4781^{11} 5901^2
Dolphin Bay (IRE) *J G Burns* 87
7 b g Dolphin Street(FR) —Stella Ann (Ahonoora)
2067a^6
Dolphin Jo (AUS) *Terry & Karina O'Sullivan* 111
5 b g Dolphin Street(FR) —High Rent (AUS) (Belligerent (AUS))
(6033a) 6712a^5
Dolzago *G L Moore* a67 38
7 b g Pursuit Of Love—Doctor's Glory (USA) (Elmaamul (USA))
88^{13} (291) 457^{10} 691^7
Domalinoise (FR) *Robert Collet* 75
2 b f Gold Away(IRE) —La Frandiere (FR) (Kaldoun (FR))
7048a^0
Dome Blonde *W J Musson* a11
2 ch f Domedriver(IRE) —Proud Titania (IRE) (Fairy King (USA))
6234^{13} 6591^{12} 6933^9
Domenico (IRE) *J R Jenkins* a53 59
9 b g Sadler's Wells(USA) —Russian Ballet (USA) (Nijinsky (CAN))
16^4 134^6 508^4 792^8 1229^7 4297^2 4859^6
Dome Rock (IRE) *L M Cumani* a72 71
2 ch c Domedriver(IRE) —My American Beauty (Wolfhound (USA))
1919^6 2349^7 4506^5 5216^8 6120^8 6438^2
Domesday (UAE) *W G Harrison* a52 53
6 b g Cape Cross(IRE) —Deceive (Machiavellian (USA))
3012^{13} 3376^8 4333^{12} 4580^7 4891^3 5503^2 5756^4 6629^8
Domestic Fund (IRE) *D K Weld* 103
2 b c Sadler's Wells(USA) —Market Slide (USA) (Gulch (USA))
5845a^2 6484a^5
Dominante (GER) *A Wohler* 109
3 ch f Monsun(GER) —Dea (GER) (Shareef Dancer (USA))
2294a^2 4013a^3 6042a^8
Domingues *Edward Lynam* 106
2 b c Danetime(IRE) —Lindfield Belle (IRE) (Fairy King (USA))
5070a^5 5456a^2 (6136a) 6631a^6
Dominican (USA) *Darrin Miller* a106
3 ch g El Corredor(USA) —First Violin (USA) (Dixieland Band (USA))
1486a^{11}
Domino Dancer (IRE) *J Wade* 89
3 b g Tagula(IRE) —Hazarama (IRE) (Kahyasi)
1851^4 2862^4 (3093) 3753^{11} 4523^6 4749^{19}
Dona Alba (IRE) *J L Dunlop* 83
2 b f Peintre Celebre(USA) —Fantastic Fantasy (IRE) (Lahib (USA))
4094^4 (5063) 5746^2
Donaldson (GER) *P Rau* 118
5 b g Lando(GER) —Daytona Beach (GER) (Konigsstuhl (GER))
1190a^4 1872a^4 2706a^5
Donatello (GER) *W Baltromei* 111
6 b h Auenadler(GER) —Devika (Alzao (USA))
1800a^2 2100a^3 2953a^8
Donegal (USA) *A M Balding* a92 97
2 bb g Menifee(USA) —Vickey's Echo (CAN) (Clever Trick (USA))
2632^2 (3510) 4057^3 5004^5 6001^4 6650^6
Don Jose (USA) *N J Vaughan* a41 50
4 bb g Dynaformer(USA) —Panthera (USA) (Storm Cat (USA))
2312^{10} 3035^{11} 3610^3 4025^6 4253^7 7285^8
Dono Da Raia (BRZ) *I Mohammed* 106
5 ch h Hibernian Rhapsody(IRE) —Outra Arumba (BRZ) (Henri Le Balafre (FR))
412a^6 598a^{12}
Donoma (IRE) *A & G Botti* 102
3 ch f Beat Hollow—Green Tern (ITY) (Miswaki Tern (USA))
1701a^9 6221a^3
Don Pasquale *J T Stimpson* a55 59
5 br g Zafonic(USA) —Bedazzling (IRE) (Darshaan)
804^8 1380^3 1715^4 1750^2 2145^6 2370^4 (2582) (2795) 3204^8 3280^{10} 3805^5 4161^9 4517^7 4660^{10} 5569^9 6096^6 6529^4 6627^{10}
Don Pele (IRE) *R A Harris* a93 96
5 b g Monashee Mountain(USA) —Big Fandango (Bigstone (IRE))
1971^{11} 2187^6 3528^3 3802^2 3859^3 4122^{20} 4389^9 4664^2 (5722) 5923^3 6173^6
Don Picolo *P A Blockley* a26 39
2 b c Bertolini(USA) —Baby Come Back (IRE) (Fayruz)
3283^9 3712^6 4293^8 6051^{10}
Don Pietro *D J Coakley* a79 85
4 b g Bertolini(USA) —Silver Spell (Aragon)
2469^{11} 2995^3 4268^8 4631^2 5539^5 6145^9 6774^3
Dont Call Me Derek *J J Quinn* a70 81
6 b g Sri Pekan(USA) —Cultural Role (Night Shift (USA))
1822^{12}
Don'Tcallmeginger (IRE) *M H Tompkins* a48 64
4 ch g Fruits Of Love(USA) —Scotia Rose (Tap On Wood)
1263^9 2430^{11} 2770^9 3177^5 3403^2 (4040) 4493^2 4708^4
Dont Denie It (IRE) *H Rogers* 5
2 ch f Elnadim(USA) —Aljay (IRE) (Balla Cove)
3438a^{17}
Don't Desert Me (IRE) *R Charlton* a63
3 b g Desert Style(IRE) —Eye View (USA) (Distant View (USA))
157^8 196^5
Dont Dili Dali *J S Moore* a89 108
4 b m Dansili—Miss Meltemi (IRE) (Miswaki Tern (USA))
174a^8 250a^3 401a^4 546a^3 648a^6 938^2 1472^3 1777a^{11} 3434^8 3628^9 4149^5 5351^7 5444^3 6299^{16}
Don't Forget Faith (USA) *C G Cox* 100
2 b f Victory Gallop(CAN) —Contredance (USA) (Danzig (USA))
(3055) 4400^2 5353^7 6040a^5
Don't Mind Me *T Keddy* a64 59
4 b m Mutamam—Dynamic Dream (USA) (Dynaformer (USA))
559^2 712^2 903^2 2582^{14} (3217)
Dont Panic (IRE) *P W Chapple-Hyam* 101
3 ch g Fath(USA) —Torrmana (IRE) (Ela-Mana-Mou)
1097^7 1500^9 2213^6 3857^3 (5114) 5635^5 (6203)
Don't Tell Anna (IRE) *R Hannon* a58 58
2 b f Choisir(AUS) —Zinnia (Zilzal (USA))
1896^9 2997^6 3687^{11} 4254^4 4453^{12} 5089^{10} 5529^2 5887^8 6263^9
Don't Tell Sue *Miss J R Tooth* 89
4 ch g Bold Edge—Opopmil (IRE) (Pips Pride)
1242^{13} 1630^{12} 3086^8
Dooneen (IRE) *C Bocksai* 64
5 b g Imperial Ballet(IRE) —Tiffany Victoria (IRE) (Taufan (USA))
356a^2 438a^3
Doon Haymer (IRE) *I Semple* 79
2 b c Barathea(IRE) —Mutige (Warning)
3013^3 4037^3 4495^2 5397a^{13} (6634)
Doonigan (IRE) *A M Balding* a47 53
3 b g Val Royal(FR) —Music In My Life (IRE) (Law Society (USA))
1399^{11} 2262^9 4550^5 5421^{11} 6060^2
Dora Explora *D J Wintle* a65 88
3 br f Vettori(IRE) —Fredora (Inchinor)
939^{12} 1106^8 1603^4 1920^{10} 2400^{13} 2881^{12} 2942^6 4686^{10} 5189^{10}
Dora's Green *S W Hall* a41 51
4 b m Rambling Bear—Compradore (Mujtahid (USA))
2366^5 2798^{12} 5752^{11}
Dorchester *W J Musson* a60 31
10 b g Primo Dominie—Penthouse Lady (Last Tycoon (IRE))
2190^8 3064^7 3408^8 5016^9
Doric Dream *B Smart* a46 60
2 ch f Ishiguru(USA) —Generous Share (Cadeaux Genereux)
4041^6 5501^4 7216^5
Doric Lady *J A R Toller* a68 69
2 b f Kyllachy—Tanasie (Cadeaux Genereux)
5595^6 6228^3 6721^2
Dories Dream *Jane Southcombe* a38 34
3 b f Foxhound(USA) —Milliscent (Primo Dominie)
6901^7 7076^7
Dorn Dancer (IRE) *D W Barker* 71
5 b m Danehill Dancer(IRE) —Appledorn (Doulab (USA))
992^4 1459^3 1748^4 (1940) 2072^8 2256^{10} 2864^4 3053^7 3345^5 (3784) 4381^5 4822^6 5253^{10} 5556^7 5934^4 6467^3
Dorset Square (IRE) *John Joseph Murphy* 72
3 b g Fantastic Light(USA) —Albula (FR) (Anabaa (USA))
4035a^6
Dorso Rosso (IRE) *Mrs C A Dunnett* 47
2 b g Redback—Baraloti (IRE) (Barathea (IRE))
4293^{13} 4916^6 5541^{11}
Do The Trick (AUS) *M Halford* 93
6 b g Favorite Trick(USA) —Verscay (AUS) (Marscay (AUS))
(3577a) 6366a^6
Dot's Delight *R A Harris* a58 58
3 b f Golden Snake(USA) —Hotel California (IRE) (Last Tycoon (IRE))
2359^7 2836^{11} 3800^3 4340^{10} 5542^2 5739^2 6801^4 6971^4 7009^{11}
Dotty's Daughter *Mrs A Duffield* a55 58
3 ch f Forzando—Colonel's Daughter (Colonel Collins (USA))
1317^5 1707^7 2301^5 2560^5 2895^4 3180^5 3588^7 4935^{11} 6390^{10}
Double Attack (FR) *M Johnston* 80
2 b f Peintre Celebre(USA) —Salome's Attack (Anabaa (USA))
(2562) 2855^{11} 3841^9 4991^{10} 5443^2 5746^6 6650^4
Double Banded (IRE) *J L Dunlop* a73 92
3 b g Mark Of Esteem(IRE) —Bronzewing (Beldale Flutter (USA))
3150^{11} 3652^{10} 4172^6 (4894) (5486) 5779^3 (6308) (6622) 6744^2
Double Bay (USA) *Jane Chapple-Hyam* a51 65
4 b m War Chant(USA) —Once To Often (USA) (Raise A Native (USA))
63^8
Double Bill (USA) *P F I Cole* a79 74
3 bb g Mr Greeley(USA) —Salty Perfume (USA) (Salt Lake (USA))
(1923) 2570^4 2881^{13} 3418^{10} 4574^{12}
Double Carpet (IRE) *G Woodward* a48 65
4 b g Lahib(USA) —Cupid Miss (Anita's Prince)
1349^8 3914^3 4177^{12} (5934) 6239^{12} 7107^7
Double Deputy (IRE) *J J Quinn* 67
6 b g Sadler's Wells(USA) —Janaat (Kris)
3027^5 4490^6
Double Doors *J H M Gosden* a88 83
3 b c Grand Lodge(USA) —Daring Miss (Sadler's Wells (USA))
3710^6 4275^2 4641^3 (5045) (5334) 6230^3
Double Duty (IRE) *B J Meehan* 63
2 b f Danehill Dancer(IRE) —Taking Liberties (IRE) (Royal Academy (USA))
6130^5
Double Harness (USA) *H Morrison* a78
3 ch c Horse Chestnut(SAF) —Lover's Lover (USA) (Woodman (USA))
(2666)
Double M *Mrs L Richards* a58 45
10 ch g First Trump—Girton Degree (Balliol)
83^5 189^2 653^5 687^4 722^6
Double Mix (FR) *Rod Collet* 93
4 b m Sagamix(FR) —Double Melody (FR) (Double Bed (FR))
6953a^0
Double Mystery (FR) *K J Burke* a31 62
7 ch g Starborough—Chene De Coeur (FR) (Comrade In Arms)
74^6 100^6
Double On Red *J M P Eustace* a56 75
2 b f Red Ransom(USA) —Rosy Outlook (USA) (Trempolino (USA))
3895^5 4564^{10} 5682^8 6233^{12} 6571^2
Double Precedent *M Johnston* a28 33
3 b f Polish Precedent(USA) —Jolies Eaux (Shirley Heights)
1361^8 3376^{14}
Double R *A B Haynes* a10
2 b f Fraam—Bint Albadou (IRE) (Green Desert (USA))
7097^{10}
Double Rainbow (IRE) *Jamie Poulton*
4 b h Sadler's Wells(USA) —Rain Flower (IRE) (Indian Ridge)
4630^{15}
Double Spectre (IRE) *Jean-Rene Auvray* a63 72
5 b g Spectrum(IRE) —Phantom Ring (Magic Ring (IRE))
651^{11} (1002) 1295^7 1609^4 2403^8 4015^5 4458^5 4878^6
Double Valentine *R Ingram* a57 53
4 ch m Primo Valentino(IRE) —Charlottevalentina (IRE) (Perugino (USA))
86^{11} 2108^3 2334^{12} 2592^7 2665^{12} 3425^6 4182^U 4471^9 (4741) 5090^6 5336^6 5425^6 6429^2 6706^5 6968^4 7098^9 7278^8
Doubloon *J Gallagher* a28 25
2 b g Umistim—Glistening Silver (Puissance)
5880^{14} 6725^9 6828^{11}
Doubly Guest *G G Margarson* 74
3 b f Barathea Guest—Countess Guest (IRE) (Spectrum (IRE))
1289^{11} 1722^9 2727^8 2940^4 3107^2 3469^{10} 5865^8 6235^5 (6421)
Doubtful Sound (USA) *T D Barron* a76 67
3 b c Diesis—Roam Free (USA) (Unbridled (USA))
222^2 (678) 1108^7 7212^6
Doubtless *D W Chapman*
2 ch f Redoubtable(USA) —Some Like It Hot (Ashkalani (IRE))
3297^7 3410^7 3833^9 4002^{10} 4559^8 4669^{10} 4923^{12}
Doughty *M Mullineaux* a49 32
5 b g Bold Edge—Marquante (IRE) (Brief Truce (USA))
183^9 282^4 339^3 448^8 622^9
Douro Valley (AUS) *Danny O'Brien* 114
6 b g Encosta De Lago(AUS) —Opaque (AUS) (Lord Seymour)
6354a^2 6712a^{11}
Dove (IRE) *Saeed Bin Suroor* a58 81
2 b f Sadler's Wells(USA) —Golden Digger (USA) (Mr Prospector (USA))
6140^8 6414^2
Dove Cottage (IRE) *W S Kittow* a65 74
5 b g Great Commotion(USA) —Pooka (Dominion)
1638^8 2621^4 3385^3 4194^7 4909^5 6253^4
Dovedale *Mrs S D Williams* a49 55
7 b m Groom Dancer(USA) —Peetsie (IRE) (Fairy King (USA))
3901^6 4544^7
Dovedon Hero *P J McBride* a72 79
7 ch g Millkom—Hot Topic (IRE) (Desse Zenny (USA))
29^4 88^6 195^2 332^2 515^4
Dower House *Andrew Turnell* a92 73
12 ch g Groom Dancer(USA) —Rose Noble (USA) (Vaguely Noble)
205^4 (799) (921)
Dowlleh *T T Clement* a78 82
3 b g Noverre(USA) —Al Persian (IRE) (Persian Bold)
1009^6 1202^{12} 1660^5 2415^4 2837^6 4029^P 6854^5 7073^8 7164^{13}
Downhiller (IRE) *J L Dunlop* 81
2 ch c Alhaarth(IRE) —Ski For Gold (Shirley Heights)
4508^{11} 5344^2 5749^2 6451^2
Downing Street (IRE) *Jennie Candlish* 83
6 b g Sadler's Wells(USA) —Photographie (USA) (Trempolino (USA))
(4179) 4569^{11} 4893^4
Down The Brick (IRE) *B R Millman* a61 75
3 b g Daggers Drawn(USA) —Damezao (Alzao (USA))
719^9 1972^{11} 2362^3 2653^5 3469^3 (4019) (4253) 4458^4 5006^8 5333^9 6235^{12}
Downtown (IRE) *David Wachman* 104
3 b f Danehill(USA) —User Friendly (Slip Anchor)
2702a^4 (4238a) 6367a^8
Doyles Lodge *H Candy* a69 74
3 b g Prince Sabo—True Bird (IRE) (In The Wings)
1587^2 2083^4 2601^2 3475^6 3948^3 4610^{11} 5339^6 5783^{10} 6102^{14}
Dragon Dancer *G Wragg* a66 118
4 b h Sadler's Wells(USA) —Alakananda (Hernando (FR))
4117^{10} (4825) 5467a^3 6043a^9
Dragon Fire (JPN) *T Kubota* a105
3 ch c Brian's Time(USA) —Magical Woman (JPN) (Paradise Creek (USA))
6942a^6
Dragon Flame (IRE) *M Quinn* 57
4 b h Tagula(IRE) —Noble Rocket (Reprimand)
2186^2 2606^4 3102^8 6537^{13}
Dragon Flower (USA) *B W Hills* a64 74
3 b f Gulch(USA) —Rawabi (Sadler's Wells (USA))
2998^7 4530^5 4908^3
Dragon Fly (GER) *Frau Jutta Mayer* 112
5 ch g Acatenango(GER) —Diana's Quest (IRE) (Rainbow Quest (USA))
1689a^5 (2409a) 3565a^6 4957a^5 5821a^8
Dragon Slayer (IRE) *P A Blockley* a86 85
5 ch g Night Shift(USA) —Arandora Star (USA) (Sagace (FR))
(205) 256^3 355a^5 493a^8 4814^8 5539^4 6067^7 6475^{14} 7018^4 7075^2 7163^6
Drama Kid (IRE) *Daniel Mark Loughnane* 44
4 b m Mull Of Kintyre(USA) —Bold Feather (Persian Bold)
4771^5
Dramatic *Sir Mark Prescott* a83 82
3 ch c Pivotal—Red Passion (USA) (Seeking The Gold (USA))
60^6 222^4 505^6 (2260) (2594) (2750) 3108^5
Dramatic Review (IRE) *J Barclay* 51
5 b g Indian Lodge(IRE) —Dramatic Shift (IRE) (Night Shift (USA))
956^7
Dramatic Solo *K R Burke* a67 70
2 ch f Nayef(USA) —Just Dreams (Salse (USA))
5100^4 5395a^{16}
Dramatic Touch *G Wragg* a51 64
3 b f Royal Applause—Sismique (Warning)
2219^{11} 2693^5 3652^{14}
Dramatic Turn *Mrs A J Perrett* 81
3 b f Pivotal—Eveningperformance (Night Shift (USA))
1900^{10}

Drastic Measure *Sir Mark Prescott* 65
2 ch f Pivotal—Danse Classique (IRE) (Night Shift (USA))
2109[2] 2997[8] 3200[9] 3838[6]

Drawback (IRE) *R A Harris* a65 77
4 b g Daggers Drawn(USA) —Sacred Heart (IRE) (Catrail (USA))
1921[2] 2143[4] (2336) (2656) (2980) 3567[6] 3905[5] 4266[10] (4686) 4909[10] 5921[4] 6475[12]

Drawnfromthepast (IRE) *J A Osborne* 98
2 ch c Tagula(IRE) —Ball Cat (FR) (Cricket Ball (USA))
1652[6] (2271) (2737) 4120[5] 4743[14]

Drawn Gold *R Hollinshead* 71
3 b g Daggers Drawn(USA) —Gold Belt (IRE) (Bellypha)
5915[4] 6286[4] (6623)

Drayton (IRE) *M F De Kock* 111
3 bb c Danetime(IRE) —Exponent (USA) (Exbourne (USA))
644a[4] 1473[21] 2857[5] 3506[11] 3894[9] 4196[5] 5325[5]

Dr Dream (IRE) *J G M O'Shea* a60 50
3 b g Dr Fong(USA) —Only In Dreams (Polar Falcon (USA))
919[4] 1166[6] 1904[10] 2662[5] 3843[2] 4961[3] *5235[7]*
6060[3] *6480[5]*

Dreadnaught (USA) *T Voss* 115
7 b g Lac Ouimet(USA) —Wings Of Dreams (USA) (Sovereign Dancer (USA))
6771a[7]

Dream Bee *E A L Dunlop* 57
2 b f Oasis Dream—Chief Bee (Chief's Crown (USA))
3435[18] 4094[12] 4683[4] 5298[8] 5914[9]

Dream Catcher (SWE) *R A Kvisla* a95 40
4 b h Songline(SWE) —Queen Ida (SWE) (Diligo (FR))
353[8] 488[4] 587[10] 3416[11] 3641[6] 5568[7] 5983[9]

Dream Day *R Hannon* a76 95
2 b f Oasis Dream—Capistrano Day (USA) (Diesis)
(5201) 5592[2] 6008[6]

Dream Eater (IRE) *A M Balding* a78 103
2 gr c Night Shift(USA) —Kapria (FR) (Simon Du Desert (FR))
1990[3] *2353[2]* 2737[4] 3459[6] 4048[3] 4372[3] (5324)
5975[6]

Dream Express (IRE) *M Dods* 71
2 b c Fasliyev(USA) —Lothlorien (USA) (Woodman (USA))
1743[6] 2166[4] 2889[2] 4278[3] 4892[12] 5550[8]

Dream Forest (IRE) *J Balding* a67 56
4 b g Raise A Grand(IRE) —Theresa Green (IRE) (Charnwood Forest (IRE))
78[2] 148[10]

Dream Green (IRE) *M R Channon* 54
2 b c Fasliyev(USA) —Queen Chief (IRE) (Grand Lodge (USA))
4362[15] 4777[13]

Dream Impact (USA) *L Riccardi* a93 108
6 b h Royal Academy(USA) —One Fit Cat (USA) (Storm Cat (USA))
1876a[4] (6686a)

Dreaming Of Liz (USA) *W Catalano* a97
2 gr f El Prado(IRE) —Silver Maiden (USA) (Silver Buck (USA))
(5247a)

Dream Lodge (IRE) *J G Given* a98 97
3 ch c Grand Lodge(USA) —Secret Dream (IRE) (Zafonic (USA))
1228[3] 1439[2] 2010[2] 2577[5] 3514[5] 3785[3] *(4429)*
4672[2] (6053) *6359[2]*

Dream Master (IRE) *J Ryan* a48 48
4 b g Priolo(USA) —Pip's Dream (Glint Of Gold)
1671[11] 2154[8] 4860[2] *5530[4]* 5886[10] *6292[3] 6569[4]*
6697[P] 7150[6]

Dream Mountain *Ms J S Doyle* a59 62
4 b g Mozart(IRE) —Statua (IRE) (Statoblest)
(23) 291[9] 2996[13] 3217[8] 3457[6] *5204[6]*

Dream Of Fortune (IRE) *J Noseda* a72 64
3 b c Danehill Dancer(IRE) —Tootling (IRE) (Pennine Walk)
1522[5] 3710[9] *5494[4] (6272)*

Dream Of Gold (GER) *D K Richardson* 80
4 b h Tertullian(USA) —Dubana (GER) (Suave Dancer (USA))
881a[7] 4838a[12]

Dream Of Paradise (USA) *Mrs L Williamson* a48 66
4 ch m Atticus(USA) —Scrumptious (USA) (Slew O'Gold (USA))
1090[12] 1258[12] *1906[12]* 2531[15]

Dream On Dreamers (IRE) *R C Guest* 49
3 b g Iron Mask(USA) —Harifana (FR) (Kahyasi)
1303[15] 2763[5] 2842[6] 3840[9] 3956[7] 4156[14]

Dream Passport (JPN) *H Matsuda* 124
4 br h Fuji Kiseki(JPN) —Grace Land (JPN) (Tony Bin)
6943a[14]

Dream River (USA) *Patrick Martin* a55 56
6 ch m Irish River(FR) —Pallava (USA) (Lyphard (USA))
(285) 1732[3]

Dream Rush (USA) *R Violette Jr* a116
3 bb f Wild Rush(USA) —Turbo Dream (USA) (Unbridled (USA))
6483a[5]

Dream Scheme *E A L Dunlop* 84
3 b f Machiavellian(USA) —Dream Ticket (USA) (Danzig (USA))
2883[8] 3797[6]

Dream Sea *M R Channon* a62 76
2 b f Barathea(IRE) —Countess Sybil (IRE) (Dr Devious (IRE))
3643[3] 4169[4] 5524[3]

Dreams Jewel *C Roberts* a49 59
7 b g Dreams End—Jewel Of The Nile (Glenstal (USA))
3365[15] 4003[2] 4253[9] *4463[4]* 6056[12] *7198[4]*

Dream Theme *D Nicholls* a80 106
4 b g Distant Music(USA) —Xaymara (USA) (Sanglamore (USA))
1082[3] 5616[20]

Dream West (IRE) *Liam Roche* a71 78
4 b g Zafonic(USA) —Dona Royale (IRE) (Darshaan)
4114a[15]

Dresden Doll (USA) *M L W Bell* a44 77
2 ch f Elusive Quality(USA) —Crimson Conquest (USA) (Diesis)
2000[7] 2478[2] *3648[10]* (4756) 5322[10]

Dressed To Dance (IRE) *N Tinkler* a68 71
3 b f Namid—Costume Drama (USA) (Alleged (USA))
(69) (478) 1965[5] 2515[4] *3066[6]* 3583[2] (3875)
4450[6] 5330[8] 5907[6] 6256[8]

Dressmaker (USA) *John M Oxx* a88 85
3 ch f Elusive Quality(USA) —Scarlet Velvet (USA) (Red Ransom (USA))
4237a[7] 6216a[14]

Dress To Impress (IRE) *G A Butler* a79 75
3 b c Fasliyev(USA) —Dress Code (IRE) (Barathea (IRE))
280[2] 4429[9] 6836[9]

Dr Faustus (IRE) *Sir Michael Stoute* 85
2 gr c Sadler's Wells(USA) —Requesting (Rainbow Quest (USA))
3856[5] 4656[2] (5227)

Drift Away (USA) *J J Lambe* a31 55
7 b m Dehere(USA) —Flying Blind (IRE) (Silver Kite (USA))
285[9]

Drift Ice (SAF) *M F De Kock* a96
6 b g Western Winter(USA) —Donya (SAF) (Elliodor (FR))
249a[10] 324a[2] 396a[5] 543a[2]

Drifting Gold *C G Cox* a77 74
3 ch f Bold Edge—Driftholme (Safawan)
17[4] 336[2] (511) 1948[2] 2260[2] (2444) *2950[5]* 3688[7]
(4186) 5029[8] 5418[6]

Drifting Snow *D K Weld* 84
3 b f Danehill Dancer(IRE) —Ma N'leme Biche (USA) (Key To The Kingdom (USA))
6553a[3]

Drill Sergeant *M Johnston* 89
2 br c Rock Of Gibraltar(IRE) —Dolydille (IRE) (Dolphin Street (FR))
5903[3] 6126[2] 6468[7]

Drink To Me Only *J R Weymes* a45 56
4 b g Pursuit Of Love—Champenoise (Forzando)
7[12] 217[8] 339[6] 524[9] 721[7] 1028[12] 3017[7] (3376)
3497[10] 4042[3] 4477[10] 5525[13] *6505[7] 6532[10]*

Driven (IRE) *Mrs A J Perrett* 73
2 b c Domedriver(IRE) —Wonderful World (GER) (Dashing Blade)
5919[4] 6451[7] 6616[4]

Driven Snow *R Charlton* 62
2 ch f Choisir(AUS) —Thermal Spring (Zafonic (USA))
3962[7]

Driving Miss Suzie *A M Balding* a65 62
3 br f Diktat—Santa Isobel (Nashwan (USA))
1203[11] 1659[6] 2274[2] 2940[6] 3427[7] *4277[3]* 4766[11]
5342[3] 5898[U] 6430[4]

Drizzi (IRE) *P T Midgley* a72 72
6 b g Night Shift(USA) —Woopi Gold (IRE) (Last Tycoon (IRE))
5497[2] (5835) *6175[7]* 6253[11] *6501[3] 6999[2] 7123[3]*

Dr Light (IRE) *S Kirk* a56 51
3 b g Medicean—Allumette (Rainbow Quest (USA))
1204[13] 1972[12] *3082[7]*

Dr Livingstone (IRE) *C R Egerton* a71 75
2 b g Dr Fong(USA) —Radhwa (FR) (Shining Steel)
4508[10] 5010[3] *5780[4]*

Dr McFab *J A Osborne* a72 70
3 ch g Dr Fong(USA) —Barbera (Barathea (IRE))
208[5] 370[3] 738[2] 937[2] 1059[4]

Drosia (IRE) *C Laffon-Parias* a100 103
4 b m King's Best(USA) —Eriza (Distant Relative)
31a[6]

Dr Sharp (IRE) *T P Tate* 92
7 ch g Dr Devious(IRE) —Stoned Imaculate (IRE) (Durgam (USA))
1300[9] 1582[10] 2170[6] 3090[9] 3533[3] 5808[3] 6335[10]
6622[2] 6760[6]

Dr Synn *J Akehurst* a67 73
6 br g Danzero(AUS) —Our Shirley (Shirley Heights)
1507[3] 1787[5] 2689[5] 3056[2] *3422[5]* 3943[18] 4505[2]
4807[12] 5917[16] 6413[5]

Drumalee Lass (IRE) *P M Mooney* 62
2 b f Quws—Grange Clare (IRE) (Bijou D'Inde)
779a[14] 2392[8] (3681)

Drum Dance (IRE) *M Hill* a60 56
5 b g Namid—Socialite (IRE) (Alzao (USA))
1596[9] 2091[3] (2304) 2979[12] *3618[3] 6608[9] 6718[2]*
6957[9]

Drumfire (IRE) *M Johnston* 110
3 b c Danehill Dancer(IRE) —Witch Of Fife (USA) (Lear Fan (USA))
3463[2] 4119[F]

Drumhallagh (IRE) *Tom Dascombe* 60
2 b g Barathea(IRE) —Nashua Song (IRE) (Kahyasi)
4755[9] 5591[7] 6246[7]

Drumin Orpen (IRE) *Joseph Crowley* 80
4 b m Orpen(USA) —Fancied (Dominion)
1171a[6]

Drumming Party (USA) *A M Balding* a64 70
5 bb g War Chant(USA) —Santaria (USA) (Star De Naskra (USA))
1885[5] 2972[6] *3212[3]* 4236[5] 4396[6] *5130[4]* 5349[8]

Drumossie (AUS) *R C Guest* 52
7 ch g Strategic(AUS) —Migvie (NZ) (Sir Tristram)
2537[6] 4280[6] (Dead)

Drury Lane (IRE) *Miss A Stokell* a50 52
7 bb g Royal Applause—Ghost Tree (IRE) (Caerleon (USA))
83[6] 307[6] 337[9] 448[13] 463[9] 1596[11] 1893[12] 2143[10]
2556[14] 3345[17] 3567[9] 3971[7] 4610[12] 4713[11]

Dryandra (IRE) *John Joseph Murphy* a89 81
4 b m Desert Prince(IRE) —Goldilocks (IRE) (Caerleon (USA))
693[3] 756[3] 1330a[8] *5788a[14]*

Dry Speedfit (IRE) *G G Margarson* 93
2 b g Desert Style(IRE) —Annmary Girl (Zafonic (USA))
(2941) 3504[7] 4225[5] 5974[22]

Dualagi *J S Moore* a60 71
3 b f Royal Applause—Lady Melbourne (IRE) (Indian Ridge)
(798) 958[4] 1269[3] 1373[5] 3000[3] 3237[2] 4269[4]
(4546) 4896[6] 5418[7] 6103[5] 6239[10]

Dual Faith (IRE) *B J Meehan* a58 52
2 b g Almutawakel—Cosa Deasa (IRE) (Barathea (IRE))
5575[10] 5880[10] *6119[11] 6433[5]*

Dubai Ace (USA) *Miss Sheena West* a70 70
6 b g Lear Fan(USA) —Arsaan (USA) (Nureyev (USA))
1959[11] *5948[9] 6271[2] 7004[10]*

Dubai Dynamo *J S Moore* a73 95
2 b c Kyllachy—Miss Mercy (IRE) (Law Society (USA))
1680[5] 1832[11] *2147[2]* (2447) 2732[18] 4501[3] 4695[5]
(5374) (6017) 6495[6]

Dubai Honor *Doug Watson* a104 73
8 gr h Highest Honor(FR) —Lovely Noor (USA) (Fappiano (USA))
175a[DSQ] 399a[6] 529a[7] 601a[5]

Dubai Jewel (AUS) *S Seemar* a68 53
4 b m Fusaichi Pegasus(USA) —Steal My Love (AUS) (Marauding (NZ))
246a[4] 476a[11] 527a[6]

Dubai Land *M R Channon* 68
2 ch c Vettori(IRE) —Sundial (Cadeaux Genereux)
4764[10] 5186[8] 5485[4] 5858[7]

Dubai Magic (USA) *C E Brittain* a81 84
3 ch g Rahy(USA) —Dabaweyaa (Shareef Dancer (USA))
111[4] 433[4] 2213[5] 3078[8] *3188[6] 4360[6]* 4710[5]

Dubai Meydan (IRE) *Miss Gay Kelleway* 74
2 b c High Chaparral(IRE) —Miss Golden Sands (Kris)
5880[3] 6333[10]

Dubai Petal (IRE) *J S Moore* a64 72
2 b f Dubai Destination(USA) —Out Of Egypt (USA) (Red Ransom (USA))
5856[12] 6126[4] 6432[7] 6756[4]

Dubai Power *C E Brittain* 84
2 b f Cadeaux Genereux—Garmoucheh (USA) (Silver Hawk (USA))
4506[2] 5164[4] 6126[3]

Dubai Princess (IRE) *J A Osborne* a81 97
2 b f Dubai Destination(USA) —Blue Iris (Petong)
(814) 1821[4] (5713) 5973[10] 6167[6] 6619[2]

Dubai Samurai *J W Hills* a42 77
2 b c Dubai Destination(USA) —Eishin Eleuthera (IRE) (Sadler's Wells (USA))
3435[17] 3896[4] 4540[3] *5680[7]*

Dubai Shadow (IRE) *C E Brittain* a56 58
3 b f Cape Cross(IRE) —Farista (USA) (Alleged (USA))
2766[7] 3079[6] 3803[4] 4104[5] 4518[5]

Dubai's Touch *M Johnston* a109 112
3 b c Dr Fong(USA) —Noble Peregrine (Lomond (USA))
(839) 4045[9] (4148) 4600[8] 5265a[10] 6045a[2] 6372a[4]

Dubai Sunday (JPN) *P S McEntee* a56 70
6 b g Sunday Silence(USA) —Lotta Lace (USA) (Nureyev (USA))
(615) 691[12] 1271[5]

Dubai's Wonder (IRE) *B W Hills* 62
2 b c Galileo(IRE) —Sena Desert (Green Desert (USA))
6616[11]

Dubai Time *K A Ryan* 101
2 b c Dubai Destination(USA) —Time Saved (Green Desert (USA))
4487[2] (4930) 5217[4] 5660a[2]

Dubai Twilight *B W Hills* a76 97
3 b c Alhaarth(IRE) —Eve (Rainbow Quest (USA))
(864) 1243[2] 1835[3] 2788[16] 3460[17] 4799[11] 5830[3]
6169[4] 6302[7]

Dubai World *Rae Guest* 65
3 b g Mtoto—Windmill Princess (Gorytus (USA))
3248[3] 3800[5] (Dead)

Dubonai (IRE) *G M Moore* a50 43
7 ch g Peintre Celebre(USA) —Web Of Intrigue (Machiavellian (USA))
182[2] 372[11]

Ducal Pip Squeak *M Dods* a38 67
3 b f Bertolini(USA) —Creeking (Persian Bold)
1746[3] 2763[3] 3382[2] 3997[6] 5555[3] 5966[8] *6361[10]*
6638[9]

Ducal Regancy Red *C J Teague* a20 37
3 ch f Bertolini(USA) —One For Jeannie (Clantime)
678[12] 2032[9] 3202[10] 4801[6] 5231[8]

Duchess Royale (IRE) *Sir Michael Stoute* 90
3 b f Danehill(USA) —Fantasy Royale (USA) (Pleasant Colony (USA))
1632[2] 2693[3] (3387) 3960[3] 4665[2] (6236)

Dudley Docker (IRE) *C R Dore* a82 75
5 b g Victory Note(USA) —Nordic Abu (IRE) (Nordico (USA))
14[4] (63) 102[2] 308[6] 424[4] 525[2] (533) (895) *1264[7]*
(4129) 5330[3] *5532[2]* 5840[10]

Dueling B'Anjiz (USA) *E J Creighton* a37 36
8 b g Anjiz(USA) —Stirling Gal (USA) (Huckster (USA))
87[8]

Duelling Banjos *J Akehurst* a72 66
8 ch g Most Welcome—Khadino (Relkino)
1249[4] 1521[12] 2218[9] (2967) 6132[12]

Duetto (IRE) *M Scudamore* 15
4 b m Exit To Nowhere(USA) —Chopins Revolution (Rakaposhi King)
4659[9]

Duff (IRE) *Edward Lynam* 115
4 b g Spinning World(USA) —Shining Prospect (Lycius (USA))
2586a[4] 4237a[3] (4747) 5409[2] 6332[9]

Duke Of Marmalade (IRE) *A P O'Brien* 123
3 b c Danehill(USA) —Love Me True (USA) (Kingmambo (USA))
1473[4] 2051a[4] 2734[2] 4693[4] 5243a[2] 5798[3]

Duke Of Milan (IRE) *G C Bravery* a74 73
4 ch g Desert Prince(IRE) —Abyat (USA) (Shadeed (USA))
724[5] 1200[10] *2350[5]* 2664[9] *2799[4] 3408[6]* 4296[6]
5191[5] *5564[9] 6542[9] 6718[3] 6773[5]*

Duke Of Touraine (IRE) *P C Haslam* a69 72
2 gr g Linamix(FR) —Miss Mission (IRE) (Second Empire (IRE))
2803[7] 2983[5] 3834[3] 4364[5] 4892[11] 5081[6] *6750[4]*

Duke Of Tuscany *R Hannon* a99 99
3 b c Medicean—Flawless (Warning)
1126[4] 1476[3] 1835[2] 2231[7] 3458[6] 4059[13] *4887[3]*
5351[5]

Dukestreet *D Shaw* a41
6 ch g Cadeaux Genereux—El Rabab (USA) (Roberto (USA))
1755[13] 1946[12] 2221[8] 3185[13]

Dulce Sueno *I Semple* 61
4 b m Lahib(USA) —Graceland Lady (IRE) (Kafu)
2937[2] 3375[8] 3787[17]

Dumaran (IRE) *W J Musson* a80 82
9 b g Be My Chief(USA) —Pine Needle (Kris)
444[5] 634[7]

Dumas (IRE) *A P Jarvis* a59 74
3 b g Iron Mask(USA) —Bucaramanga (IRE) (Distinctly North (USA))
931[14] 2545[17] 4223[13] *4591[12]* 5062[14]

Dunaskin (IRE) *Karen McLintock* a96 110
7 b g Bahhare(USA) —Mirwara (IRE) (Darshaan)
608[6] 940[13] 1767[6] (2906) 3899[3] 4376[8] 4690[2]
5618[2] 6153[8] *6645[8]*

Dundry *G L Moore* a86 88
6 b g Bin Ajwaad(IRE) —China's Pearl (Shirley Heights)
(226) (488) 1148[3] 1794[3] 3153[4] 5574[7] *6545[5]*

Duneen Dream (USA) *W J Musson* a56 14
2 ch g Hennessy(USA) —T N T Red (USA) (Explosive Red (CAN))
6237[11] *6454[8] 6791[4] 7117[7]*

Dunelight (IRE) *C G Cox* 113
4 ch h Desert Sun—Badee'A (IRE) (Marju (IRE))
1104[8] 1392[3] (2442) 3523[5] 4045[3] 4805[4] 5112[2]
6009[9]

Dune Melody (IRE) *J S Moore* a59 82
4 b m Distant Music(USA) —Desert Gift (Green Desert (USA))
979[9] 1357[13]

Dunmore Dodger (IRE) *R A Fahey* a69
2 b c Tagula(IRE) —Decrescendo (IRE) (Polish Precedent (USA))
7270[3]

Dunn Deal (IRE) *J Balding* a46 76
7 b g Revoque(IRE) —Buddy And Soda (IRE) (Imperial Frontier (USA))
896[7] *1165[11] 1436[10]* 1492[6] 2608[5] 3106[6] 3203[5]
3837[3] 4583[6] 5930[5] *6735[9] 7108[6] 7138[5]*

Dunn'o (IRE) *C G Cox* 79
2 b g Cape Cross(IRE) —Indian Express (Indian Ridge)
5003[3] 5910[4] 6419[2]

Duntulm *H Candy* a52 73
2 b c Sakhee(USA) —Not Before Time (IRE) (Polish Precedent (USA))
4273[8] 6650[7]

Durova (IRE) *T D Easterby* a47 73
3 b f Soviet Star(USA) —Taroudannt (IRE) (Danehill (USA))
1108[10] *1351[5]* 1577[4] *2950[9]* 4452[3] 4896[12] 5139[9]
5507[11]

Dushstorm (IRE) *M Botti* a62
6 b g Dushyantor(USA) —Between The Winds (USA) (Diesis)
6293[10] 6996[7]

Dusk *J L Dunlop* 68
2 b g Fantastic Light(USA) —Dark Veil (USA) (Gulch (USA))
4362[5] 5206[8] 5599[7] 6233[5]

Dusk Ballet *S C Williams* a46 29
2 b f Alhaarth(IRE) —Curfew (Marju (IRE))
5063[10] *5644[4] 6099[7] 6828[10] 6880[5]*

Dustoori *Saeed Bin Suroor* 92
3 b c In The Wings—Elfaslah (IRE) (Green Desert (USA))
(4630) 5677[2] (5941) 6490[9]

Dusty Moon *W J Knight* a80 73
2 ch f Dr Fong(USA) —Dust Dancer (Suave Dancer (USA))
(3453) 4804[7]

Dutch Art *P W Chapple-Hyam* 124
3 ch c Medicean—Halland Park Lass (IRE) (Spectrum (IRE))
1147[2] 1473[3] 2734[4] 3506[2] 4214a[2] 6029a[6]

Dutch Key Card (IRE) *C Smith* a56 80
6 b g Key Of Luck(USA) —Fanny Blankers (IRE) (Persian Heights)
1074[14] 1221[6] 3257[11] (Dead)

Duty (IRE) *K F O'Brien* a42 100
4 b g Rainbow Quest(USA) —Wendylina (IRE) (In The Wings)
6366a[9] (Dead)

Duty Doctor *S Kirk* a70 56
2 ch f Dr Fong(USA) —Duty Paid (IRE) (Barathea (IRE))
4254[5] *6119[2]* 6535[8]

Duty Free (IRE) *H Morrison* a78 91
3 b g Rock Of Gibraltar(IRE) —Photographie (USA) (Trempolino (USA))
649[5] 2801[4] 3367[2] *(3624)* (4113) 4511[2] 5006[5]
5955[2]

Dvinsky (USA) *P Howling* a80 81
6 b g Stravinsky(USA) —Festive Season (USA) (Lypheor)
(67) 276[9] 367[7] 513[10] 621[3] 803[3] 902[4] *(1252)*
1431[2] 2139[7] 2546[8] *2993[2] 3623[3] 4024[5]* 4320[9]
5119[5] 5648[2] 6122[3] 6273[4] 6568[5] 6818[9] 6946[7]
(7033) 7164[6]

Dyanita *B W Hills* a71 62
4 b m Singspiel(IRE) —Dance Clear (IRE) (Marju (IRE))
381[5]

Dylan (IRE) *M A Doyle* a50 15
4 b g Mull Of Kintyre(USA) —Rose Of Shuaib (IRE) (Caerleon (USA))
425[11]

Dylan Thomas (IRE) *A P O'Brien* a64 131
4 b h Danehill(USA) —Lagrion (USA) (Diesis)
(1050a) (1340a) 2064a[2] 2754[2] (3942) 4693[2] (5243a) (6043a) 6513a[5] 7090a[7]

Dynaforce (USA) *A Fabre* 105
4 b m Dynaformer(USA) —Aletta Maria (USA) (Diesis)
4652a[3]

Dynamic Saint (USA) *Doug Watson* a104
4 b h Sweetsouthernsaint(USA) —Le Nat (USA) (Dynaformer (USA))
329a[9] (529a) 643a[7]

Dynamo Dancer (IRE) *G M Lyons* a105 104
4 ch g Danehill Dancer(IRE) —Imperial Graf (USA) (Blushing John (USA))
1184a[5] 4211a[13] 5242a[5] *(5761a)* 6038a[9] *6920a[2]*

Dynamo Dave (USA) *B J Meehan* a63
2 b c Distorted Humor(USA) —Nothing Special (CAN) (Tejabo (CAN))
6948[6] 7266[8]

Dysonic (USA) *J Balding* a59 39
5 b g Aljabr(USA) —Atyab (USA) (Mr Prospector (USA))
8[5] 251[4] 318[3] 729[7] 892[2] 1384[9] 1902[5] 2221[4] 2418[7] 2711[11] *3169[2] 6340[4] 6773[7] 6887[5]*

Dzesmin (POL) *R C Guest* a81 89
5 b g Professional(IRE) —Dzakarta (POL) (Aprizzo (IRE))
256[10] 587[9] 693[4] 1244[3] 1582[7] 2236[4] 3093[3] 3509[8] 3978[2] 4637[5] (5623) 6759[19]

Ea (USA) *Sir Michael Stoute* 113
3 br c Dynaformer(USA) —Enthused (USA) (Seeking The Gold (USA))
(1075) 1617[6] 2788[2] 3503[7] 3940[2]

Eager Diva (USA) *K A Ryan* a71 71
2 bb f More Than Ready(USA) —Divine Diva (USA) (Theatrical)
952[2] 1101[6] *1945[5]* 4923[6] 5294[6] 5773[2] 6384[6] 6741[6] *(6998)*

Eager Igor (USA) *Eve Johnson Houghton* a83 83
3 bb g Stravinsky(USA) —Danube (USA) (Green Desert (USA))
931[3] 1091[3] 1359[3] 1956[3] (2453) 2627[7] *3215[3]* 3553[5] 4268[10] 4510[9] 5208[5] 5539[8] 5885[2]

Eagle Mountain *A P O'Brien* 124
3 b c Rock Of Gibraltar(IRE) —Masskana (IRE) (Darshaan)
1473[5] 2235[2] 3142a[3] 3566a[U] 3974[2] (4435a) 6334[2]

Eagle's Pass (IRE) *T J O'Mara* 100
5 b g Brave Act—Cd Super Targeting (IRE) (Polish Patriot (USA))
6366a[19]

Earl Compton (IRE) *Stef Liddiard* a57 51
3 b g Compton Place—Noble Story (Last Tycoon (IRE))
5495[9] 5752[10] 7118[6] 7162[2]

Earl Kraul (IRE) *G L Moore* a62 46
4 b g Imperial Ballet(IRE) —Bu Hagab (IRE) (Royal Academy (USA))
(18) 51[2] 129[3] 315[3] 616[9] 7028[4]

Earl Marshal (USA) *Sir Michael Stoute* 82
3 b g Kingmambo(USA) —Fairy Godmother (Fairy King (USA))
3244[2] 3685[2] 4229[2]

Earl Of Fire (GER) *W Baltromei* 66
2 ch c Aerion—Evry (GER) (Torgos)
6324a[9]

Earl's Court *E Charpy* 76
5 b h King's Best(USA) —Reine Wells (IRE) (Sadler's Wells (USA))
645a[7]

Earlsmedic *S C Williams* a66
2 ch g Dr Fong(USA) —Area Girl (Jareer (USA))
5337[6]

Early March *J H M Gosden* 113
5 br h Dansili—Emplane (USA) (Irish River (FR))
2396[6]

Early Promise (IRE) *Mrs A L M King* a63 58
3 b f Abou Zouz(USA) —Habla Me (IRE) (Fairy King (USA))
1151[7] 1269[4] *1903[3]* 2061[7] *2571[7] 3066[8]* 4164[6] *4361[11] 5098[9] 5386[7]*

Earthling *D W Chapman* a48 37
6 b g Rainbow Quest(USA) —Cruising Height (Shirley Heights)
524[4] 812[12] 1066[6] 1229[8] 1362[6] 4099[12]

Easement *C A Cyzer* a54 38
4 b g Kayf Tara—Raspberry Sauce (Niniski (USA))
5754[6] 6054[7]

Easibet Dot Net *I Semple* a64 74
7 gr g Atraf—Silvery (Petong)
6697[5] (6875) 7081[5] 7226[2]

Eastbourne *Eve Johnson Houghton* a47 47
2 ch c Compton Place—Glascoed (Adbass (USA))
2569[7] 4016[10] *4962[10]* 5429[6] *5818[12] 6263[11]* 6595[12]

East Coast Girl (IRE) *S W Hall* a32 59
2 ch f Captain Rio—Toledana (IRE) (Sure Blade (USA))
4028[8] 4733[3] 5901[8] *6812[10]*

Easterly Breeze (IRE) *W R Muir* a67 77
3 b c Green Desert(USA) —Chiang Mai (IRE) (Sadler's Wells (USA))
864[2] 1246[5] 1812[5] 5045[2] 5346[3] 5450[4]

Eastern Anthem (IRE) *Saeed Bin Suroor* 103
3 b c Singspiel(IRE) —Kazzia (GER) (Zinaad)
1475[3] 1957[2]

Eastern Appeal (IRE) *M Halford* 113
4 br m Shinko Forest(IRE) —Haut Volee (Top Ville)
(1548a) 2053a[7] 2586a[3] 4648a[2] 5241a[4] (6038a)

Eastern Emperor *W R Swinburn* a72 73
3 ch g Halling(USA) —B Beautiful (IRE) (Be My Guest (USA))
1204[7] 2320[4] 2836[4] *3416[9]* 4587[5]

Eastern Gift *R Hannon* a82 95
2 ch c Cadeaux Genereux—Dahshah (Mujtahid (USA))
3479[4] 3733[5] 4048[2] 4571[2] (5033) 5414[2] 5974[8] 6171[4] *6974[4]*

Eastern Pride *P A Blockley* a3 52
2 b f Fraam—Granuaile O'Malley (IRE) (Mark Of Esteem (IRE))
5267[5] *6734[8]*

Eastern Princess *G H Yardley* a54 60
3 b f Almutawakel—Silvereine (FR) (Bering)
786[3] 974[8] *1248[6]* 2195[2] *2948[7]* 3869[4] 4226[7] *6402[7]*

Eastern Romance *K A Ryan* 107
2 b f Oasis Dream—Ocean Grove (IRE) (Fairy King (USA))
1285[6] 2134[3] 2869[4] 3200[5] 5216[3] (5521) 5766[9] 6182[4] (6525a)

Eastfields Lad *S R Bowring* 29
5 b g Overbury(IRE) —Honey Day (Lucky Wednesday)
2535[9]

Eastwell Smiles *R T Phillips* a69
3 gr g Erhaab(USA) —Miss University (USA) (Beau Genius (CAN))
2455[6] 3084[3] 4392[10]

Easy Laughter (IRE) *A King* a73 69
6 b g Danehill(USA) —All To Easy (Alzao (USA))
117[6] 515[10]

Easy Target (FR) *B Smart* 98
2 ch c Danehill Dancer(IRE) —Aiming (Highest Honor (FR))
(2575) (3157) 4721[8] 5630[5] 6017[4]

Easy Wonder (GER) *I A Wood* a69 71
2 b f Royal Dragon(USA) —Emy Coasting (USA) (El Gran Senor (USA))
2961[6] 4097[3] 4837a[4] 5462a[4] 5848a[3] 6324a[7] *(6734)*

Eat Pie (USA) *M J Wallace* a70 94
2 bb f Thunder Gulch(USA) —Millie's Choice (IRE) (Taufan (USA))
(3187) 3432[7] *5247a[10]*

Eau Good *B G Powell* a86 89
3 ch g Cadeaux Genereux—Girl's Best Friend (Nicolotte)
184[5] 433[2] 584[2] 939[9] (1202) 2400[8] 2943[3] 3335[8] 3709[5] 4603[10] 4847[12]

Eau Sauvage *J Akehurst* a24
3 ch f Lake Coniston(IRE) —Mo Stopher (Sharpo)
128[9] 7282[11]

Ebenholz (IRE) *Mrs John Harrington* 74
4 b g Namid—Pretext (Polish Precedent (USA))
873a[6]

Ebert *P J Makin* a71 95
4 b g Polish Precedent(USA) —Fanfare (Deploy)
1962[2] 2446[4] 5012[6] 5419[3] 5717[4]

Ebn Malk (IRE) *M A Jarvis* 65
2 ch c King's Best(USA) —Auntie Maureen (IRE) (Roi Danzig (USA))
6571[7]

Ebn Reem *M A Jarvis* a95 88
3 b c Mark Of Esteem(IRE) —Reematna (Sabrehill (USA))
(943) 1298[9] 1817[4] 2659[2]

Ebn Zahr (UAE) *Miss J E Foster*
3 ch g Halling(USA) —Ginger Tree (USA) (Dayjur (USA))
1177[13] 2909[10]

Eboracum Dream *T D Easterby* 54
2 b f Diktat—Bollin Jeannie (Royal Applause)
1285[7] 1848[12] 2739[13] 3398[11] 4522[6] 5477[5] 6305[10]

Ebraam (USA) *D Shaw* a98 72
4 b g Red Ransom(USA) —Futuh (USA) (Diesis)
516[7] 686[13] 1064[6] 1226[6] 3064[4] (3408) 3852[2] 4394[3] 4884[3] 5387[2] 5753[7] (6360) (6707) 6876[2] 7112[6] (7255)

Ecclesiastic (USA) *M D Wolfson* a55 102
6 br h Pulpit(USA) —Starry Dreamer (USA) (Rubiano (USA))
6375a[6]

Echelon *Sir Michael Stoute* 118
5 b m Danehill(USA) —Exclusive (Polar Falcon (USA))
(1472) (2207) 2753[5] 3117a[6] (4805) (5241a) 6010[3]

Echoes Rock (GER) *A Fabre* 109
4 ch g Tiger Hill(IRE) —Evening Breeze (GER) (Surumu (GER))
3780a[4] 4520a[6]

Echo Of Light *Saeed Bin Suroor* a121 121
5 b h Dubai Millennium—Spirit Of Tara (IRE) (Sadler's Wells (USA))
3523[4] (4520a) (5142) 6031a[5] 6372a[3]

Echostar *Stef Liddiard* a34 52
2 ch f Observatory(USA) —Anqood (IRE) (Elmaamul (USA))
1156[3] (1255) 1674[4] 2087[4] 6722[13] *6881[11]*

Eclipse Park *M J McGrath* a67 40
4 ch g Rainbow Quest(USA) —Gino's Spirits (Perugino (USA))
52[8]

Eco Centrism *W J Haggas* 78
3 ch c Selkirk(USA) —Way O'Gold (USA) (Slew O'Gold (USA))
5915[3] 6286[2]

Ecology (IRE) *M Robertz* 98
9 b h Sri Pekan(USA) —Ecco Mi (IRE) (Priolo (USA))
2131a[5]

Economic (IRE) *M Botti* a73 37
4 b h Danehill Dancer(IRE) —Warusha (GER) (Shareef Dancer (USA))
488[11] 726[9] 1819[12]

Eco Sympathy *M L W Bell* 49
3 b g Dansili—Tigwa (Cadeaux Genereux)
5304[5]

E'Cusson *M A Jarvis* a53
2 b f Singspiel(IRE) —Indian Love Bird (Efisio)
6944[8]

Edaara (IRE) *W J Haggas* 89
4 ch m Pivotal—Green Bonnet (IRE) (Green Desert (USA))
1651[14] 2207[6] 2835[9]

Edas *J J Quinn* a71 73
5 b h Celtic Swing—Eden (IRE) (Polish Precedent (USA))
2935[3] 3260[3] 4284[6] 4843[3]

Eddie Dowling *M R Channon* 51
2 b c High Chaparral(IRE) —Dans Delight (Machiavellian (USA))
6493[11]

Eddie Jock (IRE) *M L W Bell* 113
3 ch g Almutawakel—Al Euro (FR) (Mujtahid (USA))
1095[3] 1544[3] (2788) 3463[7] 4148[9] 5412[3]

Eden Rock (IRE) *Pat Eddery* 100
6 b g Danehill(USA) —Marlene-D (Selkirk (USA))
331a[4] 2755[24]

Ede's *P M Phelan* a39
7 ch g Bijou D'Inde—Ballagarrow Girl (North Stoke)
7069[9]

Ede's Dot Com (IRE) *P M Phelan* a74 79
3 b g Trans Island—Kilkee Bay (IRE) (Case Law)
483[6] 815[5] 2629[7] *3644[14]* 4538[4] *5136[7] 5495[2] 6406[8]*

Edge Closer *R Hannon* a106 96
3 b c Bold Edge—Blue Goddess (IRE) (Blues Traveller (IRE))
2942[2] (3483) (3944) *(4950)* 5765[7]

Edge End *R A Farrant* a39 61
3 ch g Bold Edge—Rag Time Belle (Raga Navarro (ITY))
4808[5] 5315[5] 5741[10] *6101[10]*

Edgefour (IRE) *B I Case* a35 53
3 b f King's Best(USA) —Highshaan (Pistolet Bleu (IRE))
3387[8] 4205[15] 4684[11]

Edge Of Gold *B Palling* 79
2 ch f Choisir(AUS) —Beveled Edge (Beveled (USA))
2968[2] 3796[2] (4254) (4775) 6128[12]

Edge Of Light *B Palling* 93
2 b f Xaar—Bright Edge (Danehill Dancer (IRE))
(2997) 3988[5] 4573[4]

Edie Superstar (USA) *M A Magnusson* a67 62
2 b f Forestry(USA) —Just Out (USA) (Forty Niner (USA))
1285[5] *6140[3] 6849[6]*

Edin Burgher (FR) *T T Clement* a55 46
6 br g Hamas(IRE) —Jaljuli (Jalmood (USA))
82[10] 161[9] 562[8] 722[8] 797[10] 5121[10] 6831[9]

Educated Risk *W J Haggas* 66
2 b g Royal Applause—Tantalize (Machiavellian (USA))
4810[8] 6237[3]

Edward (IRE) *M Madgwick* a33 56
5 b g Namid—Daltak (Night Shift (USA))
6927[10] 7014[12] 7167[12]

Effective *A P Jarvis* a82 82
7 ch g Bahamian Bounty—Efficacy (Efisio)
190[10] 323[2] 717[8] 774[2] 1121[2] 1252[3] 1977[4] 2318[3] 2394[3]

Efficient (NZ) *G Rogerson* 123
4 gr g Zabeel(NZ) —Refused The Dance (NZ) (Defensive Play (USA))
(6712a)

Effigy *H Candy* a66 71
3 b g Efisio—Hymne D'Amour (USA) (Dixieland Band (USA))
1606[7] 2834[11] 3689[3] 4015[6] *5122[8]* 6132[5] 6380[3]

Effingham (IRE) *B W Hills* 72
2 b c Celtic Swing—Deemeh (IRE) (Brief Truce (USA))
3878[2] 4286[8] 5772[4] 6058[11]

Efidium *N Bycroft* a54 74
9 b g Presidium—Efipetite (Efisio)
1132[7] 1287[7] 1747[9] 2117[5] 2311[6] (2842) 3194[5] 3381[6] 3556[2] 3754[8] 3971[5] 4176[10] 4408[4] 4820[3] 5228[3] 5737[5] 6016[16]

Efisio Princess *J E Long* 69
4 br m Efisio—Hardiprincess (Keen)
1766[7] (6239) 6575[2]

Efistorm *C R Dore* a86 95
6 b g Efisio—Abundance (Cadeaux Genereux)
79[8] 155[6] (254) 810[6] (1061) 1363[6] 1754[6] 2025[5] 2399[3] (2673) 3080[4] 3298[10] 4489[2] 4696[9] (4780) 5810[2] *6142[5]* 6472[7]

Eforetta (GER) *D J Wintle* a71 66
5 ch m Dr Fong(USA) —Erminora (GER) (Highest Honor (FR))
685[3] 909[4] 1222[3] *1526[5] (1752) 2148[6]* 3033[8] 3467[9]

Egerton (GER) *P Rau* 119
6 b h Groom Dancer(USA) —Enrica (Niniski (USA))
(882a) 1340a[5] 1872a[2] 3778a[5] 4442a[5] 5077a[3] 5671a[5] (6353a) 7090a[6]

Eglevski (IRE) *J L Dunlop* 93
3 b g Danehill Dancer(IRE) —Ski For Gold (Shirley Heights)
1010[6] 1827[2] 2999[3] 3883[6] 5724[4]

Egregius Max *C F Wall* 45
3 b c Royal Applause—Singed (Zamindar (USA))
1398[14] 1838[9] 2878[13]

Egyptian (USA) *R Bouresly* a97 83
8 b g Green Desert(USA) —Link River (USA) (Gone West (USA))
105a[10] *599a[14]*

Egyptian Lord *Peter Grayson* a83 57
4 ch g Bold Edge—Calypso Lady (IRE) (Priolo (USA))
8[9] 82[5] 251[3] (317) 465[4] (521) (626) 727[2] (810) 1121[12] 1754[5] 1991[10] 3086[4] *3452[5]* 4101[10] 4734[9] *6405[9] 6708[6] 6860[9] 6938[8] 7005[6]*

Eidsfoss (IRE) *T T Clement* a27 31
5 b g Danehill Dancer(IRE) —Alca Egeria (ITY) (Shareef Dancer (USA))
52[6]

Eight Up (IRE) *Edward P Harty* 86
4 b g Old Vic—Square Up (IRE) (Up And At 'Em) (4114a)

Eighty Twenty *M W Easterby* 2
2 b f Diktat—Stonegrave (Selkirk (USA))
1285[14] *2147[11]* 4565[12]

Eijaaz (IRE) *G A Harker* 61
6 b g Green Desert(USA) —Kismah (Machiavellian (USA))
1554[2] 1967[4] 2201[2] 2431[2] 3840[7] 4096[7] 4582[11] 5286[3] 5704[5] 6558[5]

Eileen's Violet (IRE) *P D Evans* 90
2 b f Catcher In The Rye(IRE) —Brave Cat (IRE) (Catrail (USA))
1585[2] (1897) 2812[12] 3432[13] 4573[8] 4991[4] 5217[2]

Eishin Lombard (USA) *K Kozaki*
5 ch h Victory Gallop(CAN) —Pacific City (USA) (Carson City (USA))
6942a[13]

Eisteddfod *P F I Cole* a111 114
6 ch g Cadeaux Genereux—Ffestiniog (IRE) (Efisio)
(841) 1034[3] 1651[27] (2111) 3500[9] 4871a[4] (5359) 6332[10]

Eiswind *P Schiergen* 91
3 b c Monsun(GER) —Eiszeit (GER) (Java Gold (USA))
3146a[8]

Ejeed (USA) *J H M Gosden* 64
2 b c Rahy(USA) —Lahan (Unfuwain (USA))
6724[8]

Ekhtiaar *J H M Gosden* a91 101
3 b g Elmaamul(USA) —Divina Mia (Dowsing (USA))
2231[5] 2788[5] 3460[11] 4566[2] 5950[4]

Ektimaal *E A L Dunlop* a98 91
4 ch g Bahamian Bounty—Secret Circle (Magic Ring (IRE))
(49) (191) (300) (657) 840[8] 3437[5] 3943[15] 4990[8] 5413[9] *7254[2]*

Elaala (USA) *J T Stimpson* a54 47
5 ch m Aljabr(USA) —Nufuth (USA) (Nureyev (USA))
4380[9]

Ela Enta *Kevin Prendergast* 91
3 b f Royal Applause—Hasanat (Night Shift (USA))
1694a[4]

Ela Figura *A W Carroll* a44 56
7 ch m The West(USA) —Chili Bouchier (USA) (Stop The Music (USA))
36[5] 135[8] 201[10] 523[9]

El Alamein (IRE) *Sir Mark Prescott* a75 67
4 ch g Nashwan(USA) —El Rabab (USA) (Roberto (USA))
4297[6] 4638[9] 5257[8] 6056[15]

Elamar *D G Bridgwater* a25
3 b f Rainbow High—Night Transaction (Tina's Pet)
418[12]

Ela Mario (CYP) *Mrs H Sweeting*
3 ch g Ela-Aristokrati(IRE) —Forgotten Times (USA) (Nabeel Dancer (USA))
6975[10]

Elas Child (IRE) *M Halford* a54 33
2 ch f Noverre(USA) —Lady Ela (IRE) (Ela-Mana-Mou)
6392a[10]

Elasos (FR) *D Sepulchre* 111
5 b h Pythios(IRE) —Shikasta (IRE) (Kris)
663a[2] 880a[5] 1571a[6] 3665a[5] 4520a[5] 6095a[2]

Elata *N Sauer*
3 b f Zieten(USA) —Elafonissos (FR) (Exit To Nowhere (USA))
1515a[5]

El Biba D'Or (IRE) *P Giannotti* 107
8 b h Common Grounds—Quiet Awakening (USA) (Secreto (USA))
1874a[5] 3893a[6]

El Bosque (IRE) *B R Millman* a94 106
3 b g Elnadim(USA) —In The Woods (You And I (USA))
943[2] 1124[10] 1502[3] *(1930)* 2395[3] (3380) 3975[8] 4607[9] 5355[7]

El Capitan (FR) *Miss Gay Kelleway* a61 64
4 b g Danehill Dancer(IRE) —Fille Dansante (IRE) (Dancing Dissident (USA))
1167[8] 1406[8] 1671[7] *(1906) 2176[6]* 2582[12] *2875[10]* 3610[9] 4031[11]

El Cerro *Joseph Crowley* 71
3 b g Compton Place—Arndilly (Robellino (USA))
6555a[10]

El Comodin (IRE) *A Fabre* 107
3 ch c Monsun(GER) —Elle Danzig (GER) (Roi Danzig (USA))
(3361a) 4627a[4] 6376a[9]

El Coto *K A Ryan* a89 97
7 b g Forzando—Thatcherella (Thatching)
1480[5] 4176[8] 4581[10] (4713) 5255[4] 5479[2] 5737[3] 5838[5] 6253[16] 6732[6] *6882[4]*

El Dececy (USA) *D J Murphy* a56 82
3 b g Seeking The Gold(USA) —Ashraakat (USA) (Danzig (USA))
1044[3] (1412) 1843[3] 2506[3] 4332[6] 4847[10] 5296[10] 5703[11] *6314[7]* 6475[6]

El Dee (IRE) *D Carroll* a49 46
4 b g Brave Act—Go Flightline (IRE) (Common Grounds)
503[6] 4124[11]

Eldest (IRE) *V Caruso* 100
2 ch c Indian Ridge—Lara's Shock (IRE) (Caerleon (USA))
2684a[7] 6222a[6]

Eldon Endeavour *B Storey* 38
3 b g Hunting Lion(IRE) —La Noisette (Rock Hopper)
2759[9]

Eldorado *G L Moore* a71 76
6 b g Hernando(FR) —Catch (USA) (Blushing Groom (FR))
578[5] 1470[5] 1959[9] 2544[2] 3617[2]

El Dottore *M L W Bell* 63
3 b c Dr Fong(USA) —Edouna (FR) (Doyoun)
2477[4] 3415[6] 4858[12] *6260[14]*

El Duende (USA) *W Jarvis* 66
2 bb c Elusive Quality(USA) —Brianda (IRE) (Alzao (USA))
5880[5] 6251[6]

Eleanor Eloise (USA) *J R Gask* a48
3 b f Minardi(USA) —Javana (USA) (Sandpit (BRZ))
6877[6] 7029[5]

Electric Beat *C Sprengel* 110
4 b h Shinko Forest(IRE) —Divine Grace (IRE) (Definite Article)
3506[14] (4869a)

Electric Warrior (IRE) *K R Burke* a92 92
4 b g Bold Fact(USA) —Dungeon Princess (IRE) (Danehill (USA))
842^2 1179^5 1682^7 2466^9 2771^2 (3420) 4068^2 4385^2 5221^5

Electron Pulse *M Dods* a45 61
4 ch m Dr Fong(USA) —Lost In Lucca (Inchinor)
1918^{16} 2121^{13}

Elegans *Mrs C A Dunnett* a27 7
3 b f Montjeu(IRE) —Aymara (Darshaan)
977^{14} 4738^7 6286^9 6716^{12} 6858^9

Elegant Hawk *W J Knight* a95 86
3 b f Generous(IRE) —Mexican Hawk (USA) (Silver Hawk (USA))
1606^4 (3651) 4205^9 4766^2 (5500) 5725^4 6605^5

Elegant Step *A P Jarvis* 67
2 b f Xaar—Lady's Walk (IRE) (Charnwood Forest (IRE))
2039^9 2468^{15} 4293^2 4852^6 5600^6 6379^{11}

Elemental Hero (FR) *Jane Chapple-Hyam* 45
2 ch c Kyllachy—Suerte (Halling (USA))
6246^9

El Fuser *P J Makin* 62
2 ch c Zamindar(USA) —Nimble Fan (USA) (Lear Fan (USA))
2539^7 3550^8 4181^5

Elhamri *S Kirk* a85 106
3 bb c Noverre(USA) —Seamstress (IRE) (Barathea (IRE))
1394^6 2352^8 2672^5 3990^{17} 4726^9 5212^{13} 6541^6

Elijah Pepper (USA) *T D Barron* a76 68
2 ch g Crafty Prospector(USA) —Dovie Dee (USA) (Housebuster (USA))
952^3 2984^5 3673^2 4175^7 (6312) 6699^5

Elite Land *N Bycroft* 57
4 b g Namaqualand(USA) —Petite Elite (Anfield)
1301^7

Elizabeth Garrett *M J Gingell* a50 44
3 b f Dr Fong(USA) —Eleonor Sympson (Cadeaux Genereux)
103^5 194^6 357^7 469^{10} 602^9 790^{13} 900^{10} 3824^6 4943^{13} 5542^5

Elizabeth Spirit (IRE) *E S McMahon* a33
3 b f Invincible Spirit(IRE) —Generate (Generous (IRE))
6339^9 6963^6 7134^5

Elizabeth's Quest *R Simpson* a53 60
2 b f Piccolo—Reina (Homeboy)
3424^5 3850^7 4823^4 5729^{11}

Elizabeth Swann *R Hannon* 81
2 ch f Bahamian Bounty—Last Exhibit (Royal Academy (USA))
5313^2 5550^2 5949^2

Elkhorn *Miss J A Camacho* a69 89
5 b g Indian Ridge—Rimba (USA) (Dayjur (USA))
1299^7 1806^2 (3014) 3585^6 3954^2 4227^9 5332^4 5667^3 6173^7 6381^{13}

Elk Trail (IRE) *T P Tate* 73
2 ch g Captain Rio—Panpipes (USA) (Woodman (USA))
2889^6 4841^4 5485^2 6051^6

Ellablue *Rae Guest* a59 62
3 ch f Bahamian Bounty—Elabella (Ela-Mana-Mou)
36^3 511^2 894^2 1207^4 5234^{10}

Ella Junior (USA) *B J Meehan* a40 60
2 ch f Hennessy(USA) —More Ribbons (USA) (Dynaformer (USA))
5882^5 6138^{11} 6998^7

Ella Woodcock (IRE) *E J Alston* a65 92
3 b g Daggers Drawn(USA) —Hollow Haze (USA) (Woodman (USA))
348^2 446^3 3924^3 4326^2 (4538) (5046) (5508) (5664) 6053^2 6474^2

Ella Y Rossa *P D Evans* a64 55
3 ch f Bertolini(USA) —Meandering Rose (USA) (Irish River (FR))
21^4 (122) 284^3 348^{11} 577^5 744^2 (834) 1131^6 1310^7 4429^6 4918^3 6146^8 6272^4 6387^{11} 6801^5 7083^8

Ellcon (IRE) *J A Osborne* a68 43
4 b m Royal Applause—Carranita (IRE) (Anita's Prince)
311^2 489^5 1404^5

Ellemujie *D K Ivory* a84 90
2 b g Mujahid(USA) —Jennelle (Nomination)
2333^8 (2569) 3462^{10} 3925^3 4364^2 4812^6 5350^3 5597^5 5974^{14} 6291^3 6471^4

Elleno (IRE) *F & L Camici* 97
3 b c Celtic Swing—El Gran Love (USA) (El Gran Senor (USA))
1875a^6

Ellens Academy (IRE) *E J Alston* a67 86
12 b g Royal Academy(USA) —Lady Ellen (Horage)
1134^{12} 1678^3 1847^{17} 3053^{14} 3569^9 3998^{11} 4140^6 (4351) 4583^4 (4934) 4999^5 (5356) 5638^7

Ellen's Girl (IRE) *R Hannon* a42 80
4 b m Desert Prince(IRE) —Lady Ellen (Horage)
741^{11} 1025^3 1206^5 1539^{10} 1740^5 2179^7 3352^{11} 4317^2 (4532) (4632) (4828) 5166^5 (5917) 6423^5

Elle Of A Star (FR) *P Laloum* a43 48
2 b c Fly To The Stars—Claretelle (IRE) (Ela-Mana-Mou)
6879a^7

Elle Runaway (USA) *M Pierce* 114
5 rg m El Prado(IRE) —Runaway Venus (USA) (Runaway Groom (CAN))
6373a^{10}

Elle's Angel (IRE) *E J O'Neill* a26 37
3 b f Tobougg(IRE) —Stamatina (Warning)
1750^{10}

Ellesappelle *R A Harris* a67 73
4 b m Benny The Dip(USA) —Zizi (IRE) (Imp Society (USA))
(497) 605^9 610^8 665^{13} 825^6

Elletelle (IRE) *G M Lyons* 102
2 b f Elnadim(USA) —Flamanda (Niniski (USA))
(2756) 3432^3 4437a^3 5973^6

Ellies Faith *N Bycroft* 46
3 ch f Sugarfoot—Star Dancer (Groom Dancer (USA))
2116^3 3377^5 3640^6 3792^{14} (4036) 4426^4 4521^7 4943^5 5487^{11} 5698^9

Elliots World (IRE) *E Charpy* a39 104
5 b h King's Best(USA) —Morning Welcome (IRE) (Be My Guest (USA))
176a^9

Elliwan *M Johnston* 69
2 b c Nayef(USA) —Ashbilya (USA) (Nureyev (USA))
6417^{13} 6593^3

Ellmau *E J O'Neill* a76 100
2 ch c Dr Fong(USA) —Triple Sharp (Selkirk (USA))
(2147) 3504^3 4057^5 5324^{17}

Elmaleeha *J L Dunlop* 70
2 b f Galileo(IRE) —Winsa (USA) (Riverman (USA))
6649^2

Elmasong *J J Bridger* a43 48
3 ch f Elmaamul(USA) —Annie's Song (Farfelu)
1784^{11} 2140^5 2445^{11} 2978^8 3349^9 4470^2 4684^8 5728^{11} 6429^{11} 7014^{10} 7094^{12} 7185^8 7277^7

Elms Schoolboy *P Howling* a53 44
5 ch g Komaite(USA) —Elms Schoolgirl (Emarati (USA))
156^4 349^6 425^4 616^{11} 789^{11} 804^7 1362^9 7277^6

Elna Bright *R Hannon* 86
2 b c Elnadim(USA) —Acicula (IRE) (Night Shift (USA))
1762^3 2103^2 (2410) (3909) 4364^6 4812^8 5705^2

Elopement (IRE) *W M Brisbourne* a48 85
5 ch m Machiavellian(USA) —Melanzane (Arazi (USA))
286^9 496^{11} 1206^8 (1761) 1944^5 2157^4 2254^5 (2721) 4019^8 4128^5 (5482) (5676) (5769) (5968)

Eloquent Isle (IRE) *Mrs A Duffield* a42
2 b f Mull Of Kintyre(USA) —County Girl (IRE) (Prince Rupert (FR))
6903^5

Eloquent Rose (IRE) *Mrs A Duffield* a64 81
3 b f Elnadim(USA) —Quintellina (Robellino (USA))
1108^{12} 1577^{11} 1820^7 6907^4

Elounda (IRE) *H R A Cecil* 61
3 b f Sinndar(IRE) —Gaily Grecian (IRE) (Ela-Mana-Mou)
1077^7 2981^{12} 3913^7 4472^7

El Palmar *M J Attwater* a60 58
6 b g Case Law—Aybeegirl (Mazilier (USA))
1027^{14} 1374^3 1569^{12}

El Potro *J R Holt* a59 66
5 b g Forzando—Gaelic Air (Ballad Rock)
46^8 135^4 201^2 281^5 523^8 581^2 680^2 766^3 3259^2 3608^2 (4008) 4180^{14} 4881^6 (6287) 6860^5

El Puerto (FR) *M Boutin* a70 67
2 gr c Verglas(IRE) —Miss Margaux (FR) (Script Ohio (USA))
6879a^2

El Rey (IRE) *F Castro*
3 b c Lend A Hand—Surfing (Grundy)
2548a^8

El Shenandoah (FR) *C Boutin* a75 78
2 b f Trempolino(USA) —Magic Motion (USA) (Green Dancer (USA))
7048a^5

El Soprano (IRE) *K A Ryan* 88
3 b f Noverre(USA) —Lady Of Kildare (IRE) (Mujadil (USA))
3158^7 3430^7 3940^{15} 5954^{13}

El Tango (GER) *P Schiergen* 107
5 bb h Acatenango(GER) —Elea (GER) (Dschingis Khan)
990a^5 1689a^6 (2976a) 4722^6 (5849a) 6518a^4 (6941a)

Eltanin (IRE) *J Howard Johnson* 66
3 gr g Linamix(FR) —Housatonic (USA) (Riverman (USA))
1482^5 (Dead)

El Tato *T D Easterby* 63
2 b c Diktat—Villa Via (IRE) (Night Shift (USA))
1992^5 4173^5 4611^7 (Dead)

El Toreador (USA) *G A Butler* a86 80
3 ch f El Corredor(USA) —Marsha's Dancer (USA) (Northern Dancer (CAN))
1838^3 (2693) 3111^2 3645^7 4976^4 5218^5

Elusive Beau (IRE) *James Bernard McCabe* 47
2 bb c Iron Mask(USA) —Theroseofloughrea (IRE) (Lake Coniston (IRE))
5516a^7

Elusive Deal (USA) *R A Fahey* a58 58
2 ch f Elusive Quality(USA) —Peacefally (IRE) (Grand Lodge (USA))
1585^3 2039^{12} 3750^4 4126^7 5153^5 5423^6 6066^2 6478^4 6750^9 7007^8

Elusive Dreams (USA) *J H M Gosden* a71 68
3 ch g Elusive Quality(USA) —Bally Five (USA) (Miswaki (USA))
1282^5 4275^{11} (4541) 5122^7 5768^{16}

Elusive Flash (USA) *P F I Cole* a85 96
3 b f Freud(USA) —Giana (USA) (Exclusive Era (USA))
1146^3 2914^{10} 3961^7 5047^5 6852^{11} 7049a^{11}

Elusive Hawk (IRE) *A P Stringer* a44
3 bb g Noverre(USA) —Two Clubs (First Trump)
7159^5

Elusive Lady (IRE) *J R Weymes* a70 55
2 b f Clodovil(IRE) —Bella Vie (IRE) (Sadler's Wells (USA))
3013^4 3635^5 3812^6 4405^2 4770^6 5081^3 5477^3 6503^2 6698^4 (6912) (7234)

Elusive Warrior (USA) *R A Fahey* a69 64
4 b g Elusive Quality(USA) —Love To Fight (CAN) (Fit To Fight (USA))
4581^{17} 5253^{17} 5489^4 5840^{11} 6290^4 6610^2 6677^2 7025^{12} 7107^5

Elusory *J L Dunlop* 60
3 b c Galileo(IRE) —Elude (Slip Anchor)
1011^{10} 1611^4 5005^8 5938^8

Elva (IRE) *J-C Rouget* 102
3 b f King's Best(USA) —Evora (IRE) (Marju (IRE))
1339a^2 2290a^4

Elvina *A G Newcombe* a54 52
6 b m Mark Of Esteem(IRE) —Pharaoh's Joy (Robellino (USA))
(201) 680^4 1902^{10} 4635^5 4973^8 5564^5

Elyaadi *M R Channon* a76 85
3 b f Singspiel(IRE) —Abyaan (IRE) (Ela-Mana-Mou)
655^2 836^2 (1237) 1663^5 3883^5

Elysee Palace (IRE) *M A Jarvis* a77
2 b f King's Best(USA) —Noble Rose (IRE) (Caerleon (USA))
6140^5 (6434)

Ely Une (IRE) *J S Moore* a51 46
2 ch f Choisir(AUS) —D D's Jakette (USA) (Deputy Minister (CAN))
2969^8 3404^9 4311^2 4359^P 6425^3 6586^6 6734^6 6828^8

Emaara *J L Dunlop* 73
3 b f Fasliyev(USA) —Shuruk (Cadeaux Genereux)
1737^3

E Major *Sir Michael Stoute* a66
2 ch c Singspiel(IRE) —Crystal Cavern (USA) (Be My Guest (USA))
6694^3

Embossed (IRE) *Niall M O'Callaghan* a76 114
5 b h Mark Of Esteem(IRE) —L-Way First (IRE) (Vision (USA))
4415a^6

Embra (IRE) *T J Etherington* a21
2 b g Monashee Mountain(USA) —Ivory Turner (Efisio)
6912^8

Emefdream *E J O'Neill* a60 62
3 b g Efisio—Alkarida (FR) (Akarad (FR))
65^4 122^8 224^{10} 390^9 910^{10} 1210^{10}

Emef Princess *K A Ryan* a38 46
2 b f Mind Games—Woore Lass (IRE) (Persian Bold)
3812^3 4310^{11} 4702^7 5015^8 5901^5 6454^6 6624^8

Emerald Bay (IRE) *I Semple* 90
5 b g King's Best(USA) —Belle Etoile (FR) (Lead On Time (USA))
(969) 1494^{14} 1599^3 1939^3 2466^4 2871^8 3813^{11} 4497^4 5585^6 6637^2 6746^5

Emerald Crystal (IRE) *B J Meehan* 76
2 b c Green Desert(USA) —Crystal Spray (Beldale Flutter (USA))
6493^{12} 6618^4

Emerald Rock (CAN) *N J Vaughan* 57
2 b c Johannesburg(USA) —Classic Jones (CAN) (Regal Classic (CAN))
6723^6

Emerald Sky *R Brotherton* a24
3 b f Diktat—Dekelsmary (Komaite (USA))
429^7 1008^{14}

Emerald Toffee (IRE) *J T Stimpson* 14
2 ch c Tagula(IRE) —Spirit of Hope (IRE) (Danehill Dancer (IRE))
5772^{12} 6285^{10}

Emerald Wilderness (IRE) *E A L Dunlop* a81 98
3 b g Green Desert(USA) —Simla Bibi (Indian Ridge)
456^3 649^2 745^2 968^2 1111^2 (1365) 1835^4 2627^2 (3386) (3672) 4092^{10} 4640^2 4922^3 5419^7 5639^3

Emilio *R A Kvisla* a76 87
6 b g Kris—Easter Moon (FR) (Easter Sun)
211^8

Emilion *W R Muir* a63 64
4 ch m Fantastic Light(USA) —Riberac (Efisio)
89^{10} 220^3 369^{10}

Emily's Dens Joy (IRE) *Miss D A McHale* 31
2 b f Daggers Drawn(USA) —Cross Dall (IRE) (Blues Traveller (IRE))
1101^{13} 3801^6 4027^6

Emily's Place (IRE) *J Pearce* a70 74
4 b m Mujadil(USA) —Dulcinea (Selkirk (USA))
48^{12} 2748^5 (3156) 3571^5 3793^5 4404^6 4880^4 5189^8 5733^{11} 5983^2 6146^2 6342^2 6612^7 6982^4 7237^4

Emily's Rainbow (IRE) *W J Haggas* a49 54
3 b f Rainbow Quest(USA) —Showering (Danehill (USA))
5335^7 6005^8 6238^5 6590^9 6968^6

Emirates Gold (IRE) *E Charpy* a66 95
4 b h Royal Applause—Yara (IRE) (Sri Pekan (USA))
105a^6 331a^2

Emirates Skyline (USA) *Saeed Bin Suroor* 108
4 b h Sunday Silence(USA) —The Caretaker (Caerleon (USA))
(1767) 2815^5 4043^6

Emirati (IRE) *Robert Collet* a64 88
2 b c Dubai Destination(USA) —Kobalt Sea (FR) (Akarad (FR))
5260a^5

Emir Bagatelle *H Morrison* 34
2 gr g Dubai Destination(USA) —Giorgia Rae (IRE) (Green Desert (USA))
5428^{16} 5872^{11} 6105^8

Emma Gee *J Gallagher* a38
5 ch m Sure Blade(USA) —Elusive Star (Ardross)
699^{11} 825^7 2084^{11}

Emma Jean Lad (IRE) *J S Moore* a68 57
3 ch g Intikhab(USA) —Swing City (IRE) (Indian Ridge)
700^2 974^9 2545^9 3475^2 3752^{12} 4919^5 5134^6 5900^2 (6100) 6533^2

Emma's Secrets *Miss M E Rowland* 40
2 b f Fraam—Hopping Higgins (IRE) (Brief Truce (USA))
1528^7 2109^6 6093^{12}

Emmpat (IRE) *C F Swan* a100 94
9 b g Bigstone(IRE) —Nordic Abu (IRE) (Nordico (USA))
(4867a)

Emmrooz *Saeed Bin Suroor* 105
2 b c Red Ransom(USA) —Nasmatt (Danehill (USA))
5010^2 (5417) 5795^7 6297^3

Emotive *F P Murtagh* a59 66
4 b g Pursuit Of Love—Ruby Julie (Clantime)
1488^{15} 2714^{14} 4246^3 5626^8 6561^8

Emperor Cat (IRE) *Mrs N S Evans* a37 49
6 b g Desert Story(IRE) —Catfoot Lane (Batshoof)
2619^{11} 4256^{15}

Emperor Court (IRE) *P J Makin* a68 65
3 ch c Singspiel(IRE) —Tarquina (USA) (Niniski (USA))
1468^7 2542^3 3454^4 6005^4 6766^3 7282^2

Emperors Jade *A P Jarvis* a72 45
2 b c Averti(IRE) —Bliss (IRE) (Statoblest)
5550^9 6234^{10} 6641^2

Emperor's Well *M W Easterby* a55 74
8 ch g First Trump—Catherines Well (Junius (USA))
2431^{12} 2714^3 3195^3 3376^2 (3754) (4042) 4177^2 4353^8 4817^6 5557^{10} 5905^{12} 6598^{13}

Empire Dancer (IRE) *I W McInnes* a73 73
4 b g Second Empire(IRE) —Dance To The Beat (Batshoof)
3396^{11} 3599^6 3926^4 (4295) 4731^3 5114^{10} 5532^{11} 5893^6 6413^{10} 6955^4 7024^4 7104^6

Empire Seeker (USA) *B J Meehan* 65
2 b c Seeking The Gold(USA) —Lady From Shanghai (USA) (Storm Cat (USA))
6494^8

Empirical Power (IRE) *Edward Lynam* 105
6 b g Second Empire(IRE) —Rumuz (IRE) (Marju (IRE))
5242a^6 5842a^{10} 6036a^4

Empreinte Celebre (IRE) *J-C Rouget* a84 94
3 ch f Peintre Celebre(USA) —Arlesiana (USA) (Woodman (USA))
989a^6

Empress Jain *M A Jarvis* a87 100
4 br m Lujain(USA) —Akhira (Emperor Jones (USA))
1372^3 2352^7

Empress Olga (USA) *E A L Dunlop* a72 66
3 b f Kingmambo(USA) —Balistroika (USA) (Nijinsky (CAN))
689^2 908^2 1131^5

Emulate *B W Hills* a76 69
3 b f Alhaarth(IRE) —Aquarelle (Kenmare (FR))
1929^8 2767^6

Enactment *Sir Michael Stoute* 78
2 ch c Pivotal—Live Your Dreams (USA) (Mt. Livermore (USA))
2303^{10} 3733^4 4285^2 (5167) 5629^4

Enchanted Lady *H J L Dunlop* a42 46
2 b f Dr Fong(USA) —Enchanted Princess (Royal Applause)
3187^8 4683^9 5126^{10} 5442^7 5706^4 6586^8

Encinas (GER) *K McLaughlin* 90
6 br g Lomitas—Epik (GER) (Selkirk (USA))
412a^{10} 6771a^{10}

Encircled *D Haydn Jones* a69 86
3 b f In The Wings—Ring Of Esteem (Mark Of Esteem (IRE))
1722^8 (2475) 3058^3 3691^8

Encores *M G Quinlan* a76 71
3 b g Tobougg(IRE) —Western Applause (Royal Applause)
901^3 1177^4 1440^{10} 2456^5 (3056) 3384^3 3622^7 5645^4 6413^2 (6533) 6749^3

Endeavor *P Monteith* 10
2 ch g Selkirk(USA) —Midnight Mambo (USA) (Kingmambo (USA))
5904^{14}

Endiamo (IRE) *M P Tregoning* a79 96
3 ch g Indian Ridge—Aldafra (Spectrum (IRE))
(456) 2671^2 3334^5

Endless Luck (USA) *M Johnston* 88
2 bb c Giant's Causeway(USA) —Endless Parade (USA) (Williamstown (USA))
6252^2 (6740)

Endless Night *A M Hales* a64 65
4 ch g Dracula(AUS) —La Notte (Factual (USA))
379^9 4416^{16} 4915^8

Endless Power (IRE) *J S Goldie* a35
7 b g Perugino(USA) —Charroux (IRE) (Darshaan)
537^6

Endless Summer *A W Carroll* a45 73
10 b g Zafonic(USA) —Well Away (IRE) (Sadler's Wells (USA))
1681^{10} 2664^7 3594^5 4635^2 4881^3 5191^3 5349^6 5726^6 6239^6 6424^2 6608^8

End Of An Error *G F Bridgwater* 25
8 b m Charmer—Needwood Poppy (Rolfe (USA))
3036^6

Enflame *T T Clement*
3 b f Mtoto—Eternal Flame (Primo Dominie)
505^8

Enforce (USA) *E A L Dunlop* a88 95
4 bb m Kalanisi(IRE) —Kinetic Force (USA) (Holy Bull (USA))
1472^6 3028^6 6604^5 6757^4

English Archer *W M Brisbourne* 54
4 b g Rock City—Fire Sprite (Mummy's Game)
2156^6 2721^6 3035^8 (3679) 4156^6 4534^2 4972^{10} 6259^9 6453^8 6558^{14}

English Channel (USA) *T Pletcher* 124
5 ch h Smart Strike(CAN) —Belva (USA) (Theatrical)
862a^{12} 4415a^2 (5853a) (6513a)

English City (IRE) *Mrs L B Normile* a45 61
4 ch h City On A Hill(USA) —Toledana (IRE) (Sure Blade (USA))
3815^{12}

English Colony *A Penna* 111
3 b r Rock Of Gibraltar(IRE) —Jemima (Owington)
5823a^5

English Way (FR) *S-A Ghoumrassi*
2 ch c Gold Away(IRE) —Sogno (Rudimentary (USA))
6888a^0

Engrupido (ARG) *M F De Kock* a85 98
4 gr h Potrillon(ARG) —Una Gata (ARG) (Equalize (USA))
178a^8 410a^7

Enjoy The Buzz *J M Bradley* a50 62
8 b h Prince Of Birds(USA) —Abaklea (IRE) (Doyoun)
1212^{11} 1405^9 2108^6 2555^6 2982^9 3086^6 3368^6 3449^8 4390^8 4594^7 5090^7 5349^{13} 5861^{10} 6199^{16}

Enjoy The Moment *J A Osborne* 106
4 b g Generous(IRE) —Denial (Sadler's Wells (USA))
1244[10] 1582[3] 2736[14] (2860) 3898[8] 4569[4] 6335[20]

Enodoc *W R Muir* a67 84
2 b g Efisio—Raindrop (Primo Dominie)
1058[7] (1469) 1897[5] 2737[12] 4046[15] *4358[4]* 4991[11] 5480[8] *6004[7]*

Enrisy (FR) *Mme L Audon* a63
2 b c Enrique—Miss Adelaide (FR) (Exit To Nowhere (USA))
7027a[7]

Enroller (IRE) *W R Muir* 77
2 b c Marju(IRE) —Walk On Quest (FR) (Rainbow Quest (USA))
4362[12] 5813[5] 6130[4]

Ensign's Trick *W M Brisbourne* a26 70
3 b f Cayman Kai(IRE) —River Ensign (River God (USA))
1091[14] 1430[5] (1561) 1766[9] 2080[2] 2515[9] 2750[6] 3588[5] 4855[8] 5191[15] 5627[7]

Ensis (SPA) *O Rodriguez* 95
2 b f Zieten(USA) —Come Along (FR) (Exit To Nowhere (USA))
4653a[6] 6630a[4]

Enthralled *Sir Mark Prescott* a25
4 br m Zafonic(USA) —Artifice (Green Desert (USA))
13[6]

Enthusius *G L Moore* a60 51
4 b g Generous(IRE) —Edouna (FR) (Doyoun)
(416) 612[4] 1026[7] *7012[3]*

Enticing (IRE) *W J Haggas* a95 115
3 b f Pivotal—Superstar Leo (IRE) (College Chapel)
(1372) 2733[5] 3344[4] 4090[2] 5632[2]

Entranced *L Lungo* a69 64
4 b m Saddlers' Hall(IRE) —Vent D'Aout (IRE) (Imp Society (USA))
1627[13] 1892[8] 2302[12] *3173[10]*

Entre Chat *M Botti* a51 53
3 b f Green Desert(USA) —Dance Sequence (USA) (Mr Prospector (USA))
1045[7] 1639[16] 2137[6]

Envisage (IRE) *Saeed Bin Suroor* 88
3 b g Singspiel(IRE) —Truly A Dream (IRE) (Darshaan)
(6109) 6490[6]

Ephesian (IRE) *C L Popham* a23 50
2 b f Efisio—Maddie G (USA) (Blush Rambler (USA))
1079[7] *1727[11]* 3200[8] 3673[7] *5017[8]* 6194[6]

Ephorus (USA) *Sir Michael Stoute* a63
2 b c Galileo(IRE) —No Frills (IRE) (Darshaan)
6855[8]

Epices *R Ingram* a38 21
5 b g Mtoto—French Spice (Cadeaux Genereux)
123[F] (Dead)

Epicurean *Mrs K Walton* a46 71
5 ch m Pursuit Of Love—Arminda (Blakeney)
1258[11] 3956[5] 5255[12]

Epidaurian King (IRE) *D Shaw* a59
4 b g King's Best(USA) —Thurayya (Nashwan (USA))
36[7] 311[9] 1232[3] 1350[8] 6339[8] 6706[14] 6809[8] 7034[4] (7278)

Epona Miss (AUS) *D Saxon* 82
6 ch m Jeune—Candy Blue (AUS) (Bluebird (USA))
6711a[10]

Epsom Salts *P M Phelan* a53 55
2 b g Josr Algarhoud(IRE) —Captive Heart (Conquistador Cielo (USA))
5720[8] *6403[8] 6820[10]*

Equiano (FR) *M Delcher* 105
2 b c Acclamation—Entente Cordiale (IRE) (Ela-Mana-Mou)
6631a[3]

Equilibria (USA) *G L Moore* a52 57
5 b g Gulch(USA) —Julie La Rousse (IRE) (Lomond (USA))
278[4] 482[10] 3448[11]

Equip Hill (SWE) *B Bo* 107
5 b g Homme D'Honneur(FR) —Energiya Sacc (SWE) (Exceller (USA))
(4218a) 5263a[6] 6353a[8]

Equuleus Pictor *J L Spearing* a63 71
3 br g Piccolo—Vax Rapide (Sharpo)
2197[8] (3583) 3885[7] 4574[11] 5662[8] 6103[4] 6575[4]

Eradicate (IRE) *M Johnston* 104
3 b g Montjeu(IRE) —Coyote (Indian Ridge)
849[2] 1093[3] (1369) 2057[2] (2448) 2790[4] 3461[12] 4059[15] 4690[16] 5631[6] 5978[4]

Ergo (FR) *James Moffatt* 58
3 bb c Grand Lodge(USA) —Erhawah (Mark Of Esteem (IRE))
5906[12]

Eridani (IRE) *M L W Bell* a44 35
3 ch f Daggers Drawn(USA) —Rorkes Drift (IRE) (Royal Abjar (USA))
3351[11] 3803[10]

Erimo Harrier (JPN) *H Tadokoro* 111
7 b g Generous(IRE) —Erimo Hustler (JPN) (Bravest Roman (USA))
6943a[12]

Erin Thomas (IRE) *M G Quinlan* a53
2 ch f High Yield(USA) —Lyric Theatre (USA) (Seeking The Gold (USA))
2797[4] 3378[8] 4026[9] *5096[6] 6022[9] 6225[10] 6312[6]*

Ermine Grey *A W Carroll* a48 71
6 gr g Wolfhound(USA) —Impulsive Decision (IRE) (Nomination)
2194[8] 2603[4] 2716[2] 2980[3] (3571) 3907[9] 4481[3] 4878[11] *5391[6] 5569[10] 5890[6]*

Ernie Owl (USA) *B J Meehan* a91 87
2 b c Tale Of The Cat(USA) —Capitol View (USA) (Sports View (USA))
2732[16] (4335) 5048[9] 5350[5] *6001[5] 6270[2]* 6488[10]

Ernmoor *J R Jenkins* a41 51
5 b g Young Ern—Linpac North Moor (Moorestyle)
3186[12] 4707[3] 5188[8] 6238[6] *6713[10] 7069[14]*

Erra Go On *Adrian McGuinness* a83 83
6 ch g Atraf—Pastelle (Tate Gallery (USA))
32[6] 44[7]

Errigal Lad *K A Ryan* 81
2 ch g Bertolini(USA) —La Belle Vie (Indian King (USA))
4076[2] (5194) 5974[17]

Erte *W Storey* 51
6 ch g Vettori(IRE) —Cragreen (Green Desert (USA))
64[10] 3815[11] 4179[5] (4451) 4925[5] 5283[11] 5626[9]

Escape Route (USA) *J H M Gosden* a98 104
3 b g Elusive Quality(USA) —Away (USA) (Dixieland Band (USA))
1124[3] *1930[3]* 4851[6] (5419) 6011[15]

Escayola (IRE) *Grant Tuer* a85 90
7 b g Revoque(IRE) —First Fling (IRE) (Last Tycoon (IRE))
1300[4] 1654[8] 2449[P] (Dead)

Esclarmonde (IRE) *L M Cumani* a74 71
3 b f In The Wings—Questina (FR) (Rainbow Quest (USA))
1785[8] 2620[6] 3366[4] 4172[2] 4758[6] 5573[8] 6276[3] *6878[2] 7076[3] 7282[4]*

Escobar (POL) *Mrs P Townsley* a10 48
6 b g Royal Court(IRE) —Escola (POL) (Dixieland (POL))
2055[7] *7012[13]*

Escoffier *M Appleby* a64 32
5 b g Entrepreneur—Gooseberry Pie (Green Desert (USA))
88[4] 767[3] 6501[7] 6564[10] 6815[12]

Eseej (USA) *B W Hills* 63
2 ch g Aljabr(USA) —Jinaan (USA) (Mr Prospector (USA))
4725[10] 5313[6]

Eskimo Queen (NZ) *M Moroney* 111
4 b m Shinko King(IRE) —Cold Type (NZ) (Icelandic)
6712a[15]

Esoterica (IRE) *J S Goldie* 75
4 b g Bluebird(USA) —Mysterious Plans (IRE) (Last Tycoon (IRE))
967[8] 1459[9] 1892[10] 2117[4] 2823[4] 3816[7] 4100[2] (4137) 4353[5] 4931[4] (5159) (5228) 5556[4] 5840[9] 5905[5] 6463[4] 6701[4] 6746[2]

Espartano *R McGlinchey* a85 86
3 b g Vettori(IRE) —Talighta (USA) (Barathea (IRE))
1604[9] 5460a[18]

Especially (IRE) *M Johnston* a67 66
2 b f Fantastic Light(USA) —Esperada (ARG) (Equalize (USA))
2888[4] 5720[3] *6140[9] 6584[10] (7176)*

Espejo (IRE) *W J Musson* 70
3 b g City On A Hill(USA) —Beechwood Quest (IRE) (River Falls)
1131[8] 1684[8] 2110[12] 2200[7] 3843[6] 4550[6]

Espoir De Lumiere *C F Wall* 51
3 b f Mark Of Esteem(IRE) —Lumiere D'Espoir (FR) (Saumarez)
1812[10]

Esprit De Corps *P J Hobbs* a56 79
5 b g Hernando(FR) —Entente Cordiale (USA) (Affirmed (USA))
4056[4] 6131[10]

Esprit De Nuit (IRE) *Mrs A Duffield* a47 17
3 b g Invincible Spirit(IRE) —Night Spirit (IRE) (Night Shift (USA))
222[13] 1240[9] 1426[10] 2895[9]

Essential Edge (CAN) *E Coatrieux* a88 106
4 ch m Storm Cat(USA) —Rose Of Tara (IRE) (Generous (IRE))
6373a[6]

Establishment *John A Harris* a83 83
10 b g Muhtarram(USA) —Uncharted Waters (Celestial Storm (USA))
844[7] 1148[13] *3216[7]* 3533[6] 3976[3]

Estate *E J O'Neill* a82 80
5 b g Montjeu(IRE) —Fig Tree Drive (USA) (Miswaki (USA))
4582[16] (6200) *(6341)* 6473[8] (6733) *6802[4] 6875[2]*

Esteem *W Jarvis* a74 77
4 b g Mark Of Esteem(IRE) —Please (Kris)
2004[15] *3215[7]*

Esteemed Prince *D Shaw* a52 44
3 b g Mark Of Esteem(IRE) —Princess Alaska (Northern State (USA))
711[8] 894[6] 4078[10] *4977[11] 5175[5] 5752[6]*

Esteem Machine (USA) *R A Teal* a78 96
3 b c Mark Of Esteem(IRE) —Theme (IRE) (Sadler's Wells (USA))
311[3] 456[4] 826[2] 1606[5] 2059[2] 2542[2] (3948) 4574[2] (4816) 5449[2] 5765[3] 6205[13]

Estejo (GER) *R Rohne* 102
3 b c Johan Cruyff—Este (GER) (The Noble Player (USA))
6223a[7]

Esthlos (FR) *J Jay* a89 94
4 ch g Limnos(JPN) —Cozzie (Cosmonaut)
675[11] (770) (850) *1180[3]* 6014[6] (6158) 6302[3]

Estimator *Pat Eddery* a77 64
3 b c Auction House(USA) —Fresh Look (IRE) (Alzao (USA))
1108[11] 1660[8] *5684[6] 6231[9]*

Estoille *Mrs S Lamyman* a56 58
6 b m Paris House—Nampara Bay (Emarati (USA))
239[10] 320[6] 523[3] 626[9] 680[10] (Dead)

Estrela Brono (BRZ) *C Morgado* a68 80
5 b h Roi Normand(USA) —Miss Dourness (BRZ) (Ghadeer (FR))
330a[10] 473a[8] *532a[12]*

Estrela Brynhild (USA) *C Morgado* 85
4 bb m Lion Cavern(USA) —Sunset Song (USA) (Dixieland Band (USA))
174a[9] 397a[11] 546a[9]

Etain (IRE) *W R Swinburn* a63 75
3 b f Alhaarth(IRE) —Brogan's Well (IRE) (Caerleon (USA))
1282[3] 1639[7] 2219[4] (2940) 3964[6]

Et Dona Ferentes *T D Barron* a56 58
4 b m Green Desert(USA) —Sister Golden Hair (IRE) (Glint Of Gold)
77[6] 217[2] (393) 518[3]

Etenia (USA) *S Wattel* 95
2 ch f Hennessy(USA) —Eternally (USA) (Timeless Moment (USA))
4653a[4] 5373a[5]

Eternal Legacy (IRE) *E J Alston* a5 63
5 b m Monashee Mountain(USA) —Tender Time (Tender King)
1197[7] 1596[4] 1625[2] 2711[6] (3051) 3345[13] 3765[3] 3999[5] 4129[9] 4705[2] 5907[4] 6467[12] 6638[2]

Eternal Luck (IRE) *M A Jarvis* 81
2 b c Tagula(IRE) —Erne Project (IRE) (Project Manager)
(2510) 3025[2]

Eternally *R M H Cowell* a45 36
5 ch g Timeless Times(USA) —Nice Spice (IRE) (Common Grounds)
143[7]

Eternal Optimist (IRE) *C W Thornton* a56 56
2 b f Bahri(USA) —Shore Lark (USA) (Storm Bird (CAN))
4041[8] 4522[9] 4924[12] 5154[9] 5502[3] 5965[6] *6066[8] 6478[5] 6750[6] 7007[3]*

Eternal Path (USA) *Sir Michael Stoute* 81
3 ch f Theatrical—Houdini's Honey (USA) (Mr Prospector (USA))
1127[3] 1785[4]

Eternity Boy (IRE) *G Colella* 69
3 b c Monashee Mountain(USA) —Mindy Girl (IRE) (Last Tycoon (IRE))
1875a[14]

Ethereal Flame *H R A Cecil* 64
2 b f Red Ransom(USA) —Running Flame (IND) (Steinbeck (USA))
5913[8] 6411[7]

Etmaam *S Seemar* a71 73
6 b g Intikhab(USA) —Sudeley (Dancing Brave (USA))
104a[5]

Etoile D'Or (IRE) *M H Tompkins* 63
3 ch f Soviet Star(USA) —Christeningpresent (IRE) (Cadeaux Genereux)
2008[9] 2834[13] 3804[6] 4894[7] 5640[6] 6108[2] (6408)

Etoile Nocturne (FR) *F Rohaut* a84 90
3 b f Medicean—Nachtigall (FR) (Night Shift (USA))
6224a[7]

Etoile Russe (IRE) *P C Haslam* a46 67
5 b g Soviet Star(USA) —To The Skies (USA) (Sky Classic (CAN))
913[11]

Eton Fable (IRE) *W J H Ratcliffe* 66
2 b c Val Royal(FR) —Lina Story (Linamix (FR))
3977[5] 4487[9] 5904[4] 6379[7] 6593[5]

Etosha (IRE) *Saeed Bin Suroor* 73
2 b c Cape Cross(IRE) —Zibilene (Rainbow Quest (USA))
6295[7]

Etruscan (IRE) *Saeed Bin Suroor* 70
2 b g Selkirk(USA) —Maddelina (IRE) (Sadler's Wells (USA))
6107[2] 6592[7]

Ettrbee (IRE) *H Alexander*
5 bb m Lujain(USA) —Chief Ornament (USA) (Chief's Crown (USA))
374[11] 1376[9]

Etxalar (FR) *Miss Lucinda V Russell* 74
4 b g Kingsalsa(USA) —Tender To Love (Old Vic)
6257[9]

Eumene (IRE) *C C Bealby* a91 86
4 ch g Grand Lodge(USA) —Pelagic (Rainbow Quest (USA))
6995[4] 7147[2]

European Dream (IRE) *R C Guest* 108
4 br g Kalanisi(IRE) —Tereed Elhawa (Cadeaux Genereux)
(846) 1145[19] 1583[6] (1860) (2891) 3026[8] (3513) 6655[8]

Eu Tambem (BRZ) *Saeed Bin Suroor* a107
4 b h Wild Event(USA) —Charmosa (ARG) (Fain (ARG))
(601a) 859a[7]

Evaluator (IRE) *A Al Raihe* a56 74
6 b g Ela-Mana-Mou—Summerhill (Habitat)
471a[13] 541a[9]

Eva Soneva So Fast (IRE) *J L Dunlop* a100 86
5 ch g In The Wings—Azyaa (Kris)
(95) 345[2] 608[2] 698[4] 829[4] 1844[9] 2859[8] 3509[12] 4171[5] 4572[7] 5870[9] *(6230)*

Eva's Request (IRE) *M R Channon* a79 100
2 ch f Soviet Star(USA) —Ingabelle (Taufan (USA))
2364[8] *(2992) 3642[4]* 4202[5] 4804[3] 5395a[8] (5843a)

Even Bolder *R Simpson* a79 78
4 ch g Bold Edge—Level Pegging (IRE) (Common Grounds)
2242[4] 2673[9] *3190[4] 3852[5] (4066) 4944[2]* 5160[2] 5447[2]

Evening Affair *Saeed Bin Suroor* 64
3 b f Kingmambo(USA) —Neptune's Bride (USA) (Bering)
4549[3] (4845)

Evening Time (IRE) *Kevin Prendergast* 112
3 gr f Keltos(FR) —Shadow Casting (Warning)
3575a[3] 4438a[2] 5241a[8] 5842a[6]

Evens And Odds (IRE) *K A Ryan* a100 97
3 ch c Johannesburg(USA) —Coeur De La Mer (IRE) (Caerleon (USA))
760[3] 1473[23] 5355[6] 6301[7] *6852[3] 6932[10] 7074[7] 7223[3]*

Evenstorm (USA) *B Gubby* a61 61
2 ch f Stephen Got Even(USA) —Summer Wind Storm (USA) (Storm Cat (USA))
1896[8] 2271[3] 2630[5] 2756[17] *3648[6] 4065[7]* 4152[10] *4737[3]* 5357[10] *7280[8]*

Event Music (IRE) *M R Channon* 73
3 ch f Distant Music(USA) —Evening Set (GER) (Second Set (IRE))
1359[8] 1684[4] 2061[11] 2545[10]

Event Open (GER) *W Hefter* 63
2 b c Orpen(USA) —Evening Set (GER) (Second Set (IRE))
6324a[8]

Ever Bright (NZ) *P O'Sullivan* 113
4 b g Cape Cross(IRE) —Anna's Choice (NZ) (Vice Regal (NZ))
7090a[8]

Ever Cheerful *A B Haynes* a75 58
6 b g Atraf—Big Story (Cadeaux Genereux)
132[9] 183[4] 536[4] 622[5] 734[2] 3045[3] 3549[6] *3852[8]* 4312[7] 4689[11] *6210[3] (6607) 6825[2] 6870[2] 6925[3] 7119[3]*

Ever Dreaming (USA) *A M Balding* a61 58
2 bb f Dynaformer(USA) —Slept Thru It (USA) (Sunny's Halo (CAN))
4402[9] 4852[9] *7145[6]*

Everest (IRE) *B Ellison* a76 86
10 ch g Indian Ridge—Reine D'Beaute (Caerleon (USA))
932[8] 1040[11] 1308[9] 1744[7] 2027[3] 2709[2] 3049[9]

Evergrey (FR) *P Khozian* 88
2 gr f Verglas(IRE) —Eretria (USA) (Dynaformer (USA))
4626a[5]

Ever Hopeful *H J L Dunlop* a41 62
2 br f Noverre(USA) —Heather Mix (Linamix (FR))
2468[14] 4310[6] 4629[3] *5097[7]* 5429[2] 6104[3] 6419[10]

Ever Special (IRE) *J T Stimpson* a32
4 b g Fruits Of Love(USA) —El Corazon (IRE) (Mujadil (USA))
683[9]

Everybody Knows *M L W Bell* a64
2 b c King's Best(USA) —Logic (Slip Anchor)
5116[6]

Every Day (GER) *Mario Hofer* 90
2 b f Sholokhov(IRE) —En Vogue (GER) (Dashing Blade)
5028a[5] 6371a[6]

Everygrainofsand (IRE) *J R Best* a79 83
4 b g Desert Sun—Serious Delight (Lomond (USA))
901[5] *1117[4] 1447[3]* 1541[2] *1931[4]* (2242) 2458[4] (3802) 4140[5] *5119[6]*

Everyman *A W Carroll* a52 57
3 gr g Act One—Maid To Dance (Pyramus (USA))
2079[9] 2653[P] 2915[5] 4333[8] 5698[3] (6090) 6250[4] *6292[4] 6590[5] 7109[8]*

Everymanforhimself (IRE) *J G Given* 96
3 b c Fasliyev(USA) —Luisa Demon (IRE) (Barathea (IRE))
1124[13] 1298[11] 1667[5] 2044[4] 3078[9] 4374[9] 4898[3] 5168[10] (5473) 5765[4] 6205[3]

Everything *P T Midgley* 70
2 bl f Namid—Flight Sequence (Polar Falcon (USA))
1993[P] 3200[7] 3812[4] 4076[4] 4923[3]

Evette *M Johnston* a43 42
2 b f Loup Solitaire(USA) —La Scarlet (FR) (Highest Honor (FR))
5727[12] 5901[6] 6303[8] *6775[5]*

Evident Pride (USA) *B R Johnson* a104 89
4 b g Chester House(USA) —Proud Fact (USA) (Known Fact (USA))
870[2] 1568[7] (4068) 4455[4] *5221[2] 5685[3] (6669) (7163)*

Evil Knievel (BRZ) *Christian Wroe* a36 107
8 b h Legal Case—Rhana (BRZ) (Sharannpour)
176a[12] 330a[5] 544a[10]

Evinado (GER) *Werner Glanz* 83
8 ch g Zinaad—Evry (GER) (Torgos)
2409a[6]

Evita *L M Cumani* a72 64
3 b f Selkirk(USA) —Darara (Top Ville)
1296[5] 1685[4] *6314[2] 6506[7] 7046[4] 7173[3]*

Evolution Ex (USA) *I W McInnes* a53 73
5 bb g Bahri(USA) —Zoe's Gold (USA) (St Jovite (USA))
12[9] 1086[13] 2307[9] 2795[12]

Evolve (USA) *M Botti* a61 50
4 ch m With Approval(CAN) —Conical (Zafonic (USA))
(84) 369[6] 903[7]

Excape (IRE) *D R C Elsworth* 63
2 b c Cape Cross(IRE) —Viscaria (IRE) (Barathea (IRE))
2600[9] 2885[4] 3435[15]

Excelerate (IRE) *Edward Lynam* 108
4 b g Mujadil(USA) —Perle D'Irlande (FR) (Top Ville)
3140a[3] 4211a[15] 5242a[2] 6038a[2]

Excellent Art *A P O'Brien* 124
3 b c Pivotal—Obsessive (USA) (Seeking The Gold (USA))
1703a[4] (2734) 4058[2] 5798[2] 6511a[2] 7091a[8]

Excessive *W Jarvis* a72 63
3 ch f Cadeaux Genereux—Show Off (Efisio)
1635[2] 2242[2] (3031) 3713[5] 4545[6] *5136[2] (5643) 6232[7]*

Excitement (IRE) *R A Fahey* 82
2 b f Xaar—Sunny Slope (Mujtahid (USA))
4733[4] (5252) 6154[3]

Exclamation *B J Meehan* 98
2 br c Acclamation—Summer Siren (FR) (Saint Cyrien (FR))
4198[5] (5772) (5974)

Exclusionist *J Noseda* 71
3 ch c In The Wings—Groom Order (Groom Dancer (USA))
2726[4] 4771[3]

Excusez Moi (USA) *C E Brittain* a97 111
5 b h Fusaichi Pegasus(USA) —Jiving (Generous (IRE))
415a[9] *597a[14] 762[9]* 1102[9] 1294[2] 1656[2] 2184[7] 3088[8] 6491[7]

Executive Paddy (IRE) *I A Wood* a63
8 b g Executive Perk—Illbethereforyou (IRE) (Supreme Leader)
89[14] 195[14] 548[9] 610[12]

Exhibition (IRE) *N A Callaghan* 100
2 b c Invincible Spirit(IRE) —Moonbi Ridge (IRE) (Definite Article)
3435[3] (3712) 4120[3]

Exhibit One (USA) *V Valiani* 110
5 b m Silver Hawk(USA) —Tsar's Pride (Sadler's Wells (USA))
1192a[2] (1874a) 2706a[3]

Exit Fast (USA) *P T Midgley* a48 30
6 ch g Announce(USA) —Distinct Beauty (USA) (Phone Trick (USA))
464^{10} 630^{6} 730^{2} 909^{10} 966^{12} 1554^{9}

Exit Smiling *P T Midgley* a76 81
5 ch g Dr Fong(USA) —Away To Me (Exit To Nowhere (USA))
63^{7} 732^{3} (1040) 1264^{2} 2374^{2} 2986^{8} 3556^{7} 4176^{9} 4820^{5} 5339^{11} 5559^{6} 6016^{13}

Exit Strategy (IRE) *R A Harris* a52 70
3 b g Cadeaux Genereux—Black Belt Shopper (IRE) (Desert Prince (IRE))
1850^{5} 2224^{6} 2545^{3} (3342) 3713^{4} 3872^{4} 5711^{10} 6455^{8} 6818^{13}

Exit To Luck (GER) *S Gollings* a74 52
6 b g Exit To Nowhere(USA) —Emy Coasting (USA) (El Gran Senor (USA))
1997^{9} 2348^{2} 2839^{6}

Exodia *Jane Chapple-Hyam* a69 62
2 b f Dr Fong(USA) —Fenella's Link (Linamix (FR))
3055^{10} 3706^{12} 4883^{6} 5308^{6}

Exotic Venture *R M Beckett* a56 53
4 b m Piccolo—Bay Risk (Risk Me (FR))
1973^{3} 2878^{12} 3409^{6} 4023^{4} 5094^{10}

Expected Bonus (USA) *Jamie Poulton* a51 46
8 bb g Kris S(USA) —Nidd (USA) (Known Fact (USA))
187^{3} 273^{3} 495^{11} 610^{10}

Expedience (USA) *Sir Michael Stoute* a61 72
3 gr f With Approval(CAN) —Promptly (IRE) (Lead On Time (USA))
1639^{5} 2261^{6} (2962)

Expediter *H Candy* 54
2 b f Bahamian Bounty—Iris May (Brief Truce (USA))
5003^{9} 6281^{10}

Expensive *C F Wall* a98 101
4 b m Royal Applause—Vayavaig (Damister (USA))
$174a^{3}$ $397a^{6}$ $546a^{6}$ (938) 1466^{2} (2507) 2753^{9} 5354^{14}

Expensive Art (IRE) *N A Callaghan* a86 70
3 b f Cape Cross(IRE) —Walnut Lady (Forzando)
1175^{2} 1403^{3} 1737^{4} (3649) 3872^{2} 4295^{5} 5495^{7} (6559) 6794^{3} 6930^{9}

Expensive Detour (IRE) *Mrs L Stubbs* 75
3 b g Namid—Sail With The Wind (Saddlers' Hall (IRE))
(1679) 4222^{7} 5635^{15}

Expensive Dream (GER) *P Vovcenko* 110
8 b g Lomitas—Eurydike (GER) (Anfield)
$1190a^{6}$ $1872a^{7}$ $2924a^{6}$

Experimental (IRE) *John A Harris* a57 50
13 b g Top Of The World—Brun's Toy (FR) (Bruni)
64^{2} 242^{9} 372^{6} (1362) 1730^{7} 2307^{4}

Explode *Miss L C Siddall* a40 54
10 b g Zafonic(USA) —Didicoy (USA) (Danzig (USA))
3204^{9} 3638^{3} 4580^{12}

Explosive Fox (IRE) *S Curran* a64 66
6 gr g Foxhound(USA) —Grise Mine (FR) (Crystal Palace (FR))
665^{9} 3598^{6} 5426^{10}

Exponential (IRE) *J M Bradley* a21 72
5 b g Namid—Exponent (USA) (Exbourne (USA))
(1212) 1405^{8} 2390^{5} 2805^{5} 3859^{5} 4233^{13} 4734^{8} 4853^{14} 5861^{11} 6149^{11}

Express Princess (IRE) *M Botti* a60
2 b f Desert Prince(IRE) —Nashwan Star (IRE) (Nashwan (USA))
5727^{7} 5984^{3} 6626^{3} 6912^{3} 7031^{12}

Express Way (BRZ) *M F De Kock* 108
5 ch h Royal Academy(USA) —Night Fall (BRZ) (Roi Normand (USA))
$247a^{7}$ $411a^{3}$ $542a^{2}$

Express Wish *J Noseda* a77 95
3 b c Danehill Dancer(IRE) —Waffle On (Chief Singer)
1037^{2} (1737) (2395) 3431^{10} 5356^{9}

Extractor *J L Dunlop* 57
3 b g Siphon(BRZ) —Tri Pac (IRE) (Fairy King (USA))
1155^{13} 1634^{6} 2186^{4}

Extraterrestrial *Kevin Prendergast* a63 98
3 b g Mind Games—Expectation (IRE) (Night Shift (USA))
$2324a^{8}$ $4211a^{11}$

Extravagance (IRE) *L M Cumani* a53 68
3 b f King's Best(USA) —Meritxell (IRE) (Thatching)
2012^{3} 2472^{9}

Extreme Measures *Saeed Bin Suroor* 79
4 b h Montjeu(IRE) —Fade (Persepolis (FR))
6185^{7}

Extreme North (USA) *Miss V Haigh* a57
2 b g Stravinsky(USA) —North Dream (USA) (Unbridled's Song (USA))
7264^{9}

Eye Catching *J R Jenkins* 58
2 b f Diktat—Fifth Emerald (Formidable (USA))
2122^{7} 2364^{6} 2717^{5} 5089^{16} 5529^{12} 6234^{8} 6414^{13}

Eyshal (IRE) *John M Oxx* 105
3 b c Green Desert(USA) —Ebadiyla (IRE) (Sadler's Wells (USA))
$1547a^{3}$ $2066a^{3}$

Ezdeyaad (USA) *G A Swinbank* 50
3 b g Lemon Drop Kid(USA) —August Storm (USA) (Storm Creek (USA))
4997^{3}

Ezdiyaad (IRE) *M P Tregoning* a61 87
3 b c Galileo(IRE) —Wijdan (USA) (Mr Prospector (USA))
3743^{10} 4275^{9} (4815) 5724^{3}

Ezima (IRE) *J S Bolger* a98 108
3 b f Sadler's Wells(USA) —Ezilla (IRE) (Darshaan)
$2066a^{8}$ $4867a^{3}$ (6367a)

Ezthegezza *J S Moore* a65 64
2 b g Tobougg(IRE) —Salvezza (IRE) (Superpower)
2596^{9} 3550^{5} 3902^{3} 4154^{3} $4832a^{21}$ 5509^{5} 5896^{4} 6379^{14}

E Z Warrior (USA) *B Baffert* a104
3 bb c Exploit(USA) —Carson Jen (USA) (Carson City (USA))
$5852a^{5}$

Fa A Mezz *A & G Botti* 101
4 b g Halling(USA) —Sispre (FR) (Master Willie)
$1518a^{7}$

Faber Hall Flyer *Mrs C A Dunnett* 76
2 b g Danetime(IRE) —Pinini (Pivotal)
3823^{5} 4335^{5} 4854^{3} 5470^{13} 6104^{2} 6409^{3}

Fabine *B J Meehan* a70
3 b f Danehill Dancer(IRE) —Waypoint (Cadeaux Genereux)
(1452)

Fabled (IRE) *Ms Joanna Morgan* 67
3 b c Mull Of Kintyre(USA) —Fable (Absalom)
$5460a^{20}$

Fabreze *P J Makin* 74
2 ch c Choisir(AUS) —Impulsive Decision (IRE) (Nomination)
5194^{4}

Fabrian *R J Price* a76 84
9 b g Danehill(USA) —Dockage (CAN) (Riverman (USA))
1922^{10} 2180^{6} 2401^{9} 2660^{4} 3882^{7} 4072^{2} 4419^{6} 4587^{2} 5012^{10} 5383^{7} 5472^{4} 5916^{13}

Fabuleux Cherie *W R Muir* a70 64
2 b f Noverre(USA) —Ashover Amber (Green Desert (USA))
1533^{6} 1993^{5} 2651^{9} 4016^{7} (4824) (5096) 5534^{3} 5715^{3} 5887^{2} 6227^{2} (6588) 6756^{16} 6834^{4} 7072^{3}

Fabuleux Millie (IRE) *R M Beckett* a81 83
3 ch f Noverre(USA) —Flying Millie (IRE) (Flying Spur (AUS))
2373^{7} 2769^{2} 3944^{3} 4360^{3} 4574^{9} 6900^{12}

Fabulous Strike (USA) *Todd M Beattie* a122 79
4 bb g Smart Strike(CAN) —Fabulous Find (USA) (Lost Code (USA))
(5852a)

Facchetti (USA) *A P O'Brien* 100
3 ch c Storm Cat(USA) —Twenty Eight Carat (USA) (Alydar (USA))
$1461a^{3}$ $2050a^{7}$ $2324a^{9}$

Factual Lad *B R Millman* a17 66
9 b g So Factual(USA) —Surprise Surprise (Robellino (USA))
2275^{3} 3048^{6} 4266^{6} 4878^{10}

Fadansil *J Wade* 55
4 b g Dansili—Fatah Flare (USA) (Alydar (USA))
1569^{9} 2254^{13} 3675^{10} 4526^{11} 4802^{3} (5000) 5482^{7} 5676^{10}

Fadhb Ar Bith (IRE) *John A Quinn* a73
2 b g Tagula(IRE) —Teodora (IRE) (Fairy King (USA))
(7217)

Fahed *J R Jenkins*
2 gr c Cool Jazz—Glowing Light (IRE) (Contract Law (USA))
2152^{5}

Fair Along (GER) *P J Hobbs* a67 103
5 b g Alkalde(GER) —Fairy Tango (FR) (Acatenango (GER))
1582^{2} 6335^{3}

Fair Breeze (GER) *Mario Hofer* 107
4 br m Silvano(GER) —Fairwind (GER) (Andrang (GER))
$1421a^{5}$ $2296a^{2}$ $3075a^{3}$ $4838a^{4}$ $6046a^{2}$ $6524a^{2}$ (6781a)

Fairdonna *D J Coakley* a64 67
4 ch m Bertolini(USA) —Shamrock Fair (IRE) (Shavian)
272^{3} 548^{10} (2257) 3110^{5}

Fairfield Princess *M S Saunders* a81 83
3 b f Inchinor—Cool Question (Polar Falcon (USA))
1520^{3} 1900^{11} 2494^{9} 3528^{8} 4574^{14} 5722^{17}

Fair Gale *S Kirk* a71
2 b g Storming Home—Triple Green (Green Desert (USA))
6262^{7} 6456^{2} 7070^{3} (7181)

Fairgame Man *J S Wainwright* a12 54
9 ch g Clantime—Thalya (Crofthall)
743^{8} 1423^{11} 3347^{11} 4038^{9} 4583^{14}

Fairly Honest *P W Hiatt* a70 71
3 b g Alhaarth(IRE) —Miller's Melody (Chief Singer)
1722^{3} 2598^{9} 3057^{5} 3629^{5} 3824^{4} 4270^{7} 4491^{7} 5310^{6} 5557^{11}

Fairmile *Saeed Bin Suroor* a100 117
5 b g Spectrum(IRE) —Juno Marlowe (IRE) (Danehill (USA))
(244a) $544a^{3}$ $645a^{3}$ 5326^{2} (6153) 6653^{2}

Fairmont (IRE) *M Johnston* 52
2 b f Kingmambo(USA) —Fiaafy (USA) (Gone West (USA))
4854^{5}

Fairnilee *Sir Mark Prescott* a67
3 b f Selkirk(USA) —Fantastic Belle (IRE) (Night Shift (USA))
(127) 520^{5}

Fair Sailing (IRE) *J W Hills* a58
3 ch f Docksider(USA) —Fair Of The Furze (Ela-Mana-Mou)
5390^{4} 6229^{4} 6704^{4}

Fair Shake (IRE) *Karen McLintock* a52 74
7 b g Sheikh Albadou—Shamrock Fair (IRE) (Shavian)
1040^{4} 1223^{11} 1747^{13} 3343^{8} 3765^{2} 3999^{13} 5556^{9} 5905^{13}

Fairson (TUR) *K Tekdogan* a107
4 b h Royal Abjar(USA) —Fair Tail (TUR) (Cossack Guard (USA))
$399a^{4}$ $5265a^{13}$

Fairy Dress (USA) *Robert Collet* a92 100
3 b f Fasliyev(USA) —Sun Spray (USA) (Woodman (USA))
$1006a^{5}$ $1702a^{9}$ $6940a^{0}$

Fairy Festival (IRE) *J S Moore* a50 48
3 b f Montjeu(IRE) —Escape To Victory (Salse (USA))
5894^{6} 6206^{5} 6315^{5}

Fairyland (GER) *S Wegner* 98
4 ch m Tertullian(USA) —Fairy Tango (FR) (Acatenango (GER))
$1517a^{4}$

Fairy Monarch (IRE) *P T Midgley* a52 58
8 b g Ali-Royal(IRE) —Cookawara (IRE) (Fairy King (USA))
1090^{9} 1132^{4} 1381^{5} 1413^{8} 1893^{9} 3814^{5} 4099^{3} 4449^{7} 4797^{8} 5255^{7} 5503^{17} 5966^{11} 6152^{7} 6261^{8}

Fairy Slipper *Jedd O'Keeffe* 38
3 b f Singspiel(IRE) —Fairlee Mixa (FR) (Linamix (FR))
1412^{8} 2299^{5}

Fairy Wood (IRE) *J L Dunlop* 38
2 b f Fasliyev(USA) —Fantasy Wood (IRE) (Charnwood Forest (IRE))
4662^{11}

Faith And Reason (USA) *B J Curley* a89 82
4 b g Sunday Silence(USA) —Sheer Reason (USA) (Danzig (USA))
850^{13} 1083^{8} 1638^{6} 2512^{11} 3042^{9} 4019^{12} 4610^{10} 5514^{12}

Faithful Ruler (USA) *M A Magnusson* a67
3 bb g Elusive Quality(USA) —Fancy Ruler (USA) (Half A Year (USA))
456^{11} 700^{5} 1282^{6} 6779^{4} (6895) 7269^{3}

Faiths Perfection (IRE) *John Rafferty* a30 58
4 ch m Docksider(USA) —Wrapitraise (USA) (Raise A Man (USA))
1750^{6}

Fajr (IRE) *Miss Gay Kelleway* a111 110
5 b g Green Desert(USA) —Ta Rib (USA) (Mr Prospector (USA))
(56) 197^{5} 993^{5} 1145^{8} 1818^{2} 2111^{3} 2817^{2} 3098^{3} 3505^{16} 6541^{4} 6726^{2} 6932^{2} 6992^{3} (7074) 7267^{3}

Falcativ *L M Cumani* 61
2 b c Falbrav(IRE) —Frottola (Muhtarram (USA))
5971^{12}

Falcolnry (IRE) *J R Fanshawe* 80
2 b f Hawk Wing(USA) —Fear And Greed (IRE) (Brief Truce (USA))
4102^{6} (4565) 5973^{14}

Falcon Flyer *J R Best* a46 45
3 br f Cape Cross(IRE) —Green Danube (USA) (Irish River (FR))
3950^{13} 4327^{6} 4914^{9} 6830^{4} 7029^{7} 7166^{4}

Falcon's Fire (IRE) *Mrs A Duffield* a56 63
3 b g Orpen(USA) —Tres Chic (USA) (Northern Fashion (USA))
1135^{2} (1425) 1538^{9} 2829^{10} 3411^{7} 4223^{3} 4894^{4} 5300^{2} 5482^{2}

Falcon Speed *P T Midgley* 44
2 b f Hunting Lion(IRE) —Efficacious (IRE) (Efisio)
3750^{7} 4002^{7} 4285^{6} 4715^{9} 5331^{10} 5520^{10}

Falimar *Miss J A Camacho* a59 64
3 b f Fasliyev(USA) —Mar Blue (FR) (Marju (IRE))
370^{7} 603^{3} 1256^{3} 2299^{2} 3722^{9} 4081^{9} 4846^{9} 5487^{5} 5967^{3}

Fallon (SAF) *S Seemar* 27
7 b g Model Man(SAF) —Miss Pennyfeather (SAF) (Only A Pound)
$244a^{12}$

Falmassim *Miss J A Camacho* a23 74
4 b g Mozart(IRE) —Scostes (Cadeaux Genereux)
717^{9} 895^{11} 1597^{12} 2576^{2} 3408^{12} 4083^{13} 4773^{10} 5085^{9} 5284^{6} 5966^{13}

Falpiase (IRE) *J Howard Johnson* a75 98
5 b g Montjeu(IRE) —Gift Of The Night (USA) (Slewpy (USA))
2170^{2} 3412^{2} 4091^{10} 4569^{12}

Familiar Affair *A Berry* a45 33
6 b g Intikhab(USA) —Familiar (USA) (Diesis)
6732^{11}

Familiar Territory *Saeed Bin Suroor* a105 112
4 br h Cape Cross(IRE) —Forever Fine (USA) (Sunshine Forever (USA))
(2351) 3899^{2} 4588^{3}

Famous Name *D K Weld* 101
2 b c Dansili—Fame At Last (USA) (Quest For Fame)
(3438a) $5458a^{6}$ $6549a^{2}$

Famous Seamus (IRE) *T J O'Mara* 79
4 b g City On A Hill(USA) —Sposa (USA) (St Jovite (USA))
$4836a^{15}$ $6553a^{16}$

Fanatical *E F Vaughan* 92
2 b f Mind Games—Mania (IRE) (Danehill (USA))
(2468) 2756^{8} 3988^{7} 4573^{5} 4992^{2} 5974^{7}

Fan Club *D W Chapman* a81 95
3 ch g Zamindar(USA) —Starfan (USA) (Lear Fan (USA))
5355^{11} 5776^{11} 6067^{8} 6463^{11} 6816^{9}

Fancy (IRE) *R A Farrant* a53 53
4 bb m Key Of Luck(USA) —Forbidden Pleasure (Pursuit Of Love)
1521^{11} 1671^{10} 1918^{9} 2336^{16} 4673^{2} 5121^{P} (Dead)

Fancy Groom *B Grizzetti* 50
2 ch c Groom Dancer(USA) —Fancy Shawl (Polish Precedent (USA))
$6523a^{8}$ $6767a^{11}$

Fancy Woman *J L Dunlop* 32
3 b f Sakhee(USA) —Fancy Wrap (Kris)
1816^{9} 2620^{11}

Fancy You (IRE) *A W Carroll* a46 31
4 b m Mull Of Kintyre(USA) —Sunset Park (IRE) (Red Sunset)
22^{12} 83^{12} 337^{11} 403^{9} 2622^{9} 2972^{10} 3612^{6} 5690^{7} 6537^{11} 6716^{9}

Fandangerina *Sir Mark Prescott* a79 75
2 b f Hernando(FR) —Fantastic Belle (IRE) (Night Shift (USA))
5540^{11} 5682^{9} 5965^{2} 6449^{2} (6611)

Fangorn Forest (IRE) *R A Harris* a63 75
4 br m Shinko Forest(IRE) —Edge Of Darkness (Vaigly Great)
1251^{5} 1352^{6} 1534^{9} 1761^{3} 2181^{2} 2512^{10} 2654^{5} 3107^{5} 3826^{14} 4112^{11} 4257^{3} 4504^{6} 4632^{7} 4878^{12}

Fann (USA) *C E Brittain* a83 102
4 b m Diesis—Forest Storm (USA) (Woodman (USA))
765^{2} 1013^{7} 1649^{6} 2207^{8} 2507^{4} 2753^{4} 3271^{7} 3897^{2} 4503^{5}

Fantadot *D J S Ffrench Davis* a55
2 b g Fantastic Light(USA) —Bardot (Efisio)
6990^{5} 7129^{4}

Fantastic Cee (IRE) *J Noseda* a72 39
3 b f Noverre(USA) —Tee Cee (Lion Cavern (USA))
418^{6} (573) 744^{6} 1484^{7}

Fantastic Delight *B G Powell* a54 51
4 b m Fantastic Light(USA) —Putout (Dowsing (USA))
1044^{11} 1529^{8} 1966^{4} 3584^{8} 4426^{3} 5366^{4} 5782^{5} 6152^{2} 6212^{3} 6505^{3}

Fantastic Lass *R A Fahey* 42
2 b f Fantastic Light(USA) —Shaanara (IRE) (Darshaan)
3977^{9} 4565^{11} 5140^{8}

Fantastic Love (USA) *A Al Raihe* a89 94
7 b g Peintre Celebre(USA) —Moon Flower (IRE) (Sadler's Wells (USA))
$248a^{12}$ $412a^{8}$ $598a^{8}$

Fantastic Morning *M Johnston* a60 83
3 ch g Fantastic Light(USA) —Gombay Girl (USA) (Woodman (USA))
745^{4} 2376^{2} (3365)

Fantastic Star *Michael P Hourigan* a15 32
5 b m Lahib(USA) —Fervent Fan (IRE) (Soviet Lad (USA))
$1760a^{12}$

Fantastic View (USA) *J Noseda* 102
6 ch h Distant View(USA) —Promptly (IRE) (Lead On Time (USA))
2755^{9} 3505^{6}

Fantasy Believer *J J Quinn* 113
9 b g Sure Blade(USA) —Delicious (Dominion)
1102^{11} 1474^{21} 1651^{17} 2237^{4} 2463^{7} 3104^{8} 3586^{5} 3990^{6} 4150^{8} 4614^{8} 5050^{2} 5407^{13} 5810^{9} 6472^{11}

Fantasy Crusader *R M H Cowell* a58 61
8 ch g Beveled(USA) —Cranfield Charger (Northern State (USA))
(2990) 3419^{3} 3907^{7} 4266^{4} 4355^{5} 4850^{5} (4945) 5280^{6} 5636^{7} 6096^{10}

Fantasy Defender (IRE) *R M H Cowell* a56 57
5 b g Fayruz—Mrs Lucky (Royal Match)
20^{4} 156^{3} 271^{4} 402^{6} 2556^{3} 4029^{13} 4319^{7} 4685^{3} 5275^{12} 5708^{12}

Fantasy Explorer *J J Quinn* a71 96
4 b g Compton Place—Zinzi (Song)
1195^{6} 2234^{15}

Fantasy Fighter (IRE) *J J Quinn* a46
2 b g Danetime(IRE) —Lady Montekin (Montekin)
5558^{8} 6022^{6}

Fantasy Legend (IRE) *N P Littmoden* a48 26
4 ch g Beckett(IRE) —Sianiski (Niniski (USA))
5542^{7}

Fantasy Parkes *K A Ryan* a79 87
3 ch f Fantastic Light(USA) —My Melody Parkes (Teenoso (USA))
1096^{7} 1496^{17} 2044^{13} 4898^{10} 6002^{10}

Fantasy Princess (USA) *G A Butler* a75
2 ch f Johannesburg(USA) —Fantasy (Cadeaux Genereux)
(6847)

Fantasy Ride *J Pearce* a78 61
5 b g Bahhare(USA) —Grand Splendour (Shirley Heights)
256^{5} 353^{7} 726^{7} 1385^{8} 1819^{13} 2833^{13} 4610^{4} 5422^{3} 5640^{5} 6056^{5} 6583^{5} 6719^{6} 6871^{2} 7186^{8}

Fantoche (BRZ) *M J Wallace* a93 90
5 ch h Roi Normand(USA) —Diet Lark (BRZ) (Roy (USA))
43^{5} 197^{9} 608^{8} 693^{7} 1083^{2} (1438) $2067a^{9}$ 2474^{11}

Faraami (IRE) *Pat Eddery* a37 30
2 ch f Fraam—Maraami (Selkirk (USA))
5201^{11} 5428^{15} 6262^{13}

Faraday (IRE) *A P Stringer* a59
4 b g Montjeu(IRE) —Fureau (GER) (Ferdinand (USA))
242^{12} (4673) 6529^{3} 6832^{8} 6979^{5}

Fara's Kingdom *Miss J A Camacho*
3 ch g Groom Dancer(USA) —Kingdom Ruby (IRE) (Bluebird (USA))
5335^{10}

Fardi (IRE) *K W Hogg*
5 b g Green Desert(USA) —Shuruk (Cadeaux Genereux)
966^{13} 1032^{13} 1239^{8}

Fareeha *J H M Gosden* a59 62
2 b f King's Best(USA) —Shatarah (Gulch (USA))
4102^{10} 4402^{7} 5301^{11} 6715^{8}

Farefield Lodge (IRE) *C G Cox* 76
3 b g Indian Lodge(IRE) —Fieldfare (Selkirk (USA))
2012^{2} (2366) 2942^{5} 3944^{11} 4574^{4} 5662^{4} 6103^{8}

Fareham Creek *D K Ivory* a42 27
3 b g Amrak Ajeeb(IRE) —Mummy's Chick (Mummy's Pet)
149^{11} 231^{11} 574^{6} 894^{11} 1281^{8} 1750^{13}

Fares (IRE) *C E Brittain* a98 89
3 b c Mark Of Esteem(IRE) —Iftitan (USA) (Southern Halo (USA))
113^{2} 760^{6} (1035) $1336a^{7}$ 2752^{10} 3431^{18} 3941^{24} 4420^{3} 5355^{4}

Farewell Gift *Carl Llewellyn* a81 76
6 b g Cadeaux Genereux—Daring Ditty (Daring March)
652^{13}

Far Gone *M L W Bell* a72 68
2 b f Diktat—Fairy Jackie (IRE) (Fairy King (USA))
1193^{2} 1636^{2} 2717^{4} 4065^{2} 4274^{4} 4733^{2} 5496^{8}

Farinelli *John M Oxx* 107
4 br g Selkirk(USA) —Melodica (Machiavellian (USA))
$1049a^{5}$ $3138a^{14}$

Farleigh House (USA) *M H Tompkins* 89
3 b c Lear Fan(USA) —Verasina (USA) (Woodman (USA))
1471^{4} 2045^{4} 2578^{3} 2788^{10} 6013^{12}

Farley Star *R Charlton* a83 78
3 b f Alzao(USA) —Girl Of My Dreams (IRE) (Marju (IRE))
1228^{5}

Farmer Brown (IRE) *P Hughes* 89
6 b g Bob Back(USA) —Magic Moonbeam (IRE) (Decent Fellow)
(4371a)

Farne Island *Micky Hammond* a62 65
4 ch g Arkadian Hero(USA) —Holy Island (Deploy)
4582^{10} 5086^{2} 5286^{6}

Farne Isle *G A Harker* 52
8 ch m Midnight Legend—Biloela (Nicholas Bill)
2567[10] 3193[7]
Farnesina (FR) *E Danel* a94 85
5 b m Anabaa(USA) —Wardara (Sharpo)
352[5] 656[4] 4012a[5] 6954a[12]
Far Note (USA) *S R Bowring* a61 44
9 ch g Distant View(USA) —Descant (USA) (Nureyev (USA))
77[14] 145[11] 374[10] 448[12] 581[3] 632[10] 668[7]
Farouge (FR) *Yvonne Durant* 105
6 gr h Croco Rouge(IRE) —Fablimixa (FR) (Linamix (FR))
5263a[8]
Farpedon *H Candy* a63 67
2 b g Auction House(USA) —Shining Oasis (IRE) (Mujtahid (USA))
4962[5] 5771[4] 6998[5]
Farrel (IRE) *B Grizzetti* 105
2 b c Fruits Of Love(USA) —Folcungi (IRE) (Mukaddamah (USA))
6222a[3]
Far Seeking *R A Harris* a62 59
3 b c Distant Music(USA) —House Hunting (Zafonic (USA))
1433[5] 5129[4] 5781[3] 7025[10] 7174[6]
Farsighted *J M P Eustace* 72
2 b f Where Or When(IRE) —Classic Vision (Classic Cliche (IRE))
3465[5] (3884) 4453[8] 5509[3] 6128[13]
Far Song (IRE) *A M Balding* a54 35
2 ch f Distant Music(USA) —Charlene Lacy (IRE) (Pips Pride)
2724[9] 3417[9] 7216[7]
Farthermost (IRE) *R Hannon* a77 77
2 ch c Fath(USA) —Matila (IRE) (Persian Bold)
2447[5] 2941[5] 3424[3] 3850[2] 4121[12] 4764[4]
Faruffini (ITY) *L Ledda*
2 ch c Dr Devious(IRE) —Famagosta (USA) (Whitney Tower (USA))
6527a[11]
Fascinatin Rhythm *V Smith* a69 77
3 br f Fantastic Light(USA) —Marguerite De Vine (Zilzal (USA))
1127[5] 1499[6] 2786[12] 3877[7] 4147[14]
Fashion Accessory *M Appleby* 2
3 b f Muthahb(IRE) —Queen Of Fashion (IRE) (Barathea (IRE))
5304[6] 5859[10] 6090[9]
Fashion Model *M A Jarvis* 74
3 b f Rainbow Quest(USA) —Gracious Beauty (USA) (Nijinsky (CAN))
1246[2]
Fashion Rocks (IRE) *B J Meehan* a73 96
2 b f Rock Of Gibraltar(IRE) —La Gandilie (FR) (Highest Honor (FR))
3648[2] (4061) 4744[6] (5164)
Fashion Statement *M A Jarvis* 104
3 b f Rainbow Quest(USA) —Shabby Chic (USA) (Red Ransom (USA))
1581[3] (2707a) 6524a[11]
Faslen (USA) *J-C Rouget* 93
3 b f Fasliyev(USA) —Ellen (IRE) (Machiavellian (USA))
3147a[3] 5373a[8]
Fast Bowler *J M P Eustace* a81 86
4 b g Intikhab(USA) —Alegria (Night Shift (USA))
1121[9] 1357[8] 2189[7]
Fast Company (IRE) *B J Meehan* 124
2 b c Danehill Dancer(IRE) —Sheezalady (Zafonic (USA))
(3552) (4694) 6333[2]
Fastella (IRE) *G A Butler* a71
2 b f Fasliyev(USA) —Ela Athena (Ezzoud (IRE))
6225[4] 6926[2]
Fast Feet *K A Ryan* a75 89
2 b g Statue Of Liberty(USA) —Landowska (USA) (Langfuhr (CAN))
926[3] 1454[2] 1580[2] 2024[7] 4175[10] 4743[20] 6326[4] 6721[4] 6897[2] (7000) 7072[4] 7280[6]
Fast Freddie *D J Murphy* a69 59
3 b g Agnes World(USA) —Bella Chica (IRE) (Bigstone (IRE))
1161[4] 4546[8] 5174[9] 5282[11] 5420[7] 5897[6] (6886) (6957) (7013) 7107[9]
Fast Heart *A Berry* a75 89
6 b g Fasliyev(USA) —Heart Of India (IRE) (Try My Best (USA))
66[4] 154[9] 236[5] 403[2] 442[9] 622[3] 654[2] (Dead)
Fastmambo (USA) *F Head* 92
4 b g Kingmambo(USA) —Slow Down (USA) (Seattle Slew (USA))
1389a[10]
Fastnowfast (IRE) *F Costello* a17 57
3 b f Fasliyev(USA) —Printaniere (USA) (Sovereign Dancer (USA))
5460a[29]
Fastrac Boy *J R Best* a63 45
4 b g Bold Edge—Nesyred (IRE) (Paris House)
251[6] 5340[10] 5726[11] 6528[2] 6773[6] 6890[7] 7082[2]
Fasuby (IRE) *P D Evans* a28 51
3 b f Fasliyev(USA) —Sue's Ruby (USA) (Crafty Prospector (USA))
6060[4] 6408[4] 6583[11]
Fasylitator (IRE) *D K Ivory* a86 76
5 b g Fasliyev(USA) —Obsessed (Storm Bird (CAN))
314[8]
Fat Boy (IRE) *R Hannon* a77 104
2 ch c Choisir(AUS) —Gold Shift (USA) (Night Shift (USA))
(942) 1390[7] 2737[6] 3459[7] (3910) 4120[2] (4899)
Fateful Attraction *I A Wood* a74 58
4 b m Mujahid(USA) —Heavens Above (FR) (Pistolet Bleu (IRE))
91[11] 1885[13] 2716[16] 3191[3] 3455[7] 4272[4] 4856[9] 5118[8] 5733[4] 6260[4] 6458[7] (6866) 6951[7]
Fateh Field (USA) *Saeed Bin Suroor* 102
2 b c Distorted Humor(USA) —Too Cool To Fool (USA) (Foolish Pleasure (USA))
(6125) 6488[2]
Fathayer (USA) *P Paciello*
2 ch c Volponi(USA) —Bright Generation (IRE) (Rainbow Quest (USA))
(6523a)
Fathom Five (IRE) *B Smart* 103
3 b g Fath(USA) —Ambria (ITY) (Final Straw)
1108[9] (1820) (2659) (2884) 3531[2] 4726[13]
Fathoming (USA) *E A L Dunlop*
2 ch f Gulch(USA) —Ocean Ridge (USA) (Storm Bird (CAN))
5063[P]
Fathsta (IRE) *S Kirk* a76 74
2 b c Fath(USA) —Kilbride Lass (IRE) (Lahib (USA))
1990[10] 2398[6] 2941[3] 3841[2] (4193) 4762[6] 5053[3] 5350[8] 5828[7] 6017[16] 6756[7] 6899[6] (7095) (7280)
Faversham *M Wigham* a71 79
4 b g Halling(USA) —Barger (USA) (Riverman (USA))
488[16] 620[9] 1301[2] 1609[5] 2084[7] 2582[6]
Favorita (GER) *C Bocksai*
7 b m Gold And Ivory(USA) —Flying Lady (GER) (Script Ohio (USA))
439a[7]
Favouring (IRE) *M C Chapman* a57 58
5 ch g Fayruz—Peace Dividend (IRE) (Alzao (USA))
144[5] 430[2] 519[6] 580[2] 632[3] 729[3] 892[4] 1349[6] 1753[2] 2831[13] 3608[11] 4042[4] 5546[9]
Faynita (IRE) *Adrian McGuinness* 68
5 bb g Fayruz—Miss Anita (IRE) (Anita's Prince)
873a[19]
Fayr Jag (IRE) *T D Easterby* 116
8 b g Fayruz—Lominda (IRE) (Lomond (USA))
1159[3] 1770[8] 2319[6] 2857[20] 3088[10] 3894[10] 4150[7] 4614[13] 4798[5] 5254[9]
Fealeview Lady (USA) *H Morrison* a75 75
3 b f Red Ransom(USA) —Alice White (USA) (Thunder Gulch (USA))
510[6] (1903) 2309[2] 2623[4] 3430[17] 4338[3] 5339[3] 5703[8] 6343[4]
Feared In Flight (IRE) *B W Hills* 111
2 b c Hawk Wing(USA) —Solar Crystal (IRE) (Alzao (USA))
(1792) 2855[3] 3504[6] 5397a[7] 6489[3]
Fearless Warrior *J L Dunlop* 68
2 b g Erhaab(USA) —Princess Genista (Ile De Bourbon (USA))
5088[4] 5599[4] 6593[6]
Fear To Tread (USA) *Mrs P Sly* a43 83
4 ch m Peintre Celebre(USA) —Pleine Lune (IRE) (Alzao (USA))
1591[P] 3844[2] 4288[9] 5225[15]
Feasible *J G Portman* a60 67
2 ch g Efisio—Zoena (Emarati (USA))
2447[4] 2876[5] 3404[5] 5268[2]
Featherlight *Jamie Poulton* a79 69
3 b f Fantastic Light(USA) —Feathers Flying (IRE) (Royal Applause)
224[5] 572[7] 893[3] (1397) 2456[4] 3082[2] 4069[8] 5120[3] (5426) (5820) 6622[6]
Featherstone *N Tinkler* 41
2 b g Umistim—Summer Passion (Pennekamp (USA))
1674[6] 1857[7]
Feelin Foxy *J G Given* a70 73
3 b f Foxhound(USA) —Charlie Girl (Puissance)
1151[8] 1286[10] 1738[3] 1820[4] 2119[3] 2255[3] 2513[6] (2950) 3493[6] 4158[9] 4432[2] 4759[4] 5139[8] (5662) 6089[5] 6559[2]
Feeling (IRE) *P W Chapple-Hyam* 75
3 b g Sadler's Wells(USA) —La Pitie (USA) (Devil's Bag (USA))
1191a[P] 1659[7] 1998[5] 2436[3] 3248[4] 3908[10] 5807[11] 6235[15]
Feeling Fresh (IRE) *Paul Green* a66 58
2 b c Xaar—Oh'Cecilia (IRE) (Scenic)
2432[7] 5329[8] 5813[9] 6066[9] 6456[7] 6692[5] 6881[4] (7042) 7260[4]
Feeling Lucky (IRE) *W Jarvis* 24
2 b c Namid—Toldya (Beveled (USA))
5772[10]
Feeling Peckish (USA) *M C Chapman* a43 41
3 ch g Point Given(USA) —Sunday Bazaar (USA) (Nureyev (USA))
1177[7] 1937[10] 2118[11] 2420[6] 3244[8] 3710[16] 3908[8] 6055[9]
Feeling Proud (USA) *Jane Chapple-Hyam* a68 74
2 b f More Than Ready(USA) —Proud Heart (IRE) (Caerleon (USA))
(1445) 1821[8] 2134[8] 3462[7] 4022[6] 5974[27]
Feeling Wonderful (IRE) *M Johnston* a70 67
3 b f Fruits Of Love(USA) —Teodora (IRE) (Fairy King (USA))
1297[7] 1531[11] 2767[3] 3034[4] 3286[3]
Feelin Irie (IRE) *J R Boyle* a59 67
4 b g Key Of Luck(USA) —Charlotte's Dancer (Kris)
310[6] 479[6] 625[6] 723[7] (812) 1027[8] 2145[3] 2798[6] 3405[6] 4294[10] 5546[6] 5946[7] 6587[10]
Feels Like Heaven *T D Easterby* a24
3 b f Mull Of Kintyre(USA) —Gargren (IRE) (Mujtahid (USA))
711[6] 807[10]
Feet So Fast *S Seemar* a86 98
8 ch g Pivotal—Splice (Sharpo)
245a[9] 472a[8] 547a[8]
Feisty Royale *M Johnston* 80
2 b f Royal Applause—Hawait Al Barr (Green Desert (USA))
2039[2] 2983[3] 3834[2] 5216[14] (5692) 6012[3] (6128) 6486[11]
Felicia *S C Williams* a58 58
2 b f Diktat—Gracia (Linamix (FR))
6535[10] 7264[7]
Fellow Ship *P Butler* a28
7 b g Elmaamul(USA) —Genoa (Zafonic (USA))
26[7] 887[8]
Fellrunner (IRE) *A Berry*
2 b c Traditionally(USA) —Via Splendida (IRE) (Project Manager)
3761[14] 4784[RR] 6698[12]
Feminist (IRE) *J M Bradley* a47 21
5 b m Alhaarth(IRE) —Miss Willow Bend (USA) (Willow Hour (USA))
368[11] 441[6] 523[13] 653[12] 1065[8] 1317[12]
Fenice (IRE) *S Seemar* a92 104
4 gr h Woodman(USA) —Venize (IRE) (Kaldoun (FR))
248a[7] 475a[7] 544a[4] 643a[4]
Fenners (USA) *M W Easterby* a72 69
4 ch g Pleasant Tap(USA) —Legal Opinion (IRE) (Polish Precedent (USA))
(1966) 2342[3] 3371[7] 3888[6] 4352[8] 5000[3] 5300[5] 6056[3] 6583[2] 6871[3] (7157)
Feolin *H Morrison* a68 75
3 b f Dr Fong(USA) —Finlaggan (Be My Chief (USA))
889[3] 1407[10] 4112[10] (4684) 5166[3] 5860[4]
Ferneley (IRE) *Francis Ennis* 110
3 b c Ishiguru(USA) —Amber Tide (IRE) (Pursuit Of Love)
1185a[2] 2051a[11] 2752[9] 5240a[4] 6009[8]
Fern House (IRE) *Garry Moss* a54 59
5 b g Xaar—Certain Impression (USA) (Forli (ARG))
2712[12] 3345[15] 3921[5] (4252) 4773[7] 4942[7] 5930[13] 6637[8] 6886[5] 7111[4] 7284[3]
Fernlawn Hope (IRE) *J A Osborne* a59 54
2 b f Danehill Dancer(IRE) —Hana Marie (Formidable (USA))
3213[9] 4796[9] 5309[8] 5896[8] (6775)
Fervent *J M Bradley* a42 53
3 b g Kyllachy—Romancing (Dr Devious (IRE))
1215[5] 1403[6] 1923[7] 2622[11] 4529[10] 5900[14] 6100[11]
Fervent Prince *H Morrison* 74
2 b g Averti(IRE) —Maria Theresa (Primo Dominie)
1970[12] 3967[8] 4500[5] 4903[3] 5207[3] 5705[3] 6201[8]
Festival Dreams *Miss J S Davis* a42 55
2 ch g Largesse—Bright Spangle (IRE) (General Monash (USA))
4876[10] 6530[11] 6737[5]
Festivale (IRE) *J L Dunlop* 90
2 b f Invincible Spirit(IRE) —Cephalonie (USA) (Kris S (USA))
2039[6] (2457) 6619[5]
Festive Chimes (IRE) *N B King* a63 66
6 b m Efisio—Delightful Chime (IRE) (Alzao (USA))
537[3] 913[4] 2770[6] 4030[7]
Festive Tipple (IRE) *P Winkworth* a54 43
3 b g Tipsy Creek(USA) —Gi La High (Rich Charlie)
1561[14] 1899[6]
Festoso (IRE) *H J L Dunlop* 104
2 b f Diesis—Garah (Ajdal (USA))
(1814) 2812[11] 3432[2] 4744[5] 5973[3]
Fever *R Hannon* a79 89
3 b g Dr Fong(USA) —Follow Flanders (Pursuit Of Love)
719[3] (1153) (1722) 2231[2] 2790[13]
Fez (SAF) *S Seemar* a53 74
6 b g National Emblem(SAF) —Salaadims Pride (SAF) (Salaadim (USA))
394a[7]
Ficoma *C G Cox* a69 78
3 b f Piccolo—Hemaca (Distinctly North (USA))
1837[6] 4163[2] 4848[12] 5537[7] 6429[7]
Fictional *E J O'Neill* 102
6 b h Fraam—Manon Lescaut (Then Again)
1474[29]
Fiddlers Creek (IRE) *R Allan* a70 63
8 b g Danehill(USA) —Mythical Creek (USA) (Pleasant Tap (USA))
618[5] 685[6] 2810[11] 4580[6] 4713[12]
Fiddlers Spirit (IRE) *J G M O'Shea* a27 45
3 b g Invincible Spirit(IRE) —Coco Ricoh (IRE) (Lycius (USA))
1232[9] 1782[11]
Fidelia (IRE) *G Wragg* a93 98
3 b f Singspiel(IRE) —Rosse (Kris)
1127[4] 1581[7] 2597[6] 3992[3] 4549[2] (4901) 5799[4] 6604[2]
Fidelias Dance *M Johnston* a69 70
2 b f Danehill Dancer(IRE) —Fidelio's Miracle (USA) (Mountain Cat (USA))
1150[11] 1814[5] 3648[3] 4168[8] 4923[4] 5837[5] 6434[3]
Fiefdom (IRE) *I W McInnes* a93 91
5 br g Singspiel(IRE) —Chiquita Linda (IRE) (Mujadil (USA))
953[4] 1223[4] 1458[9] 2458[2] 2936[4] 3350[6] 3813[5] 4295[2] 4515[6] 4990[6] 5031[3] 5413[11] 5712[5] 5804[10] 6209[5] 6435[2] 6674[3] 6765[7] 6949[7] 7165[11]
Field Rouge (JPN) *M Nishizono* a116
5 b h Croco Rouge(IRE) —Mejiro Romer (JPN) (Lindo Shaver (USA))
6942a[2]
Fields Of Green *M Halford* 67
4 b m Royal Applause—Ishona (Selkirk (USA))
4836a[3]
Fifteen Love (USA) *R Charlton* 95
2 bb c Point Given(USA) —Nidd (USA) (Known Fact (USA))
3435[2] (3957) (5920) 6495[11]
Fifth Zak *S R Bowring* 38
3 b g Best Of The Bests(IRE) —Zakuska (Zafonic (USA))
4659[7]
Fifty (IRE) *R Hannon* a67 77
2 b f Fasliyev(USA) —Amethyst (IRE) (Sadler's Wells (USA))
4061[4] 4402[2] 5164[8] 5766[11] 6228[4]
Fifty Cents *R Charlton* 83
3 ch g Diesis—Solaia (USA) (Miswaki (USA))
(1995) 3900[8] 5617[5]
Figaro Flyer (IRE) *P Howling* a87 91
4 b g Mozart(IRE) —Ellway Star (IRE) (Night Shift (USA))
163[3] (269) 480[2] 554[4] 575[9] 692[4] 810[2] 1061[6] 1121[3] 1357[7] 1607[8] 1977[3] 2318[4] 2882[13] 3528[5] 3802[9] 4367[7] 4780[7] 5160[13] 5879[5] 6533[4] (6671) 6869[9] 7119[8] (7271)
Figaro's Quest (IRE) *C N Kellett* a63 66
5 b g Singspiel(IRE) —Seren Quest (Rainbow Quest (USA))
2839[4] 3300[6] 3927[9] 4352[6] 4859[7] 5235[5] 6697[10]
Fighting Johan (GER) *H Blume* 95
3 b c Johan Cruyff—Fireglow (FR) (Glow (USA))
1875a[9] 5464a[6] 5929a[7] 6781a[8]
Figjam *S Seemar* a69 63
4 b g Groom Dancer(USA) —Sheila's Secret (IRE) (Bluebird (USA))
105a[8]
Filey Buoy *R M Whitaker* a56 46
5 b g Factual(USA) —Tugra (FR) (Baby Turk)
682[9] 1423[7] 1715[8] 2091[8] 2619[4] 2893[7] 3257[5] 4449[14] 4488[8]
Filigree Lace (USA) *Sir Michael Stoute* 57
2 ch f Seeking The Gold(USA) —Yafill (USA) (Nureyev (USA))
6649[10]
Filios (IRE) *L M Cumani* a77 103
3 b c Kutub(IRE) —Karlinaxa (Linamix (FR))
1289[3] (1827) 2790[2]
Filliemou (IRE) *A W Carroll* a45 30
6 gr m Goldmark(USA) —St Louis Lady (Absalom)
181[9] 495[7] 1011[14] 1152[14] 1368[8]
Filligree (IRE) *Rae Guest* a47 59
2 b f Kyllachy—Clunie (Inchinor)
6105[3] 6595[5] 6897[6]
Film Festival (USA) *M Halford* a70 99
4 ch g Diesis—To Act (USA) (Roberto (USA))
3138a[26] 4867a[11]
Film Maker (IRE) *B J Meehan* 89
2 b c Danetime(IRE) —Alexander Anapolis (IRE) (Spectrum (IRE))
6295[5]
Filthygorgeous (IRE) *J R Weymes*
2 ch f Bahamian Bounty—Quick Flight (Polar Falcon (USA))
2739[15] 3378[7] 3788[8] (Dead)
Final Bid (IRE) *M G Quinlan* a58 56
4 b g Mujadil(USA) —Dusky Virgin (Missed Flight)
1026[6]
Final Desire *M Brittain* 11
4 b m Grey Desire—Call Me Lucky (Magic Ring (IRE))
3561[6] 3914[14] 5041[13]
Final Dynasty *Mrs G S Rees* a71 98
3 b f Komaite(USA) —Malcesine (IRE) (Auction Ring (USA))
2867[2] 3344[2] (3720) 4196[6] 4639[6] 5666[7] 6487[10]
Final Esteem *R A Harris* a69 68
4 ch g Lomitas—Fame At Last (USA) (Quest For Fame)
298[2] 364[10] 620[8] 825[8]
Final Flashback (IRE) *D K Weld* 83
2 ch c Singspiel(IRE) —Early Memory (USA) (Devil's Bag (USA))
1508a[6]
Finalmente *N A Callaghan* a106 112
5 b g Kahyasi—Sudden Spirit (FR) (Esprit Du Nord (USA))
1477[3] 1844[4] 2787[4] 3333[3] 4091[3] 5376[5]
Final Overture (FR) *H R A Cecil* 52
3 b f Rossini(USA) —Final Moment (Nishapour (FR))
3349[8] 4492[3]
Final Tune (IRE) *Miss M E Rowland* a81 79
4 ch g Grand Lodge(USA) —Jackie's Opera (FR) (Indian Ridge)
509[3] 672[4] 865[6] 930[4] 1283[2] 1751[3] (2865) 3346[5] 4153[9]
Final Verse *J S Moore* 113
4 b g Mark Of Esteem(IRE) —Tamassos (Dance In Time (CAN))
1104[3] 1305[5] 1723[4] 3103[4] (4167) 4543[6]
Financial Times (USA) *Stef Liddiard* a86 72
5 b g Awesome Again(CAN) —Investabull (USA) (Holy Bull (USA))
163[2] 269[2] 566[3] 835[4] 1363[2] 6708[3] 6794[2] (6829) 7078[6]
Find It Out (USA) *B J Llewellyn* a3 48
4 b g Luhuk(USA) —Ursula (VEN) (Phone Trick (USA))
6505[12]
Fine Art World (IRE) *N A Callaghan* 42
3 br g Agnes World(USA) —Foreign Relation (IRE) (Distant Relative)
3044[5] 4416[8] 4778[6] 4961[4]
Fine Deed *Ian Williams* a16
6 b g Kadeed(IRE) —Kristis Girl (Ballacashtal (CAN))
45[10]
Fine Edge *H E Haynes*
6 ch m Keen—Cap That (Derek H)
3366[14]
Fine Ruler (IRE) *M R Bosley* a71 70
3 b g King's Best(USA) —Bint Alajwaad (IRE) (Fairy King (USA))
492[6] 694[6] 904[3] 1039[10] 6695[5] 6838[4] 7143[2]
Finicius (USA) *Eoin Griffin* a111 106
3 b c Officer(USA) —Glorious Linda (FR) (Le Glorieux)
3144a[5] 4045[6] 4805[8]
Finished Article (IRE) *K J Burke* a64 71
10 b g Indian Ridge—Summer Fashion (Moorestyle)
(35) (107) 332[8] 481[3] 578[9] 617[6] 792[12] 891[5]
Finlay's Footsteps *G M Moore* a36 4
3 ch g Dr Fong(USA) —Bay Shade (USA) (Sharpen Up)
1375[7] 2909[6]
Finmore Queen (USA) *J R Fanshawe* a68 60
2 ch f Grand Slam(USA) —Slew City Slicker (USA) (Slew City Slew (USA))
6648[14]
Finnegans Rainbow *M C Chapman* a44 56
5 ch g Spectrum(IRE) —Fairy Story (IRE) (Persian Bold)
1011[11] 1271[8] 2118[8] 6569[5]
Finsbury *J M Bradley* a86 80
4 gr g Observatory(USA) —Carmela Owen (Owington)
1917[7] 3515[5] 1845[11] 2180[4] 2512[7] 3056[5] (4416) 4807[3] 4999[9] 6081[6]

Finsceal Beo (IRE) *J S Bolger* 121
3 ch f Mr Greeley(USA) —Musical Treat (IRE) (Royal Academy (USA))
(1496) 1702a[2] (2065a) 2814[8] 5243a[6] 6042a[5]

Fiona's Wonder *R A Harris* a40
3 b g Inchinor—Wondrous Maid (GER) (Mondrian (GER))
386[11] 791[13] 1782[15]

Fire Alarm *Miss Lucinda V Russell* a40 34
3 b g Smoke Glacken(USA) —Brandywine Belle (USA) (Trempolino (USA))
253[4] 454[7] 676[7] 1712[11]

Fire And Rain (FR) *Miss E C Lavelle* 108
4 b g Galileo(IRE) —Quatre Saisons (FR) (Homme De Loi (IRE))
2182[7]

Fire At Will *A W Carroll* a45 45
5 b g Lugana Beach—Kahyasi Moll (IRE) (Brief Truce (USA))
630[12] 768[10] 907[8] 1210[7] 1380[4] 2331[8] 2412[3] 3286[5] 3428[9] 3868[8] 4685[4] 5864[8]

Firebird Annie (IRE) *A Bailey* a50 51
3 b f Mujadil(USA) —Missing Virgin (IRE) (Mujtahid (USA))
619[2] 745[6] 919[6] 1716[5] 1943[15] 2565[5] 2747[2] 3040[7] 7034[11]

Fire In Cairo (IRE) *P C Haslam* a55 55
3 b f Barathea(IRE) —Ibiza (GER) (Linamix (FR))
224[6] 373[3] 3722[2] 5980[3]

Firello (NOR) *W Togersen* 85
7 br g Muhab(USA) —Fillippika (NOR) (Dalby Jaguar)
4874a[9]

Firenza Bond *G R Oldroyd* 79
2 b g Captain Rio—Bond Stasia (IRE) (Mukaddamah (USA))
1528[8] 2934[6] (3532) 4098[7] 4476[6] (6326)

Firenze *J R Fanshawe* a69 109
6 ch m Efisio—Juliet Bravo (Glow (USA))
(1670) 2184[3] 2857[9] 3511[6] 4813[7]

Fire One (IRE) *M P Tregoning* a62
3 b g Bahri(USA) —Iviza (IRE) (Sadler's Wells (USA))
293[5] 499[5]

Fireside *P W Chapple-Hyam* 92
2 b c Dr Fong(USA) —Al Hasnaa (Zafonic (USA))
5397a[6] (5971)

Firespin (USA) *M Botti*
2 ch f Luhuk(USA) —Happy Numbers (USA) (Polish Numbers (USA))
7258[8]

Firestorm (IRE) *C W Fairhurst* 59
3 b g Celtic Swing—National Ballet (Shareef Dancer (USA))
1659[8] 1917[11] 2552[9] 2840[8] 3379[4] 3792[10] 4821[8] 5906[13]

Firestreak *R Hannon* 82
2 b g Green Desert(USA) —Flash Of Gold (Darshaan)
(2632) 3938[5] 4991[6] 5410[7]

Fire Up The Band *D Nicholls* a100 103
8 b g Prince Sabo—Green Supreme (Primo Dominie)
(927) 1102[12] 1456[4] 1788[14] 2234[13] 4122[25] 4696[5] 5195[8] 5505[10]

Firewalker *B Smart* a59 66
2 b f Bertolini(USA) —Crystal Canyon (Efisio)
1963[6] 2297[3] 2934[2] 6729[4] 7129[2] 7170[2]

Firework *E A Wheeler* a54 50
9 b g Primo Dominie—Prancing (Prince Sabo)
22[10] (557) 723[6] 2336[8] 2665[15] 4319[10]

First Abode *M Brittain* 37
2 br f First Trump—Villa Del Sol (Tagula (IRE))
4041[7] 4174[8] 4897[4]

First Among Equals *D G Bridgwater* a9 38
4 b m Primo Valentino(IRE) —Margarets First (Puissance)
2104[15]

First Avenue *M A Jarvis* 80
2 b c Montjeu(IRE) —Marciala (IRE) (Machiavellian (USA))
5951[6] (6574)

First Bloom (USA) *P F I Cole* a66 51
3 br f Fusaichi Pegasus(USA) —Shy Princess (USA) (Irish River (FR))
1203[10] 1364[9]

First Boy (GER) *D J Wintle* a33 51
8 b g Bering—First Smile (Surumu (GER))
524[14] 1570[12] 3047[3] (Dead)

First Buddy *W J Haggas* a73 84
3 ch g Rock Of Gibraltar(IRE) —Dance Treat (USA) (Nureyev (USA))
(2581) 3463[9] 4331[4] 5382[3] 5978[8]

First Defence (USA) *R J Frankel* a115
3 b c Unbridled's Song(USA) —Honest Lady (USA) (Seattle Slew (USA))
5852a[7]

First Friend (IRE) *M Hill* a77 62
6 b g Mark Of Esteem(IRE) —Bustira (Busted)
212[5] 381[10] 445[6] 594[10] 634[2] 1249[3] 1761[8] 2106[6] 2492[5] 6316[9] 6598[14]

First Frost *M J Gingell* a39 13
3 ch f Atraf—Bless (Beveled (USA))
128[8] 222[12] 357[11] 577[11] 676[8] 794[6] 6108[10] 6408[6] 6570[13]

First Generation *P D Evans* a22 51
5 b g Primo Dominie—My Cadeaux (Cadeaux Genereux)
42[12]

First In Command (IRE) *Daniel Mark Loughnane* a24 61
2 b c Captain Rio—Queen Sigi (IRE) (Fairy King (USA))
5516a[10]

First In Show *A M Balding* 40
2 b f Zamindar(USA) —Rose Show (Belmez (USA))
6617[10]

First Look (FR) *P Monteith* 75
7 b g Acatenango(GER) —First Class (GER) (Bustino)
5933[3]

First Mate (IRE) *M Johnston* 80
3 b g Desert Style(IRE) —Sail Away (GER) (Platini (GER))
5383[14] 5703[10] 6110[9]

First Order *I Semple* a96 92
6 b g Primo Dominie—Unconditional Love (IRE) (Polish Patriot (USA))
41[5] 344[8] 660[4] 1088[8] 1854[9] 2244[10] 2989[2] 3500[8] 4140[8] 5039[12] 5379[7] 6313[2] 6743[3] (7078)

First Princess (IRE) *J S Moore* a64 64
3 b f King's Best(USA) —Try To Catch Me (USA) (Shareef Dancer (USA))
21[3] 93[3] 157[10] 370[6] 1345[5] 1731[2] 2077[2] 2150[5] 3384[14] 3490[7]

First Rhapsody (IRE) *T J Etherington* a38 63
5 b m Rossini(USA) —Tinos Island (IRE) (Alzao (USA))
1038[10] 1918[10] 2302[6] 2714[6] 3247[10] 3754[12] 4477[9]

First Show *R A Harris* a79 82
5 b g Cape Cross(IRE) —Rose Show (Belmez (USA))
1395[15] 1984[10] 2514[9] 3571[8] 4023[10]

First Slip *Jonjo O'Neill* a69 31
4 b g Slip Anchor—Nanouche (Dayjur (USA))
3473[9] 5187[11]

First Stream (GER) *Mario Hofer* 114
3 ch c Lomitas—First Class (GER) (Bustino)
2102a[3] 3778a[3] 4442a[2] 5077a[6] 5671a[4] 6689a[6]

First Time (GER) *Karin Suter* 103
4 br m Silvano(GER) —First Wings (IRE) (In The Wings)
355a[2] (493a)

First To Call *P J Makin* a88 83
3 ch c First Trump—Scarlett Holly (Red Sunset)
1447[5] (2196) 5099[5] 5724[8] 6144[2]

First Trim (IRE) *B J Meehan* a59 81
2 b g Acclamation—Spanker (Suave Dancer (USA))
1832[5] 5042[3] 5448[3] 5856[7] 6004[11]

First Valentini *N Bycroft* 53
3 b f Bertolini(USA) —Oscietra (Robellino (USA))
3752[5] 4226[6] 4616[6] 4842[6] 5041[3] 5488[4] 6057[5]

Fisberry *M S Saunders* a58 68
5 gr g Efisio—Elderberry (Bin Ajwaad (IRE))
2318[13] 2725[9] 3388[7] 3682[8] 3851[8] 5879[14]

Fish Called Johnny *Peter Grayson* a65 86
3 b g Kyllachy—Clare Celeste (Coquelin (USA))
1202[11] 1782[3] (2171) 2395[11] 2518[5] 2867[6] 3493[5] 3568[3] 3885[3] 4127[5] 6360[12] 6695[9] 6910[8] 6993[8] 7192[7]

Fisher Bridge (IRE) *W R Swinburn* a70 83
4 ch g Singspiel(IRE) —Kristal Bridge (Kris)
3399[2] 3854[3] (4421) 5892[7]

Fishforcompliments *R A Fahey* a92 104
3 b c Royal Applause—Flyfisher (USA) (Riverman (USA))
760[7] 1097[3] 1473[18] 2124[4] 2789[12]

Fistral *Ollie Pears* a43 50
3 b g Piccolo—Fayre Holly (IRE) (Fayruz)
1712[8] 2248[4] 2759[4] 3535[2] 4354[9] 4714[3] 5084[8] 6247[8] 6537[5] 6908[7]

Fitasabuckstoat (IRE) *K W Hogg*
4 b g Fayruz—Bardia (Jalmood (USA))
968[12] (Dead)

Fitolini *Mrs G S Rees* a69 61
2 ch f Bertolini(USA) —Miss Fit (IRE) (Hamas (IRE))
1029[5] (1727) 3077[6] 3925[4] 4126[9] 4775[8] 4975[8] 5932[6]

Fits Of Giggles (IRE) *J G Given* a65 70
2 b f Cape Cross(IRE) —Itsibitsi (IRE) (Brief Truce (USA))
(4428) 4899[6]

Fit The Cove (IRE) *H Rogers* a88 97
7 b g Balla Cove—Fit The Halo (Dance In Time (CAN))
3140a[6]

Fitzroy (IRE) *R Donohoe* 88
6 ch g Grand Lodge(USA) —Spa (Sadler's Wells (USA))
2018a[4]

Fitzroy Crossing (USA) *M Johnston* 89
2 gr c Cozzene(USA) —Jaded Lady (USA) (Afleet (CAN))
1487[3] 1652[2] 1938[7] (4328) 5216[12] (5691)

Fiulin *M Botti* 76
2 ch c Galileo(IRE) —Fafinta (IRE) (Indian Ridge)
6723[2]

Fiume *R Hannon* 66
2 ch c Medicean—River Abouali (Bluebird (USA))
5919[15] 6493[8]

Fiumicino *M R Channon* a87 98
3 b f Danehill Dancer(IRE) —Valhalla Moon (USA) (Sadler's Wells (USA))
838[2] 1499[5] 1809[4] 2926a[6] 3434[11]

Five A Side *M Johnston* 86
3 b g Lomitas—Fifth Emerald (Formidable (USA))
2305[7] 3959[10] 4228[2] 5218[8] 5623[6]

Five Satins (IRE) *M J Grassick* 61
2 b f Invincible Spirit(IRE) —Manarah (Marju (IRE))
4832a[15]

Five Two *A J Martin* 76
4 ch g Mark Of Esteem(IRE) —Queen's Gallery (USA) (Forty Niner (USA))
5184a[3] 5460a[21]

Five Wishes *M Dods* 61
4 b f Bahamian Bounty—Due West (Inchinor)
1197[5] 1625[3] 1943[2] 2713[2] 2829[2] 4480[12] 4931[8] 5935[10]

Fixateur *J G Given* a51 42
5 b g Anabaa(USA) —Fabulous Account (USA) (Private Account (USA))
1181[7] 1745[7] 2084[8]

Fixation *Mrs A J Perrett* a66 56
3 ch g Observatory(USA) —Fetish (Dancing Brave (USA))
4666[6] 5499[4] 6204[5]

Fixboard *F Poulsen* 106
6 b g Bluebird(USA) —Military Tune (IRE) (Nashwan (USA))
3505[8]

Fizzlephut (IRE) *Miss J R Tooth* a79 84
5 b g Indian Rocket—Cladantom (IRE) (High Estate)
47[7] 269[5] (835) 1004[4] 1080[6] 6708[7] 6829[6] 6976[6] 7059[2] 7116[2] 7215[5]

Fizzy Bella *M G Quinlan* a61 55
3 b f Efisio—Tetravella (IRE) (Groom Dancer (USA))
1440[11] 1716[3] 1904[9] 2801[6] 3041[5] 3629[2] 3804[10] 4550[2] 4891[4] (Dead)

Fizzy Lizzy *H E Haynes* a51 38
7 b m Cool Jazz—Formidable Liz (Formidable (USA))
22[4]

Fizzy Lover *T D Easterby* 5
2 b f Kyllachy—In Love Again (IRE) (Prince Rupert (FR))
1087[15]

Flag Of Honour (IRE) *D T Hughes* 71
2 b c Alhaarth(IRE) —Polyandry (IRE) (Pennekamp (USA))
5397a[16]

Flagstone (USA) *G A Swinbank* 57
3 ch g Distant View(USA) —Navarene (USA) (Known Fact (USA))
1529[6] 1968[3] 2581[4] 3183[8]

Flam *J R Fanshawe* 74
2 b f Singspiel(IRE) —Delauncy (Machiavellian (USA))
5596[5] 6470[6]

Flame Creek (IRE) *E J Creighton* a89 79
11 b g Shardari—Sheila's Pet (IRE) (Welsh Term)
434[5] 829[6] 1148[10] 2675[6] 2860[10] 3279[6] 6819[2] 6875[3] 7110[3] 7154[7]

Flamestone *A E Price* a45 54
3 b g Piccolo—Renee (Wolfhound (USA))
202[4] 454[8] 619[8] 912[11] 1750[7] 2661[6] 2978[3] 3540[3] 4106[8] 4337[6] 5508[9] 6108[9]

Flaming Cat (IRE) *F Watson* 49
4 bb g Orpen(USA) —Brave Cat (IRE) (Catrail (USA))
3675[6] 4771[4] 5179[13] 5553[9] 5739[11]

Flamingo Guitar (USA) *David Wachman* 91
4 ch m Storm Cat(USA) —Lotta Dancing (USA) (Alydar (USA))
5240a[7]

Flamingo Rainbow (GER) *H Rogers* 69
5 ch g Rainbow Quest(USA) —Flamingo Road (GER) (Acatenango (GER))
6555a[9]

Flare Star *T Hogan* 92
4 ch m Nashwan(USA) —Flame Cutter (USA) (Miswaki (USA))
1582[17] 2067a[14]

Flash Harry *M G Quinlan* a42 52
3 ch g Fantastic Light(USA) —Woodyousmileforme (USA) (Woodman (USA))
6999[4]

Flashin Amber *Peter Grayson* a16
3 ch g Kyllachy—Shebasis (USA) (General Holme (USA))
6339[12] 6877[12] 7032[8]

Flashing Feet (IRE) *Mrs L C Jewell* a43 35
3 b g Soviet Star(USA) —Delphini (IRE) (Seattle Dancer (USA))
68[7] 2140[7] 2454[10]

Flashing Floozie *A W Carroll* a49 51
4 ch m Muhtarram(USA) —High Habit (Slip Anchor)
133[9] 558[14] 804[5] 1206[9] 1888[16] 2142[6] 2708a[3] 5235[3] 5427[7] 5698[8]

Flash McGahon (IRE) *John M Oxx* a70 100
3 b g Namid—Astuti (IRE) (Waajib)
1171a[2] 1461a[5] 2050a[4] 2324a[5] 3139a[9] 4864a[14] 5394a[4] 5841a[9] 6363a[10]

Flash Of Colour *Mrs A J Perrett* a68 22
2 b c Averti(IRE) —Big Pink (IRE) (Bigstone (IRE))
2687[6] 6948[4] 7114[2]

Flash Of Fire (USA) *J M P Eustace* 57
2 b g Fantastic Light(USA) —Mistle Thrush (USA) (Storm Bird (CAN))
2041[15] 2473[11] 3478[8]

Flashy Max *Jedd O'Keeffe* a50 48
2 b c Primo Valentino(IRE) —Be Practical (Tragic Role (USA))
3833[8] 4285[8] 4612[8] 5038[4] 6307[11] 6814[5] 7007[2]

Flashy Photon *H Candy* 73
2 b g Compton Place—Showboat (USA) (Theatrical)
3962[11] (4537)

Flashy Wings *M R Channon* 113
4 ch m Zafonic(USA) —Lovealoch (IRE) (Lomond (USA))
862a[6] 2753[6]

Flavius (IRE) *Sir Michael Stoute* 76
3 b c Montjeu(IRE) —Stitching (IRE) (High Estate)
1659[5] 2005[4] (2909)

Flawed Genius *Sir Michael Stoute* 87
2 b c Fasliyev(USA) —Talented (Bustino)
2832[6] (3551) 4152[4] 4695[9]

Flaxby *Mrs J L Le Brocq* a62 63
5 b g Mister Baileys—Harryana (Efisio)
2708a[4] 5643[3]

Flaxton (UAE) *M Brittain* 29
2 b c Halling(USA) —Yasmeen Valley (USA) (Danzig Connection (USA))
3510[10] 4448[13] 4782[11]

Fleche Brisee (USA) *A Fabre* 89
3 br f Dynaformer(USA) —Affirm Miss (USA) (Sky Classic (CAN))
6953a[6]

Fleeting Shadow (IRE) *D K Weld* 109
3 b c Danehill(USA) —Rain Flower (IRE) (Indian Ridge)
1047a[4] 2051a[10] 2586a[8] 4412a[9] 5392a[5]

Fleeting Spirit (IRE) *J Noseda* 116
2 b f Invincible Spirit(IRE) —Millennium Tale (FR) (Distant Relative)
(2365) (4046) 4744[3] (5377) 5973[2]

Fleetway (IRE) *F Watson*
2 ch f Fleetwood(IRE) —Eponine (Sharpo)
4076[12]

Fleetwood Image *J R Weymes* a42 55
3 b g Fleetwood(IRE) —Change Of Image (Spectrum (IRE))
956[5]

Flemish Art (IRE) *M J Wallace*
2 b c Marju(IRE) —Danalia (IRE) (Danehill (USA))
4782[12]

Fleur De Montjeu (IRE) *W R Swinburn* 57
2 b f Montjeu(IRE) —Dancing Sensation (USA) (Faliraki)
4402[10] 5063[8] 6470[16]

Fleuret *Eve Johnson Houghton* 78
3 bb f Diktat—Forthwith (Midyan (USA))
2196[4] 2693[7] 4164[2] (4808) 5303[3] 5954[6]

Fleurina (FR) *Robert Collet* 94
2 b f Le Triton(USA) —Florfilla (FR) (Nombre Premier)
6416a[7] 6630a[8] 6939a[2]

Flex *D J Murphy* a19 47
2 b g Averti(IRE) —Floppie Disk (Magic Ring (IRE))
5363[11] 5521[10] 5699[5]

Flexible Friend (IRE) *D K Weld* 78
3 b c Danehill(USA) —Ripple Of Pride (IRE) (Sadler's Wells (USA))
4114a[11]

Flight Dream (FR) *M G Quinlan* a62
4 gr h Highest Honor(FR) —Flight Night (Night Shift (USA))
6766[10] 7174[4]

Flight Of The Hawk (IRE) *Miss Martina Anne Doran* a50 77
2 ch c Hawk Wing(USA) —Majestic Role (FR) (Theatrical)
6443a[10]

Flight Plan *C A Cyzer* a85 84
2 ch g Best Of The Bests(IRE) —Cyclone Connie (Dr Devious (IRE))
(4325) 4598[7] 4964[5] 5323[7] 6120[11]

Flight To Quality *M Johnston* 73
2 ch c Where Or When(IRE) —Southern Psychic (USA) (Alwasmi (USA))
4764[7] 5038[2] (5702)

Flighty Fellow (IRE) *T D Easterby* a69 85
7 ch g Flying Spur(AUS) —Al Theraab (USA) (Roberto (USA))
930[6] (1198) 2038[5] 2871[5] (3721) 4039[2] 4716[3] 4900[4] 5196[2] 5775[7] 6180[7]

Flint River *H Morrison* a80 82
9 b g Red Ransom(USA) —She's All Class (USA) (Rahy (USA))
235[7]

Flipando (IRE) *T D Barron* 106
6 b g Sri Pekan(USA) —Magic Touch (Fairy King (USA))
1157[6] 1480[12] 1767[4] (1915) (2093) 2755[2] 3558[11] 4385[3] 4745[7] 5412[7] 5631[15] 6155[15]

Floodlight Fantasy *Jedd O'Keeffe* a73 71
4 b g Fantastic Light(USA) —Glamadour (IRE) (Sanglamore (USA))
1090[14] 1263[5] 4003[8] 4717[11] 5983[8] 6801[9]

Flop (IRE) *M Brittain* 55
2 b f Fraam—Confidential (Generous (IRE))
2739[5] 3510[6] 3884[3]

Florado (GER) *H Hesse* 95
4 br h Dashing Blade—Florilla (GER) (Big Shuffle (USA))
6370a[6]

Floral Guest *G G Margarson* 36
2 b f Barathea(IRE) —Datura (Darshaan)
6080[11] 6254[7]

Floral Pegasus (AUS) *A S Cruz* 120
4 b h Fusaichi Pegasus(USA) —Crown Crest (Mill Reef (USA))
7091a[4]

Florentine Lady *D Shaw*
4 b m Medicean—Polytess (IRE) (Polish Patriot (USA))
4616[12] 5231[RR] 5567[11] 5981[13]

Florentino *C W Thornton* 31
3 b f Efisio—Sirene Bleu Marine (USA) (Secreto (USA))
4000[10] 4641[10] 4771[9]

Flores Sea (USA) *T D Barron* a64 80
3 ch g Luhuk(USA) —Perceptive (USA) (Capote (USA))
1228[8] (1484) 1802[4] 2577[7] 3196[6] 3707[10] 6492[10] 6727[15]

Florimund *Sir Michael Stoute* a89 87
4 b g Sadler's Wells(USA) —Valentine Girl (Alzao (USA))
1477[5] 1844[18] 2314[7]

Florista Gg (URU) *J S Moore* 75
4 ch m Gulpha Gorge(USA) —Flor De Fango (URU) (Villon (ARG))
3527[7] 4399[6]

Floristry *Sir Michael Stoute* 104
2 b f Fasliyev(USA) —Zaeema (Zafonic (USA))
3245[7] 4487[3] (5442) (6154) (6488)

Flor Y Nata (USA) *Sir Mark Prescott* a79 99
4 b m Fusaichi Pegasus(USA) —Rose Of Zollern (IRE) (Seattle Dancer (USA))
3028[5] 3628[8] 4060[11] 4814[12]

Flower *C A Cyzer* a60 55
2 ch f Zamindar(USA) —Time For Tea (IRE) (Imperial Frontier (USA))
5944[11] 6140[7] 6448[4]

Flower Appeal *M W Easterby* 41
2 br f Diktat—Flower O'Cannie (IRE) (Mujadil (USA))
3092[10] 3761[8] 4578[10]

Flower Haven *M J Gingell* a53 28
5 b m Dr Fong(USA) —Daisy May (In The Wings)
200[10] 443[7]

Flower Of Cork (IRE) *I A Wood* a61 47
3 b f Noverre(USA) —Scarlet Ribbons (Anabaa (USA))
1091[11] 1538[16] 2553[7] 2844[6] 4397[14] 4471[4] 4635[9] 5090[16] 5716[12]

Flower Of Kent (USA) *J H M Gosden* a74 69
3 b f Diesis—Apple Of Kent (USA) (Kris S (USA))
1407[6] 2354[12]

Flower Song *A King* a27 57
2 b f Act One—Sweet Pea (Persian Bold)
6093[11] 6418[10] 6601[12]
Flowing Cape (IRE) *R Hollinshead* 89
2 b c Cape Cross(IRE) —Jet Lock (USA) (Crafty Prospector (USA))
5143[4] 5587[2] 5910[7] 6486[2]
Fluffy *K A Ryan* a57 56
4 b m Efisio—Sirene Bleu Marine (USA) (Secreto (USA))
2520[4] 4106[2] 5907[15]
Flushed *A J McCabe* a51 35
3 b g Foxhound(USA) —Sweet And Lucky (Lucky Wednesday)
60[5] 304[8] 373[8] 619[10] 667[2] 910[6] 1164[11] 1266[8] 2110[10] 3605[4] 4842[14] 5041[9]
Fluters House *S Woodman* a21 39
3 b g Piccolo—Little Tumbler (IRE) (Cyrano De Bergerac)
1633[8] 2173[10] 2560[8] 2962[5] 3366[11]
Fluttering Rose *R M Beckett* a70 61
3 gr f Compton Place—Bethesda (Distant Relative)
188[4] 3688[8] 4269[5] 4740[9] 5433[11]
Fly By Jove (IRE) *Jane Southcombe* a55 49
4 b g Fasliyev(USA) —Flyleaf (FR) (Persian Bold)
92[6] 274[13] 1001[6] 1559[6] 2077[11] 4532[16]
Fly By Magic (IRE) *Patrick Carey* a56 83
3 b f Indian Rocket—Travel Tricks (IRE) (Presidium)
5841a[5]
Flying Applause *A King* a69 68
2 b g Royal Applause—Mrs Gray (Red Sunset)
1970[10] 3363[6] 3962[9] 4762[7] 5117[3] 5314[3] (6665)
Flying Bantam (IRE) *R A Fahey* a83 75
6 b g Fayruz—Natural Pearl (Petong)
70[5] 243[3] 367[2] (468) 609[10] 673[3] 771[6] (1133) 1458[6] 1892[3] 2190[2] (2550)
Flying Blue (FR) *R Martin-Sanchez* 95
2 b c Fly To The Stars—Viking's Cove (USA) (Miswaki (USA))
4653a[5] 5660a[5]
Flying Clarets (IRE) *R A Fahey* 99
4 b m Titus Livius(FR) —Sheryl Lynn (Miller's Mate)
(1083) 1414[2] 1767[2] 2236[15] 3558[2] 4005[4] 4849[6] 5142[7] 5631[12] (6185) 6499[9]
Flying Doctor *N G Richards* 37
4 b g Mark Of Esteem(IRE) —Vice Vixen (CAN) (Vice Regent (CAN))
4096[13]
Flying Encore (IRE) *W R Swinburn* a73 78
3 b f Royal Applause—Come Fly With Me (Bluebird (USA))
2010[6] 2369[5] 3087[6] 3852[9] 4317[3] 4884[5] 5136[8]
Flying First Class (USA) *D Wayne Lukas* a100
3 b c Perfect Mandate(USA) —Flying In Style (USA) (Flying Sensation (USA))
1882a[9]
Flying Goose (IRE) *L M Cumani* a86 84
3 ch c Danehill Dancer(IRE) —Top Of The Form (IRE) (Masterclass (USA))
2312[3] (3447) 4170[3] 4811[5] 5473[3] 6209[13] 6391[3]
Flying Grey (IRE) *P A Blockley* a57 58
3 gr g Desert Prince(IRE) —Grey Goddess (Godswalk (USA))
1538[13] (2978) 3040[4] 3274[5]
Flying Indian *A M Balding* a65 63
2 ch f Hawk Wing(USA) —Poppadam (Salse (USA))
1123[7] 1503[5] 2590[2] 2997[7] 3426[6] 4737[7] 5096[7] 5529[4]
Flyingit (USA) *Thomas Mullins* a76 90
4 b m Lear Fan(USA) —Byre Bird (USA) (Diesis)
101[2] 233[6] 299[6] 4240a[7]
Flying Pass *R J Price* a65 51
5 b g Alzao(USA) —Complimentary Pass (Danehill (USA))
4108[9]
Flying Princess (IRE) *A Berry* 17
3 ch f Bad As I Wanna Be(IRE) —Baltic Beach (IRE) (Polish Precedent (USA))
2032[11] 3639[13] 3994[10] 4938[9] 7019[13]
Flying Sommelier (USA) *T D Barron* 61
2 b g Dixieland Band(USA) —Charming Lauren (USA) (Meadowlake (USA))
2562[5]
Flying Spirit (IRE) *G L Moore* a72 76
8 b g Flying Spur(AUS) —All Laughter (Vision (USA))
232[5] 316[4] 640[9] 1741[2] 2055[2]
Flying Spud *A J Chamberlain*
6 ch g Fraam—Lorcanjo (Hallgate)
1347[13]
Flying Tackle *I W McInnes* a45 56
9 ch g First Trump—Frighten The Life (Kings Lake (USA))
201[6] 441[10] 2386[10]
Flying Time *M R Channon* 65
2 b f Mark Of Esteem(IRE) —Seagreen (IRE) (Green Desert (USA))
4852[8] (5294) 6092[4]
Flying Valentino *G A Swinbank* 76
3 b f Primo Valentino(IRE) —Flying Romance (IRE) (Flying Spur (AUS))
1108[13] 2119[4] 2577[6] 3158[5] 4080[3] 4291[7] 4940[2] 6331[7] 6623[5] 6701[12]
Fly In Johnny (IRE) *R Hannon* 68
2 b c Fasliyev(USA) —Goodness Gracious (IRE) (Green Desert (USA))
5868[4] 6125[4] 6419[12]
Fly Kiss *C E Brittain* a46 82
2 b f Arkadian Hero(USA) —Kiss Me Kate (Aragon)
1087[9] 1680[9] 2768[10] (4265) (4524) 4804[5]
Flylowflylong (IRE) *I Semple* a70 71
4 b m Danetime(IRE) —Jellybeen (IRE) (Petardia)
967[4] 1459[10] (1626) 2169[8] 2564[2] 2988[8] 3539[7]
Fly My Dream (GER) *Mario Hofer* 4
2 ch f Big Shuffle(USA) —Fly To Win (IRE) (Ali-Royal (IRE))
4837a[9] 5848a[7]

Flyng Teapot (IRE) *C Boutin* a91 93
3 ch c King Charlemagne(USA) —Joyfullness (USA) (Dixieland Band (USA))
695a[7] 1005a[5]
Flyoff (IRE) *Mrs N Macauley* a40 53
10 b g Mtoto—Flyleaf (FR) (Persian Bold)
134[7] 333[6]
Fly Society (DEN) *S Jensen* 107
6 b h Flyinfact(FR) —Pollenca (IRE) (Law Society (USA))
2131a[10] 4874a[13]
Fly So Free (IRE) *D Nicholls* 60
3 b f Fath(USA) —Xania (Mujtahid (USA))
2844[13] 3535[11] 3752[15] 4226[10]
Fly Time *Mrs L Williamson* a48 62
3 b f Fraam—Kissing Time (Lugana Beach)
1763[3] 2029[7] 2895[5] 3281[4] 3870[2] 4314[8] 4529[12]
Fly With The Stars (USA) *M Johnston* 77
2 ch g Fusaichi Pegasus(USA) —Forest Key (USA) (Green Forest (USA))
5813[10] 6285[5] 6725[3]
Focus Group (USA) *J J Quinn* 95
6 b g Kris S(USA) —Interim (Sadler's Wells (USA))
846[7] 1575[5]
Folga *J G Given* a91 99
5 b m Atraf—Desert Dawn (Belfort (FR))
1372[2] 1670[11] 2379a[7] 3746[10] 4798[11] 5403[7]
Fol Hollow (IRE) *D Nicholls* a64 92
2 b g Monashee Mountain(USA) —Constance Do (Risk Me (FR))
845[2] 1706[2] 2147[4] 2710[2] 3092[3] (3370) (4152) 4695[6] (4921)
Folio (IRE) *W J Musson* a77 93
7 b g Perugino(USA) —Bayleaf (Efisio)
995[6] 1543[9] 2906[8] 3558[15] 4166[9] 4551[5] 5362[6] 5775[2] 6110[11] 6576[4]
Folk (USA) *Saeed Bin Suroor* a114
3 b f Quiet American(USA) —Polish Style (USA) (Danzig (USA))
(476a) (647a) 859a[10] 3810a[3] 4628a[7]
Folk Opera (IRE) *Saeed Bin Suroor* a76 92
3 ch f Singspiel(IRE) —Skiphall (Halling (USA))
(1127) 1663[3]
Follingworth (IRE) *A D Brown* a22 40
4 ch m Midhish—Pennine Way (IRE) (Waajib)
273[9] 372[13]
Following Flow (USA) *R Allan* a60 77
5 bb g King Of Kings(IRE) —Sign Here (USA) (Private Terms (USA))
298[6] 366[5] 605[11] 768[4] 1627[11] 1893[10] 2091[10] 2563[14] 3180[9] 3674[6] 3814[11] 3996[4] 4891[5] 5083[4] 6908[11]
Followmyfootsteps (USA) *David Wachman* 114
3 bl c Giant's Causeway(USA) —Lady Carson (USA) (Carson City (USA))
1703a[6] 2051a[5]
Follow On *A P Jarvis* a79 73
5 b h Barathea(IRE) —Handora (IRE) (Hernando (FR))
192[4] 265[3] 458[3] 1526[3] 1793[14] 2430[8] 3217[9] 3945[11] 4067[6] 4297[3] 5204[5] 5573[5]
Follow The Band *R Hannon* a34 60
2 b c Prince Sabo—Pea Green (Try My Best (USA))
2510[8] 4571[10] 5126[12] 5417[7] 5939[10] 6478[10]
Follow The Colours (IRE) *J W Hills* a74 72
4 b g Rainbow Quest(USA) —Gardenia (IRE) (Sadler's Wells (USA))
6628[8] 7056[8]
Follow The Flag (IRE) *C F Wall* a70 71
3 ch g Traditionally(USA) —Iktidar (Green Desert (USA))
342[2] 498[5] 737[5] 1117[7] 1297[8] 2545[6] 7269[12]
Follow Your Spirit *B Palling* 53
2 b g Compton Place—Ymlaen (IRE) (Desert Prince (IRE))
4876[11] 5720[13] 6246[8]
Folly Lodge *B W Hills* a75 93
3 ch f Grand Lodge(USA) —Marika (Marju (IRE))
(1837) 3430[13] 3745[6] 4601[2] 5355[12] 6497[9]
Fonce De (FR) *Rod Collet* a97 90
5 gr m Smadoun(FR) —Pro Lina (FR) (Linamix (FR))
31a[3]
Fondled *J R Fanshawe* 91
3 b f Selkirk(USA) —Embraced (Pursuit Of Love)
1639[4] 2153[3] 2998[2] 4608[3] (5545)
Fondness *B G Powell* a56 72
4 ch m Dr Fong(USA) —Island Story (Shirley Heights)
112[7] 270[2] 1888[15] 4131[4] 4531[4]
Fongs Gazelle *M Johnston* a71 89
3 b f Dr Fong(USA) —Greensand (Green Desert (USA))
(772) (1211) (1576) 1827[5] 2506[5] 2906[4] 3335[9] (4060) 4147[4]
Fongster *A M Hales* a10
2 b g Dr Fong(USA) —First Lite Of Dawn (Green Adventure (USA))
5200[11] 5721[10] 6723[12]
Font *J R Fanshawe* 95
4 b g Sadler's Wells(USA) —River Saint (USA) (Irish River (FR))
1842[3] 2840[2] (3476) 4720[3] 5764[4] 6169[15]
Fontana Amorosa *K A Ryan* a83 96
3 ch f Cadeaux Genereux—Bella Lambada (Lammtarra (USA))
(755) 1298[12] 1808[2] (Dead)
Fontcia (FR) *D Sepulchre* 103
3 b f Enrique—Fontaine Guerard (FR) (Homme De Loi (IRE))
989a[4] 1388a[4] 2501a[9] 5058a[5] 5719a[3] 6460a[12] 6889a[10]
Fonthill Road (IRE) *R A Fahey* a77 111
7 ch g Royal Abjar(USA) —Hannah Huxtable (IRE) (Master Willie)
1657[3] 1770[7] 2463[12] 3088[3] 3529[2] 3894[7] 4438a[6] 4747[6] 5616[5] 5797[9] (6183) (6363a)
Foodbroker Founder *D R C Elsworth* 78
7 ch g Groom Dancer(USA) —Nemea (USA) (The Minstrel (CAN))
2512[9] 4365[7]

Foolin Myself *B W Hills* 83
2 b c Montjeu(IRE) —Friendlier (Zafonic (USA))
5977[5] (6618)
Foolish Groom *R Hollinshead* a64 67
6 ch g Groom Dancer(USA) —Scared (Royal Academy (USA))
976[6] 1539[4] 1673[3] 2214[3] 2716[7] 3615[8] (4259) 4532[5] 4880[10] 5348[9]
Fool Me (IRE) *E S McMahon* 87
3 b c Mull Of Kintyre(USA) —Dawn's Folly (IRE) (Bluebird (USA))
1009[5] 1298[14] 1825[11]
Fools Gold *T D Easterby* a56
2 b c Ishiguru(USA) —Sally Green (IRE) (Common Grounds)
6156[13] 7139[3]
Fool's Wildcat (USA) *B J Meehan* a79 94
2 bb c Forest Wildcat(USA) —Nine Flags (USA) (Forty Niner (USA))
3958[6] 4571[3] 5135[4] (5628) 5972[5]
Forbidden (IRE) *Daniel Mark Loughnane* a65 68
4 ch g Singspiel(IRE) —Fragrant Oasis (USA) (Rahy (USA))
6121[2] 6579[3] 6874[9] 6894[14]
Force Celebre (IRE) *M H Tompkins* a71
3 ch g Peintre Celebre(USA) —Two Shonas (IRE) (Persian Heights)
386[5] 1566[3] 1937[5] 2610[11] 4069[12] 4292[10]
Forced Upon Us *P J McBride* a68 58
3 ch g Allied Forces(USA) —Zing (Zilzal (USA))
974[4] 1155[12] 2177[5] 2668[3] 4272[7] 4856[7] 5299[7] (5900) 6210[2] 6415[12] 6831[7] 7227[12]
Force Group (IRE) *M H Tompkins* a59 71
3 b g Invincible Spirit(IRE) —Spicebird (IRE) (Ela-Mana-Mou)
1194[2] 1827[6]
Forefathers (USA) *W Mott* a104 63
3 b c Gone West(USA) —Star Of Goshen (USA) (Lord At War (ARG))
6510a[10]
Foreign Affairs *Sir Mark Prescott* a93 110
9 ch h Hernando(FR) —Entente Cordiale (USA) (Affirmed (USA))
1833[5] 2409a[7]
Foreign Edition (IRE) *Miss J A Camacho* a82 86
5 b g Anabaa(USA) —Palacegate Episode (IRE) (Drumalis)
1223[13] 1847[11] 2088[11] 2508[12] 4768[7] 5330[9] 5701[12] 5964[11] 6582[3]
Foreigner (IRE) *C W J Farrell* a61 73
4 b g Montjeu(IRE) —Northumbrian Belle (IRE) (Distinctly North (USA))
6920a[10]
Foreign Language (USA) *N A Callaghan* a74
4 ch m Distant View(USA) —Binary (Rainbow Quest (USA))
38[4] 96[10]
Foreign Music (FR) *H J Groschel* 101
3 b f Tiger Hill(IRE) —Foreign Affair (GER) (Goofalik (USA))
6046a[3]
Foreign Rhythm (IRE) *N Tinkler* 76
2 ch f Distant Music(USA) —Happy Talk (IRE) (Hamas (IRE))
2869[2] 3532[2] 4016[2] 4447[3] 5521[3] 5802[6] 6282[11]
For Eileen *G C H Chung* a50 33
3 b f Dinar(USA) —Dreams Of Zena (Dreams End)
162[7] 3455[10] 3873[11] 4530[13] 5710[10]
Foreland Sands (IRE) *J R Best* a58 40
3 b g Desert Sun—Penrose (IRE) (Wolfhound (USA))
290[3] 360[3] 786[6] 1119[3] 5276[8] 5606[5] 6176[4] 6402[2]
Foreplay (IRE) *E A L Dunlop* a82 71
4 b m Lujain(USA) —Watch Me (IRE) (Green Desert (USA))
28[8]
Foresight *Mrs A J Perrett* 77
2 ch c Observatory(USA) —Avoidance (USA) (Cryptoclearance (USA))
6494[3]
Forest Dane *Mrs N Smith* a88 88
7 b g Danetime(IRE) —Forest Maid (Thatching)
(1023) 1653[8] 1971[5] 2440[3] 2688[2] 3464[5] 4122[24] 6231[3] 6437[2] 6606[11] 6900[10]
Forest Emerald (IRE) *J W Mullins* a39
5 b m Desert Sun—Moonbi Range (IRE) (Nordico (USA))
6261[11]
Forest Viking (IRE) *J S Wainwright* 61
5 b g Orpen(USA) —Berhala (IRE) (Doyoun)
4488[11]
Forever Autumn *D G Bridgwater* a29 61
4 b g Sinndar(IRE) —Photo Call (Chief Singer)
4757[4] 5235[6]
Forever Bold *J G Portman* a36 43
3 b g Bold Edge—Still In Love (Emarati (USA))
4018[7] 4666[10] 5129[10]
Forever Changes *L Montague Hall* a52
2 gr f Bertolini(USA) —Days Of Grace (Wolfhound (USA))
6425[10] 6705[4] 6820[6]
Forever My Lord *W A Murphy* a15
9 b g Be My Chief(USA) —In Love Again (IRE) (Prince Rupert (FR))
4475[10] 5283[17]
Forfeiter (USA) *C Gordon* a60 70
5 ch g Petionville(USA) —Picabo (USA) (Wild Again (USA))
39[9] 148[5] 5820[8] 7083[2] 7168[7]
Forget It *R Hannon* 68
2 b c Galileo(IRE) —Queens Way (FR) (Zafonic (USA))
6494[6]
Forgive Me *C E Brittain* 57
2 ch f Mark Of Esteem(IRE) —Francia (Legend Of France (USA))
5596[10]
Forgotten Voice (IRE) *J Noseda* a77
2 b c Danehill Dancer(IRE) —Asnieres (USA) (Spend A Buck (USA))
(6436)

For Life (IRE) *J E Long* a79 78
5 b g Bachir(IRE) —Zest (USA) (Zilzal (USA))
144[10] 254[8] (4029) 4395[2] (5064) (5711) (6273)
Formal Decree (GER) *Saeed Bin Suroor* 119
4 b g Diktat—Formida (FR) (Highest Honor (FR))
(176a) (330a) 600a[2] 862a[7] 2617a[S] 4013a[2] 4387[2] 5142[6] 5723[5]
Formation (USA) *E A L Dunlop* a77 66
2 ch g Van Nistelrooy(USA) —Miss Valedictorian (USA) (With Approval (CAN))
2885[6] 5200[3] 5702[3] 6436[2] (6675)
Formax (FR) *M P Tregoning* 101
5 gr g Marathon(USA) —Fortuna (FR) (Kaldoun (FR))
4043[15] 4601[8] 5419[2] 5950[11]
Formidable Guest *J Pearce* a58
3 b f Dilshaan—Fizzy Treat (Efisio)
1840[12] 2153[10] 5728[7] (6590) 6804[2] 6808[3] 6896[8] 7088[4]
Formidable Will (FR) *D Shaw* a71 39
5 b g Efisio—Shewillifshewants (IRE) (Alzao (USA))
14[6] 367[5] 466[4] 1718[7] 2516[6] 3408[11] 5897[3] 6735[12] (Dead)
Forrest Flyer (IRE) *Miss L A Perratt* 56
3 b c Daylami(IRE) —Gerante (USA) (Private Account (USA))
2312[8] 3015[6] 3587[10] 4718[4] 5000[9] 5906[7] 6561[3]
Forrest Star *Miss L A Perratt* 32
2 ch f Fraam—Starfleet (Inchinor)
5550[11]
Forroger (CAN) *M A Jarvis* 92
4 bb h Black Minnaloushe(USA) —Count On Romance (CAN) (Geiger Counter (USA))
(1288) 1771[10] 2209[7] 6110[2]
Forsters Plantin *J J Quinn* 37
3 ch f Muhtarram(USA) —Ischia (Lion Cavern (USA))
2341[5] 3611[12] 4156[12]
Forsyte Saga *M Johnston* a49 72
2 br f Machiavellian(USA) —First Of Many (Darshaan)
5306[2] 5524[2] 5913[5] 6471[14] 7190[7]
Fort Amhurst (IRE) *E A L Dunlop* 81
3 ch g Halling(USA) —Soft Breeze (Zafonic (USA))
(1062) 1987[U] 3960[9]
Fort Churchill (IRE) *B Ellison* a71 94
6 b g Barathea(IRE) —Brisighella (IRE) (Al Hareb (USA))
846[13] 995[5] 1245[6] 1822[8] (2218) 4043[7] 4153[4] 4720[15] 5748[4] 6011[26]
Forthefirstime *John M Oxx* 98
2 ch f Dr Fong(USA) —Gazebo (Cadeaux Genereux) (5435a)
Forthe Millionkiss (GER) *U Ostmann* 101
3 br c Dashing Blade—Forever Nice (GER) (Greinton)
2705a[3] 4874a[12]
Fort Hull (IRE) *Mrs A J Perrett* a35 56
2 b c Indian Lodge(IRE) —Pagan Princess (Mujtahid (USA))
5274[13] 5918[6] 6202[9] 6775[11]
Fortress *E J Alston* a59 63
4 b m Generous(IRE) —Imperial Bailiwick (IRE) (Imperial Frontier (USA))
376[8] 750[9] 1227[2] 1626[2] 1944[8] 2564[5] 2905[3] 3534[4]
Fortuitous (IRE) *I W McInnes* 13
3 ch g Tobougg(IRE) —Shallop (Salse (USA))
2118[10]
Fortuity (IRE) *J H M Gosden* a78 75
2 b c Xaar—Lucky Bet (IRE) (Lucky Guest)
1990[8] 2349[3] 2832[2] 3205[10] (3642)
Fortunate Isle (USA) *R A Fahey* a91 95
5 ch g Swain(IRE) —Isla Del Rey (USA) (Nureyev (USA))
264[3] 608[9] 1494[8] 1862[2] (2136) (2807) 3558[13] 4566[17] 4814[11]
Fortunate Isles (USA) *P Bary* 85
2 b f Seeking The Gold(USA) —Dragonada (USA) (Nureyev (USA))
6939a[7]
Fortune Dancer (USA) *G L Moore* a47 60
12 ch g Rahy(USA) —Abeesh (USA) (Nijinsky (CAN))
134[10] 288[5]
Fortunella *P Howling* 26
2 b f Polish Precedent(USA) —Hazy Heights (Shirley Heights)
4875[14]
Fortune Point (IRE) *A W Carroll* a51 63
9 ch g Cadeaux Genereux—Mountains Of Mist (IRE) (Shirley Heights)
2141[7] 2490[12] 3616[8] 6096[5] 6529[12]
Fortunes Maid (IRE) *M H Tompkins* a21
2 b f Raise A Grand(IRE) —Where's The Money (Lochnager)
6912[6]
Forty Hablador (ARG) *S Seemar* a78 63
6 b g Roar(USA) —La Charlatana (ARG) (Kasteel (FR))
104a[8]
Forty Licks (ARG) *I Jory* a117 107
5 br h Not For Sale(ARG) —Bailesa (ARG) (Equalize (USA))
863a[5]
Forzacurity *P D Evans* 35
8 ch g Forzando—Nice Lady (Connaught)
3403[8]
Forzarzi (IRE) *A Berry* 53
3 b c Forzando—Zarzi (IRE) (Suave Dancer (USA))
1625[10] 2393[7]
Fossgate *J D Bethell* a81 79
6 ch g Halling(USA) —Peryllys (Warning)
1771[15] 2342[2] 2987[7] 3412[7] 4421[3] 4817[5] 5334[7] 5777[10]
Four Dancers (GER) *Frau E Mader* 79
2 b c Seattle Dancer(USA) —Four Roses (IRE) (Darshaan)
6324a[2]

Four Kings *Karen McLintock* a11 59
6 b g Forzando—High Cut (Dashing Blade)
954[7] 1221[4] 1527[8] 1711[9] 4478[3] 4822[14] 4996[10] 5836[11]

Four Miracles *M H Tompkins* a64 76
3 b f Vettori(IRE) —North Kildare (USA) (Northjet)
1746[2] 2389[4] 2763[2] (3176) 3469[9] 4960[2] 6021[3] 6276[2]

Fourpenny Lane *Ms Joanna Morgan* a82 90
2 b f Efisio—Makara (Lion Cavern (USA))
3071a[6]

Four Sins (GER) *John M Oxx* 110
3 b f Sinndar(IRE) —Four Roses (IRE) (Darshaan)
946a[2] (1777a) 2211[4] 3576a[7] (5396a) 6373a[8]

Foursquare Flyer (IRE) *J Mackie* a68 73
5 ch g Tagula(IRE) —Isla (IRE) (Turtle Island (IRE))
(45) 153[8]

Fourteenth *Sir Michael Stoute* 86
3 b c Rainbow Quest(USA) —Valentine Girl (Alzao (USA))
2320[2] (2726) 3590[2] 4147[10] 5006[2]

Four Tel *N J Vaughan* a73 56
3 gr g Vettori(IRE) —Etienne Lady (IRE) (Imperial Frontier (USA))
2312[9] 3079[7] *(5781)* 5905[9] *6749[2] (7143)*

Fourth Dimension (IRE) *Miss T Spearing* a30 76
8 b g Entrepreneur—Isle Of Spice (USA) (Diesis)
2321[8] (3630) 4576[3]

Fowey (USA) *Sir Mark Prescott* a55
3 bb f Gone West(USA) —Kumari Continent (USA) (Kris S (USA))
106[4] 193[6] 6206[10] 6695[6]

Foxhaven *P R Chamings* 111
5 ch h Unfuwain(USA) —Dancing Mirage (IRE) (Machiavellian (USA))
1664[3] 2216[3] 2907[5] 3461[6] 4091[12] 5402[2] 5976[5] 6538[4]

Foxies Bychance *R D E Woodhouse* 14
2 ch f Zaha(CAN) —Strath Kitten (Scottish Reel)
1848[14] 2115[10] 2739[10]

Fox's Den *R M Beckett* 67
2 b g Foxhound(USA) —Milly's Lass (Mind Games)
898[3] 1882[5] 2241[7] 3947[4] 5706[5]

Foxxy *J R Norton* a51 67
3 b f Foxhound(USA) —Fisher Island (IRE) (Sri Pekan (USA))
99[3] 267[8] 1531[10] 1964[7] 2538[7] 3159[5] 3379[9] 4139[9] 4925[3] 5283[7] 5906[14]

Foxy Diplomat *Miss J R Tooth* a54
3 b g Foxhound(USA) —Diplomatist (Dominion)
3394[3] 6229[8] 6457[7] 6873[11]

Foxy Music *E J Alston* a45 85
3 b g Foxhound(USA) —Primum Tempus (Primo Dominie)
219[7] 1161[2] 1616[3] 2029[3] 2529[8] 3493[4] (3568) 4452[9] 4726[19]

Fraamington *M R Channon* a39 46
2 b g Fraam—Patandon Girl (IRE) (Night Shift (USA))
2193[11] 2410[6] 2605[5] *3065[8] 3392[5]* 4405[11] 5274[12] 5520[3] 5863[5] 6722[11] *7096[7]*

Fraamtastic Too *Jamie Poulton* a39 41
3 gr f Fraam—Jilly Woo (Environment Friend)
498[13] 1606[10] 2219[F]

Fracas (IRE) *David Wachman* 114
5 b h In The Wings—Klarifi (Habitat)
1050a[2] 1550a[2] 2064a[5] (2483a) (3983a) 4647a[2]

Fractured Foxy *J J Quinn* a74 74
3 b f Foxhound(USA) —Yanomami (USA) (Slew O'Gold (USA))
(34) 216[6] 433[3] 606[2] 1108[5] *1383[3]* 1710[5] *2146[2]* 2200[6] 4071[5]

Fragrancy (IRE) *M A Jarvis* a71 96
3 ch f Singspiel(IRE) —Zibet (Kris)
1257[2] 1956[5] (3591) 4060[5] 4785[4] 5156[2] 5537[2] (6016)

Frammenti *A J McCabe* a52 40
2 br f Fraam—Blushing Victoria (Weldnaas (USA))
2590[12] 2904[8] *3109[5] 4428[6] 5423[14] 5601[8]* 6329[7] *7007[9] 7136[7]*

Francesca D'Gorgio (USA) *J Noseda* 98
2 b f Proud Citizen(USA) —Betty's Solutions (USA) (Eltish (USA))
2364[9] 2756[4] 3432[5] (3962)

Francescas Boy (IRE) *P D Niven* a39 46
4 b g Titus Livius(FR) —Mica Male (ITY) (Law Society (USA))
4249[7] *5389[6]*

Francesco *Evan Williams* a56 55
3 ch g Vettori(IRE) —Violet (IRE) (Mukaddamah (USA))
1224[5] 2105[14] 5472[6]

Franchoek (IRE) *A King* 80
3 ch g Trempolino(USA) —Snow House (IRE) (Vacarme (USA))
3367[5] 3876[3] (4104) 4391[3] (4877) (5111)

Francis *Niels Petersen* 73
9 b g Emperor Jones(USA) —Bint Damascus (USA) (Damascus (USA))
(5262a)

Frankalbert (IRE) *E Pellegrino* a61
3 b c Fasliyev(USA) —Faribole (IRE) (Esprit Du Nord (USA))
6024[9]

Frank Crow *J S Goldie* 79
4 b g Josr Algarhoud(IRE) —Belle De Nuit (IRE) (Statoblest)
969[2] 1198[14] (1455) 1939[5] 2397[10] 2822[5] 3346[7] 3813[7] 4228[8] (4479) 4704[4] 5035[7] 6021[12]

Franksalot (IRE) *I W McInnes* a66 76
7 ch g Desert Story(IRE) —Rosie's Guest (IRE) (Be My Guest (USA))
70[7] 130[5] 236[3] 292[4] 310[2] 1064[4] (1260) (1492) 1597[9] 2272[5] (2508) 2550[5] 2985[10] 3534[5] 3816[11] 3999[9] 4797[6] 5303[11] 5701[11]

Frank's Quest (IRE) *A B Haynes* a51 60
7 b g Mujadil(USA) —Questuary (IRE) (Rainbow Quest (USA))
273[P] 6968[12] 7167[10] 7276[8]

Franky'N'Jonny *M J Attwater* a49 47
4 b m Groom Dancer(USA) —Bron Hilda (IRE) (Namaqualand (USA))
2963[6] 3175[4] 3868[12] *5128[5] 5338[5]* 5864[7] *6361[8] 6642[11] 6774[8] 6893[2] 6991[9] 7125[6] 7247[5]*

Fraternal *R Charlton* a58 72
3 ch g Dr Fong(USA) —Abbey Strand (USA) (Shadeed (USA))
1398[8] 1812[9] 2127[6] 4357[3] *4951[5]*

Fraternity *J A Pickering* a49 38
10 b g Grand Lodge(USA) —Catawba (Mill Reef (USA))
20[2] 129[9] 271[6] 364[5] 450[10]

Fratt'n Park (IRE) *J J Bridger* a65 69
4 b m Tagula(IRE) —Bouffant (High Top)
30[6] 85[14] (Dead)

Fr Dominic (USA) *R M Beckett* 82
2 bb c Arch(USA) —Collodia (USA) (Leo Castelli (USA))
(5598)

Freda's Choice (IRE) *Patrick Morris* a56 62
4 b m Shinko Forest(IRE) —Marimar (IRE) (Grand Lodge (USA))
(94) 200[7] 570[6]

Freddy (ARG) *D K Ivory* a59 71
8 ch h Roy(USA) —Folgada (USA) (Lyphard's Wish (FR))
844[10] 1813[14] 2471[8] 2887[9] *3598[8] 4025[4]* 4660[14]

Fred's Lad *M W Easterby* a92 102
2 b g Warningford—Lawless Bridget (Alnasr Alwasheek)
(926) 1772[3] (2024) 2737[10] 4724[3] 5032[2] *5219[8]*

Freedom Song *R Charlton* a69
2 b f Singspiel(IRE) —Girl Of My Dreams (IRE) (Marju (IRE))
5681[2] 6140[4] 6855[4]

Freedonia *J E Hammond* 115
5 b m Selkirk(USA) —Forest Rain (FR) (Caerleon (USA))
663a[11] 4215a[6]

Free Fallin *P W Chapple-Hyam* 68
2 b f Desert Prince(IRE) —Dixielake (IRE) (Lake Coniston (IRE))
3706[9] 4796[7] 5596[14] 5883[9]

Freeloader (IRE) *R A Fahey* a88 90
7 b g Revoque(IRE) —Indian Sand (Indian King (USA))
1180[8] 1767[7]

Freemusic (IRE) *L Riccardi* 108
3 b c Celtic Swing—Favignana (GER) (Grand Lodge (USA))
1336a[2] 6687a[5]

Free Offer *J L Dunlop* 92
3 b f Generous(IRE) —Proserpine (Robellino (USA))
1089[6] 1929[9] 3058[10] (4205) (5067) 5445[3] 5978[2]

Free Roses (IRE) *J G Given* 97
4 b m Fasliyev(USA) —Ghanaj (Caerleon (USA))
4090[17] 4196[10] 4373[10]

Free To Air *A M Balding* a80 84
4 b g Generous(IRE) —Petonica (IRE) (Petoski)
753[6] 5334[6]

Fregate Island (IRE) *J G Given* a85 89
4 gr g Daylami(IRE) —Briery (IRE) (Salse (USA))
1083[3] (1470) 1844[11] 2238[2] *2994[5] 7236[7]*

Fremen (USA) *D Nicholls* a87 104
7 ch g Rahy(USA) —Northern Trick (USA) (Northern Dancer (CAN))
657[3] 697[2] 1458[13] 2807[6] 3138a[7] (3813) (4049) 4745[5] 5031[4] (5615) 6011[7]

French Art *D R C Elsworth* 78
2 ch c Peintre Celebre(USA) —Orange Sunset (IRE) (Roanoke (USA))
5951[5]

French Gallery (FR) *J-P Gallorini* a61
2 ch c Gallery Of Zurich(IRE) —Swiss Native (IRE) (Be My Native (USA))
6879a[6]

Frenchgate *I W McInnes* a44 46
6 br g Paris House—Let's Hang On (IRE) (Petorius)
1210[13] 1271[14]

French Opera *N J Henderson* a52 69
4 b g Bering—On Fair Stage (IRE) (Sadler's Wells (USA))
3448[3] 5111[3]

French Riviera *Sir Michael Stoute* 80
2 b c Montjeu(IRE) —Arietta's Way (IRE) (Darshaan)
6725[2]

Fresh Bread (USA) *Maria Rita Salvioni* 89
4 b m Mr Greeley(USA) —Lo Cal Bread (USA) (Native Prospector (USA))
6221a[6]

Fresh Mint (IRE) *M J Wallace* a84 54
3 b f Sadler's Wells(USA) —Valley Of Song (Caerleon (USA))
(6780) (6967) 7046[2]

Fretwork *R Hannon* a94 86
3 b f Galileo(IRE) —Celtic Cross (Selkirk (USA))
1391[4] (1785) 2305[3] 3590[4] 4185[4] 5006[3] 5955[4] *(6356)*

Freudian Slip *S Curran* a66 65
2 b f Ishiguru(USA) —Perle D'Azur (Mind Games)
3751[4] 3835[2] *4273[4] 4882[4]* 5313[3] *5603[11] 6432[9] 6828[7] 6928[10]*

Freya Tricks *I Semple* 68
3 b f Noverre(USA) —Trick Of Ace (USA) (Clever Trick (USA))
1804[2] 2464[3] 2760[5] 4139[5]

Friction *J G Portman* 43
2 b f Auction House(USA) —Frisson (Slip Anchor)
1960[13] 2723[8] 3296[4] 4363[6] 5186[10] *5984[13]*

Friendly Island (USA) *T Pletcher* a115 102
6 ch h Crafty Friend(USA) —Island Queen (USA) (Ogygian (USA))
860a[2]

Friends Hope *P A Blockley* a80 62
6 ch m Docksider(USA) —Stygian (USA) (Irish River (FR))
(7109) (7237)

Frigid *L M Cumani* 34
3 b f Indian Ridge—Frangy (Sadler's Wells (USA))
4908[8]

Fri Guy (USA) *Dale Romans* 115
4 ch h Theatrical—Stormy Squall (USA) (Summer Squall (USA))
4415a[7] 6513a[7]

Frimley's Matterry *R E Barr* 55
7 b g Bluegrass Prince(IRE) —Lonely Street (Frimley Park)
1527[3] 2390[13] 2893[8] 4141[3] 4706[15] 4822[11] 5083[9] 5284[5] 5503[15]

Fringe *Jane Chapple-Hyam* a76 90
4 ch m In The Wings—El Jazirah (Kris)
365[2] 3978[4] 4765[2] *5500[3]* (6204)

Frisbee *T D Easterby* a50
3 b f Efisio—Flying Carpet (Barathea (IRE))
908[5]

Frisky Talk (IRE) *B W Hills* a80 77
3 b f Fasliyev(USA) —Happy Talk (IRE) (Hamas (IRE))
1520[4] 1825[9] 3061[9] 3637[4] 4123[17] 4396[12] 5139[7] 5418[5]

Friston Forest (IRE) *A Fabre* 114
3 ch c Barathea(IRE) —Talented (Bustino)
1057a[3] 6028a[4]

Frith (IRE) *Mrs L B Normile* 51
5 b g Benny The Dip(USA) —Melodist (USA) (The Minstrel (CAN))
270[10] 966[5] 1532[11] 3538[2] 5482[12] 5553[11]

Frivolous (IRE) *J H M Gosden* 76
2 b f Green Desert(USA) —Sweet Folly (IRE) (Singspiel (IRE))
4402[8] 4602[4]

Frizzini *N Tinkler* a58 52
2 b g Bertolini(USA) —Charming Lotte (Nicolotte)
2021[10] 2818[6] 3812[11] *4459[8] 5176[5] 5365[10] 6023[8]*

Froissee *N A Callaghan* a81 82
3 b f Polish Precedent(USA) —Crinkle (IRE) (Distant Relative)
2203[4] 2607[2] (2748) (2905) 3100[2] 3855[3] 4166[10] *4949[4]* 5537[4] 6497[3]

Fromsong (IRE) *D K Ivory* a85 83
9 b g Fayruz—Lindas Delight (Batshoof)
79[11] 419[12] 1061[2] 1464[9] 2318[5] 2673[4] *(3212) 3623[11]* 4204[6] 4664[3] *4965[3] 5119[4]* 5379[5] *6141[7] 6273[6] 6589[6] 7279[8]*

Frontline In Focus (IRE) *K R Burke* a63 86
3 ch f Daggers Drawn(USA) —Christan (IRE) (Al Hareb (USA))
6355[10]

Front Rank (IRE) *Mrs Dianne Sayer* a72 66
7 b g Sadler's Wells(USA) —Alignment (IRE) (Alzao (USA))
2431[6] 3012[5] 4096[8] 5087[8]

Frosty Night (IRE) *M Johnston* 87
3 b g Night Shift(USA) —Abla (Robellino (USA))
1110[6] 2231[14] 3691[10] 3959[7] 4248[4] 4735[7] 5385[10] 6077[3] 6380[13]

Frozen Fire (GER) *A P O'Brien* 94
2 b c Montjeu(IRE) —Flamingo Sea (USA) (Woodman (USA))
6489[8]

Frynia (USA) *C Laffon-Parias* a63 81
2 br f Cat Thief(USA) —Wayward Bound (USA) (Mr Prospector (USA))
7048a[10]

Fueguino (ARG) *M Kettle* a39 65
9 ch g Luhuk(USA) —Fontina (ARG) (Salt Marsh (USA))
477a[12]

Fuel Cell (IRE) *J O'Reilly* a59 42
6 b g Desert Style(IRE) —Tappen Zee (Sandhurst Prince)
126[4] 288[7] 431[5] 500[5] (682) 1227[9] *1350[5] 1906[5]* 2027[10] *4739[9]*

Fujin Dancer (FR) *R A Fahey* 61
2 ch c Storming Home—Badaayer (USA) (Silver Hawk (USA))
5745[11] 6281[9]

Fulford *M Brittain* a59 62
2 ch g Elmaamul(USA) —Last Impression (Imp Society (USA))
1792[9] 3977[2] 4279[7] 4612[3] 4923[11] 5582[11]

Fullandby (IRE) *T J Etherington* a90 109
5 b g Monashee Mountain(USA) —Ivory Turner (Efisio)
1088[5] 1474[12] 1651[3] 2463[4] 3089[8] (3586) 3975[11] 4614[10] (5407) 5616[15] 6338[15]

Full House (IRE) *P R Webber* a71 98
8 br g King's Theatre(IRE) —Nirvavita (FR) (Highest Honor (FR))
(1959) (2736) 4056[10] 6335[26]

Full Marks *J Noseda* a63 85
2 b f Dansili—Flying Wanda (Alzao (USA))
6087[2] *6543[4]*

Full Of Gold (FR) *Mme C Head-Maarek* 107
2 ch c Gold Away(IRE) —Funny Feerie (FR) (Sillery (USA))
(6782a)

Full Of Promise (USA) *Mrs A J Perrett* a62 42
3 b f Street Cry(IRE) —Believe It Beloved (USA) (Clever Trick (USA))
1665[11] 1961[11] 5013[11] *6206[4] 6407[11] 6871[9]*

Full Of Zest *Mrs L J Mongan* a65 53
5 ch m Pivotal—Tangerine (Primo Dominie)
278[13] 1342[10]

Full Spate *J M Bradley* a35 68
12 ch g Unfuwain(USA) —Double River (USA) (Irish River (FR))
1640[9] 2187[5] 2619[6] 2652[5] 3873[12] 5062[13]

Full Speed (GER) *G A Swinbank* 73
2 b g Sholokhov(IRE) —Flagny (FR) (Kaldoun (FR))
5321[9] 5904[2] 6307[5]

Full Victory (IRE) *R A Farrant* a85 89
5 b g Imperial Ballet(IRE) —Full Traceability (IRE) (Ron's Victory (USA))
1209[8] *1401[10]* 1765[3] 2107[3] (2180) 2401[5] 2807[2] 3002[4] 3556[3] 3900[6] 4049[6] 5776[5] *6067[2]* 6180[17] 6539[4] *6674[7] 7002[8]*

Fulminant (IRE) *W Kujath* 101
6 b g Big Shuffle(USA) —Flagny (FR) (Kaldoun (FR))
1189a[4] 2811a[6] 4190a[13]

Ful Of Grace (IRE) *M G Quinlan* 56
3 b f Marju(IRE) —Mitawa (IRE) (Alhaarth (IRE))
3079[5] 3436[6] 3710[13] 4339[12] 4821[10] 5774[8] 6408[2] (6570)

Fulvio (USA) *P Howling* a61 21
7 b g Sword Dance—One Tuff Gal (USA) (Lac Ouimet (USA))
26[3] 180[3] 379[7] 440[6] 637[3] 801[7] 1360[6] 1906[10] 2258[6] 2591[4] 2798[10] 3730[4] 4294[8] *4673[10] 4914[7] 5310[9]*

Funatfuntasia *Ms Joanna Morgan* a70 79
3 b g Dansili—Guntakal (IRE) (Night Shift (USA))
7037a[5]

Funfair Wane *D Nicholls* a89 87
8 b g Unfuwain(USA) —Ivory Bride (Domynsky)
9[7] 32[11] 727[10] 992[7] 2711[9] 3053[2] 3185[8] (3498) 3636[4] 3787[2] 4038[3] (4498) 4734[6] 5552[6] 5908[3] 6157[4] 6283[5]

Fungible *E A L Dunlop*
2 ch c Compton Place—Highly Liquid (Entrepreneur)
6080[12]

Fun In The Sun *P D Evans* a46 55
3 b g Piccolo—Caught In The Rain (Spectrum (IRE))
1001[9] 1782[2] 2545[8] 3178[5] 3487[11] 3965[12] 3997[9] 4321[5] 4416[15] 4760[7] *5121[6]* 5269[3] *5497[4]* 6464[7] *6505[5]*

Funny Legend (NOR) *Wido Neuroth* 98
6 b m Funambule(USA) —Leap Day Legend (NOR) (Petorius)
(2131a) (4874a)

Funny Me *P W Chapple-Hyam* 83
2 ch c Dr Fong(USA) —Goodie Twosues (Fraam)
3478[3] 5010[7] 5227[2] (5721)

Funseeker (UAE) *M Johnston* a64 69
2 bb f Halling(USA) —Silversword (FR) (Highest Honor (FR))
5812[5] 6080[2] *6262[3] 6543[5] 6978[6] 7130[2]*

Fun Thai *A J Chamberlain* a36 46
3 ch f Fraam—Thailand (Lycius (USA))
6807[8]

Furbeseta *L M Cumani* a82 81
3 b f Danehill Dancer(IRE) —Fafinta (IRE) (Indian Ridge)
2137[2] 2579[6] *(3455) 4276[5]* 4848[5] 5545[8] *6208[8]*

Furia Ceca *L Brogi* 95
3 b c Mujahid(USA) —St Edith (IRE) (Desert King (IRE))
1335a[4] 1875a[8]

Furioso (JPN) *M Kawashima* a91
3 ch c Brian's Time(USA) —Fursa (USA) (Mr Prospector (USA))
6942a[10]

Furmigadelagiusta *L M Cumani* a95 89
3 ch c Galileo(IRE) —Sispre (FR) (Master Willie)
1974[4] (3236) 3883[3] 5619[9] *(6389)*

Furnace (IRE) *M L W Bell* 94
3 b g Green Desert(USA) —Lyrical Dance (USA) (Lear Fan (USA))
1500[3] 2788[8] 3503[4]

Furstenberg (IRE) *C Von Der Recke* 75
5 b h Monashee Mountain(USA) —Flagny (FR) (Kaldoun (FR))
438a[2]

Further Outlook (USA) *Miss Gay Kelleway* a71 73
13 gr g Zilzal(USA) —Future Bright (USA) (Lyphard's Wish (FR))
59[4]

Furusato (USA) *M Delzangles* 94
3 b f Sendawar(IRE) —Plaisir Des Yeux (FR) (Funambule (USA))
1339a[7] 2547a[4]

Fusaichi Ho O (JPN) *K Matsuda* 119
3 b c Jungle Pocket(JPN) —Admire Sunday (JPN) (Sunday Silence (USA))
6942a[11]

Fusaichi Pandora (JPN) *T Shirai* 116
4 ch m Sunday Silence(USA) —Lotta Lace (USA) (Nureyev (USA))
6943a[9]

Fusaichi Richard (JPN) *K Matsuda* a99 117
4 gr h Kurofune(USA) —Fusaichi Airedale (JPN) (Sunday Silence (USA))
858a[6]

Fuschia *R Charlton* a76 78
3 b f Averti(IRE) —Big Pink (IRE) (Bigstone (IRE))
(1386) 1837[4] 2363[3] 3475[3]

Fushe Jo *J Howard Johnson* 82
3 gr g Act One—Aristocratique (Cadeaux Genereux)
1773[10] 3919[2] 4749[18]

Fusili (IRE) *N P Littmoden* a99 96
4 ch m Silvano(GER) —Flunder (Nebos (GER))
57[4] (119) 264[7] 552[5] 701[7] 4849[11] 5327[5] 5543[3] 6576[3] *6765[9] 7086[3] 7163[7]*

Fustaan (IRE) *A G Newcombe* a73 67
3 b f Royal Applause—Alhufoof (USA) (Dayjur (USA))
(311) 7026[12] 7221[9]

Futoo (IRE) *D W Chapman* a54 44
6 b g Foxhound(USA) —Nicola Wynn (Nicholas Bill)
78[5] 305[6] 393[4] 431[4] 508[10] 1934[11]

Futun *L M Cumani* a93 107
4 b h In The Wings—Svanzega (USA) (Sharpen Up)
940[14] 1477[10] 1767[5] 2859[5] 4388[2] 4690[13] 5574[6] 6538[3]

Futune (IRE) *B J Meehan* a46 53
2 gr f Night Shift(USA) —Splendida Idea (IRE) (Kenmare (FR))
4565[8] *4883[10]* 5110[13] *5751[8]* 6449[3]

Future Deal *C A Horgan* a53 60
6 b m First Trump—Katyushka (IRE) (Soviet Star (USA))
315[6] 4945[13] 5421[6] 6212[6] 6532[4] 7034[6]

Future's Dream *K R Burke* a99 88
4 b g Bertolini(USA) —Bahawir Pour (USA) (Green Dancer (USA))
(809) (1180) 1651[20] 2208[10] 6465[4]

Futuristic Dragon (IRE) *D Shaw* a41 58
3 b g Invincible Spirit(IRE) —Calvia Rose (Sharpo)
1136[3] 1635[5] 3038[6] 4336[14] 4919[10] 5174[12] 6957[12]

Fu Wa (USA) *M W Easterby* a57 23
2 ch f Distant View(USA) —Fire And Shade (USA) (Shadeed (USA))
3750[6] 4077[9] 5363[6] 5751[12]

Fyodor (IRE) *W J Haggas* a105 105
6 b g Fasliyev(USA) —Royale Figurine (IRE) (Dominion Royale)
762[5] 5953[12] 6487[5] 6851[11]

Fyodorovich (USA) *J S Wainwright* 76
2 b c Stravinsky(USA) —Omnia (USA) (Green Dancer (USA))
1411[6] 2021[7] 3625[11] (4781) 5331[11]

Gaabal (IRE) *C E Brittain* 61
2 ch f Frenchmans Bay(FR) —Jazz Up (Cadeaux Genereux)
5162[5] 5949[14]

Gabier *G L Moore* a73 88
4 b g Galileo(IRE) —Contare (Shirley Heights)
2675[3] 5800[2]

Gaelic Princess *A G Newcombe* a84 88
7 b m Cois Na Tine(IRE) —Berenice (ITY) (Marouble)
1649[5] 2469[3] 3001[2] 3437[12] 3943[9] 4551[11] 5163[7] 5985[8] 6025[2] (6293) 6646[4] 7017[4] (7193) 7287[5]

Gaelic Roulette (IRE) *J Jay* a57 57
7 b m Turtle Island(IRE) —Money Spinner (USA) (Teenoso (USA))
1402[2] (1590) (1925) 2770[3]

Gaggia (GER) *P Rau* 34
3 br f Monsun(GER) —Ghashia (GER) (Prince Ippi (GER))
5669a[11]

Gagnoa (IRE) *Y De Nicolay* 102
2 b f Sadler's Wells(USA) —Gwynn (IRE) (Darshaan)
6040a[10] (6416a)

Gaia Prince (USA) *Mrs A J Perrett* 60
2 bb c Forestry(USA) —Castlebrook (USA) (Montbrook (USA))
4201[5]

Gainsborough's Art (IRE) *D R C Elsworth* a64
2 ch g Desert Prince(IRE) —Cathy Garcia (IRE) (Be My Guest (USA))
6602[6]

Gainsbury (GER) *P Vovcenko* 99
3 ch g Dashing Blade—Glorissima (GER) (Second Set (IRE))
6370a[8]

Gain Share *T D Barron* a72 68
2 b g Lend A Hand—Red Shareef (Marju (IRE))
1528[4] 2297[6] 5772[6] 6722[3] (6812)

Gaitskell *R Hollinshead* a54 72
2 b c Auction House(USA) —Lady-Love (Pursuit Of Love)
1007[4] 4459[10] 6675[3] 6884[6] 7022[11] 7177[5] 7272[7]

Gala Casino King (IRE) *Jennie Candlish* 60
4 ch g Elnadim(USA) —Fashion Scout (IRE) (Thatching)
1556[12] 1764[9]

Gala Casino Star (IRE) *R A Fahey* 67
2 ch c Dr Fong(USA) —Abir (Soviet Star (USA))
3977[10] 4612[5] 5143[2] 5828[12]

Galactic Star *Sir Michael Stoute* 115
4 ch h Galileo(IRE) —Balisada (Kris)
3899[5] 4166[2] (4690) (5411) (5976) 6496[4]

Gala Evening *J A B Old* a84 69
5 b g Daylami(IRE) —Balleta (USA) (Lyphard (USA))
(1526) 1794[9]

Gala Jackpot (USA) *W M Brisbourne* a18 41
4 bb g Crafty Prospector(USA) —True At Heart (USA) (Storm Cat (USA))
1210[15] 1562[7] 1742[4] 2157[10] 2372[8] 3063[8] 4961[8]

Galaktea (IRE) *C Laffon-Parias* 93
2 br f Statue Of Liberty(USA) —Granadilla (Zafonic (USA))
5373a[3] 6136a[5] 6888a[5]

Galantos (GER) *Jane Southcombe* a63 57
6 b g Winged Love(IRE) —Grey Metal (GER) (Secret 'n Classy (CAN))
23[5] 213[2] 389[7] 775[2] 1888[5] 5204[10]

Gala Sunday (USA) *M W Easterby* a52 76
7 b g Lear Fan(USA) —Sunday Bazaar (USA) (Nureyev (USA))
3155[11] 3539[6] 3755[4] 3955[8] 4383[11] 4610[3] 4998[3] 5300[6] 5704[6] (6304) 6598[2]

Galaxie Des Sables (FR) *Mme N Rossio* a92 100
3 b f Marchand De Sable(USA) —Kruguy Dancer (FR) (Groom Dancer (USA))
1006a[4] 1702a[13]

Galaxy Of Stars *D Shaw* a60 54
3 b f Observatory(USA) —Divine Secret (Hernando (FR))
219[10] 6428[12]

Galaxy Stars *P J Makin* a72
3 b g Golden Snake(USA) —Moly (Inchinor)
1450[9] 2570[7] 3622[5]

Galeota (IRE) *R Hannon* 112
5 b g Mujadil(USA) —Refined (IRE) (Statoblest)
4183[2] (4485) 4907[3] (5325) 5416[2] 5832[16] 6338[3] (6758)

Galianna (IRE) *Pat Eddery* 83
3 b f Galileo(IRE) —Ann's Annie (IRE) (Alzao (USA))
1127[7] 1812[3] (2436) 3458[3] 3993[6] 4511[9] 5594[4] 6186[5]

Galient (IRE) *M A Jarvis* a97 105
4 b g Galileo(IRE) —Endorsement (Warning)
944[3] 1582[11] 1844[15] 4637[4] 5030[8]

Galilean (IRE) *Eoin Griffin* 93
4 b g Galileo(IRE) —Darina (IRE) (Danehill (USA))
2067a[17]

Galingale (IRE) *Mrs P Sly* a48 63
3 b f Galileo(IRE) —Urban Sky (FR) (Groom Dancer (USA))
1127[13] 1576[4] 2132[6] 3624[10] 4104[11]

Galipette *H R A Cecil* 75
3 b f Green Desert(USA) —Arabesque (Zafonic (USA))
1632[5] 2393[3] 3046[5] 4186[3] 5740[7]

Galistic (IRE) *Patrick J Flynn* 103
4 ch m Galileo(IRE) —Mockery (Nashwan (USA))
875a[9] 2067a[5] (3664a) 5437a[6] 6367a[5]

Gallantry *D Shaw* a94 92
5 b g Green Desert(USA) —Gay Gallanta (USA) (Woodman (USA))
259[4] 351[4] (576) 657[4] 759[4] 840[12] 1480[13] 1818[11] 2239[9] 2528[2] 3650[4] 3941[13] 4195[2] 4990[9] 5221[9] 5638[5] 5804[13] (6391) 6674[6]

Gallas (IRE) *S Lycett* a51 66
6 b g Charnwood Forest(IRE) —Nellie's Away (IRE) (Magical Strike (USA))
45[4] 126[3] 203[2]

Gallego *R J Price* a65 71
5 br g Danzero(AUS) —Shafir (IRE) (Shaadi (USA))
1638[4] 1997[6] 2194[5] 2467[6] 2868[5] 3457[3] 4481[2] 4660[2] (5001) 5198[4] 5563[5] 5636[2] 5769[10] (6196) 6500[12] 6598[7] 6727[8]

Gallery Girl (IRE) *T D Easterby* a85 97
4 ch m Namid—September Tide (IRE) (Thatching)
1088[15] 1861[2] 2339[3] (2866) 3586[2] 3990[23] 4567[8] 4696[17] 5379[12] 5891[4]

Galley Law *W M Brisbourne* a56 22
7 ch g Most Welcome—Miss Blitz (Formidable (USA))
126[6] 372[9] 721[10]

Galley Slave (IRE) *M C Chapman* a62 60
2 b g Spartacus(IRE) —Cimeterre (IRE) (Arazi (USA))
2086[4] 2303[7] 2941[14] 3246[6] 3841[7] 4130[8] 4364[7] 4584[9] 5298[10] 5541[7] 6074[11] 6536[12] 6800[3] 7106[6] 7176[8] 7243[2]

Gallic Charm (IRE) *D R C Elsworth* a58
2 b f Key Of Luck(USA) —Kimash (IRE) (Woodman (USA))
6827[6] 7097[7]

Gallileo Figaro (USA) *N B King* a68 74
4 b m Galileo(IRE) —Temperence Gift (USA) (Kingmambo (USA))
(2252) 2887[7] (3300) (3976) 6181[6]

Galloise (IRE) *C G Cox* 54
3 b f Val Royal(FR) —Spring Daffodil (Pharly (FR))
2359[8] 3365[13]

Gallo's Wells (IRE) *J-P Gallorini* a83 78
4 b h Sadler's Wells(USA) —Rafina (USA) (Mr Prospector (USA))
6941a[0]

Gallows Hill (USA) *R A Fahey* a47 47
3 b g Stravinsky(USA) —Verinha (BRZ) (Baronius (BRZ))
1282[7] 1712[9] 3997[8] 4480[10] 4971[3] 5525[11] 6026[7]

Galway Girl (IRE) *T D Easterby* 53
3 b f Namid—Cherry Falls (IRE) (Ali-Royal (IRE))
1111[8] 1531[9] 3917[12]

Galway Nellie (IRE) *Luke Comer* a45
9 ch g Karaar—Mother Nellie (USA) (Al Nasr (FR))
489[7]

Gambara (IRE) *B Grizzetti* 90
3 b f Xaar—Gioia Infinita (Salse (USA))
2070a[10] 6519a[5]

Gambling Jack *A W Carroll* 59
2 b g First Trump—Star Of Flanders (Puissance)
1919[7]

Game Lad *T D Easterby* a61 99
5 b g Mind Games—Catch Me (Rudimentary (USA))
1041[10] 1179[8] 1480[11] 1818[9] (3091) 3559[5] 3941[10]

Game Lady *I A Wood* a73 68
3 b f Mind Games—Highland Gait (Most Welcome)
1151[5] (1383) 1766[10] 2444[5] 3237[3] 3870[3] 6239[11] 6762[10]

Game Park (USA) *J R Fanshawe* a66 61
2 ch g Elusive Quality(USA) —Carefree Cheetah (USA) (Trempolino (USA))
4070[5] 5771[5] 6267[5]

Gamesters Lady *W M Brisbourne* a70 61
4 br m Almushtarak(IRE) —Tycoon Tina (Tina's Pet)
6068[2] 6583[8] (6672) 6856[9] 7046[5] (7249)

Ganache (IRE) *P R Chamings* a64 51
5 ch g Halling(USA) —Granted (FR) (Cadeaux Genereux)
758[5] 1166[4] 1714[7] 2802[6] 3799[10] 4592[7] 5132[9] 5730[6] 5900[4] 6100[2] 6582[6] 6809[3]

Ganderas (GER) *M Weiss* 89
3 b c Dashing Blade—Giralda (IRE) (Tenby)
2503a[3]

Gandolfini (IRE) *H Rogers* a62 60
4 b g Rossini(USA) —Persian Myth (Persian Bold)
6916a[6]

Gandolfino (GER) *W Baltromei* a104 79
5 br h Alwuhush(USA) —Gentle Rock (GER) (Archway (IRE))
882a[7]

Ganymede *Mrs L J Mongan* a65 61
6 gr g Daylami(IRE) —Germane (Distant Relative)
23[3] 213[8] 291[8] 1026[5] 1451[9] 1732[7] (2176) 2430[2] 2770[7] 3448[9]

Gap Princess (IRE) *R A Fahey* a64 69
3 b f Noverre(USA) —Safe Care (IRE) (Caerleon (USA))
2255[5] 2553[5] 3302[6] (3920) 4407[3] 4848[4] 5238[5] 5556[12] 5907[8]

Garafena *Pat Eddery* a69 80
4 b m Golden Snake(USA) —Eclipsing (IRE) (Baillamont (USA))
5816[4] 6109[3] (6430)

Garda (USA) *Mme C Head-Maarek* 103
3 b c Lemon Drop Kid(USA) —Gilded Leaf (USA) (Lyphard (USA))
2751a[3]

Gardasee (GER) *T P Tate* 62
5 gr g Dashing Blade—Gladstone Street (IRE) (Waajib)
1942[6] (2810) (3155) 3403[7]

Garden City (FR) *Y De Nicolay* 94
2 b f Majorien—Green Delight (IRE) (Green Desert (USA))
3147a[4] 6525a[2]

Garden Party *Sir Michael Stoute* a69 65
3 b g Green Desert(USA) —Tempting Prospect (Shirley Heights)
1523[13] 2320[7] 2944[5] 5178[4] 5819[6]

Gardes (IRE) *Jane Chapple-Hyam* a60 62
2 b c Xaar—Golden Honor (IRE) (Hero's Honor (USA))
4656[5] 5222[6] 5771[8] 6252[10]

Gare Du Nord (IRE) *E Lellouche* 91
3 b f In The Wings—Gamine (IRE) (High Estate)
3564a[10]

Garibaldi (GER) *J O'Reilly* a65 71
5 ch g Acatenango(GER) —Guanhumara (Caerleon (USA))
631[5] 732[6] 982[4] 1579[4] 2007[13] 4493[8] (5286) 5704[13] 5750[14] 6019[4] 6304[11] 6713[7] 6832[7] 6969[8]

Garland *R Hannon* 62
2 ch f Hawk Wing(USA) —Al Persian (IRE) (Persian Bold)
5628[6] 5949[9]

Garlogs *R Hollinshead* a73 70
4 b g Hunting Lion(IRE) —Fading (Pharly (FR))
8[4] 317[3] 465[3] 521[2] 626[6] 668[3] 1436[6] 1729[6]

Garnett (IRE) *D E Cantillon* a76 75
6 b g Desert Story(IRE) —In Behind (IRE) (Entitled)
578[3] 640[2] 691[6] 2375[3] (2839) 3473[5]

Garnica (FR) *J-C Rouget* 118
4 gr h Linamix(FR) —Gueridia (IRE) (Night Shift (USA))
(2100a) 3445a[2] 4214a[4] (4871a) 6029a[8]

Garrulous (UAE) *G L Moore* a69 60
4 b g Lomitas—Friendly (USA) (Lear Fan (USA))
342[9] 459[9] (1347) 1609[9]

Garrya *B P J Baugh* a33 45
3 ch c Mark Of Esteem(IRE) —Sherkova (USA) (State Dinner (USA))
6569[12] 6751[9]

Garstang *Peter Grayson* a88 79
4 ch g Atraf—Approved Quality (IRE) (Persian Heights)
190[7] 419[9] 452[8] 513[2] 575[5] 660[11] 692[3] 827[3] 1121[7] 1401[9] 2529[6] (2866) 3536[6] 3954[4] (4233) 4489[4] 5039[11] 5332[12]

Gary's Indian (IRE) *B P J Baugh* a38 48
4 b m Indian Danehill(IRE) —Martino (Marju (IRE))
1995[9] 2433[8] 3067[12] 4532[14] 5606[13]

Gasmanfightsback *Evan Williams* 72
2 b c Primo Valentino(IRE) —Bint Baddi (FR) (Shareef Dancer (USA))
2424[5] 2651[2] 2737[19] 4255[F] (Dead)

Gaspar Van Wittel (USA) *N A Callaghan* 97
2 bb c Danehill Dancer(IRE) —Akuna Bay (USA) (Mr Prospector (USA))
(2103) (2618) 3459[9] 5048[3] 5974[6]

Gat (FR) *Mme C Dufreche* 104
3 gr c Nombre Premier—Gondwana (FR) (Hours After (USA))
5258a[4] 6028a[7]

Gatecrasher *G H Yardley* a57 45
4 gr g Silver Patriarch(IRE) —Girl At The Gate (Formidable (USA))
1231[5] 1396[4] 2430[10] 2770[11] 4246[U] 4670[12] 6798[8] 7004[11]

Gateland *B J Llewellyn* a63 45
4 br g Dansili—Encorenous (USA) (Diesis)
6501[11]

Gaudalpin (IRE) *J McAuley* a54 28
5 b m Danetime(IRE) —Lila Pedigo (IRE) (Classic Secret (USA))
3873[9]

Gaudeamus (USA) *J S Bolger* 100
3 b f Distorted Humor(USA) —Leo's Lucky Lady (USA) (Seattle Slew (USA))
1548a[5] 1694a[10] 2065a[8] 3576a[12]

Gavanello *M C Chapman* a33 47
4 bb g Diktat—Possessive Artiste (Shareef Dancer (USA))
630[8] 1376[10] 5698[7]

Gavarnie Beau (IRE) *M Blanshard* a70 89
4 b g Imperial Ballet(IRE) —Mysticism (Mystiko (USA))
486[8] 621[11] 1252[5] 1607[5] 1847[6] 2626[8] 3234[5] 3647[12] 3906[5] 4075[5] 4884[8] 5339[9] 5731[11]

Gavroche (IRE) *J R Boyle* a97 103
6 b h Docksider(USA) —Regal Revolution (Hamas (IRE))
1304[5] 2236[11] 4376[5] 5030[7]

Gayanula (USA) *Miss J A Camacho* a53
3 b f Yonaguska(USA) —Betamillion Bock (USA) (Bet Twice (USA))
7058[7] 7288[4]

Gazboolou *David Pinder* a78 80
3 b g Royal Applause—Warning Star (Warning)
(954) 1202[6] 1768[10] 3607[5] 4222[3] 4785[6] (6121) 7017[8] 7158[2]

Gee Ceffyl Bach *R C Guest* a52 58
3 b g Josr Algarhoud(IRE) —Miletrian Cares (IRE) (Hamas (IRE))
418[9] 492[10] 635[3] 731[5] 1538[4] (1782) 2905[5] 3384[4] 3965[13] 6955[6] 7028[13]

Gee Dee Nen *M H Tompkins* a85 92
4 b g Mister Baileys—Special Beat (Bustino)
316[3] 1300[3] (1677) 1959[4] 3090[7] 3748[5] (5034) 5800[3] 6335[13] (6744)

Gee Kel (IRE) *Francis Ennis* 96
3 b f Danehill Dancer(IRE) —Shir Dar (FR) (Lead On Time (USA))
946a[11]

Geestring (IRE) *R Hannon* 77
2 b f Diktat—Change Of Heart (IRE) (Revoque (IRE))
2000[5] (2968) 4775[4] 5322[12] 6012[4]

Geezers Colours *K R Burke* a82 59
2 b c Fraam—Konica (Desert King (IRE))
3781[5] 4247[4] 5902[5] 6312[2] 6503[9] (6823) (6898) 7016[2] (7232)

Gem Bien (USA) *D W Chapman* a61 41
9 b g Bien Bien(USA) —Eastern Gem (USA) (Jade Hunter (USA))
7[11] 51[8] 435[4] 519[12] 800[2] 1066[9] 1284[9] 1715[5] 1906[7] 2343[7]

Gemini Gold (IRE) *Joseph G Murphy* 94
4 b m King's Best(USA) —Wakria (IRE) (Sadler's Wells (USA))
782a[9]

Gemology (USA) *Saeed Bin Suroor* a77 87
3 b c Horse Chestnut(SAF) —Miners Girl (USA) (Miner's Mark (USA))
527a[3] 5390[2] 5781[7]

Gemstone Lass (FR) *Pat Eddery* 43
3 b f Peintre Celebre(USA) —Mutual Consent (IRE) (Reference Point)
2597[10]

Genari *P F I Cole* a90 90
4 b g Generous(IRE) —Sari (Faustus (USA))
1308[5] (1751) 1962[5] 2452[8] 3215[10] 4587[11]

General Blucher (IRE) *P W Chapple-Hyam* a71
2 br g Marju(IRE) —Restiv Star (FR) (Soviet Star (USA))
7191[3]

General Eliott (IRE) *P F I Cole* 83
2 b c Rock Of Gibraltar(IRE) —Marlene-D (Selkirk (USA))
(6294)

General Feeling (IRE) *S T Mason* a61 70
6 b g General Monash(USA) —Kamadara (IRE) (Kahyasi)
67[8] 803[6] 923[4] 1227[3] 1382[5] 2741[6] 3161[6] 3814[3] 4137[13] 4250[4] 4701[2] 5391[9] 5964[9] 6316[3] 6629[2]

General Flumpa *Miss Tor Sturgis* a59 63
6 b g Vettori(IRE) —Macca Luna (IRE) (Kahyasi)
976[4] 1199[6] 1406[11] 1924[4] 2089[5] 2745[3] 3047[11] (3250) 3805[3] 4253[12] 4959[4] 5514[10] 5704[10] 5886[6]

General Knowledge (USA) *B G Powell* a87 91
4 ch g Diesis—Reams Of Verse (USA) (Nureyev (USA))
197[10] 264[6] 488[9] 593[7] 1060[10] 1308[2] (1434) 1842[10] 2401[15] 3672[9] 6175[6] 6504[10] (6642) 6806[9]

General Ting (IRE) *Sir Mark Prescott* a58
2 b c Daylami(IRE) —Luana (Shaadi (USA))
5498[12] 5780[8] 6022[5]

General Tufto *R Charlton* 65
2 b g Fantastic Light(USA) —Miss Pinkerton (Danehill (USA))
5206[7] 5599[6] 6106[5]

Generator *Dr J D Scargill* a74 60
5 ch g Cadeaux Genereux—Billie Blue (Ballad Rock)
(560)

Generous Boy *T D Easterby* 55
2 b g Fantastic Light(USA) —Supersonic (Shirley Heights)
4037[13] 6051[7] 6698[7]

Generous Jem *G G Margarson* a57 91
4 b m Generous(IRE) —Top Jem (Damister (USA))
1396[3] 1926[2] 2890[7] 4131[3] (4766) (5144) (5229) 5504[2] 5767[6]

Generous Lad (IRE) *A B Haynes* a77 76
4 b g Generous(IRE) —Tudor Loom (Sallust)
195[4] 422[3] 539[3] 799[3] 813[3] 1295[2] 2106[3] 2194[2] 3177[6] 3554[2] 4318[2] (6709) 6819[4] 7055[4] 7147[3]

Generous Thought *P Howling* 91
2 b c Cadeaux Genereux—Rosie's Posy (IRE) (Suave Dancer (USA))
2041[5] 4014[3] (5745) (6756)

Genethni *K A Ryan* a64 61
2 b f Primo Valentino(IRE) —Mujadilly (Mujadil (USA))
(3410) (5081) 5751[6] 5887[3] 6151[11]

Genios (GER) *Dr A Bolte* a85 101
6 br h Oxalagu(GER) —Glacial Star (Royal Academy (USA))
4217a[6] 6691a[8]

Genki (IRE) *R Charlton* a53 106
3 ch g Shinko Forest(IRE) —Emma's Star (ITY) (Darshaan)
(899) 1658[2] (2044) 4006[2] (4374) 5209[2] (5765)

Genoa Star *D J Murphy* a23
4 b m Woodborough(USA) —Naval Dispatch (Slip Anchor)
5750[15] 6904[10] 7150[5]

Gentle Audrey (USA) *Melody Conlon* a104
2 b f Elusive Quality(USA) —Fatat Alarab (USA) (Capote (USA))
5826a[4]

Gentle Guru *R T Phillips* 83
3 b f Ishiguru(USA) —Soft Touch (IRE) (Petorius)
2631[2] 3164[2] (3688) 4123[6] 4848[7] 5360[3]

Gentleman Jeff (USA) *D K Weld* a65 80
3 ch g Mr Greeley(USA) —Wooing (USA) (Stage Door Johnny (USA))
4035a[4]

Gentleman's Deal (IRE) *M W Easterby* a115 93
6 b h Danehill(USA) —Sleepytime (IRE) (Royal Academy (USA))
(6) (352) (761) 848[15] 6155[12] 6931[2] (7225)

Geoffdaw *M J Wallace* a75 68
2 b g Vettori(IRE) —Talighta (USA) (Barathea (IRE))
890[3] (1021) 4461[7] 4964[10] (5496) 5629[14] 5974[21]

Geojimali *J S Goldie* a82 89
5 ch g Compton Place—Harrken Heights (IRE) (Belmez (USA))
(957) 1195[9] 1653[16] 2463[13] 2841[12] 3720[6] 4006[5] 4389[6] 4567[2] 4816[6] 5584[7] 5809[7] 6243[7] 6753[4]

Geordie Dancer (IRE) *A Berry* a14 40
5 b g Dansili—Awtaar (USA) (Lyphard (USA))
4251[9] 5083[13]

Geordie Girl *R C Guest* a33 66
2 b f Tobougg(IRE) —Chiltern Court (USA) (Topsider (USA))
1130[2] 3024[15] 3507[11] 4560[8] 5251[3] (6075) 6328[12] 6665[11]

Geordieland (FR) *J A Osborne* a96 119
6 gr h Johann Quatz(FR) —Aerdee (FR) (Highest Honor (FR))
756[2] 929[5] 1823[2] 2787[2] 4091[5] 5376[2] 6054[2]

Georgie's Pool *J W Hills* a64 48
3 b c Dilshaan—Last Result (Northern Park (USA))
1587^{3} 2177^{12} 3620^{10} 5019^{5} 5341^{3} 5755^{5} 6257^{8} 6430^{6}

Georgebernardshaw (IRE) *A P O'Brien* a81 53
2 b c Danehill Dancer(IRE) —Khamseh (Thatching)
779a^{7}

George's Flyer (IRE) *R A Fahey* a62 60
4 b g Daggers Drawn(USA) —Winged Victory (IRE) (Dancing Brave (USA))
42^{11} 4477^{11} 5237^{4} 6179^{11} 6627^{7} 6859^{11} 6979^{13}

Georges Pride *J M Bradley* 48
3 b c Averti(IRE) —Thaw (Cadeaux Genereux)
1207^{7} 1373^{6} 2104^{14} 2622^{13}

George The Best (IRE) *Micky Hammond* a24 69
6 b g Imperial Ballet(IRE) —En Retard (IRE) (Petardia)
1299^{13} 2711^{7} 3017^{12} 3185^{3} 3535^{8} 3676^{4} 4706^{7} 5672^{5} 6720^{2}

George The Second *Mrs H Sweeting* a80 70
4 b h Josr Algarhoud(IRE) —Pink Champagne (Cosmonaut)
(161) 361^{2} 513^{6} 803^{4} 2088^{10} 2217^{3} 3106^{9} (3190) 3396^{2} 3452^{2} 3906^{3} 4095^{16} 4594^{8} 4965^{11} 6231^{2} 6405^{4} 6589^{7} 6970^{8} 7054^{6}

George Washington (IRE) *A P O'Brien* a116 131
4 b h Danehill(USA) —Bordighera (USA) (Alysheba (USA))
2735^{4} 3331^{3} 5261a^{3} 6514a^{P} (Dead)

Georgie The Fourth (IRE) *E J O'Neill* a70
2 b f Cadeaux Genereux—Septembers Hawk (IRE) (Machiavellian (USA))
3213^{2}

Gertie (IRE) *E J Creighton* a46 44
3 b f Redback—Rosalia (USA) (Red Ransom (USA))
69^{9} 209^{6} 357^{6} 676^{5} 776^{5} 2454^{5} 3274^{3} 4914^{14}

Gesture *F Bruni* 87
5 b g Bahri(USA) —Stark Ballet (USA) (Nureyev (USA))
1876a^{9}

Getaway (GER) *A Fabre* 124
4 b h Monsun(GER) —Guernica (Unfuwain (USA))
(4655a) 5469a^{2} 6043a^{4}

Get Jealous (IRE) *R Hannon* 26
2 ch f Intikhab(USA) —Bauci (IRE) (Desert King (IRE))
1960^{12}

Getrah *N Wilson* 77
3 ch g Barathea(IRE) —Sahara Shade (USA) (Shadeed (USA))
1098^{6} 1841^{5} (3382) 3889^{3} 5508^{2} 6492^{13} 6636^{6}

Ghafeer (USA) *B Ellison* 73
3 b g War Chant(USA) —Hasheema (IRE) (Darshaan)
4079^{2} 4479^{8} 5156^{3} 5625^{7} 6310^{14}

Ghaill Force *P Butler* a45 15
5 b g Piccolo—Coir 'A' Ghaill (Jalmood (USA))
496^{12} 615^{10} 1344^{11} 2557^{5} 4259^{13} 7168^{6}

Gharir (IRE) *E Charpy* a98 108
5 gr h Machiavellian(USA) —Summer Sonnet (Baillamont (USA))
541a^{6} 642a^{2} 858a^{10}

Ghetto *R Hannon* a94 95
2 b c Auction House(USA) —Ellway Queen (USA) (Bahri (USA))
2596^{4} (3095) 5109^{4} 5350^{11} 6001^{3} 6297^{2}

Ghizlaan (USA) *M Johnston* 60
2 b f Seeking The Gold(USA) —Golden Ballet (USA) (Moscow Ballet (USA))
6184^{9}

Ghost Dancer *L M Cumani* a75 77
3 ch c Danehill Dancer(IRE) —Reservation (IRE) (Common Grounds)
1228^{7} 1684^{3}

Giant Love (USA) *M Johnston* 79
2 ch c Giant's Causeway(USA) —Morning Devotion (USA) (Affirmed (USA))
4725^{9} (5140) 5536^{7} 6201^{7}

Giant Slalom *W J Haggas* a80 88
3 b g Tomba—Fallara (FR) (Tropular)
1815^{2} 1936^{2} 2305^{4} 4004^{4} 4429^{3} 4811^{3} (5238) 6006^{5} (6492)

Giant Star (USA) *J S Goldie* 68
4 b g Giant's Causeway(USA) —Vogue Star (ARG) (Ringaro (USA))
5036^{5}

Gib (IRE) *B W Hills* a61 79
3 ch f Rock Of Gibraltar(IRE) —Saucy Maid (IRE) (Sure Blade (USA))
2177^{4} 2727^{3} 3150^{8} (3652) (3871) 5210^{7} 5941^{2} 6236^{6}

Gibsons *P A Blockley* a53 26
3 ch g Tipsy Creek(USA) —Amy Leigh (IRE) (Imperial Frontier (USA))
11^{6} 378^{6}

Giddywell *R Hollinshead* a57 57
3 b f Ishiguru(USA) —Understudy (In The Wings)
258^{5} 484^{4} 655^{6} 1256^{6} 1731^{9} 2008^{4} 2259^{12} 2579^{9} (3714) 3871^{3} 5755^{12} 6803^{3} 6937^{6} 7060^{6}

Gifted Flame *Miss A Stokell* a55 77
8 b g Revoque(IRE) —Little Lady Leah (USA) (Shareef Dancer (USA))
2007^{7} 2302^{9} 3422^{7} 3816^{0} 4219^{5} 4701^{13} 4966^{8} 5284^{12} 5525^{6} 5756^{9} 6152^{5} 6956^{7} 7001^{11} 7127^{7} 7153^{7} 7233^{5}

Gifted Gamble *K A Ryan* a89 97
5 b g Mind Games—Its Another Gift (Primo Dominie)
218^{2} 351^{7} 509^{2} 657^{6} 699^{5}

Gifted Glori *T D Barron* a50 47
4 ch g Vettori(IRE) —Azira (Arazi (USA))
715^{2}

Gifted Heir (IRE) *A Bailey* a59 61
3 b c Princely Heir(IRE) —Inzar Lady (IRE) (Inzar (USA))
2798^{11} 3394^{2} 4337^{2} 4735^{8} 5083^{5} 6573^{6} 7001^{2}

Gifted Lass *J Balding* a71 12
5 b m Bold Edge—Meeson Times (Enchantment I)
(8) 154^{3} 214^{3} 905^{3} 1067^{4} 6244^{7} 6752^{10} 7238^{10}

Gifted Musician *H Morrison* a59 73
5 b g Sadler's Wells(USA) —Photogenic (Midyan (USA))
1752^{6} 2201^{8}

Gift Horse *D Nicholls* 109
7 ch g Cadeaux Genereux—Careful Dancer (Gorytus (USA))
1770^{12} 2022^{3} 2858^{24} 3089^{5} 3505^{11} 3975^{7} 4567^{5} 5407^{5} 5584^{10} 6205^{5} 6472^{14}

Giganticus (USA) *B W Hills* 109
4 ch g Giant's Causeway(USA) —Shy Princess (USA) (Irish River (FR))
(1041) 1619^{4} 2528^{3} (3505) 3941^{4} (4401) 5031^{10} 5797^{12}

Giggling Monkey *P D Evans* a45 49
2 b f Fraam—Rewardia (IRE) (Petardia)
2078^{2} 2663^{8} 3174^{4} 4559^{3} 4875^{7} 6591^{4} 6775^{13} 6814^{6} 7101^{4} 7156^{5} 7286^{9}

Gigi Glamor *W M Brisbourne* 53
5 b m Secret Appeal—Gilboa (Shirley Heights)
1998^{6} 2491^{4} 3803^{12} 5626^{14}

Gigs Magic (USA) *M Johnston* a66 70
4 ch g Gulch(USA) —Magic Of Love (Magic Ring (IRE))
(1162) 1347^{3} 1720^{2} 1918^{4} 2157^{6} (2201) 2338^{2} (2567)

Gilded Cove *R Hollinshead* a74 77
7 b h Polar Prince(IRE) —Cloudy Reef (Cragador)
8^{7} 66^{2} 1165^{3} (2655) 2912^{5} 3472^{5} 4024^{8} 5177^{11} 6103^{10} 6671^{6} 6764^{3} 7020^{3} 7271^{7}

Gilded Youth *H Candy* a68 76
3 b g Gorse—Nisha (Nishapour (FR))
1923^{2} 4808^{3} (5129) 5532^{10}

Gillans Inn *J M Bradley* 54
2 b c Rambling Bear—Strat's Quest (Nicholas (USA))
1882^{9} 2103^{6} 2724^{5}

Gimme Some Lovin (IRE) *D W P Arbuthnot* a66 64
3 b f Desert Style(IRE) —Licence To Thrill (Wolfhound (USA))
2470^{3} 2878^{6} 4066^{6} 4759^{7} 5134^{2} (5386) 6625^{3} 6870^{4} 6946^{4} 7269^{7}

Gimmy (IRE) *B Grizzetti* 108
3 b g Lomitas—Pursuit Of Life (Pursuit Of Love)
1335a^{3} 5821a^{2} 6223a^{5}

Gin Genereux *M Johnston* a76 76
2 b c Cadeaux Genereux—Lady Gin (USA) (Saint Ballado (CAN))
1622^{8} 1889^{8} (2758) 3256^{5} 4154^{9} (4975) 5167^{8} 6462^{14}

Ginger Fountain *H Candy* a41 17
2 ch f Generous(IRE) —Gift Fountain (Greensmith)
5881^{13} 6432^{13} (Dead)

Ginger Minx (IRE) *N J Vaughan* a55
2 ch f Raise A Grand(IRE) —Glenmalure (IRE) (Night Shift (USA))
7258^{3}

Ginger Pickle *J R Weymes* 76
2 ch g Compton Place—Spice Island (Reprimand)
2889^{8} (3606) 4484^{3} 4844^{3} 5582^{4} 5665^{5}

Ginger Pop *G G Margarson* a65 25
3 ch g Mark Of Esteem(IRE) —Norcroft Lady (Mujtahid (USA))
128^{2} 311^{5} 502^{9} 752^{9} 1022^{13} 1541^{9} 7029^{4} 7118^{7}

Ginger Princess (IRE) *Oliver McKiernan* a57 54
5 b m Pistolet Bleu(IRE) —Palm Lake (IRE) (Spectrum (IRE))
7143^{3}

Ginger Punch (USA) *R J Frankel* a119
4 ch m Awesome Again(CAN) —Nappelon (CAN) (Bold Revenue (CAN))
5854a^{3} (6512a)

Gingham *L M Cumani* 69
2 b f Barathea(IRE) —Sianema (Persian Bold)
4774^{12} 6015^{3}

Gio Ponti (USA) *Christophe Clement* 100
2 b c Tale Of The Cat(USA) —Chipeta Springs (USA) (Alydar (USA))
6484a^{8}

Giores (IRE) *R Feligioni*
4 b h Montjeu(IRE) —Mistress Thames (Sharpo)
1192a^{7}

Giorgiolito *P Nicot* a97 107
6 b g Priolo(USA) —Alchimia (FR) (Darshaan)
437a^{4}

Giovanni D'Oro (IRE) *Miss M E Rowland* a54 58
3 b g Johannesburg(USA) —Maddie G (USA) (Blush Rambler (USA))
1022^{14} 1164^{4} 1317^{6} 2796^{2} 3469^{11}

Gipson Dessert (USA) *J-C Rouget* 99
2 br f Orientate(USA) —Gypsy Hollow (USA) (Dixieland Band (USA))
(4625a) 6416a^{2}

Gipsy Prince *M G Quinlan* a73 63
2 b g Millkom—Habla Me (IRE) (Fairy King (USA))
3465^{7} 3962^{10} 4279^{6} 5314^{4} (6098) 6263^{4}

Girardii *K C Bailey* a53
4 ch g Sinndar(IRE) —Armeria (USA) (Northern Dancer (CAN))
640^{8}

Girl Of Pangaea (GER) *E A L Dunlop* a76
2 b f Soviet Star(USA) —Genevra (IRE) (Danehill (USA))
6777^{2}

Girl Power (IRE) *Edward Lynam* 90
3 b f Key Of Luck(USA) —Rumuz (IRE) (Marju (IRE))
5394a^{5} 5841a^{7} 6036a^{5}

Gist (IRE) *W J Martin* a42 87
4 b m Namid—Ali Dreamer (IRE) (Ali-Royal (IRE))
5842a^{12}

Give Back Calais (IRE) *Miss A Casotti* 38
9 b g Brief Truce(USA) —Nichodoula (Doulab (USA))
356a^{8} 438a^{4}

Give Evidence *A P Jarvis* a67 48
3 b g Averti(IRE) —Witness (Efisio)
2335^{13} 2601^{8} 4109^{7} 4337^{12} 4595^{5} 4961^{2} 5310^{7} 5511^{4} 5739^{6} 6060^{12}

Give Her A Whirl *G A Swinbank* a37 64
3 b f Pursuit Of Love—Peggy Spencer (Formidable (USA))
1923^{8} 2435^{6}

Give Me A Break *P W Chapple-Hyam* 81
3 b c Danehill Dancer(IRE) —Cream Jug (IRE) (Spectrum (IRE))
1143^{10} 4815^{9} (5113) 5941^{4}

Give Me A Reason (IRE) *Daniel Mark Loughnane* a53 49
3 b f Daggers Drawn(USA) —Nacote (IRE) (Mtoto)
7037a^{6}

Give Me The Night (IRE) *B Smart* a84 88
4 b m Night Shift(USA) —There With Me (USA) (Distant View (USA))
1013^{10} 1861^{4} 2744^{8} 3014^{6}

Given A Choice (IRE) *J G Given* a92 79
5 b g Trans Island—Miss Audimar (USA) (Mr. Leader (USA))
3346^{4} 3955^{2} 6253^{14} 6806^{3}

Gizmo *B Smart* 51
4 b g Fasliyev(USA) —Sly Baby (IRE) (Dr Devious (IRE))
2581^{8} 3917^{6}

Gizmondo *M L W Bell* a60 66
4 ch g Lomitas—India Atlanta (Ahonoora)
1167^{4} 1347^{5} 2370^{2} 2745^{8}

Gladiatorus (USA) *Maria Rita Salvioni* 109
2 b c Silic(FR) —Gmaasha (IRE) (Kris)
2684a^{6} 6222a^{2}

Glad Star (GER) *D W Chapman*
4 br g Big Shuffle(USA) —Glady Sum (GER) (Surumu (GER))
1030^{8} 1937^{12} 4229^{10} 4817^{RR} 6383^{10}

Glad To Be Fast (IRE) *Mario Hofer* a108 86
7 ch g Big Shuffle(USA) —Glad To Be Here (IRE) (Waajib)
396a^{7} 471a^{8}

Glamaraazi (IRE) *R A Fahey* a66 61
4 b m Orpen(USA) —Raazi (My Generation)
(77) 150^{7} 376^{6} 485^{7} 686^{4} 1404^{2} 1597^{10}

Glamoroso (IRE) *D W Barker* 20
2 b c Mull Of Kintyre(USA) —Tuneful (Pivotal)
1706^{7} 5903^{12}

Glasshoughton *M Dods* 89
4 b g Dansili—Roseum (Lahib (USA))
1574^{5} 1854^{13} 2394^{10} 2866^{6} 2989^{8} (3298) 3720^{4} 3954^{3} (4703) 5581^{6} 6173^{18}

Gleaming Spirit (IRE) *A P Jarvis* a64 77
3 b g Mujadil(USA) —Gleam (Green Desert (USA))
1976^{5} 2444^{2} 2631^{4} 4127^{3} (4336) 5051^{5} 5552^{19} 6575^{13}

Glenargo (USA) *S T Lewis* a58 64
4 ch g Concerto(USA) —Her Gift (USA) (Saint Ballado (CAN))
254^{3} 368^{10} 403^{7} 2221^{10} 2652^{13} 5368^{13} 7169^{13}

Glen Avon Girl (IRE) *T D Easterby* a54 53
3 b f Mull Of Kintyre(USA) —Sandystones (Selkirk (USA))
237^{4} 336^{6} 404^{5} 894^{12}

Glenbuck (IRE) *A Bailey* a81 94
4 b g Mujadil(USA) —Bryna (IRE) (Ezzoud (IRE))
509^{5} 629^{7} 953^{3} (1268) 1474^{13} 1619^{6} 3091^{5} 3943^{5}

Glencairn Star *R A Fahey* a67 83
6 b g Selkirk(USA) —Bianca Nera (Salse (USA))
873a^{3}

Glencal *H Morrison* a69 64
3 ch f Compton Place—Raindrop (Primo Dominie)
1541^{4} 1973^{5} 3046^{3} 3853^{3} 4336^{2} (4529) 5136^{3} 5731^{3} 6123^{8}

Glencalvie (IRE) *J Akehurst* a79 82
6 ch g Grand Lodge(USA) —Top Of The Form (IRE) (Masterclass (USA))
576^{7} 697^{11} 865^{5} 1060^{7} 1446^{7} (1931) 2358^{6} 2877^{3} 3420^{12} (4234) 5114^{9} 5712^{10} 6081^{10}

Gleneagles (IRE) *T Wall* a61 82
3 ch g Pivotal—Embassy (Cadeaux Genereux)
1197^{2} 1904^{5} (2913) (3605) 4080^{2} 5585^{5} 5737^{6} 6726^{5}

Glenisland *Mrs L Williamson* 52
3 br f Diktat—Glider (IRE) (Silver Kite (USA))
2196^{6} 2763^{6} 3365^{9}

Glenluji *J S Goldie* 64
2 b g Lujain(USA) —Glenhurich (IRE) (Sri Pekan (USA))
1706^{6} 1938^{6} (2247) 4098^{6}

Glenmore Lodge *P T Midgley* a13
4 b m Indian Lodge(IRE) —In The Highlands (Petong)
908^{7} 1175^{8} 1301^{11}

Glenmuir (IRE) *B R Millman* 85
4 b g Josr Algarhoud(IRE) —Beryl (Bering)
1060^{8} 2469^{9} 2722^{3} 4234^{8} 5383^{16} 5693^{7} 5885^{8} 6199^{8}

Glen Nevis (USA) *Saeed Bin Suroor* a42 98
3 bb c Gulch(USA) —Beating The Buzz (IRE) (Bluebird (USA))
173a^{9} 641a^{3} 2789^{13}

Glenridding *J G Given* a69 31
3 b g Averti(IRE) —Appelone (Emperor Jones (USA))
3399^{8} 4036^{9} 4718^{6} 5019^{4} 5366^{5} 5945^{14} 6979^{2} 7115^{10} (7247)

Glenshee (IRE) *J J Quinn* a47 61
2 b g Mujadil(USA) —Ancient Secret (Warrshan (USA))
2337^{9} 2804^{5} 4002^{3} 4461^{8} 4783^{7}

Glentimon (IRE) *S Kirk* a44 8
3 br g Mull Of Kintyre(USA) —Eliade (IRE) (Flash Of Steel)
1250^{9} 1725^{15} 3621^{6} 4528^{7}

Glentire (GER) *H J Groschel* 91
2 bb c Pentire—Glacial Star (Royal Academy (USA))
6222a^{8}

Glenveagh (IRE) *K A Ryan* 60
2 b c Catcher In The Rye(IRE) —Limone (IRE) (Catrail (USA))
4125^{7} 4636^{3}

Glenviews Youngone (IRE) *Peter Grayson* a83 85
4 b m Namid—Baltic Beach (IRE) (Polish Precedent (USA))
5^{5} 155^{10} 490^{10} 810^{8} 1067^{10} 1565^{5} 2244^{6} 2933^{8}

Glitter Baby (IRE) *M G Quinlan* 96
4 b m Danehill Dancer(IRE) —Gifts Galore (IRE) (Darshaan)
875a^{4} 1805^{7} 2720^{3} 3628^{5} 4142a^{3} 4238a^{6} 5544^{10} 6367a^{10}

Glittering Prize (UAE) *M Johnston* a68 68
2 bb f Cadeaux Genereux—Tanami (Green Desert (USA))
4781^{8} 5033^{4} 5770^{5} 6079^{2} 6282^{2} 6572^{12} (7288)

Global Achiever *M J Gingell* a45 9
6 b g Key Of Luck(USA) —Inflation (Primo Dominie)
743^{7} 1119^{6} 1719^{10} 7069^{10} 7197^{11}

Global Champion *Mario Hofer* 94
3 b c Elnadim(USA) —Craigmill (Slip Anchor)
1387a^{6} 6691a^{7}

Global Dream (GER) *U Ostmann* 102
3 b c Seattle Dancer(USA) —Goonda (Darshaan)
1054a^{2} 1516a^{8} 2502a^{6} 3146a^{15}

Global Guest *A J Chamberlain* a49 71
3 b c Piccolo—By Arrangement (IRE) (Bold Arrangement)
3475^{7} 3682^{10} 5177^{9} 5602^{10}

Globalization (USA) *R Violette Jr* a88
2 bb c Touch Gold(USA) —In The Limelight (USA) (Polish Navy (USA))
6508a^{11}

Global Strategy *Rae Guest* a83 67
4 b g Rainbow Quest(USA) —Pleasuring (Good Times (ITY))
(64) (148) (585) 955^{6} 1793^{6} (2148) 2715^{6} 6276^{7} 6666^{7}

Global Traffic *P D Evans* a70 68
3 br c Generous(IRE) —Eyes Wide Open (Fraam)
(37) (140) (267) 370^{5} 904^{7} 1205^{7} 1355^{5} 1927^{13} 3155^{10} (3901) 4976^{6} 6027^{6} 6259^{5} 6598^{8} 6673^{5} 7175^{3}

Globe *Mrs H Sweeting* a40 28
4 b m Agnes World(USA) —Hoist (IRE) (Bluebird (USA))
567^{10} 653^{7} 687^{10} 751^{10} 2104^{12}

Gloria De Campeao (BRZ) *P Bary* 102
4 b h Impression(ARG) —Audacity (BRZ) (Clackson (BRZ))
6031a^{6}

Glorious Gift (IRE) *P W Chapple-Hyam* 82
2 b c Elnadim(USA) —Queen Of Arabia (USA) (Wild Again (USA))
4725^{4} 5194^{2}

Glorious View *M W Easterby* 46
3 b g Observatory(USA) —Prime Property (IRE) (Tirol)
2609^{10} 3183^{12} 4036^{10}

Glory Be (ITY) *J L Spearing* a50 47
5 ch m Dashing Blade—Hasana (USA) (Private Account (USA))
1590^{5}

Glory Days (GER) *E A L Dunlop* a61
4 b m Tiger Hill(IRE) —Glorosia (FR) (Bering)
338^{4} 443^{6}

Gloucester *J J Quinn* a77 77
4 b g Montjeu(IRE) —Birdlip (USA) (Sanglamore (USA))
2743^{5} 3301^{6} 4040^{6} 4582^{3} 4772^{5} (5296)

Gloved Hand *R M Beckett* a91 101
5 b m Royal Applause—Fudge (Polar Falcon (USA))
1836^{4} 2239^{8} (2835) (3059) 3511^{2} 4118^{14}

Gnillah *B R Johnson* a55 59
4 b m Halling(USA) —Dimakya (USA) (Dayjur (USA))
3950^{16} 4161^{12}

Go Amwell *J R Jenkins* a59 61
4 b g Kayf Tara—Daarat Alayaam (IRE) (Reference Point)
71^{7} 416^{15} 558^{3} 4914^{8} (5453) (5948) 6200^{3} 6561^{11}

Go But Go *E J O'Neill* a72 77
3 b g Tobougg(IRE) —Faraway Lass (Distant Relative)
2376^{4} (2763) 4197^{4} 4597^{3} 4917^{6} 6186^{14}

Go Dancing *P W Chapple-Hyam* a57 39
3 b f Golan(IRE) —Torrid Tango (USA) (Green Dancer (USA))
469^{4} 1039^{9}

Godfrey Street *K A Ryan* a88 94
4 ch g Compton Place—Tahara (IRE) (Caerleon (USA))
5195^{9} 5581^{14} (6173) 6381^{9} 6876^{11} 7112^{4} 7179^{5}

Go Dude *J Ryan* a62 49
3 b g Mujahid(USA) —Miss Doody (Gorytus (USA))
2609^{P} 4858^{7} 5342^{7} 6060^{8} 6250^{P}

Go East (GER) *P Schiergen* 98
3 ch f Highest Honor(FR) —Golden Time (GER) (Surumu (GER))
6046a^{4} (6519a)

Go For Gold (IRE) *S Seemar* 92
6 b h Machiavellian(USA) —Kithanga (IRE) (Darshaan)
248a^{10} 328a^{14} 475a^{5} 545a^{4}

Go Free *J G M O'Shea* a56 38
6 gr g Easycall—Miss Traxdata (Absalom)
1980^{3} 2764^{6}

Go Imperial (IRE) *M G Quinlan* a61 51
3 b g Imperial Ballet(IRE) —Miss Divot (IRE) (Petardia)
1022^{11} 2750^{5} 2826^{5}

Going Ballistic (USA) *D Von Hemel* a116 106
3 rg c Lite The Fuse(USA) —Holy Lightning (USA) (Holy Bull (USA))
4412a^{3}

Going Public (IRE) *D K Weld* a100 100
2 b c Night Shift(USA) —Gifts Galore (IRE) (Darshaan)
5070a^{7} 5845a^{3} 6161a^{2}

Going Skint *M Wellings* a71 54 4 b g Elnadim(USA) —Prospering (Prince Sabo) *124[12] (222) 323[3] 468[4] 717[7]* 992[11] 1562[10] 1673[11] 1899[3] 2334[10] 2652[9]

Going To Work (IRE) *D R C Elsworth* a85 85 3 b f Night Shift(USA) —Firesteed (IRE) (Common Grounds) (1024) 1407[3] 1649[9] 2181[7] 2475[3] 3555[4] 5210[4] 5725[5] *(5943)* 6129[2]

Golan Knight (IRE) *K A Ryan* 88 2 bb c Golan(IRE) —Night Rhapsody (IRE) (Mujtahid (USA)) (2303) 2855[10] 3157[3] 3841[3] 4613[6] (4991) 6251[3]

Golano *P R Webber* a75 60 7 gr g Linamix(FR) —Dimakya (USA) (Dayjur (USA)) *5732[4] 6241[3] 6459[3] 6802[6] 6875[7] 7008[5]*

Golan Way *I A Wood* a72 75 3 b g Golan(IRE) —Silk Daisy (Barathea (IRE)) 4960[6] 5405[3] *5943[4] 6272[5] 6878[5]*

Golband *J O'Reilly* a76 53 5 b m Cadeaux Genereux—Hatheethah (IRE) (Machiavellian (USA)) *8[13]* 5297[13] 6078[13]

Goldacre *Miss D A McHale* a17 2 bb f Warningford—Elsie Bamford (Tragic Role (USA)) *3392[6]*

Goldan Jess (IRE) *D Carroll* a49 72 3 b g Golan(IRE) —Bendis (GER) (Danehill (USA)) *1348[5] 1749[6]* 4423[15]

Gold Digger Miss (USA) *J Noseda* a80 79 3 ch f Gulch(USA) —Jaramar Miss (USA) (Risen Star (USA)) *73[4] 689[4] (1175) 1978[2]* (2415)

Golddigging (IRE) *J G Portman* a35 24 2 b f Acclamation—On The Make (IRE) (Entrepreneur) *3643[9]* 4028[9]

Golden Acer (IRE) *Doug Watson* a99 95 4 ch h Elnadim(USA) —Shifty Lady (IRE) (Night Shift (USA)) *326a[12] 409a[12] 474a[7]*

Golden Alchemist *M D I Usher* a76 74 4 ch g Woodborough(USA) —Pure Gold (Dilum (USA)) *49[3] 228[10] 610[5] 888[8]* 2006[5]

Golden Applause (FR) *Mrs A L M King* a52 78 5 b m Royal Applause—Golden Circle (USA) (Theatrical) 1765[13] 2194[3] 2579[8]

Golden Arrow (IRE) *I Mohammed* a101 110 4 b h Danehill(USA) —Cheal Rose (IRE) (Dr Devious (IRE)) *177a[3] 399a[8] 529a[4]* 642a[9]

Golden Asha *G G Margarson* a78 95 5 ch m Danehill Dancer(IRE) —Snugfit Annie (Midyan (USA)) *551[8]* 1670[10] 1861[7] 2240[5]

Golden Banjo (IRE) *Ms Joanna Morgan* 47 3 b g Goldmark(USA) —Banjo Island (IRE) (Warcraft (USA)) 5696a[6]

Golden Brown (IRE) *David Pinder* a63 64 3 b g Kyllachy—Sand Grouse (USA) (Arctic Tern (USA)) *1278[5]* 1633[4] 2242[3] 2982[10] *3622[11] 4919[6]* 5275[5] *5602[3] 6266[7] (6431)*

Golden Dagger (IRE) *K A Ryan* 89 3 ch f Daggers Drawn(USA) —Santarene (IRE) (Scenic) 1581[9] 1835[8] 2231[3] 2790[19] 3460[13] 6185[12]

Golden Dane (IRE) *I A Wood* a68 58 2 b g Danetime(IRE) —Golden Charm (IRE) (Common Grounds) 2723[11] 4198[8] 4629[6] 5706[2] *(6023) 6977[4]*

Golden Desert (IRE) *T G Mills* a94 84 3 b g Desert Prince(IRE) —Jules (IRE) (Danehill (USA)) *1450[2]* 1817[6] *3418[5]* 3944[4] *(4360)* 5051[7] *5684[3] 6209[4] (6900)*

Golden Dixie (USA) *R A Harris* a98 101 8 ch g Dixieland Band(USA) —Beyrouth (USA) (Alleged (USA)) 1464[8] 1971[7] 2494[3] (2694) 3268[2] 3526[8] 3990[14] 4122[17] 4456[3] (4567) (4806) 5212[14] 5407[20] 6183[13] 6472[9] *6676[4]*

Golden Doc A (USA) *B Abrams* a93 93 2 ch f Unusual Heat(USA) —Penpont (NZ) (Crested Wave (USA)) *5826a[9]*

Golden Dynamic (IRE) *G Di Chio* 103 3 b c Danetime(IRE) —Golden Vizcaya (USA) (Alydeed (CAN)) 1336a[4]

Golden Feather *Miss Venetia Williams* 82 5 ch g Dr Fong(USA) —Idolize (Polish Precedent (USA)) 4184[4]

Golden Folly *Lady Herries* a50 53 3 ch g Polish Precedent(USA) —Height Of Folly (Shirley Heights) 3804[13] 4491[3] *5426[7]* 6257[5] *6534[7]*

Golden Groom *C W Fairhurst* 64 4 b g Groom Dancer(USA) —Reine De Thebes (FR) (Darshaan) 3193[5] 3677[3] 4280[4] 4717[3] (4925) (5283)

Golden Hare (IRE) *Aidan Anthony Howard* 67 6 ch g Bahhare(USA) —Ela's Gold (IRE) (Ela-Mana-Mou) 6368a[12] 6555a[13]

Golden Hope (IRE) *T G McCourt* 49 3 b g Iron Mask(USA) —Ivory Dawn (Batshoof) 5834[14]

Golden Horus (USA) *P J O'Gorman* a56 2 ch g Buddha(USA) —Sunburst (Gone West (USA)) *6990[7] 7070[8]*

Golden Measure *B P J Baugh* a42 43 7 b g Rainbow Quest(USA) —Dawna (Polish Precedent (USA)) *1279[9] 1590[10]*

Golden Peacock *M Appleby* 3 ch g Forzando—Flamingo Times (Good Times (ITY)) 2083[12] *3113[10]* 3476[12]

Golden Penny *H Morrison* 77 2 b g Xaar—Dog Rose (SAF) (Fort Wood (USA)) 1832[14] 2138[4] 3383[4] 4121[10] 5002[3] 5871[3] 6379[5]

Golden Platitude (IRE) *W R Swinburn* a61 63 4 ch g Spinning World(USA) —Rainbow Dream (Rainbow Quest (USA)) 1215[2] 1606[8] 2077[14] *2667[6]* 5280[7]

Golden Prospect *J W Hills* a58 73 3 b g Lujain(USA) —Petonellajill (Petong) (1538) (1850) 2598[8] 3900[4] 4515[2] 4807[10] 5475[5]

Golden Quest *M Johnston* a85 102 6 ch g Rainbow Quest(USA) —Souk (IRE) (Ahonoora) 2462[3] 2860[3] 4375[4] 4569[9] 5375[7] 6335[11]

Golden Ribbons *J R Boyle* a38 20 3 ch f Compton Place—Mim (Midyan (USA)) *786[11] 1119[12]* 1213[5] 1739[14]

Golden Spectrum (IRE) *R A Harris* a69 62 8 ch g Spectrum(IRE) —Plessaya (USA) (Nureyev (USA)) *757 124[5] 200[3] 286[10] (426) 462[5] 538[10] 571[3] 650[4] 770[4] 830[3] 933[3] 1069[11] 1162[3] 1366[4]* 1673[9] 1886[3] *2225[7] 2521[9]* 3067[3] (3173) 3419[2] 3600[3] 4023[2] 4272[5] 4433[12] 4880[9] 5020[5] 5307[8]

Golden Sprite *B R Millman* a64 68 4 b m Bertolini(USA) —Shalad'Or (Golden Heights) 4015[3] 4504[8]

Golden Square *A W Carroll* a65 57 5 ch g Tomba—Cherish Me (Polar Falcon (USA)) *131[2] 200[2] 462[12]* 975[12] 1673[15] 2492[11] *3600[11]* 4880[8] *5094[7] 5817[10] 5900[13] 6311[12]*

Golden Strategy (USA) *M D Wolfson* a95 95 4 ch h Strategic Mission(USA) —Glacial Lake (USA) (Marquetry (USA)) 6771a[11]

Golden Surprice (IRE) *Aldo Locatelli* a79 5 b h Indian Lodge(IRE) —Sorpresa (ITY) (Miswaki (USA)) *(6873) 7020[11]*

Golden Titus (IRE) *A Renzoni* 118 3 ch c Titus Livius(FR) —Oraplata (USA) (Silver Hawk (USA)) (1336a) 3362a[3] 5261a[9] 6372a[2]

Golden Topaz (IRE) *J Howard Johnson* 62 3 b f Almutawakel—Miss Champagne (FR) (Bering) 2299[7] 2742[5] 4079[6] 5082[6]

Golden Trophy (IRE) *L Ficuciello* 66 3 b c Key Of Luck(USA) —Believing (Belmez (USA)) 1873a[6]

Golden Velvet (USA) *Saeed Bin Suroor* a88 101 4 br m Seeking The Gold(USA) —Caress (USA) (Storm Cat (USA)) *175a[3]* 397a[7] 541a[5]

Golden Virginy (IRE) *M & G Fratini* 2 ch f Namid—Westside Girl (USA) (Way West (FR)) 2684a[8]

Golden Wave (IRE) *D M Simcock* a68 62 3 b f Green Desert(USA) —Gold Bust (Nashwan (USA)) *1166[5]* 2118[4] *3284[2] 5224[4] 5980[4] 6672[8]*

Gold Express *P J O'Gorman* a73 75 4 b g Observatory(USA) —Vanishing Point (USA) (Caller I.D. (USA)) 2479[3]

Gold Flame *H Candy* a64 71 4 b g Gorse—Uaeflame (IRE) (Polish Precedent (USA)) *1587[4] (1976)* 2725[10] 3686[10] 4351[10]

Gold For Sale (ARG) *I Jory* a99 5 ch h Not For Sale(ARG) —Lava Gold (USA) (Java Gold (USA)) *599a[10] 858a[9]*

Gold Guest *P D Evans* a41 59 8 ch g Vettori(IRE) —Cassilis (IRE) (Persian Bold) *525 115[9]* (Dead)

Gold Gun (USA) *K A Ryan* a68 52 5 b g Seeking The Gold(USA) —Possessive Dancer (Shareef Dancer (USA)) *95[8]*

Goldhill Fair *W G M Turner* a39 41 2 gr g Bertolini(USA) —May Queen Megan (Petorius) 845[11] 2539[14] 3174[6] *3423[10]* 5302[13]

Gold Hush (USA) *Sir Michael Stoute* a75 96 3 ch f Seeking The Gold(USA) —Meniatarra (USA) (Zilzal (USA)) (1676) (2543) 4060[6] 4799[6] 5445[2] 5794[5] 6299[13]

Golding Star (FR) *J C Lopera-Fernandez* 102 3 b f Gold Away(IRE) —Lencloitre (FR) (Noblequest (FR)) 5058a[11]

Gold Option *J H M Gosden* 90 3 ch c Observatory(USA) —Minskip (USA) (The Minstrel (CAN)) 1835[9] 2669[4]

Gold Prospect *M L W Bell* a85 81 3 bb g Rainbow Quest(USA) —Grain Of Gold (Mr Prospector (USA)) 1011[4] 1204[5] 2402[10] *2767[2] (3113)* 3709[7] 4419 [5] 5218[4]

Gold Response *D Shaw* a58 54 3 ch g Intikhab(USA) —Razor Sharp (Bering) *68[3] 140[3] 267[3] 370[4]* 893[6] *1361[6]* 2133[7] 2796[10] (Dead)

Gold Sound (FR) *C Laffon-Parias* a91 109 5 ch g Green Tune(USA) —Born Gold (USA) (Blushing Groom (FR)) *437a[8] 4012a[8]*

Gold Sovereign (IRE) *Saeed Bin Suroor* a91 96 3 b g King's Best(USA) —Sassenach (IRE) (Night Shift (USA)) *(5494)* 5978[3]

Go Mo (IRE) *R M H Cowell* a82 81 5 b g Night Shift(USA) —Quiche (Formidable (USA)) *292[12] 374[12]*

Gone Fast (USA) *J R Fanshawe* 90 2 ch f Gone West(USA) —Abita (USA) (Dynaformer (USA)) 3245[2] (3796) 4400[6] 5614[7] 5973[12]

Gone Gold (USA) *J Noseda* a63 77 3 ch c Seeking The Gold(USA) —Gioconda (USA) (Nijinsky (CAN)) 1358[5] *2261[3]* (3015)

Gone'N'Dunnett (IRE) *Mrs C A Dunnett* a67 68 8 b g Petardia—Skerries Bell (Taufan (USA)) *892[7]* 1640[13] 1673[8] 2966[2] 3106[7] *3618[10]* 3829[9] (4296) 4397[5] 4689[12] 5576[13] 5711[11] *5778[8] 6542[7] 6718[5] 6887[4] 7111[5] (7137) 7265[5]*

Gongidas *Saeed Bin Suroor* 97 3 b c Big Shuffle(USA) —Gonfalon (Slip Anchor) 2153[2] (2477) (3470) 3940[6] (4785) 6155[9]

Goochie (IRE) *John Joseph Murphy* a56 60 3 b f Montjeu(IRE) —Royal Ulay (FR) (Selkirk (USA)) *6577[10] 6967[4]*

Good Article (IRE) *D K Ivory* a65 69 6 b g Definite Article—Good News (IRE) (Ajraas (USA)) 1002[3]

Good Ba Ba (USA) *A Schutz* 124 5 b g Lear Fan(USA) —Elle Meme (USA) (Zilzal (USA)) (7091a)

Goodbye *G A Swinbank* 85 3 ch f Efisio—Blow Me A Kiss (Kris) 1841[4] 2137[3] 2881[4] 3466[3] (3914) (5907) 6465[3] 6651[12]

Goodbye Cash (IRE) *P D Evans* a78 79 3 b f Danetime(IRE) —Jellybeen (IRE) (Petardia) *(1520)* 1604[7] (2060) 2306[4] 3164[4] 3240[3] *5684[4] 6006[10]* 6639[8] *7279[4]*

Goodbye Mr Bond *E J Alston* a62 97 7 b g Elmaamul(USA) —Fifth Emerald (Formidable (USA)) 846[11] 1287[5] (1599) 1842[2] 2093[9] 2755[14] 3513[5] 4176[4] 4385[5] 4922[5] 5641[5] 6180[12]

Good Cause (IRE) *Mrs S Lamyman* a31 62 6 b g Simply Great(FR) —Smashing Pet (Mummy's Pet) 1077[5] 1296[6] *7239[9]*

Good Effect (USA) *A P Jarvis* a70 78 3 ch g Woodman(USA) —River Dreams (USA) (Riverman (USA)) 3150[12] *3620[3] (4064)* (4510) 4847[4]

Goodenough Mover *Andrew Turnell* a94 87 11 ch g Beveled(USA) —Rekindled Flame (IRE) (Kings Lake (USA)) 1847[15] 2458[8] 2982[2] 3368[3] (4075) 4594[3] 5711[4] 6088[12]

Good Etiquette *Mrs S Lamyman* 12 3 b g Tipsy Creek(USA) —Aliuska (IRE) (Fijar Tango (FR)) 916[8] 1075[8]

Good Gorsoon (USA) *B W Hills* a82 86 2 b c Stravinsky(USA) —Alwaysinbloom (USA) (Unbridled (USA)) 2600[5] 4537[3] (4755) 5207[8] 6195[4] *6544[3]*

Good Intentions *P W Hiatt* a41 30 5 ch m Bien Bien(USA) —Level Headed (Beveled (USA)) *18[12]*

Good Investment *Miss Tracy Waggott* a43 53 5 b g Silver Patriarch(IRE) —Bundled Up (USA) (Sharpen Up) *240[11]* 2252[13]

Good Luck Chip (IRE) *I A Wood* a28 21 3 b f Princely Heir(IRE) —Surabaya (FR) (Galetto (FR)) 1763[11] (Dead)

Good Return *Jane Chapple-Hyam* 57 2 b g Fasliyev(USA) —Fickle (Danehill (USA)) 6106[7] 6724[12]

Good Wee Girl (IRE) *S Woodman* 28 5 b m Tagula(IRE) —Auriga (Belmez (USA)) 2273[7] 2559[7]

Goodwood Spirit *J M Bradley* a44 71 5 b g Fraam—Rechanit (IRE) (Local Suitor (USA)) 1133[8] 1318[7] 1507[9] 2108[8] 2334[8] 2619[12] 3615[5] 4256[2] 4319[3] 4532[12] 4998[12] *5179[7]* 5189[11] *6152[11]*

Goodwood Starlight (IRE) *J L Dunlop* 80 2 br c Mtoto—Starring (FR) (Ashkalani (IRE)) (4539) (5109)

Go On Be A Tiger (USA) *M R Channon* 93 3 br g Machiavellian(USA) —Queen's Logic (IRE) (Grand Lodge (USA)) 1126[8] 1662[7] 2001[2] 3463[10] 4601[10] 5209[4] 5923[15]

Go On Green (IRE) *E A L Dunlop* a85 82 3 b c Kyllachy—Colouring (IRE) (Catrail (USA)) *(423) 584[3] 725[4]* 1108[3] 1660[4] 2114[5] *2993[3] 3418[8]*

Goose Bay (GER) *P Schiergen* 94 2 b f Groom Dancer(USA) —Golden Time (GER) (Surumu (GER)) 5028a[3] 6371a[4]

Goose Chase *B J Llewellyn* a73 39 5 b g Inchinor—Bronzewing (Beldale Flutter (USA)) *38[6] 130[6] 235[12] 805[9]* 1562[12] 1739[8]

Goose Green (IRE) *R J Hodges* a67 68 3 b g Invincible Spirit(IRE) —Narbayda (IRE) (Kahyasi) *624[10]* 1359[7] 1684[2] 2079[7] 2545[15] 2601[4] 2916[14] *3620[4]* 3875[2] 4326[9] 5687[8] 6083[5] *6387[2] (6567) 6816[3] 6993[9]*

Gordonsville *A M Balding* a81 88 4 b g Generous(IRE) —Kimba (USA) (Kris S (USA)) *3084[2]* 3415[2] *5311[2] (6070)*

Go Red *M W Easterby* 51 3 b g Best Of The Bests(IRE) —Boulevard Rouge (USA) (Red Ransom (USA)) 1850[11] 3918[9] 4078[15]

Gorgeous Girl *P W D'Arcy* a44 41 3 b f Generous(IRE) —Zielana Gora (Polish Precedent (USA)) *5980[12]*

Go Solo *D E Pipe* 93 6 b g Primo Dominie—Taza (Persian Bold) 4047[14]

Go Tech *T D Easterby* a89 88 7 b g Gothenberg(IRE) —Bollin Sophie (Efisio) 993[11] 4408[5] 4922[2] 5229[5] 5593[3] 6185[10]

Got Green (FR) *R Hannon* a48 57 2 ch f Green Tune(USA) —Aphrodisias (FR) (Double Bed (FR)) 1680[11] 2504[12] 5344[7] *6433[9]*

Go The Distance (IRE) *Adrian Sexton* a26 71 5 b m Cape Cross(IRE) —Law Student (Precocious) *609[12]*

Gothenburg (UAE) *M Johnston* 102 2 b c Halling(USA) —Poised (USA) (Rahy (USA)) 3199[2] (3781) (4202)

Gottcha Gold (USA) *E Plesa Jr* a114 4 b h Coronado's Quest(USA) —Gottcha Last (USA) (Pleasant Tap (USA)) *6485a[2]*

Got The Last Laugh (USA) *W Mott* a105 89 3 br c Distorted Humor(USA) —Theresa's Tizzy (USA) (Cee's Tizzy (USA)) 5823a[10]

Gouranga *A W Carroll* a45 70 4 b m Robellino(USA) —Hymne D'Amour (USA) (Dixieland Band (USA)) *270[4] 7076[6] 7262[4]*

Govenor Eliott (IRE) *M Johnston* 69 2 ch g Rock Of Gibraltar(IRE) —Lac Dessert (USA) (Lac Ouimet (USA)) 5143[5] 5502[5] 6246[5]

Government (IRE) *M C Chapman* a54 53 6 b g Great Dane(IRE) —Hidden Agenda (FR) (Machiavellian (USA)) *524[8] (627) 729[9] 812[9] 1379[4] 1569[2] (1715) 1933[7] 2145[2]* 2370[16] 3907[15] 4177[7] 4427[4] *4668[9]* 6412[13] *7113[8] 7244[7]*

Gower *Ms F M Crowley* a76 82 3 b c Averti(IRE) —Alashaan (Darshaan) *(802) 943[6]* 1616[5] 1900[4] 2513[8] 3179[2] 5841a[11]

Gower Belle *W R Muir* a69 65 2 b f Fantastic Light(USA) —Polish Belle (Polish Precedent (USA)) *3213[6]* 3796[4] 4310[4] *5097[2] 5601[4] 6228[5]*

Gower Song *D R C Elsworth* a94 107 4 b m Singspiel(IRE) —Gleaming Water (Kalaglow) 1506[3] *6605[6]* (6757)

Gowna's Hope (IRE) *J W Mullins* 47 4 br g Distant Music(USA) —Embolden (Warning) 4256[12]

Grace Anatomy (USA) *Doug O'Neill* a104 2 b f Aldebaran(USA) —Propriety (USA) (Storm Cat (USA)) *6507a[7]*

Grace And Power (USA) *Steven B Klesaris* a106 99 2 br f More Than Ready(USA) —Lady In Power (USA) (Defensive Play (USA)) 6482a[3]

Grace Bay *Bob Jones* 4 ch m Komaite(USA) —Canova's Grace (Ron's Victory (USA)) *49[7] 125[10] 282[9]*

Gracechurch (IRE) *R J Hodges* a58 82 4 b g Marju(IRE) —Saffron Crocus (Shareef Dancer (USA)) 1208[9] 1765[10] 2107[13] 5917[12] 6196[6] *6583[4] 6911[7]*

Graceful Descent (FR) *R A Fahey* a74 71 2 b f Hawk Wing(USA) —Itab (USA) (Dayjur (USA)) 3884[2] 4448[2] 4852[3] *5236[2]* (5551) 5974[28]

Graceful Flight *P T Midgley* a15 44 5 gr m Cloudings(IRE) —Fantasy Flight (Forzando) 1625[12]

Gracefull Model *Mrs C A Dunnett* 3 b f Erhaab(USA) —Bedtime Model (Double Bed (FR)) *5728[14]* 6412[16]

Graceful Star (IRE) *D K Weld* a85 73 2 b f Soviet Star(USA) —Amandian (IRE) (Indian Ridge) 5395a[15]

Graceful Steps (IRE) *E J O'Neill* 79 3 b f Desert Prince(IRE) —Ghassak (IRE) (Persian Bold) (1155) 1320[2] (1708) (1927) 2547a[9] 3555[7] 3964[12]

Gracie's Gift (IRE) *A G Newcombe* a67 69 5 b g Imperial Ballet(IRE) —Settle Petal (IRE) (Roi Danzig (USA)) *130[9]* 1507[2] 1969[5] 2831[3] 3571[6] 4505[4] 5166[10] 5917[8]

Gracious Girl (IRE) *Enda Kelly* 67 2 b f Invincible Spirit(IRE) —Supportive (IRE) (Nashamaa) 779a[11]

Gradetime (IRE) *M Halford* a79 82 3 b f Danetime(IRE) —Grade A Star (IRE) (Alzao (USA)) 3140a[17]

Graduation *E A L Dunlop* 97 3 ch f Lomitas—Ceremonial (Lion Cavern (USA)) 1128[3] (1537) 1824[3] 2757[15] 3430[2] 5799[5] 6300[9]

Graft *Mrs P Townsley* a60 70 8 b g Entrepreneur—Mariakova (USA) (The Minstrel (CAN)) *279[11]*

Grafton (IRE) *J O'Reilly* a65 56 4 b g Desert Style(IRE) —Gracious Gretclo (Common Grounds) *217[4] 339[4] 448[5] 504[3] 627[11] 729[8]*

Grafton Street (IRE) *A P O'Brien* 92 4 b h Danehill(USA) —Bells Are Ringing (USA) (Sadler's Wells (USA)) 2736[20] 3143a[16] 6368a[19]

Graft Versus Host (IRE) *L Ficuciello* 98 4 b h Key Of Luck(USA) —Megalythe (FR) (Akarad (FR)) 1874a[7]

Grafty Green (IRE) *W M Brisbourne* a54 56 4 b g Green Desert(USA) —Banafsajee (USA) (Pleasant Colony (USA)) *5754[9]* 6109[5] *6458[12]* 6728[4] *6867[4] 6969[13]*

Graham Island *G Wragg* a87 79
6 b g Acatenango(GER) —Gryada (Shirley Heights)
2692[5] 3609[6]

Graham Two (IRE) *G P Kelly*
3 b g Agnes World(USA) —Night At Sea (Night Shift (USA))
1375[P]

Grail Knight *Miss Gay Kelleway* a37
2 ch g Carnival Dancer—Nashkova (Nashwan (USA))
7152[6]

Grain Of Truth *I Mohammed* a100 101
4 b m Gulch(USA) —Pure Grain (Polish Precedent (USA))
329a[14]

Granakey (IRE) *M Wigham* a63
4 b m Key Of Luck(USA) —Grand Morning (IRE) (King Of Clubs)
(7) 238[7] (462) 539[6] 686[5] 712[3] 6123[12] 6993[10] 7207[5]

Granary *H Candy* a62 65
3 b f Singspiel(IRE) —All Grain (Polish Precedent (USA))
4235[7] 4765[4] 5335[4] 7174[2]

Granary Girl *J Pearce* a56 57
5 b m Kingsinger(IRE) —Highland Blue (Never So Bold)
3946[13] 4327[2] 4558[4] 6452[3] 6713[6] 6866[4] 7009[12] 7056[7] 7277[3]

Gran Clicquot *G P Enright* a41 45
12 gr m Gran Alba(USA) —Tina's Beauty (Tina's Pet)
1331[0]

Grandad Bill (IRE) *J S Goldie* a47 55
4 ch g Intikhab(USA) —Matikanehanafubuki (IRE) (Caerleon (USA))
674[8] 932[12] 2370[9] 3042[3] (5503) 5964[4] 6304[8]

Grand Art (IRE) *M H Tompkins* a49 81
3 b g Raise A Grand(IRE) —Mulberry River (IRE) (Bluebird (USA))
1155[3] 1964[2] 2248[5] (3800) (4197) 5405[6] 6422[8]

Grand Assault *G C Bravery* a58
4 b g Mujahid(USA) —As Mustard (Keen)
6706[2] (7134)

Grand Court (IRE) *Evan Williams* a34 53
4 b m Grand Lodge(USA) —Nice One Clare (IRE) (Mukaddamah (USA))
1038[11] 1562[8] 2157[8] 3803[13]

Grand Couturier *R Ribaudo* 120
4 b h Grand Lodge(USA) —Lady Elgar (IRE) (Sadler's Wells (USA))
(4415a) 5250a[3] 6513a[6]

Grand Cuvee *D M Simcock* 71
2 b g Efisio—Bel Tempo (Petong)
4537[11] 5541[9] 5720[4] 6201[4] 6572[2]

Grand Diamond (IRE) *J S Goldie* a65 65
3 b g Grand Lodge(USA) —Winona (IRE) (Alzao (USA))
1289[14] 1624[9] 1964[3] 2829[3] 3816[9] 4701[7] (4971) 5840[14] 6245[4] 6738[4] 6874[8]

Grand Dream (IRE) *J G Given* 48
3 ch g Grand Lodge(USA) —Tamaya (IRE) (Darshaan)
1303[6] 1964[14] 3400[7] 3722[12]

Grande Caiman (IRE) *R Hannon* a97 75
3 ch c Grand Lodge(USA) —Sweet Retreat (Indian Ridge)
5685[12] 5724[6] 6132[6] (6666) (6819) (7086)

Grand Emporium (SAF) *S Seemar* a72 91
7 b g National Assembly(CAN) —Whistling Dixie (SAF) (Raise A Man (USA))
177a[15] 411a[10] 601a[9]

Grand Entrance (IRE) *C R Egerton* a59 76
4 b g Grand Lodge(USA) —Alessia (GER) (Warning)
3943[10]

Grande Rousse (FR) *P Bary* 97
3 gr f Act One—Geriba (CAN) (Gone West (USA))
1339a[6] 3148a[7]

Grand Fleet *M Johnston* 81
2 b g Green Desert(USA) —Janaat (Kris)
(1073) 2009[3] 5624[2]

Grand Heights (IRE) *J L Dunlop* 77
3 br c Grand Lodge(USA) —Height Of Fantasy (IRE) (Shirley Heights)
1012[2] 1290[4] (5474) 5955[7]

Grand Jour (IRE) *B P J Baugh* a84 60
4 b g Grand Lodge(USA) —Reveuse De Jour (IRE) (Sadler's Wells (USA))
4462[7] 4634[7]

Grand Lucre *G A Butler* a69 53
3 b f Grand Slam(USA) —Naughty Crown (USA) (Chief's Crown (USA))
(635) 935[8] 1345[8] 2422[4] 3286[9] 5136[6] 5528[2] 6123[2] 6343[10]

Grand Officer (IRE) *D J S Ffrench Davis* a39 48
3 b g Grand Lodge(USA) —Sheer Bliss (IRE) (Sadler's Wells (USA))
1397[7] 2110[11]

Grand Opera (IRE) *J Howard Johnson* 74
4 b g City On A Hill(USA) —Victoria's Secret (IRE) (Law Society (USA))
1481[4] 3201[4] 4281[7] 5035[3]

Grandos (IRE) *Karen George* a33
5 b g Cadeaux Genereux—No Reservations (IRE) (Commanche Run)
699[10]

Grand Palace (IRE) *D Shaw* a68 39
4 b g Grand Lodge(USA) —Pocket Book (IRE) (Reference Point)
7[9] 145[6] 181[3] (268) 485[2] 560[8] 2799[6] 2947[10] 3064[P] 4978[7] 5730[8] 6563[2] 6629[10] 6886[2] (6927) 7014[3] 7107[2] (7188) 7271[2]

Grand Passion (IRE) *G Wragg* a109 108
7 b g Grand Lodge(USA) —Lovers' Parlour (Beldale Flutter (USA))
352[2] 552[8] 761[2] 941[2] 1550a[4] 3097[5] 3912[3] 5220[5] 6298[8] (6931) 7225[2]

Grand Place *J G Portman* a54 41
5 b g Compton Place—Comme Ca (Cyrano De Bergerac)
2490[P]

Grand Rebecca (IRE) *G A Huffer* 37
4 ch m Namid—Krayyalei (IRE) (Krayyan)
2154[12]

Grand Revival (IRE) *David P Myerscough* 80
5 ch g Grand Lodge(USA) —Romancia (USA) (Woodman (USA))
3143a[9]

Grand Sefton *Stef Liddiard* a57 52
4 br g Pivotal—Nahlin (Slip Anchor)
3217[14] 3619[6] 3732[8] 3868[2] 4533[8]

Grand Show *W R Swinburn* a96 86
5 b g Efisio—Christine Daae (Sadler's Wells (USA))
4507[3] 5722[3] 6142[9] 7112[7]

Grand Silence (IRE) *W R Swinburn* a48 67
4 ch g Grand Lodge(USA) —Why So Silent (Mill Reef (USA))
4686[8]

Grand Strategy (IRE) *M A Jarvis* a78 63
2 bb c Singspiel(IRE) —Game Plan (Darshaan)
6130[8] 6436[4]

Grand Symphony *W Jarvis* a69 69
3 ch f Zamindar(USA) —Gitane (FR) (Grand Lodge (USA))
128[3] 489[2] 583[4] 1131[2] 1370[3] 1979[5] 2317[3] 2834[12] 5508[5] 6121[9] 6573[4]

Grand Value (USA) *T D Barron* 60
2 b f Grand Slam(USA) —Privyet Nadya (USA) (Cure The Blues (USA))
3884[5] 4769[6] 5226[2]

Grand View *J R Weymes* a51 37
11 ch g Grand Lodge(USA) —Hemline (Sharpo)
33[4] 281[4] 337[6] 442[6] 622[6] (653) 687[8] 1400[12] 4768[11]

Grand Vista *A Fabre* 104
3 b c Danehill(USA) —Revealing (Halling (USA))
2499a[3] 3362a[7] 4216a[2] 5259a[10]

Grand Vizier (IRE) *C F Wall* a80 69
3 b g Desert Style(IRE) —Distant Decree (USA) (Distant View (USA))
1812[13] (2261) 2633[9] (3926) 5693[6]

Grand Welcome (IRE) *E J Creighton* a48 47
5 b g Indian Lodge(IRE) —Chocolate Box (Most Welcome)
372[12] 887[3] 1119[7] 1311[9]

Grangehurst *Miss J R Gibney* a56 57
3 ch f Inchinor—My Way (IRE) (Marju (IRE))
3428[6]

Grange Lili (IRE) *Peter Grayson* a73 73
3 b f Daggers Drawn(USA) —Lili Cup (FR) (Fabulous Dancer (USA))
34[4] (103) 188[5] (219) (280) 387[3] 1067[7] 1351[6] 1825[8] 2513[9] 2672[7] 2867[7] 3568[5] 4432[5] 4712[4]

Grange Poppy (IRE) *Peter Grayson* a52
2 b f Choisir(AUS) —Columbine (IRE) (Pivotal)
883[3]

Granston (IRE) *J D Bethell* a99 98
6 gr g Revoque(IRE) —Gracious Gretclo (Common Grounds)
848[12] 1524[3] 1860[3] 2891[3] 4176[3] 4566[5] 5221[10] 5776[9]

Grantley Adams *M R Channon* a86 109
4 b g Dansili—Noble Peregrine (Lomond (USA))
415a[4] (472a) 528a[4] 1474[3] 2858[5] 3505[9] 4150[11] 4614[17] 5416[3] 5616[22] 6338[12] 6491[6]

Grapes Of Wrath (UAE) *M Johnston* a51
2 ch f Halling(USA) —Muscadel (Nashwan (USA))
5679[7] 6456[3] 6868[9] 7022[10] 7149[2] 7245[10]

Grasp *G L Moore* a62 57
5 b g Kayf Tara—Circe (Main Reef)
302[5] 2770[5]

Gravitas *Saeed Bin Suroor* 113
4 ch h Mark Of Esteem(IRE) —Bombazine (IRE) (Generous (IRE))
248a[2] 412a[5] 645a[9] 5351[4] 6198[7]

Graylyn Ruby (FR) *J Jay* a46 59
2 b c Limnos(JPN) —Nandi (IRE) (Mujadil (USA))
4273[9] 4584[10] 5344[8] 5736[5]

Graze On *Peter Grayson* a93 89
5 b g Factual(USA) —Queens Check (Komaite (USA))
5[6] 554[2] 818[6] 1363[P] (Dead)

Graze On And On *J J Quinn* 33
2 ch f Elmaamul(USA) —Laena (Roman Warrior)
6384[11] 6698[8]

Grazeon Gold Blend *J J Quinn* 94
4 ch g Paris House—Thalya (Crofthall)
1088[18] 1853[8]

Grazie Mille *R Brotherton* a29 55
3 b f Bertolini(USA) —Daintree (IRE) (Tirol)
974[11] 1154[15] 2196[13]

Great As Gold (IRE) *B Ellison* a59 85
8 b g Goldmark(USA) —Great Land (USA) (Friend's Choice (USA))
808[2] 994[2] (1196) 1793[2] (2505) 2908[2] 3609[3] 4056[6] 4569[5] 5256[8] 6335[14]

Great Barrier Reef (USA) *A P O'Brien* 109
2 ch c Mr Greeley(USA) —Song To Remember (USA) (Storm Cat (USA))
4721[2] 5070a[3] 5458a[5]

Great Britain *Saeed Bin Suroor* 117
5 b h Green Desert(USA) —Park Appeal (Ahonoora)
547a[2] (644a)

Great Charm (IRE) *M L W Bell* a62 66
2 b g Orpen(USA) —Briery (IRE) (Salse (USA))
5599[14] 6574[5] 6884[4]

Great Explorer (IRE) *E J O'Neill* a75 60
3 b c Indian Danehill(IRE) —Ninth Wonder (USA) (Forty Niner (USA))
(152) (Dead)

Great Future *H R A Cecil* 47
2 ch f Fantastic Light(USA) —Silvernus (Machiavellian (USA))
6248[14] 6470[15]

Great Hawk (USA) *Sir Michael Stoute* a103 106
4 b h El Prado(IRE) —Laser Hawk (USA) (Silver Hawk (USA))
2236[16] (3939) 4720[7] 5220[7] 5634[4]

Great Hunter (USA) *Doug O'Neill* a117
3 bb c Aptitude(USA) —Zenith (USA) (Roy (USA))
1486a[13]

Great Man (FR) *Noel T Chance* a68
6 b g Bering—Great Connection (USA) (Dayjur (USA))
142[4] 507[3] 594[12] 1347[8]

Great Plains *E Charpy* a89 104
5 b h Halling(USA) —West Dakota (USA) (Gone West (USA))
244a[3] 401a[7] 544a[5]

Great Quest (IRE) *James Moffatt* 73
5 b m Montjeu(IRE) —Paparazzi (IRE) (Shernazar)
914[7] 1042[2] 2434[4] 3027[2] 3976[9] 4717[6] 5283[6]

Great Rhythm (SAF) *H J Brown* 112
6 gr g I'm Great(SAF) —Gallo's Girl (SAF) (Steady Beat (USA))
(247a) 413a[2] 600a[9] 646a[3]

Great Rumpuscat (USA) *A P O'Brien* 93
2 b c Storm Cat(USA) —Monevassia (USA) (Mr Prospector (USA))
5456a[6] 6549a[9]

Great Uncle Ted (USA) *A Renzoni* 100
4 gr h Running Stag(USA) —One Smooth Dancer (USA) (Vigors (USA))
1876a[11]

Great View (IRE) *Mrs A L M King* a71 83
8 b g Great Commotion(USA) —Tara View (IRE) (Wassl)
1149[10] 1470[7] 2011[4] 2833[5] 3155[5] (3232) 3567[2] 3978[3] 4421[4] 4597[13] 5725[8]

Greatwallofchina (USA) *A P O'Brien* 105
2 b c Kingmambo(USA) —Dietrich (USA) (Storm Cat (USA))
4725[7] 6041a[6] 6333[8]

Great War Eagle (USA) *David Wachman* a100 98
2 br c Storm Cat(USA) —Cash Run (USA) (Seeking The Gold (USA))
(6161a) 6549a[4]

Grecian Dancer *Charles O'Brien* a100 101
4 b m Dansili—Pizzicato (Statoblest)
873a[9] 2379a[4] 3139a[3] 4438a[3]

Grecian Slave *B Smart* a62 63
2 ch c Spartacus(IRE) —Grecian Halo (USA) (Southern Halo (USA))
3760[8] 4578[4] 5735[8] 6291[5]

Greek Easter (IRE) *David P Myerscough* a78 73
4 bb m Namid—Easter Heroine (IRE) (Exactly Sharp (USA))
1288[17] 1813[10] 2181[11] 7194[2] (7224)

Greek Envoy *T P Tate* 109
3 br g Diktat—South Shore (Caerleon (USA))
(2305) 3513[2] 4690[18] (6302)

Greek God *W Jarvis* a57 57
3 b g Grand Lodge(USA) —Cephalonia (Slip Anchor)
37[4] 224[2] 373[5] 1194[8] 1937[6]

Greek Mythology (USA) *A P O'Brien* 89
2 b c Mr Greeley(USA) —Tell Me Now (USA) (A.P. Indy (USA))
1832[3] 2732[12]

Greek Renaissance (IRE) *Saeed Bin Suroor* a91 119
4 b h Machiavellian(USA) —Athene (IRE) (Rousillon (USA))
249a[7] (409a) 547a[3] 644a[8] (5512) (6338) 6758[5]

Greek Secret *J O'Reilly* a64 78
4 b g Josr Algarhoud(IRE) —Mazurkanova (Song)
8[10] 992[10] 1675[15] 3608[9] 4008[6] (4180) 4423[8] 4706[11] 4822[12] 5284[17] (5489) 5747[11] 5909[5] 6210[9]

Greek Theatre (USA) *Mrs A J Perrett* a67 64
2 ch c Smoke Glacken(USA) —Theatre Flight (USA) (Theatrical)
5003[5] 5448[5] 5720[12] 6449[5] 6715[2] 6868[U] 6973[5]

Greek Well (IRE) *Sir Michael Stoute* 102
4 b g Sadler's Wells(USA) —Hellenic (Darshaan)
1288[2] 1771[6] (2403) (2634) 3558[4] 4043[5] (4720) 5631[3] 6011[20]

Green Ascot (IRE) *R Gibson* a53 50
2 b c Barathea(IRE) —Dirigeante (FR) (Lead On Time (USA))
6879a[5]

Greenbelt *G M Moore* a77 77
6 b g Desert Prince(IRE) —Emerald (USA) (El Gran Senor (USA))
228[9] (319) 377[2] 453[8] 631[10] 733[7] 997[5] 1042[11]

Green Birdie (NZ) *C Fownes* 109
4 b g Catbird(AUS) —Mrs Squillionaire (AUS) (Last Tycoon (IRE))
7089a[7]

Green Coast (IRE) *Saeed Bin Suroor* 95
4 b h Green Desert(USA) —Oriental Fashion (IRE) (Marju (IRE))
105a[3] 395a[2]

Green Day Packer (IRE) *P C Haslam* a63 63
3 br g Daylami(IRE) —Durrah Green (Green Desert (USA))
140[6] 731[4] 893[7] 4491[4] 5626[7]

Green Diamond *M Johnston* a75 79
2 b g Green Desert(USA) —Balisada (Kris)
4048[9] 4784[2] 5541[3] 7084[3]

Green Earrings (IRE) *R Charlton* 58
2 ch f Captain Rio—Kitty Kildare (USA) (Seattle Dancer (USA))
4074[5] 4875[5] 5329[7]

Green Girl (FR) *Christophe Clement* 103
5 b m Lord Of Men—Green Sails (IRE) (Slip Anchor)
4652a[5] 5853a[6] 6790a[4]

Green Ideal *Ferdy Murphy* 68
9 b g Mark Of Esteem(IRE) —Emerald (USA) (El Gran Senor (USA))
1654[9]

Green Lagonda (AUS) *J G Given* a73 52
5 gr g Crown Jester(AUS) —Fidelis (AUS) (John's Hope (AUS))
2418[14] 2972[7] 3408[7] 6287[9] (6428) 6870[10] 6890[4] 7020[7] (7077) 7183[10]

Green Lyons (IRE) *Mme C Head-Maarek* 99
3 b f Green Desert(USA) —Spinnette (IRE) (Spinning World (USA))
1055a[6]

Green Manalishi *K A Ryan* a106 113
6 b g Green Desert(USA) —Silca-Cisa (Hallgate)
(1125) 2234[5] 2733[9] 3139a[6] 3990[19] (4196) 4746[13] 5325[4] 5407[6] 5953[5]

Greenmeadow *S Kirk* a66 62
5 b m Sure Blade(USA) —Pea Green (Try My Best (USA))
2194[12] 3191[5] 3451[4] 4023[11] 4327[7] 5094[3] 6260[13] 6627[8] 6866[6] 7009[10]

Green Oasis (USA) *E J O'Neill* a73 93
2 b f Green Desert(USA) —Class Kris (USA) (Kris S (USA))
(3109) 3432[8] 3988[6]

Green Park (IRE) *R A Fahey* 98
4 b g Shinko Forest(IRE) —Danccini (IRE) (Dancing Dissident (USA))
1088[3] 1474[23] 1788[5] 1853[3] 2440[14] (3050) 3573a[8] 3975[3] 4696[11] 5407[19] 5584[15] 5810[6]

Green Pirate *W M Brisbourne* a66 64
5 b g Bahamian Bounty—Verdura (Green Desert (USA))
124[6] 206[8] 313[2] 1740[13] 2117[7] 2492[4] 2947[4] 3173[3] 3409[2] 4433[9] 4978[8] 5016[3] 5237[5] 5503[12] 5643[2] 5981[4] 6476[4] 7207[2] 7233[3]

Green Room (FR) *J L Dunlop* 109
4 b m In The Wings—Scarlet Plume (Warning)
1144[9] 2036[3] 2702a[8] 3744[2]

Green's Delight *M W Easterby* 36
2 gr f Hunting Lion(IRE) —Beat Time (Lion Cavern (USA))
3834[8] 4770[9] (Dead)

Greenslades *P J Makin* a97 104
8 ch h Perugino(USA) —Woodfield Rose (Scottish Reel)
1836[7] 2440[5] 2835[5] 3489[4] 4806[3] 5209[8] 6472[13]

Green Wadi *M R Channon* 88
2 b c Dansili—Peryllys (Warning)
5417[2] 5813[3] 6194[3]

Greenwich Meantime *R A Fahey* a77 105
7 b g Royal Academy(USA) —Shirley Valentine (Shirley Heights)
(1582) 3090[19] 4091[11] 4375[7] 5215[9] 5375[4] 6335[25] 6744[3]

Green Wonder (GER) *D M Simcock* a37
2 b f Big Shuffle(USA) —Green Water (Suave Dancer (USA))
6626[6]

Greenwood *P G Murphy* a71 79
9 ch g Emarati(USA) —Charnwood Queen (Cadeaux Genereux)
(750) (866) 1200[8] 1252[8] 1666[6] 1931[10] 1969[9] 3422[8] 3644[5] 3965[3] 4395[10] 5917[11] 6226[5] 6579[7]

Greetings (BRZ) *P Nickel Filho* a102 95
4 br m Choctaw Ridge(USA) —Groupie (IRE) (Great Commotion (USA))
(246a) 476a[2] 647a[3] 859a[13]

Greg's Gold (USA) *D Hofmans* a117
6 gr g Lake George(USA) —Lake Windermere (USA) (Fit To Fight (USA))
6510a[8]

Gremlin *A King* 87
3 b g Mujahid(USA) —Fairy Free (Rousillon (USA))
(1504) 1810[2] 3460[14]

Grenane (IRE) *P D Evans* a49 62
4 b g Princely Heir(IRE) —Another Rainbow (IRE) (Rainbows For Life (CAN))
7158[9]

Grethel (IRE) *A Berry* a33 65
3 b f Fruits Of Love(USA) —Stay Sharpe (USA) (Sharpen Up)
1620[6] 1964[12] 2206[9] 2713[7] 3181[13] 3611[8] 4220[5] 4282[4] 4579[3] 4902[3] 4936[8] (5299) 5405[7] 5555[4] 5774[3] 5936[3] 6055[7] 6343[9] (6464) 6638[7]

Grey Boy (GER) *A W Carroll* a83 88
6 gr g Medaaly—Grey Perri (Siberian Express (USA))
56[4] 218[4] 427[4] 699[2] 1209[7] 1682[8] 2626[10] 4606[3] 4880[12] 5254[2] 5909[11]

Greyfriars Abbey *M Johnston* a66 76
3 b g Fasliyev(USA) —Mysistra (FR) (Machiavellian (USA))
3032[4] 3539[5] 3997[5] (4159) (4902)

Grey Gurkha *I W McInnes* a61 60
6 gr h Kasakov—Royal Rebeka (Grey Desire)
5915[6] 6100[8] 6804[7] (7166)

Greylami (IRE) *T G Mills* a77 75
2 gr g Daylami(IRE) —Silent Crystal (USA) (Diesis)
5011[5] 5679[2] 6138[6]

Grey Light (IRE) *L Lungo* a56 64
3 b g Namid—Flying Clouds (Batshoof)
222[8] 342[7] 954[6] 1289[6] 1624[7]

Grey Outlook *Miss L A Perratt* 68
4 ch m Observatory(USA) —Grey Galava (Generous (IRE))
955[4] 1457[5] 1490[5] 1793[12] 2250[6] 2567[4] 2824[4] 2935[4] 4499[6] 4717[9] 5001[3] 5586[9]

Grey Report (IRE) *Simon Earle* a64
10 gr g Roselier(FR) —Busters Lodge (Antwerp City)
443[5]

Grey Samurai *B Ellison* 66
7 gr g Gothenberg(IRE) —Royal Rebeka (Grey Desire)
2810[3] (3610) 3901[5] 4096[10]

Greyside (USA) *C A Mulhall* a68 79
4 gr g Tactical Cat(USA) —Amber Gold (USA) (Mr Prospector (USA))
515[6] 709[5] 994[11] 3927[P] (Dead)

Greystoke Prince *W R Swinburn* a66 58
2 gr g Diktat—Grey Princess (IRE) (Common Grounds)
2086[6] 3465[4] 4527[7] 5117[2] 6201[10]

Greyt Big Stuff (USA) *Miss Gay Kelleway* a71 76
3 gr g Aljabr(USA) —Dixie Eyes Blazing (USA) (Gone West (USA))
1205[13] 3707[8] 4073[11]

Grey Vision *M Brittain* a30 51
4 gr m Grey Desire—Brief Star (IRE) (Brief Truce (USA))
3917[11] 4178[4] 4427[9] 4705[10] 5299[12] 5487[9]

Grimes Faith *K A Ryan* a89 91
4 b g Woodborough(USA) —Emma Grimes (IRE) (Nordico (USA))
(28) 384[6] 575[11] 657[7] 699[6] 833[2] 5617[10] 6243[6] 6753[3] 7045[11] 7261[8]

Grimes Hope (IRE) *R Hannon* 56
2 ch c Daggers Drawn(USA) —Sharkiyah (IRE) (Polish Precedent (USA))
3552[12] 4363[4] 4824[2]

Gris De Gris (IRE) *J-M Capitte* a102 105
3 gr c Slickly(FR) —Deesse Grise (FR) (Lead On Time (USA))
(436a) *695a*[3] 2952a[5]

Grisham *Michael John Phillips* 90
9 b g Emarati(USA) —Shibui (Shirley Heights)
3138a[20]

Grizebeck (IRE) *R F Fisher* a62 68
5 b g Trans Island—Premier Amour (Salmon Leap (USA))
1231[2] 2253[4] 2987[6] 4124[6] 5478[5] *7125*[3]

Grizedale (IRE) *J Akehurst* 83
8 ch g Lake Coniston(IRE) —Zabeta (Diesis)
(1845) 2427[4] 3234[6] 3943[16] 4548[10] 5115[5] 6081[9] 6203[9] 6651[13]

Grooms Affection *K A Morgan* a49 88
7 b g Groom Dancer(USA) —Love And Affection (USA) (Exclusive Era (USA))
7277[5]

Groomsman *Ms V S Lucas* 76
5 b g Groom Dancer(USA) —Trois Heures Apres (Soviet Star (USA))
2708a[2]

Gross Prophet *Tom Dascombe* a88 87
2 b g Lujain(USA) —Done And Dusted (IRE) (Up And At 'Em)
2349[9] 3363[4] 4181[3] *(4459)* *4916*[3] *4975*[2] (5207) 5691[3] 5922[5] 6171[5] *(7202)*

Ground Patrol *W G M Turner* a57 63
6 b g Ashkalani(IRE) —Good Grounds (USA) (Alleged (USA))
3616[10] *3946*[7] *4739*[6] *5120*[13]

Group Captain *R Charlton* a104 116
5 b g Dr Fong(USA) —Alusha (Soviet Star (USA))
929[7] 1571a[3] 1833[3] 2216[9] 3097[6] (3989) 4722[10] 5618[9]

Group Force (IRE) *M H Tompkins* a62 61
3 b f Montjeu(IRE) —Allspice (Alzao (USA))
1092[5] *5531*[3] 5906[5] 6330[3] 6561[10] *6817*[10]

Group Therapy *J A Osborne* 98
2 ch c Choisir(AUS) —Licence To Thrill (Wolfhound (USA))
999[6] (1150) (1478) 1897[2]

Grove Creek *Niall Moran* a38 47
4 ch m Observatory(USA) —Maze Garden (USA) (Riverman (USA))
558[13]

Growler *T D Walford* 69
6 ch g Foxhound(USA) —Femme Femme (USA) (Lyphard (USA))
6717[9] *7119*[9]

Grudge *D W Barker* 69
2 b c Timeless Times(USA) —Envy (IRE) (Paris House)
1422[7] 1706[5] 2071[2] 3370[5] 4175[4] 4937[2] 5802[7]

Grylls (USA) *R Hannon* 82
2 br c Labeeb—Soupremacist (USA) (Lord Carlos (USA))
1832[17] (2398) 3077[4] 4743[17] 5324[19] 5713[2]

Guacamole *B W Hills* a79 90
3 ch f Inchinor—Popocatepetl (FR) (Nashwan (USA))
2369[8] *3645*[5] (4404) 4608[4] 5431[2] *6359*[9]

Guadaloup *M Brittain* a60 58
5 ch m Loup Sauvage(USA) —Rash (Pursuit Of Love)
2254 *1349*[3] 1596[6] *1933*[6] (2937) 3195[9] 3375[11] 4137[6] 4223[10] 4705[9]

Guadiana (GER) *A W Carroll* a47 49
5 b m Dashing Blade—Gamberaia (IRE) (Konigsstuhl (GER))
1406[12] *5606*[11] 6452[4] *6569*[7]

Guarantia *C E Brittain* a64 90
3 ch f Selkirk(USA) —Maskunah (IRE) (Sadler's Wells (USA))
3332[9] 3961[9] (4530) *4950*[9]

Guardia (GER) *J Hirschberger* 92
3 ch f Monsun(GER) —Guernica (Unfuwain (USA))
5669a[4]

Guardian Of Truth (IRE) *W J Knight* a80 78
3 ch g Barathea(IRE) —Zarara (USA) (Manila (USA))
764[3] 1062[2] 1505[3] 2185[7] 2628[2] *3284*[4] 4113[9]

Guerilla (AUS) *R C Guest* 42
7 bb g Octagonal(NZ) —Partisan (AUS) (Canny Lad (AUS))
3402[5]

Guertino (IRE) *B Smart* a57 94
2 ch c Choisir(AUS) —Isana (JPN) (Sunday Silence (USA))
952[5] 1487[2] 1889[2] (2710) 4695[4] 5216[6] 6154[7]

Guest Connections *D Nicholls* a91 91
4 b g Zafonic(USA) —Llyn Gwynant (Persian Bold)
1157[12] 1852[12] 2202[4] 2744[7] 3723[3] 3911[8] 4895[3] 5155[2] 5505[2] 5581[9] 6331[8]

Guilded Warrior *W S Kittow* a82 92
4 b g Mujahid(USA) —Pearly River (Elegant Air)
(1589) 2088[3] (2623) (3239) (3488) *4068*[13] 5413[8] 6013[11] *6606*[10]

Guildenstern (IRE) *P Howling* a80 88
5 b g Danetime(IRE) —Lyphard Abu (IRE) (Lyphard's Special (USA))
575[7] *757*[5] 1268[2] 1653[14] 2189[6] 2546[6] 2882[12] *3599*[9] 3802[4] *4024*[11] 4296[7] *5130*[6] *5234*[5] 5642[10] *6064*[7] 6239[8] *6581*[11] *7227*[5]

Guilia *Rae Guest* a101 104
4 ch m Galileo(IRE) —Lesgor (USA) (Irish River (FR))
4748[7] 5352[9] 6299[6] *6605*[3]

Guiseppe Verdi (USA) *J H M Gosden* a92 88
3 ch g Sky Classic(CAN) —Lovington (USA) (Afleet (CAN))
1076[8] *(1365)* (1916) 2426[4] *(2767)* 4147[7]

Gulf Coast *M Johnston* a65 65
2 ch c Dubai Destination(USA) —Lloc (Absalom)
1478[5] 1859[3] 2889[5] *3642*[3] 4121[14] *4461*[5] *4964*[4] 5298[5] *6388*[8]

Gulf Express (USA) *Sir Michael Stoute* a83 101
3 b c Langfuhr(CAN) —Wassifa (Sure Blade (USA))
(1166) 1603[2] 2476[6] 2788[15] 4603[2] (5208) (5748)

Gull Wing (IRE) *M L W Bell* a64 101
3 ch f In The Wings—Maycocks Bay (Muhtarram (USA))
1293[2] 1663[6] 2246[2] 2971[3] (3972) 4748[4] 6757[5]

Gumlayloy *G H Jones* a33
8 ch g Indian Ridge—Candide (USA) (Miswaki (USA))
3407[11]

Gunfighter (IRE) *J S Wainwright* a82 92
4 ch h Machiavellian(USA) —Reunion (IRE) (Be My Guest (USA))
1177[3] *1714*[4] 1995[7] (2390) 2985[2] 3512[5] 5585[4] *(6243)* (6753) *7061*[4]

Gunga Din (IRE) *A Kinsella* 76
3 b c Green Desert(USA) —Caumshinaun (IRE) (Indian Ridge)
5842a[13]

Gunnadoit (USA) *C G Cox* 51
2 bb g Almutawakel—Gharam (USA) (Green Dancer (USA))
4539[6] 5720[11] 6417[12]

Gunner Fly (IRE) *R A Fahey* a65 45
2 b c Noverre(USA) —Anne-Lise (Inchinor)
5143[9] *6022*[2] *6477*[4] *6812*[4] *7031*[6] *7149*[5]

Gunner's View *A Ennis* a65 73
3 ch c Medicean—Stark Ballet (USA) (Nureyev (USA))
1001[2] 1259[7] 1504[2] 3056[7] *3420*[10] *6971*[10]

Guto *W J H Ratcliffe* a63 99
4 b g Foxhound(USA) —Mujadilly (Mujadil (USA))
1601[13] 1788[8] 2237[16] 4696[15] 5083[2] 5505[6] 6020[4] 6702[2] 6743[14] *7020*[5]

Gwenseb (FR) *C Laffon-Parias* a95 109
4 ch m Green Tune(USA) —La Popesse (USA) (St Jovite (USA))
897a[5] 1389a[4] 2753[8] 4652a[9] 6614a[5]

Gwilym (GER) *D Haydn Jones* a73 81
4 b h Agnes World(USA) —Glady Rose (GER) (Surumu (GER))
(1200) 2479[2] 3528[7] 3594[3] 4233[5] 4396[2] 5009[3] 5381[2] 5722[10]

Gwyllion (USA) *B J Meehan* a68 67
3 bb f Red Ransom(USA) —Lady Angharad (IRE) (Tenby)
2393[5] *3110*[7] *6993*[7] *7104*[5] *7248*[8]

Gypsum (IRE) *W R Swinburn* a15
3 gr g Desert Style(IRE) —Sassania (IRE) (Persian Bold)
635[9]

Gypsy Baby (IRE) *R Hannon* a84 92
2 b f Modigliani(USA) —L-Way First (IRE) (Vision (USA))
2468[2] *2768*[2] (3043) 3880[7] 4372[2] 4743[2]

Gyration (IRE) *J G Given* a44 46
3 ch g Spinning World(USA) —Tomori (USA) (Royal Academy (USA))
977[10] *1278*[8] 4340[9] 4901[3] *5817*[8]

Gyroscope *Sir Michael Stoute* a69 94
3 b f Spinning World(USA) —Far Across (Common Grounds)
(1203) 1837[3] 2633[2] 3555[2] 4060[14] 4827[4] (5543) 5978[7]

Haajes *D J Murphy* 81
3 ch g Indian Ridge—Imelda (USA) (Manila (USA))
(4486) 4999[3] 5356[5] 5379[8]

Haarth Sovereign (IRE) *W R Swinburn* 76
3 b g Alhaarth(IRE) —Summer Queen (Robellino (USA))
1062[3] 1369[2] 2127[5] 2945[3] 5454[7]

Haasem (USA) *J R Jenkins* a68 68
4 b h Seeking The Gold(USA) —Thawakib (IRE) (Sadler's Wells (USA))
977[6] 1995[6] 2433[3] 4365[6] 4707[4] *5424*[13] 6447[3] 6727[12] *(6854)* *7073*[9] *7257*[9]

Haatef (USA) *Kevin Prendergast* 116
3 b c Danzig(USA) —Sayedat Alhadh (USA) (Mr Prospector (USA))
1473[10] (3768a) 4648a[3] (5832)

Haatmey *P R Chamings* a63 78
5 b g Josr Algarhoud(IRE) —Raneen Alwatar (Sadler's Wells (USA))
5820[6] 6200[8] *6643*[4] 6811[2] 7012[2] 7172[4]

Habalwatan (IRE) *C E Brittain* a91 103
3 b c In The Wings—Mureefa (USA) (Bahri (USA))
1842 *839*[5] 1243[4] 1617[3] 1875a[12] 2789[9] 3460[18] 3940[8] 4523[3] 4799[3] 5504[4] (5978)

Habanero *A King* a71 47
6 b g Cadeaux Genereux—Queen Of Dance (IRE) (Sadler's Wells (USA))
3215[11]

Habbie Heights *R Bastiman* 56
2 b f Josr Algarhoud(IRE) —Hello Hobson'S (IRE) (Fayruz)
4041[2] 4378[9]

Habshan (USA) *C F Wall* a87 92
7 ch g Swain(IRE) —Cambara (Dancing Brave (USA))
1395[10] (2469) 5545[5] *6067*[4]

Hadaf (IRE) *M P Tregoning* a87 78
2 b c Fasliyev(USA) —Elhida (IRE) (Mujtahid (USA))
1781[14] 2337[3] 3363[13] (4173) *(6004)*

Hada Men (USA) *M P Tregoning* 71
2 b g Dynaformer(USA) —Catchy (USA) (Storm Cat (USA))
5011[12] 5417[5] 6051[3]

Hadron Collider (FR) *R Hannon* 68
2 ch c Dubai Destination(USA) —Liver De Saron (USA) (Mt. Livermore (USA))
4362[6] 4876[7] 6058[8]

Haedi *Saeed Bin Suroor* 56
3 b f King's Best(USA) —Star Express (Sadler's Wells (USA))
2137[4] 3051[7] (5231)

Haiban *J J Lambe* a41 70
5 b g Barathea(IRE) —Aquarela (Shirley Heights)
4380[8]

Haifa (IRE) *Mrs A Duffield* a70 66
4 ch m Spectrum(IRE) —Mrs Fisher (IRE) (Salmon Leap (USA))
1090[4] 1627[7] 2714[7] 4383[10]

Hail The Chief *R Hannon* a95 93
10 b h Be My Chief(USA) —Jade Pet (Petong)
255[3] *352*[6] *658*[12] *759*[9] *941*[10] 1060[13] 1962[11]

Half A Tsar (IRE) *Mark Gillard* a19 48
3 b g Soviet Star(USA) —Villarica (IRE) (Fairy King (USA))
3349[10] 3794[12] 4182[5] 5090[5] *5386*[11] 5861[13] *5947*[9]

Halfsong (SWE) *K P Andersen* a63 98
7 br m Songline(SWE) —Half And Half (DEN) (Muthhil (IRE))
1648a[8]

Halfwaytoparadise *W G M Turner* a58 64
4 b m Observatory(USA) —Always On My Mind (Distant Relative)
2556[13] 2877[13] 3247[9] 3636[8] 4416[5] 4595[3] 4685[2] (5864) *6311*[2] 6537[8] *7006*[7]

Halicarnassus (IRE) *M R Channon* 117
3 b c Cape Cross(IRE) —Launch Time (USA) (Relaunch (USA))
1147[3] 1473[17] (1957) 2293a[15] 3458[5] 4092[12] (4387) 5142[2] 5451[5] (5589) 6943a[17]

Halkerston *C G Cox* a47 63
3 ch g Medicean—Summer Daze (USA) (Swain (IRE))
2077[3] 2477[10] *5783*[9] *6534*[12]

Halland *T J Fitzgerald* a71 64
9 ch g Halling(USA) —Northshiel (Northfields (USA))
709[6]

Halla San *R A Fahey* 99
5 b g Halling(USA) —St Radegund (Green Desert (USA))
(914) 1300[2] 1822[14] 3090[18] 3989[8]

Hallhoo (IRE) *D Selvaratnam* a60 95
5 gr h Indian Ridge—Nuit Chaud (USA) (Woodman (USA))
244a[2] 398a[5] 477a[2] 541a[4]

Hallingdal (UAE) *M Johnston* 77
2 b f Halling(USA) —Saik (USA) (Riverman (USA))
(6254)

Hallings Overture (USA) *C A Horgan* a66 60
8 b g Halling(USA) —Sonata (Polish Precedent (USA))
89[6] *212*[2] *363*[4] *740*[10] *1451*[8] 2332[4] 2572[6] 3217[10] *4161*[8] *4592*[10]

Hall Of Fame *R C Guest* a69 69
3 b g Machiavellian(USA) —Petrushka (IRE) (Unfuwain (USA))
392[3] 5472[7] (5774) 6703[5]

Halsion Challenge *J R Best* 46
2 b c King's Best(USA) —Zaynah (IRE) (Kahyasi)
4293[11] 4709[8] 5470[9]

Halsion Chancer *J R Best* a92 41
3 br g Atraf—Lucky Dip (Tirol)
(343) *(502)* *639*[4] 2631[10] *6406*[6] *(6794)* *6829*[2] *(7087)*

Halton Castle *E J Alston* 41
2 ch g Zamindar(USA) —Chilly Start (IRE) (Caerleon (USA))
4487[14] 5033[7] 5328[9]

Hamaasy *D Nicholls* a78 53
6 b g Machiavellian(USA) —Sakha (Wolfhound (USA))
(3) *66*[7] *306*[5] *(463)* *521*[5] *581*[4] *717*[3] 967[13] 5507[13]

Hamalka (IRE) *B W Hills* a55 66
2 br f Alhaarth(IRE) —Night Owl (Night Shift (USA))
3643[6] 5091[2] 5399[2] 5734[3]

Hamburg Springer (IRE) *C J Teague* 28
5 b g Charnwood Forest(IRE) —Kyra Crown (IRE) (Astronef)
2[7]

Hamilton House *M H Tompkins* a38 62
3 b g Bahamian Bounty—Grove Dancer (Reprimand)
1632[7] 1841[7] 2749[7] 4109[5] 4337[3] 4580[9] 4961[5] *5310*[10] 5917[15]

Hamish McGonagall *T D Easterby* 82
2 b g Namid—Anatase (Danehill (USA))
845[8] 5192[3] 5550[4] 5903[2] 6156[2] (6729)

Hammadi (IRE) *K A Ryan* 102
2 b c Red Ransom(USA) —Ruby Affair (IRE) (Night Shift (USA))
4285[4] 4725[3] 5192[2] (5621) 6167[4] 6631a[9]

Hammer Of The Gods (IRE) *P S McEntee* a85 65
7 ch g Tagula(IRE) —Bhama (FR) (Habitat)
28[11] *190*[5] *277*[4] *575*[4] *727*[6] *923*[6] *1165*[2] *1589*[5]

Hamoody (USA) *P W Chapple-Hyam* 104
3 ch c Johannesburg(USA) —Northern Gulch (USA) (Gulch (USA))
1095[7] 2857[21]

Hampstead Heath (IRE) *M Johnston* 75
2 gr c Daylami(IRE) —Hedera (USA) (Woodman (USA))
2632[6] 4487[4] 5344[5]

Hampton Court *M Johnston* 52
2 ch g King's Best(USA) —Rafting (IRE) (Darshaan)
6255[7] 6494[14]

Hamsat Elqamar *J H M Gosden* 66
2 b f Nayef(USA) —Moon's Whisper (USA) (Storm Cat (USA))
5596[8] 5912[6]

Hanbrin Bhoy (IRE) *R Dickin* a73 70
3 b g Cape Cross(IRE) —Sea Of Stone (USA) (Sanglamore (USA))
5768[13] 6235[10] *6997*[4]

Hand And Seal (ARG) *M Grassi* 68
5 b h Fortunate Joe(USA) —Hesilea (ARG) (Hesical (ARG))
6686a[8]

Hand Chime *Miss J Feilden* a58 48
10 ch g Clantime—Warning Bell (Bustino)
151[8] *206*[11] *313*[8] *346*[5] *533*[13] *866*[2] *932*[11] *1118*[13] *1344*[10]

Hando *F Head* a65 99
3 b c Hernando(FR) —Featherquest (Rainbow Quest (USA))
4216a[9]

Hand Of Fate (IRE) *M Johnston* a39
3 b f Jade Robbery(USA) —Destiny Dance (USA) (Nijinsky (CAN))
684[6]

Handset (USA) *H R A Cecil* a53 72
3 ch f Distant View(USA) —Call Account (USA) (Private Account (USA))
1203[5] 1685[6] 2581[2] 4659[2] *5728*[3] (6057)

Handsinthemist (IRE) *P T Midgley* 51
2 b f Lend A Hand—Hollow Haze (USA) (Woodman (USA))
1963[13] 2371[8] 2549[3] 3341[6] 3788[6] 4783[8] 5281[7] (5484) 6326[10]

Handsome Cross (IRE) *D Nicholls* a80 94
6 b g Cape Cross(IRE) —Snap Crackle Pop (IRE) (Statoblest)
957[2] 1242[4] 1941[2] 2234[11] 2463[10] 3464[11] 3836[10] 5029[12] 5481[10]

Handsome Falcon *R A Fahey* 79
3 b g Kyllachy—Bonne Etoile (Diesis)
1257[7] 1658[8] 2373[3] 3029[4] 3299[4] (3790) 4176[13] 5635[11]

Haneen (USA) *R W Price* a35 66
4 b m Bahri(USA) —Tamgeed (USA) (Woodman (USA))
980[13] 2154[11] *3600*[9] *4915*[12]

Hanella (IRE) *R M Beckett* 89
4 b m Galileo(IRE) —Strutting (IRE) (Ela-Mana-Mou)
(1371) 2082[2]

Hanging On *W R Swinburn* a88 92
3 b f Spinning World(USA) —Lydia Maria (Dancing Brave (USA))
1277[4] 1581[5] 2786[8]

Hang Loose *S W Hall* a61 47
4 b g Agnes World(USA) —My Cadeaux (Cadeaux Genereux)
1025[14] *1280*[10] 1991[16] (Dead)

Hanicor (IRE) *Ms F M Crowley* 85
6 b g Mukaddamah(USA) —Tadasna (IRE) (Thatching)
6553a[19]

Hannahbecc *S C Williams* a57 51
3 ch f Singspiel(IRE) —Encorenous (USA) (Diesis)
2836[6] 3248[6] 3881[11] *4918*[7] *5528*[10] 5710[8] *6272*[9] *6706*[3] *6825*[8] *6950*[11]

Hannicean *M A Jarvis* a52 78
3 ch c Medicean—Hannah's Music (Music Boy)
(1077) 1504[7] *2354*[10] 3960[8] 4603[5] 5620[7] 6423[14]

Hannouma (IRE) *D Smaga* 103
2 b c Anabaa(USA) —Red Blossom (USA) (Silver Hawk (USA))
6377a[2] 6782a[2]

Hanover Lady (GER) *Frau Lucie Vondrova* 93
3 b f Dashing Blade—Hanover Princess (GER) (Esclavo (FR))
5850a[2]

Hansinger (IRE) *B I Case* 78
2 b g Namid—Whistfilly (First Trump)
1970[3] 2510[5] (3465) 4121[13] 4775[12] 5374[3]

Hansomelle (IRE) *Miss Sheena West* a66 90
5 b m Titus Livius(FR) —Handsome Anna (IRE) (Bigstone (IRE))
1592[7] 1740[3] 2275[8] *2572*[10] *2990*[6] 3690[3] (3950) *4161*[3] 4395[3] (4596) 5047[10] 5114[8]

Hansomis (IRE) *B Mactaggart* 67
3 b f Titus Livius(FR) —Handsome Anna (IRE) (Bigstone (IRE))
1625[7] 2167[2] 2713[9] 3051[6] 3583[14]

Haoin An Bothar (IRE) *Adrian Sexton* a59 15
3 b g Bishop Of Cashel—Drefflane Ann (IRE) (Petorius)
602[11]

Ha'Penny Beacon *D Carroll* a68 70
4 ch m Erhaab(USA) —Beacon (High Top)
1263[2] *1567*[3] 1794[12] *2148*[5] 4040[5] *4463*[6] *5018*[2] *5364*[3] *5647*[6] *5779*[8] 6330[2] (6561)

Happy As Larry (USA) *D J Murphy* a93 74
5 bb g Yes It's True(USA) —Don't Be Blue (USA) (Henbane (USA))
119[5] *197*[8] *701*[8] 850[16] 1083[9] 5559[8] 5693[10] 5862[8] *6359*[4] *6900*[14] *6972*[7] *7087*[10] *7126*[5] *7241*[3]

Happy Go Lily *W R Swinburn* a87 84
3 b f In The Wings—Lil's Jessy (IRE) (Kris)
1122[9] (1407) 2126[5] *2574*[2] 4147[13]

Happy Hacker (IRE) *P D Evans* 51
2 ch f Captain Rio—Darling Clementine (Lion Cavern (USA))
1367[6] 2103[8] 2488[7] 3680[8] 4311[4] 4897[9]

Happy Moments (IRE) *Reginald Roberts* a70 70
5 b g Desert Sun—Rusti La Russe (Rusticaro (FR))
4865a[4]

Happy Town (FR) *Robert Collet* a93 88
4 b m Anabaa(USA) —Hope Town (FR) (Sillery (USA))
31a[12]

Hapsburg (FR) *E Libaud* 106
3 b f Anabaa(USA) —Magical Hawk (USA) (Silver Hawk (USA))
3148a[4] 4055a[4] (5058a) 6460a[4]

Harald Bluetooth (IRE) *J R Fanshawe* 67
2 b c Danetime(IRE) —Goldthroat (IRE) (Zafonic (USA))
3462[6]

Harar (GER) *Andreas Lowe* 100
5 ch h Acatenango(GER) —Hosea (GER) (Lagunas)
1874a[6]

Harare *R J Price* a83 83
6 b g Bahhare(USA) —Springs Eternal (Salse (USA))
72[6] *124*[3] (206) *426*[6] *516*[2] *538*[2] (675) *770*[2] *(1283)* *1905*[7] 1996[3] 2452[2] 3525[5] 3900[5] 4455[7]

Harbore (FR) *E Lellouche* 107
3 b g Raintrap—Harmonique (FR) (Exit To Nowhere (USA))
6028a[5]

Harbour Blues *A W Carroll* a77 71
2 ch c Best Of The Bests(IRE) —Lady Georgia (Arazi (USA))
3037[2] 3348[2] *4273*[6] 5314[11] 6379[4] *6748*[3] *(6872)* *6973*[11]

Harcourt (USA) *M Madgwick* a54 66
7 b g Cozzene(USA) —Ballinamallard (USA) (Tom Rolfe)
1026[3] *1451[12]* 4253[13] 4534[10] 6200[10]

Hard As Iron *M Blanshard* a63 10
3 b g Iron Mask(USA) —Runs In The Family (Distant Relative)
624[5] 738[10] 1399[10] 2224[9] 3966[8] 4763[7] 6090[8]

Hard Rock City (USA) *M J Grassick* 112
7 b g Danzig(USA) —All The Moves (USA) (A.P. Indy (USA))
2586a[6] 3144a[2] 3575a[2] (4211a) 6038a[5]

Hard Spun (USA) *J Larry Jones* a122
3 b c Danzig(USA) —Turkish Tryst (USA) (Turkoman (USA))
1486a[2] 1882a[3] 2487a[4] (5827a) 6514a[2]

Hard To Catch (IRE) *Mike Murphy* a63 53
9 b g Namaqualand(USA) —Brook's Dilemma (Known Fact (USA))
1885[11] 2334[14] *3618[8]*

Hard Top (IRE) *Sir Michael Stoute* 114
5 b g Darshaan—Well Head (IRE) (Sadler's Wells (USA))
1664[2] 1985[6] 3097[2] 3912[5] 4117[4] 4803[7]

Hardy Eustace (IRE) *D T Hughes* 74
10 b g Archway(IRE) —Sterna Star (Corvaro (USA))
6366a[11]

Hardy Norseman (IRE) *Madeleine Smith* a65 67
4 b g Mull Of Kintyre(USA) —Miss Willow Bend (USA) (Willow Hour (USA))
1647a[7]

Hareem (IRE) *J A Osborne* a71 52
3 b g King's Best(USA) —Knight's Place (IRE) (Hamas (IRE))
5346[6] *(5754)*

Harland *M A Jarvis* 117
3 b c Halling(USA) —White Star (IRE) (Darshaan)
(849) 2813[8] (3271) (3987a)

Harlech Castle *P F I Cole* a91 87
2 b c Royal Applause—Ffestiniog (IRE) (Efisio)
1123[4] 2526[7] 4201[2] (4762) *5135[3]*

Harlem Shuffle (UAE) *M Johnston* a74
2 br f Halling(USA) —Badraan (USA) (Danzig (USA))
(6119)

Harlequinn Danseur (IRE) *N Tinkler* a45 55
2 b g Noverre(USA) —Nassma (IRE) (Sadler's Wells (USA))
3592[11] 4002[5] 4174[6] 4781[7] 5227[7] *5423[11]* 5904[11]

Haroldini (IRE) *J Balding* a68 35
5 b g Orpen(USA) —Ciubanga (IRE) (Arazi (USA))
131[10] 463[2] 516[5] 681[2] 806[3] 1064[3] 1280[6] 5909[9] *6148[8] 6476[6] 7003[5] (7153)*

Harrington (IRE) *Noel Furlong* 95
5 b h Sadler's Wells(USA) —Our Hope (Dancing Brave (USA))
1050a[5] 3143a[5]

Harrington Bates *J J Lambe* a45 52
6 ch g Wolfhound(USA) —Fiddling (Music Boy)
6311[11] 6340[5]

Harrison George (IRE) *R A Fahey* a72 75
2 b c Danetime(IRE) —Dry Lightning (Shareef Dancer (USA))
3092[2] 4611[4] 4930[2] 5393a[4] 6156[3] *6403[4]*

Harrison's Flyer (IRE) *J M Bradley* a67 76
6 b g Imperial Ballet(IRE) —Smart Pet (Petong)
1321[2] 1405[4] 1681[6] (1885) 1991[3] 2411[6] 2655[2] 2805[2] (2966) 3536[5] 3594[6] 3906[2] 4103[5] 4204[4] 4507[8] 4634[8]

Harrison's Star *G M Moore* 47
2 gr g Erhaab(USA) —Gentle Gypsy (Junius (USA))
5904[8] 6303[6]

Harry Gee *W R Muir* 79
2 b g Averti(IRE) —Mentro (IRE) (Entrepreneur)
3363[9] 4048[11] (4733) 5207[5] 5400[4] 6201[2] 6486[14]

Harry The Hawk *T D Walford* 71
3 b g Pursuit Of Love—Elora Gorge (IRE) (High Estate)
2796[3] 3411[6] 3721[3] 5704[2] (6259)

Harry Tricker *Mrs A J Perrett* a69 97
3 b g Hernando(FR) —Katy Nowaitee (Komaite (USA))
2402[3] *3621[3]* 5005[3] (5454) (5724) 6091[2]

Harry Up *K A Ryan* a96 91
6 ch g Piccolo—Faraway Lass (Distant Relative)
5[4] (155) 344[9] 1853[6] 2463[8] 3464[6] 3586[11] 4095[17] 4386[3] 5039[2] 5379[4] 5969[2] 6743[8] *6972[3] 7078[2] 7279[5]*

Harting Hill *M P Tregoning* 55
2 b g Mujahid(USA) —Mossy Rose (King Of Spain)
4764[13]

Hartmann (USA) *B J Meehan* a67
3 b g El Corredor(USA) —Fearless Wildcat (USA) (Forest Wildcat (USA))
1522[9] 2175[3] 3062[5]

Hart Of Gold *R A Harris* a74 86
3 b g Foxhound(USA) —Bullion (Sabrehill (USA))
1476[7] 1956[11] *2570[5] 4024[13]* 4940[4] (5062) 5303[2] 5635[16] *6891[6] 7020[8]*

Hartshead *G A Swinbank* a84 103
8 b g Machiavellian(USA) —Zalitzine (USA) (Zilzal (USA))
178a[6] 331a[14] 3500[7] 3953[10] 4408[2] 4566[11] 4922[10] 6016[14]

Harts In Mo Shun (IRE) *A Berry* 46
3 b g Spectrum(IRE) —Offshoot (Zafonic (USA))
1625[6] 2012[14] 3372[8] 3639[8] 4082[10] 4713[14] 5041[11]

Harvard Avenue (USA) *Doug O'Neill* a109
6 bb g You And I(USA) —Carrie Can (USA) (Saratoga Six (USA))
860a[4]

Harvest Joy (IRE) *J Gallagher* a55 89
3 b f Daggers Drawn(USA) —Windomen (IRE) (Forest Wind (USA))
838[9] 1581[10] 2691[U] 2971[7] 3590[6] 4185[5] 5539[9]

Harvest Queen (IRE) *P J Makin* a63 110
4 ch m Spinning World(USA) —Royal Bounty (IRE) (Generous (IRE))
(1466) 2207[5] 3897[10] (5213) 6010[5]

Harvest Warrior *T D Easterby* 85
5 gr g Mujahid(USA) —Lammastide (Martinmas)
(1655) 2023[2] 2338[2] 2906[6] (3258) 3513[4] 4039[5] 4228[4] 4523[4] 4922[12] 5623[7]

Hasanka (IRE) *John M Oxx* 103
3 b f Kalanisi(IRE) —Hasainiya (IRE) (Top Ville)
1185a[7] 4238a[2] 4830a[2]

Hashbrown (GER) *C Sprengel* 99
3 b f Big Shuffle(USA) —Haraplata (GER) (Platini (GER))
1338a[4] 3121a[4] 5850a[4]

Hassaad *W J Haggas* a93 90
4 b g Danehill(USA) —Ghazal (USA) (Gone West (USA))
(1395) 2093[6] 2401[6] 3558[10] 3959[5] 5327[6] 6185[8]

Has To Be Abacus (IRE) *A B Haynes* a54 48
2 br c Indian Lodge(IRE) —No Way (IRE) (Rainbows For Life (CAN))
3043[14] 5344[11] *6865[5] 7114[9]*

Hasty Lady *K A Ryan* 68
2 b f Dubai Destination(USA) —Hasten (USA) (Lear Fan (USA))
3718[11] 4102[5] 4611[3] 5301[9] 5624[6] 6306[2]

Hasty Retreat *E A L Dunlop* a67
2 b g King's Best(USA) —Madame Maxine (USA) (Dayjur (USA))
6944[3] 7130[3]

Hatch A Plan (IRE) *Mouse Hamilton-Fairley* a66 74
6 b g Vettori(IRE) —Fast Chick (Henbit (USA))
594[14] 753[8] 1002[9] 1216[4] 1811[3] 2321[7] 2544[3] 2967[6] 3554[7] 4019[6] 4458[10] *6102[6] 6577[2] (6867) 7186[9]*

Hathaal (IRE) *E J Creighton* a74 53
8 b g Alzao(USA) —Ballet Shoes (IRE) (Ela-Mana-Mou)
16[8] 100[5] 775[8] 829[2] 2874[2] 3232[7] 3617[9] 3684[2] (3795)

Hatherden *R A Kvisla* a67 53
3 b g Tobougg(IRE) —Million Heiress (Auction Ring (USA))
(498)

Hatria (IRE) *A Renzoni* 39
5 b m Royal Applause—Conca Peligna (Persian Bold)
1337a[13]

Hatta Fort *M R Channon* 109
2 b c Cape Cross(IRE) —Oshiponga (Barathea (IRE))
1919[5] (2316) 2737[3] (3504) 6041a[4] 6333[6]

Hattan (IRE) *C E Brittain* a109 116
5 ch h Halling(USA) —Luana (Shaadi (USA))
(43) 177a[16] 248a[4] 412a[3] 545a[3] *761[10]* (1109) 1600[4] 2210[5] 2706a[2] 4013a[4] 4693[6] (5402) 5831[4] 6689a[10]

Hatton Flight *A M Balding* a68 66
3 b g Kahyasi—Platonic (Zafonic (USA))
1220[3] 2096[3] 3825[4] 4391[5] (4758) 5333[6] *5755[3] 6102[8] (6534)*

Havanavich *S Kirk* a65 70
2 b c Xaar—Queen Of Havana (USA) (King Of Kings (IRE))
4273[7] 4883[4] 5721[3] *6585[7]*

Have A Nice Day (GER) *S Smrczek* 63
2 b f Black Sam Bellamy(IRE) —Haraplata (GER) (Platini (GER))
5462a[6]

Having A Ball *P D Cundell* a55 52
3 b g Mark Of Esteem(IRE) —All Smiles (Halling (USA))
2083[6] 2304[2] 4711[2] *6587[4]*

Hawaana (IRE) *B W Hills* 79
2 b c Bahri(USA) —Congress (IRE) (Dancing Brave (USA))
3991[4] (4417) 5397a[14]

Hawaass (USA) *M Johnston* 82
2 b c Seeking The Gold(USA) —Sheroog (USA) (Shareef Dancer (USA))
1792[12] (5538)

Hawaii Prince *S T Mason* 70
3 b g Primo Valentino(IRE) —Bollin Rita (Rambo Dancer (CAN))
(2029) 3054[7] 3637[3] 4101[5] 4452[4] 5139[11] 5506[4] 5834[12]

Hawa Khana (IRE) *N P Littmoden* a59 59
2 br f Indian Danehill(IRE) —Anearlybird (USA) (Sheikh Albadou)
5540[8] 5868[5] *6225[8]* 6572[8] *6881[6] 7010[4]*

Hawk And I (IRE) *R A Kvisla* 7
2 ch c Hawk Wing(USA) —Dos Talas (USA) (You And I (USA))
4593[9]

Hawk Arrow (IRE) *G L Moore* a68 72
5 ch g In The Wings—Barbizou (FR) (Selkirk (USA))
48[4] 212[3] 332[6] 623[9] 740[2] 819[2] 1249[8]

Hawkes Bay *D Hall* 112
5 b h Vettori(IRE) —Nordico Princess (Nordico (USA))
7090a[10]

Hawk Eyed Lady (IRE) *J A Osborne* a68 71
2 b f Hawk Wing(USA) —Danccini (IRE) (Dancing Dissident (USA))
4232[10] 4662[5] 5042[2] 5322[17] 5707[8] *6799[3] 6897[7]*

Hawk Flight (IRE) *W R Muir* a66 64
2 b c Hawk Wing(USA) —Rapid Action (USA) (Quest For Fame)
6593[7] *6855[6]*

Hawk Gold (IRE) *M D I Usher* 40
3 ch g Tendulkar(USA) —Heiress Of Meath (IRE) (Imperial Frontier (USA))
6090[6] 6277[12]

Hawk House *B W Hills* a62 58
2 gr g Alhaarth(IRE) —Arinaga (Warning)
3551[7] *3850[6]* 6080[6]

Hawk Island (IRE) *G Wragg* a67
2 b c Hawk Wing(USA) —Crimphill (IRE) (Sadler's Wells (USA))
6602[4]

Hawkit (USA) *P Monteith* a72 78
6 b g Silver Hawk(USA) —Hey Ghaz (USA) (Ghazi (USA))
1627[12] 2254[2] 2865[4] 3049[8] 3502[3] 3783[8] 4159[3] (4382) (4497) 4933[6] 5674[6] 6465[8] 6636[2]

Hawk Mountain (UAE) *J J Quinn* 52
2 b g Halling(USA) —Friendly (USA) (Lear Fan (USA))
5902[4] 6384[9]

Hawksmoor (IRE) *L A Dace* a1 60
5 b g In The Wings—Moon Cactus (Kris)
18[13] 134[14]

Hawkstar Express (IRE) *J R Boyle* 56
2 b g Hawk Wing(USA) —Band Of Angels (IRE) (Alzao (USA))
6127[10] 6296[9]

Hawk Wood (IRE) *G M Lyons* 70
2 b c Hawk Wing(USA) —Mille Miglia (IRE) (Caerleon (USA))
1508a[3]

Hawridge King *W S Kittow* a65 88
5 b g Erhaab(USA) —Sadaka (USA) (Kingmambo (USA))
(4352) 4910[2] 5404[4] 5884[2] 6131[11]

Hawridge Miss *B R Millman* 71
3 b f Piccolo—In The Stocks (Reprimand)
4541[9] 5269[4] 5688[3] 6062[3] (6424)

Hawridge Prince *B R Millman* 115
7 b g Polar Falcon(USA) —Zahwa (Cadeaux Genereux)
929[4] 1393[4] 4825[4] 5829[7] 6337[6]

Haybrook *E J O'Neill* a87
2 b c Xaar—Miss Brooks (Bishop Of Cashel)
6403[2] (6799) (7015)

Haydens Mark *W J Haggas* a67
2 b g Efisio—Lady In Colour (IRE) (Cadeaux Genereux)
5337[5]

Haydock Express (IRE) *Peter Grayson* a52
3 gr g Keltos(FR) —Blusienka (IRE) (Blues Traveller (IRE))
60[7] 152[7] 336[7] 404[8] 832[6] 1008[13] *7185[7]*

Hayfield Flyer *Paul Green* a7 23
3 b f Wizard King—Diamond Rouge (Puissance)
2951[11] 3914[11] 5045[7]

Hayley's Flower (IRE) *J C Fox* a57 45
3 b f Night Shift(USA) —Plastiqueuse (USA) (Quest For Fame)
157[7] 267[11] 689[6] (1232) 2178[9] 2668[8] 5098[3] 5602[9] 6429[10] 6642[10] 7218[7]

Hayley's Pearl *Mrs P Ford*
8 b m Nomadic Way(USA) —Pacific Girl (IRE) (Emmson)
7174[7]

Hay Luz Delsol (BRZ) *M D Wolfson* a67
5 b m Astor Place(IRE) —Hay Luz (BRZ) (Minstrel Glory (USA))
249a[U] 324a[7] 543a[6]

Hayward's Heath *B W Duke* 58
3 ch f Allied Forces(USA) —Penny Gold (IRE) (Millfontaine)
1784[6] 2597[11] 2970[5] 3367[6] 3876[9]

Hazarayna *P D Evans* 68
3 b f Polish Precedent(USA) —Hazaradjat (IRE) (Darshaan)
1665[2] 2308[4] 3160[2] 3800[4] 4878[7]

Hazelhurst (IRE) *J Howard Johnson* 72
4 b m Night Shift(USA) —Iktidar (Green Desert (USA))
1892[9] 2905[7] (4083) 4942[5] 5560[5] 6560[12]

Hazelnut *J R Fanshawe* a63 73
4 b m Selkirk(USA) —Cashew (Sharrood (USA))
(3705) 4542[3] 6475[3]

Hazelwood Ridge (IRE) *Joseph Fox* a32 66
4 b g Mozart(IRE) —Aguilas Perla (IRE) (Indian Ridge)
4836a[9] *7024[10]*

Hazeymm (IRE) *D Selvaratnam* a67 109
4 b g Marju(IRE) —Shimna (Mr Prospector (USA))
330a[7] 545a[8] 645a[8]

Hazy Days *Sir Mark Prescott* a59 79
3 ch f Lomitas—Organza (High Top)
(2520) (3848) 4185[U] (Dead)

Hazytoo *N A Callaghan* a76 76
3 ch c Sakhee(USA) —Shukran (Hamas (IRE))
1100[4] *1398[3]* 4457[12] 4905[2] 5714[2] 6062[11]

Hazzard County (USA) *D M Simcock* a94 87
3 ch c Grand Slam(USA) —Sweet Lexy May (USA) (Danzig (USA))
(826) 1500[4] 2313[2] *3650[3]* 4785[7] *6143[3]* 6654[13]

Headache *B W Duke* 33
2 b c Cape Cross(IRE) —Romantic Myth (Mind Games)
2041[17]

Headland (USA) *D W Chapman* a43 9
9 bb g Distant View(USA) —Fijar Echo (USA) (In Fijar (USA))
303[8] 337[10] 463[7]

Head Of The River (IRE) *Charles O'Brien* 85
3 b c Galileo(IRE) —Vignelaure (IRE) (Royal Academy (USA))
6368a[8]

Head To Head (IRE) *Peter Grayson* a56
3 gr g Mull Of Kintyre(USA) —Shoka (FR) (Kaldoun (FR))
378[9] 404[7] 512[6] 659[3] 713[4] 778[5] 798[4] 1313[4] 2262[8] 2668[10] 2948[6] 3281[11]

Head To Kerry (IRE) *D J S Ffrench Davis* a46 52
7 b g Eagle Eyed(USA) —The Poachers Lady (IRE) (Salmon Leap (USA))
416[12] 578[13]

Heart Alone (BRZ) *I Mohammed* a115 65
6 b g Music Prospector(USA) —Sylicon Purple (BRZ) (Purple Mountain (USA))
597a[16]

Heart And Hand (IRE) *M G Quinlan* 49
3 b f Bertolini(USA) —Alchi (USA) (Alleged (USA))
253[12] 390[8]

Heart Beat (SAF) *S Seemar* a80
4 b g Jet Master(SAF) —Hear My Heart (NZ) (Personal Escort (USA))
173a[5] 526a[6]

Hearthstead Dream *D K Weld* 78
6 ch g Dr Fong(USA) —Robin Lane (Tenby)
3577a[8] 6555a[3]

Hearthstead Maison (IRE) *M Johnston* 114
3 b c Peintre Celebre(USA) —Pieds De Plume (FR) (Seattle Slew (USA))
1097[5] (1476) 1662[2] 2042[3] 2816[15] (3460) 4092[15] 4387[4] 4692[7] (5240a) 5671a[6]

Heart Of Dubai (USA) *C E Brittain* a53 55
2 b c Outofthebox(USA) —Diablo's Blend (USA) (Diablo (USA))
4916[5] 5536[8]

Heart Of Glass (IRE) *M L W Bell* 54
3 ch f Peintre Celebre(USA) —Sallanches (USA) (Gone West (USA))
1045[6] 1408[9] 1917[12]

Heathyards Joy *R Hollinshead* a49 39
6 ch m Komaite(USA) —Heathyards Lady (USA) (Mining (USA))
126[10]

Heathyards Pride *R Hollinshead* a89 84
7 b g Polar Prince(IRE) —Heathyards Lady (USA) (Mining (USA))
226[3] (608) 1621[3] 2011[3] (4318) 4637[9] 5334[5] *5892[3] 6357[4] 6739[2]*

Heaven *P J Makin* 63
2 ch f Reel Buddy(USA) —Wedgewood Star (Bishop Of Cashel)
3947[6] 4755[3] (5267)

Heaven Knows *W J Haggas* a76 103
4 ch g Halling(USA) —Rambling Rose (Cadeaux Genereux)
4720[11] 5326[6] 5830[4] (6499) 6759[6]

Heavenly Saint *S Parr* a58 58
2 b f Bertolini(USA) —Heavenly Glow (Shavian)
2663[6] 3446[3] 4968[4] *5423[10] 5727[10] 6150[10]* (6591) *6693[3]*

Heaven Sent *Sir Michael Stoute* 111
4 ch m Pivotal—Heavenly Ray (USA) (Rahy (USA))
1145[3] (1649) 2053a[2] 2815[2] 3523[3] 4652a[6] 5047[2] 6009[3]

Heaven's Gates *K A Ryan* a59 53
3 ch g Most Welcome—Arcady (Slip Anchor)
(223) 348[7] 454[3] 535[4] 3540[8] 4073[6] 4902[6] 4936[9] 5967[7]

Heavens Walk *P J Makin* a78 77
6 ch g Compton Place—Ghost Dancing (Lion Cavern (USA))
163[6] 1630[11] *2350[4] 3212[4] 3452[8] 4944[10]*

Heavenward *Sir Michael Stoute* 67
3 ch c Pivotal—Heavenly Ray (USA) (Rahy (USA))
5384[9] 5873[8] 6109[2] 6474[13]

Hebenus *T A K Cuthbert* a6 29
8 b g Hamas(IRE) —Stinging Nettle (Sharpen Up)
2561[13] 2711[15] 3782[15]

Heidi Hi *J R Turner* a5 48
3 b f High Estate—Alwal (Pharly (FR))
3202[3] 3639[9] 4787[10] 5041[5] 5627[12] *7108[8]*

Height Of Esteem *W M Brisbourne* a47 38
4 b g Mark Of Esteem(IRE) —Biscay (Unfuwain (USA))
1906[13] 2121[12] 3076[9] 4099[9] 4488[5]

Height Of Fury (IRE) *J L Dunlop* 83
4 b g Sadler's Wells(USA) —Height Of Fantasy (IRE) (Shirley Heights)
1668[6] 2367[5] 5415[8]

Height Of Spirits *T D McCarthy* a60 52
5 b g Unfuwain(USA) —Kimono (IRE) (Machiavellian (USA))
22[8] 51[5] 210[3] 273[2] 350[5] 637[2] 3149[3] 4850[10] *6532[5] 6792[9]*

Heights Of Golan *I A Wood* a71 66
3 br g Golan(IRE) —Nemesia (Mill Reef (USA))
1722[7] 2445[10] 3150[13] *3620[8] 4742[7] 5647[2] 5755[2] 6027[5] (6069) 6241[5] 6564[12]*

Held Captive (USA) *E A L Dunlop* 80
3 b f Red Ransom(USA) —Furajet (USA) (The Minstrel (CAN))
1839[4] (2886) 3514[4] 4060[13]

Helen Wood *D E Pipe* 64
4 b m Lahib(USA) —Last Ambition (IRE) (Cadeaux Genereux)
2491[5]

Heliostatic (IRE) *J S Bolger* 114
4 ch h Galileo(IRE) —Affianced (IRE) (Erins Isle)
1050a[3] 1184a[2] 2064a[9]

Hellfire Bay *K A Ryan* a64 55
2 b c Diktat—Composition (Wolfhound (USA))
6246[6] 6540[3] *6912[2] 7140[5]*

Hello Deauville (FR) *J Akehurst* a27 37
4 ch m Alhaarth(IRE) —Pulpeuse (IRE) (Pursuit Of Love)
207[13] 310[10]

Hello It's Me *D McCain Jnr* 69
6 ch g Deploy—Evening Charm (IRE) (Bering)
2505[5] 3533[8]

Hello Man (IRE) *Eamon Tyrrell* a89 72
4 b g Princely Heir(IRE) —Mignon (Midyan (USA))
6972[2] (7026)

Hello Morning (FR) *Mme C Head-Maarek* 116
2 gr c Poliglote—Hello Molly (FR) (Sillery (USA))
6615a[2]

Hello My Lord (FR) *Mme C Head-Maarek* a89 107
3 gr c Anabaa Blue—Hello Molly (FR) (Sillery (USA))
4627a[6] 6614a[10]

Hello Nemo *T E Powell* 42
3 b c Hello Mister—Marisa's Pet (Petong)
1429[6] 2470[10] 2878[16]

Hello Nod *Miss J A Camacho* a44 52
3 b g Polish Precedent(USA) —Nordan Raider (Domynsky)
728[13] 1282[9] 2012[10] 3639[5] 4137[10] 5525[12]

Hello Roberto *R A Harris* a58 80
6 b m Up And At 'Em—Hello Hobson'S (IRE) (Fayruz)
1525[7] 1766[12] 2315[6] *2799[8]* 3368[12] *3853[7]* 4689[3] 4734[4] 4881[5] 5191[9] 5349[4] *5565[7]* (5861) *6064[13] 6424[9] 6752[3] 7005[3] 7082[4] 7206[9] 7283[6]*

Hello Sunday (FR) *R J Frankel* a109 111
4 b h Poliglote—Hello Molly (FR) (Sillery (USA))
5824a[6]

Hellvelyn *B Smart* 117
3 gr c Ishiguru(USA) —Cumbrian Melody (Petong)
3506^{8} (4798) 5214^{14}
Hellzapoppin *B W Hills* 62
2 b c Mtoto—Pure (Slip Anchor)
5971^{14} 6294^{8}
Help (IRE) *Mrs P N Dutfield* a36 43
2 b f Lend A Hand—Lala Salama (IRE) (College Chapel)
3423^{12} 3681^{6} 4539^{11} *6714^{12} 6928^{9}*
Helvetio *Micky Hammond* a18 101
5 b g Theatrical—Personal Love (USA) (Diesis)
944^{6} 1300^{10}
Hemispear *Miss J R Tooth* a64 64
3 ch f Lear Spear(USA) —Milladella (FR) (Nureyev (USA))
1355^{13} 3166^{5} 4104^{12}
Hennalaine (IRE) *P F I Cole* a59
2 b f Lujain(USA) —Daralaka (IRE) (The Minstrel (CAN))
3417^{7}
Hennessy Island (USA) *T G Mills* a51
2 ch c Hennessy(USA) —Heavenly Dawn (USA) (Holy Bull (USA))
6267^{12} 6850^{10} 7084^{10}
Henry Bernstein (USA) *H R A Cecil* a43 70
3 bb c Bernstein(USA) —Hidle (USA) (Unbridled (USA))
1440^{12} 1841^{6} 2535^{3} 2893^{11}
Henry Hall (IRE) *N Tinkler* 78
11 b h Common Grounds—Sovereign Grace (IRE) (Standaan (FR))
1134^{11} 1299^{8} 1914^{4} 2418^{3} 2509^{6} 3014^{7} 3627^{7} 4008^{9} 4252^{3} 4642^{9} 4773^{4} 5297^{9} 5507^{8} 5836^{6} 5908^{7}
Henry Holmes *Mrs L Richards* a53
4 b g Josr Algarhoud(IRE) —Henrietta Holmes (IRE) (Persian Bold)
5530^{7} 6096^{9} 6832^{4} 6896^{5} 7168^{3} 7256^{4}
Henry James (IRE) *M Botti* a55 64
2 b c Iron Mask(USA) —Izibi (FR) (Saint Cyrien (FR))
7181^{3}
Henrythenavigator (USA) *A P O'Brien* 110
2 bb c Kingmambo(USA) —Sequoyah (IRE) (Sadler's Wells (USA))
(1508a) (2732) 4437a^{2} 4833a^{3}
Henry The Seventh *J W Hills* a77 48
3 b c Royal Applause—Bombalarina (IRE) (Barathea (IRE))
21^{2} 260^{3} 382^{3} 1359^{12} 2317^{13} *3622^{2} 3926^{6} 4277^{10}* 4858^{9} *5338^{4} (5733) 6121^{4} 6547^{11}*
Hepburn Bell (IRE) *J R Fanshawe* 57
2 ch f Intikhab(USA) —Borsalino (USA) (Trempolino (USA))
5937^{9}
Hephaestus *Peter Grayson* a71 67
3 b g Piccolo—Fragrant Cloud (Zilzal (USA))
510^{7} 671^{6} 925^{11} *1313^{6} 3281^{6} 5564^{3} 6718^{8} 6864^{11}*
Herb Paris (FR) *P M Phelan* a69 65
3 ch f Halling(USA) —Yaya (USA) (Rahy (USA))
6101^{2} 6533^{11} 6870^{9} 7013^{8} 7192^{10}
Here And How *M H Tompkins* a40 44
2 b f Where Or When(IRE) —Qilin (IRE) (Second Set (IRE))
5061^{12} *5527^{9}*
Hereditary *Mrs L C Jewell* a47
5 ch g Hernando(FR) —Eversince (USA) (Foolish Pleasure (USA))
2425^{5} 6643^{8}
Hereford Boy *D K Ivory* a82 77
3 ch g Tomba—Grown At Rowan (Gabitat)
188^{3} 387^{5} 778^{4} 925^{4} 1004^{8} 1373^{2} (1738) *1948^{4}* 2276^{3} 5066^{7} 5642^{13} (5942) 6157^{14} *(6405) 6589^{8}*
Here's Blue Chip (IRE) *P W D'Arcy* a64 54
3 b g Barathea(IRE) —Blasted Heath (Thatching)
149^{3} 304^{5} 731^{6} 1399^{5} 1672^{4} *2224^{4}* 2534^{11}
Heritage Coast (USA) *Sir Michael Stoute* a74 68
2 b f Dynaformer(USA) —Bristol Channel (Generous (IRE))
4565^{4} *6140^{2} 6857^{2}*
Hermanita *G Wragg* a45 59
3 b f Hernando(FR) —Subjective (USA) (Secretariat (USA))
1024^{8} 1784^{8} 2360^{6} 3427^{9} 4139^{7} (5068) *5531^{13}* 6056^{8}
Her Name Is Rio (IRE) *J S Moore* a57 68
2 ch f Captain Rio—L'Harmonie (USA) (Bering)
2968^{10} 3152^{2} 3718^{10} 5516a^{5} 5871^{11} 6282^{4} *7030^{6} 7177^{2} 7272^{5}*
Hernando Cortes *A P O'Brien* 75
3 b c Sadler's Wells(USA) —Houseproud (USA) (Riverman (USA))
1693a^{5}
Hernando Royal *H Morrison* a90 96
4 b g Hernando(FR) —Louis' Queen (IRE) (Tragic Role (USA))
(1591) 2236^{5} 3509^{4} 4047^{4} 4690^{10} 6014^{8}
Hernando's Boy *K G Reveley* 74
6 b g Hernando(FR) —Leave At Dawn (Slip Anchor)
6186^{11} (6703)
Herninski *M C Chapman* a36 39
4 b m Hernando(FR) —Empress Dagmar (Selkirk (USA))
181^{4} 1011^{12} 1271^{11}
Heroes *G A Huffer* 95
3 b g Diktat—Wars (IRE) (Green Desert (USA))
1768^{9} 2212^{7} 2788^{12} 4366^{3} 4827^{2} 5617^{2} 5950^{2} 6053^{5} 6301^{13}
Hero Heart *Jane Chapple-Hyam* a48
2 ch c Kyllachy—Rainy Day Song (Persian Bold)
6820^{9} 6926^{9}
Herolds Bay *M W Easterby* 18
2 b f Bertolini(USA) —Prime Property (IRE) (Tirol)
1193^{13} 1302^{11} 1636^{11}
Heron (IRE) *N P Littmoden* a65 42
2 b g Invincible Spirit(IRE) —Alexander Express (IRE) (Sri Pekan (USA))
5097^{5} 6177^{3} 6595^{8} 6813^{9}

Heron Bay *G Wragg* 103
3 b c Hernando(FR) —Wiener Wald (USA) (Woodman (USA))
1011^{6} 1605^{2} 1998^{3} (2790) 4044^{9} 4692^{8} 6759^{14}
Heros Reward (USA) *D Capuano* 110
5 b g Partner's Hero(USA) —Lifes Passage (USA) (Caveat (USA))
(6375a)
Herotozero (IRE) *Gerard O'Leary* a77 72
3 b g Mull Of Kintyre(USA) —Free To Trade (IRE) (Royal Academy (USA))
6916a^{2}
Herrbee (IRE) *M P Tregoning* a42 53
2 b g Mark Of Esteem(IRE) —Reematna (Sabrehill (USA))
4048^{14} 4500^{11} *4963^{7}*
He's A Decoy (IRE) *David Wachman* 116
3 b c In The Wings—Allegheny River (USA) (Lear Fan (USA))
1103^{4} 2051a^{3} 2734^{8}
Hesaguru (IRE) *J O'Reilly* a18 34
3 ch g Ishiguru(USA) —Lady Kinvarrah (IRE) (Brief Truce (USA))
1381^{9} 2116^{10} 2200^{10} (Dead)
He's A Humbug (IRE) *K A Ryan* a73 88
3 b g Tagula(IRE) —Acidanthera (Alzao (USA))
(1009) 3431^{16} 3749^{11} 4122^{15} 4726^{18} 5358^{7} *5684^{7}*
He's A Rocket (IRE) *John R Upson* a49 54
6 b g Indian Rocket—Dellua (IRE) (Suave Dancer (USA))
46^{6} 254^{7} 1163^{4} 1594^{11} (3667) 3921^{13} *4973^{6} 5564^{8}*
Hesivorthedriver (GER) *Mrs A J Perrett* a71 77
3 b c King's Best(USA) —Homing Instinct (Arctic Tern (USA))
764^{6} 3236^{4} 3908^{6} *5683^{3}* 5938^{12} 6275^{4}
He's Mine Too *D G Bridgwater* a73 69
3 b g Indian Ridge—Screen Idol (IRE) (Sadler's Wells (USA))
1111^{3} 1913^{3} 3785^{7} *7263^{2}*
He's My Best (USA) *J Noseda* a61 53
3 ch c Elusive Quality(USA) —Fair Settlement (USA) (Easy Goer (USA))
1267^{3} *2173^{6} 6546^{8}*
Hessian (IRE) *P Howling* a78 55
3 b f Barathea(IRE) —Red Letter (Sri Pekan (USA))
193^{3} 293^{2} 449^{3} 2749^{6} 3826^{8} 4321^{7} *(4591) 4889^{4} (5312) 6208^{6} (6610) 6677^{7}*
Hester Brook (IRE) *J G M O'Shea* a38 61
3 b f Soviet Star(USA) —Keen To Please (Keen)
1008^{10} 1782^{4} 2557^{LFT} *3394^{10}* 6090^{2} 6452^{11}
Heureux (USA) *J Howard Johnson* 81
4 b h Stravinsky(USA) —Storm West (USA) (Gone West (USA))
1555^{7} 2311^{2} 2985^{7} 3998^{12} 5228^{11}
Hewaar (IRE) *J O'Reilly* 22
4 b g Mujadil(USA) —Corynida (USA) (Alleged (USA))
1374^{5} 1849^{10} *1937^{13}*
Hey Presto *R Rowe* a46 43
7 b g Piccolo—Upping The Tempo (Dunbeath (USA))
2336^{14} *2802^{5}* 4395^{17} 4959^{9} *6407^{12} 7088^{8} 7186^{10}*
Heywood *M R Channon* a89 92
3 b g Tobougg(IRE) —Owdbetts (IRE) (High Estate)
939^{8} 1298^{3} (1604) 2212^{8} 3380^{8} 4093^{12} 4374^{6} 4990^{4} 5765^{9}
H Harrison (IRE) *I W McInnes* a71 91
7 b g Eagle Eyed(USA) —Penrose (IRE) (Wolfhound (USA))
561^{10} (672) 750^{4} 793^{12} 895^{6} 953^{7} 1223^{2} 1458^{4} (1555) 2419^{3} (2466) (2528) 3813^{13} 4195^{9} 4851^{13} (4990) 5031^{5} 5413^{12} 5449^{9} 5512^{5} 5804^{7} *6209^{12}*
Hiats *R Craggs* a53 20
5 b g Lujain(USA) —Naulakha (Bustino)
627^{2} 3764^{10} 4706^{17}
Hiawatha (IRE) *A M Hales* a54 69
8 b g Danehill(USA) —Hi Bettina (Henbit (USA))
19^{5} 416^{5}
Hibiki (IRE) *J S Moore* 82
3 b c Montjeu(IRE) —White Queen (IRE) (Spectrum (IRE))
4018^{3} 4235^{2} (5137) 5594^{5} 5941^{3} (6422)
Hi Calypso (IRE) *Sir Michael Stoute* 111
3 b f In The Wings—Threefold (USA) (Gulch (USA))
1898^{5} (2602) (2999) (4089) (5352)
Hiccups *M Dods* 89
7 b g Polar Prince(IRE) —Simmie's Special (Precocious)
(1223) 1682^{3} 2030^{6} 2528^{10} 3239^{3} 4581^{4} 4990^{7} 5617^{9} 6560^{14}
Hi Dancer *P C Haslam* a58 64
4 b g Medicean—Sea Music (Inchinor)
733^{9} (2890) 3280^{3} 5087^{3}
Hiddensee (USA) *M Wigham* a89 88
5 b g Cozzene(USA) —Zarani Sidi Anna (USA) (Danzig (USA))
1253^{12}
Hieroglyph *M Johnston* a71 77
2 b f Green Desert(USA) —Mighty Isis (USA) (Pleasant Colony (USA))
5194^{6} *5498^{4}* 5881^{2} *6358^{3}* (6742) *7016^{5}*
Hi Fi *Ian Williams* a56
9 b g Homo Sapien—Baroness Orkzy (Baron Blakeney)
230^{5} 458^{9} 603^{6}
Higgy's Boy (IRE) *R Hannon* a73 75
2 b c Choisir(AUS) —Pagan Rhythm (USA) (Joanie's Chief (USA))
999^{11} 1058^{6} 1990^{4} *2353^{4}* 5374^{8} *6120^{12}* 6379^{2} *6585^{5}*
High Ambition *R A Fahey* a60 84
4 b g High Estate—So Ambitious (Teenoso (USA))
1^{6} 186^{2} 770^{7} (980) *1118^{7}* (2190) 2414^{2} 5253^{8}
Highband *M Madgwick* 32
4 b m Band On The Run—Barkston Singer (Runnett)
4504^{12}
Highbourne Lady *B N Pollock* 25
3 b f Rainbow High—Lady Godiva (Keen)
1409^{8} 1816^{7} 2308^{11} 3035^{14}

High Bray (GER) *J D Frost* 89
6 b g Zieten(USA) —Homing Instinct (Arctic Tern (USA))
4184^{13} 5062^{5}
High Class Problem (IRE) *P Winkworth* a72 71
4 b g Mozart(IRE) —Sarah-Clare (Reach)
1629^{6} 2107^{14} 2514^{8} 2721^{7} *3191^{2}* 3352^{15} *3732^{5} 4272^{6}* 4505^{10} *6579^{6} 6831^{5} 7115^{12}*
High Country (IRE) *Micky Hammond* a50 93
7 b g Danehill(USA) —Dance Date (IRE) (Sadler's Wells (USA))
121^{6} 215^{9}
High Curragh *K A Ryan* a95 96
4 b g Pursuit Of Love—Pretty Poppy (Song)
840^{4} 1651^{25} 1852^{5} 2566^{9} 2841^{6} 3557^{7} 4195^{3} (4389) 5195^{3} 5505^{4} 5584^{16} 6472^{15}
High Days (IRE) *H-A Pantall* a75 75
2 ch f Hennessy(USA) —Hi Dubai (Rahy (USA))
2122^{2} 2658^{6} *3648^{4} (4274)* 5053^{5} *7048a^{6}*
High Dee Jay (IRE) *R Hannon* 48
2 b c High Chaparral(IRE) —Brogan's Well (IRE) (Caerleon (USA))
5721^{9} 5918^{15} 6127^{11}
High Dream (USA) *J-C Rouget* a99 99
3 br c High Yield(USA) —Bahama Dream (Machiavellian (USA))
695a^{2}
Highest Esteem *G L Moore* a74 58
3 b g Mark Of Esteem(IRE) —For More (FR) (Sanglamore (USA))
4541^{5} 5450^{7} *5728^{9} 6534^{4} (6807) (6871)*
Highest Height (FR) *D Smaga* 99
3 gr f Highest Honor(FR) —Largesse (FR) (Saumarez)
1006a^{0} 4873a^{10}
Highest Regard *N P McCormack* a64 69
5 b g Mark Of Esteem(IRE) —Free As A Bird (Robellino (USA))
1042^{16} *1385^{9}* (Dead)
High Finance (USA) *R Violette* a105
4 ch h Talk Is Money(USA) —Margay (USA) (Conquistador Cielo (USA))
6485a^{8}
High Five Society *S R Bowring* a48 65
3 b g Compton Admiral—Sarah Madeline (Pelder (IRE))
931^{7} 1155^{6} 1850^{12} 2538^{5} 4071^{2} 4658^{2} 5284^{8} *6505^{4} 6609^{8}*
High Frequency (IRE) *A Crook* a56 50
6 ch g Grand Lodge(USA) —Freak Out (FR) (Bering)
1556^{10} 2417^{3} 3193^{11} 4475^{8} 5561^{7}
High Heel Sneakers *P F I Cole* a109 107
4 b m Dansili—Sundae Girl (USA) (Green Dancer (USA))
1650^{7} 2441^{2} 2702a^{11} 4089^{7} 4748^{6} 5352^{14}
High Hope (FR) *G L Moore* a73 53
9 ch g Lomitas—Highness Lady (GER) (Cagliostro (GER))
1342^{8}
Highland Daughter (IRE) *C G Cox* 96
2 b f Kyllachy—Raysiza (IRE) (Alzao (USA))
(2658) 3096^{3} 3988^{8} 5614^{3}
Highland Harvest *D R C Elsworth* a80 85
3 b c Averti(IRE) —Bee One (IRE) (Catrail (USA))
(27) 184^{7} 638^{7} 1544^{2} 2045^{10} 2943^{4} 4455^{2} 5014^{4} 5620^{8} 6081^{7} *6269^{6}*
Highland Homestead *B R Millman* 66
2 b g Makbul—Highland Rossie (Pablond)
2575^{7} 2876^{6}
Highland Laddie *C R Egerton* 63
2 ch g Lomitas—Sirena (GER) (Tejano (USA))
4198^{4} 5011^{8}
Highland Legacy *M L W Bell* 95
3 ch c Selkirk(USA) —Generous Lady (Generous (IRE))
1044^{10} (1355) 1624^{3} 2808^{3} (6131) (6284)
Highland Love *Jedd O'Keeffe* a64 50
2 b g Fruits Of Love(USA) —Diabaig (Precocious)
3718^{8} *4459^{3} 5363^{4}*
Highland Song (IRE) *R F Fisher* a50 73
4 ch g Fayruz—Rose 'n Reason (IRE) (Reasonable (FR))
1226^{9} 1597^{13} 3347^{5} 3498^{2} 3839^{9} 4996^{3} 5085^{3} 5908^{13} *7026^{7}*
Highlands Skye *L Montague Hall* a5
3 b f Diktat—Manhattan Sunset (USA) (El Gran Senor (USA))
6807^{7}
Highland Warrior *P T Midgley* 90
8 b g Makbul—Highland Rowena (Royben)
1134^{5} 1483^{7} (2805) 3053^{13} 3197^{4} 3464^{13} (3515) 3720^{9} 5044^{10} 5379^{15} 5581^{4} 5806^{9} 6157^{16}
Highliner *Mrs L Williamson* a55 49
5 b h Robellino(USA) —Bocas Rose (Jalmood (USA))
1152^{11}
High Lite *M L W Bell* 51
3 ch f Observatory(USA) —Shall We Run (Hotfoot)
2192^{10} 2607^{10}
Highly Regal (IRE) *R A Teal* a57 52
2 b c High Chaparral(IRE) —Regal Portrait (IRE) (Royal Academy (USA))
5680^{5} 6202^{5} 6451^{8}
High 'n Dry (IRE) *M A Allen* a74 75
3 ch f Halling(USA) —Sisal (IRE) (Danehill (USA))
1105^{4} 3349^{4} 3961^{4} 4338^{7} 4575^{5} (6062) 6300^{13} *6795^{6} 6929^{5} 6997^{8} 7094^{4}*
Highness (GER) *W Baltromei* 84
3 ch f Samum(GER) —Honni By (IRE) (Be My Guest (USA))
2294a^{9} 6046a^{5} 6690a^{8}
High Plains (FR) *R Hannon* a59 71
2 ch c Golan(IRE) —Perusha (USA) (Southern Halo (USA))
3991^{10} 6126^{6} 6469^{4} *6868^{5}*
High Point (IRE) *G P Enright* a81 79
9 b g Ela-Mana-Mou—Top Lady (IRE) (Shirley Heights)
844^{4} 1148^{8} 1654^{5} 1959^{7} 2908^{5} *3216^{8}* 4576^{2} 5573^{3}

High Profit (IRE) *D R C Elsworth* a71
3 ch g Selkirk(USA) —Spot Prize (USA) (Seattle Dancer (USA))
6337^{9} 816^{2}
High Reach *T D Barron* a78 93
7 b g Royal Applause—Lady Of Limerick (IRE) (Thatching)
957^{4} 1292^{7} 1574^{4} 1854^{12} 2025^{6} 2249^{4} 2744^{2} 3053^{9} 3585^{3} 3762^{8} 4251^{7} 4800^{11} 5747^{6} 5934^{9} 6283^{12} 6562^{11} *6910^{7}*
High Reef (FR) *C F Swan* 92
9 b m Shareef Dancer(USA) —Debate (High Line)
4849^{10}
High Ridge *J M Bradley* a78 81
8 ch g Indian Ridge—Change For A Buck (USA) (Time For A Change (USA))
1545^{5} 2394^{12} 2494^{4} *3188^{7}* 3802^{7} 4767^{4} 4942^{2} 5064^{9} 5272^{9} 5909^{8} *6406^{7}*
High Rock (IRE) *J-C Rouget* 103
2 ch c Rock Of Gibraltar(IRE) —Hint Of Silver (USA) (Alysheba (USA))
(6377a)
High Seasons *A J Chamberlain* a66 70
4 b g Fantastic Light(USA) —El Hakma (Shareef Dancer (USA))
48^{8} 2980^{7}
High Standing (USA) *N A Callaghan* a79 59
2 bb g High Yield(USA) —Nena Maka (Selkirk (USA))
3589^{14} 3823^{8} *4160^{7}* 5541^{5} *(6263) (6388)*
High Stepping (USA) *E A L Dunlop* 59
2 ch c High Yield(USA) —Dance Colony (USA) (Pleasant Colony (USA))
6107^{7}
Hight Blue Sails (FR) *P Demercastel* a79 98
3 gr c Chichicastenango(FR) —Green Sails (IRE) (Slip Anchor)
1736a^{5}
High Treason (USA) *W J Musson* a70 92
5 ch g Diesis—Fabula Dancer (USA) (Northern Dancer (CAN))
1288^{3} 1771^{2} (1822) 3509^{10} 3989^{6} 4690^{12} 6158^{8}
High Tribute *Sir Mark Prescott* a76
3 ch c Mark Of Esteem(IRE) —Area Girl (Jareer (USA))
(160) 312^{2} 2769^{7} 3418^{12} 3646^{9}
Highway (IRE) *F Castro* a96 75
4 b g King's Theatre(IRE) —Havinia (Habitat)
1648a^{4} 2131a^{13} 4218a^{15}
Highway To Glory (IRE) *M Botti* a84 103
4 br m Cape Cross(IRE) —Anita Via (IRE) (Anita's Prince)
938^{4} 1661^{5} *6965^{7}*
High Window (IRE) *G P Kelly* a28 65
7 b g King's Theatre(IRE) —Kayradja (IRE) (Last Tycoon (IRE))
2027^{11} 5231^{9} 6475^{15} 6701^{9} *6955^{9} 7239^{8}*
Hi High *D K Ivory* a41
2 b f Tumbleweed Ridge—High Finale (Sure Blade (USA))
1728^{9} 2517^{6}
Hilbre Court (USA) *B J Meehan* a83
2 bb c Doneraile Court(USA) —Glasgow's Gold (USA) (Seeking The Gold (USA))
(6543) (6960) (7145)
Hildegarde (IRE) *T D Easterby* 51
2 b f King Charlemagne(USA) —Rose Society (Caerleon (USA))
3024^{5} 3532^{5} 3951^{13} 4279^{9} 4524^{5} 4897^{6} 5153^{13} (Dead)
Hillbilly Cat (USA) *R Ingram* a66 39
4 ch g Running Stag(USA) —Flashy Cat (USA) (Mountain Cat (USA))
221^{6} 687^{11} 722^{9} 1719^{6}
Hill Cloud *W M Brisbourne* a50 40
5 gr g Cloudings(IRE) —Hill Farm Dancer (Gunner B)
4334^{7} 4563^{5} *4948^{13} 6911^{9} 7203^{7} 7262^{2}*
Hill Farm Shanty *J T Stimpson* a20
5 b g Slip Anchor—Hill Farm Blues (Mon Tresor)
7125^{9}
Hill Of Almhuim (IRE) *Peter Grayson* a71 73
4 b g City On A Hill(USA) —Kitty Kildare (USA) (Seattle Dancer (USA))
51^{3} 187^{10} 271^{5} 557^{4} 653^{11} 751^{7} 1381^{13}
Hill Of Clare (IRE) *G H Jones* a17 41
5 gr m Daylami(IRE) —Sarah-Clare (Reach)
1435^{12} 2913^{8} 4200^{6} 6420^{15} *6766^{9}*
Hill Of Lujain *Ian Williams* a64 67
3 b g Lujain(USA) —Cinder Hills (Deploy)
2363^{9} 2912^{8} *7026^{9} 7158^{3} 7261^{9}*
Hill Queen (IRE) *L M Cumani* a69 66
3 b f Montjeu(IRE) —Minodora (IRE) (Marju (IRE))
2177^{7} 3166^{4} *4069^{3}*
Hillside Smoki (IRE) *A Berry*
3 b f Soviet Star(USA) —Najeyba (Indian Ridge)
1913^{15} 2565^{7} 2909^{5} 3377^{11} 4036^{11} 4283^{7} 4891^{11}
Hills Of Aran *W K Goldsworthy* 55
5 b g Sadler's Wells(USA) —Danefair (Danehill (USA))
4576^{14}
Hills Place *J R Best* a58 49
3 b g Primo Valentino(IRE) —Moxby (Efisio)
360^{5} 636^{3} 1320^{4} *6100^{3} 6266^{4} 6431^{6}*
Hilltime (IRE) *J S Wainwright* a45 58
7 b g Danetime(IRE) —Ceannanas (IRE) (Magical Wonder (USA))
2201^{5}
Hilltop Fantasy *V Smith* a46 45
6 b m Danzig Connection(USA) —Hilltop (Absalom)
83^{7} 579^{5} 625^{9} 1344^{4}
Hilversum *Miss J A Camacho* a48 27
5 ch m Polar Falcon(USA) —Silky Heights (IRE) (Head For Heights)
(1311) 2258^{13}
Himba *Mrs A J Perrett* 64
4 b g Vettori(IRE) —Be My Wish (Be My Chief (USA))
(1216) 1683^{8} 2686^{6} 3448^{12} 4030^{13} 4576^{12}

Hi Me *M G Quinlan* 51
2 b f Auction House(USA) —Roller Girl (Merdon Melody)
1485a[5]

Hindu Kush (IRE) *A P O'Brien* 84
2 b c Sadler's Wells(USA) —Tambora (Darshaan)
6443a[9]

Hinterland (IRE) *Saeed Bin Suroor* 109
5 bb h Danzig(USA) —Electric Society (IRE) (Law Society (USA))
331a[13] 2368[3] 3887[5]

Hint Of Spring *Saeed Bin Suroor* a52 64
3 b f Seeking The Gold(USA) —Cherokee Rose (IRE) (Dancing Brave (USA))
527a[5] 1676[3] 5678[3] (6597)

Hinton Admiral *M Johnston* a105 106
3 b g Spectrum(IRE) —Shawanni (Shareef Dancer (USA))
(760) 847[5] 1095[4] 1394[2] 1876a[10]

Hip *E A L Dunlop* 77
2 b f Pivotal—Hypnotize (Machiavellian (USA))
(4232)

Hippolyte (USA) *J G Given* a48 38
4 b m Monarchos(USA) —Liberty School (USA) (Pine Bluff (USA))
393[9] 466[5] 630[11]

Hiraboku Royal (JPN) *R Okubo* 112
3 b c Tanino Gimlet(JPN) —Mars Violet (USA) (Mr Prospector (USA))
6943a[16]

His Master's Voice (IRE) *D W P Arbuthnot* a82 81
4 ch h Distant Music(USA) —Glen Of Imaal (IRE) (Common Grounds)
234[6] 614[2] (697) 902[2] *1931[2] 2573[10]* 3481[6] 3943[20] 4134[9] 5874[13] *6232[13]*

Hiss And Boo *P Howling* a47
2 ch g Starborough—Royal Lady (IRE) (Royal Academy (USA))
7181[4]

Histoire De Moeurs (FR) *Y De Nicolay* 109
4 b m Kaldounevees(FR) —Vero De Moeurs (FR) (Double Bed (FR))
4652a[10]

Historic Place (USA) *J A Geake* 48
7 b g Dynaformer(USA) —Captive Island (Northfields (USA))
6131[14] 6473[17]

History Boy *D J Coakley* a89 84
3 b g Dr Fong(USA) —Goldie (Celtic Swing)
1230[7] 2354[9] (3170) 3407[8] *5101[5]* 5594[9] 5921[7] *6501[8]*

History Prize (IRE) *A G Newcombe* a47
4 b g Celtic Swing—Menominee (Soviet Star (USA))
98[4] 503[8] 607[12] 6815[3] 7187[8]

Hitchcock (USA) *A P O'Brien* 108
4 ch h Giant's Causeway(USA) —Beware Of The Cat (USA) (Caveat (USA))
2859[3] 3558[14] 4722[11]

Hitchens (IRE) *G L Moore* 101
2 b c Acclamation—Royal Fizz (IRE) (Royal Academy (USA))
3878[4] (4323) 4695[3] 5397a[2] 6167[5]

Hits Only Cash *J Pearce* a73 73
5 b g Inchinor—Persian Blue (Persian Bold)
306[7] 479[5] 570[2] 806[6] 1284[3] 1366[2] 1918[2] 2748[4] *4433[5]* (4856) *5237[9] (5645) 5889[6] 6293[9]*

Hits Only Heaven (IRE) *D Nicholls* a92 91
5 ch g Bold Fact(USA) —Algonquin Park (High Line)
6[U] (Dead)

Hits Only Jude (IRE) *J Pearce* a63 76
4 gr g Bold Fact(USA) —Grey Goddess (Godswalk (USA))
6290[5] 6533[7] 7003[7]

Hits Only Life (USA) *J Pearce* a54 56
4 b g Lemon Drop Kid(USA) —Southern Day (USA) (Dixieland Band (USA))
243[11] 503[10] 1906[8] 2372[2]

Hit's Only Money (IRE) *J S Goldie* a71 62
7 br g Hamas(IRE) —Toordillon (IRE) (Contract Law (USA))
(1597) 2561[8] 2864[6] 3585[8] 3787[4] 3998[10] 4281[6] 4706[6] 4931[9] 5284[14] 5935[11]

Hits Only Time *J Pearce* a54 55
2 ch c Bertolini(USA) —South Wind (Tina's Pet)
5595[11] 6107[9] 6295[11] *6530[8]*

Hits Only Vic (USA) *D Carroll* a43 57
3 bb g Lemon Drop Kid(USA) —Royal Family (USA) (Private Terms (USA))
336[9] 469[7] 4845[3]

Hit The Road (IRE) *Michael McElhone* a54 58
3 gr g Carrowkeel(IRE) —Order Of Success (USA) (With Approval (CAN))
512[7]

Hit The Roof *R Hannon* a72 69
2 b c Auction House(USA) —Rave On (ITY) (Barathea (IRE))
4201[6] 4761[7] *5200[4] 5680[3]* 6058[3] *6665[3]*

Hla Tun (USA) *W R Swinburn* a57
2 b g Johannesburg(USA) —Sophie (USA) (Pulpit (USA))
6267[8] 6602[9]

Hobby *R M Beckett* 90
2 b f Robellino(USA) —Wydah (Suave Dancer (USA))
(3471) 3880[3] 5536[2] 6498[10]

Hobson *Eve Johnson Houghton* a73 74
2 b g Choisir(AUS) —Educating Rita (Emarati (USA))
1428[2] 1762[5] 2398[2] 4046[9] (4629) 5207[6] 5534[5] *6004[4]*

Hocinail (FR) *P Winkworth* 50
3 ch g Majorien—Flamme (FR) (Shining Steel)
2105[15] 2362[10] 4534[11]

Hoffman (IRE) *T Stack* 93
5 ch g Dr Devious(IRE) —Morale (Bluebird (USA))
3138a[11]

Hogan's Heroes *Eoin Doyle* a50 63
4 b g Alhaarth(IRE) —Icicle (Polar Falcon (USA))
3805[8] 4319[9] 4920[7]

Hogmaneigh (IRE) *S C Williams* a72 111
4 b g Namid—Magical Peace (IRE) (Magical Wonder (USA))
1788[3] (2234) 2858[12] 3573a[4] 3990[15] 5325[7] 6039a[17]

Hoh Hoh Hoh *R J Price* a63 111
5 ch g Piccolo—Nesting (Thatching)
1292[4] 1474[6] 1826[7] 2197[5] (2529) 3080[3] 3526[2] 3990[2] 4386[8] 4696[2] 5050[4] 5212[3] 5407[18] 5700[3] 5953[6] 6183[2] 6338[8]

Hoh Me Hoh You (IRE) *S Kirk* a48 56
3 ch g Redback—Eastern Aura (IRE) (Ahonoora)
122[7] 295[4]

Hoh Mike (IRE) *M L W Bell* 112
3 ch c Intikhab(USA) —Magical Peace (IRE) (Magical Wonder (USA))
(1394) 2035[2] (2672) 3088[9] (3329) 4746[6] 6039a[13]

Hoh Wotanite *R Hollinshead* a90 77
4 ch h Stravinsky(USA) —West One (Gone West (USA))
424[6] 609[5] 803[5] 1226[4] 2007[5] 2576[11] *3067[2] 3173[2] (3286)* 3534[3] *(3926)* 4129[3] 4353[6] 4566[9] *4672[5] 5568[5] 5889[4] 6293[4] 6359[5] (6816) (6885) (7002) (7287)*

Holbeck Ghyll (IRE) *A M Balding* a81 88
5 ch g Titus Livius(FR) —Crimada (IRE) (Mukaddamah (USA))
1464[4] 1854[7] 2234[4] 2399[9] 2694[3] 3749[4] 4095[19] 4389[2] 5447[4] 5806[5] *6141[5]*

Holbien (IRE) *Liam Roche* a78 91
4 b g Orpen(USA) —Fading With Music (IRE) (Thatching)
551[7] 3140a[15] *5761a[14]*

Holborn (UAE) *S Seemar* a76 77
6 b g Green Desert(USA) —Court Lane (USA) (Machiavellian (USA))
326a[11] 409a[11] *532a[11]*

Holden Caulfield (IRE) *Mouse Hamilton-Fairley* 35
2 b g Catcher In The Rye(IRE) —God Speed Her (Pas De Seul)
4539[10] 6126[11] 6448[6]

Holden Eagle *A G Newcombe* 57
2 b c Catcher In The Rye(IRE) —Bird Of Prey (IRE) (Last Tycoon (IRE))
6468[12]

Hold That Call (USA) *R Hannon* a55 67
2 ch g Hold That Tiger(USA) —Rainbow Master (USA) (Entropy (USA))
1652[8] 2316[7] 2630[3] 3823[6] *4274[9]* 6409[5] *6892[7]*

Hold The Gold (IRE) *E J O'Neill* a81 75
2 b c Danehill Dancer(IRE) —Ashkirk (Selkirk (USA))
3510[5] 4192[2] *4431[2] 6138[2] (7084)*

Holiday Camp (USA) *M Al Muhairi* a93 109
5 b h Chester House(USA) —Arewehavingfunyet (USA) (Sham (USA))
177a[7]

Holiday Cocktail *J J Quinn* a69 69
5 b g Mister Baileys—Bermuda Lily (Dunbeath (USA))
538[9] (605) 675[2] 1413[9] (2302) 2603[2] *4023[8]* 6380[7]

Holiday Rock *A J McCabe* a38 18
3 b g Rock City—Angie Gold (Mesleh)
1716[8] 1937[9] 2308[9] 2909[9]

Hollow Dream (IRE) *R A Harris* a40
2 b f Beat Hollow—Sarah's Dream (IRE) (Lion Cavern (USA))
6799[10] 7058[9] 7208[7]

Hollow Hill (IRE) *Brian Nolan* a19 75
2 b f Orpen(USA) —Caladira (IRE) (Darshaan)
5395a[17]

Hollow Jo *J R Jenkins* a81 53
7 b g Most Welcome—Sir Hollow (USA) (Sir Ivor (USA))
28[5] (47) 190[9] 261[9] 513[13] 1401[7] 1931[12] 2771[6] 2993[6] 3396[9] 4594[9] *(5130)* 5387[9] 6103[7] *6406[10] 6810[10] 6890[2] 7054[5] 7253[8]*

Hollow Point (IRE) *M Johnston* a57
2 b c Cherokee Run(USA) —Squeak (Selkirk (USA))
6694[8] 7121[9] 7288[3]

Hollow Ridge *B W Hills* 91
3 b f Beat Hollow—Bolas (Unfuwain (USA))
1581[6] 2757[14] 4503[6] 6185[6]

Holly Golightley *K A Ryan* a56 60
2 b f Choisir(AUS) —Breakfast Bay (IRE) (Charnwood Forest (IRE))
1193[7] 1422[6] 1848[13] 5770[7] 6535[9] *6813[7] 7042[4] 7195[3]*

Hollywood George *K A Ryan* a73
3 b c Royal Applause—Aunt Tate (Tate Gallery (USA))
275[3] 478[2] 584[4] 935[6] (1281)

Hollywood Starlet (FR) *Y De Nicolay* a93 89
4 b m Marchand De Sable(USA) —Private Quest (USA) (Quest For Fame)
31a[16]

Holocene (USA) *P Bary* 114
3 bb c Lemon Drop Kid(USA) —Witching Hour (FR) (Fairy King (USA))
1593a[2] 4445a[2] 5261a[6] 6031a[9]

Holy Affairs (IRE) *Liam Roche* a21 49
3 b g Bishop Of Cashel—Zelda (USA) (Sharpen Up)
553[7]

Holyfield Warrior (IRE) *I A Wood* a49 28
3 b g Princely Heir(IRE) —Perugino Lady (IRE) (Perugino (USA))
2913[12] *3454[6]* 4292[11] *5095[8]* 6277[11] *6532[6]*

Holy Storm (IRE) *Eve Johnson Houghton* 49
2 b g Mujahid(USA) —Slupia (IRE) (Indian Ridge)
3383[11] 3866[8] 4201[10] 5268[12] 5470[8]

Home *J R Boyle* a71 71
2 b c Domedriver(IRE) —Swahili (IRE) (Kendor (FR))
3552[9] 4070[3] 4500[7] *5601[7]* 6379[3] 6572[3] *6868[4] 6933[3] 7156[2] 7259[2]*

Homebred Star *G P Enright* a51 21
6 ch g Safawan—Celtic Chimes (Celtic Cone)
349[9] 699[9] 887[7] 1368[7] 2412[6]

Home Call (USA) *C Von Der Recke* 99
5 b h Chester House(USA) —Call Account (USA) (Private Account (USA))
493a[5]

Homecroft Boy *P D Evans* a50 42
3 ch g Kyllachy—Quiz Time (Efisio)
136[6] 223[4] 360[6] 1119[2] 1210[6] *1397[6]* 2110[8] 2298[11] 3843[3] 4256[6] *4673[11] 6815[11] 7169[8]*

Homes By Woodford *R A Harris* a72 62
3 ch g Tumbleweed Ridge—Partenza (USA) (Red Ransom (USA))
(25) 113[5] 216[5] 382[5] 591[9] 744[3] (937) 1084[6] *1230[4]* 1927[8] 2916[10] 3429[5] 3640[5] 3804[7]

Home Sweet Home (IRE) *L M Cumani* a69 97
4 b m Danehill(USA) —Jungle Moon (IRE) (Sadler's Wells (USA))
2507[5] 3016[2] 4060[7] 5210[10]

Hometomammy *P W Hiatt* a51 39
5 b g Diktat—Catania (USA) (Aloma's Ruler (USA))
203[5] 266[9] 435[11] 462[4] 519[7] 664[5] 715[5] 812[5] 1011[16] 1206[11] *1402[9]*

Honduras (SWI) *G L Moore* a92 95
6 gr g Daylami(IRE) —High Mare (FR) (Highest Honor (FR))
6230[7] 6490[12] *6802[11] 6819[6]*

Honest Prospector (USA) *Sir Michael Stoute* a68 81
3 b c Distorted Humor(USA) —Star Nurse (USA) (Eastern Echo (USA))
2433[4] 2880[6] *3454[2]* (4138) 4640[6]

Honest To Betsy (USA) *Dale Romans* a84
2 br f Yonaguska(USA) —Hard Freeze (USA) (It's Freezing (USA))
5247a[5]

Honest Value (IRE) *Mrs L C Jewell* a42 56
2 b g Chevalier(IRE) —Sensimelia (IRE) (Inzar (USA))
3849[11] 4325[7] 4823[7] 5715[6] *6426[8]*

Honest Yankee (USA) *Mrs L C Jewell* a12 35
2 ch c Yankee Gentleman(USA) —Tresor (USA) (Pleasant Tap (USA))
2569[11] 2876[11] 3270[10] *6857[11]*

Honeycott (IRE) *J D Bethell* 49
2 ch f King's Best(USA) —Kingsridge (IRE) (King's Theatre (IRE))
3718[14] 4448[11] 5483[5] 6075[10]

Honey Monster (IRE) *Miss V Haigh* a72 72
2 ch c Choisir(AUS) —Caribbean Escape (Pivotal)
3423[3] 3812[9] 4286[3] 5324[21] 5665[8] *6502[6]*

Honey Ryder (USA) *T Pletcher* 119
6 rg m Lasting Approval(USA) —Cuando Quiere (USA) (Affirmed (USA))
861a[11] 4413a[6] 6509a[2]

Honeystreet (IRE) *D Burchell* a44
7 b m Woodborough(USA) —Ring Of Kerry (IRE) (Kenmare (FR))
1066[8] (Dead)

Honky Tonk Sally *M L W Bell* 83
2 b f Dansili—Flower Girl (Pharly (FR))
3055[3] 3507[5] 4744[10] 5357[2] (5801)

Honolulu (IRE) *A P O'Brien* 121
3 b c Montjeu(IRE) —Cerulean Sky (IRE) (Darshaan)
(2851a) 4722[2] 5408[3] 5831[3] 6374a[8]

Honorable Love *M Dods* 79
3 ch f Highest Honor(FR) —Everlasting Love (Pursuit Of Love)
1303[5] 1659[3] 2253[2] 2808[2] 3379[7] 3785[5] (4128) 5218[7]

Honoured Guest (IRE) *A P O'Brien* 113
3 b c Danehill(USA) —Wind Silence (USA) (A.P. Indy (USA))
(1047a) 1703a[3]

Honour Fulfilled (CAN) *Michael J Doyle* 79
2 br f Honour And Glory(USA) —Fulfilled Promise (USA) (Red Ransom (USA))
5293a[6]

Honour High *Lady Herries* a35 49
5 gr g Cloudings(IRE) —Meant To Be (Morston (FR))
1590[6] 2493[5] 5453[8]

Hoober *A W Carroll* 3
6 b g Mind Games—Chlo-Jo (Belmez (USA))
5873[13]

Hook Money (IRE) *A J McCabe* a53 53
3 b g Orpen(USA) —Toi Toi (IRE) (In The Wings)
3084[12] 3847[9] 4528[3] *5235[2] 5422[7] 5647[5]* 5906[9] 6250[6] 6325[11] *6815[7]*

Ho Pang Yau *J S Goldie* 51
9 bb g Pivotal—La Cabrilla (Carwhite)
966[11] 1527[9] 1893[7] 2298[9] 2563[3] 3376[4] 3497[12] 3814[10] 4972[11]

Hopeful Isabella (IRE) *Sir Mark Prescott* 43
3 ch f Grand Lodge(USA) —Hopeful Sign (Warning)
1579[13] 1894[6] 3035[13]

Hopeful Purchase (IRE) *W J Haggas* a94 101
4 ch g Grand Lodge(USA) —Funoon (IRE) (Kris)
244a[8] 331a[8] 477a[6] *759[7]* 993[7]

Hope Island (IRE) *E F Vaughan* a62 55
3 b f Titus Livius(FR) —Chapka (IRE) (Green Desert (USA))
(6704)

Hope Road *J R Fanshawe* a75 76
3 ch g Sakhee(USA) —Bibliotheque (USA) (Woodman (USA))
1863[4] 2320[8] 3058[9] 3567[3] 4815[10] *5732[3] 6124[5]*

Hope's Eternal *C L Popham*
4 ro g Highest Honor(FR) —Tennessee Moon (Darshaan)
1888[17]

Hope Your Safe *J R Best* a55 51
3 b f Tobougg(IRE) —Sunday Night (GER) (Bakharoff (USA))
3384[11] 3949[4] 4326[4] 4596[9] *5528[7]*

Hopsider (IRE) *M Gasparini* 73
4 b m Dockside(USA) —Hope Of Pekan (IRE) (Sri Pekan (USA))
6519a[10]

Hora *Sir Mark Prescott* a60 63
3 b f Hernando(FR) —Applecross (Glint Of Gold)
5533[2] (5906) *6341[9] 7178[3]*

Horatio Carter *K A Ryan* 74
2 b c Bahamian Bounty—Jitterbug (IRE) (Marju (IRE))
5771[10] 6156[4] 6754[6]

Hornpipe *M Hill* a65 73
5 b g Danehill(USA) —Dance Sequence (USA) (Mr Prospector (USA))
47[6] 154[7] 465[2] 521[6] 626[10] 746[10] 2104[17] 2652[16] *6311[5] 6609[5] 6864[7] 7218[5]*

Horologist *M W Easterby* 23
2 ch g Timeless Times(USA) —Georgia (Missed Flight)
2739[12] 3199[9]

Horseford Hill *D R C Elsworth* 86
3 b g In The Wings—Love Of Silver (USA) (Arctic Tern (USA))
2005[6] (2836) 3883[7] (4609) 5141[6] 5955[11]

Horticulture (USA) *R Charlton* a64 55
2 ch f Forest Wildcat(USA) —Substance (USA) (Diesis)
5061[9] *6434[6]*

Host (CHI) *T Pletcher* a87 116
7 ch h Hussonet(USA) —Colonna Traiana (CHI) (Roy (USA))
861a[12] 6511a[5]

Hostage *M L W Bell* a74 72
3 b f Dr Fong(USA) —Catatonic (Zafonic (USA))
(21) 1407[7] 2045[15] 2475[6] 3156[7]

Hostess (USA) *H J Bond* 111
4 bb m Chester House(USA) —Charge Daffaires (USA) (Vice Regent (CAN))
5822a[4] 6373a[7]

Host Nation *A Fabre* 108
4 b g Grand Lodge(USA) —Hunt The Sun (Rainbow Quest (USA))
990a[2] (1341a)

Hot Agnes *H J Collingridge* a61 61
4 b m Agnes World(USA) —Hot Tin Roof (IRE) (Thatching)
243[5]

Hot Cherry *J M P Eustace* 39
3 b f Bertolini(USA) —Cribella (USA) (Robellino (USA))
996[9] *1232[11]*

Hotchpotch (USA) *J R Best* a62 61
4 b g Dayjur(USA) —Anagram (USA) (Farma Way (USA))
131[7] 236[4] 292[10] 548[7] 654[8] 734[5] 920[6]

Hot Diamond *D R C Elsworth* a62 89
3 b g Desert Prince(IRE) —Panna (Polish Precedent (USA))
1840[6] 2320[11] 2880[8] 3705[4] *4069[6]* (4504) 4858[4] 5640[3] 5955[3] 6473[3]

Hotel Du Cap *G Wragg* a92 103
4 br h Grand Lodge(USA) —Miss Riviera Golf (Hernando (FR))
4117[9] 4826[7] (5588) 6614a[9]

Hotel Felix *Miss Gay Kelleway* 34
2 ch c Best Of The Bests(IRE) —Jaljuli (Jalmood (USA))
5951[17] 6294[11]

Hotham *N Wilson* a79 76
4 b g Komaite(USA) —Malcesine (IRE) (Auction Ring (USA))
1074[7] 1557[6] 2386[7] (2509) 2712[6] 3791[4] 4038[4] 4498[4] 4800[3] 5297[3] 5552[2] (5747) *6667[2] 6708[4] 6762[2]*

Hot Property (IRE) *W R Muir* a12 58
3 ch g Cadeaux Genereux—Tropical Lass (IRE) (Ballad Rock)
2059[7] 2542[4] 3151[4] 4073[4] *5422[11]* 5739[7] 6060[14]

Houghton (IRE) *Sir Michael Stoute* 71
2 b c Sadler's Wells(USA) —Love And Affection (USA) (Exclusive Era (USA))
5361[9]

Houri (IRE) *R M Beckett* 73
2 b f Alhaarth(IRE) —Witching Hour (IRE) (Alzao (USA))
5596[11] 6470[7]

House *M R Channon* 80
2 b c Elusive Quality(USA) —Eurolink Raindance (IRE) (Alzao (USA))
4048[10] 4604[2] 5448[4] 5920[3]

House Arrest *A J McCabe* a53 53
3 ch f Auction House(USA) —Mentro (IRE) (Entrepreneur)
99[7] 390[6] 577[10] 619[9] 667[7]

House Maiden (IRE) *D M Simcock* a61 63
3 b f Rudimentary(USA) —Dahoar (Charnwood Forest (IRE))
996[7] *1386[3]* 2181[4] 2475[8] 4579[8] *5102[4]* (5803) 6129[9]

House Of Tudor *J H M Gosden* 67
2 b g Medicean—Wrong Bride (Reprimand)
5321[10] 5721[5] 6051[5]

Houston Dynimo (IRE) *Kevin Prendergast* 87
2 b c Rock Of Gibraltar(IRE) —Quiet Mouse (USA) (Quiet American (USA))
4832a[3]

Hovering (IRE) *M G Quinlan* a85 96
4 ch m In The Wings—Orlena (USA) (Gone West (USA))
756[4] 929[6] 1518a[4] 2462[5] 2720[7]

Hovman (DEN) *Ms C Erichsen* a87 99
8 ch g Kateb(IRE) —Skee The Feen (Viking (USA))
4874a[0]

Howard Le Canard (FR) *J-M Capitte* a111 104
6 b g Hamas(IRE) —No Exit (FR) (Exit To Nowhere (USA))
437a[0]

Howards Dream (IRE) *D A Nolan*
9 b g King's Theatre(IRE) —Keiko (Generous (IRE))
955[13] 2764[12]

Howards Hope *I Semple* a59 60
2 ch g Kyllachy—Howards Heroine (IRE) (Danehill Dancer (IRE))
3582[5] 4378[5] 4930[6] *6022[3] 6388[7]*

Howards Prince *D A Nolan* a6 63
4 gr g Bertolini(USA) —Grey Princess (IRE) (Common Grounds)
1493[10] 1891[9] 2386[13] 2561[14]

Howards Princess *J O'Reilly* a61 73
5 gr m Lujain(USA) —Grey Princess (IRE) (Common Grounds)
77[8] 430[8] 912[12] *1163[6]* 1594[17] 2249[U] 5155[9] 5297[11]

Howards Rocket *J S Goldie* a32 52
6 ch g Opening Verse(USA) —Houston Heiress (USA) (Houston (USA))
3539[3] 3675[3] 4081[10] 4496[4] 4704[9] 4998[15] 5676[9]

Howards Tipple *I Semple* a59 73
3 b g Diktat—Grey Princess (IRE) (Common Grounds)
954[4] 1219[3] 1530[8] 2387[2] 2761[3] 3180[3] 3537[2] 4157[5] (4384) 4719[3] 5552[3] 5934[6] 6256[4] 6639[12]

Howards Way *I Semple* 62
2 b g Bertolini(USA) —Love Quest (Pursuit Of Love)
952[4]

Howdigo *J R Best* a78 78
2 b c Tobougg(IRE) —Woodrising (Nomination)
2241[11] 2632[7] 3669[3] 4076[3] *4964[3]* 5471[2] 5828[11] *6585[2] (6805)*

Howe's Jack (IRE) *M C Chapman* a33 32
2 b g Fasliyev(USA) —Berenique (IRE) (Bering)
4016[12] 4454[16] 4586[8] 5699[6] 5901[9] 6698[11] *7122[4] 7176[10]*

How's Business *C A Cyzer* a62 60
3 b f Josr Algarhoud(IRE) —Love And Kisses (Salse (USA))
4392[8] 4630[6] *4948[6] 5533[3]* 5857[3] 6054[4]

How's She Cuttin' (IRE) *T D Barron* a50 94
4 ch m Shinko Forest(IRE) —Magic Annemarie (IRE) (Dancing Dissident (USA))
(964) 2244[2] (2461) (3197) 3586[15] 6327[3] 6487[8]

Hows That *K R Burke* a45 51
5 ch m Vettori(IRE) —Royalty (IRE) (Fairy King (USA))
2716[15] 2809[8] 3257[10]

Howya Now Kid (IRE) *G M Lyons* 102
3 b c Daggers Drawn(USA) —Lear's Crown (USA) (Lear Fan (USA))
1047a[3] 1808[3] (2212)

Hoy Soy Usted (BRZ) *Christian Wroe* a50
6 b h Music Prospector(USA) —Touch Girl (BRZ) (Restless Jet (USA))
474a[14]

Hubble Bubble (USA) *M Johnston* 61
3 ch g Giant's Causeway(USA) —Vana Turns (USA) (Wavering Monarch (USA))
954[3] 1236[5] 1665[6] 1916[7] 2530[12]

Hucking Harkness *J R Best* a63
2 ch c Dr Fong(USA) —Dalaauna (Cadeaux Genereux)
6813[5] 6926[5]

Hucking Harmony (IRE) *J R Best* a63 62
2 b f Spartacus(IRE) —Gute (IRE) (Petardia)
814[3] 1033[2] 2134[9] 2746[2] 3152[6] *3426[9]* 4026[5] 5452[3] *5887[11]*

Hucking Harrier (IRE) *J R Best* a33
2 ch c Hawk Wing(USA) —Dangerous Mind (IRE) (Platini (GER))
5895[11]

Hucking Heat (IRE) *J R Best* a73 67
3 b g Desert Sun—Vltava (IRE) (Sri Pekan (USA))
290[6] (738) 889[6] 1359[4] 1634[17] 2335[8] 3178[6] *3620[2]* 4137[14] *4884[11]* 5708[8] *5819[3] 6894[6] 6997[2] 7099[5] 7251[3]*

Hucking Heist *J R Best* 74
3 b g Desert Style(IRE) —Oriental Queen (GER) (Big Shuffle (USA))
(5315)

Hucking Hero (IRE) *J R Best* a74 64
2 b c Iron Mask(USA) —Selkirk Flyer (Selkirk (USA))
3424[10] 4028[3] *(6401) 6823[6] 6899[3] 6973[7] (7016)*

Hucking Hill (IRE) *J R Best* a77 71
3 ch g City On A Hill(USA) —Con Dancer (Shareef Dancer (USA))
2689[7] *3649[4]* 4236[9] *4740[4] 4885[2] 5684[2] 6122[8] 6232[10] 6970[10]*

Hucking Hope (IRE) *J R Best* a68 69
3 b f Desert Style(IRE) —Amarapura (FR) (Common Grounds)
2750[2] 3000[2] 3087[4] 3872[3] 4141[8] 4324[5] *5495[8] 6810[4] 7119[6] 7183[5]*

Hue *B Ellison* a64 76
6 ch g Peintre Celebre(USA) —Quandary (USA) (Blushing Groom (FR))
2860[11] 3027[3] 3577a[13] 4153[6] 4717[5] 5145[5] 5257[3] 5807[3] 6077[6]

Hughmanbean (IRE) *D Carroll*
4 ch g Elnadim(USA) —Madam Baileys (IRE) (Doulab (USA))
802[6] (Dead)

Hugo Quick *T M Jones* a52 49
3 b g Zaha(CAN) —Skedaddle (Formidable (USA))
3394[7] 3881[12] 4707[5] *5728[10]*

Hugs Destiny (IRE) *M A Barnes* a64 64
6 b g Victory Note(USA) —Embracing (Reference Point)
965[2] 1239[3] 1406[10] *(1732)* 1966[8] 2250[2] 2431[8] 3012[10] *3598[10]* 3815[3] 3840[6] (4558) *4670[4]* 4994[3] 5144[3] 5257[10] 6056[10]

Hugs 'n Kisses (IRE) *John Joseph Murphy* a71 81
3 ch f Noverre(USA) —La Dolores (GER) (Surumu (GER))
(7135)

Hujum (IRE) *J E Hammond* a85 102
3 b c Rock Of Gibraltar(IRE) —Clara Bow (FR) (Top Ville)
6614a[6]

Hula Ballew *M Dods* 86
7 ch m Weldnaas(USA) —Ballon (Persian Bold)
969[5] 1287[16] 1915[3] (2311) 2742[4] 3813[10] 4176[11] 4581[13] 4820[8] 5230[7] 5559[5] 5885[7]

Hula Hula *E A L Dunlop* a39 19
2 ch f Cadeaux Genereux—Eurolink Sundance (Night Shift (USA))
6409[14] *6734[7]*

Human Touch *E A L Dunlop* a21 42
2 b f Oasis Dream—Seltitude (IRE) (Fairy King (USA))
6295[12] *6998[10]*

Humble Janet (USA) *S Asmussen* a105
3 b f Humble Eleven(USA) —Humble Retha (USA) (Siberian Pine (USA))
3810a[4]

Humungous (IRE) *C R Egerton* a98 111
4 ch g Giant's Causeway(USA) —Doula (USA) (Gone West (USA))
550[8] 658[10] 1307[2] (2476) 2755[23] 4119[2] 4745[11] 5412[4] 6011[8] 6491[3]

Hunting Girl (GER) *T Reineke* 71
4 b m Key Of Luck(USA) —Helgalill (IRE) (Bering)
5850a[8]

Hunting Haze *Miss S E Hall* 64
4 b g Foxhound(USA) —Second Affair (IRE) (Pursuit Of Love)
1968[4] 3415[3] 5286[16] 6259[12]

Hunting Lodge (IRE) *H J Manners* a21 29
6 ch g Grand Lodge(USA) —Vijaya (USA) (Lear Fan (USA))
3903[5] 4421[5]

Hunting Tower *R Hannon* a86 89
3 b c Sadler's Wells(USA) —Fictitious (Machiavellian (USA))
1202[2] 1773[7] 2669[7] (3553) 4331[5] 4847[7] 5385[5] *6439[6]*

Hunt The Bottle (IRE) *B W Hills* 74
2 b c Bertolini(USA) —Zanoubia (USA) (Our Emblem (USA))
3462[3] 3878[3] 5042[4] (5771) 6128[10]

Hurlingham *M W Easterby* a92 87
3 b g Halling(USA) —Society (IRE) (Barathea (IRE))
(149) (275) 754[5] 1230[2] 4720[13] 5218[2] 6474[11]

Hurricane Coast *K McAuliffe* a68 74
8 b g Hurricane Sky(AUS) —Tread Carefully (Sharpo)
650[8] 5237[11]

Hurricane Dennis *Mike Murphy*
3 ch g Silver Wizard(USA) —Thatcher's Era (IRE) (Never So Bold)
3274[9]

Hurricane Fly (IRE) *J-L Pelletan* 112
3 b c Montjeu(IRE) —Scandisk (IRE) (Kenmare (FR))
1056a[8] 1593a[4] 2952a[7] 3987a[7]

Hurricane Harriet *R M H Cowell* 54
2 b f Bertolini(USA) —Cold Blow (Posse (USA))
4077[4]

Hurricane Hymnbook (USA) *B J Meehan* 88
2 b c Pulpit(USA) —April Squall (USA) (Summer Squall (USA))
(5428) 5828[2]

Hurricane James (IRE) *E Charpy* a79 90
5 bb h Night Shift(USA) —Ginger Candy (USA) (Hilal (IRE))
178a[11] 325a[15] 473a[10]

Hurricane Spirit (IRE) *J R Best* a106 77
3 b c Invincible Spirit(IRE) —Gale Warning (IRE) (Last Tycoon (IRE))
118[3] 760[2] 1473[24]

Hurricane Thomas (IRE) *M Johnston* a75 77
3 b g Celtic Swing—Viola Royale (IRE) (Royal Academy (USA))
3502[4] 3722[11] 4172[12] 4821[2] (5040) 5333[8] 5839[3]

Hurstpierpoint (IRE) *R A Fahey* a62 59
2 b f Night Shift(USA) —Double Gamble (Ela-Mana-Mou)
2371[4] 2758[7] 3205[5] 3838[7] 4524[6] 5298[9] *5644[2] 5818[2] 6150[13] 6566[2] 6814[2] 6933[6]*

Hustle (IRE) *R Hannon* 77
2 ch c Choisir(AUS) —Granny Kelly (USA) (Irish River (FR))
3478[9] 4201[3] (5091) 5597[4]

Huxley (IRE) *D J Wintle* a43 46
8 b g Danehill Dancer(IRE) —Biddy Mulligan (Ballad Rock)
18[7] 742[12] 1206[16] 4685[6] 5189[9] 6199[9]

Huzzah (IRE) *B W Hills* a87 87
2 b c Acclamation—Borders Belle (IRE) (Pursuit Of Love)
1201[4] 1832[7] 3552[4] 4121[2] *4946[2]* 5374[5] (5919) *6120[3]* 6486[4]

Hyde Lea Flyer *E S McMahon* 74
2 b c Hernando(FR) —Sea Ridge (Slip Anchor)
3957[4] 4547[9] 6106[2]

Hyde Park Flight (IRE) *C P Donoghue* a61 44
3 b g Tendulkar(USA) —Quaver (USA) (The Minstrel (CAN))
6555a[14]

Hyper Viper (IRE) *C Grant* a47 58
2 b g Atraf—Double Letter (IRE) (M Double M (USA))
1882[7] 2539[8] 3043[12] 3680[3] *4022[7]* 5268[3] 5572[2] 5904[7] 6379[15]

Hypnosis *D W Barker* a79 85
4 b m Mind Games—Salacious (Sallust)
(465) 964[2] (1427) 1854[10] 1861[3]

Hypnotic *D Nicholls* a71 87
5 ch g Lomitas—Hypnotize (Machiavellian (USA))
6571[1] 842[9] 2986[16] 5737[11]

Hypocrisy *Garvan Donnelly* a85 79
4 b m Bertolini(USA) —Glensara (Petoski)
(424) 590[3] 692[5] 5460a[19] *6997[3] 7158[4]*

Hypoteneuse (IRE) *Sir Michael Stoute* a52 81
3 b f Sadler's Wells(USA) —Phantom Gold (Machiavellian (USA))
1816[2] *2766[11]* (3367) 3719[3] 5229[3]

Hystericalady (USA) *J Hollendorfer* a116
4 ch m Distorted Humor(USA) —Sacramentada (CHI) (Northair (USA))
6512a[2]

Hythe Bay *J R Best* a77 74
3 b f Auction House(USA) —Ellway Queen (USA) (Bahri (USA))
1450[8] 2243[10] 2335[7] *2594[3]* 3086[3] 3449[5] 3879[4] 4712[2] 5066[5] 6279[8] *6976[7] 7054[2] 7119[7]*

Iamagrey (IRE) *J S Moore* a60 65
2 gr f Clodovil(IRE) —Xania (Mujtahid (USA))
942[3] 2122[3] *2349[8]* 3947[5] 5393a[7] 5706[6] *6242[7]*

Ibis (USA) *Saeed Bin Suroor* 17
2 bb f Empire Maker(USA) —Sunlit Silence (USA) (Trempolino (USA))
6306[13]

Ibn Khaldun (USA) *Saeed Bin Suroor* 118
2 ch c Dubai Destination(USA) —Gossamer (Sadler's Wells (USA))
4854[4] (5306) (5828) (6170) (6489)

Ibrox (IRE) *R M Whitaker* 61
2 b g Mujahid(USA) —Ling Lane (Slip Anchor)
5551[7] 6303[4] 6723[4]

Icannshift (IRE) *T M Jones* a54 64
7 b g Night Shift(USA) —Cannikin (IRE) (Lahib (USA))
615[4] (1026) 1319[6] *1590[8] 2176[5] 2595[9]* (3047) 4019[9] (4708) *5341[8]*

Icansingarainbow *R Hollinshead* a64 51
3 b g Rainbow High—Carole's Choir (Primo Dominie)
5346[8] *5754[3]* 6109[13]

Icaros (SWE) *Wido Neuroth* a78 99
4 b h Zafonic(USA) —Impetuous Air (Warning)
1648a[5] 2131a[4]

Ice And Fire *J T Stimpson* a61 69
8 b g Cadeaux Genereux—Tanz (IRE) (Sadler's Wells (USA))
146[9] 389[11] 6330[15] *6835[6] (7012) 7081[7]*

Ice Bellini *J M P Eustace* 61
2 ch f Erhaab(USA) —Peach Sorbet (IRE) (Spectrum (IRE))
6648[13]

Ice Box (IRE) *M Johnston* a57 69
3 ch f Pivotal—Thaisy (USA) (Tabasco Cat (USA))
93[4] 348[13] 1432[3] *2224[3]* (3540)

Ice Choice (IRE) *Mark Gillard* 68
2 b f Choisir(AUS) —London Pride (USA) (Lear Fan (USA))
4875[16] 5206[9] 5592[8] 6058[7] 6254[2]

Ice Cool Kitty (USA) *R Dutrow Jr* a74
4 ch m Tomorrows Cat(USA) —Icy Chris (USA) (Dispersal (USA))
5854a[7]

Iced Diamond (IRE) *S Wynne* a52 63
8 b g Petardia—Prime Site (IRE) (Burslem)
806[8] 1280[8] 1739[9] *3173[12]* 3414[7] 3534[8] 4685[13] *6859[12]*

Iced Tango *F Jordan* a37 44
3 gr g Verglas(IRE) —Tangolania (FR) (Ashkalani (IRE))
1297[10] 2341[3] 2697[10] 3686[13] 4337[13]

Icelandic *Frank Sheridan* 107
5 b g Selkirk(USA) —Icicle (Polar Falcon (USA))
2295a[2] (6767a)

Icemancometh (IRE) *Edward Lynam* a83 74
2 b g Marju(IRE) —Irina (IRE) (Polar Falcon (USA))
3438a[7]

Iceman George *D Morris* a67 68
3 b g Beat Hollow—Diebiedale (Dominion)
2836[12] (3248) 3709[10] 4365[11] 4735[6] *5604[5]* 6235[4] *6673[6]*

Ice Mountain *B Smart* 86
3 br g Kyllachy—Sulitelma (USA) (The Minstrel (CAN))
1160[8] 2119[2] 3493[7] 5039[14] 5473[8]

Iceni Princess *P Howling* a35 10
3 b f Victory Note(USA) —Swing Job (Ezzoud (IRE))
3387[14] 3800[9] *4392[13] 6147[9] 6583[9] 6817[8] 7120[11]*

Iceni Warrior *P Howling* a49 24
5 b g Lake Coniston(IRE) —Swing Job (Ezzoud (IRE))
18[5] 84[4] 558[2] 615[9] 716[12] 792[9] 1271[12] *1362[8]*

Ice Planet *D Nicholls* 98
6 b g Polar Falcon(USA) —Preference (Efisio)
1474[15] 1653[10] 2566[6] (2841) 3089[4] 3500[4] 4614[12] 5044[4]

I Certainly May *S Dow* a62 62
2 b g Royal Applause—Deep Ravine (USA) (Gulch (USA))
2539[13] 3471[13] 4151[15] *5127[12] 5423[2]* 5736[6] *5896[6] 7117[9]*

Icicariba (IRE) *F Losani* 62
3 b f Titus Livius(FR) —Ivy Cascade (IRE) (Sadler's Wells (USA))
6519a[11]

Icklingham (IRE) *C F Swan* 85
7 b g Sadler's Wells(USA) —Braiswick (King Of Spain)
4142a[5]

Icy Atlantic (USA) *T Pletcher* 110
6 b h Stormy Atlantic(USA) —Frosty Promise (USA) (Frosty The Snowman (USA))
5823a[7] 6511a[9]

Idarah (USA) *L Lungo* 94
4 gr g Aljabr(USA) —Fatina (Nashwan (USA))
5933[7]

Idealist (GER) *J Hirschberger* 102
5 b h Tiger Hill(IRE) —I Go Bye (GER) (Don't Forget Me)
5670a[4] 6045a[8] 6691a[3]

Ideally (IRE) *B W Hills* a74 88
3 ch g Mark Of Esteem(IRE) —Ideal Lady (IRE) (Seattle Slew (USA))
973[2] 2340[8] (3366) (4419) 4993[7] *5686[8]*

Idesia (IRE) *W R Swinburn* 65
3 b f Green Desert(USA) —Indaba (IRE) (Indian Ridge)
2693[11] 3387[5]

Idiot Proof (USA) *Clifford Sise Jr* a115
3 b c Benchmark(USA) —Perfectly Pretty (USA) (Bertrando (USA))
6510a[2]

Idle No More (USA) *J H M Gosden* a92 84
3 ch c Mr Greeley(USA) —Idle Rich (USA) (Sky Classic (CAN))
(1375) 2669[6] 4523[8]

Idle Power (IRE) *J R Boyle* a91 100
9 b g Common Grounds—Idle Fancy (Mujtahid (USA))
1242[9] 1474[9] 1653[18] 2237[7] 2688[4] 3104[3] *3623[2]* 4122[12] 4816[5] 5923[3] 6205[8] *6667[3]*

Idonea (CAN) *Mario Hofer* 97
2 ch f Swain(IRE) —Ivastar (CAN) (Alwasmi (USA))
(5463a)

I Dont Do Walkin (USA) *B J Meehan* a61 65
2 bb f Orientate(USA) —Impeachable Affair (USA) (Colonial Affair (USA))
1993[2] 2468[4] 2651[7] 5470[7] *5895[7] 6151[2] 6438[5] 6586[5]*

Idun *P W Chapple-Hyam* a44 50
3 b f Robellino(USA) —I Do (Selkirk (USA))
5803[5] *6211[5] 6904[5] 7268[9]*

Ifatfirst (IRE) *M P Tregoning* a65
4 b g Grand Lodge(USA) —Gaily Grecian (IRE) (Ela-Mana-Mou)
(212)

If Paradise *M Halford* a70 102
6 b g Compton Place—Sunley Stars (Sallust)
3573a[7] 5394a[3] 5841a[10] 6363a[19]

Iftikhar (USA) *S Wynne* a58 60
8 b g Storm Cat(USA) —Muhbubh (USA) (Blushing Groom (FR))
2595[P]

Ignition *W M Brisbourne* a61 64
5 ch m Rock City—Fire Sprite (Mummy's Game)
1534[12] 2168[12] (2760) 2938[7] (3675) 4159[10] 4219[9] 5086[7] 5674[9] 5964[10]

Igor Protti *A Wohler* 99
5 b h Opening Verse(USA) —La Busona (IRE) (Broken Hearted)
5670a[6]

Iguacu *J L Spearing* 57
3 b g Desert Prince(IRE) —Gay Gallanta (USA) (Woodman (USA))
4541[6] 4908[7] 5510[8]

Iguazu Falls (USA) *Saeed Bin Suroor* a90 106
2 ch c Pivotal—Anna Palariva (IRE) (Caerleon (USA))
4725[2] *(5337)* 5972[2] 6495[3]

I Have Dreamed (IRE) *T G Mills* a96 94
5 b g Montjeu(IRE) —Diamond Field (USA) (Mr Prospector (USA))
(726) 868[4] 1244[9] *2351[5] 2994[2]* 3509[5] *4888[2] 5205[8]* 5870[12]

Ikat (IRE) *D Sepulchre* 101
3 ch f Pivotal—Burning Sunset (Caerleon (USA))
1006a[0]

Ike Quebec (FR) *R Hannon* a76 65
2 ch c Dr Fong(USA) —Avezia (FR) (Night Shift (USA))
3967[7] 4500[3] *4963[2] 6898[2] (6973) 7202[2] (7246)*

Il Cadetto *L Di Dio* 105
3 b c Zieten(USA) —Nirvana (USA) (Green Dancer (USA))
1875a[5] 5821a[6] 6687a[3]

Il Castagno (IRE) *B Smart* a42 89
4 ch g Night Shift(USA) —Cartesian (Shirley Heights)
1133[3] 1555[2] 2311[3] (2536) 2936[2] 3813[12] 4176[7] 6016[8] 6560[8]

Ile Facile (IRE) *B De Haan* a74 75
6 b g Turtle Island(IRE) —Easy Pop (IRE) (Shernazar)
48[3] 263[8]

Ile Michel *Lady Herries* a69 60
10 b g Machiavellian(USA) —Circe's Isle (Be My Guest (USA))
1886[3] 2423[6] *(2875) 5132[3]* 5916[9] *6260[10]*

Ile Royale *C N Allen* a54 60
2 b f Royal Applause—Island Destiny (Kris)
2992[8] 3962[13] 4402[16] 5534[11] 5949[11] *6227[8] 6426[4] 6624[6] 6812[9] 7022[U] 7117[3] 7182[3] 7245[7]*

Ilie Nastase (FR) *R Gibson* a98 100
3 b c Royal Applause—Flying Diva (Chief Singer)
695a[4] 4216a[6]

I'll Do It Today *J M Jefferson* a60 63
6 b g Mtoto—Knayton Lass (Presidium)
618[4] (913) 1222[8] *5364[11] 6797[4]*

Illimani (GER) *A Trybuhl*
2 b c Next Desert(IRE) —Illamira (GER) (Local Suitor (USA))
6219a[8]

Illusionary *J G Portman* 43
2 b c Observatory(USA) —Tease (IRE) (Green Desert (USA))
2539[9] 2941[8] 3902[8]

Illustrious Blue *W J Knight* a112 113
4 bb h Dansili—Gipsy Moth (Efisio)
(413a) *761[3]* 1104[4] 1392[2] (1985) 5723[4] 6298[13] *6645[3]*

Iloveturtle (IRE) *M C Chapman* 45
7 b g Turtle Island(IRE) —Gan Ainm (IRE) (Mujadil (USA))
1196[6]

Ilviz (FR) *Ollie Pears* a57
5 gr g Medaaly—Move The Mouse (IRE) (Foxhound (USA))
7060[2] 7273[8]

Il Warrd (IRE) *M P Tregoning* 90
2 b c Pivotal—Demure (Machiavellian (USA))
1832[6] (3522) 4057[6]

I'm Agenius *C Roberts* a35 40
4 b m Killer Instinct—I'm Sophie (IRE) (Shalford (IRE))
4275[14] 4659[6] *5390[11] 5900[9]* 6420[P] *6642[8]*

Imagine (USA) *J Shirreffs* 102
4 bb m Giant's Causeway(USA) —Smooth Player (USA) (Bertrando (USA))
5825a[5]

Imaginemysurprise *J A Geake* a58 55
2 b f Mujadil(USA) —Anabaa's Music (Anabaa (USA))
3596[12] 4310[9] 4755[4] 5298[14] *6478[2] 6775[6] 6933[7] 7031[13] 7171[7]*

Imawildandcrazyguy (USA) *W Kaplan* a110 91
3 rg g Wild Event(USA) —Frosty Cupcake (USA) (Top Account (USA))
1486a[4] 2487a[6]

I'm In Love (USA) *K McLaughlin* a83 98
4 bb m Zafonic(USA) —Bank On Her (USA) (Rahy (USA))
6772a[2]

Immaculate Red *R Bastiman* a54 54
4 ch g Woodborough(USA) —Primula Bairn (Bairn (USA))
1349[9] 1719[9] 2206[7] 3752[7]

Imminent Victory *R M H Cowell* a52
4 b g Benny The Dip(USA) —Brave Vanessa (USA) (Private Account (USA))
6807[5] (6893) 7123[6]

Imonso (GER) *J Hirschberger* 106
4 br h Monsun(GER) —I Go Bye (GER) (Don't Forget Me)
881a[2] 4929a[5]

Im Ova Ere Dad (IRE) *D E Cantillon* a87 77
4 b g Second Empire(IRE) —Eurolink Profile (Prince Sabo)
(243) (461) 549[6] 2990[4] 3711[12] (4272) (4880) 5339[5] 6063[5] (6547) 6795[13] 6997[6] 7141[2]

Impeller (IRE) *J S Moore* a103 103
8 ch g Polish Precedent(USA) —Almaaseh (IRE) (Dancing Brave (USA))
175a[5] 329a[8] (398a) 544a[2] 701[3] 817[4] 940[7] 1245[5] 1477[8] 3899[7] 4720[10] (5049) 5631[7] 6011[17]

Impenetrable (USA) *Saeed Bin Suroor* a47 41
3 ch c Mr Greeley(USA) —Hard Knocker (USA) (Raja Baba (USA))
4666[11] 5499[7]

Imperial Amber *Karen George* a56
5 ch m Emperor Fountain—Bambolona (Bustino)
769[4] 1068[6] 6670[6] 6904[8]

Imperial Beach (USA) *T D Barron* 62
3 b g Coronado's Quest(USA) —Millie's Trick (USA) (Phone Trick (USA))
916[6] 1238[4] 1531[7] 1943[14] 2206[8]

Imperial Decree *John Berry* 71
2 b f Diktat—Docklands Princess (IRE) (Desert Prince (IRE))
3747[12] (4293) 4832a[9] 5571[4] 6410[10]

Imperial Echo (USA) *T D Barron* 91
6 b g Labeeb—Regal Baby (USA) (Northern Baby (CAN))
1157[2] 1458[8] 2744[4] 3091[3] 3559[2] 5584[11] 5617[6] 5804[4] 6301[14] 6560[6] 6753[20]

Imperial Forum *A Peraino*
2 gr c Mizzen Mast(USA) —Crockadore (USA) (Nijinsky (CAN))
6523a[11]

Imperial Gain (USA) *J M Bradley* a71 81
4 ch g High Yield(USA) —Empress Jackie (USA) (Mount Hagen (FR))
2088[8] 2546[7] 2725[8] 3350[10] 3828[8] 4395[16] 5190[15] 5982[9]

Imperial Harry *V Smith* a71 76
4 b g Alhaarth(IRE) —Serpentara (Kris)
1470[10] 1609[2] 1813[7] 2505[7] 2833[14] 4019[2] 4630[3]

Imperial Hills (IRE) *W P Mullins* 73
3 b g Imperial Ballet(IRE) —Sixhills (FR) (Sabrehill (USA))
6368a[13]

Imperial Ice (SAF) *H J Brown* a92 88
5 ch m Western Winter(USA) —Imperial Conquest (SAF) (Royal Chalice (SAF))
174a[5] 397a[13] 532a[15]

Imperialista (BRZ) *I Mohammed* a106
4 b h Voando Baixo(BRZ) —Zarumba Bis (BRZ) (Be My Chief (USA))
(177a) 399a[9] 599a[15]

Imperial Lucky (IRE) *D K Ivory* a76 64
4 b m Desert Story(IRE) —Irina (IRE) (Polar Falcon (USA))
150[4] 233[2] 358[5] 980[14] 1036[5] 1588[3] 4361[12] 4665[4] 4828[6]

Imperial Mark (IRE) *P J O'Gorman* a26 45
2 b c Mark Of Esteem(IRE) —Farhana (Fayruz)
4962[11] 5313[8] 6202[10]

Imperial Mint (IRE) *K A Ryan* 100
2 ch c Tagula(IRE) —Escudo (IRE) (Indian Ridge)
3192[2] (3589) 4046[7] 4721[4] (5032)

Imperial Quest *J R Fanshawe* 59
3 ch f Rainbow Quest(USA) —Imperial Bailiwick (IRE) (Imperial Frontier (USA))
5873[3] 6238[11]

Imperial Star (IRE) *J H M Gosden* a114 114
4 br h Fantastic Light(USA) —Out West (USA) (Gone West (USA))
(941) 1104[9] 1985[3] 4117[2] 4825[3] 5220[4]

Imperial Stride *Saeed Bin Suroor* 126
6 b h Indian Ridge—Place De L'Opera (Sadler's Wells (USA))
598a[10]

Imperial Sword *T D Barron* a48 93
4 b g Danehill Dancer(IRE) —Hajat (Mujtahid (USA))
3569[10] 4006[10] 4581[12] 4895[8] 6467[16] 7180[6]

Imperium *Jean-Rene Auvray* a73 68
6 b g Imperial Ballet(IRE) —Partenza (USA) (Red Ransom (USA))
70[2] 234[2] 346[2] 556[5] 650[6] 724[2] 793[4] (1564) 1969[8] 2492[6] 3396[6] 5348[4] 5711[8] 6476[8] 6950[2] 6993[5] 7183[9] 7268[3]

Impetious *Eamon Tyrrell* 100
3 b f Inchinor—Kauri (USA) (Woodman (USA))
1694a[S] 1958[3] 2926a[5] 3744[6] 4238a[8] 5794[10] 6216a[10]

Imply *J H M Gosden* a80 66
3 b c Beat Hollow—Insinuate (USA) (Mr Prospector (USA))
1100[7] (1440)

Impossible Dream (IRE) *A Kinsella* 84
3 b c Indian Danehill(IRE) —Recoleta (USA) (Wild Again (USA))
5460a[22]

Impossible Ski (BRZ) *A Cintra Pereira* a108
5 b h Ski Champ(USA) —Zapara (BRZ) (Restless Jet (USA))
177a[2] 599a[4]

Impostor (IRE) *R A Harris* a25 77
4 b g In The Wings—Princess Caraboo (IRE) (Alzao (USA))
7242[7]

Impressionnante *C Laffon-Parias* 114
4 b m Danehill(USA) —Occupandiste (IRE) (Kaldoun (FR))
4010a[8] 5259a[5] 6029a[11]

Imprimis Tagula (IRE) *A Bailey* a79 83
3 b g Tagula(IRE) —Strelitzia (IRE) (Bluebird (USA))
(505) (520) 1099[3]

Impromptu *R M Beckett* a69 86
3 b g Mujadil(USA) —Pie In The Sky (Bishop Of Cashel)
899[5] (3102) 3797[3] (4634) 4885[5] 5923[11]

Impure Thoughts *J R Best* a42
2 b c Averti(IRE) —Blooming Lucky (IRE) (Lucky Guest)
6850[11] 6926[10] 7264[10]

Im Spartacus *Evan Williams* a60 79
5 b g Namaqualand(USA) —Captivating (IRE) (Wolfhound (USA))
1578[2] (1638)

I'm Well (IRE) *Tracey Collins* a54 73
2 ch f Traditionally(USA) —See Me Well (IRE) (Common Grounds)
3659a[8]

Inaminute (IRE) *K R Burke* a76 81
4 ch m Spectrum(IRE) —Phantom Ring (Magic Ring (IRE))
979[2] 1157[11] 2085[8] (2988) 3670[5] 3953[5] 4589[8] 5907[10] 6560[4] 6753[21]

In A Pickle *H J L Dunlop* a57 50
2 ch f Piccolo—Magic Hanne (Magic Ring (IRE))
3874[7] 4761[13] 5126[5] 5815[5] 6065[2] 6386[5]

Inasus (GER) *M Johnston* 63
3 ch c Kornado—Instinctive Dancer (USA) (Spend A Buck (USA))
1491[2] 4563[2]

Incanto Dream *C Lerner* 99
3 ch c Galileo(IRE) —Atlantic Blue (USA) (Nureyev (USA))
2751a[5] 6941a[3]

Incarnation (IRE) *J G Given* 53
2 b f Samum(GER) —River Patrol (Rousillon (USA))
5328[5] 5801[8]

Inca Soldier (FR) *R C Guest* a65 70
4 br g Intikhab(USA) —Chrysalu (Distant Relative)
467[9] 586[7] 682[7] 812[3] 1132[10] (1360) 1933[10] 2033[4] 2302[7] 2762[3] (2864) 3017[8] 3414[2] 3723[6] (4423) 4562[5] 4942[3] 7158[6] 7271[4]

Inch By Inch *P J Makin* a78 80
8 b m Inchinor—Maid Welcome (Mummy's Pet)
262[2] 486[3] 774[9]

Inchcape Rock *W K Goldsworthy* 39
5 ch g Inchinor—Washm (USA) (Diesis)
3365[12]

Inchdhuaig (IRE) *P C Haslam* 54
4 ch g Inchinor—Be Thankfull (IRE) (Linamix (FR))
1671[3] 2372[10]

Inchigeelagh (IRE) *H Morrison* a51 50
3 ch f Inchinor—Thank One's Stars (Alzao (USA))
535[10]

Inchinata (IRE) *B W Hills* a76 81
3 b f Inchinor—Caviare (Cadeaux Genereux)
2625[7] (3214) 3993[3] 4617[5] 5415[11] 6422[3]

Inching West *C J Down* 22
5 ch m Inchinor—Key West (FR) (Highest Honor (FR))
4357[8]

Inchlaggan (IRE) *B W Hills* 71
3 ch g Inchinor—Lakatoi (Saddlers' Hall (IRE))
1077[2] 1659[4] 4568[5] 5450[3]

Inchloch *B G Powell* a89 91
5 ch g Inchinor—Lake Pleasant (IRE) (Elegant Air)
587[5] 5870[5] 6490[4] 6759[13]

Inch Lodge *Miss D Mountain* a83 72
5 ch h Grand Lodge(USA) —Legaya (Shirley Heights)
652[14]

Inchloss (IRE) *S Parr* a37 52
6 b g Imperial Ballet(IRE) —Earth Charter (Slip Anchor)
2145[12] 2370[8] 2810[6] 3397[13] 5300[12]

Inchmahome *E F Vaughan* a62 67
4 b m Galileo(IRE) —Inchmurrin (Lomond (USA))
1312[8] (1926) 2692[7] 4131[9]

Inchmarlow (IRE) *T H Caldwell* a43 51
4 b g Cape Cross(IRE) —Glenstal Priory (Glenstal (USA))
5625[8] 7103[10]

Inchnadamph *T J Fitzgerald* a53 93
7 b g Inchinor—Pelf (USA) (Al Nasr (FR))
1794[10] 2736[12] (3412) 4569[3] 5215[12] 6335[5] (6760)

Inchpast *M H Tompkins* a84 72
6 ch g Inchinor—Victor Ludorum (Rainbow Quest (USA))
5574[8] 6014[15] 6383[3] 6622[5] (6802) (7008)

Inchwall *Peter Grayson* a50
3 ch g Inchinor—Spoilt Again (Mummy's Pet)
295[7] 633[9] 832[12]

Inchwood (IRE) *M A Jarvis* 71
2 b f Dubai Destination(USA) —Inchiri (Sadler's Wells (USA))
5912[5] 6414[5]

Incline (IRE) *R McGlinchey* a102 106
8 b g Danehill(USA) —Shalwar Kameez (IRE) (Sadler's Wells (USA))
(4051a)

Incoming Call (USA) *Sir Michael Stoute* 53
3 b f Red Ransom(USA) —Private Line (USA) (Private Account (USA))
1482[3]

Incomparable *A J McCabe* 77
2 ch c Compton Place—Indian Silk (IRE) (Dolphin Street (FR))
2832[4] 6281[5] 6595[2] (6754)

Indanehill (IRE) *P Monfort* a84 85
5 b m Indian Danehill(IRE) —English Rose (FR) (Caerleon (USA))
6923a[0]

Indared *M Mullineaux*
3 ch c Daggers Drawn(USA) —Bogus John (CAN) (Blushing John (USA))
5781[10] 6070[8]

Indecision *M W Easterby* a28 58
2 b g Muhtarram(USA) —Emma Amour (Emarati (USA))
1087[11] 1713[11] 1857[3] (2838) 3296[2] 3751[3] 3835[4] 4136[7] 4783[6]

In Decorum *J A Geake* a41 51
2 gr f Averti(IRE) —Decorous (IRE) (Runnett)
814[8] 1960[9] 2539[10] 3446[11] 5715[10] 6812[13] 7182[4]

In Deep *Mrs P N Dutfield* a46 45
6 b m Deploy—Bobbie Dee (Blakeney)
2770[8] 4067[11]

Independent George (USA) *H G Motion* 104
4 rg g Cozzene(USA) —Daylight Ridge (USA) (Dayjur (USA))
6924a[8]

Indiana Gal (IRE) *Patrick Martin* 93
2 b f Intikhab(USA) —Genial Jenny (IRE) (Danehill (USA))
5843a[3]

Indian Blessing (USA) *B Baffert* a114
2 bb f Indian Charlie(USA) —Shameful (USA) (Flying Chevron (USA))
(6507a)

Indian Chase *Dr J R J Naylor* a55 55
10 b g Terimon—Icy Gunner (Gunner B)
1229[11]

Indian Choice (USA) *P Bary* a92 111
3 b g With Approval(CAN) —Cheyenne Dream (Dancing Brave (USA))
5661a[2]

Indian Days *J G Given* 79
2 ch c Daylami(IRE) —Cap Coz (IRE) (Indian Ridge)
2575[8] 2941[10] 3712[4] 4776[7] (5053) 5828[10] 6471[8]

Indian Diva (IRE) *P A Blockley* a79 68
2 b f Indian Danehill(IRE) —Katherine Gorge (USA) (Hansel (USA))
6082[4] (6403) 6756[13]

Indian Edge *B Palling* a69 79
6 ch g Indian Rocket—Beveled Edge (Beveled (USA))
1064[5] (1366) 1765[6] 2107[4] 2722[2] 2979[2] (3487) 4657[7] 6203[12] 6423[16]

Indian Ink (IRE) *R Hannon* 121
3 ch f Indian Ridge—Maid Of Killeen (IRE) (Darshaan)
1146[2] 1496[5] (2814)

Indian Lady (IRE) *Mrs A L M King* a43 64
4 b m Namid—Lady Eberspacher (IRE) (Royal Abjar (USA))
1309[11]

Indiannie Moon *M R Channon* 18
3 b f Fraam—Ajig Dancer (Niniski (USA))
2962[6]

Indian Princess (IRE) *P Van De Poele* a96 81
4 b m Mujadil(USA) —Mary Linda (Grand Lodge (USA))
31a[4]

Indian's Feather (IRE) *N Tinkler* a80 82
6 ch m Indian Ridge—Mashmoum (Lycius (USA))
1265[8] (1352) 1568[3] 1979[3] (2347) 2568[2] 2883[5] (3247) 3715[3] 3943[8] 4665[6] 5223[3] 5532[7] 5907[3] 6232[12]

Indian Skipper (IRE) *M H Tompkins* 66
2 b c Indian Danehill(IRE) —Rosy Lydgate (Last Tycoon (IRE))
6294[7]

Indian Spark *J S Goldie* 77
13 ch g Indian Ridge—Annes Gift (Ballymoss)
3345[10] 3787[15] 4379[4] 4934[5] 5284[11] 5930[9] 6467[17]

Indian Spring (IRE) *D Smaga* a89 105
3 bl c Indian Danehill(IRE) —Lille Hammer (Sadler's Wells (USA))
2293a[10]

Indian Sundance (IRE) *K R Burke* a53 36
4 b g Namid—Can't Afford It (IRE) (Glow (USA))
281[2] 580[10] 746[8] 5782[8] 6266[12]

Indian Trail *D Nicholls* a93 113
7 ch g Indian Ridge—Take Heart (Electric)
1041[12] 1474[25] 1826[10] 2237[13] 2817[13] 3481[3] 3720[7] 4095[8] 4122[3] 4614[3] (5050) (5212) 5616[8]

Indian Vale (CAN) *T Pletcher* a117 116
5 ch m A.P. Indy(USA) —Marley Vale (USA) (Forty Niner (USA))
5854a[2] 6512a[9]

Indigo Blue (FR) *J-P Gallorini* 94
2 b c Night Shift(USA) —Eye Witness (IRE) (Don't Forget Me)
6939a[4]

Indigo Dancer *C F Wall* a51 49
4 b g Groom Dancer(USA) —Violet (IRE) (Mukaddamah (USA))
187[2] 309[8]

Indigo Mail (IRE) *M Brittain*
2 b g Modigliani(USA) —Vieux Carre (Pas De Seul)
5226[8]

Indigo Rose (IRE) *J H M Gosden* a62 64
3 b f Cadeaux Genereux—Colourfast (IRE) (Spectrum (IRE))
4457[6] 4765[5] 5271[7]

Indochine (BRZ) *A De Royer-Dupre* a86 107
4 ch m Special Nash(IRE) —Binoche (BRZ) (Kenetico (BRZ))
(174a) 476a[12] 4012a[6] 4929a[4]

Indonesia *T D Walford* a68 82
5 ch g Lomitas—Idraak (Kris)
2047[2] 2505[3] 3412[4] 3748[8] 4786[2] (5561) 6335[27]

In Dream's (IRE) *G M Moore* 34
5 b g Dr Fong(USA) —No Sugar Baby (FR) (Crystal Glitters (USA))
913[12]

In Dubai (USA) *D Selvaratnam* a80 84
4 ch m Giant's Causeway(USA) —Bahr (Generous (IRE))
397a[14]

Industrial Star (IRE) *Micky Hammond* 74
6 ch g Singspiel(IRE) —Faribole (IRE) (Esprit Du Nord (USA))
(2375) 3027[7] 4179[2] 4490[5] 5256[4]

Indy Driver *J R Fanshawe* 19
2 ch c Domedriver(IRE) —Condoleezza (USA) (Cozzene (USA))
4130[13]

Indy Wind (USA) *Amy Tarrant* a94 105
5 ch h A.P. Indy(USA) —Zagora (USA) (Kingmambo (USA))
5855a[6]

Infallible *J H M Gosden* 75
2 b f Pivotal—Irresistible (Cadeaux Genereux)
(6649)

Infidel (IRE) *J R Best* a35 20
7 b g Spectrum(IRE) —Implicit View (Persian Bold)
1347[11] 1925[9]

Infinite Patience *J S Moore* a15 66
2 bb f High Chaparral(IRE) —Idma (Midyan (USA))
2768[12] 3796[5] 4094[13] 6012[6] 6379[10] 6572[7]

Inflagrantedelicto (USA) *D W Chapman* a63 18
3 ch g Gentlemen(ARG) —Imprudent Love (USA) (Foolish Pleasure (USA))
284[6] 684[8] 1030[6] 3377[12] 3411[12]

Ingleby Arch (USA) *T D Barron* a92 102
4 b g Arch(USA) —Inca Dove (USA) (Mr Prospector (USA))
1826[5] 2058[3] 2566[3] 2817[12] 3500[3] 3941[9] 4401[11] 5254[8] 5356[4] 6836[12] 6981[5] (7126)

Ingleby Hill (IRE) *T D Barron* a51 50
3 b g Averti(IRE) —Living Daylights (IRE) (Night Shift (USA))
910[2] 1579[7] 2096[7] 2538[9] 3159[10] 4821[12] 4943[11]

Ingleby Princess *T D Barron* 78
3 br f Bold Edge—Bob's Princess (Bob's Return (IRE))
1658[4] 3557[6] 3952[6] 4940[5] 5232[12] 6020[9] 6559[5]

Ingleby Star (IRE) *T D Barron* a67 78
2 b g Fath(USA) —Rosy Scintilla (IRE) (Thatching)
1107[10] (1454) 1772[7] 6977[9] 7106[4]

Ingratitude (IRE) *N J Henderson* 94
4 ch g Inchinor—Merci (IRE) (Cadeaux Genereux)
3002[3]

In Honour (IRE) *E S McMahon* 85
2 b c Spartacus(IRE) —Andkit (USA) (Alleged (USA))
1150[4] 1454[3] 3718[3] (4181) 4695[10]

Inimical *W S Kittow* a42 53
3 b f Daggers Drawn(USA) —Mara River (Efisio)
1731[11] 2489[5] 3490[5] 4071[7]

Inka Dancer (IRE) *B Palling* a64 70
5 ch m Intikhab(USA) —Grannys Reluctance (IRE) (Anita's Prince)
1118[10] 2217[5] (4397) 4545[2] 5741[8] 6239[14] 6476[5] 6747[6] 6927[2] 7033[6]

Inkjet (IRE) *P D Evans* a54 25
3 b f Beckett(IRE) —Aussie Aisle (IRE) (Godswalk (USA))
(108) 202[8] 6402[12] 6608[13] 6796[12]

Ink Spot *M L W Bell* 77
2 b g Diktat—Good Girl (IRE) (College Chapel)
1201[8] 1938[2] 2303[2] 3192[3] 5613[10]

Inner Voice (USA) *J J Lambe* a52 57
4 gr g Cozzene(USA) —Miss Henderson Co (USA) (Silver Hawk (USA))
5285[3]

Inn For The Dancer *J C Fox* a54 38
5 b g Groom Dancer(USA) —Lady Joyce (FR) (Galetto (FR))
1254[4] 1592[6]

Inontime (IRE) *K R Burke* a59
2 ch f Golan(IRE) —Phantom Ring (Magic Ring (IRE))
6799[6] 7058[3]

Inourthoughts (IRE) *Francis Ennis* a79 103
3 b f Desert Style(IRE) —Inourhearts (IRE) (Pips Pride)
1171a[7] 5392a[2] 5841a[2]

Inquisitress *J J Bridger* a69 75
3 b f Hernando(FR) —Caribbean Star (Soviet Star (USA))
27[5] 382[6] 502[7] 737[9] 885[8] 1316[3] 1634[11] 2178[4] 2571[4] 2668[2] 3620[6] 4064[7] 4269[6] 4474[3] 4684[9] 5420[5] (5528) 6123[11] 6226[6] 6579[9] 6716[3] 6894[8] 6945[9]

Insaaf *W J Haggas* 90
2 b f Averti(IRE) —Molly Brown (Rudimentary (USA))
5766[4] (6295) 6619[9]

In Safe Hands (IRE) *C G Cox* 94
3 ch f Intikhab(USA) —Safiya (USA) (Riverman (USA))
(1639) 1809[2] 2757[5] 3028[2] 3460[19] 5047[14] 6216a[7]

Inscribed (IRE) *G A Huffer* a53 51
4 b m Fasliyev(USA) —Fay (IRE) (Polish Precedent (USA))
186[4] 557[9] 680[5] 798[3] 3393[7] 3667[5] 4029[15] 5090[2] 5336[9]

Inside Story (IRE) *M W Easterby* a76 82
5 b g Rossini(USA) —Sliding (Formidable (USA))
142[3] 297[10] 2338[5] 2527[3] 2822[6] (3922) (4353) 4577[4] 5255[3] 5838[3] 6121[5] 7018[6] 7160[4]

Insignia (IRE) *W M Brisbourne* a52 53
5 b g Royal Applause—Amathea (FR) (Exit To Nowhere (USA))
321[5] 425[3] 620[11] 666[6]

Insiyaabi (USA) *J L Dunlop* 74
3 b c Aljabr(USA) —Elle Seule (USA) (Exclusive Native (USA))
2880[4] 3710[8]

Insomnitas *M G Quinlan* a52 51
2 b c Lomitas—Sleepless (Night Shift (USA))
1846[8] 2151[5] 2618[4] 3642[6] 4524[7] 6202[8] 6433[8]

Inspainagain (USA) *T D Barron* 75
3 ch g Miswaki(USA) —Counter Cat (USA) (Hennessy (USA))
1403[4] 2844[4] (2939) 4001[2] 4452[8] 6743[7]

Inspector Clouseau (IRE) *T P Tate* 73
2 gr g Daylami(IRE) —Claustra (FR) (Green Desert (USA))
3510[4] 4890[2] (5502)

Inspirina (IRE) *R Ford* 73
3 b c Invincible Spirit(IRE) —La Stellina (IRE) (Marju (IRE))
6731[7]

Instantly (IRE) *W Jarvis* a33 46
3 b f Dansili—Wigging (Warning)
2429[9] 6005[10]

Instant Recall (IRE) *M Al Muhairi* a96 80
6 ch g Indian Ridge—Happy Memories (IRE) (Thatching)
597a[11]

Instinct *Micky Hammond* a37 35
6 b g Zafonic(USA) —Gracious Gift (Cadeaux Genereux)
1423[10]

Institute *Sir Michael Stoute* 77
2 ch c Pivotal—Constitute (USA) (Gone West (USA))
6468[6]

Instructor *R A Fahey* a88 87
6 ch g Groom Dancer(USA) —Doctor's Glory (USA) (Elmaamul (USA))
1149[3] 1494[4] 3989[10] 6180[15]

Insubordinate *J S Goldie* a27 66
6 ch g Subordination(USA) —Manila Selection (USA) (Manila (USA))
3783[9] 4099[7] 5479[7] 6732[13]

Insured *A J McCabe* a46 41
2 ch g Intikhab(USA) —Self Assured (IRE) (Ahonoora)
1201[10] *2569[8]*

Intabih (USA) *C E Brittain* 65
2 bb c More Than Ready(USA) —Lookaway Dixieland (USA) (Dixieland Band (USA))
5140[7]

Intavac Boy *S P Griffiths* a61 65
6 ch g Emperor Fountain—Altaia (FR) (Sicyos (USA))
7424 997[3] 1042[5] 1532[7] *4025[2]* 4340[4] 4972[5] 5286[14] 5750[7] 6056[6] 6330[11] 6558[2] *6613[2] 6937[8] 7060[5] 7219[6]*

Integral (GER) *P Rau* 55
3 b c Lando(GER) —Incenza (GER) (Local Suitor (USA))
4958a[6]

Integration *Miss M E Rowland* a44 44
7 b g Piccolo—Discrimination (Efisio)
64[7] 203[4] 615[7] 2946[7] 6797[7]

Intensifier (IRE) *P A Blockley* a61 56
3 b c Sinndar(IRE) —Licorne (Sadler's Wells (USA))
149[5] 304[6] 893[11] *1353[3]* 2105[9] 4156[2] 4339[7] *6387[4] 6506[5] 6534[2]*

Interactive (IRE) *Andrew Turnell* a75 40
4 b g King's Best(USA) —Forentia (Formidable (USA))
1001[11] 5873[11] *6546[4] 6858[4] 7269[4]*

Interest (USA) *T D Barron* a29 41
3 ch g Banker's Gold(USA) —Princess Kris (Kris)
373[9]

Inter Mondo (GER) *P Rau* 105
4 ch g Hondo Mondo(IRE) —In Natura (GER) (Monsun (GER))
5821a[10]

Internationaldebut (IRE) *D J Murphy* 93
2 b c High Chaparral(IRE) —Whisper Light (IRE) (Caerleon (USA))
5323[2] 5580[13] 6489[9]

Interpatation (USA) *Robert Barbara* 114
5 b g Langfuhr(CAN) —Idealistic Cause (USA) (Habitony)
5853a[3]

Intersky Charm (USA) *R M Whitaker* a44 71
3 ch c Lure(USA) —Catala (USA) (Northern Park (USA))
1412[4] 1863[5] *7282[9]*

Intersky Melody (USA) *R M Whitaker* a68 41
2 b g Sky Mesa(USA) —Mayan Maiden (USA) (Lyphard (USA))
3596[5] 4192[8] 4448[10] *5601[10]*

Intersky Music (USA) *Jonjo O'Neill* 53
4 b g Victory Gallop(CAN) —Resounding Grace (USA) (Thunder Gulch (USA))
1012[6] 4334[6]

Intersky Sports (USA) *K J Burke* a69 63
3 gr g Chester House(USA) —Nightlong (Night Shift (USA))
(76) 335[4] 491[2] 694[8] 7057[6] 7104[7]

Inter Vision (USA) *A Dickman* a96 99
7 b g Cryptoclearance(USA) —Fateful (USA) (Topsider (USA))
3050[11] 3515[8] 3720[11] 3953[11] 4227[2] 4581[9] 4696[12] 5044[6] (5379) (5505) 5804[8] *5891[5]*

In The Fashion (IRE) *H Rogers* 90
4 b m In The Wings—Tropical Lass (IRE) (Ballad Rock)
3578a[10]

In The Light *A Fabre* a91 100
3 b f Inchinor—Exclusive Approval (USA) (With Approval (CAN))
6889a[2] *7049a[3]*

Intimate Friend (USA) *Miss Diana Weeden* a33 40
6 b m Expelled(USA) —Intimate (USA) (Topsider (USA))
22[11] 210[11] 4336[6] 4596[4]

Intiquilla (IRE) *Mrs A J Perrett* 88
3 b f Galileo(IRE) —Orinoco (IRE) (Darshaan)
(1505) (2112) 2999[10] 4113[7] 5940[3] 6757[7] 6953a[0]

Inti Raimi (JPN) *S Sasaki* 121
5 b h Special Week(JPN) —Andes Lady (JPN) (Northern Taste (CAN))
6943a[10]

Into Action *R Hannon* a66 73
3 b c Sendawar(IRE) —Syrian Dancer (IRE) (Groom Dancer (USA))
553[2] 1012[8] 1205[8] 2628[11] 3473[4] 3653[2] *3945[13]* 4322[8] 4531[9] 4809[8] *6271[7]*

Into The Dark *Saeed Bin Suroor* a108 116
6 ch g Rainbow Quest(USA) —Land Of Dreams (Cadeaux Genereux)
1985[5] 2216[4] 5618[8] *6645[2]*

Intrepid Jack *H Morrison* a112 112
5 b h Compton Place—Maria Theresa (Primo Dominie)
1836[2] *2352[2]* 2858[2] 3505[17] 4150[10]

Intricate Dance (USA) *B W Hills* 43
3 b f Aptitude(USA) —Clog Dance (Pursuit Of Love)
1128[12] 1425[6]

Intricate Web (IRE) *E J Alston* a60 20
11 b g Warning—In Anticipation (IRE) (Sadler's Wells (USA))
481[4] 674[4]

In Uniform *E S McMahon* 88
2 b c Royal Applause—Scarlet Plume (Warning)
(1367) 2316[3] 3147a[6] 3910[5] (5699)

Invasian (IRE) *P W D'Arcy* a96 93
6 ch g Desert Prince(IRE) —Jarrayan (Machiavellian (USA))
3002[8] 3899[6] (4171) 4690[7] *5205[3]* 5631[5] 6014[9] 6337[7] *6765[6] 6994[3] (7147)*

Invasor (ARG) *K McLaughlin* a132
5 br h Candy Stripes(USA) —Quendom (ARG) (Interprete (ARG))
(863a)

Invention (USA) *Miss E C Lavelle* a89 93
4 b g Lear Fan(USA) —Carya (USA) (Northern Dancer (CAN))
763[4] 940[9] 2123[4] 3002[7] 4153[12]

Inventor (IRE) *B J Meehan* 79
2 b c Alzao(USA) —Magnificent Bell (IRE) (Octagonal (NZ))
5011[9] 5599[3] (5858)

Inverted *Mrs A J Duffield* a47
3 b g Averti(IRE) —Indian Silk (IRE) (Dolphin Street (FR))
222[9] 713[11]

Investment Pearl (IRE) *D R Gandolfo* a23 67
4 b m Desert Sun—Superb Investment (IRE) (Hatim (USA))
1378[8] 2721[9] 3901[14] 4757[3] *5389[11]* (Dead)

Investor (IRE) *G Martin* a95 81
8 b g Marju(IRE) —Shine On Me (Machiavellian (USA))
356a[10]

Invincible Ash (IRE) *M Halford* 79
2 b f Invincible Spirit(IRE) —Fully Fashioned (IRE) (Brief Truce (USA))
4832a[2]

Invincible Force (IRE) *Paul Green* a100 101
3 b g Invincible Spirit(IRE) —Highly Respected (IRE) (High Estate)
1656[9] 2035[8] 3529[7] 3975[6] 4196[3] 4374[7] 4726[17] 5212[8] (5394a) 5810[5] 6183[11] 6327[7] *6676[3] 6876[9]*

Invincible Hero (FR) *A Wohler* 74
3 ch c Lomitas—Indiaca (GER) (Sanglamore (USA))
3146a[14]

Invincible Lad (IRE) *E J Alston* 56
3 b g Invincible Spirit(IRE) —Lady Ellen (Horage)
2393[9] 3537[4] 3846[2] 4224[14] 4384[9]

Invincible Rose (IRE) *M Brittain* 45
2 b f Invincible Spirit(IRE) —Yorkshire Rose (IRE) (Sadler's Wells (USA))
1848[8] 2818[5] 3560[5] 3951[6] 5226[6]

Invincible Star (IRE) *Peter Casey* a47 68
3 b f Invincible Spirit(IRE) —Feather Star (Soviet Star (USA))
5696a[3]

Invincible Woman (IRE) *Ms F M Crowley* a78 92
2 b f Invincible Spirit(IRE) —Lady Helen (IRE) (Salse (USA))
3071a[7]

Inwaan (IRE) *P R Webber* a68 71
4 b g King's Best(USA) —Balaabel (USA) (Sadler's Wells (USA))
211[12] 548[6] 751[2] 803[12] 1080[3] 1681[3] *1946[10]* 2664[4] 6424[7] *6607[8]*

Inwood (IRE) *Paul Magnier* 84
4 b h Bluebird(USA) —Hardshan (IRE) (Warrshan (USA))
4836a[18]

Inxile (IRE) *D Nicholls* 86
2 b g Fayruz—Grandel (Owington)
(5192)

Inzone (IRE) *K J Condon* a85 85
2 b f Fayruz—Royal Interlude (IRE) (King's Theatre (IRE))
1546a[4] 2049a[6] 6392a[6]

Io (IRE) *J L Dunlop* 58
2 b f King's Best(USA) —Callisto (IRE) (Darshaan)
5592[7] 5937[8] 6494[11]

Ioannina *J Hirschberger* 111
4 br m Rainbow Quest(USA) —Iora (GER) (Konigsstuhl (GER))
4651a[2] 5671a[3] 6030a[8] 6781a[7]

Iolanthe *B J Meehan* a72 72
3 ch f Vettori(IRE) —Shakalaka Baby (Nashwan (USA))
1127[12] 1355[8] *1628[2]* 1887[9] 3351[2] *3731[5]* 4112[3] 4632[9] 5279[9]

Ionian *Pat Eddery* a69 63
4 b g Piccolo—Aegean Flame (Anshan)
1904[3] 2581[6] 2913[5] 3711[7] *4462[8] 5019[7]*

Ionian Spring (IRE) *D Carroll* a68 86
12 b g Ela-Mana-Mou—Well Head (IRE) (Sadler's Wells (USA))
35[5] 305[2] (464)

Ioweyou *J S Moore* a58 62
3 ch f Noverre(USA) —Cuore Di Aliante (Alhijaz)
34[6] 348[12] 574[2] 786[2] 798[2] 970[5] *1248[2] 1313[2]* 1738[5] 2444[4] *2950[6]*

I Predict A Riot (IRE) *J W Hills* a51 75
3 b g Danehill Dancer(IRE) —Manon's Song (IRE) (Sadler's Wells (USA))
1062[5] 1611[3] 2628[5] 3473[2] 4511[6] *4951[6]* 5637[2] 6235[8]

Ireland Dancer (IRE) *P M Phelan* a55 65
3 ch g Trans Island—Come Dancing (Suave Dancer (USA))
655[8] 924[5] 2178[6] 2545[13]

Ireland's Call (IRE) *Peter Casey* a88 97
6 gr g King's Theatre(IRE) —Tarikhana (Mouktar)
1184a[8] 1461a[6] 3140a[16] *4864a[5]* 5242a[7] *5761a[4]*

Irene Watts *F Folco* 101
4 ch m Miswaki Tern(USA) —Iregirl (IRE) (Simply Great (FR))
2296a[3]

Irish Artist (FR) *R Hannon* a58 70
2 b c Orpen(USA) —Anchusa (IRE) (Nashwan (USA))
2624[6] *4882[8]* 5010[6] 6410[6]

Irish Cape *Mrs N Smith* a40
4 br m Cape Cross(IRE) —Praglia (IRE) (Darshaan)
6546[9]

Irish Conection (IRE) *T McLaughlin* a51
4 b g Bold Fact(USA) —Trojan Girl (IRE) (Up And At 'Em)
7019[4] 7239[5]

Irish Dancer *J L Dunlop* 66
3 b f Danehill Dancer(IRE) —Gaelic Swan (IRE) (Nashwan (USA))
1024[3] 1536[5] 2112[5] 2445[4] 3150[10] 5347[5] 5865[7]

Irish Jig (IRE) *G M Lyons* 100
2 b c Celtic Swing—Siem Reap (USA) (El Gran Senor (USA))
779a[3] 2232[8] 3141a[3]

Irish Mayhem (USA) *B J Meehan* 85
2 bb c Woodman(USA) —Adventurous Di (USA) (Private Account (USA))
5010[13] 5538[3] 6296[2]

Irish Mickey *James Moffatt* 14
3 b g City On A Hill(USA) —Game Leader (IRE) (Mukaddamah (USA))
1197[15] 2826[8]

Irish Music (IRE) *A P Jarvis* a64
2 b c Namid—Kelly's Tune (Alhaarth (IRE))
7264[6]

Irish Pearl (IRE) *K R Burke* 89
2 b f Statue Of Liberty(USA) —Helen Wells (IRE) (Sadler's Wells (USA))
3916[5] (4662) 5614[9] 6619[6]

Irish Plane (IRE) *K R Burke* 31
3 b g Barathea(IRE) —Stem The Tide (USA) (Proud Truth (USA))
1290[11] 1804[10]

Irish Quest (IRE) *M A Jarvis* 88
3 b c Galileo(IRE) —No Quest (IRE) (Rainbow Quest (USA))
2127[13] 2402[8] 2726[9] 3367[3] 4113[2] (4809) (5333) 5574[2] 5955[8]

Irish Relative (IRE) *T D Barron* a47 47
3 b g Indian Lodge(IRE) —The Good Life (IRE) (Rainbow Quest (USA))
76[5] 223[5] 469[6] 708[4] 1301[3] 1712[13] 2116[4] 2796[7] 3377[3]

Irish Secret (CZE) *G J Smith* a13
3 ch g Secret 'n Classy(CAN) —Irska Sipka (IRE) (Mukaddamah (USA))
769[11] 1566[13]

Irish Smoke (USA) *F Parisel* a82 108
2 rg f Smoke Glacken(USA) —Added Time (USA) (Gilded Time (USA))
6507a[12]

Irish Wells (FR) *F Rohaut* 120
4 b h Poliglote—Sign Of The Vine (FR) (Kendor (FR))
880a[3] 1340a[2] 2292a[4] 2925a[4] (4872a) 6374a[10]

Irish Whispers (IRE) *B G Powell* a60 63
4 b g Marju(IRE) —Muneera (USA) (Green Dancer (USA))
775[10]

Iron Cross (IRE) *Sir Mark Prescott* 46
2 b g Cape Cross(IRE) —Alithini (IRE) (Darshaan)
5541[12] 5904[12] 6451[10]

Iron Dancer (IRE) *P A Blockley* a50 43
3 b c Iron Mask(USA) —Sin Lucha (USA) (Northfields (USA))
900[8] *1164[2] 1281[6] 5528[11]* 6408[7]

Iron Lips *C Laffon-Parias* 103
3 b f Iron Mask(USA) —Icelips (USA) (Unbridled (USA))
1055a[8] 1702a[11] 4871a[8]

Iron Mola (IRE) *M O Quigley* 67
2 b c Iron Mask(USA) —Mola (IRE) (Robellino (USA))
779a[RR]

Iron Pearl *J Ryan* a57 51
3 b f Iron Mask(USA) —Fast Tempo (IRE) (Statoblest)
219[8] 589[5] 679[12] 7014[11]

Iron Ruler (IRE) *P A Blockley* 5
3 b g Invincible Spirit(IRE) —Blushing Queen (IRE) (Desert King (IRE))
1737[7]

Irony (IRE) *A M Balding* a90 93
8 gr g Mujadil(USA) —Cidaris (IRE) (Persian Bold)
1818[4] 2239[6] 2670[3] *3650[10]* 4134[10] 4401[8] 5012[4] 5383[4]

Irridescence (SAF) *M F De Kock* 118
6 b m Caesour(USA) —Meretricious (SAF) (Dancing Champ (USA))
600a[3] 862a[10] 3433[2] 4413a[2]

Irving Place *M L W Bell* 78
2 ch g Compton Place—Prince's Feather (IRE) (Cadeaux Genereux)
1073[2] 1411[2] 2021[2] 3508[11] (4484) 5331[9] 6052[4]

Isa'Af (IRE) *P W Hiatt* a57 78
8 b g Darshaan—Shauna's Honey (IRE) (Danehill (USA))
10[6] 107[3] 333[8] 464[3] 585[9] 628[7] 6811[7] *6971[6] 7135[6]*

Isabella Glyn (IRE) *J Noseda* 69
2 b f Sadler's Wells(USA) —Questina (FR) (Rainbow Quest (USA))
6649[3]

Isabella's Best (IRE) *E J O'Neill* a8 51
3 ch f King's Best(USA) —Spanish Quest (Rainbow Quest (USA))
1154[5] *1361[11]*

Isander (USA) *Mrs A J Perrett* a62 66
2 b c Grand Slam(USA) —Let Fly (USA) (Flying Paster (USA))
2241[9] *2991[8]* 3958[7] 5571[8] *5896[12] 6207[3] 6433[6]*

Ischka (GER) *M Sowa* 46
2 bl f Sholokhov(IRE) —Itza (GER) (Local Suitor (USA))
5462a[7]

Isent She Rich (IRE) *M G Quinlan* 68
2 ch f Dubai Destination(USA) —Rahika Rose (Unfuwain (USA))
2969[2] 3706[10] 3760[4] 5914[13] 6233[13]

Ishetoo *A Dickman* 100
3 b g Ishiguru(USA) —Ticcatoo (IRE) (Dolphin Street (FR))
(1943) (2205) (2435) 3054[4] 3413[8] 3885[2] (4452) (5506) 5806[3] 6487[3]

Ishi Adiva *Tom Dascombe* 93
3 b f Ishiguru(USA) —Nightingale Song (Tina's Pet)
1900[3] 2672[6] 3344[10] (3749) 4386[5] 4806[11] 5689[8] 6197[10]

Ishibee (IRE) *J J Bridger* a61 63
3 b f Ishiguru(USA) —Beauty (IRE) (Alzao (USA))
1426[4] 2300[3] (2560) 2910[9] 3636[2] 3786[4] 4224[13] (4471) 4853[17] 5866[4] *(5897) 6101[7]* 6279[3] *6581[5] 6993[11] 7013[5]*

Ishimagic *J J Bridger* a53 43
3 ch f Ishiguru(USA) —Triple Tricks (IRE) (Royal Academy (USA))
3087[7] 3353[5] 3872[7]

Ishismart *R Hollinshead* a30 36
3 ch f Ishiguru(USA) —Smartie Lee (Dominion)
2654[8]

I Should Care (FR) *F Rodriguez Puertas* 98
3 ch f Loup Solitaire(USA) —No Exit (FR) (Exit To Nowhere (USA))
1702a[12]

Isidore Bonheur (IRE) *G A Swinbank* a73 91
6 b g Mtoto—Way O'Gold (USA) (Slew O'Gold (USA))
4105[7] 4228[S] 4716[5] 4932[5] 5775[6] *6145[8]*

Isily (GER) *Andreas Lowe* 82
2 b f Dansili—Ice Dream (GER) (Mondrian (GER))
6371a[11]

Isinkso (IRE) *R M Beckett* 46
2 gr c Clodovil(IRE) —Storm Pearl (IRE) (Catrail (USA))
2724[8]

Is It Me (USA) *A W Carroll* a57 79
4 ch g Sky Classic(CAN) —Thea (GER) (Surumu (GER))
354[10] 4421[2] 4910[6] 5725[6]

Is It Time (IRE) *Mrs P N Dutfield* a61 57
3 b f Danetime(IRE) —Ishaam (Selkirk (USA))
973[5] 5873[12] 6239[16] *6582[4] 6809[7] 7013[4] (7138)*

Islandbane (IRE) *H Rogers* 69
5 b m Orpen(USA) —Bayazida (Bustino)
5184a[6]

Island Green (USA) *D Carroll* a66 46
4 b g Cozzene(USA) —Legend Of Spring (Night Shift (USA))
156[10] (664) (729) 895[10] *1064[11]* 1527[13] *6873[4]*

Island King (IRE) *R Bastiman* a38 41
4 br g Turtle Island(IRE) —Love Of Paris (Trojan Fen)
4007[5] 4641[9] 5157[5] *6815[8] 7199[3]*

Island Music (IRE) *J J Quinn* 67
2 b f Mujahid(USA) —Ischia (Lion Cavern (USA))
4818[7] 5903[5] 6306[3] 6742[3]

Island Odyssey *E A L Dunlop* a91 90
4 b m Dansili—Tetravella (IRE) (Groom Dancer (USA))
1783[7] *2994[10]*

Island Vista *M A Jarvis* a72
2 b f Montjeu(IRE) —Colorvista (Shirley Heights)
5202[2]

Isle De Maurice *D M Grissell* a65 52
5 b g Sinndar(IRE) —Circe's Isle (Be My Guest (USA))
6131[9]

Isle Dream *R F Marvin* a6 12
5 ch m Forzando—La Volta (Komaite (USA))
183[11]

Isobel Rose (IRE) *J L Spearing* a67 71
3 b f Royal Applause—Total Love (Cadeaux Genereux)
1345[12] 2242[9] 2607[6] *3110[4]* 6594[14] *6809[4] 6894[11] 7113[10]*

Isphahan *A M Balding* a71 79
4 b g Diktat—Waltzing Star (IRE) (Danehill (USA))
757[7] 1013[8] 1787[6] 2877[12] 3828[11] 4879[4] 5189[6] 5348[3] *6226[7] 6577[9]*

Istead Rise (IRE) *P A Blockley* a54 49
3 b g Mull Of Kintyre(USA) —Tommys Queen (IRE) (Ali-Royal (IRE))
1348[4] 3276[7] 3365[8]

Istibian (IRE) *Mrs H Sweeting* a49 62
3 b g Sakhee(USA) —Cap Coz (IRE) (Indian Ridge)
5113[5] *5816[7] 6206[P] 6804[P]*

Istria (USA) *R M Beckett* a62
2 b f Zavata(USA) —Estri (USA) (Conquistador Cielo (USA))
6664[5] 6903[6]

Italian Art (IRE) *R M Beckett* 84
2 b c Captain Rio—Sallwa (IRE) (Entrepreneur)
5771[3] (6281)

Italian Girl *A P Jarvis* 103
3 b f Danehill Dancer(IRE) —Little Italy (IRE) (Common Grounds)
(1391) 2757[4] 4148[6] 5047[6] 5799[6] 6299[14]

Italian Goddess *M L W Bell* a48 66
2 ch f Medicean—Little Italy (IRE) (Common Grounds)
5301[7] 5913[4] *6434[12]*

Italian Romance *J W Unett* a79 45
4 b g Medicean—Polish Romance (USA) (Danzig (USA))
(186) (933) 7263[4]

Italian Stallion (IRE) *E Schweigert* 94
3 b c Grand Lodge(USA) —Belle Allemande (CAN) (Royal Academy (USA))
6518a[5]

Italstar (IRE) *H Morrison* a45
3 ch f Galileo(IRE) —Jorghinia (FR) (Seattle Slew (USA))
3792[13]

Itcanbedone Again (IRE) *Ian Williams* a61 47
8 b g Sri Pekan(USA) —Maradata (IRE) (Shardari)
426[9] 685[7] 932[3] 1206[6] 1673[6] *2258[4]* 2656[11] *2946[5] 3063[3] 3595[5]*

Itsabeautifulday (IRE) *M Halford* a33 68
3 b g King Charlemagne(USA) —Amiela (FR) (Mujtahid (USA))
5460a[9]

It's A Date *A King* 67
2 b c Kyllachy—By Arrangement (IRE) (Bold Arrangement)
4362[8]

It's A Dream (FR) *M W Easterby* a79 83
4 b g Kaldounevees(FR) —Bahia Mar (USA) (Arctic Tern (USA))
1395[5] 1842[5] 2401[7] 2835[10] 4039[7] 4581[11] 5228[10] 5559[15]

Itsawindup *W J Knight* a54 20
3 b g Elnadim(USA) —Topwinder (USA) (Topsider (USA))
1117[11] 1634[15] 2425[14] 6871[12] 7098[11] 7276[10]

It's Josr *I A Wood* a65 22
2 b g Josr Algarhoud(IRE) —It's So Easy (Shaadi (USA))
2876[15] 5895[10] 6262[8] 6978[2] 7121[3]

Its Moon (IRE) *T D Walford* 76
3 b f Tobougg(IRE) —Shallat (IRE) (Pennekamp (USA))
(1092) 1576[2] 1827[8] 2579[2] 3058[6] (3719) 4511[8] 4843[5] 5523[3] 6077[4]

It's My Day (IRE) *Jane Chapple-Hyam* a64 59
2 ch c Soviet Star(USA) —Ezana (Ela-Mana-Mou)
2569[10] 3625[16] 5274[5] (5818) 6584[8] 6960[6]

It's No Problem (IRE) *M Salaman* a58 59
3 b f Averti(IRE) —Polar Rock (Polar Falcon (USA))
157[3] 267[7] (572) 790[11] 1211[3] 1637[3] 1972[10] 2181[9] 3904[7] 4632[5] 4766[10] 5269[13] 5497[10]

It's Rumoured *Jean-Rene Auvray* a46 67
7 ch g Fleetwood(IRE) —Etourdie (USA) (Arctic Tern (USA))
23[7] 291[10]

Its Sensational *K R Burke*
2 b f Okawango(USA) —Syringa (Lure (USA))
4405[10] 5869[14]

It's The Limit (USA) *W K Goldsworthy* a60
8 b g Boundary(USA) —Beside (USA) (Sportin' Life (USA))
457[9] (Dead)

It's Unbelievable (USA) *P T Midgley* a58 75
4 bb g Stravinsky(USA) —Churn Dat Butter (USA) (Unbridled (USA))
793[11] 967[11] 2508[10] 3816[8] 4081[7] 4289[5] 4561[6] 4800[14] 5507[14]

Itsy Bitsy *W J Musson* a47
5 b m Danzig Connection(USA) —Cos I Do (IRE) (Double Schwartz)
5754[7] 6501[6] 6774[9]

Itzmo (GER) *G Sybrecht* 101
5 b g Mark Of Esteem(IRE) —Itza (GER) (Local Suitor (USA))
6045a[5] 6370a[5]

Ivana Illyich (IRE) *J S Wainwright* 45
5 ch m Tipsy Creek(USA) —Tolstoya (Northfields (USA))
2554[8] 2905[9] 3051[3] 3372[6] 3914[8] 4219[11] 4449[13] 4580[13]

Ivanasbo *C G Cox* a46 37
3 gr g Cloudings(IRE) —Vonispet (Cotation)
4066[11] 4530[7] 5915[11] 6311[6]

Ivans Ride (IRE) *M F Harris* a38 45
4 b g Night Shift(USA) —Ride Bold (USA) (J O Tobin (USA))
356a[4] 439a[4] 494a[8]

Ivestar (IRE) *D Nicholls* 76
2 b g Fraam—Hazardous (Night Shift (USA))
4611[6] 4818[6] 5551[2]

Ivory Gala (FR) *B J Meehan* 98
4 b m Galileo(IRE) —Rubies From Burma (USA) (Forty Niner (USA))
1789[6] 3893a[7]

Ivory Lace *S Woodman* a88 97
6 b m Atraf—Miriam (Forzando)
28[3] 261[8] 486[5] 592[5] 1004[9] 1431[4] 2272[3] (2458) (2626) 3154[3] 3670[3] (4134) 4851[11] (5115) 5359[8] 5799[9] 6437[6] 6604[10] 6929[9] 7165[12]

Ivory Silk *D K Ivory* a66
2 b f Diktat—Ivory's Joy (Tina's Pet)
7097[3] 7266[3]

Ivorys Song *D K Ivory* a20
3 b f Averti(IRE) —Katy Ivory (IRE) (Night Shift (USA))
17[11] 90[5]

Ivy Bridge (IRE) *P A Blockley* a7 47
4 b m Namid—Chinon (IRE) (Entrepreneur)
60[10] 210[14]

Ivy Creek (USA) *G Wragg* 115
4 b h Gulch(USA) —Ivy Leaf (IRE) (Nureyev (USA))
1104[6] 1600[3] (2216) (2907) 3461[5] 4803[4] 5618[3] 6496[2]

I Will If You Will *K A Ryan* a50 52
3 ch f Pursuit Of Love—Los Alamos (Keen)
522[6] 661[6] 1913[8] 6979[9] 7157[8]

Izabela Hannah *R M Beckett* a51 68
3 ch f Kyllachy—Papita (IRE) (Law Society (USA))
1151[10] 2080[4] 3000[5] 5602[7] 6268[5]

Izarra (USA) *R McAnally* a110 101
2 b f Distorted Humor(USA) —Arlucea (USA) (Broad Brush (USA))
5826a[2] 6507a[10]

Izzibizzi *E A L Dunlop* a74 80
2 b f Medicean—Sleave Silk (IRE) (Unfuwain (USA))
3507[9] 3874[2] 4916[2] 5766[2]

Jaadull *M Johnston* 62
2 b c Dubai Destination(USA) —Saafeya (IRE) (Sadler's Wells (USA))
3479[6]

Jaady (USA) *J H M Gosden* a77
3 b g Coronado's Quest(USA) —Aljawza (USA) (Riverman (USA))
(795) 1122[11] 2177[2] 2574[5]

Jaamid *Noel Meade* 72
5 b g Desert Prince(IRE) —Strictly Cool (USA) (Bering)
6368a[2]

Jaasoos (IRE) *M A Jarvis* a62 87
3 ch c Noverre(USA) —Nymphs Echo (IRE) (Mujtahid (USA))
1124[2] 2040[5] 4811[4]

Jaassey *P T Midgley* a38 65
4 b g Josr Algarhoud(IRE) —Saaryeh (Royal Academy (USA))
1675[14] 2007[12] 2431[10] 2893[10] 4082[9]

Jabal Tariq *B W Hills* 79
2 ch c Rock Of Gibraltar(IRE) —Sueboog (IRE) (Darshaan)
3435[19] 4110[5] 5011[6] 5735[3]

Jabbara (IRE) *C E Brittain* a63 68
4 b m Kingmambo(USA) —Isle De France (USA) (Nureyev (USA))
50[9] 485[6] 555[2] 586[6] 1748[8] 3829[11] (4324) (4525) 5191[16]

Jabraan (USA) *D W Chapman* a44 43
5 b g Aljabr(USA) —Miss Zafonic (FR) (Zafonic (USA))
504[13] 1086[14] 1311[5] 3534[6] 3675[4] 4966[12] 5752[9] 6738[9]

Jacaranda (IRE) *P J Hobbs* 68
7 ch g Bahhare(USA) —Near Miracle (Be My Guest (USA))
(3907) 4909[6]

Jacaranda Ridge *M A Jarvis* a61 83
3 ch f Indian Ridge—Celtic Fling (Lion Cavern (USA))
1203[4] 1639[3] 2428[5] (3827) 4589[7] 6006[11] 6497[4] 6753[5]

Jackadandy (USA) *B Storey* 28
5 b g Lear Fan(USA) —Chandra (CAN) (Morning Bob (USA))
3840[10] 4246[P]

Jack Aubrey *F Folco* 111
5 b h Alzao—Asmita (Efisio)
1874a[3]

Jack Dawkins (USA) *H R A Cecil* 97
2 b c Fantastic Light(USA) —Do The Mambo (USA) (Kingmambo (USA))
3095[5] 3625[8] 4130[4] (5350) (6471)

Jack Dawson (IRE) *John Berry* a67 81
10 b g Persian Bold—Dream Of Jenny (Caerleon (USA))
3112[5] 3653[5] 4322[3]

Jackday (IRE) *T D Easterby* 65
2 b g Daylami(IRE) —Magic Lady (IRE) (Bigstone (IRE))
4037[11] 4448[6] 5735[7] 6328[11]

Jack Frost Nipping (USA) *Seamus Fahey* 74
4 b g Miswaki(USA) —Sulalat (Hamas (IRE))
6368a[18]

Jack Got Even (USA) *B J Meehan* a52 74
2 ch c Stephen Got Even(USA) —Nara (USA) (Green Forest (USA))
4947[8] 5217[8] 5951[7] 6471[16]

Jackie Kiely *R Brotherton* a79 74
6 ch g Vettori(IRE) —Fudge (Polar Falcon (USA))
100[2] 226[4] 377[3] 568[5] 669[5] 811[3] (1263) 1922[9] 2106[8] 4610[5] 4850[7] 5307[3] 5557[3] 6196[8] 6380[2] 7110[4]

Jack Junior (USA) *B J Meehan* a102 110
3 bb c Songandaprayer(USA) —Ra Hydee (USA) (Rahy (USA))
859a[2] 2734[7] 3436[2] 6298[10]

Jack Of Trumps (IRE) *G Wragg* a80 91
7 b g King's Theatre(IRE) —Queen Caroline (USA) (Chief's Crown (USA))
3060[7] 4194[9] 4843[9]

Jack Oliver *B J Meehan* a69 77
3 ch g Compton Place—Glascoed (Adbass (USA))
725[8] 843[6] (1634) 2335[12] 2662[2] 3237[4] 4538[8] 4778[8] 6429[6]

Jack Rackham *B Smart* a77 93
3 ch g Kyllachy—Hill Welcome (Most Welcome)
(1161) (1577) 2135[3] 3952[5] 4567[3] 5212[12] 5891[9]

Jack Rolfe *G L Moore* a81 81
5 b g Polish Precedent(USA) —Haboobti (Habitat)
30[9] 195[6] 617[2] (747) 1813[6] 5145[2] (5594) 6007[3]

Jackson (BRZ) *A Selvaratnam* a67 67
5 ch h Clackson(BRZ) —More Luck (BRZ) (Baynoun)
598a[9]

Jack Sullivan (USA) *G A Butler* a113 105
6 ch g Belong To Me(USA) —Provisions (USA) (Devil's Bag (USA))
656[2] 4747[7] (4907) 6018[5] 6198[5] 6942a[12] (7223)

Jaconet (USA) *T D Barron* a48 64
2 ch f Hussonet(USA) —Radiant Rocket (USA) (Peteski (CAN))
4125[3] 4611[5] 5780[9]

Jacquart (NZ) *C G Cox* a77 59
5 b g Zabeel(NZ) —She Wishes (NZ) (Kenfair (NZ))
5012[14] 5532[5] 6122[5] 6568[8]

Jadaara *M Johnston* 83
2 b f Red Ransom(USA) —Beraysim (Lion Cavern (USA))
(4796)

Jadalee (IRE) *I Mohammed* 113
4 b g Desert Prince(IRE) —Lionne (Darshaan)
412a[9] 545a[5]

Jadan (IRE) *E J Alston* 60
6 b g Imperial Ballet(IRE) —Sports Post Lady (IRE) (M Double M (USA))
4252[14] 4706[13] 4996[9] 5085[2] 5552[17] 5667[5] 5672[2] 5836[3] (5930) 6562[9] 6594[9]

Jade Mountain *D K Weld* 72
2 br c Efisio—Tessara (GER) (Big Shuffle (USA))
779a[5]

Jafaru *G A Butler* a15 70
3 b g Silver Hawk(USA) —Rafha (Kris)
1256[5] (1624) (2105) 2445[2] 3150[3] 3450[P] 6733[7]

Jaffal (USA) *A Al Raihe* a103
5 ch h Conquistador Cielo(USA) —Savina (USA) (Nijinsky (CAN))
177a[4] 327a[3] (396a) 599a[6]

Jaffna *R T Phillips* 30
5 b m Makbul—Pondicherry (USA) (Sir Wimborne (USA))
1537[9] 1749[13] 3113[11]

Jafra (IRE) *R M Whitaker* 58
2 ch g Choisir(AUS) —Polish Saga (Polish Patriot (USA))
2337[7] 2869[7] 4002[8] 5298[7] 5965[4]

Jagger *G A Butler* a78 91
7 gr g Linamix(FR) —Sweetness Herself (Unfuwain (USA))
7086[5]

Jago (SWI) *A M Hales* a67
4 b g Brief Truce(USA) —Jariyah (USA) (It's The One (USA))
6102[10] 6603[2] 6848[2]

Jagodin (IRE) *B Neuman* 94
7 b g Be My Guest(USA) —Native Joy (IRE) (Be My Native (USA))
2976a[6] 5263a[3]

Jahash *Simon Earle*
9 ch g Hernando(FR) —Jalsun (Jalmood (USA))
1402[U]

Jajoleen (IRE) *P A Blockley* 47
4 ch m Titus Livius(FR) —Radeda (IRE) (Great Commotion (USA))
5187[8]

Jakam (IRE) *E J O'Neill* a48
2 b g Diktat—Key Virtue (USA) (Atticus (USA))
7139[5]

Jakeini (IRE) *E S McMahon* a53 77
4 b g Rossini(USA) —Talita Kumi (IRE) (High Estate)
1483[2] 1999[5] 2529[9] 3594[11] 4289[11] 4857[4]

Jalamid (IRE) *M A Barnes* 97
5 b g Danehill(USA) —Vignelaure (IRE) (Royal Academy (USA))
1971[18] 2559[3] 3056[13] 3873[7] 4294[5] 4580[11] 5503[10]

Jalandy (IRE) *S Curran* a47 43
4 b m Desert Millennium(IRE) —Jaldini (IRE) (Darshaan)
7098[7]

Jaleela (USA) *W J Haggas* a79 84
3 b f Kingmambo(USA) —Sultana (USA) (Storm Cat (USA))
1391[3] (2046) 2369[6] 6002[9]

Jalil (USA) *Saeed Bin Suroor* a98 87
3 br c Storm Cat(USA) —Tranquility Lake (USA) (Rahy (USA))
1812[2] (2376) 6143[2]

Jalmira (IRE) *C F Swan* a95 107
6 b m Danehill Dancer(IRE) —Jaldini (IRE) (Darshaan)
1050a[6] 2851a[5] 3578a[9] 4051a[12] 5998a[4] (6655)

Jal Music *L M Cumani* 61
2 ch c Ishiguru(USA) —Musica (Primo Dominie)
3687[13] 4070[4]

Jalons Bridewell *M Quinn* a45
2 b c Compton Place—Inflation (Primo Dominie)
6404[10]

Jalta (GER) *H Steinmetz* 101
4 b m Platini(GER) —Juschika (Salse (USA))
1517a[2]

Jalwada *John Queally* 91
5 b m Cadeaux Genereux—Wedoudah (IRE) (Sadler's Wells (USA))
3143a[2] 3577a[3]

Jamaahir (USA) *S Lycett* 66
4 b g Bahri(USA) —Elrehaan (Sadler's Wells (USA))
1811[6] 2218[8] 3487[8] 3794[6] 4019[13] 4544[11]

Jamaali (USA) *M P Tregoning* 48
2 ch f Langfuhr(CAN) —Raajiya (USA) (Gulch (USA))
5949[15]

Jamaar *C N Kellett* a63 23
5 ch g Nashwan(USA) —Kissogram (Caerleon (USA))
1222[11]

Jamaican Flight (USA) *Mrs S Lamyman* a26 44
14 b h Sunshine Forever(USA) —Kalamona (USA) (Hawaii)
333[7] 994[9] 1196[7] 2505[6] 6802[P]

Jambalaya (CAN) *Catherine Day Phillips* 116
5 b g Langfuhr(CAN) —Muskrat Suzie (USA) (Vice Regent (CAN))
(4414a)

Jamboretta (IRE) *Sir Michael Stoute* 91
3 b f Danehill(USA) —Jiving (Generous (IRE))
1409[3] (1988) 4111[8] 4847[2] 5385[2]

James Caird (IRE) *M H Tompkins* a86 95
7 ch g Catrail(USA) —Polish Saga (Polish Patriot (USA))
353[4] 850[10] 1060[5] 2003[9]

James Dean (IRE) *P F I Cole* a77
2 b c Clodovil(IRE) —Karenaragon (Aragon)
5780[2]

James's Lass (IRE) *R A Fahey* 20
2 ch f Daggers Drawn(USA) —Kyra Crown (IRE) (Astronef)
4522[11] 5042[16] 5558[7] 5932[9]

James Street (IRE) *Peter Grayson* a76 77
4 b g Fruits Of Love(USA) —Humble Mission (Shack (USA))
1629[8] 2358[7] 2603[9] 3036[4] 5234[9] 5565[11] 6226[9] 6266[8] 6431[11] 6706[6] 7153[6]

Jamieson Gold (IRE) *B W Hills* 95
4 b g Desert Style(IRE) —Princess Of Zurich (IRE) (Law Society (USA))
1842[7] 2670[9] 3525[9] (4548) 4601[4] 4990[13] 6301[26]

Ja Myford *P T Midgley* a59 59
3 b g Auction House(USA) —Daleside Ladybird (Tolomeo)
1111[14] 1303[11] 1676[7] 2909[2] 3159[3] 3792[9] 4229[4] 5341[7] 6257[10]

Jane Blue (FR) *B Halley Des Fontaines* 94
2 b c Indian Rocket—Rastella (FR) (Funambule (USA))
6525a[3]

Jane Of Arc (FR) *J S Goldie* 71
3 ch f Trempolino(USA) —Aerleon Jane (Caerleon (USA))
1414[7] 1898[6] 3587[11] 4078[6] 4450[5] 4579[7] 4936[3] 5286[11] 6464[9]

Jane's Delight (IRE) *G R Oldroyd* a63 65
2 br f Namid—Revolving (USA) (Devil's Bag (USA))
972[9] 1728[4] (3751) 4126[6] 4669[4]

Jane's Payoff (IRE) *Mrs L C Jewell* a60
2 b f Danetime(IRE) —Alimony (IRE) (Groom Dancer (USA))
7196[5]

Janet's Delight *S Curran* a55 55
2 b f Erhaab(USA) —Ishona (Selkirk (USA))
3238[4] 3874[11] 4417[6] 5313[7] 5603[4] 5895[5] 6503[6] 6775[8]

Janina *B W Hills* 94
2 b f Namid—Lady Dominatrix (IRE) (Danehill Dancer (IRE))
(1285) (1821) 2812[6]

Jardines Bazaar *T D Easterby* 54
3 b g Halling(USA) —Alumisiyah (USA) (Danzig (USA))
2538[4] 3640[11]

Jarvo *I W McInnes* a58 57
6 b g Pursuit Of Love—Pinkie Rose (FR) (Kenmare (FR))
18[4] 133[4] 203[8] 1206[2] (1271) (1380) 1592[2] 1967[3] 2027[9] 2275[6] 7115[13]

Jaser *P W Chapple-Hyam* a70 60
2 ch c Alhaarth(IRE) —Waafiah (Anabaa (USA))
5598[9] 5951[13] (6944)

Jasmine Joli (IRE) *Mafalda Osthaus* 75
3 b f Cape Cross(IRE) —Rose Jasmine (ITY) (Sikeston (USA))
6688a[14]

Jasmines Hero (USA) *J S Moore* a69 66
2 b c War Chant(USA) —Ryn (USA) (Mr Prospector (USA))
2600[6] 3479[5] 4323[4] 4964[11] 6201[5]

Jasoora *M P Tregoning* a61
2 b f Mark Of Esteem(IRE) —Kotdiji (Mtoto)
6119[8] 6456[4] 6805[10]

Jastaanhi *J A Pickering* a32 59
2 b f Superior Premium—Cavern Breeze (Lion Cavern (USA))
2717[7] 3465[2] 3606[4] 4026[3] 7170[6] 7258[7]

Jaufrette *Dr J R J Naylor* a48 39
4 b m Kayf Tara—Jucinda (Midyan (USA))
3084[8] 4253[10] 5820[11] 6832[16]

Jawaab (IRE) *M A Buckley* 77
3 ch g King's Best(USA) —Canis Star (Wolfhound (USA))
1111[5] 1722[10] 2453[6] 2749[3] 3707[7] 4079[4] 4778[4] (5330) 5693[3] 5768[4] 6253[2]

Jawaaneb (USA) *J L Dunlop* 85
3 ch f Kingmambo(USA) —Khazayin (USA) (Bahri (USA))
1143[14] 1632[6] 2219[6] (2915) 3427[2] 3848[2] 4511[3] 5034[2] 5404[2] 5911[4]

Jawad (IRE) *Ms Joanna Morgan* 77
6 b g Kahyasi—Mystic Charm (Nashwan (USA))
6366a[3]

Jayanjay *P Mitchell* a75 94
8 b g Piccolo—Morica (Moorestyle)
1242[12] 1630[9] 1946[11] 2139[8] 2972[9] (3613) 3859[8] 4320[8] 4594[4] 5340[3] 5731[6] 5867[5] 6174[4] 6279[6] 6428[10]

Jayer Gilles *Dr J R J Naylor* a59 62
7 br g Busy Flight—Jadidh (Touching Wood (USA))
1683[11] (2493) 4030[12] 4576[4]

Jay Gee Wigmo *A W Carroll* 21
2 b c First Trump—Queen Of Shannon (IRE) (Nordico (USA))
2086[9] 2510[11] 4454[14] 6274[10]

Jayzee (IRE) *P D Deegan* a31 52
3 b f Iron Mask(USA) —Golden Concorde (Super Concorde (USA))
99[9]

Jazabelle (IRE) *Tracey Collins* 77
4 gr m Monashee Mountain(USA) —Lingdale Lass (Petong)
5460a[28]

Jazamataz *Tom Dascombe* a37 40
2 ch f Compton Admiral—Tough Nell (IRE) (Archway (IRE))
3213[13] 3446[9] (Dead)

Jazenio *K A Ryan* a49
2 b f Auenadler(GER) —Jade Chequer (Green Desert (USA))
7058[8] 7216[4]

Jazrawy *D Carroll* a83 59
5 b g Dansili—Dalila Di Mare (IRE) (Bob Back (USA))
(305) (453) (507) 693[8] 811[4]

Jazz At The Sands (USA) *D Shaw* a35 21
4 ch g Forest Wildcat(USA) —Dahlia's Krissy (USA) (Kris S (USA))
137[10]

Jazzing About (USA) *P A Blockley* 39
2 bb c Dixie Union(USA) —Erstwhile (USA) (Arts And Letters (USA))
1150[7]

Jazz Jam *P F I Cole* 92
2 ch f Pivotal—Applaud (USA) (Rahy (USA))
3796[3] 4102[7] 5061[3] (5746) 6652[2]

Jazz Romance (IRE) *D Shaw* a26
2 ch f Choisir(AUS) —Music In My Life (IRE) (Law Society (USA))
5097[13] 5201[9] 5363[12]

Jazz Stick (IRE) *D A Nolan* 63
2 ch c Choisir(AUS) —Basin Street Blues (IRE) (Dolphin Street (FR))
3582[10] 4136[6] 4715[3] 5081[8] 5477[8] 6462[11] 6729[5]

Jazzy (ARG) *M Hennig* a99 99
5 b m Mutakddim(USA) —Jollie Fille (ARG) (Southern Halo (USA))
6483a[10]

Jebel Ali (IRE) *B Gubby* a81 79
4 b g Fruits Of Love(USA) —Assertive Lass (USA) (Assert)
501[3] 593[2] 693[9] 870[3]

Jebel Tara *C E Brittain* 97
2 b c Diktat—Chantilly (FR) (Sanglamore (USA))
1094[5] 2151[2] (2604) 2785[9] 3504[9] 5324[20] 5630[6] 5974[13]

Jedburgh *J L Dunlop* 109
6 b h Selkirk(USA) —Conspiracy (Rudimentary (USA))
1305[7] 2396[7] 3505[18] 4062[6] 4851[8] 5413[3] 6013[9] 6301[20]

Jedediah *A M Balding* 98
2 b g Hernando(FR) —Penelewey (Groom Dancer (USA))
2855[5] 3856[2] (4547) 5217[5] 6170[5]

Jeepstar *S C Williams* a81 82
7 b g Muhtarram(USA) —Jungle Rose (Shirley Heights)
457[8] 662[5] 709[4] 1272[5] 1683[2] 1949[5]

Jeer (IRE) *E A L Dunlop* 91
3 ch g Selkirk(USA) —Purring (USA) (Mountain Cat (USA))
(1303) 1773[2] 2231[12]

Jelly Mo *J W Hills* a68 66
2 b f Royal Applause—Flawless (Warning)
2241[12] 3895[14] 4593[5] 5883[10] 6584[5]

Jellytot (USA) *J O'Reilly* a64 67
4 b m Minardi(USA) —Dounine (Kaldoun (FR))
150[5] 681[13] 980[8] 1379[6] 1640[2] 2033[11] 3636[9] 4008[11] 4180[15]

Jember Red *B Smart* a46 33
4 b m Polish Precedent(USA) —Arabellajill (Aragon)
271[11] 435[13] 670[5] 714[2] 906[2] 1594[9] 6702[7] 6877[8] 7239[6]

Jemiliah *B J Meehan* a60 44
2 b f Dubai Destination(USA) —Cape Cod (IRE) (Unfuwain (USA))
1960[11] 2590[7] 4539[8] 6432[11]

Jemima Godfrey *M J Gingell* a52
3 b f Ishiguru(USA) —Quantum Lady (Mujadil (USA))
208[13] 357[5] (417) 534[2] 572[3] 791[11] (Dead)

Jemima's Art *M W Easterby* 46
2 bb f Fantastic Light(USA) —Subya (Night Shift (USA))
3510[8] 3916[7] 4422[12]

Jendas Jem *Mrs A Duffield* 30
2 b f Josr Algarhoud(IRE) —Miss Hit (Efisio)
4559[5] 5477[10]

Jeninsky (USA) *P J McBride* a83 68
2 ch f Stravinsky(USA) —Don't Ruffle Me (USA) (Pine Bluff (USA))
5770[3] (6177)

Jenise (IRE) *Mark Campion* a44 22
4 b m Orpen(USA) —Griqualand (Connaught)
271[9]

Jennie Jerome (IRE) *B J Meehan* 66
2 br f Pivotal—Colourfast (IRE) (Spectrum (IRE))
5949[8]

Jennie R. (USA) *Michele Boyce* 106
6 b m Awesome Again(CAN) —Petrouchka (CAN) (Red Ransom (USA))
4413a[5]

Jennifer's Dream (IRE) *K A Ryan* 78
2 b f Statue Of Liberty(USA) —Elara (USA) (Spinning World (USA))
4074[7] (4924) 5692[5] 6619[11]

Jennifers Joy (IRE) *M R Channon* a72 77
2 b f Green Desert(USA) —Perils Of Joy (IRE) (Rainbow Quest (USA))
1285[3] (1533) 1821[9] 4098[8] 4737[5] 5322[13] 5624[4] 6012[10] (Dead)

Jennverse *D K Ivory* a55 50
5 b m Opening Verse(USA) —Jennelle (Nomination)
22[6]

Jenny Soba *Lucinda Featherstone* a48 61
4 b m Observatory(USA) —Majalis (Mujadil (USA))
1090[13] 1301[5] 1579[5] 1671[4] 2008[10] 4082[6] (4426) 4615[8] 4920[6] 5626[4] 6076[5] 6341[11] 6569[8] 6797[10] 6835[3] 7219[5]

Jentris Girl (IRE) *T D Easterby* 57
3 b f Golan(IRE) —Carranza (IRE) (Lead On Time (USA))
1111[4] 1303[8] 1849[8] 2796[14] 3561[3] 3639[7] 3997[14]

Jeremy (USA) *Sir Michael Stoute* 121
4 b h Danehill Dancer(IRE) —Glint In Her Eye (USA) (Arazi (USA))
(1305) 1834[5] 2735[2] 4058[3] 6029a[7] 6511a[10]

Jermajesty (IRE) *J R Boyle* a50 33
2 b c Touch Of The Blues(FR) —Mystic Dispute (IRE) (Magical Strike (USA))
2232[13] 2590[11] 3850[11] 4547[12] 6079[10] 6585[11]

Jerry Hamilton (USA) *M Johnston* a70 28
2 bb c Cherokee Run(USA) —Helsinki (Machiavellian (USA))
2863[5] 6436[12] 6748[2] 6936[4]

Jessica Wigmo *A W Carroll* a52 46
4 b m Bahamian Bounty—Queen Of Shannon (IRE) (Nordico (USA))
3277[8] 4324[9] 4545[11] 4881[12] 4974[5] 5566[13] 6361[3] (6778) 6809[5] 7028[8]

Jet Express (SAF) *H J Brown* a102 96
5 b g Jet Master(SAF) —Outback Romance (SAF) (Sharp Romance (USA))
178a[7] 250a[14]

Jet Past (SAF) *S Seemar* a88 99
5 b m Jet Master(SAF) —Rather Rich (NZ) (Star Way)
397a[4] 546a[7]

Jet Propulsion (USA) *Daniel C Hurtak* 106
4 b h Double Honor(USA) —Her Jet (USA) (Northjet)
5823a[9]

Jetta Joy (IRE) *Mrs A Duffield* 41
2 b f Hawk Wing(USA) —Woopi Gold (IRE) (Last Tycoon (IRE))
4448[9] 5580[11] 5749[9]

Jeu De Roseau (IRE) *A P Stringer* a49 77
3 b g Montjeu(IRE) —Roseau (Nashwan (USA))
7198[6]

Jeu D'Esprit (IRE) *J G Given* a71 72
4 b m Montjeu(IRE) —Cielo Vodkamartini (USA) (Conquistador Cielo (USA))
(1567) 1980[5] 2361[8] 3754[2] 4615[6] 6856[5]

Jevington Star (IRE) *R M Flower* a40
2 ch g Noverre(USA) —Khalisiyn (Shakapour)
4593[10] 4882[9] 5498[13]

Jewaar (USA) *M A Jarvis* 88
4 ch m Diesis—Ringshaan (FR) (Darshaan)
1649[11]

Jewelled Dagger (IRE) *I Semple* a63 92
3 b g Daggers Drawn(USA) —Cappadoce (IRE) (General Monash (USA))
1220[6] 1489[2] (1712) (1894) (2248) 2862[2] 3299[8] 4222[2] 4672[11] (6180)

Jibajaba (USA) *R A Fahey* 75
3 gr g Aljabr(USA) —Mary's Joy (USA) (Woodman (USA))
1913[4] 2554[5] 2792[2] 3196[3] 3785[2] 3889[4] (4411) 5043[8] 5620[5]

Jidaar (IRE) *P W Hiatt* a63 82
4 b g Grand Lodge(USA) —Banaadir (USA) (Diesis)
488[14] 501[12] (Dead)

Jill Dawson (IRE) *John Berry* 67
4 b m Mull Of Kintyre(USA) —Dream Of Jenny (Caerleon (USA))
(1539) 2514[3] 4112[4]

Jilly Why (IRE) *Paul Green* a70 81
6 b m Mujadil(USA) —Ruwy (Soviet Star (USA))
8[6] 1557[7] 1999[4] 2529[2] 2870[5] 3515[3] 3569[6] 3853[4] 3921[3] 4140[4] 4525[2] 4668[5] (4836a) 5460a[16] 6064[2] (6149) 6610[8] 6677[3] 6762[4] 6885[4] 7026[3] 7078[4] 7161[7] 7271[10]

Jiminor Mack *W J H Ratcliffe* a48 51
4 bl m Little Jim—Copper Trader (Faustus (USA))
42[2] 121[4] 271[10] 514[10] 2253[11] 2795[3] 3714[6] 3789[2] 5782[9] 6250[8]

Jim Martin *J R Weymes* 79
2 b g Auction House(USA) —Folly Finnesse (Joligeneration)
(3951) 4482[4]

Jimmy Dean *M Wellings* a45 28
2 b c Ishiguru(USA) —Sister Sal (Bairn (USA))
3866[14] 4077[10] 4417[11] 6289[6] 6748[8]

Jimmy Falabella (IRE) *N A Callaghan* a38 22
2 b g Mull Of Kintyre(USA) —Super Value (Polar Falcon (USA))
3962[16] 6503[12]

Jimmy Styles *C G Cox* 97
3 ch g Inchinor—Inya Lake (Whittingham (IRE))
2393[2] 2878[4] (4182) (4574) 5765[10] 6472[10]

Jimmy The Guesser *N P Littmoden* a90 84
4 ch g Piccolo—Brush Away (Ahonoora)
81[3] 227[3]

Jim's Boy (USA) *M Johnston* 33
2 ch g Street Cry(IRE) —Ella Eria (FR) (Bluebird (USA))
6740[9] 6857[12] (Dead)

Jo'Burg (USA) *Mrs A J Perrett* a98 99
3 b g Johannesburg(USA) —La Martina (Atraf)
1473[16] 2124[3] 2368[4] 2788[20] 3463[6] 4062[10] 4420[6]

Jocheski (IRE) *A G Newcombe* a65 63
3 b g Mull Of Kintyre(USA) —Ludovica (Bustino)
53[2] 140[5] 392[5] (4516) 4757[2] 5980[5] 6421[5]

Jockser (IRE) *J W Mullins* a50 72
6 b g Desert Story(IRE) —Pupa Fiorini (ITY) (Indian Ridge)
5453[5] 5820[10]

Jodhpur *A Fabre* a96 96
3 ch c Pivotal—Khumbla Mela (IRE) (Hero's Honor (USA))
6954a[6]

Jodrell Bank (IRE) *J Ryan* a24 60
4 ch m Observatory(USA) —Aravonian (Night Shift (USA))
1280[11] 1753[13] 2334[16] 2555[8] 2791[13]

Joe Jo Star *B P J Baugh* a57 50
5 b g Piccolo—Zagreb Flyer (Old Vic)
42[7] 179[8] 1210[3]

Joe Louis (ARG) *I Jory* a82 94
4 br h Lode(USA) —Jolie Caresse (USA) (Septieme Ciel (USA))
414a[5] 859a[8]

Joe Rich *Mrs L C Jewell*
3 b g Piccolo—Lady Lacey (Kampala)
7223[5] 7282[12]

Joffe's Run (USA) *B J Meehan* 93
2 ch f Giant's Causeway(USA) —Laguna Seca (USA) (Seattle Slew (USA))
3895[8] (5162) 6008[7] 6482a[10]

Johannes (IRE) *E J O'Neill* a85 99
4 b g Mozart(IRE) —Blue Sirocco (Bluebird (USA))
6013[10] 6205[9]

Johar Jamal (IRE) *M R Channon* 86
2 b f Chevalier(IRE) —Miss Barcelona (IRE) (Mac's Imp (USA))
1636[6] (1960) (4168) 4743[7] 5324[10] 5837[4]

John Dillon (IRE) *P C Haslam* a59 69
3 ch g Traditionally(USA) —Matikanehanafubuki (IRE) (Caerleon (USA))
149[4] 449[6] 991[5] 2759[3] (3181) 4004[2] 4332[3]

John Keats *J S Goldie* a53 83
4 b g Bertolini(USA) —Nightingale (Night Shift (USA))
967[12] 1597[11] 2394[2] 2509[5] 2864[2] 3345[11] 3782[4] 3921[8] 4390[2] (4583) 4934[3] (5155) 5581[11] 6313[11]

Johnny Friendly *K R Burke* a3 53
2 b g Auction House(USA) —Quantum Lady (Mujadil (USA))
1622[9] 2983[9] 3256[6] 5251[4] 6150[12]

John O'Groats (IRE) *T T Clement* 62
9 b g Distinctly North(USA) —Bannons Dream (IRE) (Thatching)
1492[7] 1594[14] 3686[3] (3905) 6575[15]

John Potts *B P J Baugh* a59 32
2 b g Josr Algarhoud(IRE) —Crown City (USA) (Coronado's Quest (USA))
5193[9] 5880[13] 6358[9] 6761[5] 6881[5] 7245[4]

Johnston's Diamond (IRE) *E J Alston* a67 92
9 b g Tagula(IRE) —Toshair Flyer (Ballad Rock)
1999[8] 5934[11] 6103[11] 6639[14] (Dead)

Johnston's Glory (IRE) *E J Alston* a58 52
3 b f Desert Sun—Clos De Tart (IRE) (Indian Ridge)
4290[4] 4736[7] 5231[10] 5781[5] 6464[8] 6904[2] 7079[4] 7144[5]

Johnstown Lad (IRE) *Niall Moran* a86 92
3 b g Invincible Spirit(IRE) —Pretext (Polish Precedent (USA))
3140a[11] 3573a[11] 5392a[7]

John Terry (IRE) *Mrs A J Perrett* 98
4 b g Grand Lodge(USA) —Kardashina (FR) (Darshaan)
1543[3] 2209[5] 3105[6] (3509) 3989[9] 4376[2] 5030[9] 6490[5] 6759[12]

Joinedupwriting *R M Whitaker* 77
2 b g Desert Style(IRE) —Ink Pot (USA) (Green Dancer (USA))
3582[7] 4076[5] 4612[2] (5153) 5613[13] 6194[4]

Joint Agency (IRE) *N Wilson* a36 36
2 b f Captain Rio—Prima Marta (Primo Dominie)
3750[9] 4522[7] 5521[11] 6023[5]

Joint Expectations (IRE) *Mrs C A Dunnett* a38 44
3 b g Indian Rocket—Jenny Spinner (IRE) (Bluebird (USA))
1311[10] (2747) 3040[8] 3918[6] 5128[9] 5338[9] 6412[12]

Jojesse *Jennie Candlish* a61 59
3 ch g Compton Place—Jodeeka (Fraam)
378[2] 671[3] (786) (970) 1240[6] 2120[4] 4001[4] 4226[3] 4561[12] 4935[3] 5507[3] 5834[5] 6886[12] 7138[7]

Jokipur *Patrick Cody* 64
3 b g Act One—Additive (USA) (Devil's Bag (USA))
6443a[13]

Jolie Fleur *C Tinkler* a36 35
2 b f Josr Algarhoud(IRE) —Jenny Rocket (Minster Son)
4273[11] 4875[12]

Jollyhockeysticks *M R Channon* 77
2 b f Fantastic Light(USA) —Between The Sticks (Pharly (FR))
5162[8] 5721[4] 6418[3] 6652[10]

Jollys Joy *K F Clutterbuck* a6
3 b f Averti(IRE) —Nest Egg (Prince Sabo)
5637[5]

Jolly Tipsy *M W Easterby* a19 20
2 ch f Tipsy Creek(USA) —Busy (IRE) (In The Wings)
1636[10] 1963[14] 2344[9]

Jomus *L Montague Hall* a64 59
6 b g Soviet Star(USA) —Oatey (Master Willie)
48[9] 130[8] 6579[11] 6968[9] 7167[4]

Jonny Behave *I A Wood* a40
3 b g Erhaab(USA) —Bunty (Presidium)
162[4] 572[9] 661[10] 1381[7] 2697[P]

Jonny Ebeneezer *K McAuliffe* a46 86
8 b g Hurricane Sky(AUS) —Leap Of Faith (IRE) (Northiam (USA))
5391[12]

Jonny Lesters Hair (IRE) *T D Easterby* 72
2 b c Danetime(IRE) —Jupiter Inlet (IRE) (Jupiter Island)
3712[5] 3977[4] 4784[3]

Jontobel *Jedd O'Keeffe* 34
2 b g Tobougg(IRE) —Belinda (Mizoram (USA))
6307[10]

Jools *D K Ivory* a66 70
9 b g Cadeaux Genereux—Madame Crecy (USA) (Al Nasr (FR))
94[6] 364[4] 616[10] 975[13] (1381) 1740[4] 2179[6] 2514[5] 2722[5] 3615[3] 3922[9] 4685[12] 5062[4] (5336) 5946[3] 6179[3] 6431[7] (6647) (6869) 6993[6] 7164[5]

Jord (IRE) *A J McCabe* a78 58
3 b f Trans Island—Arcevia (IRE) (Archway (IRE))
147[7] 510[5] 725[3] 843[7] 1176[3] (1437) 1978[7] 2363[7] 2910[8] 3920[10] 4885[4] 5238[7] 5495[5] 6747[8] 6962[5] 7026[4] (7155) 7213[2]

Jordans Elect *P Monteith* a24 74
7 ch g Fleetwood(IRE) —Cal Norma's Lady (IRE) (Lyphard's Special (USA))
1488[4] 1967[8] 2169[3] 2391[10] 3182[8] 3343[6]

Jordan's Light (USA) *T J Pitt* a77 68
4 rg g Aljabr(USA) —Western Friend (USA) (Gone West (USA))
975[11] 1198[4] 1295[10] 1378[4]

Jordans Spark *P Monteith* a39 60
6 ch g Opening Verse(USA) —Ribot's Pearl (Indian Ridge)
1459[13] 1944[11] 2168[10] 2563[5] 2820[7] 3376[13]

Josama *R Bastiman* a23 11
3 br f Desert Sun—Edge Of Darkness (Vaigly Great)
4795[8] 6309[13] 6904[9]

Joseph Henry *D Nicholls* 94
5 b g Mujadil(USA) —Iris May (Brief Truce (USA))
1619[5] 4122[2] 5356[8]

Josephine Malines *C G Cox* 78
3 b f Inchinor—Alrisha (IRE) (Persian Bold)
2693[2] 3992[6] 5210[9] 5385[9]

Josh *K A Ryan* a87 94
5 b g Josr Algarhoud(IRE) —Charlie Girl (Puissance)
44[5] 191[5] 261[3] 384[4] 2573[9] 2936[6] 3549[5] 6907[10] 6982[11] 7224[9]

Joshua *D E Cantillon* a45
2 b g Josr Algarhoud(IRE) —Magic Flute (Magic Ring (IRE))
6419[16] 7096[8] 7235[6]

Joshua's Gold (IRE) *D Carroll* a71 74
7 b g Sesaro(USA) —Lady Of The Night (IRE) (Night Shift (USA))
1413[3] 1755[6] 2033[9] 4141[6] (4562) (4931) 5253[11] 5701[2] 6025[8] 6331[10] 6423[13]

Joshua's Princess (SAF) *J E Hammond* 90
6 b m Joshua Dancer(USA) —Princess Daisy (SAF) (Pedlar (SAF))
4652a[11]

Josh You Are *D E Cantillon* a71 64
4 b g Josr Algarhoud(IRE) —Cibenze (Owington)
(134) 291[2] 369[4] 2748[6] (3397) 4030[3] 4463[2] 4925[7]

Josr's Magic (IRE) *H J Collingridge* a57 73
3 b g Josr Algarhoud(IRE) —Just The Trick (USA) (Phone Trick (USA))
1238[3] 1484[6] 1912[2] 2146[3] 3056[12] 4272[9] 4397[13] 4742[9] 6968[5] 7098[3]

Joss Stick *P J Makin* a66 61
2 b g Josr Algarhoud(IRE) —Queen's College (IRE) (College Chapel)
3589[10] 4629[14] 5888[6] 6263[7] 6426[3] 6722[8] 6977[3] (7071)

Jost Van Dyke *J W Unett* a63 65
3 b g Foxhound(USA) —Interregnum (Interrex (CAN))
68[4] 139[6] 280[4] 679[7] 974[12]

Jousting *V Smith* a48
3 b g Josr Algarhoud(IRE) —Sweet Wilhelmina (Indian Ridge)
73[8] 141[11] 708[2] 910[7] 1266[13]

Joy And Pain *M J Attwater* a61 75
6 b g Pursuit Of Love—Ice Chocolate (USA) (Icecapade (USA))
1377[7] 1755[12] 2190[3] 2334[13] 2576[6] 2665[8] 3101[2] 3388[5] 3735[4] 4180[10] 5909[10] 6412[9] 6587[6] (6706) 6895[7] (6950)

Joyeaux *J Hetherton* a71 74
5 b m Mark Of Esteem(IRE) —Divine Secret (Hernando (FR))
2870[7] 3184[2] 3466[5] 3676[3] 4008[2] 4498[3] 4719[2] 4999[2] (5667) 5747[2] 6157[18] 6313[4] 6594[6]

Joyful Tears (IRE) *M G Quinlan* a57 70
3 ch f Barathea(IRE) —Perils Of Joy (IRE) (Rainbow Quest (USA))
1588[6] 2317[14] 4855[6] 5347[4] 5865[12] 6057[4] 6567[5] 6695[10]

Joyful Winner (AUS) *J Moore* 119
7 br g El Moxie(USA) —Northern Tycoon (AUS) (Last Tycoon (IRE))
7091a[5]

Joy In The Guild (IRE) *W S Kittow* a41 59
4 b m Mull Of Kintyre(USA) —About Face (Midyan (USA))
616[7] 976[14] 2491[2] 3047[5] 5427[5] 5886[11] 6250[5]

Jubilation *F Reuterskiold* a86 110
8 b h Zamindar(USA) —Jubilee Trail (Shareef Dancer (USA))
4874a[10]

Jubilee Dream *Mrs L J Mongan* a53 52
5 b g Bluebird(USA) —Last Dream (IRE) (Alzao (USA))
5007[14]

Jubilee Street (IRE) *Mrs A Duffield* a42 89
8 b g Dr Devious(IRE) —My Firebird (Rudimentary (USA))
1682[5] 1915[6] 4195[8]

Jucebabe *J L Spearing* 64
4 b m Zilzal(USA) —Jucea (Bluebird (USA))
1766[8] 2459[5] 2982[4] 3368[5] 3859[6] 4314[3] 4545[7] 4635[4] (4881) 5009[9] 5726[8] 5867[4] 6287[10] 6424[4]

Juce Of Hearts *J L Spearing* 46
3 b g Zilzal(USA) —Jucea (Bluebird (USA))
1207[9] 1429[4] 1541[10] 2195[10] 2652[15]

Judda *R F Marvin* 32
6 b g Makbul—Pepeke (Mummy's Pet)
180[11]

Judd Street *Eve Johnson Houghton* a102 113
5 b g Compton Place—Pudding Lane (IRE) (College Chapel)
3464[3] 4196[7] (4386) 4696[6] 5212[2] 5407[10] 5632[3] (5953)

Judge Neptune *J S Goldie* 60
3 b g Ocean Of Wisdom(USA) —Princess Louise (Efisio)
1531[2] 3785[8] 4891[8]

Judgethemoment (USA) *Jane Chapple-Hyam* a71 81
2 br c Judge T C(USA) —Rachael Tennessee (USA) (Matsadoon (USA))
4162[6] 4946[3] 5590[3] 6092[3] 6585[3]

Julatten (IRE) *D J Murphy* a43 54
3 b f Alhaarth(IRE) —Istibshar (USA) (Mr Prospector (USA))
3752[9] 4319[14] 4361[6] 4741[9] 5750[3] 5980[10]

Julian Joachim (USA) *G A Swinbank* 53
3 b g Officer(USA) —Seeking The Jewel (USA) (Seeking The Gold (USA))
2012[6] 3382[8] 4000[2] 4157[8]

Jumbajukiba *Mrs John Harrington* 115
4 b g Barathea(IRE) —Danseuse Du Soir (IRE) (Thatching)
(3138a) 4051a[8] (4237a) (5459a) 6009[7]

Jump For You (FR) *W Baltromei* 105
5 b g Montjeu(IRE) —Polly's Wika (USA) (Miswaki (USA))
2409a[9] 2976a[5] 4957a[2] 5849a[RR]

Jumpin Johnnie *R T Phillips* a36 40
2 ch g Compton Place—Trump Street (First Trump)
6469[10] 6754[7] 6998[8]

Juncea *H Morrison* a71 57
3 b f Elnadim(USA) —Strelitzia (SAF) (Fort Wood (USA))
3466[7] 4740[11] 6174[11]

Junebug Symphony (IRE) *V Smith* a38 58
5 b m Indian Lodge(IRE) —Ladies View (IRE) (Turtle Island (IRE))
46[12]

Jun Fan (USA) *B Ellison* a58 64
5 br g Artax(USA) —Ringside Lady (NZ) (Clay Hero (AUS))
154[10] 1241[5] 1493[6] 2509[8] 3636[5] 4101[11] 4478[5] 4773[8] 4939[8]

Junior *B J Meehan* a93 87
4 ch g Singspiel(IRE) —For More (FR) (Sanglamore (USA))
(1148) 1654[3] (3216)

Juniper Berry (IRE) *John Joseph Murphy* 86
2 b f Galileo(IRE) —Lucky Achievement (USA) (St Jovite (USA))
5073a[8]

Juniper Girl (IRE) *M L W Bell* 104
4 b m Revoque(IRE) —Shajara (FR) (Kendor (FR))
1844[8] 2736[2] (3090) 4691[7] 6044a[5]

Jupiter Pluvius (USA) *A P O'Brien* 103
2 b c Johannesburg(USA) —Saratoga Honey (USA) (Boundary (USA))
(6549a)

Juror (USA) *I Mohammed* a94 89
4 rg h Royal Academy(USA) —Paper Princess (USA) (Flying Paster (USA))
327a[6] 473a[2]

Just A Dancer (IRE) *B W Hills* 76
2 b f Choisir(AUS) —New Foundation (IRE) (College Chapel)
999[2] (2109) 2650[3]

Just A Flash (IRE) *B R Johnson* a40
3 b g Redback—Just Deserts (Alhijaz)
128[10] 1343[11] 2454[11]

Just A Gigolo *P D Niven* 19
7 b g Inchinor—Courtisane (Persepolis (FR))
891[11]

Just An Angel (IRE) *A P Jarvis* a45 43
3 b f Namid—Changing Partners (Rainbow Quest (USA))
1250^{6} 1396^{8} 1812^{12} 2697^{9} 3186^{11}

Just Bond (IRE) *G R Oldroyd* a93 78
5 b g Namid—Give Warning (IRE) (Warning)
(38) 444^{3} 501^{8} 2452^{4} 2986^{11} (3111) 3530^{9} 4177^{3} (4672) 5099^{7} 5196^{3} (6067) 6359^{7} 7074^{6} 7287^{2}

Justcallmehandsome *D J S Ffrench Davis* a64 55
5 ch g Handsome Ridge—Pearl Dawn (IRE) (Jareer (USA))
2141^{2} 2275^{11} 2721^{4} 3035^{6} 4577^{14} 5606^{3} (5782) (6179) 6316^{4} 6716^{7} 6956^{3}

Just Chrissie *G Fierro*
3 b f Classic Cliche(IRE) —Marsh Marigold (Tina's Pet)
1012^{9}

Just Crystal *B P J Baugh* a47 33
3 b f Polar Prince(IRE) —Grandads Dream (Never So Bold)
5567^{7} 5915^{10} 6385^{10} 7034^{5} 7133^{6} 7248^{9}

Just Dust *M W Easterby* 87
3 b g Makbul—Dusty Bankes (Greensmith)
2536^{10} 3052^{8} 3682^{11} 3971^{6} 4581^{15} 4998^{8} 5563^{10} 5936^{8}

Justenjoy Yourself *R W Price* a45 27
5 b m Tipsy Creek(USA) —Habibi (Alhijaz)
1317^{8}

Just Fly *Dr J R J Naylor* a70 52
7 b g Efisio—Chrysalis (Soviet Star (USA))
117^{10} 213^{6} 389^{6} 793^{5} 888^{4} 1002^{8} 2179^{5}

Just Intersky (USA) *V Smith* a64 83
4 gr g Distant View(USA) —Hexane (FR) (Kendor (FR))
67^{7} 4891^{12} 5964^{7} 6951^{6} (7083)

Just James *D Nicholls* a66 99
8 b g Spectrum(IRE) —Fairy Flight (IRE) (Fairy King (USA))
(2) 629^{12} 912^{8} (1374) 1423^{2} (1527) 1711^{11} 2563^{15}

Just Jimmy (IRE) *P D Evans* a45 63
2 b g Ashkalani(IRE) —Berkeley Hall (Saddlers' Hall (IRE))
3479^{8} 3760^{7} 4417^{9} 5268^{9} 6418^{9} 6478^{7}

Just Joey *J R Weymes* 87
3 b f Averti(IRE) —Fly South (Polar Falcon (USA))
1160^{9} 1577^{3} 1900^{9} 2867^{8} 3637^{6} 4726^{20} 4898^{6} 5155^{7} 5232^{8}

Just Julie (USA) *N A Callaghan* a53 68
3 ch f Gulch(USA) —Julie Jalouse (USA) (Kris S (USA))
1012^{3} 1217^{3} 1950^{4} 2690^{7} 3847^{8} 4339^{10}

Just Like A Woman *M L W Bell* a70 74
2 b f Observatory(USA) —Always On My Mind (Distant Relative)
5363^{3} 5949^{5} (6329)

Just Lille (IRE) *Mrs A Duffield* 87
4 b m Mull Of Kintyre(USA) —Tamasriya (IRE) (Doyoun)
1040^{14} 1258^{7} (1488) (1997) (2027) (3016) 3755^{5} 4637^{3} 4933^{2} 5145^{6}

Just Little (FR) *J-C Rouget* 104
3 b f Grand Slam(USA) —Just Wood (FR) (Highest Honor (FR))
(1339a) 2290a[3]

Just Matty *J G M O'Shea* 30
4 b g Bertolini(USA) —Frisson (Slip Anchor)
1001^{10} 1177^{10}

Just Mossie *W G M Turner* a54 34
2 ch g Ishiguru(USA) —Marinsky (USA) (Diesis)
4027^{5} 4136^{12} 5869^{12} 7096^{2} 7171^{3} 7286^{4}

Just Observing *P T Midgley* a78 81
4 ch g Observatory(USA) —Just Speculation (IRE) (Ahonoora)
966^{2} 1158^{3} (1416) 2314^{6} 2551^{4} 3959^{4} 4228^{6} 4365^{4}

Just Oscar (GER) *W M Brisbourne* a60 68
3 b g Surako(GER) —Jade Chequer (Green Desert (USA))
931^{12} 1297^{4} 1726^{12} 1903^{8} 2489^{2} 2759^{5} 3491^{2} 3875^{3} 4354^{2} 4480^{8} 4731^{5} 5330^{7} 5781^{4} 6361^{6} 6567^{7}

Just Puddie *W G M Turner* a14 48
2 b f Piccolo—Miss Laetitia (IRE) (Entitled)
2949^{13} 3681^{2}

Just Rob *R Hollinshead* 69
2 b c Robellino(USA) —Scapavia (FR) (Alzao (USA))
6107^{3} 6593^{2}

Just Sam (IRE) *D Carroll* 53
2 b f Mull Of Kintyre(USA) —Strawberry Sands (Lugana Beach)
4448^{12} 4781^{5} 5154^{7} 5520^{8}

Just Sort It *W Jarvis* 80
2 b g Averti(IRE) —Lady Kris (IRE) (Kris)
(1291) 1772^{10} 4168^{7} 4812^{11} 6052^{11}

Just Spike *B P J Baugh* a59
4 ch g Cayman Kai(IRE) —Grandads Dream (Never So Bold)
802^{4} 1262^{11} 1904^{6} 7105^{8} 7271^{9}

Just Superb *P A Pritchard* a42 24
8 ch g Superlative—Just Greenwich (Chilibang)
203^{7} 285^{8} 6999^{6}

Just Two Numbers *W Jarvis* 81
3 b g Bahamian Bounty—Khadino (Relkino)
1077^{4} (2944) 3689^{6} 6236^{4} 6576^{6}

Just Waz (USA) *R M Whitaker* a38 65
5 ch g Woodman(USA) —Just Tops (USA) (Topsider (USA))
913^{7} 1966^{14} 2372^{5} (2537) 2890^{2} 3193^{2} 3467^{6} 4124^{10} 6076^{7} 6308^{11}

Juxta Pose *P Winkworth* a38
4 b g Josr Algarhoud(IRE) —Shi Shi (Alnasr Alwasheek)
1120^{9} 1435^{11}

Juzilla (IRE) *W R Swinburn* a64 55
3 b f Marju(IRE) —Mizillablack (IRE) (Eagle Eyed (USA))
4666^{7} 5567^{2} 5917^{7}

Kaateb (IRE) *W J Haggas* a89 76
4 b g Alhaarth(IRE) —Muhaba (USA) (Mr Prospector (USA))
4530^{11} 4815^{7} (5384) 6007^{2} (6439)

Kaballero (GER) *S Gollings* a53 73
6 ch g Lomitas—Keniana (IRE) (Sharpo)
1915^{8} 2346^{6}

Kabeer *A J McCabe* a91 47
9 ch g Unfuwain(USA) —Ta Rib (USA) (Mr Prospector (USA))
96^{8} 592^{9} 739^{7} 915^{7} (7141) (7200) 7241^{4}

Kabis Amigos *D Nicholls* a80 76
5 ch g Nashwan(USA) —River Saint (USA) (Irish River (FR))
308^{2} 564^{8} (609) (673) (771) 915^{3} 1063^{7} 1133^{2} 1481^{9} 3999^{6} (4219) 4479^{6} 4820^{7} 5035^{8}

Kabuku *M H Tompkins* a45 67
2 b c Dr Fong(USA) —Premier Night (Old Vic)
4584^{13} 5599^{5} 5749^{5} 6410^{14} 6566^{5}

Kadia *P T Midgley* a48 49
4 ch m Arkadian Hero(USA) —Soba Up (Persian Heights)
559^{12} 728^{9} (906) 1349^{7} 1596^{12} 1933^{12} 3381^{5} 3754^{10} 5035^{9}

Kadouchski (FR) *Miss E C Lavelle* a58 58
3 b g Ski Chief(USA) —Douchka (FR) (Fijar Tango (FR))
1725^{5} 6991^{2} 7183^{11}

Kafuu (IRE) *J Noseda* 86
3 b c Danehill Dancer(IRE) —Nausicaa (USA) (Diesis)
6013^{8} 6301^{25}

Kahara *L M Cumani* 93
3 b f Sadler's Wells(USA) —Kithanga (IRE) (Darshaan)
(4765) (5415) (5955) 6473^{2}

Kahlua Bear *Miss K B Boutflower* a57 59
5 b g Mister Baileys—Crystal Magic (Mazilier (USA))
123^{4} (217) 268^{3} 1436^{8} (Dead)

Kahlua Kiss *W R Muir* a85 102
4 b m Mister Baileys—Ring Queen (USA) (Fairy King (USA))
6757^{9} 6931^{9} 7225^{6}

Kaichou (IRE) *N A Callaghan* 15
3 b f Peintre Celebre(USA) —Lipica (IRE) (Night Shift (USA))
3244^{7}

Kailasha (IRE) *C F Wall* a73 63
3 br f Kalanisi(IRE) —Snow Peak (Arazi (USA))
1312^{5} 1725^{3} 2666^{2} 3421^{5}

Kairaba *J Pearce* 58
2 ch c Storming Home—Heaven-Liegh-Grey (Grey Desire)
1007^{9} 1201^{6} (Dead)

Kalamkar (IRE) *S Donohoe* 62
5 gr h Daylami(IRE) —Kalamba (IRE) (Green Dancer (USA))
1760a[6] 4114a[13]

Kalanda Kurl (IRE) *J J Quinn* 33
2 ch f Hernando(FR) —Kalanda (Desert King (IRE))
3761^{9} 4796^{12} 5193^{10}

Kalankari (IRE) *A M Balding* a102 103
4 b h Kalanisi(IRE) —Stately Princess (Robellino (USA))
(178a) 394a[5] 540a[3] 1082^{2}

Kalasam *W R Muir* a82 77
3 ch g Noverre(USA) —Spring Sixpence (Dowsing (USA))
1081^{3} 1277^{8} 1929^{6} 2425^{4} 3913^{6} 4450^{4} 4686^{3} 5043^{2} (5307) 5539^{3} 5636^{3} 6293^{2} 6481^{2}

Kalatime (IRE) *M F Harris* a73 71
4 bb m Kalanisi(IRE) —Dream Time (Rainbow Quest (USA))
85^{13} 115^{7} 279^{3} 665^{5} 747^{8}

Kal Barg *M A Jarvis* a77 91
2 b c Medicean—Persian Air (Persian Bold)
4782^{4} (5222) 5828^{3} (6486)

Kaldoun Kingdom (IRE) *E A L Dunlop* a47 90
2 b c King's Best(USA) —Bint Kaldoun (IRE) (Kaldoun (FR))
2991^{11} 3592^{2} 3967^{4} 4484^{4} 4903^{6} (5705) 6282^{3} (6462)

Kaleo *A Wohler* 100
3 ch c Lomitas—Kazoo (Shareef Dancer (USA))
1054a[3] 2502a[7]

Kalgoorlie (USA) *I Mohammed* a68 98
3 br c Gone West(USA) —Fair Kris (USA) (Kris S (USA))
414a[7]

Kalhan Sands (IRE) *G A Swinbank* 78
2 b g Okawango(USA) —Night Spirit (IRE) (Night Shift (USA))
2983^{10} (3834) 4613^{7}

Kalinina (IRE) *Miss A M Winters* 75
4 b m Sinndar(IRE) —Kaliana (IRE) (Slip Anchor)
6555a[16]

Kalken (FR) *L Planard* 98
4 b h Kendor(FR) —Super Vite (USA) (Septieme Ciel (USA))
437a[0]

Kalligal *R Ingram* a54 73
2 br f Kyllachy—Anytime Baby (Bairn (USA))
4810^{4} 5357^{3} 5872^{2} 6177^{5} 6425^{4}

Kalmez (IRE) *D Broad* 98
4 b g Kalanisi(IRE) —Sidelined (IRE) (In The Wings)
3577a[7]

Kalokairi (IRE) *J L Dunlop* 59
2 b f Galileo(IRE) —Naziriya (FR) (Darshaan)
5162^{14} 5596^{9} 6106^{9}

Kaloura (IRE) *A Fabre* 104
3 b f Sinndar(IRE) —Kalamba (IRE) (Green Dancer (USA))
(2384a) 2926a[2] 4215a[5] 6030a[7]

Kamal *W R Muir* a64 47
2 ch g Bahamian Bounty—Star Tulip (Night Shift (USA))
1975^{4} 3341^{10} 6880^{3} 7042^{7} (7182) 7280^{5}

Kamanda Laugh *K A Ryan* a89 99
6 ch g Most Welcome—Kamada (USA) (Blushing Groom (FR))
2807^{4} 3258^{6} 4228^{10} 4566^{12} 5776^{12} 6674^{8} 7100^{6} 7241^{7}

Kames Park (IRE) *Mrs H O Graham* a98 93
5 b g Desert Sun—Persian Sally (IRE) (Persian Bold)
153^{2} (698) (763) 1244^{14} 1575^{2} 1805^{5} 2245^{5} 2861^{11} 4893^{7} 5664^{7}

Kandahar Run *H R A Cecil* 103
2 gr c Rock Of Gibraltar(IRE) —Kenmist (Kenmare (FR))
4547^{2} (5321) (6297)

Kandidate *C E Brittain* a118 118
5 b h Kabool—Valleyrose (IRE) (Royal Academy (USA))
(399a) 863a[6] 1274^{3} 1877a[5] 3331^{6} 4387^{5} 5142^{3} 6942a[15]

Kankakee (USA) *J E Pease* a96 104
4 br m Cozzene(USA) —Kool Kat Katie (IRE) (Fairy King (USA))
1421a[8] 4215a[4] 5150a[9] 6376a[7] 7128a[0]

Kannon *W J Knight* a51
2 b f Kyllachy—Violet (IRE) (Mukaddamah (USA))
6948^{10}

Kanonkop *Miss J R Gibney* a54 53
3 b f Observatory(USA) —Camcorder (Nashwan (USA))
924^{7} 1039^{7} 2105^{5} 3083^{5}

Kansas Feather (IRE) *B S Rothwell*
4 b m Darnay—Kissimmee Bay (IRE) (Brief Truce (USA))
186^{9} 365^{10}

Kansas Gold *J Mackie* a72 71
4 b g Alhaarth(IRE) —Star Tulip (Night Shift (USA))
1718^{11} 1847^{9} 2576^{15} 5330^{2} (5569) 5983^{3} (6146) 6342^{10} 6982^{5} 7173^{6}

Kapellmeister (IRE) *M S Saunders* a68 85
4 b g Mozart(IRE) —March Hare (Groom Dancer (USA))
652^{11} 6568^{11} 7046^{10}

Kapera (FR) *Noel Lawlor* a79 88
4 gr m Linamix(FR) —Kentucky Kaper (USA) (The Prime Minister (USA))
875a[10] 2067a[7] 4051a[18]

Kapil (SAF) *M F De Kock* 121
5 b g Jallad(USA) —Outstanding Star (AUS) (Bletchingly (AUS))
530a[3] (646a) 862a[5] 6338^{9} 6655^{4}

Karagan (FR) *T G McCourt* 40
5 b g Alamo Bay(USA) —Kalitita (FR) (General Holme (USA))
5696a[11]

Karaoke Queen *G C Bravery*
3 ch f Tumbleweed Ridge—Sodelk (Interrex (CAN))
6597^{15}

Kara Tau *M P Tregoning* 55
2 b g Efisio—Donna Anna (Be My Chief (USA))
3233^{6}

Karate Queen *A M Balding* a57 51
2 b f King's Best(USA) —Black Belt Shopper (IRE) (Desert Prince (IRE))
5162^{11} 5919^{14} 6401^{4}

Karayel (IRE) *R Hannon* a85 91
3 b c Fasliyev(USA) —Madamaa (IRE) (Alzao (USA))
841^{P} (Dead)

Kareeb (FR) *P A Blockley* a67 63
10 b g Green Desert(USA) —Braari (USA) (Gulch (USA))
367^{6} 440^{8} (Dead)

Karine Girl (IRE) *Nicola De Chirico*
2 b f King Charlemagne(USA) —Mindy Girl (IRE) (Last Tycoon (IRE))
6527a[9]

Karky Schultz (GER) *J M P Eustace* a45 68
2 gr g Diktat—Kazoo (Shareef Dancer (USA))
2241^{5} 2604^{3} 3024^{4} 6201^{9} 6486^{8} 6750^{11}

Karlani (IRE) *G A Swinbank* 77
4 bb g Fantastic Light(USA) —Karliyka (IRE) (Last Tycoon (IRE))
1598^{6} 2026^{2} 2095^{2} 2908^{6} 3412^{6} 4179^{3} (4280) 4925^{4} 5257^{7}

Karma Llama (IRE) *B Smart* a39 67
3 b f Intikhab(USA) —Ustka (Lomond (USA))
1684^{7} 2313^{7} 2713^{4} 5643^{8} 5907^{12} 6310^{6}

Karmei *J W Hills* a51 62
2 b c Royal Applause—Lafite (Robellino (USA))
5143^{7} 5380^{7} 6903^{4}

Karmest *A D Brown* a58 59
3 ch f Best Of The Bests(IRE) —Karmafair (IRE) (Always Fair (USA))
1312^{10} 1749^{3} 2300^{7} (2718) 3342^{10} 5602^{8} 5907^{7} 6467^{11} 6638^{4} 6896^{2} 6969^{3} 7098^{12}

Karoo Blue (IRE) *C E Brittain* a94 94
3 b c Cape Cross(IRE) —Red Conquest (Lycius (USA))
754^{3} 1662^{6} 2243^{7} 2671^{4} 3503^{15} (4080) 4276^{2} 4608^{7} 5221^{8} 6016^{3}

Karrumba (IRE) *B J McMath* a8
3 ch f Desert Prince(IRE) —Royal Bossi (IRE) (Spectrum (IRE))
1024^{9} 6751^{8}

Kasatana (IRE) *A De Royer-Dupre* 100
3 b f Hernando(FR) —Kassiyda (Mill Reef (USA))
5150a[5]

Kasban *E A L Dunlop* 74
3 b c Kingmambo(USA) —Ebaraya (IRE) (Sadler's Wells (USA))
1011^{5} 1560^{9} 2112^{3} 2628^{4}

Kaseema (USA) *Sir Michael Stoute* 92
3 bb f Storm Cat(USA) —Onaga (USA) (Mr Prospector (USA))
1096^{4} 1496^{19} 3897^{12}

Kashimin (IRE) *G A Swinbank* 77
2 b c Kyllachy—Oh So Misty (Teenoso (USA))
(6384)

Kashmina *M R Channon* 69
2 ch f Dr Fong(USA) —Lady Melbourne (IRE) (Indian Ridge)
3706^{7} 4094^{16} 4774^{10} 5314^{7} 5746^{5} 6075^{2} 6328^{10} 6572^{9}

Kashmir Lady (FR) *H Candy* a68 76
3 ch f Rock Of Gibraltar(IRE) —Persian Walk (FR) (Persian Bold)
1345^{6} 1726^{4} 2571^{3} 3474^{2} 3798^{2} 4257^{4} 4848^{9} 5701^{8}

Kashoof *J L Dunlop* 84
2 b f Green Desert(USA) —Khulood (USA) (Storm Cat (USA))
2364^{5} 3507^{2} 4061^{9} 4605^{2} (5380)

Kassuta *John A Harris* a65 57
3 b f Kyllachy—Happy Omen (Warning)
678^{4} 1437^{4} 2571^{6} 2916^{15} 3163^{2} 3605^{8} 4071^{3} 4416^{9} 5098^{8} 6088^{9} 6277^{2} 6464^{3} (6573)

Kastan *B Palling* a20 46
3 ch g Auction House(USA) —Cashiki (IRE) (Case Law)
1725^{13} 2077^{7} 3175^{3} 4256^{13} 4591^{11} 5310^{12} 6537^{15}

Kasthari (IRE) *J D Bethell* 108
8 gr g Vettori(IRE) —Karliyka (IRE) (Last Tycoon (IRE))
1823^{9} 2449^{6} 2736^{18} 4569^{6} 4893^{2} 5375^{2} 5800^{4} 6335^{6} 6760^{2}

Kasumi *H Morrison* a87 88
4 ch m Inchinor—Raindrop (Primo Dominie)
1666^{4} (2877) 4049^{2} (4268) 5950^{3} 6208^{4}

Katalak (IRE) *J P Broderick* 65
4 b h Desert Prince(IRE) —Katiykha (IRE) (Darshaan)
4582^{17}

Katelynstar (IRE) *Liam Roche* 8
2 b f Lend A Hand—Halse Copse (Robellino (USA))
6392a[11]

Kates Guest (IRE) *B G Powell* a55 32
5 b g Be My Guest(USA) —Kates Choice (IRE) (Taufan (USA))
230^{7} 425^{10}

Katesville (IRE) *R Ford* 57
3 b f King's Theatre(IRE) —Great Days (IRE) (Magical Strike (USA))
5622^{2}

Kathleen Kennet *C Tinkler* a59 62
7 b m Turtle Island(IRE) —Evaporate (Insan (USA))
2381^{0} 3950^{6} 4533^{4} 4945^{7} 5756^{6} 6532^{3} 6908^{9}

Katie Boo (IRE) *A Berry* a54 84
5 br m Namid—Misty Peak (IRE) (Sri Pekan (USA))
432^{8} 964^{6} 1241^{6} 1596^{5} 1748^{2} 1940^{3} (2386) 2712^{4} 2870^{2} (3184) 3536^{3} 3569^{4} 3784^{4} (4390) 4498^{2} 4703^{10} 4999^{6} 5403^{6} 5666^{6} 6300^{14} 6753^{14}

Katie Coniston *Dr J R J Naylor* a38 37
3 b f Lake Coniston(IRE) —Lycius Touch (Lycius (USA))
3062^{11} 3425^{8} 4541^{8} 5861^{7} 6094^{6} 6429^{9}

Katie Killane *M Wellings* a53 33
5 ch m Komaite(USA) —Efficacy (Efisio)
46^{2} 201^{9} 289^{4} 581^{7} 2174^{7}

Katie Kingfisher *M Wigham* a46 42
3 b f Fraam—Sonic Sapphire (Royal Academy (USA))
1538^{14} 2110^{9} 4526^{15} 6797^{5} 7012^{14}

Katie Lawson (IRE) *D Haydn Jones* a51 38
4 b m Xaar—Idle Chat (USA) (Assert)
516^{10} 1886^{12} 2142^{5} 3868^{13} 6859^{10} 7006^{6}

Katies Tuitor *B W Duke* a74 74
4 b g Kayf Tara—Penny Gold (IRE) (Millfontaine)
4572^{5} 5769^{6}

Katimont (IRE) *B W Hills* 76
2 b f Montjeu(IRE) —Katiyfa (Auction Ring (USA))
5811^{2} 6296^{4}

Katirisa (IRE) *John M Oxx* 89
3 b f Spinning World(USA) —Katiykha (IRE) (Darshaan)
5460a[2]

Katiypour (IRE) *B R Johnson* a91 90
10 ch g Be My Guest(USA) —Katiyfa (Auction Ring (USA))
56^{2} 259^{2} 384^{2} 576^{6} 765^{4} 1121^{10} 1446^{3} 2573^{4} 2995^{5} 3420^{6} 4266^{7} 5339^{4} 6268^{2} 6894^{12} 7251^{6}

Katoomba *H-A Pantall* a95 78
3 b f Forest Wildcat(USA) —Elizabeth Bay (USA) (Mr Prospector (USA))
6940a[9]

Katrina Bee (IRE) *R Hannon* a48 63
2 ch f Captain Rio—Way Of Truth (Muhtarram (USA))
2651^{3} 2997^{9} 4160^{4}

Katsumoto (IRE) *A J McCabe* a18 53
4 ch g Muhtarram(USA) —Self Assured (IRE) (Ahonoora)
833^{U} 1750^{9} 1934^{12}

Katy Carr *M J Wallace* a64
3 b f Machiavellian(USA) —Khalafiya (Darshaan)
257^{7}

Ka'u Mauna Kea *J A Geake* a8 52
3 ch f Observatory(USA) —Musical Twist (USA) (Woodman (USA))
4018^{5} 4575^{10} 6097^{8} 6826^{12}

Kavachi (IRE) *G L Moore* a67 80
4 b g Cadeaux Genereux—Answered Prayer (Green Desert (USA))
1401^{11} 1655^{8} 2218^{3} 2512^{3} (3048) 3705^{10} 4184^{4} 4667^{6} 5001^{2} 5862^{3} (6576)

Kavafi (IRE) *C Laffon-Parias* a100 107
5 b h Zafonic(USA) —Loxandra (Last Tycoon (IRE))
897a[4] 4012a[11] (4873a) 5823a[8]

Kavaloti (IRE) *G L Moore* a83 83
3 b g Kahyasi—Just As Good (FR) (Kaldounevees (FR))
4511^{4} 4951^{2}

Kaveri (USA) *C E Brittain* a86 87
4 bb m War Chant(USA) —Valid Bonnet (USA) (Valid Appeal (USA))
44^{10} 384^{7} 590^{5} 2240^{7} 3828^{2} 4515^{9}

Kavi (IRE) *Simon Earle* a78 61
7 ch g Perugino(USA) —Premier Leap (IRE) (Salmon Leap (USA))
29^{3} 232^{2} 316^{2} 691^{3}

Kavinsky *M Johnston* 42
2 b c Stravinsky(USA) —Khamsin (USA) (Mr Prospector (USA))
5226^{7} 6469^{12}

Kayah *R M Beckett* 104
3 b f Kahyasi—Kristina (Kris)
(1663) 2211[9] 5352[6] 6168[9]

Kayd Kodaun (IRE) *J S Bolger* 86
2 b f Traditionally(USA) —Danaskaya (IRE) (Danehill (USA))
3659a[4]

Kay Es Jay (FR) *B W Hills* a79 98
2 b f Xaar—Angel Rose (IRE) (Definite Article)
2768[4] (3213) 3880[5] 4400[3] 4626a[8] 5322[9] 5796[5] 6336[5]

Kayf Aramis *J L Spearing* a66 79
5 b g Kayf Tara—Ara (Birthright)
1003[5] 1148[9] (1793) 1959[13] 2908[3] 3279[2] 3609[4] 3976[5] 4056[12] 5884[4] 6181[2] 6622[8]

Kayflaa (IRE) *M R Channon* 51
2 b f Dubai Destination(USA) —Arhaaff (IRE) (Danehill (USA))
5812[9] 6411[9]

Kay Gee Be (IRE) *M J Wallace* a100 86
3 b c Fasliyev(USA) —Pursuit Of Truth (USA) (Irish River (FR))
(1076) *(1439)* 2037[12] 2578[5] *(6002)*

Kaymich Perfecto *R M Whitaker* a59 82
7 b g Sheikh Albadou—Manhattan Diamond (Primo Dominie)
4820[12] 5228[12] 5737[12]

Kay One (IRE) *R J Price* a47 39
2 ch f Court Cave(IRE) —Miss Tricks (IRE) (Eagle Eyed (USA))
2488[15] *3171[8] 3453[9]* 3841[8] *7010[8] 7149[8]*

Kaystar Ridge *D K Ivory* a65 31
2 b c Tumbleweed Ridge—Kayartis (Kaytu)
2630[10] *3283[2]* 4181[15] *5176[6] 6312[8] 6966[2] 7031[9]*

Kay Two (IRE) *R J Price* a87 93
5 ch g Monashee Mountain(USA) —Tricky (Song)
1242[2] 1601[3] 1788[11] 3104[11] 3990[21] 5379[9] (5689) (6197) 6487[U] *6676[7] 6876[12]*

Kazakstan *Mrs L C Jewell* a50 59
3 b g Kyllachy—Niseem (USA) (Hennessy (USA))
7279[11]

Keagles (ITY) *J E Long* a41 32
4 b m Indian Danehill(IRE) —Athens Belle (IRE) (Groom Dancer (USA))
1250[7] 1926[8] 4859[11] *5898[11] 6266[13] 6807[6] 7189[9]*

Keel Castle Maine (IRE) *Patrick Joseph Hayes* 86
6 b g Blue Ocean(USA) —Nice Mover (IRE) (Lashkari)
6555a[17]

Keelings Donabate *K R Burke* a67 34
4 b g Desert Style(IRE) —Sideloader Special (Song)
1595[10]

Keenes Day (FR) *M Johnston* a83 76
2 gr g Daylami(IRE) —Key Academy (Royal Academy (USA))
4037[6] 4586[5] (4841) 5463a[6] *6120[4]*

Keen Look (IRE) *Gerard Keane* a79 90
8 b g Key Of Luck(USA) —Killone Lady (IRE) (High Estate)
5184a[2] 5788a[4]

Keeparryappy (IRE) *K R Burke* a44 64
2 b g Fath(USA) —Coppelia (IRE) (Mac's Imp (USA))
1087[10] 1706[3] *4459[12] 5199[12]*

Keep A Welcome *S Parr* a20
4 ch g Most Welcome—Celtic Chimes (Celtic Cone)
60[12] 1573[6] 1895[9]

Keep Discovering (IRE) *Saeed Bin Suroor* 76
2 b c Oasis Dream—Side Of Paradise (IRE) (Sadler's Wells (USA))
(5277) 6052[9]

Keep Shining *J S Goldie* 42
2 b f Tomba—Turf Moor (IRE) (Mac's Imp (USA))
2451[11] 2758[5] 4097[6]

Keep Your Distance *K R Burke* a64 64
3 b g Distant Music(USA) —Queen G (USA) (Matty G (USA))
139[8]

Keep Your Head (USA) *J A Osborne* a64 53
2 b f Successful Appeal(USA) —Tudor Guest (USA) (Medieval Man (USA))
5100[5] 5727[6] 5882[8] *6903[7]*

Keidas (FR) *C F Wall* a76 76
3 b f Lomitas—Kahina (GER) (Warning)
(1410) 2834[5] 3798[5] 4170[8] *6343[5]*

Keisha Kayleigh (IRE) *B Ellison* a68 66
4 b m Almutawakel—Awtaar (USA) (Lyphard (USA))
819[5] (1301) 3156[5] 3497[4] 4582[4] 5563[2] (5738) 6021[2] 6380[6] *6837[2] 7023[3] 7249[7]*

Kelamon *M D I Usher* a74 77
3 b g Keltos(FR) —Faraway Moon (Distant Relative)
429[5] 583[3] 678[2] 1176[5] 2061[3] 2622[2] *2769[6]* (2942) (3164) 3278[4] *4950[8]* 5874[7] *6243[4] 6355[6] 6568[10]*

Kelly's Landing (USA) *E Kenneally* a117
6 bb g Patton(USA) —Best Game (USA) (Great Above (USA))
(860a) 6510a[5]

Kempes (IRE) *Ms F M Crowley* 106
4 b g Intikhab(USA) —Unicamp (Royal Academy (USA))
2067a[2]

Kempsey *J J Bridger* a69 75
5 ch g Wolfhound(USA) —Mockingbird (Sharpo)
479[9] (82) 161[3] 276[4] 561[4] 626[4] 787[3] 1004[11]

Kenmore *J G Given* 95
5 b g Compton Place—Watheeqah (USA) (Topsider (USA))
1653[9] 1941[4] 2566[11] 2744[11] 2841[13] (3180) 3557[8] 3791[8] 4581[2] 4932[7] 6331[9]

Kennington *Mrs C A Dunnett* a74 75
7 ch g Compton Place—Mim (Midyan (USA))
803[10] 1309[9] 1640[15] 2879[9] *3285[12]* 3829[12] 4296[2] 4397[3] *(4973) 5174[4]* 5576[4] *5778[10]* 6415[4] *6608[6] 6779[3] 6957[11]* 7107[3] *7265[2]*

Ken's Girl *W S Kittow* a64 76
3 ch f Ishiguru(USA) —There's Two (IRE) (Ashkalani (IRE))
(1207) 2060[2] 3528[11] 4127[7] *6273[7] 6747[7]*

Kensington (IRE) *P D Evans* a64 67
6 b g Cape Cross(IRE) —March Star (IRE) (Mac's Imp (USA))
6749[5] 6993[4] 7073[5] (7180)

Kenton Street *J A R Toller* 66
2 ch c Compton Place—Western Applause (Royal Applause)
6617[4]

Kentucky Boy (IRE) *Jedd O'Keeffe* a48 67
3 b g Distant Music(USA) —Delta Town (USA) (Sanglamore (USA))
2259[3] 3183[2] (3792) (4638) 5906[6]

Kentucky Bullet (USA) *A G Newcombe* a50 56
11 b g Housebuster(USA) —Exactly So (Caro)
503[9] 1570[3] 1934[8]

Kentucky Dynamite (USA) *A De Royer-Dupre* 117
4 b h Kingmambo(USA) —Chelsey Flower (USA) (His Majesty (USA))
1389a[7] 2500a[4] 3665a[2]

Kenwyn *K Bishop* 55
5 b g Efisio—Vilany (Never So Bold)
2107[8]

Keon (IRE) *R Hollinshead* a60 60
5 b g Rossini(USA) —Lonely Brook (USA) (El Gran Senor (USA))
144[4] 518[5] 605[2] 932[6] 1066[7] 6906[9] 6979[11] 7169[7]

Kerama (GER) *H Rogers* 66
6 b m Waky Nao—Kalila (USA) (Gulch (USA))
5460a[17]

Kerayasi (FR) *G L Moore* a66 71
5 b g Kahyasi—Good Blend (FR) (Darshaan)
4544[4] *5093[6]*

Kerriemuir Lass (IRE) *M A Jarvis* a94 95
4 b m Celtic Swing—Shabby Chic (USA) (Red Ransom (USA))
1621[6] (2474) 3959[9] 4376[7] *4888[4] 5686[3] 6605[7]*

Kerry's Blade (IRE) *Micky Hammond* 49
5 ch g Daggers Drawn(USA) —Treasure (IRE) (Treasure Kay)
4451[5] 4638[7] 4925[6] 5283[13] 5561[4]

Kerry's Dream *T D Easterby* 80
3 ch f Tobougg(IRE) —Jetbeeah (IRE) (Lomond (USA))
3885[10] 4703[11] 5662[11] 6020[3] 6157[19]

Kersaint (IRE) *K A Ryan* 86
2 b c Catcher In The Rye(IRE) —Quivala (USA) (Thunder Gulch (USA))
(1007) 1390[3] 2232[6] 3077[2] 3492[3] 4695[7] 5374[7] 6017[11]

Kerswell *B R Millman* a56 57
3 b f Komaite(USA) —Polgwynne (Forzando)
2696[10] 4071[10]

Kervriou (FR) *A M Balding* a37 80
4 ch g Pennekamp(USA) —Good Blend (FR) (Darshaan)
2003[13] 2512[8] 4551[8] *5225[14]*

Keshya *N P Littmoden* a69 55
6 b m Mtoto—Liberatrice (FR) (Assert)
107[4] 182[8]

Kestrel Cross (IRE) *Declan Gillespie* a19 96
5 b g Cape Cross(IRE) —Lady Rachel (IRE) (Priolo (USA))
250a[4] 325a[8]

Kew Green (USA) *P R Webber* a111 113
9 bb g Brocco(USA) —Jump With Joy (USA) (Linkage (USA))
(1082) 1651[26] 1791[11] 2368[6] 4167[5] 5049[11]

Kew The Music *M R Channon* a68 63
7 b g Botanic(USA) —Harmonia (Glint Of Gold)
313[11] 426[7] 560[4] (686) 718[4] 729[2] 831[4] 902[10] (Dead)

Keyaki (IRE) *C F Wall* a83 92
6 b m Shinko Forest(IRE) —Woodie Dancer (USA) (Green Dancer (USA))
1063[3] 1431[3] *(1525)* 1847[2] (2240) 2688[8] 3670[4] 4373[7] 5168[9] 5560[7]

Keycavern *M Botti* 55
3 b f Key Of Luck(USA) —Cavernista (Lion Cavern (USA))
(4292) (Dead)

Keynes (JPN) *E J Creighton* a27
5 ch g Gold Fever(USA) —Eternal Reve (USA) (Diesis)
887[9] 2176[13] 3730[8]

Key Of Destiny (SAF) *M F De Kock* a111 108
9 b g Qui Danzig(USA) —Twist Of Fate (SAF) (Secret Prospector (USA))
245a[6] *326a[9]* 470a[12]

Key Partners (IRE) *P A Blockley* a67 64
6 b g Key Of Luck(USA) —Teacher Preacher (IRE) (Taufan (USA))
88[9] 428[8] 1314[8] 1720[3] 2145[7] 2519[5] 3035[2] 3243[10] 4383[12] *5422[5] 6265[13] (6583) 6719[5] 6911[11]*

Key To Pleasure (GER) *Mario Hofer* 109
7 b h Sharp Prod(USA) —Key To Love (FR) (Alzao (USA))
(3122a) 4213a[3] 4869a[12] 6370a[4] 6767a[7]

Kezia (FR) *C Laffon-Parias* a93 97
4 b m Spectrum(IRE) —Kresna (FR) (Distant Relative)
31a[13]

Khabfair *S Seemar* a87 103
6 b g Intikhab(USA) —Ruby Affair (IRE) (Night Shift (USA))
105a[2]

Khana Ras (IRE) *E J O'Neill* a64 61
2 b c Fasliyev(USA) —Siamoise (Caerleon (USA))
1680[8] 4904[6] 5343[14] *6099[5] 6433[7] (6566)*

Khandala (IRE) *M L W Bell* a67 60
2 b f Soviet Star(USA) —Khatela (IRE) (Shernazar)
4232[8] 4968[3] 5595[8] 6075[4] *(6478)*

Khanjar (USA) *J Pearce* a81 76
7 ch g Kris S(USA) —Alyssum (USA) (Storm Cat (USA))
39[8] 180[2] 278[2] 302[3] 1732[5]

Khetaab (IRE) *E J Alston* a54 62
5 b g Alhaarth(IRE) —Liberi Versi (IRE) (Last Tycoon (IRE))
1133[7] 1260[6] 1539[15] 2298[7] 2563[4]

Khibraat *E A L Dunlop* 51
2 ch f Alhaarth(IRE) —Nafhaat (USA) (Roberto (USA))
3874[8] 4796[11] 5812[8]

Khun John (IRE) *B J Meehan* a85 87
4 b g Marju(IRE) —Kathy Caerleon (IRE) (Caerleon (USA))
2003[3] 2397[3]

Khuzdar (IRE) *Mrs A Malzard* 46
8 ch g Definite Article—Mariyda (IRE) (Vayrann)
(2708a)

Khyberie *G Wragg* a65 45
4 b m Kahyasi—Reading Habit (USA) (Half A Year (USA))
499[8] 603[5] 1364[6] 1950[2] 2176[4]

Kiama *B G Powell* a50 62
5 b m Dansili—Catriona (Bustino)
16[10] 279[9] 416[7] 496[6]

Kibaar (USA) *J E Hammond* a72 93
4 b m Red Ransom(USA) —Elanaaka (Lion Cavern (USA))
1421a[10] 6770a[5]

Kibitzer *J W Hills* a54
2 b c Diesis—Kitza (IRE) (Danehill (USA))
7191[10]

Kick And Prance *J A Geake* a58 63
4 ch g Groom Dancer(USA) —Unerring (Unfuwain (USA))
6797[11]

Kick Back (GER) *P Schiergen* 88
3 ch f Royal Dragon(USA) —Kimberly Lake (GER) (Alkalde (GER))
1338a[13]

Kid Creole (IRE) *T M Walsh* 81
9 b g Royal Abjar(USA) —Milly's Song (Millfontaine)
5841a[16]

Kid Mambo (USA) *T G Mills* a76 112
3 b c Lemon Drop Kid(USA) —Spring Pitch (USA) (Storm Cat (USA))
1126[2] 1662[3] 2235[7] 2789[4]

Kid'Z'Play (IRE) *J S Goldie* 46
11 b g Rudimentary(USA) —Saka Saka (Camden Town)
1490[8] 2764[8] 3012[7] 3679[5] 3815[8]

Kielty's Folly *B P J Baugh* a45
3 gr g Weet-A-Minute(IRE) —Three Sweeties (Cruise Missile)
6597[13] *6858[6] 7103[6]*

Kiho *Eve Johnson Houghton* 68
2 b c Dashing Blade—Krim (GER) (Lagunas)
6418[6]

Kilburn *C G Cox* 84
3 b g Grand Lodge(USA) —Lady Lahar (Fraam)
1275[10] 2788[28] 3553[8] 4111[11] 5014[9] 5218[6]

Kildare Sun (IRE) *J Mackie* a83 79
5 b g Desert Sun—Megan's Dream (IRE) (Fayruz)
256[6] 1288[6] 1862[5] 3093[10] 4228[5] *5099[2]* 5383[15] 5905[8] *6293[8]*

Kili Links (IRE) *R Hannon* 45
2 b f Bahri(USA) —Hatheethah (IRE) (Machiavellian (USA))
4232[9] 4774[16] 5110[18]

Kilimandscharo (USA) *P J McBride* a86 92
5 b g Rahy(USA) —Landaria (FR) (Sadler's Wells (USA))
(72) 263[3] (568) (1575) 1822[3] 2474[2]

Killala (IRE) *D J Wintle* 8
7 b g Among Men(USA) —Hat And Gloves (Wolver Hollow)
3795[7]

Killcara Boy *H Candy* a53
2 b g Tobougg(IRE) —Barakat (Bustino)
6948[12]

Killena Boy (IRE) *W Jarvis* a93 98
5 b g Imperial Ballet(IRE) —Habaza (IRE) (Shernazar)
1524[4] (2123) 2401[3] 3330[9] 4119[13] *5221[12] 6143[10]*

Killer Class *J S Goldie* 42
2 ch f Kyllachy—Class Wan (Safawan)
3582[12] 3781[8] 5483[7] 6462[8]

Killybegs (IRE) *Saeed Bin Suroor* a69 119
4 b h Orpen(USA) —Belsay (Belmez (USA))
530a[4] *858a[13]*

Kilmannin (IRE) *H Rogers* 69
7 b g College Chapel—Bea's Ruby (IRE) (Fairy King (USA))
5460a[12] 6553a[4]

Kilmeena Dream *J C Fox* a31
3 b f Foxhound(USA) —Kilmeena Glen (Beveled (USA))
7029[9]

Kilmeena Magic *J C Fox* a52 47
5 b m Fumo Di Londra(IRE) —Kilmeena Lady (Inca Chief (USA))
133[12] 187[6] 273[8] 789[3] 1380[5] 2656[9] *3730[6]* 3868[4] *4739[10] 6896[6]*

Kilmiston Saturn *A M Hales* a34 35
3 ch g Trifolio—Sunley Solaire (Aragon)
1062[10] *1950[10]*

Kilometre Neuf (FR) *F Doumen* a105 105
4 b h Double Bed(FR) —Mary Astor (FR) (Groom Dancer (USA))
2617a[P] 3665a[6] 4873a[4] 6031a[10]

Kilvickeon (IRE) *Peter Grayson* a47 49
3 b g Daggers Drawn(USA) —Queen Of Sweden (IRE) (Solid Illusion (USA))
360[9] 713[6] 786[4] 970[2] *1248[5]* 2301[8] *2594[8]* 2939[3] *3281[9]* 4384[6] 4536[3] 4935[9] 5716[11] 5970[4] *6773[10] 7019[8] 7284[7]*

Kilworth (IRE) *Saeed Bin Suroor* a99 105
4 gr h Kalanisi(IRE) —Perugia (IRE) (Perugino (USA))
5444[2] 6018[7]

Kimono My House *J G Given* a54 56
3 ch f Dr Fong(USA) —Roselyn (Efisio)
2607[7] 3429[13] 3825[6] 4846[2] *5388[7]*

Kimpton Carer *J A Geake* a42 45
3 b g Groom Dancer(USA) —So True (So Blessed)
3847[13] 4535[2]

Kims Rose (IRE) *R A Harris* a54 59
4 br m Desert Prince(IRE) —Pinta (IRE) (Ahonoora)
337[13] (3904) 4257[11] 4545[12] *6677[10] 6957[6] 7024[11]*

Kindallachan *G C Bravery* a64 45
4 b m Magic Ring(IRE) —Moore Stylish (Moorestyle)
2242[8] 2791[7] 3627[12] 4336[13] 4689[9] *5175[2] 5425[2] (5778) 6101[6] 6581[8] 6747[11]*

Kindkintyre (IRE) *R A Fahey* a51
3 b g Mull Of Kintyre(USA) —Sweet Nature (IRE) (Classic Secret (USA))
152[9] 222[11] 484[10] 7034 [3] 7153[2]

Kindlelight Blue (IRE) *N P Littmoden* a80 71
3 gr g Golan(IRE) —Kalimar (IRE) (Bigstone (IRE))
655[9] 1531[5] 2133[2] 2601[10] *3456[4]* 4172[9] *(4592) 4742[2]* 5557[6] *6272[3] 6506[4] (6848) 7018[2]*

Kindlelight Debut *N P Littmoden* a103 90
7 b m Groom Dancer(USA) —Dancing Debut (Polar Falcon (USA))
119[6] 197[6] 255[6]

Kind Of Fizzy *Rae Guest* a61 66
3 b f Efisio—Kind Of Light (Primo Dominie)
1923[4] *2175[5]* 2622[10] (3038) 3474[7] 4326[10] *5130[9]* 5741[3] 6239[4] (Dead)

Kineta (USA) *W R Muir* a56 55
4 b m Miswaki(USA) —Kibitzing (USA) (Wild Again (USA))
160[5] 296[9] 479[9] 1260[14] 2309[4] 2581[7]

Kinfayre Boy *K W Hogg*
5 b g Grey Eagle—Amber Gambler (ITY) (Nijin (USA))
3538[7] 3638[14]

King After *J R Best* a63 56
5 b g Bahamian Bounty—Child Star (FR) (Bellypha)
26[2] 292[2] 313[5] 379[2] 461[3] 549[3] (651) 691[8] 740[5] 799[2] 813[4] (887) 1036[4] 1118[8] 1318[4] 2665[9] *4394[4] 5094[2] (5118)* 6226[8] 6607[12] 6825[6] 6945[7] 7085[4] (7268)

King And King (AUS) *S Burridge* 117
6 b g Celestial Dancer—Merriang Road (AUS) (Persian Heights)
1877a[9]

King Bathwick (IRE) *B R Millman* a60 67
2 b g Golan(IRE) —Princess Sabaah (IRE) (Desert King (IRE))
1631[6] 2303[5] 3043[3] 3508[6] 4202[8] 5002[4] *5423[5]* 5858[5]

King Cannavaro (IRE) *Eoin Griffin* a85 81
3 b g Val Royal(FR) —Tycoon Aly (IRE) (Last Tycoon (IRE))
(5788a)

King Canute (IRE) *M J Wallace* a27 59
3 b g Danehill(USA) —Mona Stella (USA) (Nureyev (USA))
633[10] 1399[13] 2456[14]

King Charles *E A L Dunlop* a88 99
3 b g King's Best(USA) —Charlecote (IRE) (Caerleon (USA))
1467[4] 2092[2] 3460[9] 3959[2] 4814[3] 5208[3] (5764)

King Columbo (IRE) *Miss J Feilden* a70 84
2 ch c King Charlemagne(USA) —Columbian Sand (IRE) (Salmon Leap (USA))
5222[5] (6262) 6650[5]

Kingdom Of Dreams (IRE) *J Mackie* a70 78
5 b g Sadler's Wells(USA) —Regal Portrait (IRE) (Royal Academy (USA))
1862[12] 2397[5] 2660[7] 6132[8] 6253[10] 6475[9]

Kingdom Of Fife *Sir Michael Stoute* 71
2 b c Kingmambo(USA) —Fairy Godmother (Fairy King (USA))
6616[5]

Kingdom Of Naples (USA) *A P O'Brien* 90
2 b c Sadler's Wells(USA) —Inkling (USA) (Seeking The Gold (USA))
(6443a)

King Egbert (FR) *R J Price* a50 61
6 b g Fasliyev(USA) —Exocet (USA) (Deposit Ticket (USA))
1991[11] 2334[6] 3203[4] 3869[10] 4594[6] (4857) *4944[7]* 5349[9] 5430[7] 5687[10] *5947[4] 6264[10] 6528[8]*

King Etoil (ITY) *S Saggiomo* 96
3 b c Miswaki Tern(USA) —Arisqueen (Merdon Melody)
1336a[13] 1873a[7]

King Gabriel (IRE) *Andrew Turnell* a62 43
5 b g Desert King(IRE) —Broken Spirit (IRE) (Slip Anchor)
279[6] 976[11]

King Hafhafah *I A Wood* a80
2 ch c King Charlemagne(USA) —Hafhafah (Shirley Heights)
(6404) 6823[2]

King Harson *J D Bethell* a66 85
8 b g Greensmith—Safari Park (Absalom)
1458[11] 1747[2] 2466[10] 3201[7] 3682[6] 4195[10] 5253[6] 5840[3] 6331[2] 6560[11] 6701[11]

King In Waiting (IRE) *John M Oxx* 101
4 b g Sadler's Wells(USA) —Ballerina (IRE) (Dancing Brave (USA))
1550a[7] 2161a[3] 4142a[2] 4647a[7]

King Jock (USA) *R J Osborne* a74 113
6 b g Ghazi(USA) —Glen Kate (Glenstal (USA))
247a[2] *327a[8]* 530a[5] 646a[4] 1699a[3] 2233[4] 2586a[5] 5259a[2] 5409[4] 6038a[3]

King Joshua (IRE) *D R C Elsworth* a61 83
3 b g King's Best(USA) —Lady Joshua (IRE) (Royal Academy (USA))
1010[5] 1246[3] 1898[3] 2376[3] 3964[9] (Dead)

King Kasyapa (IRE) *P Bowen* 72
5 b g Darshaan—Ezana (Ela-Mana-Mou)
4231[13] 5334[8]

King Kenny *D J Murphy* a76 79
2 ch c Lomitas—Salanka (IRE) (Persian Heights)
6468[4] *6960[2]*

Kingkohler (IRE) *K A Morgan* a62 59
8 b g King's Theatre(IRE) —Legit (IRE) (Runnett)
3567[8] *6666[6] 6819[3] 7154[5]*

King Luna (FR) *A Fabre* 103
4 ch m King's Best(USA) —Luna Caerla (IRE) (Caerleon (USA))
(3893a) (5150a)

King Marju (IRE) *K R Burke* a88 88
5 b g Marju(IRE) —Katoushka (IRE) (Hamas (IRE))
480[5] 657[10] 881a[9] (1423) 1931[9] 2030[7] 2419[5] 3201[8]

King Of Argos *E A L Dunlop* a91 110
4 b g Sadler's Wells(USA) —Wannabe Grand (IRE) (Danehill (USA))
842[3] (1060) 1651[21] (2446) 3505[2] 3941[7] 4119[3] (4851) 6009[5]

King Of Cadeaux (IRE) *M A Magnusson* a52
2 br g Cadeaux Genereux—Purple Haze (IRE) (Spectrum (IRE))
6850[9] 6998[9] 7140[7]

King Of Charm (IRE) *G L Moore* a53 62
4 ch g King Charlemagne(USA) —Pumpona (USA) (Sharpen Up)
337[8] 379[6] 562[5] 690[4] (722) 1120[10] 1400[6] 2143[15] 2555[11] 6390[12] 6542[6] 6950[7] 7013[6]

King Of Chav's (IRE) *A Bailey* a56 45
4 ch g Beckett(IRE) —La Paola (IRE) (Common Grounds)
1311[7] 2745[11]

King Of Connacht *M Wellings* a37 62
4 b h Polish Precedent(USA) —Lady Melbourne (IRE) (Indian Ridge)
2433[5] 5102[8] 7125[5]

King Of Dalyan (IRE) *D Nicholls* 26
2 ch c Desert Prince(IRE) —Fawaayid (USA) (Vaguely Noble)
814[9] 3751[10] 3835[8] 4136[14]

King Of Dixie (USA) *W J Knight* 80
3 ch c Kingmambo(USA) —Dixie Accent (USA) (Dixieland Band (USA))
4258[2]

King Of Knight (IRE) *G Prodromou* a61 39
6 gr g Orpen(USA) —Peace Melody (IRE) (Classic Music (USA))
19[7] 121[2] 500[2] 612[10] 3173[8] 3419[10] 4161[4] 4533[7] 5179[8] 5421[9]

King Of Legend (IRE) *Miss Gay Kelleway* a51 63
3 b c King Charlemagne(USA) —Last Quarry (Handsome Sailor)
2083[7] 3349[7] 3710[10]

King Of Music (USA) *G Prodromou* a71 69
6 ch g Jade Hunter(USA) —Hail Roberta (USA) (Roberto (USA))
(52) 117[11] 212[10] 3946[12]

King Of Pentacles *H Morrison* 41
2 b c King's Best(USA) —Maid To Perfection (Sadler's Wells (USA))
6493[15]

King Of Prussia (IRE) *Ms F M Crowley* a56 64
3 b g Sinndar(IRE) —Likely Story (IRE) (Night Shift (USA))
6555a[11]

King Of Redfield (IRE) *J P Broderick* 60
3 b g King's Theatre(IRE) —Jazzy Refrain (IRE) (Jareer (USA))
6555a[12]

King Of Rhythm (IRE) *D Carroll* a66 72
4 b g Imperial Ballet(IRE) —Sharadja (IRE) (Doyoun)
1440[5] 4282[3] (4933) 6021[5] 6180[10]

King Of Rome (IRE) *A P O'Brien* 92
2 b c Montjeu(IRE) —Amizette (USA) (Forty Niner (USA))
6489[11]

King Of Swords (IRE) *Tracey Collins* 95
3 b c Desert Prince(IRE) —Okey Dorey (IRE) (Lake Coniston (IRE))
2324a[7] 3573a[13] 5841a[14]

King Of The Beers (USA) *C Roberts* a71 55
3 rg c Silver Deputy(CAN) —Pracer (USA) (Lyphard (USA))
37[10] (157) 267[6] 294[5] 460[6] 731[2] (790) 1039[5] 1194[4] 1353[2] 2105[7] (2259) 2558[4] 2915[7] 3901[13]

King Of The Moors (USA) *T D Barron* a53 87
4 b g King Of Kings(IRE) —Araza (USA) (Arazi (USA))
953[10] 1198[7] 1655[4] (2117) 2338[8] 3052[3] 3346[2] 3556[5] 3764[6] 4382[4] 4672[12] (6021) 6465[5] 6727[9] 6744[6]

King Of The Roxy (USA) *T Pletcher* a107
3 b c Littleexpectations(USA) —Marrakesh (USA) (Bold Forbes (USA))
1882a[6]

King Of Tory (IRE) *Edward Lynam* 99
5 b g Giant's Causeway(USA) —Across The Ice (USA) (General Holme (USA))
3138a[4] 4211a[5] 5242a[9]

King Of Tricks *M D I Usher* a49 53
3 b g First Trump—Antithesis (IRE) (Fairy King (USA))
1346[7] 1932[10] 2108[11] 3611[4] 3949[6] 4226[14] 4471[2] 4529[7] 4685[7] 4853[15]

King Of Westphalia (USA) *A P O'Brien* 84
2 b c Kingmambo(USA) —Quarter Moon (IRE) (Sadler's Wells (USA))
3435[5]

King Orchisios (IRE) *K A Ryan* a114 103
4 ch g Tagula(IRE) —Wildflower (Namaqualand (USA))
(551) (762) 2733[17] 3500[11] 3990[11] 4150[23] 5407[16] 5616[21] 6183[5] (6327) 6487[14]

King Quantas (IRE) *B Bo* 82
9 b h Danehill(USA) —Palacegate Episode (IRE) (Drumalis)
5262a[5] 6370a[9]

King Rama (USA) *John E Kiely* a60 99
6 ch g Kingmambo(USA) —Marozia (USA) (Storm Bird (CAN))
(2067a) 3143a[3] 4867a[13] 6366a[12]

King Roy (IRE) *N I M Rossiter* 39
3 b g Fruits Of Love(USA) —Meranie Girl (IRE) (Mujadil (USA))
3102[6] 4182[7] 4530[14]

King's Account (USA) *S Gollings* a54 57
5 ch g King Of Kings(IRE) —Fighting Countess (USA) (Ringside (USA))
28[14] 928[8] 2027[4] 2370[6] 2810[10] 5525[16] 5886[13]

King's Alchemist *M D I Usher* 64
2 b c Slickly(FR) —Pure Gold (Dilum (USA))
6130[7]

King's Apostle (IRE) *W J Haggas* a90 104
3 b c King's Best(USA) —Politesse (USA) (Barathea (IRE))
(700) 843[2] 1851[15] (2373) (3418) 4374[3] (4607) (5254)

Kings Art (IRE) *W M Brisbourne* a48 56
3 b g King's Best(USA) —Descant (USA) (Nureyev (USA))
1410[8] 2105[13] 2530[14] 4533[2] 4858[11] 5710[11] 5967[2] 6096[11]

King's Attitude *R A Harris* 48
3 b c King's Theatre(IRE) —Sarah's Dream (IRE) (Lion Cavern (USA))
3639[10] 4530[12] 4757[8]

King's Bastion (IRE) *M L W Bell* a66 86
3 b g Royal Applause—Aunty Mary (Common Grounds)
1099[10] 1660[2] 1820[5] 2243[5] 3099[2] 3278[3] 3797[8] 4574[5] 5168[8] 5473[5] 6025[5] (6310)

Kingscape (IRE) *J R Fanshawe* a83 85
4 br g King Charlemagne(USA) —Cape Clear (Slip Anchor)
928[6] 1318[5] 1819[7] (2157) 2660[5] (3249) 4609[3] 5225[3] (5725) 6144[6]

King's Caprice *J A Geake* a102 108
6 ch g Pursuit Of Love—Palace Street (USA) (Secreto (USA))
656[3] 759[13] 2396[9] 2858[21] 3941[26] 4601[13] 5413[7] 6301[15] 6472[6] 6668[2] 6851[2] 6932[12] 7053[6]

Kings College Boy *R A Fahey* a72 83
7 b g College Chapel—The Kings Daughter (Indian King (USA))
957[7] 1565[4] 1754[8] 1806[7] 2191[2] 2461[8] 2529[4] 2712[7] 3184[4] 3585[7] 3791[2] 4038[5] 4289[6] 4703[8] (4800) 5160[4] 5297[10] 5381[7] 5552[15] 6562[2] 6860[7]

Kings Confession (IRE) *D Carroll* a67 35
4 b g Danetime(IRE) —Night Rhapsody (IRE) (Mujtahid (USA))
1440[9]

Kingscross *M Blanshard* a78 89
9 ch g King's Signet(USA) —Calamanco (Clantime)
91[8] 1200[15] 2088[7] 2318[12] 2993[10] 3569[5] 4585[13] 5130[10] 5687[3] 6088[10] 6533[8]

Kingsdalemillenium (IRE) *W M Roper* 62
2 b f Hawk Wing(USA) —Jinsiyah (USA) (Housebuster (USA))
5395a[20]

Kingsdale Ocean (IRE) *Ms Florence Mills* 97
4 b g Blue Ocean(USA) —Madmosel John (IRE) (Martin John)
3573a[12] 3768a[6]

Kingsdale Orion (IRE) *Ms Florence Mills* 100
3 bb c Intikhab(USA) —Jinsiyah (USA) (Housebuster (USA))
1047a[8] 2051a[8]

King's Envoy (USA) *Mrs J C McGregor* a11 37
8 b g Royal Academy(USA) —Island Of Silver (USA) (Forty Niner (USA))
965[3] 2715[8] 2825[10]

King's Event (USA) *Sir Michael Stoute* 94
3 b c Dynaformer(USA) —Magic Of Love (Magic Ring (IRE))
1100[3] 4457[2] (4666) 5641[3] 6499[3]

King's Gait *T D Easterby* 101
5 b g Mujahid(USA) —Miller's Gait (Mill Reef (USA))
1653[4] 1826[8] 2841[3] 3089[7] 3401[10] 3911[6]

Kingsgate Castle *J R Best* a67
2 b c Kyllachy—Ella Lamees (Statoblest)
7015[5] 7266[6]

Kingsgate Native (IRE) *J R Best* 115
2 b c Mujadil(USA) —Native Force (IRE) (Indian Ridge)
2737[2] 4046[2] (4746) 6039a[2]

King's General (USA) *Mrs A J Perrett* 81
2 ch c Langfuhr(CAN) —Jeanie's Gift (USA) (Gulch (USA))
1781[2]

King's Head (IRE) *G L Moore* a91 103
4 b g King's Best(USA) —Ustka (Lomond (USA))
944[4]

Kings Heir (IRE) *Peter Grayson* a53 83
4 b g Princely Heir(IRE) —Unimpeachable (IRE) (Namaqualand (USA))
181[5] (Dead)

Kingsholm *I W McInnes* a82 91
5 ch g Selkirk(USA) —Putuna (Generous (IRE))
1524[10] 1791[12] 5203[5] 5664[6] 6203[11] 7002[6] 7100 7173[2] 7263[3]

King's Icon (IRE) *M P Tregoning* 78
2 b g King's Best(USA) —Pink Sovietstaia (FR) (Soviet Star (USA))
1990[2] (2424) 3459[13] 4152[14]

King's Kazeem *B W Hills* 73
2 b f King's Best(USA) —Kazeem (Darshaan)
5592[4] 6493[7]

Kingsmaite *S R Bowring* a68 45
6 b g Komaite(USA) —Antonias Melody (Rambo Dancer (CAN))
70[10] 228[4] 371[7] 450[4] 466[3] 533[3] 605[3] 681[11] 806[7] 932[7] 1027[3] 1221[11] 1379[8] 7124[7] 7153[8]

King's Majesty (IRE) *V R A Dartnall* a81 79
5 b g King's Best(USA) —Tiavanita (USA) (J O Tobin (USA))
842[7] 1395[13] 1962[14] 4107[6] 5307[6] 5916[2] (7189)

Kingsmead (USA) *Miss J Feilden* a49 58
3 b g Kingmambo(USA) —Astor Place (USA) (Deputy Minister (CAN))
834[4] 1224[7] 2096[5] 2610[9] 3825[8] 5273[5] 5647[9] 5980[7]

King's Minstrel (IRE) *R Rowe* a48 31
6 b g Cape Cross(IRE) —Muwasim (USA) (Meadowlake (USA))
133[5] 349[11]

Kings Point (IRE) *R A Fahey* a91 109
6 b h Fasliyev(USA) —Rahika Rose (Unfuwain (USA))
43[6] 331a[11] 411a[12] 477a[13] 540a[10] 1480[4] 1791[8] 3026[4] 4119[10] 4385[7] 4745[12] 5196[5] (5479)

Kings Quay *J J Quinn* a95 105
5 b h Montjeu(IRE) —Glen Rosie (IRE) (Mujtahid (USA))
763[2] 940[8] 2209[10] 2859[7] 6302[6]

King's Ransom *S Gollings* a70 73
4 b g Daylami(IRE) —Luana (Shaadi (USA))
24[2] (230) 740[7] 928[7] 1249[13] 1764[6] 2307[3] 2511[3] 3177[3] 3448[6] (4267) 4732[6] 5144[6] 5777[12] 6269[4] 6547[7] 6816[8] 7023[2] 7109[2]

Kings Shillings *D Carroll* a57 34
3 br g Superior Premium—The Kings Daughter (Indian King (USA))
223[3] (253) 454[6] 535[6] 624[11] 676[4] 832[9] 1059[10] 1224[13] 1921[10] 4071[9] 4416[14]

King's Spear (IRE) *Miss J R Tooth* a70 64
4 b g Lear Spear(USA) —First Veil (Primo Dominie)
445[3] 685[12] 805[8] 5093[8] 5188[14] 6385[9]

Kings Story (IRE) *W R Swinburn* 68
3 b c Royal Applause—Poppy Carew (IRE) (Danehill (USA))
1812[8] 2402[11] 3366[5] 4687[6]

Kings Topic (USA) *A B Haynes* a65 53
7 ch g Kingmambo(USA) —Topicount (USA) (Private Account (USA))
4464[10] 4592[3] 5237[13] 6867[10]

Kingstyle (IRE) *M Brittain* 52
2 b c King Charlemagne(USA) —Stylish Clare (IRE) (Desert Style (IRE))
1801[4] 2532[9] 3205[6] 3951[12] 4279[8] 5526[8]

King Supreme (IRE) *R Hannon* a68 62
2 b c King's Best(USA) —Oregon Trail (USA) (Gone West (USA))
3233[3] 3522[8] 4777[12] (5127) 5423[9] 6715[13]

King's Wonder *W R Muir* 73
2 ch c King's Best(USA) —Signs And Wonders (Danehill (USA))
1989[5] 5306[3] 5977[6]

Kingvati (FR) *Y De Nicolay* a93 97
5 b h Alamo Bay(USA) —Vatipan (FR) (Trepan (FR))
7128a[9]

King Verti *P C Haslam* 23
3 b g Averti(IRE) —Proudfoot (IRE) (Shareef Dancer (USA))
2116[9] 2563[12]

King Zeal (IRE) *M Wigham* a65 68
3 b c King's Best(USA) —Manureva (USA) (Nureyev (USA))
2880[9] 4815[12] 5045[3] 6387[6]

Kinlochard *Eve Johnson Houghton* 49
2 b f Efisio—Rainbow D'Beaute (Rainbow Quest (USA))
3668[4] 4016[11]

Kinnego Bay (IRE) *B W Hills* 76
2 ch c Hennessy(USA) —New Music (USA) (Prospector's Music (USA))
4132[5] 5977[8] 6234[3]

Kinout (IRE) *K A Ryan* a43 73
2 b g Invincible Spirit(IRE) —Kinn (FR) (Suave Dancer (USA))
1498[5] 2199[3] 2526[4] 3925[10] 5153[3] 5582[5] 6017[18]

Kinsman (IRE) *T D McCarthy* a52 34
10 b g Distant Relative—Besito (Wassl)
20[5] 129[6] 207[3] 350[6] 721[3] (1119) 2875[7] (6532) 6968[8]

Kinsya *M H Tompkins* a98 103
4 ch g Mister Baileys—Kimono (IRE) (Machiavellian (USA))
5012[12] 5615[2] 5833[12] 6155[5] (6539) 6654[2] 6931[5]

Kintbury Cross *P D Cundell* a54 77
5 b g Kylian(USA) —Cebwob (Rock City)
769[5] 4072[2] 4597[7]

Kintyre Lass (IRE) *B R Millman* a24 54
2 b f Mull Of Kintyre(USA) —Bold Doll (IRE) (Dolphin Street (FR))
2488[12] 2876[3] 3465[10] 4265[4] 5089[17] 5302[6] 6586[9]

Kiowa Princess *M Dods* 38
2 ch f Compton Place—Sunley Stars (Sallust)
4522[12] 5192[10] 5550[10]

Kip Deville (USA) *R Dutrow Jr* a107 122
4 rg h Kipling(USA) —Klondike Kaytie (USA) (Encino (USA))
(6511a)

Kiribati King (IRE) *M R Channon* a62 53
2 b g Kalanisi(IRE) —Everlasting (Desert King (IRE))
6130[12] 6574[9] 6805[6]

Kirkby's Treasure *G A Swinbank* a50 71
9 gr g Mind Games—Gem Of Gold (Jellaby)
1280[5] 1747[15] 2714[5] 2985[4] 3376[3] 3497[5] (4099) (4427) 4931[3] 5035[2] (5476) 5840[5] 6021[11]

Kirkhammerton (IRE) *A J McCabe* a62 48
5 ch g Grand Lodge(USA) —Nawara (Welsh Pageant)
1027[5] 1178[10] 1350[2] 1717[6] 2145[9] 2258[5] 2519[6] 3241[3] 3714[8] 3922[4] 4355[9] 4713[5] 5497[6]

Kirkinola *C Laffon-Parias* 98
2 b f Selkirk(USA) —Spinola (FR) (Spinning World (USA))
4626a[9]

Kirklees (IRE) *Saeed Bin Suroor* 119
3 b c Jade Robbery(USA) —Moyesii (USA) (Diesis)
(5351) (5723)

Kirk Michael *H Candy* a94 82
3 b g Selkirk(USA) —Pervenche (Latest Model)
1839[5] (7159)

Kirstys Lad *M Mullineaux* a63 50
5 b g Lake Coniston(IRE) —Killick (Slip Anchor)
5330[11] (6480) 6627[2] 6804[3] 6955[8] (7079) 7146[4]

Kiss Chase (IRE) *J S Goldie* a52 65
3 br g Val Royal(FR) —Zurarah (Siberian Express (USA))
1632[9] 2697[11] (3175) (3918) 4382[6] 4936[7] 5555[13]

Kissi Kissi *M J Attwater* a51 43
4 b m Paris House—Miss Whittingham (IRE) (Fayruz)
22[9] 320[5] 430[9] 801[11] 4324[10] 6537[14] 7137[4] 7238[6]

Kissing *Sir Mark Prescott* a81 54
3 ch f Grand Lodge(USA) —Love Divine (Diesis)
5499[6] 6286[5] (6766)

Kiss The Kid (USA) *Amy Tarrant* 108
4 bb h Lemon Drop Kid(USA) —Black Tie Kiss (USA) (Danzig (USA))
5853a[4]

Kiss The Ring (USA) *B J Meehan* 51
2 ch f Touch Gold(USA) —Act Devoted (USA) (A.P. Indy (USA))
3747[13]

Kitchen Sink (IRE) *Jean-Rene Auvray* a65 62
5 ch g Bold Fact(USA) —Voodoo Rocket (Lycius (USA))
125[2] (282) 654[7] 743[6] 2221[11] 2334[15] 3428[14] 4312[10] 6864[9] 7077[8]

Kitebrook *Mrs Mary Hambro* a34 42
6 b m Saddlers' Hall(IRE) —Neptunalia (Slip Anchor)
3847[10] 4630[12] 4738[6] 5979[5] 6341[8] 6798[7]

Kiton (GER) *P Rau* 108
6 b h Lando(GER) —Key West (GER) (In The Wings)
1571a[9] 4838a[2] 6095a[4]

Kitty Matcham (IRE) *A P O'Brien* 105
2 b f Rock Of Gibraltar(IRE) —Imagine (IRE) (Sadler's Wells (USA))
5843a[9] (6336)

Kiwi Bay *M Dods* 77
2 b g Mujahid(USA) —Bay Of Plenty (FR) (Octagonal (NZ))
3718[2] 4279[5] (5901) 6486[6]

Kiwi Des Mottes (FR) *E Lellouche* 89
9 b g Africanus(FR) —Princess Crystel (FR) (Crystal Glitters (USA))
6923a[7]

Kiwi Princess *M Brittain* a39 55
2 b f Vettori(IRE) —The Kings Daughter (Indian King (USA))
2532[8] 4247[8] 4784[8] 4968[5] 5298[3] 6750[10]

Kiwi The Clown (IRE) *R A Fahey* a58
3 ch g Fruits Of Love(USA) —Tenby Bay (IRE) (Tenby)
69[7] 258[6] 423[6] 535[5]

Klarity *J Pearce* a46 67
2 b f Acclamation—Clarice Orsini (Common Grounds)
5540[4] 6073[3] 6409[12] 6892[6] 7000[8]

Klassen (USA) *A King* a28 55
4 bb g Pine Bluff(USA) —One Great Lady (USA) (Fappiano (USA))
1609[11] 1741[7] 2990[12]

Knapton Hill *R Hollinshead* a61 90
3 b f Zamindar(USA) —Torgau (IRE) (Zieten (USA))
122[3] 224[7] 535[2] (974) 1091[6] 1903[4] 2043[6] 2914[6] 3239[4] 3897[13] 4005[6] 4907[5] 6596[4] 6757[13]

Knead The Dough *A E Price* a56 63
6 b g Wolfhound(USA) —Ridgewood Ruby (IRE) (Indian Ridge)
2221[12] 2622[12] 4336[4] 4583[9] 4881[14] 5276[2] (5510) 5716[5] 5947[5] 6587[7] 6720[6]

Knickyknackienoo *T T Clement* a31 3
6 b g Bin Ajwaad(IRE) —Ring Fence (Polar Falcon (USA))
4515[10] 6563[11] 6718[9] 6867[8] 6956[13]

Knight Of Kintyre (IRE) *Barry Potts* 38
4 b m Mull Of Kintyre(USA) —Ar Hyd Y Knos (Alzao (USA))
1594[6] 2563[6] 4099[8]

Knight Valliant *J Howard Johnson* 62
4 bl g Dansili—Aristocratique (Cadeaux Genereux)
1406[7] 1966[11]

Knot In Wood (IRE) *R A Fahey* a99 110
5 b g Shinko Forest(IRE) —Notley Park (Wolfhound (USA))
1788[6] 2858[10] (3500) 4150[3] 5616[23] 5832[7] 6338[6] 6758[3] 6930[5]

Knowledge (FR) *Y De Nicolay* a84 100
3 gr c Kaldounevees(FR) —Radio Mesnil (FR) (Nashamaa)
1056a[9] 2499a[6]

Know No Fear *J J Quinn* a70 75
2 b g Primo Valentino(IRE) —Alustar (Emarati (USA))
3030[4] 3297[2] 4020[2] 4702[2] (5480)

Know The Law *D R C Elsworth* a85 79
3 b g Danehill Dancer(IRE) —Mackenzie's Friend (Selkirk (USA))
2046[8] 2554[2] 3349[3] 3881[2] 4457[4] 4815[2] 5562[3] 6061[6] (6545) 6709[4] 6853[7] 7055[7]

Kocab *A Fabre* 116
5 b h Unfuwain(USA) —Space Quest (Rainbow Quest (USA))
2330a[2] 3665a[4] 4520a[3] 5719a[2] 6376a[3] 7090a[5]

Kocham Cie (GER) *M Trybuhl* 66
2 b c Sholokhov(IRE) —Knightly Manner (GER) (Alkalde (GER))
6952a[5]

Kocooning (IRE) *Robert Collet* a81 97
4 b m King's Best(USA) —Zelding (IRE) (Warning)
4190a[5] 5468a[6] 6039a[11]

Kodiak Kowboy (USA) *S Asmussen* a105
2 b c Posse(USA) —Kokadrie (USA) (Coronado's Quest (USA))
6508a[3]

Kokkokila *Lady Herries* a54 62
3 b f Robellino(USA) —Meant To Be (Morston (FR))
1988[4] 5450[6] 6204[3] 6821[6]

Kolibre *T T Clement* a8 33
4 br g Mtoto—Eternal Flame (Primo Dominie)
272[8] 1928[10]

Kompete *V Smith* a78 92
3 b f Komaite(USA) —Competa (Hernando (FR))
1096[8] 6013[16] 6301[22] 6731[3] 6929[11]

Komreyev Star *R E Peacock* a50 56
5 b g Komaite(USA) —L'Ancressaan (Dalsaan)
716[10] 1539[16] 1944[4] 2168[9] 3721[4] 4129[6] 6804[5] 7169[2] 7213[6] 7274[5]

Kondakova (IRE) *M L W Bell* a73 82
3 b f Soviet Star(USA) —Solar Star (USA) (Lear Fan (USA))
1228^11 1837^12 (2515) 3038^4 *3649^9* 4017^6 4546^5 *5134^9* 5403^3

Kong (IRE) *J L Dunlop* 105
5 b g Sadler's Wells(USA) —Hill Of Snow (Reference Point)
1650^6 2216^8 3271^6 5976^7

Kongo Rikishio (IRE) *K Yamauchi* 123
5 b h Stravinsky(USA) —Principium (USA) (Hansel (USA))
7091a^9

Konig Concorde (GER) *C Sprengel*
2 b c Big Shuffle(USA) —Kaiserin (GER) (Ile De Bourbon (USA))
6219a^4

Konig Turf (GER) *C Sprengel* 109
5 b h Big Shuffle(USA) —Kaiserin (GER) (Ile De Bourbon (USA))
881a^3 1699a^4 (2903a) 3581a^3 4217a^2 4929a^3 (5670a)

Kool Katie *Mrs G S Rees* a56
2 b f Millkom—Katie Komaite (Komaite (USA))
7216^2

Koraleva Tectona (IRE) *Pat Eddery* a61 49
2 b f Fasliyev(USA) —Miss Teak (USA) (Woodman (USA))
5681^6 6248^11

Korcula *M J Wallace* a51 44
2 ch g Tomba—Misty Goddess (IRE) (Godswalk (USA))
898^9 1857^9 3246^8 *5133^6* 6591^5 *6814^8*

Korolieva (IRE) *K A Ryan* a41 49
4 b m Xaar—Dark Hyacinth (IRE) (Darshaan)
94^11

Korty *W J Musson* a51 34
3 b g Averti(IRE) —Promissory (Caerleon (USA))
977^8 *1447^9 3620^13* 4336^11 *7166^2*

Kostar *C G Cox* a100 109
6 ch g Komaite(USA) —Black And Amber (Weldnaas (USA))
759^8 (1195) 1657^8 2319^7 4150^22 (4614)

Kotsi (IRE) *E F Vaughan* 104
2 b f Nayef(USA) —Ingozi (Warning)
(4774) 5353^2 5796^4

Kourka (FR) *J-M Beguigne* 100
5 b m Keos(USA) —Kuneitra (FR) (Lead On Time (USA))
1704a^3 3445a^4 5468a^3 6071a^6 6954a^2

Kova Hall (IRE) *M F Harris* a76 89
5 ch g Halling(USA) —My Micheline (Lion Cavern (USA))
96^12 256^8 605^12

Krakatau (FR) *D J Wintle* a66 35
3 b g Noverre(USA) —Tomanivi (Caerleon (USA))
17^5 520^4 937^4 (1266) 1672^5 *2150^3* 5879^13 *6695^8 6869^11 7028^5 7268^4*

Krasivaya (IRE) *J R Boyle* 11
3 b f Soviet Star(USA) —Damiana (IRE) (Thatching)
2219^14

Krasivi's Boy (USA) *G L Moore* a57 48
5 bb g Swain(IRE) —Krasivi (USA) (Nijinsky (CAN))
416^2 (496) 6832^12 6969^10 7256^5

Krataios (FR) *C Laffon-Parias* 120
7 b g Sabrehill(USA) —Loxandra (Last Tycoon (IRE))
1389a^6

Krikket *W J Haggas* a58 52
3 ch f Sinndar(IRE) —Star Of The Course (USA) (Theatrical)
1452^6 2079^13

Krisman (IRE) *M Ciciarelli* 101
8 ch h Kris—Corn Circle (IRE) (Thatching)
1876a^7 6224a^8

Krisnando *W J Knight* a52 50
2 b f Hernando(FR) —Kris Mundi (Kris)
5498^9 5882^11 6414^9

Kristalchen *D W Thompson* 48
5 b m Singspiel(IRE) —Crystal Flite (IRE) (Darshaan)
966^6 1239^6 1554^8 1942^7 2417^5 3204^10

Kristal Glory (IRE) *J L Dunlop* 57
2 ch c Night Shift(USA) —Kristal's Paradise (IRE) (Bluebird (USA))
1989^9 2624^3 3551^10 4501^4 5268^5

Kristensen *Karen McLintock* a41 79
8 ch g Kris S(USA) —Papaha (FR) (Green Desert (USA))
628^10 (955) (1457) 1793^10

Kristiansand *P Monteith* 67
7 b g Halling(USA) —Zonda (Fabulous Dancer (USA))
1942^2 2252^2 2825^3 5586^2

Kristoffersen *Ian Williams* a63 52
7 ch g Kris—Towaahi (IRE) (Caerleon (USA))
976^13 1152^7 2204^P

Krugerrand (USA) *W J Musson* a80 94
8 ch g Gulch(USA) —Nasers Pride (USA) (Al Nasr (FR))
993^9 1356^10 1862^6 2906^9 3386^4 3513^7 4184^7 4909^9 *5225^6* 5620^F

Kryptonite (IRE) *J W Hills* a65 38
2 b c Kris Kin(USA) —Brockton Saga (IRE) (Perugino (USA))
1989^11 3551^11 *3849^6 (7022) 7204^7*

Kudbeme *N Bycroft* 66
5 b m Forzando—Umbrian Gold (IRE) (Perugino (USA))
2023^5 (2422) 2741^8 2988^9 3414^10 3764^4 3793^6 3971^3 4081^6 4562^15 4846^11 5737^14 6019^11

Kumakawa *N P Littmoden* a54 16
9 ch g Dancing Spree(USA) —Maria Cappuccini (Siberian Express (USA))
393^2 579^4 627^9 716^3 1347^6 1592^11 2145^4 2348^5 2745^7

Kung Hei *Mrs L Stubbs* a37 24
4 b g Primo Valentino(IRE) —Cast A Spell (Magic Ring (IRE))
125^6 282^8

Kunte Kinteh *D Nicholls* a69 69
3 b g Indian Lodge(IRE) —Summer Siren (FR) (Saint Cyrien (FR))
1749^2 2740^3 3029^8 (3639) *4064^3* 4480^4 5555^10

Kuriyama (IRE) *M H Tompkins* 61
2 ch c Raise A Grand(IRE) —Gobolino (Don)
6296^7

Kurumda *C R Egerton* a40 26
3 b g Montjeu(IRE) —Susun Kelapa (USA) (St Jovite (USA))
4630^13

Kuster *L M Cumani* 84
11 b g Indian Ridge—Ustka (Lomond (USA))
1542^8 2307^6 3250^2 3485^5 4108^3

Kwazulu (USA) *J H M Gosden* a51 80
3 br c Dynaformer(USA) —De Aar (USA) (Gone West (USA))
2726^6 *3284^6* 3908^3

Kyber *J S Goldie* a37 60
6 ch g First Trump—Mahbob Dancer (FR) (Groom Dancer (USA))
716^9 (965) 1457^3 1895^6 2250^4 2567^6 (2824) 3584^3 4096^2 (4475) 4969^5 5478^7 5839^6

Kyburg *P F I Cole* a36 34
3 b f Silver Patriarch(IRE) —Native Thatch (IRE) (Thatching)
1128^15 *1523^10 1749^4* 2489^9 2661^5 *3186^9* 4270^12 5269^8

Kylayne *P W D'Arcy* a83 96
2 b f Kyllachy—Penmayne (Inchinor)
(972) 2756^16 3432^6 3988^9 4329^2 4400^5 4992^3 5164^5 5583^7 *(6270)*

Kyle (IRE) *R Hannon* a89 87
3 ch g Kyllachy—Staylily (IRE) (Grand Lodge (USA))
1037^3 (1501) (1994) 2400^4 2881^3 *3418^3* 4093^10 4607^4 5382^6 5635^14 6205^6

Kyle Of Lochalsh *Miss Lucinda V Russell* a56 59
7 gr g Vettori(IRE) —Shaieef (IRE) (Shareef Dancer (USA))
1457^7 2764^10 3815^7 4096^11 4972^12 5000^11

Kyles Bay (IRE) *Ms Caroline Hutchinson* a96 96
4 b g Fruits Of Love(USA) —Zuleika (IRE) (Lucky Guest)
3138a^24 5242a^8

Kyles Prince (IRE) *P J Makin* a86 75
5 b g In The Wings—Comprehension (USA) (Diesis)
164^2 593^8

Kylkenny *H Morrison* a82 76
12 b g Kylian(USA) —Fashion Flow (Balidar)
95^7 226^7 (377) 669^6 811^7 1263^7 1980^4 2967^4 3155^2 3403^4 6598^3 *(7123) 7242^2*

Kyllachy Storm *R J Hodges* a61 63
3 b g Kyllachy—Social Storm (USA) (Future Storm (USA))
1211^6 1634^13 1763^9 2622^6 2978^2 4758^8

Kyllis *B Smart* a65 46
2 b f Kyllachy—Princess Latifa (Wolfhound (USA))
5154^3 *5888^2 6477^6*

Kyloe Belle (USA) *Mrs A J Perrett* a51 63
3 b f Elusive Quality(USA) —Besha (USA) (Turkoman (USA))
1039^8 (1320) 2362^15 4205^7 4472^4 4766^14 5710^5 *6178^10*

Kyniska (IRE) *Tracey Collins* 98
2 b f Choisir(AUS) —Lunadine (FR) (Bering)
5843a^2

Kyoto Summit *M W Easterby* a94 97
4 ch g Lomitas—Alligram (USA) (Alysheba (USA))
1304^4 1822^11 3558^8 3753^3 4105^6 4690^11 5256^7 5807^2 6158^5

Kyrenia Girl (IRE) *T D Easterby* a6 54
3 b f King Charlemagne(USA) —Cherry Hills (IRE) (Anabaa (USA))
916^2 *1175^10* 2713^5 3918^11

Kyrhena *C W Thornton* a24 42
3 b f Desert Prince(IRE) —Kyle Rhea (In The Wings)
3640^12 4821^11 5487^15 5622^4

Kyrie Eleison (IRE) *R Hannon* a68 68
2 b c Kalanisi(IRE) —Peratus (IRE) (Mujadil (USA))
2600^4 *2991^4* 3435^12 *3849^3* 4121^9 5002^6

Kyzer Chief *R E Barr* 40
2 b g Rouvres(FR) —Payvashooz (Ballacashtal (CAN))
4818^12 5281^9 5501^9 6073^9

Laa Baas (IRE) *M A Jarvis* 48
2 b f Green Desert(USA) —Baaderah (IRE) (Cadeaux Genereux)
6409^10

Laa Rayb (USA) *M Johnston* a87 105
3 b c Storm Cat(USA) —Society Lady (USA) (Mr Prospector (USA))
(1714) 2400^5 (2633) 3330^15 3503^12 (4062) 5031^2 5431^3

Labelled With Love *Jean-Rene Auvray* a62 9
7 ch g Zilzal(USA) —Dream Baby (Master Willie)
86^4 310^5 383^3 2179^2 2331^2 2540^14

La Belle Joannie *S Curran* a53 49
2 b f Lujain(USA) —Sea Clover (IRE) (Ela-Mana-Mou)
845^15 3296^3 3751^5 4136^2 *4883^7* 5302^5 *6928^8*

La Blue Hill *H Steinmetz* 76
3 b f Tiger Hill(IRE) —La Blue (GER) (Bluebird (USA))
1855a^7

Labor Day (IRE) *J H M Gosden* a68 61
3 b f Pivotal—Late Summer (USA) (Gone West (USA))
1203^8 1901^4 2998^8 *6546^6 6929^8*

La Boum (GER) *Robert Collet* a92 103
4 br m Monsun(GER) —La Bouche (GER) (In The Wings)
5150a^4 (6460a)

Lacadena (USA) *Josie Carroll* a76 86
2 b f Fasliyev(USA) —Butterfly Blue (IRE) (Sadler's Wells (USA))
5293a^4

Lacala (IRE) *Jane Chapple-Hyam* a65 47
2 ch f Alhaarth(IRE) —Gazar (Kris)
4656^9 *5646^4 7252^9*

Lacework *Sir Michael Stoute* a76 92
3 ch f Pivotal—Entwine (Primo Dominie)
1202^7 (1610) (2092) 2862^3

La Chicaluna *J G Given* 80
2 ch f Cadeaux Genereux—Crescent Moon (Mr Prospector (USA))
1285^11 2251^2 (2504) (3494) 4121^16 5251^2 5322^15 6075^7

La Colline (GER) *W J Haggas* a75 61
4 ch m Ocean Of Wisdom(USA) —La Laja (GER) (Be My Guest (USA))
102^4 191^U

La Columbina *R Hannon* a68 76
2 ch f Carnival Dancer—Darshay (FR) (Darshaan)
3895^15 4547^3 4875^3 *5527^2* (5914)

La Conquistadora *J S Bolger* 95
3 b f Pivotal—Camaret (IRE) (Danehill (USA))
782a^4 946a^6

La Conseillante (USA) *J-C Rouget* 96
3 b f Elusive Quality(USA) —Stormin Winnie (USA) (Storm Cat (USA))
3148a^8

La Coveta (IRE) *B J Meehan* 76
2 b f Marju(IRE) —Colourful Cast (IRE) (Nashwan (USA))
5881^7 (6648)

La Cuvee *B G Powell* a43 47
3 b f Mark Of Esteem(IRE) —Premiere Cuvee (Formidable (USA))
1782^6 2489^4 3351^8 *4673^4*

Ladak *B Grizzetti* 98
3 b c Agnes World(USA) —Lyonette (IRE) (Royal Academy (USA))
1336a^5 1873a^4

La Dancia (IRE) *P Rau* 108
4 b m Mull Of Kintyre(USA) —La Constancia (Dominion)
1190a^5 2165a^4 4651a^7 (6046a) 6460a^6 6781a^6

Ladies Best *Sir Michael Stoute* 104
3 b c King's Best(USA) —Lady Of The Lake (Caerleon (USA))
2057^3 2790^8 3460^3 4092^14 5326^3 5830^2 6169^14

Lady Alize (USA) *R A Kvisla* a55 87
3 b f Indian Charlie(USA) —Marina Duff (Caerleon (USA))
1537^3 1784^10 3384^10 3826^15

Lady Althea *Mrs C A Dunnett*
4 ch m Danzig Connection(USA) —Lady Keyser (Le Johnstan)
981^4

Lady Ambitious *D K Ivory* a46 42
4 ch m Pivotal—Ambitious (Ardkinglass)
1210^8 *1907^6 2332^5 2800^2 5120^11 5389^9 6212^5 6292^8* 6570^9

Lady Amy *Miss J Feilden* a14
2 b f Fleetwood(IRE) —Hartest Rose (Komaite (USA))
4882^11

Lady Aquitaine (USA) *B J Meehan* a97 97
2 gr f El Prado(IRE) —Chalamont (IRE) (Kris)
1814^6 *2768^3* (3592) 3988^13 *5219^3* 5973^7

Lady Asheena *J Jay* a49
2 gr f Daylami(IRE) —Star Profile (IRE) (Sadler's Wells (USA))
6578^9 6737^4

Lady Aspen (IRE) *Ian Williams* a58 80
4 b m Elnadim(USA) —Misty Peak (IRE) (Sri Pekan (USA))
2258^2 2657^4 2870^10 3277^9 4632^4 5330^15

Lady Avenger (IRE) *J M P Eustace* 94
2 ch f Namid—Shioda (USA) (Bahri (USA))
(1896) 2183^2 2756^7 5614^6 5973^13

Lady Aviator *T D Easterby* a15
2 b f Averti(IRE) —Flying Carpet (Barathea (IRE))
1713^8

Lady Bahia (IRE) *Peter Grayson* a73 78
6 b m Orpen(USA) —Do The Right Thing (Busted)
47^2 163^8 269^8 368^6 521^4 613^2 (668) (787)

Lady Benjamin *P C Haslam* a58 75
2 b f Spinning World(USA) —Fresh Look (IRE) (Alzao (USA))
1422^2 *1727^4* (2385) 3398^2 (3499) 4154^2 4364^10 5665^2 5932^2 6699^4 6756^17

Lady Bid *B Palling* a12
3 ch f Auction House(USA) —Lady Ploy (Deploy)
3732^7

Lady Bower *J Ryan* a58 62
2 b f Bertolini(USA) —Noble Water (FR) (Noblequest (FR))
2949^12 3213^7 3874^10 4136^3 *4669^7* (4968) *5127^6 6958^3 7182^11*

Lady Calido (USA) *Sir Mark Prescott* a51 51
2 bb f El Prado(IRE) —Hydro Calido (USA) (Nureyev (USA))
2904^7 *3109^4* 3834^10

Lady Carollina *C F Wall* 56
2 b f Bertolini(USA) —Carollan (IRE) (Marju (IRE))
6234^5

Lady Cartuccia *J J Quinn* a44
3 b f Fasliyev(USA) —Cartuccia (IRE) (Doyoun)
3018^6 6193^6 8321^10

Lady Cat (FR) *P Bary* a76 76
2 b f Enrique—Heat Storm (USA) (Storm Cat (USA))
7048a^4

Lady Charlemagne *N P Littmoden* a50 11
2 b f King Charlemagne(USA) —Prospering (Prince Sabo)
2457^12 *6262^10 6433^10*

Lady Cobra *C E Brittain* a36 22
2 ro f Golden Snake(USA) —Little Emily (Zafonic (USA))
4537^10 *5527^11*

Lady Deauville (FR) *P A Blockley* 101
2 gr f Fasliyev(USA) —Mercalle (FR) (Kaldoun (FR))
3055^5 3880^2 4626a^3 5061^2 5614^4 (6498) 6630a^2 (6888a)

Lady Dedlock *C A Cyzer* a36 84
3 b f Josr Algarhoud(IRE) —Ideal Candidate (Celestial Storm (USA))
1068^10 1364^10 4235^4 4809^2 5352^11 5938^6 *6271^9* 6421^4

Lady Diktat *Mouse Hamilton-Fairley* a44 65
5 b m Diktat—Scared (Royal Academy (USA))
1396^6 1764^3 2142^3

Lady Docker (IRE) *H J L Dunlop* a58 37
2 ch f Docksider(USA) —Copper Creek (Habitat)
5313^9 5881^12 *6403^12 6664^7*

Lady Duxyana *M D I Usher* a47 55
4 b m Most Welcome—Duxyana (IRE) (Cyrano De Bergerac)
1210^2 *1380^6* 1507^4 1673^4 2143^2 *2257^4* 2556^7 2696^3 3149^7 *3455^4* 3615^12 4321^11 4469^4 4596^6 *6825^11 6945^8*

Lady Edge (IRE) *A W Carroll* a60 60
5 ch m Bold Edge—Lady Sheriff (Taufan (USA))
85^10 358^8 712^6 729^11 975^10 2412^4 2556^2 2965^6 3615^14 4317^7 4474^2 4688^6 5303^9 5433^5 5708^7

Lady Fas (IRE) *A W Carroll* a15 25
4 b m Fasliyev(USA) —Lady Sheriff (Taufan (USA))
4258^9 *6609^10*

Lady Fifer *Jane Chapple-Hyam* a61
3 ch f Efisio—Amarice (Suave Dancer (USA))
127^5 423^8 573^5 689^13

Lady Firecracker (IRE) *J R Best* a45 55
3 b f Almutawakel—Dazzling Fire (IRE) (Bluebird (USA))
4078^13 *7167^9*

Lady Florence *A B Coogan* 52
2 gr f Bollin Eric—Silver Fan (Lear Fan (USA))
5977^15 6648^17

Lady Friend *J W Hills* a80 81
5 gr m Environment Friend—Lady Prunella (IRE) (Supreme Leader)
1068^5 2726^2 3079^4 (3799) 4108^2 *4976^3* 5814^6

Lady From Westow *P T Midgley*
2 b f Cadeaux Genereux—Dot Com Dot (Monsun (GER))
2803^8 4522^13

Lady Georgette (IRE) *E J O'Neill* a61 63
4 b m Fasliyev(USA) —Georgia Venture (Shirley Heights)
19^11

Lady Gloria *J G Given* a88 101
3 b f Diktat—Tara Moon (Pivotal)
304^3 (522) 1672^2 *(1979)* (2181) 2369^2 2578^2 2757^7 3503^17 4060^3 5794^2 6249^2 (6889a)

Lady Grace (IRE) *W J Haggas* a89 101
3 b f Orpen(USA) —Lady Taufan (IRE) (Taufan (USA))
(2306) 2757^9 3511^3 4118^8 (6300)

Lady Grantley *M W Easterby* a18 32
2 ch f Bertolini(USA) —South Shore (Caerleon (USA))
1859^7 *2147^10 2344^10* 3510^7

Lady Hopeful (IRE) *Peter Grayson* a55 54
5 b m Lend A Hand—Treble Term (Lion Cavern (USA))
137^4 201^3 287^2 441^8 613^5 690^5 746^5 1384^5 2174^4 2459^4 2791^6 *3169^4* 4712^5 *4974^8 5566^9* 5716^7 *6864^5 7005^7 7284^4*

Lady In Blue *T D McCarthy* a40 35
3 b f Dr Fong(USA) —Dodona (Lahib (USA))
4275^13 4666^12 5013^13

Lady In Chief *Miss J A Camacho* 51
2 ch f Fantastic Light(USA) —Risque Lady (Kenmare (FR))
6015^6 6470^14

Lady In The Bath *P C Haslam* 28
3 b f Forzando—Dicentra (Rambo Dancer (CAN))
6019^9

Lady Jane Digby *M Johnston* 98
2 b f Oasis Dream—Scandalette (Niniski (USA))
(4564) 5353^5 5843a^6 6416a^8

Lady Jinks *M D I Usher* a52 55
2 ch f Kirkwall—Art Deco Lady (Master Willie)
3902^5 4527^9 4761^10 *5984^5 6427^11*

Lady Joanne (USA) *C Nafzger* a115
3 b f Orientate(USA) —Oatsee (USA) (Unbridled (USA))
(4628a) 6512a^4

Lady Johanna (USA) *K R Burke* 42
3 bb f Johannesburg(USA) —Bloomin Thunder (USA) (Thunder Gulch (USA))
2740^8 3914^9 4736^8

Lady Josh *W G M Turner* a42 22
4 b m Josr Algarhoud(IRE) —Dee-Lady (Deploy)
887^5 1368^6

Lady Killer Queen *D Carroll* 48
3 b f Killer Instinct—Princess Of War (Warrshan (USA))
5562^6 6109^6

Lady Kintyre *M W Easterby* a25 4
3 b f Mull Of Kintyre(USA) —Lady Sheriff (Taufan (USA))
6537^16

Lady Korrianda *R Curtis* a43 23
6 ch m Dr Fong(USA) —Prima Verde (Leading Counsel (USA))
558^11 2874^4 4535^9

Lady Lafitte (USA) *M Wellings* a59 67
3 b f Stravinsky(USA) —Ready For Action (USA) (Riverman (USA))
843^9 1429^2 2242^5 3046^8 *3853^9 5778^5 5982^6* 6424^14 *6608^11*

Lady Lella (ITY) *B Grizzetti*
2 b f Shantou(USA) —Laura Vinci (ITY) (Mummy's Game)
6527a^4

Lady Lily (IRE) *H R A Cecil* a93 91
3 ch f Desert Sun—Sheila Blige (Zamindar (USA))
1099^7 1372^5 2044^10 2884^4 (4425) 5356^12 (5560) 5954^10 *6142^6*

Lady Livius (IRE) *R Hannon* a101 97
4 b m Titus Livius(FR) —Refined (IRE) (Statoblest)
(828) 1372^9 1670^4 2450^9 3268^11 3481^5 4122^22 5047^9 5354^6 *6604^9*

Lady Lochinver (IRE) *Micky Hammond* a47 54
4 ch m Raise A Grand(IRE) —Opening Day (Day Is Done)
2302^17 2795^13

Lady Lorins *Andrew Turnell* a43 17
3 ch f Tomba—Charleigh Keary (Sulaafah (USA))
4530^10 *5129^9 5816^8 6546^10*

Lady Lucas (IRE) *E J Creighton* a28 35
4 b m Night Shift(USA) —Broadfield Lass (IRE) (Le Bavard (FR))
84[7] 204[10] 1537[7] 1761[9] 1884[7] 2176[14]

Lady Marmelade (ITY) *D Ducci* 95
4 b m Diktat—Ridge Reef (IRE) (Indian Ridge)
1337a[9] 1876a[6] 6686a[6]

Lady Marquet (IRE) *Jarlath P Fahey* 50
2 b f Atraf—Marqueterie (USA) (Well Decorated (USA))
3438a[12]

Lady Maya *Dr J R J Naylor* a36 49
2 br f Prince Sabo—Monte Mayor Lady (IRE) (Brief Truce (USA))
4026[7] 4500[10] 5110[16] 5818[10] 6418[14]

Lady Namid (IRE) *Patrick Morris* 46
2 b f Namid—Keshena Falls (IRE) (Desert Prince (IRE))
779a[12]

Lady Needles (IRE) *M Rolland* a74 95
5 b m Sri Pekan(USA) —Creme Veloutee (IRE) (Law Society (USA))
6953a[7]

Lady Nimue (FR) *J Jay* a31
3 gr f Medaaly—Concert (Polar Falcon (USA))
7125[7]

Lady Nova (IRE) *J S Moore* 79
2 b f Noverre(USA) —The Woodstock Lady (Barathea (IRE))
2241[8] 2968[4] 3152[5] 3680[7] 4121[17] 5516a[8]

Lady Of Kintyre (IRE) *E J Alston* 54
2 b f Mull Of Kintyre(USA) —Tartan Lady (IRE) (Taufan (USA))
2115[4] 2717[6] 3761[7]

Lady Of Passion (IRE) *M R Channon* 35
2 b f Fruits Of Love(USA) —Chatsworth Bay (IRE) (Fairy King (USA))
3085[8] 3446[10] 5065[8]

Lady Of The Park (IRE) *P A Blockley* a59 41
2 ch f Okawango(USA) —Rainstone (Rainbow Quest (USA))
4428[3] 4968[6] 6082[6]

Lady Of Venice (FR) *P L Biancone* 115
4 ch m Loup Solitaire(USA) —Lacewings (USA) (Forty Niner (USA))
4413a[3]

Lady Peanut (IRE) *D Gambarota* 74
2 b f Mull Of Kintyre(USA) —Lady Rath (IRE) (Standiford (USA))
6047a[10]

Lady Petrus *H J L Dunlop* a61 53
2 b f Oasis Dream—Odalisque (IRE) (Machiavellian (USA))
6432[10] 6649[14]

Lady Pickpocket *F P Murtagh* a55 49
3 b f Benny The Dip(USA) —Circe (Main Reef)
1566[6] 2759[7] 3824[3] 4036[4] 4528[6] 4663[2] (5622) 6259[14]

Lady Pilot *Jim Best* a72 55
5 b m Dansili—Mighty Flyer (IRE) (Mujtahid (USA))
19[9] 115[3] 291[4] 380[5] 495[12] (792) (909) (1032)

Lady Pomerol *Lady Herries* a28 8
3 b f Josr Algarhoud(IRE) —Queen's College (IRE) (College Chapel)
4018[10] 4392[9] 5137[6]

Lady Rangali (IRE) *Mrs A Duffield* 81
2 b f Danehill Dancer(IRE) —Promising Lady (Thunder Gulch (USA))
1087[5] (1422) 3256[2] (3562) (4126) 4406[5] (5766)

Lady Rochbonne *Mrs G S Rees* a68 72
2 b f Superior Premium—French Project (IRE) (Project Manager)
3404[4] 3951[2] 4192[3] 4428[5] 5601[2] 5883[4] 6075[5] 6312[4]

Lady Romanov (IRE) *D G Bridgwater* a77 79
4 br m Xaar—Mixremember (FR) (Linamix (FR))
1181[8] 1794[11] 2833[4] (3042) 3243[9] 7175[6]

Lady Sandicliffe (IRE) *Miss Jo Crowley* a65 65
2 b f Noverre(USA) —Tigava (USA) (Machiavellian (USA))
1636[4] 2193[3] 2658[8] 3642[5] 4022[8] 4783[2] 5729[4] 6427[9] 7117[6]

Lady Schmuck (IRE) *Tracey Collins* 57
2 b f Clodovil(IRE) —Merrily (Sharrood (USA))
5393a[9]

Lady See (IRE) *T D Easterby* 41
2 b f Spartacus(IRE) —Antigonel (IRE) (Fairy King (USA))
3192[9] 3635[7] 4405[8] (Dead)

Lady Selkirk *R Charlton* 55
2 ch f Selkirk(USA) —Hyde Hall (Barathea (IRE))
5162[17] 5633[8]

Lady Shirley Hunt *A D Smith* a32 35
3 ch f Zaha(CAN) —Kathy Fair (IRE) (Nicholas Bill)
1537[6] 2540[11] 2696[8] 3904[9]

Lady's Law *Rae Guest* a44 57
4 b m Diktat—Snugfit Annie (Midyan (USA))
180[7] 278[8] 728[5] 1381[6] 1666[8] 2055[5] 2467[9] 2810[7] 6797[6] 6902[10] 7100

Lady Songbird (IRE) *W R Swinburn* 79
4 b m Selkirk(USA) —Firecrest (IRE) (Darshaan)
1011[8] 1295[3] (1813) 2987[2] 3671[5]

Lady Sorcerer *A P Jarvis* a70 79
2 b f Diktat—Silk Law (IRE) (Barathea (IRE))
5201[3] 5580[2] (5944) 6297[4]

Lady Splodge *C G Cox* 56
3 b f Mark Of Esteem(IRE) —La Victoria (GER) (Rousillon (USA))
5859[3] 6420[7]

Lady Stardust *J R Fanshawe* a70 94
4 b m Spinning World(USA) —Carambola (IRE) (Danehill (USA))
1524[12] 2883[6] (3100) 3437[11] 3897[3] 6172[8]

Lady Suffragette (IRE) *John Berry* a45 45
4 b m Mull Of Kintyre(USA) —Miss Senate (IRE) (Alzao (USA))
133[11] 203[3] 285[10] 615[6] 2345[5]

Lady Tilly *W G Harrison* 2
10 b m Puissance—Lady Of Itatiba (BEL) (King Of Macedon)
1493[13] 1595[12]

Lady Toyah (IRE) *Mrs L Williamson* a25 23
3 ch f Titus Livius(FR) —Secur Pac (FR) (Halling (USA))
4671[7]

Lady Traill *B W Hills* a56 53
3 b f Barathea(IRE) —Halska (Unfuwain (USA))
1364[8] 2105[6] 2793[3] 3792[4] 4104[8] 4877[11]

Lady Valentino *M Dods* 54
3 b f Primo Valentino(IRE) —Mystery Night (FR) (Fairy King (USA))
1136[4] 1425[8] 3639[4] 4078[5] 4842[2] 5084[2]

Lady Van Gogh *R Hannon* 39
2 b f Dubai Destination(USA) —Sweet Revival (Claude Monet (USA))
5003[11] 5538[9] 5912[10]

Lady Vibeeka *Mrs H Sweeting* a65 67
2 b f Josr Algarhoud(IRE) —Indian Flag (IRE) (Indian Ridge)
1652[11] 2103[7] 2651[6] 3947[2] 4629[11] 5065[7] 5815[2] 6425[8]

Lady Warning *W G M Turner* a37
3 b f Averti(IRE) —Lady Smith (Greensmith)
17[10]

Lady Zabeen (IRE) *D M Simcock* 71
2 b f Singspiel(IRE) —Britannia House (USA) (Diesis)
3055[6] 4094[6] 5801[6]

Lady Zia (IRE) *J G Burns* 51
3 b f Dilshaan—Gift Box (IRE) (Jareer (USA))
1620[9]

La Esperanza *Miss A Stokell* 51
3 b f Mind Games—Chantilly Myth (Sri Pekan (USA))
574[7] 918[8] 1161[7]

La Estrella (USA) *D E Cantillon* a92 92
4 b g Theatrical—Princess Ellen (Tirol)
955[5] 1438[5] 1771[4] (2011) 2236[6] 2861[5] 3090[16] 4288[7] 4637[8] 5933[4] 6186[7] (6357) 6759[7] 7236[4]

Laetare (AUS) *E Martinovich* 105
7 ch g Serheed(USA) —Magdela (AUS) (Is It True (USA))
15a[8]

Laetitia (IRE) *C Byrnes* 65
7 b m Priolo(USA) —Licimba (GER) (Konigsstuhl (GER))
4371a[3]

Laeya Star (GER) *U Ostmann* 101
3 b f Royal Dragon(USA) —Linton Bay (GER) (Funambule (USA))
1338a[11] 1855a[2] 6690a[3]

Lafalda Saint Mar (GER) *P Bradik* 86
5 b m Tannenkonig(IRE) —La Nikosia (GER) (Nebos)
1517a[5]

La Famiglia *H Candy* 56
2 ch f Tobougg(IRE) —Sea Isle (Selkirk (USA))
5470[3]

Lafontaine Bleu *I Semple* 65
3 b f Piccolo—Russell Creek (Sandy Creek)
958[8] 1219[13] 5662[13]

La Fortalesa (IRE) *K A Ryan* 73
2 b c Rock Of Gibraltar(IRE) —Another Legend (USA) (Lyphard's Wish (FR))
5734[6] 6184[4]

Lagan Legend *Dr J R J Naylor* 6
6 gr m Midnight Legend—Piecemeal (Baron Blakeney)
4357[9]

La Gazzetta (IRE) *D R C Elsworth* a54 54
2 b f Rossini(USA) —Shining Creek (CAN) (Bering)
6649[12] 6847[9]

Lago D'Orta (IRE) *D Nicholls* 78
7 ch g Bahhare(USA) —Maelalong (IRE) (Maelstrom Lake)
1915[7] 2985[14] 5255[6] 5479[5] 6732[9]

La Grande Dame (GER) *A Wohler* 81
5 br m Monsun(GER) —La Bouche (GER) (In The Wings)
4957a[9] 5669a[8]

La Guancha *D A Nolan* 60
2 b f Timeless Times(USA) —Westcourt Ruby (Petong)
1302[3] 1889[5] 2247[4] 2533[3] 3341[12] 3370[6] 3812[10] 4097[7] 4715[8] 4970[3] 5480[7] 5965[7]

Laheen (IRE) *J R Best* a58 46
4 b m Bluebird(USA) —Ashirah (USA) (Housebuster (USA))
500[8] 616[13]

La Hernanda (IRE) *H-A Pantall* a55 105
3 b f Hernando(FR) —La Peregrina (FR) (Shirley Heights)
2270a[2] 2926a[4] 4557a[11]

Lahudood *K McLaughlin* 116
4 b m Singspiel(IRE) —Rahayeb (Arazi (USA))
4413a[7] (5822a) (6509a)

Laish Ya Hajar (IRE) *P R Webber* a68 72
3 ch g Grand Lodge(USA) —Ya Hajar (Lycius (USA))
1468[3] 1815[12] 2453[2] 3299[7] 5383[10] 6795[11] 6997[12]

Laith (IRE) *Miss V Haigh* a65 66
4 b g Royal Applause—Dania (GER) (Night Shift (USA))
3[8] 63[13] 722[3] 800[3] 1120[4] 1400[3] 1596[7] 2220[10] 5276[12] 5513[6] 5711[7] 6702[8] 6735[10]

Lake Carezza (USA) *N J Hawke* a48 60
5 b g Stravinsky(USA) —May Wedding (USA) (French Deputy (USA))
94[8] 217[10] 466[7]

Lake Chini (IRE) *M W Easterby* a81 82
5 b g Raise A Grand(IRE) —Where's The Money (Lochnager)
1565[10] 1852[3] 2339[5] 2762[8] 3180[6] 3498[3] 3837[7] (4379) (4706) 4773[2] 5297[2] 5522[6] 5934[3] 6283[8] 6594[4]

Lake Hero *M J Wallace* a66 27
4 b m Arkadian Hero(USA) —Inya Lake (Whittingham (IRE))
91[9] 276[7] 465[5] 3853[6] 4101[12] (Dead)

Lake Nayasa *H Morrison*
2 b f Nayef(USA) —Lady Of The Lake (Caerleon (USA))
6723[11]

Lake Poet (IRE) *C E Brittain* a83 108
4 ch h Galileo(IRE) —Lyric (Lycius (USA))
96[6] 353[6] (1244) (2209) 2815[8] 4043[2] 4722[8] 5411[6] 5830[10]

Lake Pontchartrain (IRE) *John Geoghegan* a93 89
3 b f Invincible Spirit(IRE) —Sunny Slope (Mujtahid (USA))
5761a[5]

Lake Sabina *E S McMahon* a72 70
2 b f Diktat—Telori (Muhtarram (USA))
1193[3] 1727[6] 2504[2] 3712[3] 6502[3]

Lake Toya (USA) *Saeed Bin Suroor* a106 106
5 b m Darshaan—Shinko Hermes (IRE) (Sadler's Wells (USA))
5544[6] 5767[7] 6757[2]

Lake Wakatipu *M Mullineaux* a65 65
5 b m Lake Coniston(IRE) —Lady Broker (Petorius)
5087[12] 5807[P] 6259[13]

Lakshmi (IRE) *M R Channon* a81 76
3 b f Efisio—Effie (Royal Academy (USA))
838[6] 1407[8] 1610[7] 5230[11]

La Lunete *R Charlton* a61 74
3 b f Halling(USA) —Miss Pinkerton (Danehill (USA))
4275[7] 4815[4]

La Madonetta (IRE) *Robert Collet* a70 72
2 gr f Night Shift(USA) —Venize (IRE) (Kaldoun (FR))
6525a[9] 7048a[8]

La Marmotte (IRE) *R E Barr* a60 62
3 b f Mujadil(USA) —Zilayah (USA) (Zilzal (USA))
162[5] 357[2] 1091[5] 1238[8] 1850[7] 2205[4] 2892[6] 4078[8] 4561[15]

La Matanza *T D Barron* 82
4 b m Hunting Lion(IRE) —Lawless Bridget (Alnasr Alwasheek)
(1710) 2466[8] 4479[2] 5560[6]

Lambda (USA) *Sir Michael Stoute* 56
2 br f Empire Maker(USA) —South Of Saturn (USA) (Seattle Slew (USA))
6093[7]

Lambency (IRE) *J S Goldie* a51 61
4 b m Daylami(IRE) —Triomphale (USA) (Nureyev (USA))
2121[5] 2390[9] 2827[6] 3497[8] 4141[2] 4390[4] 4583[8] (4768) 5037[5] 5489[3] 5552[7]

Lambrini Lace (IRE) *Mrs L Williamson* a60 61
2 br f Namid—Feather 'n Lace (IRE) (Green Desert (USA))
2651[4] 3030[2] 4924[7] 5932[14] 6281[8] 6624[3] 6813[3] 7170[3]

Lamentation *M Gasparini* 100
3 ch f Singspiel(IRE) —Dark Veil (USA) (Gulch (USA))
6688a[12]

Lamirel (CZE) *M Weiss* 28
6 br g Rainbows For Life(CAN) —Lamina (CZE) (Arcaro)
356a[9]

Lamistrelle (IRE) *Mrs A Duffield* 59
2 b f Barathea(IRE) —Samriah (IRE) (Wassl)
4002[6] 4564[13] 5281[8]

Lancaster Lad (IRE) *A B Haynes* a33 35
2 b c Piccolo—Ruby Julie (Clantime)
3552[13] 4904[13] 5344[14] 7121[6]

Lancaster's Quest *R Ingram* a56 54
3 ch g Auction House(USA) —Gabibti (IRE) (Dara Monarch)
758[8] 924[6]

Land Ahoy *D W P Arbuthnot* a62 75
3 b c Observatory(USA) —Night Haven (Night Shift (USA))
1948[8] 2470[5] 2631[9] 3062[10] 4186[7] 4529[11] 4759[11] 5134[8] 6264[5]

Landed Gent (IRE) *Miss V Haigh* a41 17
2 b c Kyllachy—Land Ahead (USA) (Distant View (USA))
4537[13] 4852[11] 7196[4]

Landikhaya (IRE) *D K Ivory* a65 72
2 ch g Kris Kin(USA) —Montana Lady (IRE) (Be My Guest (USA))
2596[5] 5011[10] 5337[7] 5883[3] 6233[4] 6449[9] 6899[9]

Land 'n Stars *R A Fahey* a91 109
7 b g Mtoto—Uncharted Waters (Celestial Storm (USA))
412a[7] 648a[8] 2125[7] 4091[9] 4599[3] 4803[3] 5165[4] 5376[7] 5829[6] 6335[29]

Land Of Light *G L Moore* a72 66
4 ch g Fantastic Light(USA) —Russian Snows (IRE) (Sadler's Wells (USA))
4917[2] 5204[9] 5500[5]

Land's End (IRE) *J Noseda* 57
3 b g Danehill Dancer(IRE) —Statistic (USA) (Mr Prospector (USA))
1923[5] 3102[4] 5510[5] 6309[5]

Landucci *J W Hills* a86 84
6 b g Averti(IRE) —Divina Luna (Dowsing (USA))
1984[8] 2573[8] 2965[3] 4268[11] (4884) 5223[2] 5788a[2] 6209[7] 6646[5]

Lanfredo *Miss M E Rowland* a55 55
4 b g Fraam—Lana Turrel (USA) (Trempolino (USA))
148[11]

Lang Field (USA) *Art Sherman* 110
4 gr g Langfuhr(CAN) —Out Field (USA) (Metfield (USA))
(6924a)

Langford *M H Tompkins* a94 104
7 ch g Compton Place—Sharpening (Sharpo)
264[4] 420[7] 1245[7] 1494[6] 1915[2] 2401[10] 4153[10] 4827[13] 5338[2] 5838[4] (6175)

Langham House *J R Jenkins* 63
2 ch g Best Of The Bests(IRE) —Dafne (Nashwan (USA))
3991[11] 5274[4] 6107[4] 6572[10]

Lang Shining (IRE) *Sir Michael Stoute* 96
3 ch c Dr Fong(USA) —Dragnet (IRE) (Rainbow Quest (USA))
(3710) 5012[2] 5764[6]

Lan Kwai Fong *T D Easterby* 43
3 ch f Dr Fong(USA) —Lady Pahia (IRE) (Pivotal)
3051[2] 3561[4] 4492[5] 5627[15]

Lansdown *R Johnson* 51
3 b f Lomitas—Reamzafonic (Grand Lodge (USA))
5487[14] 5739[12] 5907[14] 6256[10]

Lanterns Of Gold *Mrs A Duffield* 71
2 b f Fantastic Light(USA) —Reason To Dance (Damister (USA))
4796[6] 5227[4] (5485) 5914[12]

La Nuage *T J Etherington*
3 gr f Tobougg(IRE) —Cole Slaw (Absalom)
4229[7]

Laphonic (USA) *T J Etherington* a56 51
4 b g Labeeb—Speechless (USA) (Hawkin's Special (USA))
1436[11] 1892[11] 3839[6] 4223[6] 5336[2] 5730[9] 5897[5] 6266[9]

Lapina (IRE) *Pat Eddery* a70 71
3 ch f Fath(USA) —Alpina (USA) (El Prado (IRE))
1155[15] (1370) 2413[3] 2727[9] 3082[3] 3876[2] 4339[3] 4859[2] 5279[6] 5533[4] 5924[3]

Lap Of Honour (IRE) *N A Callaghan* a63 90
3 b g Danehill Dancer(IRE) —Kingsridge (IRE) (King's Theatre (IRE))
1076[10] 1563[2] 2010[3] 2530[11] 3048[2] 3249[5] 3689[2] (3793) 4107[2] (4608) (4811) 5431[4]

Lap Of The Gods *Miss Z C Davison* a35 39
3 b g Fleetwood(IRE) —Casarabonela (Magic Ring (IRE))
6408[3] 6570[7] 6808[4]

La Presse (USA) *I Mohammed* a79 106
3 b f Gone West(USA) —Journalist (IRE) (Night Shift (USA))
246a[3]

La Quinta (IRE) *B J Meehan* a68 65
3 ch f Indian Ridge—Peneia (USA) (Nureyev (USA))
(54)

Larad (IRE) *J S Moore* a41 40
6 br g Desert Sun—Glenstal Priory (Glenstal (USA))
4200[4] 6798[6] 6896[10]

Laredo Sound (IRE) *Mario Hofer* a103 106
5 ch g Singspiel(IRE) —Lanelly (GER) (Shining Steel)
437a[2]

Larella (GER) *P Rau* 89
2 br f Anabaa(USA) —Laurella (Acatenango (GER))
5463a[2] 6371a[9]

Larkfield *T D Easterby* 32
2 b f Catcher In The Rye(IRE) —Dominelle (Domynsky)
5042[15] 5483[11] 5904[9]

Larky's Lob *J O'Reilly* a72 55
8 b g Lugana Beach—Eucharis (Tickled Pink)
306[9] 1755[9] 4561[4] 4706[4] 5295[7] 5576[7] 5981[7] 6244[2]

La Roca (IRE) *R M Beckett* 84
3 b f Rock Of Gibraltar(IRE) —Zanella (IRE) (Nordico (USA))
1076[6] 1610[11] 2243[3] 2671[5] 2971[6]

La Rosa Nostra *W R Swinburn* a68 74
2 ch f Dr Fong(USA) —Rose Quantas (IRE) (Danehill (USA))
4882[6] 5681[3] (5912)

L'Art Du Silence (IRE) *J R Boyle* a69 55
2 b c Xaar—Without Words (Lion Cavern (USA))
1762[4] 2590[3] 2941[13] 3642[13]

Las Beatas *W R Swinburn* 76
4 b m Green Desert(USA) —Dora Carrington (IRE) (Sri Pekan (USA))
5873[6]

Lascaux (AUS) *Y Choy* a107 103
6 ch g Lion Cavern(USA) —Mutual Fund (AUS) (Zeditave (AUS))
177a[13] 245a[3] 400a[4] 470a[11] 597a[3] 644a[7]

Lascelles *J A Osborne* a75
3 b c Halling(USA) —Poppy's Song (Owington)
5494[8]

Lasciatelapassare (IRE) *R Brogi* 95
3 b f Celtic Swing—Pyjama Girl (USA) (Night Shift (USA))
1701a[10] 6688a[5]

La Spezia (IRE) *M L W Bell* a81 94
3 b f Danehill Dancer(IRE) —Genoa (Zafonic (USA))
(836) 1499[3] 2070a[5] 3744[5] 4849[9]

Last Angel (IRE) *M Wigham* a39
2 b f King Charlemagne(USA) —Magdalene (FR) (College Chapel)
1727[13] 2041[18] 5888[7]

Last Dance *J H M Gosden* 53
3 b f Sadler's Wells(USA) —Pink Cristal (Dilum (USA))
1816[5]

Last Flight (IRE) *J L Dunlop* 76
3 b f In The Wings—Fantastic Fantasy (IRE) (Lahib (USA))
1092[12] 1972[6] 2610[2] (3279) 3976[2] 5561[3] 6131[6] 6421[2]

Last Of The Line *H J L Dunlop* a70 56
2 b c Efisio—Dance By Night (Northfields (USA))
5587[7] 6080[7] 6436[10] 6736[2] (6868) 6973[6]

Last Pioneer (IRE) *R Ford* 62
5 b g New Frontier(IRE) —Toordillon (IRE) (Contract Law (USA))
2531[11]

Last Sovereign *R Charlton* a79 80
3 b c Pivotal—Zayala (Royal Applause)
222[3] (1238) 1399[2] 2354[5] 4313[6]

Last Three Minutes (IRE) *E A L Dunlop* 74
2 b c Val Royal(FR) —Circe's Isle (Be My Guest (USA))
6248[4]

La Sylvia (IRE) *Desmond McDonogh* a74 84
2 b f Oasis Dream—Hawas (Mujtahid (USA))
6392a[2]

Latanazul *J L Dunlop* 86
3 b f Sakhee(USA) —Karamah (Unfuwain (USA))
1303[2] (1816) 2999[6] 3963[3] 4570[6]

Lateral *P Schiergen* 118
4 b h Singspiel(IRE) —Ligona (Aragon)
1389a[5]

Laterly (IRE) *T P Tate* 76
2 b g Tiger Hill(IRE) —La Candela (GER) (Alzao (USA))
2432[8] 4578[F] 5904[3] 6307[3] (6723)

Latif (USA) *Ms Deborah J Evans* a79 79
6 b g Red Ransom(USA) —Awaamir (Green Desert (USA))
1997[8] 2338[6] 2527[6] 3926[12]

Latimer House (IRE) *Dr J D Scargill* a46 20
2 ch f Observatory(USA) —Tramonto (Sri Pekan (USA))
4028[10] 4428[11] 5308[9]

Latin Class (USA) *M Johnston* 61
2 b f Carson City(USA) —Latin Lynx (USA) (Forest Wildcat (USA))
1801[2] 2103[11]

Latin Dancer *B S Rothwell* 44
2 b c Averti(IRE) —Pieta (IRE) (Perugino (USA))
1528[9] 1963[12] 5281[12] 5501[7]

Latin Lad *R Hannon* 100
2 b c Hernando(FR) —Decision Maid (USA) (Diesis)
(4151) 4598[2] 6382[2]

Latin Mood (FR) *P Demercastel* 107
4 b h Acatenango(GER) —Baranciaga (USA) (Bering)
3893a[3] 4655a[7] 5469a[4] (6137a) 6526a[9] 6941a[4]

Latino Magic (IRE) *D K Weld* a90 111
7 ch h Lion Cavern(USA) —Tansy (Shareef Dancer (USA))
3144a[4] 4237a[5] (6920a)

Latin Scholar (IRE) *A King* a65 72
2 ch g Titus Livius(FR) —Crimada (IRE) (Mukaddamah (USA))
1989[10] 2977[2] 3383[6] 4364[13] 4964[9]

La Traviata (USA) *F Parisel* a106
3 bb f Johannesburg(USA) —Piedra Negras (USA) (Unbridled (USA))
6483a[6]

La Troupe (IRE) *J H M Gosden* 67
2 b f King's Best(USA) —Passe Passe (USA) (Lear Fan (USA))
6649[4]

Lattice (USA) *W Mott* 105
3 br c Arch(USA) —Lateral (USA) (Rahy (USA))
4412a[7]

Lauder *J Balding* a46 30
3 ch f First Trump—Madam Zando (Forzando)
4178[9] 4658[5] 5625[10] 5982[8]

Laughing Game *M L W Bell* a57 41
3 b f Classic Cliche(IRE) —Ground Game (Gildoran)
1012[7] 1250[8] 1396[2] 2259[8] 2610[12] 3159[12] 3624[6]

Laugh 'n Cry *Eoin Doyle* a55 51
6 b m In The Wings—The Kings Daughter (Indian King (USA))
274[7] 455[4] 616[8] 649[4] 702[5] 887[4] 1066[5] 1279[5] 3083[3] 6175[5] 6261[4] 6719[11]

Laughter (IRE) *Sir Michael Stoute* 86
2 b f Sadler's Wells(USA) —Smashing Review (USA) (Pleasant Tap (USA))
(6087)

Launch It Lily *W G M Turner* a45 61
3 br f Kyllachy—Bermuda Lily (Dunbeath (USA))
231[10] 343[6]

Laura's Best (IRE) *W J Haggas* a74 66
3 b f Green Desert(USA) —Lassie's Gold (USA) (Seeking The Gold (USA))
3914[10] 4164[3] 4514[2] 5315[2] 5494[3] 6094[3] 6343[11]

Laurel Dawn *Miss A Stokell* a53 31
9 gr g Paris House—Madrina (Waajib)
97[8] 143[8] 254[9] 281[9] 317[6] 403[8]

Laureldean Breeze (USA) *R A Fahey* a43 37
2 ch f Good And Tough(USA) —Cozwhy (USA) (Cozzene (USA))
5558[5] 6065[7] 6557[7] 7022[8] 7176[7]

Laureldean Dream (USA) *P W Chapple-Hyam*
2 b f Stravinsky(USA) —Classy Women (USA) (Relaunch (USA))
3055[P]

Laureldean Gale (USA) *Saeed Bin Suroor* 110
2 bb f Grand Slam(USA) —Ravnina (USA) (Nureyev (USA))
(3507) 4626a[2] 6040a[8]

Laurentian Lad *Rae Guest* 49
3 ch c Medicean—Cup Of Kindness (USA) (Secretariat (USA))
2726[11] 3244[5]

Laurentina *B J Meehan* a85 91
3 b f Cadeaux Genereux—Trois Heures Apres (Soviet Star (USA))
838[4] 1275[11] 1466[3] 2757[17]

Lauro *Miss J A Camacho* a64 69
7 b m Mukaddamah(USA) —Lapu-Lapu (Prince Sabo)
3381[4] (3765) 4998[11] 5738[5] 6640[7]

Laurollie *B P J Baugh* a49 41
5 b m Makbul—Madonna Da Rossi (Mtoto)
78[6] 126[5] 266[6] 372[5]

Lava Man (USA) *Doug O'Neill* a127 124
6 bb g Slew City Slew(USA) —Li'l Ms. Leonard (USA) (Nostalgia's Star (USA))
862a[16]

Lavana (GER) *Werner Glanz* 85
4 br m Silvano(GER) —Lady Lilac (GER) (Konigsstuhl (GER))
6220a[7]

Lavande *M J Wallace* a59 62
2 b f Tipsy Creek(USA) —Skara Brae (Inchinor)
2663[4] 2992[7] 4097[2] 5176[2] 6386[12]

Lavarone (ARG) *H J Brown* a79 76
4 ch h Sekari—Siusi (ARG) (Engrillado (ARG))
470a[10] 532a[9] 641a[9]

La Varrosa *Mrs P N Dutfield* a52 7
2 b f Josr Algarhoud(IRE) —Ebony Anne (IRE) (Danetime (IRE))
3162[5] 3424[7] 3866[12] 5644[9] 6404[8] 6714[7] 6793[4] 7096[5] 7240[6]

La Vecchia Scuola (IRE) *R Johnson* a39 69
3 b f Mull Of Kintyre(USA) —Force Divine (FR) (L'Emigrant (USA))
679[11] 1943[11] 2200[4] (2826) 3054[3] 3413[2] 3763[9] 3954[9] 4158[6] 4423[3] (4579) 4894[2] 5405[5] 5805[9]

Lavemill (IRE) *R F Fisher* a26 36
2 ch f City On A Hill(USA) —Mackem Beat (Aragon)
2028[5] 2251[9] 2533[4] 4461[9] 5477[12] 5902[6] 6566[11]

Lavender And Lace *Sir Michael Stoute* a63 44
2 b f Barathea(IRE) —Summertime Legacy (Darshaan)
4402[15] 5308[7]

Lavender Moon (IRE) *K A Ryan* 49
2 b f Anabaa(USA) —Kirana (Niniski (USA))
2039[8] 2738[2] 3751[2]

Lavenham (IRE) *R Hannon* a75 86
4 b m Kalanisi(IRE) —Antigonel (IRE) (Fairy King (USA))
1401[5] 2181[8] (2472) 2883[2] 3100[3] 3488[4] 3970[3] 4589[9] 5115[2]

Laverock (IRE) *Saeed Bin Suroor* 122
5 b h Octagonal(NZ) —Sky Song (IRE) (Sadler's Wells (USA))
412a[2] 598a[5] 861a[14] 3461[2] 3942[4] 4442a[4] 5264a[3] 5831[5] 6223a[3] 6689a[9]

La Voile Rouge *B J Meehan* a77 92
2 ch g Daggers Drawn(USA) —At Amal (IRE) (Astronef)
2632[5] (2991) 3504[8]

Lawaaheb (IRE) *M J Gingell* a51 37
6 b g Alhaarth(IRE) —Ajayib (USA) (Riverman (USA))
3610[8] 3705[12]

Lawdy Miss Clawdy *D W P Arbuthnot* a50 49
3 ch f Bold Edge—Long Tall Sally (IRE) (Danehill Dancer (IRE))
3046[7] 3924[4] 4801[9] 5276[4] 5716[10] 6240[2] 6927[9] 6963[4] 7265[3]

La Wildcat (CAN) *B Flint* a75
2 ch f Forest Wildcat(USA) —Zambia (USA) (Theatrical)
5247a[11]

Law Lord *A Fabre* 105
3 br c Diktat—First (Highest Honor (FR))
1056a[10] 2100a[7] 3445a[5] 5259a[8]

Law Maker *A Bailey* a79 66
7 b g Case Law—Bo' Babbity (Strong Gale)
835[8] 1121[11] 1557[3] 1681[U] 2993[12] 3108[7] 3396[8] 5085[7] 5234[7]

Lawman (FR) *J-M Beguigne* 119
3 b c Invincible Spirit(IRE) —Laramie (USA) (Gulch (USA))
1056a[4] (1593a) (2293a) (3362a) 4445a[6]

Law Of The Land (IRE) *W R Muir* a63 64
3 b g Trans Island—Bella's Dream (IRE) (Case Law)
2317[9] 3429[8] 3482[5] 4109[6] 4416[11] 4763[3] 5095[9] 5542[6]

Lawton *Miss J R Tooth* 41
2 b c Lear Spear(USA) —First Veil (Primo Dominie)
5633[12]

Lawyer Ron (USA) *T Pletcher* a128
4 ch h Langfuhr(CAN) —Donation (USA) (Lord Avie (USA))
(5059a) 5855a[2] 6514a[7]

Lawyers Choice *Pat Eddery* a83 64
3 b f Namid—Finger Of Light (Green Desert (USA))
2515[10] (3066) 3798[6] (5339) 5819[2] 6822[4] 6929[2]

Lawyer To World *Mrs C A Dunnett* a64 62
3 gr c Marju(IRE) —Legal Steps (IRE) (Law Society (USA))
21[6] 312[3] 520[7] 737[8] 1154[10] 1320[5] 2490[10] (2963) 3652[7] 3825[10] 5508[6] 5640[4] 6147[5] 6315[10]

Lay Down Darling *N Tinkler* 2
2 b f Presidium—Scoffera (Scottish Reel)
2021[11] 2838[8] 3751[9] 4405[14] 4897[11]

Layed Back Rocky *M Mullineaux* a56 53
5 ch g Lake Coniston(IRE) —Madam Taylor (Free State)
268[12] 337[12] 462[8] 617[11] 716[5] 804[11]

Lay The Cash (USA) *J S Moore* a66 48
3 ch g Include(USA) —Shanade (USA) (Sentimental Slew (USA))
2594[9] 3649[2] 4326[12] 4740[8] 4885[10] 5269[11]

Lazer Sharp (AUS) *D Hayes* 107
4 b g Zariz(AUS) —Scadabba (AUS) (Scenic)
6712a[10]

Lazio (GER) *S J Mahon* a91 110
6 b h Dashing Blade—Leontine (GER) (Selkirk (USA))
4867a[8]

Lazy Darren *R Hannon* a79 87
3 b g Largesse—Palmstead Belle (IRE) (Wolfhound (USA))
111[6] 638[4] 939[4] 1106[7] (1563) 2045[7] 2452[3] 3503[9] 3745[8] 4234[5] 4608[11] 5114[4] 5383[5] 5768[3] 6055[3]

Lazy Days *D R C Elsworth* 79
2 ch c Bahamian Bounty—Vivianna (Indian Ridge)
5971[5]

Lazzaz *P W Hiatt* a28 16
9 b g Muhtarram(USA) —Astern (USA) (Polish Navy (USA))
3063[7] 3282[7]

Lazzoom (IRE) *Miss Tracy Waggott* 40
4 b g Zilzal(USA) —Bring On The Choir (Chief Singer)
6728[8]

Leading Edge (IRE) *M R Channon* a70 70
2 gr f Clodovil(IRE) —Ja Ganhou (Midyan (USA))
1079[6] 1680[6] 3834[5] 4453[10] 4903[4] 5089[14] 5314[5] 5529[6] (5939) 6052[6] 6462[12] (6722) 6812[3] 6892[4]

League Champion (USA) *S Seemar* 34
4 b g Rahy(USA) —Meiosis (USA) (Danzig (USA))
394a[10]

Leah's Pride *Miss D A McHale* a54
6 b m Atraf—First Play (Primo Dominie)
1065[11]

Leamington (USA) *M Johnston* a69 41
2 b f Pleasant Tap(USA) —Muneefa (USA) (Storm Cat (USA))
5944[3] 6202[7] 7208[2]

Leander *K J Burke* a56 76
3 b c Kalanisi(IRE) —Guest Of Anchor (Slip Anchor)
1250[4] 1505[2] 2235[14] 2816[14]

Leandros (FR) *G M Lyons* a89 88
2 br c Invincible Spirit(IRE) —Logjam (IRE) (Royal Academy (USA))
3438a[5] 5324[8]

Leap The Liffey (IRE) *Mrs Valerie Keatley* a66 72
4 ch g Carrowkeel(IRE) —Golden Leap (Salmon Leap (USA))
4865a[5]

Lear Cavern *Laura Grizzetti* 99
3 ch c Muhtarram(USA) —Ghost Dancing (Lion Cavern (USA))
6863a[5]

Lear's Princess (USA) *K McLaughlin* a115
3 b f Lear Fan(USA) —Pretty City (USA) (Carson City (USA))
3810a[2] 4628a[2] 6512a[10]

Leaving Alone (BRZ) *M D Wolfson* a86 77
4 b h Vettori(IRE) —Que Normand (BRZ) (Roi Normand (USA))
175a[9] 329a[12] 529a[12]

Le Cadre Noir (IRE) *A Renzoni* 115
3 b c Danetime(IRE) —Rinass (IRE) (Indian Ridge)
4871a[2] (6224a) 6686a[2]

Lecanvey *R A Fahey* 69
2 b c Where Or When(IRE) —Catch The Flame (USA) (Storm Bird (CAN))
1792[8] 4002[4] 4447[5] 5008[3] 5216[11]

Lechero (IRE) *P A Blockley* a50 16
2 ch c Millkom—Lovely Ali (IRE) (Dunbeath (USA))
5621[7] 6855[9] 6980[6]

Le Chiffre (IRE) *S Curran* a77 75
5 br g Celtic Swing—Implicit View (Persian Bold)
300[3] 513[5] 710[8] 766[5] (1317) 1729[9] 2220[5] 2798[4] 3172[3] (3405) 3644[3] (4063) 4272[3] 5203[2] 6025[6] 6293[11]

Le Citadel (USA) *P D Deegan* 67
2 b g Stravinsky(USA) —Halholah (USA) (Secreto (USA))
3438a[8]

Le Corvee (IRE) *A W Carroll* a73 88
5 b g Rossini(USA) —Elupa (IRE) (Mtoto)
362[8] 501[11] (2006) 4231[8] 4284[8]

Ledgerwood *J W Hills* a51 62
2 b g Royal Applause—Skies Are Blue (Unfuwain (USA))
1781[12] 3383[10] 3592[12] 5707[3] 6449[7] 6715[11] 7117[14]

Ledicea *P Rau* 99
3 ch f Medicean—Lacatena (GER) (Acatenango (GER))
6690a[6]

Lee Applause *Edward P Harty* a67 88
5 bb m Royal Applause—Ferghana Ma (Mtoto)
6216a[11]

Left Nostril (IRE) *P S McEntee* a46 44
4 b m Beckett(IRE) —Baywood (Emarati (USA))
13[7] 125[5] 282[7] (714) 1719[12]

Legal Eagle (IRE) *J H M Gosden* 84
2 b c Invincible Spirit(IRE) —Lupulina (CAN) (Saratoga Six (USA))
2596[3] (3233) 4695[11]

Legal Lover (IRE) *R Hollinshead* a67 71
5 b g Woodborough(USA) —Victoria's Secret (IRE) (Law Society (USA))
75[5] 975[6] (1740) 2979[9] 4469[2] 5330[10]

Legal Set (IRE) *Miss A Stokell* a51 64
11 gr g Second Set(IRE) —Tiffany's Case (IRE) (Thatching)
442[4] 536[5] 622[12] 912[15] 1065[5] 1594[4] 1707[5] 1891[5] 2357[5] 2555[7] 3347[4] 3536[7] 3569[3] 3782[7] 3886[3] 4038[6] 4606[12] 4719[8] 5930[4] 6078[10] 6773[12] 6826[11]

Legendary Guest *M R Channon* 78
2 b c Bahamian Bounty—Legend Of Aragon (Aragon)
1123[2] 1291[6] 3551[4] (4076) 4695[13] 4823[3] 5053[12] 5400[6] 5773[4] 6128[5] 6282[5]

Legend Erry (IRE) *Jane Chapple-Hyam* a81 57
3 b g Act One—Azure Lake (USA) (Lac Ouimet (USA))
2836[5] 3399[5] 6238[13] 6612[8] 6831[13] (7120)

Legend In Hand (IRE) *Seamus Fahey* a51 67
5 b m Lend A Hand—Living Legend (ITY) (Archway (IRE))
148[6]

Legerete (USA) *A Fabre* 116
3 b f Rahy(USA) —Sea Hill (USA) (Seattle Slew (USA))
1055a[4] (2270a) (2926a) 4654a[7] 5465a[4] 6042a[3]

Leghila (ITY) *P Giannotti* 41
3 b f Tenbyssimo(IRE) —Libra (ITY) (Solar Wind (USA))
1701a[14]

Legion D'Honneur (UAE) *M Johnston* 71
2 b c Halling(USA) —Renowned (IRE) (Darshaan)
5880[9] 6106[3]

Legislation *J H M Gosden* a75 85
2 b c Oasis Dream—Kite Mark (Mark Of Esteem (IRE))
(3747) 4694[6] 6644[5]

Leg Spinner (IRE) *A J Martin* 109
6 b g Intikhab(USA) —Road Harbour (USA) (Rodrigo De Triano (USA))
2736[4] 3090[20] (4375) (6335)

Leg Sweep *D R C Elsworth* a69 60
3 ch g Compton Place—Radiant Bride (USA) (Blushing Groom (FR))
55[4] 160[2] 342[3] 498[4] 591[7] 1098[7] 3099[7] 4170[10] 4505[11] 5510[7]

Leicester Square (IRE) *E Charpy* 91
6 ch g Gone West(USA) —Stage Manner (In The Wings)
172a[12]

Leighton (IRE) *M S Saunders* a59
7 b g Desert Story(IRE) —Lady Fern (Old Vic)
6260[11] 6577[11] 6803[4] 6911[P] (Dead)

Leighton Buzzard *N B King* a58 68
5 b g Cyrano De Bergerac—Winsome Wooster (Primo Dominie)
278[3] 369[5] 482[9]

Leitmotif (USA) *J L Dunlop* 63
2 rg c Linamix(FR) —First Melody (Vettori (IRE))
5091[6] 6127[8] 6592[8]

Leitmotiv (IRE) *Saeed Bin Suroor* 101
4 b h Sadler's Wells(USA) —Moselle (Mtoto)
328a[2] 545a[2] 648a[7]

Leitra (IRE) *M Halford* 105
4 b m Danehill Dancer(IRE) —Glenmara (USA) (Known Fact (USA))
2050a[6] 2379a[9] 5075a[9] 5394a[9]

Lekin Sedona (IRE) *J M Saville* a50 50
2 ch g Namid—Abrahamsdotter (IRE) (College Chapel)
3297[3] 3833[6] 4636[4] 5167[11] 6255[8] 6388[3]

Lekita *W R Swinburn* a65
2 b f Kyllachy—Tender Moment (IRE) (Caerleon (USA))
6434[5]

Lella Beya *S Kirk* a60 45
2 b f Diktat—Seamstress (IRE) (Barathea (IRE))
1896[11] 5110[15] 5682[5] 5944[6] 6626[4] 6812[12] 7031[10] 7182[5]

Le Louvre (IRE) *John M Oxx* a51 45
3 ch f Barathea(IRE) —Lysirra (USA) (Lyphard (USA))
6920a[11]

Le Masque *B Smart* a66 60
3 b g Iron Mask(USA) —Red Millennium (IRE) (Tagula (IRE))
60[2] 237[3] 423[4] 6938[10] 7020[12]

Le Miracle (GER) *W Baltromei* 117
6 bb g Monsun(GER) —L'Heure Bleue (IRE) (Kendor (FR))
1341a[2] 1881a[4] 2787[3] 3565a[7] 4655a[4] 5469a[3] (6044a) 6526a[4]

Lemonette (USA) *J W Hills* a86 94
4 ch m Lemon Drop Kid(USA) —Believability (USA) (Southern Halo (USA))
499[4] 603[DSQ] 702[2] 868[2] 1470[2] 1949[2] 2474[7] 4203[5] (4909) 5669a[3] 6220a[4]

Lemon N Sugar (USA) *J Noseda* a72 60
2 b f Lemon Drop Kid(USA) —Altos De Chavon (USA) (Polish Numbers (USA))
4094[8] 5498[3]

Lemon Silk (IRE) *K J Burke* a57 72
3 ch g Barathea(IRE) —Bois De Citron (USA) (Woodman (USA))
1827[7] 2862[10] 3299[3] 3607[3] 4127[9] 5342[11] 6235[11]

Lempicka *J J Quinn* 57
3 b f Bahamian Bounty—Dress Design (IRE) (Brief Truce (USA))
3031[5] 3302[3] 3537[3] 4157[3]

Lenard Frank (IRE) *M D I Usher* 38
3 b g Daggers Drawn(USA) —Princess Sofie (Efisio)
390[11] 491[5]

Lennoxtown (IRE) *J Ryan* a62 61
4 ch g Selkirk(USA) —Pump (USA) (Forli (ARG))
88[14] 431[9] (Dead)

Lenouska (IRE) *B De Haan* a11 54
2 b f Montjeu(IRE) —Crystal City (Kris)
3152[11] 4662[8] 5186[6] 6150[11]

Leonard Charles *C R Dore* a79 52
3 b g Best Of The Bests(IRE) —Iris May (Brief Truce (USA))
113[7] 184[3] 591[8] 1887[12] (2331) 3299[6] 4354[11] 5238[11]

Leonardo's Friend *B G Powell* a57 87
4 b g Polish Precedent(USA) —Glider (IRE) (Silver Kite (USA))
48[10] 212[8] 3448[7] 4030[6] 4451[8]

Leon Knights *G A Butler* a77 75
3 b g Inchinor—Valnerina (IRE) (Caerleon (USA))
954[2] 1246[4] 2010[5] 4015[7] 4277[11] 4865a[11]

Leopoldine *H Morrison* a74 95
4 br m Desert Prince(IRE) —Beaming (Mtoto)
1372[6] 1661[2] 2450[5] 2817[20] 4118[10] 4373[6] 5954[5]

Le Paradis (FR) *F Head* 103
3 b c Montjeu(IRE) —Real Wow (USA) (Woodman (USA))
2751a[2]

Lepido (ITY) *L M Cumani* 92
3 b g Montjeu(IRE) —Luv Is For Sharing (USA) (Miswaki (USA))
1475[6]

Leprechaun's Gold (IRE) *B J Llewellyn* a62 56
3 ch g Spectrum(IRE) —Ashirah (USA) (Housebuster (USA))
1558[3] 1850[4] 2133[11] 2759[6] 3182[5] 3379[8] 4309[7] 4528[4] 4920[4] 5235[12] 5698[2] 6090[3] 6250[13]

Leptis Magna *D R C Elsworth* a55 82
3 ch g Danehill Dancer(IRE) —Dark Eyed Lady (IRE) (Exhibitioner)
(1726) 2425[10] 3056[8] 3900[2] 4502[3] 5012[13] 5545[11] 6236[9] 6824[8]

Le Riche *Miss J R Gibney* a49 49
3 ch f Pivotal—Courtlandt Queen (USA) (Deputy Minister (CAN))
2470[7] 3062[8]

Le Royal (GER) *K Schafflutzel* 19
7 b g Royal Solo(IRE) —Liebste (GER) (Nebos (GER))
355a[8]

Les Allues (IRE) *H S Howe* a43 43
2 b f Chevalier(IRE) —Cwm Deri (IRE) (Alzao (USA))
4875[9] 5186[12] 6664[8]

Les Arcs (USA) *T J Pitt* a113 122
7 bb g Arch(USA) —La Sarto (USA) (Cormorant (USA))
1770[13]

Les Fazzani (IRE) *M J Wallace* a89 104
3 b f Intikhab(USA) —Massada (Most Welcome)
1610[5] 1958[8] (3645) (3889) 6524a[6] (6688a)

Le Singe Noir *M Botti* a72 50
3 b g Averti(IRE) —Prends Ca (IRE) (Reprimand)
1117[2] 1920[9] 2951[3] 3406[3] 5102[6] 5819[8] (6176)

Leslingtaylor (IRE) *J J Quinn* 85
5 b g Orpen(USA) —Rite Of Spring (Niniski (USA))
2236[8] 4637[7] 5334[2] 6169[8]

Le Soleil (GER) *B J Curley* a61 84
6 b g Monsun(GER) —La Blue (GER) (Bluebird (USA))
(1042) 2403[2] (2833) 3978[5] 5543[4] 6110[10]

Lesson In Humility (IRE) *K R Burke* 86
2 b f Mujadil(USA) —Vanity (IRE) (Thatching)
(3995) 4613[2] 4899[4] 5583[4]

Lethal *R A Fahey* a96 93
4 ch g Nashwan(USA) —Ipanema Beach (Lion Cavern (USA))
28[12] (190) 575[3] (757) 840[3] 1474[16] 1986[3] 2237[15] 3104[9] 3464[15] *7112[10]*

Letham Island (IRE) *R M Stronge* a70 77
3 b f Trans Island—Common Cause (Polish Patriot (USA))
1089[2] 1218[3] 1827[10] 2985[9] 4542[8] *7178[6]*

L'Etincelle (IRE) *H R A Cecil* a47 63
2 b f Observatory(USA) —Fine Detail (IRE) (Shirley Heights)
4564[9] 5063[5] *5527[8]*

Let It Be *K G Reveley* a57 69
6 ch m Entrepreneur—Noble Dane (IRE) (Danehill (USA))
1225[2] 1532[4] 1745[5] 2095[3] 2434[5] 2890[3] 4409[4] 4941[5] (5158) 5486[2] (5626) 6076[2] 6308[9]

Let Me Shine (USA) *J S Bolger* 78
2 b f Dixie Union(USA) —Thislillightofmine (USA) (Kingmambo (USA))
1546a[5]

Le Toreador *K A Ryan* 68
2 ch c Piccolo—Peggy Spencer (Formidable (USA))
3915[5] 4279[4] 4781[4]

Lets Get Cracking (FR) *A E Jones* a72 70
3 b c Anabaa Blue—Queenhood (FR) (Linamix (FR))
3058[12]

Lets Go Jo *Mrs L Stubbs*
2 b g Barathea(IRE) —Living Daylights (IRE) (Night Shift (USA))
6106[12]

Let's Rock (GER) *P Rau* 80
2 b c Dashing Blade—Les Intimes (IRE) (Be My Guest (USA))
6324a[3]

Lets Roll *C W Thornton* 97
6 b g Tamure(IRE) —Miss Petronella (Petoski)
1304[2] 1805[6] 2245[3] 2861[6] 3753[7] 4375[6] 5215[10] 5619[4] 5933[2] 6473[4]

Lettre Spirituelle *J-C Rouget* a81 81
2 b f Invincible Spirit(IRE) —Epistole (IRE) (Alzao (USA))
(7048a)

Let Us Prey *N A Callaghan* 105
2 b c Hawk Wing(USA) —Entail (USA) (Riverman (USA))
2056[3] 3504[4] (3718) 5406[5] 5795[8] 6382[6]

Levera *A King* a113 110
4 b g Groom Dancer(USA) —Prancing (Prince Sabo)
(1034) 1656[5] 1723[3] 2111[2] 3098[7] 4045[13] 5588[7]

Lewis Island (IRE) *K J Burke* a69 68
8 b g Turtle Island(IRE) —Phyllode (Pharly (FR))
891[10]

Lewis Lloyd (IRE) *R E Barr* a49 52
4 b g Indian Lodge(IRE) —Sandy Fitzgerald (IRE) (Last Tycoon (IRE))
1744[12] 2091[11] 2893[4] 3345[9] 3764[9] 3996[2] 4410[5] 4920[13]

Lewis Michael (USA) *W Catalano* a118 101
4 b h Rahy(USA) —Justenuffheart (USA) (Broad Brush (USA))
5824a[4] 6485a[5]

Lexicon *Mrs J C McGregor*
7 ch m Weldnaas(USA) —Swift Move (Move Off)
4157[10] 5036[8]

Liameliss *M A Allen* 37
5 ch m Dr Fong(USA) —Ivory Palm (USA) (Sir Ivor (USA))
1925[11] 4356[7]

Liang Kay (GER) *U Ostmann*
2 b c Dai Jin—Linton Bay (GER) (Funambule (USA))
6219a[2]

Liani (IRE) *J R Norton* a51 49
2 b f Modigliani(USA) —Well Wisher (USA) (Sanglamore (USA))
2723[2] 3246[5] *3923[5]* 4192[7] *4428[4] 5015[2]* 5706[3] *6023[4] 6242[5] 6693[6] 7195[2] 7243[4]*

Liberman (IRE) *R Curtis* a36 70
9 br g Standiford(USA) —Hail To You (USA) (Kirtling)
1196[12] 3653[6] 4576[10]

Liberode (IRE) *K A Ryan* 11
2 b f Statue Of Liberty(USA) —Phyllode (Pharly (FR))
5042[14]

Liberty Belle (IRE) *J R Best* a61 82
2 bb f Statue Of Liberty(USA) —Enaya (Caerleon (USA))
1821[5] (2000) 2812[13] 3096[9] 5480[5] *6823[7] 7280[9]*

Liberty Island (IRE) *B J Meehan* 56
2 b c Statue Of Liberty(USA) —Birthday (IRE) (Singspiel (IRE))
1846[6] 2600[8]

Liberty Run (IRE) *Mouse Hamilton-Fairley* a71 61
5 ch g Grand Lodge(USA) —Bathe In Light (USA) (Sunshine Forever (USA))
29[5] 89[5] 634[4] 1319[3] (1742) 2140[P] (Dead)

Liberty Ship *J D Bethell* 74
2 b g Statue Of Liberty(USA) —Flag (Selkirk (USA))
1992[3] 2984[2] 4221[2] 4844[5]

Libertytyne *S Kirk* a48
2 br f Statue Of Liberty(USA) —Coffee Time (IRE) (Efisio)
5888[10] 6177[7] 6693[4] 6990[9]

Liberty Valance (IRE) *S Kirk* a65
2 b g Statue Of Liberty(USA) —Tabdea (USA) (Topsider (USA))
7130[5] 7235[3]

Libre *F Jordan* a72 73
7 b g Bahamian Bounty—Premier Blues (FR) (Law Society (USA))
3381[8] 3799[7] 4107[4] 4259[2] 4856[2] 5188[4] (5348) *5569[2]* 5885[10] *6342[12]*

Lickety Lemon (USA) *M Casse* 88
2 ch f Lemon Drop Kid(USA) —Tustarta (USA) (Trempolino (USA))
5293a[3]

Lidanski (IRE) *W P Mullins* 93
4 b m Soviet Star(USA) —Lidanna (Nicholas (USA))
3573a[2] 3768a[4]

Lieutenant Pigeon *T D Easterby* a69 73
2 ch c Captain Rio—Blue Velvet (Formidable (USA))
(1801) 2232[10] 3025[6] 4175[9] 6154[11] 6722[2] *6977[5]*

Life Is Sweet (USA) *W Mott* 91
2 b f Storm Cat(USA) —Sweet Life (USA) (Kris S (USA))
6482a[6]

Life's A Whirl *Mrs C A Dunnett* a51 65
5 b m Machiavellian(USA) —Spinning Top (Alzao (USA))
980[15] *1366[7]* 1673[13] 2877[2] 3247[8] (3826) 4295[7] 5546[13] 6413[6] *6816[6] 7009[6]*

Liffey Bank (IRE) *J T Gorman* 72
3 b c Invincible Spirit(IRE) —Rachel Pringle (IRE) (Doulab (USA))
4836a[4]

Light Impact (IRE) *C Laffon-Parias* 97
3 b f Fantastic Light(USA) —Ganga (IRE) (Generous (IRE))
3564a[3]

Lightning Lad *J R Jenkins* 23
2 b c Cool Jazz—Cappucino Lady (Prince Sabo)
1540[11] 3085[9] 3823[10] 4512[5]

Lightning Queen (USA) *B W Hills* a50 54
3 b f Thunder Gulch(USA) —Fairy Dancer (USA) (Nijinsky (CAN))
1205[9] 1972[8] 2558[3] 3640[7] 4391[7] 4531[6] *5782[2] 6292[12]*

Lightning Strike (GER) *Miss Venetia Williams* a82 98
4 ch g Danehill Dancer(IRE) —La Capilla (Machiavellian (USA))
6335[28]

Light Sea (IRE) *M R Channon* 47
2 ch f King's Best(USA) —Bint Al Balad (IRE) (Ahonoora)
6414[7]

Light Sentence *G A Swinbank* a71 72
4 b g Fantastic Light(USA) —Almela (IRE) (Akarad (FR))
1090[2] 1532[2] *1730[2]* (3815) 4230[4]

Light Shift (USA) *H R A Cecil* 121
3 b f Kingmambo(USA) —Lingerie (Shirley Heights)
(1126) (1581) (2211) 3576a[2] 4149[3] 6042a[6]

Lights Of Vegas *B J Meehan* 71
3 b c Traditionally(USA) —Catch The Lights (Deploy)
1098[4] 1359[P] 1974[11] 2598[14] 3429[14]

Light Vision (NZ) *R Smerdon* 107
4 b g Zerpour(IRE) —Switched (AUS) (Naturalism (NZ))
6033a[3]

Ligne D'Eau *P D Evans* a44 41
6 ch g Cadeaux Genereux—Miss Waterline (Rock City)
51[7] 182[5] 425[5] 533[9]

Lii Najma *C E Brittain* a76 72
4 b m Medicean—Opari (IRE) (Night Shift (USA))
(102) (371) 609[7] 757[9] 1382[6] 1747[16] *2149[2]* 2654[2] *3285[8]* 3826[3] *4361[4]* 4807[4] 5711[5]

Like A Gem (CAN) *D Vella* 93
4 rg m Tactical Cat(USA) —Its A Ruby (USA) (Rubiano (USA))
(6772a)

Like To Golf (USA) *Mrs A J Perrett* a43 55
3 bb g Bianconi(USA) —Like To Shimmy (USA) (Shimatoree (USA))
2456[13] 3652[6] 3876[10]

Lilac Moon (GER) *N J Vaughan* a63 57
3 b f Dr Fong(USA) —Luna De Miel (Shareef Dancer (USA))
1913[6] 2312[6] 3997[4] (4220) *6315[3] 6713[3] 6951[2] 7146[13]*

Lilac Star *T T Clement* a58 71
4 ch m Observatory(USA) —La Sorrela (IRE) (Cadeaux Genereux)
612[6] 1227[4] 4449[9] 5052[7] *5132[8]*

Lilburn (IRE) *J R Fanshawe* 17
2 b g Statue Of Liberty(USA) —Vahine (USA) (Alysheba (USA))
4130[15]

Lille Ida *M P Tregoning* a72 65
2 br f Hawk Wing(USA) —Fur Will Fly (Petong)
3187[2] 4061[7] *(6477)*

Lilleshall (IRE) *K J Condon* 79
2 ch f Spectrum(IRE) —Celebrated Smile (IRE) (Cadeaux Genereux)
(5516a)

Lille Tuva *B R Millman* 66
2 ch f Alhaarth(IRE) —Dipple (Komaite (USA))
2977[4] 3796[10] 5061[4] 5443[5]

Lily La Belle *A W Carroll* a47 42
3 b f King Charlemagne(USA) —Corniche Quest (IRE) (Salt Dome (USA))
4905[9] *5390[13] 5567[5] 6706[12]*

Lilymay *B P J Baugh* 33
7 b m Sovereign Water(FR) —Maysimp (IRE) (Mac's Imp (USA))
1998[15] 2436[9] 4334[8] 4989[6]

Limatus (GER) *P Vovcenko* 87
6 br g Law Society(USA) —Limaga (Lagunas)
1689a[9]

Limbo King *J R Fanshawe* a68 79
3 b g Barathea(IRE) —Ermine (IRE) (Cadeaux Genereux)
2944[3] 4072[4] 4667[9] *5131[7]*

Limehouse (SAF) *M F De Kock* a91
4 b h Rich Man's Gold(USA) —Biloxi Blue (SAF) (Al Mufti (USA))
414a[6] (526a)

Limelight (USA) *Sir Mark Prescott* 50
2 gr f Dalakhani(IRE) —Last Second (IRE) (Alzao (USA))
1960[10] 2371[10] 3916[8]

Limerence (USA) *H-A Pantall* a85 100
3 b f Seeking The Gold(USA) —Nijinsky's Lover (USA) (Nijinsky (CAN))
436a[2]

Limestone *J R Weymes* 48
2 b g Lujain(USA) —Moneymore (IRE) (Bigstone (IRE))
952[10] 1255[4] 1553[6] 3024[10] 3499[5] 5477[11]

Lime Tree Valley (IRE) *Kevin Prendergast* a82 82
2 b g Val Royal(FR) —Khayrat (IRE) (Polar Falcon (USA))
3438a[6]

Limit Down (IRE) *John Berry* a48 49
6 b g Desert Story(IRE) —Princess Raisa (Indian King (USA))
207[12]

Limonia (GER) *Mike Murphy* a60 60
5 b m Perugino(USA) —Limoges (GER) (Konigsstuhl (GER))
1534[11] 2143[6] *2257[9]* (2657) 2870[6] 3686[5] 4324[4] 4545[4] (4712) 5576[9] 5866[8] 6089[10] *6264[8]* 6720[7]

Linas Selection *M Johnston* 112
4 ch h Selkirk(USA) —Lines Of Beauty (USA) (Line In The Sand (USA))
5402[4]

Lincolneurocruiser *Mrs N Macauley* a73 80
5 b g Spectrum(IRE) —Rush Hour (IRE) (Night Shift (USA))
1568[8] 2189[10] 2458[5] 2877[10] 3525[11] 3828[14] 4407[12] 4587[9] 5159[4] 5253[7] 5546[3] 5916[12] *6859[8] 7024[9] 7143[8]*

Linda Green *M R Channon* a78 80
6 b m Victory Note(USA) —Edge Of Darkness (Vaigly Great)
1063[9] 1357[3] (1766) 2240[6] 2472[6] *2993[9]* 3154[4] 3784[2] 4017[5] 4396[4] 4816[10] 5722[9] 5874[6] 6089[7] 6239[5] 6575[8] *6962[10]*

Linda's Colin (IRE) *R A Harris* a77 73
5 b g Xaar—Capable Kate (IRE) (Alzao (USA))
38[5] 115[5] 288[2] (341) 461[2] 697[5] 770[8] 4577[8] 4731[10] *5020[7]* 5189[12] *6025[7] (6123)*

Linda's Lad *E Kenneally* 110
4 b h Sadler's Wells(USA) —Colza (USA) (Alleged (USA))
1495[5] 6374a[11]

Lindbergh *A J Lidderdale* a54 82
5 b g Bold Edge—Halland Park Girl (IRE) (Primo Dominie)
4021[10] 4507[9] 4664[10] 5430[9] 5535[5] 5942[9] *6428[6] 6531[9]*

Lindelaan (USA) *Sir Michael Stoute* a73 63
2 ch f Rahy(USA) —Crystal Symphony (USA) (Red Ransom (USA))
6595[4] *6799[2]*

Linden Lime *Jamie Poulton* a76 69
5 ch m Double Trigger(IRE) —Linden Grace (USA) (Mister Baileys)
(192) 457[7] 6473[19]

Linden's Lady *J R Weymes* a21 62
7 b m Compton Place—Jubilee Place (IRE) (Prince Sabo)
2938[2] 3376[5] 4099[2] 4469[9] 4701[8] (4966) *5368[10]* 5503[13] 5627[13]

Lindhoven (USA) *C E Brittain* a61 55
3 gr c Monarchos(USA) —Bevel (USA) (Mr Prospector (USA))
764[7] 1375[5] 2224[5] 2609[8] 4326[5]

Lindoro *W R Swinburn* 89
2 b g Marju(IRE) —Floppie (FR) (Law Society (USA))
(1990) 2732[19] 3462[5] 5048[8] 5324[5] 6017[15] 6167[12]

Lindy Lou *C A Cyzer* a48 66
3 b f Hernando(FR) —Daylight Dreams (Indian Ridge)
1217[2] 4542[6] 4763[6] 5279[8]

Linkslade Lad *W R Muir* a9 64
3 b g Mujahid(USA) —Goodwood Lass (IRE) (Alzao (USA))
3425[11]

Linlithgow (IRE) *J L Dunlop* a46 58
3 gr g Linamix(FR) —Diarshana (GER) (Darshaan)
904[6] 1224[2] 1972[4] 2628[8]

Linnet Park *J G Given* a45 62
2 b f Compton Place—Shifty Mouse (Night Shift (USA))
1727[10] 2365[6] 3200[3] 4349[7] 5484[4] *5887[9]* 6722[9]

Linngari (IRE) *A De Royer-Dupre* a89 124
5 ch h Indian Ridge—Lidakiya (IRE) (Kahyasi)
(530a) 862a[2] 5261a[4] 6029a[9] (6372a)

Linsalata (IRE) *J S Bolger* a86 95
2 b f Soviet Star(USA) —Nordic Pageant (IRE) (Nordico (USA))
3438a[4] 6549a[5]

Linton Dancer (IRE) *J R Weymes* a51 56
4 b m Mujadil(USA) —Daisy Grey (Nordance (USA))
425[6] 954[8]

Lion Ridge (IRE) *L M Cumani* 62
3 b c Montjeu(IRE) —Guardiagrele (IRE) (Persian Heights)
2274[5] 2840[5]

Lion Sands *L M Cumani* a111 114
3 b c Montjeu(IRE) —Puce (Darshaan)
(1998) 2813[4] 4044[5] *5220[3]* (5952)

Lipizza (IRE) *N A Callaghan* a72 80
4 b m Spinning World(USA) —Lipica (IRE) (Night Shift (USA))
4585[5] 5064[6] 5638[9] 6537[9]

Lipocco *R M Beckett* 109
3 br g Piccolo—Magical Dancer (IRE) (Magical Wonder (USA))
(1502) 2044[2] 3431[17] 4374[2] 5254[2] 5407[17]

Lips Arrow (GER) *Andreas Lowe* 91
2 b f Big Shuffle(USA) —Lips Plane (IRE) (Ashkalani (IRE))
4837a[7] (5848a) 6630a[6]

Lips Lion (IRE) *Robert Collet* 93
8 ch h Lion Cavern(USA) —Glamour Model (Last Tycoon (IRE))
437a[0]

Liquidity (USA) *Doug O'Neill* a106
3 b c Tiznow(USA) —Boa (USA) (Rahy (USA))
1486a[14]

Liquid Lover (IRE) *W M Brisbourne* a54 42
5 b g Night Shift(USA) —New Tycoon (IRE) (Last Tycoon (IRE))
443[8]

Lisathedaddy *B G Powell* a94 88
5 br m Darnay—Erith's Chill Wind (Be My Chief (USA))
(501) (702) 1414[3] 1783[5] 2218[2] 2543[3] 4060[4] 4551[9] 5327[3] 5593[2] 5940[6]

Liscanna (IRE) *David Wachman* 104
3 b f Sadler's Wells(USA) —Lahinch (IRE) (Danehill Dancer (IRE))
946a[4] 1694a[5] (2379a) 5842a[8] 6038a[6]

Li Shih Chen *A P Jarvis* a74 59
4 ch g Dr Fong(USA) —Mad Annie (USA) (Anabaa (USA))
191[11] 486[10] 902[7] 1666[10] *3619[10] 4025[8]*

Liskaveen Beauty *T J Fitzgerald* a38 42
4 gr m Danehill Dancer(IRE) —Smooth Princess (IRE) (Roi Danzig (USA))
721[8] 2592[10]

Liss Ard (IRE) *John Joseph Murphy* 89
6 b h In The Wings—Beguine (USA) (Green Dancer (USA))
2736[19]

Lisselan Dancer (USA) *J R Weymes* 28
3 b f Outflanker(USA) —Sambacarioca (USA) (Irish Tower (USA))
1573[5] *1937[11]*

Lisselan Prospect (USA) *Mrs A J Perrett* 61
2 b c Suave Prospect(USA) —Right Again Rose (USA) (Royal And Regal (USA))
2215[12] 2424[8] 2624[5] 4501[12]

Listed Art *B J Meehan* a54 36
2 ch g Night Shift(USA) —Saturnalia (Cadeaux Genereux)
2590[8] 5872[9] *6151[7]*

Listen (IRE) *A P O'Brien* 115
2 b f Sadler's Wells(USA) —Brigid (USA) (Irish River (FR))
(3071a) 4440a[2] 5073a[2] (5796)

Lisvale (IRE) *David Wachman* 101
2 b c Danehill Dancer(IRE) —Farthingale (IRE) (Nashwan (USA))
5397a[4] 5845a[5]

Litalia (IRE) *P W Chapple-Hyam* 99
4 b m Monsun(GER) —Libertad (GER) (Lagunas)
1618[6]

Literato (FR) *J-C Rouget* 124
3 ro c Kendor(FR) —La Cibeles (FR) (Cardoun (FR))
(1057a) 2293a[2] (4627a) (5661a) (6334)

Lit Et Mixe (FR) *Noel T Chance* a57 34
4 gr g Linamix(FR) —Lit (IRE) (Danehill (USA))
117[13] 5862[9]

Lithaam (IRE) *J M Bradley* a59 42
3 ch g Elnadim(USA) —Elhida (IRE) (Mujtahid (USA))
1501[8] *3062[6]* 4258[7] *5177[12] 6101[11]*

Litigious *B P J Baugh* a19
10 b m Mtoto—Kiomi (Niniski (USA))
7157[10]

Little Angel (IRE) *Miss V Haigh* a50 42
2 bb f Auction House(USA) —Green Sea (Groom Dancer (USA))
1945[8] 2188[3] 2663[9]

Little Big Boy (IRE) *R Hannon* 78
2 b g Danetime(IRE) —Beverley Macca (Piccolo)
(1992) 3486[2] (4605) 5216[7]

Little Bob *J D Bethell* 66
6 ch g Zilzal(USA) —Hunters Of Brora (IRE) (Sharpo)
1944[6] 6258[15] (6640)

Little Bones *J F Coupland* a53 56
2 ch f Tobougg(IRE) —City Gambler (Rock City)
2510[12] 3245[9] 4027[3] 4363[7] 4897[2] 6329[5] *6800[4]*

Little By Luck (IRE) *W G M Turner* a42 42
2 b f Key Of Luck(USA) —Concept (Zafonic (USA))
2651[8] *3065[4]* 3364[7] 3614[3]

Little Carmela *S C Williams* a70 62
3 gr f Beat Hollow—Carmela Owen (Owington)
1541[8] 3881[9] 4472[2] 4687[2] *(5132) 5899[6]* 6235[7]

Little Cascade *E S McMahon* a51
2 b f Forzando—Dash Cascade (Absalom)
5017[4] 5603[7]

Little Darlin *G J Smith* 9
3 b f Mujahid(USA) —Distant Cheers (USA) (Distant View (USA))
3282[10] 3683[3] 4588[4] 5378[4] 6249[7] 6538[7] 6726[6] *6935[9]*

Littledodayno (IRE) *M Wigham* a70 76
4 b m Mujadil(USA) —Perfect Welcome (Taufan (USA))
424[7] 621[13] 1165[6] 1681[9] 1885[12] 2418[9] 4165[7] 4423[4] 4855[5] 5284[7] *5947[2] 6542[4] 6608[2] (6779)*

Little Edward *R J Hodges* a96 98
9 gr g King's Signet(USA) —Cedar Lady (Telsmoss)
3268[6] 3526[9] 4095[12] 4507[4] *(4965) 5119[2]* (5447) 5689[11] 6197[2] 6327[11] *6668[3] 6851[6] 6930[7] 7053[7]*

Little Evie *R J Hodges* 46
2 b f First Trump—Cedar Lady (Telsmoss)
4756[10] 5091[8] 5442[4] *5887[12]*

Little Finch (IRE) *R C Guest* a49 54
2 b f Acclamation—Hard To Lay (IRE) (Dolphin Street (FR))
1043[7] 1302[6] 1422[9] (2028) 2247[7] 2310[4] 2533[5] 3398[13] 4405[5] 4559[7] 5520[U] *6566[6] 7030[2] 7096[8] 7182[7] 7243[7]*

Little Firecracker *Miss M E Rowland* a59 62
2 b f Cadeaux Genereux—El Hakma (Shareef Dancer (USA))
(2738) 5199[8] 5692[6] 6379[12] 6872[5] 7042[6] 7142[3] 7259[3]

Little Hotpotch *M J Gingell* a20 39
3 b f Erhaab(USA) —Berzoud (Ezzoud (IRE))
2718[10] 6792[13]

Little Iris *L M Cumani* a52 48
3 ch f Inchinor—Galanthus (USA) (Rahy (USA))
2262[7] 2940[8]

Little Jimbob *R A Fahey* a75 84
6 b g Desert Story(IRE) —Artistic Licence (High Top)
604[7] 651[6] 1040[2] 2374[10] (2709) 2828[2] 4228[9] 4922[6] 5296[2] 5838[2]

Little Knickers *Andrew Reid* a71 74
2 b f Prince Sabo—Pants (Pivotal)
2349[6] (3363) 3988[10] 4274[8] 6004[10] 6270[5]

Little Lily Morgan *R Bastiman* 42
4 gr m Kayf Tara—Cool Grey (Absalom)
62[7]

Little Lovely (IRE) *A G Newcombe* a58 53
2 ch f Mizzen Mast(USA) —Copper Play (USA) (Fast Play (USA))
6419[8] 6820[3]

Littlemadgebob *J R Norton* a19 32
3 b f Primo Valentino(IRE) —Midnight Orchid (IRE) (Petardia)
728[8] 1912[12] 4226[20] 5041[15]

Littlemissdynamite *S W Hall* a32 41
4 b m Observatory(USA) —Once In My Life (IRE) (Lomond (USA))
2153[6] 2766[12] 3800[7] 4736[5] 6212[12]

Little Miss Lili *Miss Z C Davison*
6 b m Danzig Connection(USA) —Little Miss Rocker (Rock Hopper)
1368[12]

Littlemisssunshine (IRE) *J S Moore* 96
2 b f Oasis Dream—Sharp Catch (IRE) (Common Grounds)
1101[4] 1390[2] 2199[2] 2756[6] (3668) 4046[5] 4573[7] 6167[7] 6392a[5]

Little Miss Tara (IRE) *A B Haynes* a57 74
3 b f Namid—Circled (USA) (Cozzene (USA))
864[5] 2317[12] 2940[9] 3826[7] 4472[3] 4686[6] 5454[6] 6196[13] 7103[8] 7144[6] (7277)

Little Neck (GER) *K Aga* a49 43
6 gr g Dashing Blade—Lindia (GER) (Konigsstuhl (GER))
411a[13] 471a[14]

Little Nipper *W J H Ratcliffe* a45 49
3 b g Conclude(USA) —Emma May (Nicholas Bill)
1236[9] 1716[6] 2253[13] 3257[2] 3377[6] 3789[11]

Little Paso (FR) *B N Pollock* a64 63
7 b g Jeune Homme(USA) —Seguedille (FR) (Lou Piguet (FR))
3172[8] 3405[8]

Little Pete (IRE) *R A Farrant* a67 81
2 ch g City On A Hill(USA) —Full Traceability (IRE) (Ron's Victory (USA))
1007[7] (1586) 1882[2] 2737[17] 3077[5]

Little Red Roaster (USA) *P D Evans* a34 59
3 b f Red Ransom(USA) —Pine Rob (USA) (Pine Bluff (USA))
4736[6] 5916[11] 6147[8]

Little Richard (IRE) *M Wellings* a66 59
8 b g Alhaarth(IRE) —Intricacy (Formidable (USA))
220[2] 515[9] 631[11] 767[10] 6069[4] 6407[6] 6564[3] 6883[5] (7172) 7285[5]

Little Rutland *E J O'Neill* a54
3 ch g Mark Of Esteem(IRE) —Prickly Poppy (Lear Fan (USA))
3804[15] 4491[11]

Little Task *J S Wainwright* a20 27
9 b g Environment Friend—Lucky Thing (Green Desert (USA))
2764[9]

Little Tiny Tom *C N Kellett* a28 46
3 b g Tobougg(IRE) —Villa Del Sol (Tagula (IRE))
667[11] 832[11] 2978[12] 3274[12]

Littleton Aldor (IRE) *Mark Gillard* a41 47
7 b g Pennekamp(USA) —Belle Etoile (FR) (Lead On Time (USA))
3428[7] 3795[2] 4267[9] 4460[6]

Littleton Telchar (USA) *S W Hall* a78 83
7 ch g Atticus(USA) —Miss Waikiki (USA) (Miswaki (USA))
424[9] 592[3] 673[5] 6553a[13]

Little Toto *C G Cox* a58 64
2 b c Mtoto—Moonlight Seas (Sabrehill (USA))
3866[10] 4761[3] 5274[7] 6202[4] 6715[7]

Little White Lie (IRE) *G M Lyons* 103
3 b g Orpen(USA) —Miss Informed (IRE) (Danehill (USA))
2213[2] 4211a[3]

Little Wing (IRE) *J A Osborne* 66
2 b c Hawk Wing(USA) —Hartstown House (IRE) (Primo Dominie)
2424[7] 3479[9] 3878[6]

Little Wishes *S Parr*
4 b m Most Welcome—Zac's Desire (Swing Easy (USA))
270[9]

Littonfountain (IRE) *K R Burke*
2 b g Desert Style(IRE) —Idle Chat (USA) (Assert)
6156[14]

Litzinsky *Mrs L J Young*
9 b g Muhtarram(USA) —Boulevard Girl (Nicholas Bill)
1032[12] 1402[11]

Livalex *M Dods* 51
3 b f Zamindar(USA) —Evie Hone (IRE) (Royal Academy (USA))
1529[4] 1913[13] 2300[11]

Livia (IRE) *B J Llewellyn* a43 50
6 b m Titus Livius(FR) —Passing Beauty (Green Desert (USA))
4267[10]

Living On A Prayer *T McLaughlin* a51 51
4 b m Josr Algarhoud(IRE) —Denton Lady (Inchinor)
4475[2] 5426[5] (6728) 7004[8]

Livvy Inn (USA) *Miss Lucinda V Russell* 54
2 ch g Woodman(USA) —London Be Good (USA) (Storm Bird (CAN))
2166[7] 4495[6] 4930[5]

Lizarazu (GER) *R A Harris* a50 82
8 b g Second Set(IRE) —Lilly (GER) (Motley (USA))
1200[11] 1564[6] 1787[9] 1886[8] 2107[9] 2619[10] 2979[4] 3352[13] 3873[5] 4256[9] 5062[11] 5121[7]

Lizard Island (USA) *A P O'Brien* 110
2 b c Danehill Dancer(IRE) —Add (USA) (Spectacular Bid (USA))
(3141a) 4057[2] 5458a[4] 5845a[6]

Liz Long *P Howling* a45 45
2 b f Reel Buddy(USA) —Surrealist (ITY) (Night Shift (USA))
3796[13] 4181[13] 5015[6] 5644[10] 6705[6]

Lizzie Rocket *J O'Reilly* a21 13
7 gr m Paris House—Jane's Affair (Alleging (USA))
296[11] 632[11] 666[10]

Lizzy's Girl (FR) *R Crepon* a73 75
4 b m Enrique—Lizzysue (USA) (Prospect Bay (CAN))
6923a[6]

Llab Nala *M R Channon* a54 54
2 gr g Tobougg(IRE) —Zilkha (Petong)
2876[17] 2961[7] 3866[13] 4136[9] (4311) 4405[3] 5089[5] 5534[10] 5818[3] 6066[5] 6449[13] 6584[4] 6776[4] 6928[3]

Llamadas *C Roberts* a83 66
5 b g Josr Algarhoud(IRE) —Primulette (Mummy's Pet)
95[10] 192[6]

Llizaam *J T Stimpson* 43
3 b f Foxhound(USA) —Mazilla (Mazilier (USA))
4430[11] 5019[9] 5335[9]

Loa Loa (GER) *A Wohler* a24 84
3 b f Anabaa Blue—Lorenza (GER) (Top Ville)
2294a[11] 6220a[14]

Lobby *Mrs A J Perrett* 64
2 ch c Dr Fong(USA) —Real Trust (USA) (Danzig (USA))
3551[5] 3896[11]

Lobengula (IRE) *I W McInnes* a92 71
5 b g Spectrum(IRE) —Playwaki (USA) (Miswaki (USA))
72[10] (180) 315[5] 363[14] 3765[8] 4477[5] 4966[5] (5704) 5916[7] 6342[3] (6458) (6612) (6982) (7160) 7287[6]

Local Poet *I Semple* a76 65
6 b g Robellino(USA) —Laugharne (Known Fact (USA))
424[11] 672[8] 771[2] 967[7] 1597[5] 2390[10] 2561[4] 2762[2] 3185[2] 3675[2] 3996[8] 4381[11] 5233[7] 6024[6] 6385[6] 6882[5]

Loch Awe *R E Barr* 48
4 b m Inchinor—Lochbelle (Robellino (USA))
1529[7] 2095[5] 2372[7]

Lochiel *Mrs S C Bradburne* 68
3 b g Mind Games—Summerhill Special (IRE) (Roi Danzig (USA))
1804[4] 3015[7] 3678[2] 6257[3] 6745[3]

Loch Jipp (USA) *J S Wainwright* 98
2 b f Belong To Me(USA) —Miss Keyonna (USA) (Septieme Ciel (USA))
(1193) 1821[6] (2134) 2812[9] 3432[4] 3988[4] 5614[8] 6182[8]

Lochstar *A M Balding* a78 63
3 b c Anabaa(USA) —Lochsong (Song)
1207[5] (2173)

Loch Tay *M L W Bell* a69 76
3 b g Cape Cross(IRE) —Taysala (IRE) (Akarad (FR))
1359[6] 2133[16] 2834[15]

Loch Verdi *A M Balding* 100
4 b m Green Desert(USA) —Lochsong (Song)
1986[2] 2234[12] 3464[7] 3990[9] 4373[4] 4567[4] (5278) (5666) 5953[9]

Lockerley Man *W S Kittow* a57 57
4 b g Man Among Men(IRE) —Branston Lucy (Prince Sabo)
498[12] 1001[5] 1560[13] 2492[9]

Lockstock (IRE) *M S Saunders* a65 66
9 b g Inchinor—Risalah (Marju (IRE))
121[8] 148[12] 741[9] 1562[13] 2107[7] 2492[10]

Locum *M H Tompkins* a66 58
2 ch g Dr Fong(USA) —Exhibitor (USA) (Royal Academy (USA))
2746[7] 5526[5] 5895[2]

Loda (FR) *C Baillet* a89 98
4 b m Zieten(USA) —Lois (IRE) (Be My Guest (USA))
5259a[7] (6071a) 6633a[6] 6954a[5]

Lodi (IRE) *B J Meehan* a79 78
2 ch g Bertolini(USA) —Lady Of Leisure (USA) (Diesis)
4362[4] 4764[3] (5126) 5629[13] 6486[5]

Logsdail *G L Moore* a74 81
7 b g Polish Precedent(USA) —Logic (Slip Anchor)
902[9] (1612) (2423) 2986[13] 4153[11] (5338) 5685[9]

L'Oiseau De Feu (USA) *Mrs K Waldron* a73 73
3 b g Stravinsky(USA) —Off You Go (USA) (Seattle Slew (USA))
382[2] 569[3] 633[6] 1084[7] 2079[11] 3405[13] 5886[9] 7100

Lokaloka *B Grizzetti* 105
3 b f Pursuit Of Love—Lovina (ITY) (Love The Groom (USA))
(1701a) 2707a[6] 4010a[12]

Lone Star (GER) *M Trybuhl* a66
2 ch c Kalatos(GER) —Luzelia (GER) (Stanford)
7027a[5]

Lone Wolfe *Jane Chapple-Hyam* a70 100
3 b c Foxhound(USA) —Fleet Hill (IRE) (Warrshan (USA))
(208) 1276[3] 2400[3] 3463[4] 3707[2] 4216a[3] 5588[8] 6301[23]

Long Distance (FR) *J R Fanshawe* 72
2 bb g Storming Home—Lovers Luck (IRE) (Anabaa (USA))
4584[7] 5702[2] 6303[2]

Longevity *W Jarvis* 63
2 b c Olden Times—Gevity (Kris)
6127[9] 6468[11]

Long Gone *John A Harris* a6 34
4 b m Mtoto—Absentee (Slip Anchor)
1296[7] 2084[10] 3684[4] 4859[12] 6250[9] 7199[7]

Longhill Tiger *G G Margarson* a64 72
4 b h Tiger Hill(IRE) —Lauren (GER) (Lightning (FR))
981[3] 1526[9] 1924[8] 2355[3] 2833[9] 3250[7]

Longing To Dance *David Wachman* 97
2 b f Danehill Dancer(IRE) —Palacegate Episode (IRE) (Drumalis)
5435a[2] 5843a[10]

Longoria (IRE) *M G Quinlan* a67 68
2 bb f Fasliyev(USA) —Shangri La (IRE) (Sadler's Wells (USA))
1533[7] 1848[7] (2188) 4098[3] 4315[4] 4560[6] 5692[7] 6977[6] (7122) 7272[2]

Longquan (IRE) *P J Makin* 101
3 b g Invincible Spirit(IRE) —Pipers Pool (IRE) (Mtoto)
(1817) 3431[8] 4122[11]

Longspur *Saeed Bin Suroor* a75 84
3 br g Singspiel(IRE) —Bunting (Shaadi (USA))
3685[3] 4403[2] (4948)

Longville (GER) *Mario Hofer* 99
3 br c Lando(GER) —La Paz (GER) (Roi Dagobert)
6400a[2]

Longy The Lash *Paul Murphy* 20
4 b g Contract Law(USA) —Hello Hobson'S (IRE) (Fayruz)
6732[14]

Look Busy (IRE) *A Berry* 92
2 b f Danetime(IRE) —Unfortunate (Komaite (USA))
1302[P] 1992[4] 2526[2] 2869[3] 3077[3] (3812) (4175) 4349[2] 4921[2] 4992[4] 5583[2] 6182[3] 6488[5]

Looker *J Gallagher* a49 73
4 b m Barathea(IRE) —Last Look (Rainbow Quest (USA))
620[7] 6129[8]

Look Far *N J Vaughan* a67
3 ch f Observatory(USA) —Marani (Ashkalani (IRE))
4430[3] (Dead)

Look Here *R M Beckett* 79
2 b f Hernando(FR) —Last Look (Rainbow Quest (USA))
(5918)

Looking Good (ARG) *Allan Smith* a96 72
6 br h Hidden Prize(USA) —La Pagoda (ARG) (Southern Halo (USA))
172a[10] 396a[3] 471a[11] 543a[7]

Look Of Eagles *C J Mann* a67 66
5 b m Fraam—Dreamtime Quest (Blakeney)
851[2] 3946[2]

Looks Could Kill (USA) *A B Haynes* a60 88
5 bb g Red Ransom(USA) —Mingling Glances (USA) (Woodman (USA))
1747[11] 1921[12] 2741[2] (2806) 3106[10] 3851[6] 4462[12] 6083[2] 6647[6] 6869[12]

Look So *R M Beckett* a34 81
3 b f Efisio—Last Look (Rainbow Quest (USA))
1522[12] (1839) (2662) 2914[7] 3430[16] 3889[5]

Looks The Business (IRE) *W G M Turner* a69 69
6 b g Marju(IRE) —Business Centre (IRE) (Digamist (USA))
3250[6] 3407[6] 4915[2]

Looktheotherway (IRE) *J G M O'Shea* 61
3 br f Val Royal(FR) —Gold Stamp (Golden Act (USA))
2360[5] 2620[7] 3794[5] 5040[6]

Loose Caboose (IRE) *A J McCabe* a67 68
2 b f Tagula(IRE) —Tama (IRE) (Indian Ridge)
2904[11] 3171[7] 3916[10] (4359) 5117[5] 5751[2] 6074[2] 6388[4] (6624) 6722[5]

Looter (FR) *J L Dunlop* 55
2 b g Red Ransom(USA) —Water Echo (USA) (Mr Prospector (USA))
4540[7] 5306[5] 6058[6]

Lopinot (IRE) *M R Bosley* a90 77
4 br g Pursuit Of Love—La Suquet (Puissance)
49[2] (272) (592) (765) 842[8] 1962[12] 2469[7] 3525[12] 4827[12] 7165[7] 7281[8]

L'Orage *J Ryan* 43
2 b f Storming Home—Rosa Canina (Bustino)
2756[20] 3152[9] 4774[15]

Lord Admiral (USA) *Charles O'Brien* 113
6 b h El Prado(IRE) —Lady Ilsley (USA) (Trempolino (USA))
530a[6] 600a[6] 646a[2] 1696a[2] (2586a) 3983a[3] 4648a[4] 5459a[3]

Lord Adonis (IRE) *S A Brookshaw*
4 b g Galileo(IRE) —Flaming June (USA) (Storm Bird (CAN))
7219[9]

Lord Areion (GER) *C Sprengel* 101
5 b h Areion(GER) —Luciana (GER) (Experte (GER))
6045a[6] 6691a[6]

Lord Blue Boy *W G M Turner* a26 49
3 gr g Atraf—Flair Lady (Chilibang)
4685[14] 4974[9]

Lord Chamberlain *J M Bradley* a69 65
14 b g Be My Chief(USA) —Metaphysique (FR) (Law Society (USA))
32[8] 124[11] 179[12] 369[9] 447[7] 721[12] 1210[11]

Lord Conyers (IRE) *G Woodward* a36 29
8 b m Inzar(USA) —Primelta (Primo Dominie)
3723[10] 4410[7] 5159[14]

Lord Deevert *W G M Turner* a65 63
2 br g Averti(IRE) —Dee-Lady (Deploy)
942[10] 1123[11] 1315[4] 2087[3] (2356) 4358[3] 4737[8] (5015) 5496[7] 6099[4] 6151[8] 6591[2] 6693[7] 7177[3] 7272[3]

Lord Du Sud (FR) *J-C Rouget* 119
6 gr h Linamix(FR) —Marseillaise (FR) (Esprit Du Nord (USA))
(1881a) 2787[6] 4655a[2] 6526a[10]

Lord Ego (BRZ) *M D Wolfson* a86
4 bb h Choctaw Ridge(USA) —La Rosita (BRZ) (Mannsfeld (ITY))
326a[5] 471a[10]

Lord Elrond *Miss A Casotti* 54
5 b g Magic Ring(IRE) —Cactus Road (FR) (Iron Duke (FR))
439a[6]

Lord Hill (GER) *C Zeitz* 106
3 b c Tiger Hill(IRE) —Lady Fox (GER) (Monsun (GER))
1387a[5] 2102a[5] 4958a[2] 5464a[7] 6781a[4]

Lord Laing (USA) *H J Collingridge* a65 42
4 bb g Chester House(USA) —Johanna Keene (USA) (Raise A Cup (USA))
89[4] 265[8] 1732[11] 3630[7] 4108[12] 5341[5] 6265[6] (6613) 6969[7]

Lord Mayor *B N Pollock* a104 95
6 b g Machiavellian(USA) —Misleading Lady (Warning)
297[9] (Dead)

Lord Nellsson *Andrew Turnell* a52 54
11 b g Arctic Lord—Miss Petronella (Petoski)
482[8] 677[6] 1003[4] 1888[9] 2493[3] 3927[6]

Lord Of Dreams (IRE) *G L Moore* a71 53
5 ch g Barathea(IRE) —The Multiyorker (IRE) (Digamist (USA))
805[3] 1069[4] 2521[4] 3056[11] 3600[2] 3926[10] 4433[4] 5020[4] 5310[4] (5497) 6124[3] 6837[5]

Lord Of Esteem *J Ryan* a54 51
2 ch c Mark Of Esteem(IRE) —Lady Rockstar (Rock Hopper)
3957[11] 4946[4] 5599[11] 6536[16]

Lord Of The East *I W McInnes* a81 89
8 b g Emarati(USA) —Fairy Free (Rousillon (USA))
4462[10] 4895[9] (Dead)

Lord Of The Lake *P J McBride* a26 50
3 b g Lake Coniston(IRE) —Loriner's Lass (Saddlers' Hall (IRE))
3436[7] 6751[7]

Lord Of The Reins (IRE) *D Shaw* a73 55
3 b g Imperial Ballet(IRE) —Waroonga (IRE) (Brief Truce (USA))
1976[8] 2366[9] 2948[3] 3763[7] (3846) 4661[5] (4919) (5134) 5549[3] 6810[2] 6905[3] 7033[7] 7271[8]

Lord Of The Wing *P T Midgley* a35 55
2 b c Daggers Drawn(USA) —Brangane (IRE) (Anita's Prince)
1367[8] 1631[4] 2103[5] 3925[8] 4315[11] 4527[13] 5932[7] 6326[12] 6812[8] 7022[9] 7101[9]

Lord Oroko *J G M O'Shea* a70 78
3 ch g Lord Of Men—Wannaplantatree (Niniski (USA))
141[7] 3722[4] 5006[9] (5273) 5911[2] 6421[2] 6622[3]

Lord Orpen (IRE) *Patrick Morris* a20 51
3 b g Orpen(USA) —Kenyane (IRE) (Kahyasi)
469[9]

Lord Orpheus *B W Hills* a22 36
3 b g Auction House(USA) —Lady Of The Realm (Prince Daniel (USA))
360[11]

Lord Peter Flint (IRE) *B J Meehan* 78
2 b c Cadeaux Genereux—Bibi Karam (IRE) (Persian Bold)
4777[5] 5633[2] (5880)

Lord Sandicliffe (IRE) *B W Hills* 80
2 ch c Spartacus(IRE) —Devious Miss (IRE) (Dr Devious (IRE))
5587[6] 5910[6] 6281[2] (6540)

Lord's Bidding *R Ingram* a54 35
2 b c Auction House(USA) —Lady Ploy (Deploy)
2398[10] 2876[12] 5895[12] 6585[10] 6776[2] 6857[8]

Lordship (IRE) *A W Carroll* a58 69
3 b g King's Best(USA) —Rahika Rose (Unfuwain (USA))
1684[9] 2489[16] 2916[2] 3178[3] (3475) 3570[3] 3913[9] 4073[10] 4538[3] (4710) 5360[11] 5703[7] 6278[6] 6492[6] 6623[10]

Lord Snooty (IRE) *P W Chapple-Hyam* 67
2 b c Traditionally(USA) —Actualite (Polish Precedent (USA))
5595[7]

Lordswood (IRE) *J J Bridger* a63 62
3 b g Mark Of Esteem(IRE) —Dinwood (Charnwood Forest (IRE))
162[3] 348[8] 460[9] 737[11] 2545[14] 2697[12] 3237[6] 3483[6] 4163[7] 4760[9] 6100[9] 6206[6] 6590[6] 6792[5] 6896[11]

Lord Theo *N P Littmoden* a79 80
3 b g Averti(IRE) —Love You Too (Be My Chief (USA))
1099[15] (1535) 1930[6] 2373[4] 3944[7] 4133[6] 4811[6] 5218[3] 5475[2] 5703[13] 6067[3]

Lorikeet *Noel T Chance* a79 77
8 b g Rainbow Quest(USA) —Destiny Dance (USA) (Nijinsky (CAN))
(29) 195[3] (232) 354[3] 578[2] (691) 1003[3] 7075[5]

Los Nadis (GER) *P Monteith* 78
3 ch g Hernando(FR) —La Estrella (GER) (Desert King (IRE))
5677[9] 5933[6] 6733[3]

Lost All Alone *D M Simcock* a55 49
3 b c Bertolini(USA) —Wandering Stranger (Petong)
253[9] 360[2] 2560[3] 3178[10] 5576[5] 5946[6] (6925)

Lost Ark (IRE) *E Lellouche* a98 98
3 b c Zamindar(USA) —L'Etoile De Mer (FR) (Caerleon (USA))
2499a[5]

Lost In Wonder (USA) *Sir Michael Stoute* 90
3 b f Galileo(IRE) —Arutua (USA) (Riverman (USA))
1581[11] 1958[4] 2786[11]

Lost Soldier Three (IRE) *D Nicholls* 111
6 b g Barathea(IRE) —Donya (Mill Reef (USA))
176a[5] 248a[9] 398a[8] 545a[6] 598a[3]

Lough Neagh (USA) *Miss D Mountain* a65
4 b g Giant's Causeway(USA) —Saytarra (USA) (Seeking The Gold (USA))
260[5] 492[5] 573[10] 650[12] 2154[13]

Loughsider (IRE) *H Rogers* a76 76
3 ch g Docksider(USA) —Thakhayr (Sadler's Wells (USA))
6363a[20]

Louisiade (IRE) *John A Harris* a66 65
6 b g Tagula(IRE) —Titchwell Lass (Lead On Time (USA))
75^{4} 123^{7} 252^{2} (366) (450) 497^{5} (718) 895^{5} (932) 7197^{9}

Louis Seffens (USA) *G A Swinbank* 72
2 b c Elusive Quality(USA) —Miss Seffens (USA) (Dehere (USA))
6469^{2}

Loulwa (IRE) *J Noseda* a99 98
3 b f Montjeu(IRE) —Refined (IRE) (Statoblest)
1499^{4} 3236^{2} (3678) 6168^{7} (6605)

Lounamix (FR) *J-C Rouget* a88 74
3 gr f Linamix(FR) —Luanda (IRE) (Bigstone (IRE))
6953a^{0}

Loup Breton (IRE) *E Lellouche* 115
3 b c Anabaa(USA) —Louve (USA) (Irish River (FR))
2293a^{8} (2952a) 3987a^{4} 4627a^{3} 6032a^{2}

Loup De Mer (GER) *W Baltromei* 112
5 b g Law Society(USA) —L'Heure Bleue (IRE) (Kendor (FR))
882a^{4} 6526a^{11} 6941a^{2}

Louphole *P J Makin* a81 78
5 ch g Loup Sauvage(USA) —Goodwood Lass (IRE) (Alzao (USA))
(132) (361) 1121^{6} 1357^{6} 1545^{4} 3188^{2} 3613^{4} 4024^{10} 5064^{5} 6762^{5}

Louviere *Pat Eddery* a63 74
3 b f Alhaarth(IRE) —Binche (USA) (Woodman (USA))
2005^{3} 2970^{2} 3476^{3} 4630^{4} 5333^{5} 5779^{9} 6005^{9}

Love Academy (GER) *P Schiergen* 101
2 ch f Medicean—Laurencia (Shirley Heights)
(6371a)

Love Always *S Dow* 78
5 b m Piccolo—Lady Isabell (Rambo Dancer (CAN))
(903) 1371^{2} 1783^{8} 2321^{14} 2692^{2} 3692^{3} 4171^{7} 4542^{4} 4909^{7} 5211^{2} 5514^{9} 5924^{10}

Love And Affection *Miss K B Boutflower* a50 37
4 b g Groom Dancer(USA) —Fox Star (IRE) (Foxhound (USA))
2055^{14} 2831^{8} 4031^{12}

Love And Glory (FR) *G L Moore* a54
2 b c Intikhab(USA) —La Splendide (FR) (Slip Anchor)
6419^{15} 6641^{6} 6820^{7}

Love Angel (USA) *J J Bridger* a63 65
5 bb g Woodman(USA) —Omnia (USA) (Green Dancer (USA))
354^{9} 775^{7} 1888^{13}

Love Boat Captain *John A Quinn* 56
2 b g Tobougg(IRE) —Monte Calvo (Shirley Heights)
3438a^{11}

Love Brothers *M R Channon* a76 76
3 b g Lomitas—Morning Queen (GER) (Konigsstuhl (GER))
719^{7} 1084^{2} 1237^{3} 1827^{15} 3416^{10} (4309) 4558^{7} 5006^{6} 5224^{3} 5523^{6} 5911^{5} (6054) 6383^{9}

Love Buzz (USA) *Dale Romans* a86 86
2 rg f Silver Charm(USA) —Open Story (USA) (Open Forum (USA))
5247a^{4}

Love Cat (USA) *K A Ryan* 50
2 bb g Stormin Fever(USA) —Remuda (USA) (Gilded Time (USA))
4819^{7} 5329^{11} 6469^{9}

Love Dancer (IRE) *M L W Bell* 50
2 b g Fasliyev(USA) —L'Amour (USA) (Gone West (USA))
4014^{12} 4417^{8} 4593^{8} 6107^{8}

Love Dubai (USA) *Michael J Maker* a84 99
3 bb c E Dubai(USA) —Omnia (USA) (Green Dancer (USA))
(294) 4412a^{5}

Love Empire (USA) *M Johnston* a50
2 b c Empire Maker(USA) —Gioconda (USA) (Nijinsky (CAN))
7051^{12} 7152^{7}

Love Galore (IRE) *M Johnston* 85
2 b c Galileo(IRE) —Lobmille (Mill Reef (USA))
5206^{4} (5663)

Loveinanelevator *M L W Bell* 57
2 ch f Dr Fong(USA) —Londonnetdotcom (IRE) (Night Shift (USA))
1814^{7}

Love In May (IRE) *J S Moore* a77 58
3 ch f City On A Hill(USA) —May Hinton (Main Reef)
199^{2} 385^{3}

Lovelace *M Johnston* 112
3 b c Royal Applause—Loveleaves (Polar Falcon (USA))
1202^{5} 1817^{3} (2040) (4420) (4601) (5112) 5797^{7} 6332^{11}

Lovely Doyoun (TUR) *A K Aksoy* 64
4 b m Doyoun—Castle Blaze (USA) (Lac Ouimet (USA))
5265a^{12}

Lovely Tiger (GER) *P Schiergen* 100
3 b c Tiger Hill(IRE) —Lupita (GER) (Niniski (USA))
3146a^{12}

Love Of Dubai (USA) *C E Brittain* 95
2 b f More Than Ready(USA) —Diamond Kris (USA) (Prospect Bay (CAN))
4924^{2} 5252^{4} (5882) 6336^{6}

Loveofmylife *R M Beckett* a35
2 gr f Dr Fong(USA) —True Love (Robellino (USA))
6748^{5}

Love On Sight *A P Jarvis* a62 98
3 b f Beat Hollow—Greek Dream (USA) (Distant View (USA))
919^{2} 1105^{10} 2040^{3} 3480^{9} 4093^{13} 5067^{7} 5585^{12}

Lovers Kiss *N Wilson* a50 49
3 b f Night Shift(USA) —Evening Promise (Aragon)
1219^{7} 2829^{11} 3259^{6} 3786^{14}

Loves Bidding *R Ingram* a39 73
3 b g Auction House(USA) —Charlottevalentina (IRE) (Perugino (USA))
1820^{8} 2335^{15} 2601^{9} 3164^{3} 3879^{5} 4759^{9} 5643^{9} 5879^{9} 6101^{9} 6415^{13}

Love Valentine (IRE) *M Johnston* a68 61
2 b f Fruits Of Love(USA) —Ridotto (Salse (USA))
5328^{8} (5527) 6154^{8} 6379^{9} 6715^{6}

Love You Always (USA) *Miss J Feilden* a47 61
7 ch g Woodman(USA) —Encorenous (USA) (Diesis)
179^{3} 278^{7} 496^{10} 1225^{6} 1742^{5} 2055^{12} 2214^{10} 2716^{11} 3149^{11} 4031^{14}

Low Cloud *J J Quinn* a68 51
7 b g Danehill(USA) —Raincloud (Rainbow Quest (USA))
205^{11}

Lowenherz (GER) *A Wohler* 99
3 b c Silvano(GER) —Lutte Marie (GER) (Frontal)
1054a^{4} 1593a^{6}

Low Flyer (USA) *T D Barron* 63
2 rg g Runaway Groom(CAN) —To The Right (USA) (Saint Ballado (CAN))
3024^{3} 3951^{5} 4612^{10}

Lowry's Art *R M Beckett* a52 60
2 b f Night Shift(USA) —Creme Caramel (USA) (Septieme Ciel (USA))
1781^{4} 2468^{6} 3796^{12} 5818^{4}

Loyal Focus (IRE) *D K Weld* 88
6 ch g Definite Article—Temporary Lull (USA) (Super Concorde (USA))
3577a^{11}

Loyalist (SAF) *S Seemar* 94
6 ch g Dominion Royale—Court Belle (SAF) (Royal Prerogative)
409a^{7} 528a^{8}

Loyal Knight (IRE) *S Kirk* a72 76
2 ch g Choisir(AUS) —Always True (USA) (Geiger Counter (USA))
4048^{8} 4508^{3} 5186^{3} 5974^{15} (6289)

Loyal Royal (IRE) *J M Bradley* a68 96
4 b g King Charlemagne(USA) —Supportive (IRE) (Nashamaa)
1653^{11} 2427^{7} 5923^{18} 6355^{8}

Loyal Tycoon (IRE) *D K Ivory* a71 84
9 br g Royal Abjar(USA) —Rosy Lydgate (Last Tycoon (IRE))
3^{7} 132^{5} 234^{11}

Luberon *M Johnston* a109 108
4 b g Fantastic Light(USA) —Luxurious (USA) (Lyphard (USA))
248a^{11} 328a^{7} 529a^{16} (940) 1245^{17} 1805^{8} 3558^{16} 4388^{10} 4720^{17} 5049^{10}

Lucarno (USA) *J H M Gosden* a89 121
3 b c Dynaformer(USA) —Vignette (USA) (Diesis)
1143^{2} (1522) (2042) 2235^{4} 2813^{2} 3461^{4} (4692) (5408)

Lucayan Dancer *D Nicholls* a72 89
7 b g Zieten(USA) —Tittle Tattle (IRE) (Soviet Lad (USA))
765^{9} 850^{3} 995^{3} 1245^{10} 1480^{8} 1583^{10} 1862^{7} 2906^{5} (3530) 4153^{7} 4690^{15} 5052^{5} 5327^{12} 6180^{9}

Lucayos *Mrs H Sweeting* a98 90
4 ch g Bahamian Bounty—Indian Flag (IRE) (Indian Ridge)
91^{3} (262) 419^{2} (575) (692) 828^{6} 1023^{2} 1357^{9} 1971^{6} (2139) 2237^{12} 2688^{7} 3104^{6} 3481^{9} 4456^{9} 6450^{13} 6851^{7} (6972) 7053^{2} 7255^{8}

Lucefer (IRE) *G C H Chung* a23 47
9 b g Lycius(USA) —Maharani (USA) (Red Ransom (USA))
1742^{8} 2745^{2}

Lucidor (GER) *Frau E Mader* 104
4 b h Zafonic(USA) —La Felicita (Shareef Dancer (USA))
4217a^{7}

Lucies Pride (IRE) *M Halford* 84
2 b f Noverre(USA) —Ghassak (IRE) (Persian Bold)
(5393a)

Lucifer Sam (USA) *A P O'Brien* 97
2 b c Storm Cat(USA) —Rafina (USA) (Mr Prospector (USA))
4694^{2} 5406^{7} 5845a^{8}

Lucius Verrus (USA) *D Shaw* a68 8
7 b g Danzig(USA) —Magic Of Life (USA) (Seattle Slew (USA))
144^{2} 221^{2} (239) (339) 467^{2} 548^{3} 621^{7} 724^{9} 793^{6} 1280^{2} 1755^{7} 1947^{9} 2225^{2} 2665^{17} 2947^{7} 3409^{7} 7085^{12} 7113^{4}

Luck Be A Lady (IRE) *J Noseda* 69
3 b f Alhaarth(IRE) —Khamseh (Thatching)
1105^{8} 3743^{4}

Luck Money (IRE) *P F I Cole* 107
2 b c Indian Ridge—Dundel (IRE) (Machiavellian (USA))
(2041) 2732^{3} (5397a) 6333^{5}

Luck Will Come (IRE) *M J Wallace* a68 61
3 b f Desert Style(IRE) —Petite Maxine (Sharpo)
3425^{5} (4157) 4514^{4} 4919^{3} 5602^{2}

Lucky Bee (IRE) *G A Swinbank* a16 73
3 b f Indian Danehill(IRE) —All Laughter (Vision (USA))
1176^{9} 1530^{11} 2387^{4}

Lucky Choice (ITY) *A Candi* 97
3 br c Shantou(USA) —Native Choice (IRE) (Be My Native (USA))
1875a^{7}

Lucky Clio (IRE) *M J Grassick* a55 56
3 gr f Key Of Luck(USA) —Special Lady (FR) (Kaldoun (FR))
7003^{3}

Lucky Dance (BRZ) *M D Wolfson* a88 89
5 b h Mutakddim(USA) —Linda Francesa (ARG) (Equalize (USA))
177a^{10} 331a^{12} 473a^{3}

Lucky Danceuse (IRE) *H J L Dunlop*
2 bb f Mujadil(USA) —Kristal Dancer (IRE) (Charnwood Forest (IRE))
5061^{13}

Lucky Find (IRE) *M Mullineaux* 44
4 b m Key Of Luck(USA) —Recherchee (Rainbow Quest (USA))
1573^{4} 1968^{8} 3193^{9} 4040^{7}

Lucky It Is (HOL) *A Trybuhl* 99
3 bl c Dashing Blade—Ballykissangel (GER) (Lagunas)
4213a^{9}

Lucky Kyllachy (USA) *David Wachman* 96
3 bb c Kyllachy—Intangible (USA) (Diesis)
1547a^{8} 3140a^{8} 3768a^{7}

Luckylover *M G Quinlan* a98 80
4 b h Key Of Luck(USA) —Hang Fire (Marju (IRE))
48^{5} (228) 334^{2} 427^{7} 809^{2} (1264) (1568) 1751^{2} 2189^{4} 2719^{3} 3039^{4}

Lucky Ray (ARG) *Doug Watson* a62
4 b h Halo Sunshine(USA) —Rubia Blonde (USA) (Candy Stripes (USA))
526a^{7}

Lucky Stream *M Brittain* 45
2 b f Tamayaz(CAN) —Call Me Lucky (Magic Ring (IRE))
1528^{7} 1859^{11} 2710^{9} 5521^{9}

Lucky Strike *A Trybuhl* 112
9 br g Petong—Urania (Most Welcome)
1189a^{2} (1800a) (4213a) 4869a^{6}

Lucky Tern *J M Bradley* 11
4 b g Sooty Tern—Miss Money Spider (IRE) (Statoblest)
901^{8} 1317^{13}

Lucy Babe *G Prodromou* a38 55
4 ch m Groom Dancer(USA) —La Puce Volante (Grand Lodge (USA))
6570^{6}

Lucy Rebecca *M R Channon* 60
3 b f Diktat—Crown Water (USA) (Chief's Crown (USA))
991^{7} 1153^{8} 1637^{9}

Ludovico *J M Bradley* a90 53
4 b g Zilzal(USA) —Devastating (Bluebird (USA))
1996^{9} 2494^{F} (Dead)

Ludwigshafen (IRE) *John Geoghegan* a74 80
3 b f Cape Cross(IRE) —Cape Clear (Slip Anchor)
4836a^{14} 5460a^{13}

Luisant *F Doumen* 113
4 ch h Pivotal—La Legere (USA) (Lit De Justice (USA))
2500a^{5}

Lujano *Ollie Pears* a60
2 b g Lujain(USA) —Latch Key Lady (USA) (Tejano (USA))
6693^{8} (7021) 7210^{3}

Lujiana *M Brittain* a51 41
2 b f Lujain(USA) —Compact Disc (IRE) (Royal Academy (USA))
972^{5} 5252^{9}

Lula (IRE) *M Quinn* a37 20
3 ch f Tagula(IRE) —Sodfahh (Lion Cavern (USA))
934^{2} 3846^{5}

Lullaby Lady *B W Hills* a72 57
2 b f Piccolo—Musetta (IRE) (Cadeaux Genereux)
6105^{5} 6432^{3}

Luloah *J G M O'Shea* a45 49
4 b m Mujahid(USA) —Bangles (Chilibang)
97^{4} 239^{11} 2104^{3} 2761^{2} 3368^{9} 3869^{11} 4974^{3} 6531^{7} 7137^{8}

Lumen (FR) *O Larsen* 100
5 gr m Verglas(IRE) —La Le Lu (FR) (Exit To Nowhere (USA))
4218a^{7}

Lumiere Noire (FR) *R Gibson* a85 89
3 ch f Dashing Blade—Lumiere Rouge (FR) (Indian Ridge)
5850a^{5}

Luminous Gold *C F Wall* 66
2 b f Fantastic Light(USA) —Nasaieb (IRE) (Fairy King (USA))
3706^{16} 5720^{6} 6082^{2}

Luminous One (IRE) *J S Bolger* a72 91
3 b f Galileo(IRE) —Smaoineamh (Tap On Wood)
875a^{8} 3117a^{8} 6555a^{6}

Luna Danza *B J Meehan* a51 51
3 gr f Danehill Dancer(IRE) —Sita (IRE) (Indian Ridge)
1128^{13} 1606^{12} 1988^{7} 2456^{12}

Luna Landing *Jedd O'Keeffe* a74 85
4 ch g Allied Forces(USA) —Macca Luna (IRE) (Kahyasi)
1385^{5} 1771^{11} (2314) 2861^{8} 4194^{2} 4288^{5} 4732^{10} 5504^{5} 6357^{6}

Luna Nel Pozzo *L Riccardi* 94
2 b f Choisir(AUS) —Luna D'Estate (IRE) (Alzao (USA))
6047a^{11}

Lunar Lass *G Woodward* 36
2 b f Fraam—Easter Moon (FR) (Easter Sun)
3833^{10} 5154^{6} 5931^{6} 6722^{14}

Lunar Limelight *P J Makin* a49 53
2 b c Royal Applause—Moon Magic (Polish Precedent (USA))
2398^{9} 3085^{5} 4777^{10} 5729^{9}

Luna Royale (IRE) *H-A Pantall* 95
2 b f Royal Applause—Lunaska (FR) (Ashkalani (IRE))
4626a^{7} 6416a^{6}

Lunar Promise (IRE) *Ian Williams* a81 70
5 b g Mujadil(USA) —Lunadine (FR) (Bering)
(117)

Lunar River (FR) *David Pinder* a71 71
4 b m Muhtathir—Moon Gorge (Pursuit Of Love)
1078^{9} 1521^{9} 1628^{4} (1951) 2579^{10} 3455^{11} 3731^{3} 4112^{8} 4472^{5} 5020^{3} 5178^{8} 5569^{3} 5983^{10}

Lunatico (GER) *S C Williams* 28
2 b g Bertolini(USA) —La Playa (Shavian)
3037^{9} 3383^{12} 3842^{8}

Lunces Lad (IRE) *M R Channon* a79 87
3 gr g Xaar—Bridelina (FR) (Linamix (FR))
1124^{8} 1500^{6} 2213^{4} 2881^{11} 3480^{2} 3707^{4} 4170^{4} 4811^{10} 5115^{3} 5360^{8}

Lundy's Lane (IRE) *A M Balding* a94 106
7 b g Darshaan—Lunda (IRE) (Soviet Star (USA))
327a^{10} 411a^{4} 473a^{9} 544a^{6} 2755^{7} 3330^{6} 3939^{2} 4388^{4} 5030^{2} 5402^{3} 5830^{8} 6759^{9}

L'Unico Erede *B Grizzetti*
2 b c Cadeaux Genereux—L'Ereditiera (Alzao (USA))
6527a^{2}

Luscious Lips *R Hannon* 76
2 b f Mujahid(USA) —Zing (Zilzal (USA))
1540^{7} 1814^{3} 2724^{2} (3162) 4152^{15} 4823^{5} 5939^{4} 6195^{7}

Luscivious *A J McCabe* a81 94
3 ch g Kyllachy—Lloc (Absalom)
1616^{4} 1817^{2} 2044^{5} 2884^{7} 3431^{13} 4123^{15} 4726^{8} 4950^{6} 6487^{12}

Lush (IRE) *R Hannon* 76
2 b f Fasliyev(USA) —Our Hope (Dancing Brave (USA))
1960^{3} 2969^{5}

Lush Lashes *J S Bolger* 97
2 b f Galileo(IRE) —Dance For Fun (Anabaa (USA))
(5395a)

Lu's Woman *M W Easterby* 56
2 b f Lujain(USA) —Business Woman (Primo Dominie)
5521^{4} 5902^{7} 6254^{5}

Luxurix (FR) *P R Webber* a79
6 gr g Linamix(FR) —Luxurious (USA) (Lyphard (USA))
263^{5} (623)

Lynford Lady *P W D'Arcy* a52 50
4 b m Zaha(CAN) —Little Miss Rocker (Rock Hopper)
4327^{10} 4534^{8} 4670^{9} 5132^{10}

Lyon's Hill *M Mullineaux* 49
3 ch g Generous(IRE) —New Abbey (Sadler's Wells (USA))
6257^{7} 6700^{2}

Lyrical Symphony *W J Knight* a48 55
2 b f Captain Rio—Musical Key (Key Of Luck (USA))
3874^{6} 5498^{10} 6065^{6} 6426^{10}

Lysander's Quest (IRE) *R Ingram* a54 59
9 br g King's Theatre(IRE) —Haramayda (FR) (Doyoun)
134^{2} 354^{6} 416^{4} 607^{6} 792^{5} 4322^{7} 5453^{7} 5533^{8} 6643^{9} 6811^{9}

Lytham (IRE) *D J Wintle* a56
6 b g Spectrum(IRE) —Nousaiyra (IRE) (Be My Guest (USA))
1755^{10} 2149^{12} 2519^{4} (3186) 6479^{11}

Lytton *W R Swinburn* a93 88
2 b c Royal Applause—Dora Carrington (IRE) (Sri Pekan (USA))
(4454) 5219^{7} 6182^{5}

Maahe (IRE) *R A Fahey* 43
2 b f Namid—Almond Flower (IRE) (Alzao (USA))
3200^{10} 3606^{10} 3995^{9} 5502^{7}

Maal (IRE) *David Marnane* 71
4 b g Mozart(IRE) —Dalayil (IRE) (Sadler's Wells (USA))
6368a^{5}

Ma Al Salamah (IRE) *C E Brittain* 60
2 ch f Noverre(USA) —Tres Sage (Reprimand)
5357^{6} 5540^{7}

Mabaahej (USA) *B W Hills* a62 39
3 b f Belong To Me(USA) —Tabheej (IRE) (Mujtahid (USA))
1128^{14} 1522^{3} 2083^{10} 4064^{6}

Mabel (IRE) *S C Williams* 75
4 b m In The Wings—Ma N'leme Biche (USA) (Key To The Kingdom (USA))
2047^{5} 2675^{7} 3630^{2} 5573^{9} 6056^{4} 6330^{8}

Macademy Royal (USA) *H Morrison* a75 34
4 b g Royal Academy(USA) —Garden Folly (USA) (Pine Bluff (USA))
(588) 717^{6} 1999^{13} 3212^{7} 3906^{10} 6340^{2} 6581^{2} 6993^{13}

Macaroni Gin (IRE) *J Howard Johnson* 67
3 b g Grand Slam(USA) —Polyandry (IRE) (Pennekamp (USA))
1659^{9} 4499^{9} 5157^{4}

Macarthur *A P O'Brien* 116
3 b c Montjeu(IRE) —Out West (USA) (Gone West (USA))
1185a^{3} 1693a^{3} 4692^{3} 5408^{6}

Maccabeus *P J O'Gorman* a50 54
2 b c Bold Edge—Birthday Venture (Soviet Star (USA))
3823^{7} 4132^{9} 4604^{6} 5096^{4} 5252^{8}

Mac Dalia *M G Quinlan* a68 70
2 b f Namid—Maugwenna (Danehill (USA))
2746^{5} 3423^{8} (3947) 5452^{6} 5932^{12} 7106^{3} (7240)

Mac Don (IRE) *Eamon Tyrrell* 73
3 b g Soviet Star(USA) —Sharena (IRE) (Kahyasi)
6553a^{14}

Macedon *J S Moore* 88
4 b g Dansili—Hypnotize (Machiavellian (USA))
1145^{4} 1996^{7} 2469^{14} 3943^{4} 4566^{6} 6753^{12}

Macellya (FR) *X Nakkachdji* 95
2 ch f Testa Rossa(AUS) —Macellum (IRE) (Machiavellian (USA))
6187a^{3}

Mac Federal (IRE) *Miss Sheena West* a65
5 b g In The Wings—Tocade (IRE) (Kenmare (FR))
458^{5}

Mac Gille Eoin *J Gallagher* a93 100
3 b c Bertolini(USA) —Peruvian Jade (Petong)
1022^{2} 1604^{5} 1948^{3} 2395^{2} (2629) (2769) 3749^{7} 4123^{7} 4806^{2} 4950^{5} (5449) 5797^{18}

Macheera (IRE) *Robert Collet* 93
3 b f Machiavellian(USA) —Caerlina (IRE) (Caerleon (USA))
6940a^{0}

Machinate (USA) *W M Brisbourne* a65 58
5 bb g Machiavellian(USA) —Dancing Sea (USA) (Storm Cat (USA))
179^{7} 402^{8} 517^{2} 570^{4} 625^{10} 932^{2} 975^{9} 1232^{2} 1366^{8} 2143^{3} 2550^{6} 3067^{5} 3195^{10} 4223^{5} 5190^{8} 5890^{2} 6100^{6} 6479^{2} 6629^{6} (6859) 6955^{2} 7079^{2} 7214^{7} (7248)

Machinist (IRE) *D Nicholls* a97 106
7 br g Machiavellian(USA) —Athene (IRE) (Rousillon (USA))
249a^{9} 474a^{4} 828^{5} 1195^{3} 1651^{16} 2234^{10} (2566) (3140a) 4150^{13} 4747^{11}

Mach Ride (USA) *Steve W Standridge* a103 109
4 b h Pentelicus(USA) —April Invitation (USA) (Formal Dinner (USA))
5852a[4]

Machynleth *M Al Muhairi* a96 83
7 b g Machiavellian(USA) —Tanami (Green Desert (USA))
105a[11] *249a[5] 324a[5]*

Macleya (GER) *A Fabre* 113
5 b m Winged Love(IRE) —Minaccia (GER) (Platini (GER))
990a[4] (1421a) 2165a[2] 3565a[3] (4215a) 5465a[5] 6526a[2] 7090a[11]

Mac Lough (USA) *Eamon Tyrrell* 38
5 br g Exploit(USA) —Bundle Of Gold (USA) (Seeking The Gold (USA))
1590[9]

Mac Love *J Noseda* a105 110
6 b g Cape Cross(IRE) —My Lass (Elmaamul (USA))
245a[2] 400a[5] 547a[4] 1656[3] 3098[10] 3941[6] 4401[6] 5112[4] 5409[5] 6332[14]

Macorville (USA) *G M Moore* 113
4 b g Diesis—Desert Jewel (USA) (Caerleon (USA))
1109[6] 1300[6] 1822[6] 3090[2] 3973[2] 5437a[4] 6335[33]

Macuna *C Sprengel* 75
4 br m Acatenango(GER) —Midnight Society (USA) (Imp Society (USA))
6220a[9]

Madaarek (USA) *E A L Dunlop* a57 86
3 b c Kingmambo(USA) —Hachiyah (IRE) (Generous (IRE))
649[3] (1256) 1810[4] (2185) 3533[5] 4572[6] *5686[7]*

Mad About You (IRE) *D K Weld* 108
2 b f Indian Ridge—Irresistible Jewel (IRE) (Danehill (USA))
3659a[2] 5073a[3] 6040a[3]

Madam Carwell *J G Given* 54
2 b f King's Best(USA) —Delirious Moment (IRE) (Kris)
4565[9] 5483[4] 5766[19]

Madame Bountiful *A King* a49 52
2 ch f Bahamian Bounty—Madame Crecy (USA) (Al Nasr (FR))
6087[9] *6403[7]* 6535[15]

Madame Esperance *A & G Botti* 68
3 b f Halling(USA) —Donostia (Unfuwain (USA))
6688a[13]

Madame Hoi (IRE) *M R Channon* 73
2 ch f Hawk Wing(USA) —Lindesberg (Doyoun)
5592[5] 5913[2] 6461[2]

Madame Montom (USA) *S W Hall* a39
2 b f French Envoy(USA) —Sticky Fingers (USA) (Crafty Prospector (USA))
5815[8] 6438[11] 6814[9]

Madame Rio (IRE) *K R Burke* a25 61
2 b f Captain Rio—Glenviews Purchase (IRE) (Desert Story (IRE))
2869[9] 4328[6] 5801[4] *6263[12] 6388[12]*

Madam Patti *R Ingram* a44 40
4 b m Monashee Mountain(USA) —Thabeh (Shareef Dancer (USA))
1737[6] 3046[6] 3968[5]

Madam Superior *D J S Ffrench Davis* 43
2 b f Superior Premium—Amy Leigh (IRE) (Imperial Frontier (USA))
1533[9] 1680[10] 1919[8] 4293[14]

Madam Vouvray *B J Meehan* a67 59
3 ch f Vettori(IRE) —April Stock (Beveled (USA))
2429[7] *2766[4] 3214[10]* 4510[10] 4877[12]

Madam Zorro *S Parr* a37 32
2 gr f Weet-A-Minute(IRE) —Capponicus (IRE) (Woodborough (USA))
2517[8] 2838[4] *3065[6]*

Maddie's Pearl (IRE) *M R Channon* 33
2 gb f Clodovil(IRE) —Perle D'Irlande (FR) (Top Ville)
1807[7] 2447[8]

Mad Dog Slew (USA) *F Reuterskiold* a101 84
4 br h Slew City Slew(USA) —Skep (USA) (Fappiano (USA))
2131a[12]

Maddy *R M Beckett* a63 63
2 b f Daggers Drawn(USA) —Summer Lightning (IRE) (Tamure (IRE))
2663[5] *(3423) 4065[4]* 4453[7] 6052[5] *6584[9]*

Mademoiselle *R A Harris* a62 56
5 b m Efisio—Shall We Dance (Rambo Dancer (CAN))
115[2] 266[2] 358[3] 431[3] 462[7] 532[2] 570[5] 664[2] (712) 732[8] 1038[5] 3405[4]

Made To Ransom *J H M Gosden* 84
2 b c Red Ransom(USA) —Maid For The Hills (Indian Ridge)
5951[3]

Madiba *P Howling* a69 58
8 b g Emperor Jones(USA) —Priluki (Lycius (USA))
213[13] 389[4] 1216[2] 1745[3] 2686[2] 3448[8] *3927[2]* 4322[6] *4463[5] 5426[6]*

Madison Heights (IRE) *J Howard Johnson* 67
2 ch g Monashee Mountain(USA) —Stormchaser (IRE) (Titus Livius (FR))
1963[5] 2889[4] 3205[2] 4278[2] 4892[9]

Mad Man Will (IRE) *S C Williams* a53
2 b g Namid—Native Queen (FR) (Desert King (IRE))
5097[9] 7129[5]

Madresal (GER) *P Schiergen* a101 106
8 gr g Lomitas—Midnight Society (USA) (Imp Society (USA))
881a[5] 1699a[6] 2903a[4]

Madrigale *G L Moore* a67 63
3 b f Averti(IRE) —Shy Minstrel (USA) (The Minstrel (CAN))
160[3] 231[2] 342[5] 498[2] (689) 1345[4]

Mad Rush (USA) *L M Cumani* 96
3 b c Lemon Drop Kid(USA) —Revonda (IRE) (Sadler's Wells (USA))
1153[3] (1659) 2305[2] 2999[2]

Mae Cigan (FR) *M Blanshard* a66 74
4 gr g Medaaly—Concert (Polar Falcon (USA))
1451[11] 1638[2] 1761[4] 2106[5] 2660[6] 3567[4] 4504[4] *5132[2] 5531[6]* (5777) *6102[5]* 6422[6]

Maeve (IRE) *E J Creighton* a51 45
3 b f Tomba—Boozy (Absalom)
8997 1763[6] *2146[5] 2260[6] 7148[9]*

Mafaheem *A B Haynes* a73 85
5 b g Mujahid(USA) —Legend Of Aragon (Aragon)
550[13] 1524[14] 1630[6] 1852[13] (2652) (3163) 3762[5] 3869[5] 3965[4] *(5981) 6938[7] 7077[4]*

Mafasina (USA) *Christian Wroe* a69
2 b f Orientate(USA) —Money Madam (USA) (A.P. Indy (USA))
(6849) 7016[4]

Mafeking (UAE) *M R Hoad* a89 79
3 b g Jade Robbery(USA) —Melisendra (FR) (Highest Honor (FR))
1122[2] 1987[5] 2627[13] *4276[4]* 4889[3] *5889[2] 6145[3] 6669[2] 7018[3] (7075)*

Mafioso *M Johnston* a77 75
2 b c Red Ransom(USA) —Lamarque (IRE) (Nureyev (USA))
1858[9] 5910[3] *6530[2] (6748)*

Magdalene *Rae Guest* a70 73
3 ch f Act One—Three Terns (USA) (Arctic Tern (USA))
3176[4] 3611[2] 3789[4] (4858) *5604[4] 6245[7]*

Maggie Kate *R Ingram* a61
2 b f Auction House(USA) —Perecapa (IRE) (Archway (IRE))
6964[6] 7258[2]

Magical Fantasy (USA) *J Nicol* a76 55
2 ch f Diesis—Kissing Gate (USA) (Easy Goer (USA))
4402[11] *5308[4] 6578[2] 6763[2] (6948)*

Magical Music *J Pearce* a91 68
4 b m Fraam—Magical Flute (Piccolo)
185[4] 501[7] 702[3] 979[7] *1524[8]* 2831[15] (3161) 3711[14] 4107[3] 4632[3] *(5221)* 5905[7] *6208[5] 6674[5] 7002[7]*

Magicalmysterytour (IRE) *W J Musson* 97
4 b g Sadler's Wells(USA) —Jude (Darshaan)
2002[7] 2474[3] 3060[2] 3509[7] (4572)

Magical Song *P A Blockley* a50 39
2 ch c Forzando—Classical Song (IRE) (Fayruz)
3424[6] 5470[12] *5888[8] 6899[8]*

Magical Speedfit (IRE) *G G Margarson* 78
2 ch g Bold Fact(USA) —Magical Peace (IRE) (Magical Wonder (USA))
1540[2] 1721[2] 2737[16] 3085[2] 3823[3] 4181[4] 5065[2] 5802[9] 5974[25]

Magical World *J M Bradley* 16
4 b m Agnes World(USA) —Otaru (IRE) (Indian Ridge)
403[11] 901[9]

Magic America (USA) *Mme C Head-Maarek* 111
3 ch f High Yield(USA) —Shoofha (IRE) (Bluebird (USA))
(1006a)

Magic Amigo *J R Jenkins* a68 77
6 ch g Zilzal(USA) —Emaline (FR) (Empery (USA))
89[2] 212[7] 503[7] 982[7] 2157[5] *2572[7]* 2745[4] 3249[4] 4517[5] *4945[5]* 5421[4] *6096[4] 6896[9] 7120[3]*

Magic Amour *P A Blockley* a69 60
9 ch g Sanglamore(USA) —Rakli (Warning)
3[3] (143) 252[4] 442[2] (743) (766) 1065[3] 1163[3]

Magic Box (ITY) *F & L Brogi* 102
4 ch h Namid—Bodiniyeh (IRE) (Persian Heights)
6767a[8]

Magic Carpet (IRE) *David Wachman* 100
3 b f Danehill(USA) —Paper Moon (IRE) (Lake Coniston (IRE))
4649a[2] 5998a[9]

Magic Clover (ARG) *P R Webber* 84
6 ch h Candy Stripes(USA) —Magnanimity (ARG) (Babas Fables (USA))
5594[8]

Magic Echo *M Dods* 82
3 b f Wizard King—Sunday News'N'Echo (USA) (Trempolino (USA))
1672[3] 1916[3] (2579) (2794) 3495[5] 4080[10] 5620[2] 6129[6]

Magic Glade *Peter Grayson* a94 95
8 b g Magic Ring(IRE) —Ash Glade (Nashwan (USA))
(79) 155[3] 277[5] (388) (554) 660[10] 1242[7] 1630[3] (1853) 1986[4] 2463[9] 3080[8] 3464[10] 4095[3] *6288[2] (6531) (6735) 6876[3] 7112[8]*

Magic Master (SAF) *S Seemar* a81
8 b g National Assembly(CAN) —Mystique (SAF) (Jungle Cove (USA))
324a[14]

Magic Moth *M Johnston* a79 76
4 b h Mtoto—Majoune (FR) (Take Risks (FR))
1208[4] *1438[3]* 1598[7] 2391[7]

Magic Mountain (IRE) *R Hannon* a69 82
3 b c Dr Fong(USA) —Hard Task (Formidable (USA))
1276[5] 1603[5] 2126[4] 2633[7] 3966[2] 4234[7] 4550[3] 4763[4] *5225[11] 5422[6] 6261[2]*

Magico Marco *B Grizzetti*
2 ch c Ekraar(USA) —Sopran Martha (IRE) (Thatching)
6523a[2]

Magic Rush *Mrs Norma Pook* a88 83
5 b g Almaty(IRE) —Magic Legs (Reprimand)
816 765[7] 865[2] 1121[8]

Magic Show *Jane Chapple-Hyam* a71 81
3 b c Marju(IRE) —White Rabbit (Zilzal (USA))
2402[13] 4018[6] *4275[10]* 4858[2] *(5120)* (5514)

Magic Sting *B S Rothwell* a35 88
6 ch g Magic Ring(IRE) —Ground Game (Gildoran)
2136[8] 2374[12] 2987[15] 3093[7] 3755[6] 3955[12] 4081[12] 5738[9]

Magic Warrior *J C Fox* a74 65
7 b g Magic Ring(IRE) —Clarista (USA) (Riva Ridge (USA))
48[11] 211[7] 538[5] 594[3] 773[2] 830[2] 1036[3] 1612[6] 2568[5] 3416[5] 3644[6] 4063[8] 5733[9] 6628[9] 6716[5] *6894[3] 7083[6] (7214) 7257[4]*

Magna Cum Laude (IRE) *A P O'Brien* a92 89
2 b c Danehill Dancer(IRE) —Miss Kinabalu (Shirley Heights)
5458a[8]

Magna Graduate (USA) *T Pletcher* a115
5 bb h Honor Grades(USA) —Peacock Alley (USA) (Fast Play (USA))
5059a[8]

Magnet For Money (USA) *A J Martin* 79
5 b g Sahm(USA) —Deer Ambi (USA) (Deerhound (USA))
6368a[10]

Magnifico (FR) *Mrs K Waldron* a33
6 b g Solid Illusion(USA) —Born For Run (FR) (Pharly (FR))
270[6]

Magnifico Rettore (IRE) *J Heloury*
2 b g Captain Rio—Chocolate Souffle (IRE) (Magic Ring (IRE))
6527a[8]

Magnol *J G M O'Shea* a47 52
2 gr f Tobougg(IRE) —Magnolia (Petong)
2086[7] *2344[6]* 2838[2] *6099[9] 6433[11]* 6591[6]

Magnum Opus (IRE) *D J Murphy* a33 73
5 b g Sadler's Wells(USA) —Summer Breeze (Rainbow Quest (USA))
3901[15] 4638[6] 4859[5] 5273[3] *5426[12]* 5557[7] 5704[8] 6304[14]

Magnus (AUS) *P Moody* 122
5 b h Flying Spur(AUS) —Scandinavia (AUS) (Snippets (AUS))
2733[3] 2857[14] 4746[9]

Magnushomestwo (IRE) *A Berry* a50 31
2 b g Val Royal(FR) —Classy Act (Lycius (USA))
2984[12] 3582[14] 4221[7] 5550[14] 6072[9] *6386[11]*

Magritte (ITY) *R Menichetti* 106
2 b f Modigliani(USA) —Star Of Siligo (USA) (Saratoga Six (USA))
(2684a) 3779a[2]

Magroom *R J Hodges* a67 64
3 b g Compton Place—Fudge (Polar Falcon (USA))
116[10] 919[7] 1062[11] 1317[7] (1739) (2273) 2965[2] 3178[4] 3949[3] 4270[5] 4313[8] *(5118) 5528[4]* 5860[2] (6199) *6695[2] 6997[9]*

Mahadee (IRE) *C E Brittain* 67
2 br g Cape Cross(IRE) —Rafiya (Halling (USA))
4192[10] 4487[10] 5502[2] 5883[7] 6410[13]

Mahara (USA) *J E Hammond* 100
3 ch f Diesis—Siyadah (USA) (Mr Prospector (USA))
3564a[2] 5058a[2] 6042a[11]

Mahler *A P O'Brien* 119
3 b c Galileo(IRE) —Rainbow Goddess (Rainbow Quest (USA))
2235[11] (2816) 4692[5] 5408[2] 6712a[3]

Mahmjra *C N Allen* a82 62
5 b g Josr Algarhoud(IRE) —Jamrat Samya (IRE) (Sadler's Wells (USA))
242[2] 369[8] 453[3] (503) 631[4] (811) 1181[3] 1378[3] 1819[11] 2047[8] *(2348)* 3243[5] 3496[6] 3671[8] 4030[8] 4458[11] *5205[9] 6007[8]* 6453[7]

Mahusay (IRE) *L M Cumani* 79
2 b c Noverre(USA) —Saada One (IRE) (Polish Precedent (USA))
(2086) 3025[5] 3398[4] 3909[7] 6471[13]

Maia *D Nicholls* 67
3 ch f Observatory(USA) —Preference (Efisio)
1161[3] 1620[12] (2032) 2910[7] (3413)

Maidanni (USA) *J R Gask* a64
5 bb g Private Terms(USA) —Carley's Birthday (USA) (Marfa (USA))
7099[8]

Maiden Investor *Stef Liddiard* a51 50
4 b m Orpen(USA) —Actress (Known Fact (USA))
1312[13] 1749[11] 2878[11] 3031[6] *7057[5] (7144) 7275[5]*

Maiden Miss (IRE) *M R Channon* a42 55
2 b f Xaar—Cheeky Weeky (Cadeaux Genereux)
4074[6] 4265[5] 4537[5] *5818[6]*

Maid In Bloom *B Smart* a44 59
2 b f Averti(IRE) —Fille De Fleurie (Whittingham (IRE))
1422[4] 4221[3] 4924[6] *7195[5]*

Maid Of Ale (IRE) *A King* 59
3 b f Barathea(IRE) —Borders Belle (IRE) (Pursuit Of Love)
3798[7] 4257[10] 4960[12]

Maid Ofiron (IRE) *M O Quigley* a59 68
3 b f Iron Mask(USA) —Balance The Books (Elmaamul (USA))
5841a[18] *6916a[13]*

Maid Of Lamancha *J R Weymes*
2 ch f Bahamian Bounty—Golden Fortune (Forzando)
5901[11]

Maid Of Lorn (USA) *Tracey Collins* 77
3 b f Catienus(USA) —Kutira (USA) (Dixieland Band (USA))
3576a[9]

Maid To Believe *J L Dunlop* 103
3 b f Galileo(IRE) —Maid For The Hills (Indian Ridge)
1289[13] (1722) 2971[4] 3590[3] (4185) (5006) 5767[4]

Maimoona (IRE) *W J Haggas* 77
2 ch f Pivotal—Shuruk (Cadeaux Genereux)
4810[2] 5770[2]

Mairead's Boy (IRE) *P Butler* a59 39
2 ch c Noverre(USA) —Welltold (IRE) (Danehill (USA))
1762[11] 2193[8] 4014[13] 4363[10] 4824[7] *5133[3] 6388[9] 6586[2] 6793[2] 6828[4] 7030[4] 7117[2]*

Maison Dieu *E J Alston* a66 68
4 bb g King Charlemagne(USA) —Shining Desert (IRE) (Green Desert (USA))
(896) *1226[3]* 2033[6] 2508[5] 3017[11] *3409[10]* 4141[12] *4250[2]* 4423[12] 4731[4] 5433[8] 5964[8] *6288[11] 6608[3]*

Majeen *W J Haggas* 76
2 ch c Rock Of Gibraltar(IRE) —Guilty Secret (IRE) (Kris)
5951[9] 6246[2] 6574[2]

Majehar *A G Newcombe* a69 53
5 b g Marju(IRE) —Joonayh (Warning)
243[2] (431) 650[5] 809[3] 2467[7] 2802[4] 3286[4] *(3946) (4739)* 5307[4] *(6260) 6780[3]*

Majestas (IRE) *Evan Williams* 64
3 b g Val Royal(FR) —Pantera Piceno (IRE) (College Chapel)
1672[9] 3795[12]

Majestical (IRE) *V Smith* a61 59
5 b g Fayruz—Haraabah (USA) (Topsider (USA))
158[10] 236[9] 337[5] 403[4] 442[5] 562[4] 622[7] 688[8] 722[11] (1902) 2509[10] 2966[5] (3045) *3618[4]* (3829) 4474[4] 4768[5] *5016[12] 6264[4]* 6415[7] *6587[2] 6779[2] 6825[3]* 6895[3]

Majestic Cheer *E A L Dunlop* a73 70
3 b g Royal Applause—Muwasim (USA) (Meadowlake (USA))
755[3] 1108[6] 1286[11] 1484[4] 2444[9] *5819[12] 6122[7]*

Majestic Chief *P D Niven* a61 66
3 b g Xaar—Grand Splendour (Shirley Heights)
1075[4] 1415[7] *1936[6] 3407[5]* 3907[2]

Majestic Concorde (IRE) *D K Weld* 93
4 b g Definite Article—Talina's Law (IRE) (Law Society (USA))
6366a[17]

Majestic Eviction (IRE) *M Halford* 86
3 b f King's Theatre(IRE) —Evictress (IRE) (Sharp Victor (USA))
1694a[6]

Majestic Marauder (USA) *Sir Michael Stoute* 75
2 bb c War Chant(USA) —Rose Bourbon (USA) (Woodman (USA))
3896[7]

Majestic Roi (USA) *M R Channon* 115
3 ch f Street Cry(IRE) —L'Extra Honor (USA) (Hero's Honor (USA))
(1146) 2290a[2] 2814[7] 4118[5] 5354[4] (6010)

Majestic Times (IRE) *Liam McAteer* a98 109
7 b g Bluebird(USA) —Simply Times (USA) (Dodge (USA))
2050a[10] 3140a[10] 3575a[4] 3768a[3] 4211a[4] *4864a[4]* 5616[7] 5842a[11] 6036a[7]

Majigal *M W Easterby* 49
2 b f High Estate—Face The Judge (USA) (Benny The Dip (USA))
1255[5] 1636[8] 2504[7] 3199[7]

Majik *P T Midgley* a65 67
8 ch g Pivotal—Revoke (USA) (Riverman (USA))
9[2] 143[2] 241[7]

Majofils (FR) *M Weiss* 72
4 ch h Majorien—Lias Creek (Lahib (USA))
4957a[10]

Majolica *N P Littmoden* a35 41
3 br f Lujain(USA) —Marjorie's Memory (IRE) (Fairy King (USA))
343[8]

Major Cadeaux *R Hannon* 117
3 ch c Cadeaux Genereux—Maine Lobster (USA) (Woodman (USA))
(1147) 1473[6] 3098[2] 4214a[5]

Major D'Helene (FR) *F-X de Chevigny* 92
2 ch c Majorien—Sparkbulle (FR) (Bulrush (FR))
6939a[6]

Major Eazy (IRE) *B J Meehan* 103
2 b c Fasliyev(USA) —Castilian Queen (USA) (Diesis)
1094[3] 1390[4] 2183[5] 2737[7] (3085) 3779a[7] 4046[8] (5922) 6182[12]

Major Grace (FR) *Y De Nicolay* a100 105
4 b h Majorien—Grace Royale (IRE) (Marignan (USA))
897a[7] 4520a[4] 4873a[7] *7128a[2]*

Major League (USA) *D Morris* a71 65
5 b g Magic Cat(USA) —Quick Grey (USA) (El Prado (IRE))
993[12] 1295[9] 2154[3] 2189[3] 2748[9] *3286[8]* 4319[5] 4731[11] 5303[10]

Major Magpie (IRE) *M Dods* 89
5 b g Rossini(USA) —Picnic Basket (Pharly (FR))
915[2] (1287)

Major Melody (IRE) *J J Lennon* a18 49
5 b g Fayruz—Chiming Melody (Cure The Blues (USA))
5696a[10] *7218[9]*

Major Willy *W Jarvis* 96
2 b c Xaar—Dame Blanche (IRE) (Be My Guest (USA))
1498[4] 3962[2] 4593[3] 5397a[3] 6171[6]

Majounes Song *M Johnston* 105
3 gr f Singspiel(IRE) —Majoune (FR) (Take Risks (FR))
1257[5] 1855a[3] 2599[3] 2786[6] 3744[7] (4651a) 6042a[10]

Majuro (IRE) *M R Channon* a101 100
3 b c Danetime(IRE) —First Fling (IRE) (Last Tycoon (IRE))
(922) 1035[6] 1516a[6] 2037[6] 2788[27] 4062[5] 4601[5] *4950[2]* 5355[3] 5765[5] *6003[9] 6437[5]*

Makaan (USA) *F Head* 108
3 b c Swain(IRE) —Khassah (Green Desert (USA))
1056a[5] 2100a[10] 4216a[5]

Makaaseb (USA) *M A Jarvis* 95
2 b f Pulpit(USA) —Turn And Sparkle (USA) (Danzatore (CAN))
(5596) 6336[7]

Makabul *B R Millman* a71 82
4 b g Makbul—Victoria Sioux (Ron's Victory (USA))
827[5] 1061[10] 1357[4] (1899) 2394[9] 2694[2] (3106) (3388) 4664[7] 5232[9] 5356[11] 5874[2] *6273[8]*

Makai *J J Bridger* a71 68
4 ch g Cayman Kai(IRE) —Young Sue (Local Suitor (USA))
459[7] 594[4] 631[12] 740[9] 799[4] 1249[12] 1609[10] 1741[3] 2141[11] 2275[2] *2572[13]* 2967[9] 3352[12] 3854[7]

Make A Bid *J R Norton*
2 b f Superior Premium—Make Ready (Beveled (USA))
6557[9] *6880[7]*

Make Acquaintance *M Mullineaux* 18
2 ch f Reel Buddy(USA) —Spindara (IRE) (Spinning World (USA))
5770[10] *6675[5]*

Make Haste (IRE) *R Charlton* 88
3 b g Sadler's Wells(USA) —Mosaique Bleue (Shirley Heights)
1129[5] 1812[7] (4003) (4843) 5911[3]

Make My Dream *J Gallagher* a69 70
4 b g My Best Valentine—Sandkatoon (IRE) (Archway (IRE))
86[12] 2576[10] 2878[2] 3612[2] 4165[3] 4397[2] 4808[4] 5130[5] 5867[2] 6279[4] (6594) 6794[6] 6829[7] 6946[8] 7119[4]

Make My Hay *J Gallagher* a2 6
8 b g Bluegrass Prince(IRE) —Shashi (IRE) (Shaadi (USA))
134[13]

Maker's Mark (IRE) *H Candy* 87
3 b g Invincible Spirit(IRE) —Certain Impression (USA) (Forli (ARG))
(4204) 4726[11] 5356[7] 5689[5] 6197[7] 6381[6]

Makfly *R Hollinshead* a52 80
4 b g Makbul—Flying Flip (Rolfe (USA))
1655[11] 1918[15] 2531[14] 3035[9]

Making Music *T D Easterby* 72
4 b m Makbul—Crofters Ceilidh (Scottish Reel)
1260[8] 1534[7] 2711[14] 3608[10] 4642[4] (4773) (4996) (5297) 5747[4]

Makshoof (IRE) *K A Ryan* 87
3 b g Kyllachy—Tres Sage (Reprimand)
(1658) 2884[9] 4726[6] 5584[19] 6753[6]

Maktavish *R Brotherton* a72 58
8 b g Makbul—La Belle Vie (Indian King (USA))
8[2] 79[7] 432[6] 465[8] 521[7] 905[8] 1065[9] 5349[11] 6720[16] 7137[9]

Malaath (IRE) *E A L Dunlop* a71 62
3 b f Green Desert(USA) —Mouwadh (USA) (Nureyev (USA))
1684[6] 4317[5] 4855[12]

Malakiya (IRE) *Jonjo O'Neill* a57 76
4 b g Sadler's Wells(USA) —State Crystal (IRE) (High Estate)
994[3]

Malande (IRE) *J S Bolger* 75
3 b f Beat Hollow—Masnada (IRE) (Erins Isle)
6368a[6]

Malapropism *M R Channon* a84 90
7 ch g Compton Place—Mrs Malaprop (Night Shift (USA))
1004[6] 1214[6] 1999[7] 2025[10] 2411[7] 2879[3] 2972[3] 3259[4] 3449[2] (3594) 4101[2] 4204[3] 4233[3] 4507[5] 4967[3] 5160[5] 5278[4] (5522) (5642) (5726) 5806[10] 6173[8] 6381[4] 6743[6]

Malcheek (IRE) *T D Easterby* a92 96
5 br g Lend A Hand—Russland (GER) (Surumu (GER))
1157[3] (1481) 1651[8] 2030[5] 2528[9] 2817[21] 3941[18] (4227) 4614[4] 5044[2] 5195[7] 6472[22]

Malech (IRE) *K G Reveley* 75
4 b g Bahhare(USA) —Choral Sundown (Night Shift (USA))
4772[9] 5307[7] 5487[8]

Malguru *G A Swinbank* 56
3 b g Ishiguru(USA) —Vento Del Oreno (FR) (Lando (GER))
968[9] 1111[11] 1412[6] 2096[11] 3159[8]

Malibu (IRE) *S Lycett* a66 44
6 b g Second Empire(IRE) —Tootle (Main Reef)
39[6] 3598[5] 3927[11]

Malibu Girl (USA) *E A L Dunlop* a78
2 b f Malibu Moon(USA) —Gale The Queen (USA) (Dr Blum (USA))
(6432)

Malibu Moonshine (USA) *G Contessa* a110
5 ch h Malibu Moon(USA) —Time To Coast (USA) (Coastal (USA))
5855a[7]

Malinsa Blue (IRE) *B Ellison* 84
5 b m Desert Style(IRE) —Talina's Law (IRE) (Law Society (USA))
915[8] 1199[4] (1413) (1578) 2008[5] 3052[6] 3502[8] 4526[7] 5159[3] (5559) 5885[13]

Malt Empress (IRE) *B W Duke* a21
2 b f Second Empire(IRE) —Sunset Malt (IRE) (Red Sunset)
7084[12]

Maltese Falcon *P F I Cole* a111 99
7 b g Mark Of Esteem(IRE) —Crime Ofthecentury (Pharly (FR))
5[8] 198[2] 344[2] 490[2] 762[4] (867) 1125[11] 2688[10] 6205[16] 6851[4] (6930) 7255[4]

Malt Or Mash (USA) *R Hannon* a85 107
3 gr c Black Minnaloushe(USA) —Southern Tradition (USA) (Family Doctor (USA))
2354[2] (2627) (3691) 4059[4] 4749[7] (6014) (6759)

Malyana *M A Jarvis* a77 84
3 b f Mtoto—Pass The Peace (Alzao (USA))
(1247) 1610[6] 2369[10] (4615) 5014[7] 6180[16]

Mama Leo *J G M O'Shea* a52 57
2 ch f Forzando—Milady Lillie (IRE) (Distinctly North (USA))
883[4] 972[4] 1285[8] 2152[4] 3364[2] 3626[2] 5017[7] 6586[7] 7136[6]

Mambazo *S C Williams* a84 46
5 b g Dansili—Kalindi (Efisio)
67[5] 91[6] 269[9] 480[7] 566[6] 1165[10] 1946[3] 2350[7] 2516[3] (2799) (3064) 3188[3] (3218) 3396[7] 3667[7] 4397[12] 4965[9] 6589[6] 6829[9] 7221[6]

Mambo King (DEN) *L Kelp* 92
5 b h Diktat—Gypsy Singer (USA) (Kingmambo (USA))
4218a[10]

Mambomoon *T D Easterby* 54
3 b c Zaha(CAN) —Moontime (FR) (Habitat)
1136[5] 1679[7] 2120[7] (2300) 3583[12] 4330[4]

Mamborock (FR) *J-L Pelletan* 90
3 b c Milford Track(IRE) —Lady Smythe (FR) (Moulin)
2503a[12]

Mambo Spirit (IRE) *J G Given* a92 89
3 b g Invincible Spirit(IRE) —Mambodorga (USA) (Kingmambo (USA))
(1270) 2044[11] 2659[4] 3418[2] 3637[2] 4123[16] 4950[4] 5356[6] 5765[6] 6141[8]

Mambo Sun *P A Blockley* a68 70
4 b g Superior Premium—The Manx Touch (IRE) (Petardia)
205[10] 371[8] 525[5] 732[4]

Mamichor *B R Johnson* a54 52
4 br g Mamalik(USA) —Ichor (Primo Dominie)
1254[12] 1742[3] 2143[7] (2412) 2990[11] 3616[6] 4294[6] 4469[7] 5310[5]

Mamlook (IRE) *Kevin Prendergast* 87
3 br g Key Of Luck(USA) —Cradle Brief (IRE) (Brief Truce (USA))
3143a[12]

Mamonta *M J Wallace* a61 61
4 b m Fantastic Light(USA) —Mamoura (IRE) (Lomond (USA))
23[2] 291[5]

Manaal (USA) *Sir Michael Stoute* a89 85
3 b f Bahri(USA) —Muwakleh (Machiavellian (USA))
(1110) 1414[4] 2883[7] 3350[5] (6435)

Manalito *M R Channon* 71
2 b c High Chaparral(IRE) —Brush Strokes (Cadeaux Genereux)
6294[5] 6592[6]

Man Appeal *B J Meehan* 18
2 ch f Mark Of Esteem(IRE) —Emma Peel (Emarati (USA))
5313[10]

Manassas (IRE) *B J Meehan* 99
2 b c Cape Cross(IRE) —Monnavanna (IRE) (Machiavellian (USA))
4604[3] (5575) 6041a[7]

Manathon (FR) *A E Jones* a67 75
4 b g Marathon(USA) —Fleurissante (FR) (Legend Of France (USA))
5178[9] 7173[4]

Manbar (USA) *Sir Michael Stoute* 82
3 bb c Dynaformer(USA) —Devil's Nell (USA) (Devil's Bag (USA))
1296[3] (1611) 3882[10]

Mancebo (GER) *R Curtis* 26
4 b g Acambaro(GER) —Marsixa (FR) (Linamix (FR))
3901[11]

Manchurian *M J Wallace* a94 91
3 b g Singspiel(IRE) —Royal Passion (Ahonoora)
2040[6] 3960[4] 4166[5] 4799[13] 5635[9] 6143[7]

Manda Honor (GER) *A Wohler* 77
4 gr m Highest Honor(FR) —Mandamou (GER) (Ela-Mana-Mou)
6220a[11]

Mandalay King (IRE) *Jane Chapple-Hyam* a49
2 b c King's Best(USA) —Mahamuni (IRE) (Sadler's Wells (USA))
2991[10] 6242[12]

Mandalay Prince *W J Musson* a56 61
3 b g Tobougg(IRE) —Autumn Affair (Lugana Beach)
635[4] 973[11] 1166[10] 2668[9] 2796[5] (3150) 3400[5] 4277[9] 6506[8] 6837[8] 7060[4]

Mandali (FR) *A De Royer-Dupre* 96
3 ch c Sinndar(IRE) —Mandalara (IRE) (Lahib (USA))
1593a[7]

Mandarinka *P Winkworth* a56 56
2 ch g Kyllachy—Lihou Island (Beveled (USA))
3363[7] 4016[9] 4593[6] 5089[15] 5529[5] 5751[13] 6227[7] 6426[11]

Mandarin Rocket (IRE) *Miss L A Perratt* 58
4 ch g Titus Livius(FR) —Two Thousand (IRE) (Polish Patriot (USA))
1595[9] 2168[2] 2388[6] 2820[8] 2865[6] 3182[2] 3497[2] 3675[9] 4159[5] 4383[9] 4802[5] 4997[2] 5286[7] 5674[7] (5964)

Mandarin Spirit (IRE) *G C H Chung* a87 79
7 b g Primo Dominie—Lithe Spirit (IRE) (Dancing Dissident (USA))
190[3] 218[3] 384[5] (509) 657[5] 697[7] 1023[5] 1223[10] 4965[4] 5064[4] 5381[6] 6006[9] 6391[6] 6707[4] 6795[9] 6949[12]

Mandela (NZ) *R Yuill* 112
6 br g Ebony Grosve(NZ) —Wairongoa Belle (NZ) (Sea Anchor)
6354a[11]

Mandelieu (IRE) *W J Haggas* a59 73
2 b g Acclamation—Notley Park (Wolfhound (USA))
3363[14] 3823[2] 5575[6] 6073[4] 6692[4] 7000[5]

Mandesha (FR) *A De Royer-Dupre* 121
4 b m Desert Style(IRE) —Mandalara (IRE) (Lahib (USA))
(2165a) 2925a[2] 4149[2] 5467a[2] 6043a[7]

Mandobi (IRE) *D Selvaratnam* a56 104
6 ch h Mark Of Esteem(IRE) —Miss Queen (USA) (Miswaki (USA))
172a[5]

Mandragola *B W Hills* a88 85
3 b g Machiavellian(USA) —Viz (USA) (Kris S (USA))
(884) 1277[7] 1584[4] 5725[7] 6061[3] 6357[2]

Mandriano (ITY) *D W Barker* a48 31
3 b g Averti(IRE) —My Penny (USA) (Gulch (USA))
1031[9] 1135[5] 1236[10] 1489[5] 4226[12] 4384[5] 4714[8]

Mandurah (IRE) *D Nicholls* a58 74
3 b g Tagula(IRE) —Fearfully Grand (Grand Lodge (USA))
679[3] (894) 918[2] 970[7] (1286) 1820[3] 1994[3] 2435[4] (4001) 4896[2] 5662[10]

Manduro (GER) *A Fabre* 133
5 br h Monsun(GER) —Mandellicht (IRE) (Be My Guest (USA))
(1104) (1879a) (2754) (4445a) (5467a)

Mandy's Maestro (USA) *R M Whitaker* 66
3 br g Brahms(USA) —Belle Masque (USA) (Devil's Bag (USA))
1286[9] 1595[11] 2534[9] 2910[5] 3302[11] 3752[8] 4226[5] 4478[10] 4842[10]

Maneki Neko (IRE) *E W Tuer* a75 79
5 b g Rudimentary(USA) —Ardbess (Balla Cove)
1158[5] 1490[9] 1794[5] 1890[2] 2342[7] 5486[6] 5807[7]

Mangano *A Berry* a41 55
3 b g Mujadil(USA) —Secret Dance (Sadler's Wells (USA))
136[9] 429[2] 505[4] 918[10] 970[8] 1595[2] 1943[7] 2029[4] 2205[3] 2301[6] 2844[8] 2910[2] 3342[2] 3583[8] 3752[3] 3999[5] 4224[2] 4330[5] (4480) 4714[5] 4971[4] 5299[11] 5936[6]

Mangham (IRE) *B Smart* 69
2 b c Montjeu(IRE) —Lovisa (USA) (Gone West (USA))
3761[2] 5735[5] 5965[3]

Mango Masher (IRE) *J L Flint* a65 60
3 ch g Danehill Dancer(IRE) —Shariyfa (FR) (Zayyani)
1037[8] 1282[4] 1452[4] 1936[4] 2635[7] 2945[7] 3825[5] 4246[2] 4879[12] 5188[11] 5347[13] 6798[4] 6883[6] 7012[4]

Mango Mischief (IRE) *M R Channon* 106
6 ch m Desert King(IRE) —Eurolink Mischief (Be My Chief (USA))
1650[5] 2036[5] 2720[4] (3028) 3628[7] 3974[5] 4652a[8] 5396a[8] 5998a[8]

Mango Music *M R Channon* a70 91
4 ch m Distant Music(USA) —Eurolink Sundance (Night Shift (USA))
1372[8] 1861[5] 3489[7] 5356[14] 5560[2] 5722[3] 5954[4] 6205[12] 6735[3] 6826[7]

Mango Piccle *L Wells*
3 ch g Piccolo—Starliner (IRE) (Statoblest)
6402[11]

Mangrove Cay (IRE) *A J Lockwood* a56 51
5 b g Danetime(IRE) —Art Duo (Artaius (USA))
98[2] 431[7] 1027[12] 1222[5] 1556[8] 1934[2] 4249[5] 4521[10]

Manhattan Boy (GER) *P J Hobbs* 60
5 ch g Monsun(GER) —Manhattan Girl (USA) (Vice Regent (CAN))
6132[11]

Manhattan Dream (USA) *B W Hills* 70
2 b f Statue Of Liberty(USA) —Vallee Des Reves (USA) (Kingmambo (USA))
3895[10] 4774[8] 5595[3]

Manipulate *L M Cumani* a67 80
4 b h Machiavellian(USA) —Balalaika (Sadler's Wells (USA))
1288[16] 1905[9]

Manipura (GER) *A Wohler* 89
2 b f Dansili—Macara (GER) (Acatenango (GER))
(4837a) 6047a[5]

Mannello *Jim Best* a61 61
4 b m Mamalik(USA) —Isle Of Sodor (Cyrano De Bergerac)
896[14] 1404[7] 2108[9] 2540[2] 2619[2] 3247[6] 3422[10] 3647[9] 4336[15] 5716[8] 6429[5] 6826[2] 6957[4] 7014[5] 7077[5] 7188[10]

Man Of Aran *M Halford* a70 81
7 b g Green Desert(USA) —Tahdid (Mtoto)
4865a[7]

Man Of Gwent (UAE) *G A Huffer*
3 b g In The Wings—Welsh Valley (USA) (Irish River (FR))
2005[13]

Man Of Vision (USA) *M R Channon* a84 100
3 b c Kingmambo(USA) —Nalani (IRE) (Sadler's Wells (USA))
193[2] 484[2] (638) (1293) 2790[10] 3460[2] 4059[3]

Man On The Nile (IRE) *W P Mullins* 85
7 b g Snurge—Spirit Of The Nile (FR) (Generous (IRE))
6366a[4]

Manor Park (IRE) *C G Cox* 73
2 b c Hernando(FR) —Campiglia (IRE) (Fairy King (USA))
5011[11] 5813[7]

Mansii *C E Brittain* a67 78
2 b c Dr Fong(USA) —Enclave (USA) (Woodman (USA))
1123[5] 1498[3] 2353[8] 4201[4] 4923[2] 5277[4] 5496[6] 5910[2]

Manuka Bee *J Howard Johnson* 67
2 b g Xaar—Legend (Belmez (USA))
3510[3] 5580[12] 6255[4]

Many Colours *J S Bolger* 105
3 b f Green Desert(USA) —First Of Many (Darshaan)
5998a[2]

Manyriverstocross (IRE) *A King* 55
2 b c Cape Cross(IRE) —Alexandra S (IRE) (Sadler's Wells (USA))
5919[5]

Many Volumes (USA) *H R A Cecil* 111
3 b c Chester House(USA) —Reams Of Verse (USA) (Nureyev (USA))
(1296) 1662[4] 2042[5] 3460[7] 4092[5] (4366) 5351[2] 5748[2]

Manzila (FR) *F Head* 98
4 ch m Cadeaux Genereux—Mannsara (IRE) (Royal Academy (USA))
1704a[6] 2291a[6] 2733[16] 3445a[14] 6071a[13]

Maraagel (USA) *S C Williams* a50 22
4 b h Danzig(USA) —Hasnaael Reef (USA) (Seattle Slew (USA))
5499[8] 6773[9] 7148[5] 7239[3]

Maraahel (IRE) *Sir Michael Stoute* a99 125
6 b h Alzao(USA) —Nasanice (IRE) (Nashwan (USA))
(1144) (1600) 2210[3] (2856) 3942[3] 5243a[5] 6334[10]

Maraca (IRE) *J H M Gosden* a76 18
3 b c Danehill Dancer(IRE) —Marasem (Cadeaux Genereux)
1230[6]

Maracana Boy (IRE) *M Dods* 68
2 ch g Captain Rio—Mary's Way (GR) (Night Shift (USA))
952[6] 1585[4] 2934[3] 3680[6] 4098[11] 5365[13]

Marajaa (IRE) *W J Musson* a97 93
5 b g Green Desert(USA) —Ghyraan (IRE) (Cadeaux Genereux)
197[4] 550[6] 658[4] 840[5] 1145[5] 1524[7] 2401[8] 3437[3] 4049[11] 4548[5] 4949[5] 5221[7]

Marakai *C Grant* 8
2 b g Cayman Kai(IRE) —Emmajoun (Emarati (USA))
4286[9]

Maramba (USA) *Sir Michael Stoute* a67 94
2 ch f Hussonet(USA) —Coco (USA) (Storm Bird (CAN))
3417[4] (5483) 6498[3]

Mara Spectrum (IRE) *B Grizzetti* 103
4 b m Spectrum(IRE) —Mara Dancer (Shareef Dancer (USA))
2296a[4] 6524a[8]

Marbaa (IRE) *S Dow* a70 76
4 b g Peintre Celebre(USA) —Bahareeya (USA) (Riverman (USA))
24[5] 499[3] 594[7] 685[10] 2004[7] 2214[8] 2875[9] 3428[12] 3730[5] 3868[6] 4473[3] 4595[7]

Marbeuf (USA) *Noel Meade* 60
6 b g Bahri(USA) —Salon Prive (USA) (Private Account (USA))
2067a[16]

Marchand D'Or (FR) *F Head* a95 121
4 gr g Marchand De Sable(USA) —Fedora (FR) (Kendor (FR))
860a[8] 1389a[8] (2953a) 3506[4] (4214a) 5214[2] 6029a[3] 7089a[6]

Marching Sandy (IRE) *Edward Lynam* 73
2 b g Peintre Celebre(USA) —Tiavanita (USA) (J O Tobin (USA))
6443a[8]

March Mate *B Ellison* 56
3 b g Warningford—Daira (Daring March)
968[5] 3639[6] 4138[3] 5045[5]

Marchpane *R M Beckett* 70
2 b f Olden Times—Ecstasy (Pursuit Of Love)
3866[11] (4761) 5592[6] 6012[12]

Marcus Andronicus (USA) *A P O'Brien* 116
4 b h Danehill(USA) —Fiji (Rainbow Quest (USA))
1049a[3] 1834[8]

Mardi *W J Haggas* a73 72
3 b g Montjeu(IRE) —Portorosa (USA) (Irish River (FR))
2635[9] 2945[5] 4277[12] 4960[3] 5640[8] 6250[7]

Mardood *W J Haggas* 71
2 b g Oasis Dream—Gaelic Swan (IRE) (Nashwan (USA))
6248[9] 6571[3]

Marend (FR) *D Sepulchre* 112
6 ch g Green Tune(USA) —Marende (FR) (Panoramic)
2330a[6] 3565a[5]

Marfeng *W M Brisbourne* a30 42
2 ch f Mark Of Esteem(IRE) —Chilly Waters (Polar Falcon (USA))
5766[14] 6289[8] 6649[19]

Maria Antonia (IRE) *P A Blockley* a66 60
4 ch m King's Best(USA) —Annieirwin (IRE) (Perugino (USA))
(12) 148[2] 369[9] 903[4] 1026[10] 1178[7] 4297[7] 5132[6] 6069[8] 6250[2] 6453[3] 6832[6] 7050[5] 7135[7]

Maria Gabriella (IRE) *C Laffon-Parias* 103
3 ch f Rock Of Gibraltar(IRE) —Celestial Lagoon (JPN) (Sunday Silence (USA))
3148a[2]

Marias Buddy *Eamon Tyrrell* a55 66
2 b f Reel Buddy(USA) —Mitsuki (Puissance)
1586[2]

Mariaverdi *P G Murphy* a51 34
3 b f Diktat—Belinda (Mizoram (USA))
4513[5] 4918[5] 5894[8] 6896[3] 7168[5]

Ma Ridge *T D McCarthy* a52 52
3 ch c Tumbleweed Ridge—Ma Barnicle (IRE) (Al Hareb (USA))
1928[8] 2593[4] 4321[U] 7167[13]

Marie Camargo *R A Fahey* 55
2 b f Kyllachy—Wheeler's Wonder (IRE) (Sure Blade (USA))
2364[7] 2888[5] 3582[8] 4278[7] 6572[13]

Marie Claude *J Noseda* a22
2 b f Where Or When(IRE) —Lalique (IRE) (Lahib (USA))
7216[9]

Marie Rossa *P Demercastel* 107
3 b f Testa Rossa(AUS) —Marie De Ken (FR) (Kendor (FR))
2501a[7]

Marieschi (USA) *H R A Cecil* 68
3 b g Maria's Mon(USA) —Pennygown (Rainbow Quest (USA))
1665[4] 2127[10] 4018[4]

Marie Tempest *B W Hills* 54
2 b f Act One—Hakkaniyah (Machiavellian (USA))
6648[16]

Marikhar (IRE) *Seamus Fahey* a74 90
5 b g Alzao(USA) —Marilaya (IRE) (Shernazar)
3143a[8]

Marino Lil (IRE) *J S Bolger* a68 73
3 b f Lil's Boy(USA) —Marino Waltz (Thatching)
4865a[6]

Marino Prince (FR) *T Wall* a70
2 b c Dr Fong(USA) —Hula Queen (USA) (Irish River (FR))
5780[6] 6119[10] 6503[8] (6693) (6814) (6933) 7204[3]

Mariol (FR) *Robert Collet* 103
4 b g Munir—La Bastoche (IRE) (Kaldoun (FR))
6071a[2] 6633a[3] 6954a[3]

Mariotto (USA) *Saeed Bin Suroor* 108
3 b c Swain(IRE) —Shamaat Hayaaty (IRE) (Sadler's Wells (USA))
(3272) 4059[14] 6169[P]

Marist Madame *T J Pitt* a48 43
3 ch f Tomba—Linda's Schoolgirl (IRE) (Grand Lodge (USA))
1164[3] 1281[2] 1739[4] 2560[4] 2591[10] 3286[11] 7250[9]

Marju's Gold *E J O'Neill* a52 61
3 b c Marju(IRE) —Dubious (Darshaan)
193[7] 304[9] 1224[3] 1536[3] 1972[14] 2248[3] 2653[7]

Markab *K A Morgan* a83 95
4 b h Green Desert(USA) —Hawafiz (Nashwan (USA))
5031[P] 7254[7]

Marker *J D Frost* a47 74
7 ch g Pivotal—Palace Street (USA) (Secreto (USA))
2217[8] 3487[7] 4505[8] 5425[9]

Markestino *T D Easterby* a50 55
4 b g Mark Of Esteem(IRE) —Mademoiselle Chloe (Night Shift (USA))
2576[3] 2864[10] 3839[8]

Market Forces *H R A Cecil* a98 105
3 b f Lomitas—Quota (Rainbow Quest (USA))
(1573) 2112[4] 3058[2] (3963) (6186) 6284[2] *6605*[2]

Market Watcher (USA) *Seamus Fahey* a80 58
6 b g Boundary(USA) —Trading (USA) (A.P. Indy (USA))
153[3] *6875*[9] *6883*[10]

Markmanship (FR) *C Gourdain* 41
2 b c Mark Of Esteem(IRE) —Miss Dish (IRE) (Marju (IRE))
6377a[6]

Mark Of Love (IRE) *M R Channon* a76 73
3 ch g Mark Of Esteem(IRE) —Dazilyn Lady (USA) (Zilzal (USA))
208[14] *293*[7] *661*[8] *738*[8] *924*[2] 1155[2] *(1399)* 1531[3] 1672[8] 2079[10] 2916[4] (3235) 3384[7] 3570[2] 3964[7] 4502[6] 5046[3] 5156[4]

Mark Of The Fen *Rae Guest* a55 54
3 b g Mark Of Esteem(IRE) —Krisalya (Kris)
5390[10] 5728[6] 6070[5] 6458[9] 6570[2]

Marko Jadeo (IRE) *R A Harris* a86 80
9 b g Eagle Eyed(USA) —Fleeting Quest (Rainbow Quest (USA))
44[6] *(183)* *227*[6] *359*[5] *480*[4] *614*[8] *771*[3] 1063[11] 1200[2] 1465[3] 1607[7] 2139[6] 2623[3] *3623*[6] *4024*[7] 4236[4] 4351[3] 5064[12]

Marlena (IRE) *T D Easterby* 54
2 bb f Marju(IRE) —Red Rosie (USA) (Red Ransom (USA))
3718[6] 4125[13] 4422[5] 5251[7]

Marlyn Ridge *D K Ivory* a58 64
3 b g Tumbleweed Ridge—Kayartis (Kaytu)
1399[4] 2727[4] *3624*[13]

Marmite (IRE) *E F Vaughan* a58 51
2 bb f Vettori(IRE) —Marliana (IRE) (Mtoto)
1533[11] *2344*[5] 3043[7] (3614) *(3923)* *5127*[7] *6150*[4] *6427*[5]

Marmooq *M J Attwater* a70 80
4 ch g Cadeaux Genereux—Portelet (Night Shift (USA))
366[8] *516*[6] *605*[13] *681*[10] *(734)* 980[7] *1118*[5] *1344*[2] 1739[3] 1921[6] 2336[6] 4395[18] *5391*[4] *5890*[3] *6179*[4] 6415[8] *6607*[10] *6706*[8] *6873*[9]

Marning Star *M R Channon* 73
2 b c Diktat—Mustique Dream (Don't Forget Me)
2510[10] 2739[2] 3238[7] 4121[15] 4892[3] 5109[5]

Maromito (IRE) *R Bastiman* a53 56
10 b g Up And At 'Em—Amtico (Bairn (USA))
(1707) *2174*[2] 2830[8] 3837[10] 4101[3] 4773[9] 5836[5] 6078[12] 6270[12] *6864*[3]

Maroussies Rock *P C Haslam* 37
3 b f Rock Of Gibraltar(IRE) —Maroussie (FR) (Saumarez)
1045[14]

Maroussies Wings (IRE) *P C Haslam* 108
4 b m In The Wings—Maroussie (FR) (Saumarez)
1789[4] 2036[4]

Marozi (USA) *M A Jarvis* a72 92
3 ch c Forest Wildcat(USA) —Chitka (USA) (Jade Hunter (USA))
(3395) 3797[4] (4123) 5050[9]

Marquee (IRE) *P A Blockley* a65 60
3 b c Mark Of Esteem(IRE) —Queen's Ransom (IRE) (Last Tycoon (IRE))
1358[11] 1894[3] 3035[3] 3183[3] *4429*[4]

Marraasi (USA) *M P Tregoning* a67 31
2 ch f Rahy(USA) —Bashayer (USA) (Mr Prospector (USA))
6087[13] *6432*[6] *6849*[2]

Marramed *E J O'Neill* 24
2 ch f Medicean—Marrakech (IRE) (Barathea (IRE))
4422[11]

Marriaj (USA) *B Smart* a76 77
3 bb c Giant's Causeway(USA) —Be My Sweetheart (USA) (No Robbery)
1075[6] 2862[8] *3622*[3]

Marron Flore *A J Lidderdale* a42
4 ch m Compton Place—Flore Fair (Polar Falcon (USA))
51[6] *2731*[1] *3211*[1]

Marryl *M W Easterby*
3 b g Warningford—Nordico Princess (Nordico (USA))
3714[10] 4488[13]

Marsam (IRE) *M G Quinlan* a78 95
4 gr g Daylami(IRE) —Dancing Prize (IRE) (Sadler's Wells (USA))
5717[5] 6186[8] *6669*[13] *7123*[2]

Marshman (IRE) *M H Tompkins* a93 96
8 ch g College Chapel—Gold Fly (IRE) (Be My Guest (USA))
1747[10] 1984[7] 3828[12] 5701[9]

Marsh Side (USA) *M Dickinson* 107
4 b h Gone West(USA) —Colonial Play (USA) (Pleasant Colony (USA))
5250a[7] 6374a[12]

Martinet (IRE) *P D Evans* 61
3 b g Jade Robbery(USA) —Insistent (USA) (Diesis)
1605[7] 2081[5] 2726[13] 3175[6]

Martingrange Boy (IRE) *D J Murphy* a69
2 b g Danetime(IRE) —Coloma (JPN) (Forty Niner (USA))
6926[7] *7139*[2] *(7220)* *7240*[2]

Martyr *R Hannon* a79 61
2 b c Cape Cross(IRE) —Sudeley (Dancing Brave (USA))
6130[11] 6468[10] *6855*[2] *(7204)*

Marvin Gardens *John Berry* a33 47
4 b g Largesse—En Grisaille (Mystiko (USA))
4294[3] 4972[13]

Marwah *E A L Dunlop* 73
2 f King's Best(USA) —Mubkera (IRE) (Nashwan (USA))
3706[3] 4564[4]

Mary D'Or (FR) *N Clement* a92 100
3 gr f Verglas(IRE) —Miss Bio (FR) (River Mist (USA))
6940a[2]

Maryfield (CAN) *Doug O'Neill* a113 100
6 b m Elusive Quality(USA) —Sly Maid (USA) (Desert Wine (USA))
(6483a)

Mary From Maryhill (IRE) *Miss L A Perratt* 33
3 b f Fath(USA) —Kentucky Wildcat (Be My Guest (USA))
1625[11] 2032[7] 3051[8]

Mary Louhana *Leigh Delacour* 106
4 b m Loup Solitaire(USA) —Miss Daisy (FR) (Shirley Heights)
1571a[4] 4215a[7] 6790a[7]

Mary Montagu (IRE) *J W Hills* a68 60
2 b f Danehill Dancer(IRE) —Epistoliere (IRE) (Alzao (USA))
5766[10] *6432*[5]

Maryolini *N J Vaughan* a73 68
2 b f Bertolini(USA) —Mary Jane (Tina's Pet)
2526[6] *(3596)* 4255[2] *4669*[5] *6892*[3] *(7260)*

Maryqueenofscots (IRE) *M L W Bell* 67
2 b f Fantastic Light(USA) —Marie De Blois (IRE) (Barathea (IRE))
(5328)

Marzelline (IRE) *W R Swinburn* a94 105
3 ch f Barathea(IRE) —Juno Marlowe (IRE) (Danehill (USA))
1203[6] (2360) 2786[5] 3628[6] 4203[4] *4887*[2] 5544[12] 6249[3]

Marzipan (GER) *P Schiergen* 74
3 ch c Acatenango(GER) —Murnau (IRE) (Rudimentary (USA))
1387a[8]

Masaalek *M P Tregoning* 82
2 b c Green Desert(USA) —Hammiya (IRE) (Darshaan)
1832[2]

Masada (IRE) *B J Meehan* 88
2 br f Key Of Luck(USA) —Desert Bloom (IRE) (Pilsudski (IRE))
(6419) 6619[7]

Masai Moon *B R Millman* 92
3 b g Lujain(USA) —Easy To Imagine (USA) (Cozzene (USA))
1081[4] 1660[3] (1920) 2400[2] 4811[12] 5635[8] (5923) 6301[4] 6472[8]

Masamiyr (IRE) *M Halford* 81
6 b g Dr Devious(IRE) —Masafiya (IRE) (Shernazar)
6368a[16]

Mascarpone (GER) *M Weiss* 83
3 b c Monsun(GER) —Mamourina (IRE) (Barathea (IRE))
2503a[6]

Mashaahed *B W Hills* 115
4 b h In The Wings—Patacake Patacake (USA) (Bahri (USA))
1274[2] 2182[3] 3461[8] 3974[7] 6298[2] (6653)

Mashrai (IRE) *M R Channon* 64
2 b c Dubai Destination(USA) —Largo (IRE) (Selkirk (USA))
5206[6] 6051[8]

Masiyma (IRE) *John M Oxx* 78
2 ch f Dalakhani(IRE) —Masilia (IRE) (Kahyasi)
6443a[2]

Masked (IRE) *R M Beckett* a81
6 b g Soviet Star(USA) —Moon Masquerade (IRE) (Darshaan)
7194[3]

Maslak (IRE) *P W Hiatt* a83 80
3 b g In The Wings—Jeed (IRE) (Mujtahid (USA))
735[2] 1077[3] 1804[3] *2354*[11] 4707[2] *5101*[3] *5500*[6] *5604*[2] *6124*[2] 6475[4] *6739*[3] *6875*[8] *(7151)* *7242*[3]

Mason Ette *C G Cox* a64 82
3 br f Grand Lodge(USA) —Karlaska (Lashkari)
1228[10] (1786) 2044[9] 2629[3] 5722[14] 5923[14]

Masra *G A Swinbank* 51
4 b g Silver Patriarch(IRE) —Go Sally Go (IRE) (Elbio)
6257[6]

Masriyna's Heiress (IRE) *Daniel J P Barry* 57
6 b m Princely Heir(IRE) —Masriyna (IRE) (Shahrastani (USA))
5696a[5]

Massams Lane *G C Bravery* a58 55
3 b g Lahib(USA) —Night Trader (USA) (Melyno)
1117[12] 1267[4] 1501[6] *6457*[4] *6704*[5]

Masseuse (USA) *James J Toner* 106
5 bb m Dynaformer(USA) —Pedicure (USA) (Mr Prospector (USA))
5822a[9]

Massey *C R Dore* a49 13
11 br g Machiavellian(USA) —Massaraat (USA) (Nureyev (USA))
239[8] *321*[9]

Massif Centrale *D R C Elsworth* a31 97
6 ch g Selkirk(USA) —Madame Dubois (Legend Of France (USA))
159[8]

Massive (IRE) *M R Channon* 103
3 b c Marju(IRE) —Khatela (IRE) (Shernazar)
1097[6] (2124) 3103[8] 3940[17]

Masta Plasta (IRE) *D Nicholls* 101
4 b g Mujadil(USA) —Silver Arrow (USA) (Shadeed (USA))
1242[8] 1788[15] 2022[4] 3708[3] 4190a[4] 4485[3] 5512[2] 5616[9] 6071a[12] 6363a[16]

Master At Arms *Daniel Mark Loughnane* a68 62
4 ch g Grand Lodge(USA) —L'Ideale (USA) (Alysheba (USA))
6102[3] *6583*[3] *(6883)*

Master Ben (IRE) *S R Bowring* a41 25
4 b g Carrowkeel(IRE) —Java Jive (Hotfoot)
666[8] *715*[8] *802*[2] *1261*[6] *6569*[10]

Master Chef (IRE) *J H M Gosden* a83 94
2 b c Oasis Dream—Miss Honorine (IRE) (Highest Honor (FR))
1540[5] 1846[3] *2353*[3] (3478) 4120[6] 4812[5] *5219*[11] 5597[6] 6059[3] 6488[6]

Master Halling *R Charlton* 77
3 ch g Halling(USA) —Red Empress (Nashwan (USA))
1358[3] 1998[7] 2320[9] 6061[7]

Master Jobs *S C Williams* a53
3 b g Singspiel(IRE) —Pure Misk (Rainbow Quest (USA))
703[5] *1522*[14] *1950*[12]

Master Malarkey *Mrs C A Dunnett* a52 58
4 b g Tipsy Creek(USA) —Girl Next Door (Local Suitor (USA))
978[6] 3163[9] 3829[6] 4164[9] 4689[2] 4857[2] *5425*[3] *5897*[7] *6528*[9]

Master'n Commander *C A Cyzer* a66 56
5 ch g Zafonic(USA) —Magical Retreat (USA) (Sir Ivor (USA))
265[6] *458*[2] *602*[3] *651*[9] *3217*[3]

Master Nimbus *J J Quinn* a53 52
7 b g Cloudings(IRE) —Miss Charlie (Pharly (FR))
2764[4] 4230[3] *5389*[2]

Master Of Arts (USA) *Sir Mark Prescott* a50 34
2 bb g Swain(IRE) —Grazia (Sharpo)
4733[10] *4962*[8] *5126*[11]

Masterofthecourt (USA) *H Morrison* a87 82
4 ch g Horse Chestnut(SAF) —Great Verdict (AUS) (Christmas Tree (AUS))
3641[2] 3989[11] 4631[6] *5685*[13] 6278[3] 6651[6] *6848*[6] *7141*[U] *7241*[2]

Master Of The Race *Tom Dascombe* a79 86
5 ch g Selkirk(USA) —Dust Dancer (Suave Dancer (USA))
1962[7] 2403[11]

Master O'Reilly (NZ) *Danny O'Brien* 117
5 br g O'Reilly(NZ) —Without Remorse (NZ) (Bakharoff (USA))
(6354a) 6712a[8]

Master Pegasus *C F Wall* a91 90
4 b g Lujain(USA) —Seeking Utopia (Wolfhound (USA))
1013[4] 1962[6] 2401[2] *2771*[5] 3900[9] 4827[10] *5099*[3] 6110[6] *(6674)* *7061*[3] *7281*[5]

Mastership (IRE) *C E Brittain* a101 99
3 ch g Best Of The Bests(IRE) —Shady Point (IRE) (Unfuwain (USA))
27[2] *(385)* *760*[4] 1147[4] 1703a[14] 2212[4] 3431[7] 4150[24] 4607[8] *6003*[7] *6437*[11]

Master Spy *J H M Gosden* a62
2 br c Cape Cross(IRE) —Secret Seeker (USA) (Mr Prospector (USA))
6850[6]

Master Wells (IRE) *J D Frost* 68
6 b g Sadler's Wells(USA) —Eljazzi (Artaius (USA))
(3485)

Mataram (USA) *W Jarvis* a90 72
4 b g Matty G(USA) —Kalinka (USA) (Mr Prospector (USA))
(96) *353*[3] *652*[7] *777*[2] 4068[3] 4797[7] *5221*[14] *6949*[6] *7165*[4]

Matarazzo (IRE) *G L Moore* a50 65
5 gr g Linamix(FR) —Altamira (FR) (Highest Honor (FR))
5095[6] *5531*[14] 6276[8]

Material Witness (IRE) *W R Muir* a80 93
10 b g Barathea(IRE) —Dial Dream (Gay Mecene (USA))
1984[12] 2427[6] 2626[3] *3191*[9] 3239[2] 3682[9] 4134[8] 4807[6] 5303[5]

Mathool (IRE) *C W Thornton* 27
2 b f Alhaarth(IRE) —Mathaayl (USA) (Shadeed (USA))
6306[15] 6461[7]

Matinee Idol *Mrs S Lamyman* 63
4 ch m In The Wings—Bibliotheque (USA) (Woodman (USA))
1554[10] 3193[8] 4563[3] 5561[5] 6383[7] 6558[11] 6700[4]

Matloob *D Selvaratnam* a79 92
6 b h Halling(USA) —Belle Argentine (FR) (Fijar Tango (FR))
178a[9] 331a[15] 395a[6]

Matrix (GER) *Frau Y Vollmer* 110
6 b h Big Shuffle(USA) —Massena (GER) (Konigsstuhl (GER))
1704a[10] 3122a[2] 3445a[8] 4869a[11] 6633a[0]

Matsunosuke *A B Coogan* a104 104
5 b g Magic Ring(IRE) —Lon Isa (Grey Desire)
1464[5] 2025[7] 2244[8] 2733[18] 3464[14] 3921[6] 4103[7] 4233[8] (4507) 4585[9] 5009[2] 5278[3] (5381) 5642[2] 5689[3] *(5891)* *(6141)* 6327[6] 6487[4]

Matterofact (IRE) *M S Saunders* a58 73
4 b m Bold Fact(USA) —Willow Dale (IRE) (Danehill (USA))
1309[7] 1766[2] (1991) 2315[3] (2459) 2655[6] 3086[5] *5643*[11] 5726[12] 5942[8] *6244*[6] *6752*[4] *7005*[10]

Matty Tun *J Balding* a61 77
8 b g Lugana Beach—B Grade (Lucky Wednesday)
1854[16] 2673[3] 3014[8] 3197[5] 3515[9]

Matuza (IRE) *W R Muir* a92 86
4 ch h Cadeaux Genereux—Aoife (IRE) (Thatching)
1013[5] *1179*[3] 1653[19] (2197) 2318[10] *3108*[2] *3623*[7] 4133[4] 4827[9]

Maud's Cat (IRE) *A P Jarvis* a59 59
4 b m Black Minnaloushe(USA) —Tree House (USA) (Woodman (USA))
2423[8]

Maunby Roller (IRE) *K A Morgan*
8 b g Flying Spur(AUS) —Brown Foam (Horage)
1376[12]

Mauralakana (FR) *P L Biancone* a89 112
4 b m Muhtathir—Jimkana (FR) (Double Bed (FR))
5825a[6]

Mawaared *M P Tregoning* a58 44
3 b f Machiavellian(USA) —Inaaq (Lammtarra (USA))
342[6] *492*[4] 2674[3]

Maximix *G L Moore* a70 45
4 gr g Linamix(FR) —Time Will Show (FR) (Exit To Nowhere (USA))
89[7] *5500*[15]

Maxim's (ARG) *L Reuterskiold* a88
6 br g Lode(USA) —Mari's Ballerina (USA) (Mari's Book (USA))
344[10] *(1647a)*

Maximus Aurelius (IRE) *J Jay* 73
2 b c Night Shift(USA) —Dame's Violet (IRE) (Groom Dancer (USA))
1990[6] 4454[7] 5343[3] (5624) 5974[24] 6233[14]

Maxolini *J J Quinn* 25
4 ch g Bertolini(USA) —Evening Falls (Beveled (USA))
2121[11]

Max One Two Three (IRE) *Tom Dascombe* 99
2 b f Princely Heir(IRE) —Dakota Sioux (IRE) (College Chapel)
(5003) 5592[3] (6182)

Maxwil *G L Moore* 78
2 b c Storming Home—Lady Donatella (Last Tycoon (IRE))
4151[17] 4547[6] 5536[4] (6448)

Mayaar (USA) *P W Chapple-Hyam* 67
2 ch f Grand Slam(USA) —Kovna (USA) (Seattle Slew (USA))
3245[6] 3750[3] 5380[4] 6104[7]

Mayadeen (IRE) *I Semple* a53 77
5 b g King's Best(USA) —Inaaq (Lammtarra (USA))
767[9] 966[10] 1627[6] 1893[3] 2388[4] 2564[7] (3182) 3497[6] 3816[13] 4383[6] 4580[5] 5000[4] 5676[8] *(7102)*

Mayano Sophia (IRE) *J E Hammond* 97
3 b f Rock Of Gibraltar(IRE) —Tarascon (IRE) (Tirol)
3148a[5] 6770a[8]

Maybach *B Bo* a98 98
6 gr h Machiavellian(USA) —Capote Line (USA) (Capote (USA))
1648a[2] 2131a[8] 4874a[2]

Maybe (GER) *H Blume* 80
2 b f Dashing Blade—Mamourina (IRE) (Barathea (IRE))
5463a[3]

Maybe Better (AUS) *B Mayfield-Smith* 111
5 b g Intergaze(AUS) —Amarula (AUS) (Rubiton (AUS))
6354a[9]

Maybe I Will (IRE) *R Hannon* a66 66
2 b f Hawk Wing(USA) —Canterbury Lace (USA) (Danehill (USA))
1970[6] *2590*[4] *(3643)* 5053[11] 5109[6] 5314[12] 6449[8]

Maybe I Wont *R M Stronge* a69 72
2 b c Kyllachy—Surprise Surprise (Robellino (USA))
1970[11] 2473[3] 2687[2] 2961[2] *3426*[4] 4152[8] *4274*[6] 4537[7] 4737[6] 5534[9] *5887*[7] *6227*[4] *(6438)* *6584*[6] *6828*[5] *6928*[2] *7021*[2] *(7096)* *7142*[2]

May Day Queen (IRE) *R Hannon* a74 91
2 b f Danetime(IRE) —Birthday Present (Cadeaux Genereux)
1896[3] 2325a[3] 2812[16] 3152[4] *(3648)* *6270*[7]

Mayireneyrbel *J Akehurst* a45 57
3 ch f Auction House(USA) —Travel Secret (Blakeney)
737[10] 1059[8] (1368) 4472[6] 5068[5] 5279[4] 5865[10] 6060[11] 6452[13]

Mayonga (IRE) *Sir Mark Prescott* a104 81
4 ch m Dr Fong(USA) —Mayara (IRE) (Ashkalani (IRE))
31a[10]

Maysarah (IRE) *G A Butler* a74 52
3 b f Green Desert(USA) —Royale (IRE) (Royal Academy (USA))
(1625) 3369[11] *4740*[3] *5893*[4] *6406*[3] *6854*[2] *7033*[3]

Mays Louise *B P J Baugh* a29
3 ch f Sir Harry Lewis(USA) —Maysimp (IRE) (Mac's Imp (USA))
301[9] *745*[8] *6385*[12] *6766*[11]

Maysridge Ofkuwait *A Berry* 29
3 b f Tumbleweed Ridge—Kuwait Dawn (IRE) (Pips Pride)
2032[10] 2387[9] 2761[11] 3675[8] 4079[12]

Mayview *Rae Guest* a29 44
2 b f Royal Applause—Just Ice (Polar Falcon (USA))
6104[6] *6425*[9]

Mayyas *C C Bealby* a52
7 b g Robellino(USA) —Amidst (Midyan (USA))
45[5] *240*[10]

Mazaaya (USA) *M Johnston* 84
2 b f Cozzene(USA) —Mariamme (USA) (Verbatim (USA))
(5735) 6154[6] 6471[4]

Mazara (IRE) *J L Dunlop* 41
2 ch g Alhaarth(IRE) —Azdihaar (USA) (Mr Prospector (USA))
5628[12] 5919[8]

Maze (IRE) *B Smart* 101
2 ch c Dr Fong(USA) —Aryadne (Rainbow Quest (USA))
(2251) (2855) 5048[6] 5406[10] 6182[2] 6488[7]

Mazel Baby (FR) *Mlle C Azzoulai* a74 77
4 gr m Medaaly—Rain Follow (FR) (Baillamont (USA))
6923a[0]

Mazoran (FR) *D G Bridgwater* 24
3 ch g Majorien—Isgala (FR) (Galetto (FR))
1812[15] 2081[7]

Mazzanti *K A Ryan* 89
2 b c Piccolo—Feather Boa (IRE) (Sri Pekan (USA))
1919[4] 2297[2] (2934) 3910[6] 4743[9] 5410[6] 6182[13]

McCartney (GER) *M Johnston* 115
2 b c In The Wings—Messina (GER) (Dashing Blade)
3856[3] (4495) (5004) (5406) 6333[7]

Mcconnell (USA) *J R Best* a72 69
2 ch c Petionville(USA) —Warsaw Girl (IRE) (Polish Precedent (USA))
4325[4] 5595[5] 6080[4] *7252*[2]

Mccormack (IRE) *Micky Hammond* a7 53
5 b g Desert Story(IRE) —La Loba (IRE) (Treasure Kay)
2795[11] 3994[8] 4424[9]

Mceldowney *M Johnston* a76 94
5 b g Zafonic(USA) —Ayodhya (IRE) (Astronef)
2011[2] 2170[3] 2736[15] 3090[14] 3501[3]

Mchepple *W Storey* 50
2 b f Fleetwood(IRE) —Roleover Mania (Tragic Role (USA))
4422^{8} 4783^{10} 5734^{11} 6254^{8} 6729^{3}

Mcnairobi *P D Cundell* a89 86
4 b m Josr Algarhoud(IRE) —Bonita Bee (King Of Spain)
(590) 1649^{4} 2239^{3} 2670^{5}

Mcqueen (IRE) *J T Stimpson* a53 63
7 ch g Barathea(IRE) —Bibliotheque (USA) (Woodman (USA))
4380^{2} 4906^{5} 5257^{4} 5426^{11} 6076^{6} (6330) 6558^{15}

Meadfoot *B R Millman* a49 47
3 b f Averti(IRE) —Rivermead (USA) (Irish River (FR))
69^{6} 301^{7} 573^{11} 790^{10} 1175^{7} 1782^{10} 2195^{8} 4109^{3} 4591^{4} 5269^{10} 5945^{11} 6108^{5}

Meadow Soprano (IRE) *M P Sunderland* 49
5 b m Imperial Ballet(IRE) —Good Aim (IRE) (Priolo (USA))
5838^{7}

Meantime (USA) *G Prodromou* a42 61
4 b g Point Given(USA) —Interim (Sadler's Wells (USA))
6265^{9} 6453^{11} 6613^{10}

Measured Response *J G M O'Shea* a28 59
5 ch g Inchinor—Seal Indigo (IRE) (Glenstal (USA))
3487^{3} 4959^{2} 5188^{9} 5366^{9} 6598^{12}

Measured Tempo *Saeed Bin Suroor* 101
3 b f Sadler's Wells(USA) —Allez Les Trois (USA) (Riverman (USA))
(1809) 2211^{13} 4849^{8}

Meathop (IRE) *R F Fisher* a44 46
3 b g Imperial Ballet(IRE) —Jacobina (Magic Ring (IRE))
152^{5} 619^{7} 1232^{10} 1381^{11} 2200^{5} 3636^{11}

Mecca's Mate *D W Barker* a67 107
6 gr m Paris House—Clancassie (Clantime)
847^{10} 1125^{7} 1474^{28} 3050^{2} 3089^{6} (3344) 3511^{5} 3990^{12} 4746^{14} 5616^{26} 5810^{8}

Media Hora (CHI) *F Castro* a58 24
7 ch g Somersham(USA) —Membrana (CHI) (The Great Shark (USA))
$249a^{13}$ $474a^{13}$ $1647a^{2}$

Media Stars *J A Osborne* a59
2 gr c Green Desert(USA) —Starine (FR) (Mendocino (USA))
6530^{6}

Medicea Sidera *E F Vaughan* a89 87
3 b f Medicean—Broughtons Motto (Mtoto)
1398^{7} 1620^{2} 2428^{2} 3430^{6} (3743) (4589) 5355^{5} 5954^{7} 6391^{5}

Medici Code *H Morrison* a86 108
3 ch g Medicean—Fivefive (IRE) (Fairy King (USA))
(224) (284) (322)

Medici Gold *B J Meehan* a31 44
2 ch f Medicean—Silence Is Golden (Danehill Dancer (IRE))
3643^{11} 4232^{12} 4683^{6}

Medicine Path *E J O'Neill* 110
3 b c Danehill Dancer(IRE) —Indian Mystery (IRE) (Indian Ridge)
1126^{6} $2293a^{20}$ $2952a^{6}$ (6726)

Medici Pearl *T D Easterby* a39 79
3 b f Medicean—In Love Again (IRE) (Prince Rupert (FR))
670^{3} 1620^{4} 1913^{2} (2137) 2872^{4} 3078^{4} 3411^{4} (3607) 4222^{8} 4640^{7} 5776^{10} 6474^{10} 6753^{15}

Medici Time *T D Easterby* 55
2 gr c Medicean—Pendulum (Pursuit Of Love)
2889^{11} 3951^{8} 4448^{5} 4892^{8}

Medieval Maiden *W J Musson* a70 67
4 gr m Zaha(CAN) —Brillante (FR) (Green Dancer (USA))
110^{6} 299^{5} 445^{5} 1167^{5} (1907) 2089^{13} 2572^{3} 3385^{8} 3803^{6} 5732^{9} 6124^{6} 6780^{12} 7273^{5}

Medieval Mercy (IRE) *P E I Newell* 33
8 b m Leading Counsel(USA) —Medieval Beauty (IRE) (Prince Regent (FR))
$4371a^{11}$

Meditation *I A Wood* a82 84
5 ch m Inchinor—Trojan Desert (Troy)
28^{13} 191^{4} 261^{10} 384^{8} 509^{10} 590^{6} 614^{12} 3851^{10} (4361) 4855^{7} 5303^{8} 5893^{8} 5985^{3} 6232^{11} 6269^{8} 6547^{10} 6710^{2} 6795^{10} (6824) 7017^{5} 7099^{2} 7193^{2} 7224^{6}

Medley *R Hannon* 96
3 ch f Danehill Dancer(IRE) —Marl (Lycius (USA))
1394^{3} 2306^{2} 3059^{2} 3430^{3} (3961) 5163^{6} (5354)

Mednaya (IRE) *R Gibson* 105
4 b m Anabaa(USA) —Sopran Dandy (IRE) (Doyoun)
$3445a^{6}$ $4190a^{14}$

Meeriss (IRE) *M R Channon* a93 96
2 b c Dubai Destination(USA) —Bless The Bride (IRE) (Darshaan)
(1622) 2232^{7} 4121^{3} 4776^{9} (5135) (5414) 6170^{6}

Meer Kat (IRE) *R Charlton* 90
2 b c Red Ransom(USA) —Bush Cat (USA) (Kingmambo (USA))
3551^{8} 4876^{2} 5227^{3} 5919^{2} (6194)

Meeting Of Minds *W Jarvis* a53 46
3 b f Mind Games—Turn Back (Pivotal)
73^{5} 2607^{8} 3918^{7} 4337^{4} 4684^{4} 5497^{9} 6806^{12} (7197)

Me Fein *A P Stringer* a67 32
3 gr g Desert Prince(IRE) —Attachment (USA) (Trempolino (USA))
(4914) 6056^{13} 6808^{5} 7157^{3}

Mega Dame (IRE) *D Haydn Jones* a63
3 b f Iron Mask(USA) —Easter Girl (Efisio)
2261^{8} 2520^{6} 3406^{2} 4205^{P} 4430^{9} 5019^{10}

Megalala (IRE) *J J Bridger* a40 59
6 b g Petardia—Avionne (Derrylin)
1400^{11} 1612^{8} 2143^{11} 3644^{9} 5864^{4} 6212^{7} 6452^{2} 7166^{9}

Megalo Maniac *R A Fahey* a73 62
4 b g Efisio—Sharanella (Shareef Dancer (USA))
(1349) (1569) 1755^{3} 2827^{8} 3185^{4} 3572^{8} 4701^{4} (5233) 6463^{5} 6747^{13}

Megaton *P Bowen* a34 78
6 ch g Nashwan(USA) —Pan Galactic (USA) (Lear Fan (USA))
(2367) 3216^{9}

Mega Watt (IRE) *W Jarvis* 64
2 b c Acclamation—Kilshanny (Groom Dancer (USA))
3991^{8} 4448^{3}

Meikle Barfil *J M Bradley* a53 67
5 b g Compton Place—Oare Sparrow (Night Shift (USA))
1074^{12} 1405^{7} 1991^{13} 3618^{12} 4312^{8} 4561^{5} 4881^{10} 4973^{2} 5564^{10} 5897^{8}

Meisho Samson (JPN) *S Takahashi* 123
4 b h Opera House—My Vivien (JPN) (Dancing Brave (USA))
$6943a^{3}$

Meisho Tokon (JPN) *I Yasuda* a107
5 b h Mayano Top Gun(JPN) —Lunar Sphere (JPN) (Jade Robbery (USA))
$6942a^{4}$

Mejhar (IRE) *E J Creighton* a61 47
7 b g Desert Prince(IRE) —Factice (USA) (Known Fact (USA))
5835^{6} 6407^{8} 6719^{12} 6878^{8}

Melalchrist *K A Ryan* a72 91
5 b g Almaty(IRE) —Lawless Bridget (Alnasr Alwasheek)
566^{10} 621^{4} 905^{2} 992^{2} 1074^{3} 1299^{3} 1565^{6} 1718^{4} 3053^{6} (3536) 3608^{4} (3791) 4038^{2} (4489) 5401^{5} 5689^{7} 6381^{12}

Melandre *M Brittain* a47 45
5 b m Lujain(USA) —Talighta (USA) (Barathea (IRE))
8^{8} 251^{11} 964^{9} 1241^{8} 4101^{9} 4252^{12}

Melanosporum (USA) *I Jory* 91
5 bb h Royal Anthem(USA) —Innes (USA) (A.P. Indy (USA))
$642a^{6}$

Mellifluous (IRE) *J W Hills* a33
2 b f Noverre(USA) —Danestar (Danehill (USA))
6434^{13} 6649^{20}

Melodramatic (IRE) *R Charlton* 89
2 b f Sadler's Wells(USA) —My Branch (Distant Relative)
4598^{4}

Melpomene *M Johnston* a93 91
4 ch m Peintre Celebre(USA) —Lady Joyce (FR) (Galetto (FR))
(153) 192^{8} 345^{6} 2449^{3} 2736^{9}

Melt (IRE) *R Hannon* a53 61
2 b f Intikhab(USA) —Kindle (Selkirk (USA))
5872^{5} 6281^{6} 6425^{2} 6578^{13}

Melvino *T D Barron* a77 71
5 b g Josr Algarhoud(IRE) —Safe Secret (Seclude (USA))
142^{2} (297) 428^{5} 568^{4}

Melwood Dreams *Paul Green* a55 52
2 ch g Domedriver(IRE) —Hertha (Hernando (FR))
4733^{9} 5042^{12} 5194^{10} 5736^{10} 6066^{7} 6242^{3} 6736^{6} 6750^{12} 7130^{7} 7286^{8}

Me Me Me *M J Wallace* a25
2 b g Red Ransom(USA) —Jalousie (IRE) (Barathea (IRE))
3823^{11} 4070^{8} 4946^{6}

Memorata *R Charlton* a42 24
3 b f Montjeu(IRE) —Polish Lake (Polish Precedent (USA))
1312^{11} 1685^{7}

Memorette (USA) *W Currin* a99 112
5 br m Memo(CHI) —Forever Fondre (USA) (Shahrastani (USA))
$5825a^{4}$

Memphis City (USA) *J Noseda* a81 66
2 ch g Langfuhr(CAN) —Fleet Wahine (CAN) (Afleet (CAN))
4362^{19} 4604^{5} 4810^{3}

Memphis Kate *M L W Bell* 54
2 ch f Bahamian Bounty—Halloa (Wolfhound (USA))
2663^{7} 3687^{12} 5558^{P} (Dead)

Memphis Man *P D Evans* a81 75
4 b g Bertolini(USA) —Something Blue (Petong)
1074^{8} 1493^{3} 1597^{3} 2108^{14} 2762^{7} 3172^{6} 3597^{5} 3686^{12} 4706^{9} (5866) 6247^{4} (6415) (6467) 6575^{3} 6639^{9} (6910) 7026^{8} 7215^{2} 7261^{4}

Memphis Marie *C N Allen* a60 46
3 b f Desert Sun—Spirito Libro (USA) (Lear Fan (USA))
2951^{6} 3651^{4} 4340^{7} 4518^{8} (4977) 6455^{6} 6762^{9}

Menadha (USA) *M R Channon* a86 81
2 ch c Carson City(USA) —Wiedniu (USA) (Danzig Connection (USA))
1970^{5} 2451^{4} 2949^{3} (3958) 4501^{10} 5153^{6} (6291)

Menelaus *K A Morgan* a54 56
6 b g Machiavellian(USA) —Mezzogiorno (Unfuwain (USA))
4531^{8} 5948^{11}

Menkaura *John R Upson* a37 79
4 b g Pivotal—Nekhbet (Artaius (USA))
6766^{8} 6937^{12}

Me No Puppet *E J Alston* a41 12
3 b f Mtoto—Puppet Play (IRE) (Broken Hearted)
991^{9} 7174^{5}

Menorca (IRE) *Jane Chapple-Hyam* a15
2 b f Hawk Wing(USA) —Saskya's Dream (IRE) (Ashkalani (IRE))
6857^{10}

Meon Mix *J R Fanshawe* a43 54
3 b f Kayf Tara—Millennium Dash (Nashwan (USA))
1725^{4} 4392^{7} 5346^{5} 6204^{4}

Mercator (GER) *K Woodburn*
2 br c Dashing Blade—Miskinissa (GER) (Esclavo (FR))
$6219a^{7}$

Merchant Bankes *W G M Turner* a54 68
4 b h Observatory(USA) —Lady Bankes (IRE) (Alzao (USA))
1886^{9} 2106^{10} 2890^{11} 3969^{6} 5007^{7} 5273^{7} 5820^{12}

Merchant Navy *E A L Dunlop* a70 77
2 b g Green Desert(USA) —Khalkissa (USA) (Diesis)
1858^{11} 2215^{6} 2575^{4} 4065^{12} 4964^{6} (6052) 6328^{3}

Merchant Of Dubai *G A Swinbank* 75
2 b c Dubai Destination(USA) —Chameleon (Green Desert (USA))
2575^{6} 2863^{2} (3582) 4278^{4}

Mercury Blue *S Kirk* 69
3 b f Montjeu(IRE) —Rowan Flower (IRE) (Ashkalani (IRE))
1785^{2} 2274^{7} 2981^{9} 4542^{7}

Merdiff *W M Brisbourne* a66 37
8 b g Machiavellian(USA) —Balwa (USA) (Danzig (USA))
138^{9} 350^{7} 447^{5} 627^{8} 715^{7} 768^{5}

Meridia (GER) *J Hirschberger* 97
3 b f Monsun(GER) —Montserrat (GER) (Zilzal (USA))
$1515a^{3}$ $2294a^{6}$

Meridian Grey (USA) *K A Ryan* 61
3 gr c More Than Ready(USA) —Love Rhythm (CAN) (Seeking The Gold (USA))
916^{4} 1091^{10} 1850^{14} 2661^{9} 3583^{11} 4078^{14}

Meridian Line (IRE) *J G Portman* 81
2 b f Trans Island—Meranie Girl (IRE) (Mujadil (USA))
2468^{11} 3162^{2} 3550^{10} 3866^{2} (4310) 4844^{7} 5692^{3} 5766^{16}

Merlerault (USA) *P Demercastel* a111 101
4 b g Royal Academy(USA) —Jungle Rhythm (USA) (Rhythm (USA))
(437a) $858a^{8}$ $4012a^{4}$ $4520a^{9}$

Merlin's Dancer *S Dow* a103 104
7 b g Magic Ring(IRE) —La Piaf (FR) (Fabulous Dancer (USA))
(818) 1125^{6} 1456^{5} 2234^{8} 2858^{23} 3749^{10} 4122^{5} 4386^{6} 4696^{16} 5401^{3} 5891^{12} 6231^{10}

Merlins Dreams *P C Haslam* a27
4 b g Dansili—Red Leggings (Shareef Dancer (USA))
186^{8} 338^{9} 2563^{13}

Merlins Quest *J M Bradley* a32 60
3 b c Wizard King—Wonderland (IRE) (Dolphin Street (FR))
713^{12} 899^{8} 974^{7} 1561^{9} 2196^{15} 6894^{13} 6963^{10}

Merrymadcap (IRE) *M Blanshard* a84 81
5 b g Lujain(USA) —Carina Clare (Slip Anchor)
1209^{4} 1385^{3} 1765^{4} 2107^{2} 2401^{14} 2979^{5} 3487^{10} 3855^{6} 4433^{7} 4672^{4} 4889^{10} (5178) 5568^{4}

Merrymaker *W M Brisbourne* a79 80
7 b g Machiavellian(USA) —Wild Pavane (Dancing Brave (USA))
5034^{4} 5404^{6} 5807^{8} 6077^{2} 6341^{7} 6561^{4} (6817) (6961) 7081^{8}

Merry Moon (IRE) *R J Osborne* a50 55
3 b f Night Shift(USA) —Adaja (Cadeaux Genereux)
$5696a^{9}$

Mersey Sound (IRE) *D R C Elsworth* a79 86
9 b g Ela-Mana-Mou—Coral Sound (IRE) (Glow (USA))
1272^{8}

Meru Camp (IRE) *P Winkworth* 57
3 ch g Loup Sauvage(USA) —Morgan Le Fay (Magic Ring (IRE))
1921^{7} 2273^{11}

Merveilles *Mrs John Harrington* a52 91
4 b g Vettori(IRE) —Finlaggan (Be My Chief (USA))
$4867a^{14}$

Mesbaah (IRE) *M A Jarvis* 102
3 b g Noverre(USA) —Deyaajeer (USA) (Dayjur (USA))
3463^{3} 3940^{7} 4566^{3} 5419^{5} 6198^{6}

Meshugah (IRE) *R Gibson* a82 107
3 ch c Grand Lodge(USA) —Posta Vecchia (USA) (Rainbow Quest (USA))
(2503a) $4655a^{9}$ $6400a^{7}$

Mesmerize Me *E S McMahon* 89
2 b g Mind Games—Exotic Forest (Dominion)
3589^{7} (3866) 5277^{2} 5583^{5} (6059)

Messiah Garvey *M R Channon* a74 70
3 b g Lear Fan(USA) —Maid Of Camelot (Caerleon (USA))
4940^{9} 5360^{6} 5768^{17} 6278^{13} 7164^{4}

Messias Da Silva (USA) *J Noseda* a83
2 bb f Tale Of The Cat(USA) —Indy Power (USA) (A.P. Indy (USA))
6225^{2} (6544)

Metal Guru *R Hollinshead* a70 73
3 ch f Ishiguru(USA) —Gemtastic (Tagula (IRE))
1207^{2} 2198^{5} (3168) 4525^{7} 4759^{8} 6089^{3} 6283^{9} 6747^{4} 6962^{6} 7206^{8}

Metal Madness (IRE) *M G Quinlan* 54
2 b c Acclamation—Dosha (Touching Wood (USA))
2604^{5} 3037^{5} 4323^{8}

Metaphoric (IRE) *M L W Bell* 107
3 b g Montjeu(IRE) —Virgin Hawk (USA) (Silver Hawk (USA))
(1106) 1602^{4} 2816^{6} 3883^{4} 4749^{3} 5574^{3} 5952^{6}

Metaphorical *M Johnston* 67
2 b c Bahri(USA) —Shinko Hermes (IRE) (Sadler's Wells (USA))
4656^{6} 5011^{7} 5599^{P} (Dead)

Methaaly (IRE) *M Mullineaux* a77 77
4 b g Red Ransom(USA) —Santorini (USA) (Spinning World (USA))
234^{8} 424^{5} 560^{3} (724) 1074^{4} 1357^{5} 1589^{8} 2155^{2} 3852^{6} (4021) 4734^{2} (4967) 5160^{9} 5387^{3} 5648^{8} 6020^{5} 6157^{10} 6313^{3} 6677^{5} 6762^{3} 6938^{3} 7161^{2}

Methodical *B G Powell* a30 31
5 b m Lujain(USA) —Simple Logic (Aragon)
4531^{12}

Methusaleh (IRE) *D Shaw* a69 79
4 b g Mutamam—Madamaa (IRE) (Alzao (USA))
32^{10} 191^{12} 334^{6} 445^{9} 666^{4} 729^{12} 866^{11} 912^{3} 1132^{8} 1360^{2} 1673^{5} 1740^{7} 1933^{8} 2893^{6} 3195^{7}

Metropolitan Chief *P Burgoyne* a67 63
3 b g Compton Place—Miss Up N Go (Gorytus (USA))
919^{5} 1432^{5} 2178^{8} 2545^{5} 3057^{3} 4270^{4} 4538^{5} 5275^{3} (5602) 6123^{6} 6455^{3} 7269^{13}

Metropolitan Man *D M Simcock* 111
4 ch h Dr Fong(USA) —Preceder (Polish Precedent (USA))
$531a^{3}$ $646a^{8}$ 3098^{9} 4167^{2} 5213^{4} 5412^{2} 6009^{6}

Metternich *M Johnston* a81
3 b c Machiavellian(USA) —Jomana (IRE) (Darshaan)
(338)

Mexican Bob *A King* a68 71
4 b g Atraf—Eskimo Nel (IRE) (Shy Groom (USA))
3416^{6} 4333^{2} 5273^{4}

Mexican Pete *A King* a76 83
7 b g Atraf—Eskimo Nel (IRE) (Shy Groom (USA))
3407^{3}

Mexican Venture *W Jarvis* 38
2 b c Tobougg(IRE) —Nacho Venture (FR) (Rainbow Quest (USA))
5595^{12}

Mexilhoeira *C G Cox* 41
3 ch f Observatory(USA) —With Music In Mind (Mind Games)
4808^{6}

Mey Blossom *R M Whitaker* 82
2 ch f Captain Rio—Petra Nova (First Trump)
3200^{6} 3915^{2} (4522) 4921^{4} 5322^{14} 6182^{6} 6619^{10}

Meydan Dubai (IRE) *J R Best* 91
2 b c Alzao(USA) —Rorkes Drift (IRE) (Royal Abjar (USA))
2443^{3} 2855^{6} 3995^{3} 4823^{2}

Meydan Princess (IRE) *J Noseda* a77 71
2 b f Choisir(AUS) —Miss Assertive (Zafonic (USA))
5540^{5} 5949^{6} (6228)

Meynell *M A Jarvis* a68 74
3 br f Sakhee(USA) —In Full Cry (USA) (Seattle Slew (USA))
2455^{5} 3214^{7} 4007^{2} 5013^{2} 5499^{3}

Mezel (USA) *S Seemar* a102 98
4 b h Grand Slam(USA) —Spankin' (USA) (A.P. Indy (USA))
$325a^{9}$ $410a^{14}$ $532a^{13}$

Mezuzah *M W Easterby* a57 92
7 b g Barathea(IRE) —Mezzogiorno (Unfuwain (USA))
846^{5} 1041^{3} 1179^{9} 1826^{9} 1860^{7} 2891^{4} 3091^{2} 3559^{6} 3715^{2} 3943^{7} 4745^{14} 5031^{12} 5585^{2} 5804^{11} 6539^{6}

Mezzanisi (IRE) *M L W Bell* 66
2 b g Kalanisi(IRE) —Mezzanine (Sadler's Wells (USA))
5951^{14} 6285^{3}

Mganga *M R Channon* 64
2 b g Dr Fong(USA) —Hannalou (FR) (Shareef Dancer (USA))
4110^{10} 4656^{7} 4904^{9} 5298^{13} (5736) 5914^{5}

Mharadono (GER) *P Hirschberger* 108
4 b h Sharp Prod(USA) —Monalind (GER) (Park Romeo)
$881a^{4}$ $3122a^{5}$ (6045a) (6691a)

Miacarla *A Berry* a36 66
4 b m Forzando—Zarzi (IRE) (Suave Dancer (USA))
1384^{11} 1493^{9} 1595^{4} (2844) 2933^{3} 3203^{3} 3569^{8} 3608^{15} 4498^{7} 4787^{2} 4939^{5} 5297^{4} (5507) 5565^{10} 5740^{9} 6287^{16}

Mia Diletta *B Grizzetti*
2 b f Selkirk(USA) —Maschera D'Oro (Mtoto)
$6047a^{3}$

Mia Haria *B R Millman* a47 44
2 b f Dr Fong(USA) —Pantita (Polish Precedent (USA))
4232^{15} 4875^{8} 5308^{8}

Mia Kross (IRE) *B Grizzetti* 97
4 b m Cape Cross(IRE) —Waku Waku (ITY) (Big Reef)
$6221a^{5}$ $6688a^{4}$

Miami Tallyce (IRE) *E J O'Neill* a57 54
3 b f Montjeu(IRE) —Altishaan (Darshaan)
1092^{8} 1628^{8}

Mia's Boy *P W Chapple-Hyam* a65 74
3 b c Pivotal—Bint Zamayem (IRE) (Rainbow Quest (USA))
1452^{3} 2320^{6} (2740) 4608^{6}

Michabo (IRE) *P Bowen* a71 93
6 b g Robellino(USA) —Mole Creek (Unfuwain (USA))
3858^{7} 4398^{5}

Michaels Dream (IRE) *N Wilson* a39 39
8 b g Spectrum(IRE) —Stormswept (USA) (Storm Bird (CAN))
3300^{8}

Michikabu (IRE) *R Gibson* 96
4 b m Grand Lodge(USA) —Mood Indigo (IRE) (Indian Ridge)
$6095a^{7}$

Michita (USA) *J H M Gosden* 82
2 bb f Dynaformer(USA) —Thunder Kitten (USA) (Storm Cat (USA))
(6414)

Mickey Pearce (IRE) *J G M O'Shea* a20
5 b g Rossini(USA) —Lucky Coin (Hadeer)
464^{9}

Mick Is Back *G G Margarson* a57 65
3 b g Diktat—Classy Cleo (IRE) (Mujadil (USA))
40^{2} 116^{4} 209^{5} 335^{3} 478^{6} 534^{3} 572^{4} (832) 900^{2} 1297^{2} 1903^{6} (2110) (2619) (3057) 3475^{5} (4109) 4858^{10} 6413^{4} 6623^{4} 6716^{6} 7028^{7}

Mick Jerome (IRE) *Rune Haugen* 97
6 b h Kahyasi—Acquilata (USA) (Irish River (FR))
$2976a^{3}$ $4218a^{13}$ $6137a^{9}$

Mickleberry (IRE) *J D Bethell* a55 60
3 b f Desert Style(IRE) —Miss Indigo (Indian Ridge)
1281^{4} 1932^{3} 2255^{8} 4001^{6} 5282^{2} (5752) 6720^{4} 7005^{4} 7284^{2}

Mickmacmagoole (IRE) *Seamus G O'Donnell* 81
5 b g Sadler's Wells(USA) —Musk Lime (USA) (Private Account (USA))
(2434) (4297) 4691^{9} 6422^{11}

Mick's Dancer *W R Muir* a64
2 b c Pivotal—La Piaf (FR) (Fabulous Dancer (USA))
6850^{7} 7051^{4}

Micky Mac (IRE) *T D Walford* a50 50
3 b g Lend A Hand—Gazette It Tonight (Merdon Melody)
7118[5] 7248[4]
Midas Way *P R Charnings* a81 103
7 ch g Halling(USA) —Arietta's Way (IRE) (Darshaan)
7635 5800[9]
Middle Eastern *P A Blockley* a65 66
5 b g Mujahid(USA) —Swissmatic (Petong)
681[4] 896[13] (1379) 2145[5] 4884[10] 5177[10]
Middlemarch (IRE) *J S Goldie* a81 86
7 ch g Grand Lodge(USA) —Blanche Dubois (Nashwan (USA))
1040[7] 1145[23] 1747[5] 2564[6] 2842[5] 2891[6] (3943) (4581) 6016[15]
Middleton Grey *A G Newcombe* a71 76
9 gr g Ashkalani(IRE) —Petula (Petong)
3572[6] 4606[8] 5303[6] 6024[7] 6882[11]
Midmaar (IRE) *M Wigham* a59 70
6 b g Cape Cross(IRE) —Khazinat El Dar (USA) (Slew O'Gold (USA))
86[5] 158[8] 268[2] 292[9] 440[9] 632[13] 800[10] 920[2] 1120[2] 1344[3] 1436[3] 6887[3] 6945[6] 7192[4] 7278[12]
Midnight Fling *R Charlton* 71
2 b f Groom Dancer(USA) —Perfect Night (Danzig Connection (USA))
1882[3] 2488[3]
Midnight Lute (USA) *B Baffert* a126
4 bb h Real Quiet(USA) —Candytuft (USA) (Dehere (USA))
(6510a)
Midnight Muse (USA) *T D Barron* 82
2 b c Swain(IRE) —Witching Hour (FR) (Fairy King (USA))
3199[3] (3760)
Midnight Mystique (IRE) *T D Barron* 43
2 b f Noverre(USA) —Dark Hyacinth (IRE) (Darshaan)
4422[13] 4782[9]
Midnight Oasis *Rae Guest* 45
2 b f Oasis Dream—Midnight Shift (IRE) (Night Shift (USA))
4522[5] 4756[9] 6595[13]
Midnight Sky *Rae Guest* a51 54
3 b f Desert Prince(IRE) —Midnight Shift (IRE) (Night Shift (USA))
3846[3] 4616[8] (4795) 4935[7] 5295[8]
Midnight Traveller *Thomas Cooper* a54 84
4 b g Daylami(IRE) —Swift Dispersal (Shareef Dancer (USA))
2067a[13]
Midnite Blews (IRE) *A B Haynes* a30 66
2 gr g Trans Island—Felicita (IRE) (Catrail (USA))
1021[4] 2193[4] 3043[2] 3238[5] 4316[5] 5268[15] 5498[14]
Mid Ocean *P W D'Arcy* a62 52
3 ch f Sakhee(USA) —Wavy Up (IRE) (Brustolon)
624[6] 1022[7] 1151[12]
Midships (USA) *Mrs A J Perrett* 86
2 gr c Mizzen Mast(USA) —Interim (Sadler's Wells (USA))
(2596) 3938[7] 4199[3]
Midsummer Fun (USA) *Saeed Bin Suroor* 56
3 b f Gone West(USA) —Windsharp (USA) (Lear Fan (USA))
4235[3] 4630[8]
Mid Valley *J R Jenkins* a61 53
4 ch g Zilzal(USA) —Isabella D'Este (IRE) (Irish River (FR))
22[7] 129[2] 210[6] 350[11] (435) 519[4] 637[5] 812[2] 1206[14] 1350[6] 2179[8] 3286[10] 4739[8] 4945[9] 6407[4] 6832[13] 7168[2] 7187[4]
Mi Emma (GER) *A Wohler* 111
3 b f Silvano(GER) —Mi Anna (GER) (Lake Coniston (IRE))
(1338a) 2814[2] 4010a[7] (4929a)
Miesko (USA) *M Johnston* a76 85
2 b c Quiet American(USA) —Polish Style (USA) (Danzig (USA))
4247[2] 4571[6] 5042[10] 5363[2] 5705[5] (6073) (6195)
Miesque's Approval (USA) *M D Wolfson* 124
8 b h Miesque's Son(USA) —Win Approval (USA) (With Approval (CAN))
862a[15]
Might Be Magic *P W Chapple-Hyam* 46
2 b g Fraam—Modelliste (Machiavellian (USA))
5977[14]
Mighty *Jane Chapple-Hyam* a105 115
4 ch h Pivotal—Miswaki Belle (USA) (Miswaki (USA))
(120) (340) (420) 552[3] 761[4] 1144[2] 1495[3] 2182[2] 2856[3] 5437a[5]
Mighty Alfred (IRE) *M R Channon* 55
2 gr c Kendor(FR) —Night Shifter (IRE) (Night Shift (USA))
2424[12]
Mighty Kitchener (USA) *P Howling* a72 55
4 br g Mighty(USA) —Libeccio (NZ) (Danzatore (CAN))
1[2] 84[3] 204[8] (270) 1907[2] 2332[3] 2519[2] 3217[11] 3705[17] 3946[8] 4534[4] (4670) (5018) 5283[9] 5779[5] 6069[10] 6459[8] 6697[11] 7132[6] 7273[11]
Mighty Missouri (IRE) *W R Swinburn* 66
3 b g Danehill(USA) —Pietra Dura (Cadeaux Genereux)
1155[9] 1410[2]
Mighty Moon *J O'Reilly* a91 89
4 gr g Daylami(IRE) —Moon Magic (Polish Precedent (USA))
914[4] 1621[5] 1794[6] 2011[7] 3467[7] 3609[5] 4105[4] 4248[3] 5144[2] 5623[4] 5808[7] 6186[4] 6473[15] 6703[2]
Mighty Mover (IRE) *B Palling* a61 30
5 ch g Bahhare(USA) —Ericeira (IRE) (Anita's Prince)
2981[10] 5018[8] 5709[10] 6152[4] 6315[2] (6627) 6801[2] 7046[8]
Migration *Mrs S Lamyman* a42 64
11 b g Rainbow Quest(USA) —Armeria (USA) (Northern Dancer (CAN))
220[7] 891[7] 997[6]
Mikao (IRE) *M H Tompkins* a55 97
6 b g Tagula(IRE) —Oumaladia (IRE) (Waajib)
1844[2] 2859[13] 5030[4] 5830[12] 6014[12] 6302[8]
Mikhail Fokine (IRE) *A P O'Brien* a70 79
2 b c Sadler's Wells(USA) —Rain Flower (IRE) (Indian Ridge)
5321[7]
Milanollo *M L W Bell* a51 45
2 b f Soviet Star(USA) —Military Tune (IRE) (Nashwan (USA))
3446[8] 5527[7]
Mileaminutemurphy *R Hannon* 30
2 b g Fasliyev(USA) —Shining Hour (USA) (Red Ransom (USA))
3383[14] 4316[7]
Miles Gloriosus (USA) *Maria Rita Salvioni* 108
4 b h Repriced(USA) —Treasure Coast (CAN) (Foolish Pleasure (USA))
2295a[3] 3780a[5] 6372a[6] 6687a[2]
Military Cross *L M Cumani* a104 102
4 b g Cape Cross(IRE) —Tipsy (Kris)
2755[20] (6852)
Military Power *J W Hills* 77
2 b c Dubai Destination(USA) —Susun Kelapa (USA) (St Jovite (USA))
4110[3] 5140[5]
Milk And Sultana *G A Ham* a59 53
7 b m Millkom—Premier Princess (Hard Fought)
19[4] 121[9] 279[4] 496[2]
Millachy *B W Hills* 64
3 b f Kyllachy—Millazure (USA) (Dayjur (USA))
1207[3] 1923[9] 2718[13]
Millagros (IRE) *I Semple* a70 68
7 b m Pennekamp(USA) —Grey Galava (Generous (IRE))
112[5]
Milla's Rocket (IRE) *K A Ryan* a75 82
3 b f Galileo(IRE) —Tenable (Polish Precedent (USA))
149[2] 257[2] 392[2] (569) (3196) 3495[2] 3960[6] 4640[5]
Millbag (IRE) *D Selvaratnam* a91 94
6 bb h Cape Cross(IRE) —Play With Fire (FR) (Priolo (USA))
104a[11] 325a[13]
Millbrook Star (IRE) *M C Chapman* a42 32
4 b g Orpen(USA) —Lady Bodmin (IRE) (Law Society (USA))
504[12]
Mill By The Stream *A M Hales* a66 49
5 b g Lujain(USA) —Lonesome (Night Shift (USA))
50[10] 145[2] (221) (241) 306[10] 450[5] 536[7] 710[6] 1739[10] 1947[12]
Mill Creek *B Smart* 33
2 ch f Ishiguru(USA) —Hollia (Touch Boy)
2115[7] 3370[U] 3915[9] 4405[4] 4897[3] 5520[4]
Mille Feuille (IRE) *R M Beckett* 69
2 b f Choisir(AUS) —Watch The Clock (Mtoto)
5110[3]
Millenium Sun (IRE) *E J Creighton* a33 65
3 b g Tendulkar(USA) —Millenium Love (IRE) (Great Commotion (USA))
3452[9] 3613[11] 4064[13] 4536[9] 4635[11]
Millennium Storm (GER) *M F Harris* a50 35
2 b c Samum(GER) —Millennium Dawn (IRE) (Cadeaux Genereux)
3471[10] 4527[11] 6585[12] 6775[12]
Millers Jewel *K G Wingrove*
4 b m Sly—Old Castle Liziann (The Dissident)
1904[12]
Millestan (IRE) *H R A Cecil* 89
3 b f Invincible Spirit(IRE) —Atnab (USA) (Riverman (USA))
2578[7] 3430[14] 3960[5] 4509[3] 4848[3] 5230[3] 6053[7]
Millfield (IRE) *P R Chamings* a73 77
4 br g Elnadim(USA) —Eschasse (USA) (Zilzal (USA))
1280[4] 1947[8] 2331[6] 2556[6] (4474) 4978[2] 5190[11] 5433[10] 6123[10] 6429[3] (6831) 6955[3] (6993) 7094[2] 7160[3]
Millfields Dreams *M G Quinlan* a73 69
8 b g Dreams End—Millfields Lady (Sayf El Arab (USA))
(66) 158[9] 262[3] 276[5] 4233[4] 4396[9] 4944[11] 5535[4] 5981[3] 6288[10]
Mill House Girl (IRE) *S Donohoe* a68 68
6 ch m Basanta(IRE) —Karalee (IRE) (Arokar (FR))
1760a[4] 5184a[7]
Milliegait *T D Easterby* 78
3 b f Tobougg(IRE) —Miller's Gait (Mill Reef (USA))
1851[8] 2369[9] 3400[3] 3972[3] 4579[6] 5405[8] 6474[7] 6746[8]
Millie's Rock (IRE) *M R Channon* 52
2 b f Rock Of Gibraltar(IRE) —Miletrian (IRE) (Marju (IRE))
6723[7]
Millinsky (USA) *Rae Guest* a79 81
6 ch m Stravinsky(USA) —Millyant (Primo Dominie)
79[10]
Million Percent *C R Dore* a78 74
8 b g Ashkalani(IRE) —Royal Jade (Last Tycoon (IRE))
233[7] (381) 697[6] 980[2] 1507[14] (2033) 2331[3] 3422[3] 3851[2] 4137[2] 4353[3] 5233[4]
Million Spirits (IRE) *Kevin Prendergast* 87
3 b f Invincible Spirit(IRE) —Multicolour Wave (IRE) (Rainbow Quest (USA))
2379a[6]
Millisecond *M A Jarvis* a72 81
3 b f Royal Applause—Milligram (Mill Reef (USA))
1961[5] 3649[3] (4164) (5066) 5418[4] 6381[7]
Milloaks (IRE) *E J Creighton*
2 b f Tamayaz(CAN) —Jaldini (IRE) (Darshaan)
5313[12]
Millsini *Rae Guest* a46 51
3 b f Rossini(USA) —Millyant (Primo Dominie)
1883[5] 2242[6] 3281[12] 5752[5] 5970[7] 6240[8] 6565[6]
Millville *M A Jarvis* a115 102
7 ch g Millkom—Miss Top Ville (FR) (Top Ville)
57[2] 437a[5] 5830[13] 6169[16] 6538[5] 6931[3] 7225[4]
Millyjean *John Berry* a52 33
3 ch f Whittingham(IRE) —Taken Aback (IRE) (Robellino (USA))
231[8] 577[12] 2607[11] 3394[11] 4337[7] 4778[7]
Milne Bay (IRE) *D M Simcock* 10
2 b g Tagula(IRE) —Fiction (Dominion)
2604[12]
Milne Graden *J Noseda* 95
3 b g Montjeu(IRE) —Glen Rosie (IRE) (Mujtahid (USA))
(4492) (6474)
Milongo (FR) *Brigitte Renk* 104
5 b h Blush Rambler(USA) —Madeleina (FR) (Top Waltz (FR))
2330a[7] 3893a[4]
Milson's Point (IRE) *I Semple* a69 66
3 b g Fasliyev(USA) —Hilbys Brite Flite (USA) (Cormorant (USA))
958[6] 1658[7] 2453[10] 2910[6] 3345[2] 3540[2] 3997[10] 4381[13] 4931[11] (5084) (Dead)
Miltons Choice *J M Bradley* a44 64
4 b g Diktat—Starosta (Soviet Star (USA))
750[8]
Milton's Keen *M Salaman* a41 61
4 gr g Largesse—Not A Word (Batshoof)
2336[9] 3045[2] 3487[2] 3905[2] 4259[6] 4606[9] 4879[3] 5094[9] 5348[7]
Mimetico (IRE) *B Grizzetti* 101
3 b f Monsun(GER) —Liza (IRE) (Lycius (USA))
6221a[2] 6524a[9] 6688a[2]
Mimi Mouse *T D Easterby* 92
5 br m Diktat—Shifty Mouse (Night Shift (USA))
1134[2] 1427[3] 1854[5] (2315) 3197[3] 3515[5] 4567[16] 5332[2] 5666[10]
Mimisel *Rae Guest* a42 90
3 ch f Selkirk(USA) —Milly-M (Cadeaux Genereux)
2043[5] 2914[3] 3332[8] 5850a[10] 6940a[10] 7184[12]
Mimton (IRE) *N Wilson* a29 38
2 b f Shinko Forest(IRE) —Playa Del Sol (IRE) (Alzao (USA))
1029[7] 3192[10] 3606[9] 4136[11] 4405[7] 5017[6]
Mina *Rae Guest* a70 68
5 ch m Selkirk(USA) —Midnight Shift (IRE) (Night Shift (USA))
132[3]
Mina A Salem *C E Brittain* a96 81
5 b g Singspiel(IRE) —Amber Fizz (USA) (Effervescing (USA))
7591[0] 1268[4] 3650[8]
Minaash (USA) *D M Simcock* a81 80
3 b c Dixie Union(USA) —Metanoia (USA) (Seeking The Gold (USA))
113[6] 216[4] 4360[9] (4885) 5648[3] 6232[2] 6900[9]
Minar Salam (IRE) *F Poulsen* 72
3 b f Danehill Dancer(IRE) —Greek Moon (IRE) (Shirley Heights)
6889a[0]
Mind Alert *D Shaw* a59 41
6 b g Mind Games—Bombay Sapphire (Be My Chief (USA))
77[2] 225[2] 241[3] 337[3] 430[4] 448[14] 687[7] 723[2] 797[3] 866[3] 1753[9] 2664[10] 6809[11] 6887[11] 6925[7] 7014[4] 7276[5]
Mind How You Go (FR) *J R Best* a81 80
9 b g Hernando(FR) —Cos I Do (IRE) (Double Schwartz)
(640) 1148[5] 1654[6] 1793[7] 5256[6] 6131[4]
Mind That Fox *T Wall* a46 1
5 b g Mind Games—Foxie Lady (Wolfhound (USA))
33[10] 125[4] 201[5] 254[10] 441[7] 680[13] 1065[13] 1163[5] 2104[16] 5752[4] 6565[10] 6864[10] 6955[12] 7100
Mind The Style *W G M Turner* a74 78
3 b g Mind Games—Sioux Lady (Petong)
885[5] 1004[12] (1213) 1520[6] 1763[4] 2195[5] 3597[6] 4226[15]
Mine (IRE) *J D Bethell* 116
9 b h Primo Dominie—Ellebanna (Tina's Pet)
1791[9] (2396) 3098[6] 3505[12] 4119[8] 4747[4] 5412[6] 5797[17]
Mine Behind *J R Best* a77 92
7 b g Sheikh Albadou—Arapi (IRE) (Arazi (USA))
1601[11] 1619[11] 2494[10] 2688[3] 2882[14] 3911[14] 4122[23] 6406[2] 6826[6] 6946[6] 7073[4]
Mineral Rights (USA) *I Semple* a59 57
3 ch g Gulch(USA) —Long Vacation (IRE) (Thatching)
1964[10] 2829[4] 4931[7] 5476[11] 5982[2]
Mineral Star (IRE) *R Donohoe* a74 79
5 b g Monashee Mountain(USA) —Summit Talk (Head For Heights)
(3039) 4107[7] 4820[9] 5737[4] 6024[5] 6268[4] 6412[8] 7037a[8]
Mine'sasmallone (IRE) *D T Hughes* 75
4 b g Imperial Ballet(IRE) —Lakes Of Killarney (IRE) (Ahonoora)
4114a[2] (Dead)
Mine The Balance (IRE) *H J Manners* a66 48
4 b g Desert Style(IRE) —Dia (IRE) (Astronef)
131[12] 161[2] 292[6] 361[8] 497[2] 609[11] 732[9] 770[6] 866[5] 932[10] 1118[6] 1507[10] 1899[5] 2258[8] 2619[7] 3218[3] 3619[5] 3869[9] 4416[10]
Minewander (USA) *D Vance* a89
2 ch f Mineshaft(USA) —Wander Storm (USA) (Storm Bird (CAN))
5247a[3]
Ming Vase *P T Midgley* a51 55
5 b g Vettori(IRE) —Minstrel's Dance (CAN) (Pleasant Colony (USA))
789[6] 966[9] 1350[4] 1750[4] 2307[5] 2843[5] 3161[3] 3381[10] 3793[3] 4129[4] 4713[7] 5330[13] 5563[8] 6019[3]
Mini Mosa *J H M Gosden* a71 71
3 b f Indian Ridge—Baldemosa (FR) (Lead On Time (USA))
3881[8] 4575[2] 5013[10] 6546[3] 6623[9] 6901[4]
Minimum Fuss (IRE) *M C Chapman* a57 58
3 b f Second Empire(IRE) —Jamis (IRE) (Be My Guest (USA))
147[5] 713[9] 918[3] 1031[11] 1240[8] 2205[8] 2418[6] 2553[12] 3203[12] 4939[12] 5700[8] 6565[9] 7238[7]
Ministerofinterior *C F Wall*
2 b g Nayef(USA) —Maureen's Hope (USA) (Northern Baby (CAN))
5813[11]
Minjim *C E Brittain* a49 45
2 b c Kyllachy—Sarabah (IRE) (Ela-Mana-Mou)
5135[5] 5541[13]
Minkowski *J E Hammond* 99
4 b g Galileo(IRE) —Abitara (IRE) (Rainbow Quest (USA))
4722[4]
Minneapolis *A P O'Brien* a102 97
2 b c Sadler's Wells(USA) —Teggiano (IRE) (Mujtahid (USA))
3980a[4] 5458a[7] 6041a[8] 6161a[4]
Minnie Mill *B P J Baugh* a60 53
3 b f Mind Games—Sometime Never (IRE) (College Chapel)
69[5] 336[10] 1219[11] 1437[7] 4529[4] 5191[12] 5386[5] 5946[8] 6311[10]
Minnis Bay (CAN) *E F Vaughan* a84 81
3 b g Royal Academy(USA) —Aly's Daylite (USA) (Dayjur (USA))
2402[9] 3058[11] 3646[6] (4313) 4889[2] 5114[5] 5685[8]
Minnow *S C Williams* a71 50
3 b f Averti(IRE) —Tharwa (IRE) (Last Tycoon (IRE))
2508[11] 3886[7] 4314[6] 4536[10] 4885[6] 5420[4] 6174[5] 6428[2] 6528[7] 6927[6] 7003[8] 7082[3] 7265[7]
Minority Report *L M Cumani* 108
7 b g Rainbow Quest(USA) —Queen Sceptre (IRE) (Fairy King (USA))
1480[3] 2755[18] 4062[3] 4851[7] 5413[10] 5797[23] 6198[3] 6491[8]
Minos (IRE) *R Hannon* a54 80
3 ch c Grand Lodge(USA) —Miniver (IRE) (Mujtahid (USA))
5014[11] 5208[9] 5768[15] 6063[11] 6269[11]
Minshar *L M Cumani* 83
2 ch f Noverre(USA) —Reine De Neige (Kris)
3152[3] 3884[4] (6535)
Minstrel Flyer (IRE) *E J Creighton* 22
5 b m Brave Act—Miss Sabre (Sabrehill (USA))
1673[10] 2257[10] 3616[7] 4267[8] 5835[11]
Mint *D W Barker* 77
4 b m Bahamian Bounty—Tick Tack (Primo Dominie)
964[8] 1241[7] 1404[9] 4768[12] 5507[17] 5930[2]
Minted (FR) *A Fabre* 80
2 gr c Clodovil(IRE) —Mintly Fresh (USA) (Rubiano (USA))
5373a[7]
Mint Slewlep (USA) *W Robert Bailes* a93 89
3 b c Slew City Slew(USA) —Cry Me A River (USA) (Gilded Time (USA))
1882a[7]
Minus Fifteen (IRE) *K A Ryan* 73
2 ch c Trans Island—Bumble (Rainbow Quest (USA))
6295[8] 6755[2]
Minwir (IRE) *M A Jarvis* 68
2 b c Green Desert(USA) —Elshamms (Zafonic (USA))
4335[7] 4854[6] 5428[9] 5939[3]
Mi Odds *Mrs N Macauley* a42 4
11 b g Sure Blade(USA) —Vado Via (Ardross)
80[9] 242[8] 305[4] 464[12] 665[12] 1934[9] 3714[11]
Mio Fiore *M Blanshard* a45 35
2 b f Bertolini(USA) —Queenie (Indian Ridge)
4540[9] 5126[8] 5720[16] 6566[7]
Miracle Baby *A J Chamberlain* a37 43
5 b m Atraf—Musica (Primo Dominie)
106[10] 183[7]
Miracle Card (FR) *R Donohoe* 66
4 b m Green Tune(USA) —Poudriere (FR) (Trempolino (USA))
4114a[18]
Miracle Moment (USA) *B Tagg* 35
4 b m Chester House(USA) —Rejoyced (USA) (Relaunch (USA))
6790a[8]
Miracle Ridge (IRE) *Adrian McGuinness* a81 76
12 ch g Indian Ridge—Highly Delighted (USA) (Verbatim (USA))
(33) 41[4] 480[8]
Miracle Seeker *C G Cox* 80
2 br f Rainbow Quest(USA) —Miracle (Ezzoud (IRE))
5812[2] 6470[3]
Miraculous Miss (USA) *Steven B Klesaris* a111
4 ch m Mr Greeley(USA) —No Small Miracle (USA) (Silver Deputy (CAN))
6483a[2]
Miramare (GER) *B J Curley* a99
3 ch f Rainbow Quest(USA) —Minaccia (GER) (Platini (GER))
6645[4]
Miranda's Girl (IRE) *Thomas Cleary* 69
2 b f Titus Livius(FR) —Ela Tina (IRE) (Ela-Mana-Mou)
5516a[6]
Mirin *G Wragg* a65 83
3 b f Generous(IRE) —Musetta (IRE) (Cadeaux Genereux)
1024[7] (2970) 4203[6] 5594[3]
Mirjan (IRE) *L Lungo* 98
11 b g Tenby—Mirana (IRE) (Ela-Mana-Mou)
3898[3] 4375[8] (4893) 6181[5]
Mirko *B R Millman* a52 40
3 b c Dansili—Marithea (IRE) (Barathea (IRE))
3395[6] 3968[7] 4530[4] 5095[11]
Mirthful (USA) *B W Hills* 83
3 b f Miswaki(USA) —Musicanti (USA) (Nijinsky (CAN))
1127[6] 2308[3] (2981) (4332) 4779[3] 5197[5]
Misaine (IRE) *T J Etherington* a54 55
3 b g Fasliyev(USA) —Rose Paille (FR) (General Holme (USA))
1248[3] 2711[10] (Dead)
Misaro (GER) *R A Harris* a92 89
6 b g Acambaro(GER) —Misniniski (Niniski (USA))
318[2] 368[2] 463[5] 566[5] 1212[3] (1321) (1681) (1806) 2139[3] 2655[7] (3623) 3911[4] 3990[10] 4095[11] 4567[13] 5029[4] 5278[8] 5447[5] 5722[7] 6141[9]
Mis Chicaf (IRE) *D Carroll* a49 49
6 b m Prince Sabo—Champagne Season (USA) (Vaguely Noble)
4038[8] 4141[17] 4525[11] 4966[9] 5228[8] 5701[10] 5935[3] 6311[3] 6609[12]

Mischief Making (USA) *E A L Dunlop* a57
2 br f Lemon Drop Kid(USA) —Fraulein (Acatenango (GER))
6944[9]

Mise En Place *J Morrison* 67
6 b m Dr Fong(USA) —Oleana (IRE) (Alzao (USA))
1760a[3]

Mis Fancy That (IRE) *W P Mullins* 59
2 bb f Trans Island—Mega Tassa (IRE) (Foxhound (USA))
5516a[9]

Misima Sunrise (IRE) *Timothy Doyle* 60
5 b m Tagula(IRE) —Marmaga (IRE) (Shernazar)
5460a[26]

Misk Hills *P T Midgley* a8 7
2 b g Warningford—Classical Jazz (FR) (Celtic Swing)
1858[12] 2838[6] *3065[10]*

Misphire *M Dods* 84
4 b m Mister Baileys—Bombay Sapphire (Be My Chief (USA))
957[12] 1940[5] 2085[3] 2744[17] (2870) 3158[3] 3784[5] 5954[3] 6205[10]

Misplaced Fortune *N Tinkler* 65
2 b f Compton Place—Tide Of Fortune (Soviet Star (USA))
2904[6] 4125[5] 4818[4] 5143[3] 5745[12] 6254[3]

Missabeat (IRE) *T D Easterby* 36
2 b f Distant Music(USA) —Dear Catch (IRE) (Bluebird (USA))
2364[10] 2904[12] 4076[13]

Miss Admiral *S R Bowring*
3 ch f Compton Admiral—Frisky Miss (IRE) (Fayruz)
1261[7]

Miss Andretti (AUS) *Lee Freedman* 125
6 b m Ihtiram(IRE) —Peggie's Bid (AUS) (Marooned)
(2733) 2857[15] 7089a[10]

Miss Annaleo (IRE) *I Bugattella* 101
3 b f Alzao(USA) —Monkey Business (Warning)
1701a[2] 2707a[U] 6524a[12]

Miss Antropist (IRE) *R A Harris* a43 46
2 b f Fath(USA) —Perfect Welcome (Taufan (USA))
883[6] 971[5] *1728[5]* 2078[3] 2310[3] *2517[10]* *3065[7]*

Miss Beatrix (IRE) *Kevin Prendergast* 109
3 b f Danehill Dancer(IRE) —Miss Beabea (IRE) (Catrail (USA))
1496[18]

Miss Bootylishes *A B Haynes* 85
2 b f Mujahid(USA) —Moxby (Efisio)
(2961) 3550[4] 3734[3] 4819[5] 5322[7] 5597[7] 6498[5]

Miss Bouggy Wouggy *M Blanshard* a60 40
2 b f Tobougg(IRE) —Polly Golightly (Weldnaas (USA))
2039[10] 3446[12] 5811[9] *6289[5]* *6626[2]* *6934[5]* *7022[6]*

Miss Bronte *R Hollinshead* a60 23
2 b f Ishiguru(USA) —Gemtastic (Tagula (IRE))
4020[4] 4522[10]

Miss Brush *J R Fanshawe* a45 57
4 b m Foxhound(USA) —Tattinger (Prince Sabo)
7279[10]

Miss Capricorn *K A Ryan* 38
3 b f Forzando—Miss Flirtatious (Piccolo)
1403[7] 2205[6] 2895[7]

Miss Chatty (ARG) *H J Brown* a90 92
4 ch m Halo Sunshine(USA) —Pomme D'Or (ARG) (Fort De France (ARG))
476a[5] *647a[5]*

Miss Clem's (FR) *P Bary* 96
4 b m Barathea(IRE) —Erinys (FR) (Kendor (FR))
5150a[7]

Miss Cruisecontrol *J R Best* a27 42
2 b f Hernando(FR) —Wenda (IRE) (Priolo (USA))
3643[13] 3874[13] 4547[10]

Miss Daawe *B Ellison* 60
3 b f Daawe(USA) —Feiticeira (USA) (Deposit Ticket (USA))
996[6] 1136[6] 1639[15] 3054[5] 3342[5] 4008[3] 4224[4] 4525[3] 4773[3] 5295[3] 5576[2] 5908[4]

Miss Deeds (IRE) *N P Littmoden* 34
2 b f Invincible Spirit(IRE) —Aseelah (Nashwan (USA))
2812[18] 3200[12] 4810[9] 5252[11]

Miss Delila (USA) *K A Ryan* 53
2 bb f Malibu Moon(USA) —Staraway (USA) (Star De Naskra (USA))
3706[15] 4169[8]

Miss Donovan *Patrick J Moloney* 97
4 b m Royal Applause—Cumbrian Melody (Petong)
3573a[14] 6954a[11]

Miss Emma May (IRE) *D R C Elsworth* 80
2 b f Hawk Wing(USA) —For Example (USA) (Northern Baby (CAN))
1814[4] 2365[2] 2812[8] 4402[4] 4774[4] 5353[12] 5882[2] (6411)

Miss Fancy Pants *Noel Meade* a62 61
3 gr f Act One—Sweetness Herself (Unfuwain (USA))
4035a[12]

Miss Firefly *M R Channon* 70
2 b f Compton Place—Popocatepetl (FR) (Nashwan (USA))
1993[3] 2447[2] 2869[6] 4121[4] 4364[9] 4755[5] 5167[3] 5322[16] 5705[8]

Miss Gibraltar *L M Cumani*
3 b f Rock Of Gibraltar(IRE) —Photogenic (Midyan (USA))
2542[10]

Miss Glory Be *C J Down* a56 39
9 b m Glory Of Dancer—Miss Blondie (USA) (Stop The Music (USA))
266[12] *517[6]* 5187[12] 5886[14]

Miss Gorica (IRE) *Ms Joanna Morgan* a96 96
3 b f Mull Of Kintyre(USA) —Allegorica (IRE) (Alzao (USA))
2757[12] 5242a[3] *5761a[2]*

Miss Habershon *A King* 63
3 b f Baryshnikov(AUS) —Mighty Squaw (Indian Ridge)
4549[4] 5005[6] 5384[7] 5859[8] 6060[6]

Miss Havisham (IRE) *J R Weymes* a39 56
3 b f Josr Algarhoud(IRE) —Agony Aunt (Formidable (USA))
893[13] 1968[7] 2709[4] (3040) 3587[9] (4156) 4582[12] *5388[10]* 5676[13]

Miss Highjinks (USA) *E J O'Neill* a93 79
4 ch m Stravinsky(USA) —Ready For Action (USA) (Riverman (USA))
31a[14]

Miss Holderness *J O'Reilly* 29
2 ch f Millkom—Miles (Selkirk (USA))
4487[13] 5485[7] 5702[9]

Miss Holly *D Carroll* a69 36
8 b m Makbul—Seraphim (FR) (Lashkari)
12[2] *(146)* *302[4]* *389[3]* *585[12]*

Miss Hoolie *W G M Turner* a28 39
3 b f Danehill Dancer(IRE) —Silky Dawn (IRE) (Night Shift (USA))
7159[6] *7239[7]*

Missie Baileys *Mrs L J Mongan* a63 63
5 ch m Mister Baileys—Jilly Woo (Environment Friend)
634[3] *767[7]* 982[2] *1342[5]* *1730[6]* *1951[6]* 2140[3] (2511) *2800[4]* *3397[6]* 4267[2] 5187[9] *5421[5]* *6265[10]* 6452[8] *6971[5]* *7069[3]*

Miss Imperious *B Smart* a48 49
4 b m Imperial Ballet(IRE) —Birthday Belle (Lycius (USA))
138[8]

Miss Invincible *Mrs A L M King* a48 43
3 b f Invincible Spirit(IRE) —Zagaleta (Sri Pekan (USA))
689[7] *864[6]* 2360[8] *3732[4]* 4292[3] *5754[11]*

Mission Apollo (FR) *J-L Pelletan* 71
3 b c Lomitas—Lune Rouge (IRE) (Unfuwain (USA))
2503a[13]

Mission Approved (USA) *G Contessa* 109
3 b c With Approval(CAN) —Fortunate Find (USA) (Fortunate Prospect (USA))
5853a[5]

Mission Control (IRE) *J R Boyle* a61
2 ch c Dubai Destination(USA) —Stage Manner (In The Wings)
5780[7] *(7286)*

Missioner (USA) *M Johnston* 80
2 b c Rahy(USA) —Magic Mission (Machiavellian (USA))
3896[3] 4151[3]

Mission Impossible *P C Haslam* a70 73
2 gr g Kyllachy—Eastern Lyric (Petong)
1087[2] 1792[4] 2371[3] 3838[5] 6052[12] 6328[8] *6813[2]* *(7129)* *7210[4]*

Mission Man *M G Rimell* a61 83
6 b g Revoque(IRE) —Opopmil (IRE) (Pips Pride)
110[11] *300[6]* *468[10]* (Dead)

Mission To Mars *P G Murphy* a79 40
8 b g Muhtarram(USA) —Ideal Candidate (Celestial Storm (USA))
57[6] *488[12]* *587[8]* *662[11]* (Dead)

Miss Ippolita *J R Jenkins* a65 78
3 b f Diktat—Isabella D'Este (IRE) (Irish River (FR))
1610[12] 2060[4] *2570[6]* 3038[2] 3278[2] 3688[10] 4574[13] 6621[6]

Missisipi Star (IRE) *I Mohammed* 98
4 b m Mujahid(USA) —Kicka (Shirley Heights)
250a[2]

Missit (IRE) *M R Channon* 104
2 b f Orpen(USA) —High Spot (Shirley Heights)
1101[2] (5313) 5973[5] 6336[2] 6498[2]

Miss Jenny (IRE) *B J Meehan* a79 83
3 b f Desert Prince(IRE) —Please Believe Me (Try My Best (USA))
2369[7] 3430[19] *4462[11]*

Miss Jolyon (USA) *M A Jarvis* a64 62
2 b f Johannesburg(USA) —Konvincha (USA) (Cormorant (USA))
4454[9] 5063[4] *5682[2]* 6233[11]

Miss Kin (IRE) *T J Pitt* 21
2 b f Kris Kin(USA) —Pipewell (IRE) (Lake Coniston (IRE))
1193[12] 1285[15]

Misskinta (IRE) *M J Grassick* 82
4 b m Desert Sun—Darabaka (IRE) (Doyoun)
2018a[3]

Miss Ladybird (USA) *T J Etherington* a16 23
6 bb m Labeeb—Bird Dance (USA) (Storm Bird (CAN))
124[13] *616[14]*

Miss Latina (IRE) *P J Prendergast* 71
4 b m Mozart(IRE) —Tidal Reach (USA) (Kris S (USA))
4836a[13]

Miss Lightning *R Bastiman* a6 35
4 b m Mujahid(USA) —Salu (Ardross)
1045[15] *1716[10]* 2376[5] 2839[7]

Miss Lorella (IRE) *L Camici* 84
4 b m Orpen(USA) —Lodema (IRE) (Lycius (USA))
6688a[16]

Miss Lovat *W M Brisbourne* a37 45
4 b m Wizard King—Cantina (Tina's Pet)
1360[10] 1596[16] *2257[7]* 2760[10] 4249[6] 4426[6] 4920[5] 5487[10]

Miss Lucifer (FR) *B W Hills* 118
3 b f Noverre(USA) —Devil's Imp (IRE) (Cadeaux Genereux)
1500[2] 2040[2] 4093[4] 4420[2] 5163[2] 5355[2] (5799) (6332)

Miss Macy Sue (USA) *Kelly Von Hemel* a110
4 bb m Trippi(USA) —Yada Yada (USA) (Great Above (USA))
6483a[3]

Miss Marvellous (USA) *J R Fanshawe* a37 73
3 ch f Diesis—Sue Warner (USA) (Forli (ARG))
1408[8] (3244) 3871[6] 5067[4]

Miss Maximus (IRE) *C A Murphy* 76
3 bb f Golan(IRE) —Lady Lucre (IRE) (Last Tycoon (IRE))
4240a[4]

Miss Modesty (IRE) *Paul Magnier* 71
4 ch m Monashee Mountain(USA) —Truly Modest (IRE) (Imp Society (USA))
873a[18]

Miss Monica (IRE) *P W Hiatt* a56 50
6 ch m Grand Lodge(USA) —Bea's Ruby (IRE) (Fairy King (USA))
402[9] *495[2]* *558[3]* *651[5]*

Miss Mozart *H Morrison* 55
2 b f Bahamian Bounty—Papillon De Bronze (IRE) (Marju (IRE))
4662[12] 5110[11]

Miss Mujahid Times *A D Brown* a57 57
4 b m Mujahid(USA) —Stealthy Times (Timeless Times (USA))
1384[2] 1596[17] *1902[9]* 2553[13] 3180[11] 3814[9] *4741[2]* *5566[4]* *6390[11]* *6609[9]*

Miss Mujanna *J Akehurst* a69
2 b f Mujahid(USA) —Robanna (Robellino (USA))
6964[3] *7190[2]* *7266[2]*

Miss Odd Sox *W M Brisbourne* a59
4 ch m Primo Valentino(IRE) —Dam Certain (IRE) (Damister (USA))
805[6]

Miss Okaloosa *D M Simcock* a56 4
2 b f Hawk Wing(USA) —Shalimar (IRE) (Indian Ridge)
5116[12] 5811[10] *6601[7]*

Miss Olivia *P W Chapple-Hyam* 51
2 ch f Dr Fong(USA) —Beleaguer (Rainbow Quest (USA))
4293[7] 4924[9] 5252[6]

Missoula (IRE) *M H Tompkins* 90
4 b m Kalanisi(IRE) —Medway (IRE) (Shernazar)
1288[8] 1771[8] 2987[14] 4288[6] 5256[2] (5404) 5857[4] (6181)

Missouri (USA) *M A Barnes* a50 46
4 b g Gulch(USA) —Coco (USA) (Storm Bird (CAN))
278[9] 1559[8] 3815[13] 4772[8] 5087[11]

Miss Percy *R A Fahey* 59
3 b f Mark Of Esteem(IRE) —Anabaa's Music (Anabaa (USA))
2133[15] 3159[9] 3765[5] 4128[6] 4735[4] 5084[10]

Miss Phoebe (IRE) *S Kirk* a69 58
2 b f Catcher In The Rye(IRE) —Stroke Of Six (IRE) (Woodborough (USA))
5868[7] *6119[5]* *6503[7]* *7031[3]* *7114[6]* *(7258)*

Miss Poland *J G Given*
3 b f Polish Precedent(USA) —Robellino Miss (USA) (Robellino (USA))
1863[13]

Miss Poppy *P R Chamings* a66 69
2 b f Averti(IRE) —Pretty Poppy (Song)
5110[9] 5856[3] *6225[6]* *6386[8]*

Miss Porcia *P A Blockley* a58 60
6 ch m Inchinor—Krista (Kris)
3868[3] 3965[6] *4464[4]* 4663[4] 4966[2] 4998[13] *5310[11]* *6096[12]*

Miss Redactive *M D I Usher* a43 50
4 b m Whittingham(IRE) —Gold And Blue (IRE) (Bluebird (USA))
20[9] *125[7]* *145[10]* *272[4]* *310[9]* *549[11]* *571[9]*

Miss Red Eye (IRE) *Luke Comer* 71
2 b f On The Ridge(IRE) —Wayne's Gal (IRE) (Karaar)
5073a[9]

Miss Rochester (IRE) *Sir Michael Stoute* 58
2 b f Montjeu(IRE) —Pilgrim's Way (USA) (Gone West (USA))
4774[11]

Miss Saafend Plaza (IRE) *R Hannon* a76 79
3 b f Danetime(IRE) —Coup De Coeur (IRE) (Kahyasi)
58[2] *591[5]* *611[2]* *884[3]* 1355[11] 2475[5] 2940[7]

Miss Salvador (FR) *S Wattel* a97 108
4 ro m Smadoun(FR) —Miss Recif (IRE) (Exit To Nowhere (USA))
663a[10] 5719a[5] 6376a[5] *7128a[5]*

Miss Shop (USA) *H A Jerkens* a114 106
4 b m Deputy Minister(CAN) —Shopping (USA) (Private Account (USA))
5854a[6]

Miss Silver Spurs *M D I Usher* a38 38
3 gr f Mujahid(USA) —Wakeful Night (FR) (Linamix (FR))
720[8] 3274[10] 3490[9]

Miss Skycat (USA) *T D Barron* 49
2 rg f Tale Of The Cat(USA) —Gigi's Skyflyer (USA) (Skywalker (USA))
2983[7] 4422[7] 5483[10]

Miss Solo *P C Haslam* a46 54
2 bb f Intikhab(USA) —American Rouge (IRE) (Grand Lodge (USA))
3092[4] 3718[7] *6793[5]* *6865[8]*

Miss Spirit (IRE) *Michael Mulvany* a15 57
4 b m King Charlemagne(USA) —Joyfullness (USA) (Dixieland Band (USA))
873a[7] *6288[13]*

Miss St Albans *G C H Chung* 26
6 b m Robellino(USA) —Alieria (IRE) (Lomond (USA))
6858[11]

Miss Sudbrook (IRE) *A W Carroll* a49 27
5 ch m Daggers Drawn(USA) —Missed Opportunity (IRE) (Exhibitioner)
18[3] *84[8]* *187[12]* *341[6]* *497[11]* 1002[12] *1068[13]*

Miss Sultin (IRE) *B Grizzetti* 93
3 b f Celtic Swing—Miss Caerleon (Caerleon (USA))
2070a[6] 2707a[9]

Miss Sunshine *J S Goldie* 46
2 b f Piccolo—Rhinefield Beauty (IRE) (Shalford (IRE))
3341[11] 3582[13] 3781[7] 5484[7] 6306[8]

Miss Sure Bond (IRE) *G R Oldroyd* a57 65
4 ch m Danehill Dancer(IRE) —Desert Rose (Green Desert (USA))
2256[12] 3752[6] 4802[4] 5086[6] *5366[3]* *5890[10]* 6558[13] *6906[12]*

Miss Taboo (IRE) *P T Midgley* a22 53
3 b f Tobougg(IRE) —Miss Croisette (Hernando (FR))
1135[3] 1679[2] 2032[4] 2894[2] 3342[11] 3639[2] 4178[2] 5284[13] 5625[4] *5946[13]*

Miss The Boat *A Lund* 98
5 b m Mtoto—Missed Again (High Top)
5263a[7]

Miss Tilen *V Smith* 44
2 ch f Tipsy Creek(USA) —Ashleen (Chilibang)
845[F] 972[6] 1235[2] 2115[6] 2271[5]

Miss Una (IRE) *Patrick Martin* a49 76
5 b m Spectrum(IRE) —Fer De Lance (IRE) (Diesis)
4836a[12]

Missus Molly Brown *R A Fahey* a44 51
3 b f Mind Games—Prim N Proper (Tragic Role (USA))
106[5] *375[6]* *567[9]* *910[3]* 1432[6] 1943[3] 2300[2] 2844[7] 3752[4] (4224) 4706[10] 5627[6] 5935[14]

Miss Versatile (IRE) *J S Moore* 93
2 b f Alhaarth(IRE) —Liberi Versi (IRE) (Last Tycoon (IRE))
1354[2] 2468[3] 2812[10] 3269[3]

Missvinski (USA) *J-C Rouget* a103 116
3 b f Stravinsky(USA) —Miss U Fran (USA) (Brocco (USA))
1055a[2] 2814[5] 4010a[2] 5248a[7]

Miss Wedge *Tom Dascombe* a63 63
4 b m Fraam—Tough Nell (IRE) (Archway (IRE))
1534[6] *1947[7]*

Miss Willoughby *J Ryan* a48 48
2 b f First Trump—Jeanette Romee (Victory Note (USA))
971[3] 1156[5] 1235[6] *1975[6]* 2188[4] *2517[3]* (2605) 2838[3] *3065[3]* 3246[3] 3626[4] *3923[11]* 4027[7] *4359[5]* *5015[10]* 5081[7] 5571[11] 6591[11]

Miss Wolf *G H Jones* a27 23
7 b m Wolfhound(USA) —Jussoli (Don)
537[8] *769[10]* *936[8]* 3549[12] 4961[7] *5982[11]*

Mist And Stone (IRE) *G M Lyons* a88 94
4 b m Xaar—Daunting Lady (IRE) (Mujadil (USA))
3140a[20] 5394a[2] 5841a[4] 6363a[5]

Mista Rossa *H Morrison* 62
2 br c Red Ransom(USA) —Cloud Hill (Danehill (USA))
5919[12] 6130[10] 6417[7]

Mistblack *B P J Baugh*
7 b m Wizard King—Dear Heart (Blakeney)
4989[8]

Mister Always *I W McInnes* a57 51
3 b g Titus Livius(FR) —Pieta (IRE) (Perugino (USA))
25[10] *202[3]* 4224[3] *4742[11]* 4842[7] *5564[4]* *6886[3]* *6950[8]* *7107[4]* *(7250)*

Mister Arjay (USA) *B Ellison* a60 81
7 b g Mister Baileys—Crystal Stepper (USA) (Fred Astaire (USA))
(1239) 1457[4] 1794[4] 2026[4] (2095) 2465[2] *3112[7]* 3412[9] 4490[3] 4893[6] (5256) 5839[8] 6473[12]

Mister Beano (IRE) *R J Price* a59 59
2 b g Mull Of Kintyre(USA) —Subtle Move (USA) (Known Fact (USA))
2041[13] 2832[12] 3246[2] *5096[5]* *5751[10]* *6426[5]* *6693[2]* *6958[2]* *7152[5]* *7245[6]*

Mister Becks (IRE) *M C Chapman* a29 49
4 b g Beckett(IRE) —Cappuchino (IRE) (Roi Danzig (USA))
145[7] *225[5]* *320[11]* *504[11]*

Mister Benedictine *B W Duke* a78 81
4 b g Mister Baileys—Cultural Role (Night Shift (USA))
191[8] *314[6]* 4577[2] 5001[7]

Mister Benji *B P J Baugh* a63 53
8 b g Catrail(USA) —Katy-Q (IRE) (Taufan (USA))
7[5] *80[3]* *(479)* *570[7]* *686[8]* *806[5]* *2225[10]* *3172[4]* 3534[7] *3922[10]* *7169[5]* *7250[5]*

Mister Cafnex (IRE) *B W Duke* a30 46
2 b c Royal Applause—Makelovelast (IRE) (Darshaan)
999[12] *1586[8]* 1781[15] 4683[8] 5268[13] 6051[U] *6775[9]* *7101[8]*

Mister Castlefield (IRE) *Mrs A M O'Shea* 58
3 gr g Mujahid(USA) —Woodland Garden (Godswalk (USA))
1185a[8] 6055[10]

Mister Christie *J G Given* a49 65
2 b g Auction House(USA) —Dazzling Quintet (Superlative)
3024[8] 3341[4] (3788) 4193[8] *6872[8]*

Mister Completely (IRE) *Ms J S Doyle* a76 70
6 b g Princely Heir(IRE) —Blue Goose (Belmez (USA))
(16) *159[3]* *354[12]* 1152[3] *(2222)* *2770[2]* *2996[10]* 3279[5] *3598[11]* (3653) *4067[5]* 4322[2] *(4463)* 4576[6] 4906[3] 5138[2] 5404[5] 5884[8] 6131[2] *6356[3]* 6473[9] 6622[7] *7178[5]*

Mister Conway (FR) *P Van De Poele* 113
6 b h Exit To Nowhere(USA) —Cordial Lady (USA) (The Minstrel (CAN))
663a[8] 1571a[2] (2330a)

Mister Des Aigles (FR) *Mme C Barande-Barbe* 92
4 b g Sendawar(IRE) —Baliyna (USA) (Woodman (USA))
6923a[4]

Mister Elegant *J L Spearing* a64 61
5 b g Fraam—Risky Valentine (Risk Me (FR))
131[4] *485[11]* *556[8]* *729[10]* *920[U]* *4021[3]* 4853[5] 5090[12] *5897[2]* *6264[3]* *6718[6]* *6779[11]* *6891[5]* *7020[4]* *(7108)* *7209[3]*

Mister Fips (IRE) *Jane Chapple-Hyam* a83 88
2 b c Chevalier(IRE) —Blue Holly (IRE) (Blues Traveller (IRE))
1652[7] 2056[6] 2333[2] 2737[9] 4335[2] (4636) 5410[8] *6004[3]*

Mister Fizzbomb (IRE) *J S Wainwright* a62 62
4 b g Lend A Hand—Crocus (IRE) (Mister Baileys)
2537[7] 3204[13] 5487[2] (5698) 6056[7] (6325) *7056[4]*

Mister Hardy *R A Fahey* 93
2 b c Kyllachy—Balladonia (Primo Dominie)
(845) (1043) 2232[11] 3938[3] 4743[5] 5324[9] 6017[5] 6182[7]

Mister Incredible *J M Bradley* a61 57
4 b g Wizard King—Judiam (Primo Dominie)
86[9] 252[8] 303[3] (374) (504) 622[10] 710[5] 1028[6] 1349[2] 1753[3] 2108[10] 2664[5] (2791) 3163[4] 3368[13] 3498[8]

Misterisland (IRE) *J A Osborne* 52
2 b c Spectrum(IRE) —Carranita (IRE) (Anita's Prince)
4733[8]

Mister Jingles *R M Whitaker* a50 67
4 ch g Desert Story(IRE) —Fairy Free (Rousillon (USA))
1594[12] 1976[3] 2343[3] 3286[6] 3381[12] (3814) (4223) 4479[3] (4797) 5563[9] 5966[12] 6463[9]

Mister Maq *A Crook* a54 64
4 b g Namaqualand(USA) —Nordico Princess (Nordico (USA))
80[10] 271[3] 402[5] 997[8] 2091[6] 2709[8] 3257[4] 3789[9] 4082[11] 5698[10]

Mister Marmaduke *D A Nolan* 46
6 b g Marju(IRE) —Lalique (IRE) (Lahib (USA))
1492[11] 2244[12] 2461[13] 3184[8] 3374[9] 3498[11] 3814[13] 5969[7]

Mister Minister (GER) *C Von Der Recke* 79
2 ch c Artan(IRE) —Misniniski (Niniski (USA))
6324a[5]

Mister Minty (IRE) *Mrs S Lamyman* 54
5 b g Fasliyev(USA) —Sorb Apple (IRE) (Kris)
1013[11] 1259[4] 1579[12] 2023[10] 3257[9]

Mister New York (USA) *Noel T Chance* a61
2 b c Forest Wildcat(USA) —Shebane (USA) (Alysheba (USA))
6897[10] 7015[4] 7266[4]

Mister Pete (IRE) *W Storey* 52
4 b g Piccolo—Whistfilly (First Trump)
1301[4] 5737[9] 6304[4] 6732[8]

Mister Right (IRE) *D J S Ffrench Davis* a82 83
6 ch g Barathea(IRE) —Broken Spirit (IRE) (Slip Anchor)
693[2] 1148[11] 1959[12] 4667[7] (5211) 5415[4]

Mister Troubridge *J A Geake* a43
5 ch g Mister Baileys—So True (So Blessed)
6069[5]

Mistral Sky *Stef Liddiard* a74 71
8 b g Hurricane Sky(AUS) —Dusk In Daytona (Beveled (USA))
91[5] 132[2] 234[9] 276[3] 361[9] 513[4] 536[3] 609[4] 621[9] 673[8] 766[2] 1226[2] 1382[9] 1899[4] (2220) 2334[9] 2576[4] 2799[3] 2947[5] 3064[9] 3735[3] 4021[2] 4075[3] 5016[8] 5778[3] (6101) 6671[10] 6747[3] 6869[5]

Mistress Bailey (IRE) *Nicholas Cox* a54 97
4 b m Mister Baileys—Carson Dancer (USA) (Carson City (USA))
1649[13] 1751[8] 3578a[8]

Mistress Cooper *W J Musson* 69
2 bb f Kyllachy—Litewska (IRE) (Mujadil (USA))
2630[7] 3589[5] 4016[6] 4484[6] 4903[2] 5167[2] (5534)

Mistress Eva *P Winkworth* 71
2 b f Diktat—Foreign Mistress (Darshaan)
(4709) 5883[6]

Mistress Greeley (USA) *Sir Michael Stoute* 82
2 ch f Mr Greeley(USA) —My Reem (USA) (Chief's Crown (USA))
(4102) 4804[6]

Mistress Rio (IRE) *J G Given* 18
2 ch f Captain Rio—Bu Hagab (IRE) (Royal Academy (USA))
4102[12] 4611[11]

Misty Dancer *Miss Venetia Williams* 97
8 gr g Vettori(IRE) —Light Fantastic (Deploy)
1542[4] 2236[2] (2861) 3989[4] 4388[3] 5215[15]

Misu Bond (IRE) *B Smart* 114
4 b h Danehill Dancer(IRE) —Hawala (IRE) (Warning)
3088[6] 3529[4] 4045[12]

Miswadah (IRE) *Kevin F O'Donnell* a63 58
4 b m Machiavellian(USA) —Khulan (USA) (Bahri (USA))
(796) 1212[12] 1946[5] 2324a[11]

Mitanni (USA) *Mrs A J Perrett* a61 72
4 b g Lear Fan(USA) —Maria Dolores (USA) (Prized (USA))
2514[4] 3042[4] 3711[3] 3965[8]

Mith Hill *Ian Williams* 84
6 b g Daylami(IRE) —Delirious Moment (IRE) (Kris)
1654[4] 2860[7]

Mixing *J Akehurst* a57 65
5 gr g Linamix(FR) —Tuning (Rainbow Quest (USA))
1612[9] 2214[13] 3799[11] (6453) 6719[4] 6832[2] 6969[2] 7256[7]

Mix N Match *R M Stronge* a42 57
3 b c Royal Applause—South Wind (Tina's Pet)
1403[8] 1913[7] 2173[8] 2796[4] 4287[6] 4532[17]

Miyasaki (CHI) *Rune Haugen* a66 94
5 bb h Memo(CHI) —Cantame Al Oido (CHI) (Yendaka (USA))
1648a[9] 5588[3] 6071a[14] 6370a[13]

Mizooka *R M Beckett* 74
2 b f Tobougg(IRE) —Tetravella (IRE) (Groom Dancer (USA))
2122[5] 2658[5] 3866[3] (4501) 5002[2] 5613[11]

Mizzle (USA) *M Johnston* a61 61
3 ch f Rahy(USA) —Loving Claim (USA) (Hansel (USA))
569[4] 661[2] 834[8] 1068[11]

Mo (USA) *R A Kvisla* a70 69
3 br c Cherokee Run(USA) —Mambo Mate (USA) (Kingmambo (USA))
2079[8] 2548a[7]

Moayed *N P Littmoden* a95 85
8 b g Selkirk(USA) —Song Of Years (IRE) (Shareef Dancer (USA))
198[8] 550[7] 658[7] 759[5] 828[4] 1223[9] 1448[11] 4134[7] 4515[8] 4949[10] 5312[7]

Mocha Java *B G Powell* a43 74
4 b g Bertolini(USA) —Coffee Cream (Common Grounds)
461[12] 5001[14] 5275[13] 6809[14]

Mo Cheoil Thu (IRE) *Desmond McDonogh* a72 74
3 b f In The Wings—Amizette (USA) (Forty Niner (USA))
4865a[3]

Mo Chroi *J J Bridger* a32
4 ch m Observatory(USA) —Away To Me (Exit To Nowhere (USA))
349[12] 455[7] 500[10] 869[10]

Mo Cuishle (USA) *B Tagg* a115
4 bb m Saint Ballado(CAN) —Officiate (USA) (Deputy Minister (CAN))
5854a[5]

Modarab *Mrs L B Normile* 61
5 b g Barathea(IRE) —Jathaabeh (Nashwan (USA))
1529[3] 1998[8] 2253[10] 2824[6] 5553[10]

Modeeroch (IRE) *J S Bolger* 109
4 gr m Mozart(IRE) —Majinskaya (FR) (Marignan (USA))
1548a[2] 2053a[3] 2586a[2] 3222a[3] 5241a[6]

Modern Look *D Smaga* 107
2 b f Zamindar(USA) —Prophecy (IRE) (Warning)
(6630a)

Modern Practice (IRE) *Miss V Haigh* a51
2 br c Modigliani(USA) —Practice (USA) (Diesis)
7246[4]

Modern Verse (USA) *G A Swinbank* a64 59
4 b g Pleasant Tap(USA) —Sandalwood (USA) (El Gran Senor (USA))
670[4] 758[6] 916[3] 1491[4] 2149[5] 2714[8]

Modhana (IRE) *M G Quinlan*
2 bb f Modigliani(USA) —Stridhana (Indian Ridge)
3874[14]

Mofarij *Saeed Bin Suroor* a92 95
3 ch c Bering—Pastorale (Nureyev (USA))
(595a) 1544[4] 2212[6] 6606[7]

Mogok Ruby *L Montague Hall* a76 71
3 gr g Bertolini(USA) —Days Of Grace (Wolfhound (USA))
6708[5] 6829[4] 6976[3] 7221[4]

Mohandas (FR) *W Hefter* 110
6 b h Lomitas—Mille Espoir (FR) (Mille Balles (FR))
1872a[5] 3665a[8] 6045a[7]

Moheebb (IRE) *D W Chapman* a63 78
3 b g Machiavellian(USA) —Rockerlong (Deploy)
3302[2] 3382[7] 3786[5] 4137[11] 4480[2] (4704) 5046[7] 5177[5] 5367[7] (5703) (5936) 6465[11] 6738[7] 7200[4]

Moi Non Plus *B Grizzetti* 101
3 b f Singspiel(IRE) —Di Moi Oui (Warning)
2070a[2] 2707a[2] 4055a[P]

Moksi *P W Chapple-Hyam* 54
2 b c Olden Times—Yasalam (IRE) (Fairy King (USA))
5872[6]

Molly Ann (IRE) *T D Easterby* a67 52
2 b f Medicean—Molly Mello (GER) (Big Shuffle (USA))
6470[17] 6724[10] 6903[2] 7140[2] 7288[2]

Mollyatti *Miss V Haigh* a72 66
2 b f Medicean—Tolyatti (Green Desert (USA))
4564[7] 4784[11] 5202[4] 5496[3] 5692[8]

Molly Max (GER) *Frau K Haustein* 108
3 ch c Big Shuffle(USA) —Molly Dancer (GER) (Shareef Dancer (USA))
1516a[2] 6370a[11] 6691a[5]

Moluccella *H Morrison* a48
2 b f Marju(IRE) —Pine Needle (Kris)
6601[9] 6857[7]

Momaha *J M Bradley*
3 b g Dinar(USA) —Virginia Stock (Swing Easy (USA))
7001[13]

Moment Of Clarity *R C Guest* a72 57
5 b g Lujain(USA) —Kicka (Shirley Heights)
2531[10] 3155[8] 3403[3] 3722[5] 4424[4] 4802[2] 5300[7] 5557[4] 5750[5] 6380[5] (6937) (7056) 7146[2]

Moment's Notice *S Kirk* a77 61
2 ch g Beat Hollow—Figlette (Darshaan)
4709[4] 5116[3] 5707[4] 5901[7] 6578[3] (6750)

Momix *B Grizzetti* 89
4 b m Selkirk(USA) —Savignano (Polish Precedent (USA))
2295a[8]

Monaazalah (IRE) *B W Hills* a78 80
2 b f Green Desert(USA) —Karamah (Unfuwain (USA))
(2039) 2756[15] 3508[8] 4152[12] 6588[5]

Monachello (USA) *Mrs A J Perrett* a58 77
3 b g Lemon Drop Kid(USA) —Antoniette (USA) (Nicholas (USA))
1467[5] 1810[9] 2426[7] 3629[4]

Monachesi (IRE) *F & L Camici* 115
4 b h Key Of Luck(USA) —O'Keefe (IRE) (Be My Guest (USA))
4520a[0] 6689a[2]

Monadreen Flyer (IRE) *Daniel Mark Loughnane* a76 79
2 b g Atraf—First Kiss (GER) (Night Shift (USA))
4769[4]

Monashee (USA) *L Tracy McCarthy* a109
5 gr m Wolf Power(SAF) —Avide (USA) (Wall Street Dancer (USA))
6772a[8]

Monashee Brave (IRE) *R A Harris* a63 78
4 b g Monashee Mountain(USA) —Miss Butterfield (Cure The Blues (USA))
79[12] 269[7] 1299[2] 1574[13] 2744[15] 3298[5] 3836[5] 4289[8] 4800[13] 5476[7] 5908[6] 6287[2] (6730) 7011[6] 7094[5] (7209)

Monasheemini (IRE) *Mrs N Macauley*
4 gr m Monashee Mountain(USA) —Ivory's Promise (Pursuit Of Love)
4795[10]

Monashee Prince (IRE) *J R Best* a69 69
5 ch g Monashee Mountain(USA) —Lodema (IRE) (Lycius (USA))
130[13] 158[5] 3667[4] 4083[12] 5576[10] 5897[4] (6210) 6415[5] 6717[8] (6818) 6870[6] 7183[8]

Monashee River (IRE) *Miss V Haigh* a58 54
4 b m Monashee Mountain(USA) —Dixie Jazz (Mtoto)
733[10] 812[11] (2214) 2431[13] 2467[12] 2716[6] 3647[11]

Monashee Rock (IRE) *M Salaman* a70 75
2 b f Monashee Mountain(USA) —Polar Rock (Polar Falcon (USA))
5161[3] 5633[3] 6127[5] 6535[3] 6664[2]

Monash Lad (IRE) *Mrs K Waldron* a11 70
5 ch g General Monash(USA) —Story Time (IRE) (Mansooj)
4246[10]

Monda *Miss J A Camacho* a56 59
5 b m Danzig Connection(USA) —Fairey Firefly (Hallgate)
77[9] 241[2] 339[2] 448[7] 3920[4] 4583[2] 5741[2] 6149[6] 6467[8] 6886[11]

Monday Morning (IRE) *M J Wallace* a32 55
2 b f Touch Of The Blues(FR) —Thats Your Opinion (Last Tycoon (IRE))
1636[5] 4020[6]

Mondovino (FR) *Rod Collet* a96 99
4 b h Black Minnaloushe(USA) —Divinite (USA) (Alleged (USA))
7128a[7]

Monet's Lady (IRE) *R A Fahey* a43 49
3 gr f Daylami(IRE) —Wide Range (IRE) (Spectrum (IRE))
1044[9] 1361[5] 2096[2]

Monets Masterpiece (USA) *G L Moore* a79 74
4 b g Quiet American(USA) —Math (USA) (Devil's Bag (USA))
24[3] 363[11] 458[4] 634[6]

Money Bags (SAF) *M F De Kock* a80 103
5 ch h Rich Man's Gold(USA) —Maiden Lady (SAF) (Sportsworld (USA))
325a[6] 413a[5] 541a[3] 601a[6]

Mon Image (IRE) *F Turner*
2 ch f Bold Fact(USA) —Fingertip (Alhijaz)
6527a[5]

Monkey Glas (IRE) *K R Burke* a84 81
3 b c Mull Of Kintyre(USA) —Maura's Pet (IRE) (Prince Of Birds (USA))
1076[9] 1851[7] 2425[5] 3689[9] (4287) 4331[3] 6016[7] 6053[6] 6949[5] 7017[6] 7289[3]

Monkstown Road *C N Kellett* a58 66
5 b g Makbul—Carolside (Music Maestro)
126[9] 203[10]

Monmouthshire *R J Price* a49 64
4 b g Singspiel(IRE) —Croeso Cariad (Most Welcome)
445[13] 631[9] 716[8] 808[6] 1032[8] (1206) 1592[5] 1761[6] 2490[7] 2656[12]

Monolith *L Lungo* 91
9 b g Bigstone(IRE) —Ancara (Dancing Brave (USA))
(1490) 2170[4] 2908[4] 3090[12] 3898[6] 5933[9] 6181[7]

Mon Petite Amour *D W P Arbuthnot* a64 63
4 b m Efisio—Food Of Love (Music Boy)
94[2] 274[2] (495) 612[8] (742) 903[3] 1025[13] 1521[7] 1628[5] 1951[4] 6866[10] 6951[9] 7088[3] 7257[2]

Mon Plaisir (USA) *J L Dunlop* 74
2 bb c Pleasant Tap(USA) —Coquine (USA) (Gone West (USA))
4584[3] 5274[3] 6107[10]

Monreale (GER) *T Horwart* 85
3 b c Literat(GER) —Maratea (USA) (Fast Play (USA))
3146a[11] 4958a[5]

Monroe Gold *Jennie Candlish* 26
7 ch g Pivotal—Golden Daring (IRE) (Night Shift (USA))
4891[9]

Monsheramie (IRE) *T G McCourt* a11 47
5 b g Desert Style(IRE) —Sheramie (IRE) (Shernazar)
6999[9]

Monsieur Dumas (IRE) *R Bastiman* a64 63
3 b g Iron Mask(USA) —Serenity (Selkirk (USA))
1415[4] 2506[8] 3640[8] 4526[9] 5299[2] 6026[8]

Monsieur Reynard *B J Meehan* 70
2 ch g Compton Place—Tell Tale Fox (Tel Quel (FR))
3967[3] 4328[10] 4775[9]

Monsignor Fred *H Candy* 59
5 b g Fraam—Monsoon (Royal Palace)
1924[7] 2582[9]

Monsoon Wedding *M Johnston* 74
3 b f Monsun(GER) —Hyabella (Shirley Heights)
1479[3] 3722[3] 4072[8] (5678) 6258[14] 6746[10]

Montagne D'Or (IRE) *M Johnston* 87
2 b c Montjeu(IRE) —Muschana (Deploy)
(3635) 3938[9]

Montalegre (IRE) *A & G Botti* 103
5 b h Montjeu(IRE) —Alma Alegre (IRE) (Lahib (USA))
(1518a) 5821a[3] 6518a[3] 6863a[3]

Montalembert (USA) *J S Moore* a83 93
3 bb g Kalanisi(IRE) —Garendare (Vacarme (USA))
1387a[7] 1516a[7]

Montana Sky (IRE) *R A Harris* a50 61
4 b g Peintre Celebre(USA) —Catch The Lights (Deploy)
6529[2] 6713[11] 6969[11]

Montaquila *J Howard Johnson* 84
2 b g Hawk Wing(USA) —Intellectuelle (Caerleon (USA))
1792[3] 2166[3] (3025) 3504[10] 5613[6]

Montare (IRE) *J E Pease* 115
5 b m Montjeu(IRE) —Contare (Shirley Heights)
663a[7] 1881a[3] 2787[5] 4215a[3] 5465a[6] (6376a)

Montbretia *H R A Cecil* 69
2 b f Montjeu(IRE) —Bayswater (Caerleon (USA))
6414[4]

Montchara (IRE) *G Wragg* a75 66
4 b g Montjeu(IRE) —Mochara (Last Fandango)
1069[3] (1314) 1813[8] 2621[7] 3705[8] 4708[6] 5280[11]

Monte Alto (IRE) *L M Cumani* 108
3 b c Danehill Dancer(IRE) —Peruvian Witch (IRE) (Perugino (USA))
(1633) 1920[3] 2633[3] 3335[3] (3877) 4184[2] 4799[2] (5631) 6011[6]

Monte Cassino (IRE) *J O'Reilly* 50
2 ch c Choisir(AUS) —Saucy Maid (IRE) (Sure Blade (USA))
6468[14] 6721[10]

Montecristo *Rae Guest* a48 69
14 br g Warning—Sutosky (Great Nephew)
134[8] 349[4] 558[10] 615[3] 907[6] 1362[5] 2345[8]

Montefiore (IRE) *M Botti* a44 52
2 b c Orpen(USA) —Tokurama (IRE) (Mtoto)
5901[4] 6578[12]

Monte Major (IRE) *D Shaw* a78 67
6 b g Docksider(USA) —Danalia (IRE) (Danehill (USA))
82[7] (135) 281[3] 368[4] 654[5] 746[2] 896[9] (1163) 1669[3] 1991[7] 2350[6] (2516) 2712[3] 2972[2] 3184[5] 4103[10] 6360[3] 6671[8] 6860[2] 7054[3] 7206[2]

Monte Mayor Birdie (IRE) *D Haydn Jones* a38 66
2 b f Captain Rio—Ascoli (Skyliner)
2949[11] 3733[2] 4074[4]

Montemayorprincess (IRE) *D Haydn Jones* a62 57
3 b f Fath(USA) —Blonde Goddess (IRE) (Godswalk (USA))
2080[5] 2950[10] 3869[6] 4312[6] 4759[10] (5688) 6247[10] 7009[4]

Monterrico *G Wragg* 67
2 b c Dubai Destination(USA) —Mezzogiorno (Unfuwain (USA))
4132[7] 6252[3]

Mont Etoile (IRE) *W J Haggas* a64 112
4 b m Montjeu(IRE) —Troyes (Troy)
2507[2] 3434[5] 4203[3] 5544[5] 5767[8]

Mont Fay (NZ) *Danny O'Brien* 81
5 u m — (Diesis)
6033a[12]

Montgomery *A G Newcombe* 47
6 b g In Command(IRE) —Lightening Reef (Bon Sang (FR))
2493[4] (4535)

Montiboli (IRE) *K A Ryan* a60 60
2 ch f Bahamian Bounty—Aunt Sadie (Pursuit Of Love)
1859[2] 2115[3] 3109[3] 4077[7] 4775[14]

Monticelli (GER) *J R Gask* 32
7 b g Pelder(IRE) —Marcelia (GER) (Priamos (GER))
5917[14]

Montillia (IRE) *J W Unett* a49 52
5 b m Monashee Mountain(USA) —Steel Tap (IRE) (Flash Of Steel)
2174[8]

Montiona *John A Harris* a6
3 b g Montjoy(USA) —Lady Iona (Weldnaas (USA))
149[13] 258[9] 390[10]

Montjeu's Melody (IRE) *J W Hills* a66 71
3 b f Montjeu(IRE) —Pride Of Place (IRE) (Caerleon (USA))
1988[3] 2766[5] 3351[4] 4019[7] 5007[5]

Montosari *P Mitchell* a72 65
8 ch g Persian Bold—Sartigila (Efisio)
1949[8] 2355[4] 2996[4] 3397[14]

Montparno (FR) *B De Montzey* a93 101
7 ch g Starborough—Star Des Evees (FR) (Moulin)
437a[0]

Montpellier (IRE) *E A L Dunlop* a97 95
4 b g Montjeu(IRE) —Ring Of Esteem (Mark Of Esteem (IRE))
848[16] 1149[8] (1524) 2208[2] 2755[13] 3330[10] 3650[2] 4049[5] 4119[5] 5221[15]

Montrachet *M L W Bell* 83
3 ch f Singspiel(IRE) —Riberac (Efisio)
1127[15] 2580[4] 2873[2] (3490) (3798) 4497[2] 6180[4] 6497[5] 6637[6]

Montreal (GER) *H R A Cecil* 55
2 b f Boreal(GER) —Margie's Darling (USA) (Alydar (USA))
6470[12]

Montrose Man *B J Meehan* a71 55
3 ch g Foxhound(USA) —Don't Jump (IRE) (Entitled)
6597[11] 6901[3]

Montzando *B R Millman* a43 58
4 b g Forzando—Clashfern (Smackover)
746[6] 1212[5] 1899[9] 1969[13] 2652[7] 2972[5]

Monzante (USA) *R Charlton* a105 105
3 gr g Maria's Mon(USA) —Danzante (USA) (Danzig (USA))
1126[3] 1617[4] 2042[6]

Mood Music *Mario Hofer* 99
3 b c Kyllachy—Something Blue (Petong)
4213a[8] 4869a[9] 6224a[5] 6954a[9]

Moody Tunes *K R Burke* a45 93
4 b g Merdon Melody—Lady-Love (Pursuit Of Love)
1040[10] 1287[2] 2038[4] (2189) 2446[7] (2871) 3026[2] 3330[16] 4051a[4] 5615[7] 6011[31] 6155[7]

Mookhlesa *B W Hills* 80
2 bb f Marju(IRE) —Ikhlas (IRE) (Lahib (USA))
(1101)

Moon Bird *C A Cyzer* a69 37
5 b m Primo Dominie—Time For Tea (IRE) (Imperial Frontier (USA))
158[7] 235[6] 359[8] 650[3] 888[7] 1038[8] 3191[4]

Moon Bound (IRE) *W R Muir* a74
2 b c Observatory(USA) —Inspiring (IRE) (Anabaa (USA))
7043[4] 7264[2]

Moon Catcher (USA) *T F Ritchey* a109
3 b f Malibu Moon(USA) —Smartster (USA) (Smarten (USA))
4628a[4]

Moone Cross (IRE) *Mrs John Harrington* 98
4 b m Cape Cross(IRE) —Cannikin (IRE) (Lahib (USA))
3768a[2] 4639[11] 5075a[6] 5436a[7] 5841a[6] 6036a[8]

Moon Emperor *J R Jenkins* a68 50
10 b g Emperor Jones(USA) —Sir Hollow (USA) (Sir Ivor (USA))
(482) 607[3] 691[5] 1925[8] 2996[7] 6811[4] 7012[8] 7178[4]

Moon Empress (FR) *W R Muir* a69 79
4 gr m Rainbow Quest(USA) —Diamoona (FR) (Last Tycoon (IRE))
229[2] 443[2] 537[2] (869) (1783)

Mooner (ARG) *S Seemar* a108
6 br h Mutakddim(USA) —Luna Extranjera (ARG) (Siberian Express (USA))
327a[2] 399a[5] 529a[2] 643a[5]

Moonfinder (IRE) *J L Dunlop* 53
3 b f Galileo(IRE) —Callisto (IRE) (Darshaan)
1784[7] 2359[10] 2970[6] 4172[13]

Moon Forest (IRE) *J M Bradley* a62 62
5 br g Woodborough(USA) —Ma Bella Luna (Jalmood (USA))
1027[11] 1309[4] 1564[3] 2108[2] 2190[4] 2623[6] 3409[8] 3965[9] 4562[11] 4668[4] 4807[5] 5190[12]

Moonhawk *J Howard Johnson* 73
4 b g Montjeu(IRE) —Enclave (USA) (Woodman (USA))
1804[6] 3194[4] 3764[2] 5620[6]

Moonlight Angel *W R Swinburn* a68 66
2 b f Kyllachy—Far Post (USA) (Defensive Play (USA))
2457[7] 3453[3]

Moonlight Applause *T D Easterby* a53 58
3 b f Royal Applause—Antonia's Choice (Music Boy)
583[6] 713[3] 918[5] 1031[2] 1595[5] 1943[9] 2301[2] 2895[2] 3281[3] 3588[6] 4384[3] (4616)

Moonlight Fantasy (IRE) *Lucinda Featherstone* a62 55
4 b g Night Shift(USA) —County Girl (IRE) (Prince Rupert (FR))
1199[7] 1435[8] 1967[13] 3956[9] 4426[2] 4580[3] (4920) 5179[6] 5704[12] 6179[13] (6804) 6837[3] 7146[5] (7274)

Moonlight Gambler (IRE) *T D Easterby* 46
2 ch c Captain Rio—Bound To Glitter (USA) (Boundary (USA))
1422[8] 1963[10] 2869[5] 4524[8] 4995[6]

Moonlight Man *C R Dore* a85 96
6 ch g Night Shift(USA) —Fleeting Rainbow (Rainbow Quest (USA))
840[10] 2123[5] 2476[4] 2670[4] 3525[2] 3971[4] 4886[6] 6142[12] 6391[8]

Moon Melody (GER) *M E Sowersby* 63
4 b g Montjeu(IRE) —Midnight Fever (IRE) (Sure Blade (USA))
4246[8] 4521[9]

Moon Mix (FR) *D K Weld* 90
4 gr g Linamix(FR) —Cherry Moon (USA) (Quiet American (USA))
2067a[15]

Moon Quest (IRE) *Saeed Bin Suroor* 92
3 ch g Rainbow Quest(USA) —Midnight Line (USA) (Kris S (USA))
(2320) 2999[4]

Moonshine Beach *P W Hiatt* a63 55
9 b g Lugana Beach—Monongelia (Welsh Pageant)
5779[10] 5884[10] 6200[4] 6383[4] 6643[7] 6875[5] 7012[5]

Moonshine Bill *P W Hiatt* a46 54
8 ch g Master Willie—Monongelia (Welsh Pageant)
39[7] 220[8] 496[13] 618[12]

Moonshine Creek *P W Hiatt* a42 56
5 b g Pyramus(USA) —Monongelia (Welsh Pageant)
1671[2] 2089[11] 2370[3] 3617[4] 4031[9] 4802[9] 4945[11]

Moonshine Vixen *P W Hiatt* 8
6 ch m Deploy—Monongelia (Welsh Pageant)
3236[9] 4948[12] 5187[15]

Moon Sister (IRE) *W Jarvis* 48
2 b f Cadeaux Genereux—Tanz (IRE) (Sadler's Wells (USA))
6617[8]

Moon Spray (USA) *K A Ryan* 51
2 ch g Malibu Moon(USA) —Sun Spray (USA) (Woodman (USA))
2562[6] 4247[7] 4818[10]

Moon Star (GER) *A M Hales* 57
6 b g Goofalik(USA) —Maria Magdalene (GER) (Alkalde (GER))
1609[8]

Moonstreaker *R M Whitaker* a63 63
4 b g Foxhound(USA) —Ling Lane (Slip Anchor)
2338[7] 3161[4] 4081[8] 4998[14] 5737[7] 6247[2] 6640[10] 6882[2] 7127[4]

Moon Valley *W J Haggas* a35 79
4 ch m Halling(USA) —Crescent Moon (Mr Prospector (USA))
3107[3] 3881[10] 4266[3] 4686[2] 5018[10]

Moonwalking *Jedd O'Keeffe* 78
3 b g Danehill Dancer(IRE) —Macca Luna (IRE) (Kahyasi)
1010[4] 1415[3] 1827[3] 4617[8] 5229[7] 6158[10]

Mooretown Boy (IRE) *M P Cash* a78 89
7 b g Lapierre—Tender Always (Tender King)
5788a[6]

Mooretown Lady (IRE) *H Rogers* a77 94
4 b m Montjeu(IRE) —Chaturanga (Night Shift (USA))
3138a[9] 6216a[9] 6363a[2]

Moorhouse Lad *B Smart* a91 116
4 b g Bertolini(USA) —Record Time (Clantime)
(5) 344[7] 1242[3] 1853[2] 2234[2] 2733[10] (3464) (4090) 4746[11]

Moorlander (USA) *Mrs A J Perrett* a27 67
3 ch g Cozzene(USA) —Forest Key (USA) (Green Forest (USA))
4502[10] 5166[7] 5738[6] 5943[10]

Moors Myth *B G Powell* a20 37
6 b g Anabaa(USA) —West Devon (USA) (Gone West (USA))
183[10]

Moosley (IRE) *P W Chapple-Hyam* a71
2 b c Marju(IRE) —Shauna's Honey (IRE) (Danehill (USA))
7217[2]

Mootamaress (IRE) *Mrs A L M King* 79
3 b g Fath(USA) —Perle D'Irlande (FR) (Top Ville)
1635[9] 1923[15] 3713[9] 5433[13]

Moothir (USA) *M Johnston* a70
2 gr c Elusive Quality(USA) —Alattrah (USA) (Shadeed (USA))
6850[3]

Moquette (USA) *H-A Pantall* 93
3 ch f Maria's Mon(USA) —Eternal Reve (USA) (Diesis)
1006a[0]

Moraine *R Charlton* 68
3 br f Rainbow Quest(USA) —Cantilever (Sanglamore (USA))
(1217) 2602[11]

Moral Code (IRE) *E J O'Neill* a71 51
3 ch c Danehill Dancer(IRE) —Scruple (IRE) (Catrail (USA))
141[3] 4815[RR] 6109[7] 6858[3] 6959[5]

Moral Duty (USA) *Pat Eddery* 75
2 ch c Silver Deputy(CAN) —Shoogle (USA) (A.P. Indy (USA))
3991[5] 4454[6] 5428[5] (6237)

Morbick *W M Brisbourne* a56 55
3 ch g Kyllachy—Direcvil (Top Ville)
1976[4] 2312[5] 2554[7] 3181[11] 3783[12] 6906[5] 7275[3]

Morestead (IRE) *B G Powell* 70
2 ch c Traditionally(USA) —Itsy Bitsy Betsy (USA) (Beau Genius (CAN))
3896[9] 4761[14] 5306[6] 5883[11]

Mores Wells *Kevin Prendergast* 115
3 b c Sadler's Wells(USA) —Endorsement (Warning)
(1185a) 1693a[4] 3142a[5] 4044[7] (4647a) 5437a[3] 6028a[6]

More Votes (IRE) *Eoin Doyle* a35 65
6 b g Victory Note(USA) —Mardi Gras Belle (USA) (Masked Dancer (USA))
539[7]

Morforwyn *A Bailey* a43 21
2 br f Averti(IRE) —Rash Gift (Cadeaux Genereux)
2539[16] 3109[7] 3423[11] 3923[8] 7204[8]

Morghim (IRE) *E Charpy* a91 100
4 b h Machiavellian(USA) —Saleela (USA) (Nureyev (USA))
(175a) 329a[6] 529a[8]

Morinqua (IRE) *J G Given* a38 99
3 b f Cadeaux Genereux—Victoria Regia (IRE) (Lomond (USA))
(1151) 1286[2] 1616[2] (1825) (2135) 2884[3] 3344[3] 3493[2] 4123[2] 4726[4] 5325[8] 5666[12]

Moriwood (ITY) *A & G Botti* 101
3 b c Morigi—Black Wood (USA) (Woodman (USA))
1336a[11] 1873a[3] 2295a[6]

Mormeatmic *M W Easterby* a33 80
4 b g Orpen(USA) —Mimining (Tower Walk)
1134[14] 1299[9] 1565[9] 1669[6]

Morna (FR) *S Wattel* 100
4 b m Spectrum(IRE) —More Magic (GER) (Dashing Blade)
663a[9] 990a[6] 1689a[7]

Morning Farewell *P W Chapple-Hyam* a76 80
3 br g Daylami(IRE) —Got To Go (Shareef Dancer (USA))
569[2] 764[5] (1205) 1584[5] 6669[10]

Mornin Reserves *W G Harrison* 62
8 b g Atraf—Pusey Street Girl (Gildoran)
1464[10]

Morocchius (USA) *R M Beckett* a68 65
2 b c Black Minnaloushe(USA) —Shakespearean (USA) (Theatrical)
5720[5] 6119[4] 6436[7]

Morristown Music (IRE) *J S Wainwright* 69
3 b f Distant Music(USA) —Tongabezi (IRE) (Shernazar)
1135[4] 2255[4] 2553[14] (3054) 4158[10] 4525[16] 5522[9] 5834[8] 6287[5] (6466)

Morse (IRE) *J A Osborne* a83 56
6 b g Shinko Forest(IRE) —Auriga (Belmez (USA))
190[2] 277[3] 774[6] 1252[10] 5874[11] 6283[13]

Morshdi *D Selvaratnam* 97
9 b g Slip Anchor—Reem Albaraari (Sadler's Wells (USA))
400a[10] 544a[8]

Mosaic *A Al Raihe* a98 112
5 bb h Singspiel(IRE) —Ela Romara (Ela-Mana-Mou)
475a[14]

Moscow Oznick *N J Vaughan* 60
2 bb c Auction House(USA) —Cozette (IRE) (Danehill Dancer (IRE))
5904[10] 6574[7]

Mossmann Gorge *R A Harris* a59 66
5 b g Lujain(USA) —North Pine (Import)
10[8] 78[3] 182[10] 242[11]

Moss Vale (IRE) *D Nicholls* 123
6 b h Shinko Forest(IRE) —Wolf Cleugh (IRE) (Last Tycoon (IRE))
1770[10] 2050a[2] 2184[2] 2291a[3] 2733[14] 4214a[8] 5075a[3] 5436a[2] 6039a[4]

Moss Way *W J Musson* a32 24
2 b g Zaha(CAN) —Ruwaya (USA) (Red Ransom (USA))
2147[9] 2569[9] 4854[12]

Mostacolli Mort (USA) *J Canani* 100
3 b g Hold For Gold(USA) —Quiet Whisper (USA) (Quiet American (USA))
4412a[6]

Mostanad *R A Harris* a45 59
5 b g Alhaarth(IRE) —Jeed (IRE) (Mujtahid (USA))
83[9] 273[10] 320[14] 4164[7] 4905[8] 5368[12] 5861[9]

Mostarsil (USA) *G L Moore* a67 77
9 ch g Kingmambo(USA) —Naazeq (Nashwan (USA))
2403[15] 2692[8] 3273[8] 3692[5] 4318[7] 5111[4] 5453[9]

Mostashaar (FR) *Doug Watson* a104 107
5 b h Intikhab(USA) —Nasanice (IRE) (Nashwan (USA))
395a[9] 542a[4]

Most Becoming *S Parr* a27
4 b m Most Welcome—Bertie's Girl (Another Realm)
186[7] 338[8]

Most Definitely (IRE) *R M Stronge* a82 90
7 b g Definite Article—Unbidden Melody (USA) (Chieftain)
753[11] 1253[3] 1677[5] 1959[5] 2471[6] 2887[8] 4544[5]

Motafarred (IRE) *Micky Hammond* a72 78
5 ch g Machiavellian(USA) —Thurayya (Nashwan (USA))
1967[14] 2338[9] 2550[2] 2823[5] (3422) 3644[2] 3999[4] (4418) 4820[2] 5296[6] 6016[9]

Motarjm (USA) *H J Collingridge* a66 69
3 br g Elusive Quality(USA) —Agama (USA) (Nureyev (USA))
1011[7] 1177[11] 1863[8] 3349[6] 4029[5] 4354[4] 4858[5] 5342[2]

Moth Ball *J Cassidy* 103
5 b g Royal Applause—Chrysalis (Soviet Star (USA))
6375a[4]

Mother's Day *L A Dace* a24 68
4 b m Foxhound(USA) —Compact Disc (IRE) (Royal Academy (USA))
873a[17] 4828[9] 5130[12]

Motherwell *M Brittain* 34
2 b f Tamayaz(CAN) —Mother Corrigan (IRE) (Paris House)
1858[7] 2739[7] 3760[13]

Motive (FR) *J Howard Johnson* 100
6 ch g Machiavellian(USA) —Mistle Song (Nashwan (USA))
1822[5] 2093[10]

Motu (IRE) *I W McInnes* a67 73
6 b g Desert Style(IRE) —Pink Cashmere (IRE) (Polar Falcon (USA))
560[10] 673[7] (806) 967[2] 1133[6] 1459[2] 1488[2]

Mounafes *G A Butler* a62 57
3 ch c Barathea(IRE) —Guilty Secret (IRE) (Kris)
4568[10] 4948[5] 5137[3] 5482[10] 5755[7] 6421[7]

Mountain Cat (IRE) *W J Musson* a82 73
3 b g Red Ransom(USA) —Timewee (USA) (Romanov (IRE))
661[5] (2224) 2834[10] (3620) (4433) (5367) 6002[8] 6623[7]

Mountain Climb (IRE) *J D Frost* a50 52
5 ch g Monashee Mountain(USA) —Fancied (Dominion)
721[5] (1210) 3186[6] 5782[6] 6152[3] 7001[7]

Mountain Fairy *B S Rothwell* a44
4 gr m Daylami(IRE) —Mountain Spirit (IRE) (Royal Academy (USA))
602[8] 709[P]

Mountain High (IRE) *Sir Michael Stoute* 123
5 b h Danehill(USA) —Hellenic (Darshaan)
1274[5] (1650) 2292a[3] (2925a) 5077a[8]

Mountain Pass (USA) *B J Llewellyn* a66 64
5 b g Stravinsky(USA) —Ribbony (USA) (Dayjur (USA))
(235) 516[4] 866[6] 1564[5] 2331[10] 6806[8] 6950[5] (7006) 7251[5]

Mountain Pride (IRE) *J L Dunlop* 82
2 b c High Chaparral(IRE) —Lioness (Lion Cavern (USA))
4777[3] 5633[5] (6248)

Mount Eliza (IRE) *Charles O'Brien* a99 100
5 b m Danehill(USA) —Siamoise (Caerleon (USA))
437a[3] 1777a[7] 2702a[6] 4649a[8]

Mount Hadley (USA) *Saeed Bin Suroor* a85 101
3 b c Elusive Quality(USA) —Fly To The Moon (USA) (Blushing Groom (FR))
173a[3] (641a) 5378[3]

Mount Hermon (IRE) *H Morrison* a81 75
3 b g Golan(IRE) —Machudi (Bluebird (USA))
(807) 1228[6] (5122) 5768[9]

Mount Kilimanjaro (IRE) *J L Dunlop* 104
4 b h Sadler's Wells(USA) —Hill Of Snow (Reference Point)
(929) 2125[4]

Mount Lavinia (IRE) *R M Beckett* 54
2 b f Montjeu(IRE) —Havinia (Habitat)
5162[10] 6106[10]

Mount Nelson *A P O'Brien* 113
3 b c Rock Of Gibraltar(IRE) —Independence (Selkirk (USA))
6334[11]

Mount Pleasure (USA) *J A Osborne* a78 100
2 ch c Mt. Livermore(USA) —Private Beach (USA) (Unaccounted For (USA))
(1201) (1390) 2232[3] 2732[5]

Mount Usher *G A Swinbank* a71 80
5 br g Polar Falcon(USA) —Division Bell (Warning)
1040[8] 1455[2] 2038[3] 2136[4]

Moura Praia (IRE) *M Halford* 71
2 b f Intikhab(USA) —Mistress Ellie (Royal Applause)
5393a[5]

Mouseen (IRE) *R J Price* a52 63
4 ch g Alhaarth(IRE) —Marah (Machiavellian (USA))
77[5] 145[3] 241[6] 430[11] 1562[14] 2194[7]

Mouse White *H Candy* 28
2 br g Auction House(USA) —Petinata (Petong)
2977[12] 3842[7]

Mousse Au Chocolat (USA) *J-C Rouget* 102
2 br f Hennessy(USA) —Muskoka Dawn (USA) (Miswaki (USA))
5493a[2]

Move Over Darling (IRE) *P F I Cole* a64 58
4 b m Singspiel(IRE) —Darling Harbour (USA) (Candy Stripes (USA))
1566[2] 1884[6]

Moves Goodenough *Andrew Turnell* a70 73
4 ch g Woodborough(USA) —Rekindled Flame (IRE) (Kings Lake (USA))
1283[3] 1629[7] 1886[10] (2979) 3352[2] 3799[4] 5983[12] 6423[15] 6677[8]

Movie Mogul *M L W Bell* a57 57
3 bb f Sakhee(USA) —Norfolk Lavender (CAN) (Ascot Knight (CAN))
1068[7] 1639[10] 2261[9]

Moville (IRE) *B W Hills* 79
2 b g Alhaarth(IRE) —No Sugar Baby (FR) (Crystal Glitters (USA))
3896[10] 4586[2] 5321[5]

Moving Story *P T Midgley* 52
4 b g Desert Story(IRE) —Arianna Aldini (Habitat)
2582[5] 2795[6] 3721[14] 4704[12] 5255[8] 5487[6] 6452[10]

Moving Target (IRE) *Luke Comer* a62 41
8 ch g Karaar—Lucky Noire (Aragon)
229[6] 458[6] 610[4] 685[11] 2275[10] (Dead)

Mowadeh (IRE) *J R Gask* a38 73
3 ch g In The Wings—Jazmeer (Sabrehill (USA))
1129[7] 1505[4] 1849[2] 2690[6] 3367[13] 3848[5] 4172[4] 4809[9] 5034[6] 6612[9]

Moyenne Corniche *G Wragg* 67
2 ch c Selkirk(USA) —Miss Corniche (Hernando (FR))
6593[4]

Moynahan (USA) *P F I Cole* 94
2 ch c Johannesburg(USA) —Lakab (USA) (Manila (USA))
4048[4] (4725)

Moyne Pleasure (IRE) *R Johnson* a50 50
9 b g Exit To Nowhere(USA) —Ilanga (IRE) (Common Grounds)
148[3] 240[3] 585[13] 1570[4] 1934[4] 3204[4] 3840[2] 6076[10]

Moyoko (IRE) *M Blanshard* a62 55
4 b m Mozart(IRE) —Kayoko (IRE) (Shalford (IRE))
85[4] 130[7] 313[6] 3419[8] 3904[5] 4319[4] 4532[4] 5280[5] (5756) 6096[7] 6529[10] 6801[8]

Mozakhraf (USA) *K A Ryan* a76 67
5 b g Miswaki(USA) —Anakid (USA) (Danzig (USA))
70[11] (236) 361[11] 513[7] 1597[4] 2827[9] 3194[8] (3676) (4024) 4381[10] 5556[11] 5753[5] 6064[6] 6268[6] 6947[7] 7020[6] 7209[2]

Mr Aitch (IRE) *R T Phillips* a78 84
5 b g Soviet Star(USA) —Welsh Mist (Damister (USA))
4194[5] 4732[8]

Mr Aviator (USA) *R Hannon* a76 95
3 bb c Lear Fan(USA) —In Bloom (USA) (Clever Trick (USA))
1275[8] (1956) 2426[2] 3503[11] 3940[4] 4092[2] 5631[11] 6172[3] 6499[11]

Mr Belvedere *A J Lidderdale* a48 29
6 b g Royal Applause—Alarming Motown (Warning)
1366[6] 2595[7] 5368[8] 6175[10]

Mr Bountiful (IRE) *C J Teague* a49 49
9 b g Mukaddamah(USA) —Nawadder (Kris)
320[10] 435[7] 450[3] 524[6] 664[7] 682[8] 715[9]

Mr Cellophane *J R Jenkins* a81 83
4 ch g Pursuit Of Love—Fresh Fruit Daily (Reprimand)
1063[2] 1252[2] 1545[9] 2155[3] 2882[4] 3623[10] 4295[4] 4657[6] 5064[8] 6283[2] 6575[14] 7033[4]

Mr Chocolate Drop (IRE) *Miss M E Rowland* a56 34
3 b g Danetime(IRE) —Forest Blade (IRE) (Charnwood Forest (IRE))
11[2] 224[9] 322[4] (390) 469[8] 910[4] 1232[4] 1266[7] 2796[12] 3950[11] 5688[12] 6570[12] 7124[5] 7197[8]

Mr Crystal (FR) *Micky Hammond* a41 60
3 ch g Trempolino(USA) —Iyrbila (FR) (Lashkari)
807[6] 1303[9] 1917[6] (2552) 3159[6] 4409[3] 4821[3]

Mr Darec (IRE) *M Grassi*
4 b h Indian Danehill(IRE) —Most Of People (Horage)
1700a[6]

Mr Ed (IRE) *P Bowen* 78
9 ch g In The Wings—Center Moriches (IRE) (Magical Wonder (USA))
2449[7] 4398[6]

Mr Excel (IRE) *G A Ham* a82 59
4 b g Orpen(USA) —Collected (IRE) (Taufan (USA))
6961[6] 7102[6] 7226[7]

Mr Fantozzi (IRE) *Miss J Feilden* 63
2 br c Statue Of Liberty(USA) —Indian Sand (Indian King (USA))
2151[4] 2832[10] 4130[11]

Mr Forthright *J M Bradley* a51 56
3 b c Fraam—Form At Last (Formidable (USA))
899[9] 974[10] 1561[12] (1883) 2363[6] 3369[4] (3870) 4186[5] 4536[6] 4759[6] 6424[13] 6779[8] 7003[11]

Mr Funshine *Mrs P N Dutfield* a50 62
2 b g Namid—Sunrise Girl (King's Signet (USA))
2977[10] 3363[16] 3589[9] 5529[11] 6072[4] 6386[10]

Mr Garston *M P Tregoning* a89 91
4 b g Mull Of Kintyre(USA) —Ninfa Of Cisterna (Polish Patriot (USA))
1682[2] 1962[8]

Mr Grand Lodge (FR) *L M Cumani* a77 47
3 ch c Grand Lodge(USA) —Legende D'Or (FR) (Diesis)
1452[7] 1863[10] 2261[4] 3003[7] (3600) 4429[2]

Mr Joe Platinum (IRE) *E J Creighton*
5 b g Pierre—Hurgill Lady (Emarati (USA))
7262[6]

Mr Keppel (IRE) *J A Osborne* 87
2 b c Royal Applause—Oh Hebe (IRE) (Night Shift (USA))
3478[7] 3962[5] 4323[3] (4683) (5216) (5629) 6017[7]

Mr Klick (IRE) *N Wilson* 83
3 b g Tendulkar(USA) —Lake Poopo (IRE) (Persian Heights)
1994[10] 2821[7] 3094[5] 3568[7]

Mr Lambros *Miss Gay Kelleway* a98 78
6 ch g Pivotal—Magical Veil (Majestic Light (USA))
396a[P] 5513[7] 6142[10] 6391[10] 6743[10] 7078[5] (7261)

Mr Loire *A J Chamberlain* a76 76
3 b g Bertolini(USA) —Miss Sancerre (Last Tycoon (IRE))
199[3] 385[5] (606) 843[8] 1450[7] 2144[4] 2276[2] 2769[5] 3179[6] 3879[6] (4312) 4634[9] 5387[6] 5753[10] 6148[10] 6424[15] 6720[11] 6927[7] 7192[5]

Mr Lu *G A Swinbank* 50
2 b g Lujain(USA) —Libretta (Highest Honor (FR))
2071[6] 3465[11] 5621[3]

Mr Medici (IRE) *Kevin Prendergast* a79 98
2 b c Medicean—Way For Life (GER) (Platini (GER))
5397a[5] 6549a[6]

Mr Mini Scule *S Wynne* a47 54
3 b g Piccolo—Courtisane (Persepolis (FR))
360[7] 900[9] 974[6] 1317[11] 1763[13] 3843[5] 4220[10]

Mr Mischief *M C Chapman* a73 65
7 b g Millkom—Snow Huntress (Shirley Heights)
628[2] (1376) 1793[11] 2117[8] 3249[6] 3885[7] 3705[5] 4019[3] 4231[5] 4638[3] 4925[2] 5158[3] 5300[4] 6076[4] (6564) 6802[3]

Mr Mylerstown (IRE) *Joseph Crowley* 57
2 b g Orpen(USA) —Tifosi (IRE) (Mujadil (USA))
5516a[11]

Mr Napoleon (IRE) *G L Moore* a73 62
5 gr g Daylami(IRE) —Dathuil (IRE) (Royal Academy (USA))
3705[7] 4340[3] 4517[10] 5310[3] 6260[12] 6452[7] 6951[10] (7115) (7257)

Mr Napper Tandy *M R Channon* a93 108
3 ch c Bahamian Bounty—Starfleet (Inchinor)
754[2] 1110[2] 1547a[2] 2043[2]

Mr Plod *Andrew Reid* a31
2 ch g Silver Patriarch(IRE) —Emily-Mou (IRE) (Cadeaux Genereux)
6850[12]

Mr Rooney (IRE) *D Nicholls* a34 79
4 b g Mujadil(USA) —Desert Bride (USA) (Key To The Kingdom (USA))
1061[13] 1112[2] 1321[6] 2805[10] 2989[9] 4141[16] 4942[6] 5507[4] 5740[2] 5908[2] 6287[7]

Mr Sandgroper (AUS) *D A Edwards* 104
6 ch g Peintre Celebre(USA) —Game Warrior (AUS) (Rancher (AUS))
15a[7]

Mrs Gillow (IRE) *Eoin Griffin* a44 96
6 b m Danzero(AUS) —Belladera (IRE) (Alzao (USA))
6366a[5]

Mrs Lindsay (USA) *F Rohaut* 116
3 ch f Theatrical—Vole Vole Monamour (USA) (Woodman (USA))
(989a) 2501a[2] 4557a[6] (5465a) (6373a)

Mrs Snow *Mario Hofer* 100
4 ch m Singspiel(IRE) —Shining Vale (USA) (Twilight Agenda (USA))
1472[5] 6221a[7]

Mrs Solese (IRE) *J R Boyle* a59 64
4 b m Imperial Ballet(IRE) —Sugar (Hernando (FR))
7257[13]

Mrs Summersby (IRE) *H Morrison* a63
2 ch f King's Best(USA) —Kournikova (SAF) (Sportsworld (USA))
6944[2] 7252[5]

Mr Velocity (IRE) *E F Vaughan* a54 72
7 b g Tagula(IRE) —Miss Rusty (IRE) (Mukaddamah (USA))
830[8]

Mr Wall Street *M W Easterby* a43 49
3 b g Efisio—La Suquet (Puissance)
2538[12] 3540[9] 3605[6]

Mr Whoppit *T D Easterby* a53 53
3 b g Lake Coniston(IRE) —Miss Runaway (Runnett)
583[5] 670[9] 916[5] (Dead)

Mr Wolf *D W Barker* a89 100
6 b g Wolfhound(USA) —Madam Millie (Milford)
1195[2] 1601[8] 2841[7] 3089[11] 3401[5] 3720[3] 4095[13] 5039[5] 5379[14] 5584[21]

Ms Victoria (IRE) *M Halford* a82 86
3 b f Fasliyev(USA) —Musical Refrain (IRE) (Dancing Dissident (USA))
5841a[3] 6363a[6]

Mtoto Girl *Ms J S Doyle* a38
3 b f Mtoto—Shalati (FR) (High Line)
5728[12] 6005[11] 6429[12]

Muara *D W Barker* a67 61
5 ch m Wolfhound(USA) —Darussalam (Tina's Pet)
8[3] (296) 376[4] 1067[5] 1404[4] 1748[7] 2315[9] 2553[6] 4141[10] 4423[10] 5016[11]

Mubaashir (IRE) *E A L Dunlop* a95 96
3 ch c Noverre(USA) —Birdsong (IRE) (Dolphin Street (FR))
1124[11] 1500[8] 1930[5] 2835[15] 4502[7] 5685[14]

Mubher *J L Dunlop* a18 56
2 b c Bahri(USA) —Hawriyah (USA) (Dayjur (USA))
3435[14] 3957[8] 4946[7] 5736[8]

Mucho Loco (IRE) *R Curtis* a59 64
4 ch g Tagula(IRE) —Mousseux (IRE) (Jareer (USA))
1227[6] 1906[11] 2467[10] 3047[7] 7098[6]

Mudawin (IRE) *Jane Chapple-Hyam* a99 101
6 b g Intikhab(USA) —Fida (IRE) (Persian Heights)
995[9] 1477[6] 1844[3] 3898[5] 4722[12] 5469a[5] 6335[21]

Mudhish (IRE) *C E Brittain* a77 77
2 b c Lujain(USA) —Silver Satire (Dr Fong (USA))
2241[6] 3596[2] 3962[4] (4316) 4964[12] 5629[11] 6756[3] 7052[3]

Mud Monkey *B G Powell* a68 58
3 ch g Muhtarram(USA) —Tenderfoot (Be My Chief (USA))
1218[4] 1724[10] 1927[12] 2259[9] 6453[5]

Mufasa *Miss L A Perratt* 53
2 ch c Cayman Kai(IRE) —Petticoat Rule (Stanford)
6634[7] 6740[8]

Muffett's Dream *J A Geake* a56 57
3 b f Fraam—Loveless Carla (Pursuit Of Love)
1355[9] 1785[10] 2105[10] 2628[9]

Muga (SPA) *E J Creighton* a19
2 ch f Ski Wells—Hot Doris (IRE) (Fayruz)
4946[9] 5644[11] 6151[12]

Mugeba *Miss Gay Kelleway* a49 65
6 b m Primo Dominie—Ella Lamees (Statoblest)
980[3] 1377[4] 2190[6] 2336[11] 2608[2] 2870[3] (3101) 3247[4] 3466[4] 3950[2] 4494[8] 4856[8] 5546[2] 6415[2] 6575[11] (6638)

Muhajaar (IRE) *L M Cumani* 67
2 b c Cape Cross(IRE) —Ya Hajar (Lycius (USA))
2432[3]

Muhannak (IRE) *G A Butler* a87 84
3 b g Chester House(USA) —Opera (Forzando)
1343[2] (3406) 3926[3] (4184) 4510[4] 4799[10] 5725[9] (6007) 6144[3]

Muharjam *C E Brittain* 63
2 b c Diktat—Elsie Plunkett (Mind Games)
5541[14] 6079[6] 6451[P]

Mujaadel (USA) *E A L Dunlop* 80
2 ch c Street Cry(IRE) —Quiet Rumour (USA) (Alleged (USA))
2885[2] 3435[4] (5088) 5590[6]

Mujada *M Brittain* a49 38
2 b f Mujahid(USA) —Catriona (Bustino)
1029[2] 1302[7] 1713[6] 2710[6]

Mujadil Draw (IRE) *B Grizzetti*
2 b f Daggers Drawn(USA) —Mujadil Shadow (IRE) (Mujadil (USA))
(1485a)

Mujahaz (IRE) *J L Dunlop* 70
3 b g Act One—Sayedati Eljamilah (USA) (Mr Prospector (USA))
(1810) 2602[10]

Mujahope *M Botti* a67
2 b g Mujahid(USA) —Speak (Barathea (IRE))
4883[9] 5116[9] 6814[3] 6933[2] 7121[4]

Mujamead *P C Haslam* a50 28
3 b g Mujahid(USA) —Island Mead (Pharly (FR))
373[7] 1224[10]

Mujart *J A Pickering* a58 56
3 b f Mujahid(USA) —Artifact (So Factual (USA))
925[8] 1238[6] 1538[15] 2366[4] (2661) 2718[8] 3608[8] 4661[8] 5303[12] 7138[9]

Mujinda *M Brittain* 29
2 b f Mujahid(USA) —Arminda (Blakeney)
1156[6] 2888[11] 3951[14] 5526[7]

Mujma *Sir Michael Stoute* a65 68
3 gb g Indian Ridge—Farfala (FR) (Linamix (FR))
1081[5] 1810[10] 2530[3] 2915[10]

Mujobliged (IRE) *J R Best* a49 53
4 b g Mujadil(USA) —Festival Of Light (High Top)
5817[13] 6268[11] 7186[5]

Mujood *Eve Johnson Houghton* a87 96
4 b g Mujahid(USA) —Waqood (USA) (Riverman (USA))
827[7] 1023[3] 1179[6] (1465) 1653[6] 2058[8] 2440[4] 2771[4] 2993[7] 3240[6] 3941[23] 4122[6] 4389[10] 4806[9] 5449[6] 5712[2] 5923[12] 6450[7]

Mukhber *J H M Gosden* 88
2 br g Anabaa(USA) —Tarbiyah (Singspiel (IRE))
(6296)

Muktasb (USA) *D Shaw* a65 52
6 b g Bahri(USA) —Maghaarb (Machiavellian (USA))
47[4] 82[3] 161[4] 214[5] 368[3] 613[4] 668[6] 690[3] 797[4] 1120[5] 1384[6] 1729[7] 3829[10] 4668[7] 6390[2] 6565[2] 6609[6] (6864) 6957[3] 7013[7] 7192[3] (7265)

Mulaazem *J Mackie* a70 85
4 b g King's Best(USA) —Harayir (USA) (Gulch (USA))
1438[8] 2011[8] 2397[8] 2906[10] 4230[5] 5198[2] 5916[8]

Mulaqat *D Selvaratnam* a85 119
4 b g Singspiel(IRE) —Atamana (IRE) (Lahib (USA))
399a[11] 598a[4] 648a[5]

Mulberry Lad (IRE) *P W Hiatt* a63 54
5 b g Entrepreneur—Taisho (IRE) (Namaqualand (USA))
50[5] 161[6] 268[7] (310) 383[2] 467[7] 479[4] 548[5] 710[7] 750[6] (797) 866[7] 1064[10] 6607[9] 6826[9] 6891[4] 6925[8] 6945[5] 7014[7] 7094[6] 7192[2] 7276[9]

Mullach Na Si *W P Mullins* 74
3 b g Poliglote—Fatale (IRE) (Bluebird (USA))
4035a[7]

Mullagh Abu (IRE) *M O Quigley* a18 51
2 b f Mull Of Kintyre(USA) —Sarah (IRE) (Hernando (FR))
779a[15]

Mullein *R M Beckett* 71
2 b f Oasis Dream—Gipsy Moth (Efisio)
3895[7]

Mulligan's Gold (IRE) *T D Easterby* a57 72
4 b g Fasliyev(USA) —Magic Lady (IRE) (Bigstone (IRE))
1914[5] 2202[2] 2419[2] 2712[10] 3203[9] 4251[4] 4642[4] 4800[9] 5232[4] 5908[11] 6608[5]

Mulligan's Pride (IRE) *James Moffatt* 59
6 b g Kahyasi—Babs Mulligan (IRE) (Le Bavard (FR))
913[3] 1222[7] 1556[7] 2825[5]

Mulligans Pursuit (IRE) *M D I Usher* a53 68
3 b g Musical Pursuit—Anna Mong Men (Man Among Men (IRE))
2518[7] 2995[8] 6344[9] 6671[11]

Mullins Bay *M F De Kock* a112 112
6 b h Machiavellian(USA) —Bella Colora (Bellypha)
399a[2] 858a[3] 5142[5] 5451[3] 6334[8]

Mull Of Dubai *J S Moore* a49 98
4 b g Mull Of Kintyre(USA) —Enlisted (IRE) (Sadler's Wells (USA))
1208[3] 1575[4] 1771[3] (3165) (3242) 3989[2] 4690[4] 5574[9]

Mullzima (IRE) *M A Doyle* a13
4 b m Mull Of Kintyre(USA) —Habaza (IRE) (Shernazar)
285[13]

Multahab *M Wigham* a73 72
8 bb g Zafonic(USA) —Alumisiyah (USA) (Danzig (USA))
1321[5] 1991[8] 2555[4] 3627[2] 4233[9] 4689[10] (5174) 5642[8] 6174[3] 6360[7]

Multakka (IRE) *M P Tregoning* a77 89
4 b g Alhaarth(IRE) —Elfaslah (IRE) (Green Desert (USA))
6097[2] (6670)

Multicultural *D M Simcock* a77 80
4 bl g Singspiel(IRE) —Three Piece (Jaazeiro (USA))
492[2] (769) 1356[8] 1819[3] 5205[6] 5808[10] 6007[7] 6612[6]

Multidimensional (IRE) *H R A Cecil* 115
4 b h Danehill(USA) —Sacred Song (USA) (Diesis)
(5634) 6334[5]

Multiplex *A Fabre* 113
4 b h Danehill(USA) —Shirley Valentine (Shirley Heights)
2500a[2] 3780a[3]

Multitude (IRE) *T D Easterby* a3 68
3 b g Mull Of Kintyre(USA) —Sea Modena (IRE) (Mac's Imp (USA))
1219[6] (1530) 2120[6] 2910[3] 3491[5] 4127[8] 4898[12] 5893[12] 6310[7]

Mumaathel (IRE) *M A Buckley* a78 86
4 b g Alhaarth(IRE) —Alhufoof (USA) (Dayjur (USA))
6062[15] 6795[14] 6946[10]

Mumbleswerve (IRE) *W Jarvis* a69 44
3 b c City On A Hill(USA) —Dolcezza (FR) (Lichine (USA))
114[5]

Mumbling (IRE) *B G Powell* a67 71
9 ch g Dr Devious(IRE) —Valley Lights (IRE) (Dance Of Life (USA))
29[6] 213[12] 232[3] 380[4] 578[12] 617[12] 677[13] (Dead)

Mum's Memories *W J Musson* a40
3 ch g Zaha(CAN) —Trevorsninepoints (Jester)
373[12] 791[10] 910[8] 1381[10]

Mums The Best *A B Coogan* 16
2 ch f Best Of The Bests(IRE) —Super Sally (Superlative)
1540[12] 1814[8]

Munaddam (USA) *E A L Dunlop* 118
5 ch g Aljabr(USA) —Etizaaz (USA) (Diesis)
(245a) (528a) 644a[2] (1656) 3098[8] 4058[7]

Muncaster Castle (IRE) *R F Fisher* a60 58
3 b g Johannesburg(USA) —Eubee (FR) (Common Grounds)
202[5] 301[6] (624) 790[9] 1410[6] 3497[3] 5084[3] 7023[8]

Munching Mike (IRE) *K M Prendergast* 60
4 br g Orpen(USA) —Stargard (Polish Precedent (USA))
6380[12]

Mundo's Magic *G M Moore* 76
3 b g Foxhound(USA) —Amber's Bluff (Mind Games)
1577[2] 1802[3] 2171[2] 2373[5] 3413[4] 3952[7] 4291[6] 4425[7] 4940[3] 5155[6] 5522[7]

Mungo Jerry (GER) *B N Pollock* a55 66
6 b g Tannenkonig(IRE) —Mostly Sure (IRE) (Sure Blade (USA))
792[13]

Munnings (IRE) *A J Martin* 85
4 b g Selkirk(USA) —Silly Goose (IRE) (Sadler's Wells (USA))
6366a[8]

Munsef *J L Dunlop* 117
5 b g Zafonic(USA) —Mazaya (IRE) (Sadler's Wells (USA))
1144[3] 1823[6] (2441) 3097[3] 4117[11] 5165[2] 5976[2]

Munster Mountain (IRE) *James Moffatt* a36 54
3 ch g Monashee Mountain(USA) —The Voice (ITY) (Catrail (USA))
5098[11]

Muntami (IRE) *John A Harris* a74 73
6 gr g Daylami(IRE) —Bashashah (IRE) (Kris)
(508) (631) 811[8] 1263[6] 1668[3] 2887[2] 3963[4] 4490[4]

Muqadam (IRE) *Sir Michael Stoute* 74
3 b c Rock Of Gibraltar(IRE) —Onereuse (Sanglamore (USA))
1303[7] 3365[3] 4492[2] 4845[2] 5678[2]

Muqarrar (IRE) *T J Fitzgerald* a23
8 ch g Alhaarth(IRE) —Narjis (USA) (Blushing Groom (FR))
1934[13] 2176[10] 2595[14]

Muraco *R M Beckett* a58 74
3 b g Bertolini(USA) —Miss Honeypenny (IRE) (Old Vic)
1665[9] 2127[8] 2726[3] 3367[9] (4356) 4910[5] 5500[14]

Muraqeb *Mrs Barbara Waring* a47 43
7 ch g Grand Lodge(USA) —Oh So Well (IRE) (Sadler's Wells (USA))
683[6]

Murbek (IRE) *M A Jarvis* a19 82
3 b c Dansili—Flagship (Rainbow Quest (USA))
1093[8] 1606[2] 2118[2] 2886[2] 3914[2]

Murdoch *E S McMahon* a34 73
3 b g Mutamarkiz(IRE) —Miss Pharly (Pharly (FR))
849[9] 991[4] 1440[13] 2196[7]

Murdol (IRE) *C R Dore* a40 48
3 ch g Traditionally(USA) —Rock Abbey (IRE) (College Chapel)
284[4] 373[11] 2454[8]

Muree Queen *Miss J S Davis* a48 48
3 b f Diktat—Bright Future (FR) (Akarad (FR))
37[11] 149[9] 667[5] (676) 708[3] 893[9] 1266[10]

Murfreesboro *K J Burke* a98 98
4 b h Bahamian Bounty—Merry Rous (Rousillon (USA))
4864a[10] 5392a[4] 5841a[15] 6003[11] 6198[8] 6930[6] 6992[4]

Murrin (IRE) *T G Mills* a75 83
3 bb g Trans Island—Flimmering (Dancing Brave (USA))
886[4] 1247[6] (2425) 3689[8] 5114[7] 6236[8]

Murrisk *Eamon Tyrrell* a69 53
3 ch g Groom Dancer(USA) —Food Of Love (Music Boy)
4529[6] 5016[5] 5602[4] 6778[4]

Murrumbidgee (IRE) *J W Hills* a61 68
4 gr g Bluebird(USA) —Blanche Neige (USA) (Lit De Justice (USA))
1251[4] 1539[2] 1612[2] 2214[5] 2467[4] 2990[5] 3615[10] 4319[12] 4850[8] 5299[4]

Murtaad *W J Haggas* a75
3 b c Soviet Star(USA) —Zulfaa (USA) (Bahri (USA))
1343[6]

Musaalem (USA) *W J Haggas* 58
3 gr g Aljabr(USA) —Atyab (USA) (Mr Prospector (USA))
(4908)

Musadif (USA) *R A Kvisla* 102
9 ch g Shadeed(USA) —Tadwin (Never So Bold)
1836[13] 4566[16]

Musa Golosa *B Grizzetti* 104
4 b m Mujahid(USA) —Maid In The Shade (Forzando)
1337a[11]

Musango *Miss Gay Kelleway* a73 13
4 b g Night Shift(USA) —Imbabala (Zafonic (USA))
549[5] 612[2] (740) 921[5] 1451[3] 2321[15] 2667[3] 3945[8] (4915) 5422[9] 6819[5] (6971) 7050[3] 7150[3] 7226[4]

Musashi (IRE) *J S Moore* a48 72
2 ch c Hawk Wing(USA) —Soubrette (USA) (Opening Verse (USA))
4198[7] 4500[6] 5628[4] 6233[10]

Musca (IRE) *J Wade* 84
3 b g Tendulkar(USA) —Canary Bird (IRE) (Catrail (USA))
1768[3] 2373[6] 3094[4] 3607[4] 4581[6] 5505[8]

Muscari *S Woodman* a67 67
5 ch m Indian Ridge—Desert Serenade (USA) (Green Desert (USA))
132[10]

Muscovado (USA) *L M Cumani* a60
3 bb f Mr Greeley(USA) —Only Royale (IRE) (Caerleon (USA))
6420[14] 6975[5]

Musette (IRE) *R E Barr* a32 49
4 b m Mujadil(USA) —Repique (USA) (Sharpen Up)
1426[8] 1679[11] 2206[3] 2535[5] 3914[7] 3994[6] 4426[10] 4920[15]

Mushtaaq (USA) *M A Jarvis* 86
2 b c Dynaformer(USA) —Siyadah (USA) (Mr Prospector (USA))
5206[3] 5570[4] 6051[2]

Musical Affair *F Jordan* a24 51
3 b f Alflora(IRE) —Song For Jess (IRE) (Accordion)
1432[8]

Musical Beat *Miss V Haigh* a81 83
3 ch f Beat Hollow—Warbler (Warning)
838[8] 1045[3] (1131) 1247[5] 1610[4] 1649[8] 1979[2] 2010[4] 2578[4] 2691[3] (3411) 3645[4] 3972[7] 4566[18] (4940) 5230[8]

Musical Box *G Prodromou* a42 21
3 b f Ballet Master(USA) —Houston Heiress (USA) (Houston (USA))
1267[6] 1587[5] 1749[12] 2747[5]

Musical Charm (IRE) *T D Easterby* a30 66
2 b f Distant Music(USA) —Fairybird (FR) (Pampabird)
1193[4] 1848[4] 4459[9]

Musical Chimes *W M Brisbourne* a46 46
4 br m Josr Algarhoud(IRE) —Sally Slade (Dowsing (USA))
1537[5] 2137[11] 3032[3] 3277[6] 4000[6] 4336[7] 4736[10]

Musical Feud (IRE) *Jane Chapple-Hyam* a31
2 b g Distant Music(USA) —Family At War (USA) (Explodent (USA))
7191[12]

Musical Giant (USA) *J Wade* a29 55
4 ch g Giant's Causeway(USA) —Music House (USA) (Sadler's Wells (USA))
1455[4] 1967[15] 2348[6] 3497[11] 5678[9]

Musical Gift *M Hill* a51 43
7 ch g Cadeaux Genereux—Kazoo (Shareef Dancer (USA))
9[5] 129[4] 2980[6] 5606[12]

Musical Land (IRE) *J R Weymes* a36 69
3 ch g Distant Music(USA) —Esquiline (USA) (Gone West (USA))
1529[5] 1708[7] 4411[2] 4845[4] 4997[4] 5482[8] 5755[11] 6019[7] 6315[12]

Musical Locket (IRE) *J C Fox* a56 24
3 b f Distant Music(USA) —My Lucy Locket (IRE) (Mujadil (USA))
208[3] 565[4] 736[3] 1782[8] 5366[10] 5900[12] 6532[12]

Musical Mirage (USA) *G A Swinbank* a55 84
3 b f Royal Anthem(USA) —Fantasy (Cadeaux Genereux)
1110[5] 1414[6] 1851[10] 1979[7]

Musical Parkes *W J H Ratcliffe* a29 55
3 b f Piccolo—Top Of The Parkes (Mistertopogigo (IRE))
1679[6] 2012[9] 2366[3] 3168[13] 3537[7] 4525[17] 4661[10] 6247[17] 6702[13]

Musical Romance (IRE) *B J Meehan* a63 75
4 b m Mozart(IRE) —Dear Girl (IRE) (Fairy King (USA))
1372[11] 2240[9]

Musical Script (USA) *Mouse Hamilton-Fairley* a69 64
5 b g Stravinsky(USA) —Cyrillic (USA) (Irish River (FR))
1200[12] 1681[5] 1991[5] 2350[3] 2546[9] 3064[11] 3613[10] 4236[6] 4767[3] 5009[5] 5191[7] 5340[2] 5866[2] 6174[2] 6428[4] 6581[6] 7014[2] 7119[5]

Musical Way (FR) *P Van De Poele* a80 114
5 ch m Gold Away(IRE) —Mulika (FR) (Procida (USA))
2165a[3] 2617a[8] 3117a[7] 4652a[4] (5719a) (6032a) 6524a[3] 7092a[3]

Music Box Express *D J Murphy* a64 21
3 b g Tale Of The Cat(USA) —Aly McBe (USA) (Alydeed (CAN))
6309[11] 6877[3] (7019) 7206[3]

Music Celebre (IRE) *S Curran* a66 79
7 b g Peintre Celebre(USA) —Marwell (Habitat)
195[13] 263[10] 610[13] 1539[3] 2716[4] 3600[5] 4319[11] 5338[7] 6412[7]

Music In Exile (USA) *B W Hills* 61
2 ch f Diesis—Royal Occasion (USA) (El Gran Senor (USA))
6648[12]

Musicmaestroplease (IRE) *S Parr* a85 70
4 b g Rossini(USA) —Who Told Vicky (IRE) (Anita's Prince)
895[2] 933[6] 1892[13] 2550[11] 2947[11] 4427[8] 4701[9] 5098[5] 5890[5] 6316[11] 6613[8]

Music Note (IRE) *Miss Gay Kelleway* a79 86
4 b g Indian Ridge—Samara Middle East (FR) (Marju (IRE))
765[8] 1060[3] 1395[4] 1842[13] 3420[7] 3682[7] 4268[6] 4548[7] 5114[6]

Music Review *R A Fahey* a83 80
3 b f Singspiel(IRE) —Vivid Concert (IRE) (Chief Singer)
1045[5] 2118[3] 2840[4] 3379[2] 3719[4] (4493) 4717[4] 5131[3] (5523) 6091[6] 6389[2] 6822[2]

Muskateer Steel (IRE) *B Bo* 91
6 b h Indian Rocket—Lady Of The Mist (IRE) (Digamist (USA))
5262a[6] 6370a[10]

Musketier (GER) *P Bary* 107
5 gr h Acatenango(GER) —Myth And Reality (Linamix (FR))
4520a^{8} 6095a^{5} 6771a^{3}

Mussoorie (FR) *J H M Gosden* a95 108
4 gr m Linamix(FR) —Fascinating Hill (FR) (Danehill (USA))
1421a^{9} 4748^{3} 5352^{13} 6299^{5} 6605^{8} 6757^{8}

Mustajed *B R Millman* a87 92
6 b g Alhaarth(IRE) —Jasarah (IRE) (Green Desert (USA))
353^{11} 488^{15} 850^{2} 1356^{3} 1542^{6} 2002^{4} (2692) 3090^{13} 4047^{8} 4376^{4} (4888) 5225^{4} 5830^{11}

Mustakhlas (USA) *B P J Baugh* a54 46
6 ch g Diesis—Katiba (USA) (Gulch (USA))
285^{3} 607^{8} 792^{10} 2434^{9} 7172^{9}

Mustamad *Miss A M Newton-Smith* a51 76
4 b g Anabaa(USA) —Nasanice (IRE) (Nashwan (USA))
1356^{11}

Mustameet (USA) *Kevin Prendergast* 121
6 b h Sahm(USA) —Hamasah (USA) (Irish River (FR))
(1049a) 1550a^{6} 2064a^{6}

Mustammer *D Shaw* a61 42
4 b g Fasliyev(USA) —Alazima (USA) (Riverman (USA))
13^{5} 339^{10} (403) 441^{5} 2664^{13} 2799^{10} 3169^{12}

Mustanfar (USA) *K McLaughlin* a107 107
6 ch h Unbridled(USA) —Manwah (USA) (Lyphard (USA))
5853a^{7}

Mustang Du Gueslan (FR) *D W Thompson* 36
7 b g Passing Sale(FR) —Arzel Du Marais (FR) (Djarvis (FR))
3684^{5} 4460^{9}

Mustard Benn *Mouse Hamilton-Fairley* a41
4 b g Golden Snake(USA) —Mysterious Maid (USA) (L'Emigrant (USA))
120^{6} 458^{12} 559^{10} 723^{11} 2141^{10} 2962^{7} 3868^{14}

Must Be Keen *Miss Diana Weeden* a55 56
8 b g Emperor Jones(USA) —As Mustard (Keen)
46^{5} (189) 281^{6} 337^{7} 1933^{11} 2972^{4} 3218^{7} 3906^{11} 4296^{9} 5090^{17} 5566^{11}

Mut'Ab (USA) *C E Brittain* 84
2 b c Alhaarth(IRE) —Mistle Song (Nashwan (USA))
3270^{3} 4110^{2} 4694^{7}

Mutabayen (USA) *B Smart* a54 98
2 bb c Doneraile Court(USA) —La Frou Frou (IRE) (Night Shift (USA))
(2532) 3504^{5} 4199^{4}

Mutadarek *Eoin Griffin* a58 89
6 b g Machiavellian(USA) —Nasheed (USA) (Riverman (USA))
3577a^{9}

Mutadarrej (IRE) *J L Dunlop* 88
3 ch c Fantastic Light(USA) —Najayeb (USA) (Silver Hawk (USA))
1106^{5} 1773^{11} 2126^{2} 2790^{15} 3993^{12} 4609^{8} 5718^{2}

Mutafanen *E Charpy* a68 106
6 gr h Linamix(FR) —Doomna (IRE) (Machiavellian (USA))
250a^{6} (328a) 475a^{10}

Mutajarred *W J Haggas* 109
3 ch g Alhaarth(IRE) —Bedara (Barathea (IRE))
(2873) (3514) (3715) 5615^{4} 6172^{2}

Mutakarrim *D K Weld* 110
10 ch g Mujtahid(USA) —Alyakkh (IRE) (Sadler's Wells (USA))
2161a^{2} 3119a^{5}

Mutamaasek (USA) *Lady Herries* a73 68
6 bb g Swain(IRE) —Tamgeed (USA) (Woodman (USA))
5531^{8} 6259^{16} 6866^{3} (7088) (7194)

Mutamared (USA) *K A Ryan* a110 109
7 ch g Nureyev(USA) —Alydariel (USA) (Alydar (USA))
245a^{12} 415a^{7} 841^{3} 1102^{5} 1474^{2} 2858^{20} 4150^{17} 4886^{7} 5392a^{6} 6472^{18}

Mutamarres *Doug Watson* a94 99
4 b g Green Desert(USA) —Injaad (Machiavellian (USA))
105a^{9}

Mutanaseb (USA) *M A Jarvis* a89 100
3 b g Mr Greeley(USA) —Rose Rhapsody (USA) (Pleasant Colony (USA))
(1398) (2671) 3330^{5} 4420^{4} 5797^{10} 6301^{21}

Mutasallil (USA) *Doug Watson* a98 94
7 bb h Gone West(USA) —Min Alhawa (USA) (Riverman (USA))
175a^{7} 328a^{10} 643a^{2}

Mutawaajid (AUS) *M R Channon* 115
4 b h Redoute's Choice(AUS) —Elated Lady (AUS) (Vain (AUS))
3506^{9} 4045^{11} 5214^{4} 5632^{4}

Mutawaffer *R A Fahey* 96
6 b g Marju(IRE) —Absaar (USA) (Alleged (USA))
848^{3} 1822^{2} 4722^{17}

Mutawassel (USA) *B W Hills* a93 93
6 b h Kingmambo(USA) —Danzig Darling (CAN) (Danzig (USA))
3002^{5} 4166^{4} 4888^{6}

Mutayam *D A Nolan* 54
7 b g Compton Place—Final Shot (Dalsaan)
2830^{9} 3374^{7} 3782^{13} 4498^{6} 4719^{10} 4967^{7} 5085^{5} 5481^{8} 5667^{9}

Muthabaie (FR) *R Pritchard-Gordon* a89 83
3 ch f Muhtathir—Slew Bay (FR) (Beaudelaire (USA))
7049a^{4}

Muthabara (IRE) *J L Dunlop* 100
2 b f Red Ransom(USA) —Hureya (USA) (Woodman (USA))
(2969) (3880)

Mutoon (IRE) *S C Williams* a65 59
3 b f Erhaab(USA) —Nafhaat (USA) (Roberto (USA))
114^{2} 492^{7} 591^{11} 684^{3} 1345^{7} 1538^{5} 3804^{2} 4339^{8}

Mutual Friend (USA) *E A L Dunlop* a81 82
3 gr g Aljabr(USA) —Dubai Visit (USA) (Quiet American (USA))
1117^{5} 1343^{5} (2177) 2413^{2} 2767^{4} 3165^{3}

Muzmin (USA) *M Johnston* 72
2 bb c Seeking The Gold(USA) —In On The Secret (CAN) (Secretariat (USA))
5227^{5}

Mwindaji *Mrs P Sly* 64
2 b g Hunting Lion(IRE) —Gayane (Nureyev (USA))
4571^{13} (5302) 6410^{5}

My Arch *K A Ryan* 93
5 b g Silver Patriarch(IRE) —My Desire (Grey Desire)
1013^{9} 1621^{9} (1862) 2236^{9} 3143a^{4} 3509^{14} 4388^{11}

My Aunt Fanny *A M Balding* a71
2 b f Nayef(USA) —Putuna (Generous (IRE))
5202^{3}

My Beautaful *Miss J S Davis* a57
3 ch f Classic Cliche(IRE) —Ginger Rogers (Gildoran)
152^{2} 661^{3} 5783^{11} 6147^{10}

Myboycharlie (IRE) *T Stack* 118
2 b c Danetime(IRE) —Dulceata (IRE) (Rousillon (USA))
(3574a) (4653a) 5458a^{3}

My Causeway Dream (IRE) *J S Wainwright* 40
4 ch m Giant's Causeway(USA) —Meritorious (USA) (St Jovite (USA))
1967^{17} 2254^{11} 2935^{6} 4156^{10} 4409^{9}

Mycenean Prince (USA) *R C Guest* a45 44
4 b g Swain(IRE) —Nijinsky's Beauty (USA) (Nijinsky (CAN))
445^{12} 468^{7} 4526^{8} 6642^{4} 6792^{4} 6956^{12}

My Dolly Madison *A Kinsella* 77
3 ch f In The Wings—Play With Fire (FR) (Priolo (USA))
6367a^{11}

My Drop (IRE) *E J O'Neill* a72 68
3 b c Danetime(IRE) —Notluckytochange (IRE) (King Of Clubs)
(237) 1176^{6} 1577^{6} 1738^{4} 2144^{3} 2761^{4}

My Flame *J R Jenkins* a40 53
2 b c Cool Jazz—Suselja (IRE) (Mon Tresor)
5868^{11} 6079^{7} 6540^{7} 6966^{8} 7042^{9}

Myfrenchconnection (IRE) *P T Midgley* 65
3 b g Tendulkar(USA) —Papinette (IRE) (Maelstrom Lake)
1236^{7} 1425^{4} 1894^{7} 3918^{3} 4220^{3} 4491^{5} (4842) (5525) 6199^{2} 6447^{2}

My Friend Fritz *P W Hiatt* a50
7 ch g Safawan—Little Scarlett (Mazilier (USA))
159^{6} 305^{3}

My Gacho (IRE) *T D Barron* a54 93
5 b g Shinko Forest(IRE) —Floralia (Auction Ring (USA))
(1852) 2339^{8} 4122^{21} 4389^{7} 5209^{7} 5638^{10}

My Girl Sophie (USA) *J S Bolger* a66 85
2 b f Danzig(USA) —Just Fly (USA) (Capote (USA))
779a^{8}

My Jeanie (IRE) *J C Fox* a55 26
3 ch f King Charlemagne(USA) —Home Comforts (Most Welcome)
93^{5} (7167)

My Kaiser Chief *W J H Ratcliffe* a58 67
2 bl c Paris House—So Tempted (So Factual (USA))
4173^{4} 4447^{4} 6721^{13} 7106^{5} 7243^{6}

My Learned Friend (IRE) *A M Balding* a73 84
3 b g Marju(IRE) —Stately Princess (Robellino (USA))
754^{6} 1202^{13} 5360^{12} 5874^{10} 6610^{5}

My Legal Eagle (IRE) *E G Bevan* a40 56
13 b g Law Society(USA) —Majestic Nurse (On Your Mark)
1152^{4} 1406^{3} 2089^{2} 2595^{12} 2890^{6} 3485^{2} 3901^{7} 4352^{5} 4906^{7} 5187^{3} 5427^{2} 5857^{5} 6200^{6}

My Love Thomas (IRE) *E A L Dunlop* a73 82
3 b f Cadeaux Genereux—Flanders (IRE) (Common Grounds)
1786^{4} 2363^{2} 4360^{7} 5051^{8}

My Maite Mickey *R C Guest* a31 37
3 b g Komaite(USA) —Mrs Plum (Emarati (USA))
2844^{12} 3786^{10} 4141^{18} 4938^{8}

My Mate Max *R Hollinshead* a72
2 b g Fraam—Victory Flip (IRE) (Victory Note (USA))
(7130)

My Mate Pete (IRE) *R M Beckett* a78 60
2 b g Captain Rio—Lady Peculiar (CAN) (Sunshine Forever (USA))
6105^{7} 6692^{3} (7264)

My Mentor (IRE) *Sir Mark Prescott* a74
3 b g Golan(IRE) —Vanille (IRE) (Selkirk (USA))
1587^{10} 1749^{8} 1904^{7} 2456^{2} (2668) 3622^{8}

My Michelle *B Palling* a70 63
6 b m Ali-Royal(IRE) —April Magic (Magic Ring (IRE))
(156) 266^{3} 445^{4} (571) 805^{2} 1069^{8} 1284^{4} 1765^{11} 2257^{6} 2521^{7} 4464^{2} 4532^{2} 5020^{8} 6343^{6} 6612^{2} 6816^{2} (6874) 7047^{6}

My Mirasol *D E Cantillon* a68 68
3 ch f Primo Valentino(IRE) —Distinctly Blu (IRE) (Distinctly North (USA))
76^{4} 139^{2} 284^{2} 446^{2} (534) 572^{6} 1122^{13} 1628^{10} 1927^{5} 2490^{13} 6935^{3} 7083^{11}

My Monna *Miss Sheena West* a53 42
3 b f Josr Algarhoud(IRE) —Albarsha (Mtoto)
116^{9} 5709^{8} 6206^{2} 6529^{11} 6590^{4} 6832^{4} 6975^{8} 7012^{12}

Mymumsaysimthebest *R Hannon* 91
2 b c Reel Buddy(USA) —Night Gypsy (Mind Games)
2215^{8} 3551^{2} 4110^{4} 4743^{6}

Mynd *B Palling* a56 67
7 b g Atraf—Prim Lass (Reprimand)
1065^{10} 2104^{8}

My Paris *K A Ryan* a90 109
6 b g Paris House—My Desire (Grey Desire)
658^{8} 848^{5} 1145^{9} (1480) 1860^{2} 2755^{6} 3138a^{5} 3505^{7} 4119^{11} 4745^{9} 5615^{8} 6011^{11}

My Pin Up *Christian Wroe* a69
2 b f Forzando—Victoria Sioux (Ron's Victory (USA))
6820^{5} 6964^{2} 7216^{6}

My Portfolio (IRE) *J J Lambe* a2 50
5 b g Montjeu(IRE) —Elaine's Honor (USA) (Chief's Crown (USA))
3677^{8} 6341^{12}

My Rachel (USA) *T Pletcher* 100
5 ch m Horse Chestnut(SAF) —Preserver (USA) (Forty Niner (USA))
6790a^{3}

My Rascal (IRE) *J Balding* a38 47
5 b g Imperial Ballet(IRE) —Derena (FR) (Crystal Palace (FR))
1933^{14} (Dead)

Myriola *B Palling* a53 62
2 ch f Captain Rio—Spaniola (IRE) (Desert King (IRE))
1193^{5} 1553^{7} 2147^{6} 2818^{3} 4527^{6} 5365^{3} 5751^{9} 6388^{13}

Myrtle Bay (IRE) *J C Tuck* a57
4 bl g Pennekamp(USA) —Moneypenny (GER) (Neshad (USA))
309^{4} 495^{5} 792^{11} 1342^{6} 2656^{15} 6212^{13} 6866^{11}

My Sara *R A Fahey* a65 49
3 b f Mujahid(USA) —Ancestry (Persepolis (FR))
136^{7} 224^{4} 267^{4} (373) 469^{5} 893^{12} 1092^{9} 1194^{3} 6672^{7} 7109^{5} 7211^{6}

My Sea Of Love *A & G Botti* 101
4 b m King's Best(USA) —Scent Of Success (USA) (Quiet American (USA))
6767a^{3}

My Secrets *M Johnston* a82 82
3 b c Fantastic Light(USA) —St Radegund (Green Desert (USA))
1084^{4} 1289^{2} 1415^{2} 1898^{7} 2246^{5} 2602^{14} 3170^{3} 3407^{2}

My Shadow *S Dow* a68 58
2 b c Zamindar(USA) —Reflections (Sadler's Wells (USA))
5702^{4} 6289^{7} 7070^{7} 7252^{4}

My Sheilas Dream (IRE) *W G M Turner* 50
2 b f Acclamation—Triphibious (Zafonic (USA))
(1235) 1674^{U} 2549^{5} 3174^{3} 3788^{5} 4311^{8} 4824^{5}

My Silver Monarch (IRE) *H S Howe* a16 39
3 b f Bertolini(USA) —April View (USA) (Distant View (USA))
1501^{9} 2196^{11}

My Spring Rose *J R Jenkins* a38 61
3 b f Lake Coniston(IRE) —Diamond Jayne (IRE) (Royal Abjar (USA))
2477^{11} 2880^{7} 3387^{10} 4742^{13} 5528^{12} 5873^{7} 6453^{10} 7167^{8}

Mysterious World (IRE) *Mrs K Walton* a52 63
3 ch c Desert Prince(IRE) —Salligram (Salse (USA))
4641^{8} 5335^{5} 5562^{5} 6259^{U} 6883^{9} 6999^{13}

Mystery Ocean *R M Beckett* a87 86
3 b f Dr Fong(USA) —Tiriana (Common Grounds)
838^{3} 1768^{7} 2213^{9} 3235^{5} 3845^{3}

Mystery Pips *N Tinkler* a67 65
7 b m Bin Ajwaad(IRE) —Le Shuttle (Presidium)
251^{10} 317^{9} 521^{9} 680^{9} 892^{10} (1594) 1902^{12} 2553^{4} 3169^{6} 4525^{8} 4561^{9} 4787^{4} 4973^{7} 5295^{14} 5564^{7}

Mystery River (USA) *B J Meehan* a73 74
3 ch f Dr Fong(USA) —Bacinella (USA) (El Gran Senor (USA))
1068^{3} 1439^{4} 1815^{10} 2530^{5} (3451) 3705^{14} 4631^{5}

Mystery Sail (USA) *Mrs A J Perrett* 73
2 b f Mizzen Mast(USA) —Questonia (Rainbow Quest (USA))
(5633)

Mystery Star (IRE) *M H Tompkins* a83 80
2 ch c Kris Kin(USA) —Mystery Hill (USA) (Danehill (USA))
5599^{2} 6184^{3} (6763)

Mystic *D W Barker* 37
3 ch f Bahamian Bounty—Sweet Myrtle (USA) (Mutakddim (USA))
1558^{5} 2300^{12} 4938^{7}

Mystical (IND) *S Ganapathy* 113
5 b g Alnasr Alwasheek—Mystic Memory (IND) (Malvado (CAN))
(477a) (645a) 862a^{14}

Mystical Ayr (IRE) *Miss L A Perratt* 72
5 br m Namid—Scanno's Choice (IRE) (Pennine Walk)
1488^{6} 1627^{2} 1944^{10} 2168^{3} 2564^{4} 2760^{2} 2823^{2} 3049^{5} 3343^{2} 3502^{5} 3783^{4} 4159^{7} (4383) 4477^{2} 4716^{2} 5556^{3} 5674^{2} 5905^{2} 6465^{9} 6638^{6}

Mystical Lady (IRE) *Joseph Crowley* 72
2 b f Halling(USA) —Lady Icarus (Rainbow Quest (USA))
5843a^{12}

Mystical Moon *Lady Herries* a62 64
3 b g Medicean—Moon Carnival (Be My Guest (USA))
1887^{6} 2490^{8} 4518^{9} 5120^{7} 5426^{8} 5899^{7}

Mystic Art (IRE) *C R Egerton* a73 52
2 b g Peintre Celebre(USA) —Mystic Lure (Green Desert (USA))
3592^{9} 4571^{14} 5498^{5}

Mystic Dancer *Sir Michael Stoute* a85 78
3 ch c Machiavellian(USA) —Mystic Goddess (USA) (Storm Bird (CAN))
1204^{4} 1851^{14}

Mystickhill (IRE) *D J Murphy* a65 53
2 ch f Raise A Grand(IRE) —Lady Eberspacher (IRE) (Royal Abjar (USA))
890^{4} 972^{3} 1130^{3} 1291^{8} 5751^{4} 6312^{3} 6388^{2}

Mystic Lips (GER) *Andreas Lowe* 115
3 b f Generous(IRE) —Majorata (GER) (Acatenango (GER))
1338a^{2} (2294a) 4654a^{4} 6042a^{4} 6524a^{5}

Mystic Lipstick (IRE) *J Heloury* 89
2 b f Kalanisi(IRE) —Art Fair (Alzao (USA))
6047a^{4}

Mystic Man (FR) *I W McInnes* a84 73
9 b g Cadeaux Genereux—Shawanni (Shareef Dancer (USA))
32^{4} 131^{6} 235^{2} 313^{4} 359^{3} 455^{5} (556) 672^{9} 793^{9}

Mystic Spin (IRE) *K J Burke*
3 b c Tendulkar(USA) —Mystical Jumbo (Mystiko (USA))
6704^{8}

Mystic Spirit (IRE) *N Clement* 97
2 b f Invincible Spirit(IRE) —Mirina (FR) (Pursuit Of Love)
5373a^{9}

Mystic Storm *Lady Herries* a77 75
4 b g Medicean—Mrs Nash (Night Shift (USA))
3416^{13} 4015^{8} 4231^{2} 4597^{4} 5007^{9} 5769^{7}

Mystified (IRE) *R F Fisher* a62 54
4 b g Raise A Grand(IRE) —Sunrise (IRE) (Sri Pekan (USA))
1222^{4} 1895^{2} 2537^{5} 2715^{5} 3193^{12} (4246) 6076^{12} 6703^{8}

Mystik Megan *M Mullineaux*
6 gr m Wizard King—Sian's Girl (Mystiko (USA))
4334^{11}

My Summer Of Love (FR) *K Woodburn* 66
2 b f Dashing Blade—Mlle Angelique (GER) (Law Society (USA))
4837a^{3} 5848a^{6}

Mythical Charm *J J Bridger* a62 64
8 b m Charnwood Forest(IRE) —Triple Tricks (IRE) (Royal Academy (USA))
85^{7} 130^{10} 2214^{6} 2423^{7} 2696^{7} (3149) 3422^{12} (3965) 4577^{7} 4850^{11} 5166^{9} 5862^{4} 6278^{8} 6431^{4} 6717^{7} 6796^{3} 7028^{9} 7115^{6} 7278^{3}

Mythical Fosroc (USA) *J S Moore* 35
2 b f Najran(USA) —Green Boulevard (USA) (Green Forest (USA))
5357^{12} 6384^{10}

Mythical Kid (USA) *Saeed Bin Suroor* 106
3 bb c Lemon Drop Kid(USA) —Myth To Reality (FR) (Sadler's Wells (USA))
1662^{5} 2042^{4}

Mythical Story (IRE) *J R Fanshawe* 71
3 br f Alhaarth(IRE) —Dreams (Rainbow Quest (USA))
5384^{6} 6286^{3} 6745^{4}

Myths And Verses *K A Ryan* a64 63
4 b m Primo Valentino(IRE) —Romantic Myth (Mind Games)
85^{9}

My Tiger Lilly *R A Teal* a52 56
3 ch f Tobougg(IRE) —Ashantiana (Ashkalani (IRE))
1430^{2} 2198^{6} 2560^{7} 3455^{9} 4317^{9} 5276^{14}

Mytton's Dream *Miss Joanne Priest* a50 21
5 br m Diktat—Courtisane (Persepolis (FR))
109^{8} 206^{13} 450^{9}

Mytton's Pride *A Bailey* a50 63
4 b g Tagula(IRE) —Pictina (Petong)
1360^{12} 1594^{15}

My Two Girls (IRE) *P T Midgley* 61
3 b f Danetime(IRE) —Sanctuary Line (IRE) (Lake Coniston (IRE))
970^{9} 1161^{5} 1240^{5} 1426^{9}

My Typhoon (IRE) *W Mott* a104 118
5 ch m Giant's Causeway(USA) —Urban Sea (USA) (Miswaki (USA))
5822a^{8} 6511a^{13}

Naayla (IRE) *B J Meehan* a77 81
3 br f Invincible Spirit(IRE) —Pink Cashmere (IRE) (Polar Falcon (USA))
199^{4}

Nabati (USA) *H-A Pantall* 83
3 ch f Rahy(USA) —Wajd (USA) (Northern Dancer (CAN))
2547a^{5}

Nabir (FR) *P D Niven* a72 64
7 gr g Linamix(FR) —Nabagha (FR) (Fabulous Dancer (USA))
1178^{5}

Nabra *M Brittain* a53 53
3 b f Kyllachy—Muja Farewell (Mujtahid (USA))
1346^{6} 3000^{8} 4896^{7} 5282^{8} 5627^{11}

Nacho Libre *B W Hills* 98
2 b c Kyllachy—Expectation (IRE) (Night Shift (USA))
1123^{6} (2473) 3157^{2} 4721^{5} 5032^{3} 5324^{22} 6488^{3}

Nadawat (USA) *J L Dunlop* 88
3 bb f Kingmambo(USA) —Tashawak (IRE) (Night Shift (USA))
(1045) 1610^{9} 2881^{8} (4163) 4589^{4} 5092^{2} 5560^{4} 6651^{4}

Nahlass *Ms J S Doyle* a49 22
4 ch m Bluegrass Prince(IRE) —Nahla (Wassl)
1217^{6} 1402^{7} 1590^{13}

Nahoodh (IRE) *M R Channon* 105
2 gr f Clodovil(IRE) —Mise (IRE) (Indian Ridge)
3432^{12} 3895^{3} (4744)

Naipe Marcado (URU) *I Mohammed* a93 95
4 ch h Timbero(URU) —Nadinka Foss (URU) (Full Toss (ARG))
532a^{2} 643a^{6}

Naked Spark (IRE) *W G M Turner* 30
2 b f Spartacus(IRE) —Naked Poser (IRE) (Night Shift (USA))
1896^{13} 4192^{11}

Nakheel *M Johnston* a95 106
4 b h Sadler's Wells(USA) —Matiya (IRE) (Alzao (USA))
941^{8} 1109^{3} 1477^{2} 1822^{4} 2236^{13} 2859^{12} 3468^{3} 3939^{4}

Naledi *J R Norton* a48 63
3 b g Indian Ridge—Red Carnation (IRE) (Polar Falcon (USA))
6094^{4} 6597^{7} 7103^{5} 7244^{4}

Namarian (IRE) *T D Easterby* a39 52
3 b f Namid—Zalamera (Rambo Dancer (CAN))
2224^{8} 3611^{5} 4036^{2} 4391^{15} 5698^{5}

Namaste's Wish (USA) *W Mott* 94
2 b f Pulpit(USA) —Copelan's Bid Gal (USA) (Copelan (USA))
6482a^{5}

Namaya (IRE) *J S Bolger* a105 108
4 ch g Namid—Touraya (Tap On Wood)
4864a^{8} 5242a^{12} 5459a^{5}

Named At Dinner *Miss Lucinda V Russell* 48
6 ch g Halling(USA) —Salanka (IRE) (Persian Heights)
2391[6] 4380[4] 5087[7]

Namibian Pink (IRE) *R M Beckett* a57 57
3 b f Cape Cross(IRE) —Sky Pink (Warning)
4541[3] 6057[6] *6882[9]*

Namid Reprobate (IRE) *P F I Cole* a82 86
4 br g Namid—Morning Surprise (Tragic Role (USA))
2771[11] 4657[4] *4949[9]* (5383) *5685[11]* 6203[13] 6596[6]

Namiguest (IRE) *Paul Green* a28 48
3 b f Namid—Gentle Guest (IRE) (Be My Guest (USA))
7079[10] 7157[9] 7248[7]

Naming Problems *K J Burke* a45 28
2 ch f Forzando—Basheera (Bahhare (USA))
2717[8] *3171[9] 3923[4] 4359[3] 7058[6] 7142[7]*

Namir (IRE) *D Shaw* a61 83
5 b g Namid—Danalia (IRE) (Danehill (USA))
1165[5] (1669) 1914[6] (2025) 2399[6] 2673[2] 2989[5] 3298[8] 3720[2] 4122[9] 4489[6] *5648[13]* 5747[7]

Namorado (BRZ) *S Seemar* a73 48
6 gr g Belo Colony(BRZ) —Telekina (ARG) (Equalize (USA))
395a[11]

Namroud (USA) *R A Fahey* a76 91
8 b g Irish River(FR) —Top Line (FR) (Top Ville)
4513 525[4] 629[11] 833[3] 1066[3]

Nancymay *J Ryan* 40
2 b f Millkom—Just Eliza (Hector Protector (USA))
5442[6] 5706[9]

Nando's Dream *J Noseda* a78
4 ch m Hernando(FR) —Dream Quest (Rainbow Quest (USA))
95[6]

Nanita Bonita (IRE) *Francis Ennis* a48 32
3 ch f Tagula(IRE) —Shun (Selkirk (USA))
7037a[7]

Nan Jan *R Ingram* a79 23
5 b m Komaite(USA) —Dam Certain (IRE) (Damister (USA))
1933[2] (2179) 2521[5] (2802) 3110[2] (3191) (3644) 4068[12] 4672[9]

Nannina *J H M Gosden* 119
4 b m Medicean—Hill Hopper (IRE) (Danehill (USA))
2207[3] (2753) 3433[4] 4149[8] 6010[2]

Nanny McPhee (IRE) *Dermot Murphy* 74
3 b f Invincible Spirit(IRE) —Ostwahl (IRE) (Waajib)
5392a[10] (Dead)

Nanosecond (USA) *N A Callaghan* a49 59
4 ch g Kingmambo(USA) —Easyngold (USA) (Slew O'Gold (USA))
7159[7] 7257[10]

Nanotech (IRE) *Jarlath P Fahey* a72 88
3 ch c Fath(USA) —Wing And A Prayer (IRE) (Shalford (IRE))
3573a[5] 5841a[13] 6363a[11]

Nans Best (IRE) *Liam McAteer* a70 75
3 b g Rock Of Gibraltar(IRE) —Hawas (Mujtahid (USA))
(5555) 6553a[10]

Nans Joy (IRE) *E J O'Neill* a72 95
3 b f In The Wings—True Joy (IRE) (Zilzal (USA))
737[2] 886[3] 935[4] 1407[4] (1804) 2207[4] 2914[2]

Nans Lady (IRE) *E J O'Neill* a58 78
4 b m Mozart(IRE) —Embers Of Fame (IRE) (Sadler's Wells (USA))
702[7] 3828[10] 4296[4] 4545[3] 4938[3] *5234[8]*

Nanton (USA) *N Wilson* a85 91
5 rg g Spinning World(USA) —Grab The Green (USA) (Cozzene (USA))
1041[8] 1145[15] 1862[3] 2536[4] 4176[5] 4720[5] 5554[11] 6016[6] *6359[6]*

Naomh Geileis (USA) *M Johnston* a91 97
2 ch f Grand Slam(USA) —St Aye (USA) (Nureyev (USA))
3895[2] (4286) 4626a[4] *5219[5]* 6170[4]

Naomia (GER) *P Rau* 100
3 br f Monsun(GER) —Nagoya (GER) (Goofalik (USA))
(1855a) 2294a[5]

Napoleon Dynamite (IRE) *J W Hills* a79 66
3 b c Danetime(IRE) —Anita's Contessa (IRE) (Anita's Prince)
1022[5] *1383[2] 1437[2] (2593) 4394[6] (5177) 5238[4] 5753[2] 6122[6] 6568[4]*

Napoletano (GER) *S Dow* a62 57
6 b g Soviet Star(USA) —Noble House (GER) (Siberian Express (USA))
381[9] 549[7] 686[12] 1212[7] 1507[7] 1612[5] 1740[8] 1921[5] 2273[3] 2336[3] 2556[4] (2665) 2877[7] *3419[14] 3615[7] 7268[2]*

Narmeen *M R Channon* a66 66
2 b f Royal Applause—Protectorate (Hector Protector (USA))
2365[4] *3213[3] 3453[6]* 4126[8] 4890[3] 5331[8] 5621[4]

Nasaq (USA) *M P Tregoning* a75
2 b c Gulch(USA) —Irtahal (USA) (Swain (IRE))
6436[3]

Nashharry (IRE) *S Kirk* a65 57
3 b f Ishiguru(USA) —Abbey Park (USA) (Known Fact (USA))
1345[9] 1726[10] *(2262) 2571[2] 3168[8]* 4163[8] *4740[12] 5136[11]*

Nashoba's Key (USA) *Carla Gaines* a113 113
4 b m Silver Hawk(USA) —Nashoba (IRE) (Caerleon (USA))
(5825a) 6509a[4]

Nasrawy *J J Lambe* 34
5 b g Grand Lodge(USA) —By Charter (Shirley Heights)
3678[8]

Nassar (IRE) *G Prodromou* a56 67
4 b h Danehill(USA) —Regent Gold (USA) (Seeking The Gold (USA))
616[2]

Nassau Style *J R Fanshawe* a70 76
3 ch g Bahamian Bounty—Art Deco Lady (Master Willie)
2913[4] (3276) 4080[5] *4889[11]*

Nassmaan (IRE) *P W Chapple-Hyam* a79 76
3 b c Alhaarth(IRE) —Just In Love (FR) (Highest Honor (FR))
(382) 719[4] 1089[4] 2627[10]

Nastrelli (IRE) *M Halford* a86 94
4 b g Mozart(IRE) —Dawnsio (IRE) (Tate Gallery (USA))
3140a[2] 4211a[6] 6363a[9] *6916a[8]*

Natagora (FR) *P Bary* 117
2 gr f Divine Light(JPN) —Reinamixa (FR) (Linamix (FR))
(3147a) (3779a) 4653a[2] (5973)

Natal Lad (IRE) *M G Quinlan* 88
2 b c Acclamation—Gentle Guest (IRE) (Be My Guest (USA))
6495[9]

Natco *M Johnston* a29 46
3 b f Cois Na Tine(IRE) —Young Sue (Local Suitor (USA))
4178[12] 4641[6] 4901[4] *6532[11]*

Nathan Dee *Mrs H Sweeting* a51 55
2 ch c Guys And Dolls—Blu Air Flow (ITY) (Entrepreneur)
1540[15] 2138[6] *2517[4] 3642[9] 4461[6]* 5721[6]

Nathan Jones *M G Quinlan* 57
8 b g Emperor Jones(USA) —Brightside (IRE) (Last Tycoon (IRE))
6864[12]

National Captain (SAF) *S Seemar* a76 107
5 b h Captain Al(SAF) —National Secret (SAF) (Secret Prospector (USA))
178a[4] *396a[12]* (542a) 645a[4]

National Colour (SAF) *S Tarry* a114
5 gr m National Assembly(CAN) —Rainbow Cake (SAF) (Mr Eats (IRE))
(474a) 860a[16]

National Day (IRE) *D R C Elsworth* a41
3 b f Barathea(IRE) —Rise And Fall (Mill Reef (USA))
7282[8]

National Icon (SAF) *A Manuel* a79 88
7 ch g National Emblem(SAF) —Royal Fields (SAF) (Northfields (USA))
245a[11] 409a[9]

Native American *T D McCarthy* a58 59
5 b g Indian Lodge(IRE) —Summer Siren (FR) (Saint Cyrien (FR))
19[8] 309[9]

Native Talent *B W Hills* 45
2 b c Beat Hollow—Native Justice (USA) (Alleged (USA))
2632[9] (Dead)

Native Title *D Nicholls* a84 85
9 b g Pivotal—Bermuda Lily (Dunbeath (USA))
155[6] 388[5] 536[6] 766[9]

Natmana *M R Channon* a75 74
2 b c Alhaarth(IRE) —Gracious Gift (Cadeaux Genereux)
2473[6] 3013[2] 3478[5] 4315[2] 4844[2] *5199[4]* 5582[10] 6052[3] *6502[2]*

Natural Action *W Jarvis* a71 71
3 b c Diktat—Naskhi (Nashwan (USA))
1100[9] *1440[4]* 1928[3] 2727[6] 3041[2] (4357) *4951[7]* 5955[13]

Natural Force (IRE) *R P Burns* a45 30
4 b g King's Best(USA) —Wolf Cleugh (IRE) (Last Tycoon (IRE))
3138a[18]

Natural Rhythm (IRE) *D W Chapman* a65 67
2 ch c Distant Music(USA) —Nationalartgallery (IRE) (Tate Gallery (USA))
1411[5] 1622[3] 1963[11] 3673[6] 4077[5] 4349[8] (4559) 4783[3] 4892[6] 5251[9] 5298[2] 5736[2] 5914[15] 6379[6] *6736[3] 7007[5] 7149[6] 7176[2] 7234[4]*

Naughty Frida (IRE) *E A L Dunlop* a75 73
2 b f Royal Applause—Nausicaa (USA) (Diesis)
4061[14] 5003[4] 5575[2] *(6225)* 6525a[6]

Naughty Nod (IRE) *K R Burke* a46 57
4 b g Intikhab(USA) —Quelle Celtique (FR) (Tel Quel (FR))
1178[8] 1301[6] 1942[4] 2367[4] *6875[10]*

Naughty Thoughts (IRE) *Andrew Turnell* a72 70
3 b f Grand Lodge(USA) —Gentle Thoughts (Darshaan)
1408[5] 2133[12] 2534[10] *6547[3] 6856[8] 7073[7] 7257[12]*

Naukos (GER) *H Blume* 99
4 br h Kallisto(GER) —Nagoya (GER) (Goofalik (USA))
2976a[4]

Nautical *A W Carroll* a76 86
9 gr g Lion Cavern(USA) —Russian Royal (USA) (Nureyev (USA))
846[18] 1063[10] 1200[9] 1962[13] 2414[5] 2982[3] 3388[6] 3686[4] 4390[9] 4606[6] *5130[2] 5340[4] 5731[9] 6064[3] 6344[12]*

Navajo Joe (IRE) *B J Meehan* 64
2 ch c Indian Ridge—Maid Of Killeen (IRE) (Darshaan)
6616[8]

Navajo Moon (IRE) *David Wachman* 100
3 b f Danehill(USA) —Star Begonia (Sadler's Wells (USA))
1694a[11] 4237a[4] 5396a[9]

Naval Review (USA) *Sir Michael Stoute* 73
2 bb c Storm Cat(USA) —Arutua (USA) (Riverman (USA))
(6469)

Navene (IRE) *C F Wall* a44 59
3 b f Desert Style(IRE) —Majudel (IRE) (Revoque (IRE))
1840[10] 2470[6] 3031[2] *3647[8]* 6309[2]

Navigation (IRE) *T J Etherington* a52 59
5 ch g Bahamian Bounty—Bridge Pool (First Trump)
337[2] 441[4] 1384[10] 1596[15] 2509[7] 2791[10] 4939[13] 5969[3] *6264[9]*

Navio (FR) *J-C Rouget* 98
3 b c Priolo(USA) —Neriella (Darshaan)
1057a[4]

Nawaaff *M R Channon* a65 82
2 ch c Compton Place—Amazed (Clantime)
1792[2] 2215[3] 2983[2] 3781[2] (4174) 5207[7] *6004[8]* 6699[7]

Nawamees (IRE) *G L Moore* a91 94
9 b g Darshaan—Truly Generous (IRE) (Generous (IRE))
457[3] 662[3] 1244[7] 3509[3] 4690[5] 5415[9] *(6501) (7050) (7226)*

Nawaqees *J L Dunlop* 87
4 b h Danehill(USA) —Elrafa Ah (USA) (Storm Cat (USA))
1287[13] (1962) 2469[2] 3002[6] 3437[15] 4049[17]

Nawayea *C N Allen* a51 48
4 b m Lujain(USA) —Shallat (IRE) (Pennekamp (USA))
282[6] 421[6] 580[11] 1883[3] *2174[3]* 2791[2] *3597[2]* 3829[7] 4336[5] 4471[11] *4974[6]* 5276[6] *5566[6] 5782[12] 6361[2] 7124[3] 7144[7] 7209[8] 7278[11]*

Nawow *P D Cundell* a81 83
7 b g Blushing Flame(USA) —Fair Test (Fair Season)
(316) 488[3] 593[3] 1148[6] (1668)

Nayarna *Mrs A Duffield* 47
2 b f Nayef(USA) —Dimakya (USA) (Dayjur (USA))
4247[6]

Nayef Star *J Noseda* 70
2 b c Nayef(USA) —Satin Bell (Midyan (USA))
6618[6]

Nayodabayo (IRE) *Evan Williams* a59 70
7 b g Definite Article—Babushka (IRE) (Dance Of Life (USA))
10[2] 146[7]

Nayyir *G A Butler* a112 115
9 ch g Indian Ridge—Pearl Kite (USA) (Silver Hawk (USA))
646a[7] 2442[5] 4043[11]

Ndola *B J Curley* a57 39
8 b g Emperor Jones(USA) —Lykoa (Shirley Heights)
(6292) 6583[6]

Neander (GER) *P Van Kempen* a95 93
5 ch g Devil River Peek(USA) —Night On Earth (GER) (Galetto (FR))
437a[7]

Neardown Beauty (IRE) *R E Barr* a88 88
4 br m Bahhare(USA) —Habla Me (IRE) (Fairy King (USA))
817[6] 846[16] 1209[6] 1395[3] 1710[2] 1962[4] 2507[6] 3100[6] *4068[5]* 4268[13] 6746[9] *6981[7]*

Near Germany (IRE) *R Curtis* 64
7 b g Germany(USA) —Night Year (IRE) (Jareer (USA))
1025[2] 1295[5] 2089[3] 2660[9]

Nebdi (IRE) *E J Alston* a58 54
6 b g Fayruz—Miss Nutwood (IRE) (Prince Rupert (FR))
33[9]

Nebiola (GER) *W Hickst* 97
3 b f Acatenango(GER) —Narola (GER) (Nebos (GER))
5669a[9]

Neboisha *P Howling* a53
3 ch f Ishiguru(USA) —Mariette (Blushing Scribe (USA))
2593[2] 4392[11] 4977[10] 5528[8] 6587[12]

Neckar Valley (IRE) *J G Portman* a47 50
8 b g Desert King(IRE) —Solar Attraction (IRE) (Salt Dome (USA))
2946[6] 4534[5] 5453[6]

Ned Kelly (SAF) *Christian Wroe* a40 70
6 b g Goldkeeper(USA) —Assemblance (SAF) (Complete Warrior (USA))
244a[13] 398a[14] *532a[16]*

Ned Ludd (IRE) *J G Portman* 92
4 b g Montjeu(IRE) —Zanella (IRE) (Nordico (USA))
1148[2] 1654[2] 2860[4] 5938[4] 6335[18] 6760[7]

Neele (IRE) *H Steinmetz* 108
3 ch f Peintre Celebre(USA) —Night Teeny (Platini (GER))
3075a[2] 4055a[5] 4651a[5]

Negramaro (IRE) *A & G Botti*
2 b c Orpen(USA) —Pinky Mouse (IRE) (Machiavellian (USA))
6527a[3]

Negrito (GER) *Dagmar Geissmann* 10
8 br g Protektor(GER) —Nordsee (IRE) (Kings Lake (USA))
356a[7]

Negus (GER) *A Wohler* 76
3 ch c Samum(GER) —Noble House (GER) (Siberian Express (USA))
6781a[9]

Neideen (IRE) *J Akehurst* a43 51
5 ch m Elnadim(USA) —Mynador (USA) (Forty Niner (USA))
235[13] (Dead)

Neige Eternel (FR) *Robert Collet* 86
2 gr c Verglas(IRE) —Frenchtreska (FR) (French Stress (USA))
4009a[5] 4625a[9]

Neil's Legacy (IRE) *Miss L A Perratt* a61 72
5 br m Second Empire(IRE) —Eliade (IRE) (Flash Of Steel)
1488[13] 1627[9] 1944[9] 2168[4] 2254[6] 2563[2] 2760[9] (3343) 3539[2] (3783) 4382[5] 4772[3] 4933[4] 5296[9] (5674) 6258[7] 6465[6] 6638[3] 6746[6]

Nell Gwyn (IRE) *A P O'Brien* a53 94
3 b f Danehill(USA) —Offshore Boom (Be My Guest (USA))
946a[10] 1694a[2] 2211[12] 6216a[16]

Nellie *R M Whitaker*
3 b f Lake Coniston(IRE) —Boomerang Blade (Sure Blade (USA))
1482[8] *3924[12]*

Nell Tupp *G Woodward* a2 24
4 b g Killer Instinct—Eternal Triangle (USA) (Barachois (CAN))
1413[11] 5739[10]

Nelly's Glen *R Hannon* 70
3 b f Efisio—Ravine (Indian Ridge)
1523[14] 2477[3] 2693[6] (3178) 3904[3] 6497[10]

Nelore Pora (BRZ) *P Nickel Filho* a110
5 b h Romarin(BRZ) —Factory Of Dream (BRZ) (Lupin (ARG))
(327a) 599a[8] 858a[7]

Nelsons Column (IRE) *G M Moore* 94
4 b g Benny The Dip(USA) —Sahara Rose (Green Desert (USA))
995[11] 1575[6] 2011[11] 3753[4] 4171[11] 4843[4] 5478[8] 5968[4]

Nemo Spirit (IRE) *W R Muir* 80
2 gr c Daylami(IRE) —La Bayadere (Sadler's Wells (USA))
5919[3] 6494[2]

Neon *J W Hills* a58 64
3 b f Fantastic Light(USA) —River Saint (USA) (Irish River (FR))
1403[10] *2456[7]*

Neon Blue *R M Whitaker* a54 79
6 bb g Atraf—Desert Lynx (IRE) (Green Desert (USA))
1747[3] 1845[2] 2239[4] 2536[9] 3512[3] 3828[9] 4281[5] 4407[4] (5253) 5556[6] 6651[14]

Nepos *A J McCabe* a56 57
3 b g Piccolo—Blushing Victoria (Weldnaas (USA))
2146[6] 2826[7]

Nepotista (BRZ) *A Cintra Pereira* 104
5 b g Know Heights(IRE) —Wekilinda (BRZ) (Kenetico (BRZ))
328a[2] 475a[9] 545a[7] 598a[7] 648a[10]

Nepro (IRE) *E J Creighton* a75 62
5 b g Orpen(USA) —My Gray (FR) (Danehill (USA))
465[7] 621[2] 672[6] 774[4] 927[8] 1063[13] 1214[P] (Dead)

Nero's Return (IRE) *G L Moore* a77 88
6 b g Mujadil(USA) —Snappy Dresser (Nishapour (FR))
891[2] 1470[6] *1949[6]* 2238[6] 2511[9]

Nero West (FR) *I Semple* 76
6 ch g Pelder(IRE) —West River (USA) (Gone West (USA))
2391[4] 2567[2] (3027) (3533) 4056[16] 4969[4] 5586[4] 5933[5] 6733[9]

Neshla *C E Brittain* a45
4 ch m Singspiel(IRE) —Nordica (Northfields (USA))
98[3] 402[7] 517[9]

Nesnaas (USA) *M G Rimell* a48
6 ch g Gulch(USA) —Sedrah (USA) (Dixieland Band (USA))
3191[11] 3945[14]

Nesno (USA) *J D Bethell* a72 83
4 ch g Royal Academy(USA) —Cognac Lady (USA) (Olympio (USA))
850[15] 1638[10] 2038[6] 2434[10] 3204[7] 3955[7]

Nestor Protector (IRE) *A B Haynes* a3 57
2 b g Bold Fact(USA) —Irma La Douce (IRE) (Elbio)
(971) 1882[8] 2618[3] 3734[4] *4461[10]*

Networker *P J McBride* a81 81
4 ch g Danzig Connection(USA) —Trevorsninepoints (Jester)
650[10] 737[7] 980[4] (1918) (2154) (2388) 2985[3] *3215[2]* 3437[4] *4068[4]* 4268[9]

Neutrino *P C Haslam* a64 76
5 b g Mtoto—Fair Seas (General Assembly (USA))
4333[4]

Nevada Desert (IRE) *R M Whitaker* a89 92
7 b g Desert King(IRE) —Kayanga (Green Desert (USA))
1287[12] 1480[7] 1915[4] *2346[3]* 3813[9] (3971) (4039) 4176[2] 4385[4] 4745[8] 4900[5] 5615[5] 5776[3] 6155[8] 6539[9]

Neve Lieve (IRE) *M Botti* a54 62
2 b f Dubai Destination(USA) —Love Of Silver (USA) (Arctic Tern (USA))
3213[10] 3916[3] 4796[10] 5443[4]

Never Catcher (IRE) *P A Blockley* 62
2 b f Catcher In The Rye(IRE) —Never End (Alzao (USA))
6535[6]

Never Green (IRE) *C Laffon-Parias* 102
3 b f Halling(USA) —Brooklyn's Dance (FR) (Shirley Heights)
6770a[9]

Never Say Deya *M J Wallace* a50 55
4 b m Dansili—Dream On Deya (IRE) (Dolphin Street (FR))
1596[10] *2519[7]*

Never So Easy *E S McMahon* a42
4 b g Easycall—Polistatic (Free State)
559[8]

Never Sold Out (IRE) *J G M O'Shea* a58 45
2 ch c Captain Rio—Vicious Rosie (Dancing Spree (USA))
1058[10] 1680[12] *2356[2] (3065) 5117[12] 6150[9] 6584[12]*

Never Without Me *J F Coupland* a59 73
7 ch g Mark Of Esteem(IRE) —Festival Sister (Belmez (USA))
905[4] 1299[12] 1493[2] *1718[10]* 2805[8] 4423[2] (4642) 4800[4] 5297[12] 5747[14] 6594[13]

Nevinstown (IRE) *C Grant* a53 58
7 b g Lahib(USA) —Moon Tango (IRE) (Last Tycoon (IRE))
2397 320[2] 430[10] 519[9] 1527[6] 1744[5] 1893[2] 2298[3] 2809[4] 3195[8] 4223[11] 5935[7] *6311[9]*

New Approach (IRE) *J S Bolger* 125
2 ch c Galileo(IRE) —Park Express (Ahonoora)
(3980a) (4833a) (5458a) (6333)

New Balls Please (IRE) *P M Phelan* a56 54
2 ch g Titus Livius(FR) —Kilkee Bay (IRE) (Case Law)
883[5] 1033[4] 1781[11] 3524[9] 5089[7] 5715[2] *6227[6] 6426[9]* 6722[4]

New Beginning (IRE) *Mrs S Lamyman* a78 103
3 b c Keltos(FR) —Goldthroat (IRE) (Zafonic (USA))
111[2] 184[4] 584[5] (1010) 1293[3] 1773[8] 2340[3] 2506[4] 3271[5] 3912[2]

Newcastle Sam *J J Bridger* a6 15
2 b g Atraf—Ballyewry (Prince Tenderfoot (USA))
4160[8] 4500[13] *4946[8]* 5313[11]

Newcastles Owen (IRE) *R Johnson* a48 57
4 b g Elnadim(USA) —Brittas Blues (IRE) (Blues Traveller (IRE))
728[4] 1719[8] 2509[12] 3053[8] 3180[2] 3498[10]

New Colossus *E J O'Neill* 46
2 b g Statue Of Liberty(USA) —Daisy Do (IRE) (Danehill (USA))
1622^{7} 2138^{8}

Newcorp Lad *Mrs G S Rees* a59 42
7 b g Komaite(USA) —Gleam Of Gold (Crested Lark)
110^{9} 242^{10} 2007^{14} 3497^{9} 3721^{6} 4333^{6} 4717^{7} 5000^{5} 5750^{11} 6672^{6}

New Diamond *Mrs P Ford* a22 42
8 ch g Bijou D'Inde—Nannie Annie (Persian Bold)
4880^{16} 5179^{10} 5916^{15} 6459^{10}

New Edition (USA) *J Larry Jones* 102
3 ch f Stormy Atlantic(USA) —Sashay Away (USA) (Farma Way (USA))
$5248a^{9}$

New Freedom (BRZ) *P Nickel Filho* a96
6 b g Burooj—Beautiful Maria (BRZ) (Ghadeer (FR))
$249a^{14}$ $474a^{3}$

Newgate Lodge (IRE) *M Halford* 95
3 b f Namid—Oh'Cecilia (IRE) (Scenic)
$946a^{7}$ $1047a^{7}$ $5242a^{4}$ $6363a^{15}$

Newgate Parisien *Mark Campion* a14 34
4 gb g Paris House—Gemgem (Lochnager)
4157^{11} 4659^{8} 5567^{10} 6565^{13}

New Girlfriend (IRE) *Robert Collet* 113
4 b m Diesis—New Story (USA) (Dynaformer (USA))
$1389a^{9}$ $1704a^{7}$ $2291a^{4}$ $4214a^{9}$ $4869a^{10}$ $6039a^{9}$

New Guinea *Saeed Bin Suroor* a93 110
4 b g Fantastic Light(USA) —Isle Of Spice (USA) (Diesis)
5411^{2} 5829^{4} (6538) 6759^{5}

New Jersey (IRE) *K A Ryan* 95
2 br c Statue Of Liberty(USA) —Shinkoh Rose (FR) (Warning)
1107^{4} 1478^{2} (1772) 2183^{4} 3269^{2} $3779a^{6}$ 4743^{15} 5583^{6} 6017^{9}

Newkeylets *I Semple* a60 61
4 b m Diktat—Jay Gee Ell (Vaigly Great)
296^{5} 448^{3} 668^{11} 1595^{3} 1940^{6} 3017^{14} 4157^{4} 4494^{3} 4996^{5} 5930^{15}

Newlands North (IRE) *M J P O'Brien* a17 72
6 ch g Goldmark(USA) —Park Cottage (IRE) (Thatching)
$6555a^{18}$

New Light *Eve Johnson Houghton* a35 53
3 ch f Generous(IRE) —May Light (Midyan (USA))
1973^{8} 3151^{3} 3804^{9} 4073^{9} 4532^{15} 5304^{3} 5530^{6} 6204^{7} 6597^{10}

Newly Elected (IRE) *C G Cox* 91
2 b c Acclamation—Assafiyah (IRE) (Kris)
(4571) (5323)

New Minerton (IRE) *B R Millman* 43
2 b f Trans Island—Irish Lover (USA) (Irish River (FR))
1079^{8} 2969^{7} 4593^{7}

Newnham (IRE) *J R Boyle* a87 87
6 ch g Theatrical—Brief Escapade (IRE) (Brief Truce (USA))
142^{8} 297^{7} 457^{4} (578) 617^{7} (844) 1253^{2} 1959^{15} 3216^{5} (4067) 4779^{2}

New Options *Peter Grayson* a61 40
10 b g Formidable(USA) —No Comebacks (Last Tycoon (IRE))
82^{8} 154^{11} 254^{11} 289^{2} 368^{7} 403^{3} 613^{10} 688^{9} 1163^{7} 1729^{11} 1902^{8}

Newpark Spirit (IRE) *Patrick Morris* a43 25
4 b g Desert Style(IRE) —Newpark Lady (IRE) (Foxhound (USA))
46^{7} 83^{11}

Newport Boy (IRE) *R A Harris* a62 62
4 b g Montjeu(IRE) —Dream Chaser (Record Token)
64^{6} 180^{10}

Newport Lass (IRE) *K R Burke* a35 48
3 b f Mull Of Kintyre(USA) —Mari-Ela (IRE) (River Falls)
454^{10} 2200^{9}

New Proposal (IRE) *A P Jarvis* a58 51
5 b g Orpen(USA) —Woodenitbenice (USA) (Nasty And Bold (USA))
1118^{4} 1753^{14} 1947^{11} 2357^{2} 2665^{5} 4021^{8}

New Realm (USA) *R A Farrant*
5 b g Red Ransom(USA) —Mystery Rays (USA) (Nijinsky (CAN))
1167^{11}

New Seeker *P F I Cole* 114
7 b g Green Desert(USA) —Ahbab (IRE) (Ajdal (USA))
(1294) 1723^{5} 2396^{10} 4747^{14} 5634^{5}

News Of The Day (IRE) *P Monteith* a61 70
3 ch f Diesis—Etoile Ascendante (USA) (Arctic Tern (USA))
(68) 224^{8} (357) 937^{3} 1059^{2} 1256^{2} 2389^{2} 3016^{3} 3501^{6} 4499^{5} 4936^{10} 6258^{13}

New Spirit (IRE) *John Joseph Murphy* a36 80
3 b f Invincible Spirit(IRE) —Rainbow Java (IRE) (Fairy King (USA))
7162^{5}

Newsround *D W Chapman* a22 54
5 ch g Cadeaux Genereux—Ring The Relatives (Bering)
1596^{8} 3375^{10} 3754^{7} 3787^{9} 4427^{14}

New Star (UAE) *W M Brisbourne* a51 80
3 b g Green Desert(USA) —Princess Haifa (USA) (Mr Prospector (USA))
1605^{9} 2261^{11} 3079^{3} (4993) 5432^{9} 6110^{5} 6474^{9}

Newtonian (USA) *M Brittain* a67 31
8 ch g Distant View(USA) —Polly Adler (USA) (Housebuster (USA))
997^{7} 1376^{4} 1717^{4} (1980) 2348^{7}

New Wave *R Lee* a35 40
5 b g Woodman(USA) —Vanishing Point (USA) (Caller I.D. (USA))
5636^{8} 6344^{11}

New World Order (IRE) *K R Burke* a80 84
3 b c Night Shift(USA) —Kama Tashoof (Mtoto)
152^{3} 301^{2} 483^{3} 2045^{13} 2862^{7} 3495^{4} 3919^{7} 5178^{2} (5390) 5664^{2} 6067^{10} 6949^{2} 7189^{3}

New Year (IRE) *T P Tate* 51
3 ch g Traditionally(USA) —Zelah (IRE) (Alzao (USA))
2094^{6} 2393^{8} 2873^{4} 3381^{11} 4137^{12}

New York Oscar (IRE) *A J McCabe* a88 69
3 b g Tobougg(IRE) —Special Dissident (Dancing Dissident (USA))
54^{2} (90) 1176^{7} 1286^{5} 1530^{14} 1729^{4} (1948) 2205^{7} 2518^{6} 2837^{3} 3054^{10} 4432^{4} (6406) (6589) 6707^{5} 6876^{6} 6970^{6} 7112^{5} 7212^{5}

New Zealand (IRE) *A P O'Brien* a77 102
2 ch c Galileo(IRE) —Worlds Apart (Darshaan)
$6782a^{4}$

Next Best *A Berry* a50 50
2 b f Best Of The Bests(IRE) —Lone Pine (Sesaro (USA))
1487^{6} 2310^{5} 2517^{2} 2738^{3} 3410^{3} 3788^{7} 4476^{3} 4970^{5}

Next Flight (IRE) *R E Barr* 51
8 b g Woodborough(USA) —Sans Ceriph (IRE) (Thatching)
1556^{4} 4451^{7} 4925^{9}

Next King (ITY) *A & G Botti* 101
3 gr c Shantou(USA) —Nissan (ITY) (Sharrood (USA))
$6863a^{4}$

Next Of Kin (IRE) *G A Swinbank* 56
2 b g Kris Kin(USA) —Lady Of Shalott (Kings Lake (USA))
4125^{6} 4611^{10} 5663^{5}

Neyraan *M Johnston* a55
2 b f Lujain(USA) —Zaynaat (Unfuwain (USA))
6805^{12} 7097^{6}

Nezami (IRE) *B J Meehan* 86
2 b g Elnadim(USA) —Stands To Reason (USA) (Gulch (USA))
3866^{7} 4162^{2} 4584^{4} 5274^{2} (5665)

Nhecolandia (BRZ) *A Cintra Pereira* 86
5 ch m Purple Mountain(USA) —Information Phone (BRZ) (Minstrel Glory (USA))
$174a^{6}$

Nibbles (IRE) *D W Chapman*
5 b g Soviet Star(USA) —Tumbleweed Pearl (Aragon)
2222^{5}

Nicada (IRE) *Stef Liddiard* a78 70
3 ch g Titus Livius(FR) —Rhapsani (IRE) (Persian Bold)
2317^{4} 2943^{2} 3235^{4} 3570^{5} 4313^{2} 5122^{4} 5860^{5} 6272^{6} 6996^{2} 7045^{4} 7164^{9}

Nice Applause (IRE) *M Gentile* 103
4 b h Royal Applause—Mona Em (IRE) (Catrail (USA))
$437a^{0}$

Nice Dream *C E Brittain* a40
2 b f Oasis Dream—Have Fun (Indian Ridge)
2344^{8}

Nice To Know (FR) *G L Moore* a78 78
3 ch f Machiavellian(USA) —Entice (FR) (Selkirk (USA))
1838^{4} 2541^{4} 3156^{6} (4326) (4848) 5537^{6} 6929^{4}

Nice Wee Girl (IRE) *S Kirk* a67
2 b f Clodovil(IRE) —Neat Dish (CAN) (Stalwart (USA))
3596^{4} 6404^{6} 6734^{3} 6827^{3} 6980^{4} 7097^{2} 7232^{2}

Nickelle (FR) *J-P Gallorini* 106
4 b m Sagamix(FR) —N'Avoue Jamais (FR) (Marignan (USA))
$1421a^{3}$ $2165a^{5}$

Nickel Silver *B Smart* 73
2 ro c Choisir(AUS) —Negligee (Night Shift (USA))
1858^{2} 2371^{2} 4286^{5} 5931^{4}

Nick's Nikita (IRE) *M Halford* 108
4 ch m Pivotal—Elaine's Honor (USA) (Chief's Crown (USA))
$1050a^{4}$ $1777a^{3}$ (2702a) $3119a^{2}$ $4238a^{3}$ $4647a^{4}$

Nicomedia (IRE) *R Hannon* a75 73
3 br f Key Of Luck(USA) —Ladylishandra (IRE) (Mujadil (USA))
27^{3} 633^{3} 689^{3} 1024^{2} (1310) (1628) 1887^{4} 2579^{7} 3048^{5} 3731^{6} 4205^{6}

Nigella *E S McMahon* a75 85
4 b m Band On The Run—Yabint El Sham (Sizzling Melody)
2399^{12} 3749^{9}

Night Crescendo (USA) *Mrs A J Perrett* a85 103
4 bb g Diesis—Night Fax (USA) (Known Fact (USA))
1145^{20} 1494^{3} 4043^{16} 6011^{29} (6172) 6499^{6} 6759^{3}

Night Cru *C F Wall* a89 103
4 b g Night Shift(USA) —Jouet (Reprimand)
1198^{17} 2004^{2} (2512) 2765^{2} (3060) 3882^{4} (4814) 6011^{27}

Night Cruise (IRE) *J A Osborne* a89
4 b g Docksider(USA) —Addaya (IRE) (Persian Bold)
192^{3} (457) 844^{5}

Night Falcon *H Morrison* a44 44
3 b f Act One—Original Spin (IRE) (Machiavellian (USA))
649^{7} 790^{8} 1353^{5} 1973^{6} 2489^{7}

Night Groove (IRE) *P Butler* a48 63
4 b g Night Shift(USA) —Taysala (IRE) (Akarad (FR))
212^{11} 315^{10} 982^{5} 1342^{7} 7120^{7} 7256^{8}

Night Hour (IRE) *J H M Gosden* a90 97
5 b g Entrepreneur—Witching Hour (IRE) (Alzao (USA))
1244^{5} 2236^{3} 4047^{5} 4637^{2} 5686^{4} (6490)

Nightime (IRE) *D K Weld* 116
4 ch m Galileo(IRE) —Caumshinaun (IRE) (Indian Ridge)
$2064a^{8}$

Night In (IRE) *N Tinkler* a59 76
4 b g Night Shift(USA) —Sherannda (USA) (Trempolino (USA))
992^{5} 1675^{8} (3017) 3345^{12} 4083^{15} 4562^{9} 4978^{5} 5741^{12} 6149^{5}

Nightmare Affair (USA) *G Marano* a121
6 rg h Out Of Place(USA) —Beaux Arts Ball (USA) (Black Tie Affair)
$860a^{15}$

Night Mystery *T D Easterby* 23
2 ch c Observatory(USA) —Highland Gait (Most Welcome)
3712^{9} 4077^{11}

Night Premiere (IRE) *R Hannon* 61
2 b f Night Shift(USA) —Star Studded (Cadeaux Genereux)
5110^{6} 5357^{8}

Night Prospector *R A Harris* a91 91
7 b g Night Shift(USA) —Pride Of My Heart (Lion Cavern (USA))
41^{7} 81^{4} 227^{7} (289) 419^{7} 480^{3} 575^{8} 1134^{9} 1431^{7} 2411^{8} 2655^{10} 4024^{9} 4312^{12} 4689^{4} 4853^{13}

Night Rainbow (IRE) *P G Murphy* a55 60
4 ch m Night Shift(USA) —Teresita (Rainbow Quest (USA))
4416^{17}

Night Reveller (IRE) *M C Chapman* a31 26
4 b m Night Shift(USA) —Tir-An-Oir (IRE) (Law Society (USA))
630^{7} 728^{11} 807^{8} 3593^{8} 4426^{12} 4920^{14}

Night Rider *Miss J Feilden* a28
3 b g Night Shift(USA) —Lady Emmaline (IRE) (Charnwood Forest (IRE))
6240^{10} 6778^{14}

Night Robe *P D Evans* a47 49
2 b f Robellino(USA) —Camp Fire (IRE) (Lahib (USA))
3162^{6} 3486^{3} 3902^{7} 4255^{7} 6312^{5} 6536^{11} 6736^{10} (7136) 7210^{6}

Night Skier (IRE) *J L Dunlop* a68 78
2 ch f Night Shift(USA) —Ski For Me (IRE) (Barathea (IRE))
2000^{9} 2457^{5} (3874) 4364^{11} 6120^{10}

Nightspot *Eve Johnson Houghton* a82 80
6 ch g Night Shift(USA) —Rash Gift (Cadeaux Genereux)
(1811) 2106^{2} 2397^{2} 3386^{3} 4015^{4} (4271) 4523^{5} 5454^{5} 5870^{2} 6500^{13}

Nightstrike (IRE) *Luke Comer* a58 67
4 b m Night Shift(USA) —Come Together (Mtoto)
381^{8} 486^{9} 614^{10} 2592^{2} 3950^{17}

Night Wolf (IRE) *Jamie Poulton* a63 63
7 gr g Indian Ridge—Nicer (IRE) (Pennine Walk)
274^{4} (549) 614^{13} (1318) 2414^{7} 6854^{4} 6993^{3} 7268^{10}

Nijoom Dubai *M R Channon* 103
2 b f Noverre(USA) —Aileen's Gift (IRE) (Rainbow Quest (USA))
1807^{2} 2241^{3} (2812)

Nikindi (IRE) *J S Moore* 84
2 b g Mull Of Kintyre(USA) —Alma Latina (IRE) (Persian Bold)
(898) 1094^{4} $4832a^{4}$ 5324^{11} 6488^{11}

Nikinoo *B Palling* a22
4 b m Averti(IRE) —Tzarinassilouhette (Puissance)
711^{7} 1068^{12} 1739^{13} 1921^{13}

Nikki Bea (IRE) *Jamie Poulton* a69 64
4 ch m Titus Livius(FR) —Strong Feeling (USA) (Devil's Bag (USA))
233^{4} 313^{9} 358^{7} 497^{3} 699^{3} 734^{6} 1038^{2} (1344) 1629^{5} (1947) 2771^{8} 3191^{10} 3851^{11} 4236^{11} 4361^{3} 5118^{5} 6210^{7} 6825^{14} 7269^{5}

Nikolaievich (IRE) *P F I Cole* a67 66
2 b c Xaar—Seren Quest (Rainbow Quest (USA))
3551^{9} 4876^{6} 5200^{7} 5858^{10}

Nimbelle (IRE) *T F Lacy* 50
2 bb f Namid—Bellissi (IRE) (Bluebird (USA))
6721^{8}

Nimello (USA) *A G Newcombe* a62 78
11 b g Kingmambo(USA) —Zakota (IRE) (Polish Precedent (USA))
242^{3} 508^{2} (665) 733^{5} 1178^{6}

Nimra (USA) *G A Butler* a74 82
4 rg m Cozzene(USA) —Purity (USA) (Fappiano (USA))
1793^{13} 2620^{5} 3371^{2} (3473) 3963^{6} 5478^{6}

Nimrana Fort *J S Wainwright* a46 59
4 b g Indian Ridge—Ninotchka (USA) (Nijinsky (CAN))
741^{10} 968^{10} 1301^{8}

Nina Blini *B J Meehan* a77 89
3 b f Bertolini(USA) —Film Buff (Midyan (USA))
1009^{7} 1096^{10}

Ninefineirishmen (IRE) *K R Burke* 70
2 bb c Statue Of Liberty(USA) —Tallassee (Indian Ridge)
6156^{7} 6634^{2}

Nine Stories (IRE) *J Howard Johnson* 83
2 b g Catcher In The Rye(IRE) —Irinatinvidio (Rudimentary (USA))
1743^{4} (1938) 3838^{2} 4495^{3} 4743^{16} 5582^{6}

Ninetyninetreble (IRE) *Grant Tuer* a66 61
4 b g Grand Lodge(USA) —Licorne (Sadler's Wells (USA))
769^{2} 1566^{4} 1716^{9} 2118^{5} 4003^{6} 5158^{11} 5626^{12}

Nini De Paris (FR) *J-P Gallorini* 89
3 b f Lord Of Men—N'Avoue Jamais (FR) (Marignan (USA))
$3148a^{9}$

Nino Cochise (IRE) *C R Egerton* a70
2 b g High Chaparral(IRE) —Lady Scarlett (Woodman (USA))
6948^{9} 7084^{9} 7140^{3}

Ninth House (USA) *N P Littmoden* a91 78
5 b h Chester House(USA) —Ninette (USA) (Alleged (USA))
185^{2} 351^{8} 4135^{13} 4587^{8} 4889^{9} 5128^{7} 6024^{4} 6385^{2} 6824^{5} (7057) (7251)

Niqaab *W J Musson* a66 70
3 ch f Alhaarth(IRE) —Shanty (Selkirk (USA))
2127^{4} 3160^{3} 4458^{9} 6856^{7} 6967^{5}

Nisbah *C E Brittain* a41 41
2 ch f Kyllachy—Amazing Bay (Mazilier (USA))
2504^{10} 3648^{11}

Niska (USA) *A Fabre* a69 66
2 b f Smart Strike(CAN) —Lady Of Talent (USA) (Siphon (BRZ))
$6525a^{8}$

Nistaki (USA) *D Shaw* a70 70
6 ch g Miswaki(USA) —Brandywine Belle (USA) (Trempolino (USA))
442^{7} 6428^{9}

Nite In Rome (CAN) *M Casse* 92
2 b f Harlan's Holiday(USA) —Ascot Wedding (CAN) (Ascot Knight (CAN))
$5293a^{2}$

Niteowl Lad (IRE) *J Balding* 72
5 ch g Tagula(IRE) —Mareha (IRE) (Cadeaux Genereux)
4486^{9} 4800^{12} 5507^{6} 5740^{6} 5836^{4} 6287^{3} 6594^{5}

Niza D'Alm (FR) *A Crook* a13 31
6 bb m Passing Sale(FR) —Bekaa II (FR) (Djarvis (FR))
365^{8} 1849^{9} 6561^{15}

Nizza (GER) *P Schiergen* 94
3 br f Acatenango(GER) —Nanouska (GER) (Dashing Blade)
$6046a^{6}$

Nkosi Reigns (USA) *S Seemar* a103
6 bb g Out Of Place(USA) —Ms Jiles (USA) (Tejano (USA))
$471a^{5}$ $643a^{9}$

Noah Jameel *A G Newcombe* a55 49
5 ch g Mark Of Esteem(IRE) —Subtle One (IRE) (Polish Patriot (USA))
98^{6} 274^{9} 4533^{5} 5421^{3} (7186)

Nobelix (IRE) *J R Gask* a86 92
5 gr g Linamix(FR) —Nataliana (Surumu (GER))
2736^{10} (3748) 4375^{9} (5640) 6230^{5} 6545^{3}

Nobilissima (IRE) *J L Spearing* a56 86
3 b f Orpen(USA) —Shadow Smile (IRE) (Slip Anchor)
1219^{2} 1404^{3} (2080) 2629^{8} (3240) 3797^{5} 4585^{10} 4816^{2} 6006^{12}

Nobiz Like Shobiz (USA) *B Tagg* a114 116
3 b c Albert The Great(USA) —Nightstorm (USA) (Storm Cat (USA))
$1486a^{10}$ $6511a^{4}$

Noble Calling (FR) *R J Hodges* a46 40
10 b g Caller I.D.(USA) —Specificity (USA) (Alleged (USA))
1206^{13} 2493^{8}

Noble Citizen (USA) *D M Simcock* a82 82
2 b c Proud Citizen(USA) —Serene Nobility (USA) (His Majesty (USA))
3095^{8} 4130^{6} 4882^{2} (5597) 6120^{5}

Noble Edge *Karen McLintock* a46 64
4 ch g Bold Edge—Noble Soul (Sayf El Arab (USA))
1744^{13} 2298^{4} 3956^{13} 4177^{11} 5000^{8}

Noble Ginger (FR) *J E Pease* 98
3 ch f Generous(IRE) —Nataliana (Surumu (GER))
$2384a^{6}$ $5058a^{8}$ $6460a^{3}$ $6889a^{7}$

Noble Minstrel *S C Williams* a77 78
4 ch g Fantastic Light(USA) —Sweetness Herself (Unfuwain (USA))
88^{5} (213) (354) 1959^{2} 2887^{12} 3963^{2} 4056^{13} 4569^{10} 5256^{9} 6802^{2} 7236^{5}

Noble Mount *A B Haynes* a46 48
6 b g Muhtarram(USA) —Our Poppet (IRE) (Warning)
4471^{13} 5866^{12} 7278^{10}

Noble Nova *G A Swinbank* a58 67
4 br m Fraam—Noble Destiny (Dancing Brave (USA))
462^{10}

Noble Plum (IRE) *Sir Mark Prescott* a79
3 b f King's Best(USA) —Perfect Plum (IRE) (Darshaan)
3113^{8} 3214^{2} (7076) 7205^{3}

Noble Prince (GER) *A Fabre* 111
3 b c Montjeu(IRE) —Noble Pearl (GER) (Dashing Blade)
$5258a^{5}$ $6028a^{2}$

Noche De Reyes *E J Alston* 31
2 b c Foxhound(USA) —Ashleigh Baker (IRE) (Don't Forget Me)
6595^{11}

No Commission (IRE) *R F Fisher* 29
5 b g General Monash(USA) —Price Of Passion (Dolphin Street (FR))
4249^{12}

Noddies Way *J F Panvert* a64 71
4 b g Nomadic Way(USA) —Sharway Lady (Shareef Dancer (USA))
640^{3} 691^{4} 1196^{2} 1959^{3} 2026^{8} 3653^{3} 4056^{3} 5111^{5} 5453^{2} 6383^{8}

Noddledoddle (IRE) *J Ryan* a48 41
3 b f Daggers Drawn(USA) —En Retard (IRE) (Petardia)
3163^{6} 3464^{16} 3708^{13} 3824^{8} 4109^{4} 4337^{8} 4661^{6} 6607^{13} 6730^{8} 6910^{10} 7137^{10}

No Dream (USA) *C Laffon-Parias* 109
3 b c Anabaa(USA) —Quiet Dream (USA) (Seattle Slew (USA))
$2293a^{6}$ $2952a^{4}$ $3987a^{6}$

Nodservatory *Miss J A Camacho* a23
2 ch f Observatory(USA) —Nordan Raider (Domynsky)
7058^{10}

Nod's Star *Mrs L C Jewell* a59 27
6 ch m Starborough—Barsham (Be My Guest (USA))
(87) 240^{2} 285^{2} 482^{11} 677^{2} 792^{2} 1032^{5} 4322^{11} 5138^{7}

No Greater Love (FR) *Ian Williams* a53 81
5 b g Take Risks(FR) —Desperate Virgin (BEL) (Chief Singer)
(98)

No Grouse *E J Alston* a63 69
7 b g Pursuit Of Love—Lady Joyce (FR) (Galetto (FR))
2033^{8} 2561^{3} 3017^{3} 3535^{5} 4083^{7} 4180^{16} 4562^{2} (5037) 5253^{14} 5966^{7} 6290^{8} 6610^{7}

No Guilt (IRE) *J L Spearing* 27
2 b f Viking Ruler(AUS) —Icefern (Moorestyle)
2604^{9} 3246^{7}

No Inkling (IRE) *Miss M E Rowland* a35 32
4 b m Xaar—No Tippling (IRE) (Unblest)
61^{6} 321^{8} 467^{10} 2795^{9} 6801^{12}

Noisy Silence (IRE) *E F Vaughan* 85
3 b c Giant's Causeway(USA) —Golightly (USA) (Take Me Out (USA))
(4457) 4993^{4} 6180^{11}

Nok Twice (IRE) *D Carroll* a66 51
6 b g Second Empire(IRE) —Bent Al Fala (IRE) (Green Desert (USA))
4075[8] 5935[6] *6316[2]* *6749[8]*
Nolas Lolly (IRE) *U Suter* 94
3 b f Lomitas—Holy Nola (USA) (Silver Deputy (CAN))
1006a[7]
Nomoreblondes *P T Midgley* a57 70
3 ch f Ishiguru(USA) —Statuette (Statoblest)
752[5] 958[3] 1453[4] 2029[2] 2205[2] (3811) (4896)
Nomoretaxes (BRZ) *A Al Raihe* a100 8
5 b h First American(USA) —Raghida (BRZ) (Roi Normand (USA))
105a[12]
Nona *S Dow* a45 57
4 ch m Halling(USA) —Zarma (FR) (Machiavellian (USA))
229[9] *416[13]*
Non Compliant *J W Hills* a84 82
3 b c Lujain(USA) —Flourish (Selkirk (USA))
1450[3] 1817[7] 2689[6] (Dead)
No Nines *B W Hills* a56 63
2 b g Noverre(USA) —Amber Mill (Doulab (USA))
1123[10] *1519[6]* *1975[3]* *5199[10]* 5736[3] *5896[9]*
No No Ninette *C R Egerton* a35 17
2 b f Oasis Dream—Madam Ninette (Mark Of Esteem (IRE))
4232[16] 4454[13] *6099[12]*
Non Sucre (USA) *P A Blockley* a73 73
2 bb c Minardi(USA) —Vieille Rose (IRE) (Dancing Spree (USA))
898[7] 1021[2] *3171[2]* 4202[3] (4527) 6017[21]
No Nukes *P D Evans* a31 42
2 b g Where Or When(IRE) —Intellibet One (Compton Place)
6456[6] 6593[10] *6737[7]*
Noojoom (IRE) *M P Tregoning* a79 85
3 ch f Machiavellian(USA) —Abeyr (Unfuwain (USA))
(193) 1974[7] 2971[2] (3993) 4572[8] (Dead)
No One Tells Me *Mrs John Harrington* 58
2 ch f Dr Fong(USA) —Bajan Blue (Lycius (USA))
6443a[11]
Noora (IRE) *C G Cox* a79 85
6 ch m Bahhare(USA) —Esteraad (IRE) (Cadeaux Genereux)
2543[4] *2994[6]* *3731[7]* 4112[7] *4915[3]* (5187) *5533[6]* *(6241)*
No Page (IRE) *B W Hills* 77
2 b f Statue Of Liberty(USA) —Esligier (IRE) (Sabrehill (USA))
4232[4] 5192[4] (5770) 6052[13]
Noplace For A Lady *N Tinkler* 41
2 ch f Compton Place—Pusey Street Girl (Gildoran)
1858[10] 2432[11] 4422[6]
No Point (IRE) *P A Blockley* a43 47
2 ch f Point Given(USA) —Youngus (USA) (Atticus (USA))
(1000) 1235[5] 1857[4] 4824[4] *5017[2]* 5520[7] *6881[12]*
Nora Chrissie (IRE) *Niall Moran* a62 62
5 bb m Bahhare(USA) —Vino Veritas (USA) (Chief's Crown (USA))
6803[5]
Noravana (IRE) *Miss V Haigh* a51 41
3 b f Namid—Kirvana (IRE) (Lycius (USA))
149[10] *456[13]* *661[4]* *731[7]* 2299[6] 2489[15] 2657[7] 3917[7] 4109[10] 4596[8]
Norcroft *Mrs C A Dunnett* a76 78
5 b g Fasliyev(USA) —Norcroft Joy (Rock Hopper)
774[5] *1252[4]* *1382[3]* 1678[4] *3285[6]* *3396[5]* *4024[2]* 4296[3] 4594[5] *5130[3]* *5234[2]* 5576[11] 6415[9] *(6747)* *6810[11]* *7261[6]*
Nordhal *B Grizzetti* 106
8 br g Halling(USA) —Nord's Lucy (IRE) (Nordico (USA))
1192a[4]
Nordic Affair *D R C Elsworth* a86 54
3 b g Halling(USA) —Affair Of State (IRE) (Tate Gallery (USA))
113[4] 1106[9] 2426[8] 3165[7] 6199[15]
Nordic Commander (IRE) *E A L Dunlop* a66 50
2 b c Viking Ruler(AUS) —Rising Lady (Alzao (USA))
6252[8] *6503[4]* *6827[5]*
Nordic Light (USA) *P W Chapple-Hyam* a73 81
3 bb g Belong To Me(USA) —Midriff (USA) (Naevus (USA))
456[10] *(679)* (1022) 1658[5] 2114[4]
Nordic Thunder (GER) *A Fabre* 105
4 b h Singspiel(IRE) —Navona (GER) (Leone (GER))
880a[8]
Nordtanzerin (GER) *P Schiergen* 105
4 gr m Danehill Dancer(IRE) —Nona (GER) (Cortez (GER))
3075a[5] 4838a[13]
Nordwind (IRE) *W R Swinburn* a79 94
6 b g Acatenango(GER) —Narola (GER) (Nebos (GER))
1244[6] 1582[12] 1844[10] 5415[6] 5884[7]
Norisan *R Hannon* a97 97
3 ch c Inchinor—Dream On Deya (IRE) (Dolphin Street (FR))
839[4] *1035[3]* 1306[8] 2788[30] 3463[8] (3966) 4509[5] (4778) *5128[2]*
Norman Invader (USA) *K J Condon* 108
2 b c War Chant(USA) —Enthused (USA) (Seeking The Gold (USA))
3980a[3] (5070a) 6631a[2]
Norman Norman *W S Kittow* a32
5 b g Double Trigger(IRE) —Nour El Sahar (USA) (Sagace (FR))
2519[8] 3047[12]
Norman The Great *Jane Chapple-Hyam* a78 80
3 b g Night Shift(USA) —Encore Du Cristal (USA) (Quiet American (USA))
720[2] *884[2]* 1075[3] 2153[7] *2455[4]* 3058[5] 4015[2] *(4277)* 4631[4] 4909[11] 6253[7] *6439[8]*
Norman Tradition *A M Balding* a50
3 ch f Traditionally(USA) —Normandy (CHI) (Great Regent (CAN))
4977[4] *5728[13]*
Nortelco (IRE) *Micky Hammond* 34
4 ch g Titus Livius(FR) —Irish Moss (USA) (Irish River (FR))
1301[9] 4580[10] 4920[10] 5503[18]
Norther Bay (FR) *Eoin Griffin* 72
4 b g Alamo Bay(USA) —Northern Mixa (Linamix (FR))
3138a[21]
Northern Bolt *D Nicholls* 85
2 b c Cadeaux Genereux—Shafir (IRE) (Shaadi (USA))
5042[11] (5550)
Northern Boy (USA) *M W Easterby* a70 83
4 ch g Lure(USA) —Catala (USA) (Northern Park (USA))
969[6] 1198[3] 1413[5] 2023[9] 2388[7] 2935[5] 3155[12] 3571[7] *6148[2]* *6476[2]* *(6749)* *6869[4]* *7047[5]*
Northern Candy *A Dickman* 39
3 ch g Sugarfoot—Thalya (Crofthall)
2387[8] 2826[4] 3837[13] 4226[19]
Northern Chorus (IRE) *J O'Reilly* a55 76
4 ch g Distant Music(USA) —Nationalartgallery (IRE) (Tate Gallery (USA))
432[9] 1557[9] 1669[11] 4008[10] 4083[6] 4561[3] 4822[8] 4939[4] 5507[7]
Northern Dare (IRE) *D Nicholls* a30 95
3 b g Fath(USA) —Farmers Swing (IRE) (River Falls)
670[8] (1136) 1453[3] 1965[10] (3588) 3786[3] (3885) 4127[2] 4607[3] 5584[2]
Northern Desert (IRE) *S Curran* a77 61
8 b g Desert Style(IRE) —Rosie's Guest (IRE) (Be My Guest (USA))
38[3] *865[3]* (975) *1446[9]* *3215[12]* 3675[5] *4063[14]* *7143[4]* *7251[2]*
Northern Dune (IRE) *B J Curley* a45
3 b g Dilshaan—Zoudie (Ezzoud (IRE))
53[7] *257[9]* *469[12]*
Northern Empire (IRE) *K A Ryan* a91 94
4 ch g Namid—Bumble (Rainbow Quest (USA))
1125[10] 1788[16] 4696[4] 5212[11] 5584[17] 5810[10] *6876[5]* *(7112)*
Northerner (IRE) *J O'Reilly* a53 63
4 b h Mark Of Esteem(IRE) —Ensorceleuse (FR) (Fabulous Dancer (USA))
631[13]
Northern Fling *D Nicholls* a80 100
3 b g Mujadil(USA) —Donna Anna (Be My Chief (USA))
1009[3] 1099[16] (1298) 1623[2] 2035[6] 4123[10] (4726) 5584[26]
Northern Jem *G G Margarson* 87
3 b g Mark Of Esteem(IRE) —Top Jem (Damister (USA))
977[3] 1204[3] (1863) 3460[10] 3877[2] 4228[7] 5805[10]
Northern Spy (USA) *S Dow* a90 81
3 b c War Chant(USA) —Sunray Superstar (Nashwan (USA))
(5915) 6465[10] *7163[2]*
North Fleet *J M Bradley* a55 63
4 b g Bertolini(USA) —Rhiann (Anshan)
751[4] 1112[13] *1400[2]* 1640[10] 3106[11] *4668[11]* *4974[11]* 5062[12] 5864[12] (Dead)
Northgate (IRE) *Joseph G Murphy* a87 83
2 b c Mujadil(USA) —Arcevia (IRE) (Archway (IRE))
3438a[9] *6161a[8]* 6549a[12]
Northgate Lodge (USA) *M Brittain* 53
2 ch c Hold That Tiger(USA) —Sabaah Elfull (Kris)
8451[4] 1043[6] 1130[4] 4278[10] 5153[12] 5251[10]
Northgate Maisie *Jedd O'Keeffe* 40
2 b f Sugarfoot—Chasetown Cailin (Suave Dancer (USA))
6107[12] 6303[7]
North Parade *B J Meehan* 89
2 b c Nayef(USA) —Queen Sceptre (IRE) (Fairy King (USA))
5217[6] 5590[2]
North South Divide (IRE) *R A Teal* a68
3 b g Namid—Bush Rose (Rainbow Quest (USA))
6097[U] *6546[7]* *7029[3]*
North Stars (IRE) *J O'Reilly* a41
3 b g Soviet Star(USA) —Rania (Aragon)
5157[6] 5488[8] *6240[6]*
North Walk (IRE) *Jennie Candlish* a79 84
4 b g Monashee Mountain(USA) —Celtic Link (IRE) (Toca Madera)
2800[3] *3063[6]* *3600[8]* *3922[11]*
Northwest *A Berry* 49
2 b g Reel Buddy(USA) —Adorable Cherub (USA) (Halo (USA))
2710[10] 3606[12] 5675[5] 6329[6] 6698[10]
Nortune (USA) *B Smart* 49
2 b c Street Cry(IRE) —Gilded Leaf (USA) (Lyphard (USA))
6468[13]
No Rules *M H Tompkins* 67
2 b c Fraam—Golden Daring (IRE) (Night Shift (USA))
6296[8] 6571[5]
Norwegian *Ian Williams* a69 57
6 b g Halling(USA) —Chicarica (USA) (The Minstrel (CAN))
42[4] *(124)* *206[3]* *(425)* *570[3]* *666[2]* *674[2]* *(741)* (1025) *1167[2]* 1295[6] 1539[11] 2006[6] 2423[5] *2521[10]* 6199[10] *6342[11]* *6859[6]* *7080[4]* *7146[10]* *7274[4]*
Nosferatu (IRE) *Mrs A J Perrett* 97
4 b g In The Wings—Gothic Dream (IRE) (Nashwan (USA))
(1542) (2236) 3090[11] 4047[13] 4722[9] 6169[7]
Nota Bene *D R C Elsworth* 97
5 b g Zafonic(USA) —Dodo (IRE) (Alzao (USA))
2463[16] 2858[18]
Notability (IRE) *Saeed Bin Suroor* a111 115
5 b h King's Best(USA) —Noble Rose (IRE) (Caerleon (USA))
177a[12] 413a[6] 2735[8] 3780a[6]
Nota Liberata *G M Moore* a64 69
3 b g Spinning World(USA) —Kyda (USA) (Gulch (USA))
931[8] 1091[9] 1424[2] *1936[3]* 2340[5] 2829[5] 3181[5] (3587) 4197[5] 5557[9]
Not Another Cat (USA) *K R Burke* a72 67
3 ch g Hennessy(USA) —Isle Be Loving You (USA) (Stuka (USA))
3710[7]
Notepad *W Jarvis* 59
2 b f King's Best(USA) —Petite Epaulette (Night Shift (USA))
2056[5] 2457[11]
Note Perfect *M W Easterby* 45
2 b f Diktat—Better Still (IRE) (Glenstal (USA))
1285[10] 2021[8] 3092[7]
Nothing Is Forever (IRE) *Mrs A J Perrett* a63 64
3 b g Daylami(IRE) —Bequeath (USA) (Lyphard (USA))
1887[11] *4069[7]* 4391[9] *5120[8]*
Nothing Likea Dame *D J Coakley* a62 66
2 ch f Bahamian Bounty—Dame Jude (Dilum (USA))
2488[2] *3187[4]* 3507[15] *4459[7]* 5063[9] *6966[12]* *7142[6]* *7286[6]*
Nothing To Add *K A Ryan* a45 20
2 b g Noverre(USA) —Gaijin (Caerleon (USA))
3560[9] *4020[8]* 5033[6] *7177[4]*
Nothingtodeclaire *G A Huffer* a68 33
3 b c Tobougg(IRE) —Double Fault (IRE) (Zieten (USA))
977[7] 2153[12] *3084[4]* 3651[10] 3800[6] 5510[6] *5816[12]*
Noticeable (IRE) *M R Channon* a73 89
3 b c Night Shift(USA) —Nawaji (USA) (Trempolino (USA))
1143[13] (1433) 1987[2] 2790[9] 3460[12] 3877[8] 4147[12] 4993[2] 5208[8] 5445[6] 5717[2] 5978[9] *6389[6]*
No Time (IRE) *A J McCabe* a76 69
7 b h Danetime(IRE) —Muckross Park (Nomination)
91[10] *163[7]* *276[8]* *787[4]* 1074[2] (1214) 1299[6] 1557[2] 1669[2] 1914[3] 1999[2] 2202[6] 3921[12] 4252[8] *4944[5]* *5130[7]* 5507[2] 5836[2] (5908) 6078[6] *6360[10]* 6562[4] *6890[9]* *6927[3]* *7011[8]* *(7054)* *7183[6]* *7253[3]*
Not Just Swing (IRE) *A Fabre* 103
3 b c King's Best(USA) —Misbegotten (IRE) (Baillamont (USA))
1736a[4] 5661a[5] 6400a[4]
Not My Choice (IRE) *D J Murphy* a63 82
2 ch c Choisir(AUS) —Northgate Raver (Absalom)
845[4] 1580[5] 5192[8] (5802) 5939[6] *6004[9]* 6326[6]
Notnowcato *Sir Michael Stoute* 126
5 ch h Inchinor—Rambling Rose (Cadeaux Genereux)
1274[4] (2064a) 2754[3] (3331) 4693[3] 6334[6]
Not Now Lewis (IRE) *J A Osborne* a66
3 b g Shinko Forest(IRE) —Pearl Egg (IRE) (Mukaddamah (USA))
127[3] *222[5]* *423[3]* *589[3]* *776[4]* *6642[2]* *6833[5]* *7057[7]*
Not Only One (FR) *Robert Collet* 43
2 b c Muhtathir—Highway One (FR) (Mtoto)
6952a[10]
No To Trident *P D Evans* a67 76
2 b g Zilzal(USA) —Charmante Femme (Bin Ajwaad (IRE))
4755[10] 5186[2] *5605[5]* *5984[2]* 6184[2]
Not To Know *John A Quinn* a74 66
3 b g Mujahid(USA) —Little Tramp (Trempolino (USA))
69[4] 6555a[8]
Not Too Taxing *G A Ham* a67 11
3 b g Forzando—Areish (IRE) (Keen)
69[2] *116[2]* *312[8]* *635[8]* *694[11]* 1410[10] *4064[14]* *4272[13]*
N'Oubliez Jamais (GER) *H Blume* 108
4 br h Poliglote—Night Green (GER) (Green Forest (USA))
5849a[7]
Nou Camp *N A Callaghan* a57 54
3 ch g Compton Place—Real Popcorn (IRE) (Jareer (USA))
636[9] *778[3]* *1031[13]* 1213[3] 2205[5] 2444[6] 2750[4] *3599[5]* 4336[9] 4685[10] *5945[4]* 6277[5]
Nouveau (GER) *R Hannon* a79 81
3 b g Desert Style(IRE) —Night Care (GER) (Caerwent)
1587[9] 2944[10] 3102[5] 3369[2] *3644[4]* (3872) (4330) 4574[6] *4885[3]* *5495[4]* (5874) *6232[4]*
Nouvelle Europe (GER) *P Rau* 97
3 b f Spectrum(IRE) —Nouvelle Fortune (IRE) (Alzao (USA))
2294a[7] 5669a[10]
Nouvelle Nova (IRE) *G G Margarson*
2 b f Noverre(USA) —Uhud (IRE) (Mujtahid (USA))
5308[11]
Novas (IRE) *M R Channon* 15
2 b c Noverre(USA) —Coolrain Lady (IRE) (Common Grounds)
5306[10] 5591[9]
Nova Tor (IRE) *Peter Grayson* a22 75
5 b m Trans Island—Nordic Living (IRE) (Nordico (USA))
251[9] *318[9]*
Novellen Lad (IRE) *E J Alston* 62
2 b c Noverre(USA) —Lady Ellen (Horage)
6755[6]
Novestar (IRE) *G J Smith* a29 60
2 ch c Noverre(USA) —Star Of Cayman (IRE) (Unfuwain (USA))
3833[4] 4378[7] 4818[11] 5302[3] 5572[4] *6933[8]* *7140[9]*
Novikov *J H M Gosden* 88
3 ch g Danehill Dancer(IRE) —Ardisia (USA) (Affirmed (USA))
1606[13] 1840[5] 2046[3] (2880) 3514[2] 4603[5]
Novista (IRE) *M H Tompkins* 70
3 b g Anabaa Blue—Bistranova (USA) (Torrential (USA))
6576[9]
Now Again (GER) *W Hickst*
3 ch f Lomitas—Notre Dame (GER) (Acatenango (GER))
6889a[0]
Nowaira (IRE) *M Johnston* 74
2 b f Daylami(IRE) —Shallat (IRE) (Pennekamp (USA))
5010[8] (5301) 5828[14]
Now Look Out *E S McMahon* a43 74
3 gr g Bahamian Bounty—Where's Carol (Anfield)
1577[9] 2119[6] 4233[14] 5970[9] *6244[8]*
Nownownow (USA) *F Parisel* 109
2 b c Whywhywhy(USA) —Here And Now (FR) (Exit To Nowhere (USA))
(6484a)
No Worries Yet (IRE) *J L Spearing* 67
3 b f Orpen(USA) —Charming Victoria (IRE) (Mujadil (USA))
(1763) (1912) 2198[7] 3369[7] (3869)
Now You See Me *K McAuliffe* a55 10
3 b f Anabaa(USA) —Bright Vision (Indian Ridge)
689[5] 2542[9]
Nowzdetime (IRE) *M G Quinlan* a47
2 b c Statue Of Liberty(USA) —Sensitive (IRE) (Posen (USA))
7266[7]
Nufoudh (IRE) *Miss Tracy Waggott* 65
3 b g Key Of Luck(USA) —Limpopo (Green Desert (USA))
1530[13] 2012[5] 2301[4] 3786[15] 3885[8] 4224[7] 4423[5] 4480[3] 4562[3] 4822[4] 4940[6] 5155[5] 5253[16] 5966[4]
Nuit Sombre (IRE) *G A Harker* a45 83
7 b g Night Shift(USA) —Belair Princess (USA) (Mr Prospector (USA))
(1559) 2511[6] 3258[5] 3470[5] 4891[7] (5701) (6331) 6560[3] (6701) *7045[9]*
Nujoma (GER) *C Von Der Recke* 83
2 ch f Samum(GER) —New Berlin (IRE) (Greinton)
6371a[10]
Numerical (IRE) *J L Dunlop* 56
3 ch g Numerous(USA) —Conspiracy (Rudimentary (USA))
3276[9]
Numerieus (FR) *Y De Nicolay* 94
3 br f Numerous(USA) —Northern Mixa (Linamix (FR))
1704a[5] 4190a[10]
Numide (FR) *J-C Rouget* 115
4 b g Highest Honor(FR) —Numidie (FR) (Baillamont (USA))
2617a[4] 4520a[10]
Nuqoosh *F Head* 100
3 ch f Machiavellian(USA) —Al Ishq (FR) (Nureyev (USA))
1055a[7]
Nurenberg (IRE) *Edward Lynam* a79 84
5 b g Giant's Causeway(USA) —Peneia (USA) (Nureyev (USA))
5788a[5]
Nur Tau (IRE) *M P Tregoning* 89
3 b g Peintre Celebre(USA) —Litchfield Hills (USA) (Relaunch (USA))
4147[6] (5014) 5639[6]
Nusoor (IRE) *Peter Grayson* a79 81
4 b g Fasliyev(USA) —Zulfaa (USA) (Bahri (USA))
91[7] *214[2]* *269[2]* *361[7]* *432[3]* *465[9]* *566[2]* 1061[4] 1483[3] 1630[5] 1941[5] 2244[4] 2673[7] 3014[4] 3515[6] 3836[6] 4734[3] 5085[4] *(5234)* *5648[11]* *6273[9]* *6625[7]* *6938[11]* *7221[8]*
Nutkin *J R Fanshawe* a65 73
3 gr f Act One—Cashew (Sharrood (USA))
3710[15] *4275[4]* (4707) 5738[4]
Nylla *M R Channon* a72 73
2 b f Bertolini(USA) —Eljariha (Unfuwain (USA))
3245[5] *3417[3]* (3750) 4762[9] 5692[4]
Oakbridge (IRE) *R Brotherton* a68 55
5 b g Indian Ridge—Chauncy Lane (IRE) (Sadler's Wells (USA))
123[8] (402) *7213[7]*
Oakfast (BRZ) *A Cintra Pereira* a74
5 b h Fast Gold(USA) —Oakville (BRZ) (Baronius (BRZ))
175a[8] 328a[16] *529a[11]*
Oakley Absolute *J C Fox* a64 63
5 ch g Bluegrass Prince(IRE) —Susie Oakley VII (Damsire Unregistered)
1249[11] *1521[10]* *6801[10]*
Oakley Heffert (IRE) *R Hannon* a80 81
3 b g Titus Livius(FR) —Daftiyna (IRE) (Darshaan)
1467[2] 1898[2] 2999[7] 3385[4] 4510[3] 6236[7] 6422[7] *6669[7]* *6848[4]* *7193[3]*
Oarsman *R Charlton* a70
2 ch c Selkirk(USA) —Felucca (Green Desert (USA))
5337[2]
Oasis Davis *K A Ryan* a49 70
2 b c Oasis Dream—Panarea (FR) (Highest Honor (FR))
4378[6] 4921[6] 5745[7] *6477[5]*
Oasis Sun (IRE) *J R Best* a57 35
4 ch m Desert Sun—Albaiyda (IRE) (Brief Truce (USA))
18[9] *92[3]* *(187)* *309[6]* *495[6]* *4161[7]* 4533[9] *4739[7]* *6212[8]* *6792[6]* *6832[3]* *(6969)* *7187[3]*
Oasis Wind *P F I Cole* 99
2 b c Oasis Dream—Haibah (Rainbow Quest (USA))
3383[3] (4070) 4695[2] 5324[6] 5922[3]
Oat Cuisine *M L W Bell* a62
3 b f Mujahid(USA) —Gazebo (Cadeaux Genereux)
5390[7] *5728[2]* *(6229)*
Obe Bold (IRE) *A Berry* a62 63
6 b m Orpen(USA) —Capable Kate (IRE) (Alzao (USA))
135[9] *320[13]*
Obe Brave *M R Channon* 109
4 b g Agnes World(USA) —Pass The Rose (IRE) (Thatching)
(172a) 394a[9] 472a[9] 4614[2] 5616[28] 6183[10] 6338[17]
Obe Gold *M R Channon* a100 106
5 b g Namaqualand(USA) —Gagajulu (Al Hareb (USA))
415a[5] 470a[4] 1041[11] 1195[12] 1653[17] 3481[7] 3802[6] 4122[4] 4367[2] 4456[6] 5209[5] 5617[12] 5804[9] (6205) 6450[6] 6472[5]
Obe One *A Berry* a53 61
7 b g Puissance—Plum Bold (Be My Guest (USA))
1492[8] 1711[10] 2390[11] 2561[11] 2937[9] 3996[5] 4381[7] 4719[7] 4768[3] *5566[3]* 5935[4] 6467[10] *7107[8]*
Oberlin (USA) *M Johnston* a79 59
2 ch c Gone West(USA) —Balanchine (USA) (Storm Bird (CAN))
5646[2] 5904[5] 6451[6]

Obe Royal *P D Evans* a74 74
3 b g Wizard King—Gagajulu (Al Hareb (USA))
5565[4] 5879[8] 6256[2] 6413[3] 6463[2] *6610[4] 6677[4] 6838[5] 7025[7] 7233[2]*

Obezyana (USA) *A Bailey* a88 85
5 ch g Rahy(USA) —Polish Treaty (USA) (Danzig (USA))
1480[14] 1599[7] 2528[12]

Objeto De Arte (BRZ) *P Bary*
4 ch h
6071a[5]

Obrigado (USA) *Karen George* a94 93
7 b g Bahri(USA) —Glorious Diamond (USA) (His Majesty (USA))
6669[11] 7075[3] 7193[7]

Obscene *A J McCabe* a69 47
4 b g Key Of Luck(USA) —Scene (IRE) (Scenic)
19[14] 72[12]

Observatory Ridge *M D I Usher* a51 61
2 ch f Observatory(USA) —Chiasso (USA) (Woodman (USA))
1469[7] 3902[4] 4074[3] 4501[9] *4964[13] 6066[6] 6207[6] 6433[4]*

Observatory Star (IRE) *T D Easterby* 84
4 br g Observatory(USA) —Pink Sovietstaia (FR) (Soviet Star (USA))
2421[2] 3472[3] 3998[6] 4407[2] (4820) 5776[2] 6016[2] 6539[5]

Obstructive *Andrew Reid* a73 96
3 ch g Zilzal(USA) —Emily-Mou (IRE) (Cadeaux Genereux)
1117[3] 2173[2] (2513) 3061[2] (3493) 4123[19] 5810[12]

O'Casey (IRE) *J G M O'Shea* 47
2 b g Bold Fact(USA) —Miss Scott (IRE) (Be My Guest (USA))
999[13] 1235[3] 1857[6] 2078[6] 3364[6]

Oceana Blue *A M Balding* a66
2 b f Reel Buddy(USA) —Silken Dalliance (Rambo Dancer (CAN))
4962[6] 5605[3] 5944[5] 6664[6] 7097[5] 7245[5]

Oceana Gold *A M Balding* 90
3 ch g Primo Valentino(IRE) —Silken Dalliance (Rambo Dancer (CAN))
(1815) 2598[3] 3553[6] (4111) 4566[4] 5768[2]

Ocean Avenue (IRE) *C A Horgan* a77 82
8 b g Dolphin Street(FR) —Trinity Hall (Hallgate)
753[3] 1542[7] (2321) 3554[6] 4231[6] *5225[7] 6124[4] 6709[5]*

Ocean Blaze *B R Millman* 81
3 b f Polar Prince(IRE) —La Belle Vie (Indian King (USA))
1151[9] 1373[3] (2198) 2513[2] 3277[2] 3870[4] 5160[8] (5418) 5642[5] (6020)

Ocean Gift *N Tinkler* a59 82
5 b g Cadeaux Genereux—Sea Drift (FR) (Warning)
1133[11] 1483[4] 1678[6] 2394[5] 2725[7] 3873[4] 4822[9] *5233[6] 5981[5] 6290[11] 6608[10] 6886[6]*

Ocean Glory (IRE) *Peter Grayson* a46 63
2 b g Redback—Finty (IRE) (Entrepreneur)
(5429) 5802[10] *6004[12] 6502[12] 6715[12] 6881[13] 7195[6]*

Oceanico Dot Com (IRE) *A Berry* a53 44
5 br m Hernando(FR) —Karen Blixen (Kris)
137[9]

Ocean Legend (IRE) *Miss J Feilden* a72 11
2 b c Night Shift(USA) —Rose Of Mooncoin (IRE) (Brief Truce (USA))
4132[11] *4883[3]*

Ocean Of Champagne *Micky Hammond* a12 57
3 ch f Arkadian Hero(USA) —Champagne Grandy (Vaigly Great)
1175[9] 2300[6] 2713[10] 3342[7] 3636[10] 5487[12] 5622[5]

Ocean Of Dreams (FR) *J D Bethell* a78 59
4 b g Ocean Of Wisdom(USA) —Tifosa (USA) (Hickman Creek (USA))
300[5] 509[6] 672[3] 933[7] 1262[9] 1755[11]

Ocean Pride (IRE) *D E Pipe* a81 82
4 b g Lend A Hand—Irish Understudy (ITY) (In The Wings)
316[5] 3083[6]

Ocean Transit (IRE) *W G M Turner* a31 80
2 b f Trans Island—Wings Awarded (Shareef Dancer (USA))
890[9] 999[7] 1087[8] (2078) 3550[2] 4152[U] (4453) 5164[6] 5692[2] 6251[4]

Ocean Valentine *J T Stimpson* a43 13
4 gr g King Charlemagne(USA) —Dolly Bevan (Another Realm)
5886[15] *6315[7] 6629[11] 6896[12] 7001[8] 7102[4] 7203[6]*

Ocean Waves (IRE) *Miss Tor Sturgis* a49 48
4 ch m Barathea(IRE) —We've Just Begun (USA) (Huguenot (USA))
6429[8] 6991[8] 7103[3]

Ochenvay *M Quinn* a48 36
2 gr f Tobougg(IRE) —Bogus Mix (IRE) (Linamix (FR))
3055[11] *3923[3] 4428[9]* 5572[6] *6099[8] 6427[6]* 6591[7]

Ochoa (IRE) *C G Cox* 69
2 b f Okawango(USA) —Karakorum (IRE) (Fairy King (USA))
4527[10] 5110[2] 5395a[21]

Ochre (IRE) *R A Fahey* a82
3 br f Diktat—Cox Orange (USA) (Trempolino (USA))
418[5] 720[3] 836[3] 1399[3] 1903[5] 6387[9] 6856[3] (6956) 7104[3] (7241) 7281[9]

Ochre Bay *R Hollinshead* a78 72
4 b h Polar Prince(IRE) —Cloudy Reef (Cragador)
102[9] 2719[6] *3285[2]* 3599[7] *4462[4]* 6385[3] *6735[5]*

Octave (USA) *T Pletcher* a115
3 rg f Unbridled's Song(USA) —Belle Nuit (USA) (Dr Carter (USA))
(3810a) 4628a[3] 6512a[3]

October Ben *M D I Usher* a71 69
4 b m Killer Instinct—Birmania (IRE) (Rainbow Quest (USA))
2568[6] 2990[10] 3422[6] 3644[8] 4063[5] 4577[3] 5237[2]

Oddsmaker (IRE) *M A Barnes* a61 84
6 b g Barathea(IRE) —Archipova (IRE) (Ela-Mana-Mou)
914[6] 955[3] 1090[6] (2465) (2987)

Odessa Star (USA) *J G Portman* a74 69
4 gr m Stravinsky(USA) —Cryptocari (USA) (Cryptoclearance (USA))
299[8] 358[6] 712[5] 1002[5] *5569[8]* 6196[14]

Odiham *H Morrison* a104 101
6 b g Deploy—Hug Me (Shareef Dancer (USA))
(944) 1393[5] 1582[8] 2736[5] 3090[8] (3898) 4375[5] 5800[7] 6335[8]

O'Dwyer (IRE) *A D Brown* a53 59
3 ch g Namid—Leopardess (IRE) (Ela-Mana-Mou)
194[3] 295[6] 1248[8] 1711[6] 2203[11] *2591[9]* 3257[7] 4000[7]

Oedipuss (IRE) *K J Burke* a45 45
3 b c Mujadil(USA) —Evrobi (IRE) (Grand Lodge (USA))
2520[7] 3186[13] 3595[9]

Oeuf A La Neige *Miss L A Perratt* a50 61
7 b g Danehill(USA) —Reine De Neige (Kris)
1459[8] 1493[4] 1596[2] 1711[3] 1806[3] 2390[6] 2561[6] 2711[4] 2864[9] 2937[5] 3345[6] 3498[6] 3535[4] 3674[5] 3787[12] 4449[7] 4719[6] 4934[2] (4998) 5037[9] 5284[3] 5476[4] 5552[13] (5838) 5964[3] 6463[3] 6640[6] 6732[2]

Ofaraby *M A Jarvis* a94 106
7 b g Sheikh Albadou—Maristax (Reprimand)
1449[6] 4720[18] 6172[10]

Offbeat Fashion (IRE) *D K Weld* 93
3 b f Rock Of Gibraltar(IRE) —Triple Try (IRE) (Sadler's Wells (USA))
1548a[6] 2065a[10] 4649a[6]

Officer *Sir Michael Stoute* a83 88
3 b c Medicean—Appointed One (USA) (Danzig (USA))
1077[8] 1412[2] 2402[7] 3691[5] (4018) *(5203)* 5545[3] *6067[6]*

Officer Material (IRE) *C G Cox* a53 53
3 b g Barathea(IRE) —Alserna (IRE) (Alhaarth (IRE))
1635[8] 1838[6] 2077[9] 4073[12] *6026[4] 6387[7]*

Offshore Star (IRE) *P A Blockley* a25
2 b c Spartacus(IRE) —Alvilda (IRE) (Caerleon (USA))
6312[9]

Off Stage (IRE) *Carl Llewellyn* a24 53
4 ch m Danehill Dancer(IRE) —Safe Exit (FR) (Exit To Nowhere (USA))
1178[9]

Off The Record *J G Given* a92 103
3 b c Desert Style(IRE) —Record Time (Clantime)
(1176) (1351) (1754) 3431[2] 3720[10] 4607[2] 5407[14] 5765[8]

O Fourlunda *C E Brittain* 62
3 b f Halling(USA) —Lunda (IRE) (Soviet Star (USA))
4513[3] 5270[2] 5510[3] 5915[8] 6415[10]

Ogee *Sir Michael Stoute* a99 99
4 ch g Generous(IRE) —Aethra (USA) (Trempolino (USA))
1477[9] *2351[4]* 2859[4] (3153) 3898[4] 4722[15] 5030[6] 5375[5]

Ogmore Junction (IRE) *P D Cundell* a59 44
2 b c Catcher In The Rye(IRE) —Fairy Berry (IRE) (Fairy King (USA))
3550[12] *6578[7]*

Ogre (USA) *J A Osborne* a67 59
2 bb f Tale Of The Cat(USA) —Soverign Lady (USA) (Aloha Prospector (USA))
5042[8] 5428[10] 5881[9] *6736[4] 7010[2] (7117)*

Ohana *Miss Gay Kelleway* a72 46
4 b g Mark Of Esteem(IRE) —Subya (Night Shift (USA))
7[4] 144[8]

Oh Danny Boy *M C Chapman* a63 65
6 b g Cadeaux Genereux—Final Shot (Dalsaan)
1199[11] *1717[7]* 2831[9] 5704[14] *6804[6]*

Oh Glory Be (USA) *R Hannon* a41 98
4 b m Dixieland Band(USA) —Long View (USA) (Damascus (USA))
2236[7] 3002[2] 4089[6] *5686[6]* 5940[4] 6302[4] (6620)

Oh Gracious Me (IRE) *P A Blockley* 42
3 b c Traditionally(USA) —Classic Jenny (IRE) (Green Desert (USA))
1838[10]

Oh Mary (IRE) *W J Haggas* a56 54
3 b f Anabaa(USA) —Contradictive (USA) (Kingmambo (USA))
758[4] 2046[9] 2606[12]

Oh So Saucy *C F Wall* a60 59
3 b f Imperial Ballet(IRE) —Almasi (IRE) (Petorius)
1346[3] 2262[5] 2592[3] 3612[3] 4326[11] 5546[4]

Oi Vay Joe (IRE) *W Jarvis* a57 87
3 b g Namid—Nuit Des Temps (Sadler's Wells (USA))
2243[8] 4806[10] 5358[8] *5684[10]*

Okafranca (IRE) *W R Muir* 56
2 b g Okawango(USA) —Villafranca (IRE) (In The Wings)
4162[7] 4764[14] 6274[8]

Okikoki *W R Muir* a72 80
3 b g Ishiguru(USA) —Crofters Ceilidh (Scottish Reel)
1535[3] 2045[5] 2881[7] 3491[3] 3940[14] 4502[4] 4710[7] 5360[2] 5768[6] *6435[11]* 6701[2] *7045[6]*

Old Etonian (UAE) *Peter Grayson* a84 47
3 ch g Jade Robbery(USA) —Favoured (Chief's Crown (USA))
764[2] 956[4] *7282[10]*

Oldjoesaid *H Candy* 109
3 b g Royal Applause—Border Minstral (IRE) (Sri Pekan (USA))
1502[2] 5050[14] (5810) 6327[2]

Old Kippin (IRE) *V T O'Brien* 42
6 ch m Old Vic—Pippin (IRE) (Pips Pride)
1760a[8]

Old Man Buck (USA) *K McPeek* a104 99
2 ch c Hold That Tiger(USA) —Victorian Woman (USA) (Jeblar (USA))
6508a[6]

Oldrik (GER) *P J Hobbs* 74
4 b g Tannenkonig(IRE) —Onestep (GER) (Konigsstuhl (GER))
2106[7] 2621[3] 2980[2]

Old Romney *M W Easterby* a77 89
3 br c Halling(USA) —Zaeema (Zafonic (USA))
2126[9] 2448[5] *3189[3]* 3709[9] 4135[8] 4197[2] 4993[5] 5774[10] 6253[15] 6727[14]

Olgarena (IRE) *T D Easterby* 46
3 b f Xaar—Copine (Selkirk (USA))
1092[11] 1489[7]

Oli James (USA) *P F I Cole* a59 66
2 ch c Officer(USA) —Post It (USA) (Notebook (USA))
4151[12] *5498[8]* 6058[10] *6454[7] 6775[4] 6928[5]*

Olimpo (FR) *B R Millman* 88
6 ch g Starborough—Emily Allan (IRE) (Shirley Heights)
1813[11] 2321[2] (2621) (3243) (3692) 4483[2] 5197[7] 6335[22]

Olivia Pielak (IRE) *Miss A M Winters* 41
4 b m Sendawar(IRE) —Khaytada (IRE) (Doyoun)
4142a[8] 4830a[8]

Ollie George (IRE) *A M Balding* a69 93
4 ch g Fruits Of Love(USA) —The Iron Lady (IRE) (Polish Patriot (USA))
(1208) 1506[2] 1844[5]

Olympian Odyssey *Saeed Bin Suroor* 117
4 b h Sadler's Wells(USA) —Field Of Hope (IRE) (Selkirk (USA))
330a[4] 600a[5] 4543[3] 5213[6] 5634[3] 6009[10]

Omasheriff (IRE) *W Baltromei* 103
5 ch h Shinko Forest(IRE) —Lady Of Leisure (USA) (Diesis)
1189a[7] 1800a[10]

Ombrageux (IRE) *H-A Pantall* 103
3 b c Anabaa(USA) —Ombrie (Zafonic (USA))
1057a[6]

Ommadawn (IRE) *J R Fanshawe* a68 65
3 b f Montjeu(IRE) —Bonheur (IRE) (Royal Academy (USA))
1784[5] 2726[10] 4858[6] *(5899)*

Omnicat (USA) *Saeed Bin Suroor* 77
2 br c Storm Cat(USA) —Onaga (USA) (Mr Prospector (USA))
6754[U]

On Air (USA) *J W Hills* a43 61
4 rg m Cozzene(USA) —Cumulate (USA) (Gone West (USA))
571[8]

On A Jeune (AUS) *A Payne* 114
7 b g Jeune—Chandada Rose (AUS) (King's High (AUS))
6712a[6]

Onatopp (IRE) *T D Easterby* a51 70
3 b f Soviet Star(USA) —Blueprint (USA) (Shadeed (USA))
2032[2] 2312[2] 2534[7] (3202) 3920[8] 4291[4] 4705[3] 5230[4] 5555[12] 6021[13]

Once More Dubai (USA) *Gianluca Bietolini*
2 b c E Dubai(USA) —Go Again Girl (USA) (Broad Brush (USA))
6523a[5]

Once Upon A Grace (IRE) *Ms F M Crowley* 94
3 b f Spinning World(USA) —Adamparis (Robellino (USA))
946a[5]

One And Gone (IRE) *Miss M E Rowland* a3 61
3 b g Machiavellian(USA) —Bright Smile (IRE) (Caerleon (USA))
1155[16] 1531[12] 3181[9] 4156[9] 4426[11] *7153[10]*

One Called Alice *J R Holt* a57 43
2 gr f Zilzal(USA) —Boadicea The Red (IRE) (Inchinor)
4459[4] 5015[3] 5603[5] 6066[3] 6536[8]

One For Gretta (IRE) *J Hetherton* 30
5 ch m Timeless Times(USA) —Bay Of Bengal (IRE) (Persian Bold)
630[14]

Onefourseven *Lucinda Featherstone* 44
14 b g Jumbo Hirt(USA) —Dominance (Dominion)
6798[11]

One Giant Leap (IRE) *H Morrison* 71
3 ch f Pivotal—Petite Epaulette (Night Shift (USA))
1633[3] (4000) 4880[14] 6088[3] 6310[4]

One Great Cat (USA) *A P O'Brien* 105
2 br c Storm Cat(USA) —Blissful (USA) (Mr Prospector (USA))
4120[3] 5406[3]

One Hour *M P Tregoning* a83 95
3 b c Halling(USA) —Mingora (USA) (Mtoto)
(293) 2001[3] (2669) 3272[5] 3939[3]

One Little David (GER) *P Vovcenko* 100
7 bb g Camp David(GER) —Open Heart (GER) (Sure Blade (USA))
882a[5] 1192a[5] 4838a[10]

One More Round (USA) *Ollie Pears* a101 106
9 b g Ghazi(USA) —Life Of The Party (USA) (Pleasant Colony (USA))
344[5] 490[7] 660[3] 759[3] 1474[7] 1651[23] 2058[9] 4456[7] 4614[15] (5195) 5407[11] *6003[12] 6668[9] (6826) 6947[2] 7279[2]*

Onenightinlisbon (IRE) *J R Boyle* a87 82
3 br f Bold Fact(USA) —Mickey Towbar (IRE) (Mujadil (USA))
4360[10] 5223[9] 6385[4] 6854[3] (6947) 7073[2] 7269[6]

One Night In Paris (IRE) *M J Wallace* a78 49
4 bb m Danetime(IRE) —Forget Paris (IRE) (Broken Hearted)
(85) (358) 590[7] 4949[8] 5223[7] *(6504)* 6696[2]

One Putra (IRE) *M A Jarvis* 111
5 b h Indian Ridge—Triomphale (USA) (Nureyev (USA))
2858[14] 3526[10]

One To Follow *C G Cox* 84
3 b g Mtoto—Becalmed (Dilum (USA))
2426[9] 5724[7] 6186[15] 6421[8]

One Tou Many *C W Fairhurst*
2 b f Tobougg(IRE) —Reine De Thebes (FR) (Darshaan)
1043[9]

On Every Street *R Bastiman* a31 55
6 b g Singspiel(IRE) —Nekhbet (Artaius (USA))
1934[10] 2825[8] 3371[8] 5158[5] 5835[2] *6797[9]*

One Way Ticket *J M Bradley* a60 89
7 ch h Pursuit Of Love—Prima Cominna (Unfuwain (USA))
1321[3] 1557[11] *2221[2]* 2411[3] 4233[2] 4320[3] 5009[15] 5160[12] 5272[8] 5349[5] *5947[3] 6149[9] 6773[3] 6890[12]*

One White Sock *J L Spearing* a46 50
3 b f Compton Admiral—Night Gypsy (Mind Games)
36[6] 108[5] 5270[10] 5688[13]

On Instinct (IRE) *B Smart* 63
2 b f Clodovil(IRE) —Julius (IRE) (Persian Bold)
2416[6] 4522[3] 5281[4] 6075[6] 6635[7]

Oniz Tiptoes (IRE) *J S Wainwright* 66
6 ch g Russian Revival(USA) —Edionda (IRE) (Magical Strike (USA))
3402[4] 3630[6] 4096[6] 5300[10]

Only A Game (IRE) *Miss M E Rowland* a69 66
2 b c Foxhound(USA) —Compendium (Puissance)
(3392) (3801) 4995[2] 5167[9] *6973[2] 7260[2]*

Only A Grand *R Bastiman* a59 61
3 b f Cloudings(IRE) —Magic Orb (Primo Dominie)
1238[10] 1748[9] 2255[7] 3342[9] 3786[9] 4224[6] 5935[12] 6537[2] *6908[3] (7201) 7244[2]*

Only Answer *A Fabre* 104
3 b f Green Desert(USA) —Occupandiste (IRE) (Kaldoun (FR))
1006a[0] (4190a) 5468a[4]

Only A Splash *D W Chapman* a44 47
3 b g Primo Valentino(IRE) —Water Well (Sadler's Wells (USA))
2205[9] 2938[13] 3786[13]

Only Hope *Miss Diana Weeden* a53 64
3 b f Marju(IRE) —Sellette (IRE) (Selkirk (USA))
2335[16] 5636[9] 6412[10] *7168[4]*

Only If I Laugh *M J Attwater* a65 62
6 ch g Piccolo—Agony Aunt (Formidable (USA))
383[4] 485[8] 800[9] 3422[13] 4397[16] 5276[7] *5368[6] 6947[6] 7124[4] 7166[7] 7278[9]*

Only In Jest *W G M Turner* a53 74
2 br f Averti(IRE) —Silver Purse (Interrex (CAN))
883[2] 1727[7] (1919) 2650[4] 3492[4] 4046[14] 4315[10] *5365[12]* 6195[11]

On The Map *A P Jarvis* a62 57
3 b f Agnes World(USA) —Noor El Houdah (IRE) (Fayruz)
1045[10] *1399[12] (2571) 3647[5]* 4224[15] 4514[3] 4853[8] *6385[11]*

On The Trail *D W Chapman* a51 39
10 ch g Catrail(USA) —From The Rooftops (IRE) (Thatching)
339[13] 1262[13]

On Watch *H Candy* 56
3 b f Josr Algarhoud(IRE) —Sole Control (Jupiter Island)
1785[7] 2981[11] 3876[8] 4877[10]

Onyergo (IRE) *J R Weymes* 68
5 b g Polish Precedent(USA) —Trick (IRE) (Shirley Heights)
1745[DSQ]

Opal Haze (USA) *J H M Gosden* a90 90
3 rg f With Approval(CAN) —Summer Mist (USA) (Miswaki (USA))
3244[3] *(3621) (5101)* 5619[4] 5940[5]

Opal Noir *I Semple* 83
3 b g Lujain(USA) —Wrong Bride (Reprimand)
2171[4] 2744[16] 4999[10] 5556[10] 6466[6]

Opal Warrior *Jane Southcombe* a46 32
4 b m Orpen(USA) —Indian Wardance (ITY) (Indian Ridge)
94[10] 289[9] 350[13]

Opatja *L Camici* 100
5 b m Nashwan(USA) —Thundercloud (Electric)
2296a[6]

Openide *B W Duke* a55 84
6 b g Key Of Luck(USA) —Eyelet (IRE) (Satco (FR))
16[5] 291[7] 4531[5]

Opening Act *P F I Cole* a48
2 bg c Daylami(IRE) —Bluebelle (Generous (IRE))
6934[6]

Opera Cape *Saeed Bin Suroor* 107
4 b g Barathea(IRE) —Optaria (Song)
3529[5] 3887[4] (5673) 6338[14]

Operachy *B R Millman* 60
2 b g Kyllachy—Sea Music (Inchinor)
5003[10] 5591[6] 6104[5]

Opera Crown (IRE) *P F I Cole* a49 80
3 b g Grand Lodge(USA) —Silly Goose (IRE) (Sadler's Wells (USA))
1504[6] 1887[10] 2558[6] *3189[7]* 4603[7] 4960[13] *5755[8] 6178[9]*

Opera Music *S Kirk* 93
3 b g Kirkwall—Optaria (Song)
1276[4] 2212[9] 2788[17] 3480[8] 5208[4] 5385[4] 5979[3]

Opera Prince *S Kirk* 54
2 b c Kyllachy—Optaria (Song)
5206[10] 6617[7]

Operation Red Dawn (USA) *Christophe Clement* 91
5 bb h Miswaki(USA) —Afaladja (IRE) (Darshaan)
6771a[9]

Opera Writer (IRE) *R Hollinshead* a74 55
4 b g Rossini(USA) —Miss Flite (IRE) (Law Society (USA))
74[3] 100[4] 142[9] 453[6] 507[7] 6672[3] 6883[3] 7046[6] 7285[2]

Oporto (UAE) *D M Fogarty* a11 50
4 b m Jade Robbery(USA) —Potentille (IRE) (Caerleon (USA))
2018a[6]

Opportunist (IRE) *Doug Watson* a103
8 b h Machiavellian(USA) —Fatefully (USA) (Private Account (USA))
177a[11] 327a[4] 410a[2] 543a[4] 599a[9]

Oprah Winney (USA) *R Dutrow Jr* a105
4 rg m Royal Academy(USA) —Mere Presence (USA) (Woodman (USA))
6483a[8]

Optical Illusion (USA) *I Semple* a64 74
3 b g Theatrical—Paradise River (USA) (Irish River (FR))
1246[6] *1452[5]* 2335[11] 3276[3] 4282[5] 4971[8] 5082[7] 5678[8]

Optical Seclusion (IRE) *T J Etherington* a56 58
4 b g Second Empire(IRE) —Theda (Mummy's Pet)
125[3] 282[5] 421[4] 892[12] 5282[12]

Optimistic Alfie *B G Powell* a52 53
7 b g Afzal—Threads (Bedford (USA))
5474[2] 5754[8] 5938[11] 6271[8]

Optimum (IRE) *J T Stimpson* a67 56
5 br g King's Best(USA) —Colour Dance (Rainbow Quest (USA))
585[8]

Optimus (USA) *B G Powell* a84 85
5 ch g Elnadim(USA) —Ajfan (USA) (Woodman (USA))
1308[8] 1542[5] 2003[5] 2403[10] 2621[5] 3076[4] (3690) 4418[2] 4850[2] 5383[2] 5885[3] (6603) 6853[5]

Opus Magnus (IRE) *P J Makin* a57 32
4 b g Mozart(IRE) —Bold As Love (Lomond (USA))
124[9] 6809[13] 7009[13]

Oracle West (SAF) *M F De Kock* 120
6 b g Western Winter(USA) —Noble Prophet (SAF) (Noble Ambition (USA))
330a[3] 598a[2] 861a[2] 1877a[6] 5634[2] 6374a[5]

Orama's Ghost *Sir Michael Stoute* a55 74
3 b f Golan(IRE) —Orange Sunset (IRE) (Roanoke (USA))
1203[3] 1685[3] 2359[3] 2981[8] 4392[5]

Orange *W J Haggas* 55
3 ch f Giant's Causeway(USA) —Shopping For Love (USA) (Not For Love (USA))
4575[9]

Orange Pip *R Hannon* 66
2 ch f Bold Edge—Opopmil (IRE) (Pips Pride)
6754[2]

Oranges And Lemons (FR) *C E Brittain* a35 61
4 b m Zafonic(USA) —Tarte Aux Pommes (USA) (Local Talent (USA))
66[10]

Orange Square (IRE) *R Hannon* a67
2 br c King Charlemagne(USA) —Unaria (Prince Tenderfoot (USA))
6827[9] 6944[3] 7071[2]

Orange Touch (GER) *Mrs A J Perrett* a86 102
7 b g Lando(GER) —Orange Bowl (General Assembly (USA))
345[4]

Oranmore Castle (IRE) *R A Fahey* 86
5 b g Giant's Causeway(USA) —Twice The Ease (Green Desert (USA))
957[11] (1483) 1853[9] 2461[12] 4095[18] 4122[8] 5009[8] 5232[2] 5379[6] 5722[8]

Oratory (SAF) *S Seemar* 77
10 b g Centenary(USA) —Leah The Lark (USA) (Lear Fan (USA))
328a[12]

Orbital Orchid *W S Kittow* a51 46
2 b f Mujahid(USA) —Carati (Selkirk (USA))
1727[8] 2488[8] 3648[9] 5344[10]

Orbit O'Gold (USA) *Noel Meade* 92
5 ch g Kingmambo(USA) —Lily O'Gold (USA) (Slew O'Gold (USA))
6366a[2]

Orcadian *J M P Eustace* a83 112
6 b g Kirkwall—Rosy Outlook (USA) (Trempolino (USA))
1823[8]

Orchard House (FR) *J Jay* a61 38
4 b g Medaaly—Louisa May (IRE) (Royal Abjar (USA))
1376[3] (2345) 2890[9] 3795[13]

Orchard Supreme *R Hannon* a107 93
4 ch g Titus Livius(FR) —Bogus Penny (IRE) (Pennekamp (USA))
119[4] 487[4] 550[4] (658) 761[8] 817[3] 1307[8] 1449[5] (5833) 6203[5] 6852[4] 6965[4] 6992[2] 7074[5] 7267[2]

Orchestration (IRE) *S Parr* a55 58
6 ch g Stravinsky(USA) —Mora (IRE) (Second Set (IRE))
77[4] 317[10] 430[13] (441) 562[9] 680[6] 690[7] 892[13] 1400[9] 1719[2] 2174[6] 7284[6]

Orchestrator (IRE) *T G Mills* a68 69
3 b g Docksider(USA) —Summerhill (Habitat)
2625[5] 3044[2] 3646[8] 4671[2] 5175[12]

Orchestrion *G A Swinbank* 63
2 ch f Piccolo—Mindomica (Dominion)
5281[3]

Ordinance (USA) *T G Mills* a80 85
2 b c Orientate(USA) —Moody's Cat (IRE) (Alzao (USA))
2687[4] 2991[2] 3522[3] 3896[6] 4372[4] (5200)

Ordnance Row *R Hannon* 113
4 b g Mark Of Esteem(IRE) —Language Of Love (Rock City)
1651[7] 1818[3] 2208[3] 2233[5] 2446[3] (3001) (3330) 4543[2] 4826[5] 5723[2] 6298[5]

Organizer (NOR) *Christian Wroe* a97 98
7 b g Zafonic(USA) —Orange Walk (IRE) (Alzao (USA))
178a[12] 327a[12]

Oriental Gift (FR) *J R Norton* 23
3 ch g Orientate(USA) —Golden Queen (USA) (Gold Fever (USA))
3382[9] 4334[9] 4901[6] 5488[6]

Oriental Girl *J A Geake* a55
2 b f Dr Fong(USA) —Zacchera (Zamindar (USA))
6262[11] 6601[8] 6847[8]

Oriental Hero (GER) *Frau K Haustein* 92
3 ch c Seattle Dancer(USA) —Oriental Pearl (GER) (Big Shuffle (USA))
2705a[5]

Orientalist Art *P W Chapple-Hyam* 83
2 b c Green Desert(USA) —Pink Cristal (Dilum (USA))
2041[2]

Oriental Tiger (GER) *U Ostmann* 114
4 b h Tiger Hill(IRE) —Oriental Flower (GER) (Big Shuffle (USA))
2924a[3] 3778a[6]

Orientor *J S Goldie* a87 111
9 b h Inchinor—Orient (Bay Express)
2034[5] 2463[11] 3050[5] 3586[3] 3990[18] 5039[4] 5407[8] 5616[17] 5810[7]

Orion Girl (GER) *H-A Pantall* 97
3 br f Law Society(USA) —Okocha (GER) (Platini (GER))
(2547a) 4557a[9]

Orkney (IRE) *Miss J A Camacho* a65 44
2 b g Trans Island—Bitty Mary (Be My Chief (USA))
6303[9] 6857[4]

Oronsay *B R Millman* a38 54
2 ch f Elmaamul(USA) —Glenfinlass (Lomond (USA))
3465[13] 4540[6] 5267[9] 5818[11]

Orotund *T D Easterby* a30 61
3 b g Orpen(USA) —Soyalang (FR) (Alydeed (CAN))
910[9] 2791[5] 2844[2] 3302[5] 3588[3] (3752) 4180[4] 4583[11] 4714[2] (5041) 5489[7] 6256[6]

Orpailleur *Ms Joanna Morgan* a92 97
6 gr g Mon Tresor—African Light (Kalaglow)
3140a[13] 5761a[7]

Orpen Bid (IRE) *A M Crow* 50
2 b f Orpen(USA) —Glorious Bid (IRE) (Horage)
6461[5] 6634[6]

Orpen Fire (IRE) *E S McMahon* a69
2 b f Orpen(USA) —Feet Of Flame (USA) (Theatrical)
(6503) 6960[4]

Orpenindeed (IRE) *M Botti* a96 86
4 bb h Orpen(USA) —Indian Goddess (IRE) (Indian Ridge)
6606[4] 6932[6] 7053[3] 7255[6]

Orpenlina (IRE) *Peter Grayson* a34 51
4 b m Orpen(USA) —Westlife (IRE) (Mind Games)
2830[10] 3169[9] 3597[8] 4379[7]

Orpen Quest (IRE) *M J Attwater* a64 63
5 b g Orpen(USA) —Pursuit Of Truth (USA) (Irish River (FR))
610[11] 976[5] 1167[10] 1227[10] 1715[12] 2370[13] 2980[4] 3035[4] 3280[7] 3595[6] (3868) 4161[11] 4463[8]

Orpen's Art (IRE) *N A Callaghan* a54 54
2 b c Invincible Spirit(IRE) —Bells Of Ireland (UAE) (Machiavellian (USA))
1094[6] 1919[11] 2575[11] 4098[5] 4315[8] 4605[8] 5089[4] 5365[2] 5534[12] 6828[12] 7106[7]

Orpen's Astaire (IRE) *Jedd O'Keeffe* 59
4 b g Orpen(USA) —Rhythm And Style (USA) (Keen)
928[10] 2168[11] 2714[10] 2809[7]

Orpen Wide (IRE) *M C Chapman* a87 93
5 b g Orpen(USA) —Melba (IRE) (Namaqualand (USA))
1859 451[4] 509[7] 1013[2] 1157[10] 1568[2] 2189[3] 2346[4] 2835[2] 3386[8] 4134[2] 4367[5] 4585[4] 4922[9] (5196) 5950[13] 6155[4] 6539[2]

Orphan (IRE) *E J Alston* 78
5 b g Orpen(USA) —Ballinlee (IRE) (Skyliner)
2072[9] 2390[12] 3381[S]

Orphan Boy *M G Quinlan* a8
2 b g Tipsy Creek(USA) —Miss Jingles (Muhtarram (USA))
7240[7]

Orphina (IRE) *B G Powell* a55 63
4 b m Orpen(USA) —Keralba (USA) (Sheikh Albadou)
230[6] 402[11] 1002[7] 1206[4] 1562[9] 4253[5] (4534) 4766[7] 5709[9]

Orphir (IRE) *Mrs N Macauley* a39 43
4 b g Orpen(USA) —Silver Moon (Environment Friend)
1[8] 134[9] 775[12] 1030[5] 2537[9] 2843[8] 3684[6]

Orpsie Boy (IRE) *N P Littmoden* a99 98
4 b g Orpen(USA) —Nordicolini (IRE) (Nordico (USA))
(1121) (1971) (3481) 4614[9] 4990[14] 5407[4] 6003[5] 7255[3]

Orton Park *Mrs P Sly* 69
2 ch c Bahamian Bounty—Whittle Woods Girl (Emarati (USA))
2724[4] (Dead)

Oscar Ireland (IRE) *R M Beckett* a49
6 bb g Oscar(IRE) —Distinctly Scarlet (IRE) (Import)
2874[3] 3282[5]

Oscar Night (IRE) *Adrian Maguire* 78
8 b g Oscar(IRE) —Laridissa (IRE) (Shardari)
1760a[2]

Oscar Pride (IRE) *V T O'Brien* 39
8 b m Oscar(IRE) —Contract Miss (IRE) (Contract Law (USA))
1760a[9]

Oscarshall (IRE) *M H Tompkins* a59 75
3 ch g Halling(USA) —Mafaatin (IRE) (Royal Academy (USA))
1634[3] (2061) 2662[4] 4111[14] 5532[9] 6055[8] 6501[4]

Oscar Snowman *M P Tregoning* a80 82
4 b g Selkirk(USA) —Chilly Start (IRE) (Caerleon (USA))
260[4] (422) 587[6] 2512[2] 3039[7]

Oscillator *G A Butler* a79 77
4 b g Pivotal—Craigmill (Slip Anchor)
1385[2]

Osiris Way *P R Chamings* a89 89
5 ch g Indian Ridge—Heady (Rousillon (USA))
1166[8] (1946) (2217) (2882) 3489[3] 6141[2] 6589[3] 6970[7]

Osolomio (IRE) *G A Swinbank* a83 89
4 b g Singspiel(IRE) —Inanna (Persian Bold)
1042[4] (1158) 1490[3] 2031[2] (2342) 3748[3] (4248) 4917[5] 5623[3]

Ossun (FR) *J-C Rouget* 102
2 br f Anabaa(USA) —Lamballe (USA) (Woodman (USA))
6630a[7]

Osteopathic Remedy (IRE) *M Dods* 86
3 ch g Inchinor—Dolce Vita (IRE) (Ela-Mana-Mou)
1298[8] 1768[6] 2040[7] 2841[8] 3196[2] 3885[5] 4222[6] 4785[2] 5558[3] 5776[4] 6492[7] 6637[4]

Osterhase (IRE) *J E Mulhern* a86 118
8 b g Flying Spur(AUS) —Ostrusa (AUT) (Rustan (HUN))
1171a[4] 2324a[6] 4864a[13] 5075a[8]

Ostfanni (IRE) *M Todhunter* 71
7 b m Spectrum(IRE) —Ostwahl (IRE) (Waajib)
9131[0] (2825) 4179[9]

Ostinata (IRE) *B W Duke* a51 52
2 ch f Spartacus(IRE) —Poly Dancer (Suave Dancer (USA))
1832[18] 1960[8] 2193[5] 4393[8] 5268[8] (7010)

Otaared *M A Jarvis* 81
2 bb c Storm Cat(USA) —Society Lady (USA) (Mr Prospector (USA))
4725[6]

Otaki (IRE) *Sir Mark Prescott* a40
3 gr f King's Best(USA) —On Call (Alleged (USA))
69[10] 149[12] 7186[6]

Otriad (RUS) *B J Curley*
4 b g Dotsero(USA) —Oshma (RUS) (Observation Post)
812[10]

Our Acquaintance *W R Muir* a73 75
2 ch g Bahamian Bounty—Lady Of Limerick (IRE) (Thatching)
3085[3] 3687[4] 3947[3] 4537[2] 4775[11] (5176) 5773[8] 6059[7]

Our Archie *M J Attwater* a41 38
3 b g Kyllachy—Oriel Girl (Beveled (USA))
2541[10] 3597[9] 5270[7] 5535[8] 5867[7] 7019[7] 7138[11]

Our Blessing (IRE) *A P Jarvis* a83 84
3 b g Lujain(USA) —Berenice (ITY) (Marouble)
(188) 385[4] 2395[9] 3418[11] 3688[4] 4222[9] 4585[3] 5356[18]

Our Chairman (IRE) *R Hannon* a73 72
2 b c Okawango(USA) —Lucky For Me (USA) (King Of Kings (IRE))
3383[8] 4527[2] 5720[10] 6267[2] 6328[5]

Our Choice (IRE) *C J Mann* a71 73
5 b g Indian Danehill(IRE) —Spring Daffodil (Pharly (FR))
5204[12]

Our Dolly *S Parr* a43
2 b f Lomitas—Amidst (Midyan (USA))
6694[6]

Our Faye *S Kirk* a72 95
4 b m College Chapel—Tamara (Marju (IRE))
(2696) (3154) (3970) (4373) 4633[5] 5163[5] 5354[2] 5799[7]

Our Flossie (IRE) *A D Brown* 7
4 b m Midhish—Buckalgo (IRE) (Buckskin (FR))
1086[15] 1376[13]

Our Fugitive (IRE) *A W Carroll* a73 85
5 gr g Titus Livius(FR) —Mystical Jumbo (Mystiko (USA))
1061[5] 1669[10] 1999[9] 3594[2] (3906) 4486[10] 5565[5] 5942[7] 6860[3] (7005)

Our Georgia *T D Barron* a32
4 b m Mind Games—Our Krissie (Kris)
511[4]

Our Glenard *J E Long* a49 57
8 b g Royal Applause—Loucoum (FR) (Iron Duke (FR))
1331[4] 203[9]

Our Herbie *J W Hills* a79 78
3 b g Tobougg(IRE) —Trevillari (USA) (Riverman (USA))
1076[11] 1815[14] 2633[5] 3384[6] 3732[2] 4109[2] 4505[3] 4591[8] 5338[8] 5690[4] 6261[6]

Our Jaffa (IRE) *H Rogers* a79 82
6 br m Bin Ajwaad(IRE) —Griddle Cake (IRE) (Be My Guest (USA))
3143a[15] 6368a[14]

Our Joan *P T Midgley* 31
2 ch f Starborough—Aonach Mor (Anabaa (USA))
2009[5] 5527[13] 5745[14]

Our Jo Jo (IRE) *J C Hayden* 80
2 b f Soviet Star(USA) —Torretta (IRE) (Indian Ridge)
5393a[2]

Our Kally *M D I Usher* a45 57
2 b f Kyllachy—Rendition (Polish Precedent (USA))
2122[8] 2630[6] 3532[4] 4065[8] 5096[11] 5357[11]

Our Kenny *C W Thornton* 16
5 b g Overbury(IRE) —Auntie Alice (Uncle Pokey)
1044[13]

Our Kes (IRE) *P Howling* a74 65
5 gr m Revoque(IRE) —Gracious Gretclo (Common Grounds)
30[7] 235[11] 371[5] (570) (610) 685[4] 712[4] 888[3] 933[5] (2194) 2490[6] 2665[16] 2979[6] 3455[2] 3851[14] 4856[5] 5188[3] (5983) 6146[5] 6764[4] 6874[4] 7080[2] 7237[5]

Our Lament *G C Bravery* a52 48
2 ch g Compton Place—Glider (IRE) (Silver Kite (USA))
5126[7] 5470[11]

Our Little Secret (IRE) *A Berry* a52 100
5 ch m Rossini(USA) —Sports Post Lady (IRE) (M Double M (USA))
964[7] 1999[6] 2315[4] (2418) 2805[4] (3080) 3344[5] (3531)

Our Monogram *R M Beckett* a57 81
11 b g Deploy—Darling Splodge (Elegant Air)
1253[10] 2375[6] 2996[8] 4030[10]

Our Monty (IRE) *K F O'Brien* 71
4 b g Montjeu(IRE) —She's Our Mare (IRE) (Commanche Run)
1760a[5]

Ournina *C R Wilson*
2 b f Hunting Lion(IRE) —Ella's Charm (Charmer)
5735[11] 6305[14]

Our Piccadilly (IRE) *W S Kittow* a70 74
2 b f Piccolo—Dilys (Efisio)
4074[2] 4662[2] (5603)

Our Putra *M A Jarvis* a85 78
4 b g King's Best(USA) —Prima Volta (Primo Dominie)
1845[18] 2239[12]

Our Ruby *P W Chapple-Hyam* 71
3 b f Diktat—Almost Amber (USA) (Mt. Livermore (USA))
1359[5] 1815[15] 3056[15] 4073[3] 4395[6] 6083[3] 6413[16]

Ours (IRE) *John A Harris* a65 66
4 b g Mark Of Esteem(IRE) —Ellebanna (Tina's Pet)
1280[9] 2225[6] 2947[9] 3414[5] 3999[12] 4223[7] 5525[2] (6266) 6598[6] 6859[2] 6979[3] 7127[2] 7218[3]

Our Sion *G C H Chung*
7 b g Dreams End—Millfields Lady (Sayf El Arab (USA))
3906[12]

Our Sunnie *D Nicholls* a45 65
2 b g Averti(IRE) —Barawin (FR) (Fijar Tango (FR))
2337[6] 2804[2] 3024[7] 3499[3] 3812[2] 4065[10]

Our Tallulah (IRE) *C G Cox* 44
2 b f Piccolo—Savannah Belle (Green Desert (USA))
4755[11] 5110[17] 5766[15]

Our Teddy (IRE) *P A Blockley* a83 91
7 ch g Grand Lodge(USA) —Lady Windley (Baillamont (USA))
353[9] 1208[7] 2031[3]

Our Toy Soldier *B Smart* a53 59
3 gr g Forzando—The Wild Widow (Saddlers' Hall (IRE))
2110[13] 2363[10]

Out After Dark *C G Cox* 108
6 b g Cadeaux Genereux—Midnight Shift (IRE) (Night Shift (USA))
1195[15] 1836[3] 2858[17] 3268[5] 3526[7] 4150[21] 5050[15] 5584[12] 6472[21]

Outer Hebrides *J M Bradley* a88 78
6 b g Efisio—Reuval (Sharpen Up)
1666[5] 2088[5] 2394[8] 2655[3] 2725[5] 2982[7] 3472[7] 3549[9] 3828[6] 4259[3] (4505) 4731[9] 5166[13] 5687[9] 6199[13]

Out For A Stroll *S C Williams* a67 73
8 b g Zamindar(USA) —The Jotter (Night Shift (USA))
70[6] 346[8] 571[4] 2190[7] 2514[7] (2568) 3101[5] 3711[5] 4063[7] 4319[6] 4474[5] (4515) 4880[7]

Outlook *P T Midgley* a49 66
4 ch g Observatory(USA) —Area Girl (Jareer (USA))
7158[8]

Out Of Court *C A Cyzer* a72 74
3 b g Hernando(FR) —Shot At Love (IRE) (Last Tycoon (IRE))
4457[7] 4948[3] 5113[7]

Out Of Nothing *F J Bowles* a52 72
4 br m Perryston View—Loves To Dare (IRE) (Desert King (IRE))
6553a[17]

Out Of The Red (IRE) *Lester Winters* a51 86
3 ch g Redback—Art Duo (Artaius (USA))
5761a[12]

Out Of Town *R C Guest* a31
3 ch g Namid—Superstore (USA) (Blushing Groom (FR))
4426[15] 5688[17]

Outside Edge (IRE) *W R Swinburn* 66
2 b g Danetime(IRE) —Naraina (IRE) (Desert Story (IRE))
1150[6] 1469[5] (1989)

Overbay *E J Alston*
3 b f Overbury(IRE) —On The Bay (Carlton (GER))
6286[12]

Overextended (USA) *Doug O'Neill* a95 83
2 rg c Monarchos(USA) —Way Of Life (USA) (Gulch (USA))
6508a[7]

Overfields *G J Smith* a38
7 b g Overbury(IRE) —Honey Day (Lucky Wednesday)
603[7] 628[6]

Over Ice *Karen George* a41 67
4 b m Mister Baileys—Oublier L'Ennui (FR) (Bellman (FR))
1761[5] 2194[9] 3427[6] 5366[8]

Overrule (USA) *J Noseda* 91
3 b g Diesis—Her Own Way (USA) (Danzig (USA))
(1204) 1476[5] 3460[6] 5805[7]

Oversighted (GER) *Mrs Y Dunleavy* a44 79
6 b g Selkirk(USA) —Obvious Appeal (IRE) (Danehill (USA))
6907[9]

Overstayed (IRE) *M Mullineaux* a65 84
4 ch g Titus Livius(FR) —Look Nonchalant (IRE) (Fayruz)
1601[9] 2234[14] 3050[8] 4696[18] 5039[7] 5379[16] 7078[7] 7206[7]

Over The Tylery (IRE) *Eamon Tyrrell* 63
3 b f Swallow Flight(IRE) —Ivory Turner (Efisio)
4836a[11]

Over To You Bert *R J Hodges* a57 61
8 b g Overbury(IRE) —Silvers Era (Balidar)
(51) 156[2] 274[2] 402[2] 637[4] 690[2] (800) 1251[6] 1969[11] 2273[2] 2798[7] 2979[7] 3405[2] 3647[6]

Overwing (IRE) *R M H Cowell* a79 77
4 b m Fasliyev(USA) —Sierva (GER) (Darshaan)
1067[2] 1525[6] 2191[6] 2399[8] 2933[5] 3627[8] 4017[3] 4324[3] 4712[3] 4787[7] 5387[12] 5642[4] 6089[2] 6287[12] 6671[7] 6962[8]

Ovthenight (IRE) *Mrs P Sly* a54 61
2 b c Noverre(USA) —Night Beauty (King Of Kings (IRE))
3471[12] 3842[6] 4547[7] 5127[10] 5914[4] 6427[10]

Owed *R Bastiman* a79 43
5 b g Lujain(USA) —Nightingale (Night Shift (USA))
(303) 468[2] 718[3] 896[12] 1265[2] (1377) 1935[4] 1977[7]

Own Boss (USA) *M A Jarvis* 80
3 b c Seeking The Gold(USA) —Ameerat (Mark Of Esteem (IRE))
2944[7] 3349[2] 3743[3] 4258[3] (4905)

Own Gift *S Parr* 18
3 b f Rahy(USA) —Zahrat Dubai (Unfuwain (USA))
2580[11] 4178[10] 5625[12]

Oxbridge *B J Meehan* 59
2 ch c Tomba—Royal Passion (Ahonoora)
4761[8] 5329[6] 6058[4] 6410[15]

Oystermouth *R Charlton* a47 65
3 b f Averti(IRE) —Alessia (Caerleon (USA))
1883[2] 4066[5] (5270)

Pab Special (IRE) *K R Burke* a80 81
4 b g City On A Hill(USA) —Tinos Island (IRE) (Alzao (USA))
427[2] 459[5] 604[5] 1413[2] 1655[3] 1997[4] 2311[7] 6504[5] 6628[2] 6997[7] 7241[6] 7253[6]

Paceman (USA) *R Hannon* 92
3 b c Diesis—Innes (USA) (A.P. Indy (USA))
1277^{5} 1929^{3} (2943) 3745^{5} 5776^{13} (Dead)

Pachello (IRE) *J M Bradley* a29 81
5 b g Priolo(USA) —Most Charming (FR) (Darshaan)
1200^{14} 1459^{12} 2108^{13} 3497^{13} 4880^{15}

Pacific Pride *J J Quinn* 106
4 b g Compton Place—Only Yours (Aragon)
1788^{7} 2237^{10} 3240^{7} 4095^{15} 4122^{26} 4806^{14} 5584^{13}

Pacifism (UAE) *M A Jarvis* a85 62
2 ch g Halling(USA) —African Peace (USA) (Roberto (USA))
6248^{10} 6618^{7}

Packers Hill (IRE) *G A Swinbank* 74
3 b g Mull Of Kintyre(USA) —Head For The Stars (IRE) (Head For Heights)
(1531) 2092^{7} 3607^{7}

Paco Boy (IRE) *R Hannon* a72 94
2 b c Desert Style(IRE) —Tappen Zee (Sandhurst Prince)
5126^{3} (5591) (6621)

Paco Jack (IRE) *Joseph Crowley* 71
3 b g Soviet Star(USA) —Tocade (IRE) (Kenmare (FR))
4035a^{3}

Pactolos Way *P R Chamings* a70 65
4 b g Docksider(USA) —Arietta's Way (IRE) (Darshaan)
1385^{7} 1811^{10} 2321^{5} *2667^{4}* 3907^{5} *4271^{2}* 4504^{5} *5733^{2} 6344^{8}*

Paddy Jack *J R Weymes* a9 70
2 ch g Rambling Bear—Bayrami (Emarati (USA))
3341^{3} 4076^{6} 4285^{3} 4702^{3} *5365^{11}* 5558^{2} 6072^{2}

Paddymctume *H J Manners* a31
5 b m Overbury(IRE) —Esterelle (USA) (Trempolino (USA))
499^{10} 603^{8}

Paddy Moon *J G Given* a45 41
4 b g Lujain(USA) —Tara Moon (Pivotal)
393^{10} 466^{9}

Paddy Rielly (IRE) *P D Evans* a47 55
2 b g Catcher In The Rye(IRE) —The Veil (IRE) (Barathea (IRE))
890^{7} 3842^{5} 4876^{12}

Paddy's Day (IRE) *T J O'Mara* 69
4 b h Imperial Ballet(IRE) —Shifting Shadow (IRE) (Mujadil (USA))
4114a^{8}

Paddy's Isle (IRE) *A J McCabe* 30
4 b g Trans Island—Remember Mulvilla (Ballad Rock)
6801^{11}

Paddywack (IRE) *D W Chapman* a69 69
10 b g Bigstone(IRE) —Millie's Return (IRE) (Ballad Rock)
803^{7} 992^{13} 1074^{11} (1112) 1260^{9} 1914^{8} 2509^{2} 2712^{9} 3259^{11} 3608^{6} 3791^{5} 3921^{9} 4289^{4} 4642^{2} 4800^{6} *5016^{7} 5174^{6}* 5297^{7} (5741) 6287^{13} *6476^{10} 7105^{4} 7180^{7}*

Padlocked (IRE) *D M Simcock* a77 94
3 b c Key Of Luck(USA) —Accelerating (USA) (Lear Fan (USA))
(1523) (1929) 2426^{5} (4502) 5382^{2} 5764^{7}

Padrao Lima (BRZ) *J S Moore* a65 83
4 ch g Exile King(USA) —Karakatu (BRZ) (Minstrel Glory (USA))
324a^{10} 472a^{12} 4990^{11} 5449^{10}

Padre Nostro (IRE) *M Sheppard* a65 63
8 ch g Grand Lodge(USA) —Meglio Che Posso (IRE) (Try My Best (USA))
64^{5} 665^{4} 716^{4} 907^{9} 1570^{7} 3485^{3} 3901^{9} 5427^{11}

Pagan Belief *J A R Toller* a70 69
3 b g Fraam—Au Contraire (Groom Dancer (USA))
1840^{7} (2541) 3707^{9} 5360^{7} *6232^{6}*

Pagan Crest *Mrs A J Perrett* a50 78
4 ch g Indian Ridge—Maria Theresa (Primo Dominie)
1470^{12} 5593^{10} 5870^{8} 6253^{13} *6603^{11}*

Pagano (IRE) *A King* a81 83
4 b g Night Shift(USA) —Frippet (IRE) (Ela-Mana-Mou)
1083^{4} 1668^{2}

Pagan Rose (IRE) *J A R Toller* a37 40
3 ch f Medicean—Countess Sybil (IRE) (Dr Devious (IRE))
3710^{14} 5013^{12} 5474^{3} *6026^{9}*

Pagan Rules (IRE) *Mrs A J Perrett* 64
3 b g Desert Prince(IRE) —Fernanda (Be My Chief (USA))
1972^{9} 2558^{2} 2945^{4} 3150^{7}

Pagan Starprincess *G M Moore* 61
3 b f Robertico—Pagan Star (Carlitin)
1111^{9} 1303^{10} 2133^{10} 2793^{6} 3379^{3} 4104^{10} (6076)

Pagan Sword *Mrs A J Perrett* a94 95
5 ch g Selkirk(USA) —Vanessa Bell (IRE) (Lahib (USA))
420^{3} 701^{4} 1245^{14} 2003^{2} 2397^{9} 3672^{6} 4153^{2} 4419^{2} *4888^{5}* 5049^{5} 5362^{8} 5631^{8} *6439^{3}*

Paging The King (FR) *B Dutruel* a82 73
7 ch g Spectrum(IRE) —Page Bleue (Sadler's Wells (USA))
6923a^{5}

Pain In The Neck (IRE) *M J Wallace* a57
4 br g Orpen(USA) —Ravishing (IRE) (Bigstone (IRE))
86^{13}

Painted Sky *R A Fahey* a80 75
4 ch g Rainbow Quest(USA) —Emplane (USA) (Irish River (FR))
6500^{8} *(7045)*

Paint In Green (IRE) *A & G Botti* 97
3 b f Invincible Spirit(IRE) —Theory Of Law (Generous (IRE))
6688a^{10}

Paint Stripper *W Storey* 61
2 b g Prince Sabo—Passing Fancy (Grand Lodge (USA))
3024^{13} 3192^{7} 3995^{10} 6255^{6} 6462^{2} (6635)

Paint The Town (IRE) *A P O'Brien* a66 72
2 b f Sadler's Wells(USA) —Minnie Habit (Habitat)
3659a^{9}

Paint The Town Red *H J Collingridge* 56
2 b c Mujahid(USA) —Onefortheditch (USA) (With Approval (CAN))
6106^{8}

Pairumani Princess (IRE) *E A L Dunlop* a66 70
3 b f Pairumani Star(IRE) —Persian Fantasy (Persian Bold)
1628^{6} 3166^{3} 3427^{3} 3876^{4} 4859^{3} *5364^{6}*

Pajada *M D I Usher* a52 39
3 b f Bertolini(USA) —Last Ambition (IRE) (Cadeaux Genereux)
348^{14} 460^{7} 577^{9} 1119^{4} 1381^{4} 2489^{10} 2697^{7} 2916^{12} 6062^{10} *6206^{8}* 6277^{4} 6497^{11} *6778^{10} 6831^{6} 6950^{10} 7088^{10}*

Pakama (GER) *Mario Hofer* 87
3 br f Kalatos(GER) —Puntilla (GER) (Acatenango (GER))
1338a^{12}

Pakhoes (IRE) *R Bouresly* a86 98
7 b h College Chapel—Park Charger (Tirol)
324a^{8} 474a^{11}

Paktolos (FR) *A King* a94 80
4 b g Dansili—Pithara (GR) (Never So Bold)
256^{2} (593) 698^{3} 1477^{11} 3105^{7}

Palace Episode (USA) *Saeed Bin Suroor* 110
4 bb h Machiavellian(USA) —Palace Weekend (USA) (Seattle Dancer (USA))
5823a^{3} 6924a^{6}

Palace Princess (GER) *U Ostmann* 55
3 b f Tiger Hill(IRE) —Pasca (GER) (Lagunas)
2294a^{12}

Palafamix (FR) *N Clement* a65 99
4 gr g Linamix(FR) —Palafairia (FR) (Always Fair (USA))
1879a^{5} 3780a^{7}

Palais Polaire *J A Geake* a60 60
5 ch m Polar Falcon(USA) —Palace Street (USA) (Secreto (USA))
4257^{8} *5730^{7} 5817^{2} 6431^{5} 6587^{11} 6717^{2} 6809^{6} 6950^{4} 7278^{5}*

Palamoun *B W Hills* a81 80
3 b c Mtoto—Princess Minnie (Mistertopogigo (IRE))
(816)

Palanoverre (IRE) *D J S Ffrench Davis* a49 72
3 ch f Noverre(USA) —Palavera (FR) (Bikala)
873a^{13} *3421^{13}* 3871^{4} 4259^{7} 4766^{6} 5347^{7} *5945^{5}*

Palladia Directa (GER) *C Bocksai* 44
7 b m Roi Danzig(USA) —Pasadena (GER) (Esclavo (FR))
439a^{5} 494a^{6}

Palm Court *R Charlton* a88 78
2 b c Green Desert(USA) —Amenixa (FR) (Linamix (FR))
2215^{10} 2473^{4} 3592^{3} *(4022)* 4364^{4} 4812^{12} (5268) 5571^{6} *6120^{2} 6291^{6}*

Palm Cove (UAE) *M Kettle* a47 85
4 b m Jade Robbery(USA) —Temora (IRE) (Ela-Mana-Mou)
473a^{12} *532a^{14}*

Palmerin *R Hannon* a77 79
2 b c Oasis Dream—Armorique (IRE) (Top Ville)
4151^{13} 4540^{4} *(4946) 5222^{4}* 6092^{2}

Palmer's Green *Mrs C A Dunnett* 11
2 b g Mujahid(USA) —Moss (Alzao (USA))
5570^{6} 6571^{10} *6805^{14}*

Palmetto Point *H Morrison* a71 74
3 ch g Bahamian Bounty—Forum (Lion Cavern (USA))
1266^{11} 2203^{3} (2916) 3429^{4} 3997^{3} (4760) *(4918)* 5559^{4} 6199^{3}

Palmistry *John G Carr* a76 53
4 br g Lend A Hand—Divina Mia (Dowsing (USA))
6920a^{5}

Pamir (IRE) *P R Chamings* a74 74
5 b g Namid—Mijouter (IRE) (Coquelin (USA))
626^{7} 787^{6} 6174^{10} 6279^{9} *6428^{7}*

Pampas (USA) *R Charlton* a72 57
2 ch f Distant View(USA) —Alvernia (USA) (Alydar (USA))
2768^{5} 3446^{6} *6777^{3}*

Pamper Mee (IRE) *C F Swan* 65
3 b f King Charlemagne(USA) —Courtier (Saddlers' Hall (IRE))
4035a^{13}

Panadin (IRE) *Mrs L C Jewell* 35
5 b g Desert King(IRE) —Strident Note (The Minstrel (CAN))
4355^{10} *4914^{P}*

Panamar Besar (IRE) *J Howard Johnson* 29
2 b g Bahri(USA) —Paradise Blue (IRE) (Bluebird (USA))
2888^{8}

Panamericano (IRE) *Enda Kelly* 61
2 b g Orpen(USA) —Turntable (IRE) (Dolphin Street (FR))
3438a^{10}

Panda Power *S C Williams* 46
3 b f Pursuit Of Love—Golden Panda (Music Boy)
2477^{13} 2836^{8} 3387^{13} 4340^{13} 4516^{6}

Pango's Legacy *H Morrison* a60 73
3 ch g Bertolini(USA) —Sans Egale (FR) (Lashkari)
1786^{3} 2335^{9} 3797^{7} 4236^{7} (Dead)

Panshir (FR) *Mrs C A Dunnett* a52 56
6 ch g Unfuwain(USA) —Jalcamin (IRE) (Jalmood (USA))
980^{11} *1360^{9} 1592^{10}* 2745^{6} 3034^{5} 3101^{9} *3644^{12}* 3828^{15} 4294^{11}

Pantani (NZ) *R Laing* 107
8 gr g Pentire—Dewamar (AUS) (Marscay (AUS))
15a^{6}

Pantherii (USA) *P F I Cole* 60
2 ch f Forest Wildcat(USA) —Saraa Ree (USA) (Caro)
1807^{4} 2365^{5} 5063^{7} 5746^{8}

Pantomime Prince *John Berry* a55 62
4 b g Royal Applause—Floppie (FR) (Law Society (USA))
92^{5} 210^{7} 350^{12}

Panty Raid (USA) *T Pletcher* a114 111
3 bb f Include(USA) —Adventurous Di (USA) (Private Account (USA))
4628a^{5}

Papal Bull *Sir Michael Stoute* 120
4 b h Montjeu(IRE) —Mialuna (Zafonic (USA))
1495^{4} 2182^{5} (3461) (4599) 5589^{3} 6943a^{7}

Paparaazi (IRE) *I W McInnes* a71 78
5 b g Victory Note(USA) —Raazi (My Generation)
109^{2} 364^{3} 464^{4} 612^{3} 2023^{4} 3249^{9} 4031^{8} (4249) 4972^{9} *5341^{11}* 5835^{4} 6056^{11} 6325^{7}

Papa's Princess *J S Goldie* 51
3 b f Mujadil(USA) —Desert Flower (Green Desert (USA))
3372^{4} 3994^{7} 4713^{4} 5299^{5} 5967^{8}

Papeete (GER) *Mrs N Smith* a69 74
6 b m Alzao(USA) —Prairie Vela (Persian Bold)
291^{11} 5120^{10}

Paper Talk (USA) *Saeed Bin Suroor* 103
5 gr h Unbridled's Song(USA) —Journalist (IRE) (Night Shift (USA))
394a^{3} 6013^{17}

Papillio (IRE) *K R Burke* 73
2 b c Marju(IRE) —Danish Gem (Danehill (USA))
2562^{2} 4132^{3} 4832a^{20}

Pappas Image *A J McCabe* a53
3 b g Arkadian Hero(USA) —Fair Attempt (IRE) (Try My Best (USA))
17^{6} 65^{3} 103^{3} 378^{5} 671^{7} 1031^{7} 1266^{9} 7209^{4}

Pappas Ruby (USA) *R M Beckett* a61 59
4 b m Red Ransom(USA) —Pappa Reale (Indian Ridge)
1175^{3} 1569^{11} (1933) 2257^{5} 2576^{5} 2657^{5}

Papradon *J R Best* a64
3 b g Tobougg(IRE) —Salvezza (IRE) (Superpower)
2456^{3} 3082^{10} 5095^{4} (5894) 6178^{6} *6459^{2} 6817^{3} 6871^{5}*

Papuan Prince (IRE) *S Kirk* 56
2 b c Tagula(IRE) —Pussie Willow (IRE) (Catrail (USA))
4571^{12}

Para-Choque (BRZ) *C Morgado* a47 94
5 b h New Colony(USA) —Freluche (USA) (Ogygian (USA))
249a^{11} 409a^{10}

Paradise Dancer (IRE) *J A R Toller* a74 68
3 b f Danehill Dancer(IRE) —Pintada De Fresco (FR) (Marignan (USA))
2913^{3} 3276^{5} 4575^{3} *5568^{2}* 6057^{3} *6232^{9} 6975^{2} 7224^{3} 7282^{6}*

Paradise Expected *C Grant* a63 47
4 ch m North Briton—Phenomenon (Unfuwain (USA))
1258^{13}

Paradise Island (IRE) *E A L Dunlop* 66
2 b f Green Desert(USA) —Meadow Pipit (CAN) (Meadowlake (USA))
6093^{4}

Paradise Isle *C F Wall* 113
6 b m Bahamian Bounty—Merry Rous (Rousillon (USA))
415a^{2} 547a^{5} 1102^{3} 1497^{8} 2450^{6} 5407^{2} 6300^{8}

Paradise Walk *E W Tuer* a55 73
3 b f Sakhee(USA) —Enclave (USA) (Woodman (USA))
826^{3} 1726^{9} 2475^{7} 4139^{8} (4491) (4846) 5523^{4}

Paraguay (USA) *Miss V Haigh* a82 89
4 b g Pivotal—Grisonnante (FR) (Kaldoun (FR))
765^{5} 842^{6} 1040^{3} 1133^{5} 1543^{7} 2004^{9} 2218^{4} 2423^{10} 4200^{5} 4577^{9} 4850^{9} 5253^{13} 5476^{14}

Para Siempre *B Smart* a98 93
3 b f Mujahid(USA) —Miriam (Forzando)
(65) (147) 3059^{5} 5354^{9} 5833^{5} 6301^{24}

Parasol (IRE) *Doug Watson* a107 74
8 br g Halling(USA) —Bunting (Shaadi (USA))
175a^{6} 329a^{11} 413a^{9} *529a^{9}*

Parbyblos (FR) *John Allen* 12
4 b m Milford Track(IRE) —Biblos (FR) (Vorias (USA))
3593^{12} 3795^{9}

Parchment (IRE) *A J Lockwood* 67
5 ch g Singspiel(IRE) —Hannalou (FR) (Shareef Dancer (USA))
2027^{6} 3610^{5} 4493^{6} 4941^{3} 5158^{4} (5300) 5486^{7} 5704^{7} 6330^{13} 6558^{10}

Par Excellence *W G M Turner* a53 21
4 gr m Wizard King—Great Intent (Aragon)
359^{11} 622^{11} 690^{8}

Parfaite (IRE) *A & G Botti* 86
2 ch c Daggers Drawn(USA) —Shwe Dragon (Generous (IRE))
6523a^{4}

Paris Bell *T D Easterby* 85
5 gr g Paris House—Warning Bell (Bustino)
1292^{9} 1678^{10} 2508^{7} (2912) 3053^{10} 3401^{6} 3557^{2} 3762^{6} 4006^{6} 4606^{13} 5044^{9} 6157^{6} (6639)

Paris Heights *Mrs A M Thorpe* a18 57
5 gr g Paris House—Petra Nova (First Trump)
109^{9}

Parisian Dream *B W Hills* 90
3 b c Sakhee(USA) —Boojum (Mujtahid (USA))
1839^{3} (2542) 4135^{2} (4640) 5327^{8} 5805^{11}

Parisian Gift (IRE) *Tom Dascombe* a72 59
2 b g Statue Of Liberty(USA) —My Micheline (Lion Cavern (USA))
6409^{8} *(7191)*

Parisienne Gem *Miss L A Perratt*
2 b f Rock City—Miss Pigalle (Good Times (ITY))
6461^{8}

Paris Sue (IRE) *Marcus Callaghan* a63 74
7 gr m Paris House—Lady Carbron (IRE) (Elbio)
5841a^{19}

Park Avenue Ball (USA) *James T Ryerson* a111 109
5 ch h Citidancer(USA) —Road To The Ball (USA) (Cahill Road (USA))
5852a^{6} 6485a^{7}

Park Royal (UAE) *M Johnston* a57 73
2 bb f Cape Cross(IRE) —Shbakni (USA) (Mr Prospector (USA))
4094^{3} 4725^{13} 5428^{4} 6449^{11} *6665^{9}*

Parkside Pursuit *J M Bradley* a49 72
9 b g Pursuit Of Love—Ivory Bride (Domynsky)
1991^{14} 2386^{6} *3618^{6}* 3667^{10} 4853^{18} *6891^{10} 6925^{10}*

Park's Prodigy *P C Haslam* a53 53
3 b g Desert Prince(IRE) —Up And About (Barathea (IRE))
149^{8} 449^{12} 991^{6} 1224^{4} 2096^{4} 2552^{3} *7081^{6}*

Park Valley Prince *W R Muir* a59 44
3 ch c Noverre(USA) —Santorini (USA) (Spinning World (USA))
2059^{8} 5113^{6} *5499^{9} 6706^{7} 6831^{3} (6945) 7085^{3} 7207^{4}*

Parkview Love (USA) *D Shaw* a77 70
6 bb g Mister Baileys—Jerre Jo Glanville (USA) (Skywalker (USA))
80^{2} 151^{5} 200^{5} 463^{3} 525^{3} 609^{2} (650) 718^{5} (739) 773^{3} 895^{3} *1036^{2} 1162^{5} 1382^{2}* 1666^{7} 1847^{8} 2256^{2} *6568^{7} (6677) 7045^{7} 7141^{5}* 7261^{3}

Parliamentary (JPN) *M Johnston* 70
2 b c Diktat—Rebuff (Kris)
2739^{6} 3205^{3} 4417^{4} 5613^{12} 6329^{3}

Parma (IRE) *M Botti* a9
3 ch f Grand Lodge(USA) —Braari (USA) (Gulch (USA))
569^{12} 864^{7}

Parnassian *J A Geake* a65 76
7 ch g Sabrehill(USA) —Delphic Way (Warning)
1811^{4} 2403^{3} 3386^{7} 3955^{6} 4481^{4} 5917^{9}

Parnassus (SAF) *S Seemar* a98 95
5 b g Baroon—Belle Of Athens (SAF) (Foveros)
250a^{7} 398a^{12}

Parole Board (USA) *S Seemar* a114
5 bb g Dynaformer(USA) —Forget About It (IRE) (Be My Guest (USA))
177a^{8} (543a) 858a^{2}

Parsonagehotelyork (IRE) *R A Fahey* 58
3 b f Danehill(USA) —Makarova (IRE) (Sadler's Wells (USA))
4007^{3}

Parson's Punch *P D Cundell* a63
2 b g Beat Hollow—Ordained (Mtoto)
6868^{3}

Parthenope *J A Geake* a54 54
4 gr m Namid—Twosixtythreewest (FR) (Kris)
1120^{11} 1507^{17} *2592^{4}* 3149^{12} (4469) *5336^{3}*

Partners In Jazz (USA) *T D Barron* a101 108
6 gr g Jambalaya Jazz(USA) —Just About Enough (USA) (Danzig (USA))
1179^{4} 1651^{4} 2670^{8} 3941^{19} 4401^{3} 4601^{3} 5254^{6} 5616^{13} 5797^{15} 6155^{11} *6932^{11}*

Party (IRE) *R Hannon* a67 97
3 ch f Cadeaux Genereux—Forty Belles (USA) (Forty Niner (USA))
2384a^{2} 2786^{10} 4055a^{9} 6168^{11}

Party Boss *C E Brittain* a109 80
5 gr h Silver Patriarch(IRE) —Third Party (Terimon)
118^{6} 197^{2} 352^{3} (391) (487) 552^{4} 656^{11} 1448^{9} 6852^{7} 6932^{14}

Party Girl (FR) *R Pritchard-Gordon* 101
3 ch f Bering—Voodoo Lounge (GER) (Turfkonig (GER))
1339a^{3} 2290a^{7}

Party In The Park *R Hannon* 77
2 b g Royal Applause—Halland Park Girl (IRE) (Primo Dominie)
1123^{3} 1498^{2} 1781^{3} 2737^{20} 4762^{13} 5452^{7}

Party Palace *H S Howe* a52 52
3 b f Auction House(USA) —Lady-Love (Pursuit Of Love)
37^{5} 139^{4} 209^{4} 791^{3} 1059^{7} 1211^{5} *1397^{4}* 6060^{10} *6261^{7} 6534^{6} 6697^{2} 6817^{2}*

Party Ploy *K R Burke* a47 50
9 b g Deploy—Party Treat (IRE) (Millfontaine)
89^{13}

Paso Doble *R Bastiman* a66 46
9 b g Dancing Spree(USA) —Delta Tempo (IRE) (Bluebird (USA))
2^{2} (80) 228^{7} 243^{4} (466) 579^{7} 650^{11} 768^{8} 1027^{9} 1086^{16}

Passage Of Time *H R A Cecil* 115
3 b f Dansili—Clepsydra (Sadler's Wells (USA))
(1769) 2211^{8} 5465a^{3} 6509a^{3}

Passager (FR) *Mme C Head-Maarek* 117
4 bb g Anabaa(USA) —Passionnee (USA) (Woodman (USA))
897a^{3} 1389a^{3} 1834^{3} 2500a^{3}

Passarelle (USA) *M J Grassick* a74 76
3 b f In The Wings—Kitza (IRE) (Danehill (USA))
6368a^{9} 6555a^{7}

Passing Hour (USA) *G A Butler* a69 77
3 b f Red Ransom(USA) —Timely (Kings Lake (USA))
1620^{3} (2219) 3003^{2} *3421^{9}* 4205^{13} *6293^{7}*

Passing True (IRE) *M Johnston* a45 56
3 b f Barathea(IRE) —Nambucca (Shirley Heights)
3214^{11} 4334^{5} 5157^{3} 6423^{12} *6766^{5}*

Passionate Girl (IRE) *A & G Botti* 82
3 ch f Grand Lodge(USA) —Isticanna (USA) (Far North (CAN))
2070a^{9}

Passionately Royal *M Brittain* a25 49
5 b g Royal Applause—Passionelle (Nashwan (USA))
1132^{13} 1527^{12} 2938^{14} 4099^{4} 4449^{2} 4891^{10} 5503^{6}

Passion Fruit *C W Fairhurst* a72 92
6 b m Pursuit Of Love—Reine De Thebes (FR) (Darshaan)
1157^{8} 1626^{3} 1845^{6} 2085^{7} 2507^{3} 2742^{3} 2988^{2} 3512^{10} 3953^{4} (4407) 4581^{8} 5354^{3} 5794^{8} 6018^{9}

Pass The Port *D Haydn Jones* a87 81
6 ch g Docksider(USA) —One Of The Family (Alzao (USA))
226^{5} (428) 662^{2} 1438^{4} 7055^{2} 7236^{2}

Pasta Prayer *N A Callaghan* 3
2 b c Bertolini(USA) —Benedicite (Lomond (USA))
3592^{14}

Pastellrosa (IRE) *Timothy Doyle* 75
2 ch f Captain Rio—Papaha (FR) (Green Desert (USA))
3438a^{2}

Patavellian (IRE) *R Charlton* a41 110
9 bb g Machiavellian(USA) —Alessia (Caerleon (USA))
927[3] 1657[5] 2291a[7] 2695[7] 5616[3] 6039a[5] 6338[7] 6633a[0]

Patavian (IRE) *I Semple* 68
3 b g Titus Livius(FR) —Five Of Wands (Caerleon (USA))
968[6] (1491) 2246[8] 2565[4] 3183[9] 3538[3] 4036[7]

Patavium (IRE) *E W Tuer* a55 63
4 b g Titus Livius(FR) —Arcevia (IRE) (Archway (IRE))
1579[3] 1966[3] 2391[3] 2810[5] 3300[7] 4003[3] 4493[9]

Patavium Prince (IRE) *Miss Jo Crowley* a59 78
4 ch g Titus Livius(FR) —Hoyland Common (IRE) (Common Grounds)
3101[10] 6283[14] *6428[11] 6950[9] 7188[8]*

Pathos (GER) *D R C Elsworth* 91
3 b g Danehill Dancer(IRE) —Panthere (GER) (Acatenango (GER))
2005[5] (2464) 3058[4] 3709[2] (4166)

Path To Glory *Miss Z C Davison* a50 58
3 b c Makbul—Just Glory (Glory Of Dancer)
2415[6] 2878[10] 3469[2] 4073[8] *4277[8] 5528[5] 5945[7] 6178[11]*

Pathway To Glory *M Quinn* a42
3 bb c Auction House(USA) —Nopalea (Warrshan (USA))
3425[10] 3924[11] 5270[13] *5752[7] 6240[12]*

Patio *Mrs A J Perrett* 75
2 b f Beat Hollow—Maze Garden (USA) (Riverman (USA))
2658[4] 3895[12] 5063[3] (5524)

Patitiri (USA) *Mrs C A Dunnett* a18 36
4 ch m Rahy(USA) —Dharma (USA) (Zilzal (USA))
129[14] 2748[11] 3163[10]

Patkai (IRE) *Sir Michael Stoute* 73
2 ch c Indian Ridge—Olympienne (IRE) (Sadler's Wells (USA))
5538[6] (6107)

Patsymartin *J Ryan* 27
2 ch g Bertolini(USA) —Souadah (USA) (General Holme (USA))
1498[9] 2333[12]

Patternmaker (USA) *A M Hales* a67 44
5 b g Elnadim(USA) —Attasliyah (IRE) (Marju (IRE))
33[7]

Patthepainter (GER) *K R Burke* 53
2 ch c Alhaarth(IRE) —Picturesque (Polish Precedent (USA))
4725[11] 5772[9] 6255[9]

Pat Will (IRE) *P D Evans* a51 56
3 b f Danetime(IRE) —Northern Tara (IRE) (Fayruz)
108[4] 295[8] 512[8] 1008[2] 1269[2] 1763[5] 1899[12] 2104[6] 2304[7] 2652[10] 4561[8] 5688[15]

Patwish *Enda Kelly* a40 57
3 b f Best Of The Bests(IRE) —Sagina (Shernazar)
2259[6]

Paula Lane *R Curtis*
7 b m Factual(USA) —Colfax Classic (Jareer (USA))
5120[15]

Pauline's Prince *R Hollinshead* a64 64
5 b h Polar Prince(IRE) —Etma Rose (IRE) (Fairy King (USA))
7180[4] 7248[2]

Pauls Plain *S Curran* 37
6 b g Young Buster(IRE) —On The Wagon (Then Again)
3236[8]

Paul The Carpet (UAE) *P F I Cole* a42 27
2 ch c Halling(USA) —Favoured (Chief's Crown (USA))
3471[11] *4393[11]* 5186[14]

Pauvic (IRE) *Mrs A Duffield* a48 67
4 b g Fayruz—Turntable (IRE) (Dolphin Street (FR))
79[13] 155[11] 1226[10] 1299[10] *1377[8] 6870[11] 7111[9]*

Paveroc *J S Moore* a85 93
2 b c Royal Applause—Take Liberties (Warning)
1652[5] 2316[4] 2737[5] 4048[6] (4500) 4721[6] 5324[7] 5972[6] 6170[7]

Pavershooz *N Wilson* 71
2 b g Bahamian Bounty—Stormswept (USA) (Storm Bird (CAN))
6156[5] 6634[4]

Pavlovia *M Dods* a61 62
3 b f Diktat—Waseyla (IRE) (Sri Pekan (USA))
1994[9] 2299[8]

Pawan (IRE) *Miss A Stokell* a91 104
7 ch g Cadeaux Genereux—Born To Glamour (Ajdal (USA))
5[3] 79[5] 227[8] 419[3] 575[6] 810[5] 1159[8] 1574[7] *1754[7] 1977[5]* 2139[2] *2347[3]* 2688[9] 3240[2] *6836[11] 7112[2] 7179[3]*

Pawn In Life (IRE) *D W Chapman* a49 60
9 b g Midhish—Lady-Mumtaz (Martin John)
75[6] 144[6] (321) 435[3] 519[11] 579[12] 715[3] 3470[6] 4797[11]

Paymaster General (IRE) *M D I Usher* a78 69
3 b g Desert Style(IRE) —Khawafi (Kris)
728[2] (1039) 1722[13] 1835[12] *2150[4]* 2727[12] 3150[5] 3469[5] 4355[8] 5068[4] *5500[2] 5892[6] 6144[10]*

Payne Relief (IRE) *M L W Bell* a50 53
2 bb f Desert Prince(IRE) —Saffron Crocus (Shareef Dancer (USA))
4854[9] 5540[10] *6432[12]*

Pay On (IRE) *A C Whillans* a38 49
4 ch g Danehill Dancer(IRE) —Richly Deserved (IRE) (Kings Lake (USA))
124[10]

Pay Or Pay *P S McEntee* 3
5 b g Atraf—Petinata (Petong)
2763[8]

Pay Parade *T D Easterby* 55
2 b f Mujahid(USA) —Bollin Sophie (Efisio)
1478[3]

Pay Pay Pay *P D Evans* 57
2 ch f Reel Buddy(USA) —Marabela (IRE) (Shernazar)
2968[8] 3275[4] 3977[6] 5766[21] 6410[12] 6591[8]

Pays D'Amour (IRE) *D A Nolan* a22 18
10 b g Pursuit Of Love—Lady Of The Land (Wollow)
1596[18] 2390[14] 3498[12] 4934[9]

Pay The Grey *R Hannon* 36
2 gr f Daylami(IRE) —Dance Clear (IRE) (Marju (IRE))
4852[10] 5858[9]

Pay Time *R E Barr* a55 69
8 ch m Timeless Times(USA) —Payvashooz (Ballacashtal (CAN))
2033[13] 2422[3] 2842[4] 3375[9] (3999) 4407[9] 4562[4] (4705) 5159[9] 5476[13]

Peace Dream (FR) *J-C Rouget* 106
3 gr f Linamix(FR) —Peace Talk (FR) (Sadler's Wells (USA))
1702a[5]

Peace Offering (IRE) *D Nicholls* a101 115
7 b g Victory Note(USA) —Amnesty Bay (Thatching)
1497[2] (1704a) 2291a[2] 3139a[4] 3531[4] 4798[3] 5325[2] 6039a[12]

Peace Royale (GER) *A Wohler* 100
2 b f Sholokhov(IRE) —Peace Time (GER) (Surumu (GER))
5028a[2] (5462a) 6040a[6]

Peak District (IRE) *David Wachman* 98
3 b c Danehill(USA) —Coralita (IRE) (Night Shift (USA))
4726[3] 5075a[7]

Peak Seasons (IRE) *M C Chapman* a52 58
4 ch g Raise A Grand(IRE) —Teresian Girl (IRE) (Glenstal (USA))
812[7] 1570[13] 1750[8]

Pearl (IRE) *W J Haggas* a74 71
3 b f Daylami(IRE) —Briery (IRE) (Salse (USA))
4007[4] 5335[2] 5803[2] (6420) *6673[3] 6856[4] (7032)*

Pearl Dealer (IRE) *Saeed Bin Suroor* a78 37
2 b c Marju(IRE) —Anyaas (IRE) (Green Desert (USA))
(5780) 6201[12]

Pearl Farm *C A Horgan* a61 55
6 b m Foxhound(USA) —Trinity Hall (Hallgate)
687[2] 797[8] (1038) 1947[3] 2592[8] 4395[7] *6100[13]*

Pearl Island (GER) *Frau J Meyer* 74
5 br m Law Society(USA) —Prairie Flame (IRE) (Marju (IRE))
6220a[10]

Pearl Of Esteem *Mrs C A Dunnett* a18 53
4 ch m Mark Of Esteem(IRE) —Ribot's Pearl (Indian Ridge)
5237[12] 5546[15] *5898[7] 6211[8]*

Pearl's Girl *W J Haggas* 80
4 gr m King's Best(USA) —Karsiyaka (IRE) (Kahyasi)
2883[3] 3103[7]

Pearl Sky (FR) *Y De Nicolay* 114
4 b m Kahyasi—Patissima (FR) (Lightning (FR))
(663a) 880a[2] 1340a[6] 4215a[2] 4872a[4] 6030a[10]

Pearl Trader (IRE) *M Johnston* 63
2 ch f Dubai Destination(USA) —Vintage Tipple (IRE) (Entrepreneur)
4930[3] 5485[5]

Pearl Valley *R A Fahey* a24 37
3 b f Indian Rocket—Indigo (Primo Dominie)
916[7] 1136[7] *1749[5]* 2759[10]

Pearly Jack *D E Fitzgerald* 76
9 ch g Weld—Pearly Lady (Tycoon II)
4371a[7]

Pearly King (USA) *I Mohammed* 105
4 br h Kingmambo(USA) —Mother Of Pearl (IRE) (Sadler's Wells (USA))
244a[5] 475a[2] 648a[3]

Pearly Wey *C G Cox* 103
4 b g Lujain(USA) —Dunkellin (USA) (Irish River (FR))
2058[5] 2440[9] (2688) 3481[14] 3911[3] (4122) 5407[3] 5616[27]

Pearo (IRE) *J S Moore* a38 55
2 b f Captain Rio—Westlife (IRE) (Mind Games)
2028[3] (2152) *2356[3]* 5869[13] *6438[12]*

Pearson Glen (IRE) *James Moffatt* 16
8 ch g Dolphin Street(FR) —Glendora (Glenstal (USA))
1199[10]

Peas And Carrots (DEN) *L Reuterskiold* 95
4 b g Final Appearance(IRE) —Dominet Hope (Primo Dominie)
4218a[5] 5263a[2]

Peas In A Pod *J R Fanshawe* 40
2 ch g Kyllachy—Entwine (Primo Dominie)
4454[10] 4854[11] 5595[13]

Peas 'n Beans (IRE) *T Keddy* a60 64
4 ch g Medicean—No Sugar Baby (FR) (Crystal Glitters (USA))
121[12] 1966[13] 2156[8] 2430[13]

Pecoiquen (CHI) *F Castro* a71 77
6 ch g Hussonet(USA) —Tonguie (ARG) (Big Play (USA))
331a[16] 400a[11] *1648a[6]*

Peculiar Prince (IRE) *Liam McAteer* a86 88
5 b g Desert Prince(IRE) —Lady Peculiar (CAN) (Sunshine Forever (USA))
5554[6]

Pediment *J R Fanshawe* a69 53
2 b f Desert Prince(IRE) —White Palace (Shirley Heights)
4882[7] 5274[6] *5727[2]*

Pee Jay's Dream *M W Easterby* a71 63
5 ch g Vettori(IRE) —Langtry Lady (Pas De Seul)
1178[2]

Peephole *M A Allen* a9
4 ch g Pursuit Of Love—Goodwood Lass (IRE) (Alzao (USA))
215[12] 6937[11]

Peeping Fawn (USA) *A P O'Brien* 124
3 b f Danehill(USA) —Maryinsky (IRE) (Sadler's Wells (USA))
2065a[3] 2211[2] (3117a) (3576a) (4149) (4723)

Peeress *Sir Michael Stoute* a89 122
6 ch m Pivotal—Noble One (Primo Dominie)
1834[6]

Peer Pressure *P Mitchell* a54 64
2 gr c Verglas(IRE) —Mystery Quest (IRE) (Rainbow Quest (USA))
3856[8] *4962[7]* 5274[10] *5818[7]* 6237[4] 6536[13]

Pegasus Again (USA) *T G Mills* a79 95
2 b c Fusaichi Pegasus(USA) —Chit Chatter (USA) (Lost Soldier (USA))
2855[2] *(4393)* 5048[5]

Pegasus Dancer (FR) *K A Ryan* a76 76
3 b g Danehill Dancer(IRE) —Maruru (IRE) (Fairy King (USA))
1160[4] 1802[5] 2313[6] 2821[3] 3413[DSQ] 4452[10] 4896[3] 5332[10] 5506[3] 6702[9] *6826[3] 7077[2] (7221)*

Pegasus Prince (USA) *Miss J A Camacho* a53 51
3 b g Fusaichi Pegasus(USA) —Avian Eden (USA) (Storm Bird (CAN))
678[11] 1712[3] 2538[8] 5084[5] *6026[3]*

Pegasus Prospect (USA) *Terry Gestes* a51
2 br f Fusaichi Pegasus(USA) —Fine Prospect (USA) (Mr Prospector (USA))
5247a[9]

Peggle *M H Tompkins* a21
2 b f Tobougg(IRE) —Grove Dancer (Reprimand)
6847[11]

Peggys First *D E Cantillon* a52 32
5 b g Wolfhound(USA) —Peggys Rose (IRE) (Shalford (IRE))
46[3] 189[4] 207[5] 320[4]

Peggys Flower *M Wigham* a58 61
3 b f Arkadian Hero(USA) —Peggys Rose (IRE) (Shalford (IRE))
894[10] *1164[6] 1281[3]*

Peintre Bleu (FR) *S Seemar* 85
5 ch h Spectrum(IRE) —Pacy (USA) (Manila (USA))
328a[13] 475a[4]

Peintre's Wonder (IRE) *E J O'Neill* 66
3 b f Peintre Celebre(USA) —Ring The Relatives (Bering)
1639[9] 2760[4] 3677[7] 4936[4]

Peking Beauty *J De Roualle* a93 96
5 br m Kendor(FR) —Intrum Morshaan (IRE) (Darshaan)
31a[11]

Pelham Crescent (IRE) *B Palling* a73 64
4 ch g Giant's Causeway(USA) —Sweet Times (Riverman (USA))
288[4] 612[11] 741[6] 1366[5] 1562[2] 1666[11] 3034[3] *(4464) 4592[4]* 5708[3] 6088[5] *(6316) 6628[3] 6816[5]*

Pelican Key (IRE) *D M Simcock* a76 79
3 b f Mujadil(USA) —Guana Bay (Cadeaux Genereux)
1160[10] *2769[8]* 3154[2] 3670[6] 4017[7]

Pelican Prince *K R Burke* 87
2 b c Fraam—Nightingale Song (Tina's Pet)
1528[2] (1963) 3025[3] (3524) 4743[10] 5216[13] 6017[3]

Pelican Waters (IRE) *E F Vaughan* a88 90
3 b f Key Of Luck(USA) —Orlena (USA) (Gone West (USA))
5392a[9] *(7174)*

Pelleas *R Charlton* 71
3 b g Mark Of Esteem(IRE) —Questabelle (Rainbow Quest (USA))
1204[8] 2436[6]

Peltre *M Brittain* 18
2 b f Bertolini(USA) —Pewter Lass (Dowsing (USA))
1713[10] 3025[7] 4328[11]

Pembo *B Palling* 29
2 b g Choisir(AUS) —Focosa (ITY) (In The Wings)
3404[11] 6591[10]

Penang (IRE) *C E Brittain* a54 56
3 b f Xaar—Badawi (USA) (Diesis)
764[8] 4568[7] 4989[4] 5710[9]

Penang Cinta *P D Evans* a71 80
4 b g Halling(USA) —Penang Pearl (FR) (Bering)
182[3] (445) 539[5] 741[2] (1069) (1924) 2106[4] *3112[6]* 4597[8] 4994[2] 5415[7]

Penchesco (IRE) *Pat Eddery* a71 70
2 b c Orpen(USA) —Francesca (IRE) (Perugino (USA))
2303[11] 5628[5] *6138[5] 6884[2]*

Pencil Hill (IRE) *Tracey Collins* 105
2 b c Acclamation—Como (USA) (Cozzene (USA))
(2049a) 2732[4] 6549a[10]

Pendulum Star *W R Swinburn* a86 67
3 gr f Observatory(USA) —Pendulum (Pursuit Of Love)
1537[2] 1901[6] 2428[6] *(6269) 6646[2]*

Penel (IRE) *P T Midgley* a59 57
6 b g Orpen(USA) —Jayess Elle (Sabrehill (USA))
9[3] 77[3] 144[7] 430[3] 450[2] 519[10] 729[6] 912[5] *1028[3]* 1260[3] 1744[2] *2149[8]* 2550[8] 2806[4] 2937[6] 3257[3] 3789[8] 4180[5] 4223[8] (4891) 5704[3]

Penicuik *M Johnston* a40
3 b f Hernando(FR) —Barari (USA) (Blushing Groom (FR))
936[6]

Penkinella (FR) *A Couetil* 94
4 b m Pennekamp(USA) —Pimpinella (FR) (Highest Honor (FR))
6460a[5] 6953a[9]

Penmara *Miss J E Foster* 58
4 b m Mtoto—Pendulum (Pursuit Of Love)
2431[17] 3800[10] (Dead)

Penmon Point (IRE) *R Johnson* 40
4 b g Foxhound(USA) —Brandon Princess (Waajib)
3497[14] 5739[13] 6561[14]

Penny (FR) *Mme C Head-Maarek* 70
2 br g Anabaa(USA) —Passonaria (FR) (Sillery (USA))
6952a[3]

Penny Arcade *M E Sowersby* 17
2 ch f Arkadian Hero(USA) —Concentration (IRE) (Mind Games)
3297[6] 4041[11] 4559[6] 5154[10] 5484[13]

Pennyforurthoughts (IRE) *James McAuley* 72
5 b m Almutawakel—Hirasah (IRE) (Lahib (USA))
5184a[8]

Penny From Heaven (IRE) *E A L Dunlop* a67 67
3 b f Machiavellian(USA) —Flying Kiss (IRE) (Sadler's Wells (USA))
1203[9] 2079[6] 3351[3] *4069[P]* (Dead)

Pennygee *S R Bowring*
3 b f Bertolini(USA) —Samadilla (IRE) (Mujadil (USA))
6877[13] 7239[13]

Penny Glitters *S Parr* a51 86
4 br m Benny The Dip(USA) —Lucy Glitters (USA) (Cryptoclearance (USA))
2257[8] 4029[12] 4177[8] *5368[11]* 6541[5] *6869[10]*

Penny Post (IRE) *M Johnston* a86 80
3 b f Green Desert(USA) —Blue Note (FR) (Habitat)
606[4] 755[2] 943[8] 1604[3] 1710[4] 2060[5]

Pennyrock (IRE) *J J Quinn* a54 62
3 b c Rock Of Gibraltar(IRE) —Inforapenny (Deploy)
140[9] 1091[4] 1236[2] (1558) 1965[7] *3168[10]* 4224[9] 4450[3] 4842[3]

Pennyspider (IRE) *M S Saunders* 45
2 b f Redback—Malacca (USA) (Danzig (USA))
2724[11] 3085[7] 3363[8] 3867[3]

Penrice Castle *R Hannon* a66 69
2 br f Averti(IRE) —Stormont Castle (USA) (Irish River (FR))
2193[10] *2569[4] (2797) 4065[11]* 4453[2] 5167[7] 5534[8] 6282[14]

Pentandra (IRE) *J G Given* 59
2 b f Bahri(USA) —Miss Willow Bend (USA) (Willow Hour (USA))
5329[10] 6649[9]

Pentasilea *H J L Dunlop* a67 70
4 b m Nashwan(USA) —Isabella Gonzaga (Rock Hopper)
(1364) 1811[9] 2434[2] *2770[10] 3598[3]* 4766[13]

Pentathlon (IRE) *M Johnston* a60
2 b g Storming Home—Nawaiet (USA) (Zilzal (USA))
7191[7]

Pentatonic *L M Cumani* 99
4 b m Giant's Causeway(USA) —Fascinating Rhythm (Slip Anchor)
1922[7] 2543[2] (3671) 4089[5]

Pentecost *A M Balding* a69 105
8 ch g Tagula(IRE) —Boughtbyphone (Warning)
172a[4] 325a[12] 1651[6] 2755[11] 3001[7] 3527[3] 4377[3] 5444[4] 5833[10]

Penthouse Serenade (IRE) *M Massimi Jr* 98
3 br f Val Royal(FR) —Misty Peak (IRE) (Sri Pekan (USA))
1701a[4] 6688a[3]

Penwell Hill (USA) *Miss M E Rowland* a54 27
8 b g Distant View(USA) —Avie's Jill (USA) (Lord Avie (USA))
7[6] 238[8] 431[10] 666[9] 789[13] 2946[4] 3598[13]

Penzo (IRE) *J Wade* 69
4 gr g Shinko Forest(IRE) —Thatchabella (IRE) (Thatching)
2256[13] 3502[9] 3783[10]

Peopleton Brook *J M Bradley* a79 93
5 b h Compton Place—Merch Rhyd-Y-Grug (Sabrehill (USA))
1464[7] 1630[10] 1854[6] (1999) 2191[3] 2694[5] 4095[22] 4204[8] 5009[12] 5332[9] *6360[8] 6708[10] 6794[8]*

Pep In Her Step (IRE) *Eamon Tyrrell* a27 59
4 b m Cape Cross(IRE) —Monzitta (GER) (Monsun (GER))
296[13]

Peppermint Green *L M Cumani* 72
3 b f Green Desert(USA) —One So Wonderful (Nashwan (USA))
2693[9] 3826[10] 4687[7]

Pepper Road *R Bastiman* a44 50
8 ch g Elmaamul(USA) —Floral Spark (Forzando)
435[9] 625[8] 1086[5] 2938[3] 4099[11]

Pepper's Ghost *Miss J Feilden* a52 57
2 gr c Act One—Mill On The Floss (Mill Reef (USA))
4028[7] *4947[9]* 5599[8]

Peppertree *E F Vaughan* a85 92
4 b m Fantastic Light(USA) —Delauncy (Machiavellian (USA))
1506[4] 2047[6] (5593) *6605[9]*

Peppertree Lane (IRE) *M Johnston* 112
4 ch h Peintre Celebre(USA) —Salonrolle (IRE) (Tirol)
990a[9] (1304) 1618[4] (1833) 2907[3] (3119a) 4830a[6] 5849a[5]

Pepperwood (IRE) *Noel Meade* a62 31
7 ch g Barathea(IRE) —Nishan (Nashwan (USA))
6366a[20]

Peppin's Gold (IRE) *B R Millman* a57 58
3 b f King Charlemagne(USA) —Miss Senate (IRE) (Alzao (USA))
99[8] 390[3] 708[5] (794)

Pequeno Dinero (IRE) *C W Fairhurst* a34 59
2 b f Iron Mask(USA) —Mrs Kanning (Distant View (USA))
890[8] 1302[8] (3296) 3838[3] 4524[12] 5736[4]

Percussionist (IRE) *J Howard Johnson* 117
6 b g Sadler's Wells(USA) —Magnificient Style (USA) (Silver Hawk (USA))
1823[4] 4691[6]

Percy Douglas *Miss A Stokell* a43 56
7 b g Elmaamul(USA) —Qualitair Dream (Dreams To Reality (USA))
8[12] 97[7] 225[7] 287[9] 318[6] 441[9] 581[11] 7138[12] 7238[8] 7283[7]

Perdono (USA) *A Wohler* 94
3 b c Lear Fan(USA) —Chateaumist (USA) (Trempolino (USA))
1387a[9]

Peregrine Falcon *M Johnston* a74
3 b c In The Wings—Island Race (Common Grounds)
111[3] 582[3]

Perez Prado (USA) *W Jarvis* 54
2 b c Kingmambo(USA) —Marisa (USA) (Swain (IRE))
6618[8]

Perfect Act *C G Cox* 87
2 b f Act One—Markova's Dance (Mark Of Esteem (IRE))
(4764) 5374[2] 5974[5] 6498[4]
Perfect Cause (USA) *J H M Gosden* 48
3 bb f Giant's Causeway(USA) —Possibly Perfect (USA) (Northern Baby (CAN))
5013[8] 5637[4]
Perfect Courtesy (IRE) *G A Swinbank* a4 70
3 ch g Danehill Dancer(IRE) —Kate Maher (IRE) (Rainbow Quest (USA))
931[2] 1726[8] 2453[5] 3029[9]
Perfect Flight *M Blanshard* 79
2 b f Hawk Wing(USA) —Pretty Girl (IRE) (Polish Precedent (USA))
1354[5] 1960[4] 2651[5] (4349) 5008[2] 5331[3] 5629[8] 6128[2]
Perfect Paula (USA) *B J Meehan* a83 97
2 bb f Songandaprayer(USA) —Ra Hydee (USA) (Rahy (USA))
1897[4] 2756[13] 3363[2] 4046[12] 4573[3] (4737) 5325[9]
Perfectperformance (USA) *Saeed Bin Suroor* 109
5 ch h Rahy(USA) —Balistroika (USA) (Nijinsky (CAN))
(3468) 4117[5] 6172[4]
Perfect Picture *P T Midgley* 36
8 b g Octagonal(NZ) —Greenvera (USA) (Riverman (USA))
1554[6] 2431[16]
Perfect Polly *Andrew Oliver* 104
2 b f Efisio—Nashira (Prince Sabo)
5070a[2] 5973[4] 6631a[8]
Perfect Practice *C G Cox* a59 19
3 ch f Medicean—Giusina Mia (USA) (Diesis)
208[6] 577[6] 924[8] 2008[12] 6809[2] 7166[6]
Perfect Punch *K G Reveley* a57 58
8 b g Reprimand—Aliuska (IRE) (Fijar Tango (FR))
4521[6]
Perfect Reflection *A Berry*
3 b f Josr Algarhoud(IRE) —Surrealist (ITY) (Night Shift (USA))
1709[5] 2200[12]
Perfect Reward *Mrs A J Perrett* a72 76
3 b c Cadeaux Genereux—Maid To Perfection (Sadler's Wells (USA))
4667[2] 5342[4] 5899[2] (6235)
Perfect Silence *C G Cox* 54
2 b f Dansili—Perfect Echo (Lycius (USA))
6649[13]
Perfect Star *C G Cox* 99
3 b f Act One—Granted (FR) (Cadeaux Genereux)
2971[5] (3555) 3857[2] 4509[2] (5163) (5794)
Perfect Storm *W G M Turner* 57
8 b g Vettori(IRE) —Gorgeous Dancer (IRE) (Nordico (USA))
5187[6] 5427[6] 5835[3]
Perfect Story (IRE) *J A R Toller* a92 95
5 b m Desert Story(IRE) —Shore Lark (USA) (Storm Bird (CAN))
277[2] 1292[2] 1670[2] 2450[7] 2835[14] 3511[8] 4373[9]
Perfect Stride *Sir Michael Stoute* 91
2 b c Oasis Dream—First (Highest Honor (FR))
(5011) 5691[2]
Perfect Treasure (IRE) *J A R Toller* a79 82
4 ch m Night Shift(USA) —Pitrizza (IRE) (Machiavellian (USA))
2411[4] 3613[3] (4317) (4688) 5012[8] 5560[3] 6081[5] 6450[12] 6795[5]
Per Incanto (USA) *J L Dunlop* 118
3 bb c Street Cry(IRE) —Pappa Reale (Indian Ridge)
(1876a) 4600[6] 5214[13]
Perks (IRE) *J L Dunlop* 69
2 b g Selkirk(USA) —Green Charter (Green Desert (USA))
3896[12] 4777[8] 5598[4]
Perlachy *Mrs N Macauley* a65 71
3 b g Kyllachy—Perfect Dream (Emperor Jones (USA))
17[3] 127[9] 219[5] 387[4] 713[5] 925[9] 1031[4] 1219[4] 4538[7] 4801[3] 5066[6] 6149[3] 6339[2] 6581[4] 6877[2] 7019[3] 7105[2] (7227)
Permesso *L Camici*
2 b c Sakhee(USA) —Persian Filly (IRE) (Persian Bold)
6523a[3]
Perry's Pride *Mrs G S Rees* a37 27
3 b f Perryston View—Caspian Morn (Lugana Beach)
2951[9] 3406[12] 3924[7] 4741[7] 5915[13] 6467[14]
Persian Express (USA) *B W Hills* a94 94
4 b m Bahri(USA) —Istikbal (USA) (Kingmambo (USA))
938[6] 1494[10] 1649[10] 4049[13] (4455) (5641) 5950[7] 6437[10] 6604[7]
Persian Fox (IRE) *A G Juckes* 72
3 b g King Charlemagne(USA) —Persian Mistress (IRE) (Persian Bold)
3804[5] 4270[8] 5511[3] 6060[5] 6247[11]
Persian Peril *G A Swinbank* a74 79
3 br g Erhaab(USA) —Brush Away (Ahonoora)
1827[4] 2506[7] 4332[5] 4617[9]
Persian Storm (GER) *J Hirschberger* 111
3 ch c Monsun(GER) —Private Life (FR) (Bering)
(2102a) 3146a[6] (4958a) 5464a[2]
Persistent (IRE) *P T Midgley* a57 36
2 b c Cape Cross(IRE) —Insistent (USA) (Diesis)
6139[6] 6754[8] 7140[6]
Persona (IRE) *B J McMath* a65 65
5 b m Night Shift(USA) —Alonsa (IRE) (Trempolino (USA))
12[3] 6577[12]
Personal Choice *M Brittain* 56
2 ch f Choisir(AUS) —Bonkers (Efisio)
2818[4] 3024[12] 3718[9] 4328[8]
Personal Column *T G Mills* a73 72
3 ch g Pursuit Of Love—Tromond (Lomond (USA))
582[4] 719[10] 1205[4] 1724[4] 2610[7] (3456) 4069[10]
Personify *C G Cox* a49 80
5 ch g Zafonic(USA) —Dignify (IRE) (Rainbow Quest (USA))
1209[5] 3900[7] 4234[9] 4880[3] 5559[12]

Pertemps Green *Stef Liddiard* a50 66
4 b g Green Desert(USA) —Pure Misk (Rainbow Quest (USA))
3644[11] 3965[10] 4395[15] 5690[8] 5864[11]
Pertemps Networks *M W Easterby* a62 42
3 b g Golden Snake(USA) —Society Girl (Shavian)
3260[5] 5704[9] 7211[2]
Pertemps Power *A D Smith* a55 51
3 b g Zaha(CAN) —Peristyle (Tolomeo)
2981[6] 3621[4] 4357[5] 4877[9] 5364[4] 5755[4]
Pertinence (IRE) *K Borgel* 82
3 b f Fasliyev(USA) —Peace Signal (USA) (Time For A Change (USA))
436a[8]
Peruvian Prince (USA) *R A Fahey* a88 97
5 b g Silver Hawk(USA) —Inca Dove (USA) (Mr Prospector (USA))
256[7] 652[10] 1771[12] (2397) 3242[3] 4043[3] 4153[3] 4720[2] 5631[13] 6169[12]
Peruvian Style (IRE) *J M Bradley* a56 66
6 b g Desert Style(IRE) —Lady's Vision (IRE) (Vision (USA))
2555[5] 3368[11] 3869[3] 4312[3] 4853[9] 4881[9] 5191[8] 5866[7] 5947[8]
Petara Bay (IRE) *T G Mills* 108
3 b c Peintre Celebre(USA) —Magnificient Style (USA) (Silver Hawk (USA))
(1097) 1306[7] 2235[15]
Peter Island (FR) *J Gallagher* a82 84
4 b g Dansili—Catania (USA) (Aloma's Ruler (USA))
1121[4] 1357[11] 1607[3] 1971[13] 2993[8] 3528[10] 4204[2] (4320) 4567[18] 5029[5] 5401[4] 6450[10] 6589[10] 6708[9] 6794[7]
Peter's Joy (USA) *Jean-Rene Auvray* a11
2 b g Stravinsky(USA) —Jadarah (USA) (Red Ransom (USA))
2398[13] 7266[14]
Peter's Storm (USA) *K A Ryan* a80 67
2 ch c Van Nistelrooy(USA) —Fairy Land Flyer (USA) (Lyphard's Wish (FR))
5772[5] (6386) 6756[14]
Petidium *N Bycroft* 41
2 b f Presidium—Efipetite (Efisio)
5501[8] 6306[10]
Petite Arvine (USA) *M L W Bell* a20 44
3 b f Gulch(USA) —Grapevine (IRE) (Sadler's Wells (USA))
1409[7] 1863[9] 1937[7]
Petite Cherie (IRE) *G M Lyons* 95
3 b f Fasliyev(USA) —Diamant (IRE) (Bigstone (IRE))
946a[8]
Petite Mac *N Bycroft* a27 71
7 b m Timeless Times(USA) —Petite Elite (Anfield)
895[7] 1748[6] 2072[6] 2315[7] 2711[13] (2893) 3194[7] 3762[7] 3920[5] 4083[9] 4180[9] 4768[2] 5159[6] 5489[2] 5741[6] 5908[9] 6563[12]
Petite Music (IRE) *T D Easterby* 35
2 b f Distant Music(USA) —Petite Maxine (Sharpo)
6156[12] 6306[12]
Petito (IRE) *J L Spearing* 66
4 b g Imperial Ballet(IRE) —Fallacy (Selkirk (USA))
3165[6] 3722[7] 4107[U] 4515[3] 4879[7] 5546[16]
Petit Parc *R A Teal* a69 69
2 b f Bahamian Bounty—Alkarida (FR) (Akarad (FR))
1945[4] 2457[4] 6403[11]
Petomic (IRE) *Christian Wroe* a58
2 ch c Dubai Destination(USA) —Petomi (Presidium)
7191[9]
Petrograd (IRE) *E Lellouche* 101
6 b h Peintre Celebre(USA) —Palmeraie (USA) (Lear Fan (USA))
1571a[7]
Petrosian *M Johnston* a70 67
3 b g Sakhee(USA) —Arabis (Arazi (USA))
469[3] (731) 1205[12] 1624[5]
Petrovich (USA) *Jane Chapple-Hyam* a68 108
4 ch h Giant's Causeway(USA) —Pharma (USA) (Theatrical)
6175[12] 6726[4] 7055[8]
Pevensey (IRE) *J J Quinn* a91 102
5 b g Danehill(USA) —Champaka (IRE) (Caerleon (USA))
1767[12] (2859) 3558[9] 4722[19] 5554[5] 6169[10]
Pha Mai Blue *W J Knight* a48 77
2 b c Acclamation—Queen Of Silk (IRE) (Brief Truce (USA))
3551[3] 4151[11] 4539[5] 5428[2] 5856[9] 6270[8]
Phantom Income (USA) *R Violette* a90 30
2 rg f Montbrook(USA) —Catch The Ghost (USA) (Silver Ghost (USA))
6507a[13]
Phantom Whisper *B R Millman* a91 98
4 br g Makbul—La Belle Vie (Indian King (USA))
828[7] 1363[3] 1653[7] 1971[12] 2399[2] 3104[2] 3268[3] 3911[9] (4456) 5050[10] 5689[9] 6205[7]
Pharaoh Prince *G Prodromou* a59 60
6 b g Desert Prince(IRE) —Kinlochewe (Old Vic)
133[3] 203[11] 496[9] 558[9] 721[6]
Pharaohs Justice (USA) *Jane Chapple-Hyam* a74
2 br c Kafwain(USA) —Mary Linoa (USA) (L'Emigrant (USA))
6855[7] 7051[5] (7208)
Pharaohs Queen (IRE) *E A L Dunlop* a63
2 b f Bahri(USA) —Medway (IRE) (Shernazar)
6401[3] 6868[2]
Pheidias (IRE) *Mrs P Sly* a52 44
3 ch g Spectrum(IRE) —Danse Grecque (IRE) (Sadler's Wells (USA))
499[9] 611[7] 6109[11]
Philanthropy *K A Ryan* 96
3 ch g Generous(IRE) —Clerio (Soviet Star (USA))
1843[8] 3105[3] 4749[17] (5141) 5504[3] 5805[4] 6759[21]
Philario (IRE) *K R Burke* a104 104
2 ch c Captain Rio—Salva (Grand Lodge (USA))
(2297) 3910[2] 4743[12] (5219) 5630[4]

Philatelist (USA) *M A Jarvis* a76 95
3 b c Rahy(USA) —Polent (Polish Precedent (USA))
1129[6] 1605[3] (1950) 2448[2] 2790[7] 4059[6] 4799[5]
Philharmonic *R A Fahey* a95 109
6 b g Victory Note(USA) —Lambast (Relkino)
3975[4] 4614[16] (5700) 6183[18] 6932[8] 7279[3]
Phinerine *Miss J E Foster* a58 66
4 ch g Bahamian Bounty—Golden Panda (Music Boy)
143[3] 254[4] 403[5] (442) 622[4] 2220[4] 2387[5] 2576[14] 3535[12] 6288[6] 6608[7] 6957[5] 7020[10] 7108[2] 7138[4]
Phluke *Eve Johnson Houghton* a90 95
6 b g Most Welcome—Phlirty (Pharly (FR))
1013[3] (1682) (2030) 2239[11] 2528[6] 3650[6] 3941[22] 4195[11] 4601[7] 5115[8] 5804[6] 6006[7]
Phoenix Bay *J J Quinn* 20
2 b f Reel Buddy(USA) —Bollin Victoria (Jalmood (USA))
5521[13] 6023[9]
Phoenix Eye *M Mullineaux* a20 59
6 b g Tragic Role(USA) —Eye Sight (Roscoe Blake)
39[12]
Phoenix Factor (IRE) *J S Moore* a56 68
4 b m Indian Ridge—Alassio (USA) (Gulch (USA))
263[11] 525[7]
Phoenix Flight (IRE) *Sir Mark Prescott* a74 58
2 b g Hawk Wing(USA) —Firecrest (IRE) (Darshaan)
2889[3] (3171)
Phoenix Hill (IRE) *D R Gandolfo* a63 44
5 b g Montjeu(IRE) —Cielo Vodkamartini (USA) (Conquistador Cielo (USA))
775[6] 2430[9] 2996[5] 3598[7] 7120[5] 7285[11]
Phoenix Nights (IRE) *A Berry* 41
7 b g General Monash(USA) —Beauty Appeal (USA) (Shadeed (USA))
2417[6] 2709[6] 2843[7] 4410[6]
Phoenix Tower (USA) *H R A Cecil* a80 103
3 b c Chester House(USA) —Bionic (Zafonic (USA))
(1124) (1544)
Phone Call *Mouse Hamilton-Fairley* a61 80
4 b m Anabaa(USA) —Phone West (USA) (Gone West (USA))
5732[13] 6132[13]
Phone In *R Brotherton* a66 70
4 b g Sinndar(IRE) —Patria (USA) (Mr Prospector (USA))
1406[13] 1671[6] 2089[9] 3617[7] 7151[5]
Photographer (USA) *S Lycett* a52 88
9 bb g Mountain Cat(USA) —Clickety Click (USA) (Sovereign Dancer (USA))
153[6] 291[12]
Phreeze *G A Swinbank* a73 84
3 gr c Sadler's Wells(USA) —Showdown (Darshaan)
954[11] 1177[2] 1605[10] 1937[3] (3058) 3883[8] (4570)
Pianoforte (USA) *E J Alston* a68 69
5 b g Grand Slam(USA) —Far Too Loud (CAN) (No Louder (CAN))
2117[9] 2311[11] 2809[6] 3195[12] 4082[2] 4427[6] 4820[10] 4933[3] 4998[6] 5330[6] 5539[6] 5664[3] 5905[11] 6016[10] 6304[10] 6732[10] 6806[2] 6996[10] 7143[6]
Piano Key *M D I Usher* a47 50
3 ch f Distant Music(USA) —Ivorine (USA) (Blushing Groom (FR))
1203[12] 1541[14] 2259[7] 2697[6] 2916[3] 3611[6] 3871[5] 4104[6] 4596[3] 4914[6] 7125[4] 7203[3]
Piano Man *B G Powell* a59 62
5 b g Atraf—Pinup (Risk Me (FR))
1761[2] 2141[4] 2275[4] 2875[6] 3616[4] 3868[11]
Piano Sonata *B W Hills* 55
2 b f Observatory(USA) —Matinee (Sadler's Wells (USA))
6649[11]
Picacho (IRE) *P J Hobbs* 71
4 b m Sinndar(IRE) —Gentle Thoughts (Darshaan)
3033[3] 3273[4]
Picador *Sir Mark Prescott* a85 39
4 b g Pivotal—Candescent (Machiavellian (USA))
(200) (238) 286[7] 334[P] (Dead)
Piccleyes *A J McCabe* a57 56
6 b g Piccolo—Dark Eyed Lady (IRE) (Exhibitioner)
145[5] 241[10] 430[7] 448[4] 586[3] 632[6] 668[8] 680[7] 1569[4] 1719[4] 2145[10] 2343[11]
Piccolo Diamante (USA) *D J Murphy* a59 45
3 bb g Three Wonders(USA) —Bafooz (USA) (Clever Trick (USA))
4616[9] 5282[6] 5716[4] 5982[4] 6563[8] (6718) 6869[5] 6945[3] 7113[6] 7207[3]
Piccolomini *E W Tuer* a43 50
5 b g Diktat—La Dama Bonita (USA) (El Gran Senor (USA))
909[8] 1222[6] 1556[6] 1895[4] 2345[4] 2890[14] 4409[10]
Piccolo Pete *J J Quinn* 49
2 b c Piccolo—Goes A Treat (IRE) (Common Grounds)
4221[8] 4770[11] 5154[4] 5484[10] 5903[4]
Piccolo Pride *B G Powell*
2 ch g Piccolo—Jaycat (IRE) (Catrail (USA))
7264[11]
Piccolo Prince *Mrs Marjorie Fife* a58 64
6 ch g Piccolo—Aegean Flame (Anshan)
3[11] 225[3] 462[11] 479[11] 1719[7] 2791[8]
Piccostar *A B Haynes* a64 72
4 b m Piccolo—Anneliina (Cadeaux Genereux)
751[5] 1212[10] 1534[3] 1947[6] 2336[12] 2414[4] 2696[4] (3618) 4397[10] 4881[13] 5191[10] 5867[6] 5947[6] 7082[8]
Pick A Nice Name *R M Whitaker* a46 81
5 ch m Polar Falcon(USA) —Opuntia (Rousillon (USA))
1565[8] 1847[12] 2553[3] 3101[7] (3158) 3466[2] 3557[5]
Pickering *E J Alston* a65 80
3 br g Prince Sabo—On The Wagon (Then Again)
(925) 1108[4] 1286[8] 3475[4] 3885[11] 4291[2] 4898[11] 5232[6]
Pickledallnuts *Miss J A Camacho* a9 29
3 ch f Piccolo—Salinas (Bay Express)
728[12] 1045[16] 1281[9]

Pick Of The Crop *J R Jenkins* a16 6
6 ch g Fraam—Fresh Fruit Daily (Reprimand)
20[12]
Picky *C Tinkler* a62 49
3 b g Piccolo—Passerella (FR) (Brustolon)
106[3] 484[5] 611[6] 776[3] 2362[9] 4266[9] 4516[3] 4742[5] (5095) 5531[12] (6206)
Picot De Say *C Roberts* a13 50
5 b g Largesse—Facsimile (Superlative)
5779[12] 5886[12]
Picture Frame *J T Stimpson* 66
3 ch g Fraam—Floral Spark (Forzando)
925[6] 1286[4] 2508[14]
Pic Up Sticks *B G Powell* a92 96
8 gr g Piccolo—Between The Sticks (Pharly (FR))
1242[11] 1464[3] 1971[14] 2197[6] 2237[11] 2494[6] 2694[6] 4095[10] 4606[7] 5009[4] (5160) 5272[3] 5381[4] 6405[8]
Piddies Pride (IRE) *Miss Gay Kelleway* a57 63
5 b m Indian Lodge(IRE) —Fairybird (FR) (Pampabird)
(723) 1212[6] 1400[5] 2334[5] 2657[3] 3613[9] 4324[6]
Piece Of My Heart *P F I Cole* a66 75
2 b f Fasliyev(USA) —Cultured Pearl (IRE) (Lammtarra (USA))
(1079) 1721[3] 2756[18] 7048a[7] 7202[4]
Pie O My (IRE) *J Jay* a37
2 gr c Nayef(USA) —Sea Drift (FR) (Warning)
6763[9]
Piermarini *M Johnston* 77
2 b c Singspiel(IRE) —Allespagne (USA) (Trempolino (USA))
4482[5] 5321[4] 6723[8]
Pieter Brueghel (USA) *D Nicholls* a87 96
8 b g Citidancer(USA) —Smart Tally (USA) (Smarten (USA))
5[2] 81[9] 554[6] 810[3] 1292[5] 1754[11] 1852[9] 3954[12] 5535[3] 6639[2] 6730[2]
Pietersen (IRE) *T D Barron* a74 71
3 ch g Redback—Faye (Monsanto (FR))
122[2] (136) 336[3] (535) (1091) 1410[4] 1965[4] 2133[6] 3066[4] 6310[10] 7045[8] 7164[2]
Pigeon Flight *M L W Bell* 65
3 ch g Compton Admiral—Fervent Fan (IRE) (Soviet Lad (USA))
(981) 1194[6] 1916[4] 2530[10] 3381[7]
Pikaboo *S C Williams* a46 61
4 ch m Pivotal—Gleam Of Light (IRE) (Danehill (USA))
268[10] 376[5]
Pillar Of Hercules (IRE) *H R A Cecil* 88
3 b c Rock Of Gibraltar(IRE) —Sabreon (Caerleon (USA))
2880[2] 3827[2] (4290) 5382[7]
Pimlico Dralliv (FR) *J-P Gauvin* a51
2 b g Arnaqueur(USA) —Nayana (FR) (Zayyani)
7027a[8]
Pinacotheque (IRE) *E Lellouche* 96
3 b f In The Wings—Palmeraie (USA) (Lear Fan (USA))
5058a[6]
Pinchbeck *M A Jarvis* a89 79
8 b g Petong—Veuve Hoornaert (IRE) (Standaan (FR))
81[5] 277[8] 419[8]
Pinch Of Salt (IRE) *A M Balding* a98 77
4 b g Hussonet(USA) —Granita (CHI) (Roy (USA))
2474[10] 3854[5] (5732) (6124) 6645[7] 6995[2] 7147[4]
Pindar (GER) *B J Curley* a58
3 b g Tertullian(USA) —Pierette (GER) (Local Suitor (USA))
60[9] 152[8] (6152)
Pineapple Poll *P L Gilligan* a1 7
3 b f Josr Algarhoud(IRE) —Petrovna (IRE) (Petardia)
11[7] 141[9]
Pine Cone (IRE) *M Weiss* 92
5 ch m Dr Fong(USA) —Pine Needle (Kris)
439a[3] 493a[6]
Pinewood Lulu *R C Guest* a7 64
2 b f Lujain(USA) —Lucy Glitters (USA) (Cryptoclearance (USA))
6093[5] 6384[4] 7139[6]
Pinkabout (IRE) *J S Moore* a80 83
3 br f Desert Style(IRE) —Dinka Raja (USA) (Woodman (USA))
2060[3] 2914[5] 5850a[9] 6300[15]
Pink Bay *K F Clutterbuck* a39 58
5 b m Forzando—Singer On The Roof (Chief Singer)
2331[13] 3056[14] 4294[9] 4686[7]
Pinkindie (USA) *E A L Dunlop* 80
2 ch c Smart Strike(CAN) —Only Princesses (USA) (Chief's Crown (USA))
3958[3] 5011[3] (5570)
Pink Notes *R J Hodges* 27
3 ch g Bandmaster(USA) —Pink Petal (Northern Game)
3794[10] 4630[14]
Pink Salmon *Mrs L J Mongan* a37 55
3 ch f Dr Fong(USA) —West Humble (Pharly (FR))
55[8] 5013[6] 5280[12] 7029[12] 7189[8]
Pinnacle Point *G L Moore* 61
2 ch g Best Of The Bests(IRE) —Alessandra (Generous (IRE))
5010[14] 5361[12] 5937[11]
Pinot Noir (GER) *L Ottofulling* 93
4 b h Dictator's Song(USA) —Princesse Aga (IRE) (Acatenango (GER))
6334[12]
Pinpoint (IRE) *W R Swinburn* a76 116
5 b g Pivotal—Alessia (GER) (Warning)
(1145) 1494[2] 2182[4] 4119[12] 6011[16] 6653[3]
Pintano *J Howard Johnson* 72
2 ch g Dr Fong(USA) —Heckle (In The Wings)
4350[3] 4818[5] 5745[13]
Pintle *J L Spearing* a67 98
7 b m Pivotal—Boozy (Absalom)
(2401) 4119[16] (4633) 5047[15] 5794[11]
Pionero (GER) *E Kurdu* 41
2 b c Sternkoenig(IRE) —Princesse Aga (IRE) (Acatenango (GER))
6324a[13]

Pipedreamer *J H M Gosden* 116
3 b c Selkirk(USA) —Follow A Dream (USA) (Gone West (USA))
1143[6] (1606) (2506) 3460[4] (4092) (6011)

Piper General (IRE) *J Balding* a53 21
5 br g General Monash(USA) —Pipewell (IRE) (Lake Coniston (IRE))
507[9] 685[5] 732[7] 1069[9] 4025[9]

Piperman *M Dods* 50
3 b g Zamindar(USA) —Heather Mix (Linamix (FR))
1303[14] 2012[7] 2535[12]

Piper's Song (IRE) *H Candy* a69 84
4 gr g Distant Music(USA) —Dane's Lane (IRE) (Danehill (USA))
1078[2] 1638[7] 2194[6] 3705[6] 4234[3] 4587[7] 5166[2] (5687) 6209[9]

Pipoldchap (CHI) *F Castro* a75 97
7 bb g The Great Shark(USA) —Tiquitiquiti (CHI) (Cresta Rider (USA))
324a[6] 396a[15] 1647a[4]

Pippa Greene *P F I Cole* a85 101
3 b c Galileo(IRE) —Funny Girl (IRE) (Darshaan)
(764) (4603) (6091) 6759[8]

Pippbrook Gold *J R Boyle* a61
2 ch g Golden Snake(USA) —Chiaro (Safawan)
7266[5]

Pippins Corner *M A Allen*
5 b m Piccolo—Newlands Corner (Forzando)
6121[11]

Pips Assertive Way *A W Carroll* a38 39
6 ch m Nomadic Way(USA) —Return To Brighton (Then Again)
5606[6]

Piquet *J J Bridger* a51 67
9 br m Mind Games—Petonellajill (Petong)
20[3] 51[4] 129[11] 6792[10] 6896[13] 7094[9] 7166[8]

Pirner's Brig *M W Easterby* a68 61
3 b g Warningford—Loch Maree (Primo Dominie)
147[4] 295[3] 520[3] 659[4] (707) 925[7] 1351[4] 1932[9] 2172[6] 2948[5] 3203[13]

Pirouetting *B W Hills* a75 79
4 b m Pivotal—Jitterbug (IRE) (Marju (IRE))
2527[5] 3711[11] 4828[4] 5424[11] 6063[4] 6423[4]

Piscean (USA) *T Keddy* a78 80
2 bb c Stravinsky(USA) —Navasha (USA) (Woodman (USA))
2832[15] 3589[4] 4173[3] 4812[9] (5452) 6004[2] 6182[10] 6756[12]

Pitbull *Mrs G S Rees* a61 65
4 b g Makbul—Piccolo Cativo (Komaite (USA))
1226[7] 2203[6] 3185[6] 3414[3] 4023[5] 4562[7] (4701) 5568[6] 6316[6] (6380) 6878[6]

Pittori (IRE) *J S Bolger* 91
2 b g Vettori(IRE) —Pirie (USA) (Green Dancer (USA))
5397a[9]

Piverina (IRE) *T D Barron* 53
2 b f Pivotal—Alassio (USA) (Gulch (USA))
5550[5] 6306[7]

Pivotal Answer (IRE) *J Noseda* a102 91
3 ch f Pivotal—Begueule (FR) (Bering)
2581[3] 3113[2] (3366) 3731[2] (5225) 5686[2] 5940[2] 6605[4] 6994[2]

Pivotal Era *Jim Best* a65 59
4 ch g Pivotal—Femme Savante (Glenstal (USA))
1995[8] 2175[4] 2877[8] 6148[12] 6268[7] 6581[10] 6826[5] 6947[S] (Dead)

Pivotal Flame *E S McMahon* 114
5 b h Pivotal—Reddening (Blushing Flame (USA))
847[9]

Pivotalia (IRE) *W R Swinburn* a73 61
3 b f Pivotal—Viscaria (IRE) (Barathea (IRE))
2261[2] 3066[2] 3455[3] 4073[7] 4889[5] 5367[3] (5783)

Pivotal Point *P J Makin* 117
7 b g Pivotal—True Precision (Presidium)
2695[4] 2733[13] 5416[5]

Pivotal Queen (IRE) *L M Cumani* 78
2 ch f Pivotal—Queen Of Norway (USA) (Woodman (USA))
3245[3] 4102[3]

Pivotal's Princess (IRE) *E S McMahon* 106
5 ch m Pivotal—Art Princess (IRE) (Fairy King (USA))
(1088) (2022) 3344[6] 4798[8] 5325[6] 5666[2] 5953[7]

Pivotal Truth *B W Hills* a69 55
3 ch f Pivotal—Home Truth (Known Fact (USA))
1398[4] 1961[8] 3743[9] (5567) 5819[11]

Pix *Michael McElhone* a54 39
4 b m Bertolini(USA) —Fair Kai (IRE) (Fayruz)
5425[11]

Pixie Princess (IRE) *Miss V Haigh* a30 32
3 b f Imperial Ballet(IRE) —Tereed Elhawa (Cadeaux Genereux)
1620[13] 2083[11] 3425[9] 4337[9] 4488[7] 4718[10] 5511[6]

Pixie's Blue (IRE) *J H M Gosden* a69 78
2 br f Hawk Wing(USA) —Isle Of Flame (Shirley Heights)
1445[8] 1814[2] 2000[2] 2768[6] 4169[5] 4453[5]

Place In Line *Gianluca Bietolini* 108
5 b h Docksider(USA) —Balwa (USA) (Danzig (USA))
1874a[4] 5821a[7] (6863a)

Place Vendome (FR) *Mlle S-V Tarrou* a93 99
3 gr f Dr Fong(USA) —Mediaeval (FR) (Medaaly)
2291a[9] 5468a[5] 6071a[9]

Plaisir Bere (FR) *A Junk* 102
4 b h Verglas(IRE) —Belisonde (FR) (Gay Mecene (USA))
6614a[8]

Plaka (FR) *W M Brisbourne* a57 57
2 gr f Verglas(IRE) —Top Speed (IRE) (Wolfhound (USA))
4254[7] 4963[4] 5110[10] 5729[10] 6799[8] 6966[10] 7245[8]

Plane Painter (IRE) *M Johnston* a77 83
3 b g Orpen(USA) —Flight Sequence (Polar Falcon (USA))
1365[4] 2092[3] 2340[6] 2862[5] 3215[9] 3877[5] 4309[3] 4570[2] 4732[2] 5224[5] 5478[4] (5857)

Planetarium *M Johnston* 90
2 gr c Fantastic Light(USA) —Karsiyaka (IRE) (Kahyasi)
5858[2] (6051) 6650[2]

Planet Paradise (IRE) *D Shaw* a23 34
2 b f Spinning World(USA) —Just Heavens Gate (Slip Anchor)
1727[12] 2349[11] 3364[3] 3788[4]

Planet Queen *K R Burke* 47
2 ch f Bahamian Bounty—Ash Moon (IRE) (General Monash (USA))
2115[5] 2758[6] 3492[7]

Planters Punch (IRE) *N G Richards* a52 63
6 b g Cape Cross(IRE) —Jamaican Punch (IRE) (Shareef Dancer (USA))
665[8] 3012[12]

Plateau *C R Dore* a77 86
8 b g Zamindar(USA) —Painted Desert (Green Desert (USA))
63[9] 218[5] 367[3] 556[4] 614[9] 1223[8] 1845[3] 2190[5] 2458[7] 3409[3] 3644[10] 4396[5] (4822) 5711[6] 5909[3] 6083[7] 6671[5] 6810[8] 6946[9] 7271[11]

Platinum Charmer (IRE) *K R Burke* a64 67
7 b g Kahyasi—Mystic Charm (Nashwan (USA))
1890[6] 2342[5] 2537[4]

Plato's Republic (USA) *E Charpy* 83
3 b c Catienus(USA) —Life Of The Party (USA) (Pleasant Colony (USA))
527a[2] 595a[2]

Plausabelle *G G Margarson* a61 53
6 b m Royal Applause—Sipsi Fach (Prince Sabo)
86[8]

Plavius (USA) *Saeed Bin Suroor* 41
2 br c Danzig(USA) —Sharp Minister (CAN) (Deputy Minister (CAN))
6252[9]

Players Please (USA) *M Johnston* a92 103
3 ch g Theatrical—Miss Tobacco (USA) (Forty Niner (USA))
(141) (563) 1106[4] 1835[11] 2788[7] 3650[5] 4092[4] 4720[9] 5049[6] (5504) 5631[14] 6169[3]

Playful *R M Beckett* a83 86
4 b m Piccolo—Autumn Affair (Lugana Beach)
2352[11] 6197[8] 6876[8]

Playful Dane (IRE) *K A Ryan* 81
10 b g Dolphin Street(FR) —Omicida (IRE) (Danehill (USA))
1088[10] 1574[6] 2025[8] 2419[6]

Playing Star (FR) *C Boutin* a89 97
3 b f Starborough—Playing Havoc (Distant Relative)
7049a[10]

Play Master (IRE) *C Roberts* a63 60
6 b g Second Empire(IRE) —Madam Waajib (IRE) (Waajib)
4878[9] 5779[4] 5886[4]

Play Straight *I W McInnes* a62 43
3 ch f Piccolo—Align (Petong)
535[9] 834[9] 1091[12] 1894[10] 2116[8] 2557[4] 3377[8] 4292[8]

Play The Ball (USA) *J J Lambe* a77 58
5 ch g Boundary(USA) —Copper Play (USA) (Fast Play (USA))
256[9]

Playtotheaudience *R A Fahey* a56 71
4 b g Royal Applause—Flyfisher (USA) (Riverman (USA))
1198[10] 2072[11] 3408[5] 3647[7] 4156[7] 4383[8] 5037[4] 5487[7] 5739[8] 6019[2] 6265[14] 6304[7]

Play Up Pompey *J J Bridger* a64 49
5 b g Dansili—Search For Love (FR) (Groom Dancer (USA))
19[3] (315) 363[8] 610[6] 651[8] 2980[8] 3641[7] 4108[13] 6179[5] 6260[9] 6577[7] 6719[9] 6867[7] 7083[4] (7098) 7257[6]

Pleasant Strike (USA) *T Pletcher* 103
3 bb c Smart Strike(CAN) —Colonella (USA) (Pleasant Colony (USA))
4412a[8]

Please The King (IRE) *T Hogan* 64
3 b g King Charlemagne(USA) —Placate (Rainbow Quest (USA))
4865a[14]

Pleasing *C E Brittain* a62 98
4 b m Dr Fong(USA) —Trounce (Barathea (IRE))
1661[7]

Pleasing Gift *J M P Eustace* a49 53
4 b m Largesse—Pleasure Dome (Most Welcome)
4517[8]

Pleasure Pursuit *K A Ryan* 25
3 b g Pursuit Of Love—Glen Falls (Commanche Run)
1012[10]

Plenty Cried Wolf *R A Fahey* a66 65
5 b g Wolfhound(USA) —Plentitude I (FR) (Kaldoun (FR))
503[3] 623[3] 683[3] 909[5] (Dead)

Plenty Of Action (USA) *M J Wallace* a52
2 bb f Hennessy(USA) —Mary Had A Lot (USA) (Double Zeus (USA))
7071[4] 7235[4]

Plucky *J H M Gosden* 88
3 b f Kyllachy—Pizzicato (Statoblest)
2998[3] 3743[2] (4258) 4848[2] 5954[2] 6300[6] 6497[6]

Plumage *M Blanshard* a53
2 b f Royal Applause—Cask (Be My Chief (USA))
7051[9]

Plum Pudding (IRE) *R Hannon* a95 102
4 b g Elnadim(USA) —Karayb (IRE) (Last Tycoon (IRE))
701[5] 1145[11] (1842) 2208[14] 2755[12] 3330[8] 4720[16] 5833[11] 5950[10] 6499[13]

Plush *B P J Baugh* a57 38
4 ch g Medicean—Glorious (Nashwan (USA))
4351[9]

Plutonik Rock (IRE) *A & G Botti* 33
3 b c Galileo(IRE) —Paesanella (Seattle Song (USA))
1191a[5]

Pochard *J M P Eustace* a56 58
4 br m Inchinor—Pomorie (IRE) (Be My Guest (USA))
903[6] 2156[7]

Pocket Too *M Salaman* a65 72
4 b g Fleetwood(IRE) —Pocket Venus (IRE) (King's Theatre (IRE))
(159) 291[3] 677[11] 3901[2] 4056[9] 6500[2] 6811[5] 7123[5]

Pocketwood *Jean-Rene Auvray* a72 78
5 b g Fleetwood(IRE) —Pocket Venus (IRE) (King's Theatre (IRE))
844[9] 1148[14] 1813[2] (2238) 2987[11] 3385[10] 5732[11] 6500[6] 7004[4]

Poet Laureate *A Fabre* 115
3 gr c Highest Honor(FR) —Desired (Rainbow Quest (USA))
4872a[2]

Point Of Origin (IRE) *John A Harris* a19 41
10 b g Caerleon(USA) —Aptostar (USA) (Fappiano (USA))
107[6] 240[8]

Points Of View *Sir Mark Prescott* a87 60
2 b g Galileo(IRE) —On Point (Kris)
5734[8] 5880[7] 6138[8] (6584) (6715) 6750[2]

Poisiedon (IRE) *Liam McAteer* a74 74
3 b g King's Best(USA) —Lizanne (USA) (Theatrical)
5581[13]

Polar Annie *M S Saunders* a71 62
2 b f Fraam—Willisa (Polar Falcon (USA))
3592[5] 3866[4] 4629[7] (5729) 6584[2]

Polar Circle (USA) *P W Chapple-Hyam* 94
2 b f Royal Academy(USA) —Polar Bird (Thatching)
(1807) 2756[11] (3096) 3988[12] 5973[11]

Polar Force *Mrs C A Dunnett* a69 69
7 ch g Polar Falcon(USA) —Irish Light (USA) (Irish River (FR))
158[4] 251[5] 803[9] 1436[7] 3106[2] 3388[2] (3735) 4083[11] 6287[6] 6575[12] 7011[5] 7227[9]

Polar Fox *D Shaw* a20 73
4 ch g Pivotal—Niseem (USA) (Hennessy (USA))
727[9] 905[9] 1065[12] 1280[12]

Polar Magic *I Mohammed* a84 109
6 ch g Polar Falcon(USA) —Enchant (Lion Cavern (USA))
396a[9] (540a) 646a[9]

Polar Wind (ITY) *Maria Rita Salvioni* 93
3 ch c Rob's Spirit(USA) —Miss Buffy (Polar Falcon (USA))
6224a[6]

Pole Dancer *W S Kittow* a11 35
4 b g Polish Precedent(USA) —Pounelta (Tachypous)
2194[10] 4253[11] 4914[13]

Police Officer *W J Musson* a47 21
2 b c Mark Of Esteem(IRE) —No Rehearsal (FR) (Baillamont (USA))
6409[15] 6694[7] 6791[5]

Polish Emperor (USA) *D W Barker* a69 84
7 ch g Polish Precedent(USA) —Empress Jackie (USA) (Mount Hagen (FR))
81[7] 424[12] 566[7] 621[12] 915[9] 2509[15] 3347[15] 3787[6] 4180[18] 4223[9] 4583[12] 5083[10]

Polish Index *J R Jenkins* a48 74
5 b g Polish Precedent(USA) —Glossary (Reference Point)
1946[7]

Polish Magic *Z Koplik* 98
7 gr g Magic Ring(IRE) —Petitesse (Petong)
1800a[7]

Polish Myth *J G Given* 39
3 b c Polish Precedent(USA) —Myth (Troy)
3415[4]

Polish Power (GER) *J S Moore* a93 83
7 br h Halling(USA) —Polish Queen (Polish Precedent (USA))
95[3] 226[2] (587) 698[6] 868[3] 1771[14] 2474[9] 2692[4] 3105[4] 3577a[5] 3882[5] 4597[12] 5225[12] (6144) 6500[3] 6853[2] 7086[2]

Polish Priory (IRE) *P D Evans* a43 63
2 b f Polish Precedent(USA) —Glenstal Priory (Glenstal (USA))
1201[7] 1354[11] 4602[8] 4832a[17] 5442[3] 5692[10] 6242[4] 6438[10] 6462[7] 6958[9] 7021[11]

Polish Prize *W R Swinburn* a51 50
3 b g Polish Precedent(USA) —Forest Prize (Charnwood Forest (IRE))
2944[9] 3454[7] 3827[8] 4919[7] 5420[6] 7013[12] 7137[12]

Polish Prospect (IRE) *H S Howe* a37 41
3 ch f Elnadim(USA) —Always True (USA) (Geiger Counter (USA))
1560[12] 2998[9] 3365[11] 3619[9] 5129[8] 5269[5] 5690[6] 6642[3] 6833[7]

Polish Red *G G Margarson* 83
3 b g Polish Precedent(USA) —Norcroft Joy (Rock Hopper)
1205[6] 2602[9] (2945) (3385) 3993[10]

Polish Star *J S Wainwright* a52 54
3 b g Polish Precedent(USA) —Apennina (USA) (Gulch (USA))
567[7] 678[6] 954[12] 1676[5] 1850[9] 2759[RR]

Polish Welcome *S C Williams* a54 54
4 ch m Polish Precedent(USA) —Three White Sox (Most Welcome)
3805[7]

Polish World (USA) *T J Etherington* a73 69
3 b g Danzig(USA) —Welcometotheworld (USA) (Woodman (USA))
1037[6] (1346) 1432[2] 1994[8] 5134[7] 5339[8]

Politeia (USA) *R Hannon* 65
2 bb f Mr Greeley(USA) —Ujane (USA) (Theatrical)
3507[10] 4094[11] 5162[9]

Polite Society (IRE) *M Johnston* a39 70
2 b f Seeking The Gold(USA) —Born Something (IRE) (Caerleon (USA))
2122[6] 2575[3] 3453[10]

Political Force (USA) *H A Jerkens* a118
4 rg h Unbridled's Song(USA) —Glitter Woman (USA) (Glitterman (USA))
5059a[5] 5855a[3]

Polly Jones (USA) *G L Moore* a46 35
3 b f Lear Fan(USA) —Polly's Link (USA) (Phone Trick (USA))
25[7] 162[6]

Polly Rocket *P D Niven* a38 32
3 ch f Tendulkar(USA) —Celts Dawn (Celtic Swing)
295[5] 390[7] 1426[11] 1912[4]

Polmaily *B J Meehan* 77
2 b c Hawk Wing(USA) —Hampton Lucy (IRE) (Anabaa (USA))
4132[2] 6294[3]

Polochon (FR) *J-M Beguigne* a61 88
2 b c Marchand De Sable(USA) —Fairdane (FR) (Always Fair (USA))
6879a[3]

Polonius *G J Smith* a85 1
6 b g Great Dane(IRE) —Bridge Pool (First Trump)
608[10] 629[13] 770[9] 895[13]

Poltava (FR) *D Smaga* 104
3 b f Victory Note(USA) —Passiflore (FR) (Sillery (USA))
1055a[9]

Polychrome *John Berry* a43
2 b f Polish Precedent(USA) —Pantone (Spectrum (IRE))
6998[6]

Polygonal (FR) *Miss Gay Kelleway* a34 97
7 b g Octagonal(NZ) —Sectarine (FR) (Maelstrom Lake)
6999[8]

Polygraph (IRE) *A M Balding* 78
2 ch g Pivotal—Dear Girl (IRE) (Fairy King (USA))
1832[8] 2977[5] 3478[2] 3909[5] 5828[15]

Polyquest (IRE) *G A Butler* a71 57
3 b f Poliglote—Seren Quest (Rainbow Quest (USA))
37[8] (2008) 2246[7] 2915[6] 3502[7] 4742[4] 5095[3] (6178) (6265) 6673[7] 6808[2] 7194[5]

Pomellato (GER) *P Schiergen* 117
2 br c Big Shuffle(USA) —Passata (FR) (Polar Falcon (USA))
(5028a) 6222a[4] (6631a)

Pomfret Lad *J J Quinn* a56 82
9 b g Cyrano De Bergerac—Lucky Flinders (Free State)
14[5] 323[9]

Pompeii Ruler (AUS) *Mick Price* 121
5 ch g Genuine(JPN) —West With Night (NZ) (Pompeii Court (USA))
862a[8]

Pom Pom *J G Given* 49
3 ch f Polish Precedent(USA) —Slipper (Suave Dancer (USA))
3399[6]

Pondapie (IRE) *R M Whitaker* 67
2 b g Highest Honor(FR) —Fruhling Feuer (FR) (Green Tune (USA))
5551[5] 6184[7]

Ponder Anew (IRE) *K R Burke* 65
2 b f Namid—Luisa Demon (IRE) (Barathea (IRE))
1354[12] 2109[4] 2984[4]

Poniard (IRE) *D W Barker* a61 64
3 b g Daggers Drawn(USA) —It's Academic (Royal Academy (USA))
223[6] (454) 667[3] 834[7] 1266[12] 1712[5] 1894[8]

Pont Des Arts (FR) *K Schafflutzel* 100
3 b c Kingsalsa(USA) —Magic Arts (IRE) (Fairy King (USA))
2503a[5] 6353a[5]

Pont Des Soupirs (USA) *Saeed Bin Suroor* 63
2 b c Harlan's Holiday(USA) —Flirted (USA) (Relaunch (USA))
5868[8]

Pontefract Glory *M Dods* a47 44
4 b g Lujain(USA) —Final Glory (Midyan (USA))
252[5] 321[4] 435[5] 557[12] 1221[14]

Ponte Tresa (FR) *Y De Nicolay* 112
4 gr m Sicyos(USA) —Ponte Brolla (FR) (Highest Honor (FR))
1341a[3] 1881a[2] 2925a[6] 3565a[4] 4655a[3] 6526a[3] 6941a[10]

Ponte Vecchio (IRE) *J R Boyle* a44 39
3 b g Trans Island—Gino Lady (IRE) (Perugino (USA))
93[6] 4918[6] 6532[8] 7133[2]

Pont Wood *Mrs N S Evans* a59 1
3 b g Iron Mask(USA) —Bajan Rose (Dashing Blade)
128[4] 3237[9] 4163[10] 5175[8] 5390[9] 5817[7] 6642[7] 6806[11] 6858[8]

Ponty Rossa (IRE) *T D Easterby* a78 97
3 ch f Distant Music(USA) —Danish Gem (Danehill (USA))
1298[6] 1768[2] 2037[11] (2914)

Pop Music (IRE) *Miss J Feilden* a76 60
4 b g Tagula(IRE) —Easy Pop (IRE) (Shernazar)
(110) (334) 539[2] 604[6] 675[12] 1385[4] 1434[4] 1905[6] 6603[9] 6874[11] 7023[5] (7263)

Popolo (IRE) *P W Chapple-Hyam* a68 65
3 b f Fasliyev(USA) —Delisha (Salse (USA))
65[2] 348[5] 505[2] 583[2]

Poppets Sweetlove *A B Haynes* 68
3 b f Foxhound(USA) —Our Poppet (IRE) (Warning)
973[8] 1913[9] 2693[10] (3032) 4395[9] 5433[4] (5860) 6199[4]

Poppy Dean (IRE) *J G Portman* a58 57
2 ch f Night Shift(USA) —Miss Devious (IRE) (Dr Devious (IRE))
1896[7] 2624[4] 5895[4] 6478[6]

Poppyfield (GER) *H Rogers* a60 78
6 b m Waky Nao—Pretty Su (IRE) (Surumu (GER))
(6553a)

Poppy Perfect *J M P Eustace* a14 41
2 b f Lujain(USA) —Sea Jade (IRE) (Mujadil (USA))
2410[7] 2723[10] 3614[4] 3923[9] 5017[9]

Poppy Red *Miss J R Tooth* a25
2 ch f Lear Spear(USA) —Pooka's Daughter (IRE) (Eagle Eyed (USA))
6289[9]

Poppy's Rose *I W McInnes* a53 69
3 b f Diktat—Perfect Peach (Lycius (USA))
752[6] (996) 1634[8] 2515[6] (2892) 4291[5] 4642[7] 5556[5] 5662[2] 6089[6]

Pop Rock (JPN) *Katsuhiko Sumii* 123
6 b h Helissio(FR) —Pops (JPN) (Sunday Silence (USA))
861a[6] 6943a[2]

Porjenski *A B Haynes* a45 35
3 ch f Piccolo—Stygian (USA) (Irish River (FR))
2489[13] 3175[5]

Portal *J R Fanshawe* a93 107
4 b m Hernando(FR) —White Palace (Shirley Heights)
1789[3] 2720[P] 3434[3] 3744[4] *4887[4]*

Porthole (USA) *B W Hills* 77
2 rg c Mizzen Mast(USA) —Privity (USA) (Private Account (USA))
5977[3]

Port Luanda (IRE) *R M Flower* a22 29
3 ch g Docksider(USA) —Lady Angola (USA) (Lord At War (ARG))
1928[11] 2962[4] 3044[6]

Port Macquairie (IRE) *J W Mullins* a54
3 b g Val Royal(FR) —Hishmah (Nashwan (USA))
114[10] 267[13] 5647[10]

Portmeirion *S C Williams* a73 87
6 b m Polish Precedent(USA) —India Atlanta (Ahonoora)
2034[3] 2450[11]

Port 'n Starboard *C A Cyzer* a70 67
6 ch g Polar Falcon(USA) —Sally Slade (Dowsing (USA))
30[4] 651[3] 1069[6] 3063[9] 4592[8] 4915[11]

Portodora (USA) *H R A Cecil* 70
2 b f Kingmambo(USA) —High Walden (USA) (El Gran Senor (USA))
6093[3]

Porto Marmay (IRE) *K J Condon* 100
2 ch f Choisir(AUS) —Nordicolini (IRE) (Nordico (USA))
779a[4] 2325a[7] 3071a[4] 3659a[6]

Port Quin *G Wragg* a75 75
2 ch c Dr Fong(USA) —Saphila (IRE) (Sadler's Wells (USA))
4362[20] (6246) *6974[6]*

Portrush Storm *D Carroll* 71
2 ch f Observatory(USA) —Overcast (IRE) (Caerleon (USA))
845[3]

Portway Lane *W G M Turner* a20 42
2 ch f Tobougg(IRE) —Interregnum (Interrex (CAN))
898[10] 1000[2] 1156[4] *1728[7]* 2188[6]

Posamina (FR) *A Fabre* 72
3 gr f Linamix(FR) —Posadas (USA) (Miswaki (USA))
1388a[6] 4055a[10]

Poseidon Adventure (IRE) *W Figge* 115
4 b h Sadler's Wells(USA) —Fanny Cerrito (USA) (Gulch (USA))
1872a[8] 2924a[2] 4013a[7] 4838a[11] 5671a[2] 6353a[6]

Poseidon's Bride (USA) *Saeed Bin Suroor* a85 90
4 ch m Seeking The Gold(USA) —Neptune's Bride (USA) (Bering)
471a[4] 532a[7]

Poseidon's Secret (IRE) *Pat Eddery* a78 63
4 b g Night Shift(USA) —Chita Rivera (Chief Singer)
(537) 753[5] 921[4] 1208[6] *1438[7]* 4231[14] *6007[11]*
6500[9]

Positano (IRE) *M Scudamore*
7 b h Polish Precedent(USA) —Shamaya (IRE) (Doyoun)
4200[9]

Positive Profile (IRE) *J J Quinn* a76 45
9 b g Definite Article—Leyete Gulf (IRE) (Slip Anchor)
4[5] (283) 457[5] 955[10]

Postage (USA) *K A Morgan* a54
4 bb g Chester House(USA) —Nimble Mind (USA) (Lyphard (USA))
887[6]

Postage Stampe *D M Simcock* a94 83
4 b m Singspiel(IRE) —Jaljuli (Jalmood (USA))
2003[10] 2543[5] 5067[3] 6620[3]

Postgraduate (IRE) *W J Knight* a92 87
5 b g Almutawakel—Institutrice (IRE) (College Chapel)
1060[9] 1962[15]

Postmaster *R Ingram* a61 56
5 b g Dansili—Post Modern (USA) (Nureyev (USA))
379[5] 440[5] (517) (637) 742[9] 888[2] 1025[4] 1612[4]
2154[6] *2990[7] 3173[6]* 3965[7] *4272[2]* 4395[4] *5094[12]*
5546[7] *6179[2] 6431[10] 6859[5] 6956[4] 7085[7]*

Postsprofit (IRE) *N A Callaghan* a71 70
3 b g Marju(IRE) —Housekeeper (IRE) (Common Grounds)
1218[2] *1365[3]* 1815[16] *2177[11]* 2965[5] 3705[3] 4270[11]
4858[8] 5280[4] 5508[4] *5985[5]* 6413[12]

Potemkin (USA) *A King* 54
2 bb g Van Nistelrooy(USA) —Bolshoia (USA) (Moscow Ballet (USA))
4417[7] 4904[10] 5328[7] 6536[10]

Potentiale (IRE) *J W Hills* a77 69
3 ch g Singspiel(IRE) —No Frills (IRE) (Darshaan)
(1579) 1917[2] 2653[2] 3825[2] 4283[2] 4878[8] *(5342)*
6027[2]

Pothos Way (GR) *P R Chamings* a68 57
4 ch g Wadood(USA) —Evropi's Way (Sanglamore (USA))
1249[2] 1521[5] (2572) 4458[7] *5093[7] 5732[12] (6342)*
6780[9]

Potro Tell (ARG) *W Hefter* a56 76
7 br g Potrillon(ARG) —Telletin (ARG) (Cautin (ARG))
104a[4] 244a[10] 4957a[13]

Potwash *Andre Hermans* a53 84
7 b m Piccolo—Silankka (Slip Anchor)
688[4]

Pound Sign *Evan Williams* a84 16
4 ch g Singspiel(IRE) —Profit Alert (IRE) (Alzao (USA))
3242[6]

Power Again (GER) *P R Chamings* a36 61
6 b m Dashing Blade—Pik Konigin (GER) (Konigsstuhl (GER))
1764[2] 3448[2] *4463[9]*

Power Alert *B R Millman* a53 37
3 b g Averti(IRE) —Crystal Power (USA) (Pleasant Colony (USA))
390[2] 512[3] 667[4]

Power Ballad *W J Knight* a59 63
3 ch f Titus Livius(FR) —Sea Music (Inchinor)
(5728)

Power Broker *P F I Cole* a41 23
4 b g Mark Of Esteem(IRE) —Galatrix (Be My Guest (USA))
1446[12]

Power Desert (IRE) *M Johnston* 34
2 b g Anabaa(USA) —Legende D'Or (FR) (Diesis)
5903[9]

Power Of Future (GER) *H R A Cecil* a85 91
4 ch m Definite Article—Pik Konigin (GER) (Konigsstuhl (GER))
(1272) 1794[7] 2047[7]

Power Player *D J Coakley* a66 48
3 b g Diktat—Royal Patron (Royal Academy (USA))
3651[5] *5019[2] 5311[4] 6480[2] 6975[3]*

Power Politics (USA) *M Al Muhairi* a94 93
4 b h Seeking The Gold(USA) —Stormy Pick (USA) (Storm Creek (USA))
474a[8]

Power Shared (IRE) *P G Murphy* a67 68
3 gr g Kendor(FR) —Striking Pose (IRE) (Darshaan)
5683[4] 6235[9]

Power Trip (IRE) *Miss V Haigh*
3 b g Namid—Graten (IRE) (Zieten (USA))
5625[14]

Powys Lad *K R Burke* a53 58
2 b c Diktat—Cheyenne Squaw (IRE) (Night Shift (USA))
2443[10] 2863[4] 3192[12] 5298[15] 5932[11] *6099[10]* 6305[7]

Poyle Kiera *M Blanshard* a50 51
3 b f Diktat—Poyle Amber (Sharrood (USA))
5530[5] 5859[6] 6250[16]

Poyle Ruby *M Blanshard* a50 10
3 b f Josr Algarhoud(IRE) —Poyle Jezebelle (Sharpo)
116[7] 293[9] 924[11] 3622[9] 4292[9] 4684[13]

Practical Joke (IRE) *W J Knight* a40 63
3 b g Alhaarth(IRE) —Trick (IRE) (Shirley Heights)
1398[11] 2625[9]

Practicallyperfect (IRE) *P D Evans* a65 79
3 b f King Charlemagne(USA) —Morningsurprice (USA) (Future Storm (USA))
1851[5] 2577[3] 4111[3] 4847[6] *6269[9]*

Pragmatism *M Johnston* 70
2 b c Kingmambo(USA) —Sheer Reason (USA) (Danzig (USA))
4683[3] 6493[5]

Pragmatist *P Winkworth* a60 67
3 b f Piccolo—Shi Shi (Alnasr Alwasheek)
2428[9] (2878) 3735[5] (4545) *5134[5]* 6089[8]

Praia (GER) *A Wohler* 94
3 b f Big Shuffle(USA) —Prada (GER) (Lagunas)
1338a[8]

Prairie Law (GER) *B N Pollock* a11 52
7 b g Law Society(USA) —Prairie Charm (IRE) (Thatching)
514[9] 628[9]

Prairie Moon *C E Brittain* a48
3 ch f Halling(USA) —Warning Shadows (IRE) (Cadeaux Genereux)
758[9]

Prairie Storm *A M Balding* 68
2 b g Storming Home—Last Dream (IRE) (Alzao (USA))
6418[5] 6725[5]

Prairie Sun (GER) *Mrs A Duffield* a40 80
6 b m Law Society(USA) —Prairie Flame (IRE) (Marju (IRE))
3027[6] 3412[8]

Prairie Tiger (GER) *N J Vaughan* a74 83
3 b c Tiger Hill(IRE) —Prairie Lilli (GER) (Acatenango (GER))
5304[4] *(6005)* 6474[6]

Pravda Street *P F I Cole* a75
2 ch c Soviet Star(USA) —Sari (Faustus (USA))
6827[2]

Praxiteles (IRE) *Sir Michael Stoute* a91 72
3 b c Sadler's Wells(USA) —Hellenic (Darshaan)
1812[6] *(6821)*

Preachin Man (USA) *R Werner* a104 80
2 bb c Songandaprayer(USA) —Sweet Cameron (USA) (Devil's Bag (USA))
6484a[12]

Precept *H Candy* a41 69
3 b f Polish Precedent(USA) —Anna Of Brunswick (Rainbow Quest (USA))
2726[8] 3847[2] 4403[5] *5311[5] 6007[10]*

Precious Boy (GER) *W Hickst*
2 br c Big Shuffle(USA) —Pretty Su (IRE) (Surumu (GER))
(6219a)

Precious Kitten (USA) *R J Frankel* a107 118
4 bb m Catienus(USA) —Kitten's First (USA) (Lear Fan (USA))
6509a[8]

Precious Mettle *H R A Cecil*
3 gr f Golden Snake(USA) —Silver Fan (Lear Fan (USA))
2308[10] (Dead)

Precipice *Declan Gillespie* a67 79
2 b f Observatory(USA) —On The Brink (Mind Games)
5395a[12]

Precocious Star (IRE) *K R Burke* a87 91
3 ch f Bold Fact(USA) —Flames (Blushing Flame (USA))
246a[11] 476a[10] (838) 1096[9] 2757[10] 3222a[5]
3430[12] *6604[8] 6852[9] 7165[9]*

Pre Eminance (IRE) *L R James* 40
6 b g Peintre Celebre(USA) —Sorb Apple (IRE) (Kris)
1849[11] 2843[6] 3381[13] 5835[8] 6308[12] *7081[12]*

Prelude *W M Brisbourne* 73
6 b m Danzero(AUS) —Dancing Debut (Polar Falcon (USA))
1258[6] 1926[5] 2089[10] (2531) 2810[8] (3496) 3719[2]
4194[3] (4732) 5034[5] 5807[4]

Premier Class (IRE) *J S Wainwright* 56
2 b g Indian Danehill(IRE) —Shams Wa Matar (Polish Precedent (USA))
2024[8] 2532[13] 2888[7] 3951[7] 5572[8] 6305[13]

Premier Cru *Andrew Turnell* a38 37
4 b g King's Best(USA) —No Rehearsal (FR) (Baillamont (USA))
5816[9] 6537[7]

Premier Danseur (IRE) *M Johnston* 75
2 b c Noverre(USA) —Destiny Dance (USA) (Nijinsky (CAN))
6557[2] (6755)

Premier Yank (USA) *J A Osborne* 34
2 b c Johannesburg(USA) —Sallybrooke (USA) (Dehere (USA))
5856[11]

Premio Loco (USA) *C F Wall* a91 98
3 ch g Prized(USA) —Crazee Mental (Magic Ring (IRE))
977[5] *(1343)* 2045[9] (5635)

Premium Port *A Berry* 60
2 b g Superior Premium—The Barnsley Belle (IRE) (Distinctly North (USA))
2385[5] 2934[7] 3341[7] 3673[5] (Dead)

Premium Tap (USA) *J Kimmel* a128
5 b h Pleasant Tap(USA) —Premium Red (USA) (Thirty Six Red (USA))
863a[2]

Presbyterian Nun (IRE) *J L Dunlop* 85
2 b f Daylami(IRE) —Conspiracy (Rudimentary (USA))
3706[13] 4169[2] (5061) 6012[11]

Present *M J Gingell* a48 53
3 ch f Generous(IRE) —Miss Picol (Exit To Nowhere (USA))
991[8] 1092[7] 1637[6] 2192[15] *3170[6] 3421[10]* 4172[11]
5388[9] (5542) *5899[12]*

Present Oriented (USA) *M C Chapman*
6 ch g Southern Halo(USA) —Shy Beauty (CAN) (Great Gladiator (USA))
4458[13]

President Dan *M R Channon* a56 59
3 b c Polish Precedent(USA) —Mill Line (Mill Reef (USA))
386[12] 553[6] 703[4] 1194[9] 2609[6] *2801[7]* (3876)
4322[5] 4391[4] 4687[4] 4894[6] 4943[9] 5906[8] *6271[13]*

President Elect (IRE) *T D Barron* 75
2 b c Imperial Ballet(IRE) —Broadway Rosie (Absalom)
4173[6] 6073[2] 6326[3]

Presidium Star *G M Moore* 36
2 b f Presidium—Pagan Star (Carlitin)
4174[9] 4636[9] 4937[5]

Presious Passion (USA) *Mary Hartmann* 113
4 ch g Royal Anthem(USA) —Princesa's Passion (USA) (Marquetry (USA))
6771a[5]

Preskani *Mrs N Macauley* a57 38
5 b g Sri Pekan(USA) —Lamarita (Emarati (USA))
243[13] 1569[8] 2343[4] 7153[11] 7233[9]

Presque Perdre *K G Reveley* 35
3 ch g Desert Prince(IRE) —Kindle (Selkirk (USA))
2580[7] 3611[7] 4283[5]

Press Express (IRE) *R A Fahey* 81
5 ch g Entrepreneur—Nawaji (USA) (Trempolino (USA))
915[6] 1413[6] (2084) 2743[2] 3204[5]

Pressing (IRE) *M A Jarvis* 118
4 b h Soviet Star(USA) —Rafif (USA) (Riverman (USA))
(1192a) 1700a[2] 2754[5] 4414a[7] 5264a[2] (5821a)
(6689a)

Press The Button (GER) *J R Boyle* a82 92
4 b g Dansili—Play Around (IRE) (Niniski (USA))
1395[16] 2209[9] 3039[3] 3672[3] 4049[9] (4631) 4814[4]
5362[2] (5717) 6172[5] 6499[7]

Presto Levanter *R Hannon* 73
2 b f Rock Of Gibraltar(IRE) —Presto Vento (Air Express (IRE))
1503[2] 1821[10] (2122) 3269[7] 4168[9] 5008[9]

Presto Shinko (IRE) *R Hannon* a110 117
6 b g Shinko Forest(IRE) —Swift Chorus (Music Boy)
1497[4] 2291a[10] 2695[3] 2857[12] 3445a[10] 3708[7]
(4183) 4813[4] 5112[10]

Presumptive (IRE) *R Charlton* a98 102
7 b g Danehill(USA) —Demure (Machiavellian (USA))
840[6] (1448) 2123[3] 2528[7] 3091[9] 3943[3] 5413[2]
5797[4]

Pret A Porter (UAE) *P D Evans* a72 71
3 br f Jade Robbery(USA) —Velour (Mtoto)
(58) 196[3] 1084[5] 1211[4] (1536) 2602[7] 2816[8]

Pret A Tout *P J McBride* 45
2 ch f Ishiguru(USA) —Pretiosa (IRE) (Royal Abjar (USA))
3747[16] 4335[8] 5294[8]

Prettilini *A W Carroll* a62 62
4 ch m Bertolini(USA) —Pretiosa (IRE) (Royal Abjar (USA))
150[6] 243[9] 463[6] 580[4] 625[5] 710[2] 801[10] 1902[6]
2108[7] *2343[6]* 2657[6] 3594[10] 4324[7]

Pretty Ballerina (USA) *John Joseph Murphy* a40 88
2 b f Swain(IRE) —Hawzah (Green Desert (USA))
2325a[4] 4833a[5] *7015[6]*

Pretty Bonnie *J G Portman* a53 54
2 b f Kyllachy—Joonayh (Warning)
2122[9] 2416[3] 2746[4] *3424[8] 4428[7]* 5089[6] 5706[7]
6438[6] 6693[5]

Pretty Demanding (IRE) *M G Quinlan* a40 81
3 b f Night Shift(USA) —Absolute Glee (USA) (Kenmare (FR))
1024[6] *1278[7]* 1537[8] 2192[5] (2362) (2609) 4035a[8]
4114a[5] 4240a[3] 4843[2] 5211[4] 5777[5] 6368a[4]
6555a[15]

Pretty Game *K A Ryan* a38 36
3 b g Mind Games—Catwalk Girl (Skyliner)
258[7] 454[4] 7201[6]

Pretty Majestic (IRE) *M R Channon* 91
3 b f Invincible Spirit(IRE) —Cheeky Weeky (Cadeaux Genereux)
1096[6] 3431[15] 4389[12] 4848[13] 5356[10] 5638[4] 5954[11]

Pretty Miss *H Candy* 79
3 b f Averti(IRE) —Pretty Poppy (Song)
(1429) 1900[7] 2444[3] 3688[2] 4233[6] 5066[3] 5418[2]
5642[6]

Pretty Officer (USA) *Rae Guest* a43 40
2 b f Deputy Commander(USA) —La Samanna (USA) (Trempolino (USA))
5126[9] 6138[10] 6535[12]

Pretty Orchid *G C H Chung* 57
2 b f Forzando—Dunloe (IRE) (Shaadi (USA))
6087[7]

Pretty Persuasion (USA) *M Stidham* a81 82
2 br f Cape Town(USA) —Courageous Maiden (USA) (Broad Brush (USA))
5247a[7]

Pretty Posey *J G M O'Shea* 25
3 b f Dolpour—Aegean Glory (Shareef Dancer (USA))
2873[8] 3366[12] 3794[11]

Pretty Selma *R M H Cowell* a48
3 b f Diktat—Brave Vanessa (USA) (Private Account (USA))
103[4] 378[3] 506[2] 659[6] (713) 918[9]

Prevailing Wind *J R Fanshawe* 76
2 b c Gone West(USA) —Royal Alchemist (USA) (Royal Academy (USA))
4132[4]

Prianca (GER) *Mario Hofer* 100
3 b f Diktat—Palanca (Inchinor)
1338a[5] 6221a[4]

Priceless Melody (USA) *Mrs A J Perrett* a54 40
3 bb c Orientate(USA) —Regatta Queen (USA) (Danzig Connection (USA))
136[2] 360[8] 574[3] 786[9] 894[8] 1429[5]

Priceless Speedfit *G G Margarson* 59
2 b f Barathea Guest—Princess Speedfit (FR) (Desert Prince (IRE))
4709[7] 4968[2] 5226[3] 6410[11] 6536[15]

Priceoflove (IRE) *P J Makin* a67 65
4 ch m Inchinor—Piaf (Pursuit Of Love)
92[2] 358[4] 555[5]

Pride Of India (USA) *J Noseda* 66
2 b c Johannesburg(USA) —How Could You (USA) (Boundary (USA))
2041[9]

Pride Of Joy *M A Buckley* a70 60
4 ch m Pursuit Of Love—Ivory's Joy (Tina's Pet)
(36) 154[5] 368[9] 521[8] (688) 787[2] 1067[9] 1729[5]
1991[9] *2350[8] 3190[5] 3853[10] 5174[11]*

Pride Of Nation (IRE) *L M Cumani* 116
5 b h Danehill Dancer(IRE) —Anita Via (IRE) (Anita's Prince)
1791[3] 2817[6] 3330[4] (3887) (4543) 6031a[7] 6332[13]

Pride Of Northcare (IRE) *G A Huffer* a58 62
3 gb g Namid—Pride Of Pendle (Grey Desire)
311[6] 684[4] 826[4] 5546[5] 6088[13]

Prigsnov Dancer (IRE) *J O'Reilly* 71
2 ch g Namid—Brave Dance (IRE) (Kris)
1674[5] 2247[2] 2392[2] 3788[2] 4560[10] 4770[5] (5520)
6074[6] 6326[2] 6756[9]

Prima Ballerina *J H M Gosden* 67
3 b f Pivotal—Kirov (Darshaan)
1203[7] 1639[13]

Prima Luce (IRE) *J S Bolger* 88
2 b f Galileo(IRE) —Ramona (Desert King (IRE))
4440a[5] 5353[9]

Primarily *Peter Grayson* a57 66
5 b g Mind Games—Prim N Proper (Tragic Role (USA))
(46) 281[7] 441[2] 562[6] (680) 797[5] 892[5] 1120[3]
1400[4] 1902[3] 2798[8]

Prime Aspiration (USA) *Christian Wroe* a77 76
2 bb c Tale Of The Cat(USA) —Bank On Her (USA) (Rahy (USA))
4500[8] *5337[10]* 5856[2] 6234[4] *6544[4]*

Prime Contender *G L Moore* a82 75
5 b g Efisio—Gecko Rouge (Rousillon (USA))
353[5] 693[6] 726[10] 1434[6] 2003[11] *6145[11]* 6422[12]
7194[7]

Primed And Poised (USA) *J W Hills* a74 70
2 bb f More Than Ready(USA) —Sierra Madre (USA) (Mr Prospector (USA))
1631[5] *1945[3]* 2443[2] *2992[2]*

Prime Defender *B W Hills* a105 115
3 ch c Bertolini(USA) —Arian Da (Superlative)
839[2] (1095) 1473[20] (2035) 2695[2] 3506[13] 4090[5]
5436a[3] 5832[11]

Prime Exhibit *R Charlton* 80
2 b c Selkirk(USA) —First Exhibit (Machiavellian (USA))
5813[4] (6252)

Prime Number (IRE) *J Akehurst* a75 81
5 gr g King's Best(USA) —Majinskaya (FR) (Marignan (USA))
2670[11] 3001[6] 3437[16] 4108[4] 5211[3] 5307[2] (5916)
6727[7] *7194[6]*

Prime Performer (IRE) *B Smart* 73
2 b f Acclamation—Storming Kate (IRE) (Lion Cavern (USA))
(2021) 5699[3]

Prime Powered (IRE) *R M Beckett* a78 80
6 b g Barathea(IRE) —Caribbean Quest (Rainbow Quest (USA))
593[6] 753[7] 921[6] 1470[4] 1813[13] 2218[10] 3385[5]
3799[3] (4667) 5620[F] (Dead)

Prime Recreation *P S Felgate* a48 20
10 b g Primo Dominie—Night Transaction (Tina's Pet)
46[11] 317[5] 523[12] 4857[6] *7137[6]*

Primer Lugar *W J H Ratcliffe* a23 42
2 b f Primo Valentino(IRE) —Up Front (IRE) (Up And At 'Em)
5501[11] 5734[9] *7021[8]*

Primeshade Promise *J L Flint* a49 63
6 ch m Opening Verse(USA) —Bonnie Lassie (Efisio)
3904[4] 4259[11] 5756[10] 6532[2] 6956[10]

Primitive Academy *J R Holt* a67 64
5 b h Primitive Rising(USA) —Royal Fontaine (IRE) (Royal Academy (USA))
1295[11]

Primo Heights *J S Goldie* 87
2 b f Primo Valentino(IRE) —Harrken Heights (IRE) (Belmez (USA))
(952) 1580[4] 2134[2]

Primondo (IRE) *A W Carroll* a68 68
5 b g Montjeu(IRE) —Tagiki (IRE) (Doyoun)
354[7] 617[10] (Dead)

Primos Dream *Ollie Pears* a24
2 b g Primo Valentino(IRE) —Compton Amber (Puissance)
7000[10] 7122[6]

Primo Way *I Semple* a76 87
6 b g Primo Dominie—Waypoint (Cadeaux Genereux)
256[4] 1490[6] 1744[4] (1939) 2169[6] 2564[8] 2828[4] 3346[12] 4082[7] (4496)

Primus Inter Pares (IRE) *N Wilson* a74
6 b g Sadler's Wells(USA) —Life At The Top (Habitat)
451[7]

Prince Afram *R M Beckett* 55
2 b c Fraam—Miletrian Cares (IRE) (Hamas (IRE))
5003[7]

Prince Among Men *N G Richards* 57
10 b g Robellino(USA) —Forelino (USA) (Trempolino (USA))
1888[4] 5087[10]

Prince Charlemagne (IRE) *N P Littmoden* a86 87
4 br g King Charlemagne(USA) —Ciubanga (IRE) (Arazi (USA))
95[5] 340[5] 444[4] 501[4] 652[6] 726[5] 1356[5] 1591[8] 2003[8] 2987[8]

Prince Dayjur (USA) *J Pearce* a81 10
8 bb g Dayjur(USA) —Distinct Beauty (USA) (Phone Trick (USA))
44[8] 211[11] 359[6] 455[3] 533[5] 673[2] 770[5] 3922[7] 4595[10]

Prince Desire (IRE) *B W Hills* 77
2 b c Fasliyev(USA) —No Quest (IRE) (Rainbow Quest (USA))
2424[9] 3095[7] 4192[6] 4776[6] 5251[8] (5749) 5974[20]

Prince Des Neiges (FR) *M R Hoad* a57 81
4 b g Milford Track(IRE) —Miss Smith (FR) (Grand Lodge (USA))
564[9] 1368[2] 2084[2] 2140[2] 2511[4] 2715[2] 3047[10] 4067[8] 4473[2] 5886[RR] 7120[10]

Prince Erik *D K Weld* 105
3 gr g Indian Ridge—Miracle (Ezzoud (IRE))
3142a[6] 4647a[6]

Prince Evelith (GER) *G A Swinbank* 87
4 b g Dashing Blade—Peace Time (GER) (Surumu (GER))
2452[5] 2822[3] 2986[2] 3346[8] 4039[4]

Prince Fasliyev *H-A Pantall* 103
3 b c Fasliyev(USA) —Malaisienne (FR) (Saumarez)
6071a[11]

Prince Flori (GER) *S Smrczek* 122
4 b h Lando(GER) —Princess Liberte (GER) (Nebos (GER))
1190a[3] (1872a) 2925a[3] 3942[7] 5077a[7] 6353a[4]

Prince Forever (IRE) *M A Jarvis* 105
3 b c Giant's Causeway(USA) —Routilante (IRE) (Rousillon (USA))
2043[3]

Prince Golan (IRE) *K A Ryan* 94
3 b c Golan(IRE) —Mohican Princess (Shirley Heights)
1790[6] 2862[6] 3495[8] 3919[6] 6999[12]

Prince Hamlet (IRE) *B Smart* a74
2 b c Fantastic Light(USA) —Hamsaat Hi Haat (USA) (Hennessy (USA))
6903[3] (7152)

Prince Kalamoun (IRE) *G A Swinbank* 71
2 ch g Desert Prince(IRE) —Grenouillere (USA) (Alysheba (USA))
3951[3] 4578[2] 4930[4] 5294[4]

Princelet (IRE) *N J Henderson* 90
5 b g Desert Prince(IRE) —Soeur Ti (FR) (Kaldoun (FR))
(1654) 2736[7]

Prince Livius (IRE) *B P Galvin* a61 77
4 ch g Titus Livius(FR) —Lisa's Pride (IRE) (Pips Pride)
4836a[2] 6916a[14]

Princely Green (IRE) *I A Wood* a48 41
2 b g Princely Heir(IRE) —Greenmount Lady (IRE) (Mac's Imp (USA))
2911[4] 3392[3]

Princely Hero (IRE) *D K Weld* 85
3 b g Royal Applause—Dalu (IRE) (Dancing Brave (USA))
5696a[2]

Princely Royal *J J Bridger* a33 57
3 b g Prince Sabo—Premium Princess (Distant Relative)
1248[10] 1346[11] 1782[12] 2276[6]

Princely Ted (IRE) *D Burchell* a62 62
6 b g Princely Heir(IRE) —Just Out (IRE) (Bluebird (USA))
3428[2] 3616[DSQ] 4267[3] (4972) 5000[6] 5424[6] 5569[6] 6027[3] 6196[12] (6697) 6961[5]

Princely Vale (IRE) *W G M Turner* a22 57
5 b g Princely Heir(IRE) —Lomalou (IRE) (Lightning Dealer)
1899[2] 2104[10] 2806[5] 3636[7] 4471[7] 5090[14]

Prince Namid *Mrs A Duffield* a80 100
5 b g Namid—Fen Princess (IRE) (Trojan Fen)
1363[10] 1788[4] 2237[2] 2566[10] 3050[6] 3298[7] 3557[4] 3762[3] 3953[7] 4367[4] 6381[14] 6560[7] 6701[5]

Prince Noel *N Wilson* a73 57
3 b g Dr Fong(USA) —Baileys On Line (Shareef Dancer (USA))
974[13] 1266[4] 1712[2] 2203[5] 2248[6] 3611[9] 4354[6] 4920[2] 5553[5] 5739[5] (5967) (6315) 6627[3] (6695) (6837) 6885[2]

Prince Nureyev (IRE) *B R Millman* a85 86
7 b g Desert King(IRE) —Annaletta (Belmez (USA))
501[10] 726[4] 1149[7] 1543[2] 2403[4] 2634[4] 3385[2] 4572[10] 5225[13]

Prince Of Charm (USA) *R A Teal* a72 73
3 ch g Mizzen Mast(USA) —Pretty Clear (USA) (Mr Prospector (USA))
737[3] 843[3] 1247[13] 1634[14] (2545) 3167[6] 3646[12] 7099[7]

Prince Of Delphi *R M Beckett* a74 75
4 b h Royal Applause—Princess Athena (Ahonoora)
1501[2] 2088[9] 5510[2] 6122[2]

Prince Of Elegance *Mrs A J Perrett* a74 90
3 b c Cape Cross(IRE) —Elegant Lady (Selkirk (USA))
3334[9] 3940[16] 4092[17] 4847[13] 5360[13]

Prince Of Eulleup (TUR) *A Guven* 93
4 b h Monashee Mountain(USA) —Floria (IRE) (Petorius)
5264a[6]

Prince Of Gold *R Hollinshead* a59 52
7 b g Polar Prince(IRE) —Gold Belt (IRE) (Bellypha)
(138) 252[7] 366[2] 440[4] 801[2] 1086[7]

Prince Of Light (IRE) *M Johnston* 111
4 ch g Fantastic Light(USA) —Miss Queen (USA) (Miswaki (USA))
1184a[7] 1494[7] 2093[8] 2755[15] 2815[9]

Prince Of Medina *J R Best* a65 62
4 ch g Fraam—Medina De Rioseco (Puissance)
2006[7] 2686[3] 4030[11] 4534[6] 5007[2] 6719[10] 6832[11] 6911[4] 7120[6] (7203)

Prince Of Thebes (IRE) *J Akehurst* a71 103
6 b g Desert Prince(IRE) —Persian Walk (FR) (Persian Bold)
1145[22] 1307[3] 1651[10] 2208[7] 3001[5] 3330[13] 4049[19] 4377[8] 4851[12] 5413[4] 5833[7] 6155[2] 6301[9] 6654[4]

Prince Rossi (IRE) *J D Bethell* a57 78
3 b g Royal Applause—Miss Rossi (Artaius (USA))
1108[15] 1965[11] 2373[8] 2892[5] 3411[2] 3713[2] 4224[16] 5741[5] 6764[10] 7025[3]

Prince Sabaah (IRE) *R Hannon* a87 93
3 b c Spectrum(IRE) —Princess Sabaah (IRE) (Desert King (IRE))
(1230) 1835[10] 2506[2] 3993[2] 4483[4] 5415[2] 5830[6] 6091[5] 6473[6]

Prince Samos (IRE) *D Nicholls* a85 90
5 b g Mujadil(USA) —Sabaniya (FR) (Lashkari)
846[4] 1480[15] 1583[9] 1860[4] 2209[8] 4049[15] 4153[5] 4496[6] 4713[2] 5585[11] 6475[2]

Prince's Decree *G M Moore* 60
2 br c Diktat—Rock Face (Ballad Rock)
1859[5] 3238[8] 3833[7]

Princess Aimee *D Burchell* a47 47
7 b m Wizard King—Off The Air (IRE) (Taufan (USA))
1560[8] 3365[10] 4430[6] 5018[9] 5187[7]

Princess Arwen *Mrs Barbara Waring* a48 15
5 b m Magic Ring(IRE) —Absolutelystunning (Aragon)
339[8] 447[2] 557[8] 637[9] 686[14] 801[12] 2472[13] 2870[9] 5472[8]

Princess Augusta (USA) *A M Balding* a35 32
2 b f Silic(FR) —Tri Anytime (USA) (Tri Jet (USA))
6535[14] 7070[10] 7266[12]

Princess Charlmane (IRE) *C J Teague* 34
4 b m King Charlemagne(USA) —Bint Alreeys (Polish Precedent (USA))
2554[11] 3302[8] 4795[5]

Princess Cleo *T D Easterby* a63 74
4 ch m Mark Of Esteem(IRE) —Classy Cleo (IRE) (Mujadil (USA))
626[5] 1718[14] 1940[4] 2553[2] 2805[7] 2933[6] 4252[6] 4525[15] 4787[3] 5284[10]

Princess Cocoa (IRE) *R A Fahey* a79 79
4 b m Desert Sun—Daily Double (FR) (Unfuwain (USA))
2794[3] 3301[5] 4419 [3] 4615[2] 5814[3] (6343) 6475[5] 7002[2]

Princess Coup (AUS) *M Walker* 111
4 ch m Encosta De Lago(AUS) —Stoneyfell Road (AUS) (Sovereign Red (NZ))
6354a[3] 6712a[13]

Princess Danehill (IRE) *P F I Cole* a53 47
3 b f Indian Danehill(IRE) —A La Longue (GER) (Mtoto)
3387[11] 5390[3] 5898[8] 6704[6] 6963[11]

Princesse Dansante (IRE) *F Doumen* 107
4 b m King's Best(USA) —Vallee Dansante (USA) (Lyphard (USA))
1571a[8] 4215a[8] 4872a[7] 6030a[2]

Princess Ellis *E J Alston* 80
3 ch f Compton Place—Star Cast (IRE) (In The Wings)
894[5] 996[2] 1219[4] (1595) 1943[4] 2301[7] 2435[3] 2718[6] 3763[3] 4158[4] 4935[2] 5430[3] (5834) (5970) (6157) 6487[11]

Princess Flavia (IRE) *M Quinn* 1
3 ch f Redback—Malacca (USA) (Danzig (USA))
1541[12]

Princess Gee *B J McMath* a30 43
2 b f Reel Buddy(USA) —Queen G (USA) (Matty G (USA))
6414[10] 6763[8]

Princess Ileana (IRE) *K R Burke* a65 74
3 b f Danetime(IRE) —Uhud (IRE) (Mujtahid (USA))
1748[5] 2172[3] 2515[11] 2895[6] 3369[6]

Princess India (IRE) *P Winkworth* a72 71
2 ch f Hawk Wing(USA) —Litchfield Hills (USA) (Relaunch (USA))
2658[7] 3648[7] 4662[6] (5117) 5516a[3]

Princess Jones *J-L Guillochon* 98
7 b m Emperor Jones(USA) —Nationalvelvetgirl (Alhijaz)
1421a[7] 2100a[6] 2953a[9]

Princess Kai (IRE) *R Ingram* a49 48
6 b m Cayman Kai(IRE) —City Princess (Rock City)
143[4] 225[9] 442[10] 978[5] 2104[13] 3045[5]

Princess Kiotto *W M Brisbourne* 70
6 b m Desert King(IRE) —Ferghana Ma (Mtoto)
1598[3] 3300[4] 3584[4] 4280[5] 4576[7] (4906)

Princess Lavinia *G Wragg* a71 72
4 ch m Fraam—Affaire De Coeur (Imperial Fling (USA))
1251[3] (1521) 2008[8] 2544[4] 3451[3] (4517) 5086[5] 5559[13]

Princess Lomi (IRE) *E J O'Neill* 67
2 b f Lomitas—Athlumney Lady (Lycius (USA))
4162[3]

Princess Maria (USA) *R A Fahey* 48
2 b f Giant's Causeway(USA) —Passive Action (USA) (Double Negative (USA))
5580[8] 5903[8] 6306[11]

Princess Nala (IRE) *M Halford* 98
5 b m In The Wings—Adjisa (IRE) (Doyoun)
875a[7] 2067a[3] 3143a[11] 3664a[3]

Princess Namid (IRE) *R A Harris* 2
2 br f Namid—Banutan (IRE) (Charnwood Forest (IRE))
2488[13]

Princess Of Aeneas (IRE) *Peter Grayson* a48 60
4 b m Beckett(IRE) —Romangoddess (IRE) (Rhoman Rule (USA))
6431[13] 6835[13]

Princess Palatine (IRE) *K R Burke* a63 67
3 b f Iron Mask(USA) —Kitty Kildare (USA) (Seattle Dancer (USA))
908[4] 1238[12] 2905[11] 3605[10]

Princess Rhianna (IRE) *Mrs G S Rees* a59 66
2 ch f Fath(USA) —Persian Sally (IRE) (Persian Bold)
4522[2] 4924[8] (6072) 6388[6] 6722[15]

Princess Taylor *M Botti* a77 79
3 ch f Singspiel(IRE) —Tapas En Bal (FR) (Mille Balles (FR))
3087[3] 4338[2] 4579[2] (5475) 6929[3] 7017[7]

Princess Valerina *B W Hills* a84 87
3 ch f Beat Hollow—Heart So Blue (Dilum (USA))
838[5] 1124[14] 1496[14] 2306[3] 3480[3] 4509[4] 4848[15] 6209[11] 6497[8] 6900[11]

Princess Zada *B R Millman* 72
3 ch f Best Of The Bests(IRE) —Barnacla (IRE) (Bluebird (USA))
1155[8] (2079) 2317[7] 3087[5] 3490[2] 3904[2] 4502[5] 5360[5] 5860[9]

Princess Zaha *A G Newcombe* a41 33
5 b m Zaha(CAN) —Otaru (IRE) (Indian Ridge)
2307[8] 3619[7] 7133[4]

Princess Zhukova (IRE) *R J Price* a20
2 b f Terroir(IRE) —Miss Bussell (Sabrehill (USA))
7217[6]

Prince Tamino *Saeed Bin Suroor* a95 113
4 b g Mozart(IRE) —Premiere Dance (IRE) (Loup Solitaire (USA))
324a[12] 472a[4] 547a[7] 4183[4] 4886[8]

Prince Tum Tum (USA) *D Shaw* a93 92
7 b g Capote(USA) —La Grande Epoque (USA) (Lyphard (USA))
41[2] 227[4] 307[3] 452[6]

Prince Valentine *G L Moore* a48 62
6 b g My Best Valentine—Affaire De Coeur (Imperial Fling (USA))
1118[9] 1318[6] 1740[9] 2141[6] 3149[4] 3352[7] 3615[4] 4319[2] 4469[3] 5121[3] (5708) 6607[6]

Prince Vector *A King* a90 89
5 b g Vettori(IRE) —The In-Laws (IRE) (Be My Guest (USA))
340[7] 514[6]

Prince Vettori *Mrs Norma Pook* a63 41
5 b g Vettori(IRE) —Bombalarina (IRE) (Barathea (IRE))
124[8]

Prince Woodman (USA) *B J Meehan* 105
4 bb g Woodman(USA) —Queen Mama (USA) (Seattle Slew (USA))
1657[6] 2319[9]

Prince Zafonic *Miss Gay Kelleway* 83
4 ch g Zafonic(USA) —Kite Mark (Mark Of Esteem (IRE))
2006[8] 2531[13] 2810[2] 3047[4] 3858[2] 5273[2] 5573[2] 5800[5] 6181[3]

Prinz (GER) *A Wohler* 105
3 b c Lando(GER) —Prairie Darling (Stanford)
3566a[6]

Priors Hill (IRE) *E Charpy* a86 103
4 b g Danehill(USA) —Lailati (USA) (Mr Prospector (USA))
475a[12]

Prior Warning *D Smaga* a102 107
3 ch c Barathea(IRE) —Well Warned (Warning)
(695a) 1005a[2] 2100a[8]

Priory Rock (IRE) *J S Bolger* 67
3 ch f Rock Of Gibraltar(IRE) —Priory Belle (IRE) (Priolo (USA))
4035a[10]

Private Code *B J Meehan* a65 54
2 br f Fasliyev(USA) —Aunt Pearl (USA) (Seattle Slew (USA))
942[6] 1123[8] 5309[3] 6584[7]

Private Peachey (IRE) *B R Millman* a69 72
3 b g Shinko Forest(IRE) —Adamas (IRE) (Fairy King (USA))
893[10] 1154[8] (1432) 1538[2] 2079[3] (2489) 2668[4] 4313[P] (Dead)

Private Reason (USA) *K A Ryan* a66 73
3 b c Red Ransom(USA) —Sultry Lass (USA) (Private Account (USA))
2464[5] 3170[5] 3640[10]

Private Soldier *N J Vaughan* a59 34
4 gr g Dansili—Etienne Lady (IRE) (Imperial Frontier (USA))
4000[9] 4258[8] 4492[4] (5606) 5756[3] 5782[3]

Prize Fighter (IRE) *H R A Cecil* a48 87
5 b g Desert Sun—Papal (Selkirk (USA))
444[8] 1356[7] 1862[8] (2660) 3242[4] 4184[3] 4814[5] 5052[2]

Procrastinate (IRE) *R F Fisher* a47 52
5 ch g Rossini(USA) —May Hinton (Main Reef)
364[7] 1744[3] 2709[7] 2937[10] 4250[8] 5479[6] 5782[4]

Professor Twinkle *W J Knight* a76 70
3 ch c Dr Fong(USA) —Shining High (Shirley Heights)
196[4] (460) 591[2] 638[5] 1247[10] 1722[6] 2748[2] 3400[6] 3877[4] 5454[9] 5943[8] 6547[9]

Profound Beauty (IRE) *D K Weld* 106
3 b f Danehill(USA) —Diamond Trim (IRE) (Highest Honor (FR))
3576a[5]

Prohibit *J H M Gosden* a77 82
2 b c Oasis Dream—Well Warned (Warning)
5222[2] 5498[6] (5910)

Project Dane (IRE) *L Polito* 103
3 ch c Dane Friendly—Sweet College (IRE) (College Chapel)
1336a[6]

Project Sunshine (GER) *C P Morlock* a59 64
4 b g Xaar—Prada (GER) (Lagunas)
3217[13]

Promised Gold *J A Geake* 59
2 ch g Bahamian Bounty—Delphic Way (Warning)
5918[16] 6417[9] 6592[9]

Promising Lead *Sir Michael Stoute* 116
3 b f Danehill(USA) —Arrive (Kahyasi)
(1128) 1824[2] 3028[4] (4503) 6042a[2]

Propaganda (IRE) *L M Cumani* a64 67
3 b f Sadler's Wells(USA) —Pearly Shells (Efisio)
2970[3] 3847[5] 5859[U] 6275[3] 6745[2] 6959[2] 7199[2]

Proper (IRE) *M R Channon* a71 80
3 b g Rossini(USA) —Pardoned (IRE) (Mujadil (USA))
199[6] 312[4] 725[5] 935[2] (1316) (1424) 1603[8] 1978[6] 2243[11] 3350[8] (3646) 3851[4] 4276[8] 4884[6] 5122[6] 5203[8] 5508[7] 5819[9] 6055[4] 6148[5] 6455[2]

Proper Article (IRE) *Miss J E Foster* a61 68
5 b g Definite Article—Feather 'n Lace (IRE) (Green Desert (USA))
74[4] 453[4] 7004[12]

Propinquity *Liam McAteer* 94
5 b g Primo Dominie—Lydia Maria (Dancing Brave (USA))
3138a[8]

Prop Me Up (USA) *G Sacco* a109 109
5 ch m Reparations(USA) —Natural Prop (USA) (Proper Reality (USA))
6512a[12]

Proponent (IRE) *R Charlton* 97
3 b g Peintre Celebre(USA) —Pont Audemer (USA) (Chief's Crown (USA))
1790[5] 4092[7] 5141[4] 5615[6]

Proposal *A W Carroll* a43 56
3 b f Tobougg(IRE) —Patiala (IRE) (Nashwan (USA))
1205[11] 1972[3] 2362[4] 3177[4] 3652[3]

Prospect Court *A C Whillans* a37 83
5 ch g Pivotal—Scierpan (USA) (Sharpen Up)
1379[7] 1597[8] 2256[5] 2711[2] (3053) (3259) (3557) (3886) 5806[7] 6363a[14] 6639[4]

Prospect Place *M Dods* a17 85
3 b g Compton Place—Encore My Love (Royal Applause)
1298[10] 1577[7] 1994[4] 2171[3] 2821[6] 3061[5] 3278[5] 3885[9] 4934[8] 5662[12]

Protector (SAF) *Miss Gay Kelleway* a94 109
6 b g Kilconnel(USA) —Mufski (SAF) (Al Mufti (USA))
(105a) 415a[8] 542a[7] 2858[8] (3089) 3500[2] 4150[9]

Prototype *P Bary* 90
3 b f Beat Hollow—Tuning (Rainbow Quest (USA))
989a[9]

Proudance (GER) *R Suerland* 109
5 b h Tannenkonig(IRE) —Proudeyes (GER) (Dashing Blade)
881a[8]

Proud Boris (GER) *J Hanacek* 96
3 b c Silvano(GER) —Parista (Armistice Day)
5821a[5]

Proudinsky (GER) *R J Frankel* 108
4 b h Silvano(GER) —Proudeyes (GER) (Dashing Blade)
6924a[3]

Proud Killer *J R Jenkins* a71 73
4 b g Killer Instinct—Thewaari (USA) (Eskimo (USA))
2719[8] 3388[10] 4594[2] 4767[8] (6083) 6239[9] 7179[4]

Proud Linus (USA) *D Carroll* 94
2 b c Proud Citizen(USA) —Radcliffe Yard (USA) (Boston Harbor (USA))
4724[4] 5975[9]

Proud Scholar (USA) *M A Magnusson* a59 58
5 br m Royal Academy(USA) —Proud Fact (USA) (Known Fact (USA))
369[7] 496[8] 5179[4] 5389[10]

Proud Spell (USA) *J Larry Jones* a107
2 b f Proud Citizen(USA) —Pacific Spell (USA) (Langfuhr (CAN))
6507a[2]

Provence *B W Hills* 86
2 b f Averti(IRE) —Prowse (USA) (King Of Kings (IRE))
5949[4] 6295[3] 6535[2]

Provision *A M Balding* 61
2 ch f Cadeaux Genereux—Brand (Shareef Dancer (USA))
5633[7]

Proviso *A Fabre* 113
2 b f Dansili—Binche (USA) (Woodman (USA))
(4626a) 5796[2]

Provost *M Johnston* 86
3 ch g Danehill Dancer(IRE) —Dixielake (IRE) (Lake Coniston (IRE))
(977)

Prunes *A Berry* a50 59
2 ch f Cadeaux Genereux—Sahara Shade (USA) (Shadeed (USA))
1858[3] 2138[5] 5477[4] 5644[3] 5837[6] 5932[4] 6075[8] 6305[3] 6566[9] 6635[4] 6881[9] 7021[9] 7044[5]

Prussian (USA) *W Mott* 98
2 b c Danzig(USA) —Crystal Downs (USA) (Alleged (USA))
6484a^{10}

P. S. U. Grad (USA) *Craig Dollase* a91
2 bb f Harlan's Holiday(USA) —Lo Cal Bread (USA) (Native Prospector (USA))
5826a^{10}

Psychic Star *Miss Lucinda V Russell* a72 86
4 b m Diktat—Southern Psychic (USA) (Alwasmi (USA))
1455^5 1626^6 1890^7

Psycho Cat *S T Lewis* a42 62
4 b g Hunting Lion(IRE) —Canadian Capers (Ballacashtal (CAN))
142^{10} 2225^9 2656^{14}

Ptarmigan Ridge *Miss L A Perratt* 84
11 b h Sea Raven(IRE) —Panayr (Faraway Times (USA))
957^5 1299^5 1941^7 2244^5 2461^6 2866^8 3014^3 3374^2 3536^4 4498^5 4703^7

Public Eye *L A Dace* a44 54
6 b g Zafonic(USA) —Stardom (Known Fact (USA))
133^8 187^9

Public Forum *Doug Watson* a81 99
5 b h Rainbow Quest(USA) —Valentine Girl (Alzao (USA))
401a^9

Puggy (IRE) *R A Kvisla* 102
3 b f Mark Of Esteem(IRE) —Jakarta (IRE) (Machiavellian (USA))
1146^{13} 1496^8 2207^7 2814^{11} 4118^{12} 4639^5

Pugnacious Lady *J W Hills* a55 66
3 b f Hernando(FR) —Simacota (GER) (Acatenango (GER))
1784^2 2436^5 2981^3 4809^6 *5388^{11}* 5938^{10} *6430^3*

Pugnacity *S C Williams* a36 48
3 b f Zilzal(USA) —Attention Seeker (USA) (Exbourne (USA))
208^{12} 1841^{13} *2951^7* 3057^6 3274^2

Puissant Princess (IRE) *J W Hills* a66 64
3 bb f Rock Of Gibraltar(IRE) —Toroca (USA) (Nureyev (USA))
1447^{10} 1961^7 2472^7 *3393^2 4064^{10}* 4684^{10} 5348^5

Pukka Tique *Miss J S Davis* a61 68
4 b g Groom Dancer(USA) —Surf Bird (Shareef Dancer (USA))
204^7 443^4 4463^{11}

Pull The Plug (USA) *Rod Collet* 90
2 b f Pulpit(USA) —Margay (IRE) (Marju (IRE))
6525a^4 6888a^{10}

Pulsate *Mrs A J Perrett* 52
3 ch f Inchinor—Salanka (IRE) (Persian Heights)
2429^8 2944^8 3447^{10}

Pulse *Miss J R Tooth* a50 51
9 b g Salse(USA) —French Gift (Cadeaux Genereux)
46^4 201^4 1080^9 1405^{12} 1885^{16} 2966^4

Punching *Eve Johnson Houghton* a65 60
3 b g Kyllachy—Candescent (Machiavellian (USA))
1143^{16} 1501^4 1923^{13} 2631^7 *2799^{11}* 5270^4 5714^3 *6123^{13} 6339^5 (6608) 6747^5 6779^6 7082^5*

Punisher (FR) *S Loeuillet* a93 90
3 ch c Until Sundown(USA) —Fitness Queen (USA) (Gilded Time (USA))
695a^5

Punta Galera (IRE) *Paul Green* a91 91
4 br g Zafonic(USA) —Kobalt Sea (FR) (Akarad (FR))
1356^{12} *1524^{13}* 2218^7 2512^{12} 3076^3 3241^4 3530^5 3971^8 4353^{11} *6883^2 7046^3 7132^3 7249^6*

Purde (NZ) *D Hayes* 109
4 br m Bahhare(USA) —Dupre (NZ) (Masterclass (USA))
15a^{10}

Pure Bluff (IRE) *Saeed Bin Suroor* a70 69
3 ch c Indian Ridge—Agnetha (GER) (Big Shuffle (USA))
595a^4

Pure Imagination (IRE) *J M Bradley* a75 79
6 ch g Royal Academy(USA) —Ivory Bride (Domynsky)
1060^2

Pure Passion (IRE) *A Maggi* 89
3 b c Tobougg(IRE) —Celtic Wing (Midyan (USA))
1336a^{14}

Pure Scandal *M W Easterby* a53 49
2 b g Barathea(IRE) —Sharena (IRE) (Kahyasi)
4725^{12} *5337^{13} 5680^9*

Pure Velvet (IRE) *S Kirk* a48 46
3 b f Mull Of Kintyre(USA) —Velvet Slipper (Muhtafal (USA))
2196^9 2620^8 *2951^5 5728^8 6097^6 6361^5 6505^{11}*

Purim (USA) *T Proctor* a97 116
5 bb h Dynaformer(USA) —Kirsteena (USA) (Lord At War (ARG))
6511a^{11}

Puro (CZE) *M Weiss* 53
5 ch g Rainbows For Life(CAN) —Pulnoc (CZE) (Shy Groom (USA))
494a^2

Purple Emperor (USA) *Saeed Bin Suroor* 95
3 b c Red Ransom(USA) —Checkerspot (USA) (Affirmed (USA))
2005^2 2402^2 (3151) 4147^5

Purple Moon (IRE) *L M Cumani* 120
4 ch g Galileo(IRE) —Vanishing Prairie (USA) (Alysheba (USA))
2815^4 (4117) (4722) 6354a^6 6712a^2

Purple Ransom (IRE) *I A Wood* a32 55
2 b g Intikhab(USA) —Brittas Blues (IRE) (Blues Traveller (IRE))
1033^6 2604^{10} 2961^4 4198^{10}

Purple Sands (IRE) *J Hetherton* a54 43
3 b g Desert Prince(IRE) —Violet Spring (IRE) (Exactly Sharp (USA))
535^{11} 713^{13}

Purus (IRE) *R A Teal* a77 93
5 b g Night Shift(USA) —Pariana (USA) (Bering)
102^{10} 191^9 1431^5 1845^{13} *1931^3* (2414) (2965) 3525^3 4049^{14} 5712^3 6013^5 6301^5 (6651)

Pusey Street Lady *J Gallagher* a81 89
3 b f Averti(IRE) —Pusey Street Girl (Gildoran)
1037^5 (1541) (2363) 3059^3 3746^6 *4360^8* 4639^4 5403^9 5584^{14}

Puskas (IRE) *J M Bradley* a54 84
4 b g King's Best(USA) —Chiquita Linda (IRE) (Mujadil (USA))
1464^6 *1754^{10}* 2461^3 2673^6 3179^4 3594^{12} 4103^9 4233^{12} 5009^{11} 5726^{10} 5909^U 6287^8 *6870^7 7011^7*

Pussycat Bow *M W Easterby* 7
2 ch f Bertolini(USA) —Bow Peep (IRE) (Shalford (IRE))
1919^{12} 2904^{13} 3297^5

Put It On The Card *J S Wainwright* a66 57
3 ch r Bertolini(USA) —Madame Jones (IRE) (Lycius (USA))
108^2 (295) (335) 478^3 1238^{11} 5834^{10} 6256^9 *7006^{10} 7209^7*

Putney Bridge (USA) *Mme C Head-Maarek* 103
2 b c Mizzen Mast(USA) —Valentine Band (USA) (Dixieland Band (USA))
6782a^3

Putra Laju (IRE) *J W Hills* a74 51
3 b c Trans Island—El Corazon (IRE) (Mujadil (USA))
1247^{12} 2133^{13} 4111^{13} 4960^{11} *5424^{10}* 5862^7 *6226^2 6567^2 6874^3 (7047)*

Putra Square *P F I Cole* a83 87
3 b g Cadeaux Genereux—Razzle (IRE) (Green Desert (USA))
939^6 1093^2 1293^7 1605^4 2231^{13} *5816^3 6211^2*

Puy D'Arnac (FR) *G A Swinbank* 62
4 b g Acteur Francais(USA) —Chaumeil (FR) (Mad Captain)
5482^6 5738^8

Puzzle Book (USA) *M Kettle* a38 63
3 b f Distant View(USA) —Questonia (Rainbow Quest (USA))
527a^4 595a^5

Pyro (USA) *S Asmussen* a113
2 bb c Pulpit(USA) —Wild Vision (USA) (Wild Again (USA))
6508a^2

Qaasi (USA) *M Brittain* a63 71
5 ch g Rahy(USA) —Recording (USA) (Danzig (USA))
12^4 286^{13} 369^2 482^4 2764^2 2890^4 3677^4 3888^5 4179^6 *4670^6* 5486^8 5626^5 *6069^9*

Qadar (IRE) *N P Littmoden* a109 100
5 b g Xaar—Iktidar (Green Desert (USA))
(41) 118^4 (198) 307^2 344^3 490^5 551^3 660^2 762^7 828^2 1647a^6 4150^{25} 4567^6 4990^{10} 5407^9 *6003^3* 6197^3 *7255^5*

Qasayed (USA) *C E Brittain* a58
2 b f Diesis—Bright And Cheery (USA) (Event Of The Year (USA))
5309^5

Qatar Way (GR) *P R Chamings* a31 23
3 ch f Harmonic Way—Sea Shell (IRE) (Unfuwain (USA))
1587^8 2541^9 *6830^7*

Quaglino Way (GR) *P R Chamings* a64 65
3 b g Mark Of Esteem(IRE) —Pringipessa's Way (Machiavellian (USA))
2625^{10} 4457^9 4666^5 6063^9 *6229^3 (6457)*

Quai Du Roi (IRE) *D Nicholls* a82 89
5 ch g Desert King(IRE) —Emly Express (IRE) (High Estate)
657^8 765^3 969^4 1040^{RR} 4566^{19} *(5184a)* 5585^{RR}

Quaker Boy *A C Whillans* 60
4 b g Agnes World(USA) —La Brise (IRE) (Llandaff (USA))
2298^{12} 3017^{13} 3347^{17}

Qualify *Miss Sheena West* 74
4 b g Mark Of Esteem(IRE) —Raneen Alwatar (Sadler's Wells (USA))
4708^3 5539^2

Qualitair Wings *J Hetherton* a65 66
8 b g Colonel Collins(USA) —Semperflorens (Don)
1627^5 1819^5 2006^4

Quality Son (ITY) *V Oriani* 103
6 b h Shantou(USA) —Quack Secret (USA) (Secreto (USA))
5821a^{11} 6518a^6

Quality Street *P Butler* a79 83
5 ch m Fraam—Pusey Street Girl (Gildoran)
91^2 236^2 361^{10} 1991^6 2217^7 *3190^3 (3396) (3852)* 4024^4 *4965^6 5119^8* 5381^9

Quam Celerrime *P A Blockley* a76 97
2 b c Xaar—Divine Secret (Hernando (FR))
5200^5 5680^2 (6080) 6631a^7

Quantum Leap *S Dow* a74 78
10 b g Efisio—Prejudice (Young Generation)
28^7 556^7 614^7 1666^2 (1787) *1931^6* 2272^2 2414^3 2546^5 3101^8 3350^{11} *4394^7* 4688^3 *4884^{12}* 5687^7 *5900^{11} (6587) (6825) 7085^2 7269^{10}*

Quaroma *Jane Chapple-Hyam* 69
2 ch f Pivotal—Quiz Time (Efisio)
6595^3 (6721)

Quarrymaster (IRE) *J Howard Johnson* 50
2 b g Captain Rio—Partenza (USA) (Red Ransom (USA))
1454^5 2247^8 4350^9

Que Beauty (IRE) *R C Guest* 26
2 b f Val Royal(FR) —Ardbess (Balla Cove)
5745^{15} 6087^{14} 6384^{12}

Quebec Citizen (BRZ) *Saeed Bin Suroor* a91 59
4 b h Know Heights(IRE) —Importanza (BRZ) (Basim (USA))
410a^{10}

Queen Althea (IRE) *Noel Meade* 72
3 b f Bach(IRE) —Countess Marengo (IRE) (Revoque (IRE))
6555a^2

Queen Be *I W McInnes* 29
2 ch f First Trump—Madam Zando (Forzando)
3245^{10} 3681^8 4026^8

Queen Excalibur *C Roberts* a21
8 ch m Sabrehill(USA) —Blue Room (Gorytus (USA))
2946^9

Queen Jock (USA) *Tracey Collins* a86 91
2 b f Repent(USA) —My Special K'S (USA) (Tabasco Cat (USA))
3438a^3 5073a^7 *6161a^7*

Queen Noverre (IRE) *J W Hills* a77 82
3 b f Noverre(USA) —Tafrah (IRE) (Sadler's Wells (USA))
2601^7 *3646^{13}* (4079) *4429^5 5178^3* (5539) *6145^{10}*

Queen Of Diamonds (IRE) *Mrs K Walton* a38 48
4 b m Fruits Of Love(USA) —Royal Jubilee (IRE) (King's Theatre (IRE))
907^5 1032^{10}

Queen Of France (USA) *David Wachman* 93
3 b f Danehill(USA) —Hidden Storm (USA) (Storm Cat (USA))
5998a^6

Queen Of Naples *J H M Gosden* 99
2 b f Singspiel(IRE) —Napoleon's Sister (IRE) (Alzao (USA))
5596^2 6040a^7 6652^3

Queen Of Stars (FR) *M Delzangles* 86
4 br m Fly To The Stars—Piuazza Caballini (FR) (Stay For Lunch (USA))
6137a^7 6953a^0

Queen's Best *Sir Michael Stoute* a93 110
4 b m King's Best(USA) —Cloud Castle (In The Wings)
1449^3 2123^2 2720^2 (4203) (4826) 5396a^2 6168^2

Queen Scarlet (IRE) *B J Meehan* 93
2 b f Redback—Hill Hopper (IRE) (Danehill (USA))
(3706) 4400^4 (Dead)

Queen's Composer (IRE) *B Smart* a41 79
4 b g Mozart(IRE) —Queen Leonor (IRE) (Caerleon (USA))
1747^{17} 3764^7 4137^8 6088^8 6463^6

Queen's Echo *P Monteith* a36 68
6 b m Wizard King—Sunday News'N'Echo (USA) (Trempolino (USA))
1527^2 1711^2 1944^3 2168^7 2388^9 6638^8

Queensgate *M Blanshard* a59 58
3 b f Compton Place—Ring Queen (USA) (Fairy King (USA))
1022^{10} *1346^{10}* 1766^{13} 3667^8

Queen's Lodge (IRE) *I W McInnes* 65
7 ch m Grand Lodge(USA) —Manilia (FR) (Kris)
3158^8 3686^7 4029^{14}

Queens Mantle *P J Makin* a54 28
2 b f Bold Edge—Queen Shirley (IRE) (Fairy King (USA))
5868^{12} *6225^9 6425^6 6813^4 7071^3*

Queens Quay *R Hannon* 46
3 b f Grand Lodge(USA) —Nirvana (Marju (IRE))
1560^7 1784^9 2105^{11}

Queen's Speech (IRE) *J H M Gosden* a62
2 bb f Medicean—Jazan (IRE) (Danehill (USA))
6611^5

Queen's Treasure (IRE) *M P Tregoning* a11 46
2 b f Bahamian Bounty—Daltak (Night Shift (USA))
2316^8 4014^9 4500^{12}

Quel Fontenailles (FR) *L A Dace* a39
9 b g Tel Quel(FR) —Sissi Fontenailles (FR) (Pampabird)
496^{14} 617^9 677^8

Quelle Amore (GER) *A Wohler* 106
4 b m Monsun(GER) —Qelle Amie (CAN) (Beau Genius (CAN))
1421a^{12}

Querglas Bere (FR) *Robert Collet* a80 80
3 gr c Verglas(IRE) —Ajab Alzamaan (Rainbow Quest (USA))
695a^8

Quest For Honor *A Fabre* 106
3 gr c Highest Honor(FR) —Quest For Ladies (Rainbow Quest (USA))
963a^4 (1736a) 2293a^{13} 4627a^F

Quest For Success (IRE) *R A Fahey* 85
2 b c Noverre(USA) —Divine Pursuit (Kris)
2984^3 3781^3 4378^2 4743^{13} 5324^{13} (5931)

Quetzalcoatl (IRE) *John Joseph Murphy* a64 69
2 b c Efisio—Be Thankfull (IRE) (Linamix (FR))
3438a^{16}

Quezon Sun (GER) *S Wattel* a73 99
4 br m Monsun(GER) —Quezon City (GER) (Law Society (USA))
1421a^{11}

Quicklime *Jamie Poulton* a21
3 b f Gorse—Linden Grace (USA) (Mister Baileys)
3948^6 *5494^{11}*

Quick Off The Mark *J G Given* a64 46
2 b f Dr Fong(USA) —Equity Princess (Warning)
3404^3 4125^8

Quick Release (IRE) *D M Simcock* a82 78
2 b c Red Ransom(USA) —Set The Mood (USA) (Dixie Brass (USA))
2575^2 (4192) 5004^7 5691^4 *6644^3*

Quick Sands (IRE) *R Hannon* 70
2 b f Redback—Winning Note (IRE) (Victory Note (USA))
1101^8 1533^5 2969^4 3446^2 4202^2 4501^7 5443^3 5871^{12} 6233^8

Quicks The Word *T A K Cuthbert* a28 63
7 b g Sri Pekan(USA) —Fast Tempo (IRE) (Statoblest)
1596^3 2563^8 2711^3 (3345) 3787^8 4706^5 (5284) 5935^9

Quicuyo (GER) *P Monteith* 48
4 ch g Acatenango(GER) —Quila (IRE) (Unfuwain (USA))
3015^9 3678^4 4156^8 4380^7 5586^5

Quidor Way (GR) *P R Chamings* 26
3 br g Harmonic Way—Jollity Way (GR) (Wadood (USA))
3651^8

Quiet Elegance *E J Alston* 75
2 b f Fantastic Light(USA) —Imperial Bailiwick (IRE) (Imperial Frontier (USA))
(6105)

Quietly Mine (USA) *Christophe Clement* 107
3 ch g Belong To Me(USA) —Quiet (CAN) (Roar (USA))
6375a^2

Quiet Reading (USA) *M R Bosley* a62 32
10 b g Northern Flagship(USA) —Forlis Key (USA) (Forli (ARG))
80^7

Quiet Times (IRE) *K A Ryan* a94 64
8 ch g Dolphin Street(FR) —Super Times (Sayf El Arab (USA))
81^8 198^9 419^5 452^5 (536) 710^3 766^7 1163^{RR} 6735^2 6891^2 7108^3

Quijano (GER) *P Schiergen* 122
5 ch g Acatenango(GER) —Quila (IRE) (Unfuwain (USA))
(248a) (412a) (598a) 861a^7 3665a^{10} (5077a) 6374a^3 7090a^2

Quince (IRE) *J Pearce* a93 90
4 b g Fruits Of Love(USA) —Where's Charlotte (Sure Blade (USA))
362^2 488^2 608^4 698^2 940^{11} 1477^7 2003^4 2397^6 *3112^4* 6014^{13} 6490^{13}

Quinmaster (USA) *M Halford* 114
5 gr g Linamix(FR) —Sherkiya (IRE) (Goldneyev (USA))
1184a^4 1696a^4 4051a^{16} 4237a^8

Quirina *J H M Gosden* 70
2 b f Red Ransom(USA) —Qirmazi (USA) (Riverman (USA))
6648^4

Quiron (IRE) *Carmen Bocskai* 107
6 b g Desert King(IRE) —Quebra (GER) (Surumu (GER))
(355a) 493a^2

Quite A Splash (USA) *S Curran* a31 62
3 b g Smart Strike(CAN) —Easy Sunshine (IRE) (Sadler's Wells (USA))
1011^{15} 1204^9 1560^{10} 2105^{12} 2796^8 *5945^{12} 6096^{13}*

Quito (IRE) *D W Chapman* a107 119
10 b r Machiavellian(USA) —Qirmazi (USA) (Riverman (USA))
1102^7 1656^6 1770^{11} 2396^4 2857^{17} 3506^{16}

Quorn Master *Mrs P Ford* a47
5 b g Bal Harbour—Queen Of The Quorn (Governor General)
5915^{15} *6385^8*

Quorum (GER) *M Al Muhairi* a94 38
4 b h Acatenango(GER) —Quest Of Fire (FR) (Rainbow Quest (USA))
329a^2 532a^6 598a^{11}

Quotation *Sir Michael Stoute* 75
2 b f Medicean—Eloquent (Polar Falcon (USA))
4564^2 6411^4

Qwertyuiop (IRE) *K J Burke* a19 10
2 ch c Noverre(USA) —French River (Bering)
2911^6 *3171^{11}*

Raaqia *B J Meehan* 34
2 b f Sakhee(USA) —Crown Water (USA) (Chief's Crown (USA))
6411^{12}

Rabatash (USA) *David Wachman* 108
3 bb c Johannesburg(USA) —Attasliyah (IRE) (Marju (IRE))
1047a^{10}

Rabbit *M Sheppard* a38 46
6 b m Muhtarram(USA) —Ninia (USA) (Affirmed (USA))
4544^{10}

Rabbit Fighter (IRE) *D Shaw* a80 91
3 ch c Observatory(USA) —Furnish (Green Desert (USA))
(745) 1106^{10} 3299^5 3556^8 *5223^{12} 5568^{11} 5985^{10} 6455^9 6764^2 6869^3 6993^2 7025^6 (7119) (7183)*

Rabbit Montjeu (IRE) *V Luka Jr* 57
3 b f Montjeu(IRE) —Iles Piece (Shirley Heights)
6046a^9

Rabeera *A M Balding* 66
2 b f Beat Hollow—Gai Bulga (Kris)
5596^7

Raccoon (IRE) *D W Chapman* 86
7 b g Raphane(USA) —Kunucu (IRE) (Bluebird (USA))
(1405) (1557) 1640^{12} 1806^5 (2244) 2461^4 2866^9 3749^5 4095^5 4379^2 (4561) 5029^{13} 5297^8 5740^3 6020^8

Race Driver (IRE) *E Leenders* a81 81
2 ch f Domedriver(IRE) —Remedy (Pivotal)
7048a^2

Racer Forever (USA) *J H M Gosden* a110 113
4 b g Rahy(USA) —Ras Shaikh (USA) (Sheikh Albadou)
1448^3 2817^8 3505^5 3941^2 4747^3 5112^7 5359^4 6018^6

Race The Moon (IRE) *V Smith* a69 66
2 b c Danetime(IRE) —Arbitration (IRE) (Bigstone (IRE))
2056^7 3037^7 3270^7 3909^6 4584^{12} *5896^3 (6150)*

Racey Rachel (IRE) *E F Vaughan* a39 44
2 b f Marju(IRE) —Paris Song (IRE) (Peintre Celebre (USA))
4537^9 *5201^8* 5869^5 6591^9 *6865^9 6958^7*

Racie Gracie *John Berry* 53
2 gr f Dr Fong(USA) —Maxizone (FR) (Linamix (FR))
5595^9 6295^{14}

Racinger (FR) *F Head* 118
4 b h Spectrum(IRE) —Dibenoise (FR) (Kendor (FR))
(897a) (1389a) 2735^6 3523^7 6031a^2

Racing Stripes (IRE) *K O Cunningham-Brown* a65 77
3 ch g Night Shift(USA) —Swan Lake (IRE) (Waajib)
1270^4 *6406^{11} 6996^{11} 7164^{14}*

Racing Times *W J Knight* a76 74
3 b g Danetime(IRE) —Cartesian (Shirley Heights)
27^4 76^2 752^3 1117^6 4163^9

Radhakunda *S Billeri* 82
2 b f Galileo(IRE) —Nawasib (IRE) (Warning)
6047a^8

Radiator Rooney (IRE) *Patrick Morris* a69 68
4 br g Elnadim(USA) —Queen Of The May (IRE) (Nicolotte)
47^8 361^3 467^8 4478^2 4494^{10} *6344^7 7024^5 7206^4*

Radical Views *B W Hills* a89 76
3 ch g Machiavellian(USA) —Nawaiet (USA) (Zilzal (USA))
1062[7] (1978) 2577[4] 3495[6] 4603[8] 6435[12]

Raffaas *M P Tregoning* a93 85
3 b g Green Desert(USA) —Felawnah (USA) (Mr Prospector (USA))
(2445) (3189) 4059[7] 4570[4]

Rafferty (IRE) *S Dow* a65 58
8 ch g Lion Cavern(USA) —Badawi (USA) (Diesis)
138[2] 359[10] 455[2] 497[7] 681[6] 830[7] 1344[7] 1720[7] 1933[4] 2179[3] 2331[5] 2591[3] 2798[3] 2990[8] 3241[6] 3428[13] 3730[11] 6268[9] 6587[5] 6831[4] 6873[6] 6950[6] 7188[6]

Raffish *M Scudamore* a40 74
5 ch g Atraf—Valadon (High Line)
1924[5] (3280) 3467[2] (3888) 4124[5] 4544[2]

Ragad *W Jarvis* a69 8
4 b h Alhaarth(IRE) —Waafiah (Anabaa (USA))
306[3]

Ragamuffin Man (IRE) *W J Knight* 75
2 gr c Dalakhani(IRE) —Chamela Bay (IRE) (Sadler's Wells (USA))
5538[7] 5918[3] (6418)

Ragazza Mio (IRE) *A De Royer-Dupre* 94
4 b m Generous(IRE) —Via Saleria (IRE) (Arazi (USA))
2330a[3] 6953a[0]

Rageman *M Cheno* 106
7 b g Desert King(IRE) —Subasta (FR) (Kendor (FR))
6614a[11]

Ragheed (USA) *W J Haggas* a46 105
3 ch c Rahy(USA) —Highbury (USA) (Seattle Slew (USA))
160[8] (1482) 2400[6] (3960) (4408) 4900[2] (5431)

Raglan Copenhagen *B R Millman* 67
3 b g Lahib(USA) —Peperonata (IRE) (Cyrano De Bergerac)
2878[3] (3968) 4574[8]

Rags To Riches (USA) *T Pletcher* a123
3 ch f A.P. Indy(USA) —Better Than Honour (USA) (Deputy Minister (CAN))
(2487a)

Rag Tag (IRE) *A M Balding* a44 83
4 b g Tagula(IRE) —Lovat Spring (USA) (Storm Bird (CAN))
4974[4] 5522[10]

Raguany (IRE) *B Mactaggart* 30
5 ch m Pennekamp(USA) —Roots Sister (USA) (Green Dancer (USA))
2828[5] 3538[4] 4426[14]

Rahaan (USA) *C E Brittain* 62
2 b f Forestry(USA) —Jordanesque (USA) (Mr Prospector (USA))
5913[7]

Rahere (IRE) *M Johnston* 67
2 ch c King's Best(USA) —Ascot Cyclone (USA) (Rahy (USA))
2385[3]

Rahiyah (USA) *J Noseda* 113
3 ch f Rahy(USA) —Meiosis (USA) (Danzig (USA))
1702a[3] 2814[10] 4148[5] 5354[5] 6018[2]

Raiding Party (IRE) *J W Hills* a78
2 b f Orpen(USA) —Lady Angola (USA) (Lord At War (ARG))
4962[4] (5363) (6502)

Raihanah *D Shaw* a5
3 b f Dr Fong(USA) —Al Shadeedah (USA) (Nureyev (USA))
6457[8] 6877[11]

Railings (AUS) *Roger James* 119
6 b g Zabeel(NZ) —La Suffragette (NZ) (Palace Music (USA))
6354a[14] 6712a[20]

Railway Express (IRE) *Bernard Lawlor* a45 46
3 br g Lend A Hand—Deerussa (IRE) (Jareer (USA))
6796[6] 6825[10]

Rainaldino (IRE) *O Pessi*
3 b c Kahyasi—Regina Aldi (IRE) (Dowsing (USA))
(1191a)

Rain And Shade *E W Tuer* a76 63
3 ch g Rainbow Quest(USA) —Coretta (IRE) (Caerleon (USA))
258[2] 386[2] 553[8] 1089[7] 1415[8]

Rainbow Bay *P D Evans* a70 77
4 b g Komaite(USA) —Bollin Victoria (Jalmood (USA))
896[4] 992[8] (1426) 1946[8] 2108[4] (2202) (2419) 2494[5] 3481[12] 3836[2] 4095[7] 4251[6] 4703[15] 5381[5] 5648[4] 5753[6] 6594[8] 6891[9] 7020[2] 7271[12]

Rainbow Crossing *Kevin Prendergast* a79 86
2 b f Cape Cross(IRE) —Rainbows For All (IRE) (Rainbows For Life (CAN))
3659a[5] 4440a[9]

Rainbow Flame *Tom Dascombe* a56 60
3 b g Alhaarth(IRE) —Rainbow D'Beaute (Rainbow Quest (USA))
1665[8] 1950[6] 2308[5] 3177[7] 3824[2] 4758[7] 4915[9] 6458[5]

Rainbow Fox *R A Fahey* a70 77
3 b g Foxhound(USA) —Bollin Victoria (Jalmood (USA))
1176[8] 1535[7] 2114[3] 2534[6] 2910[4] 3413[6] (3786) 4330[2] 4381[3] 4895[2] (4999) 5473[4] 5662[5] 6256[3] 6559[7] 6818[5]

Rainbow Mirage (IRE) *E S McMahon* a89 95
3 b c Spectrum(IRE) —Embers Of Fame (IRE) (Sadler's Wells (USA))
2395[8] 3431[11] 4093[15] 5168[3] 5635[10] 5923[2] 6355[3] 6707[6] 6981[2]

Rainbow Prince *M J Gingell* a29 43
4 b g Desert Prince(IRE) —Eve (Rainbow Quest (USA))
6212[11] 6570[11]

Rainbow Promises (USA) *B J Meehan* a92 91
3 bb f Came Home(USA) —To Be A Lover (USA) (The Minstrel (CAN))
4118[11] 4633[8]

Rainbow Rising (IRE) *Adrian McGuinness* a101 100
5 bb g Desert King(IRE) —Fantastic Bid (USA) (Auction Ring (USA))
(3573a) (4864a) 6363a[17]

Rainbow's Classic *P Beaumont* a39 70
4 b g Muhtarram(USA) —Legend Of Aragon (Aragon)
426[11] 504[10] 664[9]

Rainbows Guest (IRE) *A M Balding* a72 58
4 ch m Indian Lodge(IRE) —Maura's Guest (IRE) (Be My Guest (USA))
150[2]

Raincoat *J H M Gosden* 113
3 b c Barathea(IRE) —Love The Rain (Rainbow Quest (USA))
(1243) 1790[2] 2293a[11] 4044[3] 5408[10]

Rainer (FR) *F Losani* 72
8 br h Saumarez—Regina Aldi (IRE) (Dowsing (USA))
1192a[6]

Raines Boy *N P Littmoden* a16 29
2 ch c Dr Fong(USA) —Come To The Point (Pursuit Of Love)
3205[8] 6566[10]

Rainstar (IRE) *J Stadelmann* 42
5 b g Real Quiet(USA) —Restikarada (FR) (Akarad (FR))
356a[6] 438a[5]

Rain Stops Play (IRE) *M Quinn* a74 96
5 b g Desert Prince(IRE) —Pinta (IRE) (Ahonoora)
701[11] 848[19] 1082[5] 1307[6] 1842[8] 2208[13] 2891[8] 3711[2] 4107[8] 4587[6] 5950[5] 6539[8] 6654[9] 6816[4]

Raise Again (IRE) *Mrs P N Dutfield* a54 66
4 b g Raise A Grand(IRE) —Paryiana (IRE) (Shernazar)
4063[12] 4660[12] 6100[4] 7098[8] 7244[5]

Raise The Goblet (IRE) *W J Haggas* a80 78
3 b g Almutawakel—Saninka (IRE) (Doyoun)
(2192) 2609[2] 3159[11] (4069) 4518[2] 5131[2]

Raise The Heights (IRE) *B J Llewellyn* a71 61
4 b g Orpen(USA) —Blue Heights (IRE) (Persian Heights)
279[2] 453[2] 585[11] 1314[9] 2355[2] 6250[15]

Raja (IRE) *Kevin Prendergast* a90 84
2 b f Pivotal—Limpopo (Green Desert (USA))
2325a[6] 5843a[8]

Rajam *P C Haslam* 64
9 b g Sadler's Wells(USA) —Rafif (USA) (Riverman (USA))
4409[6] 5000[10]

Rajayoga *M H Tompkins* a53 54
6 ch g Kris—Optimistic (Reprimand)
775[4] 913[6] 1229[4] 4030[5] (4531) 5573[7]

Rajeh (IRE) *J L Spearing* 90
4 b g Key Of Luck(USA) —Saramacca (IRE) (Kahyasi)
4690[3]

Rakata (USA) *P F I Cole* a87 82
5 b m Quiet American(USA) —Haleakala (IRE) (Kris)
938[3] 1472[7] 1649[12] 3591[4] 5230[6] 6208[9]

Rakeekah *J H M Gosden* a58 64
2 b f Bahri(USA) —Amanah (USA) (Mr Prospector (USA))
5937[6] 6411[6] 6849[7]

Rakiza (IRE) *F Head* 98
3 bb f Elnadim(USA) —Filfilah (Cadeaux Genereux)
1006a[10] 2811a[3] 3445a[7] 4190a[8] 6071a[7] 6633a[8]

Rallying Cry (USA) *Saeed Bin Suroor* a106 113
3 bb c War Chant(USA) —Turning Wheel (USA) (Seeking The Gold (USA))
414a[3] 596a[3] 859a[4] 3683[2] 4148[8]

Ramaad *W J Haggas* 76
2 ch g Dr Fong(USA) —Artifice (Green Desert (USA))
5595[2]

Ramatni *M Johnston* a83 85
2 b f Green Desert(USA) —Wardat Allayl (IRE) (Mtoto)
1079[2] 1533[2] 1848[5] 3833[2] 4560[3] (4995) 5207[11] 6052[2] 6544[2] (6699)

Ramazutti (USA) *T Pletcher* a103 111
5 ch g Honor Grades(USA) —Mine Inning (USA) (Mining (USA))
4415a[8]

Ramblin Bob *W J Musson* a60 68
2 b c Piccolo—Bijan (IRE) (Mukaddamah (USA))
1540[9] 1970[4] (2539) 3508[10] 4255[5] 5167[12] 6099[3] 6586[3] 6978[9] 7182[9]

Rambling Light *A M Balding* a84 64
3 b g Fantastic Light(USA) —Rambler (Selkirk (USA))
293[3] (655) 3420[4]

Rambling Socks *S R Bowring* a40 39
4 ch m Rambling Bear—Cledeschamps (Doc Marten)
106[7] 271[7] 620[12] 2206[5] 2535[10]

Ramona Chase *S Kirk* 96
2 b c High Chaparral(IRE) —Audacieuse (Rainbow Quest (USA))
1970[2] 2855[4] 4598[6] (5161) 5590[U] 6170[8] 6495[10]

Ramonti (FR) *Saeed Bin Suroor* 125
5 b h Martino Alonso(IRE) —Fosca (USA) (El Gran Senor (USA))
1834[2] (2735) (4058) 5261a[2] (5798) (7092a)

Rampallion *Saeed Bin Suroor* 105
4 b g Daylami(IRE) —Minute Waltz (Sadler's Wells (USA))
5411[5] 5830[5] 6759[18]

Rampant Ronnie (USA) *P W D'Arcy* a65 62
2 b r Honor Glide(USA) —Jalfrezi (Jalmood (USA))
4028[11] 4947[5] 5428[12] 5896[11] 6478[3]

Ramvaswani (IRE) *N B King* a52 41
4 b g Spectrum(IRE) —Caesarea (GER) (Generous (IRE))
5898[4]

Ranavalona *C Smith* a55 52
3 br f Diktat—Syrian Queen (Slip Anchor)
25[2] 93[8] 577[2] 636[2] 711[4] 832[4] 991[3] 1220[9] 1412[9] 3593[3] 4366[7] 4568[9] 4920[3] 5187[10] 5487[4] 5698[6]

Randama Bay (IRE) *I A Wood* a71 46
2 bb c Frenchmans Bay(FR) —Randama (Akarad (FR))
2876[14] 4201[9] 6404[2] 6714[5]

Randomity (IRE) *M Guarnieri* 67
3 b f King's Best(USA) —Oskarberg (Warning)
6688a[17]

Rangali Belle *C A Horgan* a44 61
3 b f Diktat—Dalaauna (Cadeaux Genereux)
2429[11] 3651[9] 4575[7] 4918[10] 6704[7] 6963[8]

Rankayo Hitam (USA) *J S Moore* a72
2 b c Yonaguska(USA) —Catala (USA) (Northern Park (USA))
7084[5] 7252[3]

Rann Na Cille (IRE) *P T Midgley* a67 66
3 br f Agnes World(USA) —Omanah (USA) (Kayrawan (USA))
375[2] 505[3] 567[4] 2594[7] 2829[8] 3168[3] 3411[3] 3605[5] 4021[6] (4226) 4525[13] 4714[6] 4935[6] 5507[4] 5834[2] 5934[7] 6244[3] 6810[12]

Rannoch *Miss D A McHale* a34 40
2 ch c Best Of The Bests(IRE) —Concubine (IRE) (Danehill (USA))
1586[7] 2876[16] 3392[4] 3801[7] 4027[4]

Ransom Captive (USA) *M A Magnusson* a83 93
3 b f Red Ransom(USA) —Cap Rouge (USA) (Summer Squall (USA))
1035[7] 1809[3] 2599[6] 3028[3] 5047[12] 5419[9]

Ransom Strip (USA) *R A Fahey* a64 69
4 b g Red Ransom(USA) —L'Extra Honor (USA) (Hero's Honor (USA))
1457[8]

Rapid City *Miss J Feilden* a93 84
4 b g Dansili—West Dakota (USA) (Gone West (USA))
96[2] (164) 340[2] 842[4] 1145[12]

Rapid Flow *J W Unett* a51 36
5 b g Fasliyev(USA) —Fleet River (USA) (Riverman (USA))
6390[3] 6565[8] 7103[4]

Rapidity *E J O'Neill* 61
2 b c Mind Games—Lunasa (IRE) (Don't Forget Me)
2604[6] 3760[6] 4578[6]

Raptor (GER) *K R Burke* a106 104
4 b h Auenadler(GER) —Royal Cat (Royal Academy (USA))
848[4] 6011[12] 6541[3] 6965[3] 7223[2]

Raquel White *J L Flint* a68 64
3 b f Robellino(USA) —Spinella (Teenoso (USA))
139[3] 478[4] 624[4] 790[12] 834[3] 1310[6] 2105[3] 2362[5] (2793) 3901[3] 4231[7] 6803[2] 6902[3] 7004[6] 7249[3]

Rare Breed *Mrs L Stubbs* a16 84
4 b g Foxhound(USA) —Rare Indigo (Timeless Times (USA))
957[10] 1363[11] 1914[15] 3829[13] 4635[3] 4773[6] 4996[15]

Rare Coincidence *R F Fisher* a71 76
6 ch g Atraf—Green Seed (IRE) (Lead On Time (USA))
909[3] (1225) (1406) 3584[2] 3679[2] 3840[3] 4463[7] (5087) 5300[3] 5769[8] 6077[8] 6564[2] 7008[3]

Rare Cross (IRE) *D Shaw* a78 90
5 b m Cape Cross(IRE) —Hebrides (Gone West (USA))
2411[9] 2879[5] 3086[2] 3836[9] 3921[7]

Rasaman (IRE) *M A Jarvis* a83 87
3 b g Namid—Rasana (Royal Academy (USA))
(1037) (1450) 2518[3] 3418[4] 4123[4] 4726[14] 5358[3] 5806[12]

Rascasse *Garry Moss* 26
2 b c Where Or When(IRE) —Sure Flyer (IRE) (Sure Blade (USA))
5621[6]

Rashida *S Lycett* a68 50
5 b m King's Best(USA) —Nimble Lady (AUS) (Fairy King (USA))
3485[6] 4356[5]

Rash Judgement *W S Kittow* 87
2 b c Mark Of Esteem(IRE) —Let Alone (Warning)
3687[3] 4181[2] (4823) 5974[16] 6756[2]

Rasierra (USA) *Ray E Tracy Jr* a93
2 b f Kafwain(USA) —Sierras Kiara (USA) (Moscow Ballet (USA))
5247a[2]

Ras Laffan *E S McMahon* a57 58
2 b c Vettori(IRE) —Supreme Angel (Beveled (USA))
2889[7] 4028[5] 4784[6] 5423[8] 6150[5]

Raslan *D E Pipe* 91
4 b g Lomitas—Rosia (IRE) (Mr Prospector (USA))
2736[8] 6335[23]

Rasmani *Miss Gay Kelleway* a34
3 ch f Medicean—Rasmalai (Sadler's Wells (USA))
6778[11] 6991[10] 7125[8] 7247[7]

Rathgowney Lad (IRE) *Patrick Martin* a46 97
7 b g Up And At 'Em—Tara's Delight (Dunbeath (USA))
5761a[13]

Rathmolyon *D Haydn Jones* a58 74
2 ch f Bahamian Bounty—Feather Circle (IRE) (Indian Ridge)
3109[6] 3796[6] 4310[2] 4756[2] 5176[3] 6059[8]

Rationale (IRE) *S C Williams* a56 91
4 b g Singspiel(IRE) —Logic (Slip Anchor)
2474[6] 2861[10] 3748[6] 4419 4 6158[9]

Rattan (USA) *H R A Cecil* 77
2 ch c Royal Anthem(USA) —Rouwaki (USA) (Miswaki (USA))
4508[2] 5361[2] 6202[2]

Rattle And Hum (ITY) *F & L Camici* 104
4 b h Celtic Swing—Scuola Genovese (IRE) (Ela-Mana-Mou)
2295a[4]

Raucous (GER) *T P Tate* 87
4 b g Zinaad—Roseola (GER) (Acatenango (GER))
(1300) 1844[6] 2736[13]

Raul Sahara *J W Unett* a52 52
5 b g Makbul—Sheraton Heights (Deploy)
1311[2] 1539[8]

Rava (IRE) *J-C Rouget* 87
2 b f Nayef(USA) —Lucky Date (IRE) (Halling (USA))
4625a[7]

Ravarino (USA) *Sir Michael Stoute* a85 91
3 ch f Unbridled's Song(USA) —Sous Entendu (USA) (Shadeed (USA))
1312[3] 1863[2] 2360[2] 3113[3] (3731) (4523) 5327[10]

Ravenhill Ralph (IRE) *J G M O'Shea* a44 54
3 b g Raphane(USA) —Winter Dolphin (IRE) (Dolphin Street (FR))
2542[8] 2873[5] 3365[14] 5347[3] 5945[8]

Ravenna *M P Tregoning* a72 79
3 ch f Compton Place—Cultural Role (Night Shift (USA))
498[3] 635[5] 2079[12] 2545[12] (3083) (3421) (3803) (4139) 4597[5] 5229[2] 5523[5] 5892[8]

Raven Rascal *J F Coupland* a45 19
3 b f Zaha(CAN) —Eccentric Dancer (Rambo Dancer (CAN))
667[9] (708) 1301[12] 1489[6] 2008[13] 2116[7]

Raven's Pass (USA) *J H M Gosden* 118
2 ch c Elusive Quality(USA) —Ascutney (USA) (Lord At War (ARG))
(3625) (3938) (5048) 6333[3]

Ravinia (USA) *B J Meehan* a60 59
3 ch f Rahy(USA) —Reverie (USA) (Nijinsky (CAN))
1837[8] 2061[13] 3455[6]

Ravi River (IRE) *J R Boyle* a85 83
3 ch c Barathea(IRE) —Echo River (USA) (Irish River (FR))
886[2] 1110[7] 3334[7] 3857[6]

Rawaabet (IRE) *P W Hiatt* a60 66
5 b g Bahhare(USA) —Haddeyah (USA) (Dayjur (USA))
732[11] 1592[9] 2321[4] 2603[6] 2967[8] 3035[7]

Rawdon (IRE) *M L W Bell* a66 83
6 b g Singspiel(IRE) —Rebecca Sharp (Machiavellian (USA))
1288[13] 1638[5] 2238[4] 3042[6] 3799[6] 4333[3] 4517[3] (5198) 5916[3] 6253[3] 6727[4]

Raw Possibility (CAN) *Don Pleterski* 68
2 b f Not Impossible(IRE) —Lions Raw (CAN) (War Deputy (USA))
5293a[9]

Raydan (IRE) *D R Gandolfo* a60
5 b g Danehill(USA) —Rayseka (IRE) (Dancing Brave (USA))
(1592) 6719[13] 6871[11]

Ray Diamond *N P Littmoden* 51
2 ch g Medicean—Musical Twist (USA) (Woodman (USA))
4508[12] 5343[11] 6574[13]

Rayhani (USA) *M P Tregoning* a92 105
4 b g Theatrical—Bahr Alsalaam (USA) (Riverman (USA))
(2002) 4091[14] 4803[5] 5411[4]

Raymi Coya (CAN) *M Botti* 98
2 b f Van Nistelrooy(USA) —Something Mon (USA) (Maria's Mon (USA))
(2663) 4329[3] 5164[3] (6008)

Razaana (USA) *J L Dunlop* 56
3 ch f Dixieland Band(USA) —Jinaan (USA) (Mr Prospector (USA))
1128[8]

Raza Cab (IRE) *Karen George* a83 67
5 b g Intikhab(USA) —Laraissa (Machiavellian (USA))
699[8] (827) 1283[6] 1401[2] 1984[11] 2573[7] 2877[15] 4259[12]

Razed *P L Gilligan* a58 60
4 b g King's Best(USA) —Key Academy (Royal Academy (USA))
14[8] 278[6] 402[10]

Razzano (IRE) *A M Hales* a57 57
3 b f Fasliyev(USA) —Shewillifshewants (IRE) (Alzao (USA))
162[2] 295[2] 348[6] 417[5] 832[3] 1928[5] 2362[13] 3175[2] 3690[8] (4321) 5083[3] 5627[3] 6210[6] 6542[5]

Reaching Out (IRE) *N P Littmoden* a70 75
5 b g Desert Prince(IRE) —Alwiyda (USA) (Trempolino (USA))
117[4] 263[2] 428[3] 594[6] 651[4] 928[9] 2214[17] 3282[6]

Ready To Crown (USA) *Andrew Turnell* a55
3 b f More Than Ready(USA) —Dili (USA) (Chief's Crown (USA))
7103[2] 7282[7]

Real Chief (IRE) *Miss M E Rowland* a50 25
9 b g Caerleon(USA) —Greek Air (IRE) (Ela-Mana-Mou)
615[8]

Realism (FR) *M W Easterby* a97 95
7 b g Machiavellian(USA) —Kissing Cousin (IRE) (Danehill (USA))
1583[11] (3076) 3939[5] 4388[9] 4690[9] (5255) 5623[2] 6014[10] 6759[15]

Really Really Wish *J R Best* a77 72
2 b c Bertolini(USA) —Shanghai Lil (Petong)
1897[6] 2333[5] (5815)

Real Pearl *T D Easterby* 43
2 ch g Reel Buddy(USA) —Pearls (Mon Tresor)
5321[11]

Realt Na Mara (IRE) *H Morrison* a80 57
4 bb g Tagula(IRE) —Dwingeloo (IRE) (Dancing Dissident (USA))
(6580) 6946[3] (7161)

Realy Naughty (IRE) *B G Powell* a68 68
3 b c Night Shift(USA) —Naughty Reputation (IRE) (Shalford (IRE))
127[7] 456[7] 591[4] 738[3] 1022[4] 1634[12] 2061[14] 2545[2] 2560[2] 3178[7] 3350[4] 3646[11] 4029[9] 4321[4]

Reason (IRE) *D W Chapman* a21 52
9 b g Sadler's Wells(USA) —Marseillaise (Artaius (USA))
2176[11] 2345[12] 2795[2] 3012[4] 3193[4]

Reballo (IRE) *J R Fanshawe* a81 67
4 b g King's Best(USA) —Lyrical Dance (USA) (Lear Fan (USA))
3827[6] 4275[6] 4884[2] 5339[10] 6269[5]

Rebel Aclaim (IRE) *M G Quinlan* 65
2 b f Acclamation—Tribal Rite (Be My Native (USA))
1150[2] 1636[3] 2460[2] 3096[8] 4254[3] 5167[14] 5484[8]

Rebel Duke (IRE) *D W Barker* a82 82
3 ch g Namid—Edwina (IRE) (Caerleon (USA))
199[5] (387) 1160[2] 1820[9] 3278[6] 6173[5] 6340[3] 6730[3] 6905[5]

Rebellion *H G Motion* a98 107
4 b h Mozart(IRE) —Last Resort (Lahib (USA))
6511a[8]

Rebellious Spirit *P W Hiatt* a90 74
4 b g Mark Of Esteem(IRE) —Robellino Miss (USA) (Robellino (USA))
(14) 63[2] (211) 314[2] 509[4] 576[2] 657[9] 842[5] 1543[11] 3470[7] 4068[11] 4418 [7] 6642[6] (6806) 6997[13] 7141[3] 7241[9]

Rebel Pearl (IRE) *M G Quinlan* a63 68
3 b f Barathea(IRE) —Rebel Clan (IRE) (Tagula (IRE))
633[5] 1155[14] 2110[2] 2607[3] (2829) 3181[3] 3490[8] 6310[8] 6463[10] 7127[8] 7233[8]

Rebel Raider (IRE) *B N Pollock* a53 69
8 b g Mujadil(USA) —Emily's Pride (Shirley Heights)
496[3]

Recalcitrant *S Dow* a61 61
4 b g Josr Algarhoud(IRE) —Lady Isabell (Rambo Dancer (CAN))
89[3] 458[10] 616[4] 1026[2] 1319[2] (1764) 2089[7] 2471[7] 2964[3] 3617[5] 4019[4] (4266) 4686[5] 4959[3] 5280[9] 5636[4] 6265[3] 6577[8] 6719[2] 6871[6] 7083[10]

Recast (IRE) *R Hannon* a40
2 ch f Traditionally(USA) —Rag Top (IRE) (Barathea (IRE))
5527[12] 6140[11]

Recent Times *T D Easterby* 70
2 b f Dansili—Forever Times (So Factual (USA))
4782[3] 6105[2] 6721[6]

Reciprocation (IRE) *K McAuliffe* a75 56
3 ch c Singspiel(IRE) —Tekindia (FR) (Indian Ridge)
257[3] 484[3] (603) 703[2] 1231[4] 1950[3] 2628[10]

Reclamation (IRE) *Sir Mark Prescott* a62 53
2 b f Red Ransom(USA) —Overruled (IRE) (Last Tycoon (IRE))
5770[6] 6140[6] 6414[8]

Recoaro (IRE) *B Grizzetti* 62
3 b c Regal Archive(IRE) —Melting Gold (USA) (Cadeaux Genereux)
6767a[9]

Recoil (IRE) *Christian Wroe* 57
2 b c Red Ransom(USA) —Dazilyn Lady (USA) (Zilzal (USA))
3957[7] 5011[14] 5343[8] 5736[U] 5896[13]

Record Breaker (IRE) *M Johnston* 97
3 b g In The Wings—Overruled (IRE) (Last Tycoon (IRE))
(968) (1987) 2790[6] 3993[5] (4637) 4799[8] 5215[11]

Recovery Mission *G M Moore* 30
3 b g Foxhound(USA) —Have Fun (Indian Ridge)
2012[11] 2312[12] 3202[8] 3605[7]

Red *R M Stronge* a66 66
3 ch f Fraam—Great Tern (Simply Great (FR))
1092[4] 1637[10] 3166[2] 4877[8] 7203[4]

Red Alert Day *N A Callaghan* a101 107
2 b c Diktat—Strike Hard (IRE) (Green Desert (USA))
2041[3] 3479[2] 3915[3] (4364) 4812[3] 5219[2] 5975[4]

Red Amaryllis *H J L Dunlop* a61 70
2 ch f Piccolo—Passiflora (Night Shift (USA))
3417[11] 5110[5] 5428[3] 5707[10] 6535[4] 6761[2] 6964[11]

Red And Black (IRE) *G Angellotti* 97
3 ch f Efisio—Astoria (Primo Dominie)
2070a[8]

Red And White (IRE) *M Johnston* 83
2 b f Red Ransom(USA) —Candice (IRE) (Caerleon (USA))
2658[2] (3013)

Red Army Commander (IRE) *Christian Wroe*
2 b g Soviet Star(USA) —Penny Fan (Nomination)
4539[12]

Redarsene *M G Quinlan* a62 50
2 ch c Sakhee(USA) —Triple Zee (USA) (Zilzal (USA))
5679[6] 6079[9] 6618[9]

Redbackcappuchino (IRE) *J L Spearing* 49
2 b f Redback—Cappuchino (IRE) (Roi Danzig (USA))
1586[9] 1848[10] 2152[3] 2605[3]

Red Barnet *M W Easterby* a38 52
3 ch g Tipsy Creek(USA) —Heather Valley (Clantime)
2606[6] 3202[6] 3917[5] 4250[9] 5098[10] 5299[8] 6627[11]

Red Birr (IRE) *P R Webber* a82 76
6 b g Bahhare(USA) —Cappella (IRE) (College Chapel)
56[9] 259[5] 381[7] (538) 594[8] 675[4] 921[3] (5568) 5889[5]

Red Blooded Woman (USA) *J Noseda* a58 68
3 b f Red Ransom(USA) —Maskaya (IRE) (Machiavellian (USA))
(4736) 5303[4] 5943[7]

Red Blossom *Sir Mark Prescott* a75 70
3 b f Green Desert(USA) —Red Camellia (Polar Falcon (USA))
2554[3] 3051[9] 3454[5] 3994[2] 4575[4] 5036[2] 5315[3] 6238[2] 6597[3] 6858[2] (7103) 7184[9]

Redbrick Girl *K A Ryan* a57 53
2 b f Bahamian Bounty—Once Removed (Distant Relative)
890[5] 1156[2] 1255[6] 6066[10] 6828[6] 6977[11]

Red Brick Road (IRE) *A J Lidderdale* a42 48
3 ch g Medicean—Dacian (USA) (Diesis)
1398[10] 1838[7] 2077[8] 2916[7] 3652[8]

Red Cape (FR) *Jane Chapple-Hyam* a105 93
4 b g Cape Cross(IRE) —Muirfield (FR) (Crystal Glitters (USA))
118[2] 452[4] 551[4] 660[8] (759) 1034[4]

Red Cauldron *E J O'Neill* 67
2 ch c Choisir(AUS) —First Musical (First Trump)
2739[3] 3761[3] 4448[4]

Red Chairman *R Johnson* a60 68
5 br g Red Ransom(USA) —Chine (Inchinor)
2714[12] 3053[12] 3093[6] (3502) 3721[2] 4156[3] 4230[7] 4772[2] 5086[3] 5283[5] 5807[10]

Redchete *C E Brittain* 12
2 b f Red Ransom(USA) —Zacheta (Polish Precedent (USA))
6082[7]

Redcliff (GER) *M W Easterby* 68
3 ch g Lomitas—Rhode Island (GER) (Waajib)
1672[7] 2116[11]

Red Clubs (IRE) *B W Hills* 122
4 br h Red Ransom(USA) —Two Clubs (First Trump)
1770[2] 2184[8] 2857[4] 3506[3] 4746[4] (5214) 6029a[13]

Red Contact (USA) *A Dickman* a86 46
6 b g Sahm(USA) —Basma (USA) (Grey Dawn II)
451[8] 2827[11] 3195[11] 4462[9] 4672[3] 5177[4] 5893[10] 6738[8] 7155[3] 7213[8]

Red Current *R A Harris* a61 72
3 b f Soviet Star(USA) —Fleet Amour (USA) (Afleet (CAN))
977[4] 1297[3] 2061[16] 2607[12] 3057[2] (3394) 3731[10] 4591[9] 5188[2] (5347) (5750) 5865[3] 6245[8] 6833[2] 7032[4] 7056[9] 7237[6]

Red Delight (IRE) *R A Fahey* 60
2 b f Redback—Lindas Delight (Batshoof)
3192[5] 3673[4] 4279[10]

Red Diva *Mario Hofer* 103
3 ch f Zinaad—Royal Cat (Royal Academy (USA))
1855a[4] 2707a[7] 3564a[4] 4651a[3] 6046a[8]

Red Dune (IRE) *M A Jarvis* 77
2 b f Red Ransom(USA) —Desert Beauty (IRE) (Green Desert (USA))
6470[4]

Red Duster (USA) *S Seemar* a97 75
4 bb g Red Ransom(USA) —Logiciel (Known Fact (USA))
175a[4] 329a[5] 410a[13]

Reddy Ronnie (IRE) *D Carroll* a41 45
3 b g Redback—Daffodil Dale (IRE) (Cyrano De Bergerac)
4138[6] 4641[7] 5567[9]

Redeemed *B J Meehan* a57 73
2 b f Red Ransom(USA) —Pastel (Lion Cavern (USA))
3055[8] 4402[3] 5682[7]

Redesdale *P W D'Arcy* a60 59
2 b g Pursuit Of Love—No Candles Tonight (Star Appeal)
2832[8] 3043[6] 5605[7] 5914[11] 6427[4]

Redesignation (IRE) *R Hannon* 82
2 b c Key Of Luck(USA) —Disregard That (IRE) (Don't Forget Me)
1832[9] (4584) 5551[F]

Red Evie (IRE) *M L W Bell* 117
4 b m Intikhab(USA) —Malafemmena (IRE) (Nordico (USA))
(1834) 2735[7] 3433[7] (4600) 5241a[2] 6029a[10]

Red Expresso (IRE) *M L W Bell* 78
2 ch g Intikhab(USA) —Cafe Creme (IRE) (Catrail (USA))
1058[3] 1540[8]

Red Flare (IRE) *M R Channon* 54
3 b g Redback—Cwm Deri (IRE) (Alzao (USA))
1432[4] 1712[4] 1964[15] 2697[2] 3150[2] 3450[3] 3652[5] 4104[9]

Redflo *Ms J S Doyle* a52 7
3 b f Redback—Button Hole Flower (IRE) (Fairy King (USA))
17[9] 404[4] 502[10] 574[5] 778[8] 786[10] 798[9] 1031[14] 1151[14] 1248[7] 2195[11] 3277[10]

Red Flyer (IRE) *B P J Baugh* a49
8 br g Catrail(USA) —Marostica (ITY) (Stone)
1350[9]

Redford (IRE) *M L W Bell* 83
2 b c Bahri(USA) —Ida Lupino (IRE) (Statoblest)
4130[14] 4656[4] (5904)

Red Gala *Sir Michael Stoute* a84 109
4 b h Sinndar(IRE) —Red Camellia (Polar Falcon (USA))
(1149) (5326) 6169[5] 6496[5]

Red Giant (USA) *T Pletcher* 118
3 ch c Giant's Causeway(USA) —Beyond The Sun (USA) (Kingmambo (USA))
4412a[2]

Red Icon *R M Beckett* a74 70
2 b f Red Ransom(USA) —Blue Icon (Peintre Celebre (USA))
5308[2] 5812[4]

Red Key (IRE) *Edward Lynam* 61
2 br f Key Of Luck(USA) —Remiss (IRE) (Indian Ridge)
5393a[DSQ]

Red Kiss (IRE) *Rod Collet* a95 94
4 b m Fasliyev(USA) —Avatara (IRE) (Kris)
31a[8]

Red Lancer *D Nicholls* a93 102
6 ch g Deploy—Miss Bussell (Sabrehill (USA))
1245[11] 1480[9] 1922[5] 2209[6] 2527[2] 3143a[6] 4732[11] 6185[5]

Red Lantern *M W Easterby* a45 49
6 ch g Young Ern—Croft Sally (Crofthall)
579[11] 800[12] 1221[5] 1527[4] 2302[15] 4042[7] 4802[11]

Red Leaves *P F I Cole* 60
2 b g Rock Of Gibraltar(IRE) —Brigadiers Bird (IRE) (Mujadil (USA))
5161[4] 6252[5]

Red Lily (IRE) *J R Fanshawe* 59
2 b f Red Ransom(USA) —Panna (Polish Precedent (USA))
4564[14] 5749[8] 6107[6]

Red Lord (AUS) *A Cummings* 102
4 b g Redoute's Choice(AUS) —Dame Cath (NZ) (Zabeel (NZ))
6033a[14] (6711a)

Red Mantilla (UAE) *David Marnane* 30
5 ch m Timber Country(USA) —Sanchez (Wolfhound (USA))
4114a[14]

Red Merlin (IRE) *C G Cox* 70
2 ch g Soviet Star(USA) —Truly Bewitched (USA) (Affirmed (USA))
3896[14] 4508[5] 5971[10]

Red Moloney (USA) *Kevin Prendergast* a99 109
3 b g Sahm(USA) —Roja (USA) (L'Enjoleur (CAN))
(4830a)

Redolent (IRE) *R Hannon* 107
2 ch c Redback—Esterlina (IRE) (Highest Honor (FR))
3552[2] (4508) 5397a[8] 6170[2] 6615a[3]

Red Opera *D E Pipe* 64
5 ch g Nashwan(USA) —La Papagena (Habitat)
5087[4] 5857[8]

Red Petal *Sir Mark Prescott* a78 60
3 ch f Medicean—Red Garland (Selkirk (USA))
141[8] (392) 582[2] 1724[9] 3653[7]

Red Racketeer (USA) *A Al Raihe* a74 101
5 b h Red Ransom(USA) —Furajet (USA) (The Minstrel (CAN))
401a[11] 601a[7]

Red Raptor *J A Geake* a56 57
6 ch g Polar Falcon(USA) —Star Precision (Shavian)
94[3] 274[6] 393[5] 524[7] 4533[14] 6792[14]

Red River Boy *C W Fairhurst* 45
2 ch g Bahamian Bounty—Riviere Rouge (Forzando)
2337[10] 3812[8]

Red River Rebel *J R Norton* a62 59
9 b g Inchinor—Bidweaya (USA) (Lear Fan (USA))
10[7] 585[10] 1222[9] (2089) (3260) 3610[2] 4040[8]

Red River Rock (IRE) *T J Fitzgerald* a52 26
5 b g Spectrum(IRE) —Ann's Annie (IRE) (Alzao (USA))
(240) 389[5] 683[7] 808[4] 909[6] 1402[6] 2345[9]

Red Rock Canyon (IRE) *A P O'Brien* 118
3 b c Rock Of Gibraltar(IRE) —Imagine (IRE) (Sadler's Wells (USA))
2790[14] 3983a[2] 5243a[3]

Red Rocks (IRE) *B J Meehan* 125
4 bb h Galileo(IRE) —Pharmacist (IRE) (Machiavellian (USA))
861a[9] (1274) 2754[4] 5243a[4] 6513a[3] 7090a[9]

Red Romeo *N Wilson* a91 91
6 ch g Case Law—Enchanting Eve (Risk Me (FR))
3091[4] 3512[9] 4134[4] 4585[12] 5889[3] 6243[2] 6701[6] 6981[8] (7289)

Red Rudy *A W Carroll* a71 75
5 ch g Pivotal—Piroshka (Soviet Star (USA))
2107[10] 2623[5] 3149[9] 4418 [3] 4657[5] (4879) 5189[2] 5568[10]

Red Rumour (IRE) *R M Beckett* 83
2 b c Redback—Church Mice (IRE) (Petardia)
4500[9] (5595) 6621[5]

Red Sail *Dr J D Scargill* a61 60
6 ch m Dr Fong(USA) —Manhattan Sunset (USA) (El Gran Senor (USA))
85[5] 309[5] (4131)

Redsensor *R Hannon* a74 76
2 b c Redback—Xtrasensory (Royal Applause)
4198[2] 4500[2] 4725[8] 5587[5] 6329[4] 6586[4] (6793) 6899[5]

Red Skipper (IRE) *N Wilson* 61
2 ch g Captain Rio—Speed To Lead (IRE) (Darshaan)
3915[8] 4328[4] 4818[9] 5582[7] 6066[12] 6379[13] 6635[2]

Red Somerset (USA) *R J Hodges* a78 97
4 b g Red Ransom(USA) —Bielska (USA) (Deposit Ticket (USA))
1307[3] 1619[8] 1962[10] 3165[8] 3527[4] 4184[10] 5012[7] (5693) 6081[2] 6423[2] (6596)

Red Spell (IRE) *R Hannon* a109 101
6 ch g Soviet Star(USA) —A-To-Z (IRE) (Ahonoora)
43[2] 119[2] (197) 352[4] 487[3]

Redstone Dancer (IRE) *Miss S Collins* 113
5 ch m Namid—Red Affair (IRE) (Generous (IRE))
(3222a) (3575a) 4118[3]

Red Sun *R C Guest* a42 63
10 b g Foxhound(USA) —Superetta (Superlative)
3012[6] 3371[5] 3840[4] 4521[4] 4941[7] 5561[6] 6241[7] 6341[10]

Red Tarn *B Smart* 66
2 gr g Fraam—Cumbrian Melody (Petong)
5734[4] 6255[5] 6634[8]

Red Tune (FR) *C Boutin* 94
6 ch g Green Tune(USA) —Born Gold (USA) (Blushing Groom (FR))
6923a[3]

Red Twist *H Morrison* a68 68
2 b c Red Ransom(USA) —Spinning The Yarn (Barathea (IRE))
6127[6] 6494[9] 6855[5]

Red Vixen (IRE) *C N Allen* a51 58
4 b m Agnes World(USA) —West Escape (Gone West (USA))
129[13]

Red Wine *A J McCabe* a73 69
8 b g Hamas(IRE) —Red Bouquet (Reference Point)
226[6] 434[6] 844[6] 1668[7] 2055[10] 2572[8] 3888[DSQ] 4124[3] 4717[2] 5500[4] 5779[7]

Red Wings (IRE) *G A Swinbank* 71
2 ch f Titus Livius(FR) —Canosa (IRE) (Catrail (USA))
3812[5] 4173[2] 4522[4] 4937[4]

Redwood Rocks (IRE) *B Smart* a73 72
6 b g Blush Rambler(USA) —Crisp And Cool (USA) (Ogygian (USA))
70[12] 1892[6] 4477[6] 4931[10]

Reebal *B J Meehan* a79 83
3 b c Danehill(USA) —Applaud (USA) (Rahy (USA))
943[4] 1520[7] 1900[8]

Reel Buddy Blaze *T P Tate* 69
2 ch g Reel Buddy(USA) —Hope Chest (Kris)
2532[12] 3951[4] 5294[3] 5702[6]

Reel Buddy Star *G M Moore* 75
2 ch g Reel Buddy(USA) —So Discreet (Tragic Role (USA))
4770[2] (5902) 6328[2]

Reel Classy *M A Peill* 14
2 ch f Reel Buddy(USA) —Classy Lassie (IRE) (Goldmark (USA))
5526[10] 5770[12]

Reel Cool *B Smart* 44
2 b f Reel Buddy(USA) —Waterfowl Creek (IRE) (Be My Guest (USA))
6015[8] 6254[10] 6742[7]

Reel Gift *R Hannon* a82 103
2 b f Reel Buddy(USA) —Its Another Gift (Primo Dominie)
(3417) 3988[2] 5219[10] 5324[4] 5766[8] 6167[10]

Reeling N' Rocking (IRE) *B W Hills* a78 71
4 b m Mr Greeley(USA) —Mystic Lure (Green Desert (USA))
865[8] 1382[8] 2004[4] 2472[4] 3422[2] (3851) 4394[8] 5339[2] 6269[2] 6646[8] (7253)

Reel Madam *K A Ryan* 19
2 b f Reel Buddy(USA) —Prim N Proper (Tragic Role (USA))
5302[12] 5477[6]

Reel Man *R Hannon* a58 52
2 ch g Reel Buddy(USA) —Yanomami (USA) (Slew O'Gold (USA))
4328[7] 5591[8] 5895[9]

Reel Star *S Kirk* a61 64
2 ch c Reel Buddy(USA) —Waltzing Star (IRE) (Danehill (USA))
4761[12] 5605[6] 6274[6]

Refik (FR) *M Cesandri* 98
4 bb h Hawker's News(IRE) —Joly Coeur (IRE) (Mtoto)
2330a[4]

Refinement (IRE) *Jonjo O'Neill* 48
8 b m Oscar(IRE) —Maneree (Mandalus)
5335[8] 6420[9]

Reflecting (IRE) *A W Carroll* a70 65
4 gr m Daylami(IRE) —Church Light (Caerleon (USA))
1534[P] 1886[11] 2472[12]

Reflective Glory (IRE) *J S Wainwright* a27 53
3 ch f City On A Hill(USA) —Sheznice (IRE) (Try My Best (USA))
2299[4] 2552[10] 2905[6] 4220[8] 4449[12] 7199[6]

Reflex Blue *R J Price* a39 29
10 b g Ezzoud(IRE) —Briggsmaid (Elegant Air)
2493[9]

Reform Act (USA) *D K Weld* 107
4 b m Lemon Drop Kid(USA) —Solar Colony (USA) (Pleasant Colony (USA))
1330a[2] 1777a[5] 2702a[5] 3664a[2]

Regal Best (IRE) *Mrs A J Perrett* 64
2 b c King's Best(USA) —Carranza (IRE) (Lead On Time (USA))
6252[4]

Regal Bird (USA) *M A Magnusson* a79 79
2 bb f Grand Slam(USA) —Storm Ring (USA) (Storm Bird (CAN))
1960[2] 6974[2] 7084[2]

Regal Cheer *C F Wall* a46 44
3 b f Royal Applause—Local Abbey (IRE) (Primo Dominie)
998[6] 3395[7] 4066[9] 5930[16]

Regal Curtsy *P R Chamings* a57 63
3 b f Royal Applause—Giant Nipper (Nashwan (USA))
1345[13] 4549[5] 6278[12]

Regal Dream (IRE) *J W Unett* a64 79
5 b g Namid—Lovely Me (IRE) (Vision (USA))
1064[7] 2225[8] 4023[6] 4353[9] 4731[2] 5391[7] 5433[9] 6088[4]

Regal Estate *M A Jarvis* 37
3 b f Pivotal—Lady High Havens (IRE) (Bluebird (USA))
1901[11]

Regaleya (IRE) *H Rogers* a76 79
4 b m Mujadil(USA) —Probable (IRE) (Selkirk (USA))
4836a[17] 6553a[5] 7037a[4]

Regal Flush *Sir Michael Stoute* 117
3 b c Sakhee(USA) —Ruthless Rose (USA) (Conquistador Cielo (USA))
1106[2] 1835[6] 2231[8] (4059) (5215) 5408[4]

Regalline (IRE) *Kevin Prendergast* 78
3 b f Green Desert(USA) —Rebelline (IRE) (Robellino (USA))
6216a[17]

Regal Ovation *W R Muir* a51 59
3 b g Royal Applause—Briggsmaid (Elegant Air)
1154[11] 1972[13] 4592[9] 4877[6] 5364[5] 5622[3] 5980[11] 6271[11]

Regal Parade *M Johnston* a92 97
3 ch g Pivotal—Model Queen (USA) (Kingmambo (USA))
(301) (584) (1500) 2037[7] 2788[14] 3334[4] 3941[17] 4093[9] 4900[6] 5419[4] 5805[12]

Regal Quest (IRE) *S C Williams* a86 83
3 b f Marju(IRE) —Princess Sceptre (Cadeaux Genereux)
3334[6] 3845[2] 4502[9] 4848[10] 5163[3] 5635[13] 5907[2] 6929[6] 7184[6] 7254[4]

Regal Raider (IRE) *A M Hales* a80 70
4 b g King's Best(USA) —Alegranza (IRE) (Lake Coniston (IRE))
1287[15] 1747[12] 2390[8] 3345[8] 3674[2] 3814[8] 4719[4] 5083[8] 5233[5] 5981[8] 6288[3] 6531[5] 6826[4] (6946) (7073)

Regal Rhythm (IRE) *B J Meehan* a66 81
2 b g Namid—King Of All (IRE) (King Of Clubs)
1058[5] 1291[5] (1762) 4274[7] 4762[3] 5773[3] 6128[15]

Regal Royale *Peter Grayson* a89 100
4 b g Medicean—Regal Rose (Danehill (USA))
259[7] 419[6] 576[8] 697[13] 757[6] 1165[9] 1252[11] 1545[6] 2725[3] 2864[5] 3396[4] 3585[10] 3852[10] 6749[12] 6925[9] 7118[3] 7188[3] 7265[10] 7276[7]

Regal Step *R M H Cowell* 83
2 b f Royal Applause—Two Step (Mujtahid (USA))
(2364) 2756[14] 3269[5]

Regal Sunset (IRE) *D E Cantillon* a71 68
4 b g Desert Prince(IRE) —Sunsetter (USA) (Diesis)
2833[12] 3600[10] (4031) 4517[6]

Regal Tradition (IRE) *P A Blockley* a66
2 b c Traditionally(USA) —Dathuil (IRE) (Royal Academy (USA))
6065[9] 6289[3] 6503[3]

Regal Veil *S C Williams* a40 39
2 b f Royal Applause—Shararah (Machiavellian (USA))
4854[10] *5201[7] 6503[11]*

Regency Red (IRE) *W M Brisbourne* a61 61
9 ch g Dolphin Street(FR) —Future Romance (Distant Relative)
481[6] 514[2] 767[6] 891[3] *1279[4] 1314[5]* 1741[6] *1907[7]* 2764[3] *(2946)* 4231[4] *4464[8]* (4521) 4972[6] 5482[3] *5647[4] 6937[3] 7060[9] 7219[3] 7273[3]*

Regent's Secret (USA) *J S Goldie* a85 88
7 br g Cryptoclearance(USA) —Misty Regent (CAN) (Vice Regent (CAN))
953[9] 1245[15] 1599[8] 2388[8] 2564[3] (2714) 2986[9] 3813[8] 4159[2] 4716[9] 4933[7] 5296[5] 5674[5]

Regime (IRE) *M L W Bell* 115
3 b c Golan(IRE) —Juno Madonna (IRE) (Sadler's Wells (USA))
(1306) 2235[13] 3987a[2] 4627a[5] 5240a[3] 6496[3]

Regional Counsel *Kevin Prendergast* a75 100
3 b c Medicean—Regency Rose (Danehill (USA))
948a[9] 3139a[8] 5242a[17] *5761a[10]*

Registrar *Mrs C A Dunnett* a60 62
5 ch g Machiavellian(USA) —Confidante (USA) (Dayjur (USA))
930[9] *1251[11]* 1675[10] 3388[4] 3829[3] 4165[10] *5016[4] 5340[9]* 6415[11] 6594[3] (6720) *6910[9]*

Regulus Way (GR) *P R Chamings* a44
2 ch c Harmonic Way—Exotic Way (GR) (Flash N Thunder (USA))
6543[8]

Rehearsed (IRE) *H Morrison* a74 83
4 ch m In The Wings—Emilia Romagna (GER) (Acatenango (GER))
1526[12] (3554) 3969[2] 4483[5] (5924) (6500) 6744[4]

Reigning Monarch (USA) *Miss Z C Davison* a64 61
4 b g Fusaichi Pegasus(USA) —Torros Straits (USA) (Boundary (USA))
2153[9] 2878[8] 3101[4] 3905[4] (4165) 4397[9] 5275[11]

Reine De Coeur (IRE) *David Marnane* 74
2 b f Montjeu(IRE) —Tip Tap Toe (USA) (Pleasant Tap (USA))
2325a[9]

Rekaab (IRE) *Martin Brassil* 108
4 b g In The Wings—Za Aamah (USA) (Mr Prospector (USA))
(4142a)

Relampago Plus (ARG) *B Bo*
7 gr g Alpha Plus(USA) —Taos Ski Valley (USA) (J O Tobin (USA))
1647a[5]

Relative Order *J R Best* 80
2 b c Diktat—Aunt Ruby (USA) (Rubiano (USA))
2510[7] 2941[6] 3669[4] (4372) 5374[6]

Relative Strength (IRE) *A M Balding* a70
2 ch c Kris Kin(USA) —Monalee Lass (IRE) (Mujtahid (USA))
(7114)

Relinquished *J Noseda* a71 79
2 b f Royal Applause—Marl (Lycius (USA))
2000[4] 2457[8] 2888[2] 3508[3] (4037) *4461[3]* 4892[4] 5600[4] (6449) 6652[9]

Relix (FR) *A M Crow*
7 gr g Linamix(FR) —Resleona (Caerleon (USA))
6076[11]

Reload (IRE) *Thomas Mullins* a77 75
4 b g Minardi(USA) —Rapid Action (USA) (Quest For Fame)
5460a[6] 6553a[2]

Relocation (IRE) *J J Lambe* 52
6 b g Grand Lodge(USA) —Olean (Sadler's Wells (USA))
3679[3] (Dead)

Remaadd (USA) *D Selvaratnam* a109 103
6 gr g Daylami(IRE) —Bint Albaadiya (USA) (Woodman (USA))
175a[12] (329a) 529a[15] 643a[8]

Remark (IRE) *M W Easterby* a38 71
3 b g Machiavellian(USA) —Remuria (USA) (Theatrical)
661[9] 3159[14] 4491[10] 4920[11]

Remarkable News (VEN) *A Penna Jr* 119
5 ch h Chayim(USA) —Unreachable (VEN) (Alhajras (USA))
6511a[7]

Remarkable Remy (USA) *J Kimmel* 86
2 b f Hennessy(USA) —Most Remarkable (USA) (Marquetry (USA))
5293a[5]

Reminiscent (IRE) *B P J Baugh* a61 48
8 b g Kahyasi—Eliza Orzeszkowa (IRE) (Polish Patriot (USA))
39[2] (220) 369[3] 607[7] 1152[10] *1730[8] 2222[4] 7172[8] 7285[9]*

Remis Velisque *B G Powell* a31
4 ch m Fraam—Charming Tina (IRE) (Indian Ridge)
229[7] 265[9]

Renegade (IRE) *Mrs L J Mongan* a43 58
6 b g Fasliyev(USA) —Arcade (Rousillon (USA))
265[3] 978[8]

Ren's Magic *E J Creighton* 20
9 gr g Petong—Bath (Runnett)
3795[8] 4200[7] 4267[11] *4914[15]*

Replicator *Pat Eddery* a69 71
2 b c Mujahid(USA) —Valldemosa (Music Boy)
1033[7] 1519[4] 1882[6] *3423[5]* 3734[5] *4274[2] 5496[4]* (5863)

Requisite *Jane Chapple-Hyam* a71 58
2 ch f Pivotal—Chicarica (USA) (The Minstrel (CAN))
6721[5] *6998[2]*

Resaass (USA) *J O'Reilly* a26 46
4 bb g Seeking The Gold(USA) —Sheroog (USA) (Shareef Dancer (USA))
4563[6] *5754[10]* 6109[10]

Rescue Me *R Hannon* a59 67
2 b f Red Ransom(USA) —Duchcov (Caerleon (USA))
(1519) 3880[10] 4776[10]

Resolute Defender (IRE) *J Howard Johnson* 57
2 b g Namid—Snowspin (Carwhite)
3192[11] 4076[7] 4775[17]

Resonate (IRE) *A G Newcombe* a80 92
9 b h Erins Isle—Petronelli (USA) (Sir Ivor (USA))
2209[3] 3558[6] 4399[3] *4888[3]* 5327[4] 6499[4] *7018[5]*

Resounding Glory (USA) *R A Fahey* 77
2 b c Honour And Glory(USA) —Resounding Grace (USA) (Thunder Gulch (USA))
4076[8] 5558[3] (5903) 6486[9]

Respect (NZ) *P Cave* 108
8 b g Zabeel(NZ) —Kindness (NZ) (Star Way)
(15a)

Resplendent Ace (IRE) *P Howling* a79 67
3 b c Trans Island—Persian Polly (Persian Bold)
456[5] 565[2] (720) 1122[3] 1956[9] 2635[10] *4276[10] 5122[11] 5532[6] 5819[10] 6272[2] 6603[7] 6848[10] 7018[7] 7257[5]*

Resplendent Alpha *P Howling* a98 88
3 ch g Best Of The Bests(IRE) —Sunley Scent (Wolfhound (USA))
695a[6] 922[3] 1099[13] 4183[6] 4374[8] *4950[7]* 5416[8] 5512[4] *6668[6] 6851[9] 6972[9] 7126[2] 7212[2] 7289[6]*

Resplendent Light *W R Muir* a64 81
2 b c Fantastic Light(USA) —Bright Halo (IRE) (Bigstone (IRE))
2855[12] *3849[4]* 4508[6] (6379)

Resplendent Nova *P Howling* a93 85
5 b g Pivotal—Santiburi Girl (Casteddu)
657[2] 757[2] 846[10] 1308[11] 1845[9] *2573[2] 2771[3]* 3056[9] 3350[2] (3828) 4268[12] *(4949)* 5545[10]

Restless Genius (IRE) *A M Balding* 45
2 b c Captain Rio—Mainmise (USA) (Septieme Ciel (USA))
3592[10]

Restless Soul *C A Cyzer* a65 92
3 b f Singspiel(IRE) —Seasonal Splendour (IRE) (Prince Rupert (FR))
884[5] 1364[7] 3652[4] 3876[P] 4748[8] 5113[4] 5859[4] 6299[9] 6420[6] 6757[6] *(6959) 6994[8]*

Restless Swallow *C J Down* 15
2 gr g Bandmaster(USA) —Pink Petal (Northern Game)
5343[16]

Resurge (IRE) *J Noseda* 72
2 b c Danehill Dancer(IRE) —Resurgence (Polar Falcon (USA))
5977[7]

Retaliate *M Quinn* a55 73
3 br f Wizard King—Retaliator (Rudimentary (USA))
754[7] 935[10] 1820[11] *2146[4]* 2750[8] 3845[4] 4514[8]

Retirement *R M Stronge* a44 32
8 b g Zilzal(USA) —Adeptation (USA) (Exceller (USA))
18[2] 129[8] 187[11] 558[6] 674[10]

Rettorical Lad *Jamie Poulton* 45
2 rg c Vettori(IRE) —Reciprocal (IRE) (Night Shift (USA))
6127[13]

Reunite (IRE) *Saeed Bin Suroor* 113
4 ch m Kingmambo(USA) —Allez Les Trois (USA) (Riverman (USA))
5544[3]

Revelino (IRE) *Mrs N S Evans* a46
8 b g Revoque(IRE) —Forelino (USA) (Trempolino (USA))
623[10] 5426[9] 5948[14]

Reve Lunaire (USA) *S Seemar* a104 103
4 bb h Hennessy(USA) —My Dream Castles (USA) (Woodman (USA))
331a[3] 398a[13] 541a[10]

Reverence *E J Alston* 121
6 ch g Mark Of Esteem(IRE) —Imperial Bailiwick (IRE) (Imperial Frontier (USA))
3329[5] 3894[6] 4746[16]

Reveur *M Mullineaux* a55 66
4 b m Rossini(USA) —Without Warning (IRE) (Warning)
806[4] 1038[6] 1284[6] 1539[6] 2760[7] *3173[7]* 4533[6] *5946[5] 6458[4]* (6505) *6629[3]* 6906[6] *6979[12]*

Reve Vert (FR) *A W Carroll* 49
2 b c Oasis Dream—Comme D'Habitude (USA) (Caro)
5470[10] 5910[13] 6246[11]

Revisionist (IRE) *R Hannon* a62 66
3 b g Indian Danehill(IRE) —Lady Of Dreams (IRE) (Prince Rupert (FR))
1355[10] 1724[11] 2362[12] *(2456) 2572[11]*

Revivalism *J H M Gosden* 64
2 b c Where Or When(IRE) —Revival (Sadler's Wells (USA))
1832[10]

Revolve *Mrs L J Mongan* a66 61
7 b g Pivotal—Alpine Time (IRE) (Tirol)
610[3] 799[5] 1025[5] *1347[9] 1521[2]* 1612[3] *2572[14] 6260[7]* 6447[13]

Revolving World (IRE) *L R James* a34 56
4 b g Spinning World(USA) —Mannakea (USA) (Fairy King (USA))
(2372) 4521[5] 5839[9]

Revue Princess (IRE) *T D Easterby* 68
2 b f Mull Of Kintyre(USA) —Blues Queen (Lahib (USA))
2021[5] 3378[3] 3750[2] (4041)

Rewski (IRE) *Ms Deborah J Evans* a44 44
2 b g Beckett(IRE) —Miraculous (IRE) (Marju (IRE))
3596[9] 3995[8] (Dead)

Rey Davis (IRE) *Robert Collet* 98
2 b c King Charlemagne(USA) —San Luis Rey (Zieten (USA))
3779a[4] 4009a[4] 4625a[6] 5373a[6]

Reykon (IRE) *A Renzoni* 96
3 b c Invincible Spirit(IRE) —Realt Dhun Eibhir (Indian Ridge)
6686a[7]

Rhaam *B W Hills* 84
3 b c Fantastic Light(USA) —Elhilmeya (IRE) (Unfuwain (USA))
1093[6] 1290[3] 1998[4] (3402) (4194) 4749[14] 5334[9]

Rhadegunda *J H M Gosden* a65
2 b f Pivotal—St Radegund (Green Desert (USA))
6847[7]

Rhapsilian *J A Geake* a66 55
3 br f Dansili—Rivers Rhapsody (Dominion)
752[8] 1973[4] 2470[8] 4186[6] 4545[8] 5866[5] 6278[7] *(6542) 6825[4] 6925[6] 7183[2]*

Rhapsody In Blue (GER) *D K Richardson* 93
4 b m Winged Love(IRE) —River Patrol (Rousillon (USA))
2409a[3] 5669a[6] 6953a[8]

Rhenus *A Fabre* 113
4 b g Montjeu(IRE) —Roseate Wood (FR) (Kaldoun (FR))
6032a[5]

Rhode Island Red (USA) *B J Meehan* a51 33
2 ch f Tale Of The Cat(USA) —Miss Sobriety (CAN) (Temperence Hill (USA))
3643[8] 4402[17] 4756[14]

Rhodesian Winner (GER) *Frau Marion Rotering* 106
8 ch h Snurge—Rhodesia (GER) (Solo Dancer (GER))
4957a[12]

Rhondda Valley *Mrs A J Perrett* a33 57
3 ch f Inchinor—Morgannwg (IRE) (Simply Great (FR))
2360[7] *3214[12]*

Rhuby River (IRE) *R Dickin* a43
5 b m Bahhare(USA) —Westside Flyer (Risk Me (FR))
7167[5]

Rhuepunzel *G A Butler* a69 82
3 b f Elnadim(USA) —Fairy Story (IRE) (Persian Bold)
(2792) (3474) 4060[10] (4665) 5230[10] *6243[10]* 6497[12]

Rhyming Slang (USA) *J Noseda* a83 76
3 bb c Street Cry(IRE) —Purr Pleasure (USA) (El Gran Senor (USA))
4275[12] 4666[2] *(5499) 6145[6]*

Rhythm 'N' Blues (IRE) *John M Oxx* 83
4 b m Sinndar(IRE) —Cadence (Cadeaux Genereux)
2067a[10] 3577a[14]

Rhythm'n Roots (IRE) *Allan Smith* 107
4 b h Daggers Drawn(USA) —Saana (IRE) (Erins Isle)
247a[5]

Ribella (IRE) *S Tasbek* 108
8 b m Revoque(IRE) —Tajarib (IRE) (Last Tycoon (IRE))
5265a[2]

Riblad (ITY) *A Renzoni* 89
2 b f Dashing Blade—Bianca Maria (ITY) (Acatenango (GER))
6047a[9]

Ricci De Mare *Sir Mark Prescott* a48 43
2 b f Cadeaux Genereux—Procession (Zafonic (USA))
6540[5] *6799[7] 6897[9]*

Richards Claire (IRE) *D P Keane* a22 56
6 b m Darazari(IRE) —Loquacious (IRE) (Distinctly North (USA))
187[14]

Richardthesecond (IRE) *R M Beckett* a62 65
2 b g Acclamation—Tahlil (Cadeaux Genereux)
1992[7] 2819[3] 3532[6] 4762[5] 5089[2] *5365[6] 6098[4] 6426[2]*

Richcar (IRE) *R M Beckett* 58
2 b c Almutawakel—Gerobies Girl (USA) (Deposit Ticket (USA))
3991[9] 4764[9]

Richelieu *J J Lambe* a64 81
5 b g Machiavellian(USA) —Darling Flame (USA) (Capote (USA))
251[8] 286[12] 806[9] 3676[2] *6290[3] 6344[6]*

Rich Harvest (USA) *A P Jarvis* a38
2 bb c High Yield(USA) —Mangano (USA) (Quiet American (USA))
7266[10]

Rich James (IRE) *J D Bethell* a47 60
2 b g Ishiguru(USA) —Mourir D'Aimer (USA) (Trempolino (USA))
1859[6] 2371[7] 3297[4] 4154[6] 5477[7] *6812[6] 7136[2]*

Rich Kid (IRE) *R A Harris* a65 66
2 b c Spartacus(IRE) —Sea Glen (IRE) (Glenstal (USA))
3363[12] 4014[11] 4198[6] (5471) *6880[2]*

Rich Lord *J D Bethell* a72
3 b g Zamindar(USA) —Al Corniche (IRE) (Bluebird (USA))
(449) 744[8] 1672[10] *1936[5]*

Richtee (IRE) *I W McInnes* a39 76
6 ch m Desert Sun—Santarene (IRE) (Scenic)
1158[4] *1907[8]* 2201[6] 2531[7] 3012[8] 3155[3] 3610[7] 3956[10] 4031[10] *6152[12] 6292[11]*

Ricine (IRE) *F Rohaut* 108
5 b m Titus Livius(FR) —Rince Deas (IRE) (Alzao (USA))
1876a[3] 2953a[7] 4873a[2] (6370a) 6767a[4]

Rickety Bridge (IRE) *P R Chamings* a75 62
4 ch g Elnadim(USA) —Kriva (Reference Point)
(936) 1591[3] 2994[4] 3554[8] 6276[6] *(6797) 6961[2]*

Ridaar (FR) *J-P Gallorini* 108
7 ch g Starborough—Ridiyara (IRE) (Persian Bold)
2100a[2] 2953a[3]

Ride A White Swan *P A Blockley* 67
2 gr c Baryshnikov(AUS) —The Manx Touch (IRE) (Petardia)
3551[12] 4110[9] 4764[11]

Ridge Boy (IRE) *Kevin Prendergast* 89
6 b g Indian Ridge—Bold Tina (IRE) (Persian Bold)
3138a[3] 4051a[13]

Ridge Dance *J H M Gosden* 107
2 b c Selkirk(USA) —Pearl Dance (USA) (Nureyev (USA))
4132[6] 4571[7] (5010) (5509) 5795[4] 6489[12]

Ridge Rose *L M Cumani* 71
3 b f Sadler's Wells(USA) —Fig Tree Drive (USA) (Miswaki (USA))
3160[4] 3685[5] 4229[5]

Ridgeway Jazz *M D I Usher* a49
2 b f Kalanisi(IRE) —Billie Holiday (Fairy King (USA))
1029[4] 6312[10] 6693[10] 6865[7] 7022[3] (7149)

Ridgeway Place *A B Haynes* a26 29
3 br f Compton Place—Rockstine (IRE) (Ballad Rock)
1452[9] 1633[9] *2455[13]*

Ridgeway Star *R Ingram* a54
3 b g Tumbleweed Ridge—Princess Starla (Stetsen)
208[9] 569[9] 720[9] 5421[12] 6271[14]

Ridgewell (USA) *B J Meehan* a69 66
3 b f Rahy(USA) —Voladora (USA) (Hickory Ridge (USA))
73[3] 193[5] (661) 2598[6] *3110[10]*

Ridge Wood Dani (IRE) *E J Alston* 68
2 b g Invincible Spirit(IRE) —Dani Ridge (IRE) (Indian Ridge)
1150[10] 2451[5] 2977[7] 3560[4] 4126[5] (4903) 5331[4] 5534[2] 5802[5] 6756[11]

Ridley Didley (IRE) *N Wilson* 14
2 b g Tagula(IRE) —Dioscorea (IRE) (Pharly (FR))
5550[15]

Rievaulx Valentino *K A Ryan* a66 74
2 b c Primo Valentino(IRE) —Distinctly Blu (IRE) (Distinctly North (USA))
1130[6] 2021[3] 2818[2] 3370[2] (4221) *4669[8]* 5331[7] *6872[6] 7122[2] 7220[6]*

Rifleman (IRE) *D W Thompson* a51 58
7 ch g Starborough—En Garde (USA) (Irish River (FR))
3204[3] 3638[11]

Rigat *T D Barron* a68 72
4 b g Dansili—Fudge (Polar Falcon (USA))
2256[3] 2842[8] 3194[12] 3999[11] 4583[7] 4822[10] 5433[7] 5964[5] 6258[5] 6558[3] 6728[2] *6906[2] (7009) 7173[7]*

Riggins (IRE) *L M Cumani* a92
3 b c Cape Cross(IRE) —Rentless (Zafonic (USA))
(1282)

Rightcar Ellie (IRE) *Peter Grayson* a61 61
2 b f Namid—Maid To Order (IRE) (Zafonic (USA))
2797[6] 3532[3] *4020[7] 5365[9]* (5715) *5887[4]* 6074[7] *6227[3] 6624[12]*

Rightcar Lewis *Peter Grayson*
2 ch f Noverre(USA) —Abeyr (Unfuwain (USA))
5888[12] 6177[9]

Rightful Ruler *N Wilson* a59 47
5 b g Montjoy(USA) —Lady Of The Realm (Prince Daniel (USA))
2825[6] 3677[6] *3927[5] 6802[10]*

Right Option (IRE) *J L Flint* a70 66
3 b g Daylami(IRE) —Option (IRE) (Red Ransom (USA))
776[2] 1039[6] 1397[3] (2454) 3083[8] 3593[6] 3795[3] 4259[9] 4528[2] 4877[2] (5138) *5533[5] 5980[2]* 6259[2] *(6506) 6739[5] 6802[5] 7008[4] 7242[6]*

Right Or Wrong (IRE) *Noel Meade* 89
3 b g Key Of Luck(USA) —Sarifa (IRE) (Kahyasi)
3577a[15]

Right Ted (IRE) *T Wall* a63 78
4 b m Mujadil(USA) —Islandagore (IRE) (Indian Ridge)
742[11] 1227[11] 1435[10] 2370[12]

Right To Play (USA) *J H M Gosden* a92 98
4 bb h Kingmambo(USA) —Possibly Perfect (USA) (Northern Baby (CAN))
(1012) *1438[2]* (2047)

Riguez Dancer *P C Haslam* a63 76
3 b g Dansili—Tricoteuse (Kris)
449[4] 849[4] 2530[7] 3155[6] (4230) 5197[3]

Riki Wiki Wheels *P T Midgley* a42 19
2 b c Elmaamul(USA) —Madam Wurlitzer (Noble Patriarch)
3065[5] 6557[8] *6880[6]*

Rikochet *Mrs A L M King* a47 63
3 ch g Generous(IRE) —Narva (Nashwan (USA))
4069[13]

Riley Boys (IRE) *J G Given* a70 94
6 ch g Most Welcome—Scarlett Holly (Red Sunset)
2536[13] 3258[2] 4039[6] 4523[9] 4900[9] 5296[8] *5985[9]* 6727[13]

Rimrock (IRE) *J Noseda* 62
2 gr g Royal Applause—Hotelgenie Dot Com (Selkirk (USA))
1846[7] 2041[12] 2473[7]

Rinconada (GER) *Dr A Bolte* 96
6 bl m Lavirco(GER) —Risen Raven (USA) (Risen Star (USA))
5669a[2] 6519a[9]

Ringo (IRE) *R Johnson* 32
7 b g Norwich—Fairly Lively (IRE) (Remainder Man)
2253[14]

Ring Of Charm *C J Down* a35 28
5 b m Magic Ring(IRE) —Pink Petal (Northern Game)
4905[11] 5270[9] *5752[8] 6670[7]*

Ringsider (IRE) *Declan Gillespie* a91 73
6 ch g Docksider(USA) —Red Comes Up (USA) (Blushing Groom (FR))
2765[6] 2994[8]

Rinterval (IRE) *R Hannon* 93
2 ch f Desert Prince(IRE) —Interpose (Indian Ridge)
3895[4] (4602) 5395a[2]

Rio (IRE) *J Balding* a68 73
5 ch g Namid—Renashaan (FR) (Darshaan)
1167[3] 1385[6] 1967[16] *2521[11]*

Riodan (IRE) *J J Quinn* 77
5 ch m Desert King(IRE) —Spirit Of The Nile (FR) (Generous (IRE))
1793[16] 2204[5] 6186[13]

Rio De Janeiro (IRE) *Miss E C Lavelle* a74 75
6 b g Sadler's Wells(USA) —Alleged Devotion (USA) (Alleged (USA))
5924[5]

Rio De La Plata (USA) *Saeed Bin Suroor* 119
2 ch c Rahy(USA) —Express Way (ARG) (Ahmad (ARG))
2832[3] (3435) (4057) 5458a[2] (6041a) 6333[4]

Riolo (IRE) *K F Clutterbuck* a45 65
5 ch g Priolo(USA) —Ostrusa (AUT) (Rustan (HUN))
2831[12] 4296[8] 4688[5] 5090[8] *6955[7] 7100 7248[5]*

Rio L'Oren (IRE) *N J Vaughan*
2 ch f Captain Rio—Princess Sofie (Efisio)
4254[8]

Rio Novo *J Howard Johnson*
2 b g Nayef(USA) —Dead Certain (Absalom)
4495[7]

Rio Princess (IRE) *T G Mills* a70 69
2 ch f Captain Rio—Prince's Passion (Brief Truce (USA))
1807[3] *2349[2] 3187[3] 3417[8]* 4605[4] 5008[8] *5601[9]*

Rio Riva *Miss J A Camacho* a91 109
5 b g Pivotal—Dixie Favor (USA) (Dixieland Band (USA))
848[2] 1860[5] 2208[12] (3026) 3330[12] 3887[3] 5412[8] 6011[24]

Rio Rocket (IRE) *Tom Dascombe* a51 54
2 bb f Captain Rio—Special One (Aragon)
2392[6] 3582[6] 4097[4] 4715[6] *5887[6] 6426[7] 6958[5] 7021[5]*

Riorun (IRE) *J G Portman* a47 57
2 b g Captain Rio—Sulaka (Owington)
2977[11] 3592[8] 4181[8] *5818[9] 6099[11]*

Rio Sabotini *G A Swinbank* 56
2 ch c Captain Rio—Sabotini (Prince Sabo)
2451[10] 2818[7] 5771[9] 6462[4]

Rio Sands *R M Whitaker* 70
2 b g Captain Rio—Sally Traffic (River Falls)
4636[5] 5042[9] 5745[5] 6156[10] 6326[9]

Rio Taffeta *Peter Grayson* a63 63
2 b g Diktat—Taffeta (IRE) (Barathea (IRE))
942[5] 1021[3] 1150[3] 1315[5] *1728[2]* 1857[2] 2087[2] 2392[7] (2723) 3494[3] (3835) 4136[8] *5015[9] 7044[6]*

Riotous (IRE) *A Dickman* 70
3 b g Royal Applause—Takarna (IRE) (Mark Of Esteem (IRE))
2120[8]

Riotous Applause *J R Fanshawe* 103
4 b m Royal Applause—Wiener Wald (USA) (Woodman (USA))
1670[9] 2450[3] 5305[3] 5666[4] 5954[15]

Ripples Maid *J A Geake* a96 106
4 b m Dansili—Rivers Rhapsody (Dominion)
660[7] 867[3] 1474[8] (1836) 2058[6] 2450[2] 2858[25] 4150[26] (4639) 5403[5] 5832[13] 6300[7]

Riqaab (IRE) *E A L Dunlop* 61
2 b c Peintre Celebre(USA) —Jeed (IRE) (Mujtahid (USA))
6469[7]

Riquewihr *J S Wainwright* a71 81
7 ch m Compton Place—Juvenilia (IRE) (Masterclass (USA))
796[6] 2202[5] 2508[13] 2657[2] 2870[4] 3259[5] (3512) 3723[8] (3920) 4137[3] 4407[13] 4639[7] 4747[12]

Rising Cross *J R Best* a93 113
4 bb m Cape Cross(IRE) —Woodrising (Nomination)
1823[7] 2210[4] 2787[12] 3434[9] 4215a[9] 5849a[6] 6168[8] 6790a[5]

Rising Force (IRE) *J L Spearing* a63 72
4 b g Selkirk(USA) —Singing Diva (IRE) (Royal Academy (USA))
7080[6]

Rising Shadow (IRE) *N Wilson* a81 113
6 b g Efisio—Jouet (Reprimand)
(847) 1770[4] 2857[19] 3088[4] 3506[15] 4813[6] 5616[12] 6018[8] 6183[14] 6758[6]

Risk (IRE) *J E Hammond* a92 97
4 ch g Acatenango(GER) —Belua (GER) (Lomitas)
6137a[6]

Risk Challenge (USA) *C J Price* a33 38
5 ch g Mt. Livermore(USA) —Substance (USA) (Diesis)
1995[13]

Riskie Blue (IRE) *J S Moore* 37
2 b f Iron Mask(USA) —Riskie Things (Risk Me (FR))
971[6] 1000[3] 2078[8]

Risky Nizzy *C Lerner* 87
4 b m Cape Cross(IRE) —The In-Laws (IRE) (Be My Guest (USA))
7128a[0]

Risque Heights *G A Butler* a92 81
3 b g Mark Of Esteem(IRE) —Risque Lady (Kenmare (FR))
2317[6] 2601[5] 3032[2] 3372[7] *4069[2] (4392)* 4603[4] 5014[3] *(6145) 6357[3] 6853[4] 6995[8] 7165[8] 7281[7]*

Ristant (IRE) *A & G Botti*
2 b c Distant Music(USA) —Rosa Royale (Arazi (USA))
2684a[5]

Rita Petite *D W Chapman*
3 gr f Primo Valentino(IRE) —Most Uppitty (Absalom)
4659[10] 4938[10] *5175[13]*

River Alhaarth (IRE) *P W Chapple-Hyam* 100
5 b h Alhaarth(IRE) —Sudden Interest (FR) (Highest Honor (FR))
1844[7] 2449[2] 3090[5]

River Ardeche *P C Haslam* 78
2 b g Elnadim(USA) —Overcome (Belmez (USA)) (3977)

River Bounty *A P Jarvis* a70 70
2 b f Bahamian Bounty—Artistic Merit (Alhaarth (IRE))
3213[5] 3849[5] (4125) 4762[4] 5207[4] 5828[13] 6756[10] *6892[5] 6977[2] (7030)*

River Bravo (IRE) *P W Chapple-Hyam* 77
4 b h Indian Ridge—Sheer Spirit (IRE) (Caerleon (USA))
1041[13] 3240[5]

River City (IRE) *Noel T Chance* a62 70
10 b g Norwich—Shuil Na Lee (IRE) (Phardante (FR))
6131[15] *6709[6]*

River Club *G A Swinbank* 59
3 ch g Kyllachy—Amused (Prince Sabo)
2012[8] 2554[9] 2939[2] 3342[8] 4706[14] 4938[6] (Dead)

River Cry (FR) *P Lenogue* 42
2 b c Freedom Cry—Preambuel (Environment Friend)
6952a[9]

River Deuce *M H Tompkins* a79 58
3 b g Zaha(CAN) —Light Hand (Star Appeal)
1289[8] *5311[3] 5530[2]* 5750[10] *(6211) 6709[3]*

River Falcon *J S Goldie* a93 104
7 b g Pivotal—Pearly River (Elegant Air)
1125[2] 1456[2] 2034[2] 2463[14] 3050[4] 3586[6] 3975[10] 4386[7] (4696) 5407[7] 5616[6] 5809[6] 6183[4] 6472[16]

River Gleam (IRE) *A P Jarvis* a66 66
2 b f Trans Island—Gleam (Green Desert (USA))
3417[5] 4293[3] 4611[2] 5582[12] *6177[6]*

River Gypsy *J D Frost* a51 55
6 b g In The Wings—River Erne (USA) (Irish River (FR))
134[11] 3901[10]

Riverhill (IRE) *J Howard Johnson* a37 62
4 b g Mull Of Kintyre(USA) —Thrill Seeker (IRE) (Treasure Kay)
1459[4] 2714[4]

River Hunter (IRE) *S Kirk* a30 36
3 b f Desert Prince(IRE) —Carmenta (IRE) (Unfuwain (USA))
1928[9] *2261[12]* 3176[10]

River Kent *Mrs A Duffield* 48
2 b g Fantastic Light(USA) —Ciboure (Norwick (USA))
6107[11]

River Kirov (IRE) *M Wigham* a70 88
4 b g Soviet Star(USA) —Night Shifter (IRE) (Night Shift (USA))
1023[4] 1357[2] 1607[9] 2744[14] 2882[15] 3911[15] 5722[18] *6313[6] 6938[6]*

River Logic (IRE) *A D Brown* a53 64
4 b g Fasliyev(USA) —Grey Again (Unfuwain (USA))
508[8] 1966[12]

River N' Blues (IRE) *Dr J R J Naylor* a55 65
2 ch f Touch Of The Blues(FR) —Feather River (USA) (Strike The Gold (USA))
4761[11] 6417[8] 6649[5] *6897[5]*

River Prince *A B Haynes* a70 49
3 br g Riverwise(USA) —Princess Penny (King's Signet (USA))
(194) (512)

River Proud (USA) *P F I Cole* 111
2 b c Proud Citizen(USA) —Da River Hoss (USA) (River Special (USA))
(2600) 3459[2] 5406[8] (5972) 6489[7]

Riverscape (IRE) *Mrs A J Perrett* a74 74
2 ch f Peintre Celebre(USA) —Orinoco (IRE) (Darshaan)
5308[3] 5912[2] 6411[5]

Riverside *M Brittain* 17
2 b f Kyllachy—My Cadeaux (Cadeaux Genereux)
5550[12]

Riverside Dancer (USA) *G A Huffer* a70 81
3 ch f Stravinsky(USA) —Odori (USA) (The Minstrel (CAN))
1108[14] 1920[5] 2200[2] (2387) 4029[2] 4326[6] *4740[7] 5134[4]*

River Thames *K A Ryan* a83 88
4 b g Efisio—Dashing Water (Dashing Blade)
1134[4] 1465[7] 1854[17] 2744[6] 3184[6] (3585) 3762[4] 4140[9] 5806[2] *6676[8] 7126[6]*

River Tiber *L M Cumani* 108
4 b g Danehill(USA) —Heavenly Whisper (IRE) (Halling (USA))
244a[14] (3527) 4119[4] 4720[14] 5833[2] 6011[9]

Riviera Red (IRE) *L Montague Hall* a51
7 b g Rainbow Quest(USA) —Banquise (IRE) (Last Tycoon (IRE))
20[6] 210[4] 273[7] 7278[4]

Rivington Pike (IRE) *J J Quinn* 67
2 b g Catcher In The Rye(IRE) —Bean Island (USA) (Afleet (CAN))
4286[4] 4764[12] 5813[8]

Road Home *Mrs John Harrington* 78
4 ch g Grand Lodge(USA) —Lady In Waiting (Kylian (USA))
6368a[11]

Road To Love (IRE) *M Johnston* 115
4 ch g Fruits Of Love(USA) —Alpine Flair (IRE) (Tirol)
413a[10] 531a[8] 1305[4] 1392[5] 1985[2] 2815[10]

Road To Mandalay (IRE) *Kjell Ivar Brekstad* 104
4 b h Galileo(IRE) —Child Prodigy (IRE) (Ballad Rock)
4218a[12]

Road To Recovery *A M Balding* a46 62
3 b g Mujahid(USA) —Legend Of Aragon (Aragon)
885[7] 1541[5] 2110[6]

Roaring Forte (IRE) *W J Haggas* a82 79
2 b c Cape Cross(IRE) —Descant (USA) (Nureyev (USA))
5977[4] *(6791)*

Robbie Scott *M Johnston* a33 62
3 b g Robellino(USA) —Milly Of The Vally (Caerleon (USA))
4424[10] 5676[14]

Robbmaa (FR) *M A Jarvis* a30 55
2 bl c Cape Cross(IRE) —Native Twine (Be My Native (USA))
5680[8] 5880[6]

Robby Bobby *M Johnston* 85
2 ch c Selkirk(USA) —Dancing Mirage (IRE) (Machiavellian (USA))
5570[2] (6130)

Robema *J J Quinn* 86
4 b m Cadeaux Genereux—Germane (Distant Relative)
3158[2] 3961[3] (4195) 5031[7] 5585[10] 5950[8]

Robert Burns (IRE) *J H M Gosden* 65
2 b c Invincible Spirit(IRE) —Double Red (IRE) (Thatching)
6571[6]

Robert The Brave *P R Webber* a82 27
3 b g Primo Valentino(IRE) —Sandicliffe (USA) (Imp Society (USA))
937[5] 1289[12] *(6344) (6387) (6878) 7236[6]*

Robinzal *A W Carroll* a68 70
5 b g Zilzal(USA) —Sulitelma (USA) (The Minstrel (CAN))
2708a[5] *5643[4] 6504[2] 6677[6] 7045[10]*

Robscarvic (IRE) *G A Swinbank* 89
2 b g Statue Of Liberty(USA) —Calypso Run (Lycius (USA))
(3092) 3635[3]

Robslastcall *A Berry*
2 br f Timeless Times(USA) —Lavernock Lady (Don't Forget Me)
2385[6] 4715[10] 4968[7]

Rob's Love (ITY) *R Menichetti* 104
3 b c Rob's Spirit(USA) —Eros Love (ITY) (Love The Groom (USA))
1335a[2] 1875a[3]

Robustian *Eve Johnson Houghton* a79 91
4 b g Robellino(USA) —Pontressina (USA) (St Jovite (USA))
(993) 1149[5] 1543[6] 2003[6] 2374[4] 3672[7] *4068[8]* 4566[7] 4909[2] (5052) 5432[7] 5748[3]

Robybat (IRE) *B Grizzetti* 82
2 b c Marju(IRE) —Dark Dancer (FR) (Danehill (USA))
2684a[10]

Rocamadour *M R Channon* 111
5 b h Celtic Swing—Watch Me (IRE) (Green Desert (USA))
1145[18] 1494[13] 1860[8]

Roca Redonda (IRE) *V Smith* a45 60
3 b f Fasliyev(USA) —Devil's Crown (USA) (Chief's Crown (USA))
193[11] 357[8] 893[8] 1092[10] 1579[9] 2116[5] 2747[8]

Rochdale *A Al Raihe* a102 99
4 ch g Bertolini(USA) —Owdbetts (IRE) (High Estate)
415a[3] 472a[5]

Rochefort (IRE) *J H M Gosden* a74 81
2 b c Red Ransom(USA) —Sombreffe (Polish Precedent (USA))
4777[2] 5321[3] *5679[3]* (6058)

Rocheport *J Howard Johnson* 63
2 ch g Reel Buddy(USA) —Just A Gem (Superlative)
1801[3] 2532[4] 3370[3] 3834[7] 4702[6] 5484[12]

Rochester Falls (IRE) *Kevin Prendergast* 67
2 gr f Spectrum(IRE) —Night Life (IRE) (Night Shift (USA))
4832a[13]

Rock Anthem (IRE) *J L Dunlop* 79
3 ch g Rock Of Gibraltar(IRE) —Regal Portrait (IRE) (Royal Academy (USA))
1246[7] 1726[2] (2426) 3691[6] 4318[4] 5014[6] 5941[8]

Rockazar *G M Lyons* a80 95
6 b g Opening Verse(USA) —Final Rush (Final Straw)
4051a[14] *5788a[7]*

Rock Diva (IRE) *P C Haslam* a41 56
3 ch f Rock Of Gibraltar(IRE) —Merlannah (IRE) (Shy Groom (USA))
998[10] 3917[2] 4705[4] *5098[7]*

Rockellio (IRE) *B W Hills* 56
2 b f Rock Of Gibraltar(IRE) —Lillibits (USA) (Kingmambo (USA))
3507[12]

Rocker *B R Johnson* a74 74
3 b g Rock Of Gibraltar(IRE) —Jessica's Dream (IRE) (Desert Style (IRE))
502[2] (639) 755[5] 2513[5] 2629[5] 3061[3] 3179[3] 4123[8] 4233[10] 4546[3] 5066[2] *5312[10]* 5642[12] *6794[9]*

Rocket Force (USA) *N Wilson* a49 79
7 ch g Spinning World(USA) —Pat Us (USA) (Caucasus (USA))
3638[6] 4493[7]

Rocketry *T Keddy* 39
2 ch c Desert Prince(IRE) —Moon Search (Rainbow Quest (USA))
6125[12] 6595[10]

Rockets 'n Rollers (IRE) *Doug Watson* a95 71
7 b h Victory Note(USA) —Holly Bird (Runnett)
471a[12]

Rockfield Lodge (IRE) *J A Osborne* a71 76
2 b g Stravinsky(USA) —La Belle Simone (IRE) (Grand Lodge (USA))
3171[4] 3849[2] 4350[2] *(4962)* 5509[6]

Rockfield Tiger (IRE) *J A Osborne* a64 71
2 b c Dubai Destination(USA) —Aljazeera (USA) (Swain (IRE))
1846[4] 2432[5] 2600[7] *4947[6]*

Rock Haven (IRE) *G H Yardley* a59 63
5 b g Danehill Dancer(IRE) —Mahabba (USA) (Elocutionist (USA))
1906[2] 2519[9] 2656[4] *3067[10]* 3149[2] 3907[14] 4253[6] 4526[6] *5235[11]* 6452[5]

Rockie *T Hogan* a77 98
4 b g Bertolini(USA) —Breezy Louise (Dilum (USA))
3138a[22] 4211a[9] *5761a[8]*

Rocking *W J Haggas* 80
2 b f Oasis Dream—Council Rock (General Assembly (USA))
2337[4] (2724) 3668[3] 4573[9] 5207[10]

Rockjumper *H Morrison* 42
2 br c Cape Cross(IRE) —Bronzewing (Beldale Flutter (USA))
6248[13] 6592[11]

Rock Lily *Charles O'Brien* 82
3 b f Rock Of Gibraltar(IRE) —Persian Song (Persian Bold)
1694a[9]

Rock Me (IRE) *N A Callaghan* a34 41
2 ch c Rock Of Gibraltar(IRE) —Final Farewell (USA) (Proud Truth (USA))
4947[10] 5951[16] 6106[11] 6572[6] *6775[7] 7176[5]*

Rock Moss (IRE) *J S Bolger* a91 99
2 b g Rock Of Gibraltar(IRE) —Raghida (IRE) (Nordico (USA))
5070a[4] *6161a[9]*

Rock Music *E Charpy* a99 88
5 ch h Singspiel(IRE) —Stack Rock (Ballad Rock)
396a[14]

Rocknest Island (IRE) *P D Niven* a59 66
4 b m Bahhare(USA) —Margin Call (IRE) (Tirol)
808[10] (1229) 1556[5] (1745) 1895[3] 2505[4] 2839[2] 3300[2] 3976[6] 4638[5]

Rock 'N' Roller (FR) *W R Muir* 82
3 bb g Sagacity(FR) —Diamond Dance (FR) (Dancehall (USA))
1129[4] (1968) 5808[9] 6131[12]

Rock N Roll Kid (NZ) *M C Tam* a96 99
8 b g Justice Prevails(AUS) —Winters Tale (NZ) (Icelandic (IRE))
178a[2] 395a[7] *543a[3]*

Rock Of Rochelle (USA) *A Kinsella* 99
2 b c Rock Of Gibraltar(IRE) —Recoleta (USA) (Wild Again (USA))
(5456a) 5975[7]

Rock Of Tarik (IRE) *M J Grassick* a56 70
3 ch g Rock Of Gibraltar(IRE) —Molasses (FR) (Machiavellian (USA))
6838[6]

Rock Of Veio (IRE) *P W Chapple-Hyam* 90
3 b c Rock Of Gibraltar(IRE) —Al Saqiya (USA) (Woodman (USA))
5378[2] 6653[6]

Rock Opera (SAF) *S Seemar* a77 95
5 b m Lecture(USA) —Drummer Girl (SAF) (Al Mufti (USA))
174a[7]

Rock Peak (IRE) *H Morrison* 76
2 b c Dalakhani(IRE) —Convenience (IRE) (Ela-Mana-Mou)
5361[4]

Rocky Mistress *Y De Nicolay* 80
3 br f Rock Of Gibraltar(IRE) —Vadsagreya (FR) (Linamix (FR))
6889a[8]

Rocky Reppin *J Balding* a48 44
7 b g Rock City—Tino Reppin (Neltino)
61[4] 145[8] 321[2] 374[6] 519[8]

Rockys Choice (IRE) *Peter Casey* a85 86
4 b g Indian Danehill(IRE) —La Traviata (Spectrum (IRE))
(6368a) (6555a)

Rodeo *C W Thornton* 83
4 ch g Pivotal—Flossy (Efisio)
2822[8] 3258[3] 3556[9] 3764[3] 3790[2] 4039[8]

Rogers Lodger *J Akehurst* a56 51
3 b g Cyrano De Bergerac—Bertrade (Homeboy)
127[6] 231[9] 456[12] 636[5] 899[6] *1346[9] 4394[11]* 4595[8]

Roger's Revenge *B Smart* 58
2 ch g City On A Hill(USA) —Resemblance (State Diplomacy (USA))
3951[9] 6698[5]

Rogue *Jane Southcombe* a50 70
5 b m Royal Applause—Mystique (Mystiko (USA))
561[11] 1973[2] 2334[4] 2696[2]

Rohaani (USA) *Doug Watson* a105 108
5 ch h High Yield(USA) —Strawberry's Charm (USA) (Strawberry Road (AUS))
398a[3] 541a[8]

Roi De L'Odet (FR) *N J Henderson* 27
7 b g Grape Tree Road—Fanfare Du Roi (Rusticaro (FR))
2833[15]

Rojabaa *M Mullineaux* 30
8 b g Anabaa(USA) —Slava (USA) (Diesis)
3610[10]

Roker Park (IRE) *K R Burke* 91
2 b g Choisir(AUS) —Joyful (IRE) (Green Desert (USA))
(2337) 2785[7] 4120[8] 4724[8]

Rolexa *C F Wall* a62 71
3 b f Pursuit Of Love—Dunkellin (USA) (Irish River (FR))
2428[3] 3387[7] 4575[6] *6229[2]* 6420[5]

Roll Em Over *C W Thornton* a5 25
4 b m Tamure(IRE) —Miss Petronella (Petoski)
1804[11] 1998[14] *2946[11]* 3538[5] 3638[12]

Rolling Home (GER) *A Wohler* 104
3 b c Dashing Blade—Roma Libera (GER) (Pharly (FR))
1516a[9]

Rollin 'n Tumblin *W Jarvis* a64
3 ch c Zaha(CAN) —Steppin Out (First Trump)
5129[11] 5494[9] 6670[5] 6896[7] 7185[3] 7282[3]

Roman Army (IRE) *James Moffatt* 57
5 b g Trans Island—Contravene (IRE) (Contract Law (USA))
1491[3] 2252[14]

Roman Boy (ARG) *Stef Liddiard* a65 51
8 ch g Roy(USA) —Roman Red (USA) (Blushing Groom (FR))
72[7] 130[2] 200[8] 238[2] 313[3] 381[4] 461[7] 462[6] 556[11] 5094[4] 5280[8] 5708[6] *6096[3] 6266[6]*

Roman Empire *P A Blockley* a62
7 b g Efisio—Gena Ivor (USA) (Sir Ivor (USA))
228[12] 306[11]

Roman Fun (IRE) *I Semple* 43
3 b f Peintre Celebre(USA) —Tuscaloosa (Robellino (USA))
4155[7] 4718[8] 5835[12]

Roman History (IRE) *Miss Tracy Waggott* 58
4 b g Titus Livius(FR) —Tetradonna (IRE) (Teenoso (USA))
2254[14] 3783[11] 4082[8] 4410[2] 4582[8] 4972[4] 5286[4] 5479[9] 6019[10]

Roman Legion (IRE) *P A Blockley* 70
2 gr c Spartacus(IRE) —Singhana (IRE) (Mouktar)
6255[3] 6417[2] 6634[3]

Roman Maze *W M Brisbourne* a88 95
7 ch g Lycius(USA) —Maze Garden (USA) (Riverman (USA))
(1357) 1682[4] 1971[10] (2494) 2528[5] 3481[2] 3911[2] 4122[10] 4614[20] 5031[9] 5254[5] 6197[4] *6437[9] 6606[5] 6836[8] 6981[9]*

Roman Quest *H Morrison* a68 82
4 b g Lujain(USA) —Roma (Second Set (IRE))
1063[14] 2399[5] 2882[8] 3481[11] 3965[2] 4295[6] 4505[13] *5223[8]* 5722[5] 6239[2] 6283[6]

Roman Quintet (IRE) *R J Price* a76 78
7 ch g Titus Livius(FR) —Quintellina (Robellino (USA))
1507[11] 1969[3] (2394) 3549[2] 4390[5] 5160[6] 5430[5] 5879[10] *6148[11]*

Romantic Destiny *K A Ryan* 95
2 b f Dubai Destination(USA) —My First Romance (Danehill (USA))
2109[3] 2432[2] 2904[2] 3499[2] 3838[4] 4329[5] 4744[7] 5164[9] 5583[9]

Romantic Gift *Mrs C A Dunnett* a34
5 b m Cadeaux Genereux—Last Romance (IRE) (Last Tycoon (IRE))
977[13] *1400[8]* 2878[P] (Dead)

Romantic Verse *W J Haggas* a60 60
2 b f Kyllachy—Romancing (Dr Devious (IRE))
6409[6] *(6694)*

Roman Villa (USA) *Mrs John Harrington* 76
5 b g Chester House(USA) —Danzante (USA) (Danzig (USA))
4371a[5]

Romany Nights (IRE) *Miss Gay Kelleway* a80 92
7 b g Night Shift(USA) —Gipsy Moth (Efisio)
132[7] (276) 774[10] 1545[7] *1931[5]* 2058[7] 2528[11] *(2993) 3218[2] 3623[8]* 4133[9] 4320[4] *5119[9]* 5505[5] 5722[16] 6103[12] *7033[8]*

Romany Princess (IRE) *R Hannon* a74 74
2 b f Viking Ruler(AUS) —Fag End (IRE) (Treasure Kay)
1101[10] 1608[3] 2138[2] 3524[3] 4152[9] *(5309)* 5828[9]

Romeo's On Fire (IRE) *G M Lyons* a78 85
3 b c Danehill(USA) —Fighting Countess (USA) (Ringside (USA))
6916a[3]

Romford Car Two *Miss J Feilden* a53 50
2 b c Josr Algarhoud(IRE) —Film Buff (Midyan (USA))
5222[7] 6079[8] 6571[9]

Romil Star (GER) *M Wellings* a74 38
10 b g Chief's Crown(USA) —Romelia (USA) (Woodman (USA))
12[5] 64[4] 146[6] 240[6]

Ronaldsay *R Hannon* a80 100
3 gr f Kirkwall—Crackling (Electric)
838[7] 1407[2] 2543[8] 3555[3] 4060[2] 4849[4] 5210[2] (5814) 6299[2]

Rondeau (GR) *P R Chamings* a68
2 ch g Harmonic Way—Areti (GR) (Wadood (USA))
6262[5] 6578[11] 6827[7]

Rondo *T D Barron* a32 72
4 b g Piccolo—Flourish (Selkirk (USA))
1753[11] 2937[7] 3375[4] (3535) 3787[3] 4494[4] 4583[LFT] 4719[9]

Ron In Ernest *J A Geake* a41 62
3 ch g Medicean—Viewfinder (USA) (Boundary (USA))
3475[9] 3950[15] 4758[9] *5310[8]*

Ronnie From Donny (IRE) *C J Teague* a7 6
7 b g Eagle Eyed(USA) —New Rochelle (IRE) (Lafontaine (USA))
9[8] 303[9]

Ronnie Howe *M Dods* a71 72
3 b g Hunting Lion(IRE) —Arasong (Aragon)
237[2] (429) 707[4] 958[5] 1286[6] 2172[2] 3054[8] 3637[7]

Ronnies Girl *C J Teague*
3 b f Tobougg(IRE) —Tryptonic (FR) (Baryshnikov (AUS))
2740[13] 3917[15]

Ronnies Lad *J R Norton* a54 41
5 b g Lake Coniston(IRE) —Lycius Touch (Lycius (USA))
42[8] 109[6] 630[5] 730[7] 804[10]

Ronsai (USA) *R Hannon* a52 65
2 bb f Black Minnaloushe(USA) —Roundtree (IRE) (Night Shift (USA))
2468[10] 3668[2] 4016[4] 4310[12] 5267[4] *5815[7]*

Ronsard (IRE) *P D Evans* a64 67
5 b g Spectrum(IRE) —Touche-A-Tout (IRE) (Royal Academy (USA))
496[16] 1206[3] *1380[11]* 1406[2] 1764[8] (1888) 1925[2] 2204[4] 2434[6] 3012[3] 3279[3] 3467[3] (3903) 3976[4] 4179[7] 4576[11] 5007[10] *5948[12] 6271[10] 6341[4] 6643[3] 6811[6] (7004) 7081[10] 7135[3] 7172[5] 7285[7]*

Rood Boy (IRE) *Simon Earle* a61 31
6 b g Great Commotion(USA) —Cnocma (IRE) (Tender King)
242[7] 1570[11]

Roodolph *Eve Johnson Houghton* a81 79
3 ch g Primo Valentino(IRE) —Roo (Rudimentary (USA))
843[4] 1535[4] 2243[12] 4574[7] 5092[5] 6063[2]

Rookwith (IRE) *T G McCourt* a62 71
7 b g Revoque(IRE) —Resume (IRE) (Lahib (USA))
205[9] 5460a[23] *7002[11]*

Roonah (FR) *Karen McLintock* a10 44
4 b m Xaar—Caer Mecene (FR) (Caerwent)
966[7] 1222[12] 1554[4]

Rope Bridge (IRE) *T D Easterby* a40 60
2 b c Orpen(USA) —Carhue Journey (IRE) (Barathea (IRE))
890[11] 3606[11] 3788[3] 4560[11] 4715[4] (4970) *5887[10]* 6074[3]

Rory Boy (USA) *E A L Dunlop* 61
2 b g Aldebaran(USA) —Purr Pleasure (USA) (El Gran Senor (USA))
3625[17] 5951[10]

Rosa De Mi Corazon (USA) *Sir Mark Prescott* a83
3 ch f Cozzene(USA) —Rose Of Zollern (IRE) (Seattle Dancer (USA))
(60) (433) (510)

Rosa Grace *Rae Guest* 98
2 ro f Lomitas—Night Haven (Night Shift (USA))
(4784) (5592) 6008[5] 6336[4]

Rosaker (USA) *Noel Meade* 59
10 b g Pleasant Tap(USA) —Rose Crescent (USA) (Nijinsky (CAN))
6366a[16]

Rosaleen (IRE) *B J Meehan* a64 87
2 b f Cadeaux Genereux—Dark Rosaleen (IRE) (Darshaan)
3213[4] (3916) 4804[4] 6012[7]

Rosandwil (IRE) *A D Brown*
3 b f Muhtarram(USA) —Anne-Sophie (First Trump)
7125[11]

Rosbay (IRE) *T D Easterby* 90
3 b g Desert Prince(IRE) —Dark Rosaleen (IRE) (Darshaan)
1110[4] 1773[3] (3495) 4059[8] 4617[2] 5141[5] 5554[8] 5805[8]

Rosberg (USA) *E Charpy* a90
6 br h A.P. Indy(USA) —Bosra Sham (USA) (Woodman (USA))
529a[6]

Ros Cuire (IRE) *W A Murphy* a53 14
2 br c Expelled(USA) —Haven Island (IRE) (Revoque (IRE))
6912[5] 7130[6]

Rose Bien *P J McBride* a65 69
5 bb m Bien Bien(USA) —Madame Bovary (Ile De Bourbon (USA))
775[5] 1152[9] 1793[4] 2375[5] 2887[4]

Rosecliff *Heather Dalton* a68 61
5 b g Montjeu(IRE) —Dance Clear (IRE) (Marju (IRE))
3407[9] 3976[8] 4493[10]

Rose De Rita *L P Grassick* 4
2 br f Superior Premium—Rita's Rock Ape (Mon Tresor)
5770[13] 6104[9] 6721[14]

Rose Hip (IRE) *Joseph G Murphy* a71 71
3 b f Rossini(USA) —Rose Tint (IRE) (Salse (USA))
6553a[20]

Rosein *Mrs G S Rees* a86 66
5 b m Komaite(USA) —Red Rosein (Red Sunset)
810[11] 1977[2] 2347[2] 3108[8] 3920[9] *4965[12]*

Rosemary And Thyme *Mrs S Lamyman* a15 12
3 ch f Medicean—Marie La Rose (FR) (Night Shift (USA))
1452[10] 2477[14] 5562[8] 6597[14]

Rose Muwasim *S Parr* a62 66
4 ch m In The Wings—Muwasim (USA) (Meadowlake (USA))
309[10] 425[2] 620[5] 825[4] 1371[5] *1906[3]* 2307[10] 2582[13] 2795[10] 3714[9] *3730[7]* 4802[7] *5310[14]*

Rosenkreuz (JPN) *K Hashiguchi* 110
5 br h Sunday Silence(USA) —Rose Colour (USA) (Shirley Heights)
6943a[15]

Rosentraub *H J L Dunlop* a61 58
2 b c Dansili—Ambrosine (Nashwan (USA))
5091[7] *6436[8]*

Rose Of Inchinor *R E Barr* 69
4 b m Inchinor—Rosa Canina (Bustino)
1679[8] 2032[6] 2121[14] 4141[15] 5231[12]

Rose Of Petra (IRE) *Sir Michael Stoute* a81 91
3 b f Golan(IRE) —Desert Beauty (IRE) (Green Desert (USA))
1275[7] 1929[4] (2691) 3672[4] 4185[3]

Rose Row *Mrs Mary Hambro* a56 59
3 gr f Act One—D'Azy (Persian Bold)
700[LFT] 1093[9] *7282[5]*

Rose Siog *R A Fahey* 78
2 ch f Bahamian Bounty—Madame Sisu (Emarati (USA))
(1889) 2134[5] 3562[2] (4098) 4775[3]

Rose Street (IRE) *M A Jarvis* a81 88
3 b f Noverre(USA) —Archipova (IRE) (Ela-Mana-Mou)
(2766) 6576[2]

Roshanak (IRE) *B J Meehan* a73 78
3 b f Spinning World(USA) —Desert Bloom (IRE) (Pilsudski (IRE))
1450[4] 1837[11] *2570[8]*

Rosie Cross (IRE) *Eve Johnson Houghton* a67 64
3 b f Cape Cross(IRE) —Professional Mom (USA) (Spinning World (USA))
924[3] 1345[10] 2415[3] 2966[6] *(3281) 3649[7]* 4536[2] 4759[3] *5174[3] (5420) 5731[10] 6174[6] 6810[7] 6890[5] 6962[11]*

Rosie's Attitude (USA) *T Bush* a70
3 br f Aptitude(USA) —Irving's Baby (USA) (Quiet American (USA))
3810a[7]

Rosie Says No *R M H Cowell* a56 51
2 b f Catcher In The Rye(IRE) —Curlew Calling (IRE) (Pennine Walk)
6535[11] *6761[4] 6964[8]*

Rosie's Glory (USA) *B J Meehan* a64 75
3 bb f More Than Ready(USA) —Cukee (USA) (Langfuhr (CAN))
2472[11] *3421[7]* 4205[8] 4843[11] 5187[5] 5472[3]

Rosie's Result *M Todhunter* a18 53
7 ch g Case Law—Precious Girl (Precious Metal)
2386[12] 2418[12] 2712[13] 2830[7] 3347[8] 3782[12] 3921[11] 4768[9] 4967[12] 4996[8]

Rosinka (IRE) *H G Motion* 113
4 b m Soviet Star(USA) —Last Drama (IRE) (Last Tycoon (IRE))
5822a[2]

Rossall Point *Karen McLintock* 46
6 b g Fleetwood(IRE) —Loch Clair (IRE) (Lomond (USA))
3815[9]

Rossam (AUS) *M Sheehy* 105
6 br m Scenic—Rosie's Wonder (NZ) (Gold And Ivory (USA))
15a[3]

Rossin Gold (IRE) *P Monteith* a56 55
5 b g Rossini(USA) —Sacred Heart (IRE) (Catrail (USA))
2764[7] 3371[6]

Rossini Byline (IRE) *J L Spearing* 54
2 b f Rossini(USA) —Byliny (IRE) (Archway (IRE))
5540[9]

Rossini's Dancer *R A Fahey* a60 58
2 b c Rossini(USA) —Bint Alhabib (Nashwan (USA))
5745[9] *6386[6]*

Ross Is Boss *C J Teague* a17 16
5 gr g Paris House—Billie Grey (Chilibang)
321[7] 956[6] 1676[10] 2298[15]

Ross Moor *Mike Murphy* a77 72
5 b g Dansili—Snipe Hall (Crofthall)
153[4] 332[10] 515[2] 623[2] 747[6] 1451[2] 1949[4] 2321[9] 4108[11] 4609[2] *5093[3]* 5415[10] *6241[6]*

Rosy Alexander *N A Callaghan* a57 70
2 ch f Spartacus(IRE) —Sweet Angeline (Deploy)
3213[8] 3706[6] (4028)

Rosy Anne *J R Turner*
5 b m Paris House—Common Rock (IRE) (Common Grounds)
630[13]

Rosy Dawn *Ms J S Doyle* a53 52
2 ch f Bertolini(USA) —Blushing Sunrise (USA) (Cox's Ridge (USA))
2539[15] 3446[4] 4162[8] *5117[11]* 5727[8] *6099[6] (6433) 6776[11] 6865[2]*

Rotation (IRE) *J W Hills* 62
3 b g Galileo(IRE) —Termania (IRE) (Shirley Heights)
2192[14] 3040[6]

Rothesay Dancer *J S Goldie* a66 74
4 b m Lujain(USA) —Rhinefield Beauty (IRE) (Shalford (IRE))
964[4] 1557[13] 1748[3] 1891[3] 2249[6] 2461[11] 2761[6] 2830[3] 2933[2] 3203[2] 3347[7] (3374) 3536[2] 3784[3] 3920[7] (4158) 4787[5] 4967[6] 5481[9] 5552[14] 5581[8] 5934[2] 6157[7] 6467[7] 6639[16]

Rotuma (IRE) *M Dods* a40 62
8 b g Tagula(IRE) —Cross Question (USA) (Alleged (USA))
1967[6] 2254[8] (2843) 3343[9] 3956[4] 4580[8] 4972[7]

Rough Rock (IRE) *Miss Gay Kelleway* a58 70
2 ch g Rock Of Gibraltar(IRE) —Amitie Fatale (IRE) (Night Shift (USA))
1123[9] 1540[4] 1781[5] 3508[7] *3642[7]* (4027) 4775[6] 5277[7] 6282[13]

Rough Sketch (USA) *Sir Mark Prescott* a52 41
2 b g Peintre Celebre(USA) —Drama Club (IRE) (Sadler's Wells (USA))
5498[11] 5771[12] *6139[7]*

Roundthetwist (IRE) *K R Burke* a69
2 b g Okawango(USA) —Delta Town (USA) (Sanglamore (USA))
7235[2]

Rourke Star *B Storey* 39
5 b g Presidium—Mirror Four Sport (Risk Me (FR))
3678[6] 4229[6] 4496[8]

Rovana Jowe (GER) *A Wohler* 95
4 b m Silvano(GER) —Rovana (GER) (Dashing Blade)
1517a[7]

Rowaad *M P Tregoning* a67
2 ch c Compton Place—Level Pegging (IRE) (Common Grounds)
6119[7] 6530[4]

Rowanberry *R M H Cowell* a56 48
5 b m Bishop Of Cashel—Raintree Venture (Good Times (ITY))
135[3]

Rowan Dancer *J R Boyle* a51 22
2 b f Medicean—Golden Seattle (IRE) (Seattle Dancer (USA))
5202[6] 6082[5] *6601[11]*

Rowan Lodge (IRE) *J R Boyle* a79 77
5 ch g Indian Lodge(IRE) —Tirol Hope (IRE) (Tirol)
1264[3] 1568[5] 2084[4] 2748[3] 2831[4] 3241[2] 4860[4] (5345) 5862[2] *6226[10]* 6412[6] *6710[8]*

Rowan Pursuit *E A Wheeler* a57 30
6 b m Pursuit Of Love—Golden Seattle (IRE) (Seattle Dancer (USA))
20[13] 51[11] 349[5] 1026[13] *1344[5]* 2412[5] 2559[6] 4685[8]

Rowan River *M H Tompkins* a64 77
3 b f Invincible Spirit(IRE) —Lemon Tree (USA) (Zilzal (USA))
1310[4] 1927[4] 2635[3] 4205[3] (4610) 5385[7] 5725[11]

Rowan Warning *J R Boyle* a63 67
5 b g Diktat—Golden Seattle (IRE) (Seattle Dancer (USA))
130[3] 315[4] 363[12] 612[7] 740[3] 1347[7] 1521[4] 2572[5]

Rowe Park *Mrs L C Jewell* a101 118
4 b g Dancing Spree(USA) —Magic Legs (Reprimand)
154[2] (432) 692[2] 1023[6] (1630) (1986) *2352[3]* 5050[3] (5632) 5953[2]

Roxie Princess (IRE) *J A R Toller* a63 63
3 b f Inchinor—Pagan Princess (Mujtahid (USA))
1841[12] 2219[3] 2625[8] 3176[7] *5733[8] 6272[10] 6866[9]*

Roxy Singer *W J Musson* a26 46
3 b f Erhaab(USA) —Rainy Day Song (Persian Bold)
2445[7] *2801[9]* 3040[2] 4036[5] 4535[5] *4914[10]* 6108[6]

Roya *Miss Gay Kelleway* a29 70
4 b h Daylami(IRE) —Aegean Dream (IRE) (Royal Academy (USA))
3705[16] 4108[10] *4464[11]*

Royal Acclamation (IRE) *G A Harker* 66
2 b c Acclamation—Lady Abigail (IRE) (Royal Academy (USA))
6326[7] 6557[5] 6755[4]

Royal Admiral (NZ) *L Laxon* 105
5 b g Starjo(NZ) —Kilmaghenny (NZ) (Lord Ballina (AUS))
1877a[7]

Royal Alchemist *I Mohammed* a101 107
5 b m Kingsinger(IRE) —Pure Gold (Dilum (USA))
397a[9] (546a)

Royal Amnesty *G C H Chung* a83 36
4 br h Desert Prince(IRE) —Regal Peace (Known Fact (USA))
96[7] 205[5] 351[6] 2665[13] *2995[7] 3422[9] 3851[5]* 4340[12] *5020[9] 5422[8] 6226[4] 6710[5] 6951[5]*

Royal And Regal (IRE) *A Fabre* 115
3 b c Sadler's Wells(USA) —Smart 'n Noble (USA) (Smarten (USA))
1572a[2] 3142a[8] 5258a[3] 6028a[3] (6337)

Royal Applord *K A Ryan* 74
2 b c Royal Applause—Known Class (USA) (Known Fact (USA))
4247[3] 5033[5] 5745[2] 6255[10] 6740[4]

Royal Auditon *T T Clement* a44 58
6 ch m First Trump—Loriner's Lass (Saddlers' Hall (IRE))
434[7] 578[14] 982[3] 1926[6] *2595[10]*

Royal Axminster *Mrs P N Dutfield* a48 47
12 b g Alzao(USA) —Number One Spot (Reference Point)
1402[10] 2176[9] 3186[3] 4914[12] 6583[12]

Royal Becky (IRE) *Patrick Morris* a54 55
3 gr f Beckett(IRE) —Annahala (IRE) (Ridgewood Ben)
360[4] 567[5] 679[4] 6340[10]

Royal Challenge *I W McInnes* a74 91
6 b g Royal Applause—Anotheranniversary (Emarati (USA))
1088[11] 1574[10] 1826[11] 2399[7] 4133[7] 4507[6] 4703[6] 5029[9] 5168[13] 5747[12] *6122[4]* 6288[5] *6531[3] 6818[6] 6910[2] (7105) 7161[5] 7261[7]*

Royal Choir *C E Brittain* a72 31
3 ch f King's Best(USA) —Harmonic Sound (IRE) (Grand Lodge (USA))
5494[6] 5714[9] 6413[14]

Royal Citadel (IRE) *Mrs L B Normile* a10 73
4 b m City On A Hill(USA) —Royal Baldini (USA) (Green Dancer (USA))
1488[16] 1967[5] 2431[9] 2820[2] 3343[4] 3816[6] 4383[3] 4846[8] 5286[8] 5678[6]

Royal Composer (IRE) *T D Easterby* 72
4 b g Mozart(IRE) —Susun Kelapa (USA) (St Jovite (USA))
1675[11] 2121[2] 4423[7] (4801) 5522[2] 6562[3]

Royal Confidence *B W Hills* 102
2 b f Royal Applause—Never A Doubt (Night Shift (USA))
2997[2] 3363[5] 4061[2] (4506) (5322) 6008[4] 6336[3]

Royal Dagger (IRE) *Rae Guest* a51 46
3 gr g Daggers Drawn(USA) —September Tide (IRE) (Thatching)
429[3] 574[4] 798[8] 1031[8] 2195[6] 2826[6] *3169[10]*

Royal Degree *B Smart* 77
2 b c Royal Applause—First Degree (Sabrehill (USA))
4174[2]

Royal Delight (AUS) *C Fownes* 120
5 br g Commands(AUS) —Conquered (NZ) (Star Watch (AUS))
7089a[3]

Royal Dignitary (USA) *D Nicholls* a91 97
7 br g Saint Ballado(CAN) —Star Actress (USA) (Star De Naskra (USA))
629[5] 827[2] 953[6] 1458[3] 1651[19] (2374) 2466[3] 3138a[17] 4049[20] 4745[4] 5615[10]

Royal Embrace *D Shaw* a62 47
4 b g Bertolini(USA) —Tight Spin (High Top)
42[3] 6431[8] (6579) 6859[3] 7028[2] 7143[7]

Royal Encore *J R Fanshawe* 47
3 b f Royal Applause—Footlight Fantasy (USA) (Nureyev (USA))
5231[4]

Royal Engineer *M Johnston* a60 69
4 b g Royal Applause—Iris May (Brief Truce (USA))
198[10] 384[9] 2762[6]

Royal Envoy (IRE) *D Shaw* a69 79
4 b g Royal Applause—Seven Notes (Zafonic (USA))
673[10] 771[7] 1165[4] 1589[3] 1847[16] *2516[13] 2947[3] 3285[9] 3419[12]* 5386[13] *5730[2] 6266[2] (6582) 7023[6]*

Royal Fantasy (IRE) *J R Fanshawe* a79 82
4 bb m King's Best(USA) —Dreams (Rainbow Quest (USA))
(979) 1395[12] 4404[5] 5210[6] 5979[2] *6603[3] 6738[5]*

Royal Fire (GER) *Miss A Casotti* 18
8 b h Bin Ajwaad(IRE) —Royal Future (IRE) (Royal Academy (USA))
355a[7] 494a[9]

Royal Flynn *M Dods* 82
5 b g Royal Applause—Shamriyna (IRE) (Darshaan)
928[3] (1967) 2254[7] 2467[5] (2868) 3049[3] (3301) (3567) 3955[9] 4072[5]

Royal Game *M Todhunter* 9
5 b g Vettori(IRE) —Ground Game (Gildoran)
4972[14]

Royal Guest *J R Jenkins* a66 55
3 b g Royal Applause—Bajan Blue (Lycius (USA))
573[4] 738[9] 1247[8] *3066[5] 3622[10]* 3875[7] 3950[14] 4270[3] 4529[2] 4759[12] 5062[10] 5275[9] *5420[11]* 5688[9] 5861[2] 6078[4] 6279[10] 6466[5] *6968[2] 7276[11]*

Royal Highness (GER) *Christophe Clement* 116
5 b m Monsun(GER) —Reem Dubai (IRE) (Nashwan (USA))
(4413a) 5822a[6] 6790a[6]

Royal Indulgence *W M Brisbourne* a43 66
7 b g Royal Applause—Silent Indulgence (USA) (Woodman (USA))
2117[6] 2582[4] 2820[6] 3530[7] 4577[6] 4660[5] (4878) (4959) 5188[7] 5307[9] 5636[5] 5750[4]

Royal Intruder *R Hannon* 87
2 b c Royal Applause—Surprise Visitor (IRE) (Be My Guest (USA))
2478[7] (3878) 5008[4]

Royalist (IRE) *M A Jarvis* 79
2 b c King's Best(USA) —Nebraas (Green Desert (USA))
4048[5]

Royal Jasra *E A L Dunlop* 78
3 b c Royal Applause—Lake Pleasant (IRE) (Elegant Air)
4771[2] (5335)

Royal Jet *M R Channon* a102 92
5 b g Royal Applause—Red Bouquet (Reference Point)
(345) 763[3] 940[12]

Royal Manor *N J Vaughan* 46
2 b f King's Best(USA) —She's Classy (USA) (Boundary (USA))
5306[7]

Royal Master *P C Haslam* a60 60
5 b g Royal Applause—High Sevens (Master Willie)
1579[8] 4802[6]

Royal Melbourne (IRE) *A D Brown* a65 62
7 ch g Among Men(USA) —Calachuchi (Martinmas)
(5389) 5647^8 6068^6 6330^5 6697^3

Royal Miswaki (IRE) *Wido Neuroth*
3 b c Royal Academy(USA) —Driving Miswaki (USA) (Miswaki (USA))
2548a^2

Royal Musketeer (IRE) *T D Easterby* 44
2 b g Chevalier(IRE) —Cayman Expresso (IRE) (Fayruz)
2739^14 6184^10 6329^8

Royal Oath (USA) *J H M Gosden* a102 116
4 b h Kingmambo(USA) —Sherkiya (IRE) (Goldneyev (USA))
1145^2 1494^12 (2755) 3523^2 4045^8 5142^4

Royal Orissa *D Haydn Jones* a63 69
5 b g Royal Applause—Ling Lane (Slip Anchor)
371^3 521^3 1165^7 1377^6 1885^9 (2225) 2947^8 3064^3 3388^9 3735^6 4394^10 5016^10 5890^11 6579^8 6809^9 7013^9 7148^4

Royal Pardon *M Dods* 58
5 b m Royal Applause—Miss Mercy (IRE) (Law Society (USA))
2937^3 3185^10 3414^12 3675^7

Royal Pennekamp (FR) *H-A Pantall* a93 99
4 b h Pennekamp(USA) —Lead Cora (FR) (Lead On Time (USA))
7128a^8

Royal Power (IRE) *M R Channon* a95 107
4 b h Xaar—Magic Touch (Fairy King (USA))
247a^11 411a^9 542a^3 1305^8 4747^8 5359^7 5797^16 6301^11

Royal Premier (IRE) *H J Collingridge* a62 73
4 b g King's Theatre(IRE) —Mystic Shadow (IRE) (Mtoto)
215^6 (982) (1609) 2321^11 4365^10 5018^5 5514^4 6102^11 6564^7 6911^10 (7187)

Royal Prince *A S Cruz* 110
4 ch h Mark Of Esteem(IRE) —Pelagia (IRE) (Lycius (USA))
7092a^7

Royal Rainbow *P W Hiatt* 42
3 ch g Rainbow Quest(USA) —Royal Future (IRE) (Royal Academy (USA))
4707^8 6109^12

Royal Rationale (IRE) *W J Haggas* a76 84
3 b g Desert Prince(IRE) —Logic (Slip Anchor)
1440^2 (1928) 2669^2

Royal Rock *C F Wall* a89 99
3 b g Sakhee(USA) —Vanishing Point (USA) (Caller I.D. (USA))
977^9 1278^3 (1632) 1965^2 (2570) (3797) 4607^6

Royal Rumble (IRE) *G Miliani* 15
3 ch c Shantou(USA) —Fedina (Shaamit (IRE))
1191a^6

Royal Sailor (IRE) *J Ryan* a53 36
5 b g Bahhare(USA) —Old Tradition (IRE) (Royal Academy (USA))
87^5 372^4 1279^7 1888^14 2006^11 2603^10 2716^5 3036^5 3149^8 4284^9 4994^8 5087^13 6728^7 6798^5 6902^7 7004^7 7100

Royal Secrets (IRE) *E A L Dunlop* 74
3 b f Highest Honor(FR) —Marble Maiden (Lead On Time (USA))
1685^5 2219^2 (2625) 3591^8

Royal Senga *C A Horgan* a43 54
4 b m Agnes World(USA) —Katyushka (IRE) (Soviet Star (USA))
866^10 2334^17 5090^10

Royal Shakespeare (FR) *S Gollings* a45
8 b g King's Theatre(IRE) —Persian Walk (FR) (Persian Bold)
6102^13

Royal Sovereign (IRE) *J Howard Johnson* 55
2 b g Invincible Spirit(IRE) —Ombry Girl (IRE) (Distinctly North (USA))
1622^6 2199^6 4173^8 5081^11

Royal Storm (IRE) *Mrs A J Perrett* a73 89
8 b h Royal Applause—Wakayi (Persian Bold)
2440^15 2817^17 2858^16 3623^5 3941^27 4062^9 4601^11 4806^8 5115^11

Royal Straight *A M Balding* 65
2 ch g Halling(USA) —High Straits (Bering)
6130^9 6417^5

Royal Tartan (USA) *G L Moore* 30
2 b f Lemon Drop Kid(USA) —Castellina (USA) (Danzig Connection (USA))
5536^9

Royal Tavira Girl (IRE) *M G Quinlan* a57 63
4 b m Orpen(USA) —Just Like Annie (IRE) (Mujadil (USA))
3826^5 4319^8 4469^8 5348^6 5546^8 5864^5

Royal Tender (IRE) *B G Powell* a61 2
3 gr f Woods Of Windsor(USA) —Tender Guest (IRE) (Be My Guest (USA))
116^5 370^2 1536^10 2259^11 2456^10 3082^11 3624^9 4534^12 4739^11

Royalties *M A Allen* a20
5 b m Mujahid(USA) —Rock Face (Ballad Rock)
2222^6 3730^9 6971^9

Royle Dancer *R Hollinshead* a57 64
4 b g Makbul—Foxtrot Pie (Shernazar)
72^13

Roymar *M Appleby* 41
3 b f Muthahb(IRE) —Tapper (IRE) (Elbio)
2693^14 3176^8 3476^5 4473^4 4757^9

Roy's Delight (IRE) *Edward P Harty* a73 68
3 b g Indian Lodge(IRE) —Allurah (IRE) (Goldmark (USA))
(4865a)

Rsmiya *C E Brittain* a32 39
2 b f Diktat—Scenic Venture (IRE) (Desert King (IRE))
5984^8 6448^5

Rubber Duck (IRE) *Peter Grayson* a27
3 b f Daggers Drawn(USA) —Dhuhook (USA) (Dixieland Band (USA))
34^7 335^8 429^6

Rubenstar (IRE) *M H Tompkins* a84 85
4 b g Soviet Star(USA) —Ansariya (USA) (Shahrastani (USA))
1395^9 1845^5 2427^3 2986^10 4135^11 4889^6 5115^6 5693^2 6121^6 6435^10

Rubilini *M R Channon* a58 55
3 ch f Bertolini(USA) —Aunt Ruby (USA) (Rubiano (USA))
573^7 737^4 924^10 3000^7 3490^4 3950^4 4270^6 4596^2 4684^7 5817^9 6108^4 6277^3 6607^11

Rubirosa (IRE) *M Dods* 86
2 b c Acclamation—Bendis (GER) (Danehill (USA))
(1859) 2151^3 3398^5 4168^2 4695^8 5582^2 6154^13

Rub Of The Relic (IRE) *P A Blockley* a75 75
2 b c Chevalier(IRE) —Bayletta (IRE) (Woodborough (USA))
1150^8 1713^2 2147^3 3024^2 3275^3 3341^2 3712^2 3841^4 5613^9 5888^3 6065^3 6448^3

Ruby Brown *C A Cyzer* a65 63
5 b m Polar Falcon(USA) —Raspberry Sauce (Niniski (USA))
263^9

Ruby Delta *P D Cundell* a66 69
2 b g Delta Dancer—Picolette (Piccolo)
2241^10 2398^4 2876^2 3423^4 3842^2 4202^4 4709^6 5314^15

Ruby Legend *K G Reveley* 63
9 b g Perpendicular—Singing High (Julio Mariner)
1199^8 1416^9 1967^12 2254^3 2582^3 2843^9 3714^2 (4580) 5750^8 6258^U

Ruby Light *Sir Michael Stoute* a54 62
2 b f Fantastic Light(USA) —Rumpipumpy (Shirley Heights)
4169^6 5100^7

Ruby's Dream *J M Bradley* a51 61
5 b m Tipsy Creek(USA) —Sure Flyer (IRE) (Sure Blade (USA))
746^4 1112^11 1384^7 1729^3 2104^7 2652^6 2791^11 3169^3 3667^2 4561^11 4973^9

Ruby's Rainbow (IRE) *J Balding* a22 11
2 b f Fayruz—Sweet Finesse (IRE) (Revoque (IRE))
5154^11 5501^13 6023^7

Ruby's Smile *R Brotherton*
2 b f Bold Edge—Funny Wave (Lugana Beach)
1285^16 2333^13 4311^10

Ruby Sunrise (IRE) *B P J Baugh* a48 21
5 ch m Polish Precedent(USA) —Kinlochewe (Old Vic)
1^3 98^7

Rubytwosox (IRE) *W R Muir* a53 57
2 b f Redback—Policy (Nashwan (USA))
1445^9 2109^5 2410^4 3642^14 4265^7 5117^6 5869^7 6242^6

Rudebox (IRE) *A Peraino*
2 b c Choisir(AUS) —Windy Gulch (USA) (Gulch (USA))
2684a^11

Rudi's Pet (IRE) *D Nicholls* a1 74
13 ch g Don't Forget Me—Pink Fondant (Northfields (USA))
1557^14 1707^6 1891^6 4252^11

Rudry Dragon (IRE) *P A Blockley* a78 89
3 b c Princely Heir(IRE) —Jazz Up (Cadeaux Genereux)
(1359) 2045^12 3480^6 3689^4 3877^3 4111^4 4387^6 5043^5 6002^6 6236^2 6465^2 6636^3

Rudry World (IRE) *M Mullineaux* a72 78
4 ch g Spinning World(USA) —Fancy Boots (IRE) (Salt Dome (USA))
788^3 1028^4 1221^3 (1279) 1376^5 3063^2 3260^2 (3457) 3901^8 4096^4 4352^3 (4499) (4717) 5777^2 6158^4 6481^4

Rue Soleil *J R Weymes* a29 62
3 ch f Zaha(CAN) —Maria Cappuccini (Siberian Express (USA))
998^9 1240^2 1530^12 1709^3 2094^7 2895^3 3202^4 (3537) 3786^6 4001^5 6466^2 6562^10

Ruff Diamond (USA) *J R Best* 85
2 bb c Stormin Fever(USA) —Whalah (USA) (Dixieland Band (USA))
1652^4 (2241) 2732^20 3522^4

Ruffie (IRE) *Miss Gay Kelleway* a71 51
4 b m Medicean—Darling Lover (USA) (Dare And Go (USA))
299^4 497^6 (732) 1069^10 1352^3 1567^5 1740^11 3966^4 6537^10 7006^3 7124^2 7197^4

Ruggtah *M G Rimell*
6 gr m Daylami(IRE) —Raneen Alwatar (Sadler's Wells (USA))
3653^8

Rule For Ever *I W McInnes* a78 70
5 br g Diktat—Tous Les Jours (USA) (Dayjur (USA))
213^9 (607) 640^4 (709) 994^5 1196^4 1556^2 2026^6 2825^4

Rule Of Life *B W Hills* a79 90
3 br c Dansili—Prophecy (IRE) (Warning)
(1278) 1920^7 2598^2 3235^3 4111^9 (4551) 4847^3

Ruman (IRE) *M J Attwater* a77 58
5 b g Fayruz—Starway To Heaven (ITY) (Nordance (USA))
1640^7 2664^3 (6264) 6581^3 (6870)

Rumbled *J A Geake* a68 61
3 b f Halling(USA) —Tatanka (IRE) (Lear Fan (USA))
1345^3 2061^10 3525^14 3875^8 4309^4 4708^5

Rum Jungle *H Candy* 60
3 b g Robellino(USA) —Anna Karietta (Precocious)
6238^4

Rumpus (GER) *T P Tate* 65
3 ch g Medaaly—Roseola (GER) (Acatenango (GER))
(1220) 1637^7 2246^9

Runaway *R Pritchard-Gordon* 111
5 b h King's Best(USA) —Anasazi (IRE) (Sadler's Wells (USA))
663a^3 880a^6 5264a^7 6032a^6

Run For Ede'S *P M Phelan* a68 66
3 b f Peintre Celebre(USA) —Raincloud (Rainbow Quest (USA))
1606^3 1988^8 2691^6 3393^5 4505^6 4918^2 5342^8 6824^2 7103^9

Runforthemoneybaby (USA) *Jeff Mullins* a107 94
2 ch f Unusual Heat(USA) —Andover The Money (USA) (Dynaformer (USA))
5826a^3

Run Free *N Wilson* a64 71
3 b g Agnes World(USA) —Ellie Ardensky (Slip Anchor)
1111^6 1850^2 2453^8 3785^6 4450^7 5555^8 5968^7 6245^3 6567^4 7056^6 7180^3

Run From Nun *J A Osborne* a48
2 b f Oasis Dream—Nunatak (USA) (Bering)
5780^10 6228^8 6358^6 6736^5

Running Buck (USA) *N P Littmoden* 54
2 b c Running Stag(USA) —Dinghy (USA) (Fortunate Prospect (USA))
3283^11 3878^7 4181^11 4903^13 5534^6

Running On Empty *P D Evans* 17
4 b g College Chapel—Abstone Queen (Presidium)
2535^11 2800^8

Running Rings *P W D'Arcy* 34
3 br f Synefos(USA) —Madame Gehenne (IRE) (Lord Americo)
3621^7 3908^9 4357^7

Runs Riot (IRE) *Andrew Oliver* 48
3 b g Spinning World(USA) —Chasing Rainbows (Rainbow Quest (USA))
6330^7

Runswick Bay *G M Moore* 84
2 b c Intikhab(USA) —Upend (Main Reef)
845^5 1087^3 1743^3 2251^3 (2888) (3398) 3909^4 4812^7

Ruse *J R Fanshawe* a61 64
4 b m Diktat—Reuval (Sharpen Up)
1^4 6102^7

Russian Consort (IRE) *A King* a98 85
5 ch g Groom Dancer(USA) —Ukraine Venture (Slip Anchor)
1149^13

Russian Desert (IRE) *A Fabre* 109
3 ch c Desert Prince(IRE) —Dievotchka (Dancing Brave (USA))
1593a^5 3987a^3 4627a^8

Russian Dream (IRE) *W R Swinburn* a72 66
4 b g Xaar—Summer Dreams (IRE) (Sadler's Wells (USA))
195^10 507^6 1002^4

Russian Epic *M A Jarvis* 80
3 b g Diktat—Russian Rhapsody (Cosmonaut)
1358^7 1840^2 (2083) 2669^3 3165^4 4111^5

Russian Gift (IRE) *C G Cox* 68
3 b f Soviet Star(USA) —Birthday Present (Cadeaux Genereux)
2198^2 2515^12 3369^10 4546^4 5009^10

Russian Invader (IRE) *A King* a16 84
3 ch g Acatenango(GER) —Ukraine Venture (Slip Anchor)
4334^2 4948^10 5335^3 (6061)

Russian Mist (IRE) *M J Wallace* a65 59
4 gr g Xaar—Cape Mist (USA) (Lure (USA))
92^7 313^10 637^10

Russian Reel *K A Ryan* a49 90
2 b c Reel Buddy(USA) —Charlie Girl (Puissance)
1938^3 (2371) 2737^15 3494^2 4193^5 4743^11 5331^2 5480^4 6017^19 7202^3

Russian Rocket (IRE) *Mrs C A Dunnett* a78 81
5 b g Indian Rocket—Soviet Girl (IRE) (Soviet Star (USA))
1634 774^7 1074^5 1589^6 3627^9 3852^7 6103^9 6360^11 6575^5 7005^2 7227^10

Russian Rosie (IRE) *J G Portman* 101
3 b f Traditionally(USA) —Pink Sovietstaia (FR) (Soviet Star (USA))
1146^9 1824^4 2599^2 3332^7 4503^3 4849^3 5544^8 6772a^5

Russian Silk *Jedd O'Keeffe* 73
3 b f Fasliyev(USA) —Queen Of Silk (IRE) (Brief Truce (USA))
1577^12 2435^7 4330^11 4773^14

Russian Symphony (USA) *C R Egerton* a85 81
6 ch g Stravinsky(USA) —Backwoods Teacher (USA) (Woodman (USA))
1545^8 1971^15 2689^4 3350^7 3943^13 5312^2 6006^8 6836^5 7087^4

Russki (IRE) *D M Simcock* a91 87
3 b c Fasliyev(USA) —Rose Of Mooncoin (IRE) (Brief Truce (USA))
2400^10 2633^6 3553^7 4276^3 4608^10 (5128) (5885) 6053^3 (6359)

Rustenberg *E F Vaughan* 41
3 b f Dr Fong(USA) —River City Moon (USA) (Riverman (USA))
2219^13

Rust En Vrede *J J Quinn* a54 26
8 b g Royal Applause—Souveniers (Relko)
1378^5

Rustic Flame (IRE) *C R Egerton* 81
3 b f Danehill Dancer(IRE) —Soviet Artic (FR) (Bering)
1839^6 2693^4 (2998) 3430^15

Rustic Gold *J R Best* a64 71
3 ch g Tobougg(IRE) —Suave Shot (Suave Dancer (USA))
1039^4 1927^9 2425^8 2727^2 (3003) 3048^3 3450^5 (4015) 5941^5 6132^7

Rustler *N J Henderson* 78
5 b g Green Desert(USA) —Borgia (Machiavellian (USA))
3671^3

Rusty Roof *Rae Guest* a39
4 ch m Zaha(CAN) —Parisian Lady (IRE) (Paris House)
49^4 272^6 6480^7 6798^9

Rutba *M P Tregoning* a38
2 b f Act One—Elhilmeya (IRE) (Unfuwain (USA))
6585^13 6805^13

Rutherienne (USA) *Christophe Clement* 113
3 bb f Pulpit(USA) —Ruthian (USA) (Rahy (USA))
5248a^10

Ruthles Philly *G L Moore* a51 58
3 b f Primo Valentino(IRE) —Compton Amber (Puissance)
1238^2 1424^3 1850^16 4078^4 4291^8 4480^6 4787^11 6580^5 6809^10

Ruwain *W J Musson* a43 46
3 b g Lujain(USA) —Ruwaya (USA) (Red Ransom (USA))
6597^9 6778^8 6858^5 7186^7

Ruwi *D Koh* 110
5 b h Unfuwain(USA) —Ma Paloma (FR) (Highest Honor (FR))
1877a^13

Ryan (IRE) *J Hanacek* 100
4 b h Generous(IRE) —Raysiza (IRE) (Alzao (USA))
6518a^2

Ryan's Future (IRE) *J S Moore* a62 77
7 b h Danetime(IRE) —Era (Dalsaan)
5870^10 6490^10 7189^4 7277^4

Ryan's Rock *T D McCarthy* a43 25
2 b g Lujain(USA) —Diamond Jayne (IRE) (Royal Abjar (USA))
4508^14 4946^5 6079^11 7084^11

Rydal (USA) *J A Osborne* a76 73
6 ch g Gilded Time(USA) —Tennis Partner (USA) (Northern Dancer (CAN))
4351^2 5535^2 5726^4 5874^9 5981^2 6288^9 6531^2

Rydal Mount (IRE) *W S Kittow* a79 79
4 b m Cape Cross(IRE) —Pooka (Dominion)
1588^2 2085^6 2725^2 3472^6 5223^13 (6088) 6753^18

Rye Beau (IRE) *Mrs A Duffield* a19 29
2 b g Catcher In The Rye(IRE) —Belle Of Honour (USA) (Honour And Glory (USA))
1073^7 1728^8 3681^7 3751^11

Ryedale Ovation (IRE) *M Hill* a68 83
4 b g Royal Applause—Passe Passe (USA) (Lear Fan (USA))
9154 1223^5 2550^7 2989^7 3791^6 4038^7 (6719)

Ryedane (IRE) *T D Easterby* a75 77
5 b g Danetime(IRE) —Miss Valediction (IRE) (Petardia)
1074^9 1299^4 1557^5 2516^4 3408^3 3839^2 4251^3 4289^3 4822^2 (4942) (5387) 5753^3 6313^9

Ryhope Chief (IRE) *M Sheppard* a36 35
4 b g Indian Danehill(IRE) —Rachel Pringle (IRE) (Doulab (USA))
107^5 285^11

Ryono (USA) *S Smrczek* a108 109
8 ch h Mountain Cat(USA) —Racing Blue (Reference Point)
4217a^8 4873a^11

Rythm N Rhyme (IRE) *John A Harris* a29 8
8 ch g Danehill Dancer(IRE) —Valley Heigh (IRE) (Head For Heights)
3684^7 4492^6

Saafend Geezer *B J Meehan* 58
2 ch g Kyllachy—Kindred Spirit (IRE) (Cadeaux Genereux)
5343^10 5720^14 6295^10

Saameq (IRE) *D W Thompson* a59 52
6 b g Bahhare(USA) —Tajawuz (Kris)
369^12 514^5 5389^3

Saaratt *J W Hills* a60 71
3 ch f Mark Of Esteem(IRE) —Cambara (Dancing Brave (USA))
2429^4 3113^6 4106^5 4470^3 5733^12 6206^3 6458^6

Sabah *A M Balding* 87
4 ch m Nashwan(USA) —Massorah (FR) (Habitat)
2207^10

Sabana Perdida (IRE) *A De Royer-Dupre* 108
4 b m Cape Cross(IRE) —Capriola (USA) (Mr Prospector (USA))
2100a^9 2753^3 (5259a)

Sabancaya *W J Haggas* 62
2 b f Nayef(USA) —Serra Negra (Kris)
6648^11

Sabasha (FR) *Mlle S-V Tarrou* a93 104
4 b m Xaar—Saba (ITY) (Kris)
1337a^4 2100a^4 2953a^4 4012a^3 4871a^6 5259a^9 6633a^8

Sabirli (TUR) *C Kurt* 113
6 b h Strike The Gold(USA) —Free Trade (TUR) (Shareef Dancer (USA))
(5265a)

Sabo Prince *J M Bradley* a48 21
5 ch g Atraf—Moving Princess (Prince Sabo)
710^10 1028^11

Sabre Light *G L Moore* a57 62
2 b g Fantastic Light(USA) —Good Grounds (USA) (Alleged (USA))
4508^9 4883^8 5091^5 5871^9 6449^15

Sabre's Edge (IRE) *R J Hodges* a30 69
6 b g Sadler's Wells(USA) —Brave Kris (IRE) (Kris)
2799^9

Sac A Puces (FR) *J-P Gallorini* 91
10 ch g Jeune Homme(USA) —Scandaleuse (FR) (Groom Dancer (USA))
6941a^0

Sacho (GER) *W Kujath* 108
9 br g Dashing Blade—She's His Guest (IRE) (Be My Guest (USA))
(1189a) 2811a^2 3445a^12 4190a^6 6071a^10

Sacota *E Kurdu* 64
2 b f Black Sam Bellamy(IRE) —Scota (GER) (Marju (IRE))
4837a^8 5462a^5 5848a^4

Sacre Coeur *J L Dunlop* 83
3 b f Compton Place—Take Heart (Electric)
1670^7 2060^7 2629^9 4269^2 5051^10 5473^2 6450^9

Sacred Kingdom (AUS) *P F Yiu* 129
4 b g Encosta De Lago(AUS) —Courtroom Sweetie (AUS) (Zeditave (AUS))
(7089a)

Sacrilege *D R C Elsworth* a65
2 ch g Sakhee(USA) —Idolize (Polish Precedent (USA))
7191^6

Sacrosanct (IRE) *Joseph Crowley* 96
4 b m Sadler's Wells(USA) —Tambora (Darshaan)
875a^6 1330a^5 1777a^12 2161a^5

Saddex *P Rau* 121
4 b h Sadler's Wells(USA) —Remote Romance (USA) (Irish River (FR))
(1190a) (2292a) (4442a) 6043a^6 6943a^11

Saddlers' Queen (IRE) *J J Lennon* 20
5 b m Saddlers' Hall(IRE) —Black Queen (IRE) (Bob Back (USA))
1760a[10]

Sadeek *B Smart* 99
3 ch c Kyllachy—Miss Mercy (IRE) (Law Society (USA))
5355[8] 5809[11] 6472[20]

Sadler's Hill (IRE) *M J McGrath* a46 30
3 b g Sadler's Wells(USA) —Dedicated Lady (IRE) (Pennine Walk)
791[7] 1361[10] 4322[12] 4473[6] 7032[6] 7187[9]

Sadler's Kingdom (IRE) *R A Fahey* a54 96
3 b c Sadler's Wells(USA) —Artful Pleasure (USA) (Nasty And Bold (USA))
338[5] 484[11] 569[10] 1579[6] (1917) 2246[4] 3159[2] (3469) (4035a) 4332[4] 5197[2] (5677) 6366a[10]

Sadler's Leap (IRE) *Pat Eddery* a51 63
4 b m Sadler's Wells(USA) —Leaping Flame (USA) (Trempolino (USA))
2127[9] 2620[2] 3236[5] 4738[3] 5754[5] 6643[10]

Sadler's Star (GER) *B G Powell* a64 84
4 b g Alwuhush(USA) —Sadlerella (IRE) (King's Theatre (IRE))
488[13]

Sad Times (IRE) *W G M Turner* a57 57
3 b f Tendulkar(USA) —Mrs Kanning (Distant View (USA))
1921[3] 2200[8] 2747[3] 2978[5]

Safari *A J Chamberlain* a25 34
4 b m Namaqualand(USA) —Breakfast Creek (Hallgate)
2357[9] 2540[13] 3035[12] 3241[7]

Safari Dancer (IRE) *I Semple* 59
2 b g Indian Danehill(IRE) —Umlani (IRE) (Great Commotion (USA))
4578[8] 4890[5] 5550[6]

Safari Mischief *P Winkworth* a85 86
4 b g Primo Valentino(IRE) —Night Gypsy (Mind Games)
1885[3] (2411) 2879[6] (3452) 4095[6] 5278[5] 5381[3] 6141[4]

Safari Queen (ARG) *T Pletcher* a113 111
5 ch m Lode(USA) —Safari Girl (ARG) (Sonus (IRE))
6373a[9]

Safari Sundowner (IRE) *P Winkworth* a63 66
3 b g Daggers Drawn(USA) —Acadelli (IRE) (Royal Academy (USA))
2079[14] 6102[9] 6407[9]

Safari Sunup (IRE) *P Winkworth* a67 89
2 b c Catcher In The Rye(IRE) —Nuit Des Temps (Sadler's Wells (USA))
2991[5] (3733) 4501[2] (5871) 6471[10]

Safari Time (IRE) *P Winkworth* a59 59
2 b f Danetime(IRE) —Laurel Delight (Presidium)
4358[2] 4756[4]

Safebreaker *N Tinkler* a74 70
2 b g Key Of Luck(USA) —Insijaam (USA) (Secretariat (USA))
5675[3] 5931[2] 6289[2] 6884[3] (7140)

Safe Investment (USA) *B N Pollock* a88 89
3 b g Gone West(USA) —Fully Invested (USA) (Irish River (FR))
939[5] 1106[11] 1929[7] 5950[14] 6232[14]

Safin (GER) *F Jordan* a51
7 b g Pennekamp(USA) —Sankt Johanna (GER) (High Game)
685[8] 6342[9] 6583[10] 6803[9]

Safiyeh *M J Attwater* a31 12
2 b f Golden Snake(USA) —Safinaz (Environment Friend)
2768[11] 3733[7] 4325[8]

Safranine (IRE) *Miss A Stokell* a42 63
10 b m Dolphin Street(FR) —Webbiana (African Sky)
1534[5] 1710[6] 2309[5] 2343[9] 3277[4] 3474[4] 3784[6] 4907[6] 5627[10] 6078[11] 6962[13] 7265[9]

Safwa (IRE) *Sir Michael Stoute* 81
3 b f Green Desert(USA) —Nasanice (IRE) (Nashwan (USA))
2219[5] 2998[4] 3992[2] (4549) 5382[4] 6497[7]

Saga Celebre (FR) *John M Oxx* a85 95
3 b f Peintre Celebre(USA) —Saga D'Ouilly (FR) (Linamix (FR))
6367a[4]

Sagamihara (FR) *R Chotard* 79
2 b f Sagacity(FR) —Dontbetonme (Kris)
6187a[6]

Sagara (USA) *J E Pease* 123
3 b c Sadler's Wells(USA) —Rangoon Ruby (USA) (Kingmambo (USA))
1736a[2] 2293a[7] 3566a[3] 4872a[5] 5466a[2] 6043a[3]

Sagarich (FR) *C F Swan* 76
3 gr f Sagamix(FR) —Baranciaga (USA) (Bering)
4035a[9]

Sagassa *W De Best-Turner* a47 47
3 b f Largesse—Sally's Trust (IRE) (Classic Secret (USA))
869[7] 3794[8] 4015[13] 4828[7]

Sageburg (IRE) *A Fabre* 112
3 bb c Johannesburg(USA) —Sage Et Jolie (Linamix (FR))
5466a[4] 6032a[4]

Sagredo (USA) *Sir Mark Prescott* a84 108
3 b g Diesis—Eternity (Suave Dancer (USA))
2574[6] 3495[3] (4004) (4105) 5030[3] 5215[8] 5952[8] 6400a[6]

Sagunt (GER) *S Curran* a51 67
4 ch g Tertullian(USA) —Suva (GER) (Arazi (USA))
3350[9] 4236[12] 4884[13] 5433[6] (6447) 6780[11] 7186[11]

Sahaadi *R Hannon* 72
2 b f Dansili—Shardette (IRE) (Darshaan)
3967[5] 4774[5] 5162[4] (5707)

Sahara Boy (GER) *A Wohler* 89
2 br c Big Shuffle(USA) —Script Girl (GER) (Lavirco (GER))
6219a[5] 6888a[6]

Sahara Dawn (IRE) *D Carroll* a9 49
3 b f Desert Sun—Sharadja (IRE) (Doyoun)
1119[11] 4220[4] 4842[9] 5046[10] 5228[9] 6108[8]

Sahara Lady (IRE) *H-A Pantall* 86
3 b f Lomitas—Sagamartha (Rainbow Quest (USA))
2547a[6]

Sahara Prince (IRE) *K A Morgan* a53 49
7 b g Desert King(IRE) —Chehana (Posse (USA))
22[2] 274[12] 315[2] 500[7] 4395[12] 4532[3] 5497[5]

Sahara Silk (IRE) *D Shaw* a78 71
6 b m Desert Style(IRE) —Buddy And Soda (IRE) (Imperial Frontier (USA))
190[8] (2553) 2657[10] 3197[7]

Sahf London *G L Moore* a53 37
4 b g Vettori(IRE) —Lumiere D'Espoir (FR) (Saumarez)
(133) 187[7]

Sahnur (TUR) *Enver Mutlu* 97
3 b f Ocean Crest(USA) —Tamerinkizi (IRE) (Petorius)
5265a[7]

Sahrati *C E Brittain* a70 96
3 ch c In The Wings—Shimna (Mr Prospector (USA))
591[6] 694[4] 1010[3] 1293[4] (2126) 2790[16] 3335[2] (3959) 4092[13] 4749[10] 5805[3]

Sailing By *B R Millman* 48
2 b g Mull Of Kintyre(USA) —Rainbow Spectrum (FR) (Spectrum (IRE))
1540[13] 2078[5] 2723[3] 3364[3] 4311[5]

Sailor At Sea (USA) *R Charlton* 89
2 b c Mizzen Mast(USA) —Merida (Warning)
3085[6] (3687) (3867) 4724[6] 5032[6] 5410[10]

Sailor King (IRE) *D K Ivory* a86 86
5 b g King's Best(USA) —Manureva (USA) (Nureyev (USA))
190[6] 361[6] 513[11] 614[5] 793[3] 1063[8] (1382) 1629[2] 1845[7] (2573) 2771[7] 3215[4] 3682[2] 4548[6] 4657[8] 5223[5] 6006[3] 6391[7]

Sainglend *H Candy* 77
2 b c Galileo(IRE) —Verbal Intrigue (USA) (Dahar (USA))
3856[4] 4876[3] 5361[6] 5871[4]

Saint Alebe *D R C Elsworth* 106
8 b g Bishop Of Cashel—Soba Up (Persian Heights)
1844[16]

Saint Andrew (IRE) *Peter Casey* a66 90
3 b g Desert Prince(IRE) —Champs Elysees (USA) (Distant Relative)
4864a[12]

Saintly Place *A W Carroll* a40 51
6 ch g Compton Place—Always On A Sunday (Star Appeal)
137[7] 287[4] 440[11] 632[12] 1065[7] 2104[5] 2555[12] 2652[4] 3163[5] 4256[10] 4397[11] (Dead)

Saintly Rachel (IRE) *C F Swan* a65 97
9 b m Religiously(USA) —Ursha (IRE) (Shardari)
3138a[25] 4051a[17] 4867a[12]

Saintly Thoughts (USA) *R J Hodges* a43 52
12 bb g St Jovite(USA) —Free Thinker (USA) (Shadeed (USA))
285[7] 792[14]

Saint Remus (IRE) *Peter Grayson* a43
3 b g Diktat—Fur Will Fly (Petong)
4974[10] 5175[6] 5368[9] 6240[9] 6905[9] 7134[6]

Saitama *A M Hales* a17 7
5 b m Pursuit Of Love—Sea Ballad (USA) (Bering)
23[8] 1032[11]

Sake (IRE) *N Tinkler* 78
5 b g Shinko Forest(IRE) —Drosera (IRE) (Thatching)
1845[12] 2311[10] 2842[3] 3194[10] 3512[2] 3790[4] 4281[4] 4820[14] 5253[15]

Sakhacity *J R Jenkins* 67
2 b f Sakhee(USA) —Subtle One (IRE) (Polish Patriot (USA))
2000[6] 2968[3] 5003[6] 6237[2]

Sakhee's Secret *H Morrison* 126
3 ch c Sakhee(USA) —Palace Street (USA) (Secreto (USA))
(1099) (1808) (2695) (3506) 5214[5]

Sakhee's Song (IRE) *B Grizzetti* 109
3 b f Sakhee(USA) —Show Me The Money (IRE) (Mujadil (USA))
1337a[2] 1876a[2] 6224a[2]

Sa Kin (IRE) *A Renzoni*
2 ch c Kris Kin(USA) —Sa Magica (IRE) (Desert King (IRE))
6523a[6]

Sakkaline (IRE) *F Chappet* a89 88
7 b h Pennekamp(USA) —Shardazar (Shardari)
6923a[10]

Sakkara Star (IRE) *M Halford* 94
4 b m Mozart(IRE) —Sun Silk (USA) (Gone West (USA))
1777a[13] 3222a[6]

Salaam Dubai (AUS) *A Selvaratnam* a111
6 b g Secret Savings(USA) —Gulistan (AUS) (Rubiton (AUS))
(326a) 597a[7] 860a[3]

Salaasa (USA) *M Johnston* 89
3 ch c Swain(IRE) —Jawla (Wolfhound (USA))
(991) 1277[9] 2092[5]

Salawat *T T Clement* a15
4 b m Tomba—Galadriel (Fairy King (USA))
6070[6] 6875[11]

Salazaar (IRE) *Francis Ennis* a69 80
3 b c Xaar—Dance Ahead (Shareef Dancer (USA))
5788a[10]

Saldario (GER) *P Vovcenko* 97
5 b h Areion(GER) —Saldengeste (IRE) (Be My Guest (USA))
3122a[6] 6370a[14]

Saleima (IRE) *J Noseda* 80
2 b f Rock Of Gibraltar(IRE) —Lumber Jill (USA) (Woodman (USA))
5596[3] 6127[2] 6652[8]

Salermo (CZE) *M Weiss* 88
6 ch g Rainbows For Life(CAN) —Sapina (CZE) (Lincoln (CZE))
(438a) (494a)

Salerosa (IRE) *Mrs A Duffield* 58
2 b f Monashee Mountain(USA) —Sainte Gig (FR) (Saint Cyrien (FR))
6742[4]

Sales Tax (USA) *H A Smith* 92
2 ch f High Yield(USA) —Snit (USA) (Fit To Fight (USA))
6482a[7]

Salford Mill (IRE) *D R C Elsworth* a74 115
3 b c Peintre Celebre(USA) —Razana (IRE) (Kahyasi)
(53) 1097[2] (1475) 2235[6] 2813[7] 5351[3] 5589[4]

Salient *J Akehurst* a94 93
3 b c Fasliyev(USA) —Savannah Belle (Green Desert (USA))
939[10] 1202[3] 2213[3] 2881[5] 3553[2] 3940[12] 4268[3] 5114[2] (5360) 6013[7] 6301[18] 6606[2] 6932[5] 7074[2] 7254[3]

Salinger (USA) *Mrs L J Mongan* a61
5 b g Lear Fan(USA) —Sharp Flick (USA) (Sharpen Up)
496[7] 558[12]

Salingers Star (IRE) *G A Swinbank* 76
2 b f Catcher In The Rye(IRE) —Head For The Stars (IRE) (Head For Heights)
(2904) 4819[4]

Salisburgo (ITY) *V di Napoli* 102
4 b h Big Shuffle(USA) —Exy Girl (IRE) (Alzao (USA))
6767a[5]

Salisbury Plain *N I M Rossiter* a56 53
6 b h Mark Of Esteem(IRE) —Wild Pavane (Dancing Brave (USA))
1612[11] 1787[8] 2665[10] 2831[7] 3167[4] 3487[12] 4945[14]

Salisbury World (IRE) *J F Coupland*
4 ch g Spinning World(USA) —Dinka Raja (USA) (Woodman (USA))
2795[14] 4410[9]

Salishan (IRE) *Adrian McGuinness* a30 67
5 ch m Namid—Lancea (IRE) (Generous (IRE))
873a[15]

Salonga (IRE) *C F Wall* a73 73
4 b m Shinko Forest(IRE) —Alongside (Slip Anchor)
2004[13] 2521[3] 3249[2]

Salontiger (GER) *A Kleinkorres* 91
5 b g Tiger Hill(IRE) —She's His Guest (IRE) (Be My Guest (USA))
1189a[6]

Saloon (USA) *Sir Michael Stoute* 73
3 b c Sadler's Wells(USA) —Fire The Groom (USA) (Blushing Groom (FR))
6275[2]

Salsadar *J H M Gosden* a63 26
3 ch f Zamindar(USA) —Flaming Salsa (FR) (Salse (USA))
1030[2] 1396[9]

Salsalava (FR) *P Demercastel* a96 104
4 b h Kingsalsa(USA) —Lavayssiere (FR) (Sicyos (USA))
437a[6]

Salsalavie (FR) *P Demercastel* 99
2 b c Fly To The Stars—Lavayssiere (FR) (Sicyos (USA))
5660a[4] 6377a[5]

Salsa Steps (USA) *H Morrison* a75 80
3 ch f Giant's Causeway(USA) —Dance Design (IRE) (Sadler's Wells (USA))
3387[4] 3992[5] (5714) 6300[10]

Salsa Time *Miss J A Camacho* 65
2 b f Hernando(FR) —Kabayil (Dancing Brave (USA))
5734[2]

Salsa Verdi (USA) *Saeed Bin Suroor* a78
3 b f Giant's Causeway(USA) —Cape Verdi (IRE) (Caerleon (USA))
2766[2] 3214[3] (4430)

Saltagioo (ITY) *A & G Botti* 91
3 b c Dr Devious(IRE) —Sces (Kris)
1335a[5]

Salto Chico *W M Brisbourne* a43 54
3 b g Fraam—Miss Tango (Batshoof)
1224[9] 2259[5] 4339[6] 4877[7] 5040[4]

Salt Of The Earth (IRE) *T G Mills* a75
2 b c Invincible Spirit(IRE) —Get The Accountant (Vettori (IRE))
6897[3]

Salt Track (ARG) *Niels Petersen* a100 95
7 b h Salt Lake(USA) —Astralisima (ARG) (Fitzcarraldo (ARG))
172a[11] 327a[7] 410a[6] 532a[5] (1648a) 4874a[5]

Saluscraggie *K G Reveley* 61
5 b m Most Welcome—Upper Caen (High Top)
(2370) 2579[4] 2868[4] 3584[5] 3719[7]

Salute (IRE) *P G Murphy* a89 89
8 b g Muhtarram(USA) —Alasib (Siberian Express (USA))
(662) 944[2] 1148[7] 1506[5] 3216[4] 3748[4] 4483[3] (5427) 5769[9] 6356[2] 6739[4] (6999)

Salute Him (IRE) *A J Martin* 97
4 b g Mull Of Kintyre(USA) —Living Legend (ITY) (Archway (IRE))
2067a[11]

Salute The General *Micky Hammond* 86
4 ch g Mark Of Esteem(IRE) —Oiselina (FR) (Linamix (FR))
6475[13]

Salute The Sarge (USA) *Eric J Guillot* a112 112
2 b c Forest Wildcat(USA) —Dixie Ghost (USA) (Silver Ghost (USA))
6508a[9]

Salute The Sun (FR) *L Urbano-Grajales* 92
4 b m Fly To The Stars—Fulcrum (Pivotal)
2811a[5]

Salut L'Africain (FR) *Robert Collet* 104
2 b c Ski Chief(USA) —Mamana (IRE) (Highest Honor (FR))
3147a[5] 4625a[5] 5260a[4] 6136a[2] 6631a[4] 6888a[4]

Salut Saint Cloud *G L Moore* a79 64
6 b g Primo Dominie—Tiriana (Common Grounds)
4[4] 232[7] 354[4] 640[5] (775) 844[2] 1253[6] 1793[8] 6902[11] 7018[11] 7194[9]

Salvestro *A W Carroll* a47 65
4 b g Medicean—Katy Nowaitee (Komaite (USA))
976[7] 1435[9] 1539[9] 1671[5] 2979[8] 3617[8] 4321[8] 4532[6] 5269[12] 5345[5] 6452[6]

Salym (FR) *D J S Ffrench Davis* a43 26
6 ch g Limnos(JPN) —Tina's Crest (FR) (Ocean Falls)
372[3] 665[10] 730[4] 5820[9]

Samahir (USA) *T T Clement* a48 55
3 b f Forest Wildcat(USA) —Saabga (USA) (Woodman (USA))
6094[5] 6597[5] 6895[6] 6975[6]

Samarinda (USA) *Mrs P Sly* a99 93
4 ch g Rahy(USA) —Munnaya (USA) (Nijinsky (CAN))
117[2] 422[4] (604) 1395[7] (2995) (3215) (3650) 5221[3] 5833[3] 6143[12]

Sambalando (SWE) *Annike Bye Nunez*
3 b c Ashkalani(IRE) —Clois Mor (IRE) (Ela-Mana-Mou)
2548a[P]

Samba Reggae (ARG) *I Mohammed* a106
4 ch m Mutakddim(USA) —Rapper (ARG) (Southern Halo (USA))
476a[3] 647a[2]

Sambatiger (GER) *T Horwart* 79
2 b c Tiger Hill(IRE) —Samambaia (GER) (Ti Amo (GER))
6939a[8]

Samdaniya *C E Brittain* a51 83
3 b f Machiavellian(USA) —Cloud Castle (In The Wings)
2369[11] 2606[9] 4079[5] (4327) 5067[5] 5514[13]

Samira Gold (FR) *L M Cumani* 107
3 ch f Gold Away(IRE) —Capework (USA) (El Gran Senor (USA))
(2433) (2862) 3628[2] 4059[9] (4849) (5544) 6168[3]

Samizdat (FR) *James Moffatt* 72
4 b g Soviet Star(USA) —Secret Account (FR) (Bering)
1152[15] 3412[10]

Sam Lord *J H M Gosden* a69 80
3 ch g Observatory(USA) —My Mariam (Salse (USA))
1202[8] 1974[8] 2340[4]

Sammy The Snake (IRE) *B W Duke* 86
2 b c Diktat—Love Emerald (USA) (Mister Baileys) (779a)

Sammy Van Ammy (USA) *R Dutrow Jr* 87
2 br f Van Nistelrooy(USA) —Sammy Ammy (USA) (Henbane (USA))
6482a[9]

Samorra (IRE) *M P Tregoning* a46 76
3 b f In The Wings—Walesiana (GER) (Star Appeal)
1956[7] 2627[12]

Sam P. (USA) *T Pletcher* a102
3 ch c Cat Thief(USA) —Affirmed Legacy (USA) (Affirmed (USA))
1486a[9]

Samsa (FR) *R Gibson* a98 98
4 b m Zafonic(USA) —Everlasting Love (Pursuit Of Love)
31a[2]

Sam's Cross (IRE) *W R Swinburn* 86
2 b c Cape Cross(IRE) —Fancy Lady (Cadeaux Genereux)
4286[2] (5448) 6171[3] 6488[8]

Samsons Son *J R Best* a55 90
3 b g Primo Valentino(IRE) —Santiburi Girl (Casteddu)
1117[10] 1343[7] 1632[3] 2400[9] (2749) (3707) 3913[3] 4093[8] 4847[5] (5718)

Sam's Secret *G A Swinbank* a69 83
5 b m Josr Algarhoud(IRE) —Twilight Time (Aragon)
(1893) (2091) 2550[4] (3816) (4081) (4100) 4407[6] 5230[2] 5545[6]

Samuel *J L Dunlop* 106
3 ch c Sakhee(USA) —Dolores (Danehill (USA))
1129[3] 1998[2] 3458[3] 4803[2] 5408[9]

Samuel Charles *C R Dore* a86 84
9 b g Green Desert(USA) —Hejraan (USA) (Alydar (USA))
185[7] 427[8] (455) 592[6] 674[5] (830) 933[4] 1066[2] 1638[11] 2258[3] (3172) 3619[2] 3922[2] (5020) 5424[3] (6024) (6268) 6710[4] 6806[5] 7269[8]

Samurai Warrior *P J Makin* a73 63
2 br g Beat All(USA) —Ma Vie (Salse (USA))
4764[8] 5605[2] 6404[7]

Samurai Way *L M Cumani* 108
5 b g Darshaan—Truly Special (Caerleon (USA))
1149[2] (1849) 3509[2] 4047[2] 5215[2] (5800) 6335[24]

Samya *E Borromeo* 101
3 b f Invincible Spirit(IRE) —Special Society (IRE) (Imp Society (USA))
1701a[5] 4118[13]

San Antonio *Mrs P Sly* a96 86
7 b g Efisio—Winnebago (Kris)
119[8] 765[10] 2004[3] 2469[13] 2722[6]

Sa Nau *T Keddy* a57 64
4 b g Generous(IRE) —Trellis Bay (Sadler's Wells (USA))
747[5] 2367[6] 3630[3] 4030[4] 4297[4] 4638[2] 4906[4] 5283[4] 6131[8]

Sanaya (IRE) *A De Royer-Dupre* 114
4 b m Barathea(IRE) —Sanariya (IRE) (Darshaan) (397a) 600a[11]

Sanbuch *L M Cumani* a86 108
3 b c Tobougg(IRE) —Monte Calvo (Shirley Heights)
1230[3] 1987[4] 2448[4] (4147) 5141[2] 6014[2] 6759[2]

Sanchi (IRE) *E Charpy* 101
5 b h Darshaan—Samara (IRE) (Polish Patriot (USA))
412a[4] 545a[10]

Sandalphon (USA) *J A Geake* a12
4 b g King Cugat(USA) —Noumea (USA) (Plugged Nickle (USA))
736[4]

Sandarkan (USA) *G A Swinbank*
3 b g Rahy(USA) —True Fantasy (USA) (Seeking The Gold (USA))
4290[6]

Sand Cat *G L Moore* a85 97
4 b g Cadeaux Genereux—Desert Lynx (IRE) (Green Desert (USA))
172a[9] 409a[4] 472a[3] 3329[9] 4062[12] 4122[27] 6142[8] 6589[5] 6900[7] 6970[3] 7087[9]

San Deng *Micky Hammond* a68 70
5 gr g Averti(IRE) —Miss Mirror (Magic Mirror)
1239[4]

Sander Camillo (USA) *J Noseda* 116
3 b f Dixie Union(USA) —Staraway (USA) (Star De Naskra (USA))
1096[2] 1702a[8] 3506[18] 4118[16]

Sanders Boy *J R Norton* a48 15
4 gr g Arkadian Hero(USA) —Rising Of The Moon (IRE) (Warning)
42[9]

Sandies Choice *M Brittain* 30
2 ch f Tobougg(IRE) —Nijmah (Halling (USA))
1528[5] 1859[9] 2803[9] 5501[12]

Sand Maiden (IRE) *T D Easterby* 54
2 ch f Desert Prince(IRE) —Maka (USA) (Diesis)
3718[13] 4448[8] 4784[5] 5298[6]

San Domenico *P Bary* a101 103
3 b c Zamindar(USA) —Guarded (Eagle Eyed (USA))
1056a[7]

Sand Repeal (IRE) *Miss J Feilden* a73 71
5 b g Revoque(IRE) —Columbian Sand (IRE) (Salmon Leap (USA))
585[3] 631[3] 775[3] 994[6] 1222[2] (2686) 3279[4] 3630[4] 4708[7] 5769[4] 6200[5] 7135[4]

Sandrey (IRE) *P W Chapple-Hyam* a83 92
3 b g Noverre(USA) —Boudica (IRE) (Alhaarth (IRE))
(1660) 2044[14] 3431[12] 6437[13]

Sandro Chia (IRE) *M Colombi* 100
5 b h Rudimentary(USA) —Frida Khalo (Unfuwain (USA))
1518a[3]

Sands Crooner (IRE) *D Shaw* a74 66
4 b g Imperial Ballet(IRE) —Kurfuffle (Bluebird (USA))
163[5] 262[4] 371[10] 480[9] 626[11] 787[7] 1669[4] 1946[6] 2516[5] 2712[11] (3368) 3627[6] 4103[8] 4635[10] (7082) 7206[5]

Sands Of Barra (IRE) *I W McInnes* a72 78
4 gr g Marju(IRE) —Purple Risks (FR) (Take Risks (FR))
1539[12] 1675[9] 2556[5] 2827[2] 3375[7] 3414[9] 4042[8] 4250[7] 4562[10] (4731) 5476[2] (5556) 5840[6] 5893[5] 6463[13]

Sandtime (IRE) *John M Oxx* 86
3 b f Green Desert(USA) —Key Change (IRE) (Darshaan)
6216a[12]

Sandwith *J S Wainwright* a70 70
4 ch g Perryston View—Bodfari Times (Clantime)
566[4] 787[8] 1134[13] 1806[8] 2386[5] 2830[6] 5552[11] (5836) (6244) 6743[5] 6860[4] 7005[5]

Sandymount Earl (IRE) *Mrs John Harrington* 93
4 ch g Hernando(FR) —Joleah (IRE) (Ela-Mana-Mou)
3664a[DSQ] (6366a)

Sandy Par *P Winkworth* a51 62
2 ch g No Excuse Needed—Nesting (Thatching)
2103[3] 2687[3] 3687[7] 4903[9] 6098[7]

Sangfroid *Sir Mark Prescott* a31 53
3 gr g With Approval(CAN) —Affaire D'Amour (Hernando (FR))
3183[4] 3792[7] 4821[5] (4943) 5158[10] 5899[13]

Sangreal *K R Burke* a65 62
3 ch f Medicean—La Belle Dominique (Dominion)
1676[4] 2453[12] 2829[9] 3611[10] 3918[4] 4526[14] 5967[9]

Sanjida (IRE) *A De Royer-Dupre* 97
2 b f Polish Precedent(USA) —Sanariya (IRE) (Darshaan)
6377a[3]

San Moritz (POL) *A Walicki* 78
3 b c Roulette—Santa Monika (POL) (Who Knows)
5929a[10]

Sanripoli (IRE) *V Valiani* 74
3 b c Danehill Dancer(IRE) —Wooderine (USA) (Woodman (USA))
1336a[9]

San Roque (USA) *Ms F M Crowley* 51
2 ch c Thunder Gulch(USA) —Elegant Asset (USA) (Lord At War (ARG))
6443a[12]

San Salvador (USA) *S Seemar* a93 104
10 bb g Dayjur(USA) —Sheer Gold (USA) (Cutlass (USA))
396a[13]

San Silvestro (IRE) *Mrs A Duffield* 68
2 b c Fayruz—Skehana (IRE) (Mukaddamah (USA))
(6698)

Sans Souci Island (CAN) *R L Attfield* 106
3 b f Chester House(USA) —Faux Pas (IRE) (Sadler's Wells (USA))
6373a[5]

Santa Clara *Jane Chapple-Hyam* a57 59
2 b f Night Shift(USA) —Mena (Blakeney)
5428[11] 6082[3] 6434[10] 7136[4]

Santa Gertrudis (IRE) *Kevin Prendergast* a63 62
3 b f Machiavellian(USA) —Tani (USA) (Theatrical)
4865a[9]

Santaverti *G L Moore* a62
4 br g Averti(IRE) —Santa Vida (USA) (St Jovite (USA))
611[5] 788[2] 869[5] 1609[15] 2140[10] 2357[8]

Santera (IRE) *Mrs A Duffield* a40 43
3 br f Gold Away(IRE) —Sainte Gig (FR) (Saint Cyrien (FR))
2420[4] 2840[9] 6904[6] 7133[7]

Santero (GER) *N Sauer*
2 b c Black Sam Bellamy(IRE) —Strofa (POL) (Winds Of Light (USA))
6219a[5]

Santiago (GER) *H Blume* a113 112
5 gr h Highest Honor(FR) —Serenata (GER) (Lomitas)
5670a[3] 6045a[3] (6687a)

Santiago Atitlan *A Wohler* 103
5 gr g Stravinsky(USA) —Sylvette (USA) (Silver Hawk (USA))
1189a[4] 1876a[5] 4213a[6] 4869a[2]

Saoirse Abu (USA) *J S Bolger* 110
2 ch f Mr Greeley(USA) —Out To Late (USA) (Future Storm (USA))
2325a[2] 3071a[5] 3659a[3] (4437a) (5073a) 5796[3]

Saoodah (IRE) *M A Jarvis* a61 37
2 b f Green Desert(USA) —Saeedah (Bustino)
2630[8] 3187[5] 4329[6]

Sapphire Dream *A Bailey* 30
5 b m Mind Games—Bombay Sapphire (Be My Chief (USA))
2657[9]

Sapucai (ARG) *S Seemar* a79 51
7 b g Lode(USA) —Saint Donatila (ARG) (Saint Sever (FR))
329a[13] 410a[15]

Sarah Park (IRE) *B J Meehan* a51 56
2 ch f Redback—Brillano (FR) (Desert King (IRE))
2569[5] 2876[9] 3550[7] 5423[7]

Sarah's Art (IRE) *Stef Liddiard* a61 74
4 gr g City On A Hill(USA) —Treasure Bleue (IRE) (Treasure Kay)
132[12] 214[8] 1321[7] (5817) 6895[12]

Sarah's Boy *S Dow* 36
2 ch g Nayef(USA) —Bella Bianca (IRE) (Barathea (IRE))
5919[10] 6294[10]

Sarah's First *E A L Dunlop* a57 67
2 ch f Cadeaux Genereux—Band (USA) (Northern Dancer (CAN))
5912[7] 6296[5] 6601[6]

Sara Mana Mou *J G Portman* a45 39
4 b m Medicean—Sarabah (IRE) (Ela-Mana-Mou)
808[8]

Saranome (IRE) *R Charlton* 70
2 b c Statue Of Liberty(USA) —My Gray (FR) (Danehill (USA))
6125[9] 6419[4] 6721[7]

Saratee *C E Brittain* 56
2 b f Mark Of Esteem(IRE) —Salalah (Lion Cavern (USA))
5524[6] 5881[6]

Sargentos (GER) *M F Harris* 6
5 gr g Linamix(FR) —Subia (GER) (Konigsstuhl (GER))
355a[10] 438a[8] 493a[9]

Saricana (IRE) *John M Oxx* 75
3 b f Invincible Spirit(IRE) —Sarenara (IRE) (Darshaan)
782a[6]

Sarkando (GER) *E Kurdu* 83
2 ch f Black Sam Bellamy(IRE) —Solita (GER) (Lomitas)
5463a[4]

Sarraaf (IRE) *I Semple* a60 63
11 ch g Perugino(USA) —Blue Vista (IRE) (Pennine Walk)
3539[4] 4159[4] 4477[7] 5037[2] 5479[4] 5838[8] 5966[9] 6479[10] 6732[4] 6873[2] 7079[3] 7218[10]

Sarrera (AUS) *M Moroney* 105
7 b g Quest For Fame—Zamsong (NZ) (Zabeel (NZ))
6712a[18]

Sarwin (USA) *W J Musson* a75 59
4 rg g Holy Bull(USA) —Olive The Twist (USA) (Theatrical)
110[2] (539)

Sasphee (GER) *E Kurdu* 89
3 b f Lomitas—Suanita (GER) (Big Shuffle (USA))
6690a[7]

Sassoaloro (GER) *A Wohler* 96
3 ch c Acatenango(GER) —Spartina (USA) (Northern Baby (CAN))
2102a[4]

Sassy Gal (IRE) *John Joseph Murphy* a72 88
2 ch f King's Best(USA) —Dancing Prize (IRE) (Sadler's Wells (USA))
5843a[7] (6578)

Satan's Sister *Ian Williams* 9
6 ch m Tout Ensemble—Winter Greeting (Hello Gorgeous (USA))
3847[12] 4334[10]

Satin Braid *D R C Elsworth* a75 71
3 b f Diktat—Beading (Polish Precedent (USA))
1409[4] 1920[4] 5013[4] 5475[10] 6547[8] (6710) 7047[2] 7164[10]

Satindra (IRE) *John A Harris* a65 60
3 b g Lil's Boy(USA) —Voronova (IRE) (Sadler's Wells (USA))
6245[6] 6570[3] 6833[3] 7032[3] (7199) 7242[5]

Satinspin (NZ) *R Smerdon* 95
6 ch g Spinning World(USA) —Satin Blush (NZ) (Tawfiq (USA))
6711a[11]

Satri (IRE) *J-M Beguigne* 113
5 b h Mujadil(USA) —Laramie (USA) (Gulch (USA))
2953a[5] 3780a[2] 4214a[6] 5259a[4] 6614a[7]

Satulagi (USA) *J S Moore* a80 100
3 b f Officer(USA) —Shawgatny (USA) (Danzig Connection (USA))
246a[2] 476a[8] 1496[9] 1824[5] 2757[18] 3940[9] 5047[7] 6168[12]

Saturday Boy *Paul Green* a59 48
2 b c Josr Algarhoud(IRE) —Prideway (IRE) (Pips Pride)
2432[9] 3977[7] 4125[10] 4524[11] 5605[8] 5984[11] 7022[4]

Satwa Baron *D J Daly* a31
3 b c Singspiel(IRE) —Crown Of Spring (USA) (Chief's Crown (USA))
160[9] 311[11] 3176[11]

Satwa Queen (FR) *J De Roualle* 119
5 ch m Muhtathir—Tolga (USA) (Irish River (FR))
1421a[2] 2753[2] (4652a) (6042a)

Satyricon *M Botti* a79 81
3 b c Dr Fong(USA) —Belladera (IRE) (Alzao (USA))
(348) 591[3] 694[2] 843[5] 1815[9] 2335[3] (2534) 4170[9] 5092[6] 5819[5] 6795[4] 7094[10]

Saucy *Daniel Mark Loughnane* a56 69
6 b m Muhtarram(USA) —So Saucy (Teenoso (USA))
(274) 500[2] 616[12] 1038[3] 6096[14] 6906[7]

Saunders Encore *M S Saunders* a4
2 b f Piccolo—Magical Dancer (IRE) (Magical Wonder (USA))
7043[6]

Sauze D'Oulx *B R Millman* 88
2 b g Makbul—Bewails (IRE) (Caerleon (USA))
898[4] (1058) 1390[6] 1882[4] (3680) 4126[2] 5053[6] 5217[7]

Savanagh Forest (IRE) *M Quinn* a43 44
3 b f Shinko Forest(IRE) —Adieu Cherie (IRE) (Bustino)
343[7] (934) 4226[16] 4514[6] 5716[2] 6402[10]

Savannah *Luke Comer* a83 103
4 b h Sadler's Wells(USA) —La Papagena (Habitat)
57[5]

Savannah Bay *B Ellison* a85 92
8 ch g In The Wings—High Savannah (Rousillon (USA))
5215[14] 5677[8] 6335[31]

Savarain *L M Cumani* 79
2 b c Rainbow Quest(USA) —Frangy (Sadler's Wells (USA))
5951[4] 6493[4]

Savethisdanceforme (IRE) *A P O'Brien* a80 111
2 b f Danehill Dancer(IRE) —Bex (USA) (Explodent (USA))
5435a[8] 6040a[4]

Savile's Delight (IRE) *Tom Dascombe* a45 64
8 b g Cadeaux Genereux—Across The Ice (USA) (General Holme (USA))
66[8] 368[8] 448[9] 519[14] 715[4] 1569[7] 2104[4] 2619[9] 7107[6]

Saviour Sand (IRE) *D R C Elsworth* a74 76
3 b g Desert Sun—Teacher Preacher (IRE) (Taufan (USA))
160[6] 2046[2] 2880[5] 3420[11] 6975[4] 7174[3]

Saviours Spirit *T G Mills* a95 84
6 ch g Komaite(USA) —Greenway Lady (Prince Daniel (USA))
198[6] 452[2] 550[5] (1063) 1465[2] 2494[8]

Savoisien (FR) *J-V Toux* 98
7 b h Mansonnien(FR) —La Vie Immobile (USA) (Alleged (USA))
6941a[0]

Savoy Chapel *A W Carroll* a54 43
5 br g Xaar—Royal Gift (Cadeaux Genereux)
51[U] 129[7] 210[2] 350[8] 447[9] 497[4] 557[3] 721[4] 789[7] 887[2] 1210[12] 2331[11] 2557[2] 2963[3] 3428[5] 3868[9]

Sawherfirstandknew (IRE) *Miss Martina Anne Doran* 81
2 b f Statue Of Liberty(USA) —Salsicaia (Pursuit Of Love)
779a[10]

Sawpit Solitaire *J L Spearing*
2 gr f Daylami(IRE) —Balleta (USA) (Lyphard (USA))
6725[10]

Sawpit Sunshine (IRE) *J L Spearing* 65
2 b f Mujadil(USA) —Curie Express (IRE) (Fayruz)
2416[4] 2977[8] 3465[3] (3841) 5939[12]

Sawwaah (IRE) *Tom Dascombe* a76 86
10 b g Marju(IRE) —Just A Mirage (Green Desert (USA))
605[4] 664[4] (768) (825) (912) 1086[4] 1559[2] 2113[3] (2275) (2467) (2559) 7057[2] 7189[2]

Saxon Saint *M D I Usher* a25 49
4 b g Josr Algarhoud(IRE) —Antithesis (IRE) (Fairy King (USA))
2399[14] 2725[12]

Sayedati Elhasna (IRE) *J L Dunlop* 69
2 b f Alhaarth(IRE) —Sayedati Eljamilah (USA) (Mr Prospector (USA))
2969[3] 6093[6] 6648[6]

Sayyedati Symphony (USA) *C E Brittain* 88
2 b f Gone West(USA) —Sayyedati (Shadeed (USA))
5801[2] 6130[3] 6652[6]

Scalded Cat (IRE) *Daniel William O'Sullivan* 70
4 b m Raise A Grand(IRE) —Piccolo Rose (Piccolo)
873a[2]

Scamperdale *B P J Baugh* a83 78
5 br g Compton Place—Miss Up N Go (Gorytus (USA))
206[4] 286[6] (805) 1069[2] (1284) 1655[5] 2521[2] 3111[3] 3416[4] 3926[5] 4418 [5] 5178[5] (7173)

Scanno (IRE) *K R Burke* 59
2 b c Captain Rio—In Denial (IRE) (Maelstrom Lake)
3606[5]

Scaramoushca *G C Bravery* a56
4 gr g Most Welcome—Kinraddie (Wuzo (USA))
1[5] 270[3] 603[4] 808[5] 6807[4] 7120[9]

Scarlet Flyer (USA) *G L Moore* a78 83
4 b g Gilded Time(USA) —Tennis Partner (USA) (Northern Dancer (CAN))
1023[8] 1308[7] 1666[9] (1984) 2626[4] 3350[3] 4268[7] 5383[6] 5712[9] 6269[3]

Scarlet Knight *P Mitchell* a82 82
4 b g Lujain(USA) —Gem (Most Welcome)
1971[17] 2318[8] 2725[6] 3218[8] 3906[8] 4236[3] 4807[9] 5275[4] 5733[3] 5917[13]

Scarlet Oak *D J S Ffrench Davis* a68 73
3 b f Zamindar(USA) —Flamenco Red (Warning)
293[6] 456[8] (574) 679[2] 2515[8] 3168[5] 3369[3] 4361[7] 5136[9] (6089) 6283[10] 6423[7]

Scarlet Royal *Mrs Marjorie Fife* 46
2 b f Red Ransom(USA) —Royal Future (IRE) (Royal Academy (USA))
3761[13] 4173[7] 4522[8]

Scarlet Runner *J L Dunlop* 106
3 b f Night Shift(USA) —Sweet Pea (Persian Bold)
(1096) 1496[7] 2814[6] 4118[6] 5214[8] 5832[17]

Scarlett Heart (IRE) *J G Burns* a68 68
3 b f Lujain(USA) —Scarlett Ribbon (Most Welcome)
343[3] 588[2] 786[5] (1248) 1948[6] (2195) 2515[5] 3649[5] 4186[2] 4314[4] 4759[5] 4944[9] 6174[9] 6340[9] (6402) 7161[4]

Scarrabus (IRE) *A Crook* a39 52
6 b g Charnwood Forest(IRE) —Errazuriz (IRE) (Classic Music (USA))
913[9] 1479[5] 1745[8]

Scar Tissue *E J Creighton* a53 58
3 ch f Medicean—Possessive Lady (Dara Monarch)
1901[5] 3730[2] 4205[12] 4742[10]

Scartozz *A & G Botti* 94
5 b h Barathea(IRE) —Amazing Bay (Mazilier (USA))
2295a[5]

Scary *P F I Cole* a60
3 ch g Peintre Celebre(USA) —Danlu (USA) (Danzig (USA))
6807[3] 7199[5]

Scat Daddy (USA) *T Pletcher* a119
3 b c Johannesburg(USA) —Love Style (USA) (Mr Prospector (USA))
1486a[18]

Scatina (IRE) *Mario Hofer* 101
3 b f Samum(GER) —Silvassa (IRE) (Darshaan)
(1515a) 2707a[3] 3434[10] 4651a[4] 5849a[2] 6781a[2]

Scene Three *J J Quinn* a23 45
3 gr f Act One—Ferber's Follies (USA) (Saratoga Six (USA))
2032[8] 6152[10] 6570[8]

Scenic Shot (AUS) *D Morton* 115
5 b g Scenic—Sweepshot (AUS) (Dr Grace (NZ))
15a[4] 6354a[10] 6712a[16]

Sceptre Rouge (IRE) *A De Royer-Dupre* 100
2 b c Red Ransom(USA) —Marque Royale (Royal Academy (USA))
6615a[6]

Schermuly (IRE) *M Johnston* a46
3 b g Fruits Of Love(USA) —Express Account (Carr De Naskra (USA))
114[8]

Schiaparelli (GER) *P Schiergen* 119
4 ch h Monsun(GER) —Sacarina (Old Vic)
1190a[8] 1872a[3] (2924a) (3778a) (5671a) (6223a)

Schoenberg (USA) *C R Egerton* a44 69
3 ch c Johannesburg(USA) —Bahia Gold (USA) (Woodman (USA))
973[6] 4258[4] 5873[10] 6806[14]

Schutzenjunker (GER) *U Ostmann* 85
2 b c Lord Of Men—Schutzenliebe (GER) (Alkalde (GER))
(6324a)

Scientific *R A Fahey* a56 45
2 b g Fraam—Lady Butler (IRE) (Puissance)
4174[7] 4578[13] 5081[5] 5477[9] 6305[5] 6880[4] 7101[2] 7286[2]

Scintillation (AUS) *C S Shum* 120
7 b g Danehill(USA) —Subterfuge (Machiavellian (USA))
7089a[4]

Scintillo *R Hannon* 110
2 ch c Fantastic Light(USA) —Danseuse Du Soir (IRE) (Thatching)
1990[5] 2855[7] (3270) 4057[4] 4598[3] 5004[2] 5795[3] (6222a)

Scorpion (IRE) *A P O'Brien* 123
5 b h Montjeu(IRE) —Ardmelody (Law Society (USA))
1618[2] (2210) 2856[2] 3942[5] 5437a[2]

Scotch Bonnet (IRE) *R Gibson* 101
3 b f Montjeu(IRE) —Valley Of Hope (USA) (Riverman (USA))
3564a[5] 6953a[4]

Scotch Pancake *E A L Dunlop* a70 81
4 ch m Selkirk(USA) —Galette (Caerleon (USA))
1352[7]

Scotland The Brave *J D Bethell* 76
7 ch m Zilzal(USA) —Hunters Of Brora (IRE) (Sharpo)
2256[9] 2719[5] 3194[6] (3572) 3790[5]

Scotland Yard (UAE) *D E Pipe* a76 93
4 b g Jade Robbery(USA) —Aqraba (Polish Precedent (USA))
2736[16]

Scots W'Hae *S C Williams* a45
2 b c Piccolo—Ionian Secret (Mystiko (USA))
6897[10]

Scott *J Jay* a50 53
6 gr g Polar Falcon(USA) —Circled (USA) (Cozzene (USA))
1378[6] 1752[8] 5389[12]

Scottish River (USA) *M D I Usher* a70 69
8 b g Thunder Gulch(USA) —Overbrook (Storm Cat (USA))
(179) 206[5] 279[5] 1027[4] (1167) (1227) 1284[2] 1811[5] 2467[8] 2603[3] 3036[2] 3232[5] 3600[6] 3907[10]

Scottish Spirit (IRE) *J S Haldane*
3 b g Invincible Spirit(IRE) —Triphibious (Zafonic (USA))
1625[13] 6730[10]

Scott Summerland (HOL) *Mervyn Torrens* a54 65
4 b g Bretigny(FR) —Licence Summerland (Lion Cavern (USA))
7146[6]

Scotty's Future (IRE) *A Berry* a43 69
9 b g Namaqualand(USA) —Persian Empress (IRE) (Persian Bold)
617[8] 891[8] (3257) 3403[5] 3571[9] 3789[3] 4042[10] 4219[8] 4526[13] 4704[5] 5704[11] 6304[12] 6380[15] 6637[5]

Scoubidou (GER) *H Blume* 100
3 b f Johan Cruyff—Simply Red (GER) (Dashing Blade)
1515a[2] 2294a[4] 3148a[6] 6690a[4]

Scrap N'Dust *W G M Turner* a43 24
2 b f Averti(IRE) —Happy Lady (FR) (Cadeaux Genereux)
1000[4] 2078[7] 2517[5] 2723[9]

Screaming Reel *M Wellings* a12 52
4 b g Dr Fong(USA) —Heart Of India (IRE) (Try My Best (USA))
1995[10] 2433[6] 4018[9] 4856[15] *5235[10]*

Screenplay *G L Moore* a69 69
6 ch g In The Wings—Erudite (Generous (IRE))
2430[7] 2887[5] 3692[4] 4056[11] 5138[6]

Screen Star (IRE) *M Johnston* 99
2 gr f Tobougg(IRE) —Actoris (USA) (Diesis)
(4819)

Scripted (USA) *L M Cumani* 65
3 br c Theatrical—Val Gardena (CHI) (Roy (USA))
2046[7] 3685[6]

Scriptwriter (IRE) *Saeed Bin Suroor* 112
5 b g Sadler's Wells(USA) —Dayanata (Shirley Heights)
(1805) 2859[6] (4047) 4722[3]

Scroll *P Howling* a73 58
4 b g Mark Of Esteem(IRE) —Bella Bellisimo (IRE) (Alzao (USA))
131[9] 235[8] 612[9] 742[5] 1025[8] 1318[8] 2004[8] 2336[7] *2591[2]* 2665[11] *2798[5] 3405[10]*

Scruffy (IRE) *C J Teague* 24
3 b g Second Empire(IRE) —Karakapa (FR) (Subotica (FR))
2740[12] 3639[12] 3994[9] 4411[6] *6315[13] 7148[11]*

Scruffy Skip (IRE) *M Dods* 64
2 b g Diktat—Capoeira (USA) (Nureyev (USA))
2710[7] 4125[4] 4769[5] 5932[10] 6329[11]

Scuba (IRE) *H Morrison* a73 72
5 b g Indian Danehill(IRE) —March Star (IRE) (Mac's Imp (USA))
70[4] 724[11] 1640[14] *2149[3] 2802[2] 3191[6] 4394[5] 4978[3] 5643[6]*

Scuffle *R Charlton* 76
2 gr f Daylami(IRE) —Tantina (USA) (Distant View (USA))
6493[3]

Sculptor (NZ) *P McKenzie* 108
5 b h His Royal Highness(NZ) —Betelgeuse (NZ) (Full Out (USA))
6712a[9]

Scupio *Kevin Prendergast* 84
2 ch g Intikhab(USA) —Real Flame (Cyrano De Bergerac)
779a[2]

Scurra *A C Whillans* a43 46
8 b g Spectrum(IRE) —Tamnia (Green Desert (USA))
126[8] 3012[9] 4475[7] 5835[9]

Scutch Mill (IRE) *P C Haslam* a70 65
5 ch g Alhaarth(IRE) —Bumble (Rainbow Quest (USA))
976[3] 2201[9] *6459[6] 6883[8]*

Scuzme (IRE) *M A Barnes* a55 58
4 br g Xaar—Decatur (Deploy)
52[4] 159[4] 288[6] 481[7] 1402[4] 1590[7] 2176[8] 3840[11]

Sea Admiral *R Charlton* 66
2 b g Sinndar(IRE) —Overboard (IRE) (Rainbow Quest (USA))
5091[3] 5880[8] 6418[13]

Seabow (USA) *Saeed Bin Suroor* 99
4 b h Rainbow Quest(USA) —Dream Bay (USA) (Mr Prospector (USA))
3882[3] 4166[6] (5362) 6011[14] 6499[12]

Sea Chanter (USA) *T Pletcher* 101
2 b f War Chant(USA) —Smooth Charmer (USA) (Easy Goer (USA))
(6482a)

Sea Cookie *W De Best-Turner* a44 46
3 b f Largesse—Maylan (IRE) (Lashkari)
4200[8] 4828[5] 5774[6] 6060[7]

Sea Cove *G A Swinbank* a33 29
7 b m Terimon—Regal Pursuit (IRE) (Roi Danzig (USA))
240[5]

Seafield Towers *Miss L A Perratt* 48
7 ch g Compton Place—Midnight Spell (Night Shift (USA))
1493[12] 1892[12] 3347[13] 3585[11] 3782[10] 4478[7] 4773[11] 4934[6] 4967[10] 4996[7] 5295[5] 5507[16] 5552[12] 5672[10] 5836[13]

Seaflower Reef (IRE) *A M Balding* a63 63
3 b f Robellino(USA) —Sankaty Light (USA) (Summer Squall (USA))
3798[4] 4505[7]

Sea Frolic (IRE) *Jennie Candlish* a48 46
6 b m Shinko Forest(IRE) —Centre Travel (Godswalk (USA))
2149[11] 2302[14] 2716[9] *4464[5]* 5159[13] 5916[14] *6569[6] 6817[5] 6835[9]*

Sea Land (FR) *B Ellison* a76 64
3 ch g King's Best(USA) —Green Bonnet (IRE) (Green Desert (USA))
(342) 2354[8] 2943[7] 3388[11] 4141[5]

Seal Bay (IRE) *D Smaga* 95
2 ch f Hernando(FR) —Torrealta (In The Wings)
6416a[4]

Seal Point (USA) *Christian Wroe* a87 89
3 ch c Point Given(USA) —Maudie May (USA) (Gilded Time (USA))
(527a) *859a[11]* 4601[14] 5049[9] 5833[6] 6236[10] *6435[9] 6669[9]*

Sealy Hill (CAN) *M Casse* a109 112
3 bb f Point Given(USA) —Boston Twist (USA) (Boston Harbor (USA))
6373a[2]

Sea Map *Miss Sheena West* a62 51
5 ch g Fraam—Shehana (USA) (The Minstrel (CAN))
39[4] 159[5] 291[6] 354[5] 482[7]

Sea Mark *A D Brown* a55
11 ro g Warning—Mettlesome (Lomond (USA))
1027[7] 1254[3]

Seamus Shindig *H Candy* a84 87
5 b g Aragon—Sheesha (USA) (Shadeed (USA))
1401[4] 2139[4] 2546[2] *2993[5]* 3472[4] 3911[5]

Sean Og (IRE) *E J Creighton* a31 53
5 gr g Definite Article—Miss Goodbody (Castle Keep)
18[11]

Sean Og Coulston (IRE) *John J Coleman* 58
3 b g Raphane(USA) —Classic Silk (IRE) (Classic Secret (USA))
5696a[14]

Sea Rover (IRE) *M Brittain* 76
3 b c Jade Robbery(USA) —Talah (Danehill (USA))
(1135) 1530[2] 1825[5] 2534[5]

Sea Saga (IRE) *L M Cumani* 34
4 ch m Generous(IRE) —Winter Pageant (Polish Precedent (USA))
6576[8]

Sea Salt *R A Fahey* a59 80
4 b g Titus Livius(FR) —Carati (Selkirk (USA))
2912[4] 3374[5] 3954[8] 6157[9] 6639[7] *6907[6] 7158[7]*

Seasider *Sir Michael Stoute* a85 76
2 b c Zamindar(USA) —Esplanade (Danehill (USA))
(5872) *6644[2]*

Sea Storm (IRE) *James Moffatt* a67 76
9 b g Dolphin Street(FR) —Prime Interest (IRE) (Kings Lake (USA))
4100[5] 5196[7] 5556[8]

Seaton Snooks *T D Easterby* 63
3 b g Diktat—Buck's Fizz (Kris)
918[7] 1091[13] 1238[13] 1679[4] 2094[5]

Seattle Storm (IRE) *D R C Elsworth* a68
2 b c Robellino(USA) —Seattle Ribbon (USA) (Seattle Dancer (USA))
7051[2] 7181[2]

Sea Wall *Jonjo O'Neill* 56
5 b g Giant's Causeway(USA) —Spout (Salse (USA))
1844[17]

Sea Willow (IRE) *D R C Elsworth* a29 58
3 b g Tamarisk(IRE) —Willow Dale (IRE) (Danehill (USA))
2606[14] 3276[6] 3743[11] *4064[11]* 4856[4] 5546[10] *6272[8]*

Secam (POL) *Mrs P Townsley* a45 35
8 gr g Alywar(USA) —Scytia (POL) (Euro Star)
274[14] 372[7] 1347[4] 2214[18]

Second Opinion (IRE) *J M P Eustace* 65
2 ch f Dr Fong(USA) —Second To Go (USA) (El Prado (IRE))
4102[4] 4756[7]

Second Reef *T A K Cuthbert* a64 61
5 b g Second Empire(IRE) —Vax Lady (Millfontaine)
42[5] 72[3] 286[11] 445[7] 538[8] 966[8] 1225[4] 1554[7] 2828[6] 6732[12]

Seconds Out (IRE) *Sir Mark Prescott* a61 45
2 b g Marju(IRE) —Next Round (IRE) (Common Grounds)
1975[5] 2991[13] 5343[13] *6207[2]* 6305[6]

Secret Affair *F Breuss* a85 64
5 b g Piccolo—Secret Circle (Magic Ring (IRE))
4012a[9]

Secret Asset (IRE) *W M Brisbourne* 94
2 gr g Clodovil(IRE) —Skerray (Soviet Star (USA))
1087[7] 1889[3] (2451) (4844) 5480[3]

Secret Gem (IRE) *C G Cox* 69
2 b f Cape Cross(IRE) —Orlena (USA) (Gone West (USA))
5162[6] 5913[6] 6648[7]

Secret Liaison *S Parr* a93 87
4 gr g Medicean—Courting (Pursuit Of Love)
2346[5] (2771) 3201[6] (5921) *6765[5]*

Secret Meaning *W G M Turner* 60
2 b f Mujahid(USA) —Hidden Meaning (Cadeaux Genereux)
1428[4] 2188[2] 2310[2] 2605[4] (3246) 3680[2] 4255[4] 4762[10]

Secret Night *J A R Toller* a93 88
4 gr m Dansili—Night Haven (Night Shift (USA))
198[7] 384[3] 590[2] 759[12] 1474[14] 2835[12] *6970[5] 7184[8]*

Secret Ploy *H Morrison* 80
7 b g Deploy—By Line (High Line)
(1479) 2860[6] 3467[4] (4056) 5446[3] 6335[19]

Secret Tune *Pat Eddery* 99
3 b c Generous(IRE) —Sing For Fame (USA) (Quest For Fame)
1358[2] (1746) (2246) 2816[3] 4059[10] 4803[8]

Secret Vision (USA) *R M H Cowell* a58 33
6 ch m Distant View(USA) —Secret Angel (Halo (USA))
189[12]

Secret World (IRE) *J Noseda* 111
4 ch g Spinning World(USA) —Classic Park (Robellino (USA))
1104[7] 1834[4] 3887[6] 4543[7]

Sedara (ITY) *R Menichetti* 58
2 b f Shantou(USA) —Suave Gallant (USA) (Suave Prospect (USA))
1485a[8]

Sedge (USA) *P T Midgley* a77 70
7 b g Lure(USA) —First Flyer (USA) (Riverman (USA))
831[7] 1064[2] (1675) 2033[5] 2550[9] *(3409)* 3512[7] 4137[5] 4407[7] 4797[9] 5253[2] 5701[7] *(6148) 6610[3]*

Sedgefield (USA) *Darrin Miller* a110 99
3 ch c Smart Strike(CAN) —Belva (USA) (Theatrical)
1486a[5]

Sedgwick *J G Given* a65 74
5 b g Nashwan(USA) —Imperial Bailiwick (IRE) (Imperial Frontier (USA))
106[2] 375[3] 675[10] 1251[7] (1671) 1924[6] 2169[2] 2423[2] 2822[7] 3783[6] 4582[13] 6258[2]

Sedna (IRE) *W T Farrell* 95
5 ch m Priolo(USA) —Delphinus (Soviet Star (USA))
(5460a)

Seductive Witch *M D I Usher* a50 34
2 ch f Zamindar(USA) —Thicket (Wolfhound (USA))
3162[7] 5872[8] *6425[5] 7170[5]*

Seein'Red (IRE) *P T Midgley* 55
2 b g Redback—Red Keane (IRE) (Red Sunset)
1674[3] 2071[7] 4174[10]

Seeking Star (IRE) *M R Channon* 91
2 b c King's Best(USA) —Firedrake (USA) (Kris S (USA))
2041[4] (2478) 5828[5] (6251) 6495[8]

Seeking The Best (IRE) *Hideyuki Mori* a105
6 b h Seeking The Gold(USA) —Mackie (USA) (Summer Squall (USA))
860a[11]

Seeking The Buck (USA) *M A Magnusson* 93
3 b c Seeking The Gold(USA) —Cuanto Es (USA) (Exbourne (USA))
1606[6] 1913[5] (2413) 3400[2] 3964[2] 4147[3] 4597[2] (5218) 5543[7]

Seeking The Star (CAN) *D M Simcock* a68 61
2 b g Seeking The Gold(USA) —Water Music (CAN) (Danzig (USA))
2041[10] *2353[5] 2991[7] 4065[6]*

Seesawmilu (IRE) *E J Alston* a54 51
4 b g Almutawakel—Clos De Tart (IRE) (Indian Ridge)
1360[4] 2007[15] *3172[5]* 3180[7] 3787[5] 3839[5] 4180[19] *6064[12]* 6247[5] *6390[4]*

Segal (IRE) *J Noseda* a70 38
2 b c Cadeaux Genereux—Camcorder (Nashwan (USA))
6126[10] *6602[3] 6850[2]*

Sehoya (IRE) *R C Guest* a41 60
5 bb m Second Empire(IRE) —Blue Jazz (IRE) (Bluebird (USA))
462[13]

Sehrezad (IRE) *Andreas Lowe* 104
2 b c Titus Livius(FR) —Trebles (IRE) (Kenmare (FR))
6631a[5]

Seihali (IRE) *D Selvaratnam* a98 118
8 b h Alzao(USA) —Edwina (IRE) (Caerleon (USA))
247a[3] 413a[3] 530a[2] (600a) 862a[4]

Sekula Pata (NZ) *E J Creighton* a73 83
8 b g Pompeii Court(USA) —Torquay (NZ) (Wharf (USA))
3149[13] 5188[5] *5310[2] 5569[7]* 5838[10] *6315[4] (6529) 6713[12]*

Seldemosa *M S Saunders* a61 51
6 br m Selkirk(USA) —Baldemosa (FR) (Lead On Time (USA))
123[2] 145[4] 217[5] 440[3] 519[2] 627[7] 723[5] 800[6] 1715[14] 2358[9] 2877[9]

Select Committee *J J Quinn* 70
2 b g Fayruz—Demolition Jo (Petong)
1422[3] 2090[2] 3256[3] 3606[7] 4560[12]

Selective *A W Carroll* a66 78
8 b g Selkirk(USA) —Portelet (Night Shift (USA))
1198[15]

Seleet (IRE) *M A Jarvis* a13 62
3 b c Sakhee(USA) —Summerhill Parkes (Zafonic (USA))
(1259) 1920[8] *3416[14]* 5941[7]

Selinka *R Hannon* 105
3 b f Selkirk(USA) —Lady Links (Bahamian Bounty)
1496[21] 2757[2] (3332) 4118[4] 4805[4] 5661a[6]

Selique *E A L Dunlop* a56
3 b f Selkirk(USA) —Elle Questro (Rainbow Quest (USA))
1312[9]

Selkirk Grace *K A Morgan* a63 67
7 b g Selkirk(USA) —Polina (Polish Precedent (USA))
1376[7] 2176[2] 2595[5] 3047[2] *3397[2]* (4802) *5500[13]* 6132[3] 6500[4]

Selkirk Sky *R A Fahey* 56
3 b f Selkirk(USA) —Arctic Air (Polar Falcon (USA))
(3917) 4287[4] 4705[11]

Sell Out *G Wragg* a74 99
3 gr f Act One—Nordica (Northfields (USA))
1407[5] *1979[8] 2354[7]* (2971) 3972[2] 4503[2] 5544[4] 6299[4]

Selmis *V Caruso* 95
3 ch c Selkirk(USA) —Nokomis (Caerleon (USA))
1336a[12]

Selsey *Sir Michael Stoute* 64
2 b f Selkirk(USA) —Louella (USA) (El Gran Senor (USA))
6648[9]

Semah Harold *E S McMahon* a73 77
2 b g Beat All(USA) —Semah's Dream (Gunner B)
(3404) 4482[3] *5236[3] 6120[14] 6936[6]*

Semi Detached (IRE) *J W Unett* a67 73
4 b g Distant Music(USA) —Relankina (IRE) (Broken Hearted)
381[6] 604[9] 611[4] 6342[5] 6457[5] 6904[11]

Sempre Libera (IRE) *P W Chapple-Hyam* a67
2 b f Statue Of Liberty(USA) —Lucky Oakwood (USA) (Elmaamul (USA))
6990[2] 7129[3] 7264[3]

Sendalam (FR) *J S Moore* a101 104
5 ch g Sendawar(IRE) —Alamea (IRE) (Ela-Mana-Mou)
172a[2] 395a[8] 472a[2] *597a[15]* 2817[22] 4385[9]

Sendali (FR) *J D Bethell* 67
3 b g Daliapour(IRE) —Lady Senk (FR) (Pink (FR))
1415[6] 1968[5] 2808[5] 3792[11] 4391[6] 4821[9]

Sendar (FR) *John Joseph Murphy* 74
6 b g Priolo(USA) —Sendana (FR) (Darshaan)
3577a[12]

Sendefaa (IRE) *M Botti* a56 63
2 bb f Halling(USA) —Patruel (Rainbow Quest (USA))
5301[8] *6262[9] 6585[4]*

Sendinpost *S C Williams* a76 66
4 b m Dansili—Colleville (Pharly (FR))
112[4] 2686[5] *(2996) 3216[3]*

Seneschal *A B Haynes* a75 71
6 b g Polar Falcon(USA) —Broughton Singer (IRE) (Common Grounds)
132[8] 276[10] (359) 419[10] 561[3] 793[8] 923[3] 1118[12] 1251[2] (1562) 1886[15] 2107[6] 4577[12] 4879[9] *5424[9] 5733[5] (6226)* (6413) 6447[6] *6710[7] 7164[8]*

Senora Lenorah *D A Nolan* 27
3 ch f Tumbleweed Ridge—Blue Diamond (First Trump)
1943[17] 2826[9] 3537[8] 3811[8] 4384[7] 4714[10] 4971[9] 5970[8]

Senora's Best *M W Easterby* 25
2 ch f Best Of The Bests(IRE) —Hispaniola (IRE) (Barathea (IRE))
5521[12] 5903[10]

Senor Benny (USA) *M McDonagh* a106 111
8 br h Benny The Dip(USA) —Senora Tippy (USA) (El Gran Senor (USA))
1049a[6] 3573a[3] 3768a[5] *4864a[3]* 5075a[4] 5436a[5] 5842a[2] (6036a) 6363a[13] 6758[12]

Senor Bond (USA) *A M Hales* 38
6 ch g Hennessy(USA) —Troppa Freska (USA) (Silver Hawk (USA))
2963[5]

Senor Dali (IRE) *I Mohammed* 111
4 ch h Peintre Celebre(USA) —Far Fetched (IRE) (Distant Relative)
176a[7] 330a[9] (544a) 642a[5]

Senor Eduardo *Mrs H O Graham* a45 32
10 gr g Terimon—Jasmin Path (Warpath)
4966[13]

Senorita Parkes *K A Ryan* 43
2 ch f Medicean—Lucky Parkes (Full Extent (USA))
3582[9]

Sensasse (IRE) *Mrs A J Perrett* a80
4 b m Imperial Ballet(IRE) —Vanity (IRE) (Thatching)
1034[6] 1588[4]

Sensazione World (IRE) *B Grizzetti* 37
2 b f Spinning World(USA) —Sensazione (Cadeaux Genereux)
6047a[14]

Sense Of Joy *J H M Gosden* 100
2 b f Dansili—Bonash (Rainbow Quest (USA))
(4169) (4804)

Sensible *M J Wallace* a65
2 ch f Almutawakel—Opera (Forzando)
6777[4]

Sentiero Rosso (USA) *B Ellison* a73 75
5 b g Intidab(USA) —Kheyrah (USA) (Dayjur (USA))
151[9] 895[12] *1568[6]* 1655[9] *1720[6]* 1892[4]

Sentire (NZ) *R Laing* 105
6 br g Pentire—Sent To War (NZ) (Centaine (AUS))
6033a[4]

Sentry Duty (FR) *N J Henderson* 104
5 b g Kahyasi—Standing Around (FR) (Garde Royale)
(1844) 3090[17]

Sepia *B W Hills*
2 b f Dansili—Spanish Sun (USA) (El Prado (IRE))
5592[9]

Septimus (IRE) *A P O'Brien* 124
4 b h Sadler's Wells(USA) —Caladira (IRE) (Darshaan)
(1550a) 2210[2] (4691) (5376)

Sequoia (SLO) *J P Lopez* 96
3 ch f Sebastian—Secret Success (IRE) (Law Society (USA))
2501a[1]

Serabad (FR) *J-C Rouget* 105
3 gr g Priolo(USA) —Serasia (FR) (Linamix (FR))
1572a[4]

Serenading (USA) *Josie Carroll*
3 b f A.P. Indy(USA) —Daijin (USA) (Deputy Minister (CAN))
6772a[7]

Serena's Storm (IRE) *J J Quinn* 81
2 b f Statue Of Liberty(USA) —Princess Serena (USA) (Unbridled's Song (USA))
2504[5] (3205) 3988[11] 5322[5] 5837[2] 6498[7]

Serene Dancer *Mrs P N Dutfield* a21 53
4 b m Danehill Dancer(IRE) —Bliss (IRE) (Statoblest)
2913[9] 3482[3] 4545[9] *5499[11]*

Serene Highness (IRE) *J L Dunlop* 64
3 b f Highest Honor(FR) —Dollysister (FR) (Alydar (USA))
2693[12] 3429[12]

Serengeti *M Johnston* a92 104
3 b c Singspiel(IRE) —Tanzania (USA) (Darshaan)
638[2] (1122) (1467) 2816[4]

Sergeant Cecil *B R Millman* a66 119
8 ch g King's Signet(USA) —Jadidh (Touching Wood (USA))
1144[4] (1823) 2787[14] 3942[6] 4691[5]

Sergeant Sharpe *M H Tompkins* 66
2 ch g Cadeaux Genereux—Halcyon Daze (Halling (USA))
4293[10] 5399[4] 5735[6]

Serhaaphim *N B King* a60 60
3 gr f Erhaab(USA) —Salinova (FR) (Linamix (FR))
1220[2] 1746[4] 1928[6] 2793[7] 3792[3] 4104[3] *6811[3]*

Serial Habit (IRE) *M Brittain* 22
4 b m Lahib(USA) —Satire (Terimon)
5045[8]

Serieux *D Nicholls* a75 81
8 b g Cadeaux Genereux—Seranda (IRE) (Petoski)
3[12] 303[6]

Serious Choice (IRE) *J R Boyle* a58 53
2 b g Choisir(AUS) —Printaniere (USA) (Sovereign Dancer (USA))
6080[8] 6294[9] *6578[8]*

Seriously Lucky (IRE) *D Nicholls* 41
3 b g Key Of Luck(USA) —Serious Delight (Lomond (USA))
1426[7] 1912[7]

Serpentaria *Sir Mark Prescott* a74 86
3 b f Golden Snake(USA) —French Spice (Cadeaux Genereux)
(114) 294[4] 1637[2] 1827[9] 2602[4] 3609[2] 4490[2] 4749[8] 5446[4]

Serramanna *Ms J S Doyle* a66 63
6 ch m Grand Lodge(USA) —Spry (Suave Dancer (USA))
16[6] 88[12] 232[8]

Sesaro Express (IRE) *John A Quinn* a6
6 b g Sesaro(USA) —Curie Express (IRE) (Fayruz)
6817[9]

Sesmen *M Botti* a94 104
3 gr f Inchinor—Poetry In Motion (IRE) (Ballad Rock)
1146[6] 1702a[6] 3511[7] 4118[9] 4633[2] 5354[12] *(6604)*

Set Alight *Mrs C A Dunnett* a74 59
6 b m Forzando—Me Spede (Valiyar)
63[12]

Seta Pura *Mrs A Duffield* 61
2 b f Domedriver(IRE) —Sulitelma (USA) (The Minstrel (CAN))
5328[6] 6306[5] (6557)

Seteem (USA) *N Tinkler* 72
3 ch g Diesis—Inscrutable Dancer (USA) (Green Dancer (USA))
849[6] 1256[7] 1605[8] 1964[16] 5936[9]

Setembro Chove (BRZ) *P Shaw* a104 117
6 b h Fast Gold(USA) —Setting Trends (BRZ) (Knifebox (USA))
1877a[4]

Set Fire (IRE) *M Halford* 91
4 b m Bertolini(USA) —Incendio (Siberian Express (USA))
5460a[15]

Set Play (USA) *Peter Miller* a99 108
2 ch f Van Nistelrooy(USA) —Boldy's Reflection (USA) (Bold Ruckus (USA))
5826a[7] 6507a[11]

Set The Scene (IRE) *J H M Gosden* a66 75
3 b f Sadler's Wells(USA) —Margarula (IRE) (Doyoun)
1312[6] 1685[2] (2274) 2599[8]

Settigano (IRE) *Brian Nolan* 97
4 b g Sadler's Wells(USA) —Bonita Francita (CAN) (Devil's Bag (USA))
3138a[2]

Seven Gold Rings (IRE) *J F O'Shea* a73 90
4 b m Mull Of Kintyre(USA) —Millenium Moon (Wolfhound (USA))
5394a[8] 5841a[12] *6916a[4]*

Seven No Trumps *J M Bradley* a46 65
10 ch g Pips Pride—Classic Ring (IRE) (Auction Ring (USA))
1112[6] *1384[8] 1729[10]* (2104) 2386[3] 3368[10] 3498[4] 3535[6] 3869[2] 4312[5] 4561[7] 4881[11] 4996[13]

Seventh Cloud (IRE) *A P Jarvis* a55 55
2 br f Septieme Ciel(USA) —Wana Doo (USA) (Grand Slam (USA))
1058[9] 1354[7] *1586[3]* 3152[10] *3642[10] 3925[7]* 4453[9] 4824[3] *5133[7] 6693[12]*

Seventh Hill *M Blanshard* 72
2 ch c Compton Place—Dream Baby (Master Willie)
3552[11] 5633[6] 5919[7]

Sew In Character *M Blanshard* a43 32
3 ch g Woodborough(USA) —Elegant Rose (Noalto)
1166[11] 2223[5] 3394[9] 3922[12]

Sew'N'So Character (IRE) *M Blanshard* a94 93
6 b g Imperial Ballet(IRE) —Hope And Glory (USA) (Well Decorated (USA))
185[5] 993[8] 1287[11]

Sexy Lady (GER) *P Rau* 106
4 ch m Danehill Dancer(IRE) —Sky Dancing (IRE) (Exit To Nowhere (USA))
2296a[8] 3628[4] 4217a[5] 4838a[9]

Sforzando *Mrs L Stubbs* a64 79
6 b m Robellino(USA) —Mory Kante (USA) (Icecapade (USA))
850[11] 1042[10] 1158[2] 1371[4] 1997[5] 2865[5] 3803[11] (4333) 4772[6] 5197[4] 6021[9] 6258[3] (6727) *6803[7]*

Sgt Schultz (IRE) *J S Moore* a87 85
4 b g In The Wings—Ann's Annie (IRE) (Alzao (USA))
(265) (362) 488[6] 593[4] 652[4] (693) 829[3] 995[4] 1664[4] *2994[11]* 3959[6] 4171[3] 4597[10] *(7055)*

Shaaban (IRE) *R J Price* a18 12
6 b g Woodman(USA) —Ashbilya (USA) (Nureyev (USA))
5345[12]

Shaama Rose (FR) *M R Channon* 49
2 gr f Verglas(IRE) —River Ballade (USA) (Irish River (FR))
4875[6] 5301[13]

Shabahar (IRE) *M J McGrath* 90
3 b g Hernando(FR) —Shara (IRE) (Kahyasi)
5768[8] 6203[8] 6727[6]

Shabernak (IRE) *M L W Bell* a68 102
8 gr g Akarad(FR) —Salinova (FR) (Linamix (FR))
944[5] 1844[13]

Shabiba (USA) *M P Tregoning* 82
2 b f Seeking The Gold(USA) —Misterah (Alhaarth (IRE))
5448[2] (5949)

Shabnaam *K A Ryan* a49 61
2 b f Diktat—Noble View (USA) (Distant View (USA))
1896[4] 2710[8] *3596[8] 7043[5]*

Shaded Edge *D W P Arbuthnot* a63
3 b g Bold Edge—Twilight Mistress (Bin Ajwaad (IRE))
700[4] (3425) 4919[2] (5136) 6210[4]

Shades Of Beige (UAE) *Frau E Mader* 94
5 b m Timber Country(USA) —Idrica (Rainbow Quest (USA))
5719a[6] 6220a[13]

Shades Of Blue *C J Down* 23
4 b m Bandmaster(USA) —Just Sidium (Nicholas (USA))
4258[10] 4908[11]

Shadow Aspect *Eoin Doyle* a50 60
4 b h Nashwan(USA) —Hedonic (Gone West (USA))
106[6] 186[3] 495[8] 691[10] (Dead)

Shadow Cabinet (IRE) *M L W Bell* a63 74
2 b c Noverre(USA) —Shadow Roll (IRE) (Mark Of Esteem (IRE))
3962[8] 4584[5] *4883[5]* 5314[2] 5883[2] 6233[3]

Shadow Gate (JPN) *Y Kato* 121
5 b h White Muzzle—Fabulous Turn (JPN) (Sunday Silence (USA))
(1877a) 7092a[5]

Shadow Jumper (IRE) *J T Stimpson* a54 47
6 b g Dayjur(USA) —Specifically (USA) (Sky Classic (CAN))
77[7] 241[9] 430[12] 448[10] 517[5] 579[2] 627[10] 812[4] 1066[11] 2343[2] 3017[9] 3375[5] 3497[7] 3789[13] *4945[12] 5368[4] 5606[10] 6152[6] 7057[8] 7148[2] 7250[8]*

Shadows Fall (USA) *P F I Cole* a63 62
2 b c Dynaformer(USA) —Not Bashful (USA) (Seattle Slew (USA))
4393[5] 4852[7] *5116[11]* 5858[6] *6433[12] 6715[4] 6933[4] 7010[7]*

Shadow The Wind (IRE) *E F Vaughan* 82
3 b g Val Royal(FR) —Kesh Kumay (IRE) (Danehill (USA))
2059[3] (2470) 3480[4] 5454[2] 6236[5]

Shadowy Figure *Saeed Bin Suroor* 81
3 b c Machiavellian(USA) —Renashaan (FR) (Darshaan)
(6238)

Shady Bay *D W Chapman* 2
3 b f Sure Blade(USA) —French Project (IRE) (Project Manager)
5488[7] 6286[10] 6464[11] *6817[11]*

Shady Gloom (IRE) *K A Ryan* 49
2 b c Traditionally(USA) —Last Drama (IRE) (Last Tycoon (IRE))
6724[11]

Shady Green (IRE) *M W Easterby* a46 62
3 b g Kalanisi(IRE) —Albacora (IRE) (Fairy King (USA))
684[5] 1238[15] *2223[7]* (Dead)

Shafrons Canyon (IRE) *P M Rogers* a32 74
4 b m Lend A Hand—Carroll's Canyon (IRE) (Hatim (USA))
7143[11]

Shaftesbury (IRE) *M Johnston* a60 65
2 b g Lomitas—Vivid Concert (IRE) (Chief Singer)
5721[7] 6418[8] *6948[7]*

Shaftesbury Avenue (USA) *J O'Reilly* a58 54
4 ch h Fusaichi Pegasus(USA) —Little Firefly (IRE) (Danehill (USA))
537[7] 670[2] (728) 2149[10] 4427[7]

Shaggy Mane (USA) *D Chatlos Jr* a108 116
4 bb m Bertrando(USA) —Witchy (USA) (Bel Bolide (USA))
6483a[7]

Shahadah (IRE) *R J Price* a43 36
5 b m Daylami(IRE) —Mafaatin (IRE) (Royal Academy (USA))
2433[7] 2657[11] *4023[7]* 4532[10] *4914[11]*

Shahdawar (FR) *M Pimbonnet* a85 95
4 b g Sendawar(IRE) —Shahrazad (FR) (Bering)
437a[9]

Shaheer (IRE) *J Gallagher* a61 58
5 b g Shahrastani(USA) —Atmospheric Blues (IRE) (Double Schwartz)
19[10] 425[9] (500) 610[2] 651[2] 819[6] 982[9] 1319[4] 2141[3] 2490[2] 2963[2] *6796[8] 6867[6] 6951[11] 7098[2] 7115[11]*

Shahin (USA) *M P Tregoning* a103 114
4 b h Kingmambo(USA) —String Quartet (IRE) (Sadler's Wells (USA))
2216[2] 2907[4] 3461[2] 4599[2] *5220[6]*

Shaika *G Prodromou* a41 56
4 b m Almushtarak(IRE) —Subtle Girl (Selkirk (USA))
2084[5] 2156[5] 2745[9] 3250[9] 4473[7]

Shake On It *Eve Johnson Houghton* 82
3 b g Lomitas—Decision Maid (USA) (Diesis)
(1001) 1202[10] 2313[5] 2598[4] 4163[5] 4313[3] (4960) 5208[7] 5445[5]

Shaker (IRE) *M L W Bell* 87
2 b f Key Of Luck(USA) —Gravieres (FR) (Saint Estephe (FR))
(3245) 3880[11] 5395a[10] 6251[2] 6652[7]

Shakespeare's Son *H J Evans* a62 40
2 b g Mind Games—Eastern Blue (IRE) (Be My Guest (USA))
4527[8] *5097[4] 5815[4] 6098[9] 7042[5] 7195[4]*

Shaking *A Fabre* a83 89
3 gr f Linamix(FR) —Pinkai (IRE) (Caerleon (USA))
6941a[7]

Shakis (IRE) *Doug Watson* a86 116
7 b h Machiavellian(USA) —Tawaaded (IRE) (Nashwan (USA))
176a[10] 413a[4] 600a[10]

Shakyras Melody (IRE) *M Weiss* 65
7 b m Oscar Schindler(IRE) —Chiming Melody (Cure The Blues (USA))
(356a)

Shalimar (ITY) *L Brogi* 84
5 b m College Chapel—Picadora (ITY) (Primo Dominie)
1337a[6]

Shallal *P W Chapple-Hyam* 88
2 b c Cape Cross(IRE) —First Waltz (FR) (Green Dancer (USA))
3747[3] (4048)

Shaloo Diamond *R M Whitaker* 69
2 b g Captain Rio—Alacrity (Alzao (USA))
4350[6] 4819[3] 5580[4]

Shamayel *B W Hills* a74 83
2 b f Pivotal—Mauri Moon (Green Desert (USA))
5162[2] *(5681)* 6498[6]

Shamdinan (FR) *A Penna Jr* 116
3 ch c Dr Fong(USA) —Shamdara (IRE) (Dr Devious (IRE))
2293a[3] 3142a[9] (4412a) 5250a[5] 6513a[2]

Shamrock Bay *C R Dore* a52 67
5 b m Celtic Swing—Kabayil (Dancing Brave (USA))
1254[6] 1590[3] 6835[10]

Shamrock Lady (IRE) *Pat Eddery* 75
2 b f Orpen(USA) —Shashi (IRE) (Shaadi (USA))
1079[3] 1896[2] 2398[5] (3152) 3880[9] 5164[7] 5939[7] 6621[7]

Sham Ruby *M R Bosley* a40 49
5 ch m Tagula(IRE) —Bistro (USA) (Strawberry Road (AUS))
33[5] 296[10] 442[11] 743[3] 920[8] 1317[3] 2556[9] 3873[10] 4471[6] 4685[11]

Shamwari Fire (IRE) *I W McInnes* 41
7 ch g Idris(IRE) —Bobby's Dream (Reference Point)
2275[12]

Shanafarahan (IRE) *T P Tate* 66
2 b g Marju(IRE) —Sedna (FR) (Bering)
5734[5] 6255[11] 6469[5]

Shandelight (IRE) *Mrs A Duffield* a52 54
3 b f Dilshaan—By Candlelight (IRE) (Roi Danzig (USA))
1210[4] *(1750)* 2489[12] 2759[2] 3181[7] 3587[4] 4139[2]

Shanehill (IRE) *Evan Williams* 30
5 b g Danehill(USA) —Shunaire (USA) (Woodman (USA))
4256[11]

Shannersburg (IRE) *E J O'Neill* 80
2 bb c Johannesburg(USA) —Shahoune (USA) (Blushing Groom (FR))
1652[9] 2575[5] 3635[2] 4037[2] (4482) 4495[4]

Shannon Arms (USA) *R Brotherton* a58 46
6 b g Wolf Power(SAF) —Crestasbest (USA) (Cresta Rider (USA))
364[8] 466[6] 768[6] 1210[14] *1381[2] 1906[6] 2258[11] 2874[6] 6882[13]*

Shantina's Dream (USA) *J R Boyle* a45 57
3 b f Smoke Glacken(USA) —J'Aime Jeblis (USA) (Jeblar (USA))
1738[6] 2205[10] *3281[8] 5098[12] 6542[8] 6706[11] 6968[7] (7133)*

Shanty Star (IRE) *R Bouresly* a92 109
7 gr g Hector Protector(USA) —Shawanni (Shareef Dancer (USA))
330a[6]

Shanzu *H Candy* 68
2 b f Kyllachy—Limuru (Salse (USA))
5448[6] 5720[2] 6080[5]

Shape Up (IRE) *R Craggs* a72 83
7 b g Octagonal(NZ) —Bint Kaldoun (IRE) (Kaldoun (FR))
453[7] (685) 733[2] (928) 1042[15] 1997[3] 2314[5] 2743[4]

Sharaab (USA) *D E Cantillon* a50 61
6 bb g Erhaab(USA) —Ghashtah (USA) (Nijinsky (CAN))
2493[2] 3448[4] (4030) 4451[2] 5283[3]

Sharapova (IRE) *M J Grassick* 78
4 b m Elusive Quality(USA) —Naazeq (Nashwan (USA))
1548a[8]

Sharbasia (IRE) *H J Evans* 62
4 b m King's Best(USA) —Sharbata (IRE) (Kahyasi)
3467[12]

Share The Feeling (IRE) *J W Unett* a79 59
5 b m Desert King(IRE) —Antapoura (IRE) (Bustino)
(215) 283[2] 434[3] 515[3] 662[6]

Sharleez (IRE) *John M Oxx* 90
2 b f Marju(IRE) —Sharesha (IRE) (Ashkalani (IRE))
4440a[6]

Sharmy (IRE) *Ian Williams* a70 67
11 b g Caerleon(USA) —Petticoat Lane (Ela-Mana-Mou)
2474[12] 2660[3] 2721[2] 3035[5] 4200[2] 5211[5]

Sharpattack *M Botti* a37 52
3 ch g Auction House(USA) —Sharp Decision (Greensmith)
1261[8] 1587[7] 2094[2] 2895[10] *3924[9]* 4337[14] *5121[8]*

Sharpazmax (IRE) *P J Makin* a83 82
3 b c Daggers Drawn(USA) —Amour Toujours (IRE) (Law Society (USA))
2045[6] 2400[11]

Sharp Dresser (USA) *Mrs A J Perrett* a71 69
3 ch f Diesis—A La Mode (USA) (Known Fact (USA))
5384[2] (5859)

Sharpe Image (IRE) *G Woodward* 53
4 b m Bluebird(USA) —Silvretta (IRE) (Tirol)
5474[4]

Sharp Hat *D W Chapman* a50 58
13 b g Shavian—Madam Trilby (Grundy)
46[10] 1065[4] 1112[3] 1405[13] 1557[10] 2249[2] 2418[4] 2830[4] 3203[8] 3782[9] 4478[4] 4773[12] 4939[7] *5566[12]* 6078[7] 6702[10]

Sharp Liquor (IRE) *G T Lynch* a46 42
4 br g Fruits Of Love(USA) —Pazza Idea (IRE) (Caerleon (USA))
7131[6] 7143[10]

Sharp Nephew *B J Meehan* 100
2 ch c Dr Fong(USA) —Snap Crackle Pop (IRE) (Statoblest)
(3383) (4598) 5795[9]

Sharp Reply (USA) *Mrs S C Bradburne* 82
5 b g Diesis—Questonia (Rainbow Quest (USA))
5478[2] 6733[5]

Sharps Gold *P J McBride* a56 40
2 ch f Twice As Sharp—Toking N' Joken (IRE) (Mukaddamah (USA))
2188[5] 3801[5] 4810[6] *(5133) 6270[6]* 6536[17] *6828[9] 6977[10] 7286[3]*

Sharp Susan (USA) *W Mott* 107
3 br f Touch Gold(USA) —Winter's Gone (USA) (Dynaformer (USA))
5248a[3]

Sharp Tune (USA) *J D Frost* a26 51
5 ch g Diesis—Moonflute (USA) (The Minstrel (CAN))
721[14]

Shatter Resistant (IRE) *M R Channon* a69 69
2 b g Fath(USA) —Beech Bramble (IRE) (Cyrano De Bergerac)
1367[3] 1528[3] 1762[2] 2138[3] 2410[3] 2911[2] 3370[4] *4020[3]* 4629[9] 4970[4]

Shava *H J Evans* a59 56
7 b g Atraf—Anita Marie (IRE) (Anita's Prince)
(123) 292[5] 485[4] 586[2] 797[6] 1227[5] 1753[8] 5730[5] 5946[12] 6587[8] 7153[3]

Shavansky *J H M Gosden* 74
3 b g Rock Of Gibraltar(IRE) —Limelighting (USA) (Alleged (USA))
1204[11] 1560[2] 2402[6]

Shavoulin (USA) *Christian Wroe* a76 77
3 bb g Johannesburg(USA) —Hello Josephine (USA) (Take Me Out (USA))
173a[6] 414a[8] 595a[3] 4541[10] 5315[9] *6891[8] 7033[9]*

Shawhill *Tom Dascombe* a68 96
3 b f Dr Fong(USA) —Speremm (IRE) (Sadler's Wells (USA))
386[4] 553[3] 772[2] (1059) 1355[2] 1724[2] 2547a[2] 3564a[8] 3973[3] 5952[7]

Shaydreambeliever *R A Fahey* a62 73
4 ch g Daggers Drawn(USA) —Aunt Sadie (Pursuit Of Love)
6837[6] (7150)

Shaykhan (IRE) *James Leavy* a66 76
9 ch g Polar Falcon(USA) —Shayraz (Darshaan)
4865a[10]

Shea's Round *G L Moore* a48
3 b c Josr Algarhoud(IRE) —Elms Schoolgirl (Emarati (USA))
53[5] 157[11]

Shediak (FR) *A Fabre* 112
2 b c Selkirk(USA) —Shemissa (IRE) (Fairy King (USA))
5260a[2] 6041a[3]

Sheekey (IRE) *G A Swinbank* 79
2 b c Okawango(USA) —My Darling Dodo (IRE) (Anita's Prince)
4279[2] (5038) 5613[3]

Sheer Bluff (IRE) *D R C Elsworth* 66
2 b g Indian Ridge—Sheer Bliss (IRE) (Sadler's Wells (USA))
3435[9] 4201[6] 4586[6]

Sheer Fantastic *P C Haslam* a64 32
2 b g Fantastic Light(USA) —Sheer Bliss (USA) (Relaunch (USA))
3199[8] *6814[4] (6865)*

She Floats (IRE) *Enda Kelly* a57 64
2 b f Danetime(IRE) —Miss Croisette (Hernando (FR))
4832a[14]

Sheik'N'Knotsterd *J Akehurst* a49 60
2 ch g Zaha(CAN) —Royal Ivy (Mujtahid (USA))
1428[3] 1989[6] 2447[3] 3348[6] 3734[6] *5117[8]*

Shekan Star *K G Reveley* a53 62
5 b m Sri Pekan(USA) —Celestial Welcome (Most Welcome)
1258[9] 1966[7] 2391[9]

She Knows Too Much *A M Hales* a31
3 ch f Tobougg(IRE) —How Do I Know (Petong)
6229[7] 6546[11]

Shela House *J R Fanshawe* 90
3 ch g Selkirk(USA) —Villa Carlotta (Rainbow Quest (USA))
2886[6] 3447[2] 3881[3] 4666[3] (5870) 6110[3]

Shendaya (FR) *A De Royer-Dupre* a95 98
3 b f Danehill Dancer(IRE) —Shemaya (IRE) (Darshaan)
7049a[5]

Shepherdess (USA) *D M Simcock* a54
3 ch f Stravinsky(USA) —Hushi (USA) (Riverman (USA))
219[3] 343[4] 378[4]

Shepherds Warning (IRE) *N J Vaughan* a68 66
2 ch f Vettori(IRE) —Sky Red (Night Shift (USA))
898[6] 971[2] 1255[2] (1674) *5096[9]* 5551[4] 5746[7] 6572[5] *(7142) (7272)*

Sherafey (IRE) *Edgar Byrne* a12 49
3 br f Celtic Swing—Babolna (Generous (IRE))
4836a[16]

Sheriff's Deputy *C N Kellett* a49 45
7 b g Atraf—Forest Fantasy (Rambo Dancer (CAN))
932[13] 1086[8] *1570[9]* 2307[7] 4860[8]

Sheriff's Silk *B Smart* a77 20
3 b g Forzando—Sylhall (Sharpo)
(99) 510[3] 671[2] 1176[2] 1978[5] 2881[14]

Sheriff Star *G P Kelly* 8
4 b m Killer Instinct—Westcourt Ruby (Petong)
1995[15] 2893[12] 4038[11]

Sherjawy (IRE) *Miss Z C Davison* a56 61
3 b g Diktat—Arruhan (IRE) (Mujtahid (USA))
795[4] 900[7] 1008[6] 1763[14] 2276[4] 3237[5] 3879[RR] 4529[9] 4661[4] *6402[4]*

She's A Softie (IRE) *C F Wall* 37
3 b f Invincible Spirit(IRE) —New Tycoon (IRE) (Last Tycoon (IRE))
1923[11] 2186[6] 2607[9]

She's Dunnett *Mrs C A Dunnett* a44 32
4 b m Diktat—College Night (IRE) (Night Shift (USA))
50[12] 274[10] 980[9] 1271[13] 2748[10] 4164[10] 4336[12] 5714[6] 6412[15]

Shesha Bear *W R Muir* a65
2 b f Tobougg(IRE) —Sunny Davis (USA) (Alydar (USA))
6664[4] 6827[8]

Shes Millie *J G M O'Shea* a45 54
3 b f Auction House(USA) —Wintzig (Piccolo)
253[5] 357[12] 469[11]

Shes Minnie *J G M O'Shea* a78 88
4 b m Bertolini(USA) —Wintzig (Piccolo)
1004[10] *1525[2]* 1607[4] 1940[2] 2240[3] 3158[4] (3466) 3746[7] 4017[2] 4507[2] (4664) 5168[5] 5666[8] 5673[4] 5954[9]

She's My Outsider *A W Carroll* a82 82
5 b m Docksider(USA) —Solar Flare (IRE) (Danehill (USA))
2450[13] *7281[11]*

She's Our Beauty (IRE) *S T Mason* a51 56
4 b m Imperial Ballet(IRE) —Eleonora D'Arborea (Prince Sabo)
97[5] 201[11] 523[4] 1163[8] 1594[2] 2249[5] 2791[3] 3259[3] (3837) 5930[17] 6562[5] *7138[8]*

She's Our Dream *R C Guest* a26 60
2 b f Statue Of Liberty(USA) —Mainly Sunset (Red Sunset)
1150[5] 1992[9] 4041[3] 4406[9] 5484[6] 5665[7] 6074[9] *6736[9]*

She's Our Lass (IRE) *D Carroll* a69 81
6 b m Orpen(USA) —Sharadja (IRE) (Doyoun)
771[5] 1198[11] *1720[8] 4433[10]* 4880[6] 5035[4] 5230[5] (5620) 6180[8] 6422[9] 6727[11]

She's Our Mark *Patrick J Flynn* 106
3 ch f Ishiguru(USA) —Markskeepingfaith (IRE) (Ajraas (USA))
3222a[2] 3578a[2] 4237a[2] (4648a) 5241a[7] 5998a[5]

She's So Pretty (IRE) *W R Swinburn* a65 68
3 ch f Grand Lodge(USA) —Plymsole (USA) (Diesis)
1927[7] 2490[3] 3351[5] 3826[9] 4327[4] 5068[9] *5342[9] 5899[3] 6178[3]* 6330[14]

Shevalina (IRE) *Adrian Sexton* a37 46
5 b m Blue Ocean(USA) —First Time Round (IRE) (Elbio)
4000[4] *4430[8] 4464[7]* 5716[9] (Dead)

Shevchenko (IRE) *J Noseda* a79 106
3 bb g Rock Of Gibraltar(IRE) —Hula Angel (USA) (Woodman (USA))
1098[3] *1447[2]* (2312) (3857) (4509) 5797[2]

She Whispers (IRE) *R Hollinshead* a53 39
4 b m Royal Applause—Zariyba (IRE) (In The Wings)
1719[11] 1933[13] 2619[5] 3277[7] 3837[8] 4471[5]

She Wont Wait *T M Jones* a36 54
3 b f Piccolo—Who Goes There (Wolfhound (USA))
924[12] 1763[8] 2560[6] 4536[7] 5276[11]

Shibuni's Thea (IRE) *V Valiani* 69
3 b f Barathea(IRE) —Shibuni (Damister (USA))
6688a[15]

Shifting Star (IRE) *W R Swinburn* 79
2 ch g Night Shift(USA) —Ahshado (Bin Ajwaad (IRE))
2478[3] (2832) 3524[2] 4121[6] 4695[12]

Shifty *D Carroll* a74 67
8 b g Night Shift(USA) —Crodelle (IRE) (Formidable (USA))
14[7] 681[7] 718[6] 732[2] 809[6] 1264[6] 6628[7] 6882[8] 7113[7] 7197[2]

Shiitake *Miss L A Perratt* 67
4 b m Cayman Kai(IRE) —Petticoat Rule (Stanford)
1967[2] 2865[2] 3346[9]

Shimoni *W J Knight* a81 86
3 b f Mark Of Esteem(IRE) —Limuru (Salse (USA))
1663[4] 1958[6] 2816[7] 3458[7] 3883[10] *5686[5] 6144[7]* 6422[2] 6620[7] *7055[6]*

Shindy (FR) *J A R Toller* a73 62
2 b f Intikhab(USA) —Sheriya (USA) (Green Dancer (USA))
6649[8] *6847[3]*

Shine And Rise (IRE) *C G Cox* a82 93
3 b c Marju(IRE) —Ela Cassini (IRE) (Ela-Mana-Mou)
1001[7] 1143[12] 1927[6] 2602[5] 3450[2] 4391[2] *(4951) 5224[2]* (5911)

Shine Like A Star *J L Dunlop* 59
3 b f Fantastic Light(USA) —Fallen Star (Brief Truce (USA))
1358[12] 1665[10] 2359[6] 2945[8]

Shining Armour (IRE) *D K Weld* 92
2 b c Green Desert(USA) —Perfect Touch (USA) (Miswaki (USA))
6182[14]

Shinko (IRE) *Miss J Feilden* a58 62
4 b m Shinko Forest(IRE) —Sharp Circle (IRE) (Sure Blade (USA))
796[5] 1038[12] 1740[14] *2179[10]*

Shinko Dancer (IRE) *H Rogers* a66 83
4 bb m Shinko Forest(IRE) —Bobbydazzle (Rock Hopper)
1171a[8] 3573a[9] 5394a[6]

Shinko Femme (IRE) *J O'Reilly* 40
6 b m Shinko Forest(IRE) —Kilshanny (Groom Dancer (USA))
431[13] 571[10]

Shinko's Best (IRE) *A Kleinkorres* 110
6 ch g Shinko Forest(IRE) —Sail Away (GER) (Platini (GER))
1189a[3] 1800a[3] 3122a[3] 4869a[7] 6370a[12]

Shipboard Romance (IRE) *P D Evans* a28 47
2 b f Captain Rio—In Other Words (IRE) (Lake Coniston (IRE))
1073[5] 1367[7] 2533[2] 2723[6] 3681[3] 3801[3] 4559[2] 5302[14] *6693[9]*

Ships Watch (IRE) *R Charlton* a32
3 b f Night Shift(USA) —Bel (Darshaan)
1452[8]

Shiraz (GER) *M Weiss* 81
7 br h Bigstone(IRE) —Sintenis (GER) (Polish Precedent (USA))
355a[6]

Shire (IRE) *D R C Elsworth* 35
5 br g Trans Island—Trebles (IRE) (Kenmare (FR))
3554[9] 3907[17]

Shirley A Star (USA) *B J Meehan* a51 80
3 b f Cozzene(USA) —Fashion Star (USA) (Chief's Crown (USA))
1606[11] *2455[9]* (2597)

Shirley Oaks (IRE) *Miss Z C Davison* a53 28
9 b m Sri Pekan(USA) —Duly Elected (Persian Bold)
207[8] 341[8]

Shishangaan (IRE) *M Rulec* 92
2 b f Mujadil(USA) —Irish Flower (IRE) (Zieten (USA))
(6527a) 6888a[3]

Shishio *W De Best-Turner* a45 34
2 b c Largesse—Sachiko (Celtic Swing)
4598[10] *5116[10]* 5590[8]

Shivering *T Stack* 88
2 b f Royal Applause—Snowing (Tate Gallery (USA))
1821[7]

Shmookh (USA) *J L Dunlop* 104
3 b c Green Desert(USA) —Elrafa Ah (USA) (Storm Cat (USA))
(973) (1768) 2788[29] (3431) 4093[3] 5416[6]

Shogun Prince (IRE) *A King* a81 86
4 b g Shinko Forest(IRE) —Lady Of Dreams (IRE) (Prince Rupert (FR))
6110[4] 6422[4]

Shoot Out *C W Thornton* 24
4 b g Killer Instinct—Icy (Mind Games)
1804[13] 2091[12] 2828[7]

Shoot Pontoon (IRE) *N A Callaghan* a52
2 b g Danehill Dancer(IRE) —Burmese Princess (USA) (King Of Kings (IRE))
7051[11] 7140[8]

Shopfitter *P T Midgley* a28 50
4 b g Sugarfoot—Madam Wurlitzer (Noble Patriarch)
6816[7] 7197[12]

Shore Do (USA) *Chuck Peery* a103
2 ch c Include(USA) —Dynashore (USA) (Dynaformer (USA))
6508a[8]

Shore Thing (IRE) *C R Egerton* 81
4 b g Docksider(USA) —Spicebird (IRE) (Ela-Mana-Mou)
4171[2] 4572[11]

Short Affair *M Gasparini* 95
2 b f Singspiel(IRE) —L'Affaire Monique (Machiavellian (USA))
6047a[2]

Shortcake *M R Hoad* a45 30
3 b f Sure Blade(USA) —Confection (Formidable (USA))
343[10] 574[8] 3395[10] 4324[8] 5090[11] 5708[13]

Shorthand *Sir Michael Stoute* 100
3 b f Diktat—Much Too Risky (Bustino)
1769[4] 2786[9] 4503[4] 5544[2] 6299[12]

Short Skirt *Saeed Bin Suroor* 115
4 br m Diktat—Much Too Risky (Bustino)
(6299) 6524a[7]

Shoshiba (IRE) *P Martometti* 62
4 b m Plumbird—Magic Surprise (Bluebird (USA))
1337a[12]

Shot Bless (IRE) *M Guarnieri* 102
3 b f Daggers Drawn(USA) —Kadja Chenee (Spectrum (IRE))
(2070a) 2707a[10]

Shotfire Ridge *M Wigham* 78
4 ch g Grand Lodge(USA) —Darya (USA) (Gulch (USA))
3060[9] *3732[U]* (Dead)

Shot Gun *M R Channon* a86 80
3 b g Green Desert(USA) —Wardat Allayl (IRE) (Mtoto)
758[2] 954[5] (1246) 1956[6] *2354[4] 3420[2]* 3745[7] 4176[14]

Shotley Mac *N Bycroft* 67
3 ch g Abou Zouz(USA) —Julie's Gift (Presidium)
1850[15] 1912[9] 2840[7] 3377[9] 3605[2] 4042[2] 4411[3] 4491[2] 4817[7] 5046[2] 5255[5] 5703[4] 6055[2] 6310[2]

Shot Through (USA) *P C Haslam* a40 47
2 b g Golden Missile(USA) —Halo's Gleam (USA) (Halo (USA))
4578[9] 4611[12] 5226[4] *6776[6]*

Shot To Fame (USA) *D Nicholls* a80 99
8 b g Quest For Fame—Exocet (USA) (Deposit Ticket (USA))
697[7] 846[3] 1040[5] 1223[3] 1555[4] 1939[4] 2180[3] 2528[4] 2986[14] 3052[2] 3512[8] 5617[3] 6539[10]

Shouldntbethere (IRE) *Mrs P N Dutfield* a70 56
3 ch g Soviet Star(USA) —Octomone (USA) (Hennessy (USA))
1122[10] 1359[3] *2177[6]* 2727[13] 3429[11] *4064[2]* 5166[11] *5733[10] 5943[5] 6387[8] 6894[2] 7241[8]*

Shout (IRE) *J W Hills* a80 83
4 ch m Halling(USA) —Spout (Salse (USA))
1287[8] 1922[2] 2218[6]

Show Business (IRE) *P Butler* a52 26
3 ch g Distant Music(USA) —Gertie Laurie (Lomond (USA))
99[6] 194[4] 900[11] 1739[12] 2140[9] 2697[13]

Show Me The Lolly (FR) *S W Hall* a55 16
7 b m Sri Pekan(USA) —Sugar Lolly (USA) (Irish River (FR))
19[2] 94[5] 274[8] 517[3] 4856[13] *5179[11] 6152[13]*

Showtime Annie *A Bailey* a45 43
6 b m Wizard King—Rebel County (IRE) (Maelstrom Lake)
462[9] 2823[9] 4340[8] *4460[2]* 4663[5] 4713[6] 4846[6] *5756[7]*

Showtime Ice *M J Wallace* a69 58
2 b f Lujain(USA) —Rebel County (IRE) (Maelstrom Lake)
4756[5] *5603[2] 6761[6] 7095[5]*

Show Trial (IRE) *D J S Ffrench Davis* a59 56
3 b f Jade Robbery(USA) —Court Lane (USA) (Machiavellian (USA))
202[2] 348[10]

Shraayef *M Botti* 55
2 b f Nayef(USA) —Gorgeous Dancer (IRE) (Nordico (USA))
5596[12]

Shreddy Shrimpster *A B Haynes* a53 55
3 ch f Zilzal(USA) —Empress Dagmar (Selkirk (USA))
636[10] 920[5] 1213[2] 2195[9]

Shrek (GER) *A Wohler* 112
3 b c Pelder(IRE) —Septima (GER) (Touching Wood (USA))
(1387a) 1875a[2] 3146a[6] (5464a)

Shrewd Dude *Carl Llewellyn* a53 48
3 bb c Val Royal(FR) —Lily Dale (IRE) (Distinctly North (USA))
37[2] 267[5]

Shrine Mountain (USA) *Miss J S Davis* a73 60
5 b g Distorted Humor(USA) —Fancy Ruler (USA) (Half A Year (USA))
(26) 52[3] 138[7] 252[11] 341[5] 1740[10] *1947[14] 3172[7]*

Shuaily (PER) *Lee Freedman* 102
5 b m Shuailaan(USA) — (USA) (Funambule (USA))
6033a[10]

Shujoon *A Fabre* 108
3 b c Sakhee(USA) —Marie De Blois (IRE) (Barathea (IRE))
1572a[3] 6400a[3]

Shumookh (IRE) *M A Jarvis* 109
4 b g Mujahid(USA) —Midway Lady (USA) (Alleged (USA))
2368[2] 3887[2]

Shunkawakhan (IRE) *G C H Chung* a61 60
4 b g Indian Danehill(IRE) —Special Park (USA) (Trempolino (USA))
33[6] 144[3] 462[2] 579[10] 2990[2] 3419[4] 4294[4] *5336[4] 5730[3] 6266[3] 6587[3] 6796[7] 7115[5] 7244[8]*

Shustraya *P J Makin* a93 81
3 b f Dansili—Nimble Fan (USA) (Lear Fan (USA))
(199) 2629[4] *3418[6] 4360[5]* 4848[6] 5635[7] *(6006) 6391[9]*

Shy *P Winkworth* a68
2 ch f Erhaab(USA) —Shi Shi (Alnasr Alwasheek)
5727[3]

Shybutwilling (IRE) *Mrs P N Dutfield*
2 ch f Best Of The Bests(IRE) —Reticent Bride (IRE) (Shy Groom (USA))
2569[12]

Shy Glance (USA) *P Monteith* a76 79
5 b g Red Ransom(USA) —Royal Shyness (Royal Academy (USA))
(1132) *1283[5]* 2536[5] 2822[2] 3346[6] 3955[11] 4219[2] 4716[4] 4932[6] 5664[4] 5905[14]

Siamese Cat (IRE) *B J Meehan* 100
3 ch f Rock Of Gibraltar(IRE) —Real Cat (USA) (Storm Cat (USA))
1901[2] 2914[11] 3387[2]

Siamsa Sraide (IRE) *J S Bolger* 50
2 b g Daggers Drawn(USA) —Siamsa (USA) (Quest For Fame)
779a[13]

Si Belle (IRE) *Rae Guest* a60
2 gr f Dalakhani(IRE) —Stunning (USA) (Nureyev (USA))
7152[4]

Siberian Tiger (IRE) *M R Channon* a54 101
2 b c Xaar—Flying Millie (IRE) (Flying Spur (AUS))
2432[4] *3283[5]* 3552[3] (4130) (5002) 5350[9] (6382) 6782a[5]

Sibo Baggins (IRE) *J S Moore* 59
3 ch g Docksider(USA) —Isadora Duncan (IRE) (Sadler's Wells (USA))
2625[11] 6412[3] 6573[5] *6895[13]*

Sidereus (IRE) *F & L Camici* 81
3 b c Grand Lodge(USA) —Simaat (USA) (Mr Prospector (USA))
1875a[13] 6863a[10]

Siegfrieds Night (IRE) *M C Chapman* a44 54
6 ch g Night Shift(USA) —Shelbiana (USA) (Chieftain)
716[6] 3250[8] 3610[12]

Siena *Mrs C A Dunnett* 18
2 b f Lomitas—Sea Lane (Zafonic (USA))
6574[12]

Siena Star (IRE) *Stef Liddiard* a68 72
9 b g Brief Truce(USA) —Gooseberry Pie (Green Desert (USA))
48[6] 117[12] (363) 1249[10] (2490) 3672[8] 4266[5] 5454[8] 5636[6] *5983[7]* 6196[2] *6342[6] 6612[4]* 6727[10] *6780[4] 6951[4] 7056[5] 7080[7] 7257[8]*

Sienna Storm (IRE) *M H Tompkins* 98
4 b g Peintre Celebre(USA) —Saint Ann (USA) (Geiger Counter (USA))
929[8] 1244[13] 1844[19] 3105[5] 4171[6] 4609[7] 5052[6] 5255[2] 5479[3] 5774[4] 6019[5]

Sierra Rose *P J McBride* a40 51
3 b f Auction House(USA) —Young Whip (Bold Owl)
2836[7] *4430[7]* 4815[13] *5647[12]*

Sierras Future *I Semple* 52
3 b g Fusaichi Pegasus(USA) —Sierra Virgen (USA) (Stack (USA))
3678[9] 4496[7] 4713[3]

Sierra Vista *D W Barker* a77 114
7 ch m Atraf—Park Vista (Taufan (USA))
847[2] 1102[10] (1657) (2034) (2184) 3088[5] 3329[8] 4746[8] 5214[11]

Siesta (IRE) *J R Fanshawe* a57 40
3 ch f King Charlemagne(USA) —Quiescent (Primo Dominie)
1635[12] 2186[3] *3425[2] 3924[8]* 4336[8] *5946[2]*

Si Foo (USA) *A M Balding* a90 86
3 ch g Fusaichi Pegasus(USA) —Ascension (IRE) (Night Shift (USA))
(216) (312) 385[2] 760[8] 1099[4]

Signalman *M Gasparini*
3 gr c Silver Patriarch(IRE) —Kairine (IRE) (Kahyasi)
1191a[4]

Sign Of The Cross *J R Fanshawe* a88 85
3 b g Mark Of Esteem(IRE) —Thea (USA) (Marju (IRE))
2153[4] (2580) 3196[4] 3745[9] *5685[7] 6145[2]* 6474[4]

Sign Of The Wolf *F Rohaut* 92
7 b g Loup Solitaire(USA) —Sign Of The Vine (FR) (Kendor (FR))
1340a[8] 2292a[8]

Signora (IRE) *M Johnston* 47
2 ch f Indian Ridge—Lady Catherine (Bering)
6754[5]

Signor Panettiere *A D Brown* a59 52
6 b g Night Shift(USA) —Christmas Kiss (Taufan (USA))
155[12] 277[7] 727[7] 835[9] 5522[11] 5908[16]

Signor Peltro *H Candy* a86 93
4 b g Bertolini(USA) —Pewter Lass (Dowsing (USA))
1818[6] 2817[10] (3911)

Signor Whippee *A Berry* a47 58
4 ch g Observatory(USA) —Revoltosa (IRE) (Catrail (USA))
1493[11] 2387[6] 3180[10] 3347[10] 4478[6] 5041[7]

Signs Of Love (FR) *Noel T Chance* a45
4 b g Poliglote—Severina (Darshaan)
6766[4]

Signum (GER) *Frau A Glodde* 100
4 b h Kalatos(GER) —Southern Bird (GER) (Law Society (USA))
1800a[8] 2903a[5]

Silca Chiave *M R Channon* 109
3 ch f Pivotal—Silca-Cisa (Hallgate)
1146[5] 2752[15]

Silca Destination *M R Channon* a54 55
2 b f Dubai Destination(USA) —Golden Silca (Inchinor)
4014[5] 4232[6] 4756[5] 5939[9] *6388[10]* 6536[4] *6775[2] 7117[12]*

Silca Elegance *M R Channon* 76
3 b c Selkirk(USA) —Parisian Elegance (Zilzal (USA))
1276[6] 1838[5] 2470[2] 2606[3] (2894) 3099[5] 3483[2] 3879[2] 4127[4] 4546[6]

Silca Key *M R Channon* a73 90
3 ch f Inchinor—Baalbek (Barathea (IRE))
196[6] 563[5] 694[9] 834[6] 1815[6] *2456[8] 2668[5] 3082[8]* 3429[2] (3722) (3785) 4112[6] 4615[7] *5424[4] 5943[3]* (6129) 6299[7] 6653[5] 6757[11] *6822[5]*

Silencio (IRE) *A King* 64
6 b g Sillery(USA) —Flabbergasted (IRE) (Sadler's Wells (USA))
1888[3]

Silent Applause *Dr J D Scargill* a67 76
4 b g Royal Applause—Billie Blue (Ballad Rock)
2831[2] 4135[6] 4587[3] 5166[4] 5559[7]

Silent Beauty (IRE) *S C Williams* a51 35
3 b f Intikhab(USA) —Precedence (IRE) (Polish Precedent (USA))
1635[10] 4499[7] *4673[5] 5102[3] 5366[6] 5647[11] 5945[9]* 6453[9] *6505[9]*

Silent Lucidity (IRE) *P D Niven* 64
3 ch g Ashkalani(IRE) —Mimansa (USA) (El Gran Senor (USA))
(1489) 2389[3]

Silent Master (USA) *M Johnston* a75 58
2 b c Cherokee Run(USA) —Polent (Polish Precedent (USA))
4782[6] 5580[7] *6602[2] 6899[2] 7095[3]*

Silent Name (JPN) *R J Frankel* a115 115
5 b h Sunday Silence(USA) —Danzigaway (USA) (Danehill (USA))
6511a[12] 6924a[4]

Silent Storm *Peter Grayson* a83 75
7 ch g Zafonic(USA) —Nanda (Nashwan (USA))
238[8] 381[2] (486) 697[3] 3188[4] 4716[11] *5119[10] 6273[10] 6504[8] 6646[11] 6764[6] 6894[9] 6993[12] 7111[8]*

Silent Street *K G Reveley* 47
4 b g Celtic Swing—Smart Spirit (IRE) (Persian Bold)
1225[7] 1579[14] 1966[6] 2252[9] 2890[12] 4246[7]

Silex (GER) *P Schiergen* 98
4 b h Zilzal(USA) —Shine (GER) (Sanglamore (USA))
881a[6] 1699a[7]

Silidan *M Brittain* a43 79
4 b g Dansili—In Love Again (IRE) (Prince Rupert (FR))
1678[11] 4141[11] 4353[12] 5489[9]

Silk Affair (IRE) *M G Quinlan* 89
2 b f Barathea(IRE) —Uncertain Affair (IRE) (Darshaan)
5812[6] (6461) 6939a[5]

Silk Blossom (IRE) *B W Hills* 109
3 ch f Barathea(IRE) —Lovely Blossom (FR) (Spinning World (USA))
1146[12] 2814[13] 5354[13]

Silk Dress (IRE) *John Joseph Murphy* a42 98
3 b f Gulch(USA) —Zvezda (USA) (Nureyev (USA))
1499[7] 2065a[9]

Silk Drum (IRE) *J Howard Johnson* 67
2 gr g Intikhab(USA) —Aneydia (IRE) (Kenmare (FR))
2804[3] 3199[4] 5749[7]

Silken Spell *Mrs A Duffield* 32
2 b f Tobougg(IRE) —Walsham Witch (Music Maestro)
4422[10] 5192[9]

Silk Gallery (USA) *M L W Bell* 57
2 b f Kingmambo(USA) —Moon Flower (IRE) (Sadler's Wells (USA))
5194[8]

Silk Hall (UAE) *D W P Arbuthnot* a70
2 b c Halling(USA) —Velour (Mtoto)
5116[5] 5679[4] 6119[9]

Silkie Smooth (IRE) *B W Hills* a66 74
3 b f Barathea(IRE) —Whassup (FR) (Midyan (USA))
311[4]

Silkwood *M A Jarvis* a88 117
3 b f Singspiel(IRE) —Wood Vine (USA) (Woodman (USA))
(484) 719[2] (1277) (2786) 4723[7]

Silky Steps (IRE) *P J Makin* a67 23
2 gr f Nayef(USA) —Legal Steps (IRE) (Law Society (USA))
5872[10] *6228[9] 6601[4]*

Silly Dancer (IRE) *Adrian McGuinness* a78 80
4 b m King Charlemagne(USA) —Silly Imp (IRE) (Imperial Frontier (USA))
6553a[6]

Silly Gilly (IRE) *K R Burke* a55 63
3 b f Mull Of Kintyre(USA) —Richly Deserved (IRE) (Kings Lake (USA))
910[5] 1164[8] 1530[9] 1912[8] 2304[8] 2826[2] 3568[2] (3763) 3811[3] 4226[2] *4432[3]* 4714[4] 4734[5] 5970[5]

Silmi *E A L Dunlop* a73 66
3 gr c Daylami(IRE) —Intimaa (IRE) (Caerleon (USA))
1290[7] 2602[8]

Silvabella (IRE) *D Haydn Jones* a33 52
4 gr m Monashee Mountain(USA) —Siva (FR) (Bellypha)
6457[6] 6766[7] 6935[7]

Silvanus (IRE) *W J Haggas* 81
2 b c Danehill Dancer(IRE) —Mala Mala (IRE) (Brief Truce (USA))
4725[5] 5192[7]

Silver Appraisal *Pat Eddery* a45 58
3 gr f Royal Applause—Arinaga (Warning)
1923[6] 4606[16] *5425[8]*

Silver Arrow (ITY) *Maria Rita Salvioni* 82
2 b c Silver Wizard(USA) —Eros Love (ITY) (Love The Groom (USA))
6222a[7] 6523a[7]

Silver Blue (IRE) *C R Dore* a77 99
4 ch g Indian Lodge(IRE) —Silver Echo (Caerleon (USA))
1060[12] 1395[14] 3482[4] 3690[5] 4577[5] *5128[4] 5341[12]*

Silver Cross (FR) *D Prod'Homme* 102
5 b h Kahyasi—Snowdrop II (FR) (Niniski (USA))
2330a[8]

Silver Deal *J A Pickering* a33 42
2 b f Lujain(USA) —Deal In Facts (So Factual (USA))
3681[4] 4074[9] *5176[7] 7171[8] 7240[5]*

Silver Diamond *W Jarvis* 46
2 b f Josr Algarhoud(IRE) —Silvermour (Aydimour)
5881[10]

Silver Dreamer (IRE) *H S Howe* a44 43
5 b m Brave Act—Heads We Called (IRE) (Bluebird (USA))
1396[7] 1730[10] 3397[7] 4531[10] 5138[5] 6583[7] 7256[9]

Silver Flame *A W Carroll* 50
3 ch f Dr Fong(USA) —Pastel (Lion Cavern (USA))
1151[11] 2080[8] 4529[14] 4684[14] 5270[11]

Silver Guest *M R Channon* 97
2 br g Lujain(USA) —Ajig Dancer (Niniski (USA))
898[2] 1007[2] 1546a[3] 1846[2] 2785[4] 3486[4]

Silverhay *L Corcoran* a77 79
6 b g Inchinor—Moon Spin (Night Shift (USA))
297[5] 377[7]

Silver Hotspur *M Wigham* a57 67
3 b g Royal Applause—Noble View (USA) (Distant View (USA))
147[9] 322[3] 2418[11] 2837[5] 5425[4] 5730[13] 5970[10] 6083[6] (6609) 7250[6]

Silverlord (FR) *Mme C Head-Maarek* a78 101
3 ch g Numerous(USA) —Silverware (FR) (Polish Precedent (USA))
3361a[4]

Silver Mitzva (IRE) *M Botti* a78 95
3 b f Almutawakel—Ribblesdale (Northern Park (USA))
1024[5] 1153[5] 2362[2] 2609[3] 3421[2] 4139[4] (4339) (5131) 5523[2] 6519a[2] 6953a[3]

Silver Mont (IRE) *S R Bowring* a63 57
4 b g Montjeu(IRE) —Silvernus (Machiavellian (USA))
453[9] 585[6] 683[5] 804[3] 1152[6] (1934) (2204) 2345[2] 3927[10] 4451[4] 6076[8]

Silver Navasha (USA) *John Joseph Murphy* 21
4 b m Silver Hawk(USA) —Navasha (USA) (Woodman (USA))
4142a[10] (Dead)

Silver Pivotal (IRE) *G A Butler* a73 100
3 br f Pivotal—Silver Colours (USA) (Silver Hawk (USA))
(1068) 1391[2] (1824)

Silver Prelude *D K Ivory* a87 67
6 gr g Prince Sabo—Silver Blessings (Statoblest)
1061[11] 1669[12] 1991[17] 2516[2] 2555[13] 3408[2] (3627) 4165[11] 4486[5] 4944[8] 5016[2] 5174[2] (5565) 5642[11] 6360[2] 6594[10] 6794[5] (6976) (7059)

Silver Regent (USA) *Mrs A J Perrett* 87
2 b c Silver Deputy(CAN) —Alexine (ARG) (Runaway Groom (CAN))
4571[8] 5011[4] (5361) 6471[6]

Silver Rime (FR) *R Hannon* 79
2 gr c Verglas(IRE) —Severina (Darshaan)
4362[10] 4777[4] (5720)

Silver Sail *J S Wainwright* 44
4 gr m Daylami(IRE) —Fiveofive (IRE) (Fairy King (USA))
1967[7] 2370[10] 2795[8] 3399[9] 3789[10]

Silver Snipe *John Joseph Murphy* a59 62
3 b g Piccolo—Baileys Silver (USA) (Marlin (USA))
6647[2]

Silver Sprite *D Shaw* a58
2 gr g Best Of The Bests(IRE) —Nightingale (Night Shift (USA))
5605[12] 6694[4] 6799[11] 7031[8] 7149[3]

Silver Suitor (IRE) *D R C Elsworth* 94
3 gr g Swain(IRE) —Taatof (IRE) (Lahib (USA))
1841[10] 2402[5] 3436[5] (3908) 4572[2]

Silver Surprise *J J Bridger* a46 51
3 gr f Orpen(USA) —Dim Ofan (Petong)
1203[U] 1522[13] 1961[10] 2219[10] 2697[14] 3150[16] 4205[14] 4542[9] 5007[11] 5450[5] 6534[10] 6780[7] 6832[9] 6967[6] 7256[10]

Silver Tide (USA) *M J Grassick* a61 74
3 ch f Silver Hawk(USA) —Soaring Bay (USA) (Boone's Mill (USA))
(6858)

Silver Touch (IRE) *M R Channon* 114
4 b m Dansili—Sanpala (Sanglamore (USA))
2050a[8] (3098) 4214a[3] 4600[5] 5832[12]

Silvertown *L Lungo* a87 88
12 b g Danehill(USA) —Docklands (USA) (Theatrical)
192[P]

Silver Waters *D R C Elsworth* a58
2 ro c Fantastic Light(USA) —Silent Waters (Polish Precedent (USA))
6705[3]

Silver Wind *P D Evans* 86
2 b g Ishiguru(USA) —My Bonus (Cyrano De Bergerac)
845[9] 1007[8] 2941[2] 3398[3] (3669) 4121[11] 4695[15] 5207[2] 5629[2] 5773[5]

Simbad (FR) *P Bary* 98
3 b c Danehill(USA) —Napoli (Baillamont (USA))
4216a[7]

Simba's Pride *Miss L A Perratt* 39
3 b g Dansili—Welcome Aboard (Be My Guest (USA))
3678[7] 4138[7] 4713[10] 5299[10] 5967[12]

Simba Sun (IRE) *R M Beckett* a83 84
3 b g Intikhab(USA) —Lions Den (IRE) (Desert Style (IRE))
4276[9] 4827[6] 5385[8] 5870[4]

Simonas (IRE) *A Wohler* 108
8 gr g Sternkoenig(IRE) —Sistadari (Shardari)
4838a[7] 5929a[8]

Simondiun *W J Haggas* a86 95
4 b g Hernando(FR) —Jetbeeah (IRE) (Lomond (USA))
1822[13] 3216[6]

Simone Martini (IRE) *R Charlton* 72
2 b g Montjeu(IRE) —Bona Dea (IRE) (Danehill (USA))
5918[5] 6494[4] 6723[5]

Simple Exchange (IRE) *A Savujev* a109 106
6 b h Danehill(USA) —Summer Trysting (USA) (Alleged (USA))
4838a[3] 5670a[5] 5929a[4]

Simple Jim (FR) *A D Brown* a59
3 b g Jimble(FR) —Stop The Wedding (USA) (Stop The Music (USA))
6911[6]

Simpleton *J R Best* a40 48
4 b g Easycall—Ok Babe (Bold Arrangement)
901[6] 1928[12] 2173[9] 4741[6] 5062[6] 5497[8]

Simplex (FR) *K Schafflutzel* 103
6 b h Rainbow Quest(USA) —Russyskia (USA) (Green Dancer (USA))
355a[9]

Simplified *N B King* a53 43
4 b m Lend A Hand—Houston Heiress (USA) (Houston (USA))
133[6] 187[4] (349) 416[9] 558[7] 789[8]

Simplify *T M Jones* a27 55
5 b g Fasliyev(USA) —Simplicity (Polish Precedent (USA))
1025[12] 2336[15] 2664[8] 4807[11] 6607[14] 7069[11]

Simply Perfect *J Noseda* 116
3 gr f Danehill(USA) —Hotelgenie Dot Com (Selkirk (USA))
1496[3] 2211[6] (3433) 4010a[3] 6010[4] 6509a[P]

Simply St Lucia *J R Weymes* a66 47
5 b m Charnwood Forest(IRE) —Mubadara (IRE) (Lahib (USA))
1350[7] (3538) 4003[5]

Simpsons Gamble (IRE) *R A Teal* a59 27
4 b g Tagula(IRE) —Kiva (Indian Ridge)
86[10] 383[5] 461[9] 500[4] 559[3] 795[3] 1400[7] 1612[10] 5817[5] 6579[5] 6778[2] 7167[2]

Simpsons Ross (IRE) *R M Flower* a64 65
4 br g Imperial Ballet(IRE) —Brunswick (Warning)
92[4] (Dead)

Sina (GER) *W Hickst* 91
2 b f Trans Island—Soiree De Vienne (IRE) (Marju (IRE))
4837a[2] 5462a[2] 6371a[5]

Sinaaf *M P Tregoning* a66
2 b f Nayef(USA) —Elutrah (Darshaan)
6434[9] 6847[6]

Sina Cova (IRE) *Peter Casey* 115
5 b m Barathea(IRE) —Kumta (IRE) (Priolo (USA))
4238a[7] 5396a[7]

Sinatas (GER) *P Monteith* 55
4 b g Lomitas—Sylvette (USA) (Silver Hawk (USA))
3015[5] 3584[6] 4380[5]

Sinbad The Sailor *J W Hills* 71
2 b c Cape Cross(IRE) —Sinead (USA) (Irish River (FR))
4362[11] 5010[5] 5538[8]

Sin City *R A Fahey* 83
4 b g Sinndar(IRE) —Turn Of A Century (Halling (USA))
1416[2] 2245[2]

Sinead Of Aglish (IRE) *Peter Grayson* a69 74
2 ch f Captain Rio—Final Favour (IRE) (Unblest)
972[2] 1302[2] 1533[3] 1580[3] 2115[2] 2410[2] (2717) 4762[11] 5713[4] 6017[23] 6834[3] 7052[5]

Singapore Creek (FR) *Robert Collet* a80 94
3 b f Sagacity(FR) —Lias Creek (Lahib (USA))
2384a[5] 6460a[9] 6770a[6]

Singer Of Songs (IRE) *P A Blockley* a50 62
2 ch c Spartacus(IRE) —Waratah (IRE) (Entrepreneur)
1858[8] 3095[10] 3902[6] 5127[11]

Singhalongtasveer *G A Charlton* 53
5 b g Namaqualand(USA) —Felinwen (White Mill)
(1895) 2252[7] 3193[3]

Singing Poet (IRE) *E Charpy* a107 78
6 b g Singspiel(IRE) —Bright Finish (USA) (Zilzal (USA))
399a[3] 601a[2] 858a[11]

Singleb (IRE) *T D Barron* a51 66
3 b g Intikhab(USA) —Bubble N Squeak (IRE) (Catrail (USA))
711[3] 1278[6] 1976[7] (5625) 6310[5] 6598[10]

Sintenis Mac (GER) *P J O'Gorman* a63 61
4 ch g Pivotal—Sintenis (GER) (Polish Precedent (USA))
6062[2] 6877[4] 7239[4]

Sion Hill (IRE) *John A Harris* a53 48
6 b g Desert Prince(IRE) —Mobilia (Last Tycoon (IRE))
59[6] 238[12] 3917[9] 4488[3] 4526[12] 5121[2] (5368) 6311[4] 6532[13] 6609[2] 6908[2] 7034 [2] 7197[7]

Siraj *J Ryan* a69 59
8 b g Piccolo—Masuri Kabisa (USA) (Ascot Knight (CAN))
1718[6] 2155[4] 2272[7] 4944[6] 5130[8] 5387[11] 6101[4] 6608[4]

Sir Arthur (IRE) *B Ellison* 82
4 ch g Desert Prince(IRE) —Park Express (Ahonoora)
850[14] 1890[3] 2136[2] 2403[5] 2551[2] 2987[12] 3301[3] 4072[7]

Sir Bond (IRE) *G R Oldroyd* a66 62
6 ch g Desert Sun—In Tranquility (IRE) (Shalford (IRE))
110[5] 200[9] 1132[2] 1260[7] 1675[2] 1918[12] 2311[12] 2842[7] 3534[11] 6316[7] 7079[8] (7218)

Sir Don (IRE) *E S McMahon* a59 59
8 b g Lake Coniston(IRE) —New Sensitive (Wattlefield)
6957[10] (7192)

Sir Douglas *R A Harris* a79 64
4 ch h Desert Sun—Daintree (IRE) (Tirol)
32[2] 234[5] 323[5] 371[2] 424[2] 560[2] 609[9] (621) 774[3] 1004[7] 1252[9] 6907[8] 7033[5] 7073[6]

Sir Duke (IRE) *P W D'Arcy* a64 64
3 b g Danehill(USA) —Dimanche (IRE) (Sadler's Wells (USA))
769[7] 1011[13] (2538) 2727[5] 3058[7] 3624[5] 4297[5] 4518[6] 5138[3] 5573[4] (6147)

Sir Edwin Landseer (USA) *Christian Wroe* a95 99
7 rg g Lit De Justice(USA) —Wildcat Blue (USA) (Cure The Blues (USA))
326a[3] 415a[6] 470a[6] 540a[7]

Siren Call *W J Haggas* 53
2 b f Fantastic Light(USA) —Fleet Amour (USA) (Afleet (CAN))
5061[10] 5599[10] 5912[9]

Sirene Doloise (FR) *A Bonin* a83 104
4 br m Marchand De Sable(USA) —Ramonda (FR) (Fabulous Dancer (USA))
7128a[0]

Siren's Gift *A M Balding* a99 102
3 ch f Cadeaux Genereux—Blue Siren (Bluebird (USA))
2135[2] 2672[4] 3431[5] 3746[4] (5305) 5632[6] 6003[4]

Sir George (IRE) *P W Chapple-Hyam* 71
2 b c Mujadil(USA) —Torrmana (IRE) (Ela-Mana-Mou)
2604[2] 4832a[12]

Sir Gerard *I Mohammed* a80 106
4 b h Marju(IRE) —Chapeau (Zafonic (USA))
(325a) 531a[6] 646a[10] (Dead)

Sir Gerry (USA) *J R Fanshawe* 112
2 ch c Carson City(USA) —Incredulous (FR) (Indian Ridge)
(3192) 3910[4] (4721) 5975[8]

Sir Haydn *J R Jenkins* a66 46
7 ch g Definite Article—Snowscape (Niniski (USA))
2765[7] 3042[8] 3249[11] 3805[10] 3946[4] 4592[5] 5132[4] 5341[2] 5531[7] 6068[3] 6260[6] 7083[5] (7186)

Sir Ike (IRE) *W S Kittow* 66
2 b c Xaar—Iktidar (Green Desert (USA))
3478[4] 6234[7]

Sir Jake *T T Clement* 18
3 b c Killer Instinct—Waikiki Dancer (IRE) (General Monash (USA))
3476[9] 4235[10]

Sir Joey *J T Stimpson* a50 51
2 ch g Forzando—Estabella (IRE) (Mujtahid (USA))
4160[5] 4459[11] 5771[15] 6721[9] 6881[10] 6958[4] 7156[6] 7286[7]

Sirjoshua Reynolds *N A Callaghan* a32 90
2 b c Kyllachy—Alzianah (Alzao (USA))
898[8] 1519[7] 1846[5] (2138) 2684a[4] 3269[6]

Sir Liam (USA) *P Mitchell* a77 73
3 b g Monarchos(USA) —Tears (USA) (Red Ransom (USA))
(788) 1122[5] 1987[10] 2598[7] 2767[5] 4277[6] 4510[8] 5014[8]

Sir Loin *P Burgoyne* a62 64
6 ch g Compton Place—Charnwood Queen (Cadeaux Genereux)
82[4] 254[6] 318[8] 566[11] 1405[15] 1640[8] (2221) 2516[12] 3169[8] 3347[3] 3608[13] 3921[4] 4008[4] 4180[6] 5946[9] 6264[11] 6528[3] 6773[2] 6957[7] 7082[10] 7188[4] 7265[4]

Sir Mikeale *G Prodromou* a36
4 b h Easycall—Sleep Standing (IRE) (Standaan (FR))
5336[8] 6542[10] 7124[9]

Sirmione (AUS) *J B Cummings* 114
4 b g Encosta De Lago(AUS) —World Guide (NZ) (Defensive Play (USA))
6354a[12] 6712a[12]

Sir Monty (USA) *Mrs A J Perrett* a72 86
5 ch g Cat's Career(USA) —Lady Of Meadowlane (USA) (Pancho Jay (USA))
362[7] 640[6]

Sir Nod *Miss J A Camacho* a86 87
5 b g Tagula(IRE) —Nordan Raider (Domynsky)
3762[10] 4140[2] 4703[2] 5039[8] 5481[4] 6355[2] 6836[13]

Sir Orpen (IRE) *T D Barron* a50 79
4 gr g Orpen(USA) —Yalciyna (Nishapour (FR))
(915) 1555[5] 1747[14] 2508[6] 2741[7] 3345[16] 4141[9] 4407[10] 6148[9]

Sir Percy *M P Tregoning* 121
4 b h Mark Of Esteem(IRE) —Percy's Lass (Blakeney)
861a[4] 2210[6] 2754[6]

Sir Royal (USA) *G A Swinbank* 64
2 b c Diesis—Only Royale (IRE) (Caerleon (USA))
5580[5]

Sir Sandicliffe (IRE) *W M Brisbourne* a65 71
3 b g Distant Music(USA) —Desert Rose (Green Desert (USA))
114[7] 338[2] 569[7] 3495[7] 4282[6] 4943[3] 5388[4] 5755[6] 5980[9] 6534[8] 6871[8] 6967[2] 7060[8] (7219) 7273[2]

Sir Xaar (IRE) *B Smart* a58 107
4 bb g Xaar—Cradle Brief (IRE) (Brief Truce (USA))
1041[7] 1195[11] 3953[2] 4385[8] 4745[16] 5804[12] 6013[2] 6606[13]

Siryena *E A L Dunlop* a57 48
2 b f Oasis Dream—Ard Na Sighe (IRE) (Kenmare (FR))
3507[17] 4293[6] 5309[6] 5729[13]

Sismix (IRE) *C Laffon-Parias* 105
3 ch f Diesis—Goldamix (IRE) (Linamix (FR))
989a[2] 1388a[5] 2384a[4] 3148a[10]

Sister Act *J R Fanshawe* a75 87
3 b f Marju(IRE) —Kalinka (IRE) (Soviet Star (USA))
1128[2] 2581[9] 2880[3] 3247[7] 5885[5] (6097)

Sister Agnes (IRE) *Jane Chapple-Hyam* 63
3 ch f Dr Fong(USA) —Nibbs Point (IRE) (Sure Blade (USA))
1725[14] 2308[7] 2690[3] 3367[14] 5938[5]

Sister Etienne (IRE) *J T Stimpson* a67 67
3 b f Lend A Hand—Final Favour (IRE) (Unblest)
(506) 707[5] 925[12]

Sister Gee (IRE) *R Hollinshead* a38 31
5 b m Desert Story(IRE) —My Gloria (IRE) (Saint Estephe (FR))
450[7]

Sister Maria (USA) *E A L Dunlop* a82 82
3 bb f Kingmambo(USA) —Fraulein (Acatenango (GER))
1815[4] 2181[6] 2579[3] (3107) 3972[5] 4615[3] 4976[2] (5979) 6620[5]

Sister Moonshine *W R Muir* a60 64
2 b f Averti(IRE) —Cal Norma's Lady (IRE) (Lyphard's Special (USA))
5856[5] 6225[7]

Sistos Fascination *M Botti* a55 65
2 b g Fasliyev(USA) —Sierra Virgen (USA) (Stack (USA))
3718[15] 4323[10] 5380[5] 6073[6] 6502[7] 6812[7]

Situla (IRE) *H J L Dunlop* a73 62
3 ch f Pairumani Star(IRE) —Suspiria (IRE) (Glenstal (USA))
1247[11] 1887[13] 2545[16]

Sivota (IRE) *T P Tate* 73
3 b g Sakhee(USA) —Mamara Reef (Salse (USA))
1827[13] 2808[6] (4490) 5404[3]

Six Day War (IRE) *J A Osborne* a88 74
3 b g Barathea(IRE) —Risarshana (FR) (Darshaan)
53[3] 141[5] (304) (582) 1584[6] 1843[7]

Sixfields Flyer (IRE) *Pat Eddery* a53 62
3 gr f Desert Style(IRE) —Gratclo (Belfort (FR))
689[12] 973[10] 1081[6] 1538[3] 2224[7] 2635[8] 4355[12]

Six Of Diamonds (IRE) *J A Osborne* a75 99
3 b c Redback—Villa Nova (IRE) (Petardia)
973[3] 1343[4] 1632[4] (1887) 2627[4] (3691) 4092[3] 4799[12] (5445) 5717[3]

Six Of Hearts *J A Osborne* a64 60
3 b c Pivotal—Additive (USA) (Devil's Bag (USA))
1278[2] 1714[5] 2541[3] 3066[11] 3475[8] 4064[5] 4591[3] 5528[3] 5783[7]

Six Of Trumps (IRE) *J A Osborne* a64 59
3 b g Fasliyev(USA) —Run To Jane (IRE) (Doyoun)
1976[2] 3395[4] 4321[6] 4977[2]

Six Shots *J A Osborne* a82 63
3 b c Josr Algarhoud(IRE) —Captive Heart (Conquistador Cielo (USA))
140[2] (257) 294[2] 382[4] 563[3] 638[3]

Sixties Icon *J Noseda* 123
4 b h Galileo(IRE) —Love Divine (Diesis)
(1495) 2210[7] 3461[10]

Siyabona (USA) *Saeed Bin Suroor* 74
2 b f Kingmambo(USA) —Relish (IRE) (Sadler's Wells (USA))
6093[2] 6411[2]

Siyasa (USA) *Saeed Bin Suroor* 54
2 ch f Rahy(USA) —Jood (USA) (Nijinsky (CAN))
4169[7]

Skadrak (USA) *P W Chapple-Hyam* 93
2 ch c Forest Camp(USA) —Occhi Verdi (IRE) (Mujtahid (USA))
3991[2]

Skhilling Pride *T D Barron* 44
2 ch f Kyllachy—Twilight Time (Aragon)
2451[9]

Skhilling Spirit *T D Barron* 103
4 b g Most Welcome—Calcavella (Pursuit Of Love)
847[3] 1474[22] 1651[2] 2755[8] 3559[3] 3975[RR] 4614[22] 5616[18] 6155[6]

Skiddaw Fox *Mrs L Williamson* a7 44
3 ch c Foxhound(USA) —Stealthy Times (Timeless Times (USA))
1008[12] 1403[13] 2195[7] 7137[13]

Skiddaw Jones *M A Barnes* 47
7 b g Emperor Jones(USA) —Woodrising (Nomination)
4817[3] 5300[11]

Ski For Luck (IRE) *J L Dunlop* 53
3 br g Key Of Luck(USA) —Ski For Me (IRE) (Barathea (IRE))
1154[14] 2362[6] 2801[14]

Skip Of Colour *P A Blockley* a65 61
7 b g Rainbow Quest(USA) —Minskip (USA) (The Minstrel (CAN))
5[7] 61[2] 138[10] 366[11]

Ski School (IRE) *W J Haggas* 68
2 b g Montjeu(IRE) —Teller (ARG) (Southern Halo (USA))
3625[14] 4014[10] 4335[4] 5571[9] 6052[8] 6449[4]

Ski Sunday *M A Jarvis* a52 52
2 b c King's Best(USA) —Lille Hammer (Sadler's Wells (USA))
5880[11] 6267[10]

Skodger (IRE) *G Woodward* 26
4 b h Nashwan(USA) —Ghay (USA) (Bahri (USA))
1676[9] 3382[10]

Sky Beam (USA) *J L Dunlop* a52 52
3 bb f Kingmambo(USA) —Weekend In Seattle (USA) (Seattle Slew (USA))
1364[5] 2192[9] 2552[4] 3792[5]

Sky Chart (IRE) *N J Vaughan* a20 55
3 ch g Fantastic Light(USA) —Marion Haste (IRE) (Ali-Royal (IRE))
2341[U] 2580[6] 2873[9] 3476[4] 4943[8] 7275[7]

Sky Conqueror (CAN) *Darwin D Banach* 117
5 ch h Sky Classic(CAN) —Heavenly Ballerina (CAN) (Conquistador Cielo (USA))
6374a[7]

Skycruiser (IRE) *Saeed Bin Suroor* a63 67
2 ch c Dubai Destination(USA) —Maskunah (IRE) (Sadler's Wells (USA))
5541[10] 6080[3] 6436[6]

Sky Dive *L M Cumani* a85 69
2 ch c Dr Fong(USA) —Free Flying (Groom Dancer (USA))
4777[6] (5498)

Skye But N Ben *T D Barron* a59 64
3 b g Auction House(USA) —Island Colony (USA) (Pleasant Colony (USA))
37[3] 224[3] 373[4] 676[2] 893[2] (1154) 1708[5] (2116) 2530[9] 3587[7] 4155[5] 4936[5] 5783[3] 5967[5] 6019[8]

Skyelady *T D Barron* a76 83
4 b m Dansili—Song Of Skye (Warning)
675[5] 979[4] 1198[6] 1576[3] 2023[7] (2827) (3194) 3525[6] 3970[5]

Skylarker (USA) *T A K Cuthbert* a86 86
9 b g Sky Classic(CAN) —O My Darling (USA) (Mr Prospector (USA))
2987[16]

Sky Masterson *J H M Gosden* a73 67
3 ch g Traditionally(USA) —Katina (USA) (Danzig (USA))
1100[6] 1348[2] 1716[2] 2083[13] 2749[8] 4977[6]

Sky More *M A Jarvis* a72 91
3 b c Xaar—Jathaabeh (Nashwan (USA))
(1177) (1672) 2010[F] (Dead)

Skynda *Rae Guest* 50
2 b f Domedriver(IRE) —Skimra (Hernando (FR))
5061^{11} 5301^{12}

Sky Quest (IRE) *J R Boyle* a78 80
9 b g Spectrum(IRE) —Rose Vibert (Caerleon (USA))
164^{3} 263^{4} 594^{5} 3215^{8} 3705^{2} (4108) 4365^{5} 5052^{3} 5383^{13} 6199^{11} *6603^{6}*

Sky Walk *Jamie Poulton* a56
4 b g Josr Algarhoud(IRE) —Jamrat Samya (IRE) (Sadler's Wells (USA))
230^{4} 458^{8} 691^{11}

Skywards *E Charpy* a89 47
5 b g Machiavellian(USA) —Nawaiet (USA) (Zilzal (USA))
472a^{11}

Slade (GER) *M Trybuhl* 99
5 b m Big Shuffle(USA) —Semplice (IRE) (Common Grounds)
1800a^{5} 3122a^{4} 4213a^{7} (5850a) 6633a^{4} 6954a^{10}

Slam *B W Hills* 94
2 b c Beat Hollow—House Hunting (Zafonic (USA))
4598^{5} 5206^{2} 5971^{2} 6468^{3}

Slam Dunk (USA) *G M Lyons* 96
2 b c Grand Slam(USA) —Deep In My Heart (USA) (Rahy (USA))
5456a^{4}

Slaney Rock (IRE) *J S Bolger* 86
2 b c Rock Of Gibraltar(IRE) —Dress Code (IRE) (Barathea (IRE))
1508a^{4}

Slaney Time (IRE) *J S Bolger* 94
3 b g Rock Of Gibraltar(IRE) —Aretha (IRE) (Indian Ridge)
3140a^{18}

Slate (IRE) *Miss V Haigh* 97
3 b c Rock Of Gibraltar(IRE) —Sharp Catch (IRE) (Common Grounds)
1316^{2} (1684) (2243) 2788^{26} 4566^{15}

Slavonic (USA) *B Storey* a5 52
6 ch g Royal Academy(USA) —Cyrillic (USA) (Irish River (FR))
2298^{2} 2563^{10} 3371^{9} 3638^{7} 4099^{10}

Slavonic Lake *I A Wood* a56 54
3 b g Lake Coniston(IRE) —Slavonic Dance (Muhtarram (USA))
2192^{11} *2801^{8} 3186^{2}* 4292^{4} *5121^{4} 5606^{2} 6026^{6} 7083^{9}*

Sleepy Hollow *H Morrison* 70
2 b g Beat Hollow—Crackling (Electric)
5361^{10} 5918^{9} (6285)

Slew Charm (FR) *Noel T Chance* a60 66
5 b g Marathon(USA) —Slew Bay (FR) (Beaudelaire (USA))
830^{4} 5531^{9}

Slew's Tizzy (USA) *Gregory Fox* a104 89
3 bb c Tiznow(USA) —Hepatica (USA) (Slewpy (USA))
2487a^{7}

Sling Back (IRE) *Eamon Tyrrell* a70 84
6 b m Desert Style(IRE) —Arabian Princess (Taufan (USA))
1171a^{9} 4404^{4} *5184a^{4} 5788a^{11}*

Slip *M P Tregoning* a60 59
2 b c Fraam—Niggle (Night Shift (USA))
5200^{9} 5498^{7} 5918^{4}

Slipasearcher (IRE) *P D Evans* a68 86
3 b f Danetime(IRE) —Imperialist (IRE) (Imperial Frontier (USA))
336^{5} 512^{4} 1008^{4} 1373^{4} (1404) 1561^{5} 1766^{5} 2061^{15} 2300^{4} 2421^{6} 3549^{11} 4879^{13} 5191^{4}

Slip Silver *P J Makin* a45 41
3 gr f Slip Anchor—New Wind (GER) (Windwurf (GER))
2477^{12} *3084^{9}* 4765^{7} *5388^{6} 6069^{13} 6534^{9} 6815^{6} 6999^{11}*

Slip Star *T J Etherington* a40 55
4 b m Slip Anchor—Shiny Kay (Star Appeal)
45^{6} 270^{8} 2137^{10} 3917^{3} 4178^{3} 4250^{10} 4736^{4} 5231^{2} 5627^{14}

Slo Mo Shun *H J L Dunlop* a49 52
3 b f Polish Precedent(USA) —Malvadilla (IRE) (Doyoun)
4684^{3} *5179^{5}* 5688^{6}

Slugger O'Toole *G A Huffer* 62
2 br g Intikhab(USA) —Haddeyah (USA) (Dayjur (USA))
5910^{9}

Small Fortune *R Charlton* 80
3 b f Anabaa(USA) —New Assembly (IRE) (Machiavellian (USA))
(1409) 1974^{3} 2448^{8}

Small Stakes (IRE) *P J Makin* a74 70
5 b g Pennekamp(USA) —Poker Chip (Bluebird (USA))
234^{3} 614^{6} 1607^{10} *1931^{7}* 2427^{5} 4879^{11} 6063^{10}

Smart And Mighty (AUS) *T Noonan* a85 106
8 ch h Baryshnikov(AUS) —Billies Flurry (AUS) (Pag-Asa (AUS))
(411a) *599a^{12}* 645a^{5}

Smart Angus *R A Fahey* 28
3 gr g Agnes World(USA) —She's Smart (Absalom)
1423^{13}

Smart Ass (IRE) *J S Moore* a85 89
4 b m Shinko Forest(IRE) —Jayess Elle (Sabrehill (USA))
185^{10} 3897^{6} (4135) 4404^{2} 4633^{6}

Smart Cassie *H J Evans* a45 67
4 ch m Allied Forces(USA) —Katy-Q (IRE) (Taufan (USA))
1366^{9} 1640^{16} 2553^{9} 4635^{8} 5716^{3} *6390^{8} 6565^{3} 6864^{8}*

Smart Cat (IRE) *A P Jarvis* a50 60
4 ch m Barathea(IRE) —Lioness (Lion Cavern (USA))
229^{5} 537^{5} 928^{4} *1951^{5}* 2321^{12} 2696^{5} 3690^{2} 4112^{12} *4945^{10}* 5737^{13} 6247^{9} *6429^{4}* 6573^{7}

Smart Enough *M A Magnusson* 111
4 gr h Cadeaux Genereux—Good Enough (FR) (Mukaddamah (USA))
4745^{17} 5213^{2} 6031a^{11} (6198) 6655^{6}

Smarterthanuthink (USA) *R A Fahey* 57
2 b c Smart Strike(CAN) —Dance Gaily (USA) (Nureyev (USA))
4781^{6} 5521^{7} 6072^{7}

Smart Instinct (USA) *R A Fahey* 100
3 ch g Smart Strike(CAN) —Smile N Molly (USA) (Dixieland Band (USA))
1768^{4} 2037^{5} 3558^{5} 4092^{8} 4799^{9} 5805^{6}

Smart John *H J Evans* 59
7 b g Bin Ajwaad(IRE) —Katy-Q (IRE) (Taufan (USA))
3485^{7} 4231^{10} 4910^{9}

Smart Pick *Mrs L Williamson* a47 56
4 ch m Piccolo—Nevita (Never So Bold)
49^{6} 200^{12} 296^{6} 485^{12} 1086^{10} 1491^{8} 2032^{5} 2422^{5} 2938^{12} 3534^{2} 3839^{4} 4223^{4} 4931^{5} 5503^{5} 5803^{7} *6480^{3} 6778^{9} 7079^{6} 7169^{12}*

Smarty Deb (USA) *Doris Harwood* a92
2 ch f Smart Strike(CAN) —Taste The Passion (USA) (Wild Again (USA))
6507a^{5}

Smash Hit (IRE) *David Pinder* a60 57
4 ch g Grand Lodge(USA) —Rainbow Lyrics (IRE) (Rainbow Quest (USA))
4666^{9} 5315^{7} *5567^{4}* 6196^{15} *6716^{8} 6894^{10} 7085^{11}* (Dead)

Smash N'Grab (IRE) *J R Jenkins* a58 59
3 ch f Jade Robbery(USA) —Sallwa (IRE) (Entrepreneur)
1383^{6} 1964^{9} *2260^{8}* 2713^{3} 3583^{7} 3918^{2} (4071) 4842^{12} 5627^{4} 5688^{8} *(5945)* 6277^{10} *6895^{9} 7113^{9} 7278^{6}*

Smetana *H Morrison* a58 56
2 b c Kylian(USA) —Shimmer (Bustino)
6593^{8} *6805^{9} 7121^{7}*

Smiddy Hill *R Bastiman* a70 75
5 b m Factual(USA) —Hello Hobson'S (IRE) (Fayruz)
1134^{15} 1557^{15} 1914^{10} 2933^{9} 3449^{7} 4787^{8} 5507^{12}

Smileforawhile (IRE) *K A Ryan* 69
2 b g Green Desert(USA) —Woodyousmileforme (USA) (Woodman (USA))
1411^{7} 1622^{2} 2575^{9} *4020^{10}* 4995^{5}

Smile For Us *C Drew* a61 73
4 b g Whittingham(IRE) —Don't Smile (Sizzling Melody)
235^{14} 367^{8} 1436^{5} 2334^{2} 2576^{13} 4396^{10}

Smiling Tiger *M J Gingell*
3 b g Contract Law(USA) —Nouvelle Cuisine (Yawa)
635^{10} 794^{7} 977^{12} 1353^{7}

Smilodon *A Berry* 40
2 ch f Reel Buddy(USA) —Timoko (Dancing Spree (USA))
2297^{11} 2984^{11} 3750^{8} 4041^{10} 4897^{8}

Smirfys Gold (IRE) *E S McMahon* a55 59
3 ch g Bad As I Wanna Be(IRE) —Golden Jorden (IRE) (Cadeaux Genereux)
1453^{2} *1932^{6}* 2301^{3} 4186^{4} 4661^{7} *5420^{2}*

Smirfy's Silver *E S McMahon* a31 64
3 b g Desert Prince(IRE) —Goodwood Blizzard (Inchinor)
1236^{11} (3804) 4339^{2} 4858^{3}

Smirfys Systems *E S McMahon* a53 53
8 b g Safawan—Saint Systems (Uncle Pokey)
7025^{5} 7207^{8}

Smith Esquire (USA) *W R Swinburn* a61 56
2 b g Giant's Causeway(USA) —Makam (IRE) (Green Desert (USA))
2147^{8} 2876^{4} 3471^{6} *5127^{4}* 5914^{10}

Smokejumper (GER) *Frau E Mader* 102
3 b c Big Shuffle(USA) —Shikoku (Green Desert (USA))
1516a^{5} 4213a^{5} 6370a^{3}

Smokey Oakey (IRE) *M H Tompkins* a76 98
3 b c Tendulkar(USA) —Veronica (Persian Bold)
1768^{8} (2057) 4092^{9} 4720^{6} 4993^{3} 5554^{4} 5805^{5} (6637)

Smokeyourpipe (IRE) *R M Stronge* a51 52
2 ch g Bold Fact(USA) —Gi La High (Rich Charlie)
1540^{14} (4512) *5015^{5}* 5089^{8} *5529^{10} 6242^{10} 6928^{11}*

Smokey Rye *G L Moore* a74 62
2 b f Bertolini(USA) —Another Secret (Efisio)
3383^{7} 4061^{11} 4265^{2} 5939^{11} 6449^{14} *6849^{3} (6964) 7095^{2} 7280^{2}*

Smokey Stover (USA) *Greg Gilchrist* a119 91
4 bb g Put It Back(USA) —Milady's Halo (USA) (Jolie's Halo (USA))
6510a^{9}

Smokey The Bear *Miss Sheena West* a60 27
5 ch g Fumo Di Londra(IRE) —Noble Soul (Sayf El Arab (USA))
6212^{2} 6968^{3} 7098^{5} (7168) 7256^{3}

Smokin Beau *N P Littmoden* a89 92
10 b g Cigar—Beau Dada (IRE) (Pine Circle (USA))
155^{8} 452^{7} 554^{7} 1061^{3} 1465^{8} 2197^{9} 4038^{10} 4486^{7} *4944^{4}* 6413^{13} *(6890) (7116)*

Smokin Joe *J R Best* a83 51
6 b g Cigar—Beau Dada (IRE) (Pine Circle (USA))
56^{7} 117^{9} 233^{9} 5893^{7} 6260^{2} 6547^{5} (6716) 6824^{6} 6996^{5} 7017^{3} 7099^{3} (7164) 7224^{2} 7269^{2}

Smooth As Silk (IRE) *C R Egerton* 65
2 b f Danehill Dancer(IRE) —Doula (USA) (Gone West (USA))
4232^{11} 5061^{5}

Smoothie (IRE) *E G Bevan* a50 55
9 gr g Definite Article—Limpopo (Green Desert (USA))
416^{11} (558) 716^{13} 1026^{9} *7168^{11}*

Smugglers Bay (IRE) *T D Easterby* 78
3 b g Celtic Swing—Princess Mood (GER) (Muhtarram (USA))
1131^{7} 1827^{14} 2133^{5} (2796) 3299^{2} 3755^{2} 3889^{2} 4617^{4} 5043^{4} 5296^{3}

Snaafy (USA) *B W Hills* 92
3 b c Kingmambo(USA) —Nafisah (IRE) (Lahib (USA))
(1098) 2045^{8} 4331^{2} 5012^{3} 5385^{3} 5978^{5}

Snaefell (IRE) *M Halford* 109
3 gr g Danehill Dancer(IRE) —Sovereign Grace (IRE) (Standaan (FR))
2324a^{4} (3139a) 3573a^{6} 5075a^{5} 5436a^{6} 5842a^{4}

Snake Hips *B Palling* a55 61
3 b g Golden Snake(USA) —Royal Loft (Homing)
258^{4} 484^{6} 745^{5} 1154^{7} *1361^{9}* 2084^{3} 3035^{10} *4460^{8}* 4757^{7} 5345^{8} 6090^{5} *7032^{7}*

Snake's Head *J L Dunlop* a56 80
3 b f Golden Snake(USA) —Satin Bell (Midyan (USA))
1433^{2} 1928^{2} *2666^{3}* 3367^{4} 4357^{4} 5271^{2} (6257)

Snake Skin *J Gallagher* a63 65
4 ch m Golden Snake(USA) —Silken Dalliance (Rambo Dancer (CAN))
1254^{7} 1592^{3} (2142) 2361^{2} *2572^{4}* 3803^{8} 4253^{3} 4766^{5} *5132^{7}*

Snark (IRE) *P J Makin* a82 79
4 b g Cape Cross(IRE) —Agoer (Hadeer)
96^{4} 568^{6} 1811^{12} 2004^{10} 2514^{6} 2877^{11} 3907^{4} (4284) (4850) 5198^{3} 5725^{3} 5916^{4}

Snickers First *M W Easterby* 46
2 ch f Presidium—Mirror Four Sport (Risk Me (FR))
3916^{11} 5502^{6} 6254^{9}

Snoqualmie Boy *D R C Elsworth* a77 111
4 b g Montjeu(IRE) —Seattle Ribbon (USA) (Seattle Dancer (USA))
1104^{5} 1392^{4} 4043^{4} 4366^{2} 4874a^{11} 6011^{23}

Snow Ballerina *E A L Dunlop* a53 54
3 b f Sadler's Wells(USA) —Snow Bride (USA) (Blushing Groom (FR))
1364^{4} 1611^{5} 2793^{10}

Snowberry Hill (USA) *Lucinda Featherstone* a63 68
4 b g Woodman(USA) —Class Skipper (USA) (Skip Trial (USA))
6341^{6} (6798) 7154^{4}

Snow Bunting *Jedd O'Keeffe* a66 63
9 ch g Polar Falcon(USA) —Marl (Lycius (USA))
1382^{10} 1711^{4} 1892^{5} 2508^{8} 2827^{7} 4137^{9} 4701^{6} 5037^{7} *6064^{5} (6390) 6609^{4} 6887^{12} 7006^{5}*

Snow Clad (AUS) *A Selvaratnam* a54
4 b m Nuclear Freeze(USA) —Shereen (AUS) (Cossack Warrior (AUS))
246a^{10} 476a^{9}

Snow Dancer (IRE) *A Berry* a71 72
3 b f Desert Style(IRE) —Bella Vie (IRE) (Sadler's Wells (USA))
141^{4} 745^{3} 836^{4} 1863^{11} (2133) 2453^{3} 2530^{4} 2872^{7} 3570^{10} 5405^{2} 5703^{9} (6055)

Snowed Under *J D Bethell* a79 88
6 gr g Most Welcome—Snowy Mantle (Siberian Express (USA))
1078^{6} 1416^{7} 1922^{3} (4072) 4419^{7} 4922^{4} 5432^{4} 6253^{9}

Snowflight *R A Fahey* a38 69
3 b c Danehill Dancer(IRE) —Sadler's Song (Saddlers' Hall (IRE))
1804^{9} 3196^{5} 3570^{6} 4284^{3} 4718^{5} *5132^{13}* 5482^{5} *5755^{10}*

Snow Gretel (IRE) *M Botti* a83 101
4 b m Green Desert(USA) —Snow Princess (IRE) (Ela-Mana-Mou)
590^{4} 979^{3} (1517a) 2296a^{7}

Snowy Day (FR) *Grant Tuer* a74
4 b g Pennekamp(USA) —Snow White (Polar Falcon (USA))
117^{3} 205^{2} 568^{11}

Snowy Indian *Sir Michael Stoute* a65 74
2 b f Indian Ridge—Snow Princess (IRE) (Ela-Mana-Mou)
5162^{3} 5811^{6} *6611^{3}*

Soapy Danger *M Johnston* a78 119
4 b h Danzig(USA) —On A Soapbox (USA) (Mi Cielo (USA))
5589^{2} 5976^{3} 6526a^{8}

Soaring Falcon (IRE) *D K Weld* a79 89
2 b c Hawk Wing(USA) —Schust Madame (IRE) (Second Set (IRE))
1508a^{5}

Soba Jones *J Balding* a61 67
10 b g Emperor Jones(USA) —Soba (Most Secret)
9^{4} 59^{2} 303^{4} 388^{2} 504^{4} (580) (710) 896^{10} *1028^{5} 1262^{4} 1753^{10}*

Soca Warrior (IRE) *M J Grassick* 63
2 b c Statue Of Liberty(USA) —Top Brex (FR) (Top Ville)
5393a^{8}

Soccerjackpot (USA) *G A Swinbank* 88
3 b g Mizzen Mast(USA) —Rahbaby (USA) (Rahy (USA))
1136^{2} 1482^{2} (1913) 2536^{3} 3503^{5} 6016^{4}

Socceroo *D J Murphy* a48 63
2 b f Choisir(AUS) —Silca Boo (Efisio)
1285^{4} *6022^{4}*

Social Height (IRE) *A Berry* 11
2 ch g Monashee Mountain(USA) —Yiayia's Girl (Smackover)
3341^{13} 3751^{8} 4405^{12} 4559^{9} 4770^{14} (Dead)

Social Rhythm *H J Collingridge* a76 81
3 b f Beat All(USA) —Highly Sociable (Puissance)
725^{6} (1219) 5360^{9} 5874^{5} *6313^{7}* 6450^{3} 6701^{13}

Social Spirit (IRE) *J R Weymes* 50
2 br f Auction House(USA) —Sibilant (Selkirk (USA))
4578^{7} 5663^{4} 5904^{13}

Society Music (IRE) *M Dods* 79
5 b m Almutawakel—Society Fair (FR) (Always Fair (USA))
1198^{5} (2007) 2388^{10} 2905^{4} 3156^{2} 3721^{8} 4129^{2} 4353^{2} 4932^{2} (5230) 5674^{4}

Society Venue *Jedd O'Keeffe* 69
2 b g Where Or When(IRE) —Society Rose (Saddlers' Hall (IRE))
4578^{3} 4782^{7} 5143^{6} 5883^{5}

Sofia Royale *B Palling* a35 56
3 b f Royal Applause—Once In My Life (IRE) (Lomond (USA))
1639^{11} 1901^{7} 2727^{15} 3611^{11} *4272^{12} 7079^{11}*

Sofia's Star *P Winkworth* 82
2 b c Lend A Hand—Charolles (Ajdal (USA))
1989^{4} (2443) 3669^{5} 4121^{7} 5053^{8} 6128^{4}

Sofie Tucker *T D Easterby* 58
3 b f Erhaab(USA) —Bollin Sophie (Efisio)
1995^{3} 2341^{2} 2535^{2} 2792^{3} 3722^{6}

Sofinella (IRE) *A W Carroll* a61 66
4 gr m Titus Livius(FR) —Mystical Jumbo (Mystiko (USA))
82^{11} 281^{8} 403^{6} 523^{6} 4689^{15} *4974^{2} (5564)* (5867) *6244^{10} 6752^{5}*

Softlanding (IRE) *Robert Collet* a84 84
4 b m Nashwan(USA) —Forest Rain (FR) (Caerleon (USA))
7128a^{0}

Softly Killing Me *J Gallagher* a52 56
2 b f Umistim—Slims Lady (Theatrical Charmer)
2468^{9} 3238^{3} 3842^{4} 4547^{11} *5729^{7}* 6106^{6}

Soft Morning *Sir Mark Prescott* a101 99
3 b f Pivotal—Summer Night (Nashwan (USA))
(73) 275^{2} 1835^{13} (3335) 4147^{11} 5327^{2} 6220a^{5} 6889a^{3} *(7049a) 7128a^{4}*

Soggy Dollar *M H Tompkins* 71
2 ch g Bahamian Bounty—Ninia (USA) (Affirmed (USA))
3435^{16} 4325^{2} 4709^{2} 5613^{5} 6274^{3}

So Glamorous *C F Wall* 46
2 b f Diktat—Gena Ivor (USA) (Sir Ivor (USA))
5868^{9}

Soho Square *L Lungo* a51 78
4 ch g Generous(IRE) —Stardance (USA) (Rahy (USA))
955^{12} 1488^{12} 1967^{11} 2820^{10}

Sohraab *H Morrison* a77 97
3 b g Erhaab(USA) —Riverine (Risk Me (FR))
231^{6} (421) (671) 778^{2} 885^{2} 1900^{2} 2114^{2} 2884^{2} 3528^{2} 4123^{9} 5765^{2} 6301^{8}

Soinlovewithyou (USA) *A P O'Brien* 82
2 b f Sadler's Wells(USA) —Love Me True (USA) (Kingmambo (USA))
3659a^{7} 5353^{8}

Soizic (NZ) *L A Dace* a72 34
5 ch m Istidaad(USA) —Nellie May (NZ) (Babarooom (USA))
48^{7} 3851^{9} 4355^{14} 4577^{13} *5132^{11}*

Sokoke *D A Nolan* a2 73
6 ch g Compton Place—Sally Green (IRE) (Common Grounds)
1456^{8} 1594^{16} 1806^{12} 2244^{11} 4967^{11} 4996^{12}

Solarias Quest *A King* a69 82
5 b g Pursuit Of Love—Persuasion (Batshoof)
153^{7}

Solar Spirit (IRE) *G A Swinbank* 74
2 b c Invincible Spirit(IRE) —Misaayef (USA) (Swain (IRE))
6255^{2}

Solas Na Greine (IRE) *J S Bolger* a83 91
2 b f Galileo(IRE) —Key To Coolcullen (IRE) (Royal Academy (USA))
4440a^{7} 5073a^{6} 5435a^{5} 5843a^{11}

Soldier Field *J S Wainwright* a61 45
3 b g Fantastic Light(USA) —Khambani (IRE) (Royal Academy (USA))
1522^{8} 2261^{5} 2767^{8} 4064^{4} 4354^{7} 5237^{7} *6147^{3} 6719^{7} 7032^{2} 7199^{4}*

Soldier Hollow *P Schiergen* 121
7 b h In The Wings—Island Race (Common Grounds)
880a^{4} 1700a^{3} (2705a) (4013a) 4929a^{2}

Soldier Of Fortune (IRE) *A P O'Brien* 127
3 b c Galileo(IRE) —Affianced (IRE) (Erins Isle) (963a) (1602) 2235^{5} (3142a) (5466a) 6043a^{5}

Soldiers Quest *Peter Grayson* a87 85
3 b c Rainbow Quest(USA) —Janaat (Kris)
499^{2} (602) 1293^{5} 4713^{13} *5235^{9}*

Soldiers Romance *T D Easterby* a58 42
4 b g Allied Forces(USA) —Still In Love (Emarati (USA))
338^{6} 449^{13} 681^{9} 1493^{5} *1902^{7}*

Soldier's Tale (USA) *J Noseda* 123
6 ch h Stravinsky(USA) —Myrtle (Batshoof)
1770^{3} 2396^{3} (2857)

Soledad (IRE) *G Cherel* 111
7 b g Priolo(USA) —True (FR) (Common Grounds)
990a^{8} 1341a^{4}

Solemn *Sir Mark Prescott* a61
2 b c Pivotal—Pious (Bishop Of Cashel)
6267^{9} 6477^{3}

Solent (IRE) *R Hannon* a96 108
5 b g Montjeu(IRE) —Stylish (Anshan)
1244^{2} 1506^{6} 2859^{2} 3989^{5} 4722^{13} 5030^{10} (5829)

Solent Ridge (IRE) *J S Moore* a90 84
2 b c Namid—Carrozzina (Vettori (IRE))
2539^{6} 3043^{8} *3424^{2} 3850^{3}* (4255) *(4916)* 5536^{5} *6001^{6} 6161a^{6}*

Solicitude *D Haydn Jones* a61 37
4 ch m Bertolini(USA) —Sibilant (Selkirk (USA))
32^{5} 334^{3} 517^{7} 627^{3} 1038^{9} (5730) 6179^{9} *6607^{2} 7003^{6}*

Solidgoldesyaction *P A Blockley* a46
3 b f Intikhab(USA) —Keltech Star (IRE) (Bigstone (IRE))
375^{8} 678^{8} (1164) 1281^{5}

Solid Rock (IRE) *T G Mills* a94 99
3 b g Rock Of Gibraltar(IRE) —Sheer Spirit (IRE) (Caerleon (USA))
1035^{5} 1394^{4} 2212^{2} 2752^{11} 3431^{14}

Solid Silver *K G Reveley* 52
6 gr g Pharly(FR) —Shadows Of Silver (Carwhite)
2253^{9}

Solo City *P A Blockley* a37 39
3 b g Averti(IRE) —Surakarta (Bin Ajwaad (IRE))
11^{5} 68^{6}

Solo Flight *H Morrison* a88 90
10 gr g Mtoto—Silver Singer (Pharly (FR))
340^{4} 501^{6} 4171^{9} 4597^{14} *6144^{5} 6439^{5}*

Solo River *P J Makin* a54 57
2 b f Averti(IRE) —Surakarta (Bin Ajwaad (IRE))
5267^{3} 5470^{4} *6177^{4} 6425^{7}*

Sol Rojo *J Pearce* a75 71
5 b g Efisio—Shining Cloud (Indian Ridge)
2006^{3} 2603^{8} 3907^{19} 4284^{5} 4526^{2} 5198^{6} 5916^{10}

Solvana (IRE) *Wido Neuroth* 100
5 b m Selkirk(USA) —Simmering (Mas Media)
1189a^{8} 5262a^{2}

Solzah (IRE) *L Brogi* 99
4 b m Zaha(CAN) —Solar Dawn (Soviet Star (USA))
1337a^{3} 1876a^{12}

Somarini *T T Clement* a18 44
2 b f Bertolini(USA) —Lake Pleasant (IRE) (Elegant Air)
2532^{10} 4102^{11} 4770^{10} 5302^{16} 6872^{10} 6990^{8}

Somerset Falls (UAE) *M Johnston* 69
2 b f Red Ransom(USA) —Dunnes River (USA) (Danzig (USA))
6742^{2}

Something (IRE) *T G Mills* a108 112
5 b g Trans Island—Persian Polly (Persian Bold)
2319^{3} 2858^{4} 3505^{3} 4150^{12} 5512^{3}

Something Simple (IRE) *R Ford* a44 67
4 ch g Raise A Grand(IRE) —Baccara (IRE) (Sri Pekan (USA))
332^{11} 2275^{9}

Something Stupid (GER) *Mario Hofer* 79
2 b c Big Shuffle(USA) —Salzgitter (Salse (USA))
5028a^{8}

Sommersturm (GER) *J Hirschberger* 103
3 b c Tiger Hill(IRE) —Sommernacht (GER) (Monsun (GER))
2502a^{4} 3146a^{9} 4013a^{8} 5929a^{U}

Sommertag (GER) *J Hirschberger* 115
4 b h Tiger Hill(IRE) —Sommernacht (GER) (Monsun (GER))
4013a^{9} 5077a^{9} 5467a^{4}

Somnus *T D Easterby* 115
7 b g Pivotal—Midnight's Reward (Night Shift (USA))
3529^{6} 4747^{9} 5214^{9} 6183^{12} 6491^{5}

Som Tala *M R Channon* 96
4 ch h Fantastic Light(USA) —One Of The Family (Alzao (USA))
1582^{5} 2736^{3} 4056^{5} 4569^{7} 4893^{3} 6335^{17}

Sonara (IRE) *M H Tompkins* 75
3 b g Peintre Celebre(USA) —Fay (IRE) (Polish Precedent (USA))
1154^{3} (1415) 1624^{4} 2132^{2} 2727^{10} 3825^{7} 4172^{7} (4821) 5040^{3} 5333^{4} 5839^{2} 6421^{9}

Sonar Sound (GER) *T P Tate* 79
3 b g Slickly(FR) —Samothrace (IRE) (Arazi (USA))
1863^{12} 2872^{8} 3605^{9} 4042^{9}

Sonderborg *J Mackie* a54 50
6 b m Great Dane(IRE) —Nordico Princess (Nordico (USA))
238^{11}

Song Of Hiawatha *A P O'Brien* 110
3 b c Sadler's Wells(USA) —Sabria (USA) (Miswaki (USA))
4693^{7} 5466a^{6} 6043a^{12}

Song Of Passion (IRE) *R Hannon* a91 105
4 b m Orpen(USA) —Bint Al Balad (IRE) (Ahonoora)
1034^{5} 1619^{3} (2237) 2817^{P} (3529) 4639^{10} 5403^{8}

Song Of Victory (GER) *M Weiss* 64
3 b c Silvano(GER) —Song Of Hope (GER) (Monsun (GER))
2503a^{10}

Song Of War (IRE) *F-M Cottin*
8 b g Lost World(IRE) —Seconde Bleue (Glint Of Gold)
6923a^{0}

Sonic Anthem (USA) *J T Stimpson* a65
5 b g Royal Anthem(USA) —Whisperifyoudare (USA) (Red Ransom (USA))
(666) 2145^{11} 7146^{12}

Sonning Star (IRE) *D R C Elsworth* 76
3 b g Desert Prince(IRE) —Fantazia (Zafonic (USA))
2886^{4} 3234^{3} 3710^{5} 4018^{2} 4568^{8} 5703^{3} 6057^{2}

Sonnium (IRE) *W P Mullins* 76
3 ch g Lomitas—Cutting Glance (USA) (Woodman (USA))
4035a^{11}

Sonny Mac *M J McGrath* a70 65
4 b h Pivotal—Sea Drift (FR) (Warning)
1451^{13} 1761^{10} 3397^{12}

Sonny Parkin *G A Huffer* a77 85
5 b g Spinning World(USA) —No Miss Kris (USA) (Capote (USA))
30^{5} 233^{3} 314^{4} 1268^{7} 2189^{8} 2833^{10} 3056^{3} 3711^{4} 4135^{3} 4365^{3} (4587) 5545^{7} 6439^{10}

Sonny Red (IRE) *R Hannon* 110
3 b c Redback—Magic Melody (Petong)
1103^{2} 1473^{15} 2752^{6} 3894^{3} 4869a^{4} 5832^{8} 6039a^{15}

Sonny Sam (IRE) *M H Tompkins* 53
2 b g Black Sam Bellamy(IRE) —Purple Risks (FR) (Take Risks (FR))
4890^{7} 5599^{9}

Son Of Greek Myth (USA) *G L Moore* a45 58
6 b g Silver Hawk(USA) —Greek Myth (IRE) (Sadler's Wells (USA))
691^{9}

Son Of Spartacus (IRE) *Mrs L Stubbs* a27 46
2 ch c Spartacus(IRE) —Classic Silili (ITY) (Be My Guest (USA))
4173^{11} 4784^{10} 5154^{5} 5520^{5} 6242^{9} 6305^{11}

Sonoma (IRE) *B G Powell* a36 44
7 ch m Dr Devious(IRE) —Mazarine Blue (USA) (Chief's Crown (USA))
4535^{4}

Sonsue *B Palling* 28
2 ch f Auction House(USA) —Sontime (Son Pardo)
1150^{9} 2078^{9}

Soopacal (IRE) *B Smart* a81 76
2 b g Captain Rio—Fiddes (IRE) (Alzao (USA))
(3297) 4431^{3} 4899^{5} 5624^{7} 6251^{5} 6756^{8}

Sophia Gardens *D W P Arbuthnot* a66 67
3 ch f Barathea(IRE) —Lovely Lyca (Night Shift (USA))
5312^{8} 5687^{4} 6176^{2} 6455^{10} 6825^{7} 7085^{5} 7268^{8}

Sophie's Dream *A M Hales* a61 55
3 b g Averti(IRE) —Sophielu (Rudimentary (USA))
99^{2} (209) 322^{5} 676^{9} 5084^{11} 5338^{10}

Sophie's Girl *P W Chapple-Hyam* 93
2 b f Bahamian Bounty—Merry Rous (Rousillon (USA))
2364^{4} 2663^{2} 2812^{15} (4447) (4923) 5322^{6} 5766^{3} 6619^{4}

Sophies Secret *J R Holt* 22
2 b f Superior Premium—Funky (Classic Music (USA))
3706^{17} 4286^{10} 4875^{15}

Sopran Bodar (ITY) *M Marcialis*
3 b c Daro Sopran(GER) —Sopran Bolkris (IRE) (Kris)
1191a^{10}

Sopran Gath (ITY) *J W Hills* a72 72
4 b m Galileo(IRE) —Theano (IRE) (Thatching)
1068^{4} 1352^{4} 1811^{7} 2194^{4} 2802^{10} 3352^{10} 4321^{10} 4739^{5} 5120^{4} 5709^{3} 6068^{4} 6407^{3} 6577^{3}

Sopran Promo (IRE) *B Grizzetti* 105
3 b c Montjeu(IRE) —Middle Prospect (USA) (Mr Prospector (USA))
1875a^{4} 5821a^{4} 6223a^{6} 6687a^{4}

Sopran Slam (IRE) *B Grizzetti* 95
3 b f Grand Slam(USA) —Sopran Londa (IRE) (Danehill (USA))
1701a^{12} 2070a^{7} 6519a^{7}

Sopran Wolina (IRE) *B Grizzetti* 76
2 gr f Linamix(FR) —Sopran Woog (ITY) (Grand Lodge (USA))
6047a^{13}

Sorbiesharry (IRE) *Mrs N Macauley* a43 19
8 gr g Sorbie Tower(IRE) —Silver Moon (Environment Friend)
7135^{5} 7172^{7} 7244^{3}

Sorrel Point *H J Collingridge* a60 61
4 b h Bertolini(USA) —Lightning Princess (Puissance)
6123^{7} 6413^{9}

Sortita (GER) *M A Jarvis* 77
2 b f Monsun(GER) —Sacarina (Old Vic)
6294^{2}

Sosueme Now *A B Haynes* a44 45
3 ch f Foxhound(USA) —So Discreet (Tragic Role (USA))
4267^{4} 4528^{5} 4757^{5}

So Sweet (IRE) *M R Channon* 93
3 b f Cape Cross(IRE) —Announcing Peace (Danehill (USA))
1581^{4} 1958^{7} 2757^{13}

Soterio (GER) *W Baltromei* 107
7 b h Lavirco(GER) —So Rarely (USA) (Arctic Tern (USA))
4838a^{6}

Sotik Star (IRE) *P J Makin* a85 78
4 b g Elnadim(USA) —Crystal Springs (IRE) (Kahyasi)
1751^{5} 2180^{10} 6651^{9}

Soto *M W Easterby* a59 78
4 b g Averti(IRE) —Belle Of The Blues (IRE) (Blues Traveller (IRE))
1299^{11} 1483^{5} 1678^{7} 1914^{11} (2608) 3017^{10} 3723^{5} 4083^{8} 4381^{8} 4706^{2} 4822^{7} 5522^{4} 5908^{5} 6467^{5}

Soubriquet (IRE) *M A Barnes* a10 71
4 b g Daylami(IRE) —Green Lucia (Green Dancer (USA))
956^{3} 4771^{8} 5283^{16}

Soudaine (GER) *J Hirschberger* 101
4 b m Monsun(GER) —Suivez (FR) (Fioravanti (USA))
6781a^{3}

Soul Angel *Miss S E Forster* 52
3 ch g Tipsy Creek(USA) —Over Keen (Keen)
3447^{11} 5678^{5} 5967^{4} 6259^{8} 6464^{6}

Soulard (USA) *J L Spearing* a54 76
4 b h Arch(USA) —Bourbon Blues (USA) (Seeking The Gold (USA))
515^{8}

Soul Blazer (USA) *Miss Gay Kelleway* a67 8
4 b g Honour And Glory(USA) —See You (USA) (Gulch (USA))
265^{5} 365^{4} 2004^{16} 4272^{11} 4860^{10}

Soul Mountain (IRE) *B W Hills* a82 86
3 b f Rock Of Gibraltar(IRE) —Qhazeenah (Marju (IRE))
1105^{7} 2597^{3} 3079^{2} 3399^{4} (4334) 4615^{4} (5043) 5445^{4} 6014^{7} 6389^{4}

Soul Of Magic (IRE) *Karin Suter* 102
8 b m Definite Article—Blazing Soul (IRE) (Common Grounds)
4957a^{4} 6519a^{6}

Soundasapound *I W McInnes* 56
3 b f Pursuit Of Love—Blue Nile (IRE) (Bluebird (USA))
3377^{7} 3792^{17}

Soundbyte *J Gallagher* 15
2 b g Beat All(USA) —Gloaming (Celtic Swing)
6723^{10}

Sound Of Nature (USA) *H R A Cecil* 99
4 b h Chester House(USA) —Yashmak (USA) (Danzig (USA))
(1013) 1268^{3} (1922)

Sound The Drum (USA) *S Seemar* a101 94
5 b g Stravinsky(USA) —Uhavethebeat (USA) (Unbridled (USA))
395a^{4}

Source Du Nil (FR) *Y De Nicolay* a29
2 b c Starborough—Source De Reve (FR) (Kaldoun (FR))
6879a^{8}

Sourire *Sir Mark Prescott* a84 88
2 b f Domedriver(IRE) —Summer Night (Nashwan (USA))
2949^{8} (3199) 3642^{2} 3880^{12} 4964^{2} 5135^{2} 5400^{3} (5837)

Southandwest (IRE) *J S Moore* 91
3 ch g Titus Livius(FR) —Cheviot Indian (IRE) (Indian Ridge)
1009^{2} 1298^{7} 1667^{2} 2671^{6} 2752^{14} 4123^{5} 4374^{4}

South Cape *M R Channon* a95 100
4 b g Cape Cross(IRE) —Aunt Ruby (USA) (Rubiano (USA))
846^{19} 1651^{15} (2239) 2817^{5} 3437^{7} 3941^{11} 4377^{4} 5012^{5} (5413) 5641^{2} (5804) 6013^{13} 6301^{19} 6654^{12}

South Dakota (IRE) *A P O'Brien* 101
2 b c Danehill Dancer(IRE) —Moon Drop (Dominion)
2732^{9} 3141a^{2} 3574a^{4} 5456a^{5}

Southern Bazaar (USA) *M C Chapman* a16 26
6 ch g Southern Halo(USA) —Sunday Bazaar (USA) (Nureyev (USA))
3610^{11} 5158^{12}

Southern Courage (NZ) *Mick Price* 103
5 b g Bahhare(USA) —Calm Courage (NZ) (Spectacular Love (USA))
6711a^{7}

Southern Mistral *W J Haggas* a69 59
2 b g Desert Prince(IRE) —Hyperspectra (Rainbow Quest (USA))
4285^{7} 5126^{4} 5337^{3} 5871^{5}

Southern Regent (IND) *G A Swinbank* a91 102
6 b g Razeen(USA) —Allinda (IND) (Treasure Leaf (USA))
398a^{9} 4922^{7} 5619^{8} 5892^{2}

South Hill *R J Price*
4 b m Marju(IRE) —Briggsmaid (Elegant Air)
682^{U}

South O'The Border *Miss Venetia Williams* a79 84
5 b g Wolfhound(USA) —Abbey's Gal (Efisio)
1621^{7}

Southpaw Lad *J R Best* a75
2 b c Diktat—Ashantiana (Ashkalani (IRE))
6267^{4} 6404^{3} (6714)

Southside Star *H J L Dunlop* 48
3 ch f Singspiel(IRE) —Samara (IRE) (Polish Patriot (USA))
2005^{10} 3685^{8} 4549^{6} (Dead)

Southwark Newsboy (IRE) *Mrs C A Dunnett* 19
2 b g Chevalier(IRE) —Canoe Cove (IRE) (Grand Lodge (USA))
3733^{8} 4028^{12}

Southwarknewsflash *Mrs C A Dunnett* a58 34
3 b f Danetime(IRE) —Enchanting Wood (IRE) (Woodborough (USA))
4513^{6} 4977^{3} (5175) 5602^{11}

Southwest Star (IRE) *J S Moore* a66 60
2 b g No Excuse Needed—Christeningpresent (IRE) (Cadeaux Genereux)
814^{5} 999^{5} 3423^{6} 4832a^{11} 5216^{10} 5729^{2} 6098^{2} 6263^{2} 6503^{5} 7258^{4} 7280^{4}

Souvenance *Sir Mark Prescott* 104
4 b m Hernando(FR) —Summer Night (Nashwan (USA))
(1760a) (2018a) 2976a^{9} 4691^{8} 4803^{6} (5669a)

Sovereign's Honour (USA) *Sir Michael Stoute* 65
2 ch f Kingmambo(USA) —Chiming (IRE) (Danehill (USA))
4402^{6}

Sovereign Spirit (IRE) *W R Swinburn* a74 64
5 b g Desert Prince(IRE) —Sheer Spirit (IRE) (Caerleon (USA))
29^{8} 215^{11} 4253^{2} 5018^{6} 5341^{4} 5820^{2} 6271^{3}

Sovereignty (JPN) *D K Ivory* a71 66
5 b g King's Best(USA) —Calando (USA) (Storm Cat (USA))
32^{7} 3647^{10} 4021^{7} 4978^{10} 5340^{7} 5900^{5} 6264^{6} 6563^{4} 7278^{7}

Soviet Palace (IRE) *K A Ryan* a81 86
3 b g Jade Robbery(USA) —Daisy Hill (Indian Ridge)
1124^{5} 2040^{4} 3707^{5} 4093^{16} 4898^{9} 5635^{12} 6492^{11} (7104)

Soviet Sceptre (IRE) *Evan Williams* 58
6 ch g Soviet Star(USA) —Princess Sceptre (Cadeaux Genereux)
2656^{2} 4253^{4} 5188^{13}

Soviet Sound (IRE) *Jedd O'Keeffe* a34 49
3 ch g Soviet Star(USA) —Orange Grouse (IRE) (Taufan (USA))
1530^{10} 1943^{5} 2300^{5} 2661^{3} 3285^{7} 3583^{9} 3752^{10} 4078^{11} 4449^{11}

Sovietta (IRE) *A G Newcombe* a55 61
6 b m Soviet Star(USA) —La Riveraine (USA) (Riverman (USA))
903^{8} 2721^{3} 2967^{5} 3280^{2} 3901^{4} 4124^{9} 6643^{6}

Soviet Threat (IRE) *A G Juckes* a59 52
6 ch g Soviet Star(USA) —Veiled Threat (IRE) (Be My Guest (USA))
298^{7} 425^{7} 1435^{4} 1715^{11}

Sowdrey *M R Channon* a71 75
3 b g In The Wings—Baaderah (IRE) (Cadeaux Genereux)
602^{2} 735^{3} 956^{2} 1290^{5} 1611^{2} 2274^{3} 2628^{6} 4113^{4} 4758^{2} 5007^{3}

Sowerby *M Brittain* a43
5 b g Grey Desire—Brief Star (IRE) (Brief Truce (USA))
625^{7} 715^{6} 1379^{10}

So Will I *Doug Watson* a61 98
6 ch g Inchinor—Fur Will Fly (Petong)
245a^{7} 400a^{6} 470a^{2} 528a^{7}

Soxy Doxy (IRE) *M Johnston* 47
2 ch f Hawk Wing(USA) —Feather Bride (IRE) (Groom Dancer (USA))
5912^{8}

Soylent Green *S Parr* 19
3 b f Primo Valentino(IRE) —Slipperose (Persepolis (FR))
2581^{10} 3843^{7} 4426^{9} 5102^{7} 5622^{6}

Space Oddity (BRZ) *P Nickel Filho* a81
4 ch h First American(USA) —Sweet Suspicion (BRZ) (Baligh)
396a^{6} 532a^{8}

Space Pirate *J Pearce* a34 61
2 b c Bahamian Bounty—Science Fiction (Starborough)
2041^{16} 4130^{12} 4584^{6} 5002^{5} 5509^{2} 6410^{3} 7010^{9}

Spacious *J R Fanshawe* 107
2 b f Nayef(USA) —Palatial (Green Desert (USA))
(4656) (5353)

Spanish Ace *J M Bradley* a29 93
6 b g First Trump—Spanish Heart (King Of Spain)
(1004) (1080) 1134^{6} 1754^{12} 1854^{4} 2025^{2} 2197^{4} 2463^{15} 4095^{20} 4567^{12} 5029^{10} 5168^{12} 5332^{7} 5722^{13} 6197^{12}

Spanish Affair *Jedd O'Keeffe* a38 24
3 b g Pursuit Of Love—Catalonia (IRE) (Catrail (USA))
565^{7} 708^{9} (Dead)

Spanish Air *J W Hills* a57 40
3 b f Muhtarram(USA) —Spanish Heart (King Of Spain)
624^{13} 802^{5} 1432^{10}

Spanish Bounty *J G Portman* a73 89
2 b g Bahamian Bounty—Spanish Gold (Vettori (IRE))
1781^{10} (2193) 2650^{2} (3462) 3938^{6} 4899^{7} 5219^{12}

Spanish Conquest *Sir Mark Prescott* a65 29
3 b g Hernando(FR) —Sirena (GER) (Tejano (USA))
6178^{2} (6407) 6643^{2} 6697^{6}

Spanish Diva *S C Williams* a62 81
3 b f Singspiel(IRE) —Allespagne (USA) (Trempolino (USA))
2005^{8} 3214^{8} 3743^{8} 4518^{3} 5333^{2} 5839^{5}

Spanish Don *D R C Elsworth* a83 95
9 b g Zafonic(USA) —Spanish Wells (IRE) (Sadler's Wells (USA))
1842^{6} 2208^{9} 3060^{8} 3672^{5} 4234^{4}

Spanish Harlem (IRE) *A P O'Brien* 107
3 br c Danehill(USA) —Sleepytime (IRE) (Royal Academy (USA))
1547a^{10} 2066a^{2} 3142a^{10}

Spanish Heroine *P Winkworth* a36 39
2 br f Kyllachy—Spanish Heart (King Of Spain)
2447^{9} 3187^{9} 5301^{14}

Spanish Hidalgo (IRE) *J L Dunlop* 111
3 b c Night Shift(USA) —Spanish Lady (IRE) (Bering)
3272^{3} (3753) 4059^{5} 4749^{6} 5952^{2} (6518a) 6863a^{8}

Spanish Moon (USA) *Sir Michael Stoute* 102
3 b c El Prado(IRE) —Shining Bright (Rainbow Quest (USA))
6153^{6}

Spanish Needle *P R Webber* a65 7
3 b f Green Desert(USA) —Hasta (USA) (Theatrical)
567^{3} 752^{7} 996^{8} 6476^{3} 6749^{9}

Spanish Parade (IRE) *Eoin Griffin* a73 76
3 b g Mujadil(USA) —Frenzy (Zafonic (USA))
4865a^{8}

Spanish Springs (IRE) *J H M Gosden* a67
2 b f Xaar—Crystal Gazing (USA) (El Gran Senor (USA))
6664^{3}

Spares And Repairs *Mrs S Lamyman* a67 48
4 b g Robellino(USA) —Lady Blackfoot (Prince Tenderfoot (USA))
6700^{3} 6959^{3} 7151^{4} 7242^{4}

Sparkbridge (IRE) *S C Burrough* a40 56
4 b g Mull Of Kintyre(USA) —Persian Velvet (IRE) (Distinctly North (USA))
1893^{8} 3487^{14} 3868^{7} 5187^{13}

Sparkler *P Winkworth* 56
2 b f Best Of The Bests(IRE) —Gem (Most Welcome)
4755^{7}

Sparkling Eyes *C E Brittain* a71 84
3 b f Lujain(USA) —Lady Georgia (Arazi (USA))
755^{4} 1108^{2} (1270) 1604^{2} 1808^{5} 2450^{12} 3746^{5} 3944^{13} 4489^{8} 5051^{3} 5358^{6} 6406^{4} 6731^{4}

Sparkling Montjeu (IRE) *J W Hills* a56 64
2 b f Montjeu(IRE) —Dart Board (IRE) (Darshaan)
4402^{13} 5100^{6} 5811^{4}

Sparkling Silver *D K Ivory* a21
2 gr f Silver Patriarch(IRE) —Full English (Perugino (USA))
6964^{10} 7097^{9}

Spark Up *J W Unett* a62 39
7 b m Lahib(USA) —Catch The Flame (USA) (Storm Bird (CAN))
124^{4} 206^{6} 371^{4} 555^{4}

Sparkwell *D Shaw* a69 67
5 b g Dansili—West Devon (USA) (Gone West (USA))
66^{5} 154^{8} 3190^{9} 3859^{9} 4397^{17}

Sparky Vixen *G A Swinbank* 56
3 b f Mujahid(USA) —Lucy Glitters (USA) (Cryptoclearance (USA))
1236^{3} 1894^{4} 3372^{5} 4180^{12} 5627^{8} 6537^{3}

Spartan Dance *J A Geake* a65 61
3 ch g Groom Dancer(USA) —Delphic Way (Warning)
1724^{12} 3367^{15} 3848^{7}

Sparton Duke (IRE) *E J O'Neill* 56
2 b c Xaar—Blueberry Walk (Green Desert (USA))
2215^{9} 2532^{11}

Spate River *C F Wall* 43
2 b g Zaha(CAN) —Rion River (IRE) (Taufan (USA))
6237^{9}

Spa Wells (IRE) *Barry Potts* 49
6 ch g Pasternak—La Tache (Namaqualand (USA))
5286^{15}

Speagle (IRE) *A J Chamberlain* a85 75
5 ch g Desert Sun—Pohutakawa (FR) (Affirmed (USA))
726^{8} 846^{15} 1083^{5} 1253^{11} 1819^{10} 4072^{9} 4418^{4} 4878^{5} 5000^{2} 5255^{10} 6774^{6} 6815^{2} 7046^{7} 7173^{5} 7249^{5}

Special Branch Ami (IRE) *C R Egerton* a57
2 ch c Galileo(IRE) —Helena's Paris (IRE) (Peintre Celebre (USA))
5337^{9}

Special Day *B W Hills* 95
3 b f Fasliyev(USA) —Mustique Dream (Don't Forget Me)
1658^{3} 1994^{2} 3944^{2} 4607^{5} 4726^{2} 5212^{7} 5954^{8}

Special Edition (GER) *C Von Der Recke* 65
5 br g Big Shuffle(USA) —Safrane (GER) (Mister Rock'S (GER))
(439a)

Special Feature (IRE) *C R Egerton* a43 52
2 b g Montjeu(IRE) —Starring Role (IRE) (Glenstal (USA))
6058[9] 6417[11] 6748[4]
Special Place *J A R Toller* a70 60
4 b g Compton Place—Petarga (Petong)
234[7] 461[10] 614[3] 739[2] (923) 1118[3] 1446[6] 1845[10] 2458[9] 2802[3] 3851[7] 6607[4] 6854[7]
Special Reserve (IRE) *R Hannon* 30
2 b c Sadler's Wells(USA) —Ionian Sea (Slip Anchor)
6296[10]
Special Scene (AUS) *Dan O'Sullivan* 88
9 b g Scenic—Georgia Jean (NZ) (Dahar (USA))
6033a[15] 6711a[8]
Speciano *E Borromeo* 102
4 ch h Dr Fong(USA) —Salligram (Salse (USA))
5821a[9] 6689a[8]
Speciosa (IRE) *Mrs P Sly* 114
4 b m Danehill Dancer(IRE) —Specifically (USA) (Sky Classic (CAN))
1104[2] 1834[7] 3117a[2] 4149[6] 6010[7] 6334[7]
Speckled Hen (IRE) *D Haydn Jones* a36 76
4 b m Titus Livius(FR) —Colouring (IRE) (Catrail (USA))
33[11] 183[8]
Spectaculaire *A Fabre* 110
4 ch h Spectrum(IRE) —Gold Round (IRE) (Caerleon (USA))
(990a) 1341a[5] 1881a[6]
Spectacular Joy (IRE) *Mrs A Duffield* a51 58
3 b g Spectrum(IRE) —Great Joy (IRE) (Grand Lodge (USA))
1278[9] 1712[12] 3342[13]
Spectested (IRE) *A W Carroll* a56 42
6 ch g Spectrum(IRE) —Nisibis (In The Wings)
909[9] 994[10] 1196[8]
Spectra (IRE) *M Rulec* 87
3 b f Spectrum(IRE) —Suenna (GER) (Lando (GER))
2707a[11]
Spectrana *Mrs A J Perrett* a63 64
2 b f Spectrum(IRE) —Anapola (GER) (Polish Precedent (USA))
2468[13] 3446[5] 3874[12] 5736[11] 6274[2] 6777[5]
Speed Dial Harry (IRE) *C R Dore* a81 83
5 b g General Monash(USA) —Jacobina (Magic Ring (IRE))
35[4] 191[13] 308[3] 451[5] 629[8] 5387[10] 5753[8] 6447[14] 7241[5]
Speed Dream (IRE) *David Wachman* a67 101
3 ch c Pivotal—Copper Creek (Habitat)
1461a[4] 2035[4] 3139a[7] 6036a[9]
Speed Gifted *L M Cumani* 109
3 b c Montjeu(IRE) —Good Standing (USA) (Distant View (USA))
(2690) 3753[5] (4749)
Speed Song *W J Haggas* 78
2 b f Fasliyev(USA) —Superstar Leo (IRE) (College Chapel)
2364[3] (3823) 4349[4] 4923[7]
Speed Ticket *L M Cumani* a67
3 b c Galileo(IRE) —Kassiyra (IRE) (Kendor (FR))
6005[3]
Speed Winner (AUS) *G L Moore* a43
8 b g Danehill(USA) —Think Twice (USA) (Alleged (USA))
87[2] 134[5]
Speedy Dollar (USA) *M A Jarvis* 85
2 b c Dixie Union(USA) —Kelli's Ransom (USA) (Red Ransom (USA))
5971[6] (6468)
Speedy Sam *K R Burke* a104 100
4 b h Medicean—Warning Star (Warning)
6[2] 175a[15] 401a[3] 658[5] 7611[2] 3558[7] 3899[4] 4043[9] 5631[2] 6172[9] 6995[6]
Speedy Senorita (IRE) *K R Burke* a64 65
2 b f Fayruz—Sinora Wood (IRE) (Shinko Forest (IRE))
1553[2] 1727[2] 2416[2] 2797[5] 4098[4] 4175[3] (4715) 5365[8] (5706) 6326[5] 6741[5]
Spell Caster *R M Beckett* a80 82
2 ch f Bertolini(USA) —Princess Claudia (IRE) (Kahyasi)
(4875) 5766[6] 6120[6]
Spell Casting (USA) *M H Tompkins* 89
4 b g Kingmambo(USA) —Copper Play (USA) (Fast Play (USA))
1767[9] 2002[9] (4771)
Spent *R M Beckett* 66
2 b c Averti(IRE) —Top (Shirley Heights)
3383[9] 3967[6] 4500[4] 5571[5] 6233[6]
Sphinx (FR) *Jamie Poulton* a59 96
9 b g Snurge—Egyptale (Crystal Glitters (USA))
1794[2] 3273[3] 3898[10] (4483) 5619[2] 5677[3] 6284[5]
Spice Bar *A M Balding* a63 61
3 b g Barathea(IRE) —Scottish Spice (Selkirk (USA))
1850[6] 2490[4] 3367[16] 5001[6] 6005[5] 6178[8]
Spice Gardens (IRE) *W Jarvis* a39 58
3 ch f Indian Ridge—Lime Gardens (Sadler's Wells (USA))
5873[9] 6309[3] 6582[9]
Spice Route *M L W Bell* 110
3 ch g King's Best(USA) —Zanzibar (IRE) (In The Wings)
1093[7] (1290) (1773) 2813[5] 3458[4] 4692[6] 5618[6]
Spice Trade *J Noseda* a62 73
2 ch c Medicean—Nutmeg (IRE) (Lake Coniston (IRE))
5042[7] 5772[3] 6106[4] 7217[5]
Spic 'n Span *R A Harris* a71 66
2 b g Piccolo—Sally Slade (Dowsing (USA))
3962[12] 4273[3] 5448[8] 5780[5] 5863[2] 7140[10]
Spiderback (IRE) *R Hannon* a83 82
3 ch g Redback—Geht Schnell (Fairy King (USA))
1122[6] 1205[2] (1396) 1843[4] 1987[6] 5006[4] 5205[5] 5718[4] 6007[4] 6389[3]
Spiffing (IRE) *R M Beckett* a29 66
3 b c Indian Ridge—Stunning (USA) (Nureyev (USA))
1501[5] 1737[2] 2144[2] 3237[7] 3968[6] 6339[11]
Spin Again (IRE) *R M Beckett* 70
2 b c Intikhab(USA) —Queen Of The May (IRE) (Nicolotte)
5937[4]
Spinaimanwin (IRE) *Ian Williams* a45 61
3 ch f Spinning World(USA) —Aiming Upwards (Blushing Flame (USA))
4104[7] 4809[7] 4951[4] 6069[7]
Spinal Tap (IRE) *C R Egerton* a65 54
3 ch g Selkirk(USA) —Glam Rock (Nashwan (USA))
1215[4] 1447[8] 2077[6] 2572[2] 3150[9] 5342[6] 5533[9] 5948[10]
Spinetail Rufous (IRE) *Miss Z C Davison* a50 53
9 b g Prince Of Birds(USA) —Miss Kinabalu (Shirley Heights)
289[6] 653[8] 1969[14] 2191[8] 2879[10] 3212[9] 4689[14]
Spinneret *M A Jarvis* a63 55
3 ch f Pivotal—Branston Jewel (IRE) (Prince Sabo)
1128[9] 2175[2] 2606[7] 3393[11]
Spinning *T D Barron* a77 74
4 ch g Pivotal—Starring (FR) (Ashkalani (IRE))
1132[5] 1455[3] 2169[4] 2842[2] 2985[11] 3161[8] 3711[8] 4081[4] 4481[5] 4822[5] 4931[2] 5159[12] 5476[9] (5966) (6463) 6746[4] (6838)
Spinning Coin *J G Portman* a56 83
5 b m Mujahid(USA) —Cointosser (IRE) (Nordico (USA))
5924[7]
Spinning Dancer (IRE) *J R Holt* a18 9
4 b m Spinning World(USA) —Fair McLain (IRE) (Fairy King (USA))
61[9]
Spinning Dixie (IRE) *J A Geake* a53 37
3 b f Spinning World(USA) —Dixieline City (USA) (Dixieland Band (USA))
208[7] 498[8] 573[6] 738[11] 2978[11] 4231[12]
Spinning Fun (IRE) *F Reuterskiold*
3 b g Spinning World(USA) —Fun Board (FR) (Saumarez)
2548a[4]
Spinning Game *D W Chapman* a44 57
3 b f Mind Games—Spindara (IRE) (Spinning World (USA))
390[5] 506[3] 667[8] 934[U] 1031[10] 1943[13] 2200[11] 3605[11] 3811[2] 4226[11] 4384[2] 4525[4] 4658[6] 4787[12] 5295[11] 5930[12]
Spinning Gold *Miss Gay Kelleway* a32 46
4 ch m Spinning World(USA) —Blue Birds Fly (Rainbow Quest (USA))
5756[11]
Spinning Lucy (IRE) *B W Hills* 100
2 ch f Spinning World(USA) —Dolara (IRE) (Dolphin Street (FR))
1101[3] 1469[2] 5395a[11] 5949[3] (6306) (6619)
Spinning Ridge (IRE) *R A Harris* a66 43
2 ch c Spinning World(USA) —Summer Style (IRE) (Indian Ridge)
2138[7] 2949[7] 3596[6] 4022[3] 4683[10] 5117[13] (6065) 6263[5]
Spinning Sound (IRE) *E J O'Neill* a77 89
2 ch c Spinning World(USA) —Beryl (Bering)
3095[4] (3850)
Spirito Del Vento (FR) *J-M Beguigne* a97 118
4 b g Indian Lodge(IRE) —Heavenly Song (FR) (Machiavellian (USA))
(2500a) 4873a[3] (6031a) 7091a[6]
Spirit Of Adjisa (IRE) *Pat Eddery* a77 81
3 br g Invincible Spirit(IRE) —Adjisa (IRE) (Doyoun)
973[4] 1439[5] 1887[8] 5347[6] (5865) (6102) 6878[3]
Spirit Of A Nation (IRE) *D J Murphy* 57
2 b c Invincible Spirit(IRE) —Fabulous Pet (Somethingfabulous (USA))
6156[8]
Spirit Of Arosa (IRE) *J Akehurst* a68 86
4 b m Dansili—Vettorina (IRE) (Vettori (IRE))
1013[12]
Spirit Of Coniston *D Nicholls* a74 73
4 b g Lake Coniston(IRE) —Kigema (IRE) (Case Law)
(97) 135[2] 289[5] 441[11] (581) 668[4] 892[6] (1384) 1902[2] 2249[3] 2712[5] 3203[7] 3782[5] 4101[8] 4423[13] 4973[11] 6078[2] (6528) (6562) 6752[2]
Spirit Of Ecstacy *G M Moore* 46
3 b f Val Royal(FR) —Isla Negra (IRE) (Last Tycoon (IRE))
1303[3] 1746[8] 2760[8] 5563[12]
Spirit Of France (IRE) *Christian Wroe* 98
5 b g Anabaa(USA) —Les Planches (Tropular)
477a[8]
Spirit Of Pearl (IRE) *Nicholas Cox* 94
3 b f Invincible Spirit(IRE) —Aguilas Perla (IRE) (Indian Ridge)
2324a[10]
Spirit Of Sharjah (IRE) *P W Chapple-Hyam* 109
2 b c Invincible Spirit(IRE) —Rathbawn Realm (Doulab (USA))
(1094) (1608) 2785[3] 3459[8] 4046[6] 5377[2] 6167[11]
Spirit Of The Mist (IRE) *D J Murphy* a84 88
3 ch g Trans Island—Exciting (Mill Reef (USA))
1076[3] 1243[3] 1773[13] 6002[7] 7018[10] 7200[2]
Spiritofthestorm (USA) *R A Teal* a70
2 b f Mizzen Mast(USA) —Southern Issue (USA) (Southern Halo (USA))
5527[4] 5944[2] 6578[4] 6777[9]
Spiritofthetiger (USA) *R A Teal* a65 63
2 ch f Hold That Tiger(USA) —Royal Malt (IRE) (Royal Academy (USA))
3643[2] 4316[4] 5116[4] 5682[3] 6980[2]
Spirit One (FR) *P Demercastel* 113
3 b c Anabaa Blue—Lavayssiere (FR) (Sicyos (USA))
963a[2] 1703a[7] 2293a[14] 4627a[2] 5466a[5]
Spiritonthemount (USA) *B W Hills* 64
2 bb c Pulpit(USA) —Stirling Bridge (USA) (Prized (USA))
6079[5] 6417[6]
Spirit Rising *J M Bradley* 35
3 gr g Zilzal(USA) —River's Rising (FR) (Mendez (FR))
1561[15] 2196[14] 2489[11] 3872[6] 4321[9] 5269[15] 5345[13]
Spiritual Peace (IRE) *K A Ryan* a79 85
4 b g Cadeaux Genereux—Emerald Peace (IRE) (Green Desert (USA))
957[3] 1483[8] 1941[8] 2806[3] 3180[4] (3674) 3837[4] 5552[9] 5840[12]
Spitfire *J R Jenkins* a69 98
2 b g Mujahid(USA) —Fresh Fruit Daily (Reprimand)
(1680) (2151) 3459[10] 4431[4] (5410) 6017[8] 6488[4]
Spitfire Jane (IRE) *K R Burke* a59
2 br f Xaar—Hope Of Pekan (IRE) (Sri Pekan (USA))
6849[8] 7058[4]
Splash The Cash *K A Ryan* a65 66
2 b g Lomitas—Bandit Queen (Desert Prince (IRE))
2193[6] 3085[4] 4160[2] 4737[9] 5452[9] 6195[6] 6438[3] 6665[2] 7176[9]
Splendidio *A Crook* a50 55
3 b f Zamindar(USA) —Diddymu (IRE) (Revoque (IRE))
17[7] 90[3] 194[5] 237[6] 417[7] 1976[6] 2094[4] 3588[8] 4226[4] 4478[9] 5082[5] (5716) 6720[10] 6887[10]
Splinter Group *N A Callaghan* 56
3 ch c Inchinor—Haiyfoona (Zafonic (USA))
1093[13] 2005[11]
Split Briefs (IRE) *C A Dwyer* a64 70
3 b f Mull Of Kintyre(USA) —Jay Gee (IRE) (Second Set (IRE))
2369[12] 3084[6] 3406[4] 4591[2] 5102[5] 6412[4] 6573[9] 6749[10]
Splitthedifference *D Carroll* a56 62
2 b g Hunting Lion(IRE) —Sky Light Dreams (Dreams To Reality (USA))
942[7] (1156) 1857[8]
Split The Wind (USA) *Eve Johnson Houghton* a52 61
3 ch f Just A Cat(USA) —Maple Hill Jill (USA) (Executive Pride)
1409[5] 3393[6] 3800[2] 4327[11] 4504[7] 5005[4] 5728[4] 6097[5]
Splodger Mac (IRE) *N Bycroft* 55
8 b g Lahib(USA) —Little Love (Warrshan (USA))
1578[6] 2027[12] 4410[8] 4449[15] 4488[12]
Spoilsport *G A Butler* a54 63
4 b m Muhtarram(USA) —Spoilt Again (Mummy's Pet)
120[7] 210[13] 2143[12] 2654[6]
Spoilt Madame *P D Evans* a34 32
2 b f Bertolini(USA) —Madame Jones (IRE) (Lycius (USA))
2039[11] 6242[8] 6454[11]
Spoof Master (IRE) *N A Callaghan* a83 84
3 b g Invincible Spirit(IRE) —Talbiya (IRE) (Mujtahid (USA))
943[5] 1604[8] 1900[5] 6970[9] 7112[9]
Spooky *W Storey* 41
2 br g Vettori(IRE) —Aneen Alkamanja (Last Tycoon (IRE))
5281[10] 5902[10] 6329[9] 6634[10]
Sporting Art (USA) *G L Moore* a95 94
2 b c Doneraile Court(USA) —Playful Run (USA) (Run Softly (USA))
(3479) (4613) 5219[4] 5414[4]
Sporting Gesture *M W Easterby* 80
10 ch g Safawan—Polly Packer (Reform)
1042[14] 2201[3] 2743[3] 4040[2] 4248[2] 4558[2] 4732[5] (5145) 6158[2] 6500[11] 6703[3]
Spotoncon *A J Lidderdale* a33
6 b g Contract Law(USA) —Emma Victoria (Dominion)
24[6] 109[11]
Spot The Subbie (IRE) *Jamie Poulton* a74 61
4 b g Tagula(IRE) —Agent Scully (IRE) (Simply Great (FR))
(130) (313) 422[2] 773[6] 865[7]
Spriggan *C G Cox* a70 81
3 b c Ishiguru(USA) —Hope Chest (Kris)
899[3] 1468[2] 2196[2] 4170[2] (4671) 5114[11] 6002[13]
Spring At Last (USA) *Doug O'Neill* a121
4 bb h Silver Deputy(CAN) —Winter's Gone (USA) (Dynaformer (USA))
(858a)
Spring City (GER) *Saeed Bin Suroor* 95
3 ch c Monsun(GER) —Spirit Of Eagles (USA) (Beau's Eagle (USA))
2127[2] 2674[2] (3794)
Spring Creek *M W Easterby* a38 45
3 b f Tipsy Creek(USA) —Christening (IRE) (Lahib (USA))
2535[6] 3041[6] 3402[11] 6629[12]
Spring Dream (IRE) *M R Channon* a77 75
4 gr m Kalanisi(IRE) —Zest (USA) (Zilzal (USA))
903[5] 1158[6] 1526[8] (1884) 2082[3] 2375[4] 2887[11]
Spring Glory *Sir Mark Prescott* a69
3 b f Dr Fong(USA) —Doctor Bid (USA) (Spectacular Bid (USA))
304[7] 460[2] (553)
Spring Goddess (IRE) *A P Jarvis* a83 83
6 b m Daggers Drawn(USA) —Easter Girl (Efisio)
261[6] 314[3] (865) 930[2] 2427[10] 3154[5] 3420[5] 4060[12] 6124[7] (6997)
Spring Style (IRE) *E J O'Neill* a65
2 ch f Pivotal—Clear Spring (USA) (Irish River (FR))
6855[3]
Spring Time Girl *B Ellison* a46 51
5 b m Timeless Times(USA) —Daira (Daring March)
2302[3] 2716[3] 2938[5]
Spritza (IRE) *M L W Bell* a71 72
3 b f Spectrum(IRE) —Starlight Smile (USA) (Green Dancer (USA))
795[2] 1628[3] 1968[2] 2445[5] 2940[3] 3450[4] (4718) 5120[5] (5531) 5899[11]
Sprouston (FR) *Karen George* a39 36
4 ch g Grand Lodge(USA) —River Fantasy (USA) (Irish River (FR))
3428[11]
Spume (IRE) *D J Murphy* a67 80
3 b g Alhaarth(IRE) —Sea Spray (IRE) (Royal Academy (USA))
1277[6] 1773[14] 2872[3] 3235[6] (4450) 4704[11] 4847[11] 5196[8] 5383[9] 5701[13] 6310[12] 6598[5]
Spunger *H J L Dunlop* a66 67
4 b m Fraam—Complimentary Pass (Danehill (USA))
3427[5] 4131[5] 4660[4] 4878[3] (5188) 5569[5] 6196[7] 6500[5] 6719[8] 7088[9]
Spurron (IRE) *Gerard Keane* a45 50
7 b m Flying Spur(AUS) —The Realtour (Warning)
121[7]
Spycrawler (USA) *A Fabre* 108
3 b c Red Ransom(USA) —America (IRE) (Arazi (USA))
963a[3]
Spy Game (IRE) *Jennie Candlish* a28 54
7 b g Definite Article—Postie (Sharpo)
3595[10]
Spy Gun (USA) *T Wall* a53 51
7 ch g Mt. Livermore(USA) —Takeover Target (USA) (Nodouble (USA))
42[6] 138[4] 252[3] 366[10] 374[4] 440[7] 674[9] 682[5] 833[5] 1028[10] 1715[3] 2145[8] 2343[5] 3906[9] 6088[11] 6505[10] 6735[4] 6886[9] 7105[5] 7111[7]
Squadron *Mrs A J Perrett* a64 79
3 b g Sakhee(USA) —Machaera (Machiavellian (USA))
1724[5] 2185[2] (2628) (3969) 4511[10] 5924[4] 6131[3]
Square Dealer *J R Norton* 60
6 b g Vettori(IRE) —Pussy Foot (Red Sunset)
1849[6] 2420[5] 3638[8] 4409[5] 4941[4] 5626[10]
Squiffy *P D Cundell* a51 60
4 br g Kylian(USA) —Cebwob (Rock City)
1764[7] 2345[6] (3033) 3300[3] 4067[7] 6871[7]
Squirrel Tail *E S McMahon* a38 43
4 ch g Band On The Run—Crees Sqaw (Cree Song)
3685[9] 4235[8]
Squirtle (IRE) *W M Brisbourne* a73 76
4 ch m In The Wings—Manilia (FR) (Kris)
1239[5] 1683[5] 1884[4] 2142[4] 2493[6] 2890[13] 3473[3] 3927[3] 4352[2] 4670[11] 4906[6] 5533[12] 6076[3] 6613[4] 6835[4] 7081[2] 7172[3] 7285[4]
Sri Diamond *S Kirk* a114 40
7 b g Sri Pekan(USA) —Hana Marie (Formidable (USA))
(57) 941[4]
Srikuantan (IRE) *P F I Cole* a69
3 ch c Spinning World(USA) —Miss Asia Quest (Rainbow Quest (IRE))
5683[2] 6005[6] 6211[3]
Sriology (IRE) *M R Hoad* a58 52
6 b g Sri Pekan(USA) —Sinology (Rainbow Quest (USA))
187[8] 349[7]
Sri Pekan Two *P F I Cole* a84 73
3 b g Montjeu(IRE) —Brigadiers Bird (IRE) (Mujadil (USA))
1122[7] 1365[P] 7017[10]
Staceymac (IRE) *W R Muir* a54
4 ch m Elnadim(USA) —Neat Shilling (IRE) (Bob Back (USA))
687[5]
Stafford Will (IRE) *J G M O'Shea* 53
3 b g Rossini(USA) —Firstrusseofsummer (USA) (Summer Squall (USA))
1204[12] 1560[11] 2081[8] 5347[14]
Stage Acclaim (IRE) *B R Millman* a69 76
2 b g Acclamation—Open Stage (IRE) (Sadler's Wells (USA))
1540[6] (1970) 2316[6] 3398[7] 4372[8] 5053[10] 5331[6] 5496[5] 6282[8]
Stagecoach Emerald *R W Price* a70 46
5 ch g Spectrum(IRE) —Musician (Shirley Heights)
62[2] 302[2] 3598[9] (6068) 6341[5] 6564[6]
Stagecoach Topaz (USA) *M Johnston* 70
2 b g Stravinsky(USA) —Indian Fashion (USA) (General Holme (USA))
4733[11] 6557[6] 6698[2]
Stage Gift (IRE) *Saeed Bin Suroor* a82 117
4 ch g Cadeaux Genereux—Stage Struck (IRE) (Sadler's Wells (USA))
399a[14] 600a[8] (2617a) (3974) 6032a[7]
Stagehand (IRE) *B R Millman* a75 76
3 b g Lend A Hand—Ridotto (Salse (USA))
889[5] 1247[9] 1563[5] 1887[7] 3003[3] 3652[2] 4915[7] 5345[2]
Stagnite *Karen George* a59 61
7 ch g Compton Place—Superspring (Superlative)
252[6] 1507[8] 2540[4] 3285[10] 4595[4] 6706[9] 6908[4] 7034[7]
Stainley (IRE) *Mrs S C Bradburne* 69
4 b g Elnadim(USA) —Fizz Up (Alzao (USA))
5482[11]
Staked A Claim (IRE) *T D Barron* 61
3 ch g Danehill Dancer(IRE) —Twany Angel (Double Form)
3302[4] 3917[4] 4795[4] 6467[6]
Stalking Tiger (IRE) *R Charlton* 72
3 b g King's Best(USA) —Obsessed (Storm Bird (CAN))
2127[7] 5873[5] 6238[3]
Stallone *N Wilson* a48 58
10 ch g Brief Truce(USA) —Bering Honneur (USA) (Bering)
35[6] 148[8] 804[6]
Stamford Blue *R A Harris* a46 92
6 b g Bluegrass Prince(IRE) —Fayre Holly (IRE) (Fayruz)
1436[9] 1564[8] (1787) (1969) (2108) 2414[6] (2982) (3472) 3569[7] 4389[4] 4806[5] 5168[11] 5923[16]
Stand Guard *Sir Michael Stoute* 61
3 b g Danehill(USA) —Protectress (Hector Protector (USA))
1143[9]
Stand In Black (NZ) *L A Dace* a52 20
3 br g Istidaad(USA) —Aprikot (NZ) (Iades (FR))
53[4] 386[6] 492[12] 4015[15]
Stand In Flames *Pat Eddery* a45 57
2 b f Celtic Swing—Maid Of Arc (USA) (Patton (USA))
1354[9] 1960[7] 4310[3] 4964[14] 5526[3] 5882[12]

St Andrews (IRE) *M A Jarvis* a94 111
7 b g Celtic Swing—Viola Royale (IRE) (Royal Academy (USA))
1860[6] 2446[8] 3026[3] 3437[10] 4153[8] (4827) 5776[8] 6539[3]

Stanerra's Story (IRE) *E J O'Neill* a70
6 ch g Desert Story(IRE) —Stanerra (Guillaume Tell (USA))
204[3] 265[4] (365)

Stanley George (IRE) *M A Jarvis* a77 71
3 b g Noverre(USA) —Quinzey (JPN) (Carnegie (IRE))
1815[17] 2453[9] 2834[14] 3913[8] 4135[12] *6568[6] 6824[4] 7047[7]*

Stanley Wolfe (IRE) *Garry Moss* a30 51
4 b g City On A Hill(USA) —Quatredil (IRE) (Mujadil (USA))
2711[16] 3180[8] 3345[14] 3837[5] 4351[7] 4768[8] 4939[9] 5672[6] 6637[9] *7108[5]*

Staraco (FR) *B Goudot* 104
3 ch c Loup Solitaire(USA) —Linorova (USA) (Trempolino (USA))
963a[5] 4216a[4] 4873a[12]

Star Berry *T Wall* a53 55
4 b m Mtoto—Star Entry (In The Wings)
1764[5] 1926[3] *2332[13] 2595[13]* 3428[4] 4128[9] *6501[9]*

Starbougg *K G Reveley* 70
3 b f Tobougg(IRE) —Celestial Welcome (Most Welcome)
4411[5] 4771[7] 5486[9] 5906[15]

Starcrest *Jean-Rene Auvray* a36
3 b f Soviet Star(USA) —Singer On The Roof (Chief Singer)
73[9] 386[9]

Starcross Maid *J F Coupland* a61 61
5 ch m Zaha(CAN) —Maculatus (USA) (Sharpen Up)
630[2] 685[2] 1078[5] *1376[8] (1717) 1980[2] 2348[3]* 5750[13] 6325[10] 6558[6] *7109[6] 7198[5]*

Starfala *P F I Cole* a63 77
2 b f Galileo(IRE) —Farfala (FR) (Linamix (FR))
2768[7] 3874[9] 4796[3]

Starfinch *J J Bridger* a42 41
2 b f Fraam—Mockingbird (Sharpo)
3085[10] *3417[10]* 3856[7] 4593[11]

Stargazer Jim (FR) *W J Haggas* a89 83
5 br g Fly To The Stars—L'Americaine (USA) (Verbatim (USA))
1416[4] 1819[6] 2189[5] (2564) 2831[10] 3346[10] (4107) *6359[8] 6669[4] 6765[3] 6995[3] 7160[5]*

Stargazy *W G M Turner* a58 70
3 b g Observatory(USA) —Romantic Myth (Mind Games)
679[10] 1786[7] 5191[13] 5270[12] *7279[12]*

Star Grazer *C F Wall* a53 48
2 ch f Observatory(USA) —Oatey (Master Willie)
5595[14] 6384[8] *6714[6]*

Star In Our Eyes (IRE) *M C Chapman*
3 b f Daggers Drawn(USA) —Mossy Maze (Zamindar (USA))
1177[12]

Star In The East *Peter Grayson* a54 60
2 ch f Observatory(USA) —Snipe Hall (Crofthall)
1807[6] 2488[5] *2797[7]* 3348[5] *3923[7]* 4715[7] *5017[3] 5133[8]* 5520[6]

Stark Contrast (USA) *J Akehurst* a70 78
3 ch g Gulch(USA) —A Stark Is Born (USA) (Graustark)
1081[2] 1259[2] 2464[7] 3848[8] 4197[9] 5280[3] 5865[4] 6235[14] *(6951) 7018[9] 7224[5]*

Starlight Gazer *J A Geake* 87
4 b g Observatory(USA) —Dancing Fire (USA) (Dayjur (USA))
2882[10] (3234) 3488[2] (3682) 3943[11] 6301[6] 6753[16]

Starlight Girl *T D Easterby* 65
2 ch f Fantastic Light(USA) —Intervene (Zafonic (USA))
2039[5] 2337[5] 2984[8]

Starlight Prince *R Hollinshead* 61
2 b g Forzando—Inchtina (Inchinor)
6418[11] 6724[9]

Starlit Sands *Sir Mark Prescott* 105
2 b f Oasis Dream—Shimmering Sea (Slip Anchor)
(1848) (2199) 2756[2] 4046[4] 4573[6] (5373a)

Star Magnitude (USA) *S Dow* a91 85
6 ch g Distant View(USA) —Stellaria (USA) (Roberto (USA))
501[2] 652[8]

Star Of Angels *M Johnston* a74 74
3 b g Diktat—City Of Angels (Woodman (USA))
2951[8] 3402[7] 3678[3] 4156[4] 4499[3] 4817[4] 5482[4] 5676[7] 6056[2] 6257[4] (6558) *6672[2]*

Star Of Canterbury (IRE) *A P Jarvis* a74 77
4 ch g Beckett(IRE) —Villa Nova (IRE) (Petardia)
753[2] 1253[9] 1591[6] 2471[5] *3416[3]* 4108[7]

Star Of Gibraltar *J L Dunlop* 72
2 b f Rock Of Gibraltar(IRE) —Fallen Star (Brief Truce (USA))
4774[7] 5596[4]

Star Of Jove (USA) *J Wilson* 74
2 b f Suave Prospect(USA) —Someonewhoneedsme (USA) (Northern Jove (CAN))
5293a[8]

Star Of Light *B J Meehan* a87 109
6 b g Mtoto—Star Entry (In The Wings)
1650[4] 2815[6] 3272[7] 3899[8] (4399) 4720[8] 5326[7] 6011[25]

Star Of Pompey *A B Haynes* a55 45
3 b f Hernando(FR) —Discerning (Darshaan)
5859[7] 6204[6] *6430[2]*

Star Of Rosanna *K A Ryan* a74 65
2 b f Bertolini(USA) —Etma Rose (IRE) (Fairy King (USA))
(2087) 2618[2]

Star Of The Desert (IRE) *Mrs K Walton* a62 74
4 bb g Desert Story(IRE) —Cindy's Star (IRE) (Dancing Dissident (USA))
1198[13] 6732[7] *6885[3] 7080[5] 7213[9]*

Starofthemorning (IRE) *A W Carroll* a39 38
6 ch m Foxhound(USA) —Leggagh Lady (IRE) (Doubletour (USA))
18[6] 87[4]

Starparty (USA) *Mrs A J Perrett* a68 75
3 gr f Cozzene(USA) —Cherie Yvonne (USA) (Vice Regent (CAN))
(2635) *3421[8]* 4542[5] 5955[12] 6422[10]

Star Pattern (USA) *J H M Gosden* 62
2 ch c Seeking The Gold(USA) —Starlore (USA) (Spectacular Bid (USA))
6616[10]

Starpix (FR) *H J Brown* a46 97
5 gr g Linamix(FR) —Star's Proud Penny (USA) (Proud Birdie (USA))
325a[7] 477a[4] 540a[9] 645a[10]

Starr Flyer *A Bailey* 51
3 b g Star Of Persia(IRE) —Madame Butterfly (Reprimand)
1220[4] *1566[12]* 2909[4] 4391[12]

Starry Messenger *M P Tregoning* 77
3 b f Galileo(IRE) —The Faraway Tree (Suave Dancer (USA))
2436[2] (4229) 5006[7] 5955[10]

Stars Above *M S Saunders* a45 51
3 b f Observatory(USA) —Skimra (Hernando (FR))
322[6] 2978[13] 3904[8] 4182[9]

Star Strider *A M Balding* a73 73
3 gr g Royal Applause—Onefortheditch (USA) (With Approval (CAN))
2513[3] 3061[6] 3369[9] 3688[6] 4606[5] 5270[3] 5473[9]

Start Of Authority *J Gallagher* a55 55
6 ch g Muhtarram(USA) —Heiden's Delight (USA) (Shadeed (USA))
1739[7] 4595[11] 6278[10]

Startori *B Smart* a69 83
4 b m Vettori(IRE) —Celestial Welcome (Most Welcome)
150[8]

Startswampindowski (USA) *S Asmussen* a83
2 ch f El Corredor(USA) —Yemanja (USA) (Alleged (USA))
5247a[6]

Starviet (IRE) *M Ciciarelli*
2 b f Soviet Star(USA) —Finnine (USA) (Zafonic (USA))
1485a[4]

Star Wood (IRE) *Michael Joseph Fitzgerald* 92
5 b m Montjeu(IRE) —Woodwin (IRE) (Woodman (USA))
3143a[7]

State Dilemma (IRE) *D Shaw* a65 73
6 b g Green Desert(USA) —Nuriva (USA) (Woodman (USA))
235[5] 313[7] 461[6] 549[10]

Staten (USA) *T D Barron* 56
2 b c Century City(IRE) —Lever To Heaven (IRE) (Bluebird (USA))
6634[5]

State Shinto (USA) *R Bouresly* a90 90
11 bb g Pleasant Colony(USA) —Sha Tha (USA) (Mr Prospector (USA))
104a[12] *177a[14]* 244a[15] *396a[4] 471a[7] 532a[10]*

Stateside (CAN) *R A Fahey* 47
2 b f El Corredor(USA) —Double Trick (USA) (Phone Trick (USA))
2889[10] 3916[6] 4487[8]

Station Place *A B Haynes* a23
2 b f Bahamian Bounty—Twin Time (Syrtos)
7097[8]

Statute *F J Bowles* 67
5 b g Fasliyev(USA) —Unopposed (Sadler's Wells (USA))
4142a[6] (Dead)

Stay Active (USA) *I Semple* a50 62
3 gr g Johannesburg(USA) —Mature Miss (USA) (Mi Cielo (USA))
5084[U] 5555[14] 5840[13] *6147[6]* 6464[2] *6833[4]*

Staying On (IRE) *W R Swinburn* a81
2 b c Invincible Spirit(IRE) —Lakatoi (Saddlers' Hall (IRE))
(6358)

Steady As A Rock (FR) *M Johnston* 81
3 ch c Rock Of Gibraltar(IRE) —Metisse (USA) (Kingmambo (USA))
2881[6] 3094[3] 3491[4] 4195[12]

Steak N Kidney (USA) *M Wigham* 27
4 bb g Wild Again(USA) —Top Slipper (FR) (Top Ville)
2307[11]

Steal My Fire (IRE) *E J O'Neill* a46 60
2 b c Iron Mask(USA) —Lady Of Pleasure (IRE) (Marju (IRE))
(4405) *5117[10]*

Stealth Project *A M Hales* 59
2 b c Elmaamul(USA) —Guardee (Hector Protector (USA))
5702[7] 6494[12] 6725[6]

Steam Cuisine *M G Quinlan* a70 101
3 ch f Mark Of Esteem(IRE) —Sauce Tartar (Salse (USA))
1076[12] 2243[6] (2881) 3430[4] 4589[3] 5163[4] 5799[3] (6497)

Steel Blue *R M Whitaker* a66 90
7 b g Atraf—Something Blue (Petong)
1088[9] 1852[4] 2339[9] 2744[12] 3298[11] 3585[9] 3998[2] (4140) 4227[7] 4585[7] 4999[8] 5232[7] 6103[2] 6283[3] 6639[13]

Steel City Boy (IRE) *D Carroll* a82 65
4 b g Bold Fact(USA) —Balgren (IRE) (Ballad Rock)
(1565) 1999[12] 4486[8] 5297[6] 5507[10] 5836[12] 6020[2] 6157[5] 6467[15] *6625[8]*

Steelcut *R A Fahey* 90
3 b g Iron Mask(USA) —Apple Sauce (Prince Sabo)
1160[3] 1616[7] 2044[7] 2234[18] 2884[5] 3515[7] 4123[11] 4452[7] 5747[3]

Steele Tango (USA) *R A Teal* a70
2 ch c Okawango(USA) —Waltzing Around (IRE) (Ela-Mana-Mou)
6897[4] 7084[6]

Steeley Fox *J M Bradley* a10 59
4 b g Mind Games—Foxie Lady (Wolfhound (USA))
1541[3] 1995[12] 2393[6] 4390[11] 4594[11] *5016[13]*

Steel Grey *M Brittain* a55 8
6 gr g Grey Desire—Call Me Lucky (Magic Ring (IRE))
75[3] 238[9] (715) 1260[15] 3721[12] 3765[12] *5756[12]*

Steel Silk (IRE) *B Smart* a35 60
3 b g Desert Style(IRE) —Dear Catch (IRE) (Bluebird (USA))
4106[4] 4290[3] 4902[7] *5604[8]*

Steelwolf *B Bo* 97
6 b h Fraam—Anatase (Danehill (USA))
4218a[3] 5263a[9]

Steely Dan *Mrs L C Jewell* a74 70
8 b g Danzig Connection(USA) —No Comebacks (Last Tycoon (IRE))
6900[13] 7017[11] 7251[7]

Steenberg (IRE) *M H Tompkins* 116
8 ch g Flying Spur(AUS) —Kip's Sister (Cawston's Clown)
847[6] 1770[16] 3941[25] 5616[14] 5797[21]

Steig (IRE) *Carl Llewellyn* a67 77
4 b g Xaar—Ring Of Kerry (IRE) (Kenmare (FR))
7247[2]

Stellar Rose (USA) *B J Meehan* a39 28
2 b f Royal Academy(USA) —Stellar Blush (USA) (Blushing John (USA))
4540[11] *5097[8] 5984[12]*

Stellite *J S Goldie* a71 81
7 ch g Pivotal—Donation (Generous (IRE))
953[8] 1458[7] 1747[7] 2072[3] 2466[5] 2566[13] 5934[10] 6463[8] 6639[11]

Stepaside (IRE) *A D Brown* a55 66
3 gr g Fasliyev(USA) —Felicita (IRE) (Catrail (USA))
1424[5] 1625[8] 1965[12] 4642[10] 5084[9] 5525[14] *7209[9]*

Stephenson (FR) *Frau C Barsig* 106
6 br g Platini(GER) —Sternina (IRE) (Runnett)
1689a[3]

Steph The Ref *R M Whitaker* 58
2 bb f Rossini(USA) —Fairy Ring (IRE) (Fairy King (USA))
1848[11] 5558[6] 5770[9] 6306[6]

Step In Line (USA) *Saeed Bin Suroor* a11 65
3 b c Giant's Causeway(USA) —Quiet Weekend (USA) (Quiet American (USA))
(5488) *6209[14]*

Steppe Dancer (IRE) *D J Coakley* a114 111
4 b h Fasliyev(USA) —Exemina (USA) (Slip Anchor)
(756) 1618[3] 2216[10] 3461[7] *(5220)* 5437a[7]

Step Softly *R Hannon* 97
2 b f Golan(IRE) —Step Aloft (Shirley Heights)
(3446) (4329) 5353[6] 6008[2]

Step This Way (USA) *M Johnston* a83 67
2 ch f Giant's Causeway(USA) —Lady In Waiting (USA) (Woodman (USA))
3760[10] 4565[5] *(5100) 6291[2]*

Step To The Stars (IRE) *M Johnston* 72
3 ch f Galileo(IRE) —Tudor Loom (Sallust)
(2840) (Dead)

Sterling Moll *W De Best-Turner* a37 50
4 gr m Lord Of Men—Princess Maud (USA) (Irish River (FR))
869[9] 1402[8] 1925[7] 2471[9] *4738[5] 5120[14]* 6250[11]

Stern Opinion (USA) *P Bary* 103
2 gr c Mizzen Mast(USA) —Helstra (USA) (Nureyev (USA))
4009a[2] 5260a[3] 6136a[6]

Sterope (FR) *H R A Cecil* 46
2 b f Hernando(FR) —Sacred Song (USA) (Diesis)
6087[10]

Steve's Champ (CHI) *Rune Haugen* 83
7 br h Foxhound(USA) —Emigracion (CHI) (Semenenko (USA))
3531[5] 5262a[8]

Stevie Gee (IRE) *G A Swinbank* a80 100
3 b g Invincible Spirit(IRE) —Margaree Mary (CAN) (Seeking The Gold (USA))
760[13] 1476[6]

Stevie Smurnoff *M W Easterby* 13
2 b g Mind Games—Ladycake (IRE) (Perugino (USA))
890[13] 1255[7] (Dead)

Stevie Thunder *G A Swinbank* a64 61
2 ch g Storming Home—Social Storm (USA) (Future Storm (USA))
(5477) *6454[3]*

St Expedit *R Bouresly* 57
10 b h Sadler's Wells(USA) —Miss Rinjani (Shirley Heights)
395a[12]

St Fris *J A R Toller* a54 32
4 gr g Silver Patriarch(IRE) —Fragrance (Mtoto)
2332[8] 3945[12] 4859[10] 5453[10]

Sticky Mint (IRE) *M Blanshard* a37 47
4 b m Inchinor—Creme De Menthe (IRE) (Green Desert (USA))
181[7]

Still Calm *N J Vaughan* 62
3 b g Zamindar(USA) —Shining Water (Kalaglow)
5335[6] 6057[7]

Still Crazy (IRE) *E F Vaughan* a66 63
3 ch f Fath(USA) —Miss Bagatelle (Mummy's Pet)
(446) 624[3] 744[7] 3066[7] 3455[8]

Still Dreaming *M Dods* 61
3 ch f Singspiel(IRE) —Three Green Leaves (IRE) (Environment Friend)
2118[7] 2420[3] 2840[3] 3640[9] 4391[14] 5774[7] 5967[6] 6108[3]

Stimulation (IRE) *H Morrison* 105
2 b c Choisir(AUS) —Damiana (IRE) (Thatching)
(5587) 6171[2] 6495[2]

Stir Crazy (IRE) *M R Channon* a69 70
3 b g Fath(USA) —La Captive (IRE) (Selkirk (USA))
1022[9] *1313[3]* 1561[11] 1763[7] 1912[11] *3218[6]* 3353[2] *3649[8]* 3786[11] (4536) 4661[9] 4896[11] 4939[11] 5272[2] *5420[3]* 5711[9] 5834[11] 5909[7] 6424[12]

St Jean Cap Ferrat *G Wragg* 70
2 bb c Domedriver(IRE) —Miss Cap Ferrat (Darshaan)
3747[14] 5306[4] 5598[10] 6592[2]

St Michael's Mount *M P Tregoning* a31
2 b g Mark Of Esteem(IRE) —Marithea (IRE) (Barathea (IRE))
5200[10]

Stoic Leader (IRE) *R F Fisher* a76 88
7 b g Danehill Dancer(IRE) —Starlust (Sallust)
151[3] 234[4] 300[7] 371[6] (953) 1157[7] *1382[7]* 1458[10] 2536[12] 2936[3] 2986[4] 3585[4] 3813[2] 4195[5] 4407[8] *4462[5]* 4816[8] 4999[7] 6331[12] 6701[14] *7024[8]*

Stokesies Boy *C Roberts* a31
7 gr g Key Of Luck(USA) —Lesley's Fashion (Dominion)
5894[12]

Stokesies Luck (IRE) *C Roberts* a15 40
4 gr h King Charlemagne(USA) —Lesley's Fashion (Dominion)
5894[14]

Stolen Glance *M W Easterby* a74 80
4 b m Mujahid(USA) —Stolen Melody (Robellino (USA))
811[10] 1181[5] 1352[5] (1720) (2169) *2346[2]* 2760[3] 2905[10] (3539) 3764[8] 4716[7]

Stolen Hours (USA) *J Akehurst* a70 76
7 bb h Silver Deputy(CAN) —Fasta (USA) (Seattle Song (USA))
(2355) 2692[6] *3217[7] 3946[6]* 4458[6] (Dead)

Stolen Song *J Ryan* a38 59
7 b g Sheikh Albadou—Sparky's Song (Electric)
7012[9]

Stolen Summer (IRE) *B S Rothwell* a51 84
4 ch g Spectrum(IRE) —Touche-A-Tout (IRE) (Royal Academy (USA))
75[9] 148[9] 182[4] 389[10] 481[10]

Stolt (IRE) *N Wilson* a83 86
3 b g Tagula(IRE) —Cabcharge Princess (IRE) (Rambo Dancer (CAN))
5700[7] *5891[11]* 6381[15] *6836[10] 7059[4] (7215)*

Stoneacre Baby (USA) *Peter Grayson* a29
2 ch f Stravinsky(USA) —Katiba (USA) (Gulch (USA))
6022[8] 6225[11] 6692[6]

Stoneacre Boy (IRE) *Peter Grayson* a76 36
4 ch g City On A Hill(USA) —Sans Ceriph (IRE) (Thatching)
475[5] 163[9] 432[2] 626[2] 727[8] 905[7] 1565[11] 3396[10] 5565[6] (6174) 6860[6] 7116[6]

Stoneacre Donny (IRE) *Peter Grayson* a45
3 br c Lend A Hand—Election Special (Chief Singer)
237[7] 429[8] 2593[8] 2950[7] 3583[13] *3924[10] 7019[10] 7162[6] 7283[4]*

Stoneacre Fred (IRE) *Peter Grayson* a55 51
4 br g Lend A Hand—Election Special (Chief Singer)
94[4] 156[5] 518[10] (Dead)

Stoneacre Gareth (IRE) *Peter Grayson* a74 62
3 b g Grand Lodge(USA) —Tidal Reach (USA) (Kris S (USA))
606[5] 639[2] 707[6] 885[9] 1270[6] 1577[10] 1660[7] *1948[5]* 2172[4] 2435[8] *2594[5] 2950[2] 3212[8]* 3588[4] 3811[5] 4186[9] *4944[12] 7283[10]*

Stoneacre Girl (IRE) *Peter Grayson* a38
4 ch m Rossini(USA) —Ring Of Light (Auction Ring (USA))
287[10]

Stoneacre Lad (IRE) *Peter Grayson* a95 104
4 b h Bluebird(USA) —Jay And-A (IRE) (Elbio)
490[4] 818[3] 1754[3] 3080[9] 3586[9] (3990) 5953[13]

Stoneacre Ma *Peter Grayson*
2 b f Dubai Destination(USA) —Silent Tribute (IRE) (Lion Cavern (USA))
6477[8]

Stoneacre Pat (IRE) *Peter Grayson* a8
2 b c Iron Mask(USA) —Sans Ceriph (IRE) (Thatching)
7043[7] 7220[5]

Stone Bridge (IRE) *Adrian Sexton* 42
2 b c Atraf—Cochiti (Kris)
1508a[9]

Stonecrabstomorrow (IRE) *R A Fahey* a88 87
4 b g Fasliyev(USA) —Tordasia (IRE) (Dr Devious (IRE))
1088[14] 1852[11] 2202[9] 2528[8] 3401[3] 3569[2] 4006[3] 4816[4] *5223[11]* 6020[6] *6313[8]*

Stonehaugh (IRE) *J Howard Johnson* 85
4 b g King Charlemagne(USA) —Canary Bird (IRE) (Catrail (USA))
1458[2] 2374[6] 5617[11]

Stoneside (IRE) *Rod Collet* 112
3 b c Marchand De Sable(USA) —Greenstone (IRE) (Green Desert (USA))
1005a[3] 1703a[10] 2499a[2] 3362a[2]

Stones Of Venice (IRE) *J R Fanshawe* a47 41
2 b f Barathea(IRE) —Midnight Fever (IRE) (Sure Blade (USA))
5202[7] 6414[11]

Stoop To Conquer *A W Carroll* 91
7 b g Polar Falcon(USA) —Princess Genista (Ile De Bourbon (USA))
1148[12] 1959[14] 3273[6]

Stop Making Sense *A Fabre* a101 104
5 b g Lujain(USA) —Freeway (FR) (Exit To Nowhere (USA))
4873a[9] 6614a[4] *7128a[3]*

Stop On *M R Channon* 76
2 b g Fraam—Tourmalet (Night Shift (USA))
4325[3] 4841[3] 5344[4]

Stop The Power (GER) *Ruaidhri Joseph Tierney* 35
2 ch c Platini(GER) —Stalima (GER) (Lemhi Gold (USA))
3438a[13]

Storey Hill (USA) *D Shaw* a69
2 bb g Richter Scale(USA) —Crafty Nan (USA) (Crafty Prospector (USA))
5888[4] 6386[7] (6705)

Stormbeam (USA) *G A Butler* a65
2 b c Tale Of The Cat(USA) —Broad Smile (USA) (Broad Brush (USA))
6602[5] 6850[5]

Stormburst (IRE) *S C Williams* a66 57
3 b f Mujadil(USA) —Isca (Caerleon (USA))
998^{5} 1530^{6} 2203^{8} 2718^{7} 3342^{3} 4224^{5} (5947) 6415^{6} 6779^{5} 6925^{4} 6962^{2} 7013^{2}

Stormello (USA) *W Currin* a114
3 ch c Stormy Atlantic(USA) —Wilshewed (USA) (Carson City (USA))
1486a^{19}

Storm Force (IRE) *Saeed Bin Suroor* a91
2 b c Cape Cross(IRE) —Aguinaga (IRE) (Machiavellian (USA))
(6138) (6644)

Stormiano (GER) *Dr A Bolte* a51 92
5 b h Big Shuffle(USA) —Storm Weaver (USA) (Storm Bird (CAN))
1800a^{9}

Stormingmichaelori *N Wilson* a25 46
4 b g Vettori(IRE) —Stormswept (USA) (Storm Bird (CAN))
1529^{9} 1715^{9}

Storm In May (USA) *W Kaplan* a98 94
3 rg c Tiger Ridge(USA) —Laun Shaw (USA) (Relaunch (USA))
1486a^{16}

Storm Lily (USA) *Saeed Bin Suroor* 50
3 b f Storm Cat(USA) —Crimplene (IRE) (Lion Cavern (USA))
4666^{8} 5803^{10}

Storm Mission (USA) *J Mackie* a49 65
3 bb g Storm Creek(USA) —Bemissed (USA) (Nijinsky (CAN))
807^{3} 931^{4} 1044^{12} 1266^{5} 1538^{6} 2110^{5} 3540^{6} 4220^{7} 5511^{7}

Storm Obsession (IRE) *P J Makin* 63
3 b f Val Royal(FR) —Myran (IRE) (In The Wings)
1537^{10} 1927^{11}

Storm Of Arabia (IRE) *W R Swinburn* a69 71
4 b g Intikhab(USA) —Mauradell (IRE) (Mujadil (USA))
263^{12} 623^{6}

Storm Path (IRE) *D R C Elsworth* a49 48
3 gr c Giant's Causeway(USA) —Sianema (Persian Bold)
1129^{9} 2206^{2} 3366^{10} 6529^{8} 6713^{13} 6969^{5} 7168^{9}

Storm Petrel *R M Beckett* a53 58
3 b f Xaar—Vitesse (IRE) (Royal Academy (USA))
2542^{6} 3393^{10} 4257^{12} 5576^{6} 5860^{12}

Storm Shower (IRE) *Mrs N Macauley* a44 44
9 b g Catrail(USA) —Crimson Shower (Dowsing (USA))
374^{13}

Storm Sir (USA) *J Noseda* a69 82
2 ch c Johannesburg(USA) —Robust (USA) (Conquistador Cielo (USA))
5591^{2} 6138^{7}

Storm Trooper (GER) *Rune Haugen* 100
7 ch h Monsun(GER) —So Sedulous (USA) (The Minstrel (CAN))
4218a^{11}

Stormy Journey *Mrs K Walton* 67
2 b g Mujahid(USA) —Sabonis (USA) (The Minstrel (CAN))
2297^{9} 3024^{6} 3673^{3} 3995^{2} 4611^{9} 4995^{3} 5167^{10} 6074^{8}

Stormy River (FR) *N Clement* 122
4 gr h Verglas(IRE) —Miss Bio (FR) (River Mist (USA))
862a^{9} 1879a^{3} (3780a) 4445a^{5} 5798^{5}

Stormy View (USA) *J H M Gosden* a64 45
2 bb c Cozzene(USA) —Another Storm (USA) (Gone West (USA))
4402^{14} 4947^{4}

Storybook (UAE) *M A Jarvis* a90
3 ch f Halling(USA) —Blixen (USA) (Gone West (USA))
(260) (483)

Storyland (USA) *W J Haggas* 66
2 b f Menifee(USA) —Auspice (USA) (Robellino (USA))
5949^{7}

Stotsfold *W R Swinburn* a95 113
4 b g Barathea(IRE) —Eliza Acton (Shirley Heights)
1583^{2} 2209^{11} 4117^{3} (5451)

Stow *H Morrison* a67 67
2 ch g Selkirk(USA) —Spry (Suave Dancer (USA))
6296^{6} 6592^{4} 6857^{3}

St Petersburg *J R Boyle* a90 104
7 ch g Polar Falcon(USA) —First Law (Primo Dominie)
185^{8} 259^{6} 848^{20} 5312^{12} 6203^{3} 6603^{8}

St Philip (USA) *R M Beckett* 103
3 b c Dance Brightly(CAN) —Tender Moment (USA) (Torrential (USA))
2043^{4} 2788^{3}

Strabinios King *R A Harris* a67 63
3 b g King's Best(USA) —Strawberry Morn (CAN) (Travelling Victor (CAN))
304^{4} 1111^{12} (2206) 2829^{7} 4223^{14} 5935^{2} 6476^{7} (7020) 7183^{3} 7227^{4} 7261^{2}

Straight (IRE) *M Brittain* 57
2 b c King Charlemagne(USA) —Fun Of The Fair (Mistertopogigo (IRE))
952^{9} 3192^{6} 3834^{9} 4247^{5} 5902^{8}

Straight And Level (CAN) *Miss Jo Crowley* a70 63
2 rg c Buddha(USA) —Azusa (USA) (Flying Paster (USA))
1586^{4} 1970^{7} 2410^{5} 2569^{3} 3174^{2} 6139^{4} 6543^{3} 6899^{7} (7222)

Straight Face (IRE) *M Wigham* a69 74
3 b g Princely Heir(IRE) —Dakota Sioux (IRE) (College Chapel)
73^{6} 209^{2} 725^{10} 935^{7} 2191^{9} 2837^{10} 4918^{9} 5525^{17}

Straight Gal (IRE) *Mrs N Smith* a48 48
4 br m Namid—Kazimiera (IRE) (Polish Patriot (USA))
798^{6} 1120^{12} 3044^{4} 3615^{13}

Strategic Knight (USA) *P F I Cole* a69
2 b c Johannesburg(USA) —Western Friend (USA) (Gone West (USA))
7051^{3} 7152^{3}

Strategic Mission (IRE) *P F I Cole* 85
2 b c Red Ransom(USA) —North East Bay (USA) (Prospect Bay (CAN))
2632^{3} 3435^{6} (6127)

Strategic Mount *P F I Cole* a64 102
4 b g Montjeu(IRE) —Danlu (USA) (Danzig (USA))
4047^{6} (4376) 4722^{18} 5049^{8} 6994^{7}

Strategic Mover (USA) *P F I Cole* 95
2 ch c Grand Slam(USA) —Efficient Frontier (USA) (Mt. Livermore (USA))
4417^{3} 5004^{4} 5417^{4}

Strategic Prince *P F I Cole* 117
3 b c Dansili—Ausherra (USA) (Diesis)
1473^{8} 2235^{16} 2752^{13}

Strathaird (IRE) *P C Haslam* a44 36
3 b g Medicean—Heed My Warning (IRE) (Second Set (IRE))
60^{8} 253^{3} 2389^{8} 5622^{7} 6505^{8}

Strathmore (IRE) *R A Fahey* a72 73
3 gr g Fath(USA) —In The Highlands (Petong)
679^{5} 918^{4} 1530^{4} (2120) 2363^{5} 2892^{8} 6020^{12} 6283^{11} 6671^{3} 6910^{3} 6938^{2} 7026^{6} 7161^{3} 7271^{6}

Stratn Jack *B G Powell* a47
3 b g Rambling Bear—Strat's Quest (Nicholas (USA))
6901^{5} 7029^{11} 7251^{9}

Stravara *R Hollinshead* a67 72
4 bb g Kayf Tara—Stravsea (Handsome Sailor)
215^{4} 607^{11} 976^{8} 1811^{13} 2656^{3} 2721^{5} 2868^{7} 3243^{8} 3530^{3} 4631^{3} 5775^{4}

Stravinskaya (USA) *H Rogers* 55
5 ch m Stravinsky(USA) —Lady Fairfax (Sharrood (USA))
873a^{20}

Stravinsky's Art (USA) *D R C Elsworth* 42
3 b c Stravinsky(USA) —Halo's Gleam (USA) (Halo (USA))
2059^{12} 2366^{7} 2837^{8} 3353^{6}

Stravita *R Hollinshead* a70
3 b f Weet-A-Minute(IRE) —Stravsea (Handsome Sailor)
483^{5} 1672^{F} 6982^{10} 7131^{5} 7237^{7}

Stravonian *D A Nolan* 36
7 b g Luso—In The Evening (IRE) (Distinctly North (USA))
4713^{8} 5000^{7} 6728^{5}

Strawberry Lolly *M Botti* a87 83
4 b m Lomitas—Strawberry Morn (CAN) (Travelling Victor (CAN))
1149^{14} 1414^{8} 5203^{6} (5985) 6646^{9} 6929^{10}

Strawberry Patch (IRE) *J S Goldie* 69
8 b g Woodborough(USA) —Okino (USA) (Strawberry Road (AUS))
1806^{10} 2386^{9} 2461^{7} 2830^{5} 3017^{5} 3185^{5} 3347^{12} 3535^{9} 4773^{13} 4967^{4} 5295^{10} 5552^{10} 5672^{7} 5836^{8}

Straw Boy *R Brotherton* 56
3 gr g Hunting Lion(IRE) —Sky Light Dreams (Dreams To Reality (USA))
4658^{8}

Stream Cat (USA) *P L Biancone* a108 114
4 bb h Black Minnaloushe(USA) —Water Course (USA) (Irish River (FR))
4414a^{4} 5827a^{3}

Stream Of Gold (IRE) *K McLaughlin* 119
6 b g Rainbow Quest(USA) —River Dancer (Irish River (FR))
176a^{2} 395a^{5} 541a^{2} 642a^{7} 5853a^{2} 6374a^{4}

Street Devil (USA) *P A Blockley* 68
2 gr c Street Cry(IRE) —Math (USA) (Devil's Bag (USA))
6079^{3}

Street Diva (USA) *P A Blockley* a64
2 ch f Street Cry(IRE) —Arctic Valley (USA) (Arctic Tern (USA))
5201^{6} 5681^{5} 6432^{8} 6734^{4}

Street Life (IRE) *W J Musson* a73 76
9 ch g Dolphin Street(FR) —Wolf Cleugh (IRE) (Last Tycoon (IRE))
(89) 195^{8} 459^{6} 594^{11} 805^{5} 1249^{7} 1638^{3} (1819) (2113) 2474^{8} 2833^{6} 3232^{2} 3705^{11} 4015^{12} 4610^{9} 5732^{7} 6253^{6} 6738^{6} 6982^{6}

Street Power (USA) *J R Gask* a69
2 bb c Street Cry(IRE) —Javana (USA) (Sandpit (BRZ))
7084^{7}

Street Sense (USA) *C Nafzger* a127
3 bb c Street Cry(IRE) —Bedazzle (USA) (Dixieland Band (USA))
(1486a) 1882a^{2} 5827a^{2} 6514a^{4}

Street Sounds (CAN) *M Matz* a109 104
3 bb f Street Cry(IRE) —Rare Opportunity (USA) (Danzig Connection (USA))
5248a^{8}

Street Star (USA) *J R Fanshawe* 82
2 b f Street Cry(IRE) —Domludge (USA) (Lyphard (USA))
4232^{2} 4854^{2} (5540)

Street Warrior (IRE) *G H Yardley* a83 85
4 b g Royal Applause—Anne Bonny (Ajdal (USA))
930^{5} 1060^{4} (1209) 1599^{4} 4284^{4} 4631^{7} 6423^{11} 6596^{5}

Strength 'n Honour *Karen George* a56
7 b g Hernando(FR) —Seasonal Splendour (IRE) (Prince Rupert (FR))
6261^{10} 6774^{7}

Strensall *R E Barr* a32 76
10 b g Beveled(USA) —Payvashooz (Ballacashtal (CAN))
1557^{8} 2418^{2} 3836^{7} 3954^{7} (4101) 4703^{14} 4967^{5} 5481^{2} 5740^{5} 6020^{15} 6743^{11} 7011^{9}

Stretton (IRE) *J D Bethell* a66 89
9 br g Doyoun—Awayil (USA) (Woodman (USA))
(1621) 2465^{3} 3753^{6} 4194^{8} 4732^{7} 5229^{6} 5807^{6}

Strictly Elsie (IRE) *J R Norton* 59
2 b f No Excuse Needed—Sophrana (IRE) (Polar Falcon (USA))
3192^{8} 3761^{5} 4781^{3} 6015^{7}

Strife (IRE) *W M Brisbourne* a28 55
4 b g Stravinsky(USA) —Fife (IRE) (Lomond (USA))
2820^{11} 3076^{8} 4155^{4} 4416^{2} 5037^{10} 5269^{2}

Strike A Deal (USA) *A Goldberg* 112
3 b c Smart Strike(CAN) —Shag (USA) (Dixieland Band (USA))
5823a^{6}

Strikeen (IRE) *T G Mills* a88 77
3 ch g Intikhab(USA) —Sheen Falls (IRE) (Prince Rupert (FR))
939^{11} 2126^{7} 2627^{9} 3691^{7} 3993^{8}

Strike Force *K F Clutterbuck* a66 69
3 b g Dansili—Miswaki Belle (USA) (Miswaki (USA))
140^{4} 446^{4} 512^{2} 589^{4} (619) 671^{5} 900^{4} 1008^{3} 1346^{4} 1561^{4} 1763^{2} 2262^{3} 2387^{7} 2948^{2} (3636) 3839^{7} 4416^{6} 7100 7248^{3}

Strike The Deal (USA) *J Noseda* a76 112
2 ch c Van Nistelrooy(USA) —Countess Gold (USA) (Mt. Livermore (USA))
(2590) 2785^{5} 3779a^{3} (4120) 5406^{9} 5630^{2} 5975^{2} 6484a^{4}

Strike Up The Band *D Nicholls* a112 110
4 b g Cyrano De Bergerac—Green Supreme (Primo Dominie)
245a^{10} 326a^{14} 547a^{9} 762^{3} 4798^{12} 5673^{3} 5842a^{9} 6039a^{8} 6327^{5} 6487^{15}

Striking Spirit *B W Hills* 92
2 b c Oasis Dream—Aspiring Diva (USA) (Distant View (USA))
4571^{5} (5193) 6154^{2}

Stringsofmyheart *Miss Gay Kelleway* a68 74
3 b f Halling(USA) —Heart's Harmony (Blushing Groom (FR))
499^{7} 603^{2} 869^{3} (1194) 1843^{5} (2565) 3170^{8} 7211^{3}

Striving (IRE) *Sir Michael Stoute* 59
2 bb f Danehill Dancer(IRE) —Wannabe (Shirley Heights)
4774^{14} 5881^{5}

Striving Storm (USA) *P W Chapple-Hyam* 107
3 bb g Stormin Fever(USA) —Sugars For Nanny (USA) (Brocco (USA))
1103^{5} 1306^{2} 3142a^{11} 4627a^{9} 6655^{7}

Strobe *J A Osborne* a76 81
3 ch g Fantastic Light(USA) —Sadaka (USA) (Kingmambo (USA))
2362^{7} (2801) 3624^{4} 3945^{2} (4322) 4906^{2} 5111^{2} (5224) (5561) 5911^{7}

Stronghold *J H M Gosden* a110 121
5 b h Danehill(USA) —Insinuate (USA) (Mr Prospector (USA))
4600^{3}

Strong Market *H J L Dunlop* a24
2 b g Piccolo—Bon Marche (Definite Article)
3404^{10}

Strong Survivor (USA) *P R Webber* a60 69
4 b g Kingmambo(USA) —Summer Solstice (IRE) (Caerleon (USA))
1813^{4} 3554^{3} 6314^{5}

Strong Will *J R Holt* 54
7 b g Primo Dominie—Reine De Thebes (FR) (Darshaan)
1376^{11}

Stroppi Poppi *Jean-Rene Auvray* a37
3 b f Mtoto—Capricious Lass (Corvaro (USA))
4392^{12} 5898^{5} 6821^{8}

Structura (USA) *J S Moore* a58 62
2 bb f Stormin Fever(USA) —Sisterella (USA) (Diesis)
1503^{4} 1807^{5} 1992^{8} 4016^{3} 4310^{8} 4737^{10} 5267^{7} 6023^{2} 6227^{10}

Strut The Stage (IRE) *B W Duke* a61 76
3 b g Lil's Boy(USA) —Eva Luna (IRE) (Double Schwartz)
2196^{5} 3612^{4} 4165^{6} 4396^{7} 4529^{3} 5118^{9} 6101^{3} 6247^{12} 6764^{7} 7118^{4} 7276^{2}

St Savarin (FR) *R A Fahey* a91 101
6 ch g Highest Honor(FR) —Sacara (GER) (Monsagem (USA))
4637^{6} 5619^{6} (5933) 6169^{2} 6994^{6} (7175)

Stuart Little (DEN) *P W Chapple-Hyam* 97
3 b c Esprit Du Nord(USA) —Cocco Pio (IRE) (Turtle Island (IRE))
1126^{5}

Stubbs Art (IRE) *D R C Elsworth* 90
2 ch c Hawk Wing(USA) —Rich Dancer (Halling (USA))
1970^{8} 2478^{5} 4539^{3} 5350^{2} (5600) 6650^{3}

Student Council (USA) *V Cerin* a117
5 b h Kingmambo(USA) —Class Kris (USA) (Kris S (USA))
6942a^{8}

Style Award *W J H Ratcliffe* 75
2 b f Acclamation—Elegant (IRE) (Marju (IRE))
1553^{3} (2416) 3025^{4} (3256) 3492^{6} 4175^{2} 4476^{2} 4844^{4} 5167^{4} 5802^{4} 6635^{3} (6741)

Stylistic (IRE) *J J Lambe* a65 21
6 b m Daggers Drawn(USA) —Treasure (IRE) (Treasure Kay)
268^{11}

Sualda (IRE) *Ollie Pears* a6 84
8 b g Idris(IRE) —Winning Heart (Horage)
1208^{8} 3671^{4} 4318^{10} 6999^{10}

Subadar *R Charlton* a76 60
3 b g Zamindar(USA) —Valencia (Kenmare (FR))
(1215) 5532^{12}

Subpoena *A Al Raihe* 102
5 b h Diktat—Trefoil (Kris)
325a^{10} (470a) 540a^{2} 644a^{9}

Succeed (IRE) *Mrs H Sweeting* a60 50
4 b m Elnadim(USA) —Pico (Piccolo)
82^{6} 289^{3}

Sudamy (FR) *Robert Collet* 59
2 bb c Black Sam Bellamy(IRE) —Sudaka (FR) (Garde Royale)
6952a^{7}

Sudan (IRE) *M A Jarvis* 117
4 ch h Peintre Celebre(USA) —Sarabande (USA) (Woodman (USA))
1571a^{5} (2706a) 5263a^{10}

Sudden Impact (IRE) *Paul Green* 97
2 bb f Modigliani(USA) —Suddenly (Puissance)
1848^{3} 2134^{7} 2737^{18} (3915) 4193^{6} (4832a) 5435a^{6} 6182^{9} 6619^{8}

Sudden Impulse *A D Brown* a73 78
6 b m Silver Patriarch(IRE) —Sanshang (FR) (Astronef)
1090^{7} 1258^{3} (1532) 1771^{9} 2342^{6} (2935) 3260^{4} 3719^{8} 4582^{2} 7002^{10} 7194^{8}

Su Doku (FR) *J E Pease* 75
2 br c Kahyasi—Labyrinth (FR) (Exit To Nowhere (USA))
6952a^{4}

Sudoor *J L Dunlop* 102
3 b f Fantastic Light(USA) —Wissal (USA) (Woodman (USA))
1499^{2} 1958^{2} 3897^{5} 4633^{4} 5544^{7} (6249) 6757^{3}

Sue's Hawk (IRE) *A P Jarvis* a12
2 ch f Hawk Wing(USA) —Desert Blues (IRE) (Desert Prince (IRE))
5308^{10}

Sues Surprise (IRE) *B W Hills* a68 99
3 b f Montjeu(IRE) —My Micheline (Lion Cavern (USA))
1769^{3} 2211^{14} 3992^{7} 4430^{2} (4989)

Suffolk House *M Brittain* a47 27
5 b g Paris House—Suffolk Girl (Statoblest)
80^{5} 243^{8} 533^{11} 1527^{11} 2809^{9}

Sugarbush *J R Fanshawe* a64 68
3 b f Kingmambo(USA) —Ive Gota Bad Liver (USA) (Mt. Livermore (USA))
2597^{7} 3214^{6}

Sugar Land *C A Cyzer* a75 50
3 b f Dansili—Time For Tea (IRE) (Imperial Frontier (USA))
1037^{7} 1215^{3} (3062)

Sugar Mint (IRE) *B W Hills* 101
2 b f High Chaparral(IRE) —Anna Karenina (USA) (Atticus (USA))
4565^{2} 5353^{4} 5796^{6}

Sugar Ray (IRE) *Sir Michael Stoute* 89
3 b c Danehill(USA) —Akuna Bay (USA) (Mr Prospector (USA))
3436^{3} (4235) 5014^{2} 6091^{3}

Suggestive *W J Haggas* a107 111
9 b g Reprimand—Pleasuring (Good Times (ITY))
1294^{5} 1651^{28} 2396^{5} 4012a^{10}

Sugitani (USA) *N B King* a82 43
5 b g Kingmambo(USA) —Lady Reiko (IRE) (Sadler's Wells (USA))
(1378)

Suhayl Star (IRE) *M Wigham* a68 71
3 b g Trans Island—Miss Odlum (IRE) (Mtoto)
446^{5} 589^{6} 832^{2} 1022^{12} 1238^{9} 1538^{11} 2444^{7} 5386^{3} 5688^{10} 6587^{14}

Suhezy (IRE) *J S Wainwright* a3 54
4 b m Orpen(USA) —Ervedya (IRE) (Doyoun)
2343^{12} 2657^{8} 2938^{8} 3814^{12}

Suite Francaise *Sir Mark Prescott* a51 53
2 gr f Hernando(FR) —Entente Cordiale (USA) (Affirmed (USA))
1989^{7} 2344^{3} 2768^{9} 3373^{2} 4524^{13}

Suits Me *T P Tate* a73 89
4 ch g Bertolini(USA) —Fancier Bit (Lion Cavern (USA))
604^{3} 675^{6} 870^{4} 1199^{2} 1416^{6} 2868^{3} (3755) (4922) 5296^{7} 5775^{3} 6180^{5} (6475) (6636)

Suki Bear *W R Muir* 72
3 br f Xaar—Dominion Rose (USA) (Spinning World (USA))
2400^{14}

Sularno *H Morrison* a74 57
3 ch g Medicean—Star Precision (Shavian)
1724^{13} 2150^{2} 3384^{12} 4197^{8} 5604^{9}

Sultan Of The Sand *C C Bealby* a39 34
2 b g High Estate—Desert Bloom (FR) (Last Tycoon (IRE))
3283^{6} 3712^{7} 4077^{8}

Sumarocca *J Van Handenhove* 95
3 b f Hernando(FR) —Belle D'Argent (USA) (Silver Hawk (USA))
5058a^{7}

Sumdancer (NZ) *M Madgwick* a21
5 b g Summer Suspicion(JPN) —Epic Dancer (NZ) (Epidaurus (USA))
7069^{13}

Sumi Girl (IRE) *R A Fahey* 78
3 b f Tiger Hill(IRE) —Allonia (GER) (Surumu (GER))
1089^{3} 6180^{14}

Summer Bounty *F Jordan* a59 61
11 b g Lugana Beach—Tender Moment (IRE) (Caerleon (USA))
3280^{9} 3799^{5} 4253^{8} 4860^{9} 5345^{3} 5886^{3} 6407^{5} (6569) 6713^{5} (6896) 6969^{4} 7187^{6}

Summer Dancer (IRE) *D R C Elsworth* a83 84
3 br g Fasliyev(USA) —Summer Style (IRE) (Indian Ridge)
1815^{7} 2061^{2} (2601) 3215^{6} 3553^{3} 4710^{3} 5635^{4} 6651^{3} 6900^{4} 7193^{5}

Summer Gift *J O'Reilly* a31 71
4 b m Cadeaux Genereux—Summer Exhibition (Royal Academy (USA))
2554^{13} 2894^{9} 4846^{12} 5299^{6} 5525^{9} 5625^{5} 5890^{8}

Summer Lodge *A J McCabe* a74 74
4 b g Indian Lodge(IRE) —Summer Siren (FR) (Saint Cyrien (FR))
74^{5} 204^{5} 805^{4} 1162^{4} 1284^{7} 3049^{10} 3705^{9}

Summer Of Love (IRE) *P F I Cole* a63 69
3 b f Fasliyev(USA) —Overboard (IRE) (Rainbow Quest (USA))
1092^{6} 1355^{6} 1927^{3} 2413^{4} 2653^{3} 3351^{6}

Summerofsixtynine *J G M O'Shea* a59
4 b h Fruits Of Love(USA) —Scurrilous (Sharpo)
5816^{5} 6211^{4} 6430^{5} 6893^{3} (7262)

Summer Recluse (USA) *J M Bradley* a74 76
8 gr g Cozzene(USA) —Summer Retreat (USA) (Gone West (USA))
1969^{17} 2494^{7} 3368^{4} 3613^{2} 4320^{7} 4606^{10} 4634^{5} 4942^{4} 5272^{7} 5349^{7} 5711^{3} 5866^{9} 6148^{4} 6290^{9}

Summer's Eve *H Candy* 102
4 gr m Singspiel(IRE) —Early Rising (USA) (Grey Dawn II)
1789^{5} 2441^{4} 3103^{5} 3897^{9} 4849^{5}

Summerville Star (IRE) *Michael McElhone* a41 29
3 b f Fruits Of Love(USA) —Alexandra Fair (USA) (Green Dancer (USA))
6804^10

Summer Winds *T G Mills* 39
2 ch c Where Or When(IRE) —Jetbeeah (IRE) (Lomond (USA))
4761^9

Summit Surge (IRE) *G M Lyons* a103 102
3 b g Noverre(USA) —Lady Peculiar (CAN) (Sunshine Forever (USA))
948a^3 1185a^6 2586a^10 7037a^2

Summon Up Theblood *M R Channon* 76
2 b g Red Ransom(USA) —Diddymu (IRE) (Revoque (IRE))
4151^8 4876^4 5361^3 5749^6

Sumner (IRE) *M H Tompkins* a61 79
3 b c Xaar—Black Jack Girl (IRE) (Ridgewood Ben)
(1972) 4617^6 5279^3 (5557) 5979^4

Sun *P W Chapple-Hyam* 66
2 ch c Medicean—Radiant Bride (USA) (Blushing Groom (FR))
4362^16 5971^11

Sun Bian *L P Grassick* a55 29
5 br g Makbul—Silken Dalliance (Rambo Dancer (CAN))
272^2 559^6 773^5 1227^7 1435^3 2716^13 3173^13 5817^11 7247^4

Sunburn (IRE) *Mrs A J Perrett* a21 58
3 b g Mark Of Esteem(IRE) —Sundrenched (IRE) (Desert King (IRE))
2477^7 2886^5 3456^8 4355^7

Sun Catcher (IRE) *R Hannon* a85 81
4 b g Cape Cross(IRE) —Taalluf (USA) (Hansel (USA))
28^2 (91) 191^6 261^4 351^2 576^4 697^10 757^3 1446^2 1682^6 1984^9 2573^5 3905^6 4767^5 5312^13 6406^5

Sundae *C F Wall* a57 99
3 b g Bahamian Bounty—Merry Rous (Rousillon (USA))
1267^2 (1635) (2631) (3061) (3952) 5584^3

Sundance (IRE) *H J Collingridge* a80 76
5 ch g Namid—Titchwell Lass (Lead On Time (USA))
117^14 334^8

Sunday Geisha (USA) *Martin F Jones* a100 92
2 br f Sunday Break(JPN) —Above The Table (USA) (Never Tabled (USA))
5826a^6

Sunday Symphony *S Seemar* 114
5 br g Sunday Silence(USA) —Darrery (Darshaan)
328a^15 475a^8 648a^4

Sunderland Echo (IRE) *B Ellison* a42 91
4 ch m Tagula(IRE) —La Alla Wa Asa (IRE) (Alzao (USA))
1670^5 2396^8 2841^14 3089^12 3158^9

Sundowner (IRE) *G A Butler* 78
2 b c Galileo(IRE) —Sunsetter (USA) (Diesis)
6618^3

Sundried Tomato *D W Chapman* a55 46
8 b g Lugana Beach—Little Scarlett (Mazilier (USA))
303^5 339^12 467^3 504^7 668^13 1028^7 1262^7 1596^13

Sun In Splendour (USA) *A P Jarvis* 36
2 ch c Hold That Tiger(USA) —Fit To Win (USA) (Fit To Fight (USA))
2447^7

Sunisa (IRE) *J Mackie* a66 84
6 b m Daggers Drawn(USA) —Winged Victory (IRE) (Dancing Brave (USA))
2136^3 2543^7 2794^2 3972^4 5814^2 6129^4

Sunken Rags *K R Burke* a60 49
3 b f Superior Premium—Mise En Scene (Lugana Beach)
108^3 378^8 506^6

Sun King (USA) *N Zito* a120
5 bb h Charismatic(USA) —Clever But Costly (USA) (Clever Trick (USA))
5059a^2 5855a^4

Sun Lane *W R Swinburn* a56 54
3 ro f Daylami(IRE) —Three Piece (Jaazeiro (USA))
5304^2 5683^7 5948^13

Sunley Gift *B G Powell* 69
3 b f Cadeaux Genereux—Thracian (Green Desert (USA))
2425^11 2837^9 3875^9

Sunley Peace *D R C Elsworth* 103
3 ch g Lomitas—Messila Rose (Darshaan)
1724^3 1974^5 2602^3 2816^5 3236^3 3993^4 (4398) 4749^4 5165^3 5829^3 6335^7

Sunley Smiles *D R C Elsworth* a48
2 ch f Arkadian Hero(USA) —Sunley Scent (Wolfhound (USA))
6964^7

Sunley Song *B G Powell* a43 44
4 b m Fleetwood(IRE) —Sunley Sinner (Try My Best (USA))
87^9

Sunley Sovereign *D W Chapman* a61 65
3 b g Josr Algarhoud(IRE) —Pharsical (Pharly (FR))
348^3 446^6 (667) 1313^5 1658^11 1932^8 4896^8 5139^14 5299^14 5386^12

Sunlight (IRE) *M A Jarvis* a79 90
3 ch f Sinndar(IRE) —Church Light (Caerleon (USA))
1663^7 3645^3 (4331) 5067^6 5544^11

Sun Moon Orpen (IRE) *U Stoltefuss* 80
4 m Orpen(USA) — (USA) (Big Shuffle (USA))
6220a^12

Sunny Afternoon *R Rowe* a58 35
7 ch m Atraf—Pinup (Risk Me (FR))
819^7 1507^15 3451^5 4361^10

Sunny'n Smart (USA) *Francis Ennis* 79
3 ch g Smart Strike(CAN) —Plenty Of Sunshine (USA) (Deputy Minister (CAN))
6368a^17

Sunny Parkes *M Mullineaux* a48 44
4 ch m Arkadian Hero(USA) —Janette Parkes (Pursuit Of Love)
1229^9 2531^12

Sunny Power (AUS) *K W Lui* 115
5 b g Honour And Glory(USA) —Zebra (AUS) (Palace Music (USA))
7089a^5

Sunnyside Tom (IRE) *R A Fahey* 78
3 b g Danetime(IRE) —So Kind (Kind Of Hush)
1577^5 1994^5 2395^6 2881^9 3952^3 4222^5 4898^7 5159^10 5703^2 6380^10

Sunny Sing (IRE) *J Moore* 119
5 b h Sri Pekan(USA) —Sagrada (GER) (Primo Dominie)
7089a^12

Sunny Sprite *J M P Eustace* a70 69
2 b g Lujain(USA) —Dragon Star (Rudimentary (USA))
4962^2 5313^4

Sun Of The Sea *N P Littmoden* a64 80
3 b g Best Of The Bests(IRE) —Gem (Most Welcome)
2834^4 (3429) 4184^8 6623^6 6982^7

Sunoverregun *J R Boyle* a83 81
3 b c Noverre(USA) —Jumairah Sun (IRE) (Scenic)
2570^3 2769^4 2942^3 3483^3 4127^6 6002^11 (6667)

Sunrise (SAF) *S Seemar* a79 88
6 b h Up And At 'Em—My Sunshine (SAF) (Sun Monarch (NZ))
324a^11 400a^9 547a^10

Sunrise Bacchus (JPN) *H Otonashi* a116
5 br h Hennessy(USA) —Real Sapphire (JPN) (Real Shadai (USA))
6942a^3

Sunrise Safari (IRE) *I Semple* 106
4 b g Mozart(IRE) —Lady Scarlett (Woodman (USA))
1574^8 (1941) 2566^4 3500^12 (3954) 5039^3 5584^4 (6487) 6758^4

Sunriver (USA) *T Pletcher* a116 119
4 bb h Saint Ballado(CAN) —Goulash (USA) (Mari's Book (USA))
4414a^4 5250a^2 6374a^6

Sunset Boulevard (IRE) *Miss Tor Sturgis* a75 75
4 b g Montjeu(IRE) —Lucy In The Sky (IRE) (Lycius (USA))
(229) 594^13 (1451) 1924^3

Sunset Ridge (IRE) *Miss Gay Kelleway* a44 59
4 b m Indian Ridge—Barbara Frietchie (IRE) (Try My Best (USA))
274^11

Sunshine Kid (USA) *J H M Gosden* 108
3 b c Lemon Drop Kid(USA) —Nepenthe (USA) (Broad Brush (USA))
1276^2 1736a^3 2293a^12 4826^4 5618^5 6153^2 6771a^6

Sunshine Lady (IRE) *D Haydn Jones* a58 39
2 b f Captain Rio—Damezao (Alzao (USA))
5097^12 5363^9 6237^8 6737^2 7007^4 7234^2

Suntan Lady (IRE) *Miss V Haigh* a46 52
3 b f Redback—Scarletta (USA) (Red Ransom (USA))
40^4 65^6 894^4 1008^7 1164^7 3786^16 4109^11

Sun Valley (GER) *Frau E Mader* 81
4 ch m Lando(GER) —Schalmai (GER) (Nebos (GER))
6220a^8

Supa Sal *P F I Cole* a81 76
3 b f King's Best(USA) —Supamova (USA) (Seattle Slew (USA))
(843) 1837^7 3474^6

Supaseus *H Morrison* 104
4 b g Spinning World(USA) —Supamova (USA) (Seattle Slew (USA))
(1494) 2755^4 4119^9 6011^28

Supa Tramp *G L Moore* 61
4 b g Kayf Tara—Shirley Superstar (Shirley Heights)
891^4

Supercast (IRE) *W M Brisbourne* a73 78
4 b g Alhaarth(IRE) —Al Euro (FR) (Mujtahid (USA))
424^8 513^9 561^2 621^5 724^6 831^8 4731^6 5275^8 5731^7 5879^12

Supercraft (IRE) *M Quinn*
3 ch g Indian Lodge(IRE) —Between The Winds (USA) (Diesis)
257^RR 1725^16 2454^12 2747^7 5508^10

Super Cross (IRE) *E A L Dunlop* a74 77
3 b c Cape Cross(IRE) —Super Trouper (FR) (Nashwan (USA))
1012^5 1289^5 1708^2 2425^13 2834^6 3113^4

Super Dominion *R Hollinshead* a43 47
10 ch g Superpower—Smartie Lee (Dominion)
180^5

Superduper *R Hannon* 72
2 b f Erhaab(USA) —I'm Magic (First Trump)
3507^13 4232^3 4454^5 5595^4 6128^8

Super Frank (IRE) *J Akehurst* a87 77
4 b g Cape Cross(IRE) —Lady Joshua (IRE) (Royal Academy (USA))
(131) (261) (384) 4455^3 5115^4 5885^6 6355^4 6651^7 7253^4

Supergill (IRE) *Are Hyldmo* 60
3 b c Desert Prince(IRE) —Maharani (USA) (Red Ransom (USA))
2548a^5

Superior Star *R A Fahey* a63 74
4 b g Superior Premium—Lindfield Belle (IRE) (Fairy King (USA))
850^6 1264^4 3052^7 3161^2 3381^2 3793^4 5620^4

Superjain *J M Jefferson* a44 62
3 b f Lujain(USA) —Plie (Superlative)
1238^14 1748^11 1912^6 2220^6 3605^3 4042^13 6464^10

Supermassive Muse (IRE) *E S McMahon* 75
2 br c Captain Rio—Cautionary (IRE) (Warning)
1680^7 1992^2 (2651) 3550^14 4823^6 5032^5

Super Nebula *P L Gilligan* a32 51
3 b g Fantastic Light(USA) —It Girl (Robellino (USA))
1840^11 2005^12 2609^5 3082^16

Super Sensation (GER) *G L Moore* a59
6 ch g Platini(GER) —Studford Girl (Midyan (USA))
496^4 2595^2 3397^5

Super Sifted (GER) *H R A Cecil* a61 58
3 b f Saddlers' Hall(IRE) —Sun Moon Stars (IRE) (Shahrastani (USA))
1364^2 1950^5 2610^4

Supersonic Dave (USA) *B J Meehan* 109
3 bb c Swain(IRE) —Vickey's Echo (CAN) (Clever Trick (USA))
2042^2 2442^4 2789^11

Super Starlet (IRE) *M Botti* a43 24
2 b f Statue Of Liberty(USA) —Wings To Soar (USA) (Woodman (USA))
6015^9 6601^10 7070^12

Super Tuscan (IRE) *J G Given* a71 39
2 b c Fath(USA) —Ornellaia (IRE) (Mujadil (USA))
6469^11 6754^9 6990^3 (7170)

Support Fund (IRE) *Eve Johnson Houghton* a53 69
3 ch f Intikhab(USA) —Almost A Lady (IRE) (Entitled)
998^2 1297^9 1731^12 3425^4 (3612) 4165^8 5191^2 5711^12 5879^6 (6278) 6447^5

Supporting Role (IRE) *E S McMahon* 56
2 b c Marju(IRE) —Intercession (Bluebird (USA))
5580^10 6469^8 6725^7

Supreme Charter *E S McMahon* a71 82
4 b g Diktat—Alchi (USA) (Alleged (USA))
515^7

Supreme Kiss *Mrs N Smith* a61 61
4 b m Barathea Guest—Kiss Me Again (IRE) (Cyrano De Bergerac)
796^4 1212^9 2217^6 2459^8 3212^6 3853^8 5425^5

Surbiton (USA) *A Al Raihe* a95 75
7 ch h El Prado(IRE) —Mastina (USA) (Gulch (USA))
399a^12 529a^13

Surdoue *D Morris* a58 45
7 b g Bishop Of Cashel—Chatter's Princess (Cadeaux Genereux)
1254^13 1717^2 1980^6 2348^4 2745^5 3616^3 4266^8 4945^2 5179^9 5916^16 6096^8 6412^11 6529^5 6713^14

Surely Truly (IRE) *A E Jones* a61 67
4 b m Trans Island—Londubh (Tumble Wind)
5643^10 6718^11

Surething (FR) *M Rolland* a80 95
2 b c Zieten(USA) —Moldava (FR) (Saumarez)
6136a^4 6525a^5 7027a^2

Sureyya (GER) *E Lellouche* 102
4 br m Monsun(GER) —Sankt Johanna (GER) (High Game)
1421a^4 5150a^3 6137a^2 6953a^5

Surprise Act *P R Chamings* a61 69
3 gr g Act One—Surprise Surprise (Robellino (USA))
1725^11 2320^12 3365^6 (6277) 6874^7 7155^8

Surprise Pension (IRE) *J J Quinn* 56
3 b g Fruits Of Love(USA) —Sheryl Lynn (Miller's Mate)
(2759) 3181^6 4491^6

Surrey Spinner *Mrs A J Perrett* a83 83
3 ch c Intikhab(USA) —Markievicz (IRE) (Doyoun)
418^3 (611) 1277^3 1987^8 4603^9 5718^5 5921^5 6474^3

Survival Story (IRE) *Noel Meade* a49 67
3 b f Titus Livius(FR) —Morija (IRE) (Tirol)
4865a^13

Surwaki (USA) *R M H Cowell* a69 84
5 b g Miswaki(USA) —Quinella (Generous (IRE))
629^9 1013^6 1157^5 1481^7 2189^2 2748^7 (3241) 3711^9 4499^5 4850^4

Susanna's Dance *M Botti* a57 49
3 b f Danehill(USA) —Sonja's Faith (IRE) (Sharp Victor (USA))
1901^9 4430^5 4765^8 5783^8

Susanna's Prospect (IRE) *B J Meehan* a66 79
3 ch f Namid—Substantive (USA) (Distant View (USA))
1310^2 1731^7 2224^2 (2607) 2916^6

Sushisan (AUS) *H J Brown* 119
5 ch g Fuji Kiseki(JPN) —Meine Tochter (AUS) (Bataan (USA))
531a^7 (642a) 861a^5

Susiedil (IRE) *S T Mason* a36 46
6 b m Mujadil(USA) —Don't Take Me (IRE) (Don't Forget Me)
730^8 966^3 1227^12 2008^7 2795^5 3049^11 3638^9 4249^8 7169^10

Susie May *C A Cyzer* a69 65
3 ch f Hernando(FR) —Mohican Girl (Dancing Brave (USA))
884^6 3082^9 4104^4 (4473) 5709^6 5948^2 6271^4

Suspender (IRE) *S T Mason* 38
3 b f Distant Music(USA) —Feather 'n Lace (IRE) (Green Desert (USA))
1558^4 1913^14 6702^12 7134^8

Suzieblue (IRE) *D C O'Brien* a50 48
3 b f Redback—Blue Holly (IRE) (Blues Traveller (IRE))
25^8 502^8 577^13

Suzi's Decision *P W D'Arcy* 66
2 b f Act One—Funny Girl (IRE) (Darshaan)
4293^4 4709^3 (5470)

Suzi Spends (IRE) *M Johnston* a71 72
2 b f Royal Applause—Clever Clogs (Nashwan (USA))
2504^3 4428^2 4769^7 5153^4 5471^3 (6233) 6750^7

Suzy Spitfire (FR) *J Heloury*
2 b f Josr Algarhoud(IRE) —Egerie Cherie (FR) (Lake Coniston (IRE))
1485a^7

Sven (SWE) *B I Case* a19 33
3 b g Duty Time—Last Romance (IRE) (Last Tycoon (IRE))
1566^9 1950^11

Swains Bridge (USA) *Micky Hammond* 83
5 b g Swain(IRE) —Saraa Ree (USA) (Caro)
6158^12

Swallow Forest *T D Barron* 54
2 b f Averti(IRE) —Sangra (USA) (El Gran Senor (USA))
3915^6 4447^7

Swallow Senora (IRE) *M C Chapman* a44 41
5 b m Entrepreneur—Sangra (USA) (El Gran Senor (USA))
2187^10 4938^4 6412^14 6702^5

Swallow Star *R M Beckett* a68 75
2 b f Observatory(USA) —Swift Baba (USA) (Deerhound (USA))
(2333) 3550^11 6270^4

Swanky Lady *R Hannon* 78
2 b f Cape Cross(IRE) —Lady Links (Bahamian Bounty)
4061^6 4662^7 (5881)

Swan Queen *J L Dunlop* a46 99
4 b m In The Wings—Bronzewing (Beldale Flutter (USA))
1783^2 2238^3 (2675) 3153^2 4047^7

Swayze (IRE) *M Quinn* a55 67
4 b g Marju(IRE) —Dance Of Love (IRE) (Pursuit Of Love)
675^13 6570^5 6804^9

Swaziland *J Noseda* 43
2 b c Green Desert(USA) —Susu (Machiavellian (USA))
4362^18

Sweeney (IRE) *M A Jarvis* a90 62
3 ch g Jade Robbery(USA) —Arduine (Diesis)
436a^9 1010^7

Sweepstake (IRE) *R Hannon* 96
2 b f Acclamation—Dust Flicker (Suave Dancer (USA))
(1781) (2183) 2756^19 3988^3

Sweet Afton (IRE) *M S Saunders* 98
4 b m Mujadil(USA) —Victory Peak (Shirley Heights)
1125^4 1372^7 2450^14 3526^6 4183^7 4373^8

Sweet Andromeda *T J Fitzgerald* a39 49
2 ch f Observatory(USA) —Smooth Princess (IRE) (Roi Danzig (USA))
6312^7 6698^6 6912^7 7117^13

Sweet Cherokee *C N Kellett* a38 3
4 b m Mind Games—Sioux Lady (Petong)
252^12

Sweet Clover *K R Burke* 67
3 b f Rainbow Quest(USA) —Trefoil (Kris)
1408^6 1995^4 (3561) 4579^9

Sweet Dane (IRE) *V Smith* a43 15
2 b f Danetime(IRE) —Griqualand (Connaught)
4537^12 4962^9 5309^10 6572^14

Sweeter Still (IRE) *A P O'Brien* 86
2 br f Rock Of Gibraltar(IRE) —Beltisaal (FR) (Belmez (USA))
5435a^4

Sweet Gale (IRE) *J Noseda* a82 81
3 b f Soviet Star(USA) —Lady Moranbon (USA) (Trempolino (USA))
1128^10 1343^3 (1749) (2335)

Sweetheart *Jamie Poulton* a73 73
3 b f Sinndar(IRE) —Love And Adventure (USA) (Halling (USA))
(258) 1205^10 1504^5 1810^3 2185^5 2999^9 4113^6 4951^3 5857^2 6131^7

Sweet Hope (USA) *K A Ryan* a82 75
2 bb f Lemon Drop Kid(USA) —High Heeled Hope (USA) (Salt Lake (USA))
4173^9 4992^5 5628^3 6267^3 6611^4 (7190)

Sweet Indulgence (IRE) *W J Musson* a98 88
6 ch g Inchinor—Silent Indulgence (USA) (Woodman (USA))
345^3 (Dead)

Sweet Kiss (USA) *B J Meehan* 80
2 gr f Yes It's True(USA) —Always Freezing (USA) (Robyn Dancer (USA))
3507^3 5353^10 5910^5

Sweet Lavinia *J D Bethell* 51
4 ch m Lomitas—Latch Key Lady (USA) (Tejano (USA))
2372^9 3193^6 4451^3 4925^11 6383^6

Sweet Lilly *M R Channon* a74 113
3 b f Tobougg(IRE) —Maristax (Reprimand)
1496^12 1769^2 2501a^12 3433^5 4149^4 4654a^6 (5047) 5241a^5 6299^3

Sweet Medicine *P Howling* a51 74
5 ch m Dr Devious(IRE) —Crimley Crumb (Rainbow Quest (USA))
112^8 1167^7

Sweet Mind *R A Fahey* a41 59
2 b f Mind Games—Cape Charlotte (Mon Tresor)
5194^7 5550^7 6065^8

Sweet Mischief (IRE) *J H M Gosden* a68 27
3 b f Sadler's Wells(USA) —Sneaky Quiet (USA) (Seeking The Gold (USA))
6420^12 6821^3 6959^4

Sweet Montana (GER) *A Kleinkorres* 75
3 b f Lando(GER) —Summer Beauty (Cadeaux Genereux)
1855a^8

Sweet Nicole *J R Fanshawe* 55
2 ch f Okawango(USA) —Tatora (Selkirk (USA))
4181^7

Sweet Peak (IRE) *Eamon Tyrrell* a58 77
3 b f Desert Style(IRE) —Victory Peak (Shirley Heights)
3406^6

Sweet Pickle *J R Boyle* a76 74
6 b m Piccolo—Sweet Wilhelmina (Indian Ridge)
3^2 (67) 376^3 (555) 561^5 1377^2 1525^3 1935^3 2240^4 2422^7 (4017) 4767^9 5064^10 5648^9 (6625) 6962^4

Sweet Request *R M Beckett* a68 71
3 ch f Best Of The Bests(IRE) —Sweet Revival (Claude Monet (USA))
1143^11 1606^9 2008^2 2579^5 3427^8 3871^2 4205^4 4878^2 5271^3 6070^2 6751^5

Sweet Sara *C E Brittain* a48 67
2 b f Mark Of Esteem(IRE) —Mild Deception (IRE) (Glow (USA))
5301^5 6626^5

Sweet Seville (FR) *Mrs G S Rees* 48
3 b f Agnes World(USA) —Hispalis (IRE) (Barathea (IRE))
7239^11

Sweetsformysweet (USA) *J Noseda* a61 46
3 ch f Forest Wildcat(USA) —Pent Up Kiss (USA) (Pentelicus (USA))
3395[2] 4164[5] 4616[4] *5982[7] 6339[6] (6773)*

Sweet Venture (FR) *M Weiss* 102
5 gr h Verglas(IRE) —Bitter Sweet (FR) (Esprit Du Nord (USA))
493a[4]

Sweet Wind Music *B Grizzetti* 98
3 ch f Zamindar(USA) —Sadhya (FR) (Prince Sabo)
1701a[11]

Sweet World *A P Jarvis* a64 69
3 b g Agnes World(USA) —Douce Maison (IRE) (Fools Holme (USA))
(139) 335[2] (491) 694[7] (776) 1059[3] *3622[4] 4069[9]* 4518[7] *5128[3]* (5553) 6235[6] *7175[4]*

Swift Acclaim (IRE) *K R Burke* 50
2 b f Acclamation—Swift Chorus (Music Boy)
4378[8] 5393a[11] 5770[8] 6073[5]

Swift Cut (IRE) *A P Jarvis* a74 74
3 ch g Daggers Drawn(USA) —Jugendliebe (IRE) (Persian Bold)
275[5] 2425[6] 4163[6] 4515[5] *6838[3] 6996[13] 7164[11] 7180[5]*

Swift Gift *B J Meehan* a82 73
2 b c Cadeaux Genereux—Got To Go (Shareef Dancer (USA))
4362[3] 4784[4] *(6980)*

Swiftly Addicted (IRE) *A King* a49 59
3 ch f King's Best(USA) —Swiftly (Cadeaux Genereux)
1561[6] 2080[7]

Swift Princess (IRE) *K R Burke* 86
3 b f Namid—Swift Chorus (Music Boy)
1679[3] 2032[3] 2718[2] 3752[2] (4127) (4658) 5581[2]

Swimandyouwin (IRE) *Shaun Harley*
4 b g Xaar—Mouette (FR) (Fabulous Dancer (USA))
7199[9]

Swinbrook (USA) *R A Fahey* a86 96
6 ch g Stravinsky(USA) —Dance Diane (USA) (Affirmed (USA))
1836[5] 2688[6] 3481[4] 3911[7] 4816[3] *5312[6]* 5923[6] *6385[5] 7026[11]*

Swindon Town Flyer (IRE) *A B Haynes* a65 68
2 b g Captain Rio—Baltic Breeze (USA) (Labeeb)
814[6] 1315[3] 1989[2] *2949[10]* 3524[5] *3849[7]* 5707[7] 6072[3] 6419[6]

Swing On A Star (IRE) *Miss J Feilden* a61 61
3 br f Celtic Swing—Lady Stalker (Primo Dominie)
2693[15] 3276[10] 4182[3] *4885[7] 5174[5]* 5879[7] *6101[5] 6873[10]*

Swing The Ring (IRE) *A Berry* a70 97
4 b h Rossini(USA) —Sharkiyah (IRE) (Polish Precedent (USA))
3026[7] 3529[8] 3911[12] 4389[14] 5505[9] *6288[4] 6385[7]*

Swiper Hill (IRE) *B Ellison* a72 36
4 b g City On A Hill(USA) —Alkariyh (USA) (Alydar (USA))
673[6] 3053[11] 3723[9] *5177[7] 5643[5] 6123[5] 6579[10] 6882[3] 7079[9] 7131[2] 7146[8] 7249[8]*

Swiss Act *M Johnston* 89
3 ch g Act One—Dancing Mirage (IRE) (Machiavellian (USA))
(1584) 2503a[7] 2790[18]

Swiss Cottage *Niall Madden* a55 99
5 ch g Halling(USA) —African Peace (USA) (Roberto (USA))
3143a[14]

Swiss Franc *D R C Elsworth* 107
2 br c Mr Greeley(USA) —Swiss Lake (USA) (Indian Ridge)
1652[3] (2056) 2316[2] 2732[2] 3459[3] 4721[3]

Swop (IRE) *L M Cumani* a87
4 b g Shinko Forest(IRE) —Changing Partners (Rainbow Quest (USA))
(6546)

Swords *Heather Dalton* a66 56
5 b g Vettori(IRE) —Pomorie (IRE) (Be My Guest (USA))
1032[7] 1152[8] *1314[6]* 1730[3] *3217[12]*

Swordsman (GER) *C Von Der Recke* a81 95
5 b h Acatenango(GER) —Saiga (Windwurf (GER))
1689a[10]

Sworn In (USA) *N I M Rossiter* 101
6 ch h Kingmambo(USA) —Under Oath (USA) (Deputed Testamony (USA))
1654[10] 1793[17]

Sworn Mum (GER) *W Baltromei* 95
3 ch f Samum(GER) —Sweet Tern (GER) (Arctic Tern (USA))
6953a[2]

Sybilia (GER) *J Hirschberger* 81
3 b f Spectrum(IRE) —Slawa (GER) (Polish Precedent (USA))
1338a[10]

Sydneyroughdiamond *M Mullineaux* a41 52
5 b g Whittingham(IRE) —November Song (Scorpio (FR))
2108[5] 2394[13] 2622[8] 3372[2] 3686[8] *5566[8] 5782[13]*

Sylvan (IRE) *S Kirk* 77
3 bb f Shinko Forest(IRE) —Auriga (Belmez (USA))
1837[10] 3798[8] 4257[13]

Sylvias Grove *D Carroll* 67
2 b f Royal Applause—Branston Fizz (Efisio)
5143[11] 5770[4] 6156[9]

Symbol Of Peace (IRE) *J W Unett* a84 84
4 b m Desert Sun—Rosy Lydgate (Last Tycoon (IRE))
112[2] 297[4] (564) 604[2] 675[7] (930) 938[5] 1401[6] 1905[8] 4404[7] 4922[11] 5383[12]

Sympatric Friendly *W J Haggas* 56
3 b f Danehill Dancer(IRE) —Intercede (Pursuit Of Love)
1128[7]

Synergistic (IRE) *M Johnston* 74
2 b c In The Wings—Queens Wharf (IRE) (Ela-Mana-Mou)
5294[2] 5526[4] 5858[3]

Synge Street *R Hannon* a64 59
2 b c Medicean—Keep Quiet (Reprimand)
2443[8] 2941[4] 3550[9] 4202[6] *5127[2] 5896[10] 6438[4]*

Synonymy *M Blanshard* a75 67
4 b g Sinndar(IRE) —Peony (Lion Cavern (USA))
23[4] 213[4] 607[4] (677) 844[3] 994[8] *1253[5]* 1683[7] 2089[6] *2996[3] 3945[10]* 4352[7] *4463[3]* (5007) *5364[2] 5533[11]* 5924[2] 6131[13] *6564[8]*

Synopsis (IRE) *A Fabre* 110
3 ch f In The Wings—Epitome (IRE) (Nashwan (USA))
3564a[6] (4557a) 5352[4] 6030a[4] 6770a[3]

Syriana *A Bailey* 37
2 b f Dubai Destination(USA) —Syrian Dancer (IRE) (Groom Dancer (USA))
6648[19]

Syvilla *Rae Guest* 65
2 b f Nayef(USA) —Dance Steppe (Rambo Dancer (CAN))
6087[5]

Tabadul (IRE) *E A L Dunlop* a107 101
6 b g Cadeaux Genereux—Amaniy (USA) (Dayjur (USA))
(250a) *940[5]* 1245[4] *(1449)* 2209[4] 2815[12] 4043[14]

Tabaret *R M Whitaker* 101
4 ch h Bertolini(USA) —Luanshya (First Trump)
1159[7] 1497[6] 1770[15] 3708[2] 3990[13] 4386[4] 4696[14] 4798[9] 5212[4] 5407[14] 5700[5]

Taboor (IRE) *R M H Cowell* a71 73
9 b g Mujadil(USA) —Christoph's Girl (Efisio)
154[6] 276[2] 432[4] 561[6] 787[5] 1309[8] 1669[5] 1991[18] 2509[11] 3203[10] 3627[4] 3829[14] *7283[3]*

Tabulate *P Howling* a66 59
4 b m Dansili—Let Alone (Warning)
579[3] 742[7] 1265[7] 1671[13] *(2145) 2358[4] 2568[3]* 2831[14] *3946[10] 4361[13] 4592[11] 5020[6] 5531[10] 6265[8] 6613[7]*

Tacid *Dr J D Scargill* a50 46
5 b m Diktat—Defined Feature (IRE) (Nabeel Dancer (USA))
210[8]

Tackcoat (IRE) *Eoin Doyle* a55 62
7 b g Sesaro(USA) —Damaslin (Camden Town)
156[9] 274[5] 393[8] 666[5]

Tactical Move *Mrs V Haigh* 46
2 b c Diktat—My Mariam (Salse (USA))
3833[5] 4293[12]

Tadalavil *M R Channon* 85
2 gr g Clodovil(IRE) —Blandish (USA) (Wild Again (USA))
3967[2] 4335[3] (4611) 4921[5] 5324[15] 5400[5] 6128[3] 6486[13] 6621[4] 6756[5]

Taffetas (FR) *T Doumen* 80
3 b f Nikos—Yota (FR) (Galetto (FR))
2270a[6]

Tafira (IRE) *K R Burke* 40
2 b f Invincible Spirit(IRE) —Sabayik (IRE) (Unfuwain (USA))
3995[12] 4174[5] 4636[7] 5484[11]

Tafiya *J W Hills* a66 73
4 b m Bahri(USA) —Fickle (Danehill (USA))
2521[6] 3803[2] 4458[12] *4738[4]* 5514[2] 6275[5] *6481[6]*

Taghreed (IRE) *W Jarvis* 69
3 b f Zamindar(USA) —Waafiah (Anabaa (USA))
2083[2] 2606[2] 3032[5]

Tag Team (IRE) *John A Harris* a74 53
6 ch g Tagula(IRE) —Okay Baby (IRE) (Treasure Kay)
3[10] 1718[13] 1977[9] 2220[8] 3686[6] *3852[4]* 4180[3] *(5016)* 5340[5] 5556[8] *6671[2] 6818[3] 7026[2] 7271[3]*

Tagula King (IRE) *D Carroll* 36
2 b c Tagula(IRE) —Isla (IRE) (Turtle Island (IRE))
1087[16] 4783[9]

Tagula Sands (IRE) *J C Fox* a42
3 b g Tagula(IRE) —Pomme Pomme (USA) (Dayjur (USA))
6176[8] 6778[7] 7029[10]

Tagula Song (IRE) *J A Geake* a32
3 b f Tagula(IRE) —Bouffant (High Top)
2998[10] 3992[11] 4235[11] *7189[7]*

Tagula Sunrise (IRE) *R A Fahey* 100
5 ch m Tagula(IRE) —Lady From Limerick (IRE) (Rainbows For Life (CAN))
3091[8] 3559[4] 3961[8] 4373[3]

Tahafut *R A Fahey* a41 51
3 b f Marju(IRE) —Farha (USA) (Nureyev (USA))
6764[8] 6935[8]

Tahajjum *C E Brittain* 53
2 b f Diktat—Bundle (Cadeaux Genereux)
6087[8]

Tahdeed *Sir Michael Stoute* a40 73
3 b c Green Desert(USA) —Turn Of A Century (Halling (USA))
2046[5] 3476[7] 3881[14] *4885[9]* 5348[10]

Taikoo *H Morrison* a66 53
2 b c Dr Fong(USA) —So True (So Blessed)
6725[8] *7208[4]*

Taili *D A Nolan* 9
6 b m Taipan(IRE) —Doubtfire (Jalmood (USA))
965[8]

Taine (IRE) *W J Haggas* a70
2 b c Invincible Spirit(IRE) —Farjah (IRE) (Charnwood Forest (IRE))
7000[3]

Taita (GER) *C G Cox* 92
3 ch f Big Shuffle(USA) —Tamarita (GER) (Acatenango (GER))
1338a[9] *7184[13]*

Tajaaweed (USA) *Sir Michael Stoute* 92
2 br c Dynaformer(USA) —Uforia (USA) (Zilzal (USA))
(6106) 6489[10]

Tajdeef (USA) *B W Hills* 111
2 gr c Aljabr(USA) —Tabheej (IRE) (Mujtahid (USA))
(4198) 5406[4] 5975[3]

Tajjree *H J Collingridge* a54 27
4 b m Lujain(USA) —Rateeba (IRE) (Green Desert (USA))
36[4] (125) 251[7] 1748[12] *6528[4] 6957[13]*

Tajneed (IRE) *D K Weld* 96
4 b g Alhaarth(IRE) —Indian Express (Indian Ridge)
3140a[7] 3573a[10] 4211a[10] 5242a[10] 6363a[21]

Tajseed (IRE) *A Manuel* a13 52
7 b g Bahhare(USA) —Dublah (USA) (Private Account (USA))
394a[8]

Tajweed (IRE) *M Johnston* 64
2 ch c Pivotal—Mannakea (USA) (Fairy King (USA))
5598[13] 6592[3]

Takaamul *K A Morgan* a58 54
4 ch g Almutawakel—Mafaatin (IRE) (Royal Academy (USA))
3572[9] 4530[8] 4801[8] *6670[2] 6831[14] 7278[2]*

Takafu (USA) *W S Kittow* a68 88
5 b g Lemon Drop Kid(USA) —Proper Protocol (USA) (Deputy Minister (CAN))
1208[5] (1683) 1959[6] 2675[2] (3858) 4483[6] 5884[5] 6335[12]

Takanewa (IRE) *J Howard Johnson* 67
4 b m Danetime(IRE) —Lady Ingabelle (IRE) (Catrail (USA))
1625[5] 2711[5] 3372[3] 4938[2] 5489[10]

Takaniya (IRE) *A Fabre* 78
3 ch f Rainbow Quest(USA) —Takarouna (USA) (Green Dancer (USA))
2547a[7] 5465a[10]

Take A Bow *P R Chamings* 115
6 b h Royal Applause—Giant Nipper (Nashwan (USA))
1305[3] 1723[2] (2182) 3974[3] 4826[P] (Dead)

Take A Mile (IRE) *B G Powell* a65 65
5 ch g Inchinor—Bu Hagab (IRE) (Royal Academy (USA))
4544[9]

Take Grace (FR) *Y De Nicolay* a99 100
5 b m Take Risks(FR) —Grace Royale (IRE) (Marignan (USA))
(31a)

Take It There *A J Lidderdale* a61 47
5 ch m Cadeaux Genereux—Feel Free (IRE) (Generous (IRE))
6179[8]

Taken (IRE) *J R Fanshawe* a71 71
2 b g Red Ransom(USA) —Heart's Harmony (Blushing Groom (FR))
3625[6] 3958[4] *7191[2]*

Takeover Target (AUS) *J Janiak* 125
8 b g Celtic Swing—Shady Stream (AUS) (Archregent (CAN))
2733[4] 2857[2]

Takes Tutu (USA) *C R Dore* a71 77
8 b g Afternoon Deelites(USA) —Lady Affirmed (USA) (Affirmed (USA))
110[8] 286[8] 389[8] 631[8] 808[9] 2582[8] *(3730)* 4355[11] *4592[2] (4739)* 5257[9]

Take The Gold (IRE) *M A Jarvis* a59 64
3 ch f Grand Lodge(USA) —River Missy (USA) (Riverman (USA))
2836[2] 3908[5] *4430[4]*

Take To The Skies (IRE) *A P Jarvis* a63 53
3 b c Lujain(USA) —To The Skies (USA) (Sky Classic (CAN))
752[4] 1037[9] 3646[4] 4129[10] *4884[9] 6123[14]*

Takitwo *P D Cundell* a72 74
4 b g Delta Dancer—Tiama (IRE) (Last Tycoon (IRE))
130[4] 560[5] (793) 831[3] 923[5] (2272) 2689[3] 2877[5] *3422[11]* 4029[3] 4807[8] *6869[7] 7024[3] 7164[7]*

Talamahana *S Kirk* a55 55
2 b f Kyllachy—Bahawir Pour (USA) (Green Dancer (USA))
2468[5] 2968[9] 4602[15] 5628[8] 5766[12] *6776[9] 6881[7] 7156[4] 7272[4]*

Talayeb *M P Tregoning* 78
2 bb g Nayef(USA) —Paper Chase (FR) (Machiavellian (USA))
3435[8] 4151[4] 5590[4]

Talbot Avenue *M Blanshard* a97 103
9 b g Puissance—Dancing Daughter (Dance In Time (CAN))
41[6] 490[6] 818[2] 1986[5] 3268[7] 4095[14] 4204[5] 4696[8] 5050[11]

Talcen Gwyn (IRE) *M F Harris* a50 67
5 b g Fayruz—Cheerful Knight (IRE) (Mac's Imp (USA))
2516[9] 2966[7] (3179) 3449[3] 3594[9] 4390[3] 4689[7] 4939[6] 5272[4] 5349[3] 5726[3] *6174[8]* 6424[17]

Talent Search (USA) *Mark Shuman* a115
4 ch g Catienus(USA) —Mrs K (USA) (Dixieland Band (USA))
5852a[2] 6510a[3]

Tale Of Ekati (USA) *B Tagg* a107
2 b c Tale Of The Cat(USA) —Silence Beauty (JPN) (Sunday Silence (USA))
6508a[4]

Tale Of Two Cities (IRE) *A P O'Brien* 96
2 b c Sadler's Wells(USA) —Kasora (IRE) (Darshaan)
6782a[6]

Talihoya (IRE) *M Halford* 83
4 b m Imperial Ballet(IRE) —Pasadena Lady (Captain James)
6553a[8]

Talk More (USA) *J Noseda* 70
3 b f More Than Ready(USA) —Pomarola Talk (ARG) (Confidental Talk (USA))
1128[4] 4178[7]

Talk Of Excitment *Charles O'Brien* a38 72
3 b f Cadeaux Genereux—Chameleon (Green Desert (USA))
6916a[12]

Talk Of Saafend (IRE) *R Hannon* a54 80
2 b f Barathea(IRE) —Sopran Marida (IRE) (Darshaan)
1354[8] *1586[5] 1945[6] 3642[11]* 3909[2] 4364[3] 4812[2] 5350[7] (6012)

Tallulah Sunrise *M D I Usher* a69 36
2 b f Auction House(USA) —Tallulah Belle (Crowning Honors (CAN))
3589[11] *6964[5] 7084[4] 7260[3]*

Talon (IRE) *W J Haggas* 52
2 ch g Indian Ridge—Brief Lullaby (IRE) (Brief Truce (USA))
4110[14] 4488[7] 5343[12] 6410[8]

Tamagin (USA) *K A Ryan* a107 102
4 b h Stravinsky(USA) —Luia (USA) (Forty Niner (USA))
(3762) (4367) 5356[2] 5638[2] *5891[2]* (6472) *(6668)*

Tamarack (IRE) *W R Muir* 60
3 b g Tamarisk(IRE) —Sound Tap (IRE) (Warning)
1923[10] 2470[4] 2878[17] 4079[11]

Tamara Moon (IRE) *M R Channon* a60 74
2 b f Acclamation—Non Ultra (USA) (Peintre Celebre (USA))
1503[6] 2457[10] 3152[8] (3838) 4278[9] 4991[8] (5443) 6498[9] *6644[7]*

Tamasou (IRE) *S Parr* a67 69
2 b c Tamarisk(IRE) —Soubresaut (IRE) (Danehill (USA))
5902[2] 6307[4] *6675[2] 6763[3]*

Tamatave (IRE) *M W Easterby* a71 66
5 b g Darshaan—Manuetti (IRE) (Sadler's Wells (USA))
206[9] 374[8] 466[8] 2795[15] *5336[12]*

Tamdiid (USA) *C E Brittain* a63 52
2 b f Horse Chestnut(SAF) —Ladue (USA) (Demons Begone (USA))
4169[10] *5727[4]*

Tamino (IRE) *P Howling* a66 81
4 b g Mozart(IRE) —Stop Out (Rudimentary (USA))
1214[5] 1669[9] 1969[4] 2665[3] (3549) 3828[7] (4767) 5874[3] 6450[2] *7253[11]*

Tam Lin *Saeed Bin Suroor* 118
4 b h Selkirk(USA) —La Nuit Rose (FR) (Rainbow Quest (USA))
2182[6] 3271[2] 4005[3] 4825[5]

Tamrai Dancer *R M Beckett* 71
2 b f Tamure(IRE) —Rail Cat (Catrail (USA))
1354[6] 1762[7] (2911) 3275[2] 4202[10] 5871[6]

Tamreen (IRE) *G L Moore* a84 89
6 b g Bahhare(USA) —Na-Ayim (IRE) (Shirley Heights)
693[5]

Tamworth (IRE) *E J Creighton* a66 53
5 b g Perugino(USA) —Faiblesse (Welsh Saint)
72[11] 2258[10] 3730[12] 6935[5]

Tan Bonita (USA) *M J Wallace* a55 73
2 bb f More Than Ready(USA) —Time For Hennessy (USA) (Hennessy (USA))
1354[3] (1553) 2134[10] 4098[10] *6828[3]*

Tancredi (SWE) *N B King* a76 73
5 b g Rossini(USA) —Begine (IRE) (Germany (USA))
(279) 363[6] 426[3] 459[U] 538[3] 564[5] 686[6] (831) 975[2] 1036[6] 1283[7] 1847[18] 2831[11] *7143[9]*

Tanforan *B P J Baugh* a77 87
5 b g Mujahid(USA) —Florentynna Bay (Aragon)
262[5] 4289[10] 4719[5] *5177[8] 5645[7] 6146[9] 6431[9] 6627[6] (6764) 6869[2] 7024[2] 7143[5]*

Tang *W G M Turner* a55 61
3 ch f Bahamian Bounty—Hymne (FR) (Saumarez)
54[3] 511[3] 619[5] 2652[8] 4226[8] *4974[7]* 5716[6] *6402[9]*

Tangible *Liam McAteer* a65 79
5 b m Hernando(FR) —Trinity Reef (Bustino)
5586[3] 6555a[5]

Tango Foxtrot (IRE) *W P Mullins* 90
5 bb g Foxhound(USA) —Tango Two Thousand (IRE) (Sri Pekan (USA))
4051a[6]

Tango Jack (USA) *Eve Johnson Houghton* 65
2 ch c Stravinsky(USA) —Life In Seattle (USA) (Unbridled (USA))
2596[7] (2907)

Tango Step (IRE) *Bernard Lawlor* a67 72
7 b g Sesaro(USA) —Leitrim Lodge (IRE) (Classic Music (USA))
361[4] 873a[8] *6795[8] 6854[6] 6946[5]*

Tanja Belle (GER) *W Hickst* 98
4 ch m Banyumanik(IRE) —Ta Sterna (GER) (General Assembly (USA))
6690a[5]

Tanley *J F Coupland* a49 59
2 gr g Compton Admiral—Schatzi (Chilibang)
2028[4] 2392[5] 3410[2] 4349[9] 4715[2] 6326[11] 6557[4] *6799[9]*

Tanning *M Appleby* a39 53
5 b m Atraf—Gerundive (USA) (Twilight Agenda (USA))
7157[7]

Tantien *T Keddy* a35 40
5 b m Diktat—Tahilla (Moorestyle)
431[11] 1221[9] *1311[8]* 2304[4] 3045[6] 3754[11]

Tantris (IRE) *J A Osborne* a59
2 b g High Chaparral(IRE) —Emerald Cut (Rainbow Quest (USA))
6358[5]

Tanweer (USA) *Sir Michael Stoute* 89
2 ch g Seeking The Gold(USA) —Fitted Crown (USA) (Chief's Crown (USA))
(4362) 5414[5]

Tanzanite (IRE) *D W P Arbuthnot* a96 100
5 b m Revoque(IRE) —Resume (IRE) (Lahib (USA))
658[3] 848[18] *1524[9]* 1789[7] 6299[11] *6604[12] 6929[7]*

Tapas Lad (IRE) *V Smith* a59 55
2 b c Modigliani(USA) —Missish (Mummy's Pet)
2303[8] 2604[7] 2941[12] 5869[6] 6536[3] *6775[3] 6865[3] 6978[3] 7010[3] 7149[7] 7286[5]*

Tapisserie (GER) *C Von Der Recke* 26
2 b f Second Set(IRE) —Trance Dancer (Mtoto)
5462a[8] 5848a[9]

Tapsalteerie *M W Easterby* a30 19
4 b m Tipsy Creek(USA) —Croft Sally (Crofthall)
710[9] 766[8] 1221[12]

Taqseem (IRE) *M Al Muhairi* a101 104
4 b g Fantastic Light(USA) —Elshamms (Zafonic (USA))
472a[6] 528a[6]

Tar (IRE) *Kevin Prendergast* 80
3 b c Danzig(USA) —Royal Show (IRE) (Sadler's Wells (USA))
4836a[10] 6553a[15]

Taraba (IRE) *Miss S Collins* a71 39
4 b m Inchinor—Tarabaya (IRE) (Warning)
4371a[10]

Taralaya (IRE) *John M Oxx* 93
3 b f Kahyasi—Taradiya (IRE) (Danehill (USA))
6366a^{15}

Taran Tregarth *W M Brisbourne* a42 34
3 b f Tobougg(IRE) —Little Change (Grundy)
4989^{5} 5803^{11} 6501^{5} 6815^{10} 6835^{11}

Tara's Force (IRE) *J J Quinn* 53
2 b f Acclamation—Tara's Girl (IRE) (Fayruz)
1107^{7}

Tara's Garden *M Blanshard* 56
2 b f Dr Fong(USA) —Tremiere (FR) (Anabaa (USA))
5918^{8} 6494^{10}

Tara Too (IRE) *J G Portman* a81 93
4 b m Danetime(IRE) —Gone With The Wind (IRE) (Common Grounds)
1195^{16} 1525^{4} 2085^{5} 2626^{7} 3623^{9} 4589^{5} (4855) 5115^{12} 6208^{10}

Tarbolton (IRE) *M Johnston* 63
2 b c King's Best(USA) —Golly Gosh (IRE) (Danehill (USA))
4547^{8} 4890^{9} 5749^{3}

Tarellia *Enda Kelly* a51 57
3 gr f Pivotal—Amarella (FR) (Balleroy (USA))
2259^{4}

Tariq *P W Chapple-Hyam* 118
3 ch c Kyllachy—Tatora (Selkirk (USA))
1147^{5} 1703a^{13} (2043) (2752) (4045) 6029a^{5}

Tarkamara (IRE) *P F I Cole* a70 78
3 ch f Medicean—Tarakana (USA) (Shahrastani (USA))
1610^{10} 3062^{2} 4066^{2} 4513^{2} 4801^{5} 5714^{7}

Tarkheena Prince (USA) *G A Swinbank* 79
2 b g Aldebaran(USA) —Tarkheena (USA) (Alleged (USA))
3760^{3} 4037^{7}

Tarraburn (USA) *J Howard Johnson* 73
3 ch g Eltish(USA) —Rahy's Wish (USA) (Rahy (USA))
2313^{4} 4080^{7} 4940^{8}

Tartan Bearer (IRE) *Sir Michael Stoute* 83
2 ch c Spectrum(IRE) —Highland Gift (IRE) (Generous (IRE))
6618^{2}

Tartan Special *K R Burke* a54 50
5 b g Fasliyev(USA) —Colchica (Machiavellian (USA))
94^{9} 518^{8}

Tartan Tie *M Johnston* 83
3 b c Grand Lodge(USA) —Trois Graces (USA) (Alysheba (USA))
(2118)

Tartatartufata *D Shaw* a94 71
5 b m Tagula(IRE) —It's So Easy (Shaadi (USA))
79^{3} 155^{4} 554^{5} 5806^{13} 6157^{15} 6355^{11} (6860) 7078^{3} 7179^{2} 7215^{3}

Tarteel (USA) *J L Dunlop* 99
3 b f Bahri(USA) —Elrehaan (Sadler's Wells (USA))
(2883) (3430) 4118^{15} 5047^{13}

Tarte Tatin (IRE) *J L Dunlop* a30
3 b f Sakhee(USA) —Femme Fatale (Fairy King (USA))
6766^{12} 6901^{6}

Tartouche *Mrs John Harrington* 109
6 b m Pursuit Of Love—Megan's Flight (Welsh Pageant)
875a^{3} 1330a^{7}

Tasdeer (USA) *M A Jarvis* 86
2 b c Rahy(USA) —Mehthaaf (USA) (Nureyev (USA))
5091^{4} (5541) 5972^{8}

Tasha's Miracle (USA) *J W Sadler* a104
2 b f Harlan's Holiday(USA) —Ms Cuvee Napa (USA) (Relaunch (USA))
5826a^{5} 6507a^{4}

Tasheba *P W Chapple-Hyam* 73
2 ch c Dubai Destination(USA) —Tatanka (IRE) (Lear Fan (USA))
5361^{13} 5951^{12} (6571)

Tashelka (FR) *A Fabre* 114
3 gr f Mujahid(USA) —Tashiriya (IRE) (Kenmare (FR))
(4654a) 5465a^{8} 6460a^{7} (6770a)

Task Complete *Jean-Rene Auvray* a59 53
4 ch m Bahamian Bounty—Taskone (Be My Chief (USA))
22^{3} 189^{9} 557^{6} 801^{8} 1001^{8} 1899^{8} 3031^{4} 3966^{3} 5129^{4} 6290^{7} 6895^{11}

Tasleya *B W Hills* 49
2 b c Oasis Dream—Princess Athena (Ahonoora)
3462^{11}

Tass Heel (IRE) *B J Llewellyn* a72 62
8 b g Danehill(USA) —Mamouna (USA) (Vaguely Noble)
39^{13}

Tastahil (IRE) *B W Hills* a76 86
3 ch c Singspiel(IRE) —Luana (Shaadi (USA))
1106^{12}

Tastumaki *F Caenepeel* 90
3 b c Barathea(IRE) —Dardshi (IRE) (Darshaan)
2751a^{6}

Tasweet (IRE) *T G Mills* a71 66
3 b g Mujahid(USA) —Injaad (Machiavellian (USA))
(116) 196^{6} 725^{9} 5339^{7} 5819^{7} 6121^{7} 6547^{12}

Tatbeeq (IRE) *M A Jarvis* 70
2 b f Invincible Spirit(IRE) —Announcing Peace (Danehill (USA))
2122^{4} 2658^{3}

Tathkaar *C E Brittain* 74
2 ch f Dr Fong(USA) —Royal Patron (Royal Academy (USA))
5633^{4} 6015^{2}

Tatillius (IRE) *J M Bradley* 11
4 ch g King Charlemagne(USA) —Aunty Eileen (Ahonoora)
4616^{10}

Tatsuya (FR) *J-C Rouget* a96 96
3 b c Night Shift(USA) —Lamballe (USA) (Woodman (USA))
436a^{4}

Taurian *Mrs L Stubbs* 93
2 b g Zamindar(USA) —Moon Carnival (Be My Guest (USA))
1087^{5} (1487) 2024^{4} 3550^{6} (4154) (4769) 5410^{3} 5629^{3} (Dead)

Tavalu (USA) *G L Moore* a72 68
5 b g Kingmambo(USA) —Larrocha (IRE) (Sadler's Wells (USA))
213^{10} 691^{2} 1526^{2} 3653^{4}

Tavares (IRE) *J Jay* a37 61
4 b g King Charlemagne(USA) —Tadkiyra (IRE) (Darshaan)
2580^{9} 2913^{6} 3881^{7} 4333^{11} 4660^{11} 5020^{11} 5894^{10} 6131^{16}

Tawaash (USA) *M A Jarvis* 93
2 bb c Storm Cat(USA) —Victory Ride (USA) (Seeking The Gold (USA))
6295^{2}

Tawaassol (USA) *Sir Michael Stoute* 111
4 b h War Chant(USA) —Montecito (USA) (Seeking The Gold (USA))
4090^{9} 4798^{7} 5112^{8} 5953^{4} 6183^{19}

Tawnybrack (IRE) *Jane Chapple-Hyam* 74
3 b g Rossini(USA) —Ceannanas (IRE) (Magical Wonder (USA))
2186^{7}

Tawqeet (USA) *D Hayes* 120
5 ch h Kingmambo(USA) —Caerless (IRE) (Caerleon (USA))
6354a^{5} 6712a^{14}

Tawzeea (IRE) *M Johnston* 72
2 ch c Cadeaux Genereux—Kismah (Machiavellian (USA))
5193^{3} 5621^{2}

Tax Free (IRE) *D Nicholls* a89 118
5 b g Tagula(IRE) —Grandel (Owington)
249a^{4} 597a^{8} (1159) (1497) (2324a) 2733^{11} 3139a^{2} 4090^{3} (5468a) 5953^{3}

Tayarat (IRE) *M P Tregoning* a72 80
2 b g Noverre(USA) —Sincere (IRE) (Bahhare (USA))
1781^{9} 3270^{4} 4110^{7} 4964^{7} (5571)

Tay Bridge (IRE) *G F Bridgwater* a10 24
4 ch g Tagula(IRE) —Wild Liffey (USA) (Irish River (FR))
3032^{6}

Tayman (IRE) *Carl Llewellyn* a69 70
5 bb g Sinndar(IRE) —Sweet Emotion (IRE) (Bering)
4322^{4}

Tazawud *M Johnston* 56
2 ch g Noverre(USA) —Alhufoof (USA) (Dayjur (USA))
926^{5} 1107^{9}

Tazeez (USA) *J H M Gosden* 80
3 bb g Silver Hawk(USA) —Soiree Russe (USA) (Nureyev (USA))
5915^{2} 6597^{2}

Taziria (SWI) *C Bocksai* 67
6 br m Zilzal Zamaan(USA) —Taly (GER) (Goofalik (USA))
438a^{6}

Tcherina (IRE) *T D Easterby* 85
5 b m Danehill Dancer(IRE) —Forget Paris (IRE) (Broken Hearted)
1258^{2} (1771) 2314^{3} 2987^{5} 5145^{9} 5814^{5} 6158^{7} 6620^{8}

Tea Cake (IRE) *H J L Dunlop* a60 49
2 b f Compton Place—Griddle Cake (IRE) (Be My Guest (USA))
3895^{16} 5766^{22} 6228^{6}

Teachers Choice (IRE) *Adrian McGuinness* 83
4 b g Fruits Of Love(USA) —Son Chou (Cyrano De Bergerac)
6363a^{4}

Teadancer (IRE) *J G Portman* a53 6
2 b f Traditionally(USA) —Dance Up A Storm (USA) (Storm Bird (CAN))
4709^{3} 5309^{9} 5944^{10}

Teammate (USA) *H A Jerkens* a112
4 rg m A.P. Indy(USA) —Starry Dreamer (USA) (Rubiano (USA))
6512a^{11}

Tears Of A Clown (IRE) *J A Osborne* a85 96
4 b g Galileo(IRE) —Mood Swings (IRE) (Shirley Heights)
3672^{2} (3899) 4388^{7} 5764^{3}

Teasing *J Pearce* a86 73
3 b f Lujain(USA) —Movieland (USA) (Nureyev (USA))
1009^{4} 1535^{6} 2534^{8} 3960^{10} 6024^{3} (6232) 6568^{2} 6795^{2} 7045^{2} (7158) 7289^{7}

Teatime Lady (USA) *T D Barron* 33
2 bb f Stormin Fever(USA) —Tea Service (USA) (Atticus (USA))
1193^{11}

Tebee *J H M Gosden* a74 84
3 ch f Selkirk(USA) —Massarra (Danehill (USA))
1127^{8} 2766^{6} (3400) 4185^{2} 5131^{4} 5814^{4}

Teddy Monty (IRE) *R E Barr* a51 30
4 b g Bold Fact(USA) —Mount Soufriere (IRE) (Maledetto (IRE))
61^{7} 243^{14} 1221^{13} 1527^{14}

Tedstale (USA) *K A Ryan* a77 72
9 ch g Irish River(FR) —Carefree Kate (USA) (Lyphard (USA))
730^{3} 891^{6} 966^{4} 1376^{2} 1554^{3}

Tee Jay Kassidy *P S McEntee* a61 48
7 b g Petong—Priceless Fantasy (Dunbeath (USA))
7^{8}

Teen Ager (FR) *J S Moore* a80 66
3 b g Invincible Spirit(IRE) —Tarwiya (IRE) (Dominion)
758^{3} (1117) 1930^{4} 3480^{7} 3944^{9} 4360^{2} 4965^{10} 6231^{6} 6492^{8}

Teen Spirit (IRE) *J W Hills* 20
2 b g Sinndar(IRE) —Whitefoot (Be My Chief (USA))
6130^{13}

Tejareb (IRE) *C E Brittain* a47 50
4 b m Sadler's Wells(USA) —La Pepite (USA) (Mr Prospector (USA))
3236^{10} 4948^{8} 5709^{11}

Telegonus *D McCain Jnr* a71 65
4 b g Fantastic Light(USA) —Circe's Isle (Be My Guest (USA))
869^{4} 1231^{3} 3076^{5} 5774^{9}

Telepathic (IRE) *A Berry* a33 56
7 b g Mind Games—Madrina (Waajib)
135^{7} 912^{6} 1423^{6} 1594^{13} 3674^{8} 3996^{3} 4494^{9}

Tell *J L Dunlop* 114
4 b h Green Desert(USA) —Cephalonie (USA) (Kris S (USA))
411a^{6} 544a^{9} 3103^{6} 5213^{9} (5444) 6009^{2} 6298^{4} 6655^{2}

Telling *Mrs A Duffield* a41 52
3 b g Josr Algarhoud(IRE) —Crystal Canyon (Efisio)
1232^{8} 1579^{16} 6700^{5} 7133^{5}

Tell It As It Is (USA) *James J Smith* a82 89
3 b f Chester House(USA) —Talltalelady (USA) (Naskra (USA))
6772a^{3}

Tell Me What (FR) *R Hannon* a52 44
2 b f Diktat—Galgarina (FR) (Double Bed (FR))
1945^{7} 3878^{8}

Telltime (IRE) *A M Balding* a70 78
3 b f Danetime(IRE) —Tesla (IRE) (Fayruz)
17^{2} (231) 1450^{5} (2144) 2629^{2} 3430^{5} 3961^{5} 4420^{5} 5238^{6}

Temecula (IRE) *M Halford* 81
2 b f High Chaparral(IRE) —Gujarat (USA) (Distant View (USA))
5395a^{7}

Temlett (IRE) *W P Mullins* 105
3 ch g Desert Prince(IRE) —Bering Down (USA) (Bering)
3664a^{4} 4647a^{5}

Tempelstern (GER) *H R A Cecil* 96
3 gr c Sternkoenig(IRE) —Temple Esprit (Esprit Du Nord (USA))
1129^{2} 1849^{7} 2185^{4} (3041) (3883) 4749^{16}

Temple Of Thebes (IRE) *E A L Dunlop* a73
2 b f Bahri(USA) —Franglais (GER) (Lion Cavern (USA))
2992^{3} 3417^{2}

Temple Place (IRE) *D McCain Jnr* 98
6 b g Sadler's Wells(USA) —Puzzled Look (USA) (Gulch (USA))
(1583) 1767^{17}

Templet (USA) *W G Harrison* a68 52
7 b g Souvenir Copy(USA) —Two Step Trudy (USA) (Capote (USA))
533^{6}

Templetuohy Max (IRE) *J D Bethell*
2 b g Orpen(USA) —Eladawn (IRE) (Ela-Mana-Mou)
4279^{P}

Tempsford Flyer (IRE) *J W Hills* a87 87
4 b g Fasliyev(USA) —Castellane (FR) (Danehill (USA))
1905^{4} 2469^{8} 4889^{13} 5203^{7} 5568^{9} 6088^{6} 6412^{5}

Temtation (IRE) *J A Pickering* a56 70
3 b f Trans Island—Ish (IRE) (Danehill (USA))
588^{4} 659^{2} 778^{7} 1213^{4} 1453^{5} 1709^{2} 1943^{8} 2195^{4} 2459^{6} 2826^{3} 3281^{10} 3597^{7} 3811^{9} 7108^{4}

Tenancy (IRE) *A J McCabe* a67 69
3 b g Rock Of Gibraltar(IRE) —Brush Strokes (Cadeaux Genereux)
1297^{6} 1634^{4} 2120^{5} 4291^{9} 4616^{3} 4795^{3} 5386^{8} 5890^{12} 6149^{10} 6562^{7} 6720^{15} 7137^{3}

Ten A Penny (USA) *J A Osborne* a87 100
3 b c Gulch(USA) —Dramatical (USA) (Theatrical)
(106) (591) (754) (1089) 1476^{4}

Ten Black *R Brotherton* a55 48
3 ch g Dr Fong(USA) —Pulau Pinang (IRE) (Dolphin Street (FR))
25^{6} 139^{7} 454^{5} 534^{5} 667^{10} 4256^{14} 5235^{8} 5345^{6} 6060^{9} 7133^{9}

Tencendur (IRE) *D Nicholls* a79 79
3 ch g King Charlemagne(USA) —Jallaissine (IRE) (College Chapel)
815^{4} 1110^{3} 3196^{7} 3707^{11} (4222) 4450^{2} 4785^{8} 5043^{6}

Tendalay (USA) *J A Osborne* a78
3 bb g Red Ransom(USA) —Mandalay Point (USA) (Gilded Time (USA))
(128) (589)

Tender Falcon *R J Hodges* 85
7 br g Polar Falcon(USA) —Tendresse (IRE) (Tender King)
995^{10} 1621^{12} 1959^{10} 3385^{6}

Tender Moments *C F Wall* 77
3 br f Tomba—Cherish Me (Polar Falcon (USA))
1837^{13}

Tender Process (IRE) *E S McMahon* a83 84
4 b g Monashee Mountain(USA) —Appledorn (Doulab (USA))
1565^{3} 1854^{11} 2912^{9} 5747^{16}

Tender The Great (IRE) *B G Powell* a92 84
4 br m Indian Lodge(IRE) —Tender Guest (IRE) (Be My Guest (USA))
85^{3} 211^{4} (1534) 2085^{4} (2492) 2883^{9} 3591^{3} 4268^{2} 4827^{3} 5203^{4} (5532) 5950^{9} 6208^{2} 6391^{2} 6606^{3} 6900^{6} 6970^{4} 7165^{10}

Tender Trap (IRE) *Miss J E Foster* a87 22
9 b g Sadler's Wells(USA) —Shamiyda (USA) (Sir Ivor (USA))
153^{9}

Ten Down *J A Osborne* a77 81
2 b g Royal Applause—Upstream (Prince Sabo)
926^{2} 1058^{2} (1540) 1608^{5} 2199^{4} 3426^{7} 3925^{11} 4315^{9} 6004^{6} (6977) (7072)

Tendulkar's Diva (IRE) *A Berry* 11
2 b f Tendulkar(USA) —Daring Connection (Danzig Connection (USA))
6306^{14}

Tenement (IRE) *Jamie Poulton* a57 53
3 b g Mull Of Kintyre(USA) —Afifah (Nashwan (USA))
208^{6} 293^{8} 417^{2} 1316^{4} 1634^{10} 2362^{11}

Ten For Tosca (IRE) *R A Harris* a23 54
3 b g Distant Music(USA) —Errazuriz (IRE) (Classic Music (USA))
4919^{11} 5564^{11} 7209^{12}

Tenjack King *J A Osborne* a77 77
2 b c Kyllachy—Rash (Pursuit Of Love)
4882^{3} 5344^{3} 5646^{3}

Tenjack Queen (IRE) *Miss Tor Sturgis* a64 65
2 b f Intikhab(USA) —Kooyong (IRE) (College Chapel)
2457^{9} 3109^{2} 3417^{6} 4359^{6} 5133^{5} 6151^{6} 6426^{12}

Ten Meropa (USA) *J A Osborne* a94 69
2 b c Johannesburg(USA) —Tenderly (IRE) (Danehill (USA))
2398^{3} (2949) 4152^{11} 4975^{3} 5219^{6}

Ten On Line (IRE) *J G M O'Shea* a53 55
2 ch c Rossini(USA) —Fastnet (Forzando)
2247^{5} 2356^{4} 2723^{7} 3065^{2} 3614^{2} 3835^{5} 5302^{11} 5644^{8} 6566^{8}

Ten Pole Tudor *R A Harris* a78 73
2 b g Royal Applause—Amaniy (USA) (Dayjur (USA))
4316^{6} 4904^{12} 5302^{2} 5707^{2} 6451^{5} 6750^{5} (6800) (6936) 7095^{4}

Ten Prophets (IRE) *J J Bridger* a67 30
4 b g Namid—Mrs Evans (IRE) (College Chapel)
9^{6} 33^{8} 504^{8} 866^{12} 1317^{10}

Tenraninthemist (IRE) *T D McCarthy* a38
2 gr f Tendulkar(USA) —Saranyu (IRE) (Rusticaro (FR))
6139^{8} 6777^{10} 6928^{12}

Tense (IRE) *J A Osborne* a67 64
2 b f Invincible Spirit(IRE) —Roses From Ridey (IRE) (Petorius)
4756^{8} 5201^{4} 5428^{6} 6665^{6} 6973^{3} 7190^{3}

Ten Shun *P D Evans* a79 82
4 ch g Pivotal—Mint Royale (IRE) (Cadeaux Genereux)
902^{6} 3802^{8} 4561^{10} 5981^{11}

Tension Mounts (IRE) *J A Osborne* a74
2 b g Daggers Drawn(USA) —Dazzling Maid (IRE) (Tate Gallery (USA))
4883^{2} 5222^{3} 5605^{4}

Tension Point *J A Osborne* a65 68
3 b g Hernando(FR) —Blessed (IRE) (Jurado (USA))
58^{4} 116^{3} 209^{3}

Ten Spot (IRE) *Stef Liddiard* a58 43
2 b f Intikhab(USA) —Allergy (Alzao (USA))
4265^{6} (5644) 5896^{7} 6207^{9} 6776^{5} 7031^{11} 7117^{10} 7182^{8} 7204^{4}

Tenterhooks (IRE) *A J McCabe* a49 48
3 b f Orpen(USA) —Punta Gorda (IRE) (Roi Danzig (USA))
224^{11} 357^{4} 572^{8} 832^{8} 1008^{5} 1281^{7} 1426^{3} 1912^{5} 2110^{3} 2591^{7} 2718^{9} 4842^{8} 5041^{8} 6090^{7}

Tenth Night (IRE) *P T Midgley* 49
2 b c Mujadil(USA) —Starlight Venture (IRE) (Hernando (FR))
1993^{6} 2241^{13} 2723^{5} 4136^{10} 4363^{9} 5932^{13} 6305^{4}

Ten To The Dozen *P W Hiatt* a58 62
4 b g Royal Applause—Almost Amber (USA) (Mt. Livermore (USA))
2716^{14} 3615^{6} 4042^{11} 4129^{8} 4469^{6} (4685) 5190^{4} 5433^{3} 5708^{2} 5862^{6} 6447^{7} (6537) 6749^{11}

Teodora Adivina *H R A Cecil* a61 79
3 b f Fantastic Light(USA) —Omara (USA) (Storm Cat (USA))
1364^{3} 4765^{3} (5304) 5738^{2} 6021^{7} (6253) 6474^{12}

Teorban (POL) *Mrs N S Evans* a64 46
8 b g Don Corleone—Tabaka (POL) (Pyjama Hunt)
213^{14} 482^{2} 607^{2} 677^{10} 1526^{13} 5204^{3} 5948^{5}

Tepee *L M Cumani* a62 50
2 ch f Halling(USA) —Tentpole (USA) (Rainbow Quest (USA))
5344^{9} 5682^{4} 6119^{12} 6543^{6}

Tequila Rose (IRE) *M A Buckley* a47 34
4 b m Danehill Dancer(IRE) —Enthrone (USA) (Diesis)
350^{14} 908^{6} 1175^{11}

Tequila Sheila (IRE) *M A Allen* a37 61
5 ch m Raise A Grand(IRE) —Hever Rosina (Efisio)
2302^{16} 2714^{15} (4595) 5935^{16} 7006^{8} 7148^{8}

Terandeil *J G M O'Shea* 13
3 b f Auction House(USA) —Frisson (Slip Anchor)
1197^{11} 2077^{13} 6062^{14}

Terentia *E S McMahon* 108
4 br m Diktat—Agrippina (Timeless Times (USA))
927^{4} 1456^{3} (1788) 3344^{8} 4090^{10}

Terenzium (IRE) *Micky Hammond* a61 55
5 br g Cape Cross(IRE) —Tatanka (ITY) (Luge)
1132^{9} 1918^{3} 2302^{11} 2431^{7} 2820^{5} 4219^{10} 4998^{4} 5503^{8}

Terminate (GER) *Ian Williams* a62 67
5 ch g Acatenango(GER) —Taghareed (USA) (Shadeed (USA))
4365^{9} 4667^{5} 5094^{6} 5497^{3} (5886) 6196^{4} 6458^{10}

Termsandconditions (IRE) *W J Haggas* a26
3 b f Rock Of Gibraltar(IRE) —Council Rock (General Assembly (USA))
193^{10} 260^{11}

Terracos Do Pinhal *M Johnston* 65
2 b g Selkirk(USA) —Sister Bluebird (Bluebird (USA))
3842^{9} 4930^{7} 5227^{6}

Terra Incognita *Y De Nicolay* 99
3 b f Rock Of Gibraltar(IRE) —Terre A Terre (FR) (Kaldounevees (FR))
1388a^{3} 2290a^{6}

Terrasini (FR) *J Howard Johnson* 56
2 gr g Linamix(FR) —Trazando (Forzando)
2983^{6} 3510^{9}

Terra Verde (IRE) *A Al Raihe* 56
5 ch h Indian Ridge—Vituisa (Bering)
473a^{13} 528a^{10}

Terrific Challenge (USA) *Doug Watson* a112 105
5 ch h Royal Academy(USA) —Clever Empress (Crafty Prospector (USA))
(597a) 860a^{7}

Terry Molloy (IRE) *K R Burke* a59 69
3 b g Xaar—Pile (USA) (Shadeed (USA))
1289^{9} 2565^{6} 3804^{8} 4155^{2} 4220^{2} 4526^{4} 5966^{5} 6431^{3}

Terry's Tip (IRE) *Mrs L Stubbs* 86
2 b g Namid—Kadarassa (IRE) (Warning)
2297[8] 5521[2] 5974[4] 6281[3]
Teslin (IRE) *B Ellison* 109
3 b g In The Wings—Yukon Hope (USA) (Forty Niner (USA))
1103[8] 1475[5] 1803[4] 4093[14] (4799) (5639) 6011[3]
Tessie Bear *Andrew Reid* a50
2 b f Red Ransom(USA) —Macaerleon (IRE) (Caerleon (USA))
6847[10] 6948[11] 7222[4]
Tetouan *R Charlton* a74 88
3 b c Danehill Dancer(IRE) —Souk (IRE) (Ahonoora)
633[2] 737[6] (1297) 1929[2] 2340[2] 3709[4] 4332[2]
Tetrode (USA) *M F Harris* a39 59
5 b g Quiet American(USA) —Mother Courage (Busted)
156[13] 318[7] 789[10]
Teuflesberg (USA) *Jamie Sanders* a115 106
3 b c Johannesburg(USA) —St. Michele (USA) (Devil's Bag (USA))
1486a[17]
Teutonic (IRE) *R F Fisher* a46 41
6 b m Revoque(IRE) —Classic Ring (IRE) (Auction Ring (USA))
240[9]
Tevez *M H Tompkins* a63 68
2 b c Sakhee(USA) —Sosumi (Be My Chief (USA))
3747[10] 5598[5] *6934[3] 7204[6]*
Te Voglio Bene (BRZ) *M D Wolfson* a81
4 ch h Invitato Mio(BRZ) —Alika Girl (BRZ) (Derek (BRZ))
173a[7] 410a[8] 596a[6]
Tewkesbury (IRE) *Mrs K Waldron*
3 b g King's Best(USA) —Zeferina (IRE) (Sadler's Wells (USA))
7174[8] 7239[12]
Texas Fever (USA) *M Stidham* a104 102
2 b c Victory Gallop(CAN) —Fortyniner Fever (USA) (Forty Niner (USA))
6484a[6]
Texas Gold *W R Muir* a108 106
9 ch g Cadeaux Genereux—Star Tulip (Night Shift (USA))
1986[9] 2440[11] 3268[8] 3526[11] 4095[4] 4386[11] 4806[12] 5050[8] 5278[2] 5447[3] 5689[10] *6141[3] 6231[8] 6589[2] 6707[2] 7087[4]*
Teyaar *M Wellings* a54 46
11 b g Polar Falcon(USA) —Music In My Life (IRE) (Law Society (USA))
(83) 189[7] 217[6] 337[4] 366[12] 622[8] 722[10] 920[9] 4351[11]
Thabaat *B W Hills* 90
3 ch g Pivotal—Maraatib (IRE) (Green Desert (USA))
(901) 1603[9] 4811[8] 5804[2] 6301[16]
Thajja (IRE) *Doug Watson* a103 91
6 b h Daylami(IRE) —Jawlaat (USA) (Dayjur (USA))
249a[2] 597a[4] 860a[14]
Thannaan (USA) *B W Hills* 74
2 gr c Elusive Quality(USA) —Lady Aloma (CAN) (Cozzene (USA))
5591[4] 6125[2]
Thanxforthat (USA) *J J Quinn* 60
2 gr g Alphabet Soup(USA) —Paper Princess (USA) (Flying Paster (USA))
4174[4] 4612[9] 5477[2]
Tharawaat (IRE) *B W Hills* 77
2 b c Alhaarth(IRE) —Sevi's Choice (USA) (Sir Ivor (USA))
4598[3] 5971[7] 6616[3]
Tharaya *T D Easterby* 51
2 b f Choisir(AUS) —Karlaska (Lashkari)
1743[8] 2532[7] 2804[7] 4278[11]
Tharua (IRE) *Ernst Oertel* a52 26
5 b m Indian Danehill(IRE) —Peig Sayers (IRE) (Royal Academy (USA))
558[5]
That Look *D E Cantillon* a60 60
4 b g Compton Admiral—Mudflap (Slip Anchor)
2996[6] 3448[5]
That's Blue Chip *P W D'Arcy* a50 67
4 b g Namid—Star Cast (IRE) (In The Wings)
1914[14] *3190[10]* 4252[9] 4635[12]
That's Hot (IRE) *G M Lyons* a92 110
4 b m Namid—Smoke Lady (IRE) (Barathea (IRE))
1461a[2] 2379a[2] 4150[4] *4864a[11]* 5392a[8]
Thea Di Bisanzio (IRE) *G A Butler* a55 43
3 b f Dr Fong(USA) —Tamnia (Green Desert (USA))
4908[5] *6094[4] 6339[7] 6831[8]*
The Aldbury Flyer *W R Swinburn* 85
4 b g Royal Applause—Fantasy Ridge (Indian Ridge)
1078[4] 1470[3] 1819[2] 2003[12]
Theann *A P O'Brien* 108
3 b f Rock Of Gibraltar(IRE) —Cassandra Go (IRE) (Indian Ridge)
946a[3] 1496[10] 2050a[3] 2379a[5] 2752[7] (3511)
Theatre Groom (USA) *M R Bosley* a73 59
8 ch g Theatrical—Model Bride (USA) (Blushing Groom (FR))
(443) 617[5] 747[3] 1253[13] 1813[9] 2471[P] (Dead)
Theatre Royal *Mouse Hamilton-Fairley* a59 67
4 b m Royal Applause—Rada's Daughter (Robellino (USA))
1295[4] 1609[6] 1884[2] 2430[12] 3177[8] 4131[7] 5001[10] 5708[9] *5900[7] (6096) 6780[13] 6951[12] 7115[9] 7275[6]*
The Bear *J S Wainwright* a11 63
4 ch g Rambling Bear—Precious Girl (Precious Metal)
1159[9] *1754[13]* 2025[11]
The Best Dub *Eamon Tyrrell* 66
2 gr g Best Of The Bests(IRE) —Malabarista (FR) (Assert)
6443a[14]
The Betchworth Kid *M L W Bell* a83 92
2 b c Tobougg(IRE) —Runelia (Runnett)
3043[5] (3348) 4121[5] 4776[3] 5350[4] *6291[4]* 6471[3]
The Blue Stacks (USA) *K A Ryan* a29 2
3 b g Langfuhr(CAN) —Touch Of Honor (USA) (Devil's Bag (USA))
826[5] 1135[6] 6309[14]
The Bogberry (USA) *A P O'Brien* 86
2 ch c Hawk Wing(USA) —Lahinch (IRE) (Danehill Dancer (IRE))
2855[9]
The Bonus King *J Jay* a69 58
7 b g Royal Applause—Selvi (Mummy's Pet)
(1162) 1539[17] 2154[5] *3600[7] 3946[9]* 4533[11] 5503[9]
The Borderer *M W Easterby*
4 ch g Definite Article—Far Clan (Clantime)
3399[10]
The Brat *Miss Tracy Waggott* 45
3 b f Perryston View—Kalarram (Muhtarram (USA))
970[6] 1240[3] 1595[7] 2939[7] 3811[6] 4226[13] 5969[6] 6702[14] 6730[6]
The Bronx *M J Wallace* a61 52
3 b c Dansili—Carradale (Pursuit Of Love)
713[8] 3429[10] *7207[11]*
The Card Shark (IRE) *Vivian J Noone*
7 b g Woodpas(USA) —Mountain Sue (Lyphard's Special (USA))
5696a[13]
The Carlton Cannes *G Wragg* a66 77
3 b c Grand Lodge(USA) —Miss Riviera Golf (Hernando (FR))
(7282)
The Carpet Man *A W Carroll* a53 48
3 b g Iron Mask(USA) —Yarrow Bridge (Selkirk (USA))
1207[10] 1541[11] 1763[12] 1883[7] 5270[6] 5834[6] 6720[9] *6887[8] 6963[3] 7134[4] 7162[3]*
The Cayterers *J M Bradley* 80
5 b g Cayman Kai(IRE) —Silky Smooth (IRE) (Thatching)
1607[2] 1984[6] 2197[7] 3549[8] 4122[13] 4515[4] 4767[6] 5064[7]
The Chip Chopman (IRE) *Seamus G O'Donnell* a27 73
5 b g Sri Pekan(USA) —Firstrusseofsummer (USA) (Summer Squall (USA))
4114a[3] *5779[11]*
The City Kid (IRE) *S C Williams* a66 59
4 b m Danetime(IRE) —Unfortunate (Komaite (USA))
180[4] 206[2] 286[2] 299[U] 538[11] (620) 768[2] 1069[12] 1918[6] *3173[9]* 3428[3] 3714[4] *4161[5] 4460[3] (5391) 6290[2] (6476) 7025[2]*
The Coires (IRE) *Doug Watson* a41 77
5 b g Green Desert(USA) —Purple Heather (USA) (Rahy (USA))
104a[9]
The Composer *M Blanshard* a67 78
5 b g Royal Applause—Superspring (Superlative)
1811[8] *2572[9]* 3243[6] 3969[5] 4544[6] 5857[7] 6500[7]
The Cool Sandpiper *P Winkworth* a67 60
3 ch g Piccolo—The Dark Eider (Superlative)
3044[3] 3447[8] *5136[5] 5733[6]*
The Crooked Ring *A G Newcombe* a69 73
5 b g Magic Ring(IRE) —My Bonus (Cyrano De Bergerac)
3285[11] 3873[3] 4879[10] 5861[8]
The Cube *J Balding* a53 54
3 b g Mind Games—Nite-Owl Dancer (Robellino (USA))
1635[14] 2894[6] 3302[7] 3763[4] 4661[12] 4801[2] 5282[3] 5834[9] *6240[4]* 6720[3] *6886[8]*
The Dagger *J R Best* a61
3 ch g Daggers Drawn(USA) —Highland Blue (Never So Bold)
489[6] 633[4] 790[5]
The Dandy Fox *R Bastiman* a35 53
3 b f Foxhound(USA) —Classic Storm (Belfort (FR))
1259[12] 2091[13]
The Diamond Bond *G R Oldroyd* a48 51
3 bl g Josr Algarhoud(IRE) —Alsiba (Northfields (USA))
1166[9] 1531[6] 1964[13] 3789[12] *4673[8]* 4943[4] 5158[9] *5980[6] 6070[3]* 6561[9] 6700[6] *6999[3] 7069[8] 7262[3]*
The Dragon (IRE) *M Quinn* 10
2 b f Statue Of Liberty(USA) —Noble Rocket (Reprimand)
5357[13]
The Duke (AUS) *C Fownes* 122
8 b g Danehill(USA) —Mer Du Sud (IRE) (Bluebird (USA))
7091a[7]
The Dunion *Miss L A Perratt* 53
4 br g Beckett(IRE) —Dacian (USA) (Diesis)
1942[11] 2252[11] 2567[7] 2825[7] 4475[9] 5087[5] 5283[12]
Theebah *M R Channon* 31
2 b f Bahamian Bounty—Shall We Run (Hotfoot)
1896[14] 2086[5] 2193[9]
The Ethiopian (IRE) *A P O'Brien* 91
3 b c Sadler's Wells(USA) —Kasora (IRE) (Darshaan)
1185a[9]
The Fairy (GER) *J Hirschberger* 78
3 b f Night Shift(USA) —Tucana (GER) (Acatenango (GER))
5850a[6]
The Fifth Member (IRE) *J R Boyle* a64 89
3 b c Bishop Of Cashel—Palace Soy (IRE) (Tagula (IRE))
1927[10] 2335[2] 3384[9] (4395) 4807[2] *5122[10]* (6081) 6651[8]
The Fisio *S Gollings* a72 47
7 b g Efisio—Misellina (FR) (Polish Precedent (USA))
473 161[5] (613) (654) 727[4] 905[5] 1914[13] *5565[3] 5981[9]* 6239[15] *6671[9] 6810[3]*
The Flying Cowboy (IRE) *Jane Chapple-Hyam* 74
3 b g Tagula(IRE) —Sesame Heights (IRE) (High Estate)
3710[12] 4106[3] (4660) 5777[4] 6235[13]
The Flying Peach *Miss Gay Kelleway* a32 47
4 ch m Observatory(USA) —Taffeta (IRE) (Barathea (IRE))
17 84[6] 270[7]
The Flying Phenom *J D Frost* a21
4 gr g Paris House—Miss Flossa (FR) (Big John (FR))
5731[3] 6807[10]
Theflyingscottie *D Shaw* a55 57
5 gr g Paris House—Miss Flossa (FR) (Big John (FR))
1229[3] 1406[6] *1590[2]* 2252[3] 2890[5] (3193) 3630[5] *6459[4] 6697[9] 6797[2] 7012[10] 7120[4] 7273[7]*
The Fuzz (NZ) *D Hayes* 108
5 br g Danasinga(AUS) —Drama Queen (NZ) (Prince Of Praise (NZ))
6033a[2]
The Gaikwar (IRE) *R A Harris* a64 78
8 b g Indian Ridge—Broadmara (IRE) (Thatching)
179[5] 975[8] 1318[9] (2107) 2214[9] 2492[7] 2979[10] 3487[5] 4259[5] 4418 [11] 4850[3] 5189[4] 5348[8] 5693[9] 5917[6]
The Game *J R Boyle* a82 73
2 b g Compton Place—Emanant (Emarati (USA))
2460[5] (3833) *4274[5]* 6195[9] *6588[6]* 6699[8] *(7052) 7280[3]*
The Gatekeeper *M H Tompkins* a74 76
2 b c Mujahid(USA) —Tiempo (King Of Spain)
2041[14] 6617[2] *(6884)*
The Geester *S R Bowring* a55 48
3 b g Rambling Bear—Cledeschamps (Doc Marten)
713[7] 925[10] *1031[3]* 1635[11] *1932[5] 2950[3] 3281[5]* 4661[11] *5420[6]* 6078[8] *7138[2]*
The Geezer *Saeed Bin Suroor* a58 110
5 ch g Halling(USA) —Polygueza (FR) (Be My Guest (USA))
2907[2] 3333[4] 3912[4]
The Golden Noodle (USA) *J Van Berg* a101
2 ch f D'Wildcat(USA) —Golden Genie (USA) (Beau Genius (CAN))
5826a[8]
The Graig *C Drew* a52 50
3 b g Josr Algarhoud(IRE) —Souadah (USA) (General Holme (USA))
1250[5] 1566[11] 2456[11] 3624[12] 4106[6]
The Great Delaney *K McAuliffe* a54 62
4 b g Inchinor—Top (Shirley Heights)
5366[7]
The Grey Bam Bam *R J Hodges* 46
3 gr f Baryshnikov(AUS) —Leonie Samual (Safawan)
1211[8]
The Grey Berry *T D Walford* 102
3 gr g Observatory(USA) —Elderberry (Bin Ajwaad (IRE))
(1964) (2834) (3299) 3556[6] 4640[3] (5554) 6185[2]
The Grey One (IRE) *J M Bradley* a66 70
4 gr g Dansili—Marie Dora (FR) (Kendor (FR))
714[3] 750[5] 1027[2] (1350) 1507[5] *1755[4]* 2027[7] 2214[2] 2809[2] (3034) 3487[6] 3855[4] 3965[5] 4259[4] 4880[2] *5178[6]* 5280[10] 5917[3] 6196[9] 6447[8]
The History Man (IRE) *M Mullineaux* a42 77
4 b g Titus Livius(FR) —Handsome Anna (IRE) (Bigstone (IRE))
1226[8] 1999[11] 2202[8] *2516[11]* (3347) 3549[3] (3608) 3886[5] (4289) 4489[5] 5029[11] 5552[18] 5581[7]
The Hoofer (IRE) *J L Dunlop* 59
2 b f Vision Of Night—Dance In The Sun (Halling (USA))
3967[10] 4537[6] 5110[8] 5471[7] 6536[7]
The Illies (IRE) *B W Hills* 107
3 b c Fasliyev(USA) —Velvet Appeal (IRE) (Petorius)
1471[6] 2578[6] 3503[8] 3745[4] (3940) (4745) (5412) 6011[5]
The Iron Giant (IRE) *B G Powell* a64 61
5 b g Giant's Causeway(USA) —Shalimar (IRE) (Indian Ridge)
2141[12] *2875[5] 3397[8] 7069[12]*
The Jailer *J G M O'Shea* a60 57
4 b m Mujahid(USA) —Once Removed (Distant Relative)
1210[5] 2140[4] 2559[2] 2938[4] (5269) *5368[5] (5946)* 6199[5] *6642[9] 6895[2]*
The Jay Factor (IRE) *Pat Eddery* a69 71
3 b c Bold Fact(USA) —Corn Futures (Nomination)
1561[3] 2061[9] *2594[2] 3168[2] 3646[7]* 4236[2] *4740[10]* 5360[10] 5714[5] *6176[5]*
The Jobber (IRE) *M Blanshard* a93 107
6 b g Foxhound(USA) —Clairification (IRE) (Shernazar)
3526[4] 3990[5] 4090[6] 4798[4] 5212[6] 5305[2] 5632[8] 5953[8]
The Jostler *B W Hills* 75
2 b f Dansili—The Jotter (Night Shift (USA))
4061[13] 4602[7] (5110) 5629[10]
The Keep *R E Barr* a20 44
5 ch m Shinko Forest(IRE) —Poyle Amber (Sharrood (USA))
1679[12] 2422[8] 2535[8] 2806[7] 3917[8] 4079[10] 5085[6]
The Kiddykid (IRE) *P D Evans* a94 110
7 b g Danetime(IRE) —Mezzanine (Sadler's Wells (USA))
847[11] 1102[8] 1474[11] 1619[7] 2058[10] 3489[5] 3975[5] 4456[5] 4601[12] 4990[3] 5209[9] 5804[5] *(6209) 6606[9] 6932[6]*
The King And I (IRE) *Miss E C Lavelle* a80 69
3 b g Monashee Mountain(USA) —Scrimshaw (Selkirk (USA))
1398[6] 1786[8] 2697[3] 3384[5] 4309[6] *5783[2] 5983[4] (7132) 7205[2] 7236[3]*
The Lady Granuaile (USA) *K A Ryan* 75
2 b f More Than Ready(USA) —Marlene (USA) (Theatrical)
4328[3] 5910[12]
The Lady Lapwing *G Wragg* a37
2 b f Mark Of Esteem(IRE) —Lonely Shore (Blakeney)
6641[7] 6964[9]
The Last Bottle (IRE) *W M Brisbourne* a65 65
2 ch g Hawk Wing(USA) —Mesmerist (USA) (Green Desert (USA))
1792[5] 2371[6] 4487[6] 5153[8] *6936[2]*
The Last Drop (IRE) *B W Hills* 116
4 b h Galileo(IRE) —Epping (Charnwood Forest (IRE))
929[2] 1393[3] 1823[P] 2787[11] 4117[12]
The Last Laugh *M J Grassick* a63 78
3 b f Kyllachy—Persian Air (Persian Bold)
873a[5] 5841a[8]
The Leather Wedge (IRE) *R Johnson* a62 73
8 b g Hamas(IRE) —Wallflower (Polar Falcon (USA))
143[5] 318[5] 465[11] 581[8] 1112[10] (Dead)
The Leopard (USA) *T Pletcher* a91 101
2 bb c Storm Cat(USA) —Moon Safari (USA) (Mr Prospector (USA))
6484a[7]
The Light Fandango *R A Harris* a49 48
3 ch f Kyllachy—Alifandango (IRE) (Alzao (USA))
11[4] 68[5] 357[3] 478[7] 577[8] 676[13] 708[6] 7201[7]
The Loan Express (IRE) *T Stack* 100
2 b f Choisir(AUS) —Mamma's Too (Skyliner)
1546a[2] 2325a[5] 2756[3] 4437a[4] 5377[5]
The London Gang *Miss D A McHale* a64 67
4 b g Mind Games—Nom Francais (First Trump)
33[3] 131[5] 235[10] 298[4] 495[4] 571[6] 751[8] 797[9] 980[12] *1066[10] (7043)* 3629[7]
The Loose Screw (IRE) *C W Thornton* a38 19
9 b g Bigstone(IRE) —Princess Of Dance (IRE) (Dancing Dissident (USA))
3331[0] 602[10]
The Lord (ARG) *S Seemar* a75
7 b h Southern Halo(USA) —Lourdes (ARG) (Ringaro (USA))
249a[6] 324a[9] 474a[15]
The Magic Blanket (IRE) *Stef Liddiard* a67 63
2 b g Bahamian Bounty—Zietunzeen (IRE) (Zieten (USA))
8451[0] 2746[3] 3812[7] 3995[5] 4221[4] 5065[4] *5199[3]*
Themelie Island (IRE) *A Trybuhl* 95
2 b f Montjeu(IRE) —Thelema (IRE) (Caerleon (USA))
5028a[6]
The Mighty Ogmore *R C Guest* a47 59
3 ch f Dr Fong(USA) —Welsh Dawn (Zafonic (USA))
1131[9] 1964[11] 2299[3] 2538[11] 2905[2] 3182[3] 3400[4] 3783[5] 3956[12] 4582[15] 5674[11] 6325[9] *6569[3] 6780[5] 6815[9] 7069[6] 7187[10]*
The Mighty One *P C Haslam* a69 69
2 b g Mujadil(USA) —Presently (Cadeaux Genereux)
6698[3] *(7043) 7260[5]*
The Name Is Frank *J W Mullins* 71
2 b g Lujain(USA) —Zaragossa (Paris House)
1781[7] 2103[10] 2539[3] 3687[6] (3967) 4501[13]
The Nawab (IRE) *Barry Potts* a95 94
5 ch g Almutawakel—Eschasse (USA) (Zilzal (USA))
2449[5]
The Niagara Queen (CAN) *Michael J Doyle* a83 108
4 ch m Langfuhr(CAN) —Inspirational (USA) (Lord At War (ARG))
6373a[4]
The Nifty Fox *T D Easterby* 86
3 b g Foxhound(USA) —Nifty Alice (First Trump)
1160[6] 1825[4] (2119) 2395[7] (2867) 3493[3] 3954[11] 4452[6] 4726[10] 5379[11] 5806[6] 6327[8] 6381[5] 6743[4]
Then 'n Now *C A Cyzer* a70 78
2 b f Dansili—Rise 'n Shine (Night Shift (USA))
4232[14] 4662[4] *(4963) 5496[2]* 6008[8]
The Oil Magnate *M Dods* 81
2 ch g Dr Fong(USA) —Bob's Princess (Bob's Return (IRE))
3760[2]
The Old Soldier *A Dickman* a56 59
9 b g Magic Ring(IRE) —Grecian Belle (Ilium)
1241[9] 2386[11]
Theonebox (USA) *M J Wallace*
2 ch g Johannesburg(USA) —Khalifa Of Kushog (USA) (Air Forbes Won (USA))
4454[15]
Theoretical *A J McCabe* a62 56
3 b f Marju(IRE) —Relativity (IRE) (Distant Relative)
3168[7] 5907[13] *6581[7] 6752[6] 7082[6] 7227[2]*
The Osteopath (IRE) *M Dods* 79
4 ch g Danehill Dancer(IRE) —Miss Margate (IRE) (Don't Forget Me)
930[3] 1223[7] 1747[6] 2256[6] (2719) 2741[5] 3194[3] 3470[3] 3682[3] 4107[5] 6331[13]
The Pen *C W Fairhurst* a40 65
5 ch m Lake Coniston(IRE) —Come To The Point (Pursuit Of Love)
1211[1] 242[6] 928[5] 1090[8] (1258) 1532[5] 1967[9] 3679[4] 4156[5] 4493[5] 5158[8]
The Perfect Plan (IRE) *Tom Dascombe* a47 47
4 b g Kalanisi(IRE) —Talbiya (IRE) (Mujtahid (USA))
148[7]
The Pirate (DEN) *Niels Petersen* 95
4 b h Primatico(USA) —Medinova (Mas Media)
4874a[3]
The Power Of Phil *Miss Joanne Priest* a47
3 b g Komaite(USA) —Starboard Tack (FR) (Saddlers' Hall (IRE))
423[7] 567[6] 786[7] 687[10] 7133[DSQ] 7201[2]
The Quantum Kid *T J Etherington* 61
3 b c Desert Prince(IRE) —Al Hasnaa (Zafonic (USA))
1153[6] 2464[4] 3919[5] 4902[8]
The Quiet Enforcer (IRE) *Andrew Oliver* 82
2 b c Fath(USA) —Eastern Star (IRE) (Sri Pekan (USA))
5516a[2]
The Real Guru *Mrs A Duffield* a56 71
2 b c Ishiguru(USA) —Aloma's Reality (USA) (Proper Reality (USA))
1291[3] (4002) 4476[4] 5331[13] 6195[12] 6699[2] *6834[8]*
The Real Thing (IRE) *Tracey Collins* a39 80
3 b f Traditionally(USA) —Mad Madam Mym (Hernando (FR))
246a[9] 476a[13] 5460a[25]
The Rebound Kid *J R Weymes* a61 39
5 b g Royal Applause—Hayhurst (Sandhurst Prince)
6700[8]

There's A Light (IRE) *Tracey Collins* a57 70
3 b f Fantastic Light(USA) —Last Spin (Unfuwain (USA))
6920a[9]

The Riddler (IRE) *J A Osborne* 76
2 b c Daylami(IRE) —Wimple (USA) (Kingmambo (USA))
3958[5] 4841[2] 5663[2]

The Rip *R M Stronge* a37 64
6 ch g Definite Article—Polgwynne (Forzando)
1912 8710 1590[11]

Thermidor (USA) *R Charlton* 56
4 ch g Giant's Causeway(USA) —Langoustine (AUS) (Danehill (USA))
5231[5] 5714[4]

Thermidora *J R Fanshawe* a55 46
3 b f Theatrical—Langoustine (AUS) (Danehill (USA))
2766[9] 4765[6]

The Salwick Flyer (IRE) *I Semple* a58 57
4 b g Tagula(IRE) —Shimla (IRE) (Rudimentary (USA))
430[14] 1426[6] 2938[10] 3674[3] (4494) *4668[6]* 5672[3] 5935[8] 6467[4] *6886[7] (7148)*

The Skerret *P Winkworth* 57
3 ch g Loup Sauvage(USA) —Cosmic Star (Siberian Express (USA))
1538[7] 2489[8] 2661[2] 3237[8] 4163[4] 4395[8] 4711[3]

The Slider *Mrs L C Jewell* a54 51
3 b f Erhaab(USA) —Cottage Maid (Inchinor)
676[3] 794[5] 5528[13] 6100[7] 6579[12] 6792[7] 7032[5] 7069[4]

The Snatcher (IRE) *R Hannon* a96 96
4 b h Indian Danehill(IRE) —Saninka (IRE) (Doyoun)
1145[17] *1448[5]* 1836[6] 2401[11] 2670[10] 3401[7] 4049[7] *5203[3]* 5593[7] 5870[6] *6143[5] 6435[7] 6646[3]*

The Social Drinker *F P Murtagh*
5 b g Tipsy Creek(USA) —Sanshang (FR) (Astronef)
1423[14]

The Spring Flower (GER) *Andreas Lowe* 99
5 b m Kornado—The Dashing Lady (GER) (Dashing Blade)
3121a[3]

The Stafford (IRE) *L Wells* a20
6 b g Selkirk(USA) —Bint Zamayem (IRE) (Rainbow Quest (USA))
6896[14]

The Storm (GER) *Z Koplik* 41
2 b c Monsun(GER) —Tascalina (GER) (Big Shuffle (USA))
6324a[12]

Theta *H R A Cecil* a50 67
3 b f Rainbow Quest(USA) —Self Esteem (Suave Dancer (USA))
4568[4] *4948[7]* (5346)

The Tatling (IRE) *J M Bradley* 115
10 bb g Perugino(USA) —Aunty Eileen (Ahonoora)
1125[3] (1456) 2463[5] 2733[8] 3329[4] 4090[7] 4150[19] 4614[5] 4746[15] 5050[5] 5449[8] 6197[9] 6487[13]

The Terminator (IRE) *M Mullineaux* a45 45
5 b g Night Shift(USA) —Surmise (USA) (Alleged (USA))
42[13]

The Thrifty Bear *C W Fairhurst* 60
4 ch g Rambling Bear—Prudent Pet (Distant Relative)
1862[13] 2827[10] 3259[8] 4141[7] 4583[13] 5295[9] 5740[8] 5930[8]

The Tinker Man *M D I Usher* a51 54
3 b c Killer Instinct—Sporting Affair (IRE) (Ashkalani (IRE))
128[7] 375[5] 505[5] 713[2] 1031[6] 1248[9] 1538[8] 2489[6] 2697[5] 2981[4] 3365[7] 3950[7] 4313[9]

The Tin Man (USA) *Richard E Mandella* 122
9 br g Affirmed(USA) —Lizzie Rolfe (USA) (Tom Rolfe (USA))
4414a[2]

The Tokoloshe *M A Barnes*
5 ch g Zaha(CAN) —Hay Danzig (IRE) (Roi Danzig (USA))
3914[13] 4246[P] (Dead)

The Trader (IRE) *M Blanshard* 117
9 ch g Selkirk(USA) —Snowing (Tate Gallery (USA))
2184[4] 2695[6] 3329[10] 3708[4] 4190a[2] 4871a[5] 5700[6]

The Twelve Steps *P F I Cole* a67 42
2 b c Diktat—Polygueza (FR) (Be My Guest (USA))
6493[13] *7051[10] (7139)*

The Tyke *C G Cox* a62 42
4 gr g Cloudings(IRE) —Vonispet (Cotation)
5567[6] 6424[8]

Thewayyouare (USA) *A Fabre* 117
2 b c Kingmambo(USA) —Maryinsky (IRE) (Sadler's Wells (USA))
(6187a) (6615a)

The West's Awake (USA) *E Libaud* 102
4 b h Theatrical—Saudia (USA) (Gone West (USA))
990a[10]

The Which Doctor *J Noseda* a76 73
2 b g Medicean—Oomph (Shareef Dancer (USA))
4362[2] *(6139)*

Thewhirlingdervish (IRE) *T D Easterby* 84
9 ch g Definite Article—Nomadic Dancer (IRE) (Nabeel Dancer (USA))
2375[2] (2908) 3412[3] (3609) 3898[2] 4569[8] 4893[5]

The Whistling Teal *G Wragg* a90 110
11 b g Rudimentary(USA) —Lonely Shore (Blakeney)
1144[6] 1618[5] 1833[4] 3973[4] 4599[4] 5437a[8]

The Wicked Wizard *W Storey*
4 br g Wizard King—Sallyoreally (IRE) (Common Grounds)
2[6] 61[11]

The Willowy Wigeon *P Winkworth* 53
2 b f Josr Algarhoud(IRE) —The Dark Eider (Superlative)
4537[4] 4904[7] 5302[4] 5869[3]

The Wily Woodcock *G Wragg* a65 65
3 b c Mark Of Esteem(IRE) —Lonely Shore (Blakeney)
1522[4] 2317[8] 2635[4] 4172[14]

They All Laughed *P W Hiatt* a73 73
4 ch g Zafonic(USA) —Royal Future (IRE) (Royal Academy (USA))
130[12] 200[4] 2436 286[5] 363[9] 503[5] 665[2] 909[2] 1032[2] (1178) 1683[3] (2055) 2391[2] (3177) 3677[5] 4124[DSQ] *7198[3]*

Thiella (USA) *D K Weld* 87
3 bb f Kingmambo(USA) —Theoretically (USA) (Theatrical)
1694a[8] 2599[7]

Thimble *Mme C Head-Maarek* 96
3 b f Dansili—Daki (USA) (Miswaki (USA))
5058a[10]

Thinking Positive *J H M Gosden* a75 77
3 b f Rainbow Quest(USA) —Midnight Air (USA) (Green Dancer (USA))
2580[2] *3214[4] 4277[4] 4738[2]* (5271)

Thinking Robins (IRE) *P Martometti* 93
4 b h Plumbird—Rose Jasmine (ITY) (Sikeston (USA))
1876a[8]

Third Set (IRE) *R Charlton* a89 112
4 b g Royal Applause—Khamseh (Thatching)
1653[21] 1971[2] 2817[19] (3437) (3941) (4119)

Thistle *J Howard Johnson* 70
6 ch g Selkirk(USA) —Ardisia (USA) (Affirmed (USA))
1488[8] 1893[5]

This Way That Way *Ian Williams* a61
6 b g Dr Devious(IRE) —Ellway Dancer (IRE) (Mujadil (USA))
602[6] 3284[5] 4067[3]

Thomas A Beckett (IRE) *P R Chamings* a44 50
4 b g Beckett(IRE) —Kenema (IRE) (Petardia)
273[6] 3491[0]

Thomas Lawrence (USA) *P A Blockley* a46 64
6 ch g Horse Chestnut(SAF) —Olatha (USA) (Miswaki (USA))
92[8] 276[11] 524[11] 902[3] *1064[9]* 3965[11] 4395[13] *4673[6]* 5062[3]

Thomas Malory (IRE) *Miss V Haigh* a45 63
2 b c Mujadil(USA) —Isca (Caerleon (USA))
1411[8] 1832[16] 2024[5] 2251[7] 3494[4] 3841[5] 4154[8] 4255[8] (4970) 5089[3] 5216[9] *5529[8]* 5715[4] 6074[5] *6454[9]*

Thompsons Walls (IRE) *P C Haslam* a59 79
2 b g Trans Island—Nordic Living (IRE) (Nordico (USA))
3718[4] (4279) 4819[2] 4995[7] *6800[U] 6898[4]*

Thorax *M Johnston* 57
3 br c Machiavellian(USA) —Mezzogiorno (Unfuwain (USA))
2909[3] 3399[7]

Thornaby Green *T D Barron* a65 67
6 b g Whittingham(IRE) —Dona Filipa (Precocious)
2254[10] 2582[2] 2795[4] (3049) 3783[3] 3956[6] 4383[2] (4582) 5557[5] 5750[6] 6258[11] 6598[11] *6837[4] 7056[3] 7214[5]*

Thornbill *H Candy* a49 35
4 ch g Gorse—Red Hot Dancer (USA) (Seattle Dancer (USA))
2077[10] *2593[7]*

Thorny Mandate *W M Brisbourne* a68 69
5 b g Diktat—Rosa Canina (Bustino)
1314[10] 2006[10] 2431[4] *(2519) 3217[6] 3407[7]* 3496[5] *(4025)* 4096[3] 4493[3] 4732[4] 4910[8] *5364[8] 6027[7] 6068[8]*

Thor's Echo (USA) *S Seemar* a124 105
5 ch g Swiss Yodeler(USA) —Helen Of Troy (USA) (Mr. Integrity (USA))
597a[6] 860a[6]

Thought Is Free *J S Moore* a69 94
2 b f Cadeaux Genereux—Dayville (USA) (Dayjur (USA))
1832[13] 3096[2] 3432[10] 4744[8] *5309[2]* 5974[18]

Thoughtless Moment (IRE) *D K Weld* 101
3 ch f Pivotal—Celebrity Style (USA) (Seeking The Gold (USA))
(5242a) 5459a[4] 6216a[2]

Thoughtsofstardom *G C Bravery* a63 65
4 b g Mind Games—Alustar (Emarati (USA))
214[7] (287) 613[6] 668[2] 687[3] 746[3] 892[14] 2221[6] 2555[2] (2761) 2879[2] *6244[9] 6752[8] 6890[6] 6925[2] 7013[3] 7082[7]*

Thousand Words *B W Hills* 110
3 b c Dansili—Verbose (USA) (Storm Bird (CAN))
1103[3] 1703a[5] 2752[8] 4045[4] 4543[5] 5359[5]

Thou Shalt Not *P S Felgate* a27 17
4 bb g Commands(AUS) —Soyalang (FR) (Alydeed (CAN))
2345[11] 2519[10]

Three Boars *S Gollings* a79 67
5 ch g Most Welcome—Precious Poppy (Polish Precedent (USA))
(669) (683) 733[3] 1225[8] 2887[6] *6459[7] 6739[8] (7110) 7135[2] 7178[2]*

Three Counties (IRE) *N I M Rossiter* 76
6 b h Danehill(USA) —Royal Show (IRE) (Sadler's Wells (USA))
1319[8] 2077[5] 2556[10] 2665[4] 4879[5]

Three Gold Leaves *J G Given* 40
2 ch c Zaha(CAN) —Tab's Gift (Bijou D'Inde)
6307[9]

Three Half Crowns (IRE) *P Howling* a47 39
3 b c Barathea(IRE) —My-Lorraine (IRE) (Mac's Imp (USA))
1166[13] 2046[10] 2796[13] 3244[9]

Three Mates *W G M Turner* a33 36
3 b f Auction House(USA) —Great Aim (Great Nephew)
108[6]

Three No Trumps *P S Felgate* a44 48
3 ch f First Trump—Renaissance Lady (IRE) (Imp Society (USA))
11[3] 139[5] 1928[13] 3040[5] 4337[11]

Three Ships *Miss J Feilden* a54 48
6 ch g Dr Fong(USA) —River Lullaby (USA) (Riverman (USA))
279[8] 3149[10]

Threestoneburn (USA) *J R Boyle* a55 68
2 b f Johannesburg(USA) —White Bridle (IRE) (Singspiel (IRE))
2039[3] 2904[5] 4796[8] 5746[4] *7084[8]*

Three Thieves (UAE) *M S Saunders* a76 55
4 ch g Jade Robbery(USA) —Melisendra (FR) (Highest Honor (FR))
89[11] 215[2] (332) 428[2] (618) 747[2] 813[5] 1253[7] 1752[3] 2544[6] *7046[9]*

Throw The Dice *A Berry* a29 71
5 b g Lujain(USA) —Euridice (IRE) (Woodman (USA))
892[9] 9921[5] 1492[2] 1597[2] 1806[4] 2390[4] 2712[8] 3185[7] 3674[4] 4252[5] 4996[14] (5085) 5295[6] 5552[5] 5672[4] 5930[3] 5969[5] 6562[8] 6702[4]

Thumpers Dream *I W McInnes* a68 86
4 b m Cape Cross(IRE) —Perfect Peach (Lycius (USA))
1599[6] 1862[9] 5620[9] 5907[11] 6380[14] *6628[6] 6837[7]*

Thunder Bay *M R Channon* a60 87
2 b g Hunting Lion(IRE) —Floral Spark (Forzando)
(883) 1043[2] (1130) 1390[5] 1772[8] 4193[3] 4605[5] (5008) 5324[18] 5480[2] 5802[2] 6059[5] 6167[8]

Thunderbolt Jaxon *P W Chapple-Hyam* a59 67
3 ch g Dr Fong(USA) —Composition (Wolfhound (USA))
700[3] 901[2] *1375[4] 1903[10]* 2750[7]

Thunderclap *P D Niven* 24
8 bb g Royal Applause—Gloriana (Formidable (USA))
3956[8]

Thunder Gorge (USA) *Mouse Hamilton-Fairley* a70 74
2 b c Thunder Gulch(USA) —Renaissance Fair (USA) (Theatrical)
4014[8] 4454[4] 5088[7] 5939[2] 6128[11] *6644[6]*

Thunderousapplause *K A Ryan* a68 85
3 b f Royal Applause—Trustthunder (Selkirk (USA))
1105[5] 2395[4] (3491) 3857[4] 4639[9] *6002[12]* 6300[16]

Thunder Storm Cat (USA) *M Rulec* a82 94
3 b c Storm Cat(USA) —Tenga (USA) (Mr Prospector (USA))
1124[6] 1471[3] 2037[10] 2788[25] 3514[6] *7128a[0]*

Thunderstruck *K A Ryan* 74
2 b g Bertolini(USA) —Trustthunder (Selkirk (USA))
3760[5] 5140[4] (5526)

Thunderwing (IRE) *James Moffatt* a73 75
5 bb g Indian Danehill(IRE) —Scandisk (IRE) (Kenmare (FR))
1374[2] 1554[5] 1893[6] 2431[14] 3155[4] 3721[13] 3764[5] 5676[6] 6640[2]

Thyolo (IRE) *B G Powell* a56 91
6 ch g Bering—Topline (GER) (Acatenango (GER))
3943[17] 4597[15] 4910[7] *7050[4] 7100* (Dead)

Ti Adora (IRE) *P W D'Arcy* a98 99
5 b m Montjeu(IRE) —Wavy Up (IRE) (Brustolon)
1244[8]

Tiago (USA) *J Shirreffs* a118
3 b c Pleasant Tap(USA) —Set Them Free (USA) (Stop The Music (USA))
1486a[7] 2487a[3] (5824a) 6514a[5]

Tia Jade *G Prodromou* a45 23
3 gr f Imperial Ballet(IRE) —Sunningdale (IRE) (Indian Ridge)
193[9] 418[11] 1409[9] *6206[11] 6735[13]*

Tia Mia *J G Given* 90
2 ch f Dr Fong(USA) —Giusina Mia (USA) (Diesis)
(1302) 1821[2] 2756[10] 4046[11] 4613[4]

Tiana *Mrs A J Perrett* a90 100
4 b m Diktat—Hill Welcome (Most Welcome)
3897[8] 4503[8] 5047[11] 5359[6] 5794[4] *6604[4]*

Tiana Bleu (IRE) *P S Felgate*
5 ch m Pistolet Bleu(IRE) —Bobby Hays (IRE) (Bob Back (USA))
833[8]

Tianshan (FR) *F-X de Chevigny* a100 105
4 b m Lahint(USA) —Tangshan (CAN) (Zilzal (USA))
31a[5] 4010a[10]

Tiara Princess (IRE) *Rae Guest* 39
2 b f Monashee Mountain(USA) —All Our Blessings (IRE) (Statoblest)
3681[5] 4512[4]

Tibinta *P D Evans* a49 57
3 b f Averti(IRE) —Bint Albadou (IRE) (Green Desert (USA))
1561[2] 1943[12] 2195[3] 2515[3] 2664[11] 3667[9] 4180[7] 4312[4] 5190[6] *6210[5] 6864[4] 7011[10] 7188[9]*

Tibouchina (IRE) *R M Beckett* a65 74
4 gr m Daylami(IRE) —Kalimar (IRE) (Bigstone (IRE))
1249[6] 1628[7] (2491) (2964) 3177[2] 3554[4]

Ticking *T Keddy* a26 22
4 ch g Barathea(IRE) —Tuning (Rainbow Quest (USA))
4031[13] *6968[11]*

Tidy (IRE) *Micky Hammond* a22 74
7 b g Mujadil(USA) —Neat Shilling (IRE) (Bob Back (USA))
2007[6] 2169[5] 2809[5] 3049[4] 3403[9] 3721[10] 6640[4] *7155[7]*

Tiegan An Josh *A Crook*
2 b f Lahib(USA) —Poungada (FR) (Tropular)
7208[8]

Tiegs (IRE) *P W Hiatt* a49 47
5 ch m Desert Prince(IRE) —Helianthus (Groom Dancer (USA))
(78) 242[13] 380[3] 464[7] 628[4] 730[10] 3795[4] 4230[8] 4521[2] *4914[4]* 5187[4]

Tiepie *J Akehurst* a41 41
2 ch c Tomba—Contrary Mary (Mujadil (USA))
5587[8] *5815[9]*

Tifernati *W J Haggas* a73 87
3 b g Dansili—Pain Perdu (IRE) (Waajib)
(752) 1684[5] 2061[5] 2598[5] 2834[9] 3469[4] 3848[4] 3964[4] (4172) (4597) 5141[3]

Tiger Dream *K A Ryan* 85
2 b c Oasis Dream—Grey Way (USA) (Cozzene (USA))
5321[2] 5735[2] 6468[2]

Tiger King (GER) *P Monteith* 68
6 b g Tiger Hill(IRE) —Tennessee Girl (GER) (Big Shuffle (USA))
2823[6] 3343[7] 5676[2]

Tiger Spice *W J Haggas* a65 64
2 b f Royal Applause—Up And About (Barathea (IRE))
5042[5] 5801[3] *6358[4] 6978[4] 7101[3] (7156)*

Tiger's Rocket (IRE) *R Hannon* a64 59
2 b c Monashee Mountain(USA) —Brown Foam (Horage)
1781[13] 2424[10] 3348[7] 5089[12] *5199[6] 5729[3]* 6410[7] *6899[4] 7022[5] 7117[5] (7245)*

Tiger Tee (IRE) *John A Quinn* a46 64
2 b g Spectrum(IRE) —Frill (Henbit (USA))
3438a[15]

Tiger Tiger (FR) *Jamie Poulton* a96 99
6 b g Tiger Hill(IRE) —Adorable Emilie (FR) (Iron Duke (FR))
701[6] 1449[8] 1767[15]

Tiger Trail (GER) *Mrs N Smith* a49 36
3 b g Tagula(IRE) —Tweed Mill (Selkirk (USA))
4541[11] *5129[7]*

Tiggers Touch *A W Carroll* a26
5 b m Fraam—Beacon Silver (Belmez (USA))
500[11] 730[12]

Tighnabruaich (IRE) *M A Jarvis* 77
2 b c Rainbow Quest(USA) —Miss Mistletoes (IRE) (The Minstrel (CAN))
6184[6] 6740[2]

Tikinheart (IRE) *T D Easterby* 66
2 ch g Intikhab(USA) —Inourhearts (IRE) (Pips Pride)
1528[6] 1772[6] 3092[9] 4175[8] 4560[7] 4775[16] 5153[7] 5484[3]

Tilapia (IRE) *Sir Mark Prescott* a88
3 ch g Daggers Drawn(USA) —Mrs Fisher (IRE) (Salmon Leap (USA))
(93) 216[7] (1936) (2150) 2354[3]

Tilen (IRE) *S Parr* a40 22
4 ch g Bluebird(USA) —New Sensitive (Wattlefield)
435[8] 539[8] 570[11] 730[11]

Tilly Ann (IRE) *Peter Grayson* a32
2 b f Turtle Island(IRE) —Buckland Filleigh (IRE) (Buckskin (FR))
7216[8]

Tilly's Dream *G C Bravery* a80 81
4 ch m Arkadian Hero(USA) —Dunloe (IRE) (Shaadi (USA))
1977[10] 2191[5] 2608[3] 2805[3] (2933) 3374[4] 3708[8] 3886[6] 6173[4] 6575[9] *6762[6] (6962) 7105[7]*

Tilly Shilling (IRE) *C R Egerton* 52
3 b f Montjeu(IRE) —Antiguan Jane (Shirley Heights)
4235[5] 4630[9]

Tilsworth Charlie *J R Jenkins* a62 65
4 br m Dansili—Glossary (Reference Point)
1404[6] 2334[3] 2553[10] 3247[3] 4317[6] 4545[5] 4855[2] 5190[3] 5627[2] 6089[9] 6413[8] *6717[4] 6825[13] 6945[4] 7085[6] 7118[2]*

Tilt *B Ellison* a79 94
5 b g Daylami(IRE) —Tromond (Lomond (USA))
1244[4] 1575[3] 2236[12] 2861[3] 3090[3] 3898[9] 4047[3] 5215[4] 5677[4]

Tiltili (IRE) *P C Haslam* 50
4 ch m Spectrum(IRE) —Alexander Confranc (IRE) (Magical Wonder (USA))
2372[4] 2417[2] 3638[5]

Timarwa (IRE) *John M Oxx* 109
3 b f Daylami(IRE) —Timarida (IRE) (Kalaglow)
3117a[4] 3576a[4] 4649a[9] (5998a) 6509a[6]

Timbalier (USA) *D M Simcock* a59
2 ch c Dixieland Band(USA) —Gabacha (USA) (Woodman (USA))
6578[6] 6763[5]

Timber Creek *H Candy* 39
2 b g Tobougg(IRE) —Proserpine (Robellino (USA))
6125[11] 6285[8]

Timber Treasure (USA) *H R A Cecil* 69
3 bb g Forest Wildcat(USA) —Lady Ilsley (USA) (Trempolino (USA))
3743[7] 4258[5] 4901[2] 5384[3] 5915[5]

Timbo Timbo (FR) *H-A Pantall* a82 85
2 b c Timboroa—Blaina (FR) (Caerwent)
5260a[6]

Time Control *L M Cumani* 57
2 b f Sadler's Wells(USA) —Time Away (IRE) (Darshaan)
3706[14]

Time For Change (IRE) *P G Murphy* a62 50
3 ch g Elnadim(USA) —Dance Lesson (In The Wings)
25[5] 253[2] (910) 1266[2] 1903[9] 2178[7] 4231[16] *4742[8] 5095[10] 5817[6] 5945[10] 6121[10] 6531[8] 6792[12] 7153[4] 7197[6] 7233[10]*

Time For You *J M Bradley* a14 27
5 b m Vettori(IRE) —La Fija (USA) (Dixieland Band (USA))
18[10]

Time Marches On *K G Reveley* a18 47
9 b g Timeless Times(USA) —Tees Gazette Girl (Kalaglow)
1527[10] 1744[11] 1895[7] 2252[6] 2537[3] 3638[4]

Time Over *J L Dunlop* 74
3 ch f Mark Of Esteem(IRE) —Not Before Time (IRE) (Polish Precedent (USA))
3710[3] (4106) 4510[11]

Time Share (IRE) *G C Bravery* a60 59
3 b f Danetime(IRE) —Clochette (IRE) (Namaqualand (USA))
127[4] 343[2] 421[3] 1346[8] 1430[4] 1763[15] *2357[4] (2948)* 3688[5] 3763[8] 4514[5] 4711[4] *5386[6] 5420[12] 6340[6] 6864[2] 6927[5] 7014[8] 7192[6]*

Timetable *H R A Cecil* 81
2 b c Observatory(USA) —Clepsydra (Sadler's Wells (USA))
4584[2]

Time To Beat (GER) *W Baltromei* 87
2 b f Areion(GER) —Torbay (IRE) (Surumu (GER))
5462a[3] 6371a[8]

Time To Regret *I W McInnes* a66 61
7 b g Presidium—Scoffera (Scottish Reel)
(20) (129) (181) 238[3] 461[8] 538[7] 2007[8] 2311[5] 3194[11] 3376[10] 3721[5] 4042[6] 4488[10] 5336[5] 5503[4] (6479) (6629) 6716[4] 6874[10] 7023[7] 7127[6]

Time Upon Time *W J Knight* a46 50
3 b f Groom Dancer(USA) —Watchkeeper (IRE) (Rudimentary (USA))
1725[12] 2127[11] 2801[13]

Timewatch *M Johnston* 62
2 b c Fantastic Light(USA) —Maybe Forever (Zafonic (USA))
1043[5] 1454[4] 2371[5] 4364[8] 5571[7]

Timocracy *M Johnston* 57
2 br c Cape Cross(IRE) —Tithcar (Cadeaux Genereux)
2885[7]

Tina's Best (IRE) *R Hannon* a64 72
2 b f King's Best(USA) —Phantom Waters (Pharly (FR))
2968[5] 3479[7] 3874[5] 4315[7] 5393a[3] 5856[4] 6128[7] 6404[5]

Tina's Ridge (IRE) *Miss J S Davis* a60 63
3 ch g Indian Ridge—Phantom Waters (Pharly (FR))
69[8] 449[7] 569[5] 931[10] 1154[13] 1538[12] 2978[4] 3469[7] (3843) (4073) 4287[8] 5555[9] 7263[5]

Tinsy *J L Spearing*
3 b f Groom Dancer(USA) —Arkadia Park (IRE) (Polish Precedent (USA))
5315[11]

Tinted View (USA) *Mrs H Sweeting* a51 55
3 ch f Distant View(USA) —Gombeen (USA) (Private Account (USA))
3992[10] 4596[10]

Tintorero *M J Wallace* a58 50
2 b c Kyllachy—Lady Hibernia (Anabaa (USA))
1743[9] 2876[10] 3424[4] 4154[5] 4512[3] 4824[6]

Tin Town Boy (IRE) *H Rogers* a73 73
6 b g Danehill Dancer(IRE) —Sushari (IRE) (Shardari)
6920a[7]

Tiny Tim (IRE) *A M Balding* a46 53
9 b g Brief Truce(USA) —Nonnita (Welsh Saint)
207[9] 653[4]

Tioga Gold (IRE) *L R James* a53 46
8 b g Goldmark(USA) —Coffee Bean (Doulab (USA))
(10) 146[5] 631[6] 808[3] 1032[6]

Tipsy Lad *D J S Ffrench Davis* a57 44
5 b g Tipsy Creek(USA) —Perfidy (FR) (Persian Bold)
1715[2] 1933[9] 2273[5] 2540[10] 3241[5] (3647) 3950[9] 4294[15] 5094[8] 5128[8] 5391[11] 5730[11] 5817[4] 6268[10] 6479[4] 6587[9] 6796[11] 6908[6]

Tipsy Lillie *P S McEntee* a46 50
5 ch m Tipsy Creek(USA) —Belle De Nuit (IRE) (Statoblest)
210[10]

Tipsy Me *M L W Bell* a67 66
4 b m Selkirk(USA) —Time Saved (Green Desert (USA))
85[6]

Tipsy Prince *David Pinder* a75 73
3 b g Tipsy Creek(USA) —Princess Of Garda (Komaite (USA))
885[4] 1383[5] 1920[6] 2335[5] 2601[6] (3237) 3646[10] 4538[6] 5238[8] 5874[8] 6103[6] 6239[7]

Tip The Dip (USA) *M McDonagh* a33 53
7 ch h Benny The Dip(USA) —Senora Tippy (USA) (El Gran Senor (USA))
4142a[9]

Tip Toes (IRE) *P Howling* a52 52
5 b m Bianconi(USA) —Tip Tap Toe (USA) (Pleasant Tap (USA))
87[7] 285[4] (333) 578[11] 792[4] 982[6] 1229[2] 1402[5] 1925[3]

Tip Top Style *J Mackie* a54 29
4 b g Tipsy Creek(USA) —Eliza Jane (Mistertopogigo (IRE))
80[4] 243[7]

Tirailleur (IRE) *M J Gingell* a36 31
7 b m Eagle Eyed(USA) —Tiralle (IRE) (Tirol)
240[7]

Tiramisu (TUR) *S Tasbek* 109
4 b m Marlin(USA) —Dan Dancing (FR) (Groom Dancer (USA))
5264a[4]

Tirwanako (FR) *J-L Pelletan* 108
5 b h Sin Kiang(FR) —Alhena (FR) (Kaldoun (FR))
990a[11]

Titan Triumph *W J Knight* a89 83
3 b c Zamindar(USA) —Triple Green (Green Desert (USA))
3102[3] 3851[3] 4326[8] (4807) 5114[3] 6203[7] (6795) 6949[3] 7087[3]

Titfer (IRE) *A W Carroll* a56 61
2 ch c Fath(USA) —Fur Hat (Habitat)
1762[9] 2885[5] 3363[15] 4417[10] 5127[8] 6427[3] 6750[8]

Titian Saga (IRE) *C N Allen* a53 66
4 ch m Titus Livius(FR) —Nordic Living (IRE) (Nordico (USA))
668[5] 746[9] 964[10] 1349[10] 1719[3] 2343[10] 5954[12] 6210[8] 6264[7] 6528[5]

Titinius (IRE) *Micky Hammond* 77
7 ch g Titus Livius(FR) —Maiyria (IRE) (Shernazar)
1555[10] 2256[16] 3998[8] 4177[5] 4704[3] 5228[4] 5559[2] 5905[15] 6380[4] 6727[2]

Title Deed (USA) *A P Jarvis* a74 61
3 b g Belong To Me(USA) —Said Privately (USA) (Private Account (USA))
116[6] 293[4] 522[2] 719[8] 772[3] 1122[8] 1290[10] 4277[5] 4511[7] 6848[11]

Title Role *P F I Cole* a73 46
2 b g Mark Of Esteem(IRE) —No Comebacks (Last Tycoon (IRE))
3977[8] 4328[9] 4882[5] 6750[3]

Tito (IRE) *T D Barron* 68
2 b c Diktat—T G's Girl (Selkirk (USA))
5771[7] 6384[2]

Titree *C Laffon-Parias* a94 87
3 b f Highest Honor(FR) —Timber Nymph (USA) (Woodman (USA))
6940a[5]

Tittle *H Candy* 57
2 b f Tobougg(IRE) —Poppy's Song (Owington)
5699[4] 6105[4]

Titus Lumpus (IRE) *R M Flower* a65 62
4 b g Titus Livius(FR) —Carabosse (Salse (USA))
1446[10] 1629[3] 2358[10] 2667[7] 2802[7] 3048[8] 4395[5] 4592[6] (Dead)

Titus Shadow (IRE) *B Grizzetti* 102
3 ch c Titus Livius(FR) —Mujadil Shadow (IRE) (Mujadil (USA))
6686a[3]

Titus Wonder (IRE) *J W Mullins* a34 32
4 ch m Titus Livius(FR) —Morcote (IRE) (Magical Wonder (USA))
156[8] 350[10]

Tivers Jewel (USA) *Mrs A J Perrett* a13 63
3 bb g Tiznow(USA) —Box Of Jewels (USA) (Half A Year (USA))
3454[8]

Tivers Song (USA) *Mrs A J Perrett* a69 64
3 gr c Buddha(USA) —Rousing (USA) (Alydar (USA))
2445[6] 3189[4] 4391[11] 5111[7] 5754[4]

Tiza (SAF) *A De Royer-Dupre* a91 114
5 b g Goldkeeper(USA) —Mamushka (SAF) (Elliodor (FR))
245a[8] 400a[2] 644a[3] 860a[9] (3445a) 4214a[10] 4871a[3] 6039a[6] (6633a) 7089a[8]

Tizzydore (IRE) *A G Newcombe* a48 42
3 b f Shinko Forest(IRE) —Shannon Dore (IRE) (Turtle Island (IRE))
260[6] 342[8] 708[8] 1031[12] 1782[7] 2718[11] 2978[7] 3871[7]

Tizzy May (FR) *B Ellison* a66 78
7 ch g Highest Honor(FR) —Forentia (Formidable (USA))
1893[4] 2307[2] 2467[2] 2531[5] 3093[4] (3346) 3793[2] 4716[6] 5178[7] 5553[4] 5838[9]

To Arms *K J Burke* a7 67
5 b g Mujahid(USA) —Toffee (Midyan (USA))
3033[2] 6200[2] 7008[6]

Toasted Special (USA) *B J Meehan* a45 61
2 ch f Johannesburg(USA) —Sajjaya (USA) (Blushing Groom (FR))
5442[2] 5949[10] 6267[11] 6665[10]

Tobago Bay *M R Channon* a25 54
2 b c Tobougg(IRE) —Perfect Dream (Emperor Jones (USA))
4761[15] 5088[5] 5274[11] 5729[14] 5818[13] 5863[6]

Tobago Reef *Mrs L Stubbs* a75 58
3 b g Tobougg(IRE) —Silly Mid-On (Midyan (USA))
216[3] 744[5] 935[9] 6024[8] 6873[3] 7006[9]

Toballa *H J Collingridge* a20
2 b f Tobougg(IRE) —Ball Gown (Jalmood (USA))
7181[6]

Tobaro (GER) *T T Clement*
6 gr g Acambaro(GER) —Top Girl (GER) (Park Romeo)
6337[8]

Tobar Suil Lady (IRE) *K A Ryan* a70 71
2 b f Statue Of Liberty(USA) —Stellarette (IRE) (Lycius (USA))
4924[3] 5483[2] (5888) 6635[6]

To Be Or Not To Be *W Jarvis* a58
2 b f Tobougg(IRE) —Lady Mayor (Kris)
7190[6]

Toberanthawn (IRE) *K J Condon* 72
2 ch f Danehill Dancer(IRE) —Phariseek (IRE) (Rainbow Quest (USA))
5395a[19] 6392a[3]

Tobermory (IRE) *M A Jarvis* a69 84
3 b f Green Desert(USA) —Kerrera (Diesis)
1520[5] 2119[5]

Toberogan (IRE) *W A Murphy* a47 63
6 b g Docksider(USA) —Beltisaal (FR) (Belmez (USA))
3535[7] 4583[3] 5935[13] 6363a[12] 7111[6]

Tobogganist *W Jarvis* a72 72
2 b c Tobougg(IRE) —Seeking Utopia (Wolfhound (USA))
2832[13] 3383[5] 3850[4] 4364[12] (5883) 6233[7]

Toboggan Lady *Mrs A Duffield* a46 66
3 b f Tobougg(IRE) —Northbend (Shirley Heights)
1153[7] 1579[11] 2420[2] (3183) (3640) 4104[2] 4409[7] 5906[2] (6383)

Tobosa *W Jarvis* 115
3 b c Tobougg(IRE) —Sovereign Abbey (IRE) (Royal Academy (USA))
1095[2] 1473[14] (2037) 3362a[5] 4148[3] (5378) 6009[4]

Tobouggornotobougg *D Shaw* a48
2 ch g Tobougg(IRE) —Douce Maison (IRE) (Fools Holme (USA))
5984[10] 6705[5] 6855[10] 7176[6] 7245[9]

Tobougg Welcome (IRE) *S C Williams* a48 51
3 ch g Tobougg(IRE) —Three White Sox (Most Welcome)
69[11] 342[12] 484[7] 2610[5] 3792[2] 4531[7] 4877[4] 5533[7]

To Bubbles *T D Barron* 22
2 b f Tobougg(IRE) —Effervescent (Efisio)
6281[14]

Toccata (IRE) *D M Simcock* a53 78
3 b f Cape Cross(IRE) —Sopran Marida (IRE) (Darshaan)
(1685) 2231[11] 2971[8] 5814[7]

Todber *M P Tregoning* a48 50
2 b f Cape Cross(IRE) —Dominica (Alhaarth (IRE))
3187[7] 5856[8]

Todlea (IRE) *Jean-Rene Auvray* a55 73
7 b g Desert Prince(IRE) —Imelda (USA) (Manila (USA))
268[6] 379[8] 975[4] 1209[9] 2423[11] 2514[10] 3352[14]

Todman Avenue (USA) *A Al Raihe* a61 67
5 bb g Lear Fan(USA) —Three Wishes (Sadler's Wells (USA))
104a[6] 244a[11] 330a[11]

Todwick Owl *J G Given* a59 58
3 b g Namid—Blinding Mission (IRE) (Marju (IRE))
7023[10] 7144[4]

Toga Party (IRE) *Miss Sheena West* 36
5 b g Turtle Island(IRE) —Fun Fashion (IRE) (Polish Patriot (USA))
3176[9]

Tokyo Jo (IRE) *T T Clement* a58 58
3 b f Raise A Grand(IRE) —Wakayi (Persian Bold)
624[9] 3646[14] 3826[16] 4361[9] 4596[7] 5945[3] 6249[6] 6277[7] 6706[10] 6908[8]

Toledo Sun *S Curran* a50
7 b g Zamindar(USA) —Shafir (IRE) (Shaadi (USA))
1934[5] 2345[3]

Toll Gate (IRE) *R Charlton* a32 47
2 ch f Dr Fong(USA) —Knell (IRE) (Unfuwain (USA))
6417[10] 6737[6]

Tombalina *C J Teague* a55 50
4 ch m Tomba—Ashkernazy (IRE) (Salt Dome (USA))
1594[8] 2249[7] 3259[12] 3837[12]

Tomba Maestro *J L Spearing*
2 ch g Tomba—Ashkernazy (IRE) (Salt Dome (USA))
3589[15] 4027[8] 4512[6]

Tombas Legacy *Mark Gillard*
2 ch c Tomba—Regal Academy (IRE) (Royal Academy (USA))
3364[8] 3835[9]

Tom Bell (IRE) *J G M O'Shea* a26 53
7 b g King's Theatre(IRE) —Nordic Display (IRE) (Nordico (USA))
1002[6] (Dead)

Tombi (USA) *J Howard Johnson* 95
3 b g Johannesburg(USA) —Tune In To The Cat (USA) (Tunerup (USA))
(1403) 1825[2] 4093[4] (4898) 6472[4]

Tomintoul Flyer *H R A Cecil* 85
2 br c Dr Fong(USA) —Miller's Melody (Chief Singer)
4586[3] (5599) (6092)

Tommy Tobougg *I Semple* a43 61
3 ch g Tobougg(IRE) —Celebrate (IRE) (Generous (IRE))
1290[8] 1804[8] (3372) 4080[6] 4701[10] 5035[6] 6695[7]

Tommy Toogood (IRE) *B W Hills* a92 84
4 b h Danehill(USA) —On The Nile (IRE) (Sadler's Wells (USA))
3437[14] 4814[10] 5205[4] 6110[8] 6439[2]

Tommytush (IRE) *E J Alston* a59 60
2 b c Mujadil(USA) —Zilayah (USA) (Zilzal (USA))
4221[9] 4818[8] 5081[4] 5484[5] 5751[7] 6384[7] 6813[6] 7021[3] 7171[2] 7240[4]

Tomorrow's Dancer *K A Ryan* a50 53
3 b g Danehill Dancer(IRE) —Today (IRE) (Royal Academy (USA))
894[9] 1232[6] 1531[4] 1712[7] 2300[9] 3181[4] 3540[5]

Tomorrow's Dream (IRE) *M Halford* 73
9 br g Be My Native(USA) —Quare Dream'S (IRE) (Strong Gale)
4371a[2]

Tomorrow's World (IRE) *Sir Michael Stoute* a67 70
2 b f Machiavellian(USA) —Follow That Dream (Darshaan)
3706[5] 4393[4] 6414[6]

Tom Paris *W R Muir* a76 73
3 b g Bertolini(USA) —Nom Francais (First Trump)
2598[10] 3689[7] 4313[4] 5046[6] 5238[3] 5475[3] 6269[7] 6628[5] 6824[7] 7047[3]

Toms Laughter *R A Harris* a62 65
3 ch g Mamalik(USA) —Time Clash (Timeless Times (USA))
152[4] 522[5] 633[8] 2083[9] 2262[2] 2545[7] (2622) 3411[5] 3905[3] 3950[3] 7227[6] 7271[5]

Tom Tower (IRE) *A C Whillans* 71
3 b g Cape Cross(IRE) —La Belle Katherine (USA) (Lyphard (USA))
1623[5] 1802[6]

Toni Alcala *R F Fisher* a60 58
8 b g Ezzoud(IRE) —Etourdie (USA) (Arctic Tern (USA))
618[3] 792[7] 913[2] 1196[3] 1457[6] 1745[4] 2204[6]

Tonic Star (FR) *E Lellouche* 99
4 b m Enrique—Tonic Stream (FR) (Bering)
1421a[6]

Tonnante *Sir Mark Prescott* a73 80
3 b f Hernando(FR) —Thunder Queen (USA) (Thunder Gulch (USA))
3825[3] 4339[5] (5279) 5478[3] (5839) 6356[5]

Tony James (IRE) *K O Cunningham-Brown* a93 101
5 b h Xaar—Sunset Ridge (FR) (Green Tune (USA))
118[7] 352[7] 487[5] 550[9] 841[2] 1836[16] 3104[4] 3489[2] 4183[5] 4806[6] 5797[19] 6003[10] 6851[5] 6932[9]

Tony The Tap *W R Muir* a87 89
6 b g Most Welcome—Laleston (Junius (USA))
3188[5] 3749[2] 3990[4] 4122[16] 5050[6] 5447[6] 5513[3] 5891[3] 6141[6] 6231[5] 6708[2] (6938) 6972[8]

Too Grand *J J Bridger* a61 53
2 ch f Zaha(CAN) —Gold Linnet (Nashwan (USA))
3687[8] 3866[5] 4310[5] 5117[7] 5443[6] 5818[5] (6426) 6624[7] 6828[2] 6966[9] 7031[4] 7182[10]

Too Hot To Handle (IRE) *J M P Eustace* 51
2 br f Elnadim(USA) —Tropical Zone (Machiavellian (USA))
6409[9]

Toolittleyourlate (USA) *K A Ryan* a68 93
2 bb c Harlan's Holiday(USA) —Spirit In The Sky (USA) (Gulch (USA))
3834[6] (4358) 4724[5]

To Party (IRE) *P D Evans* a66 70
3 ch f Elusive Quality(USA) —Magongo (Be My Chief (USA))
1620[10] 1973[7] 3110[11] 3763[11]

Toparudi *M H Tompkins* a49 87
6 b g Rudimentary(USA) —Topatori (IRE) (Topanoora)
930[7] 1199[9] 1745[2] 2204[2] (2250) 2715[3] 2887[10] (3273) 3858[5] (5478)

Topatoo *M H Tompkins* 108
5 ch m Bahamian Bounty—Topatori (IRE) (Topanoora)
1472[2] (1789) 3271[4] 4826[8]

Topazes *M L W Bell* 54
2 ch c Cadeaux Genereux—Topkamp (Pennekamp (USA))
5575[11] 5910[11]

Topazleo (IRE) *J Wade* 67
3 ch g Peintre Celebre(USA) —Mer Noire (IRE) (Marju (IRE))
1863[7] 3382[6] 4283[6]

Top Bid *T D Easterby* 84
3 b g Auction House(USA) —Trump Street (First Trump)
1298[5] 1825[9] 2884[6] 3380[2] 3952[3] 4608[8] 4811[7] 6331[14]

Top Class (USA) *A P O'Brien* 101
3 b c Storm Cat(USA) —Simadartha (USA) (Gone West (USA))
1547a[7]

Top Dirham *M W Easterby* a47 83
9 ch g Night Shift(USA) —Miller's Melody (Chief Singer)
1673[7] 2149[9] 2256[4] 2714[11] (3195) 3571[3] 3754[4] 4701[5] 5525[5]

Top Draw (USA) *M L W Bell* a66 61
2 br f Elusive Quality(USA) —Cala (FR) (Desert Prince (IRE))
5882[4] 6434[4]

Topflightcoolracer *Mrs G S Rees* a83 86
3 b f Lujain(USA) —Jamarj (Tyrnavos)
237[5] 3062[4] 3406[7] 3924[2] (4432) 4740[5] (5806) 6173[10] 6676[6] 6876[7]

Topflightrebellion *Mrs G S Rees* a52
2 b f Mark Of Esteem(IRE) —Jamarj (Tyrnavos)
5097[10] 7216[3]

Topflight Wildbird *Mrs G S Rees* a59 66
4 br m Diktat—Jamarj (Tyrnavos)
805[7] 1178[12] 1627[3] 3182[4] 3502[2] 3955[3] 4128[3] 4499[4] 4717[8] 5777[6] 6258[12]

Top Gear *Mrs L J Mongan* a60 71
5 b g Robellino(USA) —Bundle (Cadeaux Genereux)
1149[11] 1542[10] 3943[19] 6175[9] 6716[11]

Topiary Ted *Tom Dascombe* a79 43
5 ch g Zafonic(USA) —Lovely Lyca (Night Shift (USA))
(151) 263[7] 538[4] 675[9] (819) 6848[5]

Top Jaro (FR) *D W Barker* a72 82
4 b g Marathon(USA) —Shahmy (USA) (Lear Fan (USA))
434[8] 568[10] 669[7] 1066[4] 1198[2] 1555[9] 1720[5] 1997[7] (2298) 2709[3] 3487[4] (4082) 4408[3] 4716[8] 5553[3] 5905[6]

Topjeu (IRE) *L M Cumani* 94
4 b g Montjeu(IRE) —Arabian Lass (SAF) (Al Mufti (USA))
2002[5] 2861[2]

Topka (FR) *F Doumen* 101
3 b f Kahyasi—Tipsy Topsy (Ashkalani (IRE))
989a[3] 1880a[5] 2501a[13] 2926a[3] 4557a[7] 6400a[10]

Top Man Dan (IRE) *D Carroll* 72
2 b g Danetime(IRE) —Aphra Benn (IRE) (In The Wings)
6184[5]

Top Mark *J R Boyle* a87 86
5 b g Mark Of Esteem(IRE) —Red White And Blue (Zafonic (USA))
38[2] 211[2] (314) 444[2] 1524[5] 2004[14] (2765) 2995[2] 3855[2] 4105[2] (4481)

Topor (TUR) *B Tosun* 92
3 b c Sri Pekan(USA) —Shiero (TUR) (Castle Rising I)
5265a[9]

Top Rocker *E W Tuer* 51
3 b g Rock City—Top Hand (First Trump)
1220[8] 1491[5] 1968[6] 2389[9] 3640[3] 3840[5]

Top Seed (IRE) *A J Chamberlain* a83 92
6 b g Cadeaux Genereux—Midnight Heights (Persian Heights)
89[12] 2527[7] 3407[10]

Top Spec (IRE) *J Pearce* a79 80
6 b g Spectrum(IRE) —Pearl Marine (IRE) (Bluebird (USA))
142[6] 297[3] 3671[9] 4171[8] 5145[7] 6878[7]

Top Tenor (IRE) *W Storey* 48
7 b g Sadler's Wells(USA) —Posta Vecchia (USA) (Rainbow Quest (USA))
62[8] 3840[8] 4179[4] 5626[11]

Top Ticket (IRE) *D M Simcock* 75
2 ch c Alhaarth(IRE) —Tathkara (USA) (Alydar (USA))
5570[3] 6248[3]

Top Tiger *M H Tompkins* a68 73
3 b g Mtoto—Topatori (IRE) (Topanoora)
849[5] 3399[3] (5898) 6158[11] 6666[5]

Top Toss (IRE) *Y De Nicolay* 100
2 gr f Linamix(FR) —Tossup (USA) (Gone West (USA))
(5493a)

Top Trees *W S Kittow* a47 56
9 b g Charnwood Forest(IRE) —Low Line (High Line)
1888[6] 2493[7] 3467[5] 5138[4] 5453[3]

Top Vision *M R Channon* 69
2 ch f Medicean—Perfect Partner (Be My Chief (USA))
3507[7] 4094[5] 4564[12]

Topwell *R C Guest* 36
6 b g Most Welcome—Miss Top Ville (FR) (Top Ville)
6700[9]

Toque De Queda *M Delzangles* 100
3 b f Dansili—Bazbina (FR) (Highest Honor (FR))
3148a[3] 5058a[9]

Tora Warning *John A Harris* a45 21
3 b g Warningford—Torrecilla (General Monash (USA))
1749[7] 2304[10] 3406[11]

Torba (IRE) *Evan Williams* 71
3 b f Daylami(IRE) —Beeper The Great (USA) (Whadjathink (USA))
1560[3] 3366[7] 3794[2] 4257[6]

Torch Of Freedom (IRE) *Sir Mark Prescott* a76 70
2 b g Statue Of Liberty(USA) —Danse Royale (IRE) (Caerleon (USA))
5575^{4} (6641) 6800^{2}

Tornadodancer (IRE) *T G McCourt* a51 70
4 b g Princely Heir(IRE) —Purty Dancer (IRE) (Foxhound (USA))
873a^{11} 5460a^{10} 5836^{7}

Torquemada (IRE) *J Akehurst* a78 71
6 ch g Desert Sun—Gaelic's Fantasy (IRE) (Statoblest)
1401^{3} 1931^{8} 2458^{3} 4295^{8} (5303) 5687^{11} 6278^{9} 6547^{2} 6996^{9} 7099^{9}

Torrens (IRE) *J Hetherton* a82 86
5 b g Royal Anthem(USA) —Azure Lake (USA) (Lac Ouimet (USA))
205^{6} 377^{4} 811^{5} 1090^{3} (1199) 1434^{2} 1922^{6} (2527) 3093^{8} 3530^{6} 3978^{6} 4166^{3} 4597^{11} 5145^{4} 5664^{5} 6230^{2} 6325^{5} 6501^{2}

Torrent *J M Saville* a37 58
12 ch g Prince Sabo—Maiden Pool (Sharpen Up)
135^{6}

Torrid Kentavr (USA) *J J Lambe* a78 75
10 b g Trempolino(USA) —Torrid Tango (USA) (Green Dancer (USA))
283^{4}

Tortola (IRE) *M H Tompkins* a31
2 ch c Cadeaux Genereux—Slipper (Suave Dancer (USA))
6850^{13}

Torver *Dr J D Scargill* a50 53
3 br f Lake Coniston(IRE) —Billie Blue (Ballad Rock)
5602^{5} 6100^{10}

Tory Brae (IRE) *R M Beckett* a34
3 b g In The Wings—Solar Crystal (IRE) (Alzao (USA))
499^{13} 703^{7}

Toryt (POL) *Carl Llewellyn* a55
8 b g Beaconsfield—Torana (POL) (Dixieland (POL))
1526^{7}

Toshi (USA) *P Monteith* a57 88
5 b g Kingmambo(USA) —Majestic Role (FR) (Theatrical)
1627^{8} (1890) 2250^{7} 2391^{5} 4933^{5}

To Sir With Love (NZ) *J S Wainwright*
6 b g Turbulent Dancer(USA) —Kudos (NZ) (Kreisler)
1259^{10} 1715^{13}

Total Impact *C A Cyzer* a88 93
4 ch g Pivotal—Rise 'n Shine (Night Shift (USA))
490^{9} 692^{7} 818^{4} 1363^{8} 3080^{10} 4965^{7} 5119^{7}

Totally Focussed (IRE) *S Dow* 64
2 rg g Trans Island—Premier Place (USA) (Out Of Place (USA))
3043^{11} 3687^{5} 4323^{5}

Totally Free *M D I Usher* a66 58
3 ch g Woodborough(USA) —Barefooted Flyer (USA) (Fly So Free (USA))
90^{4} 202^{9} 360^{10} 454^{2} 636^{13} 900^{3} (1031) 1269^{6} 1763^{10} (2146) 2262^{6} 2948^{4} 3713^{7} 3870^{5} 4071^{6}

Totem Flower (IRE) *R Charlton* 69
2 ch f Indian Ridge—Tree Peony (Woodman (USA))
3895^{9} 5063^{6}

To The Dance (IRE) *E J O'Neill* a23
2 b c Fasliyev(USA) —Jules (IRE) (Danehill (USA))
5133^{9}

To The Max (IRE) *Mrs C A Dunnett* 94
3 b c Spectrum(IRE) —Pray (IRE) (Priolo (USA))
1097^{8} 2057^{5} 2671^{8} 5641^{6}

Totoman *G G Margarson* 65
2 b c Mtoto—Norcroft Lady (Mujtahid (USA))
4325^{5}

Toto Skyllachy *T P Tate* 81
2 b c Kyllachy—Little Tramp (Trempolino (USA))
1859^{RR} 2710^{4} (3238)

Toucantini *R Charlton* a62
3 b f Inchinor—French Quartet (IRE) (Lycius (USA))
160^{4} 312^{7} 6455^{5} 6810^{9}

Touch My Soul (FR) *P Schiergen* 106
3 b f Tiger Hill(IRE) —Topline (GER) (Acatenango (GER))
(3121a) 4055a^{8}

Touch Of Ivory (IRE) *P Monteith* 68
4 b m Rossini(USA) —Windomen (IRE) (Forest Wind (USA))
955^{7} 1488^{7} 3815^{6} 4096^{12} 4383^{4} 5553^{8}

Touch Of Land (FR) *H-A Pantall* a100 119
7 b h Lando(GER) —Touch Of Class (GER) (Be My Guest (USA))
330a^{8} 600a^{7} 6032a^{9} 7128a^{6}

Touch Of Pep (IRE) *Jamie Poulton* 66
2 b c Lando(GER) —Touch Of Class (GER) (Be My Guest (USA))
6130^{6}

Touch Of Style (IRE) *J R Boyle* a81 81
3 b g Desert Style(IRE) —No Hard Feelings (IRE) (Alzao (USA))
4275^{6} 4811^{15} 5129^{2} 5532^{13} (5819) 6646^{6} 6949^{10} 7018^{8} 7160^{2}

Tough Love *T D Easterby* 79
8 ch g Pursuit Of Love—Food Of Love (Music Boy)
1132^{3} 1555^{3} 2311^{4} (2741) 2936^{7} 3790^{6} 4137^{4} 4407^{11} 5228^{6} 5559^{14}

Tough Tiz's Sis (USA) *B Baffert* a117
3 b f Tiznow(USA) —Leaseholder (USA) (Taylor's Falls (USA))
4628a^{6} 6512a^{7}

Tour D'Amour (IRE) *R Craggs* a67 71
4 b m Fruits Of Love(USA) —Touraneena (Robellino (USA))
75^{2} 200^{6} 1265^{4} 1352^{2} 1626^{4} 2254^{9} 2338^{12} 4081^{2} 4427^{11} 5159^{2} 5627^{5} 5907^{5}

Tourist *B W Hills* 72
2 b c Oasis Dream—West Devon (USA) (Gone West (USA))
5628^{7} 6469^{3}

Tournedos (IRE) *D Nicholls* a64 108
5 b g Rossini(USA) —Don't Care (IRE) (Nordico (USA))
249a^{15} 415a^{10} 474a^{12} 1456^{7} 1601^{4} 1788^{9} 2237^{9} 2463^{6} 3050^{9} 3990^{24} 5700^{4} (5841a) 6183^{17}

Tournevr (IRE) *Jane Chapple-Hyam* a55 67
2 b f Danetime(IRE) —Tuft Hill (Grundy)
3417^{12} 3915^{4} 5815^{6}

Tous Les Deux *Peter Grayson* a85 71
4 b g Efisio—Caerosa (Caerleon (USA))
96^{11} 164^{6} (263) 420^{4} 552^{6} 652^{3} 701^{12} 777^{5} 1288^{11} 1543^{10} 1905^{3} 2871^{9} 3076^{6} 3452^{4} 4024^{3} 4462^{2} 5119^{3} 5648^{10} 5889^{8} 6405^{5} 6938^{4} 7026^{5} 7221^{5}

Town And Gown *J H M Gosden* a73 48
2 br f Oasis Dream—Degree (Warning)
3055^{9} 5766^{18} 6228^{2} 6799^{4} 6926^{3}

Town House *B P J Baugh* a52 52
5 gr m Paris House—Avondale Girl (IRE) (Case Law)
137^{2} 287^{6} 441^{3} 523^{14} 680^{12} 2315^{8} 2529^{10} 3782^{11} 5672^{9}

Townkab (IRE) *N P Littmoden* a49 66
2 b g Intikhab(USA) —Town Girl (IRE) (Lammtarra (USA))
3171^{6} 3850^{10} 4130^{9} 4524^{4} 4776^{2} (5109) 5314^{10} 5600^{2} 5914^{7}

Townsville (FR) *B Secly* 74
2 b c Numerous(USA) —Imerina (FR) (Cadoudal (FR))
(6952a)

Towy Boy (IRE) *I A Wood* a63 63
2 b c King Charlemagne(USA) —Solar Flare (IRE) (Danehill (USA))
2911^{3} 4201^{8} 4629^{5} 5199^{7} 6401^{2} 6715^{9} 6973^{8}

Towy Girl (IRE) *A W Carroll* a71 54
3 b f Second Empire(IRE) —Solar Flare (IRE) (Danehill (USA))
3154^{6} 4257^{P} 5129^{3} 5532^{3} 5893^{2} 6240^{5} 7029^{2}

Toylsome *J Hirschberger* 123
8 ch h Cadeaux Genereux—Treasure Trove (USA) (The Minstrel (CAN))
4213a^{2} 4445a^{4} (6029a) 6332^{3}

Toy Top (USA) *M Dods* a14 87
4 rg m Tactical Cat(USA) —I'll Flutter By (USA) (Concorde's Tune (USA))
953^{12} 1678^{9} 1854^{20} 2315^{11} 2418^{10} 2933^{4} 3374^{8} 3782^{3} 4101^{4} 4252^{2} 4525^{6} (4787) (4939) 4967^{9} 5507^{9} 5740^{4} 5908^{12}

Trace Clip *N I M Rossiter* a21 56
9 b g Zafonic(USA) —Illusory (Kings Lake (USA))
5861^{14}

Tracer *M W Easterby* a68 71
3 br g Kyllachy—Western Sal (Salse (USA))
752^{2} 1383^{4} 2061^{12} 2317^{10} 3003^{6} 5701^{5} 6310^{11} 6640^{8}

Trackattack *M Appleby* a50 44
5 ch g Atraf—Verbena (IRE) (Don't Forget Me)
5427^{4} 7102^{5} 7157^{2} 7214^{6} 7273^{10}

Traditionalist (IRE) *G A Butler* a58 71
3 ch c Traditionally(USA) —Rouberia (IRE) (Alhaarth (IRE))
1440^{8} 2132^{5}

Trafalgar Bay (IRE) *K R Burke* 100
4 b g Fruits Of Love(USA) —Chatsworth Bay (IRE) (Fairy King (USA))
1653^{5} 2058^{2} 2817^{9} 3559^{8} 3941^{12}

Trafalgar Day *W M Brisbourne* 74
4 b g Mark Of Esteem(IRE) —Rosy Sunset (IRE) (Red Sunset)
(1222) 1683^{4} 2434^{3} 2824^{2} (3036) 3243^{3} 5769^{5}

Trafalgar Square *J Akehurst* 96
5 b g King's Best(USA) —Pat Or Else (Alzao (USA))
(1818) 2755^{10} 5950^{12}

Traffic Guard (USA) *J S Moore* a100 108
3 b c More Than Ready(USA) —Street Scene (IRE) (Zafonic (USA))
173a^{2} 414a^{2} 859a^{6} 2051a^{9} 2752^{4} (3463) 4148^{2} 5265a^{8}

Traitor's Gate *M Johnston* a41 40
2 b g Machiavellian(USA) —Wilayif (USA) (Danzig (USA))
6177^{8} 6593^{11} 6698^{U}

Tralanza (IRE) *P J Prendergast* a69 76
3 ch f Traditionally(USA) —Alegranza (IRE) (Lake Coniston (IRE))
6893^{4}

Trammon Ventre (IRE) *Eamon Tyrrell* a51 51
3 b f Mujadil(USA) —Classic Line (Last Tycoon (IRE))
6779^{9} 7025^{9}

Trance (IRE) *T D Barron* a86 88
7 ch g Bahhare(USA) —Lady Of Dreams (IRE) (Prince Rupert (FR))
955^{8} 1148^{4} 1300^{7} 1677^{4} 1793^{3} (2170) 4398^{3} 4786^{4} 6186^{10} 6335^{16} 6473^{18} 6733^{6} 6744^{5}

Tranos (USA) *Micky Hammond* a65 65
4 b g Bahri(USA) —Balancoire (USA) (Diesis)
1042^{8} 1532^{6} 2254^{16}

Tranquility *J Pearce* a42 45
3 b f Barathea(IRE) —Immortelle (Arazi (USA))
253^{7} 373^{14} 790^{7} 1204^{14} 2454^{7}

Tranquilizer *D J Coakley* a86 78
5 b m Dr Fong(USA) —Tranquillity (Night Shift (USA))
153^{5} 608^{3} 1244^{11} 1783^{4} 2471^{3} 2720^{8} (3427)

Tranquil Tiger *H R A Cecil* 113
3 ch c Selkirk(USA) —Serene View (USA) (Distant View (USA))
1204^{2} (2005) 2789^{5} (3458) 4044^{8} 4722^{16} (5165) 5952^{4}

Transcend *J H M Gosden* a82 97
3 ch g Beat Hollow—Pleasuring (Good Times (ITY))
1075^{2} 1841^{3} (2059) 2671^{7} 4276^{6} 4811^{2} 5923^{8} (6450)

Transcendent (IRE) *J D Bethell* a53 50
2 b c Trans Island—Shannon Dore (IRE) (Turtle Island (IRE))
1291^{9} 2804^{8} 3687^{10} 4923^{9} 6456^{5} 6884^{7}

Transduction Gold (USA) *J Glenney* 109
4 bb g Formal Gold(CAN) —Moondust Mink (USA) (Great Above (USA))
6513a^{8}

Transfer *A M Balding* a76
2 br g Trans Island—Sankaty Light (USA) (Summer Squall (USA))
6119^{3} 6644^{4}

Transmission (IRE) *B Smart* 77
2 b g Galileo(IRE) —Individual (USA) (Gulch (USA))
2166^{6} 2888^{3} 3510^{2} 3842^{3} 4278^{5} 5350^{15}

Trans Siberian *P F I Cole* a78 65
3 b c Soviet Star(USA) —Dina Line (USA) (Diesis)
2726^{7} (2951)

Trans Sonic *A P Jarvis* a81 74
4 ch g Trans Island—Sankaty Light (USA) (Summer Squall (USA))
1470^{11} 1811^{2} 2403^{6} 6253^{8} 7017^{9}

Transvestite (IRE) *J W Hills* a93 90
5 b g Trans Island—Christoph's Girl (Efisio)
1244^{12} 1771^{7} 2238^{5} 2765^{5} 3165^{5} (3641) 4318^{5} 5052^{4} 5593^{9} 6007^{9}

Traphalgar (IRE) *P F I Cole* a80 64
2 br c Cape Cross(IRE) —Conquestadora (Hernando (FR))
3462^{9} 3896^{13} (6602) (6899) (7027a)

Traprain (IRE) *D Carroll* 82
5 b g Mark Of Esteem(IRE) —Nassma (IRE) (Sadler's Wells (USA))
6186^{3} 6473^{7}

Traumsternchen (GER) *P Hirschberger* 34
2 b f Acatenango(GER) —Traumzeit (GER) (Risk Me (FR))
5848a^{5} 6324a^{14}

Travelling Band (IRE) *J Mackie* a54 42
9 b g Blues Traveller(IRE) —Kind Of Cute (Prince Sabo)
3714^{3} 4256^{7}

Travelling Fox *Jane Chapple-Hyam* a43 48
4 b g Slip Anchor—Lola Mora (Nearly A Hand)
788^{4} 1032^{9}

Trawlerman (IRE) *M H Tompkins* 59
2 b c High Chaparral(IRE) —Forest Lair (Habitat)
5598^{11}

Treacle Noir (IRE) *Tom Dascombe* a55 49
2 b f Raise A Grand(IRE) —Exponent (USA) (Exbourne (USA))
2333^{11} 3796^{11} 3866^{9} 4629^{12} 5527^{6}

Treason Trial *Stef Liddiard* a46 62
6 b g Peintre Celebre(USA) —Pampabella (IRE) (High Estate)
220^{6} 333^{3} 481^{5} (1152) 1406^{4} 2434^{7} 2686^{4} 3033^{5} 3969^{4} 4124^{2} (4859) 5111^{6} 6186^{9}

Treasure House (IRE) *M Blanshard* a73 74
6 b g Grand Lodge(USA) —Royal Wolff (Prince Tenderfoot (USA))
830^{5} 1198^{8} 1446^{4} 1629^{4} 2004^{5} 2665^{14} 4135^{14} 4353^{7} 4797^{4} 5118^{4}

Treasure Islands (IRE) *S W Hall* a62 52
2 b f Trans Island—Gold Prospector (IRE) (Spectrum (IRE))
6571^{8} 6777^{6}

Treasure Isle *R A Fahey* a46 46
3 ch f Bahamian Bounty—South Rock (Rock City)
2740^{7} 3382^{4} 3914^{4} 4230^{6} 5388^{5} 6069^{12}

Treat *M R Channon* 110
3 b f Barathea(IRE) —Cream Tease (Pursuit Of Love)
1496^{4} 2065a^{6} 2599^{4} 3332^{3} 3897^{7}

Tredegar *P F I Cole* a87 85
3 ch c Inchinor—Ffestiniog (IRE) (Efisio)
1275^{5} 1768^{11} 2045^{11}

Trees Of Green (USA) *Saeed Bin Suroor* a42 78
3 bb c Elusive Quality(USA) —Grazia (Sharpo)
2740^{2} 3276^{2} 3710^{4} 5285^{2} 5567^{8} 6309^{6}

Treetops Hotel (IRE) *R Hollinshead* a71 60
8 ch g Grand Lodge(USA) —Rousinette (Rousillon (USA))
23^{6} 813^{7} 1026^{8} 1319^{5} 1925^{5} 2511^{2} (2874) 3083^{4} (4961) (5341) 5531^{5} 7102^{3} 7249^{9}

Trefflich (GER) *Paul Nolan* 67
6 ch g Polish Precedent(USA) —Trefula (IRE) (Rainbow Quest (USA))
3138a^{12}

Tremelo Pointe (IRE) *H Morrison* a72 66
3 b f Trempolino(USA) —Kapria (FR) (Simon Du Desert (FR))
(684) 904^{5} 5122^{2} 5555^{11} 6547^{4}

Tremoto *F & L Camici* 71
2 b f Generous(IRE) —Therese Chenu (IRE) (Local Suitor (USA))
6047a^{12}

Trenchant *J R Fanshawe* 43
2 b g Medicean—Tromond (Lomond (USA))
6574^{11}

Trenchtown (IRE) *R Charlton* 84
2 b c King's Best(USA) —Barbuda (Rainbow Quest (USA))
4110^{6} 4852^{2} (5186)

Trendy (GER) *H J Groschel* 65
2 b f Banyumanik(IRE) —Taffy (GER) (Tirol)
4837a^{5}

Trepa (USA) *W Jarvis* 70
3 ch g Hennessy(USA) —Ball Gown (USA) (Silver Hawk (USA))
1257^{9} 1660^{9} 4135^{9} 5454^{11}

Tres Bien *P R Webber* a66
5 b g Bien Bien(USA) —Zielana Gora (Polish Precedent (USA))
45^{7} 229^{10} 265^{7} 775^{9}

Tres Hombres *Tom Dascombe* a42 53
3 ch g Tobougg(IRE) —Duena (Grand Lodge (USA))
37^{9}

Tresor Secret (FR) *J Gallagher* a65 60
7 b g Green Desert(USA) —Tresor (USA) (Pleasant Tap (USA))
88^{2} 212^{4} 481^{2} 683^{4} 813^{2} 1026^{4} 1342^{4} 1907^{3} 2222^{3}

Trevian *J M Bradley* a60 61
6 ch g Atraf—Ascend (IRE) (Glint Of Gold)
1562^{6} 2023^{6} 2336^{5} 2492^{3} 3067^{4} 3352^{3} 3600^{4} 3805^{6} (4161) 4517^{9} 4878^{4} 5188^{6} 6179^{10} 6407^{10} 6796^{4}

Trew Style *M H Tompkins* a64 25
5 ch g Desert King(IRE) —Southern Psychic (USA) (Alwasmi (USA))
5623^{8} 6733^{8} 6961^{4}

Trezene (USA) *G L Moore* a102 106
5 b g Atticus(USA) —Trevilla (USA) (Lyphard (USA))
4690^{19}

Trianon *R Charlton* 75
2 ch f Nayef(USA) —Trying For Gold (USA) (Northern Baby (CAN))
5812^{7} (6494)

Tribe *P R Webber* 83
5 b g Danehill(USA) —Leo Girl (USA) (Seattle Slew (USA))
(994) 2908^{8} 3748^{7} 4398^{7}

Tribute (IRE) *John A Harris* a44 86
6 b g Green Desert(USA) —Zooming (IRE) (Indian Ridge)
143^{6} 241^{8} 374^{9} 435^{6} 800^{8}

Tri Chara (IRE) *R Hollinshead* a69 64
3 ch c Grand Slam(USA) —Lamzena (IRE) (Fairy King (USA))
1605^{6} 1998^{12} 3685^{7} 4287^{2} 5046^{5} 5703^{12} 6245^{2} 6695^{3}

Trickle (USA) *Miss D Mountain* a67 60
3 ch f Rahy(USA) —Avitrix (USA) (Storm Bird (CAN))
4338^{8} 4855^{10} 5238^{10} 5424^{14} 7003^{12} 7166^{3}

Trick Or Treat *J G Given* a100 108
4 b m Lomitas—Trick Of Ace (USA) (Clever Trick (USA))
(2036) 2702a^{9} 3434^{7} 4089^{3} 4723^{3} 5352^{7} (6168)

Tricky Causeway (USA) *J Jerkens* 95
4 br h Giant's Causeway(USA) —Commodities (USA) (Private Account (USA))
6771a^{8}

Triel *D Nicholls*
4 b h Tout Ensemble—Winter Greeting (Hello Gorgeous (USA))
537^{11}

Trifti *C A Cyzer* a84 60
6 b g Vettori(IRE) —Time For Tea (IRE) (Imperial Frontier (USA))
164^{4} 259^{3} 604^{4} 652^{4} 739^{6} 1036^{8} 3352^{4} 3690^{9} 3945^{4} 4356^{3} 4915^{6} 5093^{4} 5424^{2} 5985^{2} 6145^{5}

Trigger's Friend *Jamie Poulton* a2 20
3 b f Double Trigger(IRE) —Four-Legged Friend (Aragon)
4541^{12} 4948^{11}

Trigger Shot (IRE) *M Weiss* 39
2 b f High Chaparral(IRE) —Trigger Happy (IRE) (Ela-Mana-Mou)
5463a^{7}

Trimlestown (IRE) *H Candy* a76 89
4 b g Orpen(USA) —Courtier (Saddlers' Hall (IRE))
1651^{9} 2239^{7} 2835^{8} 4134^{5} 4548^{2} 5115^{7} 6209^{8}

Trinculo (IRE) *R A Harris* a93 99
10 b g Anita's Prince—Fandangerina (USA) (Grey Dawn II)
59^{3} 155^{9} 214^{4} 432^{5} 465^{6} 566^{9} 1669^{8} 1991^{15} 2104^{2} 2386^{4} 3106^{8} 3368^{U} 4165^{14} (5190) 5425^{7} 5687^{6} 5866^{6} 6424^{10} 6873^{7} 6957^{2} (7107) 7207^{9} 7227^{11}

Trinidad (USA) *A P O'Brien* 82
3 b c Kingmambo(USA) —Video (USA) (Nijinsky (CAN))
4035a^{14}

Trinity College (USA) *A P O'Brien* 109
3 ch c Giant's Causeway(USA) —City College (USA) (Carson City (USA))
1047a^{6} 2051a^{12} 2483a^{2} 2789^{14} 3579a^{4} 3983a^{4} 4058^{8}

Trinkila (USA) *P F I Cole* a71 73
2 b f Cat Thief(USA) —Que Belle (CAN) (Seattle Dancer (USA))
4061^{12} 4875^{4} 5301^{3} (5605)

Triple Beat *H R A Cecil* a79 77
3 b g Beat Hollow—Three More (USA) (Sanglamore (USA))
1100^{5} 1863^{3}

Triple Shadow *M A Peill* a60 71
3 ch g Compton Place—Arctic High (Polar Falcon (USA))
2120^{3} 3054^{9} 3583^{3} 4642^{6} 4896^{5} 5139^{5} 5489^{8} 5662^{9} 5834^{4} 6701^{10} 6818^{4} 7005^{9}

Trippi's Storm (USA) *S Hough* 115
4 b g Trippi(USA) —Pocket Beauty (USA) (Storm Bird (CAN))
4415a^{3} 5250a^{4} (5823a) 6511a^{6}

Trip The Light *R A Fahey* 46
2 b g Fantastic Light(USA) —Jumaireyah (Fairy King (USA))
3718^{12} 4285^{5} 5328^{10}

Trip To The Moon *M Delzangles* 112
4 b m Fasliyev(USA) —Sparkling Isle (Inchinor)
2953a^{6} 3581a^{2} 4010a^{5} 5265a^{3}

Triskaidekaphobia *Miss J R Tooth* a66 75
4 b g Bertolini(USA) —Seren Teg (Timeless Times (USA))
82^{12} 154^{4} 214^{6} 613^{3} (746) 892^{3} 1080^{11} 1405^{11} 1885^{14} 3190^{8} 5565^{2} 6244^{5} 6428^{3} 6752^{11} 6890^{10} (7011) (7284)

Triskel *T Stack* 100
2 b f Hawk Wing(USA) —Pat Or Else (Alzao (USA))
(3659a) 4440a^{8}

Tritonville Lodge (IRE) *Miss E C Lavelle* a85 85
5 b g Grand Lodge(USA) —Olean (Sadler's Wells (USA))
192^{2}

Trivia (IRE) *N A Callaghan* a81 81
3 br f Marju(IRE) —Lehua (IRE) (Linamix (FR))
1105^{11} 1840^{3} (2554) 4587^{10} 5545^{2} (6025) 6651^{11}

Troialini *S W Hall* a83 79
3 b g Bertolini(USA) —Troia (IRE) (Last Tycoon (IRE))
719^{5} 1810^{5} 2185^{6} 2448^{7} 3709^{8} 5604^{6} 5906^{11} (6250)

Trojan Flight *R A Fahey* 87
6 ch g Hector Protector(USA) —Fairywings (Kris)
(1678) 2339[4] 2566[2] 4133[3] 4703[5] 4990[2] 5356[20]
Trojan Hero (IRE) *A Dickman* 30
2 b g Royal Applause—Anne Boleyn (Rainbow Quest (USA))
3951[11] 4781[12]
Trombone Tom *J R Norton* a64 63
4 b g Superior Premium—Nine To Five (Imp Society (USA))
1902[4] 2791[12] 4561[13] 4939[3]
Tromp *D J Coakley* a79 78
6 ch g Zilzal(USA) —Sulitelma (USA) (The Minstrel (CAN))
568[3] (753) 1591[9] 2994[7] 4318[11] 4976[7] 5500[10] 5948[8] 6564[9]
Troodos Jet *K W Hogg* a6 17
6 b g Atraf—Costa Verde (King Of Spain)
3956[11]
Tropical Star (IRE) *A Al Raihe* a114 92
7 b g Machiavellian(USA) —Tropical (Green Desert (USA))
177a[9] (249a)
Tropical Strait (IRE) *D W P Arbuthnot* a91 90
4 b g Intikhab(USA) —Tropical Dance (USA) (Thorn Dance (USA))
3794[4] 4392[2] 4948[2] (5683) (5892) 6759[4]
Troque (FR) *F Doumen* a91 102
3 b g Enrique—The Trollop (FR) (Double Bed (FR))
6032a[8]
Troubadour (IRE) *W Jarvis* a103 97
6 b g Danehill(USA) —Taking Liberties (IRE) (Royal Academy (USA))
4167[4] 4566[8] 4900[8] 5554[9] (6143) 6852[2] 7225[5]
Trouble Maker *A M Balding* a58
6 b g Green Desert(USA) —River Abouali (Bluebird (USA))
2179[9]
Trouble Mountain (USA) *M W Easterby* a57 80
10 br g Mt. Livermore(USA) —Trouble Free (USA) (Nodouble (USA))
1599[5] 1922[11] 3049[7] 3567[7] 4582[6] 4772[4] 5620[3] 5738[3] 6021[4] 6258[4] 6727[2]
Troys Steps *E J Alston* 37
3 b f Cloudings(IRE) —Troys Guest (IRE) (Be My Guest (USA))
6286[11] 6700[7] 6959[6]
Truckle *C W Fairhurst* a38 22
5 b g Vettori(IRE) —Proud Titania (IRE) (Fairy King (USA))
2[5]
Trudder (USA) *P W Chapple-Hyam* 29
2 br c Zavata(USA) —Blue Talent (USA) (Local Talent (USA))
5599[16] 6080[10]
True (IRE) *Mrs S Lamyman* a52 53
6 ch m Barathea(IRE) —Bibliotheque (USA) (Woodman (USA))
913[5] 1196[5] 1556[3] 2204[3] 2537[2] 2839[5] 6054[6] 6330[10] 6561[12]
True Cause (USA) *Saeed Bin Suroor* 108
4 ch h Storm Cat(USA) —Dearly (Rahy (USA))
6771a[2]
True Companion *Miss E C Lavelle* a83 78
8 b g Brief Truce(USA) —Comanche Companion (Commanche Run)
1813[3] 2321[10]
True Magic *J D Bethell* a71 75
6 b m Magic Ring(IRE) —True Precision (Presidium)
1911[0]
True Ruby *Dr J R J Naylor* a35 50
4 b m Josr Algarhoud(IRE) —St James's Antigua (IRE) (Law Society (USA))
6430[7] 6832[15]
True Time *E A L Dunlop* 61
2 ch f Rahy(USA) —True Fantasy (USA) (Seeking The Gold (USA))
4102[8] 4662[9] 5061[7] 6075[3]
True Vision (IRE) *Saeed Bin Suroor* 13
3 b f Pulpit(USA) —Mot Juste (Mtoto)
6420[13]
True West (USA) *Miss Gay Kelleway* a53 62
4 b m Gulch(USA) —True Life (USA) (El Gran Senor (USA))
751[0] 365[7] (Dead)
Truly Enchanting (IRE) *J Noseda* 91
3 ch f Danehill Dancer(IRE) —Truly Bewitched (USA) (Affirmed (USA))
1203[2] 1639[2] (1961) (2369) 2757[6] 3430[18]
Truly Mine (IRE) *D K Weld* 101
3 ch f Rock Of Gibraltar(IRE) —Truly Yours (IRE) (Barathea (IRE))
782a[3] 2065a[5] 3117a[5] 5240a[8] 5998a[7]
Truly Royal *Saeed Bin Suroor* 102
3 b c Noverre(USA) —Her Ladyship (Polish Precedent (USA))
641a[2] 1473[19]
Trump Call (IRE) *R M Beckett* a65 73
3 b g Mull Of Kintyre(USA) —Trumped (IRE) (Last Tycoon (IRE))
498[10] 1289[7] 1815[3] 2635[2] 3003[5] 3469[6] 3964[5] 4504[3] 5898[2]
Trumpet Lily *J G Portman* a67 71
2 b f Acclamation—Periwinkle (FR) (Perrault)
4774[6] 5681[4] 6125[8]
Trust Rule *M W Easterby* a46 46
7 b g Selkirk(USA) —Hagwah (USA) (Dancing Brave (USA))
662[12]
Try Me (UAE) *C E Brittain* 61
2 bb f Singspiel(IRE) —Cunas (USA) (Irish River (FR))
5399[3]
Trysting Grove (IRE) *E G Bevan* a54 48
6 b m Cape Cross(IRE) —Elton Grove (IRE) (Astronef)
126[2] 585[4] 665[6] (804) 1254[9] 1570[8]
Tsaroxy (IRE) *J Howard Johnson* 81
5 b g Xaar—Belsay (Belmez (USA))
850[9] (1627) 2987[10] 4497[3]
Tuanku (IRE) *M R Channon* 69
2 b g Tagula(IRE) —Be My Lover (Pursuit Of Love)
1680[4] 3951[10] (4363) (4892) 5509[4] 6233[9]
Tubby Isaacs *P J Makin* a65 38
3 b g Cyrano De Bergerac—Opuntia (Rousillon (USA))
1541[6] 6580[2] (6877)
Tucker *W R Swinburn* 108
5 b g Inchinor—Tender Moment (IRE) (Caerleon (USA))
2208[4] 2815[11] 3468[2] 6198[4]
Tuckerman *F J Bowles* a46 66
6 b g Gulch(USA) —Remuria (USA) (Theatrical)
109[5] 156[11]
Tucker's Town (IRE) *Sir Michael Stoute*
2 ch c Kingmambo(USA) —Bermuda Girl (USA) (Danzig (USA))
6358[12]
Tucum (IRE) *Edgar Byrne* 48
2 br f Diktat—Standcorrected (Shareef Dancer (USA))
5393a[10]
Tudor Court (IRE) *M Johnston* 74
2 b f Cape Cross(IRE) —Rise And Fall (Mill Reef (USA))
2904[3] 3507[6] 5483[3]
Tudor Prince (IRE) *A W Carroll* a89 91
3 bb g Cape Cross(IRE) —Savona (IRE) (Cyrano De Bergerac)
2788[23] 3078[5] 3380[3] 3857[5] 4360[11] 6203[6] (6575)
Tufton *Ian Williams* a94 94
4 b g King's Best(USA) —Mythical Magic (Green Desert (USA))
550[10] 777[2] 993[4] 1449[4] 2351[12] 3482[6] 4763[2] 5472[2] 5774[11] 6175[4]
Tugalu (IRE) *K A Ryan* a78 75
2 b c Tagula(IRE) —Merci (IRE) (Cadeaux Genereux)
3995[4] 4459[2] 4782[2] 5252[2] 5931[5]
Tullyorior Glory (IRE) *Emmanuel Hughes* a38 61
3 b f Desert Style(IRE) —Cutlers Corner (Sharpen Up)
6720[8]
Tullythered (IRE) *K R Burke* a52 48
3 ch g Docksider(USA) —Marjie (IRE) (Desert Style (IRE))
1425[3] 2453[7] 2915[9] 5188[10] 5894[4]
Tumbelini *C F Wall* a49 58
3 b f Pivotal—Kundalini (USA) (El Gran Senor (USA))
2012[4] 4066[4] 5098[6]
Tumble Jill (IRE) *J J Bridger* a51 48
3 b f Dilshaan—Jack-N-Jilly (IRE) (Anita's Prince)
21[5] 157[5] 791[8] 1211[7] 1320[3] 1397[5] 2445[9] 3186[5] 4757[6]
Tumbleweed Di *G R Oldroyd* a47 43
3 ro f Tumbleweed Ridge—Peggotty (Capricorn Line)
4801[4] 5282[7] 5781[6] 6864[6] 6963[9] 7019[5]
Tumbleweed Glory (IRE) *B J Meehan* a90 84
4 b g Marju(IRE) —Tathkara (USA) (Alydar (USA))
1842[11] 2401[4] 3437[17] 3900[10] 5685[2]
Tumblin Rosie *M Blanshard* a49 11
3 ch f Tumbleweed Ridge—Myhat (Factual (USA))
25[9] 2531[1] 417[6]
Tumult (GER) *Frau E Mader* 97
3 b g Dashing Blade—Think Twice (GER) (Second Set (IRE))
4216a[8]
Tungsten Strike (USA) *Mrs A J Perrett* 118
6 ch g Smart Strike(CAN) —Bathilde (IRE) (Generous (IRE))
(1393) 2125[5] 2787[13] 4091[6] (4803) 6712a[21]
Tuning Fork *M J Attwater* a50 61
7 b g Alzao(USA) —Tuning (Rainbow Quest (USA))
7098[10] 7276[3]
Turban Heights (IRE) *E J O'Neill* 73
3 ch f Golan(IRE) —Turban (Glint Of Gold)
4106[7] (4659) 6249[5]
Turbo (IRE) *M W Easterby* 75
8 b g Piccolo—By Arrangement (IRE) (Bold Arrangement)
2170[5] 2531[4] 2908[7] 3155[9]
Turbo Linn *G A Swinbank* 113
4 b m Turbo Speed—Linns Heir (Leading Counsel (USA))
(2420) (3434) (3744) 5352[10]
Turfani (IRE) *W J Knight* 47
2 b f Danetime(IRE) —Tuhfah (Cadeaux Genereux)
6411[10]
Turfrose (GER) *P Giannotti* 109
3 b f Big Shuffle(USA) —Turfquelle (IRE) (Shaadi (USA))
1701a[3] 2070a[3] 2707a[4] 4055a[7] (6524a)
Turibius *T E Powell* a62 70
8 b g Puissance—Compact Disc (IRE) (Royal Academy (USA))
158[12]
Turkish Sultan (IRE) *J M Bradley* a60 64
4 b g Anabaa(USA) —Odalisque (IRE) (Machiavellian (USA))
1564[9] 2622[5] 3064[5] 3106[4] 3535[3] 3906[7] 4165[9] 4321[3] 4530[2] 4731[7] 4807[7]
Turklord (IRE) *D K Weld* a37 53
2 b g Fasliyev(USA) —Miss Demure (Shy Groom (USA))
6392a[8]
Turn And River (IRE) *M Brittain* 67
2 b f Viking Ruler(AUS) —Scatter Brain (Risk Me (FR))
845[6] 1007[5] 1622[5] 2758[4] 3378[4] 3606[3] 4041[5]
Turner's Touch *G L Moore* a79 66
5 ch g Compton Place—Chairmans Daughter (Unfuwain (USA))
95[4] 377[6] 488[7] 587[3] (813) 921[2] 1470[8] 1741[5] 2156[3] 2994[3] 3416[8] 3641[4] 4458[3] 4915[4] 5422[4] 5732[2] 6261[3]
Turnkey *D Nicholls* 104
5 br g Pivotal—Persian Air (Persian Bold)
927[7] 1195[13] 1826[13] 2237[5] 2841[2] 3089[10] (3401) 3500[6] 3975[2] 4062[7] 4614[18] 5616[16] 5809[8] 6183[8]
Turn Left (IRE) *R M Beckett* a72 70
2 b c Xaar—Stamatina (Warning)
6138[3] (6593)
Turn Me On (IRE) *T D Walford* a68 65
4 b g Tagula(IRE) —Jacobina (Magic Ring (IRE))
1640[11] 2033[2] 2508[2] (3067) 3999[7] 4390[7] 5159[8] 5476[12] 6716[2] 6859[4] 6956[6]
Turn 'n Burn *C A Cyzer* a73 64
6 b g Unfuwain(USA) —Seasonal Splendour (IRE) (Prince Rupert (FR))
29[10] 662[10] 3033[4]
Turn Of Phrase (IRE) *N Wilson* a68 79
8 b g Cadeaux Genereux—Token Gesture (IRE) (Alzao (USA))
2254[12] 3049[2] (3204) (3403) 3888[2] (3978) 6158[13] 6759[20]
Turn On The Style *J Balding* a109 102
5 ch g Pivotal—Elegant Rose (Noalto)
(81) (163) (490) 1601[5] 3050[7] 3464[2] 3586[4] 4090[13] 6676[2] 6851[3] (7053) 7255[2]
Turritella (IRE) *P Martometti* 75
6 br m Primo Dominie—Flimmering (Dancing Brave (USA))
1337a[7]
Turtle Bowl (IRE) *F Rohaut* a113 120
5 b h Dyhim Diamond(IRE) —Clara Bow (FR) (Top Ville)
897a[2] 1389a[2] 1879a[2] 2735[3] 4445a[3] 5261a[8]
Turtle Soup (IRE) *J J Bridger* 76
11 b g Turtle Island(IRE) —Lisa's Favourite (Gorytus (USA))
4850[12] 5769[11]
Tuscan Evening (IRE) *John Joseph Murphy* 97
2 b f Oasis Dream—The Faraway Tree (Suave Dancer (USA))
2049a[3] 2756[9] 3071a[2] 3574a[2] 4440a[3]
Tuscan Flyer *R Bastiman* a48 52
9 b g Clantime—Excavator Lady (Most Secret)
320[8] 339[11] 450[6] 580[8] 653[3] 722[5] 978[3] 2561[7] 2791[4] 4471[10] (5276)
Tuscany Rose *M Todhunter* a42 47
4 ch m Medicean—Rosewood Belle (USA) (Woodman (USA))
965[7]
Tuscarora (IRE) *A W Carroll* a72 65
8 b m Revoque(IRE) —Fresh Look (IRE) (Alzao (USA))
70[9] 85[8] 299[3]
Tusculum (IRE) *A Fabre* 113
4 b h Sadler's Wells(USA) —Turbaine (USA) (Trempolino (USA))
990a[7]
Tutor (IRE) *W J Haggas* a77 66
3 ch g Dr Fong(USA) —Glandore (IRE) (Persian Bold)
(565) 1365[5] 2872[6] 3691[11] 4491[9]
Twardowska (ITY) *G Dolfi* 105
4 gr m Daylami(IRE) —Todeschina (Sure Blade (USA))
2296a[10]
Tweed River (USA) *Miss E C Lavelle* 57
3 b c Royal Academy(USA) —Gotablush (Nashwan (USA))
3366[8] 5938[9]
Twentyfirst Dansar *A D Smith* a40 42
4 b g Zahran(IRE) —Joker's Luck (Desert Splendour)
5421[13]
Twenty Percent *P R Chamings* a38 55
3 ch g Auction House(USA) —Truly Madly Deeply (Most Welcome)
1587[11] 1928[7] 3620[11]
Twice Over *H R A Cecil* 95
2 b c Observatory(USA) —Double Crossed (Caerleon (USA))
(5951) (6650)
Twiglet (IRE) *B W Hills* 61
2 b f Choisir(AUS) —Regal Opinion (USA) (Gone West (USA))
4061[8]
Twilight Avenger (IRE) *W M Brisbourne* a50 49
4 b g Dr Fong(USA) —Asterita (Rainbow Quest (USA))
181[6] 402[3] 508[3] 665[3] 716[11] 804[4] 907[12] 1271[10] 1362[3] 1570[5] 2141[5] 2764[11] 3047[9] 3280[8] 3679[6] 5087[9]
Twilight Belle (IRE) *K R Burke* a57 58
2 b f Fasliyev(USA) —Pretty Sharp (Interrex (CAN))
1285[9] 1960[6] 2344[2] 4892[7] 6478[9] 7007[7] 7176[4]
Twilight Star (IRE) *Saeed Bin Suroor* 75
3 b g Green Desert(USA) —Heavenly Whisper (IRE) (Halling (USA))
3447[4] (4007)
Twill (IRE) *G L Moore* a80 83
4 ch g Barathea(IRE) —Khafaya (Unfuwain (USA))
192[5] 354[8]
Twinned (IRE) *M J Wilkinson* a58 45
4 ch g Soviet Star(USA) —Identical (IRE) (Machiavellian (USA))
183[6] 254[5] 2875[12] 4561[14] 4973[3] 5564[2] 6340[8]
Twin Sun's (IRE) *Timothy Doyle* 77
4 ch g Desert Sun—Allzi (USA) (Zilzal (USA))
4836a[7]
Twist Bookie (IRE) *S Lycett* a62 41
7 br g Perugino(USA) —Twist Scarlett (GER) (Lagunas)
215[3] 7219[2]
Twitch Hill *H Candy* 67
3 ch f Piccolo—Whittle Woods Girl (Emarati (USA))
1022[3] (1430) 2080[3]
Two Acres (IRE) *A G Newcombe* a61 56
4 b g Danetime(IRE) —Raise-A-Secret (IRE) (Classic Secret (USA))
787[9] 5191[14] 5535[9] 6078[3] 6424[5] 6542[2] 6886[4] 7137[2] 7188[11]
Two Dreamers *A Crook* 38
3 ch f Best Of The Bests(IRE) —Mossy Rose (King Of Spain)
1676[8]
Two Imposters (USA) *J R Best* 55
2 bb g Gulch(USA) —Queen Of Women (USA) (Sharpen Up)
2398[12] 2632[10] 4323[7]
Two Left Feet *W R Swinburn* a72
2 b g Groom Dancer(USA) —Sardegna (Pharly (FR))
6805[2]
Twosheetstothewind *C R Dore* a68 71
3 ch f Bahamian Bounty—Flag (Selkirk (USA))
1635[3] (1709) 2867[5] 4001[3] 4546[2] 6279[5] 6667[9]
Two Step Kid (USA) *J Noseda* a68 17
6 ch h Gone West(USA) —Marsha's Dancer (USA) (Northern Dancer (CAN))
41[8] 550[12] 3802[10]
Two Timer (IRE) *D R C Elsworth* a66 74
3 ch c Selkirk(USA) —Adultress (IRE) (Ela-Mana-Mou)
1093[10] 2836[10] 3847[3] 4403[4] 5637[0] 6439[12]
Tybalt (USA) *J H M Gosden* a97 108
3 b c Storm Cat(USA) —Tuzla (FR) (Panoramic)
939[2] 1275[6] 2037[8] (3503) 4148[7]
Tycoon's Hill (IRE) *Robert Collet* a80 108
9 b g Danehill(USA) —Tycoon's Drama (IRE) (Last Tycoon (IRE))
1704a[4] 2811a[4] 3445a[13] 4214a[0] 6039a[13] 6633a[0]
Tyfos *W M Brisbourne* a76 66
2 b g Bertolini(USA) —Warminghamsharpish (Nalchik (USA))
5880[12] 6616[7] (6761) 6936[7]
Tykie Two *E J O'Neill* a49 52
3 ch f Primo Valentino(IRE) —Tycoon's Last (Nalchik (USA))
2261[10] 2535[4] 3351[10] 3825[12]
Typhoon Ginger (IRE) *G Woodward* a29 70
12 ch m Archway(IRE) —Pallas Viking (Viking (USA))
5255[11] 5737[8] 6016[12] 6253[12]
Tyrannosaurus Rex (IRE) *K R Burke* a65 53
3 b c Bold Fact(USA) —Dungeon Princess (IRE) (Danehill (USA))
4157[6] 4671[3] 4808[7] 6749[6] 6963[2] 7207[7]
Tyreless Endeavour (IRE) *Peter Casey* 69
3 b g Mull Of Kintyre(USA) —Rebecca's Girl (IRE) (Nashamaa)
4836a[LFT]
Tyrone Lady (IRE) *M C Chapman* 5
4 b m Key Of Luck(USA) —Kutaisi (IRE) (Soviet Star (USA))
714[8] 5157[7]
Tyrone Sam *K A Ryan* a71 52
5 b g Mind Games—Crystal Sand (GER) (Forzando)
(86) 235[3] 359[2] 485[9] 686[9] 912[14] 1027[13]
Tyrrells Wood (IRE) *T G Mills* a63 74
2 b c Sinndar(IRE) —Diner De Lune (IRE) (Be My Guest (USA))
4110[8] 4547[4] 5361[5] 6857[5]
Tyzack (IRE) *Stef Liddiard* a77 89
6 b g Fasliyev(USA) —Rabea (USA) (Devil's Bag (USA))
44[12] 218[7] 451[6] 509[8] 629[6] 809[7] (5166) 5693[4] 5885[9] 6423[8] 6646[10]
Uace Mac *N Bycroft* 59
3 b f Compton Place—Umbrian Gold (IRE) (Perugino (USA))
998[3] 1679[10] 2120[F]
Ubenkor (IRE) *Christian Wroe* a31
2 b c Diktat—Lucky Dancer (FR) (Groom Dancer (USA))
7191[13]
Ubiquitous Bounty *G L Moore* 20
2 b g Bahamian Bounty—In A Twinkling (IRE) (Brief Truce (USA))
5380[9] 5706[8]
Ucetek (IRE) *Sir Michael Stoute* a62
2 b f Kalanisi(IRE) —Dragnet (IRE) (Rainbow Quest (USA))
6777[7]
Ugenius *R A Harris* a37
3 b g Killer Instinct—I'm Sophie (IRE) (Shalford (IRE))
136[5] 670[6] 6935[6] 7034[12]
Ugly Betty *Garry Moss*
2 b f Where Or When(IRE) —Dancing Steps (Zafonic (USA))
5328[11] 5931[7]
Uhoomagoo *K A Ryan* a97 106
9 b g Namaqualand(USA) —Point Of Law (Law Society (USA))
6[3] 325a[11] 395a[10] 656[10] 7591[1] 2208[6] 2817[24] 3941[14] 4119[B]
Uhuru Peak *M W Easterby* a61 62
6 ch g Bal Harbour—Catherines Well (Junius (USA))
179[10] 3067[9] 3765[13] 4219[4] 5159[5] 5525[3] 5890[9] 6479[9] 6629[5]
Uig *H S Howe* a63 73
6 ch m Bien Bien(USA) —Madam Zando (Forzando)
1521[6] 1951[2] (2106) 2361[5] 2543[6] 4015[9] (4112) 4551[2] 5052[9] 6129[7] 6603[10]
Uimhir A Haon (IRE) *A P O'Brien* 106
3 b f Montjeu(IRE) —Vallee Des Reves (USA) (Kingmambo (USA))
2851a[6] 3576a[6] 4238a[4] 4649a[10] 5396a[4] 5998a[3] 6367a[9]
Ultimate Akdov (USA) *P F I Cole* a26
3 ch c Two Punch(USA) —Pithy (USA) (Quiet American (USA))
1037[10]
Ulysees (IRE) *J Barclay* a52 74
8 b g Turtle Island(IRE) —Tamasriya (IRE) (Doyoun)
3787[11] 4100[9] 4496[9] 4998[7] 5676[12] 5935[5]
Umpa Loompa (IRE) *D Nicholls* 65
3 ch g Indian Lodge(IRE) —Bold Fashion (FR) (Nashwan (USA))
711[9] 3918[10] 4658[4] 4896[10] 5625[3] (6256) 6424[16] 6559[6]

Umverti *N Bycroft* 50
2 b f Averti(IRE) —Umbrian Gold (IRE) (Perugino (USA))
5735[9] 6156[11] 6303[5]

Una Auroraborealis *J Ryan* a17 52
2 br f Fantastic Light(USA) —Aly McBe (USA) (Alydeed (CAN))
9721[0] 1101[9] 2604[4] 2812[20] 3465[8] *4022[11]* 4776[12] 5089[13]

Unasuming (IRE) *J Pearce* a53 58
4 b m Orpen(USA) —Untold (Final Straw)
4131[10] 4355[6] 4533[13]

Unbreak My Heart (IRE) *R Charlton* 88
2 ch c Bahamian Bounty—Golden Heart (Salse (USA))
3747[9] 5501[3] (5868) (6201)

Unbridled Belle (USA) *T Pletcher* a117
4 bb m Broken Vow(USA) —Little Bold Belle (USA) (Silver Buck (USA))
(5854a) 6512a[5]

Uncle Harry *J J Quinn* 19
2 b g Mind Games—Lapadar (IRE) (Woodborough (USA))
2739[11]

Uncle Max (IRE) *R A Harris* 21
7 b g Victory Note(USA) —Sunset Park (IRE) (Red Sunset)
1888[12]

Under Fire (IRE) *A W Carroll* a61 59
4 b g Lear Spear(USA) —Kahyasi Moll (IRE) (Brief Truce (USA))
72[4] 86[2] 206[7] 426[5] 4686[11] *5020[10]* 5433[12] *5730[12] 6587[13] (6968) 7079[12]*

Underthemistletoe (IRE) *R E Barr* a20 46
5 b m Lujain(USA) —Christmas Kiss (Taufan (USA))
2203[7] 2422[9] 3837[9] 4178[8] 5083[14]

Under The Rainbow *B W Hills* 107
4 gr m Fantastic Light(USA) —Farfala (FR) (Linamix (FR))
929[3] 1582[4] 2125[6] 3097[4] 3434[2] 3744[3] 4723[4] 5352[5] 5767[3] 6337[5]

Under The Sun *M Rolland* a60 71
2 ch f Trempolino(USA) —Gastina (FR) (Pistolet Bleu (IRE))
7048a[9]

Undeterred *K J Burke* a74 83
11 ch g Zafonic(USA) —Mint Crisp (IRE) (Green Desert (USA))
332[3] 568[7] 618[9] 634[8] 809[5] 1368[5] 1664[5] 2006[9] *2802[9] 2946[10]*

Une Pivoine (FR) *J E Pease* 105
3 b f Pivotal—Motzki (FR) (Le Glorieux)
1339a[8] 2547a[3] 3564a[9] 6889a[6]

Unidentified Thief (FR) *J E Hammond* a67
2 gr g Daylami(IRE) —In A Silent Way (IRE) (Desert Prince (IRE))
7027a[3]

Unilateral (IRE) *B Smart* 103
2 ch f Rock Of Gibraltar(IRE) —Mira Adonde (USA) (Sharpen Up)
2364[2] (2863) 4225[3] 4744[4] (5614) 5973[9]

Union Jack Jackson (IRE) *John A Harris* a65 63
5 b g Daggers Drawn(USA) —Beechwood Quest (IRE) (River Falls)
77[12] 241[5] 632[9] (801) (1120) 1309[2] *(1753) 1947[5] 2347[4]* 2561[5] 2806[2] *3408[9]*

United Nations *N Wilson* a81 80
6 ch g Halling(USA) —Congress (IRE) (Dancing Brave (USA))
1905[2] 2397[4] 2986[12] *3926[11]* 4176[12] (4488) 4820[4] 5197[6] *7047[9] 7200[5]*

Unleashed (IRE) *H R A Cecil* 74
2 br c Storming Home—Uriah (GER) (Acatenango (GER))
6248[5]

Unlicensed *R Hannon* a69 37
2 ch g Hawk Wing(USA) —Multicolour (Rainbow Quest (USA))
6617[11] *6850[4] 6948[5]*

Unlimited *R Simpson* a64 67
5 b g Bold Edge—Cabcharge Blue (Midyan (USA))
2546[3] 3613[8] 5191[11] *7251[10]*

Unnefer (FR) *H R A Cecil* 88
2 b c Danehill Dancer(IRE) —Mimalia (USA) (Silver Hawk (USA))
2041[8] (2885) 3938[2] 4482[2] 5161[2]

Uno Dos Tres *Jane Chapple-Hyam* a52
2 ch c Night Shift(USA) —Sartigila (Efisio)
6694[5] 6868[8]

Unquenchable Fire (IRE) *D K Weld* 81
2 b c Invincible Spirit(IRE) —Tasha's Dream (USA) (Woodman (USA))
5397a[17]

Unreachable Star *Mrs A J Perrett* a54 73
3 ch f Halling(USA) —Spinning The Yarn (Barathea (IRE))
2597[5] 3476[2] 5450[2] 5941[6] 6420[4] *7076[4]*

Unshakable (IRE) *Bob Jones* a96 99
8 b g Eagle Eyed(USA) —Pepper And Salt (IRE) (Double Schwartz)
1524[2] (2208) 3330[3] 4119[6] *5221[6]* 6011[21]

Until When (USA) *B Smart* a70 71
3 b g Grand Slam(USA) —Chez Cherie (Wolfhound (USA))
6309[4] 6731[5]

Untitled Blues (USA) *D Smaga* 92
2 b f Stravinsky(USA) —Eshaarat (Zafonic (USA))
5373a[4]

Up In Arms (IRE) *P Winkworth* a73 73
3 b g Daggers Drawn(USA) —Queenliness (Exit To Nowhere (USA))
1563[8] 1887[2] *2177[8]* 2727[11] 3367[8] 4019[5] 4458[8] (4763) 5279[5] 6132[2] *(6811) 7008[2]*

Upper Class (IRE) *M Johnston* 72
2 b c Fantastic Light(USA) —Her Ladyship (Polish Precedent (USA))
(2804)

Upper Village *Joseph G Murphy* a70 72
3 ch g Bertolini(USA) —Magic Dawn (AUS) (Bletchley Park (IRE))
6916a[10]

Upstairs *D R C Elsworth* 26
3 ch g Sugarfoot—Laena (Roman Warrior)
2059[9]

Upstanding *M Brittain* 64
2 b f Acclamation—Uplifting (Magic Ring (IRE))
952[7] 1107[5] 1302[5] 1553[5] 4098[2] 4349[3] 4924[4] 5154[2] 5252[5] 6074[4]

Up Tempo (IRE) *C R Dore* a78 78
9 b g Flying Spur(AUS) —Musical Essence (Song)
228[6] 803[13] 866[13]

Up The Chimney *A P Jarvis* a61 57
3 gr g Kyllachy—Simply Sooty (Absalom)
1398[5] 2541[6] *4066[8] 4889[12]* 5738[10]

Up The Wycombe *S Dow* a44
2 b g Diktat—Mistitled (USA) (Miswaki (USA))
3849[9] 4273[10] 6138[12] 7182[14]

Upton Grey (IRE) *J H M Gosden* 89
2 gr c Dalakhani(IRE) —Rosse (Kris)
3435[7] 4151[16] (4810) 5582[3] 6154[4] 6486[3]

Urban Spirit *B W Hills* 93
3 b c Dansili—Tenuous (Generous (IRE))
1093[5] 1605[5] (3436) 4092[11] 5639[2] 5978[6]

Urban Tiger (GER) *Carl Llewellyn* 87
4 b g Marju(IRE) —Ukraine Venture (Slip Anchor)
1922[12]

Urban Warrior *Mrs Norma Pook* a72 75
3 b g Zilzal(USA) —Perfect Poppy (Shareef Dancer (USA))
886[5] 904[4] *1039[3]* (1289) 1724[6] 2126[3] 2635[6] 2877[6] 3335[5] 4909[12]

Urgente *L Brogi* 106
5 b h Halling(USA) —Persian Filly (IRE) (Persian Bold)
1700a[5]

Ursis (FR) *S Gollings* 80
6 b g Trempolino(USA) —Bold Virgin (USA) (Sadler's Wells (USA))
6153[7]

Ursus *C R Wilson*
2 ch g Rambling Bear—Adar Jane (Ardar)
5702[8]

Useful *A B Haynes* a49 48
4 ch m Nashwan(USA) —Tarf (USA) (Diesis)
416[16] 637[11] 2540[9]

Usetheforce (IRE) *M J Wallace* a43
2 ch g Black Minnaloushe(USA) —Polynesian Goddess (IRE) (Salmon Leap (USA))
7266[9]

Usk Melody *G A Huffer* a58 84
3 ch f Singspiel(IRE) —One Of The Family (Alzao (USA))
1581[8] 1785[5] 3099[6] 3743[5]

US Ranger (USA) *A P O'Brien* 122
3 b c Danzig(USA) —My Annette (USA) (Red Ransom (USA))
(1005a) 1473[7] 2752[2] (5842a) 6029a[4]

Utility (NZ) *P Carey* 88
6 b g (NZ) — (NZ) (Prince Of Praise (NZ))
6033a[16]

Utmost Respect *R A Fahey* 113
3 b g Danetime(IRE) —Utmost (IRE) (Most Welcome)
2440[8] 3431[3] (5584) 5797[8]

Utrecht *A Fabre* 107
3 ch f Rock Of Gibraltar(IRE) —Maria Isabella (USA) (Kris)
(3148a) 4010a[9] 6460a[8]

Utrillo's Art (IRE) *M W Easterby* 29
2 ch f Medecis—Theory Of Law (Generous (IRE))
2251[8] 2604[8] 2889[3] 3205[9]

Vacation (IRE) *V Smith* a94 91
4 b h King Charlemagne(USA) —Lady Peculiar (CAN) (Sunshine Forever (USA))
656[6] 846[6] *1180[5] 1449[2]* 1767[8] 2871[2] 3330[14] 3513[6] *4068[9] 4888[7]*

Vadapolina (FR) *A Fabre* 118
3 ch f Trempolino(USA) —Vadaza (FR) (Zafonic (USA))
(1388a) 2501a[8] (4055a) 5465a[9] 6042a[9]

Vadinka *N Tinkler* a73 73
3 b g Averti(IRE) —Inchalong (Inchinor)
34[2] 147[8] 1219[10] 1679[5] 2167[3] *3168[11]* 3342[12] *6240[11]*

Vadsalina (IRE) *A De Royer-Dupre* 94
2 b f Sagacity(FR) —Vadaza (FR) (Zafonic (USA))
(6939a)

Vago (IRE) *M Gasparini* 101
4 ch h Indian Ridge—Vaghezza (IRE) (Persian Bold)
6686a[5]

Vainglory (USA) *D M Simcock* a96 87
3 ch c Swain(IRE) —Infinite Spirit (USA) (Maria's Mon (USA))
2173[3] (2606) 3078[3] *4276[7]* 5615[3] 6203[4] *(6765) 6931[8]*

Valance (IRE) *C R Egerton* a89 79
7 br g Bahhare(USA) —Glowlamp (IRE) (Glow (USA))
192[9] 362[5] 457[6] 488[8] 593[9] 662[7] 2994[9] 4067[2] 4576[8] 5007[4] 5857[6]

Valart *A J Lidderdale* a57 66
4 ch m Bien Bien(USA) —Riverine (Risk Me (FR))
283[7] 1217[4] *1628[11]* 1926[4] 2467[13] 3352[8] *4161[14]* 4532[11] 4802[8]

Valassini *B G Powell* 39
7 b m Dr Massini(IRE) —Running Valley (Buckskin (FR))
5137[5] 5345[10] 6238[9]

Valatrix (IRE) *C F Wall* 47
2 b f Acclamation—Dramatic Entry (IRE) (Persian Bold)
6409[11]

Valbenny (IRE) *P Gallagher* 109
3 b f Val Royal(FR) —Dark Indian (IRE) (Indian Ridge)
5248a[6]

Valdan (IRE) *M A Barnes* a84 92
3 b g Val Royal(FR) —Danedrop (IRE) (Danehill (USA))
760[11] 839[7] 2037[9] 2788[24] 4385[6] 4898[14] 5545[12] 5905[10]

Val De Maal (IRE) *Miss J A Camacho* a65 65
7 ch g Eagle Eyed(USA) —Miss Bojangles (Gay Fandango (USA))
77[10] (144) 268[5]

Vale De Lobo *B R Millman* a81 81
5 b m Loup Sauvage(USA) —Frog (Akarad (FR))
1567[4] (2082) 2361[4] 3554[5] 4128[4] 5067[2] 6299[15] 6620[2] *7002[3] 7236[P]*

Valeesha *W G M Turner* a38 46
3 b f Erhaab(USA) —Miss Laetitia (IRE) (Entitled)
1432[9] 1912[3] 2304[3] *2948[12]* 4471[14] 5269[7] 5511[8] 6090[10]

Valentina Guest (IRE) *Peter Casey* 97
6 b m Be My Guest(USA) —Karamiyna (IRE) (Shernazar)
875a[11] 1330a[6] 4240a[5]

Valentine Blue *A B Haynes* a43 58
2 ch g Tobougg(IRE) —Blue Topaz (IRE) (Bluebird (USA))
1291[10] 5720[7] 6202[P] *6714[10]*

Valentine Hill (IRE) *Adrian Maguire* 69
2 b f Mujadil(USA) —First Nadia (Auction Ring (USA))
5516a[4]

Valentino (FR) *A De Royer-Dupre* a97 109
8 b g Valanour(IRE) —Rotina (FR) (Crystal Glitters (USA))
897a[6] *4012a[DSQ]*

Valentino Sky (USA) *N P Littmoden* a64 64
2 b c Stravinsky(USA) —Lucky Lune (FR) (Priolo (USA))
2478[9] 3747[6] 3962[15] *4461[4]* 5871[10] *6263[3]* 6536[6]

Valentino Swing (IRE) *Miss T Spearing* a74 74
4 ch g Titus Livius(FR) —Farmers Swing (IRE) (River Falls)
2719[2]

Valento *Eve Johnson Houghton* 47
2 ch g Noverre(USA) —My Valentina (Royal Academy (USA))
5720[9] 6126[8]

Vale Of Belvoir (IRE) *K R Burke* 95
3 b f Mull Of Kintyre(USA) —Sunrise (IRE) (Sri Pekan (USA))
3708[9]

Valery Borzov (IRE) *D Nicholls* 88
3 b g Iron Mask(USA) —Fay's Song (IRE) (Fayruz)
(958) 1108[8] 3197[8] 4123[3] 4726[7] 5506[2]

Valeureux *J Hetherton* a52
9 ch g Cadeaux Genereux—La Strada (Niniski (USA))
6292[7]

Valhillen *M J Wallace* a63 37
2 ch g Bertolini(USA) —Dancing Nelly (Shareef Dancer (USA))
1519[2] 1713[5] 3589[12] *4022[4] 5127[14] 5751[3] 6098[6] (6813) 7021[4] (7171)*

Valiance (USA) *J H M Gosden* a79 95
3 ch c Horse Chestnut(SAF) —Victoria Cross (IRE) (Mark Of Esteem (IRE))
1623[3]

Valiant Romeo *R Bastiman* a15 53
7 b g Primo Dominie—Desert Lynx (IRE) (Green Desert (USA))
3449[6] 3667[6] 4379[6] 4857[5] 5276[9] 5295[2] 5930[6] 6078[5] 6730[5]

Valiant Vicar (USA) *B J Meehan* 61
2 ch g Hold That Tiger(USA) —Lets Knock On Wood (USA) (Woodman (USA))
3095[11] 3957[6] *4882[12]* 5914[16]

Validity *A J McCabe* a25 30
2 ch f Forzando—Wittily (Whittingham (IRE))
1636[9] 2086[8] 6329[12] *7288[5]*

Val Jaro (FR) *S Morineau* a72 105
4 b g Le Triton(USA) —Valana (USA) (Valanour (IRE))
2291a[8] 3445a[3] 4214a[0] 4871a[7] 6633a[0]

Vallani (IRE) *W R Swinburn* a70
2 b f Vettori(IRE) —Hecuba (Hector Protector (USA))
5308[5] 5944[4]

Vallemeldee (IRE) *P W D'Arcy* a77 68
3 b f Bering—Vassiana (FR) (Anabaa (USA))
1639[6] 2475[4] *(3084) 3421[4]* 3964[11] *5101[2]* 5333[3] *6007[5]* 6308[7] *(6673) 7205[4]*

Valley Observer (FR) *W R Swinburn* a72 72
3 ch g Observatory(USA) —Valleyrose (IRE) (Royal Academy (USA))
1001[4] *1523[4]* 1929[5] 2530[8] 3167[2] *3622[6]* 4129[7] 6199[7] *7155[4]*

Valley Of The Moon (IRE) *R A Fahey* a73 78
3 b f Monashee Mountain(USA) —Unaria (Prince Tenderfoot (USA))
1484[2] 1802[2] 2373[2] 2659[3] 3637[8] 4140[7] 4425[4] 5139[2] 5747[10] 6157[2] 6743[9] *6905[4]*

Valrhona (IRE) *J Noseda* a80 71
3 bb f Spectrum(IRE) —Minerva (IRE) (Caerleon (USA))
2455[7] (5311)

Valse Des Coeurs (FR) *G Pannier* a52 70
2 b f Homere—Pacy (USA) (Manila (USA))
6888a[9] *7048a[0]*

Valtat *B R Johnson* a32
2 b g Fasliyev(USA) —Wooden Doll (USA) (Woodman (USA))
6436[14] 6793[9] 6865[10]

Value Of Time (IRE) *K J Condon* a56 73
2 b f Xaar—Astuti (IRE) (Waajib)
5395a[14]

Valuta (USA) *R A Kvisla* a71 67
4 rg h Silver Charm(USA) —Misleading Miss (USA) (Miswaki (USA))
213[11]

Valvignères (IRE) *E A L Dunlop* a70
2 gr g Dalakhani(IRE) —Albacora (IRE) (Fairy King (USA))
6857[9] 6948[3]

Vampyrus *H Candy* a30 72
4 ch g Dracula(AUS) —Anna Karietta (Precocious)
1886[13] 2580[5] 2965[7] *4023[12]*

Vanadium *G L Moore* a81 81
5 b g Dansili—Musianica (Music Boy)
28[9] 1819[14] 2088[12] 3203[11] 5009[13] *(6290) 6647[4] 6717[6] 6869[13]*

Vanatina (IRE) *Heather Dalton* 48
3 b f Tagula(IRE) —Final Trick (Primo Dominie)
3490[6] 4714[7]

Van Bossed (CAN) *D Nicholls* 82
2 ch g Van Nistelrooy(USA) —Embossed (CAN) (Silver Deputy (CAN))
3834[4] 4279[3] 4578[11] (4937)

Vancouver Gold (IRE) *K R Burke* a67 65
5 b m Monashee Mountain(USA) —Forest Berries (IRE) (Thatching)
61[3] 228[8] 374[5] 466[2] 664[6]

Vanderlin *A M Balding* a113 112
8 ch g Halling(USA) —Massorah (FR) (Habitat)
1656[4] 2586a[9] 3103[3] 3529[3] (5031) 6370a[7]

Van Gosh *A Fabre* 107
3 ch f Peintre Celebre(USA) —Winnebago (Kris) (3564a) 4557a[4]

Vanilla Delight (IRE) *J Howard Johnson* 75
4 b m Orpen(USA) —Fantastic Bid (USA) (Auction Ring (USA))
1626[5] 2893[3] 3999[2] 4705[13]

Vanishing Dancer (SWI) *Mrs D Thomas* a67 56
10 ch g Llandaff(USA) —Vanishing Prairie (USA) (Alysheba (USA))
(278) (369) 618[8] 2800[7] 2860[8] *7285[10]*

Vanquisher (IRE) *W J Haggas* a75 79
3 b g Xaar—Naziriya (FR) (Darshaan)
1166[2] 1375[2] 1937[4] 2627[5] 3367[7] 3919[4] 5137[2] (5637)

Van Ruymbeke (IRE) *D J Murphy* a54 46
3 ch g Indian Ridge—Badrah (USA) (Private Account (USA))
1605[11] 5082[4] 5231[6] *6311[8] 6569[11] 7148[7] (7239)*

Varadouro (BRZ) *D Nicholls* a66 78
5 b g A Good Reason(BRZ) —Orquidea Vermelha (BRZ) (Lucence (USA))
415a[11] 4122[19] 4567[10] 5584[23] 5806[14] 6639[10]

Varevees *J Boisnard* 112
4 b m Kahyasi—Danse Bretonne (FR) (Exit To Nowhere (USA))
3893a[2] 4655a[5] (5469a) 6044a[2] 6526a[7]

Varinia (IRE) *M Brittain* a34 62
2 b f Spartacus(IRE) —Bucaramanga (IRE) (Distinctly North (USA))
926[6] 1043[3] 1193[8] 1858[5] 3373[5] 4221[5] *5751[11]*

Varsity *C F Swan* a88 87
4 b m Lomitas—Renowned (IRE) (Darshaan)
2067a[8]

Varya *Sir Mark Prescott* a46
3 b f Diktat—Regent's Folly (IRE) (Touching Wood (USA))
55[7] 152[6] 208[10]

Veba (USA) *M D I Usher* a54 52
4 ch g Black Minnaloushe(USA) —Make Over (USA) (Time For A Change (USA))
359[12] 500[6] 570[8] 612[13] 741[8] 1271[2] *1380[2]* 1742[7] *1906[4] 2332[6] 2519[3] 3186[4]* 3805[9] 4294[16] 4577[10] 4853[16] *5310[13]*

Veenwouden *E F Vaughan* a81 109
3 b f Desert Prince(IRE) —Delauncy (Machiavellian (USA))
1610[8] 2472[5] 3056[6] 4205[5] (4542) *5101[4]* 5952[3] 6337[3]

Vegas Boys *M Wigham* a76 76
4 b g Royal Applause—Brief Glimpse (IRE) (Taufan (USA))
50[3] 896[3] 1589[2] (2143) 2217[2] (2334) 2882[3] 3101[6]

Vehari *G F Bridgwater* a35 66
4 ch g Tomba—Nannie Annie (Persian Bold)
2113[6] 4421[7] 5188[15] 6056[14]

Veidhleadoir (USA) *J S Bolger* 80
2 b f Malibu Moon(USA) —Careyes (IRE) (Sadler's Wells (USA))
6443a[3]

Veiled Applause *R M Beckett* a85 84
4 b g Royal Applause—Scarlet Veil (Tyrnavos)
1209[2] 1318[2] 2514[2] (2722) 2986[5] 3854[2] 4365[2] *(5099)* 5432[8] *6145[7]*

Velma Kelly *W R Swinburn* a54
3 b f Vettori(IRE) —Possessive Artiste (Shareef Dancer (USA))
(5102)

Velocity's Gift *Pat Eddery* 68
3 b c Kyllachy—La Piaf (FR) (Fabulous Dancer (USA))
1098[8] 1838[2] 2477[5] 3949[5]

Veloso (FR) *Ronald O'Leary* a65
5 gr g Kaldounevees(FR) —Miss Recif (IRE) (Exit To Nowhere (USA))
(6815)

Velvet Heights (IRE) *J L Dunlop* a104 91
5 b h Barathea(IRE) —Height Of Fantasy (IRE) (Shirley Heights)
1844[14] 2675[4] 3748[2] 4779[4] 5800[6] 6302[5]

Velvet Revolver (IRE) *L Riccardi* 102
4 b m Mujahid(USA) —Noble Kara (FR) (Noblequest (FR))
1337a[8] 6224a[3] 6686a[4]

Velvet Valley (USA) *C E Longsdon* a76 69
4 ch g Gone West(USA) —Velvet Morning (USA) (Broad Brush (USA))
602[4] (733) 813[6] 1181[6] 1609[14]

Veneer (IRE) *Mrs N S Evans* a50 56
5 b g Woodborough(USA) —Sweet Lass (Belmez (USA))
7133[3]

Venerable *J H M Gosden* 94
3 b g Danehill(USA) —Fragrant View (USA) (Distant View (USA))
(1560) 1987[9] (5385) 6061[4]

Vengeance Of Rain (NZ) *D Ferraris* 122
7 b g Zabeel(NZ) —Danelagh (AUS) (Danehill (USA))
(861a) 7092a[6]

Venir Rouge *M Salaman* a80 81
3 ch c Dancing Spree(USA) —Al Awaalah (Mukaddamah (USA))
1722[11] 2079[2] 3525[8] (4200) 4610[2] 5014[5] 5415[5] 5594[7] 6422[5] *6709[2]*

Ventura (USA) *Mrs A J Perrett* a109 96
3 bb f Chester House(USA) —Estala (Be My Guest (USA))
(3044) 3591^{2} 3970^{2} (5537) 5794^{6} 6497^{2} (6965)

Veracity *M A Jarvis* a73 116
3 ch c Lomitas—Vituisa (Bering)
991^{2} (1231) (1843) 2816^{2} 4091^{2} 5408^{5}

Veras Joy *T D McCarthy* 12
2 b f Piccolo—Fly South (Polar Falcon (USA))
4662^{13} 5919^{16} 6234^{12}

Verba (FR) *R Gibson* 97
2 gr f Anabaa(USA) —Tambura (FR) (Kaldoun (FR))
$6630a^{3}$

Verbal Kint *E S McMahon* 14
3 b g Lake Coniston(IRE) —Kintara (Cyrano De Bergerac)
2366^{8}

Verbatim *A M Balding* a62 66
3 b f Vettori(IRE) —Brand (Shareef Dancer (USA))
1127^{10} 4392^{3} 5131^{8} 5803^{4} 6751^{4} 6991^{5} 7185^{2}

Verification *J Howard Johnson* 38
4 ch g Medicean—Viewfinder (USA) (Boundary (USA))
1479^{4} 2169^{9}

Verite *A J McCabe* a53 38
4 b g Foxhound(USA) —Blushing Victoria (Weldnaas (USA))
3^{9} 79^{14} 234^{13} 442^{8} 1074^{13} 1260^{10}

Vermilion (JPN) *S Ishizaka* a120 104
5 br h El Condor Pasa(USA) —Scarlet Lady (JPN) (Sunday Silence (USA))
$863a^{4}$ (6942a)

Verone (USA) *M Botti* a64 43
3 b f Dixie Union(USA) —Etheldreda (USA) (Diesis)
908^{3} 1068^{9} 2137^{7} 2607^{14} 3393^{12}

Veronica Franco (ITY) *E Borromeo* 97
4 ch m Lomitas—Gravette (Kris)
$2296a^{5}$

Veronicas Way *G M Moore* 61
2 b f High Estate—Mimining (Tower Walk)
4286^{7} 4612^{4} (5226) 6075^{9} 6536^{9}

Versatile *G A Ham* a67 74
4 b g Vettori(IRE) —Direcvil (Top Ville)
212^{6} 499^{11} 775^{14} 5204^{13} 5898^{6}

Verstone (IRE) *R F Fisher* 10
5 b m Brave Act—Golden Charm (IRE) (Common Grounds)
3638^{10}

Vertigineux (FR) *Mme C Dufreche* 103
3 b c Nombre Premier—Very Gold (FR) (Goldneyev (USA))
(4216a)

Vertigo Blue *A C Whillans* 28
4 b g Averti(IRE) —Soft Colours (Presidium)
965^{5}

Very Agreeable *W R Swinburn* a68 89
4 b m Pursuit Of Love—Oomph (Shareef Dancer (USA))
1543^{5} 2002^{6} 2474^{4}

Very Green (FR) *Mrs A L M King* 63
5 b g Barathea(IRE) —Green Bend (USA) (Riverman (USA))
$3577a^{10}$ 6902^{P}

Very Very Risky (FR) *L Cendra* 94
7 b m Take Risks(FR) —Very Very Nice (IRE) (Soviet Star (USA))
$6954a^{8}$

Very Well Red *P W Hiatt* a69 74
4 b m First Trump—Little Scarlett (Mazilier (USA))
492^{11} 559^{4} 649^{6} 801^{5} 1261^{2} (1435) (1673) (2023) 2388^{5} 3034^{7} 3156^{4} 6063^{8} 6269^{10} (6423) 6696^{5} 6856^{6} 7047^{8} 7155^{5} 7213^{4}

Very Wise *W J Haggas* a98 107
5 b g Pursuit Of Love—With Care (Warning)
6^{4} 119^{3} (264) 658^{P} 701^{2} (848) 1791^{6} 4745^{18} 5554^{3} 6011^{22} (6654) 6852^{12} 6965^{9}

Very Wise Kid *P T Midgley* 21
4 b m Cloudings(IRE) —Fantasy Flight (Forzando)
3202^{7} 3561^{5} 4178^{13}

Vesuvio *C W Thornton* a57 64
3 br g Efisio—Polo (Warning)
(3302) 3885^{6} 4480^{5} 5555^{6} 6146^{11} 6859^{7} 6979^{8}

Vettori Dancer *G G Margarson* a41 37
4 b m Vettori(IRE) —Assertive Dancer (USA) (Assert)
5421^{10} 5894^{13} 6453^{12}

Veverka *J C Fox* a52 35
6 b m King's Theatre(IRE) —Once Smitten (IRE) (Caerleon (USA))
1526^{11}

Vhujon (IRE) *P D Evans* 91
2 b c Mujadil(USA) —Livius Lady (IRE) (Titus Livius (FR))
(999) 2737^{8} 3269^{8} (3550) 4152^{13} $4832a^{18}$ 5216^{4} 5400^{P} 5629^{6} 6017^{2} 6182^{11} 6488^{9}

Viable *Mrs P Sly* a63 69
5 b g Vettori(IRE) —Danseuse Davis (FR) (Glow (USA))
819^{4} 1249^{9} 2084^{6} 3714^{5} (4294) 5687^{5} 6579^{2} 6894^{5}

Via Galilei (IRE) *J S Bolger* 91
2 b c Galileo(IRE) —Manger Square (IRE) (Danehill (USA))
$5458a^{9}$ $5845a^{9}$

Viami (IRE) *J G Burns* a70 79
3 br f Daylami(IRE) —Via Splendida (IRE) (Project Manager)
(908)

Vibrato (USA) *C J Teague* a61 49
5 b g Stravinsky(USA) —She's Fine (USA) (Private Account (USA))
7^{3} 63^{5} 238^{5} 431^{8} 3414^{13} 3787^{16} 4042^{12}

Vice Admiral *M W Easterby* a39 70
4 ch g Vettori(IRE) —Queen Of Scotland (IRE) (Mujadil (USA))
1042^{13} (1556) (2026) 2531^{6} 2890^{10} 4030^{2} 4280^{3} 4638^{4} 5257^{6} 5626^{13} 6076^{9}

Vicello (NZ) *P Stokes* 98
3 br g Brahms(USA) —Palace Beauty (AUS) (Palace Music (USA))
$6711a^{4}$

Vicious Prince (IRE) *R M Whitaker* a13 57
8 b g Sadler's Wells(USA) —Sunny Flower (FR) (Dom Racine (FR))
1598^{8} 5586^{7}

Vicious Warrior *R M Whitaker* a73 92
8 b g Elmaamul(USA) —Ling Lane (Slip Anchor)
1996^{5} 2374^{7} 2871^{3} (3556) 4049^{16} 4566^{10} 4922^{8} 5585^{8} 6180^{3} (6465) 6637^{3} 7002^{9}

Vic's Charm (IRE) *D Carroll*
6 ch g Old Vic—Sapien Dame (IRE) (Homo Sapien)
305^{8}

Victoria College (FR) *D Smaga* a84 98
3 b f Rock Of Gibraltar(IRE) —Uruk (Efisio)
$6889a^{9}$

Victorian Bounty *E J O'Neill* a73 88
2 b c Bahamian Bounty—Baby Bunting (Wolfhound (USA))
2271^{4} (2460) 3426^{2} 3925^{2} 4193^{2} (4560) 5216^{5} $5456a^{7}$

Victorian Cape (IRE) *E J O'Neill* 54
2 b c Cape Cross(IRE) —Inchoate (Machiavellian (USA))
3471^{8} 4028^{6} 4363^{5} 5302^{8}

Victorian Princess (IRE) *E J O'Neill* a48 55
2 ch f Giant's Causeway(USA) —Red Zinger (USA) (Red Ransom (USA))
2758^{8} 3453^{8} 4026^{4} 4453^{13} 4970^{6}

Victoria Reel *R Hannon* 50
2 ch f Danehill Dancer(IRE) —New Assembly (IRE) (Machiavellian (USA))
6649^{17}

Victoria Valentine *B W Hills* 71
2 b f Royal Applause—Denice (Night Shift (USA))
3055^{7} 3706^{8} 4602^{14} 5167^{13} 6419^{13}

Victors Prize (IRE) *S Curran* a37
5 b m Dr Devious(IRE) —Spoken Word (IRE) (Perugino (USA))
288^{8} 616^{6}

Victor Trumper *P W Chapple-Hyam* a81 73
3 b g First Trump—Not So Generous (IRE) (Fayruz)
7075^{6}

Victory (JPN) *H Otonashi* 119
3 b c Brian's Time(USA) —Grace Admire (JPN) (Tony Bin)
$6943a^{18}$

Victory Mile (USA) *B J Meehan* a56 54
3 b c Victory Gallop(CAN) —Viva Girl (USA) (Deputy Minister (CAN))
2261^{7} 2477^{8} 3084^{7} 4391^{10} (4757)

Victory Quest (IRE) *Mrs S Lamyman* a73 61
7 b g Victory Note(USA) —Marade (USA) (Dahar (USA))
(4) (389) 709^{3} 994^{7} 1752^{7} 6054^{5} 6802^{9} 6961^{3} 7110^{2} (7154) (7178)

Victory Shout (USA) *J R Best* a42 57
2 b g Victory Gallop(CAN) —Lu Lu's Lullaby (USA) (Palace Music (USA))
1652^{10} 2333^{9} 2590^{10} 6584^{13}

Victory Sign (IRE) *P Butler* a47 64
7 b g Forzando—Mo Ceri (Kampala)
3795^{10} 3946^{11} 4463^{10}

Victory Spirit *H J L Dunlop* a52 71
3 b c Invincible Spirit(IRE) —Tanouma (USA) (Miswaki (USA))
1535^{8} 2335^{14} 3872^{8} 4919^{9} 5778^{7}

Victory Tetsuni (USA) *Hideyuki Mori* a104
3 ch c Gone West(USA) —Radu Cool (USA) (Carnivalay (USA))
$596a^{2}$ $859a^{5}$

Vicveris (ITY) *S Billeri* 76
5 ch h Kris—Vehota Vic (Old Vic)
$1518a^{6}$ $6863a^{7}$

Vietnam *G A Huffer* a53 63
3 ch g Compton Place—Mosca (Most Welcome)
2653^{8} 3082^{15} 4109^{9} (4550) 4856^{14} 5128^{6} (6108) 6408^{5}

Viewforth *M A Buckley* a59 70
9 b g Emarati(USA) —Miriam (Forzando)
8^{11} 268^{9} 383^{10} 1991^{12} 2187^{3} 2509^{4} 3608^{7} 3829^{5} 4642^{3} 4857^{3} (5090) (5295) 5576^{12} 5879^{11}

View From The Top *Sir Mark Prescott* a71 70
3 b c Mujahid(USA) —Aethra (USA) (Trempolino (USA))
2763^{7} 2951^{2} 3181^{14} 3406^{10} 4686^{4} (5019) 5347^{9} 5709^{2} 5968^{6}

Vigano (IRE) *S Kirk* a65 70
2 b g Noverre(USA) —Perugia (IRE) (Perugino (USA))
1832^{15} 2215^{7} 2630^{2} 3508^{12} 4065^{9} 6665^{4} 6805^{7} 6978^{5} 7117^{4}

Vigo Bridge *B R Millman* 11
3 ch f Bandmaster(USA) —Peapod (Krayyan)
6094^{8}

Viking Spirit *W R Swinburn* a107 108
5 b g Mind Games—Dane Dancing (IRE) (Danehill (USA))
1195^{4} 2440^{10} (3489) 4150^{18} 4886^{2} 5797^{13} 6183^{7}

Vila Velha (IRE) *Ms Caroline Hutchinson* a50 53
4 b g Bahhare(USA) —Silver Union (IRE) (Bering)
769^{8}

Villa Bianca's (IRE) *J A Osborne* a47
4 ch m Priolo(USA) —Ostrusa (AUT) (Rustan (HUN))
13^{4} 207^{4} 273^{5}

Village Storm (IRE) *C J Teague* a25 36
4 b g Mujadil(USA) —First Nadia (Auction Ring (USA))
321^{10} 714^{5} 2792^{6} 4795^{7} 6858^{10}

Vilna (USA) *N A Callaghan* a65 57
2 b g Hold That Tiger(USA) —Not To Be Outdone (USA) (Damascus (USA))
4586^{7} 4777^{11} 5277^{6} 5729^{5} 6427^{2}

Vinando *C R Egerton* 107
6 ch g Hernando(FR) —Sirena (GER) (Tejano (USA))
2860^{5} 4047^{12} 4375^{10}

Vincennes *H-A Pantall* a74 111
3 bb f King's Best(USA) —Park Appeal (Ahonoora)
193^{8} (6690a)

Vincenzio (IRE) *C R Egerton* a53 73
3 b g Galileo(IRE) —Mystic Lure (Green Desert (USA))
1278^{4} 2944^{4} 3366^{6} 4667^{4}

Vincenzio Galilei (USA) *G M Lyons* a99 99
3 ch c Galileo(IRE) —Sometime (IRE) (Royal Academy (USA))
$4867a^{4}$

Vinea Federspiel (IRE) *Werner Glanz* 101
3 b f Singspiel(IRE) —Far Fetched (IRE) (Distant Relative)
$2070a^{4}$ $6046a^{7}$ $6688a^{18}$

Vineyard *W J Haggas* 68
2 b g Alhaarth(IRE) —Abime (USA) (Woodman (USA))
4362^{13} 5872^{3} 6234^{6}

Vintage (IRE) *P Mitchell* a66 53
3 b g Danetime(IRE) —Katherine Gorge (USA) (Hansel (USA))
4066^{7} 4541^{13} 5051^{9} 5420^{9} (5982) 6100^{5}

Vintage Year (IRE) *T J O'Mara* 79
5 b g Tagula(IRE) —Shalstayholy (IRE) (Shalford (IRE))
$873a^{16}$

Viola Carlita (FR) *J-P Gallorini* 98
3 b f Kendor(FR) —Valses Pour Moi (USA) (Gate Dancer (USA))
$1006a^{6}$ $2290a^{5}$ $6889a^{0}$

Viola Rosa (IRE) *D Shaw* a42 35
2 b f Fraam—Bleu Cerise (Sadler's Wells (USA))
3171^{10} 3760^{12} 4192^{9} 7182^{6}

Violent Velocity (IRE) *J J Quinn* a79 72
4 b g Namid—Lear's Crown (USA) (Lear Fan (USA))
300^{4} 609^{6} 672^{2} 718^{7} 992^{3} (1241) (1459) 2072^{7} 2419^{4} 2936^{5} 3999^{3} 4177^{4} 4281^{2} 4704^{2} 6021^{6} 6258^{10}

Violet Sky (IRE) *C Von Der Recke* 78
2 b f Montjeu(IRE) —Miznapp (Pennekamp (USA))
$5463a^{5}$

Violet's Pride *N Tinkler* a51 57
3 b f Kyllachy—Majalis (Mujadil (USA))
1151^{6} 2418^{15} 2553^{11} 2844^{5} 4525^{9} 4616^{5} 4795^{6} 4973^{5} 5295^{12} 5970^{3} 6565^{11}

Virgilia (IRE) *R Hannon* a46
3 b f Barathea(IRE) —Lanelle (USA) (Trempolino (USA))
1278^{8} 6830^{5} 6975^{9}

Virginia Woolf *D T Hughes* 101
5 gr m Daylami(IRE) —Vice Vixen (CAN) (Vice Regent (CAN))
$3143a^{13}$ $4830a^{7}$

Virtual *J H M Gosden* 82
2 b c Pivotal—Virtuous (Exit To Nowhere (USA))
5598^{2} 5977^{2}

Virtual Paddy *M Blanshard* a26 48
2 br g Averti(IRE) —Petrovna (IRE) (Petardia)
1367^{9} 1989^{8} 2443^{9} 3465^{12} 5186^{13} 5679^{8}

Visa Parade (ARG) *J W Sadler* a108 98
4 b h Parade Marshal(USA) —Visalia (ARG) (Ahmad (ARG))
$6924a^{7}$

Viscaya (IRE) *Mrs A Duffield* 57
2 b f Xaar—Fearfully Grand (Grand Lodge (USA))
5193^{7} 5483^{6} 5621^{5} 6074^{12}

Visconti *P W Chapple-Hyam* 62
2 ch c Medicean—Now And Forever (IRE) (Kris)
3435^{11} 4781^{10}

Viscountess (IRE) *M Johnston* 64
2 b f Green Desert(USA) —Maria Isabella (USA) (Kris)
6571^{4}

Viscount Monty *N Tinkler* 40
2 b g Sugarfoot—Desert Loch (IRE) (Desert King (IRE))
3024^{11} 3751^{6} 4136^{13} 5526^{9} 6307^{8}

Visionario (IRE) *S P C Woods* 114
3 b c Spinning World(USA) —Visionnaire (FR) (Linamix (FR))
$1056a^{3}$ $1703a^{8}$ $2293a^{18}$ $7091a^{11}$

Visionist (IRE) *M Al Muhairi* a103 94
5 b g Orpen(USA) —Lady Taufan (IRE) (Taufan (USA))
$326a^{7}$ (471a) $599a^{7}$ $644a^{5}$

Vision Of Grandeur (IRE) *D K Weld* 106
3 b c Grand Lodge(USA) —Champaka (IRE) (Caerleon (USA))
$4830a^{3}$ $6367a^{12}$

Visit *Sir Michael Stoute* 107
2 b f Oasis Dream—Arrive (Kahyasi)
3055^{2} (3988) 4744^{2} 5973^{8}

Vison Celebre (IRE) *A Fabre* 114
4 gr h Peintre Celebre(USA) —Visionnaire (FR) (Linamix (FR))
$2292a^{2}$

Vista Bella *Saeed Bin Suroor* 99
5 b m Diktat—Cox Orange (USA) (Trempolino (USA))
$397a^{5}$ $546a^{10}$

Vistaria (USA) *J H M Gosden* a7
3 ch f Distant View(USA) —Stellaria (USA) (Roberto (USA))
6229^{9}

Vital Equine (IRE) *E J O'Neill* 120
3 b c Danetime(IRE) —Bayalika (IRE) (Selkirk (USA))
1473^{2} $2051a^{6}$ $6029a^{12}$

Vital King (NZ) *P O'Sullivan* 118
5 b g Almutawakel—Wauwinet (NZ) (Bassenthwaite)
$7090a^{13}$

Vital Statistics *D R C Elsworth* 105
3 br f Indian Ridge—Emerald Peace (IRE) (Green Desert (USA))
1095^{6} 1496^{13} 2752^{5} 4118^{7} 5354^{8} 5799^{8} 6300^{5}

Vital Tryst *J G Given* a14 31
3 ch g Pivotal—Splicing (Sharpo)
678^{13} 769^{12} 1008^{11}

Vitamina Plus (ITY) *R Giorgetti* 87
3 ch f Cameron(IRE) —Pammukale (IRE) (Tirol)
$1337a^{5}$ $1701a^{7}$

Vitznau (IRE) *R Hannon* a84 101
3 b c Val Royal(FR) —Neat Dish (CAN) (Stalwart (USA))
725^{2} 815^{2} (2213) (3078) 3431^{6} 4093^{2} 4851^{4} 6013^{4} 6301^{2}

Vivacita *E J O'Neill* a67 65
3 b f Medicean—Sandrella (IRE) (Darshaan)
5346^{2} 5754^{2} 6211^{7} (6751) 6817^{7}

Viva La Flag (USA) *J L Dunlop* 92
3 ch f Rahy(USA) —On Parade (USA) (Storm Cat (USA))
1961^{4} 2625^{3} (3881) 4603^{6} (5210) 5639^{4} 6653^{4}

Viva Macau (FR) *J Moore* 114
4 bl h Sendawar(IRE) —Diyawara (IRE) (Doyoun)
$7090a^{12}$

Viva Pataca *J Moore* a84 126
5 b g Marju(IRE) —Comic (IRE) (Be My Chief (USA))
$7092a^{2}$

Viva Vettori *D R C Elsworth* a82 79
3 ch c Vettori(IRE) —Cruinn A Bhord (Inchinor)
4815^{3} 5384^{5} (5816)

Viva Volta *T D Easterby* a83 84
4 b g Superior Premium—La Volta (Komaite (USA))
1133^{10} 1555^{6} 1747^{4} (2256) 2466^{2} 3194^{9} 3512^{6} (4281) 4895^{5} 6006^{6} 6391^{4} 6560^{10}

Vive La Chasse (IRE) *Eve Johnson Houghton* a21 16
4 b m Mull Of Kintyre(USA) —Erne Project (IRE) (Project Manager)
559^{11} 1901^{13} 3044^{7}

Vive Les Rouges *C F Wall* 95
2 b f Acclamation—Bible Box (IRE) (Bin Ajwaad (IRE))
3037^{6} (4593) 5164^{2} 6017^{14}

Vivi Belle *M L W Bell* a60 58
3 b f Cadeaux Genereux—Locharia (Wolfhound (USA))
36^{9} 160^{7} (3000) 3686^{9} 6256^{5} 6607^{5}

Vixens Daughter *R T Phillips* a15 50
2 b f Foxhound(USA) —Classy Relation (Puissance)
1674^{2} 1896^{10} 4454^{11} 5096^{12} 6586^{10} 6722^{16}

Vixen Virago *Jane Southcombe* a23 35
4 ch m Foxhound(USA) —Le Pin (Persian Bold)
26^{6}

Vlasta Weiner *J M Bradley* a64 35
7 b g Magic Ring(IRE) —Armaiti (Sayf El Arab (USA))
82^{2} (137) 236^{7} 317^{7} 586^{5} 687^{U}

Vlavianus (CZE) *M Weiss* 61
6 b g Rainbows For Life(CAN) —Vlnka (CZE) (Amyndas)
$356a^{3}$ $439a^{2}$

Vodka (JPN) *Katsuhiko Sumii* 119
3 b f Tanino Gimlet(JPN) —Tanino Sister (JPN) (Rousillon (USA))
$6943a^{4}$

Vogarth *B R Millman* 59
3 ch g Arkadian Hero(USA) —Skara Brae (Inchinor)
3102^{7} 3968^{3} 4182^{4} 5190^{5} 5861^{3} 6062^{7}

Voice *H R A Cecil* a68 74
3 b f Zamindar(USA) —Seven Sing (USA) (Machiavellian (USA))
1105^{9} 1312^{4} 2317^{2}

Voice Mail *A M Balding* a61 73
8 b g So Factual(USA) —Wizardry (Shirley Heights)
19^{6} 52^{2} 309^{3} 341^{3} 459^{8} 495^{3} 610^{7} 1886^{5} 2370^{11} 2656^{13} 2963^{4} 4267^{6} 4686^{9} 4959^{6} 5345^{4} 5606^{8}

Voir Dire *Mrs P N Dutfield* a47 57
5 b g Vettori(IRE) —Bobbie Dee (Blakeney)
1590^{4} 1888^{2} 4067^{10}

Volaticus (IRE) *A D Brown* a65 59
6 b g Desert Story(IRE) —Haysel (IRE) (Petorius)
286^{4} 374^{2} 570^{9} 612^{5} 2023^{8} 2820^{4} 3195^{5} 3610^{4} 3815^{4} 4156^{13} 5525^{8}

Vol De Nuit *L Brogi* 111
6 gr h Linamix(FR) —Bedside Story (Mtoto)
$1874a^{2}$ $2706a^{6}$ $3665a^{13}$ $6689a^{5}$

Voliere *S C Williams* a96 90
4 b m Zafonic(USA) —Warbler (Warning)
2401^{13} 2835^{11} 3437^{6} 4005^{5} 4404^{3} 4665^{5} 5210^{3} 5543^{2} (5889) 6208^{3} 6654^{8} 6931^{4} 6994^{5} 7225^{3}

Volvoretas Rainbow *P C Haslam* 53
2 ch f Rainbow Quest(USA) —Volvoreta (Suave Dancer (USA))
5524^{5}

Vondova *D A Nolan* 63
5 b m Efisio—Well Proud (IRE) (Sadler's Wells (USA))
3185^{12} 3344^{11} 3676^{7} 3787^{13} 4101^{7} 4158^{5} 4381^{9} 4498^{9} 4787^{6} 5284^{16} 5481^{6} 5667^{8} 5673^{7} 5836^{9}

Vonne Owen (IRE) *John Joseph Murphy* 72
3 b f Lear Spear(USA) —Sulaka (Owington)
$3576a^{8}$ $4114a^{4}$

Von Wessex *W G M Turner* a46 46
5 b g Wizard King—Gay Da Cheen (IRE) (Tenby)
3169^{11} 3873^{6} 4471^{8} 4741^{8}

Voodoo Moon *M Johnston* 91
3 b f Efisio—Lunasa (IRE) (Don't Forget Me)
(1257) 1471^{5} 2037^{4} 2862^{9} 3430^{11} 3813^{6} 4093^{11} 4401^{5} 4785^{5} 5156^{6}

Vorteeva (USA) *K R Burke* 94
3 b g Bahri(USA) —Super Supreme (IND) (Zafonic (USA))
2001^{5} 3460^{15} 4799^{14}

Vortex *Miss Gay Kelleway* a112 113
8 b g Danehill(USA) —Roupala (USA) (Vaguely Noble)
197^{3} (394a) $530a^{7}$ $599a^{2}$ $858a^{12}$ 1034^{2} 1294^{3} $1648a^{7}$ 2755^{3} 3505^{10} 3941^{8} 4119^{15} 5412^{5} 5588^{6} (7254)

Voss *M Johnston* a56 39
3 b f Halling(USA) —Valdara (Darshaan)
157^{2} 267^{9} 460^{5}

Voxna (FR) *J F Bernard* 92
3 br f Take Risks(USA) —Vouivre (FR) (Matahawk)
$6770a^{10}$

Vytinna (FR) *D Sepulchre* a77 93
2 b f Victory Note(USA) —Messini (IRE) (Ballad Rock)
$7048a^{3}$

Wabbraan (USA) *D M Simcock* a68 52
2 b c Aldebaran(USA) —Madame Modjeska (USA) (Danzig (USA))
4540^{8} 5200^{6} 6436^{11}

Wadi Raider *M R Channon* 34
2 b c Tobougg(IRE) —Dowhatjen (Desert Style (IRE))
5227^{10} 5599^{15}

Wadlia (USA) *C E Brittain* 63
2 ch f Lemon Drop Kid(USA) —Brusque (USA) (Canaveral (USA))
5796^{7}

Wadnagin (IRE) *I A Wood* a67 62
3 b f Princely Heir(IRE) —Band Of Colour (IRE) (Spectrum (IRE))
1346^{5} 1634^{7} 2198^{3} 2515^{2} 2718^{4} 3168^{6} 3786^{8} 4529^{5} (5576) (6455) 6610^{6} 6717^{5}

Wagtail *E A L Dunlop* a90 98
4 b m Cape Cross(IRE) —Dancing Feather (Suave Dancer (USA))
3897^{4} 4633^{3} 6299^{10} 6604^{3}

Wahhaj *G Prodromou* 33
3 b c Muhtarram(USA) —Scottish Royal (IRE) (Night Shift (USA))
3948^{8} 4292^{6} 4516^{7}

Wahoo Sam (USA) *D W Barker* a81 80
7 ch g Sandpit(BRZ) —Good Reputation (USA) (Gran Zar (MEX))
(32) 109^{3} (308) 364^{6} 2452^{9} 2564^{9} 2828^{3} 3814^{6} 3922^{6} 4082^{4} 4353^{10} (4477) 4820^{11} 5330^{14} 5556^{14} 6463^{12} 6732^{5} 6882^{10}

Waiheke Island *B Mactaggart* 59
3 b f Winged Love(IRE) —West Of Warsaw (Danzig Connection (USA))
2300^{13} 2713^{11} 3051^{5} 3540^{7}

Wainwright (IRE) *P A Blockley* a66 56
7 b g Victory Note(USA) —Double Opus (IRE) (Petorius)
3^{5} 556^{10} 1718^{2} 1753^{4} 2149^{6} 3185^{9} 4999^{11} 5276^{10} 5866^{10}

Wait A While (USA) *T Pletcher* a115 119
4 rg m Maria's Mon(USA) —Flirtatious (USA) (A.P. Indy (USA))
5822a^{3}

Wait For The Light *E A L Dunlop* a77 84
3 b g Fantastic Light(USA) —Lady In Waiting (Kylian (USA))
1898^{4} 2448^{9} 5718^{3} 6061^{5} 6357^{7}

Wait For The Will (USA) *G L Moore* a74 77
11 ch g Seeking The Gold(USA) —You'd Be Surprised (USA) (Blushing Groom (FR))
29^{7} (195) 332^{4} 1451^{5} 3907^{3} (4231) 4597^{6} 6666^{3} 6902^{8}

Waitingforanalibi *T J O'Mara* a75 75
4 b g Zilzal(USA) —Balsamine (Gosport)
5788a^{8} 6553a^{12}

Wait Watcher (IRE) *P A Blockley* 95
3 b f Fath(USA) —Campestral (USA) (Alleged (USA))
1146^{10} 5396a^{10} 5618^{12}

Wake Up Maggie (IRE) *C F Wall* a90 112
4 b m Xaar—Kalagold (IRE) (Magical Strike (USA))
(1661) 3222a^{4} (4118) 4600^{4} 5409^{3} 6010^{9}

Waky Love (GER) *Frau J Meyer* 103
3 b f Royal Dragon(USA) —Waky Su (IRE) (Konigsstuhl (GER))
1855a^{5} 3121a^{2} 6691a^{2}

Waldliebe (GER) *P Rau*
3 b f Kabool—Waldbeere (Mark Of Esteem (IRE))
1515a^{F}

Waldvogel (IRE) *A Wohler* 106
3 ch c Polish Precedent(USA) —Wurftaube (GER) (Acatenango (GER))
3146a^{13} 4957a^{3} 5849a^{3}

Waleria (GER) *H J Groschel* 106
4 br m Artan(IRE) —Wiolante (GER) (Lagunas)
1517a^{3} 2924a^{4} 4013a^{6} 4838a^{5} (5929a)

Walharer *B Grizzetti* 86
3 ch c Cadeaux Genereux—Lanz Roi (ITY) (Roi Danzig (USA))
1336a^{8}

Walker (CZE) *A Berry*
3 ch g Signe Divin(USA) —Wanateluthspilgrim (USA) (Pilgrim (USA))
2298^{14}

Walking Talking *H R A Cecil* 97
3 b c Rainbow Quest(USA) —Wooden Doll (USA) (Woodman (USA))
1143^{7} (2402) 2790^{3}

Walk In My Shadow (IRE) *Augustine Leahy* 65
6 b m Orpen(USA) —Be My Folly (IRE) (Astronef)
4240a^{6}

Walk In The Park (IRE) *J E Hammond* 109
5 b h Montjeu(IRE) —Classic Park (Robellino (USA))
2292a^{7} 4655a^{6}

Wally Barge *D K Ivory* a54 38
4 b g Reprimand—Linda's Schoolgirl (IRE) (Grand Lodge (USA))
616^{5} 1284^{5} 1671^{12} 1906^{9} 3847^{11} 4161^{13}

Walnut Grove *T D Barron* 65
4 b m Forzando—Final Rush (Final Straw)
1459^{7} 1675^{7} (2072) 2390^{7} 2421^{7}

Walton House (USA) *A M Balding* a36
2 ch g Mutakddim(USA) —Dominant Dancer (Primo Dominie)
7181^{5}

Wanchai Lad *T D Easterby* 89
6 b g Danzero(AUS) —Frisson (Slip Anchor)
(1574) 2744^{13} 3298^{6}

Wanderin Boy (USA) *N Zito* a116
6 ch h Seeking The Gold(USA) —Vid Kid (CAN) (Pleasant Colony (USA))
5059a^{7} 6485a^{4}

Wandle *T G Mills* a89 101
3 b c Galileo(IRE) —Artistic Blue (USA) (Diesis)
(735) 1106^{3} 2790^{17}

Wanessa Tiger (IRE) *M R Channon* a53 57
3 ch f Titus Livius(FR) —Lominda (IRE) (Lomond (USA))
1310^{5} 1731^{13}

Wannabe Free *J Noseda* a63 73
2 b f Red Ransom(USA) —Wannabe Grand (IRE) (Danehill (USA))
5540^{6} 6267^{6} 6648^{3} 7190^{4}

Wannabe Posh (IRE) *J L Dunlop* 106
4 b m Grand Lodge(USA) —Wannabe (Shirley Heights)
(1477) 2036^{2} 2702a^{3} 4089^{2} (4748) 5352^{8}

Wannarock (IRE) *E A L Dunlop* 69
2 bb g Rock Of Gibraltar(IRE) —Propensity (Habitat)
2478^{6} 5707^{5} 6723^{3}

Wanna Runner (CAN) *B Baffert* a103
4 ch g El Corredor(USA) —Shebandowana (USA) (Mt Magazine (USA))
5824a^{8}

Wanna Shout *R Dickin* a58 49
9 b m Missed Flight—Lulu (Polar Falcon (USA))
2355^{5}

Waqaarr *M R Channon* a67 60
3 b g Tobougg(IRE) —Seeking Utopia (Wolfhound (USA))
311^{8} 573^{3} 973^{7}

Waquaas *B Bo* a95 100
11 b g Green Desert(USA) —Hamaya (USA) (Mr Prospector (USA))
5262a^{7}

War Anthem *C R Egerton* a71 66
3 br g Vettori(IRE) —Lucy Boo (Singspiel (IRE))
3447^{5} 4000^{3} 4541^{2} 4902^{4} 5568^{3}

War At Sea (IRE) *A W Carroll* a72 83
5 b g Bering—Naval Affair (IRE) (Last Tycoon (IRE))
16^{2} 88^{3}

Warcat (NZ) *Y Choy* a95 95
6 bb g Felix The Cat(USA) —Tara's Joy (NZ) (War Hawk I)
409a^{8} 474a^{5}

Warden Fizz *D R C Elsworth* 25
2 b g Efisio—Miss Rimex (IRE) (Ezzoud (IRE))
5380^{8}

Warden Warren *Mrs C A Dunnett* a64 53
9 b g Petong—Silver Spell (Aragon)
207^{14} 273^{12} 625^{11}

War Feather *T D McCarthy* a55 19
5 b g Selkirk(USA) —Sit Alkul (USA) (Mr Prospector (USA))
120^{5} 229^{4} 349^{2} 416^{6} 1592^{13} 1925^{10} 2176^{3} 4535^{10} 4914^{5} 7069^{7}

War Horn (ARG) *P Shaw* 93
5 b g Festin(ARG) —Forli Vous (ARG) (Forlitano (ARG))
1877a^{10}

Warm Embraces (IRE) *D R C Elsworth* a77 87
3 ch c Halling(USA) —Zapping (IRE) (Lycius (USA))
573^{2} (758) 1122^{3} 1974^{2} 3691^{4} 4799^{7} 5208^{2} (5432) 5639^{5}

Warming Up (IRE) *C E Brittain* a61 61
2 b c Kalanisi(IRE) —Sound Asleep (USA) (Woodman (USA))
4199^{5} 4508^{7} 5526^{6} 5914^{3} 6150^{3}

Warm Tribute (USA) *J S Goldie* 63
3 ch g Royal Anthem(USA) —Gentle Mind (USA) (Seattle Slew (USA))
954^{13} 3342^{16} 3811^{7} 4935^{8}

Warners Bay (IRE) *R Bastiman* a38 60
2 b c Iron Mask(USA) —Romangoddess (IRE) (Rhoman Rule (USA))
6384^{3} 6721^{12} 6813^{8}

Warningcamp (GER) *Lady Herries* a65
6 b g Lando(GER) —Wilette (GER) (Top Ville)
6853^{8}

War Officer (USA) *J-C Rouget* a83 101
2 br c Storm Cat(USA) —Wonder Woman (USA) (Storm Cat (USA))
6136a^{3}

War Of The Roses (IRE) *R Brotherton* a74 47
4 b g Singspiel(IRE) —Calvia Rose (Sharpo)
106^{8} 567^{12} (721) (789) 1251^{8} 4108^{8} 4660^{9} 4945^{6} 5120^{2} 5389^{7} 6407^{7} (6832) (7256)

War Pass (USA) *N Zito* a123
2 bb c Cherokee Run(USA) —Vue (USA) (Mr Prospector (USA))
(6508a)

Warren Bank *Mrs Mary Hambro* a4
2 b g Nayef(USA) —Neptunalia (Slip Anchor)
5679^{9}

Warringah *Sir Michael Stoute* a64
2 ch c Galileo(IRE) —Threefold (USA) (Gulch (USA))
6944^{6}

Warriors Key (IRE) *Kevin Prendergast* a93 98
3 b c Key Of Luck(USA) —Warrior Wings (Indian Ridge)
1547a^{11} 4211a^{2} 4864a^{9} 6920a^{3}

Warsaw (IRE) *A P O'Brien* 100
2 ch c Danehill Dancer(IRE) —For Evva Silca (Piccolo)
(1546a) 2785^{10} 4437a^{5} 4833a^{4} 5377^{6}

Warsaw Waltz *J G Given* 54
2 b f Polish Precedent(USA) —Generous Diana (Generous (IRE))
3916^{12} 5329^{5} 5812^{10}

Wasalat (USA) *D W Barker* a76 76
5 b m Bahri(USA) —Saabga (USA) (Woodman (USA))
1258^{5} 1416^{5} (2338) 2985^{13} 5230^{9} 5559^{11} 6021^{8} 6343^{8}

Wasan *E A L Dunlop* a71
2 ch c Pivotal—Solaia (USA) (Miswaki (USA))
(6850)

Wasseema (USA) *Sir Michael Stoute* 114
4 br m Danzig(USA) —Vantive (USA) (Mr Prospector (USA))
1661^{4} 2753^{7}

Wassendale *J W Hills* a55 55
3 b f Erhaab(USA) —Megdale (IRE) (Waajib)
208^{4} 498^{11} 981^{2} 1220^{5} 1988^{9}

Wassfa *C E Brittain* a74 94
4 b m Mark Of Esteem(IRE) —Mistle Song (Nashwan (USA))
381^{11} 559^{7} 1025^{7} 1379^{5} 1742^{2} (2361) 2720^{6} 3434^{12} 4203^{2} 5352^{12} 6757^{12}

Wassiljew (IRE) *W Baltromei* 97
3 b c Zinaad—Wassiliki (IRE) (Night Shift (USA))
4958a^{4} 5464a^{5}

Watamu (IRE) *P J Makin* a103 91
6 b g Groom Dancer(USA) —Miss Golden Sands (Kris)
95^{2} 608^{5} (701)

Watchful (IRE) *L M Cumani* a91 91
3 b f Galileo(IRE) —Sharakawa (IRE) (Darshaan)
(5450) 6061^{2} 6620^{4} (6853)

Watchmaker *Miss Tor Sturgis* a72 28
4 b g Bering—Watchkeeper (IRE) (Rudimentary (USA))
84^{5} 265^{2} (459) 2667^{5} 3249^{12} 5093^{5} 5500^{8} 5948^{6} 6780^{2} 6866^{2} 7224^{8}

Watch Out *M W Easterby* 45
3 b g Observatory(USA) —Ballet Fame (USA) (Quest For Fame)
2609^{4} 3183^{7} 3792^{6} 4036^{6}

Watch This Place *K R Burke* 25
2 b g Compton Place—Swissmatic (Petong)
2911^{5}

Wateera (IRE) *J L Dunlop* 70
3 b f Sakhee(USA) —Azdihaar (USA) (Mr Prospector (USA))
5768^{12} 6129^{5}

Water Dragon *Mlle C Cardenne* 98
6 b h Sri Pekan(USA) —Showboat (USA) (Theatrical)
3893a^{5}

Waterline Twenty (IRE) *P D Evans* a86 86
4 b m Indian Danehill(IRE) —Taisho (IRE) (Namaqualand (USA))
56^{6} 185^{6} 444^{6} 702^{6} 2536^{7} 3670^{7} 4195^{7} 4418^{6} 5001^{3} 5228^{7} 5383^{3} 5885^{11} 6423^{3} 6628^{4} (6646) 6710^{3} 6848^{7} 6996^{3} 7193^{4} 7281^{6}

Waterloo Corner *R Craggs* a64 71
5 b g Cayman Kai(IRE) —Rasin Luck (Primitive Rising (USA))
204^{6} 377^{5} 631^{7} 3204^{11} 3722^{8} 4081^{3} 4424^{3} 4704^{6} 5286^{9} 6304^{2} (6801) 6906^{4} 7213^{3}

Waterloo Dock *M Quinn* a58 50
2 b c Hunting Lion(IRE) —Scenic Air (Hadeer)
2451^{8} 4192^{5} 6800^{5}

Water Margin (IRE) *T G Mills* a45 57
3 b g Shinko Forest(IRE) —Tribal Rite (Be My Native (USA)) 2606^{8} 3046^{2} 3667^{3}

Water Mill (USA) *A M Balding* a83
3 gr c Unbridled's Song (USA) - Capote Miss 839^{6}

Watermill (IRE) D W Chapman a30 9
4 b g Daylami(IRE) —Brogan's Well (IRE) (Caerleon (USA)) 45^{9} 1222^{10} 1942^{12}

Water Pistol *M C Chapman* 34
5 b g Double Trigger(IRE) —Water Flower (Environment Friend)
913^{15} 1196^{10} 1406^{15}

Waterside (IRE) *G L Moore* a110 96
8 ch g Lake Coniston(IRE) —Classic Ring (IRE) (Auction Ring (USA))
118^{5} 227^{2} (307) 391^{2} 550^{3} 658^{6} (840) 1448^{8} 1791^{7} 2208^{8} 2446^{6} 3527^{2} 3971^{2} 4049^{3} 4377^{5} 4851^{3} 6852^{8} 6932^{4} 6965^{6} 7074^{8}

Watt A Will *J M Bradley*
4 ch m Karinga Bay—Wilming (Komaite (USA))
2580^{10} 3102^{9}

Wattys The Craic *G Prodromou* a51
3 ch g Erhaab(USA) —La Puce Volante (Grand Lodge (USA))
4977^{7} 5390^{8} 6176^{6} 6415^{15}

Wave Hill (IRE) *B J Meehan* 59
2 b g Mujadil(USA) —Bryna (IRE) (Ezzoud (IRE))
2443^{7} 6126^{7} 6419^{9}

Waveline (USA) *B J Meehan* a65 86
2 b f Stravinsky(USA) —Teresa Ann (USA) (Boston Harbor (USA))
1445^{3} (1882) 2812^{7} 3432^{14} 4152^{3} 5293a^{10}

Wavertree One Off *J Ryan* a48 43
5 b g Diktat—Miss Clarinet (Pharly (FR))
1888^{7} 2345^{10} 2890^{8} 3250^{4} 4859^{4} 5573^{10} 7203^{2}

Wavertree Princess (IRE) *N P Littmoden* a72 74
2 gr f Invincible Spirit(IRE) —Blushing Queen (IRE) (Desert King (IRE))
4506^{6} 4755^{6} 5380^{2} 6665^{5} 6756^{6} (6926) 7072^{5}

Wavertree Warrior (IRE) *N P Littmoden* a96 96
5 br g Indian Lodge(IRE) —Karamana (Habitat)
197^{7} (550) 1448^{7} 1651^{24} 2208^{5} 2476^{7} 2670^{6} 3201^{2} 3650^{9} 4049^{10} 4548^{4} 4827^{5} 5615^{11} 6143^{4} 6669^{6} 6900^{3} 7074^{3} 7267^{4}

Waymark (IRE) *M A Jarvis* a76 72
3 ch c Halling(USA) —Uncharted Haven (Turtle Island (IRE))
1523^{2} 2005^{7} 3689^{10} 4457^{5} 4815^{14}

Wayward Shot (IRE) *M W Easterby* a56 62
5 b g Desert Prince(IRE) —Style Parade (USA) (Diesis)
266^{8} (447) 524^{13} 627^{12}

Wazir (USA) *L Reuterskiold* a49 96
5 bb g Pulpit(USA) —Top Order (USA) (Dayjur (USA))
1648a^{11} 4874a^{7}

Webbow (IRE) *T D Easterby* a69 95
5 b g Dr Devious(IRE) —Ower (IRE) (Lomond (USA))
2536^{2} (2985) 3556^{4} (4176) (4566)

Webbswood Lad (IRE) *M R Bosley* a64
6 b g Robellino(USA) —Poleaxe (Selkirk (USA))
365^{5}

Wee Buns *S Kirk* a65 59
2 b g Piccolo—Gigetta (IRE) (Brief Truce (USA))
4016^{8} 4459^{5} 4629^{4} (5751) 6502^{11} 6898^{3} 7044^{4} 7142^{4} 7220^{3}

Wee Charlie Castle (IRE) *G C H Chung* a71 73
4 b g Sinndar(IRE) —Seasonal Blossom (IRE) (Fairy King (USA))
88^{8} 319^{3} 1717^{3} 2403^{12} 3042^{7} 3457^{5} 4063^{4} 4517^{4} 6260^{5} 6577^{5} 7186^{3}

Wee Ellie Coburn *M Mullineaux* a55 53
3 ch f Bold Edge—Wathbat Mtoto (Mtoto)
3342^{15} 4219^{6} 4526^{10} 5084^{7}

Weekend Fling (USA) *M Johnston* a68 67
3 bb f Forest Wildcat(USA) —Woodman's Dancer (USA) (Woodman (USA))
(916) 1099^{18} 1979^{4} 2742^{6}

Weet A Surprise *R Hollinshead* a79 63
2 b f Bertolini(USA) —Ticcatoo (IRE) (Dolphin Street (FR))
1728^{6} (3030) 3492^{8} 3925^{5} 4175^{5} 5096^{3} 5751^{5} (5887) 6326^{8} (6834) (7106) (7243)

Weet By Far *R Hollinshead* a59 59
2 b f Bertolini(USA) —Shaiybara (IRE) (Kahyasi)
3471^{4} 4904^{5} 5603^{9} 6022^{7} 6150^{6} 6454^{4} 6936^{3} 7130^{4} 7196^{2} 7258^{5}

Weet For Ever (USA) *P A Blockley* a59 59
4 bb g High Yield(USA) —Wild Classy Lady (USA) (Wild Again (USA))
7^{10} 14^{2} 75^{8} 664^{3} 729^{13}

Weetfromthechaff *R Hollinshead* a51 61
2 gr g Weet-A-Minute(IRE) —Weet Ees Girl (IRE) (Common Grounds)
3192^{13} 4037^{10} 4417^{5} 4923^{10} 6066^{4} 7232^{4}

Weet Intolerance *B D Leavy*
2 b f Polar Prince(IRE) —Priorite (IRE) (Kenmare (FR))
1029^{6} (Dead)

Weet Yer Tern (IRE) *W M Brisbourne* a58 59
5 b g Brave Act—Maxime (IRE) (Mac's Imp (USA))
271^{2} (350) 518^{6} 571^{7} 1210^{9} 4488^{4} 4945^{3} (5179) 5421^{2} 6316^{10} 6342^{4} 6458^{3} 6804^{4} 6937^{4} 7009^{7}

Wee Ziggy *M Mullineaux* 45
4 b g Ziggy's Dancer(USA) —Midnight Arrow (Robellino (USA))
1311^{12} 1381^{12} 2108^{12} 3534^{10} 3815^{P} 4124^{7} 4499^{8}

We Have A Dream *W R Muir* a66 69
2 bb c Oasis Dream—Final Shot (Dalsaan)
2596^{11} 2941^{7} 3423^{9} (3734) 4255^{3} 4484^{2} 4762^{8} (5529) (6282)

Weight In Gold *P J McBride* a38 44
2 b f Mujahid(USA) —Golden Ciel (USA) (Septieme Ciel (USA))
2832^{16} 3245^{8} 3849^{10} 5314^{8} 5572^{7}

Weightless *N P Littmoden* a97 106
7 ch g In The Wings—Orford Ness (Selkirk (USA))
352^{8} (777) 940^{3} 1393^{6} 2351^{8} 2859^{10} 3882^{2} 4814^{9}

Welcome Approach *J R Weymes* a12 76
4 b g Most Welcome—Lucky Thing (Green Desert (USA))
1080^{7} 1806^{6} 1914^{2} 2072^{5} 2494^{11} 2866^{3} 2989^{3} 3627^{5} 3954^{5} 3998^{4} 4289^{2} 4489^{3} 4800^{2} 4967^{2} 5481^{3} 5522^{3} 5747^{5} 6020^{11}

Welcome Cat (USA) *A D Brown* a75 79
3 b c Tale Of The Cat(USA) —Mangano (USA) (Quiet American (USA))
6967^{8} 7110^{7} 7226^{3} 7285^{12}

Welcome Inn *M E Sowersby* 23
2 ch f Zaha(CAN) —Lambeth Belle (USA) (Arazi (USA))
1857^{10} 2115^{8} 2310^{6} 2838^{7} 3296^{6}

Welcome Return (IRE) *T D Easterby* 73
2 b f Mull Of Kintyre(USA) —Aiaie (Zafonic (USA))
1302^{9} 1963^{2} 2504^{6} 3884^{6} (4278) 4892^{2} 5350^{18} 5613^{7}

Welcome Spirit *J S Haldane*
4 b g Most Welcome—Valadon (High Line)
2825^{12} 3538^{P} (Dead)

We'll Come *M A Jarvis* 98
3 b g Elnadim(USA) —Off The Blocks (Salse (USA))
1471^{2} (2153) 3503^{3} 3707^{3} 4745^{3}

Well Defined *T H Caldwell*
4 b m Barathea(IRE) —Serene View (USA) (Distant View (USA))
1995^{16}

Wellinas (GER) *W Hefter* 78
3 ch c Kalatos(GER) —Well Sired (GER) (Surumu (GER))
2102a^{7}

Well Informed *K A Ryan* a75
2 b f Averti(IRE) —May Light (Midyan (USA))
(1029)

Wellington Hall (GER) *M Wigham* a65 87
9 b g Halling(USA) —Wells Whisper (FR) (Sadler's Wells (USA))
297^{8} 428^{7} 568^{12} 3457^{7} 4025^{11}

Well Placed *W J Haggas*
3 b g Compton Place—Pudding Lane (IRE) (College Chapel)
1541^{13}

Wells Lyrical (IRE) *B Smart* 62
2 b c Sadler's Wells(USA) —Lyrical (Shirley Heights)
6592^{5} 6740^{6}

Wells Of Badr (IRE) *P W Chapple-Hyam* 62
3 b f Fasliyev(USA) —Tamburello (IRE) (Roi Danzig (USA))
1105^{12} 2433^{2} 3051^{4} 3872^{5} 4736^{9} 5563^{11} 6447^{12}

Welsh Auction *K J Burke* a58 73
3 gr g Auction House(USA) —Anneli Rose (Superlative)
899^{2} 1403^{2} 1425^{2} 1635^{4} 2260^{5} 3612^{5} 4336^{16} 5041^{4} 5338^{6} 5945^{13}

Welsh Cake *Mrs A J Perrett* a60 73
4 b m Fantastic Light(USA) —Khubza (Green Desert (USA))
1534^{13} 2472^{10}

Welsh Emperor (IRE) *T P Tate* a89 118
8 b g Emperor Jones(USA) —Simply Times (USA) (Dodge (USA))
1770^{9} 2233^{3} 3098^{4} 4600^{2} 5673^{6} 6029a^{2} (6541)

Welsh Guard (USA) *G P Enright* 44
4 ch g Silver Hawk(USA) —Royal Devotion (USA) (His Majesty (USA))
3236^{7} 4357^{6} 5384^{10}

Welsh Opera *Mrs A J Perrett* a68 54
2 b f Noverre(USA) —Welsh Diva (Selkirk (USA))
6409^{7} 6601^{3} 7097^{4}

Welsh Whisper *S A Brookshaw* a47 44
8 b m Overbury(IRE) —Grugiar (Red Sunset)
364[9] 570[10] 620[4] 1362[11] 7057[9] 7169[11]

Welltraumer (GER) *A Trybuhl* 96
3 gr c Sagamix(FR) —Washira (Most Welcome)
2102a[6]

Wendy's Boy *R Hannon* a52 21
3 b c Elnadim(USA) —Tatouma (USA) (The Minstrel (CAN))
678[5] 798[7] 1248[11]

We'Re Delighted *M R Channon* a58 69
2 b c Tobougg(IRE) —Samadilla (IRE) (Mujadil (USA))
4198[3] 4761[5] 5343[5] *5605[9]* 5863[3]

Wessex (USA) *P A Blockley* a97 88
7 ch g Gone West(USA) —Satin Velvet (USA) (El Gran Senor (USA))
6[5] 227[9] 391[3] 658[11] 840[11] 1179[2] 4886[9]

Westbrook Blue *W G M Turner* a43 84
5 b h Kingsinger(IRE) —Gold And Blue (IRE) (Bluebird (USA))
1214[7] 1854[14] 2805[9] 3837[6] 3869[7]

West End Lad *S R Bowring* a51 55
4 b g Tomba—Cliburnel News (IRE) (Horage)
3922[13] 4659[5] *4977[8]* 5886[7] 6304[15] *6564[11] 7125[2]*

Westering Home (IRE) *J Mackie* a63 67
4 b m Mull Of Kintyre(USA) —Glympse (IRE) (Spectrum (IRE))
112[3] 299[7]

Western Adventure (USA) *E A L Dunlop* 93
3 b c Gone West(USA) —Larrocha (IRE) (Sadler's Wells (USA))
(1129) 1803[3] 2790[5]

Western Art (USA) *P W Chapple-Hyam* 99
2 bb c Hennessy(USA) —Madam West (USA) (Gone West (USA))
1919[2] (3269)

Western Diplomat (USA) *A Al Raihe* a46 81
7 bb h Gone West(USA) —Dabaweyaa (Shareef Dancer (USA))
178a[10] *326a[13]*

Western Land *B Smart* a54 47
3 ch g Zamindar(USA) —Landowska (USA) (Langfuhr (CAN))
728[7] 1913[12] 2894[7] *5098[2]*

Western Point (IRE) *Sir Mark Prescott* a71 73
3 ch g Pivotal—Hesperia (Slip Anchor)
1737[5] 1923[16] *2175[8]* 2759[11] *3082[4] 3456[2]* 3876[5] (4518) (4687) 5040[2] *5604[3]*

Western Roots *M Appleby* a70 55
6 ch g Dr Fong(USA) —Chrysalis (Soviet Star (USA))
334[4] 538[6] 976[15] *1366[3] 2358[3] (2521) 2802[8] 3111[4] 3926[8] 4433[13]* 4660[6] 4959[8] *7023[4] 7100 7132[5] 7274[7]*

Wester Ross (IRE) *J M P Eustace* 77
3 b c Fruits Of Love(USA) —Diabaig (Precocious)
1204[6] (1725) 2126[6] 3058[8]

Westlander (USA) *A Schennach* 45
7 b g Gone West(USA) —Woven Silk (USA) (Danzig (USA))
356a[5] 494a[7]

West Nile (IRE) *A & G Botti* 76
5 b g Trans Island—Athlumney Dancer (Shareef Dancer (USA))
1518a[5]

Westport *K A Ryan* a83 85
4 b g Xaar—Connemara (IRE) (Mujadil (USA))
1363[5] 1847[5] 2088[6] 2744[9] *(3108)* 6381[2] *6836[3] 7126[4]*

West Wind *H-A Pantall* 116
3 ch f Machiavellian(USA) —Red Slippers (USA) (Nureyev (USA))
(2501a) 3117a[3] 5465a[2]

West With The Wind *T P Tate* 81
2 b c Fasliyev(USA) —Midnight Angel (GER) (Acatenango (GER))
6468[8] 6724[2]

Westwood *D Haydn Jones* 89
2 ch g Captain Rio—Consignia (IRE) (Definite Article)
3383[13] 4014[2] 4454[3] 4755[8] (5773) 6488[12]

Westwood Dawn *Mrs N Macauley* a49
2 gr g Clodovil(IRE) —Ivory Dawn (Batshoof)
4070[9] 5910[14] *6477[7] 6714[11] 6980[8] 7170[4]*

Whaston (IRE) *J D Bethell* a42 53
2 b g Hawk Wing(USA) —Sharafanya (IRE) (Zafonic (USA))
5227[8] 5734[10] *6358[7]*

What-A-Dancer (IRE) *R A Harris* a69 68
10 b g Dancing Dissident(USA) —Cool Gales (Lord Gayle (USA))
2619[8] 4256[5] 4532[8] 4595[9]

Whatalotofbuts *B De Haan* 40
2 ch c Kirkwall—Wontcostalotbut (Nicholas Bill)
2618[5] 3043[13]

What A Treasure (IRE) *L M Cumani* a53 75
3 ch f Cadeaux Genereux—Treasure Trove (USA) (The Minstrel (CAN))
(2309) 2696[6] 3247[2] (3845) 4855[9]

What Do You Know *A M Hales* a82 78
4 b g Compton Place—How Do I Know (Petong)
486[6] 548[2] 654[3] 724[3] 793[2] 831[2] 1666[3] 1991[2] *(2350)* 2411[5] 2655[8] 3613[5] *4024[12] (4944)* 5447[7]

Whatizzit *E A L Dunlop* a86 83
4 b m Galileo(IRE) —Wosaita (Generous (IRE))
1542[3] 2527[4]

What Katie Did (IRE) *P F I Cole* a76 68
2 b c Invincible Spirit(IRE) —Chatterberry (Aragon)
1781[6] 1970[9] 2724[6] *(4065) 4461[2] (4669)* 5053[9] 5314[9] *5601[6] (6151) (6454) 7052[2]*

What's For Tea *Tom Dascombe* a64 53
2 b f Beat All(USA) —Come To Tea (IRE) (Be My Guest (USA))
3199[6] 3635[6] 3835[3] 4363[3] 5869[4] *5984[4] (6099) 6454[2] 6566[4] 6793[3] 6966[4] 7031[2] 7044[3] 7210[2]*

Whats Your Game (IRE) *A Berry* a52 47
3 ch g Namid—Tahlil (Cadeaux Genereux)
3202[9] 3537[9] 4226[9] 4384[8] 4935[10] 5282[5] *5752[2]* 5970[6] *6339[10]* 6702[6] *7019[6]* (Dead)

Whaxaar (IRE) *R Ingram* a60 46
3 b g Xaar—Sheriyna (FR) (Darshaan)
2178[5] 3620[5] 4270[9] *6991[4] 7187[2]*

Whazzis *W J Haggas* a80 107
3 br f Desert Prince(IRE) —Wosaita (Generous (IRE))
1500[7] 1837[2] 2212[3] 2914[4] 3430[10] (3897) 4873a[6] (6221a) 6524a[10]

Wheelavit (IRE) *B G Powell* a72 74
4 b g Elnadim(USA) —Storm River (USA) (Riverman (USA))
30[6] 234[10] 359[7] 461[5] 592[7] 4108[5] 4910[3]

Wheels In Motion (IRE) *T P Tate* 83
3 b c Daylami(IRE) —Tarziyana (USA) (Danzig (USA))
1773[5] 2871[7] 3094[2] 3470[4] 4006[7] 5196[4] 5776[7]

Whenever *R T Phillips* 85
3 ch c Medicean—Alessandra (Generous (IRE))
5113[3] (5938) (6473)

Whenineedyou *A Wood* a12
2 ch f Best Of The Bests(IRE) —Party Turn (Pivotal)
6401[10]

When Yer Ready (IRE) *T D Easterby* 54
2 b g Val Royal(FR) —Rachel Green (IRE) (Case Law)
3092[6] 4612[6] 5042[13]

Where's Broughton *W J Musson* a75 69
4 ch m Cadeaux Genereux—Tuxford Hideaway (Cawston's Clown)
1819[15] *3416[12]* 4112[5] 4766[8] *5178[10] 5733[7] 6603[12] 7214[8]*

Where's Killoran *Peter Grayson* a49
2 b f Iron Mask(USA) —Calypso Lady (IRE) (Priolo (USA))
6228[10] 6734[5] 6926[8] 7071[5]

Where's Susie *D K Ivory* a63
2 ch f Where Or When(IRE) —Linda's Schoolgirl (IRE) (Grand Lodge (USA))
5681[7] 6119[6]

Where To Now *Mrs C A Dunnett* 29
2 b f Where Or When(IRE) —Starminda (Zamindar (USA))
5570[7] 6411[13]

Whinhill House *D W Barker* a69 74
7 ch g Paris House—Darussalam (Tina's Pet)
668[9] (892) (1028) 1262[8] 1557[4] 1707[3] (1891) 2418[8] 2461[10] 3203[6] 3836[4] (3921) 4083[4]

Whipchord (IRE) *R Hannon* a60 60
3 ch f Distant Music(USA) —Spanker (Suave Dancer (USA))
1345[2] 1634[9] 2545[11] 2696[9] 3000[9] 6277[8]

Whiskey And Rye (IRE) *John J Walsh* 61
2 b c Catcher In The Rye(IRE) —Another Shadow (IRE) (Topanoora)
1508a[7]

Whiskey Creek *Miss Tor Sturgis* a56 56
2 ch g Tipsy Creek(USA) —Judiam (Primo Dominie)
1993[4] 2297[10] 2984[10] 5089[11] 5167[6] *5529[3]*

Whiskey Junction *A M Balding* a72 36
3 b g Bold Edge—Victoria Mill (Free State)
1520[2]

Whispered Dreams (GER) *Saeed Bin Suroor* a75
2 ch f Platini(GER) —Waconda (GER) (Pursuit Of Love)
(6267)

Whispering Death *W J Haggas* a92 94
5 br g Pivotal—Lucky Arrow (Indian Ridge)
1272[2] 1582[6] *3216[2]* 4056[14] 4569[2] 5215[6] 5375[3]

Whispering Desert *P T Midgley* a48 63
2 b f Distant Music(USA) —Nullarbor (Green Desert (USA))
2934[4] 3256[4] 3606[2] 4097[5] (4702) 5008[5] *5529[7]*

Whistful Miss *P Howling* a44 31
2 b f First Trump—Mise En Scene (Lugana Beach)
1101[12] 3446[13] *3923[6] 4359[4]* 4824[10] *6872[9]*

Whistledownthewind (SAF) *M F De Kock* a74
4 b m Al Mufti(USA) —Lone Sailor (SAF) (Hard Up (ARG))
246a[5] 476a[7]

Whistledownwind *P W Chapple-Hyam* 88
2 b c Danehill Dancer(IRE) —Mountain Ash (Dominion)
5977[9] (6493)

Whistler *Miss J R Tooth* a40 68
10 ch g Selkirk(USA) —French Gift (Cadeaux Genereux)
1405[14] 2966[9] 3368[7] 3906[6] 4635[7] 4689[5] 4881[8] 5349[12] 6720[13]

Whistleupthewind *J M P Eustace* a63 63
4 b m Piccolo—The Frog Queen (Bin Ajwaad (IRE))
66[3] 158[3] 296[7] 383[9] 555[6] 2334[11] 3101[3] 3487[13] 4029[4] 4515[7] 4855[3] (5275) 5546[11]

Whistling Fred *B De Haan* a42
8 b g Overbury(IRE) —Megabucks (Buckskin (FR))
1342[9]

Whitbarrow (IRE) *B R Millman* a87 90
8 b g Royal Abjar(USA) —Danccini (IRE) (Dancing Dissident (USA))
896[11] *(1262) (1436) (1718) (1977) 3623[4]* (3998) 4227[5] 5168[7] 5535[7] *(6288) 6907[5] 7126[7]*

Whitcombe Flyer (USA) *Jamie Poulton* a54 47
2 bb c Fusaichi Pegasus(USA) —Bakewell Tart (IRE) (Tagula (IRE))
4160[6] 5448[7] *6926[6] 6990[6] 7220[4]*

Whitcombe Minister (USA) *Jamie Poulton* a77 83
2 b c Deputy Minister(CAN) —Pronghorn (USA) (Gulch (USA))
5971[4] *(7266)*

Whitcombe Spirit *Jamie Poulton* a65 36
2 b c Diktat—L'Evangile (Danehill (USA))
5919[9] *6805[8] 7114[4]*

White Bear (FR) *C R Dore* a72 72
5 ch g Gold Away(IRE) —Danaide (FR) (Polish Precedent (USA))
(888) 1655[7] *6568[9] 6795[12] 6947[8]*

White Cockade *Ms J S Doyle*
4 gr g Compton Place—Swissmatic (Petong)
84[9]

White Deer (USA) *M Johnston* 101
3 b g Stravinsky(USA) —Brookshield Baby (IRE) (Sadler's Wells (USA))
1257[3] 1773[6] (2313) 3078[2] 3559[10] 4851[2] 4990[5] 5355[10] 5615[9]

White Ledger (IRE) *R E Peacock* a49 30
8 ch g Ali-Royal(IRE) —Boranwood (IRE) (Exhibitioner)
201[12] 4008[7]

White Lightening (IRE) *J Wade* 78
4 ch g Indian Ridge—Mille Miglia (IRE) (Caerleon (USA))
1849[4] 3501[4] 4179[10]

White Lightning (GER) *U Stech* 111
5 gr h Sternkoenig(IRE) —Whispering Grass (GER) (Konigsstuhl (GER))
5929a[6] 6353a[7] 6781a[5]

White Moss (IRE) *M H Tompkins* a60 67
3 b f Peintre Celebre(USA) —Saint Ann (USA) (Geiger Counter (USA))
1312[7] 1816[3] 2253[7] 3429[7] 3803[3] 4128[2] 4582[8] 5036[3] 5905[4] 6277[9]

Whiteoak Lady (IRE) *J L Spearing* 72
2 ch f Medecis—French Toast (IRE) (Last Tycoon (IRE))
3245[4] (3902) 5665[6]

White's Ruby *B Smart* a52 47
3 gr f Iron Mask(USA) —Negligee (Night Shift (USA))
3302[9] 4157[7] *5175[3] 5897[10]*

Whithorn *J Balding* a15 48
4 ch g Primo Valentino(IRE) —Polar Refrain (Polar Falcon (USA))
1426[5] *1749[10]* 1921[11] 2509[13] 2844[11] 3381[U]

Whittinghamvillage *J P L Ewart* 63
6 b m Whittingham(IRE) —Shaa Spin (Shaadi (USA))
(2823) (3497) 4383[5] 4705[12] 5286[13] 5964[6]

Whodouthinkur (IRE) *Mrs C A Dunnett* a30 52
2 b g Beckett(IRE) —Scarletta (USA) (Red Ransom (USA))
3625[13] 3962[14] *5605[11]*

Whodunit (UAE) *P W Hiatt* a63 47
3 b g Mark Of Esteem(IRE) —Mystery Play (IRE) (Sadler's Wells (USA))
260[12] 655[5] 1081[8] *1399[9]* 2081[2] *2801[15]* 3159[15] 4019[10] 4845[5]

Whoneedswings (IRE) *David Wachman* 92
5 b m In The Wings—Luminary (Kalaglow)
875a[5] 2702a[10] 3143a[10]

Whos Counting *R J Hodges* a43
3 ch f Woodborough(USA) —Hard To Follow (Dilum (USA))
6390[6] 6532[9]

Who's This (IRE) *W R Swinburn* a55
3 b g Xaar—Tarafiya (USA) (Trempolino (USA))
2455[10]

Who's Winning (IRE) *B G Powell* a79 86
6 ch g Docksider(USA) —Quintellina (Robellino (USA))
91[4] 1004[3] 1063[5] (1431) (1607) 1847[4] 2139[5] 2494[2] 2655[4] 2882[9] 3481[8] 3911[10] 4320[2] 5168[2] 5535[6] 5638[6] 5923[17] *6141[10]* 6450[5] *6946[11] 7094[8]*

Whozart (IRE) *A Dickman* a43 63
4 b g Mozart(IRE) —Hertford Castle (Reference Point)
1197[12] 1594[3] (2121) 2561[2] 3347[6] 3782[14] 5908[8] 6702[3] *6735[7]*

Why Be (AUS) *L Laxon* 109
5 b g Success Express(USA) —Charybdis (AUS) (Royal Academy (USA))
7089a[11]

Wibbadune (IRE) *Peter Grayson* a58
3 ch f Daggers Drawn(USA) —Becada (GER) (Cadeaux Genereux)
6905[7] 7019[2] (7162) 7284[5]

Wicked Daze (IRE) *Sir Mark Prescott* a77 84
4 ch g Generous(IRE) —Thrilling Day (Groom Dancer (USA))
2667[2] 2833[2] *3621[2]*

Wickedish *M J Gingell* a49 55
3 b f Medicean—Sleave Silk (IRE) (Unfuwain (USA))
2429[10] *3456[5]* (4337) 5546[12] 6570[10]

Wicked Lady (UAE) *J M Bradley* a50
4 b m Jade Robbery(USA) —Kinsfolk (Distant Relative)
869[8] 1344[9] 3595[11]

Wicked Style (USA) *George R Arnold II* a112
2 ch c Macho Uno(USA) —Deviletta (USA) (Trempolino (USA))
6508a[10]

Wicked Uncle *S Gollings* a73 61
8 b g Distant Relative—The Kings Daughter (Indian King (USA))
1121[5] 5379[17] *5753[11] 6671[4] 6810[6] 7011[2] 7105[3] 7206[6]*

Wicksy Creek *M G Quinlan* 50
4 b g Tipsy Creek(USA) —Bridal White (Robellino (USA))
3246[4] 3801[2]

Wickwing *A & G Botti* 102
4 b m In The Wings—Chetwynd (IRE) (Exit To Nowhere (USA))
(2296a) 6519a[12]

Wid (USA) *J L Dunlop* 100
3 rg f Elusive Quality(USA) —Alshadiyah (USA) (Danzig (USA))
1146[8] 5354[11] 6300[2] 6621[2] 6758[13]

Wi Dud *K A Ryan* 115
3 b c Elnadim(USA) —Hopesay (Warning)
2184[5] 2857[13] 3329[2] 4090[4] 4746[5] 5214[7]

Wiesenpfad (FR) *W Hickst* 115
4 ch h Waky Nao—Waldbeere (Mark Of Esteem (IRE))
897a[8] 1699a[5] (4838a) 5464a[3] 6045a[4]

Wightgar *R A Kvisla* a41 41
3 b c Carisbrooke—Main Brand (Main Reef)
1950[7] 3244[6] 3476[5] 3792[15] 4518[10]

Wigram's Turn (USA) *A M Balding* 80
2 ch c Hussonet(USA) —Stacey's Relic (USA) (Houston (USA))
(2090) 3550[3] 3938[8]

Wigwam Willie (IRE) *K A Ryan* 92
5 b g Indian Rocket—Sweet Nature (IRE) (Classic Secret (USA))
2536[11] (3052) 3437[13] 3813[4] 4827[11] (5585) 6155[14]

Wikaala (USA) *M P Tregoning* a49
2 ch g Diesis—Roseate Tern (Blakeney)
4393[9]

Wild Bill Tracey *M J Wallace* a72 72
2 b g Bahamian Bounty—Travel Secret (Blakeney)
3370[7] 4506[4] 5065[5] *6004[5] 6692[2] 6872[3] 6977[8] 7240[3]*

Wild Fell Hall (IRE) *W R Swinburn* a87 81
4 ch g Grand Lodge(USA) —Genoa (Zafonic (USA))
1036[7] 1416[3] 1924[2] (2544) *(2994)*

Wild Gams (USA) *B Perkins Jr* a112
4 b m Forest Wildcat(USA) —Diamonds And Legs (USA) (Quiet American (USA))
6483a[9]

Wild Gardenia *J H M Gosden* a57 58
3 b f Alhaarth(IRE) —Frappe (IRE) (Inchinor)
1816[4] 2308[8]

Wild Lass *J C Fox* a41 52
6 ch m Bluegrass Prince(IRE) —Pink Pumpkin (Tickled Pink)
2540[5]

Wild Pitch *P Mitchell* a94 77
6 ch g Piccolo—Western Horizon (USA) (Gone West (USA))
(48) 353[10] (444) (515) 662[8] 1438[6] *(1949)* 2238[7] *2994[12]* 3858[6] *4271[3]*

Wild Savannah *I Mohammed* a85 112
5 b h Singspiel(IRE) —Apache Star (Arazi (USA))
248a[8] 398a[6] (541a) 645a[6]

Wildwish (IRE) *Enda Kelly* 82
3 b f Alhaarth(IRE) —Wish (Danehill (USA))
873a[4] 6036a[10]

Wild Wonder (JPN) *T Kubota* a106
5 b h Brian's Time(USA) —Waltz Dancer (JPN) (Sunday Silence (USA))
6942a[5]

Wilford Maverick (IRE) *K J Burke* a54 28
5 b g Fasliyev(USA) —Lioness (Lion Cavern (USA))
20[10] 620[10] 653[10]

Wilki (FR) *A De Royer-Dupre* 101
2 b f Oasis Dream—Khumba Mela (IRE) (Hero's Honor (USA))
3147a[2] 4009a[3] 5373a[2]

Willhego *J R Best* a78 77
6 ch g Pivotal—Woodrising (Nomination)
4551[7] 5539[RR] *6439[11] 7055[3]*

Will He Shine (USA) *Dale Romans* a111 85
5 ch h Silver Deputy(CAN) —Christmas Star (USA) (Star De Naskra (USA))
5852a[8]

Will He Wish *S Gollings* a85 97
11 b g Winning Gallery—More To Life (Northern Tempest (USA))
28[4] 191[2] 261[5] (2452) 2536[6] 5012[11] 5383[11] *5685[5] 6016[18] (6568) 7287[3]*

Willhewiz *M S Saunders* a71 81
7 b g Wizard King—Leave It To Lib (Tender King)
1004[2] 1214[4] *1589[4]* 1885[2] *2350[2]* 2673[8] 2982[8] 5272[11] 6424[6] *(6581)* 6810[5] *6976[4] 7119[2] 7183[7]*

William John *B Ellison* a57 63
4 b g Foxhound(USA) —Classy Relation (Puissance)
1578[3] 2302[5] 2715[4] 3204[2] 4042[5] 4817[2] 5300[8] (Dead)

William's Way *I A Wood* a89 89
5 b g Fraam—Silk Daisy (Barathea (IRE))
(1181) (1385) 2351[7] 2906[7] 3060[3] *4888[8] 6765[4] 6995[7]*

Willie Ever *W J Musson* a29 53
3 b g Agnes World(USA) —Miss Meltemi (IRE) (Miswaki Tern (USA))
1841[9] 2477[9] *7247[6]*

Willingly (GER) *M Trybuhl* 108
8 b h Second Set(IRE) —Winara (GER) (Konigsstuhl (GER))
1699a[8] 2705a[4]

Willit (IRE) *M R Channon* 55
2 ch f Compton Place—Fingal Nights (IRE) (Night Shift (USA))
4629[8] 4924[10] 5442[5] (Dead)

Willkandoo (USA) *K A Ryan* a50
2 bb c Unbridled's Song(USA) —Shannkara (IRE) (Akarad (FR))
6763[7]

Willofcourse *H Candy* a61 53
6 b g Aragon—Willyet (Nicholas Bill)
2143[9] 2622[4] *3618[7]* 4336[3] *4668[2]* 4853[4] 5090[4] *(5425) 5778[6] 6210[11]* (Dead)

Willow Dancer (IRE) *W R Swinburn* a75 70
3 ch g Danehill Dancer(IRE) —Willowbridge (IRE) (Entrepreneur)
1075[5] 1560[6] 3881[6] *4433[3]* 4960[5] *5604[7]*

Willow O Wisp (USA) *V Cerin* 117
5 b g Misnomer(USA) —Willow Woodman (USA) (Woodman (USA))
6924a[9]

Willy (SWE) *R Brotherton* a51 30
5 ch g Heart Of Oak(USA) —Kawa-Ib (IRE) (Nashwan (USA))
182[6] 481[8] 730[6]

Willyn (IRE) *J S Goldie* a48 63
2 b f Lujain(USA) —Lamasat (USA) (Silver Hawk (USA))
1193[6] 1487[4] 2819[4] 3205[7] 3398[12] *3923[2]* (4136) 4770[7] 5153[2] 5582[8] 5837[3] 6328[7] 6462[9]

Willywell (FR) *J-P Gauvin* a107 109
5 br h Jimble(FR) —Basilissa (FR) (Gay Minstrel (FR))
1879a[4] 2617a[2] 3665a[11] 4520a[0] 6095a[6] *(7128a)*

Wilmington *Mrs J C McGregor* a69 72
3 ch g Compton Place—Bahawir Pour (USA) (Green Dancer (USA))
231[3] 312[6] 421[5] 624[12] 4971[5] 5555[7]

Wiltshire (IRE) *P T Midgley* a59 64
5 br g Spectrum(IRE) —Mary Magdalene (Night Shift (USA))
(562) 750[2] 912[9] (1221) 1459[5] 3345[3] *3647[3]* 4100[8] 4423[9] *7024[6]*

Wimoweh (IRE) *T D Easterby* 39
2 b g Intikhab(USA) —Evening Serenade (IRE) (Night Shift (USA))
5143[10] 5485[6] 6303[10]

Windbeneathmywings (IRE) *M J Grassick* a60 78
3 b f In The Wings—Moneefa (Darshaan)
1154[4] 1628[9] 1887[5] 2793[5] (3166) 3427[4] 6982[8]

Wind Chime (IRE) *A G Newcombe* a52 62
10 ch h Arazi(USA) —Shamisen (Diesis)
1562[3] 2492[8] 4031[7] 4259[8] 6261[9]

Wind Flow *C A Dwyer* a64 68
3 b g Dr Fong(USA) —Spring (Sadler's Wells (USA))
6778[6] 7083[3] 7115[2]

Windjammer *T D Easterby* 76
3 b g Kyllachy—Absolve (USA) (Diesis)
925[3] (1240) (1453) 1820[10] 2435[2] 2837[2] 3568[4] 4452[2] 5029[7] 5481[12] 6020[10] 6256[7]

Wind Shuffle (GER) *J S Goldie* 65
4 b g Big Shuffle(USA) —Wiesensturmerin (GER) (Lagunas)
4932[8] 5741[9] 5966[3] 6463[7]

Winds Of Kildare (IRE) *C N Allen* a48 19
4 b g Shaddad(USA) —Asturiana (Julio Mariner)
260[7] 977[11] 1566[8] 2343[8] 2559[P] 3732[3] 4272[8] 4961[9] 5336[7] 6266[11]

Windsor Knot (IRE) *Saeed Bin Suroor* 117
5 ch h Pivotal—Triple Tie (USA) (The Minstrel (CAN))
5723[3] (6298)

Windsor Palace (IRE) *A P O'Brien* a82 93
2 b c Danehill Dancer(IRE) —Simaat (USA) (Mr Prospector (USA))
6549a[8]

Wind Star *G A Swinbank* 94
4 ch g Piccolo—Starfleet (Inchinor)
993[3] 1480[10] 2093[2] 2755[25] 3959[3] 4388[8] 4690[6] 5049[7] 5543[5] 6185[9]

Windward Islands (USA) *M Frostad* 117
3 rg g Cozzene(USA) —Cruisie (USA) (Assert)
6374a[9]

Windy Prospect *Mrs L J Mongan* a68 59
5 ch g Intikhab(USA) —Yellow Ribbon (IRE) (Hamas (IRE))
63[6] 206[10] 303[2] 561[8] 768[3] (1027) 1311[3] 1739[2] 4592[12] 5001[12] 5864[9] 6268[8] 6431[12] 6713[9] (Dead)

Wine 'n Dine *C A Cyzer* 72
2 b c Rainbow Quest(USA) —Seasonal Splendour (IRE) (Prince Rupert (FR))
6294[4]

Winforjoe (IRE) *J J Bridger* a34 45
3 b f Anzillero(GER) —Run Or Bust (IRE) (Commanche Run)
689[11] 884[8] 3214[14] 4356[6] 4663[3] 5137[4] 5816[11] 6275[7]

Wingbeat (USA) *Saeed Bin Suroor* 86
2 b c Elusive Quality(USA) —Infinite Spirit (USA) (Maria's Mon (USA))
(6409)

Wing Collar *T D Easterby* 103
6 b g In The Wings—Riyoom (USA) (Vaguely Noble)
3753[2] (3973) 4722[5]

Winged Cupid (IRE) *Saeed Bin Suroor* 117
4 b h In The Wings—Sweet Emotion (IRE) (Bering)
(3103) 3974[4] 4826[2] 5213[7]

Winged D'Argent (IRE) *B J Llewellyn* 108
6 bb g In The Wings—Petite-D-Argent (Noalto)
1582[14] 2449[8] 2736[11] 3090[6] (3467) 3976[7] 5808[6] 6284[4]

Winged Farasi *R A Harris* a69 66
3 b c Desert Style(IRE) —Clara Vale (IRE) (In The Wings)
655[3] 807[4] 1348[3] 1815[8] 2116[2] (2697) 3620[7] 4550[4] 5750[9] 5860[6] 6749[7] 7028[3] 7201[4] 7275[2]

Winged Flight (USA) *M Johnston* a68 87
3 b g Fusaichi Pegasus(USA) —Tobaranama (IRE) (Sadler's Wells (USA))
5764[9] 6155[13] 6560[9] 6765[8]

Winged Legacy (USA) *H R A Cecil* 69
2 ch c Diesis—Fairy Glade (USA) (Gone West (USA))
5010[10]

Wing Express (IRE) *L M Cumani* 106
3 b c Montjeu(IRE) —Eurobird (Ela-Mana-Mou)
1296[4] (2308) 3458[2]

Wing Play (IRE) *H Morrison* a75 72
2 b c Hawk Wing(USA) —Toy Show (IRE) (Danehill (USA))
6418[12] 6724[5] (6855)

Wingsinmotion (IRE) *Miss Tracy Waggott* 42
3 b f Indian Lodge(IRE) —Coulisse (IRE) (In The Wings)
849[8] 1220[7] 2096[10] 3274[4] 3402[6] 4036[8]

Wings Of Morning (IRE) *D Carroll* a55 44
6 ch g Fumo Di Londra(IRE) —Hay Knot (Main Reef)
61[10]

Win In Gold *John A Harris* a36
6 b g Pivotal—Sylvan Dancer (IRE) (Dancing Dissident (USA))
98[5] 305[7]

Winker Watson *P W Chapple-Hyam* 116
2 ch c Piccolo—Bonica (Rousillon (USA))
(1123) (2785) (3459)

Winners Toast (IRE) *David Wachman* 76
3 b c Danehill Dancer(IRE) —Greenvera (USA) (Riverman (USA))
4035a[5]

Winning Pleasure (IRE) *J Balding* a82 50
9 b g Ashkalani(IRE) —Karamana (Habitat)
102[8] 323[7] 388[4]

Winning Show *R A Harris* a66 70
3 b g Muhtarram(USA) —Rose Show (Belmez (USA))
3395[3] 3743[6] 4258[6] 5122[9] 5270[5] 5714[8] 6070[7]

Winning Smile (USA) *P W Chapple-Hyam* a46 20
3 ch f With Approval(CAN) —Acquiesce (Generous (IRE))
689[8] 758[10]

Winning Spirit (IRE) *Miss Z C Davison* a22 81
3 b g Invincible Spirit(IRE) —Taisho (IRE) (Namaqualand (USA))
1160[11] 1604[10] 3637[9] 4001[8] 6174[12] 6528[10]

Winter Bloom (USA) *H R A Cecil* 81
2 b f Aptitude(USA) —Bionic (Zafonic (USA))
3874[2] (4422) 5374[4] 6012[9]

Wintercast *W R Swinburn* 85
2 ch c Spinning World(USA) —Bright Hope (IRE) (Danehill (USA))
(6724)

Winter Cruise (IRE) *Ian Williams* a59 69
3 b g Lil's Boy(USA) —Arundhati (IRE) (Royal Academy (USA))
6293[12] 6612[10] 6801[6] 6979[10] 7172[2] (7273)

Winter Fashion (FR) *F Head* a75 108
3 b f Kendor(FR) —Ontherebound (USA) (Dayjur (USA))
1006a[2] 5259a[6]

Winter Footprints (IRE) *William Hayes* 56
3 b f Lend A Hand—Mothers Footprints (IRE) (Maelstrom Lake)
3577a[17]

Winter Lane *J R Norton* a55 38
3 b g Hernando(FR) —Winding (USA) (Irish River (FR))
499[6] 1129[8] 6109[14] 6561[13] 7110[6]

Winter Sunrise *Sir Michael Stoute* 102
3 b f Pivotal—Winter Solstice (Unfuwain (USA))
(2127) (3709) 4748[5] 6168[5]

Winthorpe (IRE) *J J Quinn* a71 71
7 b g Tagula(IRE) —Zazu (Cure The Blues (USA))
3[6] 306[8] 621[6] 717[4] 896[6] (1226) 1309[5] 1681[4] 1914[7] (2421) 2762[4] 3676[5] 4024[6] 4251[5] 5522[5] 5747[15] 6467[13] 6818[7] 7003[2] (7111) 7227[3]

Wisdom's Kiss *J D Bethell* a50 58
3 b g Ocean Of Wisdom(USA) —April Magic (Magic Ring (IRE))
1111[10] 1482[4] 2224[10] 2796[11] 4223[2] 4931[13] 5900[10]

Wise Choice *Mrs L B Normile* a60 59
4 b g Green Desert(USA) —Ballykett Lady (USA) (Sir Ivor (USA))
88[10] 215[10] 5482[9]

Wise Dennis *A P Jarvis* a107 113
5 b g Polar Falcon(USA) —Bowden Rose (Dashing Blade)
(1179) (1651) 1791[2] 2817[4] 3941[16] 5797[6] 6298[11] 6965[2]

Wise Hawk *W J Haggas* a61 66
2 b c Hawk Wing(USA) —Dombeya (IRE) (Danehill (USA))
6755[5] 6980[5]

Wise Little Girl *M A Jarvis* a83 81
3 b f Singspiel(IRE) —Gretel (Hansel (USA))
1068[2] (2359) 3877[6] 4510[6] (5405) 6144[9] 6669[5]

Wiseman's Diamond (USA) *K A Ryan* a68 62
2 b f Wiseman's Ferry(USA) —Aswhatilldois (IRE) (Blues Traveller (IRE))
5176[4] 5429[5] 6242[2] (6536) 6812[2] (7007)

Wise Melody *W J Haggas* a74
2 b f Zamindar(USA) —Swellegant (Midyan (USA))
6964[4] (7216)

Wise Son *W J Haggas* a43 81
2 b g Royal Applause—Racina (Bluebird (USA))
3589[6] (4016) 4406[2] 4975[9] 5974[12]

Wiseton Dancer (IRE) *Miss V Haigh* a44 36
3 b c Danehill Dancer(IRE) —Your Village (IRE) (Be My Guest (USA))
55[5] 202[6] 1219[14]

Wishes Or Watches (IRE) *John A Quinn* a48 51
7 br g Bravefoot—Shadya's Amal (Shaadi (USA))
6569[2] 6697[4] 7168[12]

Wishing On A Star *E J O'Neill* a27 74
3 b f Fantastic Light(USA) —Sephala (USA) (Mr Prospector (USA))
2840[6] 3421[11] 4760[11]

Witchingham *R Hannon* a60
3 b g Polish Precedent(USA) —Assertive Dancer (USA) (Assert)
114[9] 257[4] 1587[6] 6229[6] 6387[12] 6480[4] 6796[10]

Witchry *A G Newcombe* a79 78
5 gr g Green Desert(USA) —Indian Skimmer (USA) (Storm Bird (CAN))
727[5] 905[6] 1080[5]

With Confidence *D R C Elsworth* a62 63
3 ch f Polish Precedent(USA) —Farhana (Fayruz)
3992[8] 4541[4] 5013[9] 5866[3] 6831[12] 7014[6]

With Ease (IRE) *P W D'Arcy*
3 br g Grand Lodge(USA) —Twice The Ease (Green Desert (USA))
2606[15] 2886[8]

Without A Prayer (IRE) *R M Beckett* a78 96
2 ch c Intikhab(USA) —Prayer (IRE) (Rainbow Quest (USA))
3404[2] (3849) 4694[3]

Without Excuse (USA) *M Botti* a79 79
3 ch g Woodman(USA) —Dixie Jewel (USA) (Dixieland Band (USA))
1126[7] 1467[6] 2305[8] (6833) 7002[4] 7193[8]

Without Precedent (FR) *Y De Nicolay* 90
2 b f Polish Precedent(USA) —Sue Generoos (IRE) (Spectrum (IRE))
4626a[6] 6187a[5]

Withywood (USA) *G L Moore* a42 41
3 bb f Woodman(USA) —Castellina (USA) (Danzig Connection (USA))
3046[9] 3395[9] 4182[6] 4918[4] 5710[4] 5865[9]

Wizardmicktee (IRE) *D G Bridgwater* a38
5 b g Monashee Mountain(USA) —Epsilon (Environment Friend)
514[7] 664[10]

Wizby *P D Evans* a46 58
4 b m Wizard King—Diamond Vanessa (IRE) (Distinctly North (USA))
975[7] 1132[12] 1564[11] 2214[12] 2938[9] 3241[8] 6250[14] 6573[11] 6642[5] 6792[8] 7169[4] 7218[6]

Wizzy Izzy (IRE) *N Wilson* 28
2 gr f Shinko Forest(IRE) —Strelitzia (IRE) (Bluebird (USA))
845[13] 3378[6] 3915[11] 4924[11]

Wodhill Be *D Morris* a55 50
7 b m Danzig Connection(USA) —Muarij (Star Appeal)
(145) 374[3] 519[3] 801[6] 980[6] 1569[3] 1933[5] 2798[9] 3826[17] 4317[8] 4855[11] 5566[2] 5900[8] 6887[7] 7034[13]

Wodhill Gold *D Morris* a67 46
6 ch g Dancing Spree(USA) —Golden Filigree (Faustus (USA))
7[2] (75) 228[2] 888[5] 1568[4] 1720[4] 3173[11] 3419[11] 4023[3] 5568[8] 6316[12] 6629[4] 6859[9] 6956[5]

Wodhill Schnaps *D Morris* a60 65
6 b g Danzig Connection(USA) —Muarij (Star Appeal)
63[10] 266[4] 393[3] 518[2] 977[15] 1350[3] 1715[6] 2154[7] (2343) 3056[10] (3285) 3828[5] 4395[11] 4978[4] 5391[8] 5946[11] 6479[8]

Wogan's Sister *I A Wood* a50 35
2 b f Lahib(USA) —Dublivia (Midyan (USA))
4198[9] 6401[9] 6714[8]

Wolds Way *T D Easterby* a43 58
5 b g Mujahid(USA) —Off Camera (Efisio)
936[7] 1030[4] 1077[6] 1532[9] 1967[10] 2582[11]

Wolfman *D W Barker* a60 56
5 ch g Wolfhound(USA) —Madam Millie (Milford)
586[10] 632[2] 1197[4] 1595[6] 2844[3] 4180[11] 4427[3] 4701[3]

Wolf Pack *D A Nolan* a23 38
5 b g Green Desert(USA) —Warning Shadows (IRE) (Cadeaux Genereux)
1311[13] 4499[10] 5083[12] 5935[15]

Wolf River (USA) *D M Simcock* a80 77
3 b c Mr Greeley(USA) —Beal Street Blues (USA) (Dixieland Band (USA))
1098[2] 3062[3] 3447[3] 4182[2] (4938) (5495) 6231[7]

Wolgan Valley (USA) *Saeed Bin Suroor* 81
2 ch c Mr Greeley(USA) —Dancing Naturally (USA) (Fred Astaire (USA))
2056[2] 2451[2] 3383[2]

Womaniser (IRE) *L M Cumani* a45
3 b g Rock Of Gibraltar(IRE) —Top Table (Shirley Heights)
1278[10] 1523[9]

Wonderful Day (GER) *Frau C Brandstatter* 95
5 b m Kahyasi—Wonderful Dreams (GER) (Dashing Blade)
6220a[3] 6691a[4]

Wonderful Luck (USA) *S Asmussen* a78
2 ch f Trust N Luck(USA) —No Small Wonder (USA) (Capote (USA))
5247a[8]

Wonder Speed (JPN) *T Hatsuki* a95
5 b h King Glorious(USA) —Wonder Heritage (USA) (Pleasant Tap (USA))
6942a[9]

Woodala (AUS) *A Mathews* 97
6 b m Woodman(USA) —Darmala (NZ) (Danehill (USA))
15a[12]

Wood Chorus *M L W Bell* 73
2 b f Singspiel(IRE) —Woodbeck (Terimon)
6411[3]

Woodcote (IRE) *C G Cox* a93 102
5 b g Monashee Mountain(USA) —Tootle (Main Reef)
1125[8] 1474[18] 1986[8] 3464[9] 3990[7] 4122[18] 4567[14] 4886[3]

Woodcote Place *P R Chamings* a20 94
4 b g Lujain(USA) —Giant Nipper (Nashwan (USA))
1818[10] 2476[3] 2755[19] 3488[5] 4049[4] 4134[6] 4548[9]

Woodcote Wildcat (USA) *N A Callaghan* a36 24
2 bb f High Yield(USA) —Zappeuse (USA) (Kingmambo (USA))
3348[8] 3589[13] 4963[8]

Woodcraft *B W Hills* 84
3 ch c Observatory(USA) —Woodwardia (USA) (El Gran Senor (USA))
(1081) 1773[4] 2627[6] 3335[6] 4004[5] 5208[6] 5870[3]

Woodcutter (IRE) *J H M Gosden* 48
2 gr c Daylami(IRE) —Cinnamon Rose (USA) (Trempolino (USA))
4362[17]

Wooden King (IRE) *P D Evans* a50 56
2 b g Danetime(IRE) —Olympic Rock (IRE) (Ballad Rock)
2151[6] 2398[7] 3270[9] 4832a[10] 5729[6]

Wood Fern (UAE) *W M Brisbourne* a57 54
7 b g Green Desert(USA) —Woodsia (Woodman (USA))
71[9]

Woodford *M W Easterby* 28
2 b g Mull Of Kintyre(USA) —Ice House (Northfields (USA))
2251[10] 2604[11] 2888[9] 3370[8]

Woodford Consult *M W Easterby* a52 50
5 b m Benny The Dip(USA) —Chicodove (In The Wings)
2252[8]

Woodford Regen *M W Easterby* a50 58
2 b f Hunting Lion(IRE) —Katie's Kitty (Noble Patriarch)
890[6] 1029[3] 3833[3] 4844[6] 5251[5] 5932[8]

Woodins Way *P J Makin* a52 59
3 ch g Danehill Dancer(IRE) —Lady Storm (IRE) (Mujadil (USA))
1839[8] 2541[5] 3881[13] 4760[8] 5860[8] 6062[9] 6590[3] 7009[5]

Woodlander (USA) *G Contessa* a68 107
5 b h Forestry(USA) —Madam Lagonza (USA) (Kingmambo (USA))
5823a[4]

Woodland Mist *M Dods* a52
2 b f Tobougg(IRE) —Aker Wood (Bin Ajwaad (IRE))
5363[7]

Woodland Traveller (USA) *N Tinkler* 63
3 b g Gone West(USA) —Iftiraas (Distant Relative)
1410[9]

Woodnook *J A R Toller* a101 86
4 b m Cadeaux Genereux—Corndavon (USA) (Sheikh Albadou)
(419) 551[2] 656[7] 762[6] 1372[4] 2450[8] 3746[11] 6930[8] 7053[9]

Woodwee *R E Barr* a51 53
4 ch g Woodborough(USA) —Evaporate (Insan (USA))
912[7] 2091[9] 4768[10]

Woodygo *J R Best* a64 45
3 ch g Tobougg(IRE) —Woodrising (Nomination)
116[8] 293[10] 456[9] 738[5] 904[10] 1355[12] 2552[8]

Woolfall Blue (IRE) *G G Margarson* a87 87
4 gr h Bluebird(USA) —Diamond Waltz (IRE) (Linamix (FR))
353[2] 940[2] (1356) 1543[4] 1767[16]

Woolfall King (IRE) *G G Margarson*
4 b g King Charlemagne(USA) —Bazaar Promise (Native Bazaar)
1350[10]

Woolfall Rose *G G Margarson* a61 63
3 b f Generous(IRE) —Rose Noble (USA) (Vaguely Noble)
2359[4] 3041[3] 3651[7] 5068[7] 5899[9]

Woolfall Treasure *G G Margarson* 86
2 gr c Daylami(IRE) —Treasure Trove (USA) (The Minstrel (CAN))
3095[6] 3625[9] 3957[2] 4625a[8] 5323[5]

Woolstone Boy (USA) *A M Hales* a44
6 ch g Will's Way(USA) —My Pleasure (USA) (Marfa (USA))
62[6] 416[14] 585[5]

Wool Zone (AUS) *Ross Price* 90
7 gr h Flying Spur(AUS) —Ashes (AUS) (Ideal Planet (AUS))
15a[13]

Woqoodd *R A Fahey* a70 72
3 b g Royal Applause—Intervene (Zafonic (USA))
958[7] 1219[12] (4291) 4896[9] 5753[4] 6313[10] 6625[6]

Word Games *A M Balding* a63
2 b g Mind Games—Salacious (Sallust)
5895[6] 6099[13]

Word Of Warning *G Wragg* 61
3 gr g War Chant(USA) —Frosty Welcome (USA) (With Approval (CAN))
2059[10] 2913[11] 4905[4]

Word Perfect *M W Easterby* a64 81
5 b m Diktat—Better Still (IRE) (Glenstal (USA))
1377[3] 1718[8] 2864[8] (3185) 3466[6] 3920[6] 4075[6] 4381[2] (4719) 5581[10]

Wordy's Girl *M J Gingell*
4 b m Little Jim—Wordy's Wonder (Welsh Captain)
7199[8]

World At My Feet *N Bycroft* 48
5 b m Wolfhound(USA) —Rehaab (Mtoto)
1423[8] 2008[11] 2893[2] 3156[10]

World Beat (GER) *M Johnston* 33
3 b f Tiger Hill(IRE) —World's Vision (GER) (Platini (GER))
5637[3]

Worldly Wise *Patrick J Flynn* a92 100
4 b g Namid—Tina Heights (Shirley Heights)
2815[7] 4211a[14] 4867a[5] 5242a[16]

World Of Choice (USA) *Saeed Bin Suroor* 68
2 b c Distorted Humor(USA) —Palace Weekend (USA) (Seattle Dancer (USA))
5361[11] 6417[3]

World's Heroine (IRE) *G A Butler* a89 86
3 ch f Spinning World(USA) —Metaphor (USA) (Woodman (USA))
3961[2] 4589[6] 5537[3] 6002[3] 6208[7] 6822[6]

World Spirit *Rae Guest* a92 80
3 b f Agnes World(USA) —Belle Esprit (Warning)
1726[3] (2654) 3100[4] 4004[3] 4828[2] (6208) 6931[6]

World Supremacy (IRE) *G A Ham* a37 12
4 b g Spinning World(USA) —Cream Jug (IRE) (Spectrum (IRE))
2656[16]

World Tour *I Semple* 60
2 b g Spinning World(USA) —Seven Wonders (USA) (Rahy (USA))
4495[5] 5663[3] 6740[7]

World View (IRE) *M P Tregoning* a45
2 br f Golan(IRE) —Athene (IRE) (Rousillon (USA))
6065[5]

Worldwind *Mrs L J Mongan*
4 b m Agnes World(USA) —Reach The Wind (USA) (Relaunch (USA))
649[10] 2084[12]

Wotashirtfull (IRE) *K A Ryan* 78
2 ch g Namid—Madrina (Waajib)
2532[3] 2863[3] 4002[2] 4447[2] 4937[3]

Wotavadun (IRE) *B P J Baugh* a37 22
4 ch g King Of Kings(IRE) —Blush With Love (USA) (Mt. Livermore (USA))
4795[9]

Wotchalike (IRE) *R J Price* a73 58
5 ch g Spectrum(IRE) —Juno Madonna (IRE) (Sadler's Wells (USA))
279[10] 733[6]

Wovoka (IRE) *M R Channon* a81 99
4 b g Mujadil(USA) —Common Cause (Polish Patriot (USA))
1245[9] 1862[11] 2209[2] 2403[13] 2891[7] 3258[4] 3482[2] (3900) 4049[18] 4377[6] 4745[15] 5196[9]

Wow Me Free (USA) *D Vella* a104
3 ch f Menifee(USA) —Double Wow (CAN) (With Approval (CAN))
3810a[5] 6772a[4]

Wraith *H R A Cecil* a83 76
3 b c Maria's Mon(USA) —Really Polish (USA) (Polish Numbers (USA))
5562[4] 6109[4] 6286[7] 6666[2] 6821[2]

Wreningham *T Keddy* a69 62
2 br g Diktat—Slave To The Rythm (IRE) (Hamas (IRE))
3283[4] 4132[8] 4527[4] 5199[2] 5705[7] 6502[5] 6834[2] 7072[6] 7270[4]

Wrighty Almighty (IRE) *P R Chamings* a78 71
5 b g Danehill Dancer(IRE) —Persian Empress (IRE) (Persian Bold)
1564[10] 1886[2] 2492[2] 2665[7] 3218[5] 3615[2] (4319) 4688[2] (5189) 5645[3] 5862[5] 6894[7] (7085)

Writ (IRE) *I Semple* a82 60
5 ch g Indian Lodge(IRE) —Carnelly (IRE) (Priolo (USA))
44[3] (218) 300[8] (699) 967[9] 1675[6] 1905[11]

Writingonthewall (IRE) *M L W Bell* 75
2 b c Danetime(IRE) —Badee'A (IRE) (Marju (IRE))
5192^{5} (5501) 6154^{10}

Wroot Danielle (IRE) *D W Whillans* 37
7 b g Fayruz—Pounding Beat (Ya Zaman (USA))
6728^{6}

Wroughton (USA) *B J Meehan* a25 57
3 b g Royal Academy(USA) —Lady Liberty (NZ) (Noble Bijou (USA))
5005^{7} 5346^{9} *5683^{8}*

Wrynoes Pass (IRE) *R F Fisher*
3 b g Bold Fact(USA) —Home To Reality (IRE) (Imperial Frontier (USA))
223^{9}

Wulimaster (USA) *D W Barker* a70 76
4 br g Silver Hawk(USA) —Kamaina (USA) (Mr Prospector (USA))
449^{5} 564^{3} 997^{2} *1263^{8}* 1621^{4} 2011^{10} 2253^{5} 2715^{7} 2987^{13} 3403^{6} 3722^{10} 5676^{3} 6077^{7} 6304^{5} 6598^{4} *6883^{4}*

Wusuul *C E Brittain* 70
2 br f Kyllachy—Cartuccia (IRE) (Doyoun)
5524^{4}

Wutzeline (GER) *A Trybuhl* 91
3 b f Waky Nao—Warwara (GER) (Nebos (GER))
5669a^{7} 6400a^{8}

Wyatt Earp (IRE) *R A Fahey* a92 100
6 b g Piccolo—Tribal Lady (Absalom)
1088^{6} 1474^{24} (1826) 2234^{6} 2817^{23} 3500^{10} 4614^{19} 4806^{4} 5254^{3} 6472^{3} *6668^{8}*

Wycherley (IRE) *F & L Brogi* 64
3 ch c Thunder Gulch(USA) —Wynsleydale (USA) (Theatrical)
1335a^{6}

Wychwood Wanderer (IRE) *M Halford* 78
4 b m Barathea(IRE) —Calamander (IRE) (Alzao (USA))
873a^{10}

Wyeth *J R Fanshawe* a59 55
3 ch g Grand Lodge(USA) —Bordighera (USA) (Alysheba (USA))
6005^{7} 6286^{8}

Wynberg (IRE) *N A Callaghan* a51 47
2 b g Danetime(IRE) —Jayzdoll (IRE) (Stravinsky (USA))
3878^{9} 4132^{10} 4285^{9} 5428^{13} *6227^{5} 7136^{8}*

Wysiwyg Lucky (FR) *J-L Gay* a84 100
4 b m Ultimately Lucky(IRE) —Les Estelles (FR) (Dress Parade)
6460a^{11}

Xaarawise *M Botti*
2 b f Xaar—Spain (Polar Falcon (USA))
4265^{8}

Xaar Too Busy *Mrs A Duffield* 54
3 b f Xaar—Desert Serenade (USA) (Green Desert (USA))
1850^{8} 2538^{6} 2713^{8} 3377^{10}

Xalted *S C Williams* a54 51
3 b f Xaar—Joonayh (Warning)
136^{3} (360) 4326^{3} 4514^{7} 5576^{8} 5688^{5} *5946^{10} 6206^{9} 6402^{8} 6532^{7}*

Xaluna Bay (IRE) *W R Muir* a79 76
4 br m Xaar—Lunadine (FR) (Bering)
1067^{8} 1357^{P} 2479^{4} 2725^{11} *3212^{5}* 3449^{9}

Xaravella (IRE) *J G M O'Shea* a40 62
2 b f Xaar—Walnut Lady (Forzando)
3796^{7} 5038^{3} *5944^{13}*

Xchanger (USA) *Mark Shuman* a112
3 rg c Exchange Rate(USA) —Saragoza (USA) (Crafty Prospector (USA))
1882a^{8} 6485a^{6}

Xenes *R Menichetti* 101
3 b c Xaar—Lucia Tarditi (FR) (Crystal Glitters (USA))
1336a^{15}

Xiloca (BRZ) *A Selvaratnam*
4 b m Torrential(USA) —Danuza (ARG) ((USA))
246a^{12}

Xinji (IRE) *John M Oxx* a79 80
3 b f Xaar—Hero's Pride (FR) (Hero's Honor (USA))
1694a^{7} *(7037a)*

Xocolatl *Peter Grayson* a36
4 b m Elnadim(USA) —Chocolate (IRE) (Brief Truce (USA))
36^{8} 125^{8} 207^{11} 296^{12}

Xpres Boy (IRE) *S R Bowring* a57 11
4 b g Tagula(IRE) —Highly Motivated (Midyan (USA))
239^{9} 393^{7} 463^{8}

Xpres Maite *S R Bowring* a76 73
4 b g Komaite(USA) —Antonias Melody (Rambo Dancer (CAN))
319^{4} 468^{6} 1638^{9} 2023^{3} 2550^{3} *3285^{5}* 3608^{12} 4075^{4} *6874^{6} 7155^{6}*

Xtra Torrential (USA) *D M Simcock* a97 100
5 b g Torrential(USA) —Offering (USA) (Majestic Light (USA))
(255)

Xtravaganza (IRE) *J W Hills* a59 60
2 b f Xaar—Royal Jubilee (IRE) (King's Theatre (IRE))
1896^{5} 2447^{6} 4181^{14} *5127^{9} 5896^{5} 6427^{7}*

Yab Adee *M P Tregoning* a66
3 b g Mark Of Esteem(IRE) —Kotdiji (Mtoto)
386^{3} 5019^{3} 5390^{5} 5898^{3} 6459^{9}

Yacht Woman (USA) *E Borromeo* 96
2 gr f Mizzen Mast(USA) —Yacht Club (USA) (Sea Hero (USA))
5493a^{5} 6047a^{7}

Yaddree *M A Jarvis* a76 82
2 ch c Singspiel(IRE) —Jathaabeh (Nashwan (USA))
4362^{14} *4947^{2}* 5538^{2} (6451)

Yahrab (IRE) *C E Brittain* 106
2 gr c Dalakhani(IRE) —Loire Valley (IRE) (Sadler's Wells (USA))
3522^{2} (4199) 5004^{3} 5795^{6} 6170^{3}

Yakama (IRE) *D J S Ffrench Davis* a36 41
2 b c Indian Danehill(IRE) —Working Progress (IRE) (Marju (IRE))
5920^{4} 6274^{9} *6530^{9}*

Yakimov (USA) *D J Wintle* a93 85
8 ch g Affirmed(USA) —Ballet Troupe (USA) (Nureyev (USA))
1751^{4} (2346) 3076^{2} 3690^{6} 4105^{8} *6981^{11} 7175^{2}*

Ya Late Maite *E S McMahon* a61 54
4 ch m Komaite(USA) —Plentitude I (FR) (Kaldoun (FR))
3393^{8} 5019^{8} (5890)

Yali (IRE) *Francis Ennis* 82
2 b f Orpen(USA) —Klang (IRE) (Night Shift (USA))
4832a^{5} 6549a^{11}

Yamanmickmccann *R Hannon* a77 48
2 b c Desert Style(IRE) —Cashel Kiss (Bishop Of Cashel)
6234^{9} *6403^{9} 6820^{2} (6990)*

Yandina (IRE) *B W Hills* a68 86
4 b m Danehill(USA) —Lughz (USA) (Housebuster (USA))
2085^{2} (2689) 3670^{2} 4589^{2} 5115^{10} 5712^{4} *6606^{12}*

Yankadi (USA) *B W Hills* 105
2 b c Johannesburg(USA) —Clog Dance (Pursuit Of Love)
(4777) 5972^{3} 6615a^{4}

Yankee Bravo (USA) *Mrs A Duffield* 82
3 bb c Yankee Gentleman(USA) —Vickey Jane (USA) (Royal Academy (USA))
(5154)

Yankee George (IRE) *Doug Watson* a87 64
4 b g Cape Cross(IRE) —Yankee Dancer (Groom Dancer (USA))
104a^{7} *410a^{11}*

Yankee Storm *M J Wallace* a69 54
2 b c Yankee Gentleman(USA) —Yes Virginia (USA) (Roanoke (USA))
3171^{5} 3625^{12} 4181^{10} *6624^{4} 6881^{2} 7042^{2} (7210)*

Yaqeen *M A Jarvis* 108
3 b f Green Desert(USA) —Lady Elgar (IRE) (Sadler's Wells (USA))
(1105) 1496^{6} 2814^{9} (3628) 4149^{7}

Yarastar *Kevin Prendergast* 89
2 b f Cape Cross(IRE) —Yara (IRE) (Sri Pekan (USA))
5843a^{5}

Yard-Arm (SAF) *S Seemar* 102
8 b g Western Winter(USA) —Fashing (SAF) (Dancing Champ (USA))
411a^{8} 531a^{10}

Yaroslav (USA) *R Charlton* a84 85
3 bb c Danzig(USA) —Always Loyal (USA) (Zilzal (USA))
1143^{4} *(1447)* 2045^{14} 3503^{10} 4093^{7} 4811^{13} *5312^{3} 6209^{10}*

Yarqus *C E Brittain* a95 100
4 b g Diktat—Will You Dance (Shareef Dancer (USA))
6^{6} 411a^{7} 477a^{3} *599a^{13} 759^{2}* 848^{17} 1307^{7} 1494^{9} 2239^{5} 2755^{5} 4049^{8} 4720^{4} 5049^{2} 5543^{6} 6011^{4}

Yasinisi (IRE) *E J O'Neill* 86
2 br f Kalanisi(IRE) —Yazmin (IRE) (Green Desert (USA))
(2115) 3096^{4} 3880^{6}

Yasoodd *D Selvaratnam* a42 116
4 br h Inchinor—Needwood Epic (Midyan (USA))
176a^{4} 411a^{2} 531a^{2} 642a^{3}

Yathreb (USA) *J L Dunlop* 72
2 bb c Kingmambo(USA) —Thawakib (IRE) (Sadler's Wells (USA))
3896^{8} 5361^{7} 5918^{7}

Yattendon *S Kirk* a61 49
2 ch g Compton Place—Arian Da (Superlative)
3991^{12} *6897^{8} 7043^{3} 7245^{11}*

Yaya Gold (FR) *P Lenogue* 88
5 b g Gold Away(IRE) —Shiguerlienne (FR) (Shining Steel)
6923a^{2}

Yazamaan *J H M Gosden* 100
3 b c Galileo(IRE) —Moon's Whisper (USA) (Storm Cat (USA))
1617^{5} 2001^{4}

Yeaman's Hall *A M Balding* 103
3 b g Galileo(IRE) —Rimba (USA) (Dayjur (USA))
(1276) 2066a^{5} 3330^{7}

Yearning (IRE) *J G Portman* a28 47
3 b f Danetime(IRE) —Hiraeth (Petong)
713^{10} 4778^{9}

Yeats (IRE) *A P O'Brien* 126
6 b h Sadler's Wells(USA) —Lyndonville (IRE) (Top Ville)
(1330a) (2161a) (2787) (5437a) 6044a^{3}

Yeldham Lady *A J Chamberlain* a23 18
5 b m Mujahid(USA) —Future Options (Lomond (USA))
109^{10} 179^{9}

Yellow Mane (IRE) *Luke Comer* a42 56
4 ch h On The Ridge(IRE) —Mother Nellie (USA) (Al Nasr (FR))
207^{7}

Yellow Ridge (IRE) *Luke Comer* a62 82
4 ch h On The Ridge(IRE) —Jonathan's Rose (IRE) (Law Society (USA))
56^{8} 1050a^{7} 3664a^{5}

Yellowstone (IRE) *A P O'Brien* 118
3 b c Rock Of Gibraltar(IRE) —Love And Affection (USA) (Exclusive Era (USA))
948a^{5} 1473^{11} 1693a^{2} 2235^{8} 2813^{3} 3331^{4} (4044) 4692^{2} 5250a^{6} 6043a^{11}

Yem Kinn *M R Channon* 92
2 b c Dubai Destination(USA) —Nova Cyngi (USA) (Kris S (USA))
(1652) 2732^{14} 3522^{7} 4199^{2} 5048^{7} 5536^{6}

Yenaled *J M Bradley* a65 59
10 gr g Rambo Dancer(CAN) —Fancy Flight (FR) (Arctic Tern (USA))
2194^{11} 2490^{9} 2656^{10} *2946^{8} 3083^{7}* 3868^{10} 4267^{5} 5345^{7} 6452^{12}

Yeoman Leap *A M Balding* a44 55
3 b g Val Royal(FR) —Chandni (IRE) (Ahonoora)
1143^{15} *1343^{10}*

Yeoman Spirit (IRE) *A M Balding* a70 74
4 ch g Soviet Star(USA) —Hollywood Pearl (USA) (Phone Trick (USA))
4072^{6} *(5530)*

Yerevan *R T Phillips* a64 81
3 b f Iron Mask(USA) —Unfuwaanah (Unfuwain (USA))
1604^{6} (2114) 2435^{5} 2942^{4} 4710^{8} *6313^{12}* 6753^{17}

Yes Eighteen (IRE) *J W Hills* 46
2 b c Diktat—Siskin (IRE) (Royal Academy (USA))
4571^{15}

Yes Meg *P F I Cole* a45 57
2 b f Sagamix(FR) —Segsbury Belle (Petoski)
2078^{4} (2310) *3642^{8} 4022^{12}* 5268^{4}

Yes Mr President (IRE) *M Johnston* a61
2 b c Montjeu(IRE) —Royals Special (IRE) (Caerleon (USA))
7208^{5}

Yes One (IRE) *J W Hills* a71 75
3 ch c Peintre Celebre(USA) —Copious (IRE) (Generous (IRE))
573^{8} 764^{9} 1665^{5} 1927^{2} (2530) 3003^{4} 3993^{9} *5943^{6} 6314^{6}*

Yippyiayippyio *Mrs C A Dunnett* a34
2 ch f Fraam—Sandy Lady (IRE) (Desert King (IRE))
6358^{11} 6958^{8} 7266^{11}

Yo Pedro (IRE) *D Carroll* a57 83
5 b g Mark Of Esteem(IRE) —Morina (USA) (Lyphard (USA))
2091^{2} *2358^{8}* 4081^{11} 4891^{2} 5479^{8} 5739^{4}

York Cliff *W M Brisbourne* a61 67
9 b g Marju(IRE) —Azm (Unfuwain (USA))
1178^{4} 1732^{4} (1942) 2252^{4} 2825^{2} 3033^{7} 3533^{2} 4475^{4} *4670^{7}* 5404^{7} 5807^{9} *6069^{3}* 6325^{4} *6564^{5} 6697^{8}*

Yorke's Folly (USA) *C W Fairhurst* a38 54
6 b m Stravinsky(USA) —Tommelise (USA) (Dayjur (USA))
3259^{10} 4141^{14} 4525^{5} 4787^{9} 5282^{4} 5861^{12}

Yorkie *J Pearce* a40 59
8 b g Aragon—Light The Way (Nicholas Bill)
1739^{11} 4294^{12}

Yorkshire Blue *J S Goldie* a43 89
8 b g Atraf—Something Blue (Petong)
1653^{13} 2339^{2} 2566^{8} 3091^{7} 3585^{5} 3953^{8} 4227^{4} 4581^{5} 4895^{6} 4999^{4} (5083) *6243^{12}* 6639^{5} 6753^{7}

Yorktown (FR) *J-C Rouget* 97
2 b c Red Ransom(USA) —Wedding Night (FR) (Valanour (IRE))
5660a^{6}

Yorokobi (BRZ) *H J Brown* a79 103
4 b g Burooj—Fancy Lady (BRZ) (Executioner (USA))
324a^{13} 394a^{11}

Yossi (IRE) *M H Tompkins* 83
3 b g Montjeu(IRE) —Raindancing (IRE) (Tirol)
1290^{2} 1843^{6} 3081^{2} 3402^{2} 3847^{4} (4563) 5334^{3} 5619^{7} 6185^{4} 6576^{5}

You Live And Learn *H Morrison* a33 59
4 ch m Galileo(IRE) —Anniversary (Salse (USA))
4660^{8} *5120^{12}* 6308^{10}

Youmzain (IRE) *M R Channon* 126
4 b h Sinndar(IRE) —Sadima (IRE) (Sadler's Wells (USA))
861a^{3} 2064a^{3} 2925a^{5} 3942^{2} 5077a^{4} 6043a^{2}

Young Bertie *H Morrison* a73 78
4 ch g Bertolini(USA) —Urania (Most Welcome)
1200^{13} *1931^{13} 3218^{4} 3422^{4}* 4165^{2} 4853^{3} 5275^{2} (5563) (5862) (6063) 6423^{6}

Young Emma *G G Margarson* 21
4 b m Vettori(IRE) —Just Warning (Warning)
1849^{12} 3041^{7} 3593^{10}

Young Ivanhoe *P J McBride* a73 65
2 b c Oasis Dream—Cybinka (Selkirk (USA))
5575^{8} *6151^{3} 6734^{2}*

Young Mick *G G Margarson* a99 116
5 br g King's Theatre(IRE) —Just Warning (Warning)
5831^{8} 5976^{8} 6538^{2} *6645^{5}*

Young Patriarch *W J Burke* 88
6 b g Silver Patriarch(IRE) —Mortify (Prince Sabo)
4142a^{4}

Young Pretender (FR) *J H M Gosden* 105
2 b c Oasis Dream—Silent Heir (AUS) (Sunday Silence (USA))
(4604) (5260a) 6041a^{5}

Young Scotton *J D Bethell* a64 57
7 b g Cadeaux Genereux—Broken Wave (Bustino)
3765^{10} 4333^{5} 4941^{2} 5283^{8} 5626^{6} 6703^{4} *(6835) 6911^{2} 7110^{5} (7285)*

Young Valentino *M Appleby* a39 13
5 ch g Komaite(USA) —Caprice (Mystiko (USA))
133^{13} 181^{8} 5427^{10}

Your Amount (IRE) *W J Musson* a73 71
4 b g Beckett(IRE) —Sin Lucha (USA) (Northfields (USA))
607^{5}

You're Beautiful (USA) *David Wachman* 97
3 b f Storm Cat(USA) —Cee's Song (USA) (Seattle Song (USA))
1777a^{U} 2702a^{7} 3578a^{5} 3983a^{6} 4649a^{7}

You're My Son *K O Cunningham-Brown* a59 39
5 b g Bold Edge—Sheer Nectar (Piaffer (USA))
941^{2} 6821^{7} 6971^{8}

You'resothrilling (USA) *A P O'Brien* 103
2 bb f Storm Cat(USA) —Mariah's Storm (USA) (Rahy (USA))
2049a^{2} (2325a) 2812^{2} (3432) 4744^{9}

Your Pleasure (USA) *A M Balding* 73
2 ch f Forest Wildcat(USA) —Pleasure Center (USA) (Diesis)
5380^{3} (5856)

Your Round (USA) *M Hubley* 99
2 b c Distorted Humor(USA) —Another Round (USA) (Affirmed (USA))
6484a^{9}

Yousaididdo (USA) *Stanley Baresich*
3 b f Broken Vow(USA) —Make A Deal (USA) (Private Terms (USA))
6772a^{6}

Yungaburra (IRE) *D J Murphy* a95 95
3 b g Fath(USA) —Nordic Living (IRE) (Nordico (USA))
1616^{8} 4386^{13} 4726^{16} 5039^{10} 5332^{3} 5379^{2} 5581^{12} 6173^{11} 6327^{10} *6876^{10} 7112^{3}*

Yurchenko *M Wellings* a37
3 b f Mamalik(USA) —Rajmata (IRE) (Prince Sabo)
1386^{6} 1923^{14} *7162^{4} 7283^{8}*

Zaafira (SPA) *E J Creighton* a58
3 b f Limpid—Hot Doris (IRE) (Fayruz)
68^{2} 99^{5} (162) 253^{8} 357^{10} 2178^{10} 2668^{6} 2948^{9} (6935) 7001^{4} 7251^{8}

Zaafran *D Selvaratnam* a87 99
4 b m Singspiel(IRE) —Roshani (IRE) (Kris)
174a^{2} 397a^{3} 546a^{4}

Zaahid (IRE) *B W Hills* 99
3 ch c Sakhee(USA) —Murjana (IRE) (Pleasant Colony (USA))
(1838) (2400) 2881^{2} 3503^{6} 4566^{14} (5776) 6155^{3}

Zabeel House *John A Harris* a79 83
4 b g Anabaa(USA) —Divine Quest (Kris)
1931^{11} 2452^{10} *3851^{13} 5118^{6} 5645^{5} 6068^{7} 6533^{9} (7275)*

Zabeel Palace *B J Curley* a76 87
5 b g Grand Lodge(USA) —Applecross (Glint Of Gold)
726^{11} 1272^{7} 1668^{5} 5725^{10}

Zabeel Tiger *M R Channon* 56
2 b c Cadeaux Genereux—Odette (Pursuit Of Love)
2596^{8} 4782^{8} 5343^{9} 5715^{11}

Zabeel Tower *R Allan* a55 57
4 b g Anabaa(USA) —Bint Kaldoun (IRE) (Kaldoun (FR))
1890^{8} 2391^{8} (2820) 3343^{3} 3816^{5} 4156^{11} 4966^{3} 5284^{4} 5476^{5} 6304^{3} *6479^{3} 6906^{11} 7250^{10}*

Zabougg *G A Swinbank* 66
2 b g Tobougg(IRE) —Double Fault (IRE) (Zieten (USA))
2532^{5} 3761^{4} 4612^{7}

Zacatecas (GER) *A J Chamberlain* a68 91
7 gr g Grand Lodge(USA) —Zephyrine (IRE) (Highest Honor (FR))
88^{11} 283^{6} 354^{11} 508^{9}

Zachary Scott *C E Brittain* 58
3 br c Inchinor—Wardeh (Zafonic (USA))
1100^{10} 1412^{7} 1840^{9}

Zach's Harmoney (USA) *B J Meehan* a69 38
3 ch c Diesis—Cool Ashlee (USA) (Mister Baileys)
1447^{4} 1904^{2} 2886^{7} *4429^{8} 4591^{6}*

Zadalla *Andrew Oliver* a64 61
3 b f Zaha(CAN) —Inishdalla (IRE) (Green Desert (USA))
147^{6} 707^{3}

Zaffeu *A G Juckes* a59 65
6 ch g Zafonic(USA) —Leaping Flame (USA) (Trempolino (USA))
78^{4} 107^{2} 333^{5} 481^{9} 6501^{10} 6817^{6} 6999^{5}

Zafonical Storm (USA) *B W Duke* a78 100
3 ch c Aljabr(USA) —Fonage (Zafonic (USA))
1471^{8} 4648a^{8} 5355^{9} 5833^{14} *7254^{8}*

Zaham (USA) *M Johnston* a91 117
3 ch g Silver Hawk(USA) —Guerre Et Paix (USA) (Soviet Star (USA))
418^{2} (649) (939) 1275^{3} (1835) (2231) (2789) 4387^{3} 5451^{2} 5831^{2}

Zaharath Al Bustan *E D Delany* a75 77
4 ch m Gulch(USA) —Cayman Sunset (IRE) (Night Shift (USA))
4865a^{2} 6916a^{9}

Zahour Al Yasmeen *M R Channon* a70 88
3 b f Cadeaux Genereux—Bareilly (USA) (Lyphard (USA))
1076^{13} 1535^{5} 1786^{5} 2415^{7} 4330^{3} (5139) (5358) 5418^{3} 6197^{5} 6743^{12}

Zahwah *J G Portman* a56 56
2 ch f Zaha(CAN) —Inishdalla (IRE) (Green Desert (USA))
972^{8} 1354^{4} *1727^{3}* 2134^{12} 2488^{14} *6098^{11} 6438^{7}* 6722^{10} *7030^{5} 7096^{9}*

Zaif (IRE) *D R C Elsworth* 94
4 b g Almutawakel—Colourful (FR) (Gay Mecene (USA))
1245^{12} 1542^{9} (2551) 3060^{6} 3882^{8} 4399^{2} 4814^{6} 5593^{5} 6014^{5} 6169^{6}

Zain (IRE) *J G Given* a49 66
3 b g Alhaarth(IRE) —Karenaragon (Aragon)
1712^{6} 2389^{7} 4641^{2} (4936) 4998^{5} *5342^{12}* 5936^{2} 6640^{3}

Zakfree (IRE) *Liam McAteer* a63 71
6 b g Danetime(IRE) —Clipper Queen (Balidar)
6920a^{8}

Zakhaaref *M Johnston* 89
2 gr c Daylami(IRE) —Shahaamah (IRE) (Red Ransom (USA))
3761^{6} (5734) 6194^{2}

Zalkani (IRE) *J Pearce* a72 47
7 ch g Cadeaux Genereux—Zallaka (IRE) (Shardari)
332^{7} 482^{6} (634) 767^{8} 4739^{3} *5120^{6} 5531^{4} 6068^{9} 6407^{2} 6798^{2} 6911^{5} 7004^{5} 7157^{6} 7273^{9}*

Zalongo *C Byrnes* 54
5 ch g Zafonic(USA) —Tamassos (Dance In Time (CAN))
1760a^{7}

Zalzaar (IRE) *R T Phillips* a40 54
5 b g Xaar—Zalamalec (USA) (Septieme Ciel (USA))
6797^{8}

Zamalik (USA) *E J Alston* 76
4 bb g Machiavellian(USA) —Ashbilya (USA) (Nureyev (USA))
1995^{14} 3194^{2} 3572^{3} 4079^{7} 4704^{8} (5082) 5489^{6}

Zamaya *K R Burke*
3 b g Zamindar(USA) —Hiwaayati (Shadeed (USA))
149^{14}

Zambezi Sun *P Bary* 123
3 b c Dansili—Imbabala (Zafonic (USA))
2293a^{4} (3566a) 5466a^{3} 6043a^{8}

Zamboozle (IRE) *D R C Elsworth* a84 79
5 ch g Halling(USA) —Blue Sirocco (Bluebird (USA))
1308^{10} 2403^{7} 2833^{11}

Zameliana *Dr J R J Naylor* a36 27
3 ch f Zaha(CAN) —Amelia's Field (Distant Relative)
1386^{5} 1782^{13} 2489^{14} 3451^{6} 4309^{P} *6893^{5}*

Zamhrear *C E Brittain* a69 55
4 b m Singspiel(IRE) —Lunda (IRE) (Soviet Star (USA))
63^{4}

Zam Zammah *Sir Michael Stoute* a89 69
4 b g Agnes World(USA) —Krisalya (Kris)
(92) 576^{3} 1818^{13}

Zanderido *B S Rothwell* a13
5 b g Forzando—Triple Concerto (Grand Lodge (USA))
303^{7}

Zando *E G Bevan* a59 50
5 b g Forzando—Rockin' Rosie (Song)
121^{3} 179^{11} 266^{11} 682^{4} *789^{9}*

Zanida (IRE) *K R Burke* 94
3 b f Mujadil(USA) —Haraabah (USA) (Topsider (USA))
2914^{9} 3430^{9} 4726^{12} 5356^{17}

Zanjeer *N Wilson*
7 b g Averti(IRE) —Cloudslea (USA) (Chief's Crown (USA))
1265^{10} 1921^{14}

Zanjero (USA) *S Asmussen* a112
3 br c Cherokee Run(USA) —Checkered Flag (USA) (A.P. Indy (USA))
1486a^{12}

Zann (USA) *M Machowsky* 110
4 b h Dynaformer(USA) —Moments Of Magic (USA) (Danzig (USA))
6924a^{2}

Zantero *K M Prendergast* a51 53
5 b g Danzero(AUS) —Cruinn A Bhord (Inchinor)
557^{13} 723^{9} 2540^{16} 2619^{DSQ} *6627^{9} 6955^{10}*

Zap Attack *M Brittain* a19 53
7 b g Zafonic(USA) —Rappa Tap Tap (FR) (Tap On Wood)
2806^{6} (4141) 4423^{11} 4701^{11}

Zaplamation (IRE) *D W Barker* 48
2 b c Acclamation—Zapatista (Rainbow Quest (USA))
1411^{9} 1792^{10} 2385^{4} 3398^{10} 5298^{16} 5932^{5} 6462^{10}

Zarabad (IRE) *K R Burke* a78 73
5 b g King's Best(USA) —Zarannda (IRE) (Last Tycoon (IRE))
(516) 609^{3}

Zarees *Miss Gay Kelleway* a41 48
2 b c Vettori(IRE) —Night Mist (IRE) (Alzao (USA))
4070^{7} 4537^{8} 5186^{11} *6775^{10} 7021^{6}*

Zarene *P W D'Arcy* a37
2 b f Zaha(CAN) —Polish Sprite (Danzig Connection (USA))
4774^{17} *5527^{10}*

Zarkava (IRE) *A De Royer-Dupre* 119
2 b f Zamindar(USA) —Zarkasha (IRE) (Kahyasi)
(6040a)

Zar Solitario *M Johnston* a93 101
3 b c Singspiel(IRE) —Ginevra Di Camelot (FR) (Alzao (USA))
304^{2} (492) (719) (1010) (1335a) 1875a^{10}

Zarzu *C R Dore* a86 83
8 b g Magic Ring(IRE) —Rivers Rhapsody (Dominion)
81^{2} 190^{11} 480^{6} 575^{2} 692^{6} 734^{3} 1063^{15} *1262^{2} 1718^{3} 6625^{10}*

Zaskar *Tom Dascombe* a67 75
2 b f Anabaa(USA) —Bezzaaf (Machiavellian (USA))
(5097) 5828^{6} (6410)

Zato (IRE) *M R Channon* a99 99
4 ch g Zafonic(USA) —Top Table (Shirley Heights)
250a^{5} 398a^{11} 473a^{6} *840^{9}* 1145^{16} 1480^{6} 1842^{9} 1996^{2} 2208^{11} (Dead)

Zaville *J O'Reilly* a68 69
5 gr m Zafonic(USA) —Colleville (Pharly (FR))
220^{9} 389^{12} 628^{5} 4409^{8} 4925^{10} 5158^{7} *6069^{6} 6241^{9}*

Zawariq (IRE) *E J O'Neill* a60 42
3 b f Marju(IRE) —Alikhlas (Lahib (USA))
5678^{7}

Zaya (GER) *A Wohler* 88
2 b f Diktat—Zayala (Royal Applause)
6371a^{7}

Zazous *J J Bridger* a67 65
6 b g Zafonic(USA) —Confidentiality (USA) (Lyphard (USA))
236^{6} 346^{6} 560^{9} 614^{4} 654^{10} 724^{4} 866^{4} 923^{7} (1507) *6647^{5} 6831^{2} 6925^{5} 7085^{9} 7269^{11}*

Zed Candy (FR) *J T Stimpson* a69 66
4 b g Medicean—Intrum Morshaan (IRE) (Darshaan)
319^{6} 6780^{6}

Zeeno (SAF) *S Seemar* 97
4 b g Count Dubois—Ice Floe (SAF) (Northern Guest (USA))
470a^{2} 641a^{6}

Zeeuw (IRE) *D J Coakley* a69 62
3 b g Xaar—Lucky Bet (IRE) (Lucky Guest)
1501^{3}

Zee Zee (USA) *W Mott* a66 94
2 rg f Exchange Rate(USA) —Emblem Of Hope (USA) (Dynaformer (USA))
6507a^{8}

Zefooha (FR) *T D Walford* a68 71
3 ch f Lomitas—Bezzaaf (Machiavellian (USA))
1974^{9} 2598^{12} 4843^{8} 5486^{3} 6308^{5} *6673^{2}*

Zell (IRE) *E J Alston* 60
4 b m Lend A Hand—Skisette (Malinowski (USA))
1534^{10} 1944^{2} 2760^{11}

Zelos (IRE) *D J S Ffrench Davis* a70 77
3 b g Mujadil(USA) —First Degree (Sabrehill (USA))
460^{3} 522^{4} 611^{8} 2413^{6} 2653^{6} 2916^{8} 3178^{2} 3429^{6} *(3732)* 3922^{3} 4071^{4} 4760^{2} *5122^{5}* 5559^{10} *6344^{2}* (6598)

Zenato (GER) *F Reuterskiold* a80 102
6 ch g Acatenango(GER) —Zephyrine (IRE) (Highest Honor (FR))
4218a^{14}

Zendaro *C C Bealby* a54 58
5 b g Danzero(AUS) —Countess Maud (Mtoto)
4433^{11}

Zen Factor *J G Portman* 61
2 b g Josr Algarhoud(IRE) —Zabelina (USA) (Diesis)
3043^{9} 4162^{4} 5918^{13}

Zen Garden *W M Brisbourne* 52
6 b m Alzao(USA) —Maze Garden (USA) (Riverman (USA))
1998^{9} 2436^{8} 3079^{9} 4019^{11} 4859^{9}

Zennerman (IRE) *Miss J E Foster* a79 85
4 b g Observatory(USA) —Precocious Miss (USA) (Diesis)
1458^{5} 1845^{4} 2986^{7} *(3599)* 4100^{6} *4672^{8}* 4797^{3} 5253^{9} *6806^{6} 7006^{2} 7141^{6}*

Zenone (IRE) *Laura Grizzetti* 102
3 b c Orpen(USA) —Luna D'Estate (Alzao (USA))
6767a^{6}

Zerky (USA) *E A L Dunlop* 65
2 b f Kingmambo(USA) —Penny's Valentine (USA) (Storm Cat (USA))
4094^{15} 4565^{7} 5811^{3}

Zero Cool (USA) *G L Moore* a73 87
3 br c Forestry(USA) —Fabulous (USA) (Seeking The Gold (USA))
4815^{6} *5499^{2}* (5873) 6236^{3} *7281^{12}*

Zero Engagement (AUS) *T Roney* 108
7 b g Woodman(USA) —Dateless (NZ) (Grosvenor (NZ))
15a^{5}

Zero Tolerance (IRE) *T D Barron* a77 111
7 ch g Nashwan(USA) —Place De L'Opera (Sadler's Wells (USA))
848^{13} 1145^{21} 1791^{4} 3026^{5} 4043^{13} 6011^{P} 6172^{6} 6654^{14}

Zeu Tin Tin (IRE) *R A Kvisla* 90
2 b f Where Or When(IRE) —Littleton Arwen (USA) (Bahri (USA))
4169^{3} 4564^{3} 5395a^{4}

Zeydnaa (IRE) *C R Wilson* a40 56
7 b g Bahhare(USA) —Hadawah (USA) (Riverman (USA))
1556^{9}

Zhebe *P J McBride* a73 47
2 br c Dr Fong(USA) —Krajina (FR) (Holst (USA))
6618^{10} *6960^{3}*

Zhitomir *M Dods* a17 68
9 ch g Lion Cavern(USA) —Treasure Trove (USA) (The Minstrel (CAN))
912^{2} 2256^{8} 2893^{5} 3195^{4} 3414^{8} 4562^{14} 5503^{3} *5756^{8}*

Zhukhov (IRE) *T G McCourt* a43 81
4 ch g Allied Forces(USA) —Karameg (IRE) (Danehill (USA))
5460a^{3} 6363a^{8}

Z Humor (USA) *W Mott* a108
2 b c Distorted Humor(USA) —Offtheoldblock (USA) (A.P. Indy (USA))
6508a^{5}

Zia Zabel (IRE) *J L Dunlop* 63
2 b f Rock Of Gibraltar(IRE) —Blu Meltemi (ITY) (Star Shareef)
6470^{11}

Zibeline (IRE) *B Ellison* a57 79
10 b g Cadeaux Genereux—Zia (USA) (Shareef Dancer (USA))
159^{2}

Zibimix (IRE) *F Head* 101
3 gr c Linamix(FR) —Izibi (FR) (Saint Cyrien (FR))
6137a^{4}

Zidane *J R Fanshawe* a94 111
5 b g Danzero(AUS) —Juliet Bravo (Glow (USA))
1448^{4} (1653) 2858^{7} (4150) 5832^{4} 6338^{11} 6758^{8}

Zifaaf (USA) *B W Hills* a61 74
3 b f Silver Hawk(USA) —Muklah (IRE) (Singspiel (IRE))
1100^{2} *1523^{5}* 1988^{2} 2597^{4} 3151^{2} 4290^{2} (4641)

Zilli *N P Littmoden* a48 30
3 ch f Zilzal(USA) —Zizi (IRE) (Imp Society (USA))
219^{9} 577^{4} 791^{4} 6108^{7} 6573^{10}

Zillione (FR) *H Billot* 79
3 b f Anabaa Blue—State Of Mind (FR) (Priolo (USA))
4557a^{12}

Zil Up *S R Bowring* a45
3 ch c Zilzal(USA) —Sharpthorne (USA) (Sharpen Up)
522^{8} 619^{4} 711^{5} 2948^{10}

Zimbali *J M Bradley* a34 52
5 ch m Lahib(USA) —Dawn (Owington)
1112^{14} 2104^{9} 2555^{3} 3277^{5} 4314^{7}

Zimon *Ms C Erichsen*
3 b g Zilzal(USA) —Clued Up (Beveled (USA))
2548a^{9}

Zinging *J J Bridger* a50 51
8 b g Fraam—Hi Hoh (IRE) (Fayruz)
1742^{6} 2141^{8} 2423^{9} 2540^{12} 4200^{3}

Zippi Jazzman (USA) *R M Beckett* a74 81
2 ch c Dixieland Band(USA) —Redeem (USA) (Devil's Bag (USA))
2724^{3} 3589^{2} *(4020) 4737^{4}* 5629^{9} 6195^{3}

Zipping (AUS) *G Rogerson* 118
6 b g Danehill(USA) —Social Scene (IRE) (Grand Lodge (USA))
6712a^{4}

Ziride (FR) *H-A Pantall* a94 95
4 b m Valanour(IRE) —Zircon Lady (FR) (Kings Lake (USA))
31a^{9}

Zirkel (IRE) *Mrs A L M King* a68 70
4 br g Highest Honor(FR) —Mythical Creek (USA) (Pleasant Tap (USA))
1591^{7} 2113^{5} 4356^{4}

Zizou (IRE) *J J Bridger* a46 56
4 b g Fantastic Light(USA) —Search Committee (USA) (Roberto (USA))
187^{13} 630^{9}

Zomerlust *J J Quinn* 103
5 b g Josr Algarhoud(IRE) —Passiflora (Night Shift (USA))
1041^{6} 1195^{5} 1651^{13} 1826^{2} 2030^{2} 3089^{2} 3505^{15} (3975) 4614^{6} 5616^{11} 6183^{9} 6472^{19}

Zonergem *Lady Herries* a95 94
9 ch g Zafonic(USA) —Anasazi (IRE) (Sadler's Wells (USA))
4523^{2} 5362^{7}

Zonic Boom (FR) *Heather Dalton* a56 51
7 bb g Zafonic(USA) —Rosi Zambotti (IRE) (Law Society (USA))
1090^{10} 1406^{9} *(3927) 4670^{13}* 4906^{8}

Zonta Zitkala *R M Beckett* 78
3 b f Daylami(IRE) —Sioux Chef (Be My Chief (USA))
(2012) 3555^{8} 4170^{6} 4848^{8} 5475^{4} 5885^{12}

Zoogina Zaid (SWE) *Vanja Sandrup*
5 gr m Troon—Kinclaith (SWE) (Miami Springs)
1647a^{3}

Zoom (GER) *C Von Der Recke* 92
4 ch m Lomitas—Zizi Top (Robellino (USA))
5850a^{7}

Zoometric (AUS) *P Giadresco* 109
7 b g Unbridled's Song(USA) —What A Joy (AUS) (Bluebird (USA))
15a^{11}

Zoom One *M P Tregoning* a45 85
3 ch c In The Wings—Seyooll (IRE) (Danehill (USA))
2426^{3} 2999^{11} 4147^{8} 4847^{8}

Zoriana (FR) *F Rohaut* 82
2 b f Danehill Dancer(IRE) —Amarige (FR) (Lesotho (USA))
6888a^{7}

Zorin (BRZ) *A Cintra Pereira* a96 85
4 b g Norba(BRZ) —Live And Love (BRZ) (Mauser (BRZ))
326a^{10} 396a^{2} 471a^{2} 526a^{4} 596a^{5}

Zowington *C F Wall* a29 97
5 gr g Zafonic(USA) —Carmela Owen (Owington)
1836^{14} 2399^{4} 2694^{4} 3268^{9}

Zuckerpuppe (GER) *Frau E Mader* 96
3 b f Seattle Dancer(USA) —Zephyrine (IRE) (Highest Honor (FR))
1515a^{4} 2294a^{8}

Zut Alors (IRE) *Robert Collet* 97
3 b f Pivotal—Zeiting (IRE) (Zieten (USA))
1006a^{9} 1702a^{10} 5850a^{3} 6071a^{3} 6633a^{0}

INDEX TO MEETINGS FLAT 2007

† Abandoned
* All-Weather
(M) Mixed meeting

Leading Turf Flat Trainers 2007

(31st March - 10th November 2007)

NAME	WINS-RUNS	2nd	3rd	4th	WIN £	TOTAL £	£1 STAKE
A P O·Brien	18-112 (16%)	27	12	6	1,666,718	3,484,026	-33.61
Sir Michael Stoute	111-489 (23%)	76	58	53	1,685,755	2,564,739	-18.95
R Hannon	134-966 (14%)	118	87	107	1,103,367	1,941,668	-172.30
P W Chapple-Hy'm	30-207 (14%)	24	15	18	1,455,334	1,852,639	-56.95
B W Hills	89-642 (14%)	75	81	68	1,206,321	1,786,857	-107.64
Saeed Bin Suroor	73-285 (26%)	51	32	28	1,234,541	1,688,115	-16.11
M R Channon	103-1009 (10%)	105	109	104	953,555	1,649,563	-137.67
J H M Gosden	66-391 (17%)	59	54	36	1,043,331	1,633,991	-75.75
M Johnston	130-865 (15%)	102	100	96	1,050,727	1,480,392	-106.70
R A Fahey	72-777 (9%)	89	87	88	609,089	1,072,974	-313.05
J Noseda	50-234 (21%)	34	27	25	707,378	1,028,245	-18.14
K A Ryan	75-719 (10%)	80	60	69	499,914	925,465	-199.00
B J Meehan	52-522 (10%)	45	48	39	557,366	860,191	-85.42
L M Cumani	54-288 (19%)	35	45	26	566,708	840,845	-22.38
H R A Cecil	45-213 (21%)	34	27	27	561,861	731,729	-30.11
W J Haggas	57-327 (17%)	41	40	33	513,159	709,813	+50.45
M L W Bell	44-330 (13%)	40	36	32	548,375	695,693	-83.42
J L Dunlop	56-422 (13%)	62	40	36	415,642	677,453	-67.95
M A Jarvis	62-355 (17%)	55	38	32	430,105	652,583	-63.36
A M Balding	32-352 (9%)	25	36	48	479,043	652,461	-100.48
H Morrison	37-305 (12%)	41	33	30	448,630	609,683	-98.21
D Nicholls	58-501 (12%)	58	50	42	345,295	565,214	+18.87
T D Easterby	58-680 (9%)	67	66	60	321,823	544,182	-286.39
J R Fanshawe	35-253 (14%)	22	36	31	401,934	543,745	-43.16
J A Osborne	46-289 (16%)	44	24	26	284,733	541,903	-20.41
E A L Dunlop	45-361 (12%)	37	50	40	254,647	536,189	-92.88
R Charlton	39-249 (16%)	29	27	22	418,666	526,037	-88.93
B Smart	36-304 (12%)	36	34	32	343,214	483,001	-47.61
K R Burke	45-475 (9%)	53	35	48	259,616	469,397	-90.20
D R C Elsworth	29-283 (10%)	31	38	31	223,111	464,064	-108.07
C E Brittain	28-350 (8%)	44	37	39	216,535	450,619	-165.27
C G Cox	29-256 (11%)	29	22	17	281,309	431,473	-74.62
M P Tregoning	25-174 (14%)	20	17	18	152,577	396,538	-21.01
J S Moore	24-347 (7%)	39	29	39	238,288	375,694	-173.47
J S Bolger	2-6 (33%)	0	1	0	348,289	375,173	-1.25
Mrs A J Perrett	33-362 (9%)	30	34	37	211,778	357,859	-88.28
B R Millman	40-337 (12%)	29	32	38	247,522	353,129	-45.72
T D Barron	41-419 (10%)	27	43	44	197,984	336,423	-89.18
J G Given	29-279 (10%)	33	21	18	181,249	332,774	-32.97
R M Beckett	40-307 (13%)	37	36	27	195,870	326,831	+119.82
A Fabre	3-6 (50%)	1	0	1	267,987	322,753	+2.38
P F I Cole	29-268 (11%)	17	26	19	214,723	319,564	-72.38
M H Tompkins	35-373 (9%)	44	45	36	183,079	311,122	-165.17
C F Wall	30-193 (16%)	19	14	20	214,241	303,502	+47.82
Sir Mark Prescott	51-258 (20%)	41	25	12	200,122	289,537	-34.38
G A Swinbank	40-296 (14%)	36	35	36	190,348	287,186	-15.41
J R Best	20-257 (8%)	24	25	32	211,780	285,945	-98.50
G A Butler	29-170 (17%)	19	20	10	218,810	276,439	+45.43
J J Quinn	17-248 (7%)	23	24	16	192,256	266,221	-115.58
Mrs A Duffield	25-211 (12%)	17	10	22	221,317	258,114	-68.29

Leading Turf Flat Jockeys 2007

(31st March - 10th November 2007)

NAME	WIN-RIDES	2nd	3rd	4th	WIN £	TOTAL £	£1 STAKE
Jamie Spencer	190-952 (20%)	140	105	103	2,046,708	2,815,933	-63.20
Seb Sanders	190-1121 (17%)	148	138	99	883,322	1,376,579	-156.48
Ryan Moore	126-667 (19%)	98	70	62	1,637,981	2,511,210	-51.45
Richard Hughes	118-769 (15%)	100	97	67	909,489	1,749,177	-99.56
Jimmy Fortune	104-679 (15%)	80	85	58	1,460,136	2,341,158	-126.19
N Callan	102-805 (13%)	109	88	82	573,575	936,664	-175.38
Ted Durcan	96-793 (12%)	96	74	81	845,572	1,373,873	-113.53
Kerrin McEvoy	93-524 (18%)	66	56	46	995,357	1,478,452	+21.78
Steve Drowne	82-763 (11%)	85	72	70	744,219	1,161,218	-135.08
Paul Hanagan	78-751 (10%)	85	80	68	569,952	883,505	-156.46
L Dettori	77-376 (20%)	52	42	40	2,359,489	3,109,182	-123.04
R Hills	72-416 (17%)	54	51	53	811,026	1,409,603	-47.72
Martin Dwyer	69-639 (11%)	68	53	57	407,298	802,509	-151.17
Chris Catlin	69-797 (9%)	78	70	91	261,201	530,972	-127.50
T P Queally	66-481 (14%)	50	35	45	411,257	617,560	+11.44
Greg Fairley	65-476 (14%)	38	37	51	329,041	439,300	+8.37
Jim Crowley	65-721 (9%)	61	72	64	322,516	550,463	-147.65
Royston Ffrench	63-687 (9%)	76	54	69	507,026	731,465	-247.93
Tom Eaves	63-791 (8%)	70	73	84	311,854	574,625	-231.80
Philip Robinson	62-387 (16%)	51	45	31	514,280	820,080	-56.36
Darryll Holland	61-606 (10%)	70	53	48	522,127	818,221	-123.90
Dane O·Neill	61-716 (9%)	68	74	71	261,372	494,446	-296.75
Eddie Ahern	61-755 (8%)	88	69	83	412,392	910,862	-294.18
K Darley	60-520 (12%)	64	58	61	390,017	757,160	-167.57
Francis Norton	55-542 (10%)	45	53	60	477,227	709,307	-44.22
David Allan	55-575 (10%)	54	58	64	319,382	503,025	-150.68
Jimmy Quinn	54-661 (8%)	59	63	66	581,559	828,904	-202.86
John Egan	53-599 (9%)	57	61	56	307,962	601,448	-205.80
Liam Jones	52-478 (11%)	41	54	41	224,268	331,053	-8.08
William Buick	51-437 (12%)	42	45	54	434,107	582,772	-110.48
Micky Fenton	51-572 (9%)	39	43	63	209,111	356,144	-90.13
Paul Mulrennan	51-644 (8%)	52	62	56	291,861	448,489	-317.32
George Baker	48-426 (11%)	49	58	45	217,985	385,454	+27.89
Michael Hills	48-445 (11%)	43	49	44	964,478	1,335,390	-169.04
Phillip Makin	43-478 (9%)	35	54	45	187,327	317,359	-110.30
Fergus Sweeney	43-542 (8%)	44	35	47	239,948	335,176	-99.52
Richard Mullen	42-512 (8%)	38	46	44	164,408	282,806	-38.34
Joe Fanning	40-300 (13%)	26	36	22	402,603	524,607	-72.61
Nicky Mackay	40-317 (13%)	36	42	23	203,270	330,531	+27.87
T P O·Shea	40-440 (9%)	32	48	41	337,982	462,684	-64.08
Pat Cosgrave	39-464 (8%)	43	38	35	212,279	343,281	-159.79
Adam Kirby	38-525 (7%)	45	42	56	211,471	349,540	-241.96
Tony Hamilton	37-497 (7%)	40	33	50	173,111	329,742	-155.73
Hayley Turner	36-483 (7%)	41	42	49	130,907	277,592	-176.93
Pat Dobbs	34-355 (10%)	27	31	37	149,611	248,811	-87.18
L P Keniry	34-541 (6%)	49	44	52	159,575	276,291	-240.79
J H Bowman	33-303 (11%)	31	41	31	227,794	371,984	-107.42
Luke Morris	33-351 (9%)	28	42	34	239,521	319,381	-104.72
T Quinn	33-436 (8%)	37	33	54	249,070	419,239	-118.29
Step'n Donohoe	33-497 (7%)	35	38	37	111,433	190,099	-204.43

Leading Flat Owners 2007

(31st March -10th November 2007)

NAME	WINS-RUNS	2nd	3rd	4th	WIN £	TOTAL £
Godolphin	73-285 (26%)	51	32	28	1,234,541	1,688,115
Hamdan Al Maktoum	96-537 (18%)	79	60	49	972,329	1,626,429
Saleh Al Homeizi & Imad Al Sagar	10-34 (29%)	5	2	5	1,263,870	1,374,841
Cheveley Park Stud	43-182 (24%)	32	28	18	882,165	1,260,254
Mrs John Magnier & M Tabor	3-20 (15%)	5	1	3	590,512	987,564
D Smith, Mrs J Magnier, M Tabor	3-23 (13%)	6	4	0	251,697	835,749
K Abdulla	66-305 (22%)	53	43	22	428,190	746,779
Sheikh Mohammed	43-277 (16%)	33	31	26	491,402	683,384
Jaber Abdullah	23-172 (13%)	11	26	21	373,434	643,552
George Strawbridge	14-58 (24%)	11	5	10	439,936	591,276
Raymond Tooth	14-71 (20%)	8	4	7	394,655	487,383
J C Smith	13-129 (10%)	14	10	19	344,503	449,150
M Tabor & Mrs John Magnier	2-14 (14%)	3	3	0	278,222	420,091
Sheikh Ahmed Al Maktoum	39-209 (19%)	30	18	15	272,168	367,066
Anthony & David de Rothschild	1-5 (20%)	0	2	1	259,314	363,890
Niarchos Family	9-31 (29%)	5	4	4	288,499	356,180
H R H Princess Haya Of Jordan	23-155 (15%)	19	31	8	125,325	353,051
Mrs J M Corbett & C Wright	5-12 (42%)	2	0	1	337,668	344,414
Gainsborough	32-186 (17%)	28	18	18	221,713	312,762
R J Arculli	2-30 (7%)	3	2	5	182,266	289,306
Miss B Swire	4-49 (8%)	5	2	2	256,380	271,493
Mrs John Magnier	3-8 (38%)	2	0	0	224,281	260,145
Saeed Suhail	14-71 (20%)	11	12	8	164,675	258,829
Mrs J Magnier, M Tabor & D Smith	1-14 (7%)	2	1	1	34,068	251,602
Mountgrange Stud	24-105 (23%)	19	8	8	114,066	251,081
Baron G Von Ullmann	2-3 (67%)	0	1	0	239,597	250,023
Mrs Fitri Hay	10-101 (10%)	6	7	10	192,796	234,199
John Livock	4-7 (57%)	0	0	0	227,836	228,511
H Morin	1-1 (100%)	0	0	0	222,350	222,350
The Searchers	5-13 (38%)	3	2	0	116,453	220,084
Phil Cunningham	1-2 (50%)	0	0	0	211,352	218,077
M A Ryan	1-4 (25%)	0	0	2	198,730	215,462
Budget Stable	1-3 (33%)	0	2	0	198,730	212,516
M Tabor, D Smith & Mrs J Magnier	2-21 (10%)	3	2	3	38,106	203,415
D Smith, M Tabor & Mrs J Magnier	2-7 (29%)	0	1	2	141,950	202,921
Saeed Manana	14-175 (8%)	20	20	20	78,881	196,224
Box 41	11-62 (18%)	6	8	8	153,116	186,539
Terry Neill	4-18 (22%)	1	2	0	168,948	172,695
John Mayne	3-21 (14%)	3	2	5	144,902	169,847
Sangster Family	6-36 (17%)	3	5	1	104,247	163,434
M Sines	8-28 (29%)	8	2	0	50,647	158,123
Mrs Elizabeth Moran	3-10 (30%)	3	3	0	56,230	156,281
R C Bond	12-118 (10%)	11	13	12	101,288	155,275
Mrs J S Bolger	1-3 (33%)	0	0	0	149,559	152,934
Mrs Sarah E Woodhead	4-7 (57%)	1	0	0	150,449	151,991
Craig Bennett	2-3 (67%)	0	0	1	141,674	144,628
Mrs S Roy and Cheveley P'rk Stud	0-4	2	1	1	0	144,544
Michael Tabor	10-50 (20%)	6	2	5	119,331	143,511
P D Savill	12-66 (18%)	5	7	7	95,398	134,876
M B Hawtin	1-4 (25%)	1	0	0	123,320	133,583

Leading All-Weather Flat Jockeys

(6th Nov 2006 - 24th March 2007)

NAME	WIN-RIDES	2nd	3rd	4th	WIN £	TOTAL £	£1 STAKE
N Callan	60-340 (18%)	48	53	33	216,537	318,182	+20.22
Joe Fanning	51-247 (21%)	31	31	22	179,230	241,939	+11.36
Dane O·Neill	41-303 (14%)	34	45	40	132,350	197,532	-16.74
Brett Doyle	38-260 (15%)	28	34	31	126,555	205,461	-23.98
Eddie Ahern	35-258 (14%)	36	26	35	189,033	267,859	-97.55
George Baker	30-160 (19%)	21	15	15	107,607	136,672	+109.92
Tony Culhane	27-233 (12%)	22	20	36	99,277	139,790	-92.40
James Doyle	26-266 (10%)	26	27	34	96,780	149,691	-82.22
Seb Sanders	25-138 (18%)	21	11	14	100,481	140,341	-40.85
Chris Catlin	25-356 (7%)	25	34	37	78,549	123,497	-162.13
Daniel Tudhope	24-133 (18%)	14	13	13	55,881	74,785	+16.25
William Buick	24-163 (15%)	22	24	16	86,482	122,000	-26.66
Richard Hughes	23-90 (26%)	15	10	6	125,720	154,458	+27.99
Robert Havlin	22-147 (15%)	12	19	13	65,445	89,092	-1.33
Steve Drowne	22-204 (11%)	29	10	29	79,787	148,086	-43.79
Jim Crowley	21-205 (10%)	24	19	23	62,830	101,712	-33.19
John Egan	20-114 (18%)	18	13	7	93,214	141,737	+8.21
Fergus Sweeney	20-170 (12%)	19	15	14	74,431	102,690	+62.00
Jimmy Quinn	20-318 (6%)	31	27	45	69,839	133,618	-168.67
Dale Gibson	19-209 (9%)	13	14	22	54,175	82,917	+10.63
Paul Hanagan	19-245 (8%)	23	30	30	68,979	114,844	-143.23
Dean McKeown	18-170 (11%)	15	14	19	63,667	84,616	-24.67
L P Keniry	18-203 (9%)	22	15	18	57,789	87,479	-71.33
Adam Kirby	18-240 (8%)	26	15	27	61,563	94,599	-123.85
Greg Fairley	16-63 (25%)	7	5	8	58,899	69,217	+16.56
Rich'rd Kingscote	16-101 (16%)	14	21	10	52,756	80,776	+45.75
Shane Kelly	16-138 (12%)	14	13	21	41,743	60,590	-45.45
Ian Mongan	15-108 (14%)	10	12	9	50,191	76,905	-9.08
Duran Fentiman	15-155 (10%)	6	13	16	45,413	58,524	-13.84
T P Queally	15-157 (10%)	13	7	10	48,680	66,809	-19.68
Rob'ie Fitzpatrick	15-163 (9%)	15	16	12	48,609	70,755	-56.47
Graham Gibbons	14-125 (11%)	17	8	13	40,730	67,041	+21.54
Paul Mulrennan	14-159 (9%)	12	10	15	115,249	135,977	-47.69
Pat Cosgrave	14-187 (7%)	19	15	20	37,619	64,347	-125.76
Hayley Turner	14-237 (6%)	23	31	19	27,108	63,572	-91.17
Micky Fenton	13-234 (6%)	29	22	19	41,929	74,531	-126.50
Jamie Spencer	12-84 (14%)	13	13	6	44,047	69,895	-42.26
Oscar Urbina	12-88 (14%)	15	11	6	35,804	60,261	+3.94
Paul Eddery	12-98 (12%)	12	7	2	26,156	37,141	-29.75
J-P Guillambert	12-138 (9%)	16	20	15	89,612	116,695	-40.25
Tom Eaves	11-90 (12%)	7	6	9	56,586	67,315	-9.72
Steph'n Donohoe	11-93 (12%)	9	8	8	24,033	35,643	+19.50
Paul Doe	11-100 (11%)	8	11	8	28,152	52,731	-13.00
Liam Jones	11-106 (10%)	8	12	14	38,447	54,063	+33.05
Francis Norton	11-120 (9%)	23	15	14	33,861	66,280	-47.13
Jerry O·Dwyer	11-122 (9%)	7	13	10	29,770	42,338	+35.00
Phillip Makin	10-93 (11%)	8	10	11	25,806	36,064	-52.73

Leading All-Weather Trainers

(6th November 2006 - 24th March 2007)

NAME	WINS-RUNS	2nd	3rd	4th	WIN £	TOTAL £	£1 STAKE
M Johnston	45-138 (33%)	22	14	14	197,724	231,700	+79.52
K A Ryan	32-232 (14%)	27	31	27	127,000	184,129	-59.55
R Hannon	14-128 (11%)	29	22	13	95,759	160,613	-39.58
C E Brittain	16-120 (13%)	14	11	14	97,978	144,972	-37.08
G L Moore	26-150 (17%)	20	12	13	99,009	139,017	+57.25
M W Easterby	15-46 (33%)	2	2	7	126,204	129,306	+24.15
D Shaw	27-288 (9%)	27	38	37	76,357	119,162	-101.58
N P Littmoden	8-136 (6%)	14	15	22	56,410	112,968	-63.50
P J Makin	21-70 (30%)	19	5	6	86,358	109,723	+1.11
W J Haggas	19-67 (28%)	13	10	5	78,314	107,517	-4.11
Peter Grayson	19-236 (8%)	29	23	21	58,503	100,064	-72.19
I Semple	14-78 (18%)	8	11	10	73,611	93,505	-6.56
R A Harris	20-200 (10%)	16	19	18	56,840	77,322	-11.96
J R Best	14-106 (13%)	8	14	12	44,747	75,662	-16.73
Sir M Prescott	18-80 (23%)	9	11	9	56,696	75,197	-11.42
C A Cyzer	7-61 (11%)	5	8	13	61,207	74,873	-17.00
D Carroll	22-110 (20%)	12	11	12	55,236	72,099	+39.96
J A Osborne	12-89 (13%)	13	23	17	39,365	71,434	-22.00
K R Burke	11-101 (11%)	13	13	10	41,318	70,410	-41.75
P D Evans	17-163 (10%)	15	16	26	45,367	70,139	-34.69
Jane C-Hyam	7-38 (18%)	5	3	5	45,678	69,491	+0.23
R A Fahey	14-131 (11%)	8	20	15	48,498	68,268	-55.23
H Morrison	16-59 (27%)	3	2	10	61,551	66,821	+35.08
T J Pitt	14-59 (24%)	10	6	5	49,831	66,687	-16.75
R Hollinshead	13-118 (11%)	14	17	10	40,101	61,966	+40.16
T D Barron	14-60 (23%)	12	9	6	48,466	61,301	-1.06
J S Moore	10-51 (20%)	8	9	7	43,353	60,848	+42.75
P Howling	16-184 (9%)	17	18	31	33,210	59,805	-32.54
W J Musson	9-44 (20%)	3	4	5	47,177	58,899	+16.25
M R Channon	8-77 (10%)	11	10	7	38,460	56,649	-26.50
J Pearce	9-105 (9%)	15	11	13	32,613	55,504	-37.25
J Balding	14-82 (17%)	10	6	9	46,302	55,381	+12.90
G A Butler	3-12 (25%)	5	2	0	34,371	54,382	+6.12
P F I Cole	6-29 (21%)	6	1	1	38,745	53,983	+10.00
J R Boyle	11-95 (12%)	14	11	15	31,411	52,245	-24.52
M A Jarvis	11-40 (28%)	6	1	3	38,650	52,145	+1.12
A M Balding	7-63 (11%)	10	10	7	34,044	50,220	-27.92
D K Ivory	14-105 (13%)	7	12	7	38,262	50,189	+25.33
E A L Dunlop	8-41 (20%)	11	8	3	29,435	48,111	-5.78
J W Hills	5-52 (10%)	8	7	7	20,357	46,868	-25.75
B Smart	9-67 (13%)	10	5	7	33,761	45,573	-34.92
Miss G Kelleway	8-73 (11%)	5	7	12	30,064	43,465	-12.42
P W Hiatt	11-113 (10%)	9	11	10	28,658	41,557	-17.47
P A Blockley	11-117 (9%)	10	11	12	25,091	40,967	-66.00
T G Mills	9-27 (33%)	3	1	4	32,314	40,748	-0.42
D Nicholls	6-72 (8%)	7	8	5	23,969	40,534	-20.25
W R Swinburn	6-34 (18%)	4	4	4	25,145	40,240	-4.09
A J McCabe	9-103 (9%)	7	9	8	27,938	38,909	-7.50
M P Tregoning	11-36 (31%)	1	4	6	33,994	38,048	-7.09

Racing Post top rated 2007

(Best performance figures recorded between 1st January and 31st December 2007)

Manduro (GER) 132
Invasor (ARG)..132
Dylan Thomas (IRE) 131
Authorized (IRE)..131
Curlin (USA) 131
Sacred Kingdom (AUS) 129
Lawyer Ron (USA).....................................128
Premium Tap (USA)...................................128
Admire Moon (JPN) 127
Soldier Of Fortune (IRE)............................127
Street Sense (USA) 127
Any Given Saturday (USA).........................127
Notnowcato..126
Viva Pataca..126
Lava Man (USA) 126
Youmzain (IRE)..126
Sakhee s Secret..126
Midnight Lute (USA) 126
Benbaun (IRE)..125
Ramonti (FR) 125
Red Rocks (IRE)..125
Miss Andretti (AUS) 125
New Approach (IRE)...................................125
Yeats (IRE) 124
Linngari (IRE) 124
English Channel (USA)...............................124
Septimus (IRE) 124
Excellent Art 124
Good Ba Ba (USA) 124
Creachadoir (IRE).......................................124
Eagle Mountain...124
Getaway (GER) 124
Cockney Rebel (IRE)...................................124
Dutch Art...124
Peeping Fawn (USA)...................................124
Literato (FR) 124
Darjina (FR) 124
Armada (NZ)..124
Fast Company (IRE) 124
Toylsome 123
Soldier s Tale (USA) 123
Cesare 123
Daiwa Major (JPN) 123
Scorpion (IRE) 123
Takeover Target (AUS) 123
Mountain High (IRE) 123
Kongo Rikishio (IRE) 123
Sixties Icon 123
El Segundo (NZ) 123
Ask..123
Bentley Biscuit (AUS) 123
Meisho Samson (JPN)................................123
Duke Of Marmalade (IRE) 123
After Market (USA) 123
Pop Rock (JPN)..123
Efficient (NZ)...123
Sagara (USA) 123
Any Suggestion (AUS)................................123
Rags To Riches (USA)................................123
Zambezi Sun 123
Erimo Expire (JPN) 123
War Pass (USA) 123
Matsurida Gogh (JPN).................................123
Vengeance Of Rain (NZ) 122
Doctor Dino (FR) 122
Delta Blues (JPN) 122
Red Clubs (IRE) 122
Dandy Man (IRE)..122
Corinthian (USA) 122
Prince Flori (GER) 122
Fabulous Strike (USA) 122
Kip Deville (USA)...122
Quijano (GER) 122
Magnus (AUS) 122
Hard Spun (USA)..122
US Ranger (USA) 122
Bullish Luck (USA)..121
Soldier Hollow...121
Spark Of Life (AUS) 121
Desert War (AUS)..121
Absolute Champion (AUS) 121
Better Talk Now (USA)..................................121
Laverock (IRE)...121
Cloudy s Knight (USA)...................................121
Asset (IRE) 121
George Washington (IRE) 121
Sir Percy 121
Inti Raimi (JPN) 121
Shadow Gate (JPN).......................................121
Surf Cat (USA)...121
Areyoutalkingtome...121
Jeremy (USA) 121
Marchand D Or (FR) 121
Molengao (BRZ) 121
Indian Ink (IRE)...121
Hello Pretty (AUS) 121

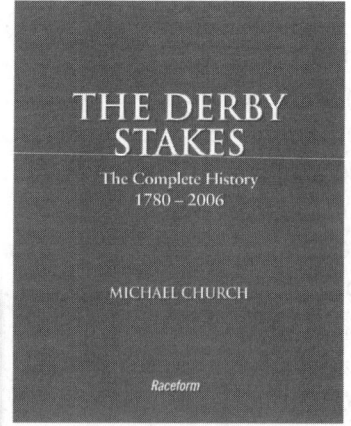

Raceform median times 2007

ASCOT

5f ...1m 1.40
6f ...1m 14.90
6f 110y...1m 22.84
7f ...1m 28.10
1m Rnd ...1m 42.10
1m Str ...1m 41.80
1m 2f ...2m 8.00
1m 4f ...2m 33.00
2m 4f ...4m 24.60

AYR

5f ...1m 0.44
6f ...1m 13.67
7f 50y ...1m 32.72
1m ...1m 43.49
1m 1f 20y ...2m 0.00
1m 2f ...2m 11.72
1m 2f 192y ...2m 23.64
1m 5f 13y ...2m 56.61
1m 7f ...3m 22.47
2m 1f 105y ...3m 54.77

BATH

5f 11y ...1m 2.50
5f 161y ...1m 11.20
1m 5y ...1m 41.10
1m 2f 46y ...2m 11.00
1m 3f 144y ...2m 30.30
1m 5f 22y ...2m 51.50
2m 1f 34y ...3m 49.60

BEVERLEY

5f ...1m 4.00
7f 100y ...1m 34.31
1m 100y ...1m 47.40
1m 1f 207y ...2m 7.30
1m 4f 16y ...2m 40.21
2m 35y ...3m 39.50

BRIGHTON

5f 59y ...1m 2.30
5f 213y ...1m 10.10
6f 209y ...1m 22.70
7f 214y ...1m 35.04
1m 1f 209y ...2m 2.60
1m 3f 196y ...2m 32.20

CARLISLE

5f ...1m 1.50
5f 193y ...1m 13.61
6f 192y ...1m 27.10
7f 200y ...1m 40.09
1m 1f 61y ...1m 57.56
1m 6f 32y ...3m 7.30
2m 1f 52y ...3m 49.90

CATTERICK

5f ...1m 0.60
5f 212y ...1m 14.00
7f ...1m 27.36
1m 3f 214y ...2m 39.00
1m 5f 175y ...3m 4.50
1m 7f 177y ...3m 31.40

CHEPSTOW

5f 16y ...59.60
6f 16y ...1m 12.40
7f 16y ...1m 23.30
1m 14y ...1m 36.00
1m 2f 36y ...2m 9.90
1m 4f 23y ...2m 38.72
2m 49y ...3m 39.40
2m 2f ...4m 0.62

CHESTER

5f 16y ...1m 2.05
6f 18y ...1m 15.65
7f 2y ...1m 28.47
7f 122y ...1m 34.75
1m 2f 75y ...2m 13.14
1m 3f 79y ...2m 25.79
1m 4f 66y...2m 40.65
1m 5f 89y ...2m 55.42
1m 7f 195y...3m 33.60
2m 2f 147y ...4m 5.57

DONCASTER

5f ...1m 1.42
5f 140y ...1m 8.00
6f 1m 14.30
6f 110y ...1m 20.48
7f 1m 27.77
1m Rnd ...1m 40.61
1m Str ...1m 41.51
1m 2f 60y ...2m 11.83
1m 4f ...2m 35.53
1m 6f 132y ...3m 9.74
2m 2f ...3m 57.93

EPSOM

5f ...55.68
6f ...1m 10.63
7f ...1m 23.95
1m 114y ...1m 45.74
1m 2f 18y ...2m 9.04
1m 4f 10y ...2m 38.73

FOLKESTONE

5f ...1m 0.80
6f ...1m 13.60
7f ...1m 27.90
1m 1f 149y ...2m 5.23
1m 4f ...2m 40.50
1m 7f 92y ...3m 27.20
2m 93y ...3m 40.70

GOODWOOD

5f ...59.05
6f ...1m 12.85
7f ...1m 28.04
1m ...1m 40.27
1m 1f ...1m 56.86
1m 1f 192y ...2m 7.75
1m 3f ...2m 27.21
1m 4f ...2m 38.92
1m 6f ...3m 3.97
2m ...3m 30.79
2m 5f ...4m 33.10

HAMILTON

5f 4y ...1m 1.20
6f 5y ...1m 13.10
1m 65y ...1m 49.30
1m 1f 36y ...1m 59.66
1m 3f 16y ...2m 26.26
1m 4f 17y ...2m 39.18
1m 5f 9y ...2m 53.40

HAYDOCK

5f ...1m 0.12
6f ...1m 13.89
7f 30y ...1m 32.06
1m 30y ...1m 45.51
1m 2f 120y ...2m 16.14
1m 3f 200y ...2m 34.99
1m 6f ...3m 6.29
2m 45y ...3m 37.90

KEMPTON (A.W)

5f ...1m 0.40
6f ...1m 13.70
7f ...1m 26.80
1m ...1m 40.80
1m 1f ...1m 54.55
1m 2f ...2m 9.00
1m 3f ...2m 22.68
1m 4f ...2m 36.90
2m ...3m 31.40

LEICESTER

5f 2y ...1m 0.90
5f 218y ...1m 13.20
7f 9y ...1m 26.10
1m 60y ...1m 45.30
1m 1f 218y ...2m 8.30
1m 3f 183y ...2m 34.50

LINGFIELD (TURF)

5f ...58.94
6f ...1m 11.67
7f ...1m 24.21
7f 140y ...1m 31.46
1m 1f ...1m 55.29
1m 2f ...2m 9.72
1m 3f 106y ...2m 29.92
1m 6f ...3m 6.92
2m ...3m 33.26

LINGFIELD (A.W)

5f ...59.78
6f ...1m 12.81
7f ...1m 25.89
1m ...1m 39.43
1m 2f ...2m 7.79
1m 4f ...2m 34.39
1m 5f ...2m 48.30
2m ...3m 28.79

MUSSELBURGH

5f ...1m 0.50
7f 30y ...1m 29.94
1m ...1m 42.50
1m 1f ...1m 53.86
1m 4f ...2m 36.90
1m 6f ...3m 5.70
2m ...3m 33.90

NEWBURY

5f 34y ...1m 2.56
6f 8y ...1m 14.32
7f ...1m 27.00
1m ...1m 40.62
1m 1f ...1m 54.59
1m 2f 6y ...2m 8.71
1m 3f 5y ...2m 22.27
1m 4f 5y ...2m 35.99
1m 5f 61y ...2m 50.99
2m ...3m 34.86

NEWCASTLE

5f ...1m 1.50
6f ...1m 15.09
7f ...1m 28.02
1m ...1m 43.48
1m 3y Str ...1m 41.90
1m 1f 9y ...1m 57.81
1m 2f 32y ...2m 11.80
1m 4f 93y ...2m 43.55
2m 19y ...3m 35.20

NEWMARKET (ROWLEY)

5f ...1m 0.47
6f ...1m 13.10
7f ...1m 26.50
1m ...1m 39.37
1m 1f ...1m 51.95
1m 2f ...2m 5.71
1m 4f ...2m 33.50
1m 6f ...3m 0.13
2m ...3m 26.92
2m 2f ...3m 54.80

NEWMARKET (JULY)

5f ...59.56
6f ...1m 13.35
7f ...1m 26.78
1m ...1m 40.43
1m 2f ...2m 6.44
1m 4f ...2m 32.91
1m 6f 175y ...3m 11.04
2m 24y ...3m 26.99

NOTTINGHAM

5f 13y ...1m 1.80
6f 15y ...1m 15.00
1m 54y ...1m 46.40
1m 1f 213y ...2m 9.70
1m 6f 15y ...3m 7.10
2m 9y ...3m 33.50

PONTEFRACT

5f ...1m 3.80
6f ...1m 17.40
1m 4y ...1m 45.70
1m 2f 6y ...2m 14.08

1m 4f 8y 2m 40.30
2m 1f 22y 3m 50.50
2m 1f 216y 4m 3.00
2m 5f 122y 5m 0.80

REDCAR

5f 58.70
6f 1m 11.70
7f 1m 24.90
1m 1m 37.80
1m 1f 1m 53.40
1m 2f 2m 6.80
1m 3f 2m 21.00
1m 6f 19y 3m 5.02
2m 4y 3m 31.50

RIPON

5f 1m 0.20
6f 1m 13.00
1m 1m 41.10
1m 1f 1m 53.85
1m 1f 170y.................2m 5.00
1m 4f 10y 2m 37.00
2m 3m 33.00

SALISBURY

5f 1m 1.59
6f 1m 14.98
6f 212y 1m 29.06
1m 1m 43.09
1m 1f 198y 2m 8.46
1m 4f 2m 36.36
1m 6f 21y 3m 7.00

SANDOWN

5f 6y 1m 2.21
7f 16y 1m 29.34
1m 14y 1m 43.95
1m 1f 1m 56.11

1m 2f 7y 2m 10.24
1m 6f 3m 4.51
2m 78y 3m 38.23

SOUTHWELL (TURF)

6f 1m 16.10
7f 1m 29.20
1m 3f 2m 28.0
1m 4f 2m 40.30
2m 3m 41.50

SOUTHWELL (A.W)

5f 1m 0.30
6f 1m 16.90
7f 1m 30.80
1m 1m 44.60
1m 3f 2m 28.90
1m 4f 2m 42.09
1m 6f 3m 9.60
2m 3m 44.54

THIRSK

5f 59.90
6f 1m 12.50
7f 1m 27.10
1m 1m 39.70
1m 4f 2m 35.20
2m 3m 31.20

WARWICK

5f 59.40
5f 110y 1m 5.89
6f 1m 14.28
7f 26y 1m 24.20
1m 22y 1m 39.60
1m 2f 188y 2m 19.40
1m 4f 134y 2m 43.60
1m 6f 213y.................3m 15.90
2m 39y 3m 32.70

WINDSOR

5f 10y 1m 1.10
6f 1m 13.67
1m 67y 1m 44.70
1m 2f 7y 2m 8.30
1m 3f 135y 2m 30.10

WOLVERHAMPTON (A.W)

5f 20y 1m 2.82
5f 216y 1m 15.81
7f 32y.........................1m 30.40
1m 141y 1m 51.76
1m 1f 103y 2m 2.62
1m 4f 50y 2m 42.42
1m 5f 194y 3m 7.37
2m 119y 3m 43.13

YARMOUTH

5f 43y 1m 2.80
6f 3y 1m 13.70
7f 3y 1m 26.60
1m 3y 1m 39.90
1m 2f 21y...................2m 8.10
1m 3f 101y 2m 27.50
1m 6f 17y 3m 5.30
2m 3m 31.41

YORK

5f 59.32
6f 1m 12.56
7f 1m 25.40
1m 1m 39.50
1m 208y.....................1m 50.99
1m 2f 88y 2m 12.50
1m 4f 2m 34.60
1m 6f 2m 59.50

Raceform Flat record times

ASCOT

Distance	Time	Age	Weight	Going	Horse	Date
5f	59.77 sec	2	9-3	Gd To Firm	Drawnfromthepast(IRE)	Jun 19 2007
5f	57.44 sec	6	9-1	Gd To Firm	Miss Andretti (AUS)	Jun 19 2007
6f	1m 12.46	2	9-1	Gd To Firm	Henrythenavigator(USA)	Jun 19 2007
6f	1m 12.46	2	9-1	Gd To Firm	Henrythenavigator(USA)	Jun 19 2007
7f	1m 26.76	2	7-12	Gd To Firm	Relative Order	Aug 11 2007
7f	1m 25.89	4	8-9	Gd To Firm	Dabbers Ridge (IRE)	Jly 29 2006
1m (R)	1m 39.14	3	9-0	Gd To Firm	Nannina	Jun 23 2006
1m (S)	1m 37.21	5	9-0	Gd To Firm	Ramonti (FR)	Jun 19 2007
1m 2f	2m 4.150	4	8-7	Gd To Firm	I m So Lucky	Jun 23 2006
1m 4f	2m 27.24	3	8-9	Gd To Firm	Linas Selection	Jun 23 2006
2m	3m 25.52	6	9-0	Gd To Firm	Tungsten Strike (USA)	May 2 2007
2m 4f	4m 18.29	8	9-1	Gd To Firm	Full House (IRE)	Jun 19 2007
2m 5f	5m 4.600	4	9-0	Gd To Firm	Baddam	Jun 24 2006

AYR

Distance	Time	Age	Weight	Going	Horse	Date
5f	56.9 secs	2	8-11	Good	Boogie Street	Sep 18 2003
5f	57.2 secs	4	9-5	Gd to Firm	Sir Joey	Sep 16 1993
6f	69.7 secs	2	7-10	Good	Sir Bert	Sep 17 1969
6f	68.9 secs	7	8-8	Gd to Firm	Sobering Thoughts	Sep 18 1993
7f	1m 25.7	2	9-0	Gd to Firm	Jazeel	Sep 16 1993
7f	1m 24.9	5	7-11	Firm	Sir Arthur Hobbs	Jun 19 1992
7f 50y	1m 28.9	2	9-0	Good	Tafaahum (USA)	Sep 19 2003
7f 50y	1m 28.2	4	9-2	Gd to Firm	Flur Na H Alba	Jun 21 2003
1m	1m 39.2	2	9-0	Gd to Firm	Kribensis	Sep 17 1986
1m	1m 36.0	4	7-13	Firm	Sufi	Sep 16 1959
1m 1f 20y	1m 50.3	4	9-3	Good	Retirement	Sep 19 2003
1m 2f	2m 4.0	4	9-9	Gd to Firm	Endless Hall	Jly 17 2000
1m 2f192y	2m 13.3	4	9-0	Gd to Firm	Azzaam	Sep 18 1991
1m 5f 13y	2m 45.8	4	9-7	Gd to Firm	Eden s Close	Sep 18 1993
1m 7f	3m 13.1	3	9-4	Good	Romany Rye	Sep 19 1991
2m 1f105y	3m 45.0	4	6-13	Good	Curry	Sep 16 1955

BATH

Distance	Time	Age	Weight	Going	Horse	Date
5f 11y	60.1 secs	2	8-11	Firm	Double Fantasy	Aug 25 2000
5f 11y	58.75 secs	3	8-12	Firm	Enticing (IRE)	May 1 2007
5f 161y	69.1 secs	2	8-7	Firm	Sibla	Aug 25 2000
5f 161y	68.1 secs	6	9-0	Firm	Madraco	May 22 1989
1m 5y	1m 39.7	2	8-9	Firm	Casual Look	Sep 16 2002
1m 5y	1m 37.2	5	8-12	Gd to Firm	Adobe	Jun 17 2000
1m 5y	1m 37.2	3	8-7	Firm	Alasha (IRE)	Aug 18 2002
1m 2f 46y	2m 5.8	3	9-0	Gd to Firm	Connoisseur Bay(USA)	May 29 1998
1m 3f144y	2m 25.74	3	9-0	Hard	Top Of The Charts	Sep 8 2005
1m 5f 22y	2m 47.2	4	10-0	Firm	Flown	Aug 13 1991
2m 1f 34y	3m 43.4	6	7-9	Firm	Yaheska (IRE)	Jun 14 2003

BEVERLEY

Distance	Time	Age	Weight	Going	Horse	Date
5f	61.0 secs	2	8-2	Gd to Firm	Addo (IRE)	Jly 17 2001
5f	60.1 secs	4	9-5	Firm	Pic Up Sticks	Apr 16 2003
7f 100y	1m 31.1	2	9-7	Gd to Firm	Champagne Prince	Aug 10 1995
7f 100y	1m 31.1	2	9-0	Firm	Majal (IRE)	Jly 30 1991
7f 100y	1m 29.5	3	7-8	Firm	Who s Tef	Jly 30 1991
1m 100y	1m 43.3	2	9-0	Firm	Arden	Sep 24 1986
1m 100y	1m 42.2	3	8-4	Firm	Legal Case	Jun 14 1989
1m 1f 207y	2m 1.8	3	9-7	Firm	Rose Alto	Jly 5 1991
1m 3f 216y	2m 30.8	3	8-1	Hard	Coinage	Jun 18 1986
1m 4f 16y	2m 35.8	4	9-3	Gd to Firm	Red River Rebel	Aug 25 2002
2m 35y	3m 29.5	4	9-2	Gd to Firm	Rushen Raider	Aug 14 1996

BRIGHTON

Distance	Time	Age	Weight	Going	Horse	Date
5f 59y	60.1 secs	2	9-0	Firm	Bid for Blue	May 6 1993
5f 59y	59.3 secs	3	8-9	Firm	Play Hever Golf	May 26 1993
5f 213y	68.1 secs	2	8-9	Firm	Song Mist (IRE)	Jly 16 1996
5f 213y	67.3 secs	3	8-9	Firm	Third Party	Jun 3 1997
5f 213y	67.3 secs	5	9-1	Gd to Firm	Blundell Lane	May 4 2000
6f 209y	1m 19.9	2	8-11	Hard	Rain Burst	Sep 15 1988
6f 209y	1m 19.4	4	9-3	Gd to Firm	Sawaki	Sep 3 1991
7f 214y	1m 32.8	2	9-7	Firm	Asian Pete	Oct 3 1989
7f 214y	1m 30.5	5	8-11	Firm	Mystic Ridge	May 27 1999
1m 1f 209y	2m 4.7	2	9-0	Gd to Soft	Esteemed Master	Nov 2 2001
1m 1f 209y	1m 57.2	3	9-0	Firm	Get The Message	Apr 30 1984
1m 3f 196y	2m 25.8	4	8-2	Firm	New Zealand	Jly 4 1985

CARLISLE

Distance	Time	Age	Weight	Going	Horse	Date
5f	60.1 secs	2	8-5	Firm	La Tortuga	Aug 2 1999
5f	58.8 secs	3	9-8	Gd to Firm	Esatto	Aug 21 2002
5f 193y	1m 12.45	2	9-6	Gd to Firm	Musical Guest (IRE)	Sep 11 2005
5f 193y	1m 10.83	4	9-0	Gd to Firm	Bo McGinty (IRE)	Sep 11 2005
6f 192y	1m 24.3	3	8-9	Gd to Firm	Marjurita (IRE)	Aug 21 2002
6f 206y	1m 26.5	2	9-4	Hard	Sense of Priority	Sep 10 1991
6f 206y	1m 25.3	4	9-1	Firm	Move With Edes	Jly 6 1996
7f 200y	1m 37.34	5	9-7	Gd to Firm	Hula Ballew	Aug 17 2005
7f 214y	1m 44.6	2	8-8	Firm	Blue Garter	Sep 9 1980
7f 214y	1m 37.3	5	7-12	Hard	Thatched (IRE)	Aug 21 1995
1m 1f 61y	1m 53.8	3	9-0	Firm	Little Jimbob	Jun 14 2004
1m 3f 107y	2m 22.46	3	8-5	Gd to Firm	Regal Connection(USA)	Aug 2 2006
1m 4f	2m 28.8	3	8-5	Firm	Desert Frolic (IRE)	Jun 27 1996
1m 6f 32y	3m 2.2	6	8-10	Firm	Explosive Speed	May 26 1994
2m 1f 52y	3m 46.2	3	7-10	Gd to Firm	Warring Kingdom	Aug 25 1999

CATTERICK

Distance	Time	Age	Weight	Going	Horse	Date
5f	57.6 secs	2	9-0	Firm	H Harrison	Oct 8 2002
5f	57.1 secs	4	8-7	Fast	Kabcast	Jly 7 1989
5f 212y	1m 11.4	2	9-4	Firm	Captain Nick	Jly 11 1978
5f 212y	69.8 secs	9	8-13	Gd to Firm	Sharp Hat	May 30 2003
7f	1m 24.1	2	8-11	Firm	Lindas Fantasy	Sep 18 1982
7f	1m 22.5	6	8-7	Firm	Differential (USA)	May 31 2003
1m 3f 214y	2m 30.5	3	8-8	Gd to Firm	Rahaf	May 30 2003
1m 5f 175y	2m 54.8	3	8-5	Firm	Geryon	May 31 1984
1m 7f 177y	3m 20.8	4	7-11	Firm	Bean Boy	Jly 8 1982

CHEPSTOW

Distance	Time	Age	Weight	Going	Horse	Date
5f 16y	57.6 secs	2	8-11	Firm	Micro Love	Jly 8 1986
5f 16y	56.8 secs	3	8-4	Firm	Torbay Express	Sep 15 1979
6f 16y	69.4 secs	2	9-0	Fast	Royal Fifi	Sep 9 1989
6f 16y	68.1 secs	3	9-7	Firm	America Calling (USA)	Sep 18 2001
7f 16y	1m 20.8	2	9-0	Gd to Firm	Royal Amaretto (IRE)	Sep 12 1996
7f 16y	1m 19.3	3	9-0	Firm	Taranaki	Sep 18 2001
1m 14y	1m 33.1	2	8-11	Gd to Firm	Ski Academy (IRE)	Aug 28 1995
1m 14y	1m 31.6	3	8-13	Firm	Stoli (IRE)	Sep 18 2001
1m 2f 36y	2m 4.1	5	8-9	Hard	Leonidas	Jly 5 1983
1m 2f 36y	2m 4.1	5	7-8	Gd to Firm	It s Varadan	Sep 9 1989
1m 2f 36y	2m 4.1	3	8-5	Gd to Firm	Ela Athena	Jly 23 1999
1m 4f 23y	2m 31.0	3	8-9	Gd to Firm	Spritsail	Jly 13 1989
1m 4f 23y	2m 31.0	7	9-6	Hard	Maintop	Aug 27 1984
2m 49y	3m 27.7	4	9-0	Gd to Firm	Wizzard Artist	Jly 1 1989
2m 2f	3m 56.4	5	8-7	Gd to Firm	Laffah	Jly 8 2000

CHESTER

Distance	Time	Age	Weight	Going	Horse	Date
5f 16y	60.06 secs	2	8-9	Gd to Firm	Not For Me (IRE)	Jly 14 2006
5f 16y	59.2 secs	3	10-0	Firm	Althrey Don	Jly 10 1964
6f 18y	1m 12.8	2	8-10	Gd to Firm	Flying Express	Aug 31 2002
6f 18y	1m 12.7	3	8-3	Gd to Firm	Play Hever Golf	May 4 1993
6f 18y	1m 12.7	6	9-2	Good	Stack Rock	Jun 23 1993
7f 2y	1m 25.2	2	9-0	Gd to Firm	Due Respect (IRE)	Sep 25 2002
7f 2y	1m 23.75	5	8-13	Gd to Firm	Three Graces (GER)	Jly 9 2005
7f 122y	1m 32.2	2	9-0	Gd to Firm	Big Bad Bob (IRE)	Sep 25 2002
7f 122y	1m 30.91	3	8-12	Gd to Firm	Cupid's Glory	Aug 18 2005
1m 2f 75y	2m 7.15	3	8-8	Gd to Firm	Stotsfold	May 7 2002
1m 3f 79y	2m 22.5	3	8-9	Gd to Firm	Rockerlong	Sep 23 2006
1m 4f 66y	2m 33.7	3	8-10	Gd to Firm	Fight Your Corner	May 7 2002
1m 5f 89y	2m 45.4	5	8-11	Firm	Rakaposhi King	May 7 1987
1m 7f 195y	3m 20.3	4	9-0	Gd to Firm	Grand Fromage (IRE)	Jly 13 2002
2m 2f 147y	3m 58.89	7	9-2	Gd to Firm	Greenwich Meantime	May 9 2007

DONCASTER

Distance	Time	Age	Weight	Going	Horse	Date
5f	58.4 secs	2	9-5	Firm	Sing Sing	Sep 11 1959
5f	58.4 secs	2	9-0	Good	D Urberville	Sep 13 1967
5f	57.2 secs	6	9-12	Gd to Firm	Celtic Mill	Sep 9 2004
5f 140y	67.2 secs	2	9-0	Gd to Firm	Cartography (IRE)	Jun 29 2003
5f 140y	65.6 secs	9	9-10	Good	Halmahera (IRE)	Sep 8 2004
6f	69.6 secs	2	8-11	Good	Caesar Beware (IRE)	Sep 8 2004
6f	69.6 secs	2	8-11	Good	Caesar Beware (IRE)	Sep 8 2004
6f 110y	1m 17.42	2	8-2	Gd to Firm	Royal Confidence	Sep 12 2007
7f	1m 22.6	2	9-1	Good	Librettist (USA)	Sep 8 2004
7f	1m 21.6	3	8-10	Gd to Firm	Pastoral Pursuits	Sep 9 2004
1m	1m 36.5	2	8-6	Gd to Firm	Singhalese	Sep 9 2004
1m (R)	1m 35.4	2	8-10	Good	Playful Act (IRE)	Sep 9 2004
1m	1m 35.3	3	9-0	Gd to Firm	Gneiss	May 2 1994
1m (R)	1m 36.6	7	9-9	Gd to Firm	Invader	Jun 29 2003
1m 2f 60y	2m 13.4	2	8-8	Good	Yard Bird	Nov 6 1981
1m 2f 60y	2m 4.81	4	8-13	Gd to Firm	Red Gala	Sep 12 2007
1m 4f	2m 27.7	3	8-12	Gd to Firm	Takwin (IRE)	Sep 9 2000
1m 6f 132y	3m 1.07	3	8-7	Gd to Firm	Hi Calypso (IRE)	Sep 13 2007
2m 2f	3m 48.41	4	9-4	Gd to Firm	Septimus (IRE)	Sep 14 2007

EPSOM

Distance	Time	Age	Weight	Going	Horse	Date
5f	55.0 secs	2	8-9	Gd to Firm	Prince Asiia	Jun 9 1995
5f	53.6 secs	4	9-5	Firm	Indigenous	Jun 2 1960
6f	67.8 secs	2	8-11	Gd to Firm	Showbrook	Jun 5 1991
6f	67.3 secs	5	8-12	Good	Loyal Tycoon (IRE)	Jun 7 2003
7f	1m 21.3	2	8-9	Gd to Firm	Red Peony	Jul 29 2004
7f	1m 20.1	4	8-7	Firm	Capistrano	Jun 7 1972
1m 114y	1m 42.8	2	8-5	Gd to Firm	Nightstalker	Aug 30 1988

Distance	Time	Age	Weight	Going	Horse	Date
1m 114y	1m 40.7	3	8-6	Gd to Firm	Sylva Honda	Jun 5 1991
1m 2f 18y	2m 3.5	5	7-13	Good	Crossbow	Jun 7 1967
1m 4f 10y	2m 32.3	3	9-0	Gd to Firm	Lammtarra	Jun 10 1995

FOLKESTONE

Distance	Time	Age	Weight	Going	Horse	Date
5f	58.4 secs	2	9-2	Gd to Firm	Pivotal	Nov 6 1995
5f	58.23 secs	3	9-4	Gd to Firm	Millisecond	Sep 2 2007
6f	1m 10.8	2	8-9	Good	Boomerang Blade	Jly 16 1998
6f	69.38 secs	4	9-8	Gd to Firm	Munaddam (USA)	Sep 18 2006
6f 189y	1m 23.7	2	8-11	Good	Hen Harrier	Jly 3 1996
6f 189y	1m 21.4	3	8-9	Firm	Cielamour (USA)	Aug 9 1988
7f	1m 25.01	2	9-0	Gd to Firm	Dona Alba (IRE)	Sep 2 2007
7f	1m 23.76	3	8-11	Gd to Firm	Welsh Cake	Sep 18 2006
1m 1f 149y	1m 59.7	3	8-6	Gd to Firm	Dizzy	Jly 23 1991
1m 4f	2m 33.2	4	8-8	Hard	Snow Blizzard	Jun 30 1992
1m 7f 92y	3m 23.1	3	9-11	Firm	Mata Askari	Sep 12 1991
2m 93y	3m 34.9	3	8-12	Gd to Firm	Candle Smoke (USA)	Aug 20 1996

GOODWOOD

Distance	Time	Age	Weight	Going	Horse	Date
5f	57.5 secs	2	8-12	Gd to Firm	Poets Cove	Aug 3 1990
5f	56.0 secs	5	9-0	Gd to Firm	Rudi s Pet	Jly 27 1999
6f	69.8 secs	2	8-11	Gd to Firm	Bachir (IRE)	Jly 28 1999
6f	69.18 secs	4	9-0	Good	Tax Free (IRE)	Sep 9 2006
7f	1m 24.9	2	8-11	Gd to Firm	Ekraar	Jly 29 1999
7f	1m 23.8	3	8-7	Firm	Brief Glimpse (IRE)	Jly 25 1995
1m	1m 37.21	2	9-0	Good	Caldra (IRE)	Sep 9 2006
1m	1m 35.6	3	8-13	Gd to Firm	Aljabr (USA)	Jly 28 1999
1m 1f	1m 52.8	3	9-6	Good	Vena (IRE)	Jly 27 1995
1m 1f 192y	2m 2.81	3	9-3	Gd to Firm	Road To Love (IRE)	Aug 3 2006
1m 3f	2m 23.0	3	8-8	Gd to Firm	Asian Heights	May 22 2001
1m 4f	2m 31.5	3	8-10	Firm	Presenting	Jly 25 1995
1m 6f	2m 58.5	4	9-2	Gd to Firm	Mowbray	Jly 27 1999
2m	3m 21.55	5	9-10	Gd to Firm	Yeats (IRE)	Aug 3 2006
2m 4f	4m 11.7	3	7-10	Firm	Lucky Moon	Aug 2 1990

HAMILTON

Distance	Time	Age	Weight	Going	Horse	Date
5f 4y	58.0 secs	3	7-8	Firm	Fair Dandy	Sep 25 1972
5f 4y	58.0 secs	5	8-6	Firm	Golden Sleigh	Sep 6 1972
6f 5y	1m 10.0	2	8-12	Gd to Firm	Break The Code	Aug 24 1999
6f 5y	69.3 secs	4	8-7	Firm	Marcus Game	Jly 11 1974
1m 65y	1m 45.8	2	8-11	Firm	Hopeful Subject	Sep 24 1973
1m 65y	1m 42.7	6	7-7	Firm	Cranley	Sep 25 1972
1m 1f 36y	1m 53.6	5	9-6	Gd to Firm	Regent's Secret	Aug 10 2005
1m 3f 16y	2m 19.8	3	8-1	Gd to Firm	McEldowney	Aug 22 2005
1m 4f 17y	2m 32.0	4	10-0	Firm	Hold Tight	Aug 22 1983
1m 4f 17y	2m 32.0	4	7-4	Firm	Fine Point	Aug 24 1981
1m 5f 9y	2m 45.1	6	9-6	Firm	Mentalasanythin	Jun 14 1995

HAYDOCK

Distance	Time	Age	Weight	Going	Horse	Date
5f	59.2 secs	2	9-4	Firm	Money For Nothing	Aug 21 1964
5f	58.2 secs	5	8-9	Good	Sierra Vista	Sep 3 2005
6f	1m 10.9	4	9-9	Gd to Firm	Wolfhound (USA)	Sep 4 1993
6f	69.9 secs	4	9-0	Gd to Firm	Iktamal (USA)	Sep 7 1996
7f 30y	1m 29.4	2	9-0	Gd to Firm	Apprehension	Sep 7 1996
7f 30y	1m 26.8	3	8-7	Gd to Firm	Lady Zonda	Sep 28 2002
1m 30y	1m 40.6	2	8-12	Gd to Firm	Besiege	Sep 7 1996
1m 30y	1m 40.1	3	9-2	Firm	Untold Riches (USA)	Jly 11 1999
1m 2f 120y	2m 22.2	2	8-11	Soft	Persian Haze	Oct 9 1994
1m 2f 120y	2m 8.5	3	8-7	Gd to Firm	Fahal (USA)	Aug 5 1995
1m 3f 200y	2m 26.4	5	8-2	Firm	New Member	Jly 4 1970
1m 6f	2m 59.5	3	8-3	Gd to Firm	Castle Secret	Sep 30 1989
2m 45y	3m 27.0	4	8-13	Firm	Prince of Peace	May 26 1984
2m 1f 130y	3m 55.0	3	8-12	Good	Crystal Spirit	Sep 8 1990

KEMPTON (A.W)

Distance	Time	Age	Weight	Going	Horse	Date
5f	60.29 sec	2	9-1	Standard	Inflight (IRE)	Aug 23 2006
5f	59.77 sec	5	8-7	Standard	Harry Up	Dec 10 2006
6f	1m 12.22	2	8-11	Standard	Dhanyata (IRE)	Sep 2 2006
6f	1m 11.49	5	9-0	Standard	Saviours Spirit	Nov 1 2006
7f	1m 25.93	2	9-0	Standard	Boscobel	Nov 22 2006
7f	1m 23.91	3	8-4	Standard	BomberCommand(US)	Nov 24 2006
1m	1m 38.56	2	9-0	Standard	Rallying Cry (USA)	Sep 30 2006
1m	1m 37.47	3	9-1	Standard	Evident Pride (USA)	Nov 29 2006
1m 2f	2m 4.44	3	8-11	Standard	Stotsfold	Sep 2 2006
1m 3f	2m 19.08	3	9-8	Standard	Acrobatic (USA)	Sep 1 2006
1m 4f	2m 32.69	4	9-4	Standard	Kandidate	Sep 2 2006
2m	3m 27.49	4	9-2	Standard	Velvet Heights (IRE)	Apr 26 2006

LEICESTER

Distance	Time	Age	Weight	Going	Horse	Date
5f 2y	58.4 secs	2	9-0	Firm	Cutting Blade	Jun 9 1986
5f 2y	59.85 secs	5	9-5	Gd to Firm	The Jobber (IRE)	Sep 18 2006
5f 218y	1m 10.1	2	9-0	Firm	Thordis (IRE)	Oct 24 1995
5f 218y	69.4 secs	3	8-12	Gd to Firm	Lakeland Beauty	May 29 1990
7f 9y	1m 22.8	2	8-6	Good	Miss Dragonfly (IRE)	Sep 22 1997
7f 9y	1m 20.8	3	8-7	Firm	Flower Bowl	Jun 9 1986
1m 60y	1m 44.05	2	8-11	Gd to Firm	Congressional (IRE)	Sep 6 2005
1m 60y	1m 42.49	3	9-2	Gd to Firm	Street Warrior (IRE)	Sep 18 2006
1m 1f 218y	2m 5.3	2	9-1	Gd to Firm	Windsor Castle	Oct 14 1996
1m 1f 218y	2m 2.4	3	8-11	Firm	Effigy	Nov 4 1985
1m 1f 218y	2m 2.4	4	9-6	Gd to Firm	Lady Angharad (IRE)	Jun 18 2000
1m 3f 183y	2m 27.1	5	8-12	Gd to Firm	Murghem (IRE)	Jun 18 2000

LINGFIELD (TURF)

Distance	Time	Age	Weight	Going	Horse	Date
5f	57.1 secs	2	8-9	Good	Emerald Peace	Aug 6 1999
5f	56.2 secs	3	9-1	Gd to Firm	Eveningperformance	Jly 25 1994
6f	68.6 secs	2	9-3	Firm	The Ritz	Jun 11 1965
6f	68.2 secs	6	9-10	Firm	Al Amead	Jly 2 1986
7f	1m 21.3	2	7-6	Firm	Mandav	Oct 3 1980
7f	1m 20.1	3	8-7	Gd to Firm	Zelah (IRE)	May 13 1998
7f 140y	1m 29.9	2	8-12	Firm	Rather Warm	Nov 7 1978
7f 140y	1m 26.7	3	8-6	Fast	Hiaam	Nov 7 1978
1m 1f	1m 52.4	4	9-2	Gd to Firm	Quandary (USA)	Jly 15 1995
1m 2f	2m 4.6	3	9-3	Firm	Usran	Jly 15 1989
1m 3f 106y	2m 23.9	3	8-5	Firm	Night-Shirt	Jly 14 1990
1m 6f	2m 59.1	5	9-5	Firm	Ibn Bey	Jly 1 1989
2m	3m 23.7	3	9-5	Gd to Firm	Lauries Crusader	Aug 13 1988

LINGFIELD (A.W)

Distance	Time	Age	Weight	Going	Horse	Date
5f	58.61 secs	2	8-12	Standard	WavertreePrincess(IRE)	Nov 24 2007
5f	57.26 secs	8	8-12	Standard	Magic Glade	Feb 24 2007
6f	1m 11.03	2	9-0	Standard	RainbowPromises(USA)	Oct 5 2006
6f	1m 9.80	7	9-2	Standard	Maltese Falcon	Nov 24 2007
7f	1m 23.96	2	9-1	Standard	Roaring Forte (IRE)	Nov 12 2007
7f	1m 22.19	4	8-7	Standard	Red Spell	Nov 19 2005
1m	1m 36.5	2	9-5	Standard	San Pier Niceto	Nov 30 1989
1m	1m 35.40	4	9-1	Standard	Mina A Salem	Dec 19 2006
1m 2f	2m 1.79	5	9-0	Standard	Cusoon	Feb 24 2007
1m 4f	2m 28.22	4	9-5	Standard	Descartes	Oct 5 2006
1m 5f	2m 42.47	3	9-2	Standard	Raffaas	July 3 2007
2m	3m 20.0	3	9-0	Standard	Yenoora	Aug 8 1992

MUSSELBURGH

Distance	Time	Age	Weight	Going	Horse	Date
5f	57.7 secs	2	8-2	Firm	Arasong	May 16 1994
5f	57.3 secs	3	8-12	Firm	Corunna	Jun 3 2000
7f 30y	1m 28.4	2	8-8	Firm	Sand Bankes	Jun 26 2000
7f 30y	1m 26.3	3	9-5	Firm	Waltzing Wizard	Aug 22 2002
1m	1m 40.3	2	8-12	Gd to Firm	Succession	Sep 26 2004
1m	1m 38.8	6	9-4	Gd to Firm	Sea Storm (IRE)	May 29 2004
1m 1f	1m 50.8	3	9-2	Firm	Short Respite	Aug 22 2002
1m 4f	2m 33.7	3	9-11	Firm	Alexandrine	Jun 26 2000
1m 5f	2m 48.9	6	8-10	Gd to Firm	Tojoneski	July 27 2005
1m 6f	2m 59.2	3	9-7	Firm	Forum Chris	Jly 3 2000
2m	3m 26.6	5	9-6	Gd to Firm	Jack Dawson (IRE)	Jun 1 2002

NEWBURY

Distance	Time	Age	Weight	Going	Horse	Date
5f 34y	59.1 secs	2	8-6	Gd to Firm	Superstar Leo	Jly 22 2000
5f 34y	59.2 secs	3	9-5	Gd to Firm	The Trader (IRE)	Aug 18 2001
6f 8y	1m 11.19	2	8-9	Gd to Firm	Mixed Blessing	Jly 23 2005
6f 8y	69.42 secs	3	8-11	Gd to Firm	Nota Bene	May 13 2005
7f	1m 23.0	2	8-11	Gd to Firm	Haafhd	Aug 15 2003
7f	1m 21.5	3	8-4	Gd to Firm	Three Points	Jly 21 2000
1m	1m 37.5	2	9-1	Gd to firm	Winged Cupid (IRE)	Sep 16 2005
1m	1m 33.59	6	9-0	Firm	Rakti	May 14 2005
1m 1f	1m 49.6	3	8-0	Gd to Firm	Holtye	May 21 1995
1m 2f 6y	2m 1.2	3	8-7	Gd to Firm	Wall Street (USA)	Jly 20 1996
1m 3f 5y	2m 16.5	3	8-9	Gd to Firm	Grandera (IRE)	Sep 22 2001
1m 4f 5y	2m 28.26	4	9-7	Gd to Firm	Azamour (IRE)	Jul 23 2005
1m 5f 61y	2m 44.9	5	10-0	Gd to Firm	Mystic Hill	Jly 20 1996
2m	3m 25.4	8	9-12	Gd to Firm	Moonlight Quest	Jly 19 1996

NEWCASTLE

Distance	Time	Age	Weight	Going	Horse	Date
5f	58.8 secs	2	9-0	Firm	Atlantic Viking (IRE)	Jun 4 1997
5f	58.0 secs	4	9-2	Firm	Princess Oberon	Jly 23 1994
6f	1m 12.18	2	9-0	Gd to Firm	Stepping Up (IRE)	Sep 5 2005
6f	1m 10.6	8	9-5	Firm	Tedburrow	Jly 1 2000
7f	1m 24.2	2	9-0	Gd to Firm	Iscan (IRE)	Aug 31 1998
7f	1m 23.3	4	9-2	Gd to Firm	Quiet Venture	Aug 31 1998
1m	1m 38.9	2	9-0	Gd to Firm	Stowaway	Oct 2 1996
1m	1m 38.9	3	8-12	Firm	Jacamar	Jly 22 1989
1m 3y	1m 37.1	2	8-3	Gd to Firm	Hoh Steamer (IRE)	Aug 31 1998
1m 3y	1m 37.3	3	8-8	Gd to Firm	Its Magic	May 27 1999
1m 1f 9y	2m 3.2	2	8-13	Soft	Response	Oct 30 1993
1m 1f 9y	1m 52.3	3	6-3	Good	Ferniehurst	Jun 23 1936
1m 2f 32y	2m 6.5	4	8-9	Fast	Missionary Ridge	Jly 29 1990
1m 4f 93y	2m 37.3	5	8-12	Firm	Retender	Jun 25 1994
1m 6f 97y	3m 6.4	3	9-6	Gd to Firm	One Off	Aug 6 2003
2m 19y	3m 24.3	4	8-10	Good	Far Cry (IRE)	Jun 26 1999

NEWMARKET (ROWLEY)

Distance	Time	Age	Weight	Going	Horse	Date
5f	58.7 secs	2	8-5	Gd to Firm	Valiant Romeo	Oct 3 2002
5f	56.8 secs	6	9-2	Gd to Firm	Lochsong	Apr 30 1994
6f	69.6 secs	2	8-11	Gd to Firm	Oasis Dream	Oct 3 2002
6f	69.64 secs	4	9-4	Gd to Firm	Asset (IRE)	Apr 19 2007
7f	1m 22.9	2	8-11	Gd to Firm	Grosvenor Square(IRE)	Sep 21 2004
7f	1m 22.2	4	9-5	Gd to Firm	Perfolia	Oct 17 1991
1m	1m 35.7	2	9-0	Gd to Firm	Forward Move (IRE)	Sep 21 2004
1m	1m 34.5	4	9-0	Gd to Firm	Desert Deer	Oct 3 2002
1m 1f	1m 47.2	4	9-5	Firm	Beauchamp Pilot	Oct 5 2002
1m 2f	2m 4.6	2	9-4	Good	Highland Chieftain	Nov 2 1985
1m 2f	2m 1.0	3	8-10	Good	Palace Music	Oct 20 1984
1m 4f	2m 27.1	5	8-12	Gd to Firm	Eastern Breeze	Oct 3 2003
1m 6f	2m 51.59	3	8-7	Good	Art Eyes (USA)	Sep 29 2005
2m	3m 19.5	5	9-5	Gd to Firm	Grey Shot	Oct 4 1997
2m 2f	3m 47.5	3	7-12	Hard	Whiteway	Oct 15 1947

NEWMARKET (JULY)

Distance	Time	Age	Weight	Going	Horse	Date
5f	58.5 secs	2	8-10	Good	Seductress	Jly 10 1990
5f	57.3 secs	6	8-12	Gd to Firm	Rambling Bear	Jan 1 1999
6f	1m 10.6	2	8-10	Gd to Firm	Mujtahid	Jly 11 1990
6f	69.5 secs	3	8-13	Gd to Firm	Stravinsky (USA)	Jly 8 1999
7f	1m 24.1	2	8-11	Good	My Hansel	Aug 27 1999
7f	1m 22.5	3	9-7	Firm	Ho Leng (IRE)	Jly 9 1998
1m	1m 39.0	2	8-11	Good	Traceability	Aug 25 1995
1m	1m 35.5	3	8-6	Gd to Firm	Lovers Knot	Jly 8 1998
1m 110y	1m 44.1	3	8-11	Good	Golden Snake	Apr 15 1999
1m 2f	2m 0.9	4	9-3	Gd to Firm	Elhayq (IRE)	May 1 1999
1m 4f	2m 25.2	4	9-2	Good	Craigsteel	Jly 6 1999
1m 6f 175y	3m 4.2	3	8-5	Good	Arrive	Jly 11 2001
2m 24y	3m 20.2	7	9-10	Good	Yorkshire	Jly 11 2001

NOTTINGHAM

Distance	Time	Age	Weight	Going	Horse	Date
5f 13y	57.9 secs	2	8-9	Firm	Hoh Magic	May 13 1994
5f 13y	57.6 secs	6	9-2	Gd to firm	Catch The Cat (IRE)	May 14 2005
6f 15y	1m 11.4	2	811	Firm	Jameelapi	Aug 8 1983
6f 15y	1m 10.0	4	9-2	Firm	Ajanac	Aug 8 1988
1m 54y	1m 40.8	2	9-0	Gd to Firm	King s Loch	Sep 2 1991
1m 54y	1m 39.6	4	8-2	Gd to Firm	Blake s Treasure	Sep 2 1991
1m 1f 213y	2m 5.6	2	9-0	Firm	Al Salite	Oct 28 1985
1m 1f 213y	2m 2.3	2	9-0	Firm	Ayaabi	Jly 21 1984
1m 6f 15y	2m 57.8	3	8-10	Firm	Buster Jo	Oct 1 1985
2m 9y	3m 24.0	5	7-7	Firm	Fet	Oct 5 2036
2m 2f 18y	3m 55.1	9	9-10	Gd to Firm	Pearl Run	May 1 1990

PONTEFRACT

Distance	Time	Age	Weight	Going	Horse	Date
5f	61.1 secs	2	9-0	Firm	Golden Bounty	Sep 20 2001
5f	60.8 secs	4	8-9	Firm	Blue Maeve	Sep 29 2004
6f	1m 14.0	2	9-3	Firm	Fawzi	Sep 6 1983
6f	1m 12.6	3	7-13	Firm	Merry One	Aug 29 1970
1m 4y	1m 42.8	2	9-13	Firm	Star Spray	Sep 6 1983
1m 4y	1m 42.8	2	9-0	Firm	Alasil (USA)	Sep 26 2002
1m 4y	1m 40.6	4	9-10	Gd to Firm	Island Light	Apr 13 2002
1m 2f 6y	2m 10.1	2	9-0	Firm	Shanty Star	Oct 7 2002
1m 2f 6y	2m 8.2	4	7-8	Hard	Happy Hector	Jly 9 1979
1m 2f 6y	2m 8.2	3	7-13	Hard	Tom Noddy	Aug 21 1972
1m 4f 8y	2m 33.72	3	8-7	Firm	Ajaan	Aug 8 2007
2m 1f 22y	3m 40.67	4	8-7	Gd to Firm	Paradise Flight	June 6 2005
2m 1f 216y	3m 51.1	3	8-8	Firm	Kudz	Sep 9 1986
2m 5f 122y	4m 47.8	4	8-4	Firm	Physical	May 14 1984

REDCAR

Distance	Time	Age	Weight	Going	Horse	Date
5f	56.9 secs	2	9-0	Firm	Mister Joel	Oct 24 1995
5f	56.01 secs	10	9-3	Firm	Henry Hall	Sep 20 2006
6f	68.8 secs	2	8-3	Gd to Firm	Obe Gold	Oct 2 2004
6f	68.6 secs	3	9-2	Gd to Firm	Sizzling Saga	Jun 21 1991
7f	1m 21.28	2	9-3	Firm	Karoo Blue	Sep 20 2006
7f	1m 21.0	3	9-1	Firm	Empty Quarter	Oct 3 1995
1m	1m 34.37	2	9-0	Firm	Mastership	Sep 20 2006
1m	1m 32.42	4	10-0	Firm	Nanton	Sep 20 2006
1m 1f	1m 52.4	2	9-0	Firm	Spear (IRE)	Sep 13 2004
1m 1f	1m 48.5	5	8-12	Firm	Mellottie	Jly 25 1990
1m 2f	2m 10.1	2	8-11	Good	Adding	Nov 10 1989
1m 2f	2m 1.4	5	9-2	Firm	Eradicate	May 28 1990
1m 3f	2m 17.2	3	8-9	Firm	Photo Call	Aug 7 1990
1m 5f 135y	2m 54.7	6	9-10	Firm	Brodessa	Jun 20 1992
1m 6f 19y	2m 59.81	4	9-1	Gd to Firm	Esprit De Corps	Sep 11 2006
2m 4y	3m 24.9	3	9-3	Gd to Firm	Subsonic	Oct 8 1991
2m 3f	4m 10.1	5	7-4	Gd to Firm	Seldom In	Aug 9 1991

RIPON

Distance	Time	Age	Weight	Going	Horse	Date
5f	57.8 secs	2	8-8	Firm	Super Rocky	Jly 5 1991
5f	57.6 secs	5	8-5	Good	Broadstairs Beauty	May 21 1995
6f	1m 10.4	2	9-2	Good	Cumbrian Venture	Aug 17 2002
6f	69.8 secs	4	9-8	Gd to Firm	Tadeo	Aug 16 1997
6f	69.8 secs	5	7-10	Firm	Quoit	Jly 23 1966
1m	1m 39.79	2	8-6	Good	Top Jaro (FR)	Sep 24 2005
1m	1m 36.62	4	8-11	Gd to Firm	Granston (IRE)	Aug 29 2005
1m 1f 170y	1m 59.12	5	8-9	Gd to Firm	Wahoo Sam (USA)	Aug 30 2005
1m 2f	2m 2.6	3	9-4	Firm	Swift Sword	Jly 20 1990
1m 4f 10y	2m 32.06	4	8-8	Good	Hearthstead Wings	Apr 29 2006
2m	3m 27.07	5	9-12	Gd to Firm	Greenwich Meantime	Aug 30 2005

SALISBURY

Distance	Time	Age	Weight	Going	Horse	Date
5f	59.3 secs	2	9-0	Gd to Firm	Ajigolo	May 12 2005
5f	59.3 secs	2	9-0	Gd to Firm	Ajigolo	May 12 2005
6f	1m 12.1	2	8-0	Gd to Firm	Parisian Lady (IRE)	Jun 10 1997
6f	1m 11.3	3	8-1	Firm	Bentong (IRE)	May 7 2006
6f 212y	1m 25.9	2	9-0	Firm	More Royal (USA)	Jun 29 1995
6f 212y	1m 24.9	3	9-7	Firm	High Summer (USA)	Sep 5 1996
1m	1m 40.4	2	8-13	Firm	Choir Master (USA)	Sep 17 2002
1m	1m 38.29	3	8-7	Gd to Firm	Layman (USA)	Aug 11 2005
1m 1f 198y	2m 4.9	3	8-6	Gd to Firm	Zante	Aug 12 1998
1m 4f	2m 31.6	3	9-5	Gd to Firm	Arrive	Jun 27 2001
1m 6f 15y	2m 59.4	3	8-6	Gd to Firm	Tabareeh	Sep 2 1999

SANDOWN

Distance	Time	Age	Weight	Going	Horse	Date
5f 6y	59.4 secs	2	9-3	Firm	Times Time	Jly 22 1982
5f 6y	58.8 secs	6	8-9	Gd to Firm	Palacegate Touch	Sep 17 1996
7f 16y	1m 26.56	2	9-0	Gd to Firm	Raven's Pass (USA)	Sep 1 2007
7f 16y	1m 26.3	3	9-0	Firm	Mawsuff	Jun 14 1983
1m 14y	1m 41.1	2	8-11	Fast	Reference Point	Sep 23 1986
1m 14y	1m 39.0	3	8-8	Firm	Linda s Fantasy	Aug 19 1983
1m 1f	1m 54.6	2	8-8	Gd to Firm	French Pretender	Sep 20 1988
1m 1f	1m 52.4	7	9-3	Gd to Firm	Bourgainville	Aug 11 2005
1m 2f 7y	2m 2.1	4	8-11	Firm	Kalaglow	May 31 1982
1m 3f 91y	2m 21.6	4	8-3	Fast	Aylesfield	Jly 7 1984
1m 6f	2m 56.9	4	8-7	Gd to Firm	Lady Rosanna	Jly 19 1989
2m 78y	3m 29.9	6	9-2	Firm	Sadeem	May 29 1989

SOUTHWELL (TURF)

Distance	Time	Age	Weight	Going	Horse	Date
6f	1m 15.03	2	9-3	Good	Trepa	Sep 6 2006
6f	1m 13.48	4	8-10	Good	Paris Bell	Sep 6 2006
7f	1m 27.56	2	9-7	Good	Hart Of Gold	Sep 6 2006
7f	1m 25.95	3	9-0	Good	Aeroplane	Sep 6 2006
1m 2f	2m 7.470	3	8-11	Good	Desert Authority(USA)	Sep 6 2006
1m 3f	2m 20.13	4	9-12	Good	Sanchi	Sep 6 2006
1m 4f	2m 34.4	5	9-3	Gd to Firm	Corn Lily	Aug 10 1991
2m	3m 34.1	5	9-1	Gd to Firm	Triplicate	Sep 20 1991

SOUTHWELL (A.W)

Distance	Time	Age	Weight	Going	Horse	Date
5f	58.89 secs	2	8-6	Standard	Egyptian Lord	Dec 15 2005
5f	57.35 secs	5	9-2	Std to Fast	Fyodor (IRE)	Jan 1 2006
6f	1m 14.00	2	8-5	Standard	Panalo	Nov 8 1989
6f	1m 13.50	4	10-02	Standard	Saladan Knight	Dec 30 1989
7f	1m 27.10	2	8-2	Standard	Mystic Crystal	Nov 20 1990
7f	1m 26.80	5	8-4	Standard	Amenable	Dec 13 1990
1m	1m 38.00	2	8-9	Standard	Alpha Rascal	Nov 13 1990
1m	1m 38.00	2	8-10	Standard	Andrew s First	Dec 30 1989
1m	1m 37.25	3	8-6	Standard	Valira	Nov 3 1990
1m 3f	2m 21.50	4	9-7	Standard	Tempering	Dec 5 1990
1m 4f	2m 33.90	4	9-12	Standard	Fast Chick	Nov 8 1989
1m 6f	3m 1.60	3	7-8	Standard	Erevnon	Dec 29 1990
2m	3m 37.60	9	8-12	Standard	Old Hubert	Dec 5 1990

THIRSK

Distance	Time	Age	Weight	Going	Horse	Date
5f	57.2 secs	2	9-7	Gd to Firm	Proud Boast	Aug 5 2000
5f	56.9 secs	5	9-6	Firm	Charlie Parkes	April 11 2003
6f	69.2 secs	2	9-6	Gd to Firm	Westcourt Magic	Aug 25 1995
6f	68.8 secs	6	9-4	Firm	Johayro	Jly 23 1999
7f	1m 23.7	2	8-9	Firm	Courting	Jly 23 1999
7f	1m 22.8	4	8-5	Firm	Silver Haze	May 21 1988
1m	1m 37.9	2	9-0	Firm	Sunday Symphony	Sep 4 2004
1m	1m 34.8	4	8-13	Firm	Yearsley	May 5 1990
1m 4f	2m 29.9	5	9-12	Firm	Gallery God	Jun 4 2001
2m	3m 22.3	3	8-11	Firm	Tomaschek	Jul 17 1981

WARWICK

Distance	Time	Age	Weight	Going	Horse	Date
5f	58.4 secs	2	9-7	Gd to Firm	Prenonamoss	Oct 9 1990
5f	57.7 secs	4	9-6	Gd to Firm	Little Edward	Jly 7 2002
5f 110y	63.6 secs	5	8-6	Gd to Firm	Dizzy In The Head	Jun 27 2004
6f	1m 11.22	2	9-3	Gd to Firm	Hurricane Hymnbook	Sep 15 2007
6f	1m 10.94	6	9-8	Good	Stamford Blue	July 12 2007
7f 26y	1m 22.9	2	9-0	Firm	Country Rambler(USA)	Jun 20 2004
7f 26y	1m 20.7	4	8-8	Good	Etlaala	Apr 17 2006
1m 22y	1m 37.1	3	8-11	Firm	Orinocovsky (IRE)	Jun 26 2002
1m 2f 188y	2m 16.2	6	7-12	Gd to Firm	Scented Air	Apr 21 2003
1m 4f 134y	2m 39.5	3	8-13	Gd to Firm	Maimana (IRE)	Jun 22 2002
1m 6f 135y	3m 7.5	3	9-7	Gd to Firm	Burma Baby (USA)	Jly 2 1999
2m 39y	3m 27.9	3	8-1	Firm	Decoy	Jun 26 2002

WINDSOR

Distance	Time	Age	Weight	Going	Horse	Date
5f 10y	58.75 secs	2	8-12	Gd to Firm	Hoh Mike (IRE)	May 15 2006
5f 10y	58.3 secs	5	7-10	Gd to Firm	Beyond The Clouds	Jun 2 2001
6f	1m 10.5	2	9-5	Gd to Firm	Cubism (USA)	Aug 17 1998
6f	1m 10.26	5	9-1	Gd to Firm	Baltic King	May 23 2005
1m 67y	1m 44.38	2	9-0	Good	Genre	Oct 3 2005
1m 67y	1m 40.27	4	9-3	Gd to Firm	Librettist (USA)	Jul 1 2006
1m 2f 7y	2m 3.0	2	9-1	Firm	Moomba Masquerade	May 19 1990
1m 3f 135y	2m 21.5	3	9-2	Firm	Double Florin	May 19 1980

WOLVERHAMPTON (A.W.)

Distance	Time	Age	Weight	Going	Horse	Date
5f 20y	61.13 sec	2	8-8	Std to Fast	Yungaburra (IRE)	Nov 8 2006
5f 20y	60.56 sec	3	8-10	Standard	King Orchisios (IRE)	Oct 29 2006
5f 216y	1m 12.61	2	9-0	Std to Fast	Prime Defender	Nov 8 2006
5f 216y	1m 13.32	5	8-12	Standard	Desert Opal	Sep 17 2005
7f 32y	1m 27.70	2	9-5	Standard	Billy Dane	Aug 14 2006
7f 32y	1m 26.86	6	9-3	Standard	Border Music	Mar 10 2007
1m 141y	1m 48.08	2	8-9	Std to Fast	Worldly	Aug 30 2006
1m 141y	1m 46.71	4	8-12	Standard	Cimyla	Nov 11 2005
1m 1f 103y	2m 0.76	2	9-0	Standard	Mr Excel (IRE)	Nov 14 2005
1m 1f 103y	1m 57.34	4	8-13	Standard	Bahar Shumaal (IRE)	Aug 31 2006
1m 4f 50y	2m 35.71	3	9-2	Std to Fast	Steppe Dancer (IRE)	Aug 30 2006
1m 5f 194y	2m 59.85	6	9-12	Std to Fast	Valance (IRE)	Aug 30 2006
2m 119y	3m 35.85	5	8-11	Std to Fast	Market Watcher (USA)	Nov 21 2006

YARMOUTH

Distance	Time	Age	Weight	Going	Horse	Date
5f 43y	60.4 secs	2	8-6	Gd to Firm	Ebba	Jly 26 1999
5f 43y	59.8 secs	4	8-13	Gd to Firm	Roxanne Mill	Aug 25 2002
6f 3y	1m 10.4	2	9-0	Fast	Lanchester	Aug 15 1988
6f 3y	69.9 secs	4	8-9	Firm	Malhub (USA)	Jun 13 2002
7f 3y	1m 22.2	2	9-0	Gd to Firm	Warrshan	Sep 14 1988
7f 3y	1m 22.12	4	9-4	Gd to Firm	Glenbuck (IRE)	Apr 26 2007
1m 3y	1m 36.3	2	8-2	Gd to Firm	Outrun	Sep 15 1988
1m 3y	1m 33.9	3	8-8	Firm	Bonne Etoile	Jun 27 1995
1m 2f 21y	2m 2.83	3	8-8	Firm	Reunite (IRE)	Jul 18 2006
1m 3f 101y	2m 23.1	3	8-9	Firm	Rahil	Jly 1 1993
1m 6f 17y	2m 57.8	3	8-2	Gd to Firm	Barakat	Jly 24 1990
2m	3m 26.7	4	8-2	Gd to Firm	Alhesn (USA)	Jly 26 1999
2m 2f 51y	3m 56.8	4	9-10	Firm	Provence	Sep 19 1991

YORK

Distance	Time	Age	Weight	Going	Horse	Date
5f	57.3 secs	2	7-8	Gd to Firm	Lyric Fantasy	Aug 20 1992
5f	56.1 secs	3	9-3	Gd to Firm	Dayjur	Aug 23 1990
6f	69.5 secs	2	9-0	Gd to Firm	Indiscreet (CAN)	Aug 22 1996
6f	68.58 secs	7	9-4	Firm	Cape Of Good Hope	Jun 16 2005
7f	1m 23.29	2	8-10	Good	Vital Equine (IRE)	Sep 9 2006
7f	1m 21.98	5	9-6	Good	Iffraaj	Sep 9 2006
1m	1m 39.20	2	8-1	Gd to Firm	Missoula (IRE)	Aug 31 2005
1m	1m 36.35	3	9-1	Gd to Firm	Mostashaar (FR)	Jun 16 2005
1m 208y	1m 46.76	5	9-8	Gd to Firm	Echo Of Light	Sep 5 2007
1m 2f 88y	2m 6.09	4	8-11	Gd to Firm	Imperial Stride	Jun 17 2005
1m 4f	2m 26.28	6	8-9	Firm	Bandari (IRE)	Jun 18 2005
1m 5f 194y	2m 51.8	3	8-7	Gd to Firm	Tuning	Aug 19 1998
1m 7f 195y	3m 18.4	3	8-0	Gd to Firm	Dam Busters	Aug 16 1988

Raceform Flat speed figures 2007

(Best time performances achieved 1st January - 31st December 2007 (min rating 105)

THREE YEAR-OLDS AND UPWARDS - Turf

A Mothers Love 107 (12f,Bev,GS,Jun 21)
Aahayson 109 (6f,Wdr,S,Jun 30)
Aajel 108 (12f,Pon,F,Aug 8)
Abandon 105 (10f,Pon,GF,May 2)
Abraham Lincoln 108 (6f,Asc,G,Sep 30)
Absolutelyfabulous 108 (6f,Leo,G,Jun 6)
Abstract Folly 108 (14f,Red,F,Aug 11)
Abunai 105 (6f,Nmk,G,Aug 18)
Acapulco 112 (12f,Yor,G,Aug 21)
Ace 117 (9f,Nad,G,Feb 1)
Ace Of Hearts 110 (8f,Rip,GF,Aug 27)
Acheekyone 105 (8f,Nby,GF,Apr 21)
Acropolis 106 (12f,Ham,G,May 18)
Adagio 110 (8f,Nmk,GF,May 5)
Adantino 109 (6f,Sal,GF,May 24)
Admiral s Cruise 110 (12f,Asc,GS,Jun 23)
Admiralofthefleet 112 (10½f,Chs,G,May 11)
Admire Moon 117 (9f,Nad,G,Mar 31)
Advanced 112 (6f,Ayr,GS,Sep 22)
Advice 106 (9f,Nad,G,Feb 9)
Aegean Dancer 108 (5f,Mus,G,Jun 9)
Aegean Prince 107 (8f,San,G,Apr 27)
Afaf 105 (8f,Nad,G,Feb 8)
Afrad 107 (20f,Asc,G,Jun 19)
Aggravation 112 (8f,Nmk,GF,May 25)
Air Bag 110 (8f,Dea,S,Aug 26)
Airmail Special 108 (12f,Lon,GS,Jly 14)
Ajaan 110 (12f,Pon,F,Aug 8)
Ajhar 108 (10f,Nby,S,Oct 27)
Ajigolo 105 (6f,Goo,GF,Sep 16)
Akarem 108 (12f,Goo,G,Jun 1)
Akua Ba 110 (8f,Cur,G,Sep 2)
Al Eile 107 (18f,Nmk,GS,Oct 20)
Al Khaleej 110 (8f,Asc,G,Jly 28)
Al Maali 105 (7½f,Nad,G,Jan 25)
Al Qasi 113 (6f,Asc,GS,Jly 27)
Al Shemali 108 (8f,Nmk,GF,May 5)
Alaghiraar 109 (10f,Lei,S,Jly 19)
Alambic 105 (17f,Pon,GF,Jun 11)
Albany Hall 110 (8f,Msn,G,Jly 22)
Aleron 106 (14f,Cat,GF,Apr 4)
Alexander Of Hales 111 (12f,Cur,SH,Jly 1)
Alexander Tango 111 (7f,Cur,G,May 7)
Alexandra Rose 110 (8f,Nad,G,Feb 8)
Alfie Flits 110 (12f,Goo,G,Jun 1)
Aliceinwonderland 111 (7f,Cur,G,May 7)
All Is Vanity 107 (8f,Cha,GS,Jun 3)
All Ivory 107 (8f,Nad,GF,Feb 1)
All My Loving 110 (12f,Cur,SH,Jly 15)
All The Good 109 (14f,Mus,G,Jun 2)
Allegretto 118 (15½f,Lon,G,Oct 28)
Allesandro 105 (12f,Cur,S,Jun 29)
Alleviate 108 (12f,Bev,GS,Jun 21)
Almaram 105 (6f,Nad,G,Feb 9)
Almuraad 108 (7½f,Nad,G,Jan 18)
Alone He Stands 107 (6f,Cur,Y,Oct 21)
Alpacco 115 (8f,Nad,GF,Feb 1)
Alpes Maritimes 105 (8f,Nmk,G,Jun 22)
Alrida 109 (14f,Mus,GF,Apr 8)
Always The Groom 107 (14f,Cur,GF,Sep 15)
Amadeus Wolf 115 (6f,Yor,G,May 16)
Amandus 107 (8f,Nad,GF,Feb 1)
Amarna 109 (8f,San,GF,Sep 14)
Amonita 107 (9f,Leo,GF,Sep 8)
Ampelio 105 (12f,Nad,G,Jan 25)
Amwell Brave 106 (12f,Yor,G,May 18)
Anabaa s Creation 110 (12f,Lon,S,Oct 21)
Ancient Culture 106 (12f,Nmk,F,Aug 11)
Angaric 107 (7f,Mus,GF,Apr 8)
Angel Sprints 107 (6f,Lei,S,May 28)
Angelonmyshoulder 107 (7f,Cur,G,May 7)
Angus Newz 108 (5f,Yar,G,Sep 18)
Anna Pavlova 116 (15½f,Lon,G,Oct 28)
Anna s Rock 107 (9f,Leo,S,Jly 18)
Annemasse 112 (8f,Hay,GF,Aug 11)
Another Jayjay 109 (10f,Leo,Y,Jly 28)
Ansells Pride 105 (8f,Mus,G,Nov 9)
Anton Chekhov 105 (12½f,Dea,S,Aug 26)
Apex 108 (8f,Bat,GF,May 21)
Appalachian Trail 111 (6f,Ncs,HY,Jun 30)
Appel Au Maitre 107 (12f,Lon,S,Oct 21)
Apply Dapply 106 (7f,Fol,G,Apr 3)
Aqaleem 109 (11½f,Lin,GS,May 12)
Aqraan 106 (9f,Cur,G,Sep 2)
Arabian Gleam 113 (7f,Don,GF,Sep 15)
Arabian Gulf 110 (12f,Chs,G,May 10)
Arabian Prince 105 (9f,Nad,G,Feb 9)
Araschan 105 (10f,Cur,GF,Jun 9)
Arch Rebel 114 (12f,Lon,S,Oct 21)
Arch Swing 113 (8f,Nmk,GF,May 6)
Archipenko 110 (8f,Lon,G,Sep 9)
Ardbrae Lady 107 (7f,Cur,G,May 7)
Arenti 109 (6f,Nad,G,Feb 9)
Areyoutalkingtome 110 (7f,Goo,GF,Sep 4)
Arminius 105 (7½f,Nad,G,Feb 8)
Army Of Angels 110 (8f,Wdr,GS,May 14)
Arqaam 110 (10½f,Yor,G,Oct 12)
Artimino 110 (8f,Nmk,GF,Jly 13)
Artless 107 (14f,Mus,G,Jly 9)
Ascot Family 106 (6f,Dea,S,Aug 26)
Ashdown Express 107 (6f,Hay,G,May 12)
Ashkazar 107 (12f,Lon,GS,Jly 14)
Asiatic Boy 111 (8f,Goo,G,Aug 1)
Ask 113 (12f,Asc,GS,Sep 30)
Asperity 108 (8f,Cha,G,Jun 10)
Assertive 114 (6f,Asc,G,Sep 30)
Asset 114 (6f,Nmk,GF,Jly 13)
Astronomer Royal 113 (8f,Lon,G,May 13)
Athanor 108 (8f,Dea,G,Aug 12)
Athlumney Lad 116 (16f,Leo,GF,Nov 4)
Atlantic Air 106 (8f,Nad,G,Feb 22)
Atlantic Coast 110 (16f,Nby,G,Aug 17)
Attercliffe 108 (12f,Cur,GY,Oct 21)
Audience 109 (8f,Goo,GF,Jun 9)
Augustine 106 (10f,Bev,GF,Apr 18)
Authorized 116 (10f,San,GS,Jly 7)
Axxos 109 (12f,Lon,GS,Jly 14)
Azarole 110 (8f,Nad,G,Feb 9)

Babodana 107 (8f,Wdr,S,Jun 30)
Baby Blue Eyes 113 (9f,Cur,G,Sep 2)
Back In The Red 107 (5f,Bat,GF,Aug 24)
Baddam 107 (22f,Asc,S,Jun 23)
Bahamian Ballet 107 (5f,Cat,GS,Jly 25)
Bahamian Pirate 110 (6f,Asc,S,May 12)
Baharah 107 (6f,Nmk,G,Nov 2)
Bahia Breeze 113 (8f,San,G,Apr 28)
Bahiano 109 (7f,Nmk,G,Nov 3)
Bailieborough 111 (10f,Red,GF,May 28)
Baizically 108 (12f,Bat,F,Apr 24)
Bajan Parkes 107 (8f,Rip,GF,Jun 6)
Balakan 108 (10f,Cur,GF,May 7)
Balakiref 109 (6f,Lei,S,May 28)
Baldoria 105 (12½f,Lon,S,Oct 6)
Balkan Knight 112 (16½f,San,GS,May 29)
Ballinteni 106 (10f,Pon,GS,Jun 24)
Ballroom Dancer 110 (8f,San,G,Aug 2)
Balthazaar s Gift 115 (6f,Asc,GS,Jly 27)
Baltic King 109 (6f,Asc,GS,Jly 27)
Balyan 107 (13f,Ham,GF,May 6)
Bandama 112 (12f,Nmk,GF,Oct 6)
Bankable 106 (8f,Asc,GS,Sep 28)
Banknote 108 (8f,Asc,G,Jly 14)
Barbirolli 106 (9f,Ham,GS,Sep 24)
Barney McGrew 107 (6f,Nmk,GS,Jun 23)
Baron De L 109 (10f,Cur,GF,Sep 15)
Baron s Pit 106 (6f,Goo,GF,Sep 16)
Baroness Richter 105 (12f,Asc,GF,Jun 21)
Barons Spy 105 (6f,War,GF,Sep 6)
Barshiba 107 (8f,Asc,GF,Jun 20)
Basaata 109 (8f,Goo,GF,Aug 4)
Battle Paint 107 (8f,Lon,G,Apr 15)
Bauer 109 (12f,Pon,F,Aug 8)
Bawaader 106 (8f,Cur,G,Sep 2)
Bazart 106 (10½f,Chs,GF,May 9)
Beatrix Kiddo 111 (10f,Dea,S,Aug 19)
Beauty Is Truth 115 (5f,Cha,GS,Jun 3)
Beaver Patrol 108 (6f,Goo,GF,Aug 4)
Beckermet 112 (6f,Nmk,S,Aug 25)
Bee Eater 114 (6f,Nmk,G,Jly 21)
Before You Go 105 (12f,Asc,GS,Sep 30)
Bel Cantor 115 (6f,Pon,GS,Jly 29)
Believe Me 111 (10f,Lon,VS,May 20)
Bellamy Cay 105 (12f,Nad,G,Mar 31)
Benandonner 110 (10f,Eps,GF,Apr 25)
Benbaun 114 (5f,Lon,GS,Oct 7)
Benedetti 113 (9f,Nad,G,Feb 22)
Bennie Blue 108 (12f,Nad,G,Feb 15)
Bentley Biscuit 112 (6f,Nmk,GF,Jly 13)
Bentong 106 (7f,Nmk,GF,Jly 13)
Benwilt Breeze 111 (6f,Ayr,GS,Sep 22)
Berlioz 106 (8f,Nad,GF,Feb 1)
Bertoliver 105 (5f,Wdr,G,May 21)
Bertranicus 111 (7f,Lon,G,Sep 9)
Best Alibi 110 (10½f,Yor,G,Oct 12)
Best Name 105 (9f,Nad,G,Mar 31)
Best Prospect 109 (10f,Ayr,GS,Sep 20)
Bicoastal 108 (8f,San,GF,Sep 1)
Bid For Glory 110 (8f,Lin,GF,Jun 13)
Bid For Gold 110 (6f,Pon,GS,Jly 29)
Bienheureux 106 (12f,Bri,G,Jly 17)
Big Robert 107 (10f,Cha,GS,Jly 8)
Bijou Dan 107 (9f,Ayr,GS,May 23)
Billy Dane 105 (8f,Hay,GF,May 26)
Binanti 109 (7f,Asc,GS,Jun 22)
Biniou 108 (5f,Not,G,Aug 14)
Binocular 107 (10f,Cha,GS,Jly 8)
Black Cat Crossing 108 (8f,Cur,GF,Sep 16)
Black Charmer 111 (8f,Yor,GS,May 17)
Black Rock 105 (8f,Nby,GF,Apr 21)
Blackat Blackitten 109 (8f,Nmk,G,Oct 4)
Blazing Heights 105 (5f,Yor,S,Jly 13)
Blue Bajan 112 (10f,Eps,GF,Apr 25)
Blue Echo 107 (6f,Chs,GF,Sep 15)
Blue Java 105 (7f,Goo,GF,Jun 15)
Blue Ksar 114 (8f,Goo,G,Aug 25)
Blue Rocket 107 (5f,Ham,G,Sep 23)
Blue Spinnaker 111 (10f,Red,GF,May 28)
Blue Tomato 110 (6f,Sal,GF,May 24)
Bluebok 110 (5f,Chs,GF,Sep 1)
Blues In The Night 107 (8f,Hay,GF,Sep 12)
Blushing King 110 (10f,Lon,HY,Apr 1)
Blythe Knight 116 (8f,Yor,GS,May 17)
Bo McGinty 105 (5f,Bev,GF,May 26)
Bogside Theatre 106 (12f,Pon,F,Aug 8)
Bold Abbott 106 (8f,San,G,Aug 2)
Bold Bibi 111 (9f,Cur,G,Sep 2)
Bold Marc 108 (8f,Crl,GS,Jun 27)
Bollin Derek 106 (16f,Rip,GF,Apr 28)
Bollin Felix 108 (12f,Pon,S,Jly 2)
Bolodenka 112 (8f,Rip,GF,Aug 27)
Bon Nuit 109 (10f,Cur,GF,May 7)
Bond Boy 106 (5f,Bev,HY,Jly 7)
Bond City 110 (5f,Nmk,GF,May 6)
Bonecrusher 106 (10f,Nad,G,Jan 25)
Bonus 107 (6½f,Nad,G,Feb 15)
Book Of Music 109 (10f,Nad,G,Feb 8)
Border Music 107 (5f,Asc,GF,Jly 14)
Borderlescott 113 (6f,Nmk,GF,Jly 13)
Boris De Deauville 115 (10f,Lon,HY,Apr 1)
Boscobel 110 (11f,Ham,G,May 18)
Boston Lodge 105 (8f,Nad,G,Feb 1)
Bouchard 106 (12f,Cur,GF,Sep 16)
Boundless Prospect 106 (8f,Red,G,Oct 6)
Brave Tin Soldier 110 (10f,Leo,GF,Sep 8)
Brides Maid 112 (8f,Msn,G,Jly 22)
Brigadore 107 (6f,Pon,G,Apr 10)
Bright Mind 108 (10f,Don,GF,Aug 17)
Brisant 117 (15½f,Lon,G,Oct 28)
Brisk Breeze 111 (12f,Asc,GS,Sep 28)
Brooklyn Boy 106 (10½f,Cha,GS,Jun 3)
Broomielaw 111 (10f,Don,GF,Aug 17)
Brut 105 (5f,Ham,GS,Sep 24)
Buachaill Dona 105 (5f,Yor,G,Aug 21)
Buccellati 109 (12f,Asc,GS,Oct 13)
Bucephalus 106 (9f,Leo,GF,Nov 3)
Bulwark 111 (16½f,San,GS,May 29)
Burning Incense 106 (6f,Asc,GS,Jun 23)
Bustan 109 (7f,Thi,F,Apr 21)
Bygone Days 111 (7f,Goo,GF,Sep 4)

Cabinet 105 (10f,San,S,Jly 26)
Cactus Rose 108 (8f,San,G,Aug 31)
Calabaza 106 (5f,War,GF,Sep 15)
Caldra 113 (8f,Nmk,G,Nov 3)
Callow Lake 107 (12f,Cur,GF,May 27)
Camps Bay 109 (12f,Goo,G,Aug 1)
Camrose 110 (12f,Don,GF,Sep 15)
Canadian Danehill 109 (5f,Yar,G,Sep 18)
Candidato Roy 109 (7f,Asc,GS,Sep 29)
Candle 107 (12f,Goo,S,Oct 4)
Candy Critic 110 (12f,Nad,G,Feb 15)
Capable Guest 113 (8f,San,G,Apr 28)
Cape 105 (6f,Fol,G,Jun 17)
Cape Of Luck 105 (7f,Fol,G,Jun 2)
Cape Royal 110 (5f,Lei,G,Sep 24)
Cape Secret 110 (16f,Nmk,F,Aug 11)
Capitalise 109 (18f,Pon,G,Oct 22)
Capricorn Run 107 (6f,Nmk,F,Sep 22)
Captain Jacksparra 108 (7f,Lin,GF,Sep 3)
Captain Marvelous 106 (7f,Nmk,GS,Oct 20)
Caracciola 109 (18f,Nmk,GS,Oct 20)
Caradak 109 (8f,Nmk,G,Nov 3)
Caravel 107 (9f,Goo,G,Aug 26)
Caribbean Coral 109 (5f,Chs,G,May 10)
Carnbridge 106 (12f,Cur,GF,Apr 15)
Carnivore 109 (7f,Mus,GS,Jun 25)
Cartimandua 108 (6f,Hay,GF,Jun 9)
Cashel Mead 108 (5f,San,S,Jly 6)
Cassandra Jade 106 (7f,Cur,SH,Aug 12)
Cassiara 106 (7½f,Bev,HY,Jly 17)
Cast In Gold 105 (7f,Nby,GF,Apr 21)
Castano 108 (5f,Fol,S,Jun 29)
Castara Bay 105 (10f,Lei,F,Sep 17)
Castle Howard 105 (11½f,Wdr,S,Jun 30)
Castlereagh 107 (10½f,Cha,GS,Jun 3)
Catherines Cafe 105 (8f,Crl,GS,Jun 18)
Caustic Wit 109 (5f,Lin,G,Jun 23)
Cavendish 107 (11f,War,GS,Jun 28)
Celestial Halo 111 (14½f,Don,GF,Sep 15)
Celtic Change 106 (8f,Nmk,G,Jun 22)
Celtic Dane 107 (8f,Cur,Y,Sep 30)
Celtic Mill 109 (6½f,Nad,G,Jan 25)
Celtic Spirit 107 (10f,Sal,GS,Jun 27)
Celtic Sultan 112 (7f,Nmk,GF,Oct 6)
Central Force 106 (9f,San,G,Aug 2)
Cesare 115 (8f,Asc,G,Jly 14)
Cesc 111 (7f,Goo,G,Aug 2)
Champain Sands 107 (7f,Mus,G,Sep 30)
Champery 107 (10f,San,GS,Jly 7)
Championship Point 111 (10f,Cur,GF,May 7)
Champs Elysees 113 (12½f,Dea,S,Aug 26)
Chantaco 105 (10f,Rip,GF,Apr 19)
Chantilly Tiffany 106 (8f,San,GF,Sep 1)
Chapelizod 106 (7f,Mus,G,Sep 30)
Chariots Of Fire 110 (7f,Cur,G,May 7)
Charles Darwin 110 (6f,Nmk,GS,May 27)
Charlie Cool 116 (9f,Nad,G,Jan 18)
Charlie Tokyo 111 (10f,Eps,GF,Apr 25)
Charlotte Vale 107 (14f,Cat,GF,Apr 4)
Charminamix 112 (9f,Leo,GF,Sep 8)
Chatila 108 (10f,Yar,G,Sep 19)
Chatshow 108 (5f,War,GF,Apr 17)
Checkit 108 (6½f,Nad,G,Feb 15)
Cheyenne Star 110 (8f,Leo,G,Jun 6)
Chichi Creasy 108 (8f,Lon,G,Apr 15)
Chill 109 (10f,Dea,S,Aug 19)
China Cherub 111 (6f,Nmk,G,Jly 21)
Chinandega 108 (8f,Dea,S,Aug 26)
Chjimes 105 (6f,Goo,S,Oct 14)
Choristar 109 (10f,Bev,GF,Apr 18)
Choysia 105 (6f,Thi,GF,May 12)
Cimyla 111 (9f,Nad,G,Jan 18)
Circuit Dancer 106 (5f,Chs,GF,Sep 15)
City Of New York 106 (10f,Leo,G,Apr 7)
City Of Tribes 109 (5f,Chs,G,May 11)
Claire Et Bleu 110 (12f,Lon,GS,Jly 14)
Classic Punch 110 (12f,Nmk,S,Jun 30)
Classical Swing 107 (7f,Leo,GF,Nov 3)
Cliche 105 (8f,San,GS,Jly 7)
Closetocrazy 112 (9f,Leo,GF,Sep 8)
Cnoc Moy 106 (8f,San,G,Jly 19)
Cockney Rebel 117 (8f,Nmk,GF,May 5)
Coconut Moon 112 (5f,Chs,GF,Sep 1)
Coeur Courageux 106 (6f,Pon,G,Jly 10)
Coeur De Lionne 107 (11f,Goo,GF,Aug 4)
Collateral Damage 110 (10f,Red,GF,May 28)
Collette s Choice 107 (14f,Mus,GF,Aug 30)
Colloquial 108 (16f,Hay,GF,Jun 9)
Colorado Rapid 115 (8f,San,GS,Jly 7)
Colorus 106 (5f,Thi,G,May 19)
Come Out Fighting 107 (6f,Asc,S,May 12)
Commando Scott 114 (6f,Nmk,GS,May 27)
Compton Classic 106 (6f,Ayr,GS,Aug 11)
Compton s Eleven 108 (6½f,Nad,G,Feb 15)
Conceal 109 (6f,Nad,G,Feb 9)
Conclave 107 (8f,Nav,YS,Jun 15)
Confuchias 112 (6f,Ncs,HY,Jun 30)
Conquest 108 (5f,Asc,GF,Jun 19)
Contemplation 106 (10f,Red,F,Sep 17)
Contentious 105 (8f,Asc,S,Sep 29)
Continent 108 (5f,Goo,G,Aug 2)
Cool Touch 114 (12f,Cur,GF,May 27)
Copernican 105 (12f,Rip,S,Jun 21)
Coquerelle 112 (10f,Lon,VS,May 20)
Cornus 108 (6f,Lei,S,May 28)
Corridor Creeper 108 (5f,Chs,G,May 10)
Cosmic Destiny 107 (5f,Chs,GF,Sep 1)
Costume 110 (7f,Goo,GF,Aug 3)
Cotton Eyed Joe 106 (14f,Mus,GF,Aug 30)
Cougar Bay 115 (8f,Cur,GF,Sep 16)
Counsel s Opinion 106 (10f,Eps,GF,Apr 25)
Count Trevisio 108 (10f,Nad,G,Feb 8)
Countdown 109 (7f,Yor,HY,Jly 14)
Counting House 105 (12f,Nby,GF,Sep 21)
Creachadoir 116 (7f,Cur,G,May 7)
Creative Mind 106 (7f,Thi,F,Apr 21)
Crime Scene 111 (12f,Nad,G,Feb 15)
Crocodile Bay 107 (8f,Hay,GF,Sep 12)
Crooked Throw 107 (8f,Leo,GF,Apr 22)
Crosby Vision 105 (7f,Thi,GF,Apr 20)
Cross The Line 105 (8f,Asc,GF,May 2)
Crossing 110 (7f,Leo,G,Apr 7)
Cupid s Bow 106 (8f,Leo,YS,Jly 4)
Curtail 106 (6f,Nmk,G,Aug 17)
Cutting Crew 110 (12f,Nmk,GF,Oct 6)

Daaly Babet 107 (10f,Dea,S,Aug 19)
Daaweitza 107 (8f,Crl,GS,Jun 27)
Dabbers Ridge 108 (6f,Hay,S,Sep 29)
Daiwa Major 112 (9f,Nad,G,Mar 31)
Dakota Rain 107 (6f,Ncs,G,Aug 27)
Dal Cais 109 (10f,Leo,G,Apr 7)
Dalle 106 (8f,Msn,G,Jly 22)
Dalvina 110 (10f,Cur,GF,Sep 14)
Damdam 111 (7f,Lon,VS,May 20)
Damika 109 (6f,Pon,G,Jly 10)
Dan Dare 110 (10f,Red,GF,May 28)
Danak 113 (8f,Leo,GF,May 13)
Danawi 105 (8f,War,GS,Jun 28)
Dance Of Light 107 (10f,Yar,GF,Jly 17)
Dancing Mystery 108 (5f,War,GF,Sep 15)
Dandy Man 120 (5f,Asc,GF,Jun 19)
Dane Blue 105 (9f,Leo,GF,Sep 8)
Danebury Hill 106 (7f,Nmk,GF,Apr 18)
Danehill Music 111 (8f,Cur,SH,Jly 1)
Danehillsundance 109 (7f,Don,GF,Sep 13)
Daniella 110 (6f,Nmk,G,Jly 21)
Dansant 105 (11f,Ham,G,May 18)
Dansili Dancer 106 (14f,Hay,GF,Sep 8)
Dansimar 107 (14f,Red,F,Aug 11)
Danzig River 106 (6f,Lei,GF,Apr 28)

Daramsar 106 (12f,Cha,GS,Jun 3)
Darjina 117 (8f,Lon,G,Sep 9)
Dark Energy 106 (10f,Ncs,GS,Oct 16)
Dark Islander 106 (7f,Goo,G,Jly 31)
Dark Missile 114 (6f,Asc,G,Sep 30)
Darrfonah 109 (12f,Yor,G,Aug 22)
Darsha 110 (12½f,Lon,S,Oct 6)
Dash To The Front 108 (11f,War,S,Jun 18)
Dawla 108 (8f,Nav,YS,Jun 15)
Day By Day 105 (5f,Ham,G,Sep 23)
Day Flight 108 (12f,Goo,G,Jun 1)
Dazed And Amazed 106 (5f,San,GS,Jly 7)
Deauville Vision 109 (8f,Cur,HY,Mar 25)
Decado 113 (9f,Cur,SH,Jly 15)
Dechiper 105 (10f,Ncs,GS,Aug 24)
Defi 107 (8f,Mus,G,Nov 8)
Del Mar Sunset 107 (10f,Nmk,GF,May 25)
Dematraf 105 (5f,Mus,G,Jun 2)
Derison 110 (5f,Lon,G,Sep 16)
Desert Chief 107 (8f,Nad,G,Feb 1)
Desert Dew 110 (8f,San,G,Apr 27)
Desert Dreamer 106 (7f,Bri,GF,Jly 8)
Desert Lord 113 (5f,Asc,GF,Jun 19)
Desert Opal 107 (5f,Not,GF,Apr 17)
Desert Sea 105 (14f,San,GS,Jly 6)
Deserted Dane 105 (5f,Crl,GS,Jun 27)
Dhaular Dhar 112 (7f,Nmk,GF,Jly 13)
Diamond Diva 113 (6f,Pon,GS,Aug 19)
Diamond Necklace 107 (8f,Cur,GF,May 27)
Diamond Quest 112 (8f,Nad,G,Feb 15)
Diamond Tycoon 113 (8f,Nby,GF,Apr 21)
Diane s Choice 107 (5f,Goo,G,Aug 2)
Dig Deep 107 (5f,Asc,GF,Jly 14)
Dig Gold 107 (12½f,War,GF,Aug 27)
Dimenticata 113 (8f,Cur,GF,May 27)
Dingaan 107 (7f,Goo,G,Aug 26)
Direct Debit 108 (7f,Nmk,G,Jun 22)
Dispol Isle 108 (7f,Mus,G,Sep 30)
Distinction 109 (16f,Goo,G,Aug 2)
Divine Night 106 (8f,Leo,GF,May 13)
Divine Spirit 106 (5f,Not,G,Aug 2)
Dixieland Boy 105 (6f,Goo,GS,Sep 26)
Diyakalanie 113 (10f,Dea,S,Aug 19)
Dizzy Dreamer 105 (5f,Lon,G,May 13)
Do The Trick 108 (14f,Cur,Y,Sep 30)
Docofthebay 115 (7f,Goo,G,Aug 2)
Doctor Dino 115 (10½f,Lon,G,Apr 29)
Doctor Scott 106 (14f,Mus,G,Jun 2)
Doe Ray Me 107 (12½f,Lon,S,Oct 6)
Dolphin Bay 112 (12f,Cur,GF,May 27)
Dominante 108 (10f,Lon,GS,Oct 7)
Domino Dancer 106 (10f,Bev,G,Aug 16)
Don Pele 106 (6f,Goo,GS,Sep 26)
Don t Panic 107 (8f,Goo,S,Oct 14)
Dono Da Raia 105 (12f,Nad,G,Feb 9)
Dont Dili Dali 106 (10f,Nad,G,Feb 8)
Down The Brick 105 (11½f,Wdr,G,Jly 30)
Downing Street 110 (16f,Thi,GF,Aug 4)
Dragon Dancer 111 (12f,Lon,GS,Oct 7)
Drayton 111 (6f,Nmk,GF,Jly 13)
Dream In Blue 108 (8f,Dea,G,Aug 12)
Drifting Snow 105 (8f,Leo,GF,Oct 29)
Drumfire 105 (8f,Nmk,GF,Jly 12)
Dubai Twilight 107 (10f,Eps,GF,Apr 25)
Dubai s Touch 110 (8f,Goo,GF,Aug 4)
Dudley Docker 107 (8f,Hay,GF,Sep 12)
Due Respect 105 (7f,Cur,G,May 7)
Duff 112 (7f,Yor,G,Aug 23)
Duke Of Marmalade 116 (10f,Leo,GF,Sep 8)
Duke Of Tuscany 105 (10f,Nby,GS,May 19)
Dukedom 107 (10f,Leo,Y,Jly 28)
Dunaskin 112 (10f,Pon,GS,Jun 24)
Dundry 106 (16f,Nby,GF,Apr 21)
Dunelight 112 (8f,Goo,G,Aug 25)
Dustoori 108 (13f,Ham,GS,Sep 24)
Dutch Art 117 (6f,Nmk,GF,Jly 13)
Dylan Thomas 120 (12f,Asc,GS,Jly 28)
Dynaforce 109 (10f,Dea,S,Aug 19)
Dynamo Dancer 108 (8f,Leo,GF,Apr 22)
Dzesmin 111 (12f,Cat,G,Sep 22)

Ea 111 (8f,Asc,G,Jly 28)
Eagle Mountain 114 (8f,Nmk,GF,May 5)
Eagle s Pass 108 (14f,Cur,GF,Sep 15)
Earl Marshal 108 (10f,Lei,S,Jly 19)
Eastern Anthem 105 (10f,Nmk,GF,May 5)
Eastern Appeal 111 (7f,Leo,G,Jun 13)
Ebert 108 (8f,Goo,GF,Jun 9)
Echelon 117 (8f,Goo,G,Aug 25)
Echo Of Light 115 (9f,Yor,GF,Sep 5)
Echoes Rock 110 (8f,Msn,G,Jly 22)
Eddie Jock 108 (7f,Nmk,GF,Apr 18)
Eden Rock 110 (8f,Nad,GF,Feb 1)
Edge Closer 105 (6f,Asc,G,Jly 28)
Effigy 105 (8f,San,G,Jly 19)
Efidium 107 (8f,Yor,HY,Jly 14)
Efistorm 105 (5f,Wdr,GF,Apr 16)
Egerton 110 (10½f,Lon,G,Apr 29)
Eglevski 106 (12f,Sal,GS,Jun 27)
Eight Up 108 (14f,Cur,GF,Sep 15)
Eisteddfod 113 (6f,Dea,S,Aug 26)
Ekhtiaar 106 (8f,Don,GF,Aug 17)
El Bosque 105 (6f,Hay,GF,Jun 7)
El Comodin 108 (10f,Cha,GS,Jly 8)
El Dececy 105 (10f,Pon,GF,Jun 11)
El Potro 105 (5f,Pon,GS,Jly 29)
El Tango 107 (14f,Yor,G,Aug 22)

Ela Enta 105 (8f,Leo,GF,May 13)
Elasos 112 (10f,Lon,HY,Apr 1)
Electric Beat 106 (6f,Nmk,GF,Jly 13)
Electric Warrior 109 (8f,Hay,GF,Aug 11)
Eliza Gilbert 108 (10f,Leo,G,Apr 7)
Elkhorn 106 (5f,Ncs,G,Jly 28)
Ellen s Girl 105 (8f,Wdr,G,Aug 25)
Elusive Flash 107 (7f,Nby,GF,Apr 21)
Emerald Wilderness 106 (10f,Fol,GF,Jly 19)
Emirates Gold 113 (8f,Nad,GF,Feb 1)
Emirates Skyline 110 (10½f,Yor,G,May 16)
Emperor s Well 109 (7½f,Bev,G,Jly 31)
Empirical Power 105 (7f,Leo,GF,Sep 8)
Empress Jain 105 (5f,Bat,F,May 1)
Endiamo 105 (7f,San,GS,Jun 16)
Enforce 105 (10f,Don,GF,Nov 10)
English Archer 108 (11f,Ham,GS,Jly 19)
Engrupido 105 (7½f,Nad,G,Jan 18)
Enjoy The Moment 109 (22f,Asc,S,Jun 23)
Enticing 116 (5f,Bat,F,May 1)
Eradicate 105 (12f,Hay,GF,Jun 9)
Erra Go On 112 (16f,Leo,GF,Nov 4)
Escape Route 109 (9f,Goo,GF,Sep 15)
Escayola 107 (16f,Rip,GF,Apr 28)
Esoterica 105 (7f,Thi,GF,Aug 3)
Estate 105 (16f,Mus,G,Nov 8)
Esteem Machine 109 (6f,Nby,G,Aug 17)
Esthlos 109 (12f,Nmk,GF,Oct 6)
European Dream 111 (8f,Red,S,Jun 23)
Evening Time 112 (6f,Leo,Y,Jly 28)
Evens And Odds 105 (7f,Nmk,S,Oct 19)
Everygrainofsand 106 (6f,Yar,GF,Jly 23)
Everymanforhimself 106 (6f,Lei,F,Sep 17)
Evil Knievel 113 (9f,Nad,G,Feb 1)
Excelerate 109 (7f,Leo,GF,Nov 4)
Excellent Art 113 (8f,Goo,G,Aug 1)
Excusez Moi 108 (7f,Hay,G,May 12)
Exit Smiling 110 (8f,Rip,GF,Jun 6)
Expensive 107 (8f,Nad,G,Feb 8)
Express Way 113 (8f,Nad,G,Feb 9)
Express Wish 106 (6f,Hay,GF,Jun 7)
Eyshal 111 (7f,Cur,G,May 7)
Ezima 111 (12f,Cur,GY,Oct 21)

Fair Along 109 (18f,Nmk,GS,Oct 20)
Fairmile 114 (10½f,Yor,G,Oct 12)
Fairy Monarch 105 (10f,Bev,GF,Apr 18)
Fajr 110 (7f,Nmk,S,Jun 30)
Falpiase 108 (16f,Goo,G,Aug 2)
Familiar Territory 108 (10f,Asc,S,Jly 27)
Fantastic View 110 (7f,Nmk,GF,Jly 13)
Fantasy Believer 107 (5f,San,GF,Sep 1)
Fantoche 108 (12f,Cur,GF,May 27)
Farefield Lodge 107 (6f,Nby,G,Aug 17)
Farleigh House 108 (8f,Not,GF,Jun 13)
Fathom Five 110 (5f,Chs,S,Jly 14)
Fayr Jag 108 (6f,Yor,G,May 16)
Fenice 107 (12f,Nad,G,Feb 15)
Ferneley 112 (10f,Leo,GF,Sep 8)
Ficoma 105 (7f,Nby,GS,May 19)
Fiefdom 106 (7f,Mus,GF,Apr 8)
Fields Of Joy 110 (9f,Leo,GF,Sep 8)
Filios 109 (12f,Asc,GF,Jun 21)
Final Dynasty 111 (5f,Ayr,G,Jly 8)
Final Verse 107 (8f,San,G,Apr 28)
Finalmente 114 (16f,Goo,G,Aug 2)
Finicius 106 (7f,Goo,G,Jly 31)
Finsceal Beo 116 (8f,Nmk,GF,May 6)
Fire Up The Band 109 (5f,Not,GF,Apr 4)
Firenze 112 (5f,San,GS,May 31)
First Buddy 107 (8f,San,GF,Sep 14)
Fishforcompliments 105 (8f,Nmk,GF,May 5)
Fiumicino 105 (10f,Nby,GS,May 18)
Fixboard 108 (7f,Nmk,GF,Jly 13)
Flamingo Guitar 107 (10f,Leo,GF,Sep 8)
Flash McGahon 107 (6f,Cur,GF,May 26)
Flashy Wings 108 (9f,Nad,G,Mar 31)
Flighty Fellow 107 (8f,Rip,GF,Aug 27)
Flipando 112 (10f,Red,GF,May 28)
Flying Bantam 107 (7f,Thi,GF,Apr 20)
Flying Clarets 110 (10½f,Yor,GS,Oct 13)
Flylowflylong 109 (8f,Ham,G,Jun 13)
Folga 108 (5f,Bat,F,May 1)
Folk Opera 108 (11½f,Lin,GS,May 12)
Followmyfootsteps 114 (8f,Cur,GF,May 26)
Folly Lodge 111 (7f,Nby,GS,May 19)
Fongs Gazelle 107 (10f,Bev,GF,May 9)
Font 108 (10f,Red,GS,Jun 22)
Fonthill Road 110 (6f,Yor,G,May 16)
Forest Dane 107 (6f,Sal,GF,May 24)
Formal Decree 118 (9f,Nad,G,Jan 18)
Formax 108 (9f,Goo,GF,Sep 15)
Fort Churchill 108 (10f,Eps,GF,Apr 25)
Forthright 105 (10f,Cur,GF,Sep 15)
Fortress 107 (8f,Ham,G,Jun 13)
Four Sins 112 (10f,Cur,GF,Sep 14)
Fourth Dimension 109 (16f,Nby,G,Aug 17)
Foxhaven 111 (12f,Goo,G,Jun 1)
Foxy Music 107 (5f,Chs,G,May 11)
Fracas 113 (10f,Leo,Y,Jly 28)
Fragrancy 108 (8f,Red,G,Oct 6)
Frank Crow 105 (7f,Mus,S,Aug 14)
Freedonia 112 (12½f,Dea,G,Aug 5)
Freeloader 106 (10½f,Yor,G,May 16)
Fremen 112 (8f,Ayr,GS,Sep 22)
Froissee 106 (8f,Yar,GS,Jun 19)
Full House 110 (20f,Asc,G,Jun 19)

Full Victory 106 (8f,San,GS,May 31)
Fullandby 106 (5f,Ayr,GS,Jly 16)
Funfair Wane 110 (5f,Ham,GS,Aug 15)
Furmigadelagiusta 105 (12f,Nby,HY,Jly 5)
Furnace 106 (8f,Nmk,GF,Jly 13)
Fuschia 105 (7f,Nby,GS,May 19)
Futun 106 (10½f,Yor,G,May 16)

Galactic Star 116 (12f,Don,GF,Sep 15)
Galeota 112 (5f,Don,GF,Sep 12)
Galistic 113 (12f,Cur,GF,May 27)
Gallantry 110 (7f,Chs,G,Jun 12)
Gallery Girl 105 (6f,Rip,G,May 20)
Game Lad 106 (7f,Ncs,HY,Jun 30)
Gap Princess 106 (7f,Red,F,Aug 11)
Gare Du Nord 107 (12f,Lon,GS,Jly 14)
Garnica 117 (6f,Dea,S,Aug 26)
Garstang 107 (5f,Wdr,GF,Aug 6)
Gaudeamus 107 (7f,Cur,G,May 7)
Gee Dee Nen 108 (16f,Rip,GF,Apr 28)
General Knowledge 106 (10f,Fol,GF,May 3)
Genki 112 (6f,Pon,GS,Jly 29)
Geojimali 109 (6f,Pon,GS,Jly 29)
Geordieland 111 (16f,Goo,G,Aug 2)
George Washington 116 (10f,San,GS,Jly 7)
Getaway 117 (12f,Lon,GS,Oct 7)
Gift Horse 107 (7f,Nmk,GF,Jly 13)
Giganticus 113 (7f,Nmk,GF,Jly 13)
Gigs Magic 108 (12f,Cat,GF,Jun 1)
Gilded Cove 106 (6f,Bat,GS,Jun 16)
Girl Power 105 (5f,Cur,GF,Sep 14)
Glasshoughton 109 (5f,Bev,HY,Jly 7)
Glenbuck 107 (7f,Mus,GF,Apr 8)
Glitter Baby 107 (10f,Yar,G,Sep 19)
Global Strategy 105 (14f,Mus,GF,Apr 8)
Gloucester 108 (10f,Bev,GF,Sep 11)
Gloved Hand 110 (7f,Nmk,G,Jun 22)
Go For Gold 108 (12f,Nad,G,Feb 15)
Golden Dixie 107 (5f,San,S,Jly 6)
Golden Quest 107 (22f,Asc,S,Jun 23)
Golden Titus 107 (8f,Lon,G,Sep 9)
Golden Velvet 106 (8f,Nad,G,Feb 8)
Gongidas 106 (8f,Yar,G,May 30)
Goodbye Mr Bond 108 (10f,Red,GF,May 28)
Gower 105 (5f,Chs,G,May 11)
Gower Song 108 (14f,Sal,GF,May 6)
Graduation 106 (7f,Nmk,G,Jly 11)
Grafton Street 107 (12f,Cur,GF,Apr 15)
Grand Passion 110 (10f,Cur,GF,May 7)
Grand Revival 106 (12f,Cur,GF,Apr 15)
Grand Show 105 (6f,Goo,GS,Sep 26)
Grand Vista 110 (7f,Lon,VS,May 20)
Granston 105 (8f,Rip,G,May 20)
Grantley Adams 109 (6½f,Nad,G,Feb 15)
Gravitas 106 (12f,Nad,G,Jan 25)
Great As Gold 106 (18f,Pon,G,Apr 10)
Great Britain 106 (6f,Nad,G,Mar 8)
Great Hawk 106 (10f,Asc,GS,Jly 28)
Great Plains 107 (10f,Nad,G,Jan 25)
Great Rhythm 111 (7½f,Nad,G,Jan 25)
Grecian Dancer 108 (6f,Leo,G,Jun 6)
Greek Envoy 108 (12f,Nmk,S,Oct 19)
Greek Renaissance 114 (6f,Nmk,GS,Oct 20)
Greek Well 108 (10½f,Yor,G,Aug 22)
Green Coast 105 (7½f,Nad,G,Feb 8)
Green Girl 108 (10f,Dea,S,Aug 19)
Green Manalishi 111 (5f,Asc,GF,Jun 19)
Green Park 111 (6f,Yor,HY,Jly 28)
Green Room 110 (12f,Nmk,G,Jly 21)
Greenwich Meantime 108 (16f,Goo,G,Aug 2)
Grey Outlook 107 (14f,Mus,GF,Apr 8)
Grizedale 106 (7f,Nmk,G,May 19)
Group Captain 108 (12f,Asc,S,Jly 29)
Guacamole 109 (8f,War,GF,Sep 15)
Guilded Warrior 112 (7f,War,S,Jly 5)
Guilia 105 (14½f,Don,GF,Sep 13)
Gulf Express 105 (10f,Nby,GS,Aug 18)
Gull Wing 108 (12f,Lei,GF,Apr 28)
Gunfighter 106 (7f,Don,GF,Nov 10)
Gunner s View 106 (8f,Bat,F,Apr 11)
Gwenseb 106 (10f,Dea,S,Aug 19)
Gyroscope 108 (8f,Wdr,G,Aug 25)

H Harrison 111 (7f,Cat,F,May 8)
Haatef 115 (6f,Asc,G,Sep 30)
Habalwatan 109 (10½f,Chs,G,May 11)
Habshan 105 (8f,Nby,GF,Jun 9)
Haifa 106 (10f,Bev,GF,Apr 18)
Halicarnassus 113 (11f,Nby,GF,Sep 21)
Halla San 111 (14f,Cat,GF,Apr 4)
Halla Siamsa 105 (12f,Leo,GF,Sep 8)
Hallhoo 108 (10f,Nad,G,Jan 25)
Hampshire 106 (7f,Leo,Y,Aug 19)
Handsome Cross 105 (5f,Eps,GF,Apr 25)
Handsome Falcon 105 (7½f,Bev,S,Jly 23)
Hansomelle 105 (8f,San,GF,Sep 1)
Hard Rock City 110 (8f,Cur,SH,Jly 1)
Hard Top 108 (10f,Lin,GS,May 12)
Harrison s Flyer 105 (6f,Bat,GS,Jun 16)
Harry Tricker 106 (10f,Goo,GF,Sep 16)
Hartshead 106 (7½f,Nad,G,Jan 18)
Harvest Queen 112 (8f,Hay,GF,Sep 8)
Harvest Warrior 108 (8½f,Bev,HY,Jly 6)
Hassaad 110 (10f,Red,GF,May 28)
Hattan 110 (12f,Asc,GS,Sep 30)
Hawkit 106 (9f,Ayr,HY,Nov 3)

Hawridge King 106 (12½f,War,GF,Aug 27)
Hazeymm 112 (9f,Nad,G,Feb 1)
He s A Decoy 115 (8f,Cur,GF,May 26)
Hearthstead Maison 115 (10f,Leo,GF,Sep 8)
Heaven Knows 109 (10f,Nby,S,Oct 27)
Heaven Sent 112 (8f,Asc,G,Jly 14)
Heliostatic 111 (8f,Leo,GF,Apr 22)
Hellvelyn 112 (6f,Nmk,GF,Jly 13)
Hernando Royal 107 (12f,Nmk,GF,Oct 6)
Heroes 110 (8f,Wdr,G,Aug 25)
Heron Bay 110 (12f,Asc,GF,Jun 21)
Heureux 105 (8f,Thi,GF,Jun 4)
Heywood 106 (7f,Goo,G,Aug 2)
Hi Calypso 110 (14½f,Don,GF,Sep 13)
High Ambition 109 (7f,Yar,G,May 31)
High Point 109 (16f,Nby,G,Aug 17)
High Treason 110 (12f,Yor,G,May 18)
Highest Height 108 (8f,Dea,S,Aug 26)
Highland Harvest 106 (8f,Wdr,G,May 7)
Highland Legacy 105 (11½f,Wdr,GF,Apr 30)
Highland Warrior 107 (5f,Yor,S,Jly 13)
Hinterland 107 (8f,Not,G,Jun 6)
Hinton Admiral 107 (7f,Nmk,GF,Apr 18)
His Master s Voice 105 (7f,Fol,G,Apr 3)
Hitchcock 110 (12f,Asc,S,Jun 23)
Hogmaneigh 109 (5f,Eps,G,Jun 2)
Hoh Hoh Hoh 109 (6f,Yor,GS,Oct 13)
Hoh Mike 113 (5f,San,GS,Jly 7)
Holbeck Ghyll 107 (5f,Eps,G,Jun 2)
Holiday Cocktail 106 (8f,Crl,G,Jun 4)
Holocene 108 (8f,Lon,G,Sep 9)
Honolulu 112 (14½f,Don,GF,Sep 15)
Honoured Guest 111 (8f,Lon,G,May 13)
Hopeful Purchase 106 (8f,Nad,GF,Feb 1)
Horseford Hill 106 (12f,Yor,GF,Sep 5)
Host Nation 105 (15½f,Lon,G,Apr 29)
Hotel Du Cap 108 (7f,Nby,GF,Sep 21)
Hotham 106 (5f,Ham,GS,Aug 15)
How s She Cuttin 108 (5f,Mus,GF,Apr 9)
Howya Now Kid 108 (7f,Eps,GS,Jun 1)
Hugs Destiny 106 (14f,Mus,G,Jun 2)
Hula Ballew 107 (8f,Thi,GF,Jun 4)
Humungous 110 (8f,San,G,Apr 28)
Hurlingham 105 (10½f,Hay,GF,Sep 8)
Hypnosis 106 (5f,Mus,GF,Apr 9)
Hypoteneuse 105 (12f,Bat,GS,Jly 9)

Ice Planet 109 (6f,Red,GS,Jun 22)
Ideally 106 (10f,Bat,GS,Jly 9)
Idle Power 107 (6f,Wdr,S,Jun 30)
If Paradise 108 (5f,Cur,GF,Sep 14)
Il Castagno 110 (7f,Cat,F,May 8)
Illustrious Blue 113 (9f,Nad,G,Feb 9)
Impeller 109 (10f,Nad,G,Feb 8)
Imperial Echo 108 (7f,Yor,HY,Jly 14)
Imperial Rose 106 (12f,Cur,S,Jun 29)
Imperial Star 111 (10f,Goo,G,May 25)
Impressionnante 108 (7f,Lon,G,Sep 9)
In Safe Hands 107 (10f,Nby,GS,May 18)
Inca Soldier 107 (6f,Red,F,Aug 12)
Inchloch 106 (12f,Don,GF,Nov 10)
Inchnadamph 109 (16½f,Don,GF,Nov 10)
Incline 110 (7f,Cur,G,May 7)
Indian Edge 109 (8f,Chp,S,Jly 13)
Indian Ink 118 (8f,Asc,GS,Jun 22)
Indian Pace 113 (16f,Leo,GF,Nov 4)
Indian Spring 105 (10½f,Cha,GS,Jun 3)
Indian Trail 110 (5f,San,GF,Sep 1)
Indochine 108 (7½f,Nad,G,Jan 18)
Ingleby Arch 112 (6f,Nmk,GS,May 27)
Inside Story 106 (8f,Hay,GF,Aug 10)
Inter Vision 108 (5f,Don,GF,Sep 14)
Into The Dark 110 (12f,Goo,G,Jun 1)
Intrepid Jack 110 (6f,Asc,GS,Jun 23)
Invasian 107 (12f,Yor,G,Aug 21)
Invention 105 (8f,San,GS,May 29)
Invincible Force 109 (5f,Cur,GF,Sep 14)
Inwood 110 (7f,Cur,G,May 7)
Iolanthe 106 (9f,San,G,Aug 2)
Ireland s Call 106 (8f,Leo,GF,Apr 22)
Irish Quest 108 (14f,Hay,GF,Sep 12)
Irish Wells 115 (10½f,Lon,G,Apr 29)
Iron Lips 108 (6f,Dea,S,Aug 26)
Irony 106 (8f,San,G,Aug 31)
Irridescence 107 (8f,Nmk,G,Jly 11)
Ishetoo 105 (5f,Hay,GF,Jun 8)
Ishibee 105 (6f,Bri,GF,Aug 14)
Italian Girl 107 (8f,Goo,GF,Aug 4)
Ivory Lace 108 (7f,Goo,GF,Sep 4)
Ivy Creek 113 (12f,Goo,G,Jun 1)

Jacaranda Ridge 106 (7f,Yar,GS,Jly 24)
Jack Junior 105 (8f,Asc,GF,Jun 19)
Jack Rolfe 106 (12f,Nby,GF,Sep 21)
Jack Sullivan 109 (7f,War,GF,Aug 27)
Jackie Kiely 107 (10f,Lei,GF,Sep 11)
Jalmira 114 (8f,Nmk,G,Nov 3)
Jalwada 107 (12f,Leo,GF,Sep 8)
Jamboretta 105 (9f,Goo,G,Aug 26)
James Caird 105 (8f,Wdr,GF,Apr 16)
Jamieson Gold 106 (7f,Nby,GS,Aug 18)
Jardin Bleu 106 (8f,Msn,G,Jly 22)
Jawaab 108 (8f,Hay,GF,Sep 12)
Jawaaneb 106 (16f,Chs,GF,Sep 15)
Jawad 106 (14f,Cur,GF,Sep 15)
Jayer Gilles 105 (16f,Nby,G,Aug 17)

Jedburgh 108 (7f,Goo,G,Aug 26)
Jeremy 115 (8f,San,G,Apr 28)
Jet Express 106 (7½f,Nad,G,Jan 18)
Jet Past 107 (8f,Nad,G,Feb 8)
Jewelled Dagger 107 (9f,Ayr,G,Jun 23)
Jilly Why 107 (6f,Thi,GF,Aug 3)
Jimmy Styles 113 (6f,Nby,G,Aug 17)
Jo Burg 106 (8f,Nmk,GF,May 5)
Johannes 106 (7f,Nmk,GF,Oct 6)
John Dillon 105 (10f,Pon,GS,Jly 29)
John Doran 105 (7f,Leo,G,Apr 7)
John Keats 107 (6f,Ncs,G,Aug 17)
John Terry 106 (12f,Don,GF,Nov 10)
Johnny Angel 105 (7f,Cur,G,May 7)
Joseph Henry 106 (6f,Goo,GF,Aug 3)
Joyeaux 107 (5f,Ham,GS,Aug 15)
Judd Street 111 (5f,Nmk,G,Oct 4)
Jumbajukiba 117 (8f,Cur,GF,Sep 16)
Junior 107 (16f,Nby,GF,Apr 21)
Juniper Girl 109 (20f,Asc,G,Jun 19)
Juror 110 (8f,Nad,G,Feb 15)
Just Lille 109 (10½f,Hay,GF,May 25)

Kabis Amigos 106 (7f,Thi,GF,Apr 20)
Kafuu 108 (7f,Nmk,GF,Oct 6)
Kalankari 109 (7½f,Nad,G,Jan 18)
Kalasam 109 (10f,Lei,GF,Sep 11)
Kaloura 112 (12½f,Dea,G,Aug 5)
Kames Park 105 (14f,Mus,G,Jun 2)
Kandidate 112 (9f,Yor,GF,Sep 5)
Kankakee 113 (12½f,Dea,G,Aug 5)
Kansas Gold 107 (8f,Hay,GF,Sep 12)
Kapera 111 (12f,Cur,GF,May 27)
Kapil 113 (8f,Nmk,G,Nov 3)
Karoo Blue 106 (8f,Red,G,Oct 6)
Kashmir Lady 105 (7f,War,G,Jly 12)
Kasthari 105 (16½f,Don,GF,Nov 10)
Kasumi 109 (8f,Goo,G,Jly 31)
Katie Boo 109 (5f,Ham,GS,Aug 15)
Katirisa 105 (7f,Cur,G,May 7)
Kavachi 106 (10f,Yar,GS,Oct 30)
Kavafi 111 (8f,Dea,S,Aug 26)
Kay Gee Be 106 (8f,Not,GF,Jun 13)
Kay Two 111 (5f,Lei,G,Sep 24)
Kayah 109 (11½f,Lin,GS,May 12)
Kayf Aramis 105 (18f,Yor,GS,Oct 13)
Keelaghan 107 (12f,Cur,GF,May 26)
Keisha Kayleigh 105 (10f,Red,GS,Sep 26)
Kempes 114 (12f,Cur,GF,May 27)
Kentucky Dynamite 107 (8f,Cha,G,Jun 10)
Kerama 109 (7f,Cur,G,May 7)
Kerriemuir Lass 107 (11½f,Wdr,G,Jun 9)
Kew Green 105 (8f,War,GF,Apr 17)
Key Of Destiny 105 (6½f,Nad,G,Jan 25)
Key Partners 106 (11f,War,GS,Jun 28)
Keyaki 105 (6f,Fol,G,Jun 2)
Kfar Yona 106 (8f,Msn,G,Jly 22)
Khun John 105 (10f,Nmk,GF,May 25)
Kid Mambo 106 (11½f,Lin,GS,May 12)
Kilimandscharo 109 (12f,Yor,G,May 18)
Killena Boy 110 (8f,San,GS,May 29)
Killybegs 105 (8f,Nad,G,Feb 22)
Kilmallock 108 (8f,Msn,G,Jly 22)
Kilmannin 105 (8f,Cur,S,Oct 22)
Kilometre Neuf 110 (8f,Dea,S,Aug 26)
Kilworth 106 (7f,Red,G,Oct 6)
King Charles 107 (10f,Asc,GS,Sep 28)
King Harson 107 (7f,Mus,G,Sep 30)
King In Waiting 107 (10f,Cur,GF,May 7)
King Jock 111 (7f,Lon,G,Sep 9)
King Of Argos 112 (8f,Wdr,GF,Apr 16)
King Of The Moors 105 (8f,Yor,HY,Jly 14)
King Of Tory 107 (8f,Cur,G,Sep 2)
King Orchisios 108 (5f,Cat,G,Oct 20)
King Rama 115 (12f,Cur,GF,May 27)
King s Apostle 110 (6f,Nmk,G,Aug 18)
King s Bastion 106 (6f,Lin,GS,May 12)
King s Caprice 105 (7f,Goo,GF,Sep 15)
King s Event 106 (10f,Nby,S,Oct 27)
King s Gait 107 (6f,Asc,S,May 12)
King s Majesty 106 (8f,Not,G,Aug 2)
Kings Point 105 (8f,Yor,GS,May 17)
Kingscape 106 (10f,Yar,S,Jly 5)
Kingscross 105 (6f,Lei,S,May 28)
Kingsdale Orion 107 (8f,Cur,GF,May 26)
Kinsya 109 (8f,Ayr,GS,Sep 22)
Kirkby s Treasure 105 (7f,Mus,GS,Sep 17)
Kirklees 110 (10f,Don,GF,Sep 13)
Knot In Wood 110 (6f,Asc,G,Sep 30)
Kocab 114 (12f,Lon,S,Oct 21)
Kocooning 106 (5f,Lon,G,Sep 16)
Kostar 113 (6f,Pon,GF,Apr 23)
Kourka 111 (5f,Lon,G,May 13)
Kristensen 110 (14f,Mus,GF,Apr 8)
Kyle 108 (7f,Goo,G,Aug 2)
Kyles Bay 113 (7f,Cur,G,May 7)
Kyoto Summit 106 (12f,Yor,G,Aug 21)

La Estrella 109 (12f,Don,GF,Nov 10)
Laa Rayb 107 (8f,War,GF,Sep 15)
Lacework 107 (10f,Red,GF,May 28)
Ladies Best 109 (10f,Don,GF,Sep 12)
Lady Gloria 109 (8f,Nmk,G,Jun 13)
Lady Grace 108 (6f,Nmk,S,Oct 19)
Lady Lily 110 (6f,Pon,F,Sep 20)
Lady Livius 105 (8f,San,GF,Sep 1)
Lady Teabing 109 (7f,Cur,G,May 7)
Lady Traill 107 (12f,Bev,GS,Jun 21)
Lake Poet 107 (10f,Eps,GS,Jun 1)
Lake Toya 109 (10f,Yar,G,Sep 19)
Land n Stars 108 (16f,Goo,G,Aug 2)
Lang Shining 107 (8f,San,G,Aug 31)
Langford 106 (10f,Eps,GF,Apr 25)
Lap Of Honour 108 (8f,Not,G,Aug 2)
Larkwing 112 (16f,Leo,GF,Nov 4)
Lascaux 109 (6½f,Nad,G,Jan 25)
Latin Mood 112 (15½f,Lon,G,Sep 16)
Latino Magic 106 (8f,Cur,SH,Jly 1)
Lavarone 106 (6½f,Nad,G,Feb 15)
Lavenham 106 (7f,Goo,GF,Sep 4)
Laverock 114 (12f,Asc,GS,Jly 28)
Law Lord 105 (7f,Lon,G,Sep 9)
Lawman 111 (10½f,Cha,GS,Jun 3)
Le Cadre Noir 115 (6f,Dea,S,Aug 26)
Le Miracle 117 (15½f,Lon,G,Oct 28)
Le Soleil 105 (12½f,Ncs,G,Apr 14)
Lee Applause 112 (9f,Leo,GF,Sep 8)
Leg Spinner 110 (18f,Nmk,GS,Oct 20)
Legerete 113 (10f,Lon,GS,Oct 7)
Leitmotiv 106 (12f,Nad,G,Feb 1)
Leopoldine 105 (7f,Lin,GS,May 12)
Leslingtaylor 105 (12f,Asc,GS,Oct 13)
Lethal 105 (5f,Goo,G,May 25)
Lets Roll 107 (14f,Mus,G,Jun 2)
Levera 109 (7f,Nmk,S,Jun 30)
Libre 107 (8f,Not,G,Aug 2)
Lidanski 108 (5f,Cur,HY,Jly 15)
Light Impact 114 (12f,Lon,GS,Jly 14)
Light Sentence 107 (10f,Bev,GF,Apr 18)
Light Shift 112 (12f,Eps,GS,Jun 1)
Linngari 116 (9f,Nad,G,Mar 31)
Lion Sands 110 (12f,Hay,GF,May 25)
Lipocco 108 (6f,Yor,GF,Sep 9)
Liscanna 110 (6f,Leo,G,Jun 6)
Literato 114 (10f,Nmk,GS,Oct 20)
Little Edward 107 (6f,Bat,F,Sep 16)
Little Eye 114 (9f,Leo,GF,Sep 8)
Little Jimbob 107 (10f,Bev,GF,Sep 11)
Little White Lie 109 (7f,Eps,GS,Jun 1)
Loch Verdi 110 (5f,Ham,G,Sep 23)
Loda 108 (7f,Lon,G,Sep 9)
Logsdail 105 (9f,Goo,GF,Jun 8)
Lone Wolfe 107 (7f,Nmk,G,Jly 20)
Longquan 105 (6f,Nmk,G,Jly 11)
Longspur 107 (10f,Lei,S,Jly 19)
Lord Admiral 114 (8f,Cur,GF,Sep 16)
Lord Du Sud 108 (15½f,Lon,G,Oct 28)
Lordship 106 (7f,Fol,HY,Aug 22)
Lost In The Rain 105 (13f,Nav,YS,Jun 15)
Lost Soldier Three 111 (9f,Nad,G,Jan 18)
Loulwa 106 (12f,Asc,GS,Oct 13)
Loup Breton 107 (10½f,Cha,GS,Jun 3)
Loup De Mer 108 (15½f,Lon,G,Oct 28)
Love On Sight 106 (7f,Goo,G,Aug 2)
Lovelace 112 (7f,Goo,GF,Sep 4)
Lucarno 114 (12f,Yor,G,Aug 21)
Lucayan Dancer 105 (10½f,Chs,GF,May 9)
Lucayos 106 (6f,Sal,GF,May 24)
Luck Be A Lady 106 (7f,Nmk,G,Jly 21)
Luck Wud Have It 105 (7f,Leo,G,Apr 7)
Lucky Dance 107 (8f,Nad,G,Feb 15)
Lucky Heroine 105 (12f,Leo,GF,Sep 8)
Lucky Kyllachy 107 (7f,Cur,G,May 7)
Luisant 105 (8f,Cha,G,Jun 10)
Lunces Lad 106 (7f,Goo,GF,Sep 4)
Lundy s Lane 113 (8f,Nad,G,Feb 9)
Luscivious 106 (5f,Chs,G,May 11)
Luzdeluna 105 (9f,Leo,GF,Nov 3)
Lykios 109 (7f,Lon,VS,May 20)

Mac Gille Eoin 109 (6f,Goo,GF,Sep 16)
Mac Love 111 (6½f,Nad,G,Jan 25)
Macarthur 113 (12f,Yor,G,Aug 21)
Macedon 106 (8f,Nby,GF,Apr 21)
Machinist 110 (6f,Cur,SH,Jly 1)
Macleya 117 (15½f,Lon,G,Oct 28)
Macorville 113 (14f,Cur,GF,Sep 15)
Mad Rush 107 (12f,Sal,GS,Jun 27)
Magdalene 106 (10f,Yar,GS,Aug 26)
Magic Carpet 114 (9f,Cur,G,Sep 2)
Magic Echo 106 (10f,Bev,GS,Jun 21)
Magic Glade 106 (5f,Thi,G,May 19)
Magic Moth 106 (12f,Bat,F,Apr 24)
Magic Show 105 (10f,Yar,GS,Aug 26)
Magical Music 107 (8f,Not,G,Aug 2)
Magicalmysterytour 107 (13f,Nby,G,Aug 17)
Magnus 119 (5f,Asc,GF,Jun 19)
Mahara 114 (12f,Lon,GS,Jly 14)
Mahler 112 (16f,Asc,GS,Jun 22)
Maid To Believe 108 (12f,Asc,GS,Sep 28)
Maison Dieu 105 (6f,Sth,G,Apr 2)
Majestic Concorde 115 (16f,Leo,GF,Nov 4)
Majestic Roi 110 (7f,Nby,GF,Apr 21)
Majestic Times 107 (6f,Ayr,GS,Sep 22)
Major Cadeaux 113 (8f,Nmk,GF,May 5)
Major Grace 108 (8f,Dea,S,Aug 26)
Majuro 106 (7f,Don,GF,Sep 13)
Maker s Mark 108 (5f,Lei,G,Sep 24)
Malande 106 (8f,Nav,YS,Jun 15)
Malapropism 109 (5f,Bev,GF,Sep 19)
Malcheek 108 (7f,Thi,GF,May 5)
Malt Or Mash 114 (12f,Nmk,GF,Oct 6)
Man Of Vision 110 (12f,Lei,GF,Apr 28)
Man On The Nile 112 (16f,Leo,GF,Nov 4)
Mandesha 114 (12f,Sai,GS,Jun 24)
Mandobi 105 (7½f,Nad,G,Jan 18)
Mandragola 108 (11½f,Wdr,G,Oct 8)
Manduro 115 (9f,Lon,VS,May 20)
Mango Mischief 111 (10½f,Yor,HY,Jly 28)
Mango Music 109 (6f,Pon,F,Sep 20)
Many Colours 115 (9f,Cur,G,Sep 2)
Many Volumes 108 (10f,Don,GF,Sep 13)
Manzila 107 (5f,Lon,G,May 13)
Maraahel 115 (12f,Asc,GS,Jly 28)
Marajaa 106 (8f,Nby,GF,Apr 21)
Marchand D Or 117 (6½f,Dea,G,Aug 5)
Marie Rossa 106 (10½f,Cha,G,Jun 10)
Marikhar 107 (13f,Nav,YS,Jun 15)
Mariotto 106 (10f,San,GS,Jly 6)
Market Forces 106 (12f,Bev,GF,May 9)
Marozi 107 (5f,Goo,GF,Aug 3)
Marquee 105 (11f,War,GS,Jun 28)
Mary Louhana 111 (12½f,Dea,G,Aug 5)
Marzelline 105 (12f,Asc,GF,Jun 21)
Masai Moon 107 (7f,Nmk,S,Oct 19)
Mashaahed 110 (10f,San,GS,May 31)
Masta Plasta 110 (6f,Yar,G,Sep 18)
Master Marvel 105 (8f,Leo,YS,Jly 4)
Masterofthecourt 105 (7f,Nmk,G,Nov 3)
Mastership 106 (6f,Nmk,G,Jly 11)
Material Witness 106 (7f,War,S,Jly 5)
Matloob 105 (7½f,Nad,G,Jan 18)
Matsunosuke 110 (5f,Lei,G,Sep 24)
Measured Response 107 (8f,Chp,S,Jly 13)
Measured Tempo 109 (10f,Nby,GS,May 18)
Mecca s Mate 112 (5f,Ayr,G,Jly 8)
Medicea Sidera 110 (7f,Nmk,G,Jly 21)
Medici Pearl 108 (7½f,Bev,HY,Jly 17)
Medley 108 (6f,Nmk,GS,Jun 29)
Melalchrist 106 (6f,Pon,G,Apr 10)
Menestrol 112 (8f,Msn,G,Jly 22)
Mesbaah 105 (8f,Asc,G,Jly 28)
Metaphoric 107 (14f,Yar,GF,Sep 20)
Metropolitan Man 110 (8f,Hay,GF,Sep 8)
Mi Emma 112 (8f,Asc,GS,Jun 22)
Mia s Boy 106 (7f,Thi,GS,Jun 19)
Mickmacmagoole 105 (12f,Cur,GF,May 26)
Middlemarch 105 (8f,Ham,G,Jun 13)
Midnight Traveller 105 (12f,Cur,GF,May 27)
Mighty 112 (14f,Cur,GF,Sep 15)
Mighty Moon 106 (14f,Cat,GF,Apr 4)
Mikao 106 (14f,Nmk,G,May 19)
Miles Gloriosus 106 (8f,Msn,G,Jly 22)
Millestan 105 (8f,Thi,GF,Sep 8)
Million Percent 106 (7f,Cat,GF,May 26)
Milton s Keen 108 (8f,Chp,S,Jly 13)
Mimi Mouse 105 (5f,Thi,G,Jun 4)
Mind How You Go 106 (16f,Asc,S,May 12)
Mine 112 (7f,Hay,GF,Jun 7)
Mine Behind 106 (6f,Fol,G,Jun 17)
Mineral Star 105 (8f,Yar,GS,Jun 28)
Minkowski 108 (14f,Yor,G,Aug 22)
Minority Report 108 (7f,Goo,G,Aug 26)
Mirin 105 (12f,Nby,S,Jun 26)
Misaro 106 (5f,Chs,GF,Sep 1)
Miss Andretti 123 (5f,Asc,GF,Jun 19)
Miss Gorica 107 (7f,Leo,GF,Sep 8)
Miss Lucifer 114 (7f,Nmk,GS,Oct 20)
Miss Salvador 109 (12f,Lon,S,Oct 21)
Missoula 111 (18f,Yor,GS,Oct 13)
Missvinski 110 (8f,Asc,GS,Jun 22)
Mist And Stone 108 (5f,Cur,GF,Sep 14)
Mister Completely 106 (16f,Chs,GF,Sep 15)
Mith Hill 106 (16f,Asc,S,May 12)
Mo Cheoil Thu 106 (7f,Leo,G,Apr 7)
Modeeroch 112 (7f,Leo,G,Jun 13)
Mojito Royale 107 (8f,Leo,GF,Nov 4)
Mombassa 106 (8f,Cur,G,Sep 2)
Money Bags 110 (9f,Nad,G,Feb 9)
Monkey Glas 105 (8f,Red,G,Oct 6)
Monolith 108 (13f,Ham,GF,May 6)
Mont Etoile 109 (10f,Yar,G,Sep 19)
Montare 115 (12f,Lon,S,Oct 21)
Monte Alto 110 (10f,Nby,GF,Sep 22)
Monteriggioni 106 (8f,Cur,Y,Sep 30)
Monthly Medal 108 (8f,Cur,Y,Sep 30)
Montpellier 112 (8½f,Eps,GS,Jun 1)
Monzante 107 (10½f,Chs,G,May 11)
Moody Tunes 108 (8f,Hay,HY,Jun 23)
Moon Quest 105 (12f,Sal,GS,Jun 27)
Mooretown Lady 111 (7f,Cur,G,May 7)
Moorhouse Lad 112 (5f,Goo,G,Aug 2)
Mores Wells 114 (14f,Cur,GF,Sep 15)
Morinqua 110 (5f,Bev,G,May 30)
Moss Vale 113 (5f,San,GS,May 31)
Motive 108 (10f,Red,GF,May 28)
Motu 105 (7f,Thi,GF,Apr 20)
Mount Eliza 106 (8f,Leo,G,Jun 6)
Mount Kilimanjaro 108 (16½f,San,GS,May 29)
Mountain High 115 (12f,Sai,GS,Jun 24)
Moves Goodenough 105 (8f,Bat,G,Jun 27)
Mr Aviator 108 (10f,Goo,G,Aug 2)
Mr Crystal 106 (14f,Red,F,Aug 11)
Mr Napper Tandy 112 (7f,Cur,G,May 7)
Mr Wolf 106 (6f,Pon,GF,Apr 23)
Mrs Lindsay 113 (12f,Lon,G,Sep 16)
Ms Victoria 105 (6f,Cur,Y,Oct 21)
Mudawin 106 (14f,Nmk,G,May 19)
Mujood 107 (6f,Goo,G,May 5)
Mull Of Dubai 108 (12f,Yor,G,Aug 21)
Mullins Bay 110 (9f,Yor,GF,Sep 5)
Multidimensional 108 (10f,Nmk,GS,Oct 20)
Multiplex 111 (8f,Cha,G,Jun 10)
Munaddam 112 (6½f,Nad,G,Jan 25)
Munnings 109 (12f,Cur,GF,May 26)
Munsef 107 (12f,Nmk,S,Jun 30)
Music Note 108 (8f,Wdr,GF,Apr 16)
Musical Beat 106 (8f,Not,GF,Jun 13)
Musical Way 109 (10f,Dea,S,Aug 19)
Mussoorie 105 (12f,Yor,G,Aug 23)
Mustajed 105 (12f,Sal,GF,Jun 17)
Mustameet 107 (10f,Cur,GF,May 7)
Mutafanen 107 (12f,Nad,G,Feb 1)
Mutajarred 108 (8f,Yor,S,Jly 13)
Mutakarrim 106 (12f,Leo,GF,May 13)
Mutamared 106 (6f,Nmk,GF,May 5)
Mutanaseb 113 (8f,San,GS,Jly 7)
Mutawaajid 113 (6f,Hay,GF,Sep 8)
Mutawaffer 109 (12f,Yor,G,May 18)
Muthara 112 (8f,Msn,G,Jly 22)
My Paris 110 (7f,Nmk,GF,Jly 13)
Mystic Lips 112 (10f,Lon,GS,Oct 7)
Mystical 110 (10f,Nad,G,Mar 8)
Mystical Ayr 108 (9f,Ham,GS,Sep 24)

Nadawat 106 (7f,Lin,GF,Sep 3)
Nakheel 107 (12f,Nmk,GF,May 5)
Namaya 110 (8f,Cur,GF,Sep 16)
Namid Reprobate 107 (8f,San,GF,Sep 14)
Namir 108 (5f,Not,GS,May 12)
Nannina 108 (8f,Nmk,GF,Oct 6)
Nans Joy 106 (8½f,Eps,GS,Jun 1)
Nanton 106 (10½f,Yor,G,Aug 22)
Nassau Style 106 (7f,War,HY,Jly 6)
Nastrelli 107 (7f,Leo,Y,Aug 19)
National Captain 107 (7½f,Nad,G,Jan 18)
Navajo Moon 114 (9f,Cur,G,Sep 2)
Nawamees 107 (12f,Yor,G,Aug 21)
Nawaqees 107 (8f,Goo,G,May 24)
Nawow 105 (16f,Nby,GF,Apr 21)
Ned Ludd 107 (16f,Asc,S,May 12)
Neil s Legacy 109 (9f,Ham,GS,Sep 24)
Nell Gwyn 107 (8f,Leo,GF,May 13)
Nell Peters 107 (7f,Cur,G,May 7)
Neon Blue 105 (7f,Yor,GF,Sep 9)
Nepotista 106 (12f,Nad,G,Feb 1)
Nero West 107 (16f,Ncs,S,Jun 28)
Nevada Desert 108 (8f,Yor,G,Aug 23)
Never Without Me 106 (6f,Red,F,Aug 12)
New Beginning 106 (10f,Lei,GF,Apr 12)
New Girlfriend 111 (6½f,Dea,G,Aug 5)
New Guinea 114 (12f,Don,GF,Sep 15)
New Seeker 109 (7f,Lei,GF,Apr 28)
Newgate Lodge 106 (7f,Leo,Y,Aug 19)
Nick s Nikita 108 (12f,Leo,Y,Aug 19)
Night Crescendo 111 (12f,Don,GF,Nov 10)
Night Cru 110 (8f,Nmk,GF,May 25)
Night Hour 107 (12f,Don,G,Oct 27)
Nightspot 107 (10f,Bev,G,Aug 16)
Nimra 106 (14f,Mus,G,Jly 9)
No Dream 107 (10½f,Cha,GS,Jun 3)
No Time 106 (5f,Not,GF,Apr 17)
Nobilissima 107 (6f,War,S,Jly 5)
Noble Minstrel 106 (16f,Goo,G,May 24)
Noddies Way 105 (16f,Goo,G,May 24)
Norisan 108 (7f,Sal,S,Jly 28)
Northern Dare 108 (6f,Nmk,G,Aug 18)
Northern Fling 105 (5f,Yor,G,Aug 22)
Northern Jem 105 (10f,Nmk,GF,Jly 12)
Northern Spy 105 (8f,Not,GF,Oct 3)
Nosferatu 107 (12f,Asc,GS,Oct 13)
Notability 106 (9f,Nad,G,Feb 9)
Noticeable 106 (11f,Goo,G,May 25)
Notnowcato 118 (10f,San,GS,Jly 7)
Nuit Sombre 106 (7f,Cat,GF,Nov 6)
Numen 105 (9f,Leo,GF,Sep 8)
Numerieus 107 (5f,Lon,G,May 13)
Nur Tau 105 (11f,Goo,GF,Aug 4)

Obe Brave 108 (7½f,Nad,G,Jan 18)
Obe Gold 109 (6½f,Nad,G,Feb 15)
Observatory Star 107 (7f,Red,F,Aug 11)
Obstructive 106 (5f,Chs,HY,Jly 13)
Ocean Blaze 105 (5f,Red,G,Oct 6)
Oceana Gold 111 (8f,San,G,Aug 2)
Oddsmaker 108 (14f,Mus,GF,Apr 8)
Odiham 108 (20f,Asc,G,Jun 19)
Off The Record 113 (6f,Nmk,G,Jly 11)
Offbeat Fashion 106 (7f,Cur,G,May 7)
Ogee 106 (12f,Asc,S,Jun 23)
Oh Glory Be 106 (10f,Sal,GS,Jun 27)
Okikoki 105 (7f,Cat,GF,Nov 6)
Oldjoesaid 109 (5f,Hay,S,Sep 29)
Olimpo 105 (14f,Not,G,Aug 14)
Ollie George 109 (12f,Bat,F,Apr 24)
Olympian Odyssey 116 (9f,Nad,G,Feb 1)
One More Round 107 (6f,Hay,GF,Sep 7)
One Way Ticket 106 (5f,Bri,F,Jun 8)
Only Answer 108 (5f,Lon,G,Sep 16)
Opera Cape 109 (6f,Ham,GS,Sep 24)
Optimus 106 (8f,San,GF,Sep 14)
Oracle West 117 (9f,Nad,G,Feb 1)
Orbit O Gold 114 (16f,Leo,GF,Nov 4)
Ordnance Row 116 (8f,San,GS,Jly 7)
Orpen Wide 109 (7f,Nmk,G,Jun 22)
Orpsie Boy 113 (6f,Sal,GF,May 24)

Osiris Way 108 (6f,Nmk,GS,Jun 23)
Osolomio 106 (13f,Ham,GF,May 6)
Osteopathic Remedy 105 (8f,Hay,S,Sep 28)
Our Blessing 105 (6f,Nmk,G,Aug 17)
Our Faye 107 (7f,Sal,GF,Sep 6)
Our Little Secret 111 (5f,Chs,S,Jly 14)
Our Monty 109 (16f,Leo,GF,Nov 4)
Out After Dark 108 (6f,Nby,GS,May 19)
Out Of The Red 106 (7f,Leo,G,Apr 7)
Outer Hebrides 106 (6f,Lei,S,May 28)
Overrule 106 (10f,Nmk,GF,Jly 12)
Overwing 106 (6f,Lei,S,Oct 9)
Own Boss 107 (7f,Nmk,G,Jly 21)

Paceman 107 (9f,Lin,GF,May 22)
Padlocked 108 (9f,Lin,GF,May 22)
Pagan Starprincess 106 (12f,Bev,GS,Jun 21)
Pagan Sword 107 (10f,San,GF,Sep 1)
Palanoverre 106 (10f,Cur,GF,May 7)
Papal Bull 113 (13f,Nby,G,Aug 18)
Paradise Isle 108 (6f,Nad,G,Feb 9)
Paraguay 105 (7f,Thi,GF,Apr 20)
Paris Bell 107 (6f,Pon,GS,Jly 29)
Parisian Dream 106 (7f,Sal,GF,Jun 12)
Partners In Jazz 107 (7f,Nby,GS,Aug 18)
Passage Of Time 112 (12f,Lon,G,Sep 16)
Passager 110 (8f,Cha,G,Jun 10)
Passion Fruit 108 (7f,Red,F,Aug 11)
Patavellian 109 (6f,Ayr,GS,Sep 22)
Pawan 106 (6f,War,S,Jly 5)
Peace Dream 107 (8f,Lon,G,May 13)
Peace Offering 115 (5f,Lon,G,May 13)
Pearl 105 (10f,Bat,G,Oct 24)
Pearl Sky 113 (10f,Lon,HY,Apr 1)
Pearly King 110 (12f,Nad,G,Feb 15)
Pearly Wey 110 (6f,Nmk,GS,May 27)
Peculiar Prince 107 (10f,Ayr,GS,Sep 20)
Peeping Fawn 117 (12f,Yor,G,Aug 22)
Peintre Bleu 109 (12f,Nad,G,Feb 15)
Pelican Waters 106 (8f,Leo,GF,Nov 4)
Pentecost 106 (7½f,Nad,G,Jan 18)
Peopleton Brook 106 (5f,Hay,GF,May 25)
Peppertree 107 (14f,Sal,GF,May 6)
Peppertree Lane 109 (12f,Pon,GS,Jun 24)
Per Incanto 107 (7f,Nby,GS,Aug 18)
Percussionist 109 (14f,Yor,G,May 18)
Perfect Casting 109 (8f,Nav,YS,Jun 15)
Perfect Reward 106 (11½f,Wdr,S,Oct 15)
Perfect Star 110 (7f,Sal,GF,Sep 6)
Perfect Story 107 (6f,Not,GS,May 12)
Perfect Treasure 105 (5f,Bri,F,Jun 8)
Perfectperformance 106 (12f,Goo,GF,Aug 3)
Perpetual Motion 108 (8f,Cur,G,Sep 2)
Peruvian Prince 107 (10½f,Yor,G,Aug 22)
Peter Island 106 (6f,Bri,F,Aug 9)
Pevensey 111 (12f,Asc,S,Jun 23)
Phantom Whisper 108 (6f,Wdr,S,Jun 30)
Philanthropy 114 (12f,Yor,GF,Sep 5)
Philatelist 105 (12f,Goo,G,Aug 1)
Philharmonic 105 (5f,Bev,G,Sep 25)
Phluke 105 (7f,Chs,G,Jun 12)
Phoenix Tower 109 (8f,Wdr,G,May 7)
Pianoforte 105 (8f,Hay,GF,Sep 12)
Pillar Of Hercules 105 (7f,Yar,GS,Jly 24)
Pinpoint 109 (8f,Nby,GF,Apr 21)
Pintle 110 (8f,Bat,G,Aug 19)
Pipedreamer 111 (9f,Nmk,GF,Oct 6)
Pippa Greene 109 (12f,Don,GF,Nov 10)
Pivotal Answer 106 (10f,Bat,GS,Jly 9)
Pivotal Point 108 (5f,Asc,GF,Jun 19)
Pivotal s Princess 108 (5f,Ham,G,Sep 23)
Place Vendome 107 (5f,Lon,G,Sep 16)
Plane Painter 107 (14f,Mus,GS,Sep 17)
Players Please 108 (10f,Goo,G,Aug 2)
Plucky 109 (7f,Nmk,G,Jly 21)
Plum Pudding 110 (8f,San,GS,Jly 7)
Poet Laureate 114 (12½f,Dea,S,Aug 26)
Pompeii Ruler 106 (9f,Nad,G,Mar 31)
Ponte Tresa 117 (15½f,Lon,G,Oct 28)
Pop Rock 105 (12f,Nad,G,Mar 31)
Poppyfield 106 (8f,Leo,GF,Oct 29)
Port Of Spain 111 (7f,Leo,GF,Nov 3)
Portal 107 (12f,Nmk,G,Jly 21)
Power Of Future 113 (16f,Leo,GF,Nov 4)
Practicallyperfect 108 (8f,San,G,Aug 2)
Prelude 105 (12f,Chs,GF,Aug 23)
Press The Button 105 (10f,Bat,G,Aug 19)
Pressing 108 (10f,Asc,G,Jun 20)
Presto Shinko 108 (5f,Nmk,GF,May 6)
Presumptive 109 (7f,Goo,GF,Sep 15)
Pretty Demanding 107 (11½f,Lin,GF,Jun 6)
Pride Of Nation 114 (8f,Yor,GS,May 17)
Prime Defender 110 (7f,Nmk,GF,Apr 18)
Prime Number 108 (10f,Lei,GF,Sep 11)
Prince Erik 106 (12f,Cur,SH,Jly 1)
Prince Evelith 107 (8f,Crl,GS,Jun 27)
Prince Fasliyev 107 (7f,Lon,VS,May 20)
Prince Flori 113 (12f,Sai,GS,Jun 24)
Prince Namid 105 (6f,Eps,G,Jun 2)
Prince Of Light 110 (10f,Red,GF,May 28)
Prince Of Thebes 108 (8f,San,GS,Jly 7)
Prince Sabaah 108 (10f,Pon,GF,Jun 11)
Prince Samos 106 (10½f,Chs,GF,May 9)
Prince Tamino 105 (6½f,Nad,G,Feb 15)
Prince Woodman 106 (6f,Hay,G,May 12)
Princelet 108 (16f,Asc,S,May 12)
Princess Ellis 105 (5f,War,GF,Sep 15)
Princess Nala 114 (12f,Cur,GF,May 27)
Princesse Dansante 111 (12½f,Dea,G,Aug 5)
Prinz 107 (12f,Lon,GS,Jly 14)
Profound Beauty 107 (12f,Cur,SH,Jly 15)
Promising Lead 113 (10f,Lon,GS,Oct 7)
Proper 106 (7f,Cat,GF,May 3)
Proponent 108 (12f,Yor,GF,Sep 5)
Prospect Court 107 (5f,Bev,HY,Jly 6)
Protector 113 (6f,Ncs,HY,Jun 30)
Provost 106 (8f,Yar,GF,Apr 9)
Ptarmigan Ridge 105 (5f,Ham,GS,Aug 15)
Puggy 107 (8f,Nmk,GF,May 6)
Pure Imagination 108 (8f,Wdr,GF,Apr 16)
Purple Emperor 106 (11f,Goo,GF,Aug 4)
Purple Moon 111 (14f,Yor,G,Aug 22)
Purus 110 (7f,Nmk,G,Nov 3)
Pusey Street Lady 108 (6f,Pon,GS,Aug 19)

Quantum Leap 105 (7f,Sal,GS,May 17)
Quartino 107 (12f,Cur,GF,May 26)
Queen Of France 111 (9f,Cur,G,Sep 2)
Queen s Best 111 (10f,Cur,GF,Sep 14)
Quest For Honor 106 (10½f,Lon,GS,Apr 8)
Quijano 109 (12f,Nad,G,Feb 9)
Quince 105 (10f,Nmk,GF,May 25)
Quinmaster 111 (8f,Leo,GF,Apr 22)
Quito 109 (7f,Hay,GF,Jun 7)

Raccoon 109 (5f,Cat,F,May 8)
Racer Forever 112 (7f,Nmk,GF,Jly 13)
Racinger 111 (8f,Asc,GF,Jun 19)
Ragged Staff 106 (7f,Cur,G,May 7)
Ragheed 111 (8f,Rip,GF,Aug 27)
Raglan Copenhagen 106 (6f,Sal,S,Jly 28)
Rahiyah 111 (8f,Lon,G,May 13)
Rainbow Bay 105 (6f,Cat,GF,Jun 8)
Rainbow Fox 106 (6f,Ham,GF,Aug 31)
Rainbow Rising 109 (5f,Cur,HY,Jly 15)
Raincoat 111 (10f,Eps,GF,Apr 25)
Rajeh 108 (12f,Yor,G,Aug 21)
Ramonti 115 (8f,Lon,G,Sep 9)
Rampallion 107 (12f,Asc,GS,Sep 30)
Ranelagh 113 (8f,Msn,G,Jly 22)
Ransom Captive 107 (10f,Nby,GS,May 18)
Raptor 105 (8f,Ncs,GS,Mar 31)
Raquel White 110 (12f,Bev,GS,Jun 21)
Rare Coincidence 107 (11f,Ham,GS,Jly 19)
Rasaman 105 (5f,Goo,GF,Aug 3)
Raslan 106 (20f,Asc,G,Jun 19)
Raucous 109 (16f,Rip,GF,Apr 28)
Ravarino 111 (10f,Bev,G,Aug 16)
Ravenna 105 (11½f,Yar,GF,Jly 23)
Rayhani 110 (12f,Don,GF,Sep 15)
Realism 110 (12f,Cat,G,Sep 22)
Record Breaker 107 (11f,Goo,G,May 25)
Red Clubs 117 (6f,Hay,GF,Sep 8)
Red Diva 113 (12f,Lon,GS,Jly 14)
Red Evie 114 (7f,Nby,GS,Aug 18)
Red Gala 111 (10f,Don,GF,Sep 12)
Red Rock Canyon 115 (10f,Leo,GF,Sep 8)
Red Rocks 113 (10f,Leo,GF,Sep 8)
Red Somerset 108 (8f,Not,GF,Oct 31)
Redeemable 108 (7f,Leo,GF,Nov 3)
Redstone Dancer 110 (7f,Cur,S,Jun 30)
Reeling N Rocking 106 (8f,Nmk,GF,May 25)
Reform Act 112 (14f,Leo,S,Jly 18)
Regal Flush 111 (14½f,Don,GF,Sep 15)
Regal Parade 109 (7f,Goo,G,Aug 2)
Regal Quest 108 (7f,Sal,GF,Sep 6)
Regent s Secret 107 (8f,Ham,G,Jun 13)
Regime 113 (10f,Leo,GF,Sep 8)
Rekaab 112 (16f,Leo,GF,Nov 4)
Reload 105 (8f,Leo,GF,Oct 29)
Relocation 107 (11f,Ham,GS,Jly 19)
Resonate 106 (10f,Nmk,F,Aug 11)
Reunite 110 (10f,Yar,G,Sep 19)
Reve Lunaire 111 (8f,Nad,GF,Feb 1)
Reverence 109 (6f,Asc,GS,Jly 27)
Rhaam 107 (12f,Pon,G,Jly 10)
Rhuepunzel 106 (7f,War,G,Jly 12)
Rhythm N Blues 108 (12f,Cur,GF,May 27)
Rhythm n Roots 107 (7½f,Nad,G,Jan 25)
Ricine 110 (8f,Dea,S,Aug 26)
Ridge Boy 110 (9f,Leo,GF,Sep 8)
Ridge Rose 105 (10f,Lei,S,Jly 19)
Rio Riva 110 (8f,Ncs,GS,Mar 31)
Riotous Applause 108 (5f,Lei,GF,Sep 11)
Ripples Maid 115 (6f,Pon,GS,Aug 19)
Riquewihr 105 (7f,Yor,S,Jly 13)
Rising Cross 109 (12½f,Dea,G,Aug 5)
Rising Shadow 111 (6f,Yor,G,May 16)
River Alhaarth 107 (16f,Hay,GF,Jun 9)
River Falcon 108 (5f,Nby,GF,Apr 20)
River Thames 106 (6f,Ayr,GS,Jly 16)
River Tiber 106 (8f,Asc,G,Jly 14)
Road To Love 111 (10f,Goo,G,May 25)
Robustian 109 (8f,Pon,G,Apr 10)
Rochdale 108 (6f,Nad,G,Feb 9)
Rock N Roll Kid 108 (7½f,Nad,G,Jan 18)
Rockie 111 (9f,Leo,GF,Sep 8)
Rockys Choice 112 (16f,Leo,GF,Nov 4)
Rohaani 105 (10f,Nad,G,Feb 8)
Roman Maze 108 (7f,Chs,G,Jun 12)
Romany Nights 108 (6f,Nmk,GS,May 27)
Rosbay 106 (12f,Yor,GF,Sep 5)
Rose Street 105 (10f,Yar,GS,Oct 30)
Rothesay Dancer 105 (5f,Ham,GF,Aug 4)
Rowe Park 110 (5f,Nmk,G,Oct 4)
Royal Dignitary 112 (8f,Rip,GF,Jun 6)
Royal Oath 113 (8f,Asc,G,Jly 14)
Royal Power 106 (8f,Nad,G,Feb 9)
Royal Rock 108 (6f,Wdr,G,Oct 6)
Rudry Dragon 107 (8f,San,G,Aug 2)
Rudry World 107 (12f,Ham,GS,Aug 15)
Runaway 111 (10f,Lon,HY,Apr 1)
Russian Epic 106 (8f,San,G,Aug 2)
Russian Invader 109 (11½f,Wdr,G,Oct 8)
Russian Rosie 108 (10f,Yar,G,Sep 19)
Ryono 108 (8f,Dea,S,Aug 26)

Sabana Perdida 113 (7f,Lon,G,Sep 9)
Sabasha 112 (6f,Dea,S,Aug 26)
Saddex 114 (12f,Lon,GS,Oct 7)
Sadler s Kingdom 109 (13f,Ham,GS,Sep 24)
Safari Mischief 108 (5f,Bri,F,Jun 8)
Safwa 105 (8f,San,GF,Sep 14)
Saga Celebre 106 (12f,Cur,GY,Oct 21)
Sagara 117 (12f,Lon,G,Sep 16)
Sageburg 112 (12f,Lon,G,Sep 16)
Sagredo 109 (10f,Pon,GS,Jly 29)
Sahrati 106 (12f,Lei,GF,Apr 28)
Sakhee s Secret 118 (6f,Nmk,GF,Jly 13)
Salford Mill 111 (11f,Nby,GF,Sep 21)
Salient 108 (7f,Nmk,GF,Oct 6)
Salonga 105 (10f,Yar,S,Jly 5)
Salute 105 (16f,Nby,GF,Apr 21)
Salute Him 107 (12f,Cur,GF,May 27)
Sam s Secret 105 (7f,Mus,GF,Aug 2)
Samira Gold 112 (10f,Yar,G,Sep 19)
Samsons Son 110 (7f,Goo,G,Aug 2)
Samuel 107 (12f,Hay,GF,May 25)
Samurai Way 106 (14f,Hay,GF,Sep 8)
San Antonio 108 (8f,Nmk,GF,May 25)
San Domenico 105 (7f,Lon,VS,May 20)
Sanaya 114 (8f,Nad,G,Feb 8)
Sanbuch 113 (12f,Nmk,GF,Oct 6)
Sanchi 106 (12f,Nad,G,Feb 9)
Sand Cat 105 (6f,Nad,G,Feb 9)
Sandrey 108 (6f,Lin,GS,May 12)
Satri 112 (6½f,Dea,G,Aug 5)
Satulagi 107 (8f,Nmk,GF,May 6)
Satwa Queen 114 (10f,Lon,GS,Oct 7)
Scarlet Oak 107 (6f,Lei,S,Oct 9)
Scarlet Runner 110 (8f,Asc,GS,Jun 22)
Scootch 107 (8f,Cur,S,Oct 22)
Scorpion 116 (14f,Cur,GF,Sep 15)
Scotch Bonnet 113 (12f,Lon,GS,Jly 14)
Scriptwriter 109 (14f,Yor,G,Aug 22)
Seal Colony 106 (7f,Cur,G,May 7)
Seasoned 112 (7f,Leo,G,Apr 7)
Secret Tune 110 (16f,Asc,GS,Jun 22)
Secret World 105 (8f,Nby,GS,May 19)
Sedge 105 (7f,Thi,GF,May 12)
Sedgwick 106 (9f,Ayr,GF,May 31)
Sedna 109 (7f,Cur,GF,Sep 16)
Seeking The Buck 108 (10½f,Hay,GF,Sep 8)
Seihali 111 (9f,Nad,G,Feb 9)
Selinka 112 (8f,Goo,G,Aug 25)
Sell Out 110 (10f,Yar,G,Sep 19)
Sendalam 107 (7½f,Nad,G,Jan 18)
Senor Benny 106 (5f,Cur,HY,Jly 15)
Senor Dali 107 (9f,Nad,G,Jan 18)
Sentinelese 111 (8f,Dea,G,Aug 12)
Sentry Duty 108 (14f,Nmk,G,May 19)
Septimus 113 (10f,Cur,GF,May 7)
Serengeti 106 (16f,Asc,GS,Jun 22)
Sergeant Cecil 111 (14f,Yor,G,May 18)
Sesmen 109 (8f,Bat,G,Aug 19)
Settigano 107 (8f,Cur,G,Sep 2)
Sexy Lady 107 (10f,Yar,GF,Jly 17)
Shahin 112 (12f,Goo,G,Jun 1)
Shaimaa 105 (12f,Leo,GF,Sep 8)
Shake On It 107 (8f,Bat,F,Apr 11)
Shakis 111 (9f,Nad,G,Feb 9)
Shamdinan 109 (10½f,Cha,GS,Jun 3)
Shanty Star 113 (9f,Nad,G,Feb 1)
Sharp Reply 108 (14f,Mus,GS,Sep 17)
Shawhill 109 (12f,Lon,GS,Jly 14)
Shaykhan 107 (10f,Cur,GF,May 7)
She s Our Mark 111 (8f,Leo,Y,Aug 19)
Shela House 105 (10f,Wdr,GS,Oct 1)
Shes Minnie 106 (6f,Nmk,G,Jly 21)
Shevchenko 108 (7f,Asc,GS,Sep 29)
Shimoni 105 (11½f,Lin,GS,May 12)
Shinko Dancer 105 (5f,Cur,GF,Sep 14)
Shmookh 114 (6f,Nmk,G,Jly 11)
Shorthand 110 (10f,Yar,G,Sep 19)
Shot To Fame 109 (7f,Chs,G,Jun 12)
Shumookh 109 (8f,Not,G,Jun 6)
Shy Glance 105 (8f,Thi,GF,Apr 20)
Sierra Vista 115 (5f,San,GS,May 31)
Signor Peltro 106 (6f,Nmk,GF,Jly 27)
Silent Lucidity 107 (8f,Ham,GF,May 6)
Silkwood 110 (12f,Asc,GF,Jun 21)
Silver Pivotal 105 (8f,Yor,G,May 18)
Silver Suitor 108 (12f,Nmk,GF,Jly 27)
Silver Touch 115 (6½f,Dea,G,Aug 5)
Silverlord 106 (10f,Cha,GS,Jly 8)
Simba Sun 107 (8f,Wdr,G,Aug 25)
Simply Perfect 112 (8f,Nmk,GF,May 6)
Sin City 108 (14f,Mus,G,Jun 2)
Sina Cova 112 (9f,Cur,G,Sep 2)
Sinsational 108 (7f,Leo,GF,Nov 3)
Sir Edwin Landseer 108 (6½f,Nad,G,Feb 15)
Sir Gerard 109 (8f,Nad,G,Feb 1)
Sir Nod 108 (6f,Thi,GF,Aug 3)
Sir Orpen 106 (7f,Cat,F,May 8)
Sir Percy 107 (12f,Eps,GS,Jun 1)
Sir Xaar 110 (7f,Nmk,GF,Oct 6)
Siren s Gift 110 (6f,Nmk,G,Jly 21)
Sivota 106 (16f,Chs,GF,Sep 15)
Six Of Diamonds 108 (10f,Goo,G,Aug 2)
Skerries 110 (7f,Leo,G,Apr 7)
Skhilling Spirit 106 (6f,Ncs,GS,Mar 31)
Sky More 108 (8f,Not,S,May 12)
Slate 107 (7f,Fol,G,Jun 2)
Sling Back 105 (7f,Leo,G,Apr 7)
Smart And Mighty 115 (8f,Nad,G,Feb 9)
Smart Ass 105 (8f,Bat,G,Aug 19)
Smart Enough 110 (8f,Hay,GF,Sep 8)
Smart Instinct 106 (10f,Goo,G,Aug 2)
Smokey Oakey 108 (10f,Ayr,GS,Sep 20)
Smugglers Bay 111 (8½f,Bev,HY,Jly 7)
Snaafy 106 (8f,San,G,Aug 31)
Snaefell 111 (5f,Cur,S,Jly 1)
So So Lucky 108 (8f,Nav,YS,Jun 15)
So Will I 110 (6½f,Nad,G,Feb 15)
Soapy Danger 115 (15½f,Lon,G,Oct 28)
Soccerjackpot 108 (8f,Red,GF,Jun 12)
Society Music 106 (8f,Thi,GF,Sep 8)
Soft Morning 106 (10f,San,G,Jly 7)
Sohraab 107 (5f,Nmk,GS,Jun 23)
Soldier Hollow 113 (10f,Lon,HY,Apr 1)
Soldier Of Fortune 118 (12f,Lon,G,Sep 16)
Soldier s Tale 114 (6f,Asc,GS,Jun 23)
Solent 110 (12f,Asc,S,Jun 23)
Solid Rock 107 (7f,Eps,GS,Jun 1)
Solsiste 107 (8f,Dea,G,Aug 12)
Som Tala 109 (20f,Asc,G,Jun 19)
Something 112 (7f,Nmk,GF,Jly 13)
Song Of Passion 110 (7f,Chs,S,Jly 14)
Sonny Parkin 105 (8f,Nmk,GF,Aug 17)
Sonny Red 112 (6f,Asc,GS,Jly 27)
Soul Mountain 107 (12f,Nmk,GF,Oct 6)
Sound Of Nature 105 (7f,Lei,GF,Apr 12)
South Cape 110 (7f,Goo,GF,Sep 15)
South Wing 106 (10f,Leo,Y,Jly 28)
Southandwest 105 (5f,Goo,GF,Aug 3)
Spanish Ace 109 (5f,War,GF,Apr 17)
Spanish Diva 107 (14f,Hay,GF,Sep 12)
Spanish Harlem 107 (7f,Cur,G,May 7)
Spanish Hidalgo 108 (12f,Rip,HY,Jly 21)
Spanish Moon 109 (10½f,Yor,G,Oct 12)
Sparkling Eyes 108 (6f,Nmk,G,Jly 21)
Special Day 107 (6f,Nmk,G,Aug 18)
Speciosa 112 (10f,Cur,S,Jun 30)
Speed Dream 105 (6f,Hay,GF,May 26)
Speed Gifted 108 (14f,Yor,G,Aug 23)
Speedy Sam 109 (10f,Nby,GF,Sep 22)
Sphinx 107 (14f,Not,G,Aug 14)
Spice Route 111 (12f,Yor,G,Aug 21)
Spirit Of The Mist 107 (10f,Eps,GF,Apr 25)
Spirit One 108 (10½f,Lon,GS,Apr 8)
Spirito Del Vento 113 (8f,Cha,G,Jun 10)
Spring Goddess 106 (8f,Not,GF,Apr 4)
Spycrawler 106 (10½f,Lon,GS,Apr 8)
Squiffy 106 (16f,War,GS,Jun 28)
St Andrews 111 (8f,Wdr,G,Aug 25)
St Philip 106 (8f,Asc,GF,Jun 21)
St Savarin 108 (12f,Asc,GS,Oct 13)
Stage Gift 115 (10½f,Yor,HY,Jly 28)
Stamford Blue 105 (7f,Sal,GS,May 17)
Star Of Light 107 (10f,Nmk,F,Aug 11)
Staraco 108 (8f,Dea,S,Aug 26)
Stargazer Jim 114 (8f,Ham,G,Jun 13)
Starlight Gazer 105 (7f,Chp,S,Jly 13)
Steam Cuisine 108 (7f,Nmk,GS,Jun 23)
Steel Blue 109 (6f,Thi,GF,Aug 3)
Steenberg 105 (6f,Ayr,GS,Sep 22)
Stef s Girl 107 (7f,Cur,G,May 7)
Step To The Stars 110 (10f,Red,GS,Jun 22)
Steppe Dancer 108 (14f,Cur,GF,Sep 15)
Still Dreaming 105 (10f,Red,GS,Jun 22)
Stoic Leader 108 (7f,Mus,GF,Apr 8)
Stolen Glance 107 (9f,Ayr,GF,May 31)
Stoneacre Lad 111 (5f,Asc,GS,Jly 29)
Stonecrabstomorrow 112 (6f,Pon,GS,Jly 29)
Stonehaugh 106 (8f,Rip,GF,Jun 6)
Stoneside 113 (7f,Lon,VS,May 20)
Stop Making Sense 108 (8f,Dea,S,Aug 26)
Stormy River 112 (8f,Msn,G,Jly 22)
Stotsfold 109 (10½f,Chs,GF,May 9)
Strategic Prince 112 (8f,Nmk,GF,May 5)
Stream Of Gold 116 (9f,Nad,G,Jan 18)
Street Warrior 107 (8f,Wdr,GF,Apr 16)
Strike Up The Band 105 (6f,Ham,GS,Sep 24)
Striving Storm 105 (8f,Nmk,GF,Apr 19)
Stronghold 112 (7f,Nby,GS,Aug 18)
Subpoena 112 (6½f,Nad,G,Feb 15)
Sudden Impulse 105 (10f,Bev,GF,Apr 18)
Sudoor 108 (10f,Yar,G,Sep 19)
Suits Me 107 (9f,Ayr,HY,Nov 3)
Summer Dancer 108 (7f,Nmk,G,Nov 3)
Summer Magic 107 (8f,Leo,GF,May 30)
Sundae 106 (5f,Nmk,GS,Jun 29)
Sunday Symphony 106 (12f,Nad,G,Feb 15)
Sunisa 105 (10f,Bev,GS,Jun 21)
Sunley Peace 113 (16f,Nmk,F,Aug 11)
Sunlight 106 (8f,Hay,GF,Aug 9)
Sunrise Safari 109 (5f,Don,G,Oct 27)
Sunshine Kid 111 (10½f,Yor,G,Oct 12)

Supaseus 106 (9f,Nmk,GF,May 6)
Supersonic Dave 105 (8f,Goo,GF,Jun 9)
Surwaki 105 (7f,Thi,F,Apr 21)
Sushisan 106 (10f,Nad,G,Mar 8)
Susie May 109 (12f,Bri,GF,Aug 14)
Sweet Lilly 109 (8f,San,GF,Sep 1)
Swift Sailing 108 (16f,Leo,GF,Nov 4)
Swiss Act 106 (12f,Chs,GF,May 9)
Symbol Of Peace 107 (8f,Not,GF,Apr 4)
Synopsis 112 (12f,Lon,GS,Jly 14)

Tabadul 109 (10f,Eps,GF,Apr 25)
Tabaret 107 (5f,Nmk,G,Jly 20)
Tajneed 105 (5f,Nav,YS,Jun 15)
Takafu 105 (15f,War,GS,May 12)
Take A Bow 113 (8f,San,G,Apr 28)
Takeover Target 118 (5f,Asc,GF,Jun 19)
Talcen Gwyn 106 (5f,Bri,GS,Jly 3)
Tamagin 106 (6f,Don,G,Oct 26)
Taralaya 109 (14f,Cur,Y,Sep 30)
Tariq 111 (7f,Goo,G,Jly 31)
Tarteel 108 (7f,Nmk,G,Jly 11)
Tashelka 115 (10f,Dea,S,Aug 26)
Tawaassol 109 (7f,Goo,GF,Sep 4)
Tax Free 111 (5f,Nmk,GF,May 6)
Teachers Choice 109 (7f,Cur,G,May 7)
Tears Of A Clown 109 (10f,Asc,S,Jly 27)
Tell 113 (8f,Nmk,G,Nov 3)
Temlett 109 (14f,Leo,S,Jly 18)
Tempelstern 106 (14f,San,S,Jly 26)
Temple Place 110 (10½f,Chs,GF,May 9)
Tencendur 105 (7f,Crl,F,Aug 6)
Tender The Great 109 (8f,Wdr,G,Aug 25)
Terentia 108 (5f,Yor,GS,May 17)
Teslin 108 (9f,Nmk,GF,Oct 6)
Tetouan 107 (9f,Lin,GF,May 22)
Texas Gold 106 (5f,Goo,G,Aug 2)
Thabaat 107 (7f,Chs,G,Sep 29)
That s Hot 109 (6f,Leo,G,Jun 6)
The Fifth Member 108 (7f,Fol,HY,Oct 9)
The Gaikwar 105 (8f,Chp,S,Jly 13)
The Geezer 111 (12f,Pon,GS,Jun 24)
The Grey Berry 112 (8½f,Bev,HY,Jly 7)
The Grey One 106 (8f,War,GS,Jun 28)
The Illies 113 (8f,Asc,G,Jly 28)
The Jobber 109 (5f,Lei,GF,Sep 11)
The Kiddykid 105 (7f,Chs,GF,Aug 31)
The Osteopath 106 (8f,Not,G,Aug 2)
The Pen 106 (11f,Ham,GS,Jly 19)
The Snatcher 105 (8f,Goo,G,Jly 31)
The Tatling 112 (5f,Asc,GF,Jun 19)
The Trader 112 (6f,Dea,S,Aug 26)
The Whistling Teal 106 (14f,Cur,GF,Sep 15)
Theann 110 (6f,Yor,S,Jly 13)
Third Set 110 (6f,Sal,GF,May 24)
Thoughtless Moment 112 (8f,Cur,GF,Sep 16)
Thoughtsofstardom 108 (5f,Lin,G,Jun 23)
Thousand Words 109 (8f,Lon,G,May 13)
Tianshan 109 (8f,Dea,G,Aug 12)
Tifernati 110 (12f,Yor,GF,Sep 5)
Tiffany Gardens 105 (7f,Cur,G,May 7)
Tigron 111 (8f,Msn,G,Jly 22)
Tilt 107 (16f,Ncs,HY,Jun 30)
Timarwa 114 (9f,Cur,G,Sep 2)
Time In Madera 112 (7f,Cur,G,May 7)
Tin Town Boy 105 (10f,Cur,SH,Aug 12)
Tis Mighty 108 (7f,Cur,S,Jun 30)
Titan Triumph 106 (7f,Goo,G,Aug 25)
Tiza 114 (6f,Dea,S,Aug 26)
To Arms 105 (16f,War,GS,Jun 28)
Toboggan Lady 110 (18f,Pon,G,Oct 22)
Tobosa 110 (8f,Nmk,GF,Oct 6)
Tombi 111 (7f,Goo,G,Aug 2)
Tonic Star 105 (8f,Dea,G,Aug 12)
Tonnante 108 (14f,Mus,GS,Sep 17)
Tony James 107 (6f,Wdr,S,Jun 30)
Tony The Tap 107 (5f,Yar,G,Sep 18)
Top Class 108 (7f,Cur,G,May 7)
Top Jaro 106 (8f,Chp,S,Jly 13)
Top Mark 107 (10f,Not,G,Aug 2)
Toparudi 109 (14f,Mus,GS,Sep 17)
Torrens 106 (10f,Bev,GF,Apr 18)
Touch Of Land 107 (9f,Nad,G,Feb 1)
Tough Love 109 (7f,Cat,F,May 8)
Tournedos 105 (5f,Chs,G,May 10)
Toylsome 110 (7f,Nmk,GS,Oct 20)
Trafalgar Bay 112 (6f,Nmk,GS,May 27)
Traffic Guard 109 (8f,Goo,GF,Aug 4)
Trance 107 (16f,Nmk,F,Aug 11)
Tranquil Tiger 105 (10f,Asc,GF,Jun 21)
Transcend 106 (6f,Bri,G,Oct 25)
Treasure House 105 (8f,Nmk,GF,May 25)
Treasure Map 108 (10f,Leo,G,Apr 7)
Treat 110 (8f,Nmk,GF,May 6)
Trees Of Green 105 (7f,War,HY,Jly 6)
Tribe 108 (18f,Pon,G,Apr 10)
Trick Or Treat 111 (12f,Yor,G,Aug 22)
Trinity College 111 (10f,Leo,Y,Jly 28)
Trojan Flight 107 (6f,Ham,G,Jun 13)
Tropical Strait 110 (12f,Don,GF,Nov 10)
Truly Enchanting 105 (8f,Not,G,Jun 6)
Truly Mine 109 (8f,Cur,GF,May 27)
Tucker 111 (8½f,Eps,GS,Jun 1)
Tufton 106 (8f,Pon,G,Apr 10)
Tungsten Strike 109 (16f,Goo,G,Aug 2)
Turbo Linn 112 (12f,Nmk,G,Jly 21)
Turn Me On 105 (7f,Cat,GF,May 26)
Turn On The Style 106 (5f,Nmk,GF,Jly 12)
Turnkey 112 (6f,Yor,HY,Jly 28)
Turtle Bowl 113 (8f,Asc,GF,Jun 19)
Twin Sun s 110 (7f,Cur,G,May 7)
Tybalt 112 (8f,Nmk,GF,Jly 13)
Tycoon s Hill 108 (5f,Lon,G,May 13)

US Ranger 113 (8f,Nmk,GF,May 5)
Uhoomagoo 108 (8½f,Eps,GS,Jun 1)
Uig 107 (9f,San,G,Aug 2)
Uimhir A Haon 110 (10f,Cur,GF,Sep 14)
Under The Rainbow 110 (12f,Yor,G,Aug 22)
Une Pivoine 108 (12f,Lon,GS,Jly 14)
Unshakable 114 (8½f,Eps,GS,Jun 1)
Usk Melody 106 (7f,Nmk,G,Jly 21)
Utmost Respect 112 (6f,Nmk,G,Jly 11)

Vacation 107 (8f,Hay,HY,Jun 23)
Vadapolina 107 (12f,Lon,G,Sep 16)
Vainglory 108 (8f,Ayr,GS,Sep 22)
Val Jaro 112 (6f,Dea,S,Aug 26)
Valentina Guest 105 (10f,Leo,Y,Jly 28)
Valery Borzov 105 (5f,Goo,GF,Aug 3)
Vallemeldee 105 (14f,Hay,GF,Sep 12)
Van Gosh 115 (12f,Lon,GS,Jly 14)
Vanderlin 106 (7f,Hay,G,May 12)
Vanquisher 106 (12f,Nmk,GF,Sep 22)
Varevees 116 (15½f,Lon,G,Sep 16)
Varsity 110 (12f,Cur,GF,May 27)
Vegas Boys 105 (7f,Bri,S,May 30)
Venerable 108 (11½f,Wdr,G,Oct 8)
Vengeance Of Rain 108 (12f,Nad,G,Mar 31)
Veracity 114 (16f,Goo,G,Aug 2)
Very Well Red 106 (8f,Bat,G,Oct 24)
Very Wise 111 (8f,Ncs,GS,Mar 31)
Vicious Warrior 108 (8f,Yor,HY,Jly 14)
Vietnam 106 (10f,Not,GS,Oct 10)
Viking Spirit 109 (6f,Chp,S,Jly 13)
Vinesgrove 105 (10f,Leo,Y,Jly 28)
Virginia Woolf 108 (14f,Cur,GF,Sep 15)
Vision Of Grandeur 108 (14f,Cur,GF,Sep 15)
Visionario 106 (8f,Lon,G,Apr 15)
Vison Celebre 109 (12f,Cha,GS,Jun 3)
Vista Bella 107 (8f,Nad,G,Feb 8)
Vital Equine 115 (8f,Nmk,GF,May 5)
Vital Statistics 105 (7f,Nmk,GF,Apr 18)
Vitznau 114 (7f,Goo,G,Aug 2)
Voodoo Moon 108 (7f,Goo,G,Aug 2)
Vortex 108 (7f,Nmk,GF,Jly 13)

Wagtail 107 (8f,Bat,G,Aug 19)
Wake Up Maggie 112 (7f,Nby,GS,Aug 18)
Walk In The Park 106 (12f,Cha,GS,Jun 3)
Walking Talking 107 (12f,Asc,GF,Jun 21)
Wanchai Lad 105 (5f,Bev,GF,May 9)
Wannabe Posh 108 (12f,Nmk,GF,May 5)
Warriors Key 107 (7f,Leo,G,Apr 7)
Wasalat 106 (10f,Rip,GF,Jun 5)
Wassfa 105 (10f,Lin,GF,Jun 6)
Watchful 108 (11½f,Wdr,G,Oct 8)
Waterline Twenty 106 (8f,San,GF,Sep 14)
Waterside 109 (8f,Yor,GS,May 17)
Wavertree Warrior 109 (8½f,Eps,GS,Jun 1)
We ll Come 111 (8f,Yor,G,Aug 23)
Webbow 108 (8f,Red,GF,Jun 12)
Welsh Emperor 113 (7f,Nby,GS,Aug 18)
West Wind 112 (12f,Lon,G,Sep 16)
Western Adventure 105 (11f,Ham,G,May 18)
Western Point 105 (11½f,Yar,GF,Aug 15)
Westlake 105 (12f,Leo,YS,Jly 4)
Westport 105 (6f,Lei,S,May 28)
What Do You Know 105 (5f,Bri,F,Jun 8)
Whatwodmyrasay 106 (7f,Cur,G,May 7)
Whazzis 109 (7f,Nby,GS,May 19)
Whispering Death 105 (14f,Hay,GF,Sep 8)
Whitbarrow 108 (6f,Crl,GF,Jly 29)
White Deer 109 (7f,Goo,G,Aug 26)
Who s Winning 105 (6f,Goo,G,May 10)
Wi Dud 112 (5f,San,GS,Jly 7)
Wid 108 (6f,Nmk,G,Nov 2)
Wigwam Willie 106 (8f,Ayr,S,Sep 21)
Wind Star 111 (10f,Red,GF,May 28)
Windbeneathmywings 107 (12f,Bev,GS,Jun 21)
Windjammer 105 (5f,Chs,GF,Sep 1)
Windsor Knot 108 (9f,Nmk,S,Oct 19)
Wing Collar 108 (14f,Yor,G,Aug 22)
Winged Cupid 112 (10½f,Yor,HY,Jly 28)
Winter Fashion 112 (7f,Lon,VS,May 20)
Winter Sunrise 108 (12f,Asc,GS,Oct 13)
Wise Dennis 115 (8f,Yor,GS,May 17)
Woodcote Place 107 (8f,Goo,G,Jly 31)
Word Perfect 106 (6f,Ham,GS,Aug 22)
Worldly Wise 105 (10f,Cur,GF,Sep 15)
Wovoka 106 (10f,Eps,GF,Apr 25)
Wyatt Earp 107 (6f,Yor,GF,Sep 9)
Wychwood Wanderer 105 (6f,Cur,G,May 27)

Yaqeen 109 (8f,Nmk,GF,May 6)
Yard-Arm 108 (8f,Nad,G,Feb 9)
Yaroslav 110 (7f,Goo,G,Aug 2)
Yarqus 110 (8f,Nad,G,Feb 9)
Yasoodd 116 (9f,Nad,G,Jan 18)
Yazamaan 106 (10½f,Chs,G,May 11)
Yeaman s Hall 111 (8f,San,GS,Jly 7)
Yeats 117 (14f,Cur,GF,Sep 16)
Yellowstone 115 (10f,San,GS,Jly 7)
Yossi 106 (12f,Pon,G,Jly 10)
You re Beautiful 108 (10f,Leo,Y,Jly 28)
Youmzain 118 (12f,Lon,GS,Oct 7)
Young Bertie 105 (8f,Wdr,G,Oct 8)
Young Mick 107 (12f,Lei,GS,Oct 29)
Yungaburra 107 (5f,Don,GF,Sep 14)

Zaafran 107 (8f,Nad,G,Feb 8)
Zaahid 107 (8f,Hay,S,Sep 28)
Zaham 111 (12f,Asc,GS,Sep 30)
Zaif 110 (12f,Nmk,GF,Oct 6)
Zakfree 107 (10f,Cur,GF,May 7)
Zambezi Sun 116 (12f,Lon,G,Sep 16)
Zar Solitario 106 (10f,Lei,GF,Apr 12)
Zato 105 (8f,Nad,G,Feb 15)
Zeeno 110 (6½f,Nad,G,Feb 15)
Zero Tolerance 112 (8f,Yor,GS,May 17)
Zhukhov 105 (7f,Cur,GF,Sep 16)
Zidane 114 (6f,Asc,S,May 12)
Zomerlust 113 (6f,Yor,HY,Jly 28)
Zonergem 110 (10f,Bev,G,Aug 16)

THREE YEAR-OLDS AND UPWARDS - Sand

Abbondanza 105 (9f,Wol,SD,Dec 7)
Abounding 108 (12f,Wol,SD,Jun 1)
Abunai 107 (6f,Wol,SD,Nov 16)
Acheekyone 107 (8f,Kem,SD,May 7)
Active Asset 107 (12f,Lin,SD,Mar 30)
Adage 106 (14f,Wol,SD,Jly 16)
Adantino 110 (6f,Lin,SD,Feb 10)
Aegean Dancer 110 (5f,Wol,SD,Nov 19)
Agnes Jedi 107 (6f,Nad,FT,Mar 1)
Ainama 107 (12f,Lin,SD,Jun 30)
Ajigolo 108 (6f,Lin,SD,Jan 20)
Al Tharib 115 (12f,Kem,SD,Sep 8)
Aleutian 108 (8f,Nad,FT,Feb 22)
Alfie Tupper 105 (10f,Kem,SD,Oct 31)
Alfresco 106 (8f,Kem,SD,Jun 6)
Aliysa 108 (6f,Nad,FT,Jan 25)
All Of Me 105 (7f,Wol,SD,Apr 24)
Almaram 109 (6f,Nad,FT,Feb 1)
Almaty Express 110 (5f,Wol,SS,Jan 26)
Alnwick 107 (13f,Lin,SD,Jly 3)
Amwell Brave 106 (16f,Lin,SD,Jan 24)
Andronikos 109 (7f,Lin,SD,Nov 24)
Another Genepi 107 (7f,Wol,SD,Apr 27)
Appalachian Trail 108 (8f,Kem,SD,Nov 28)
Arabian Prince 107 (10f,Nad,FT,Mar 8)
Arch Of Titus 111 (7f,Wol,SD,Apr 5)
Arctic Desert 106 (7f,Lin,SD,Jan 27)
Areyoutalkingtome 115 (6f,Lin,SD,Jan 13)
Art Modern 105 (12f,Lin,SD,Feb 5)
Artless 108 (11f,Sth,SD,May 22)
Ashes Regained 107 (9f,Wol,SD,May 21)
Asiatic Boy 115 (9f,Nad,FT,Mar 31)
Atlantic Quest 109 (9f,Wol,SD,Jan 19)
Atlantic Story 110 (9f,Wol,SD,Jan 19)
Audit 109 (11f,Sth,SD,May 22)
Augustine 105 (12f,Wol,SS,Jan 29)
Awatuki 106 (11f,Kem,SD,Mar 21)

Babodana 108 (8f,Lin,SD,Nov 17)
Bahamian Pirate 110 (6f,Sth,SD,Feb 13)
Bahar Shumaal 106 (12f,Kem,SD,Mar 24)
Bahiano 108 (6f,Lin,SD,Dec 7)
Baizically 107 (8f,Sth,SD,Mar 6)
Ballet Boy 106 (12f,Lin,SD,Jun 21)
Bandama 109 (10f,Kem,SD,Jun 6)
Banknote 108 (8f,Lin,SD,Mar 29)
Barathea Dreams 107 (8f,Lin,SD,May 4)
Barbirolli 108 (9½f,Wol,SD,Jan 12)
Barney McGrew 110 (7f,Lin,SD,Jan 27)
Barshiba 105 (8f,Lin,SD,Feb 10)
Bay Boy 107 (10f,Lin,SD,Feb 3)
Bazroy 108 (6f,Lin,SD,Dec 9)
Beauchamp Viceroy 108 (7f,Lin,SD,Mar 24)
Beldon Hill 106 (14f,Sth,SS,Feb 11)
Beneking 107 (7f,Lin,SD,Jan 24)
Benllech 108 (6f,Lin,SD,Dec 30)
Bennie Blue 109 (10f,Nad,FT,Mar 8)
Bertoliver 107 (6f,Lin,SD,Oct 12)
Best One 106 (6f,Lin,SD,Dec 9)
Best Selection 106 (11f,Kem,SD,Jly 4)
Billich 113 (16f,Lin,SD,Feb 14)
Binary File 108 (8f,Nad,FT,Mar 1)
Binnion Bay 112 (8f,Lin,SD,May 4)
Birkside 109 (12f,Wol,SD,Dec 26)
Birkspiel 105 (10f,Lin,SD,Feb 24)
Bishop Court Hill 112 (6f,Nad,FT,Mar 31)
Black Falcon 110 (11f,Sth,SD,Mar 28)
Blackat Blackitten 107 (8f,Kem,SD,Sep 24)
Blatant 108 (8f,Nad,FT,Mar 1)
Blue Bajan 115 (10f,Lin,SD,Feb 24)
Blythe Knight 105 (9f,Wol,SS,Jan 26)
Bobski 106 (7f,Lin,SD,Oct 14)
Bolckow 106 (12f,Sth,SD,Feb 13)
Bold Diktator 109 (9f,Wol,SD,Feb 10)
Bolodenka 106 (9f,Wol,SD,Jan 5)
Bomber Command 106 (9f,Wol,SD,Mar 10)
Bonnie Prince Blue 107 (7f,Kem,SD,May 2)
Bonus 111 (6f,Lin,SD,Jan 20)
Boo 106 (10f,Lin,SD,Mar 24)
Boot n Toot 108 (10f,Lin,SD,Mar 17)
Border Music 108 (7f,Wol,SD,Mar 10)
Borderlescott 111 (6f,Lin,SD,Nov 24)
Boscobel 110 (7f,Lin,SD,Jan 13)
Boston Lodge 110 (8f,Nad,FT,Feb 22)
Boundless Prospect 105 (8f,Sth,SW,Jan 11)
Bounty Quest 111 (6f,Nad,FT,Mar 1)
Bowl Of Cherries 107 (10f,Kem,SD,Oct 31)
Brandywell Boy 106 (6f,Kem,SD,Nov 14)
British Isles 108 (8f,Nad,FT,Feb 22)
Bugsy s Boy 106 (12f,Kem,SD,Oct 3)
Bullish Luck 112 (10f,Nad,FT,Mar 31)
Buscador 105 (9½f,Wol,SD,Jan 12)
Buxton 106 (6f,Lin,SD,Oct 15)
Buy On The Red 110 (6f,Lin,SD,Jan 20)
By The Edge 107 (5f,Wol,SD,Dec 20)

Cactus King 105 (10f,Lin,SD,Apr 1)
California Laws 112 (7f,Sth,SD,Jan 23)
Call My Bluff 108 (9½f,Wol,SD,Jan 12)
Calzaghe 107 (12f,Wol,SD,Jun 1)
Came Back 106 (6f,Sth,SD,Mar 20)
Canadian Danehill 111 (5f,Wol,SS,Jan 26)
Cantabilly 105 (16f,Kem,SD,Apr 25)
Capable Guest 108 (8f,Lin,SD,Nov 17)
Cape Hawk 112 (8f,Kem,SD,Jun 6)
Capricho 105 (8f,Lin,SD,May 4)
Capricorn Run 111 (7f,Lin,SD,Nov 24)
Captain General 106 (12f,Kem,SD,May 9)
Carcinetto 109 (6f,Wol,SD,Nov 22)
Carlitos Spirit 105 (8f,Kem,SD,Dec 5)
Carnivore 105 (7f,Lin,SD,Oct 14)
Cavallini 110 (12f,Kem,SD,May 9)
Cedar Mountain 109 (10f,Kem,SD,Jun 6)
Celtic Mill 106 (5f,Lin,SD,Mar 24)
Cerebus 106 (6f,Sth,SD,Feb 6)
Ceremonial Jade 113 (8f,Lin,SD,Feb 17)
Certain Justice 105 (7f,Lin,SD,Feb 17)
Challis 107 (9½f,Wol,SD,Jan 15)
Champery 105 (8f,Lin,SD,Apr 14)
Charlie Cool 105 (10f,Kem,SD,Apr 7)
Cherri Fosfate 108 (7f,Wol,SD,Apr 5)
Chicken Soup 111 (7f,Wol,SD,Jan 5)
Chief Commander 106 (7f,Sth,SW,Feb 8)
Chief Editor 108 (5f,Wol,SD,Nov 4)
Chief Exec 105 (7f,Wol,SD,Jan 5)
Chookie Hamilton 107 (9f,Wol,SD,Jan 19)
Chord 107 (12f,Wol,SD,Jly 6)
Cimyla 106 (10f,Lin,SD,Mar 24)
Classic Encounter 108 (5f,Lin,SD,Mar 29)
Clear Reef 108 (11f,Sth,SS,Dec 21)
Cleaver 108 (12f,Kem,SD,May 9)
Cleide Da Silva 108 (7f,Wol,SD,Jun 30)
Cleveland 106 (7f,Sth,SD,May 15)
Climate 107 (9½f,Wol,SD,Jan 12)
Coeur De Lionne 113 (12f,Kem,SD,Sep 24)
Cold Turkey 107 (12f,Kem,SD,Nov 3)
Coleorton Dancer 106 (6f,Wol,SD,Nov 22)
Colonel Flay 106 (12f,Kem,SD,Oct 3)
Come Out Fighting 106 (5f,Wol,SD,Nov 4)
Comma 111 (8f,Kem,SD,Jly 18)
Confidentiality 109 (9f,Wol,SD,Dec 4)
Conrad 105 (7f,Sth,SW,Jan 11)
Converti 106 (12f,Lin,SD,Jun 30)
Convivial Spirit 106 (7f,Wol,SD,Apr 5)
Cool Sands 108 (6f,Kem,SD,Feb 25)
Copper King 108 (7f,Lin,SD,Jan 13)
Coral Creek 105 (9½f,Wol,SD,Nov 17)
Cornus 106 (6f,Wol,SD,Nov 22)
Councellor 108 (8f,Sth,SD,Mar 6)
Counsel s Opinion 107 (10f,Kem,SD,Jun 6)
Count Cougar 107 (6f,Sth,SD,Mar 20)
Court Masterpiece 105 (8f,Nad,FT,Mar 31)
Crete 109 (12f,Lin,SD,Nov 17)
Cross The Line 109 (7f,Kem,SD,Mar 31)
Crow Wood 106 (12f,Lin,SD,Jan 6)
Curtail 108 (6f,Wol,SD,Nov 16)
Cusoon 116 (10f,Lin,SD,Feb 24)

Dado Mush 109 (8f,Sth,SD,Dec 12)
Dan Tucker 107 (12f,Kem,SD,Jun 13)
Danebury Hill 105 (8f,Kem,SD,Mar 31)
Danetime Lord 108 (7f,Lin,SD,Jan 24)
Dansant 115 (12f,Kem,SD,Dec 1)
Danzare 105 (10f,Kem,SD,Jan 3)
Dapple Dawn 106 (8f,Sth,SW,Jan 11)
Daring Affair 108 (9½f,Wol,SS,Jan 26)
Dasheena 107 (7f,Sth,SD,Dec 11)
Davenport 107 (8f,Sth,SW,Jan 11)
Day Pass 105 (9f,Nad,FT,Mar 1)
Daytona 108 (7f,Lin,SD,Mar 7)
Dazed And Amazed 106 (5f,Kem,SD,Jun 6)
Dee Cee Elle 107 (12f,Kem,SD,Jun 13)
Den s Gift 107 (8f,Kem,SD,Dec 1)
Desert D Argent 106 (11f,Kem,SD,Sep 8)
Desert Island Miss 106 (8f,Kem,SD,Sep 15)
Desert Light 105 (6f,Kem,SD,Dec 19)
Desert Lord 110 (6f,Lin,SD,Nov 24)
Desert Master 105 (6f,Wol,SD,Feb 26)
Desert Opal 106 (5f,Wol,SS,Jan 27)
Desperate Dan 108 (6f,Sth,SD,Feb 13)
Dhehdaah 107 (16f,Kem,SD,Apr 25)

Diamond Diva 106 (6f,Wol,SD,Jun 11)
Diane s Choice 109 (6f,Lin,SD,Dec 7)
Dichoh 110 (8f,Sth,SD,Mar 6)
Diktatorship 105 (14f,Wol,SD,Jly 16)
Dingaan 107 (6f,Lin,SD,Oct 12)
Discotheque 106 (9½f,Wol,SS,Jan 28)
Distinctly Game 110 (5f,Lin,SD,Feb 17)
Dixie Meister 105 (8f,Nad,FT,Mar 31)
Doctor s Cave 107 (7f,Sth,SD,May 15)
Dolzago 107 (16f,Lin,SD,Jan 29)
Dont Dili Dali 110 (8f,Kem,SD,Apr 7)
Dragon Slayer 107 (9½f,Wol,SS,Jan 26)
Dramatic 105 (6f,Wol,SD,Jun 2)
Dream Catcher 105 (9f,Wol,SD,Sep 20)
Dryandra 111 (12f,Kem,SD,Mar 24)
Dubai Twilight 105 (8f,Lin,SD,Apr 1)
Dubai s Touch 108 (8f,Kem,SD,Mar 31)
Dudley Docker 106 (7f,Sth,SW,Jan 11)
Duke Of Tuscany 108 (11f,Kem,SD,Aug 27)
Dundry 106 (12f,Lin,SD,Feb 17)
Duty Free 105 (12f,Kem,SD,Jly 17)
Dvinsky 105 (6f,Wol,SD,Mar 5)
Dynamic Saint 109 (10f,Nad,FT,Feb 22)

Ebn Reem 105 (6f,Kem,SD,Apr 7)
Ebraam 109 (5f,Wol,SD,Nov 19)
Edge Closer 108 (6f,Kem,SD,Aug 29)
Effective 107 (6f,Kem,SD,Mar 25)
Eforetta 105 (11f,Sth,SD,Mar 15)
Egyptian Lord 105 (5f,Sth,SD,Mar 28)
Eisteddfod 105 (6f,Kem,SD,Mar 31)
Ektimaal 105 (7f,Wol,SS,Jan 29)
El Toreador 105 (9f,Wol,SD,Jun 30)
Electric Warrior 109 (8f,Kem,SD,Sep 8)
Establishment 106 (16f,Kem,SD,Jly 4)
Estate 108 (16½f,Wol,SD,Nov 12)
Eu Tambem 109 (10f,Nad,FT,Mar 1)
Eumene 106 (12f,Wol,SD,Dec 14)
Eva Soneva So Fast 110 (12f,Lin,SD,Feb 3)
Even Bolder 106 (6f,Kem,SD,Aug 1)
Evens And Odds 109 (7f,Lin,SD,Mar 24)
Ever Cheerful 105 (6f,Kem,SD,Dec 12)
Evident Pride 110 (8f,Kem,SD,Sep 8)
Excusez Moi 105 (5f,Lin,SD,Mar 24)
Expensive 114 (8f,Kem,SD,Apr 7)
Expensive Art 106 (6f,Lin,SD,Jly 18)

Fairson 107 (9f,Nad,FT,Feb 8)
Faithful Ruler 106 (7f,Kem,SD,Nov 21)
Fajr 110 (7f,Lin,SD,Nov 24)
Familiar Territory 110 (10f,Kem,SD,Jun 6)
Fantoche 110 (12f,Wol,SF,May 3)
Fares 109 (7f,Lin,SD,Jan 13)
Farnesina 105 (8f,Kem,SD,Feb 4)
Fast Freddie 106 (6f,Wol,SD,Nov 20)
Featherlight 106 (12f,Lin,SD,Jun 30)
Fenice 107 (10f,Nad,FT,Mar 8)
Fidelia 106 (8f,Lin,SD,Nov 1)
Fiefdom 105 (8f,Lin,SD,Nov 26)
Figaro Flyer 108 (5f,Lin,SD,Jan 17)
Financial Times 109 (5f,Lin,SD,Jan 17)
First Order 110 (5f,Wol,SD,Dec 8)
Fishforcompliments 106 (7f,Lin,SD,Mar 24)
Fizzlephut 105 (5f,Wol,SS,Jan 27)
Flame Creek 110 (13f,Lin,SD,Nov 15)
Flint River 106 (7f,Lin,SD,Jan 24)
Flying Bantam 105 (7f,Sth,SD,Feb 15)
Flying Spirit 106 (16f,Lin,SD,Jan 24)
Flyingit 106 (8f,Sth,SW,Jan 11)
Folk 115 (9f,Nad,FT,Mar 8)
Forest Dane 107 (6f,Lin,SD,Oct 15)
Forty Licks 106 (10f,Nad,FT,Mar 31)
Fremen 105 (7f,Lin,SD,Mar 17)
Fretwork 107 (14f,Wol,SD,Oct 21)
Friendly Island 116 (6f,Nad,FT,Mar 31)
Friends Hope 108 (11f,Sth,SD,Dec 11)
Fusili 110 (10f,Lin,SD,Feb 24)
Future s Dream 109 (8f,Sth,SD,Mar 28)
Fyodor 108 (5f,Lin,SD,Mar 24)

Galient 106 (16f,Kem,SD,Apr 7)
Gallantry 108 (7f,Lin,SD,Mar 24)
Garnett 106 (16f,Lin,SD,Mar 7)
Garstang 107 (6f,Lin,SD,Feb 10)
Genari 111 (8f,Sth,SD,May 15)
Generator 106 (7f,Kem,SD,Feb 25)
Generous Lad 107 (13f,Lin,SD,Nov 15)
Gentleman s Deal 115 (8f,Sth,SD,Jan 1)
Geordieland 112 (12f,Kem,SD,Mar 24)
George The Second 107 (6f,Lin,SD,Oct 15)
Gifted Gamble 105 (7f,Wol,SD,Jan 22)
Glencalvie 106 (8f,Lin,SD,May 4)
Glenridding 108 (9f,Wol,SD,Dec 27)
Global Strategy 107 (12f,Sth,SD,Jan 7)
Golano 105 (16½f,Wol,SD,Nov 12)
Gold Digger Miss 107 (7f,Sth,SD,May 24)
Gold Prospect 107 (9½f,Wol,SD,Jun 30)
Gold Sovereign 107 (8f,Lin,SD,Sep 18)
Golden Arrow 107 (10f,Nad,FT,Feb 22)
Golden Desert 105 (7f,Lin,SD,Oct 14)
Golden Dixie 106 (5f,Wol,SD,Nov 4)
Gordonsville 106 (12f,Wol,SD,Oct 8)
Grand Passion 112 (12f,Kem,SD,Sep 8)
Grande Caiman 112 (13f,Lin,SD,Nov 15)
Granston 109 (8f,Kem,SD,May 7)
Graze On 109 (5f,Lin,SD,Feb 24)
Great Hawk 111 (12f,Kem,SD,Sep 8)
Greenbelt 107 (11f,Sth,SD,Feb 6)
Greetings 110 (7f,Nad,FT,Jan 25)
Grey Boy 105 (9f,Wol,SD,Feb 10)
Guilded Warrior 106 (6f,Kem,SD,May 9)
Guilia 105 (13f,Lin,SD,Nov 1)

Habalwatan 106 (9f,Wol,SD,Jan 19)
Hail The Chief 106 (7f,Lin,SD,Mar 24)
Halsion Chancer 110 (6f,Lin,SD,Dec 9)
Happy As Larry 105 (10f,Lin,SD,Mar 17)
Happy Go Lily 107 (12f,Kem,SD,Jun 13)
Harare 107 (9f,Wol,SF,Mar 14)
Harry Up 106 (5f,Wol,SD,Dec 8)
Harvard Avenue 113 (6f,Nad,FT,Mar 31)
Hatch A Plan 106 (10f,Kem,SD,Oct 31)
Hathaal 106 (12f,Lin,SD,Mar 30)
Hattan 110 (9f,Wol,SD,Jan 5)
Hazzard County 106 (7f,Lin,SD,Mar 30)
Heavens Walk 105 (5f,Lin,SD,Jan 17)
Hernando Royal 112 (12f,Kem,SD,May 9)
High Curragh 109 (7f,Kem,SD,Mar 31)
Highway To Glory 108 (8f,Kem,SD,Apr 7)
Hinton Admiral 111 (7f,Lin,SD,Mar 24)
His Master s Voice 107 (7f,Lin,SD,Mar 17)
Hoh Wotanite 107 (9½f,Wol,SD,Dec 31)
Holbeck Ghyll 105 (5f,Lin,SD,Oct 12)
Hollow Jo 105 (6f,Lin,SD,Dec 7)
Homes By Woodford 106 (7f,Lin,SD,Jan 13)
Hopeful Purchase 107 (7f,Lin,SD,Mar 24)
Hovering 109 (12f,Kem,SD,Mar 24)
Hucking Heat 105 (8f,Kem,SD,Dec 1)
Hucking Hope 105 (6f,Kem,SD,Dec 19)
Hurlingham 109 (8f,Kem,SD,Jan 28)
Hurricane Spirit 112 (6f,Lin,SD,Jan 13)
Hypocrisy 105 (7f,Lin,SD,Mar 1)
Hythe Bay 107 (6f,Lin,SD,Dec 7)

I Have Dreamed 107 (11f,Kem,SD,Mar 21)
Idle No More 111 (8f,Sth,SD,May 1)
Ile Michel 105 (10f,Lin,SD,Jun 23)
Illustrious Blue 112 (12f,Kem,SD,Nov 3)
Im Ova Ere Dad 107 (8f,Lin,SD,Oct 29)
Impeller 110 (10f,Lin,SD,Mar 17)
Imperial Star 114 (12f,Kem,SD,Sep 8)
Imperialista 109 (8f,Nad,FT,Jan 18)
Imperium 107 (7f,Lin,SD,Jan 24)
Impossible Ski 108 (8f,Nad,FT,Mar 1)
Inch By Inch 106 (7f,Lin,SD,Feb 17)
Inchinata 109 (11f,Kem,SD,Jly 4)
Inchpast 111 (16½f,Wol,SD,Nov 12)
Ingleby Arch 108 (6f,Sth,SD,Dec 12)
Inside Story 108 (9f,Wol,SD,Jly 27)
Into The Dark 112 (12f,Kem,SD,Nov 3)
Invasian 108 (12f,Wol,SD,Dec 14)
Invasor 120 (10f,Nad,FT,Mar 31)
Invincible Force 107 (5f,Wol,SD,Nov 4)
Italian Romance 109 (9f,Wol,SD,Jan 19)
Ivory Lace 105 (7f,Lin,SD,Jan 27)

Jack Junior 106 (9f,Nad,FT,Mar 31)
Jack Rolfe 105 (14f,Wol,SD,Mar 23)
Jack Sullivan 108 (8f,Lin,SD,Dec 22)
Jackie Kiely 105 (11f,Sth,SD,Mar 28)
Jaffal 107 (8f,Nad,FT,Feb 1)
Jalil 107 (8f,Lin,SD,Oct 12)
Jazrawy 111 (12f,Sth,SD,Feb 13)
Jebel Ali 105 (10f,Lin,SD,Feb 19)
Jilly Why 105 (5f,Wol,SD,Dec 8)
Jimmy The Guesser 107 (7f,Sth,SD,Jan 23)
Josh 109 (7f,Lin,SD,Jan 27)
Josh You Are 106 (13f,Lin,SD,Jly 10)
Junior 112 (16f,Kem,SD,Jly 4)
Just Bond 106 (9f,Wol,SD,Jun 30)

Kabeer 110 (8f,Sth,SS,Dec 20)
Kandidate 113 (9f,Nad,FT,Feb 8)
Karoo Blue 107 (8f,Kem,SD,Sep 8)
Kasumi 109 (8f,Lin,SD,Oct 14)
Katiypour 109 (8f,Lin,SD,May 4)
Kavi 106 (16f,Lin,SD,Jan 24)
Kay Two 105 (5f,Wol,SD,Nov 4)
Kelly s Landing 117 (6f,Nad,FT,Mar 31)
Kempsey 106 (6f,Kem,SD,Feb 25)
Kerriemuir Lass 107 (12f,Kem,SD,Sep 24)
Kilimandscharo 105 (9½f,Wol,SD,Jan 8)
Killena Boy 108 (8f,Kem,SD,May 7)
Kindlelight Debut 107 (8f,Lin,SD,Jan 20)
King Of Music 109 (10f,Lin,SD,Jan 6)
King Orchisios 111 (5f,Lin,SD,Mar 24)
King s Caprice 111 (6f,Lin,SD,Nov 17)
King s Ransom 105 (9f,Wol,SD,Dec 4)
Kingkohler 108 (13f,Lin,SD,Nov 15)
Kingscape 105 (11f,Kem,SD,Sep 8)
Kirk Michael 106 (7f,Wol,SD,Dec 15)
Knot In Wood 110 (6f,Lin,SD,Nov 24)
Kostar 106 (7f,Lin,SD,Mar 24)
Kylkenny 108 (11f,Sth,SD,Feb 6)

La Colline 105 (7f,Sth,SW,Jan 11)
La Estrella 106 (12f,Wol,SF,May 3)
La Presse 105 (7f,Nad,FT,Jan 25)
Laa Rayb 105 (8f,Sth,SD,May 14)
Lady Gloria 105 (8f,Sth,SD,May 24)
Lapina 106 (12f,Lin,SD,Jun 30)
Lascaux 111 (6f,Nad,FT,Mar 1)
Last Sovereign 106 (8f,Kem,SD,Jun 6)
Lemonette 109 (10f,Lin,SD,Mar 17)
Les Fazzani 112 (8f,Kem,SD,Jly 18)
Lethal 109 (6f,Kem,SD,Jan 20)
Levera 107 (7f,Lin,SD,Apr 14)
Lii Najma 108 (7f,Sth,SW,Jan 11)
Linden Lime 108 (16f,Lin,SD,Feb 14)
Lion Sands 114 (12f,Kem,SD,Sep 8)
Lisathedaddy 110 (10f,Lin,SD,Mar 17)
Little Carmela 105 (12f,Kem,SD,Oct 3)
Little Edward 109 (6f,Lin,SD,Nov 17)
Lobengula 107 (9½f,Wol,SD,Dec 15)
Longspur 106 (12f,Kem,SD,Aug 29)
Lopinot 108 (8f,Lin,SD,Mar 1)
Lorikeet 107 (16f,Lin,SD,Jan 24)
Lost All Alone 105 (6f,Lin,SD,Nov 24)
Louisiade 106 (7f,Sth,SD,Mar 20)
Loulwa 106 (13f,Lin,SD,Nov 1)
Louphole 105 (6f,Lin,SD,Feb 5)
Luberon 107 (11f,Kem,SD,Apr 7)
Lucarno 106 (8f,Kem,SD,May 7)
Lucayos 112 (6f,Lin,SD,Feb 10)
Lucius Verrus 105 (6f,Wol,SS,Feb 2)
Luckylover 109 (8f,Sth,SD,Apr 26)
Luxurix 106 (12f,Wol,SD,Mar 5)

Magic Amigo 105 (12f,Kem,SD,Jan 10)
Magic Amour 105 (6f,Wol,SF,Mar 24)
Magic Glade 112 (5f,Lin,SD,Feb 24)
Magic Moth 108 (12f,Wol,SF,May 3)
Magic Rush 106 (8f,Lin,SD,Apr 1)
Magical Music 111 (8f,Kem,SD,Sep 8)
Mahmjra 111 (11f,Sth,SD,Mar 28)
Majuro 107 (6f,Kem,SD,Aug 29)
Malt Or Mash 110 (8f,Kem,SD,Jun 6)
Maltese Falcon 112 (6f,Lin,SD,Nov 24)
Mambazo 105 (6f,Wol,SF,Jun 29)
Mandarin Spirit 106 (7f,Sth,SD,Feb 20)
Marajaa 108 (8f,Kem,SD,Sep 8)
Marchand D Or 107 (6f,Nad,FT,Mar 31)
Maria Antonia 105 (12f,Sth,SD,Jan 2)
Market Forces 105 (13f,Lin,SD,Nov 1)
Marzelline 109 (11f,Kem,SD,Aug 27)
Mastership 109 (7f,Lin,SD,Mar 24)
Mataram 105 (8f,Lin,SD,Nov 26)
Matsunosuke 109 (5f,Wol,SD,Oct 2)
Matuza 107 (6f,Wol,SD,Jun 30)
Mcnairobi 107 (7f,Lin,SD,Mar 1)
Medieval Maiden 107 (12f,Wol,SD,May 21)
Meditation 105 (7f,Lin,SD,Aug 10)
Melvino 107 (12f,Wol,SS,Jan 29)
Merlin s Dancer 113 (5f,Lin,SD,Mar 29)
Merrymadcap 106 (9f,Wol,SD,Sep 20)
Mighty 114 (10f,Lin,SD,Feb 24)
Military Cross 111 (8f,Lin,SD,Nov 17)
Millfield 105 (9½f,Wol,SD,Dec 15)
Millville 107 (12f,Lin,SD,Jan 6)
Mina A Salem 106 (7f,Lin,SD,Mar 24)
Mind How You Go 107 (16f,Lin,SD,Mar 7)
Miracle Ridge 105 (6f,Wol,SD,Jan 5)
Miramare 110 (12f,Kem,SD,Nov 3)
Misaro 107 (5f,Wol,SD,Feb 5)
Mistral Sky 105 (6f,Wol,SD,Apr 24)
Miswadah 105 (7f,Lin,SD,Mar 27)
Moayed 107 (7f,Lin,SD,Mar 24)
Monkey Glas 106 (8f,Lin,SD,Nov 26)
Monte Major 106 (5f,Wol,SD,Dec 20)
Montpellier 111 (8f,Kem,SD,May 7)
Moon Bird 106 (7f,Lin,SD,Jan 24)
Mooner 108 (8f,Nad,FT,Feb 1)
Moorhouse Lad 109 (5f,Sth,SD,Jan 1)
Morse 105 (6f,Kem,SD,Jan 20)
Most Definitely 105 (16f,Kem,SD,Apr 25)
Mountain Cat 105 (9f,Wol,SD,Sep 13)
Mountain Pass 109 (7f,Lin,SD,Jan 24)
Mr Lambros 105 (6f,Wol,SD,Dec 28)
Mr Mischief 109 (16½f,Wol,SD,Nov 12)
Mr Napper Tandy 105 (8f,Kem,SD,Mar 24)
Muhannak 107 (8f,Lin,SD,Apr 30)
Mullins Bay 110 (8f,Nad,FT,Mar 31)
Mumbling 106 (16f,Lin,SD,Jan 24)
Muntami 107 (12f,Sth,SD,Mar 6)
Murfreesboro 109 (6f,Lin,SD,Nov 24)
Musango 107 (13f,Lin,SD,Nov 15)
Musical Beat 106 (8f,Kem,SD,Jly 18)
Mutasallil 108 (10f,Nad,FT,Mar 8)
Mystic Man 108 (7f,Lin,SD,Jan 24)

Naipe Marcado 109 (8f,Nad,FT,Feb 22)
Nan Jan 107 (7f,Wol,SD,Jun 30)
Nans Joy 107 (7f,Wol,SD,Apr 5)
National Colour 109 (5f,Nad,FT,Feb 15)
Naughty Thoughts 105 (8f,Lin,SD,Oct 29)
Nawamees 112 (16f,Lin,SD,Feb 14)
Nawow 105 (12f,Lin,SD,Feb 17)
Nelore Pora 110 (8f,Nad,FT,Feb 1)
Nepro 106 (6f,Kem,SD,Mar 25)
New Freedom 105 (5f,Nad,FT,Feb 15)
New World Order 107 (8f,Lin,SD,Nov 26)
New York Oscar 105 (5f,Lin,SD,Oct 31)
Newnham 111 (16f,Lin,SD,Feb 14)
Nicada 105 (8f,Kem,SD,Dec 1)
Nicomedia 105 (7f,Lin,SD,Mar 7)
Night Cruise 114 (16f,Lin,SD,Feb 14)
Night Hour 106 (12f,Kem,SD,Sep 24)
Night Prospector 107 (6f,Lin,SD,Feb 10)
Ninth House 109 (9f,Wol,SD,Jan 19)
No Time 108 (6f,Lin,SD,Dec 7)
Noble Minstrel 110 (16½f,Wol,SD,Nov 12)
Noble Plum 108 (11f,Kem,SD,Jly 4)
Noddies Way 106 (16f,Lin,SD,Mar 7)
Norcroft 105 (6f,Kem,SD,Mar 25)
Nordic Affair 106 (7f,Lin,SD,Jan 13)
Norisan 105 (8f,Lin,SD,Apr 14)
Northern Desert 106 (8f,Lin,SD,Apr 1)
Northern Empire 105 (5f,Wol,SD,Nov 19)
Northern Spy 107 (10f,Kem,SD,Dec 16)
Nusoor 107 (5f,Wol,SS,Jan 27)

Ochre 106 (8f,Sth,SD,Dec 27)
Odiham 108 (16f,Kem,SD,Apr 7)
Off The Record 107 (5f,Sth,SD,May 15)
Ogee 109 (10f,Kem,SD,Jun 6)
Old Etonian 105 (10f,Lin,SD,Mar 24)
Ommadawn 107 (12f,Kem,SD,Oct 3)
One More Round 108 (7f,Lin,SD,Mar 24)
One Night In Paris 105 (9f,Wol,SD,Oct 27)
Only A Grand 105 (8f,Sth,SS,Dec 20)
Opal Haze 109 (12f,Kem,SD,Jly 17)
Opera Writer 105 (12f,Sth,SD,Feb 13)
Opportunist 107 (8f,Nad,FT,Feb 1)
Optimus 108 (12f,Lin,SD,Nov 17)
Orchard Supreme 110 (8f,Lin,SD,Feb 17)
Orpen Wide 106 (9f,Wol,SD,Jan 19)
Orpenindeed 110 (6f,Lin,SD,Dec 7)
Orpsie Boy 106 (6f,Lin,SD,Dec 28)
Oscar Snowman 107 (10f,Lin,SD,Feb 10)
Osiris Way 107 (5f,Lin,SD,Oct 12)
Ours 105 (8f,Sth,SD,Dec 12)

Pab Special 108 (9f,Wol,SD,Feb 10)
Pagan Sword 109 (10f,Lin,SD,Mar 17)
Paktolos 107 (9½f,Wol,SS,Jan 26)
Paparaazi 106 (9½f,Wol,SD,Jan 12)
Paradise Dancer 108 (9f,Wol,SD,Sep 20)
Parkview Love 107 (8f,Lin,SD,Mar 23)
Parole Board 111 (8f,Nad,FT,Mar 31)
Party Boss 114 (8f,Lin,SD,Feb 17)
Paso Doble 106 (8f,Sth,SD,Jan 9)
Pass The Port 108 (12f,Wol,SD,Dec 26)
Pawan 110 (6f,Lin,SD,Feb 10)
Pelican Waters 105 (9½f,Wol,SS,Dec 17)
Perfect Reward 106 (12f,Kem,SD,Oct 3)
Perfect Story 106 (6f,Kem,SD,Jan 28)
Persian Express 105 (8f,Kem,SD,Apr 7)
Pertemps Networks 106 (11f,Sth,SS,Dec 21)
Philharmonic 106 (6f,Lin,SD,Dec 30)
Phreeze 105 (11f,Sth,SD,May 22)
Picador 105 (9f,Wol,SD,Jan 21)
Pieter Brueghel 108 (5f,Sth,SD,Jan 1)
Pinch Of Salt 107 (12f,Kem,SD,Nov 3)
Pinchbeck 107 (6f,Lin,SD,Feb 10)
Pippa Greene 106 (10f,Lin,SD,Mar 24)
Pitbull 105 (9f,Wol,SD,Sep 20)
Pivotal Answer 112 (12f,Kem,SD,Sep 24)
Play Up Pompey 106 (10f,Lin,SD,Jan 31)
Players Please 108 (9½f,Wol,SD,Jan 15)
Plum Pudding 109 (10f,Lin,SD,Mar 17)
Polish Power 110 (12f,Lin,SD,Nov 17)
Pop Music 110 (9½f,Wol,SD,Jan 12)
Portal 108 (11f,Kem,SD,Aug 27)
Positive Profile 111 (16f,Lin,SD,Feb 14)
Praxiteles 109 (12f,Lin,SD,Nov 15)
Premio Loco 112 (8f,Lin,SD,Apr 30)
Premium Tap 118 (10f,Nad,FT,Mar 31)
Presumptive 106 (7f,Kem,SD,Mar 31)
Prime Defender 107 (8f,Kem,SD,Mar 31)
Primo Way 106 (9½f,Wol,SS,Jan 26)
Prince Charlemagne 105 (10f,Lin,SD,Feb 3)
Prince Of Gold 105 (7f,Wol,SD,Jan 15)
Prince Sabaah 106 (9½f,Wol,SD,Apr 24)
Prince Tum Tum 108 (6f,Wol,SD,Jan 5)
Princess Lavinia 106 (10f,Kem,SD,May 7)
Propaganda 105 (12f,Wol,SD,Nov 27)
Proper 108 (7f,Wol,SD,Apr 5)
Proper Article 107 (12f,Sth,SD,Feb 13)
Putra Square 105 (12f,Lin,SD,Oct 14)

Qadar 112 (6f,Lin,SD,Jan 13)
Quality Street 106 (6f,Lin,SD,Jan 10)
Queen s Best 109 (10f,Lin,SD,May 4)
Quiet Times 109 (6f,Lin,SD,Feb 10)
Quince 105 (12f,Lin,SD,Feb 5)
Quorum 105 (8f,Nad,FT,Feb 22)

Rabbit Fighter 111 (6f,Kem,SD,Dec 12)
Radical Views 109 (7f,Sth,SD,May 24)
Raffaas 111 (13f,Lin,SD,Jly 3)
Raise The Heights 110 (12f,Sth,SD,Feb 13)
Rakata 109 (8f,Kem,SD,Apr 7)
Rallying Cry 108 (8f,Nad,FT,Feb 9)
Rapid City 108 (10f,Lin,SD,Feb 3)
Raptor 111 (8f,Kem,SD,Nov 28)
Ravarino 109 (10f,Lin,SD,Jly 21)
Ravenna 105 (11f,Kem,SD,Jly 11)
Raza Cab 107 (7f,Lin,SD,Mar 30)

Reaching Out 106 (10f,Lin,SD,Jan 27)
Realt Na Mara 105 (6f,Lin,SD,Nov 26)
Rebellious Spirit 107 (8f,Sth,SD,Jan 2)
Red Birr 109 (9f,Wol,SD,Sep 20)
Red Blossom 105 (9f,Wol,SD,Dec 10)
Red Cape 113 (6f,Lin,SD,Jan 13)
Red Romeo 108 (7f,Wol,SD,Dec 31)
Red Spell 112 (8f,Lin,SD,Feb 17)
Regal Quest 105 (7f,Kem,SD,Dec 19)
Regal Raider 106 (6f,Lin,SD,Nov 26)
Regal Royale 109 (6f,Lin,SD,Feb 10)
Resplendent Alpha 105 (6f,Lin,SD,Nov 17)
Resplendent Nova 106 (7f,Kem,SD,Mar 24)
Restless Soul 106 (12f,Wol,SD,Nov 27)
Revolve 105 (10f,Kem,SD,May 7)
Rhapsilian 107 (6f,Kem,SD,Dec 19)
Rickety Bridge 108 (12f,Kem,SD,May 9)
Riggins 107 (7f,Wol,SD,Apr 27)
Right Option 108 (16½f,Wol,SD,Nov 12)
Right To Play 109 (12f,Wol,SF,May 3)
Risque Heights 108 (12f,Lin,SD,Nov 17)
River Deuce 107 (12f,Lin,SD,Oct 14)
Roman Boy 106 (8f,Kem,SD,Jan 14)
Rose Street 105 (10f,Kem,SD,Jun 20)
Ross Moor 105 (14f,Wol,SD,Feb 21)
Rowe Park 109 (5f,Sth,SS,Feb 11)
Royal Dignitary 106 (7f,Lin,SD,Mar 30)
Royal Jet 112 (12f,Lin,SD,Feb 3)
Royal Rock 106 (6f,Kem,SD,Jun 13)
Rule For Ever 106 (16f,Lin,SD,Mar 7)
Ruman 105 (6f,Kem,SD,Nov 19)
Russian Rocket 106 (5f,Lin,SD,Jan 17)
Russian Symphony 107 (6f,Lin,SD,Dec 9)
Russki 106 (9f,Wol,SD,Oct 21)

Safari Mischief 105 (5f,Lin,SD,Oct 12)
Sailor King 105 (7f,Kem,SD,Mar 26)
Salaam Dubai 114 (6f,Nad,FT,Mar 31)
Salient 107 (7f,Lin,SD,Nov 1)
Salsa Verdi 108 (11f,Kem,SD,Jly 4)
Salt Track 105 (8f,Nad,FT,Feb 22)
Salut Saint Cloud 105 (16f,Kem,SD,Mar 31)
Salute 109 (16f,Kem,SD,Jly 4)
Samarinda 110 (8f,Kem,SD,Sep 8)
Samba Reggae 110 (9f,Nad,FT,Mar 8)
Samuel Charles 106 (9f,Wol,SD,Jan 19)
Sands Crooner 106 (5f,Lin,SD,Dec 9)
Sarwin 109 (9½f,Wol,SD,Jan 12)
Satin Braid 106 (8f,Lin,SD,Nov 6)
Satulagi 105 (7f,Nad,FT,Jan 25)
Saviours Spirit 109 (6f,Sth,SD,Feb 13)
Scamperdale 105 (9f,Wol,SD,Jun 30)
Seamus Shindig 105 (7f,Kem,SD,May 2)
Secret Night 107 (7f,Lin,SD,Feb 7)
Selkirk Grace 105 (13f,Lin,SD,Jly 10)
Sendinpost 110 (16f,Kem,SD,Jly 4)
Seneschal 107 (6f,Kem,SD,Feb 25)
Sesmen 107 (8f,Lin,SD,Nov 1)
Sew N So Character 107 (9f,Wol,SD,Jan 19)
Sgt Schultz 106 (12f,Lin,SD,Feb 5)
Shahin 111 (12f,Kem,SD,Sep 8)
Shape Up 107 (11f,Sth,SD,Mar 15)
She s So Pretty 106 (12f,Kem,SD,Oct 3)
Sheriff s Silk 106 (6f,Sth,SD,Mar 13)
Shevchenko 107 (7f,Lin,SD,May 4)
Shine And Rise 106 (16f,Kem,SD,Aug 29)
Shot Gun 108 (8f,Kem,SD,Jun 6)
Si Foo 105 (7f,Lin,SD,Mar 24)
Silent Storm 108 (7f,Lin,SD,Feb 17)
Silver Prelude 106 (5f,Lin,SD,Nov 30)
Simondiun 106 (16f,Kem,SD,Jly 4)
Singing Poet 107 (9f,Nad,FT,Feb 8)
Sir Bond 107 (9½f,Wol,SD,Jan 12)
Sir Douglas 107 (6f,Kem,SD,Mar 25)
Sister Act 105 (8f,Kem,SD,Oct 10)
Sky Quest 105 (10f,Lin,SD,Jan 27)
Small Stakes 107 (7f,Lin,SD,Jan 24)
Smart Ass 105 (9f,Wol,SD,Jan 19)
Soft Morning 108 (8f,Kem,SD,Jan 28)
Sohraab 107 (6f,Sth,SD,Mar 13)
Solo Flight 106 (10f,Lin,SD,Feb 3)
Sopran Gath 106 (10f,Kem,SD,Oct 31)
Special Place 107 (7f,Lin,SD,Apr 4)
Speedy Sam 113 (8f,Sth,SD,Jan 1)
Spot The Subbie 109 (8f,Kem,SD,Jan 14)
Spring At Last 114 (8f,Nad,FT,Mar 31)
Spring Goddess 108 (8f,Lin,SD,Apr 1)
Sri Diamond 108 (12f,Lin,SD,Jan 6)
St Petersburg 106 (9f,Wol,SD,Jan 19)
Star Magnitude 108 (10f,Lin,SD,Feb 19)
Star Of Canterbury 106 (12f,Kem,SD,May 9)
Starcross Maid 106 (11f,Sth,SD,Mar 15)
State Dilemma 106 (7f,Lin,SD,Jan 24)
Steig 107 (9f,Wol,SD,Dec 27)
Steppe Dancer 116 (12f,Kem,SD,Sep 8)
Stoic Leader 107 (7f,Lin,SD,Jan 24)
Stoneacre Lad 111 (5f,Lin,SD,Mar 29)
Storybook 108 (9f,Wol,SD,Feb 16)
Strabinios King 106 (6f,Kem,SD,Dec 19)
Street Life 106 (12f,Kem,SD,Jan 10)
Strike Up The Band 110 (5f,Lin,SD,Mar 24)
Strobe 108 (12f,Lin,SD,Jun 21)
Sugar Land 108 (6f,Wol,SF,Jun 29)
Suits Me 106 (9f,Wol,SD,Mar 2)
Sun Catcher 111 (8f,Lin,SD,May 4)
Sunlight 106 (8f,Kem,SD,Jly 18)
Sunset Boulevard 105 (12f,Lin,SD,Jan 24)

Super Frank 112 (7f,Lin,SD,Jan 27)
Supercast 107 (6f,Kem,SD,Feb 25)
Sweet Gale 105 (8f,Lin,SD,Apr 30)
Sweet Indulgence 107 (12f,Lin,SD,Feb 3)
Sweet Pickle 106 (6f,Kem,SD,Feb 25)
Symbol Of Peace 106 (9f,Wol,SD,Mar 2)
Synonymy 105 (16f,Kem,SD,Apr 25)

Tabadul 111 (10f,Lin,SD,May 4)
Taboor 105 (6f,Kem,SD,Feb 25)
Takes Tutu 105 (9½f,Wol,SD,Jan 12)
Takitwo 109 (7f,Kem,SD,Mar 26)
Talbot Avenue 111 (5f,Lin,SD,Mar 29)
Tamagin 107 (6f,Lin,SD,Nov 4)
Tanzanite 105 (9f,Wol,SD,Mar 10)
Tarkamara 105 (6f,Wol,SF,Jun 29)
Tartatartufata 106 (5f,Wol,SD,Dec 8)
Tax Free 107 (6f,Nad,FT,Jan 25)
Ten A Penny 106 (8f,Kem,SD,Mar 24)
Tender The Great 111 (8f,Lin,SD,Oct 14)
Terrific Challenge 113 (6f,Nad,FT,Mar 1)
Tetouan 105 (7f,Lin,SD,Mar 7)
Texas Gold 107 (6f,Lin,SD,Dec 9)
Thajja 112 (6f,Nad,FT,Jan 25)
The City Kid 105 (9½f,Wol,SS,Jan 28)
The Kiddykid 107 (7f,Lin,SD,Oct 14)
The King And I 106 (12f,Wol,SD,Dec 26)
The Lord 109 (5f,Lin,SD,Mar 24)
Thinking Positive 107 (11f,Kem,SD,Jly 4)
Thor s Echo 109 (6f,Nad,FT,Mar 31)
Three Boars 107 (12f,Sth,SD,Mar 13)
Tiana 105 (8f,Lin,SD,Nov 1)
Tiger Tiger 107 (10f,Lin,SD,Mar 17)
Tilapia 109 (8f,Kem,SD,Jun 6)
Time To Regret 107 (9f,Wol,SD,Oct 26)
Titan Triumph 107 (8f,Lin,SD,Nov 26)
Tiza 105 (6f,Nad,FT,Mar 31)
Tommy Toogood 105 (11f,Kem,SD,Sep 7)
Tony James 110 (6f,Lin,SD,Nov 17)
Tony The Tap 105 (5f,Lin,SD,Oct 12)
Top Mark 108 (8f,Kem,SD,May 7)
Top Spec 105 (12f,Wol,SS,Jan 29)
Topflightcoolracer 105 (5f,Wol,SD,Aug 12)
Torquemada 106 (8f,Lin,SD,Oct 29)
Total Impact 110 (5f,Lin,SD,Mar 29)
Touch Of Style 105 (9½f,Wol,SD,Dec 15)
Tous Les Deux 107 (10f,Lin,SD,Feb 24)
Traffic Guard 108 (8f,Nad,FT,Feb 9)
Treasure House 108 (8f,Lin,SD,May 4)
Tritonville Lodge 106 (16f,Kem,SD,Jan 20)
Tropical Star 113 (6f,Nad,FT,Jan 25)
Tropical Strait 109 (12f,Kem,SD,Sep 24)
Troubadour 110 (8f,Lin,SD,Nov 17)
Tufton 107 (10f,Lin,SD,May 4)
Tumbleweed Glory 105 (8f,Kem,SD,Sep 24)
Turn On The Style 113 (6f,Sth,SD,Jan 9)
Tybalt 107 (8f,Kem,SD,Apr 7)
Tyrone Sam 107 (7f,Lin,SD,Jan 24)

Uhoomagoo 112 (8f,Sth,SD,Jan 1)
United Nations 105 (9f,Wol,SD,May 21)
Unshakable 109 (8f,Kem,SD,May 7)

Vacation 110 (10f,Lin,SD,May 4)
Valance 109 (16f,Lin,SD,Feb 14)
Vanquisher 105 (11f,Sth,SD,May 22)
Velvet Valley 105 (11f,Sth,SD,Mar 22)
Ventura 114 (8f,Kem,SD,Nov 28)
Vermilion 108 (10f,Nad,FT,Mar 31)
Very Wise 111 (10f,Lin,SD,Mar 17)
Victory Tetsuni 106 (9f,Nad,FT,Mar 1)
Visionist 105 (8f,Nad,FT,Mar 1)
Voliere 110 (8f,Lin,SD,Oct 14)
Vortex 109 (8f,Nad,FT,Mar 1)

Wagtail 105 (8f,Lin,SD,Nov 1)
Wahoo Sam 105 (7f,Wol,SD,Jan 4)
War Anthem 107 (9f,Wol,SD,Sep 20)
Warm Embraces 105 (8f,Lin,SD,Mar 24)
Watamu 114 (10f,Lin,SD,Mar 17)
Watchful 111 (12f,Lin,SD,Nov 17)
Waterline Twenty 106 (9f,Wol,SD,Jan 19)
Waterside 112 (6f,Lin,SD,Jan 13)
Wavertree Warrior 106 (8f,Lin,SD,Jan 20)
Weightless 105 (10f,Kem,SD,Jun 6)
Wessex 108 (7f,Sth,SW,Feb 8)
Western Point 106 (12f,Lin,SD,Jun 30)
Westport 109 (6f,Wol,SD,Jun 30)
What Do You Know 108 (7f,Kem,SD,Mar 26)
Whinhill House 105 (5f,Sth,SD,Apr 2)
Whispering Death 110 (16f,Kem,SD,Jly 4)
Whitbarrow 105 (6f,Sth,SD,May 14)
Who s Winning 105 (6f,Lin,SD,Jan 10)
Wicked Daze 106 (12f,Kem,SD,Jly 17)
Wild Pitch 109 (14f,Wol,SD,Feb 21)
Will He Wish 107 (7f,Lin,SD,Jan 27)
Willhewiz 105 (6f,Kem,SD,Dec 12)
William s Way 105 (10f,Kem,SD,Jun 6)
Winthorpe 107 (6f,Wol,SD,Apr 24)
Wise Dennis 111 (8f,Kem,SD,Nov 28)
Wodhill Gold 105 (8f,Sth,SD,Jan 23)
Woodnook 114 (6f,Lin,SD,Feb 10)
Woolfall Blue 105 (11f,Kem,SD,Apr 7)
World Spirit 113 (8f,Lin,SD,Oct 14)

Wraith 106 (12f,Lin,SD,Nov 15)
Wrighty Almighty 105 (8f,Lin,SD,Dec 9)
Writ 107 (7f,Wol,SD,Jan 5)

Xtra Torrential 106 (9f,Wol,SS,Jan 26)

Yakimov 106 (8f,Sth,SD,Jun 5)
Yaroslav 108 (7f,Lin,SD,May 4)
Yarqus 109 (7f,Lin,SD,Mar 24)
Young Mick 108 (12f,Kem,SD,Nov 3)
Young Scotton 105 (14f,Wol,SD,Nov 16)

Zaham 108 (8f,Kem,SD,Apr 7)
Zarzu 109 (6f,Sth,SD,Jan 9)
Zato 105 (7f,Kem,SD,Mar 31)
Zirkel 105 (12f,Kem,SD,May 9)
Zorin 105 (9f,Nad,FT,Mar 1)

TWO YEAR-OLDS - Turf

Achill Island 107 (8f,Asc,S,Sep 29)
Alan Devonshire 106 (7f,Chs,GF,Aug 31)
Albabilia 105 (7f,Nmk,F,Aug 11)
Alexander Castle 105 (7f,Don,GF,Sep 15)
Alexandros 111 (7f,Lin,GS,Jly 14)
Alfathaa 106 (8f,Asc,S,Sep 29)

Beacon Lodge 106 (6½f,Nby,GS,Oct 11)
Bett s Spirit 107 (6f,Nmk,G,Nov 2)
Billyford 105 (7f,Leo,GF,Oct 29)
Blue Chagall 105 (8f,Lon,GS,Sep 22)
Bunsen Burner 105 (7f,Leo,GF,Nov 4)

Cake 106 (5f,Asc,GS,Oct 13)
Candle Sahara 107 (6f,Goo,G,Aug 1)
Captain Gerrard 111 (5f,Chs,S,Jun 30)
Celtic Slipper 105 (8f,Don,GF,Sep 13)
City Leader 108 (8f,Asc,S,Sep 29)
Coachhouse Lady 106 (7f,Red,G,Oct 6)
Conference Call 108 (8f,Lon,GS,Oct 7)
Curtain Call 107 (8f,Cur,Y,Sep 30)
Cute Ass 106 (5f,Asc,GS,Oct 13)

Dark Angel 107 (6f,Nmk,G,Oct 5)
Declaration Of War 106 (7f,Lon,GS,Oct 7)
Donegal 105 (7f,Goo,G,Aug 1)
Drawnfromthepast 105 (5f,Asc,GF,Jun 19)
Dubai Dynamo 105 (6f,Red,G,Oct 6)
Dubai Princess 107 (6f,Nmk,G,Nov 2)

Edge Of Gold 105 (6f,Nby,S,Jun 26)
Ellemujie 105 (7f,Nmk,GF,Aug 10)
Elletelle 106 (5f,Asc,GF,Jun 20)
Emmrooz 105 (8f,Asc,S,Sep 29)
Endless Luck 106 (8f,Mus,G,Nov 9)
Eva s Request 106 (7f,Cur,Y,Sep 30)

Famous Name 106 (7f,Leo,GF,Oct 29)
Fashion Rocks 108 (6f,Goo,G,Aug 1)
Fast Company 114 (7f,Nmk,GS,Oct 20)
Festoso 105 (6f,Nmk,G,Oct 5)
Fifty 105 (6f,Goo,G,Aug 1)
Fleeting Spirit 110 (6f,Nmk,G,Oct 5)
Flying Blue 107 (7f,Lon,GS,Jly 14)
Full Of Gold 109 (10f,Sai,VS,Nov 11)

Generous Thought 107 (6f,Don,GF,Nov 10)
Golan Knight 107 (7f,Chs,GF,Aug 31)
Great Barrier Reef 107 (6f,Cur,G,Sep 2)
Greatwallofchina 105 (7f,Cur,GF,Sep 16)

Hammadi 105 (5f,Asc,GS,Oct 13)
Hannouma 107 (10f,Sai,VS,Nov 11)
Hatta Fort 107 (5f,Wdr,GF,Jun 4)
Henrythenavigator 108 (6f,Asc,GF,Jun 19)
Honky Tonk Sally 105 (7f,Chs,G,Sep 29)

Ibn Khaldun 108 (8f,Don,G,Oct 27)

Janina 105 (5f,Yor,G,May 18)
Jupiter Pluvius 107 (7f,Leo,GF,Oct 29)

Kandahar Run 106 (8f,Nmk,S,Oct 19)
Kingsgate Native 111 (5f,Yor,G,Aug 23)
Kitty Hawk Miss 105 (8f,Cur,S,Oct 22)
Kitty Matcham 106 (7f,Nmk,GS,Oct 20)
Kotsi 105 (8f,Don,GF,Sep 13)
Ksayban 107 (7f,Lon,GS,Jly 14)

Let Us Prey 105 (8f,Asc,S,Sep 29)
Listen 110 (8f,Asc,S,Sep 29)
Lizard Island 109 (7f,Goo,G,Aug 1)

Luck Money 106 (6f,Asc,GF,Jun 19)

Mad About You 107 (8f,Lon,GS,Oct 7)
Magritte 105 (5½f,Msn,G,Jly 22)
Marjalina 106 (8f,Leo,GF,Nov 3)
McCartney 108 (8f,Ham,GS,Aug 15)
Missit 105 (7f,Nmk,GS,Oct 20)
Mizooka 106 (7f,Sal,GS,Aug 15)
Myboycharlie 108 (6f,Dea,S,Aug 19)

Natagora 111 (6f,Nmk,G,Oct 5)
New Approach 115 (7f,Nmk,GS,Oct 20)
New Zealand 107 (10f,Sai,VS,Nov 11)
Norman Invader 108 (6f,Cur,G,Sep 2)

Paco Boy 109 (6f,Nmk,G,Nov 2)
Pencil Hill 105 (6f,Asc,GF,Jun 19)
Perfect Polly 107 (6f,Cur,G,Sep 2)
Plan 106 (7f,Leo,GF,Oct 29)
Planetarium 105 (10f,Pon,G,Oct 8)
Proviso 109 (8f,Asc,S,Sep 29)
Putney Bridge 107 (10f,Sai,VS,Nov 11)

Quest For Success 105 (6f,Ayr,GS,Oct 4)

Rash Judgement 105 (6f,Don,GF,Nov 10)
Raven s Pass 111 (7f,Nmk,GS,Oct 20)
Red Alert Day 107 (7f,Nmk,GF,Aug 10)
Ridge Dance 106 (8f,Asc,S,Sep 29)
Rio De La Plata 112 (7f,Goo,G,Aug 1)
River Proud 108 (6f,Nmk,GF,Jly 12)
Royal Confidence 107 (6f,Goo,G,Aug 1)

Safari Sunup 105 (7f,Sal,GS,Aug 15)
Salut L Africain 108 (7f,Lon,GS,Jly 14)
Saoirse Abu 107 (7f,Cur,G,Sep 2)
Savethisdanceforme 106 (8f,Cur,GY,Oct 21)
Scintillo 107 (8f,Asc,S,Sep 29)
Screen Star 108 (7f,Red,GF,Aug 25)
Shediak 106 (7f,Lon,GS,Oct 7)
Siberian Tiger 106 (10f,Sai,VS,Nov 11)
Simawa 107 (8f,Leo,GF,Nov 3)
Sister Act 106 (7f,Lon,GS,Jly 14)
Sophie s Girl 106 (6f,Nmk,G,Nov 2)
Spacious 106 (8f,Don,GF,Sep 13)
Spinning Lucy 109 (6f,Nmk,G,Nov 2)
Spirit Of Sharjah 106 (5f,Don,GF,Sep 14)
Starbora 105 (7f,Lon,GS,Jly 14)
Starlit Sands 105 (5f,Asc,GF,Jun 20)
Strike The Deal 106 (6f,Nmk,G,Oct 5)
Suailce 105 (8f,Leo,GF,Nov 3)
Sudden Impact 105 (6f,Cur,S,Aug 25)
Swiss Franc 107 (6f,Asc,GF,Jun 19)

Tadalavil 105 (6f,Nmk,G,Nov 2)
Tajdeef 105 (6f,Nmk,G,Oct 5)
Tathkaar 105 (7f,Red,G,Oct 6)
The Loan Express 105 (5f,Asc,GF,Jun 20)
Toirneach 106 (7f,Cur,GF,Sep 16)
Triskel 105 (7f,Leo,S,Jly 18)
Twice Over 106 (10f,Nmk,G,Nov 3)

Winker Watson 109 (6f,Nmk,GF,Jly 12)

Yahrab 106 (8f,Asc,S,Sep 29)

Zarkava 111 (8f,Lon,GS,Oct 7)

TWO YEAR-OLDS - Sand

Gin Genereux 105 (6f,Wol,SD,Aug 30)

Lady Aquitaine 106 (6f,Kem,SD,Sep 8)

Philario 108 (6f,Kem,SD,Sep 8)

Red Alert Day 106 (6f,Kem,SD,Sep 8)

Sweet Hope 105 (7f,Lin,SD,Dec 19)